PEARS

CYCLOPAEDIA

1966–67

A BOOK OF BACKGROUND INFORMATION
AND REFERENCE FOR EVERYDAY USE

EDITOR
L. MARY BARKER
B.Sc.Lond.

Seventy-fifth edition

The Editor desires to express her gratitude to readers for their criticisms and suggestions and to all those who in one way or another have contributed to the making of this edition. Correspondence is welcomed and should be addressed to the Editor at 'Middlemarch', Halstead, Sevenoaks, Kent.

First published 1897

Printed and Bound in Great Britain by Richard Clay (The Chaucer Press), Ltd., Bungay, Suffolk

Pears is revised upon reissue annually and its scope is enlarged to deal with new events and growth in knowledge. This note indicates some of the fresh topics in this issue.

The World of Science, besides giving a picture of current basic scientific ideas, has new articles by leading authorities on the philosophy of science, the study of population, the electromagnetic spectrum, the laser, micro-electronics, and the biological fixation of nitrogen.

The revised text of *Medical Matters* pays special attention to drug abuse and drug dependence and has many fresh and important things to say about the principles of first aid.

Background to Public Affairs, concerned with the changing patterns in international relations and Britain's own affairs, includes an account of recent changes in Government machinery and functions, of changes in Africa, and of " conflict studies," the new branch of university research into the causes of war.

In *Background to Economic Events*, which recounts not only events but explains the controversies about them, the story, complete with facts and figures, is brought up to the spring of 1966.

The revised text of *The Law of England* deals with recent changes in the law relating to landlord and tenant, and to husband and wife, and discusses crime and punishment in a changing society, with special reference to the young offender.

The Contemporary Theatre deals with the work of dramatists such as Brecht, Ionesco, Miller, Beckett, Pinter, and Arden and includes a glossary of dramatic terms and a note on eminent theatrical companies.

The ceramics pages have been expanded to include Chinese reign-marks in addition to English and Continental china marks.

PLAN OF VOLUME

This book of reference is divided into sections which fall into three main groups:—

I. THE WIDER WORLD

II. GENERAL REFERENCE

III. HOME AND SOCIAL

CONTENTS

I. THE WIDER WORLD

II. GENERAL REFERENCE

III. HOME AND SOCIAL

INDEX

Some of the sections are alphabetically arranged and index themselves. Their contents are not included here except where it is anticipated some special difficulty in reference may arise. Each section has a letter and, where appropriate, the column is given in brackets after the page number, *e.g.*, F8(1), G40(2). The sections " Greek Myths and Legends " and " Medical Matters " have each a separate index and glossary.

HISTORICAL EVENTS

ILLUSTRATIONS BY JACK LARKIN

CHRONICLE OF EVENTS

Note.—*For classical history and for the past millennium most dates are well established. For other periods there is sometimes considerable uncertainty. Many of the dates in ancient history are either dubious or approximate, sometimes both. For events in prehistory the reader may find it helpful to consult the Geological Time Scale and the sub-section Earliest Men in Part II of the Science Section.*

B.C. PREHISTORY

5,300,000,000 Age of Earth.

3,300,000,000 Earliest known rocks (found in Rhodesia and Manitoba).

2,000,000,000 Life appears.

600,000,000 First large-scale occurrence of fossils.

20,000,000 Early ape fossils (Miocene period—*Proconsul*, E. Africa).

10,000,000 Early ape fossils (Lower Pliocene —*Oreopithecus*, Italy).

1,700,000 Earliest known hominids (Lower Pleistocene—*Australopithecus*, and *Homo habilis* S. Africa, E. Africa.) Oldowan culture—first stage of Palaeolithic or Old Stone Age (hunting and food-gathering) which persisted until end of Ice Age, *c.* 8,000 B.C.

400,000 *Homo erectus* stage (Java, China, Africa) with crude chopping tools and early hand-axes. Heidelberg jaw (Europe).

250,000 Ancestors of Neandertalers and *Homo sapiens*, with advanced hand-axes (Europe: Steinheim and Swanscombe).

70,000 Neandertalers (Europe, Asia, N. Africa). Rhodesian Man (S. Africa). Solo Man (Java). Flake tools.

40,000 First cold phase ends. Neandertal race becoming extinct.

30,000 Second cold phase. *Homo sapiens* (modern man). Implements show significant advances: small knife-blades, engraving tools. Paintings and sculpture; magic rites and ceremonies. Cro-Magnons with Aurignacian culture.

18,000 Final culmination of last ice age. Aurignacian culture dying out to be replaced by Solutrean and then by the Magdalenian cultures. Great flowering of Palaeolithic art.

15,000 First immigrants from Asia to cross Behring Straits?

8,000 Last glaciers in Britain disappeared. Proto-Neolithic in Middle East. Agricultural settlements (*e.g.*, Jericho). Settled way of life leading eventually to such skills as weaving, metallurgy; inventions as ox-drawn plough, wheeled cart.

5,000 Britain becomes an island (land connection with continent severed by melting ice-sheets).

B.C. CIVILISATION IN THE MIDDLE EAST

4000 Susa founded.

3500 Sumerian civilisation flourishes. Cuneiform writing.

3000 First Egyptian Dynasty. Hieratic writing already perfected.
Early Minoan Age (Crete). Pictorial writing, copper, silver, gold in use. Early Mycenean civilisation begins.

2980 Memphis capital of Egypt.

B.C.

2870 First settlements at Troy.

2850 Golden Age of China begins (legendary).

2700 Great Pyramid age in Egypt begins.

2400 Aryan migrations.
Sargon founds Agade: Semitic empire.

2205 Hsia Dynasty begins in China (legendary).

2200 Middle Minoan Age: pottery, linear writing in pen and ink.

1900 Bronze Age begins in Britain.
Stonehenge (1860–1560 B.C.).

1760 Shang Dynasty begins in China (dated traditionally 1760–1122 B.C.).

1750 Aryan invasion of Mesopotamia.

1720 Hyksos conquest of Egypt. War chariots introduced.

1700 Code of Hammurabi at Babylon.

1600 Late Minoan Age: bronze in use.

1550 Sack of Babylon by Hittites.

1546 18th Dynasty in Egypt commences. Civilisation at peak (under Thotmes III, 1490). Chronology more certain.

1500 Powerful Mitanni (Aryan) kingdom in Asia Minor. Phoenicia thriving—trade with Egypt and Babylonia. Vedic literature in India.

1450 Zenith of Minoan civilisation.

1400 Ugarit (N. Syria) culture at its zenith. Cretan civilisation ends: Knossos burnt. Temple at Luxor built.

1377 Amenhotep IV (Ikhnaton), the "heretic" Pharaoh.

1350 Zenith of Hittite civilisation.

1300 Israelite oppression (Rameses II). Phoenician settlements—Hellas and Spain (Cadiz). Tyre flourishing.

1250 Assyrian conquest in Babylon: dominant in Western Asia.

1230 Exodus of Israelites from Egypt.

1200 Attacks on Egypt by "Peoples of the Sea". Downfall of Hittite kingdom. Siege of Troy (Homeric). Beginning of sea-power of independent Phoenician cities. Probably all these are connected with Achaean and other migrations in Aegean area.

1122 Chou Dynasty begins in China (870 years).

1115 Magnetic needle reputed in China.

1028 Establishment of kingship in Israel (Saul).

1000 Jerusalem capital of Israel. David king. *Rig Veda* (India).

961 Solomon begins temple at Jerusalem.

900 Probably period of writing of Homer's epics.

893 Assyrian chronological records begin.

850 Foundation of Carthage (traditional).

781 Chinese record of an eclipse.

776 First Olympiad to be used for chronological purposes.

753 Foundation of Rome (traditional).

750 Greek colonists settling in Southern Italy.

745 Accession of Tiglath-Pileser III: Assyrian Power at its height. Deportation of subject peoples (Israel 722).

683 Kingship abolished in Athens.

625 Neo-Babylonian (Chaldean) Empire (Nineveh destroyed 612).

B.C.

621 Publication of Athenian laws by Draco.

610 Spartan constitution, made rigid after Messenian Wars: later attributed to Lycurgus.

594 Athenian constitution reformed by Solon.

586 Jerusalem taken by Babylonians. Inhabitants exiled till 538.

561 Pisistratus tyrant of Athens.

560 Accession of Croesus—great prosperity of Lydia.

538 Babylon taken by Persians: Empire founded by Cyrus, soon covers almost all of civilised Middle East.

509 Foundation of Roman Republic (traditional).

508 Democratic constitution proclaimed in Athens.

500 Etruscans at height of their power in Northern Italy. Iron age beginning in Britain.

GREAT AGE OF GREECE

499 Revolt of Ionian Greek cities against Persian king Darius.

494 Secession of Plebeians from Rome. Tribunes established.

490 Battle of Marathon: Athenian repulse of Persian attack.

480 Death of Buddha. Battle of Thermopylae: Spartans under Leonidas wiped out by Persians. Battle of Salamis: Persian fleet defeated by Athenians under Themistocles; Persian invasion of Greece halted.

479 Battles of Plataea and Mycale: Greek victories by land and sea respectively destroy Persian invasion force. Death of Confucius.

477 League of Delos founded by Athens for defence against Persia; soon becomes Athenian Empire. (467 Naxos kept in by force.)

461 Pericles comes to power in Athens.

458 Cincinnatus saves Rome (traditional).

456 Death of Aeschylus.

447 Building of Parthenon begun.

431 Death of Phidias. Outbreak of Great Peloponnesian War between Athens and Sparta. Pericles "Funeral Oration" (according to Thucydides).

425 Death of Herodotus.

416 Massacre of Melos by Athenians.

415 Sicilian Expedition: flight of Alcibiades from Athens to Sparta.

413 Loss of entire Athenian expeditionary force at Syracuse.

406 Death of Euripides and Sophocles.

405 Battle of Aegospotami: Athenian navy destroyed by Sparta.

404 Athenian surrender to Sparta: beginning of Spartan hegemony in Greece.

403 Beginning of epoch of Warring States in China.

400 Death of Thucydides, Greek historian (?).

399 Execution of Socrates.

390 Occupation of Rome by Gauls under Brennus.

371 Battle of Leuctra: Spartans defeated by Thebans: beginning of Theban hegemony in Greece.

370 Death of Hippocrates of Cos (?).

347 Death of Plato.

338 Battle of Chaeronea: Greek city-states defeated by Philip II of Macedon, who becomes supreme in Greece.

336 Assassination of Philip of Macedon: accession of Alexander.

334 Alexander's invasion of Persian Empire. Battle of Granicus, first victory.

333 Battle of Issus: Alexander defeats Darius of Persia.

332 Alexander's siege and capture of Tyre, occupation of Egypt.

B.C.

331 Battle of Arbela (Gaugamela)—final defeat of Darius.

330 Death of Darius and end of Persian Empire. Alexander heir to civilisations of Middle East.

326 Battle of Hydaspes: Alexander conquers the Punjab.

323 Death of Alexander at Babylon. Beginning of Hellenistic Age in Middle East and Eastern Mediterranean. Ptolemy I founds dynasty in Egypt. Alexandria becomes intellectual centre of Hellenic world.

322 Death of Demosthenes.

321 Death of Aristotle. Maurya dynasty unites N. India.

312 Seleucus I founds dynasty in Asia.

300 Zeno the Stoic, Epicurus and Euclid flourishing.

ROME: CONQUESTS AND DECAY OF REPUBLICAN INSTITUTIONS

290 End of Third Samnite War. Rome dominates Central Italy.

275 Battle of Beneventum: Rome finally defeats Pyrrhus and the Greek cities of Southern Italy. Rome dominates all Italy.

274 Asoka becomes ruler of two-thirds of Indian sub-continent.

264 Beginning of First Punic War (Rome *v.* Carthage).

260 Battle of Mylae: first great Roman naval victory.

255 Defeat and capture of Regulus by Carthaginians.

250 "La Tène" Iron Age people invade Britain.

241 End of First Punic War. Sicily becomes first Province of Rome.

221 Kingdom of Ch'in completes conquest of all Chinese states, under Shih Huang Tih.

218 Outbreak of Second Punic War: Hannibal crosses Alps.

216 Battle of Cannae: Hannibal wipes out great Roman army.

214 Great Wall of China constructed (by linking existing walls).

213 Burning of Chinese classics.

212 Capture of Syracuse by Romans and death of Archimedes.

207 Battle of Metaurus: defeat and death of Hasdrubal. End of Hannibal's hopes of overcoming Rome.

205 Roman provinces organised in Spain.

202 Former or Eastern Han Dynasty in China. Battle of Zama: Hannibal defeated by Scipio Africanus.

201 End of Second Punic War. Rome dominates Western Mediterranean.

196 After defeating Macedon, Rome proclaims independence of Greek city-states. Death of Eratosthenes the geographer (?).

160 Death in battle of Judas Maccabaeus: Jewish revolt against Seleucids continues successfully.

149 Outbreak of Third Punic War.

146 Carthage destroyed. Roman province of Africa formed. Roman provinces of Macedonia and Achaea formed, and most of remainder of Greece reduced to vassal status.

134 First Servile War: Revolt of slaves in Sicily under Eunus. Suppressed 132.

133 Siege and destruction of Numantia by Romans. Tiberius Gracchus Tribune. Attempted land reforms. Murdered 132.

129 Roman province of Asia formed from lands bequeathed by Attalus of Pergamum.

124 Chinese Grand College to train Civil Service officials.

123 Caius Gracchus Tribune. Attempted land reforms. Murdered 121.

110 Chinese expansion to include most of south-east of modern China, under Emperor Wu Ti. Commercial activity in Indian Ocean.

B.C.

106 Jugurtha captured by Marius and Sulla.

104 Second Servile War: revolt of slaves in Sicily under Tryphon and Athenion. Suppressed 101.

102 Chinese expedition to Ferghana and possible knowledge of West.

101 Battle of Vercellae: Marius ends threat of Cimbri to Rome.

91 Social War: revolt of Italian cities against Rome. Suppressed 88. Roman franchise granted to most Italians.

88 Civil Wars of Marius and Sulla begin.

87 Massacre in Rome by Marius.

82 Proscriptions in Rome by Sulla.

75 Belgic invasion of south-eastern Britain.

73 Third Servile War: revolt of slaves in southern Italy under Spartacus the gladiator. Suppressed 71.

63 Conspiracy of Catiline exposed by Cicero.

60 First Triumvirate: Pompey, Caesar, Crassus.

58 Beginning of Caesar's conquest of Gaul.

55 Caesar's first British expedition. Repeated, 54.

53 Battle of Carrhae: destruction of Roman army under Crassus by Persians.

52 Revolt of Vercingetorix against Caesar.

50 Migration to Britain of Commius and his followers.

49 Caesar crosses the Rubicon. Beginning of war against Pompey and the Senate.

48 Battle of Pharsalus: defeat of Pompey by Caesar.

46 Caesar's calendar reforms.

44 Murder of Caesar.

43 Second Triumvirate: Antony, Octavian, Lepidus.

42 Battle of Philippi: defeat and death of Brutus and his associates.

31 Battle of Actium: naval victory of Octavian over Antony and Cleopatra. Octavian unchallenged master of the Roman world.

THE ROMAN EMPIRE

27 Octavian given the title of Augustus by the Senate.

19 Death of Virgil.

8 Death of Horace.

6 Birth of Jesus Christ. (?)

A.D.

6 Civil Service Examination system in China.

9 Radical reforms by Emperor Wang Mang. Annihilation of Roman army under Varus by Teutonic tribesmen under Arminius.

10 Cunobelinus reigning over much of south-east Britain from Colchester.

14 Death of Augustus.

17 Death of Livy.

18 Death of Ovid.

25 Beginning of Later or Eastern Han Dynasty in China.

29 Crucifixion of Christ (?).

43 Roman invasion of Britain under Aulus Plautius.

51 Caractacus taken to Rome as prisoner.

60 Revolt of Boudicca.

63 Death of St. Paul.

64 Great Fire of Rome.

65 Death of Seneca.

68 Death of Nero—end of Julio-Claudian line of Roman Emperors.

70 Jerusalem taken and Jewish revolt suppressed by Titus.

79 Destruction of Pompeii and Herculaneum by eruption of Vesuvius.

A.D.

80 Completion of Colosseum (Flavian Amphitheatre).

83 Battle of Mons Graupius: Agricola crushes Caledonians.

96 Accession of Nerva: first of the "Five Good Emperors."

97 Chinese expedition under Kang Yin (lieutenant of Pan Ch'ao) penetrates to Persian Gulf.

117 Death of Trajan, accession of Hadrian. Roman Empire at its greatest extent.

122 Beginning of Hadrian's Wall (Tyne–Solway) by Aulus Platorius Nepos.

135 Suppression of Bar-Cochba's revolt and Dispersion of Jews.

142 Construction of Antonine Wall (Forth–Clyde) by Quintus Lollius Urbicus.

180 Death of Marcus Aurelius, last of the "Five Good Emperors." Beginning of the "Decline" of the Roman Empire (Gibbon).

193 Praetorian guards murder Emperor Pertinax, sell Empire to highest bidder (Didius Julianus).

196 Clodius Albinus, governor, withdraws forces from Britain to support his attempt to become Emperor. Northern Britain overrun by barbarians.

208 Septimius Severus visits Britain to punish Caledonians (death at York 211).

212 Edict of Caracalla. Roman citizenship conferred on all free inhabitants of Empire.

220 End of Han Dynasty: China divided and frequently invaded for next three centuries.

227 Sassanid Empire in Persia.

230 Emperor Sujin—Japanese history emerging from legendary stage.

251 Goths defeat and kill Emperor Decius.

259 Break-away "Gallic Empire" set up: suppressed 273.

273 Defeat of Zenobia and destruction of Palmyra by Emperor Aurelian.

284 Accession of Diocletian, who reorganises Roman Empire (293) with rigid social laws and heavy taxation.

287 Carausius attempts to found independent "Empire of Britain": suppressed 297.

306 Constantine proclaimed Emperor at York.

313 Edict of Milan. Christianity tolerated in Roman Empire.

320 Gupta dynasty reunites India.

325 Council of Nicaea: first general Council of the Church.

367 Successful attack on Britain by Picts, Scots, Saxons.

369 Restoration of Roman authority in Britain by Theodosius.

378 Battle of Adrianople: Goths defeat and kill Eastern Roman Emperor Valens.

383 Magnus Maximus withdraws forces from Britain to support his attempt to conquer north-western part of Empire.

388 Magnus Maximus defeated and killed in Italy.

395 Death of Emperor Theodosius the Great: the division of the Empire into East and West at his death proves eventually to be the final one.

406 Usurper Constantine III withdraws forces from Britain to support his claims: probable end of Roman military occupation of Britain.

410 Sack of Rome by Alaric the Goth. Emperor Honorius tells Britons to arrange for their own defence.

THE BARBARIAN INVASIONS

415 Visigoths begin conquest of Spain.

419 Visigothic kingdom of Toulouse recognised by Roman government.

429 Vandals begin conquest of North Africa.

432 St. Patrick begins mission in Ireland.

A.D.

446 "Groans of the Britons"—last appeal to Rome (traditional).

451 Châlons: Attila the Hun repelled from Gaul by mixed Roman–Barbarian forces.

452 Attila's raid into Italy: destruction of Aquilea and foundation of Venice by refugees.

455 Rome pillaged by Vandals.

476 Romulus Augustulus, last Western Roman Emperor, deposed by Odovacar: conventionally the end of the Western Roman Empire.

481 Clovis becomes King of the Franks, who eventually conquer Gaul (d. 511).

493 Theodoric founds Ostrogothic Kingdom in Italy (d. 526).

515 Battle of Mount Badon: West Saxon advance halted by Britons, perhaps led by Arthur (?).

BYZANTIUM AND ISLAM

527 Accession of Justinian I (d. 565).

529 Code of Civil Law published by Justinian. Rule of St. Benedict put into practice at Monte Cassino (traditional).

534 Byzantines under Belisarius reconquer North Africa from Vandals.

552 Byzantine reconquest of Italy complete.

563 St. Columba founds mission in Iona.

568 Lombard Kingdom founded in Italy.

570 Birth of Mohammed.

577 Battle of Deorham: West Saxon advance resumed.

589 Reunion of China under Southern Ch'en dynasty.

590 Gregory the Great becomes Pope.

597 St. Augustine lands in Kent.

605 Grand Canal of China constructed.

618 T'ang Dynasty in China: their administrative system lasts in essentials for 1,300 years.

622 Hejira or flight from Mecca to Medina of Mohammed: beginning of Mohammedan era.

627 Battle of Nineveh: Persians crushed by Byzantines under Heraclius.

632 Death of Mohammed: all Arabia now Moslem. Accession of Abu Bakr, the first Caliph.

634 Battle of Heavenfield: Oswald becomes king of Northumbria, brings in Celtic Christianity.

638 Jerusalem captured by Moslems.

641 Battle of Mehawand: Persia conquered by Moslems.

643 Alexandria taken by Moslems.

645 Downfall of Soga clan in Japan, after establishing Buddhism: beginning of period of imitation of Chinese culture.

650 Slav occupation of Balkans now complete.

663 Synod of Whitby: Roman Christianity triumphs over Celtic Christianity in England.

685 Nectansmere: end of Northumbrian dominance in England.

698 Carthage taken by Moslems.

711 Tarik leads successful Moslem invasion of Spain.

718 Failure of second and greatest Moslem attack on Constantinople. Pelayo founds Christian kingdom of Asturias in Northern Spain.

726 Byzantine Emperor Leo III begins Iconoclast movement: opposed by Pope Gregory II, and an important cause of difference between Roman and Byzantine churches.

THE HOLY ROMAN EMPIRE AND THE TRIUMPH OF CHRISTIANITY IN EUROPE: NORSEMEN AND NORMANS

732 Tours: Moslem western advance halted by Charles Martel.

735 Death of Bede.

750 Beginning of Abbasid Caliphate (replacing Omayyads).

A.D.

751 Pepin King of the Franks: founds Carolingian dynasty. Ravenna taken by Lombards end of Byzantine power in the West.

754 Pepin promises central Italy to Pope: beginning of temporal power of the Papacy.

778 Roncesvalles: defeat and death of Roland.

786 Accession of Haroun-al-Rashid in Baghdad.

793 Sack of Lindisfarne: Viking attacks on Britain begin.

795 Death of Offa: end of Mercian dominance in England.

800 Coronation of Charlemagne as Holy Roman Emperor.

814 Death of Charlemagne: division of his empire.

825 Ellandun: Egbert defeats Mercians and Wessex becomes leading kingdom in England.

827 Moslem invasion of Sicily.

840 Moslems capture Bari and occupy much of Southern Italy.

843 Treaty of Verdun: final division of Carolingian Empire, and beginning of France and Germany as separate states.

844 Kenneth MacAlpin becomes king of Picts as well as Scots: origin of Scottish kingdom.

862 Rurik founds Viking state in Russia: first at Novgorod, later at Kiev.

866 Fujiwara period begins in Japan. Viking "Great Army" in England: Northumbria, East Anglia and Mercia subsequently overwhelmed.

868 Earliest dated printed book in China.

872 Harold Fairhair King of Norway.

874 Iceland settled by Norsemen.

885–6 Viking attack on Paris.

893 Simeon founds first Bulgar Empire in Balkans.

896 Arpad and the Magyars in Hungary.

899 Death of Alfred the Great.

900 Ghana at the height of its power in North West Africa.

910 Abbey of Cluny founded: monastic reforms spread from here.

911 Rolf (or Rollo) becomes ruler of Normandy.

912 Accession of Abderrahman III: the most splendid period of the Omayyad Caliphate of Cordova (d. 961).

928 Brandenburg taken from the Slavs by Henry the Fowler, first of the Saxon Holy Roman Emperors.

929 Death of Wenceslas, Christian King of Bohemia.

937 Battle of Brunanburh: crowning victory of Athelstan. West Saxon kings now masters of England.

955 Battle of Lechfeld: Magyars finally defeated by Otto the Great and settle in Hungary.

960 Beginning of Sung Dynasty in China.

965 Harold Bluetooth, king of Denmark, accepts Christianity.

966 Mieszko I, king of Poland, accepts Christianity.

968 Fatimids begin their rule in Egypt.

982 Discovery of Greenland by Norsemen.

987 Hugh Capet king of France: founder of Capetian dynasty.

988 Vladimir of Kiev accepts Christianity.

991 Battle of Maldon: defeat of Byrhtnoth of Essex by Vikings—renewed Viking raids on England.

993 Olof Skutkonung, king of Sweden, accepts Christianity.

1000 Leif Ericsson discovers North America.

1001 Coronation of St. Stephen of Hungary with crown sent by the Pope.

1002 Massacre of St. Brice's Day: attempt by Ethelred to exterminate Danes in England.

A.D.
1014 Battle of Clontarf: victory of Irish under Brian Boru over Vikings.

1016 Canute becomes king of England; builds short-lived Danish "empire."

1018 Byzantines under Basil II complete subjection of Bulgars.

1040 Attempts to implement Truce of God from about this time.

1046 Normans under Robert Guiscard in southern Italy.

1054 Beginning of Almoravid (Moslem) conquests in West Africa.

1060 Normans invade Sicily.

1066 Norman conquest of England under William I.

1069 Reforms of Wang An-Shih in China.

THE CRUSADES

1071 Manzikert: Seljuk Turks destroy Byzantine army and overrun Anatolia.

1073 Hildebrand (Gregory VII) becomes Pope. Church discipline and Papal authority enforced.

1075 Seljuk Turks capture Jerusalem.

1076 Kumbi, capital of Ghana, sacked by Almoravids: subsequent break-up of Ghana Empire.

1084 Carthusians founded by St. Bruno at Chartreuse.

1086 Compilation of Domesday Book.

1094 El Cid takes Valencia.

1095 Council of Clermont: Urban II preaches First Crusade.

1098 Cistercians founded by St. Robert at Cîteaux.

1099 First Crusade under Godfrey of Bouillon takes Jerusalem.

1100 Death of William Rufus in the New Forest. Baldwin I: Latin Kingdom of Jerusalem founded.

1106 Tinchebrai: Henry I of England acquires Normandy, captures his brother Robert.

1115 Abelard teaching at Paris. St. Bernard founds monastery at Clairvaux.

1119 Order of Knights Templars founded.

1120 Loss of the White Ship and heir to English throne.

1122 Concordat of Worms: Pope and Emperor compromise on the Investiture Controversy, but continue to quarrel over other matters (Guelfs and Ghibellines).

1135 Stephen takes English crown: civil wars with Matilda and anarchy ensue.

1143 Alfonso Henriques proclaimed first king of Portugal.

1144 Moslems take Christian stronghold of Edessa.

1148 Second Crusade fails to capture Damascus.

1150 Carmelites founded about this time by Berthold.

1152 Accession of Emperor Frederick Barbarossa.

1154 Henry of Anjou succeeds Stephen: first of Plantagenet kings of England.

1161 Explosives used in warfare in China.

1169 Strongbow invades Ireland: beginning of Anglo-Norman rule. Saladin ruling in Egypt.

1170 Murder of Thomas Becket in Canterbury cathedral.

1171 Spanish knightly Order of Santiago founded.

1176 Battle of Legnano: Frederick Barbarossa defeated by the Lombard League. Italian autonomy established.

1185 Kamakura Period in Japan: epoch of feudalism: until 1333.

1187 Hattin: destruction of Latin kingdom of Jerusalem by Saladin.

A.D.
1189 Third Crusade launched: leaders—Frederick Barbarossa, Philip Augustus of France, Richard Lionheart of England.

1191 Capture of Acre by Crusaders.

1192 End of Third Crusade without regaining Jerusalem. Richard I seized and held to ransom in Austria on return journey.

1198 Innocent III becomes Pope.

1202 Fourth Crusade, diverted by Venetians, takes Zara from Byzantines.

1204 Fourth Crusade captures Constantinople, founds Latin Empire. King John of England loses Normandy to France.

1206 Temujin proclaimed Gengiz Khan (Very Mighty King) of all the Mongols: soon controls all of Central Asia.

1208 Albigensian Crusade launched: the first against Christians.

1212 Battle of Las Navas de Tolosa: decisive victory of Spaniards over Moors. The Children's Crusade.

THE CULMINATION OF THE MIDDLE AGES

1215 Fourth Lateran Council: the authority of the mediaeval Church and Papacy at its zenith. Dominicans recognised by the Pope. Magna Carta extorted by barons from John.

1223 Franciscans recognised by the Pope.

1229 Emperor Frederick II, through diplomacy, recognised by Moslems as King of Jerusalem.

1230 Teutonic Knights established in Prussia.

1237 Golden Horde (Mongols) begin subjugation of Russia.

1241 Mongol incursions into Central Europe.

1250 St. Louis of France captured on his Crusade in Egypt. Mamelukes become rulers of Egypt. Mandingo king declares his independence of Ghana and embraces Islam.

1256 Conference of Baltic ports; the first form of the Hanseatic League.

1258 Provisions of Oxford: barons under Simon de Montfort force reforms on Henry III of England. Baghdad destroyed by Mongols.

1260 Kublai Khan ruling in China.

1264 Battle of Lewes: Montfort's party become rulers of England.

1265 Simon de Montfort's Parliament. Battle of Evesham: defeat and death of de Montfort.

1274 Death of Thomas Aquinas.

1281 Repulse of Mongol attack on Japan.

1282 Sicilian Vespers: rising of Sicilians against French ruler.

1284 Completion of Edward I of England's conquest of Wales.

1290 Expulsion of Jews from England. Death of Maid of Norway: Edward I begins attempts to rule Scotland.

1291 Fall of Acre: end of Crusading in Holy Land. Everlasting League of Uri: beginnings of Swiss Confederation.

1294 Death of Roger Bacon, the founder of experimental science. Death of Kublai Khan: unity of Mongol Empire now only nominal.

1295 " Model Parliament " of Edward I (anticipated in 1275).

1308 Death of Duns Scotus.

THE DECLINE OF THE MIDDLE AGES

1309 Papacy moves to Avignon: beginning of the Babylonish Captivity.

1312 Suppression of Templars by king of France and Pope.

1314 Battle of Bannockburn: victory of Robert Bruce secures Scottish independence.

1321 Death of Dante.

1325 Zenith of Mandingo Empire of Mali (North West Africa) under Mansa Musa; superseded at end of 15th century by Songhai empire.

1327 Deposition of Edward II; subsequently murdered.

A.D.

1336 Ashikaga Period in Japan: great feudal lords semi-independent of authority of Shogun.

1337 Death of Giotto.

1338 Beginning of Hundred Years' War between England and France.

1340 Battle of Sluys: English capture French fleet.

1344 Swabian League: weakness of Imperial authority in Germany obliges towns to form leagues for mutual protection.

1346 Battles of Crecy and Neville's Cross: spectacular English victories over French and Scots.

1347 Calais taken by Edward III of England. Cola di Rienzi attempts to reform government of Rome: killed 1354.

1348 Black Death reaches Europe (England 1349, Scotland 1350).

1351 Statute of Labourers: attempt by English Parliament to freeze wages.

1353 Statute of Praemunire: restraints placed on Papal intervention in England.

1354 Ottoman Turks make first settlement in Europe, at Gallipoli.

1355 Death of Stephen Dushan: collapse of Serbian Empire which he had built.

1356 Battle of Poitiers: capture of King John of France by Black Prince. "Golden Bull" regulates Imperial elections in such a way as to place power in the hands of the German princes: valid until 1806.

1358 The Jacquerie: rising of French peasants.

1360 Peace of Bretigny: Edward III makes great territorial gains in France.

1362 English becomes the official language in Parliament and the Law Courts.

1363 Timur (Tamerlane) begins his career of conquest in Asia.

1368 Ming Dynasty in China.

1370 Bertrand du Guesclin Constable of France: regains much territory from the English. Peace of Stralsund: Hansa in complete control of Baltic Sea.

1377 Pope returns to Rome: End of Babylonish Captivity.

1378 Disputed Papal Election: Beginning of Great Schism.

1380 Battle of Chioggia: decisive victory of Venice over Genoa. Battle of Kulikovo: Dmitri Donskoi of Moscow wins first major Russian victory over Golden Horde.

1381 Peasants' Revolt in England under Wat Tyler.

1384 Death of John Wyclif.

1385 Battle of Aljubarotta: Portugal safeguards independence from Castile.

1386 Battle of Sempach: Swiss safeguard independence from Habsburgs. Jagiello (Vladislav V) unites Lithuania and Poland.

1389 Battle of Kossovo: crushing defeat of Serbs and neighbouring nations by Turks.

1396 Battle of Nicopolis: "the last crusade" annihilated by Turks.

1397 Union of Kalmar: Denmark, Norway and Sweden united under one crown: dissolved 1448.

1398 Timur invades and pillages Northern India.

1399 Richard II deposed by Henry IV: first of the Lancastrian kings of England.

1400 Owen Glendower revolts in Wales. Death of Chaucer.

1401 De Haeretico Comburendo: the burning of heretics made legal in England.

1410 Battle of Tannenberg: Poles and Lithuanians break power of Teutonic Knights.

1415 Battle of Agincourt: great success of Henry V of England in France. Council of Constance ends Great Schism, burns John Hus.

1420 Treaty of Troyes: English claims to French throne recognised. Hussite Wars begin: Bohemian heretics defend themselves successfully

A.D.

1429 Relief of Orleans by Joan of Arc.

1431 Burning of Joan of Arc.

1433 Rounding of Cape Bojador: first great achievement in exploration ordered by Henry the Navigator.

1434 Cosimo dei Medici begins his family's control of Florence.

1435 Congress of Arras: Burgundians withdraw support from England, in favour of France.

1438 Albert I becomes Emperor—the first Habsburg Emperor.

1440 Death of Jan van Eyck.

1450 Rebellion of Jack Cade against government of Henry VI of England.

1453 Battle of Castillon: final English defeat and end of Hundred Years' War. Constantinople taken by Turks: end of Byzantine or Eastern Roman Empire.

RENAISSANCE, DISCOVERIES, "NEW MONARCHIES"

1454 First dated printing from movable types in Europe: Papal indulgence printed at Mainz.

1455 First battle of St. Albans: beginning of Wars of the Roses.

1458 Mathias Corvinus becomes king of Hungary. George of Podiebrad becomes king of Bohemia.

1461 Battle of Towton: Yorkist victory in a particularly bloody battle. Louis XI becomes king of France.

1467 Charles the Bold becomes Duke of Burgundy.

1469 Marriage of Ferdinand of Aragon with Isabella of Castile: union of the main kingdoms of Spain. Lorenzo the Magnificent becomes ruler of Florence.

1470 Warwick ("The Kingmaker") turns Lancastrian, dethrones Edward IV.

1471 Return of Edward IV: Lancastrians crushed at Barnet and Tewkesbury. Ivan III of Moscow takes Novgorod: Muscovy rising to supremacy in Russia.

1476 Caxton sets up his press at Westminster.

1477 Battle of Nancy: defeat and death of Charles the Bold: end of the greatness of Burgundy.

1479 Pazzi conspiracy against the Medici in Florence.

1481 Inquisition becomes active in Castile (1484 in Aragon).

1485 Battle of Bosworth Field: beginning of Tudor period in England.

1487 Lambert Simnel's rising fails.

1488 Bartholomew Diaz rounds Cape of Good Hope.

1491 Brittany acquired by King of France (by marriage).

1492 Rodrigo Borgia becomes Pope Alexander VI. Granada, last Moorish foothold in Western Europe, conquered by Spain. Christopher Columbus discovers the West Indies.

1493 Sonni Ali brings Songhai Empire to height of its prestige: Timbuktu renowned centre of literary culture.

1494 Italy invaded by French led by Charles VIII: beginning of Italian Wars and "modern" European diplomacy and international relations. Treaty of Tordesillas: Spain and Portugal agree to divide unexplored part of world; subsequently approved by Pope.

1496 Habsburg-Spanish marriages: foundation of later empires.

1497 Perkin Warbeck captured by Henry VII (hanged 1499). John Cabot discovers Newfoundland.

1498 Savonarola burned. Vasco da Gama at Calicut: the sea route to India found.

1499 Amerigo Vespucci charts part of the South American coast.

A.D.
1500 Brazil discovered by Pedro Cabral.

1503 Casa de Contratación established at Seville; beginnings of Spanish colonial government. Fall of Caesar Borgia.

1507 Affonso de Albuquerque becomes Viceroy of Portuguese Empire in the East.

1513 Accession of Pope Leo X, zenith of Renaissance Papacy. Machiavelli writes *The Prince*. Balboa discovers the Pacific (South Sea). Battle of Flodden: James IV of Scotland defeated and killed by English.

1514 Battle of Chaldiran: Turkish victory begins long series of wars between Turkish and Persian Empires.

REFORMATION, HABSBURG–VALOIS WARS

1515 Francis I becomes king of France: victory of Marignano ends legend of Swiss invincibility. Thomas Wolsey becomes Lord Chancellor of England and Cardinal.

1516 Algiers taken by Barbarossa; beginning of the Corsairs.

1517 Martin Luther nails up his Ninety-five Theses: beginning of the Reformation. Turks conquer Egypt.

1519 Charles V elected Holy Roman Emperor. Magellan begins first circumnavigation of the world. Death of Leonardo da Vinci.

1520 Suleiman the Magnificent becomes Sultan; Turkish power at its height. Field of Cloth of Gold; celebrated diplomatic meeting, spectacular but with no results.

1521 Mexico conquered by Hernando Cortes. Belgrade taken by the Turks. Diet of Worms; Luther commits himself irrevocably.

1522 Rhodes taken by the Turks; Knights of St. John move to Malta. Election of Adrian VI, last non-Italian Pope.

1523 Swedes expel Danish overlords, elect Gustavus Vasa King.

1524 Peasants' War in Germany (suppressed 1525).

1525 Battle of Pavia: defeat and capture of Francis I by Imperialists.

1526 Battle of Mohács: Turkish victory ends Hungarian independence. Battle of Panipat: Babar begins Moslem conquest of India, founds Mogul Empire.

1527 Sack of Rome by Imperialists. Italy under control of Charles V.

1529 Siege of Vienna by the Turks. Peace of Cambrai; pause in Habsburg–Valois struggle, end of serious French intervention in Italy. Diet of Speyer: origin of the name Protestant.

1532 Peru conquered by Francisco Pizarro.

1533 Ivan IV (the Terrible) becomes Czar. Marriage of Henry VIII and Catherine of Aragon declared null.

1534 Act of Supremacy: Henry VIII asserts control over English Church.

1535 Coverdale's English Bible printed. Execution of Thomas More and John Fisher.

1536 Execution of Anne Boleyn. Dissolution of smaller Monasteries by Henry VIII and Thomas Cromwell (remainder dissolved 1539). Pilgrimage of Grace: Northern rising because of religious grievances.

1538 Chibchas of Bogota conquered by Gonzalo de Quesada.

1540 Francisco de Coronado begins explorations in North America. Society of Jesus recognised by Pope.

1541 John Calvin regains authority in Geneva.

1542 First Portuguese reach Japan. New Laws of the Indies: first attempt to legislate for welfare of colonial natives, by Spanish government.

1543 Death of Copernicus.

1545 Opening of Council of Trent: the Counter-Reformation.

1547 Death of Henry VIII: Somerset Protector in the name of the boy king, Edward VI.

A.D.
1549 First English Book of Common Prayer. Kett's Rebellion in Norfolk, because of economic grievances.

1550 Deposition of Protector Somerset: Northumberland rules England.

1553 Lady Jane Grey proclaimed Queen by Northumberland on death of Edward VI: Mary I succeeds. Servetus burned by Calvin.

1555 Latimer and Ridley burned by Mary. Religious Peace of Augsburg: policy of *cuius regio, eius religio* accepted in Germany. Charles V begins his Abdications.

1556 Cranmer burned. Akbar becomes Mogul Emperor (d. 1605).

1557 Macao becomes permanent Portuguese port in China.

1558 Calais lost by English to French. Elizabeth I becomes Queen of England.

1559 Peace of Cateau-Cambrésis: end of Habsburg–Valois duel.

RELIGIOUS WARS

1561 Mary, Queen of Scots, returns to Scotland.

1562 First War of Religion in France: wars continue intermittently until 1598.

1563 Thirty-nine Articles define Elizabethan Church settlement.

1565 Malta beats off Turks.

1567 Deposition of Mary, Queen of Scots. Alva in the Netherlands: severe rule.

1568 Flight of Mary, Queen of Scots, to England: imprisonment. San Juan de Ulua: defeat of Hawkins, and end of his slave-trading voyages. Beginning of Anglo-Spanish maritime feud. Revolt of Moriscos of Granada (suppressed 1570).

1569 Rebellion of Northern Earls (Catholic) in England.

1570 Elizabeth I anathematised by Pope.

1571 Battle of Lepanto: spectacular defeat of Turkish sea-power by Don John of Austria. Bornu (or Kanem) in Central Sudan at its zenith under Idris III.

1572 Dutch "Sea Beggars" take Brill. Massacre of St. Bartholomew in France. Polish Crown elective again, after death of Sigismund II.

1576 Catholic League formed in France, led by Guise family.

1577 Drake begins voyage round world (returns 1580).

1578 Battle of Alcazar-Quivir: death of King Sebastian of Portugal. Parma re-establishes Spanish rule in Southern Netherlands.

1579 Union of Utrecht: seven northern provinces of Netherlands form what becomes Dutch Republic. Death of Grand Vizier Sokolli: decline of Turkish power begins.

1580 Philip II of Spain becomes king of Portugal.

1582 Gregorian Calendar (or New Style) introduced by Pope Gregory XIII.

1584 Assassination of William the Silent.

1585 Hidéyoshi Dictator of Japan: unification of the country. English intervention in Spanish–Dutch War.

1587 Execution of Mary, Queen of Scots. Drake "singes King of Spain's beard." Shah Abbas I (the Great) becomes ruler of Persia (d. 1629).

1588 Spanish Armada defeated.

1589 Death of Catherine de' Medici, Queen-Mother of France.

1591 Songhai Empire destroyed by troops from Morocco.

1593 Henry IV of France becomes Catholic.

1598 Edict of Nantes: French Protestants guaranteed liberty of worship. End of French Wars of Religion.

1600 English East India Company founded. Tokugawa Period begins in Japan (Ieyasu takes title of Shogun, 1603): lasts until 1868.

A.D.

1601 Rebellion and execution of Earl of Essex. Elizabethan Poor Law.

1602 Dutch East India Company founded.

1603 Irish revolts finally suppressed by Mountjoy. Accession of James VI of Scotland as James I of Britain: Union of English and Scottish Crowns.

1604 Hampton Court Conference: James I disappoints Puritans.

1605 Gunpowder Plot.

1607 Virginia colonised by London company: Jamestown founded.

1608 Quebec founded by Champlain.

1609 Twelve Years' Truce between Spain and United Provinces: Dutch independence in fact secured. Expulsion of Moriscos from Spain.

1610 Assassination of Henry IV of France.

1611 Plantation of Ulster with English and Scottish colonists. Authorised Version of the Bible in England.

1613 Michael Romanov becomes Czar: the first of the dynasty.

1614 Napier publishes his explanation of logarithms.

1616 Death of Shakespeare and Cervantes. Edict of Inquisition against Galileo's astronomy.

1618 "Defenestration of Prague": Bohemian assertion of independence begins Thirty Years' War.

1620 Pilgrim Fathers settle in New England.

1624 "Massacre of Amboina": English driven out of spice islands by Dutch. Richelieu becomes Chief Minister in France.

1628 Murder of Duke of Buckingham. Petition of Right by Commons to Charles I. Fall of La Rochelle: French Protestants lose political power. Harvey publishes his work on the circulation of blood.

1629 Charles I begins Personal Rule.

1630 Gustavus Adolphus of Sweden enters Thirty Years' War, turns tide against Imperialists.

1631 Sack of Magdeburg, one of the worst incidents of the Thirty Years' War.

1632 Battle of Lützen: death of Gustavus Adolphus.

1633 William Laud appointed Archbishop of Canterbury. Thomas Wentworth takes up his post as Lord Deputy of Ireland.

1634 Dismissal and murder of Imperialist general Wallenstein.

1635 John Hampden refuses to pay Ship Money.

1636 Japanese forbidden to go abroad.

1637 Russian pioneers reach shores of Pacific.

1638 Covenant widely signed in Scotland.

1639 First Bishops' War: Charles I comes to terms with Scots.

1640 Second Bishops' War: Charles I defeated by Scots. Long Parliament begins: abolition of Royal prerogatives. Great Elector (Frederick William) becomes ruler of Brandenburg. Revolt of Catalonia (finally suppressed 1659). Revolt of Portugal: Duke of Braganza proclaimed king.

1641 Japanese exclude all foreigners (except for small Dutch trading fleet). Massacre of Protestants in Ireland. Wentworth (Earl of Strafford) executed. Grand Remonstrance of Commons to Charles I.

1642 Charles I attempts to arrest the Five Members. Outbreak of English Civil War: first general engagement, Edgehill. Death of Richelieu.

1643 Mazarin becomes Chief Minister of France. Battle of Rocroi: French victory, end of Spanish reputation for invincibility. English Parliament agrees to Solemn League and Covenant, secures services of Scots army.

1644 Marston Moor: decisive battle of English Civil War. North lost to Charles I. Tippemuir: Montrose begins victorious Royalist campaign in Scotland. Ch'ing Dynasty (Manchu) in China.

1645 Formation of New Model Army. Naseby: main Royalist army crushed. Battle of Philiphaugh: Montrose's army destroyed.

1646 Charles I surrenders to Scots.

1647 Charles I handed over to Parliament. Charles I seized by Army. Charles I flees to Carisbrooke Castle.

1648 Second Civil War: New Model Army defeats Scots and Royalists. "Pride's Purge": Parliament refashioned by Army. Peace of Westphalia ends Thirty Years' War.

ASCENDANCY OF FRANCE

1649 Charles I executed. England governed as Commonwealth. Cromwell in Ireland. New Code of Laws in Russia completes establishment of serfdom.

1651 Battle of Worcester: Cromwell's final victory, now master of all Britain. First English Navigation Act. Hobbes' *Leviathan* published.

1652 Foundation of Cape Colony by Dutch under Van Riebeek. First Anglo-Dutch War begins (ends 1654).

1653 Cromwell dissolves Rump, becomes Protector.

1655 Major-Generals appointed to supervise districts of England. Jamaica seized by English.

1656 Grand Vizier Kiuprili: revival of Turkish government.

1658 Death of Cromwell.

1659 Peace of the Pyrenees: France replaces Spain as greatest power in Western Europe.

1660 Restoration of monarchy in Britain: Charles II. Royal Society founded.

1661 Death of Mazarin: Louis XIV now rules in person. "Clarendon Code"; beginning of persecution of Non-conformists in England.

1664 New York taken by English: Second Anglo-Dutch War ensues (ends 1667).

1665 Great Plague of London.

1666 Great Fire of London. Newton's discovery of law of gravitation.

1667 Dutch fleet in the Medway. War of Devolution begins: first of Louis XIV's aggressions.

1668 Portuguese Independence recognised by Spain.

1669 Death of Rembrandt.

1670 Secret Treaty of Dover between Charles II and Louis XIV. Revolt of peasants and Don Cossacks under Stenka Razin (suppressed 1671).

1672 Third Anglo-Dutch War begins (ends 1674). Murder of De Witt brothers: William of Orange becomes leader of Dutch against French invasion.

1673 Test Act deprives English Catholics and Non-conformists of public offices. Death of Molière.

1675 Battle of Fehrbellin: Swedes defeated by Great Elector; rise of Prussian military power.

1678 "Popish Plot" of Titus Oates utilised by Shaftesbury and the Whigs to bring pressure on Charles II.

1679 Bothwell Brig: suppression of Scottish Covenanters. Habeas Corpus Act passed.

1680 Chambers of Reunion: Louis XIV uses legal arguments to complete annexation of Alsace.

1681 Oxford Parliament: Charles II overcomes his opponents, begins to rule without Parliament.

1683 Rye House Plot. Siege of Vienna by the Turks: last major Turkish attack on Europe.

1685 Sedgemoor: Monmouth's rebellion crushed by James II. Revocation of Edict of Nantes: persecution of French Protestants by Louis XIV.

A.D.

1688 Seven Bishops protest against James II's policy of toleration, and are acquitted. William of Orange lands in England: flight of James II. "The Glorious Revolution."

1689 Derry relieved: failure of James II to subdue Irish Protestants. Killiecrankie: death of Dundee and collapse of Highland rising. Bill of Rights defines liberties established by "Glorious Revolution."

1690 Locke's *Two Treatises on Government* published. Beachy Head: French victory over Anglo-Dutch fleet. Boyne: defeat of James II by William III.

1691 Capitulation of Limerick: surrender of Irish supporters of James II on conditions which are not fulfilled.

1692 Massacre of Glencoe: Government's "lesson" to Highlanders. La Hogue: Anglo-Dutch fleet regains command of the sea.

1693 National Debt of England begun.

1694 Bank of England founded.

1695 Press licensing abandoned: freedom of the press in England.

1696 Peter the Great sole Czar.

1697 Peace of Ryswyck between Louis XIV and William III. Peter journeys "incognito" to the West.

1699 Treaty of Karlowitz: great Turkish concessions to Austrians. Death of Racine.

1700 Great Northern War, involving all Baltic powers, begins (ends 1721). Battle of Narva: Russians defeated by Charles XII of Sweden. Death of Charles II of Spain: under French influence Louis XIV's grandson Philip of Anjou named successor.

1701 War of the Spanish Succession begins. Hungarian revolt led by Francis Rakoczi against Austrians. Elector of Brandenburg receives title of King of Prussia. Act of Settlement establishes Protestant Hanoverian Succession in England.

1703 Methuen Treaty between England and Portugal. St. Petersburg founded.

1704 Gibraltar taken by Rooke. Blenheim: Marlborough prevents France from winning the war.

1706 Ramillies: Marlborough's second great victory. Turin: Eugene defeats French in Italy.

1707 Almanza: Anglo-Austrian forces in Spain defeated by French under Berwick. Act of Union: English and Scottish Parliaments united. Death of Aurungzib, last powerful Mogul.

1708 Oudenarde: Marlborough's third great victory.

1709 Pultava: Charles XII's invasion of Russia smashed by Peter the Great. Malplaquet: Marlborough's fourth great victory—at great cost in lives.

1710 Tory government in England.

1711 Dismissal of Marlborough.

1713 Peace of Utrecht: England makes advantageous peace with Louis XIV. Bourbon king of Spain grants Asiento (monopoly of Spanish American slave trade) to England.

1714 Peace of Rastatt between France and Austria. Death of Queen Anne: accession of George I. Beginning of Hanoverian Dynasty in Britain. Whig oligarchy rules.

1715 Jacobite Rising defeated at Preston and Sheriffmuir. Death of Louis XIV. France under Regent Orleans.

ENLIGHTENED DESPOTS: FIRST BRITISH EMPIRE

1716 Septennial Act: English Parliament prolongs its life from three to seven years.

1717 Belgrade taken by Austrians under Eugene.

1720 Collapse of Law's system of banking ("Mississippi Bubble") in France. "South Sea Bubble" in England.

A.D.

1721 Robert Walpole becomes first Prime Minister. Peace of Nystad: Sweden no longer a major power at end of Great Northern War. Russian gains.

1723 Death of Christopher Wren.

1727 First Indemnity Act for Non-conformists.

1729 Methodists begin at Oxford.

1730 Resignation from government of Townshend, who becomes agricultural pioneer.

1733 First Family Compact between Bourbon kings of France and Spain. Withdrawal of Walpole's Excise Bill. John Kay invents flying shuttle, first of the great textile inventions. Jethro Tell publishes *The Horse-Hoing Husbandry*, advocating new agricultural methods.

1738 Lorraine ceded to France.

1739 Nadir Shah with Persian army sacks Delhi, ruins Mogul power. War of Jenkins' Ear begins between Spain and Britain.

1740 Frederick II (the Great) becomes king of Prussia. Maria Theresa succeeds to Austrian dominions. Frederick siezes Silesia, begins War of the Austrian Succession.

1742 Fall of Walpole.

1743 Dettingen: George II, last British king to command his army in the field, defeats French.

1745 Fontenoy: Duke of Cumberland defeated by Marshal Saxe. Jacobite Rebellion under Prince Charles Edward: initial success, victory of Prestonpans, march to Derby.

1746 Culloden: Jacobites destroyed by Cumberland.

1748 Treaty of Aix-la-Chapelle: Frederick retains Silesia, elsewhere status quo.

1750 Death of J. S. Bach.

1751 First volume of the *Encyclopédie* published in France. Clive takes and holds Arcot: checks plans of Dupleix in Southern India. Chinese conquest of Tibet.

1752 Britain adopts New Style calendar.

1753 British Museum begun by government purchase of Sloane's collection.

1755 Lisbon earthquake. Braddock's defeat and death at the hands of French and Indians.

1756 Diplomatic Revolution (alliance of Austria with France) achieved by Kaunitz; Britain and Prussia perforce became allies. Seven Years' War begins. Minorca taken from British by French (Byng executed 1757). Black Hole of Calcutta: suffocation of many British prisoners.

1757 Pitt Secretary of State, main influence in British government. Rossbach: one of Frederick II's numerous victories against heavy odds. Plassey: Clive conquers Bengal.

1759 "Year of Victories" for Britain: Quebec, Minden, Lagos, Quiberon Bay. James Brindley designs Worsley–Manchester Canal: the beginning of this form of transport in Britain. Voltaire publishes *Candide*. Death of Handel.

1760 Wandewash: decisive defeat of French in India, by Coote.

1761 Panipat: Mahrattas heavily defeated by Afghans. Fall of Pitt.

1762 Catherine II (the Great) becomes Czarina. Rousseau's *Social Contract* and *Emile* published.

1763 Peace of Paris: British colonial gains, First British Empire at its height. Peace of Hubertusburg: Frederick II retains his gains. Pontiac's Conspiracy: failure of Red Indian attempt to destroy British power.

1764 John Wilkes expelled from Commons. James Hargreaves invents spinning jenny.

1766 Henry Cavendish proves hydrogen to be an element.

1768 Royal Academy of Arts founded.

1769 Richard Arkwright erects spinning mill (invention of water frame).

1770 Struensee comes to power in Denmark (executed 1772). "Boston Massacre." James Cook discovers New South Wales.

1772 First Partition of Poland between Russia, Prussia, and Austria.

A.D.

1773 Society of Jesus suppressed by Pope (restored 1814). Revolt led by Pugachov in Russia (suppressed 1775). "Boston Tea Party."

1774 Warren Hastings appointed first Governor-General of India. Treaty of Kutchuk Kainarji: great Turkish concessions to Russia. Karl Scheele discovers chlorine. Joseph Priestley's discovery of oxygen.

1775 Watt and Boulton in partnership at Soho Engineering Works, Birmingham. Lexington: first action in American War of Independence.

1776 American Declaration of Independence. Adam Smith's *Wealth of Nations* published.

1777 Saratoga: surrender of British army under Burgoyne to Americans.

1779 Beginning of great Franco-Spanish siege of Gibraltar (raised finally, 1783). Samuel Crompton invents spinning mule.

1780 Joseph II assumes sole power in Austria. Armed neutrality of maritime nations to restrain British interference with shipping.

1781 Joseph II introduces religious toleration, abolishes serfdom in Austria. Yorktown: surrender of British under Cornwallis to American and French forces.

1782 Battle of the Saints: Rodney's victory saves British West Indies.

1783 Treaty of Versailles: American independence recognised. Pitt the Younger becomes Prime Minister of Britain. First flights in hot-air (Montgolfier) and hydrogen (Charles) balloons.

1784 Death of Dr. Samuel Johnson.

1735 Edmund Cartwright invents the power loom.

1787 American Constitution drafted.

1788 Impeachment of Warren Hastings begins (ends 1795).

FRENCH REVOLUTION AND NAPOLEON

1789 Washington first President of U.S.A. French Revolution begins. Storming of the Bastille (July 14).

1790 Civil constitution of the Clergy in France.

1791 Flight of Louis XVI and Marie Antoinette to Varennes.

1792 Battle of Valmy: French Revolution saved from intervention of European kings. Denmark becomes first country to prohibit slave trade. France becomes a Republic.

1793 Louis XVI beheaded. Second partition of Poland.

1794 "Glorious First of June." Fall of Robespierre and end of Jacobin Republic. Negro revolt in Haiti led by Toussaint L'Ouverture.

1795 The Directory established. "Whiff of Grapeshot": Napoleon Bonaparte disperses Paris mob, Oct. 5. Batavian Republic set up by France.

1796 First Italian campaign of Bonaparte: victories of Lodi, Arcola.

1797 Treaty of Campo Formio: Bonaparte compels Austria to make peace. Britain left to fight France alone.

1798 Bonaparte goes to Egypt. Battle of the Nile. Vinegar Hill rebellion in Ireland suppressed.

1799 New coalition against France: Suvorov and Russians victorious in Italy. Bonaparte returns to France. *Coup d'état* of Brumaire, Nov. 9. Consulate set up.

1800 Parliamentary Union of Great Britain and Ireland.

1801 Treaty of Lunéville: Austria makes peace; great French gains in Germany.

1802 Peace of Amiens between Britain and France. *Charlotte Dundas*, first practical steamship, on Clyde.

1803 Insurrection in Ireland under Robert Emmet. Britain again at war with France.

A.D.

1804 Bonaparte becomes Emperor. Spain declares war against Great Britain. Serbian revolt against Turks under Kara George.

1805 Battle of Trafalgar, Nelson's great victory and death, Oct. 21. Battle of Austerlitz, Dec. 2.

1806 Death of Pitt, Jan. 23. Confederation of the Rhine: Napoleon's reorganisation of Germany, July 12. End of Holy Roman Empire, Aug. 6. Prussia overthrown at Jena. Napoleon declares Great Britain in a state of blockade—"Continental System."

1807 Slave trade abolished in British Empire. Treaty of Tilsit: with Alexander of Russia his friend, Napoleon controls all of Europe. Occupation of Portugal by French, to enforce Continental Blockade.

1808 Occupation of Spain by French. Spanish rising: guerrilla warfare. Peninsular War begins. Battle of Vimiero, Aug. 21.

1809 Battle of Corunna and death of Sir John Moore, Jan. 16. Attempted risings in Germany against Napoleon: Austria renews war. Treaty of Schönbruun, Oct. 14.

1810 Self-government established in Argentina: first South American state to become independent of Spain.

1811 Massacre of Mamelukes at Cairo. Luddite riots.

1812 Retreat from Moscow: destruction of Napoleon's Grand Army.

1813 War of Liberation starts in Germany. French army defeated by Wellington at Vitoria, June 21.

1814 Soult defeated by Wellington at Toulouse, April 10. Abdication of Napoleon, April 11; Louis XVIII king of France. Congress of Vienna (concluded June 1815) under guidance of Metternich. Resettlement of Europe, usually by restoration of kings. Germanic Confederation under Austrian supervision. Poland ruled by Czar. Kingdom of Netherlands to include Belgium.

THE OLD ORDER RESTORED

1815 Escape of Napoleon from Elba. Battle of Waterloo, June 18. Corn Law in Britain to safeguard agricultural interests by keeping up prices. Quadruple Alliance (Austria, Russia, Prussia, Britain) to maintain Vienna settlement and hold regular meetings ("Congress System") —frequently confused with Holy Alliance, which was simply a declaration of Christian principles. Napoleon sent to St. Helena, Oct. 16.

1818 Bernadotte made king of Sweden (Charles XIV), Feb. 6.

1819 Singapore founded by Stamford Raffles. Beginnings of Zollverein (Customs Union) in Germany under Prussian influence. Parliamentary reform meeting at Manchester dispersed by military ("Peterloo"), Aug. 16.

1820 Death of George III, Jan. 29.

1821 Death of Napoleon at St. Helena, May 5.

1822 Congress of Verona: congress system breaks down with refusal of Britain (Canning) to intervene against revolutions.

1823 "Monroe Doctrine" announced by U.S.A. President, Dec. 2.

1824 Repeal of Combination Acts in Britain which had forbidden Trades Unions. Charles X king of France.

1825 Independence of all Spanish American mainland now achieved. Nicholas I Czar of Russia. First railway, Stockton to Darlington, opened.

1826 First crossing of Atlantic under steam by Dutch ship *Curaçao*. Menai suspension bridge opened.

1827 Battle of Navarino, Turkish and Egyptian fleet destroyed. Death of Beethoven.

1828 Death of Chaka, great Zulu conqueror.

1829 Greece independent. Catholic Emancipation Act in Britain. Metropolitan Police established.

A.D.
1830 Death of George IV, June 26. Louis Philippe ousts Charles X. Belgium breaks away from Holland. Russian Poland revolts ineffectually.

1831 First Reform Bill introduced by Lord John Russell. Leopold of Saxe-Coburg becomes king of independent Belgium. British Association founded. Faraday discovers electromagnetic induction.

1832 Reform Bill passed, June 7. Walter Scott, Jeremy Bentham, and Goethe die. Electric telegraph invented by Morse.

1833 Beginning of "Oxford Movement" in English Church. First government grant made to English schools. First British Factory Act.

1834 Poor Law Amendment Act: tightening up of relief in Britain. "Tolpuddle Martyrs" victimised to discourage British working-class movement. Carlist wars begin in Spain.

1835 Municipal Reform Act revises British local government. The word "socialism" first used. "Tamworth Manifesto" of Peel defines aims of Conservative Party.

1836 People's Charter states programme of Chartists. Great Trek of Boers from British South African territory. Texas achieves independence of Mexico.

1837 Queen Victoria succeeds to the throne.

1838 National Gallery opened.

1839 First Afghan war begins. Chartist riots at Birmingham and Newport. Anti-Corn Law League founded. Aden annexed by Britain.

1840 Penny postage instituted. Queen Victoria marries Prince Albert of Saxe-Coburg-Gotha. "Opium War" with China begins. Union Act gives Canada responsible government. Last convicts landed in New South Wales.

1841 Hong Kong acquired by Britain.

1842 Chartists present second national petition and put themselves at the head of strikes.

1846 Repeal of the Corn Laws. Peel resigns.

1847 British Museum opened.

REVOLUTIONS AND NEW NATIONS

1848 Monster meeting of Chartists on Kennington Common, procession abandoned, Apr. 10. General revolutionary movement throughout the Continent. Louis Philippe abdicates: French Republic proclaimed. Swiss Federal Constitution established after defeat of Sonderbund (Catholic secession movement). Rising in Vienna: flight of Metternich, accession of Francis Joseph. Nationalist risings in Bohemia and Hungary. Frankfurt Parliament: attempt to unite Germany on liberal principles. Communist Manifesto produced by Marx and Engels. U.S.A. makes great territorial gains from Mexico. Gold discovered in California.

1849 Collapse of revolutionary movements. Rome republic besieged by French (June 3), defended by Garibaldi, holds out until July 2. Austrians take Venice, Aug. 22. Repeal of old Navigation Laws. Punjab annexed by Britain.

1850 Cavour becomes Prime Minister of Piedmont. Don Pacifico affair; privileges of British citizenship at their highest defended by Palmerston.

1851 Great Exhibition in Hyde Park. First satisfactory submarine telegraph cable between Dover and Calais laid. Gold discovered in Australia.

1852 Independence of Transvaal recognised by Britain. Napoleon III Emperor of the French.

1853 Perry lands in Japan: beginning of Western influence. Russia and Turkey at war.

1854 War declared against Russia by France and Britain. Allied armies land in Crimea, Sept. 14 (Alma, Siege of Sevastopol, Balaklava, Inkerman). Orange Free State set up.

1855 Sardinia joins Britain and France against Russia. Fall of Sevastopol and end of Crimean War. Alexander II Czar of Russia.

1856 Peace Treaty signed at Paris. Bessemer invents process for large-scale production of steel. Livingstone completes journey across Africa.

1857 Indian Mutiny. Relief of Lucknow. Canton captured by English and French.

1858 *Great Eastern* launched. Crown assumes government of India. Treaty of Aigun, by which China cedes Amur region to Russia.

1859 Darwin publishes *Origin of Species*. French support for Piedmont in war with Austria (Magenta, Solferino). Piedmont receives Lombardy. Harper's Ferry raid: John Brown hanged, Dec. 2.

1860 Garibaldi and the Thousand Redshirts in Sicily and Naples: most of Italy united to Piedmont. Vladivostok founded; Russia strongly established on N.W. Pacific.

1861 Abraham Lincoln takes office as Pres. of U.S. American Civil War commences with 11 states breaking away to form Southern Confederacy. Bull Run (July 21) Confederate success ends Federal hopes of easy victory. Victor Emmanuel proclaimed by first Italian Parliament as king of Italy. Emancipation of Serfs in Russia. Death of Prince Albert, Dec. 14.

1862 Bismarck becomes leading minister in Prussia. Garibaldi attempts to seize Rome but wounded at Aspromonte, Aug. 29. Cotton famine in Lancashire.

1863 Polish rising against Russia (suppressed 1864). French in Mexico. Battle of Gettysburg, July 1–3. Maximilian of Austria made emperor of Mexico.

1864 Cession of Schleswig-Holstein to Prussia and Austria. First Socialist International formed. Taiping rebellion in China ended. Federal army enters Atlanta, Sept. 2: General Sherman captures Savannah ("From Atlanta to the sea"), Dec. 22. Geneva Convention originated.

1865 Death of Cobden, Apr. 2. General Lee surrenders to Grant, Apr. 9. Lincoln assassinated, Apr. 14. Thirteenth Amendment to Constitution: slavery abolished in U.S. Death of Palmerston, Oct. 18. Lister introduces antiseptic surgery in Glasgow. Tashkent becomes centre of Russian expansion in Central Asia. Mendel experiments on heredity. William Booth founds Salvation Army.

1866 Austro-Prussian War over Schleswig-Holstein ("Seven Weeks War"). Prussian victory at Sadowa (July 3). Venice secured for Italy, who had, however, been defeated by Austrians at Custozza (June 24) and Lissa (July 20). Treaty of Prague, Aug. 23.

1867 North German Confederation founded. Emperor Maximilian of Mexico shot. Dominion of Canada established. Russia sells Alaska to America for $7 million. Garibaldi makes second attempt to seize Rome, but defeated by Pope with French support at Mentana, Nov. 3. Second Parliamentary Reform Bill passed (Disraeli "dished the Whigs").

1868 Shogunate abolished in Japan: Meiji period of rapid Westernisation under Imperial leadership begins. Ten Years' War (1868–78); struggle for Cuban independence from Spain. Disraeli succeeds Derby as Prime Minister but defeated in general election by Gladstone, Nov.

1869 General Grant, Pres. of U.S. Irish Church disestablished. Suez Canal formally opened.

1870 Napoleon III declares war against Prussia. French defeated at Woerth, Gravelotte, and Sedan. Paris beseiged. Rome and Papal states annexed to kingdom of Italy. Irish Land Act passed. Forster's Education Act puts elementary education within reach of all British children. Papal Infallibility announced.

1871 William I of Prussia proclaimed emperor of Germany at Versailles, Jan. 18. Paris capitulates, Jan. 28. Commune of Paris proclaimed, Mar. 28. Peace signed at Frankfurt-on-Main, May 10. Government troops enter Paris and

A.D.

crush Communards, May 28. Thiers President of the Republic, Aug. 31. Mont Cenis tunnel opened. Trade Unions in Britain legalised.

RIVAL IMPERIAL POWERS

1872 Ballot introduced in Britain. Death of Mazzini, Mar. 10.

1873 Death of Livingstone, May 4. Ashanti war.

1874 Disraeli succeeds Gladstone as Prime Minister.

1875 England purchases Khedive's shares in Suez Canal, Nov.

1876 Bulgarian massacres. Serbo-Turkish war. Bell invents the telephone. Custer defeated and killed in last large-scale Red Indian success. Porfirio Diaz in power in Mexico (until 1911).

1877 Victoria declared Empress of India. Transvaal annexed to British Empire. War between Russia and Turkey. Satsuma rebellion in Japan: final unsuccessful attempt to halt new ideas.

1878 Congress of Berlin: general Balkan settlement. Cyprus ceded to Britain. Second war with Afghanistan (ended 1880). Edison and Swan produce first successful incandescent electric light.

1879 Dual control (Britain and France) in Egypt. Zulu War. Gladstone's Midlothian Campaign. Tay Bridge destroyed, Dec. 28.

1880 Beaconsfield ministry succeeded by second Gladstone ministry. Transvaal declared a republic.

1881 British defeat at Majuba: independence of Transvaal recognised. France occupies Tunis. Gambetta becomes Prime Minister of France. Revolt of the Mahdi in the Sudan. Pasteur's famous immunisation experiment to show that inoculated animals can survive anthrax.

1882 Lord Frederick Cavendish, Irish Secretary, assassinated in Phoenix Park, Dublin, May 6. Triple Alliance (Germany, Austria, Italy) first formed. Alexandria bombarded, July 11. Cairo occupied by British troops, Sept. 14.

1883 National Insurance begun in Germany. Death of Wagner.

1884 Wolseley heads expedition to Khartoum to rescue Gordon. French establish complete protectorate in Indo-China. Evelyn Baring takes over administration of Egypt. Russians capture Merv Berlin Conference defines rights of European Powers in Africa. Third Parliamentary Reform Bill: practically all men in Britain now entitled to vote. Parsons invents his turbine. Fabian Society founded.

1885 Khartoum captured; Gordon slain, Jan. 26.

1886 Upper Burma annexed by Britain. Home Rule Bill defeated in Commons. All Indians in U.S.A. now in Reservations. Daimler produces his first motor car. Completion of Canadian Pacific Railway. Gold discovered in the Transvaal.

1887 Queen Victoria's Jubilee celebration, June 21.

1888 William II German Emperor. County Councils set up in Britain.

1889 Mayerling: tragic death of Prince Rudolf of Austria, Jan. 30. Flight of General Boulanger, after attempting to become master of France. Second Socialist International set up. Great London dock strike, Aug. 15–Sept. 16. Parnell Commission concludes sittings, Nov. 23 (129th day).

1890 Parnell ruined by divorce case: Irish politicians split. Sherman Anti-Trust Law: first attempt in U.S.A. to break cartels. Opening of Forth Bridge, Mar. 4. Bismarck resigns, Mar. 17, Caprivi succeeds. Heligoland ceded to Germany.

1891 The United States of Brazil formed.

1892 Panama Canal financial scandals in France.

1893 Home Rule Bill passes third reading in Commons, Sept. 1: Lords reject Bill, Sept. 8.

1894 Opening of Manchester Ship Canal, Jan. 1. Gladstone resigns, Mar. 3, Lord Rosebery succeeds. Armenian massacres by Turks: repeated at intervals for next quarter of century. Japan declares war against China. Dreyfus convicted of treason.

1895 Opening of Kiel canal, June 21. Rosebery resigns, June 22; Salisbury Ministry succeeds. Treaty of Shimonoseki: Japan gets Formosa, free hand in Korea. New Cuban revolution breaks out against Spanish. Marconi sends message over a mile by wireless. Röntgen discovers X-rays. Freud publishes his first work on psycho-analysis. Jameson Raid, Dec. 29.

1896 Jameson raiders defeated by Boers, Jan. 1. Adowa: Italian disaster at hands of Abyssinians, the first major defeat of a white colonising power by "natives."

1897 Cretan revolt leads to Greek–Turkish War. Hawaii annexed by U.S.A. Queen Victoria's Diamond Jubilee, June 22.

1898 Port Arthur ceded to Russia. Spanish–American War. *Maine*, U.S. warship, blown up in Havana harbour. Treaty of Paris, Dec. 10: Cuba freed, Puerto Rico and Guam ceded to U.S.A., Philippines surrendered for $20 million. Death of Gladstone, May 19. Battle of Omdurman, decisive defeat of Mahdists, Sept. 2. Empress of Austria assassinated, Sept. 10. The Curies discover Radium.

1899 Boer War begins, Oct. 10. Gold discovered in the Klondyke.

1900 Boers attack Ladysmith, Jan. 6. Battle of Spion Kop, Buller repulsed with severe losses, Jan. 24. Relief of Kimberley, Feb. 15. Ladysmith relieved, Feb. 28. Mafeking relieved May 17. Boxer outbreak in China, May. Annexation of Orange Free State, May 26. Roberts occupies Johannesburg, May 31. "Khaki Election." Annexation of the Transvaal, Oct. 25. Australian Commonwealth proclaimed, Dec. 30.

1901 Queen Victoria dies, Jan. 22. Trans-Siberian Railway opened for single-track traffic.

1902 Anglo-Japanese Alliance, Jan. 30. Death of Cecil Rhodes, Mar. 26. Treaty of Vereeniging ends Boer War, May 31.

1903 Congo scandal: celebrated case of misrule and exploitation. Royal family of Serbia assassinated, June 11. First controlled flight in heavier-than-air machine—Orville and Wilbur Wright at Kitty Hawk, U.S.A., Dec. 17.

1904 Russo-Japanese War begins, Feb. 8. Japanese victory at Yalu River, May 1. British forces under Younghusband reach Lhasa, Aug. 3. Treaty with Tibet signed at Lhasa, Sept. 7.

1905 Port Arthur falls to Japanese, Jan. 3. "Bloody Sunday" massacre at St. Petersburg, Jan. 22. Destruction of Russian fleet under Rozhdestvenski at Tsushima by Admiral Togo (May). Treaty of Portsmouth (U.S.A.) ends Russo-Japanese war. Separation of Church and State in France. Norway separates itself from Sweden.

1906 General strike in Russia. San Francisco destroyed by earthquake and fire, Apr. 18. Simplon tunnel opened for railway traffic, June 1. First Duma (Parliament with limited powers) in Russia. Liberal "landslide" majority in Britain: Labour M.P.s appear. Movement for Women's Suffrage becomes active in Britain. Algeciras Conference: Franco-German crisis resolved in favour of France. Death of Ibsen. Vitamins discovered by F. G. Hopkins.

1907 New Zealand becomes a dominion.

1908 Annexation of Congo by Belgium. Young Turk revolution. Annexation of Bosnia and Herzegovina by Austria: severe rebuff for Russia. Asquith becomes Prime Minister of Britain.

1909 Old Age Pensions in Britain. Peary reaches North Pole. Blériot makes first cross-Channel flight. House of Lords rejects Lloyd George's budget. Union of South Africa formed. Henry Ford concentrates on producing Model T chassis: beginnings of cheap motors.

A.D.

1910 King George V. Constitutional crisis in Britain over power of Lords: Liberals win two General Elections. Labour Exchanges established in Britain. Death of Tolstoy.

1911 Parliament Act: power of Lords decisively reduced. British M.P.s paid for first time. National Insurance in Britain. Great British rail strike. Second Morocco crisis between France and Germany settled by compromise. Tripoli taken from Turkey by Italy. Chinese Revolution. Amundsen reaches South Pole, Dec.14.

1912 China becomes a Republic under Sun Yat Sen. *Titanic* disaster off Cape Race, Apr. 14–15. Great British coal strike. Scott's last expedition. Outbreak of Balkan Wars.

1913 Treaty of Bucharest: most of Turkey-in-Europe divided among Balkan states.

FIRST WORLD WAR

1914 Archduke Francis Ferdinand assassinated at Sarajevo, June 28. Austria–Hungary declares war against Serbia, July 28. Germany declares war against Russia, Aug. 1. Germany declares war against France, Aug. 3. German invasion of Belgium: Great Britain declares war against Germany, Aug. 4. Great Britain declares war on Austria–Hungary, Aug 12. British Expeditionary Force concentrated before Mauberge, Aug. 20. Battle of Mons; Japan declared war on Germany, Aug. 23. Battle of the Marne, Sept. 5–9. Trench warfare began on Aisne salient, Sept. 16. Three British cruisers (*Aboukir*, *Hogue*, and *Cressy*) sunk by one U-boat, Sept. 22. First Battle of Ypres, Oct. 12–Nov. 11. Raiding of German cruiser *Emden* until destroyed, Nov. 9. Russian successes in Galicia, disasters in E. Prussia. Battle of Coronel: German cruisers *Scharnhorst* and *Gneisenau* sink British cruisers *Good Hope* and *Monmouth*, Nov. 1. Great Britain declares war against Turkey, Nov. 5. Destruction of German squadron off Falkland Is., Dec. 8. British protectorate over Egypt proclaimed, Dec. 17. First Zeppelin appeared over British coast, Dec. 29.

1915 Turkish army defeated in Caucasus, Jan 5. Great Britain declared blockade of Germany, Mar. 1. Battle of Neuve Chapelle, Mar. 10–13. Naval attack on Dardanelles called off, Mar. 22. First landing of British, Australian, New Zealand troops on Gallipoli Peninsula, Apr. 24. Second Battle of Ypres, Apr. 22–May 25: Germans first used gas. Sinking of *Lusitania*, May 4. Battle of Aubers Ridge, May 9–25. Italy declares war on Austria, May 22. British Coalition Government formed, May 26. Italian army crosses Isonzo, June 2. Zeppelin destroyed by R. A. J. Warneford, June 7. Second landing of Allied troops at Suvla Bay. Italy declares war on Turkey, Aug. 20. Turks defeated at Kut-el-Amara, Sept 28. Serbia conquered by Austria and Bulgaria, Nov. 28. French and British troops occupy Salonika, Dec. 13. British troops withdraw from Anzac and Suvla, Dec. 20.

1916 Evacuation of Gallipoli completed, Jan 8. Opening of Battle of Verdun, Feb. 21. Sinn Fein rising in Ireland, Apr. 24. First Daylight Saving Bill passed. Fall of Kut, Apr. 29. Battle of Jutland, May 31. Brusilov's offensive in Galicia begins, June 4. Kitchener drowned when *Hampshire* struck mine, June 5. Battle of the Somme, July 1–Nov. 13: British losses: 420,000. Italians capture Gorizia, Aug. 10. Hindenburg and Ludendorff chiefs of German staff, Aug. 27. Rumania declares war against Austria and Germany, Aug. 27. Tanks first used by British, Sept. 15. Lloyd George forms War Cabinet, Dec. 6. Joffre replaced by Nivelle, early Dec.

1917 Unrestricted submarine warfare begins, Feb. 1. British troops occupy Baghdad, Mar. 11. Revolution in Russia, Mar. 12. U.S.A. declares war on Germany, April 6. Battle of Arras, Apr. 9–14: Vimy Ridge taken by Canadians, Apr. 10. Pétain replaced Nivelle, May 15. Messines Ridge taken by British, June 7. First American contingents arrive in France, June 26. Allenby assumes Palestine command, June 29. Third Battle of Ypres opened, July 31. Russia proclaimed a Republic, Sept. 15. British victory on Passchendaele Ridge, Oct. 4. French victory on the Aisne, Oct. 23. Caporetto: Italians severely defeated by Austrians, Oct. 24. Balfour Declaration, Oct. 31. Bolshevik Revolution, Nov. 7 (Oct. 25 O.S.). Passchendaele captured by British, Nov. 6. Hindenburg Lines smashed on 10-mile front, Nov. 20. Fall of Jerusalem, Dec. 9. Russo-German armistice signed, Dec. 15.

1918 Treaty of Bresh-Litovsk, Mar. 3. German offensive against British opened on Somme, Mar. 21. Battle of Arras, Mar. 21–Apr. 4. Second German offensive against British, Apr. 9–25. British naval raid on Zeebrugge and Ostend, Apr. 23. Foch appointed C.-in-C. Allied armies, Apr. 14. Peace signed between Rumania and Central Powers, May 7. *Vindictive* sunk in Ostend harbour, May 9. Last German offensive against French, July 15. British, Canadians, and Australians attack in front of Amiens, Aug. 8. Allenby destroyed last Turkish army at Megiddo, Sept. 19. Bulgarians signed armistice, Sept. 29. General Allied offensive in West began, Sept. 26. Germans accepted Wilson's Fourteen Points, Oct. 23. Great Italian advance, Oct. 24. Turkey surrenders, Oct 30. Austria accepts imposed terms, Nov. 3. Popular government in Poland (Lubin), Nov. 7. Revolutionary movement begins in Germany, Nov. 8. Kaiser abdicates and escapes to Holland, Nov. 9. Armistice signed by German plenipotentiaries, Nov. 11.

THE TWENTIES AND THIRTIES

1919 Peace Conference in Paris, Jan. 18. First direct flight across Atlantic by Sir J. Alcock and Sir A. W. Brown, June 15. Interned German fleet scuttled at Scapa Flow, June 19. Treaty of Peace with Germany signed at Versailles, June 28. Treaty of St. Germain: break-up of Austrian Empire, Sept. 10.

1920 Peace Treaty ratified in Paris. First meeting of League of Nations, from which Germany, Austria, Russia, and Turkey are excluded, and at which the U.S.A. is not represented. Prohibition in U.S.A. Peace Treaty with Turkey signed at Sèvres: Ottoman Empire broken up, Aug. 10. Degrees first open to women at Oxford Univ., Oct. 14.

1921 Riots in Egypt, May 23. In complete disregard of the League of Nations, Greece makes war on Turkey. Heligoland fortresses demolished, Oct. 14. Irish Free State set up by Peace Treaty with Britain, Dec. 6.

1922 Four-Power Pacific Treaty ratified by U.S. Senate, Mar. 24. Heavy fighting in Dublin, the Four Courts blown up, July 2. Defeat of Greek armies by the Turks, Aug.–Sept. Mussolini's Fascist "March on Rome," Oct. 28. Great find of treasures in Tutankhamen's tomb, Nov. 29.

1923 French troops despatched to Ruhr, Jan. 11. Treaty of Lausanne, July 24. Earthquake in Japan, Tokio and Yokohama in ruins, Sept. 1. Rhine Republic proclaimed, Bavaria defies the Reich, Oct. 20. Turkish Republic proclaimed; Kemal Pasha, first President, Oct. 29.

1924 Lenin dies, Jan. 21. First Labour Ministry in Britain under MacDonald, Jan. 22; lasts 9 months. George II of Greece deposed and a Republic declared, Mar. 25. Dawes Plan accepted by London conference; Ruhr evacuation agreed to, Aug. 16.

1925 Hindenburg elected German President, Mar. 26. Treaty of Locarno signed in London, Dec. 1. Summer Time Act made permanent.

1926 Ibn Saud proclaimed king of the Hedjaz in Jeddah, Jan. 11. Evacuation of Cologne by British forces, Jan. 31. General strike in Britain.

1927 Canberra, the new capital of Australian Commonwealth, inaugurated, May 9. Lindbergh flies Atlantic alone, May 21.

1928 Earthquake in Greece, Corinth destroyed, Apr. 23. Capt. Kingsford-Smith flies the

A.D.

Pacific, June 9. General Nobile rescued by aeroplane from Arctic one month after disaster, June 24. Kellogg Pact accepted by Gt. Britain, July 18. German airship with 60 persons crosses Atlantic, Oct. 15. Women in Britain enfranchised.

1929 King Amanullah of Afghanistan abdicates, Jan. 14. Second Labour Ministry under MacDonald. Graf Zeppelin makes numerous successful inter-continental flights. Commander Byrd flies over South Pole, Nov. 30. American slump and Wall Street crash.

1930 *R.101* destroyed in France on first flight to India, 48 lives lost, Oct. 5—end of British interest in airships.

1931 Great floods in China. Resignation of Labour Government and formation of Coalition under MacDonald.

1932 Manchuria erected into Japanese puppet state of Manchukuo, Feb. 18. Sydney Harbour Bridge opened, Mar. 19. Ottawa Imperial Conference.

1933 Hitler appointed Chancellor by Hindenburg, Jan. 30, and step by step gains supreme control. German Reichstag set on fire, Feb. 27.

1934 Dollfuss, Austrian Chancellor, murdered by Austrian Nazis, July 25. Death of Hindenburg, Aug. 2. Hitler becomes Dictator.

1935 Saar plebiscite for return to Germany, Jan. 13. Baldwin succeeds MacDonald as Prime Minister, June 7. War begins between Italy and Abyssinia, Oct. 3. Ineffectual economic "sanctions" by League of Nations against Italy, Nov. 18.

1936 Accession of King Edward VIII, Jan. 20. Repudiation of Locarno Treaty by Germany, Mar. 7. Remilitarisation of Rhineland, Mar. 8. Italian troops occupy Addis Ababa, May 5. Civil War breaks out in Spain, July 18. King Edward VIII abdicates after a reign of 325 days, Dec. 10. The Duke of York succeeds his brother as King George VI, Dec. 12.

1937 Coalition Ministry under Chamberlain, May 28. Japanese begin attempted conquest of China—"China incident," July 7.

1938 Singapore naval base opened, Feb. 14. Austria annexed by Germany, Mar. 13. British navy mobilised, Sept. 28. Munich Agreement between Chamberlain, Daladier, Hitler, and Mussolini, Sept. 29.

1939

February 27 Great Britain recognises General Franco's Government.

March 16 Bohemia and Moravia annexed by Hitler and proclaimed a German Protectorate. 22 Memel ceded to Germany by Lithuania. 28 Anti-Polish press campaign begun by Germany.

April 1 Spanish War ends. 7 Italy seizes Albania. 14 First British talks with Russia. 27 Conscription introduced in Great Britain. 28 Hitler denounces Anglo-German Naval agreement and the Polish Non-Aggression Treaty.

May 12 Great Britain signs defensive agreement with Turkey. 22 Italy and Germany sign pact. 23 France and Turkey sign defensive agreement. 25 Anglo-Polish treaty signed in London.

July 10 Chamberlain re-affirms British pledge to Poland.

August 23 German-Soviet Pact signed by von Ribbentrop. 25 Japan breaks away from the Anti-Comintern Pact. 28 Holland mobilises. 31 British fleet mobilised.

SECOND WORLD WAR

September 1 Poland invaded by German forces. Great Britain and France mobilise. 1–4 Evacuation schemes put in motion in England and Wales: 1,200,000 persons moved. 2 Compulsory military service for all men in Britain aged 18 to 41. 3 War declared (11 a.m.) between Britain and Germany as from 5 p.m. 4 British liner *Athenia* sunk by submarine. R.A.F. raid the Kiel Canal entrance and bomb German warships. 6 First enemy air raid on Britain. 8 Russia mobilises. Russian troops on Polish border. 11 British troops on French soil. 17 Russian troops cross the Polish frontier along its entire length. Russian and German troops meet near Brest Litovsk. 27 Capitulation of Warsaw. 29 Nazi–Soviet pact signed in Moscow approving partition of Poland.

October 14 *Royal Oak* sunk in Scapa Flow with a loss of 810 lives.

November 8 Bomb explosion in the Bürgerbräukeller at Munich after Hitler's speech. Germans using magnetic mines. 29 Diplomatic relations between Russia and Finland severed. 30 Finland attacked by Russia.

December 11 Italy leaves the League of Nations. 13 Battle of the River Plate: engagement of German warship *Admiral Graf Spee* by H.M. cruisers *Exeter, Ajax,* and *Achilles.* 14 Rejection by Russia of the League of Nations' offer of mediation in the Russo-Finnish war. Russia expelled from the League of Nations. 18 *Admiral Graf Spee* scuttles herself in the entrance of Montevideo harbour.

1940

February 14 Finnish advanced posts captured by Russians. 16 299 British prisoners taken off the German Naval Auxiliary *Altmark* in Norwegian waters. 26 Finns lose the island fortress of Koivisto. Finns retreat from Petsamo.

March 12 British ships to be fitted with a protective device against magnetic mines. Finland concludes a peace treaty whereby she cedes to Russia the Karelian Isthmus, the town of Vipuri and a military base on Hango Peninsula.

April 9 Invasion of Denmark and Norway by Germany. 15 British troops arrive in Norway. 19 British soldiers land in the Faroes.

May 2 British troops withdrawn from Norway. 10 Holland, Belgium and Luxembourg invaded by German forces. Parachute troops landed near Rotterdam. British troops cross the Belgian border. British troops land in Iceland. Rotterdam bombed. 11 National Government formed under Churchill. 13 Queen Wilhelmina arrives in London. 14 Rotterdam captured. Holland ceases fighting. Allied troops land near Narvik. 17 Belgian Government moves to Ostend. 24 German forces enter Boulogne. 27 Belgian army capitulates on the order of King Leopold. British forces to be withdrawn from Flanders. Narvik captured by Allied forces. 29 Ostend, Ypres, Lille and other Belgian and French towns lost to the Germans.

June Evacuation of British army from Dunkirk (May 27–June 4): 299 British warships and 420 other vessels under constant attack evacuate 335,490 officers and men. 5 Hitler proclaims a war of total annihilation against his enemies. 8 German armoured forces penetrate French defences in the West near Rouen. 10 Italy declares war on Great Britain and France. 14 Paris captured by German forces. 15 Soviet troops occupy Lithuania, Latvia and Estonia. 22 French delegates accept terms for an Armistice. 25 Hostilities in France cease at 12.35 a.m.

July 1 Channel Islands occupied by Germany. 3 French naval squadron at Oran immobilised. 10 Battle of Britain began.

August 19 British withdrew from British Somaliland. 25 British began night bombing of Germany.

September 6 King Carol of Rumania abdicates in favour of his son Michael. 7 London sustains severe damage in the largest aerial attack since war commenced. 15 Battle of Britain ends with British victory: German aeroplanes destroyed, 1,733; R.A.F. losses, 915. 23 Japanese troops enter Indo-China.

October 7 German troops enter Rumania. 28 Greece rejects an Italian ultimatum.

November 1 Greeks repel Italian attacks. 5 H.M.S. *Jervis Bay* lost defending Atlantic convoy from German warship *Admiral Scheer.* 11 Italian fleet at Taranto crippled by Fleet Air Arm. 14 Coventry heavily attacked, the Cathedral destroyed. 22 Albanian town of Koritza captured by the Greeks.

December 2 Bristol heavily bombed. 11 Sidi Barrani captured by British forces: beginning

A.D.

of Wavell's destruction of Italian forces in Cyrenaica. 29 City of London severely burned by incendiary bombs: Guildhall and eight Wren Churches destroyed.

1941

January 5 Bardia captured. 22 Tobruk captured by Australian troops.

February 7 Benghazi captured. 26 Mogadishu, capital of Italian Somaliland, occupied by Imperial troops. German mechanised troops in Libya.

March 4 British raid Lofoten Islands. 11 U.S. Lease and Lend Bill signed by Roosevelt. 27 Keren—main battle in British conquest of Abyssinia and Somaliland. 28 Cape Matapan: Italian fleet routed by British. 30 Rommel opens attack in N. Africa.

April 4 Addis Ababa entered by Imperial troops. 6 Greece and Yugoslavia invaded by German troops. 8 Massawa capitulates. 11 Belgrade occupied by German forces. 13 Bardia given up by British. Tobruk holds out. 24 Empire forces withdrawing from Greece. 27 Athens captured by the Germans.

May 2 Evacuation from Greece completed. 10 Rudolf Hess descends by parachute in Scotland. 20 Crete invaded by German air-borne troops. 24 H.M.S. *Hood* sunk. 27 German battleship *Bismarck* sunk; British forces withdraw from Crete.

June 2 Clothes rationing commences. 4 William II (ex-Kaiser of Germany) dies. 18 Treaty of friendship between Turkey and Germany signed. 22 Germany attacks Russia. 24 Russia loses Brest Litovsk.

July 3 Palmyra (Syria) surrenders to Allied forces. 7 U.S. forces arrive in Iceland. 9 General Dentz, the French High Commissioner in Syria, asks for Armistice terms. 25 Fighting round Smolensk.

August 25 British and Russian troops enter Persia. 27 The Dnepropetrovsk dam blown up by the Russians.

September 18 Crimea cut off from mainland. 19 Kiev entered by Germans.

October 6 German attack on Moscow. 16 Soviet Government leaves Moscow. Odessa occupied by German and Rumanian troops. 19 Taganrog on Sea of Azov captured by Germans. 26 Kharkov captured by the Germans.

November 14 *Ark Royal* sunk. 18 Libyan battle opens: Eighth Army's first offensive. 23 Bardia and Fort Capuzzo captured by British. 24 H.M.S. *Dunedin* torpedoed. 25 H.M.S. *Barham* sunk. 30 Russians re-take Rostov.

December 1 Points rationing scheme in force in Britain. 4 German attack on Moscow halted. 6 Japanese attack on Pearl Harbour. 8 Japanese forces land in Malaya. 9 British forces in Tobruk relieved. 10 H.M.S. *Repulse* and *Prince of Wales* sunk off Malaya by Japanese. Philippines invaded by Japanese. 26 Hongkong surrenders to Japanese.

1942

January 2 Manila and Cavite taken by Japanese. 23 Japanese forces land in New Guinea and the Solomon Islands.

February 9 Soap rationed. 12 Escape through English Channel of German ships *Scharnhorst*, *Gneisenau*, and *Prinz Eugen*. 15 Singapore surrenders to Japanese. 27 Battle of Java Seas.

March 9 Surrender of Java to Japanese.

April 15 George Cross awarded to the island of Malta.

May 4–8 Battle of Coral Sea. 7 Madagascar invaded by British forces. 7 U.S. forces sink 11 Japanese warships off the Solomon Islands. 30 Over 1,000 bombers raid Cologne. Canterbury bombed.

June 3–7 Midway Island: U.S. naval victory turns tide in Pacific. 20 Tobruk captured by the Germans.

July 16 R.A.F. make first daylight raid on the Ruhr.

August 6 Germans advancing towards the Caucasus. 10 American forces land in the Solomon Islands. 11 Malta convoy action (loss of H.M.S. *Eagle*, *Manchester*, *Cairo*, and one destroyer). 19 Raid on Dieppe. 23–25 Battle of Solomons.

September 6 German progress halted outside Stalingrad.

October 23 El Alamein: Allied offensive opens in Egypt.

November 4 Rommel's army in full retreat. 5 Red Army holding firm at Stalingrad. Cessation of hostilities in Madagascar. 7 Allied invasion of N. Africa. 27 German forces enter Toulon. French Fleet scuttled.

December 24 Admiral Darlan assassinated.

1943

January 6 German armies in the Caucasus and the Don elbow in retreat. 18 Leningrad siege raised after sixteen months' investment. 23 Tripoli occupied by the Eighth Army. 27 American bombers make their first attack on Germany. 31 Remnants of the German army outside Stalingrad surrender.

February 9 Guadalcanal Island cleared of Japanese troops. 16 Kharkov retaken by the Russians.

March 1–3 Battle of Bismarck Sea. 23 8th Army penetrates the Mareth Line.

May 7 Tunis and Bizerta captured by Allies. 12 All organised German resistance in Tunisia ceases. 16 Dams in the Ruhr breached by the R.A.F. 22 Moscow dissolves the Comintern.

June 3 French Committee for National Liberation formed in Algiers.

July 10 Allied invasion of Sicily. 25 Mussolini overthrown. 28 Fascist Party in Italy dissolved.

August 17 Sicily in Allied hands.

September 3 Italian mainland invaded. 7 Italy surrenders. 9 British and American troops land near Naples. 10 Rome seized by the Germans. 14 Salamaua captured from the Japanese. 23 *Tirpitz* severely damaged (sunk Nov. 12, 1944). 25 Smolensk taken by the Russians.

October 1 Naples taken. 25 Russians capture Dnepropetrovsk and Dneprodzerzhinck.

November 6 Kiev taken by the Russians. 26 Second Battle of Solomons. 28 Churchill, Roosevelt, and Stalin meet in Teheran.

December 2 Men between 18 and 25 to be directed to the mining industry by ballot in Britain. 26 Sinking of German battleship *Scharnhorst*.

1944

January 22 Allied landings at Anzio. 28 Argentina breaks with the Axis Powers.

February 1 American forces land on the Marshall Islands. 2 Russians penetrate Estonia.

March 15 Cassino (Italy) destroyed by Allied bombers.

May 9 Sevastopol captured by Russians. 18 Capture of Cassino and Abbey by Allies. 19 50 Allied officers shot after escaping from a German prison camp. 30 Battle for Rome commences.

June 4 Allied forces enter Rome. King of Italy signs decree transferring his powers to Prince Umberto, his son. 6 *D-Day*: invasion of Europe (over 4,000 ships in invasion fleet). 7 Defeat of Japanese thrust at India, outside Imphal. 9 Heavy fighting near Caen. 12 First V-1 falls on England. 18 Cherbourg peninsula cut by the Americans. Russians break through the Mannerheim Line.

July 3 Minsk captured by Russians. 9 Caen captured by Allies. 20 "Bomb plot" on Hitler's life. 21 Guam captured by Americans.

August 1 Uprising in Warsaw. 4 Myitkyina falls to Allied forces. 15 Allied forces land in southern France. 23 Paris liberated. Marseilles taken. Rumania surrenders. 25 Rumania declares war on Germany.

September 3 Allies in Belgium. 4 Antwerp and Brussels taken by Allies. Holland entered. Finland "ceases fire." 6 Bulgaria asks for an armistice. 7 Boulogne entered by Allies. Bulgaria declares war on Germany. 8 First V-2 falls on England. 11 Allied forces fighting on

A.D.

Reich territory. 17 Allied air-borne troops land near Arnhem. 22 First Battle of Philippines.

October 3 Warsaw rising crushed by the Germans. 5 British troops land on the mainland of Greece. 14 Athens occupied by Allies. 15 Hungary asks for armistice terms. 20 Aachen captured by the Americans. 25 Battle of Leyte Gulf: end of Japanese sea-power. 28 Second Battle of Philippines.

December 6 Civil war breaks out in Athens. 16 German forces counter-attack in the Ardennes: last German offensive in the West. 26 Budapest encircled by Russians.

1945

January 5 Organized fighting in Athens ceases. 11 U.S. forces land on Island of Luzon. 17 Warsaw captured by the Russians. 21 Russian troops in Silesia. 23 Burma road to China reopened.

February 4 Yalta conference. 14 Bombing of Dresden. 19 Americans land on Iwojima Island.

March 6 Cologne captured by Allies.

April 1 U.S. Invasion of Okinawa. 5 Russian Government denounces the Soviet-Japan neutrality pact. Japanese Cabinet resigns. 11 Russian Army enters Vienna after 7-day battle. 12 Death of President Roosevelt. 25 Berlin surrounded by Russian troops. 27 Russians and Americans link up in Germany. 28 Mussolini and his mistress shot by Italian partisans. 30 Hitler killed himself and his mistress.

May 2 German armies in Italy surrender. Berlin captured by the Russians. 3 Rangoon captured by British. 4 German forces in N.W. Germany, Holland and Denmark surrender. 8 End of World War II against Germany officially declared to be one minute past midnight (Tuesday). 28 Naval air attacks on Japan.

June 26 United Nations Charter signed at San Francisco.

July 5 Polish Government in Warsaw recognised by Allies. 26 Labour Party remarkably successful in General Election.

August 6 Atomic bomb first used against Japan: Hiroshima laid waste. 8 Russia declares war against Japan. 9 Russia advances into Manchuria. Nagasaki target for atomic bomb No. 2. 14 Japan surrenders unconditionally to the Allies. 17 Lend-Lease terminated.

September 2 Victory over Japan celebrated: end of Second World War.

"COLD WAR": AFRO-ASIAN INDEPENDENCE

October 9 U.S.A. to keep secret of manufacture of atomic bomb. 15 Laval executed.

November 20 Trial of major war criminals opens at Nuremberg.

1946

February 1 Mr. Trygve Lie elected Secretary-General of UNO.

April 19 League of Nations formally wound up.

June 5 Italy votes for Republic. 30 United States atom bomb tests at Bikini.

July 13 United States House of Representatives approves loan to Britain. 22 Bread rationing in Britain. British H.Q. in Jerusalem blown up. 24 Underwater atom bomb test at Bikini.

August 1 Peace Conference opens in Paris.

September 6 United Nations F.A.O. considers establishment of World Food Board.

October 16 Nuremberg sentences on Nazis carried out. Goering commits suicide. 23 General Assembly of the United Nations opens in New York.

November 10 Communists head poll in French General Elections.

December 2 Agreement signed for economic fusion of British and American zones in Germany.

A.D.

1947

January 1 British coal industry nationalised. 14 M. Vincent-Auriol elected first President of Fourth Republic.

March 15 Floods in England worst recorded. 24 Netherlands Government and Indonesian Cabinet sign agreement in Batavia for a United States of Indonesia.

April 1 School leaving age raised to 15 in Great Britain.

June 5 Inauguration of "Marshall Aid".

August 3 Dutch military action in Indonesia ends. 15 India and Pakistan assume Dominion Status. Viscount Mountbatten appointed Governor-General of India and Mr. Jinnah Governor-General of Pakistan. 29 Palestine Committee agrees British Mandate should end, majority report recommends partition.

September 22 First Atlantic automatic flight by U.S. pilotless aircraft.

October 6 Cominform, new international Communist organization, set up in Belgrade.

November 20 Marriage of Princess Elizabeth. 29 Palestine Committee of U.N. Assembly votes in favour of partition of Palestine into Jewish and Arab States.

December 15 Breakdown of 4-Power Conference on Germany. 30 King Michael of Rumania abdicates; Rumania becomes a People's Republic.

1948

January 1 British Railways nationalised. 4 Burma becomes independent Republic. 30 Mahatma Gandhi assassinated in New Delhi.

February 1 New Malayan federal constitution comes into force. 4 Ceylon Independence Act. 25 New Czechoslovak Government formed under Communist leadership.

March 10 Death of Jan Masaryk.

April 1 British electricity industry nationalised. 5 First European Aid shipments sail from America. 16 O.E.E.C. established.

May 3 Mr. Rajagopalachari appointed Gov.-Gen. of India in succession to Earl Mountbatten. 14 British Mandate for Palestine ended at midnight. Jews proclaim new State of Israel.

June 28 Yugoslavia expelled from Cominform; "Titoism" denounced.

July 1 "Berlin Airlift": American, British and French zones of Berlin supplied by air. 23 Malayan Communist party outlawed. 29 Bread rationing in Great Britain ends.

August 15 Republic of Korea proclaimed.

September 3 Death of Dr. Benes. 11 Death of Mohammed Ali Jinnah. 17 Count Bernadotte, U.N. Mediator for Palestine, assassinated.

October 30 Chinese Communist forces capture Mukden.

November 3 Mr. Truman elected U.S. President. 14 Birth of a son to Princess Elizabeth.

December 21 Republic of Ireland Bill signed in Dublin.

1949

March 15 Clothes rationing ends in Great Britain. 31 Russia protests against Atlantic Pact.

April 1 Newfoundland becomes part of Canada.

May 1 Gas Industry nationalised. 3 Ten-power conference in London establishes Council of Europe. 12 Berlin blockade lifted.

August 24 North Atlantic Treaty comes into force.

September 12 Professor Theodor Heuss elected first President of West German Republic. 21 General Mao Tse-Tung proclaims People's Republic of China.

October 2 Russia recognises newly-established Chinese People's Republic. 11 Herr Wilhelm Pieck elected first President of East German Republic.

December 8 Chinese Nationalist Government leaves mainland and sets up H.Q. in Formosa. 27 United States of Indonesia come into being.

1950

January 6 Britain recognizes Communist Government of China; 24 Dr. Rajendra Prasad elected

A.D.
first President of Indian Republic; 26 New Constitution of Indian Republic comes into force.

February 14 30-year treaty of alliance between Russia and China signed in Moscow; 23 Labour Party wins General Election with narrow majority.

March 5 Lord Boyd Orr warns world that communism spreads where hunger prevails; 22 First of U.S. super-fortresses arrives in Norfolk.

April 1 Italy takes over from Britain administration of Somaliland; 13 First shipment of military aid to France under N.A. Pact unloaded at Cherbourg.

May 1 New Chinese marriage law abolishes polygamy and child marriages and gives both sexes equal rights; 19 Points rationing ends in Britain after 8 years; 25 Middle East Tripartite Declaration by Britain, France, and U.S.A.; 26 Petrol rationing ends in Britain.

June 25 N. Korean troops advance into S. Korea; Security Council calls for cease fire; 27 Pres. Truman orders U.S. air, and sea forces to support S. Korea and protect Formosa; U.N. Commission in Korea proposes neutral mediator; military assistance to S. Korea endorsed by Security Council; 30 Pres. Truman authorizes use of American ground troops in Korea.

July 2 American troops land in S. Korea; 8 Gen. MacArthur designated C.-in-C. of U.N. forces in Korea.

August 1 Security Council meets under chairmanship of M. Malik, the Soviet delegate; 7 American forces in Korea open offensive and halt drive on Pusan; 15 Princess Elizabeth gives birth to a daughter; severe earthquake in Assam; 17 independence Day in Indonesia.

September 6 British troops in action in Korea; 9 Soap rationing ends in Britain.

October 9 U.N. forces across the 38th parallel in strength; 19 Sir Stafford Cripps retires from public life on account of illness; Pyongyang, N. Korean capital, captured by U.N. forces; 21 Princess Anne Elizabeth Alice Louise christened; 26 New Chamber of House of Commons opened at Westminster; 29 King Gustav V of Sweden dies.

November 2 Death of George Bernard Shaw aged 94; 6 Chinese forces from Manchuria reported fighting in Korea.

December 3 Mr. Attlee flies to Washington for talks with Pres. Truman; 4 Pyongyang occupied by Chinese; 19 Gen. Eisenhower appointed Supreme Commander of West European Defence Forces set up by Atlantic Powers; 25 Stone of Scone stolen from Westminster Abbey.

1951

January 30 U.N. Assembly rejects resolution of 12 Asian and Arab nations calling for 7-nation conference for peaceful settlement of Korean question; 31 Decree confiscating property of Alfred Krupp cancelled.

February 15 Vesting date for Iron and Steel.

April 11 Gen. MacArthur relieved of all his commands by Pres. Truman and replaced by Lt.-Gen. Ridgway; 13 Coronation Stone returned to Westminster Abbey.

May 2 Persian oil industry nationalized; Germany admitted to Council of Europe; 3 H.M. the King opens Festival of Britain from steps of St. Paul's.

June 23 M. Malik, Russian delegate to the U.N., appeals for settlement of Korean war.

July 1 Colombo plan comes into force; 9 State of war between Britain and Germany officially ended; 10 Armistice negotiations open at Kaesong; 17 King Leopold abdicates in favour of his son Baudouin, who becomes fifth King of the Belgians; 20 King Abdullah of Jordan assassinated.

September 1 Tripartite Security Treaty between U.S.A., Australia, and New Zealand signed in San Francisco; 8 Japanese Peace Treaty—to which Russia, China, and India are not parties—signed at San Francisco; Security Pact between Japan and U.S.A., providing for retention of American forces in Japan, also signed; 23 H.M. the King undergoes successful operation; 30 Festival of Britain ends.

October 8 Princess Elizabeth and Duke of Edinburgh leave for Canadian tour; 15 Egyptian Parliament passes unanimously Bills abrogating Anglo-Egyptian treaty of 1936 and 1899 Sudan Condominion Agreement; 16 Assassination of Liaquat Ali Khan; 25 General Election won by Conservatives with small majority.

November 5 Mr. Attlee receives the Order of Merit.

December 17 London foreign-exchange market reopens after 12 years; 24 Libya becomes independent state; 31 I.R.O. closes down.

1952

January 2 Mutual Security Agency replaces Economic Co-operation Administration; 31 Princess Elizabeth and Duke of Edinburgh leave London on first stage of Commonwealth tour.

February 6 King George VI died at Sandringham aged 56; 7 Queen Elizabeth II and the Duke of Edinburgh arrive home by air from Kenya; 15 Funeral of King George VI at Windsor; 21 Identity cards abolished.

March 20 South African Supreme Court rules invalid Dr. Malan's Act which places Cape coloured voters on separate electoral register.

April 11 H.M. the Queen declares that she wishes her children and descendants to bear the name of Windsor; 21 Death of Sir Stafford Cripps in Switzerland; 28 Japan regains status as sovereign and independent power.

May 5 H.M. the Queen takes up residence at Buckingham Palace; 27 Treaty setting up European Defence Community signed in Paris.

June 23 Power plants along Yalu River attacked by U.S. aircraft in biggest raid of Korean war.

July 7 American ship *United States* wins Atlantic Blue Riband; 19 Fifteenth Olympic Games held in Helsinki; 23 Military *coup d'état* takes place in Cairo.

August 1 Ratification of Bonn Agreement, by which W. Germany again becomes independent nation, and Treaty of Paris, which sets up the European Defence Community, approved by Government against Labour opposition; 16 Severe thunderstorms in Somerset and N. Devon cause rivers to flood; W. Lyn changes course bringing devastation to Lynmouth; 26 Passive resistance campaign against racial laws in S. Africa gains momentum.

September 2 Sir William Slim appointed Gov.-Gen. of Australia (from 1953); 8 New Egyptian Cabinet appoints Gen. Neguib military Gov.-Gen. of Egypt and approves land reforms.

October 3 Britain's first atomic weapon exploded in Monte Bello Islands, off N.W. Australia; 5 Tea derationed and decontrolled; 20 State of emergency declared in Kenya as a result of Mau Mau activities.

November 1 Reported explosion of U.S. hydrogen bomb at Eniwetok atoll in mid-Pacific; 4 Gen. Eisenhower, Republican Candidate, wins sweeping victory in American Presidential election.

December 29 Fish recently caught off Madagascar confirmed as species of the prehistoric Cœlacanth.

1953

January 20 Inauguration of General Eisenhower as 34th President of the United States; 31 Violent N.E. gales combined with surging high tides caused extensive flooding with loss of life along coasts of eastern England, the Netherlands, and Belgium.

February 4 Sweet rationing ended; 23 War-time deserters in Britain granted amnesty.

March 6 Marshal Stalin died, aged 74; 24 Death of Queen Mary at Marlborough House, aged 85; 31 Mr. Dag Hammarskjöld elected U.N. Sec.-Gen. in succession to Mr. Trygve Lie.

April 15 Dr. Malan's National Party again returned to power in S. Africa with increased

A.D.

majority; 24 Mr. Churchill created a Knight of the Garter by the Queen.

May 4 Duke of Edinburgh received his pilot's "wings"; 29 E. P. Hillary and Sherpa Tenzing of the Everest Expedition led by Colonel John Hunt reached summit of Everest (29,002 ft.).

June 2 Coronation of H.M. Elizabeth II in Westminster Abbey amid scenes of magnificent pageantry; ceremony televised; 26 Republic of Egypt accorded *de facto* recognition by Britain.

July 4 German–Austrian Expedition reached summit of Nanga Parbat in the Himalayas; 13 De-nationalisation of British steel industry; 14 Royal Assent given to Central African Federation Bill; 27 Korean Armistice signed at Panmunjom.

August 9–12 Disastrous earthquakes in Greek Ionian Islands; 12 Explosion of Russian hydrogen bomb reported.

September 17 Bank rate reduced from 4 to 3½ per cent; 23 Royal Commission on Capital Punishment recommended that juries should decide whether death sentence or life imprisonment should be imposed on prisoners found guilty of murder, and that the M'Naghten Rules on insanity should be abrogated or amended; 26 Sugar rationing ended after nearly 14 years; 30 Professor Piccard in his bathyscaphe dived 10,000 ft. off Italian coast.

October 15 Sir Winston Churchill awarded 1953 Nobel Prize for Literature.

November 11 Great bell at Notre Dame rung by electricity for first time; 21 Piltdown skull, discovered in Sussex in 1911, found by anthropologists to be partial hoax; 23 The Queen and Duke of Edinburgh left in stratocruiser *Canopus* on first stage of 6-months' tour of Commonwealth.

December 1 Agreement signed for laying first transatlantic telephone cable; 23 M. René Coty elected Pres. of France at the 13th ballot; L. P. Beria, former chief of Soviet Secret Police, and six associates sentenced to death and shot; 25 The Queen gave her Christmas broadcast from Auckland; 31 Mildest December for 20 years, and before that for over 200 years.

1954

January 9 Self-government began in the Sudan; 12 M. Le Trouquer (Socialist) elected President of French National Assembly on retirement of M. Herriot; 16 M. René Coty became President of France in succession to M. Vincent Auriol; 31 Intense cold covered most of Europe.

February 3 The Queen and the Duke of Edinburgh arrived in Australia; First Parliament of newly formed Federation of Rhodesia and Nyasaland opened in Salisbury; 5 Britain's first "breeder" pile in operation at Harwell.

March 1 American hydrogen bomb exploded at Bikini; 22 London gold market reopened after 15 years.

April 1 The Queen and the Duke of Edinburgh left Australia; 3 Oxford won 100th Boat Race; 21 Russia joined UNESCO; 26 Conference on Far East opened in Palais des Nations, Geneva, Mr. Chou En-lai representing China; Russia joined I.L.O.

May 6 Roger Bannister ran the mile in under 4 min., the first man in the world to do so; 7 Fortress of Dien Bien Phu fell to Viet-Minh after siege of 8 weeks and final battle of 20 hours; 11 Bank rate reduced from 3½ to 3 per cent; 15 The Queen and the Duke of Edinburgh returned from their six-months' tour of the Commonwealth; 18 Liverpool Cotton Exchange re-opened

June 1 Television licence fee raised from £2 to £3 a year; 2 Mr. John A. Costello (Fine Gael) elected Prime Minister of Ireland; 17 Indo-Chinese crisis brought M. Mendès-France to power in France; 22 First all-African Cabinet in British Africa appointed in the Gold Coast; 27 First electric power station using atomic energy began working in Soviet Union; 30 Eclipse of the sun.

July 3 All food rationing ended in Britain; 8 Mr. Nehru opened the world's longest canal (Bhakra–Nangal hydro-electric project); 27 Agreement reached in Cairo for withdrawal of British troops from Suez Canal Zone; 31 K2 (Mount Godwin Austen), second highest peak in the world, climbed by Italian team led by Prof. Ardito Desio of Milan Univ.

August 5 Persian oil dispute settled; 11 Cessation of hostilities in Indo-China after 8 years of fighting.

September 14 Sheffield–Manchester electrified railway opened.

October 14 Mr. Anthony Eden created a Knight of the Garter by the Queen; 19 Anglo-Egyptian Suez Canal Agreement.

November 1 French settlements in India passed under Indian control; 22 Death of Andrei Vyshinsky; 30 Sir Winston Churchill celebrated his 80th birthday and was presented by both Houses of Parliament with a portrait of himself by Graham Sutherland.

1955

January 27 Bank rate increased from 3 to 3½ per cent; 31 Princess Margaret left for tour of W. Indies.

February 8 Marshal Bulganin succeeded Mr. Malenkov as chairman of the Soviet Council of Ministers; 15 Plans to build 12 atomic power stations in Britain during next 10 years announced; 17 Britain to proceed with manufacture of hydrogen bombs; 24 Bank rate raised to 4½ per cent and restrictions on hire purchase announced; Dr. Albert Schweitzer appointed honorary member of the Order of Merit; Turco–Iraqi pact signed at Baghdad (Britain, Pakistan, and Persia acceded later).

April 5 Sir Winston Churchill resigned as Prime Minister; 6 Sir Anthony Eden succeeded as Prime Minister; 18 Afro-Asian conference (29 nations) opened at Bandung; Death of Dr. Albert Einstein; 29 Signor Gronchi elected President of Italy.

May 5 Ratification of London and Paris agreements completed; Germany attained full sovereignty and Western European Union came into being; 26 British general election resulted in Conservative majority of 59.

June 15 U.S. and Britain agreed to co-operate on atomic energy; 16 Revolt against the Perón government in Argentina.

July 9 Leading world scientists issued appeal for renunciation of war because of possible effects of hydrogen bomb; 18 Four-Power conference opened in Geneva (Pres. Eisenhower, Sir Anthony Eden, M. Faure, Marshal Bulganin), the first meeting between heads of Government since Potsdam, 1945; 27 Austrian State Treaty came into force.

August 8 International conference on peaceful uses of atomic energy opened in Geneva (1200 scientists from 72 countries attended).

September 16 Universal Copyright convention came into force, bringing U.S. into agreement with European countries; 19 General Perón resigned after rebels threatened to bombard Buenos Aires; 22 Independent television service began.

October 2 City of London became a "smokeless zone"; 12 British and Soviet warships exchanged courtesy visits; 20 Syria and Egypt signed mutual defence treaty; 23 Referendum on Saar European Statute gave victory to pro-German parties.

November 5 Vienna State Opera House re-opened; 23 *Hamlet* played on Russian stage by British company, the first since Tsarist times.

December 7 Mr. Attlee announced his retirement and was created an earl; 12 Completion of 830-mile pipeline through Urals, crossing 6 rivers; 14 Mr. Hugh Gaitskell elected leader of the Parl. Labour Party; 18 Anglo–American offer of financial assistance to Egypt in building Aswan High Dam; 24 In Christmas broadcast the Pope spoke of need to suspend nuclear test explosions.

1956

January 1 Sudan proclaimed an independent republic; 27 The Queen and the Duke of Edin-

A.D.

burgh left by air for 3 weeks' tour of Nigeria; 200th anniversary of birth of Mozart celebrated; Terrorist activity in Cyprus increasing.

February 1 Britain had coldest day since 1895; **13** Referendum in Malta resulted in vote in favour of integration with Britain; **16** House of Commons rejected by majority of 31 Government motion to retain death penalty; Bank rate increased from 4½ to 5½ per cent. (highest since 1932); **23** Remarkable sunflare caused increased cosmic radiation and long-wave radio disturbances; **25** M. Khrushchev in speech to Congress of Russian Communist Party denounced Stalin.

March 2 King Hussein of Jordan discharged Lieut.-Gen. J. B. Glubb; **5** Telephone weather forecast began; **9** Archbishop Makarios with leaders of Enosis movement in Cyprus deported to the Seychelles; **23** The Queen laid foundation stone of new Coventry Cathedral; Pakistan proclaimed an Islamic Republic within the Commonwealth.

April 6 Earl Attlee created Knight of the Garter; **11** Five-day week for Civil Servants announced; **18** Cease-fire between Israel and Egypt came into force; **29** French occupation of Indo-China ended after 80 years.

May 23 First atomic power station in Britain started working at Calder Hall; **24** 2,500th anniversary of the death of Buddha celebrated in India; **31** May was the sunniest month at Kew since 1922 and the driest since 1896.

June 3 Third-class travel abolished on British Railways to conform to continental practice; **13** Last British troops left Suez; **24** Col. Nasser elected Pres. of Egypt.

July 20 Britain joined U.S.A. in withdrawing offer to help Egypt finance Aswan High Dam; **26** Pres. Nasser announced nationalisation of Suez Canal Company.

August 30 French troops arrived in Cyprus.

September 25 Newly-laid submarine telephone cable linking Britain and America opened to public service.

October 3 Bolshoi Ballet danced at Covent Garden; **15** Duke of Edinburgh left on world tour; **16** Prime Minister left with For. Sec. for Paris meeting; **17** The Queen opened Calder Hall, the world's first nuclear power station for commercial use; **19–21** New liberalised policy adopted by Central Committee of Polish United Workers' Party; M. Gomulka elected first secretary; **23** Insurrection broke out in Budapest and spread throughout country; **28** Pres. Eisenhower called upon Israel not to "endanger the peace"; **29** Israeli forces invaded Egypt and after 5 days' fighting had control of Sinai peninsula, heavy fighting at Abu Aweigila; **30** Britain and France issued 12-hour ultimatum to Israel and Egypt to cease fighting; Britain and France vetoed US resolution in Security Council calling upon Israel to withdraw behind armistice line; **31** Anglo-French offensive launched against military targets in Egypt.

November 2 UN Gen. Assembly called for immediate cease fire in Egypt; **4** Canadian resolution calling for international UN force for Middle East adopted; Soviet forces launched attack on Budapest to crush uprising; **5** Anglo-French airborne troops landed at Port Said; **6** Seaborne troops landed at Port Said; Pres. Eisenhower re-elected President with Congress controlled by Democrats; Anglo-French forces ceased fire at midnight; **7** Egypt accepted cease fire on UN conditions; **15** UN Emergency Force left Naples for Suez; **16** Suez Canal blocked by 49 ships; **17** First refugees from Hungary arrived in Britain; **22** Duke of Edinburgh opened 16th Olympic Games in Melbourne; **23** Sir Anthony Eden flew to Jamaica for rest cure; **24** UN for third time called upon Britain, France, and Israel to withdraw troops from Egypt.

December 5 140 people arrested in S. Africa for alleged treason; Anglo-French forces began to leave Port Said; **19** Lord Radcliffe's proposals for a constitution for Cyprus published; **29** Suez Canal clearing operation by UN salvage fleet began.

A.D.

1957

January 1 Anglo-Egyptian treaty of 1954 abrogated by Pres. Nasser as from October 31, 1956; Saar became tenth *Land* of German Federal Republic; Road Traffic Act came into force; **5** Eisenhower Doctrine for Middle East announced; **9** Resignation of Sir Anthony Eden as Prime Minister; **10** Mr. Harold Macmillan appointed Prime Minister; **16** Sadlers Wells Ballet group combined to form The Royal Ballet; Death of Signor Toscanini; **20** Mr. Gomulka's National Unity Front overwhelmingly returned in Polish general election; India's first atomic reactor, *Apsara*, inaugurated; **31** Trans-Iranian oil pipeline from Abadan to Teheran (600 m.) completed.

February 7 Bank Rate reduced from 5½ to 5 per cent; **15** Mr. Gromyko replaced Mr. Shepilov as Soviet Foreign Minister; **16** The Queen flew to Portugal on State visit and joined Duke of Edinburgh there who had just completed World tour; **22** Duke of Edinburgh granted title of Prince of the United Kingdom; **26** Indian resolution adopted by UN for "peaceful, democratic, and just solution" of Cyprus problem.

March 1 Mass protest in Tokio against nuclear weapon tests in Pacific; **5** Fianna Fail party under Mr. de Valera secured absolute majority in general election; **6** Ghana celebrated independence; Israeli withdrawal from Sinai completed; **11** Warning by WHO of genetic effects of radiation; **13** Anglo-Jordanian treaty of 1948 ended; **21** Homicide Act in force (death penalty retained only for five categories of "capital murder"); **25** European Common Market and Euratom treaties signed by France, Germany, Italy, and Benelux countries.

April 3 British Labour Party called for abolition of H-bomb tests; **4** No further call-ups for National Service after 1960; **8** The Queen and Prince Philip arrived in France on State visit; **9** Suez Canal cleared and opened to all shipping; **11** Agreement signed in London granting full internal self-government to Singapore from Jan. 1, 1958; **17** Archbishop Makarios arrived in Athens from exile; During the month appeals were made by the Pope, Dr. Schweitzer and Mr. Nehru for the banning of nuclear tests and weapons.

May 14 Petrol rationing (imposed 17.12.56) ended; **15** First British H-bomb exploded in Central Pacific near Christmas I.; **16** M. Spaak succeeded Lord Ismay as NATO Sec. Gen.; **18** The Queen and Prince Philip left for State visit to Denmark; **20** Death of Dr. Gilbert Murray.

June 1 New Copyright Act came into force; First drawing of Premium Bond prizes; **17** Historic decisions taken by US Supreme Court on matters relating to civil liberties; **19** Completion of British H-bomb tests in Pacific; **30** The IGY opened at midnight.

July 1 Women voted for the first time in Egypt's first general election since revolution of 1952; **17** Electricity Bill enacted appointing new Central Electricity Generating Board and Electricity Council in place of Central Electricity Authority; **18** President Mao Tse-tung's famous "Let 100 flowers blossom and 100 schools of thought contend" speech published; **25** Tunisia declared a republic; **31** Federation of Malaya Independence Act received Royal Assent.

August 1 Sir Christopher Hinton appointed chairman of new C.E.G.B., responsible for new nuclear power stations; **31** Royal Charter granted to Tangier by King of Morocco.

September 6 Disarmament discussions in London ended without agreement; **15** German general election (Dr. Adenauer re-elected Chancellor Oct. 22); **19** Bank Rate raised from 5 to 7 per cent.; **20** Death of Jean Sibelius, the Finnish composer; **30** Network Three introduced by B.B.C.

October 4 First earth satellite launched by Russia (180 lb. sphere, 23 in. diameter); **10** U.S.A. abolished fingerprinting for foreign visitors staying less than a year; **11** Largest radio tele-

A.D.
scope in world went into operation at Jodrell Bank for Manchester University; **14** The Queen opened Canadian Parliament in Ottawa; New road–rail double-decker bridge over Yangtse, one of largest in world, opened to traffic; **17** Endorsement of cheques no longer necessary save when negotiated.

November 3 Second earth satellite weighing half a ton launched into space by Russia with dog on board; **16** Russia announced construction of "scientific city" of 12 research institutes in Siberia; **20** Britain's first export order for nuclear power station for Northern Italy announced.

December 1 Latin 26-letter alphabet to be adopted in China; **4** Ninety people killed in railway accident in fog at Lewisham; **6** Attempt to launch earth satellite in the U.S.A. failed; *Sputnik I* completed its thousandth circuit of the Earth; **25** The Queen's Christmas broadcast televised for the first time; **31** The *Sputniks* were still circling the Earth, the first being expected to fall in the first days of January.

1958

January 1 Treaties establishing EEC (Common Market) and EAEC (Euratom) came into force; Metric system of weights and measures adopted throughout Japan; **3** Inauguration of West Indian Federation; Sir Edmund Hillary and New Zealand party reached South Pole; **4** *Sputnik I* disintegrated after completing 1,367 circuits of the Earth and travelling 43 million miles; **6** First non-stop flight across Antarctica by single-engine British aircraft (1,600 miles in 10 hr. 57 min.); Mr. Thorneycroft resigned from Government after disagreement in Cabinet over pruning Budget estimates; **7** Mr. Macmillan left for six-week tour of Commonwealth; **8** Summit talks proposed by Marshal Bulganin and Notes sent to 19 States; **13** Over 9,000 scientists from 44 countries petition UN Sec. Gen. to end nuclear weapons tests; **20** Dr. Vivian Fuchs, leader of Commonwealth expedition, reached South Pole; **24** Announcement that Harwell scientists working with ZETA had passed first milestone on road towards power from nuclear fusion; **28** Abolition of licensed prostitution in Italy; **31** First American earth satellite *Explorer I* (30·8 lb.) successfully launched.

February 1 Union of Egypt and Syria in the United Arab Republic; **5** Continuation of Antarctic research for at least 5 years after end of IGY announced; **8** French aircraft bombed Tunisian frontier village of Sakhiet; **14** Merger of Iraq and Jordan under name of Arab Federation; **19** Worst colliery disaster in Indian history in West Bengal; **25** Restoration plans for Stonehenge announced; Campaign for Nuclear Disarmament launched under presidency of Lord Russell.

March 2 IGY Commonwealth Trans-Antarctic Expedition, led by Dr. Vivian Fuchs, completed first crossing of Antarctic (2,200 miles in 99 days); **8** Federal union between UAR and Yemen established; **14** Birth of Prince Albert of Monaco; Small test satellite, *Beta 1958*, successfully launched by US Navy; **20** Bank rate reduced from 7 to 6 per cent; **21** Opening of London planetarium, the first of its kind in Britain; **26** Third US earth satellite, *Explorer III*, successfully launched; **27** M. Khrushchev elected Prime Minister in succession to M. Bulganin; **31** Russian resolution to suspend nuclear tests; other powers invited to follow suit.

April 1 Abolition of legalised prostitution in Japan; **4** Campaign for Nuclear Disarmament organised 50-mile protest march from London to Atomic Weapons Research Establishment at Aldermaston, Berkshire; **14** *Sputnik II* disintegrated over Caribbean, having completed 2,370 circuits of the Earth and travelled 62 million miles; **17** Nationalist Party of S. Africa returned with increased majority; Sir Grantley Adams elected first Prime Minister of the new West Indian Federation; **22** Princess Margaret opened the new Federal Parliament in Trinidad.

A.D.
May 1 Intense radiation belt in outer space discovered by US *Explorer* earth satellite; **10** Anti-government disturbances in Lebanon; **13** Military and colonist insurrection in Algeria; President of Italy paid state visit to Britain; **15** *Sputnik III* launched under IGY programme; New college to be built at Cambridge University (Churchill College); **22** Further reduction in Bank Rate to 5½ per cent.; **24** Nuclear reactor at Dounreay began working; **29** General de Gaulle accepted invitation to form a "Government of national safety."

June 1 General de Gaulle became Prime Minister of France; Clean Air Act banning emission of dark smoke came into force; **9** Gatwick Airport opened by the Queen; **19** Further cut in Bank Rate from 5½ to 5 per cent.; New British plan for Cyprus announced; **20** London bus strike ended after 7 weeks; **21** Greek Government rejected British plan for Cyprus; **23** Ghana to be declared a republic.

July 1 Conference of scientists, including Russian delegation, met at Geneva to discuss ways of detecting nuclear tests; **14** Iraq monarchy overthrown, King Faisal assassinated; establishment of Republic announced; **15** US marines landed in Lebanon; **17** British troops flown to Amman in response to King Hussein's appeal; **24** First life barons and baronesses under Life Peerages Act named; **26** H.M. the Queen created her son, Charles, Prince of Wales; **31** British Prime Minister sent appeal to all Cypriots to end violence.

August 1 British Government recognised Republic of Iraq; **5** U.S. nuclear submarine *Nautilus* surfaced after having passed under North Pole; **7** Litter Act came into force in Britain; **14** Bank Rate reduced from 5 to 4½ per cent.; **17** First attempt by America to launch moon rocket failed; Britain to resume nuclear tests on Christmas Island; **23** Bombardment by Chinese of Quemoy (Formosa Strait); **29** More American warships join Seventh Fleet in Formosa Strait.

September 1 International conference on peaceful uses of atomic energy opened in Geneva; **7** Britain successfully fired its first ballistic rocket (Black Knight) from Woomera; **15** Ambassadors of America and China met in Warsaw for discussions on Formosa crisis; **16** Relaxations in hire-purchase; **29** Referendum resulted in overwhelming victory for General de Gaulle; Lord Goddard retired as Lord Chief Justice; succeeded by Lord Justice Parker; Gen. Sir Francis Festing succeeded Field-Marshal Sir Gerald Templer as Chief of the Imperial General Staff.

October 1 India began change to metric system; **2** French Guinea proclaimed Republic of Guinea after overwhelming vote for independence in French referendum; **8** Martial law in Pakistan; **9** Death of Pope Pius XII at age of 82; **11** The London weeklies *John Bull* and *Illustrated* merged; US *Pioneer* space-rocket successfully launched (but failed to reach moon); **21** First women peers introduced to House of Lords; **28** State opening of Parliament and Queen's Speech televised; Cardinal Roncalli, Patriarch of Venice, elected as Pope John XXIII at age of 76; **31** Conference opened in Geneva (Russia, Britain, and the United States) on suspension of nuclear tests.

November 20 Bank Rate reduced from 4½ to 4 per cent.; **21** Work started on Forth road bridge, the largest suspension bridge in Europe; **27** Russian plan for withdrawal of troops and demilitarised free Berlin.

December 8 Last of four nuclear reactors at Calder Hall brought into operation; **17** Chinese leader, Mao Tse-tung, to resign as chairman of Republic but to retain party office; **18** US 4-ton missile fired into orbit; Empire Day to be known in future as Commonwealth Day; **21** General de Gaulle elected President of France; **27** Partial convertibility between £ and $ announced; UAR and Russia signed agreement on Russian co-operation in Aswan high dam project; **28** General de Gaulle announced devaluation of the franc; **31** IGY officially came to an end.

A.D.

1959

January 1 Batista Government in Cuba overthrown by revolutionary movement under Dr. Fidel Castro; **2** Russia launched planet round the sun (*Lunik I*); **3** Alaska became 49th state of American Union; **4** Mr. Mikoyan, Soviet Dep. Prime Min., arrived in Washington on 16-day visit; Rioting in Leopoldville; **7** Britain recognised new Cuban Government; **8** Gen. de Gaulle installed as first Pres. of Fifth French Republic; **10** Russian proposal for conference of 28 nations to draw up German Peace Treaty; **25** Oecumenical Council, the first since 1870, convened by Pope John XXIII.

February 1 Votes for women rejected by Swiss national poll; **9** New research reactor to be built at Windscale, Cumberland; **11** M. Vincent Auriol resigned from French Socialist Party; **21** Mr. Macmillan arrived in Moscow on official visit; **23** Archbishop Makarios returned to Cyprus after 3-year exile; Cyprus to become a republic with Greek Pres. and Turkish Vice-Pres.; **26** State of emergency declared in Southern Rhodesia; **27** Riots in Malta dockyard due to dismissal of workers.

March 3 American *Pioneer IV* went into planetary orbit round sun; State of emergency declared in Nyasaland; British scientists isolated basic molecule of penicillin; **17** Uprising in Lhasa against Chinese rule; Flight of Dalai Lama to India; **24** Iraq withdrew from Baghdad Pact.

April 5 Panchen Lama arrived in Lhasa to take over local government of Tibet; **8** Chair of Criminology founded at Cambridge; **14–16** Worst flood disaster of century in S. America; **23** British heart specialists in Moscow to demonstrate heart surgery; **27** Liu Shao-ch'i succeeded Mao Tse-tung as Chairman (President) of Chinese People's Republic.

May 1 Opening of Rajendra Bridge (6,074 ft.) over Ganges at Hathidah (Bihar); **2** First Scottish nuclear power-station opened at Chapelcross; **15** Jodrell Bank radioed message to United States via moon; **28** Opening of Mermaid Theatre in City of London; **30** Auckland Harbour Bridge officially opened; **31** World's population (2,800 millions) increasing at rate of 45 millions a year.

June 8 U.S. Post Office made first successful delivery of mail by guided missile; **17** Mr. de Valera elected Pres. of Rep. of Ireland; Serious riots in African townships in Durban; **18** Five-year plan for Scottish Highlands announced; **24** World record price (£275,000) paid at Sotheby's for Rubens' *The Adoration of the Magi*; **26** St. Lawrence Seaway formallyopened by the Queen and Pres. Eisenhower; **29** Norwegian Halden nuclear reactor in operation;

July 3 Italy to build nuclear submarine *Guglielmo Marconi*; Tancarville road bridge near Le Havre, longest suspension bridge in Europe, opened; **4** Transatlantic record flight set up by Vickers *Vanguard* turbo-prop airliner (2,500 m. in 5½ hrs.); **5** Recovery in good condition of 3 animals from outer space; **7** Litter Act passed making it an offence to drop litter (fine up to £10); **21** Launching of first nuclear merchant ship *Savannah* by Mrs. Eisenhower; **28** £100 tax-free annuity for V.C. holders.

August 16 The Street Offences Act came into force; **21** Baghdad Pact renamed Central Treaty Organisation; **22** First round-the-world service by British airliners inaugurated; **23** Announcement of plan for oil-pipeline network between Soviet Union and East European countries (completion 1963).

September 11 British loan made available for Malta dockyard. **13** Russia launched *Lunik II* which landed on moon; **15** Soviet atomic icebreaker *Lenin* made maiden voyage into Baltic; **25** Mr. Bandaranaike, Prime Min. of Ceylon, assassinated; **27** Typhoon in W. Japan (5,000 killed and missing, 1,000,000 homeless).

October 4 Russia fired *Lunik III*, which took photographs of back of moon; **8** General Election returned Conservatives with 100 overall majority; **10** End of one of longest droughts ever recorded in Britain; **24** Opening of new airport for Wellington, N.Z.; **29** Dublin's famous Abbey Theatre to be rebuilt (destroyed by fire 1951).

November 1 Basic travel allowance for British tourists ended (foreign currency up to £250 a year and further amounts on application to Bank of England); **2** First section of London-Yorkshire motorway (M1) opened to traffic; **5** Philip Noel-Baker awarded Nobel Peace Prize; **8** Sudan and U.A.R. signed agreement on distribution of Nile waters; **17** Announcement of discovery by American scientists of submarine plateau in Arctic Ocean; **19** Bank of England announced introduction of new series of bank notes (10*s*., £1, £5, £10); **14** Dounreay fast breeder reactor went into operation; **21** British book exhibition opened in Moscow; **24** CERN's proton synchrotron at Geneva went into full operation generating 24,000 million electron volts (24 GeV.); **27** Duke of Edinburgh opened Ghana's Academy of Learning in Accra; **28** Naval dockyard at Hong Kong closed after 80 years; **30** Inauguration of Italy's first nuclear research reactor; Pink Zone traffic plan went into operation in London.

December 1 Anglo-Russian cultural agreement signed in London; 12-power treaty on Antarctica signed in Washington; State of emergency in Cyprus ended; Bursting of dam at Fréjus killed 384 people; Pres. Eisenhower began tour of Europe, Asia, and Middle East; **5** Opening of 400-mile Sahara pipeline by French Prime Minister; **6** Inauguration of Panchet Hill Dam on Damodar R., Bihar; **10** Raising of school-leaving age to 16 recommended by Crowther Report; **14** Archbishop Makarios elected first Pres. of Cyprus; **15** New world speed record of 1,520 m.p.h. set up by U.S. Air Force pilot; **21** Marriage of Shah of Persia to Miss Farah Diba; **26** Soviet Antarctic expedition reached South Pole; **28** Jugoslavia's first nuclear reactor went into operation; Tokyo reported that in 1959 38 people died in hospital from 1945 Hiroshima atomic bomb attack.

1960

January 1 Republic of Cameroun (formerly French Cameroons) became independent state. **4** Albert Camus, French writer, killed in car crash. **7** Hirfanli Dam in Turkey opened, largest in Europe. **9** Work begun on Aswan High Dam. **12** State of emergency ended in Kenya after 8 years; **13** Mr. Aleksander Soldatov appointed to succeed Mr. J. Malik as Soviet Ambassador to Britain. **21** Bank rate increased to 5%. **23** M. Jacques Piccard and an American naval officer descended 7 miles under Pacific in Marianas Trench. **24** Army rising in Algeria. **29** Broadcast of Pres. de Gaulle to nation contributed to collapse of military revolt.

February 3 Mr. Macmillan addressed S. African Parliament (famous "wind of change" speech). **4** Announcement that American university had made radar contact with Sun. **13** First French atomic test in Sahara. **17** British agreement to U.S. ballistic missile early-warning system at Fylingdales Moor, Yorkshire. **19** Prince Andrew born. **29** Agadir destroyed by earthquake.

March 17 New £1 notes issued in Britain. **18** Last steam locomotive of British Railways named. **21** Sharpeville shooting in S. Africa when police fired on African gathering. **23** Mr. Khrushchev in Paris. **30** State of emergency in S. Africa.

April 1 U.N. Security Council adopted resolution deploring shootings in S. Africa. Dr. Hastings Banda, Pres. of proscribed Nyasaland African Congress, released from detention in S. Rhodesia. **5** Pres. de Gaulle on state visit to Britain. **9** Attempt on life of Dr. Verwoerd. **13** *Blue Streak* as military weapon abandoned. **27** Rep. of Togo (former Togoland) came into being as independent state.

May 1 U.S. aircraft engaged in military reconnaissance flight over Soviet territory shot down. **6** Wedding of Princess Margaret and Mr. A. Armstrong-Jones in Westminster Abbey. **7** U.S. to resume underground nuclear tests; Tal beat Botvinnik in world chess championship; Mr.

A.D.

Leonid Brezhnev succeeded Marshal Voroshilov as Pres. of Soviet Union. 16 Opening and breakdown of Summit conference in Paris. 17 Queen Elizabeth The Queen Mother officially opened Kariba Dam. 21 Earthquake disaster in Chile. 25 Everest climbed by 3 Chinese by northern slope. Army seized control in Turkey. End of U.S. foreign aid to Cuba. 30 Death of Boris Pasternak.

June 10 Britain's first guided-missile destroyer *Devonshire* launched. Britain's nuclear power programme to be slowed down. 23 Bank rate raised to 6%. 25 Completion of second Saharan oil pipe-line (Edjelé to La Skirra on Tunisian coast). 26 British rule in Somaliland ended; Madagascar became independent state within French Community. 29 House of Commons rejected Wolfenden Committee's recommendations on homosexuality. 30 Belgian Congo became independent as the Congo Republic (Pres. M. Kasavubu, Prime Min. M. Lumumba).

July 1 Ghana proclaimed a Republic; Somali Republic came into being (merging of former British Somaliland and Italian Somaliland). 6 Army mutiny in Congo. Death of Aneurin Bevan. 11 Ivory Coast, Dahomey, Niger, and Upper Volta became independent. M. Tshombe, Congolese privincial leader, declared Katanga independent. M. Lumumba asked for U.N. help in reorganising mutinous *Force publique*. 12 Congo (French), Chad and Central African Rep. became independent. 14 Sec. Council called for withdrawal of Belgian troops from Congo. 19–26 Royal Society Tercentenary celebrations.

August 2 Rawalpindi capital of Pakistan instead of Karachi. 8 Military *coup d'état* in Laos. 9 Sec. Council called on Belgium to withdraw troops from Katanga and authorised U.N. troops to replace them. 16 End of British rule in Cyprus which becomes independent Republic. 25 Olympic Games opened in Rome. 29 Prime Minister of Jordan assassinated.

September 5 Announcement by Pres. Kasavubu that he had dismissed M. Lumumba as Prime Minister of Congo. 14 M. Lumumba appealed to U.N. for protection. 19 India and Pakistan signed Indus Waters Treaty. 23 Mr. Khrushchev led Soviet delegation to U.N. General Assembly in New York and criticised U.N. operations in Congo.

October 1 Federation of Nigeria became independent state and a Member of the Commonwealth. 5 Labour Party Conference voted against Party's official defence policy. 14 Turkish trials of members of Menderes régime began. 21 Royal Navy's first nuclear submarine *Dreadnought* launched at Barrow-in-Furness by the Queen. 27 Bank rate reduced to 5½%

November 1 U.S. *Polaris* missile-firing submarines to have base on Clyde. 3 Mr. Gaitskell re-elected leader of Parliamentary Labour Party. 9 Senator John Kennedy elected Pres. of United States. 28 Islamic Republic of Mauritania proclaimed its independence.

December 1 Capture of M. Lumumba by Col. Mobutu's forces. 2 Archbishop of Canterbury visited the Pope at the Vatican. 8 Bank rate reduced to 5%. 14 Fighting in Vientiane, cap. of Laos, between right-wing and left-wing forces. 15 Marriage of King Baudouin of Belgium. 17 Revolt in Ethiopia crushed. 21 Strikes in Belgium. 27 Union of Ghana, Guinea, and Mali. 31 Farthing ceased to be legal tender.

1961

January 18 M. Lumumba, first Prime Min. of the independent Congo, sent to Katanga for imprisonment. 20 The Queen and the Duke of Edinburgh left for tour of India, Pakistan, Nepal and Iran; Mr. John Kennedy took office as 35th Pres. of the United States. 23 Portuguese liner *Santa Maria* seized in Caribbean by armed insurgents under Captain Henrique Galvão as protest against Salazar dictatorship. 26 Full diplomatic relations resumed between Britain and United Arab Republic. 31 M. Spaak resigned as Sec.-Gen. of Nato.

A.D.

February 1 Increased National Health Service prescription charges announced. 3 Capt. Galvão hands over *Santa Maria* to Commander of Brazilian Navy in Recife. 5 Riots in Angola. 13 Death of M. Lumumba announced (violent demonstrations in many countries). 15 Total eclipse of the sun visible from Europe. 21 U.N. authorised the use of force "if necessary, in the last resort" to prevent civil war in Congo; measures also to be taken for withdrawal of all foreign military personnel and mercenaries. 26 Death of King Mohammed V of Morocco; succeeded by elder son who becomes King Hassan II.

March 8 First of American nuclear-powered submarines carrying Polaris missiles arrived at Holy Loch; Death of Sir Thomas Beecham. 12 First winter ascent of the Eiger. 14 The New English Bible (New Testament) published. 15 Uprising of tribal groups in Angola, Portuguese murdered; brutal retaliation of Portuguese by burning and bombing. 25 Russian satellite with dog aboard launched and brought safely back to earth. 29 Four-year South African treason trial ended with acquittal of accused. 31 The Nore Command ceased to exist.

April 9 Death of former King Zog of Albania. 11 Opening of trial of Adolf Eichmann in Jerusalem. 12 Major Yuri Gagarin made first flight into space and back. 17 Unsuccessful invasion of Cuba by rebel forces. 22 Insurrection of part of French army in Algeria: State of emergency declared in France. 23 Census held in Great Britain. 24 Gen. de Gaulle ordered blockade of Algeria. 25 Both sides in Laos agreed to cease-fire. 26 Collapse of mutiny in Algeria. 27 Independence of Sierra Leone.

May 1 Betting and Gaming Act came into force in Britain: betting shops opened. 5 Commander Alan Shepard made first American flight into space; The Queen and the Duke of Edinburgh visited Pope John XXIII at the Vatican. 12 Botvinnik regained world chess championship from Tal. 16 International conference on Laos opened in Geneva; Army in South Korea seized power. 17 Guildford Cathedral consecrated. 19 British Trade Fair in Moscow opened (M. Khrushchev present). 20 Talks opened at Evian between French government and Algerian provincial government (broke down July 18). 31 Gen. Trujillo, dictator of Dominican Republic, assassinated; South Africa became a Republic and withdrew from British Commonwealth.

June 1 N. Cameroons became part of Nigeria. 3 Meeting of Pres. Kennedy and M. Khrushchev in Vienna. 9 Security Council voted for Afro-Asian resolution calling upon Portugal to end repressive measures in Angola. 24 Promulgation by Pope John XXIII of new constitution for the Knights of Malta. 27 Enthronement of Dr. Ramsey as Archbishop of Canterbury in Canterbury Cathedral. 30 Portuguese refused to stop repressive measures in Angola.

July 1 British forces landed in Kuwait following appeal from ruler. 2 Death of Ernest Hemingway. 7 Soviet Trade Exhibition opened in London. 11 Major Yuri Gagarin, Russian pioneer of space travel, welcomed in London. 18 Over £9 million raised in Britain for 1960 World Refugee Year. 19 Fighting began between French and Tunisian forces over Bizerta naval base; Announcement of U.K.–U.S. agreement to establish Missile Defence Alarm (Midas) Station at Kirkbride, Cumberland. 21 U.S. launched its second space traveller (Capt. V. Grissom) 118 m. high, flight time 16 mins.; New Runcorn-Widnes Bridge opened over Mersey and Manchester Ship Canal (third largest span of its kind in the world and the largest span arch in Europe). 24 Bank rate rose from 5 to 7%. 30 Israel began construction of deep-sea port at Asdod.

August 4 International Monetary Fund placed £714 million at Bitain's disposal. 6 Major Titov, Russia's second space man, circled earth 17 times before landing back near Moscow 25 hours later. 13 Soviet sector of Berlin sealed off from Western sectors. 14 Jomo Kenyatta

A.D.

became a free man again. **15** U.N. recognised M. Adoula's government as the central government of the Congo. **16** Dr. Hastings Banda's Malawi Congress Party won control in the Nyasaland Legislative Assembly. **30** No agreement reached at Geneva on banning of nuclear tests. **31** Soviet announcement of resumption of nuclear weapons tests.

September 5 International conference on preservation of wild life opened at Arusha, Tanganyika; U.S. to resume underground nuclear tests. **18** Mr. Hammarskjöld killed in plane crash when flying from Leopoldville, Congo, to Ndola, N. Rhodesia, to meet M. Tshombe in effort to arrange cease-fire between U.N. and Katanga forces. **28** Syria seceded from the United Arab Republic (the latter name to continue to be used by Egypt).

October 1 S. Cameroons gained independence as part of Cameroun. **3** Mr. A. Armstrong-Jones created Earl of Snowdon. **4** Labour Party Conference voted against Polaris bases and German troops in Britain. **5** Bank rate reduced to 6½%. **10** Volcanic eruption on Tristan da Cunha: whole population evacuated to Britain. **21** U.S. put into space, amid world-wide protest, 350 million copper needles for reflecting radio signals (they failed to disperse into orbit). **23** Nobel Peace Prize for 1960 awarded to South African, Albert Luthuli, former Zulu chief; that for 1961 posthumously to Dag Hammarskjöld. **30** Russia tested a bomb of over 60 megatons amid world-wide protest. **31** Hurricane struck British Honduras, Belize devastated; Stalin's body removed from the Lenin Mausoleum in Red Square; Australia's new radio telescope at Parkes, N.S.W. officially commissioned by Gov.-Gen.

November 1 Boy scouts permitted to wear long trousers. **2** Bank rate reduced to 6%. **3** U Thant, Burma's chief representative at U.N., elected Acting Sec.-Gen. of U.N.; Birth of son to Princess Margaret and Lord Snowdon; Government refused to save Doric arch at Euston station. **7** Dr. Adenauer re-elected Chancellor of Fed. German Rep. for fourth time. **8** Official negotiations for entry of Britain into Common Market opened in Brussels; Wales votes for Sunday opening. **9** The Queen and the Duke of Edinburgh left for tour of Ghana, Liberia, and Sierra Leone. **20** Admission of Russian Orthodox Church to World Council of Churches meeting at New Delhi. **28** South Africa's apartheid policy condemned by U.N.

December 8 Cross-Channel submarine cable linking electricity systems of England and France officially inaugurated. **9** Tanganyika became independent sovereign state within British Commonwealth; Russia broke off diplomatic relations with Albania. **15** Adolf Eichmann sentenced to death by Israeli court for crimes against the Jewish people and against humanity; Mr. Macmillan and Pres. Kennedy met in Bermuda. **17** Indian troops took over Portuguese colony of Goa. **19** Decimal coinage accepted in principle by British government. **20** Mr. Adoula and Mr. Tshombe agreed on Katanga's subordinate status. **27** Belgium and the Congo resumed diplomatic relations.

1962

January 1 Western Samoa became independent. **10** Avalanche disaster in Peru. **11** Smallpox outbreak in Britain. **15** Centigrade first used in weather forecasts. **16** Death of R. H. Tawney. **24** T.U.C. decided to join "Neddy". **27** New world record for mile by New Zealander Peter Snell (3 min. 54·4 secs.). **30** Birth of son to King Hussein of Jordan.

February 11 Death of Lord Birkett. **20** American first manned orbital flight.

March 7 Franco-Algerian negotiations began at Evian; Publication of Royal College of Physician's Report on dangers to health from cigarette smoking. **8** Bank rate reduced from 6 to 5½%. **14** Opening of 17-nation disarmament conference at Geneva. **19** End of Algerian war. **28** Inauguration of Marlborough House, built by Wren, as Commonwealth Centre.

April 1 Government's "pay pause" ended. **2** "Panda" crossings in operation in number of British towns. **5** Completion of Gt. St. Bernard road tunnel. **7** Strike in Asturias—first of many throughout Spain. **8** French people voted in referendum approving Algerian peace settlement. **11** Pres. Kennedy condemned U.S. steel industry for raising prices. **13** International agreement (40 countries) to stop oil pollution of seas and beaches. **20** Gen. Salan, O.A.S. leader, arrested by French in Algiers. **25** U.S. began new series of atmospheric nuclear tests in Pacific. **26** Britain's first satellite, *Ariel*, launched from Cape Canaveral; Bank rate down from 5 to 4½%. **30** Norway applied to join Common Market.

May 6 Signor Segni elected Pres. of Italy; Canonisation of St. Martin de Porres of Lima (d. 1639), first mulatto saint of the R.C. church. **8** Trolleybuses ran for last time in London. **13** Dr. Radhakrishnan elected Pres. of India. **25** Consecration of new Coventry Cathedral. **29** Dawley, Shropshire, designated new town. **31** Eichmann executed in Israel; Dissolution of The West Indies Federation.

June 5 Creation of University of Lagos, Nigeria. **14** Creation of European Space Research Organisation (ESRO). **15** Nuclear power station at Berkeley, Glos., began electricity supply to national grid. **18** The *Flying Scotsman* made centenary journey; Conservatives (Mr. Diefenbaker) won Canadian general election by small majority. **23** Cease-fire in Laos. **24** Opening of Punjabi University, India. **28** U.N. called for more liberal constitution for S. Rhodesia.

July 1 Burundi and Rwanda became independent; After 132 years French colonial rule in Algeria ended; Commonwealth Immigrants Act came into force. **3** Plan for British national theatre and opera house accepted by L.C.C. and Government. **5** Independence celebrated in Algeria. **8** Pres. de Gaulle and Chan. Adenauer attended Mass in Rheims cathedral. **10** *Telstar*, first experimental satellite in space communication, launched—first live television between U.S. and Europe. **20** Death of G. M. Trevelyan, the historian. **25** Opening of new civic centre at Plymouth. **26** Government announce setting up of "Nicky". **30** Archbishop of Canterbury visited Moscow. **31** Rendezvous of U.S. nuclear submarines at North Pole.

August 5 Russia began series of atmospheric nuclear tests; Death of Marilyn Monroe, at age 36. **5** Jamaica became independent. **10** Abandonment of *Blue Water* missile. **11** British mountaineers scaled Russia's highest peak (Mt. Communism). **11** and **12** Russia launched two men into orbit (64 orbits and 48 orbits). **13** British travel allowances further eased from £250 a year to £250 a journey. **14** Completion of Mont Blanc tunnel (7½ m.). **17** Pres. Kennedy's, Bill on medical care rejected by Senate. **20** Government approval for construction of new underground railway between Victoria and Walthamstow. **21** Maiden voyage of *Savannah*, world's first nuclear-powered merchant ship. **27** U.S. *Mariner II* launched towards Venus. **31** Trinidad and Tobago became independent.

September 3 Opening of Trans-Canada highway (4,800 m. from St. John's, Newfoundland, to Victoria, B.C.). **7** Life presidency for Dr. Nkrumah. **15** In exchange of Notes Iran assured Russia that no foreign rocket bases would be permitted. **20** Zimbabwe African People's Union banned in S. Rhodesia; Fighting between Chinese and Indian troops on disputed N.E. frontier. **27** Overthrow of Imamate and republic proclaimed in Yemen. **29** Canada launched her first satellite, the *Alouette*, into orbit. **30** U.S. troops enforced Fed. Government's order that Negro student should enrol at Mississippi State University.

October 3 6-orbit flight of U.S. astronaut. **9** Uganda became independent. **11** 21st Oecumenical Council opened at St. Peter's, Rome.

A.D.

17 Opening of Hyde Park Corner underpass; Electricity for national grid generated at Dounreay reactor. 24 Commencement of U.S. naval quarantine of Cuba. 28 Dismantling of missile base in Cuba agreed upon by Russia; Gen. de Gaulle won referendum for his proposal for direct election of President.

November 1 Russia sent spacecraft on 7-month journey to Mars. 6 Admiralty announced record ocean depth by H.M.S. *Cook* in Mindanao trench (37,782 ft); Opening of Commonwealth Institute (replaces Imperial Institute, S. Kensington). 18 Death of Niels Bohr. 20 Cuba blockade ended. 21 Cease-fire declaration by China on Sino-Indian border dispute (no further hostilities occurred after this date). 29 Announcement of new Indo-Pakistan negotiations on Kashmir. 30 U Thant unanimously elected Sec.-Gen. of U.N.

December 5 Soviet-American space research co-operation agreement; Uprising in British prot. of Brunei in protest to joining Fed. of Malaysia; British nuclear device exploded underground in Nevada. 9 Tanganyika became republic and Dr. Julius Nyerere its first president. 12 British troops in control of Brunei uprising. 14 Signals from *Mariner II* as it passed within 21,000 miles of Venus; Eritrea became province of Ethiopia; N. Rhodesia's first African dominated government formed. 15 Sir Edgar Whitehead's party lost to right-wing party in S. Rhodesian general election. 17 Mr. Macmillan left for meeting with Pres. Kennedy at Nassau, Bahamas. 21 U.S. decision to abandon *Skybolt*; offer of *Polaris* missiles for British submarines to form part of multilateral Nato nuclear force. 23 M. Fedorenko succeeded M. Zorin as Soviet perm. rep. at U.N. 25 Europe snowbound with freezing temperatures. 28 Agreement in principle reached between China and Pakistan defining mutual boundary. 29 Southern England swept by blizzard. 30 Worst snowstorms in England since 1881. 31 British Transport Commission replaced by British Railways Board (created by Transport Act, 1962), with Dr. Beeching as chairman.

1963

January 2 Gen. Lemnitzer succeeded Gen. Norstad as Supreme Allied Commander, Europe. 3 Bank rate reduced from 4½ to 4 per cent. 14 Gen. de Gaulle's press conference repulsing Britain's entry to EEC and rejecting U.S. Polaris offer. 15 Official ending of Katanga secession. 18 Death of Hugh Gaitskell; Aden acceded to Fed. of S. Arabia. 29 Britain was refused entry to EEC; Death of Robert Frost, the American poet.

February 1 Nyasaland became self-governing protectorate. 5 Death of Lord Samuel. 6 Shipping restrictions on Cuba announced by U.S. Government. 8 Overthrow of Iraq government and execution of Gen. Kassim. 12 Seventeen-nation disarmament conference resumed in Geneva. 14 Harold Wilson elected leader of Labour Party. 19 Bali volcano disaster (others followed March 19, May 19). Earthquake in Barce, Libya. 22 Unemployment figures showed 878,356, highest since 1947.

March 5–6 First frost-free night in Britain since Dec. 22. 8 Syrian government overthrown by military coup. 17 Typhoid broke out in Zermatt; First of Tristan de Cunha islanders returned home. 27 Publication of Beeching Report on British Railways.

April 5 Opening of Berkley and Bradwell civil nuclear power stations. 6 Polaris missile agreement signed between U.S. and Britain. 8 Mr. Diefenbaker's Conservative Party defeated by Liberals in Canadian general election. 9 Honorary American citizenship conferred on Sir Winston Churchill. 10 Pope John XXIII published his encyclical *Pacem in Terris*; New Zealand to change to decimal coinage in 1967; Loss of U.S. nuclear submarine *Thresher* with 129 lives. 17 Commissioning of Royal Navy's first nuclear-powered submarine, H.M.S. *Dreadnought*. 20 Execution of Julian Grimau, Spanish communist leader.

A.D.

May 1 End of Dutch East Indies: New Guinea (West Irian) handed to Indonesia. 15 Twenty-two-orbit flight of Major Cooper of U.S. Air Force. 16 Radio contact lost with Soviet *Mars I* launched Nov. 1962. 20 Petrosian won world chess title from Botvinnik; Life presidency for Pres. Sukarno of Indonesia.

June 1 Death of Pope John XXIII; new internal self-government constitution for Kenya came into force with Jomo Kenyatta as Kenya's first Prime Minister. 11 Iraq resumed war against Kurds. 12 Rioting on big scale in Georgetown, British Guiana. 14–19 Bykovsky-Tereshkova space flights (first woman astronaut). 16 Resignation of Mr. Ben-Gurion announced. 20 House of Commons censure on Mr. John Profumo, former Sec. of State for War. 24 Zanzibar achieved internal self-government. 28 Inauguration in Nairobi of Univ. of East Africa. 30 Pope Paul VI crowned.

July 2 Franco-German Treaty of Co-operation came into force. 5 Sino-Soviet ideological talks began. 9 State visit of King and Queen of Greece to Britain. 26 Skopje destroyed by earthquake. 29 Pres. de Gaulle rejected Moscow test-ban treaty. 31 The Peerage Bill received the Royal Assent; Security Council called on member states to impose partial arms embargo on Portugal.

August 1 Under Criminal Justice Act, 1961, minimum prison age raised to 17. 3 First successful solo climb on north wall of Eiger by Michel Darbellay, a Swiss mountain guide. 5 Partial nuclear-test-ban treaty signed in Moscow by America, Russia, and Britain. 7 Security Council resolution to stop sale and shipment of arms to S. Africa. 8 Glasgow-London mail train robbery (£2·5 million). 9 Caernarvon declared royal borough (first in Wales). 16 Announcement of American-Soviet weather- and communications-satellite programme. 20 Mr. Khrushchev visited Yugoslavia. 21 Buddhists arrested and martial law imposed in South Vietnam. 28 Great Negro "freedom march" on Washington. 31 Death of George Braque, the French painter; The "hot line" linking Kremlin with White House went into service.

September 5 Soviet-American co-operation in cosmic ray research in Antarctica announced. 15 Ben Bella elected first President of Algeria. 16 New state of Malaysia (Malaya, Singapore, North Borneo (now Sabah), and Sarawak) came into being. 17 Malaysia broke off diplomatic relations with Indonesia; Fylingdales ballistic missile early warning station came into operation. 18 New Australian decimal currency to be introduced Feb. 1966 (unit to be called the dollar). 19 Anglo-French report recommended rail tunnel as Channel link. 21 Reform of Roman Catholic Curia announced by Pope Paul VI. 23 Report on decimal currency advocated division of £1 into 100 units. 25 Denning report on Profumo affair published. 29 Reopening of Vatican Council; First buildings of University of East Anglia opened at Norwich.

October 1 Nigeria became a republic within the Commonwealth with Dr. Azikiwe its first President; Algeria nationalised French-owned land 3 Honduras government overthrown by Army. 4 Hurricane Flora struck the Caribbean. 9 Viaont dam disaster (N. Italy); the Kubaka of Buganda became first President of Uganda. 15 Dr. Adenauer retired after 14 years as Chancellor of Fed. German Republic; succeeded by Prof. Ludwig Erhard. 18 Mr. Macmillan resigned as Prime Minister; succeeded by the Earl of Home; French sent cat into space and brought it safely back. 23 Robbins report on higher education published.

November 1 Diem oligarchy of S. Vietnam overthrown by military coup; First executions in S. Africa under the Sabotage Act of 1963. 7 Eleven German miners rescued after a fortnight underground; Sir Alec Douglas-Home elected at Kinross and W. Perthshire. 9 Train and mine disasters in Japan. 13 Death of Dr. Margaret Murray, the archaeologist, at age 100. 16 Greece began to release Communist prisoners

A.D.

taken during last war. 17 Temples of Abu Simbel to be removed and re-sited. 18 Opening of Dartford–Purfleet tunnel, linking Kent and Essex under Thames. 22 Assassination of President Kennedy in Dallas, Texas; Vice-President Lyndon Johnson sworn in as new President. 27 Publication of Buchanan report.

December 3 Britain's second nuclear submarine, the *Valiant*, launched. 4 Second session of Vatican Council ended; Closure of Woolwich Arsenal announced. 10 Zanzibar became an independent state within the Commonwealth. 12 Kenya became an independent state within the Commonwealth. 22 Greek liner *Lakonia* caught fire and sank on Christmas cruise, 250 miles W. of Gibraltar. 31 Dissolution of Federation of Rhodesia and Nyasaland.

1964

January 4–6 Pope Paul made pilgrimage to Holy Land: first meeting between Pope and Patriarch of Constantinople since 1439. 9 Rioting in Panama. 12 Republican régime in Zanzibar. 20 Army mutiny in Tanganyika. 27 France recognized China; School-leaving age to be raised to 16 in 1970–71. 28 Riots in Salisbury, S. Rhodesia, after trial of Joshua Nkomo.

February 6 Anglo-French agreement on rail Channel tunnel announced. 11 Fighting between Greeks and Turks at Limassol, Cyprus. 27 Bank rate raised from 4 to 5%.

March 4 August Bank holiday in 1965 and 1966 to be moved to last Monday in month. 6 Death of King Paul of the Hellenes; son proclaimed King Constantine XIII. 10 Birth of Prince Edward. 11 S. Africa withdrew from I.L.O. 19 Opening of Great St. Bernard tunnel. 24 Stansted, Essex, provisionally chosen as site of London's third airport. 25 Plinth at Runnymede and scholarship fund for study in U.S. to be memorials to President Kennedy. 27 U.N. peacekeeping force in Cyprus operational; Britain's second space satellite, *Ariel* 2, launched in Virginia; Severe earthquake and tidal wave in Alaska.

April 4 Dr. Leakey confirmed discovery in Tanganyika of *Homo habilis*; heavy fighting in Cyprus between Greek and Turkish communities. 5 Death of General MacArthur. 8 Shaikh Abdullah, former Prime Minister of Kashmir, released by Indian Government. 9 First Greater London Council election: Labour 64, Conservatives 36. 10 Mr. Macmillan declined earldom and Order of the Garter. 13 Mr. Ian Smith became Prime Minister of S. Rhodesia on resignation of Mr. Winston Field. 16 Sentences totalling 307 years passed on 12 men found guilty in mail train robbery trial (two subsequently escaped from prison). 21 Opening of BBC-2. 23 Shakespeare quatercentenary celebrations. 27 Tanganyika and Zanzibar united (United Republic of Tanzania).

May 1 Birth of a daughter to Princess Margaret and Lord Snowdon. 9 Mr. Khrushchev's first visit to Egypt (completion of first stage Aswan High Dam). 22 State of emergency declared in British Guiana. 26 Typhoid outbreak in Aberdeen. 27 Death of Jawaharlal Nehru. 31 Mr. Harold Wilson arrived in Moscow for talks.

June 2 Mr. Lal Bahadur Shastri elected Prime Minister of India. 3 Senator Barry Goldwater of Arizona defeated Mr. Nelson Rockefeller, Governor of New York, in Republican Party's primary election in California. 5 First flight into space of Britain's *Blue Streak* rocket (fired from Woomera). 9 Death of Lord Beaverbrook. 12 Life imprisonment imposed on Nelson Mandela and others in Rivonia trial, Pretoria; 20-year treaty of friendship signed between Soviet Union and E. Germany. 24 Picturephone, whereby speakers can see as well as hear each other, in operation in U.S. 30 Last U.N. troops left Congo.

July 2 Enactment of U.S. Civil Rights Bill. 6 Nyasaland became independent state of Malawi. 8 Opening of Commonwealth Prime Ministers' Conference in London. 10 M. Tshombe succeeded M. Adoula as Prime Minister of the Congo. 12 Death of Maurice Thorez, French communist leader. 15 Mr. Mikoyan succeeded Mr. Brezhnev as President of the Soviet Union. 17 Court of Session, Edinburgh, ruled that Harris Tweed must be wholly made in Outer Hebrides; Mr. Donald Campbell broke land-speed record on Lake Eyre with 403·1 m.p.h. 27 Last appearance of Sir Winston Churchill in House of Commons. 31 American *Ranger* 7 hit moon after sending back over 4,000 pictures of surface.

August 2 U.S. destroyer attacked by N. Vietnam torpedo boats off coast of N. Vietnam. 4 Nine French miners rescued after being trapped underground at Champagnole for 8 days; Bodies of three murdered civil rights workers found near Philadelphia, Mississippi. 5 Congolese rebels captured Stanleyville; U.S. air raid on N. Vietnam. 13 General Grivas, former EOKA leader, took over supreme command of Cypriot National Guard. 13 Common Market set up by Arab League (Iraq, Jordan, Kuwait, Syria and U.A.R.) to come into force Jan. 1965. 21 Death of Togliatti, Italian Communist leader.

September 2 Indonesian landings in Malaya. 4 Opening of new Forth bridge (largest suspension bridge in Europe). 7 People's Republic of the Congo declared by Congolese rebels. 14 Third session of Vatican Council opened (closed 21 Nov.). 20 Gen. de Gaulle began his tour of S. America. 21 Malta became independent state within the British Commonwealth after 164 years of British rule. 22 Hunterston nuclear power station opened. 28 Maiden flight of supersonic TSR 2; Death of Harpo Marx, the great film comedian.

October 5 The Queen and the Duke of Edinburgh arrived in Canada on week's visit. 10 Opening of Olympic Games in Tokyo. 12 Soviet 3-man spaceship launched on 24-hour flight; First shipment of liquid methane from Saharan oil-field to Britain. 14 1964 Nobel Peace Prize awarded to Dr. Martin Luther King. 15 Mr. Khruschev replaced in posts of First Secretary of the CPSU and Prime Minister by Mr. Brezhnev and Mr. Kosygin respectively; General election in Britain: Labour won with overall majority of five. 16 Mr. Harold Wilson became Prime Minister; China exploded an atomic device. 22 M. Jean-Paul Sartre declined Nobel Prize for Literature which had been awarded him. 24 Northern Rhodesia achieved independence as Republic of Zambia with Kenneth Kaunda as its first President; S. Rhodesia became officially known as Rhodesia. 26 Government proposed 15% import surcharge and export tax rebate to deal with balance of payments crisis. 29 Nobel Prize for Chemistry awarded to Prof. Dorothy Hodgkin.

November 2 Deposition of King Saud of Saudi Arabia and accession of his brother Faisal. 3 U.S. Presidential election: sweeping victory for President Johnson over Senator Goldwater. 5 Mr. Chou En-lai in Moscow for 47th anniversary of October revolution; Cease-fire in Yemen after two years of civil strife. 10 Australia to introduce selective compulsory service for military service overseas. 12 Grand Duchess Charlotte of Luxembourg abdicated after 45 years' rule in favour of her son. 17 Government to ban export of arms to S. Africa. 23 Bank rate rose from 5 to 7%. 21 Opening of Verrazano-Narrows bridge spanning mouth of New York harbour, the world's longest bridge. 24 Belgian paratroops landed at Stanleyville to rescue rebel-held hostages. 25 £1,070 million foreign credits arranged by Bank of England for defence of sterling.

December 1 Death of J. B. S. Haldane. 2 The Pope welcomed in Bombay; U.K. to draw £357 million from I.M.F. 5 Bishopsgate railway goods depot destroyed by fire, two customs officers dying in blaze. 6 Mr. Wilson in Washington for talks with Pres. Johnson; Resignation of Pres. Segni of Italy. 8 Heavy fighting in S. Vietnam. 9 Protection from Eviction Bill published. 11 Machinery of Government Bill published. 12 Kenya became Republic within Commonwealth with Mr. Kenyatta as first President. 15 Agreement on Common

A.D.

Market cereal prices (to start 1967) reached. 16 Statement of Intent on productivity, prices and incomes signed by Government, T.U.C. and Employers' organisations. 17 Free prescriptions from 1 February 1965. 18 U.N. force in Cyprus extended until 26 March 1965. 21 Bill abolishing capital punishment given second reading in Commons. 23 Dr. Beeching returning to I.C.I. in 1965; Cyclone hit Ceylon and S. India. 28 Signor Saragat elected President of Italy. 31 Mr. Donald Campbell broke world water-speed record with speed of 276·33 m.p.h. on Lake Dumbleyung in W. Australia.

1965

January 7 Indonesia withdrew from U.N. 15 Child's body found (Dec. 11, 1964) in coffin in Stepney identified as that of Lady Anne Mowbray (1472–81), child wife of Richard, Duke of York (one of Princes in the Tower); remains reinterred in Westminster Abbey; Prime Minister of Burundi assassinated. 20 Lyndon Baines Johnson inaugurated as 36th President of U.S. 21 Prime Minister of Iran assassinated. 24 Death of Sir Winston Churchill. 26 Hindi became official language of India with English an additional official tongue. 31 National Health prescription charges ended.

February 1 The Queen and Duke of Edinburgh in Ethiopia on state visit. 4 Lysenko dismissed as Director of Institute of Genetics. 7 First U.S. retaliatory raids against N. Vietnam. 17 Pres. Johnson announced U.S. would continue "actions that are justified as necessary for defence of S. Vietnam." 18 Gambia became independent as 21st member of the Br. Commonwealth. 24 U.S. piloted jets bombed Vietcong in S. Vietnam. 25 Dr. Heenan, Archbishop of Westminster, created a cardinal.

March 3 Remains of Roger Casement, from Pentonville Prison, reburied in Dublin; Seretse Khama became Bechuanaland's first Prime Minister. 7 First of 3,500 American marines landed in S. Vietnam. 18 Alexei Leonov became first man to leave a spaceship and float in space. 19 Record price of 760,000 guineas paid at Christie's for Rembrandt's *Titus*. 23 First successful two-man manœvrable flight by Grissom and Young in *Gemini III*; Dr. Dorothy Hodgkin awarded Order of Merit. 24 Successful completion of U.S. *Ranger* moon shot programme. 25 Defeat of Mrs. Bandaranaike in Ceylon elections; Mr. Senanayake became Prime Minister. 28 Death of the Princess Royal; Earthquake in Chile.

April 1 Younger brother of King Hussein made heir to Jordan throne in place of his 3-year-old son. 2 Mr. Wilson and Pres. de Gaulle began talks in Paris. 6 Launching of *Early Bird* commercial communication satellite; Cancellation of TSR 2. 9 Fighting broke out between Indian and Pakistan forces in Rann of Kutch. 11 Tornadoes in mid-western U.S. killed 278 people. 14 Visit of Mr. Wilson to U.S. 23 Opening of 250-mile Pennine Way, Britain's first long-distance footpath from Edale in Derbyshire to Kirk Yetholm in Roxburghshire. 24 Outbreak of civil war in Dominican Republic. 27 Import surcharge of 15 per cent reduced to 10 per cent. 28 Landing of American troops in Dominican Republic. 29 Australian troops to be sent to S. Vietnam.

May 8 Arrest of Sheik Abdullah on return to India from tour abroad; Spanish confirmation that one of bodies found near Portuguese border in Feb. was that of General Delgado, Portuguese opposition leader. 11 Cyclone and tidal wave disaster in E. Pakistan killing 16,000 people. 13 Conservatives made big gains in U.K. local government elections. 14 Inauguration of Kennedy memorial at Runnymede; China exploded second atomic bomb. 15 Completion of Benmore power station and Cook Strait cable—part of New Zealand's 10-year power development scheme. 17 Britain and France to co-operate in developing two military aircraft; 31 miners killed in Welsh colliery disaster. 18 The Queen and the Duke of Edinburgh on 10-day state visit to Fed. German Republic. 20–29 Indian ascents of Everest.

A.D.

24 Britain's adoption of metric system over 10 years announced. 25 Changeover to dollar currency in Bahamas announced. 28 267 miners killed in Indian colliery disaster.

June 1 237 miners killed in Japanese colliery explosion. 3 Bank rate reduced to 6 per cent; Launching of U.S. *Gemini IV* with McDivitt and White; the latter walked in space for 20 min. 4–7 Visit of Mr. Chou En-lai to Tanzania. 7 128 miners killed in Jugoslav mine disaster. 9 World record for mile broken by M. Jazy of France (3 min. 53·6 sec.). 17 Opening of Commonwealth Prime Ministers' Conference in London. 19 Pres. Ben Bella of Algeria deposed by Revolutionary Council under Col. Boumedienne. 22 700th anniversary of Parliament celebrated. 28 *Early Bird* went into commerical service (poised 23,000 miles above Atlantic between Brazil and Africa). 30 Cease-fire agreement in Rann of Kutch signed.

July 8 Another mail train robber escaped from prison. 6 Inauguration of SRC radiotelescope at Lord's Bridge, Cambridge. 11 Mme. Furtseva, Soviet Minister of Culture, visited Britain. 14 Adlai Stevenson died in London, suddenly. 14 Mme. Vaucher climbed north wall of Matterhorn, the first woman to do so. 15 First close-up pictures of Mars successfully transmitted to earth by U.S. *Mariner IV* across 134 million miles; King Constantine of Greece dismissed his Prime Minister, Mr. Papandreou. 16 Opening of Mont Blanc tunnel. 19 Death of Syngman Rhee, former Pres. of S. Korea. 20 Malawi to become a republic on July 6, 1966. 22 Sir Alec Douglas-Home resigned as leader of the Conservative Party; succeeded by Mr. Edward Heath (July 28). 26 Maldive Islands became independent. 27 18-Nation Disarmament Conference reconvened at Geneva (adjourned Sept. 16). 29 Rebuilding of London Bridge planned; Appointment of Lord Casey as Governor-General of Australia. 30 U.S. Medical Care for for the Aged Bill passed.

August 1 Radio and television licence fees increased; Television ban on cigarette advertising. 3 Creation of a new award "The Queen's Award to Industry" for export and technological achievement; M. Malraux, French Minister of Culture, met Mao Tse-tung in Peking. 5 Clashes on Kashmir border. 6 U.S. Voting Rights Bill passed. 9 Singapore seceded from Malaysia; Marriage between Moslems and Communists forbidden in U.A.R. 11 Negro riots in Los Angeles. 12 Appointment of first woman High Court judge. 21 U.S. *Gemini V* (Cooper and Conrad) launched (landed Aug. 29 after 120 orbits). 24 Government White Paper published containing proposals for radical changes in the treatment of young offenders; Pres. Nasser and King Faisal signed cease-fire agreement in Yemen.

September 1 Pakistan forces crossed Kashmir cease-fire line. 2 Death of Sir Harry Hylton-Foster, Speaker of the House of Commons. 5 Death of Dr. Albert Schweitzer. 6 Indian forces invaded W. Pakistan and bombed Lahore. 12 American division 20,000 strong landed in S. Vietnam; General election in Norway: Labour Government defeated. 14 Second Vatican Council reconvened for 4th session. 16 Publication of Government's White Paper, *The National Plan*, covering Britain's economic development 1964–70. 21 British Petroleum oil rig *Sea Gem* struck oil in North Sea. 22 Publication of Government White Paper, *The Land Commission*, proposing a 40 per cent initial levy on development value; Cease-fire in Indo-Pakistan war. 24 Mauritius to become independent in 1966.

October 1 Attempt to overthrow Pres. Sukarno of Indonesia; reprisals against communists. 3 First international symposium on water desalination met in Washington. 4 The Pope flew to New York and addressed the U.N. Assembly; First Commonwealth Medical Conference met in Edinburgh; Independence for Rhodesia discussions opened in London. 6 Sir Robert Menzies appointed Lord Warden of the Cinque Ports. 8 Talks in London on

A.D.

Rhodesian independence ended without agreement. **11** Publication of Vinland Map, the only known example of mediæval Norse cartography. **13** Pres. Kasavubu of the Congo dismissed Mr. Tshombe. **17** Demonstrations throughout U.S. and in London against war in Vietnam. **19** Dr. Erhard re-elected Chancellor of Fed. Rep. of Germany. **22** Pakistan and India accept cease-fire call of Security Council. **26** Dr. Horace King elected Speaker of House of Commons—the first Labour Speaker. **27** Volcanic eruption in Philippines. **28** Parliament passed Bill abolishing death penalty for murder.

November 1 Severe gales swept Britain. **8** New British colony of British Indian Ocean Territory set up. **11** Mr. Ian Smith of Rhodesia signed unilateral declaration of independence; Britain declared rebel regime illegal and introduced economic sanctions. **15** New land speed record of 600·6 m.p.h. set up in Utah by jet-powered car. **20** Security Council called on all states to sever economic relations with Rhodesia, and urged oil embargo. **25** General Mobuto deposed Pres. Kasavubu. **25** France launched her first earth satellite. **27** Pres. Kaunda of Zambia asked Britain to send troops to Kariba.

December 1 R.A.F. Javelins arrived in Zambia. **4** *Gemini VII* (Borman and Lovell) launched. **6** Russia increased her defence expenditure. **8** The Second Vatican Council closed; Rent Act, 1965 came into force. **9** Mr. Mikoyan retired as President of the Soviet Union; replaced by Mr. Nikolai Podgorny. **15** Rendezvous in orbit between *Geminis VI* and *VII*; Tanzania and Guinea broke off diplomatic relations with Britain over Rhodesia. **16** Mr. Wilson addressed the U.N. Assembly; Dead Sea Scrolls exhibited at British Museum. **17** Britain imposed oil embargo on Rhodesia; New forms of service for Anglican Church published. **19** General de Gaulle re-elected French President. **22** Christmas truce in Vietnam; Death of Richard Dimbleby, the B.B.C. commentator; 70 m.p.h. speed limit on British roads came into force. **27** Oil rig *Sea Gem* collapsed in North Sea; 5 killed, 8 missing. **28** 900th anniversary of Westminster Abbey celebrated. **29** Bechuanaland (as Botswana) to become independent Sept. 30, 1966.

1966

January 3 Indo-Pakistani summit talks in Tashkent with Mr. Kosygin as host. **9** Violent rioting in Nigeria. **10** Sudden death of Mr. Shastri in Tashkent. **11** Opening of Lagos Commonwealth Conference under chairmanship of Fed. Prime Min. of Nigeria. **12** Death of Alberto Giacometti, sculptor and painter. **13** End of New York transport strike. **15** Army coup in Nigeria: Fed. Prime Min. killed. **16** General Ironsi, C.-in-C. of Nigerian army, took over command to restore law and order; Death of Sergei Korolyov, Russian space scientist. **18** Arrival in London of Sir Hugh Beadle, Chief Justice of Rhodesia, for talks with British Government. **21** Smith regime in Rhodesia rejected Royal Prerogative commuting death sentences on two Africans. **22** Opening of Volta River project in Ghana. **24** Air India *Boeing* crashed into Mont Blanc: 177 killed, including Homi Bhabha, the Indian nuclear physicist. **31** U.S. bombing of N. Vietnam resumed after 37 days; British Government banned all trade with Rhodesia; Russia launched *Luna 9*.

February 1 Queen and Duke of Edinburgh left for tour of Caribbean; Death of Buster Keaton, the silent film comedian. **3** Successful soft landing on moon by *Luna 9*: tracked by Jodrell Bank radio telescope. **4** Japanese *Boeing* crashed in Tokyo Bay: 133 killed. **5** Pres. Johnson went to Honolulu to review Vietnam with other American leaders. **9** Britain to build prototype fast reactor (PFR) at Dounreay in Caithness. **17** Britain protested to S. Africa over petrol supplies to Rhodesia. **21** British Prime Minister in Moscow for talks. **22** Defence White Paper published: Britain to buy 50 American F-111 swing-wing supersonic low-level bombers; Fleet Air Arm to be gradually run down; first of more powerful class of guided missile ships to be ordered for Navy; no more aircraft carriers to be built; Navy, with Polaris submarines, to take over full responsibility for British contribution to Nato nuclear forces from 1969–70; British forces to be withdrawn from Aden by 1968; Garrison to be withdrawn from British Guiana and from S. African territories. **23** Military coup in Damascus (ninth in Syria in 17 years); Lord Chalfont, British Disarmament Min. had talks with N. Vietnam envoy; Death of Vicky (Victor Weisz), political cartoonist; Ministry of Social Security to be established and present system of National Assistance abolished. **24** Army coup in Ghana while Dr. Nkrumah absent in Far East; U.S. to buy £107 million worth of defence equipment from Britain to offset cost of F-111s. **25** Pres. Sukarno banned all student demonstrations in Jakarta. **28** Dr. Nkrumah arrived in Moscow from Peking.

March 1 Britain to adopt decimal currency in 1971; Russian rocket landed on Venus. **2** Dr. Nkrumah arrived in Guinea from Moscow; Britain protested to Portugal over oil storage tanks being built in Mozambique to pump oil to Rhodesia. **3** Pres. Sékou Touré of Guinea appointed Dr. Nkrumah executive head of state. **4** Britain recognised new régime in Ghana; Canadian *DC 9* crashed near Tokyo: 64 killed. **5** BOAC *Boeing* crashed near Tokyo: 124 killed; Nelson pillar in O'Connell Street, Dublin, blown up. **8** Severe earthquake in Hopeh, N. China. **9** U Thant called for cessation of bombing in N. Vietnam and for participation of Vietcong in any peaceful settlement. **10** Marriage of Princess Beatrix of the Netherlands and Herr Claus von Amsberg; U.S. to establish world-wide satellite communications system by 1968, based on *Early Bird*. **11** Chi-Chi, the London Zoo's giant panda, flew to Moscow for union with An-An of the Moscow Zoo. **18** British Antarctic research station at Halley Bay sinking: new base to be built in 1967. **23** Historic meeting in Rome of Archbishop of Canterbury and the Pope. **25** Two of the team climbing north face of the Eiger reached summit. **31** British General Election: Labour victory with overall majority of 97.

General Election 1966	Votes	Seats
Labour . . .	13,057,941	363
Conservatives . .	11,418,433	253
Liberal . . .	2,327,533	12
Others . . .	452,689	1
Speaker . . .		1
	27,256,596	630

April 3 Soviet *Luna 10* became the first lunar orbiter (orbital period: 2 hr., 58 min., 15 sec.). **5** Britain warned Portugal of consequences of allowing oil to be pumped from port of Beira to Rhodesia. **6** Greek Government withdrew registration from oil-tanker *Joanna V* off Beira. **7** Recovery of U.S. hydrogen bomb lost off coast of Spain. **9** U.N. Security Council passed resolution authorising British Government " to prevent by the use of force if necessary the arrival at Beira of vessels reasonably believed to be carrying oil destined for Rhodesia." **10** C.-in-C., British Forces in Middle East, instructed to stop any ship going to Beira with oil for Rhodesia: *Manuela* intercepted and boarded by British naval party and escorted away from Beira; America's " telescope in the sky " satellite, designed to give view of universe above distorting screen of earth's atmosphere, failed; Death of Evelyn Waugh, the novelist. **11** Students and militant Buddhists intensified campaign for return to civilian rule in S. Vietnam. **13** *Manuela* entered Durban harbour. **14** *Joanna V* taken over by Beira port captain on behalf of Portuguese Government. **15** Portuguese parachute troops flown from Lourenço Marques to Beira to guard pipeline. **15** Indonesian demonstrators sacked Chinese embassy in Jakarta. **16** *Manuela* left Durban for unknown destination.

PROMINENT PEOPLE

PROMINENT PEOPLE

A

Abbot, George (1562–1633), Archbishop of Canterbury in 1611, and one of the translators of the authorised version of the Bible.

Abdullah ibn Husein (1882–1951); King of Jordan; made ruler under the British mandate in 1921 and proclaimed King in 1946 when Transjordan (renamed Hashimite Kingdom of the Jordan in 1949) was created an independent state by treaty with Britain. Assassinated.

Abelard, Peter (1079–1142), one of the most influential thinkers of the mediaeval world, b. near Nantes, pupil of Rosecelin and William of Champeaux. Living in age of great theological controversy he applied his creative and versatile mind to the problem of Christian faith and held that goodness depends upon intention and free choice. Unrivalled as a dialectician, he acquired great popularity as a teacher and attained great schclastic glory. His romance with Heloïse, niece of Canon Fulbert, has been much written about. The Canon had Abelard castrated and they retired from the world, he to the monastery at St. Denis and she to a nunnery at Argenteuil. Their bodies lie in one tomb at Père la Chaise.

Abercrombie, Lascelles (1881–1938), English poet and critic. Professor of English Literature at London University, 1929–35; Lecturer in Poetry at Queen's University, Belfast, 1931–32.

Abercrombie, Sir (Leslie) Patrick, M.A., F.S.A. F.R.I.B.A. (1879–1957), architect and town-planner. Brother of the above. Lever Prof. of Civic Design at Liverpool, 1915–35; Prof. of Town Planning at University College, London, 1935–46. Consulted on the replanning of Plymouth, Hull, Bath, the Clyde Valley, Dublin, Addis Ababa, Colombo, and Cyprus. Produced the famous plan for Greater London, 1943.

Acheson, Dean Gooderham, A.B., LL.B. (b. 1893), U.S. Secretary of State in the Truman Administration, 1949–52. Appointed 1961 to advise Sec. of State Dean Rusk on American policy in regard to Nato.

Acton, John Emerich Edward Dalberg, 1st Baron, K.C.V.O., D.C.L., LL.D. (1834–1902), English historian and brilliant scholar; Professor of Modern History at Cambridge, 1895–1902.

Adam, Robert (1728–1792), one of four Scottish brothers, all distinguished architects. Developed a characteristic style in planning and decoration and designed many important public and private buildings and interiors. His achievements include the great aristocratic houses of Harewood, Yorks; Osterley, Middlesex; Syon, Middlesex; Kedleston, Derbyshire.

Adams, John (1735–1826), succeeded Washington as President of the United States, and was the first of the Republic's ambassadors to England.

Adams, John Couch, F.R.S. (1819–92), English mathematician and astronomer. Shared credit for discovery of the planet Neptune, 1846, with the French astronomer, Leverrier (1811–77).

Adams, Samuel (1722–1803), American statesman, known as the "American Cato," who worked all his life for American Independence and signed the Declaration (1776). He organised the "Boston Tea Party."

Adams, William (*c.* 1564–1620), first Englishman to visit Japan; b. Gillingham, Kent. His knowledge of shipbuilding, navigation and European affairs proved of great value to the Japanese emperor Ieyasu at a time when he was interested in developing foreign trade.

Addams, Jane, B.A., M.A. (1860–1935), famous American sociologist who founded Hull House, Chicago, in 1889.

Addison, Christopher, 1st Viscount, K.G. P.C. M.D., F.R.C.S. (1869–1951). After joining the Labour Party held successive Ministerial offices in 3 Labour Governments and became leader of the House of Lords. Forsook his profession as professor of anatomy at Sheffield Univ. for a political career because of his great interest in public health and social reform.

Addison, Joseph (1672–1719), achieved fame both as a writer and a politician. Held many offices under various governments; contributed to the *Tatler* started by his friend Steele and with him founded the *Spectator*.

Adenauer, Dr. Konrad (b. 1876), Chancellor of the West German Federal Republic, 1949–63. Founder and Chairman of the Christian Democratic Party, 1945–66. To a defeated Germany he gave stable constitutional government, a place in the Western alliance, and provided strong, consistent leadership. He brought about reconciliation with France but resisted all attempts at accommodation with Russia. *See also* **Section C, Part I.**

Adler, Alfred (1870–1937), Austrian physician and psychiatrist and founder of the school of individual psychology. An earlier pupil of Freud, he broke away in 1911, rejecting the emphasis on sex, and regarding man's main problem as a struggle for power to compensate for feelings of inferiority. (*See* **Section J.**)

Adrian IV, Nicholas Breakspear (d. 1159), pope (1154–59), the only English pope, b. near St. Albans. Crowned Frederick Barbarossa as German emperor. Granted overlordship of Ireland to Henry II which started a dispute which raged for 800 years.

Adrian, Edgar Douglas, 1st Baron, O.M., M.A., M.D., F.R.S., F.R.C.P. (b. 1889), Prof. of Physiology, Cambridge Univ. 1937–51; Master of Trinity Coll., Cambridge, 1951–65, Pres. of the Royal Society 1950–55; Pres. of the British Association, 1954; Chancellor of Leicester University, 1958. Trustee of Rockefeller Institute, 1962. Nobel Prize for Medicine, 1932.

Æschylus (525–456 B.C.), father of Greek tragic drama. Composed seventy plays and gained the prize for dramatic excellence thirteen times.

Æsop, name famous for the fables preserved principally through Babrius (2nd century A.D.). About him nothing is known; according to legend he was a Greek slave in the 6th century B.C. who had a number of wild adventures.

Agassiz, (Jean) Louis (Rodolphe) (1807–73), Swiss-American zoologist and geologist. Author of *Researches on Fossil Fishes* (1833–43), and *Studies on Glaciers* (1840). He was an opponent of Darwin.

Agricola, Gnæus Julius (A.D. 37–93), became Roman Consul of Britain A.D. 78. Strengthened the power of the Romans in this country, corrected many abuses, and did much to encourage trade and industry. Remained in Britain 7 years.

Agrippa, Marcus Vipsanius (63–12 B.C.), the greatest military commander of Rome after Julius Cæsar.

Ahmad Khan, Sir Syed (1817–98), great Indian educationist and social reformer who founded what is now the Aligarh Muslim University.

Aird, Sir John, Bart. (1833–1911), contracting engineer of eminence, associated with many great undertakings in different parts of the world, the Aswan Dam on the Nile, completed in 1902, being one of his achievements.

Airy, Sir George Biddell, K.C.B., F.R.S. (1801–1892), Astronomer Royal (1835–1881) at Greenwich Observatory, where his brilliance and industry led to many important researches.

Akbar, Jalal-ud-din Mohammed (1542–1605), the greatest and wisest of the Mogul emperors and one of the great figures of history. He initiated economic and social reforms and succeeded in unifying his vast empire. His courts at Delhi and Agra were centres of culture and learning.

Alanbrooke, Field-Marshal Viscount, K.G., G.C.B.,

O.M., G.C.V.O., D.S.O. (1883–1963), one of the greatest soldiers of modern times; Chief of Imperial General Staff, 1941–46. Sir Arthur Bryant's *The Turn of the Tide* (1957), and *Triumph in the West* (1959), are based on the war diaries of Lord Alanbrooke.

Alaric I (376–410), the famous chief who after the death of Theodosus I led the Visigoths against the Romans, and afterwards invaded both Greece and Italy. He took Rome in 410, and died soon afterwards. It is said that he was buried with a vast treasure in the bed of the River Busento, and so that the Romans might not discover his remains, the slaves who buried him were put to death.

Alban, St., who flourished in the latter part of the 3rd century, was born at Verulamium (where St. Albans now stands) and served as a soldier under Diocletian at Rome. Later he was converted to Christianity, and was for a time a renowned preacher of that religion, finally suffering martyrdom. Offa, king of the Mercians, built a monastery to his memory near Verulamium, four or five hundred years later. St. Alban's Day: Roman Catholic Church, June 22nd; Anglican Church, June 17th.

Albani, Madame (1852–1930), stage name of Marie Louise Emma Lajeunesse, Canadian operatic soprano. Made her first appearance in England at Covent Garden in 1872 and was for many years a leading prima donna, achieving great celebrity as Elsa in *Lohengrin.*

Albert, Prince Francis Augustus Charles Emmanuel, Consort of Queen Victoria (1819–1861). On his marriage with the Queen in 1840 Parliament granted him an income of £30,000 a year. The prince adapted himself with considerable success to the difficulties of his position, and gradually secured the confidence and esteem of statesmen and public alike. The great Exhibition of 1851 owed much of its success to his efforts. He died of typhoid fever in December, 1861. The Albert Memorial forms a national tribute to his memory.

Albertus Magnus, St. (1206–80), Dominican scholastic philosopher, b. Bavaria, one of the great mediaeval university teachers and the most learned man of his time. St. Thomas Aquinas was his favourite pupil. Took scientific interest in nature and made notable botanical observations.

Alcibiades (*c.* 450–404 B.C.), treacherously killed in battle at Melissa, Phrygia, was the celebrated Athenian statesman and general, pupil and friend of Socrates.

Alcock, Sir Walter Galpin, M.V.O., Mus. Doc., F.R.C.O. (1861–1947), English musician, eminent both as organist and composer of church music. He played at the Coronations of King Edward VII, King George V and King George VI. Organist to Salisbury Cathedral, 1916–47, and Professor of Organ at Royal College of Music, 1893–1939.

Alcott, Louisa May (1832–88), American authoress; the charm and naturalness of her writings made her a favourite among children's authors, and her books are still read on both sides of the Atlantic. Her most famous book, *Little Women*, appeared in 1868.

Alcuin (735–804), scholar and ecclesiastic, a leader of the Carolingian Renaissance. His works include poems and historical and theological writings. (*See also* **J30(1)**).

Aldred (d. 1069), a powerful ecclesiastic of the 11th century in great favour with the Conqueror, whom he crowned. Bishop of Worcester (1044–60), and Archbishop of York (1060–1069).

Alekhine, Dr. (Aljechin) Alexander (1892–1946), world chess champion, 1927–35, 1937–46.

Alembert, Jean le Rond d' (1717–1783), a Parisian mathematician and philosopher who achieved great eminence by his numerous scientific works, including the *Theory of the Winds* and the *Precession of the Equinoxes.*

Alexander of Hillsborough, Earl, K.G., P.C., C.H. (1885–1965). Leader of the Labour peers in House of Lords, 1955–65; Min. of Defence, 1946–50; First Lord of the Admiralty, 1929–31, 1940–45, 1945–56.

Alexander of Tunis, Field-Marshal Earl, P.C., K.G., G.C.B., O.M., G.C.M.G., D.S.O. (b. 1891). Comm. 1st Div. at Dunkirk; C.-in-C. Southern Command, 1940–42; G.O.C. in Burma, 1942, when he conducted a masterly retreat; C.-in-C. Middle East, 1942–43, when he was largely responsible for driving the enemy out of North Africa; C.-in-C. Allied Armies in Italy, 1944; and Supreme Allied Commander, Mediterranean, 1944–45, when he successfully led a force drawn from many different nations. Gov.-Gen. of Canada, 1946–52; Min. of Defence, 1952–54.

Alexander II. of Russia (1818–1881), succeeded his father, the Emperor Nicholas, in 1855. In 1861 he emancipated 23 millions of serfs. On March 13, 1881, was assassinated by bombs thrown beneath his carriage in St. Petersburg by Nihilists.

Alexander the Great (356–323 B.C.). King of Macedon, succeeded his father Philip in 336 B.C., and from the first showed himself fitted for mighty military exploits. He conquered in turn the Thebans, the Persian Satraps, overthrew Darius, overran Syria and Phœnicia, possessed himself of all the cities along the Mediterranean, conquered Egypt, founded Alexandria, and finally retired upon Babylon, where he died eleven days later.

Alexandra, Queen (1844–1925), d. of Christian IX. of Denmark, married to the Prince of Wales (afterwards Edward VII.) on March 10, 1863. Queen from Jan. 22, 1901, to May 6, 1910.

Alfieri, Count Vittorio (1749–1803), the Italian poet, was the author of twenty-one tragedies and six comedies.

Alfonso the Wise (1221–1284), a celebrated King of León and Castile, founder of the legal code which became the basis of Spanish jurisprudence, a liberal patron of literature and science, particularly of astronomy; dethroned by his son Sancho in 1282.

Alfred the Great (849–99), king of Wessex, son of Aethelwulf; succeeded his brother as king in 871 and found himself in conflict with the Danes from the outset. After years of effort he won decisive battle of Ethandum (Edington), 878. He prepared for further attacks by the Danes by building ships, fortifications, and by reorganising the militia or *fyrd*, defensive measures which eventually withstood the invading forces. Besides being a great warrior, a very able legislator and administrator, he was also a man of letters and responsible in great measure for the revival of English scholarship.

Allenby, Field-Marshal Viscount, G C.B., G.C.M.G., G.C.V.O. (1861–1936), brilliant cavalry soldier. Served on Western front, 1914–16; commanded in Palestine, 1917–18, capturing Jerusalem on December 9th, 1917. High Commissioner for Egypt, 1919–25.

Alleyne, Edward (1566–1626), a famous actor, contemporary of Shakespeare and founder of Dulwich College.

Alma-Tadema, Sir Lawrence, O.M., R.A. (1836–1912), the son of a Netherlands notary, he came to England in 1869, where he soon made a name for himself as a painter of classical pictures of great beauty of colour and delicate design.

Ampère, André Marie (1775–1836), French mathematician who devoted himself to the study of electricity and magnetism, and was the first to propound the electro-dynamic theory.

Amundsen, Captain Roald (1872–1928). Norwegian explorer, the first to navigate the North-west Passage and the first to reach the South Pole. Sailing in the fishing smack *Gjöa*, he negotiated the North-west Passage in the 3 years, 1903–6. In 1911 he sailed south in the *Fram* and reached the Pole on December 14th, 1911, a month before his English rival Scott. He failed to complete a flight across the North Pole in 1925, but succeeded the next year. He lost his life in the Arctic while attempting to rescue Nobile, who had crashed in the *Italia.*

Anacreon (*c.* 560–475 B.C.), the celebrated Greek poet whose Odes hold a high place in poetic literature.

Anaxagoras (488–428 B.C.), Greek philosopher of Ionia who came to Athens 464 B.C. He inspired Pericles and the poet Euripides with his great love of science, and is said to have been the teacher of Socrates, who, however, differed from him. His rational theories outraged religious opinion and he retired to his native Asia Minor.

Anaximander (611–547 B.C.), Greek philosopher of Miletus in Asia Minor, pupil of Thales. He was the first among the Greeks to make geographical maps, and to speculate on the origin of the heavenly bodies; he introduced the sun-dial from Babylon or Egypt.

Anaximenes (b. *c.* 570 B.C.), the last of the Milesian school founded by Thales. For him the primal substance was air and he was the first to see the differences between substances in quantitative terms.

Andersen, Hans Christian (1805–1875), perhaps the most gifted writer of fairy tales the world has known. *Mit Livs Eventyr* (The Story of My Life) is as interesting as his fairy tales, which include *The Ugly Duckling, The Little Mermaid, The Emperor's New Clothes, The Little Matchseller.* Born and died in Denmark.

Anderson, Elizabeth Garrett, M.D. (1836–1917), one of the first English women to enter the medical profession. Practised in London for many years. In 1908–9 was Mayor of Aldeburgh, her native town, the first woman to be a mayor.

Andrea del Sarto (1487–1531). This celebrated son of a Florentine tailor was one of the great Italian artists of his time, known as the "faultless painter." Most of the famous galleries of the world contain examples of his magnificent fresco and other painting, mainly dealing with religious subjects.

Andrée, Salomon August (1854–1897), a Swedish explorer who attempted in 1897 to reach the North Pole by balloon, but, except for a message by pigeon despatched two days after his ascent, was not heard of again until in August 1930 a Norwegian scientific expedition led by Dr. Gunnar Horn discovered the remains of the Andrée expedition on White Island. The discovery included a log-book, sketch maps and the diaries kept by Andrée.

Andrew, Saint, one of the apostles of Jesus, brother of Simon Peter, whose festival is observed on November 30th. He became the patron saint of Scotland in the eighth century.

Angelico, Fra (1387–1455). Italian painter of religious subjects, mostly in the form of frescoes, of which the best examples are at Florence.

Angell, Sir Norman (b. 1874), author and publicist, whose works include *The Economic Chaos* and *The Peace Treaty* (1919), *The Great Illusion* (1910) and *The Money Game* (1928). Nobel Prize for Peace 1933.

Ångström, Anders Jöns (1814–74), Swedish physicist, whose life was devoted to the study of heat, magnetism and spectroscopy, and in all three he contributed greatly to scientific knowledge. The unit used for measuring the wavelength of light was named *Angstrom* in his honour.

Anne, Queen (1665–1714), Queen of Great Britain and Ireland from 1702 to the time of her death, was a daughter of James II., and succeeded William III., her cousin. During her reign England, in alliance with Austria, Holland, Prussia, Savoy, and Portugal, entered upon the War of the Spanish Succession. Anne's reign has been called the Augustan Age of Britain because of the many eminent men of letters who flourished during that period. She was the last of the Stuarts to occupy the British throne. The most important domestic event of her reign was the passing of the Act of Union with Scotland in 1707.

Anouilh, Jean (b. 1910), French playwright, several of whose plays have been translated into English, including *Roméo et Jeannette* (Fading Mansion), *Eurydice* (Point of Departure), *L'Invitation au Château* (Ring Round the Moon), and he has made a number of films. (*See also* **I6**).

Anselm St. (1033–1109), Archbishop of Canterbury, was a native of Aosta, and succeeded Lanfranc as English Primate. He was in serious conflict with William Rufus on the question of ecclesiastical rights, and for a time suffered exile. Under Henry I., he regained power, making a compromise with that monarch which enabled him to carry on his theological work in comparative harmony. He died at Canterbury, and was canonised in 1494, his day being celebrated in the Roman Church on April 21st.

Anson, George, 1st Baron (1697–1762), a navigator of great eminence, whose *Voyage round the World* is still a popular book of adventure. He won many victories, obtained a peerage, rose to full Admiral's rank in the Navy, and served two terms as First Lord of the Admiralty.

Antoninus Pius (86–161), Emperor of Rome from A.D. 138 to 161, the successor of Hadrian. He governed with ability and his reign brought peace and prosperity to the empire. It was during his reign that the wall between the Forth and Clyde was built.

Antonius Marcus or **Mark Antony** (*c.* 83–30 B.C.), celebrated Roman Triumvir and General; a warm supporter of Cæsar; but engaged in intrigues after the latter's death, and was opposed by Brutus and Cassius. His association with the Egyptian Queen Cleopatra is the subject of Shakespeare's play. Committed suicide after defeat by Octavian.

Antony, St. (or **Anthony**) (*c.* 251–356), was a native of Upper Egypt, and according to his own account spent much time in conflict with the devil. He is one of the best-known saints of the Roman calendar, and his festival is on January 17th. He was believed to give relief to those who appealed to him when suffering from erysipelas, from which tradition the name St. Anthony's Fire is given to the disease.

Apelles, Greek painter, the most celebrated of antiquity, who flourished in the 4th century B.C. at the time of Alexander the Great. His most famous pictures, which have not survived, are of Alexander wielding the thunderbolts of Zeus and of Aphrodite rising from the sea.

Apollinaire, Guillaume (Wilhelm Apollinaris Kostrowitzi) (1880–1918), French poet representative of the restless and experimental period in the arts before the First World War. He invented the term *surrealism.* Born in Rome of Polish extraction.

Appert, Nicholas (1752–1841), sometimes known as François Appert, invented the method of preserving animal and vegetable foods by means of hermetically sealed cans or tins. He had no scientific training, but his painstaking work and countless experiments bore the mark of a true scientist. His revolutionary methods paved the way for the creation of a vast world industry which cans millions of tons of food a year.

Appleton, Sir Edward Victor, G.B.E., K.C.B., D.Sc., F.R.S. (1892–1965), English physicist; worked under Rutherford at Cavendish Lab. (1920–24); Prof. of Physics, London Univ. (1924–36), Prof. of Natural Philosophy at Cambridge (1936–39), Sec. of D.S.I.R. (1939–49). Best known as the discoverer of the ionised region of the upper atmosphere which became known as the Appleton Layer. His researches led to the development of radar. Nobel Prize for Physics, 1947; Pres. Brit. Ass., 1953.

Apollonius of Perga (fl. 220 B.C.), Greek mathematician of the Alexandrian school, remembered for his conic sections; introduced the terms *ellipse, parabola,* and *hyperbola.*

Apollonius Rhodius (fl. 250 B.C.), scholar and poet of Alexandria and Rhodes, librarian at Alexandria. He wrote on the text of Homer and is remembered for his epic *Argonautica* about the Argonaut heroes.

Aquinas, Thomas, Saint (*c.* 1225–74), chief scholastic philosopher whose system was ruled by Leo XIII in 1879 to be the official Catholic philosophy. He was greatly influenced by Aristotle. The most important of his works are *Sumna contra Gentiles.* and *Sumna theologica.*

Arago, Dominique Francois Jean (1786–1853), French astronomer and physicist, remembered for his discoveries in electromagnetism and optics.

Archimedes (287–212 B.C.), Greek mathematician, physicist, and inventor, to whom we are indebted for his discoveries in mechanics (notably the lever), hydrostatics (floating bodies), and for the invention of the famous Archimedean screw. He lived most of his life in Syracuse, and was killed there during the siege by the Romans under Marcellus.

Argand, Aimé (1755–1803), Swiss physician, inventor of the lamp bearing his name, which was the first to admit a current of air to increase the power of the flame, by use of a chimney glass and circular wick.

Ariosto, Ludovico (1474–1533), one of the most celebrated of the Italian poets, author of *Orlando Furioso.* Besides this famous epic he wrote many comedies, satires, and poems.

Aristides (530–467 B.C.) Athenian statesman and

general who achieved fame at the battle of Marathon, 490 B.C.

Aristippus (c. 435–356 B.C.), founded the Cyrenaic school of philosophy, which taught that sensual pleasure was the only happiness. He was a native of Cyrene, in Africa, but became a pupil of Socrates, and settled in Athens.

Aristophanes (c. 444–c. 385 B.C.) was one of the foremost Athenian play-writers and the greatest of the Greek comic poets. His plays are full of satire, and deal unsparingly with the people and institutions of his time.

Aristotle (384–322 B.C.), Greek philosopher, pupil of Plato, after whose death in 347 he left Athens to become tutor to the young prince Alexander of Macedon. Subsequently at Athens he established his famous school in the garden known as the *Lyceum*, where he lectured in the *peripatos* (cloister) which gave it its name *Peripatetic*. He took the whole field of knowledge as his subject, giving it unity, and providing a philosophy which held its own for 2,000 years.

Arkwright, Sir Richard (1732–1792), was a native of Preston, and in early life a barber and travelling hairdealer. Becoming interested in mechanical problems, he set himself the task of inventing an improved cotton-spinning machine. Hargreaves' spinning-jenny was then the leading machine, but the yarn it produced could only be used for weft; it was not compact enough for warp threads. Arkwright therefore experimented until, by adopting an arrangement of rollers that moved with different velocities, he succeeded in perfecting his "spinning-frame," which successfully produced a yarn that could be used for warp as well as for weft. He took out his first patent in 1769, and entering into partnership with Mr. Jehediah Strutt, of Derby, became a manufacturer on a large scale, in 1771 establishing the first spinning-mill worked by water-power.

Arne, Dr. Thomas Augustine (1710–1778), English composer of considerable merit and of great popularity in his day. He composed numerous ballad operas, and at Drury Lane, Covent Garden, and Vauxhall organised the chief performances for long periods. His best-known opera was *Artaxerxes*, and his most popular songs were *Rule, Britannia!* and *Where the Bee Sucks*.

Arnold, Matthew (1822–1888), son of Dr. Thomas Arnold, achieved a high reputation as poet and critic. As the propounder of the principles of "sweetness and light," as well as by his graceful verse, he secured a high place amongst the literary men of the Victorian era.

Arnold, Thomas, D.D. (1795–1842), headmaster of Rugby from 1828 to his death. His influence at Rugby was such as to give that institution a supreme position among English public schools. A man of intense spiritual feeling, of a sympathetic and lovable nature, yet possessed of all the necessary attributes of scholarship, he was greatly esteemed and venerated.

Arrhenius, Svante August (1859–1927), Swedish chemist, one of the founders of modern physical chemistry. Received 1903 Nobel Prize for originating the theory of electrolytic dissociation (ionisation). Director of the Nobel Institute, 1905–27.

Arrol, Sir William (1839–1913), well-known contractor and engineer, whose firm built the Tay, Forth, and London Tower Bridges as well as the Manchester Ship Canal. Originally a piecer in a cotton-mill, and later a working blacksmith.

Artaxerxes was the name borne by several ancient Persian kings, some of whom achieved great distinction. The first Artaxerxes was the son of Xerxes, and reigned from 464 B.C. for 40 years; he was succeeded by Darius II. (424–404 B.C.), who in turn was followed by Artaxerxes II., who reigned until 358. Artaxerxes III, the last to bear the name, was a cruel and treacherous man and was poisoned in 338.

Arthur, fabled Celtic warrior of c. A.D. 600, the first reference to whom is in the 9th-cent. chronicle of Nennius, who speaks of his 12 victorious battles against the invading Saxons. His legend developed into a vast literature in mediaeval times, which was welded together by Sir Thomas Mallory in his great work *Morte d'Arthur*.

Arundel, Thomas, Archbishop of Canterbury (1353–1414), in the reigns of Richard II, and Henry IV, previously Bishop of Ely and Archbishop of York, and for a time Lord Chancellor. An active politician and bitter enemy of heresy.

Ashfield, Lord, P.C. (1874–1948), President Board of Trade, 1916–19; M.P. Ashton-under-Lyne, 1916–20; first Chairman of the London Passenger Transport Board created in 1933.

Aske, Robert, the leader of the Pilgrimage of Grace, directed against the Reformation; executed 1537.

Asoka (273–232 B.C.), Emperor of India (c. 255–c. 237 B.C.), and the most powerful ruler of his time, his Empire extending from the Himalayas to what is now Madras. He was the first ruler to embrace Buddhism and accord it recognition. Becoming a Buddhist (c. 257 B.C.) he turned aside in disgust from the thought of his earlier military conquests, and attempted by missionary propaganda to spread Buddhism throughout his lands. Many rocks and pillars are inscribed with his moral exhortations. He gave great impetus to Buddhism by organising it as the state religion.

Asquith, Herbert Henry, 1st Earl of Oxford and Asquith (1852–1928), Liberal statesman who led a great peacetime administration from 1908 until the outbreak of the First World War and the wartime coalition with the Conservatives from 1915–16 when he was displaced by Lloyd George. Home Sec. (1892–95) in Gladstone's last ministry; Chan. of the Exchequer (1904–8) under Campbell-Bannermann whom he succeeded as Prime Minister. His government enacted important social reforms including old-age pensions (1908) and unemployment insurance (1911). The death of Edward VII in 1910, the struggle over the Irish Home Rule Bill, the declaration of war on Germany, and the Easter Rising in Dublin in 1916 were among the events of his premiership. He resigned the leadership of the Liberal Party in 1926. Earldom of Oxford and Asquith conferred, 1925.

Asser, a Welsh monk of the tenth century, author of a remarkable life of King Alfred.

Astor, John Jacob (1763–1848), the founder of the Astor family of millionaires, was a native of Heidelberg, and emigrating to America, went out to the North-West and began trading in furs, soon building up a large fortune, which he invested in New York real estate.

Astor, Nancy Witcher, Viscountess, C.H. (1879–1964), the first woman M.P. to take her seat in the House of Commons, an American by birth, wife of the 2nd Viscount Astor (1879–1952).

Atatürk, Kemal (1881–1938), builder of modern Turkey. A fine soldier, he defended the Dardanelles against the British in 1915 and drove the Greeks out of Turkey in 1922. President of the Turkish Republic, 1923–38.

Athanasius, St. (296–373), was Bishop of Alexandria. He spent much of his time in bitter theological controversy, and was driven from Alexandria; taking refuge in the desert, he wrote numerous letters in support of Christian doctrine, and under Julian was recalled to Alexandria. The Athanasian creed is supposed to reflect his belief.

Athelstan (895–940), grandson of Alfred the Great, was crowned King of England in 925, and was the first ruler of all England.

Atherstone, William Guybon (1813–98), South African geologist and an originator of the South African diamond industry. He drew attention to the possibility of diamonds near Kimberley and in 1867 identified a crystal found near the Vaal River, thus helping to start mining development.

Attila (406–453), King of the Huns, was a warlike leader, who achieved many conquests over the Roman forces, committing great ravages and laying large tracts of country waste. He marched through Germany and Gaul, and died as he was preparing for another invasion of Italy.

Attlee, Clement Richard, 1st Earl, O.M., K.G., P.C., C.H. (b. 1883), Prime Minister in two successive Labour Governments, 1945–51; served as Deputy Prime Minister to Mr. Churchill, 1942–45. He was educated at Haileybury and University Coll., Oxford. Called to the Bar in 1905; tutor and lecturer in social science at the London School of Economics, 1913–23. Became Mayor of Stepney in 1919, Labour M.P. for Limehouse in 1922, and Parliamentary Leader of the Labour Party, 1935–55. During his Premiership the welfare society was established and the freedom and independence of India granted. Retired in 1955; earldom conferred. His writings include an autobiography, *As it Happened* (1954), and *Empire into Commonwealth* (1960). *See also* Section C, Part I.

Auber, Daniel François Esprit (1782–1871), a distinguished French composer of light operas, *Masaniello, Fra Diavolo, Le Domino Noir*, etc.

Auchinleck, Field-Marshal Sir Claude J. E., G.C.B., G.C.I.E., D.S.O. (b. 1884), Indian Army officer who was C.-in-C. Middle East, 1941–42, and the last British C.-in-C. in India, 1943–46.

Auden, Wystan Hugh (b. 1907), influential poet and dramatist, b. in England, naturalised American. Succeeded C. Day Lewis as Prof. of Poetry, Oxford Univ., 1956–61.

Auer, Leopold (1845–1930), the famous Hungarian violinist and teacher of the violin, among his pupils being Mischa Elman and Jascha Heifetz.

Augustine, Saint (354–430), the greatest of the Latin fathers, bishop of Hippo, b. at Tagaste in N. Africa of a pagan father and Christian mother (Saint Monica). He ranks high as a philosopher and his influence on Christianity has been second only to that of St. Paul. He was a voluminous writer, the most important works being his *Confessions*, the *City of God, On the Trinity*, and *On the Work of Monks*.

Augustine of Canterbury, Saint (d. *c*. 605), the Roman Benedictine missionary monk who was sent to Britain by Gregory the Great in 597 to convert the English peoples to Christianity. He became the first archbishop of Canterbury.

Augustus, Caius Octavianus (63 B.C.–A.D. 14), Roman emperor, succeeded Julius Cæsar. After a triumvirate of twelve years, in which he was associated with Mark Antony and Lepidus, he became supreme ruler and for forty-five years exercised a beneficent and powerful sway. He was a devoted patron of Horace and Virgil.

Aurelius, Marcus Antoninus. *See* **Marcus Aurelius Antoninus.**

Auriol, Vincent (1884–1966), French politician. Voted against surrender in 1940, was interned and escaped to London in 1943. President of the French National Assembly, 1946, and of the Fourth Republic, 1947–54.

Aurangzeb (1618–1707), Mogul emperor of India, 1659–1707, son of Shah Jehan. He was a ruler of ability, and greatly extended his empire by conquest, but his zeal for Mohammedanism aroused the hatred of the Hindus and his persecution of the Sikhs transformed them from a pacifist sect into a militant brotherhood. When he died the disruption of the vast Mogul territory rapidly followed.

Austen, Jane (1775–1817), author of *Emma, Mansfield Park, Northanger Abbey, Persuasion, Pride and Prejudice*, and *Sense and Sensibility*. Though confining herself to the personal relations of the English middle classes, she combined artistry, accuracy, imaginative power, satiric humour, sense, and genuine feeling with the ability to create a vast range of living characters, and is often considered the most perfect English novelist.

Austin, 1st Baron, K.B.E. (1866–1941), was the well-known English motor manufacturer. He was the pioneer of the small car—the 7-horsepower car—which he put on the market in 1921.

Avenzoar (Ibn Zuhr) (*c*. 1090–1162), a Moslem physician, born in Seville, the greatest of his time. His chief work was the *Tasir*.

Averroës (Ibn Rushd) (1126–98), Arab philosopher and medical writer, born in Córdova, last and most famous thinker of Moslem Spain. He studied philosophy, theology, mathematics, medicine, and jurisprudence. His greatest works are his commentaries on Aristotle. He was a friend of Avenzoar.

Avicenna (980–1037) of Bokhara, Arab philosopher and physician whose *Canon of Medicine* had an enormous influence on mediaeval Europe.

Avogadro, Amedeo (1776–1856), Italian physicist, remembered for his hypothesis, since known as Avogadro's Law, that equal volumes of gases under identical conditions of temperature and pressure contain the same number of molecules.

Avon, Earl of. (*See* **Eden, R. Anthony.**)

Ayrton, William Edward, F.R.S. (1847–1908), English electrical engineer, inventor of a number of electrical measuring instruments. His first wife, **Matilda Chaplin Ayrton** (1846–83), was one of the first woman doctors and his second wife, **Hertha Ayrton** (1854–1923), became known for her scientific work on the electric arc and sand ripples and for her work for woman suffrage.

Ayub Khan, Mohammad, Field Marshal (b. 1907), military leader and President of Pakistan since 1958; educated at Aligarh Moslem Univ. and Sandhurst. Under the 1962 constitution all executive authority is vested in the President.

Azikiwe, Rt. Hon. Nnamdi, LL.D. (b. 1904), Nigerian statesman; Gov.-Gen. of Fed. of Nigeria, 1960–; President, 1963–.

B

Baber or Babar (Zahir ud-din-Mahomet) (1483–1530), founder of the Mogul dynasty which ruled Northern India for three centuries, and a descendant of Tamerlane.

Bach, Johann Sebastian (1685–1750). Born at Eisenach, Germany, he became one of the greatest composers in history and has been called the father of modern music. During his appointment as organist at the Thomaskirche, Leipzig, he composed all his great devotional music, including the wonderful *St. Matthew Passion, The Passion according to St. John* and the Mass in B Minor. His incessant labour affected his eyes, and in 1749 he became totally blind. His family was connected with music for seven generations, of which his was the fifth.

Bach, Carl Philipp Emanuel (1714–88), third son of Johann Sebastian Bach. He is important in the history of music as founder of the symphony and sonata.

Backhaus, Wilhelm (b. 1884), German pianist, recognised as one of the most gifted, especially in the interpretation of the great classical and romantic concertos. Professor of the Piano at the Royal College of Music, Manchester, 1905.

Bacon, Francis, Lord Verulam, and Viscount St. Albans (1561–1626), was one of the greatest of English philosophers and statesmen, who was Attorney-General to Elizabeth, and under James I. became Lord Chancellor. His political career was tarnished by certain acts of corruption, for which he paid the penalty, but his writings were marked by keen insight, brilliancy of language, and a depth of thought which place them in the first rank of philosophical literature. His *Novum Organum* and his *Essays* are splendid monuments of learning and wisdom.

Bacon, Roger (1214–1294), the Franciscan friar, was a man of remarkable gifts, of great learning and inventive power. In an age of darkness he was the first to insist on the importance of experiment and can claim the title of founder of experimental science. Optics, explosives, engines, mechanical flight came within the range of his researches. The invention of gunpowder has been attributed to him, but without adequate evidence. For a long time he was looked upon as an alchemist and sorcerer, though of late his discoveries have been more truly appreciated.

Baden-Powell, Lt.-Gen. Lord, O.M., G.C.M.G., G.C.V.O., K.C.B. (1857–1941), brilliant cavalry soldier, famous for his defence of Mafeking in the South African War. Founded the organisation of Boy Scouts (1908) and Girl Guides (1910) to promote good citizenship in the rising generation. Chief Scout of the World, 1921–41.

Baer, Karl Ernst von (1792–1876), Estonian biologist, founder of the science of embryology, and discoverer of the mammalian ovum.

Baffin, William (1584–1622), navigator and explorer who in 1616 discovered the bay which separates the north-east coast of British North America from Greenland, which bears his name.

Bagehot, Walter (1826–77), English economist and journalist. Editor of the *Economist*, 1860–77. Wrote three books of lasting importance, *The English Constitution*, 1867, *Physics and Politics*, 1872, and *Lombard Street*, a description of the Money Market, 1873. He was among the first to advocate the creation of Life Peers to strengthen the House of Lords.

Baird, John Logie (1888–1946), Scottish television pioneer; inventor of the televisor and the noctovisor.

Baker, Sir Benjamin, K.C.B., K.C.M.G., F.R.S.

(1840–1907), an eminent engineer. He was consulting engineer to the Egyptian Government for the Aswan Dam, joint engineer with Sir John Fowler of the Forth Bridge, and engineer of the Central London Tube Railway.

Baker, Sir Herbert, K.C.I.E., R.A. (1862–1946) was an eminent architect who designed the Bank of England, Rhodes House, Oxford, and, with the late Sir E. Lutyens, New Delhi.

Bakst, Léon (1868–1924), Russian painter who designed scenery and costumes for the Russian Ballet of Serge Diaghilev.

Balboa, Vasco Nuñez de (1475–1517), Spanish explorer, who was the first European to set eyes upon the Pacific Ocean.

Baldwin of Bewdley, 1st Earl, K.G., P.C. (1867–1947), the leading Conservative politician between the two world wars and Prime Minister, 1923–24, 1924–29, and 1935–37.

Baldwin, James (b. 1924), American Negro writer, regarded as the most significant of his time. Novels include *Go Tell It to the Mountain* (1953) and *Another Country* (1962).

Balewa, Sir Abubakar Tafawa, K.B.E. (1912–1966), Federal Prime Minister of Nigeria, 1960–66; murdered during the crisis of January 1966.

Balfour, Arthur James, Earl of, K.G., O.M., P.C. (1848–1930), statesman, scholar, and philosopher. Entered Parliament as a Conservative in 1874. Prime Minister, 1902–5. He also served as First Lord of the Admiralty under Asquith and as Foreign Secretary under Lloyd George. His most notable action was issuing the Balfour Declaration on Palestine.

Balliol, John de, English baron whose widow in 1269 founded the college at Oxford which bears his name. Fought for Henry III. against Simon de Montfort. Died in exile in 1269.

Baliol, John (1249–1315), son of the above, competed with Robert Bruce for the Scottish throne, and Edward I. decided in his favour. Only reigned four years, when Edward deposed him, committing him to the Tower, and finally banished him from the country. He retired to Normandy. His son, Edward Baliol, recovered his father's kingdom in 1332, and was upheld by Edward III. whilst very unpopular by reason of his having given up the south of Scotland to the English. He renounced his title and throne in 1356, and retired to England on an annuity.

Ball, John (d. 1381), English priest and a leader of the Peasants' Revolt, after which he was excuted. Author of the couplet *When Adam delved, and Eve span, Who was then the gentleman?*

Balzac, Honoré de (1799–1850), one of the greatest of French novelists, and the author of over eighty novels to which he gave the covering title of *La Comédie Humaine*, depicting the appetites and passions of the new social class born of the revolution and Napoleon.

Bampton, John (1689–1751), an eminent divine, who founded the Oxford Bampton Divinity lectures.

Bancroft, Sir Squire (1841–1926), one of the best-known Victorian actor-managers.

Bandaranaike, Hon. Solomon West Ridgway Dias, B.A. (1899–1959). Socialist Prime Min. of Ceylon from 1956 until his assassination in 1959. His widow, Mrs. Sirimawo Bandaranaike, became the world's first woman Prime Minister, 1960–65.

Banks, Sir Joseph, Bt., F.R.S. (1743–1820), was president of the Royal Society for upwards of forty years. As a naturalist he was one of the most eminent men of his time, and encouraged science in every form. When Captain Cook made his voyage to the South Seas in 1768, Sir Joseph accompanied him for the purpose of observing the transit of Venus. He left very valuable botanical collections to the British Museum.

Banting, Sir Frederick Grant, K.B.E., M.C., D.Sc., M.D., F.R.S. (1891–1941). Canadian physician and discoverer of insulin. Prof. of Medical Research, Toronto University, 1923–41.

Bantock, Sir Granville, Mus. Doc. (1868–1946), Professor of Music at Birmingham University 1908–34; Chairman of Trinity Coll. of Music, London. He wrote songs, orchestral and choral music.

Barbirolli, Sir John, F.R.A.M. (b. 1899), English conductor; succeeded Toscanini as conductor of the New York Philharmonic Symphony Orchestra, 1937–42; conductor of the Hallé Orchestra since 1943.

Barbarossa (Red Beard), name given to **Frederick I** (c. 1122–90), greatest of the mediæval Holy Roman emperors who struggled (1159–77) to free the Empire from the domination of the Pope. The two brothers who were Barbary pirates also had this name: **Uruj** (c. 1482–1518) was killed by the Spaniards, and **Khaireddin** (c. 1482–1546) conquered Tunis for the Turks in 1534 and died in Constantinople.

Barbusse, Henri (1874–1935), noted French author and writer of the famous war novel *Le Feu*, which is one of the most remarkable and realistic of all war books, and portrays in a starkly vivid way the experience of the common soldier.

Barker, Dame Lilian, D.B.E. (1874–1955), governor of the Borstal Institution for Girls at Aylesbury, 1923–35; Ass. Comm. of Prisons, 1936–43.

Barnardo, Dr. Thomas John (1845–1905), the founder of the well-known homes for orphan-waifs, for some forty years devoted himself to the protection, education and advancement of destitute children.

Barrie, Sir James Matthew, Bt, O.M. (1860–1937), popular Scottish author and playwright. Among his novels are *A Window in Thrums* and *The Little Minister*, while his plays include *Quality Street*, *The Admirable Crichton*, *Dear Brutus*, *Mary Rose*, *Shall We join the Ladies?* and the children's classic, *Peter Pan*. His work is clever and entertaining and is tinged with mysticism.

Barrow, Isaac (1630–1677), a famous divine, mathematician, Greek scholar, and tutor of Sir Isaac Newton. His "Sermons" are amongst the finest in the language.

Barry, Sir Charles, R.A. (1795–1860), architect of the Houses of Parliament at Westminster which took twenty years to build. Knighted in 1852, and buried in Westminster Abbey. His son:

Barry, Sir John Wolfe Wolfe-, K.C.B., F.R.S. (1836–1918), an eminent engineer, designed and carried out some of the most prominent undertakings of the time, including Barry Dock and Tower Bridge.

Barth, Karl (b. 1886), Swiss theologian, one of the leading Protestant thinkers of the 20th century, described by the late Pope John as a Protestant St. Thomas Aquinas.

Bartok, Bela (1881–1945), Hungarian composer, one of the great figures in the music of his century. From an early age deeply interested in folk-song which inspired him in his researches into Hungarian and Rumanian peasant music. His compositions include string quartets, violin sonatas, concertos, orchestral music, a ballet and an opera, and a collection of over 7,000 melodies. Professor at Budapest Conservatory, 1907–12, when he retired into private life as a result of the opposition his compositions aroused.

Bartolommeo, Fra (1469–1517), the distinguished Florentine painter and friend of Savonarola, at whose death he became a monk.

Bartolozzi, Francesco, R.A. (1727–1815), a Florentine engraver who came to London in 1764 where he became one of the original members of the Royal Academy. He produced an enormous number of engravings and was responsible for the stipple technique.

Baruch, Bernard Mannes (1870–1965). American economist. Assisted U.S. Government in both world wars, and in 1946 was chairman of the United Nations Atomic Energy Commission.

Bashkirtseff, Marie (1860–84), Russian painter and writer of a famous autobiographical diary.

Bassi, Agostino (1773–1856), Italian amateur microscopist who first suggested that infectious diseases might be caused by the invasion of the body by micro-organisms.

Batten, Jean Gardner, C.B.E. (b. 1909) the famous New Zealand airwoman who made aviation history by her record solo flight from England to Australia in 1934.

Baudelaire, Charles Pierre (1821–67), French poet of startling originality and great sensitivity, best known for his book of verse *Les Fleurs du Mal*, also a brilliant critic. He was inordinately attached to his mother and allowed his life to be ruined by poverty, despair, and ill-health.

Bax, Sir Arnold Edward Trevor, K.C.V.O., F.R.C.M., F.R.A.M. (1883–1953), Master of the King's Musick, 1942–52; Master of the Queen's Musick, 1952–53. His work includes numerous piano compositions, songs, and chamber works.

Baxter, Richard (1615–91), a great Nonconformist divine, remarkable for the ability and boldness of his writings.

Bayard, Pierre du Terrail, Chevalier de (1475–1524), a French knight of exemplary conduct and remarkable for his chivalry. Fell at the Battle of Sesia, and was named "Le Chevalier sans peur et sans reproche."

Baylis, Lilian Mary, C.H. (d. 1937), manager of the Old Vic theatre from 1898 and of Sadler's Wells from 1931. Did great work for the British stage.

Beaconsfield, Benjamin Disraeli, Earl of, K.G., P.C. (1804–81). Son of Isaac D'Israeli (*q.v.*). Statesman and novelist; with Burke (*q.v.*) exercised most influence on Conservative political theories. His first novel, *Vivien Grey*, published when he was only twenty-one, was a brilliant success and the author was able to enter Society. *Coningsby* and *Sibyl*, published twenty years later, helped to rouse the social conscience to the evils of industrial life and of the deplorable relations existing between rich and poor (the "two nations"). Disraeli entered Parliament in 1837, but had only short periods of office before his terms as Prime Minister in 1868 and 1874–80. The second period was marked by the purchase of the Suez Canal shares, by the conferment on the Queen of the title, Empress of India, and by a diplomatic triumph at the Congress of Berlin, abroad, and by a continuation of measures for social reform, at home. He was a gifted orator, the rival and antithesis of Gladstone and the friend of Queen Victoria, who favoured his policies, honoured his wife, and called him "Dizzy."

Beardsley, Aubrey Vincent (1872–98), black-and-white artist, whose illustrations in the *Yellow Book* aroused much controversy.

Beatty, 1st Earl, Admiral of the Fleet, P.C., G.C.B., O.M., G.C.V.O., D.S.O. (1871–1936). First Sea Lord, 1919–27. From 1912 to 1916 Commander of Battle Cruiser Squadron. From Nov. 1916 to 1919 succeeded Lord Jellicoe as Admiral of the main British Fleet. On Aug. 28, 1914, fought the German fleet in the Heligoland Bight. On May 31, 1916, Lord Beatty with his battle cruisers was engaged in a great sea fight with the Germans off Jutland, for which he was granted £100,000 and an Earldom in 1919.

Beaumont, Francis (1584–1616), and **Fletcher, John** (1579–1625), joint authors of many plays, including *The Maid's Tragedy* and *Philaster*. Beaumont was buried in Westminster Abbey, and Fletcher interred in St. Saviour's, Southwark. Thought by some to be authors of plays attributed to Shakespeare.

Beaverbrook, 1st Baron (William Maxwell Aitken) (1879–1964), British newspaper owner and politician, a Canadian by birth. A man of tremendous energy and will-power, he rendered great service as Minister of Aircraft Production in the crucial years, 1940–1. He controlled the *Daily Express*, *Sunday Express*, and *Evening Standard* which sponsored his various political campaigns, notably the Empire Free Trade Movement. Known affectionately as "Max" or "The Beaver."

Becket, Thomas (1118?–70), saint and martyr, Archbishop of Canterbury under Henry II. A powerful and ambitious prelate who boldly supported the authority of the Pope against the dictates of the King, and was assassinated in Canterbury Cathedral December 29th, 1170, being canonised two years later.

Becquerel, Antoine Henri (1852–1908), French physicist who in 1896 discovered radioactivity in uranium. Shared with the Curies the 1903 Nobel Prize in Physics.

Bede, "The Venerable" (673–735), a monk of great influence and ability whose historical works cover a great range and are valuable in the outline they give of the early history of this country.

Beecham, Sir Thomas, Bt., C.H. (1879–1961), conductor and impresario. Founded the London Philharmonic Orchestra in 1931; introduced into England the operas of Richard Strauss, Russian operas, and the Diaghilev ballet; championed the music of Delius. Recognised as one of the world's greatest conductors, especially in the interpretation of Mozart and Wagner. Conductor of the Royal Philharmonic Orchestra (1946). Pub. Frederick Delius biography (1959); Memoirs: *A Mingled Chime*.

Beecher, Henry Ward (1813–1887), an eminent American preacher and lecturer, whose church at Brooklyn was for many years the most popular in the United States. Brother of Mrs. H. B. Stowe.

Beerbohm, Sir Max (1872–1956), brilliant critic and caricaturist who contributed to the *Saturday Review* during his "twelve years' bondage to dramatic criticism" (1898–1910).

Beethoven, Ludwig van (1770–1827), one of the world's greatest musicians and composers, born at Bonn of a poor but musical family, his father being a tenor singer in the service of the electoral prince at Bonn. As a child he was already remarkable for his playing of the harpsichord and violin and for his power of extemporization. Some of his compositions, sonatas, songs and pianoforte variations were published when he was only 13. At 17 he visited Vienna and played before Mozart who promptly recognised his genius. When he was about 30 he began to suffer from the worst malady that could possibly have befallen him: he became deaf. He faced his fate with indomitable courage and perhaps more than any other artist continued to develop until he reached the loftiest pinnacle of musical fame. Between the years 1805 and 1808, Beethoven composed some of his greatest works: the oratorio *Mount of Olives*, the opera *Fidelio*, and the *Pastorale* and *Eroica* symphonies besides a number of concertos, sonatas and songs. He composed four overtures to *Fidelio* at different periods: *Leonore No. 2* (1805), *Leonore No. 3* (1806), *Leonore No. 1* (1807) and *Fidelio* (1814). The *Mass in C* was first performed in 1810 and the *Mass in D* was written between the years 1819 and 1822. The symphonies, nine in number, rank as the greatest ever written and the pianoforte sonatas and string quartets are unequalled in beauty. He died at Vienna at the age of 56.

Behring, Emil von (1854–1917), German bacteriologist and father of the science of immunology. Awarded Nobel Prize in 1901.

Behring, Vitus (1680–1741), Danish navigator who entered the Russian service and in 1728 discovered Behring's Strait, afterwards being wrecked on Behring's Island, where he died.

Belisarius (505–565), brilliant Roman general under Justinian, famed for his campaigns against the Vandals, Ostrogoths, and Persians.

Bell, Alexander Graham, (1847–1922), born in Edinburgh, emigrated to Canada in 1870 and in 1871 lectured in Boston, mainly to teachers of the deaf, later becoming an American citizen. In 1876 exhibited an invention which was developed into the telephone. Invented the photophone, and devoted much attention to the education of deaf-mutes.

Bell, Gertrude Margaret Lowthian, C.B.E. (1868–1926), the "uncrowned Queen of Arabia," was a famous traveller in the East, especially in Arabia.

Bellamy, Edward (1850–1898), American journalist and author of *Looking Backward*, a utopian novel in which he foretells of many changes that have since come to pass.

Bellini, a celebrated family of Venetian painters of the Early Renaissance: **Jacopo** (*c.* 1400–70) and his two sons **Gentile** (1429–1507), whose works include the *Adoration of the Magi* (National Gallery), and **Giovanni** (*c.* 1429–1516), the most important painter of the 15th cent., brother-in-law of Mantegna, and teacher of Giorgione and Titian.

Bellini, Vincenzo (1801–35), Italian operatic composer; born in Sicily, the son of an organist. His graceful vocal melodies were much admired by his friend Chopin and he enjoyed successes in Paris and London. His best-known operas are *I Capuleti ed i Montecchi*, *La Sonnambula*, *Norma*, and *I Puritani*.

Belloc, (Joseph) Hilaire (Pierre) (1870–1953), a writer of great versatility whose works include *The Bad Child's Book of Beasts*, *The Path to Rome*, *Hills and the Sea*, *Cautionary Tales*, and historical studies of Danton, Robespierre and Richelieu.

Belzoni, Giovanni Battista (1778–1823), a renowned explorer of Egypt who settled in England at the beginning of the 19th century. After a precarious existence began to turn his attention to hydraulic experiments, and went to Egypt with a view to getting the Government to sanction a scheme of his for raising the water of the Nile. He was then attracted to the study of Egyptian antiquities, and engaged in highly successful researches.

Benedict, St. (*c*.480 – *c*.543), b. at Nursia near Spoleto, in Umbria; founded twelve monasteries, and the Order of Benedictine Monks, at Monte Cassino, near Naples. Here he wrote his celebrated Rule, a unique document of wide application. (*See* **Monasticism, J30**).

Benes, Dr. Eduard (1884–1948), Czechoslovak statesman; co-founder with Thomas Masaryk of the Czech Republic; Foreign Minister, 1918–35, and President 1935–38 and 1940–48. An all-party ministry was overthrown by a communist *coup d'état* in February 1948, and Benes, in failing health, resigned the Presidency in June, dying in September.

Benavente y Martinez, Jacinto (1866–1954), one of the greatest of Spanish dramatists. Author of *Los Intereses Creados* and other famous plays. Nobel Prizewinner, 1922.

Ben-Gurion, David (b. 1886), Zionist leader. Educated at Istanbul University. Helped to organise the Jewish Legion in 1918, and was prominently connected with the Labour movement in Palestine in between the world wars. Prime Minister of Israel, 1948–63.

Bennett, Enoch Arnold (1867–1931), author and journalist. His stories of the Pottery Towns, where he was brought up, are of high merit. *The Old Wives' Tales*, *Clayhanger*, and *Hilda Lessways* are among his most successful novels. He also wrote plays, including *Milestones*, *The Great Adventure*, and *Mr. Prohack*.

Bennett, James Gordon (1841–1918), proprietor of the *New York Herald*, and a famous yachtsman and motorist. He sent out Stanley on the expedition which resulted in the finding of Livingstone.

Bennett, Sir William Sterndale (1816–1875), English composer best known for his oratorio *The Woman of Samaria*. Schumann pronounced him to be " a thorough Englishman, a glorious artist, and a beautiful and poetic soul."

Bentham, Jeremy (1748–1832), the founder of the school of political philosophy, the tenets of which were extended by John Stuart Mill. His works on *Government*, *Usury*, and *The Principles of Morals and Politics*, expound the Utilitarian system with great lucidity.

Bentley, Richard (1662–1742), an eminent classical scholar and critic, for long Master of Trinity College, Cambridge. He was a formidable controversialist and did pioneer work in textual criticism.

Benz, Karl (1844–1929), German engineer whose motor car produced in 1885 was one of the first to be driven by an internal-combustion engine.

Béranger, Jean Pierre de (1780–1857), was the most popular song writer that France has produced. His songs were often written to serve some passing political purpose, and were invariably in harmony with popular sentiment.

Beresford, William Carr Beresford, Viscount (1768–1854), British General. Participated in capture of Cape Colony and of Buenos Aires. Reorganised Portuguese Army. Master-General of Ordnance in Wellington administration.

Berg, Alban (1885–1935), Austrian composer whose best known work is the three-act opera *Wozzeck*, based upon a drama by Büchner (*q.v.*), which has become a modern classic.

Bergson, Henri Louis (1859–1941), French philosopher, exponent of the theory of vitalism and the life force. Member of French Academy, 1941; Nobel Prize for Literature, 1927. Author of *Matter and Memory* (1896) and *Creative Evolution* (1907).

Bériot, Charles Auguste de (1802–70), Belgian violinist, whose first wife was the great operatic contralto Malibran. His son **Charles Wilfrid de Bériot** (1833–1914) was a fine pianist and the teacher of Ravel.

Berkeley, George, D.D., Bishop of Cloyne (1685–1753), the propounder of the philosophy that the only things that are real are our ideas of what is presented to our senses. In support of this philosophy he wrote several works of great ingenuity of argument, chief amongst them being his *Alciphron, or the Minute Philosopher*.

Berlin, Irving (b. 1888), American composer of popular songs, and the pioneer of both ragtime and jazz music; his songs including *Alexander's Rag-time Band*, *Always*, *What'll I Do?* were the beginning of popular jazz.

Berlioz, (Louis) Hector (1803–69), composer, born in S.E. France, the son of a country doctor; eccentric, highly-endowed, he was the greatest figure in the French romantic movement. His outstanding dramatic works are *La Damnation de Faust* and the *Roméo et Juliette* symphony. His first wife was an Irish actress, Harriet Smithson, for whom he formed a romantic attachment while she was appearing in Shakespearean parts in Rome.

Bernadotte, Count Folke (1895–1948), nephew of the late King Gustav of Sweden. As head of the Swedish Red Cross arranged for the exchange of prisoners in the second world war. In April 1945, he was the intermediary through whom Himmler attempted to capitulate. Appointed United Nations mediator for Palestine in 1947 and brought about a truce between the Arabs and Jews, but was assassinated by Jewish terrorists.

Bernadotte, Jean Baptiste (1764–1844), was a French commander of great distinction who served under Napoleon, and in 1810 was chosen heir to the throne of Sweden. In 1818 he succeeded as Charles XIV., and was a capable ruler.

Bernal, John Desmond, M.A., F.R.S. (b. 1901) Professor of Physics, Birkbeck College, 1938–1965. Author of *The Social Function of Science*, *Science in History*, *World Without War*, and of many other works on scientific and social subjects, notably crystallography, poison gases, and post-war housing.

Bernard of Menthon (923–1008), patron saint of mountaineers. Founded the alpine hospices of Saint Bernard on the famous Great Saint Bernard Pass between Switzerland and Italy.

Bernard, Saint, of Clairvaux (*c.* 1090–1153), famous French abbot of the monastery of Clairvaux whose sermons and letters had very great influence in Western Europe.

Bernhardt, Sarah (1845–1923), the most renowned tragedienne of her time. Became a member of the Comédie Française after the Siege of Paris, and thereafter occupied a specially prominent position as an actress. Her first performance in London was in 1879. Among her most conspicuous successes are *Théodora*, *Fédora*, and *La Tosca*, while she also appeared as Hamlet with distinction.

Berthelot, Marcellin Pierre Eugène (1827–1907), French chemist and politician, and the first to produce organic compounds synthetically.

Berzelius, Jöns Jakob (1779–1848), Swedish chemist, whose researches laid the foundations for modern chemical science. He devised the system of chemical symbols in use today and discovered several elements.

Bessemer, Sir Henry, F.R.S. (1813–1898), famous for his invention of the well-known process of converting cast-iron direct into steel. His invention entirely revolutionised steel manufacture, greatly reducing the cost of production and making it possible to utilise steel in many directions where previously iron only had been used.

Bevan, Rt. Hon. Aneurin, M.P. (1897–1960). British socialist politician of remarkable genius; architect of the National Health Service which came into operation in 1948. M.P. for Ebbw Vale, 1929–60; Min. of Health, 1945–51; Min. of Labour, Jan.–Apr. 1951. (*See also* **C5**.)

Beveridge, Lord, K.C.B. (1879-1963), British economist. Director of the London School of Economics, 1919–37, and Master of University College, Oxford, 1937–44. Drew up the Beveridge Plan, published in 1942, which formed the basis of the present Health and Insurance Schemes.

Bevin, Rt. Hon. Ernest, M.P. (1881–1951), Secy. of State for Foreign Affairs 1945–51; Minister of Labour and National Service, 1940–45. A British Trade Union Leader who became prominently associated with the Dockers Union, of which he was Assistant General Secretary and of the Transport and General Workers Union of which he was still General Secretary when he entered the Coalition Government as Minister of Labour. He was Chairman of the General Council of Trades Union Congress, 1937.

Bichat, Marie François Xavier (1771–1802), French physiologist and anatomist whose study of tissues founded modern histology. His theory was that life is "the sum of the forces that restrict death."

Biddle, John (1615–62), the first English Unitarian. He was fined, imprisoned and banished for his publications attacking the Holy Trinity. Under a general Act of Oblivion in 1652 he resumed his teachings, which led to further imprisonment, and as a result he died of fever.

Binyon, (Robert) Laurence, C.H. (1869–1943), English poet, art critic, and authority on Oriental art, keeper of prints and drawings at the British Museum.

Birch, (Samuel John) Lamorna, R.A. (1869–1955), English landscape painter in oils and water-colours, well known for his charming Cornish landscapes and sea studies. His pictures are hung in all the principal galleries of England.

Birkbeck, George (1776–1841), physician, philanthropist, and philosopher. A Yorkshireman who settled in London in 1804, and became the chief founder of Mechanics' Institutes.

Birkenhead, 1st Earl of, P.C., G.C.S.I. (1872–1930), Sec. for India, 1924–1928. Lord Chancellor, 1919–1922, Attorney-General 1915 to 1919. M.P. for the Walton Divn. of Liverpool from 1906 to 1918, and West Derby Divn. thereof from Dec. 1918 to Jan. 1, 1919.

Birkett, 1st Baron (William) Norman, Q.C. (1883–1962), great English advocate; Lord Justice of Appeal, 1950–7; Judge King's Bench Div. 1941–50; British Mem. (Deputy) Int. Mil. Tribunal at Nuremberg 1945–46; M.P. (L.) for East Nottingham, 1923–24 and 1929–31.

Bishop, Sir Henry Rowley (1786–1855), composer of many popular ballad operas and songs. *Maid Marian, Guy Mannering* and *The Miller and his Men*, are his best-known operas. He was also a very successful glee-writer, and was the composer of *Home, Sweet Home.* Was the first musician to be knighted in 1842.

Bismarck, Otto Eduard Leopold von, Prince Bismarck, Duke of Lauenburg (1815–98), Prusso-German statesman, chief architect of the German empire. Of Junker family he began his diplomatic career in 1851 when he was appointed Prussian member of the revived German Diet of Frankfurt. Prussian ambassador at St. Petersburg (1859–62), where he gained the confidence of the new Tsar (Alexander II), and at Paris (1862), where he had the opportunity of studying Napoleon III. Recalled to Germany by William I to head his government, from which time dates the autocratic rule which was ultimately to prove so disastrous for Germany and the world. There followed the events which led to the victory over Austria in 1866, the humiliation of France in 1871 culminating in William I being proclaimed emperor of Germany at Versailles. From 1871 until the death of William I in 1888 the rule of the "iron chancellor" dominated Europe and German domestic affairs. A struggle for supremacy developed between Bismarck and William II which ended (1890) in the "old pilot" being dropped, to use a figure of speech made memorable by one of Tenniel's cartoons. Bismarck retired to his country estates to spend the rest of his life in criticism of the emperor.

Bizet, Georges (1838–75), properly Alexandre César Léopold, French composer who gave the operatic stage several operas full of charming melody and whose immortal *Carmen* from the story by Mérimée was his greatest achievement. He also wrote some orchestral works, piano music, and songs. He died too young to enjoy popularity.

Björnson, Björnstjerne (1832–1910), the Norwegian poet, dramatist, and novelist is one of the great names in modern European literature, his poems, plays, and stories being marked by a strong intellectuality and a rich imagination.

Black, Joseph (1728–99), Scottish chemist. Prof. of anatomy at Glasgow (1756–60) and of medicine and chemistry at Edinburgh (1760). Specially known for discoveries of carbon dioxide (he called it "fixed air") and latent heat. His original work earned him the title father of quantitative chemistry.

Blackett, Patrick Maynard Stuart, C.H., F.R.S., M.A. (b. 1897), British scientist; Prof. of Physics, Imperial College of Science and Technology, 1953–64, Manchester University, 1937–52. Author of *Military and Political Consequences of Atomic Energy* (1948). Awarded 1948 Nobel Prize for his work in nuclear and cosmic ray physics. His studies also include operational research and magnetism. Pres. British Association, 1957; Pres. Royal Society, 1966.

Blackmore, Richard Doddridge (1825–1900), a novelist who in 1869 made a great reputation with his romantic story of *Lorna Doone.*

Blackstone, Sir William (1723–1780), was a Justice of the Court of Common Pleas. His great work, *Commentaries on the Laws of England*, became one of the British classics.

Blackwood, Algernon, C.B.E. (1869–1951), British author. As a young man, farmed in Canada and worked on New York newspapers. Then, from 1906, produced a steady flow of books, plays, and short stories of high quality.

Blair, Robert (1699–1746), a noted Scottish poet, whose poem, *The Grave*, entitles him to a place in all collections of British poetry.

Blake, Robert (1599–1657), Parliamentary general and an admiral in the Cromwellian navy in the Dutch and Spanish wars.

Blake, William (1757–1827), painter, poet, and mystic, whose *Songs of Innocence* and scriptural drawings reveal an intense spirituality. He was a highly independent and original thinker and has been called "the great teacher of the modern western world."

Bland-Sutton, Sir John, Bt., M.D. (1855–1936), an eminent surgeon, whose association with the Middlesex Hospital is commemorated by the Bland-Sutton Institute of Pathology.

Blasco-Ibáñez, Vicente (1867–1928), a Spanish man of letters who wrote *The Four Horsemen of the Apocalypse* and other novels which made him world-famous.

Blériot, Louis (1872–1936), French airman; the first to fly the English Channel from Calais to Dover, July 25, 1909.

Bligh, William (1754–1817), British sailor who had a noted career as a brave and able officer but who is chiefly remembered for the mutiny in 1789 on his ship *The Bounty* on a breadfruit expedition from Tahiti to the West Indies. In 1776 he had sailed with Cook as master of the *Resolution.* As Governor of New South Wales (1806) he fought to suppress the rum traffic. Promoted vice-admiral in 1814.

Blind, Karl (1826–1907), was a native of Mannheim, and in 1847 associated himself with the German revolutionary movement, but was arrested and imprisoned. Gaining his liberty, he resided in Brussels for a time, and afterwards settled in London, remaining in close touch with men like Mazzini and Louis Blanc, and by pen and speech constantly advocating political freedom.

Bliss, Sir Arthur (b. 1891), English composer, succeeded Sir Arnold Bax as Master of the Queen's Musick in 1953. His best known works are the *Colour Symphony* (1922), *Morning Heroes* (1930) and his ballet *Checkmate* (1937). Mus. Dir. B.B.C., 1941–44.

Bloch, Ernest (1880–1959), composer, whose music is characterised by its Jewish and oriental themes. He was born in Geneva, Switzerland, and became a naturalised American citizen.

Blomfield, Sir Reginald, R.A., M.A., F.S.A. (1856–1942); was a prominent architect, designer of gardens and country houses.

Blondin, Charles (Jean François Gravelet) (1824–1897), a famous French rope performer, who crossed Niagara Falls on a tight-rope.

Blücher, Field-Marshal Gebhard Leberecht von (1742–1819), was the famous Prussian commander who, after a long and brilliant military career, joined forces with Wellington in the final campaign against Napoleon, and materially helped to win the great victory of Waterloo by advancing to Wellington's support.

Blum, Léon (1872–1950), statesman and architect of French socialism. Led a "popular front" government in 1936 and a "caretaker" government for a brief period 1946–47. Served as vice-premier 1937–38. During 1940–45 was interned in Germany.

Blunden, Edmund Charles (b. 1896), English poet and critic; Prof. of Eng. Lit. at Tokyo Univ., 1924–27; Fellow and Tutor Eng. Lit., Merton College, Oxford, 1931–43; Prof. of English, Hong Kong Univ., 1953–64. Succeeded Robert Graves as Prof. of Poetry at Oxford, 1966.

Blunt, Wilfred Scawen (1840–1922), English poet and political writer who after retiring from the diplomatic service (1858–70) championed Egyptian, Indian, and Irish independence; imprisoned in 1888 for activities in the Irish Land League. His *Secret History of the English Occupation of Egypt* (1907) aroused much controversy. He married a granddaughter of Lord Byron.

Boadicea, queen of the Iceni (of Norfolk), also called **Boudicca.** She raised an army against and defeated the Roman invaders, but was afterwards vanquished by Suetonius and committed suicide in 62.

Boccaccio, Giovanni (1313–1375), an Italian author who has often been called the father of the novel. He had a lively imagination and a graceful style, and his famous *Decameron*—condemned by two Popes and by the Council of Trent—has been a fount of inspiration to poets and story-tellers from Shakespeare to Keats.

Boccherini, Luigi (1743–1805), Italian composer, contemporary of Haydn, who first gained fame as a 'cellist. Settled in Madrid in 1769 as composer to the Chapel of the Infante, which position he held until 1785. Was appointed composer to the Court of Frederick William II. of Prussia, but returned to Spain in 1797, and died in poverty in Madrid.

Bode, Johann Elert (1747–1826), German astronomer remembered mainly for his law (known as Bode's Law) for the calculation of the relative distances of the planets from the sun.

Boehm, Sir Joseph Edgar, Bt., R.A. (1834–90), British sculptor. Executed several famous monuments and statues including that of Carlyle on the Chelsea Embankment, the monument to Dean Stanley in Westminster Abbey, Darwin in the Natural History Museum, Kensington, and the equestrian statue of the Duke of Wellington at Hyde Park Corner.

Bohr, Niels Henrik David (1885–1962), Danish nuclear physicist whose researches into the structure of the atom gave him great authority in the world of theoretical physics. With Rutherford he applied the quantum theory to the study of atomic processes. Awarded Nobel Prize for Physics, 1922.

Boieldieu, François Adrien (1775–1834), French composer whose masterpiece, *La Dame Blanche*, was published in 1825. Composed many works in collaboration with Cherubini and Mehul. Succeeded Mehul as Professor of Composition at the Conservatoire, Paris, in 1817.

Boileau-Despréaux, Nicolas (1636–1711), literary critic and French poet who was contemporary with Molière, Racine, and La Fontaine. He wrote many classical imitations and is famous for his *Satires*.

Boito, Arrigo (1842–1918), Italian poet and composer. He wrote the libretti of *Otello* and *Falstaff* for Verdi, and for his own operas of *Mefistofele* and many others.

Boleyn, Anne (1507–36), queen of Henry VIII and mother of Queen Elizabeth. Originally maid-in-waiting to Catharine of Aragon and her successor when Catharine's marriage was annulled. She failed to produce a male heir and was beheaded on a charge of adultery.

Bolivar, Simón (1783–1830), South American revolutionist, b. Caracas, called the Liberator; today revered as the greatest of Latin American heroes; with some British aid freed N.W. South America from Spain, founding Grand Colombia (now Venezuela, Colombia, Panama, Ecuador); died poor, of tuberculosis, in Colombia, after Venezuela had left the Union.

Bonaventura, St. (1221–1274), a Franciscan monk of great learning and piety, and a leading Schoolman. He was called "the Seraphic Doctor."

Bondfield, Rt. Hon. Margaret Grace, C.H. (1873–1953), Min. of Labour, 1929–31. Represented Northampton, 1923–24. Wallsend, 1926–31. First woman member of a British Cabinet.

Bone, Sir Muirhead (1876–1953), Scottish artist, famous for his drawings and etchings of architectural subjects. Excelled in dry-point and drawings of intricate scaffolding. His son **Stephen Bone,** painter and critic, died in 1958 at the age of 53.

Bonheur, Rosa (1822–1899), a native of Bordeaux, and one of the most noted animal painters of the 19th century.

Boniface, St. (*c.* 675–754), a Benedictine monk, native of Devon, original name Wynfrith. Sent by Pope Gregory II. on missionary work in Germany; appointed archbishop of Mainz, 746. Attacked and killed with over 50 companions by pagans in Friesland.

Bonnard, Pierre (1867–1947), French painter of landscapes, still-lifes, and nudes, a great colourist and skilled draughtsman, acclaimed as one of the greatest painters of the century. Exhibition at the Royal Academy, 1966.

Booth, Edwin (1833–93), American Shakespearean actor, son of Junius Brutus Booth, the English tragedian, and brother of John Wilkes Booth, who assassinated President Lincoln.

Booth, William (1829–1912), founder and first general of the Salvation Army, b. Nottingham. He entered the Methodist New Connexion and was from the first interested in evangelical work. In 1865, with the help of his wife, Catherine Booth, he began mission work in the East End of London which led to the creation in 1878 of the Salvation Army on military lines. His zeal and organising ability developed it into a great religious military organisation with branches in many parts of the world. His son Bramwell (*d.* 1925) and his daughter Evangeline were among his successors. *See also* **J39.**

Borgia, Cæsar (1476–1507), the masterful and unscrupulous son of Pope Alexander VI., who paved his way to power by the murder of those who stood in his way, and aided by Louis XII. of France, became ruler of Romagna, the Marches, and Umbria. Pope Julius II. banished him from Rome, and he was imprisoned in Spain, but escaped to find a soldier's death in the Army of Navarre in the invasion of Castile.

Borodin, Alexander Porfyrievich (1834–87), Russian composer who was a professor of chemistry and founded a school of medicine for women. In a busy professional life he wrote two symphonies, three string quartets, the symphonic sketch *In the Steppes of Central Asia*, some beautiful songs, piano music, and the opera *Prince Igor*, left unfinished at his death but completed by his friends Rimsky-Korsakov and Glazunov.

Borrow, George Henry (1803–81), English author, for many years agent for the British and Foreign Bible Society; in the course of his wanderings studied gypsy life and wrote of his experiences in *Lavengro*, *Romany Rye*, *Bible in Spain*.

Bose, Subhas Chandra (1897–1945), Indian nationalist leader; killed in aeroplane crash.

Boswell, James (1740–1795), made himself famous by writing *The Life of Dr. Johnson*, spending some years in close intimacy with the great lexicographer, and producing what is probably the finest biography in the language. His own journals and letters, collected together by Yale University and published in 1949 as *The Boswell Papers*, are among the greatest literary collections ever assembled.

Botha, General the Rt. Hon. Louis (1862–1919), the Boer general who succeeded Joubert in command of the Transvaal forces in the Boer War 1899–1902. On parliamentary government being granted to the Transvaal in 1907 he became the first Prime Minister, and attended the Imperial Conference in England the same year. In 1910 made first Premier of the South African Union. After the outbreak of war with Germany took the field at the head of a Union force and, in addition to putting down a rebel movement engineered by Germany, conquered a large portion of German African Territory.

Bottesini, Giovanni (1821–89), Italian double-bass player, also famous as an opera conductor and composer.

Botticelli, Sandro (*c.* 1444–1510), Italian painter and disciple of Savonarola, the democrat. Produced many notable pictures, and assisted in the decoration of the Sistine Chapel. His illustrations to Dante's *Divine Comedy* are world-famous.

Bottomley, Horatio (1860–1933), politician, journalist, financier, and for many years one of the most notorious characters in England.

A brilliant speaker, he was twice M.P. for South Hackney. Altogether 260 petitions in bankruptcy were presented against him, mostly without effect; he was constantly in the law courts, defending himself with skilful audacity against famous K.C.s. Millions of pounds passed through his hands, much of it obtained from small investors, but he died in poverty after serving seven years' penal servitude for fraud.

Botvinnik, Mikhail (b. 1911), Russian chess player; world champion 1948–57, 1958–60, 1961–63. Retired 1965.

Boughton, Rutland (1878–1960), English composer who has also written on the history and philosophy of music. His opera *The Immortal Hour* has enjoyed great success.

Boult, Sir Adrian C., Kt., M.A., D.Mus., F.R.C.M. (b. 1889). President London Philharmonic Orchestra, 1965; and its chief conductor, 1950–57; conductor of the B.B.C. Symphony Orchestra, 1930–50, and Musical Director B.B.C., 1930–42.

Bowdler, Thomas (1754–1825), a pious English physician, who issued expurgated editions of Shakespeare and Gibbon, eliminating all expressions offensive to good taste. Hence the term "bowdlerise."

Boyce, William (1710–79), famous London organist, composer of church music, songs and cantatas, and master of the orchestra of George III.

Boyd Orr, John, 1st Baron, F.R.S., M.D., D.Sc. (b. 1880), scientist, farmer and nutritional expert. Prof. of Agriculture, Aberdeen University, 1942–45; Director-General, World Food and Agricultural Organisation, 1945–48, Chancellor of Glasgow Univ, 1946. Nobel Peace Prize, 1949. *See also* Section C, Part I.

Boyle, Hon. Robert, F.R.S. (1627–1691), English scientist who with Robert Hooke laid the foundations of the modern sciences of chemistry and physics. He established "Boyle's law," which states that the volume of a gas varies *inversely* as the pressure upon it, provided temperature be constant.

Bradley, General of the Army Omar N. (b. 1893), distinguished American soldier who was appointed chairman of the Joint Chiefs of Staff in succession to Gen. Eisenhower in 1949. Commanded 2nd U.S. Army Corps in Tunis and Sicily, the American Assault Forces in Normandy in 1944, and later the 12th U.S. Army Group. Retired 1953.

Bradman, Sir Donald George (b. 1908), Australian cricketer and one of the world's best batsmen. Captained Australia in Test matches against England, 1936–48.

Bragg, Sir Wm. (Henry), O.M., K.B.E., F.R.S., M.A., D.Sc. (1862–1942), was a brilliant scientist. Nobel Physics Prize, 1915. Was Director of the Royal Institution of Great Britain; Fullerian Prof. of Chemistry, Royal Institution, and Director of Davy-Faraday Research Laboratory, 1923–42; President of British Association, 1928. President of the Royal Society, 1936–40.

Bragg, Sir (William) Lawrence, O.B.E., M.C., F.R.S. (b. 1890), succeeded Lord Rutherford as Cavendish Prof. of Experimental Physics, Cambridge Univ., 1938–53. Dir. Royal Institution. 1954– . Shared with his father (Sir Wm. H. Bragg) the 1915 Nobel Prize for research work on X-rays and crystal structures.

Brahe, Tycho (1546–1601), a celebrated Danish astronomer, and fellow-worker of Kepler. With large sums of money put at his disposal by Frederick II. of Denmark, he built an observatory called Uraniborg on the island of Hveen, near Copenhagen, where for over 20 years he carried out a vast programme of accurate and systematic observations of the heavenly bodies and compiled tables of their motions.

Brahms, Johannes (1833–97), composer, regarded as outstanding figure of German classic-romantic school; born in Hamburg, the son of a double-bass player. His compositions are classical in form yet possess deep intensity of expression and poetic significance. He composed four symphonies which rank amongst the greatest ever written, two piano concertos, a violin concerto, a double concerto for violin and 'cello, much fine chamber music, numerous songs of great lyrical beauty, and choral work, notable among which is his *German Requiem*. Lifelong friend of the Schumanns. His life was devoted to music; he never married.

Braille, Louis (1809–52), French educationist, who, as teacher of the blind, perfected his system of reading and writing for the blind. As the result of an accident when he was three years old he was himself blind.

Bramah, Joseph (1749–1814), a Yorkshireman who devoted himself to invention, introduced numerous mechanical improvements, including the hydrostatic press, a liquid-pumping apparatus, a most ingenious series of safety locks, and bank-note printing machines.

Brampton, Lord, P.C. (1817–1907), long known to the public as Sir Henry Hawkins. Was famous as an advocate, and took part in many celebrated cases, including the Tichborne trial. His *Reminiscences*, published in 1904, was one of the books of the year.

Brandes, Georg Morris Cohen (1842–1927), Danish literary critic who exerted a vitalising influence on literature and art.

Brangwyn, Sir Frank, R.A., R.P.E. (1867–1956), artist of Welsh extraction born at Bruges; first worked for William Morris making cartoons for textiles. He was regarded as the greatest mural artist and etcher of his day.

Breakspear, Nicholas. *See* **Adrian IV.**

Brecht, Bertold (1898–1959), German dramatist and poet, whose cynical and satirical works are characteristic of the period between the two world wars. He left Germany in 1933 for Russia, went to the United States in 1941, and returned to E. Germany after the war. His plays include *Die Dreigroschenoper* (with music by Kurt Weill). *See also* **Modern Drama.**

Brennan, Louis, C.B. (1853–1932), successful inventor, born in Ireland. Paid £120,000 by the British Government for his gyro-directed torpedo; also the inventor of a mono-rail locomotive on the gyroscope principle.

Brewster, Sir David, LL.D., F.R.S. (1781–1868), Scottish physicist, a great experimenter and a prolific writer. Noted for his researches into the polarisation of light; invented the kaleidoscope Helped to found the British Association for the Advancement of Science.

Brezhnev, Leonid Ilyich (b. 1906), succeeded Nikita Khrushchev as First Secretary of the Soviet Communist Party in Oct. 1964; formerly President of the Supreme Soviet of the U.S.S.R.

Bridges, Edward, 1st Baron, K.G., G.C.B., G.C.V.O., P.C., M.C. (b. 1892), son of Robert Bridges. Permanent Secretary to the Treasury and Head of Civil Service, 1945–56. Secretary to the Cabinet, 1938–46. Chanc. Reading Univ., 1959. Chairman British Council, 1959–.

Bridges, Robert, O.M., M.A. (1844–1930), was Poet Laureate 1913–30. Practised medicine up to 1882, thenceforward devoting himself mainly to literature. He published several volumes of poems and plays, displaying refined fancy and a broad philosophic spirit. His *Testament of Beauty* was published in 1930.

Bridgewater, Francis Egerton, 3rd (and last) Duke of (1736–1803). The projector of the famous Bridgewater Canal, which was the beginning of the great English canal system, and yielded his family enormous wealth; it was absorbed in 1887 by the Manchester Ship Canal Company, who paid £1,710,000 for it.

Bridgewater, Francis Henry Egerton, 8th (and last) Earl of, F.R.S. (1756–1829), grand-nephew of the last-named, and founder of the famous *Bridgewater Treatises*, written by the most celebrated divines and scientists of the day, and devoted to demonstrating the power, wisdom, and goodness of God, as manifested in the Creation.

Bridie, James, (pseudonym of Osborne Henry Mavor), C.B.E., LL.D., M.D. (1888–1951), Scottish author and dramatist. Educated at Glasgow Academy and University. The first of his many successful plays was *The Anatomist*, produced in 1931. Others include *Tobias and the Angel, Jonah and the Whale, Mr. Bolfrey, Dr. Angelus.*

Brieux, Eugène (1858–1932), French dramatist, whose plays are satires on definite evils of society, and deal with such subjects as divorce, legal hypocrisy, social diseases, etc. Was elected a member of the French Academy in 1909.

Bright, Sir Charles Tilstone (1882–88), English telegraph engineer, who after superintending the laying of telegraph lines in many parts of Great Britain organised the Atlantic Telegraph-Company (1856), and as Engineer-in-chief supervised the laying of the first Atlantic Cable (1858).

Bright, Rt. Hon. John (1811–1889), a famous Radical Quaker statesman and orator, one of the chief promoters of the Reform movement which led to the introduction of Free Trade.

Britten, Edward Benjamin, O.M., C.H. (b. 1913), English composer of a variety of music, including song cycles, chamber music, choral works, and the operas *The Rape of Lucrezia, Peter Grimes, Albert Herring, Billy Budd, The Turn of the Screw* and *A Midsummer Night's Dream.* His great *War Requiem* was first heard at the consecration of the new Coventry cathedral in 1962. Closely associated with the Aldeburgh Festival.

Broca, Pierre Paul (1824–80), French pathologist, anthropologist, and a pioneer in neuro-surgery. He localised the seat of speech in the brain in the convolution named after him and originated methods for measuring brain and skull ratios.

Brock, Sir Thomas, K.C.B., R.A. (1847–1922), pupil of Foley, achieved a high reputation as a sculptor. The Queen Victoria Memorial in front of Buckingham Palace is his work.

Brogan, Denis William, M.A. (b. 1900), Prof. of Political Science at Cambridge. An authority on France, America, and Britain, and his works include *The Development of Modern France, Politics and Law in the United States,* and *The English People.*

Broglie, French noble family of Piedmontese origin who settled in France in the 17th cent. **Victor Maurice, comte de Broglie** (1671–1745) was marshal of France and fought in the wars of Louis XIV. **Louis Victor, prince de Broglie** (b. 1892) and **Maurice, duc de Broglie** (1875–1960) the eminent French physicists are grandsons.

Brontë, Charlotte (1816–1855), one of the most gifted novelists of the 19th century. Her *Jane Eyre,* published in 1847, attracted universal notice, and her other novels, *Shirley, Villette,* and *The Professor,* are all marked by the force of strong genius. Her sisters, **Emily** (1818–48) and **Anne** (1820–49), also wrote novels and poems, Emily's *Wuthering Heights* and some of her verse showing exceptional power.

Brookeborough, Basil Stanlake Brooke, 1st Viscount, C.B.E., M.C. (b. 1888), Prime Minister of Northern Ireland 1943–63. An Ulster Unionist.

Brooke, Rupert (1887–1915), a British poet who died during the first world war, whose works, though few, showed great promise and include the poems *Grantchester* and *If I Should Die.*

Brougham, Lord, P.C., F.R.S. (1778–1868), one of the chief legal luminaries of the 19th century, who made a great name by defending Queen Caroline against George IV., and afterwards rose to political eminence.

Brown, Sir Arthur Whitten, K.B.E. (1886–1948), together with Sir John Alcock (d. 1919) in 1919 made the first transatlantic flight, crossing from Newfoundland to Ireland in 16 hr. 12 min.

Brown, John, " of Ossawatomie " (1800–1859), the hero of Harper's Ferry, whose action in inciting certain negro slaves to rebel in 1859 struck the note of alarm which resulted in the Civil War. His attempt to take the Arsenal at Harper's Ferry was defeated, and he was hanged, being afterwards regarded as a martyr by the Abolitionists.

Browne, Charles Farrer (Artemus Ward) (1834–1867), was one of the most whimsical and entertaining humorists America has produced. In addition to his books he wrote and delivered exceedingly funny lectures, and was making an English tour with them when he was seized with a fatal illness, dying at Southampton.

Browne, Hablot Knight (1815–1882), best known as " Phiz," the illustrator of Dickens's novels, from the *Pickwick* period down to *Little Dorrit.*

Browne, Sir Thomas (1605–82), author of *Religio Medici,* was a London physician and antiquary.

Browning, Elizabeth Barrett (1806–1861), English poet, wife of Robert Browning. She was an astonishingly brilliant child, reading Homer at the age of eight. While saddling her pony she injured herself and on her father's orders spent her youth lying on her back in her room, studying and writing. Her meeting with Browning brought a remarkable recovery. In the autumn of 1846 they were secretly married and went to live in Florence. Although now regarded as a comparatively minor poet she was more read than her husband in their lifetime. Best known poems are " Cry of the Children ", *Sonnets from the Portuguese* (her own love story) and *Aurora Leigh,* a novel in verse.

Browning, Robert (1812–1889), English poet, son of artistic and cultured parents, whose money enabled him to travel and write poetry. His earlier poems and plays, though marked by singular insight and power, were far from popular, mainly because of a somewhat obscure and involved style. His *Strafford* and *The Blot on the 'Scutcheon* were both produced by Macready, and attained some measure of stage success. After the death of his wife he returned to England and wrote some of his finest work including *Dramtis Personae* and *The Ring and the Book.* He died in Venice.

Bruce, Robert (1274–1329), took part with Sir William Wallace, (*q.v.*) in the revolt against Edward I., later leading the popular cause. Achieved one victory after another, until at Bannockburn he overthrew the English army and ultimately secured Scottish independence. He reigned twenty-two years as King Robert I.

Bruch, Max (1838–1920), German composer and conductor, best known for his G minor violin concerto.

Bruckner, Anton (1824–96), Austrian composer and organist. He wrote nine symphonies, much religious music, including a *Te Deum* for chorus and orchestra, and a string quintet.

Brummell, George Bryan (1778–1840), " Beau Brummell," the fashion leader in English Society when George IV. was Prince of Wales; was a *bon vivant* and gamester whose excesses involved him in imprisonment and ultimate imbecility.

Brunel, Isambard Kingdom (1806–1859), a prominent engineer who constructed the more difficult portions of the Great Western Railways, and many other important works. He also achieved eminence as a designer of steamships.

Brunel, Sir Mark Isambard (1769—1849), father of the last-named, and constructor of the Thames tunnel, finished in 1843.

Brunelleschi, Filippo (1377–1446), Italian architect, born in Florence, pioneer of Renaissance architecture, adapting the ideals of the Roman or classic period to the conditions of his own day. Many examples of his work are to be seen in Florence—in the Pitti Palace, the Churches of San Lorenzo and San Spirito, the great cupola of the cathedral of Santa Maria del Fiore and the beautiful carved crucifix in the Church of Santa Maria Novella.

Bruno, Giordano (*c.* 1548–1600), Italian philosopher and martyr; entered the Dominican Order at Naples in his 15th year. Accused of heresy he fled from his convent and roamed over Europe. In 1592 he returned to Italy and was arrested by the Inquisition. After 7 years in prison was burned at the stake, Feb. 17, 1600. A statue to him was erected in the Campo dei Fiori, 1889.

Brutus, Marcus Jonius (85–42 B.C.), Roman Governor and one of the founders of Roman civil law.

Bryant, Arthur Wynne Morgan (b. 1899), English historian and pageant producer. Among his works are *English Saga, 1840–1940,* a life of *George V., The Story of England,* and several books on the Napoleonic war years and the Restoration period, including a balanced and informative biography of Pepys.

Buchanan, George (1506–82), Scottish humanist who spent most of his life in France lecturing and writing Latin poems, plays, and treatises. Montaigne, Mary Queen of Scots, and James VI of Scotland were his pupils at various times. He was the best Latin scholar of his age, and his most important works are *De jure regni apud Scotos* and *Rerum Scoticarum historia.*

Buchman, Rev. Frank Nathan David (1878–1961). American evangelist, founder of the movement known as Moral Re-armament. Initiated in 1920 the religious fellowship known as the Oxford Group Movement. *See* **J30**.

Buchner, Eduard (1860–1917), German chemist and professor, famous for his discovery of the enzymes within yeast cells and for his work in the chemistry of fermentation. For this he was awarded the 1907 Nobel Prize for Chemistry.

Büchner, Georg (1813–37), German dramatist

whose career was terminated by his early death at the age of twenty-four, but whose limited output (principally *Dantons Tod* and the fragment *Wozzeck*) is marked by extraordinary power and maturity.

Buckle, Henry Thomas (1821–1862), the author of *The History of Civilisation in England*, one of the most vigorous productions of the 19th century.

Budge, Sir Ernest Alfred Wallis, Litt. D., D. Litt., F.S.A. (1857–1934), a distinguished archæologist who conducted many excavations in Mesopotamia and Egypt. Was Keeper of Egyptian and Assyrian Antiquities at the British Museum, 1893–1924.

Buffon, Georges-Louis Leclerc, Comte de (1707–88), French author and naturalist who devoted his life to the study of natural history and whose great work *Histoire Naturelle* in 36 volumes appeared between 1749 and 1789.

Bulganin, Marshal Nikolai Alexandrovitch (b. 1895), Prime Minister of Soviet Russia, 1955–58. Formerly Soviet Defence Minister. Retired 1960.

Bull, John (c. 1562–1628), was organist to James I. and composed much acceptable music, including, it is supposed, our National Anthem *God save the Queen*.

Bülow, Hans Guido von (1830–94), German pianist and conductor, an outstanding figure among the musicians of his day. He married Liszt's daughter Cosima, who later left him to marry Wagner.

Bunsen, Robert Wilhelm (1811–1899), German chemist, discoverer of the metals cæsium and rubidium, and inventor of the Bunsen burner, battery, and pump. Made many important observations in spectrum analysis.

Bunyan, John (1628–1688), was originally a travelling tinker and is believed to have served in the Parliamentary army. He joined an Independent church in Bedford in 1655 and became a popular preacher. After the Restoration he was thrown into prison, and there wrote *Pilgrim's Progress*, the finest allegorical work in this or any language. Of his other works the *Holy War*, *Grace Abounding*, and *Mr. Badman* are the best known.

Burckhardt, Jacob Christoph (1818–97), Swiss historian whose *The Civilisation of the Renaissance in Italy* is one of the great classics on the subject.

Burghley, William Cecil, Lord (1520–1598), Secretary to Lord Protector Somerset, an influential statesman under Edward VI, and Queen Mary, and subsequently Queen Elizabeth's favourite Minister for forty years.

Burke, Edmund (1729–1797), the acknowledged philosopher of conservatism: son of a Dublin attorney, went to London in 1756, and made his mark in literature by his famous work on the *Sublime and Beautiful*. Later on was private secretary to the Marquis of Rockingham, then Premier, and entered Parliament, where he quickly made a name. An able and earnest debater, he took part in all the great movements of his time, and in 1795, after his retirement, was awarded a handsome pension from the Civil List.

Burnet, Bishop Gilbert (1643–1715), wrote a *History of His Own Times*, which deals with many events of which he had personal knowledge, and is a valuable legacy to historical scholars.

Burnet, Sir John James, R.A. (1859–1938), was a leading British architect, whose most important work was the King Edward VII Galleries of the British Museum, opened in May 1914. Among his many large buildings in London are Adelaide House, and the extension to Selfridge's.

Burney, Fanny (*See* **D' Arblay, Madame.**)

Burns, Robert (1759–1796), Scotland's greatest poet. Startled the world with a little book of poems in 1786 which proclaimed him a true son of the muses. With the £500 that his book yielded him he bought a farm, obtained an appointment with the Excise in 1789, and for the last five years of his life lived at Dumfries. In his career he poured forth song after song of emotional tenderness, and made his name immortal.

Burton, Sir Richard Francis, K.C.M.G. (1821–1890), explorer, orientalist, and diplomatist, who became famous after making a pilgrimage to Mecca in 1853 disguised as a Mohammedan. Later he did much exploring in Central Africa, wrote several books and made a remarkable literal translation of the *Arabian Nights* (16 vols.).

Busoni, Ferruccio Benvenuto (1866–1920), the greatest pianist of his age, and composer of 3 operas (the last, *Dr. Faust*, unfinished at his death), much orchestral and chamber music, and works for the piano. He was born in Empoli near Florence but spent much of his life in Germany.

Bustamante, Sir William Alexander (b. 1884). Prime Min. of Jamaica which gained independence in 1962; leader of the Jamaican Labour Party.

Butler, Joseph (1692–1752), an English divine who occupied an important place among 18th cent. thinkers. He declined the Archbishopric of Canterbury in 1747, but in 1750 became Bishop of Durham. In 1736 he published his *Analogy of Religion*, a reply to the deistic attacks on revealed religion.

Butler, Dr. Nicholas Murray (1862–1947), President of Columbia University, 1902–45. A well-known publicist and internationalist and one of the most honoured and distinguished leaders in the world of education. Shared with Jane Addams (*q.v.*), the noted American sociologist, the Nobel Prize for Peace, 1931.

Butler, Richard Austen, Baron, C.H., P.C. (b. 1902), British statesman; Foreign Sec., 1963–4; First Min. of State, 1962–3; Dep. Prime Min., 1961–3; Home Sec., 1957–62; Chair. Cons. Party, 1959–61; Leader of the House of Commons, 1955–61; Chan. of the Exchequer, 1951–55; Min. of Education, 1941–45; and responsible for the Education Act, 1944. A member of the distinguished Cambridge family, son of Sir Montague Butler, Master of Pembroke. Took leading part in drafting various political charters setting out Conservative policy. Chancellor of Univ. of Sheffield (1959), of Essex (1964); Master of Trinity College, Cambridge (1965). Life barony conferred 1965.

Butler, Samuel (1612–1680), renowned as the author of *Hudibras*, one of the wittiest poems in the language and one of the most quoted. His last years were spent in poverty, and he was buried in the churchyard of St. Paul's, Covent Garden, and given a memorial in Westminster Abbey, "that he who was destitute of all things when alive might not want a monument when dead."

Butler, Samuel (1835–1902), author of the satirical novel *Erewhon* and its sequel *Erewhon Revisited*. Other works include *The Fair Haven* (1873), *Life and Habit* (1877), *Evolution Old and New* (1879), in which he attacked Darwinism. *The Way of All Flesh* and his famous *Notebooks* were published posthumously. Butler was a man of great originality and scholarship. He studied painting and exhibited regularly in the Academy and was also a musician.

Butt, Dame Clara, D.B.E. (1873–1936), the famous English contralto, made her début in London in 1892. She married Kennerly Rumford in 1900.

Buxton, Sir Thomas Fowell, 1st Bart. (1786–1845), a philanthropist and zealous advocate of the abolition of slavery.

Byrd, Rear-Admiral Richard Evelyn (1888–1957), famous American aviator and Polar explorer. Was in command of the Macmillan Arctic Expedition, 1925; flew over the North Pole, 1926; with three companions flew across the Atlantic, 1927, and in 1929 made the first flight over the South Pole. Discovered Edsel Ford mountains and Marie Byrd Land on his first expedition to the Antarctic, 1928–30. He made a second expedition in 1933–5, a third in 1939, and a fourth in December 1946.

Byrd, William (1543–1623), English writer of keyboard music and the greatest musician of the 16th century. He wrote church music, sacred choral music, string music, vocal and instrumental music, and founded the school of English madrigalists. He was organist of Lincoln Cathedral at 20 and later of Queen Elizabeth's Chapel Royal.

Byron, George Gordon, 6th Lord (1788–1824), was the poet who exercised the greatest influence upon European thought during the early part of the 19th century. Educated at Harrow and Cambridge, he published his *Hours of Idleness* at twenty, a volume which was violently attacked by the *Edinburgh Review* which provoked his retaliatory *English Bards and Scotch Reviewers*, which caused a great sensation because of its unsparing criticisms of the writers of the day. His *Childe Harold's Pilgrimage*, the first two cantos of which were published in 1812, at once placed him in the front rank of poets, and thenceforward to the time of his death he continued to produce poems, most of which were marked by an intense Republican sentiment, yet full of passion and charm and beauty. He made an unhappy marriage in 1815 with the daughter of Sir Ralph Milbanke, from whom he parted after a twelvemonth. He lived abroad for the rest of his life and died at Missolonghi, whither he had proceeded with a view to aiding the Greeks in their battle for national independence.

C

Cable, George Washington (1844–1925), a well-known American author, born in New Orleans, the scene of many of his best works. Among his writings were *Ole Creole Days* (1879), *Strange Stories of Louisiana* (1889), and serious sociological studies such as *The Negro Question* (1890).

Cabot, John (*c.* 1455–*c.* 1498), Genoese explorer who settled in Bristol and sailed westwards under letters-patent from Henry VII of England in 1497. Discovered Newfoundland and Nova Scotia, believing them to be part of Asia, and may have reached the mainland of America before Columbus did. His son:—

Cabot, Sebastian (*c.* 1483–1557) was born in Venice, and in 1509 sailed in search of a north-west passage to Asia. Sailed as far as the entrance of Hudson Bay. Entered Spanish service in 1512, and in 1518 was appointed chief pilot. Spent several years exploring the Plate and Parana rivers. Re-entered English service in 1548 and organised expedition to seek a north-east passage to open up trade with India, which resulted in trade with Russia. English claim to North America is founded on the voyages of the Cabots.

Cabral, Pedro Alvarez (*c.* 1467–*c.* 1520). Portuguese navigator, friend of Vasco da Gama, and discoverer of Brazil, which he named "Terra da Santa Cruz."

Cadbury, George (1839–1922), was a prominent member of the Society of Friends, a well-known Philanthropist, and ardent Liberal, and head of the firm of Cadbury Bros., Bourneville. He took the lead in the Garden City project, and the village of Bourneville may be regarded as the first enterprise of the character to be practically completed; it has an endowment of over £200,000.

Cadogan, Rt. Hon. Sir Alexander, O.M., G.C.M.G., K.C.B. (b. 1884), entered the Diplomatic Service in 1908, and succeeded Lord Vansittart as permanent Under-Secretary of the Foreign Office in 1938. Helped to draft the Charter of the United Nations Organisation, and became Great Britain's first permanent representative on the Security Council. Chairman of the B.B.C., 1952–7.

Caedmon, the first English Christian poet, lived in the seventh century and, according to Bede, was first a cowherd and later a monk at Whitby. His poetry was based on the Scriptures.

Caesar, Caius Julius (*c.* 101–44 B.C.), Roman general. Was appointed successively military tribune, quæstor in 68, ædile in 65, and pontifex maximus in 63. A year later he was prætor, and later formed one of the first triumvirate. He invaded Gaul and Britain, in the Civil War defeated Pompey, and in the Alexandrine war met Cleopatra, and established her firmly on the throne of Egypt. On his return to Rome in 44 the crown was offered to him, a circumstance which caused the aristocratic party to compass his assassination.

Caine, Sir Thomas Henry Hall, C.H., K.B.E. (1853–1931), author of numerous novels, including *The Deemster*, *The Manxman*, *The Christian*, *The Prodigal Son*, *The Woman Thou Gavest Me*, the latter being one of the fiction sensations of 1913.

Calderón de la Barca, Pedro (1600–1681), a Spanish dramatist of great eminence whose plays number nearly 200. He was writer of court spectacles for Philip IV.

Calvin, John (1509–1564), one of the leading Reformers of the 16th century. Was born in Picardy and attained great popularity as a preacher in Paris, but was expelled, and subsequently lived at Geneva, where he continued to preach the new doctrine, giving it that special shape which resulted in the formation of the Calvinist body, distinguished by its greater austerity from that of the Lutherans. *See* J7.

Camdon, William (1551–1623), an antiquary, historian, and master of Westminster School, whose researches, especially in the field of topography, have been of the greatest value. He became Clarencieux King-at-Arms, and was buried in Westminster Abbey. The Camden Society is named after him.

Cameron, Sir David Young, R.A. (1865–1945), was one of the best known of British etchers as well as an excellent landscape-painter. King's Painter and Limner in Scotland, 1933–45.

Cameron, Richard (*c.* 1648–1680), one of the Scottish 17th-century preachers who raised the standard of revolt in defence of the Solemn League and Covenant; he was, after many vicissitudes, slain in combat near Aird's Moss, Ayrshire, in 1680. The members of the Reformed Presbyterian Church were afterwards called Cameronians.

Cameron, Verney Lovett, C.B. (1844–1894), a noted African explorer who was the first to cross the African continent from east to west. Explored Lake Tanganyika, and made many valuable geographical discoveries. In 1872 went out to find Livingstone, and in 1873 met a party of natives bearing the dead body to the coast.

Camillus, Marcus Furius (446–365 B.C.), was five times Dictator of the Roman Republic, a supporter of the patrician order, and one of the most successful of the Roman generals. He died of the pestilence, 365 B.C.

Camm, Sir Sydney, C.B.E. (1893–1966), designer of the Hawker Hurricane Fighter aeroplane.

Cammaerts, Emile, C.B.E. (1878–1953), Belgian poet, critic, historian and dramatist. Born in Brussels, he settled in England in 1908, and became Professor of Belgian Studies and Institutions in the University of London. He became widely known during the war of 1914–18 for a series of Belgian poems.

Camões, Luis Vaz de (1524–1580), the author of *Os Lusiadas*, the great epic poem of Portugal, which sets forth the adventures of the discoverers of India, and celebrates the achievements of the principal personages in Portuguese history.

Campbell, Sir Colin. *See* **Clyde, Baron.**

Campbell, Sir Malcolm (1885–1948), the racing driver who held the land-speed record of 301 m.p.h. (1935) and water-speed record 141·7 m.p.h. (1939). His son **Donald** holds the world water-speed record of 276·33 m.p.h. (1964), and the world land-speed record of 403·1 m.p.h. (1964) (the previous world record was 394·1 m.p.h. set up by the late John Cobb in 1947.)

Campbell, Beatrice Stella (Mrs. Patrick Campbell) (1865–1940), was a celebrated actress. Her first London appearance was in 1890 in *The Hunchback*. She made her film debut in 1930 in *The Dancers*.

Campbell, Thomas (1777–1844), Scottish poet who at 22 published *The Pleasures of Hope*. He was one of the founders of University College, London, and is chiefly remembered for his war songs and the poems *Ye Mariners of England*, *The Battle of the Baltic*.

Campbell-Bannerman, Rt. Hon. Sir Henry, G.C.B. (1836–1908), Prime Minister in the Liberal Ministry from December 1905 until shortly before his death in April 1908. His Government at once faced a General Election and obtained a very large majority. Notable events of his period of office were the Trades Disputes Act, 1906, the Deceased Wife's Sister Act, 1907, and the simmering quarrel between the Liberals and the House of Lords, while the settlement of the South African problem was to a great extent due to his efforts. His Ministry contained a galaxy of talent—Grey, Haldane, Lloyd George, Asquith, Morley, Churchill—and was mainly held together by his personal popularity.

Camus, Albert (1913–60), important French writer, native of Algiers, whose works show the influence of existentialism. The Nobel Prize was awarded him in 1957 for " his important literary work, which has with penetrating seriousness thrown light on the problems of human conscience in our times." His most well-known novels are *l'Etranger* (1942), *La Peste* (1947), *l'Homme Révolté* (1952). Killed in car crash.

Canaletto, Giovanni Antonio (1697–1768), Venetian artist who excelled in the art of architectural painting. Some of his work is in the National Gallery, and there is a fine collection at Windsor.

Canning, Rt. Hon. George (1770–1827), entered Parliament in 1793 and became a great orator and a devoted adherent of Pitt, under whom he served first as Under-Secretary of State and later as Treasurer to the Navy. He was Secretary for Foreign Affairs under the Duke of Portland, and in 1827 became Prime Minister, but died four months later.

Cannizzaro, Stanislao (1826–1910), Italian chemist who carried forward the work of Avogadro in distinguishing between molecular and atomic weights. He was professor of chemistry at Alexandria, Geneva, Palermo, and Rome, became a member of the Italian senate, and did much to develop scientific education.

Canova, Antonio (1757–1822), an Italian sculptor, leader of the classical revival in Italy, whose works achieved the first eminence.

Canton, John (1718–72), English physicist and schoolmaster, the first to verify in England Franklin's experiments on the identity of lightning with electricity. He was the first to demonstrate that water is compressible and produced a new phosphorescent body (Canton's phosphorus) by calcining oyster shells with sulphur.

Canute the Great (995–1035), invaded England with a Danish force, and in 1013 succeeded in dethroning Ethelred the Unready, and setting up his own father, Sweyn, in Ethelred's stead. Sweyn dying in 1014, Canute claimed the crown, but it took him some years to establish himself firmly.

Capablanca, José Raoul (1888–1942), world's chess champion, 1921–27; defeated by Alekhine.

Caractacus was the name by which a Prince of ancient Britain became famed for his resistance to the Romans in the 1st century. He was ultimately captured and taken prisoner to Rome where the Emperor Claudius was so moved by his dignity of bearing that he pardoned him.

Carey, William, D.D. (1761–1834), the first Baptist missionary to proceed to India, and from 1800 to 1830 Professor of Oriental Languages at Port William College, Calcutta. Became famed as an Oriental scholar, and published twenty-four different translations of the Scriptures.

Carissimi, Giacomo (1604–74), an Italian composer who is historically important for his development of the sacred cantata and the oratorio. Was maestro at Assisi, and later at Rome. The best collections of his works are in the National Library in Paris, and the Library of Christ Church, Oxford.

Carlyle, Thomas (1795–1881), was educated at Edinburgh University, and, after passing through some years of teaching drudgery, settled in London in 1824 and began the career of a serious man of letters; but, marrying Jane Welsh in 1826, he returned to Scotland and spent the next few years on a farm at Craigenputtoch, coming to London again in 1834. His *Sartor Resartus* was published in 1833. In 1837 he gave lectures in London, and in 1839 his *Chartism* appeared. His *French Revolution, Past and Present, Life and Letters of Oliver Cromwell, Latter-Day Pamphlets,* and *Frederick the Great* were works of noble conception.

Carnegie, Andrew (1835–1919), b. in Dunfermline, emigrated to America with his father in 1848, and after passing through much menial employment became connected with the Pennsylvania Railroad as Divisional Superintendent at Pittsburg, and ultimately established the Carnegie iron works, from which he retired in 1901 with a fortune of many millions. His munificent gifts for Free Libraries, educational work, and charitable objects are well known.

Carnot, General Lazare Nicolas Marguerite (1753–1823), was a prominent figure in the French Revolution, and author of an important work on fortification.

Caroline, Queen, wife of George IV. (1768–1821), was married to her husband in 1795 while he was Prince of Wales. The royal couple lived together only a very short time. When George succeeded to the throne in 1820 the Queen took steps to assert her position, and the King retaliated by having a Bill introduced to dissolve the marriage; the result was the famous trial before the House of Lords, when Lord Brougham distinguished himself by a most eloquent defence of the Queen. The Bill was passed by a narrow majority, but public feeling was too strong on the side of the Queen to admit of its being enforced.

Carrel, Dr. Alexis (1873–1944), American surgeon who won the Nobel Prize in 1912 for his remarkable achievements in suturing blood vessels and in the transplantation of organs. Member of the Rockefeller Institute for Medical Research 1906–44. A Frenchman by birth.

Carroll, Lewis. (*See* **Dodgson, Charles Lutwidge.**)

Carson of Duncairn, Lord, P.C. (1854–1935), had a highly successful career first at the Irish and then at the English Bar. Solicitor General for Ireland 1892; and for England 1900–6; Attorney General 1915; First Lord of the Admiralty 1917; Lord of Appeal 1921–29. Led a semi-militant organisation against the Home Rule Bill 1912–14.

Carter, Howard (1873–1939), Egyptologist and archaeologist who was associated with the 5th Earl of Carnarvon in discovering in 1922 the tomb of Tut-Ankh-Amen in the Valley of Kings, Egypt.

Cartier, Jacques (1494–1557), 16th-century navigator, born at St. Malo, whose exploration of Canada, and especially of the gulf and river of St. Lawrence, proved of great geographical importance.

Cartwright, Edmund, D.D. (1743–1823), invented the power loom, and also a wool-combing machine. Although these inventions were developed into fortune-making instruments, they benefited their inventor but little, and in 1809 Parliament made him a grant of £10,000. In 1904 a Cartwright Memorial Hall was opened at Bradford, the gift of Lord Masham.

Caruso, Enrico (1873–1921), a celebrated tenor, was born in Naples, and made his first operatic appearance in his native city. His success was unbounded.

Carver, George Washington (1864–1943), American negro agricultural chemist of world repute.

Casabianca, Louis de (*c.* 1754–1798), captain of the French flagship *L'Orient* at the Battle of the Nile. He and his ten-year-old son died together in the burning ship, refusing to quit the vessel.

Casals, Pablo (b. 1876), the famous Spanish violoncellist and conductor, who made his first appearance in Paris and London in 1898. He exiled himself from Spain in 1938 as a protest against dictatorship.

Cassatt, Mary (1845–1926), American painter and etcher. Spent most of her life in France, greatly influenced by the Impressionists and enjoyed friendship of Degas and Manet. Motherhood was her favourite subject.

Cassini, the name of a French family of Italian origin, distinguished for their services to astronomy and geography, who through four generations (1671–1793) were heads of the Paris Observatory.

Cassius, Caius Longinus, a distinguished Roman general who opposed the Dictatorship of Julius Cæsar, and took part in his murder. He died in 42 B.C., after being defeated by Mark Antony.

Castellani, Sir Aldo, Hon. K.C.M.G. (b. 1877), Italian scientist and foremost living authority on tropical diseases. Discovered the cause of sleeping sickness and other tropical diseases.

Castlereagh, Viscount, K.G., P.C. (1769–1822), British Minister of War and Foreign Secretary during the Napoleonic wars, who incurred much unpopularity because of the disastrous condition of home affairs. Succeeded to the Marquessate of Londonderry in 1821, and ended his life by suicide the following year.

Castro, Fidel (b. 1927), popular revolutionary hero of Cuba who came to power in 1959 with two main aims: (*a*) to end dictatorship, injustice and poverty, and (*b*) to end dependence on America. Far-reaching agrarian reforms are in progress, but in fulfilling the second aim he has come into conflict with American interests.

Catherine, St., was the name borne by a celebrated virgin of Alexandria, who was put to death in 307 for professing Christianity, being, according to some accounts, tortured on a spiked wheel before execution, though other authorities aver that the intended torture was miraculously prevented. From this we get the term "St. Catherine's wheel." Festival 25 Nov.

Catherine of Aragon (1485–1536), first wife of Henry VIII., was previously the wife of Arthur, Henry's elder brother, who died shortly after the marriage. She was the daughter of Ferdinand and Isabella of Spain, aunt of the Emperor, Charles V, and mother of Mary Tudor. Henry's failure to obtain papal consent to the dissolution of their marriage precipitated the Reformation crisis in England.

Catherine the Great (1729–96), Empress Catherine II of Russia. Daughter of a Prussian general, she married in 1745 the future Peter III. a weakling, later deposed and murdered. Intelligent, cultivated, autocratic, she proved herself a capable ruler for a time but was hampered and opposed by the landed interests and, despite plans for reform, her reign was marked by imperialist expansion and extension of serfdom.

Catherine de' Medici (1519–1589), wife of Henry II. of France, and a woman of commanding power and influence, especially during her Regency, which continued while her son Charles IX. was in his minority. Her antagonism to the Protestants may have led to the Massacre of St. Bartholomew. In spite of her cruelty, she was an able woman, and showed a great appreciation of art and literature.

Cato, Marcus Porcius (234–149 B.C.) a Roman statesman, soldier, and writer, of strict virtue, simplicity and wisdom, who strongly condemned the luxury of his time and carried out his duties as Censor so rigorously that he became known as "Censorious."

Catullus, Caius Valerius (87–54 B.C.), an elegant Roman poet, whose lyrics to Lesbia are amongst the finest compositions of the kind in literature.

Cavell, Edith Louisa (1865–1915), a British nurse who assisted wounded British soldiers to escape over the Dutch frontier from Belgium during the Great War. She was shot by the Germans.

Cavendish, Hon. Henry, F.R.S. (1731–1810), English chemist and physicist who made researches into the nature of gases. Is chiefly remembered for his discovery of the chemical composition of water. He also discovered hydrogen (1766).

Cavour, Count Camillo Benso (1810–1861), a distinguished Italian statesman, who, as Premier to Victor Emmanuel, did much for the unification of Italy.

Caxton, William (1422–1491), was born in Kent and employed in commerce for a time. While visiting Flanders he obtained an insight into the then new invention of printing, and afterwards set up a printing-press of his own at Westminster.

Cecil of Chelwood, 1st Viscount, P.C., Q.C., C.H. (1864–1958), third son of the third Marquess of Salisbury. Took part in the Peace Conference, 1919, and helped to draft the Charter of the League of Nations. Awarded Nobel Prize for Peace, 1937.

Cecilia, Saint, the patron saint of music, martyred in Sicily under Marcus Aurelius (*c.* 176). She became patroness of music only about the beginning of the 15th century when painters showed her with harp, organ, or other musical instruments. Her festal day is Nov. 22.

Cellini, Benvenuto (1500–71), Italian sculptor and goldsmith of the later Renaissance. Possessed remarkable talent and skill, and produced innumerable works of great accomplishment, decorative and exquisite in detail, most of which have perished. Some examples are to be found in the Vienna Museum, the Louvre, and in the Metropolitan Museum. His famous bronze statue *Perseus with the Head of Medusa* can be seen in the Loggia dei Lanzi, Florence. His fame, however, rests more on his *Autobiography*, which gives a vivid account of the period and of his own craft.

Celsius, Anders (1701–44), Swedish physicist and astronomer who became professor of astronomy at Uppsala in 1730 and worked at the new Uppsala observatory, 1740–44. He invented the Centigrade or Celsius thermometer with freezing point of water at the zero-degree and boiling point at the 100-degree point.

Cervantes Saavedra Miguel de (1547–1616), Spanish novelist, dramatist, and poet, b. at Alcalá de Henares, famous throughout the world as the author of *Don Quixote*, a wonderful study of feudalism in decay in which is to be found much social science. He had a most adventurous career, taking part in many military expeditions, and not turning to literature until his retirement from the profession of arms. In spite of the great success of his work he died in poverty and two centuries went by before he was honoured.

Cézanne, Paul (1839–1906), an outstanding figure in the world of art; b. in Aix-en-Provence, the son of a wealthy banker and tradesman. He developed a highly original style, using colour and tone in such a way as to increase the impression of depth. He said that he wanted "to make of Impressionism something solid and durable, like the art of the Museums." Like Giotto, six hundred years before, he more than any other artist determined the course European painting was to take. *La Vielle au Chapelet* and *Les Grandes Baigneuses* may be seen at the National Gallery. He was a friend of Zola.

Chadwick, Sir James, F.R.S. (b. 1891), physicist, one of Rutherford's most brilliant collaborators in the field of atomic research. Discovered the neutron in 1932, one of the main steps in the discovery of the fission process which led to the production of the atom bomb.

Chagall, Marc (b. 1889), Russian painter, born at Vitebsk of Jewish parents, the forerunner of surrealism.

Chaliapin, Fedor Ivanovich (1873–1938), a world-famous Russian opera singer, a bass with great dramatic gifts.

Chamberlain, Rt. Hon. (Arthur) Neville (1869–1940), son of Joseph Chamberlain by his second wife. Prime Minister, 1937–40. His appeasement policy, which culminated in the Munich Agreement of 1938, has been the subject of much criticism.

Chamberlain, Rt. Hon. Joseph (1836–1914), did much active municipal work at Birmingham. In 1876 he entered Parliament, and at first was an enthusiastic Liberal with Republican tendencies and served in various offices under Mr. Gladstone. When the Home Rule split occurred, he became the most active member of the Liberal-Unionist party. In 1895 he accepted office as Secretary of State for the Colonies under Lord Salisbury, and in that post won a great reputation, notwithstanding the fact that during his term of office he had the Boer War to contend with. In May, 1903, he caused great sensation by suddenly advocating a scheme of fiscal reform, involving a partial return to Protection. This policy was afterwards adopted as one of the leading planks of the Unionist platform.

Chambers, Sir William, R.A. (1726–1796), a British architect, who rebuilt Somerset House in 1775. He also laid out Kew Gardens and designed the Pagoda there.

Chaminade, Cécile (1857–1944), French pianist and composer of orchestral music, ballets, songs, and charming piano pieces.

Champlain, Samuel de (1567–1635), a French navigator who founded Quebec in 1608, and in the following year discovered the lake known by his name.

Chantrey, Sir Francis Legatt, R.A. (1781–1842), a renowned English sculptor who contributed many fine statues to Westminster Abbey and St. Paul's. His famous "Sleeping Children" tomb is in Lichfield Cathedral. He left a considerable fortune to the Royal Academy for the purchase of works of art executed in Gt. Britain. The collection is in the Tate Gallery.

Chaplin, Charles Spencer (b. 1889), the first international screen star and one of the world's greatest artists, b. in South London. His mother was a music-hall singer and he made his stage début at the age of five. In 1910 he went to the United States and there attracted the attention of Mack Sennett. It was with the Keystone Company in Los Angeles (1914–15) that he created the unforgettable figure with the minute moustache and the baggy trousers.

His most famous films include *The Tramp*, *Shoulder Arms*, *The Kid*, *The Gold Rush*, *The Circus*, *City Lights*, *The Great Dictator*, *Modern Times*, *Monsieur Verdoux*, and *Limelight*. In 1953 he decided to leave America and live in Switzerland. He is an English citizen. *My Autobiography* was published in 1964.

Chapman, Sydney, M.A., D.Sc., F.R.S. (b. 1888), mathematician and geophysicist; Chief Prof. of Mathematics, Imperial College of Science, 1924–46; Pres. Int. Comm. which organised the International Geophysical Year, 1957–8.

Chapman, George (1559–1634), an Elizabethan dramatist, who acquired more fame by his translation of Homer than by his plays. Keats's sonnet *On Reading Chapman's Homer* is a splendid tribute to the old dramatist.

Charcot, Dr. Jean Baptiste Etienne Auguste (1867–1936), a famous French explorer, who in 1903–05 and 1908–10 commanded expeditions which carried out important work in mapping, sounding, etc., in the South Polar regions. Charcot Island in the Antarctic Ocean, which he discovered in 1905, is named after him.

Chares (*c.* 300 B.C.), sculptor of the Colossus of Rhodes, a gigantic bronze statue of the sun-god, and one of the seven wonders of the world, destroyed in the earthquake of 224 B.C.

Charlemagne (" Charles the Great ") (742–814), a wise and powerful ruler, general and statesman, who from being King of the Franks became Emperor of the Romans, and governed an empire comprising Gaul, Italy, and large parts of Spain and Germany.

Charles, Jacques Alexandre César (1746–1823), French physicist, the first to use hydrogen gas in balloons and who anticipated Gay–Lussac's law of the expansion of gases on heating.

Charles Edward (Stuart) (1720–1788), the " Young Pretender " as he came to be called, grandson of James II., and the hero of 1745, lived in exile after Culloden, and his later career was mainly one of dissipation.

Charles I. (1600–1649), King of England, Scotland, and Ireland (1625–49), succeeded his father James I. in 1625. His marriage to the Catholic princess, Henrietta Maria, sister of Louis XIII. of France, displeased the English public. He was in continual trouble with his ministers and parliament; Cromwell's career began in his reign. He was beheaded in front of the Banqueting House at Whitehall, Jan. 30, 1649.

Charles II. (1630–1685), King of England, Scotland, and Ireland (1660–85), second son of Charles I. After defeat by Cromwell at Worcester (1651) escaped to France; restored to throne, 1660. During his reign Pepys was recording the great London plague of 1665, and the fire of 1666, Wren was building St. Paul's, John Bunyan was writing his *Pilgrim's Progress* and Milton his *Paradise Lost*, Newton was a fellow of the Royal Society (founded by Charles) and England was becoming a great sea power. Famed as the " Merry Monarch " because of his pleasure-loving ways. Dabbled in chemistry and probably died of mercury poisoning.

Charles V. (1500–1558), Hapsburg ruler, succeeded his grandfather, Maximilian I, as emperor of the Holy Roman Empire, and as heir to Ferdinand and Isabella succeeded to Spanish Crown. Administering such vast dominions involved him in many struggles: rivalry with Francis I of France led to four wars. Crushed revolt of peasants (1525). Augsburg settlement (1553) brought Lutherans religious equality with Roman Catholics. Retired to a monastery in Spain (1557).

Charles XII of Sweden (1682–1718), a brave but impulsive monarch whose reign was distinguished by the great Nordic War against Denmark, Poland, and Russia. Peter the Great decisively defeated him at Poltava in 1709. In 1718 he invaded Norway and was killed while besieging the fortress of Fredrikshald.

Chateaubriand, François René, Vicomte de (1768–1848), French writer and diplomat who in the midst of an adventurous and somewhat eccentric political career wrote a number of stories, poems, and essays which reflect the richness of his personality and give him a unique place in French literature. He was the friend of Mme Récamier for many years. His last years were spent in writing *Mémoires d'outre-tombe* (memoirs from beyond the tomb).

Chatham, William Pitt, Earl of (1708–1778), had a long and distinguished career as a statesman, and was the most eloquent Parliamentarian of his time. In the long conflict with France that preceded the American War of Independence, Chatham showed great resourcefulness and vigour, but his patriotic efforts were of little avail against the obstinacy of the King and his party, and he ultimately retired from contention, only making a last appearance in the House of Lords to urge a greater resistance to the war with the American Colonists, and, after a powerful speech, fell back in an apoplectic fit and died a few weeks later, being buried in Westminster Abbey.

Chatterton, Thomas (1752–1770), young English poet of remarkable talent, unappreciated until after his death. Unsuccessfully tried to pass off his writings as newly discovered ancient manuscripts and killed himself at the age of 17.

Chaucer, Geoffrey (*c.* 1343–1400). Achieved immortality by his *Canterbury Tales*, giving a most graphic description of the life and characters of his time. He was buried in Westminster Abbey.

Chekhov, Anton (1860–1904), Russian dramatist and short-story writer, whose plays *The Cherry Orchard*, *Uncle Vanya*, and *The Three Sisters* continue to delight modern audiences.

Cherubini, Maria Luigi Carlo Zenobia Salvatore (1760–1842), a Florentine musician, for many years director of the Paris Conservatoire and composer of operas and church music. Admired by Beethoven and Mendelssohn.

Chesterfield, Earl of, K.G. (1694–1773), English statesman whose fame rests upon the letters to his natural son, Philip Stanhope, under the title *Letters to his Son*, which are full of grace, wit, and worldly wisdom.

Chesterton, Gilbert Keith (1874–1936), English essayist and novelist; contributed to the *Illustrated London News*, etc., and kept himself in evidence in many literary and journalistic quarters; handled social questions, art, politics, and criticism with dexterity and audacity. Published studies of the lives and works of Robert Browning and Charles Dickens. Completed writing his own autobiography shortly before his death.

Chevalier Albert (1861–1923), English music-hall comedian of great originality; celebrated for his coster sketches and songs.

Chevalier, Maurice (b. 1888), French stage and film actor.

Chiang Kai-shek, Generalissimo (b. 1887), former President of China and member of the Kuomintang Party. Emerged from the welter of events succeeding the death of Sun Yat Sen in 1925 as the leading man in China, a position he maintained for a quarter of a century of trouble and bloodshed. The successful conclusion of the long and costly Japanese war was followed by civil war with the Communists in North China. In January 1949 he withdrew from the office of President following military defeat by the Communists and the collapse of the Kuomintang régime.

Chippendale, Thomas (*c.* 1717–1779), a celebrated designer of furniture, born in Otley, Yorkshire. His *The Gentleman and Cabinet Maker's Director* (1752) shows the wide variety of domestic furniture made in England at that time.

Chirico, Giorgio de (b. 1888), painter associated with surrealism, born in Greece of Italian parents.

Chopin, Frédéric François (1810–1849), Polish pianist and composer, son of a French father and Polish mother. He has been called " the poet of the piano " because of the originality and delicacy of his playing. His music, composed mostly for the piano, includes preludes, mazurkas, impromptus, nocturnes, études, sonatas, and a barcarolle and a berceuse. He enjoyed Paris intellectual and musical society, and played in numerous concerts all over Europe. He died of consumption and was buried in Père-Lachaise, next to his friend Bellini.

Chou-En-lai, General (b. 1898), Prime Minister of the Chinese People's Republic since 1949; Foreign Min. 1949–58. Took important part in Geneva Conference of 1954, where his talents for negotiation helped to bring to an end the 8 years' war in Indo-China and the new China into world diplomacy.

Chrysostom, St. John (347–407), a father and

saint of the Greek Church who was made Archbishop of Constantinople and was famous for his eloquent preaching and persuasive writing.

Churchill, Rt. Hon. Lord Randolph (Henry Spencer), P.C. (1849–1895), was the third son of the seventh Duke of Marlborough. Entered Parliament in 1874, and four years later became prominent on the Conservative side for his scathing attacks on what he called the "Old Gang" of his own Party, and was one of Mr. Gladstone's most severe critics. In 1885 he became Secretary for India, and in the following year was Chancellor of the Exchequer and Leader of the House of Commons, but after a few months of brilliant work resigned on a difference of opinion with his colleagues.

Churchill, Rt. Hon. Sir Winston (Leonard Spencer), K.G., O.M., C.H., C.L., (1874–1965), British statesman, soldier, and author, son of the last-named. He entered Parliament in 1900 and represented Oldham, 1900–06; N.W. Manchester, 1906–08; Dundee, 1908–22; Epping, 1924–45; Woodford, 1945–64. He served as a junior officer with the British force during the Indian frontier troubles of 1897–98 and in the Sudan Campaign, and during the Boer War as a war correspondent he had many dramatic adventures. He held the following ministerial posts: Under-Secretary for the Colonies, 1905–08; President of the Board of Trade, 1908–10; Home Secretary 1910–11. First Lord of the Admiralty, 1911–15 and 1939–40. Chancellor of the Duchy of Lancaster, 1915. Minister of Munitions, 1917; Minister of War, 1918–21; Minister of Air, 1919–21. Sec. of State for the Colonies, 1921–22. Chancellor of the Exchequer 1924–29; Prime Min. and Min. of Defence, 1940–45; Prime Min. 1951–55. Lord Rector of Aberdeen University, 1914–18; Lord Rector of Edinburgh University, 1929–32; Chancellor of Bristol University, 1930; Lord Warden of the Cinque Ports. A man of action, cast in the heroic mould, he lived a full and adventurous life, and will be remembered as the inspired war leader who expressed the determination of the British people to defeat Hitler. His numerous writings include a biography of his famous ancestor, Marlborough, and stories of the First and Second World Wars. He exhibited at the Royal Academy and was elected Academician Extraordinary in 1948. Hon. American citizenship conferred, 1963. Awarded Nobel Prize for Literature in 1953.

Chulalongkorn, Phra Paramindr Maha (1853–1910), great Siamese monarch whose appreciation of foreign institutions inspired him to carry out many reforms in his country.

Cibber, Colley (1671–1757), a London actor and dramatist of great repute in his day. *The Careless Husband*, and *Love's Last Shift* are the best of his comedies. Poet Laureate 1730–57.

Cicero, Marcus Tullius (106–43 B.C.), a Roman Republican orator and philosopher. His younger brother, Quintus Tullius Cicero (102–43 B.C.), was a Roman soldier of some note. Both were slain.

Cid (El Campeador) (*c.* 1035–1099), the name given to the famous Spanish knight, Rodrigo Diaz, Count of Vivar, whose exploits in battle and adventure made him the national hero. He drove the Moors out of Spain before he had completed his twentieth year.

Cierva, Juan de la (1895–1936), the Spanish engineer who invented the autogiro.

Cimabue, Giovanni (1240–1302), a Florentine painter whose real name was Cenni di Pepo, master of Giotto, and the leader of the movement which led to the formation of what is called the Florentine school.

Cimarosa, Domenico (1749–1801). One of the earliest Italian composers whose works in his time were as popular as they were numerous. Was composer to the Russian Court from 1789 to 1792. His most popular opera during his lifetime was *Il Matrimonio Segreto*, and it is still to-day the most frequently heard of his works.

Cimon (*c.* 507–449 B.C.), Athenian statesman and general, son of the great Miltiades who commanded at Marathon. He worked for friendship with Sparta to unite forces against Persia. Decisively defeated Persian land and sea forces at the mouth of the Eurymedon in 468 B.C. Died at the siege of Citium, in Cyprus.

Cipriani, Giovanni Battista (1727–85), Florentine painter and engraver who worked in London and was one of the foundation members of the Royal Academy. Collections of his pen-and-ink drawings are in the British Museum and Victoria and Albert Museum.

Citrine, 1st Baron P.C., G.B.E. (b. 1887), English trade-union official who rose to a prominent position in the Electrical Trades Union, of which he was Asst. Gen. Sec., 1920–23; Pres. Int. Fed. of Trade Unions, 1928–45; Gen. Sec. Trades Union Congress, 1926–46; Mem. Nat. Coal Board, 1946–47; Chair. Central Electricity Authority, 1947–57.

Clair, René, (b. 1898), French film producer, whose early films, full of wit and satire, included *Sous les Toits de Paris* and *A Nous la Liberté*.

Clarendon, Edward Hyde, 1st Earl of (1609–1674), a statesman of great ability who filled the office of Lord High Chancellor under Charles II., and for a time was in high favour but, refusing to pander to Charles's whims, was dismissed and went to live in retirement. His *History of the Rebellion* is a valuable work, having the advantage of being written by one who was a witness of, and often an important figure in, the events described. His daughter Anne was the wife of the Duke of York, afterwards James II., and it was her daughter who became Queen Anne. Clarendon died in exile at Rouen.

Clark, Sir Kenneth McKenzie, C.H., K.C.B. (b. 1903), British art critic. Director of the National Gallery, 1934–45. Chairman, Arts Council of Great Britain, 1953–60; Chairman of the Independent Television Authority, 1954–57.

Clark, Sir Wilfred Edward le Gros, M.A., M.D., D.Sc., F.R.C.S., F.R.S. (b. 1895), anatomist and anthropologist; Prof. of Anatomy, Oxford Univ., 1934–62; one of the scientists to expose the forgery of the Piltdown skull. Pres. British Association, 1961.

Clarke, Marcus Andrew Hislop (1846–81), Australian novelist, born in London. Emigrated to Australia in 1863, where he became a journalist. During his stay in Tasmania he wrote *For the Term of his Natural Life*, which has become a minor classic.

Clarkson, Thomas (1760–1846), was one of the leaders of the Negro Emancipation movement, to which he devoted the main part of his life.

Claude Lorrain (1600–1682), the most famous landscape painter of his century. His real name was Claude Gelée, and he was born at Chamange in the Vosges, going from France to Rome as a lad and there laying the foundation of his worldwide celebrity. He lived in Rome most of his life.

Claudius I. (10 B.C.–A.D. 54), Emperor of Rome, who succeeded his nephew Caligula when he was murdered. He was the grandson of Tiberius Claudius Nero, erected many imposing buildings in Rome, and visited Britain. In his later years he became the tool of favourites, and was poisoned by his wife Agrippina.

Clausewitz, Gen. Carl von (1780–1831), Germany's greatest military expert. His classic book *Vom Kriege*, which expounds his theories on war, dominated Prussia in the nineteenth century, and is still studied in military schools throughout the world.

Clemenceau, Georges Eugène (1841–1929), a prominent French statesman and editor of strong Radical tendencies who supported General Boulanger for a time and then bitterly opposed him. Was still a leading exponent of French Radicalism, though he sacrificed his independent position to become Premier and Minister of the Interior in October, 1906–1909, Prime Minister and Minister for War, France, 1917–20. Was a great orator, and a sturdy defender of Dreyfus.

Clemens, Samuel Langhorne ("Mark Twain") (1835–1910). After the Civil War drifted into journalism, making himself popular as a humorist in 1869 by his *Innocents Abroad*, the result of a trip to Europe. His other works include *A Tramp Abroad*, *Tom Sawyer*, *Huckleberry Finn*, and *Pudd'nhead Wilson*.

Cleopatra (69–30 B.C.), daughter of Ptolemy XI, the sixth queen of Egypt by that name, a brilliant, ambitious woman of captivating charm. On the death of her father in 51 she became joint sovereign with her younger brother Ptolemy XII, whom she married in accordance with Egyptian custom. She was banished to Syria, but obtaining the help of Cæsar, led a revolt and won the kingdom for herself. Cleopatra and Cæsar became lovers. In 47 she bore him a son Cæsarion (later Ptolemy XIV) and followed him to Rome. After the murder of Cæsar she returned to Egypt, where in 41 she was summoned to meet the triumvir Mark Antony. He fell in love with her and became enslaved. She bore him twins Alexander Helios and Cleopatra Selene. He deserted Octavia his wife and broke with Octavian (later Augustus), his brother-in-law, in an attempt to re-establish the power of Egypt. Antony and Cleopatra were, however, defeated at Actium in 31 B.C. and at Alexandria. Antony fell upon his sword, and Cleopatra, unable to influence Octavian, killed herself by allowing an asp to bite her. The drama of her life has been described by Shakespeare in *Antony and Cleopatra* and by Shaw in *Cæsar and Cleopatra*.

Clive, Robert, Lord (1725–1774), went out to India as a clerk in the service of the East India Company when 17, and during the diplomatic difficulties which arose between England and France attracted the attention of his superiors by some able suggestions for the curbing of the French influence. In the war that followed he was given a command and displayed such remarkable military genius that he virtually became Commander-in-Chief. In the troubles that followed with the native rulers, he was equally resourceful, and succeeded in laying the foundation of the British empire in India on a secure basis. On his return to England in 1760 he was raised to the peerage. His latter years were marked by mental disturbance and ultimately he committed suicide.

Clovis (*c.* 465–511) was the founder of the Merovingian-line of Frankish kings, and a convert to Christianity. He defeated the Burgundians and West Goths, and fixed his court at Paris.

Clyde, 1st Baron, Colin Campbell, K.C.B. (1792–1863), a British Field-Marshal who served in the Peninsular and Crimean wars and made a great reputation as Commander-in-Chief in India during the Mutiny.

Cobbett, William (1763–1835), a politician and controversialist, who, through the medium of his *Political Register*, attacked both Radical and Tory in turn. Entered Parliament in 1832. In 1830 his *Rural Rides* were published in book form.

Cobbold, 1st Baron, Cameron Fromanteel, P.C., G.C.V.O. (b. 1904), Governor of the Bank of England, 1948–61; Lord Chamberlain, 1962– .

Cobden, Richard (1804–1865), the son of a Sussex farmer, who afterwards became a commercial traveller, and during the Corn Law Agitation came into great prominence as an advocate of Free Trade. He devoted himself so completely to this cause, that for some years he entirely neglected his business affairs and in recognition of his services a subscription of £80,000 was raised for him in 1845, and in 1860 a further sum of £40,000. He entered Parliament in 1841, and except for an interval of two years remained a member till his death. In 1860 he negotiated a commercial treaty with France which was of great benefit to the trade of this country. Titles and other honours were offered to him but declined.

Cochran, Sir Charles Blake (1872–1951), a prominent English theatrical manager and producer who began as an actor in America. Among his many successes were *Bitter Sweet*, *Cavalcade*, and a number of brilliant revues.

Cockcroft, Sir John Douglas, K.C.B., O.M., C.B.E., M.A., Ph.D., F.R.S. (b. 1897), Cambridge nuclear physicist who shared with Dr. E. T. S. Walton the 1951 Nobel Prize. Dir. Atomic Energy Research Estab. at Harwell, 1946–58; Member (Research) U.K. Atomic Energy Authority, 1958–59, Member Advisory Council on Scientific Policy, 1959– ; Master of Churchill College, Cambridge.

Cocteau, Jean (1891–1963), French writer and artist whose achievements in widely varied forms of art were prodigious. Elected to the Académie Française in 1955.

Cody, Samuel Franklin (1861–1913), American aviator whose name is associated with flights at Farnborough, Hampshire, England. He was the first man to fly in Britain (1,390 feet on 16 Oct. 1908). He became a British subject in 1909. Killed while flying.

Cody, William Frederick (1846–1917), American showman, known as "Buffalo Bill," who in 1883 founded his great Wild West Show with which he toured America and Europe for many years.

Cohn, Ferdinand Julius (1828–1898), the famous German bacteriologist, of which science he was the virtual founder.

Coke, Sir Edward (1552–1634), Attorney-General under Elizabeth and Chief Justice under James I; great rival of Francis Bacon. His extensive legal erudition added many new interpretations to the Common Law system. Among his publications are his four *Institutes*, the first of which (*Coke upon Littleton*) is very famous.

Colbert, Jean Baptiste (1619–83), French statesman, who fostered new industries and encouraged commerce, endeavoured to reform the finances, and established the French Navy on a sound basis. A patron of literature, science, and art.

Cole, George Douglas Howard, M.A., (1889–1959), British economist, sociologist, and writer; Chichele Professor of Social and Political Theory at Oxford, 1944–57; Chairman Fabian Society, 1939–46; Pres. Int. Society for the Study of Socialism from 1956 until his death. Among his numerous writings on social and economic problems are *The Intelligent Man's Guide through World Chaos* (1932), *The Post-War Condition of Britain* (1956), *The Case for Industrial Partnership* (1957), *A History of Socialist Thought* (5 vols.).

Coleridge, 1st Baron (1820–94), Lord Chief Justice of England from 1880 until his death. Was a distinguished scholar, orator and barrister, his most famous case being the Tichborne trial in 1871, when his speech for the defence lasted 23 days.

Coleridge, Samuel Taylor (1772–1834), one of the great poets of the early part of the 19th century, whose *Ancient Mariner* and a few other poems stand unsurpassed for poetic beauty and originality.

Coleridge-Taylor, Samuel, A.R.C.M. (1875–1912), British composer, the son of a West African negro doctor practising in London, and an Englishwoman. He studied at the Royal College of Music where his *Hiawatha's Wedding Feast* was performed in 1898.

Colet, John (*c.* 1467–1519), humanist and divine, founded St. Paul's School, 1512. As scholar and friend of Erasmus he helped to bring the New Learning to England.

Colette (Sidonie Gabrielle Claudine Colette) (1873–1954), author of a number of highly successful novels including the famous *Claudine* stories, *Chéri* and *La Fin de Chéri*. Grand Officier de la Légion d'Honneur (1953).

Collier, Hon, John (1850–1934), English painter who became highly popular for his "problem" pictures. He is best remembered, however, as a distinguished portraitist.

Collingwood, Lord (1750–1810), British admiral whose ship the *Royal Sovereign* led the fleet to battle at Trafalgar and who on Nelson's death assumed the command.

Collins, Michael (1890–1922), brilliant and daring Irishman, leading spirit of the Sinn Fein political movement. Took part in the Easter Rebellion and organised the guerilla warfare which eventually led to the breakdown of British government and to the Anglo-Irish Peace of Dec. 6, 1921. Killed in ambush by Republicans after his return from England.

Collins, William, R.A. (1788–1847), a noted landscape and figure painter, and father of Wilkie Collins.

Collins, William Wilkie (1824–1889), the novelist, was for many years associated with Charles Dickens, and wrote *The Dead Secret*, *The Woman in White*, and *No Name*.

Colt, Samuel (1814–1862), of Hartford, Connecticut, invented the revolver and patented it in 1835. It was some time before its utility was recognised, but after being used with great effect in the war with Mexico it was universally adopted.

Columba, St. (521–597), the founder of the monastery of Iona, was a native of Ireland. From his lonely island shrine he made frequent missionary journeys to the Highlands of Scotland.

where he made many converts and was greatly revered.

Columbus, Christopher (*c.* 1446–1506), the famous Italian navigator, who, prevailing upon Ferdinand and Isabella of Spain to bear the expense of an expedition of discovery, set out on his first voyage in 1492. He first discovered the Bahamas, Cuba, and other West Indian islands, and, on his third voyage, in 1498, landed on the lowlands of South America.

Colvin, Sir Sidney (1845–1927), friend of R. L. Stevenson and biographer of Keats. Was Keeper of Prints at the British Museum, 1884–1912. Author of numerous works on art and literature.

Comenius, Johann Amos (1592–1670), famous Czech educationist. Was the first advocate of the "direct" method of teaching languages, of the use of pictures in education, and of the teaching of science.

Compton, Arthur Holly (1892–1962), American physicist whose work on X-rays led to the discovery of the so-called "Compton Effect," for which he shared with C. T. R. Wilson the 1927 Nobel Prize for Physics. He also made important cosmic-ray investigations and helped to develop the atomic bomb. His brother **Karl Taylor Compton** (1887–1954) was also a physicist who did important research on radar and the ionisation of gases.

Compton-Burnett, Ivy, British novelist, whose books deal with family relationships and include *Men and Wives, A House and its Head, Man Servant and Maid Servant, The Present and the Past, A Heritage and its History.*

Comte Auguste (1798–1857), French philosopher; founder of positivism, and father of social philosophy.

Condé, Louis II., de Bourbon, Prince de, "The Great Condé" (1621–1686), was a distinguished military commander. Victor of Rocroi, 1643.

Confucius (*c.* 551–479 B.C.), Chinese philosopher and sage, founder of the great world religion of Confucianism. He was not concerned with the supernatural but appealed to reason and taught love and respect of one's fellows, superiority to ambition, charity, forgiveness, and repentance. (*See* **Confucianism, Section J.**)

Congreve, William (1670–1729), was a famous Restoration dramatist, whose comedies of manners reflect the grossness of his age only too closely, but are redeemed by the brilliancy of his wit. He was buried in Westminster Abbey.

Conrad, Joseph (1857–1924), English novelist of Polish birth whose parents were exiled to France for political reasons. He became master mariner in the British merchant service and began to write novels after he left the sea in 1884. He has a beautiful prose style and is acknowledged to be a significant figure in English literature. His novels include: *Almayer's Folly* (1895), *Lord Jim* (1900), *Nostromo* (1904).

Conscience, Hendrik (Henri) (1812–83), the famous Flemish novelist whose historical romance, *The Lion of Flanders*, earned him a distinguished place in the world of literature.

Constable, John, R.A. (1776–1837), was a native of East Bergholt, Suffolk, and became one of the greatest of English landscape painters. He had long to wait for recognition, but ultimately attained high honour and exerted a strong influence in the development of landscape art.

Constant, Jean Joseph Benjamin (1845–1902), French portrait and subject painter; *Prisoners in Morocco, The Harem*, and *The Emir's Favourite* are among his celebrated Oriental pictures.

Constantine the Great (*c.* 272–337). Emperor of Rome from 306 to his death. Transferred the Capital of the Empire from Rome to Byzantium, thence called Constantinople after his name.

Constantine I. (1868–1923), King of Greece, 1913–17, and 1920; married Princess Sophia of Prussia, sister of the Kaiser.

Cook, Captain James (1728–1779), an adventurous navigator, whose *Voyages Round the World* is a classic. He made many discoveries in the name of Great Britain, including the Sandwich (now Hawaiian) Islands. He was murdered at Hawaii by natives.

Cooper, Sir Astley Paston, Bt., F.R.S. (1768–1841), one of the greatest surgeons of his time, and the author of several important medical textbooks.

Cooper, James Fenimore (1789–1851), was a very popular American novelist, who from about 1820 to the time of his death produced a succession of stirring stories of adventure, which enjoyed much popularity, among them *The Spy, The Last of the Mohicans, The Pathfinder*, and *The Deer Slayer.*

Cope, Sir Arthur Stockdale, K.C.V.O., R.A. (1857–1940), was a well-known portrait painter.

Copernicus, Nicholas (1473–1543), founder of modern astronomy, was born at Thorn on the Vistula, then under Polish suzerainty. Studied at Cracow and in Italy, lectured on astronomy and mathematics at Rome and in 1512 settled at Frauenburg, where he was canon of the cathedral. He also practised medicine. His beliefs concerning the universe were set forth in his great book *De revolutionibus orbium coelestium*, which was not published until his death for fear of the storm his revolutionary theories would raise. In it he proved that the planets, including the earth, revolve round the sun.

Coppée, François Joachim (1842–1908), one of the most popular of modern French writers, who as poet, novelist and dramatist, was equally successful.

Coquelin, Bonoit Constant (1841–1909), eminent French actor ("Coquelin aîné"), and **Coquelin, Ernest** ("Coquelin cadet"), his youngest brother (1848–1909), were leading lights of the Théâtre Français.

Corelli, Arcangelo (1653–1713), Italian composer and the first great violinist to enjoy universal fame; founded the present art of violin playing and gave definitive form to the *concerto grosso.*

Corneille, Pierre (1606–1684) the French tragic dramatist, whose *Cid, Polyeucte, Le Menteur*, and other plays marked a new era in French dramatic production.

Cornwallis, 1st Marquess (1738–1805), commander of the British forces which surrendered to the Americans, at Yorktown in 1781, thus ending the War of Independence; was twice Governor-General of India.

Corot, Jean Baptiste (1796–1875), a French landscape painter of great repute.

Correggio, Antonio Allegri da (1494–1534), the great Italian painter of the Lombard School, whose "Ecce Homo" is in the British National Gallery.

Cortes (or Cortez), Hernando (1488–1547), a Spanish adventurer who earned great renown by capturing Mexico for Spain, and held that country in subjection for ten years.

Cortot, Alfred (1877–1962), French pianist and conductor, best known for his playing of Chopin, Liszt, and Schumann; chorus director at Bayreuth; conducted first complete performance in Paris of Wagner's *Ring.*

Cosgrave, William Thomas (b. 1880), President of Executive Council, Irish Free State, 1922–32; Finance Min., 1923; Defence Min., 1924; Parl. Chairman Fine Gael, 1933–44.

Costello, John A., S.C. (b. 1891), Prime Minister of Irish Republic 1948–51 and 1954–57. When Attorney General, Irish Free State, 1926–32, helped to draft the Statute of Westminster.

Coulton, George Gordon, Litt. D., LL.D. (1858–1947), scholar and historian of the Middle Ages, whose main claim to fame rests upon *Five Centuries of Religion*, works in which he set forth his interpretation of monastic history in England from the Conquest to the Reformation.

Couperin. A notable family of French musicians who were organists at St. Gervais, Paris, from about 1650 until 1826. **François Couperin** (1668–1733), called "Couperin the Great," is the best known today for his harpsichord music.

Cousin, Victor (1792–1867), French educationist and philosopher, founder of the eclectic school. He was a remarkable lecturer and his writings cover nearly the whole field of philosophy.

Cousins, Samuel, R.A. (1801–1887), the greatest mezzoprint engraver of his day, whose plates after Reynolds, Millais, Landseer, and Hogarth reach the highest point of this kind of art work.

Couve de Murville, Maurice (b. 1900), French diplomat who has been Foreign Minister since Gen. de Gaulle's return to power in 1958.

Coverdale, Miles (1488–1568), one of the early English Reformers, was born in Yorkshire, and afterwards became a monk of Norwich and later Bishop of Exeter. He collaborated with Tyndale in translating the Bible; the Psalms still used in the Prayer Book are taken from their translation.

Coward, Noel (b. 1899), a successful English playwright and actor. His works include *Hay Fever, Private Lives, Blithe Spirit*, the operetta *Bitter Sweet* and the films *In Which We Serve, This Happy Breed*, and *Brief Encounter*.

Cowper, William (1731–1800), an English poet imbued with much piety of sentiment and a remarkable poetic talent. His *Task* is one of the great poems of the 18th century.

Cox, David (1783–1859), an eminent landscape painter—son of a Birmingham blacksmith—whose pictures are thoroughly English in spirit and treatment.

Crabbe, Rev. George (1754–1832), a poet of rural life and scenes, noted for his faithful pictures, characterisation and soundness of his sentiments.

Craig, Edward Gordon, C.H. (b. 1872), the son of Ellen Terry, author of several books on stage-craft. He produced many plays in England and on the Continent.

Cranmer, Thomas (1489–1556), Archbishop of Canterbury under Henry VIII, and Edward VI.; an ardent promoter of the Reformation. On Mary's accession at first consented to return to the old faith, but when called upon to make public avowal of his recantation, refused, and was burnt at the stake. His great contributions were the English Bible and Book of Common Prayer.

Crawford, Francis Marion (1854–1909), an American novelist who obtained considerable eminence by his stories of Italian life, including *A Roman Singer, Saracinesca*, and *Saint Ilario*.

Crichton, James (1560–1582). Scottish adventurer who earned considerable renown for his scholarly accomplishments and charm and was called "The Admirable Crichton." He was assassinated when only twenty-two years of age in Mantua.

Cripps, Rt. Hon. Sir (Richard) Stafford, C.H., Q.C. (1889–1952), British statesman and barrister, younger son of Lord Parmoor and nephew of Beatrice Webb. In charge of post-war Britain's economic affairs. His programme was one of purposeful austerity, but his outstanding ability and masterly exposition of the economic situation won him support from all sides. He showed that liberty and planning can be reconciled in the modern world. Labour M.P. for S.E. Bristol, 1931–50. Gave up a brilliant career at the bar to enter politics. Ambassador to Moscow, 1940–42, and Min. of Aircraft Production, 1942–45. Went on missions to India in 1942 and 1946. Resigned his seat in Parliament and as Chancellor of the Exchequer in 1950 because of broken health; was taken to Switzerland for a cure, but he did not recover.

Crispi, Francesco (1819–1901), noted Italian statesman, who aided Garibaldi and was his supporter throughout. Premier 1887–91 and 1893–96. Achieved many reforms for his country.

Crispin, St., a saint of the Roman Church and patron of shoemakers. In the 3rd century he and his brother, natives of Rome, settled in Soissons, France, and there preached Christianity, supporting themselves by shoemaking. Suffered martyrdom under Diocletian in 289, by being thrown into a cauldron of molten lead; commemorated on Oct. 25.

Croce, Benedetto (1866–1952), Italian philosopher and critic and one of the great figures of the 20th century. Devoted his long life to studying and writing, and his philosophy is expounded in the four volumes of *Filosofia dello Spirito* (which has been translated into English). He founded and edited *La Critica* in 1903, a review of literature, history, and philosophy. Strongly opposed to fascism, he was described during the war as "the grand old man who kept a torch burning in Naples which even Mussolini did not dare to extinguish."

Crœsus (died c. 546 B.C.) the last King of Lydia (560–546 B.C.), who reigned fourteen years, and acquired such immense wealth that his name has ever since been proverbial. He was a wise king, whose memory still survives in his wise sayings. Solon was his friend, and it was Solon's name that he uttered thrice while standing before the pyre on which Cyrus had condemned him to be burnt. This touched Cyrus, who spared his life and made him his companion. He succeeded his father Alyattes on the Lydian throne, 560 B.C.

Crome, John (1769–1821), known as "Old Crome," from being a humble house-painter became eminent as a painter of landscape.

Cromer, 1st Earl of, P.C., G.C.B., O.M., G.C.M.G., K.C.S.I., C.I.E., F.R.S. (1841–1917), a diplomatist who won celebrity in the post of British Comptroller-General in Egypt from 1883 to 1907. It was a stupendous task that he had imposed upon him, but he resolutely devoted himself to it, with the result that Egypt was lifted from financial difficulty and internal disorder to a condition of prosperity. In 1908 published *Modern Egypt* and *Ancient and Modern Imperialism* in 1910.

Crompton, Samuel (1753–1827), was a poor cotton worker at Bolton who invented the spinning mule, which greatly increased the power of cotton production. Received little recognition.

Cromwell, Oliver (1599–1658), Lord Protector of the commonwealth of England, Scotland and Ireland, 1653–58. Born at Huntingdon, educated at Sidney Sussex College, Cambridge, and entered parliament as member for Huntingdon in 1628. With outbreak of civil war served with the parliamentary army under Essex and won renown at Edgehill (1642). Celebrated as a great general, leader of his Ironsides, for his religious toleration, and strong foreign policy. His victories include Marston Moor (1644), Naseby (1645), Dunbar (1650), Worcester (1651).

Cromwell, Richard (1626–1712), son of the foregoing, and his successor in the Protectorate.

Cromwell, Thomas (1485–1540), originally a protégé of Wolsey, rose to high office under Henry VIII, and began the suppression of the monasteries. Executed after the failure of the Anne of Cleves marriage, which was part of his policy of alliance with the Protestant princes of Germany.

Crookes, Sir William, O.M., F.R.S. (1832–1919) eminent British scientist whose researches in chemistry and physics led to many important discoveries and inventions. He discovered the metal thallium in 1861, invented the radiometer and the Crookes' tube, which was used by J. J. Thomson and others in their researches on conduction of electricity in gases. He was also an authority on sanitation. President of the Royal Society, 1913–16.

Cruikshank, George (1792–1878), a celebrated book illustrator who was for a time associated with Charles Dickens, and later on illustrated numerous works of other novelists of his day, showing great humour and power of character-delineation.

Cummings, Bruce Frederick (1889–1917), English zoologist and man of letters. Won fame with his *Journal of a Disappointed Man*.

Cunard, Sir Samuel, Bt. (1787–1865), shipowner and co-founder of the British and N. American Royal Mail Steam Packet Co. which later became the Cunard Line and as a result of a merger in 1934, the Cunard-White Star Line, owners of the two largest liners afloat—the *Queen Elizabeth* and the *Queen Mary*.

Cunnngham of Hyndhope, Admiral of the Fleet, Viscount, K.T., G.C.B., O.M., D.S.O. (1883–1963), won the D.S.O. and two bars in the first world war, C.-in-C., Mediterranean, 1939–42 Allied Naval C.-in-C., North African campaign. First Sea Lord, 1943–46.

Cunningham, General Sir Alan Gordon, G.C.M.G., K.C.B., D.S.O., M.C. (b. 1887), brother of Viscount Cunningham. Directed Abyssinian campaign and commanded 8th Army, 1941. From 1945 served as the last British High Commissioner in Palestine.

Cunningham, Admiral of the Fleet, Sir John Henry Dacres, G.C.B., M.V.O. (1885–1962), C.-in-C., Mediterranean, 1943–46. First Sea Lord 1946–48.

Curie, Prof. Pierre (1859–1906) and **Madame Marie** (1867–1934) are names that have become famous as the discoverers of radium. M. Curie was a Frenchman, Mme. Curie a Pole; they were both indefatigable scientific investigators. Shared the Nobel Prize for Physics 1903, while their daughter, the late Mme. Irène Joliot-Curie, shared with her husband the 1935 Nobel Prize for Chemistry, awarded for their researches in radioactivity.

Curzon of Kedleston, Marquess, K.G., P.C., G.C.S.I., G.C.I.E. (1859–1925), statesman and administrator. As a young man gained distinction as traveller and author. From 1899 to 1905 was a vigorous and outstanding Viceroy of India. Foreign Secretary, 1919–23, when he played a dominant part in the reconstruction of the Middle East and was prominent at many conferences after the first world war.

Cuthbert, St. (635–687), a famous monk who became prior of Melrose, and afterwards of Lindisfarne. For a time he lived in seclusion on one of the Farne Islands, but from 684 was Bishop of Hexham.

Cuvier, Georges Léopold, Baron (1769–1832), a French naturalist who founded a system of classification in zoology, and originated the science of comparative anatomy.

Cuyp, Albert (1620–1691), a famous Dutch landscape painter, several of whose works are in our National Gallery.

Cyprian, St., was an eminent ecclesiastic of the 3rd century, who wrote several notable treatises on matters of Christian doctrine. He was beheaded in 258, at an advanced age, and the present English calendar commemorates him on Sept. 26.

Cyrus the Great (d. 529 B.C.), the founder of the Persian Empire who by his conquests of Media, Lydia, and Babylonia, made himself master of Asia Minor. He was a great warrior and a wise ruler and figures prominently in the Bible. He was slain in battle on the river Jaxartes.

D

Daguerre, Louis Jacques Mandé (1789–1851), a French artist, who acquired fame as the inventor of the earliest photographic process, and then devoted himself to scene-painting and became part-proprietor of the Diorama in Paris.

Daimler, Gottlieb (1834–1890), German inventor with N. A. Otto of Cologne of the Otto gas engine, and in his later years eminent as the inventor of the motor-car that is named after him.

Dale, Sir Henry Hallett, O.M., G.B.E., F.R.S., M.D., D.Sc., LL.D., F.R.C.P. (b. 1875). President, British Association, 1947, and of the Royal Society, 1940–45. Chairman of the Lister Institute of Preventive Medicine, 1942. Awarded Nobel Prize for Medicine, 1936.

Dalhousie, 1st Marquess of, P.C., K.T. (1812–1860). The tenth Earl and first Marquess of Dalhousie was one of the most famous of India's Governors-General. He controlled the affairs of India during a period of great difficulty, and annexed the Punjab after the second Sikh War; later on also annexing Nagpur Jhansi, Pegu and other States. He left India in 1856, the year before the Mutiny.

Dali, Salvador (b. 1904), Spanish painter whose *Persistence of Memory* with its bleak landscape and drooping watches is typical of surrealist art. In 1940 he went to live in America.

Dalton, John (1766–1844), famous chemist and mathematician, renowned for his work on the construction of matter. In 1810 published his classic *A New System of Chemical Philosophy*, in which the modern chemical atomic theory was first propounded. According to this theory the atoms of the chemical elements are qualitatively different from one another.

Damien, Father (Joseph de Veuster) (1840–1889), a Belgian missionary who, going out to Honolulu in 1864, and witnessing the terrible sufferings of the lepers confined on the Island of Molokai, obtained permission to take spiritual charge of the Government settlement, and remained there working nobly for this wretched community, until in 1889 he himself was stricken with leprosy and died.

Damocles, a Syracusan of the 5th cent. B.C., member of the court of Dionysius I. The legend related by Cicero concerning him is that he flattered his master by expressing his envy of the tyrant's riches and power, whereupon Dionysius, to demonstrate the precariousness of high estate, invited him to a banquet where he found himself sitting beneath a naked sword suspended by a hair. Hence the phrase "the sword of Damocles"—to hang by a thread.

Damrosch, Walter Johannes (1862–1950), American musician, active in the musical development of the United States. Conductor of the New York Symphony Society, 1885–1927, and composer of three operas and of incidental music to Greek plays.

D'Annunzio, Gabriele (1863–1938), Italian poet, dramatist and novelist. In Sept. 1919 he led an unofficial raid on Fiume and seized the port and town; when the Treaty of Rapallo was signed in 1920, he refused to recognise the Treaty, and declared war against Italy. Fiume was attacked and D'Annunzio, after a short resistance, surrendered.

Dante Alighieri (1265–1321), the greatest Italian poet and one of the great figures of world literature, was born in Florence in a period of political upheaval caused by the strife between Guelph and Ghibelline, which had divided mediaeval Italy for over a century. Though he saw her but once or twice, he conceived an abiding love for a Florentine lady, Bice Portinari (called by Dante Beatrice), wife of Simone di Bardi, whom he first met in 1274. She died in 1290. Some of his finest work was written after he was driven from his native city in 1301. His works include the *Vita Nuova* (written 1292–93 in memory of Beatrice), his supreme masterpiece the *Divine Comedy*, begun 1308–9 and completed shortly before his death, many beautiful lyrics, and some Latin treatises.

Danton, Georges Jacques (1759–1794), a famous member of the National Convention at the period of the first French Revolution. Was made President of the Committee of Public Safety, but Robespierre attacked and supplanted him. Danton was consigned to the guillotine shortly afterwards.

D'Arblay, Madame (1752–1840), better known as Frances (Fanny) Burney, daughter of the organist Dr. Charles Burney, made a great sensation while quite young and unmarried by her novel *Evelina*, which opened the doors of Society to her and gained her the friendship of Dr. Johnson.

Darius was the name borne by three Persian kings. The first reigned from 521 to 485 B.C., and was defeated by the Greeks at Marathon. The second was a natural son of Artaxerxes Longimanus, and having obtained the crown by the murder of his brother, reigned from 424 to 405 B.C. The third Darius was the last of the Persian kings, reigning only from 336 to 331 B.C. when Alexander the Great invaded his kingdom and defeated him in two great battles. Soon after he was assassinated.

Darling, Grace Horsley (1815–1842), English heroine who by putting off in a small boat from the lighthouse on one of the Farne Islands, of which her father was keeper, saved the shipwrecked crew of the *Forfarshire*.

Darnley, Earl of (1545–1567), was married to Mary Queen of Scots—as her second husband—in 1565. Two years later, after Mary had entered into an intrigue with Bothwell, he was murdered.

Darwin, Charles Robert, F.R.S. (1809–1882), the distinguished scientist, whose *Origin of Species* first clearly formulated and elaborated the theory of evolution. His first work (1837) described a five years' cruise in the *Beagle*, which the Government had sent out for scientific purposes. His *Origin of Species* appeared in 1859, and, though defended and supported by the scientific thought of the time generally, was much attacked by theologians. In 1871 Darwin issued his *Descent of Man*, a still further elaboration of the evolution theory. His other principal works were *The Expression Of Emotion in Man and Animals* (1872), *Insectivorous Plants* (1875), *Different Forms of Flowers* (1877), and *Worms* (1881).

Daudet, Alphonse (1840–1897), the celebrated French humorist and novelist, all of whose works have been translated into English.

Davenant, Sir William (1606–1668), a dramatist and poet of much note in his time, who filled the office of Poet Laureate in succession to Ben Jonson.

David I. (1084–1153) was King of Scotland and uncle of Matilda, daughter of Henry I.; he took up arms against Stephen on his repudiation of Matilda's claims to the English crown.

David II. (1324–1371), King of Scotland from 1330 to 1370. He was the son of Robert Bruce, and in conflict with the English Army at Neville's Cross, in 1346, was defeated and made prisoner by Queen Philippa.

David, Sir (Tannatt William) Edgeworth, K.B.E., C.M.G., D.S.O., F.R.S. (1858–1934), an Australian geologist of the first rank, who was Professor of Geology at Sydney University 1891–1924. Spent much of his time in exploration, and accompanied as geologist Shackleton's Antarctic Expedition, 1907–9, leading the party that ascended Mt. Erebus, and discovering with Sir Douglas Mawson the South Magnetic Pole.

David, Jacques-Louis (1748–1825), a celebrated French painter of classic subjects, who put his art at the service of the New Republic.

David, St., patron saint of Wales, whose festival falls on March 1st, lived in the 6th century in Wales, and founded various monasteries.

Davidson, Randall Thomas Davidson, 1st and only Baron, P.C., G.C.V.O. (1848–1930), Archbishop of Canterbury, 1903–1928. Dean of Windsor, 1883–1891; Bishop of Rochester, 1891–1895; and Bishop of Winchester, 1895–1903. Was for a long period Domestic Chaplain and Clerk of the Closet to Queen Victoria, and married in 1878 the daughter of Archbishop Tait.

Davies, Rt. Hon. Clement, Q.C., M.P. (1884–1962), lawyer and politician. Called to the Bar, 1909, took silk, 1926. He led the Liberal Party from 1945 until 1956, and represented his native Montgomery from 1929 until his death.

Davies, Sir (Henry) Walford, K.C.V.O., O.B.E., Mus.D., D.Mus. (1869–1941), Master of the King's Music, 1934–41; Director of Music and Chairman of the National Council of Music, University of Wales, 1919–41, the Gresham Prof. of Music, 1924–41.

Davies, William Henry (1871–1940), was a Welsh poet who spent his early life as a tramp and odd-job man. For six years he wandered about America, where he lost a foot "train-jumping," and for eight years followed a similar life in England, tramping, peddling and stopping in common lodging-houses. His poems reveal an intimate knowledge of and love for Nature. An account of his life is given in his *Autobiography of a Super Tramp.*

Da Vinci. *See* **Leonardo.**

Davis, Jefferson (1808–1889), an American statesman, who on the breaking out of Civil War, was made President of the Confederate States. After the war he was a prisoner in the hands of the Federals, put on his trial for treason, and subjected to much indignity, but was ultimately discharged and wrote (1881) *The Rise and Fall of the Confederate Government.*

Davis, John (*c.* 1550–1605), one of the great Elizabethan explorers and discoverer of Davis's Strait, the channel between the Atlantic and Arctic Oceans on the west of Greenland. Invented the backstaff, or Davis's quadrant.

Davitt, Michael (1846–1906), after a hard-working and precarious bringing up this ardent Irish Nationalist attracted much notice by the bitter speeches he made on behalf of the Fenian Brotherhood, and in 1870 was sentenced to fifteen years' penal servitude for treason-felony, but was released on ticket of leave in 1877. Was one of the founders of the Irish Land League 1879. In 1881 was sent back to penal servitude, but released again in the following year. Was elected to Parliament while a prisoner at Portland but disqualified. Succeeded in entering Parliament in 1892, and resigned in 1899.

Davy, Sir Humphry, Bt., F.R.S. (1778–1829), the inventor of the safety-lamp. Was an eminent chemist whose researches and discoveries were of great scientific importance. Was the first to employ the electric current in chemical decomposition and discovered that nitrous oxide was perfectly respirable.

Dawber, Sir (Edward) Guy, R.A. (1861–1938), English architect. As Chairman of the Council for the Preservation of Rural England, he did much to bring about the restoration of buildings throughout the country.

Dawkins, Sir William Boyd (1837–1929), British geologist, noted for his research on fossil mammals. Made Channel Tunnel survey in 1882.

Dawson, (George) Geoffrey (1874–1944), editor of *The Times,* 1912–19, and 1923–41; educated at Eton and Oxford; was private secretary to Lord Milner in S. Africa, 1901–5, editor of the *Johannesburg Star,* 1905–10

Deakin, Rt. Hon. Arthur, C.H., C.B.E., J.P. (1890–1955), Trade Union leader; succeeded Ernest Bevin as general secretary of the Transport and General Workers' Union in 1949 and like him was a master negotiator.

Debussy, Claude Achille (1862–1918), French composer and founder of the Impressionist school in music, whose harmonies have a vague "atmospheric" effect. Among his works are *Suite bergamasque,* containing the popular *Clair de lune, L'après-midi d'un Faune,* inspired by the poem of Mallarmé, and *La Mer.* He also wrote an opera *Pelléas et Mélisande* based on Maeterlinck's drama and many piano compositions and songs. *See* Biography by Edward Lockspeiser.

Defoe, Daniel (1660–1731), the son of a London butcher. He became a political writer and novelist, obtaining world-wide fame by his *Robinson Crusoe,* written when he was nearly sixty years of age. This was followed by several other novels, all of great merit.

De Forest, Lee (1873–1961), American inventor who was the first to use alternating-current transmission, improved the thermionic valve detector and amplifier, which revolutionised wireless and by which modern wireless and sound films (Talkies) were made possible. He designed the first high-power station for the United States Navy and was granted over three hundred patents.

De Gasperi, Alcide (1881–1954), Italian catholic politician. Founded the Christian Democrat Party and worked for European federation. Died on eve of breakdown of Brussels Conference on E.D.C. Prime Min. 1945–53.

De Gaulle, General. (*See* **Gaulle, Charles de.**)

De Havilland, Sir Geoffrey, O.M., C.B.E., F.R.Ae.A. (1882–1965), a pioneer of civil and military aviation. Began flying in 1908 and was the founder of the Stag Lane Aerodrome at Hendon and the designer of the famous Moth machines. Contributed in great measure to the advance of civil aviation since the first world war. Awarded the Guggenheim Medal in 1952. His son was killed in 1946 while testing a plane in preparation for breaking world speed record.

Delacroix, Ferdinand Victor Eugène (1798–1863), French painter of great imaginative and dramatic force, of the romantic school.

De la Mare, Walter John, O.M., C.H. (1873–1956), English poet and novelist whose work has a characteristic charm. Much of it was written for children.

Delane, John Thadeus (1817–1879), the famous editor of *The Times,* who, though he did not write himself, made his paper the greatest journal in the world. He occupied the editorial chair from 1841 to 1877.

Delaroche, Paul (Hippolyte) (1797–1856), an eminent French historical painter.

Delibes, Clément Philibert Léo (1836–91), French composer of much graceful music, including several operas, of which *Lakmé* is the most famous, and ballets, among them *Coppélia.*

Delius, Frederick, C.H. (1862–1934), English composer of German parentage. Studied at Leipzig from 1886 to 1888 where his suite *Florida* was first performed. In 1899 he went to live near Paris but became crippled and blind in his later years. Highly idiosyncratic in idiom, his music was more readily received in Germany than England until Sir Thomas Beecham's inspired performances won popularity for him in his native land. He composed operas, including *A Village Romeo and Juliet,* choral works, including *Sea Drift,* orchestral pieces, of which *On Hearing the First Cuckoo in Spring* is well known, besides chamber music, concertos, and songs.

Democritus (*c.* 460–357 B.C.), the Greek philosopher to whom the conception of the atomic theory is attributed. His cheerful disposition led to his being styled "the laughing philosopher," and the tradition tells that he put out his eyes in order not to be distracted in his speculations.

Demosthenes (385–322 B.C.), the famous Greek orator, statesman and warrior who, by his *Philippics,* roused the Athenians to resist the growing power of Philip of Macedon. Sixty-one of his orations were preserved, and are regarded as the finest examples of their kind.

De Quincey, Thomas (1785–1859), an eminent essayist and critic, the friend of Coleridge, Wordsworth, and Southey. His *Confessions of an Opium-eater* is a British classic.

De Reszke, Jean (1853–1925) and **De Reszke, Edouard** (1856–1917), Polish operatic singers, the first a tenor, the second a baritone, who achieved fame and fortune by their singing.

Derwentwater, 3rd Earl of (1689–1716), the leader of the English Jacobite movement for placing the Pretender on the English throne. The rising took place in 1715, but was completely crushed by the Battle of Preston, and Derwentwater was beheaded.

Descartes, René (1596–1650), the famous French philosopher, mathematician, and author. Unconvinced by scholastic tradition and theological dogma, he sought to get back to primary truth, to the very definition of knowledge or the reason why anything can be said to be true. The basis of his Cartesian philosophy is summed up in his own words *cogito, ergo sum* (I am thinking so I exist).

Desmoulins, Lucie Simplice Camille Benoist (1760–1794), was one of the fiercest of the French Revolutionary leaders, and from the destruction of the Bastille to the early days of the Terror was unflagging in his onslaughts upon the aristocrats and the priesthood. He fell under the displeasure of Robespierre, however, and was sent to the guillotine along with Danton.

De Valera, Eamon, LL.D. (b. New York, 1882), Pres. Rep. of Ireland, 1959– ; leader of the Fianna Fail Party; Prime Minister 1938–48, 1951–54, and 1957–59; Minister for External Affairs 1932–48. Pres. of Executive Council of Irish Free State, 1932–38; Pres. of Sinn Fein 1917–26 when Fianna Fail was founded; Delegate to Assembly and Council of League of Nations, 1932, and President thereof 1932 and 1938.

De Valois, Dame, Ninette, D.B.E. (b. 1898), Irish-born ballet dancer and choreographer. Between world wars had many triumphs as a dancer with the British National Opera company and with the Diaghilev Russian ballet. Director of the Royal Ballet School (formerly the Sadler's Wells School).

Dewar, Sir James, F.R.S. (1842–1923), physicist and chemist, a native of Kincardine. From 1875 until his death Jacksonian Prof. of Natural Philosophy at Cambridge and from 1877 Fullerian Prof. of Chemistry at the Royal Institution. Famous for his work on the liquefaction of gases and his invention of the Thermos flask. Invented, with Sir F. Abel, the explosive cordite.

Dewey, Prof. John (1859–1952), the eminent American philosopher, psychologist and educationist, who, after holding professorships at the Universities of Minnesota, Michigan, and Chicago, where he was also Director of the School of Education until 1904, was Prof. of Philosophy at Columbia University, New York, 1904–32. A follower of William James, he became well known in America as an adherent of pragmatism.

De Witt, Jan (1625–72), Dutch republican statesman, who carried on war with England and later negotiated the Triple Alliance, but was overthrown by the Orange Party and murdered.

Diaghilev, Sergei Pavlovich (1872–1929), Russian ballet impresario and founder of the Russian ballet, who selected the best dancers, musicians, and artists in his productions. Among those associated with him were Anna Pavlova, Vaslav Nijinsky, Tamara Karsavina, Leonide Massine, Michel Fokine, the choreographer, L. N. Bakst, the painter, and Igor Stravinsky, the composer.

Dick, Sir William Reid, K.C.V.O., R.A., F.R.B.S. (1879–1961), British sculptor whose works include the Livingstone statue (Victoria Falls, Africa), memorial statue of King George V. at Westminster, and the statue of Pres. Roosevelt in Grosvenor Square.

Dickens, Charles (John Huffam) (1812–1870), the most popular novelist of the 19th century, who from very humble beginnings worked himself up to the highest position in the world of letters. His literary output was enormous. From the time of the publication of the *Pickwick Papers* down to his death in 1870, covering a period of 33 years, he produced novel after novel, all possessing the original Dickensian characteristics, yet each wonderfully different from the rest and his popularity continues undiminished. He did so much for the cultivation of the true sentiment of Christmas that, whenever that season comes round, his name is recalled with honour and homage. As a public reader of his own works Dickens evinced a marvellous dramatic gift. He was buried in Westminster Abbey.

Dickinson, Goldsworthy Lowes (1863–1932), English scholar, author and philosopher; an interpreter and upholder of the Greek view of life, which is the subject of many of his books.

Dicksee, Sir Francis Bernard, R.A. (1853–1928), well known as the painter of numerous pictures, including "Harmony," "Romeo and Juliet," and "The Funeral of a Viking."

Diderot, Denis (1713–1784), the famous French philosopher and editor of the *Dictionnaire Encyclopédique*, which occupied him thirty years.

Diefenbaker, Rt. Hon. John George, M.A., Q.C. (b. 1895), Canadian lawyer and leader of the Canadian Progressive Conservative Party; Prime Min., 1957–63.

Diemen, Anthony van (1593–1645), Dutch Admiral who was Governor-General of the East Indian Colonies, 1636–45. He extended Dutch influence and trade throughout the Far East, promoted explorations to Australia, 1636–42, and on one of such explorations, Abel Tasman discovered New Zealand and named the island which we now know as Tasmania, Van Diemen's Land.

Diesel, Rudof (1858–1913), German engineer, inventor of an internal-combustion engine which he patented in 1893. The modern so-called Diesel engine represents the improvements achieved by many men and has evolved mainly from the invention of Herbert Akroyd-Stuart, patented in 1890.

Diocletian (Caius Aurelius Valerius Diocletianus) (245–313), Roman Emperor (284–305). Inaugurated the system of partnership emperors, whereby the Empire was divided into four sections (the famous tetrachy), administered by himself in the East, Maximian in Italy and Africa, Constantius in Britain, Gaul, etc., and Gallerius in Illyricum. Ruthlessly persecuted the Christians.

Diogenes (412–322 B.C.), the celebrated Greek cynic philosopher who is said to have lived in a tub wearing the coarsest clothing and living on the plainest food. Many of his sayings have been preserved.

Dionysius. Two of the tyrants of Syracuse bore this name. The first was a great soldier and statesman as well as a poet and philosopher, and lived from *c.* 430–367 B.C. The second Dionysius was his son and successor, but was of such a cruel disposition that he was driven from the throne and died in obscurity in 343.

Disney, Walter Elias ("Walt") (b. 1901), American film cartoonist; creator of Mickey Mouse. His *Silly Symphonies*, *Snow White and the Seven Dwarfs*, *Pinocchio*, and *Fantasia* brought him world-wide fame.

Disraeli, Benjamin. (*See* Beaconsfield).

D'Israeli, Isaac (1766–1848), father of Benjamin Disraeli, worked in a special literary field, and produced some interesting volumes dealing with authors and their writings. His best-known work is *Curiosities of Literature.*

Dixon, Harold Bailey (1852–1930), Professor of Chemistry at Manchester University, 1887–1922, whose work on gaseous explosions opened a new era in combustion research.

Dobson, Frank, C.B.E., A.R.A., A.R.B.S. (1888–1963), English sculptor. President of the London Group, 1923–27.

Dobson, Henry Austin, LL.D. (1840–1921), a Civil Servant from 1860 to 1901, he was the author of several volumes of Society verse and prose works, dealing chiefly with the 18th century.

Dodd, Francis, R.A., R.W.S. (1874–1949), painter, engraver and draughtsman. He was one of the official artists during the War of 1914–18, and executed a valuable series of portraits of British Admirals and Generals on active service. Appointed one of the official artists for the second world war, 1939–45.

Dodgson, Charles Lutwidge (1832–1898), a writer and mathematical lecturer at Christ Church, Oxford, who, under the pseudonym of Lewis Carroll, achieved lasting fame by his *Alice's*

Adventures in Wonderland, one of the most delightful books for children ever written.

Dolci, Carlo (1616–1686), the famous Florentine painter, examples of whose Madonnas and Saints are to be found in most National collections.

Dolci, Danilo (b. 1925), Italian architect who since 1952 has dedicated himself to the rehabilitation of the people of Sicily in their desperate poverty. He began with no resources but his own humanity, but now his work—agricultural, educational, and social—is inspiring world-wide interest.

Dominic, St. (1170–1221), founder of the Order of Dominicans, or Black Friars, who devoted much energy to the conversion of the Albigenses, but meeting with small success, instituted a policy of persecution after the manner of the later Inquisition.

Domitian (Titus Flavius Domitianus) (A.D. 51–96), Roman Emperor, son of Vespasian, who after many cruel and tyrannical acts aroused the enmity of the people and was assassinated.

Donatello (Donato di Niccolò di Betto Bardi) (1386–1466) the famous Italian sculptor, whose works are to be seen chiefly at Florence, though several examples are at South Kensington.

Donizetti, Gaetano (1797–1848), Italian operatic composer. Most popular of his sixty operas are *Lucrezia Borgia*, *Lucia di Lammermoor*, *La Fille du régiment*, *La Favorita*, and *Don Pasquale*.

Donne, John (1573–1631), an English poet and divine. As a preacher he was celebrated in his lifetime but few of his poems were printed and it was not until the 20th century that he was universally recognised as one of the most original of English poets. His writings include *Songs and Sonnets*, *Satyres*, *Elegies*, *Problems and Paradoxes*, and the *Holy Sonnets*. He took orders in 1615 and was made dean of St. Paul's in 1621. Sir Edmund Gosse's *Life and Letters* appeared in 1899 and Sir Herbert Grierson's monumental edition of Donne's poetry in 1912.

Donoghue, Stephen ("Steve") (1884–1945), in his day a famous jockey. Rode the Derby Race winner six times, and established a new record by winning this classic event in three successive years, 1921–22–23.

Doré, Gustave (1833–1883), the well-known French artist, famous for his colossal scriptural paintings and his powerful illustrations to the works of Dante, Milton, and Tennyson.

Dostoievsky, Feodor Mikhailovitch (1821–1881), one of Russia's greatest novelists. Author of *Crime and Punishment Brothers Karamazov*, *The Idiot*, *The Possessed*, etc. Dostoievsky's novels are quite exceptional for their deep psychological insight, vision and marvellous tragic and analytic power, and have had a profound influence on modern European writers.

Douglas, Marshal of the R.A.F. Lord, G.C.B., M.C., D.F.C. (b. 1893), commanded Fighter Command, 1940–42, R.A.F. Middle East, 1943–44, and Coastal Command, 1944–45. C.-in-C. and Military Governor of British Zone of Germany, 1946–47. A Labour peer.

Douglas, Norman (1868–1952), novelist and writer of witty and elegant prose. A Scot, born in Austria, he made his home on the Mediterranean and was buried on Capri. Travel books include *Siren Land* (1910). *Fountains in the Sand* (1912), *Old Calabria* (1915), *Alone* (1921), *Together* (1923); his highly entertaining novel *South Wind* was published in 1917.

Douglas-Home, Rt. Hon. Sir Alexander Frederick, M.P. (b. 1903), British statesman; Prime Minister, 1963–64; Leader of the Conservative Party, 1963–5; M.P. for Kinross and W. Perthshire, 1963–; Foreign Sec., 1960–63; Sec. of State for Commonwealth Relations, 1955–60. Formerly the 14th Earl of Home; renounced title in 1963 to stand as candidate for House of Commons.

Doulton, Sir Henry (1820–1897), famous potter and the inventor of Doulton ware.

Dowden, Edward, M.A., LL.D., D.C.L., Litt.D. (1843–1913). Well known for his critical and other writings, mainly dealing with the lives and works of the poets. Was Professor of Literature at Trinity College, Dublin, for 37 years

Dowding, Air Chief Marshal Lord, G.C.B., G.C.V.O., C.M.G. (b. 1882), Chief of Fighter Command in Battle of Britain, 1940.

Dowland, John (*c.* 1563–1626), English composer whose songs with lute accompaniment established him as the foremost lutanist of his day. His son Robert succeeded him as Court lutanist to Charles I.

Doyle, Sir Arthur Conan, M.D. (1859–1930), masterly writer of detective stories, the creator of Sherlock Holmes, the archetype of detectives, who shared a flat in Baker Street with his friend and chronicler, Dr. Watson, and conducted a long series of investigations. The immensely popular stories appeared in the *Strand Magazine* and include the *Hound of the Baskervilles* and the *Speckled Band*.

Doyle, Richard (1824–1883), an artist of much humour and fancy, who was exceedingly popular while on the staff of *Punch* from 1841 to 1850. The familiar cover of *Punch* is his work.

D'Oyly Carte, Richard (1844–1901), English theatrical manager, associated with the production of the Gilbert and Sullivan comic operas. The D'Oyly Carte Opera Companies played Gilbert and Sullivan all over the world.

Drake, Sir Francis (*c.* 1540–1596), the great admiral of Queen Elizabeth's time, who made many adventurous voyages, bent partly on discovery and partly on plunder. He was a leading figure—under Lord Howard—in the attack on and destruction of the Spanish Armada in 1588.

Draper, John William (1811–82), American chemist, b. near Liverpool, aided in the organisation of the medical school of New York university and became its professor of chemistry and physiology. He was the first to take a satisfactory photograph of the human face (1840).

Dreiser, Theodore (1871–1945), an American author whose novels of American life are written in vigorous native prose.

Dreyfus, Lt.-Col. Alfred (1859–1935), a French officer, condemned by a military secret tribunal on a charge of divulging secrets in 1894 to a foreign power, and condemned to imprisonment for life on Devil's Island in French Guiana. At a sensational new trial in 1899 he was again found guilty, and sentenced to a mitigated term of incarceration for ten years; but strenuous efforts on his behalf secured a pardon later. In 1906 he was entirely exonerated and reinstated in the army, with the rank of Major, and made a Chevalier of the Legion of Honour.

Drinkwater, John (1882–1937), was a well-known dramatist and poet. His plays *Abraham Lincoln* and *Oliver Cromwell* have had great praise and success.

Driver, Samuel Rolles (1846–1914) a distinguished Hebrew and Old Testament scholar who was Regius Prof. of Hebrew at Oxford, 1883–1914.

Drummond, William (1585–1649), a Scottish poet —laird of Hawthornden—whose works dealt largely with political matters, but revealed considerable poetic power. Ben Jonson walked from London to Scotland to pay him his respects.

Drury, (Edward) Alfred (Briscoe), R.A. (1857–1944). English sculptor who was responsible for may public monuments, including the colossal statues of Queen Victoria at Bradford and Portsmouth (1903), the decorations for the exterior of the War Office (1905) and of the Victoria and Albert Museum (1909).

Dryden, John (1631–1700), one of the most vigorous and prolific of English poets and writers, and a popular dramatist. He excelled in satire, and drew some powerful pictures of the statesmen of his day. His translation of Virgil ranks with Pope's translation of the *Iliad*. He was buried in Westminster Abbey. Originally a Parliamentarian he went over to the Royalists and was laureate and historiographer-royal, 1670–88.

Du Barry, Marie Jeanne Bécu, Comtesse (1746–1793), succeeded Mme de Pompadour as mistress of Louis XV of France. Guillotined by the Revolutionary Tribunal.

Du Chaillu, Paul Belloni (1835–1903), a noted African traveller who was chief of General Gordon's staff in 1874, and wrote many valuable books of travels, his studies of the gorilla being especially interesting.

Dufferin and Ava, 1st Marquess of, P.C., K.P., G.C.B., G.C.S.I., G.C.M.G., G.C.I.E., F.R.S. (1826–1902), was a diplomatist of great experience, a writer of brilliance, and filled many high offices with distinction and success, including those of Governor-General of Canada and Viceroy of India.

Duke-Elder, Sir William Stewart, K.C.V.O., M.A., D.Sc., M.D. (b. 1898), Scottish ophthalmic surgeon at several London Hospitals and Surgeon-Oculist to H.M. Queen Elizabeth.

Dulles, John Foster, (1888–1959), U.S. Secretary of State in the Republican Administration, 1953–59. In his foreign policy he encountered widespread criticism for his inflexible opposition to negotiation with Russia and U.S. recognition of China.

Dumas, Alexandre (1802–1870), French novelist and dramatist, who published more volumes than any man of his time. In the field of historical romance he showed wonderful power and resource and his thrilling story *Monte Cristo* is one of the great novels of the nineteenth century. He also wrote *The Three Musketeers.*

Dumas, Alexandre, Fils (1824–1895), French dramatist and novelist, son of the last-named, author of *La Dame aux Camélias.*

Du Maurier, George Louis Palmella Busson (1834–1896), one of the best known of the *Punch* artists during a long period and author of the novels of *Peter Ibbetson, Trilby,* and *The Martian.*

Dundee, John Graham of Claverhouse, 1st Viscount (1648–89), known as "Bonnie Dundee," royalist leader employed in the suppression of the Covenanters, taking part in the defeat at Drumclog and the victory of Bothwell Brig under the Duke of Monmouth in 1679. Defeated Mackay in the pass of Killiecrankie but was killed in the moment of victory.

Duns Scotus, Johannes (1266–1308), a famous scholastic who was born at Maxton, in the county of Roxburgh; joined the Franciscan Order at Dumfries in 1281, and ordained priest at Lincoln in 1291. Student and teacher at Oxford and Paris and died at Cologne. He was the great doctrinal opponent of Thomas Aquinas and has been surnamed *doctor subtilis.*

Dunstan, Saint (909–988), the famous Abbot of Glastonbury and Archbishop of Canterbury, who lived through seven reigns from Ethelstan to Ethelred and exercised great political influence.

Dupleix, Joseph François (1697–1763), was governor of the French East Indian possessions at the time when Clive was guiding the fortunes of the East India Company, and after Clive's victory at Plassey Dupleix's day was over. He returned to France, and fell into disgrace and poverty.

Dürer, Albrecht (1471–1528), the great German painter and engraver of Nuremberg, friend of Luther and Melancthon. Like his great Italian contemporary, Leonardo, he was not only a superb artist but a man of boundless intellectual curiosity and scientific insight, a true son of the Renaissance. His copper engravings include his three great masterpieces, *The Knight, Melancholia,* and *St. Jerome in His Study.* Many of his engravings are in the British Museum. He may be regarded as the founder of the German school and the inventor of etching.

Durham, John George Lambton, Earl of (1792–1840), served as Governor-General of Canada after the disturbances of 1837, and in 1839 presented the famous *Durham Report* to Parliament. This laid down the principle of colonial self-government and marks a turning-point in the affairs of the Empire.

Duse, Elenora (1861–1924), an Italian tragedienne of world-wide reputation.

Duval, Claude (1643–1670), a notorious highwayman who, coming to England from Normandy in the Duchess of Richmond's service, took to "the road," and for a few years successfully evaded capture. He was hanged at Tyburn.

Duveen, 1st and only Baron, of Millbank (1869–1939), was head of a firm of noted art dealers, and a generous benefactor to British Art.

Dvorák, Antonin (1844–1904), Czech composer whose music is rich in the folk-song melodies of his native Bohemia and has a characteristic lilt and harmony. In 1884 he conducted his *Stabat Mater* in London, where this cantata and his *Slavonic Dances* were very popular. Composed his *From the New World* symphony in New York where he was head of the National Conservatoire (1892–94). He wrote 9 symphonies besides much orchestral and chamber work, piano pieces, songs, and operas.

Dyson, Sir Frank (Watson), K.B.E., F.R.S. (1868–1939), Astronomer Royal (1910–33). Was previously (1905–10) Astronomer Royal for Scotland. Was the author of a number of works on astronomy, and widely celebrated for his interesting public lectures.

Dyson, Sir George, K.C.V.O., M.A., Mus.D., LL.D., F.R.C.M. (1883–1964), Director of the Royal College of Music 1938–53. Author of *The New Music,* in which he analyses the technique of modern schools of composition. Composed a symphony, a violin concerto, and several choral works such as *The Canterbury Pilgrims* and *Nebuchadnezzar.*

E

Eastlake, Sir Charles Lock (1793–1865), English painter of historical and religious works. Pres. of R.A. 1850.

Eastman, George (1854–1932), American inventor who invented the roll photographic film and the famous Kodak camera. He amassed a vast fortune and his philanthropies were estimated at over £60 million. After a long illness he committed suicide.

Eck, Johann von (1486–1543), one of the most vigorous opponents of the Reformation in Germany.

Eddington, Sir Arthur Stanley, O.M., F.R.S. (1882–1944), Plumian Professor of Astronomy, Cambridge, 1913; Director of the Cambridge Observatory, 1914–44. Author of *The Nature of the Physical World* (1928) and many scientific works.

Eddy, Mrs. Mary Baker (1821–1910), founder of the religion (theology and practice) which she named Christian Science, and of the Church of Christ, Scientist. Author of the Christian Science textbook, *Science and Health with Key to the Scriptures,* published in 1875. *See also* **J9**.

Edelinck, Gerard (1640–1707), French engraver, b. in Antwerp, the first to reproduce in print the colour, as well as the form, of a picture. Patronized by Louis XIV.

Eden, (Robert) Anthony, 1st Earl of Avon, K.G., M.C., (b. 1897), succeeded Sir Winston Churchill as Prime Minister in April 1955. He had been Deputy Prime Minister and Foreign Secretary since 1951. First appointed Foreign Secretary in 1935 (the youngest to hold that office for over a century), but resigned in 1938 on a difference of policy with Mr. Neville Chamberlain about relations with Italy. Entered Parliament as a member for Leamington in 1923. He has many diplomatic achievements to his credit, though his Suez policy in 1956 divided the country. Resigned because of ill-health in Jan. 1957. Memoirs, *Facing the Dictators; The Reckoning;* and *Full Circle.* Earldom conferred 1961.

Edgar (943–75), King of England 959–75, who under the influence of Dunstan was able to carry out many useful reforms.

Edgar Atheling (*c.* 1060–*c.* 1130), as grandson of Edmund Ironside, was the lawful heir of Edward the Confessor, but in the confusion of the Norman invasion he was unable to maintain his claim.

Edgeworth, Maria (1767–1849), Irish novelist, whose stories included *Castle Rackrent, The Absentee,* and *Belinda.*

Edinburgh, H.R.H. Prince Philip, Duke of, K.G., P.C., K.T., G.B.E. (b. 1921), consort of H.M. Queen Elizabeth II. Relinquished his title of Prince Philip of Greece and of Denmark on his naturalisation in 1947, taking the name of Mountbatten. He is the great-great-grandson of Queen Victoria, grandson of Admiral Prince Louis of Battenberg, and nephew of Earl Mountbatten of Burma. Educated in England and Germany and at the Royal Naval College. Served in the Royal Navy throughout the war. Pres. of the National Playing Fields Association; Pres. of the British Association, 1951–52. Chancellor of Edinburgh University, 1953.

Edison, Thomas Alva (1847–1931), an American inventor, who after an adventurous boyhood became a telegraph operator and interested in electrical problems. Established himself in New York in 1869, and invented an improved printing telegraph. In 1867 set up an elaborate laboratory and factory at Menlo Park, New Jersey, from which place he sent out many clever and some startling inventions, including a system of duplex telegraphy, afterwards improved into quadruplex and sextuplex transmission, the phonograph, and a method of preparing carbon filaments for the electric lamp; patented over 1300 inventions.

Edmund II. (Ironside) (980–1016), the son of Ethelred, after years of contention with the Danes, made a compact with Canute to divide England between them, but dying shortly afterwards the kingdom was settled on Canute.

Edward the Confessor (*c.* 1004–1066), the Anglo-Saxon king who immediately preceded—save for the brief reign of Harold of less than a year—the Norman Conquest, and founded Westminster Abbey, where a smaller church, then dilapidated, had previously for a period had a precarious existence. He was a religious-minded mystic, and was canonised in 1161, and given the shrine in the Abbey of his origination, which yet remains fairly intact, despite the ravages of time and disturbing hands.

Edward the Elder was the son of Alfred, and succeeded him as King of the West Saxons in 899. He was successful in overcoming the Danes, and became overlord of the Northern counties.

Edward the Martyr (963–979) became king in succession to Edgar, but, although supported by Dunstan, was not able to prevail against his stepmother Elfrida, who had him murdered.

Edward I. (1239–1307) was king of England from 1272 to 1307. Took part in the Crusades, completed the conquest of Wales, overcame Scottish opposition—executing Wallace and receiving the submission of Bruce, and promulgated many wise laws. He was nicknamed " Longshanks."

Edward II. (1284–1327), the son of Edward I. succeeded his father when the latter died at Burgh-over-Sands in 1307. Suffered defeat at the hands of the Scots at Bannockburn, and on account of his arbitrary disposition, cruelty and lavish concessions to favourites, was deposed in 1327, and afterwards murdered at Berkeley Castle.

Edward III. (1312–1377) was one of the ablest of English monarchs who, although much taken up with long and bitter wars with France and Scotland, did much for the commercial interests of the nation, and was the means of introducing large numbers of Flemings into the country, who laid the foundation of the English textile manufacturers. He married Philippa of Hainault, and was the father of Edward the Black Prince.

Edward IV. (1442–1483) attempted unsuccessfully to regain the lost English possessions in France, and resorted to many despotic expedients for obtaining supplies but it stands to his credit that he entered into trading treaties with the commercial merchants of the Continent which were of benefit to his people.

Edward V. (1470–1483)—son of Edward IV. and Elizabeth Woodville—was the unfortunate king who was put to death in the Tower of London, and succeeded by Richard III., his unscrupulous uncle, who had made himself " Protector " and assumed the Crown a little more than two months after the death of Edward IV., publishing the demise of the young King and his brother the Duke of York as having occurred in prison. The bones of the murdered boys were many years afterwards taken to Westminster Abbey for final burial.

Edward VI. (1537–1553), succeeded his father, Henry VIII., when in his tenth year and died in his sixteenth year. The Reformation under the Regency of Somerset first, and then of Northumberland, made considerable progress during his brief reign. He was induced during his last illness to name Lady Jane Grey his successor, with results disastrous to that unfortunate personage and many others concerned.

Edward VII. (1841–1910). Was married to Princess Alexandra of Denmark in 1863. Visited India in 1875, and from that time onward was constantly in the public eye, taking part in all kinds of functions. Succeeded to the throne on the death of Queen Victoria, Jan. 22, 1901. The Coronation, which had been planned for June 26, 1902, had to be postponed in consequence of the King's sudden illness, but eventually took place on August 9 in the same year. His Majesty was a powerful factor in the preservation of the peace of Europe, his friendly intercourse with the heads of the French, German, and other nations earning for him the title of " Edward the Peacemaker."

Edward VIII. (b. 1894), succeeded to the throne on the death of his father, George V., Jan. 20, 1936; Prince of Wales 1911–36. Abdicated in favour of his brother H.R.H. the Duke of York Dec. 10, 1936, and was created Duke of Windsor. Governor of the Bahamas 1940–45.

Edwin (585–633), King of Northumbria, killed in battle at Hatfield Chase, Yorkshire, in 633. He was baptised into the Christian faith at York in 627, and built a church there.

Egbert was a descendant of Cerdic, king of the West Saxons, and reigned from 802 to 839 in Wessex; in his later years became the first king of all England. In 835 he had to drive the Northmen away from Cornwall.

Ehrlich, Paul (1854–1914), a noted German scientist who was Director of the Royal Institute for Experimental Therapeutics at Frankfurt-on-Main, which he made famous by his experimental laboratory work in connection with cancer. His prolonged experimental researches brought him world-wide renown, his greatest triumphs being the discovery of salvarsan and neo-salvarsan. He received the Nobel Prize in 1908.

Eiffel, Alexandre Gustave (1832–1923), French engineer, one of the first to employ compressed-air caissons in bridge building. Among his notable works are the great Eiffel Tower, Paris (1887–89) and the Panama Canal Locks.

Einstein, Albert (1879–1955), one of the greatest men of science of all time, whose chief claim to fame rests upon his theories of relativity. He was born in Ulm of Jewish parents and lived for many years in Switzerland. Awarded the Nobel Prize in 1921 for his work in quantum theory. In 1933 he was driven by the Nazis to seek asylum in America and became a professor at the Institute for Advanced Study at Princeton, 1933–45. His works include *Relativity* (1920), *Zur Einheitlichen Feldtheorie* (1929), *About Zionism* (1930), *The Evolution of Physics* (1938), *The Meaning of Relativity* (1950), *Out of My Later Years* (1950).

Eisenhower, Gen. Dwight David, G.C.B., O.M. (b. 1890), Republican President of the United States, 1953–61. Supreme Commander Atlantic Forces in Europe 1950–52. U.S. Chief of Staff, 1945–48. C.-in-C. Allied Forces, European theatre of operations, 1943–45, and Allied Forces, N. Africa, 1942–43. Pres. Columbia Univ., 1948–50.

Eisenstein, Sergei Mikhailovich (1898–1948), Russian film director, whose silent film classic *The Battleship Potemkin* brought him world-wide fame. He also produced *Alexander Nevsky* and *Ivan the Terrible*.

Eleanor, Queen of Edward I. (d. 1290), was a woman of great piety and devotion. After her death the king had memorial crosses erected at the twelve places where her body rested on its way from Grantham to Westminster.

Elgar, Sir Edward, Bart., O.M., G.C.V.O. (1857–1934), English composer and Master of the King's Musick, 1924–34. Starting as a violinist and a teacher, he composed many choral-orchestral works for various festivals and sprang to fame with the *Enigma Variations*, musical portraits of his friends. Other compositions include two symphonies, the oratorios *The Kingdom*, *The Apostles* and *The Dream of Gerontius*, and the tone-poem *Falstaff*.

Elgin, Thomas Bruce, 7th Earl of, P.C. (1766–1841), a British diplomatist who brought to England from Athens the famous " Elgin marbles," now in the British Museum.

Eliot, George (1819–1880), the pen name of Marian Evans, who produced some of the most memorable novels of the 19th century, including *Adam Bede*, *The Mill on the Floss*, *Silas Marner*, *Middlemarch* and *Daniel Deronda*.

Eliot, Thomas Stearns, O.M. (1888–1965), poet and critic, one of the foremost literary figures of the 20th century. He was born in St. Louis, Missouri, came to London during the First World War, and became a British subject in 1927. His poems include *Prufrock*, *The Waste Land*, *The Hollow Men*, *Ash Wednesday*, *Four Quartets*, and *Little Gidding*; his verse dramas include *Murder in the Cathedral*, and *The Family Reunion*. He described himself as " classicist in literature, royalist in politics, and Anglo-

Catholic in religion." Awarded 1948 Nobel Prize for Literature. *See also* **Modern Drama.**

Elizabeth (b. 1900), Queen Consort of George VI., daughter of the 14th Earl of Strathmore. Before her marriage in 1923 she was Lady Elizabeth Angela Marguerite Bowes-Lyon. Chancellor, Univ. of London.

Elizabeth I. (1533–1603) came to the throne in 1558 at the age of twenty-five, and reigned forty-five years. Was a fervid Protestant, a sincere lover of her country, a masterful and enlightened ruler—fickle as far as her favourites were concerned—and added distinction to a distinguished period. The defeat of the Spanish Armada, the execution of Mary Stuart, the naval supremacy of England, the extension of her colonies, and the glory of a great new literature of which Shakespeare was the brightest ornament are features associated with her reign.

Elizabeth II. (Elizabeth Alexandra Mary of Windsor) (b. 1926), ascended the throne in February 1952 at the age of twenty-five on the death of her father George VI. Her Consort, Prince Philip, Duke of Edinburgh, is the son of Prince Andrew of Greece and a descendant of the Danish royal family. They have four children, Charles, Prince of Wales (b. 1948), Princess Anne (b. 1950), Prince Andrew. (b. 1960), and Prince Edward (b. 1964).

Ellis, (Henry) Havelock (1859–1939), literary and scientific writer and an authority on sex.

Emerson, Ralph Waldo (1803–1882), the American essayist and philosopher. His *Conduct of Life, Representative Men,* and *Essays,* are among the most brilliant literary productions of America.

Emin Pasha, the name adopted by **Eduard Schnitzer** (1840–92), a German explorer associated with Gen. Charles Gordon in the pacification of the Sudan. He joined Gordon's forces as a medical officer and showing marked administrative ability was made governor of the Equatorial Province in 1878. He was menaced by the Mahdi and rescued by Stanley in 1889. While engaged in exploration for Germany in the region of Lake Tanganyika he was murdered by Arabs.

Emmet, Robert (1778–1803), the enthusiastic youth who led the rebellion in Ireland in 1803 and was tried and executed in the same year for high treason. He is one of Ireland's patriot heroes.

Empedocles (*c.* 500–*c.* 430 B.C.), Greek philosopher, b. Agrigentum in Sicily, founder of a school of medicine which regarded the heart as the seat of life, an idea which passed to Aristotle, as did his idea that all matter was composed of four elements: earth, air, fire, and water. He was also a poet.

Engels, Friedrich (1820–1895), Socialist writer and lifelong friend of Karl Marx with whom he collaborated in producing the Communist Manifesto of 1848. *See also* **Marxism, J27.**

Epictetus of Hierapolis, the Stoic philosopher, who lived in the 1st century, and was a moral teacher of great repute and influence.

Epicurus (342–270 B.C.), the founder of the Epicurean philosophy, which taught that virtue should be followed because it leads to happiness.

Epstein, Sir Jacob, K.B.E. (1880–1959), sculptor, born in New York of Russian–Polish parents. His work includes *Rima,* the Hudson memorial in Hyde Park; *Day* and *Night* on the building of the Underground Headquarters at St. James' Park; *Genesis,* exhibited in 1931; *Lazarus,* which has a fine setting in New College, Oxford; the *Madonna and Child* group for the restored 18th cent. buildings in Cavendish Square; the figure of *Christ in Majesty,* cast in aluminium, in Llandaff Cathedral; a monumental sculpture for the T.U.C. headquarters in London, and a bronze group depicting St. Michael triumphing over the Devil for Coventry Cathedral, his last major work.

Erasmus Desiderius (1466–1536), the great Dutch philosopher and scholar, of whom it was said that he "laid the egg which Luther hatched."

Erhard, Dr. Ludwig (b. 1897), German economist and politician; succeeded Adenauer as Chanc. of the West German Federal Republic in Oct. 1963.

Ericsson, John (1803–1889), Swedish engineer who entered into competition with George Stephenson in the first famous trial of locomotives.

Ervine, St. John Greer (b. 1883), author, dramatist and critic, noted as an able controversialist.

Essex, Robert Devereux, 2nd Earl of (1566–1601), the favourite of Queen of Elizabeth in her old age, son of Walter Devereux (1541–76) and stepson of Leicester. Proved an incapable governor-general of Ireland, returning to England against the Queen's express wish. He was imprisoned and executed for organising a rebellion in London.

Ethelbert, King of Kent at the close of the 6th century and commencement of the 7th. Famous for having accepted Christianity on the entreaty of St. Augustine. Published the first code of written laws in English. Canonised later.

Ethelred II. (*c.* 968–1016), became king of England on the murder of his half-brother, Edward the Martyr (978). He was an incompetent ruler and unable to organise resistance against the Danish raids. Called "the Unready" (from Old Eng. uræd = without counsel).

Ethelwulf was the Anglo-Saxon sovereign who succeeded his father Egbert in 837. Died in 857. and was buried at Winchester.

Etty, William (1787–1848), a famous English R.A., who contributed to the Royal Academy some of its most admired pictures between 1820 and 1849.

Eucken, Rudolf Christoph (1846–1926), a famous German philosopher and theologian.

Euclid (*c.* 330–*c.* 260 B.C.), illustrious Greek mathematician whose *Elements of Geometry* remained a standard text-book until the present century.

Euler, Leonhard (1707–83), Swiss mathematician, regarded as the founder of pure mathematics. He was called by Catherine I. to St. Petersburg, where he became Professor, 1730–41.

Euripides (480–406 B.C.), the greatest of Greek tragic poets. He wrote 92 plays, 18 of which have been preserved, the most famous being *Alcestis, Medea, Iphigenia,* and *Orestes.*

Eusebius (264–340), an ecclesiastical historian whose *Chronicon* is a history of the world down to his own time, while his *Ecclesiastical History* traces the chief events of the Christian Church.

Evans, Sir Arthur John (1851–1941), distinguished archæologist, chiefly famed for his excavations at Knossos in Crete and his discovery of the pre-Phœnician script.

Evans, Dame Edith Mary, D.B.E. (b. 1888), the versatile and brilliant English actress who made her first appearance as Cressida in *Troilus and Cressida* in 1912. She has played many leading roles and has also appeared in films.

Evatt, Rt. Hon. Herbert Vere, M.A., LL.D. (1894–1965), Australian lawyer and politician; Min. for External Affairs 1941–49; leader of the Federal Labour opposition, 1951–60; Chief Justice, New South Wales, 1960–2.

Evelyn, John (1620–1706), was one of the founders of the Royal Society and wrote several scientific works, but is best remembered for his *Diary* which covers the period 1640–1706.

Eyck, Hubert van (*c.* 1366–1426), and **Eyck, Jan van** (*c.* 1386–1440), two of the greatest masters of the early Flemish School of Painters.

F

Fabius Maximus (Cunctator) (d. 203 B.C.), the Roman Consul and Dictator, saved Rome from conquest by Hannibal by deliberate and well-planned strategic evasion of battle. The term "Fabian Policy" is derived from Fabian's tactics.

Fabre, Jean Henri Casimir (1823–1915), French naturalist whose lifelong interest was the study of the habits of insects and whose observations were delightfully recorded in his *Souvenirs entomologiques,* a work of many volumes.

Faed, Thomas, R.A. (1826–1900), one of the most successful of Victorian painters, won a great reputation for his Scottish subjects.

Fahrenheit, Gabriel Daniel (1686–1736), German physicist, born in Danzig, improved construction of thermometers, notably in using quicksilver for alcohol. Devised the scale with freezing-point at 32° boiling-point at 212°.

Fairbairn, Sir William, 1st Bt., F.R.S. (1789–1874), mechanical engineer and inventor. By the first utilisation of iron in shipbuilding, became eminent and wealthy.

Fairfax, Thomas, 3rd Lord (1612–1671), a prominent leader of the Parliamentary army during the Civil War, who greatly distinguished himself at Marston Moor and Naseby.

Falla, Manuel de (1876–1946), Spanish composer whose music is highly individual with a strong folk-song element. His compositions are relatively few and comprise 2 operas, 2 ballets (*The Three-Cornered Hat* was one of Diaghilev's greatest successes), piano music, pieces for piano and orchestra, songs, harpsichord concerto, and guitar solo in memory of his friend Debussy.

Faraday, Michael, F.R.S. (1791–1867), great experimental physicist, founder of the science of electro-magnetism. He was the son of a blacksmith and at the age of 12 worked for a bookbinder, to whom he was later apprenticed. Became laboratory assistant to Sir Humphry Davy at the Royal Institution in 1813, and in 1827 succeeded him, becoming professor of chemistry in 1833. He was one of the world's most brilliant experimenters and set himself the problem of finding the connections between the forces of light, heat, electricity, and magnetism. The epoch-making discoveries he made form the basis of the modern electrical industry. He lectured superbly well and inaugurated the Christmas lectures for juvenile audiences at the Royal Institution. Standard biography by L. Pearce Williams (1965).

Farman, Henri (1874–1958), French aviator, one of the pioneers of aviation and a famous designer and builder of aeroplanes.

Farouk I (1920–65), King of Egypt, 1936–52. Forced to abdicate as a result of a military *coup d'état* in July 1952.

Farrar, Very Rev. Frederic William, D.D., F.R.S. (1831–1903), Dean of Canterbury, 1895–1903; a divine and author, some of whose writings attained a large circulation and exercised a considerable influence. His most popular publications were *The Life of Christ*, *The Life and Works of St. Paul*, and *Early Days of Christianity*. Author of the schoolboy story *Eric*.

Faulkner, William (1897–1962), American novelist, recognised as one of the great writers of the century, whose series of novels *The Sound and the Fury*, *As I Lay Dying*, *Light in August*, *Sanctuary* (which brought a Nobel Prize) give a vivid picture of the American South. Other novels include *The Hamlet*, and *The Reivers*.

Fauré, Gabriel Urbain (1845–1924), French composer and teacher; pupil of Saint-Saëns. He was much revered by his pupils at the Paris Conservatoire, among whom was Ravel. His works include chamber music, nocturnes and barcarolles for piano, an opera *Pénélope*, some exquisite songs, and *Requiem*.

Fawcett, Rt. Hon. Henry (1833–84), blind Liberal statesman and economist; Prof. of Political Economy at Cambridge. Author of *Manual of Political Economy* (1863).

Fawcett, Dame Millicent Garrett, G.B.E. (1847–1929), widow of the above; educational reformer and leader of the movement for women's suffrage; a very able writer on political economy and one of the founders of Newnham College, Cambridge.

Fawkes, Guy (1570–1606), a Yorkshire Catholic, who with Catesby and other conspirators planned the Gunpowder Plot. Although warned of the discovery of the plot, Fawkes persisted and was captured in the cellar of the Parliament House and hanged. (*See* **Gunpowder Plot**, General Information section.)

Fénelon, François de Salignac de la Mothe (1651–1715), Archbishop of Cambrai and a writer of distinction. His *Telemachus* is a French classic.

Ferdinand V. of Aragon (1452–1516), who married Isabella of Castile, and with her reigned over Spain during a period of great events. He saw the Moors expelled from Spain, equipped Columbus for the discoveries which led to Spain's vast colonial possessions, and instituted the Inquisition.

Ferguson, James, F.R.S. (1710–1776), a Banffshire man of great ability and inventiveness, who, from being a shepherd-boy, educated himself in astronomy, mathematics, and portrait painting, so that he was able to support his parents, and became eminent as a scientific lecturer. He was made a Fellow of the Royal Society.

Fermi, Enrico (1901–54), Italian nuclear physicist whose research contributed to the harnessing of atomic energy and the development of the atomic bomb. Prof. of Physics at Rome, Columbia Univ., New York, and Univ. of Chicago. He postulated the existence of the neutrino and discovered the element Neptunium. Awarded the 1938 Nobel Prize in Physics.

Festing, Field Marshal Sir Francis Wogan, G.C.B., K.B.E., D.S.O. (b. 1902), Chief of Imperial General Staff, 1958–61. During the war he commanded the 36th Division in Burma; known to his troops as the " front line general."

Feuchtwanger, Dr. Lion (1884–1958), German-Jewish author famous for his historical novels, such as *Jew Süss* and *'Tis Folly to be Wise*.

ffiorde, Sir Arthur Frederick Brownlow, G.B.E., M.A. (b. 1900), British solicitor and educationist who was Chairman of the B.B.C., 1957–64.

Fichte, Johann Gottlieb (1762–1814); was Professor of Philosophy, first at Jena and then at Erlangen, and later Rector of the University of Berlin. His works had great influence upon the thought of his time and prepared the way for the later Hegelian dialectic.

Field, John (1782–1837), composer and pianist, born in Dublin; pupil of Clementi and teacher of Glinka. At early age travelled Europe as virtuoso pianist. Composed seven concertos, three sonatas, and numerous piano pieces. Chopin's nocturnes were modelled on those of Field. The later part of his life was spent in Moscow, where he died.

Fielding, Henry (1707–1754), a celebrated English novelist, author of *Tom Jones*, *Joseph Andrews*, and *Amelia*, as well as many plays.

Fields, Gracie, C.B.E. (b. 1898), an inimitable Lancashire comedienne, and a great popular favourite with the British public. Made her first London appearance in 1915. Equally successful on the films as on the stage, she gained the affections of her music hall audiences through her abundant vitality, her Lancashire humour and her remarkably flexible voice.

Fildes, Sir Luke, K.C.V.O., R.A. (1844–1927), first attracted notice as a black-and-white artist, and illustrated Dickens' *Edwin Drood*. Exhibited at the Royal Academy in 1872, and at successive exhibitions was represented by many important works.

Finsen, Prof. Niels Ryberg (1860–1904), a Danish physician whose light-ray treatment of *lupus vulgaris* won the approval of Queen Alexandra and the aid of many philanthropists. He established in Copenhagen an institute for light therapy. Inventor of the Finsen ultra-violet lamp. Awarded 1903 Nobel Prize for Medicine.

Firdousi, *nom de plume* of **Abdul Kasim Mansur** (c. 930–1020), Persian poet whose great epic *Shahnama*, or *Book of Kings*, relates the history of Persia in 60,000 verses.

Fisher of Lambeth, Baron (Most Rev. Geoffrey Francis) P.C., G.C.V.O., M.A., Hon. D.D. (b. 1887). Archbishop of Canterbury, 1945–61, the 99th holder of the office; Bishop of London, 1939–45; Bishop of Chester, 1932–39; Headmaster Repton School, 1914–32.

Fisher, Rt. Hon. Herbert Albert Laurens, O.M., F.R.S. (1865–1940), English historian and educational reformer; author of *A History of Europe*.

Fisher, Professor Sir Ronald Aylmer, Sc.D., F.R.S. (1890–1962), one of the greatest of British scientists who revolutionised both genetics and the philosophy of experimentation by founding the modern corpus of mathematical statistics.

FitzGerald, Edward (1809–1883). English poet who gained world-wide fame by his translation of the *Rubaiyát* of Omar Khayyam (1859).

Fitzroy, Vice-Admiral Robert, F.R.S. (1805–1865) Attained celebrity as a meteorologist, and in 1854 was made superintendent of the Meteorological Department, and was the introducer of the system of storm warnings which were the beginning of weather forecasts.

Flammarion, Camille (1842–1925), French astronomer, famous for his observations on double stars, star-drift and popular lectures and books on astronomy. Founded the Astronomical Society of France in 1887. His best-known work is *L'Astronomie Populaire*.

Flamsteed, John, F.R.S. (1646–1719), was the first English Astronomer Royal, and a close friend of Sir Isaac Newton, whom he aided in many of his experiments.

Flaubert, Gustave (1821–80), one of the greatest of French novelists and creator of *Madame Bovary* which took five years to write. His perfection of style was attained only through unremitting effort. Other works were *Salammbo*, *La Tentation de Saint-Antoine* and his drama *Le Candidat*.

Flaxman, John R.A., (1755–1826), a great English sculptor who was born at York, and at 20 was employed as modeller by Josiah Wedgwood. In 1787 he went to Rome, where he stayed 7 years. In 1800 he was elected R.A. and in 1810 became professor of sculpture to the Royal Academy.

Flecker, James Elroy (1884–1915), English poet whose works include *Golden Journey to Samarkand*, *Hassan* (staged in London, 1923) and *Don Juan*, as well as many lyrics.

Fleming, Sir Alexander, F.R.S. (1881–1955), as a bacteriologist he made many original contributions, including the discovery of the antibacterial enzyme lysozyme in 1922 and penicillin in 1928. Full recognition of his discovery came only during the war, when Florey separated the drug now used for treatment from the original penicillin. Awarded Nobel Prize for Medicine jointly with Florey and Chain, 1945.

Fleming, Sir (John) Ambrose, F.R.S. (1849–1945), British scientist whose invention of the radio valve in 1904 was destined not only to revolutionise radio telegraphy but also to solve the problems which had so far prevented the successful development of radio-telephony, and eventually to make possible the transmission of high-quality speech, music, and even vision signals, and thus lead to broadcasting and television.

Fletcher, John (1579–1625), the famous collaborator with Beaumont in numerous plays which were popular in their day and take high position in the dramatic literature of the country.

Flinders, Matthew (1774–1814), an explorer and navigator, who made important discoveries in and around Australia. He sailed through Bass Strait, so called in honour of his surgeon. Sir William Matthew Flinders Petrie (*q.v.*), the archaeologist was his grandson.

Florey, Baron, Howard Walter, O.M. (b. 1898), British pathologist, b. Australia; co-discoverer of penicillin. Shared 1945 Nobel Prize with Fleming and Chain. Pres. Royal Society, 1965.

Foch, Marshal Ferdinand, O.M. (1851–1929), Generalissimo commanding the Allied Forces in France from March 1917 until after the Armistice was signed, Nov. 11, 1918. Under his direction the great German offensive was checked and turned at the Marne in July 1918. He followed up this success with a series of rapid attacks culminating in the German surrender, Nov. 11, 1918, when he imposed the conditions of the Armistice.

Fokine, Michel (1880–1944), famous Russian dancer who became choreographer to Diaghilev's company. Creator of *Les Sylphides*, *Prince Igor*, *Scheherazade*, *Firebird*, and *The Spectre of the Rose*.

Fokker, Anton Hermann Gerard (1890–1939), Dutch (naturalised American) airman and aeronautical engineer, designer and builder of the well-known Fokker triplanes and biplanes employed by the German army.

Fonteyn, Dame Margot (Mme. Roberto de Arias), D.B.E. (b. 1919), Prima ballerina of the Royal Ballet (formerly Sadler's Wells Ballet) and acclaimed foremost English dancer of to-day.

Ford, Henry (1863–1947), founder of Ford Motor Co., 1903, of which he was President until 1919, when he was succeeded by his son, Edsel B. Ford (1893–1943). Henry Ford became the world's leading industrialist and its second richest man. Was the pioneer of the cheap motor-car, of which, since 1920, more than a million have been produced annually.

Forester, Cecil Scott (b. 1899), British novelist, author of the *Captain Hornblower* series.

Forster, Edward Morgan, C.H., LL.D., C.L. (b. 1879), English novelist whose novels *A Room with a View*, *Howards End*, *A Passage to India*, have given him great authority in the world of literature.

Foscari, Francesco (*c.* 1372–1457), Doge of Venice from 1423 to 1457. A great historical character, who governed Venice with a firm hand and increased her renown.

Fosdick, Rev. Harry Emerson (b. 1878), American Baptist preacher. Professor of Theology, Union Theological Seminary, New York, and Pastor, Riverside, formerly Park Avenue, Baptist Church, New York, 1926–46.

Fourier, François Charles Marie (1772–1837), the famous French socialist, who propounded a system of associated enterprise for giving everyone ample means on a system of communal industry. He made some attempts to carry out his Utopian ideas, but they did not succeed. He is best known by his *Traité de l'Association Domestique Agricole*.

Fowler, Sir John, Bart., K.C.M.G. (1817–1898), an eminent civil engineer, son of a Sheffield land surveyor. With Sir Benjamin Baker he was the engineer of the Forth Bridge and of the Metropolitan Railway.

Fox, Rt. Hon. Charles James (1749–1806) was the second son of the first Lord Holland. Entered Parliament at nineteen, and became a Lord of the Admiralty in 1770. His opposition to the Royal Marriage Bill drew down upon him the displeasure of George III. Through the whole of Pitt's Premiership he was that statesman's most formidiable opponent. He favoured American Independence; opposed the war with France; was one of the impeachers of Warren Hastings; denounced the Slave Trade and advocated Parliamentary Reform. After the death of Pitt in 1806 he was made Foreign Secretary, but died a few months later, and was buried in Westminster Abbey.

Fox, George (1624–1691), was the founder of the Society of Friends.

Foxe, John (1516–1587), the English martyrologist, whose *Acts and Monuments* (*Book of Martyrs*) is one of the best-known books in the language. Born at Boston in Lincolnshire, he became a clergyman of the Anglican Church and died in London.

Frampton, Sir George James, R.A., F.S.A. (1860–1928). English sculptor, best remembered by his Peter Pan statue in Kensington Gardens, and the Edith Cavell Memorial in St. Martin's Place, London.

France, Anatole (Jacques Thibault) (1844–1924), one of France's notable writers of fiction, showing a great mastery of character portrayal and satire. Most of his works are translated into English.

Francis I. (1494–1547), **King of France** (1515–47). Recovered Milan from Swiss at Marignano (1515). Tried to gain support of Henry VIII (Field of the Cloth of Gold, 1520). Contested supremacy in Europe of Hapsburg emperor, Charles V; defeated and captured at Pavia (1525). French renaissance flourished during his reign.

Francis of Assisi, Saint (1181/82–1226), one of the great Christian saints, founder of the Franciscan Order. Son of a wealthy cloth-merchant of Assisi, he underwent a conversion in 1208 and turned from a life of pleasure to follow the life of the gospel, committing himself to poverty and to the complete observance of Christ's teaching. He and his friars went about preaching the gospel by word and example and the brotherhood increased rapidly in numbers. He received the stigmata (the marks of the five wounds of Christ) on Monte La Verna in Tuscany on 14 Sept. 1224. The last years were spent in illness; he was canonized by his friend Gregory IX two years after his death.

Francis, Sir Philip, K.B. (1740–1818), an English statesman, the reputed author of the famous *Letters of Junius*.

Franck, César Auguste (1822–90), composer and organist, born at Liége in Belgium. From 1872 until his death was professor of organ at the Paris Conservatoire. His music is romantic, mystical, and personal in idiom. Much of his finest composition is for the organ, and his *Symphonic Variations for Piano and Orchestra*, *Sonata for Violin* and the *Symphony in D* rank him, with his younger contemporary Debussy, among the great 19th-cent. musicians.

Franco, General Francisco (b. 1892), Spanish soldier and Dictator who served with the Spanish Forces in the Moroccan campaign of 1920–23 and was later Head of the Military Academy at Saragossa. Chief of the General

Staff 1935–36. Was Commander-in-Chief of the Nationalist Forces during the Spanish Civil War, 1936–39. President of Spain since Aug. 1939.

Franklin, Benjamin, F.R.S. (1706–1790), the famous American statesman and philosopher, who after serving an apprenticeship as a printer attracted public attention by publishing his *Poor Richard's Almanac*. He then began a series of scientific experiments, inventing among other things the lightning conductor. He was for ten years a member of the General Assembly; then lived in Britain as agent for his State for eighteen years; returning to America he took part in framing the Constitution of the United States.

Franklin, Rear-Admiral Sir John, F.R.S. (1786–1847), the famous Arctic explorer, whose final expedition in command of the *Erebus* and *Terror* ended disastrously, all the members of the expedition perishing. Many attempts were made to discover Franklin, but without obtaining anything save very fragmentary knowledge concerning his fate. He was born at Spilsby.

Franks, Rt. Hon. Sir Oliver Shewell, G.C.M.G., K.C.B., C.B.E., M.A. (b. 1905), British Ambassador to U.S.A. 1948–52; Provost of Worcester College, Oxford, 1962.

Fraser of the North Cape, Admiral of the Fleet, Lord, G.C.B., K.B.E. (b. 1888), commanded Home Fleet, Eastern Fleet, and British Pacific Fleet successively, 1943–46. First Sea Lord, 1948–51.

Fraser of Lonsdale, Ian, Baron, C.H., C.B.E. (b. 1897). Chair. St. Dunstan's since 1921; Pres. British Legion, 1947–58; B.B.C. Gov., 1937–39 and 1941–46. Life peerage conferred, 1958.

Frazer, Sir James George, O.M., LL.D., F.R.S. (1854–1941), was an eminent British anthropologist; author of *The Golden Bough* and numerous other works on his subject.

Frederick I. (*c.* 1123–90), Holy Roman emperor from 1152. Nicknamed Barbarossa. A commanding personality, he won for the empire prestige unknown since Otto the Great. Though failing to subjugate his Italian territories, for his armies suffered from the Italian climate, he dominated his German subjects, expelled the semi-independent Duke of Saxony, Henry the Lion, from his duchy, encouraged the German cities, and was a national hero. Though not an ascetic, he was remarkable for an impeccable private life, distinguished himself on the second Crusade, and was drowned in Asia Minor on his way to the third.

Frederick II. (1194–1250), Holy Roman Emperor, an enlightened ruler whose court in Sicily was a centre of culture and learning, attracting Jewish, Mohammedan, and Christian scholars. Forced by illness to return from crusade in 1227, he was excommunicated by Pope Gregory IX.; still excommunicated, he again set sail for Palestine and by skilful diplomacy gained possession of Jerusalem, Bethlehem, and Nazareth. Frederick was a philosopher and man of science and delighted in exploding superstition. He founded the university of Naples, was a patron of the medical school at Salerno, wrote a treatise on falconry, and gave Sicily a code of laws.

Frederick II. or Frederick the Great (1712–86), King of Prussia (1740–86). By his masterful government and military successes he raised Prussia to the rank of a great power. He was a scholarly potentate, composed music and played the flute.

French, Field-Marshal Sir John. (*See* **Ypres, 1st Earl of.**)

Freud, Sigmund, M.D. (1856–1939), was Professor of Neurology, Vienna University, 1902–38. An eminent psychoanalyst; author of many books on his subject. Left Austria after the *Anschluss* to take up permanent residence in England. An account of Freudian theory will be found in **Section F, Part III.**

Freyberg, 1st Baron, Lieut.-Gen. Bernard Cyril, V.C., G.C.M.G., K.C.B., K.B.E., D.S.O. (1889–1963), Gov.-Gen. of New Zealand, 1946–52. Served with distinction in both world wars. Commanded Allied troops on Crete, 1941. Won third bar to D.S.O. in Italy, 1945.

Friese-Greene, William (1855–1921), inventor of the cinematograph. His pioneer work in commercial photography brought him no profit, and for many years he lived in poverty.

Frobisher, Sir Martin (1535–1594), was the earliest of British navigators to attempt to find the North-West passage from the Atlantic to the Pacific through the Arctic seas, and his name is commemorated in Frobisher's Strait, to the south of Baffin Land. For his services in connection with the defeat of the Spanish Armada he was knighted.

Froebel, Friedrich Wilhelm August (1782–1852), was the founder of the Kindergarten system of education, the object of which is "to give children employment in harmony with their nature, to strengthen their bodies, to exercise their senses and lead them up to the original ground of all life, to the idea of unity with themselves." *See also* **J14**(2).

Froissart, Jean (1337–1410), a celebrated French writer who visited England and Scotland, and was the author of the famous *Chronicles*, which tell us so much of the achievements of the barons of old.

Frost, Robert (1874–1963), best loved of American poets. "Stopping by Woods on a Snowy Evening"; "Birches"; "The Death of the Hired Man"; "After Apple-Picking". Awarded Pulitzer Prize for poetry in 1924, 1931, 1937, and 1943.

Froude, James Anthony (1818–1894), the celebrated historian and biographer of Carlyle.

Fry, Christopher (b. 1907), English poet and dramatist of Quaker family. Author of *The Lady's Not for Burning, Venus Observed*, and *The Dark is Light Enough*. *See also* **Modern Drama.**

Fry, Elizabeth (1780–1845), a Norwich lady who devoted much of her life to the promotion of prison reform, and achieved considerable reputation as a preacher. She belonged to the Society of Friends.

Fry, Roger (1866–1934), English art critic and painter. Introduced the work of Cézanne and the post-impressionists into England. His most important book is *Vision and Design*. Biography by Virginia Woolf (1940).

Fuchs, Sir Vivian Ernest, M.A., Ph.D. (b. 1908), British geologist and explorer. Dir. of the Falkland Islands Dependencies Scientific Bureau since 1951; leader of the British Commonwealth Trans-Antarctic Expedition 1957–58, the first to cross the Antarctic continent.

Fuller, Thomas (1608–1661), the author of *Worthies of England* and a *Church History of Britain*, two well-known and valuable works.

Fulton, Robert (1765–1815), an inventive American engineer who distinguished himself by experiments in the application of steam to navigation, and finally in 1807, launched the *Clermont* on the Hudson.

Furniss, Harry (1854–1925), British caricaturist, was born in Wexford and came to London as a young man. He was a famous cartoonist and served on the staff of *Punch* from 1878–94. Illustrated the works of Dickens and Thackeray.

Furtwängler, Wilhelm (1886–1954), famous German conductor, and popular in Great Britain for his visits with the Berlin Philharmonic Orchestra, of which he succeeded Herr Nikisch as conductor.

G

Gade, Niels Vilhelm (1817–90), Danish composer. While studying at Leipzig he met Mendelssohn, whom he succeeded as conductor of the Gewandhaus orchestra. He wrote eight symphonies, chamber music, and choral works. Though characteristically Scandinavian, his work shows the influence of German romanticism.

Gagarin, Yuri Alexeyevich (b. 1934), Soviet airman who stirred the imagination of the world on 12 April 1961 by being the first man to be launched into space and brought safely back. His flight was made in the front portion of a Soviet multi-stage rocket which made a single circuit of the earth, the whole adventure taking 108 minutes.

Gainsborough, Thomas, R.A. (1727–1788), English landscape and portrait painter, whose works are remarkable for their grace and refinement. His *Duchess of Devonshire* was stolen when exhibited in 1876 and recovered in America some years later.

Gaiseric or Genseric (*c.* 390–477), king of the

Vandals, the ablest of the barbarian invaders of the Roman empire. He led his people from Spain into Africa, took Carthage, gained control of the Mediterranean by his pirate fleets, and sacked Rome in 455, thereby bringing about the fall of the western empire.

Gaitskell, Rt. Hon. Hugh Todd Naylor, C.B.E. (1906–63), statesman and economist; leader of the Labour Opposition, 1955–63; Min. of Fuel and Power, 1947–50; Min. of State for Econ. Affairs, 1950; Chan. of the Exchequer, 1950–51; M.P. (Labour) for South Leeds, 1945–63. He was succeeded as leader of the Labour Party by Harold Wilson. *See also* **Section C, Part I.**

Gale, General Sir Richard, G.C.B., K.B.E., D.S.O., M.C. (b. 1896), Commander of 6th Airborne Div. which landed in Normandy in June 1944; C.-in-C. B.A.O.R., 1952–56; Dep. Supreme Allied Commander Europe (NATO), 1958– .

Galen, Claudius (A.D. 131–201), physician, b. Pergamum (Asia Minor) of Greek parents. He lived most of his life in Rome, established a large practice, and became court physician to Marcus Aurelius. He systematised medical knowledge in accordance with his idea of purposive creation by the will of God. This unscientific attitude, by discouraging original investigation, hampered medical progress for a thousand years. Many of his treatises still survive.

Galileo (1564–1642), great Italian scientist whose experimental-mathematical methods in the pursuit of scientific truth laid the foundations of modern science. He became professor of mathematics at Pisa university when he was 25 and lectured at Padua university for 18 years. He made a number of fundamental discoveries, *e.g.*, in regard to the hydrostatic balance, thermometer, magnet, telescope, and foreshadowed Newton's laws of motion. He detected the four major satellites of Jupiter, the ring of Saturn, and the spots of the sun. He proved the superiority of the Copernican over the Ptolemaic theory, and was imprisoned for so doing. He died the year Newton was born.

Galsworthy, John, O.M. (1867–1933), an English novelist and dramatist of force and originality who wrote a great series of novels dealing with the history of an upper middle class family. Awarded Nobel Prize for Literature in 1932.

Galton, Sir Francis, F.R.S. (1822–1911), founder of eugenics, cousin of Darwin. His early work, *Meteorographica* (1863), contains the basis of the modern weather chart. He is also remembered for his device of finger-print identification and for being one of the first to apply mathematics to biological problems.

Galvani, Luigi (1737–1798), Italian physician and physiologist, whose experiments at Bologna university demonstrated the principle of animal electricity.

Gama, Vasco da (*c.* 1460–1524), the adventurous Portuguese navigator who discovered the sea route to India in 1498 by doubling the Cape of Good Hope.

Gandhi, Indira (b. 1917), daughter of Nehru, succeeded Shastri in 1966 to become India's first woman Prime Minister; formerly Pres. of Congress Party and Min. of Information.

Gandhi, Mohandas Karamchand (1869–1948), great Indian patriot, social reformer, and moral teacher. Believed in the doctrine of non-violence. In the tense situation following the granting of independence to India, he strove to promote the co-operation of all Indians but was assassinated on his way to a prayer meeting.

Garbo, Greta (b. 1905), Swedish film actress. The most arresting and poetical actress on the screen of her day.

Garcia, Manuel de Popolo Vicente (1775–1832), Spanish tenor, composer, and singing master. His son **Manuel Patricio Rodriguez** (1805–1906) was tutor to many celebrities including Jenny Lind. Both his daughters (Mme Malibran and Mme Viardot) were celebrated operatic singers. His grandsons taught at the Royal Academy of Music and the Royal College of Music in London.

Gardiner, Samuel Rawson (1829–1902), an English historian, whose works deal mainly with the period from the accession of James I. to the end of the Commonwealth. Many of his books remain the standard authorities on their subjects.

Garibaldi, Guiseppe (1807–82), Italian soldier and patriot, who with Mazzini and Cavour created a united Italy. In 1834 he was condemned to death for participating in a republican plot to seize Genoa but escaped to S. America. He returned in 1848 to fight for Mazzini but was again forced to flee. In 1851 he returned and gave his support to Cavour, taking part in the Austrian war of 1859. In 1860 with a thousand volunteers he freed Sicily, took Naples and handed over the Two Sicilies to Victor Emmanuel who was proclaimed King.

Garrick, David (1717–1779), the leading tragic actor of his time and a highly successful manager. Was buried in Westminster Abbey.

Garrison, William Lloyd (1805–1879), an eminent anti-slavery leader of America.

Gaskell, Mrs. Elizabeth Cleghorn (1810–1865), English novelist, author of *Mary Barton, Ruth Cranford*, and *Life of Charlotte Brontë.*

Gaudi i Cornet, Antonio (1852–1926), Spanish architect of great inventiveness, noted for the fantastic shape and decoration of his buildings which have many qualities in common with *Art Nouveau* (Spanish *modernismo*), He worked mainly in Barcelona.

Gauguin, Paul (1848–1903), influential French artist whose rejection of Western values led to his departure in 1891 for Tahiti where his greatest paintings were done.

Gaulle, Charles André Joseph Marie de (b. 1890), French general and statesman, chosen President of the Fifth Republic, Dec. 1958. On collapse of France in 1940 refused to surrender, but raised and led the Free French fighting forces, with headquarters in England. Took no part in parliamentary life from 1953 until June 1958, when a rebellion of colonists in Algeria brought him to supreme power. His system of government, based on personal prestige and skill in manoeuvre, has carried his country through many crises; the most serious was the army revolt in Algeria in April 1961, which he met and mastered. Repulsed Britain's attempt to enter the Common Market (1963). *See also* **Section C.**

Gauss, Johann Karl Friedrich (1777–1855), great German mathematician and astronomer. The unit of magnetic induction is named after him.

Gautier, Théophile (1811–1872) was an eminent French critic and novelist who at one time filled the position of secretary to Balzac. His romance, *Mademoiselle de Maupin*, caused a great sensation. He was also a poet.

Gay, John (1685–1732), English poet and playwright, famous for *The Beggar's Opera.* He was a writer of great wit and fancy, and much patronised by Society.

Gay-Lussac, Joseph Louis (1778–1850), a French chemist, whose experiments with gases were of much scientific importance.

Ged, William (1690–1749), was one of the inventors of the process of stereotyping. He was a goldsmith and a native of Edinburgh.

Geikie, Sir Archibald, O.M., K.C.B., F.R.S. (1835–1924), noted geologist; President of the Royal Society 1908–13. His brother **James Geikie** (1839–1915) was a specialist in glacial geology.

Geoffrey of Anjou, Duke of Brittany (1113–51), founder of the Angevin dynasty of England, was son-in-law of Henry I. and father of Henry II., the first Angevin or Plantagenet king.

Geoffrey of Monmouth (1100–1154), was the author of the famous Old English chronicle which bears his name. He was born at Monmouth, and became Bishop of St. Asaph in 1152. His *Chronicon* is a compilation from older authors, and is notable for having contained the stories of King Arthur, King Lear, and Cymbeline.

George I. (1660–1727) was King of Great Britain from 1714 to his death, ascending the throne as direct descendant of James I. His reign saw many memorable events, including the Jacobite Rebellion, the South Sea Bubble, and the beginning of Walpole's great ministry.

George II. (1683–1760), son of the last-named, was King of Great Britain from 1727 to 1760. His reign covered a prosperous period in spite of wars and rebellions, and saw the Empire extended in India and North America, though he himself was a man of limited powers.

George III. (1738–1820), grandson of George II., reigned 1760–1820. In this period came the King's clash with John Wilkes over foreign policy, the loss of the American colonies, the prolonged war with France, England's agrarian and industrial revolutions, the spread of Methodism. In 1966 two British psychiatrists published convincing evidence that the King's long mental illness was due not to insanity but to acute intermittent porphyria, an inborn error of metabolism.

George IV. (1762–1830) reigned from 1820 to his death, but filled the position of Prince Regent for some years previously. The King's personal character, in spite of the fact that he was called "The First Gentleman in Europe," showed such a want of dignity, and such an abandonment to licentiousness and frivolity, that he became very unpopular with the people.

George V. (1865–1936), was the second son of Edward VII. and Queen Alexandra. Entered the Navy as a cadet in 1877 and became second in the line of succession to the throne on the death of the Duke of Clarence in 1892. Married to Princess Mary of Teck in 1893. Succeeded to the throne May 6th, 1910, and celebrated his Silver Jubilee in 1935. Maintained the royal tradition of strenuous public engagements combined with unfailing attention to business of State.

George VI. (1895–1952), (Albert Frederick Arthur George of Windsor), second son of George V., was called to the throne in December 1936 on the abdication of his elder brother, Edward VIII. His reign was marked by the ordeal of war, by world revolution and social change and at the same time by a remarkable degree of constitutional harmony which his fine example and personal qualities did much to achieve.

George, Henry (1839–1897), American political economist whose "single tax" on land values as a means of solving economic problems is expounded in his *Progress and Poverty*, pub. 1879.

George, Saint, the tutelary saint of England, adopted by Edward III. He is believed to have been a native of Cappadocia and a vigorous champion of Christianity in the days of Diocletian, and to have suffered martyrdom at Nicomedia 303 A.D. The dragon which he is said to have slain symbolises the powers of evil over which he triumphed.

German, Sir Edward (1862–1936), English composer, best known for his incidental music and light opera *Merrie England*. (His name was originally Edward German Jones.)

Gershwin, George (1898–1937), American jazz pianist and song-writer, composer of the famous *Rhapsody in Blue* and other works including the negro "folk-opera" *Porgy and Bess*.

Gesner, Konrad von (1516–1565), a scholarly Swiss naturalist, and father of the science of zoology.

Ghiberti, Lorenzo (1378–1455), Florentine sculptor whose bronze doors, beautifying the baptistery in Florence, were described by Michaelangelo as fit for the gates of paradise.

Gibbon, Edward (1737–1794), celebrated historian of the *Decline and Fall of the Roman Empire*.

Gibbons, Grinling (1648–1720), the celebrated wood-carver and sculptor, was born at Rotterdam and was brought to the notice of Charles II. by Evelyn, the diarist. The choir stalls of St. Paul's and the carving in the Wren library at Trinity College, Cambridge, are his work.

Gibbons, Orlando (1583–1625), a noted English composer of Church music who was organist of the Chapel Royal.

Gide, André Paul Guillaume (1869–1951) French man of letters, novelist, dramatist and poet. Awarded the Nobel Prize for Literature in 1947.

Gielgud, Sir (Arthur) John (b. 1904), English actor, member of the Terry family. Began by walking on at the Old Vic, and, later, became a Shakespearian actor, making a marked success as Hamlet, Richard II., and Prospero.

Gigli, Beniamino (1890–1957), the great Italian operatic tenor of the Metropolitan Opera House New York. The possessor of a voice of great natural beauty, and one of the finest exponents of the music of Puccini and Verdi.

Gilbert, Sir Alfred, M.V.O., R.A., (1854–1934), sculptor and designer of gold and silver objects. Among his best-known sculptures are *Perseus Arming*, *Icarus*, *Eros* in Piccadilly Circus, the Shaftesbury Memorial and the Duke of Clarence Memorial at Windsor.

Gilbert, Sir Humphrey (1539–1583), knighted by Queen Elizabeth for his bravery in Ireland, later made voyages of discovery, and added Newfoundland to the British possessions.

Gilbert, Sir John, R.A. (1817–1897), one of the most prolific artists of his time. His illustrations to Staunton's edition of Shakespeare are remarkable for their picturesqueness and dramatic power.

Gilbert, William (1543–1603), physician to Queen Elizabeth I., has been called the father of electric and magnetic science. Published his great book on the magnet in 1600.

Gilbert, Sir William Schwenck (1836–1911), English humorist and playwright, is best remembered for the "Bab Ballads" and for the famous Savoy series of operas in which he collaborated with Sir Arthur Sullivan. Among the operas are *H.M.S. Pinafore*, *Patience*, *Iolanthe*, *The Mikado*, *The Gondoliers*, and *The Yeomen of the Guard*. The Gilbertian humour of plot and paradox, the kindly satire and the delightful metres combine with Sullivan's music to make the operas unforgettable and ever popular.

Gill, Arthur Eric Rowton, A.R.A. (1882–1940), English sculptor and engraver. His first piece of sculpture, *Madonna and Child*, was produced in 1910 and in 1913 he received the commission to carve the Stations of the Cross for Westminster Cathedral. In 1922–23 he carved the relief, *Christ Driving the Money-changers from the Temple*, which is placed at the entrance of Leeds University as a War Memorial. Executed the carvings on Broadcasting House, London; also worked as a designer for printing; the Gill Sans type and the George VI stamps were his designs.

Gillray, James (1757–1815), the eminent caricaturist of the time of George III., who produced upwards of a thousand political cartoons.

Giotto di Bondone (*c.* 1266–*c.* 1337), great Florentine artist, the first to break away from byzantine tradition and paint in a naturalistic way. Much of his work has perished but still surviving are the great frescoes in the churches of Assisi, Padua, and Florence. He designed the western front of the cathedral at Florence and the campanile, the lower part of which was completed from his designs before his death.

Gissing, George Robert (1857–1903), English author whose novels deal with poverty and the sociological problems of his day. *New Grub Street*, *The Unclassed*, *Charles Dickens*, *A Critical Study*, *The Private Papers of Henry Ryecroft* are among his best-known works.

Giulio Romano or Giulio Pippi (*c.* 1492–1546) was a pupil of Raphael, and himself a distinguished painter and architect.

Gladstone, Rt. Hon. William Ewart (1809–98), the great Liberal statesman of the latter part of the nineteenth century, popularly known as the Grand Old Man. Entered Parliament in 1832 as a Tory, held various offices under Peel, and joined the Aberdeen coalition in 1852. From that time he served several terms as Chancellor of the Exchequer and was Liberal Prime Minister, 1868–74, 1880–85, 1886, and 1892–94. His financial policy was able, accurate, lucidly exposed, and very successful. His first ministry was active, its legislative achievements including the Disestablishment of the Church of Ireland, the Education Act of 1870, the Ballot Act of 1872, and the Irish Land Act, but in 1873 they were aptly described by Gladstone's great rival, Disraeli, as "exhausted volcanoes." His second ministry, returned to power after the astonishing Midlothian campaign, witnessed the defeat by the Boers at Majuba, the bombardment of Alexandria, and the disaster of General Gordon at Khartoum. His last two ministries were marked by the adoption of the policy of Home Rule for Ireland, which he was unable to carry. Gladstone was a good classical scholar and an earnest high churchman, who in 1838 published the *State in its Relations with the Church*, a work of considerable interest.

Glazunov, Alexander Constantinovich (1865–1936), Russian composer, pupil of Rimsky-Korsakov. He was an accomplished and prolific composer, the first of his eight symphonies being composed when he was only 16.

Glendower, Owen (1359–1415), a famous Welsh chieftain who proved a formidable opponent to Henry IV., and gathered around him a great following of Welshmen, whom he led with much bravery, though finally defeated in 1405.

Glinka, Mikhail Ivanovich (1804–57), Russian composer whose music has a strong folk-song element. Notable among his works are his two operas, *A Life of the Tsar* and *Russlan and Ludmilla*, based on a poem by Pushkin. He is recognised as the first of the Russian national school.

Gluck, Christoph Willibald (1714–87), German composer, a figure of great historical importance in the development of the opera. He was the son of a Bohemian forester and studied in Prague, Vienna, and Italy. His first operas were in the Italian tradition, but with *Orfeo ed Euridice* (1762), inspired by classical Greek drama, he began his reform of the opera. Then followed the great operas *Alceste*, *Armide*, and *Iphigénie en Tauride* (1779), which is considered his masterpiece.

Goddard, Lord, P.C., Q.C. (b. 1877), Lord Chief Justice of England, 1946–58.

Godfrey of Bouillon (c. 1061–1100) was the leader of the First Crusade, and after the conquest of Jerusalem, exchanged the title of King for that of "Protector of the Holy Sepulchre." He liberated the Holy Land, and was buried on Mount Calvary.

Godiva, Lady (1040–1080), was the pious and beautiful wife of Leofric, Earl of Chester and Lord of Coventry. Having appealed to her lord to remit certain impositions from the inhabitants, he promised to grant her request if she would ride naked through the town. This she did, having first passed the word to have blinds and shutters drawn at the appointed hour, and so obtained the people's ransom.

Godwin, Earl of the West Saxons (990–1053), was one of the most influential noblemen of his time and gave his daughter in marriage to Edward the Confessor, against whom he was afterwards in rebellion. Godwin's son, Harold, claimed the throne after Edward's death, but was killed at Hastings.

Godwin, William (1756–1836), English Radical philosopher, author of *Political Justice* and a novel, *Caleb Williams*. Married Mary Wollstonecraft (1759–97), author of *A Vindication of the Rights of Women*, in which she pleaded for the equality of the sexes, particularly in education. Their daughter, Mary Wollstonecraft Godwin (1797–1851), married the poet, Shelley, and was the author of *Frankenstein*.

Goethe, Johann Wolfgang von (1749–1832), German poet of great gifts and versatility. Born at Frankfurt on Maine of a cultivated and well-to-do family, he was able to integrate all the powers with which nature had endowed him in one harmonious personality. Before he went to Weimar at the age of 25 he had written *Götz von Berlichingen* and *Werthers Leiden* and many beautiful lyrics. He settled at Weimar in 1775, received a Ministerial appointment and actively interested himself in the welfare of the state. *Faust*, the great dramatic poem which accompanied him from early manhood to the end, epitomises his whole life and was his crowning achievement. Not only was he a great poet, but scientist and philosopher besides.

Gogol, Nikolai Vasilievich (1809–52), one of the greatest of Russian novelists whose stories of provincial life are in the same setting as his masterpiece, *Dead Souls* (1842), of which an English translation appeared in 1906. Was also a playwright, his most successful play being *The Government Inspector* (1836), a satire on provincial bureaucracy.

Goldsmith, Oliver (1728–1774), the celebrated author of *The Vicar of Wakefield*, *The Deserted Village*, and *She Stoops to Conquer*. The son of a poor Irish curate, he found his way to London in 1756, subsequently devoting himself entirely to literature, being befriended by Dr. Johnson and held in great esteem by Reynolds, Burke and other eminent men of the time. He was buried in the churchyard of the Temple.

Goodyear, Charles (1800–1860), an American, discoverer of the art of vulcanising rubber, by which the utility of the material was greatly extended.

Goossens, Sir Eugène (1893–1962), English composer and conductor of Belgian parentage. He was associated with many famous orchestras, and his compositions include the operas *Judith* and *Don Juan de Mañara*. His brother Léon is a celebrated oboe virtuoso, both his sisters are gifted harpists, and his father and grandfather, who also bore the name Eugène, were conductors.

Gordon, Adam Lindsay (1833–1870), an Australian poet who wrote many stirring ballads and poems, his *Bush Ballads and Galloping Rhymes* being a great success.

Gordon, Major-General Charles George, C.B. (1833–1885), a distinguished soldier, administrator, and earnest Christian, who had a most adventurous, useful, and self-sacrificing career. He saw active service in the Crimea, China, and India, and in 1873 was made Governor of the Equatorial provinces of Egypt. In 1877 he went out to the Sudan for the Egyptian Government, and in 1884 again proceeded thither on behalf of the English Government to deal once more with the difficulties which had arisen consequent on the Mahdi's Rebellion. While defending Khartoum he was murdered by the Mahdi's forces on the palace staircase.

Gordon, Lord George (1751–1793), was tried for treason as the instigator of the Anti-Popery riots of 1780, but acquitted on the ground that he had no treasonable intention. Some years later he was committed to Newgate for libelling Marie Antoinette and died there of fever.

Gorky, Maxim (pseudonym of Alexey Maximovich Peshkov) (1868–1936), great Russian writer and playwright. Worked in a variety of trades from the age of ten—shoemaker's apprentice, scullion on a Volga steamboat, birdwatcher, baker, fisherman, railway guard—during which time he learned to write. His early years are described in *My Childhood* (1913). His first story was published in 1892. His works are noted for their vividly drawn characters and social realism.

Gosse, Sir Edmund, C.B., LL.D., Litt.D. (1849–1928), a distinguished poet and critic who wrote lives of Gray, Congreve and Dr. Donne, and his *History of 18th Century Literature* and *History of Modern English Literature* show great critical power and appreciation. Was librarian to the House of Lords 1904–14, and wrote a book on French literary men and a life of Sir Thomas Browne. In 1907 he published *Father and Son*, being recollections of his father.

Gould, Sir Francis Carruthers (1844–1925). Perhaps the cleverest political caricaturist of his day, and did also considerable journalistic work as assistant editor of the *Westminster Gazette*.

Gounod, Charles François (1818–93), French composer whose fame rests chiefly on his operas *Faust* and *Roméo et Juliette*, though his lyrical gifts are best shown in some of his earlier works, such as *Le Médicin malgré lui* and *Mireille*. He also wrote oratorios and church music.

Gower, John (1325–1408), an English poet of the time of Chaucer, who wrote many elegant ballads and devotional poems. His *Confessio Amantis* was his outstanding work.

Goya y Lucientes, Francisco José (1746–1828), a famous Spanish painter and etcher, and one of the greatest artists of all time, renowned for his wonderful series of etchings and satirical drawings. His portraits can only be described as ruthless in their realism, and his etchings in the *Horrors of War* tell of his hatred of the cruelty and reaction in his own country. In addition to portraits and genre he painted frescoes in the Cathedral at Saragossa. England's first exhibition of his art was held in 1963.

Grace, Dr. William Gilbert (1848–1915), renowned and almost legendary cricketer who by his character and skill dominated English cricket for over forty years, and was probably the best-known man in England. Altogether in first-class cricket he scored 54,896 runs, including 126 centuries, and took 2876 wickets. Scored 1000 runs in May 1895; and three times made over 300 runs in an innings.

Graham, John, of Claverhouse, Viscount Dundee (1643–1689). Renowned for his sturdy adherence to the Stuarts, and headed a rebellion in Scotland against William and Mary, but was killed at the Battle of Killiecrankie.

Grahame, Kenneth (1859–1932), as a writer of books for children ranks almost with Lewis Carroll. *The Golden Age*, *Dream Days*, and *Wind in the Willows*, all achieved great popularity.

Grahame-White, Claude (1879–1959), aviator and engineer, the first Englishman to gain an aviator's certificate, 1909; won the Gordon Bennett Cup with the then record speed of 60½ miles per hour in 1910, founded the first British Flying School and published many works on aircraft.

Grainger, Percy Aldridge (1882–1961), pianist and composer, b. in Australia, U.S.A. citizen. He was a brilliant player and an authority on folk-song, the influence of which is apparent in all his compositions.

Grant, General Ulysses Simpson (1822–1885), the most distinguished American general of the Civil War. President of the United States from 1869 to 1877.

Granville-Barker, Harley, D. Litt., LL.D., F.R.S.L. (1877–1946), distinguished English dramatist, producer, and actor. Introduced plays of Ibsen and Shaw to British public. His own plays reflect influence of Shaw, and are particularly notable for their realistic dialogue.

Grattan, Henry (1746–1820), an Irish orator and statesman who, first in the Irish Parliament and afterwards in the Imperial Parliament, did memorable work for the cause of his country.

Graves, Robert Ranke (b. 1895), English poet and writer. His most famous work, apart from his poems, is *Goodbye to All That*, written after the first great war. Succeeded Auden as Prof. of Poetry at Oxford, 1961–66.

Gray, Thomas (1716–1771), the English poet, whose *Elegy written in a Country Churchyard* is one of the most beautiful in the language. His other poems were not numerous but included a fine *Ode on a Distant Prospect of Eton College* and a notable *Ode to Adversity*.

Greeley, Horace (1811–1872), founder of the *New York Tribune* and a political writer of great power and influence. Was an unsuccessful candidate for the United States Presidency in 1872.

Green John Richard (1837–1883), an eminent English historian. Published a *Short History of the English People* in 1874.

Greenway, Kate (1846–1901), a gifted book illustrator and water-colour artist, whose drawings of children won her great popularity and the warm approval of no less a critic than Ruskin.

Greene, Graham, C.H. (b. 1904), English novelist and journalist whose novels (*The Heart of the Matter, Brighton Rock, The Quiet American, Our Man in Havana, A Burnt-out Case*), like his plays (*The Complaisant Lover*), and films (*Fallen Idol, The Third Man*), deal with moral problems in a modern setting from a Catholic standpoint.

Gregory, St. (257–336), was founder of the Armenian Church, and spent his last years in a cave at the foot of Mount Sebuh.

Gregory the Great, St. (*c.* 540–604), Pope 590–604. The last great Latin Father and the forerunner of scholasticism. The real founder of the temporal power and the political influence of the papacy, he also maintained the spiritual claims of Rome, enforcing discipline, encouraging monasticism, defining doctrine, and adding to the music, liturgy, and canons of the Church. Thus he exerted enormous influence on the life and thought of the Middle Ages.

Gregory VII (*c.* 1020–85), Pope from 1073. Originally called Hildebrand. Battled for papal omnipotence within the Church, stamping on simony and the marriage of priests. His victory in the conflict of empire and papacy came when the emperor, Henry IV, did penance for three days in the snow at Canossa, but had the unfortunate result of leading to further internal dissensions in Germany and to papal absorption with power politics rather than to Gregory's aim of an ideal theocracy embracing all States.

Gregory XIII (1502–85), Pope, 1572–85; introduced the Gregorian calendar.

Grenville, Sir Richard (1541–1591), the Elizabethan sea-captain, who with his one ship engaged a fleet of Spanish war-vessels off Flores, in 1591, was captured and shortly after died on the Spanish flagship *San Pablo*, an exploit celebrated in Tennyson's noble ballad, *The Revenge*.

Gresham, Sir Thomas (1519–1579), was the wealthiest London merchant and financier of his time. He built the first Royal Exchange and founded Gresham College. The son of Sir Richard Gresham (Lord Mayor of London), he succeeded his father as King's Agent at Antwerp, and proved an astute money-finder for the Court in four successive reigns, ending as Queen Elizabeth's "Royal Merchant."

Greuze, Jean Baptiste (1725–1805), French painter, whose works, especially his studies of girls, display much delicacy and beauty of handling.

Grey, Charles, 2nd Earl, K.G. (1764–1845), a great English Whig statesman under whose Premiership were passed the Reform Bill of 1832, the Bill abolishing slavery throughout the British Empire (1833), and the Poor Law Amendment Act, 1834.

Grey, Lady Jane (1537–1554), was the daughter of the Duke of Suffolk and great-granddaughter of Henry VII. On the death of Edward VI, she was proclaimed Queen, but only reigned for nine days, Queen Mary ousting her and maintaining the Tudor succession. Six months later Lady Jane and her husband, Lord Guildford Dudley, were executed.

Grey of Fallodon, 1st and only Viscount, K.G., P.C. (1862–1933). Under-Secretary for Foreign Affairs, 1892. Foreign Secy., 1905–16. He won high approval for his handling of the Balkan difficulties of 1912–13, and all through the difficult strain which preceded Germany's rush into war acquitted himself with force and dignity. Leader of Liberal Party in House of Lords until Aug. 1924. Chancellor of Oxford Univ., 1928–33.

Grieg, Edvard Hagerup (1843–1907), a Norwegian musical composer, who presented the characteristics of his country's music in numerous compositions of great melodic beauty.

Griffin, His Eminence Cardinal Bernard William (1899–1956), Roman Catholic Archbishop of Westminster from 1944 until his death.

Griffith, Arthur (1872–1922), was the first President of the Irish Free State 1921; founder and first editor of *Sinn Fein* 1906–15, and founder of the *Sinn Fein* movement.

Griffith, David Wark (1880–1948), pioneer American film producer. Noted especially for his remarkable films *Broken Blossoms* and *The Birth of a Nation*. Invented much of the technique of the modern cinema.

Grimm, the brothers **Jakob Ludwig Karl** (1785–1863) and **Wilhelm Karl** (1786–1859), German philologists and folk-lorists who wrote the world-famous *Fairy Tales*. They planned a gigantic etymological dictionary of the German language, which was completed by German scholars in 1961.

Grimond, Rt. Hon. Joseph (b. 1913), Leader of the Liberal Parliamentary Party since 1957; Liberal M.P. for Orkney and Shetlands since 1950; Liberal Chief Whip, 1951–57.

Grimthorpe, 1st Baron, LL.D. (1816–1905), long known as **Sir Edmund Beckett,** Bt., K.C., was a great authority on horology, and, with Professor Sir George Airy (*q.v.*), designed "Big Ben." He restored St. Albans Cathedral at his own cost.

Gromyko, Andrei A. (b. 1908), Russian diplomat; Foreign Minister, 1957–. Ambassador to Britain, 1952–3, and to the U.S.A., 1943–46. Representative of the Soviet Union on the U.N. Security Council, 1946–49.

Grossmith, George (1847–1912), the well-known actor and entertainer. His father, George Grossmith the elder, was also a popular entertainer and lecturer, his brother, Weedon Grossmith, was an actor and artist of considerable attainments, and his son, George Grossmith (1874–1935), was a successful comedian, and the first to introduce revue and also cabaret entertainment into England.

Grote, George (1794–1871), English historian famous for his *History of Greece*, 1846–56, an epoch-making and standard work.

Grotius, Huig van Groot (1583–1645), Dutch jurist, the founder of international law. He was condemned to life imprisonment for supporting religious toleration but made a daring escape and found refuge in Paris, where he wrote his masterpiece *De Jure Belli et Pacis*.

Grouchy, Marshal Emmanuel, Marquis de (1766–1847), a famous Napoleonic general who, at Hohenlinden, Wagram, and in the Moscow retreat rendered signal service. After Waterloo he led the defeated army back to Paris.

Grove, Sir George (1820–1900) was a distinguished engineer and bridge and lighthouse builder, but better known as an enthusiastic lover of music, the study and performance of which in England he did much to promote. His *Dictionary of Music and Musicians* is a standard work.

Guedalla, Philip, M.A. (1889–1944), was an English historian and essayist. Author of *The Partition of Europe* (1914), *The Second Empire* (1922), *Palmerston* (1926), *The Missing Muse* (1929), *The Duke* (1931), and other works.

Guido Reni (1575–1642), Italian painter of the Bolognese school whose works are characteristic of the Italian baroque art of his period and include the famous *Aurora* fresco in the Rospigliosi palace at Rome, and *Crucifixion of St. Peter* (Vatican).

Gustavus Adolphus, King of Sweden (1594–1632), the "Lion of the North," after a lengthy campaign in Poland, entered the Thirty Years' War in support of Swedish interests and Protestant distress, won the Battle of Breitenfeld in 1631, and was killed in action the next year.

Gutenberg, Johann (*c.* 1400–68), German printer, b. Mainz, the first European to print with movable types cast in moulds. The earliest book printed by Gutenberg was the Mazarin Bible (**L76**).

Guy, Thomas (1644–1724), founder of Guy's Hospital, was a dealer in Bibles, speculator and money-lender, who after making a large fortune, bequeathed £300,000 for the erection and endowment of the famous hospital.

Gwynne, Nell (1650–1687), English actress; as a girl, orange-seller near Drury Lane Theatre; favourite mistress of Charles II. Her eldest son was made Duke of St. Albans.

H

Haakon VII. (1872–1957), King of Norway. Formerly Prince Carl of Denmark, second son of Frederick VIII.; elected to the throne on the separation of Norway from Sweden in 1905. Married Princess Maud, youngest daughter of King Edward VII. in 1896.

Hadfield, Sir Robert Abbott, Bt., F.R.S. (1858–1940), English metallurgist whose discovery of manganese steel in 1882 brought him recognition from every steel-producing country.

Hadrian (76–138) was Emperor of Rome in succession to his uncle Trajan, and one of the greatest of Roman rulers. He visited Britain, and in A.D. 121 built the wall between Newcastle and Carlisle for protection of his dominions against the Picts and Scots.

Hafiz, pseudonym of Shams ad-Din Mohammed (1320–1389), great Persian lyrical poet. His principal work is the *Divan*, a collection of short sonnets called *ghazals*. The sobriquet *Hafiz*, meaning one who remembers, is applied to any one who has learned the Koran by heart.

Hahnemann, Samuel Christian Friedrich (1755–1843), the German physician who founded the system of homoeopathy. Dissatisfied with the state of medicine at the time, he set himself the task of formulating general principles governing the restoration of health. Homoeopathy is based on the principle that diseases should be treated by drugs which when given to a healthy person provoke symptoms similar to that of the disease to be treated. His second principle was that drugs should be given in almost infinitesimal doses.

Haig, Field-Marshal, 1st Earl of Bemersyde, K.T., G.C.B., O.M., G.C.V.O., K.C.I.E. (1861–1928), C.-in-C. of the British Expeditionary Forces in France and Flanders, 1915–19.

Haile Selassie I., G.C.B., G.C.M.G., G.C.V.O. (b. 1891), Emperor of Ethiopia, April 1930 to May 1936, and since May 1941.

Hakluyt, Richard (1553–1616), the first of English naval historians. By his *Divers Voyages touching the Discovery of America*, and *Principal Navigations, Voyages, and Discoveries of the English Nation*, did much to help forward the colonising spirit.

Haldane, John Burdon Sanderson (1892–1964), biologist and geneticist, noted not only for his influence in his special field of mathematical evolutionary theory but for the use he made of his great gifts in explaining science to the layman. He held the Chair of Biometry at University College, London, from 1937 until 1956. Emigrated to India in 1957. He was the son of **John Scott Haldane** (1860–1936) whose researches led to improvements in public health and industrial safety.

Haldane, Viscount, P.C., K.T., O.M., F.R.S. (1856–1928), sat for Haddingtonshire, 1885–1911. In 1901 was Vice-President of the Liberal Imperialist League, and at the close of 1905 was made War Minister and organised the Territorial Force. Lord Chancellor, 1912–15, and again in first Labour Government, 1924.

Halévy, Ludovic (1834–1903), a brilliant French writer who supplied Offenbach with libretti for some of his most famous comic operas: among them *La Belle Hélène*, *La Grande Duchesse*, and *Barbe Bleue*. In conjunction with Meilhac he wrote several notable plays of which *Frou-frou* was perhaps the most successful.

Halifax, Charles Montague, Earl of (1661–1715), seventeenth century financier who was responsible for the National Debt, the window tax, the revaluation of the currency, and the foundation of the Bank of England.

Halifax, 1st Earl of, Edward Frederick Lindley Wood, K.G., P.C., O.M., G.C.S.I., G.C.I.E., T.D. (1881–1959), filled many difficult positions with distinction and success and was especially notable as Viceroy of India, 1926–31, Foreign Secretary, 1938–40, and British Ambassador in Washington, 1940–45. He wrote a life of John Keble and was prominent in the life of the Church of England. Chancellor of Oxford University 1933–59.

Halifax, George Savile, Marquess of (1633–95), author of *Advice to a Daughter* and *Character of a Trimmer*, was a gifted and independent politician, pamphleteerist, and orator.

Hallam, Henry (1777–1859), a graceful and scholarly historian who contributed several important works. His *View of the State of Europe during the Middle Ages*, *Constitutional History of England*, and *Introduction to the Literature of Europe* are distinguished for their clearness of style and correctness of judgment.

Hallé, Sir Charles (1819–1895), a distinguished pianist and conductor who was born in Westphalia. Went to Paris to study music in 1836, and in 1848 settled in London, where he soon became known as a piano-player of the first rank. He organised an orchestra of high-class talent, and for many years conducted it in London and the provinces. He married Madam Norman Neruda (d. 1911), the celebrated violinist in 1888, and was knighted the same year.

Halley, Edmund, F.R.S. (1656–1742), English Astronomer Royal from 1720 to his death and ranked next to Newton among the scientific Englishmen of his time. Made first magnetic survey of the oceans from the naval vessel *Paramour*, 1698–1700. Discovered what is known as Halley's comet.

Hals, Franz (1584–1666), a famous painter of the Dutch School, who is represented in the leading galleries of Europe. The Wallace Collection has his world-famous picture, the *Laughing Cavalier*.

Hamilton, Alexander (1757–1804), American statesman and economist, opponent of Thomas Jefferson, served as Secretary of the Treasury in Washington's cabinet, 1789–95. Though a monarchist by predilection, he urged the adoption of the Constitution, and in conjunction with Maddison and Jay wrote the *Federalist*.

Hamilton, Emma Lyon, Lady (1761–1815), was a woman of humble birth and great personal beauty who attained prominent notice by her association with Sir William Hamilton, British Ambassador at Naples, who married her, and afterwards with Lord Nelson, who conceived an infatuation for her.

Hammarskjöld, Dag Hjalmar Agne Carl (1905–1961), Sec.-Gen. of the United Nations, 1953–61. Killed in air crash on way to the Congo to end dispute between central government in Leopoldville and M. Tshombe of Katanga province. Posthumously awarded 1961 Nobel Peace Prize.

Hammond, John Lawrence Le Breton (1872–1949), English journalist and historian whose works on social and industrial history, written mainly in collaboration with his wife, Barbara Hammond, include *The Village Labourer*, 1911; *The Town Labourer*, 1917; *The Skilled Labourer*, 1919; and *The Age of the Chartists*, 1930.

Hampden, John (1594–1643), English patriot who opposed Charles I.'s "Ship Money" tax, and by his resistance and eloquent advocacy of the wish of the people helped the Parliamentary cause.

Hamsun, Knut, pen-name of **Knut Pedersen**

(1859–1952), Norwegian author and farmer, who in his youth struggled for existence, visited America twice and earned his living by casual labour. His monumental work, *Markens Gröde* (*Growth of the Soil*), gained him the Nobel Prize in 1920.

Handel, George Frederick (1685–1759), German composer, son of a barber-surgeon to the Duke of Saxony; born the same year as Bach. He spent much of his life in England composing operas and achieving world-wide fame by his magnificent series of oratorios. His operas, of which there are over forty, include *Atalanta*, *Berenice*, and *Serse*, and his oratorios, of which there are thirty-two, include *Saul*, *Israel in Egypt*, *Samson*, *Messiah*, *Judas Maccabaeus*, and *Jeptha*. He also composed chamber music, *concerti grossi*, music for chorus and orchestra, solo cantatas, harpsichord suites, and much other beautiful and noble music. Beethoven said of Handel, "Go and learn of him how to achieve great effects with simple means." Eight years before he died he became totally blind and relied upon his old friend and copyist John Christopher Smith to commit his music to paper. He was buried in Westminster Abbey.

Hannibal (247–183 B.C.), the renowned Carthaginian general, who led an army against Rome, and achieved many notable victories over superior numbers. Was defeated by Scipio at the Battle of Zama, and afterwards suffered exile, and poisoned himself.

Harcourt, Rt. Hon. Sir William Vernon, F.R.S. (1827–1904), barrister, author, Liberal statesman, an enthusiastic supporter of Mr. Gladstone.

Hardicanute (1019–1042), son of Canute the Great, was King of England from 1040 to 1042, and imposed the tax called Danegeld. He was the last Danish sovereign of this country.

Hardie, James Keir (1856–1915), a Socialist politician and Labour representative who acted as editor of the *Miner* and the *Labour Leader* from 1887 to 1904. He is regarded as the founder of the Labour Party. During his early life he worked in a Scottish coal pit, but in 1882 became a journalist, and entered Parliament as member for West Ham (South) in 1892–95, being the first Socialist to be elected to the House of Commons. First Chairman of the Parliamentary Labour Party, 1906–8, M.P. for Merthyr Tydvil from 1900 till his death.

Hardy, Thomas, O.M. (1840–1928), was educated as an architect and practised for some time, but became known as a promising novelist in 1871 with his story *Desperate Remedies*. In 1874 his *Far from the Madding Crowd* was published, which at once made him a name. Following that, at short intervals, came a long series of powerful novels from his pen. Perhaps the most notable of his stories are *The Trumpet Major*, *The Mayor of Casterbridge*, *Tess of the D'Urbervilles*, and *Jude the Obscure*. In 1908 he completed a dramatic poem entitled *The Dynasts*, whose central figure is Napoleon.

Hargreaves, James (1720–1778), was a poor Lancashire-born mechanic who invented the spinning jenny, one of the revolutionising labour-saving contrivances of the latter half of the 18th century. It met with much opposition, however, and kept him poor, though the community afterwards reaped the advantage in a greatly improved industry.

Harkness, Edward Stephen, B.A., M.A., LL.D. (1874–1940) was a banker and one of America's greatest philanthropists. Donor of the Pilgrim's Prize of £2,000,000 to Great Britain; founded in 1930 the Pilgrim Trust in appreciation of Great Britain's acceptance of financial burdens in the Great War of 1914–18.

Harley, Robert, 1st Earl of Oxford, K.G., P.C. (1661–1724), a distinguished Tory statesman—originally, however, a Whig—of the Queen Anne period, who fell into disgrace after that Sovereign's death in consequence of being suspected of intriguing with the Stuarts. He served at different times as Speaker of the House of Commons, Chancellor of the Exchequer, and Lord Treasurer. "The Harleian Collection" in the British Museum is a reminder of his cultured literary tastes.

Harold II. (1022–1066), the last of the Saxon Sovereigns of England, and the son of Earl Godwin, was crowned King in succession to Edward the Confessor in 1066. The coming of William the Conqueror, with his great army, soon, however, put an end to the hopes of Harold and his followers; and the Battle of Hastings terminated at once his life and Saxon sway in this country.

Haroun-Al-Raschid (763–809), the famous Caliph of Bagdad, familiar to all by the references to him in the *Arabian Nights*.

Harriman, William Averell (b. 1891), American public official; under-secretary of state for political affairs, 1963; Pres. Kennedy's roving ambassador, 1961; ambassador to Russia (1943–6); and to Britain (March–Sept. 1946); special U.S. representative in Europe for Marshall Aid, 1948–52.

Harris, Joel Chandler (1848–1908), American journalist and author, famous as the creator of "Uncle Remus." The negro humour of his stories brought him world-wide popularity among adults and children alike. His Brer Rabbit in the Uncle Remus negro folk-tales was the forerunner of Mickey Mouse, impudently victorious in every contest against fearful adversaries.

Harrison, Frederic (1831–1923), as leader of the English Positivists, filled a prominent part in philosophical discussions during the last quarter of the 19th century. In 1907 he published *The Creed of a Layman* and *The Philosophy of Common Sense*, and in 1908 *Realities and Ideals*.

Harrison, John (1693–1776), the inventor of the chronometer, for which he received the Government grant of £20,000, was a mechanician of great ingenuity, who effected many important improvements in clocks, watches, and other instruments. In 1715 he made an 8-day clock with wooden wheels, which is still working in the Science Museum, South Kensington.

Harte, Francis Bret (1839–1902), the American poet and author, who leapt into popularity in the late 'sixties by his clever sketches and stories of Californian mining life.

Harty, Sir (Herbert) Hamilton, Mus. Doc. (1880–1941), was a well-known British composer and conductor. Conductor of Hallé Orchestra 1920–33; Musical Adviser and Conductor-in-Chief of London Symphony Orchestra 1932–41.

Harvey, William (1578–1657), an English doctor and scientist who rose to great eminence both as an anatomist and physiologist, and became Physician Extraordinary to James I. He immortalised himself by discovering the circulation of the blood in 1616.

Hastings, Sir Patrick, Q.C. (1880–1952), lawyer, politician, and playwright. Attorney-General in first Labour Government, 1924. Author of *The Blind Goddess*.

Hastings, Warren (1732–1818), the first Governor-General of India. On his return to England 12 years later he was impeached on charges of excessive cruelty and corruption. The trial lasted seven years, and cost Hastings £76,000. He was ultimately acquitted, and the East India Company settled an annuity of £4,000 upon him, and he lived to see his plans for the security of British rule in the Orient publicly applauded.

Hauptmann, Gerhart (1862–1946), one of the leading dramatic poets of Europe. Born in Silesia, he devoted himself first to agriculture, then to art, and subsequently to the drama, and lived in Rome, Berlin, Switzerland, and the United States. Produced many plays, including *The Weavers*. Winner of the Nobel Prize for Literature, 1912.

Havelock, Major-Gen. Sir Henry, K.C.B. (1795–1857), one of the heroes of the Indian Mutiny, who led the troops to the relief of Cawnpore and Lucknow.

Hawke, Edward, 1st Baron, K.C.B. (1705–1781), one of the great admirals of the 18th century. He won a brilliant victory over the French fleet at Quiberon in 1759 in a tremendous storm.

Hawkins, Sir Anthony Hope (1863–1933), a popular novelist and playwright. Amongst his best-known works were *The Prisoner of Zenda*, *The Dolly Dialogues*, and *Rupert of Hentzau*.

Hawkins, Sir John (1532–1595), a brilliant naval officer of the Elizabethan period, who did much sea fighting in many climes, and served as vice-admiral in the expedition against the Spanish Armada, for which he was knighted.

Hawthorne, Nathaniel (1804–1864), American novelist, author of *The Scarlet Letter* and *The Blithedale Romance.*

Haydn, Franz Joseph (1732–1809), Austrian composer, who belongs to the great classical period of Bach, Handel, and Mozart and whose style also influenced Beethoven. He has been given the title "father of the symphony." Much of his life was spent as musical director to the princely Hungarian house of Esterhazy. In 1791 and again in 1794 he visited London, where he conducted his Salomon symphonies. He composed many operatic works, string quartets, symphonies (104 in all), sonatas, songs, Masses, and chamber music. His two great oratorios, *The Creation* and *The Seasons*, were written in his old age.

Hazlitt, William (1778–1830), English essayist and critic. His *Characters of Shakespeare's Plays* and his published lectures on the poets and dramatists, besides his *Table Talks*, are still widely read. His son William (1811–1893) was also of literary tastes, though he became Senior Registrar in the Bankruptcy Court; and the son of the latter, William Carew Hazlitt (1834–1913), though originally a civil engineer, acquired celebrity as a bibliographer and numismatist.

Hearst, William Randolph (1863–1951), American newspaper proprietor who established his supremacy in sensational journalism, and built up the biggest newspaper empire in the world.

Heath, Rt. Hon. Edward Richard George, M.P. (b. 1916), Leader of the Conservative Party, 1965–; began his political career in 1950 when he entered Parliament as member for Bexley.

Hedin, Dr. Sven Anders, Hon. K.C.I.E. (1865–1952), a Swedish traveller who made discoveries in Central Asia, and wrote extensively thereon.

Heenan, His Eminence Cardinal John Carmel (b. 1905), Archbishop of Westminster (1963); member of Sacred College (1965).

Hegel, Georg Wilhelm Friedrich (1770–1831), a famous German philosopher and professor who taught that truth or reality has three aspects revealing itself in dialectical development (thesis, antithesis, synthesis) and identified reality with rationalism. Among his important works are *The Phenomenology of the Spirit, The Science of Logic, Philosophy of Right. See also* **Dialectical Materialism, J12.**

Heidenstam, Carl Gustaf Werner von (1859–1940), Swedish author and one of the most brilliant and outstanding figures in Swedish literature. Received Nobel Prize for Literature, 1916.

Heifetez, Jascha (b. 1901), Russian-born violinist who became a naturalised American. He was the first musician to win a reputation in England by gramophone records before his first personal appearance there.

Heine, Heinrich (*c.* 1797–1856), the German lyric poet, who lived for the best part of his life in Paris, and produced from time to time poems of profound beauty and subtlety of thought. Cynical, satirical, and often bitter, many of his writings excited great conflict of opinion.

Helmholtz, Hermann Ludwig Ferdinand von (1821–94), German physiologist, physicist, and mathematician who made many important contributions to the knowledge of thermodynamics, electrodynamics, and optics. His pupil Heinrich Hertz discovered electromagnetic radiation.

Helmont, Jan Baptista van (1577–1644), Belgian chemist who devoted himself to the study of gases. His chief work is *Ortus medicinae* (1648).

Héloïse (*c.* 1101–64), niece of Canon Fulbert of Notre Dame. Famed for her romantic attachment to Abelard. (*See* **Abelard.**)

Hemingway, Ernest (1899–1961), American author of some celebrated novels: *A Farewell to Arms, Death in the Afternoon, For Whom the Bell Tolls, The Snows of Kilimanjaro, The Old Man of the Sea.* Nobel Prize 1954.

Henderson, Rt. Hon. Arthur (1863–1935), President of World Disarmament Conference, 1932–35; Leader of the Labour Party, 1931–32; Foreign Secretary, 1929–31; Home Secretary, 1924. Awarded the 1934 Nobel Peace Prize.

Henrietta Maria (1609–1669), the daughter of Henry IV. of France and wife of Charles I.

Henry, Joseph (1797–1875), American physicist who invented and operated the first electromagnetic telegraph. The unit of inductance is named after him.

Henry I. (1068–1135), king of England, 1100–35; youngest son of William the Conqueror, ascended the throne during the absence on crusade of his elder brother Robert of Normandy. His long reign brought order and progress, not entirely destroyed by the anarchy under his successor Stephen.

Henry II. (1133–1189), first Angevin king of England, 1154–89, son of Matilda, daughter of Henry I, and her second husband, Geoffrey Plantagenet, count of Anjou; his lands stretched from the Solway Firth to the Pyrenees. He was a strong ruler to whom we owe the establishment of the Common law system (see **D4(1)**) and many permanent administrative reforms. His conflict with the Church brought about the murder of his archbishop Becket, a man of equally resolute character.

Henry III. (1207–1272), king of England, 1216–72; at war with his barons for the greater part of his reign; incurred unpopularity by his patronage of French favourites. Though an inept ruler his reign showed progress in many fields.

Henry IV. (1367–1413), king of England, 1399–1413, son of John of Gaunt, grandson of Edward III; called Henry Bolingbroke, first of the Lancastrian kings. He was a lover of music and poetry.

Henry IV. of France (Henry of Navarre) (1553–1610), prior to becoming king was the leader of the French Huguenots, and although going over to the Catholics on being crowned, remained in sympathy with the Protestants and protected them by the famous Edict of Nantes. Ravaillac, a religious fanatic, assassinated Henry.

Henry V. (1387–1422), king of England, 1413–22, succeeded his father Henry IV; distinguished himself in the wars with France, his victory at Agincourt (25 Oct. 1415) being his greatest triumph. Though masterful and hard, he was devout and just and made an able and energetic monarch.

Henry VI. (1421–1471), king of England, 1422–61, only son of Henry V., by nature gentle and retiring. Succeeding to the throne under a protectorship as a baby nine months old, he had a troubled reign, including a long war with France and loss of French possessions, the Jack Cade insurrection, and the beginning of the Wars of the Roses, which led to his deposition and the enthronement of Edward IV by the triumphant Yorkists. He was imprisoned in the Tower and there probably murdered. Founded Eton College (1440) and King's College, Cambridge (1441).

Henry VII. (1457–1509), the first of the Tudor line, reigned 1485–1509; succeeded Richard III, after defeating and killing him on Bosworth Field. Conspiracies and rebellions marked his reign, but he reasserted the power of the state over feudal indiscipline.

Henry VIII. (1491–1547), king of England, 1509–47, ascended the throne at the age of 18, a prince of the Renaissance, handsome, skilled in music and sports, with a love of the sea and a deep interest in theology. His marriages, the judicial murders, his quarrel with Rome and the rejection of papal supremacy, the suppression of the monasteries, the rise and fall of Wolsey, the last of England's great ecclesiastical statesmen, made his reign one of the most crucial in history. He built the royal dockyards at Woolwich and Deptford, founded Trinity House, and was the first English monarch to have a navy.

Henry "the Navigator" (1395–1460), a Portuguese Prince, son of John I. He discovered Madeira and the Azores, and was the chief instrument of the national impetus for navigation.

Henschel, Sir George, Mus.D. (1850–1934), English baritone singer, composer and conductor; born in Breslau, he became a naturalised Englishman in 1890. Founder and part conductor of London Symphony Concerts, 1886.

Hepplewhite, George (d. 1786). One of the four great English 18th-century cabinet-makers. He was a contemporary of Chippendale, Robert Adam and Sheraton. His name is identified with the style of furniture which followed the Chippendale period.

Heraclitus of Ephesus (*c.* 540–475 B.C.), a Greek philosopher. His discovery of a *changing* world (he lived in an age of social revolution when the ancient Greek tribal aristocracy was beginning to give way to democracy) influenced the philosophies of Parmenides, Democritus, Plato, and Aristotle.

Herbert, George (1593–1633), the most purely devotional of English poets.

Hereward the Wake, the last of the Saxon nobles to hold out against the Normans. Taking refuge in the Fen country, he long defied the Conqueror's forces, but was at last betrayed into the enemy's hands by monks. William afterwards honoured him with a place at Court.

Herod the Great (*c.* 73–4 B.C.), the tyrannical king of Judæa who secured the title from Marc Antony in 37 B.C. This was the Herod who was ruling when Christ was born and who ordered the massacre of the Innocents.

Herodotus (*c.* 485–425 B.C.), the great Greek historian, called by Cicero the father of history. Has also been called the father of anthropology.

Herrick, Robert (1591–1674), an English lyric poet, unrivalled in his own field. Author of *Gather ye Rose Buds, Cherry Ripe, Oberon's Feast,* etc.

Herriot, Edouard (1872–1957), French statesman; Pres. of the National Assembly, 1947–54. Mayor of Lyons for more than a generation, three times Prime Minister, the recognised spokesman of the Left-Centre party, which was for so long dominant in French politics.

Herschel, Sir John Frederick William, Bt., F.R.S. (1792–1871), a celebrated astronomer who did much to extend the power of the telescope.

Herschel, Sir William, F.R.S. (1738–1822), great astronomer, father of the last-named, discovered the planet Uranus. His sister, **Caroline Lucretia** (1750–1848), was the author of *Index to Flamsteed's Observations of the Fixed Stars* and *Errata.*

Hertz, Heinrich (1857–1894), German physicist whose laboratory experiments confirmed Maxwell's electromagnetic theory of waves.

Herzl, Theodor (1860–1904), founded modern political Zionism.

Hesiod (*floruit c.* 735 B.C.), ancient Greek nature poet, author of the poems *Work and Days,* which tells of life in the country.

Hewart, 1st Viscount, P.C. (1870–1943), **Lord Chief** Justice of England, 1922–40.

Hill, Octavia (1838–1912), a noted pioneer English social reformer who took a practical interest in the housing conditions of the poor, and a pioneer in slum clearance in London. Helped to institute the Charity Organisation Society, and was one of the first women to sit on a Royal Commission.

Hill, Sir Rowland, K.C.B., F.R.S. (1795–1879), the first propounder of the idea of the penny postal system, was secretary to the Postmaster-General from 1846 to 1854, after which he was Chief Secretary to the Post Office until 1864.

Hindemith, Paul (1895–1963), German composer and violinist. Much of his work is *Gebrauchsmusik* (workaday music written with the aim of establishing closer contact between composer and public). His works are numerous and strikingly varied, and include sonatas and chamber works, songs, operas, ballet music, symphonies, and the oratorio *Das Unaufhöriche.* Formerly Prof. of Music, Yale, and Zurich.

Hindenburg, Field-Marshal Paul von (1847–1934). President of the German Reich, 1925–34; Chief of the General Staff, 1916–18.

Hinshelwood, Sir Cyril Norman, O.M., F.R.S. (b. 1897), Pres. of the Royal Society and Dr. Lee's Prof. of Chemistry, Univ. of Oxford, 1937–. Shared with Prof. Semenov of Russia the 1956 Nobel Prize for Chemistry for researches into the mechanism of chemical reactions.

Hinton, Christopher, Baron, K.B.E., M.A., D.Eng., D.Sc(Eng.), F.R.S. (b. 1901), as Man. Dir. of the Industrial Group of the U.K. Atomic Energy Authority played important part in the building of Calder Hall. Chairman (1957–64) Central Electricity Generating Board (which owns and operates Britain's nuclear power stations); Member Transport Advisory Council (Min. of Transport) and special adviser on co-ordination of transport, 1965–.

Hippocrates of Chios (fl. *c.* 430 B.C.), a Greek business-man who specialised in mathematics and was the first to compile a work on the elements of geometry.

Hippocrates of Cos (*c.* 460–*c.* 370 B.C.), Greek physician, the father of medicine, b. on the island of Cos off the coast of Asia Minor. He established medical schools in Athens and elsewhere and separated medicine from superstition and so placed it on a scientific basis.

Hirohito, Emperor of Japan (b. 1901), acceded to the throne Dec. 1926.

Hitler, Adolf (1889–1945), German dictator, founder of National Socialism, b. in Austria, son of customs official. Worked in Vienna as artisan; already held anti-semitic views. Came to Munich in 1912; enlisted in Bavarian Infantry at outbreak of first world war. At the end of the war conditions in Germany favoured the growth of a fascist movement and under his leadership the National Socialist (Nazi) Party climbed to power. Appointed Reich Chancellor, 1933. On death of Hindenburg in 1934 became Führer. Commander-in-Chief Wehrmacht, 1935. Under the Hitler regime working class movements were ruthlessly destroyed; all opponents—communists, socialists, Jews—were persecuted and murdered. By terrorism and propaganda the German state was welded into a powerful machine for aggression. There followed the occupation of the Rhineland (1936), the annexation of Austria and Czechoslovakia (1938–39), the invasion of Poland and declaration of war by Great Britain and France (1939), the invasion of Soviet Russia (1941). Final defeat came in 1945 and on April 30 Hitler committed suicide in the Chancellery as the Russians closed in on Berlin.

Hobbes, Thomas (1588–1679), English philosopher who published his most famous work, *Leviathan,* in 1651. He favoured strong Government and therefore supported the supremacy of the State even in religion, but his arguments aroused great antagonism even among the Royalists. He was a child of his age in his enthusiasm for scientific enquiry, and his works provoked fresh thought.

Hobbs, Sir John Berry ("Jack") (1882–1963), first played for Surrey 1905; retired from first-class cricket Feb. 1935. Scored 61,221 runs including 197 centuries.

Hobhouse, Leonard Trelawney (1864–1929), English sociologist; Prof. of Sociology, London Univ., 1907–29; editor of the *Sociological Review,* 1908–10, and writer for the *Manchester Guardian,* 1897–1902. His books include *The Theory of Knowledge, Morals in Evolution,* and *Development and Purpose.*

Ho Chi-minh (b. 1892), leader of the Vietnam revolutionary nationalist party of Indo-China. Successfully led the struggle for independence during and after the second world war. President of North Vietnam.

Hodgkin, Dorothy Crowfoot, O.M. (b. 1910), Wolfson Research Professor of the Royal Society at Oxford since 1960; the third woman to receive the Nobel Prize for Chemistry, awarded in 1964 for her X-ray analysis to elucidate the structure of complex molecules, notably penicillin and vitamin B-12.

Hogarth, William (1697–1764), the celebrated engraver and painter who satirised the follies of his time in a series of engravings instinct with character, humour and power. His *Harlot's Progress,* of six engravings, was published in 1734, and gained him immediate fame. In 1735 he produced his equally celebrated *Rake's Progress,* a series of eight engravings. These were followed by *Marriage à la Mode, Industry and Idleness,* and *The March to Finchley.*

Hogben, Lancelot, M.A., D.Sc., F.R.S. (b. 1895), physiologist; Prof. Medical Statistics, 1947–61, Prof. of Zoology, 1941–47, Birmingham Univ.; Prof. Natural History, Univ. of Aberdeen, 1937–41; Prof. Social Biology in London Univ., 1930–37. Author of the great popular works *Mathematics for the Million, Science for the Citizen,* and *Mathematics in the Making.*

Hogg, Quintin (1845–1903), was an educationist and philanthropist who, purchasing the old Polytechnic Institution in 1882, turned it into a popular college, providing instruction in every department of education at moderate rates.

Hokusai, Katsushika (1760–1849), Japanese artist of the Ukiyo-e (popular school), whose work is highly original and of singular beauty and delicacy. He excelled in landscapes.

Holbein, The Elder (*c.* 1460–1524), a famous German painter, father of Hans Holbein.

Holbein, Hans—The Younger (1497–1543), was born at Augsburg, and settled in London in 1530, where he won the favour of Henry VIII.

Holden, Charles, F.R.I.B.A. (1875–1960), British architect, designer of modern public buildings, including British Medical Assen. Building, Strand, London Underground Railway Head Offices, Piccadilly Circus, University of London buildings (Senate House), Bloomsbury.

Holden, Sir Isaac, Bt. (1807–1897), an inventor and manufacturer who achieved fame and fortune in connection with wool-combing inventions.

Hölderlin, Johann Christian Friedrich (1770–1843), friend of Hegel and contemporary of Goethe and Schiller, now considered among the very greatest of German poets. His mind became unhinged in his middle years.

Holford, William Graham, Baron, M.A., F.R.I.B.A. (b. 1907), British architect and town-planner. Prof. of Civic Design, Univ. of Liverpool, 1936–47; Prof. of Town Planning, London Univ., 1949–; planned post-war redevelopment of City of London, including precincts of St. Paul's Cathedral; architect of proposed Piccadilly Circus rebuilding scheme; Member Transport Advisory Council, 1965–.

Holland, Rt. Hon. S. G., C.H. (1893–1961), New Zealand Conservative leader; Prime Minister, 1949–57.

Holmes, Oliver Wendell (1809–1894), an American doctor and author of great humour and geniality. His writings include *Autocrat of the Breakfast Table, The Professor at the Breakfast Table* and *The Poet at the Breakfast Table.*

Holst, Gustav Theodore (1874–1934), a British composer of Swedish descent whose compositions include *The Planets* suite, *The Hymn of Jesus*, an opera *The Perfect Fool*, and a choral symphony. His long career as a teacher of outstanding gifts included the appointment of musical director at St. Paul's Girls' School, London (1905–34) and at Morley College (1907–24).

Holyoake, George Jacob (1817–1906), an eminent secularist lecturer and author, who was identified with many popular movements, expecially Co-operation, of which he was the historian.

Holyoake, Rt. Hon. Keith Jacka (b. 1904), New Zealand politician and farmer; Prime Minister since 1957.

Homer (*c.* 700 B.C.), the most famous of all epic poets. Is supposed to have been a Greek who lived probably at Chios or Smyrna, and has generally been regarded as the author of the *Iliad* and the *Odyssey*, though tradition rather than ascertained fact connects his name with those great poems. *See* **H3**.

Hood, Samuel, 1st Viscount Hood of Whitley, G.C.B. (1724–1816), a successful British admiral, who in 1793 was in command of the Mediterranean fleet, and showed great capacity in that post, taking and occupying Toulon, and capturing Corsica among other exploits.

Hood, Thomas (1799–1845), an English poet, who, as a prolific writer of serious as well as humorous poems, stands in his own line unique. Of his serious verse, *The Song of the Shirt, The Dream of Eugene Aram* and *The Bridge of Sighs* may be cited as the best examples, while his comic poems, notably those of the punning order, are unequalled.

Hooke, Robert (1635–1703), English physicist, a great experimenter and inventor. He was also an architect and drew up a plan for rebuilding London after the Great Fire.

Hooker, Richard (1554–1600), Master of the Temple from 1585–91, and afterwards Rector of Boscome. Famed for his book on *Ecclesiastical Polity*, and for his exquisite choice of words, was known as "Judicious Hooker."

Hopkins, Sir Frederick Gowland, O.M., F.R.S. (1861–1947), an eminent English bio-chemist, noted for his important work on proteins and vitamins. In 1929 was awarded the Nobel Prize in Medicine for his discovery of Vitamin D. Pres. of the Royal Society 1931–36, and of the British Association, 1933.

Hopkins, Harry (1890–1946). Franklin Roosevelt's personal assistant. Particularly assisted the President at the important war-time foreign conferences, as his personal representative abroad, in working out the New Deal, and in the administration of Lend-Lease.

Hopkinson, John, D.Sc., F.R.S. (1849–98), English engineer and physicist. Senior Wrangler and Fellow at Cambridge. Studied engineering in his father's works, and set up as a consultative engineer. Specialised in electrical work, and by developing the theory of alternating current and of the magnetic current in dynamos he paved the way to the common use of electricity in daily life. Was Professor of Electrical Engineering at King's College, London, 1890–98.

Hoppner, John, R.A. (1758–1810), English portrait painter born in Whitechapel of German parents; studied at the Academy Schools, winning great distinction and painted portraits of many members of the Royal Family.

Horace, or more properly **Flaccus Quintus Horatius** (65–8 B.C.), the famous Roman satirist and poet, who was the friend of Virgil, and attained immortal fame by his *Satires, Epodes*, and *Odes*.

Horner, Arthur (b. 1894), general secretary of the National Union of Mineworkers 1946–59 and a leading British Communist.

Horniman, Annie Elizabeth Fredericka, C.H. (1830–1937). English theatre manager and founder of the repertory system in England. She was the daughter of F. J. Horniman, the traveller and collector, who founded the Horniman Museum in Forest Hill and presented it to the L.C.C. in 1901.

Houdini, Harry (1874–1926), American magician, son of a Hungarian rabbi, world-famed for his escapes from handcuffs, locked chambers, sealed cases under water, etc. His real name was Erich Weiss, and he took his stage name from the French conjuror Houdin. He was a keen student of psychic phenomena and exposed fraudulent mediums.

Housman, Laurence (1865–1959), English playwright, poet, and novelist, younger brother of **Alfred Edward** (1859–1936) also a poet of distinction, a professor of Latin at Cambridge and an eminent classical scholar, author of *A Shropshire Lad.*

Howard, John (1726–1790), earned celebrity for his philanthropic efforts on behalf of prison reform, the pursuit of which eventually exposed him to a fatal fever attack in Russia.

Howard of Effingham, Lord (1536–1624), commander of the fleet which defeated the Spanish Armada, 1588, and took part in the capture of Cadiz, 1596.

Howe, Elias (1819–1867), an ingenious American who was the inventor of the first sewing machine, by which he made a great fortune.

Howe, Julia Ward (1819–1910), American philanthropist and poetess, famous as the authoress of the *Battle Hymn of the Republic* (1861), a leader of the American Suffragette movement, and the first woman to be elected to the American Academy of Arts and Letters.

Howe, Richard, 1st (and last) **Earl** (of first creation), K.G. (1726–1799), the British admiral who in 1758 destroyed Cherbourg and in 1794 won the famous victory over the French off Brest.

Howells, William Dean (1837–1920), American novelist and author.

Hubble, Edwin Powell, B.Sc., Ph.D. (1889–1953), U.S. astronomer at Mount Wilson Observatory from 1919 until his death. Noted for his work on extragalactic nebulæ and with the aid of the 200-in. telescope at Mount Palomar made important discoveries.

Hudson, Henry (*c.* 1550–1611), was a famous English navigator who discovered the Hudson River, Hudson Strait and Bay, and his two books describing his voyages are of the greatest interest.

Hudson, William Henry (1841–1922), English author and naturalist, who spent his early years in South America, memories of which influenced much of his work. His books include *The Purple Land* (1885), *Green Mansions* (1904), *Afoot in England* (1909) and *British Birds* (1895). The Hyde Park Bird Sanctuary (opened in 1925) was established in his memory, and contains the famous figure of *Rima* by Epstein.

Huggins, Sir William, O.M., K.C.B., F.R.S. (1824–1910), British astronomer who pioneered in spectroscopic photography. Collaborated with his wife, **Margaret Lindsay Murray** (1848–1915), who was also an able astronomer.

Hughes, Thomas (1822–1896), educated at Rugby and at Oxford; practised at the Bar, and became a County Court Judge in 1882. His best-known work is *Tom Brown's Schooldays.*

Hugo, Victor Marie (1802–1885), the great poet, dramatist and novelist who headed the Romantic movement in France in the early part of the 19th century and made himself a name of the first eminence by his various writings. His dramas of *Hernani*, *Lucrèce Borgia*, *Ruy Blas*, and *Le Roi s'amuse* were in every sense great triumphs. Among his novels, *Notre Dame* belongs to his early period, and *Les Misérables*, *Les Travailleurs de la mer*, and *L'Homme qui rit*, belong to his later life, written while he was living in exile in Guernsey.

Hull, Cordell (1871–1955), U.S. Sec. of State, 1933–44. Awarded the Nobel Peace Prize, 1945.

Hull, Field Marshal Sir Richard Amyatt, K.C.B., D.S.O., B.A. (b. 1907), British Army cavalry officer, succeeded Sir Francis Festing as C.I.G.S. in 1961, and Lord Mountbatten as Chief of the Defence Staff in 1965.

Humboldt, Baron Friedrich Heinrich Alexander von (1769–1859), German naturalist and explorer whose researches are recorded in his two great books *Voyage de Humboldt et Bonpland* (23 vols., 1805–34) and *Cosmos* (5 vols., 1845–62).

Hume, David (1711–1776), the celebrated historian and philosopher whose *History of England* long held chief place in English historical literature. But Hume's enduring fame rests upon his philosophical writings. He developed the empiricism of Locke into the scepticism inherent in it. His main works are *Treatise of Human Nature* and *Dialogues Concerning Natural Religion*.

Hunt, Brig. Sir (Henry Cecil) John, Kt., C.B.E., D.S.O. (b. 1910), leader of the successful 1953 British Mount Everest Expedition.

Hunt, (James Henry) Leigh (1784–1859), an English poet, politician and essayist. In 1813 he was fined £500, and sentenced to two years' imprisonment for libelling the Prince Regent, and while in prison wrote his poem, *The Story of Rimini*, and other works. In later life he was a constant contributor to literature and from 1847 enjoyed a pension of £200 a year from the Civil List.

Hunt, Wm. Holman, O.M. (1827–1910), one of the three founders of the Pre-Raphaelite movement, and an artist who achieved distinction by several remarkable paintings, the chief of which is, perhaps, *The Light of the World*, an allegorical work.

Hunter, the brothers **William**, F.R.S. (1718–83) and **John**, F.R.S. (1728–93), were both famous Scottish physicians. William had remarkable success as a lecturer and obstetrician. His valuable anatomical collection was bequeathed to the Univ. of Glasgow. John showed real genius for anatomy, became one of the greatest surgeons of his day and made many discoveries. His surgical museum forms part of the Museum of the Royal College of Surgeons.

Huss, or Hus, John (1369–1415), the Bohemian religious reformer, was strongly influenced by Wyclif and himself urged reform both of abuses in the church and of doctrine. Sentenced to death or recantation he suffered martyrdom on July 6, 1415. His death caused a civil war which lasted for many years.

Hussein ibn Talal (b. 1934), grandson of King Abdullah, succeeded his father Talal as King of Jordan, Aug. 11, 1952.

Hutton, James, M.D. (1726–97), an Edinburgh doctor whose geological researches established the fundamental principles of modern geology. Before his time geology did not exist as a science, all was speculation. He drew his evidence from the rocks themselves, and his *Theory of the Earth* is one of the great classics of science.

Huxley, Aldous (Leonard), C.L. (1894–1963), noted modern writer, grandson of T. H. Huxley and brother of Julian; author of *Crome Yellow*, *Jesting Pilate*, *Brave New World*, *Point Counter Point*, *Ends and Means*, *Grey Eminence*, *The Perennial Philosophy*, etc.

Huxley, Sir Julian Sorrell, M.A., F.R.S. (b. 1887), biologist and writer, grandson of T. H. Huxley. Director-General of Unesco, 1946–48. Secy. of Zoological Soc. of London 1935–42.

Huxley, Thomas Henry, F.R.S. (1825–1895), an eminent scientist and author of numerous works covering a great range of research. After the publication of Darwin's *Origin of Species*, Huxley became an ardent evolutionist. His biological work, *Man's Place in Nature*, and his numerous essays were marked by great vigour and clearness of thought, and gave him a leading position. He held numerous important appointments was President of the Royal Society in 1883, and belonged to many learned societies.

Hyde, Dr, Douglas (1860–1949), the distinguished Irish scholar, historian, poet and folk-lorist. President of Eire, 1938–45.

Hypatia of Alexandria, the only woman mathematician of antiquity. She excited the enmity of Christian fanatics, who raised an agitation against her, and she was put to death in A.D. 415.

I

Ibáñez, Vicente Blasco. (*See* **Blasco-Ibáñez.**)

Ibrahim Pasha (1789–1848), an able Egyptian statesman, general, and Viceroy, who, adopted by Mohammed Ali as his son, contributed largely to the success of Egyptian policy during the quarter of a century or more of his influence. His conquest of Syria was a notable feat of generalship. He died a few months after being appointed Viceroy.

Ibsen, Henrik Johan (1828–1906), the Norwegian playwright and poet, moralist, and humanist, whose plays, though arousing considerable opposition at the time, are acknowledged as the work of one of the world's greatest dramatists. A master of technique, charging every detail with significance, fusing the comic with the tragic, Ibsen revolutionised the European theatre. His chief works are *Ghosts*, *The Master Builder*, *The Wild Duck*, *A Doll's House*, *Hedda Gabler* and the poetic drama *Peer Gynt*.

Inge, Very Rev. William Ralph, K.C.V.O., D.D. (1860–1954), English divine; Dean of St. Paul's, 1911–34; Assistant Master at Eton, 1884–88; Lady Margaret Prof. Camb., 1907–11. Earned the sobriquet "the gloomy Dean" for his incisive and somewhat pessimistic comments on contemporary affairs.

Ingersoll, Robert Green (1833–99), American lawyer, writer, and lecturer, became known by reason of his lectures directed principally against Christianity.

Ingres, Jean Auguste Dominique (1780–1867), a great French historical painter who was elected to the Institute in 1824, and at his death was a Senator of France.

Innocent III. (1160–1216), Pope from 1198, successfully asserted the power of the papacy over such secular princes as the emperor, Philip II. of France, and John of England. He promoted the 4th Crusade, initiated the crusade against the Albigensian heretics, and held the 4th Lateran Council. His pontificate marks the zenith of the medieval papacy.

Inönü, General Ismet (b. 1884), Prime Min. of Turkey; leader of the Republican People's Party founded by Kemal Atatürk whom he succeeded as Pres., 1938–50, after serving as Prime Min. from 1923 to Atatürk's death in 1938.

Iqbal, Dr. Sir Muhammad (1875–1938), poet-philosopher of the East, b. Sialkot, W. Pakistan, acknowledged as a great authority in the world of literature, both in prose and poetry. He wrote in Urdu, Persian, and English.

Ireland, John (1879–1962), English composer, best known for his settings of the poems of Thomas Hardy, A. E. Housman, and Masefield's *Sea Fever*. He also wrote chamber music, orchestral work and piano pieces.

Irving, Sir Henry (1838–1905), a great English actor who made his first appearance in London in 1866 and whose first distinct success was as Digby Grant in *Two Roses*. His record at the Lyceum Theatre from 1871 onwards covered a brilliant series of productions, including *The Bells*, his first triumph, *Charles I.*, *Eugene Aram*, and a number of Shakespearean impersonations, in some of which, notably Shylock and Hamlet, Irving gave memorable performances.

Irving, Washington (1783–1859), a writer of charming stories and miscellaneous works which won wide favour on both sides of the Atlantic.

Isabella of Castile (1451–1504), reigned jointly with Ferdinand V., her husband. During their thirty years' sway Spain was united as a single monarchy, and achieved the height of its greatness, the discovery of America, the conquest of Granada, and the expulsion of the Moors from Spain being among the events of her reign.

Ismail Pasha (1830–95), grandson of Mohammed Ali was a man of modern ideas and great public spirit, whose policy rendered Egypt practically independent of Turkey, the Sultan confirming him in the position and title of Khedive in 1873. It was his adoption of the idea of the Suez Canal that enabled that work to be successfully carried out. By reckless extravagance he involved himself in difficulties, entailing the sale of his Suez Canal shares to England, the establishment of the dual control of England and France, and his own abdication in 1879, when his son Tewfik succeeded.

Israels, Joseph (1824–1911), outstanding Dutch genre painter of the 19th century.

Ito, Hirobumi, Prince (1841–1909), one of the most enlightened statesmen of Japan. The unparalleled social metamorphosis which Japan underwent in the latter half of the nineteenth century owed much to his guidance and influence. Was four times Premier.

Ivan the Great (1440–1505), succeeded in bringing the scattered provinces of Muscovy under one supreme governmental control, and put an end to Tartar rule.

Ivan the Terrible (1530–84), crowned as first Czar of Russia in 1547, was a strong and autocratic ruler. He furthered internal consolidation and Russian eastward expansion and entered into trading relations with Queen Elizabeth.

J

Jacks, Lawrence Pearsall (1860–1955), Principal of Manchester College, Oxford, 1915–31, and Professor of Philosophy in that College, 1903–31. Entered ministry in 1887 as assistant to the Rev. Stopford Brooke. Editor of the *Hibbert Journal*, 1902–47, and author of several books of religious studies.

Jackson, Andrew (1767–1845), American general who was twice President of the United States.

Jackson, Thomas Jonathan (1824–1863), popularly known as "Stonewall Jackson," was the most brilliant general on the Southern side in the American Civil War. Was accidentally killed at the Battle of Chancellorsville. The term "Stonewall" refers to his dogged resistance at the first Battle of Bull Run.

Jacobs, William Wymark (1863–1943), novelist of quaint and peculiar humour, whose stories and sketches of East End riverside life are inimitable.

Jacquard, Joseph Marie (1752–1834), a French mechanic whose Jacquard loom provided a new and effective method of weaving designs in textile fabrics, and was an invention of the very first rank.

Jagellons, Lithuanian-Polish dynasty, ruled in Poland 1386–1572.

James I. (1566–1625), King of England (1603–25) and, as James VI., King of Scotland (1567–1625). He was the son of Mary Stuart and succeeded to the English throne on the death of Elizabeth. Numerous plots were formed against him, including the Gunpowder Plot of 1605. He persecuted the Puritans, granted many monopolies, and saw the Authorised Version of the Bible published. Described by Henry IV of France as "the wisest fool in Christendom."

James II. (1633–1701) King of England and, as James VII., of Scotland (1685–88), third son of Charles I. As Duke of York he was Lord High Admiral in the Second and Third Dutch Wars, during which New Amsterdam fell to England and was renamed New York. As a Roman Catholic he resigned his office after the Test Act of 1673, was nearly excluded from the Succession, and, when he came to the throne in 1685, aroused and united strong opposition by his attempts to obtain better conditions for his co-religionists. The unsuccessful Monmouth Rebellion, the Bloody Assize, the Declaration of Indulgence, and the Seven Bishops' Trial marked a reign which ended in the flight of the King and the Revolution Settlement of 1689.

James, Henry, O.M. (1843–1916), an Anglo-American novelist and younger brother of William James. Produced a number of notable stories, remarkable for their intellectual subtlety and careful characterisations. For the last thirty years of his life he resided mostly in London. His best-known novels are *The American, Daisy Miller, The Bostonian, The Portrait of a Lady* and *What Maisie Saw.* Became a British subject 1915.

James, William (1842–1910), the great American psychologist and philosopher, brother of Henry James, the novelist. He became Prof. of Philosophy at Harvard University, 1882, and was the founder of the philosophical system known as pragmatism. His first important work, *Principles of Psychology,* 1890, stamped him as one of the most lucid, penetrating and engaging writers of his day. *Pragmatism*, a new name for some old ways of thinking, appeared in 1907, and established him as a speculative philosopher of a high order.

Janáček, Leoš (1854–1928), Czech composer, conductor, teacher, and student of folk music, b. in Moravia, son of a village schoolmaster, creator of a national style. He wrote much choral, orchestral, and instrumental music and his best known opera is *Jenufa.*

Jeans, Sir James Hopwood, O.M., F.R.S. (1877–1946), mathematician and astronomer, author of *The Universe Around Us, The Mysterious Universe.*

Jefferies, Richard (1848–1887), an English naturalist, who, between 1873 and the time of his death, wrote some of the most beautiful descriptions of natural scenery and the customs and habits of the rural world that we possess. His *Gamekeeper at Home* and *The Life of the Fields* are books of great power and sympathy.

Jefferson, President Thomas (1743–1826), took part in the American Revolution, and drew up the Declaration of Independence. Twice U.S. Pres.

Jeffreys, George, 1st Baron of Wem (1645–1689), Lord Chief Justice of Charles II and Lord Chancellor of James II, won for himself unenviable notoriety by his harsh and cruel judgments at the Bloody Assize. He died in the Tower shortly after the flight of James II. It is now thought that the traditional view of Jeffreys is probably untrue as local records give a rather different picture of an able and conscientious judge.

Jellicoe, Adml. of the Fleet, Earl, G.C.B., O.M., G.C.V.O. (1859–1935), Commander-in-Chief of British Fleet, August 1914 to Nov. 1916; and First Sea Lord, Nov. 1916 to Dec. 1917; Gov.-Gen. of New Zealand, 1920–24.

Jenghiz Khan (1162–1227), the famous Mogul ruler who twice conquered China, and forced the Turks within European confines.

Jenner, Edward, M.D., F.R.S. (1749–1823), an English physican who became celebrated by his discovery of the vaccination system of alleviating smallpox, which has been of such incalculable benefit to mankind. Parliament made him grants amounting to £30,000 which left him still out of pocket.

Jerome, Jerome Klapka (1859–1927), a clever journalist and writer, who made his first success with his humorous book, *Three Men in a Boat.* He founded *The Idler.*

Jerome, St. (340–420), a noted theologian of the 5th century, whose Latin translation of the Scriptures (*The Vulgate*) made him famous. He died at Bethlehem.

Jesus Christ (*c.* 6 B.C.–*c.* A.D. 29), the founder of Christianity and the greatest figure of human history. The main source of information on His life and work is the New Testament. Jesus was born at Bethlehem in Judæa, and was the first-born of His mother Mary. According to Matthew, He was miraculously conceived and Joseph was His foster-father. The family home was at Nazareth in Galilee. Jesus lived at a critical period in Jewish history. His teaching is summarised in the Sermon on the Mount. So far as scholars can tell Jesus was born some six years earlier than the date which Christian tradition has chosen to fix the first year of its era.

Jiménez, Juan Ramón (b. 1881), Spanish lyric poet who was awarded the Nobel Prize for Literature in 1956.

Jinnah, Mohammed Ali (1876–1948), Indian statesman. The emergence of a separate Moslem state of Pakistan when the British left India was mainly due to his efforts. He was for many years the active President of the Moslem League, and in 1947 became the first Gov.-Gen. of Pakistan.

Joachim, Joseph (1831–1907), Hungarian violinist and composer of the classical-romantic school of

Mendelssohn, Schumann, and Brahms. He ranks as the greatest solo violinist the world has ever known.

Joan of Arc, St. (1412–1431), the girl whose heroism inspired the French to drive the English out of Orleans, and enabled Charles to be proclaimed King at Rheims. She was burned as a heretic at Rouen. Canonised at St. Peter's, Rome, 1920.

Joffre, Marshal Joseph Jacques Césaire, G.C.B., Hon. O.M. (1852–1931), Commander-in-Chief of the French Armies 1911–17. His handling of his troops during the war was eminently successful. Entered the Army in 1870, and commanded a battery during the siege of Paris.

John XXIII. (1881–1963), elected Pope in 1958 on the death of Pius XII; formerly Cardinal Angelo Giuseppe Roncalli, patriarch of Venice. The Oecumenical Council which opened in Rome in 1962 was one of the great achievements of his short reign. He sought to reform the Church to meet the needs and conditions of the times and set in train movements towards Christian unity. The principal sources of his teaching are the two enlightened encyclicals, *Mater et Magistra* (1961) and *Pacem in Terris* (1963).

John, St., the Baptist (executed A.D. 28), the forerunner of Christ.

John, St., the Evangelist, one of the twelve apostles of Jesus, a Galilean fisherman, son of Zebedee and brother of James, traditionally the author of the fourth Gospel.

John, surnamed "Lackland" (1167–1216), King of England from 1199 to his death at Newark after deposition by the Barons in 1216. One of the most detested of English monarchs, but whose reign stands out large in history because of his having granted, under compulsion, the Magna Carta, England's great bulwark of liberty.

John of Gaunt (1340–1399), Duke of Lancaster, son of Edward III. and father of Henry IV., one of the most powerful English nobles of his day. In Wat Tyler's rebellion his palace in the Savoy was destroyed.

John, Augustus Edwin, O.M., R.A. (1878–1961), outstanding British painter, especially notable for his portraits. Among others, he painted Lloyd George, Bernard Shaw, and T. E. Lawrence. His works in the Tate Gallery include *The Smiling Woman* and *Galway*.

Johnson, Amy, C.B.E. (1903–1941), was the first woman aviator to fly solo from England to Australia, when she made a record flight to India (6 days to Karachi). Lost her life when flying as a pilot of the Air Transport Auxiliary over the Thames Estuary.

Johnson, Lyndon Baines (b. 1908), American politician who as Vice-President automatically became President of the United States on the death by assassination of Kennedy on 22 Nov. 1963. In the 1964 presidential election he won a decisive victory over Senator Goldwater, the Republican candidate. Senator from Texas since 1948. *See also* **Section C, Part I.**

Johnson, Dr. Samuel (1709–1784), the great lexicographer and writer, who for a number of years was the most prominent literary man in England. His *Dictionary* was published in 1755, before which he had attained eminence by several works including the *Vanity of Human Wishes*. His *Rasselas* appeared in 1759, and for two years he published *The Idler*, a collection of essays after the style of the *Spectator*. His *Lives of the Poets* appeared in 1781. He was greatly honoured during his life, enjoyed a pension of £300 a year from 1762, at his death was buried in Westminster Abbey, and had the best biography in the language written upon him by James Boswell.

Johnston, Sir Harry (Hamilton), G.C.M.G., K.C.B. (1858–1927), was a daring and successful explorer, who led scientific expeditions into the interior of Africa. Helped to crush the Arab slave trade in East Africa and to add Nyasaland and a large part of N. Rhodesia to the British empire.

Joliot-Curie, Jean Frédéric (1900–58), French physicist. His wife **Irène** (1896–1956), daughter of Pierre and Marie Curie, was also a distinguished scientist. Their discovery of artificial radioactivity brought them a Nobel Prize in 1935. Both were dismissed from the French Atomic Energy Commission because of their sympathy for communism.

Jones, Ernest Charles (1819–69), one of the best-known leaders of the Chartist movement, was sentenced in 1848 to two years' imprisonment for his revolutionary speeches.

Jones, Sir Harold Spencer, K.B.E., F.R.S. (1890–1960). Astronomer Royal, 1933–55; H.M. Astronomer Cape of Good Hope, 1923–33. His major research was to determine the mean distance of the earth from the sun, 93,004,000 miles.

Jones, Inigo (1573–1652), a noted architect, who became known as "the English Palladio," and built, among other famous structures, the Banqueting Hall at Whitehall and the gateway of St. Mary's at Oxford. He was a Royalist, and suffered severely in the Civil War.

Jonson, Ben (1573–1637), a friend of Shakespeare and one of the great poets and dramatists of his age. Was Poet Laureate from 1619. His best plays are *Every Man in his Humour* and *The Alchemist*. Buried in Westminster Abbey.

Josephine, Empress (1763–1814), was the wife of Napoleon I. until he divorced her in 1809 and married Marie Louise. Josephine had previously been married to Vicomte Alexandre Beauharnais, by whom she had two children.

Josephus, Flavius (A.D. 38–*c.* 100), Jewish historian whose *History of the Jewish War* and *Antiquities of the Jews* contained much valuable historical evidence bearing upon Biblical history.

Joule, James Prescott, F.R.S. (1818–1889), one of the greatest of English physicists, famous for his researches on electro-magnetism and for his determination of the mechanical equivalent of heat.

Jowett, Benjamin (1817–93), English scholar remembered as the greatest Master of Balliol College, winning a great reputation for his sympathy and erudition. His outstanding works include translations of the *Dialogues of Plato* and *History of Thucydides*. His Mastership raised Balliol to a proud pre-eminence among the Colleges.

Jowitt, William Allen, Earl, P.C. (1885–1957), Lord High Chancellor in the Labour Governments, 1945–51. Pub. *The Strange Case of Alger Hiss* (1953).

Joyce, James (1882–1941), Irish author who because of the originality, daring, and range of his work exercised a great influence on the younger school of novelists, critics, and poets. Notable among his works are *Portrait of the Artist as a Young Man*, *Ulysses*, and *Finnegans Wake*.

Juin, Alphonse, Marshal of France (b. 1888), C.-in-C. of French troops in N. Africa, 1942; Res.-Gen. in Morocco, 1947–51; C.-in-C. Allied Forces, Central Europe (NATO), 1951–56.

Julian the Apostate (Flavius Claudius Julianus) (331–363) was Roman Emperor for the last two years of his life, during which period he was an avowed pagan, though previously he had professedly been a Christian. He was slain by an arrow during an expedition against Persia.

Julius Cæsar. (See **Cæsar Caius Julius.**)

Jung, Carl Gustav (1875–1961), Swiss psychiatrist, founder of the Zür School, and a former pupil of Freud (*q.v.*) until 1911, when he formulated a system of analytical psychology. (See **Section J.**)

Junot, Andoche, Duc d'Abrantès (1771–1813), one of Napoleon's great generals, brilliantly successful until defeated by Wellington at Vimeira.

Jusserand, Jean Adrien Antoine Jules (1855–1932), French author and diplomat; Ambassador to U.S.A., 1902–25. A well-known authority on English literature, his works include *The English Theatre from the Conquest to Shakespeare* (1878), *The English Novel* (1886), *The Literary History of the English up to the Renaissance* (1894).

Justinian I. (Flavius Anicius Justianianus) (483–565) was the Roman Emperor of the East whose fame rests chiefly on his laws. His *Corpus Juris Civilis* remained the accepted text-book of Roman Law to the end of the 9th century, and is still the most important of all monuments of jurisprudence. He reigned from 527 to 565.

Juvenal (Decimus Junius Juvenalis) (60–140), the famous Roman poet and rhetorician of the age of Trajan. His sixteen celebrated *Satires* are the finest in classical literature.

K

Kafka, Franz (1883–1924), Jewish writer, born in Prague, whose introspective work, the bulk of which was not published till after his early death from tuberculosis, has been widely acclaimed and discussed, and has had a notable influence on later schools, including the Surrealists.

Kálidāsa (*c.* A.D. 400), the most illustrious figure in classic Sanskrit literature and one of the greatest Oriental poets. No facts are known about his life and date, but certain evidence places him in the 5th cent. Seven of his works survive: two lyrics, *Ritu-samhara* (The Seasons), and *Megha-dūta* (Cloud Messenger); two epics, *Raghu-vamśa* (Dynasty of Raghu) and *Kumāra-sambhava* (Birth of the War-God); and three dramas, *Śakūntalā*, *Mālavikāgnimitra*, and *Vikramorvaśīya*.

Kant, Immanuel (1724–1804), German scientist and philosopher, whose *Critique of Pure Reason*, published in 1781, was the subject of fierce discussion, and involved him in trouble with the Prussian Government as to his religious belief. His speculations and the transcendental theories he worked out revealed a marvellous capacity of mind, and his works were of immense influence in shaping the philosophical thought of the 18th and 19th centuries.

Kauffmann, Angelica, R.A. (1741–1807), the famous Anglo-Swiss painter, who was one of the foundation members of the Royal Academy, and the first woman R.A.

Kaulbach, Wilhelm von (1805–1874), an eminent German painter who illustrated books by Goethe and Schiller.

Kean, Charles John (1811–1868), an English actor-manager, son of the tragedian, Edmund Kean. Charles Kean married Ellen Tree, and in the 'fifties played with her in a series of spectacular revivals at the Princess's Theatre in London.

Kean, Edmund (1787–1833), one of the greatest tragic actors in the of history the British stage.

Keats, John (1795–1821), the great English poet who, though dying at the early age of twenty-five, produced a number of poems which in richness of imagination and beauty of thought are not excelled by anything in the language. His *Odes*, his two poems, *Isabella* and *The Eve of St. Agnes*, are exquisite in form and expression.

Keble, John (1792–1866), an English clergyman and poet, whose *Christian Year* is one of the most notable works of its class.

Keene, Charles (1823–1891), one of the most talented of the *Punch* artists.

Kellogg, Frank Billings, LL.D. (1856–1937), was a Judge of the Permanent Court of International Justice, The Hague, 1930–35. American Ambassador to the Court of St. James, 1923–25. Secretary of State, U.S.A., 1925–29; chiefly remembered as the originator of the Kellogg Pact. Awarded Nobel Peace prize, 1929.

Kelvin, William Thomson, Lord, P.C., O.M., G.C.V.O., F.R.S. (1824–1907), the famous scientist and inventor, introduced the dynamical theory of heat. Shortly afterwards he interested himself in submarine telegraphy, and invented numerous important improvements, also doing splendid work in the direction of electrical invention; he covered a vast field and earned a world-wide reputation.

Kemble, Frances Anne ("Fanny") (1809–1893), was a noted actress in the early part of the 19th century. She was the daughter of Charles Kemble (1775–1854), who was also a celebrated actor, associated in many appearances with his brother, John Philip Kemble and their talented, sister, Mrs. Siddons (*q.v.*).

Kemble, John Phulip (1757–1823) was a famous tragedian, and for many years manager of Drury Lane Theatre in London. He was brother to Mrs. Siddons (*q.v.*), who first played with—and overshadowed—him in 1783.

Kempenfelt, Admiral Richard (1718–1782), an English naval officer who saw distinguished service, and sank with his ship the *Royal George* off Spithead, through a shifting of the guns when refitting which caused the vessel to capsize. Some six hundred of the ship's company perished with their admiral.

Kempis, Thomas à (1380–1471), name by which the German mystic and writer Thomas Hammerken was known, was a monk of the St. Augustine order, whose life was mainly spent at a monastery near Zwolle. He was the author of *The Imitation of Christ*, a work which has been translated into all languages.

Kennedy, John Fitzgerald (1917–63), President of the United States, 1961–63, the youngest and the first Roman Catholic ever to be elected, son of a wealthy financier. He enjoyed a world-wide personal pre-eminence and gave to the American people a new sense of purpose to meet the changes and challenges of a scientific age. He fought to end racial discrimination and though he had small success in getting his legislation through Congress, he made his mark in foreign affairs, initiating a new era in East-West relations. This youthful, talented, and mature statesman was assassinated during a motorcade drive through Dallas, Texas, on 22 November 1963. *See also* **Section C, Part I.**

Kent, William (1684–1748), a leading figure in British art, 1725 until middle of eighteenth century—architecture, landscape gardening, interior decoration, furniture, and painting. Strong Italianate influence. Surviving works: The Great Hall at Holkham, Norfolk, and lay-out at Rousham, Oxfordshire.

Kenyatta, Jomo (b. 1893), African national leader who became Kenya's first Prime Minister (1962) and first President (1964) when Kenya became a Republic within the British Commonwealth.

Kepler, Johann (1571–1630), renowned German astronomer, assistant to Tycho Brahe (1546–1601), whose measurements he used in working out his laws of planetary motion, which are: 1. The planets describe elliptic orbits, of which the sun is one focus. 2. The line joining a planet to the sun sweeps out equal areas in equal times. 3. The square of the period of revolution of a planet is proportional to the cube of its average distance from the sun. The explanation of these laws was given by Newton.

Keyes, Admiral of the Fleet, Lord, G.C.B., K.C.V.O., C.M.G., D.S.O. (1872–1945). Commodore of the submarine service during war of 1914–18, and commanded operations against Zeebrugge in 1918. Director of Combined Operations, 1940–41.

Keynes, John Maynard, 1st Baron, C.B., M.A., F.B.A. (1883–1946), British economist of international reputation. Bursar and Fellow of King's College, Cambridge. His *Treatise on Money* (1930) and *The General Theory of Employment, Interest and Money* (1936) profoundly influenced economic thought and government policy all over the world. Led the British delegation to Bretton Woods and negotiated the American loan agreement of 1945. Married Lydia Lopokova, formerly of the Russian Imperial Ballet, in 1925.

Khrushchev, Nikita Sergeyevich (b. 1894), Russian statesman who became leader of the Soviet Union soon after the death of Stalin; First Secretary of the Soviet Communist Party, 1953–64; Prime Minister, 1958–64. After the harsh years of the Stalinist régime radical changes became essential and he pursued a policy of relaxation both in home and foreign affairs. Relations with American improved but relations with China became strained. Great advances were made in scientific achievement, notably in the field of space research. In Oct. 1964 his posts were taken over by Leonid Brezhnev (First Secretary) and Alexei Kosygin (Prime Minister). *See also* **Section C, Part I.**

Kierkegaard, Sören (1813–55), Danish philosopher and religious thinker whose views have had great influence on contemporary existentialism. His main work is *Either—Or*.

King, Martin Luther (b. 1929), American clergyman and Negro integration leader; awarded 1964 Nobel Peace Prize for his consistent support of the principle of non-violence in the coloured people's campaign for civil rights.

King, Rt. Hon. (William Lyon) Mackenzie, O.M., C.M.G. (1874–1950), Prime Minister of Canada, 1921–25, 1926–30 and 1935–48.

Kingsley, Charles (1819–1875), English clergyman and novelist, best known for his historical novels *Hypatia*, *Westward Ho!*, *Hereward the Wake* and children's book *The Water Babies*.

Kipling, Rudyard (1865–1936), poet, novelist, and miscellaneous writer. Made himself celebrated while yet a youth by some exceedingly clever and characteristic sketches of Indian life written for the most part while performing journalistic duties in India. He subsequently settled in

London and produced a remarkable succession of stories, sketches, ballads, and poems, all marked by intense vigour. In 1907 was awarded the Nobel Prize.

Kirchhoff, Gustav Robert (1824–87). German physicist. He did important work in electricity and thermodynamics and put spectrum analysis on a firm basis. Published, among other scientific works, *Researches on the Solar Spectrum.*

Kitchener, of Khartoum, Field Marshal Earl, K.G., K.P., G.C.B., O.M. (1850–1916), British soldier. By his victory at Omdurman in 1898 he crushed the Sudanese dervishes and avenged General Gordon. In the early stages of the South African War he assisted Lord Roberts and took over command himself in 1900. C.-in-C. India, 1902–9; Secretary of War, 1914–16. Drowned while on his way to Russia.

Klee, Paul (1879–1940), Swiss artist, studied at Munich, Paris and Rome and later became Professor at Düsseldorf Academy. He lived in a restless, experimental period. His paintings are small-scale, delicate dream-world fantasies, full of poetical content.

Kneller, Sir Godfrey, Bt. (1646–1723), the most celebrated portrait painter of his day in England, who enjoyed the patronage in succession of Charles II., James II., William III., Anne, and George I.

Knox, John (1505–1572), the famous divine and Reformer, who stirred Scotland to mighty religious impulses in the reign of Mary Queen of Scots.

Knox, Edmund George Valpy (" Evoe ") (*b.* 1881), editor of *Punch*, 1932–48.

Knox, Rt. Rev. Mgr. Ronald Arbuthnot (1888–1957), Catholic Chaplain at the University of Oxford,1926–39, and a well-known author. His works include detective stories, among which are *The Viaduct Murder* and *Footsteps at the Lock.*

Koch, Robert (1843–1910), the most noted bacteriologist of the time, whose discoveries in connection with the bacillus of tuberculosis have greatly benefited mankind. He also closely studied the causes of Asiatic cholera and bubonic plague.

Kodály, Zoltán (b. 1882), Hungarian composer and teacher. He worked with Bartok in the collection of folk-tunes and his compositions include chamber music, sonatas, songs, the great choral work *Psalmus Hungaricus*, the orchestral suite *Háry János*, and the symphony in C, written in 1961.

Kokoschka, Oskar (b. 1886), Austrian portrait and landscape painter, ranking as one of the world's great interpretative artists. Taught (1920–24) at the Dresden academy of art, lived for a time in Prague before settling (1938) in England.

Koniev, Marshal of Soviet Union, Ivan Stepanovich (b. 1898), one of Russia's outstanding military leaders in the war against Germany, 1941–45.

Korolyov, Sergei (1907–1966), Russian space scientist who designed the world's first earth satellite, the first manned spaceship and the first moon rocket.

Kosciuzko, Tadeusz Andrzoj Bonawentura (1746–1817), a Polish general and patriot who achieved great distinction in 1794 by his gallant leading of the Polish revolutionary forces against Russia. From 1776 to 1783 took part in the American War of Independence.

Kossuth, Louis (1802–1894), a Hungarian patriot and leader, who in the struggle for his country's freedom in 1849 was for a time successful, but ultimately had to acknowledge defeat, and fled first to Turkey and afterwards to England, where he lived for some years.

Kosygin, Alexei Nikolayevich (b. 1904), succeeded Nikita Khrushchev as chairman of the Council of Ministers of the U.S.S.R. (Prime Minister) in Oct. 1964; formerly a deputy chairman of the State Economic Planning Commission, Gosplan.

Kreisler, Fritz (1875–1962), world-famed Austrian violinist, studied in Paris under Massart. First played in United States in 1888. He composed numerous violin pieces, a quartet, and some operettas. Became an American citizen in 1943.

Křenek, Ernst (b. 1900), Austrian composer of partly Czech descent. He first composed in a neo-classic or anti-romantic style, later the influence of jazz was prominent in his compositions, which include the jazz opera *Jonny spielt auf* and many instrumental works and songs. In 1938 he emigrated to the United States.

Kropotkin, Peter Alexeivich, Prince (1842–1921), anarchist, geographer and explorer, who, after a distinguished career in Russia, his native country, was imprisoned for favouring the political action of a working men's association, but escaped to England. He wrote many important books on socialistic and geographical subjects. Returned to Russia in 1917.

Krüger, Stephanus Johannes Paulus (1825–1904), the Boer leader, was one of the outstanding figures of South Africa in the last half of the nineteenth century. As a small boy he accompanied his family on the Great Trek. He was active in Transvaal politics for many years, and served as President from 1883 to 1900. His attitude towards the Uitlanders (English and other non-Boer white inhabitants of the Transvaal) produced much of the tension which led to the South African War. During the war he made unsuccessful attempts to secure help for the Boers from various European powers.

Krupp, Alfred (1812–1887), the famous German engineer, founded the great gun factories at Essen, which were the largest in the world. By his introduction of the Bessemer plan of casting steel and the steam hammer into Germany, he brought about an important development in heavy breech-loading guns, and built up factories which employed at the time of his death 20,000 workmen.

Kubelik, Jan (1880–1940), Czech violinist—son of a gardener at Michle, near Prague—who at the age of twelve played in public, and was one of the most renowned instrumentalists of his day. His son Rafael (b. 1914), a conductor of international repute, became musical director of the Royal Opera House, Covent Garden, in 1955.

Kublai Khan (1216–1294), a famous Mogul emperor and grandson of Jenghiz Khan. He greatly extended the Mogul empire by conquest, and lived in unparalleled splendour.

L

Lablache, Luigi (1794–1858), a famous bass singer and actor, especially popular in London. He held the position of singing tutor to Queen Victoria.

La Fayette, Marie Joseph Paul Roch Yves Gilbert du Motier, Marquis de (1757–1834), French soldier and humanitarian politician who fought on the side of the Colonists in the American War of Independence and on returning to France became C.-in-C. of the National Guard of Paris. By signing the demand that the king summon the States-General he became the first leader of the French Revolution, but stood out against its later excesses. In 1830 he was instrumental in setting Louis Philippe on the French throne.

La Fontaine, Jean de (1621–1695), the celebrated French poet and fabulist. His fables have been translated into all languages, and are unique.

Lagerlöf, Selma, Ph.D. (1858–1940), the famous Swedish novelist who was awarded in 1909 the Nobel Prize for literature. In 1914 was elected the first woman member of the Swedish Academy.

Lagrange, Joseph Louis, Comte (1736–1813), noted French astronomer and mathematician.

Lalande, Joseph Jerome Lefrançais de (1732–1807), a famous French astronomer and director of the Paris Observatory. He founded the Lalande yearly prize for the best astronomical work or observation and wrote a well-known treatise on astronomy.

Lamarck, Jean Baptiste Pierre Antoine de Monnet, Chevalier de (1744–1829), the prominent French zoologist who occupied important scientific posts in Paris. A precursor of Darwin, his name rests mainly on his theory of the evolution of animals, known as Lamarckism. His chief work was the *Histoire Naturelle des Animaux sans Vertèbres.*

Lamb, Charles (1775–1834), one of the most delightful of our essayists. His *Essays of Elia* are characterised by great felicity of expression, much genial humour and an ardent love both of rural life and London life. He was a clerk in the office of the East India Company for thirty-five years. In some of his writings he was assisted by his sister, Mary Lamb, to whom he was greatly devoted.

Lamb, Sir Horace, F.R.S. (1849–1934), a British scientist, was the leading authority on hydro, dynamics, and did valuable research work on wave motions and electricity.

Lambert, Constant (1905–51), English composer, conductor and critic; musical director of the Sadler's Wells Ballet. His *Rio Grande* for chorus, piano, and orchestra, shows some jazz influence.

Landor, Walter Savage (1775–1864), a writer and poet of strong genius. He wrote a fine poetic tragedy *Count Julian* in 1812, and in later life published several other volumes of poems. The work by which he is best known, however, is his *Imaginary Conversations*.

Landseer, Sir Edwin Henry, R.A. (1802–1873), the most celebrated English animal painter of his time. He designed the lions for the base of the Nelson Monument in Trafalgar Square.

Lane, Edward William (1801–1876), an English writer to whom we owe the most popular translation of the *Arabian Nights*. He was also the author of a number of books dealing with ancient Egyptian and Arabic subjects, and was one of the most prominent Orientalists of the 19th century.

Lanfranc (*c.* 1005–89), Italian churchman, b. at Pavia; Archbishop of Canterbury, 1070. Closely associated with Duke William of Normandy (William I. of England); carried out Church reforms and preserved its independence.

Lang, Andrew (1844–1912), Scottish scholar and writer of great versatility, his numerous works including poetry, fiction, history, fairy tales, folk-lore, and translations from the classics.

Lang of Lambeth, Most Rev. Cosmo Gordon Lang, 1st Baron, P.C., G.C.V.O., D.D. (1864–1945), Archbishop of Canterbury, 1928–42; and of York, 1908–28; Bishop of Stepney, 1901–08.

Langland, William (*c.* 1330–1400), author of the alliterative poem *The Vision of Piers the Plowman*.

Langton, Stephen (1151–1228), was Archbishop of Canterbury from 1213, and one of the chief instruments in forcing the Magna Carta from John.

Lansbury, Rt. Hon. George (1859–1940). British Labour politician; Chairman of Parliamentary Labour Party, 1931–35, Leader of the Labour Party, 1932–35. M.P. Bow and Bromley, 1910–12, and 1922–40.

Lao-Tzŭ, one of the ancient philosophers of China, who flourished about 600 B.C. The classic upon which his fame rests, *Tao-tê-ching*, was written many years later. (*See* Taoism. Section J.)

Laplace, Pierre Simon, Marquis de (1749–1827), French mathematician and astronomer whose researches on the motions of the solar system and the theory of probability earned him the title of "the Newton of France."

La Rochefoucauld, François, Duc de (1613–1680), a renowned French statesman and writer of the Louis XIV. period. His *Reflections and Moral Maxims* is a classic.

Lasker, Emanuel, Ph.D. (1868–1941), world's chess champion, 1894–1921—defeated by Capablanca (*q.v.*).

Lassalle, Ferdinand (1825–64), founder of the German Socialist movement, and as such exerted deep influence throughout Europe. His life story forms the basis of George Meredith's novel *The Tragic Comedians*.

Lasso, Orlando di (*c.* 1532–94), Flemish composer and choirmaster, contemporary of Palestrina, and the writer of over 2,000 compositions, including *chansons*, madrigals, and sacred music.

Laszio de Lombos, Philip Alexius, M.V.O. (1869–1937), the most fashionable portrait painter of modern times. President of Royal Society of British Artists, 1930.

Latimer, Hugh (*circa* 1485–1555), the English Reformer who became Bishop of Worcester under Henry VIII., but when Mary came to the throne was condemned as a heretic and burned at the stake.

Laud, William (1573–1645), an eminent ecclesiastic, who, after filling three minor bishoprics, was made Archbishop of Canterbury in 1633. He did much to direct the policy of Charles I., and when trouble followed, he was impeached by the Long Parliament and committed to the Tower. Was tried for treason and beheaded.

Lauder, Sir Harry (MacLennan) (1870–1950), famous singer of Scottish songs and ballads. Composed own songs and wrote own music. Knighted 1919 for services in raising money for war purposes.

Laval, Pierre (1883–1945), French politician, won notoriety over the Hoare–Laval pact in 1935. During the German occupation he was the arch French collaborator, and was afterwards tried for treason and shot.

Lavery, Sir John, R.A. (1856–1941), an eminent portrait painter; Pres. of the Royal Society of Portrait Painters, 1932–41.

Lavoisier, Antoine Laurent (1743–1794), often called the "father of chemistry," was born in Paris, and was the first to establish the fact that combustion is a form of chemical action.

Law, Rt. Hon. Andrew Bonar (1858–1923), Conservative politician. He became leader of the Opposition in 1911, joined the Coalition in 1915, and served as Prime Minister from 1922 until shortly before his death in 1923.

Lawrence, David Herbert (1885–1930), one of the most powerful and original of modern novelists, and as a poet ranked among the best this century has produced. Author of *The White Peacock*, *Sons and Lovers*, *The Plumed Serpent*, etc.

Lawrence, Sir Thomas, P.R.A. (1769–1830), one of the fashionable portrait painters of his day.

Lawrence, Col. Thomas Edward (1888–1935), known as "Lawrence of Arabia," British soldier, archaeologist and explorer. Organised and led the Arabs against the Turks in the war of 1914–18. Author of *The Seven Pillars of Wisdom* (1926), of which an abbreviated edition, *Revolt in the Desert*, was published in 1927.

Leacock, Stephen Butler (1869–1944), Head of Dept. of Economics, McGill University, Montreal, 1908–36; but best known throughout the world as a humorous writer.

Lecky, Rt. Hon. William Edward Hartpole, O.M. (1838–1903), an eminent historian. His best-known works are *The History of England in the Eighteenth Century* and *The History of European Morals*.

Leclerc (de Hautecloque), General Jacques Philippe, Marshal of France (1902–1947), French soldier of considerable personal popularity. Was Governor of the Cameroons in 1940, declared for the Free French and later led a Free French force from Lake Chad across the Sahara desert to join the Allied Forces in North Africa. Liberated Paris in 1944; commanded French troops in Indo-China, 1946. Killed in air crash in Algeria.

Le Corbusier, pseudonym of Charles-Edouard Jeanneret-Gris (1887–1965), Swiss-born French architect and town-planner whose works and theories with their emphasis on organic planning have profoundly influenced contemporary architecture. Famous for his *ville radieuse* conception of a city and architect of *L'Unité d'Habitation* at Marseilles and of Chandigarh, the new capital of East Punjab.

Lee of Fareham, Viscount, P.C., G.C.B., G.C.S.I., G.B.E. (1868–1947), First Lord of the Admiralty, 1921–22. Minister of Agriculture, 1919–21. Presented Chequers Court to the nation as a residence for British Premiers, 1917.

Lee, Robert Edward (1807–70), was one of the ablest Confederate generals in the American Civil War, and C.-in-C. when the final surrender was made at Appomattox in 1865.

Lee, Sir Sidney (1859–1926), the great authority on Shakespeare, and joint editor with Sir Leslie Stephen of the *Dictionary of National Biography*, exercising undivided control over the completion of that monumental work during the last ten years of its publication.

Leech, John (1817–1864), perhaps the most popular of all the *Punch* artists, whose sketches and cartoons were the life and soul of the paper for many years.

Lehar, Franz (1870–1948), Hungarian composer chiefly of light operas, which include *The Merry Widow*, *The Count of Luxembourg*, *Frederica*, *The Land of Smiles*.

Leibnitz, Gottfried Wilhelm, Freiherr von (1646–1716), German writer and philosopher and one of the world's supreme intellects. Invented the infinitesimal calculus which he published in 1684, independently of Newton whose previous work on the same subject was published in 1687.

Leicester, Robert Dudley, Earl of (1531–88), son of John, Duke of Northumberland (*q.v.*), was a favourite of Queen Elizabeth. He commanded the English troops in the Netherlands, 1585-87, and in England before the Armada. Married to Amy Robsart (*q.v.*).

Leighton, Frederick, Baron, P.R.A. (1830–96), English painter whose popular pictures dealt with classical subjects, characterised by delicacy of finish and splendour of colour. Among his more famous paintings are *Venus Disrobing, Clytemnestra,* and *The Garden of the Hesperides.* He was also a sculptor.

Lely, Sir Peter (1618–80), the famous painter to whom we owe so many of the portraits of the beauties of the Court of Charles II. He was born at Soest and his proper name was Van der Faes.

Lemnitzer, Gen. Lyman L. (b. 1899), American army officer who succeeded Gen. Norstad as Supreme Allied Commander, Europe, in Jan. 1963.

Lenin, Vladimir Ilyich Ulyanov (1870–1924). Russian revolutionary and statesman, architect of the Russian revolution for which cause he worked both "underground" in Russia and abroad during the years 1893–1917. It was in this period that the revolutionary Social-Democratic party was formed. An uncompromising revolutionary group, known as the Bolsheviks, developed within this party and Lenin was its leading spirit. In April 1917 Lenin and his fellow exiles returned to Russia. After the 1917 November revolution Lenin headed the new government and with intense energy consolidated the revolution, applying Marxist principles without dogmatism to the planning of Soviet social and industrial development.

Leonardo da Vinci (1452–1519), Italian painter, sculptor, architect, scientist, engineer, and musician. His creative power as an artist and scientist mark him as a supreme example of Renaissance genius. He went to Milan *c.* 1482 and worked for 16 years in the service of the powerful prince Ludovico Sforza. He was for a time with Cesare Borgia on his campaigns and died in exile as a pensioner of Francis I of France. Among his works are the famous *Last Supper, Mona Lisa, Madonna of the Rocks,* and *St. John the Baptist.*

Leoncavallo, Ruggiero (1858–1919), Italian composer of opera whose *Pagliacci* was his one outstanding success.

Leonidas was king of Sparta at the time of the invasion of Greece by Xerxes, 480 B.C., and led the defence of the Pass of Thermopylæ, where he fell.

Lermontov, Mikhail Yurevich (1814–41), great Russian poet and novelist, exiled to the Caucasus for the passionate, revolutionary poem addressed to Czar Nicholas I. written on the death of Pushkin. He has often been called the poet of the Caucasus, for the stern, mountainous country of his youth and exile had a great influence on his poetry. His novel *A Hero of Our Time* was written while he was at St. Petersburg in 1839. Lost his life in a duel.

Le Sage, Alain René (1668–1747), author of the famous stories *Gil Blas* and *Le Diable Boiteux,* also a dramatist of note.

Lesseps, Vicomte Ferdinand de (1805–94), an engineer of large ideas who, while Vice-Consul at Alexandria, conceived the plan of the Suez Canal, which work was completed in 1869. He afterwards projected the original Panama Canal, which failed.

Lessing, Gotthold Ephraim (1729–81), a noted German critic and dramatic poet, whose most celebrated work was his *Laokoon.*

Leverhulme of the Western Isles, 1st Viscount (1851–1925). Chairman and founder of the soapmaking firm of Lever Brothers, Port Sunlight, which later, by purchase and amalgamation, increased in size and importance to become Unilever Ltd. He was for many years prominent as a business pioneer and man of affairs and one of the most practical exponents of the industrial partnership movement. Presented Lancaster House to the nation, the home of the London Museum.

Leverrier, Urbain Jean Joseph (1811–77), the French astronomer, co-discoverer with John Couch Adams of the planet Neptune.

Lewis, Cecil Day, C.B.E., M.A. (b. 1904), poet and critic. Prof. of Poetry, Oxford Univ., 1951–6. Besides various poetical works has published translations of *The Georgics* and *The Aeneid* of Virgil; also detective novels under pseudonym of Nicholas Blake.

Lewis, Sinclair (1885–1951), an American author who secured his first great success in 1920 with his novel of provincial American life, *Main Street. Babbitt,* published two years later, ruthlessly satirised the 100 per cent. disciple of American *Big Business,* and added a new term, "Babbitry," to the American language. Awarded the Nobel Prize for literature, 1930.

Liaquat Ali Khan (1895–1951), leader of the Moslem League (1946) and first Prime Minister of Pakistan after independence in 1947. Assassinated at Rawalpindi.

Lidgett, Rev. Dr. John Scott, C.H., M.A., D.D. (1854–1953), founder of the Bermondsey Settlement (1891); joint editor of the *Contemporary Review*; leader of Progressive Party on L.C.C., 1918–28; a former President of the National Free Church Council.

Lie, Trygve (b. 1896), Sec.-Gen. of the United Nations 1946–52. Formerly a leading Norwegian politician and Foreign Minister, 1941–46.

Liebermann, Max (1847–1935), German impressionist painter. Among his finest pictures are *The Flax Spinner, The Woman with Goats,* and *The Net-Menders.*

Li Hung Chang (1823–1901), an enlightened Chinese statesman and general, who by sheer ability rose from a humble position to be Chief Minister, and exercised almost supreme control for a number of years.

Lilburne, John (1614–57), an English political agitator and pamphleteer, who became the leader of the Levellers, the democratic party in the English Revolution.

Linacre, Thomas (*c.* 1460–1524), humanist scholar and physician, founder of the College of Physicians. Published translations of Galen's works.

Lincoln, Abraham (1809–65), was a native of Kentucky; in early life he became a lawyer, and was returned to Congress in 1846 from Springfield, Illinois, and in 1861 was elected 16th President of the United States, when he delivered his famous anti-slavery pronouncement, which led to the Civil War of 1861–65. In 1864 he was re-elected, and in the following year was assassinated by John Wilkes Booth.

Lind, Jenny (1820–87), a famous prima donna, "the Swedish nightingale" as she was called, who made a great sensation by her wonderful voice for some seasons in Europe, London and in America, from 1837 onward.

Linnæus, Carl von Linné (1707–78), a tireless Swedish doctor and scientist who became one of the most distinguished of naturalists, and the founder of modern botany. His *Systema Naturae* was published in 1735, and other monumental works followed. First to expound the true principles for defining genera and species.

Lippi, Fra Filippo (1406–69), one of the great artists of the Italian quatrocento, whose frescoes can be seen in Prato Cathedral. His son **Filippino** (1457–1504) was equally gifted and executed many great works, including frescoes in the Carmine, Florence, and the altar-piece *Virgin and Saints* in the Uffizi Gallery.

Lippmann, Gabriel (1845–1921). French physicist, whose more important work was in the field of colour photography. His numerous inventions include the capillary-electrometer, which bears his name, and many other delicate instruments. Awarded the Nobel Prize for Physics, 1908.

Lippmann, Walter (b. 1889), American journalist, whose column in the New York *Herald Tribune* has a wide influence.

Lipton, Sir Thomas Johnstone, Bt., K.C.V.O. (1850–1931), after an adventurous early career in America, started shopkeeping in his native Glasgow, and in course of a few years became the largest shopkeeper in the world. Was renowned for his charities, and his attempts to win the America's Yachting Cup.

Lister, Lord, P.C., O.M., F.R.S. (1827–1912), achieved renown for his discovery of the antiseptic treatment which has accomplished so much on behalf of surgery. Pres. of Royal Socy. 1895–1900; and of British Assn. 1896.

Liszt, Franz (1811–86). Hungarian pianist and composer, whose brilliant playing astonished and delighted Europe and rather overshadowed his importance as a composer. He originated the symphonic poem. His daughter Cosima married Wagner.

Litvinov, Maxim Maximovich (1876–1952), Russian diplomat and statesman; Soviet Diplomatic Agent to Great Britain, 1917, Commissar for Foreign Affairs, 1929–39; Soviet Ambassador to United States, 1941–43.

Livingstone, Dr. David (1813–73), the great Scottish explorer and missionary, whose discoveries in Africa included the course of the Zambesi, the Victoria Falls, and Lake Nyasa. He opened up Central Africa to the influences of Christianity, and stirred the public conscience to the horrors of the Slave Trade. In 1871 considerable apprehension was felt in regard to his fate, but he was discovered by H. M. Stanley at Ujiji near Lake Tanganyika.

Lloyd, Marie (1870–1922), English music-hall artist and genius of Cockney comedy.

Lloyd George of Dwyfor, Earl, O.M. (1863–1945), Chairman of the Liberal Party, 1924–31. Prime Minister, 1916–22. M.P. for Caernarvon, 1890–1944. As a War Premier he displayed activity, resourcefulness, and driving power, which proved a tremendous influence in bringing about the defeat of Germany; and at the Peace Conference, in conjunction with Clemenceau and President Wilson, he was a master spirit. His daughter Lady Megan Lloyd George who was Liberal M.P. for Anglesey from 1929 to 1951 joined the Labour Party in 1955.

Locke, John (1632–1704), one of the great English liberal philosophers and founder of empiricism, the doctrine that all knowledge is derived from experience. His chief work in theoretical philosophy, *Essay Concerning Human Understanding*, was written just before the revolution of 1688 and published in 1690. Other writings include: *Letters on Toleration*, *Treatises on Government*, and *Education*.

Lombroso, Cesare, M.D. (1836–1909), famous Italian criminologist; in 1889 published his monumental work *L'uomo delinquente*, in which he put forward the theory that there was a definite criminal type which could be distinguished from the normal type, both anatomically and psychologically. He did much by his writings to hasten prison reform.

Lomonosov, Mikhail Vasilyevich (1711–65), Russian poet, philosopher, and scientist, associated with the foundation of Moscow University in the reign of the Empress Elizabeth.

London, John Griffith ("Jack") (1876–1916), an American novelist who led an adventurous life and wrote many popular novels and stirring books of adventure.

Longfellow, Henry Wadsworth (1807–82), an American poet who produced a number of volumes of poetry of great purity of thought and beauty of language. Author of *Hiawatha*.

Lonsdale, Dame Kathleen D.B.E., F.R.S. (b. 1903), Professor of Chemistry and head of the Dept. of Crystallography, Univ. College, Univ. of London. Her publications include *X-Rays and Crystals*, and *Removing the Causes of War*.

Lonsdale, 5th Earl of, K.G., G.C.V.O. (1857–1944), was a well-known sportsman whose special interests were horse-racing, hunting and boxing, the Lonsdale belts having been founded by him.

Lope de Vega Carpio, Félix (1562–1635), founder of the Spanish drama, and one of the great figures of Spanish literature. He was one of the most prolific of writers, his dramatic productions alone numbering 1500 plays, of which some 450 survive.

Louis IX. (1214–70), St. Louis, king of France, crusader, and peace-maker, fulfilled the medieval ideal of the knightly king. Memoirs by the Sire de Joinville.

Louis XIV. (1638–1715), ruled France as absolute monarch after Mazarin's death in 1661, having come to the throne at the age of 5. Asserted French supremacy but had to face coalition of European powers (League of Augsburg and the Grand Alliance). The war of the Spanish succession and his own extravagance exhausted France. Revoked Edict of Nantes (1685). The magnificent palace at Versailles is a fitting monument to one who considered himself the most powerful monarch in Christendom.

Louis XV. (1710–74), French king during whose reign France was involved in the war of the Austrian succession, and the Seven Years war which resulted in the loss of Canada, India, and Senegal to England. Among his mistresses were the celebrated Mme de Pompadour and Mme du Barry.

Louis XVI. (1754–93), king of France whose history is the history of the French Revolution. Dominated by his queen, Marie Antoinette, faced with court intrigue, the cost of French intervention in the war of American Independence and the ruin of France's credit, the French Revolution began with the calling of the States-General in 1789. Executed 21 Jan. 1793.

Louis, Joe (b. 1914), American world heavyweight boxing champion, son of a Negro sharecropper. Established a record by successfully defending his title 24 times in the years 1937–48. Retired from the ring in 1949.

Low, Archibald Montgomery, D.Sc. (1888–1956), a distinguished British scientist who had many inventions to his credit connected with wireless, television, coal and petrol engines, anti-aircraft and anti-tank rocket apparatus.

Low, Sir David Alexander Cecil (1891–1963), celebrated political cartoonist who interpreted events for the British reader for over 30 years; invented a number of stock characters, including Colonel Blimp and the T.U.C. carthorse. Born in New Zealand, he came to Britain in 1919 and joined *The Star*. Subsequently his cartoons appeared in the *Evening Standard*, the *Daily Herald*, and the *Guardian*.

Lowell, James Russell (1819–91), an American writer and poet of singular power and humour.

Lowell, Robert (b. 1917), American poet, expert on European poetry, author of the verse play *The Old Glory* and *Life Studies* (1959), an autobiographical volume in verse and prose.

Loyola, St. Ignatius (1491–1556), was the founder of the order of Jesuits.

Lucretius (Titus Lucretius Carus) (99–55 B.C.), great Roman poet of antiquity, whose life-work was the poem *On Nature* (*De rerum natura*).

Ludendorff, General Erich (1865–1937), German soldier; Chief of the General Staff to Hindenburg with whom he shared the military leadership of Germany during the Great War. Largely responsible for the victory of Tannenberg and the successes of 1915.

Lugard, Frederick, Lord (1858–1945), British colonial administrator, a man of abounding energy, initiative, tact and firmness, and possessing considerable military abilities. Helped to build up the British dominions in tropical Africa (Nyasaland, Uganda, Nigeria) and to establish the principles of British African administration, notably the system of "indirect rule" through native rulers.

Luther, Martin (1483–1546), leader of the Protestant Reformation in Germany; entered the order of Austin Friars in 1505, ordained priest in 1507, taught at Wittenburg university and preached in the town church. Until 1517 he was an orthodox Roman Catholic. His first idea of revolt occurred when he saw indulgences being sold, a practice which he openly condemned. For this he was excommunicated, and summoned before the Diet at Worms, where he made a memorable defence. He lived to see the principles of the Reformation widely established. (*See* **Lutheranism, Section J.**)

Luthuli, Albert (b. 1899), ex-Zulu chief, former Pres. of the now banned African National Congress, who has upheld non-violence in face of cruel laws against his people in S. Africa. Nobel Peace Prize, 1960; Rector Glasgow Univ., 1962.

Lutyens, Sir Edwin Landseer, O.M. (1869–1944), English architect; designed and restored many country houses and castles (e.g., Lindisfarne), architect Hampstead garden suburb, 1908. Other works include the Cenotaph in London, city plan and viceroy's house, New Delhi, British Embassy, Washington, Liverpool R.C. cathedral. Pres. Royal Academy 1938–43.

Lyell, Sir Charles (1797–1875), British geologist whose great *Principles of Geology* (1830–33) profoundly influenced 19th-century scientific thought and helped to shape Darwin's ideas. Lyell was responsible for the division of the Tertiary period into Pliocene (*Greek* = more recent), Miocene (less recent) and Eocene (dawn of recent).

Lysenko, Trofim (b. 1898), Russian biologist whose concept of genetics, that environmental experiences can change heredity, though discredited in scientific circles outside the U.S.S.R., was accepted there as dogma until 1953.

Lytton, Edward George Earle Bulwer, 1st Baron, P.C., G.C.M.G. (1803–73), a prolific novelist and dramatist, whose romantic stories included *The Last Days of Pompeii.*

Lytton, Sir Henry Alfred (1867–1936), was a noted British actor who scored many successes, chiefly playing Gilbert and Sullivan roles.

M

Macadam, John Loudon (1756–1836), Scottish engineer who invented the process of road-repairing which bears his name.

MacArthur, General Douglas, Hon. G.C.B., D.S.C., D.C.M. (1880–1964), American soldier famous for his gallant defence of the Philippines against the Japanese, 1941–42. Relieved of his commands in the Far East during the Korean campaign by President Truman in April 1951.

Macaulay, Rose, D.B.E. (1881–1958), an English authoress and literary critic. Among her literary successes are *Potterism, Dangerous Ages, Told by an Idiot, Orphan Island* and other novels noted for their keen satirical wit.

Macaulay, Thomas Babington, Lord (1800–59), the most brilliant historian of the Victorian era. His fame was assured by his *Essays* and *Lays of Ancient Rome,* and his *History* did more than confirm it. He was a son of Zachary Macaulay (1768–1838), the anti-slavery agitator, and sat in Parliament as member for Calne for some years, also serving for five years as a member of the Supreme Council of Calcutta. On his homecoming, he again entered Parliament as member for Edinburgh, and gained a new celebrity by his speeches. He at different times filled the offices of Paymaster-General and Secretary for War. Both Lord Macaulay and his father lie buried in Westminster Abbey.

Macbeth, according to Holinshed's *Chronicle,* was the usurping Scottish king who succeeded Duncan, whom he murdered. Macbeth was slain by Duncan's son Malcolm in 1056, after a reign of seventeen years. His history forms the subject of Shakespeare's celebrated tragedy.

MacCarthy, Sir Desmond, F.R.S.I., Hon. D.Litt., Hon. LL.D. (1877–1952), journalist and critic who became dramatic critic to *The Speaker,* 1904, and *The New Statesman,* 1913, where he soon made a reputation both for the substance and style of his writings. He edited *The New Quarterly,* 1907–10 and later *Life and Letters.* Latterly was literary critic to *The Sunday Times.*

MacCarthy, Justin (1830–1912), Irish politician, novelist, and historian, from 1879 to 1896 was a prominent member of the Irish Party in Parliament, succeeding Mr. Parnell in 1890 in the leadership of the party.

McCormack, (Count) John (1884–1945), was the world famous Irish tenor who became a naturalised American citizen in 1919; received a Papal peerage as Count from Pius XI in 1928.

Macdonald, Flora (1722–90), Scottish Jacobite heroine who saved the life of Prince Charles Edward after the defeat at Culloden Moor in 1746.

Macdonald, Sir John Alexander (1815–91), Canadian statesman of great vigour and imagination who became the first Prime Minister of the Dominion of Canada.

MacDonald, Rt. Hon. James Ramsay (1866–1937), Prime Minister in the first two Labour Governments, 1924, 1929–31, and in a Coalition Government dominated by Conservatives, 1931–35. His son, **Malcolm** (b. 1901), has held a number of diplomatic posts and in 1965 was appointed Special Representative of the British Government in Kenya, Tanzania, Malawi, and Zambia.

McDougall, William, F.R.S. (1871–1938), British psychologist. Professor of Psychology at Harvard University 1920–27, and Duke University, North Carolina 1927–38. His *Introduction to Social Psychology* (1908) achieved international reputation.

Machiavelli, Niccolo (1469–1527), Florentine diplomat, the first social scientist and theorist of the modern state, whose famous book *The Prince,* written in 1513, is concerned with the reality of politics. He believed that the end justifies the means.

Mackail, Prof. John William, O.M. (1859–1945), British classical scholar, Prof. of Poetry at Oxford, 1906–11, and translator of the *Odyssey.*

McKell, Sir William John, G.C.M.G., K.C. (b. 1891), Gov.-Gen. of Australia 1947–52.

Mackenzie, Sir (Edward Montague) Compton, O.B.E. (b. 1883), British novelist; literary critic to the *Daily Mail,* 1931–35; Rector of Glasgow Univ., 1931–34.

Macmillan, Rt. Hon. Harold, M.C. (b. 1894), British statesman; Prime Min., 1957–63. First entered Parliament in 1924 as Conservative M.P. for Stockton-on-Tees. He represented Bromley, Kent, from 1945 until his retirement in 1964 and served as Minister of Housing and Local Government, Min. of Defence, Foreign Sec., Chancellor of the Exchequer. He is a member of the well-known publishing family. Chanc. Oxford University, 1960. *See also* **Section C, Part I.**

McMillan, Margaret, C.H., C.B.E. (d. 1931), Scotswoman, born in America, who with her sister Rachel was a pioneer of child welfare work. Founder of open-air nursery schools. The Rachel McMillan nursery school at Deptford is a memorial to her work.

McNaughton, Gen. Hon. Andrew George Latta, C.H., D.S.O. (b. 1887), Canadian soldier, politician, electrical engineer, and representative on the U.N. Atomic Energy Commission.

Macneice, Louis (1907–63), English poet, B.B.C. script writer, and producer and director of many radio plays.

Macready, William Charles (1793–1873), English actor and manager who established himself as a tragedian of the first rank.

Maeterlinck, Count Maurice (1862–1949), Belgian man of letters whose plays include *La Princesse Maleine, Pelléas et Mélisande,* and *L'Oiseau Bleu.* Well known for his work on bees and ants.

Magellan, Ferdinand (*c.* 1480–1521), a famous Portuguese navigator, and commander of the first expedition (1519) to sail round the world.

Mahler, Gustav (1860–1911), Austrian composer and conductor; a writer of symphonies and songs, a classical romantic, much influenced by Anton Bruckner and Wagner. He completed nine symphonies (some with voices), and examples of his work in song-cycle form are *Das klagende Lied, Kindertotenlieder,* and *Das Lied von der Erde* (for solo voices and orchestra).

Maintenon, Françoise d'Aubigné, Marquise de (1635–1719), after being the wife of the poet Scarron, drifted into Court circles, and so fascinated Louis XIV. that he ultimately married her. At his death she retired to a convent.

Makarios III, Archbishop (b. 1913), Cypriot ecclesiastic and national leader. Deported by British to Seychelles, 1956–57. Pres. of Rep. of Cyprus since independence, Aug. 16, 1960.

Malibran, Marie Félivité (1808–36), was one of the most famous operatic singers of her time.

Malik, Yakov Alexandrovich (b. 1906), Soviet diplomat who has been Deputy Min. of Foreign Affairs, Permanent Rep. of U.S.S.R. to U.N., 1948–52, and Soviet Ambassador to Great Britain, 1953–60.

Malory, Sir Thomas (*c.* 1430–70), compiled the *Morte d'Arthur,* which was printed by Caxton in 1485, and relates the story of King Arthur and the Knights of the Round Table.

Malraux, André (b. 1895), French novelist whose works include *La Condition humaine* (*Man's Fate*), *L'Espoir* (*Man's Hope*), and *Psychologie de l'art* (translated into 2 vols., *Museum without Walls* and *The Creative Act*).

Malthus, Thomas Robert, F.R.S. (1766–1834), an English clergyman and economist who in his essay *The Principle of Population* contended that population growth could only be checked by war and disease and by moral restraint.

Malvern, 1st Viscount, Godfrey Martin Huggins, C.H., K.C.M.G., F.R.C.S. (b. 1893), Prime Min. of S. Rhodesia, 1933–53 and of the Federation of Rhodesia and Nyasaland, 1953–56.

Manet, Edouard (1832–83), French Impressionist painter, whose pictures *Olympia* and *Lola de Valence* have been acclaimed masterpieces.

Mann, Thomas (1875–1955), German writer who won immediate world recognition at the age of 25 with his novel *Buddenbrooks.* His liberal humanistic outlook had developed sufficiently by 1930 for him unerringly to expose the nature of National Socialism. He left Germany in 1933 to live in Switzerland and then settled in the United States. Awarded the Nobel Prize for Literature in 1929; E. and W. Germany combined to honour him with the Goethe Prize in 1948. His best-known works, apart from many volumes of essays, stories, and shorter novels, are *The Magic Mountain* (1924), the *Joseph* tetralogy (1935–43), *Dr. Faustus* (1947) and *Felix Krull* (1954).

Mann, Tom (1856–1941), was a prominent British Labour leader for more than 50 years.

Manning, Henry Edward, Cardinal (1808–92), Cardinal Archbishop of Westminster 1875–92, was a prominent Anglican Churchman up to 1851, when he joined the Church of Rome.

Mansfield, Katherine (1890–1923), short-story writer, born in Wellington, New Zealand, whose work was strongly influenced by the short stories of Chekov. Her second husband was John Middleton Murry, author and literary critic.

Manson, Sir Patrick, G.C.M.G., M.D., F.R.S. (1844–1922), an eminent physician who specialised in parasitology and became physician and medical adviser to the Colonial Office. He was the first to formulate the hypothesis that the malarial parasite was transmitted by the mosquito. The joint work of Sir Patrick Manson and Sir Ronald Ross rendered habitable vast areas of the earth hitherto closed.

Manuzio, Aldo Pio (1450?–1515), Italian printer, founder of the Aldine press in Venice, which for just over a century issued books famed for their beautiful type and bindings.

Manzoni, Alessandro Franceso Tomaso Antonio (1785–1873), Italian writer, whose romantic novel *I Promessi Sposi* ("The Betrothed") is generally regarded as the most important work in Italian literature after "The Divine Comedy."

Mao Tse-tung (b. 1893), great leader of the Chinese people. Chairman of the Central Committee of the Chinese Communist Party since 1936 and Chairman (equivalent to President) of the People's Republic of China from 1949 (when it was first established following the military defeat of the Nationalist forces) until the end of 1958 when the duties of President were relinquished. *See also* **Section C, Part I.**

Marat, Jean Paul (1743–93), one of the leading actors in the French Reign of Terror. Killed by Charlotte Corday.

Marconi, Guglielmo Marchese (1874–1937), Italian electrical engineer celebrated for his development of wireless telegraphy. With a home-made apparatus he sent long-wave signals over a distance of 1 mile in 1895. He came to England in 1896 and established the Marconi Company in 1897. Succeeded on Dec. 12, 1901 in transmitting and receiving transatlantic signals. Awarded Nobel Prize for Physics, 1909.

Marco Polo. (*See* **Polo, Marco.**)

Marcus Aurelius Antoninus (121–180), the greatest of Roman emperors and a disciple of the stoics.

Maria Theresa (1717–80), Archduchess of Austria, Queen of Bohemia and Hungary; a woman of remarkable strength of character and ability, succeeded her father Charles VI., as monarch of the Hapsburg dominions. She was an enlightened ruler and has been called a "benevolent despot."

Marie Antoinette Josephe Jeanne (1755–93) was daughter of the Empress Maria Theresa and the Emperor Francis I. of Austria, and became wife of Louis XVI. of France. She entered with spirit into the gaiety of French Court life, and drew down upon herself much popular hatred in consequence. In the terrible events which followed the outbreak of the Revolution she was one of the chief sufferers, but bore her fate with dignity and resignation, and met her death on the scaffold with unflinching courage.

Marie Louise (1791–1847), daughter of Francis I. of Austria, became wife of Napoleon in 1810, and bore him a son. (*See* **Napoleon II.**)

Marius, Caius (*c.* 155–86 B.C.), the famous Roman general of humble birth who became tribune (119 B.C.), praetor (115 B.C.), propraetor in Spain (114 B.C.) and was seven times consul. Married an aunt of Julius Caesar.

Mark Antony. (*See* **Antonius, Marcus.**)

Marlborough, John Churchill, 1st Duke of (1650–1722), brilliant soldier, the victor of Blenheim, Ramillies, Oudenarde, and Malplaquet. Married to Queen Anne's favourite, Sarah Jennings.

Marlowe, Christopher (1564–93), one of the greatest of the Elizabethan dramatists. His principal plays are *Dr. Faustus, Tamburlaine the Great, Edward II.*, and *The Jew of Malta.* He was killed in a tavern brawl at Deptford.

Marryat, Captain Frederick (1792–1848), an exceedingly popular writer of sea stories. Author of *Peter Simple, The King's Own, Jacob Faithful*, and *The Children of the New Forest.*

Marshall, General George Catlett (1880–1959), American soldier and statesman; Chief of Staff of U.S. Army, 1939–45. Initiated the American offer of aid to Europe, which led to the European Recovery Programme. Awarded Nobel Peace Prize, 1953.

Martial (Marcus Valerius Martialis) (A.D. *c.* 40–A.D. *c.* 104) was born at Bilbilis in Spain, but spent the greater part of his life in Rome, where he acquired much fame as a poet and epigrammatist.

Marvell, Andrew (1620–78), English poet, satirist and diplomatist, friend of Milton, who was best known for his many prose satires and lampoons.

Marx, Heinrich Karl (1818–83), German philosopher and socialist and lifelong partner and friend of Engels with whom he collaborated in writing many important works on socialism and in developing his theories of dialectical materialism. After being expelled from the continent he settled in London where he wrote his monumental work *Das Kapital.* Communism is based on the teachings of Marx. *See* **Marxism, J27,** *also* **Q14(2).**

Mary I. (1516–58), daughter of Henry VIII. and Catherine of Aragon. Was Queen of England from 1553 to her death. She was a strenuous Roman Catholic, and entirely reversed the religious order of things during her brief reign, persecuting, imprisoning, and burning at the stake many of the Protestant reformers, nearly three hundred persons being put to death as heretics. She married Philip of Spain in 1554.

Mary II, (1662–94), daughter of James II; came to the English throne in 1689, having married her cousin, William of Orange, in 1677. After assenting to the "Declaration of Rights," they reigned jointly until her death.

Mary, H.M. Queen, K.G., K.T., G.C.V.O. (1867–1953), Queen Consort of George V.

Mary, Queen of Scots (1542–87), daughter of James V. of Scotland, married to the Dauphin of France at sixteen years of age. On the death of her husband in 1560 she returned to Scotland, and for a time was the acknowledged Queen of the Scots. In 1565 she married Lord Darnley, who a year later was murdered and Mary married Bothwell. The Scottish nobles rebelled against Mary, and she was made prisoner and confined in Loch Leven Castle, compelled to abandon Bothwell and to sign an Act of Abdication in favour of her son. She escaped to England, sought the protection of Elizabeth, and was imprisoned for nineteen years in various castles, and ultimately beheaded on a charge of conspiracy. She was buried in Peterborough Cathedral but after her son James I. of England ascended the throne her remains were removed to Westminster Abbey.

Masaryk, Jan Garrigue (1886–1948), son of Thomas Masaryk. Served as Czech Minister in London, 1925–38 and as Foreign Secretary, 1940–48.

Masaryk, Thomas Garrigue (1850–1937), Czech philosopher and statesman, one of the greatest fighters for a democratic society; founder and first President of Czechoslovakia, 1918–35.

Mascagni, Pietro (1863–1945), Italian composer, whose brilliant one-act opera *Cavalleria Rusticana* produced in 1890 brought him sudden celebrity. None of his later operas was as successful.

Masefield, John Edward, O.M., C.L. (b. 1878), English poet laureate (since 1930), playwright, and novelist. Most popular among his poems are the *Salt-Water Ballads, Reynard the Fox*, and *Right Royal.*

Maskelyne, John Nevil (1839–1917), famous illusionist who exposed the mysteries of the Davenport spiritualistic quacks.

Mason, Alfred Edward Woodley (1865–1948), an English novelist, author of many popular stories of adventure including *The Four Feathers* and *Fire Over England*.

Massenet, Jules Emile Frédéric (1842–1912), French composer whose melodious compositions include songs, orchestral suites, oratorios, and 23 operas, among them *Manon* and *Thaïs*.

Massine, Léonide (b. 1896), a famous Russian dancer who was for some years Ballet Master at the Roxy Theatre, New York. Among his more famous ballets are *The Good Humoured Ladies*, *Boutique Fantasque*, *Pas d'Acier*, *Les Matelots*, *Le Beau Danube* and *Les Présages*.

Masters, Edgar Lee (1869–1950), American poet who occupies a permanent place in American literature by the publication in 1915 of his *Silver Spoon Anthology*, a hundred poems relating the real character as opposed to the eulogistic inscriptions on their tombstones of the dead in a typical American township.

Matisse, Henri (1869–1954), French painter, the foremost member of a group known as *les Fauves*. His work is remarkable for its use of pure and brilliant colour and its reliance on colour variations to express form and relief.

Matsys or **Metzys, Quintin** (1466–1530), a distinguished Flemish painter, who was originally a blacksmith. He excelled in Scriptural subjects.

Maugham, (William) Somerset, C.H., C.L. (1874–1965), British novelist, playwright, and short-story writer. Born in Paris, he qualified as a doctor, but soon abandoned medicine for literature, achieving a great success with his first novel in 1897, *Liza of Lambeth*, a study of slum life. He travelled widely which gave him a deep insight into human nature. As a playwright he has been equally successful. His last work *Points of View* was published in 1958.

Maupassant, Henri René Albert Guy de (1850–93), the famous French author and writer of short stories, was a friend of Flaubert, Zola, and Daudet. He was the greatest of all European short-story writers, standing alone in grace, wit and epigram.

Mauriac, François (b. 1885), French novelist whose works are regarded as among the chief literary productions of to-day. In addition to a long series of novels he has written many critical works and essays. Leader-writer for *Figaro*; Nobel Prizewinner, 1952.

Maurois, André, K.B.E. (b. 1885), French biographer, novelist and essayist who has written lives of Shelley, Disraeli, Byron, Voltaire, Fleming, and Dickens.

Maxim, Sir Hiram Stevens (1840–1916), the inventor of the famous automatic quick-firing gun.

Maxton, James (1885–1946), was a prominent Socialist politician; M.P. for the Bridgeton Divn. of Glasgow, 1926–46. Chairman of I.L.P. 1926–31 and 1934–39.

Maxwell, James Clerk (1831–79), Scottish physicist who wrote his first scientific paper at the age of 15. Was Professor of Natural Philosophy at Aberdeen, 1856, and for eight years held the same post at King's College, London, 1860–68. In 1871 he became the first holder of the new Professorship of Experimental Physics at Cambridge University. His best-known work is his treatise on electricity and magnetism, published in 1873. He made the discovery that founded the electro-magnetic theory of light, and to his electrical researches the advent of wireless is due.

Mazarin, Jules (1602–61), an Italian Cardinal who became chief Minister of State under Louis XIV., and was for a number of years the practical ruler of France. He succeeded Richelieu.

Mazeppa-Koledinsky, Ivan Stepanovich (1644–1709), the hero of Byron's poem, was a real personage, and a Pole, and was tied naked on the back of a wild horse, and so sent out across the Russian desert, for an intrigue with a noble's wife. He was liberated by Cossacks and afterwards attained an honourable position.

Mazzini, Giuseppe (1805–72), an Italian patriot, who, in his endeavours to secure the independence of Italy, incurred the disfavour of the authorities, and was compelled to leave the country. He started a newspaper called *Young Italy* at Marseilles, and in 1837 came to London, and kept up his attacks upon existing governments. In 1848 he was back in Rome and was elected dictator of the Roman Republic. He was not allowed to hold this position long, however, for the French occupied Rome and Mazzini was driven to England again. The unification of Italy was accomplished in other ways than those advocated by Mazzini, but he lived to see Victor Emmanuel King of United Italy.

Medici, the famous Florentine family who combined the career of merchants and bankers with the exercise of political power and patronage of the arts. Cosimo the Elder (1389–1464) was for over thirty years the virtual ruler of Florence. He was wealthy, cultivated, liberal, and a consummate statesman. His illustrious grandson, Lorenzo the Magnificent (1449–92), poet, friend of artists and scholars, governed the state in great munificence. His grandson, Lorenzo, was the father of Catherine de' Medici, Queen of France (*q.v.*). Then the family had some reverses until Cosimo (1519–74), one of the most able rulers of the 16th cent., became Duke of Florence and then Grand-Duke of Tuscany, which title the Medicis held until 1737.

Mehul, Etienne Nicolas (1763–1817), French operatic composer, *Joseph* being considered his masterpiece. In his early years much influenced by Gluck.

Melanchthon, Philip (1497–1560), German scholar and humanist who assisted Luther and wrote *Loci communes*, the first great Protestant work on the principles of the Reformation.

Melba, Dame Nellie, G.B.E. (1861–1931), the celebrated Australian soprano, b. in Richmond (Victoria), who made her operatic début in Brussels in 1887.

Melbourne, 2nd Viscount (1779–1848), Queen Victoria's first premier, holding office over six years, and identified with many important Liberal measures.

Mendel, Gregor Johann (1822–84), Austrian botanist. After joining the Augustinian order, he moved to the monastery at Brünn where he afterwards became Abbot and taught natural history in the school there. His main interest, however, was the study of inheritance, and his elaborate observations of the common garden pea resulted in the famous law of heredity which to-day bears his name. His hypothesis was published in 1866 but no attention was given to it until 1900. *See* **Section F, Part II.**

Mendeleyev, Dmitry Ivanovich (1834–1907), Russian chemist who made important contributions to physical chemistry and general chemical theory. First to discover the critical temperatures and formulated the Periodic Law of atomic weights. Element 101 is named after him.

Mendelssohn-Bartholdy, (Jacob Ludwig) Felix (1809–47), German composer, grandson of Moses Mendelssohn, the philosopher. He belongs with Chopin and Schumann to the early 19th century classic-romantic school, and his music has a delightful delicacy and melodic beauty. He was conductor of the famous Gewandhaus concerts at Leipzig for a time and often visited England. Frequently performed are his overtures *A Midsummer Night's Dream* and *The Hebrides* (or *Fingal's Cave*), written in his youth, two oratorios *St. Paul* and *Elijah*, the violin concerto in E minor, the piano works *Variations Sérieuses* and *Songs without Words*, and the *Scotch* and *Italian* symphonies. The name Bartholdy was added to the surname when his father abandoned Jewry.

Mendès-France, Pierre, LL.D. (b. 1907), French statesman. His skilful diplomacy and energy helped to solve the many problems that faced his country when he took office as Prime Minister in June 1954. His government was overthrown on his Algerian policy in Feb. 1955. Leader of the Radical Party minority which did not support the de Gaulle constitution. Defeated in General Election Nov. 1958.

Menuhin, Yehudi (b. 1916), violin virtuoso, one of the greatest musical prodigies of the 20th century. Born in New York of Jewish parentage; made his first London appearance in the San Francisco Orchestra, 1929.

Menzies, Rt. Hon. Sir Robert Gordon, K.T., C.H., Q.C. (b. 1894), Australian Liberal leader; Prime Minister, 1939–41, 1949–66.

Mercator, Gerhardus (1512–94), the Flemish geographer who invented a celestial and a terrestrial globe, by which he introduced his famous projection, in which meridians and parallels of latitude cross each other at right angles, both being indicated by straight lines. This greatly simplified navigation.

Meredith, George, O.M. (1828–1909), novelist and poet, " the Grand old Man of English letters." His works are rich in imagery, poetry, wit, and characterisation, and as a delineator of womanhood he is unsurpassed. Among his great novels are *Ordeal of Richard Feverel, Evan Harrington, Rhoda Fleming, The Egoist, Diana of the Crossways,* and *The Amazing Marriage.*

Mesmer, Friedrich Anton (1733–1815), was a German doctor who founded the system of mesmerism or animal magnetism.

Mestrovic, Ivan (1883–1962), a Dalmatian sculptor, recognised as one of the leading European sculptors of his day. The Tate Gallery and the Victoria and Albert Museum have examples of his work.

Metastasio, Pietro (1698–1782), the celebrated Italian librettist who provided texts for such composers as Gluck, Handel, Haydn, and Mozart. He lived in Vienna as court poet and his real name was Pietro Bonaventura Trapassi.

Metchnikov, Ilya (1845–1916), an eminent Russian biologist; Nobel Prize for Medicine, 1908.

Meyerbeer, Giacomo (1791–1864), was born in Germany, but spent most of his life in Paris, where he produced all his great operas, which include *Robert le Diable, Les Huguenots,* and *L'Africaine.*

Meynell, Alice (1849–1922), English poet and essayist, wife of **Wilfred Meynell** (1852–1948), editor of the Catholic paper *Merry England.*

Michelangelo (Michelagniolo Buonarroti) (1475–1564), the renowned Italian painter, sculptor, architect and poet, whose genius was such a power in beautifying the churches of Rome and Florence. Was the last and in some respects the greatest of the Italian sculptors; while his large paintings, particularly *The Last Judgment,* in the Sistine Chapel, are no less famous.

Michelet, Jules (1798–1874), a noted French historian and author.

Michelson, Albert Abraham (1852–1931), American physicist, born in Poland. Designer of an interferometer for estimating the diameters of stars. Collaborated with E. W. Morley in the *Michelson-Morley* experiment to measure the velocity of the earth through the " ether " which led to the conclusion that the ether is non-existent and had great value for Einstein's theory of relativity. Was the first American scientist to win the Nobel prize for Physics, 1907, in which year he was also awarded the Copley Medal.

Mickiewicz, Adam (1798–1855), greatest Polish poet and revolutionary. Chief works *The Ancestors, Pan Tadeusz.*

Mill, John Stuart (1806–73), achieved high reputation by his numerous works on philosophical questions. He was an ardent liberal and leader of the utilitarian school of philosophy. Radical M.P. for Westminster, 1865–68, died in Avignon. His chief works are *Principles of Political Economy, System of Logic, On Liberty.*

Millais, Sir John Everett, Bt., P.R.A. (1829–96), was at one time the most prominent of the English Pre-Raphaelites, but soon cast himself free from their mannerisms, and began the production of a long series of famous pictures. Among his numerous works we have room to mention only *The Eve of St. Agnes, Autumn Leaves, The Order of Release, Effie Deans, Chill October,* and *Bubbles.*

Millet, Jean François (1814–75), one of the greatest of French painters of pastoral subjects; his celebrated work *The Angelus* is universally known by its numerous reproductions.

Millikan, Robert Andrews (1868–1953), American physicist who is world famous for his researches on electrons, and for discovering the cosmic rays. Professor of Physics at Chicago University 1910–21, and Director of the Norman Bridge Laboratory of Physics at Pasadena, California 1921–45. Awarded Nobel Prize for Physics, 1923.

Milne, Alan Alexander (b. 1882), English humorist, poet, and playwright who has written much delightful verse and stories for children.

Milner, Alfred, Viscount (1854–1925), imperial statesman, who served in South Africa from 1897 to 1905 and had great influence on the history of that country. Was Secretary for War in 1918 and for the Colonies, 1919–21.

Miltiades (d. 489 B.C.), one of the leaders of the Athenian army against the Persians at Marathon.

Milton, John (1608–74), England's greatest epic poet, whose *Paradise Lost* is the greatest poem of the kind in the language. The best known of his other poems are probably the *Ode on the Morning of Christ's Nativity, L'Allegro, Il Penseroso, Lycidas,* and the sonnet *On his Blindness.* In 1652 he became totally blind, and at his death was buried in St. Giles's Church, Cripplegate, London, a monument being erected to his memory in Westminster Abbey.

Minot, George Richards, M.D. (1885–1950), an eminent American doctor who became Prof. of Medicine at Harvard in 1928, and famous for his researches in the pathology of the blood, and for his discovery of the curative properties of liver in pernicious anæmia. Shared the Nobel Prize for Medicine, 1934.

Mirabeau, Gabriel, Comte de (1749–91), one of the prominent figures of the French Revolution, and a famous orator.

Mistral, Frédéric (1830–1914), French poet who spent his whole life in Provence and wrote many works of great lyrical beauty, founded the Félibrige society (*q.v.* Gen. Inf.); completed *Lou Trésor dóu Félibrige* in 1886, a Provençal dictionary and encyclopædia of Provence. Nobel Literary Prize, 1904.

Mithridates (*circa* 132–63 B.C.), was King of Pontus from 120–63 B.C., and showed great capacity as a commander conquering a great part of Asia Minor and Greece.

Modigliani, Amedeo (1884–1920), Italian painter, b. Livorno, whose portraits and figure studies show a highly individual style. He spent most of his short life in Paris which was one of poverty, illness, and disillusionment.

Moffat, James (1870–1944), Scottish divine who translated the Bible into modern English.

Mohammed (570–632), the founder of Islam, the religion of the Moslems, fled from Mecca to Medina in 622, from which date the Mohammedan era opens. By his constant preaching and proclaiming of the one and only Deity Allah he gathered round him a small and loyal, hard, fighting band of followers and was able to return to Mecca eight years later, an acknowledged conqueror. The Sacred Book of Islam, the *Koran*—though presented by him as an original revelation from the Angel Gabriel—may in the main be traced to Biblical and Rabbinical sources. (*See* **Islam, Section J.**)

Moiseiwitsch, Benno, C.B.E. (1890–1963), Russian-born, naturalised British pianist, especially well known for his rendering of the works of the Romantics.

Molière (Jean Baptiste Poquelin) (1622–73), the greatest of French comic dramatists, who, from being a poor strolling player, became the leading dramatist of his time. His greatest comedies were *Le Tartufe, Le Misanthrope, Le Malade imaginaire* and *Le Médecin malgré lui.*

Molotov, Vyacheslav Mikhailovitch (Skryabin) (b. 1890), Russian diplomat; succeeded Litvinov as Commissar for Foreign Affairs, 1939–49. Chief representative of the Soviet Union at numerous post-war conferences. Expelled from Communist Party, 1964.

Moltke, Field-Marshal Count Helmuth von (1800–91), was responsible for the Prussian strategy in the Danish, Austrian, and Franco-Prussian wars, in all of which he was outstandingly successful.

Mond, Ludwig, Ph.D., F.R.S. (1839–1909), German chemist who in 1867 settled in England as an alkali manufacturer and in partnership with John Brunner successfully manufactured soda by the Solvay process.

Monet, Claude (1840–1926), the most representative of the French Impressionists. Exhibited in 1874 his landscape *Impression Soleil levant,* from which the word *Impressionism* was derived.

Monier-Williams, Sir Monier, K.C.I.E., LL.D., Ph.D. (1819–99), a great Sanskrit scholar who laboured with distinction in bringing westward the wisdom of the Orient.

Monk, George, 1st Duke of Albemarle (1608–69), served with distinction as general and admiral, particularly in the Anglo-Dutch wars, and in 1660 effected the Restoration of Charles II.

Monroe, James (1758–1831), Fifth President of the U.S. Was appointed Governor of Virginia in 1799, and in 1803 went to France and carried through the purchase of Louisiana. Best known as the author of the Monroe Doctrine, which he outlined in his Presidential message of 1823.

Montagu, Lady Mary Wortley (1689–1762), the greatest of English woman letter writers. The first of two volumes of her *Complete Letters* was published in 1966. *See also* **P16**(1).

Montaigne, Michel de (1533–92), a French essayist of world-wide celebrity, who may be regarded as the inventor of the essay form, and had a great influence on English writers.

Montcalm, General Louis Joseph, Marquis de (1712–59), commander of French Army against British in Canada in final struggle for possession. Defeated by Wolfe in 1759 and mortally wounded.

Montesquieu, Charles Louis de Secondat, Baron de La Brède et de (1689–1755), French philosopher and author. His works include *Les Lettres Persanes*, a witty satire on contemporary life, and his great work *L'Esprit des Lois*, setting out his ideas on politics and law. Showed a genius for generalisation and gave to history a philosophy. Greatly admired England and her constitution, which he misunderstood, and his influence on the authors of the American constitution consequently led to the impractical separation of the executive (the President) from the law-making power (Congress).

Montessori, Maria (1869–1952), educationist, whose methods for infant teaching have wide recognition. *See* **J14**(2).

Monteverdi, Claudio (1567–1643), an Italian composer of importance by reason of his pioneer work in the operatic form. His most important dramatic work was *Orfeo* (1608).

Montezuma II. (1466–1520) was Emperor of Mexico when Cortes invaded that country, and the last Aztec ruler of Mexico.

Montfort, Simon de, Earl of Leicester (1206–65), was a powerful baron, with liberal views, and a hatred of kingly tyranny. It was his bold action that forced Henry III., his brother-in-law, to grant the first English Parliament. He met his death at the Battle of Evesham.

Montgolfier, Joseph Michel (1740–1810) and **Jacques Etienne** (1745–1799), two French brothers who invented the first practical balloon.

Montgomery, Field-Marshal Viscount, K.G., G.C.B., D.S.O. (b. 1887), rose to military fame as Commander of the 8th Army in the North African and Italian campaigns, 1942–44. C.-in-C. British Forces in France and Germany, 1944–46; C.I.G.S., 1946–48. Permanent Military Chairman of the Western Union Defence Committee, 1948–51; Deputy Supreme Allied Commander Europe (NATO), 1951–58. Retired 1958. His *Memoirs* were published in 1958.

Montrose, James Graham, Marquess of (1612–50), brave and inspiring Scottish general who raised the Highland clansmen for Charles I. and again for Charles II. His lyric poetry included *My dear and only love*.

Moody, Dwight Lyman (1837–99), the American revivalist preacher, associated for many years in mission work on both sides of the Atlantic with Ira D. Sankey, the "American Singing Pilgrim."

Moore, George (1852–1933), a well-known Irish novelist; author of *Confessions of a Young Man*, *Esther Waters*, *Evelyn Innes*, etc.

Moore, Henry, O.M., C.H. (b. 1898), English sculptor, examples of whose work are to be seen in the Tate Gallery, the V. and A. Museum, and St. Matthew's Church, Northampton.

Moore, Sir John (1761–1809), British general, who trained the infantry for the Spanish Peninsular campaigns and conducted a brilliant retreat to Corunna, where he was mortally wounded after defeating the French under Soult.

Moore, Thomas (1779–1852), Ireland's greatest poet, the author of *Irish Melodies*, *Lalla Rookh*, *The Epicurean*, and many other works. He enjoyed immense popularity both in England and Ireland. Friend and biographer of Byron.

More, Sir Thomas (1478–1535), succeeded Wolsey as Lord Chancellor under Henry VIII., but fell into disgrace by refusing to take the oath of Supremacy, and was ultimately executed. His *Utopia* (*see* **J43**) is one of the world's most noted books. Canonised in 1935 along with John Fisher, Bishop of Rochester, who was similarly martyred by Henry VIII.

Morgan, Sir Henry (*c.* 1635–88), Welsh buccaneer of great skill and daring; operated in the Caribbean against the Spaniards, capturing and plundering Panama in 1671. Knighted by Charles II. and made Deputy-governor of Jamaica.

Morgan, John Pierpont (1837–1913), one of the great financiers of his time who built the family fortunes into a vast industrial empire.

Morland, George (1763–1804), a painter of English rural life.

Morley, John, Viscount, O.M. (1838–1923), Liberal statesman and author, served as Secretary for Ireland in 1886 and 1892–95, and for India, 1905–10. Biographer of Gladstone, Voltaire, Rousseau, Burke, Walpole, Cromwell, and Cobden.

Morley, Thomas (*c.* 1557–1603), English Elizabethan composer of madrigals, noted also for his settings of some of Shakespeare's songs. He was a pupil of Byrd, organist of St. Paul's Cathedral, and wrote an important theoretical work *Plaine and Easie Introduction to Practicall Music* (1597).

Morris, William (1834–96), poet and craftsman. His hatred of 19th-cent. ugliness, his belief in human equality, and in freedom and happiness for all, conspired to make him a socialist, and he accomplished much for the improvement of domestic decoration. He was a popular lecturer, founded the Socialist League and the Kelmscott Press. *See* **Arts and Crafts Movement**, **L9**.

Morrison of Lambeth, Herbert Stanley, Baron, P.C. C.H. (1888–1965), entered Parliament as Labour M.P. for S. Hackney in 1923. Leader of the L.C.C. 1933–40. Dep. Prime Min. and Leader of the House of Commons in the Labour administration, 1945–51. Life peerage conferred, 1959.

Morse, Samuel Finley Breese (1791–1872), an American artist and designer, who became the inventor of the Morse system of electric telegraphs, and of the Morse code of signals.

Moseley, Henry Gwyn-Jeffreys (1887–1915), lecturer in physics under Rutherford at Manchester Univ., 1910–12. Made great contributions to the theory of the structure of the atom. Killed at Gallipoli.

Mountbatten of Burma, 1st Earl, Admiral of the Fleet, P.C., K.G., G.C.B., G.C.V.O., D.S.O. (b. 1900), naval officer and statesman. Chief of Combined Operations, 1942–43; Supreme Allied Commdr. S.E. Asia, 1943–46; Viceroy of India, Mar.–Aug. 1947 and first Gov. Gen. of Dominion of India, Aug. 1947–June 1948. Resuming his naval career in 1948 he has served successively as Flag Officer Commanding the 1st Cruiser Squadron, Mediterranean, Fourth Sea Lord, C.-in-C. Mediterranean, C.-in-C. Allied Forces, Mediterranean, and First Sea Lord and Chief of Naval Staff, 1955–59, Chief of the Defence Staff, 1959–65.

Mountevans, Admiral Lord, K.C.B., D.S.O. (1881–1957), "Evans of the Broke," British sailor and explorer. Author of *South with Scott*.

Mussorgsky, Modest Petrovich (1839–81), Russian composer whose masterpiece is the opera *Boris Godunov* after the play by Pushkin. His piano suite *Pictures at an Exhibition* was orchestrated by Ravel.

Mozart, Wolfgang Amadeus (1756–91). The composer who bears this immortal name is universally acknowledged as the world's greatest musical genius. He was born at Salzburg, began his musical career at the age of four, toured the European courts as an infant prodigy, left the service of the Archbishop of Salzburg in his twenty-sixth year to live in Vienna, where his friendship with Haydn began and where his greatest music was written. Mozart's genius lies in the effortless outpouring of all forms of music, in the ever-flowing melodies, in the consistent beauty and symmetry of his compositions, and in the exactness of his method. Among the loveliest and grandest works in instrumental music are his three great symphonies in E flat, in G minor, and in C (called the "Jupiter"), all written in six weeks in 1788. Three of the greatest operas in musical history are his *Marriage of Figaro* (1786), *Don Giovanni* (1787), and *The Magic Flute* (1791). His last composition, written under the shadow of death, was the Requiem Mass, a work of tragic beauty.

Müller, Ferdinand von, Baron (1825–96), German botanist and explorer. Director of the Botanical Gardens at Melbourne, 1857–73. Introduced the eucalyptus into the south of Europe and other regions, and took leading part in promoting Australian exploration.

Mumford, Lewis (b. 1895), American social historian and authority on town planning and urban culture. His major work is the trilogy *Techniques and Civilization* (1934), *The Culture of Cities* (1938), *The Condition of Man* (1944).

Munkacsy, Michael von (1844–1900), a celebrated Hungarian painter of historical subjects.

Munnings, Sir Alfred James, K.C.V.O. (1878–1959), British painter whose country scenes and pictures of horses have gained him world-wide fame. P.R.A., 1944–49.

Murdock, William (1754–1839), engineer and inventor, one of the first to introduce gas lighting.

Murillo, Bartolomé Esteban (1617–82), one of the greatest Spanish painters. His chief works are altar-pieces and religious subjects.

Murray, (George) Gilbert (Aime), O.M., D.Litt., D.C.L., LL.D. (1866–1957), classical scholar and humanist whose verse translations of Euripides are known throughout the world. Became Professor of Greek at Glasgow at early age of 23; Regius Professor of Greek at Oxford, 1908–36; Chair. League of Nations Union, 1923–38; Pres. U.N. Ass. until his death.

Mussolini, Benito (1883–1945), Fascist dictator of Italy, 1922–43. From 1935 an aggressive foreign policy in Abyssinia, Spain, etc., was at first successful, and in June 1940, he entered the second world war on the side of Germany. The defeat of Italian arms in North Africa and the invasion of Sicily caused the collapse of his Government, but he was rescued from imprisonment by parachutists. Executed two years later by partisans.

N

Nansen, Fridtjof, G.C.V.O., D.Sc., F.R.G.S. (1861–1930), the Norwegian explorer who, after two or three expeditions across Greenland, in 1893 started out on his famous North Polar expedition when he reached the highest latitude until then attained—86° 14′—a feat later eclipsed by the Duke of the Abruzzi and by Peary, as well as by airship or aeroplane. He published a fascinating narrative of his exploration under the title of *Farthest North*. Active in Russian famine relief, 1921. Awarded Nobel Prize for Peace, 1922.

Napier, John (1550–1617), mathematician, who made important contribution to the advance of astronomy and other branches of science by his invention of logarithms (published 1614).

Napoleon I. (Bonaparte) (1769–1821) was born at Ajaccio in Corsica. Sent to France to receive a military education and was a captain at the age of twenty. In 1794 served in Italy with such distinction that he won a generalship, and next year was appointed Commander-in-Chief. A series of most brilliant successes followed. He defeated the Austrian forces in 1797, conducted an expedition to Syria and Egypt in 1798, returned in 1799 to find himself the most popular man in France, and in November of that year he proclaimed himself First Consul. In 1800 he was again in Italy and once more victorious. In 1804 he was made Emperor, and the following year was in the field against England, Russia, and Austria, achieving a splendid series of victories at Austerlitz and elsewhere, and practically became Dictator of Europe, distributing kingships amongst his brothers in the most profuse manner, Joseph becoming King of Naples, Louis King of Holland, and Jerome King of Westphalia. His invasion of Russia was disastrous, the Peninsular War went against him, and in 1814 the Allies entered Paris and forced him to abdicate. He was sent to Elba, but made his escape in the following year, gathered his old army about him and went forth to meet the English and Prussian armies. He was finally defeated at Waterloo on 18 June 1815, and held in captivity on the lonely island of St. Helena, where he died. His remains were removed to Paris in 1840, and rest in a magnificent tomb. Recent evidence suggests that he may have been murdered by arsenic poisoning.

Napoleon II. (1811–32) was the son of Napoleon I. and Maria Louisa. Was born in Paris and proclaimed King of Rome, but died of consumption when only twenty-one, being known at the time of his demise as the Duke of Reichstadt.

Napoleon III. (1808–73) was the son of Louis Bonaparte, King of Holland, and of Hortense, daughter of the Empress Josephine. After unsuccessful attempts to secure the French throne and years of imprisonment he took advantage of the revolution of 1848 to return to France and, following the famous *coup d'état* of December 2, 1851, emerged as master of France and was proclaimed Emperor the following year. Married Eugénie de Montijo in 1853. Dictatorial and discredited at home, unsuccessful in his foreign adventures, his surrender at Sedan in the Franco-Prussian war of 1870 brought ruin to the Second Empire, and France once again became a republic. Louis Napoleon took refuge in England and died at Chislehurst in Kent.

Nash, John (1752–1835), architect. Planned Regent Street, laid out Regent's Park, enlarged Buckingham Palace, and designed Marble Arch and the Brighton Pavilion.

Nash, Paul (1889–1946), distinguished English painter and designer. Official war artist in both world wars. Best known pictures *The Menin Road* of 1918 and *Totes Meer* of 1941.

Nash, Rt. Hon. Walter (b. 1882), New Zealand Labour politician; Prime Min., 1957–60. Resigned party leadership 1963.

Nasmyth, James (1808–90), the inventor of the steam-hammer, which became indispensable in all large iron and engineering works.

Nasir (Nasser) Col. Gamal Abd al- (b. 1918), first President of the first Egyptian Republic and influential leader of the Arab world. Fought in Palestine War of 1948–49 and organised the military *coup* of July 23, 1952, which brought the abdication of King Farouk. His two most important actions have been the nationalisation of the Suez Canal and the building, with Russian help and finance, of the Aswan High Dam.

Nehru, Pandit Jawaharlal (1889–1964), Indian statesman and one of the world's great leaders; Prime Min. and Min. of Foreign Affairs, 1947–64. Educated at Harrow and Cambridge where he studied science and law. A leading member of the Congress Party for many years, during which he was frequently imprisoned for his political activities. Played distinguished part in the final negotiations for the independence of India. Under his enlightened leadership India made dramatic technical, industrial, and social advances. *See also* **Section C, Part I.**

Nelson, Horatio, Viscount, K.C.B. (1758–1805), the great English naval commander; son of a Norfolk clergyman. Went to sea at twelve years of age, and was post-captain at twenty-one. In 1793 he was captain of the *Agamemnon* and proved his capacity and daring against the French. He lost his right eye at the siege of Calvi in 1794, and his right arm at the siege of Santa Cruz in 1797. In 1798 he achieved a great victory over the French in Aboukir Bay, in recognition of which he was created a Baron and granted a pension of £2,000 a year. Victorious at Copenhagen in 1801, he was promoted to the rank of Viscount. In 1805 the French fleet was destroyed at Trafalgar and Nelson was killed. Buried in St. Paul's Cathedral.

Nenni, Pietro (b. 1883), Italian politician and Secretary-General of the Italian Socialist Party since 1944. Minister of Foreign Affairs, 1946–47.

Nernst, Walther Hermann (1864–1941), German scientist who established the third law of thermodynamics. Nobel Prizeman, 1920.

Nero, Claudius Cæsar (A.D. 37–68), the Roman Emperor whose reign of fourteen years was rendered infamous by his cruelty and licentiousness.

Newcomen, Thomas (1663–1729), was one of the first to put a steam-engine into practical operation, and in 1705 patented his invention, which was the pumping-engine used in Cornish mines until the adoption of Watt's engine.

Newman, Ernest (1868–1959), English music critic successively of *The Manchester Guardian*, *The Birmingham Post*, *The Observer*, and of *The Sunday Times*, 1920–58. Outstanding among his numerous writings is the *Life of Richard Wagner*.

Newman, John Henry, Cardinal (1801–90). Educated at Oxford, he was incumbent of St. Mary's there from 1828 to 1843, taking an active part in the religious discussions of the time, gradually showing a tendency to adopt Roman Catholic views, and ultimately allying himself with the Romanists, resigning his living and settling at Edgbaston, Birmingham, as the head of a community of the Order of St. Philip Neri. In his *Apologia pro Vita Sua* he described the development of his religious thought. The hymn *Lead, kindly Light*, and the *Dream of Gerontius* were written by him.

Newton, Sir Isaac, F.R.S. (1642–1727), generally acknowledged as the world's greatest man of science. Achieved immortal fame for his work on the nature of white light, the calculus and gravitation Greatest published work, the *Principia*, was produced in 1687, revolutionising the scientific thought of his time. Was Member of Parliament for Cambridge in 1688, Master of the Mint in 1699, and President of the Royal Society from 1703 till his death. Honoured with knighthood in 1705.

Ney, Marshal Michel (1769–1815), was one of Napoleon's most noteworthy generals.

Nicholas II., Ex-Czar of Russia (1868–1918), son of the Emperor Alexander III. Came to the throne in 1894, and had a reign full of trouble, being unable to handle the difficulties by which he was beset. He avowed full harmony with the British and French in the war which opened in 1914, but the acts of the Empress and Court belied these pretensions, and a Revolution resulted in March, 1917, which overthrew the Romanoffs. Nicholas was detained a prisoner together with the Czarina and his children; all were probably shot on July 16, 1918.

Nicholas, St., Bishop of Myra and patron saint of Russia, flourished in the 4th century, and is popularly associated with Christmas under the corrupted name of Santa Claus.

Nicholson, Sir William (1872–1949), English painter, well known for his portraits, engravings and woodcuts as well as for his illustrations in the *Almanack of Twelve Sports* (with Kipling) and *London Types* (with Henley). His son, **Ben Nicholson** (b. 1894), also an artist, is noted for his abstract paintings.

Nicolson, Hon. Sir Harold, K.C.V.O., C.M.G. (b. 1886), author and critic, whose books include *The Congress of Vienna* (1946), *King George V.: His Life and Reign* (1952), *The Evolution of Diplomatic Method* (1954), *Good Behaviour* (1955). Married the **Hon. Victoria Sackville-West** (1892–1964), the novelist and poet.

Niemöller, Martin (b. 1892), German religious leader. A pastor in the Evangelical (Protestant) Church. Actively opposed the Nazification of the German Church and was incarcerated in a concentration camp throughout the second world war.

Nietzsche, Friedrich Wilhelm (1844–1900), German philosopher, in his younger years greatly influenced by the work of Wagner and Schopenhauer. His "superman" philosophy is eloquently expressed in his many writings, *i.e.*, *Thus spake Zarathustra, Beyond Good and Evil, The Will to Power.*

Nightingale, Florence, O.M. (1820–1910), English nurse and pioneer of hospital reform whose genius for administration was shown during the Crimean War, when she organised in face of considerable official opposition a nursing service to relieve the sufferings of the British soldiers who called her "The Lady with the Lamp." Her system was adopted and developed in all parts of the world, and she was honoured with a testimonial of £50,000, which she applied to the founding of the Nightingale Training School for Nurses, attached to St. Thomas's Hospital, London.

Nijinsky, Vaslav (1892–1950), Russian dancer, who was one of the famous company of dancers, which included Pavlova, Karsavina and Fokine, brought by Diaghilev to Paris and London just before the War of 1914–18, and was in some respects the most remarkable of them all. His sensational dancing in such Ballets as *Les Sylphides, Spectre de la Rose* and *Après-Midi d'un Faune* won him the supreme place among male dancers.

Nikisch, Arthur (1855–1922), famous Hungarian conductor, who appeared as a prodigy pianist at the age of eight, became chief conductor at the Leipzig Opera, 1879, conducted the Symphony Orchestra at Boston, 1889–93, afterwards paying visits to all the important cities of Europe.

Nimitz, Admiral of the Fleet Chester William 1885–1966), commanded the American fleet in the Pacific, 1941–45, together with army and marine forces. Chief of Naval Operations, 1945–47.

Nkrumah, Kwame (b. 1909), African leader whose country (Gold Coast) achieved independence in 1957, and in 1960 became the Republic of Ghana. Prime Min. (1957) and Pres. (1960). Deposed (1966) by military coup while absent in Far East.

Nobel, Dr. Alfred Bernhard (1833–96), the inventor of dynamite, was a Swedish engineer and chemist who amassed a large fortune from the manufacture of explosives, a great portion of which at his death in 1896 he set apart as a fund for annual prizes to such persons as during each year shall have contributed most materially to the benefit of mankind. *See* list of Nobel Prizemen, **L125–6.**

Norrie, 1st Baron Lieut-Gen. (Charles) Willoughby (Moke), G.C.M.G., G.C.V.O., C.B., D.S.O., M.C. (b. 1893), Gov.-Gen. and C.-in-C. of New Zealand, 1952–57; Governor South Australia, 1944–52. Professional cavalry officer.

Norstad, Gen. Lauris (b. 1907), succeeded Gen. Gruenther as NATO's Supreme Allied Commander, Europe, 1956–63.

Northcliffe, 1st Viscount (1865–1922), was one of the most prominent men in modern journalism. Started *Answers* in 1888 with his brother, Cecil Harmsworth. In 1894 the Harmsworths purchased the *Evening News*, and in 1896 they started the *Daily Mail*. In 1917 was special British representative in the United States.

Northumberland, John Dudley, Duke of (1502–53), an expert intriguer who dominated the Government of Edward VI. from 1549 onwards and attempted to maintain his influence when the king died by proclaiming as Queen his daughter-in-law, Lady Jane Grey, but failed and was executed.

Nostradamus or Michel de Notre Dame (1503–66), French astrologer who acquired great distinction by his labours during the plague. Publ. in 1555 *Centuries*, a book of rhymed prophecies, the fulfilment of some of which greatly added to his reputation. *Centuries* was condemned by the papal court of 1781.

Novalis, the pseudonym of **Baron Friedrich von Hardenberg** (1772–1801), German poet and novelist, representative of German romanticism. His chief work was the novel *Heinrich von Ofterdingen*, unfinished at his death.

Nuffield, 1st Viscount, William Richard Morris, G.B.E., C.H. (1877–1963), industrialist and philanthropist and until he retired in 1952 Chairman of Morris Motors, Ltd. Established the Nuffield Foundation, endowing it with £10 million, and provided large sums for the advancement of medicine in the University of Oxford.

Numa Pompilius, legendary king of Rome, to whom is ascribed Roman ceremonial law.

Nyerere, Julius (b. 1922), African statesman; President of the United Republic of Tanzania, 1964–. When Tanganyika attained independence in Dec. 1961 he was its first Prime Minister. An autobiographical account of his life is given in Lady Listowel's *The Making of Tanganyika* (1966).

O

Oaksey, Geoffrey Lawrence, 1st Baron, P.C., Q.C., D.S.O. (b. 1880), presided over the International Military Tribunal which tried the major war criminals at Nuremberg, 1945–46. A Lord of Appeal in Ordinary since 1947.

Oates, Captain Lawrence Edward Grace (1880–1912), a British explorer who, having seen active service in the South African War, joined Capt. Scott's Antarctic Expedition in 1910. He was one of the sledge party who accompanied Scott in his final dash for the South Pole. On returning, the party became stormbound, and on March 17, 1912, Oates, crippled by frost-bite, went out in the blizzard to die rather than be a burden to his starving comrades. Described in Scott's diary as a very gallant gentleman.

Oates, Titus (1649–1705), a notorious informer against Roman Catholics in reign of Charles II.

O'Casey, Sean (1883–1964), Irish dramatist of remarkable powers whose plays include *Juno and* *the Paycock, The Silver Tassie, Red Roses for Me*, and *Oak Leaves and Lavender*.

Occam (Ockham), William of (*c.* 1270–1349), English scholar and philosopher and one of the most interesting, independent and original thinkers of all time. He belonged to the Order of Franciscans, violently opposed the temporal power of the Pope, espoused the cause of nominalism and laid the foundations of modern theories of government and theological scepticism. (See **Occam's Razor, Section J.**)

O'Connell, Daniel (1775–1847), the Irish "Liberator," as he was called, was a famous orator and politician and a highly successful barrister. In Parliament he advocated the cause of Ireland with courage and audacity.

O'Connor, Feargus (1796–1855), was an Irish lawyer who became the most influential figure in the Chartist movement.

O'Connor, Rt. Hon. Thomas Power (1848–1929), sat in Parliament from 1880 until 1929, being for many years father of the house, and was one of the most successful journalists and editors of his time. He founded several publications including the *Star*.

Oersted, Hans Christian (1777–1851), the Danish physicist and chemist, whose discoveries in electrical research did much to help forward the invention of the electric telegraph.

Offa was King of Mercia from *circa* 757 to 796, and had a war-like career; he built an embankment from the Dee to the Wye, 100 miles long, which was called Offa's Dyke. He imposed "Peter's Pence" as a gift to the Pope for absolution.

Offenbach, Jacques (1819–80), French composer, born of a Jewish family at Cologne. Was the composer of many light operas, including the posthumous *Les Contes d'Hoffmann* (*Tales of Hoffmann*), the most popular of all his works.

Ohm, Georg Simon (1787–1854), was the discoverer of a law of electric current now known universally as Ohm's law. He was a native of Bavaria, professor at Munich from 1852, and gained much fame as a physicist and mathematician.

Olivier, Sir Laurence Kerr (b. 1907), British actor and director whose performances in Shakespearean and other roles have brought wide acclaim. He has also produced, directed, and played in many films, including Henry V., Hamlet, and Richard III. Director of the National Theatre.

Oman, Sir Charles (William Chadwick), K.B.E. (1860–1946), English historian who was Chichele Professor of Modern History at Oxford, 1905–46 and M.P. for the University from 1919 to 1935. His works include a popular *History of Greece*, *A Short History of England*, which is a familiar school book, and a *History of the Art of War in the Middle Ages*.

Omar Khayyám (*c.* 1050–1123), Persian poet and mathematician, called Khayyám (tent-maker) because of his father's occupation. His fame as a scientist has been eclipsed by his Rubaiyat, made known to English readers by Edward Fitz-Gerald in 1859.

O'Neill, Eugene Gladstone (1888–1953), an American playwright who, after spending his adventurous youth in such activities as sailing, gold-prospecting, and journalism, first won success in 1914 with the one-act play, *Thirst*. His later plays include *Anna Christie*, *Strange Interlude*, *Mourning Becomes Electra*, *The Iceman Cometh*. *See also* **Modern Drama.**

Orchardson, Sir William Quiller (1835–1910), an eminent R.A.; among his best-known works are *Napoleon I. on board H.M.S. Bellerophon* and *Ophelia*.

Origen (*c.* 185–*c.* 254), Christian philosopher and biblical scholar, famed for his teaching at Alexandria and Cæsarea. He attempted to synthesise Greek philosophy and Hebrew scriptures so as to prove the Christian view of the universe was compatible with Greek thought. In the persecution of Decius in 250 he was imprisoned, tortured, and pilloried.

Orpen, Sir William, K.B.E., R.A. (1878–1931), British portrait-painter; many of his celebrated war pictures were presented to the nation.

Ortega y Gasset, José (1883–1955), Spanish philosopher and essayist, one of the most eloquent men of our times. His *The Revolt of the Masses* (1932) brought him international fame.

Orwell, George (1903–50), English satirist, author of *Animal Farm* (1946) and *Nineteen Eighty-Four* (1949). His real name was Eric Blair; b. in India.

Osler, Sir William, Bt., M.D., F.R.S. (1849–1919). Canadian physician and medical historian; an authority on diseases of the blood and spleen.

Oswald, St., King of Northumbria from 625 to 642, established Christianity amongst his subjects.

Ouida, pseudonym of **Louise de la Ramée** (1839–1908), English novelist of flamboyant personality whose many romantic stories were very popular and included *Under Two Flags*, *A Dog of Flanders*, and *Moths*. Born at Bury St. Edmunds and buried at Bagni di Lucca in Tuscany. Her father was French.

Otto, Nikolaus August (1832–91). German inventor of the four-stroke cycle that bears his name.

Otto the Great (912–973), son of Henry the Fowler, crowned King of the Germans at Aachen in 936 and Emperor at Rome in 962. Overawed the papacy, checked the barbarian invasions, founded the East Mark (Austria), and considerably consolidated Germany.

Ovid (43 B.C.–A.D. 18), the famous Latin poet (Publius Ovidius Naso) whose *Metamorphoses* and *Art of Love* are among the best-known examples of Roman literature of the lighter kind.

Owen, Robert (1771–1858), socialist and philanthropist, devoted his life and fortune to the carrying out of his theories, and established socialistic colonies in Lanarkshire, Hampshire and America.

P

Pachmann, Vladimir de (1848–1923), Russian pianist, an unrivalled interpreter of the works of Chopin.

Paderewski, Ignace Jan (1860–1941), achieved unrivalled fame as a pianist and for half a century worked for the freedom of his native Poland. He represented his country at Versailles and became her first Prime Minister.

Paganini, Niccolo (1782–1840), Italian violinist and composer whose playing became a legend and brought him much fame and wealth. He ranks as first among virtuosi of the violin.

Paine, Thomas (1737–1809), English revolutionary writer, b. Thetford, Norfolk, son of a Quaker; emigrated to America (1774), becoming famous with the publication of his pamphlet *Common Sense* in favour of American independence. On return to England (1787) wrote *The Rights of Man* in reply to Burke's *Reflections on the Revolution in France*. This was extensively read but his attack on English institutions procured him a trial for sedition and he fled to France. There he wrote *The Age of Reason*, an attack on Christianity which excited great indignation in England. Returned to America where he lived his last years in solitude and ill-health.

Palestrina, Giovanni Pierluigi da (*c.* 1525–94), great Italian composer of unaccompanied church music and madrigals, among whose works are the *Missa Papae Marcelli* and the *Stabat Mater* for 8 voices, which is among the greatest musical glories of all time.

Palgrave, Sir Francis (1788–1861), English historian, best known for his *A History of Normandy and England*. His son, **Francis Turner Palgrave** (1824–97), was Professor of Poetry at Oxford, and edited the famous anthology, *The Golden Treasury*. Another son, **William Gifford Palgrave** (1826–88), was a diplomat and prose writer of ability.

Palissy, Bernard (*circa* 1510–89), a distinguished French potter, who after years of struggle and self-denial discovered the art of producing white enamel, after which he became famous and set up a porcelain factory in Paris, which was patronised by Royalty.

Palladio, Andrea (1518–80), the great Italian architect, who introduced the style of architecture known as Palladian.

Palmer, John (1742–1818), originator of the mail-coach postal service in 1784.

Palmerston, Henry John Temple, 3rd Viscount (1784–1865), English statesman, was long dominant in European affairs because of his vigorous and popular policy. He spent many years of his life in office, serving as Tory Secretary for War from 1808 till 1828 as Foreign Secretary in all the Whig cabinets between 1830 and 1851, and as Prime Minister in 1855 and from 1859 until his death. He had a lofty conception of the strength and duties of England and was the irreconcilable foe of oppression and injustice.

Pancras, St., the patron saint of children, was the son of a Roman noble, was baptised in Rome in the reign of Diocletian, where he was put to death at the age of fourteen for refusing to renounce Christianity.

Pandit, Vijaya Lakshmi (b. 1900), Gov. of Maharashtra, 1962–64; elected to Lok Sabha, 1964; Indian High Comm. in London, 1954–61. India's first Ambassador to the Soviet Union (1947–9) and to the United States (1949–51), the first woman to be elected Pres. of the U.N. General Assembly (1953–4). Sister of **Jawaharlal Nehru.**

Panizzi, Sir Anthony, K.C.B. (1797–1879), an Italian political exile, who in 1831 was appointed to the Assistant Librarianship and Keepership of the Printed Books of the British Museum. In 1856 he became Principal Librarian, retiring in 1866. The great Reading Room was constructed from his designs.

Pankhurst, Emmeline (1858–1928) was a prominent and indefatigable worker for women's suffrage, together with her daughters Dame Christabel and Sylvia.

Papin, Denis (1647–1714), a French mathematician and scientist who settled in England. He invented the condensing pump, and was a pioneer in the development of the steam engine. Not being a mechanic, he made all his experiments by means of models.

Paracelsus, Philippus Aureolus (1493–1541), a famous Swiss mystic and alchemist. He made numerous important discoveries, being the first to employ laudanum and antimony in pharmacy. The English translation of his *One Hundred and Fourteen Experiments and Cures* appeared in 1596. His real name was Theophrastus Bombastus von Hohenheim.

Park, Mungo (1771–1806), famous British traveller who in 1799 published an arresting account of his *Travels in the Interior of Africa.*

Parker, Rev. Joseph (1830–1902), a popular Nonconformist preacher and author who built the City Temple, and ministered there up to the time of his death.

Parnell, Charles Stewart (1846–91), the Irish politician, who as leader of the Nationalist Party made it more powerful than it had ever been and successfully enlisted the support of Gladstone for the policy of Home Rule. Accused by *The Times* of complicity in the crimes of the Land League on the basis of letters forged by Richard Pigott, he was completely vindicated by a Royal Commission and awarded heavy damages. Was dropped from the leadership of his party following the O'Shea divorce proceedings and died soon afterwards.

Parry, Rear-Admiral Sir William Edward (1790–1855), an Arctic explorer and naval commander of great distinction, who undertook several expeditions to the Polar regions and made numerous important discoveries.

Parsons, Hon. Sir Charles Algernon, O.M., K.C.B., F.R.S. (1854–1931), was head of the electrical and engineering works of C. A. Parsons and Co., and of the Parsons Marine Steam Turbine Co., Ltd., Newcastle-on-Tyne, and inventor of the steam turbine which has effected a remarkable improvement in the propulsion of war and mercantile vessels.

Partridge, Sir Bernard (1861–1945), began life as a stained glass designer, afterwards worked at book illustrations, and for a time was on the stage. Joined *Punch* staff 1891, and for many years was its principal cartoonist.

Pascal, Blaise (1623–62), celebrated French mathematical genius and religious philosopher whose *Provincial Letters* are one of the world's literary masterpieces. At the age of nineteen he invented an ingenious adding machine and was the first to demonstrate the barometric effects of altitude.

Pasternak, Boris Leonidovich (1890–1960), Russian poet and writer. Translations of his great novel *Dr. Zhivago* appeared in 1958, though it was forbidden in the Soviet Union. In that year he was awarded—though he declined it—the Nobel Prize for Literature "for his important contributions both to contemporary lyric poetry and to the great Russian narrative tradition."

Pasteur, Louis (1822–95), French chemist, whose work was inspired by an interest in the chemistry of life which abided with him until his death. His researches on fermentation led to the science of bacteriology and his investigations into infectious diseases and their prevention to the science of immunology. The pathological bacteriological import of Pasteur's researches came about mainly through his disciples (Lister, Roux, and others) and not directly, though all founded on his early non-medical investigations on organisms of fermentation, etc., which were of great importance in industry, and fundamentally. He spent most of his life as director of scientific studies at the Ecole Normale at Paris, where he was appointed in 1857. The Institut Pasteur was founded in 1888.

Patmore, Coventry (1823–96), poet of the Victorian era, and author of *The Angel in the House.*

Paton, Sir (Joseph) Noel (1821–1901), Scottish painter, sculptor, historical artist, archæologist, and poet.

Patrick, St. (*c.* 387–*c.* 463), the patron saint and Apostle of Ireland, was for many years a great and successful Christian missionary in that country. Few authentic facts about his life are known, but many miraculous stories, such as his alleged extermination of serpents in the island, have been associated with him.

Patti, Adelina Juana Maria (Baroness Cederström) (1843–1919), coloratura soprano, b. in Madrid of Italian parents, unsurpassed for purity of tone and style.

Pattison, Dorothy Wyndlow (1832–78), a sister of Mark Pattison, who devoted a great part of her life to hospital work in Walsall, where, as "Sister Dora," she is revered for her saintly life and devotion to the sick poor.

Pattison, Mark (1813–84), scholar and critic, rector of Lincoln College, Oxford. His wife, **Emilia Francis Strong** (afterwards Lady Dilke), was well known as a French art historian.

Paul VI, Pope (Giovanni Battista Montini) (b. 1897), elected pope in 1963 on the death of John XXIII. Formerly Archbishop of Milan. Made pilgrimage to Holy Land in Jan. 1964.

Pavlov, Prof. Ivan Petrovich (1849–1936), an eminent Russian physiologist: Director of the Physiological Institute. Foreign member of the Royal Society and Nobel Prize-winner.

Pavlova, Anna (1885–1931), one of the greatest exponents of the Russian school of dancing.

Peabody, George (1795–1869), an American merchant who lived for the greater part of his life in London, and, acquiring a large fortune, bequeathed immense sums for philanthropic purposes in England and the United States.

Peacock, Thomas Love (1785–1866), English satirist, whose novels include *Headlong Hall* and *Nightmare Abbey*, and who ranks high in English literature for the wit and grace of his style.

Pearson, Sir Cyril Arthur, Bt. (1866–1921), journalist and newspaper proprietor, who founded *Pearson's Weekly, The Daily Express*, and other publications. Retired because of blindness and devoted himself to the welfare of the blind particularly ex-servicemen; founder of St. Dunstan's.

Pearson, Lester Bowles, O.B.E., M.A. (b. 1897), Prime Min. of Canada, 1963–; Min. for External Affairs, 1948–57.

Peary, Rear-Admiral Robert Edwin (1856–1920), an American Arctic explorer who, in 1891–92, conducted a sledging expedition towards the Pole. In 1893, 1895, and 1898 was again in the Arctic regions; and in 1900–02 reached the highest latitude hitherto attained. In the spring of 1906 he touched 87 degs. 6 min. N. latitude. On April 6, 1909, making the journey by sledge over sea-ice and accompanied by only his native servant, he succeeded in reaching the Pole.

Peel, Rt. Hon. Sir Robert, 2nd Bt. (1788–1850), a prominent British statesman who entered Parliament at twenty-one years of age, and immediately exhibited great capacity, being appointed Under-Secretary for the Colonies in the following year. From 1812 to 1818 he was Secretary for Ireland; and in 1822 he became Home Secretary, introducing, whilst fulfilling that office, the new police service associated with his name. In 1834, Peel was for four months Prime Minister.

and in 1841 formed a second ministry. It was then that the Anti-Corn Law agitation became formidable, and Peel abandoned his former Protectionist attitude, and carried his Repeal measure eventually in 1846. He was thrown from his horse in Hyde Park on June 25th, 1850, and died from injuries.

Penfield, Wilder Graves, O.M., M.D., M.A., D.Sc., F.R.S. (b. 1891), Canadian brain surgeon; Dir. Montreal Neurological Institute; Prof. of Neurosurgery McGill Univ.; Pub. *The Cerebral Cortex of Man* (1950), *Epilepsy and the Functional Anatomy of the Human Brain* (1954).

Penn, William (1644–1718), became a Quaker, and wrote some powerful pamphlets supporting his new faith. He devoted himself to good works, and in 1682, having obtained a special grant from King Charles II., went to America and founded Pennsylvania.

Penney, Sir William George, K.B.E., M.A., Ph.D., D.Sc., F.R.S. (b. 1909), British scientist; Chair. U.K. Atomic Energy Authority, 1964–; Dep. Chair., 1961–64; succeeded Sir John Cockroft as Member (Scientific Research) in 1959; formerly Dir. Weapons Group, Atomic Weapons Research Estab., Aldermaston.

Pepys, Samuel, F.R.S. (1633–1703), naval administrator, sometimes called the "Father of the British Civil Service." The *Diary* was written while he was a comparatively young man and is a unique revelation of a man and his age, besides including eye-witness descriptions of the Great Plague and Fire of London.

Pergolesi, Giovanni Battista (1710–36), Italian composer, best known for his humorous opera *La Serva Padrona* and his *Stabat Mater*.

Pericles (*c.* 490–429 B.C.), the distinguished Athenian statesman, general, and orator, who raised Athens to the point of its fullest prosperity.

Perkin, Sir William Henry, F.R.S., D.Sc. (1838–1907), great organic chemist and famous for his discovery of mauve, the first synthetic dye.

Perkin, William Henry (junior) (1860–1929), foremost organic chemist of his day; Professor of Organic Chemistry at Manchester University, 1892–1912 and later at Oxford. His researches led to important industrial results.

Perrin, Francis (b. 1901), French scientist and socialist; succeeded Joliot-Curie as High Commr. for Atomic Energy in 1951. Prof. Atomic Physics, Collège de France, 1946– .

Persius Flaccus, Aulus (A.D. 34–62), a famous Stoic philosopher.

Perugino, Pietro (1446–1524), Italian artist who excelled in religious subjects and painted many fine frescoes including some in the Sistine Chapel at Rome. Raphael was his pupil.

Pestalozzi, Johann Heinrich (1746–1827), Swiss educational reformer whose theories laid the foundation of modern primary education. His teaching methods were far in advance of his time, but are now employed with outstanding success in schools in many parts of the world.

Pétain, Marshal Henri Phillipe (1856–1951), became a French national hero after the successful defence of Verdun in 1916 and was made C.-in-C. of all the French armies. In 1940 he became Prime Minister, signed an armistice with Germany, and set up a quasi-independent administration at Vichy. In 1945 he was sentenced to death for treason, the sentence being commuted to life imprisonment.

Peter I, called **The Great** (1672–1725). Czar of Russia, showed great ability and energy of character, devoting himself largely to the reorganisation of his army and navy. He spent some months at Deptford studying shipbuilding. He founded St. Petersburg (1703), which was his "window on to Europe," and gained control in the war with Sweden of Karelia, Ingermanland, and Livonia. Among the prisoners taken by him at the Battle of Poltava (1709) was Catherine Skavronsky, daughter of a Lithuanian peasant, whom he later married. By her care and understanding she did much to strengthen his power. Peter died without naming an heir, and Catherine became Empress of Russia (1725–27).

Peter, the Hermit (*c.* 1050–1115), was the main instrument of the agitation which brought about the first Crusade. He was a French monk, of great eloquence and earnestness, and lived to see Jerusalem in the hands of the Christians.

Petrarch, Francesco (1304–74), Italian poet and scholar, whose odes and sonnets *To Laura* are unmatched for their lyrical beauty and passion.

Petrie, Sir (William Matthew) Flinders, F.R.S. (1853–1942), British egyptologist; carried out excavations in Britain (1875–90), Egypt (1880–1924), and Palestine (1927–38); Prof. of Egyptology at University College, London, 1893–1935.

Phidias, the greatest of Greek sculptors, flourished from about 500 to 432 B.C., was specially famous for his work in gold, ivory and bronze. Nothing now remains to attest his genius although the sculptures in the British Museum, widely known as the Elgin Marbles, may have been from his designs.

Philip II. of France (1180–1223), was a prominent figure in the third Crusade, in which for a time he associated himself with our Richard I. Victor over a strong coalition at the momentous battle of Bouvines in 1214.

Philip II. of Macedonia (382–336 B.C.), trained in military arts in Greece, when he came to the throne instilled martial ideas into his subjects, and entered upon a career of conquest that did not end until he had become master of Greece. Father of Alexander the Great.

Philip II. of Spain (1527–98), succeeded his father the Emperor Charles V. in half his dominions. The Revolt of the Netherlands, the annexation of Portugal in 1580, and the unsuccessful attempt to subdue England by the Armada, were outstanding events of his troubled reign. He was a devout Roman Catholic, strongly supported the Counter-Reformation, built the strange Escorial, and was four times married, his second wife being Mary Tudor.

Philip V. of Spain (1683–1746), founded the Bourbon dynasty in Spain, and was the son of the Dauphin of Louis XIV. and Maria Theresa of Spain. His uncle, Charles II. of Spain, bequeathed the kingdom to him, and this led to the war of the Spanish Succession, which ultimately confirmed him in his kingship.

Phillip, Arthur (1738–1814), first governor of New South Wales. Under his command the first fleet of 717 convicts set sail from Britain to Australia, and with the founding of Sydney in 1788 colonisation of the whole country began.

Phillips, Stephen (1868–1915), dramatist and poet of distinction. Wrote popular verse dramas, including *Paolo and Francesca, Herod,* and *Ulysses.*

Piasts, first Polish dynasty in Poland until 14th century and until 17th century in Silesia.

Piazzi, Giuseppe (1746–1826), an Italian astronomer. He was the discoverer of the planet Ceres, the first known of the asteroids.

Picasso, Pablo Ruiz (b. 1881), Spanish painter who received his early training in Catalonia and settled in Paris in 1903. His influence over contemporary art is comparable with that exercised by Cézanne (*q.v.*) over the artists of his time. His work is to be found in public galleries and private collections all over the world and is represented in the Tate Gallery by *Femme Nue dans un Fauteuil Rouge*. His genius has also found scope in sculpture and etchings and he has designed décor costumes for the ballet.

Piccard, Auguste (1884–1962), Swiss physicist, noted for his stratosphere ascents in a specially constructed balloon, 1931–32, and for his submarine research. In Jan. 1960 his son, Dr. Jacques Piccard, made a descent of over 7 miles in the Marianas trench in the western Pacific in a bathyscaphe designed and built by him.

Pickford, Mary (b. 1893), was the leading film actress of the silent days and affectionately known as "the world's sweetheart."

Pilsudski, Joseph (1867–1935), Polish soldier and statesman. Led unsuccessful Polish attack on Russia in 1920 seeking the restoration of the 1772 frontiers. Exercised military dictatorship from 1926 until his death.

Pindar (522–443 B.C.), the eminent lyric poet of ancient Greece.

Pinero, Sir Arthur Wing (1855–1934), was an able English dramatist and former actor, of Portuguese descent. *Dandy Dick, The Second Mrs. Tanqueray* and *Mid-Channel* are among his plays.

Pirandello, Luigi (1867–1936), was a prominent Italian dramatist and novelist, many of whose works have been translated into English. Awarded Nobel Prize for Literature, 1934.

Pissarro, Camille (1830–1903), French Impressionist painter of landscapes; studied under Corot.

Pitman, Sir Isaac (1813–97), founded the Pitman system of phonographic shorthand.

Pitt, William (1759–1806), was the second son of the Earl of Chatham. Entered Parliament at twenty-one, and by his brilliant oratory captivated the House of Commons. In 1782, when only twenty-three, he became Chancellor of the Exchequer, and in the following year was made Premier, and held that office for seventeen years, through the trying period of the French Revolution, when war with France was almost continuous. He was undoubtedly one of the most brilliant statesmen that England has produced, and his death at the early age of forty-six was a great loss to the country. He was buried in Westminster Abbey.

Pius XII. (1876–1958), elected Pope, March 2, 1939. As Cardinal Eugenio Pacelli, he was Papal Secretary of State, 1930–39, and was outspoken in his condemnation of those aspects of the policy of the totalitarian states which he considered anti-Christian. Before he became a Cardinal he was for many years Papal Nuncio in Germany.

Pizarro, Francisco (*c.* 1478–1541), was an adventurous Spaniard who, after Columbus's discoveries in the New World, set out for South America, overthrowing the Inca empire and conquering Peru for the Emperor Charles V.

Planck, Prof. Dr. Max (1858–1947), German physicist, whose investigations into radiation of energy culminated in 1901 in his law of radiation, which laid the foundation of the quantum theory. Awarded Nobel Prize for Physics, 1918.

Plato (427–347 B.C.), great Athenian philosopher, pupil of Socrates, teacher of Aristotle. He founded a school at Athens under the name of the Academy, where he taught philosophy and mathematics. His great work is his *Dialogues*, which includes the *Republic*, the longest and most celebrated of them all. All Plato's known writings have come down to us, and they constitute one of the most influential bodies of work in history.

Playfair, Lyon (1818–98), a far-sighted Victorian who stood for the greater recognition of science in national life. He forsook his profession as professor of chemistry at Edinburgh to enter Parliament. Pres. of the British Association in 1885.

Plimsoll, Samuel (1824–98), was a native of Bristol, and while M.P. for Derby got up an agitation on behalf of merchant sailors, procuring the passing of the Merchant Shipping Act of 1876, which by defining a line above which no ship must sink in the water when loaded has ever since made the overloading of ships illegal. The line is known as the Plimsoll Mark.

Pliny the Elder (A.D. 23–79), Roman naturalist who dedicated his great work *Natural History* to the Emperor Titus. He died of fumes and exhaustion while investigating the eruption of Vesuvius. His nephew, **Pliny the Younger** (A.D. 62–113), achieved renown with his series of historical *Letters*.

Plotinus (*c.* 204–270), Greek philosopher, was the founder of Neoplatonism, which had considerable influence on early Christian thought.

Plutarch (*c.* 46–120), a pagan Hellenic writer, a contemporary of the authors of the two gospels according to St. Matthew and St. Luke. His *Lives of Agis and Cleomenes* form one of the world's most famous literary productions.

Poe, Edgar Allan (1809–49), was an American poet of unique genius, author of " The Raven," " The Bells," " Annabel Lee," and other poems of haunting melody and dainty fancy. Poe's *Tales of Mystery* are thrilling examples of their class.

Poincaré, Raymond Nicolas Landry (1860–1934), was President of France from 1913 to 1920 and won the confidence and admiration of the French people and their Allies by his services during the first world war. He was Prime Minister in 1912, 1922–24, and 1926–29.

Pole, Reginald (1550–58), archbishop of Canterbury (1556–58), cardinal of the Roman Church, antagonist of the English reformation, whose mother was Margaret Plantagenet, half-sister of Henry VII's mother. His difference with Henry VIII over the divorce of Catherine evoked his famous treatise *De Unitate Ecclesiastica*, a defence of papal supremacy and a denunciation of the king. His activity brought about his own attainder, and the execution of his brother and mother as participators in his treasonable designs.

Pollard, Professor Albert Frederick, F.B.A. (1869–1948), English historian and first director of the Institute of Historical Research; author of many authoritative works on the Tudor period.

Polo, Marco (1256–1323), the famous Venetian traveller and explorer, who made journeys through China, India, and other eastern countries, and published the record of his various wanderings, recounting the many wonders and marvels he had seen—a record which seemed for the most part beyond credence to his contemporaries, but now largely confirmed.

Pompadour, Jeanne Antoine Poisson, Marquise de, (1721–64), was for a long time the favourite of Louis XV. of France, over whom she exercised great influence.

Pompey the Great (106–48 B.C.), distinguished himself as a general while young, clearing the Mediterranean of pirates, and ultimately became, with Caesar and Crassus, triumvir.

Pope, Alexander (1688–1744), the celebrated 18th century poet and translator of *Homer*. Author of *The Rape of the Lock, Essay on Criticism*, and *Essay on Man*.

Pound, Ezra Loomis (b. 1885). American poet and scholar, famous both for the beauty of his individual verse and for his excellent translations of Provencal, Latin, Chinese, French and Italian poets.

Poussin, Nicolas (1593–1665), an eminent French painter patronised by Louis XIII.

Powys, John Cowper (1872–1963), English writer, best known for his novel *Wolf Solent* (1929) and his essays *The Meaning of Culture* (1929) and *A Philosophy of Solitude* (1933). His brothers, **Theodore Francis Powys** (1875–1953) and **Llewelyn Powys** (1884–1939), were also writers of originality.

Prasad, Dr. Rajendra (1884–1963), first President of the Indian Union, 1950; re-elected in 1952 and 1957; retired 1962; succeeded by Dr. Radhakrishnan.

Praxiteles, a great Greek sculptor who lived in the 4th century B.C.

Preece, Sir William Henry, K.C.B., F.R.S. (1834–1913), a Welsh electrician, connected with the Electric Telegraph Service from 1853, and conspicuously successful in his experiments which led to the later developments in telegraphy. He was associated with Marconi in his wireless-telegraphic schemes and introduced the block system into England.

Prescott, William Hickling (1796–1859), one of the best known of American historians.

Prichard, James Cowles, M.D., F.R.S. (1786–1848). British ethnologist and physician, whose knowledge of anatomy, psychology, and of languages enabled him to grasp the principle that people should be studied as a whole. He paved the way for future anthropological research.

Priestley, John Boynton, M.A. (b. 1894), critic, novelist, essayist, playwright and broadcaster, whose work has received great praise and includes the novels *The Good Companions, Angel Pavement*, the plays *Dangerous Corner, Time and the Conways, The Linden Tree*, and a literary history, *Literature and Western Man* (1960).

Priestley, Joseph, F.R.S. (1733–1804), was the discoverer of oxygen and other gases, and wrote *A History of Electricity*. He was also a great advocate of freedom and progress.

Priestley, Sir Raymond, M.A., D.Sc. (b. 1886), geologist. Took part in the Shackleton Antarctic Expedition of 1907–9 and Scott's Antarctic Expedition 1910–13. President of the British Association, 1956.

Prior, Matthew (1664–1721), a well-known poet and wit who acquired celebrity by writing *The City Mouse and Country Mouse*.

Prokofiev, Serge Sergeyevich (1891–1953), celebrated Russian composer, whose music has a strong folk-song element, rich in melody and invention. He has written operas: *The Love of Three Oranges, The Betrothal in a Nunnery, War and Peace*, ballets: *Romeo and Juliet, Cinderella*, symphonies, chamber music and the music for Eisenstein's films *Alexander Nevsky, Ivan the Terrible*, etc.

Protagoras (*c.* 480–411 B.C.), a Greek philosopher, chief of the Sophists, famous for his scepticism and disbelief in objective truth.

Proudhon, Pierre Joseph (1809–65), a French political economist.

Proust, Marcel (1871–1922), French psychological novelist; author of a series of 15 novels known under the title of *A la Recherche du Temps Perdu*. Proust's works have been admirably translated into English by C. K. Scott Moncrieff.

Prudhon, Pierre Paul (1758–1823), a French historical and portrait painter.

Ptolemy, Claudius Ptolemæus, a famous astronomer and geographer of Alexandria, who flourished from *c.* A.D. 90–168. He founded the Ptolemaic system, which taught that the earth was stationary and the heavenly bodies revolved around it. His great works are the *Almagest* and his *Geographical Outline*.

Puccini, Giacomo (1858–1924), Italian composer whose operas met with great success and include *Manon Lescaut, La Bohème, La Tosca, Madam Butterfly*, and *Turandot* (finished after his death).

Purcell, Henry (1658–95), one of the great figures in English music; organist of the Chapel Royal and composer to Charles II. Anthems form the greater part of his sacred music, and he wrote not only for the Court but for the stage.

Pusey, Edward Bouverie (1800–82), a famous Anglican cleric; he published *Tracts for the Times*, which inaugurated the Tractarian movement that developed into what became known as Puseyism.

Pushkin, Alexander (1799–1837), the national poet of Russia, several times exiled for his liberal views and held in high honour by contemporary Russia. Died of wounds received in a duel. His poetical tales are full of dramatic power. *Eugene Onegin* is generally considered his masterpiece and *Boris Godunov* is a fine tragedy.

Pym, John (1584–1643), a prominent statesman in the reign of Charles I. A leader of the Puritan opposition in Parliament.

Pythagoras (*c.* 582–*c.* 507 B.C.), most influential of the early Greek scientists. He was born on the island of Samos, off the Turkish mainland, which he left *c.* 530 to settle at Croton, a Greek city in southern Italy. He was a mystic and mathematician and believed in the transmigration of souls. He died in exile.

Q

Quaritch, Bernard (1819–99), a famous dealer in rare books, who was a native of Germany but settled in London, and became naturalised in 1847. His knowledge of scarce and valuable books was unique. His shop in Piccadilly was a storehouse of literary treasures.

Quasimodo, Salvatore (b. 1901), Italian poet whose greatness lies in his humanity and his rejection of the Fascist influence. He won the Nobel Prize for Literature in 1959.

Quiller-Couch, Sir Arthur Thomas (1863–1944), was a well-known novelist and essayist, who as "Q" published many delightful stories, including *Dead Man's Rock, Troy Town*, and *The Splendid Spur*. Edited the *Oxford Book of English Verse*. Professor of English Literature, Cambridge University, 1912–44.

R

Rabelais, François (*c.* 1495–1553), the great French satirist, first adopted the career of a monk, then studied medicine, and settled at Lyons as a doctor, and it was there that he published his *Gargantua and Pantagruel*, among the wittiest though coarsest books in any language.

Rachel, Mlle (stage name of **Elizabeth Félix**) (1821–58), acknowledged as the greatest tragic actress of her time and reached the height of her fame in Racine's *Phèdre* in 1843.

Rachmaninov, Sergei Vasilyevich (1873–1943), Russian pianist, composer, and conductor. He wrote operas, symphonies, piano concertos, piano pieces, and songs, and was one of the greatest pianists of his age. After the Russian revolution he made his home in America, where he died.

Racine, Jean (1639–99), a distinguished French tragic dramatist, best known by his *Andromaque, Phèdre*, and *Athalie*.

Rackham, Arthur, R. W. S. (1867–1939), a noted English artist who excelled in the illustration of books such as *Peter Pan, Alice in Wonderland*, Wagner's *Ring Librettos, Mother Goose*, Grimm's and Andersen's *Fairy Tales*.

Radhakrishnan, Sir Sarvepalli, O.M., M.A., D.Litt. (b. 1888). Pres. Indian Union, 1962– ; Vice-Pres., 1952–62; formerly Spalding Professor of Eastern Religions and Ethics at Oxford.

Raeburn, Sir Henry, R.A. (1756–1823), was a famous Scottish portrait painter, and friend and pupil of Sir Joshua Reynolds.

Raemakers, Louis (1869–1957), Dutch cartoonist, famous for his scathing satires on the Germans during the first world war. His *Cartoon History of the War* was published in 1919.

Raffles, Sir Thomas Stamford (1781–1826), an eminent naturalist. He was the founder and first President of the Zoological Society of London. Founded Singapore, 1819.

Raikes, Robert (1735–1811), a practical propounder of the Sunday School system.

Raleigh, Sir Walter (1552–1618), a scholar, courtier, soldier, sailor, and statesman. In 1584 Queen Elizabeth granted him a patent for the discovery and settlement of unknown countries in the far West. The colonisation of Virginia followed. At one time he was in great favour at Court, but quarrelled with the Queen, and suffered in fortune in consequence. When James I. came to the throne, Raleigh was supposed to be implicated in a conspiracy against that monarch, and was sentenced to death. After that he was a prisoner in the Tower of London for twelve years, and there he wrote his *History of the World*, and other works. In 1615 James set him at liberty in order to head an expedition to Guiana in the hope of finding gold, but being unsuccessful he was again imprisoned on his return, and finally beheaded in Old Palace Yard.

Raman, Sir (Chandrasekhara) Venkata, F.R.S. (b. 1888), Indian physicist whose main work has been in spectroscopy. For his research on the diffusion of light and for the discovery of the "Raman Effect" he was awarded the 1930 Nobel Prize in Physics.

Rameau, Jean Philippe (1683–1764), French composer and church organist whose *Treatise on Harmony*, 1722, and other works on musical theory profoundly influenced musical development in the 18th century.

Ramón y Cajal, Santiago (1852–1934), Spanish histologist who made many discoveries in the structure of the nervous system. Nobel Prizeman, 1906.

Ramsay, Sir William, K.C.B., F.R.S. (1852–1916), chemist and discoverer with Lord Rayleigh of the hitherto unknown constituent of air, argon. Later discovered helium and detected other inert gases, which he called neon, krypton, and xenon. With F. Soddy carried out research on radium emanation. Awarded Nobel Prize in Chemistry, 1904. President of the British Association, 1911.

Ramsey, Most Rev. Arthur Michael, D.D. (b. 1904), Archbishop of Canterbury, 1961. Archbishop of York, 1956–61; Prof. of Divinity at Cambridge, 1950–52; Lord Bishop of Durham, 1952–56.

Ranke, Leopold von (1795–1886), the painstaking and thorough German historian who laid the basis of modern historical research and demonstrated many of its methods.

Raphael Santi (1483–1520), the distinguished Italian painter whose works excel all others in their beauty of expression and inspired treatment. He lived a considerable period in Rome, where he painted his famous frescoes for the Vatican and St. Peter's and also the celebrated cartoons designed for the tapestries of the Papal chapel, which afterwards were brought to England, and are now at the Victoria and Albert Museum. His last painting was *The Transfiguration*. Examples of his work are to be found in most of the great European collections, including our own National Gallery.

Rasputin, Grigori Yefimovich (1871–1916), a "holy man" of the old Russia who lived quietly in his native village until 1904, when he became notorious for his extravagant teachings, which gave him a Messianic-like position. He was a debauchee and advocated sin in order to obtain repentance and salvation. In 1907 he was presented to the Court where he soon became all-powerful. A seeming miracle which improved the health of the Tsarevich Alexis increased his influence with the Tsar and Tsaritsa. Assassinated by a group of conspirators from the nobility.

Rathbone, Eleanor (1872–1946), social reformer, humanitarian, and independent politician. Championed widows' pensions and family allowances and laboured for political refugees, particularly children.

Ravel, Maurice (1875–1937), French composer, pupil of Fauré, one of the leaders of the impressionist movement. He wrote chiefly chamber music, piano pieces, songs, and ballet music, including *Daphnis et Chloé*, specially commissioned by Diaghilev.

Raven-Hill, Leonard (1867–1942), English artist and cartoonist, was well known for his drawings and cartoons in *Punch*, 1896–1935.

Rawlinson, Sir Henry Creswicke, Bt., G.C.B., F.R.S. (1810–95), diplomat, soldier and orientalist. For a number of years he superintended explorations in Assyria and Babylon, accumulating a valuable collection of antiquities now in the British Museum.

Ray, John (1627–1705), an English naturalist, famous for his contributions to the science of botany. He has been called the "father" of English natural history.

Rayleigh, 3rd Baron, O.M., F.R.S. (1842–1919), one of the most eminent of British physicists; an authority on sound vibrations, and the co-discoverer with Sir William Ramsay of argon. In 1904 was awarded the Nobel Prize for physics.

Read, Sir Herbert, Kt., D.S.O., M.C. (b. 1893), English poet and critic. He was assistant keeper at the Victoria and Albert Museum (1922–31), professor of fine art at Edinburgh (1931–33), and edited the Burlington Magazine (1933–39). His writings include *Poems 1914–1934, In Retreat, Reason and Romanticism, Education through Art, The Meaning of Art.*

Reade, Charles (1814–84), holds high rank amongst the Victorian novelists. His first story, *Peg Woffington*, was published in 1852. *It's Never too Late to Mend, Griffith Gaunt*, and *The Cloister and the Hearth* are his best-known novels.

Réaumur, René Antoine Ferchault de (1683–1757), an eminent French chemist, who invented the temperature scale which bears his name.

Récamier, Madame Jeanne Françoise Julie Adélaide Bernard (1777–1849), a noted society woman of the days of Napoleon.

Reeves, (John) Sims (1818–1900), was the most celebrated English tenor of his time.

Regnault, Henri Victor (1810–78), a French scientist who made highly successful experiments in regard to the physical properties of bodies and their relation to heat.

Regnault, Jean Baptiste, Baron (1754–1829), a talented French genre painter.

Reith, John Charles Walsham, 1st Baron (b. 1889), British civil engineer, the first Director-General of the British Broadcasting Corporation, 1927–38. Recognised as a man of great organising ability, he has served successively as Chairman of Imperial Airways (1938–39), Chairman of B.O.A.C. (1939–40), Min. of Information (Jan.–May 1940), Min. of Transport (May–Oct. 1940), Min. of Works and Buildings (Oct. 1940–Feb. 1942), Dir. of the Admiralty's Combined Operations Material Dept. (1943–45), Chairman Commonwealth Telecommunications Conference (1945), Chairman Commonwealth Communications Council (1946), and Chairman Colonial Development Corporation, 1950–59.

Rembrandt, Harmens van Rijn (1606–69), one of the greatest of the Dutch school of painters who produced many remarkably successful portraits, as well as numerous figure subjects, all of them distinguished by their masterly qualities. He was an etcher of high ability also, and a number of his works are in the British national collections.

Renan, Ernest (1823–92), a noted French author who wrote much upon religious subjects, and won special fame by his *Life of Jesus*, published 1863.

Reni, Guido. (*See* **Guido Reni.**)

Rennie, John, F.R.S. (1761–1821), a Scottish civil engineer. He was the constructor of the Waterloo and Southwark and new London bridges over the Thames, the London Docks, the East and West India Docks, the Plymouth breakwater, and many other works at Liverpool, Leith, Dublin, Hull, and elsewhere.

Renoir, Auguste (1841–1919), great French artist of the Impressionist school, whose vision was carefree and romantic. Some of his greatest achievements were in still-life and landscape. *La Loge, Les Parapluies, La Première Sortie* are famous pictures.

Reuter, Baron Paul Julius de (1821–99), was the pioneer of telegraphic press services.

Reymont, Vladislav Stanislav (1868–1925), Polish novelist; Nobel Prize 1924 (*The Peasants*).

Reynolds, Sir Joshua, P.R.A. (1723–92), was the first President of the R.A. from 1768 till his death, and the most eminent English portrait painter of his time.

Rhodes, Rt. Hon. Cecil John (1853–1902), born at Bishop's Stortford. Went to South Africa in 1871, entered upon a diamond-mining enterprise at Kimberley, and acquired a considerable fortune. Was a member of the Cape Legislature in 1881, and became Premier in 1890. He was at the head of the British South Africa Chartered Company, for which a vast amount of territory was annexed, the holding obtaining the name of Rhodesia. Mr. Rhodes was Cape Premier again in 1896; then followed the Jameson Raid and his retirement from political life. During the Boer War he was detained in Kimberley and did not live to see the campaign closed. He left the bulk of his fortune for the founding of scholarships at Oxford.

Ricardo, David (1772–1823), a celebrated English political economist of Hebrew descent, whose *Principles of Political Economy* gained him a high place among the exponents of the science.

Richard I. (1157–99) was King of England from 1189 to his death. He laid heavy burdens upon the people in order to equip an army for the third Crusade. At first he was victorious and did such valiant deeds that he received the name of "Cœur de Lion." Being ultimately defeated, he signed a truce with Saladin, and on his way back to England was shipwrecked. Disguised as a pilgrim, he was identified in Austria, and handed over to the Emperor of Germany, who imprisoned him in a remote castle. A large sum was demanded and paid for his ransom, and after over a year of durance he returned to England, and was crowned at Winchester. Later he was engaged in a war with France, and was mortally wounded by a bolt from a crossbow while besieging the castle of Chaluz in the province of Limousin.

Richard II. (1367–1400), son of the "Black Prince," succeeded his grandfather, Edward III., in 1377, when but ten years old, a Regency being appointed during his minority. In the Wat Tyler rising of 1381 the King confronted the rioters and promised them redress, an undertaking which he did not fulfil. For a time he was greatly under the influence of his uncle, Thomas, Duke of Gloucester, but on coming of age dismissed him, and ruled with some approach to dignity for the next seven years. After 1396 he developed a highly tyrannical disposition and banished or put to death many of the leading statesmen. The opposition against him came to a head in 1399, when Bolingbroke defeated him, and he was made prisoner and died—probably by starvation—in Pontefract Castle.

Richard III. (1452–85), last Plantagenet king of England who took the throne on the death of his brother Edward IV. in 1483, probably murdering his two younger nephews in the Tower. This led to a rebellion in favour of the Earl of Richmond (later Henry VII.) and he was slain on Bosworth Field. His character has been the subject of dissension among historians but there is no doubt that despite his unscrupulousness (not uncommon in those days) he was a brave soldier and able administrator.

Richards, Sir Gordon (b. 1904), British jockey who had one of the most successful riding records in the history of the British Turf: 21,834 mounts, 4870 winners, including the Derby (1953). Retired, 1954.

Richardson, Sir Albert Edward, K.C.V.O., P.R.A., F.S.A., F.R.I.B.A. (1890–1964), British architect and Pres. of the Royal Academy, 1954–56.

Richardson, Henry Handel, pseudonym of Henrietta Richardson Robertson (1870–1946), Australian novelist whose major work, outstanding in Australian fiction, is the trilogy *The Fortunes of Richard Mahony*.

Richardson, Sir Owen Williams, D.Sc., F.R.S. (1879–1959), distinguished English physicist. Awarded Nobel Prize in 1928 for his researches on the emission of electricity from hot bodies.

Richardson, Sir Ralph David (b. 1902), actor who has made many appearances on stage, screen, and radio.

Richardson, Samuel (1689–1761), author of *Pamela*, *Clarissa*, and *The History of Sir Charles Grandison*, exercised considerable influence on the development of the novel in England.

Richelieu, Armand Jean du Plessis, Cardinal Duc de (1585–1642), the eminent French ecclesiast and statesman, who was Minister to Louis XIII. for eighteen years. He was practically Master of France during the best part of this Cardinalate.

Ridley, Nicholas (1500–55), was Bishop of Rochester in 1547 and Bishop of London in 1550. He took an active part in the Reformation. He was burned at the stake along with Latimer.

Rienzi, Cola di (1313–54), a Roman patriot of humble birth who inflamed the people against their rulers, and aroused such enthusiasm that they proclaimed him "Tribune." During the seven months that he was permitted to exercise supreme power, he proved himself the true friend of the poor. Later murdered in a popular uprising.

Rilke, Rainer Maria (1872–1926), German lyric poet, born in Prague. His work, marked by great beauty of style, culminated in the *Duineser Elegien* and *Sonette an Orpheus*.

Rimbaud, Jean Nicolas Arthur (1854–91), French poet of great originality and friend of Paul Verlaine. All his poems were written between his sixteenth and nineteenth years.

Rimsky-Korsakov, Nikolai Andreyevich (1844–1908), Russian composer whose works include the operas *The Maid of Pskov* (also known as *Ivan the Terrible*), *The Snow Maiden*, *Le Coq d'Or*, and the symphonic suite *Scheherezade*. He was a brilliant orchestrator and rescored many works, including Borodin's *Prince Igor*.

Rizzio, David (*c.* 1540–66), was the Italian secretary of Mary Queen of Scots and an accomplished musician. Suspected of a too great attachment to Mary, he was murdered by Darnley and his friends in the Queen's presence in the Palace of Holyrood.

Robbia, Luca Della (1400–1482), a famous Florentine sculptor. He was the introducer of enamelled terra-cotta work.

Robens, Rt. Hon. Alfred, Baron (b. 1910), Chairman, National Coal Board, 1961– ; Parl. Sec. Min. of Fuel and Power, 1947–51; Min. of Labour and National Service, 1951.

Roberts, Field-Marshal Earl, V.C., K.G., P.C., K.P., G.C.B., O.M., G.C.S.I., G.C.I.E. (1832–1914), the distinguished soldier, first saw service in the Indian Mutiny, when he won the V.C. In 1880 during the Afghanistan campaign made his historic march from Kabul to Kandahar where he won a complete victory. After serving as C.-in-C., India, 1885–93, and as C.-in-C., Ireland, 1895–99, took over in South Africa in December, 1899, and entirely reversed the unhappy military situation before handing over to Kitchener a year later. C.-in-C. from 1901 until the office was abolished in 1904, and was latterly an ardent advocate of conscription.

Robertson, Sir Charles Grant, C.V.O. (1869–1948), English historian who was Vice-Chancellor of Birmingham University, 1927–38, and Principal 1920–38. His works include *The Rise of the English Nation*, 1895, *England under the Hanoverians*, 1911, and *Bismarck*, 1918.

Robertson, Field-Marshal Sir William, Bt., G.C.B., G.C.M.G., G.C.V.O., D.S.O. (1860–1933), the only British soldier to rise from Private to Field-Marshal, served as C.I.G.S., 1915–18. His son, **Brian Hubert, Lord Robertson**, G.C.B. (b. 1892), has had a distinguished military career and was Chairman of the British Transport Commission, 1953–61.

Robeson, Paul Le Roy (b. 1898), the famous Negro singer and actor, who through his singing of spirituals has increased our knowledge and understanding of the Negro. Was a great success in London in 1930 playing *Othello*.

Robespierre, Maximilien François Marie Isidoire de (1758–94), was a country advocate until the outbreak of the French Revolution, when he went to Paris, became an enthusiastic leader of the Jacobin Party, and was made a Member of the Assembly. In the Reign of Terror as President of the Committee of Public Safety he sent vast numbers to the guillotine. Then a counter-movement was set on foot and he was denounced in the Assembly, and, trying to escape, was shot and subsequently guillotined.

Robey, Sir George, C.B.E. **(George Edward Wade)**, (1869–1954), famous British comedian of the music-hall.

Robinson, William Heath (1872–1944), English book illustrator, but especially known for the fantastically comic designs of his cartoons and stage scenery.

Rob Roy (the traditional nickname of **Robert McGregor**) (1671–1734), a noted Highland outlaw who levied blackmail on the farmers and rich people of the country-side in return for certain protective services. He belonged to the clan McGregor.

Robsart, Amy (1532–1560), daughter of Sir John Robsart, and wife of Robert Dudley, afterwards Earl of Leicester. While living in seclusion at Cumnor Place under the charge of Anthony Forster, she met her death either by accident or foul play, by the latter according to common belief, Elizabeth's favourite having reason to wish her out of the way. She was discovered dead at the bottom of an old staircase.

Rockefeller, John Davison (1839–1937) was said to be the richest man in the world. Was born on a small farm in New York State, and there worked until sixteen. Migrated to Cleveland, and found employment in an office for a few years. About this time the oil trade was in a disorganised condition, owing to the reckless trading and crude methods of refining. Rockefeller saw what was wrong, and resolved upon trying to remedy it. Later he began oil-refining, and entered into the business with such vigour of purpose, and made so many improvements, that he became a millionaire in a very few years. From the exertions of himself and associates grew the Standard Oil Trust, beginning with a capital of £200,000 in 1870, and extending at such a rate that in 1892 the capital had reached twenty-two millions sterling. During his life-time he gave some 750 million dollars to education and charity.

Rodin, Auguste (1841–1917), the most celebrated French sculptor of recent days, who possessed a bold and original genius. His numerous statues and his fine historic monuments, especially that for Calais commemorating the bravery of Eustache de Saint-Pierre, brought Rodin well-deserved fame.

Rodney, 1st Baron, K.B. (1719–92), a famous English admiral who, having gained numerous victories routed the French fleet under the Comte de Grasse, whom he took prisoner, the result of this crowning success being the Peace of Versailles, 1783.

Rogers, William Penn Adair ("Will") (1879–1935) was America's foremost humorist and a famous stage and film star; was killed with Wiley Post on a holiday flight to Alaska Aug. 15, 1935.

Roland de la Platière, Madame Manou Jeanne (1754–93), was one of the leading figures of the French Revolution. Her husband, **Jean Marie Roland de la Platière** (1734–93), who was one of the Ministers during the Girondist period, escaped from Paris on the disruption of his Party, but his wife remained behind, and was sent to the guillotine. During her incarceration she wrote an *Appeal to Posterity*, remarkable for its beauty of sentiment and patriotic enthusiasm. Her husband committed suicide on receiving the news of her execution.

Rolland, Romain (1866–1944), an eminent French author whose finest work, *Jean-Christophe*, in ten vols., gained him the Nobel Prize for Literature, 1915.

Romilly, Sir Samuel, K.C. (1757–1818), a famous English lawyer who was Solicitor-General in 1806 and for many years had a distinguished career both in Parliament and at the Bar. He effected many improvements in the Criminal Law.

Rommel, Field-Marshal Erwin (1891–1944), was probably the ablest German general engaged in the second world war. His conduct of the war during the North African campaign won high praise and brought the redoubtable Afrika Corps nearly to Alexandria. He was also engaged in the campaigns in Western Europe in 1940 and 1944.

Romney, George (1734–1802), was born in North Lancashire, studied portrait painting with a Kendal artist, and for a few years obtained a living by local portrait painting. Going to London in 1762, his talent gained him speedy recognition; and after studying for a couple of years in Rome, he set up as a portrait-painter in Cavendish Square, and became highly successful. His portraits are among the finest examples of that kind of art that England has produced, and to-day realise large prices.

Röntgen, Professor Wilhelm Konrad (1845–1923), the eminent German scientist who discovered the Röntgen rays in 1895. He made other important laboratory investigations, resulting in the solution of difficult chemical problems.

Roosevelt, President Franklin Delano (1882–1945), great American statesman. Was Assistant Secretary to the Navy under Wilson and unsuccessful Democratic candidate for the vice-presidency in 1920. In 1921 was stricken with infantile paralysis, but recovered sufficiently to re-enter public life and become Governor of New York in 1929. From 1933 until his death served as President of the U.S.A., being the first American to be elected for more than two terms. His New Deal programme (see Gen. Information Section) was outstanding in his domestic policy. His "good neighbor" attitude towards the other American countries, his hamstrung efforts to restrain Axis aggression in the 1930s, his inspired and generous adoption of Lend-Lease, his war-time meetings with Churchill and Stalin, and his energetic prosecution of the war after Pearl Harbour, were the more important features of his foreign policy. His "fireside" talks on the radio brought him into close contact with the American people and his passing in the hour of victory was mourned all over the world. In 1905 married his distant cousin, **Eleanor Roosevelt** (1884–1962), who became known on her own account as a sociologist and newspaper columnist. She became Chairman of the U.N. Human Rights Commission in 1947.

Roosevelt, Theodore (1858–1919), Republican President of the U.S.A., 1901–9, and unsuccessful third party candidate in 1912 following a dispute with Taft. His daring exploits in the Spanish-American war won him wide popularity and he was elected vice-president in 1900 becoming president on McKinley's assassination. For his efforts in promoting peace, notably between Russia and Japan, was awarded the Nobel Prize in 1906. The great struggle with the Trusts marked his years of office.

Rops, Félicien (1833–98), Belgian artist, famous for drawings, etchings, and illustrations. His work is highly original, spirited, humorous and a valued commentary on the life at the time. Was an engraver of magnificent technical skill and a painter of merit.

Ross, Sir James Clark, F.R.S. (1800–62), most experienced polar explorer of the century. He accompanied his uncle, Sir John Ross, and Captain Parry on their expeditions. In the *Victory* commanded by his uncle he located the north magnetic pole in 1831. He commanded the expedition of the *Erebus* and the *Terror* to the antarctic (1839–43), discovering Victoria Land, Mounts Erebus and Terror, and the Ross ice barrier.

Ross, Rear Admiral Sir John, K.C.B. (1777–1856), the eminent explorer who made several voyages to the arctic and searched for the North-west Passage. He discovered Boothnia peninsula, and his nephew reached the magnetic pole.

Ross, Colonel Sir Ronald, K.C.B., K.C.M.G., F.R.S. (1857–1932), professor of tropical sanitation and a leading authority on tropical diseases generally, was for many years in the Indian Medical Service, and was awarded the Nobel Prize for Medicine in 1902. Discovered the malaria parasite.

Rossetti, Dante Gabriel (1828–82), was the son of Gabriele Rossetti (1783–1852), an exiled Italian author who settled in London in 1824. Dante showed great talent as a painter from boyhood, and became one of the Pre-Raphaelite Brotherhood, formed in 1848. He also distinguished himself as a poet. His sister, **Christina Georgina Rossetti** (1830–94) was also noted as a poet.

Rossini, Gioacchino Antonio (1792–1868), Italian operatic composer. His first opera *Tancredi* was produced at Venice when he was 21, and between 1816 and 1823 he wrote 21 operas, including *Il Barbiere di Seviglia*, *La Cenerentola*, *Otello*, *La Donna del Lago*, and *Semiramide*. After writing *Guillaume Tell* in 1829, which was hailed as his masterpiece, he gave up composing, producing only a *Stabat Mater* (1832–41) and a mass (1864).

Rostand, Edmond Eugene Alexis (1868–1918), French dramatist whose *Cyrano de Bergerac* created a sensation in 1898.

Rothenstein, Sir William (1872–1945), English painter and writer. Prof. of Civic Art in Sheffield University, 1917–26; Principal of Royal College of Art, 1920–35; Trustee, Tate Gallery, 1927–33. His son, **Sir John Rothenstein** (b. 1901), was until 1964 Director of the Tate Gallery and is now Rector of St. Andrews University.

Rothschild, Anselm Meyer (1743–1812), the founder of the famous financial family was born at Frankfurt-on-Main. After some experience in a bank as clerk, set up for himself first as a moneylender, then as a banker and displaying a genius for finance acquired a large fortune. His son, **Nathan Meyer Rothschild** (1777–1836), took charge of the London house, and conducted its affairs with great success, and was made an Austrian Baron in 1822. He was succeeded by his eldest son, **Baron Lionel de Rothschild** (1808–1879), who was the first Jewish member of the House of Commons.

Roubillac, Louis François (1695–1762), a French sculptor who contributed many monuments to Westminster Abbey.

Rouget de Lisle, Claude Joseph (1760–1836), a French poet who was the author of the words and the music of the *Marseillaise*, the revolutionary song and national anthem of France.

Rousseau, Jean-Jacques (1712–78), French philosopher, political writer, and composer. He was born at Geneva, and after a hard and wandering life made the acquaintance of Madame de Warens, who became his patroness and with whom he resided during the years 1731–41. He then proceeded to Paris, where he made the acquaintance of Diderot, to whose *Encyclopédie* he contributed the musical section. With the production of his pastoral melodrama *Le Devin du village* in 1722 he appeared as a successful composer. Meanwhile he had been studying social questions with great ardour, and in 1761 published his novel *Julie, ou la Nouvelle Héloïse*, which was followed in 1762 by *Emile*, a treatise on education in novel form. These two works contained so much that was at variance with convention, and so opposed to all ideas of moral restraint, that they called forth the condemnation of the orthodox, and Rousseau was obliged to leave France for a time. It was while in England that he wrote his remarkable *Confessions*, and his celebrated *Le Contrat Social*. He laid down principles of government and conduct which bore fruit in the French Revolution. (*See also* **Education, Section J.**)

Rubens, Sir Peter Paul (1577–1640), one of the most notable of Flemish painters. In 1629 he painted for Charles I., who knighted him. His *Adoration of the Magi* was sold in 1959 for the record price of £275,000.

Rubinstein, Anton Grigorovich (1829–94), a famous Russian pianist and composer and founder of the Conservatory St. Petersburg (now Leningrad). His brother Nicholas (1835–81), also a pianist, founded the Conservatory of Moscow.

Rupert, Prince (1619–82), the brilliant Royalist cavalry general opposing Cromwell and a distinguished admiral in the Dutch wars. He was also an early mezzotinter, an experimental scientist, and the first governor of Hudson's Bay Company.

Rusk, Dean, M.A., LL.D. (b. 1909), U.S. Secretary of State in the Democratic Administrations of Kennedy and Johnson, 1961–; Pres. The Rockefeller Foundation, 1952–60. Former Rhodes scholar at St. John's Coll., Oxford.

Ruskin, John (1819–1900), writer and art critic, the son of a wealthy London wine merchant. His *Modern Painters* exhibited a masterly perception of the principles of art and a boundless gift of literary expression. Other volumes appeared at intervals including *The Seven Lamps of Architecture* and *The Stones of Venice*, two memorable works which considerably enhanced the author's fame. His writings undoubtedly hastened the recognition of Turner and the Pre-Raphaelite painters. Always taking a deep interest in economic questions, Ruskin delivered and published numerous lectures on a wide range of subjects—art, pleasure, religion, war, work, and so forth; and he was acknowledged to be one of the greatest thinkers of the time. Often his views were impracticable and even eccentric, but behind them there was always evident a sincere desire to promote the well-being of the people.

Russell, Bertrand (Arthur William) 3rd Earl, O.M., F.R.S., M.A. (b. 1872), great English philosopher and mathematician, whose vigorous and sceptical writings have profoundly influenced present-day thought. He writes and speaks in a clear, witty, and elegant style and regards the task of the philosopher as one of clarification rather than speculation. In recent years Lord Russell has been actively engaged in the campaign against nuclear warfare. His numerous writings include books on mathematics, philosophy, and ethics, besides works on political and sociological subjects: *The Principles of Mathematics* (1903), *Principia Mathematica* (1910), written in collaboration with A. N. Whitehead, *Problems of Philosophy* (1911), *Marriage and Morals* (1929), *History of Western Philosophy* (1945), *Human Knowledge* (1948), *Commonsense and Nuclear Warfare* (1959). Nobel Prize for Literature, 1950.

Russell, George William (1867–1935), Irish poet generally known by his pen name of A.E. or Æ. Widely known as a leader in co-operative enterprise and a pioneer of Abbey Theatre, Dublin.

Russell, John, 1st Earl, K.G., P.C. (1792–1878), third son of the 6th Duke of Bedford. Entered Parliament as Lord John Russell on attaining his majority, and, ranging himself on the Liberal side, showed great capacity for affairs. Introduced first great measure of Reform, which was passed in 1832. Held several offices before succeeding Peel as Prime Minister in 1846. Remained in power until 1852, and was again Prime Minister from 1865 to 1866, resigning when he failed to carry a further reform bill. He also wrote lives of Thomas Moore and Charles James Fox.

Russell of Killowen, Baron, P.C., G.C.M.G. (1832–1900), Lord Chief Justice of England 1894–98. Was one of the greatest British judges and advocates of the 19th century.

Rutherford, Lord, O.M., F.R.S. (1871–1937), of New Zealand birth. Physicist, pre-eminent in the field of atomic research. Conducted his experiments at Montreal, Manchester, and at the famous Cavendish Laboratory at Cambridge, which attracted brilliant young scientists from all over the world. In 1911 announced his nuclear theory of the atom, and in 1918 succeeded in splitting the atom for the first time. His work paved the way for future nuclear research.

Ruysdael, Jacob van (*c.* 1628–82), great Dutch landscape painter, some of whose pictures are in the National Gallery.

Ruyter, Admiral Michiel Adriaanzoon de (1607–76), the Dutch admiral who in 1667 invaded England with a fleet of Dutch war vessels, advancing up the Thames and Medway and setting fire to considerable shipping. He soon saw fit to retreat, and more serious trouble was averted.

S

Sachs, Hans (1494–1576), the German shoemaker-poet of Reformation times, was an earnest worker in the Protestant cause, and wrote over 5,000 different pieces, poetry and prose.

Sadi, or Saadi (Muslih-Uddin) (*c.* 1184–1292), the Persian poet who flourished in the 13th century, and won national fame by his poems *The Garden of Roses* and *The Orchard.*

Sainte-Beuve, Charles Augustin (1804–69), French critic, and one of the most accomplished men of letters under the Second Empire. Author of *Causeries du lundi* and *Histoire de Port Royal.*

Saint-Just, Antoine (1767–94), one of the later leaders of the French Revolution closely associated with Robespierre.

St.-Laurent, Rt. Hon. Louis Stephen, Q.C. (b. 1882). Prime Minister of Canada, 1948–57.

Saint-Saëns, Charles Camille (1835–1921), French composer. His compositions have a classical style and elegance and include symphonic and chamber music and the opera *Samson et Dalila*, which was produced by Liszt at Weimar in 1877.

Saint-Simon, Claude, Comte de (1760–1825), a French scientist and socialist who had great influence upon the thought of his time.

Saintsbury, George Edward Bateman (1845–1933). Professor of Rhetoric and English Literature, Edinburgh University, 1895–1915. Author of numerous critical works on literary subjects, on which he was a leading authority.

Sala, George Augustus Henry (1828–95), journalist of high literary merit who contributed to *Household Words*, the *Illustrated London News*, and the London *Daily Telegraph* (foreign correspondent in all parts of the world).

Saladin (1137–93), the great Sultan of Egypt and Syria who led the Moslems against the Christians in the Third Crusade. In 1187 he had driven the Christians from Jerusalem after a brilliant victory at Hattin near Tiberias. This gave rise to the Third Crusade led by the Emperor Frederick I., Philip II. of France, and Richard I. of England, which achieved little. Besides being a great warrior, Saladin was a wise and cultured man, renowned for his chivalry.

Salazar, Antonio d'Oliveira (b. 1889), Prime Minister and virtual dictator of Portugal since 1932 and responsible for drafting the Portuguese constitution of 1933. Foreign Minister, 1936–47.

Salda, František (1867–1937), Czech critic, essayist, and poet whose influence on Czech thought has been profound.

Salimbene de Adamo (1221–*c.* 1288), mediæval chronicler whose vivid description of life in the 13th century is embodied in his *Cronica.*

Salisbury, Robert Arthur Talbot Gascoyne Cecil, 3rd Marquess of, K.G. (1830–1903), led the Conservative Governments of 1885–86, 1886–92, and 1895–1902. Has been considered one of the best Foreign Secretaries England has ever had, holding the office from 1878 to 1880, when he attended the Congress of Berlin, and for much of his premiership. Retired from political life after peace was declared in South Africa. His grandson, **Robert Arthur James Gascoyne-Cecil, 5th Marquess of Salisbury,** K.G. (b. 1893), was Leader of the House of Lords, 1942–45 and again 1951–57 when he resigned from the Government over its Cyprus policy. As Viscount Cranborne served as Sec. of State for the Dominions and for the Colonies.

Samuel, 1st Viscount, P.C., O.M., G.C.B., G.B.E. (1870–1963), Liberal statesman, High Commissioner for Palestine, 1920–22; Postmaster-General, 1910–14, and again May to Dec. 1915; Home Secretary, 1916, and again 1931–32. M.P. for Cleveland Division (N. Riding, Yorks), 1902–18, and Darwen Div. of Lancs., 1929–35. Chancellor of the Duchy of Lancaster, 1909–10 and 1915–16. Leader of the Liberal Party in the Commons, 1931–35, and in the Lords, 1941–55.

Sand, George (1804–76) the leading French authoress of her time—proper name, Armandine Lucile Aurore Dupin, baronne Dudevant—who, both as novelist and dramatist, achieved the highest success. A friend of men of such singular power as Alfred de Musset, Chopin and Sandeau.

Sandow, (Frederick William) Eugene (1867–1925), German "strong man"; overcame his early physical weakness to become a powerfully built man; adviser on physical culture to King George V.

Sanger, Frederick, B.A., Ph.D., F.R.S. (b. 1918), British scientist; Prof. of Biochemistry, Cambridge. Awarded 1958 Nobel Prize for Chemistry for his work in determining the chemical structure of the protein insulin.

Sankey, Ira David (1840–1908), the celebrated American evangelist, singer, and composer, associated with Dwight L. Moody, the revivalist (1837–1899) in mission-work.

San Martin, General José de (1778–1850), the principal figure in the liberation from Spanish rule of three countries: his native Argentina, Chile, and Peru.

Santayana, George (1863–1952), philosopher and poet, born in Madrid of Spanish parentage. He was Professor of Philosophy at Harvard University (where he graduated in 1886) from 1907–12, when he moved to France and thereafter spent his time wandering from country to country. His books include *The Life of Reason* (1905–6), the four volumes of *Realms of Being* (1923–40), *Persons and Places* (1945), and *The Middle Span* (1948).

Santos-Dumont, Alberto (1873–1932), Brazilian aeronaut, his most notable flights being made in Paris, and at Monte Carlo. He visited London in 1903.

Sappho of Lesbos (fl. early 6th cent. B.C.), famous lyric poetess of ancient Greece, of whose love poems only a few fragments remain.

Sardou, Victorien (1831–1908), French dramatist who had a long series of successes—*Nos Intimes*, *Séraphine*, *Rabagas*, *Divorçons*, *Fédora*, *Théodora*, *Patrie*, *La Tosca*, *Madame Sans-Gêne*, *Robespierre*, and *Dante*, the last-named written specially for Sir Henry Irving. He was elected to the French Academy in 1877.

Sargent, Sir Harold Malcolm Watts, A.R.C.O., F.R.C.M., F.R.S.A. (b. 1895), one of the best known modern British conductors. Succeeded Sir Adrian Boult as permanent conductor of the B.B.C. Symphony Orchestra, 1950–57.

Sargent, John Singer, R.A. (1856–1922). He was of American parentage and received his art education in Paris. As a portrait-painter he had few equals.

Sartre, Jean-Paul (b. 1905), French existentialist philosopher, left-wing intellectual, dramatist, essayist and novelist. Captured by the Germans in 1940, he was released on medical grounds the following year and joined the resistance movement. His major philosophical work is *L'Etre et le Néant* and his plays include *Les Mouches*, *Huis Clos*, *Crime passionnel*, *La Putain respectueuse*, and *Les Séquestrés d'Altona*. The first volume of his autobiography, *Les Mots*, was published in 1964. He was awarded (though he declined it) the 1964 Nobel Prize for Literature. *See* **Modern Drama**.

Sassoon, Siegfried (Lorraine), C.B.E. (b. 1886), English poet and writer who received the Hawthornden Prize, 1929, for *The Memoirs of a Fox-hunting Man*.

Savonarola, Girolamo (1452–98), Florentine preacher and reformer, a Dominican friar, who denounced vice and corruption not only in society but also in the Church itself, especially attacking Pope Alexander VI. He was excommunicated, imprisoned, and with two of his companions hanged in public. His passion for reform made him impatient of opposition and incapable of compromise. He understood men's hearts but not their limitations. Yet he was a noble figure rightly commanding the respect of later ages. George Eliot's historical romance *Romola* gives a fine portrait of Savonarola.

Sayce, Prof. Archibald Henry, D.Litt., LL.D., D.D. (1845–1933), a distinguished Assyriologist and philologist who was Prof. of Assyriology at Oxford University, 1891–1919. His most important works are *Introduction to the Science of Language*, 1879, *Ancient Empires of the East*, 1884, *The Principles of Comparative Philology*, 1874, and *Egypt and Babylonian Religion*, 1903.

Scarlatti, Alessandro (1659–1725), Italian musician whose influence on the history of opera has been great, founded the Neapolitan school. He composed over 100 operas, 200 masses, and over 700 cantatas and oratorios. His son **Domenico** (1685–1757) was a harpsichord virtuoso and his work has had an important influence in the evolution of the sonata. The chief years of his life were spent at the Spanish Court in Madrid.

Schiaparelli, Giovanni Virginio (1835–1910), famous Italian astronomer who was Director of the Milan Observatory, 1862–1900, and did valuable work on meteors and double stars, but is best known for his discovery of so-called canals on Mars.

Schiller, Johan Christolph Friedrich (1759–1805), the famous German dramatist and poet. Was born at Marbach in Württemberg. Educated at the military Academy at Stuttgart, and intended for a soldier, he evinced an irresistible desire for literary fame, and in 1782 had his first play, *The Robbers*, successfully produced at the Mannheim Theatre, to which he was subsequently appointed dramatic composer. Later he went to Dresden, where he completed his *Don Carlos*; from 1789 to 1793 he held the chair of history at Jena Univ. when he wrote his *History of the Thirty Years' War*, and gained the friendship of Goethe, at whose suggestion he removed to Weimar, and during the next ten years produced his greatest works—*Wallenstein*, *Mary Stuart*, *The Maid of Orleans*, and *William Tell*.

Schlegel, August Wilhelm von (1767–1845), German poet and scholar, best known for his translations of Shakespeare (which established Shakespeare in Germany), Dante, Calderón, and Camões. His *Lectures on Dramatic Art and Literature* are outstanding for their scholarship.

Schliemann, Heinrich (1822–90), German archæologist who made many notable excavations, discovered Troy and other Homeric sites.

Schnabel, Artur (1882–1951), American pianist of Austrian birth, regarded as the greatest exponent of Beethoven's pianoforte sonatas.

Schönberg, Arnold (1874–1951), Austrian composer who in 1933 was dismissed from his post as head of the Prussian Academy of Fine Arts because of his Jewish ancestry. He went to the United States, teaching first at Boston and then at Los Angeles. Among his works are the choral orchestral *Gurre-Lieder* and *Pierrot Lunaire*, a cycle of 21 poems for voice and chamber music.

Schopenhauer, Arthur (1788–1860), German philosopher of a pessimistic cast of mind, a great admirer of Plato and Heraclitus. Regarded his contemporary Hegel as a charlatan. His chief works are *The World Considered as Will and Idea* and *The Two Fundamental Problems of Ethics*.

Schreiner, Olive, pen name of Mrs. Cronwright Schreiner (1855–1920), a noted South African novelist, born in Basutoland. She first attracted attention with her *Story of an African Farm* (1883). She excelled in depicting veldt scenery and Dutch character.

Schubert, Franz Peter (1797–1828), Austrian composer, born in Vienna, the son of a schoolmaster. He was a contemporary of Beethoven and wrote not only symphonies, sonatas, string quartets, choral music, and Masses but also over 600 songs of unsurpassed lyrical beauty. It is as creator of the German *Lied* that his name is immortal. He died in Vienna at the age of 31, in poverty, before the full flowering of his musical genius.

Schumann, Robert Alexander (1810–56), composer of the early 19th-century German Romantic school. He wrote much chamber music, four symphonies, a piano concerto, and choral music, but it is his early piano pieces and songs that give constant delight. His wife **Clara** (1819–96) was one of the outstanding pianists of her time, especially as interpreter of Chopin.

Schweitzer, Albert, D.Theol., Dr. Phil., Dr. Med. (1875–1965), famous medical missionary in Lambaréné, remembered for his reverence for life. A musical critic and authority on Bach's music, a famous organist, and a noted biblical critic he became a Doctor of Medicine in order to devote his life to missionary work in Equatorial Africa. Awarded 1952 Nobel Prize for Peace and Hon. O.M. in 1955.

Scipio, Publius Cornelius (*circa* 232–183 B.C.), the greatest of the Scipios known as Scipio Africanus the elder. A distinguished Roman general in the 2nd Punic War.

Scott, Charles Prestwich (1846–1931), English journalist who was editor of the *Manchester Guardian*, 1872–1929, which under his editorship became one of the leading journals of the country.

Scott, Sir George Gilbert, R.A. (1811–78), architect who gained special fame for his restorations of Gothic churches and cathedrals, incl. Westminster Abbey, designer of the Albert Memorial, St. Pancras Station, the Martyrs' Memorial at Oxford, and St. Anne's Church in Alderney.

Scott, Sir Giles Gilbert, O.M., R.A., F.R.I.B.A. (1880–1960), architect whose work includes the great modern Gothic Liverpool Cathedral, the Bodleian Library, Oxford, and the Forth Road Bridge (opened 1964). Grandson of the above

Scott, Peter Markham, M.B.E., D.S.C. (b. 1909), son of Captain Scott, is known as yachtsman, broadcaster, and bird-artist.

Scott, Captain Robert Falcon, C.V.O. (1868–1912), commanded the National Antarctic Expeditions in 1901–4 and in 1910. His ship, the *Terra Nova*, left England on June 1, 1910. In Jan. 1911, winter quarters were established at Cape Evans, and in the following November Scott and a select party left Hut Point for the South Pole, which they reached on Jan. 18, 1912, finding there the Amundsen records. On the return journey every member of the party perished. Leading-seaman Edgar Evans died from concussion of the brain on Feb. 17; Capt. Oates from exposure on March 17; and on March 29 the rest of the party (Scott, Wilson and Bowers) died from starvation and exposure in a blizzard when only 11 miles from One Ton Depot.

Scott, Sir Walter, Bart. (1771–1832), one of the greatest of British novelists and a distinguished poet. He was educated for the Bar. His *Minstrelsy of the Scottish Border* was published in 1802. This was followed in 1805 by *The Lay of the Last Minstrel*, in 1808 by *Marmion*; *The Lady of the Lake*, *Rokeby* and *The Lord of the Isles* coming afterwards in quick succession. In 1814 he published *Waverley* anonymously, which obtained instant success. Other stories followed and the Waverley novels and their author, "The great Unknown," were everywhere the subject of discussion. *Guy Mannering*, *The Antiquary*, *Old Mortality*, *Rob Roy*, and the *Heart of Midlothian* were all published before the secret of their authorship was disclosed. The chief works of his last years were *Woodstock*, *Life of Napoleon*, and *Tales of a Grandfather*. He died at Abbotsford. Created a baronet in 1820.

Scott-Paine, Hubert (1891–1954), pioneer in the design and construction of aircraft and sea craft.

Scriabin, Alexander (1872–1915), Russian composer and pianist. He studied at the Moscow conservatoire, where he was later professor of the pianoforte, 1898–1904. He was deeply interested in theosophy, and in such works as *The Divine Poem*, and *Prometheus: a Poem of Fire* he attempted to unite music and philosophy

Seeley, Sir John Robert, K.C.M.G. (1834–95), English historian and author of *Ecce Homo*.

Segovia, Andrés (b. 1894), Spanish concert-guitarist. He has adapted works by Bach, Haydn, Mozart, and other classical composers to the guitar.

Selfridge, Harry Gordon (1858–1947), the American who revolutionised the British department store when he opened the famous shop of Selfridges in Oxford Street in 1909.

Semmelweis, Ignaz Philipp (1818–65), Hungarian physician, a pioneer in employing antiseptic methods in obstetric cases, having discovered that puerperal fever is an infection caused by germs. It was then the practice of doctors in maternity wards to examine expectant mothers with unwashed hands.

Seneca, Lucius Annaeus (*circa* 4 B.C.–A.D. 56), the famous stoic philosopher, who was tutor to Nero, and one of that emperor's most influential advisers; he was sentenced to end his own life, a sentence which he courageously carried out.

Senefelder, Alois (1772–1834), was the son of an actor at Munich, and himself engaged in dramatic composition. Being too poor to bear the cost of having his works printed, he turned his attention to inventing lithography, the main feature of the invention being discovered by accident.

Severus, Lucius Septimius (146–211), was Roman Emperor from 193 to his death. After many victories in the East he passed over to Britain with an army, subjugated the Caledonians, and repaired and partly rebuilt the famous Hadrian's wall from the Solway Firth to the mouth of the Tyne. He died at York.

Sévigné, Marie de Rabutin-Chantal, Marquise de (1626–96), French woman of letters. Her letters to her daughter Françoise written in an unaffected elegance of style give a moving picture of fashionable society in 17th-century France.

Sgambati, Giovanni (1841–1914), Italian pianist and composer who revived interest in classical instrumental music in an age of opera. Well known is his quartet in D flat.

Shackleton, Sir Ernest (Henry), C.V.O., O.B.E. (1874–1922), commander of the Nimrod Farthest South expedition of 1907–9, reached within 100 miles of the South Pole, and embarked on a new expedition in 1914. He died whilst on a scientific voyage to the Antarctic.

Shaftesbury, Anthony Ashley Cooper, 7th Earl of (1801–85), great social reformer, largely responsible for the legislation reducing the misery of the industrial revolution. He agitated for the abolition of slavery and was connected with the Ragged School Union, reformatories, refuges, and Christian associations of many kinds.

Shakespeare, William (1564–1616), England's greatest poet and dramatist, was born at Stratford-on-Avon, and was the son of a tradesman of that town who must have been at one time fairly well-off, seeing that he was made an alderman, and afterwards served as High Bailiff. Later on, however, he appears to have been unfortunate and fallen into straitened circumstances. William was the eldest son, and was probably educated at the Stratford Grammar School, but very little is known of his career up to his eighteenth year, when we have it on record that he married Anne Hathaway, who was eight years his senior. Five years after his marriage he went to London, and the next we hear of him is that he was connected with the Globe Theatre and appeared in sundry small parts. He first appeared before the public as a poet in 1593, with his *Venus and Adonis*, following this in 1594 with *The Rape of Lucrece*. Shortly afterwards he was proprietor of the Globe Theatre, and also had an interest in the Blackfriars Theatre. Then he began that remarkable career of play-writing which has since been the wonder of the world. Thirty-eight plays comprise the Shakespeare canon. Thirty-six were printed in the First Folio of 1623 (the first collected edition of his dramatic works), of which eighteen had been published during his lifetime in the so-called Quartos. *Love's Labour's Lost* and *The Comedy of Errors* seem to have been among the earliest, being followed by *The Two Gentlemen of Verona*, and *Romeo and Juliet*. Then followed *Henry VI*, *Richard III*, *Richard II*, *Titus Andronicus*, *The Taming of the Shrew*, *King John*, *The Merchant of Venice*, *A Midsummer Night's Dream*, *All's Well that Ends Well*, *Henry IV*, *The Merry Wives of Windsor*, *Henry V*, *Much Ado about Nothing*, *As You Like It*, *Twelfth Night*. Then came some of his greatest plays, *Julius Cæsar*, *Hamlet*, *Troilus and Cressida*, *Othello*, *Measure for Measure*, *Macbeth*, *King Lear*, *Timon of Athens*, *Pericles*, *Antony and Cleopatra*, *Coriolanus*, *Cymbeline*, *A Winter's Tale*, *The Tempest*, *Henry VIII*, and *The Two Noble Kinsmen*. He was able to purchase property at Stratford, and when he retired from his profession (about 1610 or 1612) he returned to his native town to live in a house which he had himself built. He was buried in Stratford Church.

Sharp, Granville (1735–1813), slavery abolitionist and founder of the colony of Sierra Leone.

Shastri, Shri Lal Bahadur (1904–66), Indian politician who became Prime Minister of India after the death of Nehru in 1964. He died of a heart attack at the end of the Soviet-sponsored Tashkent talks. *See also* **Section C. Part I.**

Shaw, George Bernard (1856–1950), brilliant Irish dramatist who conquered England by his pungent wit and devastating exposure of hypocrisy, cant and national weaknesses, and persistently expressed a highly individual opinion whether in his musical criticisms, socialist pamphlets or plays. He wrote many plays including *Man and Superman*, *Heartbreak House*, *Back to Methuselah*, *Saint Joan*, *The Apple Cart*, *Buoyant Billions*, most of which have important prefaces, sometimes equalling the play in length. Was music critic (1888–94) successively to the London *Star* and *World* and during this period wrote *The Quintessence of Ibsenism* and *The Perfect Wagnerite*. Joined the Fabian Society in 1884 and was awarded Nobel Prize for Literature in 1925. He was greatly interested in the reform of the alphabet.

Shelley, Percy Bysshe (1792–1822), one of the most brilliant poetic geniuses of the 19th century, renowned for the daring and unorthodox opinions which he held. His *Queen Mab* (written when he was nineteen), his *Alastor*, *The Revolt of Islam*, *The Witch of Atlas*, and *Adonais* all breathe the true spirit of poetry.

securing him a place in the first rank of British poets. He showed fine dramatic gifts in the *Cenci* and *Prometheus Unbound*, almost reaching sublimity in the latter masterpiece. His *Adonais* was a splendid tribute to the genius of Keats. His first wife, whom he married while very young, committed suicide. He afterwards married Mary Wollstonecraft Godwin, and formed other attachments of a complicating nature. Was always at war with his family, and finally, after spending some time with Byron and Leigh Hunt and other friends in various parts of Italy, was drowned in the Gulf of Spezia by the capsizing of his boat in a storm.

Sheppard, Very Rev. Hugh Richard Lawrie (Dick), C.H., D.D. (1880–1937), Vicar of St. Martin-in-the-Fields, London, 1914–27, where he established a reputation by his broadcast sermons and attracted large crowds of listeners. Dean of Canterbury, 1929–31; Canon of St. Paul's, 1934–37. Buried in Canterbury Cathedral.

Sheraton, Thomas (1751–1806), was the last of the great English furniture designers of the 18th cent. There is no evidence that he was a maker of furniture; his reputation rests solely on his published works which helped to create a certain trend or style, notably the *Cabinet-Makers' and Upholsterers' Drawing Book* (1791–94).

Sheridan, Rt. Hon. Richard Brinsley Butler (1751–1816), one of the greatest of English playwrights, whose comedies are frequently revived. Was born in Dublin, and educated partly at Harrow. Showing considerable capacity for dramatic composition he obtained an introduction to the Covent Garden management, and it was at the Covent Garden Theatre in 1775 that his first comedy, *The Rivals*, was produced, with such a gratifying result that Garrick, who was then at Drury Lane, opened up negotiations with the dramatist which ended in Sheridan becoming part (and ultimately sole) proprietor of Drury Lane. *The Duenna*, a musical comedy, was produced in 1775, and ran through the winter. From 1777 Sheridan managed Drury Lane, opening with an adaptation of Vanbrugh's *Relapse*. This was followed by the production of the greatest of his comedies, *The School for Scandal*, which had a wonderful success. In 1779 *The Critic* was given, and after that Sheridan wrote no more plays until 1789, when *Pizarro* was produced. In the meantime he had gained a high reputation in another sphere. In 1780 he obtained a seat in Parliament and although he only spoke on certain set occasions, he acquired a reputation for oratory which stood him in very good stead, and he filled one or two minor Ministerial offices, remaining in Parliament until 1812.

Sherman, General William Tecumseh (1820–91), a famous American soldier who, after taking part in the War with Mexico (1846–48), volunteered at the outbreak of the Civil War (1861). He took part in the battles of Bull Run and Shiloh, and was placed in command of the Army of the Tennessee (1863) and of the military division of the Mississippi with a force of 100,000. In 1864 there occurred the famous 300-mile march across Georgia to the sea. In 1865 his second march, through the Carolinas, culminated in the defeat of Johnston, which led directly to the termination of the war.

Sherrington, Sir Charles Scott, O.M., G.B.E., F.R.S., M.D., D.Sc. (1857–1952), one of the greatest of British scientists, and a leading authority on the physiology of the nervous system, whose research work over many years led to great advances in the surgery of the brain. Pres. of the British Association 1920, and of the Royal Society, 1920–25. Awarded Nobel Prize for Medicine, 1932.

Shirley, James (1596–1666), was an eminent dramatist and poet, imbued with the Elizabethan traditions.

Sholokhov, Mikhail Aleksandrovich (b. 1905), great Russian novelist who won international fame with his novel *And Quiet Flows the Don*. Nobel Prize for Literature, 1965.

Shostakovich, Dmitry Dmitryevich (b. 1906), one of the most celebrated of present-day Russian composers. His music is complex, profound, and deeply significant of the Soviet age in which he lives. His works include operas, ballets, symphonies, chamber music, and music for films.

Sibelius, Jean Julian Christian (1865–1957), Finnish composer, generally acknowledged as the greatest of the century. Works include seven symphonies, violin concerto, several tone poems, about 200 pianoforte compositions and songs.

Sickert, (Walter) Richard (1860–1942), British painter and etcher; became President of Royal Society of British Artists, 1928.

Siddons, Sarah (1755–1831), the greatest of the English tragic actresses, b. at Brecon, South Wales, eldest of the famous Kemble family. She made her first appearance in London at Drury Lane in 1775 in the part of Portia.

Sidgwick, Henry (1838–1900), Professor of Moral Philosophy at Cambridge, and besides being an eminent educationist in the broader sense, devoted himself with special success to the cause of women's education, Newnham and Girton being largely the outcome of his efforts.

Sidney, Sir Philip (1554–86), statesman, poet and soldier; was one of Queen Elizabeth's favourites, and a man of singular ability and bravery. While living in temporary retirement he composed his famous *Arcadia*, but did not allow it to be published in his lifetime. He did not lack for literary fame, however, his *Apology for Poetry* and *Defence of Poesy*, as well as numerous miscellaneous pieces all distinguished for their beauty of expression and tender sentiment, having won much favour, especially in the circle of the Court. In 1586 he was given a command in the Netherlands and was killed at Zutphen.

Siemens, Sir William, F.R.S. (1823–83), a German-born scientist and inventor, chiefly in the field of heat and electricity. Constructed many overland and submarine telegraphs. Brother of Werner v. Siemens, founder of the famous firm of Siemens-Halske.

Sienkiewicz, Henryk (1846–1916), famous Polish novelist; Nobel prizewinner, 1905 (*Quo Vadis*).

Sikorski, Wladyslaw (1881–1943), Polish general and statesman; Prime Minister during second world war.

Simpson, Sir James Young, Bt., F.R.S. (1811–70), the discoverer of the utility of chloroform as an anæsthetic, was a native of Scotland, and was a most accomplished experimental surgeon.

Sinclair, Upton (b. 1878), American novelist whose documentary novel *The Jungle* about the Chicago slaughter yards caused a sensation in 1906.

Singer, Isaac Meritt (1811–75), American mechanical engineer who devoted himself to the improvement of the early forms of the sewing-machine and patented a single-thread and chain-stitch machine.

Sisley, Alfred (1839–1899), French Impressionist painter of English origin. Painted with great delicacy and sensitivity, landscapes, villages, trees, and rivers. Influenced by Corot and Manet.

Sitwell, Edith (Louisa), D.B.E. (1887–1964), English poet whose works include *Bucolic Comedies*, *Gold Coast Customs* and *Collected Poems*. Her two brothers are **Osbert** (b. 1892), a well-known poet and novelist, and **Sacheverell** (b. 1900), a poet and critic. *See also* **M2**.

Slim, Field-Marshal Viscount, K.G., G.C.B., G.C.M.G., G.C.V.O., G.B.E., D.S.O., M.C. (b. 1891), Gov.-Gen. of Australia 1953–59. In 1943 took command of the 14th Army in Burma, later becoming commander of the Allied Land Forces, S.E.A.C., and then Commandant of the Imperial Defence College. Succeeded Lord Montgomery as C.I.G.S., 1948–52. Gov. and Constable Windsor Castle, 1964–.

Sloane, Sir Hans, Bt., F.R.S. (1660–1753), was born in County Down, Ireland, but settled in London, and became famed as a physician and naturalist. For some years he held the office of President of the Royal College of Physicians, and was elected President of the Royal Society in succession to Sir Isaac Newton. His Library of 50,000 vols., and treasures in natural history and MSS., worth from £50,000 to £80,000, were offered by his will to, and bought by the nation for £20,000, and with that nucleus the British Museum was founded.

Slowacki, Julius (1809–49), Polish romantic poet. He was a revolutionary, lived in exile and died in Paris. His tragedies include *Kordian*, *Belladyna* and *Lilli Weneda*.

Smeaton, John (1724–92), who rebuilt Eddystone Lighthouse, which had been burned down; he subsequently constructed many important works in connection with harbours and canals. He was also the inventor of an improved blowing apparatus for iron-smelting.

Smetana, Bedřich (1824–84), Czech composer, creator of a national style. He was principal conductor of the Prague National Theatre, for which he wrote most of his operas, including *The Bartered Bride* and *The Kiss*. Best known of his other compositions are the cycle of symphonic poems *My Country* and the string quartets *From My Life*. He became totally deaf in 1874, suffered a mental breakdown, and died in an asylum.

Smiles, Dr. Samuel (1812–1904), was in early life a medical practitioner; achieved wide popularity by his *Self Help*, a book that has had an enormous sale.

Smith, Adam, F.R.S. (1723–90), the father of the science of political economy. Author of *Theory of Moral Sentiments* and *Wealth of Nations*, which immediately obtained the admiration of the leading men of the day, and secured him the friendship of Gibbons, Hume, Burke, Reynolds, and Dugald Stewart.

Smith, Sir Grafton Elliot, M.A., Litt.D., D.Sc., F.R.S. (1871–1937), Australian anatomist and archaeologist who was professor of anatomy at Manchester and London Universities. His works include *The Royal Mummies* (1912), *Tutankhamen* (1923), *The Evolution of Man* (1924), and the *Diffusion of Culture* (1933).

Smith, Captain John (1580–1631), the noted seafarer and adventurer who in 1605 was the leading spirit of an expedition to Virginia, and founded Jamestown.

Smith, Joseph (1805–44), founder of Mormonism, son of a Vermont farmer. Claimed to have been granted revelation of the *Book of Mormon*, which came to be held as equal in authority and as a necessary supplement to the Scriptures. Smith, who was murdered, was not a polygamist; Brigham Young, who succeeded him, was. (*See* **Mormonism, Section J.**)

Smith, Sydney (1771–1845), an Anglican divine, who enjoyed a great reputation as a wit and writer. Founder of and contributor to the *Edinburgh Review* and author of *Peter Plymley's Letters*, supporting Catholic Emancipation.

Smith, William (1769–1839), English surveyor and geologist, the first to map the rock strata of England and to identify the fossils peculiar to each layer.

Smith, William Robertson (1846–94), Scottish biblical scholar whose contributions to the 9th edition of *The Encyclopaedia Britannica* resulted in an unsuccessful prosecution for heresy and led to the modernisation of Scottish theology.

Smollett, Tobias George (1721–71), a famous English novelist and humorist, whose *Roderick Random*, *Peregrine Pickle*, *Count Fathom* and *Humphrey Clinker* abound in fun and genial characterisation, while their pictures of sea-life are inimitable.

Smuts, Field-Marshal Rt. Hon. Jan Christiaan, O.M., C.H., K.C. (1870–1950), South African soldier and statesman, one of the dominating political figures of our century. Born in Cape Colony, studied at Cambridge University, and called to the Bar. Was an outstanding Boer commando leader during the South African War, but afterwards worked for friendship with the British and took office in Botha's Government when the Union was set up in 1910. In the first world war joined the Imperial War Cabinet. As Prime Minister, 1919–24, helped to launch the League of Nations, and later was associated with the United Nations. Prime Minister, Foreign Minister and Minister of Defence from 1939 to 1948 when he was defeated at the General Election by the Nationalists under Dr. Malan. He was a keen botanist; Pres. of British Association, 1931. Published *Holism and Evolution* in 1926.

Smyth, Dame Ethel Mary (1858–1944), English composer, the daughter of a general, and a militant suffragette. She studied in Germany, where her most important opera *The Wreckers* was first produced. She also wrote chamber music, a comic opera *The Boatswain's Mate*, and a *Mass in D*.

Snyders, Frans (1597–1657), a great Flemish still-life and animal painter who studied under Breughel.

Soane, Sir John, R.A. (1753–1837), an eminent architect who designed numerous public buildings. By his will he left his museum, library, pictures, etc., for the use of the public, and the house in which he lived at Lincoln's Inn Fields still constitutes the Sir John Soane Museum.

Sobieski, John III. (1624–96), King of Poland from 1674, and heroic defender of his country from Cossacks, Tartars, and Turks.

Socinus, Lælius (1525–62), an Italian Protestant thinker and anti-Trinitarian, founder with his nephew Faustus Socinus (1539–1604), of the Socinian system of theology.

Socrates (470–399 B.C.), Greek philosopher and great intellectual leader, was the son of a sculptor and for some time followed that calling himself, but, having other ambitions, joined the army, and was present at the battle of Potidæa, and also at the battle of Delium, saving the life of Alcibiades in the first, and of Xenophon in the second. Returning to Athens he devoted himself to study and began to exhort the people on public questions and the conduct of life. Socrates wrote nothing himself, but we know of his teachings through the writings of his pupils Xenophon and Plato. In 399 B.C. he was charged with impiety and with corrupting the morals of the young, found guilty, and sentenced to death, events immortalised in Plato's *Apology*, *Crito*, and *Phaedo*.

Soddy, Frederick, M.A., LL.D., F.R.S. (1877–1956), Prof. of Inorganic and Physical Chemistry, Univ. of Oxford, 1919–36. Nobel Laureate in Chemistry 1921. The foundation of the isotope theory was laid by him in Glasgow about 1912 before the physicists became prominent in that field.

Solatov, Alexander (b. 1917), Soviet diplomat, succeeded J. Malik as ambassador to Britain, 1960.

Solon (638–558 B.C.), was one of the Seven Sages of Greece, and became an eminent legislator, after having made a reputation as a poet. Solon's Laws were so highly esteemed that they were adopted by the Romans in the Twelve Tables.

Solyman (1490–1566), the celebrated Ottoman Sultan known as "the Magnificent," who won fame as a conqueror, law-giver, administrator, and patron of learning.

Somerset, 1st Duke of (1506–52), was Protector of England in the early part of the reign of Edward VI., but was deposed from power, tried for felony, and executed. A liberal and tolerant ruler who opposed enclosures and pursued a moderate religious policy.

Sophocles (495–406 B.C.), the famous Athenian dramatist who enjoyed the highest popularity at Athens, and in a contest with Æschylus was crowned the victor. Of the 100-odd plays of Sophocles only seven have survived: *Antigone*, *Electra*, *Œdipus*, *Ajax*, *Trachiniae*, *Philoctetes*, and *Œdipus at Colonus*.

Soult, Marshal Nicolas Jean de Dieu, Duke of Dalmatia (1769–1851), was one of Napoleon's favourite and most capable generals, distinguishing himself in the Swiss and Italian campaigns, and also in the Peninsular War, where he was Wellington's bravest opponent.

Sousa, John Philip (1854–1932), American bandmaster and composer of numerous stirring marches. His father was Portuguese and his mother German.

Soustelle, Jacques, D. ès. L. (b. 1912), French scientist and controversial figure in French politics. As leader of the U.N.R. (Union for a New Republic) he planned and carried through the revolution which brought General de Gaulle back to power in 1958. Dismissed from Government. Feb. 1960.

Southey, Robert (1774–1843), English poet and historian. In 1803 he settled near Keswick to be near Coleridge and became one of the Lake poets. He was made poet Laureate in 1813. His best work was in prose: histories of Brazil and of the Peninsular War; life of Nelson, and biographies of Wesley and others.

Southwell, Robert (1561–95), a famous Jesuit and religious poet of Elizabethan times. Beatified in 1929.

Spaak, Paul-Henri (b. 1899), Belgian statesman; first President of the U.N. General Assembly in 1946 and of the Assembly of the Council of Europe during its first session in 1949. Sec. Gen. of NATO, 1957–61.

Spaatz, General Carl Andrew (b. 1891), American soldier who held high commands in Europe, North Africa, and the Pacific, 1942–46.

Spartacus, a Thracian who became a Roman slave and gladiator in Capua, and headed an insurrection in Italy in 73 B.C. The slaves he raised routed several Roman armies, but he was eventually defeated by Crassus in 71 B.C. and slain.

Speke, Capt. John Hanning (1827–64), was the discoverer, along with Lt.-Col. J. A. Grant, of the Kagera, the main source of the White Nile, in 1862. In 1856 he discovered Lake Tanganyika and in 1858 Victoria Nyanza.

Spence, Sir Basil, O.M. (b. 1907), architect of the new Coventry cathedral, the new university of Sussex, Glasgow air terminal, Hampstead civic centre, and the new British embassy in Rome. Prof. of Architecture, Royal Academy.

Spencer, Herbert (1820–1903), was the son of a Derby schoolmaster. For some time followed the profession of civil engineer. His first book was published in 1851, under the title of *Social Statics*, when he was filling the position of sub-editor of the *Economist*. In 1855 his *Principles of Psychology* appeared, in which he seems to have anticipated Darwin's theory of Evolution. The *System of Synthetic Philosophy* began to appear in 1860, and the last of its ten volumes was issued in 1896.

Spencer, Sir Stanley, C.B.E., R.A. (1891–1959), British artist whose work shows great visionary and spiritual power. His paintings include the Resurrection pictures and the Cookham Regatta series.

Spenser, Edmund (1552–99), was born in London, educated at Cambridge, and early attracted notice by his poetic writings. After the publication of his *Shephearde's Calendar*, he was made known to Queen Elizabeth, and in 1580 received the appointment of Secretary to the Lord Deputy of Ireland, and in the division of confiscated lands that afterwards took place, Spenser received Kilcolman Castle and 3,000 acres of land. Here he wrote his *Faerie Queene*. In 1598 a rebellion broke out, and Spenser's castle was burned to the ground. He then returned to London, and there died.

Spinoza, Baruch or Benedict (1632–77), one of the greatest of modern philosophers, was born at Amsterdam, the son of a Portuguese Jew who had settled there as a merchant. He had a sceptical turn of mind and having expounded philosophical doctrines antagonistic to Judaism, was excommunicated by the rabbis as a heretic. He owed much to Descartes and in 1663 published his work on the Cartesian philosophy. The attainment of truth was his one object in life. Indifferent to money, he spent his life in study and earned his living as a lens grinder. His writings have had an extensive and enduring influence though during his lifetime some of his works, including his *Ethics*, were not allowed to be published. *See also* **J20(1)**.

Spofforth, Reginald (1770–1827), a writer of glees, including *Hail, Smiling Morn*.

Spurgeon, Rev. Charles Haddon (1834–92), a renowned Baptist who preached at The Tabernacle, near the Elephant and Castle, London, from 1861 until his death.

Staël, Madame de (Anne Louise Germaine Necker, Baronne de Staël-Holstein) (1766–1817), the daughter of Necker, the famous Finance Minister under Louis XVI., was married to Baron de Staël (Swedish Minister) at twenty. She was a brilliant woman, deeply imbued with philosophical sentiments. Two years after her marriage she made a considerable impression by her *Letters on Rousseau*, and was regarded as in sympathy with the Revolution. Later on, however, she was in disfavour, first with the Revolutionary leaders, and then with Napoleon, and was in turn exiled by both and during this time wrote *Corinne* and other able works.

Stalin, Generalissimo Joseph Vissarionovich (Djugashvili) (1879–1953), Soviet statesman who for nearly thirty years was leader of the Russian people. Studied for the priesthood at the Tiflis theological seminary. From the age of 17 was an active revolutionary and took important part in the civil war after 1917. After the death of Lenin became the outstanding figure in Russia and his aim to make Russia a great industrial power was carried into effect by modernizing agriculture on socialist lines and by a series of five-year plans, the first of which was introduced in 1929. Assumed military leadership against the German invasion, June 1941. Attended the Allied war conferences at Teheran, Yalta, and Potsdam. The denunciation of Stalin and the "personality cult" by M. Khrushchev at the Soviet Communist Party Congress in Feb. 1956 led to profound and far-reaching political consequences in Communist countries.

Stanford, Sir Charles Villiers, Mus. D. (1852–1924), Professor of Music at Cambridge University, and Professor of Composition and Orchestral Playing in the Royal College of Music. An organist and conductor of remarkable ability, and a composer of much fine instrumental choral, operatic, and other music.

Stanley, Sir Henry Morton, G.C.B., (1841–1904), British explorer, after an adventurous early career during which he fought for the Confederates in the American Civil War, joined the *New York Herald* as a correspondent in 1867 and was commissioned by Gordon Bennett to search for Livingstone. In 1871 he discovered the great missionary at Ujiji and with him explored the northern end of Lake Tanganyika. After further exploration he founded the Congo Free State in 1879. Among his books were *How I found Livingstone, Through the Dark Continent, In Darkest Africa*, and an *Autobiography*.

Steele, Sir Richard (1672–1729), b. in Dublin, founder of *The Tatler*, which made a great hit, his friend Addison contributing many papers. Two years later he and Addison were associated in *The Spectator*, Addison, however, being the leading contributor; the *Guardian* was another of Steele's ventures. He sat in Parliament for some time, and was knighted by George I.

Steer, Philip Wilson, O. M. (1860–1942), was the most distinguished of British landscape painters, and a fine portraitist.

Stefansson, Vilhjalmur (b. 1879), a famous Arctic explorer, born in Manitoba of Icelandic parents. Took part in the Anglo-American (1908–12) and Canadian (1913–18) Arctic expeditions.

Stein, Sir Aurel, K.C.I.E. (1862–1943), was a famous British archæologist who conducted expeditions, chiefly to Chinese Turkestan, resulting in priceless additions to the British Museum and the Delhi Central Indian Museum. Explored Baluchistan, 1926–28, and South Iran, 1932–33. Was Superintendent of Archæological Survey, North-West Frontier Circle, India, 1910–29.

Stendhal, *nom de plume* of the French novelist, **Marie Henri Beyle** (1783–1842), who has been an important influence in the development of the French novel and whose books show searching psychological insight. Best known for his two novels, *Le Rouge et le Noir*, and *La Chartreuse de Parme*.

Stephen (1105–54) was King of England from 1135 to his death, usurping the crown that belonged to Matilda, the daughter of Henry I.

Stephen Sir Leslie, K.C.B. (1832–1904), an eminent writer, critic and biographer. Edited the *Cornhill Magazine* (1871–82), and the *Dictionary of National Biography* (1882–91). He was the father of Mrs. Virginia Woolf.

Stephenson, George (1781–1848), was born at Wylam, near Newcastle, and up to 1804 was mainly engaged in ordinary colliery occupations. In 1804, however, an engagement as brakesman at Killingworth colliery brought him in touch with the working of Watt's steam engine, and his first efforts in invention were in improving one of those engines, showing so much ability that he was offered an enginewright's position at Killingham, which he held for some time. Then it was that he began to think seriously of producing a locomotive engine, and managed to construct an engine that would draw coal trucks at the rate of four miles an hour. In 1821, when the Stockton and Darlington Railway was undertaken, he was appointed engineer, and when the railway was opened in 1825, as a line for the transport of coal only, Stephenson won his first great triumph, by putting a locomotive on the line that was able to draw a train of thirty-eight carriages, laden with goods and passengers, at a rate of twelve miles an hour. George Stephenson, subsequently, assisted by his son Robert, constructed the Liverpool and Manchester line, and after that the railway era commenced.

Stephenson, Robert, F.R.S. (1803–59), the only son of George Stephenson, attained great eminence as a civil engineer, constructing numerous important railways and bridges, being designer and contractor for the High Level Bridge at Newcastle, the Menai and Conway Tubular Bridges, the Victoria Bridge across the St. Lawrence at Montreal, and two notable bridges over the Nile.

Sterne, Laurence (1713–68), British humourist whose *Tristam Shandy* (1759–67) brought him fame. He also wrote *The Sentimental Journey* and published some volumes of sermons.

Stevenson, Adlai Ewing (1900–65), American lawyer and politician; Ambassador to U.N., 1960–65; Gov. of Illinois, 1949–53; Democratic candidate for Presidency, 1952 and 1956.

Stevenson, Robert, F.R.S.E. (1772–1850), a native of Glasgow, famed as a builder of lighthouses, including that on Bell Rock. He invented the "flashing" system of throwing light at sea.

Stevenson, Robert Louis (1850–94), was the Scottish author of a remarkable series of essays, stories, and poems, including *Travels with a Donkey, Virginibus Puerisque, Treasure Island, Kidnapped, Dr. Jekyll and Mr. Hyde,* and *A Child's Garden of Verses.* He always suffered from delicate health and travelled extensively, finally settling in Samoa with his Californian wife, formerly Mrs. Osbourne. His literary influence was considerable, particularly on the generation which followed him.

Stinnes, Hugo (1870–1924), German industrialist who built up a huge coal-mining, iron and steel, and transport business, and also developed a large shipping concern. His group controlled the greater part of Germany's coal, iron and steel supply. In 1920 he entered the Reichstag, and later became a newspaper proprietor.

Stirling, Elizabeth (1819–95), English organist whose recitals in London exercised much influence and made Bach's music more widely known. She wrote the part-song "All among the barley."

Stoker Bram (Abraham) (1847–1912), b. in Ireland, author of *Dracula* and *Personal Reminiscences Of Henry Irving,* which records his association with the actor in managing the Lyceum Theatre.

Stokes, Sir George Gabriel, L.L.D., F.R.S. (1819–1903), Irish mathematician and physicist; Prof. of Mathematics at Cambridge from 1849; served as Sec. (1854–85) and as Pres. (1885–92) Royal Society, and as Pres. British Association (1869). Renowned for his researches in hydrodynamics and the theory of light.

Stopes, Marie Carmichael, D.Sc., Ph.D., F.L.S., F.R.L.S. (1880–1958), woman scientist who published many works on birth control.

Stowe, Harriet Elizabeth Beecher (1811–96), authoress of *Uncle Tom's Cabin* which exposed the horrors of slavery and did much to advance the cause of abolition.

Strachey, Rt. Hon. Evelyn John St. Loe (1901–63), English writer and politician; served in Attlee's cabinet, 1945–51. Author of lucid and vigorous books on the principles of democratic socialism. Son of the journalist John St. Loe Strachey and cousin of Giles Lytton Strachey, the biographer.

Stradivari, Antonio (1644–1730), an Italian maker of violins, b. Cremona, first in his art.

Strafford, Thomas Wentworth, Earl of (1593–1641), the distinguished statesman, sent by Charles I. to Ireland as Lord Deputy in 1631. Was the founder of the Irish linen manufacture. He obtained the name of "Thorough" by his sweeping measures for asserting the King's authority, but was ultimately impeached on a variety of charges, found guilty, and executed.

Strauss, David Friedrich (1808–74), German theological writer, who made a great stir in the religious world by his *Life of Jesus,* published in 1835, which attempted to prove that the evangelical history rested on a series of myths.

Strauss. Family of Viennese musicians. **Johann Strauss** (1804–49), "the elder," was a composer of dance music who with Joseph Lanner established the Viennese waltz tradition. His son, **Johann Strauss** (1825–99), "the younger," although not so good a violinist or conductor as his father, is the more famous as the composer of over 400 waltzes, which include *The Blue Danube* and *Tales from the Vienna Woods.* Two of his brothers Joseph Strauss (1827–70) and **Eduard Strauss** (1835–1916) were also composers and conductors.

Strauss, Richard (1864–1949), German composer and conductor, the son of a horn player in the opera orchestra at Munich. He succeeded von Bülow as court musical director at Meiningen. Among his compositions which are widely acclaimed are the operas *Salome, Elektra,* and *Der Rosenkavalier,* the symphonic poems *Don Juan, Till Eulenspiegel,* and *Don Quixote,* and many songs of great lyrical beauty.

Stravinsky, Igor (b. 1882), Russian composer and conductor, pupil of Rimsky-Korsakov. His early ballets *The Fire Bird* and *Petrushka* (regarded by some as his greatest work) were commissioned by Diaghilev and are representative of his early romantic style. *Pulcinella, Apollon musagète, Persephone,* and the opera *Oedipus Rex* are later works in his neo-classical style. Younger composers have been much influenced by his music. He became a French citizen in 1934, and a U.S. citizen in 1945.

Strindberg, Johan August (1849–1912), Swedish writer of intense creative energy. His work is subjective and reflects his personal conflicts. He married three times but never happily. He produced some fifty-five plays as well as novels, stories, poems, and critical essays. *Lucky Peter, Gustav Adolf, Till Damascus, The Father, Miss Julie* are some of his plays.

Strong, Leonard Alfred George (1896–1958), poet, novelist, short story writer, and critic. Author, among other books, of *Dublin Days, The Brothers,* and *The Last Enemy,* and with Cecil D. Lewis editor of *A New Anthology of Modern Verse.*

Stuart, Arabella (1575–1615), daughter of the Earl of Lennox and cousin of James I., whose next heir she was both to the English and Scottish thrones. In 1610 she married William Seymour, afterwards Earl of Hertford and Duke of Somerset, and thereby incurring the king's displeasure, she was incarcerated in the Tower of London, where she died insane.

Suckling, Sir John (1609–42), wit, courtier, and poet; served under Gustavus Adolphus and in Charles I's first Scottish war (1639). Being concerned in a plot to rescue the Earl of Strafford from the Tower, he fled to France, where he may have killed himself. He wrote poems, ballads, songs, and prose work and is said to have invented cribbage.

Sudermann, Hermann (1857–1928), German dramatist, poet and novelist. His brilliant novel, *Frau Sorge* (1887), translated into English as *Dame Care* (1892), reached its 125th edition in 1912. From 1890 he produced a succession of realistic plays and novels.

Sukarno, Achmed (b. 1901), President of Indonesia since 1945.

Sullivan, Sir Arthur Seymour, C.V.O. (1842–1900), gifted composer, gained his first musical experiences as choir-boy at the Chapel Royal, and later studied at Leipzig. He composed oratorios but at the same time cultivated a lighter vein with pronounced success. Became famous for the light operas written in collaboration with W. S. Gilbert, which include *Trial by Jury, The Sorcerer, H.M.S. Pinafore, Pirates of Penzance, Patience, The Mikado, The Yeomen of the Guard, The Gondoliers.*

Sully, Maximilien de Béthune, Duc de (1560–1641), a French Protestant statesman, a friend and companion of Henry of Navarre. His *Memoirs* made notable reading.

Sun Yat Sen, Dr. (1867–1925), Chinese revolutionary, founder and first President of the Chinese Republic, 1912, resigning almost immediately in favour of Yuan Shih-kai. Was the first graduate of medicine at Hongkong, 1891. Founded in 1905 the China Revolutionary League in Europe and Japan, and played a large part in the revolution of 1911, which overthrew the Manchu Dynasty. *See also* **Section C, Part I.**

Sutherland, Graham Vivien, O.M. (b. 1903), British artist; he painted the 80th birthday portrait of Sir Winston Churchill commissioned by Parliament and designed the vast tapestry for Coventry Cathedral.

Sutro, Alfred (1863–1933), author and dramatist.

His most successful plays were *The Walls of Jericho* (1904) and *John Glayde's Honour* (1907).

Swedenborg, Emanuel (1689–1772), Swedish philosopher, scientist, mystic. In later life he announced that Divine authority had been given him to explain natural and spiritual evidences. He published in quick succession *Arcana Coelestia*, *The Apocalypse Revealed*, *Four Preliminary Doctrines*, and *The True Christian Religion*. He also claimed that his soul had been permitted to travel into hell, purgatory and heaven. His works became the scriptures of the sect named Swedenborgians.

Sweelinck, Jan Pieterszoon (1562–1621), famous Dutch organist and composer of sacred music. In his fugues he was the first to make independent use of the pedals, and thus prepared the way for Bach.

Swift, Jonathan Dean (1667–1745), was born at Dublin, educated at Trinity College at the expense of an uncle, became secretary to Sir William Temple, and looked for political preferment, but it did not come. Entering the Church, he was made Dean of St. Patrick's in 1713. Getting entangled in political controversy, and changing his views from the Whig to the Tory side, he lost favour with the popular party, but consoled himself with a devotion to literature, which he greatly enriched by some powerful satires, poems and discourses. *Gulliver's Travels*, *A Taie of a Tub* and *The Battle of the Books* are among the best-known works. His romantic attachment to "Stella" (Hester Johnson, whom he is believed to have married privately) and "Vanessa" (Esther Vanhomrigh), and their devotion to him, are familiar stories.

Swinburne, Algernon Charles (1837–1909), was educated at Oxford, and in the early 'sixties of last century gave to the world a number of poems of singular poetic beauty and musical charm, which procured him a high rank among English poets. Swinburne's most famous productions include *Atalanta in Calydon*, *Songs before Sunrise*, *Bothwell*, and *Mary Stuart*. Perhaps the best of his writings is his essay on William Blake.

Swithin, St. (*circa* 800–862), Bishop of Winchester in 852, and on the translation of his remains to a shrine in the interior of the cathedral from the graveyard, fixed for July 15th, 971, violent rain intervened, and, it is said, continued for forty days; hence the superstition as to rain upon St. Swithin's Day.

Symonds, John Addington (1840–93), acquired fame as a poet and writer on *The Renaissance Period in Italy*.

Synge, John Millington (1871–1909), Irish poet and playwright. His best known work, *The Playboy of The Western World*, met with a hostile reception when first produced in Dublin in 1907, but English audiences were at once enthusiastic.

Szigeti, Joseph (b. 1892), famous Hungarian violinist, who made his début in 1905, toured through Europe and settled for some years in England. He made an immense reputation on the Continent, and was Prof. at the Geneva Conservatorium, 1917–24.

Szymanowski, Karol (1833–1937), Polish composer and director of the Conservatoire at Warsaw.

T

Tacitus, Caius Cornelius (55–*circa* 120). His chief claim to remembrance is that he was one of the ablest of Roman historians, and left behind him a number of works; among them a life of Agricola and his *Annales*, which have formed the ground-work of much that has since been written on the period he covered.

Tacitus, Marcus Claudius (205–276), the Roman Emperor who succeeded Aurelian in A.D. 275. His short reign was wise and marked by moderation.

Taft, Wm. Howard (1857–1930), Chief Justice United States 1921–30. President of the United States 1908–13.

Tagore, Rabindranath (1861–1941), a Bengal poet who won the Nobel Literature Prize in 1913.

Talbot, William Henry Fox, F.R.S. (1800–1877), English scientist who first discovered the principles of photography in 1833. Inventor of the calotype or Talbot-type process of which modern photography is a development.

Talleyrand-Périgord, Charles Maurice de (1754–1838), French politician and diplomat, led a mission to England in 1792 and was Foreign Minister from 1797 until 1807. He represented France at the Congress of Vienna.

Tallis, Thomas (*c.* 1510–85), a distinguished musician, who was, as organist, attached to the Chapel Royal under Henry VIII., Edward VI., Mary, and Elizabeth, and was the composer of some of the finest of our Church music.

Tamerlane or **Timur Lenk** (= **Timur the Lame**) (1336–1405), Mongol conqueror who turned his energies from deliverance of his people from barbarism to military conquest for its own sake. He made himself ruler of Samarkand in 1369 and in a series of campaigns conquered Iran, Transcaucasia, Iraq, Armenia and Georgia, invaded India and Syria, and defeated the Ottoman Turks at Angora. While preparing for the invasion of China death overtook him. His reputation is that of a ruthless and cruel conqueror who showed no mercy even to his fellow Moslems, but he was also a patron of literature and the arts. The Timurids are the line of rulers descended from him.

Tannhäuser, a mythical German minnesinger of the 13th century, who belonged, according to the legend handled so romantically in Wagner's opera, to the Salzburg family of Tanhusen, and was the beloved of Lisaura.

Tarkington, (Newton) Booth (1869–1946), American novelist whose best-known book is *Monsieur Beaucaire*, a sentimental romance which he successfully dramatised.

Tarquin Superbus (or "**the Proud**"), the last King of Rome. Was banished 510 B.C. After his deposition came the Consuls.

Tarquin the Elder, 5th King of Rome, succeeded Ancius Mastius 615 B.C., reformed the laws, embellished the city, and was assassinated.

Tartini, Giuseppe (1692–1770), great violinist and anticipator of romanticism in Italian music. In practising double stops he discovered a differential tone which modified the intonation—becoming known as Tartini's or "the third" tone—a scientific explanation of which was later given by Helmholtz. His best-known sonata is *The Devil's Trill* written after a dream in which the devil played to him.

Tasman, Abel Janszoon (*circa* 1602–59), a famous Dutch navigator; in 1642 he discovered the island of Tasmania and New Zealand shortly thereafter.

Tassigny, Jean de Lattre de, Marshal of France, Hon. G.C.B. (1890–1952), outstanding commander of the Free French Movement in Second World War; High Commissioner and C.-in-C. Indo-China, 1950–52. C.-in-C. Land Forces, Western Europe, 1948–50.

Tasso, Torquato (1544–95), one of the great Italian epic poets, author of *Jerusalem Delivered* (Ital. *Gerusalemme liberata*) which celebrates the First Crusade.

Tawney, Richard Henry, B.A. (1880–1962), great historian, pioneer of adult education, leader of socialist thought, the first critic of the affluent society; Prof. Emeritus Economic History, Univ. of London, 1931–49. Among his standard works are *The Acquisitive Society*, *Equality*, *Religion and the Rise of Capitalism*.

Taylor, Jeremy (1613–67), an English divine of great influence. The most famous of his works was his *Holy Living and Holy Dying*.

Tchaikovsky, Peter Ilich (1840–93), Russian composer. His music is melodious and intensely emotional and he excelled in several branches of composition. Amongst his works are ten operas, including *Eugene Onegin* and *The Queen of Spades* (both from stories by Pushkin), six symphonies, including the *Little Russian* and the magnificent *Pathétique*, his last completed work, ballets, including *Swan Lake*, *The Sleeping Beauty*, and *The Nutcracker*, the fantasies *Romeo and Juliet* and *Francesca da Rimini*, the piano concerto in B flat minor, the violin concerto in D, and numerous songs.

Tedder, Marshal of the R.A.F., Arthur William, 1st Baron, G.C.B., B.A. (b. 1890), was Deputy Supreme Commander under Eisenhower for the invasion of Europe, Chief of the Air Staff, 1946–48; Chairman, Western Europe Chiefs of

Staff committee, 1948–50; Vice-Chairman of the Governors of the B.B.C., 1952–54; Chancellor Univ. of Cambridge, 1950.

Telemann, Georg Philipp (1681–1767), composer of great facility and output in all fields of music. Founded Collegium Musicum at Leipzig Univ. and held appointments in many other German towns, including Hamburg. His music has vitality and originality of form and is appreciated today after long period of neglect.

Telford, Thomas (1757–1834), was a Scottish working stone-mason who became a great engineer and attained special fame as a builder of bridges, the Menai Suspension Bridge being, perhaps, his greatest work. He constructed the Ellesmere Canal, made many hundreds of miles of difficult mountain roads, was chief engineer of the Caledonian Canal, and altogether did an immense amount of public work.

Tell, William, a legendary figure in Swiss folk-lore. The story of his having been compelled by order of the imperial governor, Gessler, to shoot an apple from the head of his own son and his dramatic revenge is regarded as a legendary feat which has its origins in Teutonic myth. The Swiss hero of the Uri, however, played a great part in freeing his country from the Austrian yoke in the early part of the 14th century.

Temple, Most Rev. Frederick (1821–1902), a famous Anglican Churchman who became Headmaster of Rugby in 1858; in 1860 attained notoriety as the author of the first of the much-controverted *Essays and Reviews*, advocated the disestablishment of the Irish Church in 1868, was appointed Bishop of Exeter in 1869, translated to London in 1885, and in 1896 was raised to the Primacy. He made a strong Archbishop, and dominated the Church with his vigorous personality.

Temple, Most Rev. William, P.C., D.Litt., D.D. (1881–1944), one of the outstanding Christian leaders of his time and the son of Frederick Temple, was Archbishop of Canterbury, 1942–44, after being Headmaster of Repton, 1910–14, Bishop of Manchester, 1921–29, and Archbishop of York, 1929–42. His influence was felt among Christians of all denominations, and he strove for the unity of the Churches.

Temple, Rt. Hon. Sir William, Bt. (1628–99), English statesman and author; Ambassador to The Hague in Charles II.'s time, and instrumental in bringing about the marriage between William of Orange and the Princess Mary. William III. twice offered him the position of Secretary of State, but he declined the honour, spending the years of his retirement at Moor Park (where Swift served him for a time as private secretary). Married **Dorothy Osborne** (1627–95), the letter-writer.

Templewood, Samuel John Gurney Hoare, 1st Viscount, P.C., G.C.S.I., G.B.E., C.M.G. (1880–1959), Conservative politician; Sec. of State for Air, 1922–29; Sec. of State for India, 1931–35; Foreign Sec., June–Dec. 1935; Home Sec., 1937–39; Special Ambassador to Spain, 1940–44.

Teniers, David (the younger) (1610–94), was born at Antwerp, and his paintings of the old rustic Flemish life are unsurpassed in their humour and fidelity. He died at Brussels. His father, **David Teniers** the elder (1582–1649), was also one of the leading landscape painters of the time.

Tenniel, Sir John (1820–1914), for over fifty years leading artist of *Punch*, illustrated numerous books, including *Alice in Wonderland*.

Tennyson, Alfred Lord (1809–92), was Poet Laureate from 1850 to his death. Born at Somersby, in Lincolnshire, he showed poetic gifts while quite young, and in 1827, joined his brother Charles in the publication of *Poems by Two Brothers*. In 1847 he published *The Princess*; in 1850 *In Memoriam*, a poem of great beauty and depth of thought, in which he enshrined his affection for the memory of his dead friend Arthur Hallam; and in 1855 *Maud* appeared. His other works include *The Idylls of the Kings, Enoch Arden, Queen Mary, Harold,* and *Becket*.

Terence, Publius Terentius Afer (*c.* 184–159 B.C.), a Latin poet and dramatist, an African (Berber), who rose from the position of a slave to that of one of the most honoured men in Rome.

Teresa, St., or Theresa (1515–82), a Spanish saint and author, born at Avila, entered the Carmelite order in 1534, established a reformed order in 1562, became famous for her ascetic life and mystic visions, and died at Alba de Liste. Her religious writings include *The Way of Perfection* and *The Castle of the Soul*. She was canonised by Pope Gregory XV.

Terry, Dame Ellen, G.B.E. (**Mrs. James Carew**) (1848–1928), one of the most distinguished of English actresses. Played Shakespeare with Sir Henry Irving at the Lyceum and later appeared in plays of Bernard Shaw.

Tertullian, Quintus (*circa* 150–230), a Father and writer of the Latin Church. His chief work was his *Apologeticus*, a defence of Christianity.

Tetrazzini, Luisa (1871–1940), an Italian prima donna who sprang into prominence in 1907 by her wonderful singing at Covent Garden and hailed as a second Patti.

Tetzel, John (*c.* 1460–1519), the German Dominican monk and Inquisitor, the scandal of whose sale of indulgences roused Luther to publish his ninety-five theses at Wittenberg in 1517.

Thackeray, William Makepeace (1811–63), English novelist, author of *Vanity Fair, Pendennis, Esmond, The Newcomes, The Virginians, Philip* and *Lovel the Widower*. He edited the *Cornhill Magazine* from the first number, January, 1860, for a few years his most notable contributions being his *Roundabout Papers*. His *Yellowplush Papers* and *The Book of Snobs* (republished from *Punch*) were widely read and admired; and the lectures he delivered in America on *The Four Georges* were pungently powerful.

Thales of Miletus (*c.* 624–565 B.C.), earliest of the Greek scientists, he created a sensation by his prediction of an eclipse of the sun, which was visible at Miletus in 585 B.C. He looked upon water as the basis of all material things and in his mathematical work was the first to enunciate natural laws.

Thant, Sithu U (b. 1909), Secretary-General of the United Nations, 1962– ; Acting Sec.-Gen. after Dr. Hammarskjöld's death in 1961; Burmese Perm. Rep. to U.N. 1957–61.

Themistocles (*c.* 514–449 B.C.), Athenian soldier and statesman. By fortifying the harbour of Piræus as the port of Athens, by the remission of taxes on aliens, and by the creation of the Athenian navy, he established Athenian prosperity and made possible the later Athenian empire. Defeated the Persian fleet at Salamis in 480 B.C.

Theocritus (285–247 B.C.), one of the great Greek poets. Thirty *Idylls* have come down to us and a number of *Epigrams*.

Theodoric the Great (455–526), a celebrated King of the East Goths, born at Pannonia. In mediæval German romance he is known as "Dietrich von Bern," and had a reputation for good government, akin to that ascribed in England to King Alfred. He was the founder of the Gothic Kingdom of Italy.

Theodosius the Great (346–95) was Roman Emperor of the East for nearly twenty years. He gained victories over the Goths, and the year before his death became sole Emperor. Noted in ecclesiastical history for his conversion to Christianity, and for his submission to the penance imposed by St. Ambrose.

Theophrastus (*c.* 372–287 B.C.), succeeded Aristotle as President of the Lyceum at Athens. His *History of Plants* and his *Moral Characters* are the best known of his writings.

Thibaud, Jacques (1880–1953) famous French violinist. Killed in aeroplane crash.

Thierry, Jacques Nicolas Augustin (1795–1856), a distinguished French historian, known by his *History of the Norman Conquest*.

Thiers, Louis Adolphe (1797–1877), a French statesman and man of letters, author of *History of the French Revolution*.

Thomas, Dylan (1914–53), Welsh poet whose *Eighteen Poems* (1934) brought him instant recognition as an original and gifted artist. Other works include *Twenty-five Poems* (1936), *Deaths and Entrances* (1945), *Under Milk Wood*, a play for voices.

Thomson, James (1834–82), a Scottish poet who wrote *The City of Dreadful Night*.

Thomson, Sir (John) Arthur (1861–1933), was a well-known biologist.

Thomson, Sir Joseph (John), O.M., D.Sc., F.R.S.

(1856–1940), physicist and mathematician; Master of Trinity College, Cambridge, 1918–40; Cavendish Prof. of Experimental Physics, Cambridge, 1884–1919. Awarded Nobel Prize in 1906 for his work on conduction of electricity through gases; also discovered the electron. Pres. of the Royal Society, 1913–15. His son, **Sir George Paget Thomson,** (b. 1892) F.R.S., is also a physicist and Nobel Prizeman; former Master of Corpus Christi College, Cambridge.

Thoreau, Henry David (1817–62), American essayist and nature-worshipper. He was the friend of, and for a time lived with, Emerson. Best known for his classic *Walden, or Life in the Woods.*

Thorez Maurice (1900–64), French communist, under whose leadership the Communists became the largest single party in the French elections of 1945 and 1946; Sec.-Gen. of French Communist Party, 1930–64.

Thorndike, Dame Sybil, D.B.E., LL.D. (b. 1885), celebrated British actress who made her début with the Ben Greet players in 1904 and worked with the Old Vic from 1914–18. She won great success in the Greek tragedies, Shakespeare, Shaw, and in Grand Guignol. Both she and her husband, Sir Lewis Casson, received the honorary degree of D. Litt. at Oxford University in 1966.

Thornycroft, Sir William Hamo, R.A. (1850–1925), English sculptor whose works include the Gladstone Memorial, the statue of General Gordon in Trafalgar Square, of Queen Alexandra in the Royal Exchange, Lord Granville in the Houses of Parliament, Cromwell at Westminster, and John Bright in Rochdale.

Thorpe, Sir (Thomas) Edward, C.B., Ph.D., D.Sc., F.R.S. (1845–1925), a noted English chemist. His chief research work was done on paraffin hydrocarbons, and the derivatives of fluorine and phosphorus. Was the author of a standard *Dictionary of Applied Chemistry* and a *History of Chemistry.*

Thorwaldsen, Bertel (1770–1844), a famous Danish sculptor.

Thucydides (*c.* 460–399 B.C.), the first scientific historian, was an Athenian and took part in the Peloponnesian War, about which he wrote his *History.* Attempted an impartial account, weighing the testimony of eye-witnesses and keeping to carefully verified facts. The *History* is a graphic narrative, but Thucydides was not merely a chronicler; he saw the general significance of particular events and wished to pass on the political lessons of the past to the future. The speeches which he put into the mouths of the various actors reveal the political ideas and climate of opinion of contemporary Greece, and include the famous Funeral Oration of Pericles.

Tiberius, Claudius (42 B.C.–A.D. 37), the second Emperor of Rome, had an evil reputation but was an able ruler and successful soldier. Spent his later years in Capri.

Tillett, Benjamin (1860–1943), M.P. for North Salford 1917–24 and again 1929–31, came into prominence in the great dock strike of 1889. He was the organiser and secretary of the Dockers' Union; for several years alderman of the L.C.C.; and an active labour leader. Chairman of the General Council T.U.C. 1928–29.

Tillotson, John (1630–94), a celebrated preacher at Lincoln's Inn, "Popery" and "Atheism" being the main objects of his attacks: in 1691 became Archbishop of Canterbury.

Tindal, Matthew (*c.* 1653–1733), noted English Deist.

Tintoretto (1518–94), Venetian painter whose aim it was to unite the colouring of Titian with the drawing of Michelangelo. He is among the most original and decorative of artists whose numerous paintings, mostly of religious subjects, were executed with great speed, some of them on enormous canvasses. His real name was Jacopo Robusti, and he was called Il Tintoretto (little dyer) after his father's trade. Three of his six children were painters.

Tippett, Michael Kemp (b. 1905), English composer whose works include Concerto for Orchestra, *Midsummer Marriage, King Priam,* the cantata *Boyhood's End,* and the song-cycle *The Heart's Assurance.*

Titian, or Tiziano Vecelli (1477–1576), one of the greatest of painters. He studied under the Bellinis, and made his first essays in painting for the public in conjunction with Giorgione, whom he soon surpassed. In 1511 he was at Padua, where he painted some notable frescoes; in 1512 he was back in Venice, with a studio on the Grand Canal, employed on important commissions. From this time forward he was in great demand, and exercised his marvellous powers almost to the end of his life, dying of the plague at ninety-nine.

Titiens (or Tietjens), Teresa (1831–77), a famous German operatic prima donna and concert-room singer.

Tito, Marshal (Josif Broz) (b. 1892), Prime Minister of the Federal People's Republic of Yugoslavia since 1945. Leader of the partisan forces which successfully fought against German occupation. President National Liberation Committee, 1943.

Titus (40–81), the Roman Emperor, and son of Vespasian. Attained great renown by his successful part in the Jewish war which terminated in the capture and destruction of Jerusalem: he was deemed a profligate and a tyrant, but no sooner was he in sole power than he exerted himself to the utmost to please the people, completed the Colosseum, built splendid baths, and otherwise made himself popular.

Tizard, Sir Henry Thomas, G.C.B., F.R.S. (1885–1959), scientist and administrator; Pres. British Association, 1948. Played important part in the higher scientific direction of the second world war and as Chair. Advisory Council on Scientific Policy, 1947–52.

Tocqueville, Alexis, Comte de (1805–59), author of *De La Démocratie en Amérique* and *De L'Ancien Régime,* which set out nineteenth-century liberal ideas.

Todd, Alexander Robertus, 1st Baron, D.Sc., F.R.S. (b. 1907), British biochemist; Prof. of Organic Chemistry at Cambridge, 1944– . For his work on the structures of nucleic acids he received the 1957 Nobel Prize for Chemistry.

Tolstoy, Count Leo Nikolayevitch (1828–1910), was the most distinguished personality in modern Russian literature. Born of a good family, he was for a time in the army, but was so greatly moved by the trials and sufferings of the people that, out of pure sympathy of heart, he was impelled "to take up his pen and write." At twenty-four he published his *Childhood,* and in 1854, while in camp in the Crimea, wrote his *Tales from Sebastopol,* which procured him considerable literary fame. Later on he was a persistent advocate of progressive ideas, and, before the Emancipation Act for freeing all Russian serfs was enforced, he himself had given the serfs on his own estate their freedom. In 1862 he married, and settled down to a quiet country life, shortly afterwards publishing his *War and Peace* and *Anna Karenina.* In his latter years Tolstoy developed a sort of religious mysticism. Among his later works are *The Power of Darkness. The Kreutzer Sonata, The Cossacks, Resurrection,* and *The End of the Age.*

Tooke, John Horne (1736–1812), English politician and pamphleteer, was a supporter of Wilkes and later Pitt. His tracts advocated reform. After the French Revolution was tried for high treason, but was acquitted.

Toole, John Lawrence (1832–1906), for half a century a popular English comedian.

Torquemada, Tomás de (1420–98), the chief officer of the Spanish Inquisition.

Torricelli, Evangelista (1608–47), Galileo's pupil. He invented the barometer and improved both the microscope and the telescope.

Toscanini, Arturo (1867–1957), famous Italian conductor, La Scala Theatre, Milan, 1898–1908, and 1920–29; at the Metropolitan Opera House, New York, 1908–15; and of the Philharmonic Symphony Society of New York, 1926–36. Returned to Milan in 1946 after a ten-year exile.

Toulouse-Lautrec, Henri de (1864–1901), French painter, whose pictures portray with stark realism certain aspects of Parisian life in the nineties.

Tovey, Sir Donald Francis (1875–1940), pianist and composer who for 25 years held the chair of music at the University of Edinburgh. Outstanding among his many writings is *Essays in Musical Analysis,* and his compositions include chamber music, a piano concerto, and an opera *The Bride of Dionysus.*

Toynbee, Arnold (1852–83), after graduating at Oxford, devoted himself to practical philanthropy and social reform. From his self-denying efforts sprang the settlement in East London —Toynbee Hall.

Toynbee, Arnold Joseph, C.H., Hon.D.Litt. (Oxford, Cambridge, and Birmingham) (b. 1889), eminent scholar and historian, nephew of above. Dir. of Studies Royal Inst. of Int. Affairs, 1925–55. Major work *A Study of History*.

Trajan (*circa* 52–117) was Roman Emperor from 98 to his death. His rule was enlightened, and he was esteemed by his people.

Tree, Sir Herbert Beerbohm (1852–1917), the London actor-manager who scored successes at the Haymarket and His Majesty's Theatre.

Trenchard, Marshal of the R.A.F., Viscount, G.C.B., O.M., G.C.V.O., D.S.O. (1873–1956), Chief of Air Staff, 1918–29; Commissioner of Police of the Metropolis, 1931–35; often known as the father of the Air Force and largely responsible for the establishment of the R.A.F. College at Cranwell and the Hendon Police College.

Trent, 1st Baron, of Nottingham (Jesse Boot) (1850–1931), founder of Boots Cash Chemists, Ltd.; a great benefactor of Nottingham, especially of the University of Nottingham.

Trevelyan, George Macaulay, O.M., C.B.E. (1876–1962), English historian, son of Sir George Otto Trevelyan and great nephew of Thomas Babbington Macaulay. Regius Professor of Modern History at Cambridge 1927–40; Master of Trinity College, 1940. Chancellor of Durham University, 1949. His chief works are: *History of England*; a trilogy of books on *Garibaldi*; *England under the Stuarts*; *England under Queen Anne*; *Grey of Fallodon*; *English Social History*; *An Autobiography and other Essays*.

Trevelyan, Rt. Hon. Sir George Otto, 1st Bt., O.M. (1838–1928), Liberal statesman and historian. Became Chief Secretary for Ireland in 1882, and was later Secretary of State for Scotland. Wrote a biography of his uncle, Lord Macaulay, which was highly praised. Father of Professor G. M. Trevelyan.

Trevithick, Richard (1771–1833), a Cornish mine-manager's son, who invented the road-locomotive, putting upon the highway on Christmas Eve, 1801, the first steam-propelled vehicle for passengers.

Trollope, Anthony (1815–81), author of many novels. His Barchester series depicts a number of scenes of higher clerical life with great fidelity and success.

Trotsky, Leon, name assumed by Lev Davidovich Bronstein (1879–1940), one of the leaders of the Bolshevist revolution. War Minister of the Bolshevist Government and its leading representative at the Brest-Litovsk conference of 1917–18. He differed from the Communist Party on policy and was dismissed from office in 1925. In 1929 took up exile in Mexico where he was assassinated.

Truman, Harry S. (b. 1884), President of the United States, 1945–53. Inherited the Presidency on the death of Roosevelt in 1945 and won the Pres. election in 1948. He took the historic decision to enter Korea in 1950, dismissed Gen. MacArthur in 1951, and will perhaps best be remembered for his "Point Four" programme of raising levels of living in backward, and under-developed countries.

Tulsi Das (1532–1623), mediæval poet of India whose great masterpiece *Rām-Charit-Mānas* (popularly known as the *Rāmayana* and based on the Sanskrit epic of Vālmiki) is venerated by all Hindus just as the Bible is in the West.

Turenne, Henri de la Tour d'Auvergne, Vicomte de (1611–75), a famous French commander and Marshal of France, who was highly successful in the Thirty Years' War.

Turgenev, Ivan Serveyvich (1818–83), was a friend of Gogol and Tolstoy, and a famous Russian novelist and short-story writer. His works were frequently satirical and directed against the oppression of the peasants by the nobles. Was the inventor of the term "nihilist" to describe the Russian anarchist movement.

Turner, Joseph Mallord William, R.A. (1775–1851), was the son of a London barber, but while quite a child showed the possession of artistic genius. In 1789, after some miscellaneous schooling, he entered the Royal Academy classes, and soon began to make headway. Of his larger pictures may be mentioned *The Sun Rising through Vapour*, *Crossing the Brook*, *Dido Building Carthage*, *The Fighting Téméraire*, and *Calais Pier*. Ruskin, in his *Modern Painters*, wrote with great eloquence and critical insight regarding Turner's work, and brought about a fuller appreciation of his genius. Turner never married, and took little interest in anything outside his art. He left the oil paintings and drawings he had preserved to the National Gallery.

Tussaud, Madame Marie (1760–1850), a Swiss who while practising the art of modelling wax in Paris at the time of the French Revolution, made her escape to England and set up a small exhibition of wax figures in the Strand, later carried on by her son, grandson and great-grandson at Baker Street and in 1884 transferred to Marylebone Road.

Tut-ankh-amen (*circa* 1350 B.C.), an Egyptian Pharaoh of the 18th dynasty, whose tomb was discovered by Howard Carter in 1922, with the mummy and gold sarcophagus intact. The magnificence of the objects found aroused world-wide interest.

Twain Mark. (*See* **Clemens, Samuel L.**)

Tweedsmuir, John Buchan, 1st Baron, C.H. (1875–1940), Gov.-Gen. of Canada 1935–40, journalist, politician, and author, wrote numerous biographies, historical novels, and adventure stories, including *Montrose*, *The Path of the King*, *Greenmantle*, and *Sick-Heart River*, and an autobiography *Memory Hold the Door*. Under the pen name "O. Douglas" his sister, Anna (d. 1948), published some charming tales of domestic life.

Tyler, Wat (d. 1381), the leader of the peasants' revolt of Richard II.'s time against the iniquitous poll-tax. Over 100,000 peasants followed Tyler into London in June 1381, and the king met them in Smithfield and made promises of redress that were never fulfilled. It was at this meeting that Sir William Walworth, Lord Mayor of London, stabbed Tyler with a dagger, and afterwards handed him over to his followers to kill outright.

Tyndale, William (*c.* 1492–1536), was educated at Oxford, and conceived a strong desire to be the medium of presenting the Bible to his countrymen in their own language. He completed the translation of the New Testament at Wittenburg, where he was associated with Luther. This version was first published at Antwerp, and then found its way to England, where it was publicly burnt at St. Paul's Cross. Tyndale afterwards was associated with Miles Coverdale in a translation of the Old Testament, but only completed the Pentateuch and the book of Jonah. Antwerp was Tyndale's retreat during this later period, and in 1535 he was arrested for heresy and put to death by strangling and burning.

Tyndall, Prof. John, F.R.S. (1820–93), was an eminent scientist. His books on light, sound, and heat are well-known text-books.

U

Ulanova, Galina (b. 1910), Russian ballet dancer, made her début in 1928 and is the world's greatest living exponent of the art. She danced in Florence in 1951 and in London in 1956.

Undset, Sigrid (1882–1949), Norwegian novelist, daughter of a distinguished Norwegian antiquary, from whom she derived her knowledge of life in ancient and mediaeval Norway. Her first success came with *Jenny* (1911), and the great works based on mediaeval history, *Kristin Lavransdatter* (1920–22) and *Olav Audunsson* (1925–27), won for her the 1928 Nobel Prize for Literature.

Unwin, Sir Raymond (1863–1940), English architect and expert on Town Planning, who became known as the architect of the first garden city at Letchworth, and of the Hampstead Garden Suburb.

Ursula, St., is said to have been an English princess, who with 11,000 virgins set out on a pilgrimage, but compelled by a fierce storm to take refuge in Cologne, was there put to death with her following by an army of Huns.

Usher or Ussher, James (1581–1656), Irish prelate and scholar, one of the most distinguished theologians of his day. He worked out a system of dates setting the creation at 4004 B.C.

V

Valentine, St., was a Christian martyr of the reign of the Emperor Claudius II (d. 270 A.D.). His festival was commemorated on February 14 before Gregory the Great's time. The custom of sending valentines had its origin in a heathen practice associated with the worship of Juno about this date in the calendar, and had no connection with the saint.

Vanbrugh, Sir John (1664–1726), was a prominent architect as well as a successful dramatist.

Vancouver, George (1758–98), a British navigator who served under Captain Cook and later explored the Gulf of Georgia and the Straits of San Juan de Fuca, as also the shores of Vancouver Island.

Vanderbilt, Cornelius (1794–1877), a noted American merchant and railway speculator who accumulated a fortune of twenty millions sterling. His son William Henry Vanderbilt (1821–85) inherited and added to it.

Van Dyck (or Vandyke), Sir Anthony (1599–1641), was born at Antwerp, and after studying under Rubens went to Italy and there made a name as a portrait painter. In 1629 he came to England on the invitation of Charles I., but remained only a short time; in 1631 Charles prevailed upon him to return, made him a knight, granted him an annuity, and he became the Society painter of the day.

Vane, Sir Henry (1613–62), was a prominent statesman and diplomatist. At the Restoration he was arrested as an enemy of the State and ultimately beheaded on Tower Hill.

Van Gogh, Vincent (1853–1890), Dutch painter of some of the most colourful pictures ever created. With passionate intensity of feeling he painted without pause whatever he found around him—landscapes, still-lifes, portraits; his was a truly personal art. His life was one of pain, sorrow and often despair and in the end he committed suicide.

Van Loon, Hendrik Willem (1882–1944), Dutch-American historian, born in Rotterdam, who became famous in 1922 with the publication of *The Story of Mankind*, a picture history-book originally intended for children.

Vauban, Marshal Sebastien le Prestre de (1633–1707), a renowned French military engineer who introduced great improvements in methods of fortification, conducted fifty-three sieges, and took part in 140 battles.

Vaughan Williams, Ralph, O.M., M.A., D. Mus. (1872–1958), English composer. After Charterhouse and Cambridge he studied music in Berlin under Max Bruch and, later in Paris, under Ravel. He wrote nine symphonies besides a number of choral and orchestral works including *Sancta Civitas* and *Benedicite, Magnificat, Four Tudor Portraits, Dona Nobis Pacem*, operas including *Hugh the Drover, Riders to the Sea*, ballets, chamber music and songs. He showed great interest in folk tunes.

Velasquez, Diego (1465–1523), a Spanish soldier and companion of Columbus, sent to conquer Cuba. Velasquez founded Santiago and Havana.

Velazquez, Diego Rodriguez de Silvay (1599–1660), a famous Spanish painter, whose pictures rank among the finest in Spanish art.

Venizelos, Eleutherios (1864–1936), the Greek patriot and statesman, suffered many vicissitudes of fortune during his career. A Cretan by birth, he became Prime Minister of Greece for the first time in 1910, and again on several subsequent occasions, but died in exile. Best known probably for his activity during the Balkan wars, his finally successful attempts to bring his country into the first world war on the side of the Entente Powers, and his ambitions in Asia Minor. At the post-war conferences in 1919 he exercised more influence than anyone else outside the "Big Four."

Verdi, Giuseppe (1813–1901), Italian composer, foremost figure in 19th-century opera. Early works include *Nabucco, Ernani, I Due Foscani*, and *Macbeth*. A middle period is represented by *Rigoletto, Il Trovatore, La Traviata, Un Ballo in Maschera*, and *Don Carlo*. To the last and greatest period of his life belong *Aïda, Otello*, and his last opera *Falstaff*, produced when he was 80.

Verlaine, Paul (1844–1896), French poet, also well known for his memoirs and confessions; died in great poverty and degradation in Paris.

Vermeer, Jan (1632–75), Dutch painter and the greatest of all the "Little Masters." Jan Vermeer of Delft, as he was frequently referred to, was born in Delft, and obtained considerable recognition in his lifetime, but strangely his existence was entirely overlooked after his death, and until 1860 his paintings were attributed to other Dutch painters. *Lady at the Virginals* is in the National Gallery.

Verne, Jules (1828–1905), was one of the most popular authors of wonder-stories in Europe. The best-known of his numerous works are *Five Weeks in a Balloon, Twenty Thousand Leagues Under the Sea, Round the World in Eighty Days*.

Vernier, Pierre (1580–1637), inventor of the small sliding scale which enables readings on a graduated scale to be taken to a fraction of a division.

Veronese, Paul, or Paolo Cagliari (1528–88), a celebrated Italian painter of religious subjects. His *Marriage Feast at Cana in Galilee, The Feast in the House of Simon*, and *The Presentation of the Family of Darius to Alexander*, are paintings of world-wide celebrity, while his *Adoration of the Magi*, in our National Gallery is a grand work.

Veronica, St., a legendary woman of Jerusalem, who was said to have handed to Christ her kerchief on His way to Calvary. The old belief was that the Redeemer wiped His brow therewith, leaving on the handkerchief a miraculous impression of His face, the so-called "Veronicon." The Saint is commemorated on February 4th.

Verwoerd, Dr. Hendrik Frensch (b. 1901), succeeded J. G. Strydom as Prime Minister of South Africa in 1958. Prof. of Psychology at Stellenbosch Univ., 1928–50. An unsuccessful attempt to assassinate him was made on Apr. 9, 1960.

Vespasian (Titus Flavius Vespasinus) (9–79 A.D.) was Roman Emperor during the last nine years of his life. At one time he commanded the Roman army of occupation in Britain.

Vespucci, Amerigo (1451–1512), Florentine merchant and navigator, who settled in Spain as commercial agent of the house of Medici. He made several voyages across the Atlantic and, according to his own accounts, which are disputed by many authorities, reached the American continent on June 16, 1497. A German geographer paid him the tribute of giving the name America to what is now known as South America in a map he published in 1507.

Victor Emmanuel II. (1820–78) was King of Sardinia from 1849 to 1861, became King of Italy, according the the Proclamation of the Sardinian Senate; but it was not until 1870, when the unification of Italy was fully secured, that the title came to have its true significance.

Victoria (1819–1901), Queen of Great Britain and Ireland and Empress of India, was daughter of the Duke of Kent, and came to the throne in 1837 on the death of her uncle, William IV. In 1840 she married Prince Albert of Saxe-Coburg-Gotha, who died in 1861. Lord Melbourne was Prime Minister at the date of the Queen's accession, and for a number of years the country lived through troublesome times, the Corn Law and Chartist agitations being at times very threatening, but a more settled condition of things supervened, and for the remainder of the long and illustrious Victorian reign there was no serious home unrest. The Jubilee of Queen Victoria's accession was celebrated in 1887, and the Diamond Jubilee 10 years later.

Villeneuvre, Pierre Charles Baptiste Silvestre (1763–1806), the French naval commander who was opposed to Nelson at Trafalgar and captured along with his ship, the *Bucentaure*.

Villon, François (1431–*c.* 1485), French poet who lived at a turbulent time in French history at the close of the Hundred Years War. His extant works consist of *Le Lais* (or *Petit Testament*) and *Grand Testament*, masterpieces of French mediæval verse.

Virgil (Publius Vergilius Maro) (70–19 B.C.), the great Roman epic poet, was born near Mantua, and cultivated a farm in the adjacent village of Andes. He proceeded to Rome in his thirtieth year to obtain redress for the occupation of his lands by the military. Became known to Octavian and Mæcenas, and, having had his demand satisfied, began the writing of his *Eclogues*. *The Georgics* followed: his most famous work, the *Æneid*, comprised twelve books dealing with the story of the wanderings of Æneas after the destruction of Troy.

Vitus, St., Roman Catholic saint and martyr, who lived in the 4th century. It used to be the custom to dance before his shrine on this festival day, June 15th, in the belief that good health was thereby ensured for the next twelvemonth. The nervous ailment, St. Vitus' dance, derives its name from this practice.

Vivaldi, Antonio (*c.* 1675–1743), Venetian composer. For many years violin master at the Ospedal della Pieta there. His output of orchestral works was prolific, and their reassessment in recent years has immensely added to his reputation, long disparaged by English writers. Bach indeed arranged some of his violin pieces for the harpsichord.

Volta, Alessandro (1745–1827), Italian physicist, professor at Como and Pavia. Working on the results of Galvani, he found that the essential thing in producing an electric current was contact of dissimilar metals. He invented the voltaic pile, the first instrument for producing an electric current, and thereby laid the foundation of electrochemistry.

Voltaire, François-Marie Arouet de (1694–1778), one of the greatest of French philosophers and writers. His first essays offended the authorities, and he lived in London for a couple of years (1726–28), and there wrote some of his dramas. Returning to France he published his *Philosophical Letters*, which aroused the enmity of the priesthood. At this juncture, the Marquise du Châtelet offered him the asylum of her castle of Cirey, and for the next fifteen years he made this his home, writing there his *Discourses on Man*, *Essay on the Morals and Spirit of Nations*, *Age of Louis XIV*., &c. From 1750–53 he lived in Berlin, on the invitation of Frederick the Great.

Vondel, Joost van den (1587–1679), the greatest of the Dutch poets. Most of his dramas are on biblical subjects, and the two most famous are *Jephtha* and *Lucifer*.

Voroshilov, Marshal of the Soviet Union, Klimentiy Efremovich (b. 1881), President of the Supreme Soviet of the U.S.S.R., 1953–60; commander of the Leningrad defences in 1941.

Vyshinsky, Andrei Yanuarievich (1883–1954), Russian jurist and diplomat; conducted the prosecution of the Moscow treason trials, 1936–38; represented Russian interests at U.N.

W

Wade, George (1668–1748), military engineer who after the Jacobite rebellion of 1715 commanded the royal forces in Scotland and constructed the great military roads through the Highlands, some of which have continued to be the main lines of communication. Promoted to Field-Marshal in 1743 and in 1744 George II made him Commander-in-Chief in England. In the last Jacobite rising of 1745 his army was the first to be evaded by the Young Pretender, Charles Edward, on his famous march south.

Wagner, Richard (1813–83), German composer, born at Leipzig. He achieved a new type of musical expression in his operas by the complete union of music and drama, and his influence on later composers was immense. He made use of the *leitmotif* principle and was his own librettist. His originality and modernism aroused a good deal of opposition, and he was exiled for some years. But he was supported by many loyal friends, including Liszt, the young King Ludwig of Bavaria, and the philosopher Nietzsche. He began the music of the *Ring des Nibelungen* in 1853, finishing it a quarter of a century later. It was not until 1876 that the whole of this great drama (Rheingold, Valkyrie, Siegfried, Götterdämmerung) was performed at Bayreuth under the conductor Hans Richter. Other operas include *The Flying Dutchman*, *Rienzi*, *Tannhäuser*, *Lohengrin*, *Tristan und Isolde*, *Die Meistersinger von Nürnberg*, *Parsifal*, a religious drama. He married Liszt's daughter Cosima, formerly wife of his friend Hans von Bülow.

Waley, Arthur, C.H., C.B.E., M.A. (b. 1889), orientalist, well known for his translations of Chinese and Japanese poetry and prose, being the first to bring the literature of those countries to the western world.

Walker, George (1618–90), the hero of the siege of Londonderry, in 1688, who kept the besiegers at bay for 105 days.

Wallace, Alfred Russel, O.M., F.R.S., LL.D. (1823–1913), celebrated naturalist, a native of Usk, attracted much notice as far back as 1853 by his book *Travels on the Amazon*, detailing experiences in that region. In 1858, while down with illness in the Moluccas, the idea of the evolution theory occurred to him, and curious to say, he drafted his first notes upon it and sent them to Darwin in England while the latter was on the eve of publishing his own exposition of the theory, the result being the reading of a joint paper on the subject to the Linnean Society. The coincidence was fully acknowledged by Darwin. There are differences, however, between the points of view of the two thinkers.

Wallace, Edgar (1875–1932), English novelist and playwright, famous for his detective thrillers.

Wallace, Sir Richard, Bt. (1818–90), son of the Marquis of Hertford, and inheritor from him of a famous collection of pictures and other works of art to which he himself added largely. This was bequeathed to the nation by his widow along with Hertford House and now forms one of the most important exhibitions in London.

Wallace, Sir William (*circa* 1270–1305), the great Scottish patriot and chieftain who led the Scottish armies against Edward I., and for a time the English were kept completely in check. Later, Edward defeated him at Falkirk, and finally in 1304 he was captured, taken to London, condemned for treason, executed at Smithfield.

Wallenstein, Albrecht von (1583–1634), German soldier and statesman during the Thirty Years' War. An able administrator of his own estates, he sought the unity of Germany, but was distrusted and eventually assassinated.

Waller, Edmund (1606–87), was one of the most graceful of English poets, who tuned his lyre to suit both the Cromwellians when they were a power, and Charles II, when his turn came.

Walpole Horace, 4th Earl of Orford (1717–97), younger son of Sir Robert Walpole. He was a member of Parliament from 1741 to 1768, when he retired to his favourite house at Strawberry Hill (" a little Gothic castle ") and devoted himself to the writing of books and the accumulation of works of art. His letters give a graphic picture of Georgian England.

Walpole, Sir Hugh Seymour C.B.E., (1884—1941), a well-known British novelist, whose novels include *Fortitude*, *The Dark Forest*, *Jeremy*, and *Mr. Traill*.

Walpole, Sir Robert, K.G.(1st Earl of Orford) (1676-1745), great 18th-century Whig statesman. He sat in the House of Commons for over forty years, and was Prime Minister for the record period of twenty-one years. Although he enriched himself at the public expense, he was a great financial statesman, and his management of the national debt, encouragement of trade and industry, and his mercantilist colonial policy made England materially very prosperous.

Walter, Bruno (1876–1962), a noted conductor of German birth and American citizenship, associated especially with the opera in many different cities.

Walter, John (1776–1847), son of the founder of *The Times* and known as the second John Walter. Was the leading spirit of *The Times* from 1803 to 1847, and it was his efforts that made the journal the greatest newspaper in the world.

Walton, Izaak (1593–1683), one of the most lovable of English writers, the famous author of *The Compleat Angler, or the Contemplative Man's Recreation*. Also published lives of Donne, Hooker and George Herbert.

Walton, Sir William Turner (b. 1902), English composer, whose works include concertos for string instruments, a symphony, and coronation march, *Crown Imperial*, and an oratorio, *Belshazzar's Feast*.

Warbeck, Perkin (1474–99), a Pretender to the English Crown. The son of a Tournai Jew, he claimed to be Richard, Duke of York, supposed to have been murdered in the Tower, and therefore entitled to the throne of England in preference to its then occupant, Henry VII. The Duchess of Burgundy and Charles VIII. of France and James IV. of Scotland gave him their countenance. Warbeck was enabled in 1497 to appear in England at the head of a force of 7,000 men, but was easily defeated, tried for treason and hanged at Tyburn.

Warwick, Richard Neville, Earl of (*circa* 1428–71). "The King Maker," was the leader of the York party in the Wars of the Roses. At the battle of Northampton he made Henry VI. captive, and afterwards proclaimed Edward, Earl of March, king under the title of Edward IV. Then, when Edward showed a disposition to resent Warwick's protection, the latter drove Edward from the country and once more placed Henry VI. on the throne. He lost his life at the battle of Barnet.

Washington, Booker Taliaferro (1856–1915), a famous negro educationist who was Principal of Tuskegee Institute, Alabama, the first and greatest Institute for negro education, from 1881 until his death. He was a tireless worker for a better understanding between negroes and whites. Wrote several books, including his autobiography, *Up from Slavery*.

Washington, George (1732–99), was of English descent, and was living on his American estate at Mount Vernon when the dispute between the British home government and the colonists broke out. He became one of the leaders of the local opposition, and later was elected to the first Congress at Philadelphia. The following year, 1775, saw him Commander-in-Chief of the American army, and from that time to the end of the struggle in 1783 he was trusted and adored by the people, and on the founding of the Republic became its first President in 1789. He served a second term of office from 1793 onwards, and refused election for a third time.

Watson, John Broadus (1878–1958), American psychologist of international fame who formulated the theory known as Behavourism, in which behaviour is described in terms of physiological response to stimuli. It substantiates the work of Pavlov. *See* **J6**.

Watson-Watt, Sir Robert, F.R.S. (b. 1892), British physicist and engineer, chief of team of scientists engaged in radio location research which resulted in every aircraft and ship being equipped with radar aids enabling them to detect, locate, and shadow enemy craft with great accuracy during the Second World War.

Watt, James, F.R.S., F.R.S.E. (1736–1819). Born at Greenock, this genius was originally a mathematical instrument maker, and being brought into touch with mechanical problems, conceived the idea of the modern, that is, high-pressure steam-engine. Watt took out his first patent in 1769; the engine, however, was used only for mining operations until 1785, when it was applied to a cotton factory, Watt being greatly aided in his developments of the engine by the business ability of his partner, Matthew Boulton.

Watteau, Jean Antoine (1684–1721), a French landscape painter of transcendent ability, and especially great in *genre*. His shepherds and shepherdesses, rustic dance and fête scenes were wonderful for their harmonious brilliancy of coloration. His *chef-d'œuvre* is the *Embarkation for the Isle of Cytherus*, in the Louvre.

Watts, George Frederick, O.M., R.A. (1817–1904), occupied a unique place in English art. His works are numerous; among them may be mentioned *Love and Death*, *Hope* and *The Angel of Death*. He bequeathed to the nation a large number of his finest pictures. His portraits of Swinburne, Carlyle, Cardinal Manning, Browning, and Tennyson are especially fine.

Watts, Isaac (1674–1748), a great English hymn-writer; author of *O God, our help in ages past*.

Watts-Dunton, Walter Theordore (1836–1914), a prominent critic and close friend of Swinburne, author of *The Coming of Love* and *Aylwin*.

Waugh, Evelyn Arthur St. John (b. 1903), English satirical writer, author of *Vile Bodies*, *The Loved One*, *Brideshead Revisited*, *Life of Edmund Campion*, *The Ordeal of Gilbert Pinfold*, and an autobiography, *A Little Learning*. His brother, **Alec Waugh** (b. 1898), is also a successful writer, the author of *The Loom of Youth*.

Wavell, Field Marshal Earl, P.C., G.C.B., G.C.S.I., G.C.I.E., C.M.G., M.C. (1883–1950), Viceroy of India 1943–47; Com.-in-Chief India 1941–43; Com.-in-Chief British Forces in Middle East 1939–41; previously Southern Command 1938–39 and of troops in Palestine 1937–39. Described as one of the cleverest generals in the British Army; his strategy against the Italians in the winter campaign of 1940–41 was brilliantly successful.

Webb, Sir Aston, G.C.V.O., C.B., R.A. (1849–1930), President of the Royal Academy, 1919–24, one of our foremost architects, and the designer of the general scheme of the Victoria Memorial in front of Buckingham Palace, the new Birmingham University, the Britannia Naval College at Dartmouth and other fine structures.

Webb, Matthew (1848–83), in 1875 swam the English Channel in twenty-two hours, and was drowned eight years later in an attempt to swim through the Niagara rapids.

Webb, Rt. Hon. Sidney James, O.M. (1859–1947), eminent Socialist, one of the founders of the Fabian Society in 1884. Sec. of State for the Colonies 1929–31, and for the Dominions, 1929–30. Pres. of Board of Trade in first Labour Government, 1924. His wife Beatrice, equally with himself, was a great investigator and writer on political and economic affairs. Among their books were *History of Trade Unionism*, *English Local Government* and *Soviet Communism*. He founded (1913) and edited (till 1922) the *New Statesman*. Raised to the Peerage, 1929, as **Lord Passfield.**

Weber, Carl Maria Friedrich Ernst von (1786–1826), German composer, who is usually looked upon as the founder of the German national opera and of the German romantic movement, which found its complete musical expression in Wagner. His fame rests principally on his three great operas *Der Freischütz*, *Euryanthe*, and *Oberon*, the last being written for Covent Garden. He was an able pianist, conductor, and musical director as well as composer. He died in London after the performance of *Oberon*, and his body was taken back to Dresden in 1844.

Webster, Daniel (1782–1852), an American, who, as statesman, lawyer, and orator, exerted enormous influence on American constitutional ideas and practice. Served twice as Secretary of State and in 1842 negotiated the Ashburton Treaty which settled the Maine–Canada boundary.

Webster, Noah (1758–1843), the American lexicographer and grammarian. Author of the *Dictionary of the English Language*, and works on literary and political themes.

Wedgwood, Josiah, F.R.S. (1730–95), was the most famous of English potters. He was born at Burslem, served an apprenticeship that carried him through all the branches of the trade, and in 1759 was able to set up in business for himself with money he had saved. He persevered through failure after failure, and in a few years produced such an improved form of ware that it came into great demand. He engaged Flaxman to make classical designs for him, and his pottery became the fashion, and led to a great extension of the Staffordshire earthenware industry.

Weill, Kurt (1900–50), German composer of satirical, surrealist operas, including *Die Dreigroschenoper* (librettist Bert Brecht), and musical comedies, including *Lady in the Dark*, and *One Touch of Venus*. He left Germany in 1933 for France and went to the United States in 1935.

Weingartner, Paul Felix von (1863–1942), Austrian conductor and composer, studied at Leipzig and with Liszt. Established himself as a brilliant conductor, held several appointments in Germany, succeeded Mahler at the Vienna State Opera, and became head of the Conservatory of Music at Basle. His compositions include six symphonies, several operas, and some chamber music.

Weismann, August (1834–1914), a distinguished German biologist who was Prof. of Zoology at

Freiburg, 1866–1912. He is remembered for his theory that heredity is a question of the continuity of the germ-plasm and that acquired characteristics cannot be transmitted to descendants.

Weizmann, Chaim, D.Sc., LL.D., Ph.D. (1874–1952), Zionist leader, became provisional President of Israel in May 1948, and was elected first President in 1949. Distinguished microbiologist and organic chemist.

Wellesley, Richard Colley Wellesley, Marquess, K.G., P.C., K.P. (1760–1842) was Pitt's famous governor general of India, the son of the Earl of Mornington, the first professor of music at Trinity College, Dublin, and elder brother of the Duke of Wellington.

Wellington, Arthur Wellesley, 1st Duke of, K.G., P.C., G.C.B. (1769–1852), was the most famous British general of the 19th century. He distinguished himself in India and conducted successfully the Peninsular War. In 1814 he was British Ambassador at Paris. Then came Napoleon's escape from Elba, the short and sharp campaign which terminated at Waterloo, and the final overthrow of Napoleon. Wellington became the most prominent man in the Empire. From 1828 to 1830 he was Prime Minister. From 1842 to his death he was Commander-in-Chief. His funeral at St. Paul's was one of the great pageants of last century.

Wells, Herbert George (1866–1946), English novelist, sociologist and reformer, one of the most creative and influential writers of his time, a man with a passionate faith in progress through science. His long series of books included romances of the Jules Verne variety (*The Time Machine, The Island of Dr. Moreau, The Invisible Man*), sociological autobiography (*Love and Mr. Lewisham, Kipps, Tono-Bungay, The History of Mr. Polly, Mr. Britling Sees it Through*), and popular education (*Outline of History, The Science of Life, The Work, Wealth, and Happiness of Mankind, The Shape of Things to Come, The Fate of Homo Sapiens*). His great attempt at educating the common man proved so successful that his imitators have been legion. He was a founder member of the Fabian Society.

Wesley, Charles (1708–88), brother of John Wesley, and the poet of Methodism. Wrote a large number of hymns of enduring merit.

Wesley, John (1703–91), the founder of the great religious communion of the people called "Methodists," and the son of a clergyman of the Anglican church. Taking orders himself, in 1735, he went to Georgia as a missioner and allied himself with the Moravians, but later he abandoned all ecclesiastical traditions, and established, on a wonderfully well-devised basis, the connexion called by his name. His own open-air preaching was powerful in the extreme, his energy and depth of purpose inspiring, and his organising ability exceptional. He accomplished a great work of religions revivification, taking the world as his parish; and profound as was his conviction of his high calling as an Evangelist, John Wesley "builded better than he knew" in rearing the denominational edifice which is the monument of his faith and vigour. *See also* Methodism, Section J.

West, Rebecca, D.B.E. (Mrs. Cicily I. Andrews) (b. 1892) novelist, critic and journalist. Among her books are *Black Lamb and Grey Falcon* (a travel book and commentary on Yugoslavia, 1942), and *The Fountain Overflows*, 1957.

Westermarck, Edward Alexander, Ph.D. (1862–1939), a distinguished Finnish scientist who was Professor of Sociology at the University of London, 1907–30. Born at Helsingfors, he made an international reputation with the monumental *History of Human Marriage*, written in English and published in 1891. His *Origin and Development of the Moral Ideas*, 1906–8, was followed by many other works, including *A Short History of Marriage*, 1926; *Ethical Relativity*, 1932; and *The Oedipus Complex*.

Westinghouse, George (1846–1914), American engineer who built the dynamos for Niagara Falls, and in 1865 invented the compressed air brake known by his name and developed a compressed air system of railway signalling.

Westmacott, Sir Richard, R.A. (1775–1856), a great English sculptor who studied under Canova at Rome, and succeeded Flaxman as Professor at the Royal Academy. He executed many fine monuments in Westminster Abbey, at St. Paul's Cathedral, and elsewhere, including the statue of Achilles in Hyde Park and the pediment of the British Museum.

Wharton, Edith (Jones) (1862–1937), American novelist whose *House of Mirth* (1905) brought her fame as a social satirist. Her work was greatly influenced by her friend Henry James, and most of her fifty-four volumes were written after she was thirty-five.

Whately, Archbishop Richard (1787–1863), was for over thirty years Archbishop of Dublin, and achieved a high reputation as a writer on theology and philosophy. His treatises on *Rhetoric* and *Logic* are among the most notable books of their class.

Wheatstone, Sir Charles, F.R.S. (1802–75), was an eminent English electrician and scientist, whose experiments in association with Mr. W. F. Cooke resulted in the first application in this country of the principle of the electric telegraph. The stereoscope was also one of his inventions. He was Professor of Natural Philosophy to King's College, London, for many years.

Wheeler, Sir Charles, K.C.V.O., C.B.E., P.R.A., F.R.B.S. (b. 1892), British sculptor; P.R.A., 1956.

Whistler, James Abbott McNeill (1834–1903), was an original artist, writer, and wit, who first came to Europe from America in 1857, and made a name as an etcher both in Paris and in London. His studies of Thames scenery are especially fine. When he began to exhibit pictures in oils he greatly puzzled the critics, some of whom discovered in his "nocturnes" and other studies an impressionist of surpassing genius, while others, including Mr. Ruskin, who described one of the "nocturnes" at the Grosvenor Gallery as a "pot of paint flung in the public face," looked upon them as mere audacious eccentricities. The finest of his oil paintings are the portrait of his mother, and that of Carlyle. He brought an action against Ruskin for the criticism referred to, but only obtained a verdict of one farthing damages without costs.

White, Field-Marshal Sir George Stuart, V.C., G.C.B., O.M., G.C.M.G., G.C.I.E., G.C.V.O. (1835–1912), the heroic defender of Ladysmith in the South African War and a soldier who achieved renown at many points of a long military career.

Whitefield, George (1714–70), was for a time associated with John Wesley at Oxford in the propagation of Methodism and attracted great attention by his gifts as a preacher. He was Wesley's most powerful champion; but in 1741, differing from Wesley on a point of doctrine he left the Methodists, and thenceforward simply preached as an evangelist, allying himself with no sect, but expounding Calvinistic doctrines with fervour and eloquence.

Whitgift, John (1530–1604), a gifted Anglican prelate. Persecuted the Puritans, and was one of the authors of the famous *Lambeth Articles*. Was Archbishop of Canterbury 1583–1604.

Whitman, Walt (1819–92) was an original figure in the world of American authorship, and produced many works of striking poetic merit. He served in the Civil War, and his vigorous humanity, as expressed in his writings, made him a distinguished personality. His works include *Leaves of Grass, Drum Taps*, and *Democratic Views*.

Whittier, John Greenleaf (1807–92), America's Quaker poet, was the son of a New England farmer, and for a time followed the trade of a shoemaker. After some experience in journalism, he published his first book of poems, *Legends of New England* (1831). His best-known volumes are: *Lays of My Home* (1843), *Voices of Freedom* (1846), *Songs of Labour* (1850), and *National Lyrics* (1865).

Whittington, Richard (*c.* 1358–1423), the son of a Gloucestershire knight, Richard became a wealthy London mercer and was three times mayor of London, 1397–98, 1406–7, 1419–20. His wealth enabled him to supply large loans to Henry IV and Henry V. He was well styled "the model merchant of the Middle Ages". His fortune he bequeathed to charitable institutions. The famous legend about him lacks historical evidence, the "cat" story being a familiar theme in the folklore of almost all the nations of Europe.

Whittle, Air Commodore Sir Frank, K.B.E., C.B. (b. 1907), pioneer in the field of jet propulsion. The first flights of Gloster jet-propelled aeroplanes with Whittle engine took place in May 1941.

Whymper, Edward, F.R.S.E. (1840–1911), a wood-engraver and artist; also one of the best-known Alpine climbers, and the first to reach the summit of the Matterhorn. Author of books on mountaineering in various countries.

Wiggin, Kate Douglas (Mrs. George C. Riggs) (1856–1923), an American novelist of quaint charm and humour. Author of *Rebecca of Sunnybrook Farm.*

Wilberforce, William (1759-1833), was the son of a Hull merchant. He was educated at Cambridge, and entered Parliament in 1780. In 1789 made the first of his many proposals in the House of Commons for the abolition of the slave trade, but it was not until 1807 that the Act embodying these proposals was carried.

Wilcox, Mrs. Ella Wheeler, a popular American poetess (1855–1919). Writer of sentimental verse.

Wilde, Oscar Fingall O'Flahertie Wills (1854–1900), Irish author and dramatist, son of Sir William Wilde, a Dublin surgeon; leader of the cult art for art's sake. His works include poems, fairy-tales, short stories, and brilliantly witty comedies, *Lady Windermere's Fan, A Woman of No Importance, The Ideal Husband* and *The Importance of Being Earnest.* In 1895 he brought an action for libel against the Marquess of Queensberry, the father of his friend, Lord Alfred Douglas, but he himself was convicted of homosexual practices and sentenced to prison for two years where he wrote his famous poem, *The Ballad of Reading Gaol.*

Wilder, Thornton Niven (b. 1897), American author and playwright. Among his books are *The Bridge of San Luis Rey* and the *Ides of March.*

Wilkes, John (1727–97), a forceful and daring Whig politician who championed the cause of the people with great vigour. For a violent attack on George III's Government in his paper *The North Briton,* he was committed to the Tower, but obtained release on the ground that he was a member of Parliament. He was later expelled from the House and fled to France. He returned in 1768 and was repeatedly elected M.P. for Middlesex and as often denied his seat. A great agitation ensued, and so high was he in favour among the people, that he was made alderman, then sheriff, then Lord Mayor of London. In the end his opponents gave way, the orders against him were withdrawn, and from 1779 he was Chamberlain of the City of London.

Willcocks, Sir William, K.C.M.G. (1852–1932), a British engineer, born in India, who in 1898 planned the great Aswan Dam, which he completed in 1902. In 1911 he undertook for Turkey a vast scheme for irrigating some 31 million acres in Mesopotamia.

Willett, William (1856–1915), an English builder, noted for his long and tireless advocacy of the Daylight Saving scheme, which, however, he did not live to see put into effect. It was adopted as a war-time measure in the year Inf.)
following his death. (*See* Summer Time, Gen.

William I. (1027–87), the "Conqueror," Duke of Normandy, claimed the English throne as legally appointed successor to Edward the Confessor and, at the Battle of Hastings in 1066, defeated Harold II. who was killed. The new king crushed Saxon resistance in the North and West, transferred most of the land to his Norman followers, and drew England into closer relations with the Continent. Maintaining many old institutions such as the shire-court and the fyrd (a non-feudal army), William governed firmly, and was supported by the Church, especially by Lanfranc, Abp. of Canterbury. In 1085 he ordered the Domesday Survey (*q.v.*).

William I. of Prussia (1797–1888), the maker of modern Germany, succeeded to the throne of Prussia in 1861. It fell to him to have the control of his country during a period of mighty transition and development, with Bismarck as his chief minister. The war with Austria rendered him highly popular, and when in 1870 the war with France was entered upon the whole German people rallied round him, and after a series of brilliant achievements by his army he was proclaimed German Emperor on the 18th of January, 1871.

William II. (1056–1100), the Conqueror's son, surnamed " Rufus," King of England from 1087 to his death. Was in constant conflict with his barons, lived a life of wanton pleasure, was oppressive to his subjects, and was shot (by accident or design) while hunting in the New Forest.

William II., the Kaiser (1859–1941), King of Prussia and German Emperor 1888 until he abdicated Nov. 9, 1918, and fled to Holland, where he was subsequently interned in the castle of Doorn, living there in complete retirement until his death in June, 1941. Educated at Cassel and Bonn, afterwards entered the army and took a keen interest in military affairs. Succeeded his father, the Emperor Frederick, in 1888. His reign was marked by a strong militarism and an intense ambition to secure the dominance of Germany in the Councils of Europe —an ambition which contributed to the outbreak of the first great war in 1914.

William III (1650–1702), King of England, Scotland, and Ireland (1689–1702), son of William II of Orange (1626–50) and Mary (1631–60), daughter of Charles I. He married Mary, eldest daughter of the Duke of York (later James II) while Stadtholder of Holland. As captain-general of the Dutch forces he was successful against the French, and in 1688, when James had abdicated and fled the country, William was invited to succeed him and he and Mary afterwards became joint King and Queen. Later he was at war with France, and suffered defeats, but ultimately effected an honourable peace by the Treaty of Ryswick in 1697.

William IV of England (1765–1837) was the third son of George III., and ascended the throne in 1830 in succession to his brother, George IV. He had seen some sea service, and was flatteringly styled the "Sailor King." He showed little of kingly capacity, he was genial and pleasure-loving, and placed no obstacles in the way of government, so was, after a sort, popular. In the early part of his reign (1832) the first great Reform Bill was passed.

William the Silent (1533–84), Prince of Orange, made many attempts to secure a peaceful settlement of Netherlands' disputes with Philip II, but became the leader of the ensuing Revolt and was assassinated. He established the independence and Protestant character of the Northern Netherlands, where literary, artistic, colonising, and commercial activity flourished in the following century.

Williams, Sir George (1821–1905), the founder of The Young Men's Christian Association.

Williams, (George) Emlyn (b. 1905), Welsh actor-playwright, and producer, who has had great success in numerous plays and films, and latterly in his readings from Dickens and Dylan Thomas. Author of *Night Must Fall, The Corn is Green,* and *The Light of Heart.*

Wilson, Rt. Hon. (James) Harold, O.B.E., M.P. (b. 1916), British statesman and economist; Prime Minister 1964–; elected Leader of the Labour Party after the death of Gaitskell in 1963; Labour M.P. for Ormskirk, 1945–50; for Huyton, 1950–; Pres. of the Board of Trade, 1947–51; Chair. Public Accounts Committee, 1959–63. *See also* **Section C, Part II.**

Wilson, Richard, R.A. (1714–82), a landscape and portrait painter.

Wilson, (Thomas) Woodrow (1856–1924), President of the United States 1913–21. Was Governor of New Jersey, 1912–13. In 1916 secured from the Kaiser a promise to abandon the more inhuman forms of submarine warfare, and, on their resumption in 1917, broke off official relations with Germany and proclaimed a state of war. Entered into the conflict with the utmost vigour, bringing the full military and financial resources of the Republic into play against Germany. Was a great factor in the winning of victory and in the concluding of a just peace. Largely responsible for the setting up of the League of Nations, which was foreshadowed in his famous Fourteen Points.

Wingate, Major-Gen. Orde Charles, D.S.O. (1903–44), the leader of the Chindit forces engaged behind the Japanese lines in Burma during the second world war. Killed in an air crash.

Winifred, St., patron saint of virgins, a Welsh maiden, who was beheaded by Prince Caradoc for treating him with scorn.

Wiseman, Nicholas Patrick Stephen, Cardinal (1802–65), the first R.C. Archbishop of Westminster, created Cardinal. Much of his life was spent in the reorganisation and development of the Roman Catholic Church in Great Britain. He was one of the three great R.C. prelates of the nineteenth century, the other two being Manning and Newman.

Wodehouse, Pelham Grenville (b. 1881), English humorist, creator of the inimitable Jeeves in the Bertie Wooster stories.

Wolf, Friedrich August (1759–1824), a great German scholar, regarded by some as the founder of scientific classical philology.

Wolf, Hugo (1860–1903), Austrian song-writer. In his settings of over 300 German lyrics, including many of Mörike and Goethe, he achieved complete union of poetry and music.

Wolfe, General James (1727–59), commanded the British forces in Canada at the siege of Quebec, where he won a brilliant victory, which cost him his own life.

Wolsey, Cardinal Thomas (*c.* 1473–1530), was the son of an Ipswich butcher. Showing ability, he was sent to Oxford to be educated, later on entering the Church, where he gradually rose to a position of eminence, and was entrusted with several diplomatic missions. He was especially favoured by the King, Henry VIII., and secured rapid preferment under that monarch, being in turn Bishop of Lincoln, and Archbishop of York. He was subsequently made Cardinal and became Henry's Chancellor. For a number of years he was supreme, and by his diplomacy did much to strengthen the kingly power. But when Wolsey was unable, though willing enough, to obtain the papal sanction for Henry's divorce of Catherine, he fell into disfavour, and his decline was rapid indeed. From being a great personage, with a princely entourage, he was humbled, persecuted, and harried, and died at Leicester Abbey a broken, dejected man.

Wood, Sir Henry Joseph, C.H. (1869–1944), was the most popular English musical conductor of his day. He introduced many works and composers previously unknown to the British public and greatly stimulated and encouraged interest in classical music. His long association with the Promenade Concerts began in 1895 at the Queen's Hall, and after it was destroyed in an air raid in 1941 the concerts continued at the Albert Hall and are now named after him. He composed songs and cantatas, and his arrangement of sea shanties ends every series of Promenade Concerts.

Woodcock, George (b. 1904), succeeded Sir Vincent Tewson as secretary of the T.U.C. in 1960. Won scholarships to Ruskin College, Oxford, and Oxford Univ. and gained first-class honours in philosophy, politics, and economics. Appointed research officer of T.U.C. in 1936 and assistant general secretary in 1947.

Woodville, Elizabeth (1437–91), wife of Sir John Grey. After her first husband's death she made a secret marriage with Edward IV., and became the mother of Edward V., and his brother Prince, both of whom were put to death in the Tower by order of Richard III. She was also mother to Elizabeth, Queen of Henry VII.

Woolf, Mrs. (Adeline) Virginia (1882–1941), English novelist and essayist, daughter of Sir Leslie Stephen and wife of Leonard Woolf, writer and publisher. Together they formed the Hogarth Press. Among her best known works are *To the Lighthouse, Mrs. Dalloway, The Waves, The Years, A Room of One's Own, Orlando.*

Woolley, Richard van der Riet, Sc.D., F.R.S. (b. 1906), succeeded Sir Harold Spencer Jones as Astronomer Royal at the Royal Greenwich Observatory in 1956; formerly Commonwealth Astronomer at the Observatory at Canberra.

Wootton, Barbara Frances, Baroness, M.A., L.H.D., J.P. (b. 1897), Prof. of Social Studies, Univ. of London, 1948–52. Chair. Metropolitan Juvenile Courts. Her book *Social Science and Social Pathology* (1959) examines the state of our knowledge about social pathology, with particular emphasis on criminology and social work. Created a life peeress in 1958.

Wordsworth, William (1770–1850), the chief of the "Lake Poets," and one of the most inspired of all British bards, was a native of Cockermouth, and was educated at Hawkshead and St. John's College, Cambridge. In association with Coleridge he issued a volume of *Lyrical Ballads* in 1793. The following year saw him settled at Grasmere, and there and at Rydal Mount he passed the rest of his days. In 1802 he married Mary Hutchinson, his cousin, and the two, with the poet's sister Dorothy, formed an ideally poetic household. Here he carried out his creed of "plain living and high thinking," and produced at intervals some of the purest and noblest poetry in the language. As an interpreter of Nature in her many moods he stands unrivalled. Succeeded to the Poet Laureateship on the death of Southey in 1843.

Wren, Sir Christopher, F.R.S. (1632–1723), the most famous English architect of his time. He did not quite have all his own way with the tremendous thirty-five years' task he accepted in undertaking the reconstruction of St. Paul's after the Fire, but he produced a masterpiece of which Britain may well be proud. Chelsea and Greenwich Hospitals, and a number of London's finest churches were also his work.

Wright, Sir Almroth (Edward), K.C.B., C.B., M.D., F.R.S. (1861–1947), discovered the system of anti-typhoid inoculation, the method of therapeutic inoculation for bacterial infections (vaccinotherapy), and methods of measuring the protective substances in human blood.

Wright, Frank Lloyd (1869–1959), American architect who, with others, brought into fashion the present-day horizontal strip and all-glass design. His imaginative ideas, both as to structure and look, have influenced architecture all over the world. Early buildings were the Larkin office building, Buffalo, N.Y., and the Imperial Hotel, Tokio, which withstood the 1923 earthquake. His last building was the Guggenheim Museum in New York, based on a spiral.

Wright, Orville (1871–1948), American airman who, with his brother **Wilbur** (1867–1912), began gliding experiments on the sand dunes at Kitty Hawk, North Carolina. To the glider they built they added a petrol engine, and on 17th Dec., 1903, they made four flights, the longest being 852 ft. These flights were the first in which a man had been carried from the ground on flight by a power-driven aeroplane.

Wyatt, James, R.A. (1746–1813), a celebrated architect in his day. He built Fonthill Abbey for Beckford and the Royal Military Academy at Woolwich. Pres. of R.A. 1805–6.

Wyatt, Sir Thomas (1503–42), was the first writer of English sonnets, and a poet who did much to develop the earlier forms of verse.

Wyatt, Sir Thomas ("The Younger") (*c.* 1520–54); joined with the Duke of Suffolk in favour of Lady Jane Grey and against Queen Mary, son of the last-mentioned. Led the men of Kent in rebellion on London in 1554, but was captured and executed.

Wycherley, William (1640–1715), English Restoration dramatist, a master of satiric comedy. His plays include *Love in a Wood*, which won him the favour of the Duchess of Cleveland, mistress of Charles II, *The Plain Dealer*, and his masterpiece *The Country Wife*. His marriage to the Countess of Drogheda lost him court favour.

Wyclif, John (*c.* 1324–84), born in Yorkshire, educated at Oxford, and one of the most eminent ecclesiastics of his time. He adopted principles many of which became general at the Reformation, and brought down upon himself the bitter enmity of the Roman Catholic leaders, and would probably have been put to death but for the protection of John of Gaunt. While in comparative retirement as Rector of Lutterworth, in Leicestershire, he finished his translation of the Bible.

Wykeham, William of (1324–1404), was Bishop of Winchester from 1366 to his death, and from 1367 to 1371 Lord Chancellor. He was a man of great learning and an excellent preacher, and wielded great influence. He founded New College, Oxford, in 1379 and Winchester College in 1382.

Wyllie, William Lionel, R.A. (1851–1931), English marine painter whose *The Thames Below London Bridge* was bought by the Chantrey Bequest. Other works are *The Battle of Trafalgar*, and *The Port of London*.

Wyspianski, Stanislav (1869–1907), great Polish poet, dramatist and painter.

X

Xavier, St. Francis (1506–1552), the apostle of the Indies, was the follower of Ignatius de Loyola, and devoted his life to missionary work in the East. He was canonised in 1622.

Xenophon (444–359 B.C.), the Athenian general and follower of Socrates. His chief works are *Anabasis Hellenica*, and *Cyropœdia*.

Xerxes (*circa* 519–465 B.C.), King of Persia, was the son of the first Darius and a great commander. In 481 B.C. he started on his famous expedition against Greece when, according to Herodotus, he had a combined army and navy of over two and a half million men. He defeated the Spartans at Thermopylae, but his fleet was overcome at Salamis. He reigned from 485 to 465 B.C. and met his death by assassination.

Ximenes de Cismeros, Francisco (1436–1517), Spanish statesman and Cardinal who reformed the Franciscan Order to a great extent, and in 1502 began to direct the preparation of a polyglot bible, the *Complutensian*, which greatly influenced subsequent versions. In 1506 was made Regent for Queen Juana, and raised to the cardinalate in 1507. Personally conducted a military campaign in Africa in 1509, and afterwards became Inquisitor-General, and in 1516, Regent of Castile, but in the following year was dismissed by the Emperor Charles V.

Y

Yeats, William Butler (1865–1939), Irish lyric poet and dramatist and major figure in the Irish literary revival of the 20th century. With Lady Gregory and others founded the Abbey Theatre in Dublin, for which he wrote many plays. Interested in mysticism and the occult. Member of the Irish Senate, 1922–28; awarded Nobel Prize in Literature in 1923. Some of his best work was written in his later years in *The Tower* (1928) and *Last Poems* (1940). Plays include *Cathleen Ni Houlihan* (1902), *The Hour Glass* (1904), *Deidre* (1907).

Yonge, Charlotte Mary (1823–1901), author of over 120 novels, school books, and other works, including *The Heir of Redclyffe*, *The Daisy Chain*, *The Dove in the Eagle's Nest*, and *The History of Christian Names*.

Young, Brigham (1801–77), Mormon leader, and head of the Latter Day Saints of Salt Lake City. At his death he had seventeen wives.

Young, Francis Brett (1884–1954), British novelist. His books include *My Brother Jonathan* and *Doctor Bradley Remembers*.

Young, James, F.R.S. (1811–83), a Glasgow chemist who discovered the method of distilling oil from shale, and founded the mineral oil industry of Scotland, which led to the development of petroleum concerns.

Young, Thomas (1773–1829), one of the most versatile geniuses in history, descended from a Quaker family of Somerset. Studied languages, medicine, and held the Professorship of Physics at the Royal Institution. In 1804 elected Foreign Secretary of the Royal Society. He was very successful in deciphering Egyptian hieroglyphics and was the first to translate the inscription on the Rosetta Stone. Famous for his share in establishing the undulatory theory of light and for his work on physiological optics.

Younghusband, Lt.-Col. Sir Francis Edward, K.C.S.I., K.C.I.E. (1863–1942), soldier, explorer and writer. Wrote many works on the East. Headed the British Mission to Tibet, 1903–04. Was *Times* correspondent with the Chitral expedition. Pres. of Royal Geographical Soc., 1919–22.

Ypres, 1st Earl of, P.C., K.P., G.C.B., O.M., G.C.V.O., K.C.M.G. (1852–1925), entered Navy in 1866, afterwards passing into Army in 1874, making his mark as a Cavalry officer in the Egyptian campaign of 1884; served in South African War with brilliant success. C.-in-C. British Forces in France, 1914–15; C.-in-C. Home Forces, 1915–18; Lord Lieut. of Ireland, 1918–21.

Ysayë, Eugène (1858–1929), Belgian violinist and conductor, noted chiefly for his playing of the works of Bach and César Franck.

Yukawa, Hideki (b. 1907), Japanese physicist, who received the 1949 Nobel Prize for predicting the existence of the meson. Prof. of Physics at Kyoto Univ. since 1939.

Z

Zadkiel (the angel of Jupiter in Jewish rabbinical lore) was the name assumed by **Lilly** (1602–81) the astrologer, and also by **Richard James Morrison** (1794–1874), Hebrew scholar and amateur astronomer, in the almanack known as Zadkiel's Almanack and first issued in 1831.

Zadkine, Ossip (b. 1890), French sculptor, one of the greatest of our time, whose works include *Orpheus*, *The Return of the Prodigal Son*, *The Birth of Forms*, *Poet*, *Harlequin*. Exhibition at Tate Gallery, 1961.

Zaharoff, Sir Basil, G.C.B., G.B.E. (1849–1936), was an influential Greek banker and financier who became an armaments magnate, supplying the Allies in the first world war.

Zamenhof, Ludwig Lazarus (1859–1917), Polish linguist who was by profession an oculist, but gained fame as the inventor of Esperanto.

Zeno of Citium (*c.* 340–264 B.C.) was a Greek philosopher who founded the Stoic system.

Zeppelin, Ferdinand, Count von (1838–1917), inventor of the huge dirigible airship bearing his name. His first ascent was in 1900. He organised a Zeppelin service for the German army in the war of 1914–18, but their extreme vulnerability militated severely against their usefulness.

Zeromski, Stefan (1864–1925), great Polish novelist, poet and playwright.

Zhukov, Marshal of the Soviet Union Grigory Konstantinovich (b. 1895), led the defence of Moscow and Leningrad during second world war; served on Allied Control Commission in Germany; C.-in-C. Land Forces and Deputy Minister of Armed Forces of Soviet Union, 1946–55; succeeded Marshal Bulganin as Defence Minister, 1955–57.

Zhukovsky, Vasily Andreyevich (1783–1852), Russian poet whose original work had very important influence on Russian literature.

Zola, Emile Edouard Charles Antoine (1840–1902), was the son of an Italian engineer, and came before the public as a novelist in 1867 with *Thérèse Raquin*. He then conceived the idea of a series of novels which should depict the history of a Second Empire family in various realistic phases, and began the series with *La Fortune des Rougons*, in 1871. In 1877 he made a higher success by *L'Assommoir*. From that time every novel he published had an immense sale.

Zorn, Anders Leonhard (1860–1920), was a noted Swedish painter, etcher and sculptor.

Zoroaster, the Greek form of the name of the Persian prophet, Zarathustra, who lived about the seventh century B.C. He was a monotheist, believing in a good and holy God whom he called Ahura Mazda. Many of his teachings were absorbed by the ancient Persian religion which survives today among the Parsees in India.

Zoshchenko, Mikhail (1895–1958), Russian writer whose humorous short stories, satirising the Soviet way of life, were wildly popular throughout Russia in the 1920s. Several have been translated and published in England.

Zosimus (fl. *c.* A.D. 300), the first known alchemist. He lived in Alexandria.

Zuccarelli, Francesco (1702–88), a very celebrated Italian artist, who came to England; succeeded, made a handsome fortune, and was one of the first membersof the Royal Academy.

Zuckerman, Sir Solly, C.B., M.A., M.D., D.Sc., F.R.S. (b. 1904), British biologist; Prof. of Anatomy, Birmingham Univ., 1939–; chief scientific adviser to the Secretary of State for Defence.

Zwingli, Ulrich (1484–1531), was one of the ablest of the Swiss Reformation leaders.

Zwirner, Ernst Friedrich (1802–61), an eminent Silesian architect. Restored Cologne Cathedral.

BACKGROUND TO PUBLIC AFFAIRS

TABLE OF CONTENTS

BACKGROUND TO PUBLIC AFFAIRS

This section is in two parts. The first describes some major events since the war and carries the story to 1966. The second part describes our own political institutions, the Commonwealth, the United Nations and Western International Organisations.

I. STORY OF POST-WAR EVENTS

1. BRITAIN: POLITICAL BACKGROUND.

The End of Another War.—The way the British people greeted the end of the Second World War was markedly different from their feelings in 1918. The First World War had ended almost as suddenly as it had begun; and there was then an explosion of relief and rejoicing of a kind which has not been seen since. After all, that was a " war to end war." It could never happen again. England was to be a land " fit for heroes to live in." The outbreak of the war in 1914 had been a sudden shock to a world confident of peaceful evolution. The British people, having seen it through, were again confident that nothing like it could recur. The instant reaction when the end came was therefore one of delirious relief. The mood at the end of the last war, however, was very different. That war came gradually but relentlessly all through the 'thirties and it ended gradually too. We were in a sense at war long before it formally started; and at the end there was no clear emergence into a cloudless era of assured peace and progress. To maintain peace a continuous effort was seen to be necessary. Ideas had played a much greater part in sustaining men and women in the second great war than in the first; their sense of responsibility had grown so that the mood when the end came on 8 May 1945 was more questioning and cautious than in November 1918. Further, the second great war had touched everyone more directly—the bombing of cities, the imminence of invasion, the food shortages, the evacuation of school children, all this had spread the impact; and, when it was over, the mood was one of sober resolve.

The Age of Bewilderment.—Before we continue our narrative let us take a backward glance at the years between the wars, not to describe the events, which included the emergence of authoritarian tyrannies and a world-wide economic crisis, but to mark some of the moral characteristics. It was said to be a period of disillusionment, of moral and intellectual decay. There was the loss of faith in democracy; a sense of aimlessness reflected in the arts, a good deal of confusion and uncertainty about values, and, above all, insecurity. That there was this political apathy and bewilderment is true; but much to the contrary is true also. This was, after all, the nation which had won the war and, by resolution and will, was to win the next. The nation faces difficulties again. We shall see later that these difficulties seem hard to diagnose but we shall try to disentangle in this story the elements in what has been called our social malaise.

The First Atomic Explosion.—Momentous events were to come. The war with Japan was not yet over. Although the secret was kept at the time, the first full-scale atomic bomb explosion was made in the Mexican desert in July 1945 through the concerted efforts of a team of scientists working in America. The bomb was detonated at the top of a pylon 100 feet high and a space of ten miles cleared. Devastation inside a one-mile circle was absolute. It offered a means to a speedy end of the war with Japan. It has proved to be the first of a series of tests of increasingly powerful bombs which pose the greatest threat which has ever faced mankind and may yet destroy civilisation. A few days later the United States and Great Britain called for unconditional surrender by Japan and upon its rejection a bomb was dropped on August 6 on Hiroshima and a second on Nagasaki on August 9. The surrender terms were then accepted. Churchill in his account of the war describes his own view that there should have been no rigid insistence on " unconditional surrender." " It would be a mistake ", he writes, " to suppose that the fate of Japan was settled by the atomic bomb. Her defeat was certain before the first bomb fell."

The Face of the Post-war World.—Far-reaching changes mark the decade which ended with the Suez affair of 1956. Asian countries, driving towards independence, reached their objectives, and a similar drive in African countries was gathering momentum. The war had impoverished Britain and France, which could no longer be powers great enough to follow an independent course; and they both played rôles, although different ones, in launching Western Europe towards unity. The victors of the war quarrelled and this vitiated the working of the United Nations, which had been founded on the hope that the victors would not quarrel—not, at any rate, so profoundly that we should no longer have a state of peace but a condition given the frank but dispiriting title of " the cold war." The direct confrontation of the two great Power blocs—the United States and the Soviet Union—was therefore a cardinal feature of the decade, with the development of atomic weapons. The competition in armaments was matched by another competition in economic power. Both sides made a bid for the support of the new Afro-Asian countries; and it was seen that what attracted those countries was naturally the technical means to satisfy hunger and to secure clothing, shelter, and the materials with which to live. Russia, therefore, turned increasingly to the training of scientists and technologists in the drive towards industrialisation and economic growth, likely to comfort the peasantries of the new continents.

Estrangement between West and East.—The war had engendered friendship between Western Powers and Russia. Why did they so quickly fall apart with the defeat of the enemy—a fact which was to transform the history of the world? The fact was that relations were reverting to their pre-war state of hostility. Nazi Germany had divided the West from Russia; Russia had been suspicious of our appeasement of Germany which might liberate her for attack eastwards. And when, eventually, Russia and Germany signed a non-aggression pact in 1939, which freed Germany to turn west instead of east and to attack us, our hostility towards Russia naturally deepened. Popular feeling changed when Hitler invaded Russia in 1941 but co-operation between Western and Soviet leaders was not so close as to prevent ill-feeling—one cause of mistrust being the Russian belief that our invasion of Europe was being unjustifiably delayed. When the war ended there was still an abundance of goodwill towards Russia. But a number of political facts worked the other way. The Russians had taken a hold over a number of countries in the eastern half of Europe; and this led to the establishment in those countries of communist régimes. Were the ideas of

Russia necessarily antagonistic to the West? They were certainly incompatible. In Stalin's view, especially after his experience of Germany's invasion, there could not but be hostility from the West. This sense of suspicious defensiveness made Soviet foreign policy complex and enigmatic. Whatever the reason might be, Russia's policy followed a course which could not be easily understood; and the goodwill towards her was allowed to evaporate.

The Bomb.—In the first years of the decade the Red Army was supreme on the ground in Europe and Asia and the U.S. Air Force supreme in the air. It was the Red Army versus the atomic bomb. But in September 1949 the Soviets exploded an atomic bomb and the four years of American monopoly was over. The race for bigger bombs intensified. The United States exploded a hydrogen bomb in November 1952 and Russia followed in August 1953. The new weapon was different not only in degree but in kind. The killing effects were incalculable; and the after-effects on future generations unpredictable. Eisenhower said there was no alternative to peace; but no solution was reached on practical issues—on the two Germanys, on the status of the satellite countries in Eastern Europe, on the future of the Middle East. The post-war world disintegrated. Neutralism was seen as the only hope of survival by those countries where pent-up forces of nationalism were being released.

The Technological Race.—The race between Russia and the West was not a new one; Professor Toynbee has pointed out that it began in 1700 when Peter the Great created a strong country against invaders who had deprived her earlier of so much. Russia, defeated in the first great war, made a new start in 1917 when she threw communism (a creed borrowed from the West) into the scale. She drew ahead and after a long and bitter struggle beat the Germans in 1945 as Peter the Great had driven Russia ahead, eventually beating the French in 1812. With the American success with the atomic bomb Russia fell behind again; but she resumed the race with the West and was first with an earth satellite (1957) and a manned satellite (1961). In their technological breakthrough in 1957 the Russians developed the first inter-continental ballistic missile. The see-saw continued and, in 1961, the Americans perfected the cheap, quickfiring ICBM, the Minuteman.

The Creation of the "Satellite" States.—The satellite states, as they are known, were set up by Russia in the countries of Eastern Europe which had been occupied by Russia in the final stages of the war. This occupation had been made militarily easier when the Americans, in August 1944, had withdrawn 100,000 men from the Italian campaign for a seemingly needless invasion of the south of France. The states were Czechoslovakia, Poland, Roumania, Albania, Hungary, Bulgaria, and Yugoslavia—all, except Hungary, inhabited by peoples mainly of Slav race. Yugoslavia, however, eventually broke away under its national leader, Marshal Tito, though the country remained communist. At the Yalta conference of February 1945 attended by Roosevelt, Churchill, and Stalin, Russia had agreed that democratic governments should be set up in Eastern Europe. But the transformation of the countries to Communist régimes began very shortly afterwards and by 1948 was complete.

The Cold War and the West.—The failure of the nations to make treaties of peace or arrangements for general disarmament, and the continuing loss of confidence between Russia and the West led to an increase of armaments and defensive pacts by both sides. In the West rearmament was carried out by the U.S.A. and Western Europe on the lines of an agreement made in 1949 and known as the North Atlantic Pact. They formed the North Atlantic Treaty Organisation (NATO), the first supreme commander being Eisenhower, who afterwards became, for two terms, President of the United States (being succeeded by Kennedy in 1961). The Russians, on their side, organised the Communist countries by a "Warsaw Pact." It is refreshing to note that Austria, by agreement in 1956, established a democratic republic, to be permanently neutral like Switzerland. In Asia a number of countries which met at Bandung in Indonesia in 1955 with some African countries decided to keep neutral. Four Asian countries, however (Turkey, Iraq, Iran and Pakistan), neighbours of Russia, formed a defensive pact with Britain—the Baghdad Pact (later to become the Central Treaty Organisation or CENTO). Some countries bordering the East and South Pacific, including Australia and New Zealand, formed the South East Asia Treaty Organisation or SEATO for mutual defence against the Communists.

The General Election of 1945.—This election was quiet, conducted on an out-of-date register but with a postal vote for the Forces. A lively issue had been introduced by Churchill, who declared that if the Labour Party won the election Attlee, as Prime Minister, would be under the control of Harold Laski who was then chairman of the national executive of the Labour Party. This declaration stemmed from a statement which had been made by Laski that the Labour Party would not be bound by any commitments entered into by Attlee when, as leader of the Labour Party, he accompanied Churchill to the Potsdam conference with Stalin and Truman in June. A correspondence of increasing bitterness followed between Churchill and Attlee who asserted "The Chairman has not the power to give me instructions." Attlee seemed on surer ground in the interpretation of the constitution of his own party. The popular impression was that the matter was an election scare devised by Churchill's campaign advisers. The Labour Party had a dramatic victory, 393 Labour M.P.s being returned, with a clear majority over all other parties. They did not have a clear majority among the voters, the Liberals holding a balance. But the bias present in the constituency system worked in favour of the Labour Party.

The Resignation of Churchill.—Ordinarily Churchill might have been expected to take a few days to wind up the affairs of the Government. This would have enabled him to present the unconditional surrender of Japan to the nation. But two factors led him to resign at once and advise the King to send for Mr. Attlee. These factors were the need for Britain to be represented with proper authority at the Potsdam conference where great issues were coming to a head; and the overwhelming nature of the verdict of the electors. He thanked the nation that day for the "unflinching, unswerving support" which they had given him in his task in the war and "for the many expressions of kindness which they have shown towards their servant."

Churchill's Premonition.—There is a moving story in the last volume of Churchill's work *The Second World War* of his sudden premonition of electoral defeat. On 25 July 1945 he flew home from Potsdam and went to bed, accepting the view of the Conservative Party managers that the British people would wish him to continue his work and that it would be possible to reconstitute the National Coalition Government in the proportions of the new House of Commons. On that belief he slumbered. "However, just before dawn," he writes, "I woke suddenly with a sharp stab of almost physical pain. A hitherto subconscious conviction that we were beaten broke forth and dominated my mind. . . . The power to shape the future would be denied me. . . . I was discontented at the prospect and turned over at once to sleep again." When he awoke the first results had begun to come in and they were, as he now expected, unfavourable. By noon it was clear that the Socialists would have a majority. His wife said to him, "It may well be a blessing in disguise," to which he replied "At the moment it seems quite effectively disguised."

The Causes of the Conservative Defeat, 1945.—Looking back some twenty years after it must seem puzzling that the country could have been so ungrateful to the man who had pulled the nation through tragedy to triumph. But the people were not ungrateful. Their verdict was registered, rightly or wrongly, against the Party which had excluded Churchill from office during the pre-war years. The verdict was directed against the Conservatives despite the admiration for Churchill. It was they, not he, who were condemned for the Munich Agreement and for the pre-war unemployment. There was also an undercurrent of concern that events might follow the pattern of the First World War when the war leader, Lloyd George, was re-elected on generous promises which were not fulfilled.

Labour Faces a Financial Crisis.—On coming to office in 1945 the Labour Government was faced with the end of the financial assistance given to Britain during the war by the United States under the system known as Lend-Lease (**L69**). The Government accepted a dollar loan but the money ran out by 1947. Stafford Cripps was appointed Minister of Economic Affairs to deal with the crisis and, in the autumn, when Dr. Hugh Dalton resigned as Chancellor of the Exchequer after an indiscreet Budget disclosure to a journalist, he combined both posts. Cripps had been a brilliant lawyer before entering politics. He was now master of the economic affairs of the nation. He introduced a programme of austerity in order to reduce the demand for foreign currency; and the trade unions co-operated by accepting a policy of "wage restraint." This co-operation was willingly accorded because Cripps controlled prices, maintained an equitable taxation system and because of the social services which the Government had introduced.

The Marshall Plan.—Assistance to Britain came in a new way. In 1947 George Marshall, U.S. Secretary of State, proposed a scheme whereby his country would assist in a programme for putting Europe on a sounder economic basis. The programme would need to be a joint one, agreed to by a number, if not all European nations; and the initiative must come from Europe, the United States giving friendly aid and support. Ernest Bevin, Foreign Secretary, jumped at the offer and with fifteen other nations drew up what became known as the European Recovery Programme. The Organisation for European Economic Co-operation which, of course, is still in being, came into existence to administer the programme.

Bevin and America.—Bevin worked increasingly for effective collaboration with America and he was a prime mover in creating the North Atlantic Treaty Organisation (1949). This was the first treaty in which the U.S.A. had ever undertaken European commitments in peace time. It grew out of fear of Russian power. Bevin's policy was criticised by some members in his own party. Criticisms varied. One was that Bevin had abandoned a specifically socialist foreign policy and that he should have attempted to retain independence between the two worlds—the capitalist and communist worlds—and tried to build a bridge between them. This view was crystallised in the advocacy of a "third force" of powers standing between America and Russia and led by Britain. The group expressing this view were known as the "Keep Left" group, and it was about this group that Bevin made the often quoted remark that he had been "stabbed in the back." The members of this group of "Labour Independents" were defeated in the 1950 election.

The Work of the Labour Government, 1945–50.—The first measure was the nationalisation of the Bank of England which Churchill said did not raise any question of principle and there was little opposition. The National Coal Board, established as a public but semi-independent body, took over a very inefficient industry. The British Transport Commission was created in 1947 and took over railways, canals, and road haulage. Cable and wireless companies were nationalised and public corporations created to run airlines; in these measures the new Government were following the lines of policy accepted by earlier governments. The creation of the British Electricity Authority (1948) and the Gas Council (1949) enabled management to be taken of industries which were already under some public control. Beyond all this the Government built a "welfare state" in which the social services were no longer regarded as a form of poor relief but as a co-operative system of mutual aid and self-help provided by the whole nation and designed to ward off distress and strain wherever they may fall. At the centre of the system were the social insurance scheme and the national health service.

The Controversy over Iron and Steel.—The question of the nationalisation of this industry proved controversial and difficult. It was left to the last by the Government. The industry, which was profitable and fairly efficient, was also very complex, ownership penetrating into industries other than engineering. The nationalisation of iron and steel took effect in February 1951 (by the administration formed after the general election of 1950 when the overall Commons majority of the Labour Party was reduced to only six); but the Conservatives, returned to power in 1951, denationalised the industry.

The National Health Service.—This welfare service was created by the Labour Government's National Health Service Act of 1946 and became operative in 1948. It provided all those who take advantage of it with free medical and hospital treatment. The cost is met partly by contributions from general taxation and partly by compulsory contributions from all citizens (except certain exempted persons) and these contributions are payable whether or not advantage is taken of the service. In 1949 90 per cent of the cost was borne by taxes but by 1961 this had dropped to only 70 per cent. Aneurin Bevan who as Minister of Health had piloted this great scheme through all its stages, resigned when the Labour Government imposed charges on spectacles and teeth in 1951 although this was intended only as a temporary measure. Since then, however, governments have continued to increase general charges—on prescriptions, on contributions, on spectacles, dentures, welfare foods, and amenity beds.

The Continuing Needs of a Welfare Society.—Writing a decade and a half later we can see that social services can never be finished articles. A school of writers led by Professor Richard Titmuss have recently shown that some groups have benefited far less than others from the recent increase in production and that behind the façade of affluence there are "submerged groups." Serious social problems remain like the adequate care of the aged, housing and unemployment caused by economic and technical changes. The subject of the care of the aged becomes more urgent every year since the number of people above working age in the United Kingdom is steadily increasing (*see* **G13**).

Labour and Asia.—The granting of independence by the Attlee Government to India, Pakistan, Ceylon and Burma was of the greatest importance. Seen at the time as a historic achievement, the passage of time has confirmed its momentous nature. It is difficult to contemplate into what tragic paths we might have fallen had independence for India been further delayed. Independence to countries is very rarely given too soon. How easy it is to see now that Britain would have benefited enormously—and the wider world too—had a settlement between her and Ireland not been tragically delayed. The clock of progress was put back fatally. We were spared further conflict with our Asian dependencies by the decisive action of Attlee in sending Lord Mountbatten to India as the last Viceroy in order to transfer power to the Indians. Of the four new states in Asia only Burma elected to sever its links with the Commonwealth.

The Changing Commonwealth.—At this point we may glance ahead at the further evolution of the Commonwealth which followed the grant of independence to the Asian countries—a step criticised vehemently at the time but now seen to have been wise. As other countries in the Commonwealth reached sovereign status most of them sought full membership, so that there were welcomed to membership Ghana and Malaya in 1957, the Federation of Nigeria in 1960, Cyprus, Sierra Leone and Tanganyika in 1961, Jamaica, Trinidad and Tobago, and Uganda in 1962. Kenya and Zanzibar in 1963, Malta, Malawi, and Zambia in 1964, Gambia and Singapore in 1965, followed by Bechuanaland (Botswana), British Guiana (Guyana), and Mauritius in 1966. Thus we have a system which bears no resemblance to the empires of the past, a partnership based upon friendship between nations with a diversity of race, religion, and language. This evolution we are now beginning to take for granted; but it must not be forgotten for it is one of the most heartening features of our time. *See also* **Part II.**

Labour Faces the Country, 1950.—During the whole of its term of office, 1945–50, the Labour Government had not lost a single by-election. But the general election of 1950 gave the Labour Party only a very slight majority. They secured only 315 seats, against 298 Conservatives, 9 Liberals, and 2 Irish Nationalists. A considerable defection of middle-class voters resulted in suburban seats in London and the Home Counties returning to Conservative allegiance. Dissatisfaction with continued shortages and with rationing no doubt played a part. The redistribution of seats due to population movement had resulted, in 1950, in an electoral system with a slight bias against the Labour Party since support in working-class areas was so strong as to bank up enormous Labour majorities there, whereas the Conservative vote was more diffused and thus more effective in electoral figures. The result ended Labour's effective control of Commons. Government was scarcely possible with a majority of six and the parties renewed their fight at another election which Attlee called in October 1951.

The Conservatives Regain Power, 1951.—The Labour Party secured the highest total poll that it or any other party had received in a general election—fourteen million votes. The Conservatives received a quarter of a million less; but they secured a majority of seats. This anomaly was due to the character of the electoral system described above. The composition of the new House was 321 Conservatives, 295 Labour, 6 Liberals and 3 Irish Independents. In the atmosphere of relaxed responsibility the controversy which had begun within the Labour Party while they were in power was renewed.

Churchill at Eighty.—No Prime Minister had been so honoured as when members of both Houses assembled in 1954 in Westminster Hall to present to him a book signed by them and a portrait of him by Graham Sutherland. A memorable description of the scene is reprinted from *The Guardian* in " The Glory of Parliament " by Harry Boardman—the throng of several thousand, the drums of the Guards' band beating the opening bar of the Fifth Symphony, which Churchill had so memorably converted into a victory sign ten years earlier. He disclaimed having inspired the nation in the war. He had had only to appeal, he said, to the remorseless, unconquerable will of the people. " It was the British race that had the lion's heart. I had the luck to give the roar."

Eden Succeeds Churchill.—The new Prime Minister, Anthony Eden, who succeeded Churchill in April 1955 decided upon a general election, thus taking advantage of two factors, the controversy within the Labour Party and the economic recovery at that time. There were also, at the time, a number of strikes or threats of strikes which affected a wide public and these disputes were unfortunately due in part to inter-union rivalries. The Conservatives increased their majority from 17 in 1951 to 58.

The Election of 1955.—The Conservatives had a total of 345 M.P.s, Labour 277, Liberal 6 and Sinn Fein 2. Both the Conservative and Labour votes fell—the first by some 400,000 and the latter by over 1·5 million. When Parliament assembled four older members, including Dalton, resigned because of their age from the Labour Shadow Cabinet; and when at the end of the year Attlee resigned the leadership, Hugh Gaitskell was elected leader of the party by a substantial majority. The Labour Party was more solidified as a result of the Government's Suez adventure and Bevan was brought back as " Shadow Foreign Secretary."

Attlee's Achievement.—Attlee, who thus retired from the leadership of the Labour Party went to the House of Lords as Earl Attlee. If Churchill stood for the " finest hour " in our history, Attlee stood for the social revolution which followed it. He was the most modest man ever to engage in politics. As a young man he had gone to the East End of London to take up social work and had become Mayor of Stepney. Nobody then could possibly have imagined that he would one day become Prime Minister and Churchill's Deputy Prime Minister for five years of war. " The difference between the two," wrote Harry Boardman (who described the Parliamentary scene so brilliantly for many years for *The Guardian*), " is between genius and extraordinary ordinariness." " True there is no colour, no magnetism, but there is great concentration of purpose, a mind with a razor edge and something of harsh resolution." This simple man of few words transformed the social and economic fabric of the country and changed the face of the Commonwealth into the beneficent world-wide system it has become.

Conservatives' Third Consecutive Victory, 1959.—During the 'fifties the Labour Party had to endure the loss of three consecutive elections and a loss of increasing margins. In 1959 after eight years in office the Conservative Party secured the return of 365 Conservative members, with 258 Labour and 6 Liberal members and one Independent. It was at this election that the Liberals doubled their share of the vote partly by running more candidates and partly by the increase of votes in many of the contests in which they took a part.

Hugh Gaitskell.—In the three years preceding the death of Hugh Gaitskell Labour had lost its best orator in Aneurin Bevan and its best organiser in Morgan Phillips. It was to lose Hugh Gaitskell when, after ten years, it seemed he had won public confidence as the head of a possible alternative government. Educated at Winchester College and New College, Oxford he achieved the highest academic distinction as an economist. It was under the inspiration of Professor G. D. H. Cole at Oxford that he chose to work for the underdog; and on graduation when he became a university lecturer in economics he gave all his spare time in the service of the Workers' Educational Association, teaching economics to Nottingham miners. During the war, serving in the Civil Service, he came under the notice of Hugh Dalton. At the end of the war he chose politics as a career and won the confidence of Stafford Cripps. Upon Cripps' death, Gaitskell succeeded him as Chancellor of the Exchequer, making the spectacular rise from member to Chancellor in six years. This rapid rise was due to his intellectual powers, his gift of exposition, his industry and his character; the whole of these qualities being informed by his humanity and hatred of injustice. Disappointed by Labour's third defeat in 1959 he initiated discussion as to how the Labour Party could be modernised. In the words of a colleague, he was able to show that the Party's " socialist idealism, which is essential to it, is not static, not something writ on tablets but a constantly developing attitude of heart and mind capable of embracing and giving a new meaning to twentieth century society." At Brighton in 1962 he clearly had a united Conference behind him when he delivered a searching speech on the Common Market, setting out the criteria which needed to be satisfied before entry could be regarded as a benefit to country and Commonwealth. When struck by illness at the end of that year, Gaitskell had been acclaimed as a potential prime minister; but the greatest opportunities were lost to him. He was succeeded as leader of the Party by Harold Wilson who became Prime Minister in 1964 and for the second time in 1966.

The Macmillan Years.—Harold Macmillan succeeded Eden in January 1957 at the age of 62, in the aftermath of Suez, and he devoted himself to re-establishing the friendly relations with the United States which had been strained by the Suez affair. Early in 1959 he went to Russia for preliminary soundings for a Summit Conference, which, through no fault of his, was to collapse immediately it opened in Paris in May of the following year. In February 1960 he had shown great courage in a speech before both Houses of the Union Parliament in South Africa when he referred to " the wind of change " in the relations between Black and White in the continent of Africa. It was in July 1961 that Macmillan announced that Britain would apply for full membership of the Common Market, negotiations continuing till their breakdown in January 1963. Among other important events of his premiership were: the explosion of the first British hydrogen bomb; the settlement of the Cyprus dispute; the winning of the General Election of October 1959 with an increased majority of 100 seats; the cancellation of the *Blue Streak* missile programme, and the agreement for U.S. *Polaris* submarines to use Holy Loch; the failure in 1958 to secure free trade with the Common Market and the consequent setting up in 1960 of a European Free Trade Area with countries outside the Market; the setting up of the National Economic Development Council; the legalisation of betting shops; the winding up of the Central African Federation; the nuclear test ban treaty; and the establishment of a Federation of Malaysia.

The Resignation of Macmillan.—From the middle of 1962 the Government seemed dogged by misfortune which, it was doubtless hoped, would be changed by Britain's entry into the Common Market. Quickly following Britain's exclusion came the hardships of a severe winter and of a sudden increase in unemployment. When the spring came the Government were caught in another misfortune, the Profumo affair, involving the resignation of its War Minister. This did nothing to still the feeling in the Conservative Party that the Prime Minister should make way for a younger man, although there was a natural reluctance to press the Profumo affair as a suitable occasion for his departure. Mr. Macmillan indicated that he hoped to lead the Party at the next election. This discordant position was suddenly cut by Mr. Macmillan's illness, which compelled him to resign. By a coincidence his announcement came (10 October 1963) the day after the annual Party Conference had opened. The resignation would in any event have caused a great debate in the Party; but dropped suddenly into the excited atmosphere of a conference it caused a tumult. Many analyses have been made of the history of those days.

Lord Home Becomes Prime Minister.—Mr. Macmillan's sick-bed became the centre of the vortex in the following week. The Cabinet approved a memorandum by him as to how soundings should be taken in the Cabinet, the two Houses, and the Party Organisations. Soundings were taken and two days later they were said to show a continuing deadlock between Hailsham and Butler but a small lead for a third; and this third man was not Maudling but Lord Home, then Foreign Secretary, who had been widely regarded as a non-starter. Mr. Macmillan recommended Home to the Queen. How confused the situation was is illustrated by the fact that on the very morning when the Queen sent for Lord Home the first headline in *The Times* was "The Queen may send for Mr. Butler today."

There was an acute debate within the Party as to the way in which the leadership had been decided; and this debate resulted in a method (described below) of electing the leader of the party.

Election Results 1900 to 1964 (*see also* **C9**).

	Cons. & supporters.	Lib.	Lab.	Irish	Others
1900	402	184	2	82	—
1906	157	379	51	83	—
1910 (Jan.)	273	275	40	82	—
1910 (Dec.)	272	272	42	84	—
1918	526	28	63	73	17
1922	347	118	142	—	8
1923	261	155	191	—	8
1924	413	40	151	—	11
1929	260	59	287	—	9
1931	521	37	52	—	5
1935	431	21	158	—	5
1945	212	12	398	—	18
1950	298	9	315	—	3
1951	321	6	295	—	3
1955	345	6	277	—	2
1959	365	6	258	—	1
1964	303	9	317	—	1

Party	1950 (*Electorate* 34,269,764)		1951 (*Electorate* 34,622,891)		1955 (*Electorate* 34,852,179)		1959 (*Electorate* 35,397,304)		1964 (*Electorate* 35,917,076)	
	Votes	*Seats*	*Votes*	*Seats*	*Votes*	*Seats*	*Votes*	*Seats*	*Votes*	*Seats*
Conservatives (and allies)	12,501,953	298	13,724,418	321	13,311,938	345	13,750,935	365	11,980,783	303
Labour	13,295,736	315	13,948,385	295	12,405,246	277	12,216,166	258	12,205,581	317
Liberal	2,621,489	9	730,551	6	722,395	6	1,640,761	6	3,101,103	9
Communist	91,815	—	21,640	—	33,144	—	30,897	—	44,576	—
Others	258,454	3	177,329	3	288,031	2	223,949	1	324,106	1
	28,769,447	625	28,602,323	625	26,760,754	630	27,862,708	630	27,656,149	630

Election Year 1964.—Parliament's legal term expired in the autumn of 1964 but there remained the question whether Sir Alec Douglas-Home would go to the country in the spring or in the autumn. That decision was, of course, entirely one for him to decide; and he seemed to relish the prerogative by keeping his opponents (and the country) on the edge of uncertainty. Concealing his hand till the last moment Sir Alec decided to wait till the autumn. For many months, therefore, the country discussed the issues involved and thus went through much of the emotions of an election, which, when it came, seemed belated, the people being a little weary of worked up turmoil by politicians, press, and pollsters. Some of the fire of an election had thus been drawn prematurely from it, but no General Election can lack drama. The Government's majority dissolved and Mr. Wilson kept the lead to a photo-finish. The resultant position is examined in **Part II** with an outline of some of the far-reaching consequences. Before, however, leaving this point in our story we must note the coincidence by which, within the very two days on which the results came in, there occurred two events of world-wide importance—the fall of Khrushchev and the explosion by China of an atomic bomb. If the latter was expected, the former was certainly not. These events, which are discussed later, were more than could be assimilated and their significance will take a long time to digest.

The Balance of Payments.—Upon accession to office the new Government was faced with a prospective balance of payments deficit of £700–800 million for 1964. It was estimated that although there should be a considerable improvement in 1965 the deficit would still be at an unacceptable level. The Government therefore took measures aimed, first, to deal with the immediate and prospective deficit for 1964–65 and, second, to begin the task of dealing with the more intransigent underlying economic problem. These measures are discussed in **Section G, Part III.**

Problems Facing the New Government at Home.—Let us take a glance at the sea of troubles which immediately advanced upon the Wilson administration. The general nature of these troubles had, of course, been foreseen; but they were none the less formidable for that and their exact nature when revealed (like the Treasury's forecast of the payments deficiency) showed they were even more severe than supposed. Production needed to be raised and steadily expanded. For this a number of fundamental steps were necessary. To expand without inflation, an incomes policy (coupling incomes and wages with production) needed to be introduced; and this called for fresh attitudes by both sides of industry. Industry needed to be reinvigorated by science and technology and fresh educational foundations required to be laid. Planning, detailed in character and comprehensive in scope, required both regional, as well as national, planning. The Beeching revolution on the railways called for harmonisation with the welfare of people and with schemes for the coming revolution in our towns and our roads. Hospitals and schools needed improvement and expansion, houses to be built and pensions improved. The subject of immigration was seen to need very skilled care. There was pressure from members of all parties for the abolition of the death penalty. A promise had been made to overhaul the whole legal system and to introduce an Ombudsman. There was urgent need to look into the working not only of Trade Unions but of trade associations. "They've given me a bed of nails," said the new Minister of Labour. The metaphor could have been aptly used by the whole of the new team. Beyond all the problems cited there remained the bundle of difficulties covered by the word "Defence." This subject, described on page **C20**, brings us to the second set of troubles, the external ones.

Problems Abroad.—The problem of our security posed the question of what kind of co-operation with our allies was desirable and what, then, was possible, an enigmatic France being antagonistic to a Western alliance. How could the long deadlock on disarmament be broken? What rescue could be raced to an overstrained and threatened United Nations? The most ominous troubles seethed in Africa, in the Congo, in Rhodesia, in South Africa. In Asia, the sub-continent of India was developing all too slowly. China, estranged (through no fault of Britain) remained unpredictable as estranged people are apt to be. There was an ugly confrontation between Malaysia and Indonesia (which was soon to leave the United Nations). And beyond all these questions and many more remained perhaps the gravest of the lot—half the world underfed, ill-housed, underdeveloped, with insufficient hope. One of the mysteries which will baffle future historians is why so little popular concern was expanded on a plight fraught with so much danger for all of us.

The Passing of Winston Churchill.—When Churchill died, not long after his ninetieth birthday, on 24 January 1965 his countrymen and the whole world paid their tributes to the greatest Englishman of his time and recalled the facts of a truly astonishing career. Of all the many aspects of that career we may note here just three. First it was by a chance that Churchill did not succeed to the Marlborough dukedom. During his first twenty-one years he was an heir, but then the ninth Duchess obliged with a baby boy. We may well ponder upon the consequences if Churchill had been suffocated by a dukedom and the Commons had lost him. Second, there occurred in 1904 a campaign to restrict immigration, rather like the present campaign, but the immigration was then of Jews driven here by Russian massacres. Churchill fought that campaign with great vigour. It is amusing to recall that the *National Review* criticising Churchill for this said he was himself "half-alien and wholly undesirable." The last aspect we choose is a philosophical one. In his *Study of History*, Arnold Toynbee traces a common pattern in the lives of certain great creative figures like Moses, Saint Benedict, Peter the Great, and Lenin. They had all left the scenes of their youth, spent an interval in solitude or in entirely strange surroundings, and then returned to rise to some occasion of social crisis, to meet the challenge confronting the society to which they belonged. Churchill falls into that pattern, being for so many years, in the prime of his life, ostracised by his own Party and politically frustrated; and never more so than during the appeasement years prior to the Second World War which he so clearly foresaw and during which he returned from neglect to dominate the field at home and abroad. He is thus the most recent example in history of Toynbee's "Withdrawal-and-Return" theory.

Election of Conservative Party Leader.—A new procedure for choosing the leader of the Conservative Party was announced in February 1965 and it was first used in July of that year when Sir Alec Douglas-Home resigned. The following are the chief features of the new procedure. Ballots will be held among members of the House of Commons who receive the Conservative and National Liberal Whips; and the successful candidate will be presented to a meeting of the party for election as leader. This meeting of the party consists of:

(*a*) members of both Houses who take the Conservative Whip;
(*b*) approved prospective candidates; and
(*c*) the executive of the National Union of Conservative and Unionist Associations.

This body totalled in 1965 about one thousand. That the Conservatives in the Commons should have first say in the choice of leader is based on the fact that the leader depends on their support. In theory the meeting of the party might reject the M.P.s' choice; and in that event the M.P.s would have to ballot again.

The Ballots.—The new procedure provides for three ballots. The proposer and seconder of the written nominations stay anonymous. If one candidate receives both an overall majority and 15 per cent more of the votes cast than any other he will be elected. Failing this a second ballot will be held upon fresh nominations and any candidate receiving an overall majority will be elected. If no one does, we reach a third and final ballot. The three candidates with the highest number of votes in the second ballot will take part in this final ballot. In this last ballot each voter must indicate two preferences. The candidate with the fewest first preferences will be eliminated and his first preference votes distributed between the remaining candidates as indicated by the second preferences. This will give one candidate a majority.

The Effect of the New Procedure on the System of Government.—Mr. Edward Heath was elected leader of the party in July 1965. The new method of selecting Conservative leaders was a great change in our system of government. It marked the end of a secret ritual whereby a leader was lifted up above his colleagues by a Royal summons in which they themselves played no open part. There is thus a crucial constitutional change—power being conferred by the Parliamentary party instead of by Royal prerogative. The change from Mr. Macmillan and Sir Alec Douglas-Home to Mr. Heath marked a change from the amateur to the professional. It would be wrong to regard Mr. Macmillan as other than a professional; but he generated the Victorian view that it was best to have a well-educated gentleman at the head of affairs; and this view was realised in the image and promotion of Sir Alec. This pattern was broken in 1965. The Party seemed to be facing the view that to regain power they must narrow the social and financial gap between those who lead the Party and those who support it in the country. The traditional method of choice by "the customary processes" which had lasted for so many decades has been finally abandoned.

Wilson's Second Labour Government.—The country gave a mandate to its Government in the Election of March 1966. The result was:—

Party	Electorate: 35,900,000	
	Votes	Seats
Labour	13,057,941	363
Conservatives	11,418,433	253
Liberal	2,327,533	12
Communist	62,040	—
Others	390,649	1
The Speaker		1

There was a notable proportion of university and college lecturers and teachers among the new Labour M.P.s. *See also* **C49**.

2. SOME CURRENT TOPICS.

The University of the Air which was foreshadowed by Mr. Wilson at the Labour Party Conference in September 1963 has necessarily had to remain very much in the air in view of the serious practical problems to be resolved. In 1965 Mr. Wilson reaffirmed his intention that the University of the Air should be a serious, degree-giving, academically irreproachable enterprise and not a casual, leisure gimmick. Miss Jennie Lee who had been given responsibility for the scheme said it was not to be a "Paddy-the-next-best-thing, a dawn patrol or a midnight parade; or a patch on the working man's trousers." It was not going to be a hobby or a pastime but a social dynamic. The shape of the plan which was awaited must depend on the full intent of this potential academic revolution. Meanwhile the National Extension College has been founded, on a non-profit-making basis, by the Advisory Centre for Education to pioneer a College of the Air and to bring new standards to the neglected field of home study. Because it is non-profit making the College can spend every penny of a student's fees on providing him with the best possible home study courses. The N.E.C. is pioneering the linking of correspondence with television and radio; and students are given the opportunity to meet fellow students at day schools and residential courses. Some students have been given grants by local education authorities. Those interested in the College should write to the National Extension College, Shaftesbury Road, Cambridge.

The Coming of the Teach-in.—Most people have listened to a teach-in probably by radio or seen one on television and are thus familiar with this new affair. What precisely is it? It is a jumble or hybrid thing—part debate, part seminar, part rally or demonstration with a dash, in America, of the prize-fight. It was, of course, in America that the habit originated—sweeping across the Universities in April and May of 1965. How did it start? An argument began between faculty members at Michigan University on what to do about the Vietnam war and the threat of its extension, all protests having been made. One suggestion was to cancel all classes for a day and invite students to a daylong session on all aspects of the war. In the event the controversial proposal for a day's "work-moratorium" was dropped but the idea of a "teach-in" was developed. It was an immediate success and was adopted in many places, thousands of students and academics attending the functions. A National Teach-in was treated by press and television as an event of the first magnitude. Why the clumsy title of "teach-in"? Presumably because it was a sublimation, so to speak, of the "sit-in" when students sat on the steps of the White House and other buildings by way of protest. Teach-ins were adopted spontaneously in British universities and they seemed to fulfil a need. It was clear that both here and in the States people needed much more information about a public issue like Vietnam and they wanted to hear an account by the men at the top who were framing the decisions. The demand was so widespread that, after official refusal, high officials ultimately agreed to attend. The Oxford teach-in was attended by the Foreign Secretary himself. Thus the teach-in converted the monologue of protest into a dialogue of confrontation or debate, between the administration and an enlightened opposition.

Has the Teach-in a Future?—We must hope so. No doubt the success was due to the disquiet which did not seem to be adequately expressed in other ways. But teach-ins on other subjects would be extremely interesting—on disarmament, on foreign aid, on race discrimination. We might even reach the stage of an international teach-in—with perhaps African and Russian and even Chinese participation. Apart from such a development there is clearly the opportunity for a regeneration of public knowledge and the effectiveness of sound opinion. This is democracy at work.

Intensive Farming: the Brambell Report.—The Brambell Committee, after a year and a half's study on the welfare of farm animals and birds kept in confinement, reported at the end of 1965. Professor Brambell and his colleagues accepted the evidence that, although suffering and stress are not identical in animals and men, there were some reasons for thinking that these sensations are substantial in domestic animals, and this ought not be be disregarded. They accepted that animals can experience rage, fear, apprehension, frustration, and pleasure in varying degrees. They rejected as "an oversimplification and incomplete view" the favourite argument of intensive producers that continued production is positive evidence that an animal or bird is not suffering. They considered that it was morally incumbent on them to give the animal the benefit of the doubt and to protect it as far as possible from conditions that may be reasonably supposed to cause it suffering, though this cannot be proved. But the committee did not condemn, out of hand, such methods of farming as keeping hens in batteries or deep litter houses and beef, veal, and pig production in circumstances in which the animals are confined. The most difficult problem they had to solve was whether to recommend abolishing hen batteries as many individuals and organisations urged. They concluded "with some reluctance" that in the light of present knowledge, a modified battery system may be as good as or better than loose housing. They visualised two factors developing side by side. On one side an inevitable trend towards intensive animal husbandry. On the other a continuing development of concern for animal welfare. They recommended a progressive development of sound systems of animal husbandry to cover the welfare of animals. Existing legislation did not adequately safeguard farm animals and a new Act was needed incorporating a fuller definition of suffering and enabling ministers to make regulations. These should be enforced by the State veterinary service and a statutory farm animal welfare advisory committee. They recommended statutory standards for various classes of livestock; and it would be part of the routine work of the veterinary service, while enforcing the mandatory standards, to advise producers on more general practices and standards which are generally desirable in the interests of animal welfare but are too numerous and too complex to be given statutory force.

People who care about this subject will find a recent book by Elspeth Huxley fair, informative, and interesting: it is *Brave New Victuals (An Inquiry into Modern Production)* with a foreword by Peter Scott (Chatto and Windus). The book contains a very comprehensive bibliography.

The Robbins Report: Two Years After.—If Professor Buchanan had reason to be disappointed two years after his famous report for the reasons described below, Lord Robbins had cause for substantial satisfaction. The expansion of higher education is going upon a scale much as the report proposed. But there have been a number of departures in organisation by both Conservative and Labour Governments. The Conservative Government rejected the plan of two distinct ministries—one for higher education and one for the rest. Second, the teacher training colleges although renamed "colleges of education" have not been brought right into the university sphere. The proposed five special institutions of scientific and technical research education have not been created, although some are in the making. Again the Government is not to start new universities. The emphasis has been to expand existing institutions rather than to start new ones. The opening in October 1965 of the universities of Kent at Canterbury and Warwick at Coventry completed the group of seven new universities whose establishment was approved by the Government in the period 1958–61. The other universities in this group are Sussex at Brighton, East Anglia at Norwich, York, Essex at Colchester, and Lancaster.

Buchanan: Two Years After.—Professor Buchanan said he was very disappointed at the position two years after the publication in 1963 of his report on *Traffic in Towns*. He did not expect to bring about a change of policy overnight: but to change the attitude of Government, local authorities, and public opinion. But the light shed by the report had not penetrated very far and the attempt to inject urgency into the discussion had had no appreciable effect. He doubted whether the argument about the need to preserve our cities and towns as places where people can walk under tolerable conditions had had any influence at all on the Ministry of Transport or local highway committees. The plundering of urban environments to make more accessibility for more and more vehicles was diametrically opposed to the principles of his report. Professor Buchanan described the National Plan as schizophrenic, so far as roads are concerned. On the one hand the motor industry is exhorted to even greater efforts, which suggested that the predicted increase in traffic will take place; but little hope is expressed that we shall be able to cope with it. We have a vast private ability to invest in cars; but a complete inability to put an equivalent public investment into dealing with roads. The only way out is by investment in capital works on a coherent plan and on a continuing basis. It would be an ironical tragedy if we waited so long that we found we had lost the physical opportunities for providing ourselves with adequate urban road networks.

Cities of the Future.—It will be necessary to find room for 28 million more Britons by the end of the century. Part of this surplus will be increased population and part will be overspill from existing towns and cities. Suppose half of this surplus were catered for by building on the fringes of existing towns it would still be necessary to build 280 towns the size of Shrewsbury or 140 cities like Oxford or nearly 30 Tynesides. This illustrates the need for national planning policies quite apart from the need to consider how to make our future cities not only efficient places but beautiful and sociable.

The Threat to the Countryside.—A decade or so ago we may have felt that, by vigilance and action, what remained of the beauty of the countryside could be saved. After a hundred years of advocacy the preservation movement had seen the setting up of local planning and the creation of national parks and nature reserves. The duty of holding back the forces spoiling the countryside had at last been vested in statutory bodies and not left entirely to the endeavours of voluntary bodies. National Parks were created by official action. The optimist was tempted to feel that the danger had been diagnosed, however late in the day; and that the officially appointed watchdogs could confidently be left to stop further depredations. But events soon broke down any such assumption. Power and atomic energy stations, open cast mining, aerial masts for a variety of purposes, overhead electricity cables and pylons to carry them, coastal refineries, hydro-electric schemes, roads, houses all made their demands. He would be an exceptionally insensitive and complacent observer who could be satisfied that a fair balance had been struck between the material needs of the community and their aesthetic needs, both of which are vital. We are forced to conclude that there is a lack of will in the establishment to defend natural beauty against attack.

The Obstruction of National Parks.—That the ideal of national parks was being obstructed by lack of funds, inadequate staffing and a conflict of power between park authorities and local government were among the conclusions reached in a research report in 1965 by Mr. Arthur Blenkinsop, formerly Parliamentary Secretary of the Ministry of Health, one of the relatively few men in the country who had a detailed knowledge of the country. The ideals of the early pioneers of national parks were disappearing under the influence of post-war planning legislation; and development of those ideals are frustrated, he wrote, "all along the line by bureaucracy, shortage of money and insufficient senior men in a position to administer and plan." The Peak District is able to do more towards positive development than other national parks because it has its own offices and planning staff.

The National Parks Commission: Achievements and Proposals.—A list of the National Parks and the Areas of Outstanding Natural Beauty which have been designated so far in England and Wales will be found on **L81**, and of the Long Distance Walking Routes and Bridlepaths which have been approved on **L72**. The preservation of our countryside has been a painful subject for those who care what happens. As we have explained, it took close on a hundred years for concern for the countryside to become a statutory obligation of a government body; and when at long last we had in 1949 a National Parks Act it was soon seen to need strengthening. Minister after Minister promised to give the National Parks Commission power to tackle the problem effectually. Minister after Minister made the excuse that he could find no time to fulfil his promise. Finally the long suffering and patient Commission protested. There were thus great expectations upon the advent of a Labour Government and the creation of a Ministry of Land and Natural Resources. By that time the subject had become more complex partly because of the need for areas for intensive recreation. The new Minister affirmed the basic principles of the Commission's views on strengthening their powers and promised to make his proposals known in 1965. We may usefully outline the Commission's main recommendations:

(1.) That the present system, based as it is on the designation of National Parks and areas of outstanding natural beauty, should be supplemented by a countrywide scheme for the selection and classification of areas of special value for open-air recreation. These should be linked to development plans.

These national and regional recreation areas will often be associated with national beauty but they may not—e.g., in green belts.

(2.) Strengthening of powers by local planning authorities to make positive provision throughout the countryside and coast for amenity and open-air recreation: to acquire and manage suitable land in open country, including woods and commons; tree planting and tree preservation; improvement of derelict sites; securing of open access; creation of public footpaths and bridleways; restoration and improvement of waterways.

(3.) Grants should be improved; and the Exchequer should bear the additional administration costs due to National Park activities and the appointment of special staff.

A New Countryside Commission.—The Minister announced his proposal to reconstitute the National Parks Commission as a Countryside Commission with new powers in a speech at the second conference on "The Countryside in 1970" held in November 1965.

The country parks will vary in size from a few acres to quite large areas; and would be sited to save people from long drives on crowded roads to more distant places. Some would be designed for people with gregarious tastes, others would be left in their natural state. Many would include expanses of water for boating and swimming. These country parks would be created by local authorities with Government financial help. The promised White Paper (Cmnd. 2928) was published in March 1966 (*Leisure in the Countryside: England and Wales*).

The Natural Environment Research Council took over the responsibilities of the Nature Conservancy in June 1965. The new Council supports and undertakes research in the earth sciences and in ecology and, in addition, the Nature Conservancy took over the Geological Survey and Museum, the Hydrology Research Unit and the National Institute of Oceanography. It undertakes fisheries research, research hitherto carried out by the Meteorological Office, and long term forestry research in consultation with the Forestry Commission. The new Council thus brings together the natural life and earth scientists.

The Coastline.—The National Trust launched an appeal in 1965 to raise £2 million in an effort to preserve what was left worth preserving of the coastline of Britain. The trust owned or protected about 165 of the 3,000 miles of Britain's coastline. Of what remains only 900 miles was still unspoiled and worthy of preservation.

The Future of Common Lands.—In our overcrowded country nobody can afford to disregard 1½ million acres which make up no less than 4 per cent of the total land area of England and Wales. A Royal Commission on Common Land described these lands in 1965 as the "last reservoir of uncommitted land" which provide, as far as the public is concerned, by far the largest part of the accessible open spaces of the country. While the Report recommended substantial changes in the law relating to common land, designed to secure that the fullest practicable use of these common lands may be made in the interests of the owners, the commoners, and the public, it also recommended that common land should continue to be inviolable and safeguarded from permanent inclosure and thus continue to provide places to which the public might resort for air and exercise. The public, it said, should have a legal right of access to all commons, subject to the same conditions as apply to areas of open country which are under an "access agreement." (An access agreement under the National Parks Act, 1949, gives the public access to land, subject to conditions of behaviour.)

Registration of Commons.—The Royal Commission recommended that there be a Commons Register in which claims that land is common should be registered. They also proposed to remedy the existing state of affairs whereby there was considerable neglect of commons, and the making of individual, new, and more flexible schemes of management for each common. Under the Commons Registration Act, 1965, which resulted it will be the duty of County Councils and County Borough Councils to make a register of all common land and all town and village greens in their areas. The registers should open on 1 January 1967 and there will probably be a period of three years within which applications may be made for land and rights to be registered. What are common rights and who exercises them is a complex subject, and for more detailed information the reader is referred to a publication issued by the Common, Open Spaces and Footpaths Preservation Society, Suite 4, 166–170 Shaftesbury Avenue, London, W.C.2. entitled *Commons Their Nature, Functions and Preservation* (1*s*.). If a common or green lies in your district or parish and you wish to know how interested persons and bodies can take preliminary action you should apply to the Society for their off-print entitled *Commons Registration Act* which is an authoritative and explanatory set of notes (price 3*d*. and stamped addressed envelope).

The Council of Nature is a voluntary body which represents the naturalists and country lovers of the British Isles. It has some 350 member bodies and thus can represent the views of some 90,000 active naturalists to government departments, local authorities, and other bodies. It works for the greater appreciation of the importance of nature conservation. It is concerned with poisonous seed dressings which have killed thousands of birds; with the spoiling of the coastline; and with the enforcement of the Bird Protection Act. Its Intelligence Unit on British natural history answers questions on a wide range. The Council of Nature has Brantwood, formerly the home of John Ruskin, as a residential holiday centre on the shores of Lake Coniston, where there are courses on natural history and on ciné and still photography of wild life. It also organises the Conservation Corps which enables young people to help preserve wild life and the countryside while they enjoy a "hard work" holiday as well.

The Conservation Corps: the Hard-work Holiday.—Many more young people have volunteered for these holidays than the Corps has been able to accept; which shows that there is a large reservoir of potential public service untapped. What do these volunteers do? They undertake manual work necessary for the maintenance of nature reserves and other biologically important sites. Typical tasks include clearing scrub and undergrowth, uprooting small trees, fencing, making footpaths, digging out and planting vegetation on banks of ponds. At the same time volunteers are given talks explaining the purpose of the works and on the natural history of the area. There are over a thousand members of the Corps, some of whom spend many of their weekends working with the Corps. Volunteers make a contribution towards costs of residence and the Council pays fares for weekend work and contributes towards fares on residential work. Enquiries should be made to the Organiser of the Corps at the Council's Office, 41 Queen's Gate, London, S.W.7.

The Destruction of Britain's Buildings.—Almost every town in Britain, famous for its buildings and beauty, has had its centre cut out by speculators. This was stated by the Earl of Crawford in an address to the National Trust in 1964. It was the scandal of our generation that we should have lived to see the destruction of our country and the suicide of its beauty, worse than anything Hitler was able to do with his bombs. Our generation will be blamed and remembered for that destruction in the future.

A Land Commission.—The Government proposed to set up in 1966 a Land Commission with extensive powers of compulsory purchase, but they will work within the existing local authority planning machinery. This new body will become the major agency for supplying land for development and redevelopment; and it will also introduce a 40 per cent levy on the development value of land. The objectives of the new land policy may be stated as:

(1) to secure that the right land is available at the right time for national, regional, and local plans; and

(2) to secure that a substantial part of the development value created by the community returns to the community, and that the burden of the cost of land for essential purposes is reduced.

It is thus hoped to reduce the burden of the cost of land falling on to local authorities. The Government took the view that 40 per cent is a modest rate of levy which should give ample incentive to owners to offer their land for development. But they envisaged a progressive increase to 45 per cent and then to 50 per cent.

Other Topics.—Among other contemporary topics discussed in this section are: defence (**C20**), conflict studies (**C23**), the Ombudsman (**C29**), regional organisations (**C32**), young offenders (**C35**), and immigration (**C38**).

3. WORLD PROBLEMS AND EVENTS.

The Threat of Famine.—The world might have thought itself entitled to a little more relief from anxiety than it got. So soon after the war as 1946 famine was imminent. There was fortunately the very man at hand and ready to act—John Boyd Orr. Boyd Orr was an expert in nutrition who had long devoted his immense courage and drive to the feeding of the hungry. He had fought malnutrition in Britain in the 'thirties when destitution had followed unemployment. It was because of Boyd Orr's scientific facts and his powerful public pleading that it was possible to introduce, so early in the war, a rationing system for food. And because of fair shares and nutritional knowledge Britain came out of the war a healthier nation than she had been at its outbreak six years earlier. In 1946 however the world faced a famine situation. That, in the event, there was no widespread famine was due to Boyd Orr who, as head of the Famine Conference of that year, induced the nations to accept self-denying ordinances. Britain reimposed rationing. Out of the threat of famine, which might have cost 75 million lives, came the idea of a World Food Board.

The Idea of a World Food Board.—The Famine Conference was concerned that a similar world threat should not recur. Boyd Orr was therefore asked to plan a permanent body which would estimate in advance annual food requirements; ensure that adequate supplies were forthcoming; and see they were properly distributed. He planned such a Board which would help countries to increase food production equal to human needs; build up a reservoir of food to even out good and bad harvest years; and stabilise prices, with the Board buying surplus after bumper harvests and selling after bad. There was general enthusiasm among governments for the scheme; but it evaporated when it was seen that it entailed a sacrifice of a fraction of sovereignty. What emerged was, in the words of Professor Ritchie Calder who has told the story from personal knowledge, "a pale ghost of the original concept"—the World Food Council. The World Food Council is another name for the executive of the Food and Agricultural Organisation, which, incidentally, had been the first permanent agency of the United Nations to be established. Boyd Orr retired and was awarded the Nobel Peace Prize, a recognition of what he had tried to do.

World Poverty.—The declaration of human rights adopted by the United Nations Assembly in 1948 lays down that: "Everyone has a right to a standard of living adequate for the health and well-being of himself and of his family, including food, clothing, housing and medical care and necessary social services, and the right to security in the event of unemployment, sickness, disability, widowhood, old age, or other lack of livelihood in circumstances beyond his control." In 1962 the United Nations set as a target for attack the doubling of the standard of living of the poor countries in 25–30 years. In 1961 the General Assembly had designated the 1960s as "The Development Decade." The attack on poverty started from a position in which the gap between rich and poor countries was widening—rich getting richer faster than the rate of progress by the poor. Further there was a lack of confidence in economic matters between the West and the poor nations—neutral nations felt they were left out in the cold by the Common Market and Comecon, and India, for example, had had difficulty in raising foreign exchange for her Plans. This was not all. Other factors were running against the poor countries. All through the 'fifties they had to accept falling prices for the food and raw materials which they exported; and this was made worse by having to pay more for the manufactured goods which they imported. If they try to sell industrial goods they are confronted by protection systems. U Thant, the Secretary-General of the United Nations, has said: "The world will not live in harmony so long as two-thirds of its inhabitants find difficulty in living at all." *See also* **G36.**

Population.—At the opening of our period (1945) the total world population was about 2,500 million; today it is over 3,000 million and increasing at a rate of 2 per cent a year. Not only is world population increasing but the pace is accelerating.

In his broadcast talks on the political challenge of an overpopulated world Sir Geoffrey Vickers crystallised in the following graphic way the figures of population growth. It took about 1,650 years from the beginning of the Christian era for the world's population to double from about 250 million to 500 million. From the beginning of the industrial revolution the next double to 1,000 million took only 200 years. The next double, to 2,000 million, was reached in only another 75 years. This was in 1925; and the figure is expected to double itself again by 1975, after only 50 years. The United Nations Food and Agriculture Organisation put the rise to more than 6,000 million by the end of the century; in other words the doubling process which was taking 75 years and then 50 years would take only 25 years, namely in the last quarter of the century. Food production will need to be doubled to maintain the present inadequate *status quo*; and to be trebled to raise standards of nutrition over two-thirds of the world. *See* **Demography Today, Section F, Part IV.**

Aid for Developing Countries.—In 1964 a conference was held in London of the 21 countries (including the six principal donor states) comprised in the Colombo Plan. It was decided to continue the Plan for another five-year period when the present agreement expired in 1966. The Plan had originated in 1950 as a means of bringing the Asian nations forward to a plateau of self-sustaining economic growth and at that time there were only seven member states. The six principal donor states are now Australia, Britain, Canada, Japan, New Zealand, and the United States. In spite of serious domestic problems the British Government was determined to do its utmost to help less fortunate countries and to narrow the gap between rich and poor countries which future historians would see as the great problem of our time. The fourteen recipient countries in Asia have standards of living which are among the lowest in the world but their potentialities are in some cases among the best. The accelerating rise in population presents a serious obstacle to the abolition of poverty and a new proposal was therefore made for assistance in propagating birth control where the recipient country desires it. The imperative needs are for education, especially technical education, for experts, and for re-examination of the types of training needed by experts. It is development and economic growth, based on sound economic progress, which must be the aim and not the superficial bolstering of the prestige of new nations by prestige projects, often based on ill-drawn plans. *See* **Section G, Part III.**

Nasser and the New Egypt.—A new factor in the Middle East was introduced when the Egyptian Army revolted in 1952, overthrowing the monarchy, leading two years later to the emergence of Nasser as Prime Minister. In that year Nasser secured the agreement whereby all British forces were to leave the Suez Canal Zone by 1956. Egypt did not become a democracy in any Western sense but the government runs all the basic enterprises of the country. In 1956 Nasser internationalised the Suez Canal Company as a reply to the withdrawal by the United States of its offer to finance the High Dam at Aswan. The attack by the British and French on Egypt followed, causing serious disagreement with the United States, which inspired international action to rescue Egypt. (It was while we were bombing Egypt that Russia suppressed a revolt in the satellite of Hungary.) The nationalisation of the Suez Canal and the building, with Russian help and finance, of the High Dam are the two most important of Nasser's actions.

Egypt and Russia.—A new chapter had opened in 1955 when the Russians made an arms deal with Egypt. By that action Russia became a Middle Eastern Power. She upset the Anglo-American policy of balancing arms deliveries to Israel on the one hand and the Arab states on the other. (It was all the more creditable to the United States that she was shocked by and opposed a war upon Egypt when it came next year.) Russia's influence in Egypt penetrated a Western preserve; and she leap-frogged the " northern tier " of Turkey and Iran (which, with Pakistan, had been grouped by the United Kingdom into a defensive barrier and now known as CENTO, the Central Treaty Organisation). Russia continues to pour in money, equipment, and technicians in the building of the High Dam which was begun in 1960 and should be completed by 1970.

Israel.—This is an appropriate point to recapitulate the salient points about Israel. Palestine, formerly part of the Turkish empire, had been ruled by Britain from 1918 to 1949 under a League of Nations mandate upon the basis of the British declaration that Palestine should be " a national home " without injury to the Arab population. The Nazi persecution of Jews naturally quickened Jewish migration to Palestine and this caused strain between Arabs and Jews. After the massacre of Jews by Germany during the war itself, there was naturally a stronger flow of emigrants of Jews to Palestine; and when Britain restricted this flow and tried to curb illegal immigration, tension increased between Jews and Arabs. In 1947 Britain said she would surrender her mandate and asked the United Nations to find a solution, which they did. But their plan to divide Palestine into Jewish and Arab states was rejected by the Arabs. When Britain withdrew in May 1948 the Jews proclaimed the new state of Israel, which was at once recognised by the United States and Russia; but the country was attacked by neighbouring Arab states. The Israelis successfully defended themselves, although greatly outnumbered, and in 1949 the United Nations secured an armistice.

A Turning Point in Soviet History.—In 1961 Khrushchev publicly and dramatically completed the process which he had begun in 1956, of drawing a line under the Stalin régime and finally rejecting the cult of Stalin. This change was symbolised by the removal of Stalin's body from the mausoleum at the Kremlin. At the same time Khrushchev was confronted by an external challenge to his leadership of the Communist world—by China who believed that Russia was moving steadily away from classical communist doctrine.

Stalin had made the Soviet Union a modern industrial society and a great armed power. But the arbitrary bureaucracy through which this had been achieved had, in Khrushchev's view, overrun itself. Radical changes became essential and Khrushchev attempted various steps—the scaling down of the secret police; the rebuilding of the administrative apparatus; the opening up of virgin lands; and a new theory that war was not inevitable. The legacy of the Stalinist era had been the concept of the " monolithic " party, that is to say, a party which, however torn by internal conflict, must never allow any open division of opinion and free debate, much less the formation of any groups expounding distinctive views. This concept was challenged at the 1961 Congress.

Khrushchev Leaves the Political Scene.—The career of Nikita Khrushchev as Soviet Prime Minister and Leader of the Communist Party came to an end—to the surprise of the world—in October 1964. Stalin had died in 1953 and the struggle for succession then continued for five years, when Khrushchev emerged with supreme authority. Upon Stalin's death a triumvirate of successors, Malenkov, Molotov, and Beria had decided to give the post of party chief—First Secretary—to Khrushchev, then a relatively harmless outsider, or so he was deemed by them. Beria, the all powerful police chief, was executed as a spy in 1953, Malenkov was forced to give up the premiership in 1954 and three years later both he and Molotov were expelled from the Central Committee. Khrushchev thereupon emerged with supreme powers, and became the talkative and jocular leader whom the world knew.

The Pattern of Change in Leadership.—The student of affairs may be puzzled by the strains and dislocations which occur upon a change of leadership in Russia. But this is less surprising when it is remembered that there is no constitutional manner of embodying a change of opinion or policy in an alternative party or group of men. It will be seen from the diagram of events that after Lenin's death control was divided between the Secretary of the Party and the Premier for seventeen years, until Stalin combined both posts. After Stalin's death in 1953 control was again split (except for ten days) for another five years until, in 1953, Khrushchev who had been Secretary for five years combined the two posts again until 1964. The pattern repeated itself in 1964 Kosygin becoming Premier and Brezhnev Secretary. A meeting of the Supreme Soviet in 1965 confirmed the principle of collective leadership. At the 23rd Soviet Party Congress held in April 1966 it was decided that the Praesidium of the Central Committee should go back to being the Politburo and the First Secretary should revert to General Secretary. The new 11-man Politburo has an inner cabinet of four members: Brezhnev, General Secretary, Kosygin, Prime Minister, Suslov, the Party's theoretician, and Podgorny, the President of the Soviet Union.

Lenin 1917–24

Premier: Rykov 1924–30
Premier: Molotov 1930–41
Secretary: Stalin 1922–53

Premier and Secretary
Stalin 1941–53

Malenkov | Beria | Molotov
(*Triumvirate*)
1953

Premier and Secretary
Malenkov (10 days in 1953)

Premier: Malenkov 1953–55
Premier: Bulganin 1955–58
Secretary: Khrushchev 1953–64

Premier and Secretary
Khrushchev 1958–64

Premier: Kosygin 1964
Secretary: Brezhnev 1964

Causes of Khrushchev's Fall.—Among the deeper causes, it was said, was Khrushchev's failure in agricultural policy, which he had made his special concern but on which he had listened to bad advisers, including the geneticist Trofim Lysenko (since dismissed). Both on agriculture and trade he had set up separate regional party committees duplicating party chains of command. He was accused of extravagance and this covered first installing and then withdrawing missiles in Cuba. He violated, it was said, the principle of collective leadership, making decisions on his own.

A New System of Social Planning.—At the Supreme Soviet in 1965 Mr. Kosygin, the Prime Minister, announced a new system of Soviet planning. There have been only two movements of comparable importance since the Revolution:

(1) the beginning of Lenin's new economic policy in 1921; and
(2) the forced industrialisation through five-year plans in 1928.

Under the five-year plans the "command system" of production involving centralised planning in minute detail has held the field. It was the first object of every factory manager to reach or overreach his target and this might be regardless of profits or quality. Under the new scheme central planning is reduced. Managers are to be given broad targets and then left to produce as best they can to sell the goods and to make a profit. Sales volume and profits become the criteria of plan fulfilment. Thus the needs and desires of consumers acquire a new and effective importance. The new system seems a genuine attempt to reconcile three things:

(1) central planning;
(2) personal enterprise; and
(3) the wishes of consumers.

The State will receive interest on long-term credits for capital equipment as well as a share of the profits. The rest of the profits will be at the disposal of management for ploughing back and for incentive payments in the form of higher wages and special bonuses. This reform in the Soviet Union is clearly a compromise and like all compromises runs a risk of some instability. The student of affairs will therefore watch whether the system will issue into a greater liberalisation or to a re-imposition of the tight planning system. Another aspect of the compromise is the tension between the more flexible and empirical approach by the technocrats running the production ministries under Kosygin and the more dogmatic and traditional outlook in the Communist Party under Brezhnev.

India and China.—The independence and unity of India on the one hand and the emergence in China of the Central People's Republic on the other form the two most important political features of Asia. The two countries have lived, historically speaking, in different worlds; their experiences at the hands of the West have been different; their recent developments and their present political systems are entirely dissimilar—the one a democracy and the other authoritarian. Yet these differences had not affected India's friendship and sympathy with China. In the Cold War India had studiously refrained from being drawn to one side at the expense of the other; and this neutrality has caused her to oppose alliances such as SEATO and CENTO.

Indian Changes under British Rule.—The pattern of her development after independence had been set during British rule. The main features were: the concept of law and the rule of law; a civil service superior to any known before in Asia; a system of education introduced as far back as 1835; English as a common language; and the growth of an intelligentsia (to use a word with a Russian origin) with a humanistic outlook and responsive to Western ideals and traditions. Important consequences followed from these changes. They enabled Hindu society to reform itself on the basis of modern ideas; to create an educated leadership; to modernise Indian languages; and to introduce modern science to India.

The Leadership of Mahatma Gandhi.—That the dissolution of British rule was made so peacefully, a miracle of modern times, was due principally to Gandhi who associated nationalism with ethical concepts, summed up in the term "Gandhism" and denoting pacifism, the value of the individual soul and humane ideas. He made India conscious of the social reforms which needed to be made and created the discipline to make a democracy able to carry them through. Gandhi's ideal of religious unity, though disrupted by the partition into the two states, Pakistan and India, made it possible for the new India to be a secular state, in which all religions and minorities had equal rights.

Nehru, India's first prime minister, symbolised India's highest aspirations. As a disciple of Gandhi he revered him; but his political outlook had been different. He was an enlightened liberal working towards a modernised, rational, democratic, secular state enjoying both the benefits of large-scale scientific organisation and the spiritual good of individual liberty. Under great strains this way and that he maintained neutrality in the face of world power blocs and embodied in his politics characteristics from differing régimes. He overtowered everybody in Indian public life and was one of the few great figures on the world stage.

Shastri succeeded Nehru. Lal Bahadur was born in 1903 into a caste lower than the Brahmins but equally dedicated to learning; "Shastri" is in fact the title of the degree he received. His air of gentleness was enhanced by his small size; and even by his adversaries in India he was regarded as a good, kind, and tolerant man. He faced problems as complex as any statesman, in the world's biggest, hungriest, and restless democracy. One of his biggest decisions was not to follow China in the nuclear weapons race.

India's Gravest Problems.—The advent of Shastri justified the confidence of Nehru that, when the time came, Congress would not fail to find a successor to him. It was a great tribute to Nehru's work in building political stability over a period of seventeen years that his concept of a secular, democratic, and modern India was accepted by his successors. Shastri took over the leadership, however, when India was faced by grave internal crises. There were four serious features. (1) The first was the slow rate of economic growth. In recent years the growth in national income has been only 2·5 per cent where 5 per cent was planned; and, in 1962–63 the growth in industry was 8 per cent against 11 per cent projected; but the most acute failure was in agriculture which actually declined by 3·3 per cent in 1962–63. (2) The second difficulty was the rise in prices consequent upon inflationary pressures. (3) The third obstacle was the obstinate disparity in wealth as between the few and the masses, highlighted by increasing social consciousness but unresolved all the same, in India as elsewhere. Finally (4) India is faced by a population problem which other countries also face. In India the expectation of life in the 'forties was 32 years; it is now nearly 50. During the planning decade 1951–61 the death rate of 27 per thousand dropped to 18. The birth rate remains fairly stationary at about 40 a thousand. The net effect is that the population increases at more than 2 per cent a year.

A very readable and informative book published in 1965 was Ronald Segal's *The Crisis of India* (Cape), which provoked some controversy.

Mrs. Indira Gandhi became Prime Minister of India in January 1966 upon Mr. Shastri's death at the Tashkent conference. Her father was Nehru and she must be regarded as the only daughter in history to have succeeded her father. She is not a relation of Mahatma Gandhi. In Indian families women have always been very highly regarded and India is one of the very few countries where nothing stands in the way of a woman going to the very top. Mahatma Gandhi so far back as 1929 had been uncompromising on women's rights and after Indian independence Hindu law was changed to satisfy his requirements on the status of women. Thus it was Gandhi who took women into politics and paved the way for the election in 1966 of Mrs. Gandhi, the world's most powerful woman. (Mrs. Bandaranaike of Ceylon holds the distinction of being the first woman Prime Minister in history.) Mrs. Gandhi is more radical than both her father Nehru and Mr. Shastri but clings to no " ism " and will confront each problem individually. Among those round Shastri who helped to guide India, she was by far the most cosmopolitan. Educated in Switzerland and at Oxford, she travelled widely with her father and as his hostess met many world leaders. Her family is Hindu and there is no doubt that she shares her father's devotion to the ideal of a secular state. She faced, on election, many difficulties; she promised to honour the agreement with Pakistan reached only a few days earlier at Tashkent where Mr. Shastri died, and she announced her willingness to negotiate with China if favourable conditions are created.

India and Pakistan.—The strained relations between these two countries have formed a sorrowful chapter. The concrete problems which have recently arisen between the two countries are not, in themselves, the cause of the strain but are the result of earlier deterioration of feeling. This deterioration was most severe in the year before actual partition, when tension between Hindus and Muslims exploded into communal warfare in Calcutta and in certain provinces including the Punjab. This strife had roots which struck deep into history for the Muslims had, between the eleventh and sixteenth centuries, conquered by stages almost the whole of India. The Muslims had forestalled the British Westerners in bringing almost the whole of India under a single government. Therefore in the territories now in the Indian Union, the Hindus are masters in their own house for the first time since the beginning of the Muslim conquest of India so long ago. The partition of the sub-continent inevitably left large pockets of minorities of Muslims in India and of Hindus in Pakistan. The long history of conquest, of difference of religion and culture and the bitterness of partition itself—all this background accentuated problems which would not in themselves have been so difficult to solve. We must recall that Gandhi, Nehru and other Indian leaders did their best to heal communal strife.

Indo-Pakistani Relations.—Although a cease-fire was brought about in the Rann of Kutch in June 1965 armed clashes occurred in Kashmir during August, leading to various breaches of the cease-fire line, and were extended to other parts of the Indo-Pakistani border during September. After U Thant had not succeeded in his personal mission in persuading the two powers to stop fighting the United Nations successfully ordered a cease-fire which took effect on 22 September. Russia succeeded in inducing Mr. Shastri and President Ayub Khan to meet at Tashkent in January 1966. There an agreement was signed aimed at restoring normal and peaceful relations between India and Pakistan. It provides for the withdrawal of armed personnel in Kashmir to positions held by them before 5 August 1965. Thus another cease-fire was added to the world's collection of them: in Germany, Palestine, Korea, Vietnam, Ladakh, and now again in Kashmir.

India and the A-Bomb.—One of the sequels of the Indo-Pakistani war was the growing pressure from the Indian Parliament and public for the production of atomic weapons; and it was believed that India might explode its first atomic bomb before the end of 1966. It was claimed that India could produce 30 20-kiloton bombs for less than £20 million within a year. If, indeed, India decided to make a bomb the difficulty of getting the nuclear genie back into the bottle would become extremely difficult. It would start an arms race in Asia and weaken the present hesitations of non-aligned and neutral countries potentially capable of making the bomb. India's decision will depend in part on whether America and Russia can agree on the kind of nuclear guarantee for non-nuclear countries which would satisfy some of India's requirements.

India and China: The Frontier Dispute, 1962.—The unfortunate clash between these two countries about their border came to a head in the autumn of 1962. The Indian Government had taken the view that the 2,500-mile northern frontier drawn up when the British ruled India remained valid, whereas that alignment is not recognised by China. But the issue did not become a live one until 1959 after China had occupied Tibet. Repeated attempts to negotiate an agreed frontier failed. The disputed areas are (1) the northern region of Kashmir called Ladakh; the Ladakhis are Buddhists with intimate ties with Tibet and (2) in the north-east where the border is the so-called McMahon Line. This line was drawn on the map by a British official of that name at the time when China was weak and it has never been agreed to by China. Here too the inhabitants are more akin in religion, habits, and appearance to the Tibetans than the Indians. The area of Ladakh which the Chinese claim links Sinkiang with Western Tibet (both in China). The Chinese Government announced a cease-fire on 19 November to begin on 1 December. The situation remained quiet in 1963 and up to the time of writing (Feb. 1966). Both China and India appear to have an arguable case on historical, geographical, and judicial grounds.

China.—It is only in the last fifty years that the people of China have emerged from centuries of exploitation. It is very difficult for a Western observer to appreciate the dramatic changes which followed the overthrow of the repressive dynasty in 1911 and the advent of the Republic next year. The new leader, Sun Yat Sen, a great idealist and humanitarian, pitted himself against the age-long combination of landlords, military men, and reactionary scholars. For all his achievements Sun failed; or rather Sun's party, the Kuomintang, failed him. Power passed to the military remnants of the old Imperial army and Sun did not succeed in giving his party teeth for militant action for reform. Unfortunately, two years after Sun's death in 1925 his successor General Chiang Kai-shek opened an anti-Communist drive. That decision which drove a wedge between Kuomintang and the Communists was to be of tragic consequence.

The Emergence of Mao Tse-tung.—Sun's exhortations had been taken to heart not by Chiang Kai-shek but by Mao Tse-tung who made a completely new approach to the peasants. Mao's success in raising peasant armies established his pre-eminence as a leader. The countryside helped the Communists to develop honest government. The peasants were ready to work in field and forge. They created a people's army superior to all other armies in Chinese history. Mao takes his place as one of the four chief figures of Asia in the last decade—the others being Nehru and Vinoba Bhave of India and U Nu of Burma. He is the son of a farmer of the middle rank and this doubtless endowed him with an insight into the character of peasants. His identification with the Party was complete, whereas Chiang had called for allegiance to himself rather than to a coherent body of principles. In a sense the struggle between the two men was between a party and a person.

China and the Great Powers.—The newspaper reader may well have been puzzled by the changes in China's attitude to foreign Powers, including Russia. Since 1949 there have been seven major phases in China's foreign policy:

1. First, in 1950, an alliance with Russia, with a drawing away from the United States.
2. A desire to expand beyond her old boundaries. (The Korean War.)
3. A plan to gain Great Power status by establishing a hegemony over Asian nations.
4. Realisation of the dangers of this plan (Bandung Conference).

5. New relations with Russia.
6. Long-term firmness and patience over Formosa.
7. A disagreement with Russia in 1961.

The offensive by China's North Korean protégé against the South, a disquieting sequel to the 1950 Treaty with Russia, was followed by the two-year Korean War, an all-round tragedy; and resulted in intense bitterness between Communist China and the United States. China changed her policy and made a strenuous bid to win the friendship of Asian nations by emphasising her peaceful intentions at the Bandung Conference of Asian and African countries in April 1955. By 1954 when Manchuria came under the complete control of the Communists China felt strong enough to assert her independence and at the same time her sense of solidarity with Russia. During the last five years, however, relations with Russia have been strained.

China and Russia.—Undoubtedly the crisis in the relations between the Soviet Union and China was at the centre of the events leading to the abrupt departure of Nikita Khrushchev. Khrushchev was not himself the most wholehearted supporter of the idea of staging a massive trial of strength with China. What is the key interpretation of this dispute? Is it a schism in faith as between the relative new, ardent Communism of China and the more experienced and flexible system in Russia? Was it a clash between personalities, between Mao and Khrushchev which the fall of the latter will ease? Or are the roots of the division to be found in the differing nature of two civilisations, a common faith in Communism not proving enough to link the two countries together, after a succession of strains. What from China's point of view have those strains been? China may well have been disappointed in Russia's passivity in the off-shore islands crisis in 1958. In the following year Russia was veering towards understanding with the United States, thus appearing to China to be blind to the existence of an enemy and the true character of that country. In the same year, 1959, Russia denounced unilaterally the agreement of 1951 for technical aid for China's defence and declined to help China in making nuclear weapons. In 1963 Russia proposed a bilateral meeting but China called for a meeting of all Communist countries which Russia declined. Can these two vast countries run again in harness? How far do border questions raise serious issues and are they likely to cause open dissent?

Tensions Within a Community of Interests.—It would be unrealistic to expect that the strong community of interest between China and the Soviet Union would of itself prevent tensions. Community of interest has not, historically, prevented grave divisions within a common sphere. In his analysis *The New Cold War* (Penguin Special) Edward Crankshaw writes: "Most of the wars of which we in the West are historically conscious have been fought between powers fervently professing Christianity. Catholic has fought against Catholic. Protestant against Protestant. Christians have not hesitated to ally themselves with Muslims against fellow Christians. Catholics have allied themselves with heretics against fellow Catholics."

The Background to Border Disputes.—All the central Asian peoples—Mongols, Tibetans, and Moslem Turki peoples—were conquered by Russia and China in the eighteenth and nineteenth centuries and they drew an arbitrary line through their lands, partitioning, in effect, Central Asia. Both countries are now settling millions of people into the provinces of those people. Russian settlers in Kazak number some 40 million people, outnumbering the Kazakhs themselves. China is settling millions of Chinese in Mongol areas and Turkistan. When differences arose between Russia and China in 1960, the Chinese recalled that the Sino-Soviet frontier had been shaped by imperial Russia's pressure on a much weaker old China; and in the following years border frictions became more frequent.

Some salient facts should be noted. The Soviet Union has 220 million people increasing at the rate of 3 million a year, striving to fill and develop the empty spaces of Siberia; China has between 600 and 700 million, increasing at the rate of 20 million a year and with much less space. The Communist régime of Russia has had an innings of nearly fifty years in which to grow; China has had a mere spell of seventeen years, since she won, in 1949, the Chinese civil war, exhausted and ravaged after decades of domination, invasion, and finally the civil war itself.

China Explodes her Atomic Bomb.—China became, in October 1964, the fifth nuclear Power in the world by exploding an atomic bomb in the west of the country—probably in the Sinkiang desert. In the official announcement China gave a pledge that she would never be the first to use nuclear weapons. China would "neither commit the error of adventurism nor the error of capitulationism." The atomic device is assumed to be of the uranium or plutonium type which was used at Hiroshima and Nagasaki. Its power is likely to have been equivalent to 70,000 tons of TNT and not the million ton or megaton equivalent of the H-bomb. It was expected that the test would be followed by others on the lines of those made by the French in the Sahara in 1960. Reactions among other countries varied upon this event which had been expected for some years. Among these reactions was the view that it might be even more necessary now that China be brought into the United Nations.

At the time of the first test China did not appear to have any real means of delivering the bomb; but expert views were not unanimous, some thinking that so long as the bomb has a parachute attached to it there is no reason why it should not be tossed from a plane with the necessary range. Further it was said that Chinese submarines of a certain class were adaptable for carrying missiles with a range of 200 to 350 miles and that, within months, atomic warheads could be fitted to these missiles.

China and UNO.—The exclusion of China with a fifth of the world's population from the United Nations remained an anomaly and a folly, the gravity of which became, unfortunately, dimmed in public consciousness by the sheer continuity of the position. The China which sits at the Security Council is the island of Formosa and it has a veto. Could one detect a weakening in recent months in the China lobby—or rather the Chiang Kai-shek lobby—in Washington? Might the suggestion be revived, which Attlee made when Prime Minister, that Formosa should become UN trustee territory for perhaps 15 years, to be followed by a referendum on the island's future? *See also* **C41**.

Vietnam.—In 1941 the Vichy Government in France gave Japan, who was our fighting enemy in the Second World War, permission to use French Indo-China as a base against us. Resistance groups were formed to win back independence and to overthrow both French and Japanese fascists. Japan collapsed in 1945, when the only organised troops were controlled by Ho Chi-minh, a Communist, who set up a Democratic Republic in the northern part of Vietnam. France was bent upon restoring her colonial empire in the south and next year war broke out between the French and Ho Chi-minh. Readers will remember the dramatic seige and capture by Ho's forces of the fort of Dien Bien Phu in 1954. As a result of a 14-nation conference on Indo-China at Geneva in the same year Vietnam was partitioned after a cease-fire, the country to be united after free elections. Laos and Cambodia became independent.

A declaration taking note of the agreement was signed by the following nations who took part: U.K., France, China, Russia, Cambodia, Laos, and North Vietnam. Unfortunately the United States refused to sign the agreement and South Vietnam refused to hold elections, but both affirmed that they would not use force to upset the agreement. There was thus a crystallisation into two Vietnams—Ho Chi-minh's Hanoi régime in the North and that of the Catholic nationalist Ngo Dinh Diem at Saigon in the South. The Diem régime was corrupt but John Foster Dulles sent in men and materials to prop it up. By 1960 the Communist guerrillas in the South, known as the Vietcong, had set up a National Liberation Front. For eight or nine years a civil war was waged in South Vietnam against a very unpopular dictatorship. All that time it has received United States military support and phrases like "the defence of freedom" in Vietnam are to be construed in the light of that fact. It is true, of course, that all that time the North has been helping the rebels in the South. The position became increasingly untenable, and in 1963 the Buddhists rioted against the ruling Roman Catholic minority. The Diem régime which had savagely persecuted the Buddhists was overthrown by the military, the first of a number of military coups. In August 1964 a vessel of the U.S. fleet was attacked in the Gulf of Tonkin (off the North Vietnam coast) and American planes bombed North Vietnam installations as retaliation. This was the first of a series of bombing raids. At first the U.S. Government said that these were tit-for-tat raids but this specific basis was superseded by unrelated attacks. In March 1965 the American Ambassador in South Vietnam said that pressure against Hanoi would continue "until the enemy gives in." In June 1965 the State Department gave authority to the American military commander to use troops in offensive operations against the Vietcong.

U Thant at the United Nations, General de Gaulle in France, and important circles in the United States publicly demanded the reconvening of a conference, possibly by Russia and Britain who were co-chairmen of the Geneva conference of 1954.

A Christmas pause in the fighting was followed in the early days of 1966 by a sudden burst of diplomatic exchanges and the United States, which had earlier set out 14 points as basis of settlement, announced that it had been in direct contact with the North Vietnam Government.

Asia: the race against time.—The Vietnam crisis illustrates how the political centre of gravity in the world has changed. The most crucial division is no longer the East–West cold war. A new pattern is being traced by the spirit of Afro-Asia, comprising some seventy countries of 2,000 million people. This vast mass of people are obsessed by one overriding question: the white man brought the atomic bomb to Asia once before, twenty years ago, and exploded it: is he preparing to do so again? Can we be sufficiently understanding as to stop, before it is too late, the split of the world on racial lines: the white confronted by black, brown, and yellow united by suspicion? Can the white world, it is asked, send to Asia and Africa "teachers and technicians instead of Tommies, and books and business men instead of bombs and bases."? It is a race against time. China is finding it easier to appeal to these seventy countries to accept its leadership. The causes and consequences of this tragic polarisation need to be better understood. If China continues to be isolated, denied just entrance to the United Nations, and subjected to a trade blockade. we can scarcely wonder if she remains difficult and irreconcilable. If further we do not attack the mounting problems of racial oppression and of world poverty we cannot be surprised if the non-white population of the world is attracted by Chinese leadership. A cold war which cleaves the non-white from the white world would be a terrible situation.

War in the Congo.—Rebellion and chaos continued in the Congo throughout 1964. Unfortunately the African States had not insisted on retaining a UN presence in the Congo or themselves supplied the help needed to keep the country functioning properly. Matters were brought to a climax by killings in Stanleyville, in Orientale province, from which a Belgian–American air mission rescued a number of white people in November 1964. Tshombe's employment of white mercenaries from South Africa had added to the bitterness in the country; and the Belgian–American humanitarian intervention was used to identify the West with a white-supremacy policy which the employment of S. African mercenaries engendered. It was recalled that Tshombe had previously called in Belgian paratroops—in 1960; and the arrival of these troops had enabled him to declare the independence of Katanga and, with European support, to maintain the secession for two and a half years.

Tshombe.—It is difficult to deal adequately with Moise Tshombe in restricted space. His change in 1964 from rebel and outcast to Prime Minister of the Congo came as a shock and surprise. He had failed, as a rebel, to secure the independence of Katanga, the richest province in the Congo. It was in that province that Patrice Lumumba, the first Prime Minister of the Congo, was killed in 1962 while in detention near Elizabethville, the Katangese capital; and according to a United Nations Commission, Tshombe's Government directly or indirectly contributed to his death. At the beginning of 1963, after two outbreaks of fierce fighting with the UN, Katanga had been forcibly brought back into the Central Government and in June of that year Tshombe went into exile. Throughout Africa his name carried the same significance as Quisling's in Occupied Europe in the Second World War. Gradually, however, without once visiting the Congo he was able to attract allies to make him a strong rival to the Prime Minister, Adoula; and with the support of President Kasavubu and partly on the support of General Mobutu's Army he supplanted Adoula in 1964 and stood where Lumumba had stood just four years earlier.

Tshombe goes as Prime Minister.—President Kasavubu, Head of State throughout Congo's troubled history since independence in 1960, forced Tshombe to resign as Prime Minister in October 1965. Kasavubu invited to take his place Kimba, who was a Tshombe minister in Katanga during the three years before its secession ended in 1963. It was feared that Tshombe would return to Katanga and attempt a new secession. It was inconceivable that the UN could make a fresh intervention to prevent such a secession. President Kasavubu was himself replaced by General Mobutu soon after (November 1965). Neither man could be regarded as very competent; but Kasavubu had at any rate remained in power for five years.

The Union of South Africa.—The Nationalist Party which came to power after the Second World War was determined to maintain the supremacy of the white over the brown and black races in South Africa by a policy of separation known as apartheid (*see* **J4**). By 1961 the Union had broken with the Commonwealth on the colour question. Over the last fifteen years or more oppression had steadily grown in that country. Among the chief measures was the 1950 Suppression of Communism Act, in which the definition of communism was so wide that it was difficult to see how anyone but a few could escape the net. Three years later under the Criminal Law Amendment Act, anyone advocating even non-violent resistance to apartheid laws became liable to fine, whipping or imprisonment. Worse soon followed. In the same year the Public Safety Act gave power to the Governor-General to suspend both Parliament and the Courts with police powers in an emergency. The Unlawful Organisations Act of 1960 denied to the Africans the elementary democratic right of free association and meeting.

The United Nations and South Africa.—What can the UN do when faced by a situation like apartheid? The Charter of 1945 assumed that disputes between States would be of a territorial kind or some similar dispute which might lead to war. But "matters which are essentially within the jurisdiction of any State" were excluded from the intervention of UN. This may seem surprising, having regard to the domestic policies of dictators before the war which brought about international tensions and, in fact, war. If UN cannot intervene, can it, however, expel a country for its persistent violation of the Charter's principles? These principles include respect for human rights without distinction as to race, sex, language, or religion. The United Nations would be fully justified in expulsion. But in practice such a course might be not only unwise—especially when the United Nations is striving for universal membership—but might only strengthen S. Africa's intransigence.

UN Special Committee on Apartheid.—This Committee presented a unanimous report on the build-up of military and police forces in S. Africa and on its "repressive legislation." It emphasised the need for economic measures to be taken against that country, including an embargo on arms and petroleum products; and as a result the Security Council (which, as we have seen above, has no authority to intervene unless a threat to international peace is clearly established) did go so far, in August 1963, as to adopt a resolution calling upon S. Africa to abandon its policies of apartheid and discrimination. It called upon all States to cease forthwith the sale and shipment of arms, ammunition, and military vehicles to S. Africa. The United States immediately announced that she would allow no arms, for whatever purpose, to be supplied to S. Africa after the end of 1963. Thus, while the Charter did not authorise collective action against S. Africa, it did not absolve members from individual action and in this the United States led the way, followed by Belgium.

Cuba and the United States.—In 1961 the United States broke off diplomatic relations with Cuba with whom relations had been strained since the Castro revolution of 1959. Shortly afterwards two U.S. aeroplanes, but manned by Cubans, attacked the principal military bases near Havana, the capital. Two days later 1,500 invaders, Cuban exiles—armed, trained and largely controlled by U.S. agencies—landed on the island but were driven back. The United States intelligence service had assumed that the Cuban people would rise against Dr. Castro directly they heard of the landing. Controversy broke out in the States. Confidence in the new Kennedy administration was shaken for the affair was fundamentally alien to the American character. Relations were more bitter than ever, and, by the end of 1961, Cuba became a Communist state in the full sense.

The Cuban Crisis of the Autumn 1962.—The world came to the brink of war during the last week of October 1962. President Kennedy had pledged the United States to take measures to oppose the creation of offensive military power in Cuba. On 22 October, upon alleged evidence of offensive Soviet missile sites there, he announced a blockade of ships (or more precisely a quarantine of ships) carrying weapons to Cuba. Some Soviet ships altered course thus avoiding a direct confrontation. The United Nations made proposals to both sides in preparation for talks; and shortly afterwards Khrushchev decided to dismantle Soviet missile bases in Cuba and ship "offensive weapons" back to the Soviet Union, the United States agreeing to give assurances against an invasion of Cuba which had been threatened. The ordinary man, casting around for the salient points which emerge from this frightening position, may think these to be:

(1) the psychological dangers of foreign bases everywhere;

(2) recognition had been given to Cuba's right to her own régime;

(3) that the world was brought to the edge of war without any consultation with Britain, European countries, or the United Nations; and

(4) that the United Nations, urged on by the smaller nations, nevertheless played a great and conciliatory part.

The Dominican Revolt. The Dominican Republic which came into the news in 1965 has a population of over 3 million and occupies the eastern part of the island of Hispaniola in the Caribbean sea, 150 miles east of Cuba. The dictatorial government of President Trujillo which had ruled for 31 years ended abruptly with his assassination in May 1961. In February 1963 the first free elections for 38 years brought Juan Bosch to the presidency, but in September a civilian triumvirate headed by Senor Donald Reid Cabral and backed by military elements took office. It was the armed revolt in April 1965 against this government coupled with the demand for Dr. Bosch's reinstatement which was the occasion for President Johnson sending troops to the island. The President pleaded that he had intervened because Communist leaders had joined the revolution and he wanted to prevent another Cuba. Dr. Bosch, in exile, said that but for U.S. intervention the revolt would have succeeded. U.S. action was criticised by General de Gaulle. The Security Council which met at the request of the Soviet Union was able to arrange for a cease-fire.

France and de Gaulle.—One of the biggest changes in France after the war was the wiping out, as a serious factor, of the Radical Socialist party so powerful before the war. The newspaper reader must not be misled by the titles of foreign political parties—the Radical Socialist party was not radical and it was not socialist, giving those terms the meanings they have in England. They never regained their place in the Fourth Republic which spanned the years 1946–58. There was one hopeful spell when Pierre Mendès-France made a vigorous attempt to reform the party. In 1958 General de Gaulle, who had had a brief period of power in 1945–46, established a semi-presidential system with himself as President, taking certain powers away from Parliament and thus opening France's Fifth Republic next year.

The grant of independence to Algeria was a beneficent achievement. His dramatic refusal, however, to vote for Britain's admission to the Common Market; his refusal to accept President Kennedy's offer to share defence arrangements; and his hints of a new foreign policy imparted a novel and enigmatic pattern to the European scene.

De Gaulle: the Man.—De Gaulle's formidable height has presented cartoonists the world over with something unusual to play with and they have relished turning the image into every conceivable kind of column, pole or stick. He has created a "mystique" of a complete identity with France. He is aloof, egotistical, courageous, with a pessimistic view of human values which may be the cause of his inaccessibility and aloofness—positively lunar, as one commentator says. In public policy he has encouraged rapprochement with Germany but fear of German rearmament has strengthened his determination to have his own atomic weapons, and the French have made test explosions in the Sahara. For a character sketch of de Gaulle and the story of his veto of Britain's entry to the Common Market, the Penguin Special, *The General Says "No"* by Nora Beloff, is recommended.

De Gaulle Elected for a Second Term.—The French President's seven-year term ended in December 1965 and although he had then reached the age of seventy-five he submitted himself for re-election. He was opposed by two candidates who needed to be taken seriously (M. Mitterand and M. Lecanuet)—certainly in their combined effect—and two negligible candidates. De Gaulle took the encounter rather too casually and was forced to fight a second and straight fight with M. Mitterand, the left-wing candidate, who had secured the second position in the first ballot. De Gaulle won, as was to be expected, but had to content himself with 55·2 per cent—13 085,407 votes against M. Mitterand's 10,623,247.

What has de Gaulle achieved?—What, despite his questionable methods, did de Gaulle achieve during his first term of office? First he steadily brought the war in Algeria to an end, despite all the hopes reposed in him that he would suppress the independence movement. This was a tremendously courageous achievement; and what was equally courageous he brought France through the threat of civil war precipitated by those who were for continuing force upon Algeria. The drive to economic recovery had, it is true, commenced before he came to power. But on the political side he reasserted French spirit and struck out upon a lonely path, building his nuclear force without receiving technical knowledge from America (as we had).

The Tricolour in Space.—De Gaulle's determination that France should go into space alone was marked by the ascent in 1965 of France's *Diamant 1* with a small load—but bigger than the first American satellite *Explorer 1* over seven years earlier. It was said that the whole three-stage rocket is capable only of putting 176 lb into space and that into a low orbit. But the launching demonstrated France's technology; and on paper at any rate France ranked third behind the United States and Russia. *Diamant 2*, said to be capable of putting over 600 lb into low orbit, is expected to make its first operational flight in the next year or two. France remained committed to ELDO—the European Launcher Development Organisation—and was spending as much on space activities outside defence expenditure as Britain, some £35 million a year. Will France be able to meet the cost of her participation in the launching of the planned European vehicle (*Europa 1*) and her development of *Diamant 2*?

Adenauer and the New Germany.—A notable personal achievement of the last two decades was Dr. Konrad Adenauer's Chancellorship of the West German Federal Republic for fourteen years until his retirement in October 1963 at the age of 86. He gave to a people who had not known democratic government for 15 years a new confidence and self respect. He committed himself to constitutional government despite the fact that he was a natural autocrat. Under him Germany enjoyed the first period of stable government since the First World War. As a consequence of this new confidence Germany rebuilt prosperity from decay. His work in building a special relationship with France, culminating in a treaty of friendship, was a dramatic contrast to the long tradition of enmity with France through which he had lived. But while he succeeded in building his country into the Western community he remained intransigent over East Germany; and since a solution must be found it remains for a more imaginative successor to grapple with it.

Berlin.—The commitment to Berlin by the Western Powers is expressed in a Four-Power agreement. In 1944 the Russian, United States and British members of the European Advisory Commission (France adhered to the agreement later) agreed to divide Germany into occupation zones. This followed the defeat of Germany. They also agreed that the Berlin area would be administered separately as a fifth portion of Germany and be divided into sectors. This formally established the Western Powers' right to have their forces in what has since become West Berlin. This right carried with it the right of access by the Western Powers to their sectors in Berlin; and this was reaffirmed by the four Powers in June 1949. In October 1954 the Western Powers made a formal pledge to the people of West Berlin reaffirming their intention to keep armed forces in Berlin and that they would treat any attack on Berlin as an attack on themselves.

The Potsdam Agreement of August 1945 did not deal with rights but in essence laid down that Germany was to be treated as an economic unit and that Germany should not be dismembered politically. The Potsdam Agreement has become a dead letter by the creation of a Communist régime in the Russian zone of Germany; but this does not entail the cancellation of the rights of the Western Powers under the agreement described in the preceding paragraph.

What Khrushchev Wanted.—Soviet proposals were made many times for a German peace treaty to be signed with a confederation of the two German States, and for a Free City of West Berlin. Failing an all-German peace treaty Russia said she would sign one with the East German Republic. Thereafter countries wishing to maintain ties with West Berlin would have to agree with the East German Republic on means of access.

Western Proposals are that German reunification should take place on the basis of self determination by all Germans through free elections; and that an all-German government should negotiate a final peace treaty. This carried with it the view that the whole city of Berlin (*i.e.*, including East Berlin) should be reunified within the context of the proposals for reunifying Germany. But Russia refuses to contemplate a Germany reunited in this way since there would be no Communist influence to counter the danger which they feel of renewed German aggression. They also ask for formal recognition of the Oder–Neisse frontier line to the east of Germany.

Soviet Proposals are that the two German states should be persuaded to form a voluntary confederation on equal terms and a peace treaty should be signed with the confederation. Failing agreement between the two to confederate a peace treaty should be signed with one or both. The German States could remain "for a certain period" members of NATO and the Warsaw Pact respectively. But the Western Powers object that the four Powers cannot divest themselves of the responsibility for reunification. The East German régime has not been properly elected and a federation would preserve the division of Germany. On Berlin the Russians propose that West Berlin be converted into a neutral demilitarised Free City with token troops, including Russian. The changed status of West Berlin would need to have regard to the sovereign rights of the East German Republic and this would mean the ending of the occupation régime of West Berlin. In other words control over communications to West Berlin would pass to the East German Republic. The West object that West Berlin is already a Free City; and that a free city of Berlin should embrace East Berlin, illegally detached from four-Power administration under agreements which Russia signed.

The Assassination of President Kennedy in November 1963 at Dallas, Texas, shocked the entire world. The world recognised the growing mastery which this young man had shown during his three years of office in leadership and commitment to policies which promised increasing conciliation among nations. His youthfulness had galvanised hope in a world in which political decisions were so widely in the hands of leaders past their prime. He was the youngest American President (43) when he succeeded Eisenhower at the White House in January 1961, Eisenhower being then America's oldest President. Kennedy had had difficulties with Congress; and it was reassuring, therefore, that Lyndon B. Johnson, who as Vice-President automatically succeeded Kennedy, should have had the reputation of being a skilful negotiator in Congressional matters.

The Defeat of Goldwater.—Barry Goldwater, the Republican candidate, was decisively rejected by the American people at the Presidential election in the autumn of 1964. Lyndon B. Johnson, Democrat—"Ell Bee Jay"—had a majority of 15 million over Senator Goldwater.

In the new House of Representatives in 1964 was the largest number of Democrats since the Roosevelt New Deal years of the early 1930s. Thus President Johnson was given much greater prospects of enactment of his legislative programme. The United States is now committed to an expanding programme of civil rights for Negroes.

America's Greatest Problems.—Of the three most urgent problems which face "God's country" the first is race relations. Prosperity and education will do much, but many generations of prejudice need to be overcome, here as in other countries, before there is a conscious philosophy of acceptance. The reader is strongly recommended to read *Crisis in Black and White* by Charles E. Silberman (Cape), an unusually interesting and understanding study of the situation of the Negro in the United States today. It considers not only the history of black/white relations but also a possible solution to a crisis which menaces the future of everyone. The second problem is urban planning. Alastair Buchan in his commended book *The USA* (Oxford University Press) points out that Los Angeles flows over an area as big as one of the smaller European countries and its centre is desolated by a maze of super highways. Two out of three Americans live in big cities and these have been allowed to sprawl, their centres neglected and spoilt. The third problem is to keep the whole economy buoyant and dynamic and not dangerously dependent on a high level of defence expenditure. These three problems call for strong Federal Government; but there is still a wide Jeffersonian distrust of government. Alastair Buchan points, therefore, to the most striking anomaly in American life: a twenty-first-century attitude to scientific and economic progress with an eighteenth-century attitude to government. The President has to lead a coalition of forty-four countries of differing strength and aims; and to play a leading part in the world, unable to retreat into historic isolation or to re-fashion the world order on ideal principles.

4. THE DEFENCE CONTROVERSY.

The Defence Controversy, a supreme issue of our time, is very complex, urgent and vital. Should we build nuclear weapons or renounce them? If we keep the bomb should we use it with others or try to create a weapons system to use independently? Before we discuss the several approaches to this problem we describe various terms used in the controversy.

A deterrent is a weapons system capable of causing such a degree of destruction to an attacker that it would be too high a price for him to pay for any advantages sought. Of course, the attacker may not know what destruction the deterrent could cause, so that what is important is not the owner's estimate of his deterrent but the potential aggressor's estimate of it. Furthermore, deterrent forces must be able to strike back after an aggressor's missile attack. So there is a distinction between first and second strike weapons. The nuclear deterrent is said to be the ultimate deterrent, because nuclear weapons are the most advanced form of weapon.

The limited deterrent or minimum deterrent is the name given to a proposal first conceived by Jerome Weisner, President Kennedy's Special Assistant for Science and Technology. It has been described by Wayland Young as follows: since you can't find out exactly what nuclear stockpiles your adversary has without a great deal of hunting, you had better first ease the situation by coming down to a roughly equal low level before trying to go down to zero. The Russians' name for this idea is the "nuclear umbrella," which the Russian participants at the Pugwash Conference in 1961 broadly accepted as sound. The Americans are ahead in the crucial field of strategic missilry and the initiative taken by them at the Disarmament Conference in January 1964 for a verified freeze of nuclear weapons must be related to the idea of a limited deterrent, for you cannot come down till you stop going up.

The nuclear or thermonuclear bomb means a bomb or a missile with an explosive power measured in megatons, *i.e.*, one million times more powerful than bombs used during the Second World War. A ten megaton bomb contains the equivalent of a train of railway wagons filled with high explosive stretching from London to New York—and of course fall-out with its genetic effects.

The independent bomb. Independence, in this context, means the right and ability to launch a force alone against an aggressor. For this it is necessary to own and control thermo-nuclear weapons and be able to deliver them. The ability to deliver weapons, without which they are useless as a deterrent, raises crucial difficulties.

Other terms. *Escalation* is a term used for the belief that once a conflict begins which involves nuclear powers, the contesting parties are riding on an escalator from which there is no escape and rising to an all-out thermonuclear war. A weapon is said to be *credible* when it is trustworthy and it can be believed in for its purpose: thus it is sometimes said that the U.K. manned bomber force is credible only for a first strike. *Conventional* weapons and forces are other than nuclear. Atomic devices are described as *tactical* when they are in support of ground forces and *strategic* when they are part of an all-out major strike force.

The Approaches to the Problem.—There are broadly four approaches:

(1) that Britain should have a strong independent nuclear deterrent;

(2) that we should keep the bomb but reject the possibility of using it independently;

(3) that, for a number of political and military reasons, we should abandon the bomb;

(4) that we should abandon the bomb because it is morally wrong to make or use it.

We take these in turn.

The Independent Nuclear Deterrent.—It is argued that the bomb, like earlier types of armament, is the ultimate guarantee of the nation's security; that without it we should not reach the conference table with other great powers; that it gives us freedom of action and, as such, is a safeguard against the possibility of a change in American policies which might leave us unprotected. This policy of an independent nuclear deterrent was advocated by Sir Alec Douglas-Home when Prime Minister and he advised those who dissent to "put their heads in a bucket and think again." The layman cannot help thinking several times since contrary opinions of various kinds come to him from sources all of which must command his respect. For instance Lord Gladwyn (the former British Ambassador to France) wrote that Sir Alec "did not refer to the uncomfortable fact that Britain's 'independent deterrent' is not now completely independent, nor British, nor a deterrent and that it will become less 'credible' as time goes on." (*Encounter*, December 1963.)

Does Britain's Influence Depend Upon Nuclear Weapons?—The proposition that, without her bombs, Britain would have had no standing in the test-ban negotiations calls for some examination. However it may be true of Britain's presence at the final stage of the negotiations in Moscow the way to an agreement had been paved at Geneva over many months by the influence of what are called the lesser nations. The British delegation played, of course, an indispensable part; but the view that she was able to play that part only because she had the power to bomb is at least questionable. In regard to the generalisation that our influence is effective only because it is backed by nuclear weapons, we find that sometimes our views are accepted and sometimes they are not; and a simpler explanation is that our lead is more likely to find a response when it is soundly based upon the merits of the problem. Thus the U.S. responded to our advice on Indo-China and again on the Chinese off-shore islands. But they did not share our views on the Middle East in 1956 (when our nuclear power was stronger). If it be indeed true that political influence is made more effective by the possession of nuclear weapons then that argument is surely a direct encouragement to other countries to secure such weapons.

The Abandonment of the Right of Independent Nuclear Action.—The concept of " independence " runs counter to the military essence of the Atlantic alliance and Anglo-American co-operation; but the right to act independently was recognised in the Nassau Agreement (Clause 6) between President Kennedy and Mr. Macmillan when, in 1962, the British V-force was assigned to NATO. Thus the theoretical right of withdrawal exists. But it is argued this is only a residual independence of control and there is no case for independent nuclear action—that is, without prior consultation with our allies—in any part of the world. This conclusion was reached by the British Council of Churches, whose report is contained in a book (*The British Nuclear Deterrent*, published by the Student Christian Movement Press, 1*s.* 6*d.*). The Council recorded its belief that Britain should express her willingness to forego claim to independent nuclear action if thereby more effective machinery can be established for shared control of the deterrent in any part of the world.

The Rejection of the Bomb Itself is urged for a number of political, military and economic reasons. First, this school of thought rejects the idea that the British bomb provides Britain with a ticket of admission to the conference table. The test-ban treaty was reached in the more favourable atmosphere between Russia and the U.S.A. following the Cuba crisis; Britain's real contribution was not her presence at the conference table but her long pressure on the American Administration. And, the argument proceeds, Britain's influence in Washington has been diminished by insisting on keeping the bomb when the U.S.A. has argued the case against independent national deterrents. The second argument that the British bomb guarantees us a freedom of action which non-nuclear Powers do not have is, it is said, refuted by history; the limits of our freedom of action are set by political realities, as was demonstrated at Suez. The third argument for the independent bomb is that our interests may diverge from those of America—that is the argument used by de Gaulle for a French bomb. It is impossible, of course, to say that such a divergence cannot occur. But this possibility is transcended by larger considerations. The concept of political independence has become meaningless for we are all circumscribed by the actions of allies and others. The best safeguard for the future is to work towards a world system of security and this would be damaged by making nations more rigidly independent with their own bombs. We shall be unlikely now to persuade China and France to abandon their nuclear plans; but we reduce the chances of successfully checking the spread of nuclear weapons to other countries by ourselves retaining the bomb which, on other grounds, it is undesirable to retain. By being content for one hand alone to be on the nuclear trigger we should be better able to resist West Germany's demand for a greater say in nuclear affairs; and we could make more hopeful efforts with Russia against proliferation throughout the world. Hard thinking is more relevant to the present time than gestures of independence and more especially as such nuclear independence will be increasingly difficult to create and sustain. Those who urge these considerations would confide their nuclear defence to American control with consultation and planning between the U.S.A. and her allies.

Nuclear Disarmament.—The argument is carried further by those who form the Campaign for Nuclear Disarmament (CND). They urge that we should not only renounce nuclear weapons and stocks of atomic and hydrogen bombs and the means of delivering them, but we should go further and withdraw from NATO and abolish the American bases in this country. This, it is said, would make the country stronger not weaker. For the argument is that Russia, which has no serious quarrel with this country, would not bother to attack us if we had no nuclear weapons and were freed from association with NATO and the United States. Furthermore, say the unilateralists (the name given to those who take this view) such a renunciation would be a strong lead to other countries contemplating their own atomic weapons. This group advocate not only the abandonment of a British deterrent but resist the creation of a European deterrent. They are thus opposed to schemes like the proposed multinational nuclear force. They want disengagement in Central Europe and the creation there of a zone free from nuclear weapons and bases, as well as for nuclear-free zones elsewhere. Their ideal is not a Britain which recedes into isolation but one freed from allegiance to either of the rival power blocs and thus better able to be loyal to and effective in the United Nations.

The Pacifist Position.—Continuing across the spectrum of attitudes we reach the extreme pacifist position which is crystallised by the views of Quakers (The Society of Friends) whose opposition to nuclear weapons is bound up with opposition to all weapons. Their peace testimony expresses their whole way of life. No one, they believe, has the right to use nuclear weapons in his defence or to ask another person to use them on his behalf. " To rely on the possession of nuclear weapons as a deterrent is faithless; to use them is a sin." In 1962, Dr. Fisher, then Archbishop of Canterbury, said ". . . the danger of war comes not only from nuclear weapons but from any sort of weapon." The famous Encyclical *Pacem in Terris* issued by Pope John in Rome in April 1963 declared that " Any human society that is established on relations of force must be regarded as inhuman."

The Multilateral Force (MLF).—The components having nuclear capability earmarked for NATO, were the Bomber Command of the R.A.F., some American Polaris submarines, the F–104s of Western Germany, and a mixed-manned force of merchant ships armed with Polaris missiles. The British bombers were to remain under ultimate British control. MLF is an American plan for a NATO mixed-manned surface fleet. The idea of an integrated force is said to be a means of checking the spread of nuclear weapons to individual national forces within NATO. But it is doubtful if this hope is justified. It underestimates the West German desire for independent possession of nuclear weapons; and it has certainly not affected France's determination to have such independent possession. Moreover, it is likely to result in proliferation of nuclear forces outside NATO since Russia has repeatedly hinted that if MLF goes ahead she will create a similar MLF or give independent control of nuclear forces to Poland or Czechoslovakia since Russia regards MLF as a device for the nuclear rearming of Germany. In October 1963 Britain agreed to join in preliminary talks towards the establishment of a multilateral nuclear fleet of merchant ships armed with Polaris missiles but the Wilson Government were opposed to a multilateral surface fleet.

Britain and the MLF.—One of the first questions on the diplomatic front for the Labour Government was whether Britain should or should no join the mixed-manned nuclear sea force, the MLF, sponsored by the United States, supported by Western Germany and, with less enthusiasm by Italy. In the Labour Party's view the MLF adds nothing to the military security of the West; it would proliferate nuclear weapons; might satisfy no one completely and might even divide the Western alliance. Both MLF and Britain's attitude to European political union were discussed at the meeting, in Bonn, in November 1964 of the Western European Union. It was generally realised that mixed manning was no longer regarded either by the Americans or the West Germans as being so urgent as Washington had formerly represented it to be.

The Atlantic Nuclear Force which Mr. Wilson proposed at Washington in December 1964 contemplated four components:

(*a*) all the British V-bombers, apart from those needed outside the NATO area;

(*b*) the British Polaris submarines;

(*c*) an equal number of American Polaris submarines;

(*d*) and a mixed-manned element in which the non-nuclear members of NATO could take part.

For (*d*) the Prime Minister wanted land-based weapons, not a naval force, being opposed to a mixed-manned surface fleet.

The Political Control of ANF, it was suggested by Britain, should be vested in a single authority. This authority would not be the North Atlantic Council itself but a body linked with it. This body would issue directives to the force commander and release nuclear weapons to him in emergencies. Mr. Wilson emphasised that, within this body, a veto must be retained by each of the nations contributing nuclear weapons to the joint force. Thus the Americans and British would retain their vetos over the whole force. So would the French if they contributed "the force de frappe" to ANF. Other governments should be given a more genuine share in strategic decisions.

A New Defence Policy was crystallised in the White Paper, February 1965, and the main decisions were: completion of the already ordered four Polaris submarines (which had to be paid for anyway) but not the fifth; assignment of these four and nearly all of Bomber Command to the ANF if that can be agreed upon; a possible nuclear guarantee to the Indians and others in the Far East, using part of Bomber Command; deferment of a decision on the TSR2 bomber, cancellation of the P-1154 fighter and the HS-681 transport, development of the Kestrel fighter, purchase of the American Phantom fighter and C-130 transport, and a joint approach with France to a new jet fighter.

Strains in the Western Alliance.—It is fundamental and crucial that all the countries of the Western alliance should move together in one direction. While this dictum must have been well understood by the countries concerned their path was obstructed by sectional difficulties. During 1964 there was the estrangement between France and the United States and between France and Great Britain. There was a bid for close partnership—even for some kind of political union—between France and Germany; and for geographical reasons there seemed to be good reason for close affinity. Chancellor Erhard appointed Dr. Adenauer as his special adviser on foreign affairs and "Der Alte" set himself the task of reviving the Franco-German Alliance. But German opinion grew more and more unsure and divided as to where Germany's future lay. The Christian Democratic Party was divided upon relationship with de Gaulle and the other wing of the Government coalition, the Free Democrats, were equally disturbed.

The Fate of MLF and ANF.—The year 1965 was a period of marking time on this subject and of a slow change of attitude. There was a general election in Germany, a presidential election in France, and tension between France and the U.S.A. General de Gaulle was opposed to both MLF and ANF. It was unlikely that the Christian Democrats, if they returned to power in Germany (which they did), would accept a nuclear scheme which excluded them from direct access to nuclear weapons. (Germany is debarred by the Paris treaties from making nuclear weapons.) They had, in fact, used pressure to turn down the British draft non-proliferation treaty at the Geneva disarmament conference in 1965 on the ground that it would thwart German national nuclear ambitions. West Germany wanted a joint scheme but one which would satisfy them. Britain was impressed by the Soviet claim that a joint nuclear project would be contrary to the terms of a treaty to prevent further dissemination of nuclear weapons, such a treaty being a step in relaxing East–West tension in Central Europe. Some relaxation had already occurred with a diminishing of the belief that there was a Russian threat to Western Europe. The U.S.A. had agreed to wait until the ANF proposal had been fully discussed. Mr. Stewart, the Foreign Secretary, having told the United Nations in the autumn of 1965 that ANF was no longer among Britain's top priorities, visited Russia where he explained that Britain laid even greater stress than before on East–West disarmament talks. The problem remained, therefore, how to associate the non-nuclear powers of the alliance with nuclear decision making. And this difficulty lay at the heart of the long crisis within NATO. While de Gaulle will not allow German control of a European deterrent, German "Gaullists," like Herr Strauss, hope that the heavy cost of a French deterrent will force the French to call on German help in a European or Franco–German nuclear partnership.

De Gaulle's changed attitude to NATO in 1966 and the reasons are indicated in Part II (**C43**).

The Partial Nuclear Test-Ban Treaty was signed in Moscow in August 1963 between Britain, the U.S.A., and the U.S.S.R. who undertook not to conduct nuclear tests in three out of four possible spheres—in the atmosphere, in outer space and under water. The fourth possibility—underground tests—was not touched by the Treaty, but it declares that agreement on such tests remains a desirable aim. Within two weeks 62 further States had signed it. President de Gaulle was sceptical. Since Russia and the U.S.A. had, he said, made hundreds of tests, some quite recently, he did not see what purpose new tests could serve. He put his finger on the fact that underground tests were not covered. The Treaty was denounced by China who wanted, she said, total prohibition and destruction of nuclear weapons.

Underground Nuclear Explosions.—There has been little hope of extending the test-ban treaty to underground explosions, despite the appeal of the United States to Russia to agree. The U.S. and Britain still disagree with Russia over the question of identifying the nature of all underground explosions. The Western Powers insist that no foolproof method has yet been devised, and they cannot therefore accept a ban on nuclear underground explosions without a limited number of on the spot inspections. But this is just what Russia is opposed to, on the grounds that this would amount to espionage.

Freeze and Thaw in the Cold War.—The partial test-ban treaty is a good point from which to look back at the rise and fall in hopes for good East–West relations. The thermometer reading began low in 1948 with the Communist seizure of the régime in Czechoslovakia and with the blockade of Berlin. It rose next year when the blockade was lifted, only to fall in 1950 with the Korean War. Not till 1953 did hopes rise again with the double event of the death of Stalin (bringing the chance of a new outlook in Russia) and peace in Korea. But the thermometer reading slumped again with the fall of Dien Bien Phu in Indo-China. Russia's Treaty with Austria, a gratifying arrangement, rekindled hope but that hope disappeared again in 1956 with the double event of Russia's treatment of Hungary and the ill-fated Anglo-French invasion of Egypt. The crisis over Quemoy between China and the U.S.A. and Russia's ultimatum over Berlin kept the temperature well down; but when, at Camp David, Eisenhower and Khrushchev agreed to hold a Summit Meeting and the Foreign Ministers actually met, things looked cheerful again. Unfortunately the prospect was shattered by the U2 incident when an American intelligence service plane flew over Russia and was captured. Bad enough in itself it led to the collapse, at its very outset, of the Paris Summit Conference, 1960, for which the whole world had long been waiting with hope. Even then the thermometer was not at the lowest reading. It was, however, further depressed when Russia resumed nuclear testing; and after a good recovery, upon agreement on the neutrality of Laos by Russia, the West, and China, the reading slumped to its lowest point during the Cuba crisis in 1962. Over the last seventeen years, therefore, the graph has jumped up and down pretty frequently. The test-ban treaty rekindled hope as several times before. Experience suggests that the Cold War may well freeze again; but it would be impossible for statesmen and people to go forward without hope, however tempered it may be by experience.

The Geneva Disarmament Conference ended its 1965 session in failure. The object was to achieve a treaty designed to stop the spread of nuclear weapons to ever larger numbers of countries. Such a treaty had been thoroughly debated in 1964 when the Soviets insisted that no non-proliferation treaty was acceptable if it left the NATO powers free to set up a multilateral system of control. One cannot simultaneously think it necessary to give West Germans control of nuclear weapons and declare support for a non-proliferation treaty. The 1965 Geneva meetings began after the U.S. Government had reversed its views about MLF; but the American statement of their attitude was too much for the Russians. The U.S. said that giving nuclear weapons to an alliance would not increase the number of nuclear powers; meaning presumably that when a European political union, at present visionary, comes about, the submergence in it of Britain would make it legitimate to give nuclear arms to the new Europe. So the Conference ended in disgrace; and the countries cited in the next paragraph go on developing nuclear potentiality.

Nations and Nuclear Power.—The nuclear powers are U.S.A., Great Britain, France, Russia, and China. The powers with advanced nuclear technologies are Sweden, Israel, India, Canada, and Japan. Three other powers might obtain a nuclear capacity with external assistance; they are Western Germany, Pakistan, and the United Arab Republic.

Must the Bomb Spread? The question was examined again in a Penguin published in 1966 in association with the Institute for Strategic Studies, by Leonard Beaton. (It was a sequel to the book on the same subject a few years back by Leonard Beaton and John Maddox.) Mr. Beaton's thesis is that the spread of nuclear weapons is not an automatic process. A nation must make a definite act of will if it is to become a nuclear power. It must think hard about the implications and some have deliberately chosen to stick to conventional explosives—at least for the time being. There is the great cost not merely of the nuclear materials but of the delivery systems necessary to carry them to worthwhile targets. But this is a diminishing obstacle as nations become more competent. A more serious discouragement is that possession of nuclear weapons must increase the tensions of a country's international relations. Against this, again, is the attraction of the idea of prestige; and for this reason we may be on the verge of a spread of nuclear weapons more rapid than at any time since the war. Mr. Beaton thinks there is no simple recipe for preventing it. Technical measures—like the test-ban treaty or an effective system of safeguards under the International Atomic Energy Agency—cannot remove political reasons why some nations will want to make nuclear weapons. A proposal for a non-proliferation treaty will engender resentment of the existing nuclear monopoly unless it is accompanied by acts of drastic self-denial such as a cut-off to stockpiling. What can the countries outside the monopoly do? Mr. Beaton thinks that the potential nuclear powers—India, Canada, Sweden, Japan, Israel—should confer on a system of guarantees that will ensure Great Power support without forfeiture of the freedom of the lesser powers. The resumption of the 17-nation Geneva disarmament conference at Geneva in January 1966 ran at once into rough water as to whether an East–West treaty to prevent the spread of nuclear weapons could be achieved before NATO solves its nuclear sharing problems. Russia was expected to demand as a price for such a treaty that the Western Powers kill any plans for giving W. Germany a share in Western nuclear armaments. Thus we may make two general inductions:

(1) Existing nuclear powers must make demonstrations of self-denial before other countries will restrain their nuclear ambitions, and

(2) U.S. and the U.K. must somehow resolve Russia's objections and fears on the subject of W. Germany's share in Western nuclear armaments.

The Defence White Paper 1966 was the subject of controversy. On taking office in October 1964 the Government had decided to carry out a far-reaching examination of the nation's defence needs in the next decade, with two objectives: to relax the strain on the British economy by the defence programme which it had inherited, and to shape a new defence posture for the 1970s. The Government therefore set a financial target of £2000 million at 1964 prices to be reached in 1969–70. The cost in 1966–7 was to be limited to £2,172 million. It was decided to order 50 of the F111A aircraft (with variable sweep wings) from America by 1970 as no other aircraft can be available by that time to match it. The foreign exchange costs will be fully offset by sales of British equipment. But operationally and industrially, the Anglo-French variable-geometry aircraft was the core of our long-term aircraft programme. The present aircraft carrier force would continue well into the 1970s but Britain would not build a new carrier. A new carrier could not come into service before 1973 and by then our remaining commitments will not require her and the functions, for which we might otherwise have needed a carrier, will be performed in another way.

5. THE NEW STUDY OF CONFLICT.

Conflict studies.—A new branch of academic studies has been established here, in the United States, and elsewhere to throw light on the causes of war. It is appropriate and heartening that a new University, that of Lancaster, should start "conflict studies" as university research work. Mr. Michael Nicholson, its Director, explained in a broadcast talk something of this new inter-disciplinary study. It may seem strange, he said, in view of the mass of documents about wars of the present century—biographies, autobiographies, articles, letters, and so on—that a study of a new kind should be thought desirable. But one reply is that, despite the avalanche of material on, say, the First World War it would still be difficult to say with certainty precisely how it happened. The eruption of that war, startling as it appeared at the time, was seen later as a crisis in a series of events going back some years. What causes international tensions? Why do some escalate—to use a fashionable word—into war, while some fortunately do not? Are there clues to the way to handle disputes so as to reduce the risk of overt war—such as the Kennedy doctrine of acting so as not to corner your opponent but always to leave him some freedom of decision? What are the effects of psychological stress on the minds of those who, at a high level, take decisions in a crisis? Work has been done on analyses of arms races—for example on the psychological and financial factors in arming and disarming. At Stanford University in California an experiment has been made with diplomatic games. A game was played separately by two groups of people to simulate the 1914 crisis. One group comprised people selected by tests as having similar personality characteristics as the actual protagonists in 1914; the other group were different in type. In the game of negotiation the first group got themselves into war; the second group found other ways of resolving the crisis.

Approaches to a Science of Conflict.—Professor Rappaport of Michigan University distinguishes three approaches to the subject of tensions between nations. These are the cataclysmic, the strategic, and the ideological approaches. In the first, war is regarded very much as we regard forest fires and epidemics. It begins, spreads—like wildfire, as we, indeed, say—and runs its course. It looks as if it were self-propelled—like a dog fight—and goes to the end relentlessly unless stopped. The second approach is to discern the strategic kind of contest which nations seem to engage in all the time—so that Clausewitz was able to say that war was a continuation of policy by other means. The strategic contests which nations engage in by way of ordinary policy resemble games of chess or poker, a continuous battle of strategy to outwit the opponent. The third approach is to examine the opposition of views. Country A thinks the views of B are maleficent, and wants B to change or modify them. But A rarely goes about it in a fruitful way. Nor does B, C, and the rest of them. Verbal battles become intense but fiery speeches often have more effect on those at home than on those abroad. Professor Rappaport suggests we need to do more research on the way to conduct debates so as to achieve a real interchange of ideas. At present many political speeches at UNO and elsewhere are largely in the nature of ritualistic rhetoric; they whip up the speakers' own people and fall flat elsewhere. These three components represent the fights, games, and debates elements in conflicts. Is a science of conflict possible? It must surely be important to try to construct one. The more self knowledge we can achieve the greater the chance of enriching men. Mr. Nicholson of Lancaster says that the experience of the methods of other social sciences will be used in the exploration, from this new angle, of the causes of conflict and war in particular. From conflict studies at Chicago has come *The Study of War* by Professor Quincy Wright; from Michigan University Professor Rappaport's *Fights, Games and Debates* and the journal *Conflict Resolution*. In England, in addition to the research unit at Lancaster University, we have the Conflict Research Society, (University College, London).

What do Nations Know of Each Other?—A science of conflict will doubtless examine the nature of the information available to us about other countries. We can too easily believe that with the complete and rapid means of communication of modern times we have only to press a button and all the facts and figures will shower into our laps. The press, wireless, and radio certainly feed us very fully. But volume is no guarantee of validity. It might be supposed that if there are many voices and many writers upon an event, the composite result would contain a true picture or that the truth could be easily selected from the stream of comment. But unfortunately this may be far from correct. To illustrate this we have only to remember the totally differing public opinions created in different countries about the same event; and we may contrast the result on public opinion of reports made at the time of an event and the very different verdict of a more objective analysis made a year or two later. Whatever we choose to look at—the Suez affair, Cuba, South Africa, the Negro problem—we know that prejudiced attitudes were persistently fostered and that despite the spate of word and picture, the truth was and is hard to come by. We cannot complain that honest reporters and commentators may not succeed in the difficult task of bringing home the truth. But are they always really trying to project the truth (which would be difficult enough if they were trying)? We know that many factors prevent the truth emerging—bias, deliberate or unconscious, the pressures of interests and national policy. A grave example of this can be studied in a very readable book *A Curtain of Ignorance. China: How America is deceived* by Felix Greene (Cape). This exposes the errors and false predictions which the author maintains have been given to the American people and have seriously distorted their picture of Communist China. The book is a detailed indictment of the deliberate falsification by the American press and so-called China experts, based upon eye-witness accounts of journalists and experts from other countries who have had more opportunity than Americans to see China; and the book includes of course his own first-hand observations from three recent visits there. Mr. Greene was formerly a senior official of the B.B.C. and although he has lived most of his time in the U.S. is still technically British. He was, therefore, able to travel in China where, as he explains, he could not have gone as an American. He asserted (1965) that he is one of the very few American-based correspondents who have been to China during the previous fourteen years and the only one who had been there twice; before his book was completed he had paid a third visit. His book is a highly documented indictment of the American press and the so-called China experts there. It is not suggested that the Communist press presents a less distorted picture of the U.S. than the U.S. press presents of China; ideas about life in America in the minds of ordinary Chinese people are wildly inaccurate. This only reinforces the point we are making that there is an all-round ignorance of each other.

(Postscript: In 1966 the U.S. decided they would allow American scholars to visit China).

The Price of Deception.—We pay a colossal price for this mutual deception. Treasure is devoted to finding out the truth about the Moon or Mars. We deliberately and systematically, or so it seems, stuff ourselves with fantastic notions about our neighbours, an hour or so flight away. We may well question whether Hitler would have driven himself into war with this country if he had known anything worth knowing about the essential nature of the English people. He had never been to England. He had not seen the people at work or play. He relied upon reports from those who had moved here in very restricted circles. Considering the momentous nature of his challenge it seems an extraordinary lack of simple prudence to neglect so vital an element in the success or failure of his undertaking. "What sort of people does he think we are?" Winston Churchill asked at a certain point in the war. The answer must be that Hitler can have known nothing at any time of the essential characteristics of those he was opposing. This is an extreme and dramatic example of the neglect of psychological factors.

Human Nature and Politics.—That we do not apply psychological insights to politics is an astonishing feature of our times. So far back as forty years ago or so Professor Graham Wallas was pleading for understanding of human nature as a key to our political problems. A student of that time might have supposed that Graham Wallas's pioneer work, as exemplified in his book *Human Nature in Politics* would have been followed by systematic work on this aspect of politics. Unfortunately it has not proved to be so. There has, it is true, been increasing interest in international affairs and a large number of groups and societies founded to gather and circulate facts and ideas. (A list of a score or so of such societies is given on **C50**.) But work on psychological interpretation has been relatively slow. As we go forward the demands on our understanding and intelligence will be greater than ever. A key to all international problems is psychological. The quarrels are never really about what they seem to be about. A dramatic example of this is the long and tragic feud between India and Pakistan which is no more about Kashmir than the Second World War was about Poland. The emotional cleavage between the two communities has inevitably thrown up a number of problems extremely difficult to resolve. Even if they were solved the hostility would create other problems. No solution is therefore possible which does not analyse the emotional turmoil which smoulders beneath the outward scene. (By way of footnote President Johnson's description of the kind of society he visualises for America as "The Great Society" is the title of a book by Graham Wallas; and one does not recall that this phrase has been used hitherto.)

II. A CITIZEN'S GUIDE

This part explains the working of Central and Local Government and gives a summary of recent changes in the machinery of government and of the new regional planning organisations. It tells the story of the British Commonwealth, the United Nations, and Western International Organisations. Among the contemporary topics discussed are the Ombudsman, the upheaval in Africa, and the constitutional and political implications of the Common Market (the economic aspects being dealt with in Section G, Part III). At the end is a list of Ministers in Mr. Wilson's Second Labour Cabinet (formed April 1966), and a list of voluntary societies of particular interest to the citizen.

CENTRAL GOVERNMENT.

We devote most of our available space to recent changes in the structure of Government, but we recapitulate first a few basic facts. The skeleton of our democratic system, the way Government works (Parliament, the Civil Service, Local Government, the Judiciary) can be fairly simply described. Our constitution is not a written one so that we cannot refer to chapter and verse of an actual text. It is the actual working of the constitution that matters and this changes over the years in subtle, complex and often disguised ways. Thus the reader will find that books on this subject fall into two main groups. In the first are those which give the current outline or anatomy of Government. In the other group are a considerable number of books (all the way from Bagehot and Dicey) on how the constitution has evolved, what it needs to do, the dangers and efficacy of changes and so on. We thus have a whole range of treatises by jurists, historians, political scientists, and politicians analysing concepts, history, actual working of parts of the constitution, and comparisons with Government in other countries.

We are unique in having an unwritten constitution. Democracy is preserved by the ordinary law, by the political organisation of the people, by custom, and by rights which depend upon the capacity of the people to preserve them. The supreme law-making body is Parliament (a word which originally meant a talk). Parliament has grown from the original principle that in important matters such as making the laws the monarch ought not to act without counsel and consent, and it now consists of two Houses, the House of Lords, composed of lords spiritual and temporal, and the House of Commons representing the commoners. The principal share of parliamentary business is conducted in the Commons. Its business is divided into three branches: legislative, financial, and critical. The life of a Parliament is limited to five years, although, on the advice of the Prime Minister, the Queen may dissolve Parliament and issue a proclamation calling for election of a new Parliament. Parliament is adjourned from day to day while in session. At the end of the session it is prorogued. At the expiry of its life it is dissolved.

Legislation.—The law of this country consists of common law, statute law, and equity. One may describe the common law as that based on custom and usage as declared and expounded by judges. Statute law is the law made by Parliament, enshrined in Acts of Parliament or statutes of the realm. Parliament is thus concerned with the making of statute law. The classification of law is explained in another part of this section and more fully in **The Law of England.**

How Laws are Made.—Any member of the House of Commons may present a Bill after giving formal notice, but the principal Bills are those introduced by the Government based upon its programme outlined in the Queen's Speech.

The Bill has to pass three Readings before it can become law. The First Reading is a formality. The House gets down to discussion at the Second Reading when general principles as distinct from details are discussed. If the principles are approved, the Bill passes its Second Reading. It is then referred for detailed examination either to a standing committee or to the whole House sitting in committee. All financial Bills, such as the Finance Bill, go to a committee of the whole House of Commons. After the committee stage comes the report stage when the House considers the Bill as reported to it by the committee and decides whether further changes should be made. The final stage is the Third Reading when the House considers the Bill as a whole and whether it should or should not become law. If passed, it is sent to the Lords, where it enters on the same course. When Bills have passed through their various parliamentary stages they are sent to the Sovereign for Royal Assent.

The Lords cannot require the Commons to agree to amendments; nor can they delay a Bill indefinitely. They have no power in respect of Money Bills; and since the passing of the Parliament Act 1949 any other Public Bill which has been passed by the Commons in two successive sessions may be presented for Royal Assent without the consent of the Lords provided that a year has elapsed between the date of the Second Reading of the Bill in the Commons and the date on which it is finally passed in that House.

Bills may originate in either House, unless they deal with finance or representation when they are always introduced in the Commons. The procedure is basically the same.

Money Functions of the Commons.—The second function of the Commons (and one of its earliest in history) is to provide the State with money. The Government cannot raise money by taxation (or in any other way) or spend money without the authority of Parliament; and this power of authority belongs exclusively to the Commons. The House can vote money only on the demand and on the responsibility of a minister of the Crown.

Critical Functions of the Commons.—Parliament itself does not govern. The Queen's ministers are responsible for government and parliamentary government means that Parliament ensures that those ministers represent and have the confidence of the party which possesses a majority in the House; and further, that it controls the action of ministers by questions and criticisms. Any member may propose a motion of condemnation of any member or department of the Government, and such a motion would become a vote of want of confidence if it were made by the Leader of the Opposition.

The House of Lords is the oldest second chamber in the world and the most hereditary in its character. The House of Lords has two sets of functions, legislative and judicial. It is a party to legislation within the limits imposed by the Parliament Acts of 1911 and 1949. These limits are based on the fundamental principle that the function of the Lords, which is a non-representative assembly, is not to thwart the will of the people, but to ensure that that will is precisely and reasonably interpreted. The Conservative Party retains an overwhelming majority in the Lords and their powers of delay can limit the effective term of the life of a Labour Government. The right to run a full term of office ought not to be the privilege of the party which commands a majority in the Lords. The judicial functions of the House of Lords sprang from the fact that it is the highest Court of Appeal for the United Kingdom.

The Queen.—The Central Government is vested in the High Court of Parliament or The Queen in Parliament, consisting of the Queen and the two Houses. The Queen's tenure of the Crown holds for life (unless she abdicates), it is hereditary, and it is held by statutory right. The Queen is a constitutional monarch; she takes an oath at her Coronation to rule according to the laws and customs of the people. The Queen is the head of the Forces, which are governed by "Queen's Regulations." She is also head of the Executive, that is, all the work of the State is enacted in the name and under the authority of the Crown. Her assent is necessary before a Bill becomes an Act of Parliament. Member countries of the Commonwealth (except Malaysia, Uganda, and the Republics) owe allegiance to the Queen and she is represented by a resident Governor-General.

The Parties.—The right of a minority to oppose is an essential of democracy, and this idea means that political parties are allowed to function. The party system implies a government party (which has the largest number of candidates) and an opposition known as Her Majesty's Opposition. The system emerged in the latter half of the seventeenth century as Parliament gained the right to be the law-making bady.

The Executive.—The work of applying the law and securing obedience is called the executive work of the Government. The Executive comprises five bodies; the Queen, the Privy Council, the Cabinet, the Government Departments or Departments of State and the Civil Service.

The Cabinet was originally a committee of the Privy Council. It consists of the principal Ministers of the Crown, and is responsible for deciding the policy of the Government on all matters affecting the country, whether on foreign or home affairs. It has also complete control of the Government Departments. It is thus the central link in the whole machine of government. The Cabinet is responsible for the individual actions of its members. This follows from the requirement that a Minister's policy must be in agreement with Cabinet policy. Thus the Government have a common policy and act as one man. This is the meaning of the phrase "Ministerial responsibility."

The Prime Minister.—The office of Prime Minister, like the existence of the Cabinet, was not formally mentioned in law until recent times. He is the link between Cabinet and Queen. It is he who decides when to advise the Queen to dissolve Parliament. He is leader of the Government party in the House of Commons and gives a lead on policy. A recent writer has pointed out how the Constitution has, after long evolution, divided the functions of leadership and vested them in two personages—a Prime Minister who is temporary and removable by the will of the electorate, and the Queen, who, by contrast, embodies the principle of continuity.

The Growth of Government is illustrated by a few simple facts. In 1850 Central Government had eight departments of which only four dealt with internal affairs. By 1900 there were 13 departments which soon shot up to 24 departments. Five new ones have been added since 1962. In 1956 one in five of the whole labour force were working for Central Government, Local Government, or public bodies; and it is now about one in three.

The Life Peerage Act, 1958 was the first attempt to fulfil the promise of reform contained in the preamble of the Parliament Act, 1911. The Act provided for the creation of life peers and the introduction of women into the Lords. The first list of life peers in July 1958 included four baronesses—the first women members of the House of Lords.

The Surrender of Peerage: the Wedgwood Benn Case.—In 1962 proposals for the renunciation of peerages were made by a Parliamentary Joint Committee on House of Lords reform. This Committee was set up after a series of events involving Mr. Antony Wedgwood Benn, M.P., who declined to accept his seat in the House of Lords upon the death of his father, Viscount Stansgate, whose peerage he inherited but did not want.

The Peerage Act, 1963 legalised renunciation, the time limit for renunciation of sitting peers expiring in July 1964. Thereafter the House of Lords became a voluntary body entirely made up of those who want to be there.

The Ombudsman.—When the ordinary person is injured by unsound administration he has redress but this is limited. Sometimes there is a tribunal to which he can appeal, or he may be able to get his Member of Parliament to take up his case and perhaps ask a question in Parliament. But a question naturally tends to make a Minister defend his department rigidly; and a question cannot, in any event, deal adequately with a complex case. Sometimes the press can help to secure remedy of an injustice. The idea of a commissioner to investigate complaints has been discussed in recent years in this country and was adopted officially by the Wilson administration. The subject is treated in detail later.

CHANGES IN THE MACHINERY OF GOVERNMENT

The changes introduced by the Wilson Government in the autumn of 1964 were far-reaching and are described in the following paragraphs.

Changes in the Structure of Government, 1964.—Some of the changes in the departments of the civil service made by the Labour Government of October 1964 had been fully anticipated, but some were a surprise. A change fully expected was the appointment of a Minister for Economic Affairs, whose new office was designed, it was claimed, "to put new heart and drive into the economy." The new Ministry is responsible for framing and supervising the plan for economic development; for the general co-ordination of action to implement that plan; and for all the economic policy related to industrial expansion, allocation of physical resources and regional implications of the expansion programme. Two other new ministries of great importance were those of Technology, and of Land and Natural Resources, both described below.

Division of Responsibility between the Ministry of Economic Affairs and the Treasury.—While the former is concerned with physical resources, the Chancellor of the Exchequer at the Treasury is concerned with financial questions. The Treasury retains the traditional functions of estimates, expenditure, accounting for Government expenditure, budgetary policy, taxation policy, and all aspects, including international ones, of monetary policy. The two Ministries work closely together: programmes for capital expenditure must be related to the industrial development plan. The relation of monetary policy to the rate of expansion links the two Departments. In the previous Government the Chancellor of the Exchequer presided over the National Economic Development Council; in the Labour Government the chair was taken by the new Minister of Economic Affairs. One of the two Secretaries to the Treasury (the Economic Secretary) works in the Ministry of Economics and the other, the Financial Secretary to the Treasury, in the Treasury itself.

The Economic Advice Network between the Department of Economic Affairs and the Treasury is illustrated below:

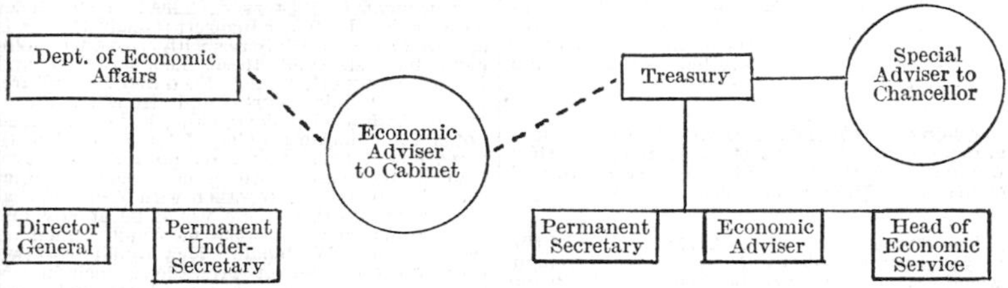

The following appointments were made in October 1964:

Economic Adviser to the Cabinet	Mr. Thomas Balogh
Special Adviser to the Chancellor	Mr. Nicholas Kaldor
Director General, Economic Affairs	Sir Donald MacDougall
Permanent Under-Secretary, Economic Affairs	Sir Eric Roll
Director General, NEDC	Sir Robert Shone
Permanent Secretary, Treasury	Sir William Armstrong
Economic Adviser, Treasury	Mr. Robert Neild
Head of Economic Service, Treasury	Prof. A. K. Cairncross

The Ministry of Technology was created by the Labour Government with a view to its being a major element in the structure of Government, its functions being partly research and development on a large scale (although pure research remains the responsibility of the Department of Education and Science). The machine-tool, computer, electronics, and telecommunications industries were among the first which the Government sought to strengthen, responsibility for them being transferred to the Ministry of Technology. The Ministry also took over responsibility for the Atomic Energy Authority, the National Research Development Corporation and research institutions of the former DSIR, including the National Physical Laboratory at Teddington. The new Ministry has a Technological Council which has been well equipped to drive ahead to advance technology in the science-based industries. The Minister is the Chairman of this Council. The first deputy chairman was Professor P. M. S. Blackett, who became President of the Royal Society in 1966, and there are ten other members representing scientific, economic, trade union, and industrial interests.

The Ministry of Technology was given more work to do by the transfer to it of the sponsoring of the whole vast complex of mechanical and electrical engineering industries from the Board of Trade in December 1965. These industries have a key place both in the National Plan and in the campaign to expand exports.

A National Computer Centre.—The Ministry of Technology announced the intention to create such a centre. It is to be an independent non-profit making company. It will store systems analyses and will possibly adopt special programmes into user programmes taking account of unique factors. It will guide and train management; and train analysts. With the support of commerce and industry, especially the computer industry, the Centre may be able in time to save the user, especially the small user, a good deal of money.

The Department of Education and Science.—To this Department was added a Minister of State with special responsibility for higher education and science and another with responsibility for schools. Within the scope of the Department fall the "pure science" research bodies:

- the Medical Research Council
- the Agricultural Research Council
- a new Natural Environment Research Council (for geology, hydrology, and oceanography)
- a new Science Research Council (for astronomy, space, university nuclear research, etc.).

A fundamental innovation is the creation of a Council of Scientific Policy (CSP) to advise the Minister on the financial priorities of science policy. It replaces the old Advisory Council on Scientific Policy; and the deletion of "Advisory" from its title denotes the basic change from an ineffective to an effective body, a change advocated by Professor Blackett in circumstances described in a later paragraph.

Why Separation of Ministry of Technology from the Department of Science and Education?—This separation was the subject of criticism and misapprehension. The problem of the machinery of Government, particularly in relation to science and technology, has been examined outside Government for the last ten years. When, ever since the early fifties, it was clear that things were going badly for us technologically, it became imperative to put things right. There was, therefore, in the view of those who created a separate Ministry, an overwhelming case for a new Ministry to give a new dynamic to industry and to technological innovation. This, it was said, could never be done if you import technology as an important but still a junior part of a large omnibus Ministry. The separation, then, can be regarded as a necessary short-term measure to advance technology so that the integration of science and technology can be made.

The Ministry of Land and Natural Resources set up in 1964 was responsible for planning and land use, the "land use" functions of the Ministry of Housing and Local Government having been transferred from that Department. The new Ministry was responsible for all town and country planning functions, for the Nature Conservancy, National Parks, Access to the Countryside, the Forestry Commission (shared with Secretary for Scotland), mineral rights, conservation of water and its availability for the community's need, the geological survey and the common land interests of the Ministry of Agriculture. Minerals under the North Sea remain the responsibility of the Ministry of Power. The Minister became responsible for the establishment of the Land Commission and for future policies relating to the community's land needs. He took part in the formulation of the national and regional plans for which the Minister of Economic Affairs has overall responsibility and in which the Ministry of Housing has an important interest.

Before the 1966 General Election Mr. Wilson announced that if the Government were re-elected he would merge the Ministry of Land and Natural Resources back again into the Ministry of Housing and Local Government.

Planning Land.—In the first decade of the century there was a Liberal election song that "God gave the Land to the People." Over fifty years later the Wilson Administration gave the planning of land to a number of Departments. First the Ministry of Land and Natural Resources, to set up a Crown Land Commission, as explained above, and to have a say in which land to buy. Decisions on land purchase are made in the Ministry of Economic Affairs or in the physical planning division of the Ministry of Housing and Local Government, or both jointly, with the first Department named above, making a triumvirate. But other Departments are also interested, like Trade and Transport.

A Ministry of Social Security.—The Government announced in February 1966 that if re-elected they would abolish the National Assistance Board and create a new Ministry of Social Security.

The Strengthening of the Cabinet.—One of the major changes made by the Labour Government was the strengthening of the position of the Prime Minister and the Cabinet by giving the Cabinet a much stronger Secretariat. The primary object of this is to ensure that the Premier and Cabinet are briefed at every significant stage of a political objective—a return, Mr. Wilson claimed, to the Churchill and Attlee position. Mr. Wilson illustrated the difference by saying that in recent years a defence proposal would go right up the Ministry of Defence where, after discussions, the majority view would be presented as the consolidated departmental view to the Cabinet who would then be expected more or less to rubber-stamp it, with the Treasury pointing out the cost—and even that factor appeared to have been somewhat ineffectual in some defence proposals. Decisions of this kind, involving five or six hundred million pounds and conditioning not only expenditure but defence policy for perhaps ten years to come should be judged at every level of the decision and not just completed within a department and then brought to No. 10. A number of other benefits flow from this earlier briefing of the Cabinet. It is easier by this means to ensure that there is co-ordination between departments, which does not always operate between strong departmental chiefs. Further, such strengthening of the Cabinet secretariat would ensure that someone is looking all the time at government as a whole. Finally, since most things have to be settled at Cabinet level, the proposal ensures that the Prime Minister is as well briefed, as he should be, as any of his colleagues, when a subject comes up for final decision for which the whole Cabinet is responsible.

The Consideration of Decisions.—In advocating a better equipped Cabinet Mr. Wilson cited instances where, he thought, decisions had been taken, in the past few years, without proper consideration. One was the sudden decision to seek entry into the Common Market. Other examples were some of the demands on our military resources. Examples of subjects which, examined departmentally, were not examined adequately at the same time by the Cabinet, were given as resale price maintenance and Rachmanism.

Scientific Advisers.—For some years, Professor P. M. S. Blackett, lately Deputy Chairman of the Advisory Council on Technology and now President of the Royal Society, had urged that a much stronger high-level body than existed was necessary to make strategic policy in the universities and in the research councils. The Advisory Council for Scientific Policy set up in 1946 had not fulfilled its rôle because of lack of powers; and when the Trend Committee in 1963 recommended its strengthening, a decision was deferred for nine months, when the setting up of a Council for Scientific Policy was announced. But it was still too weak for Professor Blackett, lacking precision as to the terms of appointment and responsibility of chairman and members. Whitehall, he said, did not want the Council to have teeth. He was sceptical as to the general usefulness of large advisory councils without executive authority: and illustrated this by the story of the prize bull sent by the Food and Agricultural Organisation of UNO to some developing country to improve the local breed of cattle. When the bull arrived it showed amiable interest but no more in the cows presented to it. When asked why it did not get on with the job the bull replied "You forget that I am an FAO bull—so my rôle is solely advisory." Professor Blackett's advice to give the Science Council teeth was carried out by the Labour Government in 1964 as explained in an earlier paragraph. Professor Blackett thought there was a strong case for Ministries with strong technological interests—and these included Fuel and Power, Transport, Health, Food and Agriculture, Housing, Public Works and Housing, etc.—having high-level policy-making bodies of mixed outside and inside people. "Supposing that 10 Government departments set up such high-level councils or boards with perhaps eight external seconded members, together with four internal civil servants, then there would be at any one time, some 80 professional men and women on secondment to Whitehall. They would be drawn from all the relevant professions, including a strong representation of natural scientists and technologists. This surely is much the quickest way to inject a more scientific and professional attitude into all the important Government departments. This cannot be done by the civil service alone as they do not now possess the people needed."

Further Changes in Planning Machinery.—Sir Richard Clarke, Second Secretary to the Treasury said after a year's experience of the Labour Government's machinery-of-government decisions of October 1964, that the Treasury and the Department of Economic Affairs had worked in very close co-operation throughout the year despite periodic revelations to the contrary in the newspapers. Although active planning of the economy was beginning to be an ingredient of Government action before October 1964, the new machinery then introduced had provided the first comprehensive reorganisation of the central economic departments. There had been very little change in the central economic machinery of government between November 1947 and the 1964 election. Sir Richard Clarke foresaw further changes in planning machinery when the full implications of the new planning tasks were appreciated. Regional developments would call for new relationships between government departments in interdepartmental regional units. And the effect of all this on not only Central but Local Government had still to be assessed. Another change must come in the Ministry of Labour's traditional rôle of "holding the ring" in wage disputes, a rôle difficult to reconcile with trying to get incomes and prices to follow a pattern prescribed by the public interest.

Control of the Executive.—The balance of power between Parliament and Whitehall has been seen in recent years to be moving in favour of Whitehall, the Executive; and the problem has become increasingly acute as to how best Parliament can effectively control the Executive. A major proposal was that almost every aspect of administration should be brought under the scrutiny of specialised sub-committees. This would be done by extending the work of the present Estimates Committee. This suggestion was made in the fourth report (1965) of the Parliamentary Select Committee on Procedure and was supported by a Study of Parliament Group, which included officers of both Houses, in a pamphlet *Reforming the Commons*, published by PEP. The Group maintained that the proposal "seek only to make party strife and parliamentary procedure combine better to provide both the general public and politicians with better argued briefs based on a more rational and objective sifting of evidence—such as select committee procedure always does." And again, the proposals "would put at last nearly all aspects of administration under the regular surveillance of Parliament and expose them to intelligent and constructive outside criticism." At present members have few of the resources available to Senators and Congressmen in Washington. They cannot call on the help of research staff nor through membership of specialist committees can they so readily examine official witnesses or study a subject in detail. In Parliament there is no equivalent of the Senate Foreign Relations Committee, the Armed Services Committee or the Joint Atomic Energy Committee.

Enquiry into the Civil Service.—In 1966 Mr. Wilson announced a fundamental and wide ranging inquiry by the Fulton Committee into Civil Service structure, recruitment, management and training. He made it clear that this did not imply that the Government had found the Civil Service lacking in its current operations; but that the time had come to ensure that the service is properly equipped for its rôle in the modern state. About the same time a reasonable, but determined attack, on Britain's senior civil servants was made in a book "Entitled to Know" by Peter Shore (MacGibbon and Kee). Mr. Shore argues that neither Parliament nor Ministers (let alone the public) have yet been told nearly as much as they are entitled to know. It was being asked whether it was fair to deny to a Minister who, after all, will be held responsible, the right to choose the Permanent Secretary of his Department.

Bringing the Law Up to Date.—A plan to codify and simplify the law was announced by the Government in 1965. The complexities and obscurity of statutes waste a great deal of time and money. Over 4,000 English statutes are said to be still extant and going back to 1235. Some of these are virtually incomprehensible even to lawyers and others contain provisions which are now irrelevant. There are some 90 volumes of delegated legislation and over 300,000 reported cases. Consultation of many Acts, perhaps up to 60 Acts, is sometimes necessary to arrive at the law on a given subject. A Law Commission, composed of whole-time members of high legal standing, was planned and this body will codify and simplify the law. In future, too, Acts of Parliament will be drafted in clearer language to enable more citizens to understand the law which governs their actions.

Speakers Conference on Electoral Law.—A new conference on electoral law has been convened and the following were the main matters relating to electoral law referred to it:

(*a*) reform of the franchise, with particular reference to the minimum age for voting;

(*b*) registration procedure generally;

(*c*) methods of election, with particular reference to preferential voting;

(*d*) conduct of elections, including problem of absent voting, polling hours, polling day as a public holiday and undue influence;

(*e*) election expenses;

(*f*) use of broadcasting.

The first Speaker's Conference was held in 1916. Another in 1929–30 failed to agree on the introduction of proportional representation and the alternative vote. There was a further Conference in 1944 but agreement was not reached on an alteration in the voting system.

Lowering the Voting Age to 18.—The Labour Party national executive expressed agreement unanimously with the idea of lowering the voting age to 18; and decided to submit its case to the Speaker's Conference on electoral reform. The addition of 18 to 21 year olds would add some two million to the electorate, being an increase of about 5 per cent. It was so far back as 1884 that Parliament decided that 21 was the right age to start voting. The law relating to the Register causes further delay and general elections take place on average every four years. In fact, therefore, the statistical chance of a voter being able to do something about his Government within a year of obtaining his majority are said to be at best one in four. Before they are twenty-one many young people are paying taxes and their disfranchisement therefore transgresses a fundamental axiom. The Liberal Party is also in favour of the step.

The United Kingdom and the Ombudsman.—Between the wars complaints were heard of the growing powers of the administration over the individual as the scope of government widened and the powers given to Government departments grew. This was the subject of a notable study, *The New Despotism* by Lord Hewart. But it was not until 1944 that so limited a step was taken as to set up a parliamentary scrutiny committee to examine ministerial rules and orders. Between 1955 and 1957 the Franks Committee re-examined the system of administrative tribunals which handle in certain cases appeals from departmental decisions. The Franks Committee also made a number of proposals for the improvement of the procedure at public inquiries. As a result there has been set up a Council on Tribunals to ventilate general grievances about both tribunal and inquiry procedure; but this is an advisory body and not an appeals body. There remained, therefore, the situation that there were many things about which a citizen could complain only through parliamentary or political channels and it was asked whether there ought not to be more facilities for complaint or appeal. This question was taken up in 1960 by the British section (called "Justice") of the International Commission of Jurists. Their report, the Wyatt Report, was published in the following year.

The Wyatt Report proposed the setting up of more tribunals where possible, including a general or miscellaneous tribunal, and then deals with the question of Ombudsman for decisions likely to remain outside the scope of tribunals and courts of inquiry. It tries to distinguish between complaints that an administrative act is "wrong policy" on the one hand and complaints that a decision is a lapse from proper standards or is oppressive or is a misuse of power on the other. It is the second group of complaints which the Report suggests should concern an Ombudsman. But this distinction can scarcely be consistently or clearly maintained; and much would need to be left to experience and sense of justice. The Report recommended a Parliamentary Commissioner who would have the same status as the Comptroller and Auditor General and be removable only by both Houses of Parliament. The proposed machinery would be supplementary to existing avenues of complaint—the parliamentary question, the adjournment debate and the *ad hoc* inquiry. In the beginning he should receive complaints only from members of either House.

Reaction to the Wyatt Report.—The Macmillan Government rejected the Report with the dictum "no derogation from ministerial responsibility to Parliament"—a statement which, with other criticisms, was answered in a memorandum by Justice in July 1962. No one, they said, suggested that the functions of the Comptroller and Auditor General conflict with ministerial responsibility. The C. and A.G. has a far wider network of agents in the departments than the Commissioner would ever have. Their function is to supply factual information for the use of Parliament. The Commissioner's functions would essentially be similar, the only difference being that they would extend to administrative standards generally and not merely to expenditure. In 1962 several members of the Royal Commission on the Police suggested Ombudsman machinery for investigating complaints alleging police misbehaviour Lord Denning's appointment to inquire into the Profumo affair was in reality something of an exercise in ombudsmanship. Eventually, in 1964, Mr. Wilson gave a pledge to give the country such a man if elected.

The Watchdog is Introduced.—In October 1965 the Government honoured their pledge by accepting an Ombudsman in a White Paper (Cmnd. 2767). It was remarkable that the official proposal when it came received so little attention. The watchdog will be called a Parliamentary Commissioner for Administration and he will act only at the instance of a member of the House of Commons. The commissioner will be an independent officer whose status and powers will be conferred by statute and secure from dismissal (except by parliamentary motion). He will have power to compel production of documents, including departmental minutes. At first he will deal solely with complaints that relate to the acts of Central Government. The Government will be willing to consider at a later stage the case for local commissioners in regard to the acts of local authorities. The Commissioner will not be allowed to investigate acts in which there are dominant considerations of national or public interest, such as investigation of crime, safety of the realm, matters affecting other countries, and administration of colonial territories. He will not pursue matters within the competence of the Courts but will have discretion to act if he thinks that the remedy open in the Courts is not one which the complainant could reasonably be expected to use. This would not limit access to the Courts. He will not pursue issues already covered by tribunals and other quasi-judicial bodies, or by the Council on Tribunals and its Scottish committee, of both of which he will be an ex-officio member.

Citizen's Defender.—The student of this subject is strongly recommended to the book *The Ombudsman: the Citizen's Defender* (published by George Allen & Unwin) which contains twenty-nine contributions including several Ombudsmen from thirteen different countries. The book, the first comprehensive treatment, is designed for laymen and expert alike and is edited by Donald C. Rowatt, who sees the ombudsman scheme as an important new addition to the defences of democracy and predicts that it will eventually become a standard part of governmental machinery throughout the democratic world. The book contains contending essays developing arguments for and against transplanting the system to specific countries.

The Principle of the Goldfish Bowl: Sweden.—A more radical Swedish rule is that all government documents must be made available for inspection by any member of the public who wants to see them. Such a person need not give any reason why he wants to see them or show that he has any personal stake in the case. The exceptions to the rule are fixed by a Secrecy Act—it is not left to the officials to decide what is to be withheld. The only part of files which government can keep private (apart from matters covered specifically by the Secrecy Act) is internal correspondence or memoranda about a case which is under discussion, in advance of an official decision. The effects of this rule are very far-reaching. The whole atmosphere and background of public debate on important issues has been changed: facts, arguments, motives, interests are brought into the open. Just as publicity in the Courts all over the world makes it possible for everybody to know how justice is administered, the publicity of documents has a similar result in the realm of public issues. The clandestine element in government is eliminated. Pressure by interested groups diminishes when the public can be aware of it. A spirit of openness prevails. Arguments are better founded and they can be more frankly made and compromises reached. But even a courteous Swedish official must find life in a goldfish bowl extremely inconvenient. Nevertheless, the advantages are regarded as outweighing the considerable drawbacks. Mr. Andrew Shonfield describes this remarkable rule in his book *Modern Capitalism* (Oxford University Press) and discusses it in his section on the political implications of active government. He is there concerned with the expanding fields of government and with the need for extra safeguards for th individual against arbitrary acts of government He pleads the case for making officials mor articulate. There are difficulties about tha especially for the British type of administrators "But," he says "on balance the disadvantage of keeping the great official inarticulate an divorced from any politics which are conducted i public view seem to be far greater."

The Council on Tribunals is the nearest thin Britain has had to an Ombudsman; but it ha insufficient powers to do much of its work. I its sixth annual report, in 1965, it complaine publicly of this handicap. The Council super vises more than 2,000 tribunals ranging fro National Assistance Appeal Tribunals to Ren Tribunals, Mental Health Review Tribunals, th Lands Tribunal, and the Air Transport Licensin Board. But they were still unable to atten certain tribunals as of right; and they had ha difficulty in seeing the report of a Governmen Department inspector when they tried to investi gate a complaint by a member of the public abou the procedure followed at a public hearing. Th Council urged that they lacked the necessar powers to carry out their statutory function adequately. The members are part-time, unpaid and their rôle is advisory, and it looks as if th Council has been deliberately handicapped fo any contest with the Administration. In 1966 Royal Commission was set up to enquire into th working of the Tribunals of Inquiry (Evidence Act, 1921.

GOVERNMENT and INDUSTRY

National Solvency.—The National Plan, th incomes policy, and the strengthened pound wer the three lines of advance in the Labour Govern ment's attempt to put Britain in a position to ear its living and pay its debts. The National Pla set out to expand output, exports, and earning over the five years to 1970. Its success depende upon the Government's ability to create a nationa sense of purpose and it was hoped that this woul be done through two channels—first by factor production committees and also by the work an advocacy of the Regional Councils.

An Incomes Policy.—The Government calle upon the trade unions to agree that they shoul not demand the fruits of higher efficiency befo they had helped to produce them. Both th Trade Union Congress and the Labour Party a their conferences in 1965 gave the Governme support in its policy. The Government had a unexpected success at the Party Conference i getting a majority of over a million votes i favour of its prices and incomes policy, 2,500,0 votes being cast against it. At the T.U. Conference a little earlier approval, in the rat of about 3 to 2, had been given for a system voluntary advance notification of wage claim This early warning system had also been e dorsed by the Confederation of British Industr the organisation of the employers.

How will the Little Neddies Grow?—It w clear that under the National Plan it was intend to make the Economic Development Committe

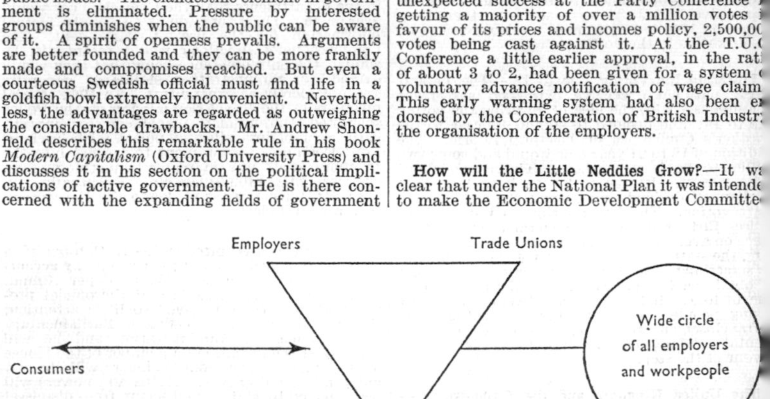

—or "Little Neddies"—a prime factor in the national economic life and administration, covering as they would most of our national industry and commerce. They are to keep the Plan under review, initiate efficiency, educate management, plan training and retraining of workers, and be concerned with investment programmes, incentives, increase of exports, and many other things. Three elements were held to give them a sporting chance of growing into sturdy Neddies: the independence of their chairmen, that they were born by agreement and not by imposition, and that the unions were involved with them. Thus we have triangular bodies (Government, employers, and unions) not just subsidiary to Government but acting as effective interlocking units of the interests involved. It was hoped that there would be two further liaisons: one, with consumers' representatives and, two, an extension of the Neddy to inform and inspire the wider circle of employers and work-people in the industry concerned and on whom in the last resort the future depends.

A New Constitutional Position.—We have said that Neddies are not just subsidiary Governmental agencies but are intended to be dynamic bodies in which the constituent elements of our economic life work together. This brings us to a fundamental change in our political life which has been insufficiently noticed. It is that the relation between Government and industry has entered a new and more permanently intimate phase. Step by step the need to manage the economy has meant advice, persuasion, and regulation by Government. With the institution of the National Economic Development Council, the spawning of little Neddies and their increasing importance in articulating the National Plan we have bodies where policy will be settled. Lord Bridges had said in 1963 that if the NEDC settled policy effectively "it would take a lot of power from Parliament." We thus meet a new constitutional situation.

The Marriage of Capitalism and Planning is thus leading to new political institutions and mechanisms in Britain as in other countries; to a new balance between public and private power; and to a possible devitalisation of Parliament. This new problem which springs from the growth during the last fifteen years of a new form of modern capitalism is studied in a book, *Modern Capitalism: the changing balance of public and private power* by Andrew Shonfield, published by Oxford University Press. In this the institutions of the new system are examined country by country. He sees France as the classic case where principles and practice have been worked out with precision. The French system is paternalistic: the premise is that bureaucrats there are so skilled that they can impose their wills upon industrialists and labour leaders. Superior knowledge, persuasion, and inducements are, it is said, driving the industrial machine ahead. (Whatever handicaps in the political field de Gaulle inherited from the Fourth Republic he had the benefit, at any rate, of the great improvement which had already been effected by the civil service in the industrial regeneration of France.) In Germany, a similar effect is obtained in a different way. Government appears to remain passive and to regard free enterprise as sacred but bureaucratic direction is given from a non-government quarter, the banks. Mr. Shonfield turning to Britain examines the dangers of the extra purposiveness of a professional bureaucracy seeking to create and sustain extra economic growth. He examines ways of easing the impact on the citizen—by changes in law and other forms of protection.

The Public Sector.—We must not overlook the fact that planning is concerned not only with the private sector of the economy but the public sector, and this includes Central and Local Government and the nationalised industries and accounted for 40 per cent of national output and 40 per cent of the country's capital assets. It absorbed 60 per cent of the nation's scientific research effort, 25 per cent of the country's man-power (and more than that indirectly) and 60 per cent of all persons who had received higher education. This large sector of our life was within the Government's direct sphere of control.

New Forms of Government Enterprise.—A revolutionary new Government agency to act as a holding company for new forms of Government commercial and industrial enterprise was announced in 1966. Armed with massive sums of capital it will have almost unlimited powers to buy up privately-owned enterprises, found new ones, and create the circumstances for big mergers between existing industrial institutions. This forms a dramatic new method of taking over—short of public ownership—firms which are falling down on their task, coupled with plans for new incentives to industry and special incentives to regions. The Government will thus be able to step into a lagging section of the economy. As a trial run for this new plan the Government set up a Government-cum-private agency for the Fairfield ship-yard. This new strategy was described as tycoonery for the benefit of the nation instead of private profit. All this will require high economic intelligence and superlative direction.

Unofficial Strikes: Their Incidence.—While we have cause to deplore these strikes and to ponder how, in everyone's interest, they can be reduced and avoided, we need to keep some better perspective than we are led to do. If we look at the figures published in 1965 by the U.N. International Labour Organisation showing the number of days lost through strikes over the previous 10 years in 18 leading industrial countries we find that Britain comes well down the list. It is twelfth—with an average of 294 days lost per 1,000 workers per year. France averaged 336 and Japan 391, both energetic and dynamic countries. Canada lost an average of 597 days and Italy which went through what was termed an Economic Miracle lost 875. America retained leadership in this, as in some other matters, since every 1,000 workers were out on an average for 1,044 days a year.

The Government and Unofficial Strikes.—In 1965 the Government firmly scotched a general idea that unofficial strikes could be made illegal. This childish notion was dissolved by the common sense view that you could not put a large number of people in prison and it would certainly not improve industrial relations if you could. Nor could you make unions pay large fines or damages if their members take part in official strikes. A proposal for weakening trade unions would be unacceptable in principle and self-defeating in practice (since unions would be tempted to call official many strikes which remain unofficial). The Government thus cleared away extremism in the preface of the advice which it submitted to the Royal Commission on Trade Unions and Employers' Associations in 1965. The Government put forward for consideration a modified view. If, it said, it is desirable in the national interest that pressure should be exerted on trade unions to give more attention to the activities of shop stewards and other subordinate bodies then the union concerned might be made subject to defined penalties, according to the time an unofficial strike lasted, unless it could show some independent tribunal that it had taken all steps open to it to prevent the strike or bring it to an end as soon as possible.

Causes of Unofficial Strikes.—Ministry of Labour figures showed that 90–95 per cent of all strikes are unofficial (not called or recognised by the unions) and that fewer than half of them are brought about by wage disputes. They are about dismissals, working conditions, demarcation disputes, and so on. Sir James Dunnett, permanent secretary to the Ministry, in his evidence to the Royal Commission, thought that the number of these strikes might be considerably reduced if the standard of personnel management in the best firms was general. Management, as well as employees, could provoke strikes; and management action over a long period could, said the Ministry, help to build up the power of unofficial leaders and weaken that of full-time trade union officials. Measures might be needed to clarify and formalise the position and duties of shop stewards within the union organisation. Some feel that there should be better negotiating machinery in the factory, with perhaps shop stewards from the various unions making up the workers' side. Another step might be for at least the more important unions involved to be represented in plant negotiations by full-time officials.

Shop Stewards have become more powerful and independent of trade union head offices in the last two decades or so. In the view of Mr. H. A. Clegg, Fellow of Nuffield College and a specialist, the main responsibility for this lies with the employers. Many firms are willing, when there is full employment, to pay above the rate; and they negotiate with shop stewards on piece rates, or bonuses. Thus stewards gain control, and their influence is spreading. The Trades Union Congress is introducing training schemes for shop stewards which should promote co-ordination between headquarters and local officials.

A New Right to Work.—There was new recognition that men have a right to work and are entitled to compensation for loss of employment which is not their fault. This principle of social justice hitherto accepted at managerial level was given statutory sanction by the Redundancy Payments Act, 1965. Apart from justice the effect of the Act will be of practical advantage. The idea of mobility of labour which became increasingly important was given concrete meaning. Pulling up roots, surrendering a house, changing children's schools, the wife losing her job—some of these factors are taken account of in the new Act, linked with programmes of retraining, longer notices, and later on perhaps unemployment benefits related to wages.

REGIONAL PLANNING AND ORGANISATION.

Planning for London and the Regions.—The Wilson Government announced its intention of establishing two planning bodies in each region of the country. One body would be an Advisory Planning Council representing both sides of industry, the local authorities, the universities and the business community. The other body a Regional Planning Board representing all Government Departments concerned with economic and social planning. The councils will have no executive authority but will be expected to advise the boards, where the decisions would be made; in their work the boards would co-operate with local authorities.

The Regions and Industry.—A new programme of Government-financed factories was introduced to stimulate industrial development in the under-employed districts. This was to correct the acute geographical anomaly whereby there was congestion and land shortage at one end of the island and waste and unemployment at the other.

What is a Region?—This proved a tricky question. There was in existence the Treasury Standard Region, a division of England into nine areas, to which some, but by no means all, Government Departments conformed. But these regions had an artificial pattern. The problem was to create a pattern of regions which had a real sense of identity and of community of interest. There are Gas Board regions, hospital regions, transport regions, further education regions, regions covered by circulation of the local weekly paper and so on. It was urged that the city region should be made the basis for regional government since it had already become a significant social entity. Each conurbation and its zone of commuting influence offered a logical unit. Regions needed to be large enough for effective, comprehensive planning yet small enough to create a real human loyalty. To meet these twin criteria the proposal was made for sub-regions with advisory councils in a satellite relationship with the main regions.

The Regions set up in England were:

Northern, North West, Yorkshire and Humberside, East Midlands, West Midlands, South West, East Anglia, Wales, and South East.

What Sort of Regional Man?—What kind of man should preside over a Regional Board? A civil servant or an outsider? An all-rounder or a specialist? If a specialist, what field—town planning, economics, sociology, production engineering? Perhaps the ideal animal does not yet exist but needs to be evolved. The chairman of the Regional Planning Board will be a member of the Ministry of Economic Affairs; but he will also be the final arbiter between the possibly conflicting views of representatives of all the other "economic and social departments."

The National Plan (1965) provided guide lines and information for regional planning. For example, one aspect among those which the regional planning bodies will be considering is how additional manpower can be brought into employment to help reach the economic expansion target. The regional offices will co-ordinate the work of Industrial Liason Officers of whom seventy are planned. Each officer, usually based on a Technical College, is responsible for maintaining contact with local firms, especially smaller firms, to promote the greater use of existing scientific and technical knowledge. The Abstract of Regional Statistics published in 1965 brought together for the first time in one publication the main economic and social statistics for regions.

LOCAL GOVERNMENT

Local Government is concerned with the domestic duties of a community as distinct from

Local Government in England and Wales

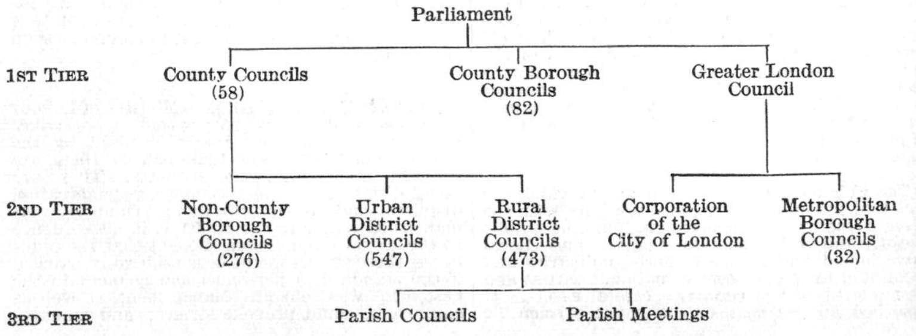

national questions like defence or taxes which must be decided by Central Government. England and Wales (exclusive of London) are divided into Administrative Counties, County Boroughs, Boroughs, Urban Districts, Rural Districts, and Parishes. The structure, as the chart shows, is split vertically: on the one side stand the county boroughs (all local government therein being in the hands of one authority—the county borough council); and on the other the organisation governing the administrative county (where there is a division of function). In Scotland there are County Councils, Burgh Councils, and District Councils; and in Northern Ireland there are County Councils, County Borough Councils, and Borough, Urban, and Rural District Councils.

London Government.—The London Government Act, 1963, involved the abolition of the London County Council and the Middlesex County Council, and parts of Essex, Surrey, Kent, and Hertfordshire have been incorporated in Greater London, which now covers the whole of the continuously developed area within the green belt. The system came fully into effect on 1 April 1965.

The London Boroughs.—There are 32 new London boroughs and the population of each is between 170,000 and 340,000. Broadly speaking the new boroughs are responsible for all the important personal services such as housing, health, and welfare. Each council has a maximum of 60 directly elected councillors, plus aldermen up to one-sixth, making a maximum of 70. The councillors also retire together every three years. The independent position of the City of London remains unchanged and it has the powers of a borough.

The Greater London Council, a directly elected body, carries out functions which need to be planned and administered over Greater London as a whole and consists of 100 councillors and up to 16 aldermen. The new councils came into existence as local authorities when they were elected in May 1964; and from that date until 1 April 1965 the new authorities and the old continued side by side. Thus the new councils took over their full functions in April 1965 when the older authorities ceased to exist.

Elections for the Greater London Council.—At the first election of the GLC, held on 9 April 1964, each borough formed a complete area and returned two, three, or four Greater London councillors. For later elections, however, each borough will be divided into electoral areas, each with a single member. These electoral areas will coincide as far as possible with parliamentary constituencies, which are being reviewed by the Parliamentary Boundary Commission to ensure that they do not span across different boroughs.

The Special Position of Education in Greater London.—The arrangements for education mark an important departure from the Government's original plan. Whereas outside the LCC area education will be a borough function, education inside the LCC area is the responsibility of a special committee of the Greater London Council. The Greater London Council as such is not the responsible education authority. Instead those members elected from the central area alone form the Inner London Education Authority and from this an Inner London Education Committee has been set up in the normal way. The ILEA decides how much money is needed for education and calls for it from the Inner London boroughs. The ILEA consists of the GLC members for the Inner London area but also one representative appointed by each Inner London borough and representatives of teachers and churches are co-opted in the usual way. Children have freedom of choice of schools not only within the Inner London area but in the Greater London area as a whole. Boundary divisions do not prevent a pupil or student from being admitted to a school or college in another area. The Government decided, in 1965, to make these temporary arrangements permanent.

The Powers of Boroughs.—Each borough is a housing authority although the Greater London Authority is the "overspill" authority. Local development plans are drawn up by the boroughs (within the framework of the overall development plan of the GLC) and the boroughs are responsible for dealing with applications for planning permission. They are wholly responsible for a wide range of personal health services and welfare services for the elderly, the sick and the handicapped, and children's services. The GLC will complete the LCC housing programme and, for the time being, inherits the LCC stock of houses (about 200,000) and will eventually transfer them to the boroughs.

Highways and Traffic.—The GLC is the traffic authority for the whole of Greater London. Thus "metropolitan roads" come under the GLC and the new boroughs take the remaining roads except trunk roads which the Ministry of Transport continues to look after.

Other Functions.—The GLC is responsible for fire and ambulance services, for refuse disposal and main sewerage. It is responsible initially for LCC Parks and open spaces and places like the Royal Festival Hall, the Crystal Palace, the LCC museums, and Kenwood House. An intelligence department was also proposed for the GLC charged with the duty of study and research into the many problems of Greater London.

The Local Government Act 1958 included the following provisions in regard to local government in England and Wales:—

1. Replacement by a general grant of a number of separate grants made for specific services. The largest to be absorbed are those for education, health, fire, and child care.
2. Rerating of industry from 25 per cent. of net annual value to 50 per cent.
3. Creation of two Commissions, one for England and one for Wales, to review the areas of counties and county boroughs, and to consider claims for extensions and also claims by large non-county boroughs or urban districts that they ought to be county boroughs. (A population of 100,000 will be regarded as establishing a presumption of adequate size.)
4. Selection of five big provincial conurbations (in England) for special review by the Commission.
5. Reviews of districts and parishes, outside these five areas, by county councils.
6. Delegation of certain health, welfare, and education functions by county councils to the larger district councils.

The Commission's Reports.—By the beginning of 1966 the Commission had issued nine final reports —West and East Midlands, the South West, Tyneside, the North East, West Yorkshire, York and North Midlands, Lincolnshire and East Anglia; and they had made draft reports on the North Western General Review area and South East Lancashire and Merseyside Special Review areas.

The End of the Local Government Commission.—It seemed in 1966 that this Commission had decided that there was little point in going on with their work. When Mr. Crossman came to office in 1964 there were hopes of a radical rethinking of Local Government patterns beyond those laid down by the Conservative Government for the Local Government Commission. Mr. Crossman said, however, there was no chance of any sweeping reform for at least ten years. But he condemned present patterns and, in September 1965, went so far as to say that county and borough councils were archaic and that the Local Government Commission could not do the job that needed to be done.

Two New Royal Commissions.—In 1966 the Government decided to be bold and appointed two Royal Commissions to review and to revise Local Government in England and in Scotland respectively. They were expected to take two years to produce a finished plan and not just a set of principles. A third year will be needed to debate legislation so that by 1970 there should be the new structure essential for a modern Britain. The Local Government Commission described above will be disbanded. The evidence which that Commission has gathered, together with the reports of the Maud and Mallaby Committees on the management and staffing of Local Government will provide an abundance of facts. It was expected that a reformed Local Government would reduce the demand for elective Regional Government. But one supreme thing was expected: that the result would be a root-and-branch reform.

LAW AND THE COURTS.

The subject of English law and its sources (comprising Common Law, Case Law, Equity, and Statute Law) is dealt with in the Section **The Law of England.**

The System of English Courts.

I. Criminal Courts.—1. *Courts of Petty Sessions.*—At the bottom of the ladder are the Courts of Petty Sessions, which can try minor offences punishable either by fine or imprisonment, with a maximum of six months' imprisonment for one offence and twelve months for two or more. These courts are presided over by not fewer than two local Magistrates, called Justices of the Peace, whose office is honorary, and who are appointed by the Lord Chancellor on the recommendation of the Lord Lieutenant of the County. Some officials, *e.g.*, Mayors during their term of office, are J.P.s *ex officio.* Most J.P.s are laymen, but all Petty-Sessional Courts are assisted by a trained magistrate's clerk, who is usually a solicitor.

These courts also act as courts of preliminary inquiry to determine whether there is a *prima facie* case (*i.e.*, a case that requires to be answered) against an accused which will require his being "indicted" for trial by jury. This they do by taking depositions from witnesses. If they decide that there is no *prima facie* case, the accused is discharged; if that there is such a case, he is committed for trial either to the Quarter Sessions or the Assizes. In many of the bigger towns a barrister known as a "Stipendiary Magistrate" is appointed to act as sole and permanent magistrate, and in London there are a number of such magistrates known as Metropolitan Police Magistrates.

2. *Quarter Sessions.*—These courts have a wide jurisdiction, but cannot try the most serious crimes, *e.g.*, murder, treason, or bigamy. Trial is by jury. The courts are of two kinds. Those which sit for the county are presided over by magistrates for the county; those for boroughs by experienced barristers known as "Recorders." Courts of Quarter Sessions also hear appeals from Petty Sessions.

3. *Courts of Assize.*—England and Wales are divided into a number of circuits of very ancient origin, each comprising a number of Assize towns. One or more judges of the High Court go on each circuit at least three times a year. Their criminal jurisdiction is unlimited, and they also deal with such civil cases as can be conveniently dealt with locally rather than at the High Court of Justice in London. A great many divorce cases are thus disposed of.

The Central Criminal Court, or Old Bailey, as it is popularly known, is the seat of the Assizes for the City and County of London and certain parts of the home counties. Because of the immense population of this area, the Sessions are held once a month, and four courts are held at a time.

4. *The Court of Criminal Appeal.*—This court is situated in the Royal Courts of Justice Building in London and usually consists of two judges of the Queen's Bench and the Lord Chief Justice. Appeals from Quarter Sessions and the Assizes lie to this court, which has powers to quash, reduce, or augment sentences on appeal.

5. *House of Lords.*—An appeal from the Court of Criminal Appeal lies to the House of Lords with the permission of the Court or of the House of Lords itself.

The constitution of the House of Lords as a judicial body is discussed on another page.

II. The Civil Courts.—1. *The County Court.*—There are about 500 County Courts in England and Wales which are grouped into circuits (not the same as the Assize Circuits). A County Court Judge visits each court at least once a month. Broadly speaking, his function is to try civil actions when the amount involved is not over £200, or in some cases £500.

2. *High Court of Justice.*—The High Court of Justice is one of the two branches of the Supreme Court of Judicature, the other being the Court of Appeal, described below. The High Court deals with all civil cases, except those dealt with by the County Courts or by the civil side of the Assizes. Since 1873 it has been divided into three divisions:—

(1) the Queen's Bench Division, which is principally concerned with common-law suits;

(2) the Chancery Division, concerned with equitable matters; and

(3) the Probate, Divorce, and Admiralty Division, whose title is self explanatory.

3. *The Court of Appeal.*—Appeal lies as of right from decisions of the County Court and from the High Court of Justice to this court. Appeals are heard by courts consisting of three appeal judges, at the head of whom is the Master of the Rolls. The court can dismiss an appeal, allow it or make a fresh order as to damages or costs, or order a new trial.

4. *The House of Lords.*—Appeal lies from the Court of Appeal to the House of Lords, with the permission of the Court or of the House of Lords. Only the "Law Lords" (or "Lords of Appeal in Ordinary"), who are eminent lawyers and life peers, and certain other high judicial appointees assist when the House of Lords is constituted as a judicial body to hear either civil or criminal appeals. They are presided over by the Lord Chancellor, who is the head of the English Judiciary. While other judges are appointed for life, his appointment is a political one, and he retains office only during the tenure of power of his party. He is, of course, always an eminent lawyer.

Judicial Committee of the Privy Council.—This is a committee of lawyers, drawn from the Privy Councillors, who hear appeals from decisions of colonial and ecclesiastical courts.

Juvenile Courts.—This is a special kind of Magistrates' Court to deal with accused persons under the age of seventeen. The magistrates chosen are specially qualified for the work, and where possible a woman is appointed as one of the three Magistrates who constitute the Court. The Court is held in private away from the ordinary court room. The object of the Juvenile Court is to introduce into the trial a plan to reform the offender by providing for the care and protection which he may need, by removal from undesirable surroundings, and by subsequent education or training. In these objectives the Court has the co-operation of social workers, including Probation Officers.

Probation Officers are attached to particular Courts, sometimes a Magistrates' or a higher court. Sometimes an offender is not sentenced to punishment, but is released "on probation," that is on the condition that he behaves well and follows directions given by the Court or by a probation officer. Such an officer is a trained man (or woman) who advises, assists, and befriends people who have been committed to his care by a court of law. The probation officer, by his assessment of the social background of the offender, can advise the court upon the wisdom of putting the offender on probation. The probation officer by his understanding can so befriend an offender as to provide a basis for his rehabilitation. He undertakes the "after care" of those released from prison or Borstal or approved schools, to which juveniles are sent.

The Welfare of the Young Offender.—Radical changes in methods of preventing and treating juvenile delinquency were proposed in a Government White Paper in August 1965 called *The Child, the Family, and the Young Offender*. These proposals emphasised the necessity of strengthening social services to the family.

The Government proposed to set up an independent committee to consider the changes necessary to mould the local authority personal services into an effective family service. This preventive work, apart from its positive social value, will expose situations which might give rise to delinquency. A high proportion of adult criminals have been juvenile delinquents; and the prospect of successful treatment is greatest with young offenders. Therefore young offenders would, in future, be divided into two categories—those under 16 and those in 16–21 age group. Those under 16 will be removed, as far as possible, from jurisdiction of courts. Thus children will be spared the stigma of criminality; and a better means will be provided for directing social inquiries, discussing treatment with parents and social workers, persuading parents to assume more personal responsibility, and to allow more flexibility in developing treatment according to the child's response. The under-16's will be dealt with by Family Councils and Family Courts. Thus there would be no Juvenile Courts as hitherto known. *See* **D36**(2).

Some Views on the Proposals.—It will be seen that deterrence in the form of fear of punishment has little part in the scheme. But prevention is aimed at both by training and by investigation of causes. This investigation offers scope for research into the root causes of crime. The proposals were broadly welcomed. But the National Association of Probation Officers, in commending much of the scheme regretted the abandonment of the existing juvenile court. They did not believe that the plan met the requirement, adumbrated by Lord Devlin, that every question affecting the liberty of the individual was one for a judicial body. The Association felt that social workers who would take part in councils' decisions and, in many cases, be charged with carrying them, would be in an "intolerable position". The Magistrates' Association in their evidence to the Royal Commission on Penal Reform had recommended that juvenile courts should be retained; the judiciary, they declared, should remain independent of the social and welfare services.

Legal Aid and Advice.—If you need help in problems, disputes, or Court cases you should know about legal aid and advice. The help of a lawyer of your own choice is within your means. You can get legal advice on questions of English law from a solicitor, whatever your means, for £1 and if your means are small such advice may be had free or for 2*s.* 6*d.* You can get legal aid, if your means are small, to make or defend a claim where there is not yet any question of taking or defending proceedings in a Court. You can also get legal aid for most Court cases in Courts of England and Wales, whatever your nationality if your means are moderate (in certain circumstances a person with an income as high as £30 a week may qualify), either free or for a contribution which you can afford. There are pamphlets *How you can get legal advice* and *Legal Aid and Advice* which can be obtained from one of the Legal Aid Local Offices or Local Committees (of which there are 110) and their addresses can be ascertained from Citizens' Advice Bureaux, Court Offices, local government offices, or the telephone directory. The No. 1 (London) Legal Aid Area Office is 29–37 Red Lion Street, London, W.C.1. The principal address in Scotland is Legal Aid Central Committee, Law Society of Scotland, 34 York Place, Edinburgh 1.

THE BRITISH COMMONWEALTH.

The Commonwealth is a free association of sovereign independent States—the United Kingdom, Canada, Australia, New Zealand, Ceylon, Malaysia, Sierra Leone, Jamaica, Trinidad and Tobago, Uganda, Malta, Gambia, Guyana, and the Republics of India, Pakistan, Ghana, Cyprus, Nigeria, Kenya, Zambia, Tanzania, Malawi, Singapore, and Botswana. So vast and complex an association has not been easy to define with precision. For a long time the term "British Empire" was used, and the self-governing countries (other than the United Kingdom) were called "Dominions." These terms have now given place to "Commonwealth" or "Commonwealth of Nations" and "Members of the Commonwealth." The last term describes the sovereign countries named in the opening of this paragraph. (*See also* **K189**.) Other parts of the Commonwealth, such as Colonies, while they may be described as "Commonwealth countries" are not *Members* of the Commonwealth.

The Nature of the Commonwealth.—The Commonwealth is not a federation, for there is no central government, defence force, or judiciary, and there are no rigid obligations or commitments between them. Nor is it a contractual association as the United Nations is. Like the United Kingdom itself the Commonwealth of Nations has no written constitution. But all its members have a broad community of interests, and they are bound together by a common sense of ideals and by a common interest in the maintenance of peace, freedom, and security. Although the Commonwealth includes about a quarter of the total population of the world about three-quarters of the Commonwealth's people live in India. The white population of the Commonwealth is only a small fraction of the whole. The diversity is further illustrated in religion, for the Commonwealth includes over 200 million Hindus, 100 million Moslems, and 80 million Christians. The same variety appears in climate and natural resources. But in spite of diversities of race, religion, language, and tradition, members share a common political heritage which has given rise to a broadly common pattern of institutions.

The Sovereign and the Commonwealth.—The Queen's legislative power in the parliaments of the Commonwealth is a formality—she reigns, though she does not rule; but she provides the element of continuity in the administration. The Queen is, therefore, Queen of the United Kingdom, Canada, Australia, New Zealand, Ceylon, Jamaica, Trinidad and Tobago, Sierra Leone, Malta, Gambia and Guyana, and she is the symbol of their free association in the Commonwealth. Malaysia, Uganda, and the Republics of India, Pakistan, Ghana, Cyprus, Nigeria, Kenya, Zambia, Tanzania, Malawi, Singapore, and Botswana do not owe allegiance to the Queen, but accept her as the symbol of the free association of the member nations of the Commonwealth and as such the Head of the Commonwealth. The Queen has, therefore, in the first group above, a relationship with the individuals comprising each country and also a relationship with the nation as a collective entity. In the case of the Malaysia, Uganda, and the Republics within the Commonwealth she has only the latter relationship.

The Colonies.—As stated in the opening passage of this outline, the United Kingdom, in common with other members of the Commonwealth, has certain dependencies which are described as "The Colonies." But this is a loose term, for "the Colonies" are not really all Colonies in the strict sense. What are loosely spoken of as Colonies are properly divided into Colonies, Protectorates, Protected States, Trust Territories etc.

Definitions.—*Colony.*—A territory belonging by settlement, conquest, or annexation to the British Crown.

Protectorate.—A territory not formally annexed, but in respect of which, by treaty, grant, usage, sufferance, and other lawful means Her Majesty has power and jurisdiction.

Protected State.—A territory under a ruler which enjoys Her Majesty's protection, over whose foreign affairs she exercises control, but in respect of whose internal affairs she does not exercise jurisdiction.

Trust Territory.—A territory administered by the United Kingdom Government under the trusteeship system of the United Nations.

Condominium.—A territory over which responsibility is shared by two administering powers.

Leased Territories.—This term applies only to that part of the mainland of China which was in 1898 leased to Great Britain for ninety-nine years and is administered by the Government of Hong Kong.

Responsibility of the British Government.—The British Government is responsible for the affairs of Colonies (properly called Crown Colonies) both internal and external, and for their defence, and their peoples are British subjects. Protectorates are governed in the same way as Colonies, but have not been annexed. The peoples of Protectorates are not British subjects but British-protected persons.

Tho Countries of the Commonwealth.—At the end of the Gazetteer is a list of all the countries of the Commonwealth showing their land area and recent estimates of population. The list distinguishes between the sovereign members and the British dependent territories, and classifies the latter according to the kind of dependency. Not all the British dependencies come exactly within the definition either of Colony of Protectorate, since, for historical reasons, many come partly under one heading, partly under another.

British Indian Ocean Territory.—The creation of a new British colony was announced in November 1965, comprising the islands of the Chagos archipelago, some 1,200 miles north-east of Mauritius, and Aldabra, Farquhar and Desroches in the western Indian Ocean. It is intended that the islands shall provide certain defence facilities for the British and United States Governments in the Indian Ocean.

The Republic of Zambia.—Northern Rhodesia became the Republic of Zambia in October 1964 on the day celebrated as United Nations Day. By good fortune Dr. Kenneth Kaunda survived the long struggle to independence. The country of 2·5 million Africans and 80,000 whites contains the rich "Copperbelt" which had been the great prize of the Federation of the two Rhodesias and Nyasaland. The economic argument for drawing these three countries together was sound; but this position had not been fortified by a willingness by white Rhodesians to make partnership with the African majority a political reality. Divided among themselves and faced by an intricately weighted franchise, Northern Rhodesia by a miracle at last received its independence. Kaunda has proved an unexpectedly strong as well as wise leader.

Malawi.—The beginnings in Malawi have been less fortunate than in Zambia. The breakup of the Federation has meant a loss of finance to Malawi and within a few weeks some of the most loyal ministers under Dr. Banda were rebelling against his authoritarian methods, the ring-leader being Mr. Henry Chipembere. Up to the beginning of 1966 Dr. Banda had been saved by his personal powers and his prestige as founder of the State. Dr. Banda has declared friendship with Portugal, an attitude which is understandable as Malawi's access to the sea is through Portuguese territory. But this does not endear him to other African countries. Malawi does not have the copper wealth of Zambia and lacks trained African talent. Malawi as a one-party State and presidential regime became a republic within the Commonwealth in July 1966.

Rebellion in Rhodesia.—The dissolution in December 1963 of the Federation of Rhodesia and Nyasaland led to the independence of Northern Rhodesia (as Zambia) and of Nyasaland (as Malawi) and left Southern Rhodesia, renamed Rhodesia, as a self-governing colony. Rhodesia's white, minority Government pressed for complete independence. The Rhodesian Front, under the Prime Ministership of both Mr. Winston Field and Mr. Ian Smith, had insisted that Rhodesia had an immediate right to independence based on (*a*) the fact that it has been self-governing for forty years, and (*b*) that this was morally, if not indeed explicitly but privately, promised by British Ministers when the Rhodesian Federation was broken up. The British Government, both under Conservative and Labour rule, specified only that while Rhodesia should move to independence like any other self-governing dependency, it should be under a constitution broadly acceptable to the people as a whole and should provide for a peaceful transition to majority rule. This principle was elaborated in a statement of five conditions set out in the following paragraph. It was not said by either party that independence could not be granted to Rhodesia until a government elected on a franchise wide enough to be described as a government "of the majority" is actually in power. But that majority rule must be the precondition was asserted by the two Rhodesian African leaders (divided, but both in prison), by the African States, by the United Nations, and by some Commonwealth countries.

Five Conditions for Independence of Rhodesia.—In the protracted negotiations between Mr. Smith and Mr. Wilson to reach a settlement in 1965 the latter took his stand on the following five conditions:—

1. a guarantee of unimpeded progress towards the majority rule already envisaged in the 1961 Constitution;
2. a guarantee of no retrogressive amendments of the 1961 Constitution;
3. an immediate improvement in the political status of the African population;
4. progress towards the elimination of racial discrimination; and
5. the overriding requirement that Britain must be satisfied that any proposed basis for independence would be acceptable to the Rhodesian population as a whole.

The British Government offered to co-operate in a crash programme of education for Africans to fit them to take an effective share in the economic and political life of the country within the span of, possibly, a decade.

The 1961 Constitution, which has been the subject of so much dispute, provided (for the first time) fifteen African members (in a Parliament of sixty-five) elected on a virtually all-African roll. The other fifty are elected on a common roll with residential and property qualifications, which were said to be low enough to enable enough Africans to become the voting majority in due course. But, even if this outcome were to be practicable, this period might be as high as twenty years. The African nationalists have largely boycotted registration on either roll; and the acceptance of the 1961 Constitution is tantamount to the indefinite continuance of minority—i.e. white—government.

Unilateral Declaration of Independence.—The long pressure for independence from 1963 to 1965 reached its climax on 11 November 1965, when

Mr. Ian Smith declared the independence of Rhodesia; and the British Government were confronted by an act of rebellion. (U.D.I. became known as I.D.I., the illegal Declaration). The rebels protested their loyalty to the Sovereign, whose commands, however, they were repudiating. African opinion was outraged, and among the countries which broke off relations with Britain were two Commonwealth countries (Ghana and Tanzania), Mauritania, Guinea, Mali, the Sudan, Algeria, and the Congo (Brazzaville). Britain ruled out, from the start, the use of force; but Mr. Wilson embarked on a policy of graduated economic sanctions, including an oil embargo; the objective being the emergence, under economic hardship, of a liberal alternative to the Smith régime. The United Nations took the view that the 1961 constitution had broken down and that the decrees signed upon I.D.I. amounted to the destruction of all safeguards for the rule of law and for human rights in the 1961 constitution and earlier legislation.

Repercussions of the Rebellion.—On the very day of the illegal declaration in Rhodesia the United Nations General Assembly in a resolution adopted by 107 votes to 2 (Portugal and South Africa), with one abstention (France), condemned the declaration. (France disapproved of the declaration and would not recognise the new government, but did not vote because, in their view, it was technically an internal British matter). Next day the Security Council by ten votes to none (France again abstaining) condemned the declaration. On 20 November the Security Council (again by ten votes to none) called upon the British Government "to quell this rebellion of the racist minority." There are many aspects of the complex position in Rhodesia, and several interpretations can be given. But one central fact must be stated simply: four million Africans remain subordinate to 220,000 whites. The implications of the rebellion go far beyond Rhodesia. It has exacerbated the whole problem of race division in Africa. As such it has aroused strong feelings in black African countries and has strained the Commonwealth (on the multi-racial character of which Britain has set such store). The rebellion exacerbates in particular the threatening confrontation between black African countries and South Africa and Portugal.

The Lagos Commonwealth Conference 1966.—Mr. Wilson agreed to attend a Commonwealth Conference called by Nigeria in January 1966. The Conference was ignored by Ghana and Tanzania, and Australia sent only a diplomatic observer, which was to be regretted in view of her involvement with coloured peoples in Asia. This was an unusual Commonwealth Conference, since the British Prime Minister appeared as a guest, and not as host. The Conference proved to be an imaginative and bold venture. It gave Mr. Wilson the opportunity to reach understanding with African countries, who undertook to study developments with Britain in the succeeding months. Students of constitutional changes will note that the Lagos Conference provided an early baptism of fire for the new Commonwealth secretariat and its secretary Mr. Arnold Smith.

Progress Towards Independence of Other Countries.—It was expected that in the summer of 1966 there would be a Conference on Basutoland at which a time-table towards independence would be agreed. In Swaziland it was expected that a programme towards a period of self-government, a preparatory stage towards independence, would be fixed in the spring of 1966. Mauritius is in a stage of constitutional transition and the Banwell Mauritius Electoral Commission was due to report in 1966 on a new electoral system. Barbados was debating in 1966 the subject of independence.

The Commonwealth Secretariat was established in 1965. This new body will act as a central source of information and preparation, independent of Britain's Commonwealth Relations Office. Thus the Commonwealth will have its own staff with no ties to any single member. There is likely to be, at least experimentally, a form of Commonwealth Assembly—an idea which originated with the British Government. It is to be hoped that meetings will not be confined to London, but that other capitals will be given an opportunity.

Arnold Smith, Canadian diplomatist, was appointed to this new post of Commonwealth Secretary General. He was a Rhodes scholar at Oxford, Canadian Ambassador in Moscow (which took him through the Cuban crisis) and a lecturer in politics and economics. The quality of paramount importance in a Secretary General of a family of 730 million is his ability to get along with people regardless of race. It was said that his indifference to the colour of skin was nothing theoretic—he just did not notice, a colour blindness of attitude. But of course his views on racial equality are strong. Just before becoming Secretary General of the Commonwealth he said: " The division of humanity between the white and other races, which coincides too closely for comfort with the division between the affluent industrialised peoples and the poor underdeveloped peoples, is, I think, the most difficult and potentially dangerous problem in the world." It was Arnold Smith who drafted at the 1964 Commonwealth Conference the Commonwealth Declaration on Racial Equality.

Britain's Special Representative in Africa.—A Special Representative dealing with Britain's relations with Kenya, Tanzania, Malawi, and Zambia was appointed in 1965. He was Mr. Malcolm MacDonald, then British High Commissioner in Kenya. He became a roving ambassador to Commonwealth countries in Eastern and Southern Africa. The British high commissioners in those countries will continue their functions in the four capitals concerned—Nairobi, Dar-es-Salaam, Lilongwe, and Lusaka; and Mr. MacDonald's responsibilities will be to co-ordinate major policy problems in which some or all of these four countries are involved, such as the Tan-Zam railway. Uganda preferred not to enter the co-ordination arrangement for the present.

Africa Scraps the Westminster Model.—The choice of many new African leaders for a one-party state has surprised and depressed many, perhaps most people of this country who have supported Africa's claims to independence. They assumed that our Westminster model of parliamentary government would serve the new Africa. The rejection of the model has come as a shock. During the course of a series of broadcasts in 1965 by Marjorie Perham called " Thinking aloud about Africa " she analysed the reasons for this rejection. The new African leaders, she explains, had no experience of parliamentary forms. Few had even sat in the colonial legislative council and that was hardly a parliament. But what they did know was the party. That was the organisation which formed the spear-head to achieve earlier independence than was planned by their rulers. From the party all political vigour sprang. Thus it is natural that it should be the party which by its momentum will create the drive towards the economic and social revolution which must follow political independence. If, in face of this, we continue to be surprised, let us remind ourselves that it took us centuries to develop our own constitution. The new African nations are only at the threshhold of their growth. African languages, it is said, cannot translate " leader of the Opposition " except as " chief of the enemies."

Upheaval in Africa. The deposition of Dr. Nkrumah in Ghana in February 1966 was the climax of a series of upheavals in Africa. In 1964 there were Army mutinies in Kenya, Uganda and Tanganyika followed by seven examples of military coups deposing Governments or leaders—in 1965, Algeria, Burundi, Congo and Dahomey, and in 1966 in the Central African Republic, Voltaic Republic and Nigeria. Add Rhodesia's illegal action and Dr. Obote's assumption of full power in Uganda and the full picture is a disturbing one of change, with more to come. Certain consequences now seem to follow inevitably from independence and these consequences would have followed even if independence had been slower than it was. (The number of independent states grew from three to 36 in the fifteen years up to 1966). Independence is achieved, as we have explained, by a strong single party which thereafter leads to a one-party State. As the new country grows differences of view naturally grow causing rifts in the single party. Suspicion and plots may grow; but whether the challenge is concealed or open the one-party State has no constitutional means for channelling peaceful change. The army comes in to do what general elections do in democracies. Mr. Colin Legum has pointed out that parliamentary democracy is not a byproduct of freedom from colonial rule. Governments are faced by two tasks on achieving independence—to establish their own authority and to achieve economic growth. Pressures emerge from tribal, regional or other sectional interests and the new Government regards it as paramount to hold the new nation–State together by whatever means are available, sometimes by coercion. Other factors must be added to the picture: poverty, breeding frustration and discontent; the rapid urbanisation which always (as in 19th century Britain) brings unemployment, crime and some break up of family life. These are problems which have occurred before and elsewhere; but coming in Africa's emotional state they are especially dangerous. The coming African revolution will need all the study and patient understanding which can be given to it.

Some New Terms in African Affairs have emerged from Pan Africanism. Perhaps the most used is "neo-colonialism," for example, by Nkrumah who has adopted it as a title of a book. It can mean the practice of granting a sort of independence with the concealed intention of making the liberated country a client-state but dominating it all the same very effectively, although not by political means. The term accuses colonial powers of subjection of African countries in a new form. Another term "balkanisation" has been borrowed from European politics; and it is applied to what is regarded as a deliberate plan to keep Africa divided so as to retain mastery of the whole Continent. It is also applied to the policy of those African countries who secede or maintain rigid independence or decline federation. "African personality" is a term for the "noble things Africa stands for" or "the basis and foundation of our humanism." "Non-alignment" is the freedom to decide each international issue on its merits without always following either West or East. "Democracy" takes many different concrete forms in Africa, as we should expect in countries of newly gained independence. Sometimes the belief is maintained in an organised opposition; sometimes only one party is allowed to exist; in others opposition parties have limited rights. An analysis of the application of modern political ideas in Africa is made by Colin Legum with a wealth of evidence in an article reprinted in a collection of papers on *The Study of Africa*, edited with notes and commentaries by Peter J. M. McEwan and Robert B. Sutcliffe, published by Methuen. The volume is strongly commended to the reader.

Immigration from the Commonwealth: the Government White Paper.—The Government's policy was set out in a White Paper (Command 2730) issued in August 1965. The Paper was published after a fact finding mission headed by Earl Mountbatten had reported, confidentially, to the Prime Minister upon return from eight Commonwealth countries. The principal features of the Government's policy were:

(1) A drastic reduction to 8,500 a year in the number of Commonwealth immigrants allowed to enter Britain (compared with the existing figure of about 20,800 a year). Of the 8,500 work vouchers to be issued annually, 1,000 would be allocated to Malta under a special arrangement for two years.

(2) New controls on entry of dependants (except wives and children).

(3) Powers to repatriate Commonwealth immigrants entering the country illegally.

(4) An obligation on immigrants to produce health certificates before admission and additional health checks on entry.

(5) A determined attack on housing shortage to prevent immigrant overcrowding, exploitation, and multi-occupation of dwellings.

(6) Measures to integrate immigrants into British life to eliminate possibility of a grade of second-class citizens.

(7) Formation of a National Committee for Commonwealth Immigrants which would take over the functions of the Advisory Council established in 1962.

It was announced that a committee, the Wilson Committee, would review the whole system of discretionary control over aliens and Commonwealth citizens alike.

Criticism of the White Paper came from the Liberals, a group of Labour M.P.s and the group of Young Conservatives known as the Bow Group. The Bow Group in the findings of its study group on immigration referred to the hardening of public attitudes and that both parties had "conducted a Dutch auction on degrees of control in a quest for electoral advantage." In 1964, they said, 42,584 alien workers were admitted to this country and, in addition, the net increase in the number of Irish residents in Great Britain was an estimated 30,000. "When these two figures are compared with those for Commonwealth immigrants it becomes clear that the colour problem, rather than a desire to limit total immigration is behind the pressure for control. . . . And if our position is to mean anything at all, we must not accept the suggestion that we have been permanently defeated by the problems of our own multi-racial society." As regards the Government's complaint of evasion by immigrants, it was replied that it was practised mainly by Australians, Canadians, and New Zealanders. The critics further complained of the proposal to give the Home Secretary power to deport any Commonwealth immigrant who has been in the country for less than six months "if he considers the public interest to require it."

The Race Relations Act, 1965.—The Government's original intention was to make racial discrimination a criminal offence. But this intention was dropped in favour of a system of local conciliatory committees which would inquire into complaints of racial discrimination and try to settle difficulties without recourse to Court procedures. Prior to the passing of the Act the Home Secretary announced that a three-man Race Relations Board would be at the centre of the new conciliatory machinery.

Earlier Stages in Immigration.—Until 1962 every Commonwealth citizen was free to enter the United Kingdom at will. It was only in the decade from 1952 onwards that a substantial number of people from the Commonwealth began to think of settling in Britain. A rough count began to be kept from 1955 of the net intake. In 1955 the net intake was some 43,000 and remained fairly steady at that level for three years. After dropping to about 30,000 in 1958 and again to under 22,000 in 1959 the number rose sharply to nearly 58,000 in 1960 and shot up to nearly 136,000 in 1961. In the first half of 1962 entry was running at the rate of some 180,000 a year.

An unusually interesting book about Immigrants in Britain written with humanity and humour is *Back Street New Worlds*, by Elspeth Huxley (Chatto and Windus).

Racial Prejudice.—A Government spokesman urged universities "to find out what make people react in the way they do to people with a different colour of the skin "—not research which would lead to a multi-thesis after a good many years but something related to the problems existing now. This seemed a strange request, and it was coupled with the defence of their policy that the Government had to face the fact of racial prejudice on a substantial scale, although they did not like it.

THE UNITED NATIONS.

Charter of the United Nations.—The Charter of the United Nations was signed on June 26, 1945. The purposes of the United Nations can be divided into four groups (security, justice, welfare, and human rights) and the nations undertook to carry out four main duties (to settle disputes peacefully, to refrain from treating or using force, to assist in carrying out the Charter, and not to assist an aggressor). The UN affirms faith in the human rights of all without distinction of race, language, sex, or religion.

Membership of the United Nations.—The UN had one hundred and seventeen member countries in 1966. They were:

Afghanistan
Albania
Algeria
Argentina
Australia
Austria
Belgium
Bolivia
Brazil
Bulgaria
Burma
Burundi
Byelorussian S.S.R.
Cambodia
Cameroun
Canada
Central African Republic
Ceylon
Chad
Chile
China (Taiwan)
Colombia
Congo (cap. Brazzaville)
Congo (cap. Leopoldville)
Costa Rica
Cuba
Cyprus
Czechoslovakia
Dahomey
Denmark
Dominican Republic
Ecuador
El Salvador
Ethiopia
Finland
France
Gabon
Gambia
Ghana
Greece
Guatemala
Guinea
Haiti
Honduras
Hungary
Iceland
India
Iran
Iraq
Ireland
Israel
Italy
Ivory Coast
Jamaica
Japan
Jordan
Kenya
Kuwait
Laos
Lebanon
Liberia
Libya
Luxembourg
Malagasy Republic
Malta
Malawi
Malaysia
Maldive Islands
Mali
Mauritania
Mexico
Mongolia
Morocco
Nepal
Netherlands
New Zealand
Nicaragua
Niger
Nigeria
Norway
Pakistan
Panama
Paraguay
Peru
Philippines
Poland
Portugal
Roumania
Rwanda
Saudi Arabia
Senegal
Sierra Leone
Singapore
Somalia
South Africa
Spain
Sudan
Sweden
Syria
Tanzania
Thailand
Togo
Trinidad and Tobago
Tunisia
Turkey
Uganda
Ukrainian S.S.R.
United Arab Republic
U.S.S.R.
United Kingdom
United States
Uruguay
Venezuela
Voltaic Republic
Yemen
Yugoslavia
Zambia

Indonesia withdrew from UNO on 21 January 1965.

Major Organs of the United Nations.—The UN have six major organs: (1) a General Assembly, (2) a Security Council, (3) an Economic and Social Council, (4) a Trusteeship Council, (5) an International Court of Justice, and (6) a Secretariat. It is especially the inclusion of the third body on this list (with all the Commissions and specialised agencies which stem from it) which makes the UN more broad and balanced than the League of Nations.

Principal Organs of the United Nations.

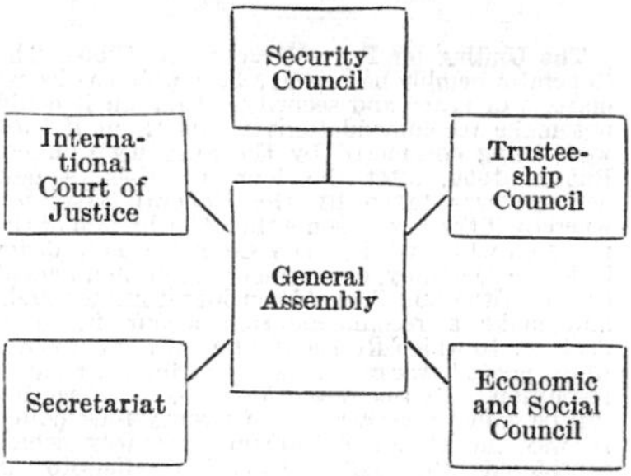

General Assembly.—The General Assembly occupies a central position in the structure of the UN. But its business is quite distinct from the Security Council. It meets once a year. The Assembly can consider the general principles of co-operation for peace and security and disarmament and regulation of armaments. It can discuss any question concerning peace and security brought before it. It makes recommendations, but any question upon which action is necessary must be referred to the Security Council. The carrying out of its humanitarian work is the function of the new Economic and Social Council (dealt with below) which it elects and supervises. Further, the Assembly controls the purse

The Security Council.—The aims of the UN are wide—from feeding starving peoples to encouraging self-government in backward areas —but it cannot advance towards the noble objectives set out in the Preambles unless peace is maintained. The principal organ to preserve peace and security is the Security Council. The size of the Security Council was enlarged from 11 to 15 with effect from January 1966. Five seats are permanently occupied by Great Britain, the U.S.A., the U.S.S.R., China, and France. The China which is represented in the UN and on the Security Council is not, however, the Republic of China (or Communist China). It is the régime of Chiang-kai-Shek, who occupies Formosa. The other seats are normally elected for two years by the General Assembly. The ten temporary members are Argentina, Bulgaria, Japan, Mali, Nigeria (these five until the end of 1966), and Jordan, Netherlands, New Zealand, Uganda, and Uruguay. The Security Council sits continuously. It has two functions: (1) to promote the peaceful settlement of disputes and (2) to stop aggression. Under the Charter, parties to a dispute have already promised not to use force, to settle their quarrels peaceably, and to refer their dispute to the Security Council if they really cannot reach a peaceful settlement. On its side the Council can call on the parties to settle disputes peacefully, it can investigate any situation likely to cause a breach of the peace, and at any stage it can recommend a solution.

The Veto.—At this point we must deal with the veto, which applies to substantive questions. The number of affirmative votes required for adopting decisions on substantive matters is 9, including the votes of the five permanent members. In other words if any one of the permanent members says "No" to the use of force, even after a full investigation, the Council cannot use force to settle the dispute. Thus when it comes to imposing sanctions for a breach of the peace the assent is required of the Great Powers, and one of them may of course be a party to the dispute. If the Great Powers imposed sanctions on each other it would mean a major war in which the present UN would disappear. Partly in order to overcome the difficulty of the veto the Assembly set up a Committee to remain in permanent session consisting of one representative of each member. It is known as the Little Assembly, its formal title being the Interim Committee.

The Uniting for Peace Resolution, 1950.—The General Assembly had always been able to discuss matters of peace and security, although it could not make recommendations about them if they were being considered by the Security Council. But in 1950, after the Korean crisis, a new decision was taken by the General Assembly whereby if there were some threat or breach of the peace on which the Security Council was in deadlock, the Assembly, on a vote of seven members of the Security Council, could consider it immediately and make a recommendation about it. This decision, to which Russia and four other countries were opposed, was called the "Uniting for Peace" resolution. By this resolution, too, the Assembly can be called together within twenty-four hours. It was the standing Interim Assembly which considered the Israeli–Egyptian dispute in November 1956.

The Economic and Social Council.—The UN pledged themselves to a broad humanitarian policy of which the following are salient points: to promote higher standards of living; full employment; the conditions of economic and social progress; solutions of international economic, social, health, and other related problems; educational co-operation; universal respect for human rights; and the fundamental freedoms for all. The main business of the Economic and Social Council is to carry out this broad policy. The size of the Council was increased from 18 to 27 with effect from January 1966. To tackle these huge problems the Council established a number of important commissions and bodies, the principal being the following:—

Regional Economic Commissions

Economic Commission for Europe (ECE)

Economic Commission for Asia and the Far East (ECAFE)

Economic Commission for Latin America (ECLA)

Economic Commission for Africa (ECA)

Functional Commissions

Disarmament
Statistics
Population
Social
Human Rights
Status of Women
Narcotic Drugs

Special Bodies

UN Children's Fund (UNICEF)

Commissioner for Refugees

Conference on Trade and Development (UNCTAD)

Organisation for Industrial Development

Intergovernment Agencies (previously called Specialised Agencies).—The agencies are organisations established by intergovernmental agreements, and their activities as a rule are co-ordinated by the Economic and Social Council. The list of the thirteen Agencies are given below.

International Atomic Energy Agency (IAEA)

International Labour Organisation (ILO)

Food and Agriculture Organisation (FAO)

UN Educational, Scientific and Cultural Organisation (UNESCO)

World Health Organisation (WHO)

World Bank (Bank)

International Finance Corporation (IFC)

International Monetary Fund (IMF)

International Civil Aviation Organisation (ICAO)

Universal Postal Union (UPU)

International Telecommunication Union (ITU)

World Meteorological Organisation (WMO)

Inter-Governmental Maritime Consultative Committee (IMCO)

General Agreement on Tariffs and Trade (GATT)

Several of these organisations were at work before the UN was set up. One such body is the ILO.

A Peace Force.—In the twenty years since its inception the UN has been called on only four times for military action—in Korea (1950), in Egypt (1956), in the Congo (1960) and in Cyprus (1964). Korea was really an American "containment" action under the covering of the UN. In the other operations, the number of troops ranged from 6,000 to 20,000. Apart from military action, the UN has sent observers or "presences" to various parts of the world, mainly to the Middle and Far East, to facilitate settlement of disputes. Thus to maintain a standby force of 20,000 men, when it might be needed so rarely, would be a waste, apart from problems of bases, control, and equipment. Two ideas about the best kind of peace force hold the field. They are:—

(1) the earmarking of national military units; and
(2) a permanent multiracial force.

The first is a pragmatic method and the second an idealistic concept.

The Dispute over Dues.—Under Article 19 of the Charter the voting rights of any nation more than two years in arrears with its dues can be challenged. When the 19th General Assembly of the United Nations opened on 1 December 1964—and the meeting had been postponed in the hope that the quarrel over dues would be reached in the interval—Russia was two years in debt, not over its general dues, but because of its refusal to pay anything towards the special fund for UN military operations in the Congo and Middle East. France was in a similar position on 1 January 1965. There was, of course, a special political background to the dispute. By the Charter the Security Council is the executive body and it is in that Council that the Great Powers, including Russia, can exercise a veto. But in 1950, at a time when Russia was boycotting the Council, the United Nations were able to take action in Korea; and then, realising that a veto in the council could prevent future peacekeeping operations, the Assembly took upon itself special powers to act where the council had failed. The Russians asserted that this was illegal and refused to contribute to the special fund for the UN forces at Gaza (put there after Suez) or in the Congo (now withdrawn).

The essence of the dispute was not a financial one but a constitutional political one. It involved the whole function and power of the Security Council and the General Assembly and the relative functions of the two. The Russians maintained that all peacekeeping should be controlled by the Security Council where the veto existed. But the rest of the membership of the UN maintained that the General Assembly had the right and duty to intervene where the Security Council had failed to act, whether owing to the veto or otherwise.

A United Nations Success: Technical Assistance.—That the United Nations is something mo than a place of talk is proved by a glance at the fifteen-year history of its programme of Technical Assistance. Those who like figures will enjoy being told that 32,000 expert years have been spent by 13,000 men and women of 90 different nationalities during the fifteen years of help in developing countries. So far 456 million dollars have been contributed and 150 countries and territories have benefited. Asia and the Far East have received 32·6 per cent of the projects, Europe 6·3 per cent, Latin America 24·1 per cent, the Middle East 13·6 per cent, and Africa 20·3 per cent. In the Congo technical assistance continued throughout the disturbances. The object of this aid is to help countries to develop their economic and political independence; and, since this must be a truly co-operative venture, receiving countries must not only invite the experts but actively participate in projects they undertake both with money and with local personnel—even the poorest being encouraged to make a contribution.

Simplification of Aid Programmes.—A major reform was made in 1966 by the simplification of the existing systems of capital and technical aid by the United Nations. The two main channels of aid were fused—the UN Special Fund and the UN Technical Assistance Board to become a single Council for a UN Development Programme.

Unicef receives Nobel Peace Prize.—Of all the United Nations agencies Unicef has most caught public imagination. In the early years of the war the attempt began to make amends to children whose early years had been shattered by war; and during the quarter century since Unicef has been bringing aid to millions all over Africa and Asia. Unicef does not draw directly on United Nations funds but voluntary help from Governments and individuals. There have been two developments of policy:

(1) a change in 1950 from post-war relief work to programmes of help for mothers and children in developing countries; and

(2) from 1960, an emphasis on education and vocational training rather than pure survival projects.

Receiving Governments contribute their share in a fixed ratio; so that the £18,000 Nobel Prize will be worth twice as much.

The Anatomy of the United Nations has undergone ironical changes since its inception. At the outset the Security Council was built as the organ through which the Great Powers would together discharge their collective responsibility as policemen. They were the superior powers. They had the authority and the means to act as the big policemen to keep others in order. But this assumed that the big five permanent members would agree and act in concert. This is just what they did not do. As a result, in 1950, by Anglo-Saxon device, the General Assembly was mobilised to ensure action when action was vetoed in the Security Council. But over the last decade the Assembly has grown both in numbers and in the independence of its views. It is not at all as interested in the conflict with Communism as those assumed who vested it with additional power: it is more interested in colonialism. So those who gave the Assembly this additional strength would like to reverse the position. But here we confront another difficulty. China, one must expect (and hope), will join the Security Council. That will make the unity in that body which is vitally necessary for peacekeeping even more difficult.

Twenty Years of the United Nations.—The aspirations of the founders in 1945 of the United Nations are still far from fulfilled. One of its chief functions was "to take effective collective measures for the prevention and removal of threats to the peace." But when dealing with one or more of the Great Powers the peacekeeping machinery of the United Nations is usually weak and inadequate. The Great Powers have failed to agree about peacekeeping. They and their associated powers provide their own military security without recourse to the world organisation. They remain judges in their own case. The paradox remains that whereas small nations need the UN, most reform of the organisation rests with the Great Powers.

Hands across the Iron Curtain.—Time brings sensational changes and one of them is the new friendliness between Russia and the United States. This was evident at the United Nations 20th Assembly. Hands were stretched across the iron curtain and emphasis given not to disagreements but to topics and areas where interests coincided and co-operation seemed possible. A new phrase "selective co-existence" was coined. Russia stressed the need to stop nuclear dissemination and supported a proposal for a world disarmament conference in mid-1966, implying that China must be present. Russia did not include Vietnam in any form of co-operation with the U.S. Russia supported the U.S. in the call to India and Pakistan for a settlement and, incidentally, Russia by her initiative in inviting those powers to meet her to discuss a settlement made a reassertion of the fact that she is an Asian power. Russia gained considerable prestige as an arbiter in Asian affairs by inducing Pakistan and India to agree not to use force for the settlement of their problems at the conference held at Tashkent in January 1966.

China Near to Admission.—In the 1965 General Assembly the voting on the admission of the Peking Government was a tie—47 to 47 with 20 abstentions. But the Assembly had decided that a two-thirds majority was needed to decide the question (56 votes to 49 with 11 abstentions). The position of Great Britain was a strange one. On the straight motion she voted that Peking should be admitted. But by agreeing with the United States that a two-thirds majority was necessary she in effect voted against the admission. While the principle of refusal is to be regretted we can draw some relief at this particular result, since China might, after all, have declined the invitation, except on conditions which were impossible. China's allegations against the United Nations and her encouragement to Indonesia on her withdrawal did not suggest co-operation. A hostile slamming back of the opening door by China might well have kept it shut tight against her for a long time. A year's interval offered hope of a less embittered situation in 1966. It will need only a few countries to change their minds on the procedural point to accept the view put forward by France that Peking should be admitted by a single majority.

Another World Disarmament Conference?—In spite of all the failure that had gone before the United Nations plunged again in 1965 into a proposal for another world disarmament conference. The Western Powers remained of the belief that nothing could result from a huge conference. Probably Russia thought the same. Most major Powers must feel that Peking must be brought into a small inner circle of negotiators. Many Powers believed that if China could be brought into a world disarmament conference it would be a way back into the United Nations itself. In the event it was decided to reconvene the 18-nation disarmament talks at Geneva in January 1966.

The International Court of Justice and the S.W. Africa Case.—Public hearings in the S.W. Africa cases (Ethiopia *v.* South Africa and Liberia *v.* South Africa) began in March 1965. In their applications, brought separately before the Court so far back as 1960, Ethiopia and Liberia held that S.W. Africa was a mandated Territory and that under the Mandate, South Africa had an obligation to submit to the United Nations reports on the administration of the Territory and petitions received from sources within the Territory. They stated that the South African Government had violated its duties by the practice of apartheid, and suppression of rights and liberties. The years since 1960 have been occupied by hearings of pleadings and objections. South Africa contested the jurisdiction of the Court but the Court decided that it did have jurisdiction to adjudicate on the merits of the dispute—but this decision was reached by the narrow vote of eight to seven.

Will U Thant go?—U Thant's term of office was due to expire in November 1966 that is, after the publication of this edition. So early as 1965 the Russians were using the initiatives taken by U Thant in putting into effect the Indo-Pakistani cease-fire resolution in order to criticise his powers; and they hinted at renewed Soviet pressure for a troika directorate—that is to say, they want not one Secretary-General but three, representing the East, the West, and the others. When they urged this originally before U Thant's election to office, the troika idea was abandoned under pressure in return for an understanding that his cabinet of advisors would reflect the geographical and ideological divisions in UN.

WESTERN INTERNATIONAL ORGANISATIONS.

1. Introduction.

This outline is an attempt to explain the various organisations through which European countries are trying to co-operate. It is hoped that the reader, with the help of the chart will find the pattern less bewildering than at first appears. The destruction in Europe in the Second World War emphasised the need for greater union, both for recovery and for defence. A bewildering array of organisations has sprung up. They differ in form, in function, and in membership. Some overlap in function. Some are much less effective than others. The edifice is not, moreover, built on a single harmonious plan. Beneath the edifice are two different kinds of foundations, that is to say, two rival theories. These two theories (the federalist and the functionalist) are explained as the story unfolds. The story traces three main streams—the military, the political, and economic developments—and describes the bodies which evolved in each stream.

Historic Origin of European Unity.—Sully, the famous Minister of Henry IV, King of France, outlined, in 1638, a proposal for achieving European unity and putting an end to war in Europe. He called it the "Grand Design." It was revived in modern dress by Monsieur Briand, the French Prime Minister, in 1929. During the War (1943) the concept of a United Europe which should be created after victory was won was outlined by Sir Winston Churchill: and he returned to the subject in his famous speech at Zurich University in 1946.

Two Starting Points: ERP and the Brussels Treaty.—There were two main sources of the present numerous European bodies. The first was the European Recovery Programme in 1947 (ERP), and the second was the Brussels Treaty of 1948.

The European Recovery Plan was popularly known as the Marshall Plan, as it was the result of the invitation made in 1947 by Mr. Marshall (then U.S. Secretary of State) to the European countries to draft a programme to put Europe on her feet economically. The U.S.A. was ready to give this aid if the countries concerned would agree on co-operation and plan their needs. In March 1948 the countries concerned created the Organisation for European Economic Co-operation (OEEC) to administer the programme of aid. This body was replaced by the Organisation for European Co-operation and Development in 1961.

The Brussels Treaty, 1948, was the other main source of the West European organisations. In March 1948 Britain, France, and the Benelux countries (Belgium, Holland, and Luxembourg), agreed at Brussels to pursue a common policy on economic, political, and military collaboration, and to promote a better understanding of the principles which form the basis of the common civilisation of Western Europe. It also provided for the creation of a Consultative Council. This Council, when formed, was the Council of Europe, and it is described below, together with an account of all the organisations which stemmed from the Treaty. Italy and the German Federal Republic joined the Brussels Treaty Organisation in May 1955, which then became the Western European Union.

2. Military Organisations.

The Brussels Treaty and the Western Union Defence Organisation.—As we have seen, under the Brussels Treaty, so far back as 1948, the five Western Powers concerned pledged themselves to military collaboration; and in the same year they formed the Western Union Defence Organisation. At that time policy was being framed by a fear of a revival of German aggression. But in time this fear was replaced by distrust of the Soviet Union. There were two developments. In the course of seven years the Western Union Defence Organisation was transformed by the inclusion of the German Federal Republic itself and of Italy into a larger body called the Western European Union. How this change came about is described in the following paragraphs, which tell the story of the creation of the new Federal Republic of Germany, the proposal for a European Defence Community (which did not materialise), and the eventual emergence of Western European Union (in 1955). The second sequel of a military character of the Brussels Treaty was the creation of the North Atlantic Treaty Organisation (NATO). Whereas WEU is a regional organisation, NATO has an even larger range, as its members include Canada and the U.S.A. An account of NATO follows the story, to which we now turn, of the emergence of the new German Republic and its eventual incorporation in WEU.

Government of Germany after the War.—As a result of Germany's unconditional surrender on June 5, 1945, all power in Germany was transferred to the Governments of the four principal Allies. By decisions at Potsdam in 1945 that power was exercised by the Commanders-in-Chief of the U.S.A., the United Kingdom, the Soviet Union, and France, each being responsible in his own zone of occupation. On matters affecting Germany as a whole, the four would be jointly responsible as members of the Control Council. Berlin was divided into four sectors of occupation.

The London Conference 1947 of the four Foreign Ministers concerned failed to agree on a joint German settlement. Unfortunately, the effect was to set in motion political and economic developments which were speedily to make Germany the battleground of the conflict of ideas between Soviet Russia and the Western Powers. The Allied Control Council could no longer function efficiently; and by the end of 1948 four-Power rule had virtually collapsed and the partition of Germany was complete. A federal Parliament and Government were formed in Western Germany. The Soviet zone prepared a rival form of Government for East Germany.

Western Germany's New Status.—In May 1952 the German problem acquired a new complexion, when the so-called "Contractual Agreements" were signed by the three Allied Powers and Western Germany at Bonn. These Agreements did not form a Peace Treaty, but they attempted to define how W. Germany and the three Allied Governments should work together. Sovereignty was to be restored to Germany and she was to enter a military alliance with France. Indeed, a Treaty called the European Defence Treaty was drawn up between the four Powers, with Italy and the Benelux countries, which was to fit German Armed Forces into a Western European system. But this system, called the European Defence Community, never came to fruition as such, owing to the refusal of France to ratify the Treaty in 1954.

Collapse of EDC.—With the collapse of EDC there was a halt to the idea of a Political Community designed to embrace both the proposed EDC and the existing European Coal and Steel Community. It was logical that these two Communities formed by the same countries should not have separate institutions but should take their place within a single political community.

The London Nine Power Conference and the Paris Agreements, 1954.—Nine Powers met in London to devise a substitute for EDC. They were Belgium, Canada, France the German Federal Republic, Italy, Luxembourg, Netherlands, United Kingdom, and the U.S.A. The Conference considered how to assure full association of the German Federal Republic with the West and the German defence contribution. All the decisions which were reached formed part of one general settlement and these were embodied in agreements signed shortly afterwards in Paris. These decisions included the following:—

1. The occupation of W. Germany by Great Britain, the U.S.A., and France should end.
2. The German Federal Republic and Italy should join the Brussels Treaty Organisation.
3. The W. German Republic was admitted to the North Atlantic Treaty Organisation (NATO).

Western European Union.—These agreements took effect on May 5, 1955, when the occupation régime in Western Germany ended and the Republic attained full sovereignty and independence. At the same time the Republic became a member of the Western European Union (the expanded Brussels Treaty Organisation), which came into formal being on May 5, 1955, and also of NATO, to which we now turn.

The North Atlantic Treaty, 1949.—The founder members of this Pact (which widened the scope of the Brussels Treaty) were Great Britain, the U.S.A., Canada, France, Holland, Belgium, and Luxembourg. The parties agreed that an armed attack against one or more of them in Europe or North America shall be considered an attack against them all and consequently they agreed that if such an armed attack occurs, each of them, in exercise of the right of individual or collective self-defence recognised by the Charter of the UN, will assist the party so attacked.

Changing Problems in NATO.—How can the North Atlantic Alliance be kept together? As time goes on the problems of cohesion become greater. Circumstances have been against finding a solution. First, for some years there has been no avowed threat from the Soviet Union to Western Europe. In the words of a wit NATO is "six powers in search of an enemy." Of course NATO comprises many more than that; but this brings us to the second great change. At the beginning of NATO there were only two substantial powers in the organisation—Britain and the United States. But now two more members have become substantial powers—France and Germany. So externally the threat has diminished and internally the difficulties of cohesion have increased. The key question has been the control of nuclear weapons. The United States is clearly not going to let control over its destiny leave its own hands. Nor will other powers leave ultimate control of their own destinies to an American President. The problem is not only how to create unity; but the really crucial question is how unity is to be made effective for, and in, a crisis. Mr. Leonard Beaton has urged that what is needed is not a committee outside governments but a committee of governments, or at least the decisive governments, with the power and advice to manage a crisis. He uses the Anglo-American relationship in the Second World War to illustrate his point. In that war Prime Minister and President decided together, the issues being defined by intelligence men working together and the military men working together. In a crisis this would now need to be achieved for at least France and Germany as well; and very more quickly—in hours rather than weeks. The technique of hammering out an agreed course is the technique of the cabinet. A crisis cabinet, urged Mr. Beaton, able to act in the face of a challenge, was surely the only way to achieve unity between substantial powers such as NATO now contains. This involves extension of the apparatus of the existing Anglo American relation.

A Crisis in NATO.—In 1966 it seemed that NATO was facing its gravest crisis since its inception in 1949. De Gaulle demanded that all foreign forces and military establishments in France should pass under French control or be withdrawn. He asked that SHAPE (NATO's military headquarters) and all other integrated headquarters then in France should be removed. In the words of *Punch* he was not only knocking SHAPE out of Europe but knocking Europe out of shape. A clause in the North Atlantic Treaty would permit France to leave NATO in 1969 and it was not certain (early in 1966) whether de Gaulle had decided to take advantage of this clause.

The Position in 1966.—The general reason for de Gaulle's action was that the position in 1966 was fundamentally changed: (1) the threat of Russian aggression in Europe had receded for several reasons, including Russia's preoccupation with China; (2) the United States' guarantee of Europe, so important in 1949, was becoming less credible since, with the development of intercontinental missiles, America was now herself threatened with instantaneous nuclear retaliation against her own territory. It was not alliance with the United States which de Gaulle appeared to be rejecting but he was questioning the further need for integrated command and American domination of the alliance.

3. Political Organisations.

Federal Union.—The development of greater political unity among the European countries may be best introduced by a word about the federalists. The Federal Union had, before the War, urged a federation of Europe as a first step in a progression towards a world federation. The Federalists advocated the surrender of absolute national sovereignty, a part of that sovereignty being vested in a federal authority. This authority, it was urged, should possess a government responsible to peoples and not to the States. It should have a Supreme Court to settle disputes between States which are members of the federation; and have an armed police force to uphold its decisions.

The Hague Congress, 1948.—Several schools of thought were represented at the Congress, one main difference being between the federalists, who want to create a real federation in Europe, and those, like the United Europe Movement, who were not committed to a federation in so far-reaching a sense. The Congress declared that the European nations must transfer some part of their sovereign rights so as to secure common action, and it demanded an early convening of a European Assembly chosen by the Parliaments of the participating nations. But in the event the political reality has not become so radical as the surrender of any sovereign rights to the Council of Europe.

The Creation of a Council of Europe.—In May 1949 the Foreign Ministers of the ten countries consisting of the five Brussels Treaty Powers and Denmark, Eire, Italy, Norway, and Sweden, concluded a formal Agreement called "The Statute of the Council of Europe." It set up a Committee of Ministers and a Consultative Assembly, forming together a Council of Europe. The Council was established twelve months after the Hague Congress, almost to a day. The Committee of Ministers provides for the development of co-operation between governments, while the Consultative Assembly provides a means through which the aspirations of the European peoples may be expressed. The seat of the Council was fixed at Strasbourg.

Council of Europe.—The Council came into existence in August 1949, and the Assembly opened at Strasbourg when M. Spaak was elected President. Mr. Churchill (as he then was) sat as an ordinary member. Procedure is a combination of British and Continental systems, but the design of the chamber follows the Continental pattern, delegates sitting at tables arranged to form a semi-circle. In November 1949 the Council of Ministers agreed to meet the wishes of the Assembly that it would not in practice exercise its right of control to fix the agenda of the Assembly.

The Consultative Assembly.—This, the deliberative organ of the Council, is empowered to debate and make recommendations upon any matter which: (i) is referred to it by the Committee of Ministers with a request for its opinion, or (ii) has been approved by the Committee. The Assembly consists of representatives of each member state appointed by national parliaments. All resolutions of the Assembly require a two-thirds majority of the representatives casting a vote. The Assembly meets annually.

The Responsibility of Members of Assembly.—The Assembly comprises over two hundred individual members of Parliament from fifteen different countries. Although they are entitled to group themselves on any particular issue if they choose, a member is in particular relationship to his country and his party or even to his constituency. There is therefore a position of some confusion and subtlety. Originally the Deputies in the Strasbourg house were seated in alphabetical order of their names: today they sit grouped in political parties.

Relations with National Parliaments.—The attempt made by the Joint Committee between Ministers and the Assembly to act as an organ of co-ordination between the two sides of the Council did not satisfy the Assembly. It therefore set up a Working Party to analyse the relations between the Assembly and national parliaments. This Party tries to see what steps can be taken in each national parliament to secure consideration of recommendations and ratification of Conventions which have been approved at Strasbourg. They have gone so far as to appoint a spokesman for each country.

What Has the Council of Europe Achieved?—The Council plays an important part in law-making. It has itself framed and launched important Conventions like that on Human Rights, and it also frames general principles and gives opinions on texts of laws. On the diplomatic side it prepared the way for a solution of the Saar problem, which had divided France and Germany since the War. It is working on the simplification of frontier formalities, and it is concerned (in common with several other international bodies) with refugees. Among other actions, it has encouraged the growth in reciprocity between countries of their social services, and established a European Court of Human Rights.

4. Economic Organisations.

The Organisation for European Economic Co-operation (OEEC).—We now turn to the third stream, the economic. We have seen that OEEC was created to administer American (Marshall) aid. But it needed also to re-create a sound European economy. The allocation of aid continued until 1952; but the practice of mutual consultation on economic matters continued in order to carry out long-term programmes. Owing to the nature of its original task of distributing Marshall Aid, the U.S.A. and Canada became associate members of the Organisation. In 1961 these two countries formed with members of OEEC the Organisation for Economic Co-operation which replaced OEEC and is described below.

European Coal and Steel Community.—A further economic development came in 1950 with the proposal for the co-ordination of coal and steel production in Germany, Belgium, France, Italy, Luxembourg, and the Netherlands. The organisation of the Community is an example of co-operation on a supra-national basis, since the governing authority is not responsible to the individual governments of member countries but only to the Community. The High Authority has the right to deal directly with the coal and steel enterprises of the Community without passing through national governments. In 1954 Great Britain formed a Standing Council of Association with the High Authority for consultations on coal and steel and for co-ordination where necessary.

The European Economic Community (EEC), or Euromarket.—In 1955 "the Six" (namely the countries in ECSC) decided to drive towards further economic integration. This decision was taken at Messina, and the six are sometimes referred to as the Messina Powers. The EEC was established by a Treaty of Rome in 1957 and is an extension to the whole economic field of the institutional method of co-operation already adopted in the European Coal and Steel Community of the Six. The principal institutions are the Parliamentary Assembly (which is common to EEC, ECSC, and Euratom), a Council of Ministers, and an executive Commission of nine members. The common Parliamentary Assembly is now called the European Parliament. The Community is merging the Six into a single economic unit by harmonising economic, social, and investment policies and establishing a common market in trade.

What is a Common Market?—A common market is a trading area with no internal tariffs (import duties) or quotas (which are quantitative restrictions on imports) and a single external tariff and quota structure. The first tariff reductions inside the Six (10 per cent.) took place on January 1, 1959. By January 1962 there had been cuts totalling 40 per cent. in internal tariffs. During 1960 the Council of the Community resolved to speed up the process of further reductions which, on original intentions, would have taken from twelve to fifteen years, so as to aim at complete liberalisation of internal tariffs by 1966.

A European Free Trade Area.—When the Six were discussing the Common Market the British Government declared (1956) that they would consider joining a free-trade area in Europe. Although she would not join the Common Market scheme itself, she would consider sharing in the stage-by-stage reduction of inter-European tariffs on all non-agricultural goods. They would not attempt (unlike the Six) to standardise their own tariff walls in relation to the world outside the European free-trade area. Such a free-trade area would be independently controlled with permanent co-ordination with EEC. In November 1958 France rejected the British proposals for linking the six European common-market nations with the eleven other OEEC countries in a free-trade area. It appeared to the French impossible to establish a free-trade area between the six treaty powers and the other eleven OEEC countries without a single customs tariff between all of them and the outside world and without measures of harmonisation in the economic and social sphere.

The European Free Trade Association.—Thereupon seven countries outside the area of the Six formed a European Free Trade Association. They were Great Britain, Austria, Denmark, Norway, Portugal, Sweden, and Switzerland, and they agreed upon a plan at Stockholm in November 1959. Inside the free-trade area comprising these seven countries it was contemplated that there would eventually be no internal tariffs or quotas, but member states would retain separate external systems. The Seven, upon the foundation of their Association, immediately offered friendly co-operation to the existing Common Market. But the problem of finding a political link—called by the diplomatists the problem of the three half-crowns (seven and six)—remained a difficult one. *See also* **G11**(1).

Britain's Application for Membership of the Common Market.—In the autumn of 1961 Britain applied for membership of the Common Market. Membership would provide this country with a much improved export opportunity but could lead equally to a sharp intensification of competition in our home market. In terms of population, purchasing power, production and growth, Western Europe is an exceptionally dynamic economy. The negotiations were stopped upon the veto of France in January 1963; and they were adjourned indefinitely. The political aspects of the Common Market are discussed below.

Organisation for Economic Co-operation and Development.—This new body has taken the place of OEEC. Canada and the United States, who were associated members of OEEC, joined with the eighteen members countries of that body to set up OECD. The convention was signed in Paris in December 1960, and the new body came into existence in the autumn of 1961. Thus Canada and the U.S.A. join in facing the broader objectives and the new tasks of today, namely to achieve in Europe the highest sustainable economic growth, employment, and standard of living; to contribute to economic development; and to expand world trade on a multilateral and non-discriminatory basis, in accordance with international obligations. The scope of OECD has been further widened by the accession to membership of Japan.

Economic Commission of Europe.—As explained in the preceding outline of the UN, ECE was the first of the great regional commissions to be set up by UNO. It was created in 1947 to concert action for the economic reconstruction of Europe, and it was hoped to strengthen economic co-operation between all European members of UNO. Russia and some of the Communist Eastern European countries are members of ECE, and it is the only European organisation where the Western bloc and Soviet powers can meet for discussion and action.

5. The Political Aspects of Membership of the Common Market.

The Treaty of Rome, 1958, which had established the European Economic Community defined (in Articles 2 and 3) the principles and objects for which the Community is to work. Those articles

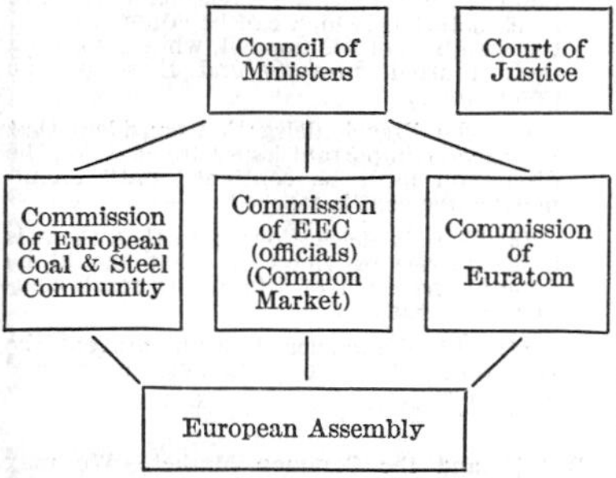

specify in detail the steps for creating a Common Market, for approximating the economic policies of member States, the promotion of harmonious development of economic activities, and raising the standard of living. But the aim of "closer relations between its member States" is stated without elaboration. It is into this gap that speculation is poured. No limit is set in the Treaty to the process of integration; on the other hand there is no commitment to join a Federation of Europe. While member States commit themselves to a common policy on a number of economic issues there will be co-ordination of national policies designed to take account of the needs of the rest of the Community.

Two Kinds of Political Aspects.—We need to distinguish between two things. First, the machinery by which the aims of the Common Market are to be achieved—the Commission, the Council of Ministers, the European Assembly, Court of Justice, and so on. This may be described as the political machinery of the Common Market. Second, we have to think of the kind of political relationship which will grow up, either by deliberate design or practical development, between member countries. We may think of the first set of facts as the engine or locomotive of the Common Market train; and we can regard the second as what sort of journey the train will take —will it take a direct run to federation or follow some other line?

The Organs of EEC.—The machinery of government of the European Economic Community consists of:

1. The Council
2. The Commission
3. The Court
4. The Parliament
5. The Economic and Social Committee; and
6. The Ambassadors of the member Governments.

The meetings of Ambassadors form unofficial permanent liaison between Council and Commission. Let us examine the five official organs.

The Council issues regulations and decisions which are, upon issue, binding in law on all member States. It consists of one member from each member State (normally a Cabinet Minister). They have votes as follows:

France	4 votes
Germany	„
Italy	„
Belgium	2 votes
Holland	„
Luxembourg	1 vote

The Commission.—Whereas the Council consists of politicians the Commission consists of permanent officials. There are nine members appointed by Governments, for a minimum term of four years and not more than two members may come from any one country. Its business is to further the general purposes of the Treaty and decisions are by majority vote. From the Commission flow two streams:—

(*a*) Proposals, which it sends to the Council.

(*b*) Under powers of its own:—

1. Decisions to named countries and binding on them.

2. Directives to named countries to achieve certain results, without specifying the means.

3. Recommendations and Opinions, which are not binding.

4. Authorisations without which many things are forbidden.

The Court, whose procedure is wholly Continental, consists of seven Judges appointed by Governments for a maximum of six years. Its word is final on the interpretation of the Treaty, on the rules made under the Treaty, and on the legality of all the actions of the organs of the Community.

The Parliament or Assembly consists of representatives of the national Parliaments. There are 142 representatives in all—36 from each of the three bigger powers, 14 from the two medium ones, and 6 from Luxembourg. It meets once a year as of right and its only power is to pass (by a two-thirds majority) a vote of censure on the Commission (the permanent officials) which must then resign. If Britain were to join its quota of members to the Assembly would presumably be 36. It is generally held that one day the Assembly will consist of representatives elected by direct universal suffrage but this will not occur until everybody is willing. In the meantime the Assembly can only consist of nominated parliamentarians.

The Working of the Organs: the Commission.—We look first at the Commission (of officials) as this is held to be by far the most powerful of the organs. Broadly speaking, it is the only body with a right of initiative, sending, as we have explained, proposals to the Council which cannot prepare its own proposals for consideration. The Commission can thus prevent the Council considering anything it does not want to be considered. Its proposals to the Council can normally be amended by the Council only by unanimous or qualified majority vote.

The Commission prepares the budget, takes member Governments into Court, runs the agricultural market and is the Monopoly and Restrictive Practices Court.

In addition to all this the Commission has its own powers as we have explained under heading (*b*) in the earlier paragraph about the Commission. By its *decisions* it can give orders to member States over a wide field. For example, it can give orders on the details of applying rules of free competition to nationalised industries or to industries with special rights. Its *directives* order the result to be achieved (for example the framework within which agricultural prices are to be negotiated). It gives (or refuses) *authorisations* over a wide range of subjects, like the postponement of the raising or lowering of a tariff in certain circumstances. The powers of the Commission are thus seen to be extensive and important and they affect, among many other matters, the running of nationalised industries and the uses of Government aid.

The Powers of the Commission contrasted with the Council.—That the Commission (of officials or "Eurocrats" as they have been called) are the real rulers of the Community is more clearly seen when that body is contrasted with the Council (of politicians), quite apart from the range and importance of the powers given to the Commission. The Commission decides by simple majority and can easily reach a decision: but the Council, which requires either unanimity or qualified majority, is often unable to make a decision. The Commission has almost all the right of initiative. It sits for a minimum of four years, while Council members come and go. The Commission meets as often as it wishes, the Council once a month. The Commission thus acquires a real personality but not the Council. It is furthermore the Commission which controls the Community Civil Service.

Is the Commission Democratic?—While Britain's application for membership of the Common Market was pending an important discussion took place in this country on the constitutional nature of the Commission and on the relative powers of Commission and Council. The main points of that discussion are not recapitulated here; but we recall that a most trenchant analysis of the Commission was made by Mr. William Pickles, Senior Lecturer at the London School of Economics and a frequent broadcaster. He described the Commission as a bureaucracy of a kind which it would be impossible to contemplate in this country, for, in his view, it was entirely undemocratic. Lord Gladwyn, the Chairman of the Common Market Campaign, did not think the Commission more important than the Council; but Mr. de la Mahotière in his book, *The Common Market* (Hodder and Stoughton), thought the power of the Commission was growing. Mr. Peter Kirk, then a Conservative M.P., an authority on the subject, thought there was a vital need for criticism of the Commission's work and that the Assembly was unworthy of the name of a Parliament at all. This discussion will, one trusts, revive if Britain reapplies; and then there will be more experience of the machinery to go on.

6. Recent Attitudes in Europe.

Proposed Merger of the Three European Communities.—The Common Market complex seemed to be advancing a further step by a proposal in 1965 for the merging of the executives of the Economic Commission, the Coal and Steel Pool, and Euratom. This meant that in 1966 there would have been a single Commission of 14 members instead of three Commissions of 23 members. It was proposed to house the new combined executive at Brussels which would have become the central point for the developing drama of political union. By July 1967 the Six would have constructed a customs union and the question would be: what kind of political system will be built to control the European Community with a unified executive? France, however, was asking in 1965 for revision or interpretation of the Rome Treaty on two important points: (1) the powers of the Commission; and (2) whether a majority voting system should replace unanimous voting in the Council of Ministers in January 1966 as laid down in the Treaty. On the second point it should be explained that the Treaty provides for a transition from unanimous agreement of the Council to weighted majority to be achieved by stages, the first stage from 1958–61, the second to the end of 1965, and the third stage ending 1970. It was the step due on 1 January 1966 which caused objection by France. France had absented herself for some time from the Council of the Six, causing a serious break between her and the other five member countries.

France and the Five Agree to Disagree.—France, which had withdrawn from the Council of Ministers in July 1965, in violation of the Treaty of Rome, returned at a critical meeting at Luxembourg in January 1966. Neither France nor the Five were prepared for their differences to lead to a total breakdown. The Treaty of Rome's provision for majority voting remained unaltered; but France's insistence on a right of veto was met by the Five agreeing that every effort should be made for a reasonable period to secure unanimity on issues of importance. The Common Market thus survives but continues in a state of nervous tension. Everything turns on de Gaulle's actions and intentions. The four-point face-saving agreement may be summarised as follows:

> (1) When very important issues of one or more partners are at stake the members of the Council will try, within a reasonable time, to reach solutions which can be adopted by all the members of the Council, while respecting their mutual interests and those of the Community.
>
> (3) The French delegation considers that where very important issues are at stake, the discussion must be continued until unanimous agreement is reached.
>
> (3) The six delegations note that there is a divergence of views on what should be done in the event of a failure to reach complete agreement.
>
> (4) This divergence does not prevent the community's work being resumed by normal procedure.

Britain and the Common Market.—We may note the five conditions which had been set out by Mr. Gaitskell to be satisfied before Britain could contemplate joining the Common Market:

> (1) proper safeguards for the Commonwealth;
>
> (2) adequate arrangements for our partners in EFTA;

(3) firm guarantees for British agriculture;

(4) freedom for Britain to pursue an independent foreign policy; and

(5) freedom to carry out national economic planning with effective powers to safeguard Britain's balance of payments.

By 1966 Britain's trade with the Commonwealth had declined and many Commonwealth countries have made other arrangements which lessen their dependence on the British market. It remains true that EFTA countries must come within any final European pattern. Agriculture in Britain remains a difficult factor as indeed French agriculture does within the Market. The fourth item about independent foreign policy is not strong since our policy is necessarily shaped by alliances and the United Nations; and it has been doubted whether our balance of payments position would be weakened if we were part of a strong European Community. But the condition which has not been firmly enunciated and is of paramount importance is that the political arrangements of the Common Market must be democratic in form. Can the commission which has large powers be made answerable to a properly elected European Parliament? Another condition would be that a European union would not jeopardise an Atlantic alliance.

The American alternative to the Common Market.—Is the only real alternative to this country joining the European block to seek closer economic ties with North America? For some time there has been study of an Atlantic free trade area as an alternative or counterpart to the European Common Market. This would comprise the U.S., Britain, Canada, and some parts of Europe and the Commonwealth; and its object would be to reduce trade obstacles with a view to complete free trade and to create a common currency system. The proposal has been given impetus by French opposition to American policies of tariff reductions, to monetary reform and to NATO. But such a scheme would lead to the very difficult point already reached by the Common Market countries. Would the members of the Atlantic free trade area, having created an economic group, be prepared to go forward and face the political integration needed to make common economic aims a success?

Will Britain Join the United States?—The BBC's Washington correspondent, invited to look ten years ahead, gave, as his first prophecy that Britain would become absorbed into the United States—perhaps in the form of half a dozen States of the Union. What are the conditions in which this could be imagined? Let us suppose that there will be no economic miracle in Britain or, at any rate, the progress will be so far less than hoped as to necessitate more financial help from the United States. Suppose too that Britain has not joined the Common Market and that it has not proved possible to rebuild NATO with an effective political and military partnership between all concerned. This will encourage in the States a tendency towards isolationism and this would be strengthened if, owing to increasing rapprochement with Russia the threat from Russia diminishes and she no longer feels the need to take such a major part in European defence. The United States would however be glad to have a foothold on Europe's western shores, and Britain might need to be a part of a larger preferably English speaking community. An increasingly prosperous America, with more and more leisure would demand the kind of cultural goods and services which Britain can supply. Such a union, it is said, might be the only way to modernise Britain and preserve British influence, even increasing it by a kind of British infiltration of the States. Equally a union might extinguish some of the quality of English life, a process which some observers already discern and thus diminish the chances of influencing America. A more realistic issue is in what concrete ways, short of political union, the two countries might effectively co-operate or merge activities. Put in that way the problem is similar to possible solutions to difficulties in other parts of the world. For example, India and Pakistan cannot live apart and cannot live together; but if they could fuse certain activities the link would be beneficial.

MEMBERSHIP OF EUROPEAN AND WESTERN ORGANISATIONS

(M is full membership, AM associate membership)

	Military			Economic			
	NATO.	WEU.	Council of Europe.	OECD.	ECSC. Euratom, and EEC.	EFTA.	ECE.†
Belgium (Benelux)	M	M	M	M	M		M
Netherlands (Benelux)	M	M	M	M	M		M
Luxembourg (Benelux)	M	M	M	M	M		M
Norway (Northern Council)	M		M	M		M	M
Denmark (Northern Council)	M		M	M		M	M
Sweden (Northern Council)			M	M		M	M
Iceland (Northern Council)	M		M	M			M
Greece (Balkan Pact)	M		M	M	AM		M
Turkey (Balkan Pact)	M		M	M	AM		M
Austria			M	M		M	AM
Finland						AM	AM
France	M	M	M	M	M		M
Western Germany	M	M	M	M	M		AM
Ireland			M	M			AM
Italy	M	M	M	M	M		AM
Portugal	M			M		M	AM
Spain				M			
Switzerland			M	M		M	AM
United Kingdom	M	M	M	M	*	M	M
Yugoslavia				AM			M
Canada	M			M			
United States	M			M			M
Cyprus			M				
Japan				M			

Note: All the countries are members of UNO except Western Germany and Switzerland.

† The U.S.S.R. and other Eastern European countries are also members of ECE.
* The United Kingdom is associated with ECSC through a Standing Council of Association.

GROWTH OF WESTERN INTERNATIONAL ORGANISATIONS

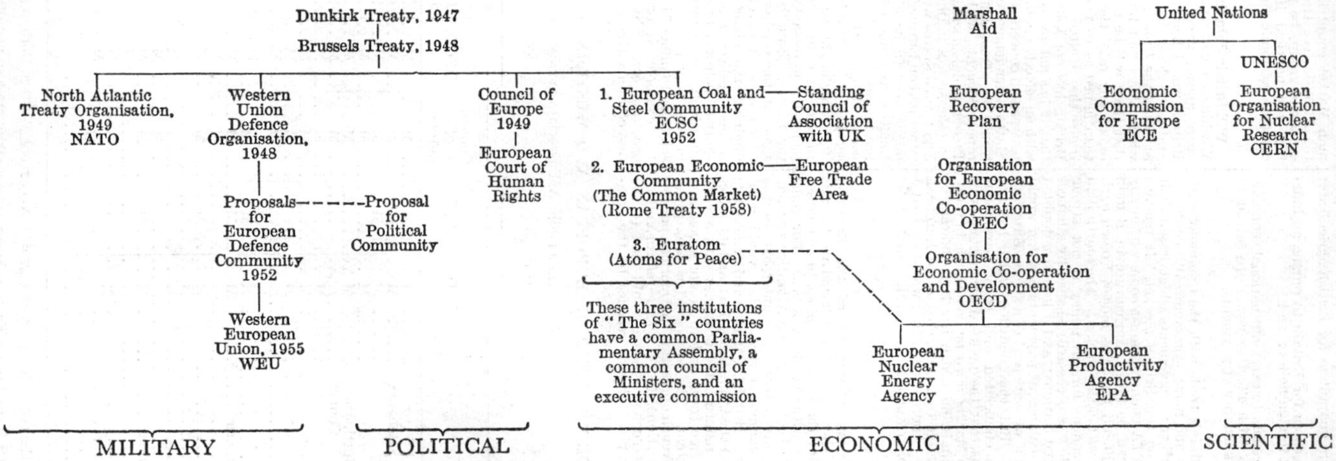

WILSON'S SECOND LABOUR CABINET
(formed April 1966)

Prime Minister and First Lord of the Treasury—Harold Wilson.
First Secretary of State and Minister for Economic Affairs—George Brown.
Lord President of the Council and Leader of the House of Commons—Herbert Bowden.
Lord Chancellor—Lord Gardiner.
Chancellor of the Exchequer—James Callaghan.
Secretary of State for Foreign Affairs—Michael Stewart.
Secretary of State for Defence—Denis Healey.
Secretary of State for Commonwealth Relations—Arthur Bottomley.
Secretary of State for Home Department—Roy Jenkins.
Secretary of State for Scotland—William Ross.
Minister without Portfolio—Douglas Houghton.
President of the Board of Trade—Douglas Jay.
Minister of Overseas Department—Anthony Greenwood.
Secretary of State for Education and Science—Anthony Crosland.
Minister of Housing and Local Government—Richard Crossman.
Lord Privy Seal and Leader of the House of Lords—Lord Longford.
Minister of Labour—Raymond Gunter.
Minister of Technology—Frank Cousins.
Minister of Agriculture, Fisheries, and Food—Frederick Peart.
Minister of Transport—Barbara Castle.
Secretary of State for Wales—Cledwyn Hughes.
Secretary of State for Colonial Affairs—Frank Lee.
Minister of Power—Richard Marsh.

SPEAKER TO THE HOUSE OF COMMONS—Dr. Horace M. King.
LEADER OF THE OPPOSITION—Edward Heath.

The composition of the House of Commons, resulting from the Election of March 1966, was Labour 363, Conservatives 253, Liberal 12, Republican Labour 1, The Speaker 1. Labour thus had a majority of 97 seats.

Changes were made in the Government. Mr. George Brown, while remaining First Secretary and Secretary for Economic Affairs, was given special oversight of Britain's economic relations with Europe. Mr. George Thomson, formerly Minister of State at the Foreign Office, was given charge of Britain's "Foreign Office" relations with Europe. Thus there were two "Ministers for Europe" in the new Government. (Mr. Thomson was appointed Chancellor of the Duchy of Lancaster and is outside the Cabinet.) It was intended that Mr. Brown should normally lead the British delegations to EFTA and other economic bodies in Europe, generally accompanied by Mr. Thomson. Mr. Thomson, under the guidance of the Foreign Secretary, was given the duty of handling all political relations with European countries and not only with the Six countries of the Common Market. Thus he became responsible for Britain's part in the Western European Union and for attending meetings of organisations like EFTA, OECD, and NATO.

To free Mr. Brown for his new task it was decided to transfer various executive functions of the Department of Economic Affairs to other Departments directly interested: the Ministry of Labour took detailed work on incomes and wages policy and the Board of Trade the subject of prices.

A LIST OF SOCIETIES.

On this page are the addresses of some of the societies working in the fields of social service and international affairs. They are only a selection from all the societies working in these and allied spheres.

What the Societies Offer.—Many of the societies offer the facility of a unique specialised library, and most of them issue not only journals and magazines but pamphlets giving the latest authoritative views and discussions of contemporary problems. Besides these facilities the associations offer the individual the opportunity of hearing experts and of discussing the subject with others interested in the same subject. Many societies hold not only lectures but conferences, covering the week-end or several days, and some of them hold Summer Schools.

Social Service.

The National Council of Social Service (26 Bedford Square, London, W.C.1) is the main promotional and co-ordinating organisation of voluntary social work in Great Britain. It publishes *Handbooks on Voluntary and Public Social Services and Directory of Organisations.*

The Annual Charities Register and Digest is a famous reference book prepared by the Family Welfare Association (address below). It is a standard guide to every branch of charitable work, giving details of Adoption Societies, Almshouses, Homes for Incurables, Convalescent Homes of all kinds, and all Welfare Institutions.

Some useful addresses are:—

British Association of Residential Settlements,
 Bishop Creighton House, 378 Lillie Rd., S.W.6.
Central Council for Health Education,
 Tavistock House, Tavistock Square, W.C.1.
Citizen's Advice Bureaux Service,
 26 Bedford Square, W.C.1.
Family Planning Association,
 231 Tottenham Court Rd., W.1.
Family Welfare Association,
 296 Vauxhall Bridge Rd., S.W.1.
Industrial Welfare Society,
 48 Bryanston Square, W.1.
Institute for the Study and Treatment of Delinquency,
 8 Bourdon St., Davies St., W.1.
National Association of Parish Councils,
 26 Bedford Square, W.C.1.
National Association of Boys' Clubs,
 17 Bedford Square, W.C.1.
Scottish Association of Boys' Clubs,
 12 Alva St., Edinburgh, 2.
National Association of Youth Clubs,
 30–2 Devonshire St., W.1.
Scottish Association of Girls' Clubs,
 13 Eglington Crescent, Edinburgh, 12.
National Council of Women,
 36 Lower Sloane St., S.W.1.
National Council of Y.M.C.A.'s,
 112 Great Russell St., W.C.1.
 10 Palmerston Place, Edinburgh, 12.
 22 Howard St., Belfast.
National Federation of Community Associations,
 26 Bedford Square, W.C.1.
National Federation of Women's Institutes,
 39 Eccleston St., S.W.1.
Federation of Women's Institutes of Northern Ireland,
 28 Bedford St., Belfast.
National Federation of Young Farmers' Clubs,
 55 Gower St., W.C.1.
National Marriage Guidance Council,
 58 Queen Anne St., Grosvenor Square, W.1.
National Union of Townswomen's Guilds,
 2 Cromwell Place, S.W.7.
Save the Children Fund,
 29 Queen Anne's Gate, S.W.1.
Scottish Council of Social Service,
 10 Alva St., Edinburgh, 2.
Northern Ireland Council of Social Service,
 28 Bedford St., Belfast.
Tavistock Institute of Human Relations,
 3 Devonshire St., W.1.
Young Women's Christian Association,
 108 Baker St., W.1.
 18 Atholl Crescent, Edinburgh, 3.
 385 Malone Rd., Belfast.

International Co-operation.

The National Peace Council (29 Great James St., W.C.1), is a federation of national societies concerned in the promotion of peace. It publishes the *Peace Year Book*, which contains a directory of societies working for peace.

United Nations Association,
 25 Charles St., W.1.
Union of Democratic Control,
 13 Prince of Wales Terrace, W.8.
Women's International League for Peace and Freedom, 29 Great James St., W.C.1.
International Voluntary Service,
 72 Oakley Square, N.W.1.
British Society for International Understanding,
 Benjamin Franklin House, 36 Craven St., W.C.2.
International Friendship League,
 Peace Haven, Creswick Rd., W.3.
Friends Peace Committee,
 Friends House, Euston Road, N.W.1.
Africa Bureau, The,
 65 Denison House, Vauxhall Bridge Rd., S.W.1.
Britain in Europe Committee,
 43 Parliament St., S.W.1.
Fabian International Bureau,
 11 Dartmouth St., S.W.1.
English Speaking Union,
 37 Charles St., W.1.
Council for Education in World Citizenship,
 25 Charles St., W.1.
Royal Institute of International Affairs,
 Chatham House, 10 St. James's Square, S.W.1.
Parliamentary Group for World Government,
 House of Commons, S.W.1.
Fellowship of Reconciliation,
 29 Great James St., W.C.1.
Campaign for Nuclear Disarmament,
 2 Carthusian St., E.C.1.
War on Want, 9 Madeley Rd., W.5.
Institute of Race Relations,
 36 Jermyn St., S.W.1.
United World Trust,
 29 Great James St., W.C.1.
Oxford Committee for Famine Relief,
 274 Banbury Rd., Oxford.
British Council of Churches,
 10 Eaton Gate, S.W.1.
World Assembly of Youth (British National Committee), 57 Charlton St., N.W.1.

Some Other Societies.

Political and Economic Planning,
 16 Queen Anne's Gate, S.W.1.
Howard League for Penal Reform,
 6 Endsleigh St., W.C.1.
Progressive League,
 13 Prince of Wales Terrace, W.8.
Ethical Union,
 13 Prince of Wales Terrace, W.8.
Electoral Reform Society,
 Albany Institute, Creek Rd., S.E.8.
Women's Co-operative Guild,
 348 Grays Inn Rd., W.C.1.
Workers' Educational Association,
 27 Portman Square, W.1.

(*Note:* Unless otherwise stated the above addresses are in London, and this is further indicated by the postal number, *e.g.*, S.W.1. Correspondents writing from places other than London should include "London," as well as the postal number, in the address.)

THE LAW OF ENGLAND

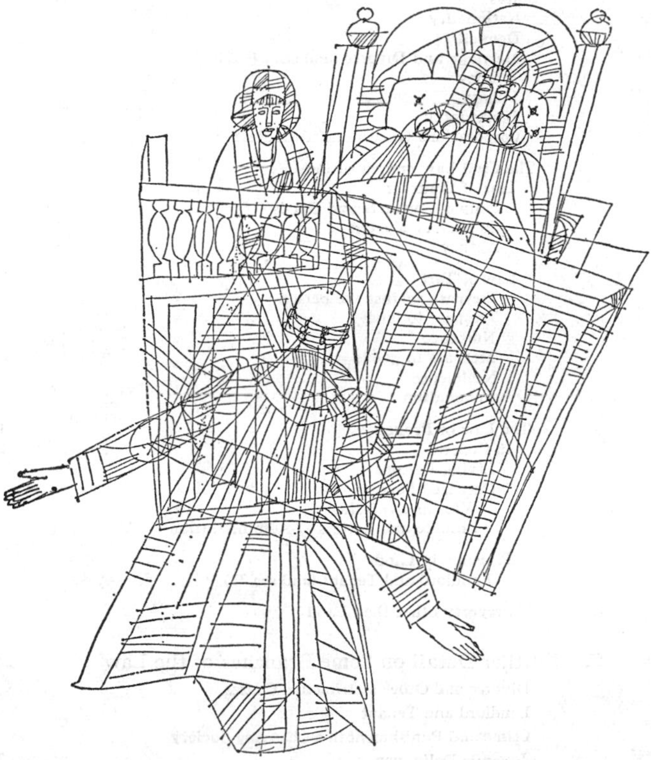

TABLE OF CONTENTS

THE LAW OF ENGLAND

A.—The Sources

Comprising

COMMON LAW — CASE LAW — EQUITY * — STATUTE LAW

B.—The Sub-divisions

I. Constitutional Law.	II. Criminal Law, dealing with the relations between the individual and the State.	III. Status.	IV. Law of Persons,* dealing with the relations between one individual citizen and another, established—		V. Law of Property.*		
Main Principles: 1. The Supremacy of Parliament. 2. The Rule of Law. (a) *The Legislature:* The franchise, elections, Parliamentary procedure, relations between Lords and Commons, Bills and Acts. (b) *The Executive:* The Crown, the Ministry, Government Departments and their powers. (c) *The Judiciary:* The Courts and their functions, the Judges, means of controlling the Executive and inferior courts. (d) *Local Government:* County, Borough, Urban and Rural District and Parish Councils and their powers. (For further details, see Section C, Part II.)	A. Grave offences against— 1. *Public Order:* Treason, sedition, riot, blasphemy, obscenity, forgery, bigamy, perjury. 2. *Persons:* Homicide, assault, sexual offences. 3. *Property:* Larceny, burglary, housebreaking, false pretences, blackmail. Subsidiary matters: (*a*) Criminal responsibility. (*b*) Unconsummated Crimes. (*c*) Joint Crimes. (*d*) Punishment and its purpose. B. *Petty Offences, e.g.,* Road Traffic, Factories and Shops, Sale of Food. etc. (dealt with by J.P.s)	1. Nationality. 2. Domicil. 3. Marriage and Divorce. 4. Infancy. 5. Lunacy. 6. Bankruptcy. 7. Corporations.	1. *By act of parties (Law of Contract):* (1) Simple Contracts. (2) Deeds: (*a*) Capacity of parties. (*b*) When writing necessary. (*c*) Mistake. (*d*) Misrepresentation. (*e*) Duress and undue influence. (*f*) Illegality. (*g*) Breach.	2. *By Law (Law of Tort):* Civil Wrongs committed against— (1) *The Person:* Trespass, assault, malicious prosecution, and false imprisonment. (2) *Land:* Trespass, Nuisance. (3) *Other Property:* Trespass, Conversion. (4) *Persons towards whom there is a duty to take care:* Negligence. (5) *Reputation:* Defamation (libel or slander). (6) *Personal and Trade Relationships:* Seduction, enticement, trade molestation *and*— (a) *Liability.* (b) *Immunity.* (c) *Effect of Death.* (d) *Remedies.*	In General: 1. *Living Persons:* (Effect of Status on Ownership). 2. *Deceased Persons:* (Wills and Intestacies, Probate and Administration).	In Land (Immoveable Property): 1. Freeholds (Settlements). 2 Leaseholds. 3. Mortgages. 4. Title. 5. Joint Ownership.	In Other Property (Moveable Property): 1. Chattels. 2. Things in action.

* *Note:* Equity is applied only in matters of civil law relating to persons and property. It has no application to constitutional or criminal law.

THE LAW OF ENGLAND

The Table set out on D3 shows in concise form—

A—the sources, and
B—the subdivisions

of the Law of England. The intention is to give a general picture of the whole system in tabular form, to explain briefly what the Table represents, and finally to deal, in slightly more detail, with a few selected subjects which may be of particular interest to the ordinary reader.

A word of warning is necessary. Learned text-books have been written on every one of the many subjects referred to in the Table, and the application of the law in any particular case is a matter for the professional expert. The following pages do not claim to do more than to make a brief survey of the whole field of English Law, for the general guidance and interest of the ordinary citizen.

A. THE SOURCES OF ENGLISH LAW

The citizen who desires to make some acquaintance with the English Legal System must begin by disabusing himself of several popular fallacies: for example, that it is a fixed and unalterable code, that it is strictly logical, that it is coldly impersonal and uninfluenced by human factors. The history and practice of the law display precisely the opposite characteristics.

1. COMMON LAW AND CASE LAW

The English Legal System is a *living organism*, not a dead, static code. The system as we know it began to develop in the twelfth century, when Henry II extended the practice of sending the royal judges about the country "on circuit," to deal with crimes and disputes, and to adapt and give official authority to the best of the local customs, some of which had been in force since Anglo-Saxon days. The judges did this by *empirical methods*—that is, by practical, commonsense decisions on the actual cases brought before them, and by setting out their reasoning in detail. Simple records of the most important decisions were kept from the earliest times; as the centuries passed, the gradual elaboration of a system of *law-reporting* ensured that the *facts* of significant cases, the *reasoned judgments* delivered on those facts, and the *principles* those judgments enshrined, should be recorded and preserved; at the same time the doctrine of *precedent*—the rule that those principles, enunciated by a superior court, should be followed by all courts inferior to it—ensured consistency throughout the country. Thus there was gradually developed a body of principles—living, growing, and adaptable to new sets of facts as they arose; principles, moreover, which rose above local differences of custom and became *common* to the whole Realm. Hence the expression *common law*.

Case Law. The system we have described is by no means a thing of the past: it is still in force today. New circumstances are continually arising; cases come before the judges for decision, and it frequently happens that the principles laid down in the past do not apply precisely, in all respects, to the particular facts in point. When this occurs it is the judge's right and duty to *interpret and adapt the principle to the new facts* before him; his judgment is reported, and his reasoning made clear. The adapted principle of that judgment becomes part of the law of England; it must be followed by all inferior courts; and it will not be ignored or abandoned by courts of the same rank, or any superior court, without reasoned argument and careful consideration. Thus the practising lawyer can never sit back with the comfortable assurance that he has "completed" his studies: he must continually keep his knowledge up to date. The practice of law is not a science, based on rigid rules, but an art—the art of *applying the known principles to the facts of new cases* as they arise.

2. EQUITY

But the English genius for practical improvisation has never excluded spiritual and *ethical motives* of conduct. For hundreds of years the Church was a great power in the land, extending its influence far beyond the strictly ecclesiastical sphere. The great church-leaders of the past took an important part in the secular activities of government and administration; from an early date the King's Chancellor was an ecclesiastic. The Chancellor was not only the King's Secretary of State and Keeper of the royal seal; as royal chaplain he was "the Keeper of the King's conscience." It was to him, therefore, that the King turned for advice on matters of state where *ethical and moral considerations* were involved.

All human institutions are fallible, and the rough-and-ready methods of the early common law sometimes fell short of those ideals of abstract justice that inspire men's minds. Despite, or perhaps because of, its practical outlook, the common law tended to become circumscribed by its own precedents. As the machinery of justice became more elaborately organised, the idealistic doctrine—"Where there is a right there is a remedy"—was apt to degenerate, in practice, into the realistic but soulless form—"Where there is a legal remedy, there is a legal right." Too close an adherence to legal formalities led sometimes to a denial of justice. This was particularly so for the weak, who could not help themselves—feeble-minded persons, tricked or cajoled into "legally" signing away their property; infants unconscionably treated by guardians who, having got legal custody (under a will or otherwise) of the infants' inheritance, refused to honour their solemn trust; borrowers who, having delayed beyond the date fixed for the repayment of a loan, found themselves deprived, under the strict terms of the mortgage deed, of property many times more valuable which they had pledged only as security. For such cases as these the common-law courts provided no remedy, since the victims had suffered *no actual illegality*. Petitions were therefore sent to the King, "the father of this people," begging him to right such wrongs; and the question of redress was delegated by the King to his Chancellor. The Chancellor had no power directly to revoke or interfere with the decisions of the royal judges by depriving the oppressive party of the property he had "legally" acquired, but he could, and did, insist that that party should not enjoy such acquisition, *unconscionably*, for his own sole advantage. The defaulting guardian, though he continued legally to hold the infant's property, was compelled to use it for the infant's benefit; the oppressive creditor, who had legally got possession of or sold the debtor's estate, was permitted to take out of the proceeds the amount of his loan, with reasonable interest and expenses, but must hand back the balance to the debtor. Thus the Chancellor administered a kind of *abstract justice*, based upon the promptings of conscience, and not on legalistic rules. He dealt with these cases in his own court—the Chancellery or *Chancery*—where the yardstick was *equity*—that which was right or fair. And over the centuries the principles on which the Court of Chancery acted became crystallised into a set of rules which followed their own precedents and made *conscientious conduct* their guiding star.

Naturally enough, the activities of the Court of Chancery were viewed with jealousy and misgiving by the royal judges of the Common Law Courts, and many were the clashes between the two. Equity, however, had come to stay, and the two systems were administered independently until as late as 1873. In that year Parliament passed the Supreme Court of Judicature Act, which (in effect) fused the two systems into one. By means of that and subsequent legislation there was constituted *one High Court of Justice*, of which the *Queen's Bench Division*, the *Chancery Division*, and the *Probate, Divorce* and *Admiralty Division* are component parts. The first-named is concerned primarily with common-law suits, the second with equitable matters; but both these Divisions must have regard to *both common law and equitable principles*. In case of a conflict of principles, those of equity are to prevail. The last-named Division (for historical reasons) deals with the diverse subjects of wills and intestacies, matrimonial suits, and disputes relating to ships at sea. Criminal cases fall within the jurisdiction of the Queen's Bench Division, but are dealt with in special courts. The criminal law (in strict fairness to accused persons) must be absolutely certain and clearly defined; it is administered on strict legalistic principles, for which the doctrines of equity are excluded. (For further details of the Courts and their functions, see Section C and D35–7.)

3. STATUTE LAW

While, as we have shown, the Courts have the function of *interpreting and adapting* the principles of law laid down in earlier times, they cannot legislate—*i.e., the Judge cannot make new laws*, or repeal or amend old laws, even when changes are rendered desirable by developing social conditions. The law-making body, or *Legislature*, is *Parliament*. *A Statute* or *Act of Parliament* is the joint act of the Queen, the House of Lords, and the House of Commons; while each of these three "Estates of the Realm" has its own functions, new law can be made, and old law repealed, only by these three Estates acting together, *i.e.*, by *Parliament*, or by some person or body of persons to whom Parliament has *delegated authority* to make *rules having the force of law*. Parliament is free to control by any written constitution or any person or body of persons whatsoever; an Act of Parliament must be enforced by all courts as the law of the land, unless and until it is repealed or amended by Parliament itself. Parliament is not bound by the Acts of a previous parliament, which it is free to repeal or amend as occasion may require. It is equally free to modify the rules of the common law and the rules of equity, however firmly entrenched; but those rules, unless and until modified by parliamentary legislation, continue to guide the Judges both in their interpretation and enforcement of *Statute Law*—*i.e.*, the body of Acts of Parliament still in force for the time being—and in their decisions on those common-law and equitable rules which the Statute Law has left untouched. For example, the Peerage Act, 1963, enables a peer to renounce his title and to become a commoner for all purposes, including voting for, and standing as, a candidate for the House of Commons.

THE ENGLISH LEGAL SYSTEM

These three main streams—*common law* (and *case law*), *equity*, and *statute law*—have flowed throughout the centuries, sometimes independently and sometimes in conjunction, to feed the waters of that great river which is the *English Legal System.*

B. THE SUBDIVISIONS OF ENGLISH LAW

I. CONSTITUTIONAL LAW

This is that part of the English Legal System which relates to four main branches of national administration:—

(a) *The Legislature*—*i.e.*, the *law-making* body known as Parliament.

(b) *The Executive*—*i.e.*, the *Government* and the functions of its various components.

(c) *The Judiciary*—*i.e.*, the *Judges*, their *Courts* and powers.

(d) *Local Government*—*i.e.*, the *Local Authorities* and their powers.

The two main principles of the Constitution are:—

1. The Supremacy of Parliament.—*I.e.*, there is nothing that Parliament cannot lawfully do, and there is no person or body of persons above Parliament. Its Acts cannot be unconstitutional, since it can itself modify the Constitution at will. Its Acts for the time being in force are the law of the land, and nobody can question their validity.

2. The Rule of Law.—This means that no person or body of persons is above the law of the land, and that there is one system of law, and one system alone, for everybody. There is not in England, as there is in some other states, a special system of law and special courts for scrutinising the acts of ministers, civil servants, or other functionaries; such persons are bound by the same rules of conduct as other citizens. (At the moment of writing (Oct. 1965), the Government is considering setting up, by Act of Parliament, an Ombudsman—an official to whom complaints of injustice by Government departments may be made. The name is borrowed from a Scandinavian institution.) A complaint by a private citizen against a Secretary of State or a Commissioner of Police is investigated by the same courts, and under the same legal rules, as a complaint against another private citizen. An apparent exception will be found to result from some special provision in an Act of Parliament itself. For example, the Army Act sets up a code of conduct for officers and soldiers, and does not apply to civilians; but that code is part of the Law of England because it is contained in an Act of Parliament—a code which (incidentally) remains valid only if it is confirmed by Parliament in every successive year. Again, the Emergency Powers (Defence) Act, 1939, conferred upon the Crown and its Ministers extensive powers, during the last War, to make Defence Regulations which should have the force of law;

but the Act itself had to be passed by Parliament with the proper formalities. Such Regulations derive their legal and binding effect solely from the *powers delegated by Parliament*; and the High Court of Justice is competent to scrutinise, and frequently does scrutinise, the wording of the Regulations and the manner in which those powers are exercised, and to satisfy itself that the Minister concerned is not attempting to exceed the authority which Parliament has vested in him—in other words, to protect the citizen against the *arbitrary abuse of lawful powers* and against their *unlawful enlargement*. *Delegated legislation* is always subject to such control; parliamentary legislation is not, since *nobody can question the validity of an Act of Parliament*. But the *interpretation* of any Act of Parliament—the ascertainment of its legal meaning and effect—is one of the proper functions of the Courts.

II. CRIMINAL LAW

This is that part of the English Legal System which deals with the relations between the individual citizen and society as a whole. Thus, if A murders or robs B, the question of redress is not one merely for B or his family; the victim cannot, in a civilised community, be permitted "to take the law into his own hands," nor can it be left to him to decide what action should be taken against the offender—otherwise blood-feuds and public disorder would result. For that reason it has been the law for centuries past that, in the case of offences (1) against public order, (2) against the person and (3) against property, *the State (representing society as a whole) itself intervenes* and *prosecutes* the offender, for the purpose of upholding public order and vindicating the rule of law by inflicting *punishment* upon him—*not* for the purpose of *compensating* the injured party (which, as will be seen below, is the contrasting function of *Civil Law*). But the *programme* of Government legislation for 1965–6 includes consideration of the payment of compensation to victims of violent crime—for the first time since Anglo-Saxon days. For offences against public order, see D38–40.

The two main categories of Crime (as the Table shows) are:—

(a) *Grave (or Indictable) Offences*, which are dealt with at Assizes, the Central Criminal Court, and Quarter Sessions, and which carry severe penalties—death or lengthy sentences of imprisonment; and

(b) *Petty Offences*, which are dealt with in *Magistrates' Courts*, and are punishable by light sentences of imprisonment or by fines (with short sentences in the alternative). Examples of this latter class are (*e.g.*, under the Road Traffic Acts) driving without due care and attention, exceeding the speed-limit, causing an obstruction, etc. (*See also* **Justices of the Peace, D37.**)

Examples of (a) *Grave (or Indictable) Offences* are set out in the Table under the three main headings of:—

(1) *Offences against Public Order*;

(2) *Offences against the Person*; and

(3) *Offences against Property*.

In connection with all these categories of offences the *Criminal Law* is concerned with the following general considerations:—

(a) **Criminal Responsibility.**—*I.e.*, the primary principles that every person is presumed (until the contrary is proved) to be sane and "to intend the natural consequence of his acts," provided that those acts themselves are *voluntary* (*i.e., intentional*) on his part. It would, for example, be absurd for a man, accused of wounding another person by shooting, to plead that he did not intend, when he discharged the firearm at the other person, to do him any bodily harm. On the other hand, it would be outrageous to convict and punish a child of four who, without understanding the wrongfulness of his behaviour, picked up and took away some attractive and valuable object from a shop-counter; a lunatic who killed somebody under an insane delusion that the victim was a wild beast; a boy (like Oliver Twist) who was compelled, by force or violent threats, to break into a house, or a man who took an overcoat from a public cloakroom, honestly but mistakenly believing it to be his own. In none of these last illustrations is the act a *voluntary* one in the sense that there was the *intention to do something wrong*. To the rule that an act is not a crime unless it is intentional in this sense there are a few rare exceptions—cases where an Act of Parliament has expressly and clearly made some form of *conduct punishable in itself*, whether it was intentional or not; for example, during the War, permitting a light to be visible in black-out hours was punishable, even if it was unintentional and involuntary on the part of the accused.

Intention must not be confused with *motive*. For example, in what has become known as "mercy-killing"—*i.e.*, taking the life of a person suffering from a painful and incurable disease—the killer is often actuated by a good *motive*—the desire to relieve hopeless suffering; but the *intention* is to kill, and the act is therefore a crime. (It is not necessary for the prosecution to prove any motive.)

The *burden of proof* in criminal cases is on the prosecution, *i.e.*, it is the duty of the prosecution to prove the accused guilty; not the duty of the accused to prove his innocence. The accused is presumed to be innocent unless and until his guilt is proved to the reasonable satisfaction of a jury. The jury are the sole judges of the true facts of the case, and their verdict must be unanimous.

(b) **Unconsummated Crimes.**—*I.e., attempts* to commit crimes which are frustrated by some outside event or by some person's intervention. For obvious reasons the *attempt* to commit a grave crime is *itself an offence* for which the offender can be prosecuted and, if convicted of the attempt, punished by fine or imprisonment. *Incitement*, by one person, of another to commit a crime, and *conspiracy* between two or more persons to commit a crime, are usually offences in themselves, whether the incitement or the conspiracy proves successful or not.

(c) **Joint Crimes** are those in which two or more persons take part. Such participation may arise in different ways. A *principal in the first degree* is the man who commits the actual offence with *guilty intention* (see (*a*) above), or who induces its commission by some other person who himself does not understand what he is doing. A *principal in the second degree* is one who *aids and abets* the guilty perpetrator at the time when the crime is committed. An *accessory before the fact* is one who *instigates* or *helps to prepare* the commission of the crime by another person, though not himself present when that other person commits it. In most cases of *grave crime* all these *three classes of participants* in a crime are *equally guilty*, and liable to the same punishment, provided that all of them shared the same *common criminal purpose*. (Thus, if two armed burglars break into a house, with their weapons drawn, and one of them shoots and kills the householder, both will be guilty of murder; while the accomplice who helped to plan the burglary will be equally guilty if the plan included the carrying of loaded weapons.) An *accessory after the fact* is one who, knowing that a *felony* (generally speaking, a grave crime involving *violence*) has been committed, shelters or receives one of the participators to enable him to elude justice. This latter kind of accessory is liable to prosecution, but the penalty in his case is less severe than that imposed upon any of the other three classes.

(*d*) **Punishment and its Purpose.**—The purpose of punishment is fourfold:—

(i) *Retribution*—to demonstrate to the community in general that crime "does not pay" and thus to uphold the rule of law and to prevent the deterioration of public morals;

(ii) *Prevention*—to restrain offenders, so far as possible, from repeating their crimes by keeping them in custody;

(iii) *Reformation*—to make them, so far as possible, better citizens by means of moral and ethical training—teaching them to "go straight"; and

(iv) *Deterrence*—to inspire among offenders and would-be offenders a fear of and a healthy respect for the law and the strength of society as a whole, which it protects.

There has been much controversy on the relative importance of these four functions of punishment. During the past half-century, *reformation* of the offender, whenever possible, has become a paramount aim.

The Murder (Abolition of Death Penalty) Act, 1965, provides that no person shall suffer death for murder; a person convicted of murder shall be sentenced to imprisonment for life. In passing sentence the Court may declare the minimum period which it recommends the Home Secretary to allow to elapse before he orders the murderer's release on licence. The few types of murder which were still subject to the death sentence under the Homicide Act,1957, (capital murder) now also fall under the same rule. Anybody under sentence of death for *capital murder* on 8 November 1965 (when the new Act took effect) is liable to imprisonment for life instead. The new Act is to continue in force until 31 July 1970, and then expire unless both Houses of Parliament pass contrary resolutions; if the new Act does expire, the law as it existed before the passing of the new Act shall again come into operation.

III. STATUS

A person's *Status*—*i.e.*, his legal position in society—affects his legal rights and duties in most civil matters and, in some few cases, in criminal matters too (see *Criminal Responsibility*, D6).

1. Nationality, in this connection, means British Nationality under the British Nationality Acts, the latest of which was passed in 1965. By the 1948 Act the term "Commonwealth Citizen" was created which can be used as an alternative to British Subject. A person may be a British subject by birth, by naturalisation, by marriage, or by registration, though under the Act of 1948 a woman who was not a British subject before marriage does not automatically acquire British nationality merely by reason of her marriage to a British subject. The law and the courts of this country can determine whether a person is a *British subject* or an *alien*; they cannot determine whether or not he is a citizen of some particular *foreign state*, since that is a matter for the law of the foreign state concerned. Generally speaking, in times of peace, an *alien* in this country has the same rights and duties as a British subject, except that an *alien* has *no right to vote* in parliamentary or municipal elections, and that some professions (*e.g.*, that of a solicitor) are closed to him. By the Act of 1964, a person who is *stateless* may apply to be registered as a citizen of the U.K. and Colonies if either parent was such a citizen when he was born, or if the place of his birth is within the U.K. and Colonies at the time of his application. By the Act of 1965 *alien wives* of those British subjects who are *not citizens of any Commonwealth country* may be *registered* as British subjects.

2. Domicil means the country where a person has his *permanent home* without any present intention of changing it. His *domicil of origin* is that of his parents while he is under twenty-one; over that age he is free to acquire a new domicil by making his permanent home elsewhere. Domicil is of particular importance in matters of—

3. Marriage and Divorce.—English law generally regards as valid a *marriage ceremony* carried out in this country after the proper preliminaries and with the proper formalities, whatever the nationality or domicil of the parties. English law also accepts the validity of a *marriage ceremony* which has been carried out abroad according to the law of the country where it took place. But if one party or the other has an *English domicil*, the *status of the marriage as an institution* must depend on English law, whether the *ceremony* was in proper form or not. For example, a man who has his permanent home in England cannot evade the English rule against consanguinity by going through a *ceremony* of marriage, in Ruritania, with his mother's sister—even if such a marriage is lawful by Ruritanian law, and even if the ceremony has been carried out with the usual Ruritanian formalities, it is still *null and void* by the law of England. The English court will *not*, generally speaking, grant a *divorce* to a man who is *domiciled abroad*, since the law of the country which is his permanent home may not recognise this divorce, or perhaps any divorce, as valid; and it is improper that he should be regarded as a single man in England and a married man in his homeland. Similarly, English law *will* generally recognise the validity of a divorce granted by the proper court of his domicil (*i.e.*, of the state where he had his permanent home at the time) or of a divorce which the law of his domicil regards as valid, even if it was granted by a court elsewhere—and that whether he is a British subject or not. But a person, whatever his nationality, whose permanent home is in England will not be regarded here as validly divorced merely because he has spent a few weeks in Barataria, where divorce procedure is simple, and has been granted a decree there. His *status*—married or single—generally *depends on the law of his domicil*—*i.e.*, the law of the country which is his permanent home. (*See also* **D24–32**.)

4. Infancy is the status of a person under the age of twenty-one. An *infant cannot vote at elections*; he *cannot hold freehold or leasehold property*, and *he cannot be made bankrupt*. (In exceptional cases where the debt is for "necessaries" (D10(1)), a bankruptcy notice may be issued against an infant.) If he enters into certain kinds of *contracts* during his infancy he *can repudiate* them, if he so desires, up to a reasonable time after his twenty-first birthday. He *cannot make a valid will*, and his rights under another person's will or settlement cannot be compromised or altered without the leave of the High Court. An infant *cannot make a valid marriage without consent* of his parent or guardian, or of the appropriate court. His rights are at all times the special care of the Chancery Division of the High Court, which will protect those rights according to the Rules of Equity (see D5).

5. Lunacy, in the broad legal sense, is the status of a person who is "incapable, by reason of unsoundness of mind, of managing his affairs." "Lunacy" in this sense is not necessarily identical with any of the mental conditions to which such psychological terms as "insanity," "imbecility," "idiocy," and the like are applied; there need be no actual mental *disease*. When a person becomes incapable, for this reason, of managing his affairs, the law, in order to protect both him and society at large, *changes his status* by putting the custody of his person, or the control of his property, or both, into reliable hands. Such matters come under the supervision of the Chancery Division, since one of the functions of Equity (see above) is to protect those who cannot help themselves. Certification of "insanity" (in the psychological sense) is not necessary; but with the proper medical certificate and legal safeguards the *patient* (as he must be called) may be removed to a mental hospital. Some reliable person (usually a near relative) may be appointed, by an Order of the *Court of Protection* (a branch of the Chancery Division), as *Receiver* of his property. The Receiver's duties are to look after the property and income of the patient, pay his debts and defray the expenses of his maintenance and medical care, and generally to deal with the patient's property on the patient's behalf. Periodical accounts must be submitted to the Court, which will scrutinise them strictly and at once intervene if there appears to be any irregularity on the part of the Receiver. If there is no relative to take the responsibility, the *Official Solicitor* at the Royal Courts of Justice will be appointed as Receiver, with the same duties and liabilities.

Apart from these matters of administration, a person of unsound mind is regarded as incapable of making a valid will, of entering into a legal agreement, or of dealing with his property. None of these transactions is valid unless the person concerned *understood the nature and effect* of what he was doing; and whether he did understand or not is a question of *evidence* in every individual case: medical and other witnesses must testify to his conduct and demeanour at the time when he entered into the transaction in question. If the Court comes to the conclusion that he was unable to understand the nature and effect of the transaction, the Court will *rescind*—*i.e.*, set aside or cancel—the transaction, even though it was in proper legal form.

If a person does an act which, if *voluntary or intentional*, would constitute a *crime* (see *Criminal Responsibility*, D6), and his legal advisers put forward a defence of insanity, the general rule is stricter; he can still be convicted unless he can prove, to the satisfaction of a jury, that he was " suffering from such a *defect of reason*, due to *disease of the mind*, as not to know the *nature and quality of the act* he was doing, or (if he *did* know this) not to know that what he was doing was *wrong*." Medical men, psychologists, and social reformers have long regarded this rule (which has been in force since 1843) as too severe. It was a rule applicable to *all crimes*; but the controversy became associated in the public mind chiefly with *murder*. As a result of a long period of agitation and discussion the rule was amended by section 2 of the Homicide Act, 1957; but *only in its application to murder cases*. It is now provided that " a person who kills (or is a party to the killing of) another shall *not* be convicted of *murder* if he was suffering from such *abnormality of mind* as substantially *impaired his mental responsibility* for his acts and omissions in doing, or being a party to, the killing." (It does not matter whether the " abnormality of mind " arises from " a condition of arrested or retarded development of mind," or from " any inherent causes," or is " induced by disease or injury.") The Act goes on to provide that a person who, under the old law, would have been convicted of murder shall instead be liable to be convicted of *manslaughter*.

In other crimes, where the accused person is clearly proved to have been insane at the time the crime was committed, the verdict in future is to be " Not guilty by reason of insanity."

6. Bankruptcy is the creation of Statute Law—there was no common law of bankruptcy. It is the status of a person (the " debtor ") who is *insolvent*—*i.e.*, who is unable to pay his debts (exceeding £50) as they fall due. By the appropriate procedure the State takes the management of the debtor's property out of his hands and places it in the hands of the *Official Receiver*, whose duty it is to realise it and (subject to certain privileged claims) to distribute it *proportionately among his creditors*. The procedure is that one of the creditors files at the Bankruptcy Court a *bankruptcy petition*, on which the Court may make a *receiving order*, which has the effect of *transferring the legal management* of the debtor's property to the Official Receiver. That official investigates the debtor's finances and draws up an account, called a *statement of affairs*, showing the debtor's liabilities and assets. There is a *meeting of creditors* and a *public examination* of the debtor in Court, as a result of which the Court may either *discharge the receiving order* (on the debtor's showing that he can pay his debts, if he is given time, or persuade the general body of creditors to accept his proposals for a *composition* of so much in the £), or the Court may *adjudicate* the debtor a bankrupt. In the latter case it is open to the creditors either to leave the management of the debtor's property in the Official Receiver's hands or themselves to appoint a *trustee in bankruptcy* (usually an accountant) nominated by some or all of them, and that trustee takes over the management of the debtor's affairs. The debtor is bound, under penalty, to give *full information* about his affairs to the Official Receiver and the trustee in bankruptcy; he cannot, while he is a bankrupt, sit or vote in Parliament or act as a Justice of the Peace or in certain other offices. He will be committing an *offence* if he conceals any property or debt or falsifies his books of account, if he obtains property on credit or secures credit of £10 or more without disclosing his status, if he trades without such disclosure or fails to keep proper books of account, or if he leaves or attempts to leave the country, taking with him property, worth £20 or more, which ought to be divided among his creditors. It is also an offence for him to transfer property with intent to defraud any creditor, and any such transaction may be set aside by the Court.

7. A Corporation or Incorporated Body is an association of persons recognised by *Act of Parliament*, or by its *Charter*, as *one single legal entity*. It may be a *chartered* or a *statutory corporation* (*e.g.*, the British Broadcasting Corporation or the London Transport Executive), a *local authority* (*e.g.*, the Greater London Council or the Westminster City Council), or a *company* incorporated under the Companies Act, 1948, or one of the earlier Companies Acts. Generally speaking, a corporation of any kind has power only to do such things as it is given power to do by its Charter or by the Act of Parliament under which it was constituted; if it goes beyond that power it is behaving *ultra vires* —" beyond its powers "—and such acts on its part will be regarded by the Courts as null and void. The Court may also restrain the corporation by *injunction*—an Order forbidding it to act in such a manner. (For *companies*, see final paragraph on this page).

Every corporation, being a single legal entity, is a legal *person* distinct from the individuals who are its members. Thus the *corporation itself* can take *proceedings*, or have proceedings brought against it, in the Civil Courts, and it may itself be *prosecuted* in the Criminal Courts, if it commits an offence, and be liable to a fine. No personal liability rests upon its individual members, directors, or officers unless they have personally done something unlawful or aided and abetted the corporation in its wrongdoing. The corporation itself can *enter into a legal agreement* with one or more of its members or a member of the public, and any person injured by its acts can enforce his legal rights against the property or assets of the corporation, which are distinct from the property or assets of the individuals who compose it.

A *company* is usually a commercial concern and generally takes advantage of the principle of *limited liability*, in which case the last word in its name must be the word " Limited." The principle is that, in the event of the company's becoming *insolvent*, none of its members can be compelled to contribute to its funds a larger sum than the sum which he agreed to pay for his *shares*, however large the indebtedness of the company itself. Every company must file at the Companies Registry a *Memorandum of Association*, setting out its *name*, the situation of its *registered office*, its *objects* (beyond which it has no power to act), its *capital*, and whether or not it is *limited*. It should also file its *Articles of Association*, setting out its *rules of management*, the method of issuing, allotting, and transferring its *shares*, the procedure for *meetings*, the powers and duties of its *directors* and other officers, and similar matters. If and when its objects have been *fully achieved*, or if it is desired to *discontinue its activities*, or if it becomes *insolvent*, it will be *wound up* and *dissolved*. The winding-up is undertaken by a *Liquidator* whose duties are similar to those of the trustee in bankruptcy (described above under *Bankruptcy*). The liquidator may be nominated by the members of the company or, in case of the company's insolvency, by some or all of the creditors, and the liquidator's appointment must be confirmed at a special meeting. If the winding-up of an insolvent company takes more than a year the liquidator must report annually to the *Board of Trade*, the Government Department which watches the interests of the persons concerned.

IV. The CIVIL LAW or LAW OF PERSONS

This deals with the relations between *one individual citizen and another*, and their mutual rights and duties. If A makes a business agreement with B, and breaks it, or if A walks without permission across B's field of new-mown hay, B will be able to secure *redress* against A by proceedings in a court of law. But in neither case is it necessary for the State to intervene, by way of prosecution, to punish A for what he has done, since no offence against society at large, and no violation of public order, or the rule of law, has arisen. The issue is one merely between A and B; B may choose to ignore the wrong done to him, or he may negotiate amicably with A for the payment of compensation or, if this fails, he may *as plaintiff sue A as defendant* in a *civil action* for *damages*. Unlike a criminal prosecution, undertaken by the State for the preservation of public order and vindication of the rule of law, with a view to punishing the offender, the *civil action* will be brought, if B so chooses, *by B himself* for the purpose of recovering *compensation* in money for the harm he has suffered and (in some cases) of obtaining an *injunction*—a Court Order prohibiting A from continuing his wrongful conduct. Again, a criminal prosecution will not be discontinued even at the request of the injured party, since the State itself is interested to see justice done; but a *civil action* can be *discontinued* by B at whatever stage he desires, with or without an agreement for the payment of *damages* in compensation.

These *relations between one individual and another*, interference with which may give rise to a *civil action for damages or injunction*, may arise in two alternative ways:—

(1) from the acts of the parties themselves, or

(2) from the operation of law.

1. Law of Contract

The relations between individuals which arise from the acts of the parties themselves are usually brought about by a *contract—i.e.*, by an agreement between them. A contract may be (a) *expressed in words*, as where A agrees to buy B's motor-car for £400, on certain stated conditions, or (b) *implied by conduct*, as where A calls a taxi and tells the driver to take him to a certain address. (*a*) In the former case, particularly if the contract is put into writing, the parties will normally have *expressed* all the necessary terms and conditions. (*b*) In the latter case it is *implied* by A's conduct, and understood by law and custom, that A will be expected to pay, at the end of the journey, the amount of the fare recorded by the taximeter; it is not necessary for the driver to stipulate those terms in advance. Everybody, several times in the course of each day, enters into an *implied contract* of this kind—when he steps on an omnibus to go to his work, when he orders a meal in a restaurant, when he tells the grocer to deliver goods to his house, and so on.

Simple Contracts and Deeds

(1) **A Simple Contract** is a contract *expressed in words* (whether in writing or not) without the formalities of a *deed* (see below), or a contract *implied by conduct*. There is no legal contract (*a*) unless there is *complete certainty* on the terms; (*b*) unless the basis of the agreement is lawful; and (*c*) unless both parties are *legally capable* of entering into it (see above, *Status*), and (*d*) in *complete agreement* on their intentions. And the agreement is not enforceable (*e*) unless there is some *consideration, i.e.*, some *quid pro quo*, expressed or implied, on either side. Thus (*a*) a promise by A that he will buy B's motor-car cannot be enforced by either side unless the price is mentioned, nor (*b*) if the car has been stolen by B, nor (*c*) if A is of unsound mind, nor (*d*) if B owns two cars, and A is thinking of the Ford, while B intends to sell the Austin. Again (*e*) a promise by C, during the course of the year's work, that he will give his employee, D, a Christmas box of £5 is not enforceable by D unless *he* has made a promise, or done something in return. If C tells D that he will give D the £5 at Christmas *on condition that* D puts in certain *extra time* over and above his normal working-hours, and D complie or promises to comply, that compliance, or promise of compliance, will be sufficient *consideration* to turn A's promise into an enforceable contract. There need be nothing at all in writing, except in a few cases laid down by law; in all other cases the only *value of a written agreement*, signed by both parties, is that it provides clear *evidence* of the terms that were agreed. A written contract requires a sixpenny revenue stamp if it is to be produced as evidence in a court of law.

(2) **A Deed** (broadly speaking) is a contract or other written document, *signed, sealed,* and *delivered* by the parties. The formalities of *affixing one's seal* to a legal document, and pronouncing the formula, "I deliver this as my act and deed," have emphasised the significance and solemnity of certain important transactions for many centuries past; and even persons who were unable to write their names were capable of carrying out the formalities of *sealing* and *delivery*. The legal requirement that deeds should also be *signed* was imposed only in 1925, by section 73 (1) of the Law of Property Act. The chief practical distinction between a simple contract and a deed is that a *deed requires no consideration* to make it enforceable. The special formalities which constitute the *execution* of a deed (*i.e.*, signing, sealing, and delivery) take the place of that moral obligation which (in a simple contract) the common law required to be satisfied by consideration on the part of the person to whom the promise was made. For this reason a *deed* is required in a case where A makes a promise to B which he desires to render enforceable without any corresponding promise by B to A, and also in a case where A desires to make to B a *gift of property* of such a nature that it cannot be physically handed over. This second case arises particularly where the subject of the gift is *land or buildings*; in fact, by a provision of the Law of Property Act, 1925, a *deed* is always necessary to *transfer the ownership* of any *freehold or leasehold* property, and also to grant a *tenancy* for a term of *more than three years*. The transfer of a *legal right* of some kind (*e.g.*, a share in a company or the claim to moneys under an insurance policy) is generally effected *by deed*.

In connection with the Law of Contract the following subsidiary matters must be considered:—

Subsidiary Matters

(a) Capacity of Parties.—The question whether a party to a contract is *legally capable* of entering into it. This question usually depends on that party's *status* (see above):—

(1) *Nationality.*—Nothing turns on this, except that *no commercial contract* can be made with an *alien enemy* in time of war.

(2) *Domicil.*—Where the two or more parties to a contract have their *permanent homes in different countries* it is a wise precaution for them to state, in the contract, under which country's law and by which country's courts, in case of a dispute, its terms are to be construed. If they omit to do so, and some dispute is brought before the English Court, it will endeavour to decide, by considering the wording of the contract, the language in which it is written, the domicil of the parties, and the general circumstances in which the contract was made, what legal system the parties intended to apply and by what court they intended is to be judged. Sometimes it will decide the dispute according to the rules of the foreign law.

(3) *Marriage and Divorce.*—There is now no practical difference in contractual capacity between single persons, married persons, and divorcees.

(4) *Infancy.*—It is not (generally speaking) impossible for a person under twenty-one to enter into a valid contract, but he will be entitled to

repudiate it at any time up to his twenty-first birthday (or a reasonable period after that) *unless* the contract is (*a*) clearly for the *infant's benefit* on the whole (*e.g.*, professional articles or an agreement for apprenticeship), or (*b*) for the provision of *necessaries—i.e.*, food, drink, clothing, or services which are necessary to the infant in his particular station in life. (The origin of this latter rule is probably the practical consideration that, in earlier times, few people would have taken the risk of providing an infant, on credit, with the bare necessities of life if they had been precluded from suing him for reasonable payment.)

(5) *Lunacy.*—A party to a "contract" who knows that the other party is of unsound mind will not be permitted to hold the latter to his bargain. See D7(2).

(6) *Bankruptcy.*—A bankrupt cannot make a valid agreement to deal with his property in a manner which contravenes the law of Bankruptcy (see above, under *Status*, D8).

(7) *Corporations.*—Whether a corporation is capable of entering into a particular contract depends upon the legal powers conferred by the Charter or Act of Parliament under which it was constituted, or (if a company) by its Memorandum of Association (see above, *Status*, D8). If the matter to which the contract relates is of grave importance it will usually signify its adherence to the contract by *affixing its seal* with the formalities laid down by its Rules or Articles of Association. If it is an everyday or trivial matter the corporation will normally enter into a contract through some agent (*e.g.*, its Town Clerk, Director, or Secretary, as the case may be) who is empowered to sign or speak on its behalf (see *Agency*, D11).

(*b*) **When Writing is Necessary.**—There are certain exceptions, laid down by Act of Parliament, to the rule (see D9 (1)) that a contract is enforceable even if made only by word of mouth or implied by conduct. The Statute of Frauds, 1677, provides that contracts of these exceptional kinds cannot be enforced by action in the Courts "unless the agreement upon which such action shall be brought, or some memorandum or note thereof, shall be in writing, and signed by the party to be charged therewith, or some other person thereunto by him lawfully authorised"—these last words mean an *agent* (see *Agency*, D11). It is *not necessary* that the *whole of the agreement* shall be formally set down in *writing*; but there must be a *written and signed record* of all the *essential terms*.

(i) *A Guarantee.—I.e.*, a promise by A to B in the form—"Please lend money (or supply goods) to C, and if C does not pay you I will." A's promise by word of mouth cannot be enforced against him.

(ii) An *agreement* for the *sale or disposition of land* (*or buildings*) or of any interest in land (or buildings). We have already stated that the actual *transfer* of a *freehold or leasehold* interest must be effected by *deed* (see *Deeds*, D9). This is not the same as an *agreement to sell or dispose of* land or buildings; a *transfer* effects an *immediate change of ownership*, while an *agreement to sell* binds the party who signs it to make a transfer of ownership at some *future time*. Such an agreement need not be in the form of a deed, but its *essential terms* must be *in writing*.

(iii) An *agreement* which *cannot be carried out within one year* from the date when it was made, either because the actual carrying out of the transaction will take more than a year or because the agreement contemplates that more than a year is to elapse before the transaction is to be done. For example, A can make, by word of mouth, an agreement to employ B from month to month, or for not more than twelve months from the date of the agreement; but if he promises to employ B for three years, or for one year commencing in six months' time, B cannot enforce that promise unless the essential terms are in writing.

(iv) An *agreement in consideration of marriage.*—*e.g.*, a promise by A, to B, to give A's daughter, C, a certain dowry or income if B will marry her. (The words do *not* cover a *promise or agreement by* B *to marry* C; the breaking of the latter agreement —"breach of promise of marriage"—can give rise to an action for damages, by C against B, even if B has put nothing at all into writing.)

(v) By the Contracts of Employment Act, 1963 (in force since July 1964), it is the *duty of an employer* (not later than 13 weeks after the employment commenced) to hand his employee a *written statement of particulars of the employment* (period, wage, working hours, and what length of notice is required for termination).

(*c*) **Mistake.**—Suppose that John Brown wants his portrait painted by a famous artist called William Brush, of whom he has heard but whom he has never met. He looks up "William Brush" in the directory and writes to him, at the address shown, offering him 100 guineas to paint the portrait. Suppose that particular "William Brush" is not the artist at all but a stockbroker of the same name. Even if that William Brush accepts Brown's offer, their apparent agreement will not constitute a valid contract, since Brown's *mistake* as to Brush's identity is so *fundamental* that it *destroys the very basis* of the agreement. Where there is a mistake of this kind, "going to the very root of the agreement," no valid contract has, in the eyes of the law, been made. In other special cases *equity* (see D4 (2)) may, on the ground of *conscience*, *relieve* one or both parties from liability under a concluded contract by *rectification* (*i.e.*, by correcting the terms they have inadvertently recorded) or by *rescission* (*i.e.*, by cancellation of the contract). It is not every mistake that will lead to these results; either the mistake must have been *fundamental* or the circumstances must have been such that it would be *unconscientious* for one party or the other to try to enforce his apparent rights.

(*d*) **Misrepresentation.**—Equity, on similar grounds, will often relieve a party from liability under a contract into which he has been induced to enter through a *representation* by the other party which is *substantially false—i.e.*, a statement which is misleading on some essential point. If it turns out that the *misrepresentation was deliberate*, the deceived party may in addition be entitled to claim *damages for fraud*. Whether the misrepresentation was *deliberate or innocent*, the deceived party will usually be able to have the contract *set aside—i.e.*, cancelled.

Suppose, for example, Jones wants to insure his life with the Markshire Insurance Company. Before issuing the policy, which is the contract between them, the Company will ask Jones—"Have you ever suffered from any serious illness?" Suppose Jones says "No," though he did in fact suffer from tuberculosis five years ago. Even if the policy contains a promise by the Company to pay Jones's widow £5000 upon Jones's death, the Company will be entitled to refuse to pay when that event happens; it has been induced to enter into the contract through Jones's misrepresentation.

(*e*) **Duress** means compulsion by *threats or force*. If a man has been compelled in this manner to put his name to a contract it is *voidable by him* at any time—*i.e.*, *he may repudiate* it on the ground of duress, and will be upheld by law in doing so. *Undue influence* means influence exerted by A upon B to such an extent that B could not have exercised any free and independent will in doing a particular act. Equity has always been jealous to protect certain classes of persons from this kind of influence; it goes so far as to *presume* that there has been undue influence where a guardian has got some benefit out of his ward, a parent from his child who is under (or only just over twenty-one, a doctor from his patient, a solicitor from his client, or a priest from his parishioner. In most of such cases the onus is upon the person in the influential position, who has obtained the benefit, to prove that there was no undue influence it is not for the other person to prove that his mind was wrongfully influenced by the former.

(*f*) Illegality of contract arises where the parties have agreed to do an act (i) forbidden by law or (ii) contrary to "public policy." (i) The former includes not only an agreement to commit a crime, but also an agreement to do an act which might be harmful to a third party and give him a right of action for breach of contract or tort. The courts will obviously not lend their assistance to a plaintiff who complains that the defendant has refused to honour his agreement to do something unlawful, whether (for example) the agreement was to burgle a house or merely to write a libellous article about another person. (ii) Even if the act agreed upon was not actually unlawful, the courts will refuse to enforce the agreement if it was to do something which is regarded as harmful to the community. It is not, for example, a crime for a man and a woman to live together without being married, nor is it even "unlawful" in the civil sense that such a way of life gives the one a right of action against the other; but no court would enforce an agreement by a woman to become a man's mistress, nor an agreement by the man to maintain her in return.

(*g*) Breach of Contract occurs when one of the parties breaks his promise and neglects or refuses to perform his duty under the contract. Breach by one party entitles the other party to sue for *damages*, the amount of which is usually assessed so as to compensate the latter for the *actual loss* he has suffered ("special damage"). In certain cases the court may award *general damages* in addition—*e.g.*, in an action for breach of promise of marriage the jilted woman may be awarded *general damages* for the distress she has suffered, her loss of reputation, etc., as well as *special damages* to cover the amount by which she is *out-of-pocket* by reason of giving up her employment, buying a trousseau, etc.

(1) *Damages* have always been the *common-law remedy* for breach of contract. In special cases, however, equity may grant two other remedies in addition to, or in substitution for, damages; but only where equity regards damages as an insufficient compensation. These additional remedies are:—

(2) *Specific Performance.—I.e.*, an order, to the party in breach, *actually to carry out* what he contracted to do. In practice this remedy is confined to: (i) contracts for the sale or letting of *land or buildings*, and (ii) contracts for the sale of some *article of a special nature* which cannot be replaced by spending money in the open market —for example, the sale of an original painting by Rembrandt. The remedy of *specific performance* is *never* granted to enforce a contract for *personal services*, since it would be impossible for the court to supervise the carrying out of such a contract.

(3) *Injunction.—I.e.*, an order by the court to the party in default *prohibiting him* from carrying out some positive act which would constitute a breach of contract. For example, where a singer has entered into a contract to work, for a certain period, only under the management of one particular impresario and no other, the court may order the singer not to offer or engage her services elsewhere during that period. Disobedience to an injunction constitutes *contempt of court*, and is punishable by fine or imprisonment.

Agency

(1) The Status of an Agent.—An *agent* is a person, who, being duly authorised, *acts on behalf of another person* who is called the *principal*. An agent is not the servant or employee of his principal. The principal tells his agent what transactions he wishes the agent to carry out, but does not exercise the control and supervision that a master exercises over his servant. Thus, for example, a solicitor is the *agent* of the client who has instructed him to attend to the purchase of a house; once instructions have been given it is left to the solicitor to carry out the work in his own way, as his skill and knowledge dictate. But the solicitor's clerk is the solicitor's *servant*; he is told what letters to write, what documents to prepare, what inquiries to make, and so forth. The two functions may sometimes appear to overlap; but the essence of agency is that there must be a *third party* with whom the principal is to be brought into relations; "the agent is the conduit-pipe connecting the principal and the third party." The agent is therefore debarred from acting for his *own benefit* without the principal's knowledge and consent.

Generally speaking, any person may do through an agent whatever he has power to do himself, except such transactions as depend upon some *personal qualification* peculiar to his own trade or profession. Thus, a man whose business is to sell or buy ordinary commercial articles can properly leave such business to an agent to perform; but an engineer, a lawyer, or a surgeon cannot entrust an agent with work that requires the exercise of *personal qualifications*, calling for special training and skill.

(2) The Contract of Agency.—Agency is brought about by *contract*—an agreement in writing, by word of mouth, or even one that may be implied from the conduct of the parties. No formal words are necessary: a request to an estate-agent to find a purchaser for your house will make him your agent for that purpose; if you ask a dealer to obtain for you a rare book or a Sheraton table, he is a purchasing agent on your behalf. The *terms* of the contract between the principal and the agent may be agreed upon in detail between them, or may depend upon the *usage* or general practice in the particular trade or profession. The parties are generally at liberty to agree upon whatever terms they please; in commercial agencies it is always desirable to set down in writing, for record purposes, the period for which the agency is to last, the area and scope of the agent's duties, his method of remuneration (usually by *commission*, at so much *per cent.* of the value of business he does), the prices at which he is empowered to sell or buy, and whether he is to be entitled to commission on sales to customers, or purchases from vendors, not introduced by him but carrying on business within his area.

In agencies of a special kind—where, for instance, a solicitor is instructed—his charges are regulated by a professional scale laid down by law; an estate-agent usually stipulates for payment of his commission on the recognised scale. Where no rate of remuneration has been agreed or implied, and after the work is done the parties cannot come to terms, the question must be decided by a court or arbitrator on the basis of *quantum meruit*—that is to say, an estimate of the *reasonable value* of his work.

(3) Rights and Duties of Principal and Agent.—These depend on the terms agreed between them; but if (as frequently happens) these terms are not on record, or are incomplete, certain legal principles apply. The first is that the relationship is one of *mutual trust*. The principal must do nothing to hinder the agent in earning his due; if he appoints a "sole agent," he must not entrust the transaction to other hands. If he does, he will have to pay the sole agent also. He must reimburse the agent for all expenses and losses properly incurred in doing what he was authorised to do. The agent must act honestly and loyally towards his principal; he must not make a secret commission or profit for himself, over and above what has been agreed; he must use proper skill and care, according to his qualifications, in his principal's business; he must keep proper accounts and pay over to his principal the money from time to time collected on the latter's behalf. If he has a *personal interest* in any transaction, he is bound to make *full disclosure*. The law will not tolerate any conduct which brings about a conflict between the agent's duty to his principal and his own *personal advantage*. The agent is therefore failing in his duty if, unknown to his principal, he buys the principal's property for himself, or sells his own property to the principal.

(4) The Principal and Third Parties.—So long as the agent has acted within the *scope* of his agency, the principal is bound by any authorised act done or agreement made between the agent and other parties. And even where the act was unauthorised, the principal is bound if he has, by words or conduct, led others to believe that the agent was authorised to do it. If the agent does something outside the scope of his agency—an act which no third party would reasonably expect the agent to have power to do—the principal is not legally bound towards the third party. These rules apply also to cases where the agent has received money or property from a third party on his principal's behalf, but fails to hand it over to him. The principal cannot claim payment over again from the third party unless the latter ought clearly to have known that the agent was not authorised to receive it. In other words, only contracts entered into and payments made by or to the agent in the *ordinary course of his business* are enforcable by and against the principal and third parties.

In cases of master and servant, similar rules apply where the servant, in the ordinary course of his business, injures some third party by a wrongful act; the servant is liable in damages, and the master also if the act (which turns out to be wrongful) was done within the *apparent scope* of the service. So, if one of the servant's ordinary duties is to deliver goods on his master's behalf by van, and while he is doing so he runs over a pedestrian through his own careless driving, the master as well as the servant will be liable to pay damages for the injury.

But the principal cannot be *prosecuted and punished*, by fine or imprisonment, for an agent's *crime* unless the principal himself authorised or took part in it.

(5) The Agent and Third Parties.—If the agent makes a contract *without disclosing* that he is merely *acting as agent*, he is *personally* liable to the other party to the contract, even though he intended to act on his principal's behalf. If he discloses that he is acting merely as an agent, but does not disclose his *principal's name*, he (the agent) will not usually be personally liable. If the contract is in writing, he can safeguard himself by signing it "as agent," "on account of," "on behalf of," or "for" a named person.

If, on the other hand, the agent gives a third party to understand that he is acting for a certain principal but has *in fact* no authority to act for him, and if the principal later refuses to accept liability, the agent is liable to the third party for his false statement or pretence. This is known as *breach of warranty*—that is, he "warranted" or guaranteed that he had authority to bind his principal, but has broken his warranty; having thus left the third party without right of redress against the principal, the agent must bear the liability himself.

2. Law of Tort

This branch of the law deals with the relations, between one individual citizen and another, which arise from the operation of the law itself, without the necessity for the parties to do any act to put them into legal relations with one another. As was pointed out above (D9 (1)), if A and B are to be linked in a contractual relationship, each of them must take some step to bring that relationship about. No such step, however, is necessary in connection with the matters dealt with by the Law of Tort. Everybody has a right to expect that his person and his property shall be inviolable by other private citizens; he also has a right to expect others to refrain from attacks upon his character and his business reputation. These rights do not arise from any agreement or other act on his part, but from the general principles of the law.

A *tort* is the violation of such a right, which entitles the injured party to bring a *civil action* for damages to *compensate* for the injury he has suffered. The word *tort* (in French "wrong") is derived from the Latin *tortus* meaning "twisted" or "distorted."

It will be seen from the Table (D3) that some torts (*e.g.*, assault) may also be crimes—that is, they may entitle the injured party *either* to bring a *civil action* for *damages* or to *prosecute* the offending party and have him *punished* by a *criminal* court in cases where the offending party's action is liable to harm the community at large; a personal assault, for example, may lead in some circumstances to general disorder, and in that event it will become a matter for intervention by the State through the criminal courts (see D39–40). This section, however, deals only with the *civil remedies* which, as in breaches of contract, are primarily *damages* and sometimes *injunction* (see D11(1)).

The main headings under which torts may be committed are shown in the Table.

Trespass is a wrongful act committed by one citizen, against the will of another citizen, either against the latter's person or in disturbance of his possession of land or other property.

(1) Trespass against the Person may be by way of *assault, battery,* or *false imprisonment.* An *assault* is an attempt to do violence to the person of another; if the act is fully consummated it becomes a *battery.* Thus it is an *assault* for one man to shake his fist in the face of another, or to adopt a threatening attitude towards another, or deliberately to set his dog on another person. If the first person actually strikes the other person, or if the dog, encouraged by the first person, actually bites or harms the other person, that is a *battery.* In order to constitute an assault or battery, and to render the trespasser liable to an action for damages, his act must be *deliberate.* It is not assault and battery if A *accidentally* knocks against B in a crowd, with the result that B falls and is injured. The act by the trespasser must also be *against the will* of the person injured. Thus an operation performed by a surgeon, though it may seriously affect the body of the other person, is not an assault or battery if the other person has consented to the operation; but such an operation, performed without the other person's consent, may amount to an assault or battery.

Certain acts which would in the ordinary way constitute assault or battery are excusable; it is recognised, for example, by the common law, that a parent or a teacher has the right to inflict reasonable chastisement upon a child or pupil in his care, and provided that the chastisement is not excessive the child or pupil has no right of action. If, however, the chastisement results in serious injury or amounts to brutal violence, then the person inflicting it will be liable to an action for damages.

False imprisonment means the *unlawful restraint* of one person by another. It need not amount to actually locking up a person in a room; it is sufficient if his freedom of movement is *totally restrained* either by confinement or by the use of force or threat of force. It should be noted that the restraint must be unlawful; it is not, for example, unlawful for a police officer to arrest a person engaged in committing a crime, or a person whom the officer has reasonable grounds for suspecting of committing, or being about to commit, a violent crime. Even a private citizen may lawfully arrest a person who has actually committed a violent crime or whose behaviour has led to a breach of the peace (see D39–40).

The tort of *malicious prosecution* is committed by a person who makes a *criminal charge* against another person where the proceedings terminate in the acquittal of the latter, where the first person was actuated by spite or ill-will, where there was no reasonable or proper cause for the proceedings, and where the second person has suffered damage as a result. The essence of the tort is *malice* on the part of the person who brought the criminal charge; it is not sufficient that he was honestly mistaken.

(2) **Trespass to Land** arises whenever one person *enters unlawfully* upon land or a building in the possession of another person. Two important points should be noted, as several popular fallacies exist about this tort. First, trespass to land is not in the ordinary case a crime, unless there is some Act of Parliament which makes the trespass a criminal offence (for example, under certain statutes it is a criminal offence for an unauthorised person to cross a railway-line or to enter a Government airfield from which considerations of security require unauthorised persons to be excluded). Secondly, it is not necessary, to constitute a trespass, that *actual damage* should be done to the land or building on which the trespasser has set foot. The essence of the tort is interference with the possession of the other party, and this may arise by merely walking across his field, or throwing refuse upon it, or placing or erecting anything on the land without the other party's consent; any act of *physical interference* suffices.

(3) **Nuisance.**—The *tort of nuisance* arises when an occupier of land or premises does something there which substantially interferes with the enjoyment by a neighbouring occupier of his land or premises. In *trespass* (see above) the interference must be *physical*; this is not so in cases of nuisance. For example, it is a nuisance if A allows his factory chimney to emit volumes of thick smoke which drifts continually into B's house or garden, or for A to carry on, in a building belonging to him, a trade or process which causes noxious smells or disturbing vibrations liable to interfere with B's enjoyment of his property. It is not, however, every such act that gives rise to an action for nuisance; there must be a certain amount of "give and take," particularly in urban areas, but people must not use their premises in an unreasonable or wilfully annoying manner. Thus it has been held that a teacher of music who had pupils singing in her house for several hours a day and on several days a week, which caused considerable disturbance to the person next door, was not committing a nuisance, since it was not unreasonable for her to use her house in this manner. On the other hand, when the person next door retaliated by clashing domestic implements and deliberately making as much noise as possible while the lessons were going on, he was held to have committed a nuisance because his conduct was unreasonable and wilfully annoying. But every case depends upon its own special facts. A building contractor who keeps a pneumatic drill going outside a private house, in connection with building operations, is not liable to an action for nuisance, provided that the use of the drill is necessary to the work, that it is confined to reasonable working hours and limited to a temporary period; but if the owner of a motor-cycle were to keep its engine running, merely to demonstrate its power, outside his own garage for several hours a day, and on several days a week, his neighbours could claim that that was (in law) a nuisance.

All the above examples may be classed as *private nuisances*, and they are torts but not crimes. There is, however, another class, known as *public nuisances*, which become criminal offences if they are liable to injure the public in general. Examples of these are leaving an unlighted obstruction on a public road, blocking a public footpath, or allowing a building to get into such a state of disrepair that it causes a danger to users of the public highway. In such cases the person causing the public nuisance may be prosecuted and punished and, moreover, any individual citizen injured by such conduct may have a right to bring a civil action for damages.

(4) **Trespass to Goods** is an unlawful disturbance by A of B's lawful possession of his goods. Such disturbance may arise by seizure or removal of the goods without the owner's consent or by conduct causing damage to the goods. It follows that every theft of goods is also a trespass; but for the preservation of public morality it is laid down that, if there is a criminal element in the conduct of the wrongdoer which makes his trespass theft, the injured party cannot bring a civil action for damages unless the thief has first been prosecuted in a criminal court.

The *tort of detinue* consists in the wrongful detention by one person of another's goods and his failure or refusal to deliver them up when demanded.

The *tort of conversion* or *trover* arises when A wrongfully appropriates the goods of B to his own use or to the use of another person, depriving the owner of them permanently or for a substantial time, or destroying them. These torts of *detinue* and *conversion* can be committed only against goods or articles of property; they cannot arise from interference with fixtures permanently attached to a building, growing crops or trees; but these torts may be committed if, after such things have been removed or cut down, the wrongdoer detains or converts them to his own use.

(5) **Negligence** in law has a very specialised meaning; it is not "neglect" or "carelessness" in the ordinary sense, but failure to take such care as the circumstances of the particular case demand. In the *tort of negligence* there are two essential elements—first, a *legal duty* to exercise proper care and, secondly, a *failure* to take such care. No action for negligence can be brought by A against B, even if B has been grossly careless, unless the relations between the parties were such that B was under that legal duty towards A. Moreover, the *degree of care* which A is entitled to expect from B will vary according to the nature of those relations.

One obvious example where the legal duty of care arises is among persons using the roads. All of us have the right to use the roads for the purpose of travelling, on foot or in some vehicle, and the manner in which each of us exercises that right will obviously affect the safety and comfort of other road-users. There is therefore a *legal duty of care* upon every road-user (under the common law, and quite apart from the provisions of Acts of Parliament relating to motor-cars) to exercise his right to walk or drive with due regard to the similar rights of other road-users. And, equally obviously, the *standard or degree of care* which it is reasonable to expect from the driver of a powerful car is higher than that which is expected from a pedestrian, since the amount of damage which will be caused by carelessness on the part of the driver is very much greater than that which the pedestrian is capable of inflicting.

We are *not* here referring to *offences* under the Road Traffic Acts, for which drivers or pedestrians may be *prosecuted and punished* under the *criminal law*. Careless or reckless driving or walking may be a criminal offence under those Acts, even if it has caused no injury to any person or property. In cases where such injury *has* been caused the *test* to be applied, in determining whether the injured person can *sue and recover damages* against the other party, is whether that other party has fallen short of the *standard of care* reasonably to be expected from him. It is true that disobedience to a provision of the Road Traffic Acts, or neglect of the Highway Code, may constitute *evidence* helping to prove that the latter party was lacking in the proper standard of care required of him; but there may be other circumstances which show that he was *negligent* in law, and liable to an action by the injured party for *damages*, even though he committed *no criminal offence*.

There are many other relationships where the *duty to take care* arises. One of these is the relation between *the occupier of premises* and persons *coming on to the premises*, whether they have a right to be there or not. Towards *trespassers* (see above) the duty of the occupier is merely a negative one—he must not "set a trap"—*i.e.*, he must not deliberately do anything calculated to cause injury, nor must he do any act which, if done carelessly, is reasonably likely to cause injury. If he knows a trespasser is on the premises he must *warn* him before he *does any dangerous act*; the fact that the trespasser has no lawful right to be there does not entitle the occupier (for example) to weaken the supports of a bridge or set off an explosion without warning. If the occupier does so, he will be liable to be sued for damages, in an action for negligence, even by a trespasser who is injured as a result.

The other rules, relating to the duty of care owed by an occupier to persons coming on to his premises, have been modified (as from January 1st, 1958) by the Occupiers' Liability Act, 1957.

The occupier's duty towards a *trespasser* remains *unchanged*. The Act, however, abolishes the former distinction between an *invitee* and a *licensee*, both of whom it describes by the new term, *visitor*. The principal rules are:—

1. The occupier owes the *same duty* ("the common duty of care") *to all his visitors*, except in so far as he is free to, and does, extend, restrict, modify, or exclude his duty, to any visitor, by agreement or otherwise.

2. The "common duty of care" means a duty to take such care as in all the circumstances is *reasonable*, to see that the visitor will be *reasonably safe* in using the premises for the purpose for which he is invited or permitted to be there.

There are *subsidiary rules*—*e.g.*, that an occupier must expect *children* to be *less careful than adults*, and that a person "in the exercise of his calling" (*e.g.*, a window-cleaner) can be expected to appreciate and guard against special risks incidental to that calling. And a *landlord* of premises, if he is under a *legal obligation towards his tenant* to keep the premises in repair, is to owe *to visitors the same duty* as if the landlord were the occupier, so far as concerns dangers arising from his default in carrying out that obligation.

Among the classes of persons upon whom the law imposes a *duty to take care* are those who practise a *profession or calling* which, from its nature, demands some special skill, ability, and experience. A man who is advised or treated by a physician, surgeon, or dentist, or who consults a lawyer or an architect, is entitled to expect him both to possess and to exercise a reasonable degree of such skill, ability, and experience. If the professional man falls short of the *proper standard*, the patient or client may bring against him an action for damages on account of his negligence. But a mere error of judgment on a difficult point does not amount to negligence, provided that the professional man possesses the proper standard of knowledge and skill and has used them carefully and conscientiously to the best of his ability. And he is not liable, by virtue of his professional status, to an action of negligence for something he has done while acting otherwise than in his professional capacity—*e.g.*, a solicitor who is asked to express an opinion on the value of a house (which is no part of his professional duty).

(6) Defamation.—The tort of *defamation* is committed by a person who *attacks the reputation* of another by "publishing" a *false and defamatory* statement concerning him to a third party. If the defamatory statement is *in writing* or some other *permanent* form (*e.g.*, a picture, a film, or a gramophone record), then the action will be for *libel*. If the defamatory statement is in *spoken words* or some other *non-permanent* form (*e.g.*, by signs or gestures) it will be *slander*.

Another important distinction must be observed at the outset. In cases of *libel* the person whose reputation has been attacked may sue for damages *without proof of "special damage"*—*i.e.*, proof that he has *suffered actual harm* from the libellous statement; while in *slander no action* can normally be brought *unless special damage* can be proved. There are, however, five exceptional cases where such proof is unnecessary, *viz.*, in slanders:—

(*a*) *disparaging* a person in the way of his *business*, *profession*, or *office of profit* (*e.g.*, saying of a doctor that "he is ignorant of the first principles of medicine");

(*b*) imputing *dishonesty* to a person holding an *office of honour* (*e.g.*, saying of a Councillor that "he gives contracts to his friends");

(*c*) imputing that a person has committed a *crime punishable by imprisonment* (*e.g.*, saying of a man "he is no better than a thief");

(*d*) imputing that a person is suffering from a *contagious disease* of a disgraceful kind (especially a venereal disease);

(*e*) imputing *unchastity* to a *woman or girl*.

In these five cases "publication" of the slander alone is sufficient to give rise to an action, without proof of special damage; for slanders of other kinds no action can be brought unless special damage can be proved.

Note also that no action can succeed, either in libel or slander, unless the statement complained of is (1) *false*, and (2) *defamatory* and unless (3) there has been *publication* to a *third party*. (1) The statement must be false "in substance and in fact"; if it is substantially true the person complaining has suffered no injury, recognised by law, to his right (see D12(1)) to the inviolacy of his reputation. (2) The statement must be *defamatory*—*i.e.*, it must be one which "tends to lower him in the estimation of right-thinking members of the community," or which is "calculated to expose him to hatred, ridicule, or contempt." (3) *Publication*, in this context, means simply *making known* the defamatory statement to at least one *third party*. If the defamatory statement is conveyed *only to the person defamed*, and to no one else, there is no "publication," and the person defamed has *no civil remedy*.

In one exceptional case—where a defamatory statement, *in writing*, is likely to lead to a *breach of the peace*—the person making it may be *prosecuted* for the offence of *criminal libel*, for the purpose not of compensating the injured party, but of upholding law and order (see D6(1)). In this exceptional case the *truth* of the statement (see above) is *no defence*, and *publication* to a third party is not necessary to secure a conviction. But there is no such offence as "criminal slander."

If a defamatory statement is made reflecting on a *class of persons* generally (*e.g.*, an attack on "Methodists" or "coloured people" or "money-lenders") that will not entitle a person who happens to belong to that class to bring an action unless he can show that *he personally* was aimed at and defamed. The family of a *deceased person* cannot bring an action for a libel or slander upon the reputation of the deceased.

The Government has, however, promised new legislation aimed against racial propaganda or discrimination generally.

If the person sued puts forward the defence that the words he used were "not published of and concerning" the person bringing the action, the question must be decided whether those to whom the statement was published could *reasonably understand* it to refer to him. If such understanding is reasonable, then it is no defence for the person who made the statement to show that he *did not in fact intend* to refer to the other person, or even that the latter's existence was unknown to him.

Some statements are defamatory in their *natural and primary sense* (*e.g.*, "John Brief is a thoroughly dishonest lawyer"); others may appear unexceptionable if looked at literally, but may have a defamatory meaning in a particular context, or in particular circumstances known to the persons to whom they are published (*e.g.*, "I hear Mrs. B has left her doctor a lot of money. A fine kind of doctor *he* is!"). In cases of the latter kind the person who claims that the published words are defamatory of him must plead an *innuendo*—*i.e.*, he must set out, in his statement of claim, the meaning in which he alleges the words complained of were used. It will be the duty of the judge to decide, as a matter of *law*, whether the words are *capable* of bearing that meaning; the jury will have to decide, as a question of *fact*, whether the words complained of did actually convey that meaning to those who heard or read them.

There are several recognised defences to an action of libel or slander:—

(1) *Justification.*—A plea that the words complained of were *substantially true.* Once the words have been shown to be defamatory, it is for the person who used them to prove their truth—not for the party injured to prove them false.

(2) *Absolute Privilege.*—By common law, or by Act of Parliament, defamatory words used on certain particular occasions, though published to third parties, cannot give rise to any right of action. The occasion is "absolutely privileged." No party to any *legal proceedings*, nor any witness, counsel, or member of the jury, nor of course the judge, can be called upon to answer for any words he has used *during the proceedings*, however spiteful, and however harmful they may have been to the reputation of any other person. The rule applies to *pleadings* (*i.e.*, allegations in writing, filed at the court) as well as to statements made in court by word of mouth.

Similar protection applies to words spoken *in Parliament* by a member of either House (though words spoken outside either House are not protected). And under the Parliamentary Papers Act, 1840, those who publish (in the ordinary sense of the word) the proceedings of either House, by its authority, are protected in the same way; so are official communications, on *affairs of State*, made by a minister to the Monarch, or by one officer of State to another in the course of his official duty. To all these *absolute privilege* applies.

(3) *Qualified Privilege.*—Apart from the cases just mentioned, there are other *occasions* which are *privileged*, not absolutely, but in a *qualified* sense. The *nature of the qualification* will be explained below; meanwhile it may be said that a *privileged occasion* of this latter kind arises whenever the person making a communication has an *interest*, or a legal, social, or moral *duty to make it*, and the person to whom it is made has a corresponding interest or duty to *receive it*. A common example is a reference given, about the character of a servant, by a former to a prospective employer; another is a report made, on the commercial credit of a trader, by one person who has dealt with him to another who intends to do so. Other occasions of *qualified privilege* are *reports* of *judicial proceedings*, of *public meetings*, and of the *proceedings* of municipal or other *public bodies*.

Such occasions are *privileged* to this extent and with this qualification—that there was no *malice* (*i.e.*, spite or other *improper motive*) in the mind of the person when he made the communication. If there was malice, then the fact that the occasion was one of qualified privilege will not protect him from an action for damages at the suit of the person defamed. In any such action it is the duty of the judge to decide, as a question of *law*, whether the occasion was one of qualified privilege; it is for the jury to decide, as a matter of *fact*, whether the defendant was malicious in what he wrote or spoke. (Contrast occasions of *absolute privilege*, where the presence or absence of *malice is immaterial.*)

(4) *Fair Comment* "on a matter of public interest."—This form of defence is most commonly employed by newspapermen, reviewers, and critics. If this defence is to succeed, the words to which it relates must be really *comment* (*i.e.*, expressions of opinion, not statements of fact): the comment must be concerned with *a matter of public interest* (*e.g.*, a book, a play, a musical performance, a political speech, or the public actions of men in the public eye—but not their private lives). Lastly, the comment must be *fair*—and it cannot be fair if it is actuated by *malice* in the mind of the commentator. If he has mingled with his comment some statement of *fact*, and that statement is inaccurate or misleading, that in itself will prevent the comment from being regarded as fair. The *onus is on the defendant* who is pleading fair comment to establish that what he is seeking to defend is really *comment*, that the matter on which he commented was one of *public interest* (not, for example, private scandal), and that the comment is *not based on any misstatement* of facts or *otherwise unfair*. Dishonest or insincere comment cannot be fair; but, on the other hand, an honest belief in the commentator's mind that his comment was fair is not enough for a successful defence. The comment must be fair *in fact*.

The usual *remedy* in actions of *libel* and *slander* is damages—a sum of money sufficient (in the jury's view) to compensate a man for the harm his reputation has suffered. In certain rare cases the Court may, in its discretion, grant an *injunction* ordering the defendant not to publish or not to repeat the publication of a libel.

The Defamation Act, 1952, reduces the risk of legal proceedings against anyone who *innocently* "published" a libel. The "publisher" may make an *offer of amends*, *i.e.*, an offer to "publish" a *correction and apology*, and to take practicable steps to *notify* those who have received copies of any defamatory document. (*a*) If the offer is *accepted* and the promise performed, the party defamed cannot bring, or continue, an action for libel or slander. (*b*) If the offer is *rejected*, then the "publisher," in any action taken against him, may plead, *in defence*, that the words were "published" innocently, and that the offer of amends was made as soon as practicable. *Innocent* publication means: (1) that the "publisher" did not intend the defamatory words to refer to the other party, and knew of no reason why they might be understood to refer to him; or (2) that the words were not in themselves defamatory, and that the "publisher" knew of no reason why they might be understood to defame the other party; also that, in either case, the "publisher" exercised all reasonable care in regard to the "publication."

V. THE LAW OF PROPERTY

I. In General

(1) **Living Persons.**—The special rights and disabilities which affect the ownership and disposal of property by certain classes of persons have been already dealt with under the heading of *Status* (D7–8). It is unnecessary to add anything here on the law of property *in general*, so far as living persons are concerned; but different rules are applicable (as will be seen below) to the ownership and disposal of *land and buildings* as compared with *property of other kinds*. The reason for this main distinction is that the former are, in their nature, *immoveable* and *cannot be physically transferred*, as can money and "chattels" (*i.e.*, animals and *tangible objects* which are capable of being owned). In addition, there is a third class—certain *intangible things* which can be owned and dealt with—for example, the right to be paid a debt, a share or stock in a company, an insurance policy, or a patent; these are known as *things in action*, and they can be transferred only in certain formal ways, which will be described below.

(2) **Deceased Persons.**—It is obvious that the law of any civilised community must make provision, not only for the *transfer by a living person of his property*, but also for the *transmission of that property* (*his "estate"*) *upon his death*. English Law permits every person who is *not disqualified by infancy or lunacy* (see D7) to *give directions, during his lifetime, as to the disposal of his estate upon his death*; he can do this by means of a *will*. If he leaves *no valid will* he is said to die *intestate*, and in that event *the law itself* lays down how his estate is to be distributed. A concise survey of the law governing the estates of deceased persons is given below. (Some of these rules have been modified, so far as *domicil* is concerned, by the Wills Act, 1963.)

Wills and Intestacies.—The law of wills is highly technical; much trouble can be caused by a "home-made" will, and it is wise to seek a solicitor's advice. It is only possible here to outline the *formalities* necessary to make a valid will, and the *procedure* to be adopted after a death. The rules stated are those under English law—applicable to England and Wales, but not Scotland or Northern Ireland.

(1) **The Nature of a Will.**—The person making a will—the *testator*—sets down how he wishes his property to be disposed of after his death, and states the names of the persons (the *executors*) who are to attend to its disposal.

The executors may be, but need not be, some or all of the persons whom the testator desires to benefit under his will. One executor alone is sufficient in law; but if that one dies before he (or she) has completed his duties, delay and difficulty may arise. It is therefore better to appoint *at least two* executors; if one dies, the other has full powers to continue the work. If the testator's *estate* (that is, his property) is large, it may be best to appoint a bank as executor; all banks have trustee departments which are experienced in such matters. They have scales of charges for executorship work, which will be supplied on request. An executor is not permitted to charge for his work, unless the will authorises him to do so—a thoughtful provision for a complicated estate. Nor is the executor bound to accept the executorship when the death occurs.

A will "speaks from death"—that is, it has no legal effect until the testator dies; it can be *revoked* (that is, cancelled) in various ways, or alterations can be made by *codicil*, which is really a supplementary will. Further, the property to which it relates is that of the testator *at the date of his death*, which may be more or less than what he owns at the date when the will is made. The will can be revoked or varied as often as desired to suit changing circumstances; its provisions are not final until death.

Generally speaking, a testator may make whatever provisions, in regard to his or her property and the persons to be benefited, he or she thinks fit. He or she may even direct that his or her wife, husband, or children are to be deprived of all benefit from the estate; but, if he or she does so, it will be well to give the reasons, either in the will itself, or in a signed, witnessed, and dated document, which should be left with the will.

Under Acts of 1938 and 1952, a husband or wife, an unmarried daughter or son under twenty-one, or a son or daughter "under disability" (that is, one who for some reason is incapable of looking after himself or herself), who is not adequately provided for under the will, may apply to the Court for "reasonable provision for maintenance" out of the estate; the Court has power either to refuse the application or to grant the applicant whatever maintenance it thinks fit. In making its decision the Court will take note of the testator's reasons for his failure to provide for the applicant in question. (See also D32(2)).

If a person dies without leaving a valid will, he is said to die *intestate*. In that case somebody (usually the husband or wife or next of kin) must apply to the Probate Registry (at Somerset House in London or in the nearest District Registry elsewhere) to be appointed *administrator*. An administrator has the same rights and duties as an executor. If there are children under twenty-one, and in certain other cases, there must be at least two administrators, and the procedure on death is more involved and troublesome than where executors have been appointed by will. Further, as the testator has not directed what is to happen to his property, the law has laid down an *order of succession*, which the administrators must observe. The intestate's husband or wife is then entitled first to the *personal effects* (furniture, household goods, motor-cars, books, etc.); next, to the whole of the estate, if there are no children or near relatives, or £5,000 if there are, and, after that, the husband or wife and children have certain rights in the remainder of the estate, if any, details of which can be found in the Intestates' Estates Act, 1952. If there is no husband or wife, or no children, or neither, the next of kin of the intestate will benefit in order of nearness of their relationship to the deceased.

It is always prudent to make a will, however simple, since by doing so the testator exercises control over the disposal of his property and saves considerable trouble for his family.

(2) **The Execution of a Will.**—The formalities must be strictly observed, except in the case of soldiers, sailors, and airmen on active service (including members of the Women's Services and nurses), for whom informal directions, even in a letter or by word of mouth, are sufficient. For all other testators, inattention to the formalities may render the will invalid, and will in any case cause considerable trouble and expense.

The will must be *in writing*—*i.e.*, not by word of mouth—handwritten, typewritten, or printed, but the wording need not be in legal or formal language, so long as it clearly identifies the testator, the executors, the various kinds of property dealt with, and the persons to be benefited. It should also state that the following formalities have been carried out when it was executed—that is, signed by the testator and *attested*—*i.e.*, witnessed by two competent persons:

(a) *The will must be signed* by the testator, or by some other person in his presence and by his direction. If the testator can write, his *usual* signature will suffice; if he is illiterate or too unwell to sign in full, he may make his "mark" or his initials alone. If he is incapable of holding a pen, someone else may sign for the testator provided he is present at the time and authorises the signature. If the testator is blind or otherwise incapable of reading the will, it should be read over to him before his signature or mark is placed on it.

(b) *The signature or mark must be at the foot or end* of the will. This means (i) nothing added *below* the testator's signature, and (ii) nothing written anywhere on the document *after the testator himself has finished signing*, will be valid, except the signatures, addresses, and descriptions of the witnesses. If, therefore, at the last minute the testator desires some addition, alteration, or deletion to be made, he and the same witnesses must sign or put their initials against the addition, alteration, or deletion, which otherwise will be ignored.

(c) *The testator's signature* must be made or (if he cannot sign) acknowledged *in the presence of two witnesses*, who must both be *present at the same time*. Any persons may be witnesses, so long as they are capable of understanding what is going on. They need not read the will or know its contents; but if either of them is a *person who is to take a benefit* under the will, he or she will *lose that benefit*. It is therefore safest to call in witnesses who are strangers to the testator. Both witnesses must be *present together* when the testator signs (or acknowledges) his signature; it will not be a valid attestation if first one witness, and then the other, is called into the room. (The wife or husband of a beneficiary must not be a witness.)

(d) *The witnesses must sign* the will *in the presence of the testator*. Either witness may, if necessary, sign by mark or initial, but no other person may sign on his behalf. For identification purposes it is usual and desirable for the witnesses to add their addresses and occupations, in case of a subsequent dispute which may necessitate their being found to give evidence.

If the will consists of several pages, they should be fastened together before execution, and the signatures of the testator and witnesses should appear at the end of every page, not to satisfy the rules set out above, but as evidence that every page formed part of the will when it was executed.

It is desirable (though not legally essential) that the will should bear, just above the signatures of the witnesses, an *attestation clause*—that is, a formal statement that these formalities have been carried out. The usual wording of this clause will be found in the example shown below.

All these rules apply in exactly the same way to a *codicil*.

(3) The Contents of a Will.—The opening words should clearly identify the testator by his full names, occupation or description, present address and (if possible) other recent addresses, and declare that this is his *Last Will*. It is sometimes found at death that a testator has a banking account or stocks and shares registered in his name at some past address, and in such cases the bank or company concerned, wishing to be sure that his identity is clear, may insist upon a sworn statement to the effect that he is the same person as the person they knew as customer or shareholder. (See the example below.)

Next follows the *revocation clause*—a declaration that the will now being made *revokes* (that is, cancels) all previous wills and codicils. If this is not inserted, doubts may arise after death as to whether the new provisions are intended to be substituted for, or merely to supplement, provisions in an older will. If it is intended that the older will is to remain valid in part, that should be clearly stated. If the document now being executed is a *codicil*, it should be described as such, and the date of the original will to which it is a codicil should be mentioned, and also which parts of the original will are being *confirmed*, to stand good, and which *revoked*.

The next clause should appoint the executors, who must be identified by their full names and descriptions or addresses. "My brother John," "my son Charles," or "my mother" will suffice, since only one person could possibly answer to any of these descriptions; but "my wife" is not enough without giving her names in full, since it does not follow that the person who is the testator's wife at the time of his death was necessarily his wife when the will was made.

Next follow the directions for disposal of the testator's property. *Bequests or legacies* of particular articles ("my pearl necklace," "my oak bedroom suite") or of particular investments ("my 3% War Stock")—these are *specific legacies*—must clearly identify exactly what is being bequeathed. In the case of land or a house, the full description should be given—"my leasehold house and grounds at 31, Acacia Road, Redhill in the County of Surrey," or "my freehold farm known as 'Newlands' at Northgate in the County of Derby." The words "I devise" are the technical words appropriate to freeholds: "I bequeath" to all other kinds of property: the effect is the same. (Bequests or legacies of *sums of money*—*pecuniary legacies*—should preferably be stated in words rather than figures; if figures are used the accidental omission of a nought may be disastrous.)

Finally, there is the clause that deals with the *residue* of the Estate—that is to say, whatever will remain after the executors have paid the funeral expenses, death duties (if any), legal and other fees, the testator's debts, and the pecuniary legacies he has bequeathed, and after the specific bequests have been handed over to those entitled. Such a clause is necessary because no testator can be sure, when he makes his will, that he has disposed exactly of everything of which he may die possessed, or that all the persons to whom he has made bequests will necessarily be alive, when he dies. In general, the death of such a person—a *legatee*—before the testator causes that person's legacy to *lapse*; but if there is a bequest of the *residue* for division among a number of persons, no harm is done: the *lapsed legacy*, being left over and undisposed of, leaves the residue to be divided among the surviving *residuary legatees*.

(4) Revocation and Revival.—A will or codicil may be *revoked* (*i.e.*, cancelled) by "burning, tearing, or otherwise destroying" it with the intention of revoking. Destruction by accident, or without the testator's desire to revoke it, is ineffective, and if a copy exists, its provisions may be put forward as still valid. The revocation clause in a later will (see above) will be equally effective to revoke an earlier will; or some part of the earlier will may be revoked by a later codicil clearly referring to that part.

A will is also *revoked*—generally speaking—by *subsequent marriage*, since the law assumes that, if the testator who is newly married had had time for or given thought to the matter, he would have altered his will. If he did not do so after marriage, he will die intestate.

If a testator makes *Will A*, and later on *Will B* containing a revocation clause, Will A is revoked —*i.e.*, cancelled. But if *Will B* is in turn revoked by *Will C*, that does *not revive*—*i.e.*, revalidate—*Will A*, unless *Will C* says, in so many words, that "*Will A* is hereby revived."

SPECIMEN WILL

I JOHN SMITH of 31 Acacia Road Redhill in the County of Surrey Company Director [1] HEREBY REVOKE [2] all wills and testamentary documents [3] heretofore made by me AND DECLARE this to be my LAST WILL.

1. I APPOINT my wife JANE SMITH [4] and my Solicitor EDWARD JONES to be jointly the Executors of this my Will.

2. I DEVISE my freehold farm known as "Newlands" situate at Northgate in the County of Derby unto my son JAMES SMITH in fee simple.[5]

3. I BEQUEATH the following specific legacies: [6]

(1) To my son THOMAS SMITH any motor-car of which I may be the owner [7] at the date of my death.

(2) To my said son JAMES SMITH all my shares in the Company known as John Smith & Sons Limited.

(3) To my said wife all my personal chattels [8] not hereby or by any codicil hereto otherwise bequeathed [9] for her own absolute use and benefit.[10]

4. I BEQUEATH the following pecuniary[11] legacies:

(1) To my daughter JULIA SMITH the sum of TWO THOUSAND POUNDS.

(2) To my secretary EVELYN ROBINSON the sum of ONE HUNDRED POUNDS.

5. I DEVISE AND BEQUEATH all the residue [12] of my real and personal estate whatsoever and wheresoever not hereby or by any codicil hereto otherwise expressly disposed of as to my freeholds in fee simple [5] and as to my personal estate absolutely unto my said wife JANE SMITH for her own absolute use and benefit.[10]

6. I DIRECT that any executor of this my Will being a Solicitor or a person engaged in any profession or business may be so employed and act and shall be entitled to make all proper professional charges [13] for any work done by him or his firm in connection with my Estate including work which an executor not being a Solicitor or a person engaged as aforesaid could have done personally.

IN WITNESS whereof I the said JOHN SMITH the Testator have to this my LAST WILL set my hand this twelfth day of April One Thousand Nine Hundred and Sixty-Five.

[14] SIGNED AND ACKNOWLEDGED by the above-named JOHN SMITH the Testator as and for his LAST WILL in the presence of us both present at the same time who at his request in his presence and in the presence of each other have hereunto subscribed our names as witnesses: } John Smith

George Matthews,
6, Elm Road,
Redhill, Surrey.
Chauffeur.

Ida Gray,
10, Oaktree Road,
Redhill, Surrey.
Children's Nurse.

Notes

[1] Profession is usually inserted for identification purposes.

[2] Revocation Clause—cancels all *previous* wills and codicils.

[3] "Testamentary documents"—includes both wills and codicils.

[4] Wife's *name* should be mentioned—he may have a different wife by the time he dies.

[5] "In fee simple"—technical words showing that the entire freehold interest is disposed of.

[6] "Specific legacies"—*i.e.*, legacies of actually specified things.

[7] Not "my motor-car"; he may sell his present car before he dies and perhaps buy a new one, in which case there might be a dispute as to whether he meant only the car he owned at the date of his will.

[8] This expression is defined in the Administration of Estates Act, 1925. It includes furniture, plate, china, wines, cigars, books, and other *personal effects*. It is better to use a word clearly *defined* by Act of Parliament than a vague word like "possessions."

[9] *i.e.*, all personal effects which the Testator has not left or will not leave to anybody else.

[10] These words show clearly that, although the wife is one of the Executors, with the duty of clearing up the estate for the benefit of *all* the persons to be benefited, these particular bequests are for *her own personal benefit*.

[11] "Pecuniary"—*i.e.*, money.

[12] "Residue"—everything left after all the other gifts have been disposed of, and debts paid.

[13] Charging Clause, without which the Executor who is a Solicitor would not be able to charge for his work on the Estate.

[14] This is the proper form of *attestation clause*—*i.e.*, the clause showing that the proper formalities for signing and witnessing were observed.

Probate and Letters of Administration.—It is a peculiarity of the English system that a deceased person's estate, upon his death, does not "vest in" (*i.e.*, fall into the possession of) the persons to whom he has left it by will, or among whom it has by law to be distributed (the "beneficiaries"); the estate vests, in the first instance, in his executor or executors, if he has appointed any such. (If he has made no such appointment, then, pending the appointment of administrator or administrators (see above), the estate vests (for the time being) in the Presiding Judge of the Probate Division of the High Court of Justice; that Judge has no duties in relation to the estate, but any notices that would, if there were executors, have to be served upon them, must be served for the time being upon him.) The generic name that applies both to executors and administrators, when their title has been lawfully recognised, is *legal personal representatives*; that is to say, they are *recognised by law as representing the deceased person*, for all purposes under the law of property, and for most purposes under the law of contract and the law of tort. Generally speaking, the deceased person's rights and liabilities are transmitted to his legal personal representatives, and can be enforced by or against them as soon as they have taken out a *grant of probate* or of *letters of administration*.

This "grant," in either case, is a document issued by one of the Registries and bearing the seal of the Probate Division of the High Court and the signature of one of its Registrars. It states the deceased's name and address, the date and place of his death, and *either* (1) that his *last will* has been *proved and registered* in the Registry concerned, or (2) that he died *intestate* (as the case may be); that (in the former case) the *executors*, or (in the latter case) the *administrators*, whose names addresses, and descriptions are given, are *entitled to administer* (*i.e.*, to deal with) all the estate which "vests in" them by law; and the document concludes by certifying that an *Inland Revenue Affidavit* has been delivered, showing the *gross and net values* of the estate and the amount of *estate duty and interest* (if any) paid. Where a will has been "proved," a photostat copy of the will is bound up inside the "grant"; if no will has been "proved" the "grant" consists of a single sheet bearing the above-mentioned particulars. It is important to note that, in either case, the *title* of the *legal personal representatives* (*i.e.*, their legal right to deal with the estate) is evidenced by the "grant"—*i.e.*, the document by which the Court's authority is conferred upon them—and not directly by the terms of the will or by their relationship (if any) to the deceased. Anybody, for example, who is *purchasing property of the deceased* from the legal personal representatives is required only to *satisfy himself that probate or letters of administration have been granted to them*; such a purchaser is not in the least concerned with the terms of the will.

Whenever any *formal transaction* has to be carried out in connection with the deceased person's estate the "grant" must be produced; this applies in particular to dealings with land or buildings, "things in action" (see D 23 (2)), the initiation, defence, or continuation of legal proceedings for the benefit of the estate, and the transfer of the deceased's contractual rights. There are, however, a number of *informal acts* which the persons (if any) appointed by the will to be executors, or the nearest relatives who intend to apply for letters of administration, may properly do before the issue of the "grant"; these include such common-sense matters as arranging the funeral, safeguarding and insuring documents and valuables, feeding livestock, locking up premises, and preserving property which would deteriorate if neglected. All persons should, however, take care *not to sell or dispose of any part of the estate before the "grant"* is issued; a person who, without lawful authority, meddles with the estate may find himself regarded as *executor de son tort*—*i.e.*, placed in the position of an executor by his own wrongdoing—and thereby bound to meet the liabilities of the deceased person, and pay the death duties (if any), for which he ought to have provided. Even a person named in the will as executor takes a risk if he does more than the most urgently necessary acts before probate, since it may turn out that that will is, for some technical reason, invalid, or some later will may come to light in which he is not named.

Not more than four persons can apply for a grant of probate or letters of administration. If therefore the will names more than four executors, the persons named will have to decide among themselves which of them are to apply. Even if there are no more than four, *none of them is compelled* to apply, unless he has already meddled with the estate; he can renounce his right by signing a form of renunciation. If the deceased has appointed no executor by will, one or more (not exceeding four) of the next-of-kin can apply for letters of administration. Apart from the special cases (see above) in which there must be at least two administrators, no grant will be made to any more distant relative of the deceased unless and until all nearer relatives have renounced their rights or been "cleared off"; this last expression means that it must be clearly shown that they are dead or for some other reason are incapable of acting as administrators. (The order of priority among the relatives entitled to take out a grant is: (1) husband or wife; (2) children and their "remoter issue" (*i.e.*, grandchildren, great-grandchildren, etc.); (3) parents; (4) brothers and sisters and issue of deceased brothers and sisters; (5) half-brothers and half-sisters and issue of deceased half-brothers and half-sisters; (6) grandparents, and so forth.)

It has been said above that the property of a deceased person "vests" on his death in his executor or executors, if any; if there are no executors it "vests" in his administrators as soon as they have been duly constituted as such by the "grant." *In law* these *legal personal representatives* (executors or administrators) have the same *powers* of disposing of the deceased's property as if they were the owners of that property in the fullest sense; but in accordance with the rules of *equity* (see D4) they must exercise their powers of disposal strictly in accordance with what is *just and conscionable*—*i.e.*, they must distribute the property itself, or sell it and distribute the net proceeds, as laid down by the terms of the *will* (if any); in case of an intestacy, as laid down by the *law of succession*, as set out in the Intestates' Estates Act, 1952. That strict exercise of their powers which conscience demands will be enforced, in case of need, by the Chancery Division of the High Court of Justice (see D5), *at the suit of any beneficiary* under the will or intestacy. But *purchasers* and persons other than the beneficiaries can safely deal with the legal personal representatives as though they were legal owners of the deceased's property, provided the "grant" is produced as evidence of their powers.

The *procedure* in applying for a *grant of probate* or *letters of administration* is that the applicants must make a *valuation* of the various kinds of property of which the estate consists; the value of each item is to be the value on the date of death. (It is not usually necessary to employ a licensed valuer, though this may be helpful if the estate includes valuable jewellery, antiques, or works of art.) An *Inland Revenue Affidavit*, for death-duty purposes, must be *completed* and *sworn before a Commissioner for Oaths*. This document is one of a number of printed forms (varying according to the nature and composition of the estate, and obtainable from Somerset House, the Estate Duty Office, and certain principal post offices). It is divided into headed columns showing (*a*) the descriptions and the values of the various parts of the estate (*e.g.*, cash at bank, Government securities, stocks and shares, furniture and effects, and so forth); a separate section shows (*b*) the funeral expenses and the debts which the deceased left owing. The *gross estate* consist of the items under (*a*); the *net estate* is calculated by deducting those under (*b*) from the gross total (the cost of a tombstone cannot be deducted).

In the simplest cases *estate duty* is payable on the *net estate*, according to a sliding scale; but no duty is payable on an estate of £5000 or less. (In all but the simplest cases it would be wise to consult a solicitor, as the law relating to estate duty is excessively complicated.)

Another part of the document sets out particulars of the deceased and of the applicants, and the kind of grant required. The document, when sworn, must be forwarded to the Estate Duty Office, who will *assess the duty payable* (if any) and interest on such duty from the date of death. This must be *paid in full* before proceeding further, *except* the part of the duty that relates to *freehold property*, which may be paid by instalments. (The deceased's bank will usually grant a loan or overdraft for the purpose of such payment.) When the duty has been paid the Inland Revenue Affidavit will be returned to the applicants receipted.

The second document required is the *Form of Oath for Executors or Administrators*. This gives particulars of the deceased and of the applicants, as before, and declares *either* (*a*) that they believe the "paper writing" before them to be the deceased's *last will*, or (*b*) that the deceased died *intestate*; in either case they declare their *relationship* (if any) to the deceased, and the *capacity* in which they apply (*e.g.*, "the executors named in the will," or "the lawful widow of the deceased," or as the case may be); and they swear *to administer* the estate (the gross amount of which they mention) *according to law*, and to produce proper accounts whenever called upon to do so. This Oath must also be sworn before a Commissioner.

If there is a will it must now be signed (for identification purposes) by the applicants and the Commissioner for Oaths. If there is no will a third document is required, known as an *Administration Bond*. This is a printed form which must be completed and signed, sealed, and delivered (see D9 (2)) by the applicants and two *sureties*—*i.e.*, independent persons who are willing to *guarantee* that the applicants will carry out their duties according to law, under the *penalty* of forfeiting double the value of the estate if there is any default. (In practice, an *insurance company* will usually undertake *the duty of surety* for a reasonable premium, and in that event no other surety is required.) The Bond must be executed (*i.e.*, signed, sealed, and delivered by the individual sureties, or sealed by the insurance company, and also signed, sealed, and delivered by the applicants) before a Commissioner for Oaths.

Finally, the applicants must take to the Principal Probate Registry at Somerset House, or to one of the District Registries outside London, (*a*) the receipted Inland Revenue Affidavit; (*b*) the duly sworn Oath for Executors or Administrators; (*c*) *either* the will (if any), duly marked with the signatures of the applicants and the Commissioner, *or* the Administration Bond, duly executed. If there is no hitch, the *grant of probate* or *letters of administration* will usually be posted to the applicants (or their solicitor) within about fourteen days.

(For the convenience of persons who have no legal adviser, there is a Personal Applications Department, situated in the Royal Courts of Justice, Strand, W.C.2, where the officials are extremely helpful in answering questions and showing applicants how to complete the forms. But in most cases trouble and delay will be avoided by employing a solicitor.)

II. Property in Land (Immoveable Property)

Although the *logical distinction* preserved in the legal systems of other countries is between property in land and buildings and property of other kinds ("immoveables" and "moveables"), English law has from an early date made the more artificial distinction between *real property* or *realty* (*i.e., freeholds*) and *personal property* or *personalty* (*i.e., leasehold* land and property of all other kinds). The reason is historical. In early times, if the possession of freehold land was withheld from its rightful owner, his remedy was an action for recovery of the actual thing withheld—*i.e.*, the freehold land itself—and that very *thing* (in Latin, *res*) would be restored to the owner under an order of the Court. On the other hand, when property of other kinds (including leaseholds) was withheld from its rightful owner, his remedy was an action against the wrongdoer, in which the remedy would be the award of *damages* against the wrongdoer *personally* (*in personam*)—not an order for the restoration of the actual goods or other property withheld. Although that distinction in the remedies is no longer generally applicable, the terms (*realty* and *personalty*) have been retained.

1. Realty or Freehold Property.—The difficulties of this branch of the law are due principally to historical reasons which go back to the Feudal System. In a very practical sense that System recognised only the Monarch as the *owner* of land; those who held it from him were *tenants* (in French, "holders"). If the tenancy was one which was not limited to expire at the end of a fixed period it was known as "an estate in fee simple"—*i.e.*, a *freehold*; a tenancy which was for a fixed period only was known as "a term of years absolute," or a *leasehold*.

When the Feudal System came to an end this distinction remained. A freehold estate in land is still an interest which has *no fixed expiry date*; and the freeholder, out of that unlimited interest, can "carve," as it were, *fixed leasehold terms*, during which tenants will hold the land of him.

The property legislation of 1925 has profoundly changed and simplified the law. Until the end of 1925 one important characteristic of the freehold estate was that of *primogeniture*—the rule that, on the death of the freeholder intestate, the freehold passed intact to his *eldest son* or (if he left no son) to his eldest male heir. This was abolished by the Administration of Estates Act, 1925, which enacted that, in the event of a person's dying intestate after December 31st, 1925, the *whole of his property* (realty as well as personalty) should devolve upon his legal personal representatives (see D18); and that it should, as one whole, be sold and converted into money so far as necessary for the payment of the deceased's funeral expenses and debts, death duties, administration expenses, and for distribution among his next of kin. The eldest son, or heir, has no longer any special privilege.

Settlements.—On the other hand, a freeholder (whom we will call Charles), having a freehold estate in land—*i.e.*, an interest which has no expiry date—can *during his lifetime* create *successive interests* to take effect one by one. Charles can, if he so desires, *settle* his freehold estate to be enjoyed by himself during his lifetime; after his own death, by his eldest son George during that son's lifetime; then by his second son John, during John's lifetime, and finally by George's son Peter "in fee simple." The successive interests of Charles, George, and John are called *life interests*; the ultimate, future freehold interest, reserved for Peter to enjoy after the deaths of his grandfather, his father, and his uncle, is called a *remainder*. Both the life interests and the remainder are *rights of property* to which Charles, George, John, and Peter become *entitled immediately* the settlement is made—that is, they are *present rights* to the *future enjoyment* of the property, and those rights can be dealt with at any time, even before they "fall into possession." Since Charles, George, and John *must* some time die, Peter knows *now* that his freehold remainder *must* come, some time, to him or his personal representatives and, through them, to his next of kin (see above); for even if he dies young, while George and John are still alive, his right will not be "defeated" but will be preserved for those to whom his property may eventually pass under his will or intestacy. Therefore that *present right* to *future enjoyment* is a piece of property which Peter can deal with *now*, unless he is under twenty-one, or unless he is restricted by the terms of the settlement from doing so. George and John can, if they are so minded, do the same with their life interests—that is, they can *now* sell to another person, for hard cash, their present rights of future enjoyment, or they can mortgage (*i.e.*, pledge) those rights against a loan, on the understanding that they will get back those rights when the loan is repaid.

To watch over these successive interests, and to preserve the rights of the ultimate successor, Charles appoints *trustees* of the settlement, whose duty it is to act impartially by all the beneficiaries. A *trust corporation* (usually one of the bank trustee companies), which never dies, or *at least two individuals*, may act as trustees. The Trustee Act, 1925, provides for the appointment, by a simple procedure, of new trustees to take the place of those who die, become unfit, or unwilling to go on acting, etc. In the last resort the Chancery Division of the High Court (the guardian of equity) has power to make such an appointment; for "equity never lacks a trustee."

In order to enable landed property to be freely disposed of, it is provided by the Settled Land Act, 1925, that the person who is for the time being enjoying the current life interest (see above) has power to *sell the entire freehold* estate if he so desires. Nevertheless, the scheme of interests under the settlement is not defeated, for the purchaser from the tenant for life must pay the purchase-money not to him but to the trustees; they must invest the money in safe investments, and carry out the provisions of the trust with the necessary modifications. Each *tenant for life* will then receive the *interest or dividends* on the investments during his lifetime, just as formerly he would have received the rents and profits of the land during his lifetime; while the *remainderman* (Peter) will ultimately come into the *capital* of the trust fund (*i.e.*, the investments themselves) in lieu of the freehold interest. (By the terms of a recent Act, half the investments may consist of stocks or shares in commercial concerns recommended by a stockbroker or other competent adviser.)

2. Leaseholds.—We have seen above that the freeholder, out of his estate which is unlimited in time, can "carve" fixed *terms of years absolute* or *leasehold* estates. These terms may be of any length; the most common are terms of 999 and 99 years. The document by which such a term is granted is called a *lease*; the person granting the term is the *landlord* or *lessor*; the person to whom it is granted is the *tenant* or *lessee*. But the lessor, by the grant of a lease, has not given up *all* interest in the land. The lessor's freehold estate is unlimited in time; when, therefore, the leasehold term (however long) comes to an end, the right to possession and enjoyment of the land will *revert* to the freeholder. That right, known as a *reversion*, is again a *present right* to *future enjoyment* and, as such, a piece of property which the freeholder can, if he wishes, dispose of *now*. The "sale of a reversion" is, in fact, equivalent to the sale of the freehold subject to an existing lease; it confers upon the purchaser the lessor's right to receive rent from the lessee throughout the leasehold term, and at the expiration of that term to *repossess and enjoy* the land without limit of time.

The *lessee* has a *legal estate* in the land for a *fixed term* of years, and he in turn (unless prohibited by the provisions of his lease) can grant *sub-terms* to expire at any time before his own *head-term*. This is a process which can be repeated, in turn, by each lessee, underlessee, sub-underlessee, and so forth, who will become respectively the underlessor, sub-underlessor, and so forth, of the person to whom the next subordinate interest is granted. Thus Michael, the freeholder, by granting to James a term of 999 years, leaves himself with a *freehold reversion* which will revert, at the expiration of the 999 years, into the possession of the then freeholder. James, by the grant of an underlease, can carve (out of his leasehold term of 999 years) a sub-term of 99 years in favour of William, whose underlessor or landlord he becomes, leaving himself with a *leasehold reversion* of 900 years. William, in his turn, can grant to Anne a sub-underlease for 21 years, leaving himself a *leasehold reversion* of 78 years, and so forth. The relationship of lessor and lessee, or landlord and tenant, subsists between William and Anne, James and William, Michael and James; this relationship is one of *privity of estate* as well as *privity of contract*. The former phrase means that each of these pairs of individuals is linked by their *mutual interest in the same term of years* as above described. The latter phrase, *privity of contract*, means that the *link is contractual*—it arises from the agreement between Michael and James contained in the headlease, the agreement in the underlease between James and William, and that in the sub-underlease between William and Anne. But between Anne and James, between William and Michael, there is no relationship of any kind, neither of contract nor of estate; Michael can look only to James, James to William, and William to Anne, to carry out the terms of the respective tenancies.

In certain circumstances, however, there may be *privity of estate* between two parties without *privity of contract*. Suppose Michael *conveys* (*i.e.*, transfers) his freehold reversion, *during the subsistence of James's lease*, to Robert. Thereby Robert will take over all Michael's rights; *i.e.*, he will become lessor, in place of Michael, to James as lessee, as well as being entitled to possession of the freehold when James's lease expires. Between Robert and James there will be *privity of estate*, arising from their mutual interest in the term of 999 years (as lessor and lessee respectively); but there is between them no *privity of contract*, for Robert and James have made *no agreement* with one another. The distinction may in certain circumstances be important.

The Form and Contents of a Lease.—A lease for a term of more than three years must be made by deed (D9 (2)) between the lessor and the lessee. It names and describes the parties, and sets forth that, in return for an annual *rent* (and sometimes on payment, in addition, of a lump sum called a *premium*), the lessor *demises* (*i.e.*, lets) to the lessee, for a term of so many years from such and such a date, the land in question with the buildings erected thereon. (In the law of property the buildings go with the land on which they stand.) Then follow the *lessee's covenants*—the promises which he is to perform: to pay the rent by stipulated instalments, on certain dates; to pay rates, taxes, and other outgoings on the property; to put and keep the property in full repair; to paint the inside and the outside of the buildings at stated times; to keep the property insured, to its full value, in the names of the lessor and himself; to permit the lessor periodically to inspect the condition of the property; to carry out repairs which the lessor, as a result of such inspections, may call upon him to carry out. These are some of the stock clauses; but every individual lease must be carefully studied in order to ascertain what the lessee's obligations are.

Next come the *lessor's covenants*—the promises which the lessor is to perform; the chief of these is that, if the lessee carries out his part of the bargain, the lessor will permit him "quiet enjoyment" of the property without disturbance during the term. Some leases also contain *stipulations* binding on both parties; for example, a *stipulation* that the rent shall be reduced or suspended if the property is damaged or destroyed by fire, and sometimes an arbitration clause. At the end of most leases comes a *proviso*, for the protection of the lessor, to the effect that he shall be entitled to expel the lessee, and to re-enter and repossess the property, if the lessee ceases to pay his rent or to perform his covenants as required, or in the event of the lessee's bankruptcy.

One copy of the lease (the *original*) is signed, sealed, and delivered (D 9 (2)) by the lessor, and handed over to the lessee as evidence of his *title* to the leasehold interest. The other copy (the *counterpart*) is signed, sealed, and delivered by the lessee, and handed over to the lessor as evidence of his entitlement to the rent and to the performance of the covenants by the lessee. The counterpart requires a stamp (impressed by the Stamp Duty Branch of the Inland Revenue) of only five shillings; but the original must be stamped at the rate of 10*s*. for every £100 of the rent (in addition to £1 for every £100 of the premium. No stamp duty is payable on rents up to £100; and the stamp on the premium under £4,500 is *nil* if the rent is £50 or less).

Statutory Reforms in Law of Landlord and Tenant.—The above text on *Leaseholds and Leases* sets out the common law rules. But, at various times since 1920, Parliament has considerably amended and added to those rules—particularly to protect (1) tenants of trade, business and professional premises, and (2) tenants of dwellings of comparatively low rateable value.

Business Tenancies.—The Landlord and Tenant Act, 1954, Part II gives security of tenure to the tenant of most business premises. Fuller details are given on D33.

Residential Tenancies.—The Rent Act, 1965 restores the security of tenure which had been undermined by the 1957 Rent Act; full securty of tenure, accompanied by rent regulation, is given to tenants of low and moderate-rented properties (*i.e.*, of rateable value up to £400 in London and £200 elsewhere). It is now an offence for a landlord to evict a tenant from premises of any value whatever without a court order. This is now a permanent part of the law of Landlord and Tenant, and replaces the temporary provisions of the Protection from Eviction Act, 1964.

The 1957 Rent Act allowed controlled rents to become decontrolled when the premises were re-let. The new Act stipulates that the vacation of a controlled property will result not in decontrol but in conversion on re-letting to a regulated tenancy under the new Act. For fuller details see D33–4.

3. Mortgages.—The word *mortgage* is Norman-French; its literal meaning is "dead pledge." The process of mortgaging land and buildings is roughly analogous to that of pawning a piece of jewellery as security for a loan of money—with the important difference that the land cannot, of course, be physically handed over to the lender (as can the jewellery) to be kept in his custody until the loan is repaid. But a pledge and a mortgage have this in common—that the parties intend no change of *ownership*; the *borrower* (the *mortgagor*) is and remains *owner* of the property *after*, as *well as before, the transaction*. In exchange for a loan of a certain sum, the *lender* (the mortgagee) temporarily enjoys a *charge* upon property worth (it may be) much more than that sum, as *security* for the repayment of the loan, with the stipulated interest, at the stipulated time. The *borrower* is still the property-*owner*.

Because of the essential immoveability of land, the mortgage transaction is effected by a *mortgage deed*, which sets out the terms on which the loan is granted. Generally speaking, the borrower (the mortgagor) is permitted to remain in *possession* of the mortgaged property unless and until he fails to pay an instalment of interest or to repay the capital when called upon, or unless and until he breaks some condition of the mortgage deed. In early times such failure was often the signal for the lender (the mortgagee) to oust him *permanently* from possession, and even to deprive him of *ownership* of the property. But the courts of equity (as we have seen, D4 (2)) gradually evolved the rule that it was unconscionable for the lender to enrich himself, at a low cost to himself, from a transaction in which the intention of the parties was to *pledge the property temporarily* as a *security*, not to sell it permanently for a small sum. Hence was evolved the concept known as the *equity of redemption*—the rule that, even *after the legal date* fixed by the deed for repayment of the loan and for freeing the property from the mortgage, the borrower should still remain entitled to *redeem* the property (*i.e.*, to free it from the charge) by tendering to the lender the balance of the loan, with all interest and costs to date; and that the lender should thereupon be *bound* to give the borrower full and unfettered rights over the property, free from all the conditions of the mortgage, and in the same state as it was in originally. The lender (the mortgagee) must get no collateral (or additional) advantage of a permanent kind once the loan, interest, and costs were paid off; and this is still the law today.

The law, as stated above, has established the principle that the borrower who mortgages his freehold or leasehold interest, as security for a loan of money, shall not be deprived of his ownership, but shall retain such ownership after the execution of the mortgage deed. That deed is, in the first place, a *contract or agreement* under which the borrower promises to repay the loan to the lender, with interest at a certain rate, in one sum or by instalments, and meanwhile, for the lender's protection, to keep the property insured, in proper repair, and so forth. But that is not all; it is clearly important that the lender (the mortgagee) should, in addition, be granted an interest *in the property itself*—an interest which will enable him to take actual *possession* of the property, if need be, to enforce his rights, much as the pawnbroker has the right to *possession* (though not *ownership*) of the pledged article until the loan is repaid.

The Law of Property Act, 1925, devised a method of giving the lender (the mortgagee) a legal estate in the property while still preserving the rights of ownership of the borrower (the mortgagor). That Act provides that the grant of a mortgage of land, in *whatever form* it is effected, shall confer upon the lender (the mortgagee) *a term of years absolute*—*i.e.*, a *legal estate* in the *land itself*, which the mortgagee can deal with by sale, and which will be transmitted, as an interest in land, to his legal personal representatives upon his death. It is further provided that, on the final discharge of the mortgage (*i.e.*, the repayment of the loan, with all interest and expenses due to the mortgagee), that term of years shall *cease and be extinguished*, the mortgagor thereafter continuing to hold his freehold or leasehold estate *free from the mortgage term of years*, and free also from all the conditions of the mortgage deed.

In such a scheme it was necessary to distinguish the term of years conferred by the mortgage from any term of years absolute which might be or might have been conferred upon a lessee or underlessee by way of a lease or tenancy (see above, *Leaseholds*). For the purpose of such distinction the Act provides that, if the mortgagor's legal estate is a *freehold*, the mortgage deed confers upon the mortgagee a *term of 3000 years*, thus leaving to the mortgagor a legal *reversion* to commence after the expiration of that term (since the freehold estate is not limited to expire at any particular time). And if the mortgagor's legal estate is a *leasehold*, due to expire at the end of a fixed period, the mortgage deed confers upon the mortgagee a *term of years to expire ten days before* the leasehold term, thus again leaving the mortgagor with a legal reversion (in this case of ten days only).

In this way each party has a legal estate in the *land itself*, quite apart from the *contractual* rights and obligations in regard to the loan, which can be enforced by and against him *personally*. The mortgagor can sell his freehold *subject to the mortgage term* and the obligations of the mortgage deed; the mortgagee can *sell his mortgage term* with the benefit of the rights that go with it. The sale of a freehold (whether subject to a mortgage or not) is effected by a deed called a *conveyance*; the sale of a leasehold is effected by a deed called an *assignment*. The mortgage term can be dealt with in a deed called a *transfer of mortgage*. In every case the purchaser takes over the vendor's legal estate in the land, subject to, or with the benefit of, the personal obligations or rights in the original deed. In case of the death of the mortgagee or mortgagor, the legal estate in question, and the rights or obligations, are transmitted to his personal representatives.

Finally, it should be mentioned that, as an additional safeguard, the *title deeds* (evidencing the mortgagor's freehold or leasehold title) must be handed over to the mortgagee when the mortgage deed is executed, as part of the latter's security. The mortgagor must take care to get them back when he *redeems* the property by paying off the loan, interest, and expenses.

4. Title.—(a) *Evidence of title.*—Before freehold or leasehold property changes hands, it is the duty of the purchaser's solicitor to *investigate title*—*i.e.*, to satisfy himself that the vendor has a proper title himself and a proper right to convey or assign. Generally speaking, the purchaser's solicitor must go through the deeds (evidencing sales, transmissions on death, grants of leases, grants and redemptions of mortgages) for at least *thirty years back*; he must check every step in the *devolution of title* (*i.e.*, every change in ownership) and make *requisitions* (*i.e.*, demand explanations) on any point which is doubtful. This is still the system over the greater part of the country. No stamp duty is payable on conveyances up to £4,500; from £4,500 to £6,000 it is 10*s*. per cent; after that it rises to £1 per cent.

(b) *Registration of Title.*—With a view, however, to simplifying such procedure the Land Registration Acts have provided for a different system. In areas to which an Order in Council has made the system applicable, *registration of title* is *compulsory* upon any sale of freeholds, or of leaseholds having more than forty years to run. Registration is effected in the following way: the Government lawyers at H.M. Land Registry, in Lincolns Inn Fields, London, W.C.2, or some District Registry, investigate the title of every freehold or leasehold sold after the appropriate date, *once and for all*. If they are satisfied that it is in order, they register the owner as *registered proprietor* of the land with *absolute title* to his freehold or *good leasehold title* to his leasehold. (These kinds of titles indicate that the title is unexceptionable, but if there is a slight doubt the proprietor may be granted a *qualified title*; and if he is in possession of the land he may be granted a *possessory title*, which signifies little more than the fact of possession. The Chief Land Registrar is empowered, however, to convert both qualified and possessory titles into absolute or good leasehold titles, after fifteen years in the case of freeholds, and after ten years in the case of leaseholds.)

The Land Registry issues to the registered proprietor a *land certificate*, certifying (on behalf of the Government) that a registered title of the appropriate kind has been granted. In any further transactions relating to that particular land the purchaser's solicitor need not concern himself with the original deeds save in exceptional cases; he can generally rely upon the certified statements made in the *land certificate*, on which the name of the new registered proprietor is entered by the Land Registry officials when a *transfer* in his favour, or the grant of a lease to him, is lodged at the Registry. There are appropriate sections in the land certificate for registration of a mortgage and the particulars of the mortgagee for the time being.

At the time of going to press, registration of title is compulsory in the Counties of London, Middlesex and Surrey, in the County Boroughs of Eastbourne and Hastings, in the City of Oxford, and in the whole of Kent and Berkshire; also the Cities of Oldham, Leicester, Manchester and Salford, Huddersfield, Blackburn, Rochdale and Reading. But any landowner elsewhere may voluntarily apply for registration of his title.

5. Joint Ownership.—If two or more persons are the owners of freehold or leasehold property, that does not mean that A owns one part of the land and buildings, and B and C other parts; the effect is that all of them *jointly own the whole*. (The analogy will be clear if the reader considers the case of a motor-car owned jointly by A, B, and C; clearly *all three own the entire car* between them; it cannot be said that A owns the engine, B the chassis, and C the body.) The Law of Property Act, 1925, recognises such joint ownership of land by means of a device known as a *trust for sale*. The respective rights of A, B, and C (equal or unequal) can be fully enforced only if and when the property is *sold* and the net proceeds of sale, in money, divided up in the proper proportions; and any or all of the joint owners can insist upon such sale or division for the purpose of obtaining their proper shares. But, while the property remains unsold, all the joint owners have rights according to the proportions of their shares; if, for example, the property is let, the net rents, after paying for repairs and other expenses, must be divided between them in those proportions. Up to four persons can jointly own a freehold or leasehold legal estate in land; if more than four are entitled to the *beneficial interest*, then four of their number only must hold the *legal* estate, and *equity* will enforce the *beneficial rights* of all against the legal owners. A purchaser from joint owners of the legal estate is concerned only with the latters' *legal title*; provided he hands over the purchase-money to them (not being less than two), or somebody authorised by them, *the purchaser is not responsible* for what they may do with that money. If those legal owners, from whom the purchaser buys, fail to pay over the proper shares to those *beneficially interested*, it is for the latter to enforce their rights against the vendors, who have sold the legal estate, by action in the Chancery Division, the guardian of equity. The purchaser's title to the land itself is not affected by the vendors' failure properly to carry out the terms of the trust for sale, so long as the *legal estate* has been properly transferred to him and he has paid the purchase-money to *not less than two* legal owners.

III. Property Other than Land (Moveables)

1. Chattels.—Chattels are *concrete things* which can be the subject of ownership, other than land or buildings, and other than objects so closely affixed to land or buildings that they are regarded as part thereof (*e.g.*, growing crops and trees, or "landlord's fixtures" built into some structure or so closely attached that they cannot be removed without serious damage to the structure).

In the ordinary way chattels can be *sold* or *given away* without any special legal formalities—merely by *physical transfer*—*i.e.*, by the owner handing them over to somebody else. If a chattel is to be *mortgaged* as security for a loan, the procedure differs according to whether the person pledging it (the borrower) is or is not to retain *possession* of the chattel. (His *ownership*, in either case is not disturbed.)

(*a*) If, as happens when an article is *pawned*, the borrower is not to keep the article in his possession, he hands it over to the pawnbroker, who hands him in exchange the agreed loan and a *pawn-ticket*. On production of the pawn-ticket, and the repayment of the loan with the stipulated interest, the borrower is entitled to receive the article back. (Provision is made by law for cases where the borrower defaults in payment, or where an unreasonable time elapses before he seeks to *redeem* what he has pledged.)

(*b*) If, however, the arrangement is that the *borrower* is to *retain possession* of the mortgaged article (as may happen if he borrows from a *moneylender* on the security of his furniture), then the borrower must execute and hand to the lender a document called a *bill of sale*. The law relating to such a document is extremely complex; but the most important provision is that the lender cannot enforce his rights unless he *registers* the bill of sale, at the Bankruptcy Court, in a register which any member of the public can inspect for a small charge. If then some member of the public desires to purchase the article from the person in whose possession it remains, but has reason to suspect that that person, though he may be the owner, has mortgaged it to a money-lender, it is open to the proposing purchaser to inspect the *register of bills of sale* to satisfy himself on the point. If he finds an entry against the owner's name, he will be wise not to proceed with the transaction. If he finds no such entry, and has no reason to believe the owner to be bankrupt, he can usually assume that there is nothing to prevent the person in possession from passing a good title to him. The proposed purchaser can also inspect the register of bankruptcies in order to see whether the vendor has the right to sell (see D8(1)).

2. Things in Action.—These (see D16 (1)) are *intangible rights* which can be owned and dealt with but, because of their abstract nature, cannot be *physically* transferred. If Brown owes Jones £50, Jones (the creditor) can transfer to Robinson the right to collect the £50 from Brown. Jones does this by a document called an *assignment* of the debt and (most important) by giving *written notice* to Brown (the debtor) that Robinson is now the creditor instead of Jones.

Similarly, if Jones owns ten shares in Brown & Co., Ltd., Jones will hold a *share certificate*—*i.e.*, a document certifying the amount of his shareholding. He has certain rights in the company, but these depend upon the company's *memorandum and articles* (D 8 (2)) and upon the *registration* of his name in the company's register of shareholders. The share certificate is only *evidence* of his rights—it is not in itself a piece of property, and the physical handing over of the certificate will effect nothing unless Jones executes a *share transfer* in Robinson's favour and Robinson sends it to the company for registration, together with the old share certificate in Jones's name. After *registration* of Robinson's name, the company will destroy the old certificate and issue a fresh one to him.

Again, if Jones has insured his life with the Brown Life Assurance Society, he will have received a *policy* which is *evidence* of the right of his legal personal representatives to be paid £1000 on Jones' death. If Jones wishes, during his lifetime, to transfer that benefit to Robinson, he can do so, but it will not suffice for him merely to hand Robinson the policy. To transfer the *rights* under the policy he must execute an *assignment* in which it is stated that Jones, being the policy-holder and entitled to certain rights thereunder, now *assigns* those rights to Robinson. But no transfer of those rights will have been effected until Robinson has *notified* the Assurance Society of what has been done and sent it the policy and the assignment for *registration* in its books.

These examples illustrate the principle, set out in the Law of Property Act, 1925, that an *unconditional assignment*, in writing, by a person (the assignor) entitled to any debt or other thing in action, in favour of another person (the assignee), if *notice in writing* is given *to the debtor* or other person on whom the obligation rests (in the above examples, to Brown, the Company, and the Assurance Society), shall entitle the assignee to all the assignor's rights, including the right to enforce those rights by action in the Courts, without calling upon the co-operation of the assignor in whom the right to the debt, or other thing in action, was originally vested.

DIVORCE AND OTHER MATRIMONIAL CAUSES

1. HISTORICAL SKETCH

The anomalies in this branch of the Law of England, and the legalistic attitude of the Courts to the subject, are principally due to historical reasons. For centuries the Church of Rome was the supreme ecclesiastical authority, and the law of that Church (Canon Law) applied to *matrimonial causes*—that is to say, disputes relating to any marriage and the mutual rights and duties of the spouses. Marriage was *indissoluble*—that is, there was no such thing as divorce in the modern sense of *breaking the legal tie*. But the Ecclesiastical Courts, which alone administered the matrimonial law before 1858, might for certain reasons grant a *decree of nullity* (a declaration that a particular "marriage" was null and void). In other cases they might grant what is now called a *legal separation* (known, in those days as a "divorce *a mensa et thoro*," *i.e.*, banishment from bed and board); this latter decree, however, *did not dissolve* the marriage bond, but merely gave judicial sanction to the spouses' living apart from each other, and regulated the terms of the separation. After the Reformation the Ecclesiastical Courts continued to deal with matrimonial causes on the same legal principles as before.

As a result of the Acts of Supremacy passed in the reigns of Henry VIII and Elizabeth I, the Sovereign was declared to be the supreme governor of the Realm in all spiritual and ecclesiastical, as well as temporal, causes. This royal supremacy, exercised constitutionally through Parliament, was part of the law of the land; since there was no limitation upon the power of Parliament (see D5), special Acts were passed, from time to time, to effect that which neither the Ecclesiastical nor the Civil Courts then had jurisdiction to do, *viz.*, to break the marriage tie itself. A divorce of this kind, known as "divorce *a vinculo matrimonii*" (a divorce from the marriage bond) was rare, for the procedure was cumbersome and expensive. Except by the passing of a special Act of Parliament, there was no means of getting a marriage dissolved before the year 1858.

The Matrimonial Causes Act, 1857, transferred the jurisdiction in matrimonial matters from the Ecclesiastical Courts to the new Civil "Court for Divorce and Matrimonial Causes"; but perpetuated the old ecclesiastical practice with regard to nullity suits and judicial separation (formerly known as "divorce *a mensa et thoro*"). Apart from this rearrangement, the Act took the revolutionary step of conferring upon this Court a new judicial power—that of granting a *divorce in the modern sense* of a complete *dissolution of marriage*. As we have seen (D5), the Supreme Court of Judicature Act, 1873, and subsequent legislation, set up one single High Court of Justice, of which the Probate, Divorce, and Admiralty Division formed part, taking over (with other work) the jurisdiction which had been conferred in 1857 upon the "Court for Divorce and Matrimonial Causes." This jurisdiction remains in the hands of the Probate, Divorce, and Admiralty Division to-day. Great changes have been effected *by statute* (notably in 1923, 1925, 1937, 1950, and 1963) extending the grounds for divorce and the jurisdiction of the Court; but in the *interpretation and adaptation of principles* the great body of *case law* (see D4), which enshrined the principles and practice of the old Ecclesiastical Courts, is not without its influence to-day. The principles of equity (see D4), however, have not modified the strict legalism of this branch of the law; *equity has no application to the law of matrimonial causes* (except for resort to *injunction* (see D11) for the protection of the wife's person or property).

2. POWERS OF INFERIOR COURTS—SUMMARY JURISDICTION

Concurrently with the jurisdiction of the Divorce Division of the High Court, Magistrates' Courts now have power (Matrimonial Proceedings (Magistrates' Courts) Act, 1960, and Rules made thereunder) to grant relief (by a *matrimonial order*) to *either spouse* (the *complainant*) in certain cases of misconduct on the part of the other spouse (the *defendant*). The procedure is simpler, quicker, and cheaper than in the High Court. A Magistrates' Court may grant a matrimonial order; if such order provides (*a*) that the complainant shall be no longer bound to cohabit with the defendant that has the same effect as a High Court decree of judicial separation (see D28). A Magistrates' Court may also provide (*b*) that the husband shall pay the wife (or (*c*) where the husband's earning capacity is impaired by age, illness, mental or physical disablement, that the wife shall pay the husband) weekly maintenance up to £7 10*s*. plus (*h*) up to 50*s*. for each dependant child; (*d*) the child's custody (up to 16 years of age) may be granted to the complainant or (*e*) to a county council or county borough council or (in special circumstances) (*f*) such child may be ordered to be placed under the supervision of an independent person (such as a probation officer) and (*g*) access to the child may be granted to either spouse or to any parent. (There are special provisions relating to (*d*), (*e*) and (*f*).)

Either spouse may apply for relief on the ground that the defendant—

(1) has *deserted* the complainant;

(2) has been guilty of *persistent cruelty* to the complainant or an infant child of the complainant or of the family;

(3) has been convicted (i) on indictment (*i.e.*, by a jury) of any *assault* on the complainant, or (ii) by a Magistrates' Court of certain offences (involving imprisonment for not less than one month) *against the person* of the complainant, or (iii) of a *sexual offence* (or an attempt thereat) against an infant child of either spouse who is a child of the family;

(4) has committed *adultery*;

(5) while knowingly suffering from *venereal disease*, has insisted upon sexual intercourse with the complainant, or permitted such intercourse without the complainant being aware of such disease;

(6) is a *habitual drunkard* or a *drug addict*;

(7) being the *husband*, has compelled the *wife*, or led her, *to submit to prostitution*;

(8) being the *husband*, has wilfully *neglected to provide reasonable maintenance* for the wife or any dependant child of the family;

(9) being the *wife* (*in case* (*c*) *above*) has *wilfully neglected to provide*, or make a reasonable contribution to, *reasonable maintenance* for the husband or any dependant child of the family, having regard to any resources of the spouses.

A Magistrates' Court has jurisdiction to hear any such complaint *if either spouse ordinarily resides in the Court district*, or (except in (3) above) *if the cause of complaint arose in that district*, or (in case (3)) if the offence or attempt arose in that district. Jurisdiction is also exercisable *if the complainant resides in England* and the parties last resided together in England (even if the defendant now resides in Scotland or Northern Ireland), or *if the defendant resides in England* though the com plainant resides in Scotland or Northern Ireland. The Court may order the *costs* of the application to be paid by either party.

The general rule is that a complaint under (4) above must be made *within six months* of the date when the act of adultery first became known to the complainant. A complaint on any other grounds must generally be made within six months of the ground of the complaint arising, unless the complainant was abroad at the time; but this time limit does not apply to such continuing offences as desertion (see below) or wilful neglect to maintain.

These "domestic proceedings," as they are termed, may be heard before one stipendiary (legally qualified magistrate) or not more than three justices of the peace, including, so far as practicable, both a man and a woman. The *hearing* is *in private*, the public being excluded, and newspapers are prohibited from publishing details; "domestic proceedings" must be dealt with separately from other matters, and reports from probation officers may be received on the subject of any attempted reconciliation or on the means of the parties. In general, the magistrates should apply the same general principles as are applied in the Divorce Division; lay justices of the peace are advised on the law by their legally qualified clerk.

A *Magistrates' Court*, however, has *no power to grant a divorce* or *to annul a marriage:* the sole jurisdiction to make such a decree is in the hands of the Divorce Division of the High Court of Justice.

An order may be enforced by committing the defendant to prison if his failure to comply with the order is shown to be due to wilful refusal or culpable neglect. (See also D32 (1)).

No order is enforceable while a wife is *residing with her husband*, and *no order* may be made on the application of a complainant where it is proved that he or she has been *guilty of adultery*, unless the defendant condoned or connived at (see below), or by his wilful neglect or misconduct conduced to (*i.e.*, tended to lead to), the adultery. An *order already granted* will be *discharged* (i.e., its effect will be terminated) on *proof of the complainant's adultery*, or *on* proof that the spouses *voluntarily resumed cohabitation.*

If a matrimonial cause is pending in the Divorce Division of the High Court, no application for a separation or maintenance order ought to be dealt with by a Magistrates' Court. And a Magistrates' Court may refuse to make any order when the suit in question would, in its opinion, be more conveniently dealt with by the Divorce Division.

Appeals. A Magistrates' Court has power "to state a case," upon *a point of law* (not a question of *fact*) arising on the application, for decision by a Divisional Court consisting of two or more judges of the Divorce Division. And an appeal from a Divisional Court lies to the Court of Appeal, by leave of either the former or the latter.

3. MATRIMONIAL CAUSES in the DIVORCE DIVISION of the HIGH COURT

(1) Constitution of the Court

The President of the Probate, Divorce, and Admiralty Division and not less than three other High Court Judges attached to that Division are the permanent judges for Matrimonial Causes. They sit both at the Royal Courts of Justice in London and at Assizes. Certain subsidiary duties are performed by the seven Registrars of the Principal Registry of the Division at Somerset House, and by District Registrars in the principal cities of England and Wales.

(2) Practice and Procedure

In contrast to "domestic proceedings" in Magistrates' Courts, the *Judges* of the Divorce Division sit normally in *open court*, though they have power to sit *in camera* (in private) where the ends of justice so require. In *nullity proceedings*, however, it is provided by statute that evidence on the question of *sexual incapacity* must be heard *in camera* unless the Judge is satisfied that the ends of justice require such evidence to be heard in open court. Press publicity is limited by statute to certain matters, and the publication of indecent matter may give rise to prosecution, in *any* matrimonial proceedings.

In general, practice and procedure in the Divorce Division are governed by statute, by rules of Court framed by a judicial committee under statutory authority, and by the principles and practice of the old Ecclesiastical Courts—except in proceedings for dissolution of marriage, which the old Courts could not entertain (see D24(1).

(3) Relief and Grounds for Relief

(a)—Nullity of Marriage. The Court has power to declare a "marriage" null and void in two main classes of case:

(i) "*Marriages*" *Void from their Inception*—*i.e.*, where one of the parties had *another husband or wife living* at the time of the ceremony; where there was a *mistake* as to the *nature* of the ceremony, or the *identity* of the other party; where one party had been declared of *unsound mind* and was detained as a lunatic at the time of the ceremony; where the parties were within the *prohibited degrees* of relationship (*e.g.*, brother and sister, or uncle and niece); or where the *ceremony was not in due form*, or was a mock "marriage."

(ii) *Marriages which are Voidable*—*i.e.*, which stand good unless and until one party or the other ("the Petitioner") successfully petitions the Court for annulment—*i.e.*, where either party was sexually *impotent at the date of the ceremony*; where either party has wilfully *refused to consummate* the marriage; where the marriage was *induced by threats* or fear or duress (*i.e.*, force), or where one spouse was *intoxicated* at the time of the ceremony.

The Act of 1950 has (somewhat illogically) added certain other grounds: (*a*) where either party was, at the time of the ceremony, in fact of *unsound mind* but had not been declared so, or was then a *mental defective*, or then subject to recurrent fits of *insanity or epilepsy*; (*b*) where the other spouse was, at the time of the marriage, suffering from *venereal disease* in a communicable form; and (*c*) where the wife was, at the time of the marriage, *pregnant by some person* other than the petitioning husband. But in these last cases (*a*), (*b*), and (*c*) the Court must not grant a decree unless it is satisfied that the petitioner was, at the time of the marriage, ignorant of the facts alleged; that the proceedings were instituted within a year of the marriage, and that there has been no sexual intercourse between the parties, with the consent of the petitioner, since he or she discovered that there were grounds for a decree of nullity.

Where a "marriage" is *void* (see above) the law regards it as *never having taken place* at all. Where it is *voidable*, the decree *annuls the marriage retrospectively* from its inception; but certain transactions between the parties while they actually remained married are validated, and the Court has power to order maintenance for the woman; and *any child* who would in the normal way have been the legitimate child of the parties *remains legitimate*, notwithstanding the annulment.

Sterility—i.e., inability to produce children—is not, in itself, a ground for annulment of the marriage. If the *impotence* of one spouse appears to be *curable* without danger the Court may, before pronouncing a decree, require that opportunity for *cure* be first given. If he or she *refuses to undergo examination or treatment* the Court may infer, after hearing the other party's evidence, that impotence exists. The petitioning husband or wife may ask for a nullity decree on the ground of *his or her own impotence*, provided he or she did not know of it at the time of the marriage. And there have been recent cases in which *both partners* have been granted decrees.

Apart from the one-year rule (mentioned in the last paragraph but two) in certain cases, delay (however long) in petitioning for nullity is no bar to the grant of a decree.

(b) **Divorce.**—(i) *Its Nature and Purpose.*—Divorce means the *breaking of the legal tie* of marriage by a decree of the Court. There is much controversy on the subject, some of it ill-informed, and much of it tinged with emotion and prejudice. It is not the purpose of this sub-section to take sides in the controversy, but (so far as possible) to remove misconceptions and to set out the various points of view.

We have to start by facing the unpalatable truth that *some marriages do break down* in fact. The symptoms of break-down may be continual strife, and sometimes violence, between the spouses, so long as they continue to live together; or there may be an actual breaking-up of the home because one or the other finds the situation intolerable and leaves. The function of the law should be to deal with this state of affairs as best it can, paying due regard: (*a*) to the interests of the children (if any), who are innocent parties to the dispute: (*b*) to the interests of the spouses and of any third party involved; (*c*) to the interests of public decency and the safeguarding of family life generally.

The problem has suffered from over-simplification by the Press and the protagonists on either side. Sometimes it is represented (quite inaccurately) as a conflict between those who want divorce to be "easier" or "harder" to obtain. Sometimes it is said that divorce as an institution is "causing the break-up of family life." This is a superficial view, ignoring the true nature of the problem, and confusing effect with cause. Happily married couples do not seek divorce. Divorce is the drastic *remedy* provided by the civil law in the case of a marriage which has already *broken down in fact*; the availability of divorce does not bring about the break-down, any more than the availability of surgical treatment can be said to bring about ill-health. A marriage may break down—that is to say, the "kernel" of the marriage, the mutual respect and affection between the spouses, has withered away; only an empty shell—the legal tie—continues to subsist between them. How should this situation be dealt with by law?

It is common ground, among both the upholders of the orthodox view and those who advocate reform, first, that every possible effort should be made, by private individuals and public institutions, to effect a reconciliation, if at all possible. Such efforts are favoured by the law, and excellent work is done to this end by religious organisations, medical men, probation officers, lawyers, and such institutions as the Marriage Guidance Council.

Secondly, it is common ground that, if such efforts are unsuccessful and the *breach proves irreparable* in fact, the interests of the children (if any) should be paramount, and no pains should be spared to secure their proper care and maintenance. This is laid down by law; the Judge in a matrimonial cause may take the initiative in providing for the custody, maintenance, and education of the children, or for placing them under the care of the Chancery Division (see D5); whether the initiative is taken by the Judge or by one of the parents, the welfare of the children is the *paramount consideration*, irrespective of the rights and wrongs as between the parents. Nobody will deny that, once the marriage has broken down *in fact*, the children will suffer to some extent; but it does not follow that they would suffer less if the legal tie between the parents were preserved, or if the home, with its atmosphere of strife, and perhaps of violence, were kept together at all costs—even assuming such a thing were possible. A divorce may not be granted unless the Judge is satisfied that all possible arrangements have been made for the care and upbringing of the children (D31).

It is at this point that the main controversy begins. Where the "kernel" of the marriage has withered away, should the "shell"—the legal tie—be preserved or discarded? And if discarded, then in what circumstances and on what conditions? The present answer of the law is a not altogether satisfactory compromise.

The Christian Churches declare that marriage is not merely a civil institution but a religious sacrament, and the Roman Church regards it as indissoluble. This last is a matter of religious dogma and belief; not a question for rational argument. It is a view as deserving of respect as any other; but, as we have seen, it was abandoned by Parliament a century ago, and is unlikely to be reinstated in the civil law of England. Many churchmen regard this view as binding on their consciences, but it is no longer the law of the land. For better or worse, a marriage can now be legally dissolved, leaving each party free to contract another union if he or she so desires. On what basis, then, ought such dissolution to be granted?

This is the second stage of the controversy. The conventional view, the attitude of the present law, is that a decree of divorce can, and ought to, be granted solely as a result of some *matrimonial misconduct* by the "guilty" party, entitling the "innocent" party—and only the "innocent" party—to go to the Court for relief. According to this view, the decree of divorce (though in law a merely civil remedy) is regarded virtually as in the nature of a *penalty* upon the "guilty" party for his or her wrongdoing—a view that has survived from biblical times. The reformers consider this an anachronism and an anomaly, pointing out: (*a*) that in those times (as is the case under Jewish and Islamic law to-day) it was only the husband who could divorce his wife (not *vice versa*)—a step which was then a very severe punishment, since divorce meant, for the woman, disgrace, degradation, and poverty; whereas there is to-day little or no economic penalty or social stigma upon the "guilty" spouse, who is frequently no less—and often more—desirous than the "innocent" spouse of obtaining his or her freedom. The reformers further emphasise: (*b*) that the matrimonial law has never pretended to identify itself wholly with the doctrines of the Church; for example, the Book of Common Prayer declares, of marriage, that "first, it was ordained for the procreation of children"; yet not even the Ecclesiastical Courts went so far as to annul a deliberately childless marriage, and under the present law a refusal to have children is not a matrimonial offence and involves no penalty. Finally, (*c*) the reformist view is that the essence of the married state—the "kernel"—is the mutual respect and affection between the spouses; once that "kernel" has withered away and the marriage has *irretrievably broken down in fact*, the preservation of the legal tie is a mere pretence; the breaking of that legal tie, from the point of view of public decency, should be regarded as the necessary and proper result of the break-down of the essence of the marriage, or the break-up of the marital home. Under the present system, a refusal by the "innocent" party to take proceedings for divorce, however malicious his or her motive for such refusal, cannot be questioned, and this makes for irregular unions and illegitimate births; on the other hand, the law's insistence that there must be an "innocent" and a "guilty" party inevitably induces two spouses, who find their union intolerable, to resort to unworthy subterfuges; under a more rational system (such as obtains, for example, in the Scandinavian states) both parties might amicably join forces to have the marriage dissolved, once it was quite clear that reconciliation was out of the question. Parliament has recently discussed the advisability of permitting a divorce where the spouses have *actually lived apart* for 7 years; but without success.

All these view-points, and others, were considered by the Royal Commission which heard evidence in 1951–55 and made certain recommendations in 1956; its Report, however, was by no means unanimous, and the law, by and large, remains unchanged. That is to say—only the "innocent" party, except in "discretion cases" (D29 (1)), can take proceedings for divorce against the "guilty" party; the law has sternly set its face against "divorce by consent" in any circumstances—if such consent comes to light.

(ii) *Grounds for Divorce.* The *Petitioner* (*i.e.*, the husband or wife who is *asking the Court for a divorce* against the other spouse) may present a petition on the ground that the *Respondent* (the other spouse):

(*a*) has since the celebration of the marriage *committed adultery*;

(*b*) has *deserted* the Petitioner *without cause* for at least *three years* preceding the presentation of the petition; but, by the Act of 1963, the 3 years' period is not to take account of any one period of 3 months during which the spouses came together again with a view to reconciliation.

(*c*) has since the celebration of the marriage treated the Petitioner with *cruelty*; or

(*d*) is *incurably of unsound mind* and has been *continuously under care and treatment for at least five years* immediately preceding the presentation of the petition. (*See also* **D31** (2).)

Further, a *wife* may petition for divorce on the grounds that:

(*e*) her husband has, since the celebration of the marriage, been guilty of *rape*, *sodomy*, or *bestiality*.

Finally, to cover those cases where one of the spouses has disappeared and not been heard of for many years:

(*f*) any married person who alleges that reasonable grounds exist for *supposing the other party to be dead* may petition the Court *to have it presumed* that the other party is dead and *to have the marriage dissolved.*

No petition for divorce on any ground may be presented *until the expiration of three years* from the date of the marriage, unless a Judge is satisfied that there is a case of *exceptional hardship* upon the Petitioner or *exceptional depravity* on the part of the Respondent. Whether there is such a case is a question for the Judge's discretion upon the evidence brought before him.

As to the above-mentioned grounds for divorce:

(a) *Adultery* means *voluntary sexual intercourse* between a husband and a woman who is not his wife, or between a wife and a man who is not her husband. (A woman who has been raped—*i.e.*, forced to have intercourse with another man against her will—is not guilty of adultery.) For obvious reasons, *direct evidence* of the act of adultery is rare, and the Court may infer from circumstantial evidence that adultery has taken place.

(b) *Desertion* means, primarily, the *intentional permanent abandonment*, by one spouse of the other, *without that other's consent*, and *without reasonable cause.* Therefore there is *no desertion* in such cases (for example) as: (i) where a husband *cannot* live with his wife because he is serving a sentence of imprisonment; (ii) where a husband leaves his wife for a *short time* for necessary business or family reasons, *intending to return to her*; (iii) while a *separation continues with the consent of both parties*; (iv) where the spouse who abandoned the other had *just cause* to do so; (v) any one period of 3 months cohabitation with a view to reconciliation does not break the period of desertion.

Indeed, in certain cases under (iv) the doctrine known as constructive desertion may apply *against the other spouse*, if he or she has (figuratively speaking) *driven the first spouse away. Constructive desertion* means, not "desertion" in the literal sense of walking out of the matrimonial home, but conduct on the part of a husband which is intended to force, and virtually forces, his wife to leave him, or *vice versa.* Thus, if a husband brings his mistress to live with him in the matrimonial home and, as a result, his wife leaves him, not only is the wife innocent of desertion in the legal sense, but the husband is himself guilty of constructive desertion; it will be presumed against him that he intended to terminate his marital association, and he has in fact *carried out that intention.* Such a case illustrates the principle that there are *two elements* in the legal meaning of *desertion*—the *act* of physical separation and the *intention* to bring normal married life to an end.

In order to bring about desertion it is not necessary that the spouses should cease to live under the same roof; "desertion is not withdrawal from a place, but from a state of things." It is sufficient that the Respondent (the "guilty" spouse) has withdrawn from, or forced the other to withdraw from, *cohabitation*—*i.e.*, from sharing a common "home" in the full sense of the word. A wife "deserts" her husband if she refuses (against his will) to share his room, to take her meals with him, and to perform the usual duties of a wife. On the other hand, the mere refusal of sexual intercourse, in itself alone, does not amount to desertion, though it *may amount to cruelty* (D28) if it has broken or is likely to break the health or spirit of the Petitioner.

It should also be noted that desertion is not a single act but a continuous state of affairs. The Petitioner must prove beyond reasonable doubt *that desertion without cause continued* during the entire period of *three years* required by law as the basis of a divorce petition. Although (see above) desertion in the legal sense must be *without the consent* of the petitioning spouse, recent judicial decisions have tended to dispense with the requirement that the deserted party must prove a *continuing desire* for the deserting party to return, and a *continuing willingness* to receive and reinstate the deserting party, during the *entire period of three years* preceding the commencement of proceedings; in other words, once the latter party's *original act and intention of deserting* has been proved, that intention is *presumed to have continued*, unless there is evidence to the contrary. (But see above (b)(v).) But any kind of *agreed separation* is fatal to the case, whether the agreement be in writing, by word of mouth, or implied by conduct. An agreement, however, by a husband, who is *already living apart* from his wife, to *maintain* her and the children does not constitute a separation by agreement, unless there is evidence that the *wife actually consented* to his leaving her. A *matrimonial order* made by a Magistrates' Court (see (D24 (2)) does not necessarily prevent the period of desertion from running, unless the order contains a clause, deliberately inserted, to the effect that "the parties shall no longer be bound to cohabit."

If the deserting party makes an *offer to return* to the matrimonial home it is the duty of the other party to receive him (or her) back and to resume normal married life together, *if the offer to return is genuine* and if no other matrimonial offence (such as adultery or cruelty) has been committed by the deserting party. Whether such an offer is "genuine" is a question of fact, to be decided on all the evidence; it will generally be a wise safeguard for a deserted party who receives such an offer to *take legal advice* before accepting or rejecting it; for if rejection of the offer subsequently proves to have been unjustified, he (or she) may become the deserting party. This situation, again, arises from the legal view that "desertion" consists of two elements—the *act* and the *intention* of deserting. (See also (b) (v), above).

An *honest and reasonable belief*, by one spouse, that the other spouse has committed, or is committing, adultery, if such a belief is induced by the other spouse's conduct, may be "just cause" for the first spouse to refuse cohabitation, and prevent him (or her) from being regarded as the deserting party.

(c) *Cruelty* is not defined by statute, but has been decided, in reported cases, to mean conduct causing danger to life, limb, or bodily or mental health, or giving rise to a reasonable apprehension of such danger. (The term "Mental Cruelty" is unknown to English law; but there may be *cruelty* in the legal sense *without physical violence.*) The Courts have refused to commit themselves to a comprehensive definition; *every case* must be considered on its *own facts* in the light of the whole history of the marriage. One single act, even of violence, can seldom be regarded as "cruelty"; but the conduct complained of must be of a *grievous nature*—not mere conduct which (however reprehensible) may be regarded as "part of the wear and tear of married life." In order to constitute cruelty, the conduct must be understood to be likely to break the latter's *health or spirit.* An *insane person*, who does not understand the nature and quality of his acts, and so cannot form the necessary "intention" (see D8), *can be guilty of cruelty* if he was warned of the probable result; for it is no longer necessary for the petitioner to prove that the respondent *intended* to be cruel or was aiming or directing his conduct against the petitioner.

Drunkenness, in itself, is *not* cruelty; but if it is so *persistent*, or its effects so inevitably *distressing* to the other spouse, as to *threaten his or her health*, it may amount to cruelty. Similar considerations apply to persistent refusal of sexual intercourse, excessive sexual demands, or sexual malpractices either forced upon the other spouse or committed with third parties.

A *divorce petition* based wholly or partly on cruelty must *set out specifically the acts* complained of, evidence of which is to be given at the trial. (This ensures that the Respondent knows the details of the case he has to meet.)

(c) Restitution of Conjugal Rights.—Either spouse may petition the Court for such a decree where the other spouse has "wrongfully withdrawn from cohabitation" (see above). *Willingness to return* to cohabitation, *if genuine*, or *proof of just cause* (see above) for refusal are good defences. If the petition succeeds, and the Court orders the erring spouse to return, his or her *non-compliance* with the order *will not lead to enforcement* by arrest or otherwise; but it will (so to speak) fix upon him or her responsibility for the separation, and *establish* his or her status as the deserting party (see above). And *non-compliance* with a restitution decree is in itself *a ground* for the other party to petition for a decree of *judicial separation* (see below).

(d) Judicial Separation.—A petition for this form of relief may be presented by either spouse on the ground last mentioned in the foregoing paragraph, or on any of the grounds for which a divorce petition (see above) might have been presented. The *effect of the decree* (as in the case of a similar order made by a Magistrates' Court) is that the Petitioner is *no longer bound to cohabit* with the Respondent, and cannot therefore be regarded as a deserting party. (The *legal bond* of marriage *remains in force*; the procedure is therefore often employed by a spouse who does not desire divorce, perhaps for reasons of conscience, perhaps merely so as not to allow the other party freedom to marry somebody else.) It is, however, open to a Petitioner, who has obtained a decree of judicial separation, to petition for divorce, on the same facts, at a later date—*provided that three years have elapsed* since the date of the marriage (see D27 (1)).

Bars to Relief.—(1) *Absolute Bars.*—It is, by statute, the duty of the Court to investigate, so far as it reasonably can, the facts alleged in any petition for divorce or judicial separation, and to inquire whether there has been any *connivance* or *condonation* on the part of the Petitioner, and whether any *collusion* exists between the parties. *The Court must dismiss* the petition, and *refuse a decree, even in an undefended suit, unless* it is satisfied: (*a*) that the *Petitioner has proved his or her case*; (*b*) that the Petitioner has not been *accessory to or connived at* the adultery (if any) of the other party; (*c*) that the Petitioner has not *condoned* the adultery (if any) or the cruelty (if any) of the other party.

(a) *The Petitioner must prove the case*—that is to say, satisfy the Court that there are *proper grounds* for a decree *according to law*; there is no such thing, in suits for divorce and judicial separation, as judgment by consent, by admission, or in default of defence (as is possible, for example, in actions for breach of contract (D11) and tort (D12)). *In matrimonial suits* the *State*, and not merely the parties themselves, must see that the provisions of the law are *strictly observed.*

(b) *There must be no connivance*—that is to say, the Petitioner must not have intended *to promote or encourage or provide opportunity for* the commencement or the continuance of the Respondent's adultery. Merely *keeping watch upon a suspected spouse*, for the purpose of obtaining evidence, is not necessarily connivance; there must be active *encouragement or acquiescence*—wilfully "shutting one's eyes" to what is going on or likely to take place. (But, if a spouse who has connived at his partner's adultery repents and withdraws his acquiescence, the connivance may be regarded as "spent," and no longer be a bar to divorce.)

(c) *There must be no condonation* of adultery or cruelty—that is to say, *forgiveness* of all such acts as are known to, or suspected by, the injured spouse, and the restoration of normal marital relations with the offending spouse. ("Forgiveness" means forgiveness *on condition* that there shall be *no further matrimonial offence.*) Condonation may be by words or conduct. The Petitioner *cannot obtain a decree* on the ground of any offence or offences which he or she has *condoned*, except in case of *revival*. But adultery or cruelty shall not (now) be deemed to have been condoned merely because of a resumption of cohabitation (for not more than three months) with a view to reconciliation.

Revival—If, subsequent to the condonation, the offending spouse again commits some matrimonial offence or offences, the former offence or offences, other than adultery, are *revived*—*i.e.*, the effect of the forgiveness and restoration (see above) is cancelled, and the former offence or offences wi again afford a ground for divorce or judicial separation. It does not matter whether or not the new offence is of the same nature as the old; condoned cruelty will be revived by new acts of cruelty or desertion; condoned cruelty will be revived by a new act of adultery, and so forth. But, by the Act of 1963, adultery, once condoned, cannot be revived.

(2) *Discretionary Bars*—(*a*) *There may be an agreement* or *bargain* between the parties (whether for financial consideration or otherwise) that the Petitioner will commence or conduct a suit for divorce or judicial separation, or that the Respondent will not defend such a suit. There is *collusion* if one party *requests or suggests* that the other *should commit adultery* in order to provide evidence for a divorce, and the other party *accedes* to the request or suggestion. But it is not necessarily collusion for the Petitioner, knowing that *adultery has already been committed*, to ask the other party *for details or for evidence* on which the Petitioner can act. The Court regards financial arrangements between the parties with suspicion, if they are entered into *before the suit is commenced*, and it will carefully investigate such arrangements, and it has a discretion, under the 1963 Act, to permit such financial arrangements if they are fully disclosed. Once the petition has been filed, there is no objection to discussion, between the parties or their advisers, of necessary financial arrangements as to alimony or maintenance (see D30(1)) or the disposal of the matrimonial home.

(*b*) Apart from connivance and condonation, either of which (as we have seen) is a *bar* to the granting of a decree, the *Court has a discretion either to refuse or to grant* a decree of divorce or judicial separation, according to circumstances, if it finds that the *Petitioner* has himself (or herself): (*i*) been *guilty of adultery* during the marriage; (*ii*) *shown unreasonable delay* in presenting or prosecuting the petition; or (*iii*) been guilty of cruelty, or desertion without reasonable cause, *before* the Respondent's acts of adultery or cruelty on which the petition is based. The Court has a similar *discretion*, where the ground for the petition is *adultery, desertion*, or *unsoundness of mind*, either to refuse or to grant a decree to a *Petitioner* who has (*iv*) been guilty of such *wilful neglect or misconduct* as has conduced to (*i.e.*, helped to bring about) the Respondent's adultery, desertion, or unsoundness of mind; and (*v*), by the 1963 Act, it has a discretion to grant a divorce where there has been an agreement between the parties, if full disclosure is made (see (*a*) above).

In a case where each party is asking for a divorce against the other, each admitting his (and her) own misconduct and asking the Court to exercise its discretion in his (and her) favour, the *Court may exercise its discretion in favour of both* and dissolve the marriage. The same applies to *nullity*.

In case (*i*) above, where the *Petitioner* has himself (or herself) been *guilty of adultery*, it is the Petitioner's duty to lodge in the Divorce Registry a *discretion statement*—*i.e.*, a written statement in a sealed envelope (to be opened by the Judge at the hearing) admitting the facts and explaining the circumstances of his (or her) adultery. The *petition* in such a case must *contain a clause praying the Court* "to exercise its discretion in the Petitioner's favour." The Petitioner's *own* adultery, admitted in open Court, may be the only such evidence available.

Decree Nisi and Decree Absolute.—When the case comes on for trial the Judge will hear the *evidence of the Petitioner* and his or her witnesses, and *legal argument* on his or her behalf; *if the case is defended* by the Respondent spouse, or by the co-respondent (*i.e.*, any *man* accused, in the petition, of adultery with a Respondent *wife*), or by any *woman named* in the petition as having committed adultery with a Respondent *husband*, the Judge will hear their evidence and legal argument on their behalf. The Judge, if not satisfied on points (*a*), (*b*), and (*c*), (D28–9) in a case of divorce or judicial separation, must *dismiss the petition*, in which event the married status of the parties will remain unchanged. If the Judge *is* satisfied on the points mentioned he will, in a suit for *judicial separation*, pronounce a *final decree*; in a *suit for restitution of conjugal rights* he will *order* the deserting spouse to *return to cohabitation* (the effect of the decree and the order is described above, D28 (1)).

In a suit for *nullity* or *divorce*, the Judge will pronounce a decree *nisi*—*i.e.*, an order that the marriage is to be *annulled* or *dissolved* unless (*nisi*), before that event takes place, *some cause* is shown to the Court *why final annulment or dissolution ought not to be permitted*. Intervention for this purpose may be made by an official known as the *Queen's Proctor*, or by any member of the public. Such interventions after decree *nisi* are rare, but may be made on the ground, for example, that there was a collusive arrangement (see above) which was not disclosed, or some other material fact, which was concealed from the Court at the hearing.

If such intervention succeeds, the decree *nisi* will be *rescinded* (*i.e.*, cancelled) and the parties will retain their former status. If there is *no such intervention*, or if such intervention is *dismissed*, then the marriage will be *finally annulled or dissolved* on application (on a special form), at the Divorce Registry concerned (not in open court), by or on behalf of the *Petitioner*, not earlier than *three months* after the decree *nisi* (unless the Court fixes a shorter time by special order). If the Petitioner does not make such an application, then the Respondent may do so after the lapse of a *further three months* (*i.e.*, six months after the date of the decree *nisi*), and the Court has power to grant or refuse such application or to deal with the case as it thinks fit.

The decree which *finally annuls or dissolves* the marriage is called a *decree absolute*. Unless and until it is granted, the marriage tie still subsists; the decree *nisi* does *not* terminate the status of husband and wife. But the *decree absolute* does terminate that status, leaving both parties free to marry again.

Incidental Matters

(1) Custody and Maintenance of Children.—Apart from the general power of the Chancery Division, as guardian of equity (D5), *to protect the person and the property of any infant* (D7) and of the Local Authority under the Children and Young Persons Act, 1963, (even though there may be no matrimonial proceedings between its parents), and apart from the additional powers of that Division and of Magistrates' Courts, under the Guardianship of Infants Act, 1925, *to appoint a guardian or guardians for any infant*, and to make orders for either parent to have *access* to the infant (*i.e.*, to see it periodically) and for the infant's *maintenance*, the Divorce Division itself may make orders for the *custody, maintenance, and education* of the *children of the family* (see D31 (1)) in any matrimonial proceedings, and give directions for placing them under the protection of the Court, and for access to them by either or both of the parents. The expression "children of the family" includes children lawfully adopted by both husband and wife, children of a bigamous "marriage" which has given rise to nullity proceedings (D25), and also children born before the marriage of their parents and legitimated by that (subsequent) marriage. The Court may make such orders and give directions at any time after proceedings have been commenced for nullity, divorce, judicial separation, or restitution of conjugal rights; it may make interim orders, and give interim directions, from time to time *during the proceedings.* It is, however, *unusual* for the Divorce Division to make orders for custody of or access to any child *over the age of sixteen* (since such orders would be difficult to enforce). (See also D31(1) for recent changes in the law.)

In all such proceedings, in *whatever court* they may be taken, the *paramount consideration* is the *welfare of the children—not the punishment of the "guilty" parent, nor any privilege* of the father as against the mother, or *vice versa.* (It is, for example, unusual for the Court to deprive the mother of the custody of a very young child, even though she has committed or is living in, adultery—unless, or course, she is neglecting the child or is a "bad mother" in the widest sense.) In some cases, for good reason, both parents may be passed over, and the custody of the child may be given to some third party.

(2) **Financial Provision.**—(a) *Alimony Pending Suit.*—On any petition for nullity, divorce, judicial separation, or restitution of conjugal rights, the Divorce Division may make such *order* for *payment by the husband to the wife* of *alimony pending suit* (*i.e.*, a periodical sum for or towards her support *during the proceedings*) as the Court thinks just. The Court may also *order a wife Petitioner*, in a suit for divorce or judicial separation on the ground of the *husband's insanity*, to pay *alimony pending suit* for or towards the *support of the husband during the proceedings.*

(b) *Permanent Alimony* is the term used for similar payments which the Court may order the husband to make to the wife *after* the pronouncement of a *decree of judicial separation* on any ground, and such an order *in favour of the wife* may be made even where a decree has been pronounced *against her.* An order for *permanent alimony* may also be made *in favour of the husband* in a case where the *wife petitioned* for judicial separation on the ground of *his insanity. Permanent alimony* may also be ordered in favour of the wife where an order for *restitution of conjugal rights* has been made in her favour.

(It will be observed that, in all the above cases, the period during which the payment of *alimony* may be ordered is *while the status of marriage remains in being.*)

(c) *Permanent Maintenance* is the provision which the Court may order the husband to make in favour of the wife *after a decree absolute* of *divorce or nullity—i.e.*, for the period *after the married status has been terminated.* (The Court may, *in exceptional cases*, make an order for *permanent maintenance* in favour of a "guilty" wife.) In *one case permanent maintenance* may be ordered *against a wife* and *in favour of a husband*—where the *wife petitioned* for divorce on the ground of *his insanity.* The order may be for payment of a *monthly or weekly sum* during the *joint lives of the parties* (*i.e.*, so long as they shall *both* live), or for a capital sum to be invested so as "to secure to the wife such gross or annual sum of money, for any term not exceeding her life," as the Court thinks reasonable, in both cases having regard to "*her fortune* (if any), to the *ability of the husband*, and to the *conduct of the parties.*" The amount of the order is therefore left to the *discretion of the Court*; and it may be varied by the Court from time to time as the circumstances of the parties change. (The words "conduct of the parties" show that, in fixing the payments, the Court does not necessarily regard the question of "guilt" or "innocence" as clear-cut on the one side or the other; it may take into consideration the *whole history of the marriage.* The Court also takes into account the *property and income* of *both parties.*) (*See also* D32(1) C.)

(d) *Periodical Payments* may be ordered to be made, *by the husband to the wife*, on or after the making of a *decree for restitution of conjugal rights*, for the joint lives of the parties. The Court may order the husband to "secure" such payments as in the case of permanent maintenance. Where the *husband successfully applied* for the decree, the Court may order the wife, if she is "in receipt of any *profits of trade or earnings*," to pay to the husband, or for the benefit of the children, such part of those profits or earnings as it thinks reasonable. See also D32 (C and D).

Where a husband has been guilty of *wilful neglect to provide reasonable maintenance* for his wife or infant children, then, in any case where the wife might have petitioned for judicial separation, the Court may (on the wife's application) order the husband to make to her such *periodical payments* as may be just, and it may order the husband to "secure" such payments (as described above). (Thus, where there has been wilful neglect to maintain, on the part of the husband, the wife may apply for financial relief in the Divorce Division instead of in the Magistrates' Court; there is *no limit* in the Divorce Division to £7 10*s.* a week, as there is in the Magistrates' Court (D24 (2)). And the wife may make such an application even if she does not wish to petition for a decree of nullity, divorce, judicial separation, or restitution of conjugal rights.)

(e) In any case where the Court has power to make a *permanent* order, it may now order the payment of a *lump sum* (1963 Act).

(f) *Settlements.*—In any case in which the Court pronounces a decree for divorce or judicial separation by reason of the *wife's adultery, cruelty, or desertion*, the Court has power to order the wife's property, or any part of it, to be *settled* (D20) for the benefit of the innocent party, or of the children of the marriage, or both.

The Court also has power, after a decree for nullity or divorce, to vary the terms of any settlement which may have been made on the parties before or after their marriage; the variation may be made to benefit the children, or the parties or either of them, as the Court thinks fit.

(g) *Damages against Co-respondent.*—A husband who is petitioning for a decree of *divorce or judicial separation*, on the ground of his *wife's adultery*, may ask for an award of *damages against the Co-respondent* (*i.e.*, the man with whom she has committed adultery). Such a claim, which is comparatively rare nowadays, is usually tried before a judge and jury; the damages should be assessed so as to *compensate the husband*, so far as possible, for the loss of his wife where she has been seduced from his side by the adulterer.

(h) *Costs.*—The costs of the proceedings are *always in the discretion of the Court*, each case depending on its own facts. Generally speaking, however, the costs "follow the event"—*i.e.*, when a decree or order is made against a husband he will usually be ordered to pay the costs incurred; costs, however, are rarely awarded against a "guilty" wife, but are not infrequently ordered to be paid by the Co-respondent (if any). An order for costs may be made, but rarely is, against the "woman named" in a petition as having committed adultery with the husband.

Note on Domicil.—It has been explained above (see D7) why the English Court will *not, generally speaking*, grant a *divorce* to a man who is *domiciled abroad.* Since the *domicil of a wife* is the same as *that of her husband* (even if she has not lived with him for many years), the refusal of the English court to accept jurisdiction has caused hardship in many cases. To mitigate this hardship the Matrimonial Causes Act, 1950, confers upon the Divorce Division an additional statutory jurisdition in the following cases, *in favour of a wife*, even if her husband is *not domiciled in England*:

(*a*) In *any* matrimonial proceedings, *other than* for a "decree of presumption of death and dissolution of marriage" (see below), if: (i) the wife has been deserted by her husband, or the husband has been deported from the United Kingdom as an alien; and (ii) immediately *before the desertion or deportation* the husband *was* domiciled in England.

(*b*) In proceedings for *divorce* or *nullity*, if: (i) the wife is *resident* (*i.e.*, actually living for the time being) in England; and (ii) has been *ordinarily resident* there for a period of *three years* immediately preceding the commencement of the proceedings; and (iii) the husband is *not* domiciled *in any other part of the United Kingdom*, or in the Channel Islands or the Isle of Man. (The two last-named territories have their own separate systems of law.)

(*c*) In proceedings for a decree of "presumption of death and dissolution of marriage": the husband is presumed by law (*for the purpose of ascertaining the wife's domicil*) to have died "immediately after the last occasion when she knew, or had reason to believe him, to be living." (Thus the wife can acquire an English domicil of her own as from that date.)

And, under the Matrimonial Causes (War Marriages) Act, 1944:

(*d*) In the special case of *marriages celebrated during the Second World War*, where: (i) the *husband* was, at the time of the marriage, domiciled *outside the United Kingdom*; (ii) the *wife* was, immediately before the marriage, *domiciled in England*; and (iii) the parties *never resided together* in the country which was the husband's domicil at the time of the marriage, the Divorce Division may deal with proceedings for divorce or nullity *as if both parties* were at all material times *domiciled in England*. (This provision was to cover the special cases of soldiers from the Dominions or Colonies, the United States or other foreign countries who, while stationed here during the War, married English girls and had to go back to their own countries, *leaving their wives behind*—in some instances without communicating with them again.)

RECENT CHANGES IN THE LAW

Since the above survey was completed, there have been certain important changes in the law, effected by Acts of Parliament:

A. By the Matrimonial Proceedings (Children) Act, 1958

1. The powers of the Divorce Division to provide r the *custody, maintenance, and education of the ildren* of the family (D29 (2)) are enlarged to pply also to a *child of one of the parties* (including n *illegitimate* or *adopted* child) "who has been ccepted as one of the family by the other party," s they apply to a child (whether legitimate or egitimate) of *both parties*. All such children re referred to as "children of the family".

2. Where a husband has been *guilty of wilful eglect to provide reasonable maintenance* for his wife infant children (D30 (2)), enabling the Divorce ivision to order the husband to make *periodical yments* to the wife, the words "infant children" e to include any *illegitimate child* of *both* parties, d the Court may make orders for *custody of and cess to* (D29 (2)) any such children. If the Court nsiders it in the *child's best interests*, it may order e periodical payments for the child's benefit to made *to the child* itself, or *to some other person* the child's behalf, instead of to the wife 30 (2)).

3. The same Act contains further enlightened and much-needed reforms for the *protection of the children* in matrimonial proceedings (whether defended or undefended). The Court, generally speaking, is *not* to pronounce a decree of *judicial separation* (D28 (2)), or make *absolute* any decree for *divorce or nullity* (D29 (2)), unless and until the Court is satisfied *either*—

(*a*) that arrangements have been made for the *care and upbringing* of every such child under 16, and that such arrangements are satisfactory or the best that can be devised in the circumstances, *or*

(*b*) that it is impracticable for the party or parties appearing before the Court to make any such arrangements.

But the Court *may* proceed without observing these requirements if: (i) there are *special reasons* against delay, and (ii) either or both of the parties have given to the Court a *satisfactory undertaking* to bring the question of such arrangements for the children before the Court within a specified time.

4. On any application to the Court for *special leave* to present a divorce petition *within three years from the date of marriage* (D27 (1)), the Judge must consider, not only the *possibility of a reconciliation* between the parties and the *interests of the children of the marriage* (which was his duty under the Act of 1950), but also the interests of any child referred to in para. A1, above.

5. Even if proceedings for divorce, nullity, or judicial separation are *dismissed*, the Court may still make provision for the custody, maintenance and education of any child referred to in para. A1 above, and may vary such orders from time to time.

6. Finally, the Court is given power, in exceptional circumstances, to commit the care of any such child *either*: (i) to a *county council* or *county borough council*, *or* (ii) to an *independent person* under the *supervision* (if the Court think fit) of a *welfare officer* or of a county council or county borough council. Further powers are conferred on *Local Authorities* by the Children and Young Persons Act, 1963.

B. By the Divorce (Insanity and Desertion) Act, 1958

1. The words "continuously under care and treatment" (in relation to a spouse of unsound mind) (D27 (1)) are to be interpreted *more liberally and more broadly* (in various ways) then has been the practice of the Court in the past.

2. A person who has *deserted* his or her spouse and is now of *unsound mind* may be regarded (for the purpose of divorce or judicial spearation) as *capable of forming the intention of continuing* the desertion, if the Court takes the view that the "deserting" party would in any event have stayed away (even if no unsoundness of mind had supervened). (*Note.* Hitherto the Petitioner has faced almost insuperable difficulties in such cases, since it is not normally possible to attribute to a person of unsound mind the capability of forming any "intention" whatsoever (D8 (1)). See also Cruelty—D27(ii) (c), and D28 (c).

3. Where the Petitioner is seeking *divorce* on the ground of the Respondent's *desertion* without cause for at least *three years* preceding the presentation of the petition (D27 (1)), any *agreement for separation* (whether in writing or not), entered into before *1st January 1938*, shall be *disregarded* by the Court if either: (*a*) the Respondent *had already deserted* the Petitioner, or (*b*) the Court is satisfied that the *circumstances* in which the agreement was made would have amounted to desertion (*without cause*) by the Respondent but for the

Petitioner's apparent consent, in the agreement, to a separation.

(*Note.* Desertion did not become a ground for divorce until *1st January 1938.* Some deserted spouses may have entered into separation agreements, inadvertently, *before* that date, and this provision is intended to mitigate hardship where there was (at that time) a genuine case of desertion but the case was ruined by the signature of a written agreement to live apart, or by some form of spoken words or conduct, on the part of the deserted party, appearing to signify consent to the separation.)

C. By the Maintenance Orders Act, 1958

1. Maintenance Orders *made by the High Court* (or a County Court) may be *registered in a Magistrate's Court,* which is given power to *vary* and to *enforce* such Orders. Maintenance Orders *made by a Magistrates' Court* may be *registered in the High Court,* which is given power to *enforce* such Orders. (The purpose of such registration is to make enforcement more easily effective; in some cases it may be more convenient for the wife to resort to High Court procedure; in others to proceed in the Magistrates' Courts.)

2. If the spouse (usually the husband) liable for payments under a Maintenance Order is a person *in employment,* and if his maintenance payments are at least four weeks *in arrear,* then the Court may make an *Attachment of Earnings Order.* This Order will *authorise and direct his employer to deduct from his earnings* certain sums (which the Court will specify), to be handed over *by the employer* to an official of the Court, who will pass them on to the wife as instalments towards the payment of: (*a*) the arrears, and (*b*) the amounts currently falling due under the original Maintenance Order. (*Note.* Hitherto the Courts have had no power to compel employers to collect such payments out of the defaulting husband's earnings; the wife's only remedy has been to ask for an order committing the defaulting husband to prison—a procedure which gave her *no financial redress* or assistance.)

The *Attachment of Earnings Order* will also specify the "protected earnings rate"—*i.e.,* the rate below which the Court thinks the defaulting husband's earnings should *not* be reduced by virtue of the authorised deductions. (*Note.* In other words, the Court will see that the defaulter is left with a reasonable part of his earnings to live on.)

D. By the Matrimonial Causes (Property and Maintenance) Act, 1958

1. The Court is given power to make an order against the Respondent (D27 (1)) for financial provision (D30 (1)) in favour of the Petitioner (D27 (1)) or the children, *either* at the time of the decree *nisi* (D29 (1)) *or* at any subsequent date; but the Court is not to disregard any delay on the part of the Petitioner in applying for such financial provision.

2. The Court is given power to set aside (*i.e.,* cancel the effect of) any disposition of property by a Respondent husband (or former husband) in favour of some third party, if that disposition of property has been made within the past three years (preceding the Petitioner's application for financial provision), and seems to have been made with the intention of defeating or frustrating the Petitioner's application. But no such disposition of property is to be set aside if it was made *for valuable consideration* in favour of a *person who acted in good faith* and without knowing of the Respondent's intention to defeat or frustrate the Petitioner's application. (*Note.* This will enable the Court to protect a wife, in certain circumstances, if the Respondent husband (or former husband) has (for example) transferred part of his property to his mistress, with the intention of defeating his wife's claim to maintenance, alimony, *etc.* Up to now the Court has had no power to remedy such action by a husband who has made a transfer of the kind *prior to* a Court Order for maintenance, *etc.*) *See also* Lump Sum orders, D30 (e), and Matrimonial Causes Act 1963 (below).

3. The power of the Court to order "reasonable provision for maintenance" out of the estate of a deceased person (D16 (2)), in a case where his will or intestacy does not leave his wife "reasonably" provided for, is now extended to benefit a *former wife* (*i.e.,* "a woman whose marriage with him was during his lifetime dissolved or annulled.") (*Note.* This definition is not limited to a former wife who was the "innocent" party in divorce proceedings; but the Court has a discretion to make or refuse the order, taking all the circumstances into account.) Such an order may be discharged, varied, suspended or revised at the suit of various interested parties.

4. The Court's powers under paras. 2 and 3 (above) are extended to protect: (*a*) a *former husband* whose former wife has divorced him, or obtained a judicial separation against him, on the ground of *his insanity* (D27 (1)), or (*b*) where the Court has ordered a settlement of the wife's property, or "periodical payments" out of her income, where there has been a decree for restitution of conjugal rights (D28 (1)).

5. The executors or administrators (D18 (2)) of the deceased spouse are not to be liable if, when a claim under para. 3 is made, they have already distributed the deceased's estate (provided they waited for 6 month after the Grant of Probate or Letters of Administration (D18 (2)); but the claimant under para. 3 can follow the property into the hands of a beneficiary and recover it (if it is still available) by means of an order under para. 3 (above).

6. Under the Married Women's Property Act, 1882, the Court was given power to decide in a *summary manner* (*i.e.,* by a rapid and simple procedure) disputes between any husband and wife about the *ownership of any property.* That power is now extended to cases where the respondent spouse *has been, but no longer* is, in control of the property, or the *claimant does not know* whether it is still in the respondent's control or not. The Court may order the necessary enquiries to be made; in appropriate cases it may also order property in the hands of the respondent, or of a third party, *to be sold,* so that the claimant may have his or her share paid out of the proceeds.

E. By the Matrimonial Causes Act, 1963

The Court is given power to grant an injunction against any person who appears likely to dispose of property so as to defeat any of the provisions of D (above) or to transfer such property abroad.

F. By the Married Women's Property Act, 1964

If any question arises as to the right of a husband or wife to money derived from any allowance made by the husband for housekeeping or any similar expenses, or to any property acquired out of such money, the money or property (in the absence of agreement to the contrary) shall be treated as belonging to them both in equal shares. (The old rule was that the wife's savings out of housekeeping allowances belonged to the husband.)

Note] Since the above section went to press Parliament has passed the Matrimonial Causes Act, 1965; this received the Royal Assent on 8 November 1965 and came into force on 1 January 1966. It does little more than to consolidate the old law as set out above; the necessary changes will be made in the next edition.

STATUTORY REFORMS IN LAW OF LANDLORD AND TENANT

(1) Business Tenancies

Under the Landlord and Tenant Act, 1954, Part II (and cases decided under it) *security of tenure* is granted (under certain conditions) to a lessee or under-lessee who *occupies premises for the purpose of a trade, business, profession or employment* carried on by him on the premises. (We shall refer to such premises as "*the holding*".) The holding may not be used as business premises, and there is no security, if the lease or tenancy agreement prohibits their use as such, unless permission has been given by the lessee's (or under-lessee's) landlord to that effect. *Tenancies excluded* from protection include agricultural holdings, mining leases, on-licensed premises (except certain hotels and restaurants) and tenancies not exceeding three months, unless the tenant and the person who carried on the same business there before him have occupied the premises for more than six months altogether.

A holding is protected by the Act by the provision that the *tenancy does not automatically come to an end* on the date specified in the original lease, but only (i) *if the landlord gives to the tenant not less than six nor more than twelve months notice* in writing to terminate the tenancy; (ii) *if the tenant gives to the landlord, within a similar period, a request for a new tenancy*; (iii) where the tenancy is for a *fixed period*, if the *tenant gives at least three months notice* (expiring at the end of the period or on any quarter day afterwards) *that he does not want the tenancy continued*; (iv) if it is a *periodic tenancy* (from month to month or year to year), the *tenant gives the landlord notice to quit*, of the full legal length; (v) if the tenancy is *surrendered* or (vi) if the tenancy is *forfeited* (which can be done by the landlord only on a Court application). In cases (*i*) *and* (*ii*), the *parties may agree* to fresh terms for a new tenancy. It is *vital* in such cases that the *time-table* laid down in the Act shall be adhered to, and the *advice of a solicitor* should be sought *at least twelve months before the end of the lease*; if any request or application is out of time, the Court cannot help the party in question. The twelve months or six months *notice of termination* (see above) *must not expire* earlier than the date of expiry of the original lease.

Where (i) the landlord serves the notice of termination: (*a*) it must require the *tenant, within two months of the notice* being given, *to notify the landlord whether or not he is willing to give up possession* on the specified date; (*b*) it must state *whether or not the landlord will oppose an application to the Court* for a new tenancy, and if so on what grounds. Four of the grounds are that the tenant has neglected repairs or payment of rent for which he is liable or committed some other breach of his lease, or that the landlord has offered reasonable alternative accommodation. Three further grounds are: (*e*) that the existing tenancy is an underlease of part of premises held under the head lease, and the separate lettings would produce a lower total rent than if the whole were let together; (*f*) that on the termination of the current tenancy the *landlord intends to demolish or reconstruct* the holding or a substantial part, and could not reasonably do so without obtaining possession of the whole; (*g*) finally, that on the termination of the current tenancy, *the landlord intends to occupy the holding* for the purposes of a business to be carried on by him, or as his residence. (But the landlord *may not oppose* the grant of a *new lease on this final ground* if his interest was purchased or created within *five years* immediately preceding the termination of the lease.)

If the *tenant* prefers *to request a new tenancy*, he must propose to the landlord that it shall commence not more than twelve nor less than six months from the date of request; but the commencement must *not be earlier than the date of expiry* of his existing lease. The tenant must also propose the period of the new lease, the rent he is willing to pay and the other particulars of the proposed new tenancy. The tenant cannot make such request (*a*) if the landlord has already served a termination notice, or (*b*) if the tenant has served notice to quit; nor can either (*a*) or (*b*) take place after the tenant's request for a new tenancy.

Within two months after the tenant's request, the landlord must serve on the tenant notice stating on which of the above grounds (if any) he will oppose the Court's grant of a new tenancy. The parties cannot make any agreement to the effect that the Act shall not apply.

The next step is for the *tenant, not less than two months nor more than four months after the landlord's termination notice or the tenant's request* for a new tenancy, *to apply to the County Court*, which *must grant him a new tenancy* on such terms as the parties may agree on or the Court thinks fit, unless the landlord establishes any of the above grounds of objection. If the *landlord's objections are false*, the Court will grant the tenant *damages*.

If the landlord establishes any of grounds (e), (f) or (g), so that the Court cannot grant a new tenancy, the Court orders the *landlord to pay to the tenant compensation for disturbance*. If the tenant has carried on *business* on the holding *for the whole of fourteen years* preceding the termination, the compensation is *twice the net rateable value:* if for a *lesser period, a sum equal to the rateable value*.

If the above procedure is carried out, the *old lease continues* in effect *until the final disposal of the case*, even if the lease has expired meanwhile. "*Final disposal*" includes any necessary *time for appeal*.

(2) Residential Tenancies

Under the Rent Act, 1965, *security of tenure* is provided for *tenants of dwellings* with *rateable value* (*a*) *up to* £400 a year in the *Metropolitan Police District* and £200 *elsewhere* (including (*b*) those still controlled by the old Rent Restriction Acts 1920 to 1939, which now apply only to very small and low-rated dwellings.) The Act imposes a *standstill on present rents* (except variations of rents including rates, cost of services and owner's improvements). *Rent officers or assessment committees* will be set up *to revise rents* in category (*a*). The protected tenancies under (*a*) are called "regulated tenancies". Certain *statutory tenancies* of *formerly requisitioned dwellings* (which would have *expired on March 31, 1966*) are continued after that date as regulated tenancies. *Occupiers who are not tenants* (*i.e.* those in occupation *necessarily because of their employment*, such as caretakers) *are included* under the term "tenants".

The task of the *rent officers and rent assessment committees* is *to fix fair rents* on application of landlord or tenant, or both, in counties, county boroughs, London boroughs and the City of London. They are *to take into account all the* circumstances, age, character, locality and state of repair of the dwelling; but *disrepair due to the tenant's neglect* and *improvements by the tenant* are to be *disregarded*, as is *also* any *great demand* (*exceeding supply*) *of dwellings in the district*. The fixed rents are to be registered, and must *include payments for furniture and services* (*if any*). *If the landlord pays rates*, that fact is to be noted, and the *registered rent plus the rates may be recovered from the tenant*. If the cost of services, or of repairs to be done by the landlord, is a variable sum, the registered terms must say so. The landlord cannot lawfully recover more than the registered rent, taking the above variations into account.

It is *unlawful for any person* (with intent to *cause the residential occupier* to *give up occupation* or to refrain from pursuing his rights or remedies) to do anything calculated *to interfere with his peace or comfort* or *persistently to withdraw or withhold services* reasonably required for occupation. "Residential occupier" means a person occupying the premises as a residence, either by contract or by any Act of Parliament. The penalty is a fine up to £100 or imprisonment up to six months or both, before the magistrates, for a first offence, and a fine up to £500 or the imprisonment, or both, for a subsequent conviction. The *occupier*, even if the premises are not "protected" (*i.e.*, not subject to the Rent Restrictions Acts or certain other statutes) *cannot lawfully be evicted even* when the tenancy has terminated and the occupier continues to reside there, *without leave of the Court. In default*, the owner is liable, on conviction before the magistrates, to a *fine up to* £100 *or six months' imprisonment or both*—unless he can prove that he reasonably believed that the occupier had ceased to reside in the premises. *Occupiers protected* are the tenant or *former tenant*, a lawful *subtenant*, and the widow or widower, or any member of the family of either, residing with the occupier at his death.

The demand for or taking of a premium as a condition of the grant, renewal, continuance or transfer of a *protected tenancy* (in addition to the rent) *is forbidden* (except in case of expenses, paid by the outgoing tenant, for a period after the transfer, or improvements he has paid for, or as a refund to the outgoing tenant of any reasonable premium which he himself paid on taking possion, or (if part of the premises are business premises) for goodwill transferred to the incoming tenant.) There are also *restrictions on the demand for, or taking of, a premium in relation to a "regulated tenancy"*; broadly speaking, a premium is lawful only if the tenancy or its continuance is for more *than seven years*—and then only if the registered rent is higher than the rent payable under the tenancy.

There are wide provisions regarding the protection of occupiers of furnished dwellings and regarding mortgages. As the Act of 1965 has only recently come into force, there is little case law on the subject, and legal advice should be sought.

(*Note*: The Queen's Speech (Nov. 1965) foreshadowed the introduction of legislation to reform the leasehold system for residential property.)

CRIME AND PUNISHMENT IN A CHANGING SOCIETY

It is a melancholy reflection that man is not naturally benevolent or tolerant towards his fellows: that humanitarian conduct is not necessarily associated with theological dogma, cultural values, or political progress, and is seldom induced by admonition or moral exhortation. In particular, we may consider the comparative lack of humanising influence, from ethical Christianity or parliamentary democracy, upon the punishment of criminals. It is only when the scientist and the philosopher begin to speculate upon and seek out the sources of conduct which fills the ignorant with horror and disgust that it becomes possible to persuade the ordinary man that such conduct is not a perverse form of wickedness, calling for passionate condemnation and savage repression, but a symptom, calling for investigation, of a deeper disorder which must be scientifically diagnosed, its causes traced and treated, unemotionally and impersonally, with a view to their mitigation or removal.

The Growth of Research.—Much the same, or similar, problems have arisen with regard to religious persecution and witch-hunting on the most barbarous scale, which survived sixteen centuries of Christianity. They gradually fell out of use, not because of the realisation that they were morally wrong, but because of the spirit of scepticism that was abroad early in the eighteenth century—reflected particularly in the *Treatise* of David Hume (1728–40). The revolting treatment of lunatics continued even longer, throughout most of the polite and sophisticated 1700s, when one of the shows available for the amusement of visitors to London was the antics of the inmates of Bethlehem Hospital, or Bedlam; such scenes were material for *The Rake's Progress* of William Hogarth (himself a socialist reformer) as late as 1735. It was not until the 1790s, when research was devoted to cerebral anatomy and physiology, that insanity was regarded as a matter rather for compassion and treatment than ridicule and contempt. Slavery owed its abolition as much to intellectuals like Steele, Pope, Thomson, Cowper, Sterne, Johnson, and Adam Smith, as to religious reformers like Wesley, Whitefield, and Granville Sharp. It received its death-blow in England (in the early 1700s) from lawyers like Mansfield. In America, as we know, slavery was nominally abolished by political action only in 1865, but racial intolerance still persists in many of the States.

Penal Reform.—Penal reform owed its inception principally to two men—the investigator and research-worker John Howard (the greatest of whose work was done between 1777 and 1784), and the Utilitarian philosopher Jeremy Bentham, whose *Principles of Morals and Legislation* (1789) laid the foundations of our present system. He advocated the prevention of crime by the scientific method of seeking out and removing its cause, and the reform of the convicted criminal by means of his classification, education, and rehabilitation in the community on his discharge. He taught that conduct is morally "good" only when it promotes the greatest happiness of the greatest number; all punishment, being in itself evil, ought to be admitted only so far as it promises to exclude some greater evil.

Until comparatively recent times the only conception of punishment, apart from sporadic experiments by reformers like Pope Clement XI (1700–21), who built a prison for the special treatment of young offenders, was by death or the infliction of physical pain. In France, the worst savageries of the criminal law were swept away by the Revolution in 1789; in our country Sir Samuel Romilly could say, as late as 1817, "the laws of England are written in blood." In his day the death penalty was still exacted for thefts of more than forty shillings in value; transportation remained a common form of punishment until 1852, when it was replaced by penal servitude, and executions might still take place in public until the 1860s. Even in our own times there have been judges who regarded deterrence as the principal function of the criminal law.

Recent Government Recommendations.—Since the 1930s the emphasis has gradually changed. The 1959 White Paper presented to Parliament by the Home Secretary, entitled *Penal Practice in a Changing Society*, contained a number of enlightened ideas for dealing with the new wave of crime which has been evident since the end of the last War, despite increase in prosperity—contrary to the beliefs of reformers like Bentham, who thought that, if poverty and starvation were removed from society, crime would diminish. That document tried to formulate scientific problems in a scientific way; the recent and continuing prevalence of offences involving violence was regarded as an opportunity for the study of symptoms, research into causes, diagnosis and selection of treatment. Panic legislation was rejected in favour of experiment, adjustment, and trial of new techniques.

In April 1964 a new White Paper was presented to Parliament by the Home Office, entitled *The War Against Crime in England and Wales—1959 to 1964*. It is written in an equally enlightened manner; it recalls that the 1959 document proposed a "fundamental re-examination of penal methods based on studies of the causes of crime, or rather the factors which cause or inhibit crime, and supported by a realistic assessment of the results achieved by existing methods." It reminds us that the increase in violent crimes, which had been evident in the years before 1959, has continued from 1959 to 1964, and so has the search for more effective remedies.

Some Statistics.—Between 1963 and 1964 there was an increase of 11 per cent in the indictable offences recorded by the police, an increase of

6·7 per cent in breaking and entering, and an increase of 17 per cent in violence against the person. Convictions on these offences fell during the period by 3·5 per cent. One-third of all those convicted each year are under 17 years of age; one-half are under 21, as are also two-thirds of those convicted of breaking and entering. Even when account is taken of the strength of the Police Force and better records, and more co-operation from the public, there has still been a substantial increase in the actual volume of crime. In 1963 the Home Secretary appointed a Committee, under the chairmanship of Mr. Wilfred Perks, to consider and report what changes, if any, are desirable for reporting and recording information about criminal offences and proceedings, and in the collection and presentation of the statistics.

Prevention and Detection of Crime: Recent Developments.—As criminals become better organised and use more efficient techniques, it is necessary for police methods to keep pace with these changes. Substantial increase in police pay has lead to an improvement in recruiting, and between 1960 and 1963 the number of policemen in England and Wales has risen from just under 70,000 to just over 77,000. In the provinces the Forces are substantially up to strength, but in London and other large cities a further 10,000 policemen could, it is estimated, help to reduce the wave of crime.

As man-power has been strengthened, more police have been engaged in the work of prevention and detection; the engagement of civilians (such as traffic wardens) has been a further aid to efficiency. New powers are being given to the Home Secretary, by Parliament, to this end; in the Home Office itself a Police Research and Planning Branch has been established to concentrate on means of combating the growing volume of serious and unsolved crime. There have been improvements in the prospects of promotion and of training at the Police College, and also in the provision of modern housing for policemen and their families, the budget for which has risen since 1959 from £1,200,000 to £5,000,000. Discussions which have taken place between the Home Secretary and persons prominent in voluntary services to the community have resulted in the establishment of representative committees to study the facts of delinquency and the best ways of using local resources against it.

Juvenile Delinquency: Emphasis on Prevention.—A strong Advisory Committee has been appointed to take into account conditions in the home, the family, at school and at work, the housing situation, and the personality of the delinquent. The Committee is concerned rather to find out the reasons why juveniles commit crimes, and what can be done about it, rather than with methods of punishment after the crimes have been committed. The 1959 proposals were very largely concerned with the *treatment* of delinquents; the 1964 White Paper lays the emphasis on *prevention*. Special importance is attached to the powers and duties of every County Council and County Borough Council " to make available such advice, guidance and assistance as may promote the welfare of children by diminishing the need to receive them into or keep them in care . . . or to bring children before a Juvenile Court." These duties are imposed by Section 1 of the Children and Young Persons Act, 1963, which also empowers Local Authorities to arrange for voluntary organisations to provide any of these services. (For the new White Paper of 1965, see D36.)

Sentencing Policy in Criminal Cases.—The Home Office has been aiming to secure full information for the courts about the background of offenders by those best qualified to supply it, full co-ordination of this information and its prompt application, to ensure that sentence follows immediately upon conviction. The Criminal Justice Act, 1962, provides that no one should normally wait more than 8 weeks, after committal, for trial; and the Home Office is giving careful guidance to Magistrates and others as to what is involved in every form of sentence, what it is designed to achieve, what it in fact achieves, and its result. On 30 May 1964, *The Times* published an important article by a well-known Criminologist on *Sentencing Policy in Criminal Cases*; on the same day the Lord Chief Justice called for group study to secure uniformity in sentencing policy and a deeper understanding of the social factors involved, and on 2 June the Lord Chancellor proposed compulsory courses for J.P.s.

Law Reform.—On 15 June 1964 the Criminal Appeal Act gave power to the Court of Criminal Appeal to order a fresh trial on new evidence, and a Committee under Lord Donovan is reviewing its constitution, powers, and procedure. Other legislation has dealt with suicide, indecent offences against children, the order of Counsel's addresses to Criminal Courts, the alteration of the verdict of " guilty but insane " to one of " not guilty because of insanity, " and provision has been made for the continuance of a trial where a juryman has died or is discharged. The Standing Committee on criminal law revision is considering the law of larceny and perjury, the attendance of witnesses at criminal trials, and the division of crimes into felonies and misdemeanours. Other Acts of Parliament have been passed, in the last five years, on Street offences, Betting and Gaming and Licensing offences.

The Need for More Research.—Further investigation is needed into the social and psychological aspects of delinquency, methods of prevention and the effects of the various kinds of " treatment " (this word is being increasingly used in place of the word " punishment "). In 1963 a Committee was appointed to examine the influence (if any) of television upon juvenile delinquency and this is being financed by the I.T.A. Full details of research are set out in the appendix to the White Paper.

Treatment of Offenders.—The Criminal Justice Act, 1961, increased the maximum fines for *juvenile offenders*, reduced the minimum age for attendance at an attendance centre from 12 to 10; altered the conditions of after-care for children released from approved schools, and permitted the temporary removal of unruly pupils, and the transfer to borstal, of those who cannot benefit from approved school training or interfere with the training of others. Power was given to the Home Secretary to give fresh directions on the management of approved schools and to regulate the constitution of voluntary managing bodies; the minimum age at which a sentence of borstal training can be imposed has been reduced from 16 to 15; imprisonment for offenders under 17 has been abolished, and borstal has become the principal form of institution for training offenders between 17 and 21 (as well as for those between 15 and 16 not suitable for approved schools). Where offenders between 17 and 21 are sentenced to imprisonment, great changes are made in the conditions; sentences must now be either not more than 6 months, or over 3 years. As detention centres will take the place of prisons for all offenders under 21, the Act provides for abolishing these sentences of imprisonment by Order (now abolished by Order of 1963).

Preventive detention and corrective training are being abolished; in their place prison sentences for those over 21 are to be drastically increased, in case of grave offences. The Prison Rules were amended in 1963 to make all prisoners already in preventive detention eligible for release after serving two-thirds of their sentences. The 1965 White Paper (Cmnd. 2742) proposes further drastic changes (see D36).

Probation Service.—The Morison Committee reported in 1962 on the Probation Service and made recommendations. Salaries have been raised to new levels; in 1963 there was a one-third increase in the number of students in training; and a Probation and Advisory Training Board has been set up. Four additional Probation Inspectors have been appointed; the strength of the service has been increased to over 2,000, and it is hoped to bring it up to 2,750 during 1966. Under the Administration of Justice Act, responsibility for the London Probation Service is transferred from the Home Secretary to a Probation Committee composed of representatives of the Courts.

Home Office Children's Department.—A great building programme for approved schools and their modernisation should provide, by 1966, 2,000 more places than were available in 1961. The Central Council for Child Care is organising the training of staff for approved schools and remand homes; in the latter there has been a 27 per cent increase in places available, and four new homes are expected to be completed by 1965.

The Home Secretary has, since 1 April 1963, been responsible for the functions formerly carried out by the Prison Commission; and the work of his Prisons Department is closely integrated with that of other departments dealing with the treatment of delinquency.

Detention Centres.—Offenders in remand homes, detention centres, borstals, and prisons have risen from 20,800 in 1956 to 29,000 in February 1964. Expenditure has increased from £822,000 in 1958–9 to £6,935,000 in 1964–5; and 27 new establishments have been opened. Eight further remand homes are under construction. Detention centres have increased since 1959 from 4 to 15, including one for girls; there is room for about 3,800 a year in those for boys of 17 to 21 and about 900 a year for boys from 14 to 17. Five new borstals for boys (accommodating 1,000) have been built since 1959 and one for girls; when the two new ones have been completed, there will be an additional 300 places for boys and 80 for girls. As a result of the recent legislation the number of offenders under 21 sent to borstal has increased and of those sentenced to imprisonment has fallen.

Prisons.—For adult offenders, 4 new open prisons for men and one for women have been opened and a number of prisons for both men and women, of various kinds, have been built or planned. Overcrowding is being reduced; the number of men sleeping three to a cell has fallen from 8,600 in April 1963 to about 6,000 in April 1964. Further relief will be obtained when the new prisons under construction are completed. The strength of the prison service has risen from just under 7,000 at the beginning of 1958 to more than 10,000 in April 1964.

Employment of Prisoners.—The Home Secretary's principal objectives are to reduce overcrowding, to improve training facilities for long-term prisoners, and to ive them proper employment; to develop the hostels which help their transition from detention to freedom, and to establish a sound after-care system.

After-Care.—Under the Criminal Justice Act, 1961, the assistance of after-care has already been applied to persons released from detention centres, and arrangements are being reviewed for organising statutory and voluntary after-care for those discharged from prisons, borstals, detention centres, and approved schools. The Advisory Council has recommended that full use should be made of the help of voluntary workers, and that those concerned with the welfare of persons in custody, and with the preparations for their release, should become members of the Prison Service. The Government has accepted these proposals, though it will take time to recruit and train the necessary staff. A great importance is attached to voluntary work.

New Royal Commission—a Scientific Approach.—In conclusion, the 1964 White Paper expresses doubts whether the existing penal methods produce sufficiently good results; for example, boys leaving approved schools seem less responsive to training than they used to be. It is questioned whether enough is being done to experiment with new methods of treatment, rather than concentrating too much on trying to improve the traditional methods. Another problem to be considered is whether the separate control of different forms of treatment is satisfactory; probation is the responsibility of Magistrates; attendance centres, detention centres, and borstals of the Government; remand homes and approved schools of the local authorities. A new Royal Commission has been set up to make a fundamental review of the whole penal system, to re-assess its value and study what we ought to be seeking to achieve, to examine the deficiencies of the present system and to consider new ideas. All these questions are to be investigated in the light of modern knowledge of crime and its causes, and of modern penal practice here and abroad; the Royal Commission is also to re-examine the concepts and purposes which underlie the treatment of offenders in England and Wales, to report how far they are realised by the methods available to the courts; and whether these, or the arrangements for selecting the sentences of particular offenders, should be changed; and also to review the work of the services themselves. Priority is to be given to offenders under 21 (who form so high a proportion of the total); improvement in the handling of young offenders would be of value in the war both against juvenile delinquency and against adult criminals.

Conclusion.—All these activities represent "a formidable armoury" for intensifying the war against crime. It seems that the mistakes of earlier generations have taught us a good deal about delinquency; the aim is still a study of symptoms, research into causes, diagnosis of causes and selection of remedial treatment rather than mere attempts at deterrence. Although the application of reformative principles has not succeeded in reducing crime during the past 20 years, and in fact, under the affluent society, violent crime has even increased, we must consider the matter dispassionately and realise that it has not been proved that the abolition of brutal punishments has necessarily been the cause of the increase in delinquency. The authorities have not reverted to panic legislation for outmoded methods of punishment; prevention of crime is now the chief Government aim, though reformation, retribution and deterrence are not forgotten. Among other things the Malicious Damage Act has given the Magistrates Courts powers to award a maximum amount of compensation to victims of violent crime of £100, plus a maximum fine of £100; and proposals are being considered for compensating victims of personal violence, and for the criminal to contribute towards such compensation.

The 1965 Proposals.—On 24 August 1965, after much ventilation in Parliament and the press, the Government published a new White Paper (Cmnd. 2742) containing proposals for further radical changes in the treatment of young offenders. They are "*provisional* proposals for practical reforms *to support* the family, *to forestall and reduce delinquency*, and to *revise the law and practice* relating to *offenders up to 21*. They are published for the *purpose* of *discussion* before legislation is prepared." Interested organizations will be consulted and the advice sought of those who will have to operate any new system.

Age Groups.—Under the system at present in force, young people under the age of 21 are dealt with in two categories: children and young persons under the age of 17 who, if they are thought to be in need of care, protection or control, or (being over the age of 10) are alleged to have committed an offence, may be brought before a Juvenile Court; and young persons between the ages of 17 and 21 who, if they are accused of committing an offence, are dealt with by the ordinary Courts, but for whom certain special sanctions are available, for instance, training at attendance centres, detention centres or borstals, or commital to remand centres for observation. It is proposed in the White Paper that there should be a new dividing age line at 16—soon to be the upper age limit for compulsory school attendance and, since it is the age at which many young people begin to earn, leave home, and are legally entitled to marry, may mark a significant stage in their lives.

There are two main purposes—(1) to take children and young persons *under 16*, as far as possible, *outside the ambit of the criminal law and the courts*, and to make arrangements for their welfare with the agreement of parents and guardians; (2) *to divorce* arrangements for the *trial and treatment* of those from *16 to 21*, so far as possible from the ordinary criminal courts and from the adult penal system. "In both cases the *determining* factor must be the welfare of the particular child or young person; the *object of training* must be to make him a *law-abiding and useful citizen*. There is no intention to deal lightly with young offenders—quite the contrary." *Firm discipline* and constructive treatment are necessary, directed to their *welfare or rehabilitation*.

(1) **Children under 16** should be spared "the stigma of criminality". In most cases the facts are not in dispute, and the *problem* is to decide the *appropriate treatment*. Present arrangements (in the Juvenile Courts) are not the best way of getting parents to take more responsibility for their children's behaviour.

(I) *Family Councils* would be appointed by the local authorities, consisting of *social workers* of the children's service, and others selected for their *understanding and experience of children*. There would be enough Councils to enable unhurried discussions with parents; in no case would they meet in a Court building. Social enquiries would be undertaken by the area children's service.

(i) Before discussing possible action with parents, the Council would consider all information available *about the child and his background*. (*a*) Sometimes the parents would be able *to deal with the situation themselves*, *or* (*b*) it might be agreed that the parents should pay compensation to victims of the child's delinquency, *or* (*c*) it might be agreed to *place the child under* the supervision of a children's officer, *or* to send him to some form of *residential training*.

(ii) *Observation Centres*, provided by the local authorities, would replace the present remand homes. Such Centres would facilitate the examination of children still living at home as well as residential observation. In cases of *long term residential training* the child would be placed in the *care of the local authority*, either in a residential school or children's home, or boarded out in a foster home. Local authorities and voluntary bodies would be encouraged to develop a *wide range of residential establishments*; the present "approved schools" would fit into this new pattern. 1,000 extra social workers would be needed.

(II) (i) *Family Courts*, staffed by *Magistrates selected for their capacity to deal with young people*, would hear any case where (*a*) the *facts* were in *dispute*, *or* (*b*) the *Family Council failed to reach agreement* on treatment. In (*a*) the Family Court would refer the case back to the Family Council after the facts were proved. If the Council still could not agree on treatment, or if the case were grave, the Family Court could make an order which can now be made by a Juvenile Court; but if long-term residential training were appropriate the child would be committed to the care of the local authority (see (ii) above).

(ii) It may be that the jurisdiction of the Family Court will later be enlarged to include other family matters.

(2) **Young Offenders over 16**—(i) Although at present the age of demarcation is 17, those over that age being dealt with by the ordinary Courts, and those under 17 by the Juvenile Courts, it is now proposed to establish *Young Offenders' Courts* to exercise criminal jurisdiction over those over 16 and under 21. The more serious cases would be committed to a superior Court (homicide at the Assizes).

(ii) The Young Offenders Courts would sit at *separate times* from both the ordinary Courts and the Family Courts to avoid contacts between accused adults and alleged young offenders. *Appeals* from the Young Offenders Courts would be heard by a court of *quarter sessions, specially constituted* if the Young Offenders Court were *not* presided over by a legally qualified chairman, and by the *Court of Criminal Appeal* if the chairman *were so qualified*.

(iii) Young Offenders, *if convicted*, could be sentenced to detention—*not exceeding* 3 *months* if the chairman were *unqualified*, and *not exceeding* 3 *years* if he *were so qualified*. Three types of custodial sentence are proposed:

(*a*) "short-term"—three or six months in a detention centre;

(*b*) "training"—for between nine months and two years in a youth training centre;

(*c*) "long-term training"—in cases where the Court now imposes a prison sentence.

(iv) *No change* is proposed in the organization and methods of *detention centres*; but *borstals and senior approved schools* are proposed to be *merged* into a comprehensive training system, under the supervision of the Home Office.

(v) *Voluntary effort* is to be *maintained* and strengthened—not lost or given up.

JUSTICES OF THE PEACE

Sentencing Policy.—The arrangements, announced at the end of May 1964, by the Lord Chief Justice, "for the purpose of achieving greater uniformity of sentencing policy and a deeper understanding of the many social factors involved," comprise the organisation of more and longer conferences of all holders of judicial office, including justices of the peace, chairmen of quarter sessions, recorders and High Court judges. Working parties, in groups, are to consider case histories of "offenders," and later meet to discuss the sentences which each group would have passed if these cases had come before them in court. On the same day it was announced from Downing Street that a Royal Commission was being appointed (under the chairmanship of Lord Amory (former Chancellor of the Exchequer)),

> "to conduct a fundamental review of penal methods, the concepts and purposes which should underlie the punishment and treatment of offenders in England and Wales; to report how far they are realized by the penalties and methods of treatment available, and whether any changes are desirable in these, or in the arrangements and responsibility for selecting the sentences to be imposed on particular offenders; and to review the work of the services and institutions dealing with offenders and the responsibility for their administration, and to make recommendations."

Compulsory Training of New J.P.s.—Early in June 1964 the Lord Chancellor announced new arrangements for the *compulsory* training and instruction of newly-appointed justices of the peace, and fresh attempts to stop "glaring instances of inadequate, excessive or inconsistent sentences." An advisory council is to re-organise the present scheme for *voluntary* training (which started in 1950), and every newly-appointed justice is to give an undertaking not to try cases, without the Lord Chancellor's authority, until he or she has been through a *compulsory* course. The course will include attending as observers in their own and other courts and at quarter sessions, and visits to prisons, borstals, and similar institutions.

General Duties of J.P.s—All these announcements have focused attention upon the work of justices of the peace—the unpaid, lay magistrates throughout the country who deal with the largest proportion of criminal offences, in various courts. Other manifold duties fall upon them—the appointment of special constables, certain matters relating to highways, the grant and renewal of licences for the sale of intoxicating liquors, "domestic proceedings" (matrimonial orders between husband and wife), custody of children and affiliation and adoption orders. Certain magistrates—both laymen and lawyers—with special qualifications sit in juvenile courts to deal with offences by and against young people, and with the committing of young people to the care of approved persons or authorities, whenever the young people are in need of care and protection.

Although, therefore, the criminal jurisdiction of J.P.s (as they are generally known) is by no means the full extent of their duties, it is this criminal jurisdiction which has been most frequently in the public eye; and the three announcements mentioned above relate only to that aspect of the J.P.s' duties. Neither historically nor currently are J.P.s expected to be lawyers; the clerk of the court, who advises them on points of law, is always a solicitor; and at quarter sessions the chairman and deputy chairman are usually barristers or solicitors of not less than ten years' standing, with special qualifications for the task.

Procedure and Powers.—For "domestic proceedings" and in juvenile courts (outside the City of London and the metropolitan stipendiary court area, where full-time, legally-qualified, paid magistrates preside), not more than three J.P.s should sit, including both a man and a woman, whenever practicable. For other duties not more than seven J.P.s (and, preferably, not more than five, and an odd, not even, number) should sit. The election of a chairman and a number of deputy-chairmen is held by the J.P.s in October; those elected hold office for one year from January 1, and are eligible for re-election. All sittings are held in public, except in "domestic proceedings," custody and adoption cases; and in these and in juvenile courts the press, though not usually excluded, are not permitted to identify the parties by name or address, or to publish evidence of an indecent character.

The powers of one single J.P., sitting alone, are restricted to adjourning a trial, remanding a prisoner in custody or on bail, and taking recognisances. An information charging an offence may be laid before him; if it is in writing, and substantiated on oath, he may issue a warrant; in a civil matter, in similar circumstances, he may issue a summons. Search warrants may, in most cases, be issued by a single J.P., and so may a summons or warrant requiring the attendance of a witness. A stipendiary (legally-qualified, paid, full-time magistrate) is not so limited; he has all the powers of a court of summary jurisdiction (*i.e.* two or more J.P.s sitting together).

Criminal Jurisdiction.—Except in those instances in which a special limit of time is prescribed by a particular Act of Parliament, no information may be laid (in regard to a criminal offence), nor complaint (in a civil case) after the lapse of six months from the date when the offence was committed or the matter of complaint arose. The J.P.s' criminal jurisdiction covers (1) the trial of "summary offences" (minor offences triable by a magistrates' court other than under (2) below) punishable by a maximum of six months imprisonment for one offence, or a fine (in general) not exceeding £25. The jurisdiction also extends to (2) certain "indictable" (more grave) offences which may be tried summarily if the accused consents; in such cases the maximum punishments are 6 months imprisonment or a fine not exceeding £100, or both, for one such offence, or 12 months imprisonment for two or more such offences. There are also (3) certain petty offences which the accused or the prosecution may elect to be tried on indictment, before a jury at quarter sessions. No offender under the age of 17 may be sentenced to imprisonment by a court of summary jurisdiction; but such young offender may be sent to a detention centre. Alternatively, he may be committed, in custody, to quarter sessions for sentence to a period of borstal training. Firts offenders should not be sent to prison; they are frequently placed on probation.

One J.P. or more may sit as a court of preliminary enquiry to determine whether there is a *prima facie* case (*i.e.* one that calls for a defence) against an accused which will require his being indicted before a jury. For this purpose the J.P.s take depositions (that is, evidence given by word of mouth, under oath, by prosecution witnesses, and reduced to writing and signed by each witness who has given it). If the J.P.s decide, at the end of the hearing, that the prosecution has disclosed no *prima facie* case, the accused is discharged; if there is such a case, then after due warning to the accused that he is not obliged to say anything but that, if he does answer the charge, anything he says will be written down and may be used in evidence at his trial, he is committed for trial, on bail or in custody (according to the gravity of the charge), at quarter sessions or assizes.

History of the Office of J.P.—The above is by no means an exhaustive account of the duties of J.P.s and of the procedure before them; but sufficient has been said to indicate the vital importance of their work. The office is both honorary and honourable; as early as 1327, in the reign of Edward III, the King appointed "conservators" of the peace within his Kingdom; and the Justices of the Peace Act, 1361, in the same reign, determined "what sort of persons should be Justices of the Peace and what authority they should have." From that day to this their duties have gradually become more difficult and extensive, as society has grown more complex. It would seem that, while there are many advantages in leaving the trial of the less grave offences to lay magistrates (as J.P.s are), the system, which for over six centuries has prominently figured in our penal practice, will be brought up to date and made more efficient by the proposed compulsory training. The only doubts have arisen on the ground that persons "of the best of reputation in the counties" (Act of 1344), who are prepared to give their time, without remuneration, to these public-spirited duties, may find it difficult, or in some cases impossible, to attend courses of training, in their spare time, in addition.

Recruitment of J.P.s.—The Lord Chancellor in his 1965 presidential address to the Magistrates' Association at Guildhall, London, said he would like to see the J.P.s recruited from more varied walks of life, a new system of training for the Bench and the abolition of the *ex officio* justices (*e.g.*, Mayors during their term of office). "The strength of the lay magistracy," he said, "is dependent on the ordinary man and woman realising that the Benches reflect all shades of opinion and are not representative of one section only." He said he would also like to see more coloured magistrates appointed. "There are now two coloured justices serving on the Bench and these appointments have both been tremendously successful."

FREE SPEECH AND PUBLIC ORDER

In the constitution of our parliamentary democracy (see **D5**) certain unwritten rules have been recognised for about three centuries past. These rules, which are not always easy to reconcile, may be summarised as follows:

(1) **Free Speech.**—Free and open discussion, *within the law*, ought to be permitted, both in private and in public, of all political, social, moral and religious questions.

(2) **Unpopular Opinions.**—Unpopular or minority opinions, *lawfully expressed*, privately or publicly, by act or word, *do not become unlawful* merely because their expression may induce *other people* to commit *unlawful* acts.

(3) **Provocation.**—Every man is presumed to *intend* the *natural consequences* of his acts; hence, the use of *threatening, abusive or insulting* language or behaviour, if it is *naturally* provocative of disorder, is *unlawful*.

(4) **Public Order.**—The *preservation of public order* is of paramount importance; a magistrate or police officer has a *right and duty* to take any

steps necessary to *stop a breach of the peace* taking place, or to prevent a breach which he reasonably apprehends.

These rules have recently been widely discussed, as a result of the activities of political extremists who make a special feature of propaganda against racial or religious minorities. Some of their meetings and marches have been accompanied by grave public disorder.

Until comparatively recent times the whole subject depended upon common law decisions (D4), not statute law (D5). For example:

Unlawful Assembly is a common law offence, constituted by an assembly of three or more persons, intending either *to commit a crime* by open force, or to carry out any *common purpose, whether lawful or unlawful*, in such manner as to give *firm and courageous persons* in the neighbourhood *reasonable grounds* to apprehend a *breach of the peace* in consequence of the assembly. (The words " any *common* purpose, *whether lawful or unlawful*," should be noted.)

Sedition is a common law crime, which includes the doing of *acts* or the speaking of *words* with the *intention* of promoting feelings of *ill-will or hostility* between different classes of the Queen's subjects. If the words or acts (whatever the intention) have a *direct tendency* to cause *unlawful meetings or disturbances*, they are seditious, since " a man is *presumed to intend* the *natural* consequences of his acts " (see (3), above). This does not mean that there must be no full and free discussion, nor that there is any prohibition upon criticism, or even censure; but there must be *no malignity*, nor any imputation of *corrupt or malicious motives*, such as to incite people *to take the law into their own hands* and to provoke them to *tumult and disorder*.

With these principles in mind, let us consider some actual cases (decided during the past eighty years) in which these rules have been applied.

Beatty v. Gillbanks (1882) arose from the activities of the newly-founded Salvation Army, which was " an association for carrying out religious exercises among themselves, and for a religious revival among certain classes of the community." Its leaders formed their followers into *processions* which marched through the streets of Weston-super-Mare, with *bands and banners*, collecting people as they marched back to their hall, where *prayer-meetings* were held. They were opposed on several occasions by an organisation calling itself the " Skeleton Army," which objected to these religious exercises. In consequence, disorders frequently arose, and the Salvation Army leaders were charged with " unlawfully and tumultuously assembling to the disturbance of the peace." The Magistrates bound them over to be of good behaviour; the Salvation Army appealed to the High Court.

The Judges decided that *the Magistrates were wrong*. " Everyone must be taken to intend the *natural* consequences of his acts " ((3), above) " and *if* this disturbance of the peace was the *natural consequence* of the Salvation Army's activities, they would have been liable, and the Magistrates would have been right to bind them over. But the evidence does not support this contention. . . . There was nothing in their conduct which was either tumultuous or against the peace; on the contrary, the evidence shows the disturbances were caused by other people, antagonistic to them. What has happened here is that an *unlawful organisation* has assumed to itself the right *to prevent* the Salvation Army from lawfully *assembling*, and the *decision of the Magistrates* amounts to this—that a man may be *convicted for doing a lawful act if he knows that his doing it may cause another to do an unlawful act*. There is *no authority* for such a proposition."

Wise v. Dunning (1902) is a contrasting case. A fanatical *Protestant clergyman* had, on several occasions, held meetings in parts of Liverpool containing a *strong Roman Catholic population*. At these meetings he had used *offensive, violent, and provocative language*, attacking the Pope and the Roman Catholic Church. In consequence, breaches of the peace had occurred, and the Liverpool Magistrate had bound him over to be of good behaviour. The Protestant clergyman appealed to the High Court, protesting that there was no evidence that he had committed or intended to commit a breach of the peace, and that the Magistrate's decision (as in the earlier case) was wrong. But the Judges *upheld the Magistrate's decision and dismissed the appeal*. The Lord Chief Justice said " there was abundant evidence that, in the public streets, he had used *language which was abusive*, which had *caused an obstruction*, and that he intended to do *similar acts* in another place." The two other Judges said that every case depends upon its own *facts* and *evidence*:

> " The law does not as a rule regard an illegal act as being the natural consequence of a temptation held out to commit it; but . . . the cases show that *the law regards the infirmity of human temper* to the extent of considering that a breach of the peace, although an illegal act, may be the *natural consequence* of *insulting or abusive* language or conduct ".

The clergyman's behaviour (unlike that of the Salvation Army leaders in the earlier case) was *in itself violently provocative;* therefore the Magistrate was justified in binding him over, " under preventive power " to stop breaches of the peace, which were the " natural result " of his behaviour.

Both the above cases, as it happened, dealt with religious controversies. But the same rules apply in controversies of other kinds.

Duncan v. Jones (1936) was concerned with provocation on a *political and social* question. There was grave unemployment at the time, and feelings between the unemployed, and their supporters, against the Government, and its policies, ran high. Mrs. Jones had held a *meeting of unemployed* men right *opposite an unemployed training-centre*; she had made a speech strongly attacking the Government's policy, and a *disturbance had followed*. Fourteen months later, when she appeared at the *same place* for the *same purpose*, the Police Superintendent forbade her to hold the meeting there. She insisted on doing so, stepped on her box, and began to address the bystanders. It was not, at that stage, suggested that she was obstructing the highway, or inciting anybody to commit a breach of the peace. Nevertheless she was *convicted of obstructing* the Superintendent *in the execution of his duty*, and her conviction was upheld by the High Court. " She must have known (from earlier experience) the *natural consequence* of holding such a meeting at that place; the Superintendent *reasonably apprehended a breach of the peace;* it therefore became *his duty to prevent it*, and she was guilty of *obstructing him in carrying out that duty*."

The Public Order Act, 1936.—In the period preceding the Second World War, extremist political organisations held meetings at which they wore political uniforms and used " strong-arm " tactics similar to those in vogue among the Italian Fascists and German Nazis. They also indulged, like the Nazis, in virulent propaganda calculated to stir up racial hatred. As a result of the exasperation of public feelings, in the existing state of international tension, grave disorders took place in London and other cities. The situation was discussed in both Houses of Parliament and it was generally agreed that the law required to be *clarified and strengthened*. On December 18, 1936, the *Public Order Act* received the Royal Assent, and came into force on January 1, 1937.

Prohibition of Political Uniforms.—Section 1 of the Act (subject to certain exceptions) *forbids the wearing*, in a *public place* or at a *public meeting*, of *uniform* signifying the wearer's association with a *political organisation*, or with the promotion of a *political object*. (The exceptions are "ceremonial, anniversary or other special occasions" on which the Chief Officer of Police may permit a relaxation of the prohibition (with the Home Secretary's consent) only if he is satisfied that no risk of public disorder is likely to be involved.)

Prohibition of Quasi-Military Organisations.—Section 2 makes it an *offence* to participate in the *control or management* of an *association* whose members are (*a*) *organised* or *trained* or *equipped* to enable them to be employed "in usurping the functions of the police or of the armed forces of the Crown," or (*b*) *organised and trained*, or *organised and equipped* as follows: either (i) for the purpose of the use or display of *physical force* in promoting a *political object*, or (ii) in such manner as to arouse *reasonable apprehension* that they are *organised*, and either *trained or equipped*, for the purpose described in (i). (It was under (*b*) (ii) that two of the leaders of a present-day extremist political organisation were convicted and sentenced to imprisonment in October, 1962, at the Central Criminal Court; their appeals, in November, were dismissed.) The consent of the Attorney-General (the Senior Law Officer of the Crown) is required before a prosecution under Section 2 can be instituted. In certain circumstances a High Court Order may be made to search the premises of the organisation and to impound its property.

Preservation of Public Order on the Occasion of Processions.—Section 3 confers powers for this purpose, as follows:

(1) On a *Chief Officer of Police*, if he has *reasonable grounds* for *apprehending* that a *procession* may occasion *serious public disorder* (having regard to time, place and circumstances), power *to impose* on the organisers or participants in the procession such *conditions* as appear *necessary for preserving public order* (including the route of the procession and power to prohibit it from entering any "public place"); but no conditions restricting the display of *flags, banners or emblems* are to be imposed unless they are *reasonably necessary to prevent risk of a breach of the peace*.

(2) On a *Borough or Urban District Council* (if the Chief Officer of Police believes that his powers under (1) (above) will not suffice to prevent serious public disorder, and on application by him) power to *make an Order* (with the consent of the Home Secretary) *prohibiting* all *public processions*, or certain classes of public processions in the area for a period *not exceeding three months*. (This power does not apply within the City of London or the Metropolitan Police Area, as to which see (3) (below).)

(3) On the *Commissioner of the City of London Police*, and the *Commissioner of Metropolitan Police*, a power similar to that described in (2) (above), and on similar conditions. Thus, within the *London Area* the *Police Authorities*, and in *urban areas outside London* the *Local Authorities*, are given *power to prohibit processions* (or "marches") on the conditions described in (2) above.

It is an *offence* for anybody *knowingly to fail to comply* with any *Order* or *condition* imposed, *or to organise* or *assist in organising* a public procession *in contravention* of the Section.

It should be noted that *this Section* deals with *processions* (or "marches")—*not meetings*. *Meetings* continue to be *governed by the common law* principles laid down in *Beatty v. Gillbanks*, *Wise v. Dunning*, etc. (as extended by Sections 4 and 5 of the Act).

Prohibition of Offensive Weapons.—By Section 4, anybody is guilty of an *offence* if he has with him any *offensive weapon* at a *public meeting* or *on the occasion of* a *public procession*, without lawful authority. (Note the words "*on the occasion of* a public procession"; it is *not only those taking part* in the procession, *but also bystanders*, who may commit this offence.) "Lawful authority" extends to servants of the Crown, Members of Parliament or of a Local Authority (acting as such), police officers, members of Fire Brigades or Cadet Corps, and so forth.

Prohibition of Offensive Conduct Conducive to Breaches of the Peace.—Section 5 reads—"Any person who in any *public place or* at any *public meeting* uses *threatening, abusive* or *insulting* words or behaviour with *intent to provoke* a *breach of the peace, or* whereby a *breach of the peace is likely to be occasioned*, shall be guilty of an offence." (This *declares and clarifies* the *common law* principles laid down in *Wise v. Dunning* and *Duncan v. Jones* (above).)

Disorderly Conduct at a Public Meeting.—Section 6 refers to the **Public Meeting Act, 1908.** Section 1 of the 1908 Act makes it an offence for a person to *act in a disorderly manner* at a *lawful* public meeting for the purpose of *preventing the transaction of the meeting's business*. Section 6 of the 1936 Act gives power to a constable, if he *reasonably suspects* an offence under the 1908 Act, *to demand* of the suspected offender his *name and address* (provided that the chairman of the meeting requests him to do so). If the suspected offender *refuses* or fails to give his name and address, or gives a *false name and address*, he *commits an offence*, and the constable may arrest him without warrant. (Note that, to qualify for protection, the public meeting must, in the first place, be *lawful*.) The **Public Order Act, 1963**, has greatly increased the penalties under Section 5 of the Act of 1936 and Section 1 of the Act of 1908; but an undertaking has been given by the Home Office that the new Act will not be used to suppress mere "heckling" at a public meeting.

Jordan v. Burgoyne (1963) was similar to *Wise v. Dunning* (1902), except that the 1963 case was concerned with section 5 of the Public Order Act, 1936. At a *public meeting* in Trafalgar Square, to an audience of 5,000, *which included many Jews*, Colin Jordan used the words—"Hitler was right. Our real enemies—the people we should have fought—were not the National Socialists of Germany, but World Jewry and its associates." There was *complete disorder* and a general surge towards the speaker by the crowd, but they were restrained by the police, under Superintendent Burgoyne; and 20 arrests were made while the crowd was being dispersed.

Before the Bow Street Magistrate Jordan was convicted and sentenced to imprisonment, for "*using at a public meeting insulting words whereby a breach of the peace was likely to be occasioned.*" He appealed to Quarter Sessions, who found as a fact that, though *the words were highly insulting*, they were *not likely to lead ordinary responsible persons to commit breaches of the peace*; they therefore allowed Jordan's appeal against conviction. The prosecution then asked for "a case to be stated" for the High Court on the question whether the words in section 5 could properly be interpreted to mean "likely to lead to a breach of the peace by ordinary citizens."

The Lord Chief Justice, with two other Judges, decided that *Quarter Sessions were wrong*. *The test was not* whether the insulting words were likely to cause a breach of the peace by a *hypothetical audience*, whatever their creed, faith, race or political views; in any case the Judges imagined that any *reasonable citizen would be provoked* beyond endurance. But this was an *Act to keep order in public places*, and "a speaker must take *his audience as he finds it*. If those words to that audience are likely to provoke a breach of the peace, the *speaker is guilty of an offence*. The right of *free speech is not in question*; he may *express his views* as *strongly* as he likes, *but he must not threaten, abuse or insult that audience*." The case was sent back to Quarter Sessions with a direction to find the offence proved, and to dismiss Jordan's appeal from the Magistrate's conviction.

EDUCATION & CAREERS

EDUCATION AND CAREERS

AUNTS and uncles can be infuriating when they insist on asking what their nephews and nieces intend being when they grow up. The fact is that very few boys and girls do know, while they are still at school, what they want to be when they leave. They often have to decide, however, as they go up the school, which courses they are going to select or which subjects they would like to drop, and these decisions, unfortunately, may well affect the careers that will be available to them. A boy or girl who, for example, drops Maths, frequently finds that he or she cannot become a draughtsman, do computor work, train for physiotherapy or even biological work.

The following pages are written in an attempt to be helpful to nieces and nephews and to their parents, whether or not the great decision has yet been made. For those still undecided there are some hints about coming to a decision, and for those who are already inclining towards some job or career, there is practical advice not only about how to prepare for entry, what sort of examinations have to be passed but also what sort of studying may be required even after starting on the job.

Another decision which boys and girls, and their parents, have to take is what is the best time to leave school. Is it better to leave at sixteen and try to qualify by part-time study at the same time as gaining practical experience on the job? Is it better to stay on in the sixth form? Should one continue full-time even after that, at a university or a technical college? These are very difficult questions but it should be remembered that more and more employers prefer to take older pupils, as they believe that education is best acquired while one is young but practical training can be gained at any time. In fact, employers increasingly feel that nothing is lost by continuing longer at school or college while irredeemable harm can be done by leaving too soon.

Once upon a time the only jobs for which the candidates needed training and testing by written examination were the Church, the Law, Medicine, and Teaching, and for all these the candidates had to go to University. Today there is hardly a trade and there is no profession which does not demand, not only a form of training, but a training which has to be tested by written examinations. These examinations may be taken while at school, but also they are often taken after leaving school, the candidate working either full-time, at a university or a technical college, or part-time, while earning. It is particularly with this sort of job that this section will deal.

CHOOSING A CAREER

Some Personal Advice.—Before starting to deal with the groups of possible jobs, it would perhaps be helpful to say a word about how to decide what sort of work to go for. An old trick is to think of the answer to this kind of question:—

Likes

E.g., " Do I like working with people? "
" Do I like working for people? "
" Do I like working with animals or plants? "
" Do I like working with things? "
" Do I like ' Paper Work '?"

Attainments

E.g., " What standard shall I reach at School? ":—

C.S.E. Examinations.
G.C.E. Ordinary levels in the subjects usually regarded as less difficult, *e.g.*, Geography, Art, Woodwork, English, General Science, Elementary Mathematics.
G.C.E. Ordinary levels in the more difficult subjects, *e.g.*, Additional Mathematics, French, Latin, German, Physics, Chemistry.
G.C.E. Advanced levels.

Talents

E.g., " Have I any special talents for figures, for writing good English, for languages, for science, for drawing, for mending things, for making things with my hands? "

Disposition

E.g., " Would I be prepared to give up some of my leisure time to working for examinations? "

Some Suggestions.

Having thought about the answers to these questions, it is now time to make a rough survey of the jobs which exist today. These are given below under three main headings, and examples are given of jobs, each of which will probably require time to be spent, after leaving school, on working for exams.

Group One. Work in an Office.

Largely concerned with problems expressed in words or in figures.

Examples:

Accountancy.
Banks and Insurance Offices.
Solicitors' Offices.
Civil Service and Local Government Service.
Building Societies.
Librarianship.

Group Two. Work with Things.

Largely concerned with studying, designing, making, and repairing things.

Examples.

Mechanical, Electrical, Civil Engineering.
Surveying and Architecture.
Draughtsmanship.
Agriculture, Forestry and Horticulture.
Dentistry or Surgery or Medical Services, *e.g.*, Physiotherapy.
Laboratory Work.
Furniture Design and Manufacture.

Group Three. Work with People.

Largely concerned with contacts with other people, teaching them, advising them, observing them, persuading them.

Examples:

Salesmanship and Purchasing.
Teaching.
The Church.
General Medical Practice, *i.e.*, ordinary doctor.
Journalism.
The Armed Services.
The Police.
Hotel Management.
Nursing and Social Work, *e.g.*, Medical Social Worker or Probation Service.

The list of examples could, of course, quite easily be multiplied by ten, but those given are enough for the moment. Here is some advice to a boy or girl as to how to use them:

You will find other suggestions in the list of booklets on E34. No. 1 in the "Choice of Careers" series of booklets sets out the basic questions which have to be answered when deciding upon a career. The *Careers Guide* published by H.M.S.O. (7*s*. 6*d*.) is very useful on opportunities in the Professions, Industry and Commerce.

Having answered the questions and studied the lists, make a list of your own, of all the occupations which you think might attract you, and then read the passage about them later in this section.

Having done this, and having read some of the recommended books or pamphlets on them, then you *must* go and get some advice. This is most important; you really cannot afford to rely merely on written advice for something so important as your future. You ought to be able to get advice from your school—from the Head, or from your House Master or House Mistress, or from the member of staff in charge of Careers—but it has to be admitted that not all schools are very up to date about these things, and not all children feel the confidence they ought to feel about the advice given them by teachers; if this is so, there is always the expert available for every young person in Great Britain, and that is the *Youth Employment Officer* whose address will be in the Post Office. Of course, you can often contact the Y.E.O. through your school, and this is preferable, but not absolutely necessary. The great thing is to get his or her advice; it won't cost you anything, and it won't be biased, and you can be sure that he will do all he can, after a good long interview, to put you on the right track to your future. Of course you may feel, and some parents may feel, that this is not enough, if so, one of the following will help you. They will give you a lengthy consultation with tests of various kinds and will charge a fee:—The National Institute of Industrial Psychology, 14 Welbeck Street, W.1. The Vocational Guidance Association, 37a Devonshire Street, W.1.

EXAMINATIONS AND COURSES.

Examinations.—Before starting on any of the detailed requirements for those who are hoping for particular jobs, a general picture of the Examination Field may be helpful. The first important point to make clear is that a boy or girl does not have to have been at a Grammar School or at an Independent School in order to enter the Examination Field. Many other schools are offering examination courses which will be useful for those who want qualifications before leaving school, but even those who are not able to benefit by these while still at school, who may be in a Secondary Modern School where no external examinations are taken, or who may not be regarded by the school authorities as "up to taking" an examination, need not feel cut off from their opportunities. There is often the chance of continuing full-time education at a College of Further Education. If it is important to earn some money, there are plenty of jobs waiting for those who are prepared to work, perhaps in the evenings, perhaps on the one day per week they are released by their employers (this system is known as the day-release scheme). By this means there are valuable qualifications that can be acquired in competition with those who have been to schools where examinations are the normal end to a school career.

It is important, too, not to be discouraged by an unsuccessful career at school; often boys or girls who have been hopeless in class will suddenly, after leaving school, begin to do work, perhaps in mathematics, which was quite beyond them at school, because they suddenly see the sense in learning the subject which only then they realise is connected with the work they want to do.

Some examinations are normally taken while at school; others, normally only after leaving. The commonest In-school examination is of course the *General Certificate of Education*, though it can also be taken by those who have left school, particularly in Technical or Further Education Colleges, but also through Correspondence Colleges (*see* below).

Apart from the G.C.E. there are certain other examinations and certificates; among these there are:—

Certificate of Secondary Education (C.S.E.). This examination is taken by pupils who have completed a five-year course in a secondary school. Not only can it be taken in single subjects but the grade of pass is noted on the certificate. Most professional bodies recognise a Grade I certificate as equivalent to an "O" level pass in the G.C.E.

Certificates of the City and Guilds Institute. The courses available through the Institute can be taken at Technical Colleges and are sometimes begun at school. More than three hundred subjects, mainly technical subjects, are available. The corresponding body (mainly for non-technical subjects) is the *Royal Society of Arts.*

It will be noticed that many correspondence colleges prepare students to take examinations of various Professional Institutions; these examinations vary with each profession, and almost all of them have separate stages. Often it will be found that if a candidate has passed the G.C.E. at Ordinary level (or has a Grade I pass in C.S.E.) in certain subjects he can start the professional course farther on, that is to say he is "exempted" from one of the early stages of the course. With Advanced level still further "exemption" is often allowed.

University Degree.

The General Certificate of Education (or C.S.E. Grade I pass) is essential for anyone wishing to take a degree at a British University, and the details for qualifying for University entry are uniform, except that Oxford and Cambridge are a law unto themselves, and every Faculty of each University has its own special requirements concerning particular subjects passed at Advanced and Ordinary level, which is only to be expected. The minimum entrance qualifications are given below, but it is important to check with the Registrar of the University whether there are any special requirements. Applications for all British Universities (except the Medical Schools) have to be made through the Universities' Central Council on Admissions. (*See* **E4**).

SOME CORRESPONDENCE COLLEGES

The Bennett College Ltd., Sheffield.

British College of Accountancy, 20 Milton Road, Harpenden, Herts.

British Institute of Engineering Technology, College House, 29 Wrights Lane, W.8.

Civil Service Correspondence School, 10 Station Parade, High Street, S.W.12.

College of Estate Management, St. Alban's Grove, Kensington, W.8.

E.M.I. Institute, 43 Grove Park, W.4.

International Correspondence Schools, Kingsway, W.C.2.

Metropolitan College, St. Albans, Herts.

Nalgo Correspondence Institute, 1 York Gate, N.W.1.

National Institute of Engineering, 148 High Holborn, E.C.1.

Pitman Correspondence College, 20 Russell Square, W.C.1.

Rapid Results College, Tuition House, S.W.19.

The School of Accountancy, 2 West Regent Street, Glasgow, C.2.

School of Careers, College House, 29 Wrights Lane, Kensington, W.8.

University Correspondence College, Burlington House, Cambridge.

Wolsey Hall, Oxford.

Minimum Entrance Requirements for University and for Colleges of Advanced Technology:—

Anyone needing help in entering a University should read *University and College Entrance, the basic facts*, published by the National Union of Teachers (4*s*.); the Handbook published by the Universities' Central Council on Admissions, 29 Tavistock Square, W.C.1; *A Compendium of University Entrance Requirements*, published by the Committee of Vice-Chancellors and Principals, 36 Gordon Square, W.C.1.

Degree.

1. The candidate usually should have passed in English Language and in either four, or five other subjects.

2. The subjects usually should include:—

(*a*) a language other than English;
(*b*) either mathematics or an approved science (ask the Registrar about this if in doubt).

3. At least two of the subjects must be passed at Advanced level.

4. In view of the increasing difficulty in obtaining a place at a University, candidates usually have to offer more than the minimum number of passes and the marks obtained should be well above the pass level.

5. A University degree is, of course, essential for doctors, dentists, surgeons; for almost all teachers of Grammar School standard; and in nearly all cases for those who hope to go into the Church of England. In nearly all other professions a degree is an advantage, and this is so even in the technical world.

Degree in Technology. However, those who are technically minded, and who are not attracted by study which has not much connection with the practical applications of their chosen field, may now study for a Degree in Technology. This usually entails full-time study sandwiched in between periods of working in the related industry. The Degree can be taken at the new Technological Universities, and at *some* Colleges of Technology and Technical Colleges.

Admission to these courses requires similar qualifications as for University entrance: advanced levels in mathematics and physics, and/or chemistry may be essential, though there may not be so much rigidity about the Ordinary levels. A *good* Ordinary National Certificate or Ordinary National Diploma also qualifies.

National Certificate and National Diploma.

The *National Diploma* is awarded at the Ordinary level to students who have successfully completed full-time courses for two years from age 16; the *Higher National Diploma* after a three-year full-time, or a sandwich, course. These diplomas are usually worked for at Colleges of Technology, and are related to technical careers. The *Ordinary National Certificate*, usually on a day-release basis, is awarded to students who successfully complete two years' part-time study. The entry to these courses is four G.C.E. O level passes (mathematics, physics, English language or technical drawing and one other) or by the completion of a general course at a College.

The *Higher National Certificate* is obtained after three years' part-time study after obtaining an O.N.C., an O.N.D., or A levels in G.C.E. In many Colleges it is now possible to take O.N.C. and O.N.D. as well as H.N.C. and H.N.D. in Business Studies as well as in a wide range of technical subjects. *See* Chart (E5).

SCHOOL SUBJECTS AND CHOICE OF CAREER.

School courses tend to become narrower after the pupil has reached the early teens, and narrower still after O level has been taken. There are some careers for which it is important to begin and to keep on with certain subjects at this stage. This does not mean that all other subjects should be dropped (on the contrary), nor does it mean that there are not a very large number of careers for which no particular specialisation is necessary, but it may be helpful to indicate the careers which are listed in this section, for which certain subjects ought to be studied seriously while at school.

For all scientific and technical careers, mathematics is important, and a fairly wide range of sciences useful. For engineering (including draughtsmanship), mathematics should be linked with physics. For the medical careers (doctor, dentist, medical auxiliary, pharmacist), chemistry, backed up by physics and perhaps by biology, is important, for optics, physics and biology are the valuable subjects. For agriculture and forestry, chemistry and biology are useful. For photography, physics or chemistry is important.

For an actuary, mathematics to a high level is essential; for an air hostess, fluency in a foreign language.

For a number of professions (*e.g.*, accountancy, surveying, chiropody, insurance), a range of four, five, or six subjects to O level is the necessary minimum and usually include English, frequently mathematics, sometimes a foreign language. But it must be borne in mind that these are *minimum* requirements only and that study beyond O level (in any subjects) makes successful passing of the professional examinations more likely. Indeed, many professions now require A level passes as well as O.

Although O level mathematics is usually required for banking, accountancy, insurance, these must not be looked on as "mathematical" careers.

There is so much emphasis on technical matters in the Forces nowadays that mathematics and physics are extremely useful here.

It will be noticed that there is a large number of careers which are described later in this section which do not figure in the above list. For most of them, a good range of subjects is important rather than one or two special ones. It is often frustrating and sometimes dangerous to assume that particular school subjects link inevitably with particular careers. For instance, English is by no means the only important subject for journalism, but ease of expression in spoken and written English is of immense value in all sorts of careers, from engineering to accountancy. Geography, history, English literature, modern and classical languages, art, music, scripture, and other similar subjects should not normally be linked to careers even when they are taken to degree level. But employers appreciate the fact that they have been studied, and are often attracted by the applicant who has studied them.

APPRENTICESHIPS.

Until now an apprentice learnt his trade while working at it; after a set period of years he became a skilled or a qualified person. Engineering is today the career where there are more apprenticeships than in any other trade, so the examples given below are taken mainly from engineering, but many other trades now run apprenticeship schemes, which are similar to that described here. *See* Chart (E5).

The Industrial Training Act (1964) is likely to change the apprenticeship system. In engineering, for example, first-year training will in future probably be given in special training centres rather than "on the job".

Craft Apprenticeship, taken up by a boy who has done reasonably well at school, usually begins at 16; after a probationary period an apprentice is set to a particular trade, such as glass-blowing, fitting and turning, printing, or plumbing, and he is expected to study the theoretical background to his craft at the Technical College, working in most cases towards a City and Guilds Certificate either on one day a week or at short periods of full-time study (block release).

TYPICAL APPRENTICESHIP SCHEMES IN ENGINEERING

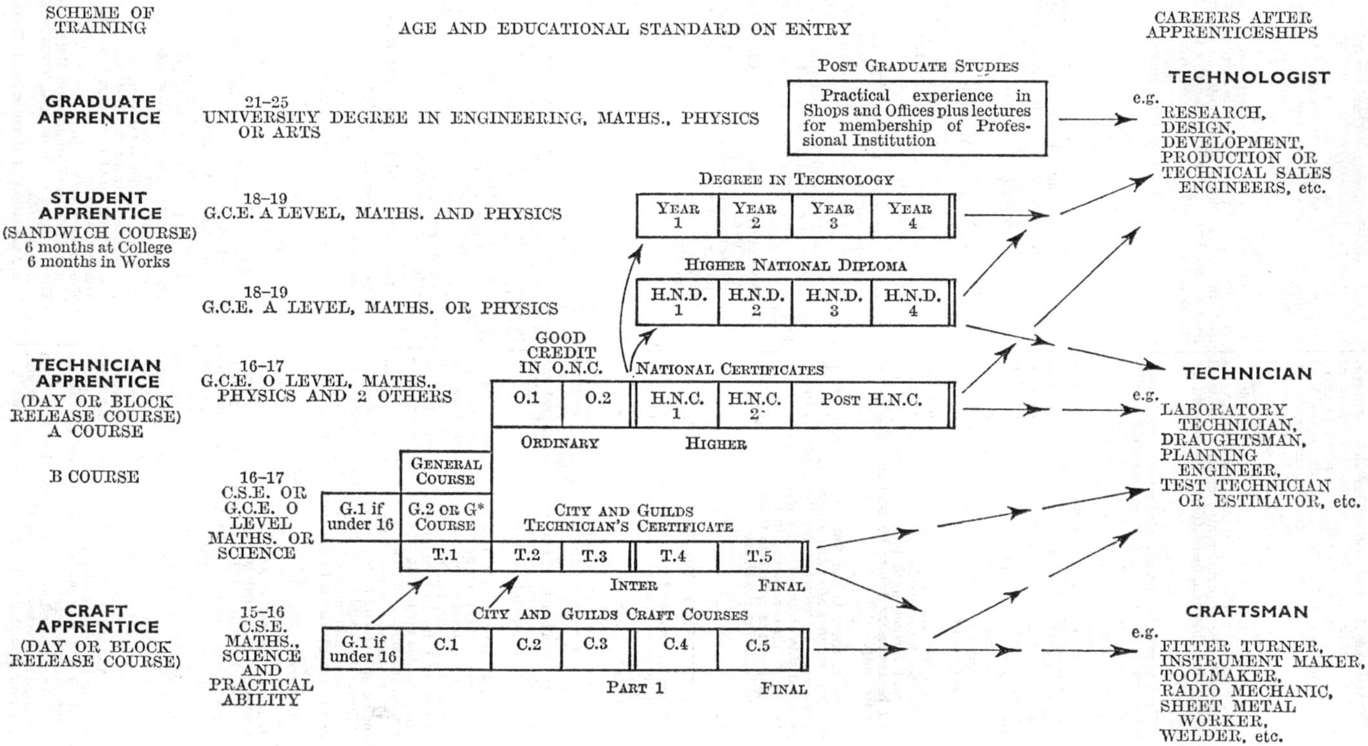
SCHEME OF TRAINING
AGE AND EDUCATIONAL STANDARD ON ENTRY
CAREERS AFTER APPRENTICESHIPS
GRADUATE APPRENTICE
21–25 UNIVERSITY DEGREE IN ENGINEERING, MATHS., PHYSICS OR ARTS
POST GRADUATE STUDIES
Practical experience in Shops and Offices plus lectures for membership of Professional Institution
TECHNOLOGIST
e.g. RESEARCH, DESIGN, DEVELOPMENT, PRODUCTION OR TECHNICAL SALES ENGINEERS, etc.
STUDENT APPRENTICE (SANDWICH COURSE) 6 months at College 6 months in Works
18–19 G.C.E. A LEVEL, MATHS. AND PHYSICS
DEGREE IN TECHNOLOGY
YEAR 1
YEAR 2
YEAR 3
YEAR 4
18–19 G.C.E. A LEVEL, MATHS. OR PHYSICS
HIGHER NATIONAL DIPLOMA
H.N.D. 1
H.N.D. 2
H.N.D. 3
H.N.D. 4
GOOD CREDIT IN O.N.C.
TECHNICIAN APPRENTICE (DAY OR BLOCK RELEASE COURSE) A COURSE
16–17 G.C.E. O LEVEL, MATHS., PHYSICS AND 2 OTHERS
NATIONAL CERTIFICATES
O.1
O.2
H.N.C. 1
H.N.C. 2
POST H.N.C.
ORDINARY
HIGHER
TECHNICIAN
e.g. LABORATORY TECHNICIAN, DRAUGHTSMAN, PLANNING ENGINEER, TEST TECHNICIAN OR ESTIMATOR, etc.
B COURSE
16–17 C.S.E. OR G.C.E. O LEVEL MATHS. OR SCIENCE
GENERAL COURSE
G.1 if under 16
G.2 OR G* COURSE
CITY AND GUILDS TECHNICIAN'S CERTIFICATE
T.1
T.2
T.3
T.4
T.5
INTER
FINAL
CRAFT APPRENTICE (DAY OR BLOCK RELEASE COURSE)
15–16 C.S.E. MATHS., SCIENCE AND PRACTICAL ABILITY
CITY AND GUILDS CRAFT COURSES
G.1 if under 16
C.1
C.2
C.3
C.4
C.5
PART 1
FINAL
CRAFTSMAN
e.g. FITTER TURNER, INSTRUMENT MAKER, TOOLMAKER, RADIO MECHANIC, SHEET METAL WORKER, WELDER, etc.

Next comes the *Technical or Technician Apprenticeship*, starting at 16–17, sometimes known as Student Apprenticeship. The standard of entry for this would be either the C.S.E., or the G.C.E. O level in four subjects including mathematics, physics and English language or the successful completion of a general course at a Technical College. The Technician Apprentice will usually study one day a week at a Technical College, either on a National Certificate course or a Technician's course. These apprenticeships can lead to such jobs as draughtsman, inspector, tester, laboratory assistant.

Next comes the proper *Student Apprenticeship* for which either G.C.E. A level including mathematics and physics or a *good* ordinary National Certificate is essential. The course will lead to a Higher National Certificate, a Higher National Diploma, or a Degree in Technology, on a day release basis or for the Diploma on a sandwich course. In the sandwich course the student spends up to six months in each year full-time at a College with a corresponding time (full-time) at work. Alternatively, after a year in industry, the student apprentice may be sent to University for a full-time degree course, occasionally at his employer's expense.

Ultimately the aim of the student will be to qualify for membership of a professional Institution and further work and practical experience will be necessary before he becomes eligible for membership.

Finally, there is the *Graduate Apprenticeship*, which is entered after the University and which serves as an introduction for the graduate to the practical side of industry, sometimes this type of apprenticeship is arranged in the form of a sandwich course, the practical training preceding as well as following the University course.

FINANCIAL AID TO STUDENTS.

Nowadays no one who is able to continue studying either at school or after leaving school should be put off by fear of financial difficulties. It may, of course, be frustrating for the fifteen-year-olds, or for the Sixth Formers, to see their contemporaries earning good money or having a good time while they are studying, but frustration turns to jubilation when the last exams are finished with, and when the much-desired and valued qualifications are leading the former victims not only to better paid but to more interesting work.

School Maintenance Grants.—It may be a question of staying on at school to take Ordinary or Advanced level examinations; students are not yet paid for this, but in some cases parents are; widows and those whose income is equally low are often eligible for maintenance grants (to maintain a child at school), which for a sixteen-year-old may be as much as £80 per annum. Application for such grants should be made to the local Education Officer. It should not be forgotten either that an income-tax allowance of £165 is granted for each child over 16 who is in full-time education.

University Grants.—After school, university grants are available from the County, or County Borough, Education Authority for most students who are good enough to be accepted by a University (*see* E4 (1)). They are normally quite sufficient to keep a student at University without relying seriously on their parents for help. Applications should be made normally in the final school year, and the Head of the School should be seen about these. Every year an increasing number of industrial and commercial concerns, including the nationalised industries, offer scholarships for University courses. Unlike Local Authorities' awards, the industrial scholarships do not always depend on a means test. A list of such scholarships is sent to schools each year by the Youth Employment Service.

State scholarships, which have hitherto been granted on the results of the G.C.E. examinations, are now available only for " mature students ".

Local Authority Grants.—There are other forms of further full-time study for which grants are available from or through Local Education Authorities, and these include grants for teacher training at Colleges of Education, and for study in Technical Colleges for qualifications in Architecture, Surveying, Librarianship; or in special training schools such as for Medical Auxiliaries or Merchant Navy Cadets. Sometimes, however, study for some of these careers is carried out on a part-time or sandwich basis, and the student is paid wages by his employer for the time he is studying as well as for the time he is working. As a general rule, if there is a choice between full-time or part-time study, full-time is the more advisable.

The Armed Services.—The Armed Services are very keen for study to be continued for as long as possible after school, and each branch of the Services runs its own Apprentice Schools (*see* E10, 11). The Navy, Army, and Air Force run their own scientifically biased Colleges, and also send selected Cadets to the University. Valuable scholarships are also offered by all three Services to selected future sixth-formers to encourage them to stay on at school before going to Dartmouth, Sandhurst, or Cranwell; and the Army has its own sixth-form course at Welbeck. All enquiries about Services should be made to the Director of Recruitment of the branch concerned, the particulars of which are given under the heading *Armed Services* below.

Where to apply for Grants.—The sources to which parents should apply for grants are varied, and to compile a list of all the available awards and allowances would obviously require a junior encyclopædia to itself, and these remarks are meant only to give an indication of what may be done. Full details from any particular body should be obtained as follows:—

(*a*) County Authority—The Chief Education Officer.
(*b*) Large Firm—The Personnel Manager.
(*c*) Arm of Service—Director of Recruitment of the Arm concerned.
(*d*) University—The Registrar.

C.S.E., G.C.E. AND THE PROFESSIONAL BODIES

Mention has already been made of the advisability of staying at school as long as possible and, in view of the possibilites of financial help for those who need it to continue their full-time education, it may be of interest to note some of the professional bodies which either *accept* the C.S.E. or the O level of the G.C.E. as providing exemption from their preliminary examination or *require* them as evidence of preliminary education.

The number of subjects required varies slightly according to the professional body—but it is usually four, five, or six and in nearly every case English Language is an essential.

The professional bodies concerned are:—

The Association of Certified and Corporate Accountants.
The Institute of Chartered Accountants.
The Institute of Company Accountants.
The Institute of Actuaries.
The Advertising Association.
The Royal Institute of British Architects.
The Incorporated Association of Architects and Surveyors.
The Chartered Auctioneers and Estate Agents Institute.
The Institute of Builders.
The Building Societies' Institute.
The Royal Institute of Chemistry.
The Institute of Cost and Works Accountants.
The Forestry Commission.
The Royal Horticultural Society.
The Chartered Insurance Institute.
The Corporation of Insurance Brokers.
The Law Society.
The Library Association.
The Institution of Mining and Metallurgy.
The Institute of Municipal Treasurers and Accountants.
The Association of Occupational Therapists.

The Institute of Quantity Surveyors.
The Society of Radiographers.
The Rating and Valuation Association.
The Chartered Institute of Secretaries.
The Corporation of Secretaries.
The Royal Institution of Chartered Surveyors.

This is not a complete list. Details for any particular professional body are set out in the Ministry of Education Circular No. 226, which also gives their addresses. An increasing number of these bodies are raising their minimum requirements to **A** G.C.E. level (notably Actuaries, Architects, Law). Others allow **A** G.C.E. passes as an alternative to a wider range of **O** G.C.E. Some offer exemptions to certain graduates. For most of them, sixth-form experience will make qualifying professionally more likely. Usually only a C.S.E. Grade I is accepted as equivalent to G.C.E. O level.

CAREERS FOR GIRLS.

Girls are difficult. They often do not like to show too much interest in their future careers, because this might make people think that they were not expecting to get married. Nothing could be more ridiculous. The girl who has a career, especially a career for which training is needed, is probably far more likely to make a good marriage, than the one who just drifts out of school into the first available job. Here are four reasons why this is so:

(1) The girl with a training will probably attract the better-educated man.

(2) If a girl has a job which holds her interest she may well find a husband who also works in the same field—a shared interest is a good basis for a marriage.

(3) The girl with a training will have something extra to give her children as they grow up, and so be a more satisfactory mother.

(4) The mother who has training qualifications can go back to her profession after her children have grown up; this not only has the advantage of adding to the family income, but means that an escape from the home to an outside interest is always available should the desire, or indeed the need, arise.

Giving advice to girls is a specialist task, and often the Youth Employment Officer, who helps girls also, either is a woman or has a qualified woman assistant who can help girls who are still at school. Further advice may be had from the Women's Employment Federation, 251 Brompton Road, S.W.3.

Careers open to girls today are no longer restricted to teaching, nursing and "secretarial," interesting and rewarding as these can be. Women can easily find jobs after being trained as accountants, engineers, and architects and, although most of us have yet to see a woman Bank Manager (a few have been appointed) and the banks are more and more turning to women to take on responsible positions behind the counter. Often, if education is continued and then capped by a secretarial course it can lead to some very interesting and rewarding positions as personal assistants or secretaries.

Finally, the advantages of a University degree to a girl who can and wants to continue her Sixth Form studies should be obvious, and no girl should be denied a University course just because it does not seem to lead to a job.

To avoid fruitless thumbing through jobs for boys only, here is a list of the jobs for girls, which are included in the next part of the section:

Accountancy, Advertising, Agriculture, Air Hostess, Architect, Banking, Beauty Culture, Catering and Hotel Management, Child Care, Chiropody, Civil Service, Dentistry, Dietetics Dressmaking, Engineering, Floristry, Hairdressing, Horticulture, Hospital Administration, Hotel keeping, Institutional Management, Insurance, Journalism, Laboratory Assistant, Laundry Management, Law, Librarianship, Local Government, Medicine, Meterology, Midwifery and Maternity Services, Museums, Music, Nursing, Occupational Therapy, Orthoptics, Personnel Management, Pharmacy, Photography, Physiotherapy, Police, Probation Service, Radiography, Science, Secretarial work, Singing, Social work, Speech Therapy, Surveying, Teaching, The Services, Veterinary Surgery.

LIST OF CAREERS AND ESSENTIAL DETAILS.

How to Use this List.

1. The careers are listed in alphabetical order; those which are available both to girls and to boys have the letters **B. G.** beside them; if only boys are eligible, **B.**, if only girls, **G.**

2. Opposite the heading "Qualifications," initials have been used to indicate the following:—

Certificate of Secondary Education	**C.S.E.***
Ordinary level of the G.C.E. .	**O**
Advanced level of the G.C.E. .	**A**
Ordinary National Certificate .	**O.N.C.**
Higher National Certificate .	**H.N.C.**

3. The indications of salary given are meant as a rough indication of what a young person may expect to start earning after qualification in the career concerned. In the rare cases where no qualification is required the starting salary is given. The upper levels of salary vary from job to job in many cases, and therefore often the upper end of the salary bracket has been omitted.

* As a qualification C.S.E. Grade I is not included as it is an alternative to O level G.C.E.

ACCOUNTANCY.

B. G.

Age of Entry. 16–18 or Graduate.

Qualifications. O or, more usually, A or Degree.

Pay. £1250–£1400.

Aptitudes. Ability in use of figures; capacity for prolonged attention to detail and clear expression.

Method of Entry.

1. Junior employment in Accountancy in either public service (*e.g.*, in local government) or industry.
2. As articled clerk (either in a firm of Accountants or in the Treasurer's Department of a Local Authority).
3. As a graduate in any of the above.

Further Study.

Intermediate Exam. of the Professional Body (after $2\frac{1}{2}$ years).

Final Exam. of the Professional Body (after 5 years).

As the name implies, the accountant is the professional concerned with accounts of all descriptions in commerce, industry, and public affairs. The young person who starts on a five-year course of part-time study combined with daytime work as an articled or non-articled clerk must be prepared for a lot of hard work with comparatively little money at the beginning. During five years of training he or she will be expected to acquire a sound knowledge of the theory and practice of Bookkeeping and Accounts, Auditing, Company Law, Law of Contract, Sales, Bankruptcy, Trusts, and related subjects.

The theoretical training is usually acquired from a correspondence course, although facilities are available in some areas at Local Technical Colleges. The cost of a complete course is about £80, although this may be lower if Technical College courses are available.

Graduates entering the profession have three years only to serve under articles. Universities offering approved degree courses in Accountancy are Birmingham, Bristol, Cardiff, Newcastle, Hull, Leeds, Liverpool, London, Manchester, Nottingham, Sheffield, Southampton.

Once an accountant is qualified, advancement is very much a matter of his own initiative, record, and personality.

Note: Before starting on a course of study, it is essential to find out from the professional body concerned the exact nature of their requirements, as the details vary considerably.

Addresses of Professional Bodies.

The Institute of Chartered Accountants in England and Wales, City House, 56–66 Goswell Road, E.C.1.

The Institute of Chartered Accountants of Scotland, 27 Queen Street, Edinburgh, 2.

The Institute of Chartered Accountants in Ireland, 7 Fitzwilliam Place, Dublin.

The Association of Certified and Corporate Accountants, 22 Bedford Square, W.C.1.

The Institute of Municipal Treasurers and Accountants, 1 Buckingham Place, S.W.1.

Institute of Cost and Works Accountants, 63 Portland Place, W.1.

Pamphlets.

Universities and the Accountancy Profession. Available from the Institute of Chartered Accountants.

Choice of Careers, No. 59 (H.M.S.O.).

ACTUARIAL WORK.

B. G.

Age of Entry. 18 or Graduate.

Qualifications. A or Degree.

Pay. £1,250 to £1,500 on qualification.

Aptitudes. Ability in Mathematics. Must be able to develop powers of analysis and clear expression.

Method of Entry. Through Life Assurance Offices or Government Actuary's Department, either straight from school or as Mathematics or Economics Graduate.

Further Study. The professional examinations of the Institute of Actuaries, *i.e.*,

Entrance Examination (Good A level G.C.E. Maths. may exempt).

Intermediate, Associateship, and Fellowship Examinations.

The Actuary is the expert on whom Insurance Companies rely for the calculations of insurance risks and the fixing of premiums. The would-be Actuary must be interested in and proficient at mathematics, which is going to provide him with the tools of the job. He (or she) must be prepared to continue part-time study in such subjects as Probability, Statistics, Finance, and Investment. For the qualified person there are plenty of openings at home and increasingly so overseas.

The Institute of Actuaries and their Scottish equivalent, the Faculty of Actuaries, run an Actuarial Tuition Service, which provides correspondence courses leading to the Associateship examinations of the bodies concerned. The cost of the tuition service amounts to about £200 including examination fees.

Addresses of Professional Bodies.

The Institute of Actuaries, Staple Inn Hall, High Holborn, W.C.1.

The Faculty of Actuaries, 23 St. Andrew Square, Edinburgh.

Pamphlets.

The Actuarial Profession. Available from the Institute of Actuaries.

The Actuarial Profession as a Career. Available from The Faculty of Actuaries.

Choice of Careers, No. 93, No. 109 (H.M.S.O.).

ADVERTISING.

B. G.

Age of Entry. 16–18 or Graduate.

Qualifications. O or A or Degree.

Pay.

Juniors, about £250.
Trainees, £400.
Junior Copywriters and other junior specialists, £400 upwards.
Graduates, £650.

Aptitudes. Imagination; ability to mix and to express ideas briefly and to the point.

Method of Entry. By direct application to firm or agency on leaving school (or University).

Further Study. Study for the Joint Intermediate examination and the Final examinations of one of the professional bodies.

There is a great deal of competition for entry into this career, and the young man or woman wishing to go far will have to be prepared to learn while working and to develop a critical and independent mind. Nowadays much advertising work is carried out by advertising agencies, and it is by and large only the biggest organisations which carry their own advertising departments.

Agencies, in particular, have openings for specialists in the many activities connected with selling, *e.g.*, statistics, market research, commercial art, photography, technical production, specialised overseas work, T.V., Cinema and Radio. These specialists are often brought into the business after qualifying or training in another field (graduates for statistics, printers for space-salesmanship). The potential recruit would therefore be well advised to think carefully whether or not it would pay to gain specialist experience elsewhere first. There is no truth in the idea that one can afford to run an expensive car in this career by virtue of the ability to think of a new catch-phrase every morning.

Although the examinations of the two Associations are not essential, the courses are a very good supplement to practical experience. The Associations have a Joint Intermediate examination, but run separate Membership examinations. In addition, the Institute of Practitioners in Advertising have an Associate Membership final examination designed for the "specialists" mentioned above.

Addresses of Professional Bodies

Advertising Joint Intermediate Examination Board, 1 Bell Yard, W.C.2.

The Advertising Association, 1 Bell Yard, W.C.2.

The Institute of Practitioners in Advertising, 44 Belgrave Square, S.W.1.

Pamphlets.

A Career in an Advertising Agency. Available from The Institute of Practitioners in Advertising.

Careers in Advertising. Available from The Advertising Association.

Choice of Careers Series, No. 44 (H.M.S.O.).

AGRICULTURE.

B. G.

Age of Entry. 17+.

Qualifications.

1. For Farm Institute Course—C.S.E. or O.
2. For Agricultural College Course—O or A.
3. For teaching and advisory service—Graduate.

Pay.

1. For Farm Managers £600+.
2. For Commercial Agricultural Representatives—about £500+ and commission.
3. For Technical Officers of Ministry—£895–£3182.

Aptitudes. Genuine interest in the country and in farming. Ability to use one's hands.

Method of Entry. Normally one year on farm, followed by:—

1 year at Farm Institute, or
2 years at Agricultural College, or
3 years at University.

Further Study. Certificate Course (at Farm Institute), Diploma Course (at Agricultural College) or Degree Course (at University).

The young person who wishes to take up Agriculture as a career has normally to choose one of three ways of gaining the necessary knowledge and experience. Whichever way is chosen, it is highly advisable to spend a year on a farm gaining practical experience and making quite sure that this *is* the life one wishes to lead.

Then for those who are interested chiefly in the practical side and who do not wish to pursue theoretical studies too far, the best choice is an apprenticeship or a 1-year course at a Farm Institute which will fit them to become skilled farm workers or smallholders.

Those who intend to become farm managers, bailiffs or commercial representatives do better to follow the 2-year course at an Agricultural College. These are both residential and non-residential, and the course leads to the National Diploma.

Those who are thinking of management, teaching or of becoming advisers in the service of the Ministry of Agriculture, Fisheries, and Food, or of County Councils, or of research, should attend a University and attain the B.Sc.(Agric.) degree.

There are, in addition to the three main methods of entry indicated above, the Agricultural Apprentice Scheme, and the "British Boys for British Farms" Scheme, which is sponsored by the Y.M.C.A. The Y.M.C.A. also arranges for boys to contact farmers for their year's practical experience.

The Apprenticeship lasts for three years. Apprentices are allotted to selected farms and, where necessary, arrangements are made for training to be carried on at more than one farm. The Y.M.C.A. scheme caters more for boys with a *town* background and has been operating successfully for more than 25 years.

Addresses.

The Agricultural Research Council, Cunard Buildings, 15 Regent Street, S.W.1.

Dept. of Education and Science, Curzon Street, W.1.

Ministry of Agriculture, Fisheries and Food Great Westminster House, Horseferry Road, S.W.1.

The Secretary, Y.M.C.A., "British Boys for British Farms," 4 Great Russell Street, W.C.1.

Pamphlets.

Choice of Careers Series:

No. 85, *Agriculture and Horticulture: Managerial and Technical Posts* (H.M.S.O.).

No. 86, *Farm and Horticultural Workers* (H.M.S.O.).

AIR HOSTESS (AIR STEWARDESS).

G.

Age of Entry. 21–28.

Qualifications. At least one foreign language.

Pay. £480 a year after preparatory training plus £2 a week flying pay. On promotion to Stewardess Class II, £671 rising to £791 upwards.

Aptitudes. Language ability, good diction, tact, and patience.

Method of Entry. Posts are advertised in National Press.

Further Study. 6 to 8 weeks preparatory training.

The girl who wishes to be an Air Hostess must be prepared to face very stiff competition. The competition is, in fact, so great that the Airlines are able to demand very high standards of turn-out, poise, and personality.

The Air Hostess's work could be described as social work, as it involves not only the congenial task of handing round drinks and the food which has been prepared by the Air Steward but also catering for the many needs of the infinite variety of passengers, from babes in arms, sometimes unaccompanied, to worried old ladies who have mislaid their passports, or simply people who are feeling or being sick.

It is a great advantage to have had nursing and catering experience when applying for these posts. There is traditionally a high "wastage rate" of hostesses through marriage, but it should not be overlooked that for those who wish to make a long career with an Airline, promotion possibilities are good—Flight Stewardesses and Senior Catering Officers are recruited from the ranks.

Addresses.

The Manager, Selection Services, B.O.A.C., London Airport, Middx.

Personnel Services Manager, B.E.A., Bealine House, Ruislip, Middx.

Pamphlet.

Choice of Careers Series, No. 116 (H.M.S.O.).

AIR PILOT (CIVIL).

B.

Age of Entry. 18–20 (23 for Graduates).

Qualifications. A.

Pay. £1,450+ on completion of training (+ allowances).

Aptitudes. Highest standards of reliability, outlook, and physical fitness essential.

Method of Entry. Acceptance by the College of Air Training, Hamble, Hants.

Further Study. 2 years at College of Air Training.

The very high cost of becoming a Civil Airline Pilot privately has, until recently, made this an impossible career for nearly all except those who have been trained by the R.A.F.

Changes in the organisation of the R.A.F. and the end of National Service have meant that the Civil Airlines have been gradually losing their main source of recruits and there are now brilliant prospects for the young man who is good enough to secure a place at the new College of Air Training. The cadet will have a two-year residential course covering all aspects of flying, as well as general education.

Those chosen will be sponsored by one or another of the Airlines, and the cost to the student's parents will be no more than what they would pay if he were attending a normal University course with Local Authority assistance.

There is no need for any air-minded young man considering this career to fear that he may be left "grounded" at a comparatively early age, as the tendency is for the ceiling age for active pilots to rise. Given physical fitness, pilots may expect to fly well on into their fifties.

It must be emphasised, however, that competition for places is very keen, and only the very best type of candidate can hope to be accepted. The cost of training one cadet is between £4,000 and £5,000, and it is only to be expected that the Government and the Airlines, who between them provide the money, should take the utmost care to ensure that the number of cadets failing the course is reduced to the absolute minimum.

Addresses.

The Chief Personnel Officer, B.O.A.C., London Airport, Middx.

The Personnel Services Manager, B.E.A., Bealine House, Ruislip, Middx.

The Ministry of Civil Aviation, The Adelphi, Strand, W.C.2.

The College of Air Training, Hamble, Southampton, Hants.

Pamphlet.

Choice of Careers Series, No. 116 (H.M.S.O.).

ARCHITECTURE.

B. G.

Age of Entry. 18+.

Qualifications. A. Otherwise Intermediate or Final exam. of R.I.B.A. or equivalent or Degree.

Pay.

1. With Intermediate qualifications, about £700–£900.
2. With Final qualifications, £900–£1,200+.

Aptitudes. Interest in people and their surroundings, artistic ability, particularly modelling, facility in mathematics.

Method of Entry.

1. As articled pupil or junior assistant to Architect.
2. 3-year full-time degree or diploma course at Technical College or School of Architecture, entering profession as assistant with Intermediate Exam. of R.I.B.A. or equivalent.
3. 5-year full-time course at School of Architecture, entering profession with Final Exam. of R.I.B.A. or equivalent.
4. 5-year sandwich course at certain Technical Colleges; students spend the first year at the College, subsequently spending alternative periods of six months at the College and in architect's offices.
5. Two years' practical work is also required, one of which must be post-graduate.

Further Study.

1. If entering as articled pupil or junior assistant: about 10 years' part-time study, leading to Final Exam. of R.I.B.A.
2. If entering after 3-year full-time course: about 4 years' part-time study, leading to Final Exam. of the R.I.B.A.

As the training is long young people should be sure about their desire to become architects. It is an advantage if they have an artistic flair as well as the ability to organise and deal with people. It is however not essential to have a pronounced artistic flair as the qualified architect will not necessarily have an exciting career of cathedral designing to look forward to. This there might possibly be at some time or another, but much of the time—especially at the beginning of a career—will be spent in routine work. Even the qualified person starts, almost without exception, in the office of an established architect or in the Architect's Department of a Local Authority. This is partly because the newly qualified have to gain 12 months' practical experience and take a final examination in order to secure registration with the Architects' Registration Council. Another reason is that Architects—like Solicitors—are not allowed to advertise, and so the young free lance would find the odds heavily against him in his initial attempts to find work.

Address of Professional Body.

Royal Institute of British Architects, 66 Portland Place, W.1.

Pamphlet.

Choice of Careers Series, No. 16 (H.M.S.O.).

THE ARMED SERVICES.

All three Services today offer exceptional opportunities to those who enjoy community life, who wish to travel, and who have a sense of adventure. Space does not permit the giving of full details for each branch, and the following should be regarded as the barest of outlines only. Dealing first with entry through Non-Commissioned Ranks:

(*a*) The Army.

Men and Boys.

Age of Entry. 15–30.

Qualifications. Ability to pass selection and education tests.

Pay.

£3 3*s.* 0*d.* per week for junior apprentice (all found) to £32 per week (all found) depending on rank, service, and married status.

Aptitudes. In general, interest in outdoor life and sense of adventure.

Method of Entry.

1. Boys at 15+:—to Junior Leader Regts. and Army Apprentice Schools.
2. Men:—Apply Army Information Office.

Further Study. Great variety of courses available. Type and degree of specialisation largely dependent on individual's ability.

There are three Army Apprentice Schools and a number of Junior Leader Regiments, which give boys of school-leaving age thorough courses of training (including general education) lasting 3 years.

When these boys join the colours they stand an excellent chance of early promotion to Warrant Officer or even commissioned rank. Their specialised training, which is developed and widened during their subsequent service, is also a very good preparation for skilled work in the civilian world when they are released.

Men under 30 (in exceptional cases 33) have similar opportunities during service of up to 22 years. Great emphasis is laid on sport and recreational facilities are available wherever the Army is, at next to no cost. The grim barrack blocks and needlessly restrictive regulations are becoming increasingly a thing of the past.

(*b*) The R.A.F.

Men and Boys.

Age of Entry. 15–40.

Qualifications. Selection, education and aptitude tests to be passed.

Pay. £3 3*s.* 0*d.* per week during first year to £32 per week (all found), depending on rank, service, and married status.

Aptitudes. As for Army.

Method of Entry.

1. Boys at 15+:—Craft or administrative apprenticeships.
2. Boys at 16+:—Technician apprenticeships.
3. Men:—Apply R.A.F. Recruiting Office.

Further Study: Unlimited opportunities for those who are able, and want, to continue specialised training.

Boys who enter the Service on Aircraft Apprenticeships or the Boy Entrant Training Scheme are trained according to ability and aptitude in a variety of trades covering all branches of R.A.F. activity. Examples are: aircraft engineering, radio, electrical, instrument and general engineering, telegraphist, photographer, catering. They are thoroughly prepared for their subsequent career in the R.A.F., and have every chance of early promotion to Senior N.C.O. and even commissioned rank. There are three R.A.F. Apprentice Schools at Halton, Hereford, and Locking.

Men who enter from the age of 17½ receive a thorough training in one of the twenty-two trade groups, and here again there is every opportunity of promotion for those who show intelligence and initiative.

As with the Army, sport and recreational facilities are outstanding, and the airman can leave the service after 22 years with a pension and a thorough knowledge of a trade which he can turn to good account in civilian life.

(*c*) Royal Navy and Royal Marines.

Men and Boys.

Age of Entry. 15–28.

Qualifications. Ability to pass education and selection tests (Artificer Apprentice—O).

Pay. £3 3*s.* 0*d.* per week (for a junior) to £32 per week (all found) depending on rank service and married status.

Aptitudes. As for Army and R.A.F.

Method of Entry.

1. Boys:—
   (i) As Junior Seaman or Junior Mechanic.
   (ii) As Artificer Apprentice.
   (iii) As Junior Marine.
2. Men (17½+):—
   (i) Apply Naval Recruiting Office.
   (ii) Direct entry as Artificer—apply Naval Recruiting Office.

Further Study. Within the framework of the Service, the new entrant is encouraged to study to as high a standard as his capabilities allow.

Although all men and boy entrants into the Royal Navy receive wide and thorough training to suit them for their eventual jobs, there is one particular type of entry requiring higher initial qualifications and larger specialist training. This is for those who become Artificers, who serve a trade apprenticeship for 4 years in the course of which they are chosen for one of the Technical Branches. Direct Entry as an Artificer (for men) is available for those who have done 4 years' civilian apprenticeship, and can pass a trade test, to become an Engine Room, Aircraft, Electrical Ordnance, or Shipwright Artificer. Royal Marines train as a Commando, on sea service or as an amphibious unit.

As with the other Services, promotion prospects up to and including command rank are good for those with keenness and determination, and many of the specialist skills acquired during service are of great use in later civilian life.

General Note on Terms of Service.

It must not be forgotten that the Forces expect a fair amount of service in return for the very expensive training they provide, and the following is an indication of how each branch of the Services arranges its terms:—

1. **Army.** Apprentices undertake to serve until 26 years of age + 4 years in Royal Army Reserve. Service may be extended to 22 years, when there is a pension.
2. **R.A.F.** Apprentices undertake to serve until 30 years old. At any time after the age of 22 an airman may be re-engaged until he is 55, but he keeps the right to leave at 40 with a pension.
3. **Royal Navy.** All recruits except Artificer Apprentices have to serve 9 years (reckoned from the age of 18). Artificer Apprentices are required to serve 12 years (reckoned from the age of 18), as their training lasts so much longer.

Addresses from which detailed information about all three Services can be obtained:—

1. *Army.* The Under Secretary of State, War Office (M.P.6), S.W.1.
2. *R.A.F.* The Careers Information Centre, Royal Air Force, Victory House, Kingsway, W.C.2.
3. *Royal Navy.* The Director of Naval Careers Service, Admiralty, S.W.1.

Pamphlets.

H.M. Forces: Openings for Boys in the Ranks:—

No. 50, *Her Majesty's Forces* (H.M.S.O.).
No. 55, *Army* (H.M.S.O.).
No. 56, *Royal Air Force* (H.M.S.O.).
No. 54, *Royal Navy* (H.M.S.O.).

Commissioned Service (All Arms).

B.

Age of Entry. 17–19.

Qualifications. Generally A, exceptionally O, for short service commission.

Pay. The basic pay on commissioning is about £600 plus allowances.

Given efficient service, promotion is automatic in the early stages in all three Services, thereafter it is by selection. The pay of a Lt. Commander, Major and Squadron Leader commences at about £1,780 p.a. plus considerable allowances *e.g.* marriage ration or flying allowances.

Aptitudes. All three Services demand the highest standards of personality and integrity. Initiative, leadership, and self-reliance are essential qualities.

Method of Entry.

1. *Army:*—
   (i) To Welbeck College (the Army's 6th Form Public School); thence to Sandhurst after good A level results in science and mathematics.
   (ii) To Sandhurst direct.
2. *R.A.F.:*—
   (i) To R.A.F. College, Cranwell.
   (ii) To R.A.F. Technical College, Henlow.
3. *Royal Navy* and *Royal Marine:*—
   (i) To Britannia Royal Naval College, Dartmouth.
   (ii) Suitably qualified candidates by interview for training and 12-year Commission in Fleet Air Arm.
   (iii) Royal Marine entry to Officers' School.
4. All three Services have scholarship schemes to assist boys to complete their sixth-form studies at school with entry to officer training assured.

Further Training. The Officer training of the Service concerned; then study for promotion examinations and a great variety of specialist courses throughout Service career.

Space does not allow the giving of detailed requirements and conditions of service. Broadly speaking, a candidate for a commission in any of the Armed Services must be of reasonable academic attainment (at least A level of the G.C.E.); must satisfy the Service Selection Board as to his suitability, and must be physically fit.

Permanent Commissions are available in the Army and the R.A.F., for graduates wishing to enter the Service. There is an ever-growing demand for entrants with scientific qualifications as the Services grow yearly more technical.

Short Service commissions for varying periods of years are also available in all three arms. They are non-pensionable, but carry a handsome gratuity at the end of the contract, and opportunities exist for converting these commissions into permanent commissions carrying the normal opportunities of advancement and pension entitlements.

No interested boy should be put off this career because of stories of the need for a private income. The vast majority of serving officers nowadays live successfully on their pay. Marriage, education, and disturbance allowances are generous.

Pamphlet.

No. 68, *H.M. Forces: Commissioned Service* (H.M.S.O.).

THE WOMEN'S SERVICES (The Women's Royal Army Corps, The Women's Royal Air Force, The Women's Royal Naval Service).

G.

Age. 17½+.

Qualifications. None laid down.

Pay. From £4 11*s.* per week on entry, all found.

Aptitudes. Liking for community life, willingness to travel, and ability to become proficient in a trade.

Further Study. In all cases, to acquire proficiency in a trade. In some cases, for promotion examinations.

The Women's Services are designed to relieve pressure on the available man-power, and there is, therefore, a variety of interesting careers within the framework of each Service. The following are examples of the main trades which can be studied and practised in each arm of the Services:—

W.R.A.C. Catering, Clerical work, Electrical work, Motor Transport, Signals, Storekeeping.

W.R.A.F. Aircraft Engineering, Radio work, Electrical work, Motor Transport, Air Traffic Control, General Engineering, Police, Radar Operating, Photography, Medical, Accounting, Supply, Catering.

W.R.N.S. Radio work, Air Mechanic, Radar, Telegraphist, Cinema Operator, Clerical, Supply, Catering, Medical.

Pay is at about three-quarters of the equivalent rating for men, and after 22 years' service women are entitled to a pension. At regular intervals they have the option of ending their Service, and can in any case withdraw on marriage if they wish.

Officers are recruited: (1) from the ranks, or (2) by direct entry. Some enter after graduation.

Terms of service for officers are somewhat complicated, and vary from branch to branch, but in essence, an officer either serves for a period of 20 years to earn a pension or has a short-service commission, which usually carries a gratuity.

Addresses.

1. *W.R.A.C.* Ministry of Defence M.P.6(B)A., S.W.1.
2. *W.R.A.F.*, Victory House, Kingsway, W.C.2.
3. *W.R.N.S.* The Director, W.R.N.S., Admiralty, Whitehall, S.W.1.

Pamphlet.

No. 63, *H.M. Forces: Women's Services* (H.M.S.O.).

AUCTIONEERING OR ESTATE AGENCY.

B.

Age of Entry. 16–18.

Qualifications. O.

Pay. £300 to £600 during training, £800 + on qualification.

Aptitudes. Ability to make clear judgments and master complicated detail.

Method of Entry.

1. As Junior Clerk.
2. As Articled pupil.
3. As Graduate in Estate Management.

Further Study. Part-time study for professional qualification.

There are two main branches of this profession, namely the urban and the rural. This is recognised in the examinations of the professional bodies, and the candidate is able to study in accordance with his own inclinations and background. Thus the young countryman will probably feel more at home studying Agricultural Science, and Husbandry and Farm Management, rather than Dilapidations and Fixtures and Domestic Sanitation.

This glimpse of a section of the candidate's studies may serve to dispel the idea that all a qualified Auctioneer and Estate Agent has to do is to earn money through exercising a big voice and a small hammer.

Indeed, through a combination of training, study, and experience, he has to become an expert in such matters as the money market, valuations, mortgages, construction and maintenance of buildings, and have more than a nodding acquaintance with the Law of Property and the Law of Contract.

The three ways into the profession are:

1. By service as a Junior Clerk combined with part-time study.
2. By taking articles, which may cost over £200 for the premium. This is a more satisfactory way than (1) above, and arrangements can often be made to pay the premium by instalments, or even to have it waived altogether.
3. By entry with a degree, which must be either the B.Sc. (Estate Management) of the University of London or the B.A. (Estate Management) of the University of Cambridge. Both these degrees provide exemption from the professional examinations.

There are no laid-down salary scales for the profession at present, but a qualified successful man could expect to earn up to about £1,500 p.a. as Manager. There are also some openings in the Civil Service for suitably qualified people.

Addresses of Professional Bodies.

The Chartered Auctioneers' and Estate Agents' Institute, 29 Lincoln's Inn Fields, W.C.2.

The Chartered Land Agents' Society, 21 Lincoln's Inn Fields. W.C.2.

The Incorporated Society of Auctioneers and Landed Property Agents, 34 Queen's Gate, S.W.7.

The Royal Institution of Chartered Surveyors, 12 Gt. George Street, S.W.1.

Pamphlet.

Choice of Careers Series, No. 87 (H.M.S.O.).

BANKING.

B. G.

Age of Entry. 16–18.

Qualifications. O (or ability to pass Entrance Exam) or A.

Pay. Juniors commence at about £360.

Aptitudes. Integrity and ability to mix.

Methods of Entry. By application to local or Staff Manager of Bank concerned.

Further Study. For Diploma Examinations of Institute of Bankers (either Banking Diploma or Trustee Diploma).

Nowadays there are many opportunities in the world of banking for the keen boy or girl who is prepared to study and take a real interest in the job. Although the starting salary is modest, some idea of the prospects may be gained from the fact that out of every three young men joining a bank one can expect to become a Manager or executive of similar status. The pre-war regulation whereby girls had to resign on marriage has now been largely withdrawn, and a keen, intelligent girl has good prospects of earning more than £1,000 p.a. The widespread belief that the promotion—if it comes at all—comes only late in a career is without foundation today, and in most banks those who are going to go ahead are noted for promotion within the first 10–12 years.

Banks are well known as good employers. Encouragement (often financial) is given to continuing study, pensions are usually two-thirds of the eventual salary, and often non-contributory. Assistance with house purchase is normally obtainable at rates which are far better than the man in the street can obtain from other sources. Girls who do leave on marriage can expect a "dowry" if they have completed a reasonable term of service.

Addresses of Professional Bodies.

The Institute of Bankers, 10 Lombard Street, E.C.3.

Institute of Bankers in Scotland, 62 George Street, Edinburgh.

Pamphlets.

Choice of Careers Series, No. 67 (H.M.S.O.)

BEAUTY CULTURE.

G.

Age. Rarely possible at 16+, as reputable firms usually wait till 23.

Qualifications. Usually previous training as a hairdresser.

Pay. £7–£8 after 2 years. (There are no fixed rates.)

Aptitudes. Ability to get on with women, tact, self-confidence, and good manner of speaking.

Method of Entry. Acceptance by private training organisation.

Further Study. 3–12 months' training.

The usual way of acquiring training is to attend a privately run school, fees for which vary, but which for a year's course are in the neighbourhood of £120 p.a. Local Authorities rarely give grants for training. The courses, which are theoretical as well as practical, lead to a diploma issued by the School, and this is useful in obtaining a post. For those who wish to run their own salons, there are often side courses in such things as Salesmanship, Display, and Management. Many firms expect candidates to have done a preliminary course in Hairdressing (*see* E20 (2)) first.

It must be emphasised that this is a tiring and often frustrating job, and the successful girls are the ones who can stand for long hours without showing strain, and who can keep even-tempered even when there is a long run of ill-mannered or inconsiderate clients.

Addresses.

The London College of Fashion, John Princes Street, Oxford Street, W.1.

The Delia Collins School of Beauty Culture, 40 Sloane Street, Knightsbridge, S.W.1.

The Academy of Beauty Culture Ltd., 72 Park Mansions, Knightsbridge, S.W.1.

The Mary Wood Training School of Beauty Culture and Salesmanship, 42 Beauchamp Place, S.W.5.

The Mary Reid School of Beauty Culture, 8 Queen Street, Edinburgh.

Pamphlet.

Choice of Careers Series, No. 104 (H.M.S.O.).

BIOLOGY / BOTANY } *See* **Science.**

CATERING, HOTEL MANAGEMENT, DOMESTIC SCIENCE.

B. G.

Age. 15+ for craft training or apprenticeships. 16 or 18 for management training.

Qualifications. C.S.E. or O. A. for management courses and teaching.

Pay. £600 upwards for managers.

Aptitudes. Interest in making other people happy and comfortable; practical efficiency; interest in food and drink extending beyond greediness; organising ability.

Method of Entry. As student in Technical College which runs a Hotel and Catering Course. (Addresses of these from Hotel and Catering Institute, or from Careers Pamphlet No. 15.) Or a post obtained through the Youth Employment Service.

Further Training. One to four years' part- or full-time study in a Technical College leading to Diploma or Certificate.

Individual Colleges (*e.g.*, Battersea College of Technology and Westminster Technical College) give their own awards on satisfactory completion of their own courses; to an increasing extent Local Authority Technical Colleges are running courses in Hotel Work, including cookery, and students are prepared for the City and Guilds Institute Certificates. Courses vary in length, and include practical experience in a hotel or restaurant; sometimes up to one year will be spent abroad. Jobs in hotels, either as chefs or as assistant managers, are readily available to those who are well qualified; the pay is good and the prospects encouraging, but hotel work of all kinds is inevitably wearing, both physically and mentally, and good health and even temper are important pre-requisites.

Girls often take the examinations of the Institutional Management Association which lead to posts in residential clubs, hostels, schools, and canteens. There is a great demand for staff in these posts as well as for domestic science and housecraft teachers. Demonstrating is not so easy to find.

Addresses.

British Hotel and Restaurant Association, 88 Brook St., W.1.

Hotel and Catering Institute, 24 Portman Square, W.1.

Institutional Management Association, 324 Grays Inn Rd., W.C.1.

Pamphlet.

Choice of Careers Series, Nos. 13, 15 and 33 (H.M.S.O.).

CHEMISTRY. *See* **Science.**

CHILD CARE. *See* **Social Work.**

CHIROPODY.

B. G.

Age. 17+.

Qualifications. O.

Pay. When qualified £625 to £1,107; more in private practice.

Aptitudes. Interest in people, good eyesight, reassuring personality.

Method of Entry. Acceptance by School recognised by Board of Registration of Medical Auxiliaries.

Further Study. 3 years' full-time course leading to Final Professional Examination.

Chiropody—care of the feet—is becoming increasingly important nowadays. This is borne out by the growing number of posts available in public service (hospitals and clinics) and large firms. Probably the majority of qualified people still prefer, however, to go into private practice. When a practice is well established it can provide a very reasonable living, but there is always the difficult period when the new practitioner is getting himself known, and the beginner must be prepared for lean times at first.

Private practice is attractive partly because one can equip oneself for the job for little more than £100.

Address.

The Society of Chiropodists, 8 Wimpole Street, W.1.

Pamphlet.

Choice of Careers Series, No. 61 (H.M.S.O.).

THE CHURCHES.

B. G.

The Ministry or priesthood can hardly be considered a career in the same sense as most of the jobs in this section. Financial reward is limited, and those who wish to enter the Church must be prepared for a lifetime of service to others and convinced of their own vocation. This applies to all the Churches, and the first thing to do is to consult the minister of the church the candidate attends. The following is the procedure where four of the main churches are concerned. Girls cannot enter the priesthood of the Church of England or Roman Catholic Church, but they can become ordained ministers of various other churches.

(*a*) **Church of England.**

Age. Normally 23.

Qualifications. Up to 25 years old, normally a Degree. After 25—A may suffice.

Method of Entry. Application through Bishop to Central Advisory Council of Training for the Ministry.

Further Study. Normally a full-time University Degree followed by 2 years at a Theological College. Modified arrangements are made for the training of those who wish to enter the Ministry later in life.

Address. The Secretary, Central Advisory Council for the Ministry, 9 Tufton St., Westminster, S.W.1.

(*b*) **Roman Catholic Church.**

Age. Candidates for ordination must notify their intention from age of 13+.

Qualifications. Usually O or A before acceptance into Seminary.

Method of Entry. Via Parish Priest.

Further Study. 6 years or longer in a seminary at home or abroad.

(*c*) **The Methodist Church.**

Age. Preferably before 30.

Qualifications. Passing the Local Preacher's written examinations.

Method of Entry. Via the Superintendent Minister of the circuit in which the candidate is a church member.

Further Study. 3 or 4 years at one of six Residential Colleges affiliated to a University Course, probably including a degree.

Address. The Secretary, Ministerial Training Committee, 1 Central Buildings, Westminster, S.W.1.

(*d*) **The Baptist Church.**

Age. Under 40.

Qualifications. Usually O.

Method of Entry. Via the Association to which candidate's Church belongs.

Further Study.

1. 3 to 6 years at a Baptist College including perhaps a degree course at University to which College is affiliated.
2. Examinations prescribed by Baptist Union.

Address. The Baptist Union of Great Britain and Ireland, The Baptist Church House, 4 Southampton Row, W.C.1.

Other Addresses.

The Careers Secretary, Conference of Missionary Societies in Great Britain & Ireland, 2 Eaton Gate, S.W.1.

The British Council of Churches, 10 Eaton Gate, S.W.1.

The Director of Education, London Board of Jewish Religious Education, Upper Woburn Place, W.C.1.

The General Secretary, Presbyterian Church House, 86 Tavistock Place, W.C.1.

Salvation Army, 73 Queen Victoria St., E.C.4.

THE CIVIL SERVICE.

B. G.

There are three main classes of the Civil Service, which are dealt with separately below. The openings in the Foreign and in the Scientific Civil Service are listed at the end of this section.

(*a*) **The Clerical Class.**

Age. 16–20.

Qualifications. At least O or appropriate Civil Service examination.

Pay. £385 at 16, rising to £975.

Aptitudes. Various, according to department involved, but in all cases a liking for general office duties.

Method of Entry.

1. By Clerical Class Examination.
2. By interview if holding O (in London and certain other towns.)

The Clerical Class makes up the largest group of Civil Servants, and the work varies according to the department concerned. Thus the Clerical Officer may have to compile statistics, prepare documents, check accounts, or to interview members of the public and deal with correspondence. Newcomers to departments are systematically trained in the work they will be doing.

Opportunities exist within the Service for promotion to the Executive Class, either by internal examination or, in the case of Civil Servants over the age of 28, on merit. Pensions are non-contributory (except in so far as dependants are concerned). There is usually a five-day week and holidays are generous. Juniors are often assisted with lunch vouchers, and even lodging allowances. Welfare and security of tenure are excellent.

(*b*) **The Executive Class.**

Age. 17½–24.

Qualifications. A or appropriate Civil Service Examination.

Pay. £549 at 18 to £1,408 (basic grade).

Aptitudes. Sound judgment, initiative, sense of responsibility.

Method of Entry.

1. By Executive Class Examination.
2. By interview if holding A or Degree.

The work of the Executive Officer might be summed up as the detailed carrying out of policy that has been decided, and thus can carry a considerable amount of responsibility. As with the Clerical Class, training is given to new entrants to fit them for their duties, and some officers are chosen for specialist training in such fields as accountancy or statistics. Those who show great ability have opportunities of promotion to the Administrative Class, and many more reach the grades of Higher Executive Officer, Senior Executive Officer, and Chief Executive Officer, with correspondingly bigger salaries.

(*c*) **The Administrative Class.**

Age. 20½–24.

Qualifications. Normally a good degree, and/or appropriate Civil Service examination.

Pay. £895 to £1,521.

Aptitudes. Creative approach, judgment of highest order, capacity for involved and protracted original work.

Method of Entry.

1. Administrative Class Examination and interviews.
2. 1st and 2nd Class Honours Degree followed by tests and interviews.

The Senior Civil Servants in this Class are the people responsible for formulation of national policy in accordance with the wishes of the Ministers. These posts are among the hardest to obtain, and any boy or girl going to University with the intention of becoming an Administrative Class Civil Servant should not be disappointed if the goal is not reached.

The work involves giving expert advice to Ministers of the Crown, planning new proposals giving flesh and blood to the wishes of Parliament and the organising of departmental work. For the very best are the rewards of a Permanent Under-Secretaryship, and the attendant heavy responsibilities.

The foregoing is an indication of the structure and possibilities of the three main classes of the Civil Service. There are in addition many ancillary and specialist departments which offer attractive careers, such as the following:—

1. (Parallel to Clerical Branch): Assistant Preventive Officers, Cartographical Draughts

men, Assistants in Scientific Civil Service, Foreign Service (Grade 6, Branch B).
2. (Parallel to Executive Branch): Officers of Customs and Excise, Assistant Experimental Officers in the Scientific Civil Service, Foreign Service (Grade 5, Branch B).
3. (Parallel to Administrative): Statisticians, Patent Examiners, Inspectors of Taxes, Inspectors of Factories, Scientific Officers, engineering posts, Foreign Service (Senior Branch).

Address.

The Secretary, Civil Service Commission, 23 Saville Row, W.1.

Pamphlets.

Choice of Careers Series

No. 31, *Civil Service Junior Posts* (H.M.S.O.).

No. 32, *The Civil Service, General, Scientific and Technical Posts* (H.M.S.O.).

DANCING.

B. G.

Age. 9–15 (for entry to a Ballet School). Otherwise not after age of 17.

Qualifications. —

Pay.

1. Corps de Ballet, £10 11*s.* per week.
2. Revue Chorus work, £11 13*s.* per week. (These are London rates. Television work, solo work, etc., may earn considerably more).

Aptitudes. Natural ability essential; determination; extremely good health; physical perfection.

Method of Entry. Acceptance by a School of dancing. Royal School of Ballet offers Scholarships for boys.

Further Training.

1. Ballet Schools: Dancing instruction combined with general education.
2. Other Schools of Dancing: 3–5 years leading to examinations of Royal Academy of Dancing and Imperial Society of Teachers of Dancing.
3. 3-year training course (for intending teachers), *e.g.*, at Royal Academy of Dancing.

There are two main divisions of dancing as a profession—theatrical and teaching. On the theatrical side many young people (girls especially) are attracted nowadays to ballet, and it must be emphasised that only those in the very highest flight can hope to win a position in a corps de ballet. It is worth noting that the Royal Ballet School itself provides 85 per cent of the ballet companies of the Royal Opera House and Sadler's Wells. There is a shortage of good male dancers, so prospects for boys are better than for girls.

Apart from ballet, revue work and television (increasingly) provide employment for those who are set on making dancing a career. Minimum pay is fixed by Actors' Equity. It is quite common for dancers to take up teaching when they retire from the stage. The teaching may be in private establishments, where the remuneration is by arrangement, or in State schools, where salary is in accordance with the terms of the Burnham Committee Report. Others prefer to go for teaching from the outset, and the Royal Academy of Dancing runs 3-year training courses.

While there are various scholarships available from the different schools, the fees are often quite stiff (for example, the Royal Ballet School fees are £153 p.a. for day pupils and £350 for boarders). Help may often be obtained, however, from the local Education Authorities, subject to means of parents.

Addresses.

The Royal Ballet School, 45 Colet Gardens, W.14.

The Royal Academy of Dancing, 15 Holland Park Gardens, W. 14.

Book.

The Making of a Dancer, by Arnold Haskel (Pub. A. C. Black), 8*s.* 6*d.*

Pamphlet.

Choice of Careers Series, No. 99 (H.M.S.O.).

DENTISTRY.

B. G.

Age. 17.

Qualifications. A.

Pay.

1. In Public Service and the Armed Forces, about £1,500–£2,260 (basic grade).
2. In private practice—dependent on size of practice, but usually commences at about £1,500.

Aptitudes. Calmness of manner, ability to instil confidence, manual dexterity.

Method of Entry. By application to approved Dental School.

Further Study.

1. A Degree course.
2. Diploma Course at dental school.

There is a great need nowadays for trained dentists of both sexes, both in private practice and public service. The course of training is long (4½ years for those holding qualifications on entry as above in chemistry, physics, and biology, which enables them to gain exemption from Part I of the training course). It is also expensive for those who cannot get substantial assistance from Local Education Authorities or other sources (£400–£500 in addition to books and living expenses). But for those who are willing to make the initial sacrifices it offers an interesting and valuable career which, for once, is well rewarded, but the work is very demanding.

One word of warning. There is considerable competition for entry, and only good candidates are accepted.

There are Dental Schools in, or attached to, the following Universities: Birmingham, Bristol, Leeds, Liverpool, London, Manchester, Newcastle, Sheffield, Wales, St. Andrews, Queens (Belfast).

Address.

The General Dental Council, 37 Wimpole Street, W.1.

British Dental Association, 13 Hill St., W.1.

Pamphlets.

Dentistry—A career and a future. Available from General Dental Council.

Choice of Careers Series, No. 96 (H.M.S.O.).

DENTAL NURSE or SURGERY ASSISTANT.

G.

Age. 16–18.

Qualifications. Preferably C.S.E. or O.

Pay. £242–£600.

Aptitudes. Neatness and pleasant, reassuring personality.

Method of Entry.

1. By application to Dental Hospital for course.
2. By application to a dentist in private practice.

Further Training.

1. Full-time course (6 months–2 years, depending on Hospital).
2. By dentist in private practice during course of work.

The Dental Nurse (or Dental Surgery Assistant, to give her her correct title) has to be a girl who can adapt herself to a variety of jobs connected with dentistry. She may be expected to look after the clerical and reception work of a practice, reassure patients before treatment (and comfort them afterwards), process X-ray photographs, and prepare materials for use by the dentist. In a hospital with a Dental Department her work will naturally tend to be more specialized.

Full-time training can be had at the following institutions:—

Guy's Hospital Dental School, S.E.1.

Eastman Dental Hospital, Gray's Inn Road, W.C.1.

London Hospital, Whitechapel, E.1.

Royal Dental Hospital, Leicester Square, W.C.1.

In the provinces at the Dental Hospitals of Bristol, Birmingham, Dundee, Manchester, Sheffield.

The details of these courses vary considerably from hospital to hospital, but in all cases, however, the students work for the Examination for Dental Nurses and Assistants, which is held annually in London.

The pay is not startlingly good, but for the girl who enjoys giving service to others and meeting different types of people Dental Nursing offers a satisfying and interesting career.

Address.

The British Dental Nurses and Assistants Society, 2 Summer Street, Leyland, Lancs.

Pamphlets.

Dental Surgery Assistants. Available from the British Dental Nurses and Assistants Society.

Choice of Careers Series, No. 96 (H.M.S.O.).

DENTAL TECHNICIAN.

B. G.

Age. 15–21.

Qualifications.

Pay. £560 upwards on qualification.

Aptitudes. Ability with hands and liking for delicate manual work.

Method of Entry. Acceptance by dentist, hospital, or firm, as apprentice.

Further Training. 5-year apprenticeship including 1 day part-time-release study per week.

The Dental Technician is the craftsman (or woman) who makes the various appliances used nowadays, such as dentures, bridges, and plates. Apprenticeships are available with private dentists, hospitals and firms manufacturing the various appliances and, together with the practical experience they gain, apprentices have to prepare themselves for the Intermediate, Final, and Advanced examinations of the City and Guilds of London Institute, which are both practical and theoretical in their scope.

There is a constant demand for the services of Dental Technicians, and no skilled person need fear unemployment, but there may be difficulty in getting taken on as an apprentice.

Addresses.

Associated Dental Technicians Section of the Society of Goldsmiths, Jewellers, and Kindred Trades, 329–331 Gray's Inn Road, W.C.1.

Union of Shop, Distributive & Allied Workers, 188 Wilmslow Road, Fallowfield, Manchester, 14.

Pamphlet.

Choice of Careers Series, No. 96 (H.M.S.O.).

DIETETICS.

B. G.

Age. 20–21.

Qualifications. (*a*) Three or four year full-time integrated course in College and Hospital. A. (*b*) 18 month diploma course: one of the following:—

1. Degree in Household Science, Nutrition, Domestic Science, or Pure Science, plus at least 3 months' training in cookery.
2. State Registration in Nursing, plus at least 3 months' training in cookery.
3. Teacher's Diploma in Domestic Science, with perhaps additional qualifications in physiology and chemistry.
4. Institutional Management Certificate plus approved educational exam.
5. Associate Membership of Hotel and Catering Institute resulting from examination, plus approved 2-year course in catering.

Pay. £685 to £1,277 or more.

Aptitudes. Interest in people, organising ability, ability to think clearly.

Method of Entry. Acceptance by one of the bodies running courses leading to one of the recognised Diplomas in Dietetics (see below).

Further Training. Usually 12–18 months full-time theoretical and practical study.

The dietician is concerned with the study of nutrition—the composition of food and how the body uses it. A lot of the work is in hospitals, where the dietician is of great value in the treatment of illness, and training therefore includes a period in a hospital kitchen (hence the need to be able to cook). In the course of the job the dietician meets all sorts and conditions of people, from doctors and food specialists to refractory patients, and so must be prepared to exercise tact and discretion and to mix easily.

The following Technical Colleges are recognised for the training of Dieticians:—

Aberdeen:	Robert Gordon's Technical College.
Dublin:	St. Mary's College of Catering.
Leeds:	College of Technology.
London:	Battersea College of Advanced Technology.
	Ealing Technical College.
Wales:	Llandaff Technical College, Cardiff.

Address.

The British Dietetic Association, 251 Brompton Road, S.W.3.

Pamphlet.

Choice of Careers Series, No. 13 (H.M.S.O.).

DOMESTIC SCIENCE. *See* **Catering and Hotel Management.**

DRAMATIC ART.

B. G.

Age. Normally 17–18 (18 for a teaching course).

Qualifications. Preferably O or A.

Pay.

1. £10–£12 per week minimum (in London).
2. As teacher—in accordance with Burnham scales.

Aptitudes. Acting ability, determination, good health.

Method of Entry. Usually acceptance by a school of drama.

Further Training. 3 year full-time course at a school of drama.

The first thing to say about acting as a career is that it is a very insecure profession, offering great rewards to the few, but very often frustration and disappointment to the majority—especially to girls. At any one time up to half the qualified actors and actresses are unable to get work in the theatre.

For those who are nevertheless determined to make a career of the stage, by far the best way of getting training is to obtain a place at one of the schools of drama; the addresses of some of these are given below.

On completion of the course, the next step is to obtain a situation with a Repertory Company, if possible, and so enlarge the field of experience. Some lucky ones, of course, get recognition and "stardom" while training or even before, but this is very much the exception to the rule.

Some of the schools of drama mentioned above run courses for teachers of dramatic art. These courses are recognised as a teacher's qualification by the Department of Education, and on this side the prospects are much brighter as there is a growing demand in educational establishments of all descriptions for dramatic work in and out of the classroom. Degree courses are available at Birmingham, Bristol and Manchester Universities.

Addresses.

The British Actors' Equity Association, 8 Harley Street, W.1.

The Royal Academy of Dramatic Art, 62–4 Gower Street, W.C.1.

The Central School of Speech and Drama, The Embassy Theatre, Swiss Cottage, N.W.3.

New College of Speech and Drama, Ivy House, North End Road, N.W.11.

The Guildhall School of Music and Drama, John Carpenter Street, Victoria Embankment, E.C.4.

The Rose Bruford Training College of Speech and Drama, Lamorbey Park, Sidcup, Kent.

Pamphlet.

Choice of Careers Series, No. 98 (H.M.S.O.).

DRAUGHTSMAN.

B. G.

Age. 15½–18.

Qualifications. Preferably O or first year of O.N.C.

Pay. Between £4 and £5 10*s.* 0*d.* at age 16.

Aptitudes. Capacity for attention to detail, sound maths., ability to think for himself.

Method of Entry. Apprenticeship.

Further Training. 5-year apprenticeship including day release study at a technical college leading to technical or professional examinations.

It is a common mistake to think that all a draughtsman needs to have in the way of natural talent is the ability to draw well. His job is the preparation of scale drawings from which the various parts of, for instance, a machine are made. He therefore needs to know enough engineering to be sure that the parts he is drawing will do their job and enough mathematics to calculate stresses by formula. Most firms insist that their apprentices should have a thorough grounding in general engineering practice in various departments before the real drawing-office training begins. The apprenticeship, including part-time theoretical study, usually leads to examinations such as the Ordinary and Higher National Certificate and those of the Institution of Engineering Designers, the Institution of Mechanical Engineers, the Institution of Electrical Engineers among others.

The work of a draughtsman is very satisfying for those who are interested in drawing and engineering, and it has very often proved a valuable stepping-stone to senior technical appointments in industry.

Address.

The Institution of Engineering Designers, 38 Portland Place, W.1.

Pamphlets.

Choice of Careers Series (H.M.S.O.), No. 16, No. 60, No. 87.

DRESS DESIGNING.

Usually G.

Age. Usually 15½–18.

Qualifications. None laid down.

Pay. No scale: salary by arrangement.

Aptitudes. Practical needlework, perseverance, knowledge of and interest in French and Art.

Method of Entry.

1. Learning while working in factory or workroom.
2. Acceptance by Technical College or School of Art for full-time course.

Further Training.

1. Training in factory or work-room supplemented by part-time technical or art college study (about 4 years).
2. Full-time course in technical or art college (2–4 years).

Dress Designing is not a well-defined career in the sense that so many in this section are. Obviously all dresses have to be designed before they are made, but the majority are designed abroad and adapted for use in this country. There are 3 fairly distinct classes of work:—

1. "Haute Couture"—the designing of models for the famous fashion houses. This is a "glamorous" job, and only very few really outstanding people achieve posts of this nature. Even for these, there is a great element of chance in the process of becoming recognised.
2. "Wholesale Couture"—the designing of models for restricted retail trade, usually based on the current fashion trends.
3. "Wholesale Manufacture"—the designing of cheaper dresses for production in large quantities.

There is no guarantee of employment for those who have successfully completed their training, and a great deal of luck is needed (being, for example, in the right place at the right time).

Mention must be made of an alternative method of training at the Faculty of Dress Design of the Royal College of Art. Candidates for the 3-year full-time course have to be between the ages of 17 and 25, and have to pass an entrance examination in five Parts. Part I is the submission of "testimonies of study" (*i.e.*, examples of candidate's original work), and Part II is a more general examination testing the candidate's interests, command of English, and critical approach to contemporary trends in fashion. There is also a practical test.

For those who are accepted, the 3-year course includes Life Drawing, History of Costume, Designing, Dressmaking, Tailoring, Millinery, Accessories, Pattern Cutting, Children's Clothing, Lingerie, Shoe Design, and Jersey Wear. Successful graduates are entitled to style themselves Designer of the Royal College of Art (Des.R.C.A.).

There is also a course of training at the London College of Fashion, Oxford Street, which is very suitable for those interested in wholesale designing.

Addresses.

The Faculty of Fashion Design, The Royal College of Art, 20 Ennismore Gardens, S.W.7.

The London College of Fashion, John Princes St., Oxford Street, W.1.

Pamphlets.

Choice of Careers Series (H.M.S.O.), No. 9, No. 103.

ENGINEERING.

B. G.

Space does not allow full treatment of this extremely complex career in all its aspects. The following should therefore be regarded as the barest outline of the main branches of the profession and, before any decision is reached, advice and full details should be obtained from the Youth Employment Officer and professional bodies concerned. These are *examples* only of engineering careers available and, it is hoped, will serve to indicate the general pattern. *See* Chart (E5).

Age. 16 (as an apprentice) and upwards, dependent on method of entry.

Qualifications. Dependent on method of training and branch concerned; C.S.E. or O for Craft, Technician or O.N.C. course, followed (if possible) by H.N.C. For H.N.D., or Dip. Tech. course, either 2 A levels or a good O.N.C.

Pay. £4 to £5 10*s.* 0*d.* per week (starting apprentice aged 16)—about £600–£800 p.a. on completion of apprenticeship. Thereafter depending on branch of profession, and the qualifications obtained. Further prospects depending on quality of individual up to £2,000 or more.

Aptitudes. All branches demand character and intellectual ability from those who are going to do well. All would-be engineers must possess qualities of patience and assiduity, and be interested as well in the special requirements of their particular field. They should have practical interest and ability.

Method of Entry. Usually—1. Apprenticeship; 2. Sandwich Course; 3. As a graduate.

Further Training.

1. *Apprenticeship.* Usually 5 years supplemented by part-time study at technical college. It sometimes includes a period of full-time training early in the apprenticeship.
2. *Sandwich Course.* Usually 4-year course leading to (for example) Degree in Technology. The course is usually alternate six-monthly periods of full-time study at a technical college (or University) and full-time engineering practice with a firm.
3. *As a Graduate.* A further period of "graduate apprenticeship" (about 2 years) is usually required. One of these years may sometimes be served *before* beginning the graduate course.

1. Aeronautical Engineering.

This covers a very wide field and includes design and construction of engines, airframes, guided weapons, and secondary equipment.

(a) *Trade Apprenticeship* (5 years) leads to jobs of Fitter, Machinist, Tool-maker, Sheet-metal Worker, Electrician, Pattern-maker. There are good opportunities for further promotion.
(b) *Engineering Apprenticeship* (for those holding O or A or equivalent) leading to posts in Design, Stressing, Aerodynamics, Laboratory, or Maintenance. Promotion prospects to executive level are excellent.
(c) *Student Apprenticeship* (for graduates and others) leading to senior technological positions.

Address.

The Royal Aeronautical Society, 4 Hamilton Place, S.W.1.

2. Automobile Engineering.

A specialised branch of mechanical engineering, sub-divided into Chassis Engineering and Body Engineering.

(a) *Trade Apprenticeship* (4–5 years) leads to skilled craftsman status in one of the following trades: Body Engineering, Body Jig-making, Carpentry, Electrical Maintenance, Fitting and Turning, Foundry Work, Machine Tool Fitting, Laboratory Work, Pattern-making, Press-tool Making, Sheet-metal Work, Tool-making, Welding.
(b) *Engineering Apprenticeship* (for those holding O or A or equivalent). These apprenticeships lead to posts in the following departments: (1) Development, Experimental, or Research; (2) Drawing Office; (3) Production; (4) Costing; (5) Service (Technical); (6) Sales.

Address.

The Institution of Mechanical Engineers, (Automobile Division), 1 Bird Cage Walk, S.W.1.

3. Chemical Engineering.

The chemical engineer's main job is the design, construction, and operation of equipment in connection with manufacturing processes where there are chemical (and sometimes physical) changes.

(a) *Student Apprenticeship* with a suitable firm, combined with part-time study for O.N.C. and H.N.C. is a common method of entry for those who do not take a degree. Regional Gas Boards offer interesting openings in Chemical Engineering.

Alternatively:

(b) *Sandwich Course* at a Technical College or University leading to Degree or Diploma in Chemical Engineering.

The two other main methods are:—

(c) *Degree Course* in Chemistry, followed by post-graduate course in Chemical Engineering.
(d) *Degree Course* in Chemical Engineering.

Universities and Colleges offering Chemical Engineering Degrees or Diplomas are: Birmingham, Cambridge, Durham, Glasgow, Glamorgan, London, Loughborough, Neath, Salford, Sheffield and Wales.

Address.

The Institution of Chemical Engineers, 16 Belgrave Square, S.W.1.

4. Civil Engineering.

The term covers the design, construction, and maintenance of railways, roads, waterways, bridges, dams, tunnels, airports, etc. Municipal Engineering is the field of Civil Engineering concerned with municipal services, such as public health, town planning, water supply, drainage, and surveying work.

(a) *Apprenticeship* is open to those with O (or who can pass the Common Preliminary Examination of the Engineering Joint Board); 3 years' practical and theoretical work, supplemented by part-time technical work to H.N.C. or a degree in engineering; 2 years' further practical experience is needed before qualifying for Associate Membership of the Institution of Civil Engineers.
(b) *Degree Course/Diploma in Civil Engineering Course.* These are available through Student Apprenticeships (sometimes Sandwich Courses) (see E6) or through full-time study at a Technical College or University. Entrance qualification A level. The courses are followed by 3 years' work (usually as a graduate assistant to an approved firm of civil engineers) before full status is gained.

Addresses.

1. The Institution of Civil Engineers, Great George Street, S.W.1.
2. Institution of Municipal Engineers, 25 Eccleston Square, S.W.1.
3. Institution of Structural Engineers, 11 Upper Belgrave Street, S.W.1.

5. Electrical Engineering.

This is a "blanket" term covering a very wide range of occupations, ranging from fundamental research and design to routine maintenance of installations.

(a) *Craft Apprentices* usually enter a works on leaving school. Those who show ability are encouraged to continue part-time studies leading to the City and Guilds of London Institute Electrician's Certificate.

(b) *Electrical Technicians* follow a course of practical training supplemented by part-time study at a Technical College, or in some cases they follow a course based on the "block-release" system (*i.e.*, 4 weeks' full-time study alternating with approximately double the period work with the firm). The great variety of courses available and specialised training involved cannot be dealt with here, but mention may be made of the City and Guilds of London Institute Electrical Technician's Certificate, towards which the training of many technicians leads.

(c) *Professional Electrical Engineers* are trained either by following a full-time degree course at a University (or a full-time diploma course at a technical college, or by taking a Student Apprenticeship which involves a Sandwich Course and leads usually to H.N.D. after 4–5 years. In both cases further study and examinations are necessary before Associate Membership of the Institution of Electrical Engineers is obtained.

Address.

The Institution of Electrical Engineers, Savoy Place, W.C.2.

6. Mechanical Engineering.

Mechanical Engineering is concerned with the design, manufacture, and maintenance of machinery. There is a tremendous variety of work which comes within the scope of the Mechanical Engineer, and many of the other branches which are mentioned in this section need a good general grounding in mechanical engineering as a prerequisite of further training.

(a) *Craft Apprenticeship.* This is for youngsters leaving school who wish to make a career as skilled craftsmen. The apprenticeship lasts 5 years, and practical experience is supplemented by day part-time-release courses, evening courses, and, in some cases, Sandwich Courses. Apprentices prepare for City and Guilds or O.N.C. and H.N.C. and even higher qualifications. Those who do not follow their studies to this level are thoroughly trained as skilled workers in trades such as Milling, Turning, Fitting, Setting, Grinding, Foundry Moulding, Sheet-metal Working.

(b) *Student Apprenticeship.* This is a 4- to 5-year course (often Sandwich) for students who have passed O or A or equivalent examination. General background training is given, and the apprentice has the opportunity of specialising. Those who complete their training satisfactorily can expect to become responsible members of the staff of an engineering concern.

(c) *Graduate Apprenticeship.* This is designed to provide the practical background for those who hold degrees or diplomas in engineering. The course lasts about 2 years and is designed to fit graduate apprentices for posts in Research, Development, Design, Estimating, Contracting, Sales, and Production.

Address.

The Institution of Mechanical Engineers, 1 Bird Cage Walk, S.W.1.

7. Mining Engineering.

(a) *Coal Mining.* The National Coal Board runs its own system of training and apprenticeship schemes, full details of which can be obtained from the address below. Of special interest to Sixth Formers leaving school are the 100 University Scholarships offered each year by the National Coal Board for suitable boys who wish to take up mining engineering. These Scholarships are tenable at any University offering a mining-degree course, and the National Coal Board assumes entire responsibility for fees and maintenance—irrespective of parents' income. It should be noted that some scholarships are also available for degree courses in mechanical, electrical and chemical engineering.

Addresses.

The National Coal Board, Hobart House, Grosvenor Place, S.W.1.

Institution of Mining Engineers, 3 Grosvenor Crescent, S.W.1 (for coal mining).

(b) *Metalliferous Mining.* Young men who wish to qualify as mining engineers in this sense of the word usually study for a degree or equivalent qualification at either the Royal School of Mines (South Kensington) or the Camborne School of Metalliferous Mining (Cornwall). It is also possible to specialise in Metalliferous Mining at some of the Universities offering Mining Engineering courses.

The work of a Mining Engineer who has specialised in this department of mining usually takes him abroad. He may be involved in discovering mineral deposits, extracting the ore from the ground, or refining. There is a limited number of scholarships available, details of which may be had from the first address below. Candidates for courses must be aged 18 and hold A or equivalent.

Addresses.

British Overseas Mining Association, 8 Great Winchester Street, E.C.2.

Institution of Mining and Metallurgy, 44 Portland Place, W.1.

8. Production Engineering.

The Production Engineer is concerned with every aspect of manufacture where planning of output in the most economical way is concerned. He is the expert on works management, production management planning, plant layout, jig and tool design, estimating, time-study, rate-fixing, motion study, process study, production control, inspection, purchasing, and stores control. He must be a man who can mix easily and command confidence and respect.

There are three main ways of becoming a production engineer:

(a) *Production Engineering Apprenticeship.* A 5-year course supplemented by part-time study for O.N.C. and H.N.C. and then for the Associate Membership Examination of the Institution.

(b) *Sandwich Course* (3–5 years) leading to H.N.D. in production engineering or Degrees.

(c) *Engineering Degree* (3–4 years), followed by 2 years' practical work with a firm.

Address.

Institution of Production Engineers, 10 Chesterfield Street W.1.

This is a selection only of the various careers available in engineering. The following is a list of the professional bodies associated with other branches of the profession, and details can be obtained from them:—

1. *Agricultural Engineering.*

Institution of Agricultural Engineers, 6 Queen Square, W.C.1.

2. *Gas Engineering.*

The Institution of Gas Engineers, 17 Grosvenor Crescent, S.W.1.

3. *Heating and Ventilating Engineering.*

The Institution of Heating and Ventilation Engineers, 49 Cadogan Square, S.W.1.

4. *Illuminating Engineering.*

The Illuminating Engineering Society, 32 Victoria Street, S.W.1.

5. *Marine Engineering.*

The Institute of Marine Engineers, The Memorial Building, 76 Mark Lane, E.C.3.

6. *Radio and Electronic Engineering.*

The British Institution of Radio Engineers, 9 Bedford Square, W.C.1.

7. *Railway Engineering.*
The Director of Training and Education, British Transport Commission, 222 Marylebone Road, N.W.1.

8. *Water Engineering.*
The Institution of Water Engineers, 11 Pall Mall, S.W.1.

9. *Welding Engineering.*
The Institute of Welding, 54 Princes Gate, Exhibition Road, S.W.7.

Pamphlets.
Choice of Careers Series (H.M.S.O.)
No. 78, *Engineering Work for Boys.*
No. 77, *Engineering Work for Girls.*
No. 92, *The Professional Engineer.*
No. 60, *Engineering Draughtsman.*
No. 64, *Fitter, Turner and Machinist.*
No. 79, *Electrician.*

Training Opportunities for Women in Engineering, 3*s.* 6*d.* Available from Women's Engineering Society.

FIRE SERVICE.

B.

Age. 18–31 (35 for ex-regulars from the Forces).
16 in certain areas where there is a junior training scheme.

Qualifications. (Adults) Ability to pass a simple education test.
(Junior scheme)—O.

Pay. Junior firemen from £295 p.a. Adults £600–£835. Divisional officers from £1,300.

Aptitudes. Ability to serve as member of team, physical strength.

Method of Entry. By application to the Chief Officer of Fire Brigade in question.

Further Training. 2–3 months' course of training at a Brigade Training School.

There are certain minimum physical requirements for a Fireman. He must be not less than 5 ft. 7 in. tall and be able to pass a fairly strenuous medical examination. Promotion to the rank of leading fireman is by examination after 2 years' service, and to the rank of sub-officer after 4 years' service.

There are opportunities for further advanced training at the Fire Service College for chosen officers. Service is pensionable, and dependants are provided for in case of death.

Address.
The Institution of Fire Engineers, 94 Southwark Bridge Road, S.E.1.

FORESTRY.

B.

Age.
1. Forest Workers, 15+.
2. Foresters, 19–30 (38, if ex-regular servicemen).
3. Forest Officer 21+

Qualifications.
1. Forest Worker —.
2. Forester—O.
3. Forest Officer—Degree in Forestry.

Pay.
1. Forest Worker, £8 10*s.* per week.
2. Forester £571 to £1,331 (+ house or cash allowance).
3. Forest Officer, from £1,032 at age 25.

Aptitudes. High standard of fitness; liking for country life; self-reliance and ability to handle men, especially in Forester grades and above.

Method of Entry.
1. Forest Worker: By application to Youth Employment Officer or direct to a Forester.
2. Forester: By application to a Forester Training School (1 year's practical experience a prerequisite).
3. Forest Officer: Acceptance by Selection Board of Forestry Commission (for those holding degree).

Further Training.
1. Forest Worker, practical training while working.
2. Forester, 2-year course at Residential Forestry School. (There may be a waiting list for these schools; 2 years' delay is not uncommon.)

Work in Forestry is varied. Forest workers are those who do the practical work in the woods, involving the care of trees, thinning, felling, and sawmill work. Foresters are in charge of areas of woodland, and Forest Officers are in overall charge of whole regions and concerned with long-term plans for development and afforestation. At present prospects of employment with the Forestry Commission in this country are limited, but there are various openings overseas for the last category through the Overseas Civil Service.

In addition to the posts available with the Forestry Commission, attractive jobs are open to graduates in Forestry as managers of privately owned land, and in the timber trade.

Addresses.
The Forestry Commission, Education Branch, 25 Saville Row, W.1.
Royal Forestry Society of England and Wales, 49 Russell Square, W.C.1.
Empire Forestry Association, Royal Empire Society, Northumberland Avenue, W.C.2.

Pamphlets.
Choice of Careers, No. 81 (H.M.S.O.).
Training as a Forester. Available from The Forestry Commission.

HAIRDRESSING.

B. G.

Age. 16+.

Qualifications. None laid down.

Pay. Apprentices: About £3 10*s.* per week.
Men: £7 12*s.* per week (minimum after 2 years).
Women: £6 11*s.* per week (minimum after 2 years).

Aptitudes. Pleasant manner, unruffled air, self-confidence, cleanliness, artistic ability, manual dexterity, ability to stand for long periods, a good skin.

Method of Entry.
1. Apprenticeship to Master Hairdresser.
2. Full-time course at School of Hairdressing under Local Education Authority auspices.
3. Full-time course at private school of hairdressing.

Further Training.
1. As apprentice, 3 years, supplemented by part-time study.
2. As student at School of Hairdressing sponsored by Local Education Authority, 2 years.
3. As student at private school. Usually 3–6 months. Some of these are not recognised by the trade, enquiries should always be made to the official bodies.

The hairdresser, whether man or woman, is nowadays a member of a highly skilled profession offering an attractive career to those who are prepared to study and have a flair for getting on with people. It is pointed out that the above are minimum rates, and take no account of tips, which are a traditional aspect of the business.

Apprentices and students at L.E.A.-directed

Schools of Hairdressing study for the examinations of the City and Guilds of London Institute or the Entrance Examination of the Hairdressers' Registration Council. The courses at private schools are much more intensive and quite expensive (*e.g.*, £70 for a six-month course), but the period of study is, of course, much shorter. Grants are rarely allowed at private schools by Local Authorities, and in some cases their training is not recognised by the trade.

L.E.A. establishments holding courses include:–

London College of Fashion, Oxford Street, W.1.

Erith Technical College, Belvedere, Kent.

Enfield Technical College, Queens Way, Ponders End, Enfield, Middx.

Watford College of Further Education, Queens Road, Watford.

Full details of courses in private schools can be obtained from the associations named below.

Addresses.

The National Hairdressers' Federation, 20 Cranbourne Gardens, N.W.11.

The Incorporated Guild of Hairdressers, 33 Great Queen Street, W.C.2.

Pamphlet.

Choice of Careers No 104 (H.M.S.O.).

HEALTH VISITOR. *See* **Nursing.**

HORTICULTURE.

B. G.

Age. 15+.

Qualifications.

1. For Horticultural Institute—C.S.E. or O.
2. For Horticultural College—O. or A.
3. For University—A.

Pay. Foremen and chargehands, technical assistants (in parks' departments), horticultural advisers—£600 upwards.

Aptitudes. Liking for working with the soil, open-air work in all weathers, patience, practical ability, organising and business ability for management.

Methods of Entry.

1. At least a year in a market garden, nursery, glasshouses or with the parks' department of a Local Authority, or
2. Preferably a three-year apprenticeship, followed by further training at an Institute, College or University.

Further Study. Full-time courses for National Certificate (one year), Diploma (two years) or Degree (three years).

There are a great variety of careers open to those who are interested in Horticulture from the worker growing and packing crops at a market garden or in glasshouses, to the Parks' Superintendent of a large Authority who may be in charge of a staff of a hundred or more, the teacher or the horticultural adviser in the Agricultural Advisory Service.

Addresses.

The Secretary, The Horticultural Education Association, Long Ashton Research Station, Bristol.

The Institute of Park and Recreation Administration, Lower Basildon, Berks.

The Royal Horticultural Society, Vincent Square, S.W.1.

Pamphlets.

Choice of Careers Series (H.M.S.O.), No. 85, No. 86.

HOSPITAL ADMINISTRATION.

B. G.

Age. 16–20.

Qualifications. O. or A.

Pay. £310 at 16 upwards.

Aptitudes. Initiative, good judgment, ability to mix.

Method of Entry.

1. As a Junior Clerk.
2. As a graduate (limited number only).

Further Training. Part-time study in preparation for professional qualifications (very often the examination of the Institute of Hospital Administrators).

Hospital Administration is a term covering the work of about 450 hospital management committees right down to the day-to-day administrative running of a particular department in a particular hospital. The clerk who gains qualifications as a result of part-time study and who is prepared to move from one part of the country to another has real opportunities for promotion.

There are two stages in the examinations of the Institute of Hospital Management:

1. *Intermediate.*

   Part I comprises papers on Public Administration, Economics, and the Hospital and Health Services.

   Part II comprises papers on Secretarial Practice, Commercial Law, Book-keeping, Statistics (3 only to be taken).

2. *Final* (Candidates must have completed at least 3 years in Hospital Administration):

   Part I comprises papers on Hospital Administration, Hospital Finance, General Law affecting Hospitals.

   Part II. 3 subjects must be offered from a comprehensive list covering many of the aspects of Hospital Administration, *e.g.*, Accountancy, Supplies, Personnel Management, Records.

All posts are pensionable, and holidays vary according to age and status.

Address.

The Institute of Hospital Administrators, 75 Portland Place, W.1.

Pamphlet.

Careers in Hospital Administration. Available from The Institute.

Choice of Career Series (H.M.S.O.) No. 28.

HOTEL RECEPTIONIST. *See* **Catering and Hotel Management.**

INSURANCE.

B. G.

Age. 16–25.

Qualifications. Usually O but increasingly A.

Pay. About £500 at 18 in London. Less outside. One in ten estimated to get £2,000 or more by 40 or above.

Aptitudes. Ability in written and spoken expression probably more important than mathematical ability. Pleasant personality and wide interests.

Method of Entry. By application to secretary or staff manager of company or firm.

Further Training. Part-time study for the examination of the Chartered Insurance Institute. Training on courses at College of Insurance and employers' own training schools. Management courses also.

Insurance work falls into four main categories, fire, life, marine, and accident. Some insurance employers deal with all branches; others specialise in one only. After preliminary training the young man has to decide whether he wishes to specialise in indoor or outdoor work. The former leads to promotion to positions as chief clerk or departmental head for those who show promise, and there is ample opportunity for specialisation. The latter, involving probably more contact with people, leads to positions such as inspector or fire surveyor.

All employers encourage employees to study for the qualifying examination of the Chartered Insurance Institute.

Ten subjects for Associateship, sixteen subjects for Fellowship. Study is spread over five winters. Day release in the first year is common among employers for half-a-day a week at a Technical College. Evening classes are arranged throughout the country in conjunction with postal tuition. Practical training for the job is given at the College of Insurance to which some employers send young men. Others have their own training schools or run their own schemes.

While it is true that girls can follow a similar indoor career in insurance and are eligible for the same examinations, the majority of jobs for girls are of a clerical or secretarial nature. Here the path of promotion is towards specialised clerical work, confidential secretarial posts, accountancy, or technical work.

An increasing number of companies have vacancies for graduate entrants in administrative and foreign posts.

With most companies, welfare and pension arrangements are excellent and employees are encouraged to join the various sports and social clubs.

Addresses.

The Chartered Insurance Institute, The Hall, 20 Aldermanbury, E.C.2.

The Corporation of Insurance Brokers, 15 St. Helen's Place, E.C.3.

Pamphlets.

Choice of Careers Series (H.M.S.O.), No. 93.

Insurance careers. (boys).
Sixth-formers in insurance. (boys).
Insurance broking as a career. (boys).
I chose insurance. (girls).
} All free from the Chartered Insurance Institute.

JOURNALISM.

B. G.

Age. 17+.

Qualifications. Usually at least O + preferably a knowledge of shorthand and typing.

Pay. Minimum rate at 16, £6 8*s.* to £8 18*s.* 6*d.* per week.

Aptitudes. Ability to mix with all types of people, adaptability, initiative, and independence.

Method of Entry. Usually by application to provincial or suburban weekly.

Further Training. 5 years made up as follows:—

1. 6 months' probation.
2. 3 years' articled apprenticeship.
3. 18 months' course leading to National Diploma.

One of the most difficult things about Journalism as a career is actually getting started. Many young people at school who develop an interest in writing feel that they would like to take up this career, only to find that it is very hard to get a job. The best method is to write to the editor of as many provincial or local papers as possible, and of course be prepared to go where the work is. Addresses of all newspapers can be found in *Willing's Press Guide.*

While waiting for a vacancy it is a good thing to work up proficiency in shorthand and typing.

It is sometimes possible to obtain a post on some newspapers as a graduate, and for graduate entrants (aged 24 or over) there is a special 2-year course leading to a Certificate of Training of the National Council for the Training of Journalists. The more normal method is, however, that outlined in the Further Training paragraph above, where, during the 3-year apprenticeship, the new entrant is trained in all aspects of reporting. At the same time the apprentice follows a part-time course (either by correspondence or at a Technical College) in English, Central and Local Government, British Life and Institutions, a special Law Course, and an optional subject.

Full details of these courses and of the final 18-month course for the National Diploma are given in the *Handbook of Training* published by the National Council.

Addresses.

The Institute of Journalists, 2–4 Tudor Street, E.C.4.

The National Union of Journalists, 22 Great Windmill Street, W.1.

The National Council for the Training of Journalists, 6 Carmelite Street, E.C.4.

Pamphlet.

Choice of Careers Series, No. 83 (H.M.S.O.).

LABORATORY WORK. *See* Science, *also* Medical Laboratory Technology.

LAUNDRY MANAGEMENT.

B. G.

Age. 16+.

Qualifications. Preferably C.S.E. or O.

Pay. Depending on age, experience, and responsibility, but minimum rates are laid down in Orders of Laundry Wages Council.

Aptitudes. Ability to handle varying types of people.

Method of Entry.

1. By application to a firm.
2. Acceptance on full-time courses (minimum age 18 years).

Further Training.

1. *Learnership Scheme.* Practical training and background instruction during work, supplemented by part-time study for appropriate examinations of City and Guilds of London Institute.
2. 3-year *Apprenticeship.* Available for boys only and in a few firms only, supplemented by part-time study as in (1) above.
3. *Trainee Manager/Manageress Scheme.* Available for suitable persons of 18 years and over.
4. *Full-time Laundry Management Course.* 2 years. Candidates must hold O and be 18 years or more.

There are over 4,000 laundries in the country, and there is considerable scope in this still-expanding industry for the ambitious boy or girl who is prepared to work hard. There are basically three processes in laundry work: sorting of articles with regard to treatment, washing or cleaning, and finishing (*i.e.*, ironing or pressing), and the would-be manager or manageress must become thoroughly acquainted with, and have practical experience of, all the processes involved. The apprentice or learner must also become familiar with business methods and management techniques. There is plenty of exacting work for an intelligent boy or girl who is prepared to study hard.

In addition to the usual Local Education Authority Grants, which may be available for many who wish to follow a full-time course, the Laundry Industry offers some scholarships. Full details can be obtained from the first address below.

Addresses.

The Laundry Industry Education Committee, 16–17 Lancaster Gate, W.2.

The Institute of British Launderers and Cleaners Ltd., 16–17 Lancaster Gate, W.2.

Pamphlet.

Choice of Careers Series, No. 70 (H.M.S.O.).

LAW.

B. G.

(*a*) **Barrister.**

Age. No person may be called to the Bar before the age of 21.

Qualifications.

1. A or degree.
2. The "keeping" of 12 terms (see below).
3. Success in Bar Examinations.

Pay.

1. In private practice, income depends on many factors, mention of which is made below.
2. In Civil Service and with private undertakings—about £900–£2,000, or even higher.

Aptitudes. Clarity of thought and language. Good health. Wide general knowledge.

Method of Entry. Acceptance by one of the Inns of Court as a student.

Further Training. At least 12 months as a pupil of a practising barrister. Then perhaps a further period of "devilling" (see below).

The Bar is the senior branch of the profession, and only a barrister can plead in the higher courts.

The profession of barrister (in private practice) while being one of the most respected is, initially, at least, one of the most precarious. First, admission to one of the Inns of Court has to be obtained and fees of about £66 have to be paid to cover tuition. There may also be certain deposits as well as dining and examination fees.

The student then has to "keep" 12 terms, *i.e.*, dine in Hall on any 6 days of each term. Students who are studying for a University degree at the same time are allowed to "keep term" by dining in 3 times a term only. The Bar Examination is divided into two parts, as follows:—

Part I. Roman Law; Constitutional Law and Legal History; the Law of Contract and Tort; the Law of Real Property; Criminal Law.

Part II. Criminal Procedure; General Principles of Equity; Company Law and either Practical Conveyancing or Divorce Law or Public International Law; Evidence and Civil Procedure; a special subject; a general paper.

The next step is to be "called," which is the slightly ritual acceptance of the student into the profession (providing the Call Fees (about £62) have been paid).

At this point the young barrister has to decide whether there is enough money available to continue into private practice. This will entail a premium of up to 100 guineas for the privilege of working for an established barrister and so learning the practical side. Thereafter the new barrister *may* be lucky enough to be asked to "devil," *i.e.*, to carry on the more humdrum and routine tasks for a nominal salary. This devilling is an important period in the barrister's career, as it is at this time that he makes the necessary contacts for establishing his own practice. (It should be remembered that advertisement is not allowed.) When finally a private practice is set up several lean years must be anticipated before the newcomer is well known by the solicitors who are to provide him with briefs.

Many barristers prefer to take appointments either with the Civil Service or with large private firms which retain legal staffs. This is indeed often the only way of making a career for those who cannot afford the substantial outlay involved in embarking on private practice.

The Scottish system is entirely different, and information can be obtained about how to become an Advocate in Scottish Law by application to the Faculty of Advocates at the address given below.

Addresses.

The Inner Temple, E.C.4.

The Middle Temple, E.C.4.

Lincoln's Inn, W.C.2.

Gray's Inn, W.C.1.

The Faculty of Advocates, Parliament House, Edinburgh, 1.

The Council of Legal Education, 4 Gray's Inn Place, W.C.1.

(*b*) **Solicitor.**

Age. No person under the age of 21 may be admitted as a Solicitor.

Qualifications. A (to commence articles), or degree.

Pay.

1. About £1000 p.a. on first qualifying as a Managing Clerk in private practice.
2. *Public Service*, about £985 (starting salary)—over £2,000 in some cases.

Aptitudes. Tact, patience, integrity, capacity for detail, interest in people.

Method of Entry. As articled clerk to solicitor, in private practice or in public service, *e.g.*, Town Clerk.

Further Training. 5 years from taking of articles (3 years for a graduate) combined with part-time study for the Law Society's Intermediate and Final Examinations.

The demand for solicitors exceeds the supply and many responsible and well-paid appointments are held by women.

The solicitor comes into contact with the public chiefly when they need legal advice or representation, especially in connection with the purchase and sale of houses, the making of wills, matrimonial affairs, and general litigation. Not so well known is the whole aspect of Company work involving the flotation of companies, bankruptcy, and company law generally.

During articles (for which a premium is less often required), a clerk must attend at a recognised law school for legal instruction on either a full-time or part-time basis. Exemption is allowed for barristers, graduates in law, and clerks with 10 years' experience or more.

The Intermediate Examination of the Law Society is in two parts, which may be taken separately. Part I consists of Real Property Law, Law of Contract and Torts, Public Law, Constitutional Law, and Criminal Law. Part II is concerned with Accounts and Book-keeping.

The Final Examination consists of Real and Property Law, Law of Trusts and Succession, Tax Law, Contract, Tort, Company Law, and Partnership Law.

Once admitted, the new solicitor has the choice of aiming for a private practice or going into Public Service. In the former case the usual thing is to secure a post as a managing clerk with a firm of solicitors with the idea of eventual partnership in mind. For those who choose Public Service, prospects of promotion and increased responsibility are very good.

The Scottish system is slightly different, and information about how to become a solicitor in Scotland can be obtained from the second address below.

Addresses.

The Law Society, 113 Chancery Lane, W.C.2.

The Law Society of Scotland, Law Society's Hall, North Bank Street, Edinburgh.

Pamphlets.

Choice of Careers Series, No. 26 (H.M.S.O.).

Lawyers in the Government Service. Available from The Civil Service Commission, 6 Burlington Gardens, W.1.

(*c*) **Legal Executives.**

Age. 16 or 18.

Qualification. O.

Aptitudes. Capacity for detail, tact, patience and an understanding of people.

Method of Entry. Work in a solicitor's office.

Further Training. Study for Associate Membership of the Institute of Legal Executives followed by the Fellowship examinations.

Many young persons taking up employment of a legal nature who do not wish to qualify as barristers or solicitors can now, by study, passing examinations and working in a solicitor's office, achieve a recognised status. By the time they are twenty-five years old they can qualify as legal executives when they may expect to become Managing Clerks in a legal office. This new qualification now offers a worthwhile career to people who are interested in the law, but who for one reason or another are unable to qualify as solicitors.

Address.

The Institute of Legal Executives, Maltravers House, Arundel Street, W.C.2.

Pamphlet.

Choice of Careers Series (H.M.S.O.) No. 26.

LIBRARIANSHIP.

B. G.

Age. 17–20.

Qualification. A. or degree.

Pay. £405 to £920 after qualification.

Aptitudes. Methodical mind, capacity for detail, good memory, friendly demeanour.

Method of Entry. By application to Librarian of a Public Library.

Further Training.

1. Professional examination. (*a*) 1 year full-time or 3 years part-time for Part I Examination. (*b*) 1 year full-time or several years part-time for Part II.
2. Post-graduate Professional examination at a University (London or Sheffield).

Librarianship is a term covering not only the services of the Public Libraries but also the University and College libraries and those of the learned and professional bodies. Very often in the case of the latter, very high academic qualifications are demanded, and in this section we are chiefly concerned with the public-library system as a career. The Junior joining a staff will find that at first a lot of time is spent in routine matters —the arranging of books, filing and indexing, and counter duties. At the same time the beginner will be expected to study for the Examinations. It is pointed out that "O" standard in one foreign language or a science subject is an advisable qualification, as this is a compulsory requirement for the Registration Examination, which has to be passed before any real promotion can be expected in the service.

Graduates who wish to acquire library qualifications can follow the Diploma Course of the London School of Librarianship and Archives (1-year, full-time).

The general salary pattern in the Library Service is that juniors and those who are not yet Chartered Librarians (*i.e.*, aged 23, with 3 years' service, having passed the Registration Examination) are not very highly paid, but for the qualified man or woman the range extends through seven grades to over £4,000 p.a. Promotion however, is slow, and very often entails moving to another part of the country in order to take a higher post.

Address.

The Library Association, 7 Ridgemont St., Store Street, W.C.1.

Pamphlets.

Choice of Careers Series, No. 4 (H.M.S.O.).

The Library Profession. Available from The Library Association.

LOCAL GOVERNMENT SERVICE.

B. G.

Age. Usually 16.

Qualification. O for entry into General Division. A or degree.

Pay. £290–£700 (General Division (unqualified). Other Divisions and grades correspondingly higher.
(Clerical officers in the Greater London Council commence at £515 at 16 or 18.)

Aptitudes. Impartiality, sense of duty.

Method of Entry. By examination, interview, in reply to advertisement, or through the Youth Employment Service.

Further Training. Part-time study for the appropriate professional or technical examinations.

Local Government is a term covering the work of the following types of local authority: County, County Borough, Borough, Metropolitan Borough, Urban District, and Rural District. These authorities are responsible for the administering of a very wide range of public services: *e.g.*, education, public health, housing, road work, police, fire services, civil defence, welfare, libraries, swimming-pools, playing fields, etc.

There are about 180,000 Local Government Servants in England and Wales. They are divided into the following classes:—

(i) General.
(ii) Clerical.
(iii) Miscellaneous.
(iv) Administrative, Professional and Technical (known as A.P.T.) which is subdivided.

The school-leaver will normally enter the General Division, and his or her subsequent career depends on record and the passing of the appropriate examinations.

It is important that one should start in a branch of Local Government in which one's own inclinations and preferences for a particular type of work can be developed.

The main departments are:—

1. **The Clerk's Department,** which looks after the legal side of Local Government. There is considerable variety of work, and it is often possible to arrange to serve under articles (*see* **Law**). Highest positions are increasingly reserved for graduates.
2. **The Treasurer's Department,** which is responsible for the finances of the authority. The ambitious beginner will study for accountancy qualifications (*see* **Accountancy**).
3. **The Housing Department,** which is in many authorities steadily increasing in importance. Architects, Surveyors, Engineers, Managers are all required, and facilities exist for acquiring professional status in many aspects of the work.
4. **The Engineer's Department.** A professional Engineering qualification, acquired either before or during service, is essential for those who seek promotion. The department is concerned with roads, drainage, sewerage, municipal buildings, and general development (*see* **Engineering**).
5. **The Public Health Department.** Under the control of the Medical Officer of Health, this is concerned with the general health of the public. School Medical and Dental Officers, Public Health Inspectors, Food Inspectors, Health Visitors, Midwives, etc., belong to this department.
6. **Education Department,** which is responsible for the administration of the Schools, Further Education Colleges, Youth Service, and Youth Employment Bureaux. The higher posts in this department offer an alternative career to those who have teaching experience (who are not themselves Local Government Officers) and indeed are usually reserved for former teachers.

All these departments, as well as the others which have been mentioned, require administrative and clerical employees in addition to the specially qualified technical people, such as doctors and engineers, and there is certainly no need for boys or girls to feel that by entering the Service at school-leaving age they are condemned to a humdrum life on a third-rate salary for the rest of their days. Posts are pensionable (contributory), and welfare arrangements are good.

Addresses.

The National and Local Government Officers Association, Nalgo House, 8 Harewood Road, N.W.1.

The Local Authorities Conditions of Service Advisory Board, 41 Belgrave Square, S.W.1.

The Director of Establishments, Greater London Council, County Hall, S.E.1.

Pamphlet.

Choice of Careers Series, No. 28 (H.M.S.O.).

MEDICAL LABORATORY TECHNOLOGY.

B. G.

Age. 16+.

Qualifications. O or A.

Pay. £390 to £725 p.a.; £885 to £1,025 when qualified with possibility of higher appointments.

Aptitudes. Patience, interest in science, attention to detail, reliability, manual dexterity.

Method of Entry. By application to the Area Pathologist of the Hospital Management Committee or to the Government Department concerned.

Further Training. Part-time study for the examinations of the Institute of Medical Laboratory Technology. Two A levels (science) allows completion of Intermediate course in two years instead of three.

Medical Laboratory Technology is the study and practice of the technical methods used in laboratory work to ascertain the nature of diseases, usually from specimens of body tissue, blood, etc. It is of great interest to the school-leaver who is interested in science and prepared to continue studies in spare time. The work is such that the pathologists under whom the technicians work must have absolute confidence in the reliability and accuracy of their juniors.

The beginner has to obtain a post as indicated above, and then apply for registration by the Institute as a student. Much of the practical instruction is by a Senior Technician in the course of duties. The Intermediate Examination of the Institute is taken after 3 years' experience and thereafter, having gained the status of a Junior Technician, the young man or woman has a further 2 years' part-time study for the Final Examination.

There is continuing development in the Health Services, and prospects for new entrants are reasonably good.

Address.

The Institute of Medical Laboratory Technology, 74 New Cavendish Street, W.1.

Pamphlets.

M.L.T. as a Career. Available from the Institute.

Choice of Careers Series, No. 57 (H.M.S.O.).

MEDICAL SOCIAL WORKER. *See* Social Work.

MEDICINE.

B. G.

Age. 17 years 9 months (minimum).

Qualifications. A in chemistry, physics, biology. Sometimes O + Pre-Medical Examination (First M.B.).

Pay.

1. Hospital Service: about £770 p.a. to over £4,445 (Consultants).
2. General Practice, depending on size of practice. In the National Health Service there is a capitation fee for every patient on doctor's list up to £3,500+.
3. In Public Health, Industry, Armed Forces, Colonial Medical Service, about £1,515 to over £4,500.

Aptitudes. Patience, calmness of manner, interest in other people, capacity for hard work, integrity.

Method of Entry. Acceptance as a student by one of the Medical Schools.

Further Training. At least 5 years' full-time study for degree or diploma, followed by one year as a "house-surgeon" in a hospital.

It is important for the would-be doctor to ensure, while still at school, that the Sixth Form syllabus being followed is the best preparation for medical training. A level in chemistry, physics, and biology (for London Hospitals, Zoology) means exemption from the First or Pre-Medical Examination, which otherwise entails a whole year's study at a Technical College or Medical School. It must also be remembered that expenses may be even heavier than in other forms of training, and although help is available from Local Education Authorities and through Scholarships, this is bound to be an anxious time for parents of moderate means.

When the student has passed the Final Examinations of the course he is following, he or she has to spend 1 year as a house-surgeon in an approved hospital or institution before starting in a practice. Doctors in general practice need to have great reserves of physical strength, patience, and endurance. Unless they can come to some sort of "duty" arrangement with other doctors practising in the locality, or unless they work in a partnership, they must expect to have little time they are certain to be able to call their own.

Many newly qualified doctors prefer to work for public authorities or in large industrial or commercial concerns, where at least work is usually in line with office hours. For those who like community life, the Armed Services offer a secure and well-paid career with the opportunity of seeing much of the world.

The following is a list of the Medical Schools which offer courses in Medicine:

Aberdeen University.
Belfast, Queen's University.
Birmingham University.
Bristol University.
*Cambridge University.
Cork, University College.
Dublin—
  Trinity College.
  University College.
  Royal College of Surgeons.
Edinburgh University.
Galway, University College.
Glasgow University.
Leeds University.
Liverpool University.
London University.
Manchester University.
Newcastle University.
*Oxford University.
St. Andrews University.
Sheffield University.
Welsh National School of Medicine, Cardiff.

* These universities offer only the pre-clinical 3-year course. Except in rare cases the clinical period of training, another 3 years, must be done elsewhere.

Addresses.

British Medical Association, B.M.A. House, Tavistock Square, W.C.1.

General Medical Council, 44 Hallam Street, W.1.

English Conjoint Board, 8 Queen Square, W.C.1.

Irish Conjoint Board, Royal College of Surgeons in Ireland, St. Stephen's Green, Dublin.

Scottish Conjoint Board, 18 Nicolson Street, Edinburgh, 8.

Pamphlet.

Choice of Careers Series No. 108 (H.M.S.O.).

MERCHANT NAVY.

B.

Age.

Navigation Officers, 16–17½.
Engineer Officers, 16+.
Radio Officers, 16½+.

Qualifications.

1. O or A.
2. Ministry of Transport Eyesight Certificate.

A level may shorten apprenticeship for Navigation Officer.

Pay.

Navigation and Engineer Officers, minimum monthly basic rate (with food found) on foreign-going general traders: Fourth Mate (uncertified) £60 17*s.* 6*d.*; Junior Engineer (with certificate) £73 10*s.*; Chief Engineer £128 2*s.* 6*d.*–£162 5*s.* 0*d.* (depending on gross tonnage) plus seniority increments.

Aptitudes. Self-reliance, capacity for unstinted work, first-class eye-sight, physical fitness, sense of adventure.

Method of Entry.

(a) *Navigation Officer.*

1. By acceptance at Training School (see address below).
2. By application to shipping line.

(b) *Engineer Officer.*

1. By apprenticeship in heavy engineering, marine works, or shipbuilding yard.
2. Acceptance by a shipping company on full-time Technical College course, combined with seagoing and workshop experience.

(c) *Radio Officer.* Acceptance in a school to train for Postmaster General's 2nd or 1st Class Certificate and the Ministry of Transport Radar Maintenance Certificate.

Further Training.

(a) *Navigation Officer.*

1. Course of pre-sea training at approved training school plus shortened apprenticeship.
2. 4 years' apprenticeship with shipping line.

(b) *Engineer Officer.*

1. 4 years' marine engineering experience ashore plus 18 months' sea service.
2. 4 years' apprenticeship with shipping company.

(c) *Radio Officer.* 12–30 months' training for the Postmaster General's Certificates and the Ministry of Transport Radar Certificates.

Careers in the Merchant Navy fall usually into the categories of Navigation, Engineer, and Radio. The future Navigation Officer has to study as an apprentice for the Certificate of Competency, which qualifies him as a Second Mate. After a further 12 months at sea he is able to sit for the First Mate's Certificate, and 2½ years later for the Master's Certificate. During this sea time he can pursue his studies by correspondence course.

The pattern for Engineer Officer is similar, except that the 4 years' apprenticeship is on land in a works preferably connected with the shipbuilding industry. On completion of his apprenticeship the young engineer spends 21 months at sea before taking the Second Engineer's Certificate and a further similar period before the Chief Engineer's Certificate. There is an alternative method for boys with O level or equivalent qualifications which comprises 2 years' full-time Technical College work followed by 18 months' practical engine-room experience at sea, and a further year in a shipyard or engineering works.

The necessary qualifications for a Radio Officer have to be obtained before the beginning of service afloat, and it is a wise precaution to ensure that one has the necessary physical requirements before starting a course, in order to avoid possible disappointment later.

Radio Officers are usually employed by the Radio Companies, but increasingly are being employed directly by Shipping Companies.

The life of a Merchant Navy Officer varies according to whether he is employed on "home" or "foreign" work (*i.e.*, short-range or long-range shipping) and according to the type of ship he is working. For example, an officer on a deep-sea oil-tanker may spend relatively long periods away from home, but this is compensated by longer home leave. The social demands on board a large passenger liner will, of course, be greater than if one is serving on a little cargo vessel. But the qualities required in every branch and on every type of ship are the same—trustworthiness, intelligence, ability to get on with others, and willingness to take responsibility. For those possessing these qualities, the sea offers a fine and interesting career.

Addresses.

The Board of Trade, St. Christopher House, Southwark Street, S.E.1.

The Marine Society, Clark's Place, Bishopsgate, E.C.2.

The Shipping Federation Ltd., Minories, E.C.3.

For Radio Officers:—

G.P.O. Radio Services Dept., St. Martins-le-Grand, E.C.1.

For Eyesight Tests:—

Mercantile Marine Office, at any big port in the United Kingdom.

Local Authorities usually make grants for training only at approved colleges, *e.g.*, (*a*) for Navigating Officers; King Edward VII Nautical College, 680 Commercial Road. E.14; School of Navigation, Southampton University; (*b*) for Radio Officers: Norwood Technical College.

Pamphlets.

How to Join the Merchant Navy. (The Board of Trade, Southwark Street, S.E.1.)

Merchant Navy Careers. (The Shipping Federation.)

Why not? An Engineer Officer in the Merchant Navy. (The Shipping Federation.)

Choice of Careers Series (H.M.S.O.), No. 72, No. 73.

MIDWIFERY. *See* Nursing.

MUSIC.

B. G.

Age. 16 (for professional training). 18 (for teacher training).

Qualifications. O, preferably A for teacher training.

Pay. As a teacher in State system—in accordance with Burnham scales. Otherwise—very varied.

Aptitudes. Natural talent and strong constitution.

Method of Entry. Acceptance by a school of music or University.

Further Training. 3–6 years at school of music, leading to a diploma or degree.

The person who studies music with a view to making a career has two courses open. He or she can study to become a professional performer or a teacher. In the former case it must be realised that competition is very great, and only those who are at the top of their "class" and able to stay there can hope for the "glamorous" solo work. There has been recently, however, an increased public demand for music, and prospects of getting an orchestral post are perhaps slightly better for the good performer than they were in the past. This growth (or revival) of interest in music in this country means that there is also more for the trained teacher to do.

The boy or girl who wishes to take up music professionally must be proficient enough to pass a entrance examination if he or she wishes to follow a full-time School of Music course. The addresses of the best known of these schools are given below.

These courses cater for both would-be performers and teachers, and for the latter there is the alternative of a University course leading to a degree in music. These degrees are offered by the Universities of Birmingham, Bristol, Cambridge, Dublin, Durham, Edinburgh, London, Manchester, Oxford, Sheffield, Wales and the National University of Ireland.

The profession of music is in many respects more of a vocation than a career, and only those who have a real determination to devote their lives to this branch of the arts and sufficient character to withstand the boredom of repeated rehearsals, and the often straitened circumstances of a musician's life, should embark on such a hazardous undertaking.

Addresses.

The Royal Academy of Music, Marylebone Road, N.W.1.

The Royal College of Music, Prince Consort Road, South Kensington, S.W.7.

The Guildhall School of Music and Drama, John Carpenter Street, E.C.4.

The Birmingham School of Music, Paradise Street, Birmingham, 1.

Trinity College of Music, Mandeville Place, Manchester Square, W.1.

The Royal Manchester College of Music, Ducie Street, Oxford Road, Manchester.

The London College of Music, Great Marlborough Street, W.1.

The Scottish Academy of Music, St. George's Place, Glasgow, C.2.

Books.

To be a Professional Musician (Methuen), 10*s*. 6*d*.

Choice of Careers Series, No. 101 (H.M.S.O.).

NURSING.

Usually G, but B much in demand.

Age. 18–30 (for beginning of training).

Qualifications. (*a*) State Registration: O or A. (*b*) State Enrolled Nurses: possibly C.S.E.

Pay. Student nurses commence at £365; Staff nurse in General hospital £690–£880; Ward sisters up to £1,205.

Aptitudes. Interest in people, good health, even temper, tact.

Method of Entry. By application to Matron of approved hospital.

Further Training. At least 3 years until State Registration.

Nursing nowadays is a profession which appeals to many young women who wish to make a career in the service of others. Training for State Registration (S.R.N.) cannot begin until the age of 18, and girls who leave school at 15 are often at a loss as to what to do with the intervening 3 years. Those who have the opportunity of staying in a Sixth Form are well advised to do so, as Sixth Form work is a useful preparation for the further study the student must tackle.

There are the alternatives of the pre-nursing courses which are run by some schools and technical colleges, and the cadet schemes which are run by some hospitals.

Training (which is resident) lasts for 3–4 years (except for Fever Nursing, which is a 2-year course). Registration may be obtained in: (i) General Nursing; (ii) The Nursing of Sick Children; (iii) Fever Nursing; (iv) Mental Nursing; (v) The Nursing of Mental Defectives; (vi) Midwifery. It is considered advisable to qualify in General Nursing as a basic training, whichever branch is taken up later.

There are alternative courses run on simpler lines for girls who feel they cannot cope with the considerable amount of study involved in the S.R.N. course. This leads to the qualification of State Enrolled Nurse. The salary scale for the S.E.N. is slightly lower than the one indicated above. No fees incurred during training although a deduction may be made for board and lodging.

Specialised Training Schemes. The General Nursing Council has approved a number of new schemes of training which enables the Student nurse to obtain a qualification in addition to State Registration. For example, combined hospital and university courses offering integrated community health courses; the combined nurse training and degree course at Edinburgh University; and the shortened nursing training available to graduates at St. Thomas's Hospital.

The qualified nurse has many interesting openings available to her. Apart from the different branches of hospital work, there are: District Nursing, Midwifery, Private Nursing, Public Health Nursing (all of which allow the nurse a more independent and less communal life), Industrial Nursing, the Nursing Services of the Crown, the Overseas Nursing Service, and the various Missionary Societies.

Male Nurses. These are nowadays quite often trained and employed under similar conditions. They work usually in the larger hospitals, and almost always live out (except in the case of Psychiatric Hospitals). There are good prospects, particularly for Male Nurses, as "Sister Tutors," when both teaching and nursing qualifications are combined.

Address.

Nursing Recruitment Service, 6 Cavendish Square, W.1.

Pamphlet.

Choice of Careers Series:—

No. 82, *Nursing and Midwifery* (H.M.S.O.).

No. 89, *Nursing for Men* (H.M.S.O.).

OCCUPATIONAL THERAPY.

B. G.

Age. 18+.

Qualifications. O or A.

Pay. Commences at £623.

Aptitudes. Interest in people, initiative, tact, practical and/or artistic ability.

Method of Entry. Acceptance for course by approved Training School.

Further Training. At least 3 years leading to the Diploma of the Association of Occupational Therapy.

The Occupational Therapist is concerned with helping the patient to recover and regain his self-confidence by guiding him into a suitable form of work, activity, or recreation. The therapy is therefore partly psychological and partly physical, and the therapist is the person who sees that the doctor's wishes in this respect are carried out and who can prescribe the necessary activities and encourage the patient to co-operate.

During training the student works for part of the time in a hospital learning how to become a member of the team concerned with the recovery of the patient. He or she also studies Anatomy, Physiology, Psychology, Medicine and Surgery, Psychiatry, and the Theory of Occupational Therapy, as well as a series of remedial techniques.

A list of the approved training schools can be had from the address below. Fees are payable, but maintenance and other grants are often available from the Local Education Authority, subject to the usual conditions.

Address.

The Association of Occupational Therapists 251 Brompton Road, S.W.3.

Pamphlets.

Choice of Careers Series, No. 53 (H.M.S.O.).

Occupational Therapy. Available from the Association.

OPTICIAN.

(1) Dispensing Optician.

B. G.

Age. 16+.

Qualification. O.

Pay. £557–£929 in the Hospital Eye Service, more in private practice.

Aptitudes. Neatness, manual dexterity, interest in people, attention to detail.

Method of Entry. Acceptance for a full-time course or employment with a registered optician.

Further Training. Two years' full-time college course or by working under an approved optician with part-time study (this takes about 4 years).

The dispensing optician is the person who dispenses the prescriptions of oculists and his work is concerned with the selection, measuring, fitting, checking and supply of spectacles and other optical appliances.

(2) Ophthalmic Optician.

B. G.

Age. 18+.

Qualification. A.

Pay. £712–£1,087 (minimum scale in Health Service).

Aptitudes. Neatness, interest in people and in the medico-sciences, attention to detail.

Method of Entry. Acceptance by a recognised training institution for a full-time course.

Further Training. 3-year full-time training course followed by 1 year of practical work with a qualified optician.

The ophthalmic optician is responsible for the examination of eyes and for the prescription of spectacles, contact lenses, etc. He or she also dispenses these prescriptions. During the twelve months' practical clinical experience which follows the full-time college course, the student may expect a salary of about £410. He or she can then join the National Health Service, either in the Hospital Eye Service or in private practice.

Addresses.

British Optical Association, 65 Brook Street, W.1.

Worshipful Company of Spectacle Makers, Apothecaries' Hall, E.C.4.

Institute of Optical Science, 23 Southampton Row, W.C.1.

The Association of Dispensing Opticians, 22 Nottingham Place, W.1.

Pamphlets.

Choice of Careers Series, No. 74 (H.M.S.O.).

The Optical Profession. Available from the Association of Optical Practitioners.

ORTHOPTICS.

B. G.

Age. 17+.

Qualifications. O, but preferably A.

Pay. £623 to £829 (minimum scale).

Aptitudes. Patience, liking for people, especially children.

Method of Entry. Acceptance on a course at an approved hospital.

Further Training. 2½ years' full-time training leading to the Diploma of the British Orthoptic Board.

The orthoptist is concerned with remedial work with patients (very often children) who suffer from squints and "lazy" eyes. She (for it is usually girls who take up this career) may work in an eye hospital, a children's hospital, a general hospital with an ophthalmic department, or a school clinic. There are also some opportunities with ophthalmic surgeons in private practice.

Those who become interested in teaching may take a course after at least 2 years' experience in order to qualify. The teaching side commands rather higher salaries. There are fourteen Orthoptic Training Schools attached to hospitals throughout the country, and a list of these and full details can be obtained from the address below.

Addresses.

The Faculty of Ophthalmologists, 45 Lincoln's Inn Fields, W.C.2.

British Orthoptic Board, Tavistock House (North), Tavistock Square, W.C.1.

Pamphlets.

Choice of Careers Series, No. 69 (H.M.S.O.).

Orthoptics. Available from British Orthoptic Board.

PERSONNEL MANAGEMENT. *See* **Social Work.**

PHARMACY.

B. G.

Age. 18.

Qualifications. A.

Pay. Retail and industrial: from £1,000 upwards. Hospital: £955 upwards.

Aptitudes. Interest in science, capacity for detail, normal colour vision.

Method of Entry. Registration with the Pharmaceutical Society as a student and acceptance by a School of Pharmacy.

Further Training.

1. Degree in Pharmacy followed by 1 year's practical training in a pharmacy, a hospital, or a manufacturing laboratory.

Pharmacy is the branch of medical work concerned with the dispensing of medicines and appliances. There are three main branches of the profession, namely retail, hospital, and manufacturing. The majority of vacancies occur on the *Retail* side, and the normal procedure is for the newly qualified person to secure employment as an assistant to an established pharmacist, with the intention of eventually taking a partnership, starting alone, or obtaining a managerial post in one of the large retail concerns. *Hospital Pharmacy* work is growing in scope and importance. There is a serious shortage of hospital pharmacists and promotion for entrants with first-class ability is rapid. *Pharmaceutical Manufacturing* provides many openings, often with the opportunity for research and travel.

It should be noted that there is nothing to stop a qualified young person gaining experience in more than one of these branches, as experience gained in one type of work is of undoubted value in the others.

Address.

The Pharmaceutical Society of Great Britain, 17 Bloomsbury Square, W.C.1.

Pamphlets.

Choice of Careers Series, No. 62 (H.M.S.O.).

Careers in the Hospital Service, *The Pharmacist*, available from the local office of the Ministry of Labour.

PHOTOGRAPHY.

B. G.

Age. Usually 16.

Qualifications. Preferably O.

Pay.

1. In commercial work, about £600 p.a. after training.
2. In National Health Service, about £540–£645 (Whitley Council Scale).
3. Civil Service, £351–£825.
4. Press Photographers (as Journalists).
5. Cinematography, from £12 18s. per week at 21.
6. Television, £500 at 18.

Aptitudes. Patience, neatness, artistic ability.

Method of Entry.

1. Apprenticeship.
2. Acceptance on full-time course at School of Photography.
3. Securing of employment as junior assistant to photographer.

Further Training.

1. 4-year apprenticeship, combined with part-time study for the exams of the Institute of British Photographers or for City and Guilds Certificate.
2. 3 years' full-time study at Art School or School of Photography.
3. As a junior assistant, part-time study for the examination of the Institute of British Photographers or the City and Guilds of London Institute.

Photography as a career has many branches of which the following are the main ones: Portraiture, Advertising, Press, Medical, Scientific.

All these branches demand skilled work, not only in the taking of pictures but on the processing side. Some, such as the Scientific or Press branches, require special aptitudes or training. Indeed, the amount of background knowledge of science needed to make a top rate Scientific Photographer is often of degree order.

Those who choose to acquire their training by apprenticeship or while working as a junior assistant must guard against the danger of getting too one-sided a practical experience while training. For an apprenticeship, this can generally be avoided by careful choice of a firm which deals with varied work, but it presents a real problem for the ordinary assistant attempting to study in his or her spare time. Even for those who wish to follow full-time courses, there is considerable difficulty in finding vacancies, as there are too few schools for the number wishing to train. Early application is therefore essential.

A full list of the Colleges providing full-time courses can be obtained from the Institute at the address below.

Addresses.

The Institute of British Photographers, 38 Bedford Square, W.C.1.

National Council for the Training of Journalists, 6 Carmelite Street, E.C.4.

Pamphlet.

Choice of Careers Series, No. 83 (H.M.S.O.).

PHYSICS. *See* **Science.**

PHYSIOTHERAPY.

B. G.

Age. 18+.

Qualifications. O or A.

Pay. £623 p.a. starting salary when trained. Possibility of rising to £1,545 p.a.

Aptitudes. Physical fitness, tact, liking for people.

Method of Entry. Acceptance for training by a school recognised by the Chartered Society of Physiotherapy.

Further Training. 3 years' full-time training at a school as above, studying for the examinations of the Society.

The physiotherapist is the person who assists the doctor to hasten the recovery of patients suffering from many types of injury or illness by using physical means. Thus massage, electrotherapy, and exercises prescribed by a doctor all come within the scope of the physiotherapist. It is obvious, therefore, that the trained person must be fully grounded in physiological matters, as well as the potentialities of the aids which are now available. It is because of the necessary thoroughness of training that the course lasts 3 years.

Grants are available from the Ministry of Health.

As is so often the case where work involving service to others is concerned, salaries are not particularly high, but the young man or woman who takes up physiotherapy as a career has at least the satisfaction of knowing that the work he or she is doing is of increasing social importance.

A detailed list of training establishments is available from the Society at the address below.

Address.

The Chartered Society of Physiotherapy, Tavistock House(South), Tavistock Square, W.C.1.

Pamphlet.

Choice of Careers Series, No. 52 (H.M.S.O.).

Physiotherapy, a career with a future. Available from the Society.

POLICE.

B. G.

Age.

Men, 19–30; Cadets, 16–18.

Women, 20–35; Cadets, 17 (when employed).

Qualifications. For Cadets: usually C.S.E. or O.

Pay.

1. Men, £700–£1,040 after nine years.
2. Women, £630–£935 after nine years.

(These are Constables' rates only and are somewhat higher in the London area.)

Aptitudes. Good health, patience, team spirit, keen observation.

Note. There are certain physical requirements:—

Men must be at least 5 ft. 8 in. tall (in some forces taller).

Women must be at least 5 ft. 4 in. tall.

Sight must be normal without glasses.

Method of Entry. By application to the local Police Station or the Chief Constable or Senior Officer of the local Police Force.

Further Training. 3 months' basic training, followed by practical training for about 2 years.

The fundamental purpose of the police is the maintenance of law and order, but there are many other ways in which they are of service to the community—from the relief of traffic congestion to the simple help and guidance of the general public.

There are 125 Police Forces in England and Wales, and thirty-three in Scotland, and they vary greatly in size and make-up. The largest and most complex are those in the large towns, and it is in these forces that the ambitious boy or girl will probably be most interested.

Specialist police work is done by the following branches: C.I.D., finger-prints and photography, motor patrol, wireless duties, river police work, registration of aliens. These departments draw on the ordinary constabulary for their recruits, and young people with special aptitudes have a good chance of being selected.

For the first 2 years new entrants are on probation, and during this time they have several courses and examinations. Promotion thereafter to the ranks of Sergeant and Inspector is by service and examination subject to vacancies being available. There is a contributory superannuation fund, and an officer may retire after 25 years' service on half the average pay of the last 3 years of service. Welfare and sports facilities are usually very good. One important thing to note is that the pay rates quoted (which are the minimum) do not show the "hidden income" of rent-free accommodation or allowance in lieu.

Boys and girls who have definitely decided on the police as a career (or who wish to find out for themselves what it is all about), but who are not old enough to join, can join the Police Cadets attached to certain police forces.

Addresses.

The Police Recruiting Department, Home Office, Horseferry House, Dean Ryle Street, S.W.1.

The Police Recruiting Department, Scottish Home Department, St. Andrew's House, Edinburgh, 1.

Pamphlets.

Choice of Careers Series, No. 80 (H.M.S.O.).

Your Career: Life in the Police. Available from the Home Office.

PRINTING.

B.

Age. 15–16.

Qualifications. It is said to be useful if the candidate for an apprenticeship has a relation in the firm which he wishes to join.

Pay. Basic minimum over £11 per week on completion of training. Real wages often considerably higher.

Aptitudes. Intelligence, good eyesight, neatness, attention to detail.

Method of Entry. Acceptance of candidature for apprenticeship by Local Apprenticeship Committee.

Further Training. 6 years' apprenticeship coupled with day part-time release and evening study at a Technical College.

Printing is a skilled occupation, and the term covers the activities of compositors, machine managers, photo-process workers, stereotypers, electrotypers, etc. It is also one of the most highly remunerated manual industries, and there is considerable competition for the available apprenticeships. It is therefore helpful to have the agreement of a master printer to accept the would-be apprentice when applying to the Local Apprenticeship Committee.

Some schools also run full-time courses for those interested in the ancillary aspects of printing, such as costing, estimating, paper, and administration, as well as the practical operative work. Such courses last from 2 to 3 years.

Printing enjoys one of the highest degrees of security as an individual career, and does not suffer from the recessions which periodically hit other industries.

Full details of this career can be obtained from the second address below.

Addresses.

The British Federation of Master Printers, 11 Bedford Row, W.C.1.

The Joint Industrial Council of the Printing and Allied Trades, 11 Bedford Row, W.C.1; *or* 60 Doughty Street, W.C.1.

Pamphlets.

Choice of Careers Series (H.M.S.O.), No. 45, No. 46, No. 47, No. 48, No. 49.

PROBATION OFFICER. *See* **SOCIAL WORK.**

RADIOGRAPHY AND RADIOTHERAPY.

B. G.

Age. 18.

Qualifications. At least O.

Pay. £623–£829 on qualification, senior posts rising to £1,391.

Aptitudes. Interest in people, tact, scientific outlook.

Method of Entry. Acceptance by training hospital recognised by Society of Radiographers.

Further Training. 2 years' full-time study at a training hospital leading to the Diploma Examination of the Society of Radiographers. Grants are available from the Ministry of Health.

Radiography is the taking of X-ray photographs, and Radiotherapy is the treatment of disease by X-ray and radium techniques. The training for both branches is the same during the first year, but thereafter those who are going in for Radiotherapy follow a different course. The radiographer is a member of one of the important teams of doctors, nurses, therapists, and almoners who are essential to the efficient running of the hospital service. At the moment the majority of workers in Radiography and Radiotherapy are women, but there is no reason why young men with an interest in this type of work should not make a satisfying career, especially as radiography services are expanding.

A list of the hospitals offering courses can be obtained from the Society at the address below.

Address.

The Society of Radiographers, 32 Welbeck Street, W.1.

Pamphlet.

Choice of Careers Series, No. 41 (H.M.S.O.).

SCIENCE.

B. G.

Age. 21 for graduates, 16 or 18 for technicians.

Qualifications. C.S.E., O., A. or Degree in appropriate science subjects, including maths.

Pay. Newly qualified graduates, about £800. Junior technicians £5 p.w. upwards.

Aptitudes. Imagination, enthusiasm, capacity for original thought, integrity, practical ability, ability to work with a team, patience, perseverance.

Methods of Entry. Either through a University, a College of Technology, or a post in a laboratory.

Further Training. In view of the increasing complexity of all the sciences it is important to continue with full-time study as long as possible, preferably to A level G.C.E. or beyond to a degree or Dip. Tech. or to Graduate membership of a professional institute. Those who attempt to qualify by evening classes or even on a day release course nowadays, seldom go as far as was originally hoped. There are however part time courses for technicians in a variety of applied sciences at many Technical Colleges. Syllabuses are arranged by City & Guilds of London Institute for: Chemical Technicians, Metallurgical Technicians, Science Laboratory Technicians, Illuminating Engineering, Papermaking, Plastics, Milk, Printing Ink Technicians, Dyeing of Textiles, Paint Technology and Leather Manufacture Dyeing and Finishing Technicians' Certificate.

As mathematics is the universal language of science, reasonable ability in this subject is essential. The basic natural sciences are physics, chemistry, and biology. All scientists need to be trained in scientific method to observe accurately and to consider objectively. Scientists may be employed in research; in the development of ideas; in production and the management of productive plant; in testing, analysis and control; in technical services; sales information; in lecturing at Universities and Colleges of Technology and in teaching in schools.

Addresses.

The Institute of Physics, 47 Belgrave Square, S.W.1.

The Royal Institute of Chemistry, 30 Russell Square, W.C.1.

The Institute of Biology, 41 Queens Gate, S.W.7.

The Institute of Metallurgists, 4 Grosvenor Gardens, S.W.1.

The Mathematical Association, 22 Bloomsbury Square, W.C.1.

Pamphlets.

Choice of Careers Series:
Nos. 100, 57, 94, and 109 (H.M.S.O.).

SECRETARIAL WORK AND OFFICE MANAGEMENT

B. G.

Age. 15, only rarely now, usually 16 or 18.

Pay. Varies widely, £6 to £8 per week to start.

Aptitudes. Tact, discretion, a good memory, facility with words and figures.

Method of Entry. By application for advertised posts or through the Youth Employment Service or an employment agency.

Further Training. If not qualified before entry, for shorthand typing and/or National Certificates or Diplomas in Business Studies. Also for professional qualifications.

(1) Office work generally. Owing to the increasing use of all kinds of office and computing machines, office work is changing very rapidly, *e.g.*, the proportion of girls using shorthand is decreasing, particularly in large offices, where the use of audio typing and machines requiring figure work is increasing rapidly.

(2) Secretaries are required mainly as personal assistants to management and so offer an interesting and well-paid career for the well educated, reliable, and intelligent girl, especially if she has good personal qualities. Training is usually by a full-time course at a private secretarial school or a Technical or Commercial College, after O. A. or a degree has been obtained. Women graduates (often with language qualifications) who take a secretarial course can look forward to very interesting careers, often involving travel and increasing responsibility as they gain experience.

(3) Management, *i.e.*, supervision, control, and organisation of staff, sales and marketing, buying, accountancy and finance, insurance and transport, planning and production. Training usually combines practical experience with study for appropriate qualifications.

Information about Accountancy, Actuarial work, Advertising, Banking, Insurance, Law, and Laundry work will be found elsewhere in this section. Other professional organisations which offer examinations leading to suitable qualifications are:—

Building Societies Institute, 6 Cavendish Place, W.1.

British Institute of Management, 80 Fetter Lane, E.C.4.

Chartered Institute of Secretaries, 16 Park Crescent, W.1

Institute of Office Management, 167 Victoria Street, S.W.1.

Institute of Personnel Management, 80 Fetter Lane, E.C.4.

Institute of Shipping and Forwarding Agents, 16 Park Crescent, W.1.

Institute of Transport, 80 Portland Place, W.1.

Institute of Travel Agents, 6 Duke Street, S.W.1.

Purchasing Officers' Association, York House, Westminster Bridge Road, S.E.1.

Institution of Works Managers, 34 Bloomsbury Way, W.C.1.

Pamphlets.

Choice of Careers Series (H.M.S.O.). *Office Work*, No. 65; *Company Secretary*, No. 29.

SOCIAL WORK.

B. G.

Age of Entry. 21+, more usually 22+ or after experience in paid employment.

Qualifications. Degree or Diploma in Social Studies or Degree followed by post graduate training.

Pay. Varies, usually between £750 and £1,400.

Aptitudes. Tact, patience, interest in people and in social conditions, emotional stability, a sense of vocation, persistence in arduous and sometimes discouraging work.

Method of Entry. Acceptance for specialised training, *i.e.*, appointment with Central or Local Government Authority or with a voluntary organisation.

Further Study. Specialised training for the chosen branch, and for membership of professional organisation.

Different branches of social work touch almost every aspect of life. Some are concerned with problems of work, recreation or accommodation, while others cater for special classes of persons with particular needs, *e.g.*, deprived children. Others help people who have special difficulties with their relations with others or who suffer from physical or mental illness. There are also social workers who deal with groups of people to prevent them getting in trouble or into emotional difficulties.

Social workers are trained to do case work with individuals but some work with people who may not have individual problems and so work with groups in clubs and centres.

Addresses.

Child Care: Central Training Council in Child Care, Home Office, Thames House South, Millbank, S.W.1.

Council for Training in Social Work, Clifton House, Euston Road, N.W.1.

Family Case Work: Association of Family Caseworkers, Denison House, 296 Vauxhall Bridge Road, S.W.1.

Health Visitor. *See* Nursing.

Housing Manager: Society of Housing Managers, 13 Suffolk Street, S.W.1.

Medical Social Worker: Institute of Medical Social Workers, 42 Bedford Square, W.C.1.

Mental Health or Mental Welfare Officer: Local Authority.

Moral Welfare Officer: Josephine Butler Memorial House, 34 Alexandra Drive, Liverpool 7.

Neighbourhood Workers: National Federation of Community Associations, 26 Bedford Square, W.C.1.

Personnel Manager: Institute of Personnel Management, 80 Fetter Lane, E.C.4.

Probation Officer: Probation Advisory and Training Board, Home Office, Whitehall, S.W.1.

Psychiatric Social Workers: Association of Psychiatric Social Workers, 71 Albany Street, N.W.1.

Welfare Workers with the Deaf: National Institute for the Deaf, 105, Gower Street, W.C.1.

Welfare Worker with the Blind and Home Teachers of the Blind: Royal National Institute for the Blind, Great Portland Street, W.C.1.

Youth Club Leader: National Association of Boys' Clubs, 17 Bedford Square, W.C.1. National Association of Youth Clubs, 32 Devonshire Street, W.1. Y.M.C.A., Great Russell Street, W.C.1. Y.W.C.A., 108 Baker Street, W.1.

Youth Employment Officer: Tutor-in-Charge, Full-time Course for Y.E.O.s, Lamorbey Park, Sidcup, Kent, or Manchester College of Commerce, Manchester, 1.

Pamphlet.

Choice of Careers Series No. 102, No. 28 (H.M.S.O.).

SPEECH THERAPY.

B. G.

Age. 18.

Qualifications. O preferably A.

Pay. £614–£1,185.

Aptitudes. Self-confidence, ability to speak clearly and well, liking for people, tact.

Method of Entry. Acceptance by approved training school.

Further Training. 3 years' full-time training for either (*a*) the Licentiate of the College of Speech Therapists or (*b*) the degree course at the University of Newcastle-upon-Tyne leading to the Bachelor of Education (Speech).

Speech Therapists are usually girls, but there is no reason why boys who are interested in people and who satisfy the other preliminary requirements should not make a rewarding career in speech therapy, even though the financial return is unexciting.

The work involves the remedial treatment of speech defects, especially in children, at school, clinics, and in hospitals. There is also a considerable amount of part-time work available, payment for which is on a sessional basis.

Address.

The College of Speech Therapists, 68 Queen's Gardens, W.2.

Pamphlets.

Choice of Careers Series, No. 51 (H.M.S.O.).

Speech Therapy as a Career. Available from the College.

SURVEYING.

Age. Generally 18.

Qualifications. O but usually A.

Pay. Depending on branch, but roughly in region of £600–£1,300 p.a. on qualification.

Aptitudes. Capacity for detail, methodical mind, ability to calculate quickly and accurately.

Method of Entry. In general:—

1. As a junior assistant or under articles in an approved Surveyor's office.
2. Acceptance by approved training school for full-time course.
3. As a graduate holding B.A., or B.Sc. (Estate Management).

Further Training.

1. If entering as junior assistant or under articles: at least 4 years' part-time study leading to the Final Examination of the Royal Institution of Chartered Surveyors.
2. Full-time study for the First and Intermediate examinations of the Royal Institute, followed by 2 years' practical work and then the Final Examination.
3. If entering as a graduate, 2 years' practical work.

All the above methods lead to membership of the Royal Institute.

Surveying is a profession with many specialised aspects. The various branches are: Building Surveying, Housing Management, Land Agency, Land and Hydrographic Surveying, Mining Surveying, Quantity Surveying, Town and Country Planning, Valuation.

Building Surveying is concerned with the supervision of building, building repairs, and the specifications for builders' work of all descriptions.

Housing Management is more specifically the development and management of housing estates.

Land Agency involves the management of country estates, and agricultural improvements valuations.

Land and Hydrographic Surveying is concerned with measuring and drawing the shape of the land, and mapping the rivers, lakes, and seas. Surveyors in this category are usually government servants.

Mining Surveying is concerned with underground surveys and preparing plans for workings. Surveyors are usually employed by the National Coal Board, but have great scope for work overseas.

Quantity Surveying is concerned with drawing up the estimates of materials and labour required in accordance with the architect's plans. The Quantity Surveyor is also concerned with the valuation of work executed.

Town and Country Planning deals with the preparation and development of planning schemes and involves the surveying of resources and needs of a particular area. Further study to gain the Diploma of the Town Planning Institute is advisable for this branch of the career.

Valuation. The Valuation Surveyor either works for the Inland Revenue and is employed to value real property for the Crown in connection with death duties, income tax, etc., or is in private practice and carries on similar work on behalf of private individuals.

The newcomer to this profession will have decided which branch of surveying he or she wishes to take up. Except for Mining and Land Surveying, all branches have a common syllabus for the First Examination of the Royal Institution of Chartered Surveyors, but thereafter the Intermediate and Final Examinations are on work appropriate to the specialisation being followed. The requirements of the other professional bodies vary in detail, and full information may be had from the addresses below.

There is at present a shortage of qualified surveyors in the country, partly because many surveyors obtain lucrative employment overseas, and the prospects for energetic ambitious young people are excellent.

Addresses.

The Royal Institution of Chartered Surveyors, 12 Great George Street, Westminster, S.W.1.

The Institute of Quantity Surveyors, 98 Gloucester Place, W.1.

The Incorporated Association of Architects and Surveyors, 75 Eaton Place, S.W.1.

Institute of Builders, 48 Bedford Square, W.C.1.

Pamphlet.

Choice of Careers Series, No. 87 (H.M.S.O.).

TEACHING (England and Wales).

B. G.

Age. 18+.

Qualifications. O, usually A.

Pay. Depending on qualifications, status and experience, basic scale £730–£1,400 with additions for qualifications and training.

Aptitudes. Patience, interest in the young, sense of humour, good health.

Method of Entry (State system).

1. Acceptance by a College of Education.
2. As a graduate followed usually but not necessarily by a year's course at a University Department of Education.

Note. At the moment it is not essential for a graduate (or person holding certain other qualifications in, *e.g.*, art, music) to hold a Diploma in Education of a University Department of Education, but in a few years' time this may be essential for new entrants.

Further Training.

1. If accepted by a College of Education, 3 years' full-time training. This can sometimes be combined with study for a degree (Bachelor of Education).
2. A post-graduate Diploma in Education course offered by University departments of Education.

The majority of posts in teaching are available in schools run by the Local Education Authorities or assisted by them. These fall into three main categories: Primary, Secondary, and Further Education.

The Primary System is made up mainly of Infant Schools (5–7 years) and Junior Schools (7–11). Teaching in Infants' and Junior Schools demands special qualities of patience and understanding, and it is usual for the Training College student to follow a slightly different programme of studies from those who are going to specialise in Secondary Teaching.

The Secondary System is being constantly modified by many Local Education Authorities, but basically there are two distinct patterns: (i) The Secondary Modern/Secondary Technical/Secondary Grammar organisation, and (ii) The Comprehensive System.

In the first of these children are sorted out at the age of 11 (or 13) according to their parents' wishes and their educational possibilities. Those who go to Grammar Schools need a more specialised and academic course, and it is to this type of school that most graduates are attracted. There are nevertheless many Modern Schools (which outnumber the Grammar by 4 or 5 to 1) offering courses leading to " O " and thus giving opportunities to graduates. Technical Schools (which sometimes recruit their children at 13+) offer as well opportunities to people qualified in industry and commerce who wish to enter the teaching profession.

The Comprehensive School aims at offering the facilities of the above three types under one roof, and is usually a large organisation affording opportunities to many different types of teacher.

The Further Education system comprises the Colleges of Technology, the Colleges of Further Education, Village Institutes, Evening Institutes, and is of interest to those who feel more drawn to work with young people and adults. Much of the very varied field of work in Further Education is done by part-time teachers and lecturers, but there are nevertheless many opportunities for full-time teaching.

Salaries and conditions of service have improved in the teaching profession, and it is now an attractive career (especially for women with the advent of equal pay). There are still many vacancies in all types of schools, and especially for qualified teachers of science and mathematics.

There is a need for teachers of mentally and physically handicapped children.

The independent schools are more and more coming into line with the State schools as regards salary, etc., and often are able to offer added inducements, such as free or cheap accommodation.

There are no fees for courses at the Training Colleges, and help with maintenance is available for those who need it.

The educational system and methods of teacher training are different in Scotland and Northern Ireland, and details can be obtained from the appropriate addresses below.

Addresses.

Department of Education and Science (Teachers' Branch), Curzon Street, W.1.

The National Committee for the Training of Teachers, 140 Princes Street, Edinburgh, 3.

The Ministry of Education, Massey Avenue, Stormont, Belfast.

Pamphlets.

Choice of Careers Series No. 117. (H.M.S.O.).

Becoming a Teacher.

Career in Education for University Graduates.

Department of Education and Science List No. 172 (List of Training Colleges).

Teaching Housecraft.

Teaching Handicraft.

Teaching in Technical Colleges.

You'd Like to Teach—A Chance for the Late Entrant.

The above are available from the Department of Education and Science.

VETERINARY WORK.

B. G.

Age. 18+.

Qualifications. A.

Pay.

1. In private practice as assistant, about £1,200 to commence.
2. In Government Service, from £1,281.

Aptitudes. Patience, capacity for detailed observation, fondness of animals.

Method of Entry. Acceptance on University course.

Further Training. 4–6 years' University Degree course.

Veterinary work is concerned with the maintenance of good health in animals and the cure of animal diseases—in other words, the " vet " is the animal doctor. The vet suffers from this disadvantage, however—that animals cannot speak about their symptoms. The young man or woman contemplating veterinary work as a career must, therefore, have a real understanding of and love for animals. This is what makes veterinary work a vocation rather than a career for many people.

In order to practise as a " vet " one must be a member of the Royal College of Veterinary Surgeons, and the necessary qualification for this is a University Veterinary Degree. Degree courses are offered by the following bodies:—

The Universities' Central Council on Admissions, 29 Tavistock Square, W.C.1.

Royal Veterinary College and Hospital, Camden Town, N.W.1.

Royal (Dick) School of Veterinary Studies, Summerhall, University of Edinburgh, 9.

University of Glasgow Veterinary School.

Veterinary Schools of the Universities of Bristol, Cambridge, Liverpool.

Veterinary College of Ireland, Ballsbridge, Dublin, S.E.4.

For the qualified person, openings are available with the Ministry of Agriculture, Fisheries, and Food, and for men in the Army (where after 1 year's service one reaches the rank of Captain). The majority of newly qualified people take a post as an assistant to an established vet in order to gain the necessary practical experience.

Address.

The British Veterinary Association, 7 Mansfield Street, Portland Place, W.1.

The Royal College of Veterinary Surgeons, 32 Belgrave Square, S.W.1.

Pamphlet.

Choice of Careers Series, No. 111 (H.M S.O.).

ZOOLOGY. *See* Science.

* * *

BOOKLETS.

Booklets in the series " Choice of Careers " are obtainable from H.M. Stationery Office at: York House, Kingsway, London, W.C.2; 423 Oxford Street, London, W.1; 13a Castle Street, Edinburgh, 2; 39 King Street, Manchester, 2; 35 Smallbrook, Ringway, Birmingham, 5; 109 St. Mary Street, Cardiff; 50 Fairfax Street, Bristol, 1; 80 Chichester Street, Belfast, or through any bookseller.

Choosing Your Career (1). 1s. 9d.

Accountant (59). 1s.

Advertising (44). 1s.

Agriculture and Horticulture:

Managerial and Technical Posts (85). 1s. 3d.

Architect (16). 1s. 6d.

Art and Design (103). 2s.

Baking (84). 1s. 6d.

Banking and the Stock Exchange (67). 1s. 3d.

Bespoke Tailoring (5). 1s. 6d.

Blacksmith (36). 1s. 6d.

Boot and Shoe Manufacture (3). 2s. 3d.

Bricklayer (24). 1s. 6d.

Building & Civil Engineering (110). 2s. 6d.

Chiropodist (61). 6d.

Civil Aviation (116). 1s. 6d.

Civil Service:

Junior Posts (31). 2s. 3d.

General, Scientific and Technical posts (32). 1s. 6d.

Clothing Manufacture (106). 1s. 6d.

Coal Mining (107). 2s.

Company Secretary (29). 1s.

Cotton Spinning (34). 1s. 6d.

Dancing (99). 1s.

Dentistry (96). 1s. 6d.

Domestic Science and Dietetics (13). 1s. 9d.

Dramatic Art (98). 1s. 3d.

Dressmaking and Millinery (9). 2s.

Electrician (79). 2s.

Engineering Draughtsman (60). 1s. 6d.

Engineering Work for Boys (78). 1s. 9d.

Engineering Work for Girls (77). 1s. 6d.

Farm and Horticultural Workers (86). 1s. 9d.

Fire Service (114). 1s. 9d.

Fishing (90). 1s. 9d.

Fitters, Turners, Machinists (64). 2s.

Forestry (81). 2s. 3d.

Foundry Industry (19). 1s. 9d.

Furniture Manufacture (38). 1s. 6d.

Glass Manufacturing (113). 1s. 9d.

Glazier (30). 1s. 3d.

Hairdressing and Beauty Culture (104). 2s.

H.M. Forces:

Openings for Boys in the Ranks (50). 2s.

Royal Navy (54). 2s. 3d.

Army (55). 2s.

Royal Air Force (56). 2s.

Commissioned Service (68). 1s. 6d.

Women's Services (63). 2s. 3d.

Hosiery, Knitwear and Lace (91). 1s. 6d.

Hotel and Catering Industry—Management (15). 1s. 3d.

Hotel and Catering Occupations (33). 1s. 6d.

Insurance (93). 2s.

Iron and Steel (105). 2s. 6d.

Journalism (83). 1s. 9d.

Laboratory Technicians and Assistants (94). 2s. 6d.

Laundry and Dry Cleaning (70). 1s. 6d.

Law (26). 1s. 3d.

Librarianship (4). 1s.

Local Government Service (28). 1s. 3d.

Mastic Asphalt Spreader (43). 1s.

Mathematician (109). 1s. 6d.

Medical Laboratory Technician (57). 6d.

Medicine and Surgery (108). 1s. 6d.

Merchant Navy Officers (72). 2s. 3d.

Merchant Navy Ratings (73). 2s.

Motor Mechanic (71). 1s. 9d.

Music (101). 1s.

Nursing and Midwifery (82). 2s. 6d.

Nursing for Men (89). 1s. 6d.

Occupational Therapist (53). 9d.

Office Work (65). 1s. 6d.

Ophthalmic Optician and Dispensing Optician (74). 1s.

Orthoptist (69). 1s.

Painter and Decorator (27). 1s. 6d.

Pharmacist (62). 9d.

Photography and Cinematography (115). 2s. 6d.

Physiotherapist and Remedial Gymnast (52). 1s. 3d.

Plastering (14). 1s. 3d.

Plumber and Gas Fitter (17). 2s.

Police (80). 1s. 9d.

Pottery (6). 1s. 6d.

Printing:

Bookbinding and Printer's Warehouse Work (49). 1s. 6d.

Composing Room Crafts (46). 1s. 3d.

Graphic Reproduction Processes (48). 1s. 9d.

Machine Room Workers (47). 1s. 3d.

Printing (45). 2s.

Professional Engineers (92). 1s. 9d.

Radio and Television Servicing (66). 1s. 9d.

Radiographer (41). 1s. 3d.

Railways (88). 2s.

Retail Selling (75). 1s. 6d.

Scientist (100). 1s. 3d.

Sheet Metal Worker and Coppersmith (97). 2s

Ship-building and Ship-repairing (95). 2s.

Silk, Rayon, Nylon and Cotton Cloth Manufactur (35). 1s. 6d.

Social Workers (102). 1s. 9d.

Speech Therapist (51). 1s.

Stonemasonry (8). 1s. 6d.

Surveyor, Land Agent, Auctioneer and Esta Agent (87). 2s.

Teaching (117). 2s.

Veterinary Science (111). 1s. [illegible]d.

Wall and Floor Tiler (7). 1s. 3d.

Welder and Cutter (37). 1s. 9d.

Wood Sawyer and Wood Cutting Machinist (18 1s. 6d.

Woodworking Craftsmen (25). 1s. 9d.

Wool Textiles & Carpets (112). 2s.

Note. The serial number given in bracke after each title should be quoted when orderin Postage 3d. to 5d. extra on single copies.

THE WORLD OF SCIENCE

TABLE OF CONTENTS

THE WORLD OF SCIENCE

SOMEONE has calculated that the world is now doubling the number of its scientists every ten years. We may greet such statements with enthusiastic approval; we may recoil in apprehension and alarm. What we cannot do is to deny that science will transform the mental and physical life of mankind even more quickly in future than it has in the past. For science brings knowledge and understanding; indeed, it is the most powerful system ever devised for accumulating knowledge and deepening understanding. Inevitably, therefore, science will stimulate and direct our thoughts and give us practical control over many aspects of nature which have always been uncontrolled.

Science is not to be confined in laboratories, nor is it exclusively the concern of highly trained specialists. Science has many links, mutually fertile ones, with technology of all kinds, and through technology science changes the aspect of cities, the way of life of peasants, the effectiveness of drugs, the routines of work, the comforts of homes. And, it must be admitted, science intensifies the horrors of war and many of the nagging strains of everyday life.

Because of its all pervasive social effects, because of the ambiguity of some of its gifts, science presents us with moral choices and therefore enters as an inescapable factor into politics and the arts. Nevertheless, for some scientists, understanding alone would be a sufficient prize to justify their patient studies and it is in this spirit that, in the following pages, a number of scientists have tried to explain in simple language how the universe appears to them at this time. For the moment, the formidable moral problems of how to use our knowledge are left to the reader; here we simply outline some of the main scientific concepts of today.

In Part I the inanimate universe is described. This is the domain of cosmology, astronomy, geology, physics, and chemistry. There are already many interesting links which join this realm to that of the living and make it difficult to say where the boundary lies. Nevertheless it is still convenient to accord to the biological and social sciences two separate chapters, Parts II and III. In Part IV our intention is to give some short accounts of recent discoveries and new developments in both science and technology. They are contributed by scientists actively engaged in these, their own special fields.

I. THE STRUCTURE AND ORIGIN OF THE UNIVERSE

The universe includes everything from the smallest sub-atomic particle to the mightiest system of stars. The scientific view of the universe (not the only view but the one we are concerned with here) is a remarkable achievement of the human mind, and it is worth considering at the outset what a "scientific view" is, and what is remarkable about it.

A scientific view of something is always an intimate mixture of theories and observed facts, and not an inert mixture but a seething and growing one. The theories are broad general ideas together with arguments based on them. The arguments are designed to show that, if the general ideas are accepted, then this, that, or the other thing ought to be observed. If this, that, or the other actually are observed, then the theory is a good one; if not, then the theoreticians have to think again. Thus theoretical ideas and arguments are continually subjected to the severe test of comparison with the facts, and scientists are proud of the rigour with which this is done. On the other hand, theories often suggest new things to look for, *i.e.*, theories lead to predictions. These predictions are frequently successful, and scientists are entitled to be proud of that too. But it follows that no theory is immutable; any scientific view of any subject may, in principle, be invalidated at any time by the discovery of new facts, though some theories are so soundly based that overthrow does not seem imminent.

A remarkable aspect of the scientific view of the universe is that same principles are supposed to operate throughout the whole vastness of space. Thus the matter and radiation in stars are not different from the matter and radiation on earth, and their laws of behaviour are the same. Therefore theories hard won by studies in terrestrial physics and chemistry laboratories are applied at once to the whole cosmos. Astronomy and cosmology are spectacular extensions of ordinary mechanics and physics.

LOOKING AT THE UNIVERSE.

The universe is observable because signals from it reach us and some manage to penetrate our atmosphere.

First, there are waves of visible light together with invisible rays of somewhat longer (infra-red) and somewhat shorter (ultra-violet) wavelengths. These waves show us the bright astronomical objects and, to make use of them, astronomers have constructed telescopes of great power and precision backed up with cameras, spectroscopes, and numerous auxiliaries. The most powerful telescope, at Mt. Palomar, California, has a 200-in.-diameter mirror. The next major advance in optical telescope performance probably awaits the erection of telescopes on satellites outside the earth's atmosphere, which at present acts as a distorting and only partially transparent curtain.

Secondly, there are radio waves of much longer wavelength than light. These can be detected by sensitive radio receivers with special aerial systems. These are the radio telescopes. The most well known is at Jodrell Bank and started working in 1957.

A third type of radiation from outer space impinges on the atmosphere. This is the cosmic radiation. It consists of very fast-moving fundamental particles, including protons (**F14**). Cosmic rays are detected by Geiger counters, by the minute tracks they leave on photographic plates, and by other means. The origin of cosmic rays is still uncertain, but many people think they must have an intimate connection with the nature and evolution of the universe itself.

By looking at, and listening to, the universe with optical and radio telescopes, astronomers have formed a remarkably detailed picture of its structure. The merest outline of this will now be given.

Great Distances and Large Numbers.—Let us start with nearby objects. This raises at once the question of what "nearness" and "distance" are in astronomy and how they are to be expressed. A convenient unit of distance is the *light-year*, *i.e.*, the distance that light, travelling at 186,000 miles per second, traverses in one year. Since vast numbers as well as vast distances will enter the question, we need a shorthand for large numbers. Ten times ten times ten will be represented by 10^3; six tens multiplied together (*i.e.*, one million) will be written 10^6, and so on. 10^{14} would mean a hundred million million. One divided by a million (*i.e.*, one-millionth) will be written 10^{-6};

the very small number obtained by dividing one by the product of fourteen tens will be written 10^{-14}. A light-year is $5{\cdot}88 \times 10^{12}$ miles; the radius of an atom is about 10^{-8} cm.

The Solar System.—The earth is the third, counting outwards, of nine planets revolving in nearly circular orbits round the sun. Their names and some other particulars are given in the table (**F7**). The sun and its planets are the main bodies of the solar system. Between Mars and Jupiter revolve numerous chunks of rock called the asteroids; the largest of these, Ceres, is 480 miles across. Apart from these, the solar system is tenuously populated with gas, dust, and small particles of stone and iron. Dust continuously settles on the earth, and frequently small fragments enter the atmosphere, glow, and evaporate; these are meteors or shooting stars. Sometimes larger rocks, called meteorites, hit the earth. Comets are relatively compact swarms of particles—containing ice according to one theory—which travel in elongated orbits round the sun. Their spectacular tails form under the sun's influence when they approach it. Not all comets stay indefinitely in the solar system; some visit us and go off into space for ever.

The sun itself is a dense, roughly spherical mass of glowing matter, 865,000 miles across. Its heat is so intense that the atoms are split into separated electrons and nuclei (*see* **F10**) and matter in such a state is called plasma. At the sun's centre the temperature has the unimaginable value of about 13 million degrees Centigrade (a coal fire is about 800° C.). Under such conditions the atomic nuclei frequently collide with one another at great speeds and reactions occur between them. The sun consists largely of hydrogen and, in the very hot plasma, the nuclei of hydrogen atoms interact by a series of reactions whose net result is to turn hydrogen into helium. This is a process which releases energy just as burning does, only these nuclear processes are incomparably more energetic than ordinary burning. In fact, the energy released is great enough to be the source of all the light and heat which the sun has been pouring into space for thousands of millions of years.

We may note in passing that the occurrence of these energy-producing reactions in sufficiently hot plasmas is the reason why so much effort is nowadays put into the study of plasma physics. There are many experiments being made to produce and contain hot plasma. They are man's attempts to imitate on earth the energy-giving processes in the sun.

Stars.—In colour, brightness, age, and size the sun is typical of vast numbers of other stars. Only from the human point of view is there anything special about the sun—it is near enough to give us life. Even the possession of a system of revolving planets is not, according to some modern views, very unusual.

No star can radiate energy at the rate the sun does without undergoing internal changes in the course of time. Consequently stars evolve and old processes in them give rise to new. The exact nature of stellar evolution—so far as it is at present understood—would be too complex to describe here in any detail. It involves expansion and contraction, changes of temperature, changes of colour, and changes in chemical composition as the nuclear processes gradually generate new chemical elements by reactions such as the conversion of hydrogen to helium, helium to neon, neon to magnesium, and so on. The speed of evolution changes from time to time, but is in any case very slow compared with the pace of terrestrial life; nothing very dramatic may occur for hundreds of millions of years. Evidence for the various phases of evolution is therefore obtained by studying many stars, each at a different stage of its life. Thus astronomers recognise many types with charmingly descriptive names, such as blue giants, sub-giants, red and white dwarfs, supergiants.

The path of stellar evolution may be marked by various explosive events. One of these, which occurs in sufficiently large stars, is an enormous explosion in which a substantial amount of the star is blown away into space in the form of high-speed streams of gas. For about a fortnight, such an exploding star will radiate energy 200 million times as fast as the sun. Japanese and Chinese (but not Western) astronomers recorded such an occurrence in A.D. 1054, and the exploding gases, now called the Crab nebula, can still be seen in powerful telescopes and form a cloud six or seven light-years across. While it lasts, the explosion shows up as an abnormally bright star and is called a *supernova*.

Groups of Stars.—It is not surprising that ancient peoples saw pictures in the sky. The constellations, however, are not physically connected groups of stars but just happen to be patterns visible from earth. A conspicuous exception to this is the Milky Way, which a telescope resolves into many millions of separate stars. If we could view the Milky Way from a vast distance and see it as a whole we should observe a rather flat wheel of stars with spiral arms something like the sparks of a rotating Catherine wheel. This system of stars is physically connected by gravitational forces and moves through space as a whole; it is called a *galaxy*.

The galaxy is about 10^5 light-years across and contains roughly 10^{11} stars. An inconspicuous one of these stars near the edge of the wheel is our sun; the prominent stars in our night sky are members of the galaxy that happen to be rather near us. Sirius, the brightest, is only 8·6 light-years away, a trivial distance, astronomically speaking.

The galaxy does not contain stars only, there are also clouds of gas and dust, particularly in the plane of the galaxy. Much of the gas is hydrogen, and its detection is difficult. However, gaseous hydrogen gives out radio waves with a wave-length of 21 cm. Radio telescopes are just the instruments to receive these, and workers in Holland, America, and Australia detected the gas clouds by this means. In 1952 they found that the hydrogen clouds lie in the spiral arms of the galaxy, and this is some of the strongest evidence for the spiral form.

Around the spiral arms, and forming part of the galaxy, are numerous globular clusters of stars. These are roughly spherical, abnormally densely packed, collections of stars with many thousands of members. Because of its form and density, a globular cluster may be assumed to have been formed in one process, not star by star. Thus all its stars are the same age. This is of great interest to astronomers, because they can study differences between stars of similar age but different sizes.

Galaxies.—One might be forgiven for assuming that such a vast system as the galaxy is in fact the universe; but this is not so. In the constellation of Andromeda is a famous object which, on close examination, turns out to be another galaxy of size and structure similar to our own. Its distance is given in the table (**F7**). The Milky Way, the Andromeda Nebula, and a few other smaller galaxies form a cluster of galaxies called the Local Group. Obviously it would not be so named except to distinguish it from other distinct groups and it is indeed a fact that the universe is populated with *groups*, or *clusters*, of *galaxies*. A cluster may contain two or three galaxies, but some contain thousands. So far as the eye of the telescope and camera can see, there are clusters of galaxies.

On a photograph a galaxy is a nebulous blob without the hard outline that a single star produces. Such nebulæ were formerly thought to be inside the Milky Way, but, after controversy, it was established that many of them were separate distant galaxies. By about 1920 it was known that there were at least half a million galaxies and with the advent of the 100-in. Mt. Wilson telescope this number rose to 10^8 and is being increased further by the 200-in. telescope which can see out to a distance of 7×10^9 light-years. Through the powerful telescopes the nearer galaxies reveal their inner structures. Photographs of galaxies are among the most beautiful and fascinating photographs ever taken, and readers who have never seen one should hasten to the nearest illustrated astronomy book. Rece careful co-operation between optical and radio-astronomers has revealed that some very remote galaxies are strong sources of radio waves. Sometimes these radio galaxies have unusual structures suggestive of violent disturbance.

The Expanding Universe.—Two discoveries about galaxies are of the utmost importance. One is that, by and large, clusters of galaxies are uniformly distributed through the universe. The other is that the distant galaxies are receding from us.

How is this known? Many readers may be familiar with the Doppler effect first discovered in 1842. Suppose a stationary body emits waves of any kind and we measure their wavelength, finding it to be L ins. Now suppose the body approaches us; the waves are thereby crowded together in the intervening space and the wavelength appears less than L; if the body recedes the wavelength appears greater than L. The Austrian physicist, J. Doppler (1803–53), discovered this behaviour in sound waves, and it explains the well-known change of pitch of a train whistle as it approaches and passes us. The same principle applies to the light. Every atom emits light of definite wavelengths which appear in a spectroscope as a series of coloured lines—a different series for each atom. If the atom is in a receding body all the lines have slightly longer wavelengths than usual, and the amount of the change depends uniquely on the speed. Longer wavelengths mean that the light is redder than usual, so that a light from a receding body shows what is called a "red shift." The speed of recession can be calculated from the amount of red shift.

It was the American astronomer, V. M. Slipher, who first showed (in 1914) that some galaxies emitted light with a red shift. In the 1920s and 1930s the famous astronomer E. Hubble (1889–1953) measured both the distances and red shift of many galaxies and proved what is now known as Hubble's Law. This states that the speed of recession of galaxies is proportional to their distance from us. This does not apply to our neighbours in the Local Group, we and they are keeping together. Hubble's Law has been tested and found to hold for the farthest detectable galaxies; they are about 7×10^9 light-years away and are receding with a speed $\frac{2}{5}$ of that of light.

Does this mean that the Local Group is the centre of the universe and that everything else is rushing away from us? No; Hubble's Law would appear just the same from any other cluster of galaxies. Imagine you are in a square on some fabulous chess board which is steadily doubling its size every hour; all other squares double their distances from you in an hour. Therefore the farther squares from you must travel faster than the nearer ones; in fact, Hubble's Law must be obeyed. But anyone standing in any other square would get the same impression.

This extraordinary behaviour of the universe is one of the most exciting discoveries of science. Let us envisage one possible implication. If the galaxies have always been receding, then in the past they must have been closer together. Following this to its conclusion, it seems that all the matter in the universe must have been packed densely together about 10^{10} years ago. Was this really so? The lack of any definite answer to this question is one of the things that makes cosmology so interesting.

Quasars.—In November 1962 Australian radio-stronomers located a strong radio emitter with ufficient precision for the Mt. Palomar optical stronomers to identify it on photographs and xamine the nature of its light. The red shift was so great that the object must be exceedingly listant; on the other hand it looked star-like, nuch smaller than a galaxy. By the end of 965 dozens of these objects had been discovered nd other characteristics established such as trong ultra-violet radiation and inconstancy, in ome cases, of the rate at which radiation is mitted. One great problem here is: how can ich relatively small objects generate such nconceivably great amounts of energy that they ppear bright at such huge distances? So far his is unanswered; these quasi-stars, or *quasars*, re a great mystery, though they are generally held to be an important pointer towards a deeper understanding of cosmology.

Close upon this discovery came another equally important. In June 1965 the discovery of "quiet quasars" was announced from Mt. Palomar. These share with quasars the property of being small, *i.e.*, like stars rather than galaxies, and of emitting enormous quantities of blue and ultra-violet light. But unlike quasars they are not remarkable sources of radio waves. An important thing about quiet quasars is that they appear to be much more numerous even at great distances than the unquiet ones.

THE ORIGIN OF THE UNIVERSE.

Errors of observation and interpretation occur of course. But there are many checks and repetitions made, so that, on the whole, the descriptive account of the universe would be generally agreed among astronomers. When it comes to inventing theoretical explanations, however, science is on less sure ground, and indeed the theory of the universe is an arena of controversy at present. In most other sciences experiments can be repeated and the same phenomena observed under differing but controlled conditions. This is very helpful. But, by definition, there is only one universe; one cannot repeat it or do experiments with it. On the other hand, it must be remembered that the light from distant galaxies has taken perhaps 10^9 years to reach us, so it tells us what the galaxies were like that number of years ago. Therefore we are not confined simply to describing the present state of the universe; by looking farther into space we are looking farther into the past as well. How, then, does the state of the universe vary with time?

Evolutionary Theories.—One answer to this can be obtained from Einstein's general theory of relativity. Some slight indication of what this theory is about is given on page **F15**, and its logical development is, of course, a matter for mathematical specialists. It turns out that, if we assume that matter is distributed uniformly throughout space (as observation strongly suggests), then the solutions of Einstein's equations show how the state of the universe may vary with time. Unfortunately there are many possible solutions corresponding to expanding, static, or contracting universes. As we have already seen, the actual universe is expanding, therefore the static and contracting solutions can be ruled out. There is still a multiplicity of expanding possibilities: some correspond to indefinite expansion from an initially very dense state, others to expansion followed by contraction to a dense state followed by expansion and so on repeatedly, *i.e.*, a *pulsating* universe. The "dense state" is presumably to be identified with the time when the receding galaxies were all concentrated near one another, possibly in some dense conglomeration of atoms. This initial state is thought by some to be the origin of the universe; they would say it has been expanding and evolving ever since. If the universe is pulsating, then sooner or later, gravitational attractions between galaxies will slow the observed recession down and turn it into a mutual approach and so back to the dense state. A straightforward application of the mathematics makes this dense state *infinitely* dense, and presumably something must happen before this inconceivable situation arises. For example, forces between atomic nuclei may play an important part and determine what the dense state (if any) is actually like.

The Steady-State Theory.—A rival theory was proposed in 1948 by Bondi, Gold, and Hoyle. They suggested that the universe is not changing with time; there was no initial dense state and no pulsations; the universe always has been, and always will be, like it is now. This does not mean that no local changes can be observed—this would clearly be contrary to the facts. But it does mean that, on the large scale, the clusters of galaxies have a distribution which is uniform in space and unchanging in time. If the numbers of clusters of galaxies in a large volume of space were counted every few thousand million years the answer would always be the same.

At first sight this appears to contradict outright

the observed expansion of the universe. For if the galaxies are receding from one another how can the number in a given volume remain constant? The situation is saved by a bold proposal. It is that matter, in the form of hydrogen atoms, is being *continuously created* throughout space. This gas accumulates in due course into new galaxies, so that as the old ones move apart the young ones appear to keep the numbers up. The necessary amount of continuous creation can be calculated and is equivalent to the appearance of one atom in an average-sized room every 20 million years. If this seems absurdly small, try calculating the rate of creation in tons per second in a sphere of radius 10^9 light-years.

The rate of creation is, however, much too small to have affected any of the laws of ordinary physics. The famous law of the conservation of matter ("matter can neither be created nor destroyed") is violated, but on such a small scale that physicists, it is said, should not complain. Nevertheless, some do complain and see in this violation a strong point against this theory.

The Formation of Galaxies and Stars.—On any theory of the universe, some explanation has to be found for the existence of clusters of galaxies. In all theories galaxies condense out from dispersed masses of gas, principally hydrogen.

According to the evolutionary theory, the "initial dense state" consisted of very hot plasma in a state of overall expansion. The expanding plasma was both cooling and swirling about. The random swirling produces irregularities in the distribution of the hot gas—here it would be rather denser, there rather less dense. If a sufficiently large mass of denser gas happened to occur, then the gravitational attraction between its own particles would hold it together and maintain its permanent identity, even though the rest of the gas continued to swirl and expand. Such a large mass would gradually condense into fragments to become galaxies, the whole mass turning into a cluster of galaxies.

The steady-state view is interestingly and significantly different, for, on this theory, galaxies have always been present, and the problem is one of finding how existing galaxies can generate new ones out of the hydrogen gas which is supposed to be continuously created everywhere. Moreover, this was to be done at just the right rate to maintain the galactic population density constant —otherwise it would not be a *steady-state* theory.

Inside galaxies there is an average density of the order of 10 or 20 hydrogen atoms per cubic inch; between galaxies, the density is 10^5 times less. Consequently we can imagine the relatively dense galaxy attracting the surrounding gas towards it by gravitation. If the galaxy were stationary the gas would presumably form an accretion to the galaxy. But imagine the galaxy to be moving through inter-galactic space. Then the combined effect of gravitation and motion is to create a region of increased gas density in the wake of the galaxy. This concentration in the wake becomes sufficiently large and dense to condense itself, by its own gravitational attraction, into a new galaxy. The offspring may either stay near the parent, forming an embryonic cluster of galaxies, or separate. In either case the process is repetitive and leads to the required stability in the number of galactic clusters.

Once a huge gas cloud becomes sufficiently condensed to be separately identifiable as a galaxy, further condensation goes on inside it. It is believed on theoretical grounds that it could not condense into one enormous star but must form many fragments which shrink separately into clusters of stars. In these clusters many stars, perhaps hundreds or thousands or even millions, are born at once. A small cluster, visible to the naked eye, is the Pleaides. The Orion nebula, visible as a hazy blob of glowing gas in the sword of Orion, is the scene of much star-forming activity at present.

The Changing Scene.—The 1960s are seeing revolutionary developments in both observational and theoretical astronomy. Already the attractive simplicity of the original steady-state theory has been obscured by modifications forced upon its protagonists by new evidence or theoretical objections. For example, if quasars are really a special feature of the very remote parts of the universe, then the universe is not uniform as the steady-state theory required. Since greater distances correspond to earlier times, any extra abundance of objects observed at the greater distance means that the universe was denser in its younger days than now. This favours an evolutionary theory of the universe. It has been suggested that the preponderance of distant quasars is only apparent; but the occurrence of many near-by ones has yet to be demonstrated.

Theoretical objections have also been raised to the proposals for the formation of galaxies from matter which is continuously created at all places as described above. New developments of the steady-state theory emphasise a postulated inhomogeneity of the universe: creation and expansion occurring to different degrees in different regions but all within an infinitely extended space. By this device it is possible to reconcile an overall steady-state universe with local regions (such as the one we observe) possessing evolutionary characteristics like a concentration of quasars at great distances.

On the observational side there has even been a suggestion that the initial dense state (postulated in the evolutionary theory) was accompanied by the generation of electromagnetic waves which can still be detected as they echo round the universe: such is the interpretation of a weak radio whisper received on the most sensitive apparatus (developed for satellite communications) and not attributable to any known cosmic or terrestrial source.

The Formation of the Chemical Elements.—A stable nucleus is one that lasts indefinitely because it is not radioactive. There are 284 known kinds of stable atomic nuclei and little likelihood of any more being found. These nuclei are the isotopes (*see* **F10**) of 83 different chemical elements; the other elements, including, for example, uranium and radium are always radioactive. Some elements are rare, others abundant. The most common ones on earth are oxygen, silicon, aluminium, and iron. However, the earth is rather atypical. It is especially deficient in hydrogen, because the gravitational attraction of our small planet was not strong enough to prevent this very light gas from escaping into space.

It is possible to examine the chemical constituents of meteorites and to infer the composition of the sun and other stars from the spectrum of the light they emit. By such means, the conclusion has been reached that 93% of the atoms in our galaxy are hydrogen, 7% are helium; all the other elements together account for about one in a thousand atoms. A glance at the Table of Elements on page **N34** will show that hydrogen and helium are two of the lightest elements; they are in fact the two simplest.

According to the steady-state theory, hydrogen atoms are constantly being created. The evolutionary theory supposes that the dense initial state was a system of very hot protons and electrons, *i.e.*, split-up hydrogen atoms. In either case, therefore, the problem is to explain how the heavier chemical elements appear in the universe at all. It is here that a fascinating combination of astronomy and nuclear physics is required.

We have already referred to the fact that the energy radiated from the sun originates in nuclear reactions which turn hydrogen into helium. Why is energy given out? To answer this question we note that nuclei are made up of protons and neutrons (*see* **F10**). These particles attract one another strongly—that is why a nucleus holds together. To separate the particles, energy would have to be supplied to overcome the attractive forces. This amount of energy is called *binding energy* and is a definite quantity for every kind of nucleus. Conversely, when the particles are brought together to form a nucleus the binding energy is *released* in the form of radiations and heat. Different nuclei consist of different numbers of particles, therefore the relevant quantity to consider is the *binding energy per particle*. Let us call this B. Then if elements of *high* B are formed out of those of *low* B there is a *release* of energy.

Now B is small (relatively) for light elements

like lithium, helium, and carbon; it rises to a maximum for elements of middling atomic weight like iron; it falls again for really heavy elements like lead, bismuth, and uranium. Consequently, energy is released by forming middleweight elements either by splitting up heavy nuclei ("nuclear fission") or by joining up light ones ("nuclear fusion").

It is the latter process, fusion, that is going on in stars. The fusion processes can be studied in physics laboratories by using large accelerating machines to hurl nuclei at one another to make them coalesce. In stars the necessary high velocity of impact occurs because the plasma is so hot. Gradually the hydrogen is turned into helium, and helium into heavier and heavier elements. This supplies the energy that the stars radiate and simultaneously generates the chemical elements.

The very heavy elements present a problem. To form them from middleweight elements, energy has to be *supplied*. Since there is plenty of energy inside a star, a certain small number of heavy nuclei will indeed form, but they will continually undergo fission again under the prevailing intense conditions. How do they ever get away to form cool ordinary elements, like lead and bismuth, in the earth? One view links them with the highly explosive supernovæ, to which we have already referred (**F4** (2)). If the heavy elements occur in these stars the force of the explosion disperses them into cool outer space before they have time to undergo the fission that would otherwise have been their fate. The heavy elements are thus seen as the dust and debris of stellar catastrophes. This view is in line with the steady-state theory, because supernovæ are always occurring and keeping up the supply of heavy elements. In the evolutionary theory some of the generation of elements is supposed to go on in the very early stages of the initial dense state and to continue in the stars that evolve in the fullness of time. It cannot be claimed that the origin of the chemical elements is completely known, but we have said enough to show that there are plausible theories. Time and more facts will choose between them.

The Formation of the Planets.—Did the sun collect its family of planets one by one as a result of chance encounters in the depths of space? Or was the solar system formed all at once in some generative process? To this fundamental question at least there is a fairly definite answer. The planetary orbits all lie in about the same plane and the planets all revolve the same way round the sun. This could hardly have happened by chance: indeed, it provides almost conclusive evidence for the alternative view. But what was the generative process?

Many ideas have been proposed, and the problem is very intricate. One view is that the sun and its planets formed in a stellar condensation, a feature of which was the pushing outwards from the central sun of a disc of matter which subsequently became the planets. Such a process would be regarded as normal in stars, and not exceptional.

On the other hand, the planets have been attributed to the effect of a passing star whose gravitational attraction drew out from the sun a jet of gaseous matter which condensed into the planets. Such an encounter between stars is very rare and, on this theory, the formation of planets must be an outside chance. This theory is not widely held now.

The connection between stellar and planetary theory is brought out again by the existence on the planets of the heavier chemical elements. How did they get there? If it be true that heavy elements are hurled into space by exploding supernovæ (see above), then at least one such explosion must have mingled its products with the widespread interstellar hydrogen before the planets condensed. At one time Hoyle put forward the view that the sun was once accompanied by another star (there are many such binary systems known to astronomers) and that the sun's partner exploded. Some of the ejected gases, captured by the sun's gravitational attraction, later condensed into planets, while the remnant of the star recoiled from the explosion and got away into space. This explanation was later modified in that the exploding star and the sun need not be a close pair but merely two of a cluster of stars formed at the same time.

Before leaving this subject, where theories are more numerous than firm conclusions, one more question may be raised: was the earth formed hot or cold? There are adherents to both opinions. One side would say that the planets condensed from hot gases, became liquid, and subsequently cooled and solidified, at the surface if not throughout. Others would say that dust, ice, and small particles formed in space first and subsequently accumulated into large bodies, whose temperature rose somewhat later on. With space exploration beginning in earnest, considerable future progress in understanding planetary formation can be anticipated. (*See also* **Section L: Mars, Venus, Planets**).

THE SOLAR SYSTEM.

Name.	Distance from Sun (millions of miles).	Diameter (thousands of miles).	Average density (water = 1).	Number of Satellites.
Sun	—	865	1·41	—
Mercury	36	3·1	3·73	0
Venus	67	7·6	5·21	0
Earth	93	7·9	5·52	1
Mars	142	4·2	3·94	2
Jupiter	484	85·0	1·34	12
Saturn	887	70·0	0·69	9
Uranus	1785	30·9	1·36	5
Neptune	2797	33·0	1·32	2
Pluto	3670	?	?	0

SOME ASTRONOMICAL DISTANCES.
(1 light-year = $5{\cdot}88 \times 10^{12}$ miles).

Object.	Distance from Earth (light-years).	Velocity of recession (miles per second).
Sun	$1{\cdot}6 \times 10^{-5}$	—
Nearest star (Proxima Centauri)	4·2	—
Brightest star (Sirius)	8·6	—
Pleiades	340	—
Centre of Milky Way	$2{\cdot}6 \times 10^{4}$	—
Magellanic clouds (the nearest galaxies)	$1{\cdot}6 \times 10^{5}$	—
Andromeda Galaxy	$1{\cdot}5 \times 10^{6}$	—
Galaxy in Virgo	$7{\cdot}5 \times 10^{7}$	750
Galaxy in Gt. Bear	10^{9}	9,300
Galaxy in Corona Borealis	$1{\cdot}3 \times 10^{9}$	13,400
Galaxy in Bootes	$2{\cdot}3 \times 10^{9}$	24,400
Very remote quasar	$\sim 1{\cdot}5 \times 10^{10}$	~150,000

THE EARTH.

Shape and Size.—The earth has the form of a slightly flattened sphere, the polar radius being 6,357 km. (3,950·4 miles) and the equatorial radius 6,378 km. (3,963·5 miles). Its mass is $5{\cdot}97 \times 10^{27}$ gm. and its volume is $1{\cdot}083 \times 10^{27}$ c.c.; hence its average density is about 5·5 grams per cubic centimetre. This is about twice the average density of the surface material, so it is inferred that there exists a large volume of high density material within the earth.

Structure.—From a study of the passage of earthquake waves through the earth and observations of such properties as magnetism, moment of inertia, temperature increase with depth, etc. it is deduced that the earth has a structure consisting of a series of shells. The central *core* has a radius of some 3,600 km. (2,250 miles); it is probably in part liquid, and is almost certainly composed of an alloy of nickel and iron. Separated from the core by a fairly sharp boundary is the *mantle*; this has a thickness of about 2,800 km. (1,750 miles) and is solid. It is probably composed of silicates of iron and magnesium with some metallic iron in the inner region. The outer 100 km. (62·5 miles) is the *crust*, which is solid under ordinary conditions but which may partially liquefy during periods of igneous activity. Under the continents it is possible to distinguish two layers in the crust; an upper, less dense one, probably granitic in character, known as the sial, and a lower, denser one, the sima, probably basaltic in character. The sial appears to be absent under the Pacific Ocean and very thin or absent under the Atlantic and Indian Oceans. The concept of the sial blocks "floating" in the sima provides an explanation for the observed vertical movements of continents and leads to the theory that they may have "drifted" to their present positions. The junction between the sima and the mantle is quite sharp, the break being known as the Mohorovičić Discontinuity. *See* **Mohole, Section L.**

Composition.—Direct observation of the crust is confined to the surface and mines or boreholes, the deepest of which reach only to about 5 miles. From analyses of the crustal rocks, the abundance of the elements in the crust can be estimated. The commonest is oxygen (46·6%), followed by silicon (27·7%), aluminium (8·13%) and iron (5%). The next four are calcium, sodium, potassium, and magnesium, ranging between 3·6 and 2%. These 8 elements total 97·57% of the whole crust. Most of the other 84 elements are present in amounts to be measured in parts per million; *e.g.*, copper occurs to the extent of 45 p.p.m., tin, 3 p.p.m. These are average proportions over the whole crust; to be workable as ores, concentrations need to be much higher—*e.g.*, both copper and tin ores have to contain a minimum of 1% metal to be economic. Locating the rare occurrences of such concentrations is the job of the prospecting geologist. Taking the earth as a whole, *i.e.*, core, mantle and crust, most authorities agree that the commonest element is iron, followed by oxygen, silicon, and magnesium in that order; after this, there is only partial agreement.

The Age of the Earth.—It is possible to make an estimate of the age of the earth's crust by considering the rate at which radioactive elements break down into inert elements. A number of methods are now available, the most important being those based on the study of the abundances of isotopes of lead and other elements. From the data obtained, estimates can be made of the following points on the time scale: Age of earth's crust about $5{\cdot}3 \times 10^{9}$ years (as a planet the earth has existed for several thousand million years); life emerged about 2×10^{9} years ago; first large-scale occurrence of fossils, 600×10^{6} years ago. Other points on the scale are given in the table on **F30** (10^{9} = thousand million; 10^{6} = million).

The Materials of the Earth's Crust.—Geologists recognise three main classes of rocks making up the crust—Igneous, Sedimentary, and Metamorphic. Rocks are aggregates of minerals, which may be regarded as simpler, homogeneous compounds, in contrast to the complex, inhomogenous mixture which is a rock. The bases of rock classification are minerals present, shape and size of the individual grains, and the mode of origin of the material.

Igneous rocks are usually regarded as having crystallised from a molten state, although certain types may have arisen in other ways, *e.g.*, by reaction between high-temperature fluids, of the right composition, and pre-existing rocks. Typical igneous rocks are granite and basalt; granite is coarse-grained, intrusive into other rocks, and contains the minerals quartz, potash or soda felspar, and usually a mica. Basalt is fine-grained, flows out as lava at the surface and contains the minerals augite, calcium felspar, and usually olivine. Between these extreme types are some thousands of intermediates, but together granite and basalt constitute 90–95% of all igneous rocks seen at the surface.

Sedimentary rocks are derived from pre-existing rocks by the processes of weathering and erosion, followed by transport to the point of ultimate deposition of the material, which is then converted from unconsolidated sediment to rock by the process of lithifaction. Typical sedimentary rocks are sandstone, limestone, and shale. Sandstone consists of particles of quartz and occasional other minerals, whereas shales are compacted clays, which may become slate if compressed very strongly during mountain building. Limestones may be chemical precipitates, but are commonly formed by the aggregation of skeletal material of animals. Some other sedimentary types of interest are conglomerates—lithified pebble beds—and evaporites, such as rock salt and gypsum beds. The bulk of the sedimentary rocks were formed under marine conditions.

Metamorphic rocks are produced by the action of heat and/or pressure upon pre-existing rocks, producing considerable changes in mineralogy and texture. Rocks subjected to heat alone are termed hornfelses (marbles if the original rock was a limestone). Pressure alone may produce slates, but often pressure results in shearing forces which crush and break up rocks to a fine powder (subsequently lithified), known as mylonite. Heat and pressure together produce the type of metamorphism known as regional, because it occurs over large areas (*e.g.*, the Scottish Highlands), where it can be seen to have been associated with mountain-building processes. Typical rocks of this kind are schist and gneiss; the former is a foliated rock, usually with much mica, while the latter is a banded rock, with dark and light bands of quartz and/or felspar and mica and/or hornblende. Some gneisses, called migmatites, were produced by the injection of granitic material along the foliation planes of schists.

Mountain Building.—There is no general agreement among geologists about the origin of mountains, despite many years of argument. It is a matter of observation that the great mountain ranges are built of sedimentary rocks—usually much metamorphosed in the deeper levels—and occur in relatively narrow belts of great length. The idea has developed that long narrow depressions known as *Geosynclines* develop in the crust, into which vast quantities of sediments are poured. The floor is slowly depressed by the weight of material, and ultimately the two sides of the geosyncline move together, folding the sediments both upwards and downwards, producing the complex structures seen in such regions as the Alps and Himalayas. It has been suggested that convection currents in crust, core, or mantle may provide the forces required, but some geologists believe that the earth is contracting and causing the skin to "wrinkle." Another possibility is that the sial blocks move about in the sima, and the Alps, for example, were formed when Africa drove northward towards Europe. It is suggested that radioactive heating of the sima layers may make them sufficiently mobile to allow movement to take place, and this seems to be an essential feature of most theories of mountain building.

Glaciation.—Within the last million years much of the northern part of the Northern Hemisphere was covered by ice-sheets, now reduced to the Arctic ice-cap. This has profoundly modified the landscape, especially in mountainous regions such as the Alps, North Wales, and the Scottish Highlands. The ice, moving first as valley glaciers and later as sheets over wide areas, scraped off all loose surface material, which was then available to abrade the bare rocks to give the characteristic scenery. In Britain the maximum advance of the ice-sheets brought them to the line Bristol Channel–Thames Estuary, passing just north of London. The great heaps of débris transported by the glaciers are known as moraines. The cause of the ice age is not fully understood, but it is worth noting that in the Permo-Carboniferous period in the Southern Hemisphere there was a widespread glaciation at the same time as the coal measures and desert sediments were being laid down in the Northern Hemisphere. Other glaciations are known from several other epochs as far back as 2×10^9 years.

The Oceans.—The oceans cover 75% of the earth's surface. They may be divided into three main types of environment—the *shelf seas*, bordering the continents, the *continental slopes*, transitional between the shelves and the *abyssal region*. Each region has its own type of sedimentation, fauna, and flora. Because of the virtual absence of a sial layer under the oceans, the study of the ocean floor yields special information about the sima and mantle, and may provide data leading to a solution of current problems relating to geosynclines and mountain building. Study of sedimentation in the oceans is important for understanding the ancient sedimentary rocks.

The Atmosphere.—The atmosphere at sea-level contains about 78·1% nitrogen and 21% oxygen, the remainder being carbon dioxide (0·03%) and the inert gases. It is thought that in the early stages of the earth's history much more carbon dioxide existed and less oxygen. When plants developed, the carbon dioxide was utilised in the building up of food substances with the release of oxygen in the process of photosynthesis (T29).

The International Geophysical Year, 1957–58.—The results of the IGY observations are still being analysed and discussed in order to exhaust their scientific content. It is certain that almost all the principal investigations in geophysics during the next half century and almost all the advances in our knowledge of the earth and of the forces acting upon it will be based upon the global data accumulated during the IGY. The oceans of the world have been so incompletely studied and present so many problems, many of which could not be investigated during the IGY, that further observations are to continue over a period of years, and a comprehensive programme of observations in the marine sciences has been planned.

THE WORLD OF PHYSICS.

Anyone compelled by curiosity or professional interest to look into contemporary journals of pure physics research is soon struck by the fact that the old text-book division of physics into "heat, light, sound, electricity, and magnetism" has become very blurred. The indispensable periodical of research summaries, *Physics Abstracts*, contains about 450 entries a month, under forty separate headings. This is very daunting even to the experienced physicist and, as a token of the human effort devoted to one single branch of science, it is impressive for variety, for degree of specialisation, and for sheer volume. How can the main features of this great work be presented to the non-specialist?

Two different, though complementary, sections can be distinguished. First, there is the physics concerned with the properties of matter in bulk, with solids, liquids, and gases, and with those odd but very important substances, such as paints, plastic solutions, and jelly-like material, which are neither properly solid nor liquid. In this vast domain of physics questions like this are asked: Why is iron magnetic, copper not? What happens when solids melt? Why do some liquids flow more easily than others? Why do some things conduct electricity well, others badly, some not at all? During the last century, particularly the last few decades, it has become clear that such questions can be answered only by raising and solving others first. In particular, we must ask: (i) Of what nature are the invisible particles of which matter is composed? and (ii) How are those particles arranged in bulk matter?

The first of these two questions has generated the second major category of modern physics: this is the physics of particles and of the forces that particles exert on each other. In this field, which represents science at its most fundamental, questions like this are asked: If matter is composed of small units or particles, what are they like? How many kinds of particle are there? Do the particles possess mass? electric charge? magnetism? How do the particles influence each other? How can their motion be described and predicted?

Once scientists became convinced that matter did indeed consist of particles, the *arrangement* of the particles in matter became an important question. This is the problem of *structure*. It was discovered, by von Laue in Germany and by W. H. and W. L. Bragg in England, that the structure of solids could be inferred from the way X-rays are reflected. It is well known that X-rays can penetrate solids. In doing so, they encounter successive layers of particles and are reflected from them. The reflections reveal how far apart the layers are and how the particles are arranged in space. This is the technique of X-ray crystallography. By now it has shown that most solid matter is *crystalline*, *i.e.*, it consists of a regular pattern of particles repeated over and over again to fill the volume of the solid—just as a wallpaper is covered by repeated units of design. The units in a crystal are very small, often about 10^{-8} cm. across, and the particles in them are very close together.

Liquids, on the other hand, have no repeated pattern, but consist of particles which are jumbled up, though still very closely packed—like marbles in a bag. In gases, the particles are widely separated and moving rapidly about; the average distance between particles in air is about 10 times that in ordinary solids, and air particles have an average speed of 5×10^4 cm. per sec. (1,000 m.p.h.).

In general, therefore, the structure of matter is fairly well understood. This does not mean that structure studies are out of date, but only that now they are devoted to elucidating the structure of particular substances, often extremely complex ones such as are found in living matter. We shall therefore say no more about structure, but turn to the major divisions of physics introduced above: (i) particles and their forces; (ii) the properties of matter in bulk.

I. PARTICLES AND FORCES.

The idea that matter is composed of small particles, or atoms, originated, it is true, in classical times. Nevertheless, the modern views need be traced back no farther than the beginning of the nineteenth century, when Dalton and his contemporaries were studying the laws of chemical combination. By that time the distinctions between elements, compounds, and mixtures were already made. Compounds and mixtures are substances which can be separated into smaller amounts of chemically distinguishable constituents. Elements (*see* N34) cannot be so divided. In a mixture the components may be mixed in any proportion and sorted out again by non-chemical means. In a compound the elements are combined in fixed proportions by weight. This last fact gives the clue to atomic theory.

Dalton and atomic theory.

Dalton pointed out that the fixed combining weights of elements could easily be explained if the elements consisted of atoms which combined in simple numerical ratios, *e.g.*, 1 atom of element A with one of B, or one of B with two of C, and so on. For instance, 35·5 gm. of chlorine combine with 23·0 gm. of sodium to make 58·5 gm. of ordinary salt. If we assume one atom of chlorine links with one of sodium, then the atoms themselves must have weights in the ratio 35·5 to 23·0. This turns out to be consistent with the combining weights of chlorine and sodium in all other compounds in which they both take part. Sometimes two elements combine in several different proportions by weight. But this is easily explained by assuming that the atoms link up in different numbers, *e.g.*, one iron atom with one oxygen, or two irons with three oxygens, or three irons with four oxygens. Then the three different combining proportions arise from the three different numbers of atoms, *using in each case the same ratio of oxygen atom weight to iron atom weight.*

Atomic weight.

Over the century and a half since Dalton, these ideas have been repeatedly tested by chemical experiments. No one now doubts that every chemical element has atoms of characteristic weight. By convention the number 12·0000 is ascribed to carbon and called its "atomic weight." The atomic weights of other atoms are expressed by giving their ratio to that of carbon, *e.g.*, hydrogen, 1·008; iron, 55·85. These numbers are only ratios; the real weight of one single oxygen atom is $2{\cdot}7 \times 10^{-23}$ gm.

J. J. Thomson and the electron.

Matter is electrically uncharged in its normal state, but there exist many well-known ways of producing electric charges and currents—rubbing amber, or rotating dynamos, for example. It is therefore necessary to have some theory of electricity linked to the theory of matter. The fundamental experiment in this field was made by J. J. Thomson when, in 1897, he discovered the electron.

If you take two metal electrodes sealed inside a glass vessel, and if the air is suitably pumped out and a high voltage applied to the electrodes, then the negative one emits a radiation which causes the walls of the tube to glow. The rays are called *cathode rays*. The discovery of the electron was essentially a clarification of the nature of cathode rays. Thomson showed that they were streams of particles with mass and negative electric charge and a general behaviour unlike any other atomic particle known at that time. The importance of this discovery for the world of science cannot be overestimated, and its technical progeny are in every home and factory in radio valves, television tubes, and other devices.

Rutherford–Bohr atom.

Since the electrons emerge from matter, they are presumably parts of atoms. The relation between the negative electrons and the positively charged constituents of matter was elucidated by the great experimenter Rutherford and the great theoretician Bohr. Their work, just before the First World War, showed that the positive charge, together with almost all the mass, is concentrated in the central core or nucleus of the atom about which the very light-weight electrons revolve. The diameter of an atom is about 10^{-8} cm., roughly one-three hundred millionth part of an inch. The central nucleus has a diameter about 10,000 times smaller still. The nucleus and the electrons hold together because of the electric attraction between them.

At this stage work could, and did, go on separately along several different lines:

(i) Electrons could be studied on their own. Nowadays the handling of beams of electrons of all sizes and intensities has become a major industry.

(ii) The nucleus could be treated as a special problem, and this led to the mid-century flowering of nuclear physics, to the atomic bomb, and to nuclear power.

(iii) The behaviour of electrons in the atom could be analysed; this is the great domain of atomic physics which spreads into many other sciences as well.

Volumes have been written about each of these three fields, but we can spare only a few lines for each.

The Electron.

Electrons are expelled from solids by light, heat, electric fields, and other influences. It has therefore been possible to study beams of electrons on their own *in vacuo*. Electrons inside matter, either as constituents, or temporarily in transit, can also be observed by their innumerable effects. These observations all show the particles to be indistinguishable one from another; all electrons are the same wherever they come from. They have a definite mass ($9{\cdot}11 \times 10^{-28}$ gm.), a negative electric charge, a magnetic moment, and a "spin" (intrinsic rotatory motion). No one has ever subdivided an electron or obtained an electric charge smaller than that on one electron. The electronic charge is therefore used as a basic unit of charge in atomic physics. The electron has come to be the best known of all the "fundamental particles."

The Nucleus.

The early research programmes in nuclear physics were greatly facilitated by the occurrence in nature of certain unstable (radioactive) nuclei which emit fast-moving fragments. The latter can be used as projectiles to aim at other nuclei as targets; the resulting impacts yield much valuable information. This technique still dominates nuclear physics, though nowadays the projectiles are artificially accelerated by one or other of the large costly machines designed for the purpose.

The most important early discovery was that the nucleus consists of two types of fundamental particle—the positively charged *proton* and the electrically neutral *neutron*. These two are of nearly equal mass (about 1,800 times that of the electron), and like electrons, have a magnetic moment and spin. The proton charge is equal to the electron charge, though opposite in sign. Consider a moderately complex nucleus like that of iron. This usually has 30 neutrons and 26 protons. Its atomic weight therefore depends on the total number of neutrons plus protons, but the total charge depends only on the number of protons—called the *atomic number*. The latter is denoted by Z while the total number of neutrons plus protons is called *mass number* and denoted by M. Z is also the number of electrons in the atom, since the atom as a whole is electrically neutral. The atomic number determines the chemical nature of the atom (see below), so that by altering the number of *neutrons* in a nucleus we do not change the chemical species. It is therefore possible to find—and nowadays to make—nuclei of the same element which nevertheless differ slightly in weight because they have different numbers of neutrons. These are called *isotopes*. Iron isotopes are known with 26, 27, 28, 29, 30, 31, 32, and 33 neutrons, but all have 26 protons. Only those with 28, 30, and 31, and 32 neutrons occur naturally; the rest have been made.

Stable Isotopes.

The protons and neutrons in a nucleus are bound together by strong forces called *nuclear forces*. In many cases, the forces are so strong that no particles ever escape and the nucleus preserves its identity. There are two hundred and eighty-four different combinations of neutrons and protons of this kind, and they are called the *stable isotopes*. The earth is largely composed of such stable isotopes, because any unstable ones have, in the course of time, spontaneously broken up into stable residues.

Nevertheless, there are some unstable nuclei left on earth. They give rise to the phenomenon of radioactivity which was discovered by Becquerel in 1893.

Unstable Isotopes: Radioactivity.

Becquerel found that certain chemicals containing uranium gave off rays capable of blackening a photographic plate, and shortly afterwards Marie and Pierre Curie discovered more substances, including radium, which produce similar but stronger effects. By now, about fifty chemical elements having radioactive properties are known to exist on earth, some, like radium, being strongly radioactive, others, like potassium, being so weak that the radiations are difficult to detect. These are called the *natural radioactive isotopes*.

The main facts about radioactivity are as follows: it is a *nuclear* phenomenon and (with minor exceptions) proceeds quite independently of whatever the electrons in the atom may be doing. Thus, the radioactivity of an atom is not affected by the chemical combination of the atom with other atoms, nor by ordinary physical influences like temperature and pressure. The radioactivity consists of the emission by the substance of certain kinds of rays. The early workers, Rutherford being the giant among them, distinguished three kinds of rays labelled α, β, and γ. These are described below. Whatever kind of ray is examined, it is found that the radiation from a given sample decreases gradually with time according to a definite law which states that the intensity of radiation decreases by half every T seconds. The number T, called the half-life, is constant for each radioactive material, but varies enormously from substance to substance. For instance, radium decreases its activity by a half every 1,622 years, whereas the half-life of one of the polonium isotopes is about $0{\cdot}3 \times 10^{-6}$ sec.

α-, β-, and γ-rays.

The three most well-known types of radioactive emission are quite distinct from one another.

(i) α-rays or α-particles consist of two protons and two neutrons bound together. They are ejected from the radioactive nucleus with one of several well-defined speeds. These speeds are high, often of the order 10^9 cm. per sec. Two protons and two neutrons are the constituents of the nucleus of helium, and α-particles are thus fast-moving helium nuclei.

(ii) β-rays are moving electrons. They may emerge from their parent nucleus with any speed from zero to a definite maximum. The maximum speed often approaches that of light, and is different for each isotope. The electron has a positively charged counterpart, the positron (see below), and β-rays are sometimes positrons. To distinguish the two cases, the symbols $\beta-$ and $\beta+$ are used. The naturally occurring β-radiations are almost all $\beta-$.

(iii) γ-rays travel with the speed of light because they are in fact electromagnetic waves differing from light only in the extreme shortness of their wavelength. They have no electric charge.

It is unusual, though not unheard of, for the same radioactive substance to emit both α- and β-rays. On the other hand, γ-rays frequently accompany either α- or β-rays.

γ-rays pass through matter easily; in fact, they are extra penetrating X-rays. α-rays can be stopped by thin sheets of tissue paper. α-rays brought to rest pick up a pair of electrons from the surrounding matter and become neutral helium atoms, and helium gas from this source is consequently found imprisoned in certain radioactive rocks. β-rays are intermediate in penetrating power between α- and γ-rays.

We must now try to interpret these observations.

Radioactive Disintegration.

A nucleus is a collection of neutrons and protons interacting with each other and possessing collectively a certain amount of energy. Just as some human organisations lose their coherence if they accept too many members, so nuclei can remain stable only if (i) the total number of particles is not too great, and (ii) neutrons and protons are there in suitable proportions. Radioactive nuclei are the ones for which either or both these conditions do not hold. Sooner or later such nuclei eject a fragment, thus getting rid of some energy they cannot contain. This is called a *radioactive disintegration*, and the fragments are the α-, β-, and γ-rays. α-emission relieves a nucleus of two neutrons and two protons and some energy; γ-emission simply carries off excess energy without altering the number or kind of particles left behind. β-emission is more complicated. There are no electrons normally present in a nucleus, but they are suddenly created and explosively emitted if a neutron changes into a proton; positive electrons are similarly generated if a proton changes into a neutron. β-emission is therefore a mechanism for changing the ratio of protons to neutrons without altering the total number of particles.

Both α- and β-emission change the Z of a nucleus, and the product, or daughter nucleus, is a different chemical element. α-emission also changes the M. It might happen that the daughter nucleus is unstable, in which case it too will disintegrate. Successive generations are produced until a stable one is reached. Part of such a family tree is shown below. The symbols above the arrows show the kind of rays emitted at each stage, the figures are the mass numbers, M, and the names and symbols of chemical elements can be found on N28.

$$U^{238} \xrightarrow{\alpha} Th^{234} \xrightarrow{\beta} Pa^{234} \xrightarrow{\beta} U^{234} \xrightarrow{\alpha} Th^{230} \xrightarrow{\alpha}$$

$$Ra^{226} \xrightarrow{\alpha} Rn^{222} \xrightarrow{\alpha} Po^{218} \xrightarrow{\alpha} Pb^{214} \xrightarrow{\beta} Bi^{214} \xrightarrow{\beta}$$

$$Po^{214} \xrightarrow{\alpha} Pb^{210} \xrightarrow{\beta} Bi^{210} \xrightarrow{\beta} Po^{210} \xrightarrow{\alpha} Pb^{206}$$

(Pb^{206} is stable lead).

This family exists naturally on earth, because the head of the family, U^{238}, has so long a half-life ($4{\cdot}5 \times 10^9$ years) that there has not yet been time enough since its formation for it to have disappeared.

Artificial Radioactivity.

Nowadays many new radioactive isotopes can be man-made. All that is required is to alter the M or Z (or both) of a stable isotope to a value which is incompatible with stability. The means for doing this is *bombardment*, *i.e.*, stable nuclei are exposed to the impacts of atomic particles such as streams of protons from an accelerator, the neutrons in an atomic reactor, or simply the α-particles from another radioactive substance. The new material is called an *artificially radioactive isotope*. Artificial radioactivity is not different in kind from that of the naturally radioactive substances, but the half-lives are usually on the short side. Indeed, the isotopes in question would exist in nature but for the fact that their short half-lives ensured their disappearance from the earth long ago.

Suppose a piece of copper is exposed to the intense neutron radiation in an atomic reactor at Harwell.

The more abundant of the two stable isotopes of ordinary copper has thirty-four neutrons and twenty-nine protons (*i.e.*, $Z = 29$, $M = 63$). In the reactor many (not all) of these nuclei absorb a neutron, giving an unstable copper nucleus with $Z = 29$, $M = 64$. When removed from the reactor the specimen is observed to be radioactive with a half-life of 12·8 hours. It is somewhat unusual in that it gives out both $\beta-$ and $\beta+$ rays. Some nuclei emit electrons, leaving a daughter nucleus with one more positive charge than copper, *i.e.*, a zinc nucleus ($Z = 30$, $M = 64$). One neutron has become a proton, and the resulting zinc nucleus is stable. The others emit positrons, leaving behind a nucleus in which a proton has been turned into a neutron ($Z = 28$, $M = 64$); this is a stable nickel nucleus. The overall process is one example of the artificial transmutation of the chemical elements which is now a commonplace of nuclear physics. It was first discovered by Irene and Frederick Joliot-Curie in 1934.

Lack of a Complete Theory.

Consider now a collection of, say, one million radioactive nuclei of the same kind. It is impossible to tell exactly when any one of them will disintegrate; it is a matter of chance which ones break up first. All we know is that, after a time equal to the half-life, only a half a million will survive unchanged. In general, the more excess energy a nucleus has, the more likely it is to break up, and therefore the shorter the half-life of that particular nuclear species. In principle, to calculate the half-life theoretically, one would have to have a reliable theory of nuclear forces and energies. This is still being sought after, so it is probably fair to say that while the laws of behaviour of radioactive isotopes are well and accurately known, the *explanation* of this behaviour in terms of the properties of protons and neutrons is by no means complete. *See also* Part IV: Radioactivity Today.

Nuclear fission—chain reaction.

A discovery important not just for nuclear physics but for the whole of mankind was made by Hahn and Strassman in 1939. This was the discovery of nuclear fission in uranium. One of the natural isotopes of uranium is an unstable one, U^{235}, with 143 neutrons and 92 protons. It normally shows its instability by emitting α- and γ-rays. If uranium is bombarded with neutrons, some U^{235} nuclei temporarily gain an extra neutron, which makes them even less stable. This they show by splitting into two roughly equal parts, called fission fragments, together with two or three neutrons. There are two highly important things about this disintegration. One is that the two or three neutrons can promote further disintegrations in other uranium nuclei, and the process can therefore be self-propagating; it is then called a *chain reaction.* The other is that the total mass of the fission products is less than that of the original nucleus. This mass difference does not disappear without trace; it turns into energy according to a formula referred to in a paragraph below (**F15(1)**).

Application of these new forces.

The world has found two uses for the energy liberated in nuclear chain reactions: the atomic bomb and nuclear power plants. In the first, conditions are arranged to promote and encourage a tremendous and rapid chain reaction leading to an explosion; in the second, the steady liberation of energy in the form of heat is controlled for use in turbines which can generate electricity or provide propulsion. Both uses represent epoch-making technical achievements, but mankind has yet to show itself capable of bearing sanely the burden of responsibility which nuclear physicists have laid upon it. One thing is certain: the discoveries will not cease. Already, other fissionable elements have been made and used; new chemical elements have been created; nuclear plants (" atomic piles ") have stimulated great demands for new materials that will stand the heat and radiation inside the reactor, and this promotes research in other fields of science; irradiation inside an atomic pile gives new and potentially useful properties to old materials; nuclear power drives ships and aircraft. It is difficult to write even briefly about contemporary nuclear physics without feeling keenly the ambiguity of its powerful promises.

Although so much is known about the behaviour of nuclei, the theory of the nucleus leaves much to be desired. What holds the neutrons and protons together? Why are some nuclei more stable than others? It is certain that the forces between neutrons and protons in a nucleus are unlike the electrical attractions between the nucleus as a whole and its surrounding electrons. Nor have they anything to do with gravitation. Indeed, the best description and explanation of nuclear forces is the objective of much of the contemporary research effort in nuclear physics.

Atoms.

A nucleus surrounded by its full complement of electrons is an electrically neutral system called an atom. Neither the atom as a whole, nor its nucleus, counts as a "fundamental particle" because either can be subdivided into more elementary parts, thus:

$$\text{atom} \longrightarrow \text{electrons} + \text{nucleus} \longrightarrow \text{electrons} + \text{neutrons} + \text{protons}$$

The chemical identity of the atoms of a given element, which was Dalton's key idea, depends entirely on the number and motion of the electrons. For example, the simplest element, hydrogen, has one proton for a nucleus, and one electron. The latter is comparatively easily detached or disturbed by the electric forces exerted by neighbouring atoms, consequently hydrogen is reactive chemically, *i.e.*, it readily lends its electron to build chemical structures with other equally co-operative elements. The second element, helium, has a nucleus of two protons and two neutrons; outside are two electrons in a particularly stable arrangement. Indeed, this pair of electrons is so difficult to disarrange that a special name has been coined to cover such cases—*closed shells.* Helium, with its closed shell, will not react chemically with anything. As the nuclear charge increases, different electron arrangements of greater or lesser stability succeed one another, with every so often a closed shell corresponding to one of the chemically inert gases neon, argon, xenon, krypton.

Such considerations, pursued in sufficient detail, enable atomic physics to account for all the differences and similarities among the chemical elements and, in principle at least, for the other facts of chemistry as well.

Ions.

It is possible to remove one or more electrons from an atom, leaving it positively charged. The atom is then said to be *ionised* and is called a *positive ion.* Alternatively, some atoms are capable of accepting electrons above their normal complement, thus becoming negative ions. The behaviour of ions is very important in many fields of physics and chemistry, and some of these will be referred to later.

Molecules.

Electrical attractions of various kinds cause atoms and ions to form compound groups. This is the basis of chemical combination, and the smallest conceivable fragment of compound which still preserves the chemical identity of that compound is called a molecule. Molecules have a wide range of complexity, from simple pairs of atoms to highly intricate spirals and chains composed of thousands of atoms.

Excited atoms.

Like the nuclei described above, atoms can be given excess energy and will then return to their ground state with the emission of radiation. The excess energy usually resides in one of the electrons which is executing unusually violent motion. The electron returns to normal by releasing its excess energy in the form of light whose colour is characteristic of the atom involved. Herein lies the explanation of innumerable natural and technical phenomena, such as the colours of glowing gases whether they exist in the sun and stars, in auroræ, or in street-lamps and neon signs. Herein also lies the reason for the importance of spectroscopy, which is the study of the characteristic radiation from excited atoms; for spectroscopy is not only a useful tool for the chemical identification of elements (" spectroscopic analysis ") but was one of the main routes along which twentieth-century physicists broke through to a knowledge of the inner nature of the atom.

Fields and Waves.

Maxwell and electromagnetic waves.

Atoms are held together by the electric attraction of the nucleus for the electrons. Finer details of atomic behaviour depend on the magnetic moments of the particles. Any region of space subject to electric and magnetic influences is called an *electromagnetic field.* Before the discovery of the electron, Maxwell had perfected a general theory of the electromagnetic field, giving to physics a celebrated set of equations which describe satisfactorily almost all electric and magnetic phenomena. *Inter alia,* he proved that disturbances in the electric and magnetic conditions at one place could be propagated to another place through empty space, with a definite velocity, just as sound waves are propagated through air. Such electromagnetic disturbances in transit are called *electromagnetic waves,* and their velocity turned out experimentally to be the same as that of light and radio waves—which was a decisive argument to show that both of these phenomena are themselves electromagnetic waves.

Einstein and photons.

In the years between about 1900 and 1920 this view was upset by Planck, Einstein, Millikan, and others, who focused attention on phenomena (radiant heat, photoelectricity) in which light behaves like a stream of particles and not at all like waves. A wave and a particle are two quite different things, as anyone will admit after a moment's contemplation of, say, the ripples on a pond and a floating tennis ball. The acute question was: is light like waves or particles? This celebrated dilemma soon multiplied its horns. In 1927 electrons were shown to be quite capable of behaving as waves instead of particles, and this is now known to be true of protons, neutrons, and all other fundamental particles as well.

Theoretical physicists have devised means of having it both ways. To say that light behaves as particles means that the waves of the electromagnetic field cannot have their energy subdivided indefinitely. For waves of a given frequency, there is a certain irreducible quantity of energy that must be involved whenever light interacts with anything. This quantity is the product $h\nu$, where ν is the frequency and h is a constant named after Planck. Each such unit is called a *quantum of the electromagnetic field* or a *photon* and is counted as one of the fundamental particles. Frequencies and wavelengths vary widely; typical wavelengths are: radio—hundreds or thousands of metres; radar—a few centimetres; visible light—5×10^{-5} cm.; X-rays—10^{-8} cm.

It is now accepted that every fundamental particle is a manifestation of the waves of one or other kind of field. Physicists speak of waves, particles, and fields in the same breath or rather the same equation. Little is to be gained by asking if electrons or photons are "really" particles or waves. All one can say is that they are things whose behaviour is predicted and described by certain equations. Those who must visualise can imagine particles in some phenomena and waves in others; neither conception contains the whole truth. Why should the ultimate invisible constituents of matter be forced into one or other category derived from everyday experience? For convenience, however, we shall continue to call these things "fundamental particles."

Quantum Theory.

The point of view of the last paragraph is characteristic of quantum theory, which is the currently accepted fundamental theory of matter and motion. One can reasonably ask at what position in space, exactly, is a particle? Or, what, exactly, is the wavelength of a wave? But the first question cannot be reasonably asked of a wave, nor the second of a particle. Since electrons have something in common with both, one question cannot be answered precisely for electrons without ignoring the other; alternatively, both questions can be given an imprecise answer. As the wavelength of electrons is intimately connected with their speed, one has to accept an accurate knowledge of the speed (wavelength) and ignorance of position, or the converse, or *inaccurate* knowledge of both. This is the famous Heisenberg Uncertainty Principle. Quantum theory is a set of mathematical rules for calculating the behaviour of fundamental particles in accordance with the Uncertainty Principle. In spite of its equivocal-sounding name, the principle has led to an enormous increase in the accuracy with which physical phenomena can be described and predicted. Quantum theory includes all that previous theories did and more.

Quantum theory grew up in the same epoch as the Theory of Relativity. Heroic attempts have been made to combine the two, but with only partial success so far. Relativity is concerned with all motion and all physical laws, but its characteristic manifestations occur only when something is moving with nearly the velocity of light. Quantum theory is likewise all-embracing, but its typical phenomena almost always occur when something on the minute atomic scale is in question. Consequently, the vast majority of everyday mechanics needs no more than the classical theory laid down by Newton, which is neither relativistic nor quantum.

Relativity.

Historically, relativity grew out of attempts to measure the speed with which the earth moved through that hypothetical medium, called the ether, which was supposed at that time to be the bearer of light waves. To take a simple analogy: sound waves travel through still air with a certain definite speed, v. If you move through the air with speed v' towards oncoming sound waves, they will pass you at the speed $v + v'$. Michelson and Morley, in their celebrated experiment of 1887, failed to find the corresponding behaviour on the part of light. This is so important an experiment that it has been repeated, and repeatedly discussed, ever since. In October 1958 the latest and most accurate confirmation of the Michelson–Morley result was announced. It seems as if light always travels with the same speed relative to an observer, however fast he moves relative to anything else. Einstein put it this way: two observers moving with any constant velocity relative to each other will always agree that light travels past them at the same speed; this speed is denoted by c, and is approximately 186,000 miles per second.

This postulate, logically developed, leads to remarkable conclusions. For instance: if you walk from tail to nose of an aircraft at 4 m.p.h. and the plane is receding from me at 300 m.p.h., then you recede from me at 304 m.p.h. "Common sense," Newton, and Einstein would all agree on this. But if you could walk at 0·25c and the plane moved at 0·5c, the Newtonian mechanics would give your recession speed as 0·75c, whereas Einsteinian relativity would give about 0·71c. Although at the everyday speed of 300 m.p.h., the disagreement, though present in principle, is absolutely negligible, at speeds near that of light it becomes very pronounced. Many experiments show that the relativity answer is right.

Equivalence of mass and energy.

Another famous consequence of relativity is the equation $E = mc^2$, connecting energy, E, with mass, m. c is so great that when mass is converted to energy a small mass gives a large energy. The grim demonstration of this was given to the world at Hiroshima; a more hopeful one at Calder Hall. The life-giving energy of the sun is derived from nuclear processes which consume mass and deliver energy according to this equation.

Mass and rest mass.

"Mass" is far from being a simple notion. The only complication we shall note here is that the mass of a body is not necessarily constant. A stationary body can be observed to have a mass called its *rest mass*. If the body moves, it has energy of motion and therefore, according to Einstein's mass–energy equation, it increases its mass. Mass thus depends on speed, but in such a way that there is very little change unless the speed approaches that of light. Many experiments on atomic particles demonstrate this. The interesting question now arises: do all fundamental particles have rest mass? or do some have mass derived solely from their energy? The answer appears to be that photons and neutrinos have no rest mass; all other particles have. The Table on **F14** gives their rest masses.

Special theory of relativity.

The mathematical development of Einstein's ideas, leading to the conclusions just referred to, constitutes the Special Theory of Relativity. Stated more generally, the theory raises the question whether two observers in uniform relative motion could ever detect, as a result of their relative speed, any difference in the physical laws governing matter, motion, and light. To this, Special Relativity answers: No. The detailed theory involves special consideration of the results the two observers would obtain when measuring (i) the spatial distance, and (ii) the time interval, between the same two events. It turns out that they would not agree on these two points. They would agree, however, on the value of a certain quantity made up jointly of the spatial distance and the time interval in a somewhat complex combination. The intimate mixture of space and time in this quantity has led to the treatment of the three space dimensions and time on an equivalent footing. Hence the frequent references to time as the "fourth dimension." Minkowski devised an extremely elegant presentation of relativity theory by using an extension of ordinary geometry to four dimensions. A line drawn in his four-dimensional space represents the path of a particle in space and time, *i.e.*, the whole history of the particle. Thus the movement of particles in the ordinary world is turned into the geometry of lines in Minkowski's four-dimensional world of "space-time."

SOME MEMBERS OF THE ATOMIC FAMILY

The numbers in brackets after the name denote first the electric charge and second, the mass. The charge on an electron is counted as −1 unit and the electron mass as +1 unit. Thus (+1, 207) means the particle has a positive charge of 1 unit and a mass 207 times that of the electron.

Photon (0, 0)	A quantum of electromagnetic radiation, *e.g.*, light, X-rays, γ-rays. The concept was introduced by M. Planck in 1900 when he described the emission of light as taking place in "packets" rather than in a steady stream. The energy of a photon is proportional to the frequency of the radiation and inversely proportional to the wavelength.
	Leptons
Electron (−1, 1)	Discovered by J. J. Thomson in 1897. The number of orbital electrons in an atom determines its chemical properties. Actual rest mass = $9{\cdot}1 \times 10^{-28}$ gm. Emitted as β-rays by some radioactive nuclei. A stable particle.
Positron (+1, 1)	Positive counterpart or, "anti-particle," to the electron. Predicted theoretically by P. A. M. Dirac in 1928 and first discovered in cosmic rays by C. D. Anderson in 1932. Emitted as β-rays by some radioactive nuclei. When positrons and electrons collide they usually annihilate each other and turn into γ-rays; consequently, positrons only last about 10^{-10} sec. within ordinary matter, but are stable in isolation.
Neutrino (0, 0) and Anti-neutrino (0, 0)	These particles travel with the speed of light and are distinguished from one another by the relation of their spin to their direction of motion. A neutrino is emitted with the positron during positive β-decay; and an anti-neutrino with the electron during negative β-decay. Their interaction with matter is extremely slight. First postulated by Pauli in 1933 and detected in 1956. π-meson decay also produces neutrinos and anti-neutrinos but in 1962 it was proved experimentally that these are a different species. Thus there are two kinds of neutrino each with an anti-neutrino. All these particles are distinguished from photons by having different spin.
Muon (±1, 207)	Similar to, but heavier than, the electron and positron; disintegrates into electron (or positron if positive) +neutrino +anti-neutrino.
	Mesons
Pion (±1, 273) or (0, 264)	The π-meson. Charged pions decay either into muons and neutrinos or into electrons and neutrinos. Neutral pions decay into γ-rays, into "positron-electron pairs," or both. Pions are intimately connected with nuclear forces, *i.e.*, with the "strong" interaction.
Kaon (±1, 967) or (0, 974)	The K-mesons. These decay in many different ways producing other mesons, electrons, and neutrinos.
	Baryons
Proton (+1, 1836·1)	The positively-charged constituent of nuclei; the hydrogen nucleus is one proton. Fast-moving protons occur in cosmic rays. Does not spontaneously disintegrate.
Anti-proton (−1, 1836·1)	Negative anti-particle of the proton. Its existence was long suspected. Artificially produced and detected for the first time in 1955. Will react with the proton to produce pions or kaons.
Neutron (0, 1838·6)	Discovered by J. Chadwick in 1932. The neutral constituent of nuclei. When free it spontaneously disintegrates into a proton, an electron, and an anti-neutrino, after an average lifetime of about 18 minutes. Passes through matter much more easily than charged particles.
Anti-neutron (0, 1838·6)	The anti-particle of the neutron from which it is distinguished by properties connected with its magnetic moment and spin. Will react with neutron to produce pions or kaons.
Lambda Particle (0, 2183)	Discovered in 1947. Decays into proton plus pion.
Sigma Particle (0 or ±1; about 2330)	Various modes of disintegration, producing neutrons, protons, mesons and lambda particles.
Omega Minus (−1, 3270)	Predicted by recent theory and discovered at Brookhaven, New York, in 1964. Still under intensive study.

Gravitation.

General theory of relativity.

The apparently innocuous extension of the preceding ideas to include observers in accelerated relative motion opened up new fields of mathematical complexity, but enabled Einstein to bring gravitation into the argument. In speaking of atoms and particles we have not yet mentioned gravity. This is because the electrical and magnetic forces acting between the particles constituting matter are much stronger than the gravitational; gravity need not enter atomic theory at all. But in the discussion of astronomical problems and the movements of large-scale, electrically uncharged bodies, it has been usual, ever since Newton, to say that two bodies of mass m_1 and m_2, separated by a distance r, attract one another with a force proportional to m_1m_2/r^2. This is Newton's inverse square law of gravitation. With this, Newton explained the movements of planets and comets and the falling to earth of the apple from his tree.

The apple's fall is accelerated, and we observe this by noting its position relative to certain marks fixed with respect to us, and by timing it with some sort of clock. This system of location in space and time may be called our "frame of reference." We therefore assert that, in our frame of reference, the apple falls down with an acceleration which Newton saw no alternative but to attribute to a thing called gravitational attraction. Galileo had shown that *all* bodies fall with the same acceleration at all points, and we can now rephrase this by saying that in our frame of reference there is a constant gravitational attraction or *uniform gravitational field*. (This last statement and Galileo's demonstration only refer strictly to points fairly near the earth's surface; at greater distances the gravitational field decreases and is therefore not uniform.)

Now suppose a collection of falling bodies is observed by an intelligent creature, designated C, who inhabits one of them. C has his own frame of reference fixed relative to him. In C's frame neither his own body, nor any of the others, is accelerated, and therefore he has no reason to suppose a gravitational force is acting on them. We have, therefore, the following situation:

(i) in our frame, fixed relative to us, we find all the bodies falling subject to a gravitational pull;

(ii) in C's frame, undergoing accelerated fall relative to us, no gravitational field is apparent.

It looks, therefore, as if one has only to choose the correct frame of reference for the measurements in order to remove the need for any assumptions about the existence of gravitational fields. This is a simple illustration of the connection between gravitation and frames of reference for the measurement of space and time. Einstein's General Theory of Relativity extends this to cover non-uniform gravitational fields and shows that what Newton taught us to call the gravitational field of material bodies is better thought of as a peculiarity of the space and time in the neighbourhood of such bodies. Since space–time, as we mentioned above, can be expressed in geometrical terms, Einstein has transformed the theory of gravitation into an exercise (a difficult one) in the geometry of space–time. Other physicists, in Einstein's tradition, are trying to turn *all* physics into geometry, but no one knows whether this is really feasible.

All this abstruse work is much more than a demonstration of mathematical power and elegance. Observable phenomena which fall outside the scope of Newton's theory of gravitation are accounted for by relativity. One is the small but definite discrepancy between the actual orbit of the planet Mercury and the predictions of Newton's theory. Another is the bending of stellar light rays as they pass close to the sun, an effect which results in the apparent displacement of the position of the star. A third is the effect of a gravitational field on the wavelength of light emitted by atoms. Similar atoms in different places in a gravitational field emit radiations with slightly different wavelengths. For example, the light from an atom in the intense field of a star should have slightly longer wavelength than the corresponding light from an atom on earth. This effect has always proved very difficult to detect with certainty. However, Einstein's prediction was verified with moderate accuracy in 1960 by a very subtle method which was purely terrestrial in its operation. The atoms being compared were placed at the top and bottom of a water tower and the difference in their emission was detected by means that belong rather to nuclear physics than to astronomy.

Particles.

Nature seems to use four different kinds of force to make one particle interact with another. The weakest force is gravity; while this dominates celestial mechanics its effect inside atoms is negligible compared with the other three. The binding forces inside atoms are *electromagnetic*, *e.g.*, the attraction of nuclei for electrons. Considerably stronger still is the nuclear force which holds the nuclei together and this is called the *strong interaction*. The fourth force is called the *weak interaction* and is intermediate in strength between electromagnetic and gravitational forces. It is responsible for a number of phenomena of which the best known is β-radioactivity.

Particles may respond to some or all of the forces. Protons are involved with all of them but electrons respond to all except the "strong interaction." When new particles are discovered physicists try to find out their fundamental properties and among these is their response (if any) to each kind of force. Some other basic properties are: electric charge (if any), mass (if any), and the speed with which the particle splits up spontaneously into other types.

In the last few years *Pears* has contained a table of "elementary particles" headed The Atomic Family. By 1965 so many of these had been discovered (about a hundred) that the whole conception of "elementary-ness" was in question. Are all the particles equally "elementary"? Are some of them excited states or combinations of others? When a family reaches a hundred it becomes difficult to believe they are *all* grandparents. One current trend is away from setting up a hierarchy in which some particles are elementary and some composite and towards treating them all as mutually dependent for their existence. This, however, is a very difficult problem, not yet solved.

A few particles are stable but most decay into products. The lifetimes of unstable particles are extraordinarily short by everyday standards but, even so, some (of about 10^{-17} sec. or upwards) are much longer than others (of about 10^{-22} sec.). The Table on page **F14** contains the stable particles and a *selection* of the moderately unstable ones with brief comments on their properties.

The Table shows a rudimentary classification into four groups: (i) the photon; (ii) leptons—which are particles, lighter than protons, which do not react to the "strong" type of force; (iii) mesons—which are particles, lighter than protons, which are subject to all the kinds of force; (iv) baryons—which include protons, neutrons, and heavier particles, all of which react to the "strong" force. Many of these particles have been produced for the first time in recent years by bombarding matter with beams of high energy particles. Much of this work is done in the large accelerating machines at Brookhaven, New York, and the European Organisation for Nuclear Research, Geneva.

Forming particles into groups is an important matter. It is comparable with arranging chemical elements into the Periodic Table. The pattern does not of itself explain anything but it strongly suggests where to look for explanations. The classification of particles currently favoured is based on the very sophisticated mathematical ideas known as *group theory*. Group theory is a branch of mathematics which is finding increasing application in physics and it had a resounding success recently which illustrates the value of grouping. It turned out that there was no known particle to occupy a vacant position in one of the family groups required by the theory. This particle, the omega minus, was sought and found with exactly the right properties in February 1964. This is reminiscent of finding the missing elements in the Periodic Table. The discovery of omega minus generated much excitement in the scientific world and many physicists believe that a new and deeper understanding of fundamental physics is just round the corner. If this turns out to be so, then the careful grouping and classification of particles according to regularities in their properties will have played a vital role.

Conclusion.

Over a century's development of the atomic ideas has brought a progressive, if jerky, increase in the mathematical precision of the theories. In some fields of particle physics, observations to one part in a million, or even better, can be explained, to that level of accuracy, by the existing theories. At the same time, however, the theories have lost visual definition. An atom as an invisible but none the less solid billiard ball was easy enough; so was a light wave conceived like a sound wave in air. Even after Rutherford, an atom consisting of a miniature solar system merely exchanged the solid billiard ball for a system of revolving billiard balls and was no great obstacle to visualisation. But since quantum theory and the Uncertainty Principle, every unambiguous visualisation of fundamental wave-particles leaves out half the picture, and although the electrons are in the atom, we can no longer represent them in definite orbits. The moral seems to be that visualisation is unnecessary, or at best a partial aid to thought. All the theoretical knowledge is in the equations, and these are very precise. Hence the non-physicists' grumble—that physics is too mathematical these days—has some justification, and hence also the growing distinction in physics between the theoreticians, who are usually mathematically trained, and the experimenters, who can rarely read the papers their theoretical colleagues write, but provide the results for them to write about.

II. THE PROPERTIES OF MATTER IN BULK.

One of the most obvious and at the same time most wonderful things about the properties of matter is their great variety. Think of air, diamond, mercury, rubber, snow, gold, pitch, asbestos. . . . Even the differences of state of the same chemical substance are remarkable enough, ice, water, and steam, for example. One of the aims of physics is to reach an understanding of all these different properties by explaining them in terms of the behaviour of the particles discussed in the previous section (**F9–15**). The widespread success with which this imposing programme has been carried out indicates the maturity of physics. It is difficult to think of any major property of matter in bulk for which there is not some attempted theoretical explanation, though future physicists will no doubt regard some present-day theories as rudimentary or incorrect.

Physics, Statistics, and Thermodynamics.

Take a number equal to the population of London, multiply it by itself, and multiply the product by another million. The answer is about the number of molecules in 1 cubic centimetre of ordinary air. They are constantly moving about and colliding with one another. Even if the nature of the molecules and their laws of motion were perfectly understood, it would clearly be impracticable to calculate the exact paths described by each particle of so vast an assembly. This difficulty brought into being a whole branch of physics concerned with calculating the overall or average properties of large numbers of particles. Just as statisticians will provide the average height, income, expectation of life, and so on, of the population of London, without knowing everything about every individual, so statistical physicists can work out average properties of molecules or atoms in large groups. This important branch of physics is called *Statistical Mechanics*. It was founded in the nineteenth century by Maxwell, Boltzmann, and Gibbs and is still being actively developed.

Consider now all the molecules in 1 cubic centimetre of air contained in a small box. They are continually bombarding the walls of the box and bouncing off. This hail of impacts (it is actually about 10^{23} impacts per square centimetre per second) is the cause of the pressure which the gas exerts against the walls of the box. Now suppose we pump air in until there is twice as much as before, though the box is still the same size and at the same temperature. This means that the density of the gas (*i.e.*, the mass of 1 unit of volume) has doubled. We should now expect twice as many impacts per second on the walls as before, and consequently twice the pressure. We therefore arrive at a conclusion that, if the volume and temperature are constant, the pressure of a gas is proportional to its density. This is one of the simplest statistical arguments that can be checked against observation; in fact, it stands the test very well.

Heat, temperature, and energy.

The proviso about the temperature remaining the same is an important one for the following reason. In the nineteenth century there was much discussion about the nature of heat. To Joule we owe the now well-established view that heat is equivalent to mechanical work. In one of his experiments, in the 1840s, the work necessary to rotate paddle wheels against the resistance of water in a tank generated heat that caused a slight rise in the temperature of the water. Joule found out exactly how much work was equivalent to a given quantity of heat. However, one can do other things with work besides generate heat; in particular, work creates motion, as when one pushes a car. Bodies in motion possess a special form of energy, called kinetic energy, which is equal to the work done in accelerating them from a state of rest. We have, then, three closely connected ideas: work, heat, and kinetic energy. Now according to the views of the nineteenth century, which are still accepted, any heat given to a gas simply increases the kinetic energy of its molecules; the hotter the gas, the faster its molecules are moving. If, therefore, the gas in our box is allowed to get hotter, there is an increase in molecular speed, and the impacts on the walls become correspondingly more violent. But this means the pressure increases, so we have another law: if the density remains the same, the pressure increases if the temperature does.

Laws of Thermodynamics.

Such considerations as these have been pursued with great elaboration and subtlety. The notions of heat, temperature, energy, and work—familiar but vague in everyday life—have been given precise definitions, and the relations between them have been enshrined in the Laws of Thermodynamics. Enshrined is perhaps a suitable word, because these laws are so soundly and widely based on experimental results that they have greater prestige than any others in physics. If any proposed physical law comes in conflict with thermodynamics, then so much the worse for that law—it has to be revised. It is sometimes asserted that no one is properly educated who does not understand the Second Law of thermodynamics. We cannot, therefore, leave this section without at least stating the two best known thermodynamic laws:

First Law: *If any physical system is given a quantity of heat, and if the system performs some work, then the energy of the system increases by an amount equal to the excess of heat given over work done.* This law asserts that heat, energy, and work are convertible one into the other, and that all such transactions balance exactly. This is one form of a principle accepted as fundamental in all science, *viz.*, the Principle of the Conservation of Energy, according to which energy can never be created or destroyed, but only changed from one form to another.

Second Law: *It is impossible to make an engine which will continuously take heat from a heat source and, by itself, turn it all into an equivalent amount of mechanical work.* In fact, all engines which produce work from heat—steam engines for example—always use only a fraction of the heat they take in and give up the rest to some relatively cool part of the machine. The Second Law makes this obligatory on all work-from-heat devices. This statement of the Second Law has an engineering ring about it and, indeed, it arose from the work of the nineteenth-century French engineer Carnot. Nevertheless, it can be rephrased in very abstract terms, and has been applied with unbroken success to all fields of science involving the transfer of heat and allied matters. It sets a definite limit to the kinds of physical process that can be conceived to take place. Nothing has been known to contravene it.

The States of Matter.

The molecular motion in gases has been referred to in the previous section. Tacitly it was assumed that each molecule acted independently of all others, except that collisions occurred between them. In reality, molecules exert attractive forces on one another and, if a gas is cooled so that molecular movements become relatively sluggish, a time comes when the attractive forces succeed in drawing the molecules close together to form a liquid. This process is called condensation.

The molecules in a liquid are packed tightly together and they impede each others' movements. On the other hand, movement still persists, and the molecules struggle about like people in a milling crowd. Besides wandering about, the molecules vibrate. These motions represent the energy contained in the liquid.

The fact that the molecules, though irregularly packed, can still slip past one another and move from place to place, explains the essential property of liquids that distinguishes them from solids—ability to flow. As a matter of fact, although the rather vague assertion that in a liquid molecules are irregularly packed would be generally accepted, there is no agreed opinion on what the irregularity is actually like. Indeed, not only the precise structure of liquids, but the theory of liquids in general, is fraught with such considerable mathematical difficulties that the liquid state is much less well understood than the solid or gaseous.

Most solids are crystals. The popular idea of a crystal is of something which has a more or less regular geometrical form with faces that glint in the light—like snowflakes or gems. However, crystallinity really depends on a regular inner pattern of the atoms, and may or may not show itself on the visible surface. A lump of lead, for example, is crystalline, though it may not look it.

The actual arrangement of the atoms in a crystal can be extremely complex. Some are quite simple, however. The largest model of a crystal structure must surely be the 400-ft. "Atomium" building in the 1958 Brussels Exhibition. This consisted of eight balls, representing atoms, situated at the corners of a cube, and one more ball exactly in the middle. Imagine this repeated in all directions so that every ball is the centre of a cube whose corners are the eight neighbouring balls. This is known to crystallographers and physicists as the "body-centred cubic structure"; it is the actual arrangement of atoms in iron, sodium, chromium, and some other metals. If every ball, instead of being the centre of a cube, were the centre of a regular tetrahedron (a solid figure with four equal triangular faces), and had its four neighbours at the corners of the tetrahedron, then we should have the "diamond structure." This is how the carbon atoms are arranged in diamonds.

In crystals the atoms are locked into a regular ordered structure by attractive forces which give the solid its rigidity and prevent it from flowing. The atoms are so close together that any attempt to press them closer involves crushing or distorting the atoms—a process they resist strongly. This explains why solids (and liquids too) are so difficult to compress. Gases can easily be compressed because there is so much space between the molecules.

The distinction between solid and liquid is not so sharp as is commonly supposed. A lump of dough will not bounce, but is plastic; a steel ball-bearing is very elastic and bounces excellently, but one cannot mould it in the fingers. Neither dough nor steel qualifies for description as a liquid. There are, however, substances which can be moulded like plasticine into a ball that will then bounce very well on the floor like an elastic solid, and finally, if left on a flat table, will spread into a pool and drip off the edge like a liquid. There is no point in trying to force such things into rigid categories. One may say instead that for short, sharp impacts the material behaves like an elastic solid, but under long-sustained forces it flows like a liquid. The properties of these, and many other anomalous materials, are increasingly engaging the attention of those who study the science of flow—*rheology*. It is interesting to see how many familiar and important materials exhibit peculiar rheological behaviour—paint, dough, ball-pen ink, cheese, unset cement, and solutions of nylon and other plastics are only a few examples.

Inside a Crystalline Solid.

We now return to our wallpaper analogy of crystal structure and give some free play to our visual imagination.

Suppose we have walls papered with a regular pattern of, say, roses, fuchsias, and green leaves. These represent the different kinds of atoms in the solid. Careful observation shows that the whole pattern is shimmering. The flowers and leaves are not stationary, but are undergoing slight random oscillations about their proper positions. In a crystal these movements are called thermal vibrations, and are never absent. The hotter the crystal, the more the vibration, and at a high enough temperature the vibrations become so great that the atoms get right out of position and the pattern disappears altogether, *i.e.*, the crystal melts. Thermal vibrations are essential to the theory of solids, and are responsible for numerous physical properties.

Next we note something extraordinary about some of the papered walls. On these the paper has been hung in irregular patches fitted together like a not very well-made jig-saw puzzle. Lines of roses which should be vertical are horizontal in some patches, oblique in others. This represents the situation in most ordinary solids, for they consist of many small pieces of crystal irregularly packed together. Such material is called *polycrystalline*, and the small pieces are *crystal grains*. Crystal grains may be almost any size, sometimes visible to the naked eye, as often on galvanised iron.

However, on one wall, we see excellent regularity and no obvious patches at all. The physicist would call this a *single crystal*, and several techniques exist for preparing them. Natural single crystals can be found, and there are some beautiful large single crystals of rock salt. But on examining the single crystal wall closely, we find a number of places where the paperhanger has failed to make adjacent pieces register perfectly—there is a slight disjointedness. This occurs in real single crystals, and the line along which the structure fails to register is called a *dislocation*. These are much studied by physicists because of their bearing on the mechanical properties of solids, on the yielding of metals under strong stress, for instance.

This by no means exhausts the possibilities of the wallpaper analogy; several other phenomena can be found. For example, in a place where there should be a fuchsia there is actually a daffodil—something completely foreign to the pattern. Or perhaps a small wrongly shaped leaf is jammed between the proper leaves in a place that should really be blank. These represent chemical impurity atoms. The first is called *substitutional*, because it occupies the position of an atom that should be there, the second is called *interstitial*, because it does not. Substitutional impurities of indium metal, deliberately added to the semi-conductor germanium, make possible the manufacture of transistors (*see* **Section L**). Some steels derive their valuable properties from interstitial carbon atoms within the iron pattern.

What physicists call a vacancy would occur if a flower or leaf were simply missing. Remembering that all the atoms are vibrating, we should not be surprised if occasionally an atom jumps into a neighbouring vacancy if there happens to be one, *i.e.*, the atom and the vacancy change places. Later this may occur again. In the course of time, a rose which was near the ceiling may make its way to the floor by jumping into vacant rose positions when they occur near enough. This process, which the physicist calls *diffusion*, is also analogous to the game in which numbers or letters can be moved about in a flat box because there is one vacant space to permit adjustment. The more vacancies there are in a crystal, the faster diffusion occurs. It is, in fact, very slow in solids, but is nevertheless evidence that apparently quiescent materials are really internally active.

Metals, Electricity, and Heat.

There is ample evidence that inside metals there are large numbers of free electrons. To illuminate this statement let us take sodium metal as an example. One single sodium atom has a nucleus with eleven protons; there are therefore eleven electrons in the atom. The outermost one is easily detached, leaving a positively charged sodium ion behind. We may think of these ions arranged in the three-dimensional pattern characteristic of sodium crystals. It is the same as the iron structure previously described. The detached electrons, one per atom, occupy the spaces in between. The usual metaphor is that the structure of ions is permeated by a "gas" of electrons. Like all visualisations of fundamental particles, this must be taken as a rough approximation. The important point is that the electrons in the gas are not bound to individual atoms but may wander freely about the crystal, hindered only by the collisions they make with the vibrating ions.

This is the picture as it appeared to physicists of the first decade of this century, and we can explain many properties of metals with it. Naturally the theory has developed greatly since then, thanks to the great work of Lorentz, Sommerfeld, and Bloch; it now relies heavily on quantum theory, but it is surprising how little violence is done to modern ideas by the simple picture we are using.

The free electrons move randomly in all directions at thousands of miles per hour. If the metal is connected across a battery it experiences an electric field. Electrons are negatively charged particles, and are therefore attracted to the electrically positive end of the metal. They can move through the metal because they are free; this flow is not possible to those electrons which remain bound to the ions. The function of the battery is to keep the flow going and, for as long as it is going, it is the electric current.

The flow of electrons is not unimpeded. They constantly collide with the ions and are deflected from the path of flow. This hindrance is what the electrician calls *electrical resistance*. The electric force, due to the battery or a dynamo, accelerates the electrons, thus giving them extra energy; but they lose this to the ions at collisions because the ions recoil and vibrate more than before. The net effect of innumerable collisions is to increase the thermal vibrations of the ions, *i.e.*, to make the metal hotter. This is the explanation of the fact well known to every user of electric irons: that electric current heats the conductor. If a strong current is passed through a wire, the heating is so great the wire glows, as in electric-light bulbs, or melts and breaks, as in blown fuses.

If one end of a metal rod is heated we soon feel the heat at the other end; metals are excellent thermal conductors. This is because the mobile free electrons carry the heat energy down the rod, passing it on to the ions by colliding with them. Substances without free electrons cannot do this, nor can they conduct electricity well; so we have, in the free electrons, an explanation of the fact that the good electrical conductors are the good heat conductors. For technical purposes, it would be useful to have electrical insulators that would conduct heat well, and *vice versa*; but this is almost a contradiction in terms, and one can only compromise.

Non-conductors and Semi-conductors.

There are some elements, and numerous compounds, in which all the electrons are so tightly bound to their parent atoms that free electron flow is impossible. These materials are electrical and thermal insulators.

Let us return to our sodium atom. It readily loses its outer electron, forming a positive ion. The ion is very stable; indeed, its electron arrangement resembles the "closed shell" belonging to the inert gas neon. The chlorine atom, on the other hand, would have a very stable structure, resembling the inert gas argon, if only it could be given one extra electron to complete the closed shell. If the outer sodium electron were given to a chlorine atom we should have two stable ions, one positive and one negative. These would then attract each other and form a compound. This is just how common salt, sodium chloride, is formed, and its crystals consist of a regular network of alternate sodium and chlorine ions. As all the electrons are bound to ions, it is not surprising that salt will not conduct electricity or heat to any appreciable extent. Not all insulating compounds are built on this pattern, but all have structures which bind the electrons tightly.

We have seen (**F17**) that Nature does not permit a hard-and-fast distinction between solids and liquids; nor does she between conductors and insulators. Over a hundred years ago, Faraday knew of substances which would conduct electricity, but rather badly. A common one is the graphite in pencils. Others are the elements selenium, germanium, and silicon, and a considerable number of compounds. Such substances are called semi-conductors.

Semi-conductors conduct badly because they have so few free electrons, many thousands of times fewer than metals. In very cold germanium—say, 200 degrees below freezing—all the electrons are tightly bound to atoms and the substance is an insulator. It differs from normal insulators in that, on warming it, the gradually increasing thermal vibration of the crystal detaches some of the electrons, for they are only moderately tightly bound. The warmer the crystal becomes, the more of its electrons become detached and the better it conducts electricity. By about the temperature of boiling water, there are so many freed electrons that conduction is moderately good, though less good than in metals. This is basic semi-conductor behaviour. Because transistors can be made of germanium, and because they are of such great technical importance, more knowledge has accumulated about germanium than about any other material. *See also* **Transistor, Section L.**

Magnetism.

The most important thing about magnetism is that it is inseparably connected with electricity. Oersted showed this in July 1820, when he deflected a magnetic compass needle by passing an electric current through a wire near it. Since then, many experiments have shown that wherever a current flows there will certainly be a magnetic field in the surrounding space. The laws of this are very well known now—they are the Maxwell equations previously referred to (**F13**). However, most people first meet magnetism when, as children, they pick up pins with a magnet. Where is the electricity here? and what is a magnet?

The explanation of magnetism exemplifies beautifully the technique of explaining the bulk properties of matter in terms of fundamental particles. In the atoms the electrons are moving and a moving electric charge constitutes an electric current. Therefore each moving electron is a tiny source of magnetism. It does not immediately follow that every atom is a source of magnetism because it might—and often does—happen that the magnetic effect of different electrons in the atom cancel out. In helium atoms, for example, the two electrons have equal but opposed magnetic effects. Nevertheless some atoms and ions have a net effect called their *magnetic moment*. This simply means they behave like tiny magnets. Crystals containing such atoms will be magnetic, though the magnetism is much weaker than in ordinary magnets because the different atoms largely annul one another's effects. In a very limited number of crystals, however, the magnetic ions act on one another in a special way which forces all the atomic magnets to point in the same direction. The total effect of many co-operating atoms is very strong and the crystal becomes what we normally call a magnet. Iron acts like this, so do cobalt and nickel, the rarer elements gadolinium and dysprosium, and a fair number of alloys. On the whole, this behaviour, which is called *ferromagnetism*, is very rare. The reason for the co-operation of all the atomic magnets is not explained to everyone's satisfaction yet, though the key idea was given by Heisenberg in 1928.

In the section dealing with the electron it was pointed out that every electron has an *intrinsic* magnetic moment. This is in addition to any effect simply due to the electron's motion round a nucleus. The net effects of ions are therefore partly due to the intrinsic magnetism of electrons. In the ferromagnetic metals the latter is by far the most important contribution. Thus we pick up pins, and benefit from magnets in other ways, because innumerable fundamental particles act in co-operation for reasons that are still somewhat obscure. It is interesting to ask whether the electrons responsible for magnetism are the same free electrons that allow the metals to conduct electricity. It is thought not.

We are accustomed to think of magnets as metallic. Actually the magnet originally discovered by the Chinese was the mineral lodestone, which is a non-metallic oxide of iron. Nowadays a number of non-metallic magnets are made. They are called *ferrites*, and some are insulators and some are semi-conductors. The combination of magnetism and insulation is technically very valuable in radio, radar, and other applications. The explanation of ferrite behaviour is related to that of metallic ferromagnetism, but is not the same.

Conclusion.

The aim of the second part of this account of physics is to show how our conception of fundamental particles allows us to build theories of the properties of matter. This very aim shows that the two "major divisions" of physics referred to at the beginning (**F9**) are divided only in the way that labour is divided by co-operating workers to lighten the task. For the task of physics is a very great one—no less than to explain the behaviour of matter; and since the universe, living and inanimate, is made of matter, physics must necessarily underlie all the other sciences.

II. BIOLOGY—THE SCIENCE OF LIFE

Biology embraces the study of all living things which exist on earth at the present time and also the recognisable remains of those which are now extinct. Living things or *organisms* range from the simplest microscopic animals and plants to the largest animals and forest trees. Although it is extremely difficult to give a comprehensive definition of life, we may attempt to distinguish the living from the non-living.

Living Processes.—All organisms when alive undergo continual physical and chemical changes. These *metabolic* processes are extremely complex, but are exhibited by even the smallest organism, however simple its structure may be. Metabolism also involves the processes of *nutrition*, *i.e.*, the intake of food materials, *excretion* or removal of the waste end products of metabolism, and also *respiration*. All organisms also exhibit *irritability*, by which is meant that they react to external stimuli and changes in their environment. *Growth* is also a characteristic of living things and involves the increase in size and complexity of the individual. Finally, all organisms *reproduce*, *i.e.*, they give rise to new individuals which enable the species to survive. It should be emphasised that non-living things may possess one or other of these properties separately, but it is only the living organism which exhibits all of them together.

The Branches of Biology.—Biology can be divided into two main subjects, *Botany*, the study of all plants, and *Zoology*, the study of all animals, but as we shall see later this separation is not clear cut. *Taxonomy* (or *Systematics*) involves the classification of organisms. *Morphology* is concerned with the size and form of whole organisms and their organs and the spatial relationships of the parts of the body to each other. *Histology* is the study of the types of cells present in the body, whereas *Cytology* deals with the minute structures within the cell. *Embryology* is the study of the development of organisms, and *Physiology* involves all the life processes and the functions of different organs and tissues. *Ecology* deals with the relationships of organisms to one another and to their environment. *Genetics* is the branch of biology devoted to the study of inheritance, and *Palaeontology* deals specifically with fossil remains.

These branches of biology have developed as our knowledge of all aspects of organisms has increased, stimulated by the application of modern techniques often borrowed from the sciences of physics, chemistry, and mathematics. However, it should be emphasised that they are not water-tight compartments but are all closely inter-related. For example, genetics and cytology are involved in the study of heredity, and embryology has both its physiological and genetical aspects. Certain branches which have developed rapidly in recent times, such as *Biochemistry*, may transcend the division between zoology and botany, whereas the study of a particular group may have become so vast and important that it has become a complete science in itself, *e.g.*, *Bacteriology*.

The fields mentioned above are essentially "pure science" aspects of biology, but they are also the foundations of many applied sciences, such as medicine, agriculture, and forestry, which are of such importance to human existence. Much of the research done in these applied fields adds to our knowledge of living things, just as many discoveries made by the academic biologist are of practical importance. In short, it is the main object of the biologist, however specialised or applied his particular field of research may be, to add to our total knowledge and understanding of life.

THE CELL.

The basic structural unit of nearly all organisms is the cell. Simple forms of life such as bacteria and protozoa are unicellular (**F22**), but with increasing complexity of organic form there is increase in number and specialisation of function of the cells. In man it has been estimated that there are approximately 10^{14}, and these are of various types, with different forms and specialised functions. Essentially each cell consists of a minute amount of living substance, the cytoplasm, which contains a single, often spherical structure, the nucleus. The nucleus is bounded by a thin membrane and contains one or more refractive bodies, the nucleoli. In animals the cell is usually bounded by a thin flexible membrane, but in most plant cells there is a rigid cell wall composed primarily of cellulose.

Cell Division.—Although exceptions occur, most organisms reproduce sexually, and in this process a new individual always begins as a single cell or zygote. This cell divides repeatedly by a process called mitosis to give rise to the complex multi-cellular body of the organism. In the first stage of mitosis, the prophase, a number of discrete double strands, the chromosomes, appear in the nucleus and gradually shorten and thicken. By the end of prophase the nucleolus has disappeared and the nuclear membrane breaks down. During the next stage, metaphase, the chromosomes become arranged across the equator of a striated spindle which appears in the cell. At anaphase the two threads of each chromosome, the chromatids, separate and move to opposite poles of the spindle. Thus in the last stage of mitosis, telophase, two daughter nuclei are formed, one at each end of the cell and each containing the same number of chromosomes as the original nucleus. Finally, a membrane or wall is formed which divides the cytoplasm into two uninucleate portions.

Thus by repeated mitotic divisions the body of the organism is built up. An important difference between most animals and most plants lies in their method of development. In animals there is a relatively short period of development and the body grows as a whole until the adult size is reached, although repair and replacement of tissues may occur throughout life. In higher plants, on the other hand, the roots and shoots are able to grow continually by means of permanently embryonic apical regions.

Chemistry of the Living Cell.—Ever since cells were first detected by Robert Hooke over 200 years ago with the aid of the optical microscope, the way in which cells grow and reproduce themselves has puzzled scientists. In this century biochemistry has made tremendous progress, and our knowledge of the chemistry of life is very rapidly expanding, due in no small measure to the availability of isotopes (**F10**). With the aid of compounds prepared in the laboratory and labelled with either radioactive or heavy isotopes of elements such as carbon, hydrogen, nitrogen, oxygen, sulphur, and phosphorus, biochemists can now follow the metabolic fate of these substances in living organisms. By these means it has been discovered that life is a dynamic process, that each part of the human body, for example, is continually breaking down and being replaced with new material. It is possible to find out just how each constituent is made and how long it stays in the body before it is replaced, and where and how this takes place. It is also possible to carry out many of the complex chemical reactions of living matter, *in vitro*, by making use of isolated enzyme preparations. It is becoming increasingly apparent that each individual process of life is a discrete chemical reaction but that life itself consists of many thousands of such reactions, all interdependent and all co-ordinated togther within the living cell, which has an average diameter of not more than a hundredth of a millimetre. The complexity of these chemical reactions and their diversity is well illustrated if one considers a single sperm cell, which by chemical reaction alone is capable of giving the necessary information to set in motion all the chain of reactions which will eventually lead to the creation of a replicate form of life.

Pattern of Chemical Organisation.—In the last decade our knowledge of the chemical organisation within the cell has also rapidly and dramatically increased. This has been brought about largely by the intense research into the cause of cancer, which is primarily a disease of abnormal cell growth. Cytochemists have been trying to find out why a cell should change its usual pattern of reproduction and rapidly grow in an uncontrolled abnormal form. The development of the electron microscope has greatly aided them in their understanding of the internal structure of the cell. With this instrument it is possible to obtain sharp images of particles as small as 20 Ångstroms (2×10^{-7} cm.) in diameter, and so, many structures within the cell which were not apparent with the optical microscope are now clearly visible. This, together with recent advances in the techniques of isolating without damage important parts of the cell, has revealed a common pattern of organisation in the majority of cells. It is now known that the protoplasm itself has a very definite structure. When suitable preparations are examined with the electron microscope numerous cylindrical or spherical particles, the mitochondria, together with a finer structure, the endoplasmic reticulum, are detected. On disintegrating the cell, the latter breaks up into a mass of fine particles which are called microsomes. Within the protoplasm there is another non-particulate section called the Golgi apparatus, named after its discoverer. Attempts to isolate these various fractions were for many years unsuccessful; the small mitochondria for example, were very easily damaged, especially by changes in osmotic pressure, and when treated with weak salt solutions much of their biochemical activity was destroyed. These difficulties have now been overcome, and it is possible to isolate nuclei, mitochondria, and microsomes uncontaminated with each other and still in a highly active biochemical state. Rat-liver cells are a very convenient source, although any soft tissue, such as lungs, heart, brain, or muscle could be used. Small pieces of the tissue are ground in a Potter–Elvehjem homogeniser, which is essentially a glass tube with a well-fitting plunger. The liver cells themselves are disrupted, but the smaller particles within the cells, and red blood cells, escape destruction. The homogenate is then centrifuged in sucrose solution. The heaviest particles, the nuclei, are deposited first on the bottom of the centrifuge tube, and the supernatant liquid is then transferred to another tube and centrifuged again at a higher speed, thus bringing down a deposit of mitochondria. On centrifuging this supernatant liquid at a very high speed which exerts a force equal to 100,000 times gravity the microsomes are obtained. These separate fractions after careful washing can then be suspended in suitable reaction media and their biochemical reactions studied separately without interference from other cell constituents.

The Nuclei.—The nuclei are of prime importance to the life of the cell, for if one dissects an amœba, a unicellular organism, so that one half contains the nucleus, this half will continue to live and reproduce normally, but the other half, which is merely a sphere of protoplasm, soon ceases to move and eventually dies. The fact that the protoplasm continues to react biochemically for some time after enucleation can be demonstrated by the way in which it utilises radioactive phosphorus. If, however, a nucleus from another amœba is placed inside this protoplasm, then it will continue to live and reproduce normally. The nucleus therefore controls the normal metabolic processes and is also essential for reproduction.

DNA and Cell Division.—The chromatids which separate and become the chromosomes of the daughter nuclei at mitosis are formed by longitudinal splitting of the chromosomes of the parent nucleus. These chromosomes must transmit in some chemical form all the information for the new cell to replicate its parent. Chemically the chromosomes consist of deoxy-ribonucleic acid, DNA, which is structurally a long polymer of smaller chemical fragments called nucleotides. Each nucleotide consists of one of the four nitrogenous bases, adenine, guanine, cytosine, or thymine, a sugar, deoxyribose, and phosphoric acid all linked to one another. DNA is the genetic material of the cell, and all the hereditary information that the genes contain is thought to be transmitted by the order in which the four bases are arranged on the long polymeric molecules of this substance. By analysing the X-ray-diffraction patterns of DNA, Watson and Crick at Cambridge have shown that the molecule consists of two long intertwined helices. At cell division it is thought that these two spirals separate, one half going to each cell; there they act either as a mould or a cast, forming a new spiral on their surface which is a replica of the one from which they have just parted. A simple analogy is to consider a toy lead soldier in a mould; if one separates the soldier from the mould and then makes a new soldier in the mould and uses the original soldier to make a new mould, one then has two identical sets of soldiers and moulds.

RNA and the Nucleolus.—The way in which DNA in the nucleus transmits its information to the rest of the cell is thought to be by means of another nucleic acid, ribonucleic acid, RNA, which also consists of chains of nucleotides. In this case the nucleotides consist of one of the four bases, adenine, guanine, cytosine, or uracil, linked with a sugar, ribose, and phosphoric acid. RNA is the chief chemical constituent of the microsomes. On studying the nucleolus with the electron microscope, numerous small particles are easily discernible, and these are very similar to the microsomes in the protoplasm. Not only are these RNA-containing particles present in the nucleolus but they are also seen to be clustered around the outer membrane of the nucleus. The electron microscope has shown that this membrane contains numerous pores which would thus enable these particles to escape into the surrounding protoplasm and so carry to the rest of the cell the information which has been genetically transmitted.

The Microsomes.—The smallest particles obtainable from a cell homogenate are the microsomes, and the electron microscope has shown that these are really very small fragments of the disintegrated endoplasmic reticulum. They consist chiefly of RNA. By means of very elegant isotope studies, Borsook in the U.S.A. has shown that these particles are in all probability responsible for protein synthesis. Proteins (*see* **Section L**) are always associated with life, but in fact they are only complex organic compounds. When pure, some proteins can be obtained in a crystalline state. All the proteins can be split up easily into their component amino-acids: there are about twenty different naturally occurring amino-acids. Proteins differ from each other by the sequence in which these simple units are joined together. There are many different kinds of proteins, such as collagen, the structural protein of the skin, and keratin, the protein of hair.

Site of Enzyme Synthesis.—One of the most important classes of proteins are the enzymes. These substances are responsible for bringing about most of the chemical reactions inside the cell; their functions are very varied, each enzyme being highly specific for any particular reaction. Before a cell can grow therefore it has to be able to make enzymes, which are not transmitted as such by the DNA of the dividing nucleus; these enzymes are made by the microsomes. When a synthetic amino-acid containing a radioactive carbon atom is ingested by a living organism it becomes incorporated fairly rapidly into all the proteins. Borsook decided to study the incorporation of an amino-acid as soon as possible after its administration in order to determine the site of protein synthesis. He injected a radioactive amino-acid into the tail vein of a rat, and after two minutes removed the liver and isolated the nuclei, mitochondria, and microsomes. He found that the proteins of the microsomes were radioactive, whereas the proteins of the other fractions were not, thus showing that the site of synthesis was probably the microsomal particles. If the microsomes are washed with a detergent-like substance, desoxycholic acid, they are further disintegrated into smaller particles; similar small particles can also be seen adhering to the endoplasmic reticulum when it is carefully studied with the electron microscope. It is these particles which Borsook showed to be the sites of synthesis of protein and, owing to their small size, it is not improbable that each is responsible for the synthesis of one enzyme or one type of protein, which is then discharged into the protoplasm. How, then, do these particles bring about the orderly synthesis of a specific protein? It is thought that the RNA which they contain, acts as a template and that amino-acids previously activated or given sufficient energy to combine easily with one another, are orientated in a definite sequence on a molecule of RNA; after all the amino-acids have joined together to form the protein molecule this is then released into the cell, leaving the RNA free to repeat the process. Variations in the structure of the RNA molecule would lead to the synthesis of different proteins.

The Mitochondria.—Some mitochondria are visible in a cell when it is examined with an optical microscope, but they become much more readily apparent under the electron microscope. They are usually cylindrical in shape, but this varies with the type of cell, and under certain conditions they are spherical. When seen in a living cell they are in constant motion. They have two outer membranes, the inner one being very convoluted. A rat-liver cell contains about a thousand mitochondria, but in other types of cells the number and distribution of these particles within the cell varies.

The Energy Source of the Cell.—The function of mitochondria is to provide energy for the reactions of the rest of the cell; they are found to be most numerous in those cells requiring most energy and, moreover, are usually grouped within the cell at strategic points for this purpose. Thus in a muscle cell they are grouped around that part of the protein fibre which contracts, and in a sperm cell they are in highest concentration in the neck of the cell where the head joins the vigorously moving tail. How do mitochondria provide this energy? When food, especially carbohydrates, enters the body it is broken down into smaller chemical fragments until some of it is converted to pyruvic acid; this can also be derived from some fats and amino-acids. These reactions take place outside the mitochondria, and the pyruvic acid then passes through the semi-permeable mitochondrial membrane to be further metabolised, within the mitochondria, by a series of enzymes. In this sequence of reactions, known as the citric acid cycle, carbon atoms are oxidised one at a time to carbon dioxide, which is then eventually exhaled from the body. In this process energy is liberated not in the form of heat but in the form of an energy-rich compound, adenosine triphosphate, ATP. The mitochondria produce far more energy than they themselves require, and the excess is passed into the cytoplasm as ATP for the use of the rest of the cell. Not all biochemical oxidations are brought about by the direct action of oxygen; the mitochondria contain enzymes for the removal of hydrogen ions and electrons, and these are passed in a series of reactions from one compound to another until they eventually combine with oxygen to form water.

Control of Cell Metabolism.—When mitochrondria are isolated in a pure state from a cell and suspended in solutions of various nutrients they swell and alter shape, this being due to the passage of these compounds through the semi-permeable membrane of the mitochondrial wall. One of the compounds which has a very marked influence on the shape of mitochondria is the hormone, thyroxine. The function of this hormone in the body is to control the rate of metabolism, *i.e.*, the rate at which energy is provided and utilised; it is possible that it achieves this by acting on the mitochondria and so controlling the formation and release of energy. The movement of the mitochondria in the living cell may be an indication of their state of activity. As they alter in shape they expose different parts of their internal structure to the available reactants and also release into the surrounding protoplasm the compounds needed for the metabolism of the rest of the cell. The mitochondria can be broken into fragments by changes in osmotic pressure or by subjecting them to ultrasonic vibrations. It is then found that the different enzyme systems that they contain are associated with certain parts of the mitochondria; some of these enzymes are soluble and escape into solution, while others, especially the hydrogen-transferring enzymes, are associated with the non-soluble fraction. This can be shown, by electron microscopy, to be similar in appearance to the structural membranes of the mitochondria. As more detailed electron-microscope studies of the mitochondria are made it is becoming increasingly apparent that they themselves have a detailed and intricate structure and that the enzymes they contain are arranged in a definite order.

Summary.—From this outline of the functions of the particulate fractions of the cell, it is clear that there is much organisation and division of labour within the living cell. The nucleus, by virtue of its DNA, controls not only the pattern of reproduction but also the general metabolic processes of the cell. It does this by sending out microsomal particles of RNA, which in turn bring about the synthesis of proteins and enzymes. None of this would be possible, however, without the source of energy which is provided by the mitochondria as ATP. Other minute structures, such as the Golgi apparatus, have also been found in living cells, but nothing definite is yet known of their biochemical functions.

THE CLASSIFICATION OF ORGANISMS.

There are many uni-cellular, microscopic animals and plants, as well as thousands of multi-cellular ones of diverse kinds. The naming and classifying of this vast assemblage of living things has received the attention of man for centuries. At first the main interest was a practical one, to recognise those which were useful as food, fuel, and medicine and also those which were harmful or poisonous to human beings. With the exploration of the earth by Western man so many new types of animals and plants were found and brought back to Europe that a uniform system of naming and classification became imperative, and over the last 300 years such a system has been slowly built up. It was soon realised that some species were very similar and could be grouped together in what are now known as genera and that these could be grouped together into recognisable families and so on. With the general acceptance of Darwin's conception of evolution a new element was introduced into the problems of classification. Obviously a satisfactory classification of a group of organisms should reflect the past history or evolution of that group. Thus the aim of the present-day taxonomist who is concerned with such matters is to produce a natural classification based on phylogeny or true relationships. Our knowledge of this must always be incomplete, even if only because of the incompleteness of the geological record. Hence there is no finality in any proposed classification, which may have to be drastically modified as new facts about all aspects of living things are discovered.

CLASSIFICATION OF ANIMALS.

As indicated in the chart, the animal kingdom is usually divided into two groups, the invertebrates and the vertebrates. The former includes a number of distinct groups which are arranged in order of complexity. However, this arrangement does not necessarily indicate close relationships between them. Strictly the invertebrates are to be distinguished from the chordates, *i.e.*, animals possessing a longitudinal skeletal structure, the notochord. In two small groups, the hemichordates and the urochordates, this structure is still present, but in the largest group, the euchordates or vertebrates, the notochord is replaced by a cartilaginous or bony backbone. The five groups of living vertebrates are clearly distinct, but the fossil record indicates that the order in the chart reflects their evolution in time. Thus the first true vertebrates were the fishes, and from these arose the amphibia. The amphibia gave rise to the reptiles, and both the birds and mammals evolved from different unspecialised reptilian stocks.

Protozoa.—These are all microscopic animals which are unicellular, though some may have more than one nucleus and others form colonies. Many are able to swim by waving hair-like flagella or cilia. Others, such as *Amœba*, exhibit a kind of flowing movement, parts of the cell putting out pseudopodia which are followed by the rest of the cell. Protozoa are found in all types of habitat, they are abundant in the soil and fresh-water, and many of the most beautiful forms occur in the floating plankton of the seas. Others are important diseases of man, and include *Trypanosoma*, which causes sleeping sickness, and *Plasmodium* the malarial parasite.

Porifera.—The sponges are fixed, multicellular aquatic animals, most of which are marine. Basically a sponge consists of a central cavity surrounded by two layers of cells, although the body may be branched and plant-like in form. Between the two layers of cells is a thin, gelatinous tissue containing calcareous or siliceous spicules which may be fused to form a rigid skeleton. Water is drawn in through many inhalant apertures and is passed out of the single apical exhalant aperture. Minute food particles present in the water are ingested by the inner wall cells.

Cœlenterata.—These are aquatic animals with a two-layered wall surrounding a central cavity which has only a single opening. This mouth is often surrounded by tentacles which bear many specialised stinging cells. A few live in fresh water, such as the solitary *Hydra*, but most are marine. The corals are colonial, and the remains of their calcareous skeletons form the large reefs and atolls common in the Pacific Ocean. Other familiar members of this group are sea-anemones, jelly-fish, and the floating Portuguese-man-of-war.

Platyhelminthes.—These are the worms which have soft, bilaterally symmetrical, and usually flattened bodies. The body tissue originates from three embryonic cell layers, and no body cavity is present. Some have a mouth and digestive tract, but these may be absent, and there is no blood system. The group includes the small fresh-water, free-living flatworms and also internal parasites, such as the liver-fluke which attacks sheep and the tape-worms which live in the gut of dogs, poultry, and man.

Nemathelminthes.—The round worms may be microscopic or up to 2 ft. in length. The body is smooth and pointed at both ends and has a digestive tract but no body cavity or blood system. Although they can move actively, they are unable to progress in any direction. The round worms occur everywhere, in water, in soil, and some, such as *Ascaris*, are parasites in the gut of various animals.

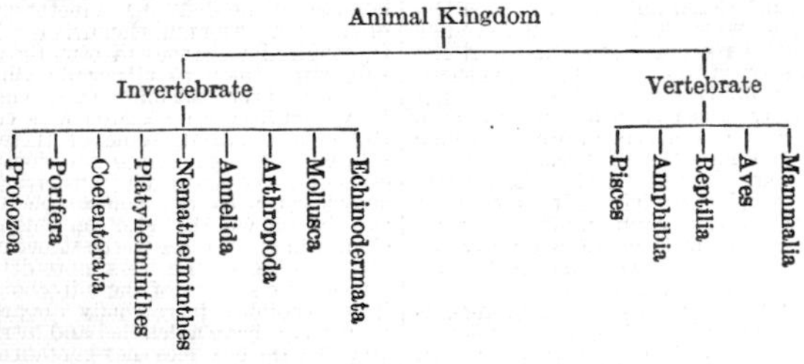

Annelida.—These are the worms with segmented bodies. Due to this feature, waves of muscular contraction can occur along the length of the body, and directional movement is possible. Usually they have a digestive tract open at both ends, a body cavity, and a blood system. The group includes the common earthworm, *Lumbricus* many marine worms, and the leeches.

Arthropoda.—This large group of animals has the general characters of the annelids, but there i usually a hard exoskeleton, each segment bears a pair of appendages which may have various functions, and the blood is contained in the body cavity. Further, they possess a simple " brain " at the front end of the body. The most important classes are:

Crustacea.—Mostly true aquatics which have two pairs of antennæ. Included here are the crabs, shrimps, wood-lice, water-fleas, and the sedentary barnacles.

Myriapoda.—These are the millepedes and centipedes which have only one pair of antennæ and numerous pairs of legs.

Insecta.—This is the largest of all animal groups with over 100,000 species. The body has a head bearing one pair of antennæ, a thorax of three segments, each bearing a pair of legs, and an abdomen. Usually the adult possesses wings. Cockroaches, locusts, grasshoppers, earwigs, lice, dragon-flies, aphids, moths, butterflies, beetles, flies, bees, wasps, and ants all belong to this vast group.

Arachnida.—These are mostly terrestrial, air-breathing forms with no antennæ and four pairs of legs, such as the scorpions, spiders, and mites.

Mollusca.—The molluscs are mostly aquatic and differ from the arthropods in having non-segmented bodies with restricted body-cavities. The exoskeleton is a shell. There are three important groups:

Lamellibranchiata.—These are the bi-valved shell-fish, such as the mussel, oyster, and scallop. The head is reduced, and no eyes are present.

Gasteropoda.—These molluscs are not symmetrical and possess a single shell. The head bears eyes and tentacles. Included here are the slugs, snails, limpets, and whelks.

Cephalopoda.—This is a group of highly specialised, free-swimming, marine molluscs which are bilaterally symmetrical. There is a definite head containing a brain and bearing a pair of large eyes similar to those of vertebrates. Cuttle-fish, the octopus, and the giant squids, which may reach 50 ft. in length and are the largest invertebrates known, are included here. The extinct Ammonites, the shells of which are commonly found in many rocks, were also cephalopods.

Echinodermata.—These marine invertebrates are all radially symmetrical and have a calcareous skeleton just beneath the surface. Included here are the star-fish, sea-urchins, and sea-cucumbers. The stalked, sedentary sea-lilies which inhabit the deep oceans are also echinoderms. They have a long geological history, and many extinct forms are known.

Pisces.—The fishes are all cold-blooded, aquatic, and possess gills by means of which they breathe. The body is covered with scales or spines and bears fins for balance and propulsion. The cartilaginous fishes, such as sharks, rays, and dogfish, have no bones in the skeleton, the gill-slits are exposed, and the skin is covered with many minute tooth-like spines. The much larger group of bony fishes have bony skeletons, the gill-slits are covered by a flap of tissue, and the body is covered with flat, overlapping scales. Many fossil fishes are known from as far back as the Silurian period.

Amphibia.—These are cold-blooded vertebrates which have to return to water for breeding. They show various advances over the fishes. Pentadactyl limbs are usually present, and the skull is jointed at its connection with the vertebral column so that the head can be moved. The eggs, which are laid in water, have no hard shell and hatch into a larval form with external feathery gills. With rare exceptions a metamorphosis takes place, the larva gradually changing into the adult, which possesses lungs. The skin of the adult is usually naked and may be important in assisting respiration. The class includes the newts and salamanders, which possess tails, and the frogs and toads, which have no tails in the adult.

Reptilia.—The reptiles were the first vertebrates to become truly land animals. They are cold-blooded but have a more completely bony skeleton and more highly organised blood system than the amphibia. The egg contains much food material, which supports the developing embryo, and there is no larval stage. The present-day reptiles, snakes, lizards, turtles, tortoises, crocodiles, and alligators are much smaller and far less numerous than those of the Mesozoic.

Aves.—The only diagnostic feature of birds is the possession of feathers, although the presence of scales on the legs, the structure of the skull, and the laying of eggs with shells are characters which indicate a reptilian ancestry. However, they show many specialised adaptations to the habit of flight. The fore-limbs are developed as wings for flapping and gliding, and the skeleton is rigid and light, with air cavities in the bones. The body is compact and streamlined and the weight is centralised beneath the wings. As there is no bladder and the rectum is short, waste materials are not retained and the weight is thereby further reduced. The power necessary for flight requires a high metabolic rate, the maintenance of which is assisted by a large heart with a high rate of beating, a very efficient respiratory system, and a constant body temperature of 38–42° C. The 19,000 or more species of birds can be divided into the perching birds, which include many of our song birds, those which scratch for their food, such as the pheasant, the waders, such as the long-legged stork and heron, the swimming birds, which include gulls, ducks, and geese, and finally, the large flightless birds, such as the emu and ostrich.

Mammalia.—The mammals are the dominant land animals of the present time. They are warm-blooded and have a glandular skin bearing hairs. The body cavity is divided into thorax and abdomen by a muscular diaphragm, the former containing the lungs and heart, which is completely divided into four chambers. The red corpuscles of the blood have no nuclei. The ear is divided into three regions, the middle ear containing three small bones. They all possess mammary glands with which they suckle their young. In the largest group of mammals, the *Eutheria*, the young develop within the uterus of the female and are born at an advanced stage. In the small group of marsupials of Australia and Central and South America, such as the kangaroos and opossums, the young are born at an early stage and transferred to a pouch round the mammary glands, where they remain for a considerable time. There are also two species of monotreme mammals, the duck-billed platypus (*Ornithorhynchus*) and spiny ant-eater (*Echidna*) of Australia, which lay eggs. It is impossible in the space available to describe the vast range of eutherian mammals, but the main orders may be briefly referred to as follows:

Edentata.—The American sloths, ant-eaters, and armadillos, which are mostly insectivorous and have incomplete dentition.

Cetacea.—These are the entirely aquatic whales, porpoises, and dolphins, which are fish-like in form and have no hind-limbs.

Ungulata.—A large group of hoofed mammals, most of which can run quickly on land. It includes the herbivorous pigs, sheep, antelopes, deer, camels, and giraffes.

Carnivores.—These are mostly carnivorous, have keen hearing, sight, and smell, and have sharp teeth and claws for killing and tearing their prey. The cats, dogs, bears, hyenas, and also the aquatic seals, sea-lions, and walruses belong to this group.

Rodentia.—The rodents are a highly successful world-wide group characterised by the possession of long, sharp, incisor teeth which are used for gnawing. The mouse, rat, squirrel, and rabbit are examples.

Insectivora.—Small, carnivorous, mostly nocturnal mammals, such as the shrews, hedgehogs, and moles.

Cheiroptera.—The bats are truly aerial mammals which have many of the adaptations to flight found in birds. The wings are, however, sheets of skin stretching between the fingers of the fore-limbs.

Primates.—Mainly arboreal, with opposable thumb and big toe for climbing. Nails instead of claws are present at the end of the digits. They have stereoscopic vision, which is important for judging distances when jumping. The brain is well developed. The primates include the small primitive lemurs, monkeys, the anthropoid apes, such as the chimpanzee, and man, *Homo sapiens.*

THE PHYSIOLOGY OF ANIMALS.

Some basic features of the physiology of cells have already been dealt with, and in unicellular animals all life processes, such as respiration, movement, growth, and reproduction, are carried on by one and the same cell. However, in multicellular animals cells are of various types, constituting distinct tissues and organs which perform special functions in the body. Although each living cell has its own complex metabolism under control of its own nucleus, there must also be co-ordination between all cells of an organism for the efficient functioning of the body as a whole. In the space available it is impossible to deal fully with all the physiological aspects of living animals, but an attempt will be made to compare some of the processes in different groups.

Feeding and Digestion.—All animals must take in and digest food materials. As well as water they require complex organic substances, proteins, fats, and carbohydrates, together with small amounts of various salts and vitamins. The insoluble organic substances are obtained from the dead bodies of other animals and plants. These must first be taken into the body and there broken down or digested by enzyme action into simpler, soluble substances. Proteins are broken down to their constituent amino-acids, insoluble carbohydrates to sugars, and fats to fatty acids and glycine. These soluble substances are then absorbed and distributed to various parts of the body where they are required, or stored for future use. Finally, the unused parts of the food are released from the body.

Diversity of Digestive Systems.—Many animals, called macrophagous feeders, take in relatively large masses of food at intervals of time. Some, such as frogs, fish, and snakes, swallow their food whole, but many break it up first. Most crustacea have appendages with which the food is torn, biting insects have cutting mouth parts, molluscs have rasp-like radulae which are used to scrape off small particles of food, and many mammals break up their food with strong jaws and teeth. In contrast, microphagous feeders collect small food particles continuously and are generally sedentary aquatic animals. They possess cilia which set up water currents from which minute food particles are filtered out, *e.g.*, lamellibranchs. A few animals, *e.g.*, *Lumbricus*, are detritus feeders which take in large quantities of soil or mud. Finally, some take in only soluble food materials. These fluid feeders include internal parasites which absorb dissolved substances over the whole surface of the body, *e.g.*, tape-worms, and insects with sucking mouth parts, *e.g.*, aphids.

Amoeba feeds by flowing around food particles, which are thus digested intra-cellularly. This type of digestion is common in the protozoa and in the amoeboid feeding cells which occur on the inner wall of the body cavity in coelenterates. Most other animals have a gut or alimentary canal in which nearly all digestion takes place extra-cellularly. This canal is basically a tube with the mouth at the anterior end and an anus at the posterior end. Food is taken in through the mouth and forced along by peristaltic action—waves of contraction of the muscles of the gut wall. Generally there is a digesting region, the stomach, and farther along an absorbing region the intestine. In worms the gut is more or less a straight tube, but in higher invertebrates it is more complex, is often coiled or twisted, and possesses diverticula which may have special functions.

In most vertebrates there is an oesophagus or delivery tube between the mouth and the stomach. Birds have an enlarged oesophagus or crop in which the food is stored before it is passed into a two-chambered stomach. The first chamber has a soft glandular wall which secretes digestive enzymes. The second chamber or gizzard has a hard muscular wall and contains stones, and it is here that the food is crushed.

Complex Digestive Systems of Mammals.—The most complex alimentary systems are found in the mammals, although much variation occurs, which can often be related to the type of diet. The carnivors have well-developed canine teeth with which the flesh of the prey is torn, and seals and sea-lions have very sharp teeth which can grip the slippery fish on which these animals feed. Rodents gnaw with their chisel-like incisor teeth, which continue to grow as they are worn away, and herbivorous ungulates have flat grinding teeth, which break up hard plant material. Some whales have no teeth, but, instead, numerous fringed plates of whalebone hang from either side of the palate. Large quantities of water are taken into the open mouth and then forced out again between the plates by the tongue. The plates form a sieve which traps the small organisms called " krill " on which the whale feeds.

In most mammals digestion of starch begins in the mouth under alkaline conditions. When the masticated food reaches the stomach proteins are broken down by enzymes which work under acid conditions. Usually the stomach is a simple curved chamber, but in ruminants such as sheep and cattle it has four chambers. The food is passed down the oesophagus and stored in the paunch. In the second chamber it is rolled into small masses or cuds which are passed up to the mouth and chewed again. When the cuds are swallowed again they enter a third chamber, and from here pass to the fourth chamber, in which the main digestion begins.

From the stomach the food enters the duodenum, in which digestion is completed. Enzymes from the pancreas continue the breakdown of carbohydrates and others digest fats. The simple soluble substances are absorbed through the walls of the long, coiled small intestine, which is richly supplied with blood vessels. In herbivorous rodents, such as the rabbit, there is a large side branch at the end of the small intestine. This is the caecum and appendix in which cellulose is digested. In carnivorous animals and man the caecum and appendix are very reduced and of doubtful function. In the colon water is removed and the waste materials are temporarily stored in the rectum before being eliminated from the body.

Respiration.—Basically respiration involves the absorption of oxygen from the environment and the oxidation of organic substances, such as sugars, resulting in the release of energy and the formation of waste carbon dioxide. All living cells respire and remain alive only if supplied with oxygen. Hence in all animals there must be an efficient respiratory system by which oxygen can be taken up and carbon dioxide released and also a circulatory system by which the oxygen is transported all over the body.

Gaseous Exchange.—In protozoa and most simple aquatic animals gaseous exchange takes place through the whole body surface. Most worms also have no special respiratory organs and are either aquatic or live in very wet surroundings. The entire body surface of *Lumbricus* secretes moisture, and atmospheric oxygen dissolves in this and is then absorbed in solution. Most molluscs are aquatic and possess gills or ctenidia contained in a mantle cavity. The gills are ciliated, and a continuous stream of water passes through the mantle cavity. Although they are primarily feeding structures, the gills are richly supplied with blood vessels and they take up dissolved oxygen from the water. In terrestrial molluscs, such as slugs and snails, the gills are reduced and the mantle cavity itself acts as a simple lung. The smaller crustacea absorb oxygen all over the body surface, but in most the thoracic appendages bear feathery gills. Continuous water currents are drawn forwards through these, and gaseous exchange takes place. In contrast, most air-breathing insects and arachnids have a system of tracheae, which are branched tubes ramifying throughout the body. They open to the exterior by lateral spiracles, and gaseous exchange takes place in the tracheoles, which terminate the ultimate branches of the tracheae.

Breathing Apparatus of Fish and Amphibia.—The respiratory systems of vertebrates are specialised parts of the anterior region of the gut. Fish have five to seven pairs of lateral gill slits, which in the bony members are covered by an operculum. Water is drawn into the mouth when its floor is lowered. Then the mouth is shut and the floor raised, thus forcing the water through the gill slits. A small group of fish, the *Dipnoi*, have simple lungs which are branches from the lower side of the oesophagus and air is forced into these by the mouth. Many bony fish also have a similar air sac which may be connected to the oesophagus, but this is a hydrostatic organ and is not used in respiration. The aquatic larvae of amphibia have external gills, but the adults usually have lungs. Air is forced into these when the floor of the mouth is raised with the mouth and nostrils shut. The moist, naked skin also allows a certain amount of surface respiration in amphibia.

Complex Breathing Systems.—Respiration is more efficient in the other vertebrate groups, as the volume of the lungs is changed by movement of the ribs, which form a box around the lungs. This is assisted in mammals by the diaphragm, a sheet of muscle which lies beneath the lungs and separates the thorax and abdomen. The lungs are spongy masses of tissue with many small air spaces, and in mammals the internal surface area may be thirty times that of the external surface of the body. The presence of nostrils and a false palate enables the animal to breathe when the mouth is full of food. Associated with the high development of a respiratory system is the formation of a sound-producing organ, the larynx and vocal chords in mammals and the syrinx at the base of the trachea in birds.

Blood Systems.—In the simpler animals there is no blood system, and the dissolved oxygen and nutrients move about the body solely by diffusion, assisted to a certain extent by streaming movements of protoplasm within the cells. Annelids have a well-developed blood system, which consists of dorsal and ventral longitudinal tubes from which capillaries supply the various organs. The blood may be pumped round the system by contractions of the dorsal vessel, but in *Lumbricus* there are five pairs of muscular, contractile "hearts." In some of the burrowing polychaete worms there is a definite two-chambered heart with an auricle into which the blood enters and a pulsating ventricle which pumps the blood round again. The mulluscs also have hearts, but these often have two auricles and a single ventricle. The heart in arthropoda consists of the long dorsal blood vessel which forces the blood along arteries. These discharge the blood into sinuses, which are cavities surrounding the various organs. From here the blood collects in the pericardial sinus surrounding the heart. The blood passes back into the heart *via* lateral perforations or ostia. Thus in the arthropoda there are no blood capillaries and the system is described as an "open" one.

Vascular System of Vertebrates.—The vascular system of vertebrates is fairly uniform, the basic pattern being very evident in fishes. They have a heart with a single auricle and a ventricle from which blood is pumped *via* arteries to the gills, where it becomes oxygenated. The blood is collected in the dorsal aorta, from which branches supply all parts of the body. The de-oxygenated blood collects in veins and eventually passes into the auricle again. One vein, the hepatic portal, runs from the intestine to the liver, where it breaks up again into capillaries. It is here that much of the digested food absorbed from the intestine is stored.

The main differences encountered in the other vertebrate groups are related to the presence of lungs instead of gills in the adult. In amphibia there are two auricles, and oxygenated blood returns to the left one from the lungs *via* the pulmonary veins. Oxygenated blood from the skin, together with de-oxygenated blood from the rest of the body, enters the right auricle. The blood passes from both auricles to the ventricle, by which it is pumped into the arterial system and into the pulmonary arteries to the lungs. Thus in the amphibia the separation of arterial and venous blood is incomplete. In most reptiles the ventricle is partly divided by a septum, and the venous blood from the right auricle enters the right side of the ventricle and is pumped to the lungs along the pulmonary arteries. The oxygenated blood from the lungs passes from the left auricle to the left side of the ventricle and thence into the arterial system. In the crocodiles and the warm-blooded birds and mammals the partitioning of the ventricle is complete. All venous blood enters the right auricle and is pumped to the lungs by the right ventricle. The oxygenated blood returns to the left auricle and is forced into the arterial system by the left ventricle. Thus, in these animals with a four-chambered heart there is complete separation of oxygenated and de-oxygenated blood.

Function of the Blood.—The blood itself is responsible for the transport of food materials and oxygen throughout the body. The nutrients are dissolved in the fluid or plasma, but oxygen is actually combined with a carrier in the blood. In most annelids this is red haemoglobin which is dissolved in the plasma, but in some of the burrowing forms it is haemerythrin contained in separate cells, the corpuscles, which are carried along in the blood stream. Crustacea and some molluscs possess blue haemocyanin as an oxygen carrier dissolved in the blood plasma. All vertebrates possess haemoglobin in minute disc-like red corpuscles. The blood also transports other substances about the body, such as hormones secreted by various glands, carbon dioxide to the lungs, and waste nitrogenous materials to the kidneys. Also present in the blood are various types of white corpuscles which are part of the defence mechanism of the body. Some ingest invading bacteria, while others produce antitoxins which counteract the poisonous substances excreted by the bacteria.

Nervous Systems.—All animals are capable of controlling their own bodies and responding to external stimuli. In the worms and higher groups control and response is mainly due to the presence of a nerve system. This consists of many cells or neurons, each of which has a number of short, thin, branched dendrites and a long axon surrounded by sheath cells. The axons may be about 1 mm. long or may extend several feet, as some do in large mammals. It is along these that nerve impulses travel. The neurons are grouped together to form nerves, and in some places ganglia or swellings are formed. They may also be massed together to form a definite brain and spinal cord.

The segmented invertebrates usually have a double, ventral, solid nerve cord lying beneath the gut, with a pair of ganglia in each segment. There is also a nerve ring round the oesophagus with a pair of cerebral ganglia above. These may be well developed in some arthropods and constitute a primitive brain. The molluscs also have a ventral nerve cord and a ring with ganglia round the oesophagus. This is particularly well developed in the cephalopods, such as *Sepia*, which has a brain comparable with that of the vertebrates.

Vertebrates.—The central nervous system of vertebrates is a hollow dorsal tube with an anterior brain protected by the skull and a backward extension, the spinal cord, enclosed in the vertebrae of the spinal column. The development of a brain is associated with the formation of a head with sense organs at the front end of the body. Masses of neurons form the nerve centres or grey matter of the brain and spinal cord. Surrounding and connecting these are millions of nerve fibres constituting the white matter. The cranial and spinal nerves which are given off by the central nervous system are composed entirely of axons. Close to the point where a spinal nerve joins the central nervous system the nerve fibres are grouped into two separate bundles or roots. The dorsal root contains the sensory fibres, which convey impulses to the brain. The ventral root contains the motor fibres, which convey impulses from the brain to the various muscles, etc. The sensory component of the nervous system can be further divided into: (*a*) *somatic*, which conveys impulses from the skin sense organs (exteroceptors) or from the muscles indicating their condition (proprioceptors); and (*b*) *visceral* which carries impulses from the mucous surfaces of the viscera (interoceptors). Thus the central nervous system receives information about both the internal and external environment of the body. The motor system can also be divided into components: (*a*) *general visceral*, which conveys impulses to the non-striated muscles and glands of the viscera, the blood vessels and iris of the eye; (*b*) *special visceral*, which supplies the voluntary striated muscles of the jaws; and (*c*) *general somatic*, which innervates all the other striated muscles of the body.

All these ingoing and outgoing impulses are controlled by the central nervous system. The simplest type of nervous behaviour occurs in reflex actions. If a finger is put on a hot plate an impulse is sent to the spinal cord. An impulse is then sent directly *via* a motor nerve to the arm muscles, which move in response, and the finger is rapidly withdrawn from the plate. Such an action is involuntary and rigid. However, a single sensory fibre makes a large number of connections with other neurons in the spinal cord and brain. These may be motor fibres connected to various effectors or neurons which carry impulses to other parts of the central system. Further, the neurons of the central nervous system are not rigidly fused, but can make new synaptic connections with each other. Thus the combinations between receptors and effectors are limitless, and the brain and spinal cord act as a flexible co-ordinating system.

The Brain.—The brain itself can be divided into three regions related basically to different sense organs: (*a*) the fore-brain (nose); (*b*) the mid-brain (eye); and (*c*) the hind-brain (ear, taste, skin). These primary centres constitute nearly the whole of the brain in fish. There is little co-ordination between these, and the behaviour of fish is mostly a series of reflex actions without much variation or modification by experience. The most important correlation centre in fish is the cerebellum in the roof of the hind-brain, which regulates the posture and movement of the body. In birds it is the floor of the fore-brain, the corpus striatum, which is well developed. This correlates reactions and movements of instinctive behaviour which are so evident in the complex life routine of many birds. In mammals it is the roof of the fore-brain, the cerebrum, which is so well developed. It deals with impulses from the sense organs, which remain separate until final co-ordination. The cerebrum judges which of many responses to make to a particular set of impulses. Thus arbitration and hesitancy in behaviour are involved. Further, impressions gained from experience are stored or learnt, and the use of this stored experience to decide on the response to a given set of stimuli results in intelligent behaviour. The cerebrum is most developed in man, and it has been estimated that there are 10 million neurons in the human cerebral cortex.

Reproduction.—A single animal may live for a short or long time, but eventually it dies, and the continuance of the species is dependent upon reproduction. Some protozoa, such as *Amoeba*, reproduce asexually by the simple division of the cell to produce two new individuals. Asexual reproduction also occurs in some coelenterates, such as jelly-fish, in which there is an alternation of sexual and asexual generations. However, the vast majority of animals only reproduce sexually. This involves the fusion of two cells, the gametes, produced by adult individuals, and each zygote thus formed develops into an individual of the next generation. The gametes are of two kinds, the large, spherical, immobile ova produced by the female gonad or ovary and the much smaller motile sperms produced by the male gonad or testis. The motility of the sperms helps them to reach the passive ovum, which contains food reserves to support the early development of the embryo.

Worms.—The flat worms, particularly parasitic forms, have complicated life cycles, and many are hermaphrodite, *i.e.*, each individual has both male and female organs. Cross-fertilisation usually occurs, the sperms from one worm being introduced into the female duct of another. The round worms are unisexual, and internal fertilisation also occurs. Of the annelids the polychaete worms are unisexual, but the ova and sperms are shed into the sea, where fertilisation takes place. However, *Lumbricus* and the leeches are hermaphrodite, cross-fertilisation takes place and the eggs are laid in cocoons.

Arthropods.—Many crustacea are unisexual, though the sedentary barnacles are hermaphrodite. Internal fertilisation may occur, but in the crabs and crayfish pairing takes place and the sperms are deposited on the tail of the female. When the eggs are shed they become fertilised and remain attached to the abdominal appendages. Most crustacea have motile larval stages into which the eggs first develop. In *Daphnia*, the water-flea, parthenogenesis sometimes occurs, *i.e.*, the eggs develop without being fertilised. The sexes are separate in the arachnida and there are usually no larval stages except in the primitive king-crabs. The insects are also unisexual, and the fertilised eggs are laid after copulation. In some, *e.g.*, dragon-flies, an immature nymph similar to the adult is formed, but in flies, beetles, moths, and many others the egg hatches into a larval form. This then develops into a pupa, from which the final adult or imago is produced. In the social ant's nest the workers are sterile females with large heads, reduced eyes, and no wings. The males and queens are winged, and insemination of the latter occurs during the "nuptial" flight.

Molluscs and Echinoderms.—Most lamellibranchs are unisexual, although some species of scallops and oysters are hermaphrodite. There are motile larval forms, and in the swan mussel, *Anodonta*, the larvae develop in the mantle cavity of the parent and when liberated become attached to the gills or fins of fish, where they remain parasitic for some time. Some gasteropods are unisexual, but the slugs and snails are hermaphrodite. In the latter cross-fertilisation occurs, the two approaching snails being stimulated to copulate by firing small sharp darts of calcium carbonate into each other. The echinoderms are unisexual, and fertilisation takes place in the sea. The egg first develops into a ciliated larval form.

Vertebrates.—The sexes are always separate in the vertebrates. In some cartilaginous fish, *e.g.*, dogfish, internal fertilisation occurs and the eggs are laid in protective sacs. In contrast, the bony fish shed ova and sperms into the water, where fertilisation takes place. Although pairing may take place in the amphibia, fertilisation occurs in water, and there is usually an aquatic larval stage. The reptiles, birds, and mammals are independent of water for fertilisation, as copulation takes place and the sperms from the male are introduced directly into the female. Most reptiles and all birds lay eggs with hard shells. Development of the embryo in marsupial mammals begins in the female uterus, but is continued in a ventral pouch which surrounds the teat of the mammary gland. In the two living species of monotreme mammals the eggs are incubated in a similar pouch. Finally, in the eutherian mammals the embryo develops in the female uterus and is born at an advanced stage.

Diversity of Sexual Reproduction.— This brief survey will give some idea of the diversity of sexual reproduction in animals. External fertilisation is very much a matter of chance, and large numbers of gametes are produced which offset the great losses of gametes and embryos that this method involves. Internal fertilisation is more certain, and is also independent of external water—an important factor in land animals. In vertebrates particularly there is increase in the care of the young by the parents, involving the development of characters of behaviour as well as those of structure. Some fish lay their eggs in holes or nests which are protected by the male. Similarly, a few frogs build nests, while others carry the eggs about. The eggs of birds require a constant high temperature for their development, and they are usually incubated by the parents. After hatching the young are fed and guarded by the parents until they can leave the nest and fend for themselves. In the eutherian mammals the embryos are attached to the uterus wall by the placenta, *via* which food materials pass from the mother. The period of gestation is long, and after birth the young are supplied with milk from the mother until they are weaned and can feed themselves. Another feature in mammals is the period of "childhood" during which they play and learn and are protected and fed by their parents. The internal fertilisation, internal development, and care and protection of the young after birth which is so conspicuous in the higher vertebrates results in the reduction of losses during the vulnerable embryonic and young stages, and in consequence relatively few progeny are produced by a pair of individuals.

CLASSIFICATION OF PLANTS.

There are various ways in which the main classes of the plant kingdom can be grouped, but a simple, up-to-date arrangement is given in the chart. Vascular plants are often known as the *Tracheophyta* because they all possess woody conducting elements. These are absent in non-vascular plants, and the bacteria, fungi, and algæ are often called *Thallophyta, i.e.,* they have a relatively simple plant body or thallus. Many of the bryophytes also possess a thallus, but in some there is a stem bearing leaves, although a true vascular system is absent. Many thallophytes are aquatic, whereas the tracheophytes are mostly land plants in which the development of woody tissues can be related to the attainment of the land habit as the plant kingdom evolved. However, the chart should not be taken as indicating the evolutionary relationships of the various groups. It is more a convenient arrangement which reflects the relative complexity of the plant body.

Bacteria.—This is a vast group of minute organisms of very simple structure. They are spherical or rod shaped and may exist as separate cells, some species being motile, or as long chains or irregular masses. Their minute size makes the elucidation of their structure very difficult. There is a wall of complex composition, and cytoplasm which contains glycogen and fat. Electron-microscope studies have revealed the presence of structures which appear to consist of nuclear material. Multiplication is by simple division, which may take place very rapidly. For example, *Bacillus subtilis* can divide every 20 minutes, so that in 8 hours a single cell may give rise to 16 millions. Recent research indicates that a sexual process may also occur. Bacteria can survive unfavourable conditions by producing a resistant spore within the cell. They do not possess chlorophyll, though a few are pigmented. Most obtain their food already formed, and are thus either saprophytes or parasites. The saprophytic bacteria occupy a vital position in the living world. They are responsible for most of the decay of dead organic matter, and it has been truly said that without them the surface of the earth would soon become completely covered with the dead bodies of animals and plants. Bacteria also play a vital part in the circulation of nitrogen in nature. By breaking down organic material, ammonia is released and ammonium carbonate is formed in the soil. This is oxidised by other bacteria to form nitrates, which can be absorbed by plants again. Yet other bacteria can "fix" atmospheric nitrogen, and one species, *Rhizobium leguminosum*, occurs in the root nodules of plants such as clover and lupins. These plants are often grown on poor soils and ploughed in, thus improving the fertility of the soil. The parasitic bacteria are also of great importance, as they are responsible for many diseases of plants, animals, and man. (*See* **P7(1)**.)

Fungi.—This is a large group of plants, none of which contain chlorophyll. Hence, like the bacteria, they are either parasites on other living plants and animals or saprophytes which live on dead organic matter. Some are unicellular aquatic plants, but many have a body called a mycelium composed of many branched threads or hyphæ. In the higher fungi (*e.g.*, toadstools, bracket fungi, and puff-balls) complex reproductive structures are formed. All fungi produce spores. In the aquatic species these may be motile, but the majority form minute, airborne spores. The spore output is often very great, and a single mushroom may produce 1,800 million spores. Some fungi are serious diseases of crop plants, such as potato blight and wheat rust.

Algæ.—These are essentially aquatic plants which contain chlorophyll. They range from microscopic forms to the large seaweeds. The green algæ (*Chlorophyceæ*) live mostly in fresh water and may be unicellular, motile or non-motile, or filamentous, though a few found in tropical seas are more complex. The brown algæ (*Phæophyceæ*) are mostly seaweeds which possess a brown pigment, fucoxanthin, which masks the green chlorophyll. They include the bladder-wracks (*Fucus*) and kelps (*Laminaria*) of our coasts and the seaweeds which form dense floating masses over hundreds of square miles of the Sargasso Sea. Other groups are the red algæ (*Rhodophyceæ*), mostly seaweeds of delicate form, the unicellular motile diatoms (*Bacillariophyceæ*), and the blue-green algæ (*Cyanophyceæ*). All algæ possess unicellular reproductive organs. Various types of life cycle occur, the most complex being found in the red algæ.

Bryophyta.—These are the liverworts (*Hepaticæ*) and the mosses (*Musci*). They are all small plants characterised by a sharply defined life-cycle. This consists of an alternation of generations, the "plant" being a gametophyte bearing

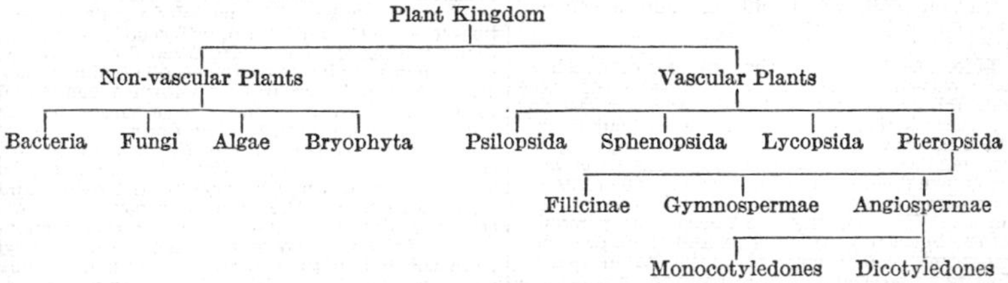

sex organs. The latter are multicellular, the female archegonium containing a single stationary ovum and the male antheridium producing many motile sperms. The latter are released and swim in water to the archegonium, where fertilisation takes place. After this a sporophyte is formed which is always dependent on the gametophyte and never becomes free living. The sporophyte usually consists of an absorbing foot buried in the tissue of the gametophyte and a stalk or seta bearing at the top a single sporangium. In many mosses this is a complex structure with hygroscopic teeth which move apart only when dry, thus releasing the minute spores only when conditions are suitable for their dissemination in the air. The bryophytes are of little economic importance, and may be looked upon as an evolutionary sideline. However, they occupy suitable "niches" in many plant communities, and species of the bog-moss *Sphagnum* cover large areas where rainfall is high.

Psilopsida.—This is a small group of primitive, vascular, spore-bearing plants. Its only living representatives are two rare genera of the Southern Hemisphere. However, a number of fossil forms are known from the Devonian period. The best known are those found in the chert at Rhynie in Scotland. The plants are excellently preserved, and their internal structure can be easily seen. They were probably marsh plants with prostrate and erect leafless stems, although *Asteroxylon* had simple leaves.

Sphenopsida.—The only living members of this group are about twenty-five species of horsetails (*Equisetum*). In the Carboniferous period many tree forms existed (*e.g.*, *Calamites*), the remains of which are very common in coal deposits.

Lycopsida.—In the Carboniferous period the tree clubmosses were also prominent members of the forests (*e.g.*, *Lepidodendron*). They often reached 100 ft. in height, were branched or unbranched, and had large simple leaves. They also had extensive root systems. The only living members belong to a few genera of small herbaceous clubmosses, such as *Lycopodium* and *Selaginella*. Like the true mosses, they have an alternation of generations, but the elaborate plant with stem, leaves, and roots is the sporophyte, and the gametophyte is very small. In *Lycopodium* only one kind of spore is produced, and the resultant gametophyte is bisexual. *Selaginella* produces numerous small microspores which give rise to the very reduced male gametophytes and motile sperms and the few large megaspores which produce the female gametophytes. The latter are formed within the megaspore wall, which splits to allow the sperms to reach the small archegonia.

Filicinæ.—These are the true ferns, which in some classifications are put with the horsetails and clubmosses in the Pteridophyta or vascular cryptogams (*i.e.*, vascular plants without seeds). The ferns have a long fossil history, and remains very similar to the living Royal ferns (*Osmunda*) are known from the Carboniferous. The ferns are widespread and particularly abundant in tropical forests. The majority are herbaceous perennial plants, but a few are aquatic, and there are some tree ferns, which may reach 20 ft. in height. Most ferns possess a stem bearing roots and large leaves or fronds. The plant is the sporophyte and produces numerous spores in sporangia borne on the fronds. Each spore gives rise to a minute green free-living gametophyte known as the prothallus, which bears the archegonia and antheridia. After fertilisation a young sporophyte develops, which at first draws nourishment from the prothallus. Thus, as in the *Bryophyta*, external water is essential for the motile sperms to swim in, and there is a clearly defined alternation of generations, but the sporophyte is a complex independent plant, and the gametophyte is reduced though free-living.

Gymnospermæ.—These were the dominant land plants in the Mesozoic era, although fossil remains are found as far back as the Devonian. The living members still form large forests in the North Temperate regions. They are mostly tall evergreen trees with roots, stems, and small leaves. The conifers include the pines (*Pinus*), larches (*Larix*), and yews (*Taxus*). The cycads are a relic group of tropical plants with thick, unbranched trunks and large fern-like leaves. The maiden-hair tree of Japan (*Ginkgo biloba*) has also had a long geological history. Another interesting Gymnosperm is *Metasequoia*, a genus well known to palæobotanists. In 1948 a few living specimens were found in a remote area of China. Seeds were collected and plants are now being grown in botanical gardens all over the world. The Gymnosperms are characterised by the production of "naked" seeds, which are usually borne on cones. The male pollen grains, which are equivalent to the microspores of *Selaginella*, are carried by wind to the ovule of the female cone. The pollen germinates and the pollen tube carries the male gametes to the reduced archegonia borne on the female prothallus, which, unlike those of the ferns, is retained within the ovule on the parent plant. After fertilisation an embryo is formed, the prothallus becomes the food store or endosperm, and the outer part of the ovule becomes the seed coat. The cycads and *Ginkgo* retain a primitive feature in that the male gametes are motile and they swim to the archegonia from the pollen tube.

Angiospermæ.—The apparent sudden rise of the Angiosperms in the Cretaceous period is still the "abominable mystery" it was to Darwin. Various suggestions have been put forward, but nothing definite is known about the origin of the group. The Angiosperms or flowering plants are now the dominant group over most of the land surface of the earth, and at least 250,000 species are known. Apart from the natural vegetation, the majority of our crop and garden plants are Angiosperms. They occur in every type of habitat and range in form from gigantic trees to minute plants, such as the duck-weeds. Some are climbers, others succulents, and a number have reverted to the aquatic habit. Although most possess chlorophyll, a few are partial (*e.g.*, Mistletoe) or complete parasites (*e.g.*, Dodder).

Flower, Fruit and Seeds.—The diagnostic feature of the group is the production of seeds, which are completely enclosed within the female part of the flower, the ovary. Basically a flower is a short reproductive shoot which bears several whorls of lateral organs. At the base are several, often green, protective sepals forming the calyx, and above this are the often brightly coloured petals of the corolla. Within this are the stamens of the andrœcium or male part of the flower. Centrally is the female gynœcium of one or more carpels containing the ovules. The parts of the flower may be free, as in the buttercup, or fused together. In many species the petals are fused (sympetalous), the stamens are borne on the corolla (epipetalous), and the carpels are fused to form a compound gynœcium (syncarpous). The stamens possess anthers, which produce pollen grains. These are shed and carried by insects or wind to the receptive stigmas of the carpels. Each produces a tube which grows down the style to the ovary and enters an ovule. The ovule is a complex structure containing an ovum and a primary endosperm nucleus. Two male nuclei are discharged from the pollen tube, one fuses with the ovum and the other fuses with the primary endosperm nucleus. After this "double fertilisation" an embryo is formed which is embedded in the nutritive endosperm and the outer tissues of the ovule form the seed coat or testa. The ovary of the carpel develops into the fruit containing the seeds. Fruits are of various kinds, being either dehiscent and opening when mature to release the seeds or indehiscent, with a succulent or dry wall. The indehiscent fruits are shed as a whole, and often contain only a single seed. Seeds and fruits show great variation in structure, and often have adaptations assisting dispersal. Some have hairs or wings which aid wind dispersal, whereas others have hooks or are sticky and are transported by animals. Some have flotation devices and may be carried a great distance from the parent plant by water. Seeds vary in size from the microscopic seeds of orchids to those of the double coconut, which may weigh 40 lb. Only about 10% of the weight of a seed is water, and the embryo, although alive, is dormant. The bulk of a seed consists of stored food material, commonly fats or starch and proteins, which may be contained in the endosperm surrounding the embryo, although in some species the endosperm is absorbed during seed development and the food is stored in the one or two swollen seed leaves or cotyledons of the embryo.

Classification of Flowering Plants.— John Ray (1627–1705) was the first botanist to recognise the two great divisions of the Angiosperms—the dicotyledons with two seed leaves and the monocotyledons with only one. This primary division of the flowering plants has stood the test of time and is still recognised. Other differences are also found between the two groups. The dicotyledons usually have net-veined leaves and the floral parts are in fours or fives, whereas the monocotyledons usually have leaves with parallel veins and the floral parts are in threes.

THE PHYSIOLOGY OF SEED PLANTS.

When a dormant seed is planted it takes up water and dissolved oxygen from the soil and germinates. Early growth is dependent on the food reserves present in the seed, but when these are exhausted the young plant becomes self-supporting. The root hairs absorb water and simple inorganic compounds of nitrogen, phosphorus, potassium, calcium, magnesium, sulphur, and iron. These, together with certain trace elements, such as boron and manganese, are essential for healthy growth. The water passes up the woody tissues of the root and shoot, and a great deal is lost by evaporation through the stomatal pores present in the leaf surfaces. In most plants the stomata are only open during the day, and it is through these that gaseous exchange also takes place. Oxygen is taken up from the atmosphere and carbon dioxide is given out due to respiration.

Photosynthesis.—In the overall process of photosynthesis carbon dioxide is taken up by the plant and oxygen given out. The living cells of all green parts of plants, particularly of leaves, contain chloroplasts, which are discoid bodies 2–20 microns across. Their structure is complicated, and they contain two green pigments, the closely related chlorophylls a and b, together with yellow xanthophylls and orange-yellow carotenes. The chlorophylls are responsible for absorbing light energy from the sun, mostly in the red and blue regions of the spectrum. This energy is ultimately used in the formation of organic compounds from the carbon dioxide and water which the plant obtains from its environment. Thus green plants are almost unique in the living world in being able to synthesise organic compounds from these simple substances, and it is upon this process that all life ultimately depends. Due to its fundamental importance, both to the living world and to man's food production, the secrets of this process are being actively studied by many research workers all over the world. By using radioactive isotopes it has been shown that the energy absorbed by chlorophyll is involved in the photolysis or splitting of water molecules. Some of the hydrogen from the water combines with carbon dioxide and oxygen is released from the plant. One of the first compounds formed appears to be phosphoglyceric acid. This substance occupies a central position in plant metabolism. It is an intermediate compound in the formation and breakdown of sugars, and it is easily converted into other substances from which fats and proteins are synthesised. Undoubtedly photosynthesis takes place in a number of steps, and a full understanding of the process has still to be reached. It cannot yet be fully demonstrated *in vitro*, but a recent advance has been made by American and German workers, who have synthesised chlorophyll in the laboratory.

Reaction to Environment.—Like all organisms, plants react to their environment in many ways. They exhibit many growth movements or tropisms. For example, stems are commonly positively phototropic and grow towards light, and they are also negatively geotropic and grow away from the centre of gravity. Many roots are positively geotropic and also positively hydrotropic and grow towards water. Some plant organs also exhibit nastic movements and can assume various positions. Thus many flowers and leaves open out during the day and close at night.

THE GEOLOGICAL RECORD.

London is an old city as cities go, although not so old as Rome, but geologically speaking it is not so long since the land upon which London stands was beneath the sea. Later in time there were tropical jungles on the banks of the Thames in which sabre-toothed tigers hunted their prey, the Thames was a tributary of the Rhine, and, still more recently (in fact only yesterday on the geological time-scale), the great Ice Ages brought sub-arctic conditions to our land.

The various stages in the history of the earth can be read by the geologists in the strata or layers of rock laid down since the planet began to solidify, and it is in these rocks, too, that the record of life upon earth may be traced.

No Life Rocks.—The earliest rocks in the record are known as the Azoic (no life) rocks, because they show no trace of living things, and these layers are of such thickness that they occupy more than half of the whole record. That is to say, for more than half of the earth's history nothing living existed upon any part of the globe. For millions of years the surface of our planet was nothing but bare rock without soil or sand, swept by hot winds exceeding in violence the wildest tornadoes of today, and drenched by torrential downpours of tropical rain, which, as we have seen elsewhere, gradually tore away the surface to form sandy sediments at the bottom of the seas. In such ancient rocks pushed above the surface by later upheavals we can still trace the marks of primeval oceans as they rippled upon the barren shores or of raindrops which left their imprint perhaps 1,500 million years ago.

Primitive Sea-life.—As we move upwards through the strata, however, traces of life begin to appear and steadily increase as we come to the more recent levels. The earliest signs appear in what is known as the Early Paleozoic Age (or by some writers as the Proterozoic Age), when we find the fossilised remains of small shellfish, seaweeds, and trilobites—the latter were creatures somewhat like the plant-lice of modern times. All these primitive animals and plants lived in the shallow tidal waters of ancient seas; for as yet life had not invaded either the dry land or the deep oceans. It is, of course, clear that these creatures of Early Paleozoic times were not the first living things: they were merely the first creatures capable of leaving fossilised remains, and without doubt must have had more primitive ancestors—amœbic-like forms, jellyfish, bacteria, and so on whose bodies were too soft to leave any traces in the record of the rocks. This problem, however, will be discussed more fully later.

The Age of Fishes.—Towards the end of the Early Paleozoic Era, in what we now know as the Silurian period (see **F30**), there arose a new form of life: the first backboned animals, primitive fishes somewhat similar to the sharks of today; and in the division of the Upper Paleozoic Era known as the Devonian, they had come to multiply so greatly that this is frequently described as the Age of Fishes.

First Land Animals and Plants.—It is about this time, too, that we begin to find traces of animal and plant life upon the dry land. Both animals and plants had acute problems to solve before it became possible for them to live out of water; for both animals and plants had hitherto been supported by the surrounding water and respired by removing oxygen dissolved in the water. In land animals this problem was solved by a long series of adaptations from gills to lungs. Plants were able to invade the land because of the evolution of an impermeable outer cuticle which prevented water loss and also the development of woody tissues which provided support and a water-conducting system for the whole plant body.

Amphibia and Spore-bearing Trees.—The first type of vertebrates (backboned animals) to live upon dry land was the group of amphibia in the Carboniferous Age, which is today represented by the newts, frogs, toads, and salamanders. In all these forms the eggs give rise to a tadpole stage with gills which lives for some time entirely in water. Later the gills give place to a primitive form of lung which enables the animal to live upon land. Even so, amphibia are restricted more or less to swampy or marshy land, and without a damp environment they would dry up and shrivel to death. The most abundant forms of plant life in the Carboniferous period were the tree-like horsetails, clubmosses, and ferns, the fossilised tissues of which are found in the coal measures and are burned as household coal. But these plants also, as in the case of the amphibia, could exist only amongst the swamps and marshes, and life, although it had freed itself from the necessity of existence in the waters of the earth, still had to return to the water in order to reproduce itself. The highlands and the deeper waters of the planet were still empty of living things. Although the Carboniferous period had been a period of warmth and abundance, the Paleozoic Era came to an end with a long cycle of dry and bitterly cold ages. Such long-term climatic changes were due, it is now supposed, to such factors as changes in the earth's orbit, the shifting of its axis of rotation, changes in the shape of the land masses, and so on. Long before the Ice Ages of more recent times, there are records in the rocks of alternating periods of warmth and cold as far back as the Azoic and Early Paleozoic Eras. This long cold spell at the close of the Paleozoic era came to an end about 220 million years ago, and was succeeded by a long era of widely spread warm conditions—the Mesozoic Era, the so-called Age of Reptiles.

The Mesozoic Era.—The reptiles first appeared in the Permian, but it was during the Mesozoic era that they became the dominant group of animals. The giant reptiles included the stegosaurus, the gigantosaurus, the diplodocus, and many other kinds which were far larger than any land animals living today. Some, for example the diplodocus, were 100 ft. long, although they were vegetarian in habit and were preyed upon by other almost equally huge flesh-eating reptiles. Some species, such as the plesiosaurs and icthyosaurs, became secondarily aquatic, while the pterodactyl possessed wings with which it could glide and perhaps fly short distances. However, they all differed from the amphibia in that they had hard, dry skins, their lungs were more efficient, fertilisation was internal due to the development of copulatory organs, and they laid eggs with hard, protective shells.

It was also during the Mesozoic era that the warm-blooded birds arose. The birds, like the reptiles, lay eggs with hard shells, and they have several internal features found in the reptiles. The fossil bird Archæopteryx, three specimens of which have been found in Germany, lived in the Jurassic period. Although it was obviously a bird, it retained many reptilian features. Earliest mammals are recognised in rocks of the late Palaeozoic but in the Mesozoic considerable evolution of the group took place. The fossil Trituberculata which are also found in the Jurassic, are believed to be related to forms from which both the marsupial and placental mammals arose. Although insects were present as far back as the Carboniferous, it was in the Mesozoic that many of the groups we know today first appeared.

Great changes also took place in the plant cover of the land during this era. The spore-bearing giant horsetails and tree clubmosses declined and were replaced by gymnosperms—trees bearing naked seeds. One large group of these, the cycadeoids, has become extinct, but the conifers and a few of the once abundant cycads still remain. The flowering plants or angiosperms also made their appearance, and towards the end of the Cretaceous their evolution was extremely rapid. In fact, many of the fossil leaves found in rocks of Cretaceous age are indistinguishable from those of some present-day flowering plants.

A New Era.—But, perhaps 150 million years later, all this seemingly everlasting warmth and sunshine, the lush tropical life, the giant reptiles who had ruled the world, were wiped out by a new period of bitter cold which only the hardy species could survive. A new Era known as the Caenozoic was beginning, ushered in by a period of upheaval and volcanic activity, following which the map of the world came to resemble more closely the picture we know today. The cold period may have lasted several million years, and the main species to survive it were those which had come into existence towards the end of the Mesozoic Era, the seed-bearing flowering plants, the birds, and the mammals. The once all-powerful reptiles from this time onwards are represented only by the comparatively few and relatively small reptilian species of today: the snakes, lizards, crocodiles, and alligators. It was at this

THE GEOLOGICAL TIME SCALE.

ERAS	PERIODS	AGE (millions of years)	LIFE
CAENOZOIC	Pleistocene	1	Man
	Pliocene		Birds, Mammals and modern plants Molluscs
	Miocene	25	
	Oligocene		
	Eocene	70	
MESOZOIC	Cretaceous	135	Dinosaurs, Cycads; Earliest Birds; Ammonites and Sea-urchins
	Jurassic	180	
	Triassic	225	
PALAEOZOIC	Permian	270	First mammals; Early reptiles
	Carboniferous	350	Amphibians, tree-ferns, first insects
	Devonian	400	Fishes, first land plants
	Silurian	440	Mainly invertebrate animals; no life on land. Trilobites and graptolites
	Ordovician	500	
	Cambrian	600	
PRE-CAMBRIAN (also PROTEROZOIC, ARCHAEOZOIC)		2,000	Life emerges
		5,300	Age of Earth's crust

time, too, that, long after the creation of the mountains of Scotland and Norway (the so-called Caledonian revolution), or even of the Appalachian mountains (the Appalachian revolution), there arose the great masses of the Alps, the Himalayas, the Rocky Mountains, and the Andes. These are the mountain chains of the most recent, the Caenozoic revolution. Initially, as we have seen, the climate of the Caenozoic Era was cold, but the weather grew generally warmer until a new period of abundance was reached, only to be followed at the end of the Pliocene by a period of glacial ages generally known as the First, Second, Third, and Fourth Ice Ages.

The Great Ice Age.—The latter was separated by interglacial periods when the climate was milder—we are, in fact, living at the moment at the end of the last Ice Age, for the retreat of ice from Europe began only about 25,000 years ago. It must be remembered, however, that even at the height of the Glacial periods the ice never extended over the whole face of the earth; it was, indeed, limited to an area which never moved farther south than what is now Northern Germany, Northern France, the larger part of the British Isles, small areas in the North of Asia, and about half of the North American continent.

THE EVOLUTION OF ORGANISMS.

Introduction.—It is commonly thought that the great 19th cent. naturalist Charles Darwin was the first person to suggest that life had continually evolved. However, the idea that species of living organisms could change over long periods of time was considered by some Greek writers and, much later, by the Frenchmen Buffon and Lamarck at the end of the 18th cent. Further, the work of the 18th cent. geologists such as James Hutton and William Smith provided a basis without which Darwin's contribution would have been impossible. Hutton showed that the earth's surface had undergone prolonged upheavals and volcanic eruptions with consequent changes in sea level. This implied that the earth was much older than had previously been supposed. Smith developed a method of dating the geological strata by means of the fossils found in them and demonstrated that widely different types of animals and plants existed at different periods of the earth's history. As described in the previous section a general picture is presented of the evolution of organisms from the simple to the complex and from the aquatic to the terrestrial environment. These discoveries were in conflict with the Biblical account in the book of Genesis and, although various attempts were made to explain them away or discredit them, it became abundantly clear that through millions of years life has been continually changing, with new species constantly arising and many dying out. Before considering Darwin's major contribution to the theory of evolution it will be appropriate to outline briefly the various lines of evidence which indicate that, in fact, evolution has taken place.

The Evidence for Evolution.—

1. *The Geological Record.*—It has already been pointed out that successively younger rocks contain fossil remains of different and relatively more complex organisms. The spore-bearing plants preceded the gymnosperms and the angiosperms arose much later. Similarly in the vertebrate series the fish appeared before the amphibia which were followed by the reptiles and later by the air breathing, warm-blooded birds and mammals. On a more restricted level the rocks provide even greater support for the occurrence of evolution. For example, the evolution of the horse has been worked out in great detail from the small Eohippus which was about a foot high and had four digits on the forefeet and three on the hind feet to the large one-toed animal living today. However, such complete series are rare and the geological record is very incomplete. There are a number of gaps, particularly between the major groups of organisms. No satisfactory fossil evidence is known of the ancestors of the angiosperms (**F28**(2)) and although some may be discovered it could be that they did not grow in conditions which favoured their preservation as fossils. On the other hand, Archæopteryx (**F30**(2)) provides an indisputable link between the reptiles and the birds.

Another important point should also be made about the geological record. Although we talk about the age of fishes, the age of reptiles and so on it must be emphasised that these are the periods during which particular groups were abundant or even dominant. Each group probably originated many millions of years before it became widespread. Further, some groups, such as the giant reptiles and the seed-ferns, died out completely whereas others, the fishes and true ferns for example, are still common today. However, even in the latter groups there is evidence that they have continued to evolve so that many fishes and ferns that exist today are very different from those of the Devonian and Carboniferous periods (**F30**). On the other hand, the geological record also shows that some species, for example the Maiden-hair tree, have remained unaltered for many millions of years.

2. *Geographical Distribution.*—Nearly all the marsupials or pouched mammals are found only in the Australian continent which was cut off from the mainland about 60 million years ago. All the fossil evidence indicates that at that time the eutherian or placental mammals did not yet exist. The marsupials are the only naturally occurring mammals in Australia but since the isolation of the continent the group has given rise to a large number of species very similar in appearance to those which evolved elsewhere in the world among the eutherian mammals (**F23**(2)). There are marsupials which look like wolves, dogs, cats and squirrels; yet they have no close biological relationships to these animals. Further, some marsupials such as the kangaroos have evolved which are unlike any other creatures in the rest of the world. Quite clearly the isolation of Australia so long ago has resulted in the evolution of these distinct types. A similar small-scale effect of isolation was studied by Darwin in the Galapagos islands where each has its own distinct flora and fauna which differ also from those of the S. American mainland.

3. *Anatomy.*—The comparative study of the development and mature structure of the mammalian body provides much evidence that all the species have evolved from a single ancestral stock. Although the arm of an ape, the leg of a dog, the flipper of a whale and the wing of a bat appear very different externally they are all built on the same skeletal plan. It would be difficult to explain such similarities unless they had all evolved from a common type. There is also evidence that the early development of an animal recapitulates its biological history to a certain extent. For example, the gill slits found in fish are formed during the early stages in the development of a mammal although later they disappear. Finally, apparently useless vestigial structures sometimes occur which would be inexplicable unless regarded in the light of an evolutionary history. In man a small appendix and vestiges of a third eyelid occur but these are functionless although in other animals such structures are well developed and functional, *e.g.*, the appendix in the rabbit.

4. *Human Selection.*—During his brief history on earth modern man has continually selected and bred animals and plants for his own use. We have only to look at the various breeds of dogs which have been developed from a single wild type to see that under certain circumstances great structural divergence can occur in a species even in a relatively short time.

The Darwinian Theory of Evolution.—Darwin amassed a great deal of information such as that outlined above which convinced him that evolution of life had taken place over millions of years. His was the first real attempt to collect all the evidence scientifically and no other satisfactory alternative explanation of all the facts he presented has been proposed. Perhaps even more important was his attempt to explain *how* evolution had actually occurred. He published his theory after many years of work in his book *The Origin of Species by Means of Natural Selection* in 1859. Some of his ideas have since been modified owing to our increased knowledge of genetics but they are so important that it is worth while recounting the main points of his theory.

1. *The Struggle for Existence.*—It is clear that in nature there is a severe struggle for existence in all animals and plants. Over a period of time the number of individuals of a species in a given community does not vary greatly. This implies that the number of progeny which survive to become mature breeding individuals more or less replaces the number of mature ones that die. Generally speaking the reproductive output of a species is much greater than this. For example, a single large foxglove plant may produce half a million seeds each one of which is potentially capable of giving rise to a new individual. Obviously nearly all the progeny die before reaching maturity and the chance of any single one surviving is very remote.

2. *Variation.*—The individuals of any generation of human beings obviously differ from one another and such differences are found in other organisms. No two animals of the same species (except perhaps for identical twins) are exactly alike and when a large number of individuals are examined it is clear that they vary considerably in structure, colour, activity and so on. Darwin also pointed out that generally these variations were passed on from one generation to the next, for example, the children of tall parents tend to grow tall.

3. *Survival of the Fittest.*—If there is an intense struggle for existence in their natural environment among individuals of a species having different characteristics, those which are best "fitted" to a given set of conditions are most likely to survive to maturity. These will reproduce and the features which enabled them to survive will be passed on to their offspring. This process is liable to continue and a species will become better adapted to its environment.

4. *Natural Selection.*—Over a long period of time the environment of a given species is never stable but will change in various ways. As it does so the characters which best fit the individuals to the changed environment will be selected (not consciously of course) and the species will change. The environment may change only in part of the range of the species and thus lead to divergence and the production of a new species alongside the old one.

Darwin and Lamarck.—Darwin pictured evolution as a slow continuous process with natural selection operating on the small inheritable variations found between the individuals of a species which are undergoing intense competition. This neglects the important effect of the environment on the growth and structure of the individual. It is obvious that external conditions will affect the development of an organism, for example the effect of various soil conditions on the growth of a plant or the amount of food material available to an animal. Lamarck maintained that the characters acquired by an individual owing to the effect of its environment could be passed on to its offspring. Undoubtedly characters are acquired by the individual during its growth but in spite of many attempts to prove otherwise no experiments have been done which prove conclusively that these are inherited by the offspring. Thus Lamarck's theory that evolution has occurred by the inheritance of acquired characters is not generally acceptable today.

Mutation Theory.—The data accumulated by Darwin showed that the variations between individuals of a species are small and graded into one another. If a particular character in a group of individuals is measured it is found that it varies symmetrically about a mean or average, with most values clustered about the mean and with few extreme ones. Darwin himself was worried about this fact because, although selection over a long period of time might shift the position of the mean, he did not see how it could bring about the discontinuity necessary for the establishment of a distinct new species. De Vries in his *Mutation Theory* published in 1901 put forward the view that evolution depends, not on the accumulation of continuous minute variations, but primarily upon large discontinuous variations or mutations. The importance of such spontaneous "sports" was considered by Darwin but he rejected the idea because when they appear they are usually "monstrous". Such individuals are less "fitted" to their environment and therefore they will not survive to reproduce and give rise to a new species. That mutations are important factors in evolution is undoubtedly true but modern work has shown that the whole problem is far more complex than either Darwin or De Vries supposed.

Mendelism.—It is remarkable that in spite of carrying out many careful experiments on inheritance in plants Darwin did not discover the simple laws which are the basis of modern genetics. Mendel investigated inheritance in the garden pea and published his results in 1865, *i.e.*, at the time that Darwin's work was being widely discussed. However, Mendel's important discoveries were not generally known until 1900. When he crossed a pure breeding tall plant with a pure breeding dwarf plant all the progeny were tall. When these plants were self-pollinated the next generation consisted of approximately one quarter dwarf plants and three quarters tall. From this and similar experiments Mendel deduced that the "factors" passed from parents to offspring were paired, only one of the pair came from each parent and that one could be dominant over the other. When he dealt with two pairs of characters, *e.g.*, tall or dwarf plants and round or wrinkled seeds, he found that they segregated and recombined independently and in predictable ratios.

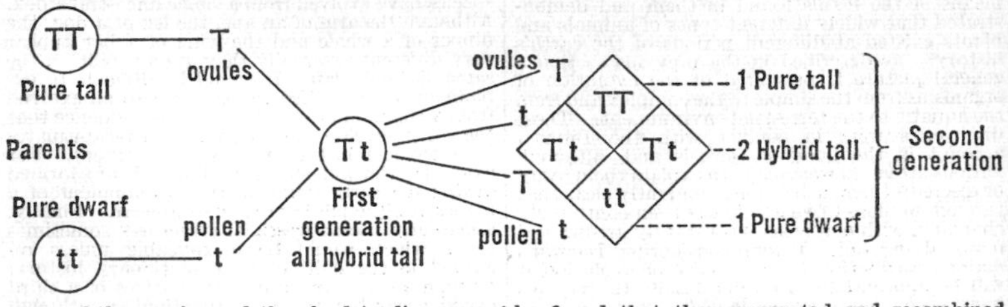

The importance of Mendel's work in relation to evolution is that it showed that there was no blending of the characters in the offspring. Mutations can be hidden as recessive characters in a population and are not diluted or lost. Although they may not be of importance when they first appear they may be so if the selection pressure changes and they become of survival value. Thus specific characters may change or diverge and evolution will take place. His investigations also showed that recombination of factors could give rise to plants with new characteristics. By crossing a pure bred tall plant having round seeds with a dwarf plant having wrinkled seeds he produced in the second generation some tall plants with wrinkled seeds and dwarf plants with round seeds. When a large number of characters are involved it is obvious that considerable variation and recombination occurs upon which natural selection can work.

Mendel was fortunate in his choice of experimental material with its easily recognisable contrasting characters. It is now known that his "factors" are the genes carried by the chromosomes in the nucleus of the cell. At the present time the biochemical basis of heredity is being vigorously investigated.

THE ORIGIN OF LIFE.

We have seen in the previous two sections that life has existed on earth for many millions of years and that it has continuously changed or evolved. This raises the obvious question of the origin of life on earth. There are three possible explanations: (*a*) that it was supernaturally created; (*b*) that living organisms arrived from some other part of the universe; or (*c*) that it arose by natural processes from inorganic matter. The first explanation is not strictly scientific, *i.e.*, it does not elucidate observations in terms of natural laws. The second possibility, if true, only pushes the problem one stage farther back. It would also require an explanation of how living organisms could survive the hazardous journey through space. There remains the third suggestion that life arose on the earth at an early stage in its long history. This view is accepted by most scientists today, and N. W. Pirie has proposed the convenient term *biopoesis* (life-making) for the origin of life. The approaches to the problem so far have been mainly speculative, but the increasing attention which it has been given in recent years culminated in a conference on the Origin of Life held in Moscow in 1957 by the International Union of Biochemists.

Chemical Conditions before Life appeared.—The earliest fossil remains found in the rocks are of relatively complex organisms. Undoubtedly life first appeared much earlier than the time when these organisms existed, and in a much simpler form. J. D. Bernal has pointed out that biopoesis involved development from the simple to the complex and that Darwin's concept of evolution has to be projected backwards to include the chemical evolution of non-living and pre-vital substances. All living things are built up from organic compounds which contain the element carbon. These compounds are extremely complex, and a single molecule of a protein may contain many hundreds of atoms. Proteins, which are the structural basis of protoplasm, consist of many simpler amino-acids linked together. Thus, before considering the formation of the complex organic compounds found in living organisms, the formation of the simplest organic substances, such as hydrocarbons, must be dealt with. Presumably at an early stage in the earth's history there were land masses, seas and rivers, an atmosphere, but no life or complex organic compounds. It seems likely that the atmosphere consisted of a mixture of nitrogen, carbon dioxide, hydrogen, ammonia, and methane, but probably no oxygen was present. Therefore the conditions on earth when life first arose were probably very different from those today, and A. Oparin and J. B. S. Haldane have concluded that these favoured the formation of energy-giving organic molecules. Recent experiments in Russia and America have shown that if mixtures of the gases mentioned above are exposed to electrical discharges or ultra-violet light many organic molecules are formed, including those of amino-acids. This suggests a way in which simple organic compounds may first have been formed on earth, as its atmosphere would have been exposed to both electrical discharges (lightning) and ultra-violet light (from the sun).

From Simple to Complex Molecules.—A further step would involve the formation of sub-vital systems which, using this energy, could grow, split, and reproduce themselves. Haldane has suggested that these may have been complex phosphates, but J. W. S. Pringle believes that they were oxidised hydrocarbons. The maintenance of these sub-vital systems poses two problems, their protection from the turbulence of their environment and an adequate concentration of their constituents. According to Pringle, they existed in the depths of the oceans, but Haldane suggests they occurred in water-logged soils. Bernal considers they may have been adsorbed on to certain clays along shores and estuaries where the clay minerals might also have acted as inorganic chemical catalysts and promoted the building of larger molecules. Pirie has made the important point that probably many sub-vital systems were formed over a long period of time and that life on earth today represents only one or a few of the most successful.

The Need for More Research.—Another crucial step would be the development of a cell membrane which would contain and protect the system within but which would allow the interchange of substances between the system and the environment. No useful hypothesis has been suggested for this, although Haldane has put forward the view that this was a highly improbable event which occurred once to form the first cell.

Obviously we are far from having an answer to this intriguing problem, which has become of even greater importance with the beginning of space exploration and the possibility of finding life on other planets. It is one which can be fully answered only by the joint efforts of scientists of many disciplines, astronomers, biologists, chemists, and physicists.

III. THE ORIGINS OF HUMAN SOCIETY

THE EARLIEST MEN.

Before describing the earliest men, it is important to try and define just what is meant by "Man." Man is a member of the Order of Primates and of the Sub-Order Anthropoidea, which includes also apes and monkeys. Both Man and the apes belong to the Super-Family Hominoidea, which is subdivided into two Families: the Pongidae or anthropoid apes; and the Hominidae, which includes all extinct and modern forms of Man. The most important anatomical difference between the two Families is that hominids walk upright, whereas pongids are dependent also on their arms for locomotion.

The common ancestral stock of these two Families is represented by such fossil forms as *Proconsul* from East Africa, which lived during the Miocene period about 20 million years ago; these early apes show certain characteristics of the "hominid" line which are not found in the great apes of today. The modern apes have specialised for life in the trees, but some of their ancestors must have left the forests and taken to life on the open plains. In this new environment, the arms no longer had to be used for swinging from tree to tree and gradually the pelvic girdle and lower limbs became adapted to an erect posture. This development had far-reaching effects: it meant that the hands were now free for tool-using and tool-making.

The Australopithecines.—The earliest known hominids are the Australopithecines of E. and S. Africa which lived over a million years ago, during the later part of the Lower Pleistocene. They are so ape-like in appearance that for many years scientists disputed that they were hominids rather than pongids. But, although they cannot be regarded as " men " in the sense that we speak of all members of the genus *Homo* as men, the shape of their pelvis and limb bones makes it certain that they had adopted the erect posture, and for this reason they are classified as hominids.

The first *Australopithecus*—a name which means " southern ape "—was found in 1924 at Taung, Bechuanaland, by Professor R. Dart; it was the skull of a child, and therefore its true position in the evolutionary scheme could not be assessed with certainty. From 1936 onwards, however, adult remains of similar creatures were found by the late Dr. R. Broom in the limestone caves of the Transvaal. These fossils were given various names, but it is now generally agreed that they are all members of one genus. Probably two species are represented: one is small and unspecialised, the other larger and more like the modern gorilla. Both had small brains, but when their size is taken into consideration the brain is relatively larger than that of modern apes.

Occasional finds of crude stone tools in the South African caves suggested that the Australopithecines might have been tool-makers. This view seemed to be supported by a discovery in East Africa in 1959. In the lowest bed of Olduvai Gorge, Tanganyika, Dr. and Mrs. Leakey found a skull which is similar to the more ape-like of the two Australopithecine species from South Africa. Known as *Australopithecus* (*Zinjanthropus*) *boisei*, it was dated by the potassium-argon method to about 1,700,000 years. It has a huge palate with enormous molars, hence its popular name " Nutcracker Man." Also at Olduvai were remains of a more advanced hominid which in 1964 was named *Homo habilis*. It seems to be transitional between the Australopithecines and *Homo erectus* and there seems little doubt that it was this hominid that made the stone tools found in Bed I and the lower part of Bed II in abundance.

This " pebble culture ", the Oldowan, is known from many parts of Africa. It is the first stage of the Palaeolithic or Old Stone Age, which persisted from about a million years ago until the end of the Ice Age about 8000 B.C.

Homo erectus.—The second stage in the evolution of the hominids is represented by *Homo erectus*, or *Pithecanthropus*, as he was formerly called. His remains have been found in Java, China, and Africa, in deposits dating from the Middle Pleistocene, about 400,000 years ago. The brain was considerably larger than it had been during the Australopithecine stage, but it was still very small compared with that of modern man. The skull is extremely thick, the forehead low and sloping, the brow-ridges very heavy, and the chin region receding. The first skull of *Pithecanthropus erectus*—" erect ape-man "—was found as long ago as 1891 at Trinil, Java, by Dr. E. Dubois. Other specimens were discovered by Dr. G. H. R. von Koenigswald during the 1930s, including a rather earlier form named *P. robustus* and a massive jaw of *Meganthropus* which probably represents the Australopithecine stage in Java.

The first remains of Pekin Man from the cave of Chou Kou Tien near Pekin were discovered in 1927 and 1929. Named *Sinanthropus pekinensis*, these specimens are now accepted as being a sub-species of *Homo erectus*. A sad fate befell the original material: it was all lost in American hands during the war as it was being evacuated from China. There are casts of the originals however and two more pieces of mandible were found in 1959. Perkin Man was accompanied by crude tools of stone and bone and hearths show that he could make fire. Large accumulations of bone prove that he was a skilful hunter and human skulls smashed to extract the marrow indicate that he was also a cannibal.

The only certain representatives of *Homo erectus* outside Asia consist of a skull from Bed II, Olduvai Gorge, and jaws found in Algeria and Morocco in 1954–5. They were named *Atlanthropus*, but are almost identical with jaws of Pekin Man. They were accompanied by Acheulian hand-axes, pear-shaped tools which persisted with very little change from the end of the pebble-culture for about 200,000 years. The Olduvai skull, found in 1960, was also associated with hand-axes. It has been dated by the potassium-argon method to about 490,000 years.

The earliest human remains from Europe consists of an isolated jaw found at Mauer, near Heidelberg in Germany in 1907. It is extremely massive and has a number of features which distinguish it from *Homo erectus*. In 1964 and 1965 some teeth and parts of a skull were found at Vertesszöllös in Hungary which may be equally ancient. Both are thought to be roughly contemporary with Pekin Man.

These remains date from the second of the four glacial advances which followed one another during the Pleistocene period. In northern Europe and North America deposits from these successive glacials and interglacials provide a means of dating fossils and implements found in them. Two human skulls dating from the Second or Great Interglacial, about 250,000 years ago, are known from Europe: from Steinheim in Germany and from Swanscombe in Kent. These are roughly contemporary with the last survivors of *Homo erectus* in North Africa. Like the latter, Swanscombe Man was associated with hand-axes.

In the Steinheim brain-case we have, for the first time, proportions not very much smaller than those of modern man. The forehead, however, is sloping and there are well-marked brow-ridges. Probably both the Steinheim skull and the fragmentary Swanscombe remains are ancestral both to modern man and the Neandertal people.

The Neandertaloids.—During the early part of the Fourth Glaciation, in Upper Pleistocene times, the Neandertal race occupied parts of Europe, western and central Asia, and North Africa. At the same time rather similar people lived in southern Africa (Rhodesian Man) and Java (Solo Man). In Europe the Neandertalers lived in caves to protect themselves from the cold. They also buried their dead in caves, with the result that many of their skeletons have been preserved. The first Neandertal remains were found before the end of the last century, in the Neander valley in Germany, as well as in Gibraltar, Belgium, and Jugoslavia. Then many others were discovered in France, and now they are known also from central Siberia and from Cyrenaica and Morocco in North Africa.

The so-called " classic " Neandertalers had a rather brutal appearance, with heavy brow-ridges, sloping foreheads, and receding chins. At Mount Carmel in Palestine these exaggerated forms were found in the Tabun cave, while close by, at Skhul, were others with features far nearer to the men of today. This may be a case of individual variation within a group, or it may mean that Neandertalers interbred with people of modern type to produce hybrids.

Rhodesian Man, though clearly not a Neandertaler, has many distinctive features which distinguish him from modern man, particularly the enormous brow-ridges which form a continuous bar above the eye sockets. The first skull of this type was found in 1921 at Broken Hill in Northern Rhodesia; in 1951, a very similar skull was discovered near Saldanha Bay in Cape Province. The associated fauna and stone tools make it probable that these human remains date from the early part of the Upper Pleistocene, not more than 50,000 years ago and perhaps less. Contemporary and rather similar in appearance is Solo Man from Java, probably a direct descendant of *Homo erectus*, whose remains were found a few miles away.

Homo sapiens.—Events during the Fourth or Last Glaciation can be dated fairly exactly by the radiocarbon method, which, by means of new techniques, can now provide absolute dates over the past 50,000 years. Such dates have supported chronologies previously obtained by studying the geological deposits, which indicate three main cold phases separated by milder periods. Neandertal Man became extinct soon after the first cold phase ended about 40,000 B.C. and was replaced by *Homo sapiens* of completely modern appearance by the beginning of the second cold phase about 30,000 B.C.

Neandertal Man's stone tools were made on flakes; they consisted of points and other weapons which were probably hafted as spears. The implements made by the men who succeeded him show significant advances; they include small knife-blades and engraving tools, specialised for different purposes. It was during this Upper Palaeolithic stage that Man began to concern himself with something more than merely hunting and searching for food. He produced very fine paintings and sculpture, adorned himself with necklaces and other ornaments, and apparently practised magic rites and ceremonies.

Europe.—The earliest known skull of completely modern type comes from Combe Capelle in south central France and was associated with an industry which represents the first stage of the

Upper Palaeolithic of western Europe. The somewhat later Cro-Magnon people, named from a rock shelter at Les Eyzies in the Dordogne, are associated with a culture known as Aurignacian, which is believed to have originated somewhere in the Middle East, perhaps in the region of Palestine. These people were rather tall, with long heads, very large brain-cases, and short, broad faces. They were responsible for very fine cave paintings depicting the animals they hunted, such as the mammoth, woolly rhinoceros, and reindeer.

Africa.—From their original homeland, these people spread westwards not only over Europe but also along the southern shores of the Mediterranean through North Africa. In East Africa too skeletons which are typical of the Mediterranean race have been found associated with an industry not unlike the Aurignacian of Western Europe but considerably later in time. Curiously enough, no skeletons showing characteristic Negroid traits have been found in Africa before post-Pleistocene times, about 8000 B.C., which suggests that the Negroid stock evolved relatively late. In southern Africa there were in Upper Pleistocene times people with very large brain-cases and yet with features reminiscent of the present Bushmen and Hottentots; the first skull of this type, from Boskop in the Transvaal, was found as long ago as 1913.

Asia.—Turning now to Asia, the most remarkable finds of early *Homo sapiens* come from the Upper Cave at Chou Kou Tien (where Pekin Man was discovered). One of the skeletons, an elderly man, is very like the "Old Man of Cro-Magnon." A skull from Niah Cave in Sarawak dated to 40,000 B.C. is the earliest known representative of *Homo sapiens* in Asia. In Java the descendants of Solo Man may be represented by the Wadjak people probably dating from around 8000 B.C., who bear a striking resemblance to the Australian aborigines. They may be roughly contemporary with a skull from Keilor near Melbourne which proves that Australia was populated in late Pleistocene or early post-Pleistocene times.

America.—The question of the date of the first peopling of the New World is very controversial; in nearly every case the geological evidence for the association of early human remains has been questioned. It seems that the first immigrants from Asia crossed the Behring Straits before the end of the Ice Age, perhaps about 15,000 B.C. They are believed to have been of an "archaic White" strain, something like the modern Ainu and Australian aborigines, and probably similar to the "old man" of the Upper Cave at Chou Kou Tien. Later immigrants were fully Mongoloid, and it seems that a mixture of these two strains gave rise to the American Indian.

The End of the Old Stone Age.—From this brief review of developments all over the world, we must return to the Upper Palaeolithic in Western Europe. We left the Cro-Magnons with their Aurignacian culture during the second cold phase of the Last Glaciation. During the time of the main advance of the ice sheets, about 18,000 B.C., the Aurignacian culture died out and was replaced first by the Solutrian and then by the Magdalenian cultures. The Magdalenians are renowned for their very fine working of bone and antler, particularly in the form of barbed harpoons, and for their artistic skill. In many ways their paintings of animals, such as those in the cave of Lascaux, surpass the ones of the Aurignacian period. As the Ice Age drew to a close, however, the Magdalenians disappeared, and with them the great flowering of Upper Palaeolithic art also died out.

Up till the end of the Ice Age, Palaeolithic people must have lived in essentially the same way all over the world. They were hunters and food-gatherers, living in small bands as the Bushmen and Australian aborigines do today. Within these small, isolated groups, certain mutations must have arisen which were advantageous in particular environments. These would have been encouraged by natural selection, thus leading to the differentiation of distinct races in different localities.

After the ice finally retreated about 8000 B.C. the way of life of people in Europe must have changed considerably. The great herds of cold-loving animals upon which Palaeolithic hunters depended for their food either became extinct or retreated as forests began to spread over the open country of former times. The Mesolithic people—living after the end of the Pleistocene and before the Neolithic stage—had to rely increasingly on fishing and collecting shell-fish to supplement their diet.

Outside the areas affected by the ice, however, certain progressive people gave up their nomadic existence and began to live in settled communities. In Palestine and other parts of the Middle East wild wheat and barley grew and there were herds of wild goats and sheep. The Mesolithic Natufians reaped these grasses and cereals and domesticated the dog to help in hunting. It was they who led the way to events which were to revolutionise Neolithic Man's way of life: agriculture and stock-keeping.

ENVIRONMENT AND CULTURE.

It is clear that no people could enter a Bronze or Iron Age unless bronze and iron were, in fact, available in their environment. Hence the Eskimos, who have no metals available to make into weapons or ornaments, still use stone, ivory (from walrus tusks), and bone. In short, their environment does not permit a higher degree of culture. The primitive races or "backward" peoples have evolved ways of life which are often well adapted to the environments in which they live. The second point is that great advances are made only upon the foundations erected by others. The quantum theory and the theory of relativity could not have been evolved by the scientists of ancient Greece or by Galileo or Newton, not because they were less intelligent than Einstein, but because every innovator can progress only a little beyond what he had received from his predecessors in many different lands and times. The house of science is not built top floor first, but slowly upon the foundations laid by earlier thinkers. "Civilisation" is not such a simple concept as we once supposed, and technological advance does not necessarily imply high moral standards. Scientists are agreed that there are no significant intellectual differences between any of the races in existence today, and that the reason why some peoples are relatively backward is either because the raw materials necessary for technological advance have been lacking in their environment, or because by a historical accident their country has been out of contact with the general flow of civilisation, so that the spread of new ideas did not reach within their boundaries. *See also* **Q14**(2).

Definition of Terms.—Anthropologists are agreed that, although it may be quite correct to speak of "national character," we cannot explain this in terms of race or heredity. The true explanation is that such traits are cultural rather than biological in origin, and, since the "culture concept" is immensely important in modern social science, we must first of all define our terms:

> A *society* is a group of people who live and work together, regarding themselves as members of the group, and feeling towards it an emotion best described as "belonging."
>
> A *culture* is the way of life followed by such a group—that is to say, its written or unwritten laws, its religious beliefs, its ideals, its art, technology, and even its pots and pans.

Without written records we are left to deduce the record of prehistoric man by the culture to which he belonged—Azilian, Magdalenian, Acheulian, and so on—and here the archæologist, who knows very little of the ideals and religious beliefs or laws of these bygone peoples is generally thinking in terms of their *material* culture, which includes objects found during excavations such as pots and pans, knives, weapons, needles, and ornaments.

But when we talk of culture in relation to present-day peoples, we are more often thinking of the way of life of the group—its ideals, incentives, and unwritten laws. Culture is what has been described as the "cake of custom," and its importance lies in the fact that it is the cement which binds the members of a group into a living organism.

Sub-Cultures.—All of us are members, not of one group only, but of many, and each group, however small, has a culture of its own, a way of life to which we must conform if we wish to retain group membership or, at any rate, the respect of the other members. As an example, let us take an imaginary individual with the name of George Campbell, who happens to be a Lowland Scot, a Presbyterian, a socialist, a coal-miner working at the coal-face in a particular pit, a pigeon-fancier, and a follower of Newcastle United football team. The interesting thing is that, knowing these facts, we already know a great deal about Mr. Campbell; for we can be sure that his membership of these groups (national, religious, political, sporting, and so on) will strongly influence his behaviour. One of the serious defects of classical psychology and of much popular thought is that it failed to notice how much of the individual's day-to-day behaviour arises, not from the depths of his unconscious or from what is ordinarily described as his "character," but simply from his need to conform to the, often unwritten, rules of his membership groups. If anyone suggested to our Mr. Campbell that he was not an entirely free agent, that he was not as independent as he prides himself on being, he would, no doubt, be very annoyed. Nevertheless, this is merely a commonplace statement of fact. Campbell has all the prejudices of the Lowland Scot—he thinks that education is a "grand thing," that Roman Catholics are a dangerous and superstitious sect, that the English are a somewhat inferior nation over the Border who regrettably lack stamina and intelligence, and that money, although the root of all evil, is a good thing to have and be careful about. But, had he been born in the South of Italy, he would have regarded education as the exclusive possession of wealthy landowners, Catholicism as the only true religion, the English would have meant little to him at all (until the last war), and his goods would be exchanged by barter rather than money. Mr. Campbell enjoys his morning porridge and bacon and eggs, but his enjoyment of them is only a prejudice learned in childhood and his opposite numbers in Africa and France enjoy locusts, frog's legs, and snails, which it has never struck him to regard as "food" at all. His grandfather might have worn a beard, but if Campbell came to work wearing one, he might find himself in difficulties; this is one of the many quite innocuous things which are "not done" in certain groups. Campbell might, on special occasions, wear a kilt, but Mr. Smith over the Border would find himself under considerable social pressure to stop doing so if he ever had the temerity to start. There is no law saying that Scots or Englishmen may not strip to the waist in a hot cinema or theatre, but they do not do so, although a miner may do so at work and other people at the seaside. In short, Mr. Campbell, like the rest of us, is for the most part a creature of custom.

Approved Patterns of Conduct.—If we take the usual analogy of the clay, the potter, and the design, then it will be seen that the newborn child (the clay) is modelled by the parents (the potter), not at random, but according to the approved pattern of a particular society (the design). Everyone, into whatever society he is born, is brought up to have specific attitudes to women or men, to sexual relations, to cleanliness, to aggressiveness, and to competition, and these attitudes are unique to each society at any given time. Most middle-class Englishmen feel that they ought to "get on" and have ambitions, that one should not strike a woman, that one ought to have a daily bath, and that it is rude to argue in public with shopkeepers, waiters, and public servants. Frenchmen and Italians have no such inhibitions about arguing in public, and Americans have a much stronger desire to succeed. Such differences in national or class character may often cause difficulties through misunderstanding. For example, the average British worker attaches more importance to sticking together with his mates than to getting on, and he rather despises the middle-class attitude that one must succeed at all costs, regardless of whom one has to overcome in order to get there. Then the average American is brought up to feel that when he has made more money than someone else, he should be proud of his achievement and make no secret of his opulence, however temporary, while on the other hand the Englishman feels that it is impolite to discuss money or speak of one's achievements. Therefore to the American the Englishman is a queer, reticent, and "stodgy" individual; to the Englishman the American is noisy and boastful. Neither accusation is true—both are judging each other in terms of how they have been taught people ought to behave.

Interaction of Group Influences.—Although we have so far spoken of the national character of such large groups as the British, American, French, and Italians, it is obvious that when dealing with groups of this size composed of many subgroups, the resulting picture will be far from clear. Our Mr. Campbell is, to the foreigner, simply "British," but he is, as we have seen, also a Scot, a Protestant, a member of the working-class, and a miner. So, although he shows many traits which are "British" in the widest sense, he differs in obvious ways from another Britisher who was born in London, is of the middle class, belongs to the Church of England, and works as an accountant. It is not only national, but also regional, religious, class, and occupational groups which influence personality, and there are other factors also at work which we must shortly discuss. Before doing so, however, the reader is asked to turn to **Section Q, Part II**, where a brief account is given of the researches of Ruth Benedict and Margaret Mead into the cultural ideals of various primitive societies. Primitive peoples are more suited to anthropological studies, because, in the first place, they can be separated into small tribal communities which are, for the most part, not subdivided into regional, class, or religious subgroups. Secondly, they are much less subject to social change, and have remained closely integrated, undivided, and in varying degrees static for considerable periods of time.

Individual Differences.—Now, as we can readily observe, individuals differ quite considerably from each other, even within the same social group, so we must now consider what factors give rise to the individual variations upon the theme set by culture; several, in fact, have already been mentioned. These are, the subgroups to which the individual belongs, his status and role, and his particular upbringing and inheritance. Social change, too, gradually brings about changes in the "basic personality type" of a society, as, for example, the changes in the Englishman's attitude to, say, music and sport which took place between Elizabethan and Victorian times.

1. *The Influence of Subgroups* in bringing about particular attitudes in the individual has already been discussed, and need not be further elaborated here.

2. *Status and Role.*—An individual's status is his position in society, not only in respect of social class, but also in occupational, marital, professional, and other spheres. His role is the behaviour which is associated in that society with a given status. Perhaps these concepts are most simply explained if we regard social life as a sort of stage-play in which each individual is an actor in particular roles: a parson has to act as a parson, a doctor as a doctor, a father as a father, and a manager as a manager. Parsons are expected to talk and dress in a particular manner, fathers to behave in a certain way (which differs in each society), and although every parson or father is an individual in his own right, many of

his acts can be understood only when we realise that he is acting in the way society expects of parsons and fathers. When people break these unwritten rules, difficulties may arise. There is no law which says that a parson may not play the saxophone, but one who did would be looked on somewhat askance by his parishioners, and, although patients sometimes complain that their physician puts on an exaggerated "bed-side manner," they are often even more distressed when he does not. Gordon Rattray Taylor tells of a factory manager who went about in a shabby old car, and who, far from being thought endearing and democratic for doing so, was regarded with disapproval by the workers, who felt that he was "letting down the side" by not behaving in a manner appropriate to his position. This is what is described as "*formal status*," since managers, parsons, fathers, and so on, occupy formal positions recognised by society as at present constituted. There is also *informal* status—that is to say, the type of status allotted to individuals in a small and intimate group such as the working group in the factory. For example, we have George, who is the one who defies management and takes the lead when complaints are to be made; Alf, the one who tells dubious funny stories; Bill, the one who knows all about First Aid; and Harry, the amiable idiot who is always teased by group members but protected from the jibes of the members of other groups. All these individuals have been allotted a certain informal status, and are supposed to act "in character," although each man in another group may play a quite different role. Alf, the joker, may be henpecked at home—a sad little man; Bill, the knowledgeable First Aider, may be a very insignificant member of the local St. John's Ambulance Brigade, to whom he may be the "silly ass"; George, the resentful, may be the kindly father. But within each group their roles are fixed and difficult to evade. Status and role, therefore, have a powerful influence upon behaviour.

3. *Differences due to Upbringing and Heredity.*—Although the influence of heredity, so far as personality is concerned, has been grossly exaggerated, it does indeed play some part. What is inherited, however, is not specific behaviour but temperament, and temperamental differences, being based on glandular and structural nervous factors, are fairly permanent features of the personality. By and large, upbringing determines *what* we do, temperament *how* we do it.

The most important differences between one individual and another in the same culture arise from the vagaries of upbringing; for, even apart from such accidents of fate as the loss of one or both parents, illness in childhood, and natural calamities, the obvious fact is that no parents ever pass on the cultural design to their children without many individual variations. If we picture the cultural design as a rough mould which supplies the main outlines of the pattern, we can also picture the parents as adding individual touches of their own (whether knowingly or otherwise) to a material which already varies for biological reasons. At this point it is necessary to say something of the work of Freud, for it is he who has given us some of our closest insights into what one might describe as the microscopic anatomy of the individual personality. Unfortunately to do so is by no means easy because Freudian theory is extremely complex, and has, furthermore, been considerably modified by later writers of the psycho-analytic school. What is given here must be taken only as a very rough outline of what Freud and later psycho-analysts have been trying to say.

FREUDIAN THEORY.

The newborn child is a young animal, with no morals or sense of reality and no "instincts" as we understand the term in the lower animals. It has only two great drives which Freud takes to be fundamental—sex and aggression. Although Freud described sex and aggression as "instincts," the word is nowadays reserved for a particular form of behaviour which, if it exists at all in man, is certainly a dying category—it should be used solely for behaviour which is inborn, relatively fixed, and automatic. Ants, bees, and wasps, for example, carry out the most detailed acts; nest-building, caring for the grubs, or food-collecting and storing; but there can be no doubt at all that none of these acts is in any way intelligent. They are based on the insect's nervous structure, and could not occur otherwise than they do. Among the higher animals, the birds and mammals, such instinctual behaviour comes to be increasingly modified by intelligence, but it is only in man that intelligence assumes its full significance, and all behaviour is modifiable and no longer automatic. The drives of sex and aggression in man do not involve any elaborate type of fixed behaviour pattern; they are simply the raw material of action, to be modified in many different ways as the child learns from its parents and others. Briefly, all animals in varying degrees (more so in the lower animals, less so among the higher) are like tram-cars moving upon fixed rails, and however complex the route they take, it is largely what has been laid down from the beginning. Human beings, on the other hand, are like motor cars, which, although making use of the same source of energy as the animals, can utilise it to drive where they please.

Sex.—Freud used the word sex in a rather specialised sense to apply, not only to sexual behaviour in the ordinary meaning of the word, but also to such behaviour as eating and drinking, excretion, and, at a higher level, to love and friendship. It might almost be said that in Freudian terminology sex and aggression are words used to describe the two poles of desire, positive (love, lust, hunger, longing, wanting) and negative (hating, fearing, avoiding, killing, getting rid of things).

The Id.—The problem of society is to modify this primitive creature which can only need and desire, hate or fear, want pleasure and avoid pain, into a civilised being, and this is the problem it delegates to the parents, who, in the long run, utilise the child's need for security or protection and care to compel it to act in approved ways. The baby learns, by imitation, by trial and error, by punishment or the threat of punishment, by love or fear of the loss of love, to conform more or less to social standards. The primitive aspect of the mind, which includes not only the innate drives of sex and aggression but also all those thoughts and emotions which, in the course of development, the individual comes to accept as forbidden, is described as the Id, and just because it contains this sort of material, thoughts and emotions within it become or remain unconscious.

When the infant is born, its mind is all Id, but sooner or later the child is confronted by stern reality when it comes to realise that desires are not satisfied automatically. Sometimes it is hungry and food is not forthcoming, sometimes it is wet and uncomfortable and has to wait to be "changed"—all these events occur even to the most fortunate baby.

The Ego.—So a part of the mind comes to be separated off from the primitive Id, whose function it is to deal with reality, and this part is known as the Ego—the conscious mind as we know it in adult life. The basic function of the Ego is to deal with life as it really is, not as we should like it to be.

The Superego.—Still later, perhaps about the age of three or four, the child is faced by another problem; for it has to start conforming to the ethical dictates of society, to what is ordinarily described as the moral code. It has to learn what is done and what must not be done, and so a further division in the mind takes place and part of the mind begins to specialise in moral control. This part is known as the Superego. The Superego arises in two distinct stages—firstly, the child comes to realise that, under penalty of punishment or disapproval, it must obey its parents; at this stage, then, compulsion comes from outside. Later, however, the child by a process of what Freud describes as "introjection" takes the parental standards within itself. One part of the mind, as it were, plays the role of the moral parent in relation to the rest. This is the fully-fledged Superego.

Character.—An individual's character is the result of a three-cornered struggle between the primitive biological drives (represented by the Id), the hard facts of reality (represented by the Ego), and the moral dictates of society (represented by the Superego). The Superego is the censor which forbids thoughts or actions not allowed by society or, more accurately, thoughts or actions which were forbidden by the parents in early childhood. As one writer says, the Superego is a sort of psychological gyroscope which places control within the mind and avoids, in varying degrees, the need for outward compulsion. When the dictates of the Superego are transgressed the individual has a sense of guilt and feels himself more or less a social outcast.

Expression of Primitive Impulses.—But the primitive drives are very powerful and cannot be totally repressed—they demand some sort of outlet, and are given it on condition that they are suitably modified or appear in socially acceptable forms or at least at socially acceptable times. Most societies, for example, permit the expression of primitive emotion at certain periods or under certain conditions; the sexual drive is permitted expression in marriage, and naked aggression in warfare. But more often the drives have to be modified by one or other of two fundamental mechanisms known as reaction formation and sublimation. In the case of reaction formation the energy of the forbidden impulse is utilised in emphasising its opposite; it is as if the individual were saying: "Of course I don't have such wicked desires—you can see I am quite another sort of person." Perhaps this mechanism will become clearer if we give some examples.

(1) Even the layman is aware that people who are excessively puritanical are frequently by their very puritanism demonstrating quite the contrary aspects of their character. We laugh at the elderly lady who is afraid of finding a man under her bed precisely because we are aware consciously or unconsciously, that she would not have the fear if she did not also have the hope. Similarly, when we read in the papers of a gentleman who so disapproves of obscene books or magazines that he buys hundreds of them to find out whether they are suitable or not for others to read, we may suspect that his own motives are not entirely devoid of suspicion. In short, the character-trait of puritanism is sometimes a reaction formation against strong sexual desires; the individual is fighting in the outer world the very problem he is unable to deal with in his own mind. *See also* **The Nature of Aggression, Q7.**

(2) The second method of dealing with primitive impulses is by sublimation—that is to say, by making them socially useful. A butcher, a surgeon, or a prize-fighter are all expressing in modified form their latent sadism, but in a way which is recognised by society. Women who have wanted children and failed to have them may become teachers, helpers in nursery schools, and so on in a valuable attempt to satisfy a frustrated need. If Freud is correct, the frustrated sexual curiosity of childhood may later take the form of a desire to know, causing the individual to become a scientist or a bookworm. Art, sculpture, and painting may all be sublimations of the infant's natural dirtiness and pleasure in messing about with mud, water, or even its own excretions. The reader may or may not accept these latter assumptions, but it is only fair to say that those who are in a position to know have found a great deal to support Freud's theories.

Mental Mechanisms.—Even in adult life the individual's adjustment to reality—the "hard facts of life"—and to moral problems is never complete, and self-deception is common. In this connection Freud describes various mental mechanisms which even those who do not accept the Freudian theory in its entirety have found valuable in understanding human behaviour. We will conclude, therefore, by describing some of these forms of self-deception here and giving examples of their influence upon human behaviour.

1. *Displacement.*—An emotion, when conditions do not permit its being directed towards a particular object, may be directed against another which originally had nothing to do with it. "Love on the rebound" is an example of this in which, when the original object of love has disappeared, another is quickly found, not because of any real qualities possessed by the new object, but rather because the emotion demands some outlet. In Nazi Germany Hitler permitted the displacement of economic and other resentments felt by the Germans after the Treaty of Versailles on to the Jews and Communists, who were thus made scapegoats for the convenience of the Nazi party. It is important to understand that this is one of the commonest types of mental mechanism which is universally, although unconsciously, used by us all.

2. *Projection.*—This is an example of a mechanism which has already been demonstrated. In brief, it means the tendency to project the objectionable qualities we refuse to recognise in ourselves upon others. "It is not I but he who is thinking and doing these wicked things." Thus, as we have seen, people who will not admit to their own impure thoughts accuse others of possessing them; those who are aggressive believe that everybody else but themselves are aggressive; the greedy accuse others of greed, and so on. Carried to an extreme degree, this is the mechanism behind persecution mania or paranoia, as the psychiatrist calls it. Projection is another very important trick of the mind, and its social effects are often all too evident.

3. *Compensation.*—Alfred Adler, one of Freud's pupils who later founded a separate system of psychology, was the first to draw attention to this important mechanism.

Briefly, Adler pointed out that those who suffer from a deep-seated sense of inferiority (whether due to physical or mental defects or to lack of affection in childhood) have a strong tendency to compensate for this either by overcoming the actual defect or by becoming superior in some other field. *See* **Individual Psychology, Section J.**

4. *Rationalisation.*—This, as Bradley said of philosophy, is "the giving of bad reasons for what we do upon impulse." Nowadays, for example, nobody ever goes to war in order to kill a lot of people or take their country from them; they go to war for the other nation's own good—because they want to help them. Rationalisation is too familiar to most of us to need further discussion.

5. *Conversion.*—This is the mechanism which most people find it least easy to understand. Whereas the other mechanisms are, in their milder forms at least, almost normal, conversion is always abnormal, and implies more or less serious disturbance of the mind. There are two types of conversion: hysterical and psychosomatic.

In the first case, a state of mental conflict produces symptoms of physical disorder which, however, are not due to any underlying physical disease. Such cases may show symptoms of blindness, deafness, complete or partial paralysis of the limbs, double personality, or loss of memory, all of which can be shown to be purely psychological in origin, and, in fact, occur because the individual in some sense does not want to be able to walk, see, hear, or remember. In short, the symptom occurs because it gets the individual out of some difficulty which he is facing at that particular period.

People with psychosomatic disorders suffer from actual physical disease as a direct result of mental stress. Within their bodies actual physical damage has resulted from prolonged exposure to emotional tensions. Elsewhere (**P46 (1)**) something has been said about the autonomic nervous system which prepares the organism for relaxation or emergency. The frustrated worker, hating his job and resenting his boss, has the raised blood-pressure normal to the angry animal; but it continues day in and day out until his arteries become thickened and the pressure can no longer return to normal. The ambitious business-man, mentally on the attack for years at a time perpetuates the associated physical changes normal to an attitude of attack; his stomach-wall is drained of proper blood-supply and the digestive juices, ordinarily neutralised by anti-enzymes in the blood, digest the lining of the stomach itself, causing an ulcer. Of course, what has been said here is inevitably over-simplified; for no disease is due to a single cause, nor is it at all clear why one patient gets one type of psychosomatic disease and a second another.

In summary, this is how views have altered:

(a) To a considerable extent we must discard the old view that sickness is always something that happens to an unsuspecting individual, like being hit on the head by a falling slate. Patients usually go to a doctor in much the same frame of mind as they would go to a watch-maker—" Here, there's something wrong with this watch—what are *you* going to do about it? " But from now on it has to be realised that the patient and the illness are one, that it is because he is the sort of person he is that he has become ill in a particular way.

(b) Fear and hate or anxiety not only cause unhappiness but also sickness and death. Hate and fear can kill.

(c) The psychosomatic diseases and the mental disorders generally are social diseases. They are strongly influenced by the stress of modern life and are on the increase.

(d) Mention must be made of the body-mind problem which these observations bring to the fore. Ultimately, of course, this problem is a philosophical one which cannot be decided by observation or experiment, but today psychologists and doctors are inclined to make use of the working hypothesis that body and mind are one—that " mind " is only a useful word to refer to certain processes occurring in the body. *See also* **Mind and Matter, Section J.**

(e) There are three types of individual who are in rebellion against society: the neurotic, the criminal, and the genius. The differences between the three are that the neurotic rebels in secret or unconsciously, the criminal openly, and the genius by his creative work is able to sublimate his conflicts in art or literature or even to change society nearer to his heart's desire. (It will be understood that this is a very loose formulation of a very complex problem.)

Now it is the modern view that such conflicts are not private and individual as has hitherto been thought (notably by Freud); for it is the conflicts latent in a particular society which are fought out in sensitive minds. Briefly each society is now regarded as a sort of electromagnetic field in which the neurotic, the criminal, and the genius are areas of high tension—in them the conflicts suffered by the society as a whole are magnified to the point of breakdown. Whereas, as was realised long ago, such diseases as cholera, typhoid, or smallpox are due to material defects of society in respect of hygiene and the application of medical knowledge, the behaviour of neurotics, criminals and those with psychosomatic disorders is due to cultural defects of the society in the psychological sphere.

Modern psychology and sociology are showing more clearly than ever before that, in the words of Donne, " no man is an island," and that for the misery or unhappiness or badness of the few we are all responsible. *See also* **Section Q, Part II.**

IV. SPECIAL TOPICS

THE PHILOSOPHY OF SCIENCE.

The Experimental Character of Science.

If we ask what distinguishes scientific work from other human activities, the first answer is that it is one form of enquiry; if we ask what distinguishes it from other enquiries, then the most striking feature is its foundation in observation and experiment. An experiment is an observation carried out to test an idea, hypothesis, or theory. This feature separates scientific work from work in theology, morals, mathematics, and philosophy. It seems natural to insist on a close relation to experiment as a condition which any theory, concept, or investigation must fulfil if it is to belong to science: a theory must be susceptible of experimental proof or disproof; for every concept there must be experimental tests to decide whether or not it applies; an investigation must include the submission of any iypotheses put forward to an experimental test. To insist strictly on this defining condition is to take a *positivist* approach to science as, for example, the physicist Ernst Mach did. Positivism, as a more general philosophy, holds that not only science but all enquiry must fulfil this condition. Positivism rules out work in theology, norals, mathematics, and philosophy as enquiries; t rules out any of the results of such work as knowledge. This attitude has aroused considerable opposition, but even in science itself positivism faces great difficulties. These difficulties re genuine problems, for the closest relation to xperiment is the most natural condition to lemand of science. The difficulties appear as oon as we ask what further characteristics an nquiry must possess if it is to count as scientific.

Explanation.

The explanation of a fact lies in another which etermined it. " Why is this valley straight nd steep-sided? " " Because it was once laciated." Glaciation would be no explanation f straightness or of steep-sidedness unless there ere a connection between these circumstances; he connection lies in a law of geology, that if a rge body of ice moves slowly down a river valley shaves off bends and cuts down into the valley oor across its whole breadth. An explanation can be challenged in two ways: the circumstance offered in explanation may not be a fact: and there may be no connection between this circumstance and the fact to be explained. Hypotheses expressing connections are of conditional form: if . . . , then. . . . In everyday life explanations of particular occurrences are offered even though no connection is known to hold universally: " What made him lose his temper? " " You laughed when he was relating his difficulties." The connection intended is that if you hadn't laughed then he would not have lost his temper, but no generalisation is known from which this conditional could be deduced. In contrast, it is characteristic of science that it is a search for connections which hold universally, such as the geological law about glaciation. The search for universal laws distinguishes science from other activities in which explanations are sought, from detective work, medical practice, and the writing of history. It constitutes the first difficulty which positivism has to face, for a universal hypothesis does not seem susceptible of experimental proof. Disproof perhaps—a man may place a piece of wood in water and watch it sink, so finding experimental disproof of the universal hypothesis that all wood floats on water —but no amount of observation will, by itself, prove that hypothesis. Observations must be brought to an end sometime, yet later observations might have proved the theory false.

Confirmation.

Some philosophers have argued that this difficulty arises from demanding an impossibly strict relation of theory to experiment. They suggest that although it is impossible to see what experimental results would be conclusive proof of a theory, yet it may be possible to see what results would count as evidence in its favour. This is all that can be demanded of a theory, but this can be demanded. However, while logic and mathematics provide rules showing, in many cases, whether one proposition implies another, they provide no rules showing whether one proposition supports another, and, if so, how strongly. Those who believe that rules of evidential support can be found, analogous to the rules of logic and mathematics, call them rules of *confirmation.* The character that rules of confirmation must share with rules of logic is complete independence of science, both of experiment and of theory; if a body of rules is to constitute the relationship between theory and experiment the rules cannot themselves, without confusion, be dependent upon theory or experiment. For example, the rule: *the observation that this is a swan and this is not white contradicts the hypothesis that all swans are white,* is itself independent of science; it derives from a rule of logic. On the other hand the rule: *the observation of a motorcyclist driving fast on ice is strong support for the conclusion that he will soon fall,* is not independent of science although it is a rule concerning evidential support; it is not a rule of confirmation. Two places where philosophers seek rules of confirmation are the classical definition of probability and the principle of induction.

The Classical Definition of Probability.

Early writers on this subject define the probability that a dice will fall with an odd-numbered side up (on the evidence that it has fallen) as the ratio of odd-numbered ways of falling to all ways of falling. The answer, in this example, seems to be 3/6, or 1/2. Some regard this figure as showing the support given by the evidence to the conclusion and regard this method of measuring probabilities as one method, perhaps *the* method, of measuring strength of confirmation. But what is counted, in the example about the dice, is not the number of ways the dice can fall, but the number of sides it can fall on: what counts as a side is definite, but a great many opinions might be held about what counts as a way. There are in fact many problems in probability for which contradictory answers can be got, according to the choice of how to count the ways. A simple example is this: we are following a man along a road and he is out of sight when the road divides into three. Two roads lead along the valley, one leads up the hill. How strongly does the evidence that he took one of the roads confirm the conclusion that he went up the hill? There are three roads altogether, he took one of them, therefore the answer is 1/3; but there are two courses he might have taken—he might have climbed the hill or he might have stayed in the valley—climbing the hill is one of these, therefore the answer is 1/2. In this form the classical definition of probability does not provide a rule of confirmation. Various attempts have been made to make the method of counting definite. Some depend on the assumption that any body of evidence can be split up into atomic pieces of evidence which cannot themselves be split. For example, the evidence that the dice has fallen on one of its faces can be split into: *Either it has fallen* 1 *spot up or* 2 *spots up or* 3, 4, 5, *or* 6 *spots up*; perhaps these alternatives could be split up into further alternatives, but if there is a limit to this process then—at least in theory—a definite method of counting the ways which make the evidence true would exist. No conclusive arguments in favour of this assumption have been found.

The Principle of Induction.

A more direct approach is to declare that a principle called the principle of induction provides a rule of confirmation. This principle gives rules such as: the evidence that of three eggs investigated, each has a yolk, provides some confirmation of the conclusion that all eggs have yolks, and evidence concerning a greater number of eggs would provide correspondingly more. Unfortunately this principle, obviously invalid for conclusive confirmation, is no more satisfactory for lesser degrees. In application it leads to contradictory conclusions.

Consider a set of experimental results concerning the variation of one variable, X, with another, Y: these are plotted as crosses on the graph in the diagram in the next column.

According to the inductive principle these results are some confirmation of the hypothesis which they all fit, that the line H gives the law by which X and Y vary. Again, according to the principle, they confirm to exactly the same degree the hypothesis that this law is given by the line K; for they all lie on K, just as they lie on H. Now consider what value Y has for a value of X (x) which is not given in the results: line H gives one value for Y, line K another. But if the results confirm one of these values for Y, they must

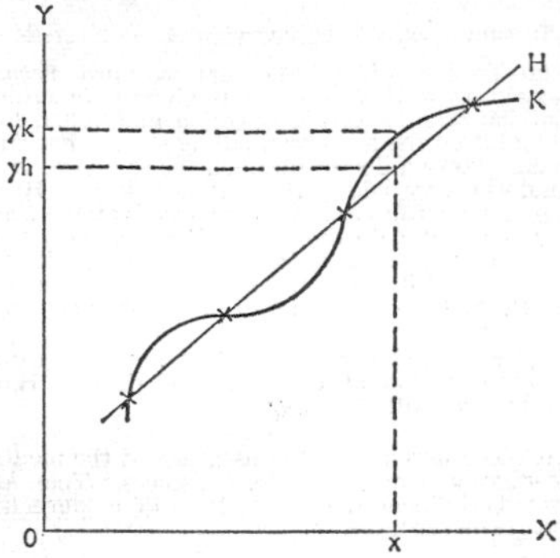

disconfirm the other for the two are inconsistent; therefore this application of the principle of induction leads to the conclusion that the results both confirm and disconfirm each of the predicted values. The principle leads to contradictory predictions: it gives, not wrong answers, but rather no answers at all.

Falsifiability and Knowledge.

In default of any convincing account of how experiments can give even inconclusive support to a universal hypothesis it is tempting to accept the view that the experimental character of a theory consists, not in the possibility of experimental proof, but rather in the possibility of experimental disproof: if a theory can be refuted by experiment, then it has experimental consequences. Sensible as this seems, it leaves the mystery of how anyone can ever come to know a theory to be true. Of course, a man might come to accept a theory which happened to be true, but if his belief were come to by accident it could hardly count as knowledge. Knowledge, it seems, demands proof, or at least very good evidence, and no evidence can count in science except experiment. It has been suggested that knowledge does not differ at all from holding a belief that happens to be true, but that there is a difference between *saying* that someone knows something and *saying* that he holds a true belief about it. On this view, saying that someone knows about a subject is to admit his right to speak on it. But there may be a difference between knowing and believing truly which does not consist in the possession, or lack, of evidence—a difference analogous to that between hitting the bull's-eye by luck and hitting it by skill. Experience brings skill to a man with talent, but experience is no part of marksmanship and it is possible, if unlikely, that a man should shoot well without it. So, perhaps, scientific knowledge is a skill, for example a skill at predicting eclipses which experiment helps a man to attain, but which, in theory at least, he might attain without it. In such views scientific work is an enquiry in which ideas, and the submission of these ideas to experimental test, play a large part; but there is besides, and this is what many find objectionable an irrational element: a choice between whatever ideas have survived experimental trial.

Explanation: Causal and Functional.

It is natural to speak of the circumstance offered in explanation of a fact as its cause. This is clearly correct in the geological example: the glaciation was the cause of the straightness and steep-sidedness of the valley. But it is not s obvious that the difference in density of mahogany and water is the cause of a piece of mahogany floating: the difference in density is not a circumstance which precedes the floating. Similarly with Newton's law relating force and acceleration, which does not tell us that if a force is applied then an acceleration of a certain value will follow: it tells us rather that if a force is applied to a body *at any time* then *at that time* the acceleration of the body will have a certain value. Such examples are typical of physics and evidently they are closely related to causal explanations, but it is a difficult task to say exactly how. Such laws are called *functional*, as opposed to causal: they enable us to argue from the value of one variable to the value of the other, but they do not enable us to make predictions unless we can first predict the future values of one of them.

Association and Causal Connection.

A distinction is often drawn between circumstances which are invariably associated with another, so that they may serve as a sign of it, and circumstances which are not only associated with another, but are causally connected with it, so that they figure in its explanation. For example, orange spots are, perhaps, a sign that a fungus is inedible, but they are unlikely to figure in the explanation of its inedibility, as, perhaps, the presence of some organic acid might do. This distinction between association and causal connection presents a further problem to positivism, for no experimental consequences distinguish the one from the other. The presence of the organic acid in an edible fungus disproves the causal connection between the two, but it also disproves the invariable association. The same difficulty appears with particular propositions: " If you were to walk on the ice, you would fall in " and " You won't walk on the ice without falling in " have a different relation to observable fact, for the latter (which is the same as "Either you won't walk on the ice or you will fall in ") is proved by the observation that you do not venture on the ice whereas the former is not, but there is no observation which will refute one without refuting the other. Those who see the scientific character of a theory in its experimental consequences must identify invariable association with causal connection, and so identify prediction with explanation.

Statistical Association.

Scientific hypotheses take not only the universal form: *All springs stretch when loaded* but also probability forms such as: *There is a probability of 3/4 that a child of brown-eyed parents will also have brown eyes.* Such probability hypotheses are most simply interpreted as frequencies, on the analogy of the frequencies with which heads turn up in a sequence of throws of a penny, but how are these frequencies themselves to be understood? One suggestion is: *In a group of* 1,000 *children of brown-eyed parents 3/4 will have brown eyes.* This gives no definite interpretation however because the proportion would depend upon how the group of children was selected from all the children of brown-eyed parents available. Another suggestion is: *In the next thousand children born of brown-eyed parents 3/4 will have brown eyes.* But this would mean that from the observation that in 500 children born of brown-eyed parents more than 3/4 were brown-eyed, it could be predicted that in the next 500 born less than 3/4 would be brown-eyed. This reasoning leads gamblers to bet on heads after a long run of tails. The frequency of 3/4 for brown-eyed children of brown-eyed parents is not intended to justify any such inference. To avoid this consequence the frequency must be interpreted as concerning not merely a long sequence of children, but an infinitely long sequence. If it does so, then even very long runs in which all children are blue-eyed will not prove the frequency of 3/4 incorrect, indeed such runs must be expected occasionally and the eye-colour of one group of children is to show no prediction of the eye-colour of another. But if the frequency concerns only what happens in an infinite sequence of children, then it has no observational consequences. Here is another difficulty for positivism.

Such frequency hypotheses, Mendel's laws are an example, show how circumstances influence one another but not how they determine one another. The fact that the hypotheses of a theory have a frequency form might be due to the undeveloped state of that branch of science, or it might be due to the absence of universal connections in that part of nature with which the theory deals. In some parts of atomic physics there are reasons for supposing that no laws of universal form hold. Not everyone regards this conclusion as established but if it is correct the possibilities of explanation are severely limited: it would not be possible to explain facts, only to state the factors which exerted an influence and assess their strength.

Inferred Entities.

Many scientific theories provide their explanations in terms of entities whose existence and whose properties are inferred from experimental results, but which are not themselves observable. Examples are the particles of the molecular theory of gases, the ether of the theory of light and of radio waves, and the genes of Mendelian genetics. Hypotheses involving the existence of such entities are neither provable nor refutable by experiment: it is indeed on the evidence of experiment that such entities are postulated, but to try to check their existence by experiment would be little better than checking one newspaper report against another. Other theories provide explanations in terms of properties which, although they belong to observable bodies, are not themselves observable. The structural strength of a wooden beam is an example. Unobservables of this type are thought to present less of a problem to positivism, for a statement about the strength of a beam may be interpreted as a statement about what would happen if the beam were subjected to various loads. Such properties are often called *dispositional*, because they concern the manner in which the body is disposed to behave under various conditions. Of course the hypothesis that a beam has a certain strength is of universal form and concerns more than a mere association between load and behaviour, so this brings us back to the other difficulties of positivism; but if all unobservables could be regarded as dispositional properties of observables, one difficulty would be overcome. The genetic constitution of a plant might be identified as its behaviour in breeding experiments, rather than considered as an unknown physical structure; the passage of an electromagnetic wave through an empty region of space might be regarded, not as the displacement of an unobservable medium, the ether, but as a variation in the accelerations which very small pieces of iron would experience if placed in that region. This policy is a modern application of Occam's Razor: regard a theory as asserting relationships between what can be observed, never as postulating entities which cannot be observed. It is not always a plausible policy. When, in the molecular theory of gases, a gas is said to consist of a large number of small particles in constant motion it is not ordinarily supposed that this is just a way of summarising the observable behaviour of the gas: that it expands when heated, combines chemically with other gases in simple proportions by weight, and so on.

Positivism requires only that an entity should be observable, not that it should be observed; the mountains on the side of the Moon hidden from the Earth were unobserved before photographs were obtained, but not unobservable. The conception of the Earth and the Moon as approximately spherical masses of rock moving at a definite distance from one another showed what would count as an observation of the hidden side of the Moon; but in more primitive cosmologies it might be impossible to see what would count. The particles of the molecular theory of gases have many of the properties of larger sized bodies—mass, size, and elasticity—and they might, though sub-microscopic, be regarded as observable but unobserved. Whether this is correct depends on whether the theory allows us to see what would count as an observation of the particles. The fact that they share many properties with larger bodies may be misleading: fairies share many properties with ordinary people, but fairy stories do not tell us what to do if we want to see one, nor how to be sure whether we have seen one or not.

Special Problems.

The problems we have considered arise over science in general; there are, besides, problems arising in particular sciences: questions about the distinction between inanimate matter and living organisms, about the nature of consciousness, or about the absolute or relational character of space.

Conclusion.

Despite the formidable difficulties which face positivism many philosophers still maintain it in some form. However, even the less strict forms—those involving confirmation by experiment, or refutation by experiment, rather than proof—face great difficulties. Recent work in the philosophy of science has failed to find a satisfactory account of the nature of science, but it has in many ways achieved a fuller and clearer understanding of the ideas and problems involved.

DEMOGRAPHY TODAY

John Graunt, one of the first Fellows of the Royal Society, founded the subject of demography with the publication in 1662 of his book *Natural and Political Observations made upon the Bills of Mortality*. Then world population was about 500 million; today it is 3,200 million and increasing at 2 per cent a year. It is not surprising therefore that within the last two decades there has been a major development of university institutes devoted to population research. The second United Nations World Population Conference held in Belgrade in 1965 provided demographers with an opportunity to take stock of their science and evaluate the progress made since the first U.N. population conference was held in Rome in 1954.

Demography—the scientific study of population—consists of the numerical and analytical portrayal of human populations viewed as aggregates of persons. Demographers are interested in the distribution of people among certain categories at any one time. For instance, the age distribution of a population will in normal circumstances give a reasonably good idea of the level of birth rates—a high fertility population having a large proportion of young people and a low fertility population a relatively small proportion. Demographers are also interested in the changes which occur to populations over a period of time, such as the age at which people marry, the extent to which people marry or remain single, average size of family, and in advances in medicine which lead to changes in the principal causes of death and to improvements in the expectation of life. They are concerned with variations in the proportion of people residing in urban and rural areas, in the way people earn their living, and in the education received as children. Many of these variables are inter-related. As an example, people living in cities frequently tend to have smaller families than people living in rural areas, and the infants of well-educated parents are less likely to die in the first year of life than those of poorly educated or illiterate parents. The relationship between population growth on the one hand, and economic and social developments on the other, is of such vital importance in the world today that demographers must have some understanding of economics, sociology and statistical techniques if they are to make worthwhile contributions to the study of population.

Present and Future World Population.

The population of the world is estimated to have passed the 3,000 million mark early in the 1960s—an increase of at least 50 per cent since 1920. If the current trend of growth continues, world population at the end of the century will be about 7,410 million. But if there is a fairly early fertility decline in the less developed countries of the world then it will probably be between the upper and lower limits of 6,800 and 5,300 million, according to recent estimates made by the United Nations. At a minimum, the increase in population, both absolutely and proportionately, seems certain to be much greater in the last 40 years of the century than in the 40 years preceding 1960, unless the world becomes engulfed in nuclear war. The current high rate of population growth is due to improved medical services and public health measures, while high birth rates have persisted in much of the world.

Population Projections

National population projections looking ahead for up to about 20 years are an essential element in the formulation of a country's plans for economic and social development. Projections covering a longer period are necessarily speculative, but they serve a purpose in providing a picture of the possible size and structure of the future population on the basis of assumptions relating to the future course of fertility, mortality and migration. The assumptions used may not be justified by events. For example, projections made in the early post-war years in respect of developing countries for the most part underestimated the rapidity with which death rates were to fall, and therefore produced figures which were consistently below the population totals actually reached in the early 1960s.

Demographers making population projections work from the existing population, subdivided by age and sex, and apply death rates specific for age and sex to determine the number of people already born who will still be alive in a given number of years. They use assumed birth rates to estimate the likely number of future births over the same period, and death rates to determine the number of those still unborn children who will survive. The possible future trend in migration also needs to be taken into account. A much wider range of data is now used in forecasting than was the case a few years ago. Considerable account is now taken of marriage rates and the duration of marriage and of the results of opinion surveys on desired family size. In considering mortality, attention is paid to specific causes of death and to specific public health programmes. The size of the reduction in death rates as the result of effective malaria eradication programmes in developing countries illustrates the importance of estimating the trend in each major cause of death separately.

It is obviously difficult to predict the future course of mortality, fertility and migration even for countries with good population statistics. The task is much greater when the data on current population are of doubtful validity or of inadequate coverage. In making projections of the world's population, the biggest uncertainty relates to China. While the 1953 census figure of 583 million is accepted as a base, there is very little reliable information which can be used to make realistic assumptions about birth and death rates. The figures for total population and estimates of birth and death rates for most of the countries of tropical Africa and for some of the other countries of Asia cannot be regarded as being even approximately accurate. It can, however, be stated categorically that whereas the population growth of Europe, America and Oceania (Australia and New Zealand) was the dominant factor in world population expansion in the late 19th century, it is the less developed regions of the world which are now growing in population at an unprecedented rate. A decline in the proportion of world population living in the areas which are now more developed seems certain to take place between now and the end of the century.

The Components of Population Growth.

(1) *Fertility.*—The range of measures of fertility includes the crude birth rate, calculated as the number of births in a year per thousand population alive in mid-year, and the gross reproduction rate, calculated as the number of live female births of the "average" mother as she lives through the reproductive period. Using either of the

measures fertility is on average about twice as high in the developing countries as in the more developed regions of the world. In Europe, North America, Japan and Oceania, the national crude birth rates are in general between 15 and 25 per 1,000 population, and the average gross reproduction rate is about 1·4; in the developing countries the average crude birth rate is rather over 40 and the gross reproduction rate nearly 3·0. Even these fertility rates are well below the upper limits of human physiological capacity.

The decline in fertility in the more developed countries, which started in France in the late 18th century and spread to other countries, can be attributed largely to the voluntary use by married couples of various methods of family limitation, including abortion, restraint in frequency of *coitus*, the use of *coitus interruptus*, and in modern times the use of contraceptives. Change in age at marriage has not been an important contributing factor except in one or two countries such as Ireland. The fertility decline has been associated with processes of modernisation and improved living standards. But the precise nature of this association is still a matter for conjecture. In those countries where birth rates are now low, the decline occurred first among the middle-class, better-educated women of over 30 years of age, and later spread to younger wives and eventually to all classes of the community.

In most of the less developed countries birth rates are still high, while death rates have fallen rapidly. The majority of the population in these countries live in rural areas, where living standards remain low and programmes of social and economic development have not as yet made much impact. If the high rate of population growth is to be reduced, however, the birth rate must drop in the rural areas as well as in the towns and cities. The governments of a number of developing countries have adopted programmes designed to accelerate fertility declines in the hope that a reduced rate of population growth will complement development efforts and make improvements in the standard of living more easily attainable. Such programmes have been adopted in India and Pakistan, and more recently in South Korea, Tunisia, Turkey, the United Arab Republic and a few smaller countries. In China men and women are being encouraged to marry late and have small families. Most of these programmes are too recent to judge of their success. The Indian programme, which is the oldest, has not yet had any marked effect on the birth rate. On the other hand, there has been a substantial drop in fertility in the last few years in Taiwan, Hong Kong and Singapore, where active family planning campaigns are in progress.

(2) *Mortality.*—The most common measures of mortality are the crude death rate, giving the deaths per annum per 1,000 of the mid-year population, and the expectation of life at birth, representing the average number of years of life for the individuals in the population, on the assumption of static death rates for every age-group of each sex. A century ago few populations enjoyed a life expectancy of more than 40 years. Now in the countries of lowest mortality a baby girl may expect to live to over 70 and a baby boy to almost that age. The picture is changing too in the developing countries. In Latin America expectation of life is now above [illegible]0 and in Asia a little under 50. Only in tropical Africa does the probable current figure average less than 40. But in these regions estimates of mortality are subject to a wide margin of error, and there are almost certainly big local and national variations in death rates. The crude death rate does not give a true picture of mortality as it ignores the age-structure of the population. In New Zealand, for instance, the crude death rate for the Maori and the non-Maori population is almost the same at about 8 to 9 deaths annually per 1,000 population. But if specific death rates for each 5-year age group up to the end of middle age) for the Maori population are computed they are found to be two to three times as high as for the non-Maori population. This is because the Maoris are a very youthful population owing to their high birth rate. Expectation of life at birth for the Maori is now about 60 years and for the non-Maori over 70 years.

Health conditions vary widely in different parts of the world. In the countries of North and Western Europe, North America, Australia and New Zealand, in many of which the expectation of life at birth reaches or exceeds 70 years, deaths from cancer and heart disease—diseases of later life—account for over half of total mortality, though accidents are the principal cause of death of teenagers and young adults. In much the larger part of the world the killing diseases of infancy and childhood, and the infectious and parasitic diseases which affect all ages, still take a heavy toll of human life.

Unfortunately accurate statistics on causes of death are not available for the majority of countries in which mortality is still at a high level. This is not surprising in view of the very low ratio of doctors to population in the rural areas of most of the countries of Asia, Africa and Latin America.

(3) *Migration.*—International migration has a considerable effect on the growth rate of some of the smaller and medium-sized countries, particularly in Europe, Oceania, North America and parts of Africa. In Australia, France, Switzerland and West Germany net immigration in recent years has not been far short of the natural increase of population, and Ghana has attracted large numbers of migrants from neighbouring African countries. Among the emigrant countries Ireland has lost more population than the gain through natural increase, while Portugal, Greece and Italy have lost substantial numbers. Labour migration is responsible for the absence of a large proportion of adult males of working age from some tribal areas of East, Central and Southern Africa.

Migration between countries in different continents now takes a form which contrasts with migration between countries within the same continent. Thus movement between southern and north-western Europe and between one African country and another is mostly of a temporary nature, with young adult males forming the majority of the migrants. Movements between continents, mainly from Europe to North America and Oceania, is more evenly balanced between males and females, with the emphasis on family units, and is of a more permanent nature. All international migration is however heavily concentrated in the younger age-groups.

Demographers who study international migration are interested not only in its dimensions and in the age–sex structure of the migrants, but also in its social and economic effects. One problem which has aroused world-wide concern stems from the fact that many of the technicians, doctors and teachers from developing countries, who go abroad for training, settle in the industrially advanced countries. The "brain drain" is in fact a very widespread phenomenon, and the United Kingdom, for instance, both gains and loses highly skilled workers through migration.

Internal migration consists largely of movement from rural areas to towns and cities. Except in parts of the Soviet Union, Brazil and Africa south of the Sahara, the frontier phase of population redistribution seems to be virtually finished. Young adults form a high proportion of the migrants, as in the case of international migration, but problems of migrational control do not arise in so far as no international boundaries have to be crossed. Better employment opportunities and more money are the main attraction for migrants from rural areas to cities. In an effort to prevent cities from growing too large, several industrialised countries attempt to guide internal migration through the locationing of new industries. In developing countries problems arising from rapid urbanisation are particularly acute, as the cities for the most part are quite unable to absorb the migrants at the rate at which they move from the rural areas. Yet, despite the difficult urban living conditions, it seems to be the ambition of most of those who have received an education in these countries to live in the towns.

Population and Employment.

Population structure plays an important part in determining the size of a country's labour force. The countries with low birth rates, which are in fact the most industrialised and urbanised countries, have the highest proportion of persons between the ages of 15 and 64, and the largely agricultural countries the lowest proportion, with the partly industrialised countries in an intermediate position. The facts that young people in the more industrialised countries tend to undergo longer periods of education and training than in agricultural countries, and that people retire from work more gradually in an agricultural community, offset this difference to some extent in so far as a higher proportion of the under 20s and over 60s work in the latter type of country.

In most developing countries the rate of population growth, and hence of labour force growth, is high, and employment opportunities have not expanded sufficiently rapidly to meet the additional demands for work. At the same time there is usually an inadequate supply of skilled workers in these countries for the implementation of economic development plans. Although economists are not agreed on the nature of the relationship between population growth and economic development, it is clear that population increases have an important effect on the trend in *per capita* product and, conversely, that economic development itself has an influence on the demographic processes.

Population and the Supply of Food and Natural Resources.

The future relation between population and food and resources is an obviously vital aspect of the world's currently high rate of population growth. Broadly speaking, there are two opposed schools of thought, the one contends that with scientifically directed exploitation the earth's resources are large enough to solve the food and population problem, the other that there is a real and early danger of the demand from increased population outstripping the supply from resources. If a much greater degree of political compatibility and fluidity of trade between nations could be achieved, the world could probably support the existing growth rate of population of 2 per cent per annum for a century or so without making too many speculative assumptions about scientific and technical developments. National boundaries and international rivalries cannot however be ignored, and serious analyses indicate that the population of some of the more crowded countries of Asia, such as India, already face the grim possibility of being condemned to a lasting state of undernourishment and malnutrition, unless successful and simultaneous action is taken both to reduce the rate of population increase and to improve agricultural and industrial productivity.

THE ELECTROMAGNETIC SPECTRUM.

The gradual development of the scientific understanding of the electromagnetic spectrum over the past two centuries provides some interesting examples of the interaction between technological progress, the collection of experimental data and the quest for mathematical laws of nature. None of these processes can occur in isolation. In order to collect experimental data it is essential that the appropriate technology shall be available; in order to construct a mathematical theory it is essential that sufficient data shall be available to stimulate our imagination and to provide some crucial tests. Both experimental data and theoretical insight are essential for progress in technology.

In the following we trace the development of our knowledge of the electromagnetic spectrum, and the interaction of radiation with matter, up to the present time, beginning in the days well before the known spectrum was thought to be electromagnetic in origin.

Light as Wave Motion.

Before 1700, at the very beginning of the scientific era, many experiments were carried out to investigate the properties of light. Some of these were aimed at finding the laws which describe the propagation of light from place to place; others were attempts to determine the composition of light. Such experiments were possible before the development of 19th-century technology because of the relative simplicity of the apparatus required.

It was Newton who made the first step along the road towards solving the problem of the composition of light. By passing a narrow beam of sunlight through a glass prism he was able to show that white light could be separated into a sequence of coloured components forming the *visible spectrum*, in which the colours grade continuously from red through orange, yellow, green, blue and indigo to violet. But this, in itself, was only a partial solution. It was still necessary to show that these coloured components were in some way simpler than the original white light.

Studies of the propagation of monochromatic light (consisting of single colour components) soon made it clear that this was indeed the case. Interference experiments, in which two beams of monochromatic light were made to interfere with one another to produce light and dark patches, showed that each colour component had to be interpreted as wave motion of a certain wavelength. White light is just a mixture of components of many different wavelengths.

In order to be able to vizualise the relationship between colour and wavelength let us consider the analogy with waves on the surface of the sea. These vary both in amplitude (the height of the wave) and in wavelength (the distance between two successive troughs). In the case of light the amplitude of the wave determines the intensity, while the wavelength determines the colour The analogue of white light is a choppy sea, in which no definite waves can be observed.

If we pursue this analogy a little further an interesting question arises. Sea waves are disturbances of water. What is the medium which is disturbed by light waves and thus can be said to be the analogue of water? We shall return to this problem later.

It can be shown by interference experiments that red light corresponds to a wavelength of $7 \cdot 7 \times 10^{-5}$ cm. and violet light corresponds to a wavelength of $3 \cdot 9 \times 10^{-5}$ cm. All the other colours of the visible spectrum have intermediate wavelengths.

Radiant Heat and Light.

It must have been realised in very early times that light and radiant heat were closely related phenomena, as they are so commonly found in association. Both of the important natural sources of light, the sun and fire, radiate heat in amounts easily detected by the skin.

Only at the beginning of the 19th century, however, did it become technologically possible to investigate the relationship between radiant heat and light in a scientific fashion. Sensitive heat detecting devices were produced which made it possible to demonstrate that heat radiation is subject to the same laws of propagation as light thus showing it to be similar in character Measurements also showed that the components of this radiation were of a longer wavelength than light. It was found that heat radiation continues the visible spectrum into an invisible region at the red end up to wavelengths of 2×10^{-3} cm for this reason it is often referred to as *infra-red* radiation.

Other experiments carried out at about the same time showed that sunlight also had components with wavelengths which were beyond the violet end of the visible spectrum, going down to 10^{-6} cm. This was called *ultra-violet* radiation.

Electromagnetic Waves.

At the time when the investigations referred to above were being carried out, nothing was known to connect the visible spectrum and its invisible extensions with the phenomena of electricity and magnetism. However, a side product of the amazing progress made in technology in the early 19th century was the continuous improvement of the experimental techniques which were available to physics. During this period it became possible to study the properties of electricity and magnetism systematically; the results of this work being summarised by Faraday and others in a series of quantitative laws of nature. Finally, in 1865, James Clerk Maxwell achieved the unification of all these laws into a single mathematical theory of electromagnetism. The resulting set of equations, known as *Maxwell's equations*, not only accounted for all the phenomena of electricity and magnetism, but also predicted the existence of an electromagnetic wave motion.

Maxwell soon realised that the known properties of light, infra-red and ultra-violet radiation corresponded precisely with the properties of the electromagnetic radiation predicted by his theory. In particular, the velocity of light which had been determined experimentally was in exact accord with the velocity of the wave motion predicted by his equations. It thus became clear that all these radiations were electromagnetic in origin. In order to be quite sure of this conclusion, however, it was still necessary to show that radiation with similar properties to light could be produced by means that were obviously electromagnetic.

This problem was solved by Hertz in 1888. He was able to show that sudden changes in the electric current flowing in a circuit were transmitted through space and could be detected by observing the resulting current in another circuit up to 20 metres away. Using this arrangement Hertz was able to show that the radiation he was producing had the same velocity as light, and propagated in a similar way, except that now its wavelength was several metres and thus in a different region of the spectrum from radiations previously known. Electromagnetic waves in this region of the spectrum are now commonly referred to as *radio waves*.

The discovery of radio waves has been followed by a long sequence of technological developments in the field of electronics which began early in the present century, and which seem likely to continue for a long time to come. At the present time standard electronic methods are available for the production and detection of electromagnetic waves over the wavelength region from 10^5 cm. down to almost 1 mm.

The Role of Maxwell's Theory in the Development of Theoretical Physics.

While it would be difficult to overstate the debt owed to Maxwell's theory by 20th-century technology, a debt of even greater magnitude is certainly owed by contemporary theoretical physics. Nearly the whole of the present conceptual framework of fundamental physics was produced as a response to the stimulus to thought provided by this theory.

As an example, let us return to the question raised previously about the medium in which electromagnetic waves are disturbances. In the original presentation of his theory Maxwell assumed the existence of an all-pervading medium which was known as the *ether*. It soon became clear, however, that most of the predictions of his theory were independent of this assumption. In 1887 the famous experiment of Michelson and Morley (**F13** (2)) was performed in order to detect the presence of the ether. This was found to be impossible. Finally, the results of this experiment, in conjunction with certain mathematical properties of Maxwell's equations, led Einstein to put forward his special theory of relativity, which denies the existence of the ether, and which is now well authenticated experimentally. Physicists have thus been forced to the conclusion that in looking for an electromagnetic analogue of water for sea waves they were trying to push the analogy too far.

The rapid development of quantum theory (**F13** (1)) has been almost entirely due to the experimental and theoretical study of the interactions between electromagnetic radiation and matter. One of the first steps was taken when it was discovered that the electrons emitted from metals due to the action of ultra-violet radiation have an energy which is not related to the intensity of the incident radiation, but is dependent on its wavelength. Einstein showed in 1905 that this could only be explained on the basis that energy is transferred between radiation and matter in finite amounts, or *quanta*, which are inversely proportional to wavelength.

The challenge to combine relativity theory, quantum mechanics and Maxwell's theory into an all-embracing theory of the interaction of electromagnetic radiation with matter has only recently been met. In 1950 the combined efforts of Feynman and Dyson produced a theory of relativistic quantum electrodynamics which is able to account for all interaction phenomena between radiation and electrons.

X-rays and Gamma Rays.

Two further sources of electromagnetic radiation were discovered in the 1890s which extended the known spectrum beyond the ultra-violet to even shorter wavelengths.

Röntgen found that extremely penetrating radiations, which he called *X-rays* because of their mysterious properties, could be produced by bombarding matter with high velocity electrons. Although Röntgen soon realised that these radiations were electromagnetic in origin, it was some years before interference phenomena could be observed and determinations of X-ray wavelengths were made. The problem was to find some way of constructing an apparatus in which the components were separated by distances about the same as the wavelength of the radiation, so that interference effects would occur. This was not solved until it was realised that ready-made apparatus was already to hand in the form of the crystalline solids, for the interatomic spacing in crystals is about 10^{-8} cm., which lies right in the centre of the X-ray spectrum (10^{-6} cm. to 10^{-10} cm.). Nowadays the properties of X-rays are well known, so the procedure has been reversed, and X-rays are an important tool for determining the atomic structure of crystals.

The penetrating power of X-rays may be explained in terms of the relationship between energy and wavelength mentioned above. X-ray quanta have very high energy and are therefore not easily stopped by matter.

Very soon after the discovery of X-rays Bequerel was able to show that similar radiations were emitted by radioactive substances. These were called *gamma rays* (**F11** (1)). The gamma-ray spectrum covers the wavelength region below 10^{-8} cm.

It follows that the spectral regions ascribed to X-rays and gamma rays overlap, so that these terms actually refer to methods of production of radiation rather than to its wavelength.

Spectroscopy.

Newton's arrangement with the prism was the first *spectroscope*; its function was to separate out the colour components of a source of light. Two hundred years elapsed before this apparatus was developed into a precise scientific instrument, capable of measuring both the wavelength and intensity of each colour component. In this form it is called a *spectrometer*.

The slow development of experimental spectroscopy in the visible region was almost entirely due to a lack of appreciation of its possible applications as a research tool, rather than to any intrinsic difficulties of construction. Progress only occurred when it became clear that all atoms and molecules had well defined characteristic spectra which could be used to recognise them. The main obstacle in the way of discovering this simple fact had been a technological one; because of the difficulty of obtaining really pure chemicals, strong effects due to certain common impurities were present in nearly all the observed spectra, thus masking the differences between them.

The outstanding feature of all atomic and molecular spectra is the existence of many well defined *lines*, corresponding to the emission or absorption of monochromatic components of radiation. Measurement of the positions and strengths of these lines not only enables us to distinguish between the various atoms and molecules but also, with suitable interpretation, gives us a great deal of information about their internal structure.

In order to produce emission spectra it is necessary to energise the material under investigation by some means, such as by heating in a flame. The resulting radiation then consists largely of sharp bright lines, characteristic of the material. Absorption spectra are produced by interposing the experimental material between a white light source and the spectrometer. Then dark lines are seen, corresponding to absorptions of energy, in exactly the same places as the bright lines are observed in the emission spectra.

Spectroscopic techniques have now been developed to such an extent that accurate measurements of wavelength and intensity are possible not only in the visible region, but over almost the whole of the electromagnetic spectrum. For example, in optical spectroscopy, which covers the region in which photographic emulsions are sensitive, between 10^{-4} cm. and 2×10^{-5} cm., it is now possible to determine wavelengths to an accuracy better than one part in a million. This makes the spectrometer one of the most accurate measuring devices available to the physicist.

Each region of the spectrum has its own characteristic type of spectrometer, and each region has specific applications in probing some particular aspects of the structure of matter.

Optical spectroscopy, for example, is of particular value in analysing the electronic structure of atoms. Interactions are possible because the quanta of radiation in this region of the spectrum have energies of the same order of magnitude as the changes of electron energy which occur in atoms. In the 1920s and 1930s the results obtained from spectroscopy in this region of the spectrum were found particularly useful for testing the predictions of quantum theory and, at the same time, provided a tremendous challenge to theoretical physicists to develop this theory further so as to be able to explain all the data obtained. Nowadays, when quantum theory has been firmly established and special theoretical techniques for dealing with atomic structure have been developed, the role of optical spectroscopy has changed. Its main application now is to tell us something about the interaction of atoms with their environment—the way in which they fit into solids and liquids.

Towards the long wavelength end of the infrared region, above 10^{-4} cm., photographic emulsions are no longer sensitive, and it becomes necessary to employ special detecting devices. For this reason infra-red spectrometers are considerably less accurate than optical spectrometers. The main application of spectroscopy in this region is to give us information about the characteristic internal vibrations of the atoms in molecules and crystals. This, in turn, enables us to get information about the atomic structure of these systems.

It is also possible to do spectroscopy in the radio wave region, where it is referred to as *magnetic resonance* because a magnetic field is applied to the system under investigation to produce the small energy differences required for the absorption and emission of radiation at these wavelengths. This type of spectroscopy can give information both on the electronic structure of atoms and on the structure of the atomic nucleus.

In the above examples we have emphasised the role of spectroscopy in probing the structure of matter. Another field of application is in astronomy, where it is possible to use spectroscopic techniques to determine such diverse things as the composition of the sun and the distance of the galaxies. During the last few years the use of radio wave spectroscopy in this field has led to the discovery of several new types of stellar object, and this data is now producing a complete reappraisal of our understanding of the universe.

Far Infra-red Spectroscopy.

Even now, when it is possible to produce and detect radio waves of wavelengths down to one millimetre by standard electronic techniques, an appreciable gap still exists between this and the longest infra-red wavelength of two hundredths of a millimetre. According to one's point of view, this part of the spectrum may be called the *far infra-red* or the *submillimetre region.*

Because there are many interesting phenomena which can only be investigated properly by means of far infra-red spectroscopy, vigorous attempts are being made at the present time to improve the methods of production and detection of radiation in this difficult intermediate region of the spectrum. Most of the techniques which have been developed so far are simple extensions of those in use in the infra-red.

For example, the most frequently used source of far infra-red radiation at present is the mercury arc discharge lamp. These lamps are designed to have a large output in the visible region of the spectrum, so it is hardly surprising that only a very small part of the total output of energy is available at far infra-red wavelengths. Although this energy is minute compared with that which can be produced in other parts of the spectrum, it is still the best source obtainable at present for far infra-red work.

Very recently some progress has been made in producing radiation of wavelengths below one millimetre by using the special properties of a continuous arc discharge to generate harmonics of a very high energy source of radio waves at 1 cm. The radiation produced in each harmonic is of very low energy, but has the advantage common to all radio wave production techniques that it is monochromatic. The main limitation of this method is that it only seems possible to cover a very small part of the far infra-red spectrum (down to about 0·05 cm.).

It should be apparent from the above remarks that an important technological advance is necessary before the available sources of far infra-red radiation can be considered adequate. The most hopeful possibility at the moment is that masers (**F47**) will be discovered which will operate satisfactorily in this region.

Turning our attention to detecting devices, we find a considerably more complicated, and at the same time more hopeful, situation. The favourite far infra-red detector in research laboratories has for a long time been the *Golay cell.* This is a crude, but effective, pneumatic device in which a volume of gas is expanded by the heating effect of the incident radiation. A simple bellows arrangement responds to this expansion and allows it to be amplified electronically.

In recent years, however, the Golay cell has been gradually giving way to a variety of more sophisticated devices which utilise certain specially prepared materials which have the property that their electrical conductivity varies with the amount of incident far infra-red radiation. These detectors can be made as much as one hundred times more sensitive than the Golay cell in some parts of the spectrum. Even so, the real technological breakthrough has yet to come; none of these devices has a sensitivity comparable with that of the best detectors available in other parts of the electromagnetic spectrum.

Experimental work in the far infra-red is also complicated by two other factors. Because wate vapour absorbs radiation strongly over much of this region it is necessary to put the spectrometers in a vacuum container. In order to obtain well defined absorption spectra it is usually necessary to cool the samples being investigated to liquid nitrogen temperatures (200° C. below freezing), and sometimes even to liquid helium temperatures (269° C. below freezing).

The reader may be wondering why physicists should be content to struggle on doing research work in the far infra-red under such difficult conditions and with such evidently inferior tools. Why not wait until technological developments make it possible to obtain far better results than those obtainable at present? The answer to this question is twofold: (1) much useful information can be gathered even with crude devices, and (2) we cannot hope for technological progress to occur in the absence of scientific effort. In other words, pure science and technology are still just as inextricably interwoven as they have been throughout the whole period of the discovery and exploration of the electromagnetic spectrum.

THE LASER

When the day comes to communicate with our neighbours on remote planets orbiting other stars our "radiotelephone" will probably make use of a beam of light from a laser. This is a new and very remarkable kind of light source that was developed only in recent years. Its full potential is yet to be realised, but even now it has great importance. With the laser we shall be able to probe the behaviour of matter under the influence of enormous energy densities, range and survey vast distances to microscopic accuracy, and send millions of telephone and television messages between any two points that can see each other with telescopes. Little wonder that the laser has achieved wide prominence within but a few years. It is a development as central to optical science and engineering as the discovery of the triode valve was to electronics.

From the time man first opened his eyes until late in 1960 when the first laser was developed most of our sources of light have been no different in principle from bodies heated to incandescence. A hot tungsten filament, a candle, a gas fire, the sun, a carbon arc, even the glowing screen of a television set are some familiar examples. All of these can be termed natural sources. They are fine, of course, for the usual purposes of illumination, but not however for the additional purposes to which the laser can be put. The reason for this restriction is a fundamental one. Natural light is inherently subject to fluctuations in intensity technically called "noise". Laser light, as we shall see, is quite different, and more closely resembles radio signals.

Light Waves and Radio Waves.

Radio waves that bring sound radio and television into our homes and light waves that bring visual perception into our lives are closely related forms of radiant energy from two regions of the electromagnetic spectrum. The relationship is not obvious because radio wavelengths are many orders of magnitude too long to be detected visually. The wavelengths of radiation we can see fall in the ranges of from 0·4 to 0·8 microns (one micron is one thousandth of a millimetre) while those of radio are from tens of thousands to millions of millions times longer. In their familiar form radio signals come from sources, like valve oscillators, that are tractable to modulation, amplification and the many other operations known for many years in the field of electronics. The result has been a versatile field rich in scientific discovery and practical application.

It has always been desirable to extend electronics to shorter and shorter wavelengths so that a greater part of the electromagnetic spectrum could be exploited in similar ways, but the idea of generating non-noisy light has been particularly attractive, for reasons that we shall discuss.

The techniques for generating and dealing with radio signals cannot be extended directly to light despite their close relationship. Even if it were possible in theory to scale electronic equipment for shorter and shorter wavelengths, by the time it would be scaled to the wavelengths of light the equipment would have to be of microscopically small dimensions. The laser is a development that avoids these difficulties but produces the desired result.

Incoherent Light.

Light from a natural source is emitted at random by agitated electrons. It is the usual case that electrons independently and spontaneously emit bits of light to add to the general glow to be seen from the source. As a result natural light is mainly what we call incoherent. Expressed as a kind of wave motion natural light has to be regarded as brief packets of energy travelling in random directions at uncorrelated times. Incoherent light therefore is neither well-directed in space nor smooth in time. The former results in the fact that illumination from our familiar light sources is proportional to the inverse square of the distance from the source which implies that only a fraction of the light energy can ever be collected and focused to a small spot or collimated and sent along a parallel beam. The latter means that ordinary light is inherently much too unsteady to be an efficient carrier of information coded in time.

Coherent Light.

Light from a laser also comes from agitated electrons, but another process dominates the kind of radiation. In effect, many electrons radiate together under the common stimulus of an incident light wave. This co-operative phenomenon, which is called stimulated emission, leads to light which is both well-directed in space and smooth in time. Laser light, in contrast to natural light, is coherent and can be expressed as a regular progression of waves carrying energy along a particular path. The essential difference, therefore, is that laser light is an orderly sort of wave motion like that of breakers falling rhythmically against the seashore, while ordinary light is a disordered and random sort not very different from the rippled surface of the sea broken by rainfall. All of the potential and actual uses for the laser stem from this difference.

Laser Action.

When a light beam encounters any transparent medium whether it be solid, liquid, or gas the normal behaviour is for some fraction of the energy in the beam to be progressively absorbed. In other words the further a light beam travels through a medium, the more attenuated it usually becomes. But in a laser the reverse happens and an incident beam becomes progressively brightened. The medium is made to give up energy and amplify an incident beam.

We are familiar with the howls and whistles (which in fact are audio oscillations) that can be produced in a public address system when too much sound from the loudspeaker reaches the microphone. In a similar way, our amplifying medium can be made to produce steady oscillations of light. What is needed is a pair of mirrors, one at each end of the medium, to reflect an amplified beam of light back upon itself. The beam is confined and has no alternative but to build up intensity with each traversal between the mirrors. The amplifier would continue this process indefinitely except that it saturates at some limiting intensity. When this happens the system produces steady oscillations around the original signal many times fed back upon itself. If both of the mirrors were perfectly reflecting none of the energy so generated would be able to leave the system. We therefore make one of the mirrors slightly transparent, and now a fraction emerges.

Dozens of different materials have worked as lasers. Common to all of them is the underlying process called stimulated emission of radiation. The same principle was originally applied to microwave devices, and the name, maser, which is the microwave parent of the laser, derives from the expression "*m*icrowave *a*mplification by the *s*timulated *e*mission of *r*adiation". Upon application to light wavelengths the microwave part of the name lost its meaning and the term maser became generally descriptive of any device in which stimulated emission dominates. Now, for lack of any standard nomenclature, the names optical maser and laser are used interchangeably, the *l* in the latter standing for *l*ight. One detailed example, the laser made from synthetic ruby, is sufficiently representative to illustrate the basic idea.

Ruby Lasers in Theory.

Synthetic ruby, like its naturally occurring counterpart, is a crystal of aluminium oxide with a small percentage of chromium atoms replacing some of the aluminium during the growth of the crystal. A strongly fluorescent material, it absorbs broad bands of blue and green light and re-radiates much of the energy in the form of a narrow band of red light. The red fluorescence gives ruby its colour, and arises from the way electrons belonging to the chromium atoms interact with radiation.

These electrons can exist only in particular energy states. Their state of lowest energy, the so-called ground state, is the normal relaxed one. The action of blue and green light when it is absorbed by the crystal is to elevate some ground state electrons indirectly to a sharply defined excited state. From here they can either give up spontaneously some of their excess energy in the form of red fluorescence light and relax back to the ground state, or they can wait for an incident light beam of the same wavelength and add their energy to it synchronously on their way back to the ground state. In either case the wavelength of the emitted light is determined by the difference in energy between the ground and excited states.

The first process is called spontaneous emission of radiation and produces ordinary thermal light. The second process is called stimulated emission of radiation and, when it dominates, it produces the conditions we described earlier which lead to amplification of light. However, electrons in the ground state are just as susceptible to the influence of an incident red beam as the excited electrons, and whereas the excited ones undergo stimulated emission and give up energy to the incident beam, the ground state ones undergo (stimulated) absorption and take some away in proportion to their numbers. For net amplification, therefore, a majority of the electrons must be in the excited state. To put them there enough energy must be supplied to the crystal in the form of blue and green light. Then so long as a population majority is maintained in the excited state the crystal will prefer to amplify any incident light of the correct wavelength. In the absence of stimulated emission the system will regain equilibrium by the spontaneous process.

Ruby Lasers in Practice.

One practical way of putting enough blue and green light into a ruby crystal to bring it to the laser condition is to bathe it with light from a very bright xenon flashtube like the kind used for ordinary flash photography. The flash will last for only about one thousandth of a second, but for a sizeable fraction of this time the crystal will be capable of amplifying light. If the crystal has the form of a right circular cylinder, with its end faces polished flat and parallel to each other, and if these faces have highly reflecting coatings one of which is slightly transparent, then conditions are right for generating coherent light. For the time that the crystal is sufficiently activated by the flash tube it will oscillate in the way we have previously described. Some fluorescence or stray light travelling along the axis of the crystal will trigger off the process. Then, since only a parallel beam of light will reflect back and forth between the two faces, only light travelling in that direction will build up to a great intensity, and a fraction of it will come out through the simi-transparent face. It will be confined to a very narrow cone, steady in brightness for as long as the oscillations can be supported by a supply of energy from the flashlamp, and it will be very nearly a single red wavelength (stabilized at the wavelength where the gain of the medium is greatest).

The output from a pulsed ruby optical laser is a tidal wave of light with kilowatts or even megawatts of peak power and, except for diffraction effects from where it emerges, nearly all of the energy appears along a well-defined wavefront. By means of lenses and telescopes this energy can be harnessed almost in its entirety. It can be beamed vast distances through a telescope, or focused to tiny spots of incredibly intense light.

Recent experiments have demonstrated what laser light from a ruby can actually do in this way. A ruby laser in one such experiment was connected to a large telescope and aimed at the moon. At a distance of a quarter of a million miles it illuminated an area of the moon no more than a few miles across. This was verified by means of another telescope trained on the same part of the moon when, not quite three seconds after each burst of laser light was sent out, a little of the reflected light was detected after its round trip. Detection back on earth was difficult because the moon is a diffuse reflector and little of the light was returned to its source. But an observer many times further away than the moon would have had no trouble seeing the direct beam. The reach of our strongest searchlight is paltry in comparison. In another experiment the output of a ruby laser was focused and brought to bear on an industrial diamond. So generated, this needle point of concentrated light had sufficient energy to vapourize a substantial portion of the diamond. Sunlight can be focussed with a magnifying glass and used to ignite paper and wood. To collect and use more of the sun's energy requires much larger optical systems, and in no case can temperatures in the focused sunlight exceed 6000° K, the surface temperature of the sun. But with comparatively simple optics the ruby laser can just as easily drill holes into the toughest of refractory materials, and achieve very much higher temperatures with its focused light.

Laser Materials.

Now that the techniques have been discovered for building lasers there is no theoretical limit to the number of substances that can be used for this purpose. Many have already been found, even at this early stage of development, and a list of them includes quite a variety of crystalline and plastic solids, fluorescent liquids, semiconductor compounds, and mixtures of gases. They operate at various wavelengths falling throughout the optical spectrum from the ultra-violet to the infra-red. Some, like our example of ruby, operate on a pulsed basis with outputs of high power. Others, like a gaseous mixture of helium and neon operate continuously and generate fractional watt output powers.

Two gas lasers currently head the list of exciting developments. The first employs ionised argon and is capable of continuously generating more than ten watts of blue-green light of unbelievable brilliance. The second employs a mixture of carbon dioxide, nitrogen and helium, also operates continuously and is reported to have generated fractional *kilowatt* beams of infra-red light.

Continuously Operating Lasers.

Continuous operation is an important development for certain applications. The first to have worked continuously is the helium-neon laser. In this device light amplification is obtained from neon atoms whose electrons are put steadily into an active state. An electrical discharge is used to do this indirectly by means of helium atoms that act as intermediaries in the energy transaction. The device in essence is a tube containing the gaseous mixture that becomes the amplifying medium, an electrical source to excite the discharge in the tube, and two mirrors (one slightly transparent) to confine the oscillations and permit a little of the light to emerge; so long as the discharge is maintained, a steady output of coherent light is developed.

A continuously operating laser has extended regularity in time. This has applications in the science of measurement. Distances can be measured in terms of wavelengths of light to a maximum of the distance that the reference light beam can travel during its brief period of regularity. This is the so-called coherence length. The best natural source in this respect is regular for no more than a few thousandths of one millionth of one second, the time it takes for light to travel about one yard. Light from a helium-neon laser has detailed regularity for much longer—one second or more—and light can travel 186,000 miles in this period. So with lasers at our disposal we can now speculate about measuring the farthest points on earth and even interplanetary distances to within a small fraction of an inch.

Possible Technical Uses.

The laser is like a radio frequency oscillator but many decades down in wavelength. The implications of this similarity are important. The pulsed laser produces light oscillations chopped into a kind of Morse code. A continuously operating one produces steady oscillations that, when modulated, are able to carry messages in the same way that radio beams do. But beams of electromagnetic energy spread out and become diffuse at great distances from their sources, the effect being proportional to wavelength, so in this respect beams of laser light are orders of magnitude more concentrated than radio beams of the same power. The bandwidth that can be carried by these beams is inversely proportional to the wavelength, so not only can the equivalent laser beam go much further, it can carry vastly more messages than a radio beam. The reach, definition and synchronism of coherent light also have obvious appeals for the idea of an optical radar system. With beams of laser light objects potentially can be detected at greater distance, located to increased accuracy, and their velocities clocked to higher precision than with traditional radar systems using radio beams.

The Laser in Research.

For the science-minded the laser holds most interest in the realms of basic research. For some of us, the intriguing questions raised by this development involve the basic nature of laser light: how it can be understood and described in detail; what it means to combine two laser beams from independent sources (like two interfering radio stations) and observe beat notes between them; what it means to produce fringes between two independent laser beams whose light waves are so well organised that they can interfere broadly with each other; why ordinary light is too disorganised in time and space for either of these effects to occur. For others of us the influence of laser light upon external things attracts our attention. New physical effects predicted theoretically about the action of this light source can be investigated. One example is an exceptional "non-linear" behaviour of quartz and other crystals that can be shown up by the intense, monochromatic light from a ruby laser; incident red light is doubled in frequency (and halved in wavelength) and both red and its harmonically related blue light emerge from a crystal so illuminated. Other effects are just as likely to be noticed first and explained afterwards. Chemists among us are measuring how laser light can affect chemical reactions, biologists and surgeons how it can affect living tissues. Metallurgists and others are planning novel ways of using it to work difficult materials, and communication engineers are speculating about limitless numbers of messages between boundless populations. Technologists of all kinds are finding their horizons broadened, and every one of us is starting to feel the consequences of increased knowledge and advanced technology which the laser is bringing.

MICROELECTRONICS.

The word microelectronics rather inadequately describes a new branch of technology which is making a major impact on the electronics industry. The key tools are semiconductor integrated circuits and thin-film circuits each of which has the capability of reducing entire electronic circuits into minute modular "chips" or substrates complete with interconnections.

While it is this extreme miniaturisation which has led to the term "micro," in fact the importance of the technology lies in its ability to make electronic systems more reliable and cheaper and faster in operation. These factors also enable far more complex electronic systems to be envisaged than were ever considered possible before. For these reasons the general term "integrated electronics" has been introduced which more nearly describes the basic technology, but without undue emphasis on the size aspect.

Historical.

The immense possibilities of electronic circuitry to perform complex tasks such as computing, switching, transmission of speech and data, and for the control of mechanical devices was becoming increasingly recognised in the early 1950s. Scientists and engineers were visualising immense computing machines capable of solving mathematical problems at lightning speed, the electronic control of mechanical motion for activities as diverse as rockets and "space" satellites and automatic machines used for the manufacture of the products used in everyday life.

The main obstacle to the realisation of the electronic machines visualised was the inadequacy of the tools available. The thermionic valve was the key tool and although it was capable of performing all the functions required it was bulky and consumed considerable power. Nevertheless the first computers were built with valves and although they occupied complete rooms their computing ability was modest compared with present day machines occupying a fraction of the space.

The first breakthrough for the pioneers of electronics came with the advent of the transistor, which was invented by the Bell Laboratories in 1947 and became a proven alternative to the valve by the mid-1950s. Compared with a thermionic valve the transistor is tiny, has fewer electrodes and operates with low voltage and current. Use of transistors resulted in much smaller equipment, which had considerably reduced power dissipation and was capable of faster operation since the length of leads carrying signals from one part of the equipment to another were much shorter.

The significant size and power reductions possible also spurred the manufacturers of all the other components used in electronic circuits to effect similar size reductions. Capacitors, resistors, inductors, connectors, and wiring systems have all been progressively reduced in size and this trend is still continuing. Such reductions have enabled far more complex electronic systems to be considered. Space vehicles, guided missiles and aircraft have provided the main outlets for this trend. As the complexity of the electronics for military and other systems has increased so has the need for increased reliability. The reliability of any system is inversely proportional to the number of components and interconnections it contains, so that the more components and interconnections, the less reliable is the system. This crucial factor placed a limitation on the complexity of systems which could be practically realised, but fortunately scientists and engineers studying new device concepts provided a major step forward by introducing the integrated circuit solution which offers a drastic reduction in the number of interconnections, greater reliability, and a further major factor not previously discussed—much lower cost. To appreciate these features, ley us briefly examine the technologies involved.

Basic Building Bricks.

The main constituents of any electronic circuit whether it be a radio or television set, a hearing aid, a high speed computer or a microwave communications system are valves or transistors, diodes, capacitors, inductors, and resistors. Each plays a part in controlling the flow of electrons so that particular electronic functions can be carried out. Valves and transistors are defined as active elements since they can generate and amplify electrical signals and act as switches similar to electromechanical relays, but at enormously high speeds. The remaining components are defined as passive elements. Capacitors and inductors can impede or store electrical energy and together they form frequency selective devices. Resistors impede electron flow and diodes have non-symmetrical properties which can impede or let flow an electrical current depending on its direction.

These are the basic building bricks which have to be fabricated and interconnected to make an integrated circuit. Only a minute fraction of the material used in their construction is actually needed for processing the electrical signal; the bulk is determined by physical limitations of fabrication and the need to connect the working element to robust terminals which usually requires at least two connection interfaces per terminal of the element. Reduction of the redundant bulk material and the number of connection interfaces are central features of integrated circuits which contribute to improved reliability and lower cost.

Let us now look at the two main technologies used for making integrated circuits.

Semiconductor Integrated Circuits.

To appreciate the important aspects of the technology a brief review of basic mechanisms and processes is useful. Semiconductor materials, such as germanium or silicon, are so designated because their properties stand midway between those of insulators and metals. These properties can be accurately determined and controlled by adding minute quantities of selected substances to highly purified material. These substances determine the conduction mechanisms in the material; for example, the addition of phosphorus creates material with an excess of conduction electrons (designated *n*-type material) whereas boron creates material with an electron deficit or excess of mobile positive charges referred to as "holes" (designated *p*-type material). Thus conduction can either be by electrons or holes. If a region of *p*-type material and a region of *n*-type material are formed in one piece of material then the boundary between them is called a *p–n* junction. Such a junction behaves as a rectifier; polarised in one direction, current flows easily, polarised in the other the junction is swept clear of conduction charges, a local electric charge called a space charge is built up and negligible current flows. This gives us our diodes and in addition the space charge can be used to provide capacitors.

Transistors.

The formation of two junctions very close together is the basis of the transistor which can be likened to the thermionic triode. Two *p–n* junctions separate the transistor into three regions called collector, base, and emitter in the diagram on the right.

In a valve the electrical signal applied between the grid and cathode controls the current flowing from the cathode to the anode. The signal on the grid controls current by affecting the electrostatic field which exists between cathode and grid.

In a transistor the electrical signal applied between the base and the emitter controls the current flow from emitter to collector. The signal on the base controls current by affecting the electrostatic potential which exists across the base region. For efficient operation of the transistor the current carriers from the emitter must not be captured in the base region *en route* for the collector circuit. In practice this entails extreme purity and crystal perfection in the semiconductor material and a very thin base region, in practice 0·0005 inches or less. A transistor requires a voltage supply of about 6 volts for operation compared with above 100 volts for a valve, and more important, requires no heated cathode which consumes considerable power and is often the cause of failure in valves.

To provide resistors the bulk resistivity of the semiconductor is utilised. Resistor value is determined by the length-to-cross-section ratio of the material. As described previously the addition of substances such as boron or phosphorus will reduce resistivity and in practice the same level of addition required to make *p–n* junctions is used to determine resistor values.

Reviewing this brief description of the technology we see that the same type of process is necessary to make all of the components, and the key step is the selective introduction of the significant substances to make *p–n* junctions for transistors, diodes, and capacitors, and to make resistors.

Introducing Impurities.

The most widely used method of introducing the substances selectively into silicon, for example, is high temperature diffusion. The silicon is placed in a furnace, held at about 1000° C in a vapour containing atoms of the required substance. Depth of penetration is determined by temperature and time in the furnace. The areas where penetration is required are determined by a convenient masking process. A surface layer of silicon dioxide which blocks the passage of atoms can be grown by exposing the silicon to an oxidising process at high temperature. Windows etched in this oxide then determine the positions where diffusion takes place.

Transistors, diodes, resistors, and capacitors then can be fabricated in a single piece of silicon by a set of compatible processes and since each of these components need only occupy an extremely small area, typically 0·0001 square inches, large numbers of these components can be accommodated in one piece of material, the provision of isolation between each component and the forming of an interconnection pattern between them completes the basic conception of the semiconductor integrated circuit.

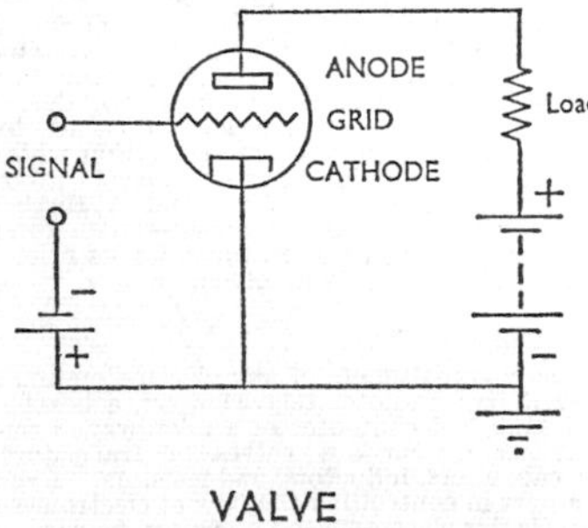

VALVE

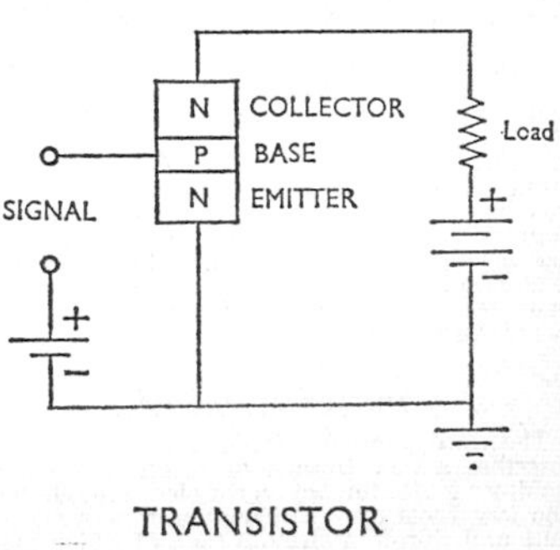

TRANSISTOR

It is necessary now to introduce dimensions nto the picture to illustrate the precision required :o carry out these operations. A suitable slice of silicon is about 1 inch in diameter and about)·010 inches thick. A 1000 transistors can be simultaneously manufactured in this slice or alternately 500 integrated circuits each containing about 30 transistors or diodes and 30 resistors. To define the microscopic regions that have to be etched in the oxide masks for making the individual elements of a circuit, precision photolithographic processes have been developed. The urface of the oxide is coated with a photoensitive compound and then exposed to ultraviolet light through a high resolution photographic mask. Where the mask prevents light rom polymerising the compound it can be dissolved away leaving areas exposed for etching the equired windows in the oxide. The photographic masks defining diffusion areas are made rom drawings 500 times actual size to minimise drafting errors and then reduced to actual size and repeated as many times as the circuit occurs n a slice.

The Manufacturing Process.

In a simplified manner let us now trace the rocess steps required for an integrated circuit.

1. Oxidise p-type silicon slice.
2. Using mask, etch windows in oxide in all areas to be occupied by transistors and diodes.
3. Carry out deep n-type diffusion which produces n–p junction between each device and the common silicon substrate. When supplied with a suitably directed voltage this junction isolates each device from the substrate.
4. Re-oxidise surface.
5. Using mask, etch windows in oxide to provide transistor base region and diodes.
6. Diffuse p-type impurity giving collector-base junction and completing diode p–n junction. This diffusion will also provide resistors.
7. Re-oxidise surface.
8. Using mask, etch windows in oxide to provide transistor emitter region.
9. Diffuse n-type impurity giving emitter-base junctions and completing transistors.
10. Re-oxidise surface.
11. Using mask, etch windows in oxide to expose contact areas.
12. Deposit by evaporation an aluminium layer to interconnect all the contact areas which complete the circuit.
13. With diamond-tipped tool scribe and break slice to form individual integrated circuit chips.
14. Mount chip in can and connect terminals to aluminium interconnection pattern by welding fine aluminium wire links.

Observe that the fabrication of integrated cuits requires repeated steps of diffusion and asking and although great precision and control required to place the p–n junctions accurately, large number of slices can be processed simulneously. Each circuit contains about 50 comnents, there may be 500 such circuits on a slice d some 20 slices may be processed at one time. will be seen therefore that theoretically over e million components are made in one manuturing cycle. In practice, of course, faults d errors occur and this theoretical figure is ver reached. Nevertheless the yield of circuits sufficient to make the cost of an integrated cuit only a little more than one of the transistors itained in it. This is one of the most significant pects of the technology and as techniques are proved, more and more complex circuits can considered without appreciable increase in t.

Observe also that due to the internal internection system, the number of external erconnection points is very much smaller than h discrete components wired together. In lition the interconnection paths are extremely rt and are made under the same rigidly itrolled conditions as the rest of the process steps. These factors are responsible for the significant increases in reliability of equipment using integrated circuits now being achieved in practice.

Thin-Film Integrated Circuits.

The technique of depositing metal and insulating films by evaporation, sputtering or electro-deposition has been known for many years and is widely used to make resistors and capacitors. The technology of thin-film integrated circuits is concerned with the sequential deposition of metals and insulators to make resistors, capacitors, and conductors on substrates of glass or ceramic. Research is also being carried out on active elements such as transistors made in film form, and although working devices have been demonstrated, it may be some time before they are a practical proposition.

As in the case of semiconductor circuits, large numbers of resistors and capacitors suitably interconnected can be processed on one substrate; interconnections are made under controlled conditions and are minimised. Active devices such as transistors are welded or soldered to the conductor film to complete the circuit. Film circuits are many orders of magnitude larger than semiconductor circuits but are still much smaller than their equivalent using conventional components.

Nickel/chromium and tantalum are widely used for making resistors and silicon monoxide, silicon dioxide, and tantalum pentoxide are used for the capacitor dielectrics. Chromium/gold and silver are used for interconnection patterns. Resistor values are determined by controlling the resistivity of the deposited film and adjusting the length/width ratio of the film. Typically a resistor of 30,000 ohms would be 0·5 inches long and 0·005 inches wide.

A capacitor consists of a dielectric film sandwiched between two conductor films, its value being determined by dielectric constant, thickness of the dielectric and the area of the film. Typically a capacitor of 0·01 microfarad would occupy an area of 1 square centimetre.

One manufacturing method used is to deposit the films sequentially through metal masks to define accurately the resistors, capacitors, and interconnection areas. Alternatively these areas can be defined after the deposition process using the photolithographic techniques mentioned previously. The tolerance to which the components can be made is largely determined by the mask accuracy; since we are dealing here with sizes many orders larger than the semiconductor circuit but using the same mask technology it is obvious that very high accuracy of component values can be achieved.

In practice a typical thin-film integrated circuit containing 4 transistors, 12 resistors, and 2 capacitors measures 1 by 0·5 by 0·1 inches.

Integrated Circuit Limitations.

Power dissipation limits the electronic functions which can be usefully achieved using integrated circuits. Power rectification and amplification for example, require large surface areas to dissipate the heat generated.

The properties of inductors, most familiar in the form of coils of wire, are determined by their size and although very small inductance values can be achieved using thin-film techniques the integration of inductors generally is not feasible. Much effort is being spent to develop circuits which do not require the use of inductors.

Semiconductor resistors and capacitors cannot be made to very close tolerances and the range of values is very limited. On the other hand, transistors are very easily made, and for these reasons designers of semiconductor circuits make liberal use of them. Also the degree of isolation possible between elements of a circuit is limited and this restricts the frequency at which semiconductor integrated circuits can be operated.

Thin-film circuits at present suffer from the disadvantage that only passive elements can be made and the active elements have to be added. On the other hand, thin-film resistors and capacitors can be made over a wide range of values with great accuracy of value.

Setting up costs for manufacturing a particular semiconductor circuit is very high and this limits the number of types which can be made economically. Computers which use large quantities of the same type of functional circuit are an ideal application for semiconductor integrated circuits.

Setting up costs of thin-film circuits are not nearly as high and this enables a very much wider range of circuits to be considered. Where precision of component values are necessary, or where only small quantities of a particular circuit are required, they have advantages over the semiconductor types.

Microelectronic Applications.

Already many complex electronic equipments have been built using integrated circuits, mostly for applications where reliability, size and weight are of extreme importance. Typical examples are computers used for command, guidance, and control of missiles and weapons systems besides equipment for receiving and transmitting information from ground stations to missiles and aircraft.

Size and weight reduction factors between 10 and 100 to 1 have been achieved compared with similar equipment built with conventional components. Size reductions of this magnitude are only possible if the whole equipment design can be miniaturised to be compatible with integrated circuits. Requirements for miniature connectors, precision printed circuit cards, new forms of compact cable harness, and adjustable components such as variable resistors have led to many new developments which form an important branch of microelectronics.

The application of integrated circuits and many of the other microelectronic parts to commercial equipment has commenced. The main incentives here are increased reliability of equipment and low cost; extreme size reduction is not so important since the equipment usually has to work in connection with mechanical machines which cannot be miniaturised. Apart from the low cost of integrated circuits great cost savings can be made through design and manufacturing simplification. System design time is reduced since the starting point for a design now is at the functional circuit level and not at the individual component level. Drafting time and numbers of drawings required are greatly reduced since again functional circuits do not have to be drawn. A circuit card which previously held say 30 components can now hold the equivalent of at east 10 times this number.

Already complex computers containing many thousands of thin-film circuits are being built and even more complex machines using semiconductor integrated circuits are in the design stage. Electronic telephone exchanges now in the research and development stages will be a very large user of integrated circuits.

The Future.

With the development of new processes and the progressive refinement of factory techniques there is no doubt that more and more complex electronic functions will be processed in a small piece of material. Already circuits have been made with 1000 transistors interconnected on one chip of material and there seems no reason why, for example, the complete logic circuits for a computer should not be made in one or two slices of material. For such a concept, new methods of extracting heat from the material and new methods of interconnection will be required.

It will be appreciated that the approach outlined offers enormous advantages and it will open up new fields for electronics never possible before. Learning machines and electronic analogues of brain mechanisms for example, require extremely complex circuits which can make full use of microelectronic techniques.

THE BIOLOGICAL FIXATION OF NITROGEN.

According to a recent report of the World Health Organisation protein deficiency, particularly in the young of underdeveloped countries, is a major cause of ill-health in the world today. This is primarily because protein is an essential constituent of all living cells, so that with increase in the world's population more is required and concomitantly less per head is available. This problem will become even more acute with time unless more edible protein becomes available. This increase will have to be in the first instance, in plant protein, for animals derive their supplies from the plant either directly or indirectly by eating other animals.

If one considers the matter a step further and breaks down the plant protein molecule into the basic chemical constituents, four elements are recognised: carbon, hydrogen, oxygen, and nitrogen. Plants obtain ample supplies of the first three from atmospheric and soil sources primarily as water, carbon dioxide, and oxygen. Nitrogen however is in a somewhat different category, for although very large quantities are available in the air (about 80 per cent by volume of the air is molecular nitrogen (N_2)) the vast majority of plants cannot use this and are dependent on the small quantities of soil nitrogen present as nitrates and ammonium nitrogen. If plant growth is to continue this supply must be continuously replenished and most people think of this as simply adding chemically produced nitrogen fertiliser from a bag. What is not generally recognised is that fertiliser from the bag accounts for only about 6 per cent of the total nitrogen requirements of the Earth and there is nothing to suggest that this proportion will increase. The bulk of combined nitrogen now in circulation has been, and is, derived from the air by the process of biological nitrogen-fixation—that is certain restricted plant groups can use the nitrogen of the air directly as a source of nitrogen for protein synthesis. When these plants die this nitrogen is released into the soil in combined form and thus made available for the growth of non-nitrogen-fixing plants. Thus continuous biological nitrogen-fixation is a basic requirement for the continuance of life on Earth.

Methods of Demonstrating Nitrogen-Fixation.

The question of which plants fix nitrogen has been the subject of a good deal of controversy in the past, but now two reliable methods of demonstrating fixation are available:

1. *Total nitrogen analysis.* This involves growing the test plant in a solution or soil containing little or no combined nitrogen, and after a suitable period (generally a matter of weeks) measuring the total nitrogen present and comparing this with a series set up at the same time but without the test organism. This latter series acts as a control and when large gains occur only in the series containing the test plant, and if the various limitations of the method are appreciated it can be accepted that the nitrogen increases are due to fixation by the test organism.

2. *The use of isotopic nitrogen.* This method which is becoming increasingly popular involves exposing the test material to an atmosphere containing molecular nitrogen suitably enriched with a nitrogen isotope (*see* **F10**(2)) and subsequently determining whether the plant incorporates isotopic nitrogen in cell synthesis. Two isotopes have been used—nitrogen-15 (^{15}N) which is stable and must therefore be measured in an instrument called a mass spectrometer and nitrogen-13 (^{13}N) a radioactive isotope. Because the half-life of the latter is so short (10·05 minutes) it is not generally suitable but the ^{15}N method is now routinely used in many laboratories.

Which Plants Fix Nitrogen?

Only a relatively small group of micro-organisms which carry out the process either alone or in symbiosis (*see* **L111**) with higher plants are known. These are:

1. Bacteria of the genus *Rhizobium* which fix nitrogen in association with the roots of plants of the angiosperm family Leguminosae. (*See* **F27(2)**.)
2. Micro-organisms of uncertain nature, but probably filamentous bacteria (actinomycetes) which fix nitrogen in association with the roots of certain woody plants such as common alder (*Alnus glutinosa*) and bog myrtle (*Myrica gale*).
3. Certain microscopic algae belonging to the class Myxophyceae (often called the blue-green algae because of their colour).
4. Certain free-living bacteria, some of which such as *Azotobacter* are common soil micro-organisms.
5. Possibly certain fungi and soil yeasts, although the evidence for these is not nearly as strong as for the above-mentioned groups.

If we now consider each of these:

The Rhizobium—Leguminosae Association.

It has been known for many centuries that legume crops such as peas, clovers, and soya beans are beneficial to subsequent crop yield and they were therefore included in the crop rotation systems devised by early civilisations, although the reason why they were beneficial was unknown until the end of the 19th century. Then, in 1886–88, the German scientists H. Hellriegel and H. Wilfarth showed that peas and clovers which developed swellings or nodules on their roots increased in nitrogen content in soils free from combined nitrogen, whereas cereals and non-nodulated legumes did not. They postulated that this was due to the root nodules fixing gaseous nitrogen from the air and that such nodules were formed by infection of the roots by bacteria, now known to be of the genus *Rhizobium*. These conclusions have since been confirmed many times for hundreds of legume species.

Rhizobium species are free-living motile, aerobic rod-like organisms, 1 to 3 $\times 10^{-4}$ cm. in length and of widespread distribution in the soil. They fix nitrogen only in the root nodule. The rhizobia enter the legume via small hair-like structures present on the roots. These root hairs, as they are called, normally serve the function of absorbing water and mineral nutrients from the soil. Having entered the root hairs the rhizobia then move inwards towards the root cortex where they penetrate disomatic cells (*i.e.*, cells with twice the chromosome complement of ordinary cells). Once these cells are penetrated they and the surrounding cells rapidly divide, a growing point becomes established, and a lateral swelling on the root which eventually forms into a nodule is produced.

In external appearance the nodules are small, spherical, club-shaped, or branched structures generally about 0·2–0·8 cm. in length. If a section is cut through a mature legume nodule an outer uninfected area, and an inner central region filled with the bacteria and which is red in colour due to the presence of haemoglobin, can be distinguished. The haemoglobin is almost identical with that which acts as an oxygen carrier in mammalian respiratory systems and this is the only place in the plant kingdom where it is present in any abundance. It surrounds the bacteria within the infected cells of the legume and is itself enclosed in a complex membrane system derived from the host cells. It is essential for fixation as nitrogen is fixed only after haemoglobin develops. It possibly functions as an oxygen carrier but the oxygen levels in the nodules are very low and it is not generally accepted that this is its rôle. According to another theory (again controversial) haemoglobin is involved in the chemical combination of nitrogen by passing electrons from the bacterium on to the host cell membrane where the nitrogen is converted to ammonia and thus fixed. It is fair to say that the exact rôle of haemoglobin, like the exact site of fixation within the nodules, is not known with certainty.

Once fixed, the nitrogen is rapidly transferred from the nodules to the remainder of the plant via the water conducting elements. It then becomes available to the farmer in the form of protein when he harvests his crop, or else if the plants die or are ploughed back into the soil it becomes available to non-nitrogen-fixing plants.

The Nodulated Non-legumes.

Although there is no doubt that on a purely economic basis the legumes are the most important nitrogen-fixing plants, the nodulated non-legumes, which are of much more restricted occurrence, fix nitrogen just as efficiently, and from an ecological and purely scientific viewpoint may be more important. Ecologically they are important early colonisers of areas low in soil nitrogen, for example *Myrica gale* is characteristic of acid bog-land, *Alnus glutinosa* is important in the recolonisation of recently deglaciated areas in Alaska, while *Hippophaë* and *Casuarina* are commonly found on sand-dune systems in temperate and tropical regions respectively. Biochemically they are important because the nodules continue to fix nitrogen for up to 24 hours after being cut from the roots (that is much longer than those of legumes). Thus they are useful tools for studying symbiotic fixation in the laboratory without having to worry about the complications of total plant growth as well.

The root nodules, unlike those of legumes, generally form coral-like masses which may be as large as tennis balls and which appear to be modified lateral roots. An interesting feature of the nodules of some species, particularly those of water-logged soils, is that the tips produce white upwardly growing rootlets which act as aerating organs and thus help supply the nodules with air (and nitrogen) under water-logged conditions.

Internally the nodules differ from those of legumes in two main respects. First, as mentioned previously, the micro-organisms which cause nodule formation are probably actinomycetes. Secondly, although they penetrate the roots via root hairs as in legumes, it is the outer regions of the nodule rather than the central region which becomes infected. The nodules are similar to the legumes, however, in that haemoglobin is present (though not in quantity), host plant membranes are present, and (unfortunately) the exact site of fixation is unknown. A stumbling block in the study of fixation by non-legume nodules is that it is not yet possible to get the micro-organisms which occur inside the nodules to grow on their own outside. Despite this, these micro-organisms must be of widespread distribution in the soil for they are not passed on from one plant generation to another in the seed, and yet in the field the plants are always abundantly nodulated. Thus to obtain nodulated plants for study in the laboratory one has to resort to brushing the seedling roots with a suspension of crushed nodules or to grow the seedlings in soil in which nodulated plants had previously been growing.

The Myxophyceae (Blue-Green Algae).

While the nodulated legumes and non-legumes are truly terrestrial plants the blue-green algae inhabit the seas, lakes, and land. Their distribution ranges from the Antarctic wastes to the arid desert soils of Arizona and from the inland lakes of Alaska to the Sargasso Sea. Despite this they are seldom very abundant although the fossil record shows they had evolved to their present level as early as the time when the first land plants appeared on the surface of the Earth.

The nitrogen-fixing blue-green algae are filamentous in appearance and at first sight many resemble strings of beads. Each "bead" is in fact a round or square cell about 2 to 10 $\times 10^{-4}$ cm. in diameter and often linked together in groups of 10–30. The individual cells show little internal differentiation under the light microscope. One can recognise an outer pigmented region which is also the site of nitrogen-fixation, and a colourless central area containing the nuclear material. The plants are characterised by the presence of two pigments not found in other plants except the red algae (Rhodophyceae). These are phycocyanin (a blue pigment) and phycoerythrin (a red pigment). Together with the green chlorophyll pigments they give the blue-green colour characteristic of these algae. Not all species fix nitrogen but those which do (and over forty are now known) contain large empty-looking cells called heterocysts inter-mingled with the ordinary cells. It was once thought that heterocysts were the nitrogen-fixing sites of blue-green algae, but this supposition now seems to be erroneous and their occurrence in nitrogen-fixing species only is probably coincidental.

Economically the algae are particularly important in South-east Asia, especially in India where they are abundant and important in rice paddy fields during the rainy season when over 40 lb. nitrogen per acre per year may be fixed and become available to the rice plant. So important is this source of combined nitrogen that Japanese workers have attempted to grow nitrogen-fixing algae in mass culture and to inoculate the paddy fields artificially with them. This method is not yet an economic proposition but it may prove useful in the future.

Finally, mention should be made that nitrogen-fixing blue-green algae form associations with other organisms, for example with fungi to form lichens (*see* **L70**), with bryophytes such as *Pellia*, with the water-fern *Azolla*, with cycads which bear root nodules containing blue-green algae as endophytes, and with the tropical angiosperm *Gunnera*. These are not strict nitrogen-fixing symbioses because the algae can fix nitrogen on their own but at the same time the associations probably ensure that the non-algal partner is supplied with an ample source of combined nitrogen.

The Bacteria.

Until about 1950 it was generally accepted that the only two bacteria which could fix nitrogen alone were *Azotobacter* and *Clostridium* but since then many other genera such as *Beijerinckia*, *Pseudomonas*, *Aerobacter*, and *Chromatium* have been shown to fix nitrogen. Most are common soil micro-organisms, but others occur associated with the leaves of certain tropical plants to form swellings on the leaves called leaf nodules. Unlike the previous groups the contribution of free-living nitrogen-fixing bacteria is not likely to be very great for the two following reasons. First they are seldom present in very high quantities and secondly the majority cannot synthesise their own carbohydrate but must have it readily supplied, and the quantities of free carbohydrate in most environments are too low to allow very high fixation rates.

Bacteria have proved to be particularly useful however in laboratory studies on the mechanism and biochemistry of fixation. Prior to 1960 such studies relied on the use of intact organisms. This had serious disadvantages because nitrogen-fixation by whole cells is closely associated with overall growth so that the reactions specially concerned with nitrogen-fixation were often obscured by general metabolism. In 1960 active nitrogen-fixing cell-free extracts of several bacteria were obtained almost simultaneously in several laboratories so that it is now possible to study the nitrogen-fixing enzyme systems *in vitro*. It may be noted that nitrogen-fixing extracts of symbiotic systems have not yet been achieved.

Fungi and Yeasts.

There have been reports from time to time that certain fungi and yeasts fix nitrogen, but some of the data are of doubtful significance. Many more positive results will have to be obtained using the sensitive isotopic method before it is generally accepted that fixation by these organisms does in fact occur.

Mineral Nutrition of Nitrogen-Fixing Plants.

All the elements necessary for healthy plant growth on combined nitrogen are required for nitrogen-fixation to proceed. It seems likely however that at least three mineral elements: cobalt, iron, and molybdenum are specifically involved in the fixation process for they are required in larger quantities when the organisms are fixing nitrogen than when they are growing on combined nitrogen. These elements are now often added to agricultural soils to improve nitrogen-fixation and encouraging results have been obtained. For example, in some Australian soils additions of 1 oz. cobalt per acre increases legume crop yield by up to 70 per cent. The laboratory scientist on the other hand looks at the effects of various elements on fixation from a slightly different angle. To him increased crop yield indicates that the elements added to the soil are involved in the nitrogen-fixing enzyme systems and careful studies by biochemists have confirmed that the two major enzyme systems in the fixation process are indeed molybdenum-containing and iron-containing proteins.

Another inorganic nutrient which markedly affects fixation is combined nitrogen. When it is available to the plant nitrogen-fixation is inhibited, the extent of inhibition being more or less inversely proportional to the quantities supplied. This is because the nitrogen is reduced to ammonia (NH_3) in the nitrogen-fixation process and when ammonia or any other form of combined nitrogen which is reduced to ammonia is present in the soil the plant uses this preferentially. In the case of symbiotic plants the effect of combined nitrogen is even more drastic, for it also inhibits nodule formation. This is probably because combined nitrogen prevents the formation by the plant of growth substances necessary for the bacteria to grow round and into the root hairs.

Biochemistry of Nitrogen-Fixation.

It is now fairly well established that the process of fixation involves the conversion, or "reduction", of molecular nitrogen to ammonia ($N_2 \rightarrow 2NH_3$) but the intermediate steps in the reduction process are uncertain. Irrespective of which are the actual steps in fixation it is obvious that there are several major requirements necessary for nitrogen-fixation to continue. These are:

(1) a reducing source for the reduction of nitrogen;
(2) an energy source;
(3) enzyme systems which will allow the reactions to proceed rapidly;
(4) carbon skeletons with which the ammonia will combine to form amino acids.

Almost all the evidence on the nature of these four basic requirements has been obtained from studies on free-living organisms rather than symbiotic systems. If we now consider these:

1. The reduction of nitrogen.—Nitrogen-fixing plants are versatile organisms and one of the ways in which this versatility is expressed is in the way they reduce nitrogen. Three possible sources of reducing power are known although they are not necessarily used by all organisms:

(a) *Pyruvic acid* ($CH_3.CO.COOH$). The first evidence that pyruvic acid could act as a source of reducing power was obtained by American workers in 1960 when they found that this substance had to be added before nitrogen-fixing cell-free extracts of the bacterium *Clostridium pasteurianum* could fix nitrogen. They observed that the organism split up the pyruvic acid enzymatically and that one of the products of this split was electrons which were then passed on to the gaseous nitrogen which was then reduced. At first this reaction was considered to be peculiar to *Clostridium* but it has since been found in other nitrogen-fixing organisms, although it is not yet known whether it is of universal occurrence in nitrogen-fixing plants.

(b) *Molecular hydrogen*. Perhaps the most obvious source of reducing power is the molecular hydrogen of the air and indeed scientists had long considered this possibility but were unable to obtain positive proof. It has recently been shown however that photosynthetic bacteria fix nitrogen almost twice as fast in the presence of gaseous hydrogen as in its absence. This has subsequently been confirmed by other workers for other organisms.

(c) *Photoreduction of nitrogen.* A third possible source of reducing power in photosynthetic organisms is the electrons made available when water (H_2O) is split up (into H^+ and OH^-) in the presence of light energy in the process of photolysis.

2. **Energy sources.**—An interesting feature of biological nitrogen-fixation is that it occurs at room temperature, yet to achieve this chemically the industrial chemist has to employ high temperatures and pressures. This suggests either that there is no energy requirement for biological fixation, or else chemical energy rather than heat energy is used. Chemical energy is generally available from the compound adenosine triphosphate (ATP) and although early workers could not demonstrate an ATP requirement it has since been shown to be necessary. (*See* **F21**.)

3. **Carbon skeletons.**—Once ammonia is formed it is incorporated into amino acids. The carbon skeletons necessary for this must come either from photosynthetic products or from a carbohydrate source such as glucose added to the medium in which the organisms are growing. The details of entry need not concern us here, but although several possible carbon skeletons are available the most commonly used is α-ketoglutaric acid which combines with ammonia to give the amino acid called glutamic acid, and other amino acids essential for growth are then formed from this by a process called transamination.

4. **The Enzymes.**—The most intriguing components of the nitrogen-fixing complex are of course the enzymes which bring the process about. It is known that in *Clostridium* there are two main enzymes: *hydrogenase* which passes the reducing power on to an electron carrier called ferredoxin. Ferredoxin is an iron-containing protein which in turn passes the electrons on to the enzyme *nitrogenase* where the nitrogen is actually reduced. It has been possible to separate the two enzyme systems in *Clostridium* extracts and to show that they cannot fix nitrogen separately but do so when combined. Now that nitrogen-fixing cell-free extracts are available it can be anticipated that in the near future much more detailed knowledge of these enzyme systems will become available.

The Quantities of Nitrogen Fixed in the Field.

Finally brief mention may be made of the quantities of nitrogen fixed by the various groups in Nature. In agricultural soils a good legume crop will fix 100–200 lb. nitrogen per acre per year, while non-legumes such as *Alnus* fix corresponding amounts in non-agricultural soils. The quantities fixed by blue-green algae differ in different regions of the world but values of 30–60 lb. per acre per year are usual in Indian paddy fields. Bacteria probably fix up to 5 lb. per acre per year in natural soils, but few data are available. One of the main aims in biological nitrogen-fixation is to exploit these various sources of combined nitrogen more efficiently.

IS THE CLIMATE CHANGING?

The Reason for Asking.

This question has been raised in many quarters in recent years following a number of extreme seasons. English summers from 1950 to 1963 yielded on average about 19 per cent more rainfall than those of the 1930s and 40s; 1954, 1956, 1958, and 1960 were notably wet. And the sequence seemed to many people to be continued by the remarkably cool summers of 1962 and 1963. The picture was relieved mainly by the particularly sunny seasons in 1955 and 1959 and the late summer of 1964. The last-named does not rank as a warm summer, however, the warmth of May and a heat wave in late August having been offset by some remarkably cold snaps: snow fell on or near the A9 road over the Scottish Highlands as late as 20 June and as early as 19 August, both dates being records. The 1962–63 winter, over most of England the longest and coldest for 223 years, was followed by another in 1963–4 that, although only marginally colder than average, was the driest for 221 years. These last are outsize extremes, beyond the limits of what the British climate had latterly been thought liable to, and both pointing to the same period in the past (the 1740s) for the closest parallel.

Recent Climatic Warming.

Among scientists the subject of climatic variations has received an extraordinary amount of attention over the last 25 to 30 years, since the discovery that climates in most parts of the world were undergoing a sustained warming, the origins of which could be traced many decades back. Between about 1880 and 1940 the average warming over the world appeared to be 0·4 to 0·5° C, from 1800 to 1940 probably almost 1° C. There were corresponding changes of average rainfall, amounting to 30 to 50 per cent in some parts of the world, and affecting agricultural prospects significantly. The length of the growing season and the frequency of snow in the English lowlands, the length of the open season for shipping in ports liable to ice (*e.g.*, Spitsbergen, Riga, Montreal), rainfall on the Argentine pampas and on the grain lands of the U.S. Middle West and Central Asia were among the things that showed important changes. The relevance to future planning of many tables of climatic statistics—which really only summarise the experience of some group of past years—began to appear doubtful.

The short answer to the question in the title is that the climate is always changing in greater or less degree. Every year, every decade, every century brings a somewhat different experience. There is clearly a need to get the facts in perspective and seek a deeper understanding of the phenomenon in physical terms.

Evidence of Climatic Changes in the Past.

It was geology that produced the first unmistakable evidence that great climatic changes had occurred, at least in the distant past. England had known epochs of tropical warmth and ice ages. But the time scale of geological epochs is counted in millions of years. Recent techniques, including for instance careful measurements of the faint traces of magnetisation of rocks remaining from the time when they were laid down (as it were a weak magnetic compass fossilised within the rock), seem to indicate that the poles, equator, and continents have wandered during geological time. The grossest changes of climate may therefore be attributable to large changes of the main geography. They are properly a separate study, different in nature from the various shorter term climatic changes that mostly concern us, and will not be further discussed here.

Ice ages and interglacial periods rather warmer than now have however alternated several times within the last half million years, during which the major geography has remained more or less unchanged. Even within historical times, and apparently in late prehistoric times also, quite severe climatic changes have several times forced themselves upon the attention of men. A great sandy desert now lies across what was in Roman times the great Silk Route through central Asia, used by regular trading caravans from China. In 1492 the Pope recorded his concern that no priest or bishop had been able to reach Greenland for eighty years because of the extensive freezing of the seas. And shortly after that the old European colony in Greenland died out. In the 1690s wet cold summers and ruined grain harvests year after year in upland parishes all over Scotland caused famine and deaths on the same scale as the Black Death, and probably made the Union with England seem inevitable.

19th Century Attitudes.

Despite all this, an idea grew up during the 19th century that the climate had become stabilised and had undergone no real change at least since Classical times. The facts mentioned in the last paragraph had never been submitted to thorough investigation, and had apparently been largely forgotten or explained away. As a corollary, it was generally believed that the values of any climatic element, such as temperature or rainfall, had only to be averaged over a long enough period of years to produce a figure of lasting validity, to which the climate would always return. This attitude doubtless expressed the natural hope of a generation to which long series of observations, made with instruments, and some of them at least stretching over more than a hundred years, were themselves a marvel of the scientific age; the computation of averages was a very great labour, and without machine aids no more elaborate statistical calculations could very well be thought of.

Growing Knowledge of Weather History.

Several things have changed the situation since. On the one hand, the recent climatic warming already referred to became so marked, especially in the 1920s and 30s, that it could no longer be ignored. At the other extreme, research in a variety of disciplines, particularly in palaeobotany (*e.g.*, by Godwin and his co-workers) and in archaeology powerfully aided in recent years by radiocarbon dating of samples used in evidence, has added greatly to our knowledge of the post-glacial climatic sequence. This has been supplemented by published compilations, from many European countries and Japan, of excerpts from documentary material relating to the nature of the seasons and weather year by year over the last one thousand years or so—a still growing source material for weather history, suitable for careful statistical treatment and meteorological analysis.

Climate Since The Last Ice Age.

The main stages of post-glacial climatic history so far clearly recognised may be briefly listed as follows:

(1) Final culmination of the last (*Würm/Wisconsin*) ice age 15,000 to 20,000 years ago. World temperature about 5° C lower than now. Mean sea level about 100 metres lower due to the accumulated ice on land.

(2) Prolonged warming, accompanied by melting of the ice sheets, and sea level rising 100 metres in 10,000 years. The Scandinavian ice sheet broke into small remnants, and the last glaciers in Britain disappeared, around 8000 B.C. The warming was however interrupted by at least two drastic climatic deteriorations around 11,500 and 8800 B.C., after the *Bölling* and *Alleröd* warm phases respectively: in the latter case prevailing temperatures are estimated to have fallen 3 to 4° C within 50 to 80 years, a rate of climatic change probably only liable to occur near the margins of existing ice sheets.

(3) By about 6000 B.C. the *Post-glacial Climatic Optimum* was beginning; prevailing temperatures were already equal to the highest levels attained in the previous interglacial periods, about 2° C higher than those of today. This warmest post-glacial climatic period lasted broadly until 3000 B.C. It was at first generally dry (the *Boreal* phase), but after the filling of the North Sea and enlarged Baltic by the rising sea waters the climate became much moister (the *Atlantic* phase). At the same time the southern half of the Sahara, probably also of Arabia and the Indian Thar desert, enjoyed a moister régime than since. There was probably no permanent pack-ice on the Arctic Ocean. By 3000 B.C. world sea level had reached its highest and appears to have undergone only very minor changes since.

(4) Between 3000 and 1000 B.C. there is evidence of unsteadiness of the climatic régime; but towards the end, in the late Bronze Age, a dry warm period occurred in western and central Europe (the *sub-Boreal*), that lasted several centuries and, judged by recovery of the former vegetation limits, was as warm as anything that had gone before.

(5) Between about 1000 and 500 B.C., in the early Iron Age, there followed a cooling of about 2° C, a more abrupt change than any other in Europe since the Würm ice sheet melted. Raininess and wetness of the ground increased all over western and northern Europe. All existing glaciers in the U.S. Rockies and most of the present extent of ice in the Alps appear to have come into being at this time (the so-called *sub-Atlantic* climatic phase, a term sometimes extended to include everything that has happened since).

(6) Partial recovery took place from perhaps 100 B.C. onwards. Here and there enough detail is known to indicate some of the ups and downs along the way. By the early Middle Ages, between about 1000 and 1300, another—rather short-lived—warm epoch was attained, with once more a higher proportion of dry summers in Britain, though annual rainfall was probably rather high and there may have been a greater liability than now to occasional heavy rains and thunderstorms. In the 1100s average temperatures seem generally to have been perhaps ½° C higher than now, and more than this in the Arctic, where the extent of sea ice was much reduced. This epoch, sometimes called the *Mediaeval Optimum* or *Little Optimum* seems to have left traces in the vegetation history of central Europe and New Zealand and in the wanderings of primitive peoples in the Arctic, in the U.S. Great Plains and central Asia. It seems to have encouraged ocean voyages in the Arctic, the Atlantic and the Pacific.

(7) Deterioration from 1250 or 1300 (a hundred years earlier in the Arctic) to 1600, with especially sharp phases around 1315, the 1430s and after 1560, is clear from the increasing frequency of wet summers, of autumnal wind storms and cold frosty or snowy winters in many parts of Europe. In some regions, and at some times, the effects upon the human economy were drastic. This period, accompanied by advancing glaciers, apparently culminated with the greatest extent of ice on land and sea since the Würm ice age. It has accordingly been called the *Little Ice Age*. World temperatures were then about 1° C lower than in recent decades. The effects can be traced in North America, China, and New Zealand as well as in Europe.

(8) From about 1700 until recent decades, through many vicissitudes, the picture was one of general recovery, particularly strong in its initial and final stages. The 1730s produced over all northern Europe a remarkable peak of warmth, affecting all seasons of the year and equal to anything in this century, but it lasted only one decade. A sharp reversion occurred in 1740 and there were several later runs of cold years, before the rapid warming between 1900 and 1930.

Climatic Change in Recent Years.

Since about 1930 the winters in Britain and Europe appear to have been getting on average colder again, and over most of the world the latest evidence (from calculations by J. M. Mitchell) suggests a downward trend of temperatures over the year as a whole. It is important to discover whether this should be viewed as just another temporary reversion or whether it marks the beginning of a more prolonged cooling tendency.

Among the new elements in the situation since the beginning of the century, fortunately, there are now possibilities of much more penetrating statistical treatment and meteorological analysis.

Laborious examination of old observation records, the exposure and behaviour of the instruments, carried out with patient attention to detail by individual workers in various countries (*e.g.*, by Manley in England), has apparently succeeded in homogenising many such records and reducing the monthly mean values to close equivalence to what would be obtained with modern instruments. Thus, we now have comparable observational material for study going back to the early 18th century or beyond for London, Berlin, Utrecht, and other places.

The Vortex Round the Poles.

The invention of the radio-sonde, a balloon-borne transmitting instrument which makes it possible to observe atmospheric pressure, temperature, humidity and winds every day regardless of cloud cover, and the employment of these instruments at a world-wide network of places since about 1945, has given us the first regular surveys of the main currents of the atmospheric circulation in depth. This has revealed that these main wind currents consist of a rather simple circumpolar whirl of generally westerly upper winds over each hemisphere. The flow around this circumpolar vortex undergoes both regular seasonal and irregular changes of strength, and is deflected into a system of waves on its way round the hemisphere. North–south mountain ranges like the Andes and the Rockies are capable of disturbing the upper wind flow in this way. The waves are a succession of troughs and ridges extending over various ranges of latitude. There tend to be upper ridges over the warm, and upper troughs over the cold, parts of the temperate and neighbouring subpolar zone. The wave-length—the spacing between neighbouring troughs and ridges—tends to be longer the stronger the flow and the higher the latitudes in which this flow is for the time being located.

The Wind Circulation and Climatic Variations.

The intensity of development and prevailing positions of, and the paths followed by, the surface weather systems, depressions and anticyclones, vary with the flow around the upper vortex. This makes it possible to interpret the condition and behaviour of the general upper wind circulation over the world from observation of the distribution of barometric pressure and winds at the surface, which also determine the surface weather. Barometric pressure and winds are closely related to each other, and observations of either or both help to complete a single picture of the wind circulation. Just as the isobars on a synoptic daily weather map provide the most convenient unified picture of what is producing the weather at any instant of time, so the mean circulation map for a month or a season is the handiest and most fundamental tool for studying the slower variations of climate.

Circulation Changes.

The barometer was early developed to a satisfactory state and its exposure presents fewer problems than with the thermometer or rainguage. Maps (due to H. H. Lamb and A. I. Johnson) of average barometric pressure extending over as much of the world as possible for each January and each July back to 1750 (and for *all* months of the year back to 1873) have reconstructed for us the changes in the prevailing wind circulation during the last great period of climatic change listed above. They reveal it as a large-scale phenomenon of apparently world-wide extent and show us some of the mechanics of how it came about. From at latest 1860 until about the 1920s, the main arms of the general atmospheric circulation in all parts of the world—the North Atlantic westerlies, the Trade Winds, the monsoon currents of Asia and the Brave West Winds (Roaring Forties) in the southern hemisphere—were all increasing in strength and prevalence, to judge by the pressure differences associated with them. In the case of the westerlies in the neighbourhood of the British Isles we can trace this increase in progress right through from 1760, and on the evidence of wind observations alone we can trace some aspects of the same process from 1680. It looks as if the whole world's wind circulation was undergoing a progressive, though fluctuating, increase of vigour during the entire period of the climatic warming lasting more than two centuries.

The circulation changes are readily apparent from the sample graphs of average pressure differences in January illustrated in fig. 1.

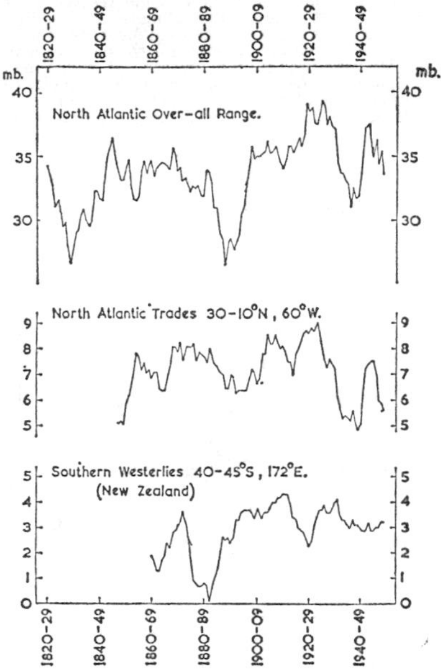

FIG. 1. Pressure difference indices of atmospheric circulation strength in January: 10-year running means.

It is scarcely surprising therefore that gradually more heat was being transported to the Arctic and melting the ice there, that the warm North Atlantic Drift conveying Gulf Stream water across the ocean seems to have become stronger and spread farther north, and that the increasing westerly winds brought an increasing rainfall right across Europe as far as central Asia. Changes of average annual rainfall in several parts of the world amounted to 30 to 50 per cent or more.

Westerly Type Weather in Britain and Recent Trends.

That this was not just a matter of the average circulation, but affected also the frequency of westerly winds in this part of the world on individual days, is shown by fig. 2, which illustrates the frequency of "westerly type weather" in Britain each year, and the 10-year moving mean of this frequency, from 1873 to 1963. And here we encounter clear evidence that this trend, like most of the others mentioned in this article, has latterly reversed. In the case of the general wind circulation a weakening tendency can be traced from about the mid-1920s and likewise with the frequency of westerly winds in Britain. The average level of winter temperatures seems to have begun to turn downwards about the same time, already 35 years ago. Signs of reversal in the other seasons in Britain, as with the trends of rainfall in various parts of the world, of sea temperatures, and of renewed increase of the Arctic sea ice, first became apparent much later in the record, mostly since 1950. But they appear to be logical concomitants of the tendency for weakening of the general atmospheric circulation, and explanations for the lag of a decade or two in their response can fairly readily be suggested.

Can We Forecast Climatic Change?

It would be a matter of some interest to be able to forecast whether these newest tendencies will continue. Already it is clear that tables of climatic figures for the early part of this century should not be used without some reserve as a guide to the future. But climatic forecasting, however great the economic need for it, must wait until the agencies responsible for the changes here studied have been fully diagnosed. A wide range of things may be at work. Several are known to have climatic effects, but in each case the magnitude of the effect and the processes which bring it about need to be established. There are, for instance, subtle variations in the composition of the radiation coming from the sun. The sluggish vertical circulation of the oceans may contribute to changes in the sea surface temperatures in regions where deep water comes to the surface. Volcanic eruptions from time to time throw up dust veils, which partially screen the earth from the incoming solar radiation for up to two or three years. Man's burning of fossil fuels (coal, natural gas, and oil) is increasing the quantity of carbon dioxide in the atmosphere. This substance should have more or less the reverse effect of volcanic dust, since it allows most of the incoming solar beam to pass but intercepts the outgoing long-wave radiation from the earth. Forest clearance and agriculture change the heating and cooling, and moisture-retaining, properties of the ground. And henceforward rocket exhausts must be expected to pollute the outer atmosphere with strange substances that also may affect the passage of solar and terrestrial radiation.

With all these and other variables, the climate cannot be expected to remain strictly constant. Some of them concern chiefly the differences between one year and another, others may bring about longer-term changes. In the case of several we see examples of how human activities could themselves cause climatic changes, either intentionally or inadvertently. Moreover, natural events such as great volcanic eruptions are liable to introduce an unpredictable element into the problem. Climatic forecasting cannot be regarded as just round the corner.

The Present State of Our Understanding.

The most promising results so far are the demonstration of interconnections—through the atmospheric circulation—between changes occurring in one part of the world and another, and of interconnection between the changes in the atmospheric and ocean circulations. It is already possible to comment on some schemes for artificial modification of climate, for instance by removal of the Arctic sea ice (if that should ever become practicable). Both on theoretical grounds, and from an extension of the analysis of changes of prevailing winds and climate over Europe back to the Mediaeval Optimum when there was much less Arctic ice, it appears that one probable result would be an increase of aridity in parts of the interior of the great continents. Analysis (by Lamb) of the distribution of warm or dry and wet or cold anomalies shown by the European records of the last thousand years not only confirms the early mediaeval warm epoch and the cold period centred on the 17th century, but suggests a westward shift of the distribution over Europe during the late mediaeval climatic decline and an eastward shift during the more recent recovery. (The latter can be amply demonstrated by the instrumental observations since 1800.) These are the changes that would be expected if the general atmospheric circulation was weakening, and the central polar cold region expanding, between 1300 and 1600 and opposite changes going on from about 1700. This might be explainable by some (single) long-period fluctuation in the intensity of the solar energy, or in the amount of that energy effectively reaching the earth, over those centuries. Modern measurements of the intensity of the solar beam, however, either from observatories at the earth's surface (*i.e.*, at the bottom of the atmosphere) or mounted on satellites, have not so far produced evidence of any corresponding change in the solar energy received since 1930 to explain the latest apparent weakening of the atmospheric circulation.

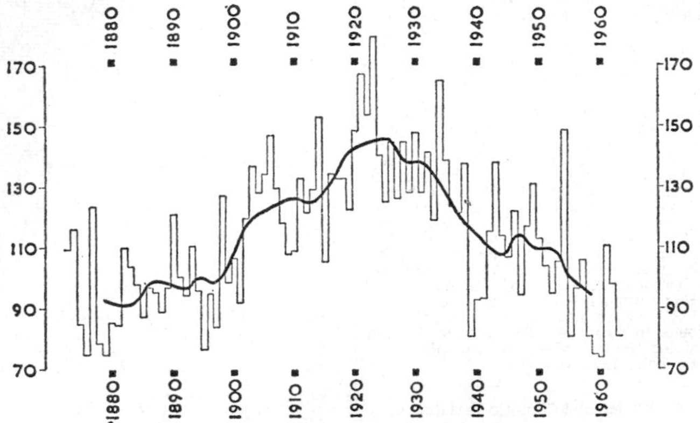

FIG. 2. Number of days per year of Westerly type weather in Britain 1873 to 1963: individual years' totals and 10-year running mean.

An interesting recent Soviet observation that may be relevant is that the deposit of dust (for the most part not volcanic) from the atmosphere on the glaciers of the Caucasus is found, from examination of the annual ice layers in which the dust gets embedded, to have been at a minimum around the 1920s and to have been increasing since. The Caucasus is fairly remote from the main sources of desert sand and industrial smoke particles, though certainly by no means immune from either—as the proximity of the Baku oilfield and arid regions in Turkey and Persia must be taken to indicate. And it doubtless receives dust consisting of minute dry soil particles from the steppes. The reported changes in the amount of dust deposited may therefore be only a matter of a change in the frequencies of winds from different directions. Something approaching a global survey of dust in the annual layers of glaciers and ice sheets would be needed to establish a sequence of changes in the overall dustiness of the atmosphere.

BACKGROUND TO ECONOMIC EVENTS

TABLE OF CONTENTS

BACKGROUND TO ECONOMIC EVENTS

THE aim in this section is to help the ordinary reader to follow economic events as they happen, and to understand the controversy that accompanies them. It is divided into three parts. Part I gives a brief description of the most important problems of economic policy. Part II is concerned with a more detailed survey of developments in the British economy up to 1960. In the course of this survey, the specialised terms used by economists are explained, and the attempt is made to present an intelligible summary of the information, facts, and figures relevant to an understanding of economic events. There are five main sub-sections: International Trade and Payments; Production, Employment, and Industry; Incomes, Wages, and Prices; Money, Banking, and Finance; and Economic Aspects of the Public Services. Some suggestions for further reading are given at the end of Part II. Part III is written as shortly before publication as possible, and contains a survey of developments in the British economy since 1960.

I. CENTRAL PROBLEMS OF ECONOMIC POLICY

Unemployment.

Between the wars, unemployment was Britain's most urgent economic problem. The level of unemployment varied with the ups and downs of the trade cycle. Quite the worst slump was that of the early 1930s: in 1932, nearly 3 million workers were without a job. But unemployment remained high even in the best years, and in no year between 1919 and 1939 were there fewer than a million workers unemployed. Economists make a distinction between *structural* unemployment and *cyclical* unemployment. Structural unemployment appears when the structure of industry gets out of line with the pattern of demand for industrial products. In Britain, unemployment was particularly severe and persistent in areas which were dependent on the coal, textile, and shipbuilding industries, and some sections of the engineering industry. These industries had been in the forefront of Britain's industrial growth in the 19th cent., and had contributed greatly to the expansion of exports. In areas like South Wales, Tyneside, Clydeside, and Northern Ireland there was little alternative work for those no longer needed in the "staple" industries: new industries were being built up in the inter-war period, but they tended to be located in the relatively prosperous Midlands and South-East England. Cyclical unemployment appears when there is a general decline in the level of demand for goods and services, which leads to a decline in the employment of workers producing those goods and services. In the slump years unemployment was so high because of a combination of structural and cyclical unemployment; in the best years, unemployment was largely structural.

Unemployment means waste. Men willing to work, who could produce valuable goods and services, are idle; the economy produces fewer goods and services than it is capable of producing. Unemployment also means hardship and low standards of living for those out of work, and for their families.

The avoidance of mass unemployment has been accepted as a primary objective of economic policy by all political parties, and there is a wide measure of agreement on the policies which must be applied to ensure that unemployment on the scale of the 1930s never occurs again. Cyclical unemployment has to be tackled by measures to increase total demand and total spending by consumers, by investors, and by the Government. Structural unemployment has to be tackled by inducing new industries to move into areas where other employment is declining, or by inducing labour to move from those areas to areas where there is a demand for its services.

There have been ups and downs in unemployment in the post-war years, but these have been very slight compared to those of the pre-war years. In most post-war years, less than 2 per cent of the working population was unemployed—a sharp contrast with the 11 per cent for 1937 and the 22 per cent for 1932. But there are still areas of the country where structural unemployment is serious. In Northern Ireland, for example, despite the efforts which have been made to attract new industries, unemployment ranged between 6 and over 10 per cent during the 1950s.

Inflation.

A characteristic of the British economy in post-war years has been a persistent rise in prices and money incomes. For example, between 1954 and 1964, retail prices went up by about 35 per cent, or—expressed as an annual rate—by 3·1 per cent per annum, export prices rose by 18 per cent (or 1·6 per cent per annum), and weekly wage rates by about 55 per cent (4·4 per cent per annum). However, these rates of increase were considerably slower than the corresponding rates in the immediately post-war decade. This inflation of prices and money incomes is considered undesirable for two main reasons. Firstly, it is associated with an arbitrary redistribution of purchasing power. Prices rise for everyone, but some members of the community are better placed than others to secure increases in their money incomes which offset, or more than offset, the rise in the price of the goods and services they buy. The feeling that particular groups are falling behind, in that their money incomes have not risen as fast as those of other groups, is a source of much unrest and discontent. Secondly, and crucially for the British economy, an inflation of prices makes it more difficult to achieve a satisfactory balance of payments. As prices of our exports rise, it becomes harder to sell them in foreign markets; and as imports become cheap in comparison with goods produced at home there is a tendency to buy more of them.

Two main explanations have been advanced to account for the inflation which has occurred. The first stresses the role of an excess of demand or spending power in the economy—of too much money chasing too few goods, and so leading to a rise in prices. The inflationary problem is seen as the obverse of the cyclical unemployment problem: the latter involves a deficiency of spending, and the former an excess. Those who consider an excess of demand (*demand-pull*) to be an important factor in the inflationary situation favour policies designed to reduce purchasing power: for example, the reduction of spendable income by levying higher taxes, or the reduction of spending financed through borrowing by making credit more expensive or more difficult to get. The second stresses the role of an excessive increase in incomes: it is argued that prices have risen mainly because costs have increased faster than productivity (*cost-push*). Those who take this view favour measures to restrain or control increases in wages, profits, rents, and other forms of income. Neither explanation excludes the other. Many would agree that both demand-pull and cost-push factors have contributed—with different strengths at different times—to the inflationary spiral in prices and incomes, and that measures both to control demand and to restrain or control incomes may be necessary.

But it is easier to specify in general terms the measures needed to combat inflation than it is to apply policies which are successful in practice. In particular, policy measures to restrain or control wage increases are difficult to reconcile with widely-accepted procedures of collective bargaining.

The Balance of Payments.

Britain is heavily dependent on imports. This country must import food: it cannot produce enough food within its borders to feed its population. Many of the raw materials necessary for its industry have to be purchased from abroad. Furthermore, some manufactured goods produced in other countries will be purchased because they are cheaper or more attractive than similar goods produced at home. All these goods, and our imports of services, have to be paid for in foreign currency. Foreign currency is earned by exporting goods and services to other countries. It is not, however, considered sufficient to earn enough foreign currency from our exports to pay for our imports. The objective is to earn considerably more than that, so that we have a surplus of foreign currency available to pay off external debts, to build up our external assets by investing abroad, to enable us to lend and give aid to underdeveloped countries, and to increase our foreign exchange resources.

Since the war, our balance of payments position has been precarious. Exports have increased considerably, but so have imports; and the margin of safety has been so narrow that unfavourable turns of events have led to crises in the balance of payments. In several years, our earnings from the export of goods and services have not even been sufficient to cover our payments for imports, and in no year has the surplus been as large as is considered necessary. With the balance of payments delicately poised even in favourable years, and with corrective action necessary in crisis years, economic policies have been much influenced by our foreign trade problems. It is easy to say that most of the problems would disappear, or would become less urgent, if we could achieve a major expansion of our exports. But most export markets are highly competitive, and we cannot expect to sell more unless the price, quality, and terms of delivery of our goods and services are at least as attractive as those of our rivals in export markets.

Economic Growth.

Taking a longer view, the most important objective of internal economic policy must be to raise the standard of living. The standard of living can increase only if more goods and services are produced per head of population. In a fully-employed economy, the main source of increased output is a higher productivity—output per person—of the working population.

Standards of living in this country have been rising: the output of goods and services per head of population increased by about 24 per cent between 1954 and 1964. Nevertheless, many economists are of the opinion that the rate of growth of output and productivity can be, and should be, increased. In particular, they point out that our rate of growth compares unfavourably with that achieved by some other countries. The potentialities for higher productivity are enormous. The U.S.A. has the highest standard of living in the world: in many industries, output per person employed is twice or more that yet attained in this country. In order to achieve a higher level of productivity in this country, more and better machinery and capital equipment will have to be installed; also, work will have to be planned, organised, and controlled in such a way as to make more effective use of labour and machinery.

Underdeveloped Countries.

Britain and the other developed countries of the world have important responsibilities towards the underdeveloped countries. The poorest two-thirds of the world's population account for only a sixth of total world income and output, while two-thirds of world income accrue to the richest sixth of world population, a category which includes Britain. The poorest two-thirds suffer from poverty, hunger, malnutrition, debilitating diseases, and widespread illiteracy. To make matters worse, most of the poor countries are experiencing a rapid growth of population. Output has to rise as fast as population just to prevent standards of living from falling, and an increase in standards of living requires an even faster growth of output.

Few underdeveloped countries can hope to solve the increasing problems they face without active and generous help from developed countries. This help must take many forms. Financial aid in the form of grants or loans, in order to place resources at the disposal of underdeveloped countries which they would otherwise not be able to obtain; technical aid to assist in the solution of the many technical problems which have to be solved; trading policies which do not hinder underdeveloped countries from getting the imports they need or from selling their exports—these are all activities in which Britain must play her part. In particular, of course, Britain must contribute to the development of the underdeveloped countries of the Commonwealth.

The Inter-relationship of Economic Problems.

Each of the problems briefly described above is extremely complex. The difficulties of achieving successful solutions are further aggravated by the fact that the problems are inter-related in such a way that measures which are helpful for one problem can make others more difficult to solve. For example, a reduction of purchasing power might be considered helpful in the control of inflation, and might ease balance of payments problems by reducing—or slowing down the increase of—imports. But it could also lead to an increase in unemployment, and to a slowing down in the rate of growth of the economy. Or again, a reduction in aid to underdeveloped countries could make it easier to balance our external accounts, but such action could hardly be reconciled with our responsibilities towards underdeveloped countries. In the next section, particular aspects of the British economy up to 1960 are considered in some detail; the final section discusses the main features of the development of the economy since 1960.

II. SURVEY OF THE BRITISH ECONOMY UP TO 1960

1. INTERNATIONAL TRADE AND PAYMENTS.

Imports and Exports.

In 1959 Britain bought from abroad goods to a value of £3,988 million, or about £77 per head. Food is the largest item in this bill, accounting for £1,522 million. Fuel, largely oil, cost about £468 million, basic materials for industry £931 million, and manufactured goods (a category that includes a large number of semi-manufactured goods bought for further processing) £1,053 million. This last category of imports had increased sharply in the previous five years; in 1954 manufactured goods cost only £679 million in a total import bill of £3,374 million. Some of the more important individual items are shown in the table.

Most of these goods are paid for by exports of manufactured goods, which accounted in 1959 for £2,813 million out of a total value of exports of £3,330 million. Any list of such goods would be almost endless, as nearly all British industries do

VISIBLE IMPORTS AND EXPORTS IN 1959.
(£ million)

Imports of goods (c.i.f.)		Exports of goods (f.o.b.)	
Food, drink and tobacco	1,522	Food, drink, and tobacco	190
Basic materials	931	Basic materials	130
Fuels and lubricants	468	Fuels	118
Semi-manufactured goods	661	Metals	455
Finished manufactures	392	Engineering products	1,468
Other	13	Textiles	248
		Other manufactured goods	643
		Other	78
TOTAL	3,988	TOTAL	3,330
		Re-exports of imports	131

MAJOR ITEMS.

Imports		Exports	
Meat	347	Drinks	71
Wheat and other cereals	231	Wool, etc.	65
Fruit and vegetables	235	Coal	24
Butter, cheese, eggs, etc.	190	Refined petrol	95
Sugar	86	Chemicals	293
Tea, coffee, cocoa, etc.	176	Iron and steel	192
Tobacco	85	Non-ferrous metals	113
Metal ores and scrap	123	Metal manufactures	150
Wood, paper, and paperboard	316	Cars, aircraft, etc.	488
Wool, cotton, etc.	285	Ships	48
Rubber	64	Electrical machinery	232
Petrol and oil	467	Other machinery	626
Chemicals	138	Textiles:	
Non-ferrous metals	206	Cotton	63
Machinery	203	Woollen	83
Textiles	98	Other	102

some exporting; again some of the more important items are shown in the table. In addition, some £131 million of imports were re-exported without being worked on in this country.

The Balance of Visible Trade.

In the table the value of imports is much higher than that of exports; but this, the normal method of valuation in the trade returns, gives an unfair picture. Imports are valued c.i.f. (cost, insurance, and freight), *i.e.*, at the prices when loaded abroad, plus the cost of transporting them to Britain; while exports are valued f.o.b. (free on board), *i.e.*, at the prices when loaded in British ports. So in order to get a fair picture of the balance of trade, the cost of transport and insurance must be subtracted from the value of imports. When both imports and exports are valued on the same f.o.b. basis, the deficit is smaller: in 1959, the value of imports exceeded that of exports by £60 million. The position of a *deficit* on the *balance of visible trade* is the normal one. Only in 1958 was a *surplus* achieved on visible trade.

In the table figures are given for the balance of visible trade since 1946. In one year, 1951, imports exceeded exports by £750 million, and in both 1947 and 1955 there were substantial deficits. In the next table we show figures to illustrate the sources of the year-to-year changes in the balance. Each figure shows the percentage change on the previous year; for instance, in 1951 the sharp deterioration may be attributed to the rise in imports, which rose 16 per cent in volume and 34 per cent in price, giving a total increase in value of over 50 per cent. The rise was far from compensated by the rise in export value of under 25 per cent, the result of a much smaller price rise of only 19 per cent for an almost unchanged volume of exports.

The Terms of Trade.

Thus the deficit for 1951 was due almost equally to two factors—a sharp rise in the volume of imports and a sharp deterioration in the *terms of trade*. The terms of trade are the ratio of the average price of exports to that of imports. An improvement in the terms of trade is shown by a rise in the price of exports relative to imports. Thus the figure of 12 per cent for the deterioration in the terms of trade between 1950 and 1951 means that in 1951 12 per cent more exports by

VISIBLE TRADE BY VALUE.
(£ million)

	1946.	1947.	1948.	1949.	1950.	1951.	Average. 1946–51.
Imports (f.o.b.).	1,082	1,560	1,794	1,978	2,390	3,501	2,051
Exports (f.o.b.).	920	1,146	1,604	1,847	2,254	2,752	1,754
Balance of visible trade	−162	−414	−190	−131	−136	−749	−297

	1952.	1953.	1954.	1955.	1956.	1957.	1958.	1959.	Average 1952–59.
Imports (f.o.b.)	2,959	2,896	3,020	3,432	3,462	3,570	3,341	3,616	3,287
Exports (f.o.b.)	2,831	2,677	2,825	3,076	3,411	3,543	3,432	3,556	3,169
Balance of visible trade	−128	−219	−195	−356	−51	−27	+91	−60	−118

VISIBLE TRADE: VOLUMES AND PRICES.
(Percentage change over previous year)

	1947.	1948.	1949.	1950.	1951.	Total change 1946–51.
Volume of imports	+13	+ 5	+ 9	—	+16	+ 50
Volume of exports	+10	+27	+10	+14	+ 4	+ 80
Price of imports .	+19	+13	+ 4	+18	+34	+125
Price of exports .	+15	+10	+ 3	+11	+19	+ 65
Terms of trade .	− 3	− 3	− 1	−11	−12	− 40

	1952.	1953.	1954.	1955.	1956.	1957.	1958.	1959.	Total change 1951–59.
Volume of imports	−8	+8	+1	+11	−1	+4	—	+7	+20
Volume of exports	−6	+2	+4	+ 7	+6	+2	−4	+4	+15
Price of imports .	−2	−9	−1	+ 3	+2	+2	−8	−1	−13
Price of exports .	+5	−4	−1	+ 2	+4	+5	−1	−1	+ 9
Terms of trade .	+6	+6	—	− 1	+2	+3	+6	—	+25

volume would have been needed to buy the same amount of imports as in 1950.

Up to 1951 the terms of trade turned against Britain every year. As a result, over the whole period an 80 per cent rise in the volume of exports was not nearly sufficient to pay for the 50 per cent rise in the volume of imports. But after 1951 the terms of trade moved nearly as consistently in Britain's favour. Price-changes were much smaller, but over the period 1951–59 import prices fell by 13 per cent and export prices rose by 9 per cent, so that there was a net improvement in the terms of trade of 25 per cent. This permitted an improvement in the balance of visible trade despite the fact that the volume of exports did not rise as much as the volume of imports. (Discrepancies in the figures are due to approximations and plurality of sources.)

The Volume of Visible Trade.

Superficially, therefore, it would appear that an improvement in the terms of trade was good for Britain's balance of visible trade in the 1950s. This, in turn, might seem to imply that faster inflation in this country, leading to a more rapid increase in export prices, would be helpful to the balance of visible trade. This argument is false, and to see why it is false we have to consider the relationship between prices and volumes in international trade. If the prices of our export goods rise faster than the prices of our competitors in overseas markets, it will become progressively more difficult to sell our exports. If the prices of the goods we import rise slower than the prices of home-produced goods, it will become progressively more attractive to buy goods produced abroad. Thus in the longer run, an improvement in the terms of trade may be associated with a faster rise in the volume of imports than in the volume of exports. It is no accident that over the period of worsening terms of trade the volume of our exports went up faster than the volume of our imports, and that over the period of improving terms of trade the volume of our exports went up slower than the volume of our imports. For a time, it is true, an improvement in the terms of trade may more than offset the slower increase in the volume of exports, so that the balance of trade improves—as it did in the 1950s. But in the longer run, improving terms of trade may be more a hindrance than a help to the balance of trade; and an improvement in the terms of trade caused by inflation in the home economy would be particularly dangerous. One of the most ominous signs in the 1950s was a persistent fall in Britain's share of world trade. Her competitors in export markets—and particularly Germany and Japan—were more successful in expanding their exports.

It will be noted from the table that the largest deficits in visible trade—in 1947, 1951, and 1955—occurred in years when there was a sharp increase in the volume of imports. The improvement which occurred in the years after each of these crisis years was in part attributable to a fall, or slower growth, in import volume. The implication is that some part of the additional imports in crisis years was not used in those years, but added to stocks. The fall or slower growth in imports in the years after was in part attributable to the running down of stocks accumulated in crisis years. Changes in holding of stocks have an important part in the explanation of ups and downs in the economy after the war: the increase and subsequent running down of stocks has been described as an *inventory cycle* to distinguish it from the more severe and pervasive *trade cycle* of pre-war years. Since some of the materials and goods going into stock are imported, the inventory cycle has had a direct impact on the balance of visible trade, an impact which was particularly serious when, as in 1951, additional imports were bought at sharply increased prices.

Invisible Trade, and the Current Balance of Payments.

For every post-war year except 1958, visible imports exceeded visible exports, so that there was a deficit on visible trade. This deficit was offset by a surplus on *invisible transactions*, as they are called. This surplus derives from four main groups of transactions. The first covers receipts from non-residents, *less* payments to non-residents, for services such as shipping and insurance. The second covers receipts from foreign governments in respect of military bases in this country, *less* payments by this country in respect of military bases abroad. The third covers receipts of gifts and grants made to this country, *less* gifts and grants—e.g. grants to some Commonwealth

THE CURRENT BALANCE OF PAYMENTS. (£ million.)

Year.	Balance on visible trade. (1)	Balance on invisible trade. (2)	Current balance of payments. (1) + (2)
1950	−136	+433	+297
1951	−749	+330	−419
1952	−128	+355	+227
1953	−219	+398	+179
1954	−195	+406	+211
1955	−356	+283	− 73
1956	− 51	+309	+258
1957	− 27	+256	+229
1958	+ 91	+254	+345
1959	− 60	+199	+139
Average 1950–54	−285	+384	+ 99
1955–59	− 81	+260	+179

countries—made by this country. The fourth covers receipts of interest, dividends, and profits earned on overseas investment, *less* interest, dividends, and profits paid out on foreign investment in this country. The table shows that in most years, the surplus on all these transactions taken together exceeded the deficit on visible trade, so that Britain earned a surplus on the *current balance of payments*. During the 1950s, it was only in the two years of exceptionally large deficits on visible trade—1951 and 1955—that there was a deficit in the current balance of payments. In the later years of the 1950s, however, there was a distinct tendency for the surplus from invisible trade to decline. Net earnings from shipping services fell; Government military expenditure abroad and grants to other countries increased; defence aid to this country fell. Britain could no longer rely on such a substantial surplus on invisible transactions to offset deficits on visible trade: but surpluses on the current balance of payments continued because the balance of visible trade improved markedly.

The Current Balance of Payments by Regions.

All the figures presented so far refer to Britain's trade with the external world as a whole. More detailed figures are also available showing the results of trade between this country and groups of other countries: data for 1959 are shown in the table. Almost 40 per cent of visible imports and exports came from or went to the countries of the overseas sterling area—comprising the Colonial Territories, independent Commonwealth countries other than Canada, British Protected States in the Persian Gulf, and a few other countries such as Burma. One reason for Britain's declining share in world trade is that trade within the sterling area has been growing less rapidly than world trade as a whole. Rather less than 30 per cent of our visible trade was done with Western Europe, and rather less than 20 per cent with North America. It will be noted that the current balance of payments surplus of £139 million was made up of a large surplus with sterling area countries, partially offset by a deficit with all other countries taken together. A deficit with non-sterling countries had persisted throughout the 1950s.

BALANCE OF PAYMENTS BY REGIONS, 1959.
(£ million.)

	With overseas sterling area.	With North America.	With Latin America.	With Western Europe.	With other countries.	With all non-sterling countries.	With all countries.
Imports	1,378	680	221	1,047	290	2,238	3,616
Exports	1,361	668	159	1,052	316	2,195	3,556
Balance on visible trade	− 17	− 12	−62	+ 5	+26	−43	− 60
Balance on invisible trade	+240	+156	−31	−81	−85	−41	+199
Current balance of payments . . .	+223	+144	−93	−76	−59	−84	+139

The Long-term Capital Account.

We have seen that Britain earned a surplus on its current balance of payments in most years of the 1950s. Yet it is not sufficient for this country to avoid deficits on its current account. The objective is to earn a substantial surplus in order to finance investment in and lending to other countries—particularly Commonwealth countries; to repay debts to foreign countries which have been incurred; and to build up the reserves of gold, dollars, and other currencies which can help to tide us over difficult periods. In fact, the objective of the Government in the late 1950s was to earn current account surpluses of £300–£400 million in normal years: and a surplus of this magnitude was only achieved in the exceptionally favourable year 1958.

Throughout the 1950s we had a considerable and growing deficit on long-term capital account, which means that we were investing in and lending to other countries more than other countries were investing in and lending to this country. As with current transactions, there were considerable regional differences. The usual pattern was of a heavy deficit in long-term capital transactions with the sterling area, and a much smaller deficit in long-term capital transactions with the rest of the world. In 1959, our deficit with the sterling area accounted for £224 million of the total deficit on long-term capital account of £317 million (excluding the subscription of £236 million to the International Monetary Fund: see **G11 (1)**). As was usual throughout the 1950s, most of the current balance of payments surplus with the sterling area was used to finance a flow of long-term capital from this country to sterling area countries.

Monetary Movements.

Taking current and long-term capital transactions together, there was in 1959 an adverse balance of £178 million: this was the amount by which the deficit of long-term capital account (again excluding the contribution to the I.M.F.) exceeded the surplus on current account. This balance has to be financed either through an increase of liabilities (for example, an increase in sterling balances held by foreigners) or by a reduction in assets (for example, a reduction in the gold and dollar reserves). Such "financing" transactions are important to an understanding of our balance of payments problems, but a complete description cannot be attempted here. We will confine ourselves to two of the most important sources of "finance": the sterling balances and the foreign exchange reserves.

The Sterling Balances.

Sterling is an international currency, and governments and individuals may hold balances in sterling for many reasons. Sterling area countries reckon to keep a high proportion of their international trade reserves in the form of sterling balances. Sterling balances will also be held to the extent that they are considered to be a convenient, profitable, or safe way of holding liquid assets. It may be convenient to hold sterling to finance trading transactions, because sterling is widely acceptable in settlement of trading debts. It may be profitable to hold sterling balances if the rate of interest paid on balances in London is higher than that paid in other financial centres. And it may be considered safe to hold sterling if the chances of a sterling devaluation (which would automatically reduce the value of the balances in terms of any currency which did not devalue) are thought to be remote.

An increase in sterling balances enables this country to finance an adverse balance on current plus long-term capital account without increasing other liabilities or reducing our reserves. Conversely, a reduction in sterling balances can impose a drain on reserves even if there is no adverse balance on the current plus long-term capital account.

At the end of 1959, sterling balances held by non-residents amounted to over £4,200 million,

£150 million higher than they had been in 1950. Nearly two-thirds of this amount was held by sterling area countries. These holdings represent a major portion of the foreign exchange reserves of the overseas sterling area countries. They can, of course, be drawn upon to finance deficits in the balance of payments of sterling area countries. Total holdings fluctuated during the 1950s, but they were somewhat higher at the end of 1959 than they had been at the end of 1950, even though some countries had substantially reduced their

STERLING BALANCES AND FOREIGN EXCHANGE RESERVES.
(£ million.)

	End-1959.	*Of which:* Official.	Unofficial.
Held by overseas sterling countries			
U.K. colonies	875	687	188
Independent countries	1,829	1,478	351
Sum	2,704	2,165	539
Held by non-sterling countries			
Western Europe	387	99	288
North and Latin America	72	13	59
Other	344	213	131
Sum	803	325	478
Held by international organisations	705	705	—
Total sterling balances	4,212	3,195	1,017
Gold and convertible currency reserves	977	—	—

ıoldings. In the longer run, it is to be expected hat the holdings of sterling area countries will be educed. Many sterling area countries are elatively underdeveloped, and an increasing umber of countries will probably find it necessary o run down their sterling balances in order to inance a part of the imports which will be re-uired for their development programmes. India, or example, has used most of the sterling holdings he accumulated during the war, for this purpose.

Sterling holdings outside the sterling area, and articularly the unofficial holdings, are very olatile, in that they may be withdrawn very apidly if for any reason it is thought less profitable or less safe to hold sterling than some other urrency. There was, for example, a large withrawal of balances in 1956, the year of the Suez ffair.

oreign Exchange Reserves.

The gold and convertible currency reserves can e used to finance any foreign currency payments hich cannot be financed in any other way: they re a last line of defence in international trade. he reserves held in London belong to the sterling rea as a whole, and not just to this country. Iembers of the sterling area are willing to pay into ıese central reserves some or all of their net arnings of gold and convertible currencies, in exchange for sterling balances. They do this on the understanding that they can, should they wish to do so, call upon the central reserves by exchanging sterling balances for gold and convertible currencies. The central reserves of gold and foreign currencies amounted to rather less than £1,000 million at the end of 1959, a level which, though higher than in many previous post-war years, was felt to be quite inadequate. There are bound to be imbalances in international trade and payments, and a very important function of international trade reserves is to tide over temporary imbalances by increasing reserves in favourable periods, and running down reserves in unfavourable periods. If reserves are not sufficient to withstand temporary pressures, measures to protect the reserves will have to be taken—e.g., raising bank rate and tightening up monetary policies generally—which may create unemployment and recession, and restrict the growth of the economy.

Fortunately, our membership of the International Monetary Fund (see **G11** (1)) gives us the right to draw on the resources of the Fund: this is an important additional source of foreign exchange in times of stress. At the time of the Suez affair in 1956, we were able to make a large drawing from the Fund, and as a consequence that crisis had a less disrupting effect on the economy and the balance of payments than would otherwise have been the case.

The Balance of Payments: Good and Bad Years.

Balance of payments statistics for five years selected from the 1950s are shown in the table. Two were good years, the other three were crisis years. The chief contrast between 1951 and 1955 on the one hand, and 1954 and 1958 on the other, is to be found in the balance of visible trade. The deficits in the former years were so great that even

THE BALANCE OF PAYMENTS IN SELECTED YEARS.
(£ million.)

	Good Years.		Crisis Years.		
	1954.	1958.	1951.	1955.	1957.
alance on visible trade	−195	+ 91	−749	−356	− 27
ılance on invisible trade	+406	+254	+330	+283	+256
ırrent balance of payments	+211	+345	−419	− 73	+229
ılance on long-term capital payments	−240	−259	n.a.	−183	−183
alance on current account *plus* long-term capital payments	− 29	+ 86	n.a.	−256	+ 46
ange in sterling balances	+175	+ 58	+ 83	−134	−173
ange in foreign exchange reserves	+ 87	+284	−344	−229	+ 13

allowing for the surplus on invisible trade, there was a deficit on current account—small in 1955, and very large in 1951. On top of these deficits on current account, there was as usual a deficit on long-term capital payments, so that a heavy adverse balance on current *plus* long-term capital account had to be financed: in both years there were considerable reductions in the foreign exchange reserves. In 1954 and 1958, however, the surpluses on current account covered, or nearly covered, the deficit on long-term capital payments; foreign exchange reserves increased in both years.

The crisis of 1957 was very different from those in 1951 and 1955. There was a substantial surplus on current account which was more than sufficient to cover the deficit on long-term capital payments, and the foreign exchange reserves rose slightly. Yet this was a year in which crisis measures—including the raising of Bank Rate to the very high level of 7 per cent—were taken to protect the £. A clue to the difficulties of that year is provided by the sharp fall in sterling balances. 1957 was a difficult year for many countries in the overseas sterling area, and there was a sharp fall in their sterling balances. But this withdrawal cannot of itself explain the severity of the crisis. Moreover, the magnitude of the fall in total balances over the whole year gives a misleading impression. Total sterling balances actually rose over the first half of 1957, and rose again at the end of the year as confidence in sterling recovered after the crisis measures. In the few months in between, there was a massive withdrawal of sterling, due to an expectation that the German Government would appreciate the value of the mark. The speculative outflow was stemmed partly by announcements by the German Government that no appreciation was contemplated, and partly by the increase in the rate of interest in this country which made the holding of sterling balances more attractive. In 1957, the trade and long-term investment position was relatively favourable: that a crisis nonetheless occurred underlined the vulnerability of sterling to speculative pressures.

Throughout the 1950s, in fact, the balance of payments position of this country was far from secure. As a consequence, economic policies were much influenced by balance of payments considerations, and many hold the view that the growth of the economy as a whole was hampered by measures imposed primarily to protect the balance of payments. The problem which faced economic policy-makers was this: As total demand for goods and services expands, it is difficult to prevent growth in the demand for imports and diversion of exports to the home market, particularly when home industries reach the limit of their productive capacity. Yet if consequent balance of payments difficulties are met by restrictions on total demand, it is difficult to maintain the investment necessary for growth in the productive capacity of the economy. The main need at the end of the 1950s was much the same as that at the beginning: to achieve an expansion of exports relative to imports so as to secure larger surpluses on the current balance of payments.

We shall now examine certain aspects of the framework within which international trade and payments took place in the 1950s.

Exchange Controls and Convertibility.

A currency is fully convertible if it can be freely exchanged for any other currency, or for gold, at the ruling official rates of exchange. Exchange controls impose restrictions on convertibility by limiting the powers of holders of a currency to exchange their holdings for other currencies or gold at the official rate of exchange. For many years after the war, for example, there was a world-wide shortage of dollars: if sterling had been convertible, there would have been a rush to convert sterling into dollars, with the consequence that the dollar reserves of the sterling area would soon have been exhausted. In fact, a premature attempt to establish sterling convertibility in 1947 led to such a drain on reserves that strict exchange controls had to be re-imposed.

Exchange controls on residents can be enforced by requiring that earnings of foreign currencies (e.g., the proceeds from the sale of exports) be handed over to the exchange control authority—the Bank of England acts as Government's agent—in exchange for sterling; and by permitting the exchange of sterling for foreign currencies (e.g., to enable the purchase of imports) only for transactions approved by the exchange control authority. Non-resident holders of sterling were, however, able to circumvent exchange controls by buying or selling in the "free" markets established in certain overseas financial centres where the "free" exchange rate for sterling was often well below the official rate. An important move towards wider convertibility was made in 1955, when the Bank of England was given power to operate in the "free" markets by selling sterling in exchange for foreign currencies or gold, or by selling foreign exchange or gold in exchange for sterling. During periods when sterling was weak, operations to support sterling involved heavy sales of gold and currencies from the reserves, and much of the loss of reserves in 1956 and 1957 was attributable to operations in the free markets. Encouraged by the greatly improved position of sterling in 1958, the Government made sterling held by non-residents fully convertible in December 1958, thus officially recognising the convertibility which had in fact been in operation for the previous three years. Residents, however, continued to be subject to exchange controls. Several other Western European countries declared their currencies convertible at the same time.

Convertibility, of course, makes it easier for funds to move into and out of sterling and other convertible currencies; and during the later years of the 1950s international movements of funds became much more important than they had been in earlier post-war years. Funds which can easily be shifted from one currency to another are particularly sensitive to rumours about possible changes in exchange rates; but provided that there is confidence that exchange rates will not in fact be changed, they tend to move towards those financial centres in which rates of interest are higher. For this reason, changes in bank-rate and other measures affecting interest rates can have a substantial effect on international monetary movements.

Exchange Rate Variation.

The exchange rate is the ruling official rate o exchange of pounds for gold and other currencies It determines the value of British goods in relatio to foreign goods. If the pound is devalued i terms of gold and the other currencies, Britis exports (which are paid for in pounds) becom cheaper to foreigners and British imports (paid fo by purchasing foreign currency) become more ex pensive to holders of pounds. Consequentl devaluation can improve the British balance o payments position by encouraging exports an discouraging imports. The case against devalua tion, however, is that the prospect of devaluatio results in a speculative outflow of foreign fund and that the rise in price of raw materials an consumption goods imported results in highe home prices and in wage demands to maintain th British standard of living, so that inflation ca neutralise the beneficial effects of devaluation.

Import Controls and Tariffs.

Import controls impose limitations on th quantity or value of goods which are permitte to enter a country: tariffs are duties levied imported goods so that the price of those goods consumers in a country is higher than the pri received by the foreigners supplying the good In the early post-war years, this country mai tained strict import controls over a wide range goods. These were gradually dismantled, until 1959 the last remaining import controls on goo were abandoned, except on habit-forming dru and some agricultural products and textil from the Far East—to give a measure of pr tection to British producers.

All countries impose tariffs. Some tariffs a primarily intended to raise revenue for the Gover ment, and others are primarily intended protect home industries by raising the price competing goods from abroad. The rights countries to raise tariffs, or to operate tariffs in discriminatory way (i.e., to offer lower tariffs goods from some sources than on similar goods from other sources), are closely circumscribed by the rules of GATT. The object of the *General Agreement on Tariffs and Trade* is to work towards free trade, especially through a reduction of tariffs. During the 1950s GATT held several major Conferences, at which bargaining to reduce tariffs was attended by modest success. But the most significant moves towards freer trade in the 1950s were on a regional basis.

The European Common Market and the European Free Trade Area.

At the end of the 1950s, Europe was divided into two major trading groups. The Common Market, or *European Economic Community* (EEC) comprised six countries: Belgium, France, Holland, Italy, Luxembourg, and West Germany. The Treaty of Rome (ratified in 1958) envisaged a rapid reduction of tariffs on industrial goods traded between member countries, the formulation of common agricultural policies, the establishment of a uniform external tariff on imports into Common Market countries from the outside world, and a movement towards a closer integration of economic and political policies. In the protracted negotiations which led up to the Treaty of Rome, Britain had argued in favour of a looser form of association in a Free Trade Area, involving, in the main, a reduction of tariffs on trade within the area. Britain felt that her special relationships with Commonwealth and Sterling Area countries would be compromised if she accepted the principle of a common external tariff; that her agricultural policies were very different from those of some European countries, so that there would be severe difficulties in subscribing to a common agricultural policy; and that proposals for the closer integration of economic and political policies should be considered very cautiously. In the end, agreement could not be reached with the six countries who signed the Treaty of Rome. The idea of a Free Trade Area, however, found support from other countries, and the *European Free Trade Association* (EFTA) was set up with a membership of seven countries; Austria, Denmark, Norway, Portugal, Sweden, Switzerland, and the United Kingdom. As will be obvious from a glance at a map, the EFTA covers a much less compact group of countries than the EEC.

The International Monetary Fund and the International Bank.

The *International Monetary Fund* was set up after the war with the objective of working towards free trade at stable exchange rates. Under the original agreement setting up the Fund, members agreed to make their currencies convertible into other currencies and gold at fixed rates of exchange, and agreed not to impose exchange or import controls without the permission of the Fund. Any alteration in the rates of exchange by more than 10 per cent also requires the permission of the Fund. For many years after the war, the imbalances in world trade—and particularly the acute shortage of dollars—were such that many countries had to invoke the clauses in the agreement which permitted them to impose restrictions during a "transitional" period. Although there is still a long way to go before the Fund reaches its objectives, considerable progress towards them was made during the 1950s. The progressive relaxation of exchange and import controls by this country was paralleled in some other countries, and most of the currencies important in world trade and payments were declared convertible.

An important function of the Fund is to make foreign exchange resources available to members who run into balance of payments difficulties. Each member country makes a deposit (called its quota) partly in gold, and partly in its own currencies, with the Fund. The size of the deposit is fixed in relation to the country's share in world trade. In return, it is granted certain automatic drawing rights, which entitle it to borrow foreign currencies from the Fund. Furthermore, the Fund has power to make larger loans, and to grant stand-by credits to be drawn on if required. Before the Fund will make such loans and credits available, it has to be satisfied that the borrowing country is taking appropriate action to correct the balance of payments disequilibrium. In 1956, at the time of the Suez crisis, Britain negotiated a loan of $561 million and an even larger stand-by credit. The stand-by credit was not required, and the loan enabled this country to ride out the crisis without a severe loss of reserves. Because it was felt that the resources of the Fund were inadequate in relation to international monetary movements, quotas were raised by 50 per cent in 1959, and each member country paid an additional subscription into the Fund.

The International Bank has the primary function of making funds available to assist development in underdeveloped countries. Member nations agree to subscribe quotas—fixed in much the same way as the quotas for the Fund—to the Bank. In fact, only a small proportion of the quotas has been called up by the Bank: the major part of the Fund's resources are borrowed—on the security of the remainder of the quotas—in financial centres: particularly in New York, but also in London and elsewhere.

Usually, loans are made to finance specific projects of investment in underdeveloped countries; and the Bank will normally make a loan only if it is satisfied that the investment will yield a revenue sufficient to enable the payment of interest on the loan, and the repayment of the sum lent. By mid-1959, the Bank had agreed to make development loans totalling $4 billion (about £1,400 million), though the total outstanding was considerably lower because loans made in earlier years had been partially repaid, and some loans agreed had not yet been disbursed. Thus a sizeable amount of lending was channelled through the Bank, but it was clear that some projects of great value to underdeveloped countries could not be financed in this way, because they would not yield returns quickly enough or large enough to meet the Bank's stringent requirements for interest and repayment. Accordingly, a new institution, the *International Development Authority*, was set up in 1960 with the power to make loans at low rates of interest and with more generous repayment conditions. The I.D.A. contributes (but only on a limited scale) towards the development of education and agriculture.

The Needs of Underdeveloped Countries.

Two-thirds of the world's population live in dire poverty—a poverty which can scarcely be imagined by those accustomed to the standards of living attained in the relatively few developed countries of the world. The alleviation of this poverty is widely recognised as the most important economic—and indeed political—task of the second half of the twentieth century.

Underdeveloped countries are predominantly agricultural countries, and "subsistance" agriculture is widespread. In subsistance agriculture, the primary object is to produce the food for your own family. Primitive tools and techniques of cultivation are used, and the margin between what can be produced and what is required to support life is narrow: the failure of crops because of drought, or the destruction of crops by floods, can lead to famine unless food is quickly supplied from outside the area affected. Because the margin is so narrow, the surplus from the agricultural sectors which can be exchanged for the products of other sectors is small—which is another way of saying that the demand for the goods and services produced by other sectors—e.g., industry or services—is low. There is a vicious circle in which low productivity is both a cause and an effect of low incomes. In many countries there is population pressure on the land and much under-employment in the sense that people have insufficient work to keep them occupied for more than part of the day or year. With the application of modern methods of disease control—e.g., the control of malaria through DDT spraying—death rates have tended to fall, while birth rates have remained high. In consequence, some countries are experiencing a very rapid expansion of population: rates of increase of 3 per cent, involving a doubling of population in as little as 24 years, have been recorded. The pressure of population on the land has therefore increased. Less productive land has had to be brought into cultivation, and erosion and loss of fertility have become major problems. A substantial increase in output is required to prevent a fall in per capita income as population grows, and an even greater increase is required if living standards are to be improved.

This is an immense problem, and one which most underdeveloped countries will not be able to solve without generous help from developed countries. There are usually considerable potentialities for increasing agricultural output: but before such increases can be achieved new skills have to be mastered and different techniques of production introduced. Schemes of irrigation and flood control, for example, can increase production: but they require heavy investment, and different crops and cropping patterns may have to be introduced if the fullest benefit is to be derived from such schemes. In most countries, too, alternative employment in industry or services has to be created to reduce pressure on land resources, and to meet the demands which higher incomes will generate. Nearly all underdeveloped countries now have development plans: but only a combined and sustained effort by developed and underdeveloped countries can ensure that the plans are successful.

Aid to Underdeveloped Countries.

One form of financial assistance to underdeveloped countries—the loans of the International Bank—has already been mentioned. Another source of funds is investment by individuals and firms from developed countries. These investments—setting up branch factories, for example—tend to be in projects which offer relatively bright prospects of profit to the investor. Prospects in the least developed countries are often not sufficiently attractive for the private investor: most of the UK private investment overseas, for example, has been concentrated in the relatively highly developed countries of the sterling area. Nonetheless, some underdeveloped countries such as India have attracted a significant amount of private investment.

Quite the most important source of financial aid to underdeveloped countries has been the loans and grants made by the Governments of developed countries. The contribution of the U.S.A. has been preponderant, though Britain and France have been important sources of aid for sterling and franc area countries respectively. Figures prepared by the United Nations show that grants and loans from the Governments of developed countries to underdeveloped countries averaged nearly $3 billion (over £1,000 million) per annum in the years 1958 and 1959, and that this aid had increased rapidly during the 1950s. Government aid can take many forms. Specific projects can be financed, or aid can take a more general form in financing some of the expenditure by the Governments of underdeveloped countries. All financial aid provides foreign currencies to underdeveloped countries, and enables them to buy more imports than would otherwise have been possible. This is particularly important, because countries in the process of development are commonly faced with rapidly rising import bills. Machinery and other capital equipment has to be imported, and often there are increased imports of food and consumer goods as incomes rise. If the underdeveloped countries were to buy only the goods which could be paid for by receipts from their exports, development would be seriously hindered. An innovation at the end of the 1950s was the scheme in which Britain, the U.S.A., and certain other countries undertook to ensure that sufficient foreign currency was available to finance the completion of India's Second Five-Year Plan. It is to be hoped that co-operative schemes of this sort will be an increasingly important feature of aid on a generous scale to underdeveloped countries. For it is certain that the level of financial aid will have to be increased if there is to be a sustained improvement in the standard of living of these nations.

Yet financial aid alone is not enough. Most underdeveloped countries need help and advice on planning their development, to ensure that development possibilities are exploited and that scarce resources are used to best advantage. Hence the many schemes for sending out experts—by the technical agencies of the United Nations, such as the Food and Agriculture Organisation, the World Health Organisation, the International Labour Organisation, the Technical Assistance Bureau, and the United Nations Educational, Scientific, and Cultural Organisation (UNESCO); by the International Bank; and by individual countries, notably by the U.S.A. under its Point Four programme. Hence also the schemes for educating and training people from the underdeveloped countries in universities and colleges in the developed countries, one of the main strands of the Colombo Plan, the Commonwealth's own scheme for help to the poorer members in South-East Asia. The list could go on, but what is being done is still far below the need.

Finally, mention must be made of an important responsibility of developed countries, which is too often overlooked. The eventual objective must be to put developing countries into such a position that they can manage without aid. This means that those countries must be able to pay for their imports with their exports. The exports of underdeveloped countries at present consist largely of primary products—food and raw materials. The prices of most of these products fluctuated considerably in the 1950s, but the general trend was of falling prices for most of the decade after 1951. This was an important cause of the improvement in Britain's terms of trade (*see* **G7** (1)), because Britain is a large importer of primary products. The reverse side of the coin was a deterioration in the terms of trade of many underdeveloped countries, who were able to buy fewer imports for a given quantity of exports. A strong case can be made for a policy on the part of developed nations designed to ensure a greater stability of prices for food and raw material exports from underdeveloped countries. Moreover, developed countries must not act in such a way as to hinder a growth of exports from developing countries. These countries will need to increase their exports of food, raw materials, and simple industrial products from their new industries. To the extent that developed countries adopt a dog-in-the-manger attitude to protect their own agriculture and industry, developing countries will be severely hindered: and the developed countries will not benefit so markedly from the rapid growth of markets for the more advanced industrial products as the wealth of all nations increases.

2. EMPLOYMENT, PRODUCTION, AND INVESTMENT.

Population.

In June 1959 the population of the United Kingdom was estimated to be 52·0 million—45·4 million in England and Wales, 5·2 million in Scotland, and 1·4 million in Northern Ireland. The total was still rising slowly, at a rate of about 1 per cent every five years. Prediction of future trends is difficult. Before the war it was common to predict that Britain's population would fall later in the century; but these predictions were made during the depression of the 'thirties, when the birth-rate was very low. Since then the birth-rate has risen sharply, and the net reproduction rate (the ratio of the birth-rate of girls less their infant mortality to the population of women of child-bearing age) has been above unity in most years since the war. There are several possible explanations of the high birth-rate, the most important being the rapidly falling age of marriage, which makes it difficult to say whether the high birth-rate will be maintained. In the near future population will certainly continue to rise slowly as improving medical services raise the average length of life, which is now 71 years, as against 61 years in 1930–32, and as the gap between generations shortens. But whether in the long run—after A.D. 1980, say—the population will continue to rise, nobody now can predict with confidence.

The Population of Working Age.

Of the total population, only some are of working age. Working age is defined as the period between the minimum school-leaving age of 1[illegible] and retiring age—65 for men and 60 for women. Of course, not all those of working age do work—some are invalids, some are still at school—and not all those above retiring age have retired; but nevertheless the ratio between the population of working age and the total is a useful statistic, as it does provide a rough guide to the numbers wh[illegible]

POPULATION BY AGE-GROUPS, 1959.
(Millions.)

Ages	Males.	Females.	As proportion of totals. Actual. 1954.	Actual. 1959.	Estimated. 1978.
Below working-age.					
0–4	2·08	1·97	22·7	23·2	22·8
5–9	1·96	1·87			
10–14	2·16	2·06			
Total	6·20	5·91			
Of working-age.					
15–19	1·76	1·70	63·4	62·3	59·9
20–24	1·71	1·66			
25–29	1·67	1·65			
30–34	1·73	1·74			
35–39	1·94	1·99			
40–44	1·58	1·64			
45–49	1·83	1·89			
50–54	1·76	1·85			
54–59	1·53	1·71			
60–64 (men only)	1·16	—			
Total	16·68	15·82			
Above working-age.					
60–64 (women only)	—	1·50	13·9	14·5	17·3
65–69	·91	1·28			
70–74	·67	1·03			
75 and above	·77	1·38			
Total	2·35	5·19			
Total	25·24	26·92	100	100	100

have to be supported out of the current national income, but who do not contribute to it. This ratio is rising, and will continue to rise. In 1954, 22½ per cent of the population was below working age and 14 per cent above. By 1978 it is fairly certain that 17½ per cent of the population will be above working age; and, much more speculatively, it is guessed that 22½ per cent will be below. So the population not of working age will rise from 36½ to 40 per cent, which means that for every 100 persons of working age there will be 67 other persons, as against 58 in 1954. The expected growth in the proportion of the old explains why the cost of pensions (see G32) is going to grow steadily: more generally, it is clear that some growth in output per head of the population of working age will be needed to meet the needs of the increasing proportion of dependants. A move to increase the school-leaving age would, of course, still further raise the proportion of dependants.

The Working Population.

Not all persons of working age actually work, although the vast majority do; but only a part are gainfully employed, *i.e.*, work for wages, salaries, or profits. And it is only those who are gainfully employed who are counted in the working population. Housewives, mothers, and those who give their services gratis to good causes are not included, unless they also do some work for cash. In 1959, when the total population of Great Britain was 52 million, of whom 32½ million were of working age, the total working population (including the unemployed who were seeking employment) was only 24½ million. Of the 16 million women of working age, only 8 million were gainfully employed. So for every gainfully occupied person there was just over one other person to be supported out of the goods and services they provided.

One feature of the post-war years, until the recession of 1958, was a steady increase in the proportion of persons going out to work. Between 1948 and 1958 this factor added well over half a million persons to the working population. Such an increase is unlikely to continue, and one has to expect that in the future increased output will have to come from increased productivity, and not, as it did to some extent in recent years, from an increase in the proportion of people who work.

Most of the working population work for wages

DISTRIBUTION OF WORKING POPULATION, JUNE 1958.
(Thousands.)

Basic industries.		Manufacturing industries.		Services.	
Agriculture and fishing	1,090	Chemicals and allied trades	538	Distribution	3,000
Mining and quarrying	858	Bricks, pottery, glass	329	Insurance, banking, and finance	523
Building and contracting	1,528	Metal manufacture	562	Professional	1,985
Gas, electricity, and water	382	Engineering and other metal goods	3,946	Public administration: National	550
Transport and communication	1,733	Textiles, leather, and clothing	1,671	Local	784
		Food, drink, and tobacco	954	Miscellaneous	1,827
		Paper and printing	591		
		Furniture and other wooden goods	309		
		Other manufacturing	447		
Total	5,591	Total	9,347	Total	8,669
As percentage	*23*		*40*		*37*

or salaries as employees. Of the total in June 1958 of 24·6 million, under 2 million were employers or self-employed, over ½ million were in the Forces, and 22·3 million were either employees or unemployed persons looking for work. The table shows the industries in which people work. About two-fifths of the total work in manufacturing industry, nearly 4 million of these in the engineering and allied industries. A quarter work in the basic industries, and the remaining 37 per cent are in the so-called service industries—3 million in distribution, 2 million in the professional services (¾ million each in education and in the health services).

Employment and Unemployment.

In June 1960, 305,000 persons—1·4 per cent of the working population—were unemployed. Even in January 1959, the worst month of the 'fifties, the rate rose only to 2·8 per cent, and in most years in the 'fifties the average was lower than 1½ per cent. This contrasts with an average figure in 1937, the best year of the 'thirties, of 11 per cent. and with a figure of 22 per cent at the bottom of the slump in 1932. Probably 1–1½ per cent is somewhere near the practicable minimum; for some unemployment is more or less inevitable. Some seasonal rise in unemployment in the winter must be expected, e.g. in seaside towns; and for this reason unemployment in January is about ½ per cent higher than in June. Moreover some unemployment is bound to be involved in job-changing and as the demands of industries change. Full employment does not mean no unemployment, but rather that there should be about as many jobs vacant as there are workers looking for jobs. A large excess of vacancies, such as occurred in 1951 and 1955, is evidence of inflation; for it means that some factories which need workers to fulfil the demands for their output cannot get them.

To some extent unemployment figures are misleading, as not all unemployed workers are eligible for unemployment benefit under the National Insurance Scheme. Most married women who go out to work normally opt not to pay the full National Insurance contributions, so that, when they lose their jobs, they just drop out of the figures for the working population unless they choose to register for work. Between June 1957 and January 1959, the worst point of the recession of 1958–59, unemployment rose by 368,000, from 250,000 to 618,000; but in the same period the numbers in employment fell by as much as 591,000. Thus unemployment figures definitely understate the seriousness of recessions, as they do not count all the persons who would like to have, but cannot find, jobs.

UNEMPLOYMENT AND VACANCIES
(Annual averages for Great Britain, thousands.)

	Unemployment.	Vacancies.	Unemployment as percentage of total employees.
1932*	2,829	n.a.	*22·1*
1937*	1,482	n.a.	*10·9*
1951	253	410	*1·2*
1952	414	275	*2·0*
1953	342	274	*1·6*
1954	285	329	*1·3*
1955	232	405	*1·1*
1956	257	357	*1·2*
1957	313	276	*1·4*
1958	457	198	*2·1*
1959	475	223	*2·2*
1960	360	314	*1·6*

* Figures relate only to population insured against unemployment.

Of the 475,000 persons unemployed in 1959, 344,000 were men and 131,000 were women. Of the men over half, 183,000, had been unemployed for over eight weeks, 75,000 between two and eight weeks, and 85,000 under two weeks. Thus long-term unemployment was about 1 per cent of the total labour force, serious enough for those affected, but not the kind of unemployment to be cured easily by reflationary measures.

Regional Unemployment.

One peculiarly dreadful feature of the inter-war years was the depressed areas—the regions of the country where a third of the men had not had a job for a year or more. Such extreme regional unemployment has not recurred since 1945; only in Northern Ireland was unemployment very high in the 1950s. In 1956, the best year since 1950, unemployment there averaged 6·4 per cent, and in 1958 it rose to 9·3 per cent on average. Nevertheless, it was disquieting that in the recession of 1958–59 unemployment did rise rather more sharply in the old depressed areas of the North-East, Scotland, and Wales. These areas are particularly dependent on the heavy industries of mining, steel, and shipbuilding, and there are unwelcome signs of a re-emergence there of depressed conditions, though on nothing like the pre-war scale.

REGIONAL UNEMPLOYMENT.
(Percentage unemployed.)

	In January 1959.	In July 1960.
Great Britain	2·8	1·3
Midlands	2·2	0·6
London and South-east	1·7	0·7
North Midlands	2·1	0·8
East and West Ridings (Yorkshire)	2·7	0·9
Eastern and Southern	2·1	0·9
South-western	2·9	1·2
Lancashire and Cheshire	3·6	1·7
North-east and North	3·9	2·3
Wales	4·6	2·1
Scotland	5·4	3·2
Northern Ireland	9·7	6·0

In 1959 the Government passed the Local Employment Act, a measure to give the Board of Trade powers to induce industry to go to the areas where unemployment shows a tendency to be permanently high. This Act does not cover Northern Ireland, which is the responsibility of the Northern Ireland Government. Under the Act some progress has been made; for instance, some motor-car manufacturers have agreed in bargains with the Board of Trade to put some of their new factories in the areas with relatively high unemployment. But, in general, it has proved difficult to persuade firms to set up new factories in Wales, Scotland, or the North-East; and even more difficult to persuade them to go to places like Falmouth, where there are isolated pockets of unemployment. But, unless the policy is fully successful, we shall continue to have the position whereby checks have to be placed on the economy before full employment is reached, because in the booming areas of London and the West Midlands vacancies far exceed unemployment.

Production and Productivity.

It is fairly easy to measure output in the main manufacturing industries, and in many of the basic industries. It is much more difficult to do so in the service industries; the output of a doctor or a shopkeeper is not easily measured. So each month the Central Statistical Office calculates an Index of Industrial Production covering the main productive industries; estimates for changes in the output of service industries are made only once a year. This tends to give a false impression of the rate of growth of output, since the productive industries—particularly manufacturing industries—are the ones best placed to raise their output per head. Much more than a doubling of the index of industrial production is needed to double the standard of living; and roughly a 5 per cent increase in industrial output is likely to be accompanied by a 3 per cent increase in the total output—or national product—on which the average standard of living depends.

In the discussion which follows, by output is meant *real output*, valued at the prices of a particular year, and not *money output*, changes in which are partly due to variation in prices. Between 1948 and 1959 total output rose by 32 per cent. Up to 1954 the average rate of growth was nearly 3 per cent per year; but after that year it dropped to less than 2½ per cent. Employment also rose, so the increase in output per head was rather lower—only 26 per cent between 1948 and 1959. Also, up to about 1954, the average working week was getting longer, in spite of cuts in the official working week. If in future years the average working week becomes shorter, the same rate of increase in output will require a rather higher rate of increase in output per hour worked.

cars, tractors, commercial vehicles, and aircraft. Paper and printing is another fast-growing industry, with general and electrical engineering not far behind. At the other end of the scale are textiles and shipbuilding, two industries which were in continuous difficulties between the wars, and continue to be so, as they lose their export markets to cheaper competitors. The timber and furniture industry did not increase its output after 1954, mainly because additional expenditure on goods for the home market was concentrated on electrical equipment.

As with industries as a whole, so within manufacturing industries, growth in productivity tends to be fastest where growth in demand is greatest. The industries where output stagnated are the ones where productivity also stagnated—notably in shipbuilding and textiles. This fairly general rule is one reason why it is so unfortunate if restrictions have, for balance-of-payments reasons, constantly to be placed on demand—and particularly on demand for goods such as cars and washing machines, of which so many are bought on hire-purchase; for the restraints tend to hinder the expansion of fast-growing industries. Manufacturers become less eager to take the risks of buying new, more productive equipment, and the growth of productivity, on which the future standard of living depends, tends to slow down.

CHANGES IN OUTPUT AND EMPLOYMENT BY INDUSTRY, 1948–59.
(1959 as percentage of 1948.)

	Proportion of total output in 1954.	Output.	Employment.	Output per head.*
Agriculture, etc.	5	132	84	157
Mining	4	101	94	107
Manufacturing	37	148	112	132
Building	6	128	104	123
Gas, electricity, and water	2	178	116	153
Transport and communication	8	122	94	130
Distribution	13	137	121	113
Insurance, banking, and finance	6	147	119	124
Professional services	7	142	135	105
Miscellaneous services	7	110	86	128
Public administration and defence	6	89	86	104
Total	100	132	105	126

* These figures are approximate, and in respect of service industries, should be taken as only rough guides.

The fastest-growing group was that of the public utilities, including the electricity industry. Next came manufacturing and finance, closely followed by the professional services—largely education and health. At the other end of the scale are miscellaneous services, which include the declining cinema industry and domestic service; mining; and public administration and defence. The last two are also ones with very slowly risihg productivity; and in general there is some relation between growing output and growing productivity—the notable exception being agriculture, in which a sharp rise in output went with a sharp fall in employment, as farms became increasingly mechanised.

Within manufacturing industry two industries have set the pace—chemicals, which includes drugs, plastics, cosmetics, detergents, and oil refining; and vehicles, which includes, besides motor cars, tractors, commercial vehicles, and aircraft.

Foreign Comparisons.

Between 1953 and 1959 British manufacturing output rose by 24 per cent. This was a greater expansion than that of the U.S.A., but it was smaller than that of all West European countries

CHANGES IN MANUFACTURING OUTPUT.

		Output as percentage of level in 1954.			1959 as percentage of 1948.		
		1957.	1958.	1959.	Output.	Employ-ment.	Produc-tivity.
Fast-growing industries.							
Chemicals	(8)	115	115	131	193	122	159
Vehicles	(10)	115	118	131	213	129	164
Engineering	(22)	111	111	118	170	142	121
Paper and printing	(7)	112	113	121	184	128	152
Slowly-growing industries.							
Food	(7)	104	108	110	139	133	106
Iron and steel	(7)	113	100	104	127	101	126
Clothing and footwear	(4)	105	101	112	127	98	129
Drink and tobacco	(4)	112	113	120	117	105	111
Static or declining industries.							
Timber, furniture, etc.	(3)	96	94	101	144	100	144
Textiles	(10)	97	82	92	108	91	119
Shipbuilding	(3)	108	109	101	87	86	101

Note. Figures in brackets refer to the percentage importance in total output in 1954.

except Sweden. In the three large members of the Common Market, output went up by 60 per cent or more. In Russia and in Japan the rate of growth was still faster, output nearly doubling in six years. Although there are good reasons for not accepting the Russian figures at their face value—a value which would imply that, while Britain added a half to her output, Russia in the same period 1948–59 quadrupled it—the contrast is broadly correct. A similar contrast between West European countries and Britain is found for the volume of exports, which suggests a link between output growth and export performance.

This phenomenon of slow growth is not new in Britain. It was there between the wars, and even before the First World War. So probably the causes lie in rather fundamental aspects of British industrial organisation. Britain may still be the second most productive large industrial nation—international comparisons of productivity cannot easily be made. But it is a fast diminishing lead, and it is not one that gives Britain any edge in the competition for foreign markets, since British standards of living are also higher than those of our main European competitors.

Capital and Automation.

Many of the growing industries are capital-intensive: they use much machinery and equipment per unit of output produced. In chemicals, steel, and, above all, electricity, the plant is extremely expensive. Most of the innovations since the war—nylon, atomic power, terylene, polythene, etc.—require a high capital investment, and cannot pay unless they are worked nearly full-out. One way to achieve this is by shift work, and it may be that a full exploitation of the potentialities of these new industries will require a great extension of this system of work. And the future holds out prospects of still more intensive requirements for capital as automation spreads. With automation, much of the manual semi-skilled work should come to an end. The new electronic computers will be able to control the machines that actually do the manufacturing operations. "Transfer" machines have been developed to pass a component from one machine to another. Control machines can read details of the work to be done off a piece of tape; they can start and stop machines at the right point; they can adjust themselves to correct mistakes or to adjust for faulty materials.

So far the impact of automation has been small. The main use has been in the office, where electronic computers can carry out far more efficiently much of the routine calculating, recording, and checking operations previously done by clerks. But it will continue to spread, and must do so if the growth in wealth is to continue. The change will come only gradually. But ultimately one can envisage that both in manufacturing industry and in office work the machine will have replaced much of the human effort in work, and even more of its drudgery. The typical manual job will become that of the skilled maintenance man.

This revolution will take many decades to effect. It raises no spectre of widespread redundancy; but it does mean that over the years more and more emphasis will need to be laid on the training of workers for skilled work, and indeed on raising the general level of education. Also over the years the average size of factory is likely to grow, as these new methods, if they are to be profitable, have to be used on a large scale. Finally, the prospect is for ever-increasing requirements of capital—and of course for the savings to finance it.

Monopoly and Competition.

This trend to increasing size and increasing capitalisation has been going on now for many decades, and in the process it has changed the face of British industry. In the early nineteenth century the typical firm was the owner-managed textile mill. Then in the 1860s and 1870s came the discovery of cheap methods of making steel, with the consequential immense growth in the engineering industries. Most of the chemical industry is still newer—some very new—and in these capital-intensive industries the big firm predominates. In some it has become almost a monopoly: no small firm can easily challenge industrial giants like Imperial Chemical Industries, the Dunlop Rubber Company, or Unilever. In others the pattern is of a few firms, all large, as in motor cars, detergents, and steel. Competition goes on, but it has changed its form. In the old days competition was largely by price. Now it is largely by advertising and by variations in the quality and other features of the product—detergents and motor cars being good examples. And in many industries groups of firms producing similar products entered into agreements which had the effect of restricting competition, for example through schemes for price-fixing.

The passage of the Restrictive Practices Act in 1956 outlawed many of the main forms of restrictive agreements to prevent competition. Collective price-fixing was declared to be illegal unless the industry could show that the practice brought substantial benefit to the public. Collective price-fixing is the system under which a central associa-

MANUFACTURING OUTPUT AND EXPORTS: SOME FOREIGN COMPARISONS.
(1953 = 100.)

	Manufacturing output.				Volume of exports 1959.
	1948.	1955.	1957.	1959.	
Western Europe.					
Common Market Countries.					
Belgium	91	120	128	128	154
Holland	70	119	126	140	167
France	77	122	148	162	165
W. Germany	36	130	149	165	222
Italy	61	120	137	159	231
EFTA Countries.					
Norway	74	118	128	130	150
Sweden *	89	111	118	121	150
U.K.	82	115	117	124	121
Eastern Europe.					
Poland *	39	124	149	178	n.a.
U.S.S.R.*	45	128	156	191	n.a.
North America.					
Canada	76	106	113	118	119
U.S.A.	77	103	107	114	104
Far East.					
Japan	30	119	174	220	285

* All output.

tion for the industry lays down minimum prices at which members may sell. Usually such a system was backed by arrangements for collective boycotts, under which members of the association would refuse to sell goods to wholesalers or retailers who broke the rules. Often the wholesalers too were in the scheme, and they would collectively refuse to buy from manufacturers who broke the rules. Collective boycotts were also found in industries without collective price-fixing, one common purpose being to make sure that retailers did not sell a manufacturer's products below his recommended price. This form of collective resale price maintenance was also outlawed by the Act. The Act did however permit the individual manufacturer to enforce resale price maintenance for his own products by securing a court order prohibiting price-cutting by retailers.

The Working of the Restrictive Practices Act.

Under the Act any restrictive agreements of several specified kinds had to be registered with the Registrar of Restrictive Practices. He then had to decide whether there was a *prima facie* case for the discontinuation of the agreement, and, if he thought there was, the case was referred to a new Restrictive Practices Court, containing both judicial and lay members. The first case was one against the Chemists' Federation, and they were ordered to abolish the rule whereby sales of certain proprietary drugs were to be made only to pharmaceutical chemists whose names were on a certain list. As a result, these drugs, which are not those for which prescriptions are needed, can be sold in other than chemists' shops. The second case was a most important one as a precedent. The Master Spinners were ordered to abolish their system of collective price-fixing for spun yarn. The case was decided this way, even though the Court felt that it had been established that marked local unemployment would be caused in a few cotton-spinning towns. This was ruled not to outweigh the general gains of the public from increased competition bringing lower prices. The defendants in several other cases brought before the Court failed to justify their agreements as being in the public interest. As a result of these adverse verdicts, a number of industries decided to abandon their existing agreements without defending them before the Court. By mid-1960 only two favourable verdicts had been given—the first in favour of a complicated scheme for sharing export markets for water-tube boilers, and the second in favour of a price-fixing agreement among the black nut and bolt makers.

In general, the Court has been tougher than anticipated; but it is still too early to assess the significance of the new law on the degree of competition in British industry. It leaves untouched the industries where one firm is dominant; these remain the responsibility of the Monopolies Commission, who report on industries referred to them by the Board of Trade, and make recommendations after investigation. Some trade associations have come up with a form of agreement for exchanging information about prices. Such an agreement is not registrable, even though its most likely purpose is to encourage manufacturers to observe a common price policy. But there have been definite signs of increased competition. In 1958–59 many shops began to sell products below their manufacturer's recommended prices, and few manufacturers chose to enforce their rights of compulsory resale price maintenance through the courts. And some expect that, as self-service shops become commoner, the practice will spread. Competition from abroad has also increased sharply; the abolition in 1960 of the last restrictions on American imports brought a sharp challenge from across the Atlantic.

Nationalised Industries.

Nationalised industry accounts for about 20 per cent of British industry. Local authorities also run some services—largely in bus transport and water provision. With the exception of coal-mining, all these industries are natural monopolies in which the provision of competing services would be obviously wasteful. They are thus obvious candidates for nationalisation. With the exception of the brief episode of steel nationalisation in 1951–53, nationalisation has not been extended into manufacturing industry, not even where the existence of a private monopoly might suggest that there was a strong case. But nationalised industries are not free from competition. The railways face competition from road transport, some publicly and some privately owned; the fuel industries compete with each other, and with the privately owned oil industry.

Nationalised industries are supposed to earn enough to cover their costs. In the first ten years the two airways corporations were granted subsidies; but these have now ceased. Costs for a nationalised industry include interest payments on capital—both on the compensation paid to the previous owners and on the rather larger amounts of capital raised since nationalisation. The electricity boards, and to a lesser extent the gas boards, earn something above their costs to finance expansion, but not even then on the scale which is normal practice in private industries. The National Coal Board had accumulated a deficit of £57 million by 1960: the increases in coal prices had not covered the increased costs of mining and distributing the coal. The British Transport Commission, which owns the railways, and supervises the running of London Transport, British Road Services, the canals, many provincial bus companies, and some port authorities, is in chronic deficit. In 1957 it was granted special dispensation to incur a deficit to be charged to capital account on the specious grounds that this was a temporary move pending the full-scale implementation of a £1,200 million modernisation scheme for the railways. In 1960 the deficit of £78 million, which is paid by the Treasury, was recognised for what it was, a subsidy, and was treated for the first time as a current charge against the Government.

Capital Requirements of Nationalised Industries.

The nationalised industries are voracious users of capital, as they are nearly all highly capitalised industries. Until 1956 they raised new capital, when they wanted it, by floating an issue on the Stock Exchange, the issue being guaranteed by the Government. In 1956 the Chancellor of the Exchequer decided to end this system, which made it more difficult to exercise control over the volume of credit, and substitute one in which the nationalised industries draw directly on the Exchequer for their capital. This sytem has been attacked from both sides. The advocates of private enterprise have pointed to the strain this puts on the Exchequer, and to the unfairness whereby the nationalised industries get their capital cheaper or more easily than private industry. A private firm raising a loan would have to pay about ½ per cent more per annum in interest, and it has been recommended that nationalised industries should be forced to borrow on the strength of their own credit. Both the coal-mines and the railways would have the gravest difficulty in raising any capital; but the others could.

From the other side, it has been pointed out that the nationalised industries have suffered from their dependence on the Exchequer. Investment in them was held back in the 'forties and early 'fifties by government fiat. No private industry has had to face the restrictions put on the railways, or even more on the Post Office, the only nationalised industry run by a Government Department and not by a public corporation. And in most balance-of-payments crises the nationalised industries have been forced by the Government to cut back their planned programmes, sometimes at a serious cost in disorganisation. And, whatever new arrangements might be made for financing the capital programmes, it is certain that capital requirements will continue to be very substantial.

Investment.

In 1959 gross investment in capital assets amounted to £3,673 million. This is about 17½ per cent of the gross national product, which is a measure of the total value of the goods and services produced by the nation. In other words, about one part in 6 of total production was used to replace old assets or to add to the nation's stock of capital equipment. The addition to the stock of capital assets (net investment) accounts for under one half of gross investment: the remainder (about 8 per cent of total output) was needed to offset the wastage of assets already in use. In several other developed countries, a rather higher proportion of output was devoted to investment: in West Germany the proportion of gross investment was 22 per cent.

Since the future rate of growth of the economy, and our ability to remain competitive in export markets, is in part dependent upon the proportion of output devoted to investment, it must be a cause for concern if our proportion is lower than that achieved by other developed countries. But some progress was made. The proportion of output invested—and, in particular, the proportion of output which was used to enlarge the stock capital assets—was higher in the late 1950s than in the early 1950s. This implies, of course, that the proportion of total output going to some other uses fell: after 1952, there was a sharp fall in the proportion of output used for military defence.

Types of Investment.

The next table shows what investment consists of. The usual classification is into four groups—plant and machinery, the products of the heavy engineering industry; vehicles (motor cars, lorries, ships, locomotives, etc.), also produced by the engineering industry; houses and flats, and other construction work, both falling in the building and contracting industry. In 1959 investment was split roughly half and half between engineering and building and contracting, although, as plant and vehicles wear out much more quickly, the proportions for net investment were different—40 : 60. In 1954 the composition of investment was rather different. House-building was then much more important, and other types of construction work (roads, railway works, factories, shops, schools) much less important. This last kind of investment is much longer-term than other kinds, and its steady growth does show the extent to which Britain neglected to bring her basic assets up to date during and for many years after the war.

KINDS OF INVESTMENT IN 1959.
(£ million.)

	Gross expenditure.	Wastage.	Net addition to assets.
Plant and machinery	1,304	811	493
Vehicles	611	402	209
Houses	646	264	382
Other construction .	1,112	474	638
Total . . .	3,673	1,951	1,722

More interesting, though more difficult, is an analysis of investment by purpose. Only a quarter of total investment is undertaken by manufacturing industry to maintain and improve its equipment; and, even if the other main productive industries (mining, agriculture, and building) are included, the proportion is still under a third, and is not much more than the requirements of transport and distribution. Even the chemical industry—the most highly capitalised of all manufacturing industries—requires much less capital than the railways. The public utilities—here widely defined—require 16 per cent of total investment, more than half of it for the electricity industry; and finally, social investment in housing, schools, hospitals, etc., takes less than a quarter of the total.

The predominance of transport is recent. The railway modernisation plans and the quintupled road-building programme combined to raise investment in transport assets by no less than 61 per cent between 1954 and 1959. Distribution—another area in which investment had tended to lag behind—rose by 30 per cent, as shop building and rebuilding increased. Social investment, on the other hand, fell off. School and hospital building went up; but public housing fell off sharply, mainly as a result of the abolition of general housing subsidies. Subsidies from the Government to local authorities for new housing were confined to houses built in connection with slum clearance schemes.

The Finance of Investment.

Any business is allowed to charge as a cost the depreciation of its assets. Normal depreciation allowances are based on the original cost of the asset and on its expected useful life. In a time of price inflation depreciation allowances will not provide sufficient finance to permit the replacement of assets at higher prices, and there are many supporters of depreciation allowances being based on replacement costs. Many firms do set aside extra funds specifically to cover these extra replacement costs. However, an official committee

GROSS INVESTMENT: ANALYSIS BY PURPOSES, 1959.
(£ million.)

Productive industry		1,137
Agriculture, etc.	144	
Mining	114	
Building and contracting . . .	59	
Engineering	248	
Chemicals	126	
Iron and steel	118	
All other manufacturing . . .	328	
Transport and distribution . . .		1,054
Railways	167	
Ships, harbours, docks, and canals .	181	
Air	34	
Roads	80	
Lorries, buses, and vans . . .	223	
Other distribution	369*	
Public utilities and services . . .		595
Electricity	340	
Gas	44	
Water and sewerage	89	
Postal, telephone, and radio . .	89	
All other	33	
Social investment		837
Housing	646	
Education.	148	
Health.	39	
Other	4	
Legal fees, etc.		5[illegible]
Total		3,673

	As percentage of total.	Percentage increase in real terms since 1954.
Manufacturing industries	23	*+15*
Other productive industries . . .	9	*+22*
Transport	19	*+61*
Other distribution	10	*+30*
Public utilities and services . . .	16	*+16*
Housing	18	*−10*
Other social services	5	*+47*
	100	*+22*

* Miscellaneous services are included here.

of enquiry recommended against a change in practice, and with prices rising less rapidly the issue became less important.

Governments have, however, adopted certain fiscal devices to encourage replacement and investment. Soon after the war initial allowances were introduced. Under this system firms were permitted to charge against profits in the first year of its life 20, or at times 40, per cent of the cost of any new equipment, and the system amounted to a loan of the tax saved in the first year, repaid over the life of the asset. This system was withdrawn in 1951, but was later reintroduced. It is still operative for ships; but for machinery it has been replaced by the system of investment allowances, under which a firm may charge against profits 20 per cent of the cost of any new machine, with the difference that all ordinary depreciation allowances are still chargeable. So the investment allowance is a grant, not a loan, of the saved tax. The allowances were introduced in 1954, withdrawn in 1958, and reinstated in 1959.

Depreciation allowances, including investment and initial allowances, were sufficient in 1959 to cover about 70 per cent of productive investment by the private sector, and to cover about 40 per cent of public productive investment. The residue of new investment, both productive and non-productive, had to be provided from savings. Companies relied mainly on retained profits, which were in fact larger, taking companies as a whole, than net investment, and so too did the profit-making nationalised industries. This course was not possible for the railways or the coal-mines, which drew all their funds for net investment from the Treasury. The table gives some idea of the load thus placed on the public sector.

Although less than half of total investment was publicly financed, a much lower proportion of this investment was covered by depreciation allowances or retained profits. The weight of public investment which had to be financed from other sources goes a long way towards explaining the difficulties the Government has in exercising monetary or fiscal control over the economy. For the necessary funds have either to be raised in taxation (a Budget surplus) or borrowed in one form or another from the private sector without unduly inflating the credit base. Monetary and fiscal measures will be discussed in later sections.

THE FINANCE OF INVESTMENT
(£ million.)

	1954.	1959.	As percentage of total. 1954.	1959.
Privately-financed				
Housing . . .	223	376	*9*	*10*
Productive assets	1,066	1,719	*41*	*47*
	1,289	2,095	*50*	*57*
Of which:				
Covered by depreciation allowances . .	639	1,194	*25*	*33*
Other . . .	650	901	*25*	*25*
Publicly-financed				
Housing . . .	421	270	*16*	*7*
Productive assets .	659	933	*26*	*26*
Other (schools, roads, etc.) .	219	375	*8*	*10*
	1,299	1,578	*50*	*43*
Of which:				
Covered by depreciation allowances . .	223	351	*8*	*10*
Other . . .	1,076	1,227	*42*	*33*

3. INCOMES, WAGES, AND PRICES.

Personal Income, Spending, and Saving.

National income is a measure of the total income accruing to residents in return for valuable services rendered. It therefore consists of the sum of wages, salaries, profits, and rents. Not all this income accrues to persons. Thus, companies do not distribute all their profits to shareholders; in 1959 undistributed profits amounted to £3,302 million. This is part of national income, but not of personal income. On the other hand, some personal incomes are not payments for services rendered. Such incomes are called "transfer payments" to emphasise that their payment does not add to the national income, but only transfers income from one recipient to another. Included in this category are retirement pensions, children's allowances, National Assistance payments, etc., amounting in 1959 to £1,637 million; and the interest on the National Debt paid out to persons. Total personal income in 1959 was £19,676 million.

DISPOSAL OF PERSONAL INCOME, 1959.

	£ million	Percentage
Total Personal income . .	19,676	100
less:		
Direct Taxes	1,791	9
National Insurance contributions	898	4½
gives:		
Disposable income . . .	16,987	86½
available for:		
Consumption	15,715	80
Saving	1,254	6½
Remittances abroad (net) .	18	—

The table shows what happened to this income. Direct taxation—income tax and surtax—took about 9 per cent of total personal income, and National Insurance contributions, which being compulsory are in effect a form of tax, took a further 4½ per cent. The remainder of personal income—called disposable income—was available for spending or saving. In 1959, total personal savings amounted to £1,254 million.

CONSUMPTION EXPENDITURE, 1959.

	£ million	Percentage
Food	4,798	30½
Drink and Tobacco . .	2,000	13
Housing, fuel, and light .	2,137	13½
Clothing	1,505	9½
Durable goods * . . .	1,301	8½
Other goods and services.	3,974	25
Total consumption .	15,715	100

* Motor-cars, furniture, television sets, refrigerators, etc.

Four-fifths of personal income was spent on consumption goods and services. Over 30 per cent of consumption spending went on food; and almost as much was spent on drink and tobacco as was spent on housing—rent, repairs, maintenance, *plus* lighting and heating. Some consumption expenditure is subject to indirect taxation, which is the name given to taxes which are levied on particular goods and services. Thus more than three-quarters of expenditure on tobacco goes to the Government. Total indirect taxation on consumers' expenditure amounted to £2,730 million in 1959, though this was offset by subsidies—payments by the Government towards the cost of particular goods and services, mainly some foods and housing—amounting to £377 million.

Types of personal income.

The sources of personal incomes are shown in the table. Incomes from employment—including employers' contributions to National Insurance and to private pension schemes—accounted for 71 per cent of the total in 1959: a substantially higher proportion than before the war. The proportion of wages has risen slightly, and the proportion of salaries has gone up sharply. The main reason is not that salaries have risen faster than wages, but rather that the number of salaried workers has increased much faster than the number of wage-earners. There has also been an increase in the proportion of personal incomes derived from grants paid out by public authorities. These include old-age pensions, war pensions, sickness benefits, childrens' allowances, student grants, and many other grants under various schemes. Some of these grants were not payable before the war; and in recent years the number of old-age pensioners has been rising quite rapidly.

PERSONAL INCOME BY TYPES OF INCOME.

	£ million.	Percentages of total.	
	1959.	1959.	1938.
Incomes from Employment.			
Wages	7,975	40·5	38
Salaries	4,585	23·3	18
Pay in cash and kind of the Forces	389	2·0	1½
Employers' contributions to National Insurance and other superannuation schemes	984	5·0	2½
	13,933	70·8	59½
Incomes from Self-employment.			
Professional persons	309	1·6	2
Farmers	442	2·2	1½
Other self-employed	1,142	5·8	9
	1,893	9·6	12½
Incomes from Property	2,213	11·3	22½
Grants from Public Authorities.			
Pensions and widows' benefits	736	3·7	n.a.
Other	901	4·6	n.a.
	1,637	8·3	5½
Total	19,676	100	100

The types of income which have fallen as a proportion of total income are the incomes of self-employed persons, and incomes from property. The number of self-employed persons has declined, and moreover the incomes of some groups have not increased as rapidly as other incomes. The fall in property incomes since before the war has been particularly striking. During the war and for several years afterwards property incomes changed little—the effects of rent control, excess profit tax, and low interest rates were such that these incomes did not rise, while other incomes increased sharply. In more recent years, property incomes have increased, as rent control on some property was lifted, and as interest rates rose; but nevertheless, the share of property incomes in 1959 was only about a half of what it had been in 1938. Over those two decades, there was a fundamental redistribution of income away from property-owners towards employees.

Incomes by Size.

In 1959 nearly half the population received incomes under £500, and nine-tenths under £1,000. The remaining 9 per cent of the population with incomes over £1,000 received 26 per cent of the total income, and the top 1 per cent received 8 per cent of the total. Thus Britain is still far from being an egalitarian society; income is still very unevenly distributed, but not so unevenly as before the war, when the top 1 per cent received 16 per cent of the total income.

Taxes on income are, of course, highly progressive, rising sharply as income increases. Those with low incomes pay no income tax, and, in so far as they are pensioners, no compulsory contributions either. Those with incomes between £250 and £500 pay about 4 per cent of their incomes in direct taxes; for them the National Insurance contributions—over £50 deducted for an adult male, *plus* another £30 paid by the employer—are far more important than any tax. Even for the prosperous working classes and lower middle classes earning over £500 but under £1,000, tax is still only 7 per cent, and it is only in the incomes above £1,500 that taxes begin to take away a substantial proportion of income. And even then those with incomes between £3,000 and £5,000 still keep two-thirds of the total. It is only on incomes above £5,000 that the share taken by the State begins to exceed that kept by the individual.

INCOMES BY SIZE IN 1959.

Range of income before tax	Percentage of total number of incomes	Percentage of total income received.	Percentage of total income after direct taxes.	Percentage paid in direct taxes.
£50–£250	19	7	8	—
£250–£500	28	17	18	4
£500–£1,000	44	49	52	7
£1,000–£1,500	6	12	12	10
£1,500–£2,000	1·4	4	3½	18
£2,000–£3,000	0·9	3½	3	26
£3,000–£5,000	0·6	3	2½	34
Over £5,000	0·03	4	2	66
	100	100	100	10

These various tax burdens somewhat change the distribution of incomes. Only 6½ per cent of the population have an income over £1,000 after tax, and the 1 per cent of population who receive the highest incomes get 5 per cent of total income after tax as compared with 8 per cent of total income before tax. But the redistributive effect of taxation must not be over-stressed; the levelling-up of incomes before tax has been very much more important in making Britain rather more egalitarian than has been any taxation policy.

Income and Spending Power.

In many ways figures for incomes alone substantially over-estimate the degree of equality to be found in Britain. First, incomes are incomes as defined for income-tax purposes. Any allowed expenses are not included, and for the self-employed and the higher ranks of management the expense allowance now adds substantially to spending power. Particularly important are cars required for business, but also used for pleasure and as tax rates have risen, it has become increasingly profitable for such classes to claim every expense to which they are conceivably entitled There is little doubt that this adds substantially to the standard of living of those in a position to claim such allowances, although it is very difficult to see any simple way in which the taxation system could be made more equitable in this respect.

Second, capital gains were not taxable (but see G42). If one buys an asset which rises in value after one has bought it, one has clearly gained extra spending power. In the U.S.A. realised capital gains are taxable, at a rather lower rate than income. In India the same object of taxing persons according to their spending power was attempted by having a tax on total expenditure so that those who spend out of capital gain rather than out of income should be taxed a heavily, but this failed due to difficulties in implementation. In Britain not only have peopl been exempt from tax on capital gains, a considerable advantage in periods of boom in Ordinar Share values, but also they have been able by a number of devices to convert income into capita gains, and thus avoid paying income tax. Th possibility arises in two ways. Certain individua whose profession is dealing in securities do hav to pay income tax on their capital gains, and the are therefore indifferent as between receivin dividends or capital gains. If therefore they bu shares from an ordinary tax-payer just before dividend is due to be paid and sell it back to hi immediately afterwards the ordinary tax-paye escapes the tax which would normally be pai and gets a tax-free capital gain instead, while th dealer is no worse off than he would have been

DISTRIBUTION OF CAPITAL: VALUE OF ESTATES FOR DEATH DUTIES IN 1957–58.

Size of estate.	Number of estates.	Value, £ million.	Percentages of total.	
			Numbers.	Value.
£3,000–£5,000	23,919	92·6	40	12
£5,000–£10,000	19,157	137·3	32	18
£10,000–£25,000	11,944	185·2	20	24
£25,000–£50,000	3,708	131·8	6	17
£50,000–£100,000	1,313	94·0	2	12
£100,000–£500,000	554	99·6	1	13
Over £500,000	24	39·5	0·04	5
	60,619	780·1	100	100

he had received an equivalent amount in capital gain. So there is a net saving in tax to be shared between the two appropriately. A rather similar racket operates with charities and other tax-exempt bodies. In the 1960 Budget the Chancellor took general powers to stop the loss of revenue that results from these practices, after previous Chancellors had tried to close the loopholes by making specific types of transaction illegal. This legislation was not intended to alter the system under which capital gains were tax-free. It applied only to capital gains which can be shown to have been deliberately substituted for income in order to avoid tax.

Distribution of Capital.

Spending power depends not only on income and capital gains but also on the sheer amount of capital owned; and in respect of capital Britain is still far from egalitarian. The only figures are those that arise in connection with the payment of death duties. In 1959 of those who at death left estates of more than £3,000—less than one-fifth of the total numbers dying—1 per cent owned 18 per cent of the total, and 10 per cent owned about half the total—and this in spite of a growing tendency for the rich to pass on their money before death in order to avoid death duties. Nor has there been all that much narrowing since before the war; in 1938 about half the total value of estates was accounted for by 6½ per cent of the total number of estates. Indeed, the main change appears to have been that the fairly rich are more numerous, and the extremely rich somewhat less numerous. The vast majority still own very little, and Britain is far from being a property-owning democracy.

Wages and Salaries.

In 1959, 66 per cent of personal income was paid to employees in the form either of wages, salaries, or Forces' pay. The distinction between the first two is very much a matter of convention; many salary-earners now earn less than wage-earners,

WAGE AND SALARY LEVELS IN MANUFACTURING INDUSTRY.
(October 1959.)

	Administrative, Clerical, and Technical Staff.			Wage-earners. Adults only.
	All.	Monthly-paid.	Weekly-paid.	
Men .	366*s*. 3*d*.	468*s*. 4*d*.	287*s*. 1*d*.	284*s*. 3*d*.
Women	150*s*. 0*d*.	197*s*. 4*d*.	141*s*. 10*d*.	141*s*. 4*d*.

and the real social division is between those salary-earners who are paid monthly and the rest. Actually in 1959 the average weekly salary in manufacturing industry was 3*s*. more than that of

AVERAGE WEEKLY EARNINGS IN CERTAIN INDUSTRIES:
(May 1960.)

Men.				Women (full-time).			
Industry.	Earnings.	Hours worked.	Earnings per hour.	Industry	Earnings.	Hours worked.	Earnings per hour.
	s. *d*.		*s*. *d*.		*s*. *d*.		*s*. *d*.
Motor vehicles .	380 5	47·4	8 0	Road passenger transport . .	207 10	46·4	4 6
Printing . . .	346 3	45·2	7 8	Motor vehicles .	189 1	40·6	4 8
Engineering . .	294 2	47·0	6 3	Engineering . .	154 8	40·8	3 10
Chemicals. . .	286 8	47·5	6 0	Local government service . .	148 5	40·6	3 8
Transport and storage . . .	274 1	50·7	5 5	Textiles . . .	143 3	41·1	3 6
Building and contracting . .	267 11	49·4	5 5	Clothing . . .	140 5	39·5	3 7
Textiles . . .	258 6	48·3	5 4	Chemicals . .	139 3	41·0	3 5
Clothing . . .	251 5	44·2	5 8	Food, drink, and tobacco . .	138 10	42·1	3 4
Local government service . . .	215 0	46·1	4 8	Laundries . .	119 4	41·5	2 10
All industries covered in enquiry . .	282 1	48·0	5 10	All industries covered in enquiry . . .	145 0	42·6	3 7
Other industries *							
Coal-mining . .	319 3 (+19 2 in kind)	n.a.	n.a.		Boys.		
				All	123 1	44·2	2 9
Docks . . .	315 5	n.a.	n.a.		Girls.		
Railways . . .	247 0	n.a.	n.a.				
Agriculture . .	199 7	51·7	3 10	All	93 1	41·9	2 3

* These figures relate to industries not covered in the Ministry of Labour's surveys of earnings, and refer to slightly different periods.

adult wage-earners for males and 6*d.* more for women. (These figures are not exactly comparable, as the salary figures include some juveniles.) Monthly-paid staff earned much more, £23 on average for men as against £14 for the weekly-paid staff. But even though the weekly-paid salaried staff do not now earn more than wage earners, they are still in effect better paid; for they work shorter hours on the whole, and they are much more likely to be covered by private superannuation schemes. Also they usually work in better conditions.

No regular statistics are collected about salary levels; but every half-year the Ministry of Labour publishes detailed figures of the actual earnings in one week of wage-earners in a wide range of industries. Some figures are shown for weekly and hourly earnings during a week in May 1960. The average weekly wage for men was £14 2*s.*, and for women a little over half this—£7 5*s.* There are some quite sharp differences between industries. In motor manufacture the average wage was £19, and in local government service (roadmen and suchlike) as little as £10 15*s.* Farm workers, not included in the survey, earn under £10 a week. For women the best-paying industry is the buses, where nearly equal pay between male and female conductors brings an average wage of £10 8*s.* In the worst industry—laundries—the average wage is as low as £5 19*s.* Boys (under 21) earn £6 3*s.* on average, and girls (under 18) £4 13*s.*

Differentials.

Women earn on average much less than men, and juveniles usually much less than adults. Before the war the gap was relatively greater. Men, for instance, earned 4·1 times as much in May 1960 as they did in October 1938; but for women the ratio was 4·5 times. Nearly all this narrowing occurred during the war, when it was the common practice for wage advances to take the form of a flat-rate increase to all employees regardless of sex. Since 1950 the practice has altered. The usual thing has been to grant roughly similar percentage increases to all grades, and there has in fact been a slight widening of the gap.

The same narrowing occurred in other differentials. Skilled workers, for instance, were during the war granted the same flat-rate advances as unskilled, and there was then and, to some extent, also in the years immediately after the war, a sharp narrowing of the reward for skill in many industries. As for the sex differential, the narrowing has now come to a halt; but it has not been reversed, and wages within the working-class are much less widely spread than they used to be. Some would say the rewards for skill were insufficient; but, on the other hand, the upgrading of the lowest-paid has, together with the reduction in long-term unemployment, been the main means by which the grinding poverty of the worst-off members of society—with all its undesirable consequences, such as malnutrition of children—has been eliminated. Today the really numerous poor are the old, the sick, and the handicapped—and not, as before the war, families with a working head who was earning too little to make ends meet.

Differentials have been a major source of industrial strife in some industries. In engineering there has been continued conflict between unions with membership largely among the skilled and those with membership largely among the semi-skilled over what form demands for wage increases should take. On the railways the strife has been even more open, with the A.S.L.E.F., representing the drivers and firemen, calling a strike in 1955 to increase their members' pay relative to that of other railway workers. Conflict over differentials also lay behind the London bus strike of 1958.

Overtime and Short Time.

The earnings of any individual worker depend on many factors, and are usually far above the minimum wage-rates payable for a week. They include overtime earnings, and overtime working is common for men. In most weeks 1½–1¾ million workers in manufacturing will be working overtime to the extent of 7½–8 hours. So for men the average working-week in May 1960 was over 48 hours, which is at least 4 hours above the average standard working-week without overtime. In the cement industry the average working-week for men was nearly 57 hours, and in no industry was it below 44 hours. Indeed, the average working-week in 1960 was higher than before the war, even though in most the standard working-week has been reduced. In most industries it was cut by 4 hours soon after the war from 48 to 44 hours, and in 1960 further widespread reductions of 1½–2 hours were made.

Short-time, the working of less than the standard week, has never been common since the war. It has been important in particular industries at particular times; but even in February 1959, at the bottom of the recession, it was far smaller than overtime. Then 132,000 workers were on an average short-time of 12½ hours—a total of 1½ million hours lost, as against 9¾ million hours of overtime in the same week.

Earnings and Rates.

Overtime is not, however, the main reason why earnings exceed minimum wage-rates; for most workers earn very much more than the minimum in the standard working-week. One reason is payment by results, the system of payment under which the worker's wage depends partly on output. The commonest form is still the piecework system, under which pieceworkers are paid a fixed low rate per hour for each hour worked *plus* a fixed piecework price for each operation performed; but increasingly employers tend to prefer as a more effective incentive some scheme under which the bonus payment is related to the output of a larger group or to that of a whole factory. With payment by results systems—these cover 38 per cent of workers in manufacturing industry—earnings rise as productivity rises, and, as usually such workers also participate in advances in wage-rates negotiated between employers and unions, the gap between earnings and wage-rates tends to widen for them. So workers not paid by results press for similar advances for themselves, and in times of booming trade get them under a wide variety of names and forms—merit payments, lieu rates, compensation bonuses, etc.

Between 1947 and 1959 wage-rates rose by 83 per cent and earnings by 111 per cent. The advance in rates was little more than the rise in prices—only 9 per cent—so that anyone who actually earned the minimum rate throughout was little better off. But earnings rose by 26 per cent more than prices, so that the main source of the extra real income of the working-class is to be found in the widening gap between earnings and rates. This was particularly so up to 1953, since between 1947 and 1953 the real value of the wage-rate fell a little. Since then there has been a slow growth in the real value of the wage-rate, as well as a continued growth in the excess of actual earnings over minimum rates.

Wage Negotiation.

In Britain 9¾ million workers belong to 653 different trade unions. Most of these unions are very small, 466 having less than 2,500 members; but 17 have a membership of over 100,000. The main job of unions is collective bargaining with employers, and in most industries most employers also belong to associations which bargain collectively on their behalf. Some big firms, however, prefer to remain outside the associations, and strike their own bargain with the unions—Ford's, for instance. Before the war many firms tried to encourage the formation of Company Unions, *i.e.*, of unions confined to employees of a single firm; but this is now uncommon. In some lowly paid trades—catering, baking, dressmaking, and others—minimum wages are fixed by Wages Boards or Councils set up by the Ministry of Labour; and representatives of the workers and employers, and independent members, meet together to reach agreement on the settlement to be recommended to the Minister. But over most of industry the aim of collective bargaining is to reach voluntary agreement, and the Ministry of Labour intervenes only when no agreement is reached. Even in the nationalised industries, the Government does not usually intervene unless negotiations between the Boards and the unions break down.

The usual pattern of negotiation is like this. First, the union puts in a claim for an all-round increase, usually much larger than it expects to get. Then after a time the employers reply, often offering a much smaller increase, and sometimes none at all. They then argue round a table until either they reach agreement or they definitely fail to reach agreement. If the latter happens the next step varies considerably from industry to industry. Many industries have their own "conciliation" machinery, in which outsiders try to help the two sides to reach agreement. Some, though not many, also have their own "arbitration" machinery, in which outsiders can recommend a solution of the dispute, which is sometimes binding and sometimes not. It depends on what the two sides have agreed on in advance. Many industries have no machinery of their own, and depend on the general facilities the Minister of Labour can offer. He may, as he did in the printing dispute, appoint an impartial conciliator; or he may, with the agreement of both parties, refer the matter to the Industrial Court, which arbitrates between the parties; or he may set up a Court of Enquiry which enquires into the dispute and makes recommendations, which are not binding on the parties; or he may decide to do nothing at all, if he judges intervention to be useless. Nor need either unions or employers call him in; the former may opt to put pressure on the employers immediately either by strike action, or by banning overtime or piecework, or by other action. Until 1956 the Minister of Labour also had the power, if he chose, to refer a dispute to the National Arbitration Tribunal, even without the consent of one of the parties; but this power has now been abolished. Thus the Government in this country has little power to control wages directly, or to impose agreements. The Minister of Labour can, for example, delay the authorisation of Wages Council recommendations; but in the main the role of the Minister is confined to mediating between independent parties. There is not even the right that exists in the U.S.A. to impose compulsorily a "cooling-off" period of 60 days, still less the fixing of wages characteristic of Communist states.

Important Negotiations.

A few negotiations are particularly important in determining how wages rise in a year; for the pattern of later settlements tends roughly to follow those of earlier settlements. Probably the most important of all are those between the Confederation of Engineering and Shipbuilding Unions—an organisation representing 3 million workers—and the Engineering Employers' Federation, as this single negotiation directly affects the wages of 3½ million workers, and indirectly many more. On several occasions since the war negotiations between these two have broken down, and only finally been settled after a Court of Enquiry had recommended a compromise wage-advance, once, in 1957, during the course of a strike. The Confederation is a special negotiating body comprising all the unions who have members working in the engineering and shipbuilding industries. These include many small skilled workers' unions, such as the Patternmakers' Union, but they also include, besides the ¾-million-strong Amalgamated Engineering Union, the two large general unions, the Transport and General Workers' Union, with over a million members, and the General and Municipal Workers' Union, with not far short of a million. These last two represent the semi-skilled and unskilled workers, and conflict between them and the skilled unions concerning differentials is common.

The other really important negotiation is that between the British Transport Commission and the three railway unions—the large National Union of Railwaymen, representing most grades, the Amalgamated Society of Locomotive Engineers and Firemen, representing the drivers and the firemen, and the Transport Salaried Staffs' Association, representing the ticket collectors, railway clerks, etc. The importance of this negotiation lies in the fact that railwaymen are comparatively badly paid; but, as the Transport Commission runs a deficit, any wage advance has effectively to be paid for by the Government. Time and time again—for example the rise in early 1960 arising out of the Guillebaud Report on railway pay—wage advances have been given to railwaymen with the purpose of trying to narrow the gap between them and other workers; but the advance given to railwaymen then acts as a guide to other settlements, so that the railwaymen remain relatively as badly paid as before.

Strikes.

The strike is the unions' weapon of last resort. Most unions maintain strike funds in order to support their members when they call them out on strike; but these funds are small, and strike pay is usually very much below normal wages—£2 to £4 a week as against an average wage of £14. So unions cannot afford to call strikes irresponsibly, and major official strikes are uncommon. In most years there will be one or two, but not more, and the total number of working-days lost is usually negligible—less than one day per head. Even in the industry affected the lost working-days are usually made up in the following weeks by overtime.

Nevertheless, the big strikes are important; for the success or failure of one big strike can affect the results of all the other collective bargaining under way at the time. They can also affect the awards of arbitration tribunals, since, in the main, arbitration awards tend to follow the pattern of settlements already made in other industries. There is no purpose in a tribunal trying to be fair if it cannot get its awards accepted. So the settlement reached as a result of a strike often determines the amount by which wage-rates will rise on average over all industries. The successful engineering strike in 1957 was the main reason why in that year most workers got a rise of 8*s*. on average. The failure of the London bus strike in 1958 and the relative failure of the printing strike in 1959 were among the factors which led to rather slower increases in wage-rates during 1958 and 1959 than in most previous years.

Most strikes are neither large nor official, nor about wages. An official strike is one called by a union, usually by decision of the national executive, and is usually the result of a breakdown in collective bargaining about wages. But unofficial strikes called by local leaders without the

STRIKES.

Industry.	In 1959.			In 1958.
	Number of strikes.	Workers involved, thousands.	Working-days lost, thousands.	Working-days lost, thousands.
Coal-mining	1,292	190	362	450
Vehicles	135	158	465	160
Engineering	111	29	97	74
Shipbuilding	78	23	315	336
Transport	88	30	96	2,116
Building	170	21	118	151
Paper and printing	7	123	3,509	4
All other	192	70	288	171
Total	2,073	644	5,250	3,462

authorisation of unions are usually about other matters. None of the big unofficial strikes which have plagued the London Docks since the war was about wages, but usually about some relative triviality that only bore witness to the thoroughly poor state of labour relations in that industry. Much the same may be said about the continual strikes in shipbuilding, many of them caused by demarcation disputes concerning which jobs should be done by which type of skilled worker. These sort of strikes are really a form of industrial protest, and the employers have to bear their share of the blame.

In 1959 there were in all 2,073 strikes. One of these, the official strike in the printing industry, led to a loss of 3½ million working-days, twice as much as all the other strikes put together. Without the printing strike, the average strike involved 250 workers and lasted just over three days. Most indeed were still smaller; in mining, the industry with much the largest number of strikes, the average strike involved 150 workers and lasted under two days.

In most industries there are very few strikes. The main strike-prone industries, apart from the mines, are vehicles, shipbuilding, and docks; but even in these the extent of strikes must not be exaggerated. In shipbuilding, with the worst record of disputes, losses are only just over one day a year and, if that were all, could safely be ignored. But, of course, strikes are also a symptom of industrial trouble; and it is no accident that in shipbuilding productivity has scarcely improved at all since the war.

Prices and Real Incomes.

The aim of a union is to get for its members a higher standard of living, and its success depends on the extent to which wage-advances exceed the rise in the cost-of-living. Until 1953 average wage-rates (though not earnings) lagged behind the rise in prices. Since then they have risen somewhat faster than prices, and the standard of living of the workers has been rising fairly steadily as a result. Much the same has been true of other groups. Salaries lagged behind the rise in prices probably even more during and immediately after the war; but since then have risen rather faster than wages, partly because of more effective negotiation on their behalf by their unions—or their professional organisations. Real incomes of pensioners and of those on National Assistance have been going up too in the 'fifties, after the serious erosion of their value in the later 'forties. The retirement pension is still inadequate for a decent life; but that is because when the National Insurance Scheme was set up in 1948 it was believed that the nation could not afford anything better, and not as in 1951 because inflation had eroded the value of the pension. Something too has been done for holders of other pensions, such as retired civil servants and postmen, so that inflation can no longer be deplored on the main ground that it leads to much hardship. The main danger is that British exports become uncompetitive, and that the balance of payments position deteriorates.

WAGES AND PRICES.
(1947 = 100.)

May.	Weekly wage-rates.*	Weekly earnings.*	Index of retail prices.	Real wage-rates.	Real earnings.
1949	108	113	109	99	104
1951	118	129	121	98	107
1953	135	149	141	96	106
1955	152	173	147	103	118
1957	169	194	160	106	121
1959	182	211	167	109	126
1960	187	226	169	111	134

* The figures for wage-rates cover a wider group of workers than the figures for earnings, and the two series are therefore not strictly comparable.

Price Changes.

In the calculation of real wages it is usual to make use of the Index of Retail Prices, commonly called the cost-of-living index. This index is calculated monthly by the Ministry of Labour, and in a few industries with sliding-scale agreements (iron and steel, building) wages are adjusted to take account of changes in the index. In other industries the change in the index naturally has a large influence on the course of negotiations. Indeed, up to 1958 it was probably the dominant influence. In no year before then had the annual rise in prices been less than 2 per cent. In most years it was rather higher, and in some years it was much more—in 1951–52, nearly 10 per cent. 1958 and 1959 were, however, years of stable average retail prices.

Price changes have not been similar for different types of goods. For instance, between January 1952 and January 1956, when the total index rose by 16 per cent, food went up by 25 per cent, rents and rates by 18 per cent, fuel and light by 28 per cent, and services by 19 per cent; but the prices of clothing, drink, tobacco, and durable household goods (furniture, TV sets, washing-machines, etc.) scarcely altered. In those years, average prices went up least for the rich, and most for the very poor, particularly for the pensioners, for whom rent, fuel, and food form a much higher proportion of total expenditure than for most households.

The Causes of Price Inflation.

Prices charged in the shops are determined by a great many factors, over many of which the Government has little or no control. First among these is the price of imports. Prices of imported food and raw materials are determined in the world markets, in which Britain is only one of many purchasers. In the raw material markets the U.S.A. is usually the dominant purchaser, and prices depend greatly on the level of economic activity there. In the food markets British

RETAIL PRICES.

	Weight.*	Percentage change (Jan.–Jan.).			
		June 1947–Jan. 1952.	1952–56.	1956–58.	1958–60.
Food	350	+50	+25	+ 5	+ 2
Clothing	106	+47	− 1	+ 3	—
Housing	87	+ 4	+18	+18	+10
Tobacco	80	} + 8	{ + 3	+ 8	—
Drink	71		+ 3	+ 6	− 7
Transport and vehicles	68	included in	other items	+13	+ 3
Durable household goods	66	+37	+ 2	+ 1	− 4
Fuel and light	55	+40	+28	+16	+ 3
Other goods	59	+37	+ 7	+12	+ 1
Services	58	+24	+19	+13	+ 4
All items	1,000	+32	+16	+ 8	+ 2

* *I.e.*, proportionate importance of item in total expenditure.

purchases are much more important, since the U.S.A. grows most of its own food, and is a large exporter of some foods. Prices in raw material markets are continually changing, and can fluctuate wildly. For instance, the average price of copper rose 40 per cent between 1954 and 1955, and then fell back in 1957 to 10 per cent below its 1954 level. Fluctuations at the time of the Korean War were even more fantastic. The price of wool rose over four times, and then came down just as abruptly to only a quarter above its earlier level; the price of rubber behaved similarly. The large rise in import prices, coming on top of the rise that had been brought about by devaluation, was the real reason why the cost-of-living index shot up sharply in 1951. Since then, however, the dominant trend of import prices has been downwards, and changes in prices of imports cannot be directly blamed for the continuing rise in prices since 1951. The source has to be looked for in the tendency of wages, salaries, profits, and other incomes to rise faster than real output, and this they have done in almost every year since the war.

Wages and Prices.

Wage increases are probably the most important—for this reason. When a trade union negotiates a wage advance for all or most of the employees in an industry, firms will immediately consider whether they should increase their prices to cover their increased wage-costs. As it is common practice for firms to fix the selling prices of their products by first calculating the direct costs of labour and of materials, and then adding on a percentage to cover overhead costs and profits, they will tend to want to raise their prices not only to cover the cost of the wage advance but also to cover their percentage addition. Moreover, in deciding whether or not their customers will stand for such increases, firms will be influenced by the knowledge that their competitors have to pay the increased wages too, and will probably therefore be raising their prices. So industry-wide wage advances—and changes in costs of materials—are particularly likely to be passed on to the consumer; and, as wage-earners are also consumers, to generate further demands for wage advances to cover the increased prices. Profits per unit also go up under this tendency to set prices on a *cost-plus* basis; but it is the wage advance which tends to set the spiral off, by providing the opportunity for price increases.

Once this spiral gets going, it is very hard to stop it. In general, the requirement is that wage earnings should not rise faster than productivity (output per man). But, as in some industries productivity is very slow to rise, and as it would be unfair and impracticable to exclude their workers from participating in any general rise in the standard of living, this requirement involves that in industries with a rapid growth of productivity wage advances should be kept well below the rate of rise of productivity. For two reasons this is rather difficult. First, rising productivity often raises the wages of some workers in these industries automatically, because they are paid by results or through some incentive scheme. The rise of wages from this source takes the form of a tendency on the part of earnings in these industries to rise faster than wage-rates; but that does not mean that all employees benefit, or that there is any likelihood that the unions in these industries will not press for the same rate of increase in wage-rates as is achieved in the slowly-growing industries. Second, employers in the rapidly-growing industries have far less reason to resist demands for wage increases than those in slowly-growing industries. Indeed, they are quite likely to bid up wages in order to get the labour they need, rather than to try to hold down wages.

There are therefore major problems in preventing a faster rise in wages than in productivity, with its consequence of rising prices. And once a wage-price spiral has started, the problems become more acute because unions and employers become accustomed to substantial annual advances in money wages. A main source of continuing price inflation has been the tendency of money wages to continue to advance at a rate that was appropriate when the cost-of-living was going up sharply, but ceased to be appropriate in later years. The trend is shown in the table, from which it will be seen that it was not until after 1958 that there was any substantial slowing-down in the rate of rise of wages per unit of output. Import prices fell sharply in 1958, and this made an important contribution to price stability in that year. 1959 was an exceptionally favourable year. Industrial output, which had increased little over the previous three years, shot up; and there was in consequence a substantially greater increase in productivity than can be looked for over a run of years. It would be dangerous to assume, on the basis of the stability of prices in 1958 and 1959, that the wage-price spiral had been finally brought under control at the end of the 1950s.

The Stopping of Price Inflation.

There are several possible methods of attack on the inflationary spiral of wages and prices. Perhaps the most fundamental, and certainly the most helpful to other objectives of economic policy, is to achieve a faster rate of productivity growth. The faster the growth of average productivity, the faster can average incomes rise without an increase in average prices. But if wages and other incomes rise more rapidly than productivity, it will be difficult to maintain price stability.

Comprehensive and detailed Government control of wages must probably be ruled out for political and institutional reasons, and so must comprehensive and detailed control of prices. Either would involve a much more "controlled" economy than we have at present, and experience suggests that such detailed control would involve a major loss of flexibility in the economy. At the other extreme, general exhortations to unions to exercise restraint on wages, and to manufacturers to exercise restraint on prices, have probably had little effect.

Various intermediate lines of approach have been or could be tried. In 1948–50, the Government secured the co-operation of the T.U.C. in the wages "freeze". For a time this was successful, but the increases in prices which followed the devaluation in 1949 made substantial increases in wages unavoidable, and the freeze was abandoned. By setting an example in the nationalised industries over which it has a more direct influence, the Government can encourage employers to take a tougher attitude towards wage claims. This

COST AND PRICE CHANGES.

Annual percentage rate of increase in:	Period.					
	1949–59.	1949–51.	1951–54.	1954–57.	1957–58.	1958–59.
Wage and salary costs per unit of output	5	5	4	6	4	2
Profits and other incomes per unit of output	4½	1	6	3	5	4
Costs of imported goods .	3	25	−4	2	−7	−1
Prices of all goods and services	4½	8	2	4	2	1

was one strand of policy in the later 1950s, and the firm line taken in the London bus dispute in 1958 probably moderated other wage claims for a time. Its disadvantage is the obvious unfairness of a policy which is most likely to be effective in nationalised industries, many of whose workers are relatively badly-paid. Another approach is to lower tariffs or remove quotas on imports, thus exposing some manufacturers at home to tougher competition from abroad. Manufacturers would be less able to raise prices without losing markets, and unions would be less willing to press wage claims if there was a real danger that some of their members would lose their jobs as a consequence. But the gains from a policy which depends for its success on higher imports have to be weighed against its effects on the balance of payments. Or again, many prices in the economy are directly influenced by Government indirect taxation which raises the price of some goods, and Government subsidies which lower the prices of other goods. By manipulating its tax and subsidy policies, the Government can exercise a powerful influence on the price level: though of course any reduction in indirect taxation or increase in subsidies would probably have to be financed by increases in direct taxation, which may in turn have undesirable effects on incentives to harder work and greater effort.

More indirectly, the Government can attempt to control the wage-price spiral by controlling purchasing power through its monetary and fiscal policies. If purchasing power is curbed, manufacturers find it more difficult to raise prices, and the bargaining power of unions may be reduced. In the 1950s, the Government relied heavily on fiscal and more especially monetary policies, the nature of which will be examined in later sections. The main danger is that curbing purchasing power is likely to curb the rise in output and productivity, so that attempts to control the wage-price spiral in this way could result in the stagnation of the economy. Furthermore, there is a danger that some wage increases will continue in periods of stagnation so that inflation cannot be entirely avoided.

It is clear that there is no easy solution—there are difficulties and disadvantages attaching to every possible measure for controlling price inflation. Certainly the problem of inflation was not solved in the 1950s; in Part III we shall discuss the solutions which have been attempted in the 1960s.

4. MONEY, BANKING, AND FINANCE.

The Radcliffe Report.

In September 1957 the Chancellor set up the Radcliffe Committee to report on the working of Britain's monetary institutions. The report of the committee, published in 1959, contains a detailed description of the monetary institutions of this country, and a systematic appraisal of monetary policies in the 1950s. It is complicated, because the monetary system is complicated; but it is written in terms which can be understood by the layman. Any reader who finds the following account inadequate should consult it.

Money.

In Britain money consists of bank-notes and coinage. Bank-notes—mainly in denominations of £5, £1, and 10*s*.—are issued by the Bank of England, which has been publicly owned since 1946, and which acts in effect as an agent of the Government.

The total size of the bank-note issue is not a good guide to the amount of purchasing power in the economy. The Bank of England stated in its evidence to the Radcliffe Committee that it was now its policy to issue bank-notes in accordance with the convenience of the public, and not to use this means of controlling the amount of purchasing power. As a result, the various checks on the size of the note issue—in particular the Parliamentary control over the fiduciary issue, *i.e.* the permitted maximum level of the note issue—have become functionless and may be ignored. An increase in the value of the note issue is now only a symptom and not a cause of inflation.

Credit and Monetary Policy.

What matters is the amount of purchasing power available to the public. Most private expenditure is financed out of income—after paying taxes—and most government expenditure out of taxes; but most investment, public and private, and a growing amount of purchase of durable goods by consumers, is not financed out of income, but out of borrowing of one kind or another. And the primary purpose of monetary policy must be to keep the total of this kind of expenditure out of credit in line with the amount of savings private individuals and profit-making companies are prepared to make out of their incomes. For if such investment expenditure exceeds the amount which the community wishes to save out of its current level of income, it means that the total demand for goods and services exceeds total current output. If output cannot be increased because men and machines are already fully-employed, prices and wages and also imports are forced up in response to the demand. If, on the other hand, investment expenditure falls short of saving out of full-employment income, production and employment are reduced below the full-employment level. There is no automatic mechanism in our economic system which ensures full-employment of resources, and it is the task of Government to balance savings and investment at the right level of employment.

The details of this task are complicated; but the main outlines are straightforward enough. First, in many fields the Government has only very restricted powers to influence behaviour. It cannot compel persons or companies to save; it can only offer them inducements to do so in the form of high interest rates or of tax concessions on receipts from interest, and their effectiveness is limited. Nor in general has it very much direct power over expenditure out of credit. It can and does control the conditions under which hire-purchase agreements are made—and this does, temporarily at any rate, make a great deal of difference to the amount of goods bought on hire-purchase. It can to a certain extent influence private companies in their investment policies by granting and withdrawing incentives to investment (see **G19(1)**); but it is doubtful quite how much influence these changes have. And it can, if it chooses, exercise direct control over building, by allowing building only on licence. This power, however, is not now used in order to control the level of investment, but only in order to encourage it in depressed areas and discourage it elsewhere. The only authorities over whose investment the Government does have real control are the nationalised industries; and, as the Radcliffe Committee pointed out, there are obvious disadvantages in any system whereby investment in public utilities is determined, not by the need for such investment, but by the need to balance savings and investment.

The two main means remaining are fiscal and monetary control. If the Government thinks there is going to be a shortage of private savings it raises more in taxation or reduces its current expenditure and so increases the Budget surplus (see **G33(2)**). The second form of control is much more complex; in principle, the aims are twofold. One is to keep the amount of credit-creation down (or up) to the required extent; the second is to ensure that the Government gets the share of savings it needs to cover its investment programmes. The complexity arises from the interrelations between these two tasks.

The Government as Borrower.

The Government is a heavy borrower from the rest of the economy. In 1958 total public borrowing—by government, nationalised industries, and local authorities—from the private sector stood at £30,727 million, equivalent to 1·68 times the annual national income. Most of this immense National Debt was built up during the war, when government expenditure far exceeded taxation; but the total continues to advance year by year, owing to the heavy capital requirements of the nationalised industries.

The Government borrows in six main ways. First, the issue of bank-notes is in effect a form of government borrowing. Second, it borrows from foreign governments. Third, it borrows from companies through tax reserve certificates, which are a means by which companies let the Government have the taxes they will have to pay on profits as the latter are earned, rather than when the taxes legally become due. Fourth, it borrows

PUBLIC DEBT IN 1958.
(£ million.)

		As percentage.
Banknotes and coins	2,199	*7*
Overseas loans	2,297	*7*
Tax reserve certificates	346	*1*
National savings	5,756	*19*
Gilt-edged securities	14,489	*47*
Treasury bills	2,938	*10*
Local authority debt	2,390	*8*
Other	312	*1*
	30,727	*100*

direct from private individuals through the various forms of national savings. In all forms of national savings, the Government pays interest—or in the case of premium bonds prizes in *lieu* of interest to the winners of the monthly draw—to the holders, who have the right either on demand or at short notice to demand the repayment of their loans.

Gilt-edged Securities and Treasury Bills.

The fifth and sixth methods of borrowing are through the market. The main method is through the Stock Exchange by the issue of fixed-interest securities, called gilt-edged securities. In 1958 the net amount owing on all such securities was £14,489 million—nearly a half of total public debt; in addition, the local authorities owed another £477 million on their issues of securities. Most gilt-edged securities are promises to repay at a specified date in the future the amount originally borrowed, and in the meantime to pay interest at a fixed rate each half-year. Some gilt-edged securities are irredeemable, and consist therefore simply of the promise to pay the interest in perpetuity.

Most gilt-edged securities are held by institutions. It is estimated—with a large margin of error—that only 21 per cent are held by private individuals, to which should be added another 6 per cent owned by trustee funds, friendly societies, and trade unions. 22 per cent appear to be held by the banks and discount houses, 18 per cent by the other major financial institutions of the country. and 12 per cent by overseas holders (corresponding to the sterling balances of overseas countries, see G8(2)), leaving 22 per cent unaccounted for. Gilt-edged securities, unlike national savings, are not liquid assets. Until they become due for repayment they can only be sold on the Stock Exchange for what they will fetch, and variations in their market value are quite considerable. In 1958 their average market value was 21 per cent below their nominal value, the degree of depreciation depending very closely on the length of time

GOVERNMENT SECURITIES:
NOMINAL AND MARKET VALUES.
(£ million in 1958.)

Securities due for repayment in:	Nominal value.	Market value.	Market value as percentage nominal value.
Less than five years (short-term)	3,772	3,670	*97*
Five to fifteen years (medium-term)	5,498	4,642	*84*
Over fifteen years (long-term)	5,694	4,147	*73*
Never	3,755	2,333	*62*
	18,719	14,792	*79*

to repayment. On short-dated bonds, due to mature in less than five years, it was only 3 per cent, and on irredeemable stock it was 38 per cent. Fluctuations in these market values play a very important part in the working-out of monetary control.

The sixth form of government borrowing is by means of Treasury Bills, of which £2,938 million were outstanding in 1958. A Treasury Bill is an extremely short-term loan to the Government—usually for three months. Each week the Treasury offers for sale some £300 million of these, and a number of specialised institutions bid for them. The difference between their bids and the value of these bonds on repayment is called discount, and is a substitute for interest. These bills play a crucial role in the monetary system, for it is by affecting the rate of discount on Treasury Bills that Bank Rate influences monetary conditions in the economy; but more of that a little later.

Government Borrowing and Liquidity.

Monetary policy consists largely in varying the way in which the Government borrows to finance its expenditure. This is because the form of borrowing affects the amount of liquidity in the economy. All financial institutions have some policy regarding liquidity. In general they all try to maintain sufficient reserves either of cash or of assets which can be immediately converted into cash to meet any foreseeable sudden increase in their commitments. But they do not hold all their assets in liquid form. The chance that all their creditors simultaneously demand their money back can be ruled out, and therefore most of them act on the principle that they should maintain cash or other liquid assets to cover some percentage of their total outstanding commitments. Whereas currency and Treasury Bills are regarded as liquid assets, government securities and most other forms of government borrowing are illiquid.

If therefore the Government borrows more by issuing currency or Treasury Bills and less by other means, this action increases the amount of liquid assets about and therefore the total lending which financial institutions think it safe to make. And, conversely, if the Government borrows less by issuing currency or Treasury Bills and more by other means, this tends to decrease the total amount of loans which financial institutions are prepared to make. However, government control over the way in which it borrows is circumscribed. The public can be persuaded to hold more government securities only if the rate of interest earned on securities is increased. In the 1950s the British Government was unable to prevent a rapid accumulation of short-term debt, even though it allowed the rate of interest earned by irredeemable government securities to rise from less than 4 per cent in 1950 to over 5 per cent in 1960.

The Commercial Banks

In the centre of the financial world stand the commercial banks, and the first purpose of any credit squeeze is to put pressure on them by reducing their liquidity. By convention, the London clearing banks—which include the five large banks with branches all over England—have a rule that they should always hold at least 30 per cent of their assets in liquid form. This rule theoretically enables the Bank of England to put heavy pressure on them when it wants to by funding debt. Actually the system does not work as easily as this would make it sound, because in practice the banks hold much of the rest of their assets in nearly liquid form (see table). In June 1960, for instance, nearly 20 per cent of their assets were in gilt-edged securities, even after a period of heavy sales, and the banks hold mainly short-dated securities. So, if the banks want to they can by selling such securities maintain their liquidity and still go on increasing their advances, which are the loans the Government really wants to squeeze. In early 1960 they did just this, and prevented the Government's credit squeeze from being effective.

The Control of the Commercial Banks.

The means by which the Bank of England puts on pressure works in two ways. The first is by open-market operations, in which the Bank deliberately sells more government stock than it otherwise would. The purchasers pay by cheque, and thus create a debt from the commercial banks to the Bank of England. Such debts have to be settled in cash, and so pressure is put on the banks' liquidity. The second is Bank Rate. If Bank Rate is raised it has the immediate effect of raising the rate of discount on Treasury Bills. A high rate of discount on these makes them appear attractive investments to those who do not normally buy them, and the commercial banks find it difficult to get as many of them as they would like. So again there is pressure on the banks' liquidity.

LONDON CLEARING BANKS: ASSETS.

	£ million.		As percentage of total deposits.		
	June 1960.	June 1958.	June 1960.	June 1958.	Average 1938.
Liquid assets.					
Cash	605	550	*8·1*	*8·2*	*10·6*
Other including Treasury Bills	1,687	1,640	*22·7*	*24·6*	*18·9*
	2,292	2,190	*30·8*	*32·8*	*29·5*
*Other assets.**					
Special deposits	70	—	*1·0*	—	—
Investments	1,349	2,181	*18·1*	*32·7*	*28·0*
Advances	3,242	2,029	*43·5*	*30·4*	*42·3*
	4,661	4,210	*62·6*	*63·1*	*70·3*

* Excluding balances with other banks, items in transit, etc.

Faced by such pressure, the banks have to take steps to restore their liquidity either by selling securities or by calling in advances. Neither method brings in much cash directly; for since the banks will be paid by cheque rather than in cash, they have to go on until the depletion of deposits caused by the paying of these cheques cuts down the total of deposits to the level where liquid assets once again represent 30 per cent of the total. To this there is one major exception; if the Bank of England buys the securities the banks sell—and the need to ensure an orderly market may force it to do so—then selling securities brings more cash into the banks, and thus enables them to replenish their liquidity.

Since 1958, the monetary authorities have had the power to call upon the banks to make "special deposits" in cash with the Bank of England. Unlike other deposits of the banks with the Bank of England, special deposits cannot be treated as forming part of the liquid assets of commercial banks. This is in effect another way of putting pressure on the liquidity position of banks: the necessity of making such deposits could force them to sell securities or reduce advances. The first calls for special deposits—amounting to 1 per cent of total deposits to begin with, but later increased to 2 per cent of total deposits—were made in 1960.

Bank Advances and Other Credit.

Bank advances are the simplest of all forms of credit; the customer is just given the right to sign cheques beyond his credit account, and interest is charged on the overdraft. In the late 1950s, a new form of advance—the personal loan—was introduced by some banks. These are granted to customers who would not earlier have been regarded as credit-worthy. A higher rate of interest is charged than on ordinary overdrafts, and more specific rules about repayment are laid down.

Most advances, however, are made to business, particularly to small business, and to farmers. An analysis is shown in the table. In business the common practice is to finance working capital —stocks and work-in-progress—out of bank advances, and to depend on more permanent forms of borrowing for the purchase of fixed capital. But there are no fixed rules; business gets its finance wherever it can, and in fact there is such a variety of other ways in which it can get capital that a squeeze on bank advances alone is not as effective as might be expected. Big businesses, in practice, scarcely suffer at all; for they are in the best position to tap other sources of credit. Quite a good example is provided by the hire-purchase finance companies. During the credit squeeze of 1956–58 the banks were asked by the Chancellor of the Exchequer to hold down advances, and in particular not to increase advances to hire-purchase finance companies. They did so; but the companies had no difficulty in getting the money they needed by borrowing direct from the public at high rates of interest. The real sufferers tend to be small businesses and professional people, who do find it hard to obtain credit elsewhere; but even they may be able to do so—by, for instance, taking out a mortgage on their property or by buying their equipment on hire-purchase where previously they had paid cash, or by cashing some national savings.

BANK ADVANCES.
(£ million.)

Advances to:	May 1960.	As percentage of total.
Manufacturing industry . .	838	*24*
Agriculture and fishing . .	350	*10*
Retail trade	369	*11*
Other trade and industry .	632	*18*
Financial institutions:		
Hire-purchase companies.	148	*4*
Other	337	*10*
Local government authorities	86	*2½*
Churches and charities . .	17	*½*
Personal and professional .	680	*20*
	3,457	*100*

The Radcliffe Committee discussed at length how effective a squeeze on the banks was likely to be, and in general their conclusion was that it was not likely to be very effective, because most borrowers would usually find other sources of credit. The other sources would usually be more expensive; but they thought this mattered very little, as interest payments form only a small part of most business costs, except in very highly capitalised industries, most of which are now publicly owned. Interest does matter in housing; the monthly interest payments due on a mortgage to a building society can go up substantially when the rate of interest goes up, although usually for existing, as opposed to new, mortgages no more money is asked for; instead the term of the mortgage in years is extended by cutting the capital repayment each month. But in hire-purchase, where service charges far exceed the interest element in any loan, interest is of trivial importance. The Committee thought that a credit squeeze could substantially increase the inconvenience of borrowing by forcing persons who wanted to borrow to have to shop around for funds instead of just going to their bank and arranging an advance, and that this would, temporarily at any rate, serve to deter a number of borrowers, and thus cut down the amount of spending out of credit. But running through the report is a scepticism concerning the likely general effectiveness of monetary policy as an anti-inflationary weapon of control—and an even greater scepticism concerning its utility as an anti-deflationary weapon. One may be able to discourage spending on credit by making it hard to get. It is bound to be far more difficult to encourage spending by making credit easily available, if business prospects are so poor that no investment looks as if it will be profitable. Before the war the limit on bank advances was not credit policy, but simply the inability of the banks to find any other credit-worthy customers.

The Stock Exchange.

The banks through their advances are the main providers of short-term credit; but most long-term credit is provided through the Stock Exchange. In 1959 the total market value of all securities traded on the Stock Exchange was £39,020 million, of which £22,588 million represented stocks or shares in public companies. There are three main types. Debenture Stock is simply a fixed-interest loan. Preference Stock is a fixed-interest loan, with provisions for waiving the interest if the company fails to earn profits. Preference shareholders cannot get a company declared bankrupt if it does not pay them a dividend; but Debenture holders can. The third type—and much the most important—is Ordinary Shares. Nominally the owner of an Ordinary Share is a part-owner of the company concerned, with most of the rights of ownership. He has no right to any particular dividend or interest payment, but only the right to participate in net profits if there are any. In 1959 Ordinary Shares on the Stock Exchange werc valued at £20,486 million. Debenture Stock amounted to £1,133 million and Preference Shares to £1,629 million—both very low figures in relation to the value of Ordinary Shares, and to the value of government securities, which stood at £14,778 million. So in effect for the ordinary investor on the Stock Exchange the main choice was between buying a fixed-interest gilt-edged security and an Ordinary Share.

Each type of holding has obvious advantages. The fixed-interest security brings in a guaranteed income; the Ordinary Shareholder has no such guarantee, though in practice during the 1950s the risk of a decline in dividend was small. But in a time of inflation the risks attached to holding fixed-interest securities are in some ways greater than those attached to holding Ordinary Shares; for, while Ordinary Shares appreciate in market value when there is inflation, fixed-interest securities tend to fall in market value, because the Government is forced to increase interest rates as an anti-inflationary measure. Furthermore, in the long run the growth of the economy tends, even without inflation, to raise the value of Ordinary Shares by increasing the amount of business done by companies. And, lastly, for investors who pay tax at heavy rates on their incomes—and most large personal investors in the Stock Exchange are rich people—capital gains are worth much more than income in dividends. So for private investors, the Ordinary Share was a much better bet in the 1950s; and because Ordinary Shares were so popular, the yield on such shares—the ratio of dividends to market value—fell below the yield obtainable on Government securities in 1959 and 1960. Historically, the greater security of gilt-edged holdings has normally been reflected in lower yields: if inflation is controlled, or if the prospect of industrial expansion became less bright, the " normal " pattern of yields may well return—and this will involve a fall in the price of Ordinary Shares relative to the price of Government securities.

The Ownership of Ordinary Shares

Most Ordinary Shares are held by private individuals; but increasingly in recent years holdings by insurance companies and pension funds have become more important, because of the growth of private superannuation schemes. Insurance companies and pension funds cannot afford to take risks, so still the main bulk of their funds are invested in fixed-interest securities; but they have been showing a growing tendency to increase the proportion of their funds invested in Ordinary Shares. This switch, by lowering the demand for gilt-edged securities relative to Ordinary Shares, contributed to the downward pressure on the prices of gilt-edged securities. Further pressure may result from the effects of the legislation to change the laws governing trustees introduced in 1960. Most trusts lay down that investment may only be made in trustee securities—gilt-edged or other virtually riskless securities—so that in general trustees were not able to invest in Ordinary Shares. But the legislation gives general permission for trustees to invest up to 50 per cent of their funds in the Ordinary Shares of large companies. Clearly it was inequitable to prevent trusts from investing in the only security which in a time of inflation was likely to maintain its value.

Monetary Control in the 1950s.

The Radcliffe Committee was required to consider the working of Britain's financial institutions, and its report is largely a factual account of how the system actually works. The activities of the main financial institutions are analysed. Representatives of each type gave evidence on the sort of work they did, and on the kind of principles they worked on in deciding how to invest their resources. In the light of this evidence the Committee made its assessment of the effectiveness of monetary policies during the 1950s.

Under the Labour Government there was no major use of monetary policy; Bank Rate, for instance, was kept at 2 per cent throughout, and the rate on Treasury Bills was only ½ per cent. Instead the Government then relied on controls and on fiscal measures to keep inflation in check. For this non-use of monetary controls there was, in fact, a very strong case; the pent-up demand for goods was so strong, and the funds available to companies and individuals so large, that monetary restriction would not have made

INTEREST RATES 1948–60.

	Bank Rate.*	Treasury bill-rate.*	Rate of yield on.	
			Irredeemable government bonds.†	Ordinary Shares.†
1948	2	½	3·2	4·6
1951	2–2½	½–1	3·8	5·8
1952	2½–4	1–2½	4·2	6·5
1953	3½–4	2–2½	4·1	6·1
1954	3–3½	1½–2	3·8	5·4
1955	3–4½	2–4	4·2	5·4
1956	4½–5½	4–5	4·7	6·3
1957	5½–7	4–6½	5·0	6·3
1958	4–7	3–6½	5·0	6·2
1959	4	3–3½	4·8	4·8
1960 (January–June)	4–6	4–5	5·3	4·4

* Range during year. † Annual average.

very much difference. When the Conservatives returned to office one of their first actions was to raise Bank Rate to 2½ per cent, and very soon after that to 4 per cent. It was then reduced, but raised again in 1955–57, to reach a peak in the crisis of 1957 of 7 per cent. Thereafter it was reduced, and was increased again during 1960. The rate on Treasury Bills followed a similar course; but it gradually crept rather nearer to Bank rate. At the same time long-term interest rates rose sharply. In 1948 the rate on irredeemable stock was 3¼ per cent; by early 1960 it stood at 5¼ per cent, and by then considerably exceeded the rate of return on ordinary shares.

In addition to influencing the cost of credit by manipulating interest rates, the Government influenced the availability of certain sorts of credit through the credit-squeeze. At times it made it more difficult for the banks to extend their lending by operating on the banks' liquidity position, and it also issued more or less strongly-worded " requests " that banks should restrict the growth of, or secure a reduction in, their advances.

A form of monetary control which was particularly important in the 1950s was the control of hire-purchase. By increasing or lowering the proportion of the price which has to be paid as a down-payment, and by reducing or lengthening the length of time over which repayments can be made, the Government was able greatly to influence the volume of hire-purchase transactions, and therefore the use of this particular form of credit. These controls, of course, only affect the rather narrow class of goods—cars, furniture, washing-machines, television sets, etc.—for which a substantial proportion of sales are on hire-purchase terms. In consequence, the output of those industries concerned with the manufacture of these goods fluctuated widely.

The Effectiveness of Monetary Controls.

This is a subject on which there is vigorous controversy among economists. Not all of them accept the conclusions of the Radcliffe Committee, which had this to say about monetary policy in the 1950s (para 469):

> " (1) The obstructions to particular channels of finance have had no effect on the pressure of total demand, but have made for much inefficiency in financial organisation;
> " (2) the controls of hire-purchase terms have had sizeable impact, of a once-for-all kind, on each major charge;
> " (3) these sizeable effects on total demand have implied major directional effects (*i.e.* effects on particular kinds of expenditure and industry), which, though sometimes deliberately sought, have in general been detrimental to industrial efficiency."

They go on to add (para. 472):

> " We are driven to the conclusion that the more conventional instruments (*e.g.* Bank rate) have failed to keep the system in smooth balance, but that every now and again the mounting pressure of demand has in one way or another (generally *via* the exchange situation) driven the Government to take action, and that the quick results then required have been mainly concentrated on the hire purchase front and on investment in the public sector which could be cut by administrative decision. The light engineering industries have been frustrated in their planning, and the public corporations have had almost equally disheartening experience. That these two should be the ' residuary legatees ' for real resources when sharp adjustments were called for is not a comforting thought. It is far removed from the smooth and widespread adjustment sometimes claimed as the virtue of monetary action; this is no gentle hand on the steering wheel that keeps a well-driven car in its right place on the road."

It is, however, important to note that the Radcliffe Committee did recognise that monetary measures had influenced " confidence " in sterling. A rise in interest rates increased the attractiveness of holding sterling balances, and stern monetary measures were taken as indicative of the Government's intention to solve its problems without recourse to devaluation. In these ways, monetary policy contributed—for example in 1957 (see **G10(1)**)—to the stemming of speculative outflows of sterling balances which threatened to impose heavy strains on our reserves. Many commentators feel that these effects provide an important justification for the use of certain forms of monetary controls.

5. ECONOMIC ASPECTS OF THE PUBLIC SERVICES.

The Cost of Public Services.

In 1959 total public expenditure—excluding expenditure by nationalised industry—was £7,833 million, about £150 per head. Some of

THE FINANCE OF PUBLIC SERVICES.
(£ million.)

	1952.	1959.	Percentage change 1952–59.	As percentage of total expenditure 1959.
Expenditure.				
Debt interest	654	920	*+41*	*12*
Military and civil defence	1,651	1,610	*− 2*	*21*
Social services *	2,328	3,656	*+57*	*47*
Other expenditure	1,200	1,647	*+37*	*21*
	5,833	7,833	*+34*	*100*
Receipts.				
Direct taxes	2,332	2,970	*+27*	*38*
Indirect taxes	1,899	2,485	*+31*	*32*
Local rates	392	710	*+81*	*9*
National Insurance contributions	476	898	*+89*	*11*
Other income	453	765	*+69*	*10*
	5,552	7,828	*+41*	*100*
Net borrowing (excluding borrowing on behalf of nationalised industries)	281	5	—	—
Social Services Expenditure * (detail).				
Pensions, benefits, and assistance grants	825	1,482	*+80*	*19*
Education and child care	478	921	*+93*	*12*
Health services	510	797	*+56*	*10*
Housing	439	369	*−16*	*5*
Welfare foods, school meals, and milk	76	87	*+14*	*1*

* Food and agricultural subsidies (£395 million in 1952, and £343 million in 1959) are not counte[d] as social services, since in 1959 their primary purpose was to support British agriculture rather than t[o] cheapen food.

the details are shown in the table. Most of the expenditure was directly incurred by the Government; but £2,028 million represented expenditure by local authorities—nearly half of it on education—and £1,038 million expenditure out of the National Insurance funds on pensions and other benefits under the National Insurance Scheme. Both local authorities and the National Insurance funds are partly financed out of grants from the Central Government, which collects in taxes considerably more than it spends itself. Overall there was a rough balance between expenditure and receipts, although if one includes the capital expenditure of nationalised industries, which is also financed by the Government, there would be a large net deficit, *i.e.*, public authorities as a whole are big borrowers from the private sector of the economy. Since 1952 total public expenditure has risen by a third; but there has been a fairly steady decline in the ratio of public to private expenditure—accompanied by a steady fall in the proportion of the national income taken in taxes.

Public Housing.

Housing expenditure consists of two quite different items. The first, housing subsidies, is a current cost, and represents the difference between the cost of housing, including the cost of borrowing, and rents received on council housing. In 1959 costs exceeded the rents of £196 million by £116 million, so that the average council-house tenant was paying about 13*s*. in the £ of the cost of his house. Most of the balance was borne by the Central Government, as up to 1957 the Government contracted to pay a flat subsidy per year on every council house built. From then onwards government subsidies have been confined to houses built in connection with certain specific schemes—largely in connection with slum clearance. The ordinary new council house receives no government subsidy, although some local authorities continue to subsidise new housing out of the rates; but the subsidies continue for housing built before the general subsidy was withdrawn.

The other part consists of the capital cost of building new houses—£252 million in 1959. This is financed out of borrowing by local authorities. Until 1953 local authorities borrowed from the Central Government through the Public Works Loan Board; but from 1956 onwards they have been increasingly forced to borrow from the market, and in 1959 repayments to the Central Government in respect of past loans exceeded new borrowing by £34 million. This practice was criticised by the Radcliffe Committee, who found that much of the borrowing was very short-term; but the Government did not modify its policy.

The two policies of cutting subsidies and making borrowing more difficult have sharply cut council housing. In 1953, the peak year, councils built 239,000 houses, in 1959 only 125,000; and in England and Wales private building now exceeds council building in the ratio 3 : 2. In Scotland, however, general housing conditions are far worse—in 1951 over half the households had three rooms or less, as against 15 per cent in England and Wales—and council house-building there still exceeds private building by 5 : 1.

Education.

Education and child care cost £921 million in 1959, 93 per cent more than in 1952. The main cause of the increase has been the sharp rise in the school population, which has risen by nearly a million pupils since 1952. As a secondary school pupil costs much more to educate than a primary school pupil—the ratio of pupils to teachers is 31 in primary schools and 21 in secondary schools—the prospects are for a continuing sharp rise in the early 1960s. And after that will come the turn of the Universities, who have just begun on their expansion scheme to cope with the bulge. Nor, when the bulge is past, is there any prospect that the pressure will relax. The needed reforms as laid down in the Education Act of 1944—smaller classes, raising the school-leaving age to 16, getting rid of the gaunt Board Schools inherited from the Victorian era, raising the standards in the secondary modern schools to something nearer parity of esteem with the grammar schools, setting up County Colleges for compulsory further education—will all be very expensive; but to this expenditure, though not to any exact timing, both political parties are committed.

The main task of providing education falls on the local education authorities: in England and Wales 91 per cent of children go to schools maintained by such authorities and only 2 per cent to schools receiving direct grants from the Ministry of Education. They also pay most of the maintenance grants to University students, although the costs of the grants to the Universities themselves are paid by the Treasury.

Social Security.

Social security benefits come from two sources. The larger part, £990 million in 1959, is paid out of the National Insurance and Industrial Injury Funds. These funds, which are administered by the Ministry of Pensions and National Insurance, are built up largely out of the compulsory weekly National Insurance contributions which most of the adult population have to pay. For employees, both employer and employee pay a contribution, in return for which employees receive rights to pensions, sickness, unemployment, and other benefits. The self-employed also pay contributions of smaller size than the sum of the employer's and employee's contribution, and are not entitled to unemployment and one or two other benefits. And most non-employed persons, other than married women and the retired, have to pay still lower contributions, and are entitled to even fewer benefits. Weekly contributions include a contribution to the cost of the National Health Service. The remaining part of the contributions in 1959 covered 75 per cent of the costs of benefits and administration, grants from the Government 20 per cent, and interest on accumulated funds 6 per cent, leaving a net surplus of a mere £19 million.

The most costly benefit is the retirement pension. The pension is paid as of right on retirement. Individuals may increase their rate of pension by staying on at work after the minimum retiring age of 65 for men or 60 for women; but the number who do so for more than a year is small—partly, but probably not mainly, because most private superannuation schemes lay down a fixed retiring age. Assistance grants, on the other hand, are given only on proof of need after a test of means. The high number of supplementary grants shows that the statutory pension remained below what the National Assistance Board regards as the minimum acceptable standard, and it was partly to improve the pensions of those able to afford higher contributions that the scheme for graduated pensions was introduced.

The Finance of Social Security.

The financial problem, however, has been important. The National Insurance Scheme is an odd mixture of insurance and tax. The levels of contributions, when the scheme started in 1948, were fixed on the actuarial principle that contributions by or on behalf of an individual *plus* a specified State contribution should on average suffice to pay for the benefits to which he was entitled. But the scheme did not allow for inflation, and a succession of increases granted in the rate of pensions has put an end to this actuarial probity. Whenever a bill is introduced to increase pensions, the Government Actuary calculates by how much contributions should be raised in order that those who contribute throughout their working lives at the new rates would just earn their right to the new benefits; but the new rates of pensions are granted to all, including those who have already retired. It was always calculated that as the number of retired persons grew the fund would move into deficit; but with each rise in pensions the estimated size of the future deficit has risen. The scheme for graduated pensions also had the objective of reducing this deficit.

Graduated Pensions.

Under this scheme, which affects only employees, there are two kinds of workers—contracted-in and contracted-out. Contracted-out workers continue under the old scheme, with the difference that their employer (on whom the decision whether to contract out rests) must institute a private superannuation scheme that gives at least as favourable terms as the new State scheme, including the provision that rights under the scheme should be transferable up to the limits of the State scheme. Transferability is the guarantee that the individual does not lose his pension rights when he changes his job, and one unsatisfactory feature of the private schemes that have existed has been their use to tie employees to their jobs. Contracted-in workers come under a new scheme, under which the weekly National Insurance contribution depends on earnings. Those earning less than £9 pay a flat-rate contribution, which is lower than that paid by contracted-out workers. Those earning more than £9 pay in addition a percentage of the amount by which earnings exceed £9 up to a limit of £15, and in return receive the right to an increased pension on retirement.

The scheme is devised partly to encourage private superannuation, which is still largely confined to salaried employees *plus* employees of the State. But one purpose is clear: in return for a promise of higher pensions when they retire, most workers who are contracted-in pay more now, and thus contribute now to the cost of the pensions of the retired. The estimated deficit is eliminated, and indeed the principle is established that the basic rates of contributions should not be fixed on acturial principles but on the principle that on balance benefits paid in a year should roughly balance receipts. No provision was made for automatically increasing pensions as the cost of living goes up or indeed as the average standard-of-living rises; all changes in rates of benefit still require a new Act of Parliament.

The Budget.

Most public services are paid for currently, whether by National Insurance contributions, taxes, rates, or out of government income from the Post Office and other sources. Most of this income and expenditure passes through the Budget, which is divided into two parts. "Above-the-line" items refer to current receipts from taxes, etc., and current government expenditure. The latter is lower than total current public expenditure, as it does not include expenditure by the National Insurance Fund or by local authorities, except in so far as these are financed by government grants. The normal practice is for receipts to exceed expenditure by a considerable margin.

Forty per cent of the total revenue comes from income tax, which is levied both on individuals and on the undistributed profits of companies, and other taxes on incomes and profits raise the proportion to nearly half. The next biggest revenue-raiser is the tobacco tax; tax multiplies the price of cigarettes and tobacco by over 3½ times, and the receipts from this one tax could pay for half of defence or all the health services. Taxes on no other goods even remotely approach this level. On drinks they add under two-thirds to the cost, and on private motoring and radio and electrical goods less than one-third. On food and fuel taxes are negligible, and on clothing under 5 per cent; and on most other goods they add somewhat over 10 per cent.

The Budget Deficit.

In 1959–60 the "above-the-line" surplus was £386 million in a total revenue of £5,630 million. There is always such a surplus on current account, though in 1952–54 it was very small; but except in 1949–51 when the "above-the-line" surplus was very large, the deficit "below-the-line" makes the Government a net debtor. In 1959–60 expenditure "below-the-line," which is expenditure on capital account, exceeded receipts by £700 million, largely owing to the voracious demands for capital of the nationalised industries. Such demands are now met directly out of the Exchequer.

Deciding on the overall deficit to aim for is the Chancellor's most difficult task when drawing up his Budget. A large deficit is inflationary; sometimes that may be required (as in 1952–53 or 1959–60) to get the economy out of a recession. A small deficit—and even more a surplus—is deflationary, and can, as in 1950–51, make a substantial contribution to holding an inflation in check. But the calculation of the precise deficit or surplus needed is a chancy business; for the level that is required depends on the amount of saving and on the amount of spending out of credit that people intend to do—and this is not easily predictable. It also depends on the change in the foreign balance. Nor can the Chancellor

BUDGET SURPLUSES AND DEFICITS.
(£ million.)

	Surplus above-the-line.	Deficit below-the-line.	Overall surplus (+) or deficit (−).
1949–50	549	486	+ 63
1950–51	722	473	+249
1951–52	380	529	−149
1952–53	88	524	−436
1953–54	94	391	−297
1954–55	433	500	− 67
1955–56	397	538	−141
1956–57	290	621	−331
1957–58	422	635	−213
1958–59	377	559	−182
1959–60	386	700	−314

be sure his figures are right; estimating next year's revenue, and even next year's expenditure, by the Government is difficult enough, but he needs in deciding on his surplus to estimate not merely these but also the likely trends of private incomes and expenditure, without really reliable information as to what they were in the past year. So it cannot be expected that fiscal policy alone can prevent inflation and deflation—even if the Chancellor could ignore, as he cannot, the likely effects on prices and savings of any changes in taxes he may make. Nevertheless, fiscal action—running large deficits when economic activity is low, and small ones when it seems to be excessively high—is the most important action through which the economy can be kept on an even keel. Monetary policy may help; but the decision the Chancellor takes each April about his surplus is the key one.

6. SOURCES OF STATISTICS, AND SOME SUGGESTIONS FOR FURTHER READING.

The non-specialist will find that most of the statistics he needs are given in the *Annual Abstract of Statistics*, published every year by Her Majesty's Stationery Office. This comprehensive document includes figures on population, social conditions, education, labour, production, trade and balance of payments, national income and expenditure, wages and prices, and many other topics. For more up-to-date information, reference should be made to the *Monthly Digest of Statistics* which has a similar coverage and gives month-by-month figures. A selection of the more important series, presented in a manner which can more easily be understood by the layman, is given in another Stationery Office publication, *Economic Trends*, also issued monthly.

Even greater detail is given in various other Government publications. The most important of these are the Blue Book on *National Income and Expenditure*, published annually; and the *Balance of Payments* White Paper, published twice a year. Both these are extremely valuable sources of information for the economist, but are difficult for the layman. Fuller information on labour problems is given in the *Ministry of Labour Gazette* and on trade in the *Board of Trade Journal*. Unlike all the other statistical sources mentioned these latter two include dicussions of the statistic presented. A comprehensive official *List of Principal Statistical Series Available* was published in 1965.

For an analysis of developments in the economy the reader is recommended to the official *Economic Report*, published just before the Budget by the Treasury. It contains a survey of the economi events of the previous year, and it is written in such a way as to be comprehensible to the ordinary reader who has some background knowledge of economics. Rather more technical is the *Economic Review*, a private publication issued by the National Institute for Economic and Social Research. And the weekly newspaper *The Economist* will keep the reader up-to-date with economic developments. For more general background reading, the reader might wish to refer to Shonfield, *British Economic Policy since the War*, published by Penguin Books; to *Growth in the British Economy* by Political & Economic Planning, published by George Allen & Unwin; to Worswick and Ady, *The British Economy in the Nineteen-fifties*, published by Blackwell; and to Dow, *Management of the British Economy*, 1945–60, (Cambridge University Press). Plans for future economic growth have been drawn up by the National Economic Development Council and embodied in its reports, which include *Conditions Favourable to Faster Growth* and *The Growth of the Economy*. In September 1965 *The National Plan* (Cmnd. 2764) was published, together with a brief outline for general readers entitled *Working for Prosperity*. The Department of Economic Affairs publishes a monthly *Progress Report*, available free of charge to the public.

III. DEVELOPMENTS IN THE BRITISH ECONOMY SINCE 1960.

1. INTERNATIONAL DEVELOPMENTS

The Balance of Payments to 1965.

The balance of payments has dominated events in the British economy since 1960. It is therefore important to analyse the balance of payments in some detail, both before the payments crisis of 1964, and during the crisis and its aftermath.

(i) The Current Account.

It is clear from the table that the deterioration in the current balance of payments of well over £400 million between 1959 and 1960 had two causes: a sharp increase in the deficit on visible trade, and a sharp reduction in the surplus on invisible trade. The increase in the deficit in visible trade was, in turn, mainly attributable to the increase of nearly £500 million in imports: exports also increased but not by enough to pay for the increased imports. As the price of imports hardly changed, the increased import bill reflects the import of a larger volume of goods than in any previous year. The main cause was the upsurge in demand and production in 1959–60. During the upsurge, productive capacity at home became strained, and some goods were imported to supplement home supplies. Stocks of imported goods were run down in 1959 and replenished in 1960. And higher incomes meant higher demands for imported goods. These developments might be interpreted as indicating the adverse effects on the balance of payments on internal expansion. No doubt imports will increase as the economy expands; but it can be argued that sudden and very rapid bursts of expansion, as in 1959–60, will have a much greater effect on imports than would a steadier and more sustained growth.

In the following two years, imports were steady at about the 1960 level—the internal economy was relatively stagnant, partly because restrictive measures (see below) had been adopted to curb demand at home and protect the balance of payments. Meanwhile there was a slow increase both in the prices and in the volume of goods imported. Imports were sharply up by over £250 million in 1963 with the rapid expansion of national expenditure, but there was a slightly larger increase in the value of exports.

The surplus on invisible trade, which had exceeded £300 million in the early and middle fifties, had declined to £120 million in 1960. There are several contributory factors in this decline: a rise in Government overseas expenditure, a fall in the net earnings of interest, profits, and dividends, and the emergence of a deficit in shipping services. Between 1960 and 1964 the surplus on invisible trade increased somewhat, but it is unlikely to return to its magnitude of the mid-fifties. It follows that if Britain is to earn a satisfactory current account surplus, it will have to earn a surplus on visible trade. In general it would be best to secure such a surplus through a faster increase in visible exports: but if a sufficient increase does not occur, it becomes necessary to restrict imports by tariffs or physical controls, or through a restriction of demand and output in the home economy. Note that even in the years when demand was held back, the current account surplus fell very far short of the £200–300 million which is considered desirable.

BALANCE OF PAYMENTS, 1959–65
(£ million)

	1959	1960	1961	1962	1963	1964	1965
Visible imports (f.o.b.)	3,638	4,137	4,041	4,092	4,366	5,006	5,044
Visible exports (f.o.b.)	3,522	3,733	3,892	3,994	4,287	4,471	4,779
Balance on visible trade	−116	−404	−149	−98	−79	−535	−265
Balance on invisible trade	+248	+131	+135	+191	+184	+129	+129
Current Balance of payments	+132	−273	−14	+93	+105	−406	−136
Balance on long-term capital transactions	−483	−185	+77	−93	−162	−363	−218
Balance on current account *plus* long-term capital transactions	−351	−458	+63	0	−57	−769	−354
Balance of monetary movements*	+366	+158	−39	−89	+125	+747	+249
Of which: change in sterling balances	+137	+397	−356	−23	+150	−6	−2
change in foreign exchange reserves	+119	−177	−31	+183	+53	+122	−246
change in IMF account with	−133	−151	+374	−379	+5	+359	+499

* A plus sign denotes a rise in liabilities or a fall in assets, and a minus sign a fall in liabilities and a rise in assets.

(ii) Flows of Long-term Capital.

The deficit on long-term capital, representing the excess of the amounts we lend, invest and reinvest abroad over the corresponding amounts lent, invested, and re-invested by foreigners in this country, is subject to abnormal fluctuations. Thus the deficit in 1959 was unusually large because it included the British subscription to the IMF (*see* **G11**), and became a small surplus in 1961 owing to receipts of a special nature. Allowing for such abnormal factors, however, the capital outflow was fairly stable over the period 1959–63 at £100–200 million per annum.

(iii) Monetary Movements.

Any deficit in long-term capital transactions, together with any deficit on current account, has to be financed either by increasing our short-term liabilities to foreigners, or by reductions in our assets. In 1960, £450 million had to be financed, but the imbalance on current *plus* capital account was very small in the following years until the crisis year of 1964. Oddly enough, the financing of the huge 1960 deficit did not raise any immediate problems, owing to a substantial inflow of short-term funds (*i.e.* additions to our short-term liabilities). The sterling balances of sterling area countries fell by over £200 million during 1960, but this fall was more than offset by an unprecedented increase of over £600 million in the sterling balances held by non-sterling area countries. The major cause of the inflow during the second half of the year was a speculation against the dollar, based on fears that it might be devalued. So great was the inflow that there was a curious combination of a very large *deficit* on current plus long-term capital account and a substantial *rise* in our reserves of gold and convertible currencies.

The dangers inherent in the financing of deficits through additions to short-term liabilities were vividly demonstrated the following year. Much of the funds which moved in during 1960 was moved out again before July 1961 in a wave of speculation against sterling. The outflow was financed partly by running down reserves of gold and convertible currencies by £280 million between end-1960 and July 1961, and partly through the Basle agreement under which European central banks undertook to build up short-term holdings in centres (London in this case) from which funds were being withdrawn. The rapid drain on the reserves had to be stopped; and the European central banks were not prepared to see their sterling holdings rise much higher. So in July 1961 a series of crises measures—including the raising of Bank Rate to 7 per cent—were taken, primarily to protect sterling. In addition, arrangements were made to withdraw over £500 million from the IMF (*see* **G11**) with provision for further credits if necessary. Partly for this reason, and partly because funds began to flow back into this country in the second half of the year, there was a modest increase in the reserves over 1961 as a whole. In 1962, speculative movements of funds were much less violent. Aided by a substantial improvement in the current balance of payments, Britain was able to complete repayment of its IMF drawing. These repayments did, however, involve a drain on the reserves; and this explains the substantial fall in the reserves over the year.

In order to increase the resources available to neutralise the massive movements of short-term funds which had so disrupted balance of payments in 1960 and 1961, the IMF initiated a scheme for a "lenders club." In December 1961 the participating countries—including most major Western trading nations—agreed to an arrangement whereby they undertook (subject to some control by lending countries over the use to be made of the funds) to make available loans totalling about £2,140 million to the IMF for re-lending to countries suffering an outflow of short-term funds.

The 1964 Crisis.

Imports in 1964 were some £640 million higher than in 1963, whereas exports were up by less than £200 million. The remarkable increase in the value of imports cannot be explained simply as a rise in import prices: imports increased by 15 per cent in value and by 11 per cent in volume. Nor can it be seen merely as a response to the expansion of the economy: if imports had done no more than rise in line with output, they would have increased in volume only by about 4 per cent. Part of the explanation lies in the fact that importers were stockbuilding after the depletion of raw material stocks during the boom of 1963. More important, however, is the fact that imports of manufactured goods rose by 28 per cent, or two-thirds of the total rise in import value. This leads us to the conclusion that home producers were losing ground in the British market to foreign competitors. In the same way, the disappointing performance of exports was due, not to lack of overseas demand—world trade in manufactures rose by about 15 per cent in 1964—but to the diminishing competitiveness of British products.

(i) Remedial Measures.

The timing of Government action on the balance of payments position was influenced by the General Election of mid-October. The out-going Government had been concerned with the impending Election, and argued that the deficit was abnormal and could be expected to improve without remedial action. On taking office, the new Government decided that immediate remedial action was necessary. Three courses were possible. It could devalue the pound and so improve the competitive position of British exports and import-substitutes (*see* **G10**). But a devaluation was seen to have disadvantages. The price of necessary imports would be increased and this would lower the British standard of living; the ensuing wage demands would make it more difficult to implement an Incomes Policy—which is an alternative method of improving the British competitive position in world markets (*see* **G39**). Furthermore, the devaluation of the pound might have necessitated the devaluation of other currencies including the dollar: this would have defeated the purpose of the devaluation. These real arguments against devaluation are not to be confused with the spurious argument that devaluation is somehow morally wrong. A second possible course of action was to reduce imports to a satisfactory level by the deflation of the economy. However, national income would have to fall by a multiple of the required cut in imports. Deflation was rejected because it would cause unemployment and because it was considered to provide only a short-term solution to Britain's economic problems: somehow the foreign imbalance had to be corrected without impeding the growth of output and productivity. A third course of action was to impose import controls or tariffs and export subsidies. Import controls were rejected: for one reason, it would take time to set up the necessary administrative machinery. So it was that the Government decided upon an additional import tariff and an export subsidy.

Within two weeks of coming to power, the Government announced its measures (which had in fact been investigated by the previous Chancellor). There was to be an immediate but temporary surcharge of 15 per cent on all imports of manufactures and semi-manufactures: the more necessary imports such as foodstuffs and basic raw materials were excluded. A new system of export rebates was introduced, representing the indirect taxes paid in Britain by British exporters, mainly duties on oil, petrol, and vehicle licenses. The value of the rebate averaged 1½ per cent of the value of exports. The import surcharge was critically received by the other EFTA members; it clashed with their objective of eliminating all tariffs by the end of 1966. In response to pressure from the EFTA countries, the Government announced that the import surcharge would be reduced by 5 per cent to 10 per cent in April 1965.

Some commentators have argued that Britain should direct its policies towards removing restraints on trade, by cutting tariffs within EFTA or GATT or even unilaterally: lowering tariff barriers will contribute to efficiency by subjecting British industries to stiffer competition. By contrast, it is also possible to argue that we should at times impose greater restraints on imports, so that economic growth can occur without being hampered by balance of payments difficulties. The Government defended its action to the GATT Council in terms of an article in the Treaty which allows Parties in balance of payments difficulties to resort to tariff restriction (*see* **G11**). Regrettably, the GATT Council declared the import surcharge a violation of the Treaty.

(ii) Speculation Against Sterling.

The long-term capital outflow in 1964 of £400 million was as remarkable as the deficit on current account. The outflow was due to an increase in private investment abroad; there was no increase in net Government lending. Part of the net private capital outflow in the first half of the year may have been abnormal and part in the second half of 1964 may have been related to the growing current account deficit: portfolio investment in this country was not an attractive proposition, and foreign firms tended to repatriate any funds available.

There was a net short-term capital inflow in the first half of 1964, which financed the growing overall deficit. The crisis arose in the second half of the year, when an outflow of short-term capital —a "flight of hot money"—took place in expectation that a British devaluation would be necessary to cure the worsening imbalance. To protect the reserves, the IMF granted Britain a stand-by credit of £330 million. However, once the feeling developed that the pound would have to be devalued, the process became cumulative: the greater the outflow the more likely it seemed that Britain would be forced to devalue. A great deal of sterling was offered for sale by speculators holding pounds—the "Gnomes of Zurich"—and by British exporters and foreign importers who would be requiring foreign currency in future. In order to prevent the price of sterling from falling below the official minimum limit to the exchange rate of £1 = $2.78 (*i.e.*, to "support sterling") the Bank of England was itself forced to buy pounds. To do this the Bank had to draw on the country's reserves of gold and foreign exchange. The vast drain on the reserves could not be allowed to continue, and in late November, Bank Rate was raised by 2 per cent to 7 per cent. The aim of this measure was to lure back short-term capital funds with the high rate of interest, and also to convince speculators that the pound would not be devalued. Speculators were not convinced, however, and the crisis continued. Two days later it was announced that an enormous loan totalling £1,070 million would be made available to Britain from all the leading Western central banks. This news was sufficient to slow down the speculative outflow, and by the close of 1964 the selling had come to an end.

After the Crisis.

Imports in 1965 were up on 1964 by only 1 per cent in value, this being entirely due to an increase in their volume. Thus imports increased a good deal more slowly than output in 1965. This was partly because the stockbuilding of 1964 had come to an end, and partly because the import surcharge held back imports of manufactured consumer goods. The value of exports was 7 per cent higher in 1965 than in 1964, and their volume 5 per cent higher. Thus the current deficit was more than halved, from the record of over £400 million in 1964 to less than £150 million in 1965. The deficit on long-term capital was also cut considerably. Nevertheless, an overall deficit amounting to £350 million in 1965 had to be financed by monetary movements.

The trade balance showed little improvement by mid-1965, and in the third quarter fear of devaluation led to yet another run on sterling, probably as severe as that of November 1964. The Government was again forced to draw on the IMF and to borrow from the United States Federal Reserve Bank. This time, however, the extent of speculation against the pound was successfully concealed. When the trade balance improved rapidly in the second half of 1965, the speculation died away.

In the course of 1964 and 1965, Britain borrowed over £1,000 million from the IMF and the Central Banks. This debt will have to be repaid over the next few years out of balance of payments surpluses. Some progress had been made in reducing the deficit by 1966; but the need to achieve a balance of payments surplus remains the dominant problem for the British Government.

Trading arrangements.

(i) Application for Membership of the Common Market.

In mid-1961 it was announced that Britain would apply for full membership of the European Economic Community, otherwise known as the Common Market. The European Economic Community (EEC) consists of six full members—Belgium, France, Holland, Italy, Luxembourg, and West Germany. The full members ratified the Treaty of Rome in 1958. The Treaty provides for the progressive elimination of tariffs on trade between members, a common agricultural and commercial policy, a common external tariff on goods imported into the Community, and some integration of fiscal and monetary policies. Britain had participated in the negotiations which led up to the Treaty, and had argued in favour of a looser "free trade area" without a common external tariff, and excluding trade in agricultural products. No compromise acceptable to the six countries which favoured a tighter economic union was found, and Britain joined with six other European countries—Austria, Denmark, Norway, Portugal, Sweden and Switzerland—in forming the European Free Trade Area (EFTA).

Later, however, when the Common Market proved to be highly successful in terms of the growth of production and trade, the British Government decided to apply for membership. There were three main problems to be solved in the negotiations. The first two—the trading links with Commonwealth countries, and the position of British agriculture—were those which had influenced the British attitude in the earlier negotiations. Now Britain also had obligations to her trading partners in EFTA. The Common Market countries welcomed the British application, but made it clear that renewed negotiations must take place within the framework of the Treaty.

(ii) The British Proposals.

The British delegation made the following proposals for the solution of Britain's special problems. For British *agriculture* there was to be a long "transition period"—that is to say, a period for adjustment before British agriculture became fully integrated into the Common Market agricultural arrangements—possibly 12 to 15 years from the date of joining the Common Market. By contrast, it was not proposed to negotiate for favourable conditions for British *industry*: on joining the Common Market, Britain was prepared to make a reduction in her tariffs equivalent to the reductions which had already been made by the Six.

Two lines of approach were suggested for protecting the trading positions of the underdeveloped countries of the Commonwealth. One involved granting those countries the status of "associated territories" which would give their products access to European markets on preferential terms. There was a precedent for this sort of arrangement, in that France had already negotiated associated status for some of her former colonies in Africa. But it was recognised that the Six might not be prepared to offer associated status to some of the larger underdeveloped countries of the Commonwealth—*e.g.*, India, and that some countries might wish to reject an offer of associated status for political reasons. As an alternative, therefore, it was suggested that the Common Market external tariff on some of the more important agricultural exports from these countries—*e.g.*, Indian tea—should be reduced or eliminated; and that arrangements should be made to ensure that the external tariff on manufactured goods exported from these countries—*e.g.*, textiles from Hong Kong—did not lead to a reduction of such exports. For the more developed countries of the Commonwealth, there were proposals that the Common Market external tariff on raw material imports should be reduced or eliminated for certain Commonwealth produced materials, such as aluminium, zinc, and woodpulp. It was also proposed that certain arrangements should be made with respect to foodstuffs—chiefly wheat, meat and dairy products—produced by developed members of the Commonwealth. The principle underlying these arrangements, it was suggested, should be that Commonwealth producers " be given in the future the opportunity for outlets for their products comparable to those they now enjoy."

(iii) **The Negotiations.**

In the course of prolonged negotiations, considerable progress towards a final agreement was gradually made: progress in reducing tariffs important in Commonwealth trade, in agreeing that Commonwealth countries in Africa and the West Indies should be offered associated status on the same terms as the ex-French territories, and in agreeing that the problems of India, Pakistan and Ceylon could best be solved by trade treaties negotiated between the Common Market and these countries. The problem of temperate foodstuffs proved the most intractable. Britain wanted specific arrangements to ensure that Commonwealth-produced temperate foods would be able to find markets in Europe, at least in the short term. France made it clear that she envisaged a reduction of food imports into Common Market countries, to permit an expansion of her agricultural output: this point of view was clearly incompatible with the British proposal for " comparable outlets " for Commonwealth producers. Nor was there agreement on the transitional arrangements for British agriculture.

Nevertheless, it was the opinion of many observers that by January 1963 the stage had been set for a final round of bargaining, and that given good-will on both sides Britain's entry could have been assured. It therefore came as a surprise when France decided that the negotiations should be broken off. Despite opposition from the other five, a French veto was imposed on the British application. Perhaps the fundamental reason for the breakdown can be inferred from a statement attributed to General de Gaulle: " The Europe I prefer is the Europe of the Six." That may be the final word for the present, but this issue could well recur in the future.

Britain and the Developing Countries.

(i) **Trade.**

An important international event of 1964 was the United Nations Conference on Trade and Development (UNCTAD), held in Geneva. It was convened to discuss the problems arising from the sluggish demand for primary products exported by the underdeveloped countries to the developed countries, and the consequent falling prices of these products (*see* **G12**). Primary commodities exported by developing countries—such as coffee, tea, cocoa, sugar, wool, cotton, jute, rubber, and mineral ores—decreased in price on average by about 16 per cent over the period 1957–62.

For the first time the poorer nations of the world —77 were represented—came together to act as a pressure group on trading matters. The Conference made the following recommendations. Developing countries should be given freer access to world markets for their manufactures and semi-manufactures by the elimination of quotas and tariffs. International commodity agreements should be made for each major primary commodity in world trade, to stabilise commodity prices. Compensation schemes—whereby countries are compensated for the declining prices of their primary products—were recommended for consideration. The Conference resolved that UNCTAD should meet regularly in future and that it should be serviced by a new permanent Trade Secretariat of the United Nations.

(ii) **Aid.**

The gap between the living standards of the underdeveloped areas of the world and of the countries already highly industrialised has tended to widen in the past few years. It was through a growing world recognition of this situation that the 1960s have been designated " The United Nations Development Decade." World inequalities have increased despite a larger flow of economic assistance from the richer to the poorer nations. The total net flow of financial resources from Western industrial countries to the developing world was over £3,300 million in 1964. Roughly £800 million of this was net private investment, and over £2,500 million official government aid. But whereas total aid increased rapidly in the 1950s, the increase has not continued in the 1960s: total aid in 1964 was no higher than the estimate for 1961. More than half of the official Government aid in 1964 was contributed by the United States; the other principal donors being France, West Germany, and Britain in that order. The figures for " aid " can be misleading, however, since part of some countries' contributions is political rather than economic in nature.

The table shows how British economic aid to underdeveloped countries has increased in recent years. It was fairly constant before 1957–58 but more than doubled to £189 million in the seven years following 1957–58. Aid per capita of the British population nearly tripled, and amounted to £3 10*s*. per head in 1964–65. However, when aid is expressed as a percentage of the Gross National Product, we see that the percentage increase from 0·42 of one per cent in 1957–58 to 0·67 of one per cent in 1960–61 and has since remained at that level. To be just one per cent of G.N.P., aid would have to be raised by about £100 million. Aid may be divided into multilateral aid and bilateral aid. Multilateral aid is given through the medium of the international institutions, such as the International Bank (IBRD) and the International Development Authority (IDA) (*see* **G11**); bilateral aid is given directly to the developing countries. Multilateral aid was still only £18 million in 1964–65. The increase in aid since 1957–58 had taken place in bilateral aid. Whereas loans were fairly negligible in 1957–58, they increased rapidly, and exceeded grants in 1963–64. It must be remembered in deciding the terms on which Government aid is provided, that the foreign indebtedness of the developing countries is increasing sharply. About four-fifth of British loans is made available for 20 years or more. Normally the rate of interest on these loans is the rate at which the

BRITISH GOVERNMENT AID, 1957–58 TO 1964–65

	Total aid			Multi-lateral aid £m	Bilateral aid		
	£m	per capita £	as a percentage of G.N.P. %		Total £m	Grants £m	Loans £m
1957–58	81	1·6	0·42	19	62	50	12
1958–59	109	2·1	0·54	24	85	48	37
1959–60	130	2·5	0·61	20	110	54	56
1960–61	151	2·9	0·67	21	130	60	70
1961–62	160	3·0	0·66	6	154	80	74
1962–63	148	2·8	0·59	10	138	70	68
1963–64	175	3·3	0·66	17	158	71	87
1964–65	189	3·5	0·67	18	172	87	85

British Government can borrow on the capital market. However, the Government decided in 1965 to make development loans free of interest in appropriate cases. About a third of expenditure on aid is formally tied to the purchase of British goods and services. Other aid is not tied formally, and may be used to finance local expenditure; but when it is used to finance imports directly, it has to be spent on British goods if these are available on competitive terms. Multilateral aid is untied. The tying of aid tends to raise the costs to developing countries; but it also enables countries with precarious foreign balances —such as Britain—to be more generous.

Aid takes the form not only of financial but also of technical assistance; underdeveloped countries lack skilled experts, administrators and teachers as well as capital resources. To co-ordinate and promote technical assistance the Department of Technical Co-operation (DTC) was set up in 1961. British Government expenditure on technical assistance amounted to £25 million in 1963–64. At the end of 1964, British technical assistance personnel overseas totalled altogether 13 thousand (excluding volunteers recruited by voluntary societies): over 5 thousand administrators, 2·5 thousand teachers, 1·3 thousand agricultural advisers, 1·5 thousand industrial and technological advisers, and a thousand doctors and medical workers.

In the past decisions on aid were made separately by a number of Government bodies—the Treasury, the DTC, the Colonial Office, Commonwealth Relations Office, Foreign Office, and so on. In October 1964 the incoming Government established an Overseas Development Ministry (ODM), through which all British aid is now channelled and co-ordinated. With a voice in the Cabinet, the new Ministry should be more effective in pressing for aid to the developing countries than has been the case in the past. The amount of aid which ought to be provided has become a political issue in some countries such as the United States; thankfully this has not occurred in Britain.

2. INTERNAL DEVELOPMENTS

Industrial Output and Employment.

In the third quarter of 1965 industrial production was 31 per cent higher than it had been in 1958. This expansion occurred largely in two spurts: during the twelve months between March 1959 and March 1960 industrial output increased by 11 per cent, and between March 1963 and March 1964 it rose by 14 per cent. The three years before March 1959 and the three years between the booms were periods of industrial stagnation. The table also indicates that the numbers employed in industry were only 4 per cent higher near the end of 1965 (allowing for seasonal variation) than in 1958, so that productivity—output per person employed—rose by about 26 per cent over the period. Here again, a very high proportion of the increase was secured in the boom periods.

INDUSTRIAL PRODUCTION, EMPLOYMENT AND PRODUCTIVITY, 1959–65]

(Quarterly averages of seasonally adjusted index numbers, 1958 × 100)

Year	Quarter	Industrial production (1)	Employment in industry (2)	Productivity in industry 100 × (1) ÷ (2)
1959 . .	I	102	100	102
1960 . .	I	112	102	110
1961 . .	I	114	104	109
1962 . .	I	114	104	110
1963 . .	I	113	101	112
1964 . .	I	127	103	123
1965 . .	I	132	104	127
1965 . .	III	131	104	126

Restriction and De-restriction.

The early years of the 1960s have witnessed several changes in the emphasis of Government monetary and fiscal policies. In the first half of 1960 the emphasis was on restrictive policies, both because of the deterioration in the balance of payments position, and because it was apparent that the very rapid expansion of output had created severe strains in the economy at home. No doubt there would have been a slowing down in the rate of growth of output even if restrictive measures had not been taken: an increase as rapid as that in 1959 was possible only because a substantial excess capacity had developed over the preceding years. But the measures taken to restrict demand reinforced this tendency, and growth in industrial output was halted.

A relaxation of restraints did help to stimulate some increase in output in the early months of 1961. But from July 1961—again primarily for balance of payments reasons—there was a phase of even sterner restrictions. The progressive relaxation of restrictions during the summer of 1962, coupled with measures designed to stimulate industrial output, had not had any major effect by the end of the year.

In some ways, the situation early in 1963 was analogous to that of early 1959. There was a substantial under-utilisation of capacity in many branches of industry, since new investment had continued in 1960–62. Labour resources for expansion were available, in that unemployment was higher than at any period since the war. Consequently the expansionist policies of 1963 helped to produce a year of boom which saw a spurt of industrial output, and a substantial increase in productivity. This progress could not be maintained in 1964, when industrial production and productivity flattened out, and the balance of payments deteriorated. However, the 1960 remedy of deflation was not repeated; it was now realised that "stop-go" policies were harmful to the growth of the economy, and that the balance of payments problem would have to be solved by other measures. But although full employment was maintained between 1964 I and 1965 III, industrial production per man rose at less than 2 per cent per annum over this period. Some commentators have attributed this slow growth in productivity to a decline in the average length of working week: output per *man-hour* increased more rapidly.

Regional Economic Problems.

(i) Regional Unemployment.

Much publicity has been given in the 1960s to the varying degrees of prosperity and levels of unemployment in different regions of the country. In February 1963—during a period of recession—the percentage of all workers unemployed in Great Britain was 3·9. But the table shows that a lower proportion of the labour force was unemployed in the Midlands and the South, and that there was a much higher percentage of unemployment in the North, in Scotland and in Northern Ireland. Furthermore the boom conditions of early 1964 or the labour shortages of early 1965 or 1966, were not shared equally: unemployment remained significant in these areas.

One of the main reasons for the regional pattern of unemployment is that certain industries and services in which big changes have been taking

PERCENTAGE OF WORKERS UNEMPLOYED, BY REGIONS

	February 1963	February 1964	February 1965	February 1966
London and South-Eastern	2·3	1·3	1·0	0·9
Eastern and Southern	3·6	1·4	1·2	1·1
South-Western	3·8	2·0	1·8	1·9
Midlands	3·4	1·2	0·8	0·8
Yorkshire and Lincolnshire	3·3	1·6	1·2	1·1
North-Western	4·1	2·5	1·8	1·4
Northern	7·1	4·1	3·1	2·8
Scotland	6·2	4·5	3·6	3·0
Wales	6·0	2·9	2·8	3·0
Northern Ireland	11·2	7·9	6·9	6·3
Great Britain	3·9	2·0	1·6	1·5

DECREASE IN EMPLOYMENT IN SELECTED INDUSTRIES, 1954–65

	Thousands	Per cent
Textiles	224	23
Mining and quarrying	242	28
Shipbuilding	77	27
Agriculture, forestry, and fishing	221	21

place, tend to be grouped in specific regions. Most of our early industrial centres had to be established close to coal, iron ore, and adequate water supplies. But employment in many long-established industries has recently been declining. The scale of this contraction can be seen from the table. On the other hand, new and growing industries, and their related offices, have been concentrated in Greater London, the South East, and the Midlands. The growth of services, too, has centred on the areas where industry is booming and population is increasing. In the absence of Government intervention, the process would tend to become cumulative, and regional inequalities would grow rather than diminish.

(ii) Regional Planning.

There are essentially two ways of tackling the problem of regional imbalances: taking jobs to the people or bringing people to the jobs. Insofar as the latter alternative is chosen, the Government should encourage the mobility of labour, *e.g.*, through retraining schemes or a housing subsidy. However, the migration of population may damage community life in the denuded areas, and cause congestion, housing shortages and overcrowding in the booming regions. The Government can create employment opportunities in the relatively depressed regions in various ways. It can try to induce expanding industries to set up new plants in these regions by offering tax incentives (*see* **G41 and G42**); it can authorise additional expenditure on public works—*e.g.*, by accelerating road-building programmes—to provide additional employment; it can place orders for the goods it needs—*e.g.*, defence contracts—where work is required. General measures to expand the economy are necessary; but they must be supplemented by more specific measures to reduce regional imbalances.

Under the Conservative Government, development plans involving high rates of public investment were prepared for the depressed areas Central Scotland and North-East England. A plan was also made for the congested South-East; the Government's *South-East Study*, published in 1964, argued that "so far as the basic problem is concerned, there is little choice; large population increases in the South-East are inevitable." The Study proposed a long-range plan for new cities and substantial expansion of existing towns, so as to contain the expansion of London itself.

On taking office in October 1964, the Labour Government made regional planning the responsibility of its Department of Economic Affairs. Britain was divided into 8 regions, with the intention of producing a regional plan for each area. The Government also established two kinds of planning body: regional economic planning Councils and Boards to advise on and co-ordinate the planning of each region. It was Government policy to even up regional imbalances; *e.g.*, the measures announced in July 1965 to defer public construction programmes and control private construction excluded the "development districts." Moreover, office building in London and Birmingham was strictly limited.

Planning for Faster Growth.

There has been an increasing dissatisfaction with the rate of growth achieved in this economy over the past decade or so. The economies of most Common Market countries have increased their industrial output at a much faster rate. Furthermore, there has been dissatisfaction with the way in which the economy has grown: the characteristic pattern has been one of sharp bursts of expansion interrupted by rather lengthy periods of stagnation.

(i) The National Economic Development Council.

To stimulate a more systematic study of the problems involved in securing a faster and more even rate of growth in the British economy, the Conservative Government established the National Economic Development Council (NEDC or "Neddy"). The two-tier organisation was similar to that of the corresponding planning council in France. The Council itself consisted of representatives from the T.U.C. and employers' organisations, Government ministers and independent members, and it was served by a group of experts. This group undertook research into the problems of securing a faster rate of growth, into the means of overcoming obstacles to growth, and into the economic policies which could be most conducive to faster growth.

In its first report, in 1963, the Council made a projection for the economy. It adopted a target rate of growth of output over the period 1961–66 equal to 4 per cent per annum, which was substantially faster than the rate of growth actually achieved in previous years. It attempted to predict how investment, exports, imports, consumption, and the output of each industry would have to grow if the target rate of growth was to be achieved. The merit of this exercise was twofold: it helped to focus Government attention on the long-term, by showing that policies designed to solve short-term difficulties might intensify the problem of raising long-term economic growth and, by bolstering expectations, it encouraged firms to invest.

A particularly interesting feature of the work of the NEDC is its study of individual industries. Seventeen major industries were surveyed detail to assess the changes in output, employment, productivity, investment and exports which were feasible in each industry. Economic Development Committees—which have come to be known as "little Neddies"—were established as part of the NEDC machinery to report on the problems of individual industries. It is impossible for an individual firm or industry to make correct decisions on future expansion without knowing how the rest of the economy will behave; by relating planning at the national level and planning at the level of individual industries the NEDC did valuable work.

Economic projections might be worthless, however, if the correct policies from growth are not pursued. Conscious of this limitation, the NEDC turned in its second report to a consideration of the conditions and policies favourable to faster growth.

(ii) The Department of Economic Affairs.

In October 1964, the incoming Government established a new Department of Economic Affairs (DEA). While short-term measures to regulate the economy or the balance of payments remained the responsibility of the Treasury, the DEA took over from the Treasury the responsibility for long-term economic policy. The DEA was charged with the task of preparing and implementing a realistic plan for economic expansion. The NEDC, now reconstituted, lost its function of making the national plan, and appears to have become a consultative and advisory body: a link between the Government and the economic community. An industrial division of the DEA was formed to work closely with the "little Neddies." Also co-operating with the "little Neddies" were a number of working parties set up by the new Ministry of Technology, to consider the application of modern technology in particular industries.

(iii) The National Plan.

The National Plan for the British economy over the period 1964–70 was published by the Government in 1965. The Plan is based on the assumption that output will rise by 3·8 per cent per annum over the period. Since the labour force is expected to grow at 0·4 per cent per annum, this means an annual growth in productivity of 3·5 per cent—considerably higher than the 2·7 per cent average over the period 1960–64. The increase in utput, and the need to increase productivity, will involve a substantial expansion in investment expenditures. The Plan requires an increase in industrial investment of 7·0 per cent and in total investment of 5·5 per cent per annum. Expenditure by consumers will have to rise more slowly—by 3·2 per cent per annum at constant prices—but even this is higher than the corresponding increase for 1960–64 of 3·1 per cent per annum. Thus the Plan does not call for "austerity"—with output increasing more rapidly, more goods and services will be available both for investment and for consumption expenditures.

In many ways, the crucial assumptions are those concerned with the balance of payments. The Plan supposes that imports will increase by 4·0 per cent per annum, and that to achieve a "satisfactory" surplus of £250 million on the overall balance of payments in 1970, exports will have to rise by 5·6 per cent per annum. If such a rapid expansion of exports is not achieved—and in the period 1960–64 the annual increase averaged only 3·1 per cent—the whole Plan could be jeopardised, and the balance of payment difficulties might, as in the past, appear to justify policies to restrict the growth in domestic output. Unlike the NEDC reports, the Plan is a full statement of Government policy.

Wages and Prices.

Retail prices have continued to edge upwards in the early years of the 1960s: in 1965 they were 21 per cent higher than in 1958. The table shows that hardly any of this increase can be attributed to an increase in import prices. To explain the inflation we must look to the behaviour of labour costs. Between 1958 and 1965 the nationally negotiated weekly wage rates rose by 29 per cent, and weekly earnings—including overtime payments and payments negotiated on the factory—by 47 per cent. Since the increase in productivity over the period was slow, income from employment per unit of output (indicating labour costs per unit of output) rose by 23 per cent.

One of the main dangers of this inflation of costs and prices is that exporters will find it more difficult to compete in foreign markets. The table shows that export prices in fact increased slowly. But this may well imply that producers were having to accept lower profit margins on exports than on sales in the home market; and this would not encourage producers to push their sales in overseas markets.

PRICES AND WAGES, 1958–65
(Index numbers, 1958 = 100)

	Retail prices	Import prices	Export prices	Weekly wage rates	Weekly earnings	Income from employment per unit of output
1959	101	99	99	103	105	100
1960	102	99	101	105	112	102
1961	105	97	101	110	118	109
1962	110	96	102	114	123	113
1963	112	100	105	118	128	115
1964	115	104	107	123	136	117
1965	121	104	109	129	147	123

Incomes Policy.

Britain's competitive position in world trade has deteriorated relative to that of her main rivals, the United States, West Germany and France; hence her balance of payments difficulties. The British share in total world exports of manufactures fell from 17·2 per cent to 13·2 per cent between 1959 and 1965. There are essentially two methods of remedying this situation. We must secure either a relative fall in the external value of the pound, or a relative rise in its internal value. In other words, either there must be a devaluation of the pound in terms of other currencies, or we must have a policy to limit the increase in the British price-level. In the 1960s efforts have been made, and are still being made, to introduce some form of "incomes policy" which will restrain increases in wages and other incomes, and so prevent inflation.

(i) The Pay Pause.

In July 1961 the Chancellor of the Exchequer called for a "pause" in wages, salaries, and dividend payments. Exhortations for restraint have been a familiar feature of ministerial statements for many years, but on this occasion the Government soon made it clear that it intended to use such power as it has to influence the amount and timing of wage and salary awards. It has power to decide when the pay awards recommended by the Wages Councils—which fix minimum wages for 3½ million workers—shall be implemented. The Government's power is strongest over workers which it directly or indirectly employs, *e.g.*, civil servants, teachers, and Post Office workers. Their pay awards were cut back. The Government also had a limited influence on awards made in nationalised industries.

The "pay pause" came to an end in April 1962. It was envisaged as a temporary policy, and its effects are difficult to assess. It certainly postponed some wage awards which would otherwise have been made in that period, and it may have contributed to a stiffening of resistance to wage claims. But this was achieved at the cost of some interference with established bargaining machinery; and, because the pause affected some groups of people more severely than others this form of incomes policy was seen to be discriminatory.

(ii) "The Next Step."

In February 1962 the Government issued a White Paper called *Incomes Policy: The Next Step* which outlined its incomes policy for the period after the pause. It stated that "the objective must be to keep the rate of increase in incomes within the long-term rate of growth of national production. In recent years national production has risen by about 2 to 2½ per cent a year. We ought to be able to do better than this, but on present trends it seems likely to increase at about this rate in 1962. It is accordingly necessary that the increase of wages and salaries, as of other incomes, should be kept within this figure during the next phase." The Government stressed that most of the arguments which had in the past been advanced in justification of wage and salary claims—for example, increases in the cost of living, trends in productivity or profits in particular industries, and comparisons with levels or trends in other employments—should be given less weight; and that "general economic considerations"—*i.e.*, the increases which the economy can afford given the prospective rate of increase in national production—should be given more weight. The document did not indicate how this policy would be implemented.

(iii) The National Incomes Commission.

Late in 1962 the Government set up the National Incomes Commission (NIC). However, the powers of this body were limited. It could not participate in, nor comment upon, wage claims while negotiations were in progress unless the parties involved consented; and as the T.U.C. did not intend to co-operate with the Commission, such consent was unlikely. It could be asked to report on inflationary settlements which had been reached (unless the settlement was reached by arbitration); but it had no power to cancel or modify an agreement. It could be asked to comment in advance on wage claims in the public sector (but not in nationalised industries), and even then only if the claims were not referred to other forms of arbitration. It could be asked to comment on profit levels.

It was curious that the Government's permissible rate of increase in money incomes (2–2½ per cent) was less than the rate of productivity increase written into the NEDC reports. It is not surprising then, that the Chancellor, in his 1963 Budget, announced a new "guiding light" of 3–3½ per cent per annum, on which NIC should base its recommendations. The fourth and final report of the Commission in February 1965 was perhaps the most interesting: NIC examined agreements in the engineering and shipbuilding industries, and found that these industries provide classic examples of "wage drift." Wage drift arises when there is an increase in the gap between wages at nationally determined rates and actual earnings (*see* **G22**). It is a phenomenon common to many industries, particularly when labour is scarce and employers have to compete with each other for labour. Wage drift may occur because of increased overtime or higher earnings on piece-rates; in these cases earnings are matched by some increase in productivity. When it results from local bargaining between managers and shop-stewards—for bonuses, merit money, and so on—wage drift need not be accompanied by increased output. NIC argued that the two sources of increased earnings—increases in nationally determined rates and wage drift—must be considered together, in the context of an incomes policy. The Commission concluded that the settlements were contrary to the national interest because they failed to take account of the average rise in earnings that had occurred as a result of wage drift.

(iv) The National Board for Prices and Incomes.

In October 1964 the Labour Government's new Department of Economic Affairs was made responsible for achieving an incomes policy. The lessons of the past had been learned; the Government recognised that a successful incomes policy would require the support of both sides of industry. Its first objective was to achieve a "Joint Statement of Intent on productivity, prices, and incomes"; this was signed in December 1964. In this document the T.U.C. and the employers' organisations undertook to co-operate with the Government in producing an effective machinery for the implementing of an incomes policy. In February 1965, the Government explained this machinery in a White Paper. There already existed a national body representing Management, Unions, and Government—NEDC. Accordingly the NEDC was given a new function: to carry out general reviews of price and income behaviour, to review the reports submitted to it, and to consider their implications for the national interest. The parties represented on the NEDC would then be expected to act in accordance with its reviews.

It was Government policy that growth in earnings per employee should equal the planned growth in national output per employee of 3–3½ per cent per annum. Thus, in those industries (*e.g.* engineering) in which productivity growth exceeds this "norm," earnings should rise less rapidly than productivity, and in those industries (*e.g.* railways) in which productivity growth falls short of the norm, earning could rise more rapidly than productivity. Moreover, prices would be expected to fall in industries such as engineering and permitted to rise in industries such as railways. Growth in earnings per employee should exceed the norm only in exceptional cases; *i.e.* as a reward for increasing productivity by eliminating restrictive working practices; if necessary to transfer labour from one industry to another if earnings are too low to maintain a reasonable standard of living; or if a group of workers have fallen seriously out of line with earnings fo[r] similar work.

To make specific recommendations on the basi[s] of this policy, the Government set up a Nationa[l] Board for Prices and Incomes. It consists of a[n] independent Chairman, a number of independen[t] experts, a businessman and a trade unionist. Th[e] Prices Review Division of the Board can investigate the price of any goods in the economy, an[d] the Incomes Review Division has power to investigate all claims and settlements relating t[o] wages, salaries and other incomes. In less tha[n] a year of operation the Board had produced [a] dozen reports on prices of printing, bread, soap, coal and electricity, and earnings in the electricit[y] industry, civil service, railways, armed forces, etc.

There is no statutory authority to enforce th[e] recommendations of the Board: reliance is place[d] on voluntary methods and the power of persuasio[n] and public opinion. However, the Governmen[t] outlined a compulsory "Early Warning" syste[m] in late 1965, whereby it will be notified in advanc[e] of any intended increase in incomes and in certai[n] prices. What this becomes law, the Board wi[ll] have enough time to consider increases before the[y] are put into effect. A voluntary Incomes Polic[y] depends on co-operation among Governmen[t,] workers and employers. It remains to be see[n] whether co-operation will last, and whether co-operation among representatives at the top wi[ll] be undermined by "wage drift" at the factor[y] level.

Restrictive Practices.

The Restrictive Trade Practices Act of 19[5?] prohibited collective boycotts for the enforceme[nt] of resale price maintenance (r.p.m.), but it also permitted individual manufacturers to enforce r.p.m. for their own products (*see* **G17**). Few suppliers would want the publicity of enforcing r.p.m. through the courts, but individual suppliers could still put some commercial pressure on price-cutters, *e.g.*, by offering less favourable terms or by refusing them supplies. The Resale Prices Act of 1964 prohibited all methods of enforcing minimum resale prices. However, goods which had been registered in due time with the Registrar of restrictive trading agreements or have been approved by the Restrictive Practices Court, were exempted, temporarily in the former case and permanently in the latter. For r.p.m. to be approved by the Court, it must be shown that some ensuing benefit to consumers (*e.g.*, of increased quality or more retail outlets) outweighed any detriment. It is also lawful to withhold supplies to retailers selling goods at a loss to attract customers. The list of applications for exemption is a long one, but the effect of the Act should be lower prices in the shops. It will also mean a more rapid decline of small retailers.

The Monopolies and Mergers Act of 1965 strengthened control over monopolies and mergers. With regard to monopolies, the Government wished to provide itself with legal powers of enforcement: previously monopolies had been expected to comply voluntarily with the findings of the Monopolies Commission. The Act also permits the Government to refer a merger or a proposed merger to the Monopolies Commission, in cases where the merger would lead to monopoly (defined as control of at least one third of the market) or would increase the power of an existing monopoly, or where the value of the assets taken over exceeds £5 million. But it would be wrong to presume that mergers are always bad: it is possible that mergers—by facilitating research and other economies of large-scale operation—will increase industrial efficiency. For this reason the Government proposed in 1966 to establish an Industrial Reorganisation Corporation to promote the grouping of firms in cases where such grouping would be beneficial to their industry.

Restrictive labour practices—which result in the "over-manning" of plant or the "under-employment" of men—are common in British industry. These stem from such causes as the fear of redundancy and unemployment, anxiety to preserve a craft skill threatened by technical progress, the desire to work at overtime rates, and sometimes just inertia. In the fully-employed economy of the 1960s, redundancy should not be a problem, and under-employed labour is urgently needed elsewhere. The elimination of these restrictive practices requires more enlightened management, more union co-operation, and more Government measures to promote the mobility of labour between occupations.

Monetary and Fiscal Policies since 1960.

There is probably no country in the world which has made fuller use than Britain of budgetary policy as a means of stabilising the economy. Since 1941, almost all adjustments to the total level of taxation have been made with the object of reducing an excess in total demand or of repairing a deficit. Whereas in the United States there is still a public clamour for "balanced budgets," British Governments have accepted Keynesian principles—first laid down by Lord Keynes—for managing the economy by adjusting the level of taxation and private saving relative to public expenditure and private investment. This does not mean to say that British policies have always been successful. Apart from the difficulty of deciding when demand is excessive or deficient, there are the difficulties that data are available only with a serious time-lag, and may be inaccurate; that economic events cannot be predicted with any certainty; and that the quantitative effects of Government measures are not easy to estimate.

1960.

In the first half of 1960 there were a series of restrictive measures designed to curb the increase in home demand and to improve the balance of payments position. Bank Rate was raised from 4 to 6 per cent. To exert pressure on the banks' liquidity positions, and so help to curb bank advances, the banks were called upon to place special deposits (*see* **G28**) with the Bank of England. Restrictions on hire purchase transactions were also imposed. Furthermore, the 1960 Budget was restrictive: the Chancellor estimated an overall deficit (*see* **G33**) for 1960–61 of only £318 million.

1961.

By contrast the Budget of April 1961 was sternly anti-inflationary in that the estimated overall deficit was reduced to a mere £69 million. Profits tax and some indirect taxes were increased, but there was a major reduction in surtax. In addition, the Chancellor was granted powers to introduce, if he considered it necessary, an economic "regulator": a surcharge on, or rebate of, indirect taxes by up to 10 per cent. This power provides greater scope for using fiscal measures to influence the economy in the periods between Budgets.

In July 1961 the Chancellor introduced a collection of restrictive measures. These measures were primarily intended to ease the critical foreign exchange situation but they were not without effect on the domestic economy. Bank Rate was raised from 5 to 7 per cent. To restrict the growth in home demand, the Chancellor imposed a 10 per cent surcharge in indirect taxation and called the banks to increase their special deposits at the Bank of England. Furthermore, the Chancellor announced that he aimed to restrict the increase in Government spending (at constant prices) in 1962–63 to 2½ per cent; and proposed a "pay pause." Not only was the outflow of funds stopped, but it was actually reversed. These measures were all too successful in restricting demand at home: there was a fall in industrial production in the second half of 1961.

1962.

The 1962 Budget was, however, no less restrictive in intention than the 1961 Budget. The estimated overall deficit, at £74 million, was virtually unchanged. The Chancellor withdrew the 10 per cent surcharge on all indirect taxes, but made changes in indirect tax rates so that the revenue from indirect taxes would not be reduced. In addition, there was a move towards uniformity of purchase tax rates. The main novelty of the 1962 Budget was a tax on speculative gains. If stocks and shares are bought and sold within a period of 6 months, any gain or profit on the transaction is now taxed as income. So is any gain or profit on purchases and sales of land and buildings (but excluding any gain from the sale of a house occupied by the owner) within a period of 3 years. These capital gains had not previously been subject to tax in this country.

From the summer of 1962 onwards, changes in monetary and fiscal policies were designed to stimulate economic activity. Bank Rate was reduced to 4 per cent, all special deposits held by the Bank of England were released, qualitative restraints on bank lending were abolished, £42 million of post-war credits were released, investment allowance for industry was increased, and the purchase tax on cars was reduced to 25 per cent.

1963.

January 1963 saw further reduction in purchase taxes, and a very considerable increase in social security payments. In the April Budget the estimated overall deficit for 1963–64 of £687 million was more than £600 million greater than that of the previous year. Tax reliefs amounting to £269 million for 1963–64 were announced. The most important benefits to individuals were derived from increases in the allowances which can be charged against income before income tax is levied. In addition, Schedule A taxes were abolished for owner-occupiers. Other changes in taxation were designed to stimulate investment spending by companies: depreciation allowances were increased for tax purposes, and companies investing in areas of high employment were permitted to charge depreciation on their assets at a rate of their own choosing. The 1963 Budget was designed to provide a fiscal boost to the economy, and in this it succeeded. National output rose by more than 5 per cent over the year, and continued to increase in the new year.

1964.

By 1964 the economy was beginning to show signs of strain, and the trade figures revealed a rapid deterioration in the balance of visible trade. The Chancellor's objective in his April budget was to slow down the rate of growth without producing deflation. He planned an overall deficit of £791 million, but provided for additional taxation amounting to £103 million. This was to be secured by increasing the duties on tobacco and alcoholic drinks by about 10 per cent.

Consumption expenditure was stagnant in the first half of 1964. However, both consumption expenditure and industrial production jumped sharply towards the end of 1964, and there were reports of a growing labour shortage. The balance of payments was heavily in deficit throughout the year. Nothing was done about it, however, until after the General Election in October. In November the Chancellor of the Exchequer presented a "little budget," aimed partly at reducing excess demand in the economy and partly at providing increased social security benefits. Petrol duties were increased immediately by 6*d*. a gallon. The following measures were to take effect from April 1965: an increase of 6*d*. in the £ in the standard rate of income tax, an increase in National Insurance contributions and payments, and a rise in pensions. Old-age pensions were increased by 12*s*. 6*d*. to £4 for a single retired person and by 21*s*. to £6. 10*s*. a week for married couples. During the sterling crisis of November (*see* **G34**) Bank Rate was raised to 7 per cent to stem the outflow of funds, but this was not accompanied by a " credit squeeze " to restrict productive investment, as in the crisis of 1961. Unlike some of his predecessors, the Chancellor had not opted for deflation as the cure for the balance of payments deficit. Instead, reliance was placed on an import surcharge and an export rebate. However, the British policy came under fire from some European Governments, who called for a deflation of the British economy.

1965.

Full employment was maintained in 1965. The Chancellor in his April Budget gave priority to two considerations: the need both to improve the external balance and to avoid deflation. To help improve the balance of payments he tried to reduce the net outflow of long-term capital by making investment abroad less attractive relative to home investment. For example, whereas companies trading abroad could previously offset taxes paid overseas against income liable to tax, this concession was to be abolished in stages; also, he introduced more stringent control of foreign exchange made available for direct investment abroad. Taxation was increased by £164 million; tobacco and alcohol being singled out yet again because a rise in their price is known to affect sales very little. However, the Budget was not particularly deflationary: the Government's overall deficit for 1965–66 was estimated at £724 million. It was the intention, rather, that consumption expenditure be reduced to free resources for export production and home investment.

The Budget contained two major fiscal innovations. A corporation tax was introduced to replace the existing company income tax and profits tax. This tax, at a rate unlikely to exceed 40 per cent, was imposed on distributed as well as undistributed profits, so as to encourage the retention of profits for the financing of business expansion. A further innovation was the introduction of a capital gains tax, far more comprehensive than the first move in this direction taken in 1962. This tax is levied on the gain realised on an asset between its purchase and sale, provided this does not exceed the gain between April 6, 1965, and sale. It applies to all assets, with limited exceptions: the most important being owner-occupied houses, and goods and chattels realised for less than £1,000. Gains realised within a period of one year are treated as ordinary income and taxed accordingly. Gains on assets held for more than a year are taxed at a flat rate of 30 per cent in the case of individuals. However, gains realised by companies over any period are taxed at corporation tax rates. There are many administrative difficulties in implementing such a tax. Nevertheless, it is an important attempt to remedy the inequality in the taxation of earned and unearned incomes.

Because the balance of payments had shown no sign of rapid improvement by July, the Chancellor found it necessary to introduce further measures. They included tighter controls on foreign exchange and on the terms of hire-purchase, and a postponement of Local Authority and Government programmes. Thankfully, these measures were not sufficient to produce deflation, and at the end of the year, unemployment was still very low.

1966.

In January the Government decided to introduce a new system of incentives to stimulate desirable sorts of investment. Initial and investment allowances on new plant and machinery were to be replaced by cash grants in some sectors (*e.g.*, export and import-substitute industries) and in the development areas these grants were to be double the national rate.

The state of the economy was such that the General Election of March 1966 was fought largely on the economic issues discussed in these pages, *e.g.*, the balance of payments, incomes policy, and entry into the Common Market.

In its first eighteen months of office, the Labour Government's policy for handling the short-term economic problem can be roughly summed up as follows: to restrict the growth of demand somewhat, but not as drastically as in the past; to use various *ad hoc* measures to deal with the immediate balance of payments; and to hope that by the time the *ad hoc* measures have to be dropped, longer term measures designed to strengthen the balance—especially productivity policy and incomes policy—will have put the situation right. The year 1966 has been described as a " make or break " year for the British economy. This it will indeed be if the protection from competition afforded by the import surcharge and the export rebate is removed in response to foreign pressures.

Some commentators would argue that the low level of unemployment in early 1966 called for a deflation of the economy: only by relaxing an acute labour shortage can the rise in money incomes and prices be restricted. However, apart from the direct harm of immediate unemployment, deflation could have damaging effects on investment and the growth of productive capacity, so making it more difficult to achieve balance of payments equilibrium in the long run. Moreover, deflation would amount to an abandonment of the National Plan, based as it is on the expectation of reasonably steady rate of growth. Also, deflation is a blunt instrument, affecting all regions and industries equally, irrespective of whether they are fully employed or slack. Measures to correct the balance of payments by cutting internal demand have been tried in the past and found wanting. An alternative policy is available: that of operating directly on the balance of payments.

Each of the various possibilities for direct operation on the external balance has its difficulties. Although devaluation is permitted by the Articles of Agreement of the IMF, there would be considerable pressure against devaluation from Britain's creditors and from politicians. The import surcharge imposed as a temporary measure in 1964—which amounts to a selective devaluation—is contrary to the rules of the GATT, and has come under pressure from Britain's trading partners. However, quantitative import restrictions are permitted by the GATT, and could be imposed selectively on goods for which British substitutes exist. With these alternatives available, even though they may be politically unpopular, there should be no need to sacrifice full employment and jeopardise economic growth on account of the balance of payments deficit, should it not be eliminated in the course of 1966.

GREEK MYTHS & LEGENDS

TABLE OF CONTENTS

GREEK MYTHS AND LEGENDS

PART I. INTRODUCTION

(*a*) **The Significance of the Myths and Legends.**

We all know how the stories and books that we knew in our youth have coloured our thought. So it is with the myths and legends of the earliest civilisation of Europe, that of the Greeks. Their stories have entered the stream of consciousness of European men and women through the ages, affecting their literature and art, and even their ways of thinking.

The Origin of Myths. True myth has been defined by Robert Graves as "the reduction to narrative shorthand of ritual mime performed on public festivals, and in many cases recorded pictorially." These rituals were, says Graves, "archaic magic-makings that promoted the fertility or stability of a sacred queendom or kingdom—queendoms having, it seems, preceded kingdoms throughout the Greek-speaking area."

The immense diversity of these myths is partly due to geographical causes, for, in the widely differing districts of Greece, different conceptions of the divinity and varying rituals of propitiation were evolved. There are also historical causes, for the Mediterranean peoples worshipping an earth goddess were conquered by successive waves of Hellenes bringing with them some form of tribal sky god.

Legends. Interwoven with the religious myths were a host of legends, traditional stories, which though not authentic had, like the tales of Troy, a substratum of fact. There were, also, all kinds of fables and anecdotes, folk-tales such as that of Perseus, and allegories and romances, which fused with the myths and legends to make a fascinating complex of stories.

Their Preservation in Literary Form. These have been preserved for us largely by the Greek poets, especially by Homer in his *Iliad* and *Odyssey*, and by Hesiod in his *Theogony*, works which probably date from about the eighth century B.C. The Greek dramatists of the fifth century B.C.—Aeschylus, Sophocles, and Euripides—who relied on myth and legend for most of their plots, also handed on the ancient tales, though often in slightly altered form. Then about five centuries later Roman writers, such as Virgil, Ovid and Horace, modelling themselves on the Greeks, refashioned and embroidered their themes. It is not surprising that we have so many variants of the same tale.

This rich and complex treasure of Greek myth and legend has become increasingly familiar in Western Europe, at first in Latin versions, then after the Renaissance in the original Greek, and today in excellent modern translations.

Their Significance Today. Because of their extraordinary vitality and pervasiveness, some familiarity with Greek myth and legend is almost indispensable to a full appreciation of our European culture.

In Art and Literature. Great painters like Botticelli, Veronese and Rubens made the ancient stories the subject of their pictures, and writers from Shakespeare to James Joyce have enriched their work by constant reference. The French dramatists from Racine to Giraudoux are notable for relying on them for the basic plot of their dramas. Today when good and inexpensive translations enable us to go direct to Homer's *Iliad*, or to see Euripides' *Medea* on the stage, it is especially useful to have some general knowledge of the mythical background to the particular epic or play.

Psychology. Not only to those who love art and literature is the knowledge of Greek mythology rewarding. Psychologists have found here suggestive symbols for the profound mental processes they are endeavouring to elucidate. Through Freud the term "Œdipus complex" is now a commonplace, and Jung has found in the myths symbolic archetypes of human response.

Philosophy and Religion. Philosophers also have found it profitable to return to the myths. Bertrand Russell emphasises the influence of Greek religion on Greek philosophy, and, through such philosophers as Pythagoras and Plato, on Christianity itself.

Anthropology. Of recent years anthropologists scrutinising the myths have been able to discern something of the way of life of primitive societies. The two-volume Penguin *The Greek Myths*, by Robert Graves, incorporates some of their interpretations.

Archæology. Perhaps the most exciting of all recent investigations are those of the archæologists working on sites once considered only legendary. The German Schliemann, trusting to the fidelity of his Homer, actually unearthed the foundations of Priam's Troy and Agamemnon's Mycenæ, finding fabulous treasure and proving to the astonished world that these antique tales were indeed rooted in fact. Through Schliemann's trust in Homer we have added an early chapter to History, that of the Mycenæan culture of pre-classical Greek which flourished from about 1550 to 1200 B.C.

Another centre of ancient story, the island of Crete, was the field of Sir Arthur Evans' enquiries, and his excavation of the magnificent Palace of Cnossos not only pushed back the frontiers of history yet further to about 3000 B.C., but also showed how many Cretan legends had some factual basis.

More recent excavations at legendary Mycenæan sites on the mainland have led to the discovery of the Palace of Nestor at Pylos, and the House of Cadmus at Thebes.

Tablets found at Mycenæan towns and in Cnossos inscribed in an entirely unknown script, "Linear B," have challenged scholars with a fascinating puzzle. After years of study Michael Vertris and others have at last been able to decipher the script. Although so far only inventories are available, it is significant that the language used is archaic Greek. We now know therefore that the Greeks of the Mycenæan age could write, and that Homer's single reference to writing is once more a faithful record of fact. (See Book VI of the *Iliad* and the reference to Bellerophon's "folded tablet.")

(*b*) **The Historical Background to the Myths and Legends.**

Our knowledge of the earliest periods of Greek history is very recent. The great historian Grote, writing in 1846, said that we must consider the First Olympiad of 776 B.C. as the starting point. Anything earlier was matter for conjecture. It is largely due to the discoveries of archæologists that scholars are now able to push back the frontiers of history. From archæological evidence they can now reconstruct the probable course of events from as early a date as 3000 B.C.

3000 B.C. Early Bronze Age. It was about 3000 B.C., when the Neolithic Age was succeeded in the Eastern Mediterranean by the Early Bronze Age, that a bronze-using people, akin to those of early Crete and the Cyclades, entered Greece and fused with the Neolithic folk already there. These invaders were not Aryans, but of Mediterranean stock, and they worshipped the Great Goddess, a fertility goddess who appeared in many guises. She was unmarried, and in many instances her lover appeared to her in the form of a bird.

2000 B.C. Coming of Hellenes. A thousand years later, in the Middle Bronze Age a very different kind of people began to enter Greece. These were the Hellenes or Greeks, an Aryan people from the North, for whom transport and conquest were easy by reason of their horses and wheeled vehicles. Unlike their predecessors, they were patriarchal, and their chief divinity was a tribal sky-god, but as they fused with the pre-Hellenic stock already in the country, so their patriarchal worship mingled with the matriarchal and the sky-god married the earth-goddess.

Minyans and Ionians. Successive waves of these Hellenes invaded the country in three main groups beginning in about 2000 B.C. with Minyans and Ionians.

Minoan Culture. Penetrating far south to the islands, and to Sicily, Southern Italy, and Asia Minor, they became expert navigators. They were much influenced by a brilliant and sophisticated Minoan culture already flourishing in Cnossos in Crete, and this began to have considerable effect on the mainland of Greece from about 1580 B.C. onwards.

1400 B.C. Achæans. In about 1400 B.C., however, Cnossos fell, destroyed either by earthquakes or by invaders, for the Achæans, the second wave of Hellenes, had now begun to enter Greece, and from about 1400 to 1100 B.C. Mycenæ on the mainland was probably the centre of civilisation in the Ægean world.

Mycenæan Culture. It is this Mycenæan culture of the Late Bronze Age which, seen through legend, is depicted in Homer's *Iliad* and *Odyssey*. Mycenæ is Agamemnon's own citadel, and other cities where archæological remains are now being found are named in the *Iliad's* "Catalogue of Ships." The Achæans as Homer shows them were a conquering feudal aristocracy and a concerted attempt probably made by them in the beginning of the twelfth century B.C. to seize the Black Sea trade may be reflected in the epic of the siege of Troy.

1200 B.C. Dorians. But the Achæans themselves were soon to be defeated, for at the end of the twelfth century B.C. the last influx of invading Hellenes, the Dorians, ancestors of the classical Greeks, entered the country. They practically destroyed the Mycenæan civilisation, and the Late Bronze Age now gave way to the Iron Age.

The Olympian Divinities. The close fusion between the early non-Aryan Mediterranean people, with their matriarchal culture, and the successive waves of patriarchal Hellenes was reflected in the Greek worship of Olympians. The ancient earth-goddess of fertility lived on in such guises as Aphrodite or Hera, and Zeus, sky-god of the Hellenes, appropriately took Hera to wife. Indeed, many deities, such as Demeter or Athene, combined, in the single divinity, both Mediterranean and Hellenic traits.

A third element in Greek Olympian religion derived from a Hittite culture flourishing in Asia Minor in about 1300 B.C. which had developed from a Hurrian culture of about 1500 B.C. Hesiod writing in about 750 B.C., incorporated some violent Hurrian myths of the cannibalism of the gods, in his *Theogony* or *Birth of the Gods*.

The "Epic Cycle." By the eighth century B.C. there was in existence a rich store of myth and legend known as the "Epic Cycle," which was drawn on by Homer and also by later poets and dramatists.

Homer's Picture. Homer, whose epics were probably completed at the end of the eighth or in the seventh century B.C. presents the composite myth and legend of Greece in highly civilised form, as the beliefs of a successful war-like aristocracy. The twelve deities dwelling on Olympus acknowledged the supremacy of Zeus, and Dionysus the god of wine and ecstasy who entered from Thrace in the eighth century B.C. was still an outsider, a god of the lower orders.

The Coming of Dionysus. But by the fifth century B.C. Dionysus had been accepted as an Olympian, taking the place of Hestia. The growing popularity of his worship which induced an ecstatic union with the god in a frenzy partly stimulated by wine, partly mystical, shows the need of the recently civilised Greeks for an impulsive religious expression which was not always satisfied by the prudent cults of the serene Olympians.

Orpheus. From the worship of Dionysus developed that of Orpheus, which aimed at mystic union with the god through enthusiasm wholly mystic, and through purification. The Orphics, believing in the transmigration of souls and an after life, had much influence on the Greek philosopher Pythagoras, and this influence was transmitted through Plato into Christianity itself.

The great influence of Greek religion on philosophy has only recently been recognised, and Bertrand Russell commends especially the study of John Burnet's *Early Greek Philosophy*, especially its second chapter, "Science and Religion."

(*c*) **Bibliography.**

There is no one book or Bible of Greek myths. Many versions exist, and in a short account it is not possible to record all variations. The reader is advised to consult the masterpieces of Greek literature now available in translation.

The Iliad. Homer, transl. E. V. Rieu. Penguin L14.
The Odyssey. Homer, transl. E. V. Rieu. Penguin L1.
The Theban Plays. Sophocles, transl. E. F. Watling. Penguin L3.
Electra and other plays. Sophocles, transl. E. F. Watling. Penguin L28.
Alcestis and other plays. Euripides, transl. P. Vellacott. Penguin L31.
Bacchae and other plays. Euripides, transl. P. Vellacott. Penguin L44.
Plays. Aeschylus, transl. G. M. Cookson. Everyman 62.
Dramas. Sophocles, transl. Sir George Young. Everyman 114.
Plays, 2 vols. Euripides, transl. A. S. Way. Everyman 63 and 271.
Greek Drama for Everyman. F. L. Lucas. J. M. Dent & Sons.

Men and Gods (Myths of Ovid). Rex Warner. Penguin 885.
Greeks and Trojans (Siege of Troy). Rex Warner. Penguin 942.
The Greek Myths, 2 vols. Robert Graves. Penguin.
The Golden Ass. Apuleius, transl. Robert Graves. Penguin L11.
The Greeks. H. D. F. Kitto. Pelican.
The Twelve Olympians. Charles Seltman. Pan.
Women in Antiquity. Charles Seltman. Pan.
The Bull of Minos. Leonard Cottrell. Pan.
Dr. Smith's Classical Dictionary. William Smith. John Murray.
A Smaller Classical Dictionary. Ed. Blakeney. J. M. Dent & Sons.

(*d*) **Guide to Pronunciation and Spelling.**

This Cyclopædia uses the long-established convention of spelling Greek names which is also used by such modern scholars as Robert Graves and E. V. Rieu.

It is helpful to remember that:—
"ch" and "c" are pronounced "k."
"œ" and "æ" are pronounced "ē," as in "see."
"eus" rhymes with "juice."

Part II. NARRATIVE OUTLINES

THE OLYMPIAN CREATION MYTHS, 1–22.

1. Uranus and Ge. The infinite and empty space which existed before creation was known as Chaos. The Earth, or Ge, sprang from Chaos, and herself gave birth to Uranus, the Heavens, and Pontus, the Sea. Ge then became, by Uranus, the mother of the hundred-handed giants, the Hecatoncheires or Centimani (Cottus, Briareus, also called Ægæon, and Gyes or Gyges); of the one-eyed Cyclopes (Brontes, Steropes and Arges); and of the twelve Titans. Greek writers give inconsistent lists of these Titans, but those most frequently mentioned are Cronus, Oceanus, Hyperion, and Iapetus, and the Titanesses Rhea, Themis, Tethys, and Mnemosyne.

2. Barbarous stories follow of Uranus' dealings with his descendants, and these have been influenced by myths from the Hittite culture which flourished in 1300 B.C. in Anatolia, or Asia Minor, and which probably embodied still earlier Babylonian material. These Hittite legends reached Greece through the Phœnicians, and Hesiod (eighth century B.C.), a poet whose family had recently come from Asia Minor incorporated them in his *Theogony*.

3. Revolt of Cronus. Uranus had thrown his rebellious sons the Cyclopes into Tartarus, in the Underworld, and Ge persuaded the Titans, with the exception of Oceanus, to rise against their father. She gave Cronus, the youngest, a flint sickle, and with this he unmanned Uranus. Drops from the wound falling upon Mother Earth, she bore the three Erinnyes or Eumenides, the furies Alecto, Tisiphone, and Megaera, and from drops that fell into the sea Aphrodite was born.

4. Uranus deposed, the Titans freed the Cyclopes, but Cronus, now supreme, consigned them again to Tartarus along with the Hundred-handed giants.

5. Cronus then married his sister Rhea, and mindful of the curse of Uranus and Ge, that he also would be deposed by his own son, he swallowed each of his children at birth.

6. Birth of Zeus. But when Zeus the youngest was born, Rhea gave Cronus a stone to swallow and saved Zeus, who, according to Minoan tradition, was brought up in the Dictæan cave in Crete. In 1900 the reputed "birth-cave" was explored by archæologists—probably the first men to enter for two thousand years, and there they found votive offerings to the god which may have been left there in the second millennium B.C. It was here that the Curetes, Rhea's priests, clashed their weapons to drown the cries of infant Zeus, while a goat, Amalthea, acted as his nurse, and was rewarded by being placed among the stars as Capricorn, while one of her horns became the Cornucopia or horn of plenty.

7. Zeus when of age was counselled by Metis, the daughter of Oceanus, and with Rhea's help gave to Cronus a potion which obliged him to disgorge first the stone and then his other children, Hestia, Demeter, Hera, Hades, and Poseidon. These now joined with Zeus in a contest against their father and the other Titans, who were led by Atlas.

8. War between Zeus and Titans. The war, known as the Titanomachia, was waged in Thessaly, and lasted ten years, until Ge promised Zeus victory if he would free the Cyclopes and the Hundred-handed giants from Tartarus.

9. The Cyclopes gave to Zeus a thunderbolt, to Hades a helmet of darkness, and to Poseidon a trident. Thus aided, the three brothers overcame Cronus, and the Hundred-handed giants stoned the other Titans, who were defeated and consigned either to an island in the West or to Tartarus, guarded by the Hundred-handed. Atlas was punished by being made to carry the sky on his shoulders, but the Titanesses were spared. The supersession of the old dynasty of Titans by the new order of gods is the theme of Keats' fine poem, *Hyperion*.

10. The Olympians. Zeus and his brothers now divided the government by lot. To Hades fell the Underworld, to Poseidon the sea, and to Zeus the sky, while the earth was common to all. Zeus, the greatest of the gods, lived on the lofty summit of Mt. Olympus between Macedonia and Thessaly, along with Poseidon and their sisters, Hestia, goddess of the hearth-fire, Demeter, goddess of agriculture, and Hera, who became the wife of Zeus. Seven other divinities, Aphrodite, Pallas Athene, Apollo, Artemis, Hephæstus, Ares, and Hermes were also numbered among the twelve great Olympians, and at a later date a new-comer, Dionysus, took the place of Hestia.

11. The Giants' Revolt. But the troubles of Zeus were not over. A post-Homeric story tells of the giants' revolt. Twenty-four giants with serpents' tails, sons of Ge, tried to avenge the imprisonment of their brothers the Titans by attacking Olympus. Led by Alcyoneus, they included Porphyrion, Ephialtes, Mimas, Pallas, Enceladus, and Polybutes. Only after terrible struggles in Olympus and on earth, were the giants defeated by the gods, who were helped by a magic herb of invulnerability found by Heracles, who always dealt the giants the final blow.

12. The story offered some explanation of huge bones found at Trapezus and volcanic fires at neighbouring Bathos and Cumæ, the reputed sites of the battles. The burial of Enceladus under Mt. Etna in Sicily, and of Polybutes under Nisyrus, likewise accounted for their volcanic nature. The inclusion of Heracles before his apotheosis indicates the late origin of the legend.

13. Ephialtes and Otus. Another version of the giants' revolt ascribes it to the gigantic Alœidæ, Ephialtes, and Otus, sons of Iphimedeia by Poseidon, but named after Alœus, whom their mother later married. At the age of nine Ephialtes and Otus first captured and imprisoned Ares, god of war, and then, vowing to outrage Hera and Artemis, they piled Mount Pelion on

Ossa in their attack on Heaven. Artemis induced them to go to the island of Naxos in the hope of meeting her, but disguised as a doe she leapt between them and they killed each other in error. Hermes then released Ares, and the spirits of the Alœidæ were tied with vipers back to back to a pillar in Tartarus.

14. Typhon. After the destruction of the giants, Ge in revenge brought forth the gigantic monster Typhon, fathered on her by her own son Tartarus. His huge limbs ended in serpents' heads and his eyes breathed fire. When he approached Olympus the gods in terror fled to Egypt disguised as animals, Zeus as a ram, Apollo a crow, Dionysus a goat, Hera a white cow, Artemis a cat, Aphrodite a fish, Ares a boar and Hermes an ibis. Athene alone was undaunted and persuaded Zeus to attack Typhon. After a fearful struggle, in which Zeus was temporarily incapacitated and only rescued by Hermes and Pan, he destroyed Typhon with his thunderbolts and buried him under Mt. Ætna, which still breathes fire.

15. The flight of the gods to Egypt serves to explain the Egyptian worship of them in animal form.

16. Prometheus and Epimetheus. The creation of mankind is often ascribed to Prometheus, whose name signifies "forethought," as that of his brother, Epimetheus, means "afterthought." These two, unlike their brother Atlas, had supported Zeus during the war with the Titans. But Prometheus, the clever benefactor of mankind, by stealing fire from Olympus and giving it to humans, brought upon himself divine vengeance.

17. The infuriated Zeus ordered Hephæstus to make a lovely woman, Pandora, the Eve of Greek myth, who was endowed by the gods with baleful powers and taken by Hermes to Epimetheus. When he had married her, she opened a box from which escaped all ills which plague mankind.

18. Zeus punished Prometheus by chaining him to a crag in the Caucasus, where all day long an eagle tore at his liver, which grew whole again during the night. Only after many generations did Heracles, with the consent of Zeus, shoot the eagle and free the heroic rebel.

19. The agony of Prometheus is the theme of Æschylus' tragedy *Prometheus Bound*; the liberator is depicted in his lost drama, *Prometheus Unbound*. Shelley's dramatic poem of the same name takes Prometheus as a symbol of those who challenge tyranny for the sake of mankind.

20. Deucalion and Pyrrha. Deucalion, the son of Prometheus, is the Noah of Greek myth. When Zeus decided to wipe out mankind by releasing a great flood on earth, Deucalion, warned by his father, made an ark which saved both himself and his wife Pyrrha, daughter of Epimetheus. After nine days the flood subsided and the ark came to rest on Mt. Parnassus.

21. Deucalion and Pyrrha then earnestly prayed at the shrine of Themis that the earth might be re-peopled. Themis appeared and commanded them to throw the bones of their mother behind them. They interpreted this as meaning the rocks of mother earth and those flung by Deucalion became men, those thrown by Pyrrha women.

22. Their son, Hellen, was the mythical ancestor of all the Hellenes.

THE OLYMPIAN DEITIES, 23–128.

ZEUS, 23–28.

23. Zeus, identified with Jupiter by the Romans, was the greatest of the Olympian divinities, omnipotent king of gods, father of men, and possibly master even of fate. Legends of his origin and supremacy are told in para. 6–20.

24. Zeus was the bright god of the sky, whom the invading Achæans introduced into Greece in about 1200 B.C., together with his consort Dione. Her worship, however, did not penetrate south of Zeus' shrine at Dodona in Epirus, where the rustling of oak leaves was interpreted as the voice of the god, and Zeus found other wives. His Olympian consort was Hera, who was in origin the Great Goddess of the pre-Hellenic matriarchal society. This marriage symbolises the fusion of the Achæans with their predecessors.

25. He first married Metis, daughter of Oceanus and Tethys, but when she was pregnant with Athene he swallowed her and brought forth Athene from his head. His second wife was Themis, daughter of Uranus and Ge, a divinity representing order, and their children were the Horæ and the Mæræ, or Fates, though some say that the Fates were daughters of Erebus and Night, and that even Zeus was subject to them. To Zeus and Hera were born the deities Ares, Hebe, and Hephæstus, unless the latter was the parthenogenous son of Hera. Zeus was also the father of Persephone by his sister Demeter, of the Charities, or Graces, by Eurynome, and of the Muses by Mnemosyne.

26. By mortal women four Olympian deities were children of Zeus; Hermes the son of Maia, Apollo and Artemis the children of Leto, and Dionysus the son of Semele. Zeus loved many mortal women, and Hera was intensely jealous and revengeful towards them and their children.

27. Although Zeus' earliest oracle was at Dodona, he was said to dwell with his fellow divinities on the summit of Olympus in Thessaly, and was also worshipped at Olympia in Elis. The Greeks dated their era from the first festival of the Olympiad in 776 B.C.

28. Zeus alone used the thunderbolt and was called the thunderer. The oak, the eagle, and mountain summits were sacred to him, and his sacrifices were usually bulls, cows, and goats. His attributes were the sceptre thunderbolt, eagle, and a figure of Victory held in his hand. The Dodonean Zeus sometimes wore a wreath of oak leaves, the Olympian Zeus one of olive.

HERA, 29–35.

29. Hera, identified by the Romans with Juno, was the Great Goddess of the pre-Hellenic matriarchal society, whom Zeus, supreme god of the Achæans, appropriately took to wife.

30. She was said to be a daughter of Cronus and Rhea and reluctantly married her brother Zeus, who in the form of a cuckoo sought her out at Cnossos in Crete, or perhaps in Argos, and their wedding night was spent on Samos. Ge gave Hera the tree with the golden apples later guarded by the Hesperides.

31. Though Hera was treated with reverence by the gods, she was greatly inferior in power to Zeus and must obey him, her subordination reflecting the attitude of the Achæans towards women. Only in her power to bestow the gift of prophecy was Hera equal to her husband.

32. She was often rebellious and jealous of Zeus' intrigues and persecuted his children by mortal women. At one time, with Poseidon and Apollo, she led a conspiracy of all the Olympians save Hestia to put Zeus in chains. He was freed by Thetis and Briareus, and punished Hera by hanging her with wrists chained to the sky and an anvil on each ankle.

33. Hera bore Zeus Ares and Hebe and annually renewed her virginity by bathing in a spring near Argos. As properly speaking, the only married goddess among the Olympians, she was worshipped as goddess of marriage and the birth of children, the Ilithyiæ being her daughters.

34. Hera was of majestic stature, and her attributes were a diadem, veil, sceptre, and peacock. Samos and Argos were seats of her worship.

35. Because of the judgment of Paris she was relentlessly hostile to the Trojans.

HESTIA, 36–37.

36. Hestia, called Vesta by the Romans, and the eldest sister of Zeus, was a divinity brought to Greece by the invading Achæans. Though Poseidon and Apollo both sought her love, she swore by Zeus always to remain a virgin.

37. She was goddess of the fire on the hearth, supremely important in those days because so difficult to rekindle, and was naturally thought of as goddess of home life. Each town or city had its sacred hearth, which, like that of the home, was an asylum for suppliants. The first part of all sacrifices offered to the gods was due to Hestia, the most peaceable and kindly of all the Olympians, but at a later date Dionysus took her place among the twelve Olympian gods.

ATHENE, 38–45.

38. Athene, whom the Romans identified with Minerva, was the embodiment of wisdom and power.

39. The Achæans brought with them a young warrior goddess, who bore the titles, Kore, Parthenos, Pallas, meaning girl, virgin, maiden, and she was in about 1700 B.C. identified with an older pre-Hellenic " Palace Goddess," worshipped in Crete. The " Palace Goddess " was one aspect of the Great Goddess, revered not for motherhood but for feminine intuition, and from pre-Hellenic times comes the name Athene.

40. The complex Pallas Athene was thus not only the patroness of women's arts such as weaving, protectress of agriculture, inventor of plough, rake, and ox-yoke, but also a warrior, a wise tactician, appearing in armour and wearing on her ægis or shield the head of Medusa, during the Trojan War the great protagonist of the Greeks. Legends of the birth of Pallas Athene reveal how the patriarchal Hellenes took over, and made their own a matriarchal divinity.

41. She was said to be a daughter of Zeus and Metis, but before her birth an oracle had foretold that she would be a girl, and that if Metis had another child it would be a son who would depose his father. Zeus therefore swallowed Metis, and later, suffered an agonising headache as he walked by Lake Triton. Hermes realising the cause, persuaded Hephæstus, or, according to some, Prometheus, to cleave open Zeus' skull, from which Athene sprang completely armed.

42. The centre of her cult was Attica and Athens, and legend said that when Athene and Poseidon contended for the possession of the city, the gods judged it should belong to Athene, who in planting the olive-tree had conferred the better gift.

43. Preferring to settle quarrels peaceably, Athene established here the court of the Areopagus, where if votes were equal, she herself gave a casting vote to free the accused, as in the trial of Orestes.

44. In 566 B.C. Pesistratus founded the great Panathenaic festival, celebrated every fourth year, and its magnificent procession was represented on the frieze of the Parthenon now in the British Museum, while the birth of Athene was represented in the gable at the east end of the Parthenon, and the contest with Poseidon at the west. Pesistratus also introduced a new coinage, with the head of Athene on one side, and the owl, her bird, upon the other.

45. Other pre-Hellenic acropolipses were sacred to Athene, and her worship flourished in Sparta, Corinth, Argos, and Thebes.

HEPHÆSTUS, 46–56.

46. Hephæstus, identified with Vulcan by the Romans, was the smith-god, a superb artist in metals.

47. He probably originated as a pre-Hellenic fire-god near the Mt. Olympus of Lycia in Asia Minor, where gaseous vapour, seeping through the soil, ignited. The Lycians emigrated to Lemnos, where they became known as Pelasgians, and again found fire issuing from the earth, and this fire became the symbol of their god Hephæstus.

48. The cult of Hephæstus spread to Athens, where his artistic genius was so venerated that in the frieze of the Parthenon where two pairs of gods are given positions of honour, Zeus appears with Hera, and Hephæstus with Athene.

49. In Homer's time Hephæstus was one of the twelve Olympians, his exalted position reflecting the importance of the smith in a Bronze Age society when weapons and tools had magical properties. He is, like other smith-gods, represented as lame, possibly because the tribe deliberately lamed their smith to prevent his running away, possibly because work at the forge developed muscular arms but feeble legs.

50. According to Homer, Hephæstus was the son of Zeus and Hera, though later tradition says that he was son of the goddess alone, just as his fire sprang mysteriously from the earth.

51. Born lame and weak, Hephæstus was so much disliked by Hera that she threw him from Olympus, when he fell into the sea and was cared for by the sea-goddesses Thetis and Eurynome in a grotto under the sea.

52. After nine years Hera took him back to Olympus, where he had a fire smithy, but on one occasion he enraged Zeus by taking Hera's part, so that he was again flung from Olympus, this time by Zeus. He was a day falling, and alighted in the evening on the island of Lemnos, as described in *Paradise Lost*, Book I, lines 740–746. Later writers diverge from Homer in making this second fall the cause of Hephæstus' lameness.

53. He again returned to Olympus and acted as mediator between Zeus and Hera, though the gods laughed at him as he hobbled about.

54. His workshop in Olympus was in his own palace, and all the palaces of the gods were made by him He also made the magnificent armour of Achilles, as is described in the eighteenth book of the *Iliad*, the necklace of Harmonia, and the bulls of Æëtes. Later accounts place his workshop on the volcanic island of Sicily, where the Cyclopes served him.

55. In the *Iliad*, Hephæstus' wife was Charis, but in the *Odyssey* she was Aphrodite, who was unfaithful to him with Ares. How Hephæstus caught the two together in an invisible net he had made, and exposed them to the ridicule of the gods, is told in a poem known as the " Lay of Demodocus," incorporated in the eighth book of the *Odyssey*.

56. Hephæstus' favourite spots on earth were Lemnos, and volcanic islands like Lipara, Hiera, Imbros, and Sicily. In Greek art he is represented as a vigorous man with a beard, carrying a hammer or similar instrument, and wearing an oval cap or chiton.

APHRODITE, 57–63.

57. Aphrodite, goddess of desire, identified by the Romans with Venus, was derived from the Great Goddess of pre-Hellenic times, her counterparts being the orgiastic Ishtar of Babylon and Astarte of Syria.

58. She was worshipped as a fertility goddess at Paphos in Cyprus, whence Phœnicians took her worship to Cythera, an island off Southern Peloponnesus. Probably as late as the eighth century B.C. her fertility cult was established on Acrocorinthus above Corinth. There was a similar sanctuary on Mt. Eryx in Western Sicily. In these places the goddess was served by young girls, but in other Greek states her worship was more that of protectress of the city.

59. According to Hesiod, Aphrodite sprang from the seed of Uranus and rose naked from the sea, as in Botticelli's picture "The Birth of Venus." Rising near the island of Cythera, she passed to Paphos in Cyprus.

60. Homer makes Aphrodite the daughter of Zeus and Dione, and represents her as wife to Hephæstus. She was, however, unfaithful to him and in love with Ares. The amusing situation when they were caught together is described in para. 55. Harmonia was one of their children.

61. Aphrodite also bore sons to Poseidon, and Priapus to Dionysus, and later stories tell that she bore Hermaphroditus to Hermes, and Eros to either Hermes, Ares, or Zeus.

62. Her love for the mortal Adonis is the theme of Shakespeare's *Venus and Adonis*, and one of the Homeric hymns tells of her passion for Anchises, cousin of Priam, to whom she bore Æneas, the hero of Virgil's *Epic*. Unfortunately Anchises, boasting of Aphrodite's love, was struck by Zeus with a thunderbolt.

63. Aphrodite possessed a magic girdle which made the wearer irresistibly lovely and desirable. Doves and sparrows were sacred to her. Her most beautiful statue was that of Praxitiles in the fourth century B.C., a copy of which is preserved in the Vatican. The Venus de Milo may be seen in the Louvre.

ARES, 64–67.

64. Ares, god of war, who was identified by the Romans with Mars, was a divinity of Thracian origin, whose worship spread through Macedonia to Thebes, Athens, and cities of the Peloponnesus, especially Sparta. Ares was, however, not popular with the Greeks, who disliked purposeless war and despised the Thracians for enjoying it, and their attitude is reflected in the myths of Ares.

65. He was the son of Zeus and Hera, and as he delighted in battle for its own sake he was hated by the other gods, except Eris, Hades, and Aphrodite, who was in love with Ares and he with her. The two were once trapped together in a net which Hephæstus had engineered, as is described in para. 55.

66. Ares was not always successful in battle. The Alœidæ conquered him and left him imprisoned in a brazen vessel for thirteen months, until he was released by Hermes. Athene twice vanquished him, and Heracles also defeated him and forced him to return to Olympus.

67. According to a late tradition, Ares once defended himself before the gods in a trial where he was accused of murdering Halirrhothius, son of Poseidon. Since he pleaded that he had saved his daughter, Alcippe, from being violated, Ares was acquitted, and the place of the trial became known as the Areopagus.

APOLLO, 68–80.

68. Apollo's worship probably derived from two sources, from the Dorians, who in about 1100 B.C. entered Greece and reached as far south as Crete, and from Ionians, living in the islands and mainland of Anatolia, or Asia Minor, who became acquainted with a Hittite divinity worshipped in Lycia, and hence called Lycius.

69. Apollo's Dorian shrine was at Delphi, near the Castalian spring on Mt. Parnassus, where he was called the Pythian, or Loxias, the Ambiguous. His Ionian shrine was at Delos, where he was called Lycius, and Phæbus, or Shining, and where he was more closely associated with his twin-sister, Artemis.

70. Legends said that Apollo and Artemis were the children of Zeus and Leto, but before their birth, jealous Hera caused Leto to wander from place to place till she gave birth to Artemis under a palm-tree at Ortygia, and to Apollo beside a palm in the isle of Delos.

71. This story is told in the Delian Homeric Hymn of 700 B.C., while the Delphic Hymn tells how Apollo, soon after his birth, sought out the she-dragon Python, on Mt. Parnassus, and there killed her, taking over the Oracle of Earth at Delphi, where his priestess the Pythoness became the mouthpiece of his oracles, which were imparted in hexameter verse. Apollo was commanded by Zeus to visit the Vale of Tempe for purification, and to preside over the Pythian games held in Python's honour.

72. Hera, still implacable, sent the giant Tityus to violate Leto, as she came with Artemis to Delphi, though some say that it was Artemis who was attacked, but the giant was killed by the arrows of Apollo and Artemis.

73. Apollo was not always subservient to Zeus. He once, with Hera, Poseidon, and other Olympians, bound Zeus with chains and was punished by being sent with Poseidon as bondman to King Laomedan, where by playing the lyre and tending the flocks he helped Poseidon to build the wall of Troy. On another occasion, furious that Zeus had slain his son Asclepius, Apollo retaliated by killing the Cyclopes. Zeus now sent him to serve King Admetus of Pheræ in Thessaly, and again he kept flocks. He also helped Admetus to win his bride Alcestis and even ensured that the kin should be restored to life if one of his family woul die in his stead.

74. Apollo loved many mortal women, includin Cyrene, mother of Aristæus, Coronis, mother of Asclepius, the healer, and Aria, mother of Miletus. The nymph Dryope was also seduced by Apollo but when he pursued the nymph Daphne she crie for help and was turned into a laurel, hencefort Apollo's tree; and the nymph Marpessa preferre his rival, Idas. Apollo loved Cassandra, daught of Priam, and conferred on her the gift of prophec but, when she disappointed him, decreed that sh should never be believed. Hyacinthus, a Sparta prince, in origin an earth deity, was beloved b Apollo, and when he was killed by the god's jealo rival, Zephyrus, the hyacinth flower sprang fro his blood.

75. Apollo had varied characteristics. He wa destroyer, as his arrows indicated, and sudde deaths were ascribed to him. It was he who se plagues among the Greeks besieging Troy. B he was also protector, warding off evil, as h fatherhood of Asclepius indicated. He protect flocks and cattle, as his service to Laomedan a Admetus showed, and later writers particular stressed this aspect.

76. As god of prophecy, Apollo could com municate the gift to gods and mortals, and of the centres of his worship Delphi was the mo famous. The shrine had probably been esta lished by pre-Hellenic people, worshipping Moth Earth, and had been seized by invading Hellen who killed Python the oracular serpent, took ov the oracles in the name of their own Apollo, a held funeral games in honour of Python to plac the original inhabitants. The shrine was su posed to contain the Omphalos, or navel stone earth, and a chasm which occasionally gave o intoxicating vapours. Over this Apollo's prie ess, Pythia, sat on a tripod, and uttered his ora after chewing intoxicating laurel leaf. She w regarded as the mystical bride of the god.

77. As god of song and music Apollo appears in the *Iliad* delighting immortals. He was said to have received the lyre from Hermes, and its seven strings were connected with the seven Greek vowels. In music none surpassed Apollo, not even Pan, nor Marsyas, the satyr who had found Athene's discarded flute which played by itself. Defeated in a contest, Marsyas was flayed alive by the victorious god. Apollo was the leader of the Muses, or Musagetes. He valued order and moderation in all things, his favourite maxims being "Nothing in Excess," and "Know thyself."

78. Apollo also delighted in the foundation of towns, and his oracle was always consulted before a town was founded.

79. In later writers he was identified with the sun god, the result of Egyptian influence, for in Homer, Helios, god of the sun, is completely distinct from Apollo.

80. The worship of Apollo, typical of all that is most radiant in the Greek mind, has no counterpart in the religion of Rome. Not till the end of the third century B.C. did the Romans adopt his religion from the Greeks.

ARTEMIS, 81–89.

81. Artemis, whose Roman counterpart was Diana, had two chief aspects. One was as 'Mistress of Animals," a goddess of the chase, worshipped in primitive matriarchal society, and probably owing something to the Britomartis and Dictynna, worshipped as huntresses in Crete. The other, originating in Asia Minor, was of the ge-old mother-goddess, and is most clearly seen n Artemis Ephesia, who was worshipped as an rgiastic goddess.

82. Legends of the birth of Artemis are told in he story of Apollo, and as his sister she shared nany of his characteristics. She carried bow and rrows, made for her by Hephæstus, and had ower to send plague and sudden death, as when he and Apollo killed the children of Niobe. She vas also protectress of children and young animals nd goddess of the chase.

83. Like Apollo, Artemis was unmarried, and ater writers stressed that she was a maiden goddess and severely punished any lapses. She hanged Actæon to a stag to be torn to pieces by is own hounds, only because he had seen her athing, and some traditions say that she killed rion because of his unchastity. The nymph allisto, who had been seduced by Zeus, was in the rm of a bear hunted down by the hounds of rtemis.

84. When Apollo was identified with the Sun, rtemis was identified with Selene, the Moon.

85. The Arcadian Artemis, early worshipped in rcadia as a huntress among the nymphs, was nconnected with Apollo.

86. Another aspect of the goddess was as the rce Artemis of Tauris, to whom all strangers ere sacrificed. Iphigeneia was once her priestess, d she and Orestes took her image to Brauron in tica, whence the goddess was called Brauronia. his Brauronian Artemis was worshipped in hens, and also in Sparta, where boys were ourged at her altar until they sprinkled it with eir blood.

87. Artemis as an orgiastic goddess had her ief centre in Ephesus, with its immensely ealthy temple, and it was this Artemis that St. ul encountered. (See Acts of the Apostles, . XIX.)

88. Though usually regarded as a rural divinity, temis was supreme in three great cities, in hesus, in Marseilles, to which Ionian Greeks m Asia Minor took her cult between 600 and) B.C., and in Syracuse, where she was known Artemis Arethusa.

89. The goddess was often portrayed as a huntress, as in the so-called Diana of Versailles, now in the Louvre. As huntress her chlamys reached only to the knees, and she carried a bow, quiver, and arrows, or a spear, and was accompanied with stags or dogs. As Selene, she wore a long robe and veil, and a crescent moon on her forehead.

HERMES, 90–98.

90. Hermes, whom the Romans called Mercurius, was originally one of the gods of the pre-Hellenic people, the divinity dwelling in the cairn, or "herma," set up by shepherds as a landmark in wild country, and so developing as a protector against predatory animals and a guide to travellers. This Hermes was identified with a similar divinity worshipped in Minoan Crete, a "Master of Animals," a son or lover of the Great Goddess, and therefore a god of fertility.

91. Legends said that Hermes was the son of Zeus and Maia, an embodiment of the Great Goddess, and a daughter of Atlas, whence Hermes' name Atlantiades.

92. The "Hymn to Hermes" of 600 B.C. tells that he was born in a cavern on Mt. Cyllene in Arcadia (from which he was sometimes called Cyllenius), and that he grew with amazing rapidity. When only a few hours old he went to Pieria and stole some of the oxen of Apollo, which he drove to Pylos, and then, returning to Cyllene, he invented the lyre by stringing a tortoise-shell with cow-gut. Apollo, on discovering the thief, accused him to Zeus, who ordered Hermes to restore the oxen. But when Apollo heard the lyre he was delighted, took it in exchange for the oxen, and became the friend of Hermes, leading him back to Zeus.

93. Zeus gave to Hermes supreme power over animals and appointed him his herald. Hermes also acted as herald to Hades, conducting shades to the underworld. (See Virgil's *Æneid*, Bk. IV, ll. 242 *sqq.*) As herald he was regarded as god of eloquence, whence St. Paul, "the chief speaker," was mistaken for him in Lystra of Asia Minor. (See Acts of the Apostles, Ch. XIV.) Heralds promote peace and therefore trade. Thus Hermes came to be looked on as god of peaceable commerce.

94. He was also god of prudence and cunning, and even of theft, and was said to have helped the Fates in composing the alphabet. Many inventions ascribed to Hermes, such as weights and measures, the musical scale, astronomy, olive-culture, and the arts of boxing and gymnastics, were pre-Hellenic, and the stories of his childhood may indicate how the Hellenes took over these arts in the name of their god Apollo. As a god of fertility and luck, Hermes presided over games of dice.

95. He played a part in such incidents as the rescue of Dionysus, the punishment of Ixion, the selling of Heracles to Omphale, the judgment of Paris, and the leading of Priam to Achilles, but his most famous exploit was perhaps the slaying of Argus, the hundred-eyed giant sent by Hera to watch Io.

96. Hermes had several sons, including Echion, herald to the Argonauts, Autolycus the thief, his son by Chione, and Daphnis.

97. His worship flourished in Arcadia, where he was to be found with Pan and the muses. It spread to Athens, and he became one of the best loved of the Olympians.

98. Hermes' attributes were the Petasus, a travelling-hat, in later time adorned with wings, the Alipes, or winged-sandals, and the Caduceus, or heralds' staff, whose white ribbons were later mistaken for serpents because he was herald to Hades. Sacred to Hermes were the tortoise, the palm-tree, the number four, and some kinds of fish, and his sacrifices were incense, honey, cakes, pigs, lambs, and kids.

POSEIDON, 99–109.

99. Poseidon, identified by the Romans with Neptune, derived from a god worshipped by the earliest Aryan invaders of Greece, the Minyans and Ionians, who entered the country in about 2000 B.C. It was with the aid of horses and wheeled vehicles that they quickly overcame any resistance, and their god Poseidon was often thought of as the horse whose hooves thunder on the earth. He is constantly spoken of in Homer as "earth-shaker," while many legends show him in equine guise. It is possible that he was originally thought of as a sky-god, a thunderer, and the mate of an earth-goddess who later developed as Demeter.

100. But when in about 1450 B.C., another wave of invading Aryans, the Achæans, entered Greece, they also brought their sky-god, a thunderer called Zeus, possibly in origin identical with Poseidon, and the latter, recognised as an older brother of Zeus, came to be revered as a sea-divinity, for the Minyans were, by now, expert in navigation.

101. According to legend, Poseidon was the eldest son of Cronus and Rhea, and when, after the deposition of Cronus, he and his brothers Zeus and Hades cast lots for sovereignty, the sea became Poseidon's share. He dwelt in an under-water palace near Ægæ in Eubœa, which is described in the beginning of the 13th book of the *Iliad*, and here he kept his horses with brazen hooves and golden manes, and when they drew his chariot over the sea it became tranquil.

102. He was said to have created the horse when disputing with Athene for the possession of Athens, and he taught men how to bridle horses. He was the protector of horse-races, and horse and chariot races were held in his honour on the Corinthian isthmus.

103. In the form of a horse he raped his sister Demeter, when she was disguised as a mare. Their offspring were the horse Arion and the nymph Despœna, and some say Persephone also, though according to another version Demeter was searching for Persephone, her daughter by Zeus, at the time of the rape.

104. Poseidon, though equal to Zeus in dignity, was less powerful and resented the pride of his younger brother. He once joined with Hera, Apollo, and other Olympians, to put Zeus in chains, and he and Apollo were punished by being sent as bondsmen to Laomedan. Here Poseidon built the walls of Troy, hence called Neptuniia Pergama. When Laomedan refused the wages due, Poseidon sent a sea-monster, which would have devoured the king's daughter Hesione if she had not been rescued by Heracles. In the Trojan War, Poseidon naturally sided with the Greeks, though he became hostile to Odysseus after he had blinded Polyphemus, son of the god.

105. Poseidon desired earthly kingdoms, his attempts to take control possibly being political myths. He disputed with Athene for the possession of Athens, but she was awarded the city because her planting of the olive was judged the better gift. When these divinities, however, disputed the possession of Troezen, Zeus judged they should share it equally. In his claim for Corinth, Poseidon received only the isthmus, where the quadrennial Isthmian games were held in his honour, while the Areopagus was awarded to Helios.

106. Poseidon first intended to marry Thetis, but when it was prophesied that her son would be greater than his father he paid court to Amphitrite, daughter of Nereus. Only after Delphinos had most eloquently pleaded his suit did Amphitrite accept Poseidon, who in gratitude placed Delphinos' image among the stars, as the Dolphin. Amphitrites' reluctance, paralleled by Hera's shrinking from Zeus, and Persephone's from Hades, probably represents the resistance of an early matriarchal society to a patriarchal system.

107. Poseidon's son by Amphitrite was Triton, but he had many more children by other divinities and mortals.

108. One of them, Scylla, was particularly hateful to Amphitrite, who is said to have turned her into a monster with six barking heads and twelve feet. Poseidon also loved the nymph Tyro, mother of his children Pelias and Neleus, and Æthra, the mother of Theseus. His offspring by Medusa were Chrysaor and Pegasus.

109. Sacrifices to Poseidon were usually black-and-white bulls. His symbol of power was the trident, possibly in origin a thunderbolt, by means of which he could shake the earth or subdue the waves, and which became in Hellenistic and Roman times a symbol of sea-power, as it is today. Poseidon's other attributes were the horse and the dolphin, and he was usually represented as accompanied by Amphitrite, Triton, Nereids, and dolphins.

DEMETER, 110–116.

110. Demeter, counterpart of the Roman Ceres, was probably in origin a divinity of the Minyans, who entered Greece in about 200 B.C., and who revered her as an earth-goddess, a mate to their sky-god, who later developed as Poseidon. Both these divinities could take the form of a horse. The worship of this earth-goddess then merged with that of the Great Goddess of the pre-Hellenic matriarchal society, and Demeter was worshipped as the corn-goddess.

111. She was daughter to Cronus and Rhea, and sister to Zeus, by whom she became the mother of Persephone, or Core, the maiden, herself another aspect of the goddess. According to the Homeric Hymn of the seventh century B.C., Hades asked Zeus' permission to marry Persephone, and as he received no downright refusal was emboldened to carry off the maiden as she was gathering flowers Demeter wandered the earth searching for her daughter until Helios told her what Hades had done. She then shunned Olympus and wandered still on earth, which she forbad to bring forth fruit Zeus finally told Demeter that her daughter migh return, provided she had eaten nothing in the Underworld, and he sent Hermes to escort her back. Hades agreed to let Persephone go, bu gave her a pomegranate to eat, and it was at las agreed that she should spend a third of the yea with him in Hades, as Queen of the Underworld and the rest of the year with Demeter, who onc more allowed the earth to bear its fruit.

112. Inconsistent accounts are given of th place of the rape. Demeter's priests said it wa Eleusis, about twelve miles from Athens, the Lati poets Enna in Sicily, where, according to Ovid Persephone was gathering poppies. Some say i was Ascalaphus who saw Persephone take food i the Underworld and that because he revealed this he was turned by Demeter into an owl.

113. It is said that during her wandering Demeter punished those, like Abas, son of Celeu who were unkind to her, but showered blessings o those like Celeus himself and his son Triptolemu who received her hospitably in Eleusis and whom she taught the art of agriculture.

114. The Eleusinian Festival in honour Demeter and Persephone was probably full established in Athens by Pesistratus at the end the sixth century B.C., probably about the tim when the cult of Dionysus was instituted. The was an annual procession from Eleusis to Athen and those who spoke Greek could be initiated in the final rite of the mysteries. The Thesmophori celebrating the foundation of laws, was also he in the goddesses' honour, in Athens and in oth parts of Greece.

115. The myth originated in the most primiti rites of seed time and harvest at a time when on women practised the arts of agriculture. Pers phone, representing the vegetation which d down during the winter, had her counterpart in t primitive corn-puppet which was buried in wint to be dug up again sprouting in spring, and la writers saw the story as an expression of t death of the body and the immortality of the so

116. In art Demeter was represented with a garland of corn or a ribbon, and holding a sceptre, corn ears, or a poppy, and sometimes a torch and basket. Pigs were sacred to her. There is in the British Museum a fine statue of Demeter of about 330 B.C., which was found at Cnidos in Asia Minor.

DIONYSUS, 117–128.

117. Dionysus, god of wine, also called Bacchus by both Greeks and Romans, was not in Homer's time one of the aristocratic Olympian deities, but a god worshipped by humble folk whom wandering bands of ecstatic worshippers brought into Greece from Thrace in the eighth century B.C. The cult, which spread through Macedonia and Thessaly, to Bœotia, Delphi, Athens, and beyond, was characterised by a mystic frenzy when the worshippers, intoxicated with wine, believed themselves to be at one with Dionysus or Bacchus, sometimes called Bromius " the Boisterous." The men who followed him were known as Bacchoi, the women Bacchæ, or Bacchantes or Mænads, or in Athens and Delphi, Thyiads.

118. The immense popularity of the Dionysian cult, especially with women, indicates that among the recently civilised Greeks there was a longing for a more instinctive and impulsive life, valuing enthusiasm rather than prudence, and during the sixth century certain wise statesmen introduced the new cult among the other state religions. Dionysiac festivals were established in Corinth, Sicyon, Delphi, and Athens. In Delphi the sepulchre of Bacchus was placed near the very tripod of Pythia, and his temple, a theatre, was at the highest point of the sacred precinct. In Athens Pesistratus founded the Dionysia and the Panathenaic Games at about the same time, and a theatre was set up where the worshippers of Bacchus enacted the first primitive drama. In the fifth century, when the Parthenon was finished, the new god had been accepted among the twelve Olympians taking the place of Hestia. This change incidentally secured a majority of gods over goddesses on Mt. Olympus, and is perhaps evidence of a society becoming increasingly patriarchal.

119. Legends said that Dionysus was the son of Semele by Zeus, who visited his beloved disguised as a mortal. When Semele was six months with child, jealous Hera, disguised as an old woman, persuaded her to ask her mysterious lover to appear in his true form. Unwillingly Zeus consented, " hapless Semele " was consumed by fire, and her unborn child sewn up in Zeus' thigh to be delivered three months later as Dionysus.

120. The child was first entrusted to Athamas and Ino of Bœotia, and reared in the women's quarters disguised as a girl, until Hera undeceived punished Athamas with madness so that he killed his own son. Hermes then took Dionysus to Mt. Nysa, where the nymphs cared for him, feeding him with honey, and where he first invented wine. Zeus later placed the images of the nymphs among the stars as Hyades.

121. When Dionysus had grown to manhood Hera drove him mad and he wandered through the world with his old tutor Silenus and a wild rout of Satyrs and Mænads. He went through Egypt, Syria, and Asia to India, overcoming military opposition, teaching the culture of the vine, founding cities and laws. He returned to Europe through Phrygia and then invaded Thrace.

122. Here Lycurgus, King of the Edones, opposed his worship, but, maddened by Rhea, he killed and mutilated his own son, and the Edones caused him to be torn to death by horses.

123. Dionysus now proceeded to Bœotia, and in Thebes was resisted by King Pentheus. But Pentheus was also driven mad and torn to pieces by the Mænads or Bacchæ, among whom were his own mother Agave and her two sisters, for in their frenzy they believed him to be a wild beast. This is the legend used by Euripides in his play, *The Bacchæ*.

124. Dionysus also visited the islands of the Adriatic. At Icaria he hired a ship bound for Naxos, but the sailors were Tyrrhenian pirates and steered towards Asia, intending to sell Dionysus into slavery. The god, however, turned himself into a lion and the oars into serpents. Ivy grew round the ship and flutes were heard. The terrified pirates, leaping overboard, were transformed to dolphins. Arrived at Naxos, Dionysus found Ariadne deserted by Theseus and at once married her. A Renaissance conception of this incident can be seen in Titian's picture " Bacchus and Ariadne " in the National Gallery, or in Tintoretto's picture in the Doge's Palace in Venice.

125. At Argos people refused at first to accept Dionysus, but when the women had been maddened by him, they admitted he was a god.

126. His worship established throughout the world, Dionysus was received into Olympus as one of the twelve great divinities, taking the place of Hestia. He brought Semele there from the Underworld, and she was henceforth known as Thyone.

127. Dionysus was worshipped as god of the vital and intoxicating powers of nature, and also, because of his close connection with tillage and early civilisation, as a law-giver. He was also god of tragic art. In art he was represented as young, handsome, and athletic, but later as slightly effeminate. He was accompanied with a wild crowd of Satyrs, and Mænads, the latter frenzied with wine and mystic exaltation, and carrying cymbals, swords, serpents, or the Thyrsus, a wand wreathed with ivy and crowned with a fir-cone. The worship of Dionysus appealed strongly to women, and many would spend the whole night on the mountain in ecstatic dancing and tearing wild animals to pieces. Sacred to the god were the ivy, laurel, and asphodel, and the dolphin, serpent, tiger, lynx, panther, and ass. His sacrifice was usually a goat or ass.

128. The myths of Dionysus are evidence that there was at first much opposition to the ritual use of wine, and the frenzy it engendered. The earlier drink of the Greeks had been a kind of beer flavoured with ivy and mead, and mead was the drink of Homer's Olympians. Wine was not invented by the Greeks, but probably first imported by them from Crete, whither vine culture had probably spread from Mt. Nysa in Libya. The use of wine spread from Thrace to Athens and other civilised cities. The story of Dionysus' wanderings in India represents the spread of vine culture there.

PERSEUS, 129–144.

129. The ancient folk-tale of Perseus, grandson of Acrisius, has been told by Kingsley in *The Heroes*.

130. Acrisius and Prœtus, the twin sons of Abas, King of Argos, eventually agreed, after much discussion, to divide their inheritance. Proetus became ruler of Tiryns, whose massive walls he built by the aid of the Cyclopes, while Acrisius ruled uneasily in Argos, for an oracle had declared that he would be killed by a son born to his daughter Danaë.

131. To prevent this disaster, Acrisius had Danaë immured in a brazen dungeon or tower, with doors of brass, but all in vain, for Zeus visited her in a shower of gold, and she became the mother of Perseus.

132. Not daring to kill Danaë, Acrisius set mother and son adrift on the sea in a chest, which floated to the isle of Seriphos, one of the Cyclades. Here it was found by the sailor Dictys, and he took Danaë and her son to the king Polydectes, who received them hospitably.

133. When Perseus was grown to manhood, however, Polydectes sought to marry Danaë and seized a pretext to send Perseus off to fetch the head of the Gorgon Medusa.

134. Medusa and her sister Gorgons, Stheno and Euryale, who were the daughters of Phorcys and Ceto, and dwelt in Libya, had once been beautiful. But Medusa lay with Poseidon in one of the temples of Athene, and the enraged goddess turned her into a winged monster with brazen claws and serpent hair, so hideous that she turned to stone all who looked upon her.

135. Athene, eager to help Perseus, against her enemy, gave him a polished shield whereby he might see Medusa only in reflection. Hermes provided him with a sickle, and told him how to procure winged sandals, a magic wallet in which to carry the decapitated head, and Hades' helmet of invisibility.

136. On Hermes' advice Perseus visited the Gorgons' sisters, the Grææ, three old women grey from birth who had only one eye and one tooth between them, and these they passed from one to another. Perseus found them on Mt. Atlas, and, by snatching the eye and tooth, forced the Grææ to tell him where he could find the sandals, wallet, and helmet. They directed him to the Stygian nymphs, who gave him what he needed.

137. Flying westward to the land of the Hyperboreans, Perseus found the Gorgons asleep. He successfully beheaded Medusa and was astonished to see, springing fully grown from her body, the winged horse Pegasus and the warrior Chrysaor, both of whom had been begotten on her by Poseidon.

138. Though pursued by Stheno and Euryale, Perseus in Hades' helmet escaped to the south. Some say that he petrified the Titan Atlas by showing him the Gorgon's head and then flew over Æthiopia.

139. Here he saw, chained naked to a rock on the sea coast, the lovely Andromeda, and at once fell in love with her. He learned the cause of her plight from her parents, Cepheus, King of Æthiopia, and his wife Cassiopeia. The latter had rashly boasted that Andromeda was more beautiful than the Nereids, and when they had complained of this to Poseidon, the sea god had sent a monster to lay waste the country. Only by the sacrifice of Andromeda, said the oracle of Ammon, could the land be delivered.

140. Perseus promptly offered to rescue the maiden, provided she would become his wife, but, after he had slain the monster, Cepheus and Cassiopeia were reluctant to keep their promise, for they said Andromeda had already been contracted to another. Their protégé and his followers, arriving at the wedding, attempted to seize the bride, but were easily circumvented by Perseus, who showed them Medusa's head and turned them all to stone. Poseidon set the images of Cepheus and Cassiopeia among the stars, the latter in a humiliating position.

141. Perseus, with Andromeda, now hastened to Seriphos, where he found that Danaë and Dictys had been obliged to take refuge in a temple, but going to Polydectes' palace, he exposed the Gorgon's head and turned the king and all his followers to stone. He then gave the head to Athene, who set it in her ægis, and Hermes restored Perseus' accoutrements to the Stygian nymphs.

142. After making Dictys King of Seriphos, Perseus, taking with him Danaë and Andromeda, returned to Argos, and Acrisius, mindful of the oracle, fled to Larissa, in vain, however, for Perseus, visiting Larissa and taking part in public games, accidentally killed his grandfather by a throw of the discus.

143. Grieved by this mishap, Perseus arranged to exchange kingdoms with his cousin Megapenthes, the son of Prœtus, who now moved to Argos while Perseus became King of Tiryns. He also founded Mycenæ, which, like Tiryns itself had mighty fortifications built by the Cyclopes.

144. The massive remains of both cities have been investigated by Schliemann and other archæologists, and remain as some of the most interesting antiquities in all Greece.

BELLEROPHON, 145–150.

145. The story of Bellerophon is told by William Morris in *The Earthly Paradise*.

146. Bellerophon, the son of Glaucus, King of Corinth, having killed one Bellerus, fled to Prœtus, King of Tiryns. Unfortunately Prœtus' wife, Anteia, fell in love with the young man, and when he refused her advances falsely accused him to her husband of trying to seduce her. Prœtus, reluctant to kill a guest, sent him instead to Anteia's father, Iobates, King of Lycia, carrying a letter which requested that the bearer be put to death.

147. Iobates also shrank from killing a guest and decided to send Bellerophon against the Chimæra, a fire-breathing monster with a lion's head, goat's body, and serpent's tail, said to be the offspring of Echidne and Typhon, which was now ravaging Lycia.

148. Bellerophon was advised to catch the winged horse Pegasus, sprung from Medusa. Pegasus, by striking his hoof on the earth of Mt. Helicon, had created the spring of Hippocrene, sacred to the Muses, and he was found by Bellerophon at another of his fountains, that of Pirene in the Acropolis of Corinth. The hero flung over the horse's head a golden bridle, which Athene had given him, and astride his flying steed he easily shot the Chimæra with his arrows.

149. The frustrated Iobates now sent Bellerophon against the Amazons, and, when the hero again returned victorious, planted an ambush of guards against his arrival. Bellerophon slew them all, and Iobates, convinced at last that there had been some mistake, produced Prœtus' letter and learned the truth. He gave his guest his daughter in marriage and made him his heir.

150. Later tradition records that Bellerophon presumptuously tried to soar to Olympus mounted on Pegasus, but that Zeus sent a gadfly which stung the horse and caused him to throw his rider to earth. Bellerophon ended his days in wretchedness, but Pegasus gained Olympus.

JASON AND THE ARGONAUTS, 151–163.

151. The story of Jason and the Argonauts was already popular in Homer's day, and has more recently been told by Kingsley in *The Heroes*, and by William Morris in *The Life and Death of Jason*.

152. Jason's father Æson, the rightful King of Iolcus, had been deprived of his kingdom by his two half-brothers, Pelias and Neleus. The mother of all three was Tyro, who, seduced by Poseidon, bore him the twins Pelias and Neleus. She exposed the twins, but they were reared by a horse-herd, and when Tyro later married Cretheus, founder and King of Iolcus, they were adopted by him.

153. Tyro's son by Cretheus was Æson, but on Cretheus' death Pelias imprisoned Æson, expelled Neleus, and made himself supreme. The life of Æson's infant son Jason was saved only because he was smuggled out of Iolcus and entrusted to the care of Cheiron, the Centaur.

154. When a young man, Jason returned to Iolcus, fearlessly demanding his kingdom, and

Pelias, to be rid of him, asked him to go to Colchis to fetch the golden fleece. This, the fleece of the ram on which Phrixus had escaped, and which he had given to King Æëtes of Colchis, was now hanging on an oak-tree in the grove of Ares, guarded night and day by a sleepless dragon.

155. Jason welcomed the enterprise and commanded Argus, the Thespian to build him a fifty-oared ship called the *Argo*, into whose prow Athene herself fitted an oracular beam. Most of the heroes of the day flocked to join Jason, and his crew included the Dioscuri, Castor and Polydeuces, Heracles, and Orpheus the musician.

156. They met many adventures on the way. After lingering too long with the women of Lemnos, they slipped through the Hellespont and reached Mysia. Here Hylas, the squire of Heracles, while fetching water was stolen away by the Naiads, leaving nothing but an empty pitcher, and Heracles left the *Argo* in a vain search for him.

157. On the island of Bebrycos the Argonauts were met by its king, Amycus, son of Poseidon, and a renowned boxer, who contrived to kill all strangers by challenging them to a boxing match, but Polydeuces met the challenge and killed the bully. In Thrace they freed the blind king and prophet Phineus from a plague of Harpies, and in gratitude he advised Jason how to navigate the Bosphorus. At its entrance were the perilous floating islands, the Symplegades. It is possible that rumours of icebergs gave rise to the fable of these islands, which clashed together and crushed any ship which attempted to pass between them. But Jason, following the advice of Phineus, released a dove, and the *Argo* slipped between the islands as they recoiled. Henceforth they remained fixed. After overcoming other dangers, the Argonauts at last reached the River Phasis and Colchis.

158. Here Æëtes promised that he would give Jason the fleece if he could yoke together two fire-breathing bulls with brazen feet, the work of Hephæstus, plough the field of Ares, and sow it with the dragon's teeth left over by Cadmus at Thebes. It was Medea who enabled Jason to perform this terrible task. This sorceress princess, the daughter of Æëtes by his first wife, fell instantly in love with Jason and promised to help him if he would swear by all the gods to marry her and be faithful. She gave him a fire-resisting lotion and he completed the task. Then when Æëtes failed to keep his promise Medea charmed the dragon to sleep while Jason took down the fleece and they fled together in the *Argo*.

159. The furious Æëtes pursued them, but Medea ruthlessly murdered the young half-brother Absyrtus she had brought with her, and cut him into pieces which she dropped one by one over the side of the boat, Æëtes, stopping to collect the fragments for burial, soon lost sight of the fugitives.

160. There are many conflicting accounts of the *Argo*'s return journey, but none of them is feasible, for the Greek knowledge of geography was at that time very limited. Tradition said that the ship reached the Western Mediterranean and visited the island of Circe, who purified Jason and Medea of murder.

161. On their return to Iolcus they found that Pelias had forced Æson to take his life, though one tradition mentioned by Ovid and by Shakespeare in *The Merchant of Venice*, says that he was renewed to youthful vigour by Medea. All agree that Medea took a terrible revenge on Pelias. She persuaded his daughters, with the exception of Alcestis, to cut their father up and boil him in a cauldron, promising falsely that this would rejuvenate him. Pelias' son Acastus, horrified at the murder, then expelled Jason and Medea and they repaired to Corinth.

162. For many years they lived happily until they were involved in the final tragedy, dramatised by Euripides in his *Medea*. Jason deserted Medea for Glauce, also called Creusa, daughter of Creon, and the sorceress sent the young bride a garment which consumed her in flames, set fire to the palace, and involved Creon also in death. Some say that Medea also killed her own children by Jason.

163. Medea then escaped in a chariot drawn by winged serpents and took refuge with Ægeus of Athens, who married her. But on Theseus' arrival in the city, Medea departed and after many wanderings became an immortal. Some say that Jason took his own life; others that he was mercifully killed when the poop of his own ship *Argo* fell upon him.

HERACLES, 164–202.

164. Heracles, the most famous of the Greek heroes, was the son of Alcmene by Zeus.

165. Alcmene's brothers having been killed by the Taphians, she would not consummate her marriage with her husband Amphitrion, son of Alcæus, until he had avenged their death. While Amphitrion was away from Thebes fighting the Taphians, Zeus visited Alcmene in her husband's likeness and told her how he had been victorious. The true Amphitrion returned the following day, and the ensuing confusion is the theme of comedies by Plautus, Molière, and Dryden.

166. Nine months later Zeus boasted that he was about to become the father of a son who would be called Heracles, or glory of Hera, and who would be ruler of the house of Perseus. The jealous Hera exacted from him a promise that any son born that day to the house of Perseus should be king. She then hastened the birth of Eurystheus, who was a grandson of Perseus, and delayed that of Heracles. Alcmene bore two children, Heracles, son of Zeus, and Iphicles, Amphitrion's son, who was a night younger. Alcmene, fearing Hera, exposed Heracles, but Hera in error nursed him, thus conferring on him immortality.

167. Returned to Alcmene, Heracles prospered, and when still in his cradle, strangled with either hand two terrible snakes which Hera had sent to destroy him. In his youth he was taught how to drive the chariot by Amphitrion, fighting by Castor, how to sing and play the lyre by Eumolpus, wrestling by Autolycus, and archery by Eurytus. Linus, who was once teaching him to play the lyre, censured him, and Heracles then promptly killed his teacher with his own lyre, so Amphitrion sent him away to keep cattle.

168. In his eighteenth year he set out to attack the lion of Mt. Cithæron which was destroying the herds of both Amphitrion and his neighbour Thespius. The chase lasted fifty days, and Thespius, who was Heracles' host all this time; rewarded him by giving up his fifty daughters to him. Heracles killed the lion with a wild-olive club and made himself a garment of the pelt, with the head as helmet, though some say that he wore the skin of the Nemean lion.

169. On his return to Thebes, Heracles challenged the Minyan heralds from Orchomenus, who had come to collect tribute of cattle, and then led a victorious campaign against the Minyans in which his foster-father Amphitrion was killed.

170. Heracles was rewarded by Creon King of Thebes, who gave him his eldest daughter, Megara or Megera, in marriage, and Heracles became by her the father of several children. Creon's youngest daughter was married to Iphicles.

171. But Hera now visited Heracles with madness, so that he killed his own children and two of Iphicles'. When he recovered his reason he went, after purification, to consult the oracle at Delphi. The Pythia, calling him, for the first time, Heracles, advised him to go to Tiryns and there serve Eurystheus King of Argos for twelve years, doing whatever he was commanded. At the end of that time immortality would be conferred on him.

172. Most reluctantly Heracles set out. The gods gave him gifts of armour, but he relied on his bow and arrows and on the olive clubs which he cut for himself. His nephew Iolaus, oldest son of Iphicles, accompanied him as his faithful charioteer and companion. Thus supported, Heracles embarked on the twelve gigantic tasks imposed on him by Eurystheus.

The Twelve Labours of Heracles.

173. **The First Labour** was to bring back the skin of the Nemean or Cleonæan lion, an enormous creature, said to be the offspring of Typhon and Echidne, which was devastating the valley of Nemea near Cleonæ. As the pelt could not be pierced by any weapon, Heracles strangled the lion with his hands. He rededicated the Nemean games to Zeus and took the lion's carcase back to Tiryns, where he flayed it with its own claws. Some say that he wore the pelt as his armour. Eurystheus was so terrified that he now took refuge in a brazen urn below the earth whenever Heracles approached.

174. **The Second Labour** was to kill the Lernean Hydra, another monster which was said to be the offspring of Echidne by Typhon, and which Hera brought up. It lived at the sevenfold source of the River Amymone and haunted the neighbouring swamp of Lerna. It had a dog-like body and nine snaky heads, one of them immortal. As soon as Heracles struck off one head with his club, two grew in its place, while an enormous crab seized the hero's foot. He crushed the crab and called on Iolaus to burn the necks of the eight heads as he crushed them. The immortal head was buried and Heracles poisoned his arrows in the monster's gall, so that henceforth any wound they caused was fatal. Hera placed the image of the crab among the signs of the zodiac.

175. **The Third Labour** was to capture alive the Ceryneian Hind. This creature had brazen feet and golden antlers, and was therefore often called a stag. Heracles pursued it tirelessly for a year, and eventually shot an arrow which pinned the forelegs together without causing bloodshed. He then carried the creature back on his shoulders.

176. **The Fourth Labour** was to capture alive the Erymanthian boar, which had come down from Mt. Erymanthus to ravage Psophis. During his journey Heracles was entertained by the Centaur Pholus, who had a cask of wine given by Dionysus. When this was opened, other Centaurs besieged the cave. Repulsed by Heracles, some of them fled to the Centaur Cheiron. Heracles accidentally wounded Cheiron, who was an old friend, with one of his poisoned arrows. Cheiron, an immortal, could not die, although he now longed to do so, and was relieved from pain only when he later surrendered his immortality to Prometheus. Heracles continued his pursuit of the boar, drove it into a snow-drift, bound it with chains, and carried it to Eurystheus, but when he heard that the Argonauts were gathering for Colchis he hastened to join them, accompanied by Hylas.

177. **The Fifth Labour** was to cleanse in one day the stables of Augeias, King of Elis, who had more cattle and sheep than any man on earth. The dung had not been cleared away for years. Heracles swore a bargain with Augeias that he would cleanse the stalls in one day in return for a tenth of the cattle, and Phyleus, son of Augeias, was a witness to their mutual oaths. Heracles then diverted the Rivers Peneius and Alphaeus through the stalls, which were thus cleansed in a day. But Augeias now learned that Heracles had been under Eurystheus' orders, and therefore refused the reward and even denied the bargain. When Phyleus was loyal to the truth Augeias banished him. Heracles later avenged himself on Augeias.

178. **The Sixth Labour** was to free the marshy lake of Stymphalia in Arcadia of the Stymphalian birds which were sacred to Ares. These man-eating creatures had brazen beaks, claws, and wings, and used their feathers as arrows. Heracles, helped by Athene, frightened the birds with a rattle and then shot them down, though some say that they flew off to the island of Aretius in the Black Sea, where they were found later by the Argonauts.

179. **The Seventh Labour** was to capture the Cretan bull. Poseidon had sent the bull to Minos for a sacrifice, but he had substituted another, and it was now raging over the island. Heracles did not avail himself of Minos' offers of help, but captured the bull single-handed and took it to Eurystheus, who set it free again. It roamed through Greece to Marathon, where Theseus captured it and took it to Athens for sacrifice to Athene.

180. **The Eighth Labour** was to bring back the mares of Diomedes, a savage King of the Bistones in Thrace, who fed his horses on human flesh. On his way Heracles visited Admetus and freed Alcestis from death. Then with a few companions he drove the mares down to the sea, and turning to repel the attacking Bistones, he left them in the charge of his friend Abderus, who was soon eaten by them. Heracles, however, killed Diomedes and threw his body to the mares. He then founded the city of Abdera in honour of his friend and drove the mares back to Eurystheus, who set them free on Mt. Olympus, where they were eaten by wild beasts.

181. **The Ninth Labour** was to fetch for Admete, daughter of Eurystheus, the golden girdle that Hippolyte, Queen of the Amazons, had received from Ares. After an eventful journey through Europe and Asia, Heracles and his companions reached the land of the Amazons, where Hippolyte, sister of Antiope, received him kindly and promised him the girdle. But Hera roused the Amazons, and they attacked Heracles. In the fight he killed their leaders and Hippolyte herself, from whom he took the girdle. On his way home Heracles came to Troy, where he rescued Laomedan's daughter Hesione from a sea monster sent by Poseidon.

182 **The Tenth Labour** was to fetch the oxen of Geryon without either demand or payment. Geryon, a powerful monster with three bodies, lived on the island of Erythia. Its site was disputed. Some said it was beyond the ocean stream. Others identified it with Gades. Heracles travelled to the frontiers of Libya and Europe, where he set up two pillars, Calpe and Abyla, on the two sides of the Straits of Gibraltar, hence called the "Pillars of Hercules." When Helios shone too brightly, Heracles shot at him with an arrow, and Helios, admiring such boldness, gave him a golden cup or boat in which he sailed to Erythia. Geryon's cattle were guarded by the two-headed dog Orthrus, said to be the offspring of Typhon and Echidne, and the herdsmen Eurytion, son of Ares. Heracles felled both of these with his club, and, after overcoming Geryon, he sailed with the cattle to Tartessus in Spain, where he returned the golden boat to Helios. On his adventurous journey back through Gaul, Italy, Illyricum, and Thrace, he resisted many attempts, such as that of Cacus, to steal the cattle and eventually handed them over to Eurystheus, who sacrificed them to Hera.

183. **The Eleventh Labour** was to fetch the golden apples of the Hesperides. These grew on the tree which Hera had received from Ge at her wedding and which she had planted in a garden on Mt. Atlas. It was guarded by the Hesperides and the dragon Ladon, another offspring of Typhon and Echidne. Heracles first consulted Proteus, or as some say Prometheus, and, following the advice he received, he persuaded Atlas to fetch the apples, while he himself upheld the celestial globe. According to some, he also shot Ladon. Atlas, returning with three apples, tried to avoid taking back the burden of the globe, but Heracles, by a ruse, transferred the globe back to the giant's shoulders, took the apples, and hastened away. On his return journey he killed the giant Antæus, and also persuaded Zeus to free Prometheus, the arrow with which Apollo shot the vulture being placed among the stars a[s]

Sagitta. Eurystheus made Heracles a gift of the apples, but the hero dedicated them to Athene, who returned them to their rightful place.

184. The Twelfth Labour was to bring back the dog Cerberus from Tartarus, the most difficult task of all. Heracles descended from Tænarum in Laconia and was guided by Athene and Hermes. After he had crossed the Styx and freed his friend Theseus and Ascalaphus, he obtained Hades' permission to carry away Cerberus, provided he could do so without using any weapon. Heracles seized Cerberus by the throat and dragged him up to show Eurystheus. He then carried the monster back to Tartarus.

185. According to most writers Heracles now returned to Thebes and gave his wife Megara to his nephew Iolaus, but Euripides, in his play *Heracles*, uses a different version. He represents the hero first killing the tyrant of Thebes, who had attempted to kill Megara and her children, and then, driven insane by Hera, himself killing his wife and family.

186. Heracles now desired to marry Iole, daughter of his friend Eurytus, King of Œchalia. Eurytus had promised her to the man who could surpass him and his sons in shooting with the bow. Though Heracles surpassed them all, Eurytus still refused to give him Iole because he had murdered his own children, and in this Eurytus was supported by all his sons except Iphitus. Later when Iphitus appeared suspicious of him, Heracles in a frenzy of rage slew him. Though purified from this murder, he was still troubled in mind, and consulted the Delphic Oracle. He was advised to serve as a slave and to give the proceeds to the family of Iphitus.

187. Heracles was purchased by Omphale, Queen of Lydia, and widow of Tmolus, and he served her either for one or for three years. Later writers say that he lived effeminately at this time, and that he used to change garments with Omphale, but others say that he continued to perform heroic deeds.

188. His period of servitude to Omphale completed, Heracles sailed against Troy. On a previous occasion, probably when returning from the land of the Amazons, Heracles and his friend Telamon had come to Troy, where they had found Laomedan's daughter, Hesione, exposed naked to a sea-monster, sent by Poseidon (*see para.* 104). Heracles had freed Hesione and killed the monster, but Laomedan had refused to give him the reward he had promised, the white horses given by Zeus in exchange for Ganymede.

189. Heracles and Telamon therefore now sailed to Troy to take their revenge. How they sacked the city is described in para. 275. Hesione was given to Telamon and bore him the son Teucer. On his return, Heracles faced a terrible storm raised by Hera and perils on the island of Cos. He was then led by Athene to Phlegra, where he helped the gods in their battle with the giants.

190. Heracles now took his revenge on Augeias, who had refused him payment for cleansing the stables. He invaded Elis and eventually killed Augeias, his sons, and their allies, the Moliones, though some say that he spared Augeias. He then founded the Olympic Games, and fetched from the source of the Danube the wild-olive tree whose leaves should crown the victor. Heracles then destroyed the city of Pylus, which had helped Elis. He killed Neleus the king and all his sons except Nestor.

191. Heracles next marched against Hippocoon who had fought against him under Neleus. Hippocoon had driven out his brother Tyndareus and seized the kingdom of Sparta. Heracles killed him and all his sons, and restored Tyndareus. He was helped in this enterprise by Cepheus and his twenty sons, but Cepheus and seventeen sons were killed. It was about this time that Heracles seduced the priestess Auge, daughter of Aleus, King of Tegea, and became by her the father of Telephus.

192. After four years in Arcadia, Heracles left for Ætolia, where Œneus was King of Calydonia and Pleuron. Heracles wished to marry Œneus' daughter Deianeira and won her by defeating Achelous, the mighty river-god, son of Oceanus and Tethys. He now sent Iolaus as leader of his sons by the daughters of Thespius to settle in Sardinia.

193. Three years later, while at a feast, Heracles accidentally killed the boy Eunomus, and went into voluntary exile, taking Deianeira and their son Hyllus.

194. They reached the River Evenus, across which the centaur Nessus carried travellers for a small fee. Heracles let Nessus carry Deianeira, while he himself swam, but the centaur galloped off with her and would have violated her if Heracles had not shot him through the breast. The dying centaur then told Deianeira to take his blood as a charm to keep Heracles' love.

195. Heracles now resided at Trachis, and from there invaded Œchalia with an army in order to avenge himself on Eurytus, who had refused to surrender his daughter Iole, even though Heracles had won her in the archery contest. The hero killed Eurytus and all his family, and sent Iole to Deianeira in Trachis while he visited Cenæum in Eubœa and prepared a thanksgiving sacrifice to Zeus.

196. He had sent Lichas to Deianeira to fetch a white shirt to wear at the ceremony. Deianeira, fearful that Iole might win Heracles' love, rubbed the shirt in Nessus' blood, not knowing that Heracles' arrow, steeped in the Hydra's blood, had poisoned it. When Heracles put the shirt on, it burned with excruciating agony into his body, and attempts to tear it off took his flesh with it. Heracles seized Lichas and flung him into the sea and then commanded his son Hyllus to take him to Trachis. Deianeira, aghast at what she had unintentionally done, hanged herself. Heracles asked Hyllus to promise to marry Iole and to build him a funeral pyre on Mt. Œta.

197. This tragic climax to Heracles' career has been dramatised by Sophocles in the *Women of Trachis*, or *Trachiniæ*, where Deianeiras' distress at Ioles' arrival and her ill-fated ruse to keep her husband's love are touchingly represented.

198. Heracles finally ascended his funeral pyre to be burned alive. To Philoctetes, who kindled the flame, he gratefully bequeathed his quiver, bow, and arrows. Thunderbolts demolished the pyre, and Heracles was carried by a cloud to Olympus. There he became immortal, Hera was persuaded by Zeus to adopt him as her son, and reconciled to her at last, he married her daughter Hebe.

The Children of Heracles, or Heracleidæ.

199. Eurystheus now determined to expel from Greece Alcmene and all the children of Heracles. Only in Athens did they find protection, and when Eurystheus attacked the city he was resisted by Theseus (or by his son Demophon), Iolaus, and Hyllus. As an oracle had demanded the sacrifice of one of Heracles' children, his daughter Macaria killed herself. Eurystheus was then defeated, by either Iolaus or Hyllus, and despatched by Alcmene.

200. These events are the theme of Euripides' play, *The Children of Heracles* or *Heracleidæ*.

201. Hyllus later, endeavouring to enter Peloponnesus, was slain in single combat by Echemus, King of Tegea. Only Tleopolemus settled in Argos.

202. Some generations later, the descendants of of Heracles conquered Peloponnesus in conjunction with the Dorians. This legend indicates the conquest of the Achæans by the later invaders.

THESEUS, 203–218.

203. Theseus, the great hero of Attica, was the son of Æthra by Ægeus, King of Athens, though he was also reputed to be the son of Poseidon. Æthra was the daughter of Pittheus, King of Troezen and here she secretly brought up her young son.

204. When he was of age, Æthra showed him the sandals, and a sword which was an heirloom of Cecrops, that Ægeus had left for him under a great rock. Theseus was able to lift the rock, recover the tokens, and proceed to Athens.

205. He insisted on going not by sea, but by the dangerous land route, and, like Heracles, he freed the country of many terrors. He killed Periphetes, whose club he afterwards carried, Sinis, the the wild sow of Crommyum, Sciron, Cercyon, and Sinis' father Polypemon, who was surnamed Procrustes.

206. Meanwhile in Athens Ægeus had married Medea, who had fled for safety from Corinth. Medea recognised Theseus, and jealous for Medus, her son by Ægeus, she attempted to poison him. But Ægeus recognised Cecrops' sword in time and welcomed his son with great rejoicing. Medea fled, taking Medus, and Theseus then scattered other rivals, the fifty sons of Pallas, nephews of Ægeus, who had hoped to succeed him to the throne.

207. Theseus next captured and sacrificed to Athene, the Marathonian bull which Heracles had brought from Crete and which had been driven to Marathon.

208. He now, of his own free will, went as one of the seven youths who with seven maidens were chosen by lot to be sent to Crete as yearly tribute, to be devoured there by the Minotaur. But Ariadne, daughter of Minos, King of Crete, fell in love with Theseus, and gave him a sword and a clue of thread by which he might find his way out of the labyrinth where the Minotaur lived. Theseus slew the monster, released his fellow Athenians, and fled with them and Ariadne, but at Naxos he deserted her and she was consoled by Dionysus, to whom the island was sacred.

209. Theseus forgot on his return to hoist the white sail which was to have been a sign of victory, and Ægeus, seeing the black sail, threw himself in despair into the sea now called Ægean. Theseus then became the King of Athens.

210. He is said to have invaded the country of the Amazons either with Heracles or later, and here he carried off Antiope, who became his wife, though according to another tradition, Theseus took not Antiope but her sister Hippolyte. It is "Hippolyta" who appears as his bride in *The Midsummer Night's Dream.* In revenge the Amazons invaded Attica, and were eventually defeated by Theseus in the midst of Athens itself.

211. Later Theseus married Ariadne's sister Phædra, another daughter of Minos, who bore him the sons Acamas and Demophon. But Phædra fell desperately in love with her step-son Hippolytus (Theseus' son by either Antiope, or Hippolyte), and when the young man rejected her advances she killed herself, after leaving a letter falsely accusing him to Theseus. The enraged Theseus prayed to Poseidon that Hippolytus might die that very day, and the god sent a sea-monster which so terrified the chariot horses of Hippolytus that they dragged him to death. The story is the theme of Euripides' tragedy *Hippolytus*, and the *Phedre* of Racine.

212. Theseus was a close friend of Pirithous, King of the Lapithæ, and attended his wedding to Hippodameia, and when a drunken Centaur attempted to carry off the bride, Theseus joined with the Lapithæ in the famous fight against the Centaurs.

213. After Hippodameia's death, Pirithous and Theseus together carried off the girl Helen of Sparta, and she fell by lot to Theseus. As she was too young to marry, he concealed her in the village of Aphidnæ, where she was cared for by his mother Æthra.

214. Theseus then, full of misgiving, fulfilled his promise to Pirithous to help carry off another daughter of Zeus, by accompanying him to the Underworld to take away Persephone. But Hades chained them both to a rock, where they languished till Heracles came to the Underworld and released Theseus only (*see para.* 184).

215. Meanwhile Helen's brothers, the Dioscuri Castor and Polydeuces, invaded Attica, and being told by Academus where Helen was hidden, they rescued her, taking Æthra as her slave.

216. When Theseus returned from Tartarus he was unable to keep order among his people, who were being stirred up against him by Menestheus. He retired to the island of Scyros, where he was treacherously killed by King Lycomedes. He nevertheless returned in spirit to help the Athenians at the Battle of Marathon, and though Menestheus succeeded Theseus as king, the sons of Theseus were afterwards restored to the throne.

217. Theseus, like Heracles, took part in the heroic enterprises of his age. He joined in the Calydonian hunt and helped Adrastus at Thebes, and he may have been one of the Argonauts.

218. Although Athenians in later times looked on Theseus as an historical figure, ascribing political institutions to him, he was in fact a legendary hero.

CRETAN MYTHS, 219–239.

219. Recent archæological discoveries have indicated that many of the ancient legends concerned with Crete have a factual basis, and a very readable book on the subject is the "Pan" Book *Bull of Minos*, by Leonard Cottrell.

220. In 1899 Sir Arthur Evans began his excavations at Cnossos and soon unearthed the remains of the magnificent, unfortified and labyrinthine so-called "Palace of Minos" with its indications of an elegant and highly artistic civilisation.

221. From the architectural evidence available, scholars now consider that there existed in Crete between 2500 and 1400 B.C., a "Minoan" pre-Hellenic culture which had affinities with that of Egypt. This maritime, commercial culture, its sea-power making fortification unnecessary, spread to the mainland of Greece, where it became known as Mycenæan. It is in fact possible that Crete may have exercised some kind of suzerainty over the mainland. The Cretans probably worshipped a goddess who was served by priestesses. The favourite sport was bull-fighting, in which men and women toreadors showed amazing skill. Cretan architects and engineers were exceptionally ingenious.

222. Discoveries such as these give special significance to such legends as that of Minos' sea power, and of Crete's exaction from Athens of a tribute of men and maidens for the Minotaur. Again the constant appearance of the bull in Cretan legend and Dædalus' building of the labyrinth appear to have foundation in historical fact.

223. It was to Crete that Zeus, in the form of a bull, brought Europa, said to be the daughter of Agenor, son of Poseidon and King of Phœnicia, and of his wife Telephassa.

224. As the lovely Europa was playing on the sea-shore with her maidens, Zeus appeared as a white bull and she dared to climb on his back, an incident depicted in the masterly painting by

Paul Veronese in the Palace of the Doges in Venice. Suddenly Zeus, plunging into the sea, carried off Europa to Crete, where he fathered on her the three sons, Minos, Rhadamanthus, and Sarpedon. When the reigning king later married Europa he adopted her three sons as his heirs.

225. The brothers quarrelled, however, over the boy Miletus, son of Apollo. As Miletus preferred Sarpedon, they both fled from Minos to Asia Minor. Here Miletus founded the kingdom that bore his name, and Sarpedon, after aiding Cilix, King of Cilicia, against the Lycians, became king of the latter and was permitted by Zeus to live for three generations.

226. Rhadamanthus, though at first ruler of part of Crete, also found it wise to flee. He went to Bœotia, and on Amphitrion's death married Alcmene. So just a ruler did he prove, that he became one of the judges of the Underworld.

227. Minos, now sole ruler of Crete, was confirmed in his power by Poseidon, who sent him a magnificent white bull. This so delighted the king that he withheld it from sacrifice, and when it later ran savage it was captured by Heracles as his Seventh Labour, and eventually slain by Theseus.

228. Minos was the law-giver to Crete and was helped in the defence of the island by Talos, a bull-headed, brazen giant and by his powerful fleet.

229. Curious legends are told of Minos' loves. One was Procris, another Britomartis, a Cretan nymph whom he pursued for nine months, until she leaped into the sea and was deified by Artemis, sharing with her the epithet Dictynna.

230. Once when Minos was besieging Nisa, the port of Megara, which belonged to King Nisus, Scylla, Nisus' daughter, fell in love with him, and killed her father by cutting off the hair on which his life depended. Although Scylla let him into the city, Minos was so horrified at her parricide that he left her, and she swam after his ship until her father's soul, changed to a sea-eagle, pounced on her, and she was turned to the bird Ciris. Others say that Minos drowned Scylla, and she was turned into the fish Ciris. She has sometimes been confused with Scylla the daughter of Phorcys.

231. The wife of Minos was Pasiphaë daughter of Helios and Persë and several of their children, as Glaucus, Androgeos, Ariadne, and Phædra were the subject of legend.

232. Glaucus when a boy was drowned in a cask of honey, and his body found by the seer Polyeidus. Unable to resuscitate Glaucus, Polyeidus was entombed with him, but here a serpent revealed a herb which restored Glaucus to life, and the seer and the boy were released.

233. Androgeos won every contest in the Panathenaic games and was slain at the instigation of Æegus. Minos in revenge exacted from Athens a yearly tribute of seven youths and maidens to be devoured by the Minotaur.

234. This monster with bull's head and man's body, was the offspring of Pasiphaë and the white bull. Dædalus the craftsman had enabled her to satisfy her desire, and afterwards built the labyrinth in which her shameful offspring was housed.

235. When Ægeus' son Theseus voluntarily joined the youths destined for the Minotaur, Ariadne fell in love with him, and enabled him to kill the monster by giving him a sword and a clue of thread by means of which he found his way out of the labyrinth. Ariadne then escaped with Theseus, but was deserted by him on Naxos, where she was found by Dionysus, as depicted in Titian's "Bacchus and Ariadne" in the National Gallery. Tintoretto's picture in the Doge's Palace in Venice shows the marriage of Ariadne to the god.

236. Her sister Phædra was later married to Theseus, and her unrequited passion for her step-son Hippolytus and its tragic outcome has been described in para. 211.

237. The cunning Dædalus, whose craftsmanship was symbolic of the latest development in sculpture and architecture, had been welcomed by Minos after his flight from Athens. The legend runs that he had been so bitterly jealous of his nephew Talos, or Perdix, inventor of the saw, chisel, and compasses, that he threw him headlong from Athene's temple on the Acropolis. Athene changed Talos into the bird "perdix" or partridge, and the Areopagus banished Dædalus.

238. Welcomed to Crete, he found his skill greatly valued by Minos, until the king discovered how he had aided Pasiphaë. Minos then imprisoned Dædalus with his son Icarus in his own labyrinth. They were released by Pasiphaë, and Dædalus made wings fastened to the shoulders with wax on which they flew away. Icarus mounted too high, the sun melted the wax and he was drowned in the Icarian Sea, but Dædalus reached Cumæ near Naples, and fled thence to Sicily. Here Cocalus welcomed him, and when Minos pursued the craftsman, Cocalus' daughters enabled him ingeniously to kill the king.

239. After Minos' death, although his son succeeded him, Cretan civilisation collapsed. Minos himself became a judge in the Underworld.

THEBAN MYTHS, 240–271.

240. The legend concerning the origin of Thebes is that of Cadmus, who according to common tradition was the son of Agenor, son of Poseidon and the King of Phœnicia, and of his wife Telephassa.

241. The sister of Cadmus, Europa, was one day carried off by Zeus, who appeared to her in the form of a bull (as is described in para. 224) and Agenor sent Cadmus in search of his sister.

242. Unable to find her, Cadmus consulted the Delphic oracle, who advised him to relinquish his search but to follow a cow and build a town where she should sink down with fatigue. Cadmus followed the cow from Phocis to Bœotia, and where she rested he built Cadmea, later the citadel of Thebes.

243. Making sacrifice to Athene, he sent his men for water from a spring of Ares not knowing that it was guarded by a dragon which killed most of his men. When Cadmus had killed the dragon Athene advised him to sow its teeth, and immediately there sprang up, fully armed, the Sparti, or "Sown Men," who fought with each other till only five survived—Echion, Udæus, Chthonius, Hyperenor, and Pelorus. These five were the ancestors of Thebes, and with their help the Cadmea was built.

244. Zeus gave to Cadmus as wife Harmonia, daughter of Ares and Aphrodite, and the Olympian deities attended the wedding. Harmonia received as a gift from Aphrodite the famous necklace made by Hephæstus, which Zeus had originally given Europa, and which conferred irresistible loveliness upon its wearer. From Athene she received a magic robe which conferred divine dignity. The children of Cadmus and Harmonia were Autonoe, Ino, Semele the mother of Dionysus, Agave, Polydorus, and later Illyrius.

245. It is said that Cadmus introduced to Thebes from Phœnicia the use of letters.

246. In old age Cadmus resigned the throne to Pentheus, his grandson, the son of Agave and Echion. But Pentheus, resisting the worship of Dionysus, was destroyed by Agave and her sisters Autonoe and Ino, as is depicted in *The Bacchæ* of Euripides.

247. Cadmus and Harmonia then left Thebes and were later, in the form of serpents, received in the Islands of the Blessed.

248. Another legend concerning Thebes is that of Amphion and Zethus the twin sons of Antiope by Zeus.

249. Antiope was divorced by her husband Lycus of Thebes, and cruelly treated by his second wife, Dirce. Meanwhile Amphion and Zethus were brought up by cattle men on Mt. Cithæron. When they were old enough to know what had happened they took their revenge. They killed Lycus and Dirce, who was tied to the horns of a wild bull and her body thrown into a fountain which henceforth bore her name, and then took possession of Thebes.

250. Amphion and Zethus now built the lower fortifications below the Cadmea, and so skilfully did Amphion play on the lyre given him by Hermes that the stones moved into place of their own accord. The brothers ruled jointly, Zethus married Thebe, who gave her name to the city, and Niobe became the wife of Amphion.

251. Niobe, the proud daughter of Tantalus and sister of Pelops, had seven sons and seven daughters, and boasted that she was superior to Leto, who had only two children. As punishment to her, Apollo killed the boys with his arrows, and Artemis the girls, and Niobe "all tears" was turned by Zeus into a stone on Mt. Sipylus. The crag of Niobe, being snow-capped, appears to weep when the sun strikes the snow. It is said the Amphion also was either killed by Apollo or that he took his own life.

252. Most famous of Theban kings was Œdipus, who claimed direct descent from Cadmus through Polydorus, Labdacus, and Laius, and all three of the great Greek tragic dramatists were inspired by the fateful story of Œdipus and his children.

253. Œdipus the son of Laius, King of Thebes, and of his wife Jocasta, was as a new-born child exposed on Mt. Cithæron, his feet tied together and pierced with a nail, for Laius had learned from the oracle at Delphi that he would be killed by his own son. Found by a shepherd of Polybus, King of Corinth, the child was called from his swollen feet Œdipus, and was reared by Polybus as his own son.

254. When Œdipus grew to manhood, he was told by the Delphic oracle that he was destined to kill his own father and marry his mother, and he resolved never to return to Corinth. But going from Delphi, he met Laius riding in a chariot, and in a quarrel killed him.

255. Laius had been on his way to ask the Delphic oracle how he could rid Thebes of the Sphinx, a winged lion with the head and breast of a woman. This monster was said to be the offspring of Typhon and Echidne, or of Orthrus and the Chimæra. Seated on a rock, she challenged each wayfarer with her riddle and strangled him when he failed to solve it.

256. Œdipus, arriving in Thebes, heard the Sphinx's riddle. "Which being, having only one voice, has sometimes two feet, sometimes three, and sometimes four and is weakest when it has most." Œdipus answered rightly that the being was man, who crawls in infancy and supports himself with a staff in old age, and the Sphinx thereupon flung herself to death.

257. As the Thebans had promised that whoever should vanquish the Sphinx should become king and marry Jocasta, Œdipus became King of Thebes and had four children by his own mother, Eteocles, Polyneices, Antigone, and Ismene.

258. Thebes, thus defiled by murder and incest, was visited by plague and the blind seer Teiresias said that the city would be saved when one of the "Sparti" (a title given also to descendants of the "Sown Men") should give his life. When he learned this, Menœceus, father of Jocasta, leapt from the walls to his death.

259. The plague still raging, Œdipus consulted Teiresias, and it is at this point that the famous *Œdipus Tyrannus* of Sophocles begins. Œdipus was horrified when at last convinced of his unconscious guilt and, after Jocasta had hanged herself, he blinded himself with a pin taken from her garment and prayed her brother Creon to banish him.

260. Eventually Œdipus went into exile accompanied by Antigone, and followed later by Ismene. At Colonos in Attica he found refuge in a grove of the Eumenides and, protected by Theseus, was received at last by the gods. These last hours of Œdipus are most touchingly presented by Sophocles in his *Œdipus at Colonos*.

261. Angered by his sons' neglect, Œdipus had cursed them, saying that they should divide their inherited land by the sword. They therefore agreed to rule in turn, but when Eteocles' term had expired he refused to abdicate. Polyneices then sought the help of Adrastus, son of Talaus and King of Argos, whose daughter Argia he married, while her sister Deipyle married Tydeus (son of Œneus of Calydon), who, on account of some murder he had committed, was also a fugitive.

262. When Adrastus prepared to restore Polyneices, his brother-in-law, the seer Amphiaraus, prophesied death for all the leaders save Adrastus. Amphiaraus had married Adrastus' sister Eriphyle, and Polyneices, following the advice of Tydeus, bribed Eriphyle, giving her the famous necklace of Harmonia on the condition that she would persuade her husband to joint the expedition.

263. Adrastus, Amphiaraus, Polyneices, and Tydeus were joined by Capaneus, Hippomedon, and Parthenopaeus, the son of Meleager and Atalanta, and these seven marched against Thebes. The war that followed was dramatised by both Æschylus, in his *Seven against Thebes*, and by Euripides, in *The Phœnician Maidens*.

264. After Thebes had suffered initial reverses, Teiresias prophesied that a royal prince must sacrifice himself, and a second Menœceus, the son of Creon, now took his own life.

265. The attackers were soon repelled. Capaneus, scaling the walls, was struck by Zeus with lightning. Tydeus, wounded by Melanippus, might have been saved by Athene with an elixir given her by Zeus, but Amphiaraus, who bore him a grudge, persuaded him to drink the brains of the dead Melanippus. This so disgusted Athene that she left him to his fate. Hippomedon and Parthenopæus also having been killed, offered to settle the dispute in single combat with Eteocles, but both were mortally wounded. Amphiaraus fled in his chariot and the earth opened and swallowed him. As the seer had prophesied, Adrastus was the only one of the seven left alive.

266. Thebes was not unscathed. The *Antigone* of Sophocles opens at the point where Creon refused to allow burial to Polyneices. The courageous Antigone dared to disobey him and he ordered that she should be imprisoned alive in a cave. Here she hanged herself, and Creon's son Hæmon, to whom she was betrothed, took his own life in despair.

267. Euripides, in *The Suppliants*, dramatises the next phase of the story. Since the Thebans had refused burial to their fallen enemies, Adrastus and the mothers of the slain went to Eleusis and secured the help of Theseus. He defeated the Thebans, and the bodies of the Argives received burial rites, but Evadne, daughter of Iphis and wife of Capaneus threw herself on to the flaming pyre and perished.

268. Thebes was again attacked ten years later when Adrastus assembled the "Epigoni," the descendants of the "Seven." His own son Ægialeus made one, and also Diomedes, son of Tydeus, with his faithful companion Sthenelеus son of Capaneus and Evadne.

269. Since Alcmæon, like his father Amphiaraus was unwilling to join the Epigoni, Thersander followed the example of his father Polyneices in once more bribing Eriphyle, this time with the magic robe of Harmonia. She then persuaded Alcmæon to join the expedition along with his brother the seer Amphilochus.

270. Ægialeus was killed before the walls of Thebes, and Teiresias then advised the Thebans to evacuate the city and himself accompanied them, though he died next dawn on drinking from the well of Tilphussa. That day Adrastus, hearing of Ægialeus' death, also died of grief, and in accordance with Teiresias' prophecy the Argives took the empty city.

271. Alcmæon, on return, slew his mother Eriphyle, in revenge for her vanity and deceit towards his father and himself. Pursued by the Erinnyes, he fled to Phlegeus, King of Psophis, who purified him and gave him his daughter Arsinoë in marriage. Alcmæon gave his wife Harmonia's necklace and robe, but was soon forced by the Erinnyes to flee once more. He was next purified by the river-god Achelous and married his daughter Callirrhoë, who soon demanded the necklace and robe. Alcmæon, daring to revisit Psophis, obtained them from Phlegeus on the pretext of taking them to Delphi, but when Phlegeus discovered that they were destined for Callirrhoë he ordered his sons to slay Alcmæon. Finally, Phlegeus himself sent the ill-fated treasures to Delphi.

LEGENDS OF TROY, 272–352.

272. One of the most romantic discoveries of modern times is that of the German Schliemann, who, trusting the descriptions of Homer, excavated a site on the coast of Asia Minor, near the entrance to the Dardanelles. Between 1871 and 1873 he unearthed the foundations not of one Troy but of seven, his most spectacular find being a hoard of exquisite gold ornaments. His work proved that Troy belonged not only to legend but also to history.

273. It is now considered that in the Bronze Age Troy was an important centre for trade. Frequently attacked, it was many times rebuilt, and Greeks, Cretans, and Phrygians all claimed to have had a hand in establishing it. In Homer's time, when the sixth Troy was standing, it had probably absorbed three small towns, Dardania, Tros or Troy, and Ilium, and was probably inhabited by three tribes, Dardanians, Trojans, and Ilians, whose names are all represented in the early legends of Troy's foundation.

274. One of these tells how Scamander of Crete founded a colony in Phrygia, and how, jumping into the River Xanthus, he changed its name to his own. The nymph Idæa bore him a son Teucer (whence the Trojans are called Teucri), and Teucer gave a piece of land to Dardanus, the son of Zeus by the Pleiad Electra, who built there the town of Dardania. The grandson of Dardanus was Tros, who became the father of Ilus and also of Ganymede, whom he relinquished to Zeus for a gift of horses. The son of Ilus was Laomedan.

275. It was to Laomedan that Zeus assigned Apollo and Poseidon as labourers. They built for him the walls of Troy, and when Laomedan refused payment, Poseidon sent the sea-monster, which would have devoured his daughter Hesione had not she been rescued by Heracles. But again Laomedan refused the agreed reward—the white horses given by Zeus in exchange for Ganymede—and Heracles returned later to sack Troy. He gave Hesione to his fellow-warrior Telamon, and killed Laomedan and all his sons save Podarces, who was ransomed by his sister Hesione, and his name changed to Priam, which means "redeemed."

276. After a few years Priam sent Antenor to demand that Telamon should send back Hesione, and the Greeks' scornful refusal was one of the causes of the Trojan War.

277. Priam had fifty sons, nineteen of them by his second wife Hecabe, or Hecuba, who bore him many famous children, including Hector, Paris, Deïphobus and the prophetic twins Helenus and Cassandra. Troilus may have been her son by Apollo.

278. Before the birth of her second son, Hecuba dreamed that she had brought forth a blazing firebrand, and the new-born child was therefore exposed on Mt. Ida. Brought up by a shepherd, he was called Paris, and later, by his courage earned the name Alexander or "defender of men." Paris was beloved by the nymph Œnone, but he deserted her as the result of a tempting suggestion of Aphrodite's.

279. The occasion of this was the famous "Judgment of Paris," of which a Renaissance version can be seen in Rubens' picture in the National Gallery.

280. The story goes that alone of all the gods, Eris was not invited to the marriage of Peleus and Thetis, and in revenge she flung in the golden apple of discord with "to the fairest" inscribed upon it. Immediately Hera, Athene, and Aphrodite disputed its possession, and Zeus commanded Hermes to lead the goddesses to Mt. Ida for Paris to judge the dispute.

281. Although Hera promised him rule in Asia, and Athene fame in war, Paris gave the apple to Aphrodite, who promised him as his wife the loveliest of all women.

282. Paris now discovered his parentage and was joyfully welcomed by Priam, and under Aphrodite's protection sailed to Sparta.

283. His sister Cassandra foretold doom, but was as usual unregarded. In her youth she had been loved by Apollo, who had taught her the art of prophecy on condition that she became his lover. But she had disappointed him, and Apollo had then ordained that her prophecy should never be believed.

284. Welcomed to Sparta by King Menelaus, Paris fell in love with his beautiful queen, Helen, and in Menelaus' absence he succeeded in carrying her off to Troy with much treasure, thus precipitating the Trojan War, now inevitable by reason of an oath sworn by the leading chieftains of Greece to defend Helen's husband.

285. Helen, the daughter of Leda by Zeus, had been brought up in the Court of Leda's husband, Tyndareus of Sparta. So lovely was she that even as a young girl she had been carried off by Theseus and Pirithous, to be rescued and brought back by her brothers, the Dioscuri. All the noblest in Greece then became rivals for her hand, and at the instigation of Tyndareus swore an oath to defend her chosen husband.

286. Helen married Menelaus, and when the Dioscuri were immortalised, he succeeded Tyndareus as King of Sparta.

287. After Helen had fled with Paris, leaving her husband and daughter Hermione, Menelaus summoned the chieftains to war. His powerful brother Agamemnon, King of Mycenæ, who had married Helen's half-sister, Clytemnestra, was leader, and from the Peloponnese came also old Nestor of Pylus, whose Palace has only recently been discovered. Nestor was the only one of Neleus' twelve sons spared by Heracles. Renowned for wisdom and eloquence, he had been a courageous fighter. He had defeated the Arcadians and Eleans and had taken part in the Calydonian hunt and the fight between Centaurs and Lapithæ. Although he had ruled over three generations, he gladly joined the expedition to Troy.

288. The courageous Diomedes, son of Tydeus, and King of Argos, also came from the Peloponnese with eighty ships. He had been one of the Epigoni who had taken Thebes, and two fellow Epigoni came with him—Sthenelus, son of Capaneus, and Euryalus, the Argonaut. Tleopolemus, son of Heracles, the Argive who had settled in Rhodes, brought nine ships, and Palamedes, son of Nauplius, joined the muster from Eubœa.

289. But Agamemnon needed more distant allies, and together with Menelaus and Palamedes, he went to Ithaca to persuade Odysseus to join them.

290. Odysseus was the son of Anticleia, a daughter of the wily thief Autolycus, and of Lærtes, King of Ithaca, though some say that his father was really Sisyphus. He had won his wife Penelope, daughter of King Icarius of Sparta, in a foot race, and when Icarius had tried to persuade Penelope to remain with him, Odysseus had told her she might do as she wished. Penelope had veiled her face to hide her blushes and had followed her husband to Ithaca.

291. An oracle had warned Odysseus not to join the expedition to Troy, and when the envoys arrived they found him ploughing and sowing salt. But the far-sighted Palmedes placed Odysseus' infant son Telemachus in front of the plough, and Odysseus was tricked into revealing his sanity and joining the expedition.

292. Agamemnon also welcomed allies from Salamis and Locris. From Salamis, bringing twelve ships, came Great Ajax, son of King Telamon, a courageous fighter, who boasted that he needed not the help of the gods. His half-brother, Teucer, son of Telamon by Hesione and the best archer in Greece, fought behind Great Ajax' shield. Little Ajax also fought with them. Son of Oileus, King of the Locrians, he was small in stature but swift of foot, and skilled in throwing the spear. He brought forty ships.

293. An important contingent from Southern Thessaly also sailed to Troy, for Calchas, a renegade prophet from Troy, foretold that the city could not be taken without the help of Achilles, son of Peleus, King of the Myrmidones at Phthia in Thessaly, and of the Nereid, Thetis.

294. By dipping her son into the Styx, Thetis had made him invulnerable, except for the heel which she was holding. Achilles had been taught by Cheiron and by his tutor Phœnix, and was renowned for strength, speed, and high courage.

295. Thetis, knowing that if Achilles went to Troy he would never return alive, sent him disguised as a girl to the Court of Lycomedes, King of Scyros, and here Lycomedes' daughter Deidamia bore him the son Neoptolemus, or Pyrrhus. When Odysseus, accompanied by Nestor and Ajax, visited Scyros, he left a spear and shield among a pile of gifts for the maidens, and Achilles, seizing these, revealed his identity.

296. Achilles joined the Greeks together with his tutor Phœnix and Patroclus, his cousin, who had come as a boy to Peleus' Court after an accidental murder and had become the inseparable friend of Achilles.

297. The Greeks were further strengthened by Idomeneus, King of Crete, who brought 100 ships and shared the command with Agamemnon. Meriones accompanied Idomeneus.

298. The fleet was fortunate in being abundantly supplied with provisions, by Anius, son and priest of Apollo in Delos, for his three daughters who had been dedicated to Dionysus received from the god power to produce at will corn, oil, and wine.

299. The expedition set out from Aulis, but first made a false landing and ravaged the country of Telephus, son of Heracles and Auge, and now King of Mysia. When he repelled the Greeks, Dionysus caused him to stumble over a vine, and he was wounded by Achilles. Told by an oracle that his wound could be cured only by him who had inflicted it, he visited the Greeks, who likewise knew through an oracle that they could not take Troy without the aid of Telephus. Achilles therefore gladly cured him with rust from the spear which had injured him, and Telephus showed the Greeks the route they should take.

300. Assembled a second time at Aulis, the Greeks were delayed by unfavourable winds, for Agamemnon, by killing a hart, had vexed Artemis. Calchas foretold that only the sacrifice of Agamemnon's daughter Iphigeneia would appease the goddess, and Agamemnon reluctantly gave his consent, though some say that Artemis snatched Iphigeneia from the altar and bore her off to Tauris (*see para.* 396). Certainly the winds changed and the fleet set sail.

301. When they landed on the island of Tenedos, in sight of Troy, Achilles killed King Tenes and his father Cycnus, and here Philoctetes, son of Poeas suffered misfortune. Most famous of the Greek archers, he had been the friend of Heracles, and had received from him the famous bow and poisoned arrows when he set fire to the hero's funeral pyre on Mt. Œta. He was now injured in the foot by one of these arrows or, as some say, by the bite of a snake, and the smell of the wound became so offensive that, on the advice of Odysseus, Philoctetes was left behind on the island of Lemnos.

302. It was probably from Tenedos that the envoys Menelaus, Odysseus and Palamedes were sent to Priam to request the return of Helen. They were courteously entertained by Antenor, the wisest of the Trojans, who advised that Helen should be sent back, but the Trojans were obdurate.

303. The Greeks then attacked the mainland, and Protesilaus of Thessaly, who was an uncle of Philoctetes, was the first to leap ashore, though he knew through an oracle that it meant death. Wordsworth, in his poem *Laodamia*, tells how Laodamia his wife, the daughter of Acastus, desolate with grief, begged the gods to let her husband return for only three hours. Hermes led Protesilaus to her, and when he died the second time she died with him.

304. Achilles, the second to land on Trojan soil, soon distinguished himself as the most courageous and formidable of all the Greeks.

305. It was through Achilles that Æneas entered the war. At first he took no part, although he was the son of Priam's cousin Anchises. But when Achilles raided his herds on Mt. Ida, he led his Dadanians against the Greeks, and distinguished himself in battle. His mother, Aphrodite, frequently helped him, and once carried him away when wounded by Diomedes, while the god Poseidon, though hostile to Troy, saved him from Achilles.

306. Many cities allied to Troy were raided by Achilles. In Thebes in Cilicia he killed King Eëtion, father of Hector's wife Andromache, while Great Ajax raided the Thracian Chersonesus and in Teuthrania killed the King Teuthras and took his daughter Tecmessa.

307. In the tenth year of the war the Greeks at last concentrated their armies before Troy itself, which was defended by the mighty Hector, by Æneas, and by many allies, including Sarpedon, a son of Zeus, who was in command of the Lycians.

308. The Greeks were hampered by rivalries between the chiefs. Odysseus took a cruel revenge on Palamedes, who had tricked him into joining the forces. He bribed one of Palamedes' servants to hide under his master's bed a letter written in the name of Priam, and then accused Palamedes of treachery. Palamedes' tent was searched, the letter was found, and he was stoned to death by the whole army. Thus perished the sage, who was said to have invented lighthouses, scales, measures, the discus, certain letters of the alphabet, and dice.

309. Then in the tenth year there broke out the notorious quarrel between Achilles and Agamem-

non with which the *Iliad* opens. Chryseis, the daughter of the Trojan priest, Chryses had been taken prisoner and assigned to Agamemnon, and when Chryses came to ransom her, Agamemnon roughly repulsed him. Apollo, in revenge, sent a plague among the Greeks, and on Calchas' advice, Agamemnon unwillingly sent Chryseis back. He recompensed himself, however, by seizing Briseis, who had been given to Achilles, and Achilles then stubbornly refused to take any further part in the fighting, though some say that his motive in this was to curry favour with Priam, for he had fallen deeply in love with Priam's daughter Polyxena.

310. The Trojans quickly seized this opportunity to attack, and Agamemnon was glad to grant a truce so that Paris and Menelaus might settle the quarrel by a duel. But when Paris was losing, Aphrodite carried him away and fighting broke out again.

311. Diomedes wounded Æneas and Aphrodite and then strove with Glaucus, a Lycian prince second in command to Sarpedon, but when they remembered the friendship between their forefathers they desisted and exchanged gifts. Hector and Ajax fought in single combat till nightfall, when they also exchanged gifts, Hector giving Ajax a sword and receiving a purple baldric.

312. The Greeks, hard-pushed, were now forced to build a wall and trench, and when they were driven back even farther, Agamemnon in alarm offered to return Briseis to Achilles, but he courteously and firmly refused.

313. Diomedes and Odysseus then made a night-raid on the Trojan lines. After killing the spy, Dolon, they slew Rhesus the Thracian and drove off his snow-white horses, for an oracle had declared that once they had drunk of Scamander, and eaten the grass of the Trojan plain, the city would not be taken. The play *Rhesus*, attributed to Euripides, dramatises these incidents from the *Iliad*.

314. Next day, however, the Trojans victoriously set fire to the very ships, and Achilles went so far as to lend Patroclus his own armour and let him lead the Myrmidones. After killing Sarpedon, Patroclus drove the Trojans back to their very walls, until he was at last himself wounded by Euphorbus, son of Panthous, and slain by Hector, who at once stripped him of his borrowed armour, though Menelaus, who had killed Euphorbus, now joined with Ajax in rescuing the body.

315. Achilles was prostrate with grief, but Thetis visited him with new armour made by Hephæstus, and he made peace with Agamemnon, who at last sent Briseis back. Achilles then drove the terrified Trojans back to the city. The noble Hector alone withstood him, though Priam and Hecuba, implored him to come in. Thrice did Achilles chase Hector round the walls of Troy, and then finally killed him, stripped him of his armour, and, tying him by the ankles to his chariot, dragged him ignominiously back to the ship, though some say that Achilles dragged Hector three times round the walls of Troy by the purple baldric that Great Ajax had given him.

316. Each day at dawn Achilles, crazed with grief, pulled the corpse three times round the tomb of Patroclus until at last, in one of the most touching scenes of the *Iliad*, Priam, led by Hermes, went to Achilles' tent and begged to ransom his son's body for burial.

317. The lovely Penthesilea now came to the Trojans' aid. She was the daughter of Otrere and Ares, and Queen of the Amazons. But Achilles killed her, and as he mourned over her, he was ridiculed by Thersites, the ugliest and most scurrilous of the Greeks, and Achilles felled him with a blow. This angered Diomedes, a kinsman of Thersites, and he flung the body of Penthesilea into the Scamander, but it was rescued and honourably buried, some say by Achilles himself.

318. Memnon the black-skinned, handsome son of Eos and Priam's half-brother Tithonus, and King of Ethiopia, now reinforced the Trojans. He killed several Greeks, including Antilochus, the gallant son of Nestor, who, too young to sail from Aulis, joined his father later.

319. The vengeful Achilles then engaged Memnon in fierce single combat while Zeus weighed their fates in the balance. Memnon was slain and, at the request of Eos, Zeus honoured him by causing birds, called Memnonides, to rise from his funeral pyre and fight above it till they fell as a sacrifice. They were said to visit yearly the hero's tomb on the Hellespont.

320. Many great monuments, called Memnonia, were supposed by the Greeks to have been erected in Memnon's honour, the most famous being the colossal statue behind the temple of Egyptian Thebes, which gave forth each sunrise a sound like the breaking of a lyre-string.

321. Achilles' own course was now run, and in a battle near the Scæan gate Paris, aided by Apollo, shot him through the vulnerable ankle.

322. Great Ajax then killed Glaucus, and he and Odysseus rescued the body of Achilles. But they quarrelled violently over the possession of the armour. Homer, in the *Odyssey*, says that Odysseus killed Ajax, and that when he summoned the spirits of the dead, Ajax held sullenly aloof. Sophocles, however, in his tragedy *Ajax*, represents Ajax thrown into madness by defeat and slaying the sheep of the Greeks, believing them to be his rivals, and finally falling on the very sword that Hector had given him.

323. So many heroes dead, the Greeks lost heart, and Calchas said they must fetch the bow and arrows of Heracles. Odysseus and Diomedes therefore sailed to the island of Lemnos, where Philoctetes had been left to languish, and Sophocles, in his play *Philoctetes*, shows how he was persuaded to return.

324. Cured of his wound by one of the sons of Asclepius, either Machaon or Podalirius, Philoctetes challenged Paris to an archery contest. Mortally wounded, Paris besought his former lover Œnone to cure him, but she refused, and then in remorse at his death took her own life, events described by Tennyson in his *Death of Œnone*.

325. Helenus and Deiphobus now quarrelled for the possession of Helen, now homesick for Sparta, and when Deiphobus forcibly married her, Helenus, as some say, fled to Mt. Ida, where either he freely joined the Greeks, or was captured or ensnared by Odysseus, for Calchas had said that only Helenus knew the secret oracles which protected Troy. Helenus said it would fall that summer, if a bone of Pelops were brought to the Greeks, if Achilles' son Neoptolemus, or Pyrrhus, joined them, and if Athene's Palladium were stolen from the citadel.

326. Agamemnon at once sent for the shoulder-blade of Pelops, while Odysseus, Phœnix, and Diomedes went to Scyros and persuaded Lycomedes to let Neoptolemus join them. Odysseus then gave Neoptolemus his father's armour.

327. It is said that Priam now sent Antenor to Agamemnon to sue for peace, but Antenor, out of hatred for Deiphobus, conspired with the Greek leader as to how they might secure the Palladium. They arranged that Odysseus, disguised as a filthy runaway slave, should gain entrance to Troy. Recognised by Helen alone, he gained much useful information, including the confession that she longed to return home. It was either on this occasion that he stole the Palladium, or later when he was accompanied by Diomedes.

328. Odysseus is said to have devised the stratagem of the wooden horse. This was built by the cowardly Epeius, son of Panopeus, under the supervision of Athene, and it bore an inscription saying that it was dedicated to the goddess. Then twenty-three or more of the bravest Greeks, including Neoptolemus, Odysseus, Sthenelus, and Thoas of Calydon, climbed into the hollow belly.

329. At nightfall, Agamemnon and the remaining Greeks burnt their camp and sailed to the island of Tenedos, leaving behind only Sinon, a cousin of Odysseus and grandson of the cunning Autolycus.

330. At dawn Priam and his sons found the wooden horse on the shore, and believing it to be sacred to Athene, had it hauled in spite of opposition up to the citadel. Cassandra declared that warriors were within it, and she was supported by Laocoön, son of Antenor, and priest to both Apollo and Poseidon, who flung a spear at the horse's flank and caused a clatter of arms. Their warning was, however, neglected, partly because Sinon, who had let himself be taken prisoner, said that the horse was the Greeks' atonement for stealing the Palladium, partly because the fate which now befell Laocoön was misinterpreted.

331. Laocoön had offended Apollo by marrying in spite of vows of celibacy, and the god now punished him by sending two enormous serpents, which crushed to death both the priest and his two sons—a disaster represented in the magnificent sculpture probably dating from the first century B.C. and now in the Vatican. Priam wrongly supposed this to be a punishment for smiting the horse, and it was now welcomed with feasting and revelry.

332. In the evening Helen with Deiphobus strolled round the horse and, imitating in turn the voice of each man's wife, she called to the heroes, who stifled their replies.

333. At night Agamemnon, warned by a beacon lit by Sinon, sailed to the shore, and as Antenor gave the word the warriors within the horse leapt down to slaughter and pillage.

334. Priam had been persuaded by Hecuba to take refuge with her and her daughters before an altar to Zeus, but their son Polites was slain before their very eyes by Neoptolemus, and when the old king feebly tried to attack the slayer, Neoptolemus butchered him also. Odysseus and Menelaus meanwhile killed and mangled Deiphobus, but Menelaus pardoned Helen, and led her safely to the ships.

335. Cassandra fled to the sanctuary of Athene, but Little Ajax roughly dragged her away, and she was claimed as booty by Agamemnon. Her sister Laodice, the wife of Helicaon, was mercifully swallowed up by the earth.

336. Hector's widow Andromache was given to Neoptolemus, and the Greeks, eager to exterminate the whole family of Priam, even killed her infant son Astyanax, by hurling him to death from the city walls, fearful lest he should one day avenge his parents.

337. At the demand of Achilles' ghost Polyxena was sacrificed to him by Neoptolemus, to ensure favourable winds. Some say this happened at Troy, others only when the Greek fleet had reached Thrace.

338. Hecuba fell to the share of Odysseus, who took her to the Thracian Chersonesus, and there she avenged the death of one of her sons. Polydorus, the youngest of Priam's sons, had, according to Homer, been slain by Achilles, but later accounts speak of another son of the same name. Just before the fall of Troy Priam had entrusted him, together with much gold, to Polymester, King of the Thracian Chersonesus, and when Troy fell Polymester murdered Polydorus for his gold and cast him into the sea. Hecuba discovered the body. She contrived to kill Polymestor and his two sons, and she then evaded the angry Thracians by turning herself into a bitch named Mæra.

339. Euripides combined this story of Hecuba's revenge with that of the sacrifice of her daughter Polyxena in his tragedy *Hecuba*.

340. Few of the inhabitants of Troy escaped death or slavery. The wise Antenor, his wife Theano, and their children were all spared, and were said to have sailed to the West Coast of the Adriatic and there to have founded Venice and Padua.

341. Æneas' carried on his back his blind father Anchises through the Dardanian gate and so to safety. The Romans said that he took with him the Palladium, that stolen by Odysseus being only a replica, and, after seven years' wandering, reached Latium, where he founded Lavinia, and became their ancestral hero.

342. Æthra, the mother of Theseus, who had served Helen as a slave, was rescued by her grandsons, Acamas and Demophon, the sons of Theseus and Phædra.

THE RETURNS FROM TROY.

343. Part of the ancient "Epic Cycle" of the Greeks was the cycle known as "The Returns," which was used both by Homer and Æschylus. It told of the adventures of the Greeks on their way home. Most suffered misfortune.

344. The fate of Agamemnon is described in para. 386–388, and that of Odysseus in para. 353–369.

345. Menelaus, who failed to sacrifice to Athene, took eight years, and only by seizing Proteus learned how to reach Sparta, where he married Hermione to Neoptolemus.

346. Neoptolemus had been accompanied by Andromache and by Helenus, who prophesied a safe route. He had abandoned his kingdom in Thessaly and settled in Epirus, part of which he gave to Helenus, who married Andromache. Neoptolemus then claimed Hermione, although her grandfather, Tyndareus, had betrothed her to Orestes, and as a result he was murdered, either by Orestes himself or at his instigation.

347. Many Greeks settled in Italy. Diomedes, hated by Aphrodite, finding on his return to Argos that his wife had been unfaithful, left for Ætolia to help his grandfather Œneus, and later settled in Daunia in Italy, where he married Euippe, daughter of King Daunus. He was buried in one of the islands since called Diomedans, and his companions were turned into gentle birds. Philoctetes also settled in Italy.

348. Idomeneus, caught by tempest on his return to Crete, vowed to sacrifice to Poseidon the first person he met on return. As this was his own son, Crete was punished by pestilence, and Idomeneus exiled. He settled in Calabria in Italy.

349. Demophon, son of Theseus visited Thrace and gained the love of the king's daughter, Phyllis, but when he left her to visit Athens, she killed herself in despair of his return and was turned into a tree.

350. Many sailors were ship-wrecked on the dangerous promontory of Caphareus, where Nauplius, King of Eubœa, eager to avenge the death of his son Palamedes, lighted misleading fires.

351. The seer, Calchas, like Amphilochus, went safely overland to Colophon. Here he contended in prophecy with Mopsus, a son of Apollo and Manto, the daughter of Teiresias, and being surpassed, he died of grief. Amphilochus joined with Mopsus in founding the city of Mallus, but they killed each other in a fight for its possession.

352. Nestor alone returned home without mishap and enjoyed a happy old age.

THE WANDERINGS OF ODYSSEUS 353–369.

353. Odysseus' journey home, lasting ten years, and his final arrival in Ithaca are the theme of Homer's epic the *Odyssey*. E. V. Rieu says that this may be thought of as a novel, and Samuel Butler argued that it might well have been written by a woman! The incidents of the *Odyssey* form the background of reference to the *Ulysses* of James Joyce.

354. After leaving Troy, Odysseus and his men visited the Cicones, where he obtained several jars of sweet wine, and then they landed on the Libyan promontory of the Lotophagi. Here lived the Lotus-eaters, who gave his men some of the fruit, inducing the enervating dreaminess described by Tennyson in *The Lotus-eaters*.

355. Next, landing on the west coast of Sicily, Odysseus, with twelve companions, entered the cave of a giant, but when the owner, the one-eyed Cyclops, Polyphemus, son of Poseidon, came in with his flocks, he blocked the entrance with a gigantic stone, and devoured two of Odysseus' companions. Next evening, by which time only six of his men survived, Odysseus made Polyphemus drunk with his sweet wine and then blinded him. At dawn the Greeks escaped by clinging under the bodies of the sheep as they went out to graze, and so reached their ship, but henceforth they had to reckon with the vengeful hostility of Poseidon.

356. Odysseus was next entertained by Æolus, who gave him a bag of winds, but when his foolish crew untied this, they were blown back to Æolus, who now refused further help.

357. In Telepylos, city of Lamus, King of the cannibal Læstrygones, Odysseus lost all his ships except one, but in this he reached Ææa, the island of the enchantress Circe, daughter of Helios and Perse. Men sent by Odysseus to explore were turned by her to swine, and only Eurylochus returned to tell the news. Odysseus, hastening to their rescue, was given, by Hermes, the plant Moly, which vanquished Circe's charms. She restored his companions and lavishly entertained them all for a year.

358. Then, on Circe's advice, Odysseus sought the counsel of the dead seer Teiresias. He sailed to the River Oceanus, and in the land of the Cimmerians summoned the spirits of the dead, who thronged to lap the blood of a libation he had prepared. First appeared Elpenor, one of his crew, who while drunk had fallen to death from Circe's roof. Later came Teiresias, who gave him prophetic advice, and then Anticleia, the mother of Odysseus, the men and women of antiquity, and his former comrades.

359. He again visited Circe, who advised him how to circumvent the Sirens and Scylla and Charybdis. Odysseus nullified the Sirens' spell by having himself lashed to the mast, and by filling the sailors' ears with wax, and he just avoided the whirlpool Charybdis, though Scylla's six mouths snatched and devoured as many of his seamen.

360. At the island of Thrinacia, against the warnings both of Teiresias and Circe, Odysseus' companions slaughtered the cattle of Helios, and when they put to sea Zeus destroyed all save Odysseus himself.

361. Clinging to wreckage, he drifted ten days until he reached the island of Ogygia. Here the nymph Calypso lovingly kept him for eight years, until at Athene's request Zeus sent Hermes to command his release.

362. On a raft that Calypso had taught him to make, Odysseus sailed for eighteen days, till it was wrecked by vengeful Poseidon. Then helped by Leucothea and Athene, Odysseus landed on the island of Scheria. Here he was led by the beautiful Nausicaa to the Court of her father Alcinous, who was the prosperous ruler of the Phæacians. Alcinous gave Odysseus a ship, and after an absence of ten years he at last landed on Ithaca. Athene disguised him as a beggar and he was hospitably welcomed by his swineherd Eumæus.

363. Odysseus' mother Anticleia had died of grief, Lærtes his father had withdrawn to the country, and his wife Penelope had been keeping at bay a crowd of unruly suitors led by Antinous. She had promised to wed one of them when she had finished a robe for Lærtes, but each night she unpicked the work of the day, until her servants betrayed her ruse, and she was now hard-pressed. Her son Telemachus had gone in search of Odysseus, and after visiting Nestor and Menelaus, he now returned to Ithaca and also visited the hut of Eumæus.

364. Here Odysseus made himself known to Telemachus and they planned revenge. First the son set out for home, followed later by Odysseus still in beggar's disguise. He was recognised only by his aged hound Argus, which at once expired, and by his nurse Eurycleia.

365. Next day Penelope announced that she would accept the suitor who could shoot with the great bow of Eurytus which only Odysseus had been able to wield. No one could bend it till Odysseus seized it and shot Antinous. Supported by Telemachus, he killed the suitors, and at last made himself known to Penelope. He then visited Lærtes, but the kinsmen of the suitors rose against him and battle ensued until Athene, disguised as Mentor effected a reconciliation.

366. At this point the *Odyssey* ends, though Teiresias had prophesied that Odysseus must again set out on a journey and propitiate Poseidon and then return to an honourable old age till death came to him from the sea.

367. Tennyson, in his poem *Ulysses*, imagines him, even in age, hungry still for travel.

368. Another tradition says that Telegonus, son of Odysseus by Circe, while searching for his father, landed on Ithaca and began to plunder for food. When opposed by Odysseus and Telemachus, all unknowing he killed his father. He then took Telemachus and Penelope back to Ææa, and there married Penelope, while Telemachus married Circe.

369. Although Homer represents Penelope as a faithful wife, other writers say that she became the mother of Pan, either by Hermes or by all the suitors. It is a tradition such as this that Joyce evidently follows in his *Ulysses*.

LEGENDS OF THE HOUSE OF PELOPS, 370–398.

370. Some of the most dramatic of all Greek stories have their setting in Mycenæ, city of the legendary hero Agamemnon. In 1876 Schliemann began excavation on this ancient site, and here he unearthed the famous shaft-graves with their precious treasures, which probably date from 1600 B.C., four centuries before the era of Agamemnon and the siege of Troy. Schliemann thus proved to the learned world that the city at all events was historical, and scholars now believe that it was the centre of a Late Bronze Age culture.

371. According to legend, Agamemnon was a descendant of Tantalus, son of Zeus and the nymph Pluto and father of Pelops, Broteas, and Niobe. Tantalus was said to be a wealthy king, but whether of Lydia, Argos or Corinth, is uncertain.

372. Highly favoured by his father Zeus, Tantalus was even invited to Olympian banquets, but he proved unworthy of such honours, divulging Zeus' secrets and stealing nectar and ambrosia from Olympus.

373. Tantalus was also said to have received from Pandareus a dog made of gold, and then to have sworn by Zeus that he had never seen or heard of it. As this dog was the one which Hephæstus had made for Rhea, and which she had set to watch the cradle of the infant Zeus, the gods were naturally incensed. Pandareus perished miserably, and his orphan daughters were carried off by Harpies, and Tantalus suffered agonising punishment for this and other crimes, the most ghastly of which was his murder of his son Pelops. Having invited the gods to a banquet, he cut Pelops into pieces and served them in a stew. Demeter, still grieving for Persephone, was the only divinity who did not notice what she was eating, and she consumed the shoulder.

374. Tantalus' punishment became proverbial. Tortured with thirst, he was placed in a lake whose waters receded whenever he attempted to drink, while above his head were laden fruit boughs which flew upwards as soon as he reached for them. Thus "tantalised," he also saw suspended above his head a huge rock which threatened to fall and crush him.

375. After punishing Tantalus, Zeus ordered Hermes to put the limbs of Pelops into a cauldron and boil them. Clotho took him from the cauldron, Demeter gave him an ivory shoulder, which became a kind of birthmark for his descendants, and Pelops was restored to life.

376. Pelops was later expelled from his kingdom of Phrygia and came with his followers to Pisa in Elis. Here Œnomaus, son of Ares, was king, and as an oracle had said that he would be killed by his son-in-law, he challenged to a chariot race all who came to woo his daughter, Hippodameia. If the young man won, he would marry Hippodameia, if not he would be killed by the spear of Œnomaus, which, like his wind-begotten horses, was a gift of his father Ares.

377. Many suitors had lost their lives when Pelops arrived in Pisa. He was already possessed of a winged golden chariot, the gift of Poseidon, but he also bribed Œnomaus' charioteer Myrtilus, the son of Hermes, with the promise of half the kingdom, to remove the lynch-pin from the chariot of his master and substitute one of wax. Œnomaus was flung out and killed, and Pelops married Hippodameia.

378. Pelops refused to keep faith with Myrtilus and flung him into the sea. Myrtilus, as he died, cursed the whole race of Pelops, and his image was set among the stars as the charioteer by his father Hermes. Pelops soon became master of Olympia and revived the Olympic Games. His wealth and power in the peninsula were so great that it was called the Peloponnesus, or "Island of Pelops."

379. The eldest sons of Pelops, Atreus and Thyestes, with the connivance of their mother, killed Chrysippus, their half-brother, and were obliged to flee their home.

380. They were kindly received at Mycenæ, and after the death of King Eurystheus, Atreus seized the kingdom in spite of the bitter rivalry of Thyestes, whom he forthwith banished.

381. Thyestes, however, who had already succeeded in seducing Atreus' second wife Ærope, now tricked his brother into killing Pleisthenes, his own son by his first wife. Atreus, planning grisly reprisals, lured Thyestes to Mycenæ by promising him half the kingdom. He then killed the sons of Thyestes and served him their flesh at a banquet. When the horror-stricken father realised what he had eaten, he laid a curse on the house of Atreus and fled once more.

382. Thyestes, seeking revenge, was advised by the Delphic Oracle to beget a son by his own daughter, and going to King Threspotus at Sicyon, where his daughter Pelopia was a priestess, he ravished her and fled.

383. Atreus now visited Sicyon, and, believing Pelopia to be a daughter of Threspotus, married her as his third wife. When she gave birth to Thyestes' son, Ægisthus, she exposed the baby, but Atreus, believing Ægisthus to be his own child, took him in and reared him.

384. When later Thyestes was seized and brought back to Mycenæ, Atreus commanded Ægisthus to slay him, but Thyestes disarmed the boy, and recognising him as his own son, ordered him to kill Atreus. Then, at last, Thyestes ruled in Mycenæ.

385. According to Homer, Atreus had two sons by Ærope, Agamemnon and Menelaus, and these two now took refuge with King Tyndareus of Sparta. Here Menelaus married Helen, daughter by Zeus of Tyndareus' wife, Leda, and some say that Agamemnon was helped by Tyndareus to expel Thyestes and gain his father's throne.

386. Agamemnon's wife was Clytemnestra (the daughter of Tyndareus and Leda), whom he forcibly married after killing her first husband in battle. But when his brother's wife, Helen, was stolen away by Paris, and the Trojan War broke out, Agamemnon was away fighting for ten years, and it was not difficult then for Ægisthus to seduce Clytemnestra.

387. Not only had Agamemnon forcibly married Clytemnestra, but he had also agreed to the sacrifice of their daughter, Iphigeneia at Aulis, and her cup of bitterness was full when she learned that he was returning from Troy, bringing with him Priam's daughter, the prophetess Cassandra, as his mistress.

388. It is at this point that Æschylus' great trilogy of the *Oresteia* begins. Clytemnestra conspired with Ægisthus to kill both Agamemnon and Cassandra. She welcomed her husband royally on his return, but while he was in his bath entangled him in a net, and after Ægisthus had twice struck him, she beheaded him with an axe. She then went out to kill Cassandra, who had refused to enter the palace because, in visionary trance, she was horrified to smell the ancient shedding of blood and the curse of Thyestes (*see para.* 381).

389. It was not difficult now for Clytemnestra to seize power, for Orestes, her young son, had been smuggled out of Mycenæ by his sister Electra, and for many years Clytemnestra and her paramour ruled in Mycenæ.

390. Ægisthus, however, lived in constant fear of vengeance. He would have killed Electra had Clytemnestra allowed, so he married her to a peasant, who was fearful of consummating their union. Orestes meanwhile had taken refuge with Strophius, King of Phocis, who had married Agamemnon's sister, and here he formed that friendship with the king's son, Pylades, which became proverbial.

391. The intensely dramatic situation at this point has inspired all three of the great Greek tragedians, and it is most interesting to compare the various interpretations given by Æschylus, in *The Libation Bearers*, the second play of his trilogy, by Sophocles, in *Electra*, and by Euripides, in *Electra*.

392. Electra, burning for revenge, sent constant messages to Orestes, and when he and Pylades were of age they came secretly to Mycenæ, and with Electra's help killed both Ægisthus and Clytemnestra.

393. The agonising punishment that Orestes now endured is portrayed in the *Eumenides*, the last play of Æschylus' trilogy, and in the *Oreste*[s] of Euripides. Although the Delphic Oracle had encouraged Orestes to avenge his father, she was powerless to prevent his being pursued by the Erinnyes, the avengers of matricide, who drove him mad and hounded him from land to land. At length, on the further advice of the Pythian Priestess, he reached Athens and embraced the image of Athene in her temple on the Acropolis. The goddess then summoned the Areopagus t[o]

judge his case. Apollo defended him against the Erinnyes on the grounds that motherhood is less important than fatherhood, and he was acquitted by the casting vote of Athene, the verdict being a triumph for the patriarchal principle.

394. The furious Erinnyes were then pacified by Athene, who persuaded them to accept a grotto in Athens, where they would be offered sacrifices, libations, and first fruits. Their name henceforward was Eumenides, or the "well-meaning."

395. According to another tradition, followed by Euripides, in his *Iphigeneia Among the Taurians*, Orestes was told by Apollo that he would be freed from madness by fetching the statue of Artemis from the Tauric Chersonese.

396. When Orestes and Pylades reached Tauris they were seized by the barbarous natives, who sacrificed all strangers to Artemis, but they found to their amazement that the priestess was none other than Orestes' own sister Iphigeneia. Orestes believed that she had lost her life when sacrificed to Artemis at Aulis (as is described in para. 300), but she had in fact been rescued by the goddess and brought to Tauris as her priestess.

397. Iphigeneia, by her ready wit, rescued Orestes and Pylades from sacrifice, and all three returned to Greece, carrying with them the image of the goddess. Here they were reunited with Electra, and returned to Mycenæ, where Orestes, by killing Ægisthus' son and becoming king, finally ended the strife between the sons of Atreus.

398. Orestes, after killing his rival Neoptolemus, married his cousin Hermione, and Electra was married to Pylades.

THE UNDERWORLD, 399–409.

399. The Greeks expected to enter after death into the cheerless nether world, the domain of Hades, known to the Romans as Orcus, or Dis, but as Hades was possessor of all the rich metals and gems of the earth, the ancients usually preferred the euphemism "Pluto," "the wealth," when speaking of one so dreaded.

400. The word "Hades" was used too of his actual domain, which was also called Tartarus, although in the *Iliad*, the word "Tartarus" had been reserved for the very lowest region of the Underworld, where the rebel Titans had been thrust.

401. Hades, son of Cronus and Rhea, won the lordship of the nether world when his brother Zeus won the sky, and Poseidon the sea. His most treasured possessions were the helmet of darkness, given him by the Cyclopes, and the staff with which he drove the ghosts.

402. He ruled with his queen, Persephone, whom he had forcibly abducted from the upper world, but he was not always faithful to her, and she once changed the nymph Minthe, whom he was pursuing into the plant mint, and the nymph Leuce, whom he loved, was afterwards changed into the white poplar.

403. The companion to Persephone was Hecate, who had once aided Demeter in her search for the lost maiden. Hecate was a mysterious divinity, a triple goddess, mighty in heaven, on earth, and in the Underworld, honoured by Zeus and all the immortal gods. She came to be regarded by the Hellenes as primarily a dread divinity of the Underworld, as one who kept company with the dead and who fostered sorcery and witchcraft. She figures as such in *Macbeth*. Worshipped where three roads met, she was represented with three bodies and three heads.

404. Also dwelling in the Underworld were the Erinnyes, winged daughters of earth or of night, with serpent hair, who punished unnatural crime. They were later known euphemistically, as the "Eumenides," or "well-meaning," and this name was said to have been given them after the acquittal of Orestes, as is portrayed in the *Eumenides* of Æschylus. Late writers named three Erinnyes, Alecto, Megæra, and Tisiphone.

405. Ghosts conducted to Hades' realm by Hermes had first to cross the Styx, the "hated" river, and supplied by relatives with a coin laid under the tongue of the corpse, they paid the surly ferryman Charon. Without this coin they were unable to cross the Styx. Arrived on the farther bank, they propitiated Cerberus, represented by later writers as a fierce dog with three heads, said to be another of the monsters born to Echidne.

406. Styx was not the only river ghosts encountered. There was also Acheron, river of woe, Phlegethon, river of flames, Cocytus, river of wailing, and Lethe, the river of forgetfulness, where ghosts drank and forgot their past.

407. The three judges of the Underworld were Æacus, Rhadamanthus, and Minos. Wicked spirits were sent by them to the place of punishment, those who had led an indifferent life to the cheerless asphodel fields, and the virtuous to Elysium.

408. Although Elysium was said to be near the Underworld, it formed no part of Hades' dominion, and Homer placed it far away to the west of the earth, near Oceanus. It was a blessed abode, without cold or snow. Later writers also spoke of the "Fortunate Isles," located by Greek geographers as beyond the pillars of Heracles, and eventually identified with the Canary and Madeira islands.

409. In their picture of life after death the Greeks combined contradictory ideas. Broadly speaking, the figures of Persephone and Hecate represent the hopes of pre-Hellenic people for an after-life, while Hades personifies the Hellenic fear of the finality of death.

PART III. INDEX AND GLOSSARY

Note: The numbers in this part refer to the numbered paragraphs in Part II.

Abas. (1) Son of Celeus and Metanira, turned by Demeter into a lizard because he mocked her when she drank too eagerly. *See also* 113.
(2) The grandson of Danaus and twelfth King of Argolis, was renowned for his sacred shield, the very sight of which subdued revolt. He was father of the twins Acrisius and Prœtus.

Abderus, 180.

Absyrtus (or **Apsyrtus**), 159.

Abyla, 182.

Academus, 215.

Acamas, a son of Theseus and Phædra, went with Diomedes to Troy to demand the surrender of Helen. *See also* 211, 342.

Acastus was the son of Pelias, King of Iolcos. He joined the Argonauts, but after Medea had caused the death of Pelias, Acastus banished her and Jason. He later received Peleus kindly, but when he falsely suspected his guest of making love to his wife, he treacherously deserted him. Acastus and his wife were later slain by Peleus. The daughter of Acastus was Laodamia.

Achelous, 192, 271.

Acheron, 406.

Achilles, 293, 294, 295, 296, 299, 301, 304, 305, 306, 309, 312, 314, 315, 316, 317, 319, 321, 322, 337, 338.

Acrisius, 129, 130, 131, 132, 142.

Actæon, 83.

Admete, 181.

Admetus, King of Pherae in Thessaly, was helped by Apollo to marry Alcestis, the beautiful daughter of Pelias. Apollo also ensured that Admetus should escape death, provided that one of his family would die in his place (*see* 73). When the time came and Hermes summoned Admetus to Tartarus, only Alcestis was willing to die in his stead, but when she descended to Tartarus, Persephone refused the sacrifice. A later version says that Heracles arrived with an olive club just in time to prevent Hades, who had arrived in person, from carrying off Alcestis. The earlier version represents a matriarchal point of view. The later was dramatised by Euripides in his *Alcestis*, translated by Browning.

Adonis, 62.

Adrastus, 261, 262, 263, 265, 267, 268, 270.

Æacides, descendants of Æacus.

Æacus, son of Zeus and Ægina, was King of the Myrmidones. He helped Poseidon and Apollo to build the walls of Troy. By his wife Endeis he had two sons, Peleus and Telamon, while Phocus was his son by a Nereid. So virtuous was the life of Æacus that he became one of the three judges of the Underworld. *See also* 407.

Ææa, 357, 368.

Ædon was the daughter of Pandareus and wife of Zethus, King of Thebes. Her son was Itylus. Ædon was jealous of Niobe, the wife of Zethus' brother, Amphion, and in an attempt to kill Niobe's eldest son she killed her own son Itylus in mistake. Zeus, in pity, turned her into a nightingale whose song still mourns for Itylus.

Æëtes, 154, 158, 159.

Ægæon, another name for Briareus.

Ægeus, 203, 204, 206, 209, 233.

Ægialeus, 268, 270.

Ægina, daughter of Asopus, mother, by Zeus, of Æacus.

Ægisthus, 383, 384, 386, 388, 390, 392.

Ægyptus, *see* **Danaides**.

Æeneas, 62, 305, 307, 311, 341.

"Æneid," 93.

Æolus. (1) Son of Hellen and ruler of Thessaly, was ancestor of the Æolic Greeks.
(2) Son of Poseidon, was ruler of the seven Æolian isles. Zeus gave him control of the winds. *See also* 356.

Ærope, wife to Atreus, 381, 385.

Æschylus, 19, 263, 343, 388, 391, 393, 404.

Æsculapius, *see* **Asclepius**.

Æson, 152, 153, 161.

Æthra, 203, 204, 213, 215, 342.

Ætna, Mt., 14.

Ætolus, son of Endymion, was King of Elis. Having accidentally killed Apis in a chariot race, he was banished across the Gulf of Corinth and conquered the country called Ætolia after him. His two sons were Pleuron and Calydon. Both these names are also names of cities in Ætolia.

Agamedes, *see* **Trophonius**.

Agamemnon, 287, 289, 291, 292, 297, 300, 309, 310 312, 315, 326, 327, 329, 333, 335, 344, 370, 371, 385, 386, 387, 388, 390.

Aganippe, a fountain at the foot of Mt. Helicon in Bœotia. It was sacred to the Muses, hence called Aganippides, and was thought to inspire those who drank it. The epithet Aganippis is also applied to the fountain of Hippocrene, also sacred to the Muses.

Agave, 123, 244, 246.

Agenor. (1) King of Phœnicia, 223, 240, 241.
(2) Son of the Trojan Antenor and Theano.

Aglaia, "the bright one," one of the charities or graces.

Agraulos. (1) Wife of Cecrops.
(2) Daughter of Cecrops. To her and her sisters, Erichthonius was entrusted.

Aides or Aidoneus, Hades.

Ajax. (1) Great Ajax, son of Telamon, 292, 306, 311, 314, 315, 322.
(2) Little Ajax, son of Oileus, 292, 335.

"Ajax" of Sophocles, 322.

Alcæus, 165.

Alcestis, *see* **Admetus** *and* 161.

Alcides, a name of Heracles, a reputed grandson of Alcæus.

Alcinous, 362.

Alcippe, 67.

Alcmæon, 269, 271

Alcmene, 164–167, 199, 226.

Alcyone or Halcyone. (1) Daughter of Atlas and Pleione, and leader of the Pleiades.
(2) Daughter of Æolus and wife of Ceyx. When her husband perished in a shipwreck, the distraught Alcyone flung herself into the sea. The gods in pity changed the pair to birds usually identified as kingfishers, which were said to breed in the "halcyon days" of the winter solstice, when Æolus forbids the winds to blow.

Alcyoneus, 11.

Alecto, one of the Eumenides, 3, 404.

Aleus, 191.

Alexander, *see* **Paris**.

Alipes, 98.

Alœus, 13.

Aloidæ, 13, 66.

Althæa, daughter of Thestius, wife of Œneus, and mother of Meleager, Gorge, and Deianira.

Amalthea, 6.

Amazons, a race of warrior women said to have come from the Caucasus and to have settled in Asia Minor. *See also* 210, 317.

Ammon, 139.

Amphiaraus, 262, 263, 265, 269.

Amphilochus, 351.

Amphion, 248, 249, 250, 251.

Amphitrion, 165, 166, 167, 168, 169, 226.

Amphitrite, 106, 107, 108, 109.

Amphitryoniades, a name of Heracles, a reputed son of Amphitrion.

Amycus, 157.

Amymone was one of the fifty daughters of Danaus. A fountain in Argolis was named after her.

Amythaon, father of Bias and the seer Melampus.

Anatolia, 2, 68.

Anchises, 62, 305, 341.

Andræmon, husband of Gorge. He succeeded Œneus as King of Calydon and was father of Thoas.

Androgeos, 231, 233.

Andromache, 306, 336, 346.

Andromeda, 139, 140, 141, 142.

Anius, 298.

Antæus, 183.

Anteia, 146.

Antenor, 276, 302, 327, 330, 333, 340.

Anticleia, 290, 358, 363.

Antigone, 257, 260, 266.

"Antigone" of Sophocles, 266.

Antilochus, 318.

Antinous, 363, 365.

Antiope. (1) The Amazon, 210, 211.
(2) Mother of Amphion and Zethus, 248, 249.

Aphareus, King of Messene, father of Idas and Lynceus, hence called Apharetidæ.

Aphidnæ, where Thesus hid Helen, *see* **Theseus**.

Aphrodite, 3, 10, 14, 55, 57–63, 65, 244, 278, 280, 281, 282, 305, 310, 311, 347.

Apis. (1) The son of Phoroneus.
(2) The sacred bull of Memphis, worshipped as a god by the Egyptians.

Arachne, a Lydian maiden who challenged Athene to compete with her in weaving. When Athene found Arachne's work faultless, she angrily tore it up, and the terrified maiden hanged herself. Athene then turned her into a spider and the rope into a cobweb.

Arcas, son of Zeus and Callisto, who was supposed to have given his name to Arcadia.

Aria, the mother of Miletus by Apollo.

Arion. (1) An actual historical character was a lyric poet and player on the lyre, who lived at the Court of Periander of Corinth at about 625 B.C. The following curious fable is told of him. On one occasion Arion visited Sicily and won the prize in a musical contest. Laden with gifts, he took ship for Corinth, and the captain and crew decided to murder him for his treasure. They gave him permission to sing one last song. Arion then invoked the gods, and leapt into the sea. Here he was rescued by one of the music-loving dolphins that had gathered to hear his song, and taken on its back to Corinth, where he told Periander of his adventures. Later, when the ship arrived, the captain and crew swore that Arion had been detained in Sicily. Periander then confronted them with Arion himself and had them executed. The images of Arion and his lyre were set among the stars.
(2) A fabulous horse, 103.

Aristæus was the son of Apollo and Cyrene, born in Libya. He went to Thrace and fell in love with Eurydice, who, fleeing from him, perished by a snake bite. As a punishment Aristæus lost his bees, and how he raised a new swarm is told in Virgil's fourth *Georgics*. After death was worshipped as a god.

Asclepius or **Æsculapius** was a son of Apollo by Coronis. He was brought up by Cheiron, who taught him healing. He once recalled a dead man to life and was killed by Zeus with a thunderbolt. At Apollo's request, however, he was placed among the stars. Another tradition says that Asclepius was a native of Epidaurus. In Homer he was not a god, but the "blameless physician," father of Machaon and Podalirius, physicians to the Greek Army. His supposed descendants were the Asclepiadæ, a caste of priests who transmitted from father to son the knowledge of medicine as a sacred secret. Epidaurus was the centre of Asclepius' worship. Cocks were sacrificed to him and serpents sacred.

Asopus, a river god, son of Oceanus and Tethys, and father of Evadne, Eubœa, and Ægina.

Astræus, a Titan, was father, by Eos, of the beneficent winds and, some say, of the stars also.

Atalanta. (1) The Arcadian Atalanta, daughter of Iasus and Clymene, was exposed by her father and suckled by a bear. She always carried arms. She joined the Calydonian hunt and bore a son, Parthenopæus, to Meleager. Reconciled to her father, she refused to marry unless a suitor should conquer her in a foot race, those who failed in the attempt being killed by her. Eventually Milanion outstripped Atalanta by dropping in her way one after the other, three golden apples given him by Aphrodite. Atalanta stopped to gather these and lost the race. *See also* 263.
(2) The Bœotian Atalanta was said to be daughter of Schœneus and to have married Hippomenes, but the same tales are told of her. See Swinburne's play *Atalanta in Calydon* and the poem *Atalanta's Race*, by William Morris.

Athamas, was the son of Æolus and King of Orchomenus in Bœotia. At Hera's command he married Nephele, and had children Phrixus and Helle. But Athamas secretly loved Ino, daughter of Cadmus and Harmonia, who bore him Learchus and Melicertes. Deceived by Ino's intrigues, Athamas would have sacrificed Phrixus, had not a ram with a golden fleece, sent by Hermes, rescued the boy and flown through the air with him and his sister Helle. Between Europe and Asia, Helle fell into the straits since called Hellespont, but Phrixus reached Colchis, where he sacrificed the ram to Zeus and gave the fleece to Æëtes, from whom it was later carried off by Jason. Meanwhile Athamas, driven mad by Hera because he had sheltered Dionysus, killed his son Learchus, and Ino flung herself into the sea with Melicertes, where both were transformed into marine deities. Ino became Leucothea, and Melicertes changed to Palæmon. Athamas, forced to flee, settled in Thessaly. *See also* 120.

Atlantis was a legendary island, west of the Pillars of Hercules. Its virtuous and powerful inhabitants, becoming degenerate, were defeated by the Athenians, and the island was swallowed up by the ocean in a day and night. *See* the *Timæus* of Plato.

Atlas, the son of Iapetus and Clymene, was father of the Pleiades, Hyades, and Hesperides. *See also* 7, 9, 16, 91, 138, 183.

Atropos, one of the Fates.

Bassareus was an epithet of Dionysus. "Bassaris" was a fox-skin which was worn by the god and also the Mænads in Thrace. Hence Bassaris means Mænad or Bacchante.

Belus, son of Poseidon and father of Ægyptus, Danaus, and Cepheus.

Bias, brother of Melampus.

Biton and **Cleobis**, sons of a priestess of Hera at Argos, in their filial devotion once dragged their mother's chariot to the temple. Their mother prayed Hera to grant them the best gift for mortals, and they both died while asleep in the temple.

Boreas, the North wind, was the son of Astræus and Eos, and brother to the other beneficent

Creon. (1) Of Corinth, 162.
(2) Of Thebes, 259, 266.

Cretan Bull, 179, 227.

Crete, 68, 81, 90, 128, 219–239.

Cretheus, 152, 153.

Creusa. (1) Daughter of Creon of Corinth, 162.
(2) Wife of Xuthus.

Crommyum, Sow of, 205.

Cronus, son of Uranus and Ge and father, by his sister Rhea, of Hestia, Demeter, Hera, Poseidon, Hades, and Zeus. *See also* 1–9.

Cumæ, 12.

Curetes, 6.

Cyclades, 132.

Cyclopes. Different accounts are given of the Cyclopes. Hesiod describes them as Titans (*see* 1, 3, 4, 8, 9). Homer speaks of them as one-eyed giant shepherds in Sicily, the Chief being Polyphemus (*see* 355). Later tradition describes them as helpers of Hephæstus living in Mt. Ætna (*see* 54). The walls of unhewn stone in Mycenæ and other ancient sites are known as Cyclopean (*see* 130, 143).

Cycnus, 301.

Cyllene, Mt., 92.

Cyllenius, 92.

Cynthus, a mountain in Delos where Leto bore Apollo and Artemis, hence called Cynthus, and Cynthia.

Cyprus, 58, 59.

Cyrene, daughter of Hypseus, was beloved by Apollo and became the mother of Aristæus. She was carried by Apollo from Mt. Pelion to Libya, where the city Cyrene was named after her.

Cythera, 58, 59.

Dactyli were beings who were supposed to have discovered iron and the art of working it by fire. Mt. Ida in Phrygia was their original abode.

Dædalus, 222, 234, 237, 238.

Danæ, 130, 131, 132, 133, 141, 142.

Danai, used in Homer of the Greeks.

Danaides were the fifty daughters of Danaus, son of Belus and King of Libya. Danaus' brother Ægyptus, the father of fifty sons, suggested a mass marriage, and Danaus in fear fled with his daughters to Argos, where he was elected king in place of Gelanor. The fifty sons of Ægyptus followed Danaus and asked for his daughters as wives. Danaus agreed, but gave each daughter a weapon with which to kill her bridegroom on the bridal night. All complied save Hypermnestra, who spared her husband Lynceus. Lynceus, after killing Danaus, became King of Argos. The story is the theme of Æschylus' play *The Suppliants*. In Hades the Danaides were condemned continually to carry water in sieves.

Danaus, *see* **Danaides.**

Daphne, a daughter of the river god Peneus in Thessaly, was pursued by Apollo in the vale of Tempe, but when she cried for help she was turned into a laurel-tree, which became the favourite tree of Apollo. The myth probably refers to the Hellenes' capture of Tempe, where the goddess Daphœne was worshipped by Mænads who chewed the laurel and thus intoxicated themselves. Afterwards only Apollo's Pythoness might chew laurel.

Daphnis was a son of Hermes and a nymph, who exposed him in a laurel grove. He was adopted by Sicilian shepherds, taught by Pan to play the pipes, and was looked on as the inventor of bucolic poetry. He was blinded by a nymph to whom he was faithless, and Hermes caused the fountain Daphnis at Syracuse to spring up in his honour.

Dardania, 273, 274.

Dardanus, 274.

Daulia or Daulis was an ancient town in Phocis It was the residence of Tereus and the scene of the story of Philomela and Procne, who are hence called Daulias.

Daunus, 347.

Deianeira, 192, 193, 194, 195, 196, 197.

Deidamia, 295.

Deiphobus, 277, 325, 327, 332, 334.

Deipyle, 261.

Delian Homeric Hymn, 71.

Delos, 69, 70.

Delphi, 69, 71, 72, 76, 117, 118, 171, 186, 242, 253, 254, 271, 382, 393.

Delphinos, 106.

Demeter, 7, 10, 25, 99, 103, 110–116, 373, 375.

Demodocus, 60.

Demophon. (1) Son of Celeus and Metaneira who received Demeter hospitably. In return the goddess tried to make their son immortal by holding him over the fire, but the scream of Metaneira broke the spell and Demophon died.
(2) Son of Theseus, 199, 211, 342, 349.

Despœna, 103.

Deucalion, 20, 21.

Diana, 81, 89.

Dictæan Cave, 6.

Dicte, a mountain in the east of Crete, where Zeus was brought up, and hence called Dictæus.

Dictynna, 81, 229.

Dictys, 132, 141, 142.

Diomedes, Mares of, 180.

Diomedes, son of Tydeus, 268, 288, 305, 311, 313, 317, 323, 326, 327, 347.

Dione, 24, 60.

Dionysia, 118.

Dionysus, 10, 14, 26, 37, 61, 95, 114, 117–128, 298, 299.

Dioscuri were the twin heroes, Castor and Polydeuces (called by the Romans Pollux). According to Homer they were sons of Leda and King Tyndareus of Sparta, but some said that they were, like Helen, children of Leda and Zeus, and that all three were born at the same time out of an egg. Another tradition held that only Helen and Polydeuces were children of Zeus and that Castor was son to Tyndareus and therefore mortal. Polydeuces, famous as a boxer, and Castor, as tamer of horses, were inseparable. They were noted for their rescue of Helen from Aphidnæ (*see* 215), for their part in the Calydonian hunt and the expedition of the Argonauts (*see* 155, 157), and for their final battle with another pair of inseparable twins, their cousins and rivals, Idas and Lynceus, sons of Aphareus. Accounts of the battle vary, but it is usually said that Idas killed Castor, that Polydeuces killed Lynceus, and that Zeus intervened by slaying Idas with a thunderbolt. Polydeuces, the only survivor, implored Zeus to let him die with Castor, but Zeus decreed that the twins should spend their days alternately under the earth and among the gods. He also set their image among the stars as Gemini. The worship of the Dioscuri as divine spread from Sparta. Poseidon giving them power over wind and wave, they were worshipped especially as protectors of sailors. They were regarded as inventors of the war-dance and patrons of bards, and they presided at the Spartan Games. In art each is represented as mounted on a magnificent white horse, carrying a spear, and wearing an egg-shaped helmet crowned with a star.

Dirce, 249.

Dis, 399.

Dodona, 24, 27, 28.

Dolon, 313.

Dorians, 68.

Doris, daughter of Oceanus and Thetis, wife of her brother Nereus, and mother of the Nereides.

Dorus, son of Hellen, was the mythical ancestor of the Dorians.

Dryades were nymphs of trees.

Dryope, the daughter of King Dryops, was seduced by Apollo. She was afterwards carried away by the Hamadryads or tree-nymphs. *See also* 74.

Echemus, 201.

Echidne, a monster half woman, half serpent, said to be the mother of many monsters, such as:

Chimæra, 147; Nemean Lion, 173; Lernean Hydra, 174; Orthrus, 182; Ladon, 183; Sphinx, 255; Cerberus, 184, 405. Her mate was Typhon. She was killed by Argus.

Echion. (1) Son of Hermes, took part in the Calydonian hunt and was herald to the Argonauts.
(2) One of the Sparti, 243, 246.

Echo was a nymph who diverted Hera's attention with incessant talking while Zeus amused himself with the nymphs. When Hera discovered the trick she took from Echo all use of her voice except in repetition of another's speech. Echo then fell in love with Narcissus, a beautiful youth, who repulsed her, and she pined away in grief until only her voice remained. Artemis, in anger at Narcissus' coldness, caused him to fall in love with his own reflection in a fountain. In despair he took his own life and was turned into the flower.

Edones, 122.

Eëtion, 306.

Elatus, one of the Lapithæ, and father of Cæneus.

Electra. (1) The Pleiad, 274.
(2) Daughter of Agamemnon and Clytemnestra, 389, 390, 392, 397, 398.

" Electra " of Euripides, 391.

" Electra " of Sophocles, 391.

Electryon, King of Mycenæ, was the son of Perseus and Andromeda. His daughter Alcmene married Amphitryon.

Eleusis, in Attica, had a splendid temple of Demeter, 112, 113, 114.

Elpenor, 358.

Elysium, 407, 408.

Empusæ, daughters of Hecate, were horrible demons, with the haunches of asses and wearing brazen slippers. They could disguise themselves as bitches, cows, or maidens, and in the latter shape they would lie with men asleep and suck their strength till they died. The idea of Empusæ was probably brought from Palestine, where the Lilim, or daughters of Lilith, had similar characteristics.

Enceladus, 11, 12.

Endymion, King of Elis, was a beautiful Æolian youth, who, while sleeping in a cave on Carian Mt. Latmus, was seen by Selene the moon, who came down and kissed him. He afterwards returned to the cave and fell into a dreamless sleep. By his wife he had four sons, one of them being Ætolus, who conquered the land now called Ætolia. The myth probably indicates the fate of one who marries the moon Goddess. See Keats's *Endymion*.

Enipeus was the river god loved by Tyro.

Enna, 112.

Eos, in Latin Aurora, was the Dawn, daughter of Hyperion and Theia. She drove her chariot each morning to announce the approach of her brother Helios, and, as Hemera, accompanied his across the sky to arrive with him in the West in the evening as Hespera. Her husband was Astræus, said by some to be father by her of the stars and all winds save the East. Eos carried off several beautiful youths, including Orion, Cephalus, and Tithonus. Her son by Tithonus was Memnon. Eos asked Zeus to grant Tithonus immortality, but omitted to ask also for perpetual youth. Tithonus therefore shrank away until he became a cicada. Among Greeks in Asia Minor the golden cicada was an emblem of Apollo the sun god.

Epaphus, son of Zeus and Io, reigned over Egypt, and was rumoured to be the sacred bull, Apis.

Epeius, 328.

Ephesia (Artemis Ephesia), 81.

Ephesus, 87, 88.

Ephialtes, 11, 13.

Epigoni, 268, 269.

Epimetheus, 16, 17, 20.

Erato, the Muse of erotic poetry and mime, sometimes carries a lyre.

Erebus, or darkness, son of Chaos, begot Æther and Hemera by his sister Night. *See also* 25.

Erichthonius. (1) Son of Hephæstus. Athene entrusted to the daughters of King Cecrops of Athens a chest which they were forbidden to open. It concealed the infant Erichthonius. According to one version, the daughters (Agraulos, Pandrosos, and Herse) were overcome with curiosity and opened the chest. Seeing a serpent within it, they leapt in madness from the Acropolis to their death. Erichthonius succeeded Cecrops as King of Athens, and was himself succeeded by Padion.
(2) Erechtheus the second was grandson of Erechtheus, son of Hephæstus, and the son of Pandion, whom he succeeded as King of Athens. He was father by Praxithea of four sons, including Cecrops, and seven daughters, Protogonia, Pandora, Procnis wife of Cephalus, Creusa, Oreithyia, Chthonia, and Otionia. When the Eleusinians under Eumolpus son of Poseidon attacked Athens, Erechtheus was told to sacrifice Otionia, whereupon her two eldest sisters, Protogonia and Pandora, also sacrificed themselves. Erechtheus slew Eumolpus, whereupon Poseidon demanded vengeance, and either he or Zeus slew Erechtheus.

Eridanus was a river god. Phæthon fell to his death here. Because amber was found here Eridanus was later supposed to be the Po.

Erigone, *see* **Icarius.**

Erinnyes or Eumenides, 3, 260, 271, 393, 394, 404.

Eriphyle, 262, 269, 271.

Eris, 65, 280.

Eros, who in Latin was named Amor or Cupid, was said to be the son of Aphrodite by either Ares, Hermes, or her own father Zeus. The early Greeks thought of him as a winged "sprite," but by the fifth century B.C. he was represented as a boy, irresponsible but lovely, flying on golden wings and carrying in his golden quiver arrows which could wound both men and gods, and torches. He was sometimes portrayed as blindfolded. He usually accompanied his mother Aphrodite. *See also* **Psyche.**

Erymanthian Boar, 176.

Erysichthon, son of Triopas, dared to cut down trees in a grove sacred to Demeter, and when he ignored protests she punished him with an insatiable hunger.

Eryx, Mt., 58.

Eteocles, 257, 261, 265.

Etna, Mt., 12.

Euippe. (1) The daughter of Cheiron, being with child by Æolus, son of Hellen, was changed into a horse. Their child was Melanippe.
(2) The daughter of Daunus, 347.

Eumæus, 362, 363.

Eumenides or Erinnyes, 3, 260, 271, 393, 394, 404.

" Eumenides," 393, 404.

Eumolpus, "the good singer," was the son of Poseidon and Chione, the daughter of Boreas and Oreithyia. His mother threw him into the sea as soon as he was born, but his father Poseidon cared for him. He was brought up in Ethiopia, and lived later at the Court of King Tegyrius of Thrace, and then came to Eleusis in Attica. Here he became the priest of the mysteries of Demeter and Persephone. He initiated Heracles into the mysteries and taught him to sing and play the lyre. Eumolpus led an expedition against Erectheus of Athens, three of whose daughters sacrificed themselves to ensure victory. Eumolpus was killed by Erectheus, who was then himself slain by either Poseidon or Zeus. Eumolpus' descendants became hereditary priests of Demeter at Eleusis.

Eunomus, 193.

Euphorbus, 314.

Euphrosyne, one of the Charities or Graces.

Euridice, *see* **Orpheus.**

Euripides, 123, 161, 185, 200, 211, 246, 263, 267, 313, 339, 391, 393, 395.

Europa, 223–224, 244.

Eurus, son of Astræus and Eos, was the South-east wind.

Euryale, 134, 138.

Euryalus, 288.

Eurycleia, 364.

Eurylochus, 357.

Horæ, goddesses of the order of nature and the seasons (*see* 25). It is said that Zeus' fatherhood of the Horæ on Themis indicates that the Hellenes took over control of the calendar.

Hyacinthus, 74.

Hyades, 120.

Hydra of Lerna, 174, 196.

Hygeia, the goddess of health, was either the daughter or the wife of Asclepius. She is represented as dressed in a long robe and feeding a serpent from a cup.

Hylas, 156.

Hyllus, 193, 196, 199, 201.

Hyperboreans, 137.

Hyperenor, one of Sparti, 243.

Hyperion, a Titan and father of Helios, Selene, and Eos. 1, 9.

Hypermnestra, *see* **Danaides.**

Hypnus, the god of sleep.

Hypseus was the father of Cyrene beloved by Apollo.

Hypsipyle was the daughter of Thoas, King of Lemnos. When the women killed all the men in the island she saved her father. She welcomed Jason on the Argonauts' landing in Lemnos and bore him twins. Later the women of Lemnos discovered that she had spared Thoas and sold her as a slave to King Lycurgus of Nemea, who entrusted his son Opheltes to her care.

Iacchus, the name of Dionysus in the Eleusinian mysteries, where the god was regarded as the son of Zeus and Demeter.

Iapetus, a Titan and father of Atlas, Prometheus, and Epimetheus, 1.

Iasion, Iasius, or **Iasus** was the son of Zeus and Electra. Demeter loved him and bore him a son Pluton or Plutus, and Zeus, in anger, slew Iasion with a thunderbolt.

Icaria, 124.

Icarius. (1) Was an Athenian who received Dionysus hospitably and learned from him the cultivation of the vine. He gave some wine he had made to shepherds who, seeing double, believed they had been bewitched and killed Icarius. His daughter Erigone was led to his grave by his dog Mæra, and she hanged herself in despair from the tree under which her father had been buried.
(2) Of Sparta, 290.

Icarus, 238.

Ida, Mt., near Troy, 278, 280, 305, 325.

Idæa, 274.

Idas, the twin brother of Lynceus, was said to be son of Aphareus. He was in love with Marpessa, whom he carried off in a chariot given him by Poseidon, who was really his father. Idas' rival Apollo fought with him for Marpessa, but Zeus separated the combatants, and she chose Idas. With his devoted twin he took part in the Calydonian hunt, and the Argonauts' expedition, and both were finally killed in a battle with their rivals, the Dioscuri.

Idomeneus, 297, 348.

"Iliad," 77, 101, 309, 313, 316, 400.

Ilithyiæ, daughters of Hera, who in the *Iliad* and early poets are represented as helping women in childbirth. In the *Odyssey* and later poets only one goddess, Ilithyia, is represented. *See also* 33.

Illyrius, son of Cadmus, 244.

Ilus, 274.

Imbros, 56.

Inachus, son of Oceanus and Tethys, was first King of Argos, and gave his name to the river.

Ino, 120, 244, 246.

Io, daughter of Inachus was beloved by Zeus, who turned her into a white heifer through fear of Hera. The goddess Hera set Argus of the hundred eyes to watch the heifer, but Hermes, at Zeus' bidding, charmed Argus to sleep and cut off his head. Hera placed Argus' eyes in the tail of her favourite bird, the peacock, and sent a gadfly to torment Io, who fled from land to land till she came to the Nile. Here she recovered her human form and bore Zeus a son Epaphus. The Ionian Sea and the Bosphorus, (or cow's ford) were said to have derived their name from Io.

Iobates, 146–149.

Iolaus, 172, 174, 185, 192, 199.

Iolcus, 152, 153, 154, 161.

Iole, 186, 195, 196, 197.

Ion, *see* **Xuthus.**

Ionians, 68, 88, 99.

Iphicles. (1) Son of Amphitrion, 166, 170, 171, 172.
(2) One of the Argonauts.

Iphigeneia, 86, 300, 387, 395, 396, 397.

"Iphigeneia Among the Taurians" of Euripides, 395.

Iphimedeia, wife of Alœus, 13.

Iphis, 267.

Iphitus, 186.

Irene, called Pax by the Romans, was goddess of peace and according to Hesiod one of the Horæ, daughters of Zeus and Themis. She was worshipped in Athens.

Iris, in the *Iliad* she appears as messenger of the gods, but in the *Odyssey* she is never mentioned. She was originally a personification of the rainbow.

Ishtar, 57.

Ismene, 257, 260.

Issa, daughter of Macareus, was loved by Apollo

Isthmian Games, 105.

Ithaca, 289, 290, 353, 362, 363, 368.

Itys was the son of Tereus and Procne.

Ixion, the son of Phlegyas, King of the Lapithæ, treacherously murdered his father-in-law. Though pardoned by Zeus, Ixion now tried to seduce Hera, but was deceived by a phantom, Nephele, who bore him a Centaur. Ixion was punished by being chained to a fiery wheel which rolled ceaselessly through the sky. His son was Pirithous. See Browning's *Ixion.*

Jason, 151–163.

Jocasta, 253, 257, 258, 259.

Juno, Roman counterpart of Hera, 29–35.

Jupiter, Roman counterpart of Zeus, 23–28.

Juventas, *see* **Hebe.**

Labdacus, 252.

Lachesis, one of the Fates.

Ladon, 183.

Lælaps, the swift dog which Procris gave t Cephalus.

Lærtes, 290, 363, 365.

Læstrygones, 357.

Laius, 252, 253, 254, 255, 258.

Lamia, daughter of Belus, loved by Zeus. Sh became one of the Empusæ.

Lamus, 357.

Laocoön, 330, 331.

Laodameia, wife of Protesilaus, 303.

Laodice. (1) Daughter of Priam, 335.
(2) Homeric name for Electra, daughter c Agamemnon.

Laomedan, 274, 275.

Lapithæ were a mythical people living in Thessal and governed by Pirithous, who, being a son Ixion, was half-brother to the Centaur Rivalry between the Centaurs and Lapith reached its climax at the celebrated struggle a the wedding of Pirithous. *See also* 212.

Larissa, 142.

Leander, a youth of Abydos, swam across th Hellespont every night to visit Hero, prieste of Aphrodite in Sestos. One night he wa drowned, and Hero then flung herself into th

to the Underworld. Here his music delighted even Hades, so that he allowed Eurydice to follow her husband back to life, provided only that he did not look round. On the very threshold of life Orpheus anxiously looked back, and so lost Eurydice. He was so desolate with grief that the jealous Thracian women tore him to pieces in an orgy of Dionysus, a god whom he had neglected to honour. The Muses collected the fragments of his body, which were buried at the foot of Olympus, but his head, thrown into the River Hebrus, was carried still singing down to sea and on to Lesbos, whither his lyre also drifted, to be placed later as a constellation in the heavens at the intercession of Apollo and the Muses.

The Greeks considered Orpheus to be the greatest poet before Homer, and fragments of poetry extant were ascribed to him.

The religion "Orphism" was characterised by a sense of sin and the need for atonement, the idea of a suffering man-god, and a belief in immortality. It had an influence on such philosophers as Pythagoras and Plato, and formed a link between the worship of Dionysus and Christianity.

Palæmon, a sea-god, originally Melicertes, son of Athamas and Ino.

Pan, the misshapen god with goat feet, horns, and tail, was said by some to be an ancient divinity coæval with Zeus, though most reported him to be the son of Hermes. He was the god of shepherds and flocks, living in rural Arcadia, hunting and dancing with the nymphs. He would also lurk in forests, startling travellers with a sudden shout and filling them with "panic." Pan loved many nymphs, including Syrinx, who fled in terror and was metamorphosed into a reed, from which Pan made the syrinx (or Pan's pipe) that he was said to have invented, for his love of music was well known. He was also said to have seduced Selene. The Olympians looked down on Pan as a rustic, uncontrolled divinity. He is the only god whose death was reported. The worship of Pan began in Arcadia, which was despised by the Greeks for its backwardness. It did not reach Athens till early in the fifth century B.C. The Romans later identified Pan with Faunus. *See also* 14, 77–97, 369.

Pandion, King of Athens, was son of Erichthonius and father of Procne, and Philomela, and of Erechtheus, who succeeded him.

Pandrosos, daughter of Cecrops. To her and her sisters, Erichthonius was entrusted.

Parnassus, Mt., a lofty mountain range north-west of the Gulf of Corinth. The name was usually limited to the two-peaked summit north of Delphi, above which the Castalian spring issued. The mountain was one of the chief seats of Apollo and the Muses, and was also sacred to Dionysus. *See also* 20, 69, 7.

Peleus, son of Æacus, King of Ægina, joined with his brother Telamon in killing their half-brother Phocus. Expelled by Æacus, he went to Phthia in Thessaly, where he was purified by the king's son Eurytion, but accompanying Eurytion to hunt the Calydonian Boar, he accidentally killed his benefactor. Peleus now fled to Acastus, King of Iolcos, who purified him, but here he was falsely accused by Acastus' wife. Acastus then took Peleus on a hunting expedition on Mt. Pelion, and while his guest was asleep secreted his sword and deserted him. Peleus would have been killed by Centaurs had not Cheiron rescued him. Zeus now decided to give to Peleus the Nereid Thetis as wife. Zeus himself would have married her had he not been warned by Themis that she would bear a son more illustrious then his father. Cheiron told Peleus how to master Thetis by holding her fast whatever form she might assume, and all the divinities save Eris came to the wedding. She in revenge cast in the golden apple, which caused, eventually, the Trojan War. Thetis bore to Peleus the hero Achilles, whose death he survived. *See also* 280, 293, 296.

Pelides, the son of Peleus, that is Achilles.

Peneus, a god of the River Peneus in Thessaly, son of Oceanus and Tethys and father of Daphne and Cyrene.

Periclymenus, the Argonaut was the son of Neleus and brother of Nestor. Though he could assume what shape he chose, he was killed by Heracles.

Periphetes, a monster at Epidaurus who used to kill passers-by with an iron club. He was killed by Theseus.

Pero, daughter of Neleus and Chloris and wife of Bias.

Persë, daughter of Oceanus and wife of Helios, by whom she became the mother of Æëtes, Circe, Pasiphaë, and Perses.

Perses, son of Helios and Persë and father of Hecate.

Phæthon, "the shining," was a son of Helios by Clymene. He gained his father's permission to drive the chariot of the sun, but his incompetence provoked Zeus to kill him with a thunderbolt, and he fell into the River Po. His mourning sisters were turned into alder- or poplar-trees, which wept tears of amber. Phæthon's fate may represent the ritual death of the boy interrex for the sacred king, who ruled for one day and was then killed, usually by horses.

During the Bronze Age amber, sacred to the king, was carried from Baltic to Mediterranean via the Po valley.

Phalanthus, a mythical Spartan said to have founded Tarentum in Italy about 700 B.C.

Pheræ was an ancient town in Thessaly, the home of Admetus.

Pheres, son of Cretheus and Tyro, was the father of Admetus and Lycurgus and the founder of Pheræ in Thessaly.

Philemon, an old man of Phrygia who, with his wife Baucis, hospitably received Zeus and Hermes.

Philoctetes, 198, 301, 303, 323, 324, 347.

"Philoctetes" of Sophocles, 323.

Philomela, *see* **Tereus.**

Phineus was the son of Agenor and ruled in Salmydessus in Thrace. He imprisoned his sons, by his first wife, Cleopatra, because of a false accusation made by their stepmother, Idæa. For this, or some other fault, he was punished with blindness, and two Harpies tormented him. When the Argonauts reached Thrace, Zetes and Calais, brothers of Cleopatra, killed the Harpies and were also said to have vindicated and freed their nephews, the sons of Phineus. In return, he advised Jason what course to take (*see* 157). Milton compares himself to Phineus (*Paradise Lost*, Book III, lines 35, 36).

Phlegethon, 406.

Phlegeus, 271.

Phocis, a country in Northern Greece, its chief mountain Parnassus and its chief river Cephissus, 390.

Phocus, son of Æacus, killed by his half-brothers Telamon and Peleus.

Phœbe, a name of Artemis as goddess of the moon.

Phœbus, 69.

"Phœnician Maidens, The," 263.

Phœnix, 294, 296, 361.

Pholus, a Centaur, 176.

Phorcys, a sea-deity, was, by Ceto, the father of Ladon, Echidne, the three Gorgons, and the three Greæ.

Phoroneus, son of Inachus and the nymph Melia, was an early mythical King of Argos.

Phrixus, son of Athamas and Nephele.

Phrygia, 121.

Phylachus, father of Iphiclus.

Phyleus, son of Augeias, 177.

Phyllis, beloved by Demophon, 349.

Pieria, on the south-east coast of Macedonia, was inhabited by Thracian people, who in early times worshipped the Muses, hence called Pierides. *See also* 92.

Pierides. (1) The Muses.
(2) The nine daughters of Pierus, a king in Macedonia, named after the Muses. They were conquered in a contest with the Muses and turned into birds.

Pirene, 148.

Pirithous, the son of Ixion and Dia, was King of the Lapithæ in Thessaly. He became a close friend of Theseus. *See also* 212, 213, 214.

Pisa, in Elis, 376, 377.

Pittheus, King of Troezen, was son to Pelops and father of Æthra, 203.

Pleiades, daughters of Atlas and Pleione were companions of Artemis. They were changed into doves and placed among the stars.

Pleione, mother by Atlas of the Pleiades.

Pleisthenes, 381.

Pluto. (1) A name for Hades, 399.
(2) The nymph, 371.

Podalirius, 324.

Podarces. (1) Original name of Priam, 275.
(2) Son of Iphiclus, who led the Thessalians against Troy.

Pœas, 301.

Polites, 334.

Pollux, Roman name for Polydeuces.

Polybus, 253.

Polybutes, 11, 12.

Polydectes, 132, 133, 141.

Polydeuces, one of Dioscuri, 155, 157, 215, 285, 286.

Polydorus. (1) Son of Cadmus and Harmonia, 244, 252.
(2) Son of Priam, 338.

Polyeidus, 232.

Polymester, 338.

Polymnia or Polyhymnia, the Muse of the sublime hymn.

Polyneices, 257, 261, 262, 263, 265, 266, 269.

Polypemon, *see* **Procurstes** *and* 205.

Polyphemus, 355.

Polyxena, 309, 337, 339.

Pontus, 1.

Porphyrion, 11.

Poseidon, *see especially* 99–109 *and also* 7, 9, 10, 13, 32, 36, 42, 44, 60, 67, 73, 110, 134, 137, 139, 140, 152, 157, 211, 223, 227, 305, 330, 348, 362, 366, 377.

Praxitiles, 63.

Priam, 275, 276, 277, 282, 302, 309, 315, 316, 318, 327, 330, 331, 334, 336, 338.

Priapus, son of Dionysus and Aphrodite, a god of fruitfulness.

Procne, *see* **Tereus.**

Procris was the daughter of the second Erectheus to be King of Athens. She married Cephalus. *See also* 229.

Procrustes or the "Stretcher" was the surname given to the robber Polypemon. He used to tie travellers to a bed, and if they were too short he would rack them, and if too tall, he would hack off their legs. He was served in the same way by Theseus. *See also* 205.

Prœtus, son of Abas, King of Argolis, inherited the kingdom jointly with his twin brother Acrisius. Soon expelled, he fled to Iobates, King of Lydia, whose daughter Anteia, also called Sthenebœa, he married. Returning to Argolis, he forced his brother to divide the kingdom and became ruler of Tiryns, whose massive walls he built by aid of the Cyclopes. *See also* **Melampus, Bellerophon.**

Prometheus, 16–20, 41, 176, 183.

Protesilaus, 303.

Proteus was the prophetic old man of the sea, subject to Poseidon, whose flocks of seals he tended. By assuming any shape he chose, he could avoid the need of prophesying, unless gripped fast, when he would at last resume his usual shape and tell the truth. He could be found at midday in the island of Pharos. *See also* 183, 345.

Psamathe, *see* **Linus** (1).

Psyche appears in late Greek literature as a personification of the soul, purified by suffering to enjoy true love. The beauty of the maiden Psyche excited the envy of Aphrodite who sent Eros to persecute her, but he fell in love with her and secretly visited her nightly. When Psyche, urged by her two sisters, sought to discover his identity, he left her. Searching for Eros, she endured further persecution, but he secretly helped her, and she finally overcame Aphrodite's hatred, to become immortal and united with Eros for ever. The story is told in *The Golden Ass* of Apuleius.

Pygmalion of Cyprus is said to have fallen in love with the ivory image of a maiden that he himself had made, and to have prayed Aphrodite to breathe life into it. When she consented, Pygmalion married the maiden, whom he called Galatea. By her he became the father of Paphus and Metharme. It is probable that the story concerns a priest of Aphrodite at Paphus who kept the image of the goddess in order to retain power. See William Morris's version in *The Earthly Paradise.*

Pylades, 390, 392, 396, 397, 398.

Pylos, 92.

Pyrrha, 20, 21.

Pyrrhus, *see* **Neoptolemus.**

Pythia, 76, 118, 171.

Pythian or Pythius, 69.

Python, 71, 76.

Rhadamanthus, 224, 225, 226, 407.

Rhea, 1, 5, 6, 7, 30, 101, 111, 122, 373.

Rhesus, 313.

" Rhesus," attributed to Euripides, 313.

Rhode or **Rhodos** was said to be the daughter of Poseidon. She was the wife of Helios.

Salmoneus, son of Æolus and brother of Sisyphus, emigrated from Thessaly and built Salmone. In his presumption he emulated Zeus, who destroyed him and his city with a thunderbolt.

Samos, 30, 34.

Sarpedon, 224, 225, 307, 311, 314.

Saturnus, a mythical King of Italy, identified by the Romans with Cronus.

Satyrs were beings who embodied the fertile power of nature. They were represented as men wearing skins and crowned with vine, fir, or ivy, with pointed ears, small horns, and a tail. They were said to be sons of Hermes, and were always connected with the worship of Dionysus. Older Satyrs were called Sileni *See also* 121, 127.

Scæan Gate, 321.

Scamander, River, 274, 313, 317.

Scheria, 362.

Sciron was a robber living on the frontier between Megaris and Attica. He robbed travellers and compelled them to wash his feet on the Scironian rock. He then kicked them into the sea, where a giant tortoise turtle devoured them. He was killed by Theseus. *See also* 205.

Scylla and **Charybdis** were two rocks between Italy and Sicily. In one dwelt Scylla, a fearful monster with six barking heads and twelve feet. Under the opposite rock lived Charybdis, who thrice daily swallowed and then regurgitated the waters of the sea. See *Odyssey* XI, ll. 85–110, *and also* 108, 359.

Scylla, daughter of Nisus, 230.

Scyros, 295, 326.

Selene, 84, 89.

Semele, 26, 119, 126, 244.

Semiramis and her husband Ninus were mythical founders of Ninus or Nineveh.

Seriphos, 132, 141, 142.

Sicily, 56, 112.

Sicyon, 118, 382, 383.

Sileni, *see* Satyrs.

Silenus was one of the Sileni who brought up Dionysus and was his constant companion. He was a jovial, bald old man usually drunk and riding on an ass. He had the power of prophecy. *See also* 121.

Sinis or **Sinnis** was a robber living on the Isthmus of Corinth, where he killed travellers by tying them to the top of a fir-tree which he tied to the earth and then allowed to spring upright. He was killed in the same way by Theseus. *See also* 205.

Sinon, 329, 330, 333.

Sirens were sea-nymphs who could allure by their songs all who heard them. When the Argonauts sailed past, Orpheus surpassed them, and Odysseus contrived to hear them unscathed.

Sirius, the dog-star.

Sisyphus, son of Æolus, married Merope, the Pleiad, who bore him Glaucus. He seduced Anticleia, daughter of Autolycus, and mother of Odysseus, and some said that Sisyphus was really the father to Odysseus. He founded Ephyra, later Corinth, and though he promoted navigation, was a notorious knave (*see Iliad* VI, 153). In the Underworld he was condemned always to roll uphill a huge stone which always toppled back again.

Smintheus, a name of Apollo.

Sophocles, 197, 259, 260, 266, 322, 323, 391.

Sparta, 45, 64, 86, 282, 284, 285, 286, 385.

Sparti or **" Sown Men,"** 243, 258.

Sphinx, 255, 256, 257.

Stentor, herald of the Greeks in the Trojan War. His voice was as loud as that of fifty men.

Steropes, 1.

Stheneboea, also called Anteia, 146.

Sthenelus. (1) Was the son of Perseus and Andromeda, and King of Mycenæ. His wife Nicippe, who bore him Alcinoe, Medusa, and Eurystheus.
(2) The son of Capaneus and Evadne, 268, 288, 328.

Stheno, 134, 138.

Strophius, 390.

Stymphalian Birds, 178.

Styx, 184, 294, 405, 406.

" Suppliants, The," 267.

Symplegades, 157.

Syrinx, *see* Pan.

Talaus, 261.

Talos. (1) Cretan giant, 228.
(2) Nephew of Dædalus, 237.

Tantalus, 251, 371, 372, 373, 374, 375.

Taphians, 165.

Tartarus, 4, 8, 9, 13, 14, 184, 400.

Tauris, 86, 300, 395, 396.

Tecmessa, 306.

Teiresias or **Tiresias**, 258, 259, 264, 270, 358, 360, 366. See Tennyson's poem *Tiresias*.

Telamon, son of Æacus, King of Ægina, joined with his brother Peleus in killing their half-brother Phocus and, expelled by his father, he went to Salamis, where he married Glauce, daughter of the king, whom he succeeded. Telamon later married Peribœa of Athens, who bore him Great Ajax. He joined in hunting the Calydonian Boar, and some say that he sailed with the Argonauts. *See also* 188, 189, 275, 276.

Telchines were variously described. It is said that Rhea entrusted the infant Poseidon to them and that they were artists in metal, making the sickle of Cronus and Poseidon's trident. But they were also said to be destructive beings, interfering with the weather, and earning the hostility of Apollo, who assumed a wolf's form to destroy some of them, and of Zeus, who overwhelmed others by flood.

Telegonus, 368.

Telemachus, 291, 363, 364, 365, 368.

Telephassa, 223, 240.

Telephus was the son of Heracles and Auge the priestess, daughter of Aleus, King of Tegea. He was abandoned as a child, but on reaching manhood questioned the Delphic Oracle as to his parentage. He was told to sail to King Teuthras in Mysia, and there found his mother married to the king. He succeeded Teuthras and was said to have married Priam's daughter Laodice. He tried to prevent the Greeks on their way to Troy from landing in Mysia. *See also* 299.

Telephylos, 357.

Tempe was a beautiful valley in Thessaly watered by the River Peneus. Apollo here pursued Daphne, daughter of the river-god Peneus. He had also purified himself here after killing the Python.

Tenedos, 301, 302, 329.

Tenes, son of Apollo, was reputedly the son of Cycnus, King of Colonæ in Troas. His stepmother, failing to seduce him, falsely accused him to Cycnus, who put Tenes, with his sister Hemithea, into a chest and threw it into the sea. The chest was driven to the island Leucophrys, whose inhabitants made Tenes king. The island was then called Tenedos. Cycnus, discovering his error, sailed to Tenedos and was reconciled with his son. When the Greeks landed on Tenedos on their way to Troy, Achilles killed both Tenes and Cycnus.

Tereus, a son of Ares, was King of the Thracians and lived in Phocian Daulis. He helped Pandion, King of Athens, and was therefore given Pandion's daughter Procne in marriage. She bore him a son, Itys. But Tereus was in love with Procne's sister, Philomela, and hiding Procne among the slaves, he told Philomela that her sister was dead, and so seduced her. He

THE CONTEMPORARY THEATRE

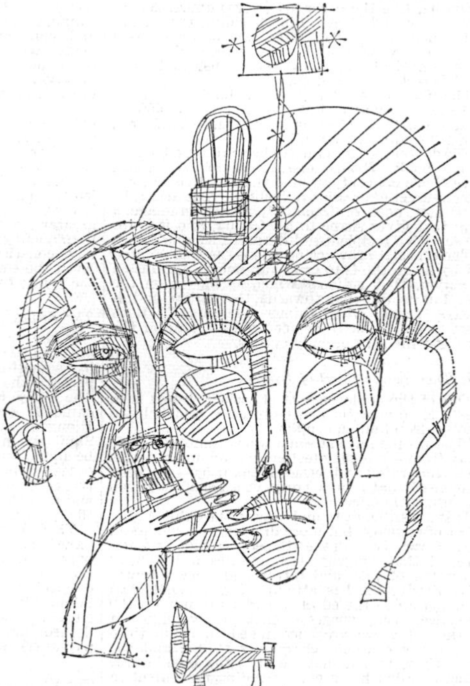

THE CONTEMPORARY THEATRE

This section concerns the English theatre since 1950 and is confined to plays produced before a live audience.

It consists of four sections:

I. Introduction
II. Eminent Theatrical Companies
III. Glossary of Dramatic Terms
IV. Dictionary of Dramatists

I. INTRODUCTION

What significance can the modern audience be expected to find in such spectacles as squalid garrets and basements, characters most unrealistically bursting into song, old tramps changing hats, or a young man trying to teach a set of weighing-machines to sing the Hallelujah Chorus?

These are some of the questions that trouble the playgoer, and since they are not always easy to answer it may be helpful first to consider what is the function of dramatic art, what are its constituents and background, and how to judge a play.

The Function of Dramatic Art.

It is not the function of art to make a statement but to induce an imaginative response, and the spectator receives not an answer to a question but an experience.

Drama, like the other arts, gives expression to that subtle and elusive life of feeling that defies logical definition. By feeling is to be understood the whole experience of what it feels like to be alive—physical sensations, emotions, and even what it feels like to think.

This flux of sensibility cannot be netted down in logical discourse, but can find expression in what Clive Bell, when discussing the visual arts, called "significant form."

The contemporary philosopher, Susanne Langer, in her book, *Feeling and Form*, has developed Clive Bell's concept, arguing that all artistic form is an indirect expression of feeling. The artist, be he painter, poet, or dramatist, creates an image, a form that gives shape to his feeling, and it is for the sensitive recipient to interpret its significance.

The especial province of drama, as was pointed out by Aristotle, is to create an image, an illusion of action, that action "which springs from the past but is directed towards the future and is always great with things to come." Both tragedy and comedy depict such action and the conflict which it normally entails.

The Therapeutic Effect of Drama.

One of the achievements of serious drama is to create an image that will objectify and help to resolve deep human conflicts.

Most people have at some time or another come away from a fine play feeling in some inexplicable way exhilarated and released, and it has long been recognised that drama can have a beneficial, even a therapeutic effect.

It is not difficult to understand the exhilarating effect of comedy, but more difficult to understand that of tragedy. In the 4th century B.C. Aristotle claimed that tragedy accomplishes a beneficial purgation of pity and terror and very recently Miss Bradbrook has attempted a psychological explanation of the effect of serious drama on the audience. She suggests that in watching a mature play we are encouraged to sympathise with many different characters at one and the same time, and it may be that the imaginative effort entailed has a corresponding movement in the unconscious mind. There, at the most primitive level, is an "internal society," the petrified infantile images of father, mother, and siblings, to which we are linked by inflexible attitudes. It may be that the sympathetic response to the playwright's images of these figures helps us to relax our rigid attitudes towards them so that the internal pattern of relationships shifts, and we experience a sense of release and a new access of energy.

It is noteworthy also that drama can be fully appreciated only in a public performance, a social event demanding the co-operation and understanding between author, players, and audience. Because it can flourish only in a community, normally a city, it has been called the metropolitan art.

The Constituents of Drama.

Drama is a complex art in that it uses two very different kinds of ingredient or material, one speech, the literary constituent, the other the gesture, movement, and confrontation of actors on an actual stage. Speech is man's most precise subtle, and mature means of expression. Gesture and confrontation, which he shares to some degree with animals, is more primitive and some of the power of drama as an art form is its fusion of civilised speech and primitive gesture into one organic whole.

It is just possible to conduct brief scenes using only one of these media. The chorus in Shakespeare's *Henry V* is virtually confined to speech and there is in Galsworthy's *Justice* a remarkable wordless scene, showing a convict in solitary confinement in his cell, that proved so moving that it led to an amendment of the penal code.

Perhaps the more primitive gesture has the greater emotional force, but it is the words made permanent in the literary script that up till now have constituted the commanding form of drama. Even the wordless mime is given permanence by the printed script.

The Ritual Element.

While speech and the confrontation of actors are essential to full drama, there is an element that has sometimes been neglected and that is ritual, perhaps the most primitive and evocative of all. The early tragedy of Greece was probably organically connected with the religious ritual of Dionysus and the matrix was song and dance. Similarly in England the origins of drama are to be found in church liturgy and ritual and civic occasion, both of which used procession, pageantry, costume, and symbolic insignia to great effect and also clowning which served as comic relief to the solemnity.

There have naturally been few dramatists who have been able to combine literary ability, a sense of stage situation and also skill in the use of ritual process. The enduring power of Shakespeare is due to his manifold genius in that he could deploy inimitable poetry, swift action, and such ritual enrichments as royal processions, crowning and dethroning, duelling and wrestling, masque and pageantry, song and dance.

The Background of Modern Drama.

The happy fusion of both literary and theatric excellence which is to be found in Shakespeare's plays is extremely rare, for it demands not only versatile genius but also a receptive audience and a suitable building. By the Restoration t delicate balance was already disturbed and by the middle decades of the 19th century popular taste had all but banished literature from the stage. The disorderly audiences of the time demanded only spectacular and sensational theatrical and musical effects, and in the vast monopoly theatres of Drury Lane and Covent Garden they could hardly have heard, let alone appreciated, good dialogue. The managers discouraged men of genius, so that poets like Browning, who had no practical knowledge of the theatre, produced wordy "closet dramas," which were virtually unactable, while the popular theatrical melodramas like *Maria Marten* or *Murder in the Red Barn*, are unreadable.

With the gradual establishment of smaller theatres, catering for a sober middle-class audience, men of talent again began to write for the stage. It was the turn of literature to take command, and more popular and traditional techniques such as music and clowning were now banished to the music-hall and pantomime.

T. W. Robertson, Henry Arthur Jones and Pinero all furthered the trend towards realism but it was the genius of Ibsen, especially in such works as *Ghosts* and *The Wild Duck*, that set a high standard of excellence for the literary and realistic play of middle-class life. He expressed his profound insight into personal and social problems in finely constructed plays, written in naturalistic prose, the overtones of poetic universality being conveyed in symbolism that was verbal.

Able writers, like Granville Barker and Galsworthy, although they lacked the poetic power of Ibsen, firmly established in England a similar type of literary play, realistic, well-constructed, serious-minded, concerned with the middle class and almost exclusively verbal.

One of the few exceptions to this preoccupation with the realistic and literary play was Shaw. Like Shakespeare, he was not only a literary genius. He was also well acquainted with stage-production and although much too wordy in old age, in his best comedies he combined some of the wittiest dialogue to be found in English drama along with the delightful shocks and surprises of total theatre. Androcles' engaging Lion belongs to the same family as Titania's Ass and Whittington's Cat.

But Shaw in his prime was unique, and between the wars the verbal, realistic play was perpetuated by such writers as Maugham and Coward. Not over-concerned with psychological or social issues, they used it to portray the leisured classes.

By the 'forties the conventional West End play ad with a few exceptions come to imitate not life but photography. Confined to the proscenium arch and realistic to the last trivial detail, it presented a prosaic picture of middle- and upper-class life, with stereotyped situation, demanding only stock responses and lacking interest in ideas, poetic intensity, and genuine wit. With the star cast and the long commercial run, theatre-going had become not an artistic experience but a social occasion.

Apart from the novel comedies of such writers as Ustinov and Rattigan and the verse plays of T. S. Eliot and Fry, it was the revivals of the classics, English and European, that were bringing genuine drama to the stage. Shakespeare could be enjoyed not only at Stratford and the Old Vic, but in the West End. It was largely due to ielgud that Shakespeare was now a box-office draw.

Gielgud's fine histrionic sense, and his highly sensitive and poetic interpretation had earned him that rare distinction of being the Hamlet of his generation and as early as 1934 his production and performance at the New Theatre had broken all records since Irving.

As actor and producer, working with other fine artists, such as Edith Evans, Peggy Ashcroft, Olivier, Guinness and Scofield, Gielgud later confirmed his success. Enthralling interpretations of plays by Shakespeare, Webster, Otway, Congreve, Sheridan, Wilde and Chekhov demonstrated that the classics could have a wide popular appeal.

Other artists followed and in a successful season at the New Theatre, Sybil Thorndike, Olivier and Richardson played to crowded houses in *Oedipus*, *Henry IV*, *The Critic* and *Peer Gynt*.

Such achievements have reminded audience and aspiring playright that there are many other dramatic styles than that of fashionable realism and so may even have helped to further the dramatic revival of the 'fifties.

The Revival in the Fifties.

It is not easy to identify the causes of this revival, but undoubtedly one reason is that young playwrights like Wesker and Delaney have injected new vigour into the jaded realistic mode by using it to express the vital stresses and conflicts of the working people whom they know. Hence the settings in basement and attic. *See* Neo-realism.

More far-reaching is the general awareness among *avant-garde* playwrights that verbalism is not enough and their readiness to experiment with the resources of "total theatre." Here the way has been shown by scholarly research into the history of the theatre which has given men confidence to revive valid techniques such as song, music and clowning that the early 20th century had exiled to the music-hall.

The most vital stimulus has been the challenge of genius. Brecht's Epic Theatre (*q.v.*) has offered a more free and fluid form than that of the well-made play, and his novel uses of traditional theatrical devices (such as song, masks, extravagant costume and settings, direct address to the audience) have been quickly adapted by dramatists like Arden, Bolt, and Osborne.

Meanwhile Ionesco, whole-hearted devotee of the Theatre of the Absurd (*q.v.*), has introduced monsters like the rhinoceros and has exploited stage properties like empty chairs to satirise man's empty existence. He has soon been followed by Saunders and by Simpson, whose weighing-machines symbolise the dominance of imagination by machinery. Monsters and machinery recently restricted to pantomime are returning to the stage.

A most pervasive influence has been that of Artaud's demand for a Theatre of Cruelty (*q.v.*). This is both the most novel and the most atavistic type of theatre, for it attempts to re-create in modern terms that primitive, even barbaric ritual from which drama evolved. In England it is best known still in translation of Genet and of Weiss.

Another interesting aspect of theatre today is a new and highly topical interpretation of Shakespeare, for some critics and producers have traced in his plays the bleak disenchantment that is typical of post-war Europe.

Peter Brook has said that his fine production in 1963 of *King Lear*, with Paul Scofield as protagonist, owed much to the critic Jan Kott, a Polish Professor of Literature, whose book *Shakespeare our Contemporary*, was published here in the following year.

Kott, who lived through the Nazi tyranny and the Stalinist occupation of Poland, urges that the power-politics, chicanery and violence of twentieth century Europe have their counterpart in the Wars of the Roses and the Tudor disturbances. He finds in Shakespeare's Histories and in the Tragedies, especially *Macbeth*, what he terms the "Grand Mechanism" of history, the blood-stained struggle for power with its terrible consequences, and he claims that Shakespeare "condemns war by showing up the Feudal butchery."

The series, "The Wars of the Roses," which was produced for the B.B.C. during 1965–6 by Peter Hall and John Barton with the Royal Shakespeare Company, vividly demonstrated the crime-ridden lust for power and the feudal butchery. Meanwhile at Stratford and the Aldwych, the production of *Henry V* neglected the traditional, royal splendour and showed the king, grimy and battle-scarred, leading a tattered army, plagued by corrupt camp-followers. Played on a bare, gaunt stage, grey, metallic and cavernous, it was strikingly similar in tone and significance to Brecht's *Mother Courage*, running concurrently at the Old Vic.

The most exciting aspect of the contemporary theatre is its catholicity of outlook and method. There is some danger that in the rediscovery of the resources of total theatre with its movement, symbolic objects and ritual, the literary aspect of drama may now be neglected. The enduring popularity of Shakespeare, the many-sided genius, may help to preserve the balance.

Criteria of Judgment.

How can the value of novel and experimental plays be estimated? The ultimate test of time is obviously impossible and some of the critical principles by which traditional drama has been interpreted are no longer relevant to the revolutionary plays of Brecht and Ionesco.

The first canon of criticism is to remember that every art form determines the criteria by which it is judged, and the good dramatic critic does not approach any play with a pontifical set of rules but endeavours to keep an open mind, and so to discover its unique significance and value.

Since artistic form is an expression of human feeling, the first encounter with a work of art should be in a mood of extreme receptivity, so that by shedding preconceived notions, the recipient may be aware of the feeling implicit in the work, however novel or even bizarre the expression may be.

The initial reaction to drama should be intuitive.

The nature and quality of the implicit feeling can then be considered. Is it an original and genuine response to experience, or perfunctory and stereotyped, is it intense or diffuse, profound or shallow, subtle or commonplace, reasoned or irrational?

Questioning its inherent feeling often reveals that a commercially successful piece, although "well-made," is valueless, while an unconventional work, like Pinter's *Dumb Waiter*, explores and reveals deep-seated anxieties and fears.

Drama is an especially complicated art, in that part of its material being words, it may also involve discussion of ideas. This discussion, however, should not be mistaken for a statement of the author's convictions. In a good play it is an expression of his characters' *feeling* about ideas, a very different thing.

Another enquiry concerns the appropriateness and beauty of the form in which the feeling is conveyed. Many consider that Beckett's *Waiting for Godot* conveys the same mood implicit in *King Lear*, and that each play is an image of man, disillusioned, adrift, assailed by despair in an alien universe. This recognised, the critic's task is to explore the form of the two plays. Apart from the fact that they both use a most improbable fable, they could hardly be more different. *King Lear* is a Renaissance verse tragedy of the fall of princes, with subtle presentation of character development and contrast, and with a coherent plot skilfully developed through arresting action up to the tragic climax. *Waiting for Godot* is a prose play about an abortive encounter, almost devoid of individual characterisation and story, with a static, circular structure and an ending as ambiguous and inconclusive as its beginning. Yet in either case the form of the play has artistic significance and appropriateness and repays analysis, and here again the critic needs to be a flexible interpreter of the artist's purpose.

The most searching question to be asked of a play is whether it is life-enhancing, whether, like the finest art, it gives delight or deepens understanding.

Most difficult to estimate are those plays like *Lear* or *Godot*, which express a mood of despair. But if man's honesty and endurance are ultimately affirmed, the play is not negative in import. Lear begs forgiveness and the tramps still wait.

Similarly a biting satire may be positive if it helps to clear away old wood to make room for new growth. A facile optimism may be a betrayal.

Ideally the best way to know a play is first to see it on the stage, when its theatrical qualities can be enjoyed, and later to read it at leisure, when its literary value can be appreciated.

II. EMINENT THEATRICAL COMPANIES

Londoners owe an incalculable debt to the Royal Shakespeare Company at the Aldwych, to the National Theatre, temporarily at the Old Vic, to the English Stage Company at the Royal Court and to enterprising theatre clubs like the Unity, the Hampstead and the Arts.

One of the most rewarding experiences for the visitor to London is to witness, at the Aldwych or Old Vic one of those superb productions which have an international reputation or to see the *avant-garde* work at the Royal Court. Such an experience is analogous to visiting the National Gallery, the Tate, or the Festival Hall.

Many provincial repertory theatres are also doing exciting work, including revivals and premières. These include the Bristol Old Vic, the Chichester Festival, the Belgrade at Coventry, the Ashcroft at Croydon, the Glasgow Citizens', the Arnaud at Guildford, the Nottingham Playhouse, not to mention the Royal Shakespeare at Stratford and the work of the Edinburgh Festival.

The Royal Shakespeare Company.

When Peter Hall was appointed Director of the Royal Shakespeare, in 1960, he decided to supplement the annual season of Shakespeare at Stratford-on-Avon by a continuous repertory of classical and contemporary plays at the Aldwych.

In 1962, after Peter Hall and Michel Saint Denis had also become Directors, a special experimental season was also held at the New Arts.

A brilliant team of over 100 actors has now been gathered together and the imaginative direction and artistic perfection of the ensemble playing has recently become more widely known through their Wars of the Roses seen on television.

Each year Shakespeare's plays, freshly interpreted, have alternated with other classics and with unorthodox and trenchant modern work. Brecht's and Beckett's plays have been seen. Whiting, Pinter, and Livings have been sponsored, with Whiting's *Devils*, 1961, and *A Penny for a Song*, 1962, Pinter's *Collection*, 1962, *The Homecoming*, 1965, and Livings' *Eh?*, 1964.

In 1964 alone twelve productions were put on, including highly experimental work: Vitrac's *Victor*, short pieces by Tardieu, Arrabel, Beckett, Whiting, and Saunders, and the *Marat-Sade* of Weiss, brilliantly produced by Peter Brook. In addition the theatre played host for the World Theatre Season.

Recently a thriving R.S. Theatre Club has been founded, very popular with the young, which provides booking facilities and concessions, discussions, and a quarterly magazine, *Flourish*.

The National Theatre.

Sixty years after Granville Barker and William Archer had formulated plans for a National Theatre, the inaugural production of *Hamlet* took place on 22 October 1963 at its temporary home, the Old Vic, pending the building of the permanent theatre on the South Bank, promised by the end of 1971.

Laurence Olivier having already been appointed Director, the nucleus of a distinguished company was formed and soon established its high reputation for fine ensemble playing, guest artists also appearing on occasion.

The intention has been to build up a large repertoire of classical and modern plays from all countries. Already a wide range of imaginative productions has been acclaimed by packed houses. The list includes *Othello*, and *Much Ado about Nothing*, Farquhar's *Recruiting Officer*, Congreve's *Love for Love*, *Hobson's Choice* by Brighouse, Shaffer's *Royal Hunt of the Sun* and *Black Comedy*, and Arden's *Armstrong*. Other countries are represented by Chekhov's *Uncle Vanya*, Feydeau's *A Flea in her Ear*, Brecht's *Mother Courage*, and Miller's *Crucible*.

Plans for the future envisage O'Casey's *Juno and the Paycock*, de Vega's *Bond Honoured*, Büchner's *Danton's Death*, Ostrovsky's *The Storm* and Jonson's *Volpone*.

A most attractive booklet is issued for each production and is available to the audience at a trifling cost. This supplies authoritative information about the author, the play, its sources and inner references, notable productions and critical estimates, together with photographs, rehearsal productions, and plans.

Productions of the National Theatre have appeared at the Chichester Festival Theatre, and have gone on provincial tours. In September 1965 the company made its first tour abroad, visiting the foremost Soviet theatre, the Kremljovesky, and the Frei Volks Buhne in West Berlin. It has played to the Berliner Ensemble, the National Youth Theatre, and the Commonwealth Festival.

The English Stage Company.

Since 1956 the English Stage Company at the Royal Court has been tireless in its discovery and support of new talent. Formed to promote contemporary drama, the company acquired in 1956 a long lease of the Royal Court with George Devine (d. 1965) as Director and Tony Richardson as Assistant. Declaring themselves a Writers' Theatre, they were extraordinarily successful in discovering and sponsoring playwrights hitherto unknown, such as Osborne, N. F. Simpson, Ann Jellicoe, and John Arden, and in persuading the novelist Nigel Dennis to write for the stage.

An offshoot of the Company, the English Stage Society, initiated in May 1957 the inexpensive Sunday night "Productions without Decor", which brought to light such successes as Wesker's *The Kitchen* and Owen's *Progress to the Park*.

Writers beginning to make their reputation elsewhere were welcomed. Beckett's *Endgame* and *Krapp's Last Tape* had their première here. Many distinguished foreign plays were seen in Britain for the first time at the Court, including Arthur Miller's *The Crucible*, Tennessee William's *Orpheus Descending*, Ionesco's *The Chairs* and *Rhinoceros*, Sartre's *Nekrassov* and *Altona*, Genet's *The Blacks*, and Brecht's *The Good Person of Szechwan*, the first Brecht ever staged in London. Revivals of the classics were also produced.

In October 1965 William Gaskill succeeded Devine and his policy is to have several plays in repertoire. The autumn season 1965 saw new plays, by Jellicoe and Simpson, and *Saved* by Bond, a new writer. In 1966 there have been revivals of Arden's *Musgrave* and of a Middleton, Cregan's *Transcending* and Keith Johnstone's *The Performing Giant*, which experiments with clowning. A teach-in concerning the controversial *Saved* was an admirable innovation, fostering understanding between audience, actors, and director.

Theatre Workshop.

Unfortunately the work of Joan Littlewood as Director of Theatre Workshop, at Stratford East, now belongs to history. From 1953 to 1961 she introduced several new playwrights, including Behan and Delaney, her work culminating in *Oh What a Lovely War*, 1963, which like so much of her work was transferred to the West End.

She looked for scripts which, however formless, had some spark of life. Spontaneity and pseudo-Brechtian techniques and not careful construction are the hallmark of her work. She and her company would work together on a meagre script so that it is sometimes difficult to judge who was responsible for the final play.

Plays evolved from a bare outline include Norman's *Fings Ain't What They Used T'Be*, Chapman's *You Can't Always Be on Top*, 1957, and Lewis's *Sparrers Can't Sing*, 1960.

Joan Littlewood's masterpiece, *Oh What a Lovely War*, paradoxically uses a period pierrot show brilliantly to satirise the tragic futility of the First World War.

The Hampstead Theatre

The Hampstead Theatre Club, now London's first Civic theatre under the energetic direction of Roose-Evans, has sponsored many aspiring playwrights. It has to its credit the premieres of several plays now widely acclaimed, including two by Pinter, one by Milner and one by Howarth.

III. GLOSSARY OF DRAMATIC TERMS

Absurd Drama.

The Theatre of the Absurd, originating in Paris, was introduced here through the plays of Beckett and translations of Ionesco, Vian, and Vitrac. It has had considerable impact on Pinter, N. F. Simpson, Saunders, and Campton, while American absurdist plays by Albee, Gelber, and Kopit and by the Swiss, Frisch, have also been produced here.

The concept of the Absurd was first formulated by Camus to indicate the discrepancy between human reason and aspiration and an indifferent and hostile universe. But like Sartre he expressed his convictions through the traditional dramatic form.

Not every playwright of the Absurd is an existentialist and many are more concerned with an irrational human society than with the universe. What they have in common is a technique. All have discarded traditional realism and express absurdity through images that are themselves absurd, including bizarre situations and objects, both sad and comic, such as aged parents consigned to dustbins.

There is in the Absurd an element of Surrealism and Miss Bradbrook has suggested that a better term might be Theatre of Dream, for it is the unconscious dream mind that juxtaposes objects and incidents that in the waking state have no connection, such as a rhinoceros in a provincial street. Pinter seems to have an intuitive awareness of the hinterland of dream, while Simpson makes a conscious manipulation of Surrealism.

Frisch has ably demonstrated that the Absurd can be an effective vehicle for satire and many absurdist writers, such as Ionesco and Simpson, have satirised the modern prostitution of language corrupted by salesmen and politicians, and have used conversation of vapid emptiness to reveal its breakdown as a means of communication.

It is partly because of their distrust of language that they have had recourse to ludicrous objects and images, thus extending the range of total theatre.

The Aristotelian Play.

Brecht and Ionesco have disparagingly referred, somewhat inaccurately, to "Aristotelianism." Strictly speaking, this means the concept of tragedy which Aristotle first analysed in his *Poetics*, basing it primarily on the tragedies of Sophocles, especially the *Oedipus Rex* (P), *c.* 425 B.C. The Aristotelian concept, revived since the Renaissance, has obviously been much modified, but certain basic principles can still be discerned.

Aristotle claims that poetry in general aims at that rational pleasure which is part of the good life. He defines tragedy as the imitation of an action complete in itself and stresses its inner coherence. Tragedy must have an intelligible beginning, a middle necessitated by the beginning and which itself necessitates the end. "The story . . . must represent one action, a complete whole, with its several incidents so closely connected that the transposal or withdrawal of any one will disjoint and dislocate the whole."

The action should be of some magnitude, with "incidents arousing pity and fear wherewith to accomplish the purgation of such emotions." Here is Aristotle's celebrated doctrine of purgation or "catharsis" which has been variously interpreted, some considering that something like a ceremonial purification is intended, with an ethical end in view, others that bodily or psychological relief from tension is meant.

Aristotle emphasised the paramount importance of action or plot, the characters being revealed in and through the action. The kind of plot recommended is one where the hero is an eminent man, neither inordinately good nor bad, whose misfortune is brought upon him by some error of judgment.

Here is the germ of the splendid Renaissance tragedy concerned with the fall of princes and also of the modern finely constructed play, such as Ibsen's *Ghosts*. Such a play has classical symmetry, the beginning, middle, and end, becoming in modern parlance the exposition, development, and climax or denouement. It has its own organic unity and inevitibility. But although many writers, such as Sartre, still work within the classical disciplines many have discarded the traditional form.

Brecht and his followers have repudiated the whole pattern in favour of a sequence of self-contained episodes strung along a narrative thread, where ironic detachment supersedes the emotional involvement and catharsis of Greek tragedy.

In this day of the common man few are concerned with the fall of princes, and it is interesting to examine some of the more striking modern plays and to ask how far they stand up to the Aristotelian canon. Should a new concept of tragedy be evolved, that of potentiality unrealised, not a fall from greatness but a failure to rise?

The Brechtian or Epic Play.

Many British dramatists have felt the pervasive influence of the Bavarian Brecht (*q.v.*), who developed a new kind of Epic or narrative play of debate, with a loose sequence of episodic scenes linked by commentary or songs. Discarding realism, Brecht attempted not to arouse the onlooker's emotions but to stimulate him to think about social issues and to take left-wing action. In the event his ambiguous central situation appealed to deeper levels of experience.

There have been several instances of the ambiguous protagonist, but English playwrights have tended to adopt not the political intentions but the style of the Epic genre. Esslin has said that Shaffer in *The Royal Hunt of the Sun* has joined " Bolt, Arden and John Whiting of *The Devils* in the select group of British dramatists who have genuinely benefited from the conception of epic . . . techniques in drama."

Theatre of Cruelty.

In 1938 Antonin Artaud published *The Theatre and its Double*, a collection of essays and letters, which forms the theoretic basis of the Theatre of Cruelty, his central purpose being a ritual of cruelty to exorcise fantasies.

Professor Brustein has described how Artaud hated industrial civilisation, believing, like Freud and D. H. Lawrence, that it stifled instinctual life. He claimed that the theatre, as the heart of a common culture, should enact a primitive ritual of cruelty, a sacrificial frenzy and exaltation. In this way it would bring to the surface and exorcise the spectator's latent anarchy, violence, and eroticism, serving as an " outlet for repressions."

Artaud envisaged a total theatre, appealing to total man, primarily visual, where the all important Director would deploy " music, dance, plastic art, pantomime, mimicry, gesticulation, intonation, architecture, scenery and lighting " to induce a state of trance. Attacking the inadequacy of a pallid conceptual language, Artaud demanded that dramatic language should have an emotional and incantatory effect.

It is Genet who most closely fulfils Artaud's demands and in England the specific Theatre of Cruelty has been best represented by his plays and the *Marat-Sade* of Weiss. But the methods of production advocated by Artaud have had a wide and pervasive influence on the movement towards total theatre.

Expressionism.

One of the most notable contemporary revivals of Expressionism is Wesker's *Chips with Everything*. The genre flourished in Germany after the First World War, where its chief exponents were Kaiser and Toller, and in Czechoslovakia in the plays of Capek. O'Neill and O'Casey have also occasionally experimented with Expressionism.

Reacting from Realism with its insistence on individual psychology and the detailed representation of actual life, Kaiser, Toller, and Capek sought to express rather the general aspirations and fears of humanity, especially man grappling with the advent of machinery. Their characters are symbolic types, as the Nameless One, representing the mob in Toller's *Man and the Masses*. The decor is stylised, the dialogue staccato, and the brief scenes are characterised by mass movement and swift action.

Naturalism.

Naturalism in drama may be regarded as a special case of Realism, and it is not easy, nor perhaps always desirable, to make a sharp distinction between the two.

Naturalistic drama attempts to record as faithfully as possible the actual experiences of life, however banal, and to present life, undistorted by the playwright's theories or too much concern for artistic form. The virtues of Naturalism are fidelity and spontaneity. Its danger is that it may keep so close to life as to lose artistic form and tension, becoming the stage version of the tape recorder. *See* **Slice-of-Life Play.**

It was Zola in the 1870s who propounded the principles of Naturalism. Distrusting both the play of ideas and the well-constructed play as tending to impose on life a falsifying and artificial pattern, he urged that drama should record as objectively as possible the actual course of man's life, especially the way it is conditioned by environment.

Strindberg's *Miss Julie*, 1888, is an essay in Naturalism but the genre is found in its most accomplished form in the Russian theatre, especially in Stanislavsky's production at the Moscow Art Theatre of the plays of Chekhov and in 1902 of Gorky's *The Lower Depths.*

Neo-Realism.

There is nothing new in dramatic Realism (*q.v.*) as such. What is novel is the realistic presentation of the shabby lodgings and streets of the underprivileged. Gorky in *The Lower Depths* was perhaps the first dramatist to reveal the wretched condition of the destitute and this play influenced O'Neill's *The Iceman Cometh.* Their recent production in London, with a starkly realistic background, had some effect on those contemporary plays where the kitchen-sink and dustbin are as much in vogue as was formerly the fashionable drawing-room.

Any worth-while play has significance far beyond its milieu and modern neo-realistic plays vary greatly in theme and purpose. Wesker Delaney, Livings, Owen, Osborne, Orton, Bond Lawler, and Seymour have all used the style in differing ways.

Several of these playwrights have themselves been workers and their plays are an authentic interpretation of their own culture, once inaccessible to the middle-class audience. The fact that their work is occasionally loose in structure may be attributable to the influence of Naturalism (*q.v.*) or to the author's unacademic background The advent of this fresh and vigorous drama from a group that has seldom been articulate is one of the most encouraging aspects of modern theatre

Realism.

Writers of realistic drama, such as Galsworthy attempt to create a stage illusion of actual life usually through the medium of the well-constructed play. It is not always easy to distinguish between Realism and Naturalism—its extreme form—but one salient difference is that the latter tends to discard organised plot as imposing a false pattern on the flux of life.

Bolt, Cooper, Mortimer, Shaffer, and Porter have all written realistic plays, and since the 'fifties there has been a succession of competently constructed realistic plays associated with the novelists, Graham Greene, C. P. Snow, and Ir Murdoch.

The Satirical Play.

Recent months have seen heartening revival of plays by Shaw, triggered off by Stage Sixty production of *Widower's Houses*, with its topical relevance to Rachmanism. This has been followed by *Too True to be Good*, from the Edinburgh Festival, *Fanny's First Play, Man and Superman* at the Arts, and *You Never Can Tell*, with Ralph Richardson.

Shaw has found few successors, for genuine satire is a most demanding art. Subjective hostility and negative criticism are not enough The motive power in Ibsen and Shaw was ration indignation, a most difficult fusion of strong emotion and objective reasoning, and their satire was constructive in that it implied and indicated positive values. It was also characterised by a precise aim at a specific target. Vague and wholesale denunciation diffuse a disagreeable tone which has a boomerang effect for it becomes associated not with the targets but with the critic himself.

The graces of satire are detachment, irony, and wit and it flourishes apparently in a stable society such as that of the 18th century, which produced Swift and Voltaire. The European upheavals of the last half century have been unpropitious for satire and it is significant that the best plays in this genre, those of Frisch and Dürrenmatt, have come from neutral Switzerland.

The English playwright nearest to Shaw is Nigel Dennis, and Giles Cooper's *Everything in the Garden* was a successful piece.

The "Slice of Life" Play.

Here is an extreme kind of Naturalism, where the author has been so anxious to preserve fidelity to the natural spontaneity of living, that he has all but discarded form, as having a cramping and distorting effect.

One of the most typical examples is Henry Chapman's *You Won't Always Be On Top*, showing the disconnected minor incident and talk of men ostensibly "at work" on a building site. Shelagh Delaney's *The Lion in Love* is also in this vein.

Verse Drama.

During the 20th century several attempts have been made to revive drama in verse—the normal vehicle for the Renaissance playwright. Although the verse plays of Shakespeare and his contemporaries, kept alive in excellent revivals, still rise like the Himalayas above the contemporary scene, the dramatist today who tries to use verse has not the benefit of an unbroken tradition. Yeats, T. S. Eliot, and Christopher Fry all succeeded for a time in getting their verse plays on to the stage but at the moment the most successful poetic drama achieves its effect through poetic prose and the theatrical poetry of its situation and stage imagery. Dylan Thomas' *Under Milk Wood* successfully used these media. For many contemporary audiences it is Beckett, Arden, and Pinter who have captured the poetry inherent in drama.

The Well-made Play.

The term "well-made play" is most frequently used in a derogatory sense. Eric Bentley has pointed out that the "well-made play" is a form of classical tragedy, degenerate in that although the plot is ingeniously contrived, with arresting situation, intrigue, and suspense, the play is mechanical and devoid of feeling. The television series, *The World of Wooster*, is an example.

The expression was frequently used disparagingly of the French plays of Scribe and of Sardou, ridiculed by Shaw for his "Sardoodledum."

IV. DICTIONARY OF DRAMATISTS

This part, alphabetical in arrangement, includes dramatists whose work, whether English or in translation, has had its British première since 1950. Unless otherwise stated the quotation of date and actor refers to the British première.

Inexpensive paperback editions are referred to thus: F: Faber and Faber. M: Methuen. P: Penguin.

Arthur Adamov (b. 1908).

Adamov first wrote plays such as *Professor Taranne* (P), which translate his own personal neuroses into images of the absurd, until with the propagandist *Paolo Paoli* he adopted a Brechtian technique. His *Spring 1871*, an epic panorama of the Paris Commune, had its world première in London in 1962.

Edward Albee (b 1928).

The American Albee, an adopted son, is a brilliant satirist of his society.

The Zoo Story. P.

An absurdist one-act dialogue reveals a schizophrenic's failure to communicate—even with a dog—and ends with his self-immolation.

The Death of Bessie Smith.

This is a realistic satire on the neurotic refusal of white hospitals in Memphis, in 1937, to admit the injured negro singer.

The American Dream.

In an absurdist satire the newly adopted son proves to be a facile young man who embodies unscrupulous materialism with inner deadness.

Who's Afraid of Virginia Woolf? 1964. P.

A brilliant and scarifying satire on sterility in an American campus uses a ritual movement. George and Martha, named after the Washingtons, are an unsuccessful and childless middle-aged couple. They cherish a fantasy "son," whom George, to spite Martha, symbolically "murders" during a liquor-ridden night party, when they attack each other and their guests (a young couple also childless) with ferocious mental cruelty.

Jean Anouilh (b. 1910).

Anouilh is a playwright of remarkable theatrical versatility and skill. Following Giraudoux, he has frequently employed classical themes, as in *Eurydice* (M), and *Antigone*, 1949 (M), with Olivier and Vivien Leigh. More recently he has treated historical figures, Saint Joan in *The Lark* and Becket in the play of that name. The play within a play is a favourite expedient of his.

Anouilh's outlook is deeply pessimistic. A recurring theme is that purity is incompatible with experience of life and many of his protagonists say, "No." His plays fall into two categories—the fatalistic *piéces noires* and the romantic fantasies, *piéces roses*.

They have been extraordinarily popular on the London stage of the 'fifties and Anouilh's amoral attitude has been reflected in many West End successes.

John Arden (b. 1930).

Arden is a vigorous and gifted playwright, who has experimented with a variety of subjects and methods, sometimes too original and complex to find quick acceptance.

His characters are full-blooded and rich in human contradictions, and he has sympathetically brought to life even such bogeys as Herod and King John. He loves to dwell on some ambiguous personality, where generosity conflicts with violence, and to consider the problems of directing man's unruly vitality.

His favourite theme is the dispute between instinctual energy and good government and he pleads the case cogently for both sides, giving no facile judgment or direct "message," unless it be "the recognition of the fallibility of man." Thus although, like Brecht, he is deeply concerned with social and political dilemmas, he remains politically "uncommitted." He is above all the dramatist of the dilemma.

There has been a fruitful cross-fertilisation of Arden's interest in current events and his literary studies; and his historical plays, like Brecht's *Mother Courage*, combine a fine sense of period and a sharp relevance to some current issue.

Arden's plays are poetic in structure, depending in part on the recurrent image and metaphor and, like Arthur Miller in *The Crucible*, he has skilfully devised for each an appropriate dialect of time and place. At the same time he has a keen sense of theatre, and has successfully adapted techniques from Miracle plays, Elizabethan drama, music-hall, puppet stage, and Brechtian epic play.

Live Like Pigs. 1958. P.

Seventeen realistic scenes, full of comic and frightening incident, reveal how tensions develop between households at different social levels in a council housing estate. The authorities—a well-meaning local official (Alfred Lynch) and a police sergeant (Stratford Johns)—fail to forestall a violent and fatal conflict.

Most of the scenes are prefaced, in Brechtian style, by verses of the old street-ballad type, sung with monotonous melancholy. This device gives a sense of the universal nature of human discord in an otherwise firmly particularised time and place.

The Happy Haven. 1960. P.

Here, in a good-tempered satirical fable, enlivened by a dash of magic, Arden touches on problems of longevity.

Doctor Copperthwaite, the superintendent of the Happy Haven, an old people's home, is, like a mediaeval alchemist, bent on producing an Elixir of Life and Youth, intending to use his five unsuspecting patients as guinea-pigs. But outwitted by them he is himself transformed into a small boy.

The theme is childishness. The egocentric demands of the very old are seen as amusing childish foibles, while Doctor Copperthwaite, so absorbed in his research as to forget ends for means, brings childishness on himself.

In form the play is an extended puppet show. The characters wear masks, the set is formalised, and there is even a dog, Hector, but unlike Dog Toby he is visible only to the dramatis personae.

Serjeant Musgrave's Dance. 1959. M.

For this fine play, which explores the ethical dilemma of war, Arden drew on two sources—contemporary events in Cyprus and a journal written by a deeply devout N.C.O. during the Crimean War. He has fused his material into vivid incidents, which he projects against the background of a fictitious colonial war of the 1880s.

In a frost-bound colliery town there arrive three private soldiers, led by the dominating Serjeant Musgrave. They claim to have come recruiting but are in fact deserters from a colonial war.

In spite of his rigid sense of military duty, Musgrave had been horrified by the terrible five-fold reprisals taken by the British for the assassination of a comrade, Billy Hicks. Believing himself to be God's agent, he has now come to Billy's town, obsessed by one purpose, to expose war's horrors.

Exhibiting Billy's skeleton in the market-place, he at first wins sympathy in his denunciation of atrocities. Then bewildered by his own confused "logic," he demands twenty-five deaths in return for the five taken by the British and turns the gatling on the astonished crowd.

Suddenly, with the thaw, the Dragoons arrive and Musgrave finds himself awaiting execution, stunned that no one has learned the lesson he yearned to teach.

Fierce incident and macabre surprise are used for a play of ideas which enunciates no facile answer. It is typical of Arden's fair and non-doctrinaire approach that the dilemma of the religious man in face of war should be embodied in the fanatical and confused Musgrave. This has sometimes misled the audience, but the spirit of compassion implicit throughout the play is clearly revealed in the gentle, pacific Private Attercliffe, who is also to be executed with Musgrave. The women's parts are also significant, especially that of Mrs. Hitchcock, the owner of the inn, who visits Musgrave in prison and shows him how he had erred in trying to use war itself to end war. In his darkest despair she gives him hope, and it is symbolic that he accepts drink from her hand.

The complex play weaves together many tensions; harsh discord between colliery owner and strikers; contention between the three privates, each of whom is strongly individualised; the discrepancy between a woman's love and the careless soldier's life; Musgrave's own bitter inner struggle.

The dialogue has a wonderful period character and the soldiers' ballads and lyrical songs occur with complete naturalness.

The Workhouse Donkey. 1963.

Styled by Arden as a "vulgar melodrama", this ample Brechtian play shows jockeying for power in a northern town between the Tory Alderman Sweetman, a wealthy brewer, and Alderman Butterthwaite (Frank Finlay), the Labour ex-mayor. Both attempt to manipulate the police and to enlist the support of the electorate, represented by the shifty turncoat Doctor Blomax, until all these four elements of the community are deeply corrupted.

Butterthwaite, called "the workhouse donkey" because born in the workhouse, is the dominating Rabelaisian character. A Dionysiac figure, he is drunken, lecherous, and amoral, yet devotedly loyal and generous. Finally in an attempt to help the treacherous Blomax he robs the Borough safe and brings disaster on himself and the town.

Arden says, "The personality of the late Mr. Joseph D'Arcy of Dublin inspired much of the play."

Armstrong's Last Goodnight. 1964. M.

The old "Ballad of Johnnie Armstrang," *c.* 1603, forms the framework of a play concerning the dilemmas of government. Armstrong of Gilnockie (Albert Finney), the Scots Border laird, freebooter and rebel, is invited to a meeting by the young Scottish King James V and then treacherously hanged. Arden has introduced into this stark story the historical character of the king's herald, Sir David Lindsay, poet and politician, and shows him at first striving by devious diplomatic expedients to persuade Armstrong to loyalty, before he finally advises force. The play is diversified by minor characters and incidents which sometimes, however, overcomplicate and obscure the impressive ballad line.

The introduction of Lindsay was suggested to Arden by his reading of Conor Cruse O'Brien's book *To Katanga and Back*, for he was struck by "a basic similarity of moral" between 20th-century Africa and 16th-century Scotland, the rôle of O'Brien being similar to that which he invents for Lindsay.

Arden makes free use of Elizabethan pageantry and of Brechtian ballad-singing and the setting is the mediaeval convention of "simultaneous mansions," Gilnockie, the Border, and the Court all being formally represented on the stage at one and the same time.

Arden "constructed" a dialect to suggest the place and period, but for the English audience it is not easy to follow, especially as Armstrong himself has a marked impediment in his speech.

Left-handed Liberty. 1965. M.

When commissioned by the Corporation of the City of London to write a play to commemorate the 750th anniversary of the sealing of Magna Carta, Arden made a careful study of the historical facts, which he presents with very little transposition and addition.

He approaches his theme of liberty from an unusual angle, showing the aftermath of Runnymede in the apparent failure of the Charter, and demonstrating that the agreement had to take place in people's minds before it could become effective.

It is typical of Arden that he does not present a clash of black and white. John is a rounded character, a slippery villain, but shrewd and energetic and gifted with the Plantagenet charm while some of the barons are coarse and unscrupulous fighters.

The use of stylised scene emblems, such as charts, maps, and views of Runnymede, give mediaeval colour to the simple stageing and Arden has again invented a suitable dialect.

James Baldwin (b. 1924).

Baldwin is an American Negro novelist and essayist, and a champion of Civil Rights.

The Amen Corner. 1965.

Acted by a Negro cast including singers of Spirituals, the successful play gently probes the genuine and the self-deluded elements in religious experience.

Samuel Beckett (b. 1906).

Beckett, an Anglo-Irishman, who has made his home in France, is the most distinguished of the English dramatists of the Absurd. His world drastically limited, peopled chiefly by old men awaiting their death, but it is the profoundly tragic world of Lear in the storm and it is conceived with the intensity and haunting power and suggestiveness of the true poet.

His work is poetic in its verbal imagery, sometimes as searching and macabre as that of Webster, and his dramatic prose has an underlying poetic rhythm often more flexible and effective than that of Eliot's verse. In structure his plays have a poetic symbolism, a latent significance, like that of the novels of James Joyce, Beckett's close friend, and their striking visual imagery has a kind of theatrical poetry, as for instance the two tramps at the foot of a bare tree in *Waiting for Godot*. It is remarkable that so literary a playwright should also have succeeded with the wordless mime play.

Beckett's chief weakness as a dramatist is that the action and visual imagery are frequently too static, as in the motionless dustbins in *End Game*, much less effective theatrically than Ionesco's movable chairs.

Waiting for Godot. 1955. F.

This tantalising and compelling tragi-comedy, Beckett's masterpiece, originally written in French and produced in Paris in 1953, was later translated and performed in more than twenty countries.

Character and incident are pared to the bone and only a skeleton situation remains. At evening, on a desolate road, bare but for a single tree, two wretched tramps, Vladimir and Estragon, wait for a mysterious Mr. Godot. As they while away the time with desultory talk and clowning, a tragi-farcical diversion is provided by the entry of Pozzo and Lucky, bullying master and wretched slave, and a boy later brings a message that Mr. Godot cannot come but will arrive the next evening. After discussing whether or not they shall hang themselves from the tree, the tramps decide to go away for the night, but remain on the spot.

Act II presents "Next day, same place," the only difference being that the tree has sprouted a few leaves, and the basic pattern of Act I is repeated.

Although by the skilful use of music-hall techniques Beckett presents his tramps in the guise of amusing clowns, they are at the same time pathetically human as they waver between suicide and irrational hope. A fretful affection has kept them together over fifty years, and their dispositions are complementary, possibly even representing different aspects of the one personality. The practical and extrovert Vladimir, nicknamed Gogo, may depict man's intellect, his executive powers, the ego, while the more poetical and introvert Estragon, nicknamed Didi, may represent the body, instinct, the id.

Pozzo and Lucky, another pair of contrasting characters, are portrayed more farcically. The loud, confident Pozzo drives Lucky in as if he were a beast of burden. Lucky carries in his mouth the whip with which he is beaten and humbly obeys every insolent command. He dances for Pozzo and even thinks for him. In their second appearance Pozzo is blind and Lucky deaf.

They may be considered personifications respectively of master and slave, worldly materialism and higher values, the physical and the intellectual, body and soul, or the two aspects of a sado-masochistic relationship.

The play as a whole is a most complex dramatic symbol expressing man's anxiety and suffering as to his origin and destination.

The uncertainty is symbolised by the characters' confusion as to even the physical actualities of time and place, but the dominating symbol is the tramps' doubt as to Godot's identity and purpose.

Such an oversimplified interpretation as to equate Godot with God is inadequate, yet the play has undoubted Christian references. A tree is frequently used as an emblem of the Cross. Beckett, questioned about its theme, quoted a wonderful sentence in Saint Augustine, . . . "Do not despair; one of the thieves was saved. Do not presume; one of the thieves was damned."

Beckett neither affirms nor denies Saint Augustine's statement but inverts it into a question, more distressing than direct denial. Can we any longer accept the existence of divine grace and judgment? It is a question such as this that gives to the play its symbolic shape of doubt, and which is cogently expressed in the theatrical image of two outcasts at the foot of a tree, a tree of life which puts forth leaves, a tree of death which they contemplate using as a gallows.

Yet the significance of the play is even deeper than an exploration of religious doubt, its appeal wider and more contemporary. The anguished uncertainty of the 20th century is whether life has any meaning whatsoever and the play shows the suffering of man, lost and anxious in an apparently meaningless universe.

Some have considered it to be written from the point of view of existentialism: continuing vainly to hope for a supernatural revelation, the tramps lack the courage to come to terms with the nothingness at the root of our being and the need to choose and create our own destiny.

A Jungian psychologist, Eva Metman, has made a similar interpretation, remarking, "Godot's function seems to be to keep his dependents unconscious."

"Habit is a great deadener," says Vladimir. If Beckett's play enables the audience to escape the drug of habit and to face this image of anguish and so find some relief, then it may have the therapeutic value of that inner knowledge advocated by Freud and Jung.

It is not a play for those who cannot bear to suffer. When performed in San Francisco Gaol, the first play there for forty-four years, it held its audience of fourteen hundred convicts spellbound. They realised that each must find his own personal message. All knew that it spoke to those who must suffer and wait.

Endgame. 1958. F.

Also translated from the French, this play again depicts a static situation. In a single, claustrophobic room, the selfish, materialistic Hamm, who keeps his senile and legless parents in dustbins, is now paralysed and blind and dependent on his servant Clov, who longs to leave him. But if Clov should leave, both would die, for Hamm owns the only store of food in a devastated and dead world. Finally Clov sees outside what may be a small boy, "a potential procreator," and he prepares for departure but remains immobile.

The play like poetry can be interpreted in several ways. Since Hamm and Clov are mutually dependent, it probably represents tension between complementary aspects of personality, Hamm sensation and emotion, and Clov intellect. As Clov has vision and sees the boy, the situation suggests the struggle of the mystic endeavouring to escape from a deadening materialism to a vital awakening of the spirit. It may also depict a period of traumatic depression when the whole external world seems dead and unreal. The play's overall impression is that of the dissolution of the personality in death, both personal and global.

Endgame lacks the wry humour of *Waiting for Godot*, and is less compelling than Ionesco's *Exit the King*, but is more potent in its latent imagery than is Ionesco's play.

Krapp's Last Tape. 1958. F.

In the briefest sketch, Krapp, a solitary, decrepit, unsuccessful old man listens to his own autobiographical tape-recording of thirty years ago, but the moment of miraculous insight it commemorates is now so meaningless to him that he switches off that section of the recording and broods on a description of his love-making.

Beckett employs a most effective stage device to pose contemporary queries as to the limitations of verbal communication and the continuity of personal identity.

Happy Days. 1962.

Here again the paralysis of later life is indicated. A woman talks ceaselessly, although progressively buried in a mound of earth until it reaches her neck.

Beckett's two "Mimeplays without Words" are in striking contrast to the plays in that all is conveyed in symbolic wordless action.

Brendan Behan (1923–64).

Behan, a Dubliner, and author of the autobiography, *The Borstal Boy*, used his own experiences in the I.R.A. and as political prisoner to give substance to his two unusual plays.

The scripts of both were sent to Joan Littlewood and considerably altered, especially in the deletion of "chunks of terrible sentimentality," while the length of *The Hostage* had to be trebled. Lacking in structure and depth of characterisation, they are vividly impressionistic, lively, and voluble. As Tynan says, "Language is out on a spree, ribald, dauntless and spoiling for a fight."

Because they are presented in comic terms, Behan's strong social convictions are fully integrated in his plays. *The Quare Fellow* is an effective plea for the abolition of capital punishment and *The Hostage* makes the business of war seem extremely childish.

The Quare Fellow. 1956. M.

The scene is an Irish gaol during the twenty-four hours immediately preceding the execution at 8 a.m. of "the quare fellow," who has brutally killed his own brother. Farcical and macabre happenings succeed one another, as the unnerving effect of impending death is shown on both prisoners and warders, while a recurring song from the punishment cell sounds a melancholy refrain. The sombre theme is presented obliquely, masked by the harsh irony of prison jests, and although the play has little plot it is remarkably tense, partly because we never see the condemned man. Much is also due to Joan Littlewood's skill in redistributing dialogue and tightening the structure.

The film version completely distorted the disciplined and claustrophobic atmosphere of the play.

The Hostage. 1958. M.

Again the basic situation is the waiting for an execution. The scene is an old Dublin house, once the refuge of the I.R.A., now a brothel. Irish patriots bring here a captured Cockney private soldier, Leslie Williams, as hostage for an Irish boy, now a political prisoner in Belfast, who is to be executed next morning.

Teresa, the gentle little Irish maid, reared in a convent, tries to save Leslie. There is touching pathos as these two orphans, neither of them understanding what the strife is about, recall their childhood, and when in a raid on the house Leslie is shot, Teresa utters her lyric lament. But the mood is only held for a moment. Leslie leaps up and sings "The bells of hell go ting-a-ling-a-ling," and the play ends.

The mood is much less consistent than that of *The Quare Fellow.* Here the comedy is chiefly a diversion supplied by a host of minor characters. The action is constantly held up for songs more or less satirical and music-hall exchanges between comedian and "feed," some of them genuine Irish inconsequence, others mediocre backchat and malapropism. All this pseudo-Brechtian trimming detracts from the growing sense of alarm as Leslie gradually realises his fate and is of doubtful value.

Robert Bolt.

Bolt has recently said, "I do like plays in which the people have ideas as well as predicaments" and he is one of the few dramatists who have scored West End successes with the play of ideas. He holds the balance of discussion so fairly that only in the outcome is it clear that he himself is committed. His earlier work, represented by *The Flowering Cherry* (1957), with Ralph Richardson, was in the naturalistic convention, but more recently he has experimented with other dramatic techniques, owing something to Brecht and to the Theatre of Cruelty and of the Absurd.

The Tiger and the Horse. 1960.

This play takes its title from Blake's "The Tygers of wrath are wiser than the horses of instruction." It is concerned with the inadequacy of detachment, the philosophy held by Jack Dean, (Michael Redgrave), the Master of an Oxbridge college, the well-balanced man who represents Blake's "horse," while his wife, Gwen, the "tiger," passionately concerned for the world's suffering, shows signs of neurosis. The action revolves round her wish to sign a petition for unconditional nuclear disarmament and Dean eventually, to save his wife from mental breakdown, bravely identifies himself with her and the cause, thereby deserting his philosophy and his career.

In its outcome the play stresses the value of social idealism, stifled as it may be by philosophic detachment and the pressures of conformity. It is typical of Bolt's dialectic that this value should be upheld by the disturbed Gwen and by Louis, an oddly irresponsible young man.

In this play Bolt departs from the realistic style by trying to make his characters larger than life in being unusually articulate about what they stand for.

A Man for All Seasons. 1960. P.

Here Bolt attempts to give his characters heroic dimensions by striking back into history.

Believing that our need today is a sense of personal individuality or "selfhood," he chooses as his hero of "selfhood" Sir Thomas More (Paul Scofield). More, described by one of his contemporaries as "a man for all seasons," was not only flexibly adjusted to Renaissance society, but also managed to preserve an inner core of unassailable integrity. Suspected of a critical attitude to Henry VIII's divorce, he used his skil in "the thickets of the law," yet resolutely refused to swear the oath to the Act of Succession that would have released him from the Tower and the block, because for him perjury meant the los of the soul, the self. His constancy is thrown into relief by the growing corruption of Richard Rich, whose final perjury sends More to his death.

More challenges comparison with Brecht's Galileo. He also is a man of supreme intelligence whose inner certitude of truth is persecuted by an absolute power. He also skilfully avoids open clash until he must eventually make a final choice between astute temporising and commitment o his life to his belief. The difference is that More opts unequivocally for constancy.

Bolt uses what he calls a "bastardized version" of Brecht's style. Episodic scenes ar strung along a strong thread of intellectual argument. There is also a commentator in the form of the Common Man, who with the aid of propert box takes a swift succession of minor parts changes of role which throw into relief the steadfast individuality of More.

Bolt, like Brecht, believing that beauty o language is a means of "alienation," matches fin passages from More himself with his own appropriate use of wit and imagery, using images of lan to suggest society and its laws and those of wate and sea the superhuman context.

Gentle Jack. 1963.

Bolt depicts the conflict between the natur spontaneity of nature, represented by the magi figure of folk-lore, Jack-of-the-Green, in his fores (Kenneth Williams) and the inhibitions of societ in the person of Miss Lazara, financier and pluto crat (Edith Evans). Since Bolt believes that th modern doctrine of the return to nature may lea to violence, Jack finally contrives two murder The play was not successful. Bolt in dealing wit this age-old conflict could not, like Euripides i *The Bacchae*, draw on a familiar and deeply fe myth, and his allegorical plot proved puzzlin while the setting was too reminiscent of *De Brutus*. The play is too cerebral, the characte are more blue-prints than flesh and blood.

Edward Bond (b. 1935).

Saved. 1965.

Saved, which did not pass the censor, was fir presented to the English State Society.

As a result of casual sexual intercourse with th promiscuous Pam, Len gets involved with h morose South London family, with Fred, th putative father of her baby, and with Fred's lew gang, which murders the baby on the stage.

Since the play is largely in delinquents' argo and is limited to a photographic study of inar culate people, it is in itself somewhat inarticulat but it constitutes a frank and compassiona social document.

Bertold Brecht (1898–1956).

Perhaps the most original and vigorous dram tist and producer of the century, the Bavari Brecht was remarkable in his command of bo literary and theatrical genius.

His practice and theory underwent constant modification. Early plays, like *Baal*, written to provide entertainment, reveal a satiric and anarchic attitude, and in 1928 the ironic *The Threepenny Opera* (P), made him famous. From 1930 onward his work became explicitly communistic, marked by the rejection of the individual in favour of a social ideal. But although Brecht always remained " committed " to Marxist ideology, most of his later plays, written after his withdrawal from Nazi Germany, are less didactic than humanist in spirit and it is by these mature works that he is best known in Britain.

After 1949 Brecht consolidated the famous Berliner Ensemble in East Berlin, where he developed his influential techniques of production.

The most permanent feature of Brecht's mature drama are the Epic form and the *Verfremdung*, or " alienation " effect, both developed in reaction to the traditional dramatic form, which he dubbed " Aristotelian." He considered that the closely constructed Aristotelian play, which encourages the audience's emotional participation in the action, syphons off the spectator's emotion, leaving him a passive and acquiescent member of society.

According to Brecht, the drama should be not ritual but debate. The spectator should be a calm and detached observer, calmly investigating the view of the world that confronts him, rationally considering arguments and stimulated to decisive social action. It is taken for granted that he will find the solution to problems in communism.

Brecht therefore developed his " Epic," or narrative play, loosely constructed with a sequence of individual scenes, functioning as independent dramatic illustrations or quotations to the narrative.

He uses a variety of techniques to establish the narrative tone, such as an actual story-teller on the stage, explanatory verses relayed before the scenes, and banner headlines which foretell the events to be portrayed. Although by throwing the action thus into the past tense, he discards the lure of suspense, his dramatic intelligence, vigour, and inventiveness excite lively interest and curiosity.

To break down the traditional identification of the spectator with the action, Brecht developed his celebrated " alienation " effect, devising techniques to keep him at a critical distance. This implies using an image that suddenly makes the familiar appear strange and novel to the onlooker, so that he is shocked into recognising its significance.

His productions were thus avowedly non-realistic and theatrical, sometimes appearing like an inspired charade. He used not only direct narration but direct address to the audience, formalised settings and properties, masks and stylised make-up, sometimes grotesque in character. His text, " scarcely more than a prompter's copy," was freely adapted during rehearsal, so that an acquaintance with the pattern of Brecht's mime and gesture is often necessary to the full understanding of his plays.

Few find in Brecht's mature work the plea for communism that he intended, and many of his protagonists, designed as exponents of capitalist villainy, appeal strongly to the sympathy. The compelling and fascinating central ambiguity can be ascribed, as Esslin has pointed out, to the tension between Brecht's conscious reason and the unconscious emotional experience on which every creative writer must intuitively draw. This profound tension is the major source of Brecht's power.

Brecht's influence has been pervasive, especially on the dramatists Arden, Bolt, Whiting, and Shaffer, and on the producer Joan Littlewood. Above all his iconoclastic attitude and his fertile experiment have been invaluable in encouraging a new and empirical approach to drama.

Baal. Written 1918.

The amoral vagabond poet, Baal (O'Toole), driven by instinct and emotion, expresses the subjective experience of the youthful Brecht.

Galileo. Written 1938–9. M.

Brecht intended Galileo's recantation as an image of the scientist's allowing the State to assume authority over science. It has also been interpreted as Galileo's cunning expedient, allowing him to continue research.

Mother Courage. Written 1939. M.

In his panorama of war's futility, Brecht designed Mother Courage—a camp follower in the Thirty Years' War—as an epitome of the haggling profiteer. But his intuitive understanding of this dynamic, maternal figure, bereaved eventually of all three children, has endowed her with an ambiguous fascination.

The Good Person of Szechwan. Written 1938–40. M.

Shen Te (Peggy Ashcroft), the benevolent prostitute, has to disguise herself as Shui Ta, the harsh task-master, in order to survive in an unjust commercial society.

Puntila. Written 1940–1.

The drunken generosity of the mean landowner, Puntila, designed by Brecht to highlight his harshness when sober, has however given him an attractive inconsistency. The chauffeur who rejects Puntila's daughter, is a Schweikian character.

The Caucasian Chalk Circle. Written 1944–5. M.

The prologue to this delightful fairy-tale constitutes an overt plea for communism rare in Brecht's later work. The rascally judge Adzak, who takes bribes from the rich and gives judgment in favour of the poor, is one of Brecht's typical contradictory characters.

David Campton (b. 1924).

Campton's brief " glimpses " or playlets use techniques of the Absurd, which he considers as " a weapon against complacency," to expose the actual dangers that threaten society, especially the bomb. His most notable works are the collections of playlets, *The Lunatic View*, 1957, and *A View from the Brink*, 1961.

Albert Camus (1913–60).

It was the French existentialist philosopher and novelist, Camus, who first enunciated the concept of the Absurd, describing it as whatever in human experience is incompatible with man's desire for reason, justice, happiness, and purpose.

Like Sartre, Camus expressed his views through the traditional dramatic form, and the plays most familiar here were those written before he had moved on to a more humanistic philosophy.

Caligula. French publication 1945.

The Roman Emperor, Caligula, suddenly decides to act in accordance with the absurdity of the universe and by his violent and perverse crimes forces on the Senators his own recognition of the absurd meaninglessness of existence.

Cross Purposes. French publication 1945.

Man's futile desire for happiness is dramatised in the legend of the mother and daughter who murder for gain the visitor to their inn, only to discover they have killed the son of the house. They then commit suicide.

Giles Cooper (b. 1918).

Everything in the Garden. 1962. P.

Cooper deftly uses sophisticated comedy for a sharp satire on the sacrifice of principle to money in an effeminate bourgeois society. Four bored middle-class wives become part-time employees in an exclusive brothel, while their complaisant husbands enjoy the tax-free profits. There is a sudden horrifying change of key when at a party a neighbour realises the position and the four men destroy this outsider in a kind of ritual murder. In Cooper's second version the play returns rather shakily to the comic vein. It is interesting to compare Pinter's *The Homecoming*.

Shelagh Delaney (b. 1939).

Shelagh Delaney is a Salford girl from a secondary modern school and her plays owe their attraction to their fresh and artless picture of a handful of workers and hangers-on known at first hand. Although produced by Joan Littlewood her plays are basically naturalistic in subject and style.

A Taste of Honey. 1958. M.

After seeing Rattigan's *Variations on a Theme*, the seventeen-year-old Shelagh Delaney decided she could do better herself and sent the script of this play to Joan Littlewood, who made several improvements without impairing the spirit.

The significance of the play lies in its unconventional and striking subject, the pregnancy of an unmarried adolescent expecting a black baby and her friendship with a homosexual lad. The setting, a cheap lodging, deserted by a raffish mother, was at the time a novel one. Joan Littlewood's production involved the entry and exit of characters to music, a device which brought out the play's introspective and dreamlike quality, but the realistic film version ignored this aspect.

The Lion in Love. 1960. M.

A more ambitious play, taking its title from Æsop's fable, again gives an uncompromising picture of an adolescent girl's first encounter with love in a home neglected by the mother. But the girl is more mature and the main interest has in fact shifted to the mother. The play is a kaleidescope of folk in indecision. They are presented with fidelity, the dialogue being so realistic as to be flat and monotonous. Although *The Lion in Love* is a more mature work it lacks the compulsive central theme of the previous play.

Nigel Dennis (b. 1912).

Dennis, also a novelist, is a hard-hitting satirist in the tradition of Voltaire and Shaw, and in a Shavian preface to his first two plays he wittily defines his favourite targets. One is the doctrine of Original Sin as preached by Saint Augustine, the other the assumptions of psychoanalysis. He argues that both of these undermine natural self-reliance, and tend to delegate power over the mind to a hierarchy, clerical or medical, which may threaten personal individuality. The Preface is a lively firework display, but Dennis' arguments are sometimes one-sided and negative, more striking than valid.

One of the few dramatists to write in a Shavian tradition, he shows considerable dramatic talent, especially in his vigorous first acts, with their strikingly novel situation and witty and intelligent dialogue. But in the middle of his plays satire gets the upper hand and discussion diverts interest from the characters and tends to hold up the action and to weaken the structure, as in some of the later plays of Shaw himself.

Cards of Identity. 1956.

The play was adapted from Dennis' own novel. The "Mallets," members of a club formed to give people a changed identity, inveigle local people to a country house, where by exploiting psychological techniques they induce them into accepting changed names, memories, and identities and then use them as servants. Only in face of their Bank Manager do the victims rediscover their original personalities.

Dennis uses the adroit situation to illustrate the thesis developed in his Preface. Arguing that the basis of personality is memory, Dennis infers that the psychologist can edit his patient's memories, inject his own viewpoint and so undermine and manipulate personality. This plausible thesis is not verified by any appeal to scientific evidence.

The Making of Moo. 1957.

Compton, a colonial civil servant, has weakened the native taboo on murder by unwittingly killing the river god. He decides to invent the new religion, of Moo (the name suggested by the lowing of cattle), complete with mythology, musical ritual, and ethical code. In this daring satire on revealed religion Dennis exposes similarities between pagan trust in the efficacy of ritual blood sacrifice and the Christian doctrine of Atonement for Original Sin. In his Preface he suggests that to conform to a religious sect is to belong to an Identity Club, which threatens the individuality of its members.

August for the People. 1961.

Opening with a satire on the admission of the public—at a fee—to private "stately homes", the play proceeds to an indictment of the tameness of the common man. It lacks the pungency and inventiveness of Dennis' early work.

Friedrich Dürrenmatt (b. 1921).

The German-Swiss Dürrenmatt acknowledges the Greek dramatists, Shakespeare, and Swift as major influences. He describes his work as "theatre of paradox," revealing "precisely the paradoxical effects of strict logic." He is an unsparing critic of contemporary society, whose dangerous tendencies he exposes in striking dramatic extravaganzas, reminiscent of the later Shaw.

The Physicists. 1963.

Dürrenmatt has said that this arresting play is not so much about the hydrogen bomb as about society itself and the impossibility of escaping the consequences of one's thinking.

The central character, attempting to suppress scientific discoveries that may lead to the hydrogen bomb, retires to a private asylum pretending to be in contact with King Solomon. There he is first in danger of two spies, pretending to the delusion that they are Einstein and Newton, and eventually of the mad proprietress whose use of his discoveries will lead to the destruction of the human race.

The Marriage of Mr. Mississippi.

An extravaganza poses the opposition between two principles carried to their logical and farcical extreme. One is a passion for the law of Moses, interpreted as retributive justice. The other is pure Marxism. The two characters embodying these principles, together with a Quixotic lover, are manipulated and destroyed by an unscrupulous politician.

T. S. Eliot (1888–1965).

In his attempt to revive poetic drama the distinguished poet, T. S. Eliot, was moved by deeply religious and social aims, modestly regarding his work as experimental, "that of the first generation only." The verse he evolved was of a flowing poetic rhythm, "close to contemporary speech" and based on natural stress. Normally he used a line with three stresses and varying length.

In his two plays of the 'thirties Eliot had adopted the ritualistic themes and patterns of Greek drama and had achieved a certain tragic intensity. But the *Cocktail Party* inaugurated a new style, the theme still being Christian redemption and the plot deriving from Greek drama, but the idiom, that of the fashionable comedy of manners. In spite of subtle organisation the liaison has been an uneasy one.

It is curious that the creator of Prufrock should seem unable fully to animate his dramatis personae. This is partly because their inspiration is literary, partly because they are used to illustrate Anglican doctrine and to convey a message. Nor do they belong to the impeccable background against which they are so carefully placed.

The wealth and subtlety of reference of these plays and the beauty of the language make them a delight to the reader, but they are less compelling on the stage.

The Cocktail Party. 1949. F.

This play has its origin in Euripides' tragicomedy *Alcestis*, the demi-god Hercules being replaced by Reilly, the psychiatrist, whose intervention breaks the back of the play, for it is not easy to sympathise with people who let their actions be so directed.

The Confidential Clerk. 1953.

Described as "high farce," this play derives from another tragi-comedy of Euripides, the *Ion*, whose theme of parents seeking their lost children reappears in Terence, Plautus, and Shakespeare.

The Elder Statesman. 1955.

Eliot here returns to a tragedy, the *Oedipus at Colonus* of Sophocles, but the youthful peccadilloes of Lord Claverton appear pallid compared with the patricide and incest of Sophocles' protagonist.

Max Frisch (b. 1911).

Frisch, a German-Swiss who has been influenced by Shaw and Brecht, dramatises current issues in ingenious, apt, and witty parables that have a lucid economy of outline.

The Fire-Raisers. 1961. M.

A delightful Absurdist satire on bourgeois self-delusion and ineptitude shows Biedermann (Alfred Marks) persuading himself that he can cajole the incendiaries about to set fire to his house by inviting them to a good dinner. The situation is analogous to that of Benes of Czechoslovakia who included communists in his government, and to that of the Germans who connived at Hitler.

Andorra. 1964. M.

An incisive and moving satire on the vicious pervasiveness of antisemitism shows the Andorrans' betrayal of the lad Andri, reputedly a Jewish foundling, to the invading totalitarian state. Andri is in fact a Gentile and his assumption of Jewish traits is an example of identity imposed from without by society.

Christopher Fry (b. 1907).

Fry was widely acclaimed in the 'forties for bringing verse back to the stage. His delightful verse, which plays over the surface of his plays like lambent flame, has been compared by Allardyce Nicol to that of the youthful Shakespeare.

Fry has written highly original comedies and religious plays and his work is informed by an implicit spirit of affirmation and hope, conveyed with gaiety and insouciance. He has a gift for devising ingenious situations in terms of poetic fable and metaphor.

Venus Observed. 1950.

Hope Wallace commented on the "dancing, glancing felicity" of this unusual comedy, in which Olivier was protagonist.

A Sleep of Prisoners. 1951.

This original religious play was commissioned for performance in churches during the Festival of Britain.

The Dark is Light Enough. 1954.

An eccentric and saint-like old countess (Edith Evans) gives asylum to men from both sides in the Hungarian rising of 1848. The theme of non-intervention is presented with a lightness and elegance which completely save the play from didacticism.

Curtmantle. 1962.

A historical play concerning Becket and Henry II concentrates on the contradictory nature of Henry. Fry deliberately uses a plainer and rougher verse and some prose.

Jack Gelber.

Gelber is one of the few Americans to attempt plays of the Absurd.

The Connection.

Beckett's theme of waiting is presented through drug addicts waiting for their dope, to the improvisations of a jazz quartet, but the realistic ending is inconsistent with the Absurdist style.

Jean Genet (b. 1910).

The French Genet, abandoned as a child, has lived as social outcast and criminal and, while politically "uncommitted," has mirrored his bitter repudiation of society in plays of frightening impact.

His dramatis personae have been the rejected murderers (*Deathwatch* (F)), despised servants (*The Maids* (F)), prostitutes (*The Balcony*), Negroes (*The Blacks*), and Algerian peasants (*The Screens*). These have realised their fantasies of sex, power, violence, and revenge only by compulsive ritual acts, so that sequences of arresting ceremonial, sometimes Absurdist, replace character study and coherent plot.

In his destructive scorn of contemporary society, his recourse to rituals of violence, and his incantatory language, Genet satisfies the requirements of Artaud's Theatre of Cruelty.

The Balcony. 1957. F.

This censored play had its world première at the Arts Theatre Club. It opens in a brothel, where the frequenters enact their fantasies of power by dressing up as bishop, judge, or general, until after an abortive revolution they are called upon by the Court to impersonate these authorities in actuality. Eventually the defeated revolutionary leader visits the brothel to enact the part of Chief of Police, who is then satisfied that his image also has been established in popular regard. The film gives a softened version of the play.

Jean Giraudoux (1882–1944).

Two plays of the French dramatist, Giraudoux, who had stimulated the return of poetry to the stage, were produced here in the 'fifties. *Duel of Angels*, 1953, with Vivien Leigh, was a posthumous work. *Tiger at the Gates*, 1955 (M), with Michael Redgrave, was a translation by Fry of a fine play of 1934. Giraudoux here used the classical legend of Troy as a vehicle for a protest against the stupidity of war.

Willis Hall (b. 1929).

In 1958 Hall was one of the few playwrights giving a candid realistic picture of the underprivileged, as in his best play *The Long and the Short and the Tall* (P) about soldiers trapped in the Malay jungle in 1942. He later collaborated with Waterhouse in North country comedies such as *Celebration* and *Billy Liar*.

David Halliwell.

Little Malcolm and His Struggle Against the Eunuchs. 1965.

A deliciously funny send-up of the angry young man cult is located in a Huddersfield garrett. Here Malcolm, a beatnik ex-art student, compensates for his inadequacies—professional and sexual—by fantasies of Hitlerian power. He imposes on his three chums his farrago of "Dynamic Insurrection", which so distorts reality that they all finally beat up the nice girl who wants to help Malcolm.

The sources of disaffection and violence are scrutinised incisively but with sympathy.

Rolf Hochhuth.

The Representative. 1963.

Using some dramatis personae who represent historical personages, this play in verse exposes the failure of Pope Pius XII, Christ's "representative," to protest against the massacre of the Jews. Film sequences of the horrors of Auschwitz are used with harrowing effect.

N. C. Hunter (b. 1908).

With a feeling for atmosphere, Hunter portrays disappointed people, ruefully accepting their limited environment, but his plays lack passion, intellectual pressure, and novelty.

His West End successes have been *Waters of the Moon*, 1951, *A Day by the Sea*, *A Touch of the Sun* and *The Tulip Tree*, all produced with star actors.

Donald Howarth.

A Lilly in Little India. 1965.

In the manner of Dylan Thomas's *Under Milk Wood*, two households are revealed simultaneously. A fatherless boy, nagged by his mother, finds some self-confidence by growing a lily bulb. This brings him into touch with a motherless girl and their hesitant friendship is indicated with some distinction and charm.

Eugene Ionesco (b. 1912).

Ionesco, one of the leading Parisian playwrights of the Absurd, differs from Camus and Sartre in that he expresses his conviction of life's absurdity, not rationally, but through images that are in themselves absurd.

In 1948, while learning English from a primer, Ionesco stumbled on his vocation, his shocked reaction to the platitudes he was memorising being dramatised in *The Bald Prima Donna*. Here he singled out aspects of contemporary life which still remain as the chief targets of his ridicule.

One is the empty, myopic existence of the petit bourgeois, his lack of passion and thought, the yielding to conventional pressures, the urge to conform. Another is the desiccation of language which, stereotyped and inadequate, has become "nothing but clichés, empty formulas and slogans."

Ionesco's sense of life's absurdity has deep roots, for he is keenly aware of the anguish of the modern world, of the flight from reason, both tragic and absurd in its potentialities. He believes that by dramatising his own inner hurt he can best reveal a universal experience. In *The Shepherd's Chameleon* he has plainly stated that for him "the theatre is the projection on to the stage of the dark world within," the world of dream, anguish, dark desires, inner contradictions, and obsessions.

It follows naturally that he is little preoccupied with specific social problems. Regarding the human condition as wider and deeper than the social condition, he dislikes any kind of political message or conformism and deliberately repudiates the "committed" and didactic play.

Iconoclastic in both his principles and technique, Ionesco—as he indicated in *Victims of Duty*—has challenged most dramatic assumptions, including realism, the concept of the "Aristotelian play," consistent characterisation, motivation, plot, and the distinction between tragedy and comedy.

Discarding so much, Ionesco has evolved a new technique of shock tactic, using most ingenious theatrical devices to express his convictions. He attempts "to go right down to the very basis of the grotesque, the realm of caricature . . . to push everything to paroxysm, to the point where the sources of the tragic lie. To create a theatre of violence—violently comic, violently tragic."

In his plays, as in those of Pinter, the traditional dividing lines between tragedy and comedy melt away, for his amusing images are at the same time poignant, expressing as they do human disappointment and folly, so that his hilarious comedy may have a tragic import.

A characteristic technique is the use of proliferating material objects, which externalise the anxieties of his characters—an accumulation of chairs or eggs, for instance, or an expanding corpse. He hopes thus "to make the stage settings speak; to translate action into visual terms; to project visible images of fear, regret, remorse, alienation."

The discarding of proved theatrical techniques is risky. Shock tactics are successful only as long as they surprise by their novelty. It is a measure of Ionesco's talent that he continues to invent the novel and arresting.

In two of his most recent plays, *Rhinoceros* and *Exit the King*, the nihilism for which Ionesco has been criticised has been relieved by the assertion of the human value of fortitude.

Ionesco's plays were introduced into England in the 'fifties and they have had a marked and specific impact on English drama, especially on Simpson and Saunders. Although Pinter has a philosophy and style all his own, his work is based on similar presuppositions.

The Bald Prima Donna. Written 1948.

Characters from an English language manual come to life and pour out their clichés in a "parody of a play," which Ionesco first considered to be a "tragedy of language," but which proved theatrically very funny. The first dialogue between husband and wife is now a classic.

Thus Ionesco, almost by accident, wrote the first of many satirical exposures of the sterile language of those who live a merely mechanical existence.

The Lesson. Written 1950. P.

A nervous old professor coaches an eager young girl. Elaborately "proving" the impossibility of communicating by words, he arbitrarily decides what various words shall mean, until he rapidly gains assurance and eventually rapes and murders his pupil, the fortieth that day.

Ionesco illustrates the prostitution of language as a means to power, the sexual element in power, and the sadism lurking in the teacher–pupil relationship and indeed in all authority.

Jack. Written 1950.

Urged by his conventional family to settle down to married life, the Bohemian son, Jack, resists Roberte, the proposed bride, because having only two noses she is not ugly enough. He eventually succumbs to Roberte II with three noses. Ionesco parodies submission to bourgeois conformity.

The Chairs. Written 1951. P.

An ancient concierge and his wife prepare for a crowd of guests who are to hear his final message to posterity. As the totally invisible guests arrive the couple fetch more and more chairs for them, until, with the entry of the professional orator who is to pronounce the message, they jump into the sea. But the orator is deaf and dumb and his writing on the blackboard is a meaningless jumble.

The empty chairs constitute a most effective theatrical image for man's failure to communicate, and the dumb orator makes the record of a lifetime seem utterly futile. It may also suggest how meaningless can be the words of author and actor. Ionesco says, "The theme of the play is nothingness made concrete."

Victims of Duty. Written 1952.

By transforming a detective into a psychoanalyst, Ionesco argues that there is little difference between the psychological drama and the mere detective play.

Amédée. Written 1953.

A corpse in the flat of a married couple, constantly growing at a frightening rate, is a gruesome and appropriate image of their dead love.

Rhinoceros. Written 1958. P.

More and more rhinoceroses appear in a small provincial town. They are the inhabitants who, one after the other, want to be turned into these thick-skinned, aggressive animals. Finally only Bérenger (Olivier) resists the urge to conform.

The terrifying lure of conformity is here skilfully and movingly illustrated.

Exit the King. Written 1963.

In an agnostic counterpart of the 15th-century *Everyman*, Ionesco shows King Bérenger (Alec Guinness), in his disintegrating palace, reluctantly submitting to the process of dying, his final resource being fortitude alone. This dramatic elegy, inspired by the final scenes of Richard II, is designed with bold simplicity, presenting man's mortal dissolution with unflinching honesty and a tenderness new in Ionesco.

Ann Jellicoe (b. 1928).

Ann Jellicoe's initial work as producer has left its mark on her plays. In an interview given soon after her unusual play, *The Sport of My Mad Mother*, she expounded what she was then trying to do.

Discounting the concept of man as a rational creature and stressing that people are driven by their emotions, fears, and insecurities, she concentrated in her early plays on people in a highly emotional and irrational condition. What is more unusual, she deliberately tried to stir up in the audience the very emotions that were being portrayed on the stage. To do this she employed violent sensory and emotional stimuli—a barrage of visual action, rhythm, sound and sheer noise. Words were reduced to a minimum and these few frequently incantatory and devoid of meaning. Ann Jellicoe wanted the audience to yield unthinkingly to the emotional impact and to refrain from asking "What does this mean?" Needless to say literary values were being sacrificed to theatrical.

While these plays were often intense and exciting, they were severely limited in range and manner and to some degree obscurantist. The emotional is only one aspect of human experience, and it is inextricably entangled with intellectual experience which is just as valid. To dwell almost exclusively on the irrational to the neglect of coherent speech—man's hard-won tool of thought—is partial and misleading.

The function of the artistic image is so to reveal aspects of experience that they can be recognised and harmonised, and to elucidate the significance of the image intelligence is necessary.

It is interesting that in her latest play, *Shelley*, Ann Jellicoe appears to have discarded her theories.

The Sport of My Mad Mother. 1957. F.

A gang of teddy boys, living in terror of another gang which never appears, is dominated by the fierce and enigmatic Greta. Exulting in their feelings of violence, they express themselves in inarticulate and disjointed words and phrases, staccato cries and incantatory songs. Flim, a commentator, emphasises these with a set of instruments, including a motor-horn, which make sounds that are often discordant and arhythmic.

All this makes a receptive audience aware of what it may feel like to belong to an adolescent gang, but Greta is not easy to accept. A mother–schoolmistress figure, she finally gives birth to a child and is evidently an embodiment of the Indian goddess, Kali. The epigraph of the play is "All creation is the sport of my Mad Mother, Kali." In 1964 Ann Jellicoe explained that the play is based on myth and uses ritual, bodying forth "fear and rage at being rejected from the womb or tribe." Such symbolism demanding an interpretation of its significance is out of key with a play so deliberately "anti-intellect" and restricted to a direct emotional impact.

The Knack. 1961.

The knack in question is that of getting girls and three out of the four characters are frankly exposed in the irrational grip of sex. The inhibited Colin struggles with the over-experienced Tolen for the possession of Nancy (Rita Tushingham) and again the action is carried forward as much by improvisation as by coherent speech. The film version, which in 1965 won the Grand Prize at Cannes, captures the spirit of the play.

Shelley. 1965.

A lucid, well-documented chronicle play illustrates incidents in Shelley's life from his expulsion from Oxford until his death. Unfortunately the simple straight-line structure is not suited to the complexity of poetic genius. One would not guess that this is the Shelley capable of writing *Prometheus Unbound.* The personality that emerges is that of the selfless social idealist and pamphleteer and the theme his theory of free love, involving two women—Harriet and Mary—in disaster. The predicament is viewed more from the women's angle and the initial germinal situation, that with Harriet, who is presented as innocently pathetic, is so oversimplified as to be false.

The frequent change of brief scenes, effective in themselves, has a fragmented effect.

Erroll John. A West Indian playwright.

Moon on a Rainbow Shawl.

This play won first prize in *The Observer* competition of 1956. It depicts life among the poor in the Caribbean islands.

Arthur L. Kopit.

Oh Dad, Poor Dad. 1961.

Described by its young American author as a "tragifarce," this play won a prize at Harvard in 1960. First produced in England in 1961, it was revived in 1965, with Hermione Gingold as Madame Rosepettle, the wealthy widow—a parody of the dominating and devouring American "Mom," who emasculates husband, suitor, and son. She travels about accompanied by her husband's dead body in a coffin and her son Jonathan, aged seventeen, whom she treats as a child of ten. When in a final wildly comic and gruesome scene a young girl offers Jonathan love, the father's body falls across the bed and he is so terrified that he strangles her. The story is a frightening Freudian phantasy, the treatment deft and farcical, but there is little latent content.

Bernard Kops (b. 1928).

Kops, who was born in Stepney, of Jewish working folk, left school at the age of thirteen.

His plays include *The Hamlet of Stepney Green*, 1958 (P), *Good-bye World*, 1959, *Change for the Angel*, 1960, *The Dream of Peter Mann*, 1960 (P), the one-act, *Stray Cats and Empty Bottles*, and *Enter Solly Gold*, 1962, chosen for performance in the provinces by Centre 42.

Kops is less successful with realism than with fantasy, diffuse and unashamed and enlivened with the gaiety of local colour and frequent Jewish folk-song.

Most of his plays are variations on a basic design—that of the idealistic dreamer-hero, with an uneasy relationship with his easy-going mother, who in some cases is courted by a suitor whom he dislikes. Eventually the hero realises that a devoted girl is his true mate. Kops' plays thus draw nourishment from a deep emotional source, that of the Oedipus–Hamlet myth, on to which he grafts the happy ending of the fairy tale.

Social criticism, especially of mass-produced goods is often a secondary theme.

The attraction of the plays is their fairy-tale charm and naïveté, their uninhibited joyousness and sense of fun and the easy way in which the rhythm of dialogue flows into verse, song, and dance. Kops is like a Jewish J. M. Barrie, with the significant difference that most of his heroes renounce their dream for reality.

The artistic tension between spontaneity of feeling and excellence of form has become so relaxed that dramatic intensity is often sacrificed. The plays are loosely constructed, often prolix, and the dialogue sometimes so naturalistic as to be feeble and banal.

Ray Lawler. An Australian playwright.

The Summer of the Seventeenth Doll.

This vigorous realistic play was directed by John Sumner both in Melbourne, 1955, and in London. The seventeenth annual "lay-off" of two cane-cutters with their girl friends in Melbourne proves a tawdry fiasco. The more local theme—the awakening from the "Australianist" dream of the virile outback hero—carries with it the universal implication of the pain of disenchantment.

The Piccadilly Bushman. 1955.

This play proved disappointing.

Henry Livings (b. 1929).

The protagonist of Livings' frank and realistic comedies of working life is normally the little man, whose unforseen reactions culminate in hilarious disaster which topples down the petty rulers. Farce and near fantasy are lightly used to suggest a plea for the disregarded people who support the social edifice.

Stop It, Whoever You Are. 1960. P.

The insignificant Perkin Warbeck, a lavatory attendant in a factory, is involved in a series of ludicrous mishaps, but indirectly gets his own back on his harsh and frigid wife and his mean, pompous landlord. The comedy, which is very funny indeed, culminates in a fantasy-like scene of Warbeck's death, a séance, and a gas explosion.

Big Soft Nellie or the Sacred Nit.

A farcical comedy has as protagonist a mother's boy who is the laughing stock of his mates.

Nil Carborundum. 1962. P.

The scene is the kitchen of an R.A.F. station and the action culminates in a riotously-funny mock commando raid, which exposes both the pilfering cook and service routines that are now an anachronism.

Eh? 1964. M.

In an ultra-modern factory the incompetent young boiler-man, Val (David Warner), need attend to the boiler for only a few minutes during the 24 hours. Since he brings his bride to sleep in the bottom bunk and gives most of his attention to growing giant mushrooms, he neglects his duties and blows the place to smithereens. Again a light-hearted farcical comedy shows the underdog confounding established authority. A further significance is a fool's lapse starting the "mushroom cloud."

Arthur Miller (b. 1915).

Arthur Miller, an admirer of Ibsen, shares his strong sense of moral purpose and of the individual's responsibility to the community. This is balanced by a sympathetic understanding of the insecurity of the individual in modern society.

Miller's characters, deeply felt and realised, are fallible men who suffer through their own errors of character or judgment in social conditions which are incomprehensible, indifferent, or even hostile to them.

A recurrent pattern is that of paternal responsibility within a patriarchal family unit, and the father's distress as he sees his errors hurting wife and sons. But the sense of responsibility flows outwards to society as a whole, of which the family is but the growing point. Significantly—apart from the benign mother-figures—Miller's most balanced characters are lawyers.

His plays are well constructed, the dialogue economic and telling, and he has progressed from the realism of *All My Sons*, published 1947, to much freer experimental techniques, while the prose style has become more fluid and eloquent.

Death of a Salesman. Published 1949. P.

A compassionate and finely-balanced play exposes the impingement of hire-purchase commercialism on the ageing salesman, Willy Loman, a weak, foolish, and deeply affectionate man, and also reveals his overwhelming sense of guilt towards wife and sons. The play is worked out on two planes, the inexorable present and Willy's past which obsessively enacts itself within his mind. The film version with Frederick March, is excellent.

The Crucible. Published 1953.

In 1949 Marion Starkey's *The Devil in Massachusetts* dealt with a witch-hunt in Salem in 1692, and pointed out its relevance to our own age, also rent by "ideological intensities." In 1952 the activities of McCarthy gave it a special urgency.

In his powerful play Miller uses this historical incident to depict not an indifferent society but one in which positive evil is unleashed. The evils he explores are the persecution of a minority and the interference of the State in the individual conscience.

Characteristically Miller focuses attention on the plain man, John Proctor, and he invents his former adultery with Abigail, so that the play is not a partisan manifesto but a study of the complex contradictions of actual life. The self-righteous fanaticism of the persecutors and Proctor's own growth in self-knowledge and courage are faithfully and poignantly portrayed.

A View From the Bridge. 1956. P.

Eddie Carbone, a Brooklyn docker, is so gripped by jealous possessiveness of his wife's niece, that he eventually betrays her two kinsmen, illegal immigrants, to the Authorities.

In a play of repressed sexual passion, with hints of incest and homosexuality, Miller shows mastery of a kind of situation new to him and the heightening tension is realised in taut and disciplined sequences.

A lawyer, Alfieri, acts as a Greek chorus but is powerless to intervene, for Eddie infringes something more primitive than the legal code and it is by the primitive vendetta that he is eventually killed.

Incident at Vichy. 1966.

Miller here turns to the responsibility of society for the individual in a play which exposes the latent racial hostility which even the best men may unconsciously harbour.

The example he takes is antisemitism, the place and time Vichy in 1942, the scene a bleak anteroom within sound of a railway, where sealed trucks are deporting Jews to the furnaces of Auschwitz. Here a group of men and a boy, Jewish suspects, await investigation. There is an atmosphere of chill horror and suspense as each tries to summon up his own pitiful defence against the premonition of the ghastly journey he must embark on, once he is summoned behind the closed door.

Eventually only two men remain, the two most aware and articulate, Doctor Leduc, a Jewish analyst (Anthony Quayle) and Von Berg (Alec Guinness), the only Gentile of the group, a cultured and humane Viennese Prince, who is horrified by the vulgarity and barbarism of the Nazis.

In their final dialogue Doctor Leduc convinces the Prince of his unconscious antisemitism and the Prince gives his safe-conduct to the doctor.

A subsidiary theme of the play is the way society imposes extrinsically an identity on the individual, in this instance, as in Frisch's *Andorra*, the rôle of victim on the Jewish people. Through Leduc, Miller also criticises the Jews' acceptance of their rôle.

This disturbing play makes the greatest demands on the emotions, intelligence and humanity of the audience, who like the Prince to some degree undergo psycho-analysis. But the play is also characterised by a fine restraint. As in Æschylus' *Agamemnon* the violence takes place behind closed doors, with the significant difference that in Miller's play the chorus and victims are identical.

Roger Milner.

How's The World Treating You? 1965.

A comedy in the nonsensical-satirical vein of Henry Livings does not maintain the conviction of its lively and amusing first Act.

John Mortimer (b. 1923).

Mortimer, a barrister, first won success with his short plays, such as *The Dock Brief*, 1957, and *Lunch Hour*, 1960 (M)., originally written for radio and television.

Here his talents are seen at their best, especially his gift for seizing on an unusual encounter between "the lonely, the neglected, the unsuccessful," whom he envisages in realistic settings of shabby gentility, and he is particularly sympathetic to those who allow their fantasy to overlap or swamp actuality.

But the moment of insight that gives pathos to his short plays is not enough to illuminate those of full length, like *What Shall We Tell Caroline?* and *The Wrong Side of the Park*, which lack substance. *Two Stars for Comfort*, 1960, is also unsatisfactory. Mortimer seems here to have inflated the situation of *Collect your Hand Baggage*, (M), where the same kind of middle-aged Bohemian is seen "conferring himself as a favour" on a plain girl. The play is flawed by sentimentality and debases the gospel of Lawrence to one of casual pleasure. Mortimer here gives an anaemic version of the theme of *The Summer of the Seventeenth Doll* devoid of the psychological insight and intensity of Lawler's work.

Eugene O'Neill (1888–1953).

Although O'Neill's work belongs to the first half of the century, three of his later works had their delayed première here in the 'fifties, two of them making a great impression.

Recognised as the greatest and most influential of American playwrights, O'Neill at his best came to close grips with the serious issues of human life, showing man battling with a harsh environment and with his own inner passions. He was deeply involved with his characters, often the flotsam and jetsam of humanity, conceived with disillusioned compassion, and he could create the powerful theatrical situation which rivets the audience. On the stage these gifts went far to compensate for a looseness of structure and a dialogue which is singularly flat, poor in vocabulary, and lacking in rhythm. His plays are better acted than read.

O'Neill, lacking the advantage of an American dramatic tradition, experimented with many European techniques before finding his own most personal style—a faithful realism with suggestive overtones of emotion and reflection.

British playwrights like Wesker and Alun Owen resemble O'Neill. They also are committed to individuals, especially to working people living insecurely. Like him they reveal the subtle and inhibiting ties that bind members of a family or gang, subjects which lend themselves to a similar rather sprawling and diffuse structure and dialect style. So far they have not matched O'Neill's passionate and gripping intensity.

The Iceman Cometh. Published 1947.

In a naturalistic play, whose prototype is Gorky's *The Lower Depths*, down-and-outs await the arrival of the dionysiac Hickey. His abortive attempt to rouse them from their " pipe dreams " leaves them sunk even more deeply than before in drink and self-deceit. The pessimistic theme is that of Ibsen's *The Wild Duck* and the situation that of Beckett's *Waiting for Godot*.

Long Day's Journey Into Night. Published 1955.

An avowed autobiographical play depicts O'Neill's family on the day when his mother (Gwen Francgon Davies) relapses into drug addiction and Eugene learns that he must leave the doomed circle for a sanatorium. As it was there that he chose his vocation, this constitutes the one note of hope in a deeply mournful reverie. The Freudian love–hate relationships are unfolded with tender understanding.

Joe Orton.

Entertaining Mr. Sloane. 1964. P.

Because the handsome and indolent lodger, Mr. Sloane, kills their father the sensual and slovenly middle-aged Kath and her homosexual brother are able to blackmail him into satisfying their demands. The amoral comedy, written in a dead-pan realistic style, was successfully transferred to the West End.

John Osborne (b. 1929).

Osborne has considerable theatrical talent, torrential eloquence and the journalist's flair for seizing the mood of the moment.

All these gifts were evident in *Look Back in Anger* which was perfectly timed and its success immediate. The protagonist, Jimmy Porter, voiced the pent-up feelings of contemporary youth, especially of the classes newly educated, now baffled by the complacency of the privileged classes who had muddled through two wars and left them without sense of security or direction. The play's pervasive mood of self-pity and strident denunciation runs, with some variation, through Osborne's later work, although with the passing of years it seems increasingly subjective and irrelevant to the current situation.

In his major plays Osborne keeps to the same basic pattern of characterisation and structure. In Jimmy Porter he created an unforgettable character, a myth. But Jimmy with some change of occupation and age is constantly reappearing, disaffected, disorganised by self-pity, articulate, and dominating. Archie Rice and Bill Maitland are older but they also are Narcissus figures driven on by sado-masochistic urges to destroy themselves and their circle. Osborne's minor characters are sketched in a perfunctory, rather stagey way, serving chiefly as audience or target to the protagonist, and there is little dramatic confrontation of equals.

Closely linked with the structure of the plays is the nature of the dialogue. Osborne's forte is rhetoric, the thinly disguised monologue, splendidly uninhibited, with some of the inebriation and excitement of the pub, and with the same coarse and bawdy jests. Sometimes it is a tirade of invective, sometimes shrill and hysterical, always commanding, always flowing exclusively from the protagonist. Minor characters are given little opportunity for repartee or discussion, their rôle being for the most part to act as " feed."

Osborne's plays appear to be satiric in intention but in comparison with the masterpieces of Ibsen and Shaw they express merely negative hostility against the " establishment " and are not based on any clear concept of the values that should be realised in a good society.

" There aren't any good, brave causes left." says Jimmy Porter. Neither here nor in any other play is there anything to suggest that Osborne does not endorse this destructive statement, one of the silliest of the century.

His invective is moreover too general, indiscriminate, and direct to be effective. His weapon is the bludgeon of sarcasm, seldom the rapier of irony. Some notable exceptions are to be found in *Luther* where the targets are limited and specific and the speech where Tetzel sells indulgences is finely ironic. In this play Osborne has learned from the intelligence of Luther and the process of history. He is in general too emotional and subjective a writer to excel in an art which demands disciplined thought and detachment.

The sameness in structure and tone in Osborne's work is cleverly mitigated by experiment in theatrical techniques. The realism of the garret scene in *Look Back in Anger* was in 1956 strikingly original. In *The Entertainer* and *Luther* he profited by the example of Brecht, and *Under Plain Cover* was influenced by Genet.

Look Back in Anger. 1956. F.

This play is concerned with misalliance in a garret. Jimmy Porter, aggressively working-class in allegiance, has married Alison, a colonel's daughter. The son of an indifferent mother, Jimmy has identified himself with his father and is now making a neurotic attack on his wife, bent on breaking her nerve by a relentless barrage of savage vituperation against her and her privileged family. When she goes home because she is pregnant, her friend Helena takes her place and somewhat improbably becomes Jimmy's mistress. Alison having lost her baby returns and only when Jimmy reduces her to grovelling before him do they resume their unstable contact.

The play was arresting in its shabby setting, at that time a novelty, and in its theme of social and sexual tension expressed in terms of furious diatribe, for it cleverly synthesises the attack on Alison with an attack on the privileged classes. Jimmy's marriage to her symbolises plunder and rape on these classes with all the excitement that rape arouses and her sensational replacement by Helena gives another fillip.

It is interesting to note that the pattern of personal and social relationship between Jimmy, Alison, and the Colonel echoes that of Jean, Julie, and the Count in Strindberg's *Miss Julie*.

The play's central weakness is in its portrayal of character. The supporting characters are too compliant to be convincing but more disturbing is Osborne's ambivalent attitude to the neurosis of Jimmy. It is impossible to escape the feeling that Jimmy is not objectively presented and that this immature and wantonly destructive figure is to some degree the mouthpiece of the author.

The play is satirical in intention but not in effect, since Jimmy's anger is plainly the outcome of jealousy. It is rather a melodrama of words, shocking the complacent and preparing for the reception of new playwrights. The film version is recommended.

The World of Paul Slickey.

This comedy with music was a failure. It was an attempt at social satire, but in its indiscriminating attack on a multitude of targets failed to maintain any consistent standard of reference.

The Entertainer. 1957. F.

Osborne here attempts to use the Brechtian device of " endistancing," employing a framework of music-hall scenes, where Archie Rice (Olivier), a seedy comedian, tries to hold the stage with tawdry patter and songs in a dubious show with nudes called " Rock'n Roll New'd Look." These are intended to " endistance " realistic scenes of Archie's shabby home. But the " endistancing " device serves little purpose for the overall mood of unquestioned disillusion " whooped up " by drink and patter is in both planes unrelieved. Querulous complaint that England has lost the glory and glamour of Edwardian days is crystallised on the realistic plane by the report of the death of Archie's son at Suez and in the music-hall by the presentation of a nude Brittania, wearing only her helmet.

Osborne turns to the music-hall because he claims it to be a folk art, with a technique that " cuts across the restrictions of the so-called naturalistic stage," with an immediate, direct contact. The film version is good.

Luther. 1961. F.

Luther, based on a recent biography, is Osborne's least subjective work, although he again takes for his hero a rebel, the son of an unsympathetic mother, and emphasises the emotional and not the intellectual sources of Luther's protests.

The play is imitative of Brecht's *Galileo* both in its loose " epic " structure and also in the attempt to present the protagonist in an equivocal light. The first two acts give a sympathetic and leisurely portrayal of Luther's early conflicts of conscience and vigorous attack on superstition while in the third act he is hurriedly presented as having treacherously let down the peasants who had been encouraged to rise against the Emperor. But the political reasons for Luther's dilemma are not even hinted at and we are invited not to think, as in *Galileo*, but to condemn while ignorant of relevant facts. Structurally this sudden *volte face* is most damaging to the play.

The most effective scenes, such as Tetzel's selling of indulgences and Martin's sermon at Wittenberg are all pure rhetoric, without a word of dialogue and directed straight at the audience.

Skilful period production and the acting of Albert Finney as Luther made the play theatrically effective.

Two Plays for England. 1962.

Two slight plays, satirical in purpose, were inflated to make a double bill.

The first, *The Blood of the Bambergs*, is a parody of a royal wedding. Monarchy is held up to ridicule along with its trappings of ceremonial and fulsome adulation by press and radio. The bridegroom having just been killed in his racing-car, an Australian press photographer is secretly passed off in his place. The final act takes the form of film with an unctuous running commentary, the film device deriving from the German Expressionist theatre, where it was first used by Ernst Toller.

The second piece, *Under Plain Cover*, is intended as an attack on sensationalism in the press. The first part shows a pretty provincial couple dressing up in rôles symbolic of sex fantasy, their activities accompanied by a thin trickle of dialogue. In the second half dramatic presentation is abandoned in favour of a charade and commentary by a reporter who tells how the press, discovering the couple to be brother and sister, break up the alliance until it is resumed even more furtively than before, a feeble presentation of the compelling theme of incest. The first scene is a pallid imitation of the brothel scene in Genet's *The Balcony*, where the assuming of symbolic rôles has powerful sexual and political implications lacking in Osborne's play.

These sketches do not profess to offer convincing studies of character in action and unlike intelligent satire they do not imply positive standards nor use the mature techniques of irony and wit, but rely on parody and mimicry.

Inadmissible Evidence. 1965.

A play, which many have praised highly, has the ingredients of a commercial success. It provides the sensational spectacle of a middle-aged solicitor, Bill Maitland, obsessed with sex, and disintegrating under the influence of drink and drugs, and, thereby, such a rôle for the star actor (Nicol Williamson) as to constitute a stage *tour de force*.

The play opens with a dream sequence as Maitland is tried in the court of his own mind. What follows is his rancid outpouring of self-pity, as during forty-eight hours, he is progressively deserted by staff, clients, and mistress. Some of the minor characters are here reduced to unheard voices on the telephone and one actress serves to impersonate three faceless clients. Maitland's flagellation of himself and his circumstances is unrelieved and monotonous.

Alun Owen (b. 1926).

Of Welsh stock but with an Irish mother, Alun Owen spent his youth in Liverpool. Most of his writing has been for television, but in 1957 he worked on two plays simultaneously, both produced in 1959.

His most characteristic style is the new naturalism used in a romantic nostalgic way to evoke the local colour of Liverpool. He seizes on the idiomatic dialects and the dramatic conflict implicit in the clash of race and religion between Welsh, Ulster folk, and Irish, while the restless ambition of some of the younger generation to get away to sea or to London gives a wider horizon to a scene otherwise parochial.

Progress to the Park. 1959. P.

This, in Owen's favourite idiom, is a leisurely enquiry into the affinities and animosities of Liverpool working folk, especially of a group of four young men and a girl as they eddy about in street, pub, and park. The clash of race and religion is always just below the surface, and what thread of story there is concerns the crossing of young love by parental prejudice. The most lively character is Teifon, the voluble Welshman, originally a kind of commentator, and the mouthpiece of Owen's views.

The Rough and Ready Lot. 1959.

A carefully constructed historical play concerns four mercenary officers in a revolutionary army in South America just after the American Civil War. In a different milieu religious strife is again the theme. The convictions of an Irish Catholic clash violently with those of a Welsh militant atheist as to whether they shall shell a Catholic monastery which blocks the pass. Eventually both men are killed, together with the vacillating English colonel, and it is the " simple and ordinary " man, Kelly, who takes command, the conflict of belief still unresolved.

Harold Pinter (b. 1930).

Pinter, formerly an actor, is now considered as one of the leading playwrights of the " Theatre of the Absurd." He exerts an almost hypnotic power over his audience, for he has an assured theatrical expertise, an uncanny sense of the novel situation and the telling pause; and, as his plays find resolution in some final surprise, they are aesthetically satisfying.

His art has developed swiftly, and two main phases can now be distinguished. The early plays, culminating in *The Caretaker* in 1960, were concerned with the underprivileged and showed a growing sense of compassion and only a passing interest in sex. More recently Pinter has explored new ground. The plays have been much concerned with sexual experience; the background has usually been sophisticated; and the attitude detached, sometimes to the point of apparent indifference.

Whatever the subject, Pinter's plays have a certain poetic resonance, an imaginative absurdity. His power is probably due to his intuitive awareness of man's sub-conscious life and most of his plays present a dream-like sequence of events, half credible, half absurd. In the early plays the dream drifts into a familiar nightmare of the most primitive kind—that of the violent invasion of personal security—a fear that must have assailed man's stone-age ancestor as he lurked in the squalid shelter of his cave, terrified of wild beasts and the inexplicable catastrophes of nature. Many of Pinter's later plays are still dream-like fantasies of sexual anxiety and gratification, especially as to marital fidelity.

The situation that first fascinated him was that of a room, a door, and two people. He has said " Obviously they are scared of what is outside the room. Outside . . . there is a world bearing upon them which is frightening." The room is normally cosy but sordid, the people insecure, for Pinter is most interested in people when they are " at the extreme end of their living, where they are living pretty much alone." The danger that breaks in on them is both comic and shocking, but bizarre as the predicament may be, the play is anchored in actual experience. " I think it is impossible," he says, "—and certainly for me—to start writing a play from any kind of abstract idea. . . . I start writing a play from an image of a situation and a couple of characters involved and these people always remain for me quite real."

But his basic situation is so novel and striking that, like poetry, it can be interpreted on more than one level, both as a revelation of those periods of intense private anxiety when the individu all but distraught, holds on precariously to some tiny foothold, and also as an image of the predicament of the whole human race whose existence is threatened by ungovernable forces. Like Kafka, whom he admires, Pinter expresses vividly the feeling of inscrutable menace from some vague hinterland invading humdrum human existence. *The Birthday Party*, in particular, has much in common with Kafka's *The Trial*.

In his first three plays the threat is left deliberately unexplained, so that an aura of mystery surrounds the action and violence actually breaks through, but in *The Caretaker* there develops a more subtle menace from within, threatening the mind rather than the body and there is no overt violence.

The theme of uncertainty has persisted throughout. In his first play, *The Room*, 1957, he mystified his audience by contradictory information about insignificant details. This trick served perhaps to heighten the atmosphere of insecurity but some critics found it irritating, and in later plays,, *The Collection*, for instance, we find instead a highly significant uncertainty as to people's veracity and motives. Pinter has explicitly stated that imprecision conveys a truer picture of our experience. "The desire for verification is understandable," he says, "but cannot always be satisfied," and he points out that it is particularly difficult to be precise about people's inner life and motives, especially if they are inarticulate. He consistently rejects the rôle of the omniscient playwright, like Ibsen, and looks at his characters through the eyes of the ordinary observer, frequently puzzled by human inconsistencies.

A related theme has been the ambiguous nature of personal identity, treated with increasing insight, from the puzzle as to who Riley may be in *The Room*, to the pathos of maimed personality in *The Caretaker*, and the possibility of divided personality in *The Lover*. Some of the disturbing fascination that Pinter exerts is due to the state of uncertainty in which he leaves his audience.

As a playwright of the Absurd Pinter is closest n feeling to Beckett, and he shares with Ionesco an awareness of the way that comedy interlocks with tragedy. "Everything is funny," says Pinter, "the greatest earnestness is funny; even tragedy is funny. And I think what I try to do in my plays is to get to this recognised reality of the absurdity of what we do and how we behave and how we speak." Occasionally, like Ionesco, he uses stage "furniture" to heighten the absurdity and both playwrights have a quick ear for the absurd clichés and *non-sequiturs* of everyday peech.

Pinter is a stylist in the use of stage dialogue, n expert in cockney dialect. It is talk rather than dialogue that he records, what Martin Buber has described as "monologue disguised as dialogue," for his characters talk at people rather than to them. They rarely listen or respond, each bolstering up his self-confidence in an intermittent "monologue" spiced with empty boasting. This is particularly appropriate to the confused and defeated people he portrays, who even n their defensive jargon shrink from human contact.

Although Pinter's dialogue appears on the urface to be little more than a tape-recording of casual talk, there is beneath the demotic prose a poetic rhythm more compelling than the carefully calculated verse rhythms of T. S. Eliot.

'he Room. 1957.

Pinter's first play, written in four days for the rama department of Bristol University, is already characteristic. Rose, left alone at night, is ervously aware of the door of her dingy room, specially when a blind Negro, Riley, enters ith a message from her father. Her husband on is return savagely kills Riley and Rose goes blind.

The murder of Riley, possibly a rather clumsy eath symbol, is melodramatic, but the lit room a vivid dramatic image of man's tiny area of omfort in an indifferent universe.

he Dumb Waiter, written 1957, produced 1960. P.

In a one-acter Ben and Gus, hired assassins orking for some mysterious "organisation," easily await their unknown victim in a basement room in Birmingham. The sudden intrusion of a grotesque Ionesco-like dumb-waiter increases their anxiety, until it is revealed that the victim is Gus himself. Situation and dialogue are both comic and taut with menace. The trite phraseology, as the killers mention "the senior partner," "the job," and "clearing up," ironically uses a business jargon. The tiny play is a microcosm of a treacherous world where violence can suddenly break up man's apparent alliances.

The Birthday Party. 1958.

In Pinter's first full-length play, the room this time is in a shabby boarding-house where Stanley, who claims to have been a concert pianist has taken refuge, until he is suddenly unnerved by the arrival of a sinister pair, the specious Goldberg and the brutal McCann who like Gus and Ben are there "to do a job." They subject Stanley to a fantastic catechism, a parody of brain-washing, and during his phoney and ludicrous birthday party he is blindfolded and his glasses broken—symbolic of destruction of vision. Next morning the pair lead Stanley away, conventionally dressed in black jacket and striped trousers, incapable of speech, his personality disintegrated.

The menace here is economically sustained through indirect means, and the fact that the identity of the three main characters is never revealed adds to the terror. Some see Stanley as the political refugee; some, since he was a pianist, as the artist who is made to conform by the pressure of society. But by its deliberate lack of definiteness, the play has a wide reference to all who seek refuge from a strange and hostile world.

The Caretaker. 1960. M.

The play is set in a junk-filled room, where the kindly Aston lives in his brother's derelict house. He brings home an old tramp, Davies, who grudgingly agrees to stay as "caretaker" and then tries to encroach further by playing off one brother against the other, until finally rejected by both.

In a naturalistic background Pinter has created two unforgettable characters, presented in psychological depth with reference to their past, and has depicted their failure to come to terms with compassion and restraint.

Davies is one who bites the hand that feeds him. His very identity is suspect for he passes under an assumed name, having "left his papers" years ago "at Sidcup." But he never retrieves them, like Beckett's Krapp repressing part of his past. Aston haltingly tells Davies how he once had periods of unique lucidity, now destroyed by a terrifying shock-treatment he was subjected to in mental hospital, but Davies' only reaction is later to threaten him. It is remarkable that when Aston finally rejects Davies' last encroachment the plight of the tramp should seem as pitiful as Aston's own, Pinter having wisely rejected his first intention to end the play with the violent death of Davies.

This mature play shows a man actually opening the door to his fears and mastering them. Aston in his long speech faces the wrong done to him by "people." His unique vision destroyed, his only creative outlet has been tinkering with his hands, but as he tries to break out of his isolation by befriending another crippled human being, he unhappily meets a man so twisted by his own suffering and resentment that he cannot respond. Some find in Aston a moving image of the mystic and artist in man whose creative insight is destroyed by an imperceptive and mechanical society. The film is excellent.

A Slight Ache. 1961.

A short play, first heard on the Third Programme in 1959, shows an elderly couple haunted by a match-seller, who stands speechless at their gate. Eventually the wife takes him into the home instead of the husband. It is possible that the silent match-seller may represent the unconscious desires of the wife and the anxieties of the husband.

A Night Out. 1961.

First broadcast and televised in 1960, this compassionate and realistic brief play shows the clerk, Albert, trying one night to escape from the retarding domination of his nagging and self-righteous mother. After threatening her with a clock, he finally finds himself in the room of a prostitute who proves equally peevish and would-be genteel. It is doubtful whether Albert's violent gestures have won him any independence.

The Collection. 1962.

In an assured, sophisticated comedy of manners, originally presented on television in 1961, Pinter makes authentic use of mystification.

Did Stella in fact sleep with a stranger, Bill, in Leeds? She tells James, her husband, that she did so, but during the course of the friendship that develops between the two men, Bill gives three contradictory accounts of what is supposed to have occurred, while Harry, an older man who has given Bill a home, becomes increasingly jealous of James.

There is irony in that Stella's story, told perhaps to pique her husband, should impel him away from her to male society and the changing of partners has the elegant formality and economy of a dance movement.

Pinterian violence is here only lightly indicated: in James' half playful throwing a knife at Bill and in Harry's ferocious account of him as a "slum slug" that he has picked up.

The Lover. 1963.

An arresting short play shows the husband (Alan Badel) and the wife (Vivien Merchant) first as affectionate but distant partners, and then with provocative change of clothes as erotic lovers. The performance of symbolic rôles, including dressing up in fetish garments, had already been used by Genet. Pinter cleverly adapts the device to discriminate between the apparently incompatible strands in the marriage relationship, a distinction analogous to that between Aphrodite Urania and Aphrodite Pandēmus, the Love Sacred and Profane of classical mythology.

The Homecoming. 1965.

Teddy (Michael Bryant), a Doctor of Philosophy in an American University, brings his wife, Ruth (Vivien Merchant), on a surprise visit to his former home in North London, where Max (Paul Rogers), his widowed father, still lives with his two younger sons, Lenny and Joey. It is gradually revealed that Ruth before her marriage had been a "model" and the family decide to keep her as their common mistress, while Lenny, a pimp, arranges that she shall earn her keep as a prostitute. The plot is underlined by Lenny's bragging anecdotes of sexual brutality—a counterpart to the more undifferentiated violence of the earlier plays.

Because this black comedy is played with clinical detachment, the audience is induced to suspend emotion. Only at the last moment is this cool acceptance shattered by an outburst of human feeling when Max, aged 70, crawls sobbing to Ruth asking to be kissed and the audience is shocked into feeling the degradation involved.

On the surface the play is a disillusioned glance at life. "It would be ridiculous to maintain that what we know merits reverence," says Lenny. It may also be interpreted as a fantasy of sexual gratification, which in a dream state escapes the taboo of ethical and humane feeling and can be indulged in without demur. The use of some accepted sex symbols and the slow and trance-like acting, especially that of Ruth, is dream-like in its effect and the final shock of degradation is analogous to waking up and realising what the dream has implied.

It is possible also to see in Teddy an acquiescent Hamlet. He returns home from a foreign university to find marital infidelity, for it is disclosed that his mother had been unfaithful with an uncle figure. Ruth is the counterpart of Ophelia, who was bidden by Hamlet, "Get thee to a nunnery"—(an Elizabethan cant term for brothel). Teddy is like Hamlet also in that he prefers "to operate on things and not in things."

The Homecoming is professionally brilliant, but it lacks the depth of reference and emotional power of Pinter's earlier plays.

Hal Porter. An Australian playwright.

The Tower. P.

Set in Hobart in 1850, this well-constructed traditional play tensely presents violent passion and incident veiled by the steely dialogue of mannered society.

The Professor. 1965.

A play set in the Far East, with a Japanese heroine, was less successful.

Terence Rattigan (b. 1912).

With a flair for witty farce and social comedy, Rattigan expertly serves up a nourishing morsel in an appetising *vol-au-vent.*

More recently he has attempted to penetrate suffering as in *The Browning Version,* 1948, and *The Deep Blue Sea,* 1952. *Variations on a Theme* was less successful and incidentally provoked Shelagh Delaney into writing her first play.

David Rudkind.

Afore Night Come. 1962. P.

In a Worcestershire orchard the fruit pickers enact the ritual murder of a freakish old tramp whom they dread as a threat to their virility. A realistic working day world is infused with the primitive terror of *The Golden Bough.*

Jean-Paul Sartre (b. 1905).

The plays of the French philosopher, Sartre, can be fully interpreted only in the light of his atheistic existentialist philosophy. Discarding conventional morality, Sartre insists that the individual must evolve his own ethical code through daring freely to choose and act for himself. He must also will this freedom for others, and by seeking to establish an interdependence of freedoms he "engages," or "commits" himself in the political struggle.

Sartre himself is a communist and his best plays, like those of Brecht, are fully "committed" to left-wing ideology. They have sought to vindicate the inevitability of violence in the struggle for freedom and to decry the "bourgeois morality" which shrinks from such crime.

Sartre is also concerned with the "absurdity" of man's predicament as a rational creature in an illogical and indifferent universe, but unlike Ionesco he presents the situation, not through absurd images but through the medium of the traditional well-made play.

Sartre has had a considerable influence on the climate of ideas, encouraging an attitude of harsh disillusion and stimulating the current discussion as to whether or not drama should be a vehicle for social and political convictions. It is interesting to contrast the views of Wesker and Pinter on this issue.

Lucifer and the Lord. Published 1951. P.

The dilemma between non-violence and force is here given greater universality by being projected back into the time of the Peasants' Revolt in Germany. The brilliant General Goetz, having failed in a policy of Christian love, unflinchingly embraces a ruthless violence as the only possible "realist" social ethic.

Nekrassov. Published 1956.

A satirical farce ridicules the sensational anti-communism of a section of the popular French press.

Altona. Published 1956. P.

This play, showing a former Nazi officer going mad in an attempt to justify his own resort to torture, is an attack on "Western morality" in its own recourse to torture, used by French colonials in Algiers. The film version well reproduces the claustrophobic horror.

James Saunders (b. 1925).

In Saunders' early work the influence of Ionesco is apparent in the satirical use of a banal dialogue, in which the characters converse without communicating, and in the reference to some concrete symbol which represents their anxieties or predicament. His later work is reminiscent o

Pirandello. Nevertheless Saunders' ingenious plays have a freshness and vigour all their own.

Alas Poor Fred.

In a one-act play a friend who had some time ago been cut in half is the symbol of a married couple's former passionate love life, long since sundered. The situation is like that of Ionesco's *Amédée.*

The Ark. 1959.

In a more direct style this full-length play of ideas re-interprets the Old Testament story.

Ends and Echoes. 1960.

This is the general title for three clever one-acters. In *Barnstable*, the most amusing one, a house is gradually collapsing around its unwitting inhabitants, a symbol of the disintegration of their conventional way of life.

Next Time I'll Sing to You. 1963.

Based on Raleigh Trevelyan's book on the hermit of Canfield, who died in 1942, this moving play uses the rehearsal style of Pirandello's *Six Characters.* Like an elegiac quintet is explores the theme of solitude.

A Scent of Flowers. 1964.

Like the previous play, this is a reconstruction of the past. It is gradually revealed that the character, Zoe, is in fact the spirit of a girl who has just committed suicide, because her love for a married man is incompatible with her religion. The play proceeds by her touching encounters with the circle of relatives and friends to whom she had turned in vain for help.

Alan Seymour. An Australian dramatist.

The One Day of the Year. P.

Like Lawler's *Summer of the Seventeenth Doll*, this realistic and moving play examines one of Australia's cherished legends—this time the celebrations of Anzac Day. It is set in Sydney in the working class home of the sentimental "digger," Alf Cook, whose son Hughie is at the university. Alf's deep anger and hurt when Hughie publishes his satirical photographs of the Anzac Day celebrations in which Alf had taken part focuses the universal clash between generation, culture, and class.

Peter Shaffer

Shaffer is an assured and ingenious dramatist whose first success was with the realistic well-made play and who has since moved on to freer modes of composition.

His plays operate successfully on two levels: they offer insight into the subtleties of personal relationships, especially into the difficulties of adjustment between people of different cultural background, and they also involve discussion of ideas. The aesthetic problem of distinguishing between genuine love of art and snobbish pretension is a recurring theme, often presented in a triangular situation.

Five Finger Exercise. 1958. P.

An alive, realistic play shows Clive, the young Cambridge student, growing away from his stifling mother, with her pretensions to modish culture, but failing to make contact with his honest philistine father. The advent of an enigmatic stranger, Walter, acts as a catalyst. Mother and son are both attracted to Walter, the father's fierce jealousy is aroused and Walter is narrowly saved from suicide.

Shaffer shows some of Ibsen's precision in his probing of a family situation where the members change and develop as they become painfully aware of their hidden drives.

The Private Ear and the Public Eye. 1962.

Two short and spare triangular plays both demonstrate the influence of artistic taste on the relationship between the sexes.

The Private Ear.

Bob, a shy music-lover, asks Ted to help him entertain a girl whom he has met at a concert. But the ignorant girl is won by the complacent Ted's vulgar patter and Bob, left alone, defaces his gramophone record and forces himself to listen to the broken music of love.

The Public Eye.

A witty, ironic comedy shows Charles, a correct and pompous dilettante, unwarrantably jealous, employing a private detective, Louis (Kenneth Williams) to spy on his wife. She becomes attracted to Louis because of their shared joy in things of beauty. With the entry of the iconoclastic Louis, a brilliant, comic invention, farce and tenderness go hand in hand with high comedy.

The Royal Hunt of the Sun. 1964.

A sweeping "epic" drama of Pizarro's fantastic conquest of Peru skilfully uses, as narrator, "old Martin", who watches his own boyhood as page to Pizarro. Shaffer deploys "total theatre" in dazzling ceremonial, processions and masks, in ritual dancing, mime and strange, metallic music.

There is rich thematic material in the clash of "two immense and joyless powers", in the conflict of Christianity and Sun worship. Personal tragedy develops in the mutual attraction felt by the grizzled Pizarro (Colin Blakeley) and the young Inca, Atahualpa (Robert Stephens). Captor and prisoner, they painfully seek for the god in each other and the Inca accepts death both as a sacrifice to friendship and the final test of his faith.

Black Comedy. 1965.

A highly successful brief comedy frankly uses an effective device of Chinese theatre. During a party the lights fail and the stage, although supposed to be in darkness, is still fully illuminated, so that the behaviour of the dramatis personae is visible only to the audience.

N. F. Simpson (b. 1919).

N. F. Simpson's plays of the Absurd are in the peculiarly English vein of Lewis Carroll and Edward Lear, a world of surrealist fantasy, *non-sequitur* and nonsense. It is almost a contradiction in terms to organise such material coherently and to do so in a full-length play is a *tour de force* which Simpson brought off in his *One Way Pendulum.* His best work ridicules the mechanical and conventional existence, the attenuation of feeling, of the little suburban home, his favourite milieu.

The Resounding Tinkle. 1957. P.

A most unusual play, which pokes fun at suburban life, discards plot, progress, and characterisation, and the uniform dialogue is one continuous flow of clever verbal paradoxes and *non-sequiturs.* The apologetic "author" appears at intervals and in the final act there is a parody discussion of the play by a panel of "critics"—devices used by Ionesco in *The Shepherd's Chameleon.*

Simpson's verbal agility is exhilarating, but some find the play over-cerebral. It is certainly at the opposite end of the spectrum from *The Sport of My Mad Mother.*

One Way Pendulum. A Farce in a New Dimension. 1959.

Here Simpson has devised a framework built of whimsy and yet firm enough to carry its own logic and to be dramatically satisfying. The characters are drawn simply, but consistently, each with his own "humour," in the manner of Ben Jonson and the dialogue is a close parody of banal family interchange.

The play concerns a suburban family, the Groomkirby's, whose son, Kirby, is teaching a collection of weighing-machines to sing the Hallelujah Chorus. His ineffectual father is combining his two favourite hobbies of law and "do it yourself" carpentry, by building an enormous model of the Old Bailey in the living-room, where the phlegmatic mother pays a charwoman to eat up the "left-overs."

Finally a trial takes place in the Old Bailey and Kirby is convicted of murdering forty-three people in order that he may wear black, the weighing-machines being part of a complicated device to cause a holocaust of death.

The main theme of the play is the tyranny of things, which is exemplified by the absurd Ionesco-like objects. These are treated with the respect due to human beings while human beings are treated as things, and father and son are so obsessed by things that they cannot get into touch with one another.

The tyranny of mechanical routine and social custom is also indicated. Kirby will only eat when a cash-register rings and will only wear black when it is sanctioned by funeral convention.

The anxiety and guilt which result from a starved and mechanical existence are finally symbolised in the nightmare parody of a trial scene in the final act.

Although the stage objects are novel and intriguing and can be assigned a clear meaning they lack the suggestive power of Ionesco's chairs or rhinoceroses. Contrived rather than intuitive, they illustrate more than they illuminate the human condition. But the play is an original and successful experiment and the implied comment on the unconscious assumptions and compulsive habits of the Groomkirbys has a wide reference.

The film version is recommended.

The Cresta Run. 1965.

A play about counter-espionage proved disappointing, partly because its mockery is directed at a schoolboy dream rather than at a general malaise, partly because it lacks the bold structural outline of *One Way Pendulum.* Even the absurd objects—keys, codes, disguises—are trivial compared with the " Old Bailey." Simpson has also lost some of the claustrophobic compulsion of his earlier plays by his constant switching of the action from the home of the suburban couple to the Ministry and back again.

It is unfortunate that a promising latent theme—the compulsion felt by the Security man to divulge his secret information—is swamped by trivia, while the best jest is only a casual aside—the suggestion that in England Intelligence should logically be in the hands of private enterprise!

The Hole, 1957, and *The Form* are one-acters in the same style as the full-length plays.

Wole Soyinka.

Soyinka, a Nigerian, is an admirer of Brecht, Arden, and Dürrenmatt.

The Road. 1965.

The Road, set in a drivers' haven in Nigeria, was successfully produced with a large cast of coloured actors.

Gwyn Thomas (b. 1913).

The Keep. 1962.

A realistic and fluent comedy of character in a South Wales home is strengthened by the sardonic twist of its surprise ending.

Jackie the Jumper. 1963.

A period play with music is set in the Chartist era.

Peter Ustinov (b. 1921).

Ustinov's versatile and ingenious comedies have proved more popular than his serious plays. Recent productions include *Romanoff and Juliet*, 1956, and *Photo Finish*, 1962.

Boris Vian (1920–59).

The French Vian was influenced by the Absurdist approach of Ionesco.

The Empire Builders. 1962.

Man's futile flight from death is imaged in a family trying to escape from a terrifying noise by moving up to a higher and higher floor and meaner quarters. Eventually the father alone reaches the attic, where he dies.

Fred Watson.

Infanticide in the House of Fred Ginger.

In spite of its being an ill-constructed piece this was described by a responsible critic as a " fascinating and immensely promising failure."

Roger Vitrac (1899–1952).

The French Vitrac, an associate of Artaud, attempted Surrealist plays which anticipate the Theatre of the Absurd.

Victor. 1964.

Victor is a boy of 9 but 7 foot tall and with a mature intelligence. He and his outsize girl-friend are the only rational beings in a farcical adult world.

Peter Weiss (b. 1916).

The German-speaking Weiss has adopted Swedish nationality and Marxist doctrine.

The " Marat Sade." 1964.

The full title of this verse play, one of the most impressive exemplifications of Artaud's Theatre of Cruelty, is *The Persecution and Assassination of Jean-Paul Marat as Performed by the Inmates of the Asylum of Charenton under the Direction of the Marquis de Sade!* As the title indicates this complex work operates on receding planes of cruelty, thus exciting in the audience that vivid experience of violence which is the aim of Artaud.

Artaud's demand for primitive ritual which shall exorcise repressed fantasy is met not only by Corday's threefold visit and murder of Marat but also by the lunatics' frenzied miming of the ceremony of the guillotine—a background motif to the whole play. Meanwhile the use of pantomime and gesticulation on the open stage satisfy Artaud's demands for spectacle, for " poetry in space."

Peter Brook, the brilliant Director, has pointed out that these elements are not inconsistent with a Brechtian " alienation "—achieved by the device of a play within a play, the protesting comments of the Director of the asylum, the intellectual debates between Sade and Marat and not least by the ribald songs of a grotesque quartet of zanies. The final effect is an inextricable blend of the comic and the violent.

The Investigation. 1965.

A documentary of the Auschwitz trials, edited by Weiss, had a multiple première in East and West Germany and at the Aldwych. Described by Weiss as an " Oratorium in 11 Cantos," after Dante's Inferno, it indicts the millions, especially the German monopoly capitalists, who tacitly supported the atrocities.

Arnold Wesker (b. 1932).

Wesker, son of a Jewish-Hungarian father and a Russian mother, first became a chef, and worked for four years in Norwich, London, and Paris, before taking a six months' course at the London School of Film Technique, where he wrote his first play.

He is known not only as a dramatist but also as a devoted socialist. Since 1962 much of his time has been given to his efforts to bring an enjoyment of good drama and art to people who would otherwise lack opportunity. To this end he has founded—under the aegis of the Trade Unions—the well-known Centre 42.

Wesker's early plays were in the naturalistic idiom, centred on the vivid portrayal of an East End Jewish family and a farm-labourer's family in Norfolk. He evidently found naturalism inadequate and there gradually appeared in his work strains of Expressionism, which in *Chips with Everything* became the dominant style. Wesker's hold on dramatic structure is erratic, but he has an exhilarating sense of movement on the stage.

The most individual characteristic of Wesker's work is his passionate concern for his characters. They are presented in the round, living, aspiring, and erring, so that they achieve an independent existence, especially the women, like Sarah Kahn and Beatie Bryant. Although male protagonists like Ronnie Kahn and Pip are seen both in their strength and weakness, Wesker does not entirely succeed in detaching himself from them, somehow conveying his personal reactions to them—a conflict of love and exasperation. He has nevertheless gone much further than Osborne, for instance, in creating a truly objective image, as his more flexible dialogue indicates. He has a keen ear for social and personal idiosyncracies, especially urban Jewish volubility and the fumbling speech of the country labourer.

Like Sartre, Wesker is deeply " committed " to social and political ideals. He is a convinced socialist but not a propagandist, for his plays explore the moral and practical difficulties of the socialist position and he shows unusual honesty in portraying Ronnie Kahn, the most vocal of socialists, as a weak if not a renegade personality.

The Trilogy—The trilogy consists of three naturalistic plays in which a discursive history of the Jewish family, the Kahns, is fused with political debate on the course of socialism.

Chicken Soup with Barley. 1958. P.

This is the springboard of the trilogy. It opens on October 4, 1936, the morning of Moseley's attempted march through the East End of London, when the curtain rises on the basement flat of the Kahns, a Jewish family dedicated to socialist activities. It is 1957 when the play ends with the disillusion of the son, Ronnie, at the Russian occupation of Hungary.

Each of the Kahns is a live human being, presented not for moral judgment but with sympathy. Especially commanding is the mother Sarah. What Jung might call an "extraverted feeling type," she is ignorant of events, contemptuous of books, a strenuous mother figure, and yet in her aggressive dynamic the most masculine person of the group, in contrast to her amiable but shiftless husband, Harry, and the vacillating Ronnie.

The central theme of the play is the conflict between attitudes of mind, "caring," or concern for the welfare of others, and indifference to it. The battle is fought on two fronts, in the home and politically, it being taken for granted that socialism is an expression of "caring." The stalwart Sarah is the centre of the two-fold conflict, for she attacks both social inertia and that of her husband and son.

Structurally the play is sprawling, but Wesker already shows his intuitive sense of theatrical movement. At the end of Scene I there is an imaginative leap forward as the little band of fighters surges from the basement to the light, the exhilaration heightened by the thronging movement and cries from the streets above. A more experienced dramatist might have placed such a triumphal movement as the final climax, but the general pattern of the play is of recoil and listlessness, held only by Sarah's unshakeable faith in caring and Ronnie's honesty with himself.

Roots. 1959. P.

There is here a skilful shift of scene to Norfolk, where Beatie Bryant (Joan Plowright), a farm-labourer's daughter on holiday from London, revisits her family. Beatie is engaged to Ronnie, who has for three years been trying to educate her, especially in the arts and in the intelligent use of words (the "bridges" of communication). She has ignored his advice but endlessly parrots his sayings to her phlegmatic family.

Preoccupied with the primal necessities of life the Bryants are the coarse "roots" from which Beatie has sprung. In spite of a rough friendliness they are ignorant, prejudiced, stubborn, and above all inarticulate.

When on the day appointed for his visit, Ronnie sends instead a letter saying their marriage would not work, Beatie is at last galvanised by shock into finding thoughts and words of her own. These folk she realises are without spiritual roots or standards. Then comes her ecstatic moment of self-realisation. She is at last thinking and speaking for herself.

Although he does not know it Ronnie has realised his ambition, "to save someone from the fire."

The play is well constructed, the characters and dialogue are convincing, Beatie delightful. The ideas discussed, about "roots," or the power of heredity, and "bridges," or the need for communication, are implicit in the situation and develop organically from it.

I'm Talking about Jerusalem. 1960. P.

In 1946 the Kahns' daughter and her husband, Dave, settle in Norfolk to put into practice the theories of William Morris, but Dave, finding that his hand-made furniture cannot compete economically with the factory product, faces their failure and in 1959 they return to London.

The theme of disillusion is here fully analysed by the voluble Kahns, but the mood escapes despair and Dave's self-respect and sober appraisal of unpalatable facts is contrasted with the embittered cynicism of a friend.

The play is weak structurally. There is insufficient action and Dave is not a sufficiently commanding figure to hold things together. Then the intimate study of tender family relationships, suitable to a novel, is embarrassing, except for brief moments on the public stage.

Two symbolic moments in Act II indicate that Wesker was realising the limitations of realism. One is the miming of a simple ritual of reconciliation, the other a ritual enactment of the story of creation.

The Trilogy as a Whole—Wesker's trilogy throws up vital questions of good and evil, both personal and social, the chief perhaps being that of heredity. Must Ronnie and Beatie inherit their parents' limitations? Is Mrs. Bryant right when she says, "The apple don't fall far from the tree"? Is man foredoomed and his struggle vain? Ironically it is the undependable Harry who suggests that giving people some love may help them to change, while of socialism he says, "It'll purify itself." Who was right and in what degree?

The Kitchen. 1959. P.

In a two-acter, Wesker draws on his experience as a chef to give a vivid impression of a day in the kitchen of Marango's restaurant. The play is notable for its skilful contrasts in pace and movement. The quiet morning quickens to a frenzy of anxiety at lunch-time, and the doldrums of the afternoon are succeeded by the sudden outburst of a German who goes beserk.

The swirling vortex is an image of the blind activity of society, and, while avoiding the rigidity of allegory, Wesker clearly indicates that the kitchen is a microcosm of the world, where men with their casual contacts find themselves in a situation beyond their grasp. The play ends with the dramatic irony of Marango's failure to perceive that work and food alone cannot satisfy man's desires.

Although it destroyed the claustrophobic atmosphere the film version caught very well the movement of the play.

Chips with Everything. 1962. P.

In *R.U.R.* (*Rossum's Universal Robots*) the Expressionist playwright, Karel Capek, used robots as dramatis personae. In *Chips with Everything* Wesker brilliantly deploys the techniques of Expressionism to illustrate the process whereby military discipline can reduce individuals to a robot-like uniformity, both the complacency of authority and the inertia of the ranks.

A squad of nine R.A.F. conscripts is subjected to a battery of bullying abuse from the corporal and psychological manipulation by the commissioned officers, until, their personal identity submerged, they learn to move as one mechanical unit and pass out to the blaring of a military band playing "God Save the Queen."

Expressionism is particularly appropriate to his purpose. He uses type characters to represent social forces—the best example being Corporal Hill—and the identity of the recruits is, with two exceptions, indicated very lightly. The dialogue is for the most part staccato, while brief, stylised, symbolic scenes, such as the square bashing and bayonet practice, succeed one another rapidly, a triumphant instance of Wesker's innate command of stage movement.

As to the two recruits presented in greater detail: the plight of the gentle Smiler, broken and suffering, is sufficiently generalised to give pathos and depth to the play without disturbing its tone, but the predicament of Thompson is treated with too much psychological detail to be in key, especially as the portrait is not entirely convincing.

The son of a general, Thompson is at first resistant to authority and appears to be trying to assume leadership of the squad, his least credible success being the sudden conversion of a Christmas party from rock 'n roll to the singing of folk-ballads. But the habits of a class that can eat "chips with everything" are too distasteful for him, and accused by the recruits of "slumming" and assailed by the blandishments of the officers, he suddenly capitulates and assumes officer's uniform.

The overall effect is tense and powerful, and scenes of moving comedy, such as the breathtaking mime of stealing coke, alternate with those where the audience, facing the same direction as the recruits themselves, cannot escape feeling the obliterating effects of the military machine.

The Four Seasons. 1965.

The course of love through the four seasons of the year is traced through the shared experience of a man and woman whose previous marriages had foundered. Wesker has unfortunately applied an Expressionist style to unsuitable material, a static situation without incident or plot and the experiment has proved unsuccessful.

John Whiting (1915–63).

John Whiting was an original playwright who was much preoccupied with the theme of self-destruction, but was slow to find his own style.

A Penny for a Song. 1951.

Written at a time of great personal happiness this is an agreeable whimsy, depicting two eccentric brothers in their Dorsetshire residence preparing to repel the armies of Napoleon. The appearance on the stage of a balloon and a home-made fire-engine give the authentic period touch of gentlemanly interest in scientific invention, and also impart to the farcical idyll a dash of pantomime.

Whiting cleverly gives a comic perspective to the recent fear of foreign invasion and so takes the sting out of terror.

Saint's Day. 1951.

This play, written before *A Penny for a Song*, won the award in a Festival of Britain Play Competition.

It concerns self-destruction, its central figure being the octogenarian Paul Southman, once a famous revolutionary poet who had long ago gone into self-imposed exile because of popular outcry against his work.

The plays opens well. Southman is a striking figure, an embodiment of the angry artist at war with society, and like Swift in his aggressive scorn of compromise, his scurrilous style and final madness. His predicament is at first sufficiently distanced to be convincing, but when the fashionable young writer Procathren introduces the glossy contemporary world it begins to seem implausible. Later Procathren accidentally kills Paul's grand-daughter, Stella, and then orders three deserting soldiers to hang Paul and Stella's husband, also an artist, and the initially powerful theme is swamped by melodrama.

The play generally is overloaded with half-developed symbolism and allusion.

Marching Song. 1954. P.

In a play which is much concerned with the Existentialist stress on the importance of choice, Whiting returns to the theme of self-destruction.

The setting is generalised—a wealthy house "above a capital city in Europe." Rupert Forster, formerly a general, who seven years previously had inexplicably lost a decisive battle, here meets his dilemma. He must either face a trial, which might cause political unrest, or commit suicide. The choices are represented by two people.

In Act II Forster encounters Dido, a young woman who revives his sense of humanity and will to live. She represents the female side of personality, the Jungian anima and her name recalls the Dido of the Æneid, who by her love deflected Æneas from the path of military duty enjoined by fate.

In Act III he has a very different meeting with Captain Bruno, the embodiment of military ambition, who represents the male aspect of personality. To him Forster at last confesses the cause of his fatal defeat. He had been so overcome with compassion for children whom he had destroyed while they were impeding his tanks that he had been unable to follow up his advance. Bruno stigmatises the delay as military error and guilt and Forster commits suicide rather than face disgrace and imprisonment.

This is a strongly constructed play, its dominating theme worked out with single-minded austerity. But it lacks thrust and momentum. Forster's reversion to his original decision to commit suicide gives it a circular movement and it is more concerned to clarify judgment of the past than to affect the future. In this it is reminiscent of Morgan's *The River Line*. In its acknowledgment of the discrepancy between military code and humane ethic it is highly topical and stimulating.

The Devils. 1962. P.

Suggested to Whiting by Peter Brook, this intricate and distinguished play is based on Aldous Huxley's *The Devils of Loudun*, which treats of an actual case of suspected diabolism in France between 1623 and 1634.

Whiting employs two focal points. One is Grandier (Richard Johnson), again a man who invites his own destruction, a worldly and sensual priest who is yet gifted with a rare religious insight and compassion. The other is a hunchback prioress (Dorothy Tutin). Although she has not met Grandier, she becomes obsessed by fantasies of his amorous adventures and her resulting hysteria, which spreads throughout the convent, is suspected as diabolical possession, instigated by Grandier. Richelieu, for political reasons, uses this as a pretext to get rid of him. Grandier, in spite of excruciating torture and degradation, the prelude to his being burnt alive, struggles to retain his faith.

In its subject and theme *The Devils* is strikingly similar to Miller's *The Crucible*. Both plays show *l'homme moyen sensuel* accused of diabolism and beset by a woman's jealousy, fanatical superstition, and malignant spite, yet still keeping his integrity in the face of death.

There are significant differences. Whiting's intricate play is not realistic but Brechtian in style, with a series of brief episodes and a commentary by a sewerman, whose ironic and sceptical remarks counterpoint Grandier's eloquence. It lacks Miller's reference to the contemporary scene and its final note is one of harsh pessimism, as the sewerman tells the prioress that Grandier's bones are being prized by the crowd as superstitious "charms."

The final act presents an almost unbearable spectacle of barbarous ritual of physical torture as the maimed and twitching Grandier is paraded in public procession through the streets.

Tennessee Williams (b. 1914).

The American Tennessee Williams is a playwright of great talent, whose freely flowing naturalistic plays combine violence and melodrama with haunting portrayal of personality, fluent dialogue, and original settings.

Of recent years the following major plays have been produced in Britain: *The Glass Menagerie*, 1948, revived 1965 (P); *A Street Car Named Desire* 1949 (P); *The Rose Tattoo* (P); *Cat on a Hot Tin Roof* (P); *Camino Real*, the least realistic play, 1957 (P); *Suddenly Last Summer* (P), and *Period of Adjustment*, 1961.

Although his plays breathe the atmosphere of the Deep South—often decadent in tone—Williams, unlike the extravert Miller, is preoccupied not with social issues but with the inner life of his characters. Compelled by their own passions and obsessions and caught in the web of family relationships, they break away only at great cost and pain to themselves and others, so that a mood of determinism, sombre but not altogether despairing, broods over much of Williams' work.

He portrays the vulnerability of those who desire or love anything intensely, humanity's sense of guilt, defiant aggression and despair, all of which he claims to find within himself. The violence characterising so much of his work reaches its climax in *Suddenly Last Summer*.

Especially poignant are Williams' penetrating psychological studies of life's pathetic failures; the crippled Laura retreating to her glass menagerie, Blanche Dubois, of *Street Car*, and the alcoholic Brick and his childless wife in the *Cat*. Less successful is the rather facile optimism of his recent "serious comedy," *Period of Adjustment*.

IDEAS & BELIEFS

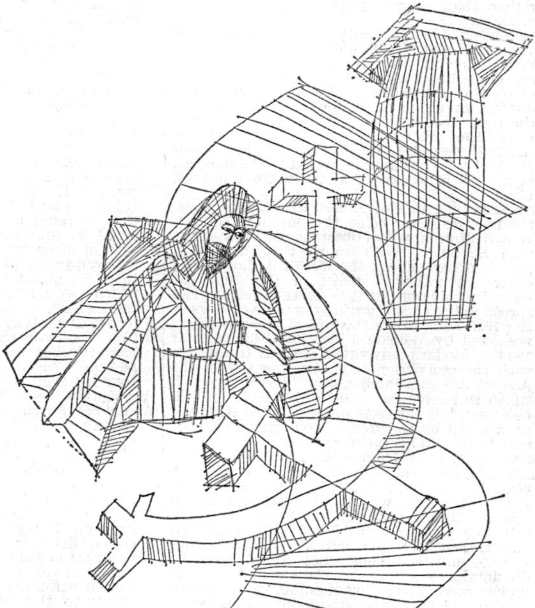

IDEAS AND BELIEFS

This section explains many of the ideas and beliefs which people have held at different periods in history. Beliefs may be true or false, meaningful or totally meaningless, regardless of the degree of conviction with which they are held. Since man has been moved to action so often by his beliefs they are worth serious study. The section throws a vivid light on human history.

Man has always felt a deep need for emotional security, a sense of "belonging." This need has found expression in the framing of innumerable religious systems, nearly all of which have been concerned with man's relation to a divine ruling power. In the past people have been accustomed to think of their own religion as true and of all others as false. Latterly we have come to realise that there is common ground for all since our need in the world today is a morality whereby human beings may live together in harmony.

There is also to be found in man an irresistible curiosity which demands an explanation of the world in which he finds himself. This urge to make the world intelligible takes him into the realm of science where the unknown is the constant challenge. Science is a developing process, always in the making, founded in observation and experiment. Basic scientific ideas and some of the results of recent scientific activity are to be found in the section "The World of Science."

In this dictionary the subjects fall broadly into three groups: religious, philosophical, and political. In writing of beliefs, especially cherished beliefs, and of how they fit into the modern picture of the world, it is difficult to avoid causing some offence but the reader is assured that the writer has tried to be fair and helpful.

A

Abecedarians, name (derived from A B C) of a small German religious sect, founded by the Anabaptist Storch in 1522, who claimed that, as knowledge of the Scriptures was communicated directly by the Holy Spirit, it was wrong to learn to read. *See* **Baptists**.

Activists, those in a political movement who insist on taking active steps towards their objectives rather than merely putting forward a programme.

Adoptionism, in Christianity, a doctrine advanced at various times which holds that Jesus was not born divine but, in virtue of his human spiritual achievements, was designated by God as the Son of God at the moment of his baptism in the Jordan, as told in all the four Gospels. Among the sects who held this "heretical" doctrine were the Paulicians (*q.v.*). The "Adoptionist" view differs from the orthodox "Conceptionist" view only in regard to the moment in the life of Jesus when the incarnation took place.

Adventists, a group of American religious sects, the most familiar being the Seventh-Day Adventist Church, which observes Saturday as the true Sabbath. With more than a million members throughout the world, it shares with other Adventists a belief in the imminent second coming of Christ (a doctrine fairly widespread in the U.S.A. during the early decades of the 19th cent. when the end of the world was predicted by William Miller for 1843, then for 1844). Modern Adventists content themselves with the conviction that the "signs" of the Advent are multiplying, the "blessed event" which will solve the world's ills. Believers will be saved, but the sects differ as to whether the unjust will be tortured in hell, annihilated, or merely remain asleep eternally.

Agnosticism. *See* **God and Man**.

Albigenses, also known as Cathari. French 12th cent. heretical sect (named after the town of Albi in Provence), who maintained that material things belonged to the realm of Satan and that salvation was to be achieved by crushing all animal instincts, particularly the sexual instinct; universal continence would end the domination of matter by the extinction of the human race. The eating of animal flesh was forbidden and vegetarianism enjoined in order to weaken the desires. Those who rigidly kept to these rules were initiated into the grade of the "Perfect"; those unable fully to comply were known as the "Believers". Condemned as heretics by Pope Innocent III, the sect was finally exterminated in the Albigensian Crusade led by Simon de Montfort towards the end of the 12th cent. (In his thoroughness, de Montfort also succeeded in destroying the high culture of the Troubadours.) *See* **Manichaeism**.

Alchemy, ancient art associated with magic and astrology in which modern chemistry has its roots. The earliest mention of alchemy comes from ancient Egypt but its later practitioners attributed its origins to such varied sources as the fallen angels of the Bible, to Moses and Aaron, but most commonly to Hermes Trismegistus, often identified with the Egyptian god Thoth, whose knowledge of the divine art was handed down only to the sons of kings (cf. the phrase "hermetically sealed"). Its main object was the transmutation of metals. Egyptian speculation concerning this reached its height during the 6th cent. in the Alexandrian school. Brought to Western Europe by the Moslems, one of its most famous Arab exponents was Jabir (*c.* 760–*c.* 815), known to the Latins as Geber, who had a laboratory at Kufa on the Tigris. One school of early Greek philosophy held that there was ultimately only one elemental matter of which everything was composed. Such men as Albertus Magnus (1206–80) and Roger Bacon (1214–94) assumed that, by removing impurities, this *materia prima* could be obtained. Although Bacon's ideas were in many ways ahead of his time, he firmly believed in the philosopher's stone, which could turn base metals into gold, and in an elixir of life which would give eternal youth. Modern science has, of course, shown in its researches into radioactivity the possibility of transmutation of certain elements, but this phenomenon has little bearing on either the methods of the alchemist or the mysteries with which he surrounded them.

Anabaptists. *See* **Baptists**.

Analytical Psychology, the name given by Carl Gustav Jung (1875–1961) of Zürich to his system of psychology which, like Adler's Individual Psychology (*q.v.*), took its origin from Freud's psychoanalysis (*q.v.*) from which both diverged in 1911. Briefly, Jung differed from Freud: (1) in believing that the latter had laid too much emphasis on the sexual drive as the basic one in man and replacing it with the concept of *libido* or life energy of which sex forms a part; (2) in his theory of types: men are either extrovert or introvert (*i.e.* their interest is turned primarily outwards to the world or inwards to the self), and they apprehend experience in four main ways, one or other of which is predominant in any given individual—sensing, feeling, thinking, or intuiting; (3) in his belief that the individual's unconscious mind contains not only repressed material which, as Freud maintained, was too unpleasant to be allowed into awareness, but also faculties which had not been allowed to develop—*e.g.*, the emotional side of the too rational man, the feminine side of the too masculine one; (4) in the importance he attaches to the existence of a collective unconscious at a still deeper level which contains traces of ancient ways of thought which mankind has inherited over the centuries. These are the *archetypes* and include vague primitive notions of magic, spirits and witches, birth and death, gods, virgin mothers, resurrection, etc. In the treatment of neuroses Jung believed in the importance of (*a*) the present situation which the patient refuses to face; (*b*) the bringing together of conscious and unconscious and integrating them.

Jung's school of thought is undeniably not popular with scientific psychologists, but his emphasis on the more spiritual side of man's nature has brought him support from those of a religious or philosophical turn of mind, notably in the Roman Catholic Church.

Anarchism, a political philosophy which holds, in the words of the American anarchist Josiah Warren (1798–1874), an early follower of Robert Owen, that "every man should be his own government, his own law, his own church." The idea that governmental interference or even the mere existence of authority is inherently bad is as old as Zeno, the Greek Stoic philosopher, who believed that compulsion perverts the normal nature of man. William Godwin's *Enquiry Concerning Political Justice* (1793) was the first systematic exposition of the doctrine. Godwin (father-in-law of Shelley) claimed that man is by nature sociable, co-operative, rational, and good when given the choice to act freely; that under such conditions men will form voluntary groups to work in complete social harmony. Such groups or communities would be based on equality of income, no state control, no property; this state of affairs would be brought about by rational discussion and persuasion rather than by revolution.

The French economist Proudhon (1809–65) was the first to bring anarchism to the status of a mass movement. In his book *What is Property?* he stated bluntly that "property is theft" and "governments are the scourge of God." He urged the formation of co-operative credit banks where money could be had without interest and goods could be exchanged at cost value at a rate representing the hours of work needed to produce each commodity. Like Godwin, he disapproved of violence but, unlike Marx, disapproved of trades unions as representing organised groups.

In communistic anarchism these ideas were combined with a revolutionary philosophy, primarily by the Russians Michael Bakunin (1814–76) and Peter Kropotkin (1842–1921) who favoured training workers in the technique of "direct action" to overthrow the state by all possible means, including political assassination. In 1868 anarchists joined the First International which broke up a few years later after a bitter struggle between Bakuninists and Marxists. Subsequently small anarchist groups murdered such political figures as Tsar Alexander II of Russia, King Humbert of Italy, Presidents Carnot of France and MacKinley of America, and the Empress Elizabeth of Austria.

Anarchism and communism differ in three main ways: (1) anarchism forms no political party, rejects all relationship with established authority, and regards democratic reform as a setback; (2) communism is against capitalism, anarchism against the state as such; (3) both have the final goal of a classless society, but anarchism rejects the idea of an intermediate period of socialist state control accepted by communism. Philosophical anarchists, such as the American writer Henry David Thoreau (1817–62), were primarily individualists who believed in a return to nature, the non-payment of taxes, and passive resistance to state control; in these respects Thoreau strongly influenced Ghandi as did the Christian anarchist Tolstoy. *See also* **Syndicalism.**

Anglicanism, adherence to the doctrine and discipline of the Anglican, as the genuine representative of the Catholic Church. *See* **Church of England.**

Anglo-Catholicism. To Queen Elizabeth I the Church of England was that of the "middle way" in which human reason and commonsense took their place beside Scripture and Church authority. The extent to which these various factors are stressed creates the distinctions between "high" and "low" church. Anglo-Catholics tend to reject the term "Protestant" and stress the term "Catholic" and, although few accept the infallibility of the Pope, some Anglo-Catholic churches have introduced much or all of the Roman ritual and teach Roman dogmas. *See* **Catholicism, Tractarianism.**

Animatism, a stage in primitive religion in which life is attributed to inanimate objects.

Animism (see above) is a more advanced stage in which it is believed that natural objects may be the *abodes* of souls or spirits.

Anthropomorphism, the ascription of human physical and moral qualities to God or gods (in psychology to gods or animals). Psychologists use the term *Anthropopathy* for the ascription of such qualities specifically to the Deity.

Anthroposophy, a school of religious philosophic thought based on the work of Rudolf Steiner (1861–1925), a German theosophist. His best known work is in education and medicine. The centre of the Anthroposophical Society is at Goetheanum, Basel, Switzerland. Schools, curative homes, and clinics are to be found in many parts of the world. Though concerned with reincarnation and destiny, anthroposophy is essentially Christian in outlook.

Anticlericalism, resentment of priestly powers and privileges, traceable in England to Wyclif's insistence in the 14th cent. on the right of all men to have access to the Scriptures. The translation of the Bible into the common tongue was a great landmark in the history of the Bible and the English language. Wyclif's principles were condemned by the Roman Church of his time but were readily accepted during the Reformation. Tudor anticlericalism arose from motives ranging from a greedy desire to plunder the riches of the Church to a genuine dislike of the powers of the priesthood whose spiritual courts still had the right to decide on points of doctrine or morals in an age when the layman felt he was well able to decide for himself. In innumerable ways the Church was permitted to extort money from the laity. It is generally agreed, says Trevelyan, that the final submission of church to state in England was motivated quite as much by anticlericalism as by Protestantism. The rise of the Reformed churches in England satisfied the people generally and anticlericalism never became the fixed principle of permanent parties as happened in France and Italy from the time of Voltaire onwards.

Antisemitism, a term first applied about the middle of the last century to those who were anti-Jewish in their outlook. Although this attitude was prevalent for religious reasons throughout the Middle Ages, modern antisemitism differed (*a*) in being largely motivated by economic or political conditions, and (*b*) in being doctrinaire with a pseudo-scientific rationale presented by such men as Gobineau (1816–82) and Houston Stewart Chamberlain (1855–1927), and later by the Nazi and Fascist "philosophers." Beginning in Russia and Hungary with the pogroms of 1882 it gradually spread south and westwards where, in France, the Dreyfus case provided an unsavoury example in 1894. Thousands of Jews from Eastern Europe fled to Britain and America during this period; for in these countries antisemitism has rarely been more than a personal eccentricity. During the last war the murder of six million Jews by the Nazis and their accomplices led to a further exodus to various parts of the world and finally to the creation of the state of Israel.

The individual Jew-hater makes unconscious use of the psychological processes of projection and displacement: his greed or sexual guilt is projected on to the Jew (or Negro or Catholic) because he cannot bear to accept them as his own emotions, and his sense of failure in life is blamed on his chosen scapegoat rather than on his own inadequacy.

But there are social causes too and politicians in some lands are well versed in the technique of blaming unsatisfactory conditions (which they themselves may have in part produced) upon minority groups and persuading others to do the same. Historically, the Jew is ideally suited for this role of scapegoat: (1) in the Middle Ages when usury was forbidden to Christians but not to Jews, the latter often became moneylenders incurring the opprobrium generally associated with this trade (*e.g.*, to the simple-minded Russian peasant the Jew often represented, not only the "Christ-killer," but also the moneylender or small shopkeeper to whom he owed money); (2) many trades being closed to Jews, it was natural that they concentrated in others, thus arousing suspicions of "influence" (*i.e.* Jews are felt to occupy a place in certain trades and professions which far exceeds their numerical proportion to the population as a whole); (3) even with the ending of ghetto life, Jews often occupy *en masse* some parts of cities rather than others and this may lead to resentment on the part of the original inhabitants who begin to feel themselves dispossessed; (4) Jews tend to form a closed society and incur the suspicions attached to all closed societies within which social contacts are largely limited to members; marriage outside the group is forbidden or strongly disapproved of, and the preservation, among the orthodox, of cultural and religious barriers tends to isolate them from their fellow citizens. Discrimination, hateful as it is, does not come from one side only and it is such barriers as these that help to maintain an old and cruel folly. *See* **Racism, Zionism, Judaism.**

Antivivisection, opposition to scientific experimentation upon live animals based, according to its supporters, both on the moral grounds of the suffering imposed, and on the less secure claim that many doctors and scientists of repute have rejected the value of information gained in this way. It is true that the protagonists of the movement during its early days in the mid-19th cent. included a number of eminent physicians and surgeons, but few today—whatever their moral scruples—would deny the value of the results obtained. The Animal Defence and Anti-vivisection Society (one of the half-dozen or more in Britain) claims to have co-ordinated medical opposition by "the foundation of various associated medical bodies and the publication of numerous articles by members of the profession whilst at the same time drawing attention to methods of prevention and cure of disease not associated with animal experimentation." These include such methods as homeopathy, nature cure, herbalism, physiotherapy, hydrotherapy, and psychotherapy of which it would be not unfair to say that the first three are long outdated and the last three are merely auxiliary methods of treatment in specific diseases. Without animal experiments we should be without vaccines, sera, or antitoxins against smallpox, tetanus, typhoid, diphtheria, poliomyelitis, and a multitude of other diseases; we should have no detailed knowledge about vitamins, or about the effects of radioactive fall-out; we would be unable to test out new drugs for safety before using them on human beings. Animal experimentation is controlled by the Cruelty of Animals Act of 1876 which makes obligatory the possession of licences by experimenters, inspection of laboratories by the Home Office, and the issue of annual returns of experiments.

Apartheid, an Afrikaans word meaning "apartness," referred to by South African Government spokesmen as "separate development" or "self-development." To others it means the system of total racial discrimination between Black and White South Africans—the permanent inhabitants of the country—as enforced by the Nationalist Party since it came to power in 1948. Some degree of racial segregation has existed in South Africa since the earliest days of colonialism in the mid-17th cent. and the policy was continued by the United Party under Smuts and Hertzog from 1934 onwards though it was never a political issue. This changed when the Nationalist Party gained power and oppressive measures against the non-White segment of the population have grown steadily under Malan, Strydon, and Verwoerd. *Apartheid* involves the beliefs in racial purity and *baaskap* or white supremacy which is maintained by discriminatory legislation. The official policy of the South African Government is to create separate self-governing Black states in which the Africans would be guided to self-government and, it is claimed, eventually to independence. The first Bantu reserve was set up in the Transkei (*see* **K171**) in 1962. But Africans with 70 per cent of the population would have only about 12 per cent of the land. Cities and mineral areas would remain the reserve of the Whites. Total *apartheid* or complete separation of the Black and White races in South Africa remains unlikely to be realised since mining, the main industry of the country, is based on relatively low-paid African labour.

Apartheid has been condemned by the General Assembly of the United Nations and the Secretary-General, U Thant, has expressed the hope "that, in response to the repeated recommendations and decisions of the United Nations organs the Government of the Republic of South Africa will abandon its policies of *apartheid*, and also implement measures aimed at bringing about racial harmony based on equal rights and fundamental freedoms for all the people of South Africa." *See also* **Section C, Part I.**

Arianism, formed the subject of the first great controversy within the Christian Church over the doctrine of Arius of Alexandria (d. 336) who denied the divinity of Christ. The doctrine, although at first influential, was condemned at the Council of Nicaea (325), called by the Emperor Constantine, at which Arius was opposed by Athanasius, also of Alexandria, who maintained the now orthodox view that the Son is of one substance with the Father. Arius was banished and the heresy had died out by the end of the 4th cent., but disbelief in the divinity of Christ has formed part of the doctrine of many minor sects since, notably in **Unitarianism** (*q.v.*).

Arminianism, the doctrine of Jacobus Arminium or Jakob Harmensen (1560–1609), the Dutch minister of a Protestant church in Amsterdam, who had trained in the universities of Leyden and Geneva where he learned the Calvinistic doctrine of predestination (*See* **Calvinism**). Later he became deeply convinced of the falsity of this belief which maintained that God had, by an eternal decree, predestined which people were to be saved and which eternally damned. In face of the bitter opposition of his opponent Franz Gomar and his party who held this view, Arminius asserted that God bestows forgiveness and eternal life on all who repent and believe in Christ. In England a modified Arminianism was later to become the theology of Wesleyan Methodism.

Assassins, a sect of Moslem Shi'ites, founded by the Persian Hasan i Sabbah (*c.* 1090), which for more than two centuries established a rule of terror all over Persia and Syria. The coming of the Mongols in 1256 destroyed them in Persia and the Syrian branch suffered a similar fate at the hands of the then Mamluk sultan of Egypt, *c.* 1270. It was a secret order, ruled over by a grand master, under whom the members were strictly organised into classes, according to the degree of initiation into the secrets of the order. The devotees, belonging to one of the lower groups, carried out the actual assassinations under strict laws of obedience, and total ignorance of the objects and ritual of the society. It is believed that the latter were given ecstatic visions under the influence of hashish, whence the term *hashshashin*, which became corrupted to "assassin."

Associationism. In psychology, the Associationist school of the 19th cent. accepted the association of ideas as the fundamental principle in mental life. It was represented in Britain by the two Mills and Herbert Spencer, in Germany by J. F. Herbart (1776–1841). To these, mental activity was nothing but the association of "ideas" conceived of as units of both thought and feeling—the emotion of anger or the perception of a chair were both "ideas"—and apart from them the self did not exist. Personality was simply a series of these units coming and going, adding to or cancelling each other out, in accordance with rigid and mechanistic scientific laws.

Assumption of the Virgin. The Roman Catholic

belief, that the Blessed Virgin ascended bodily to heaven after her death, was proclaimed by Pope Pius XII towards the end of 1950. It is now, therefore, binding on all Catholics under pain of anathema and the guilt of mortal sin. Protestants are liable to make the mistake of supposing that such dogmas are new additions to the faith invented by the pope of the moment. According to Catholic doctrine, no addition can be made to the "faith once delivered to the saints," and every dogma is justified by reference to Bible texts and the traditions of the Church. Both Eastern and Western Churches have been permitted to believe in the Assumption of the Virgin for over a thousand years, and the new dogma merely clarifies the old belief and makes it binding on the faithful.

Astrology, a pseudo-science bearing much the same historical relationship to astronomy as alchemy did to chemistry. Originally it was divided into the two branches of Natural Astrology which dealt with the movements of the heavenly bodies and their calculation, and Judicial Astrology which studied the alleged influence of the stars and planets on human life and fate. It was the former that developed into modern astronomy; the latter was, and remains, sheer superstition.

Astrology owes most to the early Babylonians (or Chaldeans) who, being largely nomadic in an environment which permitted an unobstructed view of the sky, readily accepted the idea that divine energy is manifested in the movements of the sun and planets. Gradually this concept became enlarged and the relative positions of the planets both in relation to each other and to the fixed stars became important together with the idea of omens—that, if a particular event occurred whilst the planets were in a particular position, the recurrence of that position heralded a recurrence of the same sort of event. Soon the planets became associated with almost every aspect of human life. They were bound up with the emotions, with parts of the body, so that astrology played quite a large part in medicine up to late mediaeval times. Not only was the position of the planet to be considered but also the particular sign of the zodiac (or house of heaven) it was occupying, and it was believed possible to foretell the destiny of an individual by calculating which star was in the ascendant (*i.e.* the sign of the zodiac nearest the eastern horizon and the star which arose at that precise moment) at the time of his birth. Astrology was popular among the Egyptians, the Romans (whose authorities found the Chaldean astrologers a nuisance and expelled them from time to time), and during the Middle Ages when astrologers were often highly respected. Because of people's innate desire to see into the future there are, alas, still astrologers about to exploit ignorance.

Atheism. *See* **God and Man.**

Atomism. (1) in philosophy, the atomists were a group of early Greek thinkers, the most important of whom were Leucippus (fl. *c.* 440 B.C.) and his younger contemporary Democritus (*c.* 460–370 B.C.). Prior to these men, although it had been agreed that matter must be composed of tiny ultimate particles and that change must be due to the manner in which these mingled or separated from each other, it was supposed that there existed different types of particle for each material—*e.g.* for flesh, wood, hair, bone. The atomists taught that atoms were all made of a single substance and differed only in the connections (pictured as hooks, grooves, points, etc.) which enabled them to join each other in characteristic ways. Theirs was the first move towards modern atomic theory and a predecessor of the modern concept of chemical linkages. (2) in psychology, atomism refers to any theory which holds that mental states can be analysed without loss into elementary units, *e.g.* **Associationism** and **Behaviourism** (*q.v.*).

Authoritarianism, a dictatorial form of government as contrasted with a democratic one based on popular sovereignty. Its alleged advantages are the avoidance of the delays and inefficiency said to be characteristic of the latter, but like "Bolshevism" the word is used today mainly as a form of abuse.

B

Baconian Method, the use in science and philosophy of the inductive (as opposed to the deductive or Aristotelian) method of reasoning as proposed by Francis Bacon (1561–1626). Deduction argues from supposedly certain first principles (such as the existence of God or Descartes's "I think, therefore I am") what the nature of the universe and its laws *must* be, whereas Bacon denied the possibility of proving religious or metaphysical doctrines by thought and argument. The only means of obtaining true knowledge of the universe, in his view, was by the amassing of facts and observations so that when enough were obtained the truth would be known in the same way that a child's numbered dots in a playbook joined together by a pencilled line create a picture. This method, known as induction, is essentially the method of modern science, although it is generally agreed today that Bacon underrated the importance of hypothesis and theory since the greatest possible number of observations are of little significance until the scientist's intuition makes sense of them.

Baptists, a Christian denomination whose distinctive doctrines are that members can only be received by baptism "upon the confession of their faith and sins" and that "baptism in no wise appertaineth to infants." Baptism is therefore by total immersion of adults. Modern Baptists base their doctrines upon the teaching of the Apostles and some hold that the **Albigenses** (*q.v.*) maintained the true belief through what they regard as the corruption of the Roman Church in mediaeval times. On the other hand any connection with the Anabaptist movement during the Reformation is rejected and the beginning of the modern Church is traced to John Smyth, a minister of the Church of England who in Amsterdam came under the influence of the Arminians (*q.v.*) and Mennonites. Smyth died in 1612 when the first Baptist church in England was built at Newgate. This, the "General" Baptist Church, rejected Calvinistic beliefs and held the Arminian doctrine of redemption open to all, but some years later a split occurred with the formation of the "Particular" Baptist Church which was Calvinist in doctrine. In 1891 the two bodies were united in the Baptist Union and today the sect is spread throughout the world, notably in the U.S.A.

The **Anabaptist** movements of Germany, Switzerland, and Holland also practised adult baptism in addition to a primitive communism and demanded social reforms. Persecuted by both Catholics and Protestants, their leader, Thomas Münzer, and many others were burned at the stake (1525). However, this sect was noted for its violence under a religious guise, and its taking over of the state of Münster in 1533 was characterised by wild licentiousness, since, as Antinomians, they believed that the "elect" could do no wrong. A revival begun by Menno Simons (d. 1561), a Dutch religious reformer, led to the formation of the Mennonite sect which, whilst rejecting infant baptism, gave up the objectionable features of the Anabaptists. This reformed sect still exists as small agricultural groups in the original strongholds of the movement and in the United States.

Beat Generation, a term first used by the American writer Jack Kerouac in his novel *The Town and the City* to define various groups spread across the face of the country, but notably New York and San Francisco, which, belonging to the post-war generation, represented a complex of attitudes. Briefly, these are: rejection of the values of the past and lack of conviction in the possibility of a future for humanity—hence an acceptance of nothing but the immediate present in terms of experience and sensations; rebellion against organised authority, not out of any political conviction (as in the case of anarchism), but rather from lack of any interest or desire to control events, nature, or people; contempt for the "Square"—the orthodox individual who, stuck firmly in his rut, "plays it safe" and remains confident of the rightness and decency of his moral values. The "Beatnik" has contracted out of what one of them describes as "an increasingly meaningless rat-race rigged up by and for Squares" which wastes effort and brutalises feeling. He loathes the pretences without which, he claims, the Square cannot succeed, and throwing off all masks is indifferent to the opinions of others, his dress, or the need to work, thus entering into "the inescapable truth and squalor of his own being." He "digs" (likes) everything, tries everything from drugs to sexual relationships, which have no significance outside the sensations of the moment to the advanced Beatnik or "hipster." All men are addressed as "man," all women as "chick." Of course, the above is an intellectualisation by such Beat writers as Kerouac, Allen Ginsberg, and Carl Solomon or Norman Mailer of a philosophy which for many Beatniks would be meaningless, being satisfied with any excuse for their own exhibitionism, sexual promiscuity, and psychopathic tendencies. Beards (in men), bare feet, sloppy clothes, and unwashed bodies are the familiar Beatnik uniform of today.

Beatniks exist in many European countries and are not to be confused with the British "Angry Young Man" who shares with them nothing but the qualities of belonging to the post-war generation and their rejection of certain features of modern society. Instead of creating his own world of fantasy, the Angry Young Man wants his right of entry into the real world where careers are made and ambitions realised. Such writers as John Wain, Kingsley Amis, John Osborne, and Colin Wilson are men who, unlike the Beatnik, still *care*—they speak for the working-class or lower middle-class intellectual with a red-brick education who finds that even in the Welfare State the "Establishment" and class still count.

Behaviourism, a school of psychology founded in 1914 by J. B. Watson (1878–1958), an animal psychologist at Johns Hopkins University, Baltimore. Its main tenet was that the method of introspection and the study of mental states were unscientific and should be replaced by the study of behaviour. When animals or human beings were exposed to specific stimuli and their responses objectively recorded, or when the development of a child, as seen in its changing behaviour, was noted, these alone were methods which were truly scientific. Watson contributed an important idea to psychology and did a great deal towards ridding it of the largely philosophical speculations of the past. But he also went to absurd extremes, as in his view that thought is nothing but subvocal speech, consisting of almost imperceptible movements of the tongue, throat, and larynx (*i.e.*, when we think, we are really talking to ourselves), and his further opinion that heredity is, except in grossly abnormal cases, of no importance. He claimed that by "conditioning," the ordinary individual could be made into any desired type, regardless of his or her inheritance.

The work of Ivan Pavlov had begun about 1901, but was unknown in America until about ten years later, and it was through another Russian, Vladimir Bekhterev, that the concept of "conditioning" was introduced into the country. Bekhterev's book *Objective Psychology*, describing his new science of "reflexology," was translated in 1913 and played a great part in the development of Behaviourist ideas. The conditioned reflex became central to Watson's theory of learning and habit formation (*e.g.*, he showed that a year-old child, at first unafraid of white rats, became afraid of them when they came to be associated with a loud noise behind the head). Finally all behaviour, including abnormal behaviour, came to be explained in terms of conditioned responses; these were built up by association on the infant's three innate emotions of fear, rage, and love, of which the original stimuli were, for the first, loud noises and the fear of falling; for the second, interference with freedom of movement; and for the third, patting and stroking. The Behaviourist method is widely used all over the world as a technique in psychological research, but in the Western world there remain few Behaviourists of the out-and-out Watsonian type. The work of Freud has made it impossible to ignore the importance of introspection in psychology.

Benthamism. *See* **Utilitarianism.**

Bolshevism, an alternative name for **Communism** (*q.v.*), usually used in the West in a derogatory sense. When the Russian Social Democratic Party at a conference held in London in 1903 split over the issue of radicalism or moderation, it was the radical faction headed by Lenin (who subsequently led the 1917 Revolution and became first Head of State of the Soviet Union) which polled the majority of votes. The Russian for majority is *bolshinstvo* and for minority *menshinstvo*; hence the radicals became known as Bolsheviki and the moderates as Mensheviki, anglicised as Bolsheviks and Mensheviks. *See* **Communism, Marxism.**

British Israelites, a religious group who hold the race-theory that the English-speaking peoples (of the White Race) are the lineal descendants of the "lost Ten Tribes" of Israel (deported by Sargon of Assyria on the fall of Samaria in 721 B.C.). They believe the Anglo-Saxons to be God's "Chosen People" in the literal sense of the term as it is used in the Old Testament, by whom the world will be brought in readiness for the Millennium. The official organisation is the British–Israel World Federation of which the official journal is the *National Message*. Some British Israelites have the notion that the future can be foretold by the measurements of the Great Pyramid.

Buddhism, one of the great Oriental religions. It arose against the background of Hinduism in north India in the 6th cent. B.C., its founder (real or legendary) being the Hindu prince Siddhartha Gautama, known as the Buddha or "Enlightened One." Distressed by the problem of human suffering from which even death allowed no escape—since Buddha accepted the Hindu doctrine of a cycle of lives—he left his palace and his beloved wife and child to become a religious mendicant and ascetic, studying without success for six years the beliefs of Brahmin hermits and self-torturing recluses. After this fruitless search he sat down under a tree (the Bo-tree) and finally came to understand the cause and cure of suffering. The result of his meditations are enshrined in the "four noble truths" which are: (1) that existence is unhappiness; (2) that unhappiness is caused by selfish desire or craving; (3) that desire can be destroyed; (4) that it can be destroyed by following the "noble eightfold path" whose steps are: right views; right desires; right speech, plain and truthful; right conduct, including abstinence not only from immorality but also from taking life, whether human or animal; right livelihood, harming no one; right effort, always pressing on; right awareness of the past, the present, and the future; and lastly, right contemplation or meditation. The more man acquires merit by following these rules in his chain of lives, the sooner is *Nirvana* attained; he loses his individuality, not by annihilation, but "as the dewdrop slips into the shining sea," by merging with the universal life.

Buddhism teaches the way of salvation through ethics and discipline; it preaches the law of *karma*—that a man's actions control his destiny after death as inevitably as cause follows effect, so that his future is solely in his own keeping. A universal God plays no part in this religion, and in many Buddhist nations no word exists for the concept which was neither affirmed nor denied by Buddha himself but simply ignored. Nor did Buddha claim to be other than a man, although much superstition entered the religion at a later date; prayers were made to Buddha, ritual developed, sacred relics preserved under stupas, and the belief in a succession of Buddhas introduced; the sacred writings (*Tipitaka*) are divided into three parts: for the layman, the monks, the philosophers. They were produced by devotees at three councils—the first held immediately after the death of Buddha at the age of 80, the last at the order of King Asoka in 244 B.C. The founder himself wrote nothing.

Buddhism spread to Ceylon, Nepal, Tibet, Mongolia, Indo-China, Burma, Siam, China, and Japan, although on the whole losing influence in India. In Tibet, Buddhism developed into Lamaism (*q.v.*). In Ceylon and Burma it persisted in its pure form (the Hinayana), while in

China and Japan it developed into the Mahayana with its bodhisattvas and avatars. Sects developed, one of the most important being the Chinese **Ch'an** (Japanese **Zen**) **Buddhism** (*q.v.*). Outside Asia there are active movements in many Western countries where the serenity and rational humanism of Buddhism appeals to intellectuals as diverse as staid humanists and eccentric beatniks.

Bushido, the traditional code of honour of the Samurai or Japanese military caste corresponding to the European concept of knighthood and chivalry with which it took its separate origin in the 12th cent. Even today it is a potent influence among the upper classes, being based on the principles of simplicity, honesty, courage, and justice which together form a man's idea of personal honour. *Bushido* was strongly influenced by **Zen Buddhism** (*q.v.*).

C

Calvinism, the branch of Protestantism founded basically (although preceded by Zwingli and others) by Jean Chauvin (1509–64), who was born in Noyon in Picardy. John Calvin, as he is usually called, from the Latin form of his name, Calvinius, provided in his *Institutions of the Christian Religion* the first logical definition and justification of Protestantism, thus becoming the intellectual leader of the Reformation as the older Martin Luther was its emotional instigator. The distinctive doctrine of Calvinism is its dogma of predestination which states that God has unalterably destined some souls to salvation to whom "efficacious grace and the gift of perseverance" is granted and others to eternal damnation. Calvinism, as defined in the Westminster Confession, is established in the Reformed or Presbyterian churches of France, Holland, Scotland, etc., as contrasted with the Lutheran churches, and its harsh but logical beliefs inspired the French Huguenots, the Dutch in their fight against Spanish Catholic domination, and the English Puritans. The rule set up under Calvin's influence in Geneva was marred by the burning at the stake of the anatomist Servetus for the heresy of "pantheism," or, as we should say, Unitarianism.

Perhaps its greatest single influence outside the Church was the result of Calvinist belief that to labour industriously was one of God's commands. This changed the mediaeval notions of the blessedness of poverty and the wickedness of usury, proclaimed that men should shun luxury and be thrifty, yet implied that financial success was a mark of God's favour. In this way it was related to the rise of capitalism either as cause or effect. Max Weber, the German sociologist, believed that Calvinism was a powerful incentive to, or even cause of, the rise of capitalism (*q.v.*); Marx, Sombart, and in England, Tawney, have asserted the reverse view—that Calvinism was a result of developing capitalism, being its ideological justification.

Capitalism is an economic system under which the means of production and distribution are owned by a relatively small section of society which runs them at its own discretion for private profit. There exists, on the other hand, a propertyless class of those who exist by the sale of their labour power. Capitalism arose towards the end of the 18th cent. in England where the early factory owners working with small-scale units naturally approved of free enterprise and free trade. But free enterprise has no necessary connection with capitalism; by the beginning of this century monopolies were developing and state protection against foreign competition was demanded. Capitalism is opposed by those who believe in **socialism** (*q.v.*), first, for the moral reasons that it leads to economic inequality and the exploitation of labour and the consuming public, and that public welfare rather than private profit should motivate the economic system; secondly, for the practical reason that capitalism leads to recurrent economic crises. Defenders of the system, however, maintain that it conduces to efficient production by providing the strongest incentive to enterprise and good service.

Catholicism. For those who are not Roman Catholics the term "Catholic" has two separate meanings. The more general refers to the whole body of Christians throughout the world, the more specific refers to a particular view of Christianity. In this latter sense the Church of England, the Orthodox Eastern Churches, and others consider themselves "Catholic" meaning that (*a*) they belong to Christ's Church as organised on an accepted basis of faith and order; (*b*) they insist on the necessity of "liturgical" worship through established forms (*e.g.*, baptism, holy communion); (*c*) they emphasise the continuity of Christian tradition by the use of ancient creeds (*e.g.*, the Apostles' Creed, the Nicene Creed) and regard the ministry as a succession (Apostolic succession) deriving from early practice. In this sense there is thought to be no necessary contradiction between Catholicism and Protestantism regarded as a renewal of the Church in the 16th cent. by an appeal to the Scriptures as interpreted by the early Fathers of the Church. This definition obviously excludes Quakers, Christian Scientists, and many Nonconformist sects.

The Roman Catholic Church is the religious organization of all those who acknowledge the bishop of Rome as head of the Christian Church, recognizing him as the lawful successor of St. Peter, who was the apostle appointed by Christ to be the head of the Church. Whereas in the Protestant Churches prayer and preaching play a central part (each individual soul seeking direct communication with God), in Roman Catholic worship the central service is the Mass, or Holy Eucharist, the seven sacraments (baptism, confirmation, eucharist, penance, extreme unction, orders, and marriage) being administered by a special priesthood. Church discipline and organisation are strong and authoritarian. *See* **Papal Infallibility**.

Catholic Apostolic Church, a body of Christians which originated in England *c.* 1831, founded on the teaching of Edward Irving (d. 1834). They disapprove of the term "Irvingites" by which they are sometimes known. The common doctrines of Christianity are accepted; symbolism and mystery characterise the elaborate liturgy, and lights and incense are used.

Characterology, the attempt made over many centuries to classify people into personality types on the basis of physical or psychological characteristics. The first attempt was made by Hippocrates in the 5th cent. B.C. who classified temperaments into the *sanguine* (or optimistic), the *melancholic*, the *choleric* (or aggressive), and the *phlegmatic* (or placid); these were supposed to result from the predominance of the following "humours" in the body: red blood, black bile, yellow bile, or phlegm respectively. Theophrastus, a pupil of Aristotle, described, with examples, thirty extreme types of personality (*e.g.* the talkative, the boorish, the miserly, etc.); these were basically literary and imaginative but about the same time "physiognomy" arose which attempted to interpret character from the face. Physiognomy became of importance again during the Renaissance and there are still those today who believe in it in spite of the fact that, broadly speaking, there is no connection whatever between facial features and personality (*i.e.* although it may be possible to tell from the features that a man is an idiot or some extreme abnormal type and some idea of character may be obtained from an individual's characteristic facial expressions, it is not possible to tell (as Johann Lavater, the best-known physiognomist of the late 18th cent. believed) from the shape of the nose, height of the brow, or dominance of the lower jaw, whether anyone is weak, intellectual, or determined). The contention of the 19th cent. Italian criminologist Cesare Lombroso that criminals show typical facial characteristics—prominent cheekbones and jaw, slanting eyes, receding brow, large ears of a particular shape—was disproved by Karl Pearson early this century when he found that 3,000 criminals showed no significant differences of features, carefully measured, from a similar number of students at Oxford and Cambridge.

It has, however, been noted that people in general tend to be intellectual or emotional, inward- or outward-looking, and this observation is reflected in the classifications of the Scottish psychologist, Alexander Bain (d. 1903), into intellectual, artistic, and practical; Nietzsche's Apollonian and Dionysian types; William James's "tender" and "tough-minded"; and C. G. Jung's introvert and extrovert. Careful experiments have shown that these are not clear-cut and that most individuals fall in between the extremes.

Some connection has been found between temperament and body-build. Ernst Kretschmer (b. 1888) showed that manic-depressive patients and normal people who are extroverted and tend to alternate in mood (as do manic-depressives to an exaggerated degree) are usually short and stout or thick-set in build; schizophrenics and normal people, who both show shyness, serious or introverted reactions, are usually tall and slender. The former of "pyknic" body-build are "cyclothyme" in temperament, the latter with "schizothyme" temperament are of two bodily types—the tall and thin or "asthenic" and the muscularly well-proportioned or "athletic." The American Sheldon has confirmed these observations on the whole and gone into further details. Louis Berman has classified personalities according to the endocrine glands predominating: thus the "adrenal" type is vigorous and persistent, those whose adrenal glands are less active tend to become neurasthenic; the hyperthyroid type is restless, the subthyroid listless; the individual in whom the front part of the pituitary is active is masculine to a high degree, when the posterior pituitary is active he may show feminine traits. It is quite true that in disease of these glands such traits develop but most scientists agree that Berman is over-enthusiastic in his claims so far as normal people are concerned. *See also* **Q5(1)**.

Chartism, a socialistic movement in England (1837–55) which attempted to better the conditions of the working classes. Named after "The People's Charter" of Francis Place (1838), its programme demanded: (1) universal manhood suffrage; (2) vote by ballot; (3) equal electoral districts; (4) annual parliaments; (5) payment of members; (6) abolition of their property qualifications. Chartism was supported by the Christian socialists (*q.v.*), J. F. D. Maurice (1805–72), and Charles Kingsley (1819–75) with certain qualifications.

Chauvinism, a term applied to any excessive devotion to a cause, particularly a patriotic or military one. The word is derived from Nicholas Chauvin whose excessive devotion to Napoleon made him a laughing-stock.

Chirognomy, the attempt to read character from the lines in the hand (as contrasted with **Chiromancy**, the superstitious attempt to foretell the future in the same way) has few supporters, and not many psychologists would accept that handwriting reveals character in any way that is of practical use. It is highly probable that everything about an individual's acts or productions is *potentially* capable of revealing something about his character; the practical question is whether at present we can interpret them and it is ordinarily agreed that, in the case of the hand and handwriting, we cannot.

Christadelphians, a religious denomination formed in the U.S.A. about 1848 at the time of the American Civil War by John Thomas, an Englishman from London. They claim to represent the simple apostolic faith of the 1st cent., and, in common with many other sects, hold that they alone interpret the Scriptures truly. None but those who share their beliefs will rise from the dead and enjoy immortal life when Christ returns after the battle at Armageddon when His kingdom will be established on earth with its capital in Jerusalem. The political events of our time are regarded as fulfilments of biblical prophecies preceding the millennial reign of Christ over the earth. For them heaven and hell do not exist. In social life Christadelphians keep to themselves and hold aloof from organisational activities, though they do take an interest in political events if only from the point of view of their belief in biblical prophecy.

Christianity, the religion founded by Jesus Christ whose teaching is found in the New Testament's four Gospels. Simple as His creed may seem it soon became complicated by the various ways in which Christians interpreted it, and the differences within the early Church are reflected

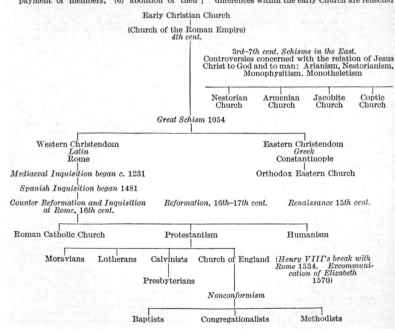

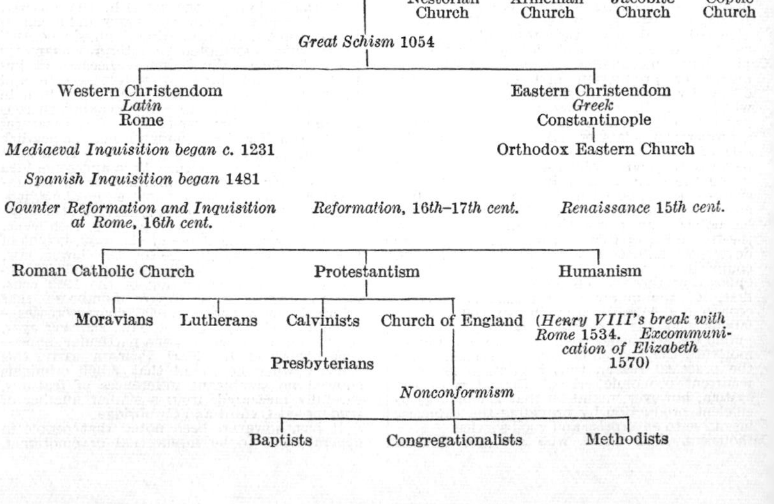

in the numerous Councils held to define truth from heresy. The Eastern Church of the Byzantine Empire from the 5th cent. onwards had differed in various ways from the See of Rome and by 1054 the breach became permanent. The 16th cent. Reformation was the other great break in the unity of the Church and once Protestantism had given in effect the right to each man to interpret the Scriptures in his own way, the tendency to fragmentation increased so that, by 1650, there were no fewer than 180 sects, mostly dogmatic and intolerant towards each other. Today there are many more, some of which are mentioned in this section under the appropriate headings. Nevertheless there are signs today that the trend of disunity is being reversed. The modern oecumenical movement, which has its roots in the great missionary movement of the 19th cent., aims to bring about a reunion of Christendom by uniting Christians throughout the world on the simple basis of the acceptance of Jesus Christ as God and Saviour, *i.e.*, on the basis of Christian fellowship. The movement finds expression in the World Council of Churches (*q.v.*). The Christian life is expressed in the words of Christ: "Thou shalt love the Lord thy God with all thy heart and thy neighbour as thyself."

Christian Democrats, a term describing the members of moderate Roman Catholic political parties existing under various names in Belgium, France, the German Federal Republic (most German Protestants are in East Germany), Italy, and the Netherlands. In several of these countries they are the largest parliamentary party, their platform being based on a programme of moderate social reform advocated by members who in many cases have been active in wartime resistant movements. In spite of efforts of Dr. Adenauer of Germany and Sr. Fanfari of Italy in 1955 a Christian Democratic International has failed to develop.

Christian Science, a religious denomination founded by Mary Baker Eddy (1821–1910), an American lady who sought to organise a church which would reinstate primitive Christianity and its lost element of healing. The sacred book of the movement is *Science and Health with Key to the Scriptures* published by Mrs. Eddy. Its main tenets are that nothing is real save God; that man's essential nature is spiritual and wholly good; that matter, evil, disease, and sickness are unreal—illusions of our mortal minds due to "wrong thinking." Therefore doctors, medicine, surgery and drugs are rejected as irrelevant, spiritual healing being the only cure for what is really mental error. Spiritual healing is claimed to have been brought about in many diseases by Mrs. Eddy herself, by the reading of her book, and, today, by Christian Science practitioners. The name of the movement is misleading since it has nothing to do with any of the natural sciences of which Mrs. Eddy had no first-hand knowledge. Mrs. Eddy was first interested in spiritualism, and afterwards, having been a patient of a faith-healer named Quimby, to whom she was indebted more than she cared to admit, she put herself forward as a mind-healer, claiming that she herself had been divinely healed. The denomination is apparently a wealthy one with widespread membership; its excellent newspaper, the *Christian Science Monitor*, read by many outside the movement, gives well-written accounts of all the world events we imagine to be going on around us.

Christian Socialism, a movement launched in 1848, a year of revolutions throughout the continent, by a group in England designed to commit the Church to a programme of social reform. The leaders, notably J. F. D. Maurice, Charles Kingsley (both Anglican clergymen), and John Ludlow were deeply moved by the wretched conditions of the British working class and the two priests had, indeed, given active support to the Chartist movement (*q.v.*). However, all insisted that socialism in its existing forms ignored the spiritual needs of mankind and must be tempered with Christianity. Tracts were written to expose the sweated industries, the consequences of unrestrained competition, and the evils following the enclosure system; but, more concretely, Christian socialism fostered co-operative workshops and distributive societies based on those of the Rochdale pioneers, organised a working-man's college and set up elementary classes for education, and supported the trade-union movement's right to organise and bargain for its members.

No longer an organised body today, Christian socialism acts through individuals who reject Marx's teaching of revolutionary change, and seek to bring it about by the methods of action through political parties, education, and encouragement of the unions. They believe that Christ's teachings can only be fully realised in a new society since Christianity implies social responsibility, and material factors are admitted to have an important bearing on the ability to lead a truly religious life. In the U.S.A. the eminent theologians Paul Tillich and Reinhold Niebuhr support these views and the Fellowship of Socialist Christians publishes quarterly *Christianity and Society* of which Niebuhr is editor. The factory-padre in Britain and the Catholic worker-priests of France bear evidence to the continuing influence of the early movement. The latter have been suspect by the Roman hierarchy whose official position is expressed in the papal encyclicals *Rerum Novarum* (1891) and *Quadragesimo Anno* (1931). These give no support to socialism in any form but reveal the Church's concern over industrial matters and labour problems.

Church of England. There is some evidence of possible continuity with the Christianity of Roman Britain, but in the main the Church derives from the fusion of the ancient Celtic church with the missionary church of St. Augustine, who founded the See of Canterbury in A.D. 597. To archbishop Theodore in 673 is ascribed its organisation in dioceses with settled boundaries, and in parishes. St. Augustine's church was in communion with Rome from the first, but the Church of England was not brought within papal jurisdiction until after the Norman conquest, and was at no time under the complete domination of Rome. It remains the Catholic Church of England without break of continuity, but during the Reformation the royal supremacy was accepted and that of the pope repudiated. It is the Established Church (*i.e.*, the official church of the realm), crowns the sovereign, and its archbishops and bishops in the House of Lords can act as a kind of "conscience of the state" at every stage of legislation. The policy of religious toleration has been accepted since the 16th cent. The Church is organised in two ecclesiastical provinces (Canterbury and York) and 43 dioceses. Its form of worship is embodied in the Book of Common Prayer, which was compiled in 1549.

The Anglican Communion comprises the churches in all parts of the world which are in communion with the Church of England. All the bishops of the Anglican Communion meet every ten years in the Lambeth Conference (last held in 1958), over which the Archbishop of Canterbury by custom presides as *primus inter pares*. The Conference has no legislative power, but in practice exercises great influence.

Church of Scotland, the established national church of Scotland, presbyterian in constitution, and governed by a hierarchy of courts—the kirk-sessions, the presbyteries, the synods, and the General Assembly. *See* **Presbyterianism.**

Clairvoyance. *See* **Telepathy.**

Communism, ideally refers to the type of society in which all property belongs to the community and social life is based on the principle "from each according to his ability, to each according to his needs." Since no such society as yet exists, the word in practice refers to the Communist Party's attempt to achieve such a society by initially overthrowing the capitalist system and establishing a dictatorship of the proletariat. The modern movement is based on Marxism as further developed by Lenin who applied Marx's analysis to the new conditions which had arisen in 20th cent. capitalist society. Noting the large trusts and combines which (according to the Marxian "theory of concentration") with their large concentrations of capital were ousting the small producers of an earlier stage, Lenin concluded that the state (representing the ruling class) and these large capital interests were collaborating in imperialist policies which would inevitably lead to recurrent wars; that the skilled worker would become more important and, receiving higher wages, would betray the proletariat by moving to the right; and that the poorer workers would continue to support revolutionary socialism. Communists believe that their first task is the establishment of socialism under which there remain class distinctions, private property to some extent, and differences between manual and brain workers. The state is regulated on the basis "from each according to his ability, to each according to his work." In time this gives place to communism as described above and the state will wither away. Marxism–Leninism develops continuously with practice since failure to apply its basic principles to changed circumstances and times would result in errors of dogmatism. Two fundamental principles of communism are (1) peaceful co-existence between countries of different social systems, and (2) the class struggle between oppressed and oppressing classes and between oppressed and oppressor nations. China, for example, holds that it is a mistake to lay one-sided stress on peaceful transition towards socialism otherwise the revolutionary will of the proletariat becomes passive and unprepared politically and organisationally for the tasks ahead. *See also* **Trotskyism.**

Confessional Church, Lutherans in Germany who, led by Pastor Niemöller (b. 1892), opposed those teachings of the Nazi regime which they found incompatible with Christianity.

Confucianism. Confucius (Latinised form of K'ung-Fu-tzu) was born in 551 B.C. in the feudal state of Lu in modern Shantung province. He was thus a contemporary of Buddha, although nobody could have been more dissimilar. Where Buddha was metaphysical in his thought, Confucius was practical; Buddha was original, Confucius had hardly an original idea in his head; Buddha wanted to convert individuals to an other-worldly philosophy, Confucius wanted to reform the feudal governments of his time, believing that in this way their subjects would be made happier. Other religions have, in their time, been revolutionary; Confucius was a conservative who wanted to bring back a golden age from the past. The only respect in which Confucius agreed with the Buddha was that neither was particularly interested in the supernatural, and God or gods played little part in their religions.

Much of his time was spent in going from the court of one feudal lord to another trying to impress them by his example. For he suffered from the curious belief that the example set by the ruler influences his subjects. He made much of etiquette, trembling and speaking in low tones before princes, at ease and polite with his equals, and behaving with "lofty courtesy" to his inferiors. Promoting the idea of "the golden mean," he was not impressed by heroic deeds or unusual people, and was greatly displeased when he heard that a truthful son had reported that his father had stolen a sheep: "Those who are upright," he said, "are different from this; the father conceals the misconduct of the son, and the son conceals the misconduct of the father." One feels that Confucius would have felt not at all out of place in an English public school. Virtue brings its own reward in this world, ceremonial is important, politeness when universal would reduce jealousy and quarrels; "reverence the spirits but keep them far off." Destiny decides to what class a man shall belong, and as destiny is but another name for Nature prayer is unnecessary, for once having received his destiny, a man can demand and obtain from Nature what he chooses—his own will determines all things.

Although not very successful in his lifetime so far as the rulers were concerned, Confucius found numerous disciples before his death at the age of 70 who collected his teachings which are found, together with those of his later follower Mencius (372–289 B.C.), in the *Wu Ching* (five classics), and the *Shih Shu* (four books) which contain the Analects, The Great Learning, The Doctrine of the Mean, and the Book of Mencius. In time Confucianism became with Taoism and Buddhism one of the main religions in China. Unlike Buddhism it had little influence elsewhere.

Congregationalists, the oldest sect of Nonconformists who hold that each church should be independent of external ecclesiastical authority. They took their origin from the Brownists of Elizabeth's days. Robert Browne (*c.* 1550–*c.* 1633), an Anglican clergyman, who had come to reject bishops, was forced with his followers to seek refuge, first in Holland and then in Scotland where he was imprisoned by the Kirk. In later life he changed his views and is disowned by Congregationalists because of his reversion to Anglicanism. His former views were spread by Henry Barrow and John Greenwood who, under an Act passed in 1592 "for the punishment of persons obstinately refusing to come to church" (and largely designed for the suppression of this sect), were hanged at Tyburn. They had preached (*a*) that the only head of the church is Jesus Christ; (*b*) that, contrary to Elizabethan doctrine, the church had no relationship to the state; (*c*) that the only statute-book was the Bible whereas the Articles of Religion and the Common Prayer were mere Acts of Parliament; (*d*) that each congregation of believers was independent and had the power of choosing its own ministers. The body fled once more to Holland and were among the Pilgrims who set sail in the *Mayflower* for America in 1620 whilst those who remained were joined by Puritans fleeing from Charles I. They became free once more to live in England under the Commonwealth only to be repressed again under Charles II. Finally full liberty of worship was granted under William III. In 1833 the Congregational Union of England and Wales was formed which has no legislative power. It has issued a Declaration of Faith by which no minster is bound; he is responsible to his own church and to nobody else. The sect is widespread both in Britain and the U.S.A. where it is held in special honour because of its connection with the Pilgrim Fathers.

Conservatism. The name "Conservative" came into general use after 1834 in place of the older name of "Tory," although "Tory democracy" is now widely used to describe Conservative social reform policy. Originally the party of the aristocracy and landed gentry, Conservatism has been supported from the end of the 19th cent. by the large business interests, and more recently by lower-income groups in the population. Although originally based upon the teachings of Burke and Disraeli, Conservative doctrine has been considerably modified, especially since 1945 after defeat by the socialists. The Party's industrial policy seeks to reconcile the need for central direction with encouragement of individual enterprise, best described perhaps as "welfare capitalism." The Conservatives increased their parliamentary strength in three successive general elections from 1951–59, but were defeated by Labour in 1964. On the continent, Conservatism has generally been identified with fear of social progress, exaggerated respect for authority, and nationalism; such parties have more often than not been extremely reactionary and anti-democratic. *See also* **Section C, Part I.**

Coptic Church, the sect of Egyptian Christians who, holding "Monophysite" opinions (*i.e.*, refusing to grant the two natures, God and Man, of Christ), were declared heretical by the Council of Chalcedon in 451. Their practice of circumcision and their language may derive from the religion of ancient Egypt, but otherwise they, like the Armenians, are regarded as heretical branches of Eastern Christianity. Their patriarch is at Alexandria.

Cynics, a school of philosophy founded in the time of Alexander the Great by Diogenes. Choosing to live like a dog by rejecting all conventions of religion, manners, or decency, and allegedly living in a tub, Diogenes unwittingly brought on his school the title "Cynic," meaning not "cynical," as the word is understood today but "canine." His teacher, Antisthenes, who had been a disciple of Socrates, decided, after the latter's death, that all philosophy was useless quibbling and man's sole aim should be simple goodness. He believed in a return t nature, despised luxury, wanted no government, no private property, and associated with working men and slaves. Far from being cynics in the modern sense, Diogenes and Antisthenes were virtuous anarchists rather like old Tolstoy (except that in the practice of their beliefs they were more consistent).

D

Darwinism. *See* **Section F, Part II.** *See also* **Vitalism.**

Deism. *See* **God and Man.**

Demonism, Demons, and the Devil. Demons are ethereal beings of various degrees of significance and power which are believed to be implicated in men's good, but especially evil, fortune. They are common to most cultures. From the anthropological point of view the demon arose as a widespread concept in the following ways: (1) as a psychological projection into the outer world of man's own good or evil emotions and thoughts; (2) as a survival of primitive animism (*q.v.*), thus spirits are believed to haunt places, trees, stones, and other natural objects; (3) when by warlike invasion the gods of the vanquished become the devils of the conquerors (as when the Jews occupied Canaan); (4) as a primitive belief that spirits of the dead continue after death to hover near their former habitation, and not always entirely welcome to the living; (5) the conception of a supreme source of evil (the Devil or Satan) which took shape among the Jews during their sojourn in Babylon under the influence of Zoroastrianism (*q.v.*), a religion in which the struggle between the two spirits, Good and Evil, reached its height in the imagination of the ancient world. The Satan of the Old Testament was first regarded as one of God's servants (in the Book of Job he goes up and down the earth to see whether God's commands are obeyed), but when the Jews returned from their captivity he had become identified with Ahriman, the spirit of evil, who was in continual conflict with Ahura Mazda, the spirit of good. As Dr. Margaret Murray has pointed out, the primitive mind ascribed both good and evil to one power alone; the division into God and the Devil, priest and witch, belongs to a higher stage of civilisation. *See also* **Witchcraft, Magic.**

Determinism and Free-will. The question of whether man is, or is not, free to mould his own destiny is one which has exercised the minds of philosophers since Greek mythology conceived of the Fates as weaving a web of destiny from which no man can free himself. Socrates emphasised that man could through knowledge influence his destiny whilst ignorance made him the plaything of fate; Plato went further in pointing out that man can, and does, defeat the purposes of the universe and its divine Creator. It is our duty to live a good life, but we can live a foolish and wicked one if we choose. Aristotle wrote " Virtue is a disposition or habit involving deliberate purpose or choice." If this were not so morality would be a sham.

The Problem for Theology. The last of the great philosophers of antiquity and one of the great influences in moulding Catholic theology was Plotinus (*c.* 204–270). Soul, he taught, is free, but once enmeshed in the body loses its freedom in the life of sense. Nevertheless, man is free to turn away from sensuality and towards God who is perfect freedom; for even when incarnated in matter the soul does not entirely lose the ability to rescue itself. This conception was carried over into the beliefs of the Early Christian Apologists because it appeared to be in line with the teaching of Jesus that He had come to save man from sin. Sin implies guilt, and guilt implies the freedom to act otherwise; furthermore an all-good God cannot be responsible for the sin in the world which must be man's responsibility and this again implies freedom. Pelagius (*c.* 355–*c.* 425), a Welsh priest, not only believed in freewill but, questioning the doctrine of original sin, said that when men act righteously it is through their own moral effort, and God rewards them for their virtues in heaven. This belief became fairly widespread and was declared a heresy by the Church, being attacked notably by St. Augustine (354–430), a contemporary of Pelagius, who believed in predestination—that, since the sin of Adam, God had chosen who in all future history would be saved and who damned. This represents one tradition in Christianity: the determinism which leads to Calvinism (*q.v.*). St. Thomas Aquinas (1227–74), the greatest figure of scholasticism and one of the principal saints in the Roman Catholic Church, compromised between the two positions in the sense that, believing man to be free, he yet held that Adam's sin was transmitted to all mankind and only divine grace can bring salvation. But even when God wishes to bestow this salvation, the human will must cooperate. God foresees that some will not accept the offer of grace and predestines them to eternal punishment.

The Problem for Philosophy. With the Renaissance, thinkers began to free themselves from the domination of the Church and to study the world objectively and freely without preconceptions. But the more man turned to science, the more he discovered that the world was ruled by apparently inexorable laws and, since the scientist must believe that every event has a cause, he was led back to determinism. Man as part of the universe was subject to law too and all that existed was a vast machine. Francis Bacon (1561–1626) separated the fields of religion and science but left man subject completely to the will of God. Thomas Hobbes (1588–1679) was a rigid determinist and materialist although, having had trouble with the church in France whence, as a royalist, he had fled, he took care to announce that the Christian God is the Prime Mover.

Modern philosophy begins with René Descartes (1596–1650), a Frenchman who tried to reconcile the mechanical scientific universe of his time with the spiritual need for freedom. He did this by separating completely mind and body; the former, he said, is free, the latter completely determined. But, by admitting that the will can produce states of body, he was left with the problem of how this could happen—a problem which the so-called Occasionists solved to their own satisfaction by stating that the will is free and God so arranges the universe that what a person wills happens. Baruch Spinoza (1632–77), a Dutch Jew whose independence of thought had led to his excommunication from the Amsterdam Synagogue in 1656, was a complete determinist. He asserted that God and Nature are one, everything that happens is a manifestation of God's inscrutable nature, and it is logically impossible that things could be other than they are. Thus both Hobbes and Spinoza were determinists for entirely opposed reasons. The former as a materialist, the latter because he believed in the absolute perfection and universality of God. Yet the great religious mystic and mathematician Blaise Pascal (1623–62) held that, no matter what reason and cold logic may indicate, we *know* from direct religious experience that we are free. John Calvin (1509–64) and Martin Luther (1483–1546) were both determinists. *See* **Calvinism, Lutheranism.**

To the more practical British philosophers, John Locke (1632–1704) and David Hume (1711–76), free-will was related to personality. Locke believed that God had implanted in each individual certain desires and these determine the will; the desires are already there, but we use our will to satisfy them. Hume argued that a man's behaviour is the necessary result of his character and if he had a different character he would act otherwise. Accordingly, when a man's actions arise from his own nature and desires he is free. He is not free when external events compel him to act otherwise (*e.g.*, if he strikes another because his own nature is such he is free as he is not if he is compelled to do so against his desire). Leibnitz (1646–1716), although as a German metaphysical philosopher holding very different general views, said much the same thing—that choice is simply selecting the desire that is strongest. But most of the 18th cent. from Voltaire onwards, with the great exceptions of Rousseau and the later German philosophers Kant, Fichte, Schopenhauer, and Hegel, who were initially influenced by him.

accepted determinism. Rousseau (1712–78) began to stem the tide by his declaration that man is a free soul striving to remain free and only prevented from being so by society and the cold science which stifles his feeling heart. Once again the will became important as Kant (1724–1804) asserted that belief in freedom is a moral necessity although it cannot be proved by reason; the moral nature of man shows that there is a "transcendental" world beyond the senses where freedom applies. Fichte and Schelling found freedom in the Absolute ego or God of whom each individual was part and thus also free. Hegel (1770–1831) saw the whole universe as evolving towards self-awareness and freedom in man although this could only be fully realised in a society that makes for freedom. Even God himself only attains full consciousness and self-realisation through the minds of such individuals as are free. This is the goal of the dialectical process. (*See* **Dialectical Materialism.**)

The Scientist's View. For the scientist the law of cause and effect is a useful hypothesis since, by and large, it is necessary for him to assume that all events are caused. Nevertheless the modern tendency is to think in terms of statistical probability rather than relentless mechanistic causality, and, although the free-will problem does not concern the scientist as such, it is clear that freedom and determinism (assuming the terms to have any meaning at all) are not necessarily opposed. In sociology, for example, we *know* that certain actions will produce certain results upon the behaviour of people in general, *e.g.*, that raising the bank rate will discourage business expansion. But this does not mean that Mr. Brown who decides in the circumstances not to add a new wing to his factory is not using his free-will. Even in the case of atoms, as Dr. Bronowski has pointed out, the observed results of allowing gas under pressure in a cylinder to rush out occur because most of the atoms are "obeying" the scientific "law" relating to such situations. But this does not mean that some atoms are not busy rushing across the stream or even against it—they are, but the general tendency is outwards and that is what we note. Lastly, the modern philosophical school of Logical Analysis would probably ask, not whether Free-will or Determinism is the true belief, but whether the question has any meaning. For what scientific experiment could we set up to prove one or the other true? The reader will note that some of the philosophers mentioned above are using the words to mean quite different concepts.

Dialectical Materialism, the combination of Hegel's dialectic method with a materialist philosophy produced by Karl Marx (1818–83) and his friend Friedrich Engels (1820–95). It is the philosophical basis of **Marxism** (*q.v.*) and **Communism** (*q.v.*). "Dialectic" to the ancient Greek philosophers meant a kind of dialogue or conversation, as used particularly by Socrates, in which philosophical disputes were resolved by a series of successive contradictions: a thesis is put forward and the opposing side holds its contradiction or antithesis until in the course of argument a synthesis is reached in which the conflicting ideas are resolved.

From Thesis through Antithesis to Synthesis. Hegel in the 19th cent. put forward the view that this process applies to the course of nature and history as they strive towards the perfect state. But to him, as to the Greeks, the conflict was in the field of ideas. The "universal reason" behind events works through the ideas held by a particular society until they are challenged by those of another which supersedes them and in turn, usually by war, becomes the agent of universal reason until the arrival of a new challenger. Hegel therefore regarded war as an instrument of progress and his Prussian compatriots found no difficulty in identifying their own state as the new agent of progress by universal conquest. Feuerbach, Lassalle, and other early socialists were impressed by some of Hegel's ideas: *e.g.*, that societies evolved (with the assumption that finally their own ideal society would be achieved) and that truth, morals, and concepts were relative so that a type of society that was "good" at one time was not necessarily so at another. But Marx and Engels in effect turned Hegel upside-down, accepted his dialectic but rejected his belief that ideas were the motive force. On the contrary, they said, ideas are determined by social and economic change as a result of materialistic forces. (*See* **Calvinism,** where it is pointed out that the Marxist view is not that Calvin changed men's economic ideas but rather that a developing capitalism unconsciously changed his.) The historical materialism of Marxism purports to show that the inexorable dialectic determines that feudalism is displaced by capitalism and capitalism by creating a proletariat (its antithesis) inevitably leads to socialism and a classless society. The state, as a tool of the dominant class, withers away. Dialectical materialism is applied in all spheres. As a philosophy there is little to be said for it save that it has shown us the close dependence of man's thoughts upon current material and social conditions. But as a battle-cry or a rationalisation of Marxism it wields immense power over the minds of men. *See* **Marxism.**

Diggers, one of the many sects which flourished under the Commonwealth (others were the Muggletonians, the Levellers, the Millenarians, and the Fifth Monarchy Men), so-called because they attempted to dig (*i.e.* cultivate) untilled land. Gerrard Winstanley, a profoundly religious man, and leader of the Diggers, believed in the economic and social equality of man and castigated the clergy for upholding the class structure of society. In his book *The True Leveller's Standard Advanced* (1649) he wrote: "Every day poor people are forced to work for fourpence a day, though corn is dear. And yet the tithing priest stops their mouth and tells them that 'inward satisfaction of mind' was meant by the declaration 'the poor shall inherit the earth'. I tell you, the Scripture is to be really and materially fulfilled. You jeer at the name 'Leveller'; I tell you Jesus Christ is the Head Leveller."

Disciples of Christ, a Protestant religious group founded in the United States early in the 19th century by Thomas Campbell, a Scot, his son Alexander, and Barton Warren Stone who had broken away from the Presbyterian church. The basis for faith and conduct is the Bible itself, each individual interpreting it for himself. The group has always had a liberal reputation and stands for racial equality and Christian unity. The Disciples of Christ Church is particularly strong in the central and western states of America.

Docetists, a Gnostic sect (*q.v.*) during the early centuries of Christianity who believed that, since it was unworthy that the Son of God should have died a humiliating death on the cross, the entity that was crucified was a mere phantom. Mohammed, who believed in Jesus as a prophet but not as divine, adopted these views. The heretical Albigenses were influenced by Docetism, Gnosticism, and Manichaeism (*qq.v.*).

Doukhobors, a religious sect of Russian origin, founded by a Prussian sergeant at Kharkov in the middle of the 18th cent., and now mainly settled in Canada. Like many other sects they belong to that type of Christianity which seeks direct communication with God and such bodies tend to have certain traits in common such as belief in the "inner light," opposition to war and authority in general, and often ecstasies which show themselves in physical ways such as shaking, speaking in strange tongues (glossolalia), and other forms of what to the unbeliever seem mass hysteria. Liturgy, ritual, or ceremony is non-existent. The Doukhobors were persecuted in Tsarist Russia, but in 1898 Tolstoy used his influence to have them removed to Canada where the government granted them uninhabited land in what is now Saskatchewan and seven or eight thousand settled down in peace which they enjoyed for many years. Recently, however, their practices have caused difficulties once more; for even the most tolerant government which is prepared to accept pacifism, total dependence on communally-owned agriculture, refusal to engage in commerce non-payment of taxes, rejection of the marriage ceremony and separation "when love ceases," finds it difficult to tolerate, as civilisation advances ever closer to Doukhobor communities, their proneness to " put off these troublesome disguises which we wear "—*i.e.*, to walk about naked in the communities of their more orthodox neighbours. What the future of the Doukhobors in their various sects (for even they have their differences) will be it is impossible to say, but it is difficult to believe that these simple people can long resist the pressure of modern civilisation.

Druidism, the religion of Celtic Britain and Gaul of which Druids were the priesthood. They were finally wiped out by the Roman general Suetonius Paulinus about A.D. 58 in their last stronghold, the island of Anglesey. There are two sources of our present beliefs in Druidism: (1) the brief and factual records of the Romans, notably Pliny and Julius Caesar, which tell us that they worshipped in sacred oak groves and presumably practised a religion doing reverence to the powers of nature which must have had its roots in early stone age times and had many cruel rites *e.g.*, human sacrifice; (2) the beliefs put forward by William Stukeley, an amateur antiquarian who from 1718 did valuable work by his studies of the stone circles at Stonehenge and Avebury. However, influenced by the Romantic movement, he later put forward the most extravagant theories which unfortunately are those popularly accepted by those without archaelogical knowledge today. Stonehenge and Avebury were depicted as the temples of the " white-haired Druid bard sublime " and an attempt was made to tie up Druidism with early Christianity, above all with the concept of the Trinity. In fact, these circles have no connection with the Druids. They may have made ceremonial use of them but recent evidence suggests that the megalithic stones at Stonehenge (**L109**) belong to a Bronze Age culture (1860–1560 B.C.). Nor have Druidism and Christianity any relationship. Almost nothing is known of the religion. Yet such were its romantic associations that, even today, one hears of " Druidic " ceremonies practised at the appropriate time of year on Primrose Hill in the heart of London (though whether seriously or with tongue in cheek one does not know).

Dualism, any philosophical or theological theory which implies that the universe has a double nature, notably Plato's distinction between appearance and reality, soul and body, ideas and material objects, reason and the evidence of the senses, which infers that behind the world as we perceive it there lies an " ideal " world which is more " real " than that of mere appearance. In religions such as **Zoroastrianism** or the **Gnostic** and **Manichaeism** heresies (*qq.v.*), it was believed that the universe was ruled by good and evil " principles "—in effect that there was a good God and a bad one. In psychology, dualism refers to the philosophical theories which believe mind and body to be separate entities. The opposite of dualism is monism which asserts the essential unity of the substance of the universe.

E

Education. Education was no great problem to primitive man, but as societies became more complex people began to ask themselves such questions as: *What* should young people be taught? *How* should they be taught? Should the aim of their education be to bring out their individual qualities or rather to make them good servants of the state?

The first teachers were priests who knew most about the traditions, customs, and lore of their societies and thus the first schools were in religious meeting places. This was notably true of the Jews who learned from the rabbis in the synagogue, and throughout the Middle Ages in Christendom as will be seen later.

The Greeks. We begin, as always, with the Greeks whose city-states, based on slavery, educated men (not women) for the sort of life described in Plato's *Dialogues*—the leisured life of gentlemen arguing the problems of the universe at their banquets or in the market-place. This made it necessary to learn debate and oratory (or rhetoric) especially for those who proposed to take up politics. The Sophist philosophy taught the need to build up convincing arguments in a persuasive manner, to learn the rules of logic and master the laws and customs of the Athenians, and to know the literature of the past so that illustrations might be drawn from it. These strolling philosophers who taught for a fee were individualists showing the student how to advance himself at all costs within his community.

Socrates had a more ethical approach, believing that education was good in itself, made a man happier and a better citizen, and emphasised his position as a member of a group. His method of teaching, the dialectic or "Socratic" method, involved argument and discussion rather than overwhelming others by rhetoric and is briefly mentioned under **Dialectical Materialism** (*q.v.*). Today this method is increasingly used in adult education where a lecture is followed by a period of discussion in which both lecturer and audience participate; for psychologists have shown that people accept ideas more readily when conviction arises through their own arguments than when they are passively thrust down their throats.

Socrates' pupil Plato produced in his book *The Republic* one of the first comprehensive systems of education and vocational selection. Believing that men are of different and unequal abilities he considered that they should be put into social classes corresponding to these differences, and suggested the following method: (1) For the first 18 years of a boy's life he should be taught gymnastics and sports, playing and singing music, reading and writing, a knowledge of literature, and if he passed this course sent on to the next stage; those who failed were to become tradesmen and merchants. (2) From 18–20 those successful in the first course were to be given two years of cadet training, the ones thought incapable of further education being placed in the military class as soldiers. (3) The remainder, who were to become the leaders of society, proceeded with advanced studies in philosophy, mathematics, science, and art. Such education was to be a state concern, state supported and controlled, selecting men and training them for service in the state according to their abilities.

Plato's pupil Aristotle even suggested that the state should determine shortly after birth which children should be allowed to live and destroy the physically or mentally handicapped; that marriage should be state-controlled to ensure desirable offspring. However, in their time the leisured and individualistic Sophists held the field and few accepted the educational views of Plato or his pupil.

Rome. The Romans were not philosophers and most of their culture came from Greece. Administration was their chief aptitude and Quintilian (A.D. *c.* 35–*c.* 95) based his higher education on the earlier classical tuition in public speaking, but he is important for emphasising the training of character and for his humanistic approach to the method of teaching that caused his *Institutio oratoria* to be influential for centuries later—indeed one might almost say up to the time of the great Dr. Arnold of Rugby. Education, he believed, should begin early but one must " take care that the child not old enough to love his studies does not come to hate them " by premature forcing; studies must be made pleasant and interesting and students encouraged by praise rather than discouraged when they sometimes fail; play is to be approved of as a sign of a lively disposition and because gloomy, depressed children are not likely to be good students; corporal punishment should never be used because " it is an insult as you will realise if you imagine it yourself." The world became interested not in *what* he taught but *how* he taught it; he was the pioneer of humanistic education and character-training from Vittorino da Feltre (1378–1446) of Mantua, through Milton and Pope who commended his works, to the modern educationists who have studied their pupils as well as their books.

The Middle Ages: The Religious View. With the development of Christianity education once more became a religious problem. The earliest converts had to be taught Christian doctrine and were given instruction in "catechumenal" schools before admission to the group, but as the religion came increasingly into contact with other religions or heresies a more serious training was necessary, and from these newer "catechetical" schools, where the method used was the catechism (*i.e.*, question and answer as known to all Presbyterian children today), the Apologists arose among whom were Clement of Alexandria and the great Origen. From this time education became an instrument of the church and in 529 the Emperor Justinian ordered all pagan schools to be closed.

As typical of the best in mediaeval education whilst the lamp of civilisation burned low during the Dark Ages, after the fall of Roman power, and survived only in the monasteries, we may mention St. Benedict (*c.* 480–*c.* 547) of Monte Cassino. There, in southern Italy, a rule was established which became a part of monastic life in general. Monastic schools were originally intended for the training of would-be monks, but later others were admitted who simply wanted some education; thus two types of school developed, one for the *interni* and the other for *externi* or external pupils. Originally studies were merely reading in order to study the Bible, writing to copy the sacred books, and sufficient calculation to be able to work out the advent of holy days or festivals. But by the end of the 6th cent. the "seven liberal arts" (grammar, rhetoric, dialectic, arithmetic, geometry, music, and astronomy) were added.

The Renaissance. The close of the Middle Ages saw the development of two types of secular school. One came with the rise of the new merchant class and the skilled trader whose "guilds" or early trade unions established schools to train young men for their trades but ultimately gave rise to burgher or town schools; the other was the court school founded and supported by the wealthy rulers of the Italian cities—Vittorino da Feltre (mentioned above) presided over the most famous at Mantua.

These Renaissance developments are paralleled in northern Europe by the Protestant reformers who, having with Martin Luther held that everyone should know how to read his Bible in order to interpret it in his own way, were logically committed to popular education, compulsory and universal. In theory this was intended for biblical study, but writing, arithmetic, and other elementary subjects were taught and Luther said that, even if heaven and hell did not exist, education was important. Universal education is a Protestant conception.

Views of Philosophers. From this period onwards people were free to put forward any ideas about education, foolish or otherwise, and to create their own types of school. Of English philosophers who theorised about, but did not practise, education we may mention the rationalist Francis Bacon (1561–1626) who saw learning as the dissipation of all prejudices and the collection of concrete facts; the materialist and totalitarian Hobbes (1588–1679) who, as a royalist, believed that the right to determine the kind of education fit for his subjects is one of the absolute rights of the sovereign power or ruler; the gentlemanly Locke (1632–1704) whose ideal was a sound mind in a sound body to be attained by hard physical exercise, wide experience of the world, and enough knowledge to meet the requirements of the pupil's environment. The end result would be one able to get on with his fellows, pious but wise in the ways of the world, independent and able to look after himself, informed but reticent about his knowledge. Classics and religious study were not to be carried to excess, since Locke held that these subjects had been overrated in the past. Locke's pupil was the well-to-do, civilised young man of the 17th cent. who knew how to behave in society.

Jean-Jacques Rousseau (1712–78) was a forerunner of the Romantic movement which despised society and put emotion at a higher level than reason. His book *Emile* describes the education of a boy which is natural and spontaneous. Society, he holds, warps the growing mind and therefore the child should be protected from its influences until his development in accordance with his own nature is so complete that he cannot be harmed by it. During the first 4 years the body should be developed by physical training; from 5 to 12 the child would live in a state of nature such that he could develop his powers of observation and his senses; from 13 books would be used and intellectual training introduced, although only in line with the child's own interests, and he would be given instruction only as he came to ask for it. Moral training and contact with his fellows to learn the principles of sympathy, kindness, and helpfulness to mankind would be given between 15 and 20. Girls, however, should be educated to serve men in a spirit of modesty and restraint.

Summary. Broadly speaking, then, there have been four main attitudes to education: (1) religious, with a view to a life beyond death; (2) state-controlled education, with a view to uniform subservience to authority; (3) "gentlemanly" education, with a view to social graces and easy congress in company; (4) the "child-centred" education, which attempts to follow the pupil's inner nature. It is unnecessary to mention the ordinary method of attempting to instil facts without any considerable degree of co-operation between pupil and teacher in order that the former may, with or without interest, follow some occupation in adult life; for this the philosophers did not consider. Today there remain the two fundamental principles: education for the advantage of the state and its ideology or education for individual development and freedom.

Four educationists of the modern period who have influenced us in the direction of freedom were Johann Pestalozzi of Switzerland (1746–1827) who, by trying to understand children, taught the "natural, progressive, and harmonious development of all the powers and capacities of the human being"; Friedrich Froebel (1782–1852) of Germany, the founder of the Kindergarten who, like Pestalozzi, was influenced by Rousseau but realised the need to combine complete personal development with social adjustment; Maria Montessori (1869–1952) whose free methods have revolutionised infant teaching; John Dewey (1859–1952) who, as philosopher and educationist, held that the best interests of the group are served when the individual develops his own particular talents and nature.

Eleatics, the philosophers of Elea in ancient Greece who, at the time when Heraclitus (*c.* 535–475 B.C.) was teaching that change is all that exists and nothing is permanent, were asserting that change is an illusion. Of the three leaders of this school, Xenophanes asserted that the universe was a solid immovable mass forever the same; Parmenides explained away change as an inconceivable process, its appearance being due to the fact that what we see is unreal; and Zeno (the best-known today) illustrated the same thesis with his famous argument of the arrow which, at any given moment of its flight, must be where it is since it cannot be where it is not. But if it is where it is, it cannot move; this is based, of course, on the delusion that motion is discontinuous. The Eleatics were contemporaries of Socrates.

Empiricism. While not a single school of philosophy, empiricism is an approach to knowledge which holds that if a man wants to know what the universe is like the only correct way to do so is to go and look for himself, to collect facts which come to him through his senses. It is, in essence, the method of science as contrasted with rationalism (*q.v.*) which in philosophy implies that thinking or reasoning without necessarily referring to external observations can arrive at truth. Empiricism is typically an English attitude, for among the greatest empirical philosophers were John Locke, George Berkeley, and David Hume. *See* **Rationalism.**

Epicureanism. The two great schools of the Hellenistic period (*i.e.* the late Greek period beginning with the empire of Alexander the Great) were the Stoics and Epicureans, the former founded by Zeno of Citium (*not* to be confused with Zeno the Eleatic) (*q.v.*), the latter by Epicurus, born in Samos in

342 B.C. Both schools settled in Athens, where Epicurus taught that "pleasure is the beginning and end of a happy life." However, he was no sensualist and emphasised the importance of moderation in all things because excesses would lead to pain instead of pleasure and the best of all pleasures were mental ones. Pleasures could be active or passive but the former contain an element of pain since they are the process of satisfying desires not yet satiated. The latter involving the absence of desire are the more pleasant. In fact, Epicurus in his personal life was more stoical than many Stoics and wrote "when I live on bread and water I spit on luxurious pleasures." He disapproved of sexual enjoyment and thought friendship one of the highest of all joys. A materialist who accepted the atomic theory of Democritus, he was not a determinist, and if he did not disbelieve in the gods he regarded religion and the fear of death as the two primary sources of unhappiness.

Epiphenomenalism. *See* **Mind and Body.**

Erastianism, the theory that the state has the right to decide the religion of its members, wrongly attributed to Erastus of Switzerland (1524–83) who was believed to have held this doctrine. The term has usually been made use of in a derogatory sense—*e.g.*, by the Scottish churches which held that the "call" of the congregation was the only way to elect ministers at a time when, about the turn of the 17th and 18th cent., they felt that Episcopalianism was being foisted on them. "Episcopalianism" (*i.e.* Anglicanism) with its state church, ecclesiastical hierarchy, and system of livings presented by patrons was to them "Erastian" in addition to its other "unscriptural practices."

Essenes, a Jewish sect which, during the oppressive rule of Herod (d. 4 B.C.), set up monastic communities in the region of the Dead Sea. They refused to be bound by the scriptural interpretations of the Pharisees and adhered rigorously to the letter of Holy Writ, although with additions of their own which cause them by orthodox Jews today to be regarded as a break-away from Judaism. Among their practices and beliefs were purification through baptism, renunciation of sexual pleasures, scrupulous cleanliness, strict observance of the Mosaic law, communal possession, asceticism. Akin in spirit, although not necessarily identical with them, were the writers of Apocalyptic literature preaching that the evils of the present would shortly be terminated by a new supernatural order heralded by a Messiah who would reign over a restored Israel. The casting out of demons and spiritual healing formed part of these general beliefs which were in the air at that time. The sect has an importance far beyond its size or what has been known about it in the past since the discovery from 1947 onwards of the Dead Sea Scrolls (*See* **Section L**) of the Qumran community occupying a monastery in the same area as the Essenes and holding the same type of belief. These scrolls with their references to a "Teacher of Righteousness" preceding the Messiah have obvious relevance to the sources of early Christianity and have given rise to speculations as to whether Jesus might have been influenced by views which, like His own, were unacceptable to orthodox Jews but in line with those of the Dead Sea communities. At the very least they seem to show that early Christianity was not a sudden development but a gradual one which had its predecessors.

Ethical Church, a movement typical of 19th cent. rationalism which attempted to combine atheism (or at any rate the absence of any belief in a God which was inconsistent with reason or based on revelation) with the inculcation of moral principles. Prayers were not used and ordinarily the service consisted in the singing of edifying compositions interspersed with readings from poems or prose of a similar nature by great writers holding appropriate views. It terminated in a talk on an ethical or scientific theme. There is an Ethical Church in London and the South Place Institution where Moncure Conway preached from 1864 to 1897 still exists.

Ethnocentrism, the exaggerated tendency to think the characteristics of one's own group or race superior to those of any others.

Evangelicanism, the belief of those Protestant sects which hold that the essence of the Gospel consists in the doctrine of salvation by faith in the atoning death of Christ and not by good works or the sacraments; that worship should be "free" rather than liturgical through established forms; that ritual is unacceptable and superstitious. Evangelicals are Low Churchmen. The Lutheran Church of Germany, formerly the Evangelical Church, was reorganised after the war and freed from state control. It is now called the Evangelical United Brethren Church.

Evangelism, the preaching of the Gospel, emphasising the necessity for a new birth or conversion. The evangelistic fervour of John Wesley and George Whitefield (*see* Methodism) aroused the great missionary spirit of the late 18th and 19th cent. George Fox, founder of the Society of Friends (*q.v.*), was also an evangelist. Evangelists can be Low, High, or Middle Churchmen.

Existentialism, a highly subjective philosophy which many people connect with such names as Jean-Paul Sartre (b. 1905) or Albert Camus (1913–60) and assume to be a post-war movement associated with disillusion and a sordid view of life. However, existentialism stems from Sören Kierkegaard (1813–55), the Danish "religious writer"—his own description of himself—in such works as *Either/Or*, *Fear and Trembling*, and *Concluding Unscientific Postscript*. Between the two wars translations of Kierkegaard into German influenced Martin Heidegger's (b. 1889) great work *Being and Time* and the other great existentialist Karl Jaspers (b. 1883); it has strongly influenced modern Protestant theology notably in Karl Barth, Reinhold Niebuhr, and Paul Tillich and beyond that field Gabriel Marcel (b. 1887), the Spanish writer Unamuno (1864–1936) in his well-known *The Tragic Sense of Life*, and Martin Buber of Israel (b. 1878) in his *I and Thou*. We have it on Heidegger's authority that "Sartre is no philosopher" even if it is to his works that modern existentialists often turn.

Existentialism is extremely difficult for the non-metaphysically-minded to understand; it deals, not with the nature of the universe or what are ordinarily thought of as philosophical problems but describes an attitude to life or God held by the individual. Briefly, its main essentials are: (1) it distinguishes between *essence*, *i.e.*, that aspect of an entity which can be observed and known—and its *existence*—the fact of its having a place in a changing and dangerous world which is what really matters; (2) existence being basic, each self-aware individual can grasp his own existence on reflection in his own immediate experience of himself and his situation as a free being in the world; what he finds is not merely a knowing self but a self that fears, hopes, believes, wills, and is aware of its need to find a purpose, plan, and destiny in life; (3) but we cannot grasp our existence by thought alone; thus the fact "all men must die" relates to the essence of man but it is necessary to be involved, to draw the conclusion as a person that "I too must die" and experience its impact on our own individual existence; (4) because of the preceding, it is necessary to abandon our attitude of objectivity and theoretical detachment when faced by the problems relating to the ultimate purpose of our own life and the basis of our own conduct; life remains closed to those who take no part in it because it can have no significance; (5) it follows that the existentialist cannot be rationalist in his outlook for this is merely an escape into thought from the serious problems of existence; none of the important aspects of life—failure, evil, sin, folly—nor (in the view of Kierkegaard) even the existence of God or the truth of Christianity—can be proved by reason. "God does not exist; He is eternal," was how he expressed it; (6) life is short and limited in space and time, therefore it is foolish to discuss in a leisurely fashion matters of life or death as if there were all eternity to argue them in. It is necessary to make a leap into the unknown, *e.g.*, accepting Christ (in the case of the Christian existentialist) by faith in the sense of giving and risking the self utterly. This means complete commitment, not a dependence on arguments as to whether certain historical events did, or did not, happen.

To summarise: existentialism of whatever type seems to the outsider to be an attitude to life concerning itself with the individual's ultimate problems (mine, not yours); to be anti-rationalist and anti-idealist (in the sense of being, as it seems to the believer, practical)—in effect it seems to say " life is too short to fool about with argument, you must dive in and become committed " to something. Sartre who calls himself an " atheist existentialist " is apparently committed to the belief that " hell is other people," but for most critics the main argument against existentialist philosophy is that it often rests on a highly specialised personal experience and, as such, is incommunicable.

Extra-sensory Perception. *See* **Telepathy.**

F

Fabian Society. In 1848 (the year of *The Communist Manifesto* by Marx and Engels) Europe was in revolt. In most countries the workers and intellectuals started bloody revolutions against the feudal ruling classes which were no less violently suppressed; hence on the continent socialism took on a Marxist tinge which to some extent it still retains. But at the same time England was undergoing a slow but non-violent transition in her political and industrial life which led the workers in general to look forward to progress through evolution. Marxism never became an important movement in England even though it took its origin here. There were many reasons for this: the agitation of the Chartists (*q.v.*); the writings of Mill, Ruskin, and Carlyle; the reforms of Robert Owen; the religious movement led by the Wesleys; the Co-operative societies; the Christian socialists. Furthermore legislation stimulated by these bodies had led to an extension of the franchise to include a considerable number of wage-earners, remedial measures to correct some of the worst abuses of the factory system, recognition of the trade unions, etc.

This was the background against which the Fabian Society was founded in 1884 with the conviction that social change could be brought about by gradual parliamentary means. (The name is derived from Quintus Fabius Maximus, the Roman general nicknamed "Cunctator," the delayer, who achieved his successes in defending Rome against Hannibal by refusing to give direct battle.) It was a movement of brilliant intellectuals, chief among whom were Sidney and Beatrice Webb, H. G. Wells, G. B. Shaw, Graham Wallas, Sidney Olivier, and Edward Pease. The Society itself was basically a research institution which furnished the intellectual information for social reform and supported all contributing to the gradual attainment by parliamentary means of socialism.

The Webbs's analysis of society emphasised that individualist enterprise in capitalism was a hang-over from early days and was bound to defeat itself since socialism is the inevitable accompaniment of modern industrialism; the necessary result of popular government is control of their economic system by the people themselves. Utopian schemes had been doomed to failure because they were based on the fallacy that society is static and that islands of utopias could be formed in the midst of an unchanging and antagonistic environment. On the contrary, it was pointed out, society develops: " The new becomes old, often before it is consciously regarded as new." Social reorganisation cannot usefully be hastened by violent means but only through methods consonant with this natural historical progression—gradual, peaceful, and democratic. The Fabians were convinced that men are rational enough to accept in their common interest developments which can be demonstrated as necessary; thus public opinion will come to see that socialisation of the land and industries is essential in the same way that they came to accept the already-existing acts in respect of housing, insurance, medical care, and conditions of work. Gradual " permeation " of the power groups—trade unions, political parties, managers, and enlightened employers—would speed the process.

The Society collaborated first in the formation of the Independent Labour Party and then with the more moderate Labour Party and the trade unions and Co-operative movement. But in general it disapproved of independent trade union action since change should come from the government and take political form. The class-war of Marx was rejected and so too was the idea of the exclusive role of the working class—reform must come from the enlightened co-operation of all classes—not from their opposition.

Fabians have not been notably internationalist in their outlook in the sense that they have no permanent affiliations with international socialist bodies and were primarily concerned with progress in Britain. So far as imperialism is concerned they have urged increasing self-government and the training of native populations until they are ready to govern; but this is a gradual process to be accompanied by the improving of social and economic conditions.

Faculty Psychology, a school of psychology, basically belonging to the early 19th cent., which sought to explain mental phenomena by referring them to the activity of certain agencies or faculties such as memory, imagination, will, etc., as if they were entities in their own right rather than merely general terms for various groups of mental phenomena. Its most extreme form was phrenology (*q.v.*) which found no less than thirty-seven so-called faculties.

Falangists. The Fascist Party of Spain founded in 1933 by José Antonio Primo de Rivera, son of the man who was dictator of the country from 1923 to 1930; he was shot by the Republicans. In 1937 the falangists who had shown unwelcome signs of social radicalism were merged with the other right-wing political groups to form the *Falange Española Tradicionalista y de las Juntas de Ofensive Nacional Sindicalistas* which replaced the Cortes (*i.e.* the Government) between 1939 and 1942 when the Cortes was reinstituted. The Falange is the only political party allowed in Spain. *See* **Fascism.**

Fascism. From the end of mediaeval times with the opening up of the world, the liberation of the mind and the release of business enterprise, a new spirit arose in Europe exemplified in such movements as the Renaissance, the Reformation, the struggle for democracy, the rise of capitalism, and the Industrial Revolution. With these movements there developed a certain tradition which, in spite of hindrances and disagreements or failures, was universally held both by right- and left-wing parties however strongly they might fail to agree on the best means of attaining what was felt to be a universal ideal. The hard core of this tradition involved: belief in reason and the possibility of human progress; the essential sanctity and dignity of human life; tolerance of widely different religious and political views; reliance on popular government and the responsibility of the rulers to the ruled; freedom of thought and criticism; the necessity of universal education; impartial justice and the rule of law; the desirability of universal peace. Fascism was the negation of every aspect of this tradition and took pride in being so. Emotion took the place of reason, the " immutable, beneficial, and fruitful inequality of classes " and the right of a self-constituted élite to rule them replaced universal suffrage because absolute authority " quick, sure, unanimous " led to action rather than talk. Contrary opinions are not allowed and justice is in the service of the state; war is desirable to advance the power of the state; and racial inequality made a dogma. Those who belong to the " wrong " religion, political party, or race are outside the law.

The attacks on liberalism and exaltation of the state derive largely from Hegel and his German followers; the mystical irrationalism from such 19th cent. philosophers as Schopenhauer, Nietzsche, and Bergson; from Sorel (*see* **Syndicalism**) came the idea of the " myth," and an image which would have the power to arouse the emotions of the masses and from Sorel also the rationale of violence and justification of force.

But these philosophical justifications of fascism do not explain why it arose at all and why it arose where it did—in Italy, Germany, and Spain. These countries had one thing in common—disillusionment. Germany had lost the 1914–18 war, Italy had been on the winning side but was resentful about her small gains, Spain had sunk to the level of a third-rate power, and people were becoming increasingly restive under the reactionary powers of the Catholic Church, the landed aristocracy, and the army. In Marxist theory, fascism is the last fling of the ruling class and the bourgeoisie in their attempt to hold down the workers.

Italian Fascism. The corporate state set up by Benito Mussolini in Italy claimed to be neither capitalist nor socialist, and after its inception in 1922 the Fascist Party became the only recognised one. Its members wore black shirts, were organised in military formations, used the Roman greeting of the outstretched arm, and adopted as their slogan "Mussolini is always right." Membership of the Party was not allowed to exceed a number thought to be suited to the optimum size of a governing class and new candidates were drawn, after strict examinations, from the youth organisations. The Blackshirts, a fascist militia, existed separately from the army and were ruled by Fascist Headquarters.

At the head of government was Mussolini, "Il Duce" himself, a cabinet of fourteen ministers selected by him and approved by the King to supervise the various functions of government, and the Grand Council or directorate of the Fascist Party, all the members of which were chosen by the Duce. Parliament, which was not allowed to initiate legislation but only to approve decrees from above, consisted of a Senate with life-membership and a Chamber of Fasci and Corporations composed of nominated members of the Party, the National Council of Corporations, and selected representatives of the employers' and employees' confederations. Private enterprise was encouraged and protected but rigidly controlled; strikes were forbidden, but a Charter of Labour enforced the collaboration of workers and employers whose disputes were settled in labour courts presided over by the Party. All decisions relating to industry were government-controlled (*e.g.*, wages, prices, conditions of employment and dismissal, the expansion or limitation of production), and some industries such as mining, shipping, and armaments were largely state-owned.

Italian fascism served as a model in other countries, notably for the German National Socialist Party, in Spain and Japan, and most European nations between the wars had their small Fascist parties, the British version led by Sir Oswald Mosley being known as the British Union which advocated the abolition of free speech, greater interest in the Commonwealth, and anti-semitism. Although fascism in all countries has certain recognisable characteristics, it would be wrong to think of it as an international movement taking fixed forms and with a clearly thought-out rationale as in the case of communism. It is doubtful, for example, whether Japanese "fascism" was entitled to be described as such, and the Spanish Falange differs in many respects both in outlook and origins from the German or Italian varieties. In fact the word "fascist," like "bolshevik," is often used as a purely emotive term of abuse. *See* **Falange, Nazism.**

Fatalism. *See* **Determinism.**

Fetichism, originally a practice of the natives of West Africa and elsewhere of attributing magical properties to an object which was used as an amulet, for putting spells on others, or regarded as possessing dangerous powers. In psychology the term refers to a sexual perversion in which objects such as shoes, brassières, hair, etc., arouse sexual excitement.

Feudalism. The feudal system took its origins from Saxon times and broadly speaking lasted until the end of the 13th cent. It was a military and political organisation based on land tenure, for, of course, society throughout this period was based almost entirely on agriculture. The activities of men divided them into three classes or estates. The First Estate was the clergy, responsible for man's spiritual needs; the Second was the nobility, including kings and emperor as well as the lesser nobles; the Third was composed of all those who had to do with the economic and mainly agricultural life of Europe. The praying men, the fighting men and administrators, and the toilers were all held to be dependent on each other in a web of mutual responsibilities.

The theory of feudalism, although it by no means always worked out in practice, was as follows: the earth was God's and therefore no man owned land in the modern sense of the word. God had given the pope spiritual charge of men, and secular power over them to the emperor from whom kings held their kingdoms, and in turn the dukes and counts received the land over which they held sway from the king. Members of the Second Estate held their lands on the condition of fulfilling certain obligations to their overlord and to the people living under them, so when a noble received a fief or piece of land he became the vassal of the man who bestowed it. To him he owed military service for a specified period of the year, attendance at court, and giving his lord counsel. He undertook to ransom his lord when he fell into enemy hands and to contribute to his daughter's dowry and at the knighting of his son. In return the lord offered his vassal protection and justice, received the vassal's sons into his household and educated them for knighthood.

The system was complicated by the fact that large fiefs might be subdivided and abbots often governed church lands held in fief from nobles. The serf or toiling man dwelt on the land of a feudal noble or churchman where he rendered service by tilling the soil or carrying out his craft for his manorial lord in return for protection, justice, and the security of his life and land. He was given a share in the common lands or pastures from which he provided for his own needs. In the modern sense he was not free (although at a later stage he could buy his freedom) since he was attached to the soil and could not leave without the lord's permission. On the other hand he could neither be deprived of his land nor lose his livelihood. Feudal tenures were abolished in England by statute in 1660, although they had for long been inoperative. In Japan a feudal system existed up to 1871, in Russia until 1917, and many relics of it still linger on (*e.g.* the *mezzadria* system of land tenure in parts of Italy).

Fourierism. *See* **Utopianism.**

Freemasonry, a secret organisation with different systems in different countries. It shares with other secret societies the characteristics of being secret, having signs by which one fellow-member can recognise another, initiation ceremonies, peculiar regalia, and various grades of enlightenment. In England freemasonry was first organised in 1717 and in France and Germany in 1725 and 1737 respectively. Masons claim to be working for the good of mankind, and carry out various charitable works. Many notable people are in the movement. Whatever their beliefs there can be no doubt that on the continent freemasons have intervened in politics and the organisation is banned by the Roman Catholic Church. Absurd attempts have been made (and quite possibly are part of Masonic belief) to trace the society back to early and even Biblical times. Historically, of course, this is absurd, nor have freemasons any connection with the masons' guilds of the Middle Ages which were intended for masons in the ordinary sense of the word.

Freudian theory. *See* **Section F, Part III.**

Friends, The Society of, or **Quakers,** a religious body founded in England in the 17th cent. by George Fox (1624–91). The essence of their faith is that every individual who believes has the power of direct communication with God who will guide him into the ways of truth. This power comes from the "inner light" of his own heart, the light of Christ. Quakers meet for worship avoiding all ritual, without ordained ministers or prepared sermons; there is complete silence until someone is moved by the Holy Spirit to utter his message.

In the early days Quakers gave vent to

violent outbursts and disturbed church services. Friends had the habit of preaching at anyone who happened to be nearby, their denunciation of "steeple-houses" and references to the "inner light," their addressing everyone as "thee" and "thou," their refusal to go beyond "yea" and "nay" in making an assertion and refusing to go further in taking an oath, must have played some part in bringing about the savage persecutions they were forced to endure. Many emigrated to Pennsylvania, founded by William Penn in 1682, and missionaries were sent to many parts of the world. The former violence gave way to gentleness. Friends not only refused to take part in war but even refused to resist personal violence. They took the lead in abolishing slavery, worked for prison reform and better education. As we know them today Quakers are quiet, sincere, undemonstrative people, given to a somewhat serious turn of mind. The former peculiarities of custom and dress have been dropped and interpretation of the Scriptures is more liberal. Although Quakers refuse to take part in warfare, they are always ready to help the victims of war, by organising relief, helping refugees in distress, or sending their ambulance units into the heat of battle.

G

Gestalt Psychology. Whilst Behaviourism (*q.v.*) was emerging in America a new school of thought was arising in Germany which has revolutionised the outlook of psychology in certain fields and is one of the most important schools of today. Basically dealing with problems of perception and learning, it took issue with the old concept of the **Associationists** (*q.v.*) that mental life was based on the "association of ideas," and one of the doctrines of the Behaviourists and others that learning is based either on a process of trial and error or conditioning. The three founders of the school were Max Wertheimer, Wolfgang Köhler, and Kurt Koffka who named it the Gestalt school—a German word which is retained because it had no definite English counterpart but may roughly be translated as "pattern" or "configuration." They meant by this that the human mind has a natural tendency to find significant patterns among sensations, contrary to the Associationist view that initially we simply experience atomised elements which we later learn to associate together as an object. The latter was described by the new school as a "brick and mortar" psychology which explained where the bricks came from but failed to explain the mortar which makes the elements a whole. (The whole is not the mere sum of its parts.) Thus a tune is made up from notes in a scale but is not present in them individually, and the tune is still present if we change the key using entirely different notes. Pattern and relationships which have significance are at the basis of mental activity, especially in learning. Thus experiments have shown that if hens are presented with grain laid on both white and grey pieces of paper and are allowed to eat from the grey but are shooed away from the white, they soon learn to go to the grey piece only. This, the Associationists would say, is a perfect example of the association of ideas: white equals punishment, grey equals food, so naturally the paper associated with food wins. But Köhler did a further experiment and substituted black for the white paper. If the theory of association were correct, the hens would still feed at the grey paper which they had learned to associate with food. In fact, they went to the grain on the black paper. The obvious explanation was that the birds were not responding to a simple association, grey equals food, but to the relationship "darker than." They took in the whole situation, not just parts of it.

Similarly the Behaviourist theory of learning was one of conditioning—the dog presented with food preceded by a whistle soon begins to salivate at the whistle alone. Other psychologists emphasised the process of trial and error showing, for example, that a cat placed in a box which could only be opened by a latch or by pulling a wire loop to reach a plate of food outside, at first made completely random movements until by chance the correct one happened to be made. On subsequent occasions the random element grew less and less and thus the cat ultimately learned to go straight for the latch. But Köhler criticised these experiments (without denying that some learning may be by either conditioning or trial and error) by pointing out that in most of the trial and error experiments where mazes or puzzle boxes were used the *whole situation* was not open to the animal's inspection. An important element in learning, even in animals, is insight. Thus a dog separated from food by a length of fencing will almost immediately run around the fence provided it can see its ends. A chimpanzee with a banana outside its cage and a suitable stick inside within the same field of vision will soon use it to poke the fruit inside. But if the stick is lying at the back of the cage the absence of a compact visual pattern of stick and banana will likely cause it to fail. Gestalt, in short, emphasises the pattern-finding and significance-seeking tendencies of the mind and its ability to learn by insight. It has also criticised the type of personality test which lists individual traits, giving the subject a rating for each trait, on the ground that such tests do not show the function of each trait in the total personality which is an organised whole rather than the sum of its individual characteristics.

Gnosticism. Among the many heresies of early Christianity, especially during its first two centuries, was a group which came under the heading of Gnosticism. This was a system or set of systems which attempted to combine Christian beliefs with others derived from Oriental and Greek sources, especially those which were of a mystical and metaphysical nature, such as the doctrines of Plato and Pythagoras. There were many Gnostic sects, the most celebrated being the Alexandrian school of Valentius (fl. *c.* 136–*c.* 160). "Gnosis" was understood not as meaning "knowledge" or "understanding" as we understand these words, but "revelation." As in other mystical religions, the ultimate object was individual salvation; sacraments took the most varied forms. Many who professed themselves Christians accepted Gnostic doctrines and even orthodox Christianity contains some elements of Gnostic mysticism. It was left to the bishops and theologians to decide at what point Gnosticism ceased to be orthodox and a difficult task this proved to be. Two of the greatest, Clement of Alexandria and his pupil Origen, unwittingly slipped into heresy when they tried to show that such men as Socrates and Plato, who were in quest of truth, were Christian in intention, and by their lives and works had prepared the way for Christ. Thus they contradicted Church doctrine which specifically said *Extra ecclesiam nulla salus*—outside the Church there is no salvation.

God and Man. The idea of gods came before the idea of God and even earlier in the evolution of religious thought there existed belief in spirits (*see* **Animism**). It was only as a result of a long period of development that the notion of a universal "God" arose, a development particularly well documented in the Old Testament. Here we are concerned only with the views of philosophers, the views of specific religious bodies being given under the appropriate headings. First, however, some definitions.

Atheism is the positive disbelief in the existence of a God. **Agnosticism** (a term coined by T. H. Huxley, the 19th cent. biologist and contemporary of Darwin) signifies that one cannot know whether God exists or not. **Deism** is the acceptance of the existence of God, not through revelation, but as a hypothesis required by reason. **Theism** also accepts the existence of God, but, unlike Deism, does not reject the evidence of revelation (*e.g.*, in the Bible or in the lives of the saints). **Pantheism** is the identification of God with all that exists (*i.e.*, with the whole universe). **Monotheism** is the belief in one God, **Polytheism** the belief in many (*see also* **Dualism**).

Early Greek Views. Among the early Greek philosophers, Thales (*c.* 624–565 B.C.) of Miletus, in Asia Minor, Anaximander (611–547 B.C.), his pupil, and Anaximenes (b. *c.* 570 B.C.), another Miletan, were men of scientific curiosity and their speculations about the origin of the universe were untouched by religious thought. They were basically materialist and atheist in thought. Heraclitus of Ephesus (*c.* 540–475 B.C.), the philosopher of change, and the founder of metaphysics, was scornful of the popular religion of his day. For him fire was the prime element—the *Logos*—the most complete embodiment of the process of Becoming. Empedocles of Agrigentum in Sicily (*c.* 500–*c.* 430 B.C.) introduced the idea of opposition and affinity. All matter is composed of the so-called four elements—*earth, water, air,* and *fire*—which are in opposition or alliance with each other. All these were materialist philosophers who sought to explain the working of the universe without recourse to the gods.

Socrates, Plato, and Aristotle. Socrates (470–399 B.C.) was primarily concerned with ethical matters and conduct rather than the nature of the universe. For him goodness and virtue come from knowledge. He obeyed an " inner voice " and suffered death rather than give up his philosophy. He believed in the persistence of life after death and was essentially a monotheist. Plato (427–347 B.C.) was chiefly concerned with the nature of reality and thought in terms of absolute truths which were unchanging, logical, and mathematical. (*See* **Mind and Matter.**) Aristotle (384–322 B.C.) took his view of matter not from Democritus (atomic view) but from Empedocles (doctrine of four elements), a view which came to fit in well with orthodox mediaeval theology. Matter is conceived of as potentially alive and striving to attain its particular form, being moved by divine spirit or mind (*nous*). (An acorn, for example, is matter which contains the form " oak-tree " towards which it strives.) Thus there is a whole series from the simplest level of matter to the perfect living individual. But there must be a supreme source of all movement upon which the whole of Nature depends, a Being that Aristotle describes as the " Unmoved Mover," the ultimate cause of all becoming in the universe. This Being is pure intelligence, a philosopher's God, not a personal one. Unlike Plato, Aristotle did not believe in survival after death, holding that the divine, that is the immortal element in man, is mind.

Among the later Greek thinkers the Epicureans were polytheists whose gods, however, were denied supernatural powers. The Stoics built up a materialist theory of the universe, based on the Aristotelian model. To them God was an all-pervading force, related to the world as the soul is related to the body, but they conceived of it as material. They developed the mystical side of Plato's idealism and were much attracted by the astrology coming from Babylonia. They were pantheists. The Sceptics were agnostics.

From Pagan to Christian Thought. Philo, " the Jew of Alexandria," who was about 20 years older than Jesus, tried to show that the Jewish scriptures were in line with the best in Greek thought. He introduced the *Logos* as a bridge between the two systems. Philo's God is remote from the world, above and beyond all thought and being, and as His perfection does not permit direct contact with matter the divine *Logos* acts as intermediary between God and man. Plotinus (204–70), a Roman, and the founder of Neoplatonism, was the last of the great pagan philosophers. Like Philo, he believed that God had created the world indirectly through emanations—beings coming from Him but not of Him. The world needs God but God does not need the world. Creation is a fall from God, especially the human soul when enmeshed in the body and the world of the senses, yet (*see* **Determinism**) man has the ability to free himself from sense domination and turn towards God. Neoplatonism was the final stage of Greek thought drawing its inspiration from the mystical side of Plato's idealism and its ethics from Stoicism.

Christianity: The Fathers and the Schoolmen. It was mainly through St. Augustine (354–430), Bishop of Hippo in North Africa, that certain of the doctrines of Neoplatonism found their way into Christianity. Augustine also emphasised the concept of God as all good, all wise, all knowing, transcendent, the Creator of the universe out of nothing. But, he added, since God knows everything, everything is determined by Him forever. This is the doctrine of predestination and its subsequent history is discussed under **Determinism.**

In the early centuries of Christianity, as we have seen, some found it difficult to reconcile God's perfection with His creation of the universe and introduced the concept of the *Logos* which many identified with Christ. Further, it came to be held that a power of divine origin permeated the universe, namely the Holy Spirit or Holy Ghost. Some theory had to be worked out to explain the relationships of these three entities whence arose the conception of the Trinity. God is One; but He is also Three: Father, Son (the *Logos* or Christ), and Holy Ghost.

This doctrine was argued by the Apologists and the Modalists. The former maintained that the *Logos* and the Holy Spirit were emanations from God and that Jesus was the *Logos* in the form of a man. The Modalists held that all three Persons of the Trinity were God in three forms or modes: the *Logos* is God creating, the Holy Spirit God reasoning, and God is God being. This led to a long discussion as to whether the *Logos* was an emanation from God or God in another form; was the *Logos* of like *nature* with God or of the same *substance*? This was resolved at the Council of Nicaea (325) when Athanasius formulated the orthodox doctrine against Arius (*q.v.*): that the one Godhead is a Trinity of the same substance, three Persons of the same nature—Father, Son, and Holy Ghost.

St. Thomas Aquinas (1227–74), influenced greatly by Aristotle's doctrines, set the pattern for all subsequent Catholic belief even to the present time. He produced rational arguments for God's existence: *e.g.*, Aristotle's argument that, since movement exists, there must be a prime mover, the Unmoved Mover or God; further, we can see that things in the universe are related in a scale from the less to the more complex, from the less to the more perfect, and this leads us to suppose that at the peak there must be a Being with absolute perfection. God is the first and final cause of the universe, absolutely perfect, the Creator of everything out of nothing. He reveals Himself in his Creation and rules the universe through His perfect will. How Aquinas dealt with the problem of predestination is told under **Determinism.**

Break with Mediaeval Thought. Renaissance thinkers, free to think for themselves, doubted the validity of the arguments of the Schoolmen but most were unwilling to give up the idea of God (nor would it have been safe to do so). Mystics (*see* **Mysticism**) or near-mystics such as Nicholas of Cusa (*c.* 1401–64) and Jacob Boehme (1575–1624) taught that God was not to be found by reason but was a fact of the immediate intuition of the mystical experience. Giordano Bruno held that God was immanent in the infinite universe. He is the unity of all opposites, a unity without opposites, which the human mind cannot grasp. Bruno was burned at the stake in 1600 at the instigation of the Inquisition (a body which, so we are told, never caused pain to anyone since it was the civil power, not the Inquisition, that carried out the unpleasant sentences) for his heresy.

Francis Bacon, who died in 1626, separated, as was the tendency of that time, science from religion. The latter he divided into the two categories of natural and revealed theology. The former, through the study of nature, may give convincing proof of the existence of a God but nothing more. Of revealed theology he said: " we must quit the small vessel of human reason . . . as we are obliged to obey the divine law, though our will murmurs against it, so we are obliged to believe in the word of God, though our reason is shocked at it." Hobbes (d. 1679) was a complete materialist and one feels that obeisance to the notion was politic rather than from conviction. However, he does mention God as starting the universe in motion, infers that God is corporeal but denies that His nature can be known.

From Descartes Onwards. Descartes (1596–1650) separated mind and body as different entities but believed that the existence of God could be deduced by the fact that the idea of him existed in the mind. Whatever God puts into man, including his ideas, must be real. God is self-caused, omniscient, omnipotent, eternal, all goodness and truth. But Descartes neglected to explain how mind separate from body can influence body, or God separate from the world can influence matter.

Spinoza (1632–77) declared that all existence is embraced in one substance—God, the all-in-all. He was a pantheist and as such was rejected by his Jewish brethren. But Spinoza's God has neither personality nor consciousness, intelligence nor purpose, although all things follow in strict law from His nature. All the thought of everyone in the world, make up God's thoughts.

Bishop Berkeley (1685–1753) took the view that things exist only when they are perceived, and this naturally implies that a tree, for example, ceases to exist when nobody is looking at it. This problem was solved to his own satisfaction by assuming that God, seeing everything, prevented objects from disappearing when we were not present. The world is a creation of God but it is a spiritual or mental world, not a material one.

Hume (1711–76), who was a sceptic, held that human reason cannot demonstrate the existence of God and all past arguments to show that it could were fallacious. Yet we must believe in God since the basis of all hope, morality, and society is based upon the belief. Kant (1724–1804) held a theory similar to that of Hume. We cannot know by reason that God exists, nor can we prove on the basis of argument anything about God. But we can form an idea of the whole of the universe, the one Absolute Whole, and personify it. We need the idea of God on which to base our moral life, although this idea of God is transcendent, *i.e.*, goes beyond experience.

William James (1842–1910), the American philosopher (*see* **Pragmatism**), held much the same view: God cannot be proved to exist, but we have a will to believe which must be satisfied, and the idea works in practice. Hegel (1770–1831) thought of God as a developing process, beginning with " the Absolute " or First Cause and finding its highest expression in man's mind, or reason. It is in man that God most clearly becomes aware of Himself. Finally Comte (1798–1857), the positivist, held that religion belongs to a more primitive state of society and, like many modern philosophers, turned the problem over to believers as being none of the business of science.

Good and Evil.

Early Philosophers' Views. The early Greek philosophers were chiefly concerned with the laws of the universe, consequently it was common belief that knowledge of these laws, and living according to them, constituted the supreme good. Heraclitus, for example, who taught that all things carried with them their opposites, held that good and evil were like two notes in a harmony, necessary to each other. " It is the opposite which is good for us." Democritus, like Epicurus (*q.v.*), held that the main goal of life is happiness, but happiness in moderation. The good man is not merely the one who *does* good but who always *wants* to do so: " You can tell the good man not by his deeds alone but by his desires." Such goodness brings happiness, the ultimate goal. On the other hand, many of the wandering Sophist teachers taught that good was merely social convention, that there are no absolute principles of right and wrong, that each man should live according to his desires and make his own moral code. To Socrates knowledge was the highest good because doing wrong is the result of ignorance: " no man is voluntarily bad." Plato and Aristotle, differing in many other respects, drew attention to the fact that man is composed of three parts: his desires and appetites, his will, and his reason. A man whose reason rules his will and appetites is not only a good but a happy man; for happiness is not an aim in itself but a by-product of the good life. Aristotle, however, emphasised the goal of self-realisation, and thought that if the goal of life is (as Plato had said) a rational attitude towards the feelings and desires, it needs to be further defined. Aristotle defined it as the " Golden Mean "—the good man is one who does not go to extremes but balances one extreme against another. Thus courage is a mean between cowardice and foolhardiness. The later philosophers Philo and Plotinus held that evil was in the very nature of the body and its senses. Goodness could only be achieved by giving up the life of the senses and, freed from the domination of the body, turning to God, the source of goodness.

Christian Views. St. Augustine taught that everything in the universe is good. Even those things which appear evil are good in that they fit with the harmony of the universe like shadows in a painting. Man should turn his back on the pleasures of the world and turn to the love of God. Peter Abelard (1079–1142) made the more sophisticated distinction when he suggested that the wrongness of an act lies not in the act itself, but in the intention of the doer: " God considers not what is done but in what spirit it is done; and the merit or praise of the agent lies not in the deed but in the intention." If we do what we believe to be right, we may err, but we do not sin. The only sinful man is he who deliberately sets out to do what he knows to be wrong. St. Thomas Aquinas agreed with Aristotle in that he believed the highest good to be realisation of self as God has ordained, and he also agreed with Abelard that intention is important. Even a good act is not good unless the doer intended it to have good consequences. Intention will not make a bad act good, but it is the only thing that will make a good act genuinely good.

In general, Christianity has had difficulties in solving the problem of the existence of evil; for even when one accepts that the evil men do is somehow tied up with the body, it is still difficult to answer the question: how could an all-good God create evil? This is answered in one of two ways: (*a*) that Adam was given free-will and chose to sin (an answer which still does not explain how sin could exist anywhere in the universe of a God who created everything); (*b*) by denying the reality of evil as some Christians have chosen to do (*e.g.*, Christian Science *q.v.*). The Eastern religions, on the other hand (*see* **Zoroastrianism**), solved the problem in a more realistic way by a dualism which denied that their gods were the creators of the whole universe and allowed the existence of at least two gods, one good and one evil. In Christianity there is, of course, a Devil, but it is not explained whence his evil nature came.

Later Philosophic Views. Hobbes equated good with pleasure, evil with pain. They are relative to the individual man in the sense that " one man's meat is another man's poison." Descartes believed that the power to distinguish between good and evil given by God to man is not complete, so that man does evil through ignorance. We act with insufficient knowledge and on inadequate evidence. Locke, believing that at birth the mind is a blank slate, held that men get their opinions of right and wrong from their parents. By and large, happiness is good and pain is evil. But men do not always agree over what is pleasurable and what not. Hence laws exist and these fall into three categories: (1) the divine law; (2) civil laws, (3) matters of opinion or reputation which are enforced by the fact that men do not like to incur the disapproval of their friends. We learn by experience that evil brings pain and good acts bring pleasure, and, basically, one is good because not to be so would bring discomfort.

Kant (*see* **God and Man**) found moral belief to be inherent in man whether or not they can be proved by reason. There is a categorical imperative which makes us realise the validity of two universal laws: (1) " always act in such a way that the maxim determining your conduct might well become a universal law; act so that you can will that everybody shall follow th principle of your action"; (2) "always act so as to treat humanity, whether in thine own person or in that of another, in every case as an end and never as a means."

Schopenhauer (1788–1860) was influenced by Buddhism and saw the will as a blind impelling striving, and desire as the cause of all suffering. The remedy is to regard sympathy and pity as the basis of all morality and to deny one's individual will. This is made easier if we realise that everyone is part of the Universal Will and therefore the one against whom we are struggling is part of the same whole as ourselves.

John Stuart Mill and Jeremy Bentham were both representatives of the Utilitarian school, believing that good is the greatest good (happiness) of the greatest number (*see* **Utilitarianism**). Lastly, there is the view held mostly by political thinkers that good is what is good for the state or society in general (*see* **State and Man**).

Guild Socialism, a British form of syndicalism (*q.v.*) created in 1906 by an architect, A. J. Penty, who was soon joined by A. R. Orage, S. G. Hobson, and G. D. H. Cole. The background to the movement was the situation that, although at that time the Labour Party had 29 members in the House of Commons, a period of severe economic crisis had shown the government unwilling and the Labourites unable to do anything about it; the workers were resorting again to direct action to secure their demands and the democratic and constitutional methods to which the Fabians had partly persuaded them seemed to have failed. The guild socialists advocated a restoration of the mediaeval guild system as was being recommended by the French syndicalists whose programme involved a return to direct economic action, a functional industrial structure, return of craftsmanship, and distrust of the state. Guild socialists believed that value was created by society as a whole rather than by individuals singly, and that capitalist economists had recommended the acquisition of wealth without emphasising the social responsibilities which wealth should bring. The trade unions were to be organised to take over and run their own industries after nationalisation. Thus guild socialists were not only against capitalism but also against state socialism in which the state took over the control of industry. Political authority was held to be uncongenial to human freedom and therefore nothing was to be gained by the substitution of state bureaucracy for capitalist control. The National Guilds League, formed in 1915, advocated the abolition of the wages system, self-government in industry, control by a system of national guilds acting in conjunction with other functional democratic organisations in the community. This body was dissolved in 1925, but the theories of guild socialism are often referred to by British Labour Party theorists and have undoubtedly influenced British socialism.

H

Hinduism, the religion and social institutions of the great majority of the people of India. Hinduism has no fixed scriptural canon but its doctrines are to be found in certain ancient works, notably the *Veda*, the *Brahmanas*, the *Upanishads*, and the *Bhagavad-gita*. The dark-skinned Dravidians invaded India between about 3250 and 2750 B.C. and established a civilisation in the Indus valley. They were polytheists who worshipped a number of nature-gods; some elements of their beliefs persisted into Hinduism. They were subdued by a light-skinned Nordic people who invaded from Asia Minor and Iran about 1500 B.C. The language of these Aryan people was Vedic, parent of Sanskrit in which their religious literature (the Vedas) came to be written after many centuries of oral transmission.

The *Veda* or Sacred Lore has come down to us in the form of mantras or hymns of which there are four great collections, the best-known being the *Rig-Veda*. These Vedic Aryans worshipped nature-deities, their favourites being Indra (rain), Agni (fire), and Surya (the sun). Their religion contained no idolatry but became contaminated by the more primitive beliefs of the conquered Dravidians. Sacrifice and ritual became predominant in a ceremonial religion.

As a reaction a more philosophic form arose (c. 500 B.C.) with its scriptures in the *Upanishads*. At its highest level, known as Brahmanism, belief is in a subtle and sophisticated form of monotheism (*Brahma* is an impersonal, all-embracing spirit), but there is a tolerant acceptance of more primitive beliefs. Thus Vishnu (a conservative principle) and Siva (a destructive principle) grew out of Vedic conceptions. The two great doctrines of Hinduism are *karma* and transmigration. The universal desire to be reunited with the absolute (the *Atman* or *Brahma*) can be satisfied by following the path of knowledge. Life is a cycle of lives (*samsara*) in which man's destiny is determined by his deeds (*karma*) from which he may seek release (*moksa*) through ascetic practices or the discipline of **Yoga** (*q.v.*). Failure to achieve release means reincarnation—migration to a higher or lower form of life after death—until the ultimate goal of absorption in the absolute is reached.

In the great Sanskrit epic poems *Ramayana* and *Mahabharata* the deity takes three forms, represented by the divine personalities of Brahma, Vishnu, and Siva. There are also lower gods, demi-gods, supernatural beings, and members of the trinity may even become incarnate, as Vishnu became identified with Krishna, one of the heroes of the *Mahabharata* and the well-known *Bhagavad-gita*.

The ritual and legalistic side of Brahmanism is the caste system based on the elaborate codes of the *Law of Manu*, according to which God created distinct orders of men as He created distinct species of animals and plants. Men are born to be Brahmans, soldiers, agriculturists, or servants, but since a Brahman may marry a woman from any of these castes, an endless number of sub-castes arises.

Hinduism has always shown great tolerance for varieties of belief and practice. Ideas pleasant and unpleasant have been assimilated: fetichism, demon-cults, animal-worship, sexual-cults (such as the rites of *Kali* in Calcutta). Today, as would be expected in a country which is in the throes of vast social change, Hinduism itself is changing. Under the impact of modern conditions new ideas are destroying old beliefs and customs. *See also* **Jainism, Sikhism.**

Humanism, the term applied to (1) a system of education based on the Greek and Latin classics; and (2) the vigorous attitudes that accompanied the end of the Middle Ages and were represented at different periods by the Renaissance, the Reformation, the Industrial Revolution, and the struggle for democracy. These include: release from ecclesiastical authority, the liberation of the intellect, faith in progress, the belief that man himself can improve his own conditions without supernatural help and, indeed, has a duty to do so. "Man is the measure of all things" is the keynote of humanism.

To the humanist, religion is an evolutionary process, just as science is, each being an expression of man's yearning to understand the world in which he finds himself. With the growth of knowledge many phenomena once mysterious have ceased to be so, and if a religion ceases to develop and keep pace with social change it no longer convinces or helps. Thus to the humanist the idea of a supernatural "God" has ceased to be scientifically tenable. "Divinity," says Sir Julian Huxley, "is the chief raw material out of which gods have been fashioned. Today we must melt down the gods and refashion the material into new and more effective organs of thought."

Humanity, Religion of. *See* **Positivism.**

Hussites, the followers of John Hus, the most famous pupil of John Wyclif. He was the rector of Prague University and, although it is now by no means certain that his beliefs were heretical, he was condemned to death for heresy and burnt at the stake in 1415 at Constance whence he had come with a safe conduct issued by the Emperor Sigismund of Hungary. The latter based his action on the doctrine that no faith need be kept with heretics, but it is obvious that the main objection to Hus was his contempt for authority of any kind. After their leader's death, the Hussites became a formidable body in Bohemia and Moravia. They took up arms on behalf of their faith, their religion being strongly imbued with political feeling (hostility to Germanism and to the supremacy of the Roman Church). Their religious struggles for reform led to the Hussite Wars during which the movement splintered into several groups.

I

Iconoclast Heresy. In 726 the Byzantine Emperor Leo III forbade the use of images in worship by Imperial decree—a decree which was continued intermittently until 843 when the heresy was abandoned. This was the Iconoclast controversy in which Emperor and Papacy were violently opposed. In the end the image-worshippers triumphed and the sacred pictures (icons) have remained to this day. This ecclesiastical conflict between the Iconoclasts and the Papacy over a matter of ritual was the first of the crises which over three centuries were finally to bring about the schism between Orthodox Christendom and Western Christendom. Though temporary, the supremacy of the State over the Church was nevertheless of supreme importance. Although the Iconoclast heresy is often given as the reason for the absence of statues in the Eastern Churches there is no evidence that they existed to any extent even before the movement began.

Idealism, in a philosophical sense, the belief that there is no matter in the universe, that all that exists is mind or spirit. *See* **Mind and Matter** and **Realism.**

Immaculate Conception, one of the important dogmas concerning the Blessed Virgin Mary, as taught by the Roman Catholic Church, is that she was conceived and born without original sin (according to a bull of Pius IX, 1854). Christians in general believe in the immaculate conception of Jesus Christ.

Immortality. The belief in a life after death has been widely held since the earliest times. It has certainly not been universal, nor has it always taken a form which everyone would find satisfying. In the early stages of human history or prehistory everything contained a spirit (*see* **Animism**) and it is obvious from the objects left in early graves that the dead were expected to exist in some form after death. The experience of dreams, too, seemed to suggest to the unsophisticated that there was a part of man which could leave his body and wander elsewhere during sleep. In order to save space, it will be helpful to classify the various types of belief which have existed in philosophical thought regarding this problem: (1) There is the idea that, although *something* survives bodily death, it is not necessarily eternal. Thus most primitive peoples were prepared to believe that man's spirit haunted the place around his grave and that food and drink should be set out for it, but that this spirit did not go on forever and gradually faded away. (2) The ancient Greeks and Hebrews believed for the most part that the souls of the dead went to a place of shades there to pine for the world of men. Their whining ghosts spent eternity in a dark, uninviting region in misery and remorse. (3) Other people, and there were many more of these, believed in the transmigration of souls with the former life of the individual determining whether his next life would be at a higher or lower level. Sometimes this process seems to have been thought of as simply going on and on, by others (*e.g.*, in Hinduism and Buddhism) as terminating in either non-sentience or union with God but in any case in annihilation of the self as self. Believers in this theory were the Greek philosophers Pythagoras, Empedocles, Plato (who believed that soul comes from God and strives to return to God, according to his own rather confused notions of the deity. If it fails to free itself completely from the body it will sink lower and lower from one body to another.) Plotinus held similar views to Plato, and many other religious sects in addition to those mentioned have believed in transmigration. (4) The belief of Plato and Aristotle that if souls continue to exist after death there is no reason why they should not have existed before birth (this in part is covered by (3)), but some have pointed out that eternity does not mean "from now on," but the whole of time before and after "now"—nobody, however, so far as one knows, held that *individual* souls so exist. (5) The theory that the soul does not exist at all and therefore immortality is meaningless: this was held by Anaximenes in early Greek times; by Leucippus, Democritus, and the other Greek atomists; by the Epicureans from the Greek Epicurus to the Roman Lucretius; by the British Hobbes and Hume; by Comte of France; and William James and John Dewey of America. (6) The thesis, held notably by Locke and Kant, that although we cannot prove the reality of soul and immortality by pure reason, belief in them should be held for moral ends. (For the orthodox Christian view *see* **God and Man, Determinism and Free-will.**) From this summary we can see that many philosophies and religions (with the important exceptions of Islam and Christianity) without denying a future life do deny the permanence of the individual soul in anything resembling its earthly form (*see* **Spiritualism, Psychic research**).

Imperialism, the practice by a country, which has become a nation and embarked upon commercial and industrial expansion, of acquiring and administering territories, inhabited by peoples usually at a lower stage of development, as colonies or dependencies. Thus the "typical" imperialist powers of the 19th cent. and earlier were Britain, Belgium, Holland, Spain, and Portugal, whilst Germany, Italy, and Japan, which either did not have unity during this period or adequate industrial expansion, tried to make good their lacks in this direction by war in the 20th cent. The term "imperialism" is not easy to define today (although often enough used as a term of abuse). Many people accuse the Soviet Union of imperialism—not only because she does not permit free elections in her satellites, but also because she still holds the vast Asiatic empire acquired by the Tsars in times past. There is also what may be described as economic imperialism exerted, not through armies, but through economic penetration and here America is by no means guiltless. The Afrikaners in South Africa pass laws to permit the exploitation of the Black and Coloured peoples in their midst. Israel, too, whatever one may think of its creation on humanitarian grounds, is surely a piece of land taken from the Arabs who formed 90 per cent of its population, by a people whose only rational claim is that their ancestors lived there two thousand years ago. Imperialism is a dangerous word and, before using it, we would do well to remember the retort of a British statesman who, when lecturing in America prior to Indian independence, was asked by an elderly matron: "What are you going to do about the Indians?" "Which Indians, madam —ours or yours?"

Individual Psychology. The term is applied to the psychological system of Alfred Adler of Vienna (1870–1937) who, together with C. G. Jung (*see* **Analytical Psychology**), broke with Freud in 1911. Adler's system of psychotherapy is based on the idea, not of sex as a driving force as in the case of Freud, but on the concept of "compensation" or a drive for power in an attempt to overcome the "inferiority complex" which he held to be universal in human beings. The child naturally feels inferior to adults, but bullying, making him feel insignificant or guilty or contemptible, even spoiling, which makes him feel important within the family but relatively unimportant outside, increases this feeling. Or the child may have physical defects: he may be small or underweight, have to wear glasses, become lame, be constantly ill, or stupid at school. In these ways he develops a sense of inferiority which for the rest of his life he develops a technique to overcome.

This may be done in several ways: he may try to become capable in the very respects in which he feels incompetent—hence many great orators have originally had speech defects; many painters poor eyesight; many musicians bec partially deaf; like Nietzsche, the weakling, he may write about the superman, or like Sandow, the strong man, be born with poor health.

On the other hand he may overdo his attempt and overcompensate. Hence we have the bully who is really a coward, the small man who is self-assertive to an objectionable degree (Hitler, Napoleon, Stalin, and Mussolini were all small men) or the foreigner who like three of these men wanted to be the hero of their adopted country—Hitler the Austrian, Napoleon the Italian, Stalin the Georgian.

But what about the man who can do none of these things, who continues to fail to compensate? He, says Adler, becomes a neurotic because neurosis is an excuse which means "I could have done so-and-so but . . ." It is the unconscious flight into illness—the desire to be ill. Thus a man who used to have a good job lost it through no fault of his own and developed a "nervous break-down," one of the symptoms of which was a fear of crossing streets. Adler would have asked: "What purpose is served by this symptom?" "Why does he unconsciously not want to cross streets?" The answer was that he had only been offered inferior jobs, and although he felt for his family's sake that he ought to take them, something inside said: "No, I have been an important man and I cannot bear to do insignificant work—if I am unable to cross streets I am unable (through no fault of my own) to go out to work." Adler's treatment involves disclosing these subterfuges we play on ourselves so that we can deal with the real situation in a more realistic way. The criticism of Adler's theory is not that it is not true. It is. But it is not the whole truth, for people are much more subtle than Adler gave them credit for; Freud recognised this element of "secondary gain" in neurosis but he knew that there was more to it than that. Nevertheless Adler's method works well in some simpler cases.

Islam, the religion of which Mohammed (570–632) was the prophet, the word signifying submission to the will of God. It is one of the most wide-spread of religions. Its adherents are called Moslems or Muslims. Islam came later than the other great monotheistic religions (Judaism and Christianity) and may be regarded in some respects as a heresy. Mohammed accepted the inspiration of the Old Testament and claimed to be a successor to Moses, and although he did not recognise Jesus as God, he did recognise Him as a prophet (*see* **Docetism**).

The sacred book of Islam is the Koran, the most influential book in the world next to the Bible. According to Islamic belief the words were revealed to the prophet by God through the angel Gabriel at intervals over a period of 20 years, first at his native Mecca and then at Medina. The book is divided into 114 *suras* or chapters: all but one begin with the words: "In the name of Allah, the Merciful, the Compassionate." It is written in classical Arabic, and Moslems memorise much or all of it. The Koran superseded the Gospel as Mohammed superseded Christ. Its ethical teachings are high.

The great advantage of Mohammedism is that, like orthodox Judaism, it is a literal-minded religion lived in everyday life. No Moslem is in any doubt as to exactly how he should carry on in the events of his day. He has five duties: (1) Once in his life he must say with absolute conviction: "There is no God but Allah, and Mohammed is His Prophet." (2) Prayer preceded by ablution must be five times daily—on rising, at noon, in mid-afternoon, after sunset, and before retiring. The face of the worshipper is turned in the direction of Mecca. (3) The giving of alms generously, including provisions for the poor. (4) The keeping of the fast of Ramadan, the holy month, during which believers in good health may neither eat nor drink nor indulge in worldly pleasures between sunrise and sunset. (5) Once in his life a Moslem, if he can, must make the pilgrimage to Mecca. In addition, drinking, gambling, and the eating of pork are forbidden and circumcision is practised. Polygamy is permitted, although decreasing; sexual relations outside marriage are disapproved of; marriage is only with the wife's consent; and divorce may be initiated by either husband or wife. A great advantage in the spread of Islam has been its lack of race prejudice.

Mohammed's main achievements were the destruction of idolatry, the welding of warring tribes into one community, the progress of a conquest which led after his death to the great and cultured empire which spread throughout the Middle East into north Africa, north India, and ultimately to Spain. That it did not spread all over Europe was due to the Muslim defeat by Charles Martel at Tours in 732 A.D.

J

Jainism. Although a wide-spread Indian sect the Jains, like the Sikhs, are regarded as heretics by the Brahmans. The movement founded by Vardhamana, called Mahavira (the great hero), in the 6th cent. B.C. arose rather earlier than Buddhism in revolt against the ritualism and impersonality of **Hinduism** (*q.v.*). It rejects the authority of the early Hindu Vedas and does away with many of the Hindu deities whose place is largely taken by Jainism's twenty-four immortal saints; it despises caste distinctions and modifies the two great Hindu doctrines of *karma* and transmigration. Jain philosophy is based on *ahimsa*, the sacredness of all life, regarding even plants as the brethren of mankind, refusing to kill even the smallest insect. The Jain temples are among the most beautiful in India.

Jansenism, the name given by the Roman Catholic Church to the heresy of Cornelius Jansen (1585–1638), a Dutch-born professor of theology at Louvain, derived from his work *Augustinus*, published after his death. This book set out to prove, by a study of the works of St. Augustine, that Augustine's teachings on grace, predestination and free-will (which, of course, Augustine denied) were opposed to Jesuit teaching. Already hostile to Jansen for forbidding them entry to Louvain university, the Jesuits were outraged and in 1653 Pope Innocent V condemned five of Jansen's propositions as heretical. This produced one of the most famous controversies in history in which the scholars and divines of the great convent of Port Royal in Paris defended the *Augustinus*, for which they were later expelled from their posts. Meanwhile the great Pascal (1623–62) had taken up his pen in their defence and exposed Jesuit hypocrisy in his *Lettres Provinciales*, one of the masterpieces of world literature for its brilliant phrasing, delicate irony, and deadly quotation from Jesuit writings. The Letters had great influence, filled the Jesuits with rage, but even Pascal could not stop the cruel persecution which followed. Another Jansenist text-book was published late in the century, Quesnel's *Moral Reflections on the New Testament*, which Pope Clement XI in his bull *Unigenitus* condemned as heretical in 1713. The French Church was split from top to bottom, the aged king Louis XIV supported the bull, and in 1720 it was made part of French law. Most Jansenists fled the country. Thus ended Jansenism in France but a small sect still exists in Holland, Catholic in everything except acceptance of the *Unigenitus*.

Jehovah's Witnesses, a religious body who consider themselves to be the present-day representatives of a religious movement which has existed since Abel "offered unto God a more excellent sacrifice than Cain, by which he obtained witness that he was righteous." Abel was the first "witness," and amongst others were Enoch, Noah, Abraham, Moses, Jeremiah, and John the Baptist. Pre-eminent among witnesses, of course, was Jesus Christ who is described in the Book of Revelation as "the faithful and true witness." Thus they see themselves as "the Lord's organisation," in the long line of those who through the ages have preserved on earth the true and pure worship of God or, as the Witnesses prefer to call Him, "Jehovah-God."

So far as other people are aware, the movement was founded by Charles Taze Russell (Pastor Russell) of Allegany, Pittsburgh, Pennsylvania, U.S.A. in 1881 under the name, adopted in 1896, of the Watch Tower Bible and

Tract Society, which has continued as the controlling organisation of Jehovah's Witnesses. Its magazine, *The Watch Tower Announcing Jehovah's Kingdom*, first published in 1879, and other publications are distributed by the zealous members who carry out the house-to-house canvassing. The movement has a strong leadership.

Their teaching centres upon the early establishment of God's new world on earth, preceded by the second coming of Christ. Witnesses believe this has already happened, and that Armageddon "will come as soon as the Witness is completed." The millennial period will give sinners a second chance of salvation and "millions now living will never die" (the title of one of their pamphlets).

The dead will progressively be raised to the new earth until all the vacant places left after Armageddon are filled. There is, however, some doubt about the "goatish souls" who have made themselves unpleasant to the Witnesses, those who have accepted (or permitted to be accepted) a blood-transfusion contrary to the Scriptures, and others who have committed grave sins.

Every belief held by the movement, it is claimed can be upheld, chapter and verse, by reference to the Scriptures. Witnesses regard the doctrine of the Trinity as devised by Satan. In both wars Witnesses have been in trouble for their refusal to take part in war and it is only fair to add that six thousand suffered for the same reason in German concentration camps.

Judaism, the religion of the Jews, the oldest of the great monotheist religions, parent of Christianity and Islam, the development of which is presented in the Old Testament. The creed of Judaism is based on the concept of a transcendent and omnipotent One True God, the revelation of His will in the *Torah*, and the special relation between God and His "Chosen People." The idea of Incarnation is rejected, Jesus is not recognised as the Messiah. The *Torah* is the Hebrew name for the Law of Moses (the Pentateuch) which, Judaism holds, was divinely revealed to Moses on Mount Sinai soon after the exodus of the Israelites from Egypt (1230 B.C.). Many critics deny the Mosaic authorship of the first five books of the Bible and believe them to be a compilation from four main sources known as J (Jahvist), E (Elohist), D (Deuteronomist) and P (Priestly Code), distinguished from each other by the name used for God, language, style, and internal evidence. From the historical point of view an important influence on Judaism may have been the monotheism of Ikhnaton, the "heretic" Pharaoh (note, for example, the derivation of Psalm 104 from Ikhnaton's "Hymn to the Sun").

The Talmud is a book containing the civil and canonical laws of the Jews and includes the Mishna, a compilation from oral tradition written in Hebrew, and the Gemara, a collection of comments and criticisms by the Jewish rabbis, written in Aramaic. There are in fact two Talmuds: the one made in Palestine (the Jerusalem Talmud), finished at the beginning of the 5th cent., and the other made in Babylon, completed at the end of the 6th cent.

Judaism at the beginning of the Christian era had a number of sects: (1) the Pharisees (whose views include the first clear statement of the resurrection of the just to eternal life and the future punishment of the wicked) who held to the *Torah* and the universality of God; (2) the Sadducees, the upper class of priests and wealthy landowners, to whom God was essentially a national God and who placed the interests of the state before the *Torah*; they rejected ideas of resurrection and eternal life; (3) the Essenes (*q.v.*) who were regarded as a puritanical break-away movement by both parties The views of the Pharisees prevailed.

Jewish writing continued through the years and some books were added to the *Torah*, among them the Three Major Prophets and certain books of the Twelve Minor Prophets. There were also the Apocalyptic writers who were unorthodox in their preaching of a divinely planned catastrophic end to the world with a "new Heaven and a new earth," preceded by a divine Messiah, and a future life—all of which beliefs influenced early Christianity. Judah Halevi of Toledo (*c.* 1085–*c.* 1140) and Moses Maimonides of Cordova (1135–1204) were the great Jewish philosophers.

Modern movements in Judaism stem from the Enlightenment, notably with Moses Mendelssohn in the 18th cent. who accepted, as was the tendency of the period, only that which could be proved by reason. He translated the Pentateuch into German thus encouraging German Jews to give up Yiddish and Hebrew for the language of the land and thereby preparing them for their vast contribution to Western civilisation. One of his disciples, David Friedländer (d. 1834) instituted "reform" Judaism behind which lay the desire for assimilation. He wanted to eliminate anything that would hamper the relationships of Jews with their neighbours or tend to call in doubt their loyalty to their adopted state. A similar movement in America (1885) called for the rejection of dietary laws, the inauguration of Sunday services, and the repudiation of Jewish nationalism. Between "reform" and orthodoxy there arose the conservative movement which, in England, includes prayers in English in the service, does not segregate men and women in the synagogue, and translates the Law in a more liberal way. (The fact is that it would be almost impossible for a strictly orthodox Jew to live in a modern industrialised community at all.)

Judaism is essentially a social and family religion which, more than almost any other, concerns itself with the observances of every aspect of daily life. As in Islam (*q.v.*) details are laid down in the most minute way for the behaviour of the orthodox.

The home is the main Jewish institution and Jews, like Catholics, cannot surrender their religion. Circumcision takes place eight days after birth, and a boy becomes a man for religious purposes at his Bar Mitzvah at the age of thirteen. Women are spared most of this because their place in the home is considered sufficiently sacred. Among festivals are Passover, recalling the Exodus; Rosh Hashanah (the Jewish New Year), the anniversary of the Creation and the beginning of ten days of penitence ending with Yom Kippur (the Day of Atonement), a day of fasting spent in the synagogue; Purim, celebrating the deliverance of the Jews from Haman; and Chanukah, celebrating their victory against the Syrians under their leader Judas Maccabeus. A new and semi-religious festival with some Jews is the Yom Haatzmaut, the anniversary of the birth of the new Jewish state of Israel.

K

Karma. *See* **Buddhism, Hinduism.**

Ku Klux Klan. After the American Civil War (1861–65) southern conservatives and ex-Confederate leaders began to fear (as they had every reason to do) both Negro and poor White rule. Taxes were rising owing to radical legislation and the tax-burdened and disenfranchised planters finally took to illegal means to achieve their ends by trying to effect an alliance with the poor White and small farmer through appealing to his anti-Negro prejudice.

Hence the Ku Klux Klan was formed in 1866 as a secret society by a small group of Confederate veterans in Tennessee with the intention of frightening Negroes by dressing in ghostly white robes in the guise of the spirits of dead soldiers. But the movement spread like wild-fire throughout the South encouraged by small farmers and planters alike. General Nathan Bedford Forrest was appointed "Grand Wizard" of the Klan "empire" and in every community armed Klansmen riding at night horsewhipped "uppity" Negroes, beat Union soldiers, and threatened carpet-bag politicians (*i.e.*, fortune-hunters from the North). Soon several similar organisations arose, many of which did not stop at torture, burning property, and murder. In fact, although claiming to be a "holy crusade" the Klan was a vicious and contemptible organisation in which former Southern leaders trying to regain control deliberately set poor and middle-class Whites against the Negroes by appeal to race-prejudice. Congress struck back with laws and intervention of Federal troops, and after a large number of convictions in South Carolina much of the violence stopped even if the feelings continued.

After the 1914–18 war the movement, dormant since 1900, revived as a sadistic anti-Negro, anti-Jewish, anti-Catholic society, spreading to the north as well as the south. By 1926, with its white-gowned hooligans and fiery crosses, the Klan began to subside once more. But it rose again after the second world war. After some cruel racial murders in Alabama during 1964–5 President Johnson denounced K-K-K terrorism and promised new criminal legislation to deal with the Klan.

Kuomintang, a Chinese Nationalist party founded in 1891 by Sun Yat Sen. It took part in the first Chinese revolution of 1911 and led the second the following year, dominating south China by 1930 and, under Chiang Kai-shek, who succeeded Sun Yat Sen on his death in 1925, conducted China's defence against Japanese invasion from 1937–45. Sun Yat Sen had attempted to found a democratic republic based on Western parliamentary democracy and in his famous *Testament* laid down the principles upon which the constitution of China should be based. In 1946, Sun Fo, the son of Sun Yat Sen, deplored the party's departure from the principles of social democracy and the welfare of the people in which his father had believed. Beginning as a movement largely inspired by Russia, the Kuomintang under Chiang Kai-shek degenerated into a reactionary and corrupt military oligarchy which, collapsing in 1949, was replaced by the Communist party, leaving Chiang and his followers to rule Formosa with American aid.

L

Lamaism, the religion of Tibet, which is to Tibetans the most genuine form of Buddhist orthodoxy, but to others a corrupt and primitive tyranny. Its beliefs and worship derive from the Mahayana form of Buddhism which was introduced into Tibet in 749 A.D. The emphasis laid by its founder on the necessity for self-discipline and conversion through meditation and the study of philosophy deteriorated into formal monasticism and ritualism. In Tibet, Mahayanian Buddhism came into contact with demon-worship which, as the original religion of the country, contaminated it to the Lamaistic form. The religion from its original unworldly form had by the 17th cent. become a form of civil government in which the Dalai Lama, as the reincarnated Buddha, was both king and high priest, a sort of pope and emperor rolled into one, who ruled despotically in both civil and religious affairs. Under him was a hierarchy of officials in which the lowest order was that of the monks who became as numerous as one man in every six or seven of the population. The main work carried out by this vast church-state was the collection of taxes to maintain the monasteries and other religious offices. When the Dalai Lama dies, his spirit is held to pass into the body of a new-born child, who is selected by a royal search party which allegedly recognises him by certain marks. Second in power to the Dalai Lama is the Panchen or Tashi Lama believed to be a reincarnation of Amitabha, another Buddha. The last Dalai Lama fled to India in 1959 when the Chinese entered his country and it remains to be seen what effects Chinese communism will have upon a land for so long secluded from strangers and whether the religion will survive the impact of dialectical materialism.

Latitudinarians, Anglican churchmen of exceedingly broad views (*e.g.*, bishops who would admit dissenters—*i.e.*, those rejecting the views or authority of the Established Church). Although still used today, the term applies especially to such eminent 17th cent. divines as Burnet, Hales, Tillotson, and Chillingworth.

Levellers, an English military-politico-religious party prominent in the Parliamentary Army about 1647 which stood for the rights of the people. *See* **Diggers.**

Liberalism. The Liberal Party is the successor to the Whigs (a nickname derived from *whiggamore* used in the 17th cent. for Scottish dissenters) of the 18th and 19th cent. Prior to the victory of the Labour Party in 1922, it was one of the two main British political parties. Liberals are moderately progressive in the sense that most appreciate the humanistic aspects of socialism while strongly disapproving of its policies of state control, and they dislike any form of monopoly, state-run or otherwise. In general, the Party advocates co-ownership in industry, electoral reform (proportional representation), protection of individual liberties, governmental reform, tax reform, strict measures against any form of monopoly, and entry to the Common Market.

Logical Positivism, a school of philosophy founded in Vienna in the 1920s by a group known as " the Vienna circle ": their work was based on that of Ernst Mach, but dates in essentials as far back as Hume. Of the leaders of the group, Schlick was murdered by a student, Wittgenstein came to Britain, and Carnap went to America following the entry of the Nazis. Briefly, the philosophy differs from all others in that, while most people have believed that a statement might be (*a*) true, or (*b*) false, logical positivists consider there to be a third category; a statement may be meaningless. There are only two types of statement which can be said to have meaning: (1) those which are tautological, *i.e.*, those in which the statement is merely a definition of the subject, such as " a triangle is a three-sided plane figure " (" triangle " and " three-sided plane figure " are the same thing); and (2) those which can be tested by sense experience. This definition of meaningfulness excludes a great deal of what has previously been thought to be the field of philosophy; in particular it excludes the possibility of metaphysics. Thus the question as to whether there is a God or whether free-will exists is strictly meaningless, for it is neither a tautological statement nor can it be tested by sense-experience.

Lollards, a body of Reformers who, under the leadership of Wyclif, were subjected to cruel persecution in the reign of Richard II. Sir John Oldcastle, a prominent Lollard, was burned at the stake.

Lutheranism. The Reformation had a long history before it became, under Luther and Calvin, an accepted fact. The mediaeval Church had held (as the Catholic Church holds today) that the sacraments were the indispensable means of salvation. Since these were exclusively administered by the clergy, any movement which attacked clerical abuses was forced by sheer necessity to deny the Church's exclusive control of the means of salvation, before it could become free from dependence on a corrupt priesthood. Hence the Albigenses and the Waldenses (*q.v.*), the followers of John Hus and Wyclif (*see* **Anticlericalism**), were bound to deny the authority of the Church and emphasise that of the Bible. Luther began his movement primarily in order to reform the Church from its gross abuses and the famous ninety-five theses nailed to the door of the Church at Wittenberg in 1517 were not primarily theological but moral complaints dealing with the actual behaviour of the clergy rather than Church beliefs. But unlike the earlier reformers, Luther had arrived at the right moment in history when economic individualism and the force of nationalism were bound, sooner or later, to cause the authorities in Germany to line up on his side. Thus he began with the support of the peasants who were genuinely shocked at the abuse of indulgences and other matters, but ended up by being supported by the noblemen who wanted to destroy the power of the pope over the German states and looked forward to confiscating the lands and property of the Church. When the peasants wanted the reform of actual economic abuses relating to the feudal system, Luther took the side of the nobles against them. The contemporary movement in Switzerland led by Ulrich Zwingli had no such secular support, and Zwingli was killed in 1531.

Martin Luther (1483–1546) was the son of a miner in Eisleben in Saxony, entered the order of Austin Friars in 1505, and later taught at the newly founded university of Wittenberg. After the publication of the theses the real issue so far as the Church was concerned was whether he was willing or not to submit to the authority of his superiors; Luther refused to compromise with his conscience in the famous words: " Here I stand; I can do no other." In a further statement Luther recommended the formation of a German national church, the abolition of indulgences and other means whereby Rome obtained money from Germany, and an end to the celibacy of the clergy. For this he was naturally excommunicated. His teaching was based on the German translation of the Bible, but he was by no means a fundamentalist: *e.g.*, he denied that the Book of Hebrews was written by Paul, would have nothing to do with the Apocalypse, and regarded the letter of James as "an epistle of straw." The Scriptures were open to all and could be interpreted by private judgment enlightened by the Spirit of God. Like Calvin, Luther was a predestinarian and determinist, but he was also a conservative and soon became alarmed about the position taken by many extremists once the Reformation was under way. He had really wanted the Church to reform itself, but when he alienated Rome he had perforce to rely more and more on the secular powers which finally resulted in the state-church form which became pronounced in Prussia and later elsewhere. Whereas Calvin wished the Church to be at least the equal of the State and in some respects its superior, Luther's rebellion resulted in the reverse, a state-controlled episcopalianism. The modern Lutheran Church is most active in Germany (where it has been freed from state control and is now called the Evangelical United Brethren Church), the Scandinavian countries (where it is the established state church) and in the United States. *See* **Calvinism, Presbyterianism.**

M

Magic, a form of belief originating in very early days and based on the primitive's inability to distinguish between similarity and identity. The simplest example would perhaps be the fertility rites in which it is believed that a ceremony involving sexual relations between men and women will bring about fertility in the harvest. Or the idea that sticking pins in an image of an individual will bring about harm or even death to the real person. Magic is regarded by some as a form of early science in that man in his efforts to control Nature had recourse to magical practices when the only methods he knew had failed to bring the desired results. It filled a gap. By others magic is regarded as an elementary stage in the evolution of religion. It can be said to have served a purpose there too. Yet magic differs from religion, however closely at times it may come to be related with it, in this important respect: religion depends upon a power *outside and beyond* human beings, whereas magic depends upon nothing but the casting of a spell or the performance of a ceremony—the result follows automatically. (We do well, as Dr. Margaret Murray reminds us, to keep in mind " that when anything regarded as out of the ordinary course of nature is brought about by human means it is called a miracle if the magician belongs to the beholder's own religion, but it is magic—often black magic—if the wizard belongs to another religion. In Grimm's words, 'Miracle is divine, Magic is devilish.' ")

The idea that " like produces like " is at the roots of imitative magic, and it is interesting to note that in some languages (*e.g.*, Hebrew and Arabic) there is no word for " resembles " or " similar to." Hence one says " All thy garments are myrrh " instead of " are *like* myrrh." It follows that an event can be compelled by imitating it. One engages in swinging, not for pleasure, but to produce a wind as the swing does; ball games are played to get rainy weather because the black ball represents dark rain-clouds; other ball games, in which one attempts to catch the ball in a cup or hit it with a stick, represent the sexual act (as some gentlemen at Lords may be distressed to hear) and bring about fertility; in medicine up till a few centuries ago herbs were chosen to cure a disease because in some respects their leaves or other parts looked like the part of the body affected (*e.g.*, the common wildflower still known as " eyebright " was used in bathing the eyes because the flower looks like a tiny eye).

Traces of these beliefs are still found today in children's games and the spells accompanying them have turned into nursery rhymes: dolls are the images of deposed gods or idols; tug-of-war was formerly a sex-conflict with men pulling one end and women the other to bring about fertility; skittles when knocked down by a ball produced the thunder-noise necessary to produce rain. There is reason to believe that the oldest words known in English, relics of our prehistoric language, are " Ena, mena, mina, mo " of the nursery rhyme.

Divination is another aspect of magic and no general of the past would have gone to war without consulting his diviners who referred to animals' livers, how the sacred chickens ate, or the way ceremonially shot arrows fell. Even Cicero wrote a book on divination discussing the significance of dreams, premonitions, and the flight of birds, which revealed the purposes of the gods. If we find it difficult to make any distinction between diviners, priests, medicine-men, rain-makers, shamans, and witch-doctors of early societies, we could perhaps say that they have crystallised out into priests, scientists, and humbugs of our own day. For it would appear that magic, like witchcraft, still exists today—not merely in the form of children's stories and fears, or grown-ups' enjoyment of creepy tales, belief in fortune-telling, omens, amulets, and our own half-embarrassed fear of walking under ladders—but as cults attracting many of those who ought to have more sense. *See* **Witchcraft.**

Malthusianism, the theory about population growth put forward by the Rev. Thomas Malthus (1766–1834) in *An Essay on Population* (1798). His three main propositions were: (1) " Population is necessarily limited by means of subsistence." (2) " Population invariably increases where means of subsistence increase, unless prevented by some very powerful and obvious checks." (3) " These checks, and the checks which repress the superior power of population, and keep its effects on a level with the means of subsistence, are all resolvable into moral restraint, vice and misery." In other words, no matter how great the food supply may become, human reproductive power will always adjust itself so that food will always be scarce in relation to population; the only means to deal with this is by " moral restraint " (*i.e.*, chastity or not marrying), " vice " (*i.e.*, birth-control methods), or misery (*i.e.*, starvation). More specifically, Malthus claimed that while food increases by arithmetical progression, population increases by geometrical progression.

It is true that these gloomy predictions did not take place in Malthus's time largely owing to the opening up of new areas of land outside Europe, the development of new techniques in agriculture, the growth of international trade to poorer areas, the increased knowledge of birth-control, and developments in medical science which reduced the misery he had predicted. Furthermore, we now know that as a society becomes industrialised its birth-rate tends to fall. Nevertheless there are very few scientists who are not perturbed by the growth in the world's population which has increased from about 465 million in 1650 to over 3,000 million today.

Manichaeism. The early Christian apologists who had not yet acquired an adequate knowledge of philosophy had little intellectual trouble in dealing with the heathen; their trouble arose when confronted with religions which had a philosophical basis. Thus Gnosticism (*q.v.*) caused them a good deal of concern, Neoplatonism (*see* God and Man) rather less, since it could never appeal to the masses, and Manichaeism considerable anxiety, because it could appeal both to the philosopher and the masses. Mithraism (*q.v.*), the only other serious contendant, was troublesome for a different reason in that it was the religion of the Roman army and bore a close resemblance to Christianity itself.

Manichaeism was an Asiatic religion which developed from Zoroastrianism (*q.v.*) and shows the influence of Buddhism (*q.v.*) and Gnosticism (*q.v.*) being founded by Mani, a Persian, who was born in Babylonia, *c.* 216 A.D. Mani presented himself to Shapur I as the founder of a new religion which was to be to Babylonia what Buddhism was to India or Christianity to the West. His aspiration was to convert the East and he himself made no attempt to interfere directly with Christianity although he represented himself as the Paraclete (the Holy Ghost or " Comforter ") and, like Jesus, had twelve disciples. His success in Persia aroused the fury of the Zoroastrian priests who objected to his reforming zeal towards their religion and in 276 Mani was taken prisoner and crucified.

Of Mani's complicated system little can be said here, save that it is based on the struggle of two eternal conflicting principles, God and matter, or light and darkness. Like the Albigenses (who followed much of this heresy) Mani divided the faithful into two clases: the " Perfect " who were to practise the most rigid asceticism, and the " Hearers " whose discipline was much less severe. After death the former went to heaven immediately, the latter reached it only through a kind of purgatory, and the unbelievers were doomed to hell. Although its founder had no intention of interfering with the West, after his death his followers soon spread the religion from Persia and Mesopotamia to India and China. (Manichaeism flourished in China until the 11th cent.) It reached as far as Spain and Gaul and influenced many of the bishops in Alexandria and in Carthage where for a time St. Augustine accepted Manichaeism. Soon the toleration accorded it under Constantine ended and it was treated as a heresy and violently suppressed. Yet it later influenced many heresies, including, as we have seen, the Albigenses, and it even had some influence on orthodox Catholicism which had a genius for picking up elements in other religions which had been shown to appeal to worshippers provided they did not conflict unduly with fundamental beliefs.

Maronites, a Roman Catholic community of Christians living in the Mount Lebanon region. Their secular clergy marry as in the Greek Church, but their bishops are celibate.

Marxism. The sociological theories founded by Karl Marx and Friedrich Engels on which modern communist thought is based. Marx and Engels lived in a period of unrestrained capitalism when exploitation and misery were the lot of the British working class, and it was their humanitarianism and concern for social justice which inspired their work. They co-operated in 1848 in writing the *Communist Manifesto*, and in his great work, *Das Kapital* (1867), Marx worked out a new theory of society. He showed that all social systems are economically motivated and change as a result of technical and economic changes in methods of production. The driving force of social change Marx found to be in the struggle which the oppressed classes wage to secure a better future. Thus in his celebrated theory of historical materialism he interpreted history in terms of economics and explained the evolution of society in terms of class struggle. (*See* **Dialectical Materialism**). " In the social production of their means of existence," he wrote, "men enter into definite and unavoidable relations which are independent of their will. These productive relationships correspond to the particular stage in the development of their material productive forces." Marx's theory of historical materialism implies that history is propelled by class struggle with communism and the classless society as the final stage when man will have emancipated himself from the productive process. Marx was the first to put socialism on a rational and scientific basis, and he foretold that socialism would inevitably replace capitalism and that in the transition period the revolutionary dictatorship of the proletariat would be necessary. His prophecy, however, came to realisation not in the advanced countries as he had envisaged but in backward Russia and China. *See also* **The Social Effects of Technical Change, Section Q, Part II.**

Matriarchy, a theory in anthropology developed by Bachofen (*Das Mutterrecht*, 1861) and followed by the American Briffault (*The Mothers*, 1927) that society was originally a matriarchate with authority invested in women. The opinion of nearly all modern anthropologists, however, is against this view. Both historically and today a genuine matriarchate is nowhere to be found, although in a few places feminine prerogatives have evolved to a marked degree in various directions. Thus there are societies which are *matrilineal* (*i.e.*, where descent is traced through the mother's side) and it is quite possible that this used to be the general state of affairs since, at a time when man's part in reproduction was unclear, one could only be certain of the individual's mother. There are other societies in which residence is *matrilocal* (*i.e.*, where the married couple live in the home of the wife's family). But neither of these has any bearing on the issue of whether women ever *ruled* society. Furthermore, there are groups where women are physically stronger than men; where agriculture is primarily in their hands; where, as in the case of the famous bodyguard of the King of Dahomey, they are even soldiers; where men, rather than women, do the cooking or sewing. Yet the question of societies ruled by women either in the past or present may be ruled out; the subject is closed.

Mennonites. *See* **Baptists.**

Mensheviks. *See* **Bolshevism.**

Methodism, the religious movement founded by John Wesley in 1738, at a time when the Anglican Church was in one of its periodic phases of spiritual torpor, with the simple aim of spreading "scriptural holiness" throughout the land. Up to that time Wesley had been a High Churchman but on a visit to Georgia in the United States he was much impressed by the group known as Moravians (*q.v.*), and on his return to this country was introduced by his brother Charles, who had already become an adherent, to Peter Böhler, a Moravian minister in England. Passing through a period of spiritual commotion following the meeting, he first saw the light at a small service in Aldersgate in May 1738 " where one was reading Luther's preface to the Epistle to the Romans " and from this time forth all Wesley's energies were devoted to the single object of saving souls. He did this for fifty years and at the end of his life confessed that he had wasted fifteen minutes in that time by reading a worthless book. Even when he was over eighty he still rose at 4 a.m. and toiled all day long.

Soon Whitefield, a follower with Calvinist views, was preaching throughout the country and Charles Wesley was composing his well-known hymns; John's abilities at this time were taken up in organising the movement described as " People called Methodists." They were to be arranged in " societies " which were united into " circuits " under a minister, the circuits into " districts " and all knit together into a single body under a conference of ministers which has met annually since 1744. Local lay preachers were also employed and to maintain interest the ministers were moved from circuit to circuit each year. These chapel services were not originally meant to conflict with the Church of England of which Wesley still considered himself a member. They were purely supplementary, and it used to be the custom (before the Methodists began to count themselves as Nonconformists) for Methodists to attend Church in the morning and Chapel in the evening.

The class-meeting was the unit of the organisation where members met regularly under a chosen leader to tell their " experiences " upon which they were often subjected to severe cross-examination. At the end of every quarter, provided their attendances were regular, they received a ticket of membership which entitled them to come to monthly sacramental services. If attendance was inadequate the name was removed from the list, without appearance on which nobody was deemed a member. The price of the ticket was " a penny a week and a shilling a quarter " but Wesley was not interested in receiving money from anyone who was not utterly devoted to the cause.

John Wesley introduced four other innovations, some of which were regarded by Churchmen who had previously been willing to commend his efforts in bringing religion to the poorer classes as dangerous: (1) He started the Sunday-school scheme and afterwards enthusiastically supported that of John Raikes, often regarded as the founder of the idea; this was of immense importance in the days before the Education Acts. (2) He reintroduced the Agapae or "love feasts" of the early Church which were fellowship meetings deepening the sense of brotherhood of the society. (3) He began to copy the open-air meetings of the eloquent Whitefield and soon unwittingly produced the most extraordinary results, finding that his sermons led to groans, tears, fainting-fits, and all sorts of emotional expression. Even his open-air lay speakers produced like results and these came to be associated with Methodism and gave significance to the proud Anglican claim that *their* services would be "without enthusiasm." (4) After some hesitation he ventured to consecrate Dr. Thomas Coke, who was being sent as a missionary to America, as a bishop of his church. In addition to Wesley's religious work he was a great educator of the common man. Thus he introduced the cheap book and the church magazine, publishing books of any sort which he thought would edify and not harm even when the views expressed were different from his own—*e.g.*, Thomas à Kempis's *Imitation of Christ* and works of history biography, science, and medicine in some cases written by himself. In this way the movement with its cheap books and reading rooms had an influence far beyond its actual membership. Both the Anglican Church and the Evangelical movement of Wilberforce and others profited from Wesley's work. Some social historians, rightly or wrongly, have claimed that it was Wesley's influence among the working classes that spared England the revolutionary activity which characterised most other European countries during the first quarter of the 19th cent.

Methodism, especially after Wesley's death in 1791, began, like other movements, to develop schisms. There were the long-standing differences which the Baptist movement (*q.v.*) had shown too between Arminian and Calvinist sections—*i.e.*, between those who did and those who did not accept the doctrine of predestination. In the case of the Methodists, this led to a complete break in 1811. Then there were differences associated with the status of the laity, or the relationship of the movement with the Anglican Church. The "Methodist New Connection" of 1797 differed only in giving the laity equal representation with the ministers but the more important break of the Primitive Methodists in 1810 gave still more power to the laity and reintroduced the "camp-meeting" type of service. In 1815 the Bryanites or "Bible Christians" were formed, and a further schism which was even brought before the law courts was ostensibly over the foundation of a theological college. The real reason, of course, was that the ministers were becoming more Tory, whilst the laity were becoming more Radical. Finally in 1932, at a conference in the Albert Hall in London, the Wesleyan Methodists, the Primitive Methodists, and the United Methodists became one Church, the Methodist Church. Including America, where Methodism under the original direction of Thomas Coke spread like wildfire, the Methodist is one of the largest Protestant Churches of today.

Mind and Matter.

Early Greek Views: Idealism and Dualism. Primitive peoples could see that there is a distinction between those things which move and do things by themselves and others, such as stones, which do not. Following the early state of **Animism** (*q.v.*), in which spirits were believed to have their abode in everything, they began to differentiate between matter or substance and a force which seems to move it and shape it into objects and things. Thus to the Greek Parmenides (fl. c. 475 B.C.), who was a philosopher of pure reason, thought or mind was the creator of what we observe and in some way not quite clear to himself it seemed that mind was the cause of everything. This is perhaps the first expression of the movement known as Idealism which says, in effect, that the whole universe is mental—a creation either of our own minds or the mind of God. But from Anaxagorus (488–428 B.C.) we have the clearer statement that mind or *nous* causes all movement but is distinct from the substance it moves. He does not, however, think in terms of individual minds but rather of a kind of generalised mind throughout the universe which can be used as an explanation of anything which cannot be explained otherwise. This is the position known as **Dualism** (*q.v.*) which holds that both mind and matter exist and interact but are separate entities.

Most people in practice are dualists since, rightly or wrongly, mind and body are thought of as two different things; it is the "common-sense" (although not necessarily the true) point of view. Plato in a much more complex way was also a dualist although he held that the world of matter we observe is in some sense not the genuine world. The real world is the world of ideas and the tree we see is not real but simply matter upon which mind or soul has imprinted the idea of a tree Everything that exists has its corresponding form in the world of ideas and imprints its pattern upon matter. Mind has always existed and, having become entangled with matter, is constantly seeking to free itself and return to God.

Plato's pupil Aristotle had a much more scientific outlook and held that, although it was mind which gave matter its form, mind is not *outside* matter, as Plato had thought, but *inside* it as its formative principle. Therefore there could be no mind without matter and no matter without mind; for even the lowest forms of matter have some degree of mind which increases in quantity and quality as we move up the scale to more complex things.

So far, nobody had explained how two such different substances as matter and mind could influence each other in any way, and this remains, in spite of attempts to be mentioned later, a basic problem in philosophy.

Two later ideas, one of them rather foolish and the other simply refusing to answer the question, are typified by the Stoics and some members of the Sceptic school. The first is that only matter exists and what we call mind is merely matter of a finer texture, a view which as an explanation is unlikely to satisfy anyone; the other, that of some Sceptics, is that we can know nothing except the fleeting images or thoughts that flicker through our consciousness. Of either mind or matter we know nothing.

Renaissance Attitude. Christian doctrines have already been dealt with (*see* **God and Man, Determinism and Free-will**), and the past and future of the soul is dealt with under **Immortality.** Nor need we mention the Renaissance philosophers who were really much more concerned about how to use mind than about its nature. When they did consider the subject they usually dealt with it, as did Francis Bacon, by separating the sphere of science from that of religion and giving the orthodox view of the latter because there were still good reasons for not wishing to annoy the Church.

17th-cent. Views: Hobbes, Descartes, Guelincx, Spinoza, Locke, Berkeley. Thomas Hobbes in the 17th cent. was really one of the first to attempt a modern explanation of mind and matter even if his attempt was crude. As a materialist he held that all that exists is matter and hence our thoughts, ideas, images, and actions are really a form of motion taking place within the brain and nerves. This is the materialist theory which states that mind does not exist.

Thus there are three basic theories of the nature of mind and body: idealism, dualism, and materialism, and we may accept any one of the three. But, if we accept dualism, we shall have to explain precisely the relationship between body and mind. In some of his later writings Hobbes seems to suggest that mental processes are the effects of motion rather than motion itself; *i.e.*, they exist, but only as a result of physical processes just as a flame does on a candle. This theory of the relationship is known as *epiphenomenalism.*

Descartes, the great French contemporary of

Hobbes, was a dualist who believed that mind and matter both exist and are entirely different entities; therefore he had to ask himself how, for example, the desire to walk leads to the physical motion of walking. His unsatisfactory answer was that, although animals are pure automatons, man is different in that he has a soul which resides in the pineal gland (a tiny structure in the brain which today we know to be a relic of evolution with no present function whatever). In this gland the mind comes in contact with the "vital spirits" of the body and thus there is interaction between the two. This theory is known as *interactionism*, and since we do not accept its basis in the function of the pineal gland, we are simply left with the notion of interaction but without the explanation of how it takes place.

One of Descartes's successors, Arnold Guelincx, produced the even more improbable theory of *psychophysical parallelism*, sometimes known as the theory of the "two clocks." Imagine you have two clocks, each keeping perfect time, then supposing you saw one and heard the other, every time one points to the hour the other will strike, giving the impression that the first event causes the second, although in fact they are quite unrelated. So it is with the body and mind in Guelincx's view, each is "wound up" by God in the beginning in such a way as to keep time with the other so that when I have the desire to walk purely unrelated physical events in my legs cause them to move at the same time. A variety of this theory is *occasionism*, which says that whenever something happens in the physical world, God affects us so that we *think* we are being affected by the happening.

The trouble about all these theories is (*a*) that they really explain nothing, and (*b*) that they give us a very peculiar view of God as a celestial showman treating us as puppets when it would surely have been easier to create a world in which mind and matter simply interacted by their very nature. Spinoza, too, believed in a sort of psychophysical parallelism in that he did not think that mind and body interacted. But since in his theory everything is God, mind and matter are simply two sides of the same penny.

John Locke, another contemporary, thought of the mind as a blank slate upon which the world writes in the form of sensations, for we have no innate or inborn ideas and mind and matter do interact although he does not tell us how. All we know are sensations—*i.e.*, sense impressions. Bishop Berkeley carried this idea to its logical conclusion: if we know nothing but sensations, we have no reason to suppose that matter exists at all. He was, therefore, an idealist.

18th cent. Views: Hume, Kant. David Hume went further still and pointed out that, if all we know are sensations, we cannot prove the existence of matter but we cannot prove the existence of mind either. All we can ever know is that ideas, impressions, thoughts, follow each other. We do not even experience a self or personality because every time we look into our "minds" all we really experience are thoughts and impressions. Hume was quick to point out that this was not the same as saying that the self did not exist; it only proved that we cannot know that it does.

Kant made it clear that, although there is a world outside ourselves, we can never know what it is really like. The mind receives impressions and forms them into patterns which conform not to the thing-in-itself but to the nature of mind. Space and time, for example, are not realities but only the form into which our mind fits its sensations. In other words our mind shapes impressions which are no more like the thing-in-itself than the map of a battlefield with pins showing the position of various army groups at any given moment is like the battlefield. This, of course, is true. From physics and physiology we know that the sounds we hear are "really" waves in the air, the sights we see "really" electromagnetic waves. What guarantee do we have that the source is "really" like the impression received in our brain? Kant was the leader of the great German Idealist movement of the 18th cent. which in effect said: "why bother about matter when all we can ever know is mental?"

19th and 20th cent. Views. The Englishman Bradley, and the Frenchman Henri Bergson in the 19th and early 20th cent. both held in one form or another the belief that mind in some way creates matter and were, therefore, idealists, whereas Comte, the positivist (*q.v.*), and the Americans William James and John Dewey, held that mind is a form of behaviour. Certain acts (*e.g.*, reflexes) are "mindless" because they are deliberate; others which are intended may be described for the sake of convenience as "minded" (*i.e.*, purposeful). But like the majority of modern psychologists—insofar as they take any interest in the subject—they regarded mind as a process going on in the living body. Is there any reason, many now ask, why we should think of mind as being any different in nature from digestion? Both are processes going on, the one in the brain, the other in the stomach and intestines. Why should we regard them as "things"? *See also* **F39.**

Mithraism, a sun-religion which originated in Persia with the worship of the mythical Mithra, the god of light and of truth. It was for two centuries one of early Christianity's most formidable rivals, particularly in the West since the more philosophical Hellenic Christianity of the East had little to fear from it. (Arnold Toynbee has described Mithraism as "a pre-Zoroastrian Iranian paganism—in a Hellenic dress"; Manichaeism as "Zoroastrianism—in a Christian dress".) Mithraism was a mystery-faith with secret rites known only to devotees. It appealed to the soldiers of the Roman Army which explains its spread to the farthest limits of the Roman empire and its decline as the Romans retreated. The religion resembled Zoroastrianism (*q.v.*) in that it laid stress on the constant struggle between good and evil and there are a number of parallels with Christianity, *e.g.*, a miraculous birth, death, and a glorious resurrection, a belief in heaven and hell and the immortality of the soul, a last judgment. Both religions held Sunday as the holy day of the week, celebrated 25 December (date of the pagan winter solstice festival) as the birthday of the founder; both celebrated Easter, and in their ceremonies made use of bell, holy water, and the candle. Mithraism reached its height about 275 A.D. and afterwards declined both for the reason given above and, perhaps, because it excluded women, was emotional rather than philosophical, and had no general organisation to direct its course. Yet even today, from the Euphrates to the Tyne, traces of the religion remain and antiquarians are familiar with the image of the sun-god and the inscription *Deo Soli Mithrae, Invicto, Seculari* (dedicated to the sun-god of Mithra, the unconquered).

Mohammedanism. See Islam.

Monasticism. When in the 4th cent. A.D. Constantine in effect united state and church there were naturally many who hastened to become Christians for the worldly benefits they expected it to bring in view of the new situation. But there were others who, in their efforts to escape from worldly involvement, went into the deserts of North Africa and Syria to live as hermits and so in these regions there grew up large communities of monks whose lives of renunciation made a considerable impression on the Christian world. They were men of all types but the two main groups were those who preferred to live alone and those who preferred a community life. Among the first must be included St. Anthony, the earliest of the hermits, who was born in Egypt *c.* 250 and who lived alone in a hut near his home for fifteen years, and then in the desert for a further twenty. As his fame spread Anthony came forth to teach and advocate a life of extreme austerity, until by the end of his life the Thebaid (the desert around Thebes) was full of hermits following his example. (Not unnaturally, he was constantly assailed by lustful visions which he thoughtfully attributed to Satan.) In the Syrian desert St. Simeon Stylites and others were stimulated to even greater austerities and Simeon himself spent many years on the top of a pillar in a space so small that it was only possible to sit or stand.

With some of these men it is obvious that ascetic discipline had become perverted into an unpleasant form of exhibitionism.

The first monastery was founded by Pachomius of Egypt *c.* 315 and here the monks had a common life with communal meals worship, and work mainly of an agricultural type. In the Eastern part of the Empire St. Basil (*c.* 360) tried to check the growth of the extreme and spectacular practices of the hermits by organising monasteries in which the ascetic disciplines of fasting, meditation, and prayer, would be balanced by useful and healthy activities. His monasteries had orphanages and schools for boys—not only those who were intended for a monkish life. But the Eastern Church in general continued to favour the hermit life and ascetic extremes. Originally a spontaneous movement, the monastic life was introduced to the West by St. Athanasius in 339 who obtained its recognition from the Church of Rome and St. Augustine introduced it into North Africa beyond Egypt. The movement was promoted also by St. Jerome, St. Martin of Tours, who introduced it into France, and St. Patrick into Ireland. The monastery of Iona was founded by St. Columba in 566. But it must be remembered that the Celtic Church had a life of its own which owed more to the Egyptian tradition than to Rome. Unlike the more elaborate monasteries of the continent those of the early Celtic Church were often little more than a cluster of stone bee-hive huts, an oratory, and a stone cross. It had its own religious ceremonies and its own art (notably its beautifully carved crosses and the illuminated manuscripts such as the Lindisfarne Gospel (*c.* 700) and the Irish Book of Kells dating from about the same time). The Scottish St. Ninian played a major part in introducing Egyptian texts and art to Britain where, mixed with Byzantine influences and the art of the Vikings, it produced a typical culture of its own. Strangely enough, it was the relatively primitive Celts who played almost as large a part in preserving civilisation in Europe during the Dark Ages as did the Italians since. It was St. Columbanus (*c.* 540–615) who founded the great monasteries of Annegray, Luxeuil, and Fontaine in the Vosges country, St. Gall in Switzerland, and Bobbio in the Apennines. So, too, it was the Anglo-Saxon Alcuin (*c.* 735–804) who was called from York by Charlemagne to set up a system of education throughout his empire; the most famous of the monastic schools he founded was at Tours. Among those influenced by him was the philosopher John Scotus Erigena.

Meanwhile from the south, as the disintegrating Roman empire became increasingly corrupt, St. Benedict of Nursia (*c.* 480–*c.* 543) fled the pleasures of Rome to lead a hermit's life near Subiaco. Here he founded some small monasteries, but *c.* 520 made a new settlement, the great monastery of Monte Cassino in southern Italy, where he established a "Rule" for the government of monks. This included both study and work and emphasised that education was necessary for the continuance of Christianity. As his influence spread his Rule was adopted by other monasteries, and schools became part of monastic life. It is not possible to describe the many different orders of monks and nuns formed since, nor the mendicant orders of friars (*e.g.*, Franciscans, Dominicans, Carmelites, Augustinians). In many ways even those outside the Roman Catholic Church owe much to the monastic movement. Monasticism, of course, is not peculiar to Christianity and forms a major aspect of Buddhism, especially in the form of Lamaism in Tibet (*q.v.*).

Monophysitism, a heresy of the 5th cent. which grew out of a reaction against Nestorianism (*q.v.*). The majority of Egyptian Christians were Monophysites (Mono-physite = one nature)—*i.e.*, they declared Christ's human and divine nature to be one and the same. This view was condemned at the Council of Chalcedon (A.D. 451) which pronounced that Jesus Christ, true God and true man, has two natures, at once perfectly distinct and inseparably joined in one person and partaking of the one divine substance. However, many continued to hold Monophysite opinions, including the Coptic Church (*q.v.*), declaring the Council to be unoecumenical (*i.e.*, not holding the views of the true and universal Christian Church).

Monopsychism, the theory of the intellect held by the Arab philosopher Averroës (1126–98) in his interpretation of Aristotle, maintaining that the individual intelligence has no existence in its own right but is part of the divine mind (*nous*) from which it emerges at birth and into which it is absorbed at death. He thus denied personal immortality, a view which was opposed by Christian philosophers.

Monothelites, a Christian sect of the 7th cent. which attempted to reconcile Monophysitism with orthodoxy. They admitted the orthodox view of Christ's two natures as God and man, but declared that He operated with one will. Monothelitism was condemned as heretical by the Council of Constantinople in 680 A.D.

Montanism, a Phrygian form of primitive Puritanism with many peculiar tenets into which the early Christian theologian Tertullian (*c.* 150–*c.* 230) was driven by his extremist views that the Christian should keep himself aloof from the world and hold no social intercourse whatever with pagans. The sect had immediate expectation of Christ's second coming and indulged in prophetic utterance which they held to be inspired by the Holy Ghost but which their enemies put down to prompting by the Devil. In seeking persecution and martyrdom they antagonised the Church and were suppressed.

Moral Re-Armament, a campaign launched in 1938 by an American evangelist of Lutheran background, Frank N. D. Buchman (1878–1961), founder of the Oxford Group Movement, and at first associated with the First Century Church Fellowship, a fundamentalist Protestant revivalist movement. On a visit to England in 1920 Buchman preached "world-changing through life-changing" to undergraduates at Oxford, hence the name Oxford Group. This revivalist movement was based on Buchman's conviction that world civilisation was breaking down and a change had to be effected in the minds of men.

Two of the Group's most typical practices were group confession of sins openly and the "quiet time" set aside during the day to receive messages from the Almighty as to behaviour and current problems. In the eyes of non-Groupers the confession (often of trivial sins) appeared to be exhibitionist and there was felt to be a certain snobbery about the movement which made it strongly conscious of the social status of its converts.

The Oxford Group gave way to Moral Rearmament, the third phase of Buchmanism. M.R.A. men and women lay stress on the four moral absolutes of honesty, purity, love, and unselfishness. They believe they have the ideas to set the pattern for the changing world and, indeed, claim to have aided in solving many international disputes—political, industrial, and racial. Theologians complained of the Group that their movement lacked doctrine and intellectual content; M.R.A. is no different in this respect. Conference centres are at Caux, Switzerland, Mackinac Island, Michigan, U.S.A., and Odawara, Japan.

Moravian Church, a revival of the Church of the "Bohemian Brethren" which originated (1457) among some of the followers of John Hus. It developed a kind of Quakerism that rejected the use of force, refused to take oaths, and had no hierarchy. It appears to have been sympathetic towards Calvinism but made unsuccessful approaches to Luther. As a Protestant sect it was ruthlessly persecuted by Ferdinand II and barely managed to survive. However, in the 18th cent. the body was re-established by Count Zinzendorf who offered it a place of safety in Saxony where a town called Herrnhut (God's protection) was built and this became the centre from which Moravian doctrine was spread by missionaries all over the world. Their chief belief (which had a fundamental influence on John Wesley—*see* **Methodism**) was that faith is a direct illumination from God which assures us beyond all possibility of doubt that we are saved, and that no goodness of behaviour, piety or orthodoxy is of any use without this "sufficient, sovereign, saving grace."

Mormons, or Latter-day Saints, one of the very numerous American religious sects; founded in 1830 by Joseph Smith, the son of a Vermont farmer, who, as a youth, had been influenced by a local religious revival though confused by the conflicting beliefs of the various denominations. He said that while praying for guidance he had been confronted by two heavenly messengers who forbade him to join any existing church but prepare to become the prophet of a new one. Soon, in a series of visions, he was told of a revelation written on golden plates concealed in a nearby hillside. These he unearthed in 1827 and with the help of "Urim and Thummim" translated the "reformed Egyptian" characters into English. Described as the *Book of Mormon*, this was published in 1830 and at the same time a little church of those few who accepted his testimony was founded in Fayette, N.Y. In addition the first of Joseph Smith's "miracles"—the casting out of a devil—was performed. The *Book of Mormon* purports to be a record of early American history and religion, the American Indians being identified as the ten Lost Tribes of Israel, whose fate has never failed to attract the attention of those who prefer myth to fact (cf. British Israelites). Jesus Christ is alleged to have appeared in America after His ascension. Yet Smith's eloquence was able to influence quite educated people, including Sidney Rigdon with whom he went into business for a time. *Doctrine and Covenants* is the title of another book dealing with the revelations Smith claimed to have received. Soon the sect was in trouble with the community both because its members insisted on describing themselves as the Chosen People and others as Gentiles and because they took part in politics, voting as Smith ordered them to. Smith was constantly in trouble with the police. Therefore they were turned out from one city after another until they found themselves a dwelling-place at Nauvoo, Illinois, on the Mississippi.

That would probably have been the end of the story had not Smith been murdered in 1844 and thereby made to appear a martyr, and had there not appeared Brigham Young, a quite extraordinary leader, who stamped out warring factions and drove out the recalcitrant. While persecutions continued Brigham Young announced that it had been revealed that he must lead the faithful to Salt Lake, then outside the area of the United States. There followed the famous trek of more than a thousand miles across desert country in which he led the way, reaching his journey's end in the forbidding valley of the Great Salt Lake on 24 July 1847. By 1851 30,000 Mormons had reached the Promised Land. Here they held their own in a hostile environment and under the practical genius of their leader carried through a vast irrigation scheme and built Salt Lake City which still serves as the headquarters of their sect. In 1850 their pioneer settlement was made Utah Territory, and in 1896 incorporated in the Union. The church was strictly ruled by its leader who also looked after affairs of state for thirty years until his death in 1877.

Polygamy, although opposed by some Mormons, and only sanctioned by Brigham Young when Salt Lake City had been built, is the best-known of Mormon doctrines. It brought the sect into much disrepute and was renounced in 1890. Mormons are millenarians, believing that some time Christ will appear and rule for a thousand years. They perform ritual ceremonies which take the form of a kind of morality play with such actors as God and Satan, Adam and Eve, and there are ablutions, hand-claspings, and anointings. "Miracles" are still performed, for the church has recovered all the powers possessed by the early church. The Old Testament was intended for the Jewish Dispensation, the New for the Christian, but the *Book of Mormon* and the *Doctrine* are for the true church—although all are equally inspired.

There are two orders of priests or leaders: the Melchizedeks, or higher order, include the apostles or ruling elders, and the high priest; the Aaronic priesthood, or lower order, attends to the temporal affairs of the church as the Melchizedeks attend to the spiritual. Members abstain from alcohol, tobacco, coffee, and tea. The church lays stress on the importance of revelation through visions, on education to meet the social, spiritual, and cultural needs of its members, and on community welfare. Members of the Church of Jesus Christ of Latter-day Saints now number over two million in congregations throughout the world.

The Reorganised Church of Jesus Christ of Latter-day Saints with its headquarters at Independence, Missouri, has been separate and distinct since 1852.

Muggletonians, one of the many sects which arose during the Commonwealth but, unlike most of the others (**Levellers** (*q.v.*), **Diggers** (*q.v.*, Fifth-Monarchy Men, and the Millenarians) which tended to have a strongly political aspect, this was purely religious. Founded by two journeymen tailors, Lodowick Muggleton and John Reeve, who interpreted the Book of Revelation in their own peculiar way, it was decided that Reeve represented Moses, and Muggleton, Aaron. They also believed that the Father, not the Son, had died on the cross (an ancient heresy) but added the strange statement that He left Elijah in control during His period on earth. Rejecting the doctrine of the Trinity, they also asserted that God has a human body. Nevertheless, for a time, they had a large number of followers.

Mysticism, a religious attitude which concerns itself with direct relationship with God, "reality" as contrasted with appearance, or the "ultimate" in one form or another. All the higher religions have had their mystics who have not always been regarded without suspicion by their more orthodox members, and, as Bertrand Russell points out, there has been a remarkable unity of opinion among mystics which almost transcends their religious differences. Thus, characteristic of the mystical experience in general, have been the following features: (1) a belief in insight as opposed to analytical knowledge which is accompanied in the actual experience by the sense of a mystery unveiled, a hidden wisdom become certain beyond the possibility of doubt; this is often preceded by a period of utter hopelessness and isolation described as "the dark night of the soul"; (2) a belief in unity and a refusal to admit opposition or division anywhere; this sometimes appears in the form of what seem to be contradictory statements: "the way up and the way down is one and the same" (Heraclitus). There is no distinction between subject and object, the act of perception and the thing perceived; (3) a denial of the reality of time, since if all is one the distinction of past and future must be illusory; (4) a denial of the reality of evil (which does not maintain, *e.g.*, that cruelty is good but that it does not exist in the world of reality as opposed to the world of phantoms from which we are liberated by the insight of the vision). Among the great mystics have been Meister Eckhart and Jakob Boehme, the German religious mystics of the 13th and 16th cent. respectively, Acharya Sankara of India, and St. Theresa and St. John of the Cross of Spain. Mystical movements within the great religions have been: the Zen (*q.v.*) movement within Buddhism; Taoism in China; the Cabalists and Hasidim in Judaism; the Sufis within Islam; some of the Quakers within Christianity.

Mystery Religions. *See* **Orphism.**

N

Nancy School of Psychotherapy. Before Freud, the only satisfactory means of treating neurosis psychologically was hypnosis (used for centuries in one form or another, but rediscovered by Anton Mesmer (1733–1815), hence the name). Also at that time the commonest neurosis was hysteria—a condition in which physical disease is mimicked unconsciously by the production of such symptoms as paralysis, loss of memory, areas of pain, or loss of feeling, even deafness and blindness. This condition was discovered by Ambrose Liébeault of Nancy in Lorraine to be particularly susceptible to treatment by hypnosis (which, unlike Mesmer who was somewhat of a charlatan, he used in a scientific way). Liébeault (1823–1904) and his colleague Hippolyte Bernheim (1840–1919) believed: (*a*) that hysteria was produced by suggestion and particularly by autosuggestion on the part of the patient; and (*b*) that suggestion was a normal trait found in varying degrees in everyone. These conclusions are true, but as Freud showed later, are far from being the whole truth. *See* **Paris School of Psychotherapy.**

Natural Law, the specifically Roman Catholic doctrine that there is a natural moral law, irrespective of time and place, which man can know through his own reason. Originally a product of early rational philosophy, the Christian form of the doctrine is basically due to St. Thomas Aquinas who defined natural law in relation to eternal law, holding that the eternal law is God's reason which governs the relations of all things in the universe to each other. The natural law is that part of the eternal law which relates to man's behaviour. Catholic natural law assumes that the human reason is capable of deriving ultimate rules for right behaviour since there are in man and his institutions certain stable structures produced by God's reason which man's reason can know to be correct and true. Thus, the basis of marriage, property, the state, and the contents of justice are held to be available to man's natural reason. The rules of positive morality and civil law are held to be valid only insofar as they conform to the natural law, which man is not only capable of knowing but also of obeying.

Protestant theologians criticise this notion. Thus Karl Barth and many others hold that sinful and fallen man cannot have any direct knowledge of God or His reason or will without the aid of revelation. Another theologian Niebuhr points out that the principles of the doctrines are too inflexible and that although they are the product of a particular time and circumstance, they are regarded as if they were absolute and eternal. In fact, as most social scientists would also agree, there is no law which can be regarded as " natural " for all men at all times. Nor does it seem sensible to suppose that all or even many men possess either the reason to discern natural law or the ability to obey it; whether or not we accept man's free-will (and all Protestant sects do not), we know as a fact of science that people are not always fully responsible for their actions and some not at all.

Nazism, the term commonly used for the political and social ideology of the German National Socialist Party inspired and led by Hitler. The term *Nazi* was an abbreviation of National Socialist. Those in the Federal Republic today sympathetic to National Socialist aims are known as neo-Nazis. *See* **Fascism.**

Neoplatonism. *See* **Determinism and Free-will** and **God and Man.**

Nestorian heresy. The 5th cent. of the Christian Church saw a battle of personalities and opinions waged with fanatical fury between St. Cyril, the patriarch of Alexandria, and Nestorius, patriarch of Constantinople. Nestorius maintained that Mary should not be called the mother of God, as she was only the mother of the human and not of the divine nature of Jesus. This view was contradicted by Cyril (one of the most unpleasant saints who ever lived) who held the orthodox view. In addition to his utter destruction of Nestorius by stealthy and unremitting animosity Cyril was also responsible for the lynching of Hypatia, a distinguished mathematician and saintly woman, head of the Neoplatonist school at Alexandria. She was dragged from her chariot, stripped naked, butchered and torn to pieces in the church, and her remains burned. As if this were not enough Cyril took pains to stir up pogroms against the very large Jewish colony of Alexandria. At the Council of Ephesus (A.D. 431) the Western bishops quickly decided for Cyril. This Council (reinforced by the Council of Chalcedon in 451) clarified orthodox Catholic doctrine (*see* **Monophysitism**). Nestorius became a heretic, was banished to Antioch where he had a short respite of peace, but later, and in spite of his weakness and age, was dragged about from one place to another on the borders of Egypt. We are assured that his tongue was eaten by worms in punishment for the wicked words he had spoken, but later the Nestorian church flourished in Syria and Persia under the protection of the rulers of Persia and missions were sent to India and China.

Nihilism, the name commonly given to the earliest Russian form of revolutionary anarchism. It originated in the early years of Tsar Alexander II (1818–81), the liberator of the serfs, who, during his attempts to bring about a constitutional monarchy, was killed by a bomb. The term " nihilist," however, was first used in 1862 by Turgenev in his novel *Fathers and Children*. *See* **Anarchism.**

Nominalism. Early mediaeval thinkers were divided into two schools, those who regarded " universals " or abstract concepts as mere names without any corresponding realities (Nominalists), and those who held the opposite doctrine (**Realism**) that general concepts have an existence independent of individual things. The relation between universals and particulars was a subject of philosophical dispute all through the Middle Ages.

The first person to hold the nominalist doctrine was probably Roscelin or Roscellinus in the late 11th cent., but very little is known of him and none of his works remains except for a single letter to Peter Abelard who was his pupil. Roscelin was born in France, accused twice of heresy but recanted and fled to England where he attacked the views of Anselm, according to whom Roscelin used the phrase that universals were a *flatus voci* or breath of the voice. The most important nominalist was the Englishman William of Occam in the 13th cent. who, once and for all, separated the two schools by saying in effect that science is about things (the nominalist view), whereas logic, philosophy, and religion are about terms or concepts (the Platonic tradition). Both are justified, but we must distinguish between them. The proposition " man is a species " is not a proposition of logic or philosophy but a scientific statement since we cannot say whether it is true or false without knowing about man. If we fail to realise that words are conventional signs and that it is important to decide whether or not they have a meaning and refer to something, then we shall fall into logical fallacies of the type: " Man is a species, Socrates is a man, therefore Socrates is a species." This, in effect, is the beginning of the modern philosophy of logical analysis which, to oversimplify, tells us that a statement is not just true or untrue, it may also be meaningless. Therefore, in all the philosophical problems we have discussed elsewhere, there is the third possibility that the problem we are discussing has no meaning because the words refer to nothing and we must ask ourselves before going any further " what do we mean by God," has the word " free-will " any definite meaning?

Nonconformism, the attitude of all those Christian bodies which do not conform to the doctrines of the Church of England. Up to the passing of the Act of Uniformity in 1662 they were called " puritans " or " dissenters " and were often persecuted. The oldest bodies of nonconformists are the Baptists, Independents, and (in England) the Presbyterians; the Methodists, although dating from 1738, did not consider themselves nonconformists until some time later. The Presbyterians are, of course, the official Church of Scotland where it is the Anglicans (known as " Episcopalians ") who are the nonconformists, although not generally described as such.

O

Occam's Razor, the philosophical maxim by which William of Occam, the 13th cent. nominalist (*q.v.*), has become best-known. This states in the form which is most familiar: " Entities are not to be multiplied without necessity " and as such does not appear in his works. He did, however, say something much to the same effect: " It is vain to do with more what can be done with fewer." In other words, if everything in some science can be interpreted without assuming this or that hypothetical entity, there is no ground for assuming it. This is Bertrand Russell's version, and he adds: "I have myself found this a most fruitful principle in logical analysis."

Occultism. *See* **Magic, Alchemy, Astrology,** and **Theosophy.**

Orangemen, members of an Irish society formed in Ulster in 1795 to uphold Protestantism. Their name is taken from King William III, Prince of Orange, who defeated James II at the Battle of the Boyne (1690), hence the enormous banners depicting "King Billy on the Boyne" and such other subjects or mottoes as appeal to the primitive mind when they are carried in procession on 12 July each year. The society has branches in many English-speaking countries but flourishes chiefly in Ulster.

Origenists, a sect of early religionists led by the Christian Father Origen in the 3rd cent., who accepted in general the doctrines of Plotinus (*see* **Neoplatonism**). They believed that men's souls are created before their bodies and are striving to enter bodies as they are born. When the soul leaves the body it enters another body if it has been sinful since justice requires punishment; but the punishment happens naturally through the driving power of the sinner's own errors. The celestial bodies are believed also to have souls, and it is asserted that Christ was the Son of God only by adoption and grace. The Council of Constantinople in 553 condemned Origen's doctrines.

Orphism. The Greeks in general thought very little of their gods, regarding them as similar to human beings with human failings and virtues although on a larger scale. But there was another aspect of Greek religion which was passionate, ecstatic, and secret, dealing with the worship of various figures among whom were Bacchus or Dionysus, Orpheus, and Demeter and Persephone of the Eleusinian Mysteries. Dionysus (or Bacchus) was originally a god from Thrace where the people were primitive farmers naturally interested in fertility cults. Dionysus was the god of fertility who only later came to be associated with wine and the divine madness it produces. He assumed the form of a man or a bull and his worship by the time it arrived in Greece became associated with women (as was the case in most of the Mystery Religions) who spent nights on the hills dancing and possibly drinking wine in order to stimulate ecstasy; an unpleasant aspect of the cult was the tearing to pieces of wild animals whose flesh was eaten raw. Although the cult was disapproved of by the orthodox and, needless to say, by husbands, it existed for a long time. This primitive and savage religion in time was modified by that attributed to Orpheus whose cult was more spiritualised, ascetic, and substituted mental for physical intoxication. Orpheus may have been a real person or a legendary hero and he, too, is supposed to have come from Thrace, but his name indicates that he, or the movement associated with him, came from Crete and originally from Egypt, which seems to have been the source of many of its doctrines. Crete, it must be remembered, was the island through which Egypt influenced Greece in other respects. Orpheus is said to have been a reformer who was torn to pieces by the Maenad worshippers of Dionysus. The Orphics believed in the transmigration of souls and that the soul after death might obtain either eternal bliss or temporary or permanent torment according to its way of life upon earth. They held ceremonies of purification and the more orthodox abstained from animal food except on special occasions when it was eaten ritually. Man is partly earthly, partly heavenly, and a good life increases the heavenly part so that, in the end, he may become one with Bacchus and be called a "Bacchus." The religion had an elaborate theology (*see* **Section H, 117–128**). As the Bacchic rites were reformed by Orpheus, so the Orphic rites were reformed by Pythagoras (*c.* 582–*c.* 507 B.C.) who introduced the mystical element into Greek philosophy which reached its heights in Plato. Other elements entered Greek life from Orphism. One of these was feminism which was notably lacking in Greek civilisation outside the Mystery Religions. The other was the drama which arose from the rites of Dionysus. The mysteries of Eleusis formed the most sacred part of the Athenian state religion, and it is clear that they had to do with fertility rites also, for they were in honour of Demeter and Persephone and all the myths speak of them as being associated with the supply of corn to the country (*see* **Section H, 110–116**). Without being provocative, it is accepted by most anthropologists and many theologians that Christianity, just as it accepted elements of Gnosticism and Mithraism, accepted elements from the Mystery Religions as they in turn must have done from earlier cults. The miraculous birth, the death and resurrection, the sacramental feast of bread and wine, symbolising the eating of the flesh and drinking of the blood of the god, all these are common elements in early religions and not just in one. None of this means that what we are told about Jesus is not true, but it surely does mean: (*a*) that Christianity was not a sudden development but had its predecessors; (*b*) that the early Church absorbed many of the elements of other religions; (*c*) that perhaps Jesus Himself made use of certain symbols which He knew had a timeless significance for man and invested them with new meaning.

Orthodox Eastern Church. There are two groups of Eastern churches: (1) those forming the Orthodox Church dealt with here which include the ancient Byzantine patriarchates of Constantinople, Alexandria, Antioch, and Jerusalem, and the national churches of Russia, Greece, Yugoslavia, Bulgaria, Rumania, etc. (although Orthodox communities exist all over the world and are no longer confined to geographical areas); (2) the churches which rejected Byzantine orthodoxy during various controversies from the 5th to the 7th cent., notably the Coptic church (*q.v.*) and the Armenian church. Although all Orthodox churches share the same doctrine and traditions they are arranged as national independent bodies each with its own hierarchy. They do not recognise the pope, and the primacy of the patriarch of Constantinople is largely an honorary one. Although claiming to be the One Holy, Catholic, and Apostolic Church its alleged infallibility rests on universal agreement rather than on any one individual, and agreement over the faith comes from the Scriptures interpreted in the light of the Tradition. The latter includes dogmas relating to the Trinity, Christology, Mariology, and Holy Icons; the testimony of the Fathers (St. Athanasius, St. Basil, St. John Chrysostom, St. Cyril of Alexandria, etc.); the canons or rules as formulated by the Councils and the Fathers. The Orthodox Church did not take part in the great Western controversies about the Bible, nor, of course, in the Reformation. Attempts have recently been made to improve relations between Rome and Constantinople: the two Churches agreed in 1965 to retract the excommunications cast on each other in A.D. 1054, which formalised the Great Schism.

Oxford Group. *See* **Moral Re-Armament.**

Oxford Movement. *See* **Tractarianism.**

P

Pantheism. *See* **God and Man.**

Papal Infallibility. The basis of papal infallibility is (*a*) that every question of morals and faith is not dealt with in the Bible so it is necessary that there should be a sure court of appeal in case of doubt, and this was provided by Christ when he established the Church as His Teaching Authority upon earth; (*b*) ultimately this idea of the teaching function of the Church shapes the idea of papal infallibility which asserts that the pope, when speaking officially on matters of faith or morals, is protected by God against the possibility of error. The doctrine was proclaimed in July 1870.

Infallibility is a strictly limited gift which does not mean that the pope has extraordinary intelligence, that God helps him to find the answer to every conceivable question, or that Catholics have to accept the pope's views on politics. He can make mistakes or fall into sin, his scientific or historical opinions may be quite wrong, he may write books that are full of errors.

Only in two limited spheres is he infallible and in these only when he speaks officially as the supreme teacher and lawgiver of the Church, defining a doctrine that must be accepted by all its members. When, after studying a problem of faith or morals as carefully as possible, and with all available help from expert consultants, he emerges with the Church's answer—on these occasions it is not strictly an answer, it is *the* answer.

Historically speaking, the Roman Catholic Church of the early 19th cent. was at its lowest ebb of power. Pope Pius IX, in fear of Italian nationalism, revealed his reactionary attitude by the feverish declaration of new dogmas, the canonisation of new saints, the denunciation of all modern ideals in the Syllabus of Errors, and the unqualified defence of his temporal power against the threat of Garibaldi. It is not too much to say that everything regarded as important by freedom-loving and democratic people was opposed by the papacy at that time. Thus in England, Lord Acton, the great historian, who was co-editor with Richard Simpson of the Catholic monthly, the *Rambler*, was forced to resign because his liberal views had given offence to Cardinal Wiseman, archbishop of Westminster. Acton's struggles against the hierarchy were in vain and the "Ultramontanes" won when in 1870, after a long and sordid struggle, the Vatican Council, convened by Pius IX, pronounced the definition of his infallibility. Döllinger, a German priest and famous historian of the Church, was excommunicated because, like many others, he refused to accept the new dogma. If, as the Catholic statement above claims, papal infallibility is a logical extension of the past history of the Church, it is strange that the greatest Catholic scholar of the age failed to observe it. It is difficult not to doubt that there was some connection between the pronouncement of the pope's infallibility and his simultaneous loss of temporal power.

Paris School of Psychotherapy. The Paris school is important because it was the school of the famous French neurologist Jean Charcot (1825–93), teacher of Sigmund Freud (1856–1939) and Pierre Janet (1859–1947). At a time when hypnosis and the neurosis known as hysteria were very much "in the air," and Liébeault and his colleagues (*see* **Nancy School**) were regarding hysteria as a condition which was produced by autosuggestion, Charcot was maintaining the opposite view. Hypnosis, or the ability to be hypnotised, was, in his view, a symptom of a hysterical personality, and hysteria had a physiological basis.

Charcot was a highly controversial figure and his demonstrations were famous, if to some verging on the notorious; he aroused much antagonism among Roman Catholics by stating that faith cures at Lourdes were actually cases of hysteria and not, therefore, miraculous since they could equally well be cured by himself. However, he regarded hysteria as a sign of hereditary degeneration. His supposed words: "You will always find sex at the root of the trouble" and his pupil Janet's evidence that forgotten (or, as we should now say, repressed) traumatic events lay behind the symptoms which would go when the event was allowed expression, had a potent influence on the young Freud who made the uncovering of the past and the importance of sex the foundations of psychoanalysis (*see* **Section F, Part III**). Janet's belief was that hysteria is due to dissociation or imperfect integration of the personality. Modern belief is that Charcot was wrong about the physical basis of hysteria, wrong about the pathological significance of hypnosis, but right on the whole about the importance of sexual problems in neurosis.

Parsees. *See* **Zoroastrianism.**

Paulicians, a Christian heretical sect which derives its name not from Paul the Apostle but from Paul of Samosata who was patriarch of Antioch, 260–72. His followers, the "Pauliani," were condemned for their "Adoptionist" (*q.v.*) attitude by the Council of Nicaea (325). Originally wide-spread in Anatolia, especially in Armenia from the 5th cent. onwards, they were cruelly persecuted by the Byzantine emperors and were deported (*c.* 755) to the Balkans to garrison that part of the East Roman empire. Elsewhere in this section the Albigenses or Cathari are mentioned; the Paulicians form part of their spiritual ancestry. It is debatable whether the "Adoptionist" doctrines professed by the Albigenses came from the Balkan Bogomils, through the Crusaders, or from the north of Spain, where there was an "Adoptionist" movement in the late part of the 8th cent. The evidence seems to be in favour of the Balkan influence but it should be noted that although the Bogomils were influenced by the Paulicians and the Manichaeans, the Paulicians themselves repudiated Manichaeanism. An authentic liturgical book of the Paulicians—*The Key of Truth*—was discovered in 1891 in Echmiadzin where the Armenian historical archives were kept. This manuscript throws new light on the heresy.

Pavlovian theory. *See* **Behaviourism.**

Pelagian heresy. *See* **Determinism and Free-will.**

Peripatetic philosophers, a name given to the followers of Aristotle derived from the philosopher's habit of walking up and down as he expounded his theories.

Phrenology, a psychological "school" founded in 1800 by two Germans, Franz Josef Gall and Johann Gaspar Spurzheim. Gall was an anatomist who believed there to be some correspondence between mental faculties and the shape of the head. He tested these ideas in prisons and mental hospitals and began to lecture on his findings, arousing a great deal of interest throughout both Europe and America, where his doctrines were widely accepted. Phrenology became fashionable, and people would go to "have their bumps read" as later men and women of fashion have gone to be psychoanalysed. Roughly speaking, Gall divided the mind into thirty-seven faculties such as destructiveness, suavity, self-esteem, conscientiousness, and so on, and claimed that each of these was located in a definite area of the brain. He further claimed that the areas in the brain corresponded to "bumps" on the skull which could be read by the expert, thus giving a complete account of the character of the subject. In fact, (*a*) no such faculties are located in the brain anywhere for this is simply not the way the brain works; (*b*) the faculties described by Gall are not pure traits which cannot be further analysed and are based on a long outdated psychology; (*c*) the shape of the brain bears no specific relationship to the shape of the skull. Phrenology is a pseudo-science; there is no truth in it whatever. But, even so, like astrology, it still has its practitioners.

Physiocrats. A French school of economic thought during the 18th cent., known at the time as *Les Economists* but in later years named physiocrats by Du Pont de Nemours, a member of the School. Other members were Quesnay, Mirabeau, and the great financier Turgot. The physiocrats held the view, common to the 18th cent., and deriving ultimately from Rousseau, of the goodness and bounty of nature and the goodness of man "as he came from the bosom of nature." The aim of governments, therefore, should be to conform to nature; and so long as men do not interfere with each other's liberty and do not combine among themselves, governments should leave them free to find their own salvation. Criminals, madmen, and monopolists should be eliminated. Otherwise the duty of government is *laissez-faire, laissez passer*. From this follows the doctrine of free trade between nations on grounds of both justice and economy; for the greater the competition, the more will each one strive to economise the cost of his labour to the general advantage. Adam Smith, although not sharing their confidence in human nature, learned much from the physiocrats, eliminated their errors, and greatly developed their teaching.

Physiognomy. *See* **Characterology.**

Pietism, a movement for reviving piety in the Lutheran Church of the 17th cent.

Plymouth Brethren, a religious sect founded by John Nelson Darby, a minister of the Protestant Church of Ireland, and Edward Cronin, a former Roman Catholic, in 1827. Both were dissatisfied with the lack of spirituality in their own and other churches and joined together small meetings in Dublin every Sunday for "the breaking of bread." Soon the movement began to spread through Darby's travels and writings and he finally settled in Plymouth, giving the popular name to the "Brethren." Beginning as a movement open to all who felt the need to "keep the unity of the Spirit," it soon exercised the right to exclude all who had unorthodox views and split up into smaller groups. Among these the main ones were the "Exclusives," the Kellyites, the Newtonites, and "Bethesda" whose main differences were over problems of church government or prophetical powers. Some of these are further split among themselves. Readers of *Father and Son* by Sir Edmund Gosse, which describes life with his father, the eminent naturalist Philip Gosse, who belonged to the Brethren, will recall how this basically kind, honest, and learned man was led through their teachings to acts of unkindness (*e.g.*, in refusing to allow his son and other members of his household to celebrate Christmas and throwing out the small tokens they had secretly bought), and intellectual dishonesty (*e.g.*, in refusing for religious reasons alone to accept Darwinism when all his evidence pointed towards it).

The original views of Darby which were perpetuated by the "Exclusive" Brethren were somewhat as follows: Christianity has fallen from New Testament purity and all Christendom and every Church is corrupt and has incurred God's displeasure, notably by establishing ministerial offices which hinder the believer's approach to God. Ministers should not be officials but possess special gifts ("Charismata") granted from above and assigned by the Holy Ghost according to his will; these Charismata have no connection whatever with any official posts although in some cases they may coincide with them. The whole doctrine of the Brethren is based on the need for *direct* access to God and the rejection of any intermediate agency such as priests, ministers or presbyters. The Exclusive Brethren adopted new harsh rules in 1965 designed to prevent "Saints" (members) from having any contact with "Sinners" (non-members). Members sharing homes with non-members were to be expelled; members must declare their bank balances; unmarried members, single or widowed, must marry as soon as possible within the sect.

Today, the majority of Brethren belong to the "Open Brethren" assemblies and, unlike the "Exclusives," hold that the Lord's Supper (a commemorative act of "breaking the bread" observed once a week) is for all Christians who care to join them. Baptism is required and Brethren believe in the personal premillenial second coming of Christ.

Poltergeist, allegedly a noisy type of spirit which specialises in throwing things about, making loud thumpings and bangings, and occasionally bringing in "apports," *i.e.*, objects from elsewhere. Most so-called poltergeist activities are plain frauds, but the others are almost invariably associated with the presence in the house of someone (often, but not always a child) who is suffering from severe mental conflicts usually of a sexual nature. The inference is that those activities which are not simply fraudulent are either due to some unknown influence exuded by such mentally abnormal people, or that they are actually carried out by ordinary physical means by such people when in a state of hysterical dissociation—*i.e.*, unconsciously. The second hypothesis is much the more probable. *See* **Psychic Research.**

Polytheism. *See* **God and Man.**

Positivism, also known as the **Religion of Humanity**, was founded by Auguste Comte (1798–1857), a famous mathematician and philosopher born in Montpellier, France. His views up to the end of the century attracted many and it would have been impossible throughout that time to read a book on philosophy or sociology that did not mention them, but today his significance is purely of historical interest. In his *Cours de Philosophie Positive* (1830) he put forward the thesis that mankind had seen three great stages in human thought: (1) the theological, during which man seeks for supernatural causes to explain nature and invents gods and devils; (2) the metaphysical, through which he thinks in terms of philosophical and metaphysical abstractions; (3) the last positive or scientific stage when he will proceed by experiment and objective observation to reach in time "positive truth."

Broadly speaking, there is little to complain of in this analysis; for there does seem to have been some sort of general direction along these lines. However, Comte was not satisfied with having reached this point and felt that his system demanded a religion and, of course, one that was "scientific." This religion was to be the worship of Humanity in place of the personal Deity of earlier times, and for it he supplied not only a Positive Catechism but a treatise on Sociology in which he declared himself the High Priest of the cult. Since, as it stood, the religion was likely to appear somewhat abstract to many, Comte drew up a list of historical characters whom he regarded as worthy of the same sort of adoration as Catholics accord to their saints. The new Church attracted few members, even among those who had a high regard for Comte's scientific work, and its only significant adherents were a small group of Oxford scholars and some in his own country. Frederic Harrison was the best-known English adherent and throughout his life continued to preach Comtist doctrines in London to diminishing audiences.

Pragmatism, a typically American school of philosophy which comes under the heading of what Bertrand Russell describes as a "practical" as opposed to a "theoretical" philosophy. Whereas the latter, to which most of the great philosophical systems belong, seeks disinterested knowledge for its own sake, the former (*a*) regards action as the supreme good, (*b*) considers happiness an effect and knowledge a mere instrument of successful activity.

The originator of Pragmatism is usually considered to have been the psychologist William James (1842–1910) although he himself attributed its basic principles to C. S. Peirce. The other famous Pragmatist is Dr. John Dewey, best-known in Europe for his works on education (for although American text-books on philosophy express opinions to the contrary, few educated people in Europe have taken the slightest interest in Pragmatism and generally regard it as an eccentricity peculiar to Americans).

The basic source of Pragmatism is William James's book *The Will to Believe* (1896) in which he points out that we are often compelled to take a decision where no adequate theoretical grounds for a decision exist; for even to do nothing is to decide. Thus in religion we have a right to adopt a believing attitude although not intellectually fully convinced. We should believe truth and shun error, but the failing of the sceptical philosopher is that he adheres only to the latter rule and thus fails to believe various truths which a less cautious man will accept. If believing truth and avoiding error are equally important, then it is a good idea when we are presented with an alternative to believe one of the possibilities at will, since we then have an even chance of being right, whereas we have none if we suspend judgment. The function of philosophy, according to James, is to find out what difference it makes to the individual if a particular philosophy or world-system is true: "An idea is 'true' so long as to believe it is profitable to our lives," and, he adds, "the true is only the expedient in our way of thinking . . . in the long run and on the whole of course." Thus "if the hypothesis of God works satisfactorily in the widest sense of the word, it is true." Bertrand Russell's reply to this assertion is: "I have always found that the hypothesis of Santa Claus 'works satisfactorily in the widest sense of the word'; therefore 'Santa Claus exists' is true, although Santa Claus does not exist." Russell adds that James's concept of truth simply omits as unimportant the question whether God really *is* in His heaven; if He is a useful hypothesis that is enough. "God the Architect of the Cosmos is forgotten; all that is remembered is belief in God, and its effects upon the creatures inhabiting our petty planet. No wonder the Pope condemned the pragmatic defence of religion."

Predestination. *See* **Calvanism.**

Presbyterianism, a system of ecclesiastical government of the Protestant churches which look back to John Calvin as their Reformation leader. The ministry consists of presbyters who are all of equal rank. Its doctrinal standards are contained in the *Westminster Confession of Faith* (1647) which is, in general, accepted by English, Scottish, and American Presbyterians as the most thorough and logical statement in existence of the Calvinist creed. The Church of Scotland is the leading Presbyterian church in the British Isles.

The Reformation in Scotland was preceded by the same sort of awareness of the moral corruption of the Roman Church as had happened elsewhere, but for various political and emotional reasons, which need not be discussed here, the majority of the Scottish people (unlike the English who had been satisfied with the mere exchange of Crown for Pope) were determined on a fundamental change of doctrine, discipline, and worship, rather than a reform of manners. The church preachers had learned their Protestantism not from Luther but from Calvin and their leader John Knox had worked in Geneva with Calvin himself and was resolved to introduce the system into Scotland. In 1557 the "Lords of the Congregation" signed the Covenant to maintain "the blessed Word of God and his congregation" against their enemies, and demanded the right to worship as they had chosen. However, the real date of the Scottish Reformation is August 1560 when Mary of Guise (the regent for Mary Queen of Scots who was not yet of age) died and the Estates met to settle their affairs without foreign pressure; the Confession of Faith was drawn up and signed by Knox and five other ministers and almost unanimously adopted by the Estates.

The ideas on which the Reformed Kirk was based are found in the *Confession*, the *Book of Discipline*, and the *Book of Common Order*, the so-called Knox's liturgy. They are strongly anti-papal, referring to the Roman Church as the "Kirk malignant"; Apostolic Succession and Transubstantiation are repudiated; Christ is the sole head of the Kirk; the papist priests are not ministers at all and the Mass is a blasphemy. Knox's liturgy, the same as that used in Geneva but translated into English, was used until Laud's attempt to force an Anglican liturgy on the Kirk led to an abandonment of both in favour of "free prayers." The Book of Discipline contains elaborate rules for everything connected with church affairs.

The Presbyterian tradition includes uncompromising stress on the Bible as the Word of God, and the value of a highly trained ministry, which has given the Church of Scotland a high reputation for scholarship and has in turn influenced the standard of education in Scotland. The unity of the Church is guaranteed by providing for democratic representation in a hierarchy of courts (unlike the Anglican Church, which is a hierarchy of persons). The local kirk-session consists of the minister and popularly elected elders (laymen). Ministers, elected by their flocks, are ordained by presbyters (ministers already ordained). Above the kirk-session is the court of the presbytery which has jurisdiction over a specified area; above that the court of synods which rules over many presbyteries; and finally the General Assembly which represents the whole church. The function of the elders is to help the minister in the work and government of the kirk. At the head of the General Assembly is the Moderator.

A number of attempts were made by England to foist episcopacy on Scotland: under James I, Charles I, and Charles II the Covenanters were hunted down, executed and dragooned over a period of nearly thirty years before William of Orange came to the throne and Presbyterianism was re-established (1690). Today Presbyterians no less than other Christian communities are looking at Christianity as a common world religion in the sense that the principles which unite them are greater than those which divide them. *See* **Church of Scotland, Calvinism.**

Protestant, the name first applied to those who favoured the cause of Martin Luther and who protested against the intolerant decisions of the Catholic majority at the second Diet of Speyer (1529), revoking earlier decisions of the first Diet of Speyer tolerating the Reformers in certain cases (1526). In general the name "Protestant" is applied to those Churches which severed connection with Rome at the time of the Reformation. The essence of Protestantism is the acceptance by the individual Christian of his direct responsibility to God rather than to the Church. *See* **Lutheranism, Presbyterianism, Calvinism.**

Psychic Research, the *scientific* study of so-called psychic phenomena as contrasted with spiritualism (*q.v.*) which is the cult of those who already believe in their supernatural nature. It is obviously impossible here to summarise work that has been carried out (in Britain notably by the Society for Psychical Research, founded in 1882) on such subjects as mediumship, apparitions, telepathy and clairvoyance (discussed here separately under the heading of Telepathy) poltergeists (also discussed separately), levitation, and precognition.

But the point at which we must begin is the human mind and the nature of scientific evidence and so far as these are concerned the following points may be made.

(1) There is little use in discussing psychic phenomena until we realise that almost no human being—least of all one with strong convictions—is a completely trustworthy witness. A person may be utterly honest in every othe respect except that in which his convictions ar involved.

(2) This does not mean that a witness is eithe telling the whole truth or is simply lying; fo the following possibilities exist: (*a*) he may b telling the truth: (*b*) he may be consciousl lying for motives of his own; (*c*) his recollection may be incorrect in discussing something tha happened in the past; (*d*) he may really believ that he saw or heard what he said he did an may be telling the truth *as he experienced it*—*e.g.*, seeing a ghost—without realising that wha he experienced is a product of his own ur conscious mind; (*e*) there are various degrees c lying, for the mind has a natural tendency t add coherence and meaning to the only partl coherent events of the day, and it is a norma trait (consciously or unconsciously) to make "good story" out of what originally wer isolated and unconnected happenings; (*f*) eve under the most favourable conditions th evidence of scientifically-trained people is not a good as it might be (cf. the psychological e periment in which a class of students is su denly exposed to a deliberately contrived scen *e.g.*, two men eccentrically dressed rush into th lecture-room, exchange words, and have quarrel—and the students are afterwards r quired to write down what they saw and hear rarely 10 per cent. being even 70 per cer correct as to what really happened).

(3) There are many aspects of "psychic phenomena which are not "psychic" at all, b based on well-known scientific principles. Ho many people, for example, know: (*a*) that *eve* physical illness has its psychological aspect, that a person with chronic arthritis, let us sa may get up and walk for the first time in yea after injection with a new drug which is lat proved to be worthless or no better th aspirin (*e.g.*, cortisone), yet if a "spiritu healer" got the same results he would acclaimed for his psychic powers; (*b*) that it possible to be completely paralysed, tota blind or deaf, have total loss of sensation some part of the body, have two or more pe sonalities, *without any physical disease bei present*, in the neurosis (cured daily by ps chiatrists without mystery) known as hyster

(4) It is possible under hypnosis, or se hypnosis, to produce stigmata—*e.g.*, marks r sembling the nail-prints of the Crucifixion hands and feet, to produce blisters at w spontaneous bleeding, and many of the ph nomena usually described as miraculous, in t consulting room and by scientific means.

(5) We all have more potent senses than ordinarily realise. We may not consciou know the number of steps leading to our fl but can be made under hypnosis to t

Furthermore, there are people who are hypersensitive in hearing and vision (often without being aware of it), so that in "thought-transference" experiments where they are sent to another room whilst others decide on some object or idea, they may subconsciously hear what is going on; or in card experiments in telepathy they may be able to read the face of the card reflected in the pupils of the "sender" opposite, or tell in a familiar pack which card is which from almost invisible differences on the backs of the cards.

(6) Most of us have no idea of the mathematical laws of probability and are therefore likely to misinterpret the "mysteriousness" of phenomena. Thus, suppose I have a "premonition" that someone has died and later find my feelings confirmed by the event, then I may not remember or know (*a*) that on many previous occasions I, in common with most other people, have had "premonitions" the vast majority of which did *not* come true; (*b*) that, on the last occasion I saw the person, or from things I may have heard, I may have unconsciously noted signs that all was not well and expected the event; (*c*) that the most "improbable" things happen quite normally (*e.g.*, during the last war a flying bomb fell through the roof of the British Museum and failed to explode, and some time later a second flying bomb fell *through the same hole* and likewise *failed to explode*); (*d*) that the chance of a pack of cards being dealt so that each of four persons receives a complete suit is exactly the same as the chance that any other combination of cards may come up.

(7) That collective hallucinosis does occur (it would be invidious to mention in detail certain "miraculous happenings" which might hurt the religious susceptibilities of many, but we are entitled to ask how it is possible for the sun to stand still in the sky in the presence of thousands of people collected in a particular area when it is seen nowhere else in the world and has been noted by no astronomical laboratory?)

(8) Mediums have been proved to be prepared to do the most extraordinary things in order to deceive a suggestible audience seated in semi-darkness—*e.g.*, the so-called "ectoplasm" (a supposedly psychic substance or materialisation) which exudes from the medium's body has been found before the séance, as have "apports" or objects apparently appearing from nowhere, half-way down the medium's throat or in the stomach ready to be regurgitated, and even in other bodily apertures.

It is not maintained that psychic phenomena do not happen, but that we must be extremely cautious in accepting the evidence of our own, or even more, other people's, senses, and much less free in our interpretation of what has been observed really means. *See* **Poltergeist, Telepathy, Spiritualism.**

Psychoanalysis. *See* **Section F, Part III.**

Pyrrhonism, a sceptical philosophy which doubts everything.

Q

Quakers. *See* **Friends, The Society of.**

Quartodecimani, an early Christian community who celebrated the Easter festival on the 14th day of the month, when the Jews celebrated their Passover. In consequence of the confusion caused, the practice was condemned by the Council of Nicaea in 325.

Quietism, a doctrine of extreme asceticism and contemplative devotion, embodied in the works of Michael Molinos, a 17th cent. Spanish priest, and condemned by Rome. It taught that the chief duty of man is to be occupied in the continual contemplation of God, so as to become totally independent of outward circumstances and the influence of the senses. Quietists taught that when this stage of perfection is reached the soul has no further need for prayer and other external devotional practices. Similar doctrines have been taught in the Moslem and Hindu religions. *See* **Yoga.**

R

Racism, the doctrine that one race is inherently superior or inferior to others, one of the bases of racial prejudice. It has no connection whatever with the study of race as a concept, or the investigation of racial differences, which is a science practised by the physical anthropologist (who studies physical differences), or the social anthropologist (who studies cultural differences). Racism is simply a vulgar superstition believed in by the ignorant or mentally unbalanced, and it may be categorically stated as a scientific fact that racial superiority is a myth believed in by no scientist of repute. There are, therefore, only two questions which it is necessary to answer: (1) If no race is superior to any other, why are there obvious differences between the backward and the technically advanced peoples? (2) If there are no inherent differences between races, then why does racial prejudice exist? Both of these are, strictly speaking, questions to which the scientists must give an answer: the former is answered in **Section F, Part III,** and **Section Q, Part II**; the latter under **Anti-semitism, J3.**

Ranters, a derisive term for the Primitive Methodists (*see* **Methodism**).

Rationalism is defined as "the treating of reason as the ultimate authority in religion and the rejection of doctrines not consonant with reason." In practice, rationalism has a double significance: (1) the doctrine as defined above, and (2) a 19th cent. movement which was given to what was then known as "free-thought," "secularism," or agnosticism—*i.e.*, it was in the positive sense anti-religious and was represented by various bodies such as the Secular Society, the National Secular Society, and the Rationalist Press Association (founded in 1899).

In the first sense, which implies a particular philosophical attitude to the universe and life, rationalism is not easy to pin down although, at first sight, it would appear that nothing could be simpler. Does it mean the use of pure reason and logic or does it mean, on the other hand, the use of what is generally called the "scientific method" based on observation (*i.e.*, the evidence of our senses) and experiment? If we are thinking in terms of the use of pure reason and logic then the Roman Catholic Church throughout most of its history has maintained, not that the whole truth about religion can be discovered by reason, but as St. Thomas Aquinas held, the basis of religion—*e.g.*, the existence of God—can be rationally demonstrated. Nobody could have made more use of logic than the schoolmen of the Middle Ages, yet not many people today would accept their conclusions, nor would many non-Catholics accept St. Thomas's proofs of the existence of God even when they themselves are religious. The arguments of a first Cause or Prime Mover or the argument from Design on the whole leave us unmoved, partly because they do not lead us to the idea of a *personal God*, partly because we rightly distrust logic and pure reason divorced from facts and know that, if we begin from the wrong assumptions or premises, we can arrive at some very strange answers. If the existence of a Deity can be proved by reason, then one can also by the use of reason come to the conclusions, or rather paradoxes, such as the following: God is by definition all good, all knowing, all powerful—yet evil exists (because if it does not exist then it cannot be wrong to say "there is no God"). But if evil exists, then it must do so either because of God (in which case He is not all good) or in spite of God (in which case He is not all powerful).

Arguments of this sort do not appeal to the modern mind for two historical reasons: (1) many of us have been brought up in the Protestant tradition which—at least in one of its aspects—insists that we must believe in God by faith rather than by logic and in its extreme form insists on God as revealed by the "inner light"; (2) our increasing trust in the scientific method by direct observation and experiment. Thus, no matter what Aristotle or St. Thomas may say about a Prime Mover or a First Cause, we remain unconvinced since at least one scientific theory suggests that the universe did not have a beginning and if scientific investigation proved this to be so, then we should be entirely indifferent to what formal logic had to say.

The secularist and rationalist movements of

the 19th cent. were anti-religious—and quite rightly so—because at that time there were serious disabilities imposed even in Britain by the Established Church on atheism or agnosticism and freedom of thought. They are of little significance now because very little is left, largely thanks to their efforts, of these disabilities.

Finally, although most people are likely to accept the scientific method as the main means of discovering truth, there are other factors which equally make us doubt the value of "pure" logic and reason unaided by observation. The first of these is the influence of Freud which shows that much of our reasoning is mere rationalising—*e.g.*, we are more likely to become atheists because we hated our father than because we can prove that there is no God. The second is the influence of a movement in philosophy which, in the form of logical positivism or logical analysis, makes us doubt whether metaphysical systems have any meaning at all. Today, instead of asking ourselves whether Plato was right or wrong, we are much more likely to ask whether he did anything but make for the most part meaningless noises. Religion is in a sense much safer today than it ever was in the 19th cent. when it made foolish statements over matters of science that could be *proved* wrong; now we tend to see it as an emotional attitude to the universe or God (a "feeling of being at home in the universe," as William James put it) which can no more be proved or disproved than being in love.

Realism is a word which has so many meanings, and such contradictory ones, in various spheres, that it is difficult to define. We shall limit ourselves to its significance in philosophy. In philosophy, "realism" has two different meanings, diametrically opposed. (1) The most usual meaning is the one we should least expect from the everyday sense of the word—*i.e.*, it refers to all those philosophies from Plato onwards which maintained that the world of appearance is illusory and that ideas, forms, or universals are the only true realities, belonging to the world beyond matter and appearance—the world of God or mind. In early mediaeval times St. Thomas Aquinas was the chief exponent of this doctrine which was held by the scholastics as opposed to the Nominalists (*q.v.*). (2) In its modern everyday meaning "realism" is the belief that the universe is real and not a creation of mind, that although all we really experience is the evidence of our senses there is a reality that causes the appearance, the "thing-in-itself" as Kant described it. Material things may not really be what they appear to be (*e.g.*, a noise is not the "bang" we experience but a series of shock-waves passing through the atmosphere), yet, for all that, we can be sure that matter exists and it is very possible (some might add) that mind does not.

Reformation, the great religious movement of the 16th cent., which resulted in the establishment of Protestantism. In the previous century Wyclif, Hus, and others had sounded the warning note, and when later on Luther took up the cause in Germany, and Zwingli in Switzerland, adherents soon became numerous. The wholesale vending of indulgences by the papal agents had incensed the people, and when Luther denounced these things he spoke to willing ears. After much controversy, the reformers boldly propounded the principles of the new doctrine, and the struggle for religious supremacy grew bitter. They claimed justification (salvation) by faith, and the use as well as the authority of the Scriptures, rejecting the doctrine of transubstantiation, the adoration of the Virgin and Saints, and the headship of the Pope. Luther was excommunicated. But the Reformation principles spread and ultimately a great part of Germany, as well as Switzerland, the Low Countries, Scandinavia, England, and Scotland were won over to the new faith. In England Henry VIII readily espoused the cause of the Reformation, his own personal quarrel with the Pope acting as an incentive. Under Mary there was a brief and sanguinary reaction, but Elizabeth gave completeness to the work which her father had initiated. *See* **Lutheranism, Calvinism, Presbyterianism, Baptists, Methodism.**

Reincarnation, the transmigration of souls. *See* **Immortality, Hinduism, Buddhism.**

Renaissance is defined in the *Oxford English Dictionary* as: "The revival of art and letters, under the influence of classical models, which began in Italy in the 14th century." It is a term which must be used with care for the following reasons: (1) Although it was first used in the form *rinascita* (re-birth) by Vasari in 1550 and people living at that time certainly were aware that something new was happening, the word had no wide currency until used by the Swiss historian Jacob Burchardt in his classic *The Civilization of the Renaissance in Italy* (1860). (2) The term as used today refers not only to art in its widest sense but to a total change in man's outlook on life which extended into philosophical, scientific, economic, and technical fields. (3) Spreading from Italy there were renaissance movements in France, Spain, Germany, and northern Europe, all widely different with varying delays in time. As the historian Edith Sichel says: "Out of the Italian Renaissance there issued a new-born art; out of the Northern Renaissance there came forth a new-born religion. There came forth also a great school of poetry, and a drama the greatest that the world had seen since the days of Greece. The religion was the offspring of Germany and the poetry that of England."

The real cause of the Renaissance was not the fall of Constantinople, the invention of printing, the discovery of America, though these were phases in the process; it was, quite simply, money. The rise of a new merchant class gave rise to individualist attitudes in economic affairs which prepared the way for individualism and humanism. The new wealthy class in time became patrons of the arts whereas previously the Church had been the sole patron and controller. Thus the artist became more free to express himself, more respected, and being more well-to-do could afford to ignore the Church and even, in time, the views of his patrons.

It is true that art continued to serve to a considerable extent the purposes of faith, but it was judged from the standpoint of art. Mediaeval art was meant to elevate and teach man; Renaissance art to delight his senses and enrich his life. From this free and questing spirit acquired from economic individualism came the rise of modern science and technology; here Italy learned much from the Arab scholars who had translated and commented upon the philosophical, medical, and mathematical texts of antiquity, while denying themselves any interest in Greek art and literature. Arabic Latin versions of Aristotle were in use well into the 16th cent. The Byzantine culture, though it had preserved the Greek tradition and gave supremacy to Plato, had made no move forward. But the Greek scholars who fled to Italy after the fall of Constantinople brought with them an immense cargo of classical manuscripts. The recovery of these Greek masterpieces, their translation into the vernaculars, and the invention of printing, made possible a completer understanding of the Greek spirit. It was the bringing together of the two heritages, Greek science, and Greek literature, that gave birth to a new vision. But it was not only Aristotle and Plato who were being studied but Ovid, Catullus, Horace, Pliny and Lucretius. What interested Renaissance man was the humanism of the Latin writers, their attitude to science, their scepticism.

The period *c.* 1400–1500 is known as the **Early Renaissance.** During this time such painters as Masaccio, Uccello, Piero della Francesca, Botticelli, and Giovanni Bellini were laying the foundations of drawing and painting for all subsequent periods including our own. They concerned themselves with such problems as anatomy, composition, perspective, and representation of space, creating in effect a grammar or textbook of visual expression. The term **High Renaissance** is reserved for a very brief period when a pure, balanced, classical harmony was achieved and artists were in complete control of the techniques learned earlier. The High Renaissance lasted only from *c.* 1500 to 1527 (the date of the sack of Rome), yet th interval included the earlier works of Michelangelo, most of Leonardo's, and all the Roman works of Raphael.

Ritualism, a tendency which, during the 19th cent., developed in the High Church section of the Church of England to make use of those vestments, candles, incense, etc. which are usually regarded as features of the Church of Rome. Since some opposition was aroused, a Ritual Commission was appointed in 1904 to take evidence and try to find some common basis on which High and Low Church could agree with respect to ceremonial. The report of 1906 in effect recommended the giving of greater powers to bishops to suppress objectionable practices. Although they are often associated together, it is worth while pointing out that there was no special connection between the Oxford Movement or Tractarians (*q.v.*) and Ritualism because Pusey disliked ritual and even Newman, who eventually went over to Rome, held extremely simple services at his church of St. Mary's.

Roman Catholic Church, the Christian organisation which acknowledges the Pope as the lawful successor of St. Peter, the apostle appointed by Christ to be the head of His Church. The reforming impulse at the Second Vatican Council (1962–5) has set in train great movements towards religious unity and the reform and modernisation of the Roman Catholic Church.

Romanticism. *See* **Section L.**

Rotarianism. The Rotary Club is primarily an American association but has many members in Britain and presumably elsewhere since all Rotary Clubs are united in an international organisation. It consists of groups of business and professional men formed with the purpose of serving their community and humanity in general. The name is derived from the clubs entertaining in rotation and its badge, the blue and gold cog-wheel, is familiar.

S

Sabellian heresy. During the 4th cent. great controversies raged within the Christian Church over the divinity of Jesus Christ. Arius (*see* **Arianism**) denied Christ's divinity and maintained that the Father alone was truly divine. This doctrine was condemned at the Council of Nicaea (325), Arius being opposed by Athanasius who held the now orthodox view of the Trinity which was reaffirmed at the Council of Constantinople (381). The Sabellians, named after their founder Sabellius (*fl.* 215), a Libyan priest and theologian, held the view that God is indivisible but with three roles, appearing successively as the Father (the creator), as the Son (the redeemer), and as the Holy Spirit (the divine spirit within men). This view, which makes the person of Jesus Christ ultimately an illusion, was condemned.

Salvation Army. The religious movement which in 1878 became known by this name arose from the Christian Mission meetings which the Rev. William Booth and his devoted wife had held in the East End of London for the previous thirteen years. Its primary aim was, and still is, to preach the gospel of Jesus Christ to men and women untouched by ordinary religious efforts. The founder devoted his life to the salvation of the submerged classes whose conditions at that time were unspeakably dreadful. Originally his aim had been to convert people and then send them on to the churches, but he soon found that few religious bodies would accept these "low-class" men and women. So it was that social work became part of their effort. Practical help, like the provision of soup-kitchens, accompanied spiritual ministration. Soon, in the interests of more effective "warfare" against social evils, a military form of organisation, with uniforms, brass bands, and religious songs, was introduced. Its magazine *The War Cry* gave as its aim "to carry the Blood of Christ and the Fire of the Holy Ghost into every part of the world." There were persecutions: mobs, sometimes encouraged by the police, assaulted the Salvationists who, although not the aggressors, were often punished by the magistrates. In a single year 56 buildings belonging to the Army were wrecked, and (excluding men) over 250 women were seriously hurt. General Booth saw with blinding clarity that conversion must be accompanied by an improvement of external conditions. Various books had earlier described the terrible conditions of the slums, but in 1809 he produced a monumental survey entitled *In Darkest England and the Way Out.* There is insufficient space to go into its proposals, but from that time forward the Army was accepted and its facilities made use of by the authorities. Today the Army's spiritual and social activities have spread to countries all over the world; every one no matter what class, colour, or creed he belongs to is a "brother for whom Christ died." After his death in 1912, the General was succeeded by his son Bramwell. *See also* **D37(1).**

Sandemanians or Glassites, an obscure religious sect whose sole claim to fame is that one of its members was the great Michael Faraday, founder of the science of electromagnetism, who never failed to attend its Sunday services.

Sceptics. From Thales of Miletus (*c.* 624–565 B.C.) to the Stoics in the 4th cent. B.C. philosophers had been trying to explain the nature of the universe; each one produced a different theory and each could, apparently, prove that he was right. This diversity of views convinced the Sceptic school founded by Pyrrho (*c.* 360–270 B.C.) that man is unable to know the real nature of the world or how it came into being. In place of a futile search for what must be for ever unknowable, the Sceptics recommended that men should be practical, follow custom, and accept the evidence of their senses.

Schoolmen. From the time of Augustine to the middle of the 9th cent. philosophy, like science, was dead or merely a repetition of what had gone before. But about that time there arose a new interest in the subject, although (since by then Western Europe was entirely under the authority of the Catholic Church) the main form it took was an attempt to justify Church teaching in the light of Greek philosophy. Those who made this attempt to reconcile Christian beliefs with the best in Plato and Aristotle were known as "schoolmen" and the philosophies which they developed were known as "scholasticism." Among the most famous schoolmen must be counted John Scotus Erigena (*c.* 800–*c.* 877), born in Ireland and probably the earliest; St. Anselm, archbishop of Canterbury (1033–1109); the great Peter Abelard whose school was in Paris (1079–1142); Bernard of Chartres, his contemporary; and the best-known of all, St. Thomas Aquinas of Naples (1225–74), who was given the name of the "Angelic Doctor."

The philosophies of these men are discussed under various headings (**God and Man, Determinism and Free-will**), but being severely limited by the Church their doctrines differed from each other much less than those of later philosophical schools. However, one of the great arguments was between the orthodox Realists (*q.v.*) and the Nominalists (*q.v.*) and a second was between the Thomists (or followers of St. Thomas Aquinas) and the Scotists (followers of John Duns Scotus—not to be confused with John Scotus Erigena). The two latter schools were known as the Ancients, whilst the followers of William of Occam, the Nominalist, were known as the Terminalists. All became reconciled in 1482 in face of the threat from humanism of which the great exponent was Erasmus of Rotterdam (1466–1536) who hated scholasticism.

Shakers, members of a revivalist group, styled by themselves "The United Society of Believers in Christ's Second Appearing," who seceded from Quakerism in 1747 though adhering to many of the Quaker tenets. The community was joined in 1758 by Ann Lee, a young convert from Manchester, who had "revelations" that she was the female Christ; "Mother Ann" was accepted as their leader. Under the influence of her prophetic visions she set out with nine followers for "Immanuel's land" in America and the community settled near Albany, capital of New York state. They were known as the "Shakers" in ridicule because they were given to involuntary movements in moments of religious ecstasy.

Central to their faith was the belief in the

dual role of God through the male and female Christ: the male principle came to earth in Jesus; the female principle, in "Mother Ann." The sexes were equal and women preached as often as men at their meetings which sometimes included sacred dances—nevertheless the two sexes, even in dancing, kept apart. Their communistic way of living brought them economic prosperity, the Shakers becoming known as good agriculturists and craftsmen, noted for their furniture and textiles. After 1860, however, the movement began to decline and few, if any, are active today.

Shamans, the medicine men found in all primitive societies who used their magical arts to work cures, and protect the group from evil influences. The *shaman* was a man apart and wore special garments to show his authority. Shamanism with its magical practices, incantations, trances, exhausting dances, and self-torture is practised even today by tribes that have survived in a primitive state of culture.

Shiites or Shia, a heretical Moslem sect in Persia, opposed by the orthodox Sunnites. The dispute, which came almost immediately after the death of the Prophet and led to bitter feuding, had little to do with matters of doctrine as such, but with the succession. After Mohammed's death, there were three possible claimants: Ali, the husband of his daughter Fatima, and two others, one of whom gave up his claim in favour of the other, Omar. The orthodox selected Omar, who was shortly assassinated, and the same happened to his successor as Ali was passed over again. The Shiites are those who maintain that Ali was the true vicar of the Prophet, and that the three orthodox predecessors were usurpers.

Shintoism, the native religion of Japan, primarily a system of nature and ancestor worship. Since the intellectual content of Shinto is negligible, it is unnecessary to go into its mythology which, very briefly, states that when heaven and earth began there were two beings—a god named Izanagi and a goddess named Izanami. These two gave birth to the islands of Japan. The goddess died, and subsequently her consort Izanagi gave birth (whilst washing his eyes and nose) to three deities: those of the Sun, Moon, and Storm. The first was named Amaterasu, the third Susanowo; after various quarrels between the brother and sister, one of the descendants of Amaterasu, Jimmu Tenno, became the first earthly emperor of Japan who acquired his position by conquest of the province of Yamato in central Japan (*i.e.*, the area south of modern Kyoto) where he set up his capital and built a palace. Thus the Japanese emperors are the ancestors of the Sun-goddess. The primary deities were, therefore, personifications of nature, and the worship of the Sun occupied a central position. After the introduction of Buddhism this crude polytheism became known as Shinto, *i.e.*, "the way of the gods." During the Tokugawa shogunate (*c.* 17th cent.) Confucianism became the orthodox religion of the state—largely because it lays so much emphasis on deference to authority, but neither Buddhism nor Shinto were set aside (by this time both had become interrelated). The authorities, however, regarded Buddhism as for the lower classes and alleged that in essentials Shinto and Confucianism were identical. Latterly, Shinto became increasingly tied up with patriotism and militarism and was increasingly taught in schools prior to the second world war. At the level of the Japanese home, Shinto is represented by the kamidana or "god-shelf" and the miniature Buddhist temple which are prayed to as enshrining the spirits of the family's ancestors. After the defeat of Japan in the second world war Hirohito disavowed his divinity.

Sikhism. The Sikh community of the Punjab, which has played a significant part in the history of modern India, came into being during a period of religious revival in India in the 15th and 16th cent. It was originally founded as a religious sect by Guru (teacher) Nanak (1469–1538) who emphasised the fundamental truth of all religions, and whose mission was to put an end to religious conflict. He condemned the formalism both of Hinduism and Islam, preaching the gospel of universal toleration, and the unity of the Godhead, whether He be called Allah, Vishnu, or God. His ideas were welcomed by the great Mogul Emperor Akbar (1542–1605). Thus a succession of Gurus were able to live in peace after Nanak's death; they established the great Sikh centre at Amritsar, compiled the sacred writings known as the *Adi Granth*, and improved their organisation as a sect. But the peace did not last long, for an emperor arose who was a fanatical Moslem, in face of whom the last Guru, Govind Singh (1666–1708), whose father was put to death for refusal to embrace Islam, had to make himself a warrior and instil into the Sikhs a more aggressive spirit. A number of ceremonies were instituted by Govind Singh; admission to the fraternity was by special rite; caste distinctions were abolished; hair was worn long; the word singh, meaning lion, was added to the original name. They were able to organise themselves into 12 *misls* or confederacies but divisions appeared with the disappearance of a common enemy and it was not until the rise of Ranjit Singh (1780–1839) that a single powerful Sikh kingdom was established, its influence only being checked by the English, with whom a treaty of friendship was made. After the death of Ranjit Singh two Anglo-Sikh wars followed, in 1845–46, and 1848–49, which resulted in British annexation of the Punjab and the end of Sikh independence. In the two world wars the Sikhs proved among the most loyal of Britain's Indian subjects. The partitioning of the continent of India in 1947 into two states, one predominantly Hindu and the other predominantly Moslem, presented a considerable problem in the Punjab, which was divided in such a way as to leave 2 million Sikhs in Pakistan, and a considerable number of Moslems in the Indian Punjab. Although they number less than 2 per cent. of the population (roughly 8 million) the Sikhs are a continuing factor in Indian political affairs because of their prolonged agitation for a separate Sikh-dominated state within the Union.

Socialism, a form of society in which men and women are not divided into opposing economic classes but live together under conditions of approximate social and economic equality, using in common the means that lie to their hands of promoting social welfare. The brotherhood of man inspires the aims of socialism in foreign, colonial, social, and economic policies alike. The word "socialism" first came into general use in England about 1834 in connection with Robert Owen's "village of co-operation" at New Lanark. About the middle of the 19th cent. Charles Kingsley and others established a form of Christian socialism, and William Morris, John Burns, and others founded a Socialist League in 1886. With the development of trade unions the socialist movement took a more practical trend. **Fabianism** (*q.v.*) associated in its early days with the names of Beatrice and Sidney Webb and George Bernard Shaw, aims at the gradual reorganisation of society by creating intelligent public opinion by education and legislation. The British Labour Party believes in peaceful and constitutional change to socialism by democratic methods based upon popular consent. A democratic programme of planned economy and public ownership of certain vital industries and services were features of socialist government from 1945–51 together with a comprehensive system of social security. Further radical reforms in the interest of social justice and industrial efficiency are in progress under the socialist government which took office in Oct. 1964. *See also* **Section C, Part I.**

Southcottians, followers of Joanna Southcott who died in 1814 shortly after announcing to them that (although aged over 50) she was about to give birth to a divine man named Siloh. In spite of the fact that she went through all the actions of a woman about to give birth it is not surprising that no Siloh appeared nor was she pregnant. She also announced that, 100 years after her death, great revelations would be made —but in 1914 people had other things to think about and no revelations were vouchsafed. Yet this unfortunate woman still has her followers who believe that Siloh will appear and that the "true" revelations will be made at some unspecified future date under the right conditions

It is difficult to decide which is the stranger phenomenon, Joanna or her followers.

Spiritualism is a religion which requires to be distinguished from **psychical research** (*q.v.*) which is a scientific attempt carried on both by believers and non-believers to investigate psychic phenomena including those not necessarily connected with "spirits"—*e.g.*, telepathy or clairvoyance and precognition. As a religion (although for that matter the whole of history is filled with attempts to get in touch with the "spirit world") spiritualism begins with the American Andrew Jackson who in 1847 published *Nature's Divine Revelations*, a book which is still widely read although it bears traces of the period in which it was written. Thus reference is made to the theories of "Mesmerism" and "magnetic influence" which really belong to the period when hypnosis was described as Mesmerism after the name of its first modern exponent, Anton Mesmer (d. 1815). The division of man into body, soul, and spirit is accepted and it is supposed that the "soul" is simply a sublimation of the body, needing food which after digestion by the body is refined into a more ethereal form. It even takes the actual form of the body which in reality is merely the covering by which soul communicates with the outer world before passing the messages on to the spirit which is a process of the Divine in which it will ultimately be absorbed. As we grow older there is a gradual separation between spirit or soul and the body—a process which Davis claimed to have observed in the clairvoyant state. According to his observations, the soul, still retaining the form of the body from which it was separating, moved above it but was still joined by a tenuous stream of "vital electricity" which Davis compared with the umbilical cord and took some time to vanish. Death in this view is literally a birth-process from a lower to a higher plane.

The earth is surrounded by a series of spheres from lower to higher, and although these are spiritual it is claimed that their actual distance from the centre of the earth can be measured in ordinary miles or metres. Davis supposed that the passage from lower to higher spheres is accompanied by an increase in moral perfection until the spirit is ultimately absorbed in God. In the lower spheres, however, it still retains something of the material which enables mediums to enter into contact with it. Therefore nearly all spiritualist meetings include a séance, and for the rest, there are prayers, sermons, and hymns. There are ministers, lay officers, and mediums; the latter usually are "freelance" and move about from one church to another. It is, as most people are well aware, perfectly possible for capable and knowledgeable men and women to be either "spiritualists" or (more commonly) interested in spiritualism, but for the most part those who attend services are people who come seeking for proof that their loved ones are not dead but have "passed on" and such are unlikely to retain a critical attitude on the subject however hard-headed they may be in other respects. In spite, or perhaps because of this, the Spiritualist Church is one with an ever-increasing membership especially in Britain and America. It is not permitted for Roman Catholics to hold or practise spiritualist beliefs.

State and Man. Most of the early civilisations such as those of Egypt and Babylonia were theocratic, that is to say, they were arranged in a hierarchy with, at the peak, a king who was also an incarnation of the god. Needless to say, in such circumstances there was no room for philosophising about the nature of the state and the relationship which ought to exist between state and citizens. As usual, we have to turn to ancient Greece for the beginnings of thought about this problem. We do so as briefly as possible since in general it is only the later philosophers whose work has much contemporary interest and, in any case, most people today realise that the political philosophy of a particular time is bound to reflect the actual conditions prevailing then and as such is of mainly theoretical interest today.

The Greek Approach. The early pre-Socratic philosophers Democritus and the Pythagorean school, for example, held that the individual should subordinate himself to the whole; they had no doubt that the citizen's first duty was to the state. The Greeks until the time of Plato were not really thinking in terms of individual rights, nor had they given much thought to what form the state should take—they simply accepted it. The first great attempt to describe the ideal state is to be found in Plato's *The Republic* which is referred to elsewhere (*see* **Education**). His pupil Aristotle did not try to form a utopia but made many comments on the nature of government. Thus, while agreeing that the state was more important than any individual person, he distinguished between good and bad states, and pointed out that to the extent that the state does not enable its citizens to lead virtuous and useful lives it is evil. A good constitution must recognise the inequalities between human beings and confer on them rights according to their abilities: among these inequalities are those of personal ability, property, birth, and status, as freeman or slave. The best forms of rule were monarchy, aristocracy, and democracy; the worst forms—tyranny, oligarchy (or rule of a powerful few), and ochlocracy (or mob-rule). The later Greek thinkers of Hellenistic times held two opposed points of view. The Epicureans (*q.v.*) taught that all social life is based upon self-interest and we become members of a group for our own convenience; therefore there are no absolute rights and laws—what is good is what members decide at that time to be good, and when they change their minds the law must change too. Injustice is not an evil in any god-given sense; we behave justly simply because if injustice became the general rule, we ourselves should suffer. The Stoics (*q.v.*), on the other hand, held that the state must dominate the individual completely and everyone must carry out, first and foremost, his social duties and be willing to sacrifice everything for it; but the state of the Stoics was no narrowly national one, but one that strove to become a universal brotherhood.

The Christian Approach. The orthodox Christian view is expressed in St. Augustine's book *The City of God*. Here it is held that the church, as the worldly incarnation of the City of God, is to be supreme over the state, and the head of the church is to be supreme over secular rulers. In addition it must be recognised that, whilst the secular ruler can make mistakes, the church does not, since it is the representative of God's kingdom on earth.

The Secular State. During the Renaissance (*q.v.*) people began to think for themselves and the results of their cogitations were not always pleasant; for it was during this time that many rulers, petty and otherwise, were seeking absolute authority. Two notable thinkers at this stage were Niccolo Machiavelli (1469–1527) in Italy and Thomas Hobbes (1588–1679) in England, where, of course, the Renaissance arrived later in history. Both supported absolute monarchy against the former domination of the church. The name of Machiavelli has become a by-word for any behaviour that is cunning and unscrupulous, but he was not really as bad as he is usually painted. It is, indeed, true that in his book *The Prince* he showed in the greatest detail the methods by which a ruler could gain absolute control and destroy civic freedom, but this despotism was intended as merely a necessary intermediate stage towards his real idea which was a free, united Italian nation wholly independent of the church. Hobbes was a materialist whose thesis was that man is naturally a ferocious animal whose basic impulse is war and pillage and the destruction of whatever stands in his way to gain his desires. But if he allowed himself to behave in this way his life would be "nasty, brutish, and short" so he creates a society in which he voluntarily gives up many of his rights and hands them over to a powerful ruler in his own interest. But having done this he must obey; even when the ruler is unjust, as he has no right to complain because anything is better than a return to his natural state. The religion of the king must be the religion of the people and the only things on ruler has the right to do is to cause a man to commit suicide or murder or to make him confess to a crime.

Views of Locke: Live and Let Live. John Locke (1632–1704) disagreed with these views. Man is naturally peaceful and co-operative and therefore social life comes readily to him. He sets up an authority in order to preserve the group and that is why laws are made; but the function of the state is strictly limited to maintaining the public good and beyond this men are to be left free. Therefore absolute power and the doctrine of the Divine Right of Kings were wrong because power ultimately rests with the people who have the right to make and break governments. It is also wrong that those who make the laws should be able to execute them. This is the important British doctrine of the separation of powers between the legislature and the executive which, in Britain and America, is regarded as one of the bases of democracy.

Rousseau's Social Doctrine. The only other views we need consider here are those of Jean-Jacques Rousseau (1712–78) and Herbert Spencer (1820–1903), since the views of the two important intervening figures, Hegel and Karl Marx, are dealt with elsewhere (*see* **Dialectical Materialism**) and after Spencer we come to a stage where political philosophy begins to merge with sociology and the social sciences. Rousseau is a puzzling figure. On the one hand he has been hailed as the prophet of freedom and on the other as the father of modern totalitarianism. His book *Social Contract* (1762) begins with the words: "Man is born free, and everywhere he is in chains." He says that he is in favour, not merely of democracy, but of direct democracy in which everyone has to give his assent to all measures as in the Greek city-states and in Geneva, of which city he was a citizen. (This method is still in force in respect of some measures in the Swiss cantons.) Natural society is based on a "social contract" or mutual agreement and Rousseau speaks of a "return to nature" which would ensure the sovereignty of the people at all times. Thus far, he seems to agree with Locke but soon we find that he is more akin to Hobbes, since (as we are learning in our own day) nothing is more tyrannical than the absolute rule of all the people. (Public opinion is more Hitlerian than Hitler.) As it turns out, then, the "social contract" consists in "the total alienation of each associate, together with all his rights, to the whole community" and "each of us puts his person and all his power in common under the supreme direction of the general will." Rousseau admired direct democracy in the small city-state, but if his doctrine is applied to large states, then the "general will" becomes absolute. It is in this sense that he is regarded as the forerunner of totalitarianism. Herbert Spencer is quoted only as an example of the inappropriate application of a biological theory to social issues. Influenced by Darwin's thesis of natural selection, he saw in society a struggle in which the fittest survived and the less fit perished. Each individual had the right to preserve himself, but in the case of human beings this depended upon group life in which, to some extent, each individual is limited by the rights of others. But this should not go too far, and he condemned the socialism of J. S. Mill which (*a*) would give over-much protection to the unfit, and (*b*) would give the state powers which it has no right to since the best government is the least government. In accordance with Darwinism free competition was essential.

Stoics, the followers of Zeno, a Greek philosopher in the 4th cent. B.C., who received their name from the fact that they were taught in the Stoa Poikile or Painted Porch of Athens. They believed that since the world is the creation of divine wisdom and is governed by divine law, it is man's duty to accept his fate. Zeno conceived virtue to be the highest good and condemned the passions. (*See* **God and Man, State and Man, Determinism and Free-will** for a more detailed account of their beliefs.)

Sunnites, the orthodox sect of Islam as contrasted with the Shiites or Shia (*q.v.*).

Swedenborgianism. The Church of the New Jerusalem, based on the writings of Emanuel Swedenborg (1688–1772), was founded by his followers eleven years after his death. The New Church is regarded by its members not as a sect but as a new dispensation bearing the same relationship to Christianity as Christianity does to Judaism.

Syndicalism, a form of socialist doctrine which aims at the ownership and control of all industries by the workers, contrasted with the more conventional type of socialism which advocates ownership and control by the state. Since syndicalists have preferred to improve the conditions of the workers by direct action, *e.g.* strikes and working to rule, rather than through the usual parliamentary procedures, they have been closely related to anarchists (*q.v.*) and are sometimes described as anarcho-syndicalists. Under syndicalism there would be no state; for the state would be replaced by a federation of units based on functional economic organisation rather than on geographical representation. The movement had bodies in the United Kingdom, where guild socialism (*q.v.*) was strongly influenced by its doctrines, in France, Germany, Italy, Spain, Argentina, and Mexico, but these gradually declined after the first world war losing many members to the communists. Fascism (*q.v.*) was also strongly influenced by the revolutionary syndicalism of Georges Sorel in making use of his concept of the "myth of the general strike" as an emotional image or ideal goal to spur on the workers; with Mussolini the "myth" became that of the state. Mussolini was also influenced by Sorel's doctrine of violence and the justification of force. Syndicalism had a certain influence in the Labour Party in its early days, but was crushed by men like Ernest Bevin who began to fear that by involving the workers in direct responsibility for their industries, it would put them at a disadvantage when bargaining for wages.

T

Taoism, a religion which, although in a degenerate state, is still one of the great Eastern creeds. Its alleged founder, Lao-tze, is said to have been born in Honan about 604 B.C.; he is also said to be the author of the bible of Taoism, the *Tao-te-ching*, or in English *The Way of Life*, and to have disapproved of Confucius. This, if true, would hardly be surprising; for Taoism is eminently a mystical religion recommending doing nothing and resisting nothing, whereas **Confucianism** (*q.v.*) is eminently a practical code of living and its founder insisted on intervening in everything to do with social life. But the truth as revealed by modern scholarship is rather different. We are told that the poems of the *Tao-te-ching* are anonymous and probably originated among recluses in lonely valleys long before the time of Confucius; they were collected and given form at some time late in the 3rd cent. B.C. and their authorship attributed to Lao-tze. It is entirely possible that no such person ever existed (unlike Confucius, who certainly did), but if there were such a man he appears to have used a pseudonym since "Lao" is not a surname but an adjective meaning "old" and it was customary to attribute important works to old men on account of their supposed wisdom. Lao-tze simply means "the old philosopher," and although the *Tao-te-ching* is one of the most remarkable and instructive books ever written it is as anonymous as the Border Ballads.

It is apparent that the religion learned both from the ancient Chinese mystics and from Brahmanism: *Tao*, the Way, is impalpable, invisible, and incapable of being expressed in words. But it can be attained by virtue, by compassion, humility, and non-violence. Out of weakness comes true strength whereas violence is not only wrong but defeats its own ends. There is no personal God and such gods as men imagine are mere emanations of *Tao* which gives life to all things. *Tao* is Being. Works are worthless and internal renunciation is far better than anything that follows from the use of force because passive resistance convinces the other from within that he is in error whereas violence only compels the external appearance of conviction whilst inwardly the individual is as before. "It is wealth to be content; it is wilful to force one's way on others."

Later Lao-tze became a divinity and indeed one of a Trinity each worshipped in the form of idols (which the founder had hated). Soon there was worship of the forces of nature: the stars, the tides, the sun and moon, and a thousand other deities among whom Confucius was one. The purest mysticism and wisdom had been utterly corrupted by contact with the world.

Telepathy and Clairvoyance. Telepathy is the alleged communication between one mind and another other than through the ordinary sense channels. Clairvoyance is the supposed faculty of "seeing" objects or events which, by reason of space and time or other causes, are not discernible through the ordinary sense of vision. Such claims have been made from time immemorial but it was not until this century that the phenomena were investigated scientifically. The first scientific studies were made by the Institute for Psychical Research. A new era in experimentation began with the work of J. B. Rhine at Duke University, North Carolina, and S. G. Soal of London University. The most common technique is card guessing using a special pack of cards with the Zener symbols (circle, square, cross, wavy lines, star), thus giving the subject one chance in five of guessing correctly. Although the results obtained have led to the conclusion that telepathic communication is a fact, scepticism still exists, partly because of criticism of the methods employed, the validity of the data obtained, and the assumptions drawn, and partly because telepathic theory appears to clash with existing scientific thought. Dr. Rhine uses the term extra-sensory perception (abbreviated to ESP) to include telepathy, clairvoyance, and precognition. His studies also include what is described as the PK effect or psychokinesis, the supposed influence of the human mind on the movements of physical bodies. The Psi force is the term used for the faculty behind ESP and PK. Reference should be made to the entry on **Psychical Research** in order to obtain the background relating to the various fallacies involved in accepting human evidence uncritically.

Theism. *See* **God and Man.**

Theosophy, a religious movement originated by Madame Helena Petrovna Blavatsky (1831–91) who founded the Theosophical Society in New York in 1875 and had as one of her main disciples Mrs. Annie Besant (1847–1933), originally an assistant of Charles Bradlaugh, the well-known 19th cent. atheist and secularist. Theosophy accepts the doctrines of *karma* and reincarnation, and, like the Swedenborgians and spiritualists, holds that there are higher and lower planes in the life after death. As in these other sects, the geography of this supernormal world is worked out in great detail.

Tractarianism, a Catholic revival movement, also known as the **Oxford Movement** (not to be confused with the so-called Oxford Group), which had its beginnings at Oxford in 1833. The leaders included the Oxford high churchmen E. B. Pusey, J. Keble and J. H. Newman. Through the *Tracts for the Times* (1833–41), a series of pamphlets which were sent to every parsonage in England, they sought to expose the dangers which they considered to be threatening the church from secular authority. The immediate cause of the movement was the Reform Act (1832) which meant that the state was no longer in the safe keeping of Tories and Churchmen but that power was falling into the hands of Liberals and Dissenters. They advocated a higher degree of ceremonial in worship nearer the Roman communion. In *Tract 90* (the last) Newman showed how the Thirty-nine Articles themselves, which were regarded as the bulwark of Protestantism, could be made to square with Roman doctrine. It was obvious which direction the movement was taking and the romanizing tendency was widely resented. In 1845 Newman went over to Rome. Pusey and Keble persisted in their efforts to secure recognition of Catholic liturgy and doctrine in the Anglican Church. Catholicism of the Anglican type (*i.e.*, Catholic in ritual, ceremony, and everything save submission to the Pope) is termed Anglo-Catholicism (*q.v.*).

Transmigration of Souls. *See* **Immortality, Buddhism, Hinduism.**

Transubstantiation, the conversion in the Eucharist of the bread and wine into the body and blood of Christ—a doctrine of the Roman Catholic Church.

Trotskyism, a form of communism supporting the views of Leon Trotsky, the assumed name of Lev Bronstein (1879–1940) who, in 1924, was ousted from power by Stalin and later exiled and assassinated in Mexico. Trotsky held that excessive Russian nationalism was incompatible with genuine international communism and that Stalin was concentrating on the economic development of the Soviet Union to an extent which could only lead to a bureaucratic state with a purely nationalist outlook.

U

Unitarianism has no special doctrines, although clearly, as the name indicates, belief is in the single personality of God, *i.e.*, anti-trinitarian. This general statement, however, can be interpreted with varying degrees of subtlety. Thus unitarian belief may range from a sort of Arianism which accepts that, although Christ was not of divine nature, divine powers had been delegated to him by the Father, to the simple belief that Christ was a man like anyone else, and his goodness was of the same nature as that of many other great and good men. Unitarianism has never been popular, and has often been held in secret by men who professed, or at least belonged to churches which professed, more orthodox views. The Toleration Act (1689) excluded Unitarians but from 1813 they were legally tolerated in England. Nevertheless attempts were made to turn them out of their chapels on the ground that the preachers did not hold the views of the original founders of the endowments. But this ended with the Dissenting Chapels Act of 1845. In America no such difficulties existed, and in the Boston of the 19th cent. many of the great literary figures were openly unitarian both in belief and name: *e.g.*, Emerson, Longfellow, Lowell, and Oliver Wendell Holmes.

Utilitarianism, a school of moral philosophy of which the main proponents were J. S. Mill (1806–73) and Jeremy Bentham (1748–1832). Bentham based his ethical theory upon the utilitarian principle that the greatest happiness of the greatest number is the criterion of morality. What is good is pleasure or happiness; what is bad is pain. If we act on this basis of self-interest (pursuing what we believe to be our own happiness), then what we do will automatically be for the general good. The serious failing of this thesis is (1) that it makes no distinction between the quality of one pleasure and another, and (2) that Bentham failed to see that the law might not be framed and administered by men as benevolent as himself. J. S. Mill accepted Bentham's position in general but seeing its failings emphasised (1) that self-interest was an inadequate basis for utilitarianism and suggested that we should take as the real criterion of good the social consequences of the act; (2) that some pleasures rank higher than others and held that those of the intellect are superior to those of the senses. Not only is the social factor emphasised, but emphasis is also placed on the nature of the act.

Utopias. The name "utopia" is taken from a Greek word meaning "nowhere" and was first used in 1516 by Sir Thomas More (1478–1535) as the title of his book referring to a mythical island in the south Pacific where he sited his ideal society. Since then it has been used of any ideal or fanciful society, and here a few will be mentioned. (The reader may recall that Samuel Butler's 19th cent. novel, describing an imaginary society in New Zealand where criminals were treated and the sick punished, was entitled *Erewhon* which is the word "no-where" in reverse.) It should be noted that not all utopias were entirely fanciful—*e.g.*, Robert Owen's and François Fourier's beliefs, although found to be impractical, were, in fact, tried out.

Sir Thomas More. More wrote at a time

when the rise of the wool-growing trade had resulted in farming land being turned over to pasture and there was a great wave of unemployment and a rise in crime among the dispossessed. More began to think in terms of the mediaeval ideal of small co-operative communities in which class interests and personal gain played a decreasing part, a society which would have the welfare of the people at heart both from the physical and intellectual points of view. His utopia was one in which there was no private property, because the desire for acquisition and private possessions lay at the root of human misery. There was, therefore, only common ownership of land and resources. Each class of worker was equipped to carry out its proper function in the economic scheme and each was fairly rewarded for its share in production so that there was neither wealth nor poverty to inspire conflict. Nobody was allowed to be idle, until the time came for him to retire when he became free to enjoy whatever cultural pleasures he wished, but, since the system was devoid of the waste associated with competition, the working day would be only six hours. There was to be compulsory schooling and free medical care for everybody, full religious toleration, complete equality of the sexes, and a modern system of dealing with crime which was free from vindictiveness and cruelty. Government was to be simple and direct by democratically-elected officials whose powers would be strictly limited and the public expenditure kept under close scrutiny. It will be seen that More was far in advance of his age, and to most democratically-minded people in advance of an earlier utopia, Plato's *Republic*, which is described under the heading of **Education**.

James Harrington. James Harrington published his book *The Commonwealth of Oceana* in 1656 and offered it to Oliver Cromwell for his consideration but without tangible results. Better than any other man of his time Harrington understood the nature of the economic revolution which was then taking place, and, like More, saw the private ownership of land as the main cause of conflict. He put forward the theory that the control of property, particularly in the shape of land, determines the character of the political structure of the state; if property were universally distributed among the people the sentiment for its protection would naturally result in a republican form of government. The Commonwealth of Oceana was a society "of laws and not of men"—*i.e.*, it was to be legally based and structured so as to be independent of the good or ill-will of any individuals controlling it. Thus there must be a written constitution, a two-house legislature, frequent elections with a secret ballot, and separation of powers between legislature and executive—all today familiar features of parliamentary democracy, but unique in his time.

Saint-Simon. The utopias of the late 18th and 19th cent. come, of course, into the period of the industrial revolution and of laissez-faire capitalism. Individual enterprise and complete freedom of competition formed the outlook of the ruling class. Naturally the utopias of this period tended to have a strongly socialist tinge since such theories are obviously produced by those who are not satisfied with existing conditions. Saint-Simon's *New Christianity* (1825) is one such, and by many, Claude Henri, Comte de Saint-Simon (1760–1825) is regarded as the founder of French socialism. His book urged a dedication of society to the principle of human brotherhood and a community which would be led by men of science motivated by wholly spiritual aims. Production property was to be nationalised (or "socialised" as he describes the process) and employed to serve the public good rather than private gain; the worker was to produce according to his capacity and to be rewarded on the basis of individual merit; the principle of inheritance was to be abolished since it denied the principle of reward for accomplishment on which the society was to be founded. Saint-Simon's proposals were not directed towards the poorer classes alone, but to the conscience and intellect of all. He was deeply impressed with the productive power of the new machines and his scheme was, first and foremost, intended as a method of directing that power to the betterment of humanity as a whole.

Fourier. Francois Marie Charles Fourier (1772–1837), although by conviction a philosophical anarchist who held that human beings are naturally good if allowed to follow their natural desires, was the originator of what, on the face of it, one would suppose to be the most regimented of the utopias. It consisted of a system of "phalanxes" or co-operative communities each composed of a group of workers and technicians assured of a minimum income and sharing the surplus on an equitable basis. Agriculture was to be the chief occupation of each phalanx and industrial employment planned and so carefully assigned that work would become pleasant and creative rather than burdensome. One of his ideas was that necessary work should receive the highest pay, useful work the next, and pleasant work the least pay. The land was to be scientifically cultivated and natural resources carefully conserved. Most of the members' property was to be privately owned, but the ownership of each phalanx was to be widely diffused among members by the sale of shares. Such "parasitic and unproductive" occupations as stockbroker, soldier, economist, middle-man and philosopher would be eliminated and the education of children carried out along vocational lines to train them for their future employment.

The strange thing was that Fourier's suggestions appealed to many both in Europe and the U.S.A. and such men (admittedly no economic or technical experts) as Emerson, Thoreau, James Russell Lowell, and Nathaniel Hawthorne strongly supported them. An American Fourier colony known as Brook Farm was established and carried on for eight years when it was dissolved after a serious fire had destroyed most of its property.

Robert Owen. Robert Owen (1771–1858), a wealthy textile manufacturer and philanthropist, established communities founded on a kind of utopian socialism in Lanarkshire, Hampshire, and America. Of his New Lanark community an American observer wrote: "There is not, I apprehend, to be found in any part of the world, a manufacturing community in which so much order, good government, tranquillity, and rational happiness prevail." The workers in Lanark were given better housing and education for their children, and it was administered as a co-operative self-supporting community in Scotland. Later in life Owen returned to sponsoring legislation that would remove some of the worst evils of industrial life in those days: reduction of the working day to twelve hours, prohibition of labour for children under the age of ten, public schools for elementary education, and so on. But he lived to see few of his reforms adopted. He also promoted the creation of co-operative societies, the formation of trades unions, labour banks and exchanges, the workers' educational movement, and even an Anglo-American federation. There can be no doubt that, if he saw little result himself, he left the imprint of his convictions to benefit future communities who may not even know his name.

V

Vitalism, the philosophical doctrine that the behaviour of the living organism is, at least in part, due to a vital principle which cannot possibly be explained wholly in terms of physics and chemistry. This belief was at one time held strongly by the late Professor C. E. M. Joad and is implicit in Henri Bergson's (1858–1941) theory of creative evolution. It was maintained by Bergson that evolution, like the work of an artist, is creative and therefore unpredictable; that a vague need exists beforehand within the animal or plant before the means of satisfying the need develops. Thus we might assume that sightless animals developed the need to become aware of objects before they were in physical contact with them and that this ultimately led to the origin of organs of sight. Earlier this century a form of vitalism described as "emergent evolution" was put forward. This theory maintains that when two or more simple entities come together there may arise a new property which none of them previously possessed. Today biologists would say that it is the *arrangement* of atoms that counts, different arrangements exhibiting different properties, and that biological organisation is an essentially dynamic affair, involving the lapse of time.

W

Wahabis, members of an Arabian sect of Islam which originated in the teaching of Muhammad Ibn 'Abd-al-Wahab, born at the end of the 17th cent. He was deeply resentful of the Turkish rule which, in addition to its tyranny, had brought about innovations in the religion which Muhammad regarded as a perversion of its original form. He proceeded to reform Islam to its primitive conditions and impressed his beliefs on Mohammed Ibn Saud, a sheikh who spread them with the aid of his sword. Under the successors of Ibn Saud the power of the Wahabis spread over much of Arabia where it is dominant today in Saudi Arabia. Its particular characteristic is that it refuses to accept symbolic or mystical interpretations of the words of the Prophet and accepts quite literally the teaching of Islam. It is, in fact, a sort of Moslem fundamentalism. Although crushed by the Turks in 1811–15, the movement remains an important element in Mohammedanism.

Waldenses, a movement also known as "The Poor Men of Lyons," founded by Peter Waldo of that city about the same time, and in the same part of southern France, as the Albigenses (*q.v.*) with whom, however, they had nothing in common. Their main belief was a return to Apostolic simplicity, based on reading the Bible in their own language; their doctrines were somewhat similar to those of the Mennonites and the Quakers. However, they did not wish to separate themselves from the Church and were originally protected by several popes until the Lateran Council of 1215 excluded them mainly for the crime of preaching without ecclesiastical permission. From this time they were subjected to persecution, yet maintained some contact with the Church until the Reformation when they chose to take the side of the Protestants. Situated mainly on the sides of the Alps, half in Piedmont and half in France, they were persecuted or not according to the contemporary political convenience of the Dukes of Savoy, and the major attempt to destroy them called forth Oliver Cromwell's intervention and the famous sonnet of Milton. In spite of torture, murder, deportation, and even the kidnapping of their children, to have them brought up in the Roman Catholic faith, the sect survived, and still exists, having been granted full equality of rights with his Roman Catholic subjects by Charles Edward of Piedmont in 1848.

Witchcraft. There are various interpretations and definitions of witchcraft from that of Pennethorne Hughes who states that "witchcraft, as it emerges into European history and literature, represents the old paleolithic fertility cult, plus the magical idea, plus various parodies of contemporary religions" to that of the fanatical Father Montague Summers who says that spiritualism and witchcraft are the same thing. The leading authority on witchcraft, however, Dr. Margaret Murray, distinguishes between Operative Witchcraft (which is really **Magic** (*q.v.*)) and Ritual Witchcraft which, she says, "embraces the religious beliefs and ritual of the people known in late mediaeval times as 'witches.'" That there were such people we know from history and we know, too, that many of them—the great majority of them women—were tortured or executed or both. Since the figures of such executions vary so enormously it would be pointless to quote them, nevertheless they must have been considerable, especially after the promulgation of the bull *Summis desiderantes* by Pope Innocent VIII in 1484. Dr. Murray points out that there have ordinarily been two theories about witchcraft: (1) that there were such beings as witches, that they possessed supernatural powers and that the evidence given at their trials was substantially correct; (2) that the witches were simply poor silly creatures who either deluded themselves into believing that they had certain powers or, more frequently, were tortured into admitting things that they did not do. She herself accepts a third theory: that there were such beings as witches, that they really did what they admitted to doing, but that they did not possess supernatural powers. They were in fact believers in the old religion of pre-Christian times and the Church took centuries to root them out. What this religion was is not quite certain, but it may have been the remains of the Druidic cult (*q.v.*) or have had much earlier origins. However, that there existed "covens" of witches who carried out peculiar rites Dr. Murray has no doubt whatever. Pope Innocent VIII who himself was "a man of scandalous life," according to a Catholic historian, appointed in his bull ". . . our dear sons Henricus Institor and Jacobus Sprenger, professors of theology . . . delegated as Inquisitors of these heretical pravities." One of the results was the *Malleus Maleficarum* ("The Hammer of Witches") published by "the dear sons" and used as a text-book of procedure of witchcraft trials.

World Council of Churches, a union of Christian Churches from all over the world (including the Churches of the Protestant, Anglican, and Orthodox traditions, but excluding the Roman Catholic Church), engaged in extending Christian mission and unity throughout the world. All Churches which "accept our Lord Jesus Christ as God and Saviour" are eligible. This modern oecumenical movement stems from the great World Missionary Conference held at Edinburgh in 1910. The World Council was founded in 1948 and meets for consultation from time to time; the third assembly met in New Delhi in 1961, when the Russian Orthodox Church was admitted.

Y

Yoga, a Hindu discipline which teaches a technique for freeing the mind from attachment to the senses, so that once freed the soul may become fused with the universal spirit (*Atman* or *Brahma*), which is its natural goal. This is the sole function of the psychological and physical exercises which the Yogi undertakes, although few ever reach the final stage of *Samadhi* or union with *Brahma* which is said to take place in eight levels of attainment. These are: (1) *Yama*, which involves the extinction of desire and egotism and their replacement by charity and unselfishness; (2) *Niyama* during which certain rules of conduct must be adopted, such as cleanliness, the pursuit of devotional studies, and the carrying out of rituals of purification; (3) *Asana*, or the attainment of correct posture and the reduction to a minimum of all bodily movement (the usual posture of the concentrating Yogi is the "lotus position" familiar from pictures); (4)–(5) *Pranayama*, the right control of the life-force or breath in which there are two stages at which the practitioner hopes to arrive, the first being complete absorption in the act of breathing which empties the mind of any other thought, the second being the ability almost to cease to breathe which allegedly enables him to achieve marvellous feats of endurance; (6) *Pratyahara* or abstraction which means the mind's complete withdrawal from the world of sense; (7) *Dharana* in which an attempt is made to think of one thing only which finally becomes a repetition of the sacred syllable OM, and perhaps by a kind of self-hypnosis, leads (8) to *Samadhi* the trance state which is a sign of the complete unity of soul with reality.

Yoga is very old, and when the sage Patanjali (*c.* 300 B.C.) composed the book containing these instructions, the *Yoga Sutras*, he was probably collecting from many ancient traditions. Some of the claims made by Yogis seem, to the Western mind, frankly incredible; but in the West and especially in recent years Yoga methods have been used at the lower levels in order to gain improved self-control, better posture, and improved health. Whether it achieves these ends is another matter, but the genuine Yogi regards this as a perversion of the nature and purpose of the discipline.

Z

Zen Buddhism, a Buddhist sect which is believed to have arisen in 6th cent. China but has flourished chiefly in Japan; for some reason it has of recent years begun to attract attention in the West thanks to the voluminous writings of Dr. D. T. Suzuki and the less numerous but doubtless much-read books of Mr. Christmas Humphreys. But the fact that these writings exist does not explain their being read, nor why of all possible Eastern sects this particular one should be chosen in our times. What is Zen's attraction and why should anyone take the trouble to read about something (the word "something" is used for reasons that will become evident) that is not a religion, has no doctrine, knows no God and no after-life, no good and no evil, and possesses no scriptures but has to be taught by parables which seem to be purposely meaningless? One of the heroes of Zen is the fierce-looking Indian monk Boddhidharma (fl. *c.* 516–534) who brought Buddhism to China, of whom it is recounted that when the Emperor asked him how much merit he had acquired by supporting the new creed, the monk shouted at him: "None whatever!" The Emperor then wished to know what was the sacred doctrine of the creed, and again the monk shouted: "It is empty—there is nothing sacred!" Dr. Suzuki, having affirmed that there is no God in Zen, goes on to state that this does not mean that Zen denies the existence of God because "neither denial nor affirmation concerns Zen." The most concrete statement he is prepared to make is that the basic idea of Zen is to come in touch with the inner workings of our being, and to do this in the most direct way possible without resorting to anything external or superadded. Therefore anything that has the semblance of an external authority is rejected by Zen. Absolute faith is placed in a man's own inner being. Apparently the intention is that, so far from indulging in inward meditations or such practices as the Yogi uses, the student must learn to act spontaneously, without thinking, and without self-consciousness or hesitation. This is the main purpose of the *koan*, the logically insoluble riddle which the pupil must try to solve. One such is the question put by master to pupil: "A girl is walking down the street, is she the younger or the older sister?" The correct answer, it seems, is to say nothing but put on a mincing gait, to *become* the girl, thus showing that what matters is the experience of being and not its verbal description. Another *koan*: "What is the Buddha?" "Three pounds of flax" is attributed to T'ung-shan in the 9th cent. and a later authority's comment is that "none can excel it as regards its irrationality which cuts off all passages to speculation." Zen, in effect, teaches the uselessness of trying to use words to discuss the Absolute.

Zen came to Japan in the 13th cent., more than five centuries after Confucianism or the orthodox forms of Buddhism, and immediately gained acceptance whilst becoming typically Japanese in the process. One of the reasons why it appealed must have been that its spontaneity and insistence on action without thought, its emphasis on the uselessness of mere words, and such categories as logical opposites, had an inevitable attraction for a people given to seriousness, formality, and logic to a degree which was almost stifling. Zen must have been to the Japanese what nonsense rhymes and nonsense books, like those of Edward Lear and Lewis Carroll, were to the English intellectuals. Lear's limericks, like some of the *koans*, end up with a line which, just at the time when one expects a point to be made, has no particular point at all, and *Alice in Wonderland* is the perfect example of a world, not without logic, but with a crazy logic of its own which has no relationship to that of everyday life. Therefore Zen began to impregnate every aspect of life in Japan, and one of the results of its emphasis on spontaneous action rather than reason was its acceptance by the Samurai, the ferocious warrior class, in such activities as swordsmanship, archery, Japanese wrestling, and later Judo and the Kamikaze dive-bombers. But much of Japanese art, especially landscape gardening and flower-arrangement, was influenced similarly, and Zen is even used in Japanese psychiatry. The very strict life of the Zen monks is based largely on doing things, learning through experience; the periods of meditation in the Zendo hall are punctuated by sharp slaps on the face administered by the abbot to those who are unsatisfactory pupils. Dr. Suzuki denies that Zen is nihilistic, but it is probably its appearance of nihilism and its appeal to the irrational and spontaneous which attracts the Western world at a time when to many the world seems without meaning and life over-regimented. However, it has influenced such various aspects of Western life as philosophy (Heidegger), psychiatry (Erich Fromm and Hubert Benoit), writing (Aldous Huxley), and painting (Die Zen Gruppe in Germany).

Zionism, a belief in the need to establish an autonomous Jewish home in Palestine which, in its modern form, began with Theodor Herzl (1860–1904), a Hungarian journalist working in Vienna. Although Herzl was a more or less assimilated Jew, he was forced by the Dreyfus case and the pogroms in Eastern Europe to conclude that there was no real safety for the Jewish people until they had a state of their own. The Jews, of course, had always in a religious sense thought of Palestine as a spiritual homeland and prayed "next year in Jerusalem," but the religious had thought of this in a philosophical way as affirming old loyalties, not as recommending the formation of an actual state. Therefore Herzl was opposed both by many of the religious Jews and, at the other extreme, by those who felt themselves to be assimilated and in many cases without religious faith. Even after the Balfour Declaration of 1917, there was not a considerable flow of Jews to Palestine, which at that time was a predominantly Arab state. But the persecutions of Hitler changed all this and, after bitter struggles, the Jewish state was proclaimed in 1948. Today Zionism is supported by the vast majority of the Jewish communities everywhere (although strongly disapproved of in the Soviet Union as "Western imperialism") and Zionism is now an active international force concerned with protecting the welfare and extending the influence of Israel.

Zoroastrianism, at one time one of the great world religions, competing in the 2nd cent. A.D. on almost equal terms from its Persian home with Hellenism and the Roman Imperial Government. Under the Achaemenidae (*c.* 550–330 B.C.) Zoroastrianism was the state religion of Persia. Alexander's conquest in 331 B.C. brought disruption but the religion flourished again under the Sassanian dynasty (A.D. *c.* 226–640). With the advance of the Mohammedan Arabs in the 7th cent. Zoroastrianism finally gave way to Islam. A number of devotees fled to India there to become the Parsees. In Persia itself a few scattered societies remain.

The name Zoroaster is the Greek rendering of Zarathustra, the prophet who came to purify the ancient religion of Persia. It is though that he lived at the beginning of the 6th cent B.C. He never claimed for himself divin powers but was given them by his followers The basis of Zoroastrianism is the age-long wa between good and evil, Ahura Mazda headin the good spirits and Ahriman the evil ones Morality is very important since by doing righ the worshipper is supporting Ahura Mazd against Ahriman, and the evil-doers will b punished in the last days when Ahura Mazd wins his inevitable victory.

The sacred book of this religion is the *Avesta* If Zoroastrianism has little authority today, it had a very considerable influence in the past Its doctrines penetrated into Judaism (*q.v.*) and, through Gnosticism, Christianity. The worship of Mithra by the Romans was an impure version of Zoroastrianism. Manichaeism (*q.v.*) was a Zoroastrian heresy and the Albigensianism of mediaeval times was the last relic of a belief which had impressed itself deeply in the mind of men.

GAZETTEER OF THE WORLD

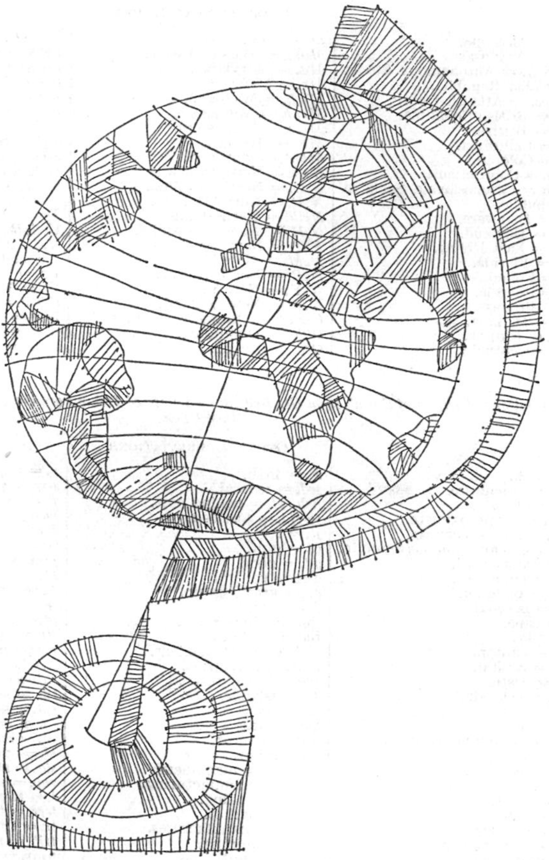

GAZETTEER OF THE WORLD

This edition of the gazetteer has been revised from standard and authoritative sources. For the population figures the latest censuses have been used, where available, and where not available, the latest official estimates.

An endeavour has been made to include all the more important places throughout the world. The small scale of the maps included in the Cyclopædia does not enable all places included in the gazetteer to be named on the maps.

In regard to the spelling of place names, the general principle followed has been to adopt national spellings. For those countries where the Latin Alphabet is not used, the principles for transliteration laid down by the "Permanent Committee on Geographical Names" of the Royal Geographical Society have been followed. Chinese entries are in the conventional English form. New official Chinese form, based on Chinese romanised alphabet adopted 1958, is in brackets. There may be a few instances where the spelling shown on the map does not conform to that used in the gazetteer.

ABBREVIATIONS USED IN THE GAZETTEER

Geographical Names

Ala. = Alabama.
Ark. = Arkansas.
A.S.S.R. = Autonomous Soviet Socialist Republic.
Atl. Oc. = Atlantic Ocean.
B.C. = British Columbia.
Brit. = British.
Cal. = California.
Col. = Colorado.
Conn. = Connecticut.
ČSSR = Czechoslovak Socialist Republic.
Del. = Delaware.
Eng. = England.
E.R. = East Riding.
Fla. = Florida.
Fr. = French.
Ga. = Georgia.
Ill. = Illinois.
Ind. = Indiana.
Kan. = Kansas.
Ky. = Kentucky.
La. = Louisiana.
Mass. = Massachusetts.
Md. = Maryland.
Me. = Maine.
Mich. = Michigan.
Minn. = Minnesota.
Miss. = Mississippi.
Mo. = Missouri.
Mont. = Montana.
N.B. = New Brunswick.
N.C. = North Carolina.
N.D. = North Dakota.
Neth. = Netherlands.
N.H. = New Hampshire.
N.J. = New Jersey.
N.M. = New Mexico.
N.R. = North Riding.
N.Y. = New York.
N.Z. = New Zealand.
O.F.S. = Orange Free State.
Okla. = Oklahoma.
Ore. = Oregon.
Pac. Oc. = Pacific Ocean.
Pa. = Pasadena.
Penns. = Pennsylvania.
R.I. = Rhode Island.
R.o.I. = Republic of Ireland.
R.S.F.S.R. = Russian Soviet Federal Socialist Republic.
S.C. = South Carolina.
Scot. = Scotland.
S.D. = South Dakota.
S.S.R. = Soviet Socialist Republic.
Tenn. = Tennessee.
U.A.R. = United Arab Republic.
U.S.S.R. = Union of Soviet Socialist Republics.
Va. = Virginia.
Vt. = Vermont.
Wash. = Washington.
W.I. = West Indies.
Wis. = Wisconsin.
Wyo. = Wyoming.

Abbreviations of names of Counties in Gt. Britain and Rep. of Ireland are those recognised by the General Post Office.

Other Abbreviations

a. = area.
agr. = agriculture.
alt. = altitude.
approx. = approximate.
arch. = archaeological.
aut. rep. = autonomous republic.
ass. = associated.
bdy. = boundary.
bldg. = building.
bor. = borough.
C. = cape.
c. = city.
can. = canton.
cap. = capital.
cas. = castle.
cath. = cathedral.
ch. = chief.
co. = county.
co. bor. = county borough.
col. = colony.
colly. = colliery.
comm. = commercial.
cst. = coast.
ctr. = centre.
cty. = country.
dep. = department.
dist. = district.
div. = division.
E. = east or easterly.
elec. = electrical.
engin. = engineering.
estd. = estimated.
exp. = exports.
F. = firth.
fed. = federal.
fish. pt. = fishing port.
fortfd. = fortified.
ft. = feet.
G. = gulf.
gd. = good.
gen. = general.
gr. = great, group.
I. = island.
impt. = important.
inc. = including.
indep. = independent.
inds. = industries.
industl. = industrial.
Is. = islands.
L. = lake.
lge. = large
lgst. = largest.
m. = miles.
machin. = machinery.
mftg. = manufacturing.
mkg. = making.
mkt. = market.
mnfs. = manufactures.
mng. = mining.
mt. = mount.
mtn. = mountain.
mun. = municipality.
mun. bor. = municipal borough.
N. = north or northerly.
nat. = national.
nr. = near.
p. = population.
par. = parish.
parlt. = parliament.
parly. = parliamentary.
prod. = products.
prot. = protectorate.
prov. = province.
pt. = port.
R. = river.
rep. = republic.
residtl. = residential.
rly. = railway.
rural dist. = rural district
S. = south or southerly.
shipbldg. = shipbuilding.
sm. = small.
spt. = seaport.
sq. m. = square miles.
St. = Saint.
st. = state.
sta. = station.
sub. = suburb.
t. = town.
terr. = territory.
tr. = trade.
trib. = tributary.
univ. = university.
urb. dist. = urban district.
vil. = village.
W. = west or westerly.
wat. pl. = watering place.
wks. = works.
wkshps. = workshops.

Land = administrative division of W. Germany approx. corresponding to "province".

A

Aabenraa, *spt.,* S.E. Jutland, Denmark; at head of Aabenraa fjord; cars, trailers, clothing; p. (1960) *14,219.*

Aachen, *t.,* N. Rhine-Westphalia, Germany; formerly Aix-la-Chapelle; one of the oldest cities in Germany, cath., famous baths; suffered badly from bombing in Second World War and was first large German town to be taken by the Allied Forces in 1944; non-ferrous metal inds. textiles, needles, footwear, elec. goods; p. (1963) *174,300.*

Aaiun, *cap.,* Saguia el Hamra region of Spanish Sahara.

Aalborg, *c., spt.* Jutland, Denmark; shipbldg., cement, textiles, machin.; airport; p. (1960) *85,800.*

Aalen, *t.,* Baden-Würtemberg, Germany; on R. Kocher; iron, textiles, lens mkg.; p. (1963) *33,700.*

Aalst, *see* **Alost.**

Aar, *R.,* Switzerland, flows through Brienz and Thun lakes, and thence into the Rhine, 181 m.; famous Aar gorges above Meiringen.

Aarau, *t.,* cap. Aargau can., Switzerland; precision tools and instruments, shoes, textiles; hydro-elec. plant; p. (1957) *14,280.*

Aargau, *can.,* N. Switzerland; a. 542 sq. m.; extensive vineyards, cereals, orchards, metal prod., textiles, salt mining; p. (1961) *360,940.*

Aarhus, *c.,* principal spt. on E. coast of Jutland, Denmark; famous Gothic cath., univ.; iron, metals, shipbldg, marine engin., textiles, paper, chemicals; p. (1960) *119,568.*

Abaco, Gt., Bahama Is., W. Indies; p. (1953) *3,407.*

Abadan, *t.,* Iran; oil refineries; exp. petroleum; p. (1960) *293,000.*

Abakan, *t.,* R.S.F.S.R., on R. Jenisei; sawmilling, food inds.; p. (1959) *56,000.*

Abbazia, *see* **Opatija.**

Abbeville, *mftg. c.,* on the R. Somme (N. France); connected with Paris and Belgium by canals; sugar-milling, carpets, biscuits, beer; p. (1954) *19,502.*

Abbeyleix, *t., rural dist.,* Laoighis, Ireland; quarries; p. (rural dist. 1961) *11,813.*

Abbotsbury, *par.,* Dorset, Eng.; world-famous swannery.

Abbots-Langley, *par.,* Herts, Eng., birthplace of Nicholas Breakspeare (Pope Adrian IV); p. (1961) *18,157.*

Abeokuta, *t.,* Nigeria; palm oil, hardwoods; p. (1953) *84,000.*

Aberavon, *t.,* Glamorgan, Wales; on R. Avon, 8 m. E. of Swansea; harbour Port Talbot; lge. coal and iron inds., metals, tinplate, cables; p. (1961) *31,226.*

Aberayron, *urb. dist.,* Cardigan, S. Wales; p. (1961) *1,220.*

Abercarn, *urb. dist.,* Monmouth, Eng.; coal and iron, tin-plate, knitting pins; p. (1961) *19,221.*

berchirder, *burgh,* Banff, Scot.; p. (1961) *755.*

bercorn, *par.,* W. Lothian, Scot.; on the Forth; Roman wall built by Antoninus began here, and extended to Kirkpatrick on the Clyde; p. (1951) *806.*

bercorn, *t.* Zambia; trading sta.; airfield; European p. (1959) *250.*

berdare, *urb. dist.,* Glamorgan, Wales, on the R. Cynon; wire cables; p. (1961) *39,044.*

berdeen, *co.,* Scot.; mtnous; agr., oats, barley, turnips, cattle; fisheries; granite, brewing, distilling, paper; a. 1,970 sq. m.; p. (1961) *298,503.*

berdeen, c., Aberdeenshire and Kincardine, Scot.; at mouth of R. Dee, 100 m. N.E. of Edinburgh; univ.; sm. shipbldg., fishing, oats, whisky, paper mkg., granite, tourism; p. (1961) *185,379* of whom *23,254* S. of R. Dee are in Kincardine co.

berdeen, *t.,* S.D., U.S.A.; chemicals, foundry; p. (1960) *23,073.*

berdeen, *spt.,* Wash., U.S.A.; lumbering, salmon canning; p. (1960) *18*,741.

berdour, *par.,* Fife, Scot.; sea-bathing noted; p. (1951) *1,939.*

berdovey, *wat. pl.,* Merioneth, Wales, on estuary of R. Dovey.

berfeldy, *burgh,* Perth, Scot., in Strath Tay, 4 m. below Loch Tay; mkt.; salmon and trout fishing resort; p. (1961) *1,469.*

berfoyle, *par.,* Perth, Scot.; tourist resort; p. (1951) *1,133.*

Abergavenny, *mun. bor., t.,* Monmouth., on R. Usk; light engin., concrete prods.; p. (1961) *9,625.*

Abergele, *urb. dist.,* Denbigh, Wales; small wat. pl.; p. (1961) *7,982.*

Aberlour, Charlestown of, *burgh,* Banff, Scot.; on R. Spey, 12 m. S. of Elgin; p. (1961) *958.*

Abernethy, *burgh,* Perth, Scot.; on R. Tay, once the cap. of the Pictish Kings; p. (1961) *601.*

Abersychan, *par.,* Monmouth, Eng.; coal, iron, and steel; p. *25,748.*

Abertillery, *urb. dist.,* Monmouth.; coal, engin., leather goods; p. (1961) *25,160.*

Aberystwyth, *mun. bor., wat. pl.,* on Cardigan Bay at the mouth of the R. Ystwyth, Cardigan, Wales; univ. college; Nat. Library of Wales; p. (1961) *10,418.*

Abidjan, *cap.,* Ivory Coast, W. Africa; palm oil, cocoa, copra, hardwood, rubber; p. (estd. 1960) *177,500.*

Abilene, *t.,* Texas, U.S.A.; univ.; food prod., oilseeds, oil-refining, cotton; p. (1960) *90,368.*

Abingdon, *mun. bor.,* Berks, Eng., on R. Thames; cars, leather goods; p. (1961) *14,283.*

Abingdon, *t.,* Va., U.S.A.; lumbering, flour milling; mnfs. condensed milk, chemicals, tobacco; tourist resort; p. (1960) *4,758.*

Abington, *t.,* Mass., U.S.A.; shoes, textile machin.; p. (1960) *10,449.*

Abitibi, *R.* and *L.,* R. flows into James Bay, Ontario, Canada; gold dist.

Abo, *see* **Turku, Finland.**

Abomey, *old cap.,* Dahomey, W. Africa; former slave mkt.; cotton; p. (estd. 1960) *18,900.*

Abovyan, *t.,* Armenian S.S.R.; 10 m. from Yerevan; new model t. founded 1963; planned p. *50,000.*

Aboyne and Glentanner, *par.,* Aberdeen, Scot.; hol. res. on R. Dee nr. Ballater; p. (1951) *1,651.*

Abraham, Plains of, nr. Quebec; Wolfe's victory over French under Montcalm, 1759.

Abram, *urb. dist.,* Lancs, Eng.; coal, engin., cotton mnfs.; p. (1961) *6,017.*

Abrantes, *t.,* Portugal, on the Tagus R.; French won battle here in Napoleonic Wars, 1807; p. (1940) *11,339.*

Abruzzi and Molise, *region* of Italy on the Adriatic, inc. provs. of Aquila, Chieti, and Campobasso, Teramo, a. 5,883 sq. m.; p. (1961) *1,584,777.*

Abu, *mtn.,* Rajasthan, India, 5,653 ft.; Jain temples.

Abukir or **Aboukir,** *vil.* on Abukir Bay, U.A.R.; site of ancient Canopus; Battle of the Nile fought in the Bay, 1798; p. *7,086.*

Abu Simbel, Nile Valley, U.A.R.; famous anc. temples carved out of solid sandstone, one to Rameses II and the other to his Queen; rescue operation from rising waters behind Aswan High Dam undertaken.

Abydos, *ruined c.,* Upper U.A.R.; celebrated for its temple of Osiris.

Abydos, *ruined castled t.,* Anatolia on the Dardanelles, which resisted Philip of Macedon; famous for the story of Leander and Hero.

Abyssinia, *see* **Ethiopia.**

Acadia or **Acadie,** French name applied to previous possessions S. of St. Lawrence R., inc. Nova Scotia and New Brunswick and part of Maine.

Acajutla, *spt.,* Salvador, Central America; exp. coffee; cement, oil refining, fertilisers; p. (1960) *15,475.*

Acambaro, *t.,* Mexico; rly. junction; p. *17,643.*

Acapulco, *spt.,* Pacific coast, Mexico; tourism; exp. hides, cedar, fruit; p. (1960) *28,582.*

Accra, *spt., cap.* Ghana, W. Africa; univ.; airport; p. (1960) *491,060* (inc. cap. dist. and rural a.)

Accrington, *mun. bor., mftg. t.,* Lancs, Eng.; 20 m. N. of Manchester; cotton ctr., coal, textile machin., engin., bricks; p. (1961) *40,987.*

Acerra, *t.,* S. Italy; destroyed by Hannibal 216 B.C.; restored 210 B.C.; olive oil, wine, hemp; p. *16,460.*

Achaia, *prov.,* Greece; a. 1,206 sq. m.; chief currant-producing dist.; spt., Patras; p. (1961) *236,770.*

Achill, *I.,* off the W. coast of Mayo, Ireland; agr., [fishing.

Achill Head, *cape,* Mayo.

Achinsk, *industl. t.,* R.S.F.S.R., on R. Chulym; impt. rly. junction; manganese, cement; p. (1956) *42,400.*

Acireale, *spt.,* Sicily; sulphur baths; p. (1961) [*43,752.*

Acklin, *island,* Bahamas, W. Indies; timber, sponges; p. (1953) *1,273.*

Aconcagua, *mtn.*, Andes, Argentine, S. America, highest peak of New World, alt. 22,835 ft.

Aconcagua, *prov.*, Chile; a. 3,939 sq. m.; cap. San Felipe; alfalfa and Mediterranean fruits; p. (1957) *154,075*.

Aconquija, Sierra de, *mtn. range*, N. Argentina, S. America; rises steeply from Chaco lowland to 18,000 ft.

Acqui, *ancient walled t.*, N. Italy, prov. Alessandria; famous cath., sulphur springs; p. *18,975*.

Acre (Akka), *c.*, *spt.*, Israel, famous for its sieges during Crusades and in 1799 withstanding Napoleon for 61 days; p. *14,000*.

Acre, *st.*, Brazil; a. 59,139 sq. m., cap. Rio Branco; rubber; p. (1960) *160,208*.

Acton, *former mun. bor.*, Middlesex, Eng.; now inc. in Ealing outer bor., Greater London, (*q.v.*).

Ada, *t.*, Oklahoma, U.S.A.; p. (1960) *14,347*.

Adamawa, *prov.*, W. Africa, divided between Nigeria and Cameroun; a. 70,000 sq. m.; ivory, groundnuts.

Adams, *mftg. t.*, Mass., U.S.A.; paper, cottons, woollens, calcium quarrying; p. (1960) *11,949*.

Adam's Bridge, ridge of sand and coral reef, 30 m., between India and Ceylon. Proposed inter-dominion rly.

Adam's Peak, *sacred mtn.*, S. Ceylon, alt. 7,352 ft.

Adana, *t.*, Turkey; on R. Seihan; wool, cotton, grain, tobacco; p. (1960) *230,024*.

Adapazari, *t.*, Turkey; rly. junction; agr. and tr. ctr., silk, linen; high grade concentrate from low grade iron ore deposits in Camdagi a.; p. (1960) *80,160*.

Adda, *R.*, N. Italy, flows through L. Como to R. Po.

Addis Ababa, *cap.* Ethiopia; terminus of Jibuti rly.; p. (1960) *450,000*.

Adelaide, *c.*, *spt.*, *cap.*, S. Australia; on R. Torrens, which flows into G. of St. Vincent; trans-continental rly. connections; inds. using wool, leather, iron; exp. wheat, wool, wine, ores; univ.; oil refinery on St. Vincent's G.; p. (with subs) (1961) *587,656*.

Adelboden, *t.* Bern can., Switzerland; 19 m. S.W. of Interlaken; health resort, mineral springs.

Adélie Land, Antarctica; French terr. and dependency of Réunion.

Adelsburg, *t.*, Jugoslavia; 20 m. N.E. of Trieste; extensive grotto and stalactite cavern.

Aden, *spt.*, *terr.*, *Crown Col.*, S. Arabia; t. stands on peninsula of Aden, is refuelling pt. and entrepôt for cotton, clothing, coffee, tobacco; salt mftg., oil refinery; Aden Terr. inc. Perim I. and Kuria Muria Is., also administers Kamaran I.; a. 75 sq. m., p. (estd. 1964) *220,000*.

Aden Protectorate, S. Arabia; comprises section of mainland stretching along G. of Aden and inland for about 100 m., also Sokotra I; a. 112,080 sq. m.; p. (estd.) *1,000,000*. Aden *Colony* and *Protectorate* joined Federation of S. Arabia, 18 Jan. 1963; renamed **Protectorate of Southern Arabia** (*q.v.*).

Aden, Gulf of, Arabian Sea; 48 m. l., 180 m. wide.

Aderno, *t.*, Sicily, Italy; at base of Mt. Etna, ancient ruins; p. *24,307*.

Adige, *R.* in N. Italy; enters Adriatic N. of Po, length 240 m.

Adirondacks, *mtns.*, N.Y., U.S.A.; highest peak, Mt. Marcy, 5,345 ft.

Adiyaman, *t.*, Turkey; p. (1960) *17,021*.

Adlington, *urb. dist.*, Lancs, Eng.; nr. Chorley; cotton, coal-mining; p. (1961) *4,281*.

Admiralty G., N.W. of Western Australia.

Admiralty I., off Alaska mainland; belongs to U.S.A.; fishing, timber.

Admiralty Is., S.W. Pac. Oc. N. of New Guinea, comprise 40 sm. is.; Australian mandate; coconuts, copra; a. 663 sq. m.; p. *13,134*.

Adonara, *I.*, one of Nusa Tenggara Is., Indonesia; p. (estd.) *25,000*. [p. (1961) *69,951*.

Adoni, *t.*, Andhra Pradesh, India; cotton market;

Adour, *R.*, S.W. France; rises in Pyrenees, enters Bay of Biscay below Bayonne; length 207 m.

Adowa, *t.*, *cap.*, Tigre prov., N. Ethiopia; alt. over 6000 ft., tr. and mkt. centre; p. (1945) *11,500*.

Adra, *spt.*, *t.*, Almeria, S. Spain; nr. Guardia Viejas salt beds and Berja lead-mines; sugar-cane, fish, fruit and veg. canning; p. (1957) *13,687*.

Adrano, *t.*, Sicily, Italy; at S.W. foot of Etna; agr. mkt.; p. (1936) *24,307*.

Adrar *oasis*, Sahara Desert, Algeria; salt, dates, grain.

Adria, *mkt. t.*, Rovigo, Italy; formerly on cst., now 14 m. inland, old Etruscan c.

Adrian, *c.*, Michigan, U.S.A.; 73 m. W. of Detroit; p. (1960) *20,347*.

Adrianople, *see* Edirne.

Adriatic Sea, branch of the Mediterranean, between Italy and Balkan Peninsula; forms G. of Venice on the N.; chief trading pts., Venice, Trieste, and Ancona on the N., Brindisi and Dürres on the S.; a. 52,000 sq. m., length 450 m.

Adullam or Aidelma, *former dist.*, Palestine; S.E. Jerusalem. Site of Canaanite city; cave, David's hiding-place from King Saul.

Adwick le Street, *urb. dist.*, W.R. Yorks, Eng.; coal; p. (1961) *18,212*.

Adzhar, *rep.*, Georgian S.S.R.; tea, citrus fruits, oil-refining, engin.; ch. t. Batumi; a. 1,100 sq. m.; p. (1959) *242,000*.

Aegades, group of rocky Is. off W. coast of Sicily; ch. t. Favignana on I. of that name.

Aegean Is., between Greece and Turkey; called the Grecian Archipelago, inc. Crete, Cyclades, Sporades, and Dodecanese; a. 1,506 sq. m.; p. (1961) *477,476*.

Aegean Sea, branch of the Mediterranean; studded with Is., between Greece and Turkey; connected through the Dardanelles with Sea of Marmara and thence through the Bosphorus Strait with the Black Sea.

Aegina, *I.*, Greece; in G. of same name, sponge fisheries.

Aerö, *I.* in the Baltic off Denmark; p. (1960) *10,109*.

Aetolia and Acarnania, *prov.*, N. Greece; cap. Missolonghi; p. (1961) *237,738*.

Afam, S. Nigeria; oilfield; pipe-line E. to Pt. Harcourt.

Affric, Glen, Inverness, Scot.; 30 m. S.W. of Inverness; hydro-elec. scheme, opened 1952.

Afghanistan, *mtn. cty.*, Asia; monarchy; cap Kabul; comm. ctrs. Kabul, Kandahar; ch. rs. Kabul and Helm; climate, intense summer heat severe winter cold, scanty rainfall; races Afghans, aboriginal hill-tribes; languages official Persian, spoken Pushtu; religion, Islam cereals, fruit, sheep, horses, camels; inds. carpets, woollens, silks; coal-mining at Dara-i-Suf natural gas at Shibarghan; rich copper, lead iron resources undeveloped; a. 250,000 sq m.; p. (est.) *13,800,000*.

Afragola, *t.*, Napoli prov., S. Italy; 5 m. N.E. o Naples; cereals, fruit, hemp; p. (1961) *45,881*

Africa, second largest *continent*; bounded on N by Mediterranean, by Red Sea and Indian Ocean on E., by Atlantic Ocean on W.; adjoin Asia at Isthmus of Suez. Deserts in N., forest in centre, and lofty plateaux and veldts in S Highest mtn., Kilimanjaro, 19,324 ft.; chie rivers, Nile, Congo, Niger, Zambesi; larges L. Victoria. Rainfall heavy near equator, al most rainless in Sahara and Kalahari, elsewher moderate. Races include Negro, Bantu Arabs, Berbers, Hottentots, Bushmen. Agri culture: wine, olives, wheat, esparto grass i N.; cocoa, oil palm, groundnuts, coffee, cotto in centre; wheat, maize, wool in S. Minerals gold, diamonds, copper. Compared with onl 4 at end of last war, 38 countries were indep. i 1966. Those still to become fully indep. are the Spanish cols. of Sp. Guinea, Sp. Sahara Ifni; the Portuguese cols. of Angola, Por Guinea, Mozambique; Fr. Somaliland; an Rhodesia, Swaziland, Basutoland; and S.W Africa; a. (approx.) 11,500,000 sq. m.; p. (estd *225,000,000*.

Afyon Karahisar *t.*, Turkey; opium; p. (196(*38,392*.

Agadir, *spt.*, S. cst. Morocco; wrecked by earth quake, 1960; new town built S. of former c. in of greater geological stability.

Agawam, *t.*, Mass., U.S.A.; engin.; p. (1960) *15,71*

Agder, E. and W., *two dists.*, Norway; (E.) 3,607 sq. m.; p. (1963) *77,639* (W.) a. 2,794 s m.; p. (1963) *112,012*

Agen, *t.*, *cap.* Lot-et-Garonne, France; 85 r from Bordeaux; cath.; p. (1954) *32,593*.

Agincourt, *vil.*, Pas-de-Calais, France; famed f battle in 1415 between English, led by Henry and French under d'Albert.

Agira, *t.*, Sicily, Italy; marble, cement, sulphu p. *15,172*.

Agra, *c.*, Uttar Pradesh, India; on Jumna R 115 m. S.S.E. of Delhi; formerly cap. of Mog Empire; famous Taj Mahal mausoleum; univ p. (1961) *508,680*.

Agri, *t.*, Turkey, p. (1960) *19,786*.

Agrigento, *t.*, S. cst. Sicily, Italy: grain, sulphur, salt; p. (1961) *47,094*. Agrigento (lately Girgenti, and formerly Agrigentum, Akragas), is also famous for its Greek temples.
Agrinion, *t.*, Greece; tobacco; p. (1951) *21,752*.
Aguadilla, *spt.*, Puerto Rico, Central America; exp. coffee and sugar; p. *13,468*.
Aguascalientes, *st.*, Mexico; cap. Aguascalientes; a. 2,499 sq. m.; p. (1960) *243,363*.
Aguascalientes, *t.*, *cap.*, Aguascalientes, Mexico; alt. over 6000 ft.; 360 m. N.W. of Mexico City; wide range of local inds.; hot springs; p. (1960) *126,617*.
Aguilar de la Frontera, *t.*, S. Spain; wine, olives; Moorish castle, p. (1957) *15,224*.
Aguilas, *t. spt.*, Murcia, on E. cst. of Spain; exp. esparto, iron ore; p. *246,462*.
Agulhas, *C.*, 100 m. E. of C. of Good Hope, most southerly point of Africa.
Ahaggar, *mtns.*, S. Algeria range 9,000–10,000 ft.
Ahlen, *t.*, N. Rhine-Westphalia, Germany; on R. Werse; coal mining, metal and engin. wks.; p. (1963) *42,200*.
Ahmedabad, *temporary cap.* Gujarat, India; Jain temple, splendid mosques, pottery, silk, gold, cotton; p. (1961) *1,149,918*.
Ahmadnagar, *c.*, Maharashtra, India; lge. trade in cotton and silk goods; p. (1961) *119,020*.
Ahmedi, *pt.*, Yemen; nr. Hodeida; oil storage.
Ahuachapán, *dep.*, Salvador; cap. Ahuachapán; trade in coffee, sugar, tobacco, cereals; p. (1960) *130,710*. [p. (1961) *20,981*.
Ahvenanmaa (Åland), *dep.*, Finland, a. 572 sq. m.;
Ahwaz, *c.*, S.W. Iran, on Karun R., cap. Khuzistan prov.; oil pipe-line passes through to Abadan; p. (1956), *119,828*.
Aigion, *t.*, Greece; currants exported; p. *11,011*.
Aigues-Mortes, *t.*, Gard, France; on R. Rhône delta; canal centre, once spt. now 3 m. from Mediterranean; salt-works; p. (1954) *3,746*.
Ailsa Craig, *rocky I.*, off Ayrshire cst., Scot., alt. 1,114 ft.; gannetry.
Ain, *dep.*, France; mainly agr., vines, grains, sheep, tobacco, silk; a. 2,248 sq. m.; p. (1962) *327,146*.
Ain Sefra, *terr.*, S. Algeria; p. *193,347*.
Aintab, *t.*, Syria, military centre in the Middle Ages; hides, morocco leather; p. (1950) *72,743*.
Aintree, *vil.*, Lancs., Eng.; nr. Liverpool; nylon plant projected 1964.
Air or Asben, *oasis* in Sudan, cap. Agades; dates, indigo, senna.
Air, *mtns.*, Niger, W. Africa; ch. t. Agadès.
Airdrie, *lge. burgh. mftg. t.*, N.E. Lanark, Scot.; 12 m. E. of Glasgow; coal-mng., iron inds., brick and concrete wks., steel tubes, pharmaceutics; p. (1961) *33,620*.
Aire, *R.*, W.R. Yorks, Eng.; trib. Ouse; l. 70 m.
Aireborough, *urb. dist.*, W.R. Yorks., Eng.; p. (1961) *27,643*.
Airlie, *par.*, Angus, Scot.; seat of the Earls of Airlie; p. (1951) *630* [tunnel.
Airolo, *vil.*, Switzerland; at S. end of St. Gotthard
Aisne, *dep.*, France; agr., timber, sugar, brewing, textiles; cap. Laon; a. 2,866 sq. m.; p. (1962) *512,920*.
Aisne, *R.*, N.E. France; trib. R. Oise; l. 150 m.
Aix, *t.*, Bouches-du-Rhône, France; 18 m. N. of Marseilles; old cap. of Provence; thermal springs; p. (1962) *72,696*.
Aix-la-Chapelle, *see* **Aachen.**
Aix-les-Bains, *health resort*, Savoy, France; p. (1954) *15,680*.
Ajaccio, *spt.*, *cap.* Corsica; timber, flour, olive oil, tobacco; p. (1962) *42,282*.
Ajmer, *t.*, Rajasthan, India; cotton, salt, opium; p. (1961) *231,240*.
Aksu (Aqsu), *t.*, Sinkiang, China; walled town, impt. trading ctr. on caravan route; textiles, carpets, jade carving, tanning, metal wkg.; p. *50,000*.
Akaroa, *t.*, S. I. New Zealand; on Akaroa Harbour; scenic and historic interest; p. *556*.
Akershus, *co.*, Norway; a. 2,064 sq. m.; p. (1963) *249,760*; Akerhus fortress (14th cent.) at Oslo.
Akhisar, *t.*, Turkey; ancient Thyatira; manganese, tobacco, olives, cotton, grain; p. (1960) *40,013*.
Akhmim, *t.*, Upper U.A.R.; linen and cotton goods; limestone quarries; p. *28,000*.
Akhtyika, *t.*, Ukrainian S.S.R.; metal wks.
Akimiski I., *I.*, James Bay, Canada.
Akita, *t.*, Japan; silk, metals, rice, oil-refining; p. (1955) *190,202*.
Akmolinsk, *see* **Tselinograd**
Akola, *t.*, Maharashtra, India; cotton; p. (1961) *115,760*.
Akpatok I., *I.* in Ungava Bay, Labrador.
Akron, *mftg. c.*, Ohio, U.S.A.; largest rubber mftg. ctr. in the world; maize mills, woollens, machin., chemicals, plastics, tools; p. (1960) *290,351*.
Akrotiri, Cyprus; British sovereign a. within Rep.
Aksaray, *t.*, Turkey; p. (1960) *20,046*.
Aksehir, *t.*, Turkey; p. (1960) *20,607*.
Aktyubinsk, *t.*, N.W. Kazakhstan S.S.R.; at S. end of Ural Mtns.; ferro-alloys, engin., lignite, elec. power, chemicals; p. (1959) *97,000*. [*9,152*.
Akureyri, *t.*, N. Iceland; herring fishery; p. (1962)
Akyab, *spt.*, Burma; at mouth of Kaladan R.; exp. rice; p. *38,094*.
Alabama, *st.*, U.S.A.; cap. Montgomery, ch. pt. Mobile; minerals, cotton, cereals, sugar, fertilisers, chemicals, mng.; a. 51,609 sq. m.; p. (1960) *3,266,740*.
Alagôas, *maritime st.*, Brazil; cap. Maceio; sugar, cotton, tobacco, rubber, rice, textiles; a. 11,016 sq. m.; p. (1960) *1,271,062*.
Alajuela, *prov.*, Costa Rica, Central America; cap. Alajuela; coffee, sugar; p. (1963) *237,568*.
Alameda, *spt.*, Cal., U.S.A.; airport; light mnfs., shipbldg., fish-canning, holiday resort; p. (1960) *61,316*.
Alamosa, *t.*, Col., U.S.A.; flour-milling, meat-packing, stockyards; p. (1960) *6,205*.
Aland Is. (Ahvenanmaa), group belonging to Finland at entrance of G. of Bothnia; a. 572 sq. m.; p. (estd. 1958) *21,967*.
Alasehir, *t.*, Turkey; ancient Philadelphia; mineral springs, wheat, tobacco, raisins; p. (1960) *13,923*.
Alaska, *st.*, U.S.A.; in Arctic N. America; mtnous.; furs, timber, salmon fishing, mng., natural gas, oil; severe earthquake, 28th March 1964; a. 586,400 sq. m.; p. (1960) *226,167*.
Alaska Highway, from Dawson Creek, B.C. to Fairbanks, Alaska, 1,527 m. long; built for Second World War programme; main supply base and H.Q., Edmonton, Alberta.
Alatau, *mtns.*, bdy. of W. Turkestan and Sinkiang, China; group of 5 ranges, outliers of Tien-Shan; alt. up to 15,000 ft.; highest peak Khan Tengri, 22,800 ft.
Alava, Basque *prov.*, N. Spain; ch. t. Vitoria; viticulture; a. 1,175 sq. m.; p. (1959) *130,887*.
Alba, *t.*, N. Italy; in Tanaro valley; mkt. for silk, cattle, grain, wine; p. (1936) *11,072*.
Albacete, *prov.*, S.E. Spain; cereals, fruit, sheep; a. 5,739 sq. m.; p. (1959) *384,849*.
Albacete, *t.*, *cap.*, Albacete, Spain; on plains of Alta Mancha; agr. mkt., fruit, saffron; p. (1959) *74,807*.
Alba-Iulia, *t.*, Romania; on R. Mures, formerly Carlsburgh; union of Transylvania with Romania proclaimed here 1918; p. (1956) *14,776*.
Alban Hills, *volcanic group*, 10 m. S.E. of Rome, Italy; circumference 35 m.; greatest alt. Monte Faete, 3,137 ft.; viticulture.
Albania, *rep.*, S. Europe; lying along Adriatic, adjacent Jugoslavia and Greece; rugged mtnous. cty., fertile Adriatic littoral and Koritsa Basin; maize, wheat, olive oil, cheese, tobacco, wool, hides, horses, bitumen; cap. Tiranë; a. 10,629 sq. m.; p. (1960) *1,625,000*.
Albano Laziale, *t.*, Italy; S. of Rome; saline springs, mud baths; p. (1936) *9,414*.
Albany, *st. cap.*, New York, U.S.A.; on R. Hudson; river pt., iron, brass, chemicals, textiles, paper, machin. tools, car equipment; p. (1960) *129,726*
Albany, *spt.*, *t.*, W. Australia; on King George Sound; agr. and pastoral; p. (1961) *10,502*.
Albay, *t.*, Luzon I., Philippines; hemp, sugar, copra.
Albemarle I., largest of the Galapagos in Pacific Ocean; alt. summit, 5,020 ft. above sea-level.
Albemarle Sound, *inlet*, N. Carolina cst. U.S.A. 60m.
Albert, *t.*, Somme, France; on R. Ancre; almost destroyed First World War and damaged again Second World War; aircraft, machin., hardware; p. (1954) *8,991*.
Albert L., Africa; great reservoir of White Nile, extreme length 100 m., general breadth 20 m., alt. 2,100 ft.; greater part in Uganda.
Alberta, *prov.*, W. Canada; Rockies, in W.; pre-eminently agr.; wheat, alfalfa, dairying, livestock; coal, gas, oil, chemicals; cap. Edmonton; a. 255,285 sq.m.; p. (1961) *1,331,944*.

Albertville, *t.*, Congo; on W. of L. Tanganyika; rly. to Kongola on L. Lualaba.
Albi, *cap.*, Tarn, France; cath.; industl. and comm. ctr. in coal mining dist.; p. (1962) *41,268.*
Albigeois, *sub-region*, Basin of Aquitaine, France; centred on Albi; rich farming, cereals and vines; sm. coalfield and associated industries.
Albion, *t.*, Mich., U.S.A.; mnfs. iron goods; p. (1960) *12,749.*
Albuquerque, *c.*, N. Mex., U.S.A.; on Rio Grande; wool, hides, timber, metals, cement; univ.; (1960) *201,189.*
Albury, *t.*, N.S.W., Australia; on Murray R.; sheep farming, currants; p. (1961) *18,617.*
Alcalá de Henares, *t.*, Spain; 20 m. E. of Madrid; univ.; p. (1957) *19,415.*
Alcalá la Real, *t.*, Andalusia, Spain; p. (1957) *29,165.*
Alcamo, *t.*, Sicily, Italy; 24 m. S.W. of Palermo; olives, oranges, lemons, wines; Saracen cas.; p. *51,200.*
Alcázar de San Juan, *t.*, nr. Ciudad Real, Spain; soap, gunpowder, wine; p. (1957) *25,139.*
Alcázar Quivir (Al Kazral Kebir), *c.*, Morocco, N. Africa; 80 m. N.W. of Fez; p. (1960) *34,035.*
Alcester, *t.*, *rural dist.*, Warwick, Eng.; needles and fish-hooks, agr. and mkt. gardening; p. (rural dist. 1961) *15,556.*
Alcoy, *t.*, Spain; textiles, farm implements, mach., elec. engin., fine paper mkg.; p. (1959) *53,031.*
Alcudia, *Roman walled t.*, Majorca I., Spain; 31 m. from Palma; site of Roman t. of Pollentia; p. (1957) *3,556.*
Aldan, *navigable R.*, Siberia, U.S.S.R.; length 300 m.
Aldeburgh, *mun. bor.*, *spt.*, E. Suffolk, Eng.; 30 m. from Ipswich; fisheries; H.Q. of gr. of Eng. writers and musicians; p. (1961) *2,972.*
Alderley Edge, *urb. dist.*, Cheshire, Eng.; p. (1961) *3,618.*
Aldermaston, Berkshire, Eng.; Atomic Weapons Research Establishment.
Alderney, most N. of Channel Is.; agr. and hort. prods., dairying; sand, grit, gravel; tourism; t. St. Anne; airpt.; a. 1,962 acres; p. (1961) *1,472.*
Aldershot, *mun. bor.*, Hants, Eng.; bricks; lge. military camp; p. (1961) *31,260.*
Aldridge, *urb. dist.*, Staffs, Eng.; plastics, packing-cases; p. (1961) *50,981.*
Aleksandrovsk, *see* **Zaporozhe.**
Alentejo Alto and Baixo, *provs.*, S. Portugal; caps. Evora and Beja; cereals, stock raising, copper, and iron; a. 9,219 sq. m.; p. (1950) *769,936.*
Alençon, *t.*, *cap.*, Orne, France; textiles, lace; p. (1954) *21,893.*
Aleppo, *c.*, ch. tr. centre N. Syria; grain, textiles, carpets, dairying, cement, sugar, brewing; p. (1961) *496,231.*
Alès, *t.*, Gard, France; trades in raw silk produced in region; coal mining, chemicals, iron-ore, pyrite, zinc; p. (1962) *43,370.*
Alessandria, *c.*, N. Italy; 46 m. E. of Turin; linen, hats, macaroni; p. (1961) *92,291.*
Alesund (Aalesund), *spt.*, W. coast Norway; fishing; p. (estd. 1960) *19,000.*
Aletsch, *glacier*, Bernese Alps, Valais can., Switzerland; lgst. in Europe; length exceeds 15 m.
Aletschhorn, *mtn.*, Bernese Alps, Valais canton, Switzerland; alt. 13,763 ft.
Aleutian Is. (U.S.A.), N. Pac. Oc., chain of Is. stretching out 1,200 m. from the most S.W. point of Alaska towards Kamchatka.
Alexander City, *t.*, Ala., U.S.A.; formerly Youngville; textiles; p. (1960) *13,140.*
Alexandretta, *spt.*, *see* **Iskenderun.**
Alexandria, *ch. pt.*, U.A.R., N.E. Africa; founded by Alexander the Great, 332 B.C.; floating dock; exp. cotton, wheat, rice, gum; p. (1960) *1,513,000.*
Alexandria, *t.*, Dunbartonshire, Scot.; on W. side of vale of Leven; cotton printing, bleaching, dyeing, torpedo wks.
Alexandria, *t.*, Louisiana, U.S.A.; rice, foundries; p. (1960) *40,279.*
Alexandria, *c.*, *spt.*, N.E. Virginia, U.S.A.; on Chesapeake Bay; mnfs. foodstuffs, thread, cotton, leather goods; p. (1960) *91,023.*
Alexandrina L., inlet, S. Australia; nr. Encounter Bay.
Alexandroupolis, *spt.*, Thrace, Greece; oak timber tr., many antiquities; p. (1961) *18,712.*
Alford, *urb. dist.*, Lindsey, Lincoln, Eng.; agr. mkt., brewing, food-preserving; p. (1961) *2,134.*
Alfortville, *t.*, Seine, France; S.E. suburb of Paris, rubber, paper, glass, hosiery, metal wks.; p; (1954) *30,195.*
Alfreton, *urb. dist.*, Derby, Eng.; coal, iron, stone, chemicals, textile, engin., hosiery, knitwear; p. (1961) *22,998.*
Algarve, *prov.*, Portugal, cap. Faro; fruit, fishing, wines, salt; a. 2,028 sq. m.; p. (1950) *325,971.*
Algeciras, *spt.*, Spain; on bay opposite Gibraltar; fishing, cork, oranges; winter health resort; p. (1959) *64,842.*
Algeria, *indep. sov. st.* (3 July 1962), N. Africa; formerly under French rule; comprises N. Algeria (divided into 12 deps.) and Saharan deps.; fertile valleys, rugged mtns., barren plateaux; warm, moist winters, hot, dry summers; Berbers, Kabyles, Arabs, Tauregs; cap. Algiers; products: wine, fruit, olive oil, timber, tobacco, minerals; oil and gas deposits; a. 919,600 sq. m.; p. (estd. 1963) *10,453,000.*
Alghero, *spt.* on western coast of Sardinia; cath.; coral fisheries, fruit, wine.
Algiers, *dep.*, Algeria, N. Africa; cap. Algiers; p. (1948) *2,765,898.*
Algiers, *cap.*, *naval port*, Algeria; strongly fortified; coaling sta.; exp. wheat, wine, olives; oil refining at Maison Carrée; p. (1963) *820,000.*
Algoa Bay, about 425 m. E. of C. of Good Hope S. Africa.
Algonquin Park, Ontario, Canada; *park*, game reserve, tourist centre. [(1957) *10,564.*
Alhama, *c.*, Granada, Spain; hot springs; p.
Alhambra, *c.*, S. Cal., U.S.A.; oil refining equipment, felt, clay, aircraft, p. (1960) *54,807.*
Alhaurin el Grande, *t.*, S. Spain; rly.; olive oil, marble quarries; p. (1957) *11,537.*
Alicante, *prov.*, S.E. Spain; ch. t. Alicante; a. 2,267 sq. m.; p. (1959) *696,165.*
Alicante, *spt.*, *t.*, E. Spain; tourism; wine, fruits, minerals; p. (1959) *117,204.*
Alice, *t.*, Cape Prov., S. Africa; health resort; timber inds.; p. (1960) *3,536* inc. *746* whites.
Alice Springs, *t.*, N. Territory, Australia; ctr. vast pastoral holdings; Stuart highway (arterial road) to Darwin; p. (1957) *3,000.*
Aligarh, *t.*, Uttar Pradesh, India; univ.; wheat, cotton, gold and silver work; p. (1961) *185,020.*
Alingsås, *t.*, Sweden, E. of Gothenburg; clothing ind.; p. (1961) *17,546.*
Aliwal North, *t.*, Cape Prov., S. Africa; sulphur springs, health resort; p. (1960) *10,706* inc. *2,629* Europeans.
Aikmaar, *t.*, Netherlands; world cheese mkt.; salt; natural gas in the Schermer Polder; p. (1960) *43,208.*
Allahabad, *t.*, Uttar Pradesh, India; univ.; Hindu pilgrimage ctr.; p. (1961) *411,955.*
Allegan, *t.*, Mich., U.S.A.; mkt. for dairy and fruit products of the district; mnfs. drugs; p. (1960) *4,822.*
Allegheny Mtns., U.S.A.; bold escarpment in the W. Section of the Appalachian system stretching from Pennsylvania to W. Virginia.
Allegheny, *R.*, U.S.A.; joins the Ohio R., Pittsburgh, Penns.; length 350 m.
Allen, Bog of, *peat morass*, Ireland; a. 372 sq. m.
Allen, Lough, *L.*, Ireland, length 5 m., breadth 3 m.; one source of R. Shannon.
Allenstein, *see* **Olsztyn.**
Allentown, *t.*, Penns., U.S.A.; on Lehigh R., furniture, silk, tobacco; lorries; p. (1960) *108,551.*
Aller, *t.*, N.W. Spain; agr. mkt.; coal-, iron-, lead-mines; p. *23,600.*
Alliance, *t.*, Ohio, U.S.A.; coal; p. (1960) *28,362.*
Allier, *dep.*, France; coal- and iron-mining, mineral springs, wine, wheat; a. 2,848 sq. m.; p. (1962) *380,221.*
Allier, *R.*, Central Massif, France; rises in Cevennes; trib. of R. Loire.
Alloa, *spt.*, *burgh*, Clackmannan, Scot.; on N. bank of R. Forth 5 m. E. of Stirling; engin. brass, bricks, tiles, woollens, glass, distilling p. (1961) *13,895.*
Alma, *R.*, Crimea, U.S.S.R.; great victory over Russia by Allies, 1854.
Alma-Ata, *cap.*, Kazakh S.S.R.; engin., textiles leather, printing inds.; p. (1962) *534,000.*
Almada, *t.*, Portugal; on R. Tagus opposite Lisbon; founded by English Crusaders.
Almaden, *t.*, Sierra Morena, Spain; ancient Sisapon; quicksilver-mines; p. (1957) *12,375.*
Almansa, *t.*, Spain; textiles, leather, shoes, soap brandy; p. (1957) 15,990.

Almelo, *t.*, Overyssel, Netherlands; 25 m. S.E. of Zwolle: cotton textile mnfs.; p. (1960) *50,548.*
Almendralejo, *t.*, Badajoz, Spain; wine, brandy; p. (1957) *21,394.*
Almeria, *prov.*, S. Spain; ch. t. Almeria; a. 3,338 sq. m.; p. (1959) *367,833.*
Almeria, *spt.*, *t.*, S.E. Spain; cath.; exp. grapes, oranges, esparto grass, lead; p. (1959) *83,653.*
Almondbury, *t.*, W.R. Yorks, Eng.; joined to Huddersfield.
Aln, *R.*, Northumberland, Eng.
Alnwick, *urb. dist.*, Northumberland, Eng.; cas.; brewing, agr. machin.; p. (1961) *7,482.*
Alor, *I.*, one of Nusa Tenggara Is., Indonesia.
Alor Star, *t.*, *cap.*, Kedah st., Malaya; on main road and rly., N. airport; p. *32,424.*
Alost (Aalst), *t.*, Belgium; 14 m. N.W. of Brussels; rly.-junc.; weaving (linen, silk), brewing, rubber goods; p. (1962) *45,196.*
Alpena, *c.*, Thunder Bay, Mich., U.S.A.; cement, paper, tanneries, sawmills; p. (1960) *14,682.*
Alpen on Rhine, *t.*, Netherlands; on Old Rhine, 10 m. S.E. of Leyden; mkt. for dairy produce; p. (1960) *24,292.*
Alpes-Maritimes, *dep.*, S.E. France; ceded by Italy in 1860; ch. t. Nice; olives, wines, fruit; a. 1,443 sq. m.; p. (1962) *618,265.*
Alps, highest mtns. in Europe; 600 m. long from G. of Genoa to near Vienna; 130 m. broad in Tyrol; principal peaks: Mont Blanc (15,784 ft.), Mont Rosa (15,217 ft.), Matterhorn (14,782 ft.).
Alps, Apuan, limestone range near Viareggio, Italy; source of Carrara marble.
Alps, Australian, mtn. range between E. Victoria and N.S.W.; highest peak, Mt. Kosciusko, 7,328 ft.
Alps, Southern, mtn. ridge between Westland and Canterbury, New Zealand, highest peak Mt. Cook 12,349 ft.
Als, *I.*, Denmark, in the Little Belt, a. 130 sq. m.
Alsace-Lorraine, *prov.*, France; industl., agr., wooded, minerals; total a. 5,601 sq. m. Taken from France, in 1871, retroceded 1919; now divided into deps. of Bas-Rhin (1,848 sq. m. and p. (1954) *707,934*); Haut-Rhin (1,354 sq. m. and p. (1954) *509,647*); Moselle (2,403 sq. m. and p. (1954) *769,388*).
Alsager, *urb. dist.*, *mkt. t.*, Cheshire, Eng.: motor vehicles; p. (1961) *7,800.*
Alsdorf, *t.*, N. Rhine-Westphalia, Germany; 10 m. N.E. of Aachen; tar-distillation plant; p. (1963) *31,900.*
Alston, *t.*, Cumberland, Eng., on S. Tyne R. in N. Pennines; limestone quarrying, hosiery; p. (1961) *2,198.*
Altai, *mtns.*, S. boundary of Siberia; extend from sources of Obi to Gobi Desert more than 2,500 m. Bieluka Peak, alt. 13,644 ft.
Altamaha, *R.*, Georgia, U.S.A.; flowing into Atlantic; length 150 m.
Altamira, *caves*, N. Spain; prehistoric shelters, paintings of animals (Magdalenian).
Altamura, *t.*, Apulia, Italy; at foot of the Apennines; wines, wool; p. (1961) *43,735.*
Altdorf, *t.*, *cap.* Uri can., Switzerland; on R. Reuss; rubber goods, wood workings; p. *5,692.*
Altena, *t.*, N. Rhine-Westphalia, Germany; site of ancient cas. of Counts von der Marck; metals, wine; p. (1963) *24,100.*
Altenburg, *t.*, Leipzig, E. Germany; lignite mining, engin., metallurgy, mnfs. playing cards, textiles; p. (1963) *46,866.*
Alton, *urb. dist.*, Hants, Eng.; breweries, light engin.; p. (1961) *9,158.*
Alton, *t.*, Illinois, U.S.A.; machinery, glass, chemicals, flour; p. (1960) *43,047.*
Altona, *t.*, part of Hamburg, Germany; iron, textiles, breweries, glasswks., soap, leather, tobacco, fish canning; p. (estd. 1954) *250,000.*
Altona, *t.*, S. Victoria, Australia, 8 m. S.W. Melbourne; oil refinery, chemicals.
Altoona, *c.*, Blair, Penns., U.S.A.; coal, rly. wks.; p. (1960) *69,083.*
Altrincham, *mun. bor.*, Cheshire, Eng.; heavy engin.; p. (1961) *41,104.*
Altus, *t.*, Okla., U.S.A.; cotton, livestock, grain mkt.; p. (1960) *21,225.*
Altyn Tagh, part of Kunlun mtns., Tibet, 14,000 ft.
Alva, *burgh*, Clackmannan, Scot.; at S. foot of Ochil Hills, 3 m. N. of Alloa; woollens, printing, fruit and fish canning; p. (1961) *3,957.*
Alvah, *par.*, Banff, Scot.; near the hill of Alva; p. (1951) *892.*
Alvin, *t.*, Texas, U.S.A.; grain mkt., oil wells; p. (1960) *5,643.*
Alvsborg, *co.*, Sweden; a. 4,919 sq. m.; p. (1961) [*375,006.*
Alyth, *mftg. burgh*, Perth., Scot.; in Strathmore, 17 m. N.E. of Perth; p. (1961) *1,862.*
Amadeus, *large salt L.*, N. Terr., Australia; 92 m. long.
Amadjuak Lake, Baffin I., Canada.
Amagasaki, *t.*, Japan; sub. of Osaka; chemicals, polyethylene; iron and steel; p. (1960) *406,000.*
Amakusa Bay, *inlet*, Kyushu, Japan; on W. cst. E. of Nagasaki.
Amakusa, *I.*, Japan; kaolin.
Amalfi, *spt.*, Italy; on G. of Salerno; tourist resort; fisheries. [p. *12,365.*
Amalias, *t.*, W. Greece; grapes, wine, currants;
Amapa, *Fed. terr.*, Brazil; a. 53,059 sq. m.; cap. Macapá; manganese ore; p. (1960) *68,889.*
Amara, *t.*, *R. pt.*, Iraq; on left bank of R. Tigris 250 m. below Baghdad; Arab t. and agr. mkt. at R. crossing; p. *18,000.*
Amarillo, *t.*, Texas, U.S.A.; oil refining, creameries; p. (1960) *137,969.*
Amasya, *t.*, Turkey; on Yeshil-Irmak; fruit, salt, silk, wine; p. (1960) *28,188.*
Amazon, *R.*, S. America; lgst basin and extent of water of any river in the world; rises among the Andes as Alto Marañon, and flows 3,900 m. to the Atlantic. Ocean steamers penetrate to Iquitos, 1,935 m. from mouth. One of its affluents, the Madeira, has an extreme length of *c.* 2,000 m. Drains nearly 3 million sq. m.
Amazonas, *st.*, Brazil; rubber, timber; a. 616,148 sq. m.; cap. Manaus (*q.v.*); p. (1960) *721,215.*
Amazonas, *dep.*, Peru; a. 13,943 sq. m.; cap. Chachapoyas; p. (1961) *117,525.*
Amazonas, *fed. terr.*, Venezuela; cap. Puerto Ayacucho on Orinoco R.; a. 70,000 sq. m.; p. (1961) *15,000.*
Ambala, *t.*, E. Punjab, India; cotton, flour; p. (1961) *105,507.*
Ambarchik, *spt.*, Yakut rep., U.S.S.R.; air base, gold-mining; p. *10,000.*
Ambato, *c.*, Ecuador, S. America; S. of Quito, on slope of Mt. Chimborazo; alt. 8,859 ft.; textiles, canned fruits, leather gds.; p. (1950) *33,908.*
Amberg, *t.*, Bavaria, Germany; on R. Vils; iron, mining, engin., textiles; p. (1963) *42,300.*
Ambert, *t.*, Puy-de-Dôme, France; paper, cheese.
Amble, *urb. dist.*, Northumberland, Eng.; exp. coal; p. (1961) *4,889.*
Amblecote, *urb. dist.*, Staffs., Eng.; glass, fireclay, iron wks.; p. (1961) *3 008.*
Ambleside, *sm. mkt. t.*, Westmorland, Eng.; nr. L. Windermere; tourist centre, slates.
Amboina, *I.*, Moluccas, Indonesia; a. 314 sq. m.; spices; p. *66,821.*
Amboina, *t.*, *cap.*, *residency*, Molucca Is., Indonesia; pt. on S. cst. of Amboina I.; shipyards; p. (estd.) *17,334.*
Amboise, *t.*, Indre-et-Loire, France; 15 m. E. of Tours; famous cas. and prison; p. (estd.) *4,500.*
Ambriz, *spt.*, Angola; sugar-cane, coffee, copper.
Ameland, *I.*, W. Frisian Is., Netherlands.
America, *continent*; a. 16¾ million sq. m., p. *215,000,000.* The two vast divs. of this continent are joined by the narrow Isthmus of Panama. The most N. point is over 9,000 m. distant from C. Horn, the extreme S. point. *See also* N. and S. America.
Amersfoort, *t.*, Netherlands; on R. Eem; textiles, leather, tobacco, steam turbines; p. (1960) *70,194.*
Amersham, *t.*, Bucks, Eng.; 17th-century mkt. hall; light inds.; Radio chemical centre of U.K. Atomic Energy Authority; p. (of rural dist.) (1961) *56,565.*
Ames, *t.*, Iowa, U.S.A.; State College of Agriculture; p. (1960) *27,003.*
Amesbury, *t.*, Mass., U.S.A.; 40 m. N. Boston; cotton; p. (1960) *9,625.*
Amesbury, *t.*, *rural dist.*, Wilts, Eng.; nr. ancient British monuments of Stonehenge; p. (rural dist. 1961) *22,594.*
Amherst, *t.*, Mass., U.S.A.; machin.; Univ. of Mass.; p. (1960) *10,306.*
Amherst, *spt.*, Nova Scotia, Canada; shipbldg.; p. (1961) *10,788.*
Amiens, *c.*, Somme, N. France; on R. Somme; fine cath.; velvet, linen, woollens, silks; p. (1962) *109,869.*
Amirante Is., British group, Indian Ocean; S.W. of Seychelles.

Amityville, *t.*, N.Y., U.S.A.; Long I. sub. of New York; seaside resort; p. (1960) *8,318*.

Amlwch, *urb. dist., wat. pl.*, Wales; N. cst. of Anglesey; p. (1961) *2,910*.

Amman, *cap.*, Jordan; site of very ancient c.; aerodrome; p. (1961) *244,599*.

Ammanford, *urb. dist.*, Carmarthen, Wales; anthracite, brick mkg.; p. (1961) *6,264*.

Ammendorf, *t.*, Saxony-Anhalt, Germany; lignite mining, chemicals; p. (estd. 1954) *20,000*.

Ammer, *R.*, Germany; joins Neckar nr. Tübingen.

Amorgos, *I.*, Grecian Archipelago: p. *3,069*.

Amoy (Xiamen) *c.*, former treaty-pt., Fukien, China; rail link to Yingtang, Kiansi; tea, fruit, bricks; p. (estd. 1953) *224,000*.

Amravati, *t.*, Maharashtra, India; textiles, timber; p. (1961) *137,875*.

Amritsar, *c.*, Punjab, India; holy Sikh city; univ.; shawls and carpets; p. (1961) *376,295*.

Amroha, *t.*, Uttar Pradesh, India; pilgrimage ctr.; p. (1961) *68,965*.

Amrum, *I.*, one of N. Frisian Is., Germany; off W. cst. of Schleswig.

Amsterdam, *spt., cap*, Netherlands; at junction of R. Amstel and the Ij; built on 96 Is. joined by 300 bridges, harbour can hold 1,000 ships; two univs., Royal Palace, Bourse; extensive tr.; exp. dairy prod., sugar, tobacco; shipbldg., diamond polishing, aeronautical, marine, elec. machin., oil refining; p. (1960) *869,602*.

Amsterdam, *t.*, N.Y., U.S.A.; woollens; p. (1960) *28,772*. [refining.

Amuay, *t.*, N. Venezuela, Paraguaná pen.; oil

Amu Darya (Oxus), *R.*, U.S.S.R.; flows from the Pamir Mtns. to Aral Sea, length 1,350 m.

Amur, *R.*, flows from Mongolia between Manchuria and E. Siberia into the Pacific, opposite Sakhalin I.; length 3,000 m.

Anaconda, *t.*, Montana, U.S.A.; copper, zinc, manganese; p. (1960) *12,054*.

Anadyr, *R.*, U.S.S.R.; flows into Bering Sea.

Anaheim, *t.*, Cal., U.S.A.; p. (1960) *104,184*.

Anahuac, *depression*, central plateau, Mexico; average alt. 7,000 ft.; surr. by higher country inc. volcano Popocatapetl (17,887 ft.); contains Mexico City, a. approx. 1,500 sq. m.

Anaiza, *t.*, Nejd, Saudi Arabia; p. *25,000*.

Ancash, *dep.*, Peru; a. 14,700 sq. m.; ch. t. Huaraz; p. (1961) *586,889*.

Ancholme, *R.* Eng.; rises in Lincolnshire and joins the Humber.

Anchorage, *t.*, Alaska, U.S.A.; timber, salmon fishing and canning; almost devastated by earthquake 28 Mar. 1964; p. (1960) *44,237*.

Ancona, *spt.*, Central Italy; on the Adriatic Sea; founded by Dorians, 1500 B.C.; sugar refineries, shipbldg.; p. (1961) *99,678*. [lead, copper.

Andalusia, *old div.*, S. Spain; citrus fruits, sherry,

Andalusian Mtns. (Baetic Mtns.), S. Spain; young Alpine fold mtns. stretching from Atl. Oc. (Cadiz) to Mediterranean (Alicante); inc. Sierra Nevada (highest peak, Mulhacén, 11,420 ft.); some minerals, esp. lead and silver.

Andaman and Nicobar Is., Bay of Bengal; constituted a Union Territory, India, 1 Nov. 1956; timber; a. 3,215 sq. m.; p. (1961) *63,548*.

Andenne, *t.*, Namur, Belgium; on the Meuse, mining, chalk quarrying, chemicals; p. (1962) *7,919*.

Anderlecht, *sub.* of Brussels, Belgium; spinning, weaving, dyeing; p. (1962) *96,454*.

Andermatt, *vil.*, Uri, Switzerland; at foot of Mt. St. Gotthard; tourist ctr., winter health resort.

Andernach, *t.*, Rhineland-Palatinate, Germany; on the Rhine, 70 m. N.W. of Coblenz; R. port; metallurgy; p. (1963) *21,200*.

Anderson, *t.*, S.C., U.S.A.; cotton, lumber; p. (1960) *41,316*.

Anderson, *c.*, Indiana, U.S.A.; p. (1960) *49,061*.

Anderson, *R.*, N.W. Terr., Canada; flows into Arctic Ocean.

Andes, *great mtn. system*, S. America; 4,500 m. long; from Panama to C. Horn, 40 m. broad; volcanic; several of the peaks are over 20,000 ft. high. Rich in minerals.

Andhra Pradesh, *state*, E. India; cap. Hyderabad; a. 106,286 sq. m., p. (1961) *35,983,447*.

Andizhan, *t.*, Uzbekistan S.S.R.; formerly residence of Khans of Khokan; cotton, metals, petroleum, engin.; p. (1959) *129,000*.

Andorra, *sm. st.*, E. Pyrenees, under joint suzerainty of Pres. of France and Bishop of Urgel (Spain), virtually indep.; livestock, wines, tobacco; a. 191 sq. m.; p. (1954) *5,664*.

Andover, *mun. bor., mkt. t.*, Hants, Eng.; prehistoric earthwks.; p. (1961) *16,972*.

Andover, *t.*, Mass, U.S.A., on R. Merrimac; woollens, rubber; p. (1960) *17,149*.

Andria, *t.*, S. Italy; wine, olive oil, cotton textiles; p. (1961) *70,831*.

Andros, *largest I.*, Bahamas; sponges, sisal hemp; p. (1953) *7,136*.

Andros, *sm. spt.*, Andros I., Cyclades, Greek Archipelago; on E. cst.; p. (estd. 1960) *2,600*.

Andujar, *t.*, Spain; on Guadalquivir R.; mineral springs, pottery, soap, textiles, tanning, uranium plant; p. (1957) *28,499*.

Angara, *R.*, Siberia, U.S.S.R.; trib. of Yenisei; navigable almost its entire length, rises nr. and flows through L. Baikal; length 1,300 m.

Angarsk, *t.*, E. Siberia; on R. Angara 20 m. N.W. Irkutsk; engin., saw milling; p. (1959) *134,000*.

Angel Falls, *waterfall*, Venezuela, nr. Ciudad Bolivar; 3,212-ft. drop. [Bothnia.

Angermanälven, *R.*, Sweden; falls into G. of

Angermanland, *old div.*, Sweden; now mainly in prov. of Vasternoorland.

Angermünde, *t.*, Frankfurt, E. Germany; 40 m. N.E. Berlin; rly. ctr.; p. (1963) *12,784*.

Angers, *t.*, *cap.*, Maine-et-Loire, France; on R. Maine; mkt. t. for local produce, fruit, vegetables, Anjou wines, Cointreau; textiles; cath.; p. (1962) *122,269*.

Anglesey, *I., co.*, N. Wales, separated from Caernarvon by Menai Straits; cattle rearing, farming; a. 276 sq. m.; p. (1961) *51,700*.

Anglet, *t.*, Basses-Pyrénées, France; airport, woodworking, cellulose mftg; p. (1954) *12,603*.

Angola (Port. W. Africa), Portuguese possession, W. Africa; cap. Luanda; ch. prod. palm oil rubber, coffee, maize, sugar, wax, diamonds; oil struck in Cabinda; a. 481, 350 sq. m.; p. (1960) *4,832,677*.

Angoulême, *mftg. t.*, Charente, France; on R. Charente; cognac, paper; fine cath.; suffered during Huguenot wars; p. (1962) *51,223*.

Angra do Heroismo, *cap.*, Azores Is.; exp. wine, pineapples, flax; p. (1960) *102,365*.

Angren, *t.*, Uzbekistan S.S.R.; lgst. ctr. of lignite mng. in C. Asia; p. (1959) *55,000*.

Anguilla I., Leeward Is., W.I.; cap. A.; a. 50 sq. m.; p. (1957) *5,109*.

Angus, *co.*, Scot., formerly Forfar; agr. and mftg.; a. 875 sq. m.; p. (1961) *278,370*.

Anhalt, *dist.*, Saxony-Anhalt, Germany; former duchy; agr. and mining.

Anholt, *I.*, Kattegat, Denmark; p. (1960) *239*.

Anhwei (Anhui), *prov.*, China; soya-beans, rice, tea, coal and iron; a. 54,319 sq. m.; cap. Hofei; p. (1953) *30,343,637*.

Anjou, *old div.*, France; on both sides of R. Loire within the Paris Basin; ch. t. Angers.

Ankara, *cap.*, Turkey; on the Sakarya R.; grain and fruit ctr.; mohair cloth; p. (1960) *646,151*.

Anking (Anqing), *c.*, Anhwei prov., China; rice, cotton, wheat, tanning; p. (1953) *105,000*.

Anklam, *t.*, Neubrandenburg, E. Germany; on Peene R.; engin., sugar, furniture; p. (1963) *19,785*.

Annaba (Bône), *spt.*, Algeria; 280 m. E. of Algiers; fertile plain; phosphates; p. (estd. 1963) *155,000*.

Annaberg, *t.*, Karl-Marx-Stadt, E. Germany; in Erz Mtns.; cobalt, tin, uranium mng.; p. (1963) *29,005*.

Annam, *region*, N. and S. Viet-Nam; formerly within French Union; divided by 17th parallel bdy. (1957); rice, cotton, cinnamon, silk, tea lacquer, minerals; a. 56,973 sq. m. ch. t. Hué.

Annan, *burgh*, Dumfries, Scot.; on R. Annan, 2 m. from its mouth in Solway Firth; cotton, ropes gloves, boiler mkg., fishing; Chapelcross reactor sta.; p. (1961) *5,572*.

Annapolis, *cap.*, Maryland, U.S.A.; naval academy; p. (1960) *23,385*.

Annapolis Valley, Nova Scotia; famous fruit growing area.

Ann Arbor, *c.*, Michigan, U.S.A.; on the Huron University of Michigan; motor lorries, farm implements; p. (1960) *67,340*. [*48,251*

An Nasiriya, *t.*, .Iraq.; on Euphrates R.; p. (1950

Annecy, *industl t.*, France, dep. of Haute-Savoie p. (1962) *45,715*. [p. *17,822*

Annen, *t.*, Germany; coal, steel, chemicals, glass

Annonay, *t.*, Ardèche, France; mnfs. paper woollens, silk, leather goods; p. (1954) *16,201*.

Ansbach, *t.*, Bavaria, Germany; machin., metallurgy, furniture inds.; rly. ctr.; p. (1963) *32,600.*
Anshan, *industl. c.*, Liaoning, N. China; at foot of Changpai Shan, 60 m. S.W. of Mukden; ctr. of ch. worked deposits of iron-ore in China; iron, steel, engin.; p. (1953) *549,000.*
Ansong, *t.*, Central Korea; 40 m. S.E. of Seoul; rice, silk cocoons; p. (estd. 1950) *20,000.*
Ansonia, *c.*, Conn., U.S.A.; machin., brass goods, cotton-braid inds.; p. (1960) *19,819.*
Antakya (Antioch), *ancient c.*, S. Turkey; on R. Orontes; tobacco, olives, maize, soap, silk; p. (1960) *45,848.*
Antarctica, *plateau continent* within Antarctic circle; 7,000–10,000 ft. high; volcanoes and several Is.; owned chiefly by Britain, Australia, New Zealand, France, Norway; penguins. *See also* Brit. Antarctic Terr.
Antarctic Ocean, lies approx. S. of 60° S.; contains Antarctica; whaling.
Antequera, *t.*, Spain; sugar, textiles; metallurgy, trade in olive oil, grain; p. (1957) *43,334.*
Antibes, *spt.*, France; Alpes-Maritimes; health resort; oranges, flowers for perfume mnfs.; p. (1954) *27,064.*
Anticosti, *barren I.*, N. of R. St. Lawrence, Canada; 140 m. by 28 m.; game preserve.
Antigua, *ch. I.*, Leeward group, W.I.; sugar, molasses, pineapples; yacht harbour; oil refinery under construction; a. 171 sq. m.; ch. t. St. Johns; p. (estd. 1965) *60,000.*
Anti-Lebanon, *mtn. range*, Syria; E. of Lebanon; length 60 m.; alt. 6,000–8,000 ft.
Antilles, Greater and Lesser, W. Indies, comprising the Archipelago enclosing the Caribbean Sea and G. of Mexico.
Antioquia, *dep.* Colombia, S. America; cap. Medellin; a. 25,402 sq. m.; maize, coffee, sugar, gold, silver, panama hats; p. (estd. 1962) *1,971,710.*
Antipodes, *Is.*, New Zealand; in S. Pacific, uninhabited.
Antisana, *volcano*, Central Ecuador, S. America.
Antofagasta, *prov.*, Chile; exp. nitrates, copper; a. 47,502 sq. m.; p. (1960) *240,537.*
Antofagasta, *spt.*, Chile; cap. of prov.; nitrates, copper, lt. inds.; p. (1960) *91,400.*
Antony, *t.*, Seine, France; brick wks., toys; p. (1962) *46,823.*
Antrim, *co.*, extreme N.E. of N. Ireland; co. t. Belfast; famous Giant's Causeway is on the N. coast; p. (1961) *273,923.*
Antrim, *t.*, N. Ireland; on Six-Mile Water; linen, nylon; p. (1961) *1,448.*
Antsirabé, *t.*, Malagasy; thermal springs; p. (1957), 18,460.
Antung (Andong), *c.*, Liaoning, China; on R. Yalu, 15 m. from mouth; Chinese frontier sta. main rly. from China into N. Korea; mkt. for agr. produce; lumbering; p. (1953) *360,000.*
Antwerp, *spt.*, Belgium; on R. Schelde; famous Gothic cath.; Franz Hals born here in 1580, and Vandyck in 1599; great petroleum port; shipbldg., textiles, tobacco, distilling, diamond cutting, chemicals; p. (1962) *251,419.*
Antwerp, *prov.*, Belgium; grain, flax; a. 1,104 sq. m.; p. (1962) *1,455,644.*
Anyang, *c.*, Honan prov., China; coal, cotton ind.; p. (1953) *125,000.*
Anzhero-Sudzhensk, *t.*, W. Siberia, U.S.S.R.; nr. Tomsk; coal-mng., mng. equipment, pharmaceutics; p. (1959) *116,000.*
Anzin, *t.*, Nord, France; chief coal-mining centre of France; p. (1954) *15,658.*
Aomori, *spt.* Honshu, Japan; on bay of same name; salmon; p. (1955) *183,747.*
Aosta, *t.*, *cap.*, Val d'Aosta, N. Italy; in valley of Dora Baltea at node of trans-Alpine routes; iron inds.; Mont Blanc road tunnel links to Martigny, Switzerland, opened 19 Mar. 64; p. (1951) *24,181.*
Apalachee Bay, Fla., U.S.A.; receives Apalachee R.
Apapa, *spt.*, sub. of Lagos, Nigeria; on mainland opposite I. on which Lagos is situated; modern pt. equipment, terminus of W. Nigerian rly. system; rly. wkshps.; exp. palm oil and kernels, hides and skins, ground-nuts, cocoa, rubber; imports cotton piece goods, machin.
Apeldoorn, *mftg. t.*, *rly. junction*, Gelderland, Netherlands; p. (1960) *103,126.*
Apennines, mtn. "backbone" of Italy; length 800 m., width 70–80 m.; highest part is in Gran Sasso, *q.v.*
Apia, *spt.*, Upolu, W. Samoa; p. *c. 10,000.*
Apiskigamish, *L.*, Labrador, Canada.
Apolda, *t.*, Erfurt, E. Germany; textiles, engin. chemicals; p. (1963) *29,313.*
Appalachian Mtns., parallel ranges between At. and Mississippi, stretching from Maine to Alabama. Highest peak, Mt. Mitchell, 6,711 ft.
Appenzell, *can.*, N.E. Switzerland; divided into the half-cantons, Appenzell Inner-Rhoden, a. 67 sq. m., cap. Appenzell; p. (1961) *12,943*; and Appenzell Ausser-Rhoden, a. 94 sq. m., cap. Herisau; p. (1961) *48,920.*
Appenzell, *t.*, *cap.*, Appenzell, Switzerland; on R. Sitter; linen tr.; p. (1957) *5,001.*
Appleby, *mun. bor.*, *mkt. t.*, Westmorland, Eng.; on R. Eden; cas.; p. (1961) *1,751.*
Appleton, *c.*, Wis., U.S.A.; paper; p. (1960) *48,411.*
Appomattox, *R.*, Virginia, U.S.A.; joins James R.
Apsheron, *peninsula* on W. side of the Caspian; petroleum wells (nr. Baku) and mud volcanoes.
Apulia, *S.E. region*, Italy; pastoral plain; grain, fruits, livestock; wine, oil; a. 7,470 sq. m.; p. (1951) *3,214,854.*
Apurimac, *dep.*, Peru, S. America; ch. t. Abancay; a. 8,187 sq. m.; sugar; p. (1961) *275,910.*
Apurimac, *R.*, Peru; joins the Ucayali; l. 500 m.
Aqaba (Akaba), *pt.*, Jordan; loading of phosphates and discharging of oil; p. (1961) *9,228.*
Aqaba, *G.*, between Sinai Peninsula and Saudi Arabia. N.E. arm of the Red Sea.
Aquila degli Abruzzi, *t.*, *cap.*, Abruzzi prov., Italy; on R. terrace of R. Aterno; mkt. and sm. inds. associated with local farming; holiday resort; cath.; p. (1961) *56,314.*
Aquitaine, Basin of, *geographical region*, S.W. France; to W. and S.W. of Central Massif, to N of Pyrenees, bordered on W. by Atl. Oc.; warm, wet, oceanic climate; rich agric. lowland; inc. Landes, reclaimed sandy area; ch. ts. Bordeaux, Toulouse.
Arabia, S.W. peninsula of Asia; mainly desert plateau; nomadic Bedouins; coffee, dates, gums, horses, camels; petroleum; divided between Saudi Arabia (most impt.), Yemen, Oman, Kuwait, Bahrein, Trucial chiefs of the Oman cst. and Aden protectorates; a. about 1,000,000 sq. m.; p. (approx.) *8,000,000.*
Arabian Desert, U.A.R., N.E. Africa; between R. Nile and Red Sea; alt. approx. 1,200–6,000 ft.; a. approx. 80,000 sq. m.
Arabian Sea, N.W. part of Indian Ocean, between Horn of Africa and India.
Aracajú, *spt. cap.* Sergipe st., Brazil; sugar soap, textiles, tanneries; p. (1960) *115,713.*
Arad, *t.*, Israel; in Negev desert, E. of Beersheba; new t. inaugurated 21 Nov. 1962; ind. to be based on gasfields at Zohar and Kanaim; chemicals, fertilisers.
Arad, *t.*, Romania; on R. Maros, wine, corn, tobacco, textiles; p. (1959) *112,139.*
Arafura Sea, N. of Australia, S.W. of Papua, and E. of Timor.
Aragon, *old prov.*, Spain; forests, coal, iron.
Araguaia, *R.*, Brazil; trib. of Tocatins; length 1,000 m.
Araish (Laraish, Larache), *spt.*, Morocco, N. Africa; on Atlantic cst., 45 m. S.W. of Tangier; tr. in grain and fruit, cork; p. (1960) *30,763.*
Arak, *t.*, Iran; carpets; p. (1956) *58,929.*
Aral Sea, large salt *L.*, Kazakhstan Rep. (U.S.S.R.); a. 26,166 sq. m.; receiving the Amu and Syr Darya Rs.; no outlet.
Aran, *Is.* group in Galway Bay, Ireland; fishing.
Aranjuez, *t.*, Spain; on R. Tagus; mkt. gardens; strawberries, asparagus; p. (1957) *24,667.*
Ararat, *mtn.*, Turkey; supposed resting-place of Noah's Ark.
Ararat, *t.*, Victoria, Australia; on Hopteins R., 131 m. from Melbourne; p. (1961) *7,930.*
Aras R. (the ancient Araxes), rising in Armenia, flows through Transcaucasia to the Kur, 500 m.
Arauan, *trading t.*, Sahara desert, N. Timbuktu.
Arauco, *prov.*, S. Chile; a. 2,222 sq. m.; cereals, alfalfa, fruit; p. (1961) *94,079.*
Aravalli Mtns., Rajasthan, India; Mt. Abu, 5,650 ft.
Araxes R., rises in Armenia, flows through Transcaucasia to Caspian Sea; bdy. between Persia and U.S.S.R.
Arbroath, *royal burgh*, Angus cst., Scot.; engin., textiles (flax, jute, cotton, woollens), fishing; holiday resort; p. (1961) *19,533.*

Arcachon, *t.*, Gironde, S.W. France; on S. side of Bassin d'Arcachon (Bay of Biscay); fish. pt.; health resort; p. (1954) *14,958.*

Arcadia, *div.* of Peloponnesus, Greece; cap. Tripolis; p. (1951) *154,318.*

Archangel (Archangelsk), *t., dist. ctr.*, U.S.S.R.; on E. side of Dvina estuary, White Sea; lge. harbour kept open in winter by ice-breakers; fishery headquarters; exp. and inds. connected with N. Russia's softwood resources; engin., hydro-elec.; p. (1961) *276,000.*

Archbald, *bor.*, Penns., U.S.A., N.E. of Scranton; anthracite, silk mills; p. (1960) *5,471.*

Arcos, *t.*, Cadiz, Spain; on R. Guadalete; famous Gothic church, ancient fortifications; cattle; cork trees; p. (1957) *21,120.*

Arcot, *t.*, India; 65 m. W. of Madras; taken by Clive 1751; p. (1961) *25,029.*

Arctic Ocean, seas in the N. polar area.

Arcueil, *sub.*, Paris, France; on both sides of Briève valley S. of Paris; varied light inds. concerned with chemicals, clothing, foodstuffs; p. (1954) *18,067.*

Ardabil, *t.*, Azerbaijan, Iran; dried fruits, carpets; p. (1956) *65,720.*

Ardèche, *dep.*, S. France; Cévennes Mtns.; olives, wine silk, minerals; cap. Privas; a. 2,144 sq. m.; p. (1962) *248,516.*

Ardennes, *dep.*, N.E. France; farming, woollens, iron; cap. Mézières; a. 2,027 sq. m.; p. (1962) *300,247.*

Ardennes, *hilly wooded dist.*, Belgium, France, [Luxembourg.

Ardmore, *t.*, Oklahoma, U.S.A.; coal, cotton, oil refineries; p. (1960) *20,184.*

Ardnacrusha, Clare, Ireland; power sta. on R. Shannon 3 miles N. of Limerick.

Ardnamurchan, most westerly point of mainland of Scotland, Argyll.

Ardres, *t.*, France; Pas de Calais; nr. site of "Field of the Cloth of Gold," where Henry VIII and Francis I met in 1520; p. (1954) *758.*

Ardrishaig, *t., spt.*, Argyll, Scot.; on Loch Fyne; holiday resort.

Ardrossan, *burgh*, Ayr, Scot.; on Firth of Clyde, 25 m. S.W. of Glasgow; shipbldg., oil storage, road bitumen, engin.; p. (1961) *9,574.*

Arecibo, *c., spt.*, N. coast of Puerto Rico; W. Indies; coffee, sugar; p. (1960) *28,460.*

Arendal, *spt.*, Norway; on Skagerrak; wood pulp, aluminium, shipping; p. (1960) *11,395.*

Arequipa, *dep.*, Peru; minerals, wool; cap. Arequipa; a. 21,947 sq m.; p. (1961) *392,352.*

Arequipa, *t.*, Peru; textiles, leather, soap, candles, canning, flour, brewing, p. (1961) *221,900.*

Arezzo, *t., cap.*, Arezzo prov., Tuscany, Central Italy; hill site in a basin within the Apennines at junction of valley routes; mkt. for silk, wine, olives; p. (1961) *74,245.*

Argentan, *t.*, Orne, France; gloves, lace; p. (1954) *8,339.*

Argenteuil, *t.*, Seine-et-Oise, France; industl.; p. (1962) *82,458.*

Argentina, *rep.*, S. America, bounded by Atlantic, Andes, and Parana, Uruguay, Paraguay and Pilcomayo Rs.; inc. Pampas and Patagonia; cap. Buenos Aires; agr. and pastoral; exp. meat, wool, wheat, maize, linseed, cotton; a. 1,079,965 sq. m.; p. (1960) *20,008,945.*

Argenton, *t.*, Indre, France; gloves, linen, lace; p. (1954) *6,109.*

Argolis, *prov.*, N.E. Morea, Greece; cap. Nauplion; [p. (1951) *85,389.*

Argonne, *hill ridge*, S.E. Paris Basin, France; composed of greensand; wooded; alt. 1,000 ft.; a. approx. 250 sq. m.

Argos, *t.*, Greece; leading Dorian city prior to the 7th century B.C.; ancient acropolis, theatre; p. (1951) *14,706.*

Argostolion, *cap.*, Cephălonia I., Greece; shipbldg.; destroyed by earthquake 1953; p. (1961) *8,205.*

Argun, *R.*, N.E. Asia; headstream of Amur; rises in Heilungkiang, China, and for 500 m. forms frontier between U.S.S.R. and China; length 1,000 m.

Argyll, *co.*, W. Scotland; mountainous, deer forests, pastoral, fishing, distilling; a. 3,165 sq. m.; p. (1961) *59,345.*

Ariano Irpino, *t.*, Italy; pottery; ancient Aequum Tuticum; p. *22,855.*

Arica, *t., free spt.*, N. Chile; exp. sulphur, copper, silver; oil pipe-line connects to Sica-Sica (Bolivia); p. (1960) *46,542.*

Arichat, *spt.*, Madame I., off Cape Breton I., Nova Scotia, p. *675.*

Ariège, *dep.*, S. France; livestock, fruit, iron, copper; cap. Foix; a. 1,892 sq. m.; p. (1962) *137,192.*

Arima, *bor.*, Trinidad, W.I.; nr. Port of Spain; cacao industry; p. (1960) *10,900.*

Arish, El, *t., cap.*, Sinai, Egypt; on Mediterranean at mouth of Wadi el Arish; p. (1947) *10,791.*

Arizona, *st.*, U.S.A.; bordering on Mexico; agr., stock-rearing, copper, silver, gold, cotton, oil; cap. Phoenix; a. 113,909 sq. m.; p. (1960) *1,302,161.*

Arjona, *t.* Colombia, S. America; sugar; p. *10,410.*

Arkadelphia, *t.*, S.W. Ark., U.S.A.; cotton, lumber, flour mills; p. (1960) *8,041.*

Arkansas, *st.*, U.S.A.; cap. Little Rock; agr., bauxite, coal, petroleum, natural gas, timber; a. 53,102 sq. m.; p. (1960) *1,786,272.*

Arkansas, *R.*, U.S.A.; navigable 650 m.; length 1,450 m.

Arkansas City, *t.*, Kan., U.S.A.; oil, flour mills, packing plant; p. (1960) *14,262.*

Arkhangelsk, *see* **Archangel.**

Arklow, *urb. dist., spt.*, Wicklow Ireland; fisheries, copper, lead, bog iron, pottery; p. (1961) *5,387.*

Arles, *ancient Roman c.*, Bouches-de-Rhône, France; on the Rhône; corn, wine, hats, silk; p. (1962) *42,353.*

Arlington, *t.*, Mass., U.S.A.; residtl. sub. of Boston; p. (1960) *49,953.*

Arlon, *cap.*, Belgian Luxembourg; p. (1962) *13,373.*

Armadale, *burgh*, West Lothian, Scot.; 10 m. S.W. of Linlithgow; coal, iron, limestone, brick and fireclay wks., engin., hosiery; p. (1961) *6,193.*

Armagh, *co.*, Ulster, N. Ireland; a. 512 sq. m.; p. (1961) *117,580.*

Armagh, *urb. dist.*, Armagh, N. Ireland; cath.; linen, whisky; p. (1961) *9,982.*

Armavir, *old ruined cap.* of Armenia, U.S.S.R.; on the slope of the extinct volcano Algaghoz; grain, engin.; p. (1959) *111,000.*

Armenia, *const. rep.* U.S.S.R., former area divided between Turkey, Russia, Iran; rich mineral deposits; agr., cattle rearing, forestry; hydro-elec. stas. under constr.; cap. Yerevan; a. 11,900 sq. m.; p (1959) *1,768,000.*

Armenia, *t.*, Colombia, S. America; coffee; p. (estd. 1959) *110,000.*

Armentières, *mftg. t.*, Nord, France; base of British operations against Lille in First World War; cloth, linen; p. (1954) *24,940.*

Armidale, *t.*, N.S.W., Australia; univ.; ctr. of wool industry, gold mining; p. (1961) *12,884.*

Arnhem, *ch. t., cap.* Gelderland, Netherlands; on R. Rhine; lge. tin smelter; light inds. using rubber and rayon; p. (1960) *124,241.*

Arnhem Land, N. part of N. Territory, Australia; with C. Arnhem.

Arno, *R.*, Central Italy; flows past Florence and Pisa into Mediterranean; Val d'Arno is the fruitful valley of the R.,; length 75 m.

Arnold, *urb. dist.*, Sherwood Forest, Nottingham, Eng.; hosiery, brick mkg.; p. (1961) *26,809.*

Arnsberg, *t.*, N. Rhine-Westphalia, Germany; on R. Ruhr; metal and wood mftg.; spa; p. (1963) *21,700.*

Arnstadt, *t.*, Erfurt, E. Germany; on R. Gera, 10 m. S. of Erfurt; artificial silk, leather goods, engin.; p. (1963) *26,929.*

Arosa, *t.*, Grisons, Switzerland; health and holiday resort.

Arpino, *t.*, Italy; textiles, paper, marble quarries; p. *10,564.*

Arrah, *t.*, Bihar, India; famous in the Mutiny; p. (1961) *76,766.*

Arran, *I.*, Bute, Scot.; in Firth of Clyde; contains many summer resorts; a. 165 sq. m.; p. (1961) *3,705.*

Arras, *t., cap.*, Pas-de-Calais, France; famous for tapestry; grain; dyeing, brewing; battle, First World War (1917); p. (1962) *45,643.*

Arroux, *R.*, France; trib. of the Loire; flows past Autun; length 75 m.

Arrow Lakes, expansions of Columbia R., Brit. Columbia.

Arta, *prov.*, Epirus, Greece; on R. Arta; p. (1961) [*82,504.*

Arta, *t., cap.*, Arta, S. Epirus, Greece; on left bank of R. Arta, 10 m. N. of G. of Arta; purely agr. interests; p. (1961) *16,399.*

Arta, *G.*, between Albania and Greece; near which the Battle of Acitum was fought, 29 B.C.
Artem, *t.*, R.S.F.S.R.; 29 m. N.E. Vladivostok; ctr. of coal-mng. a.; p. (1959) *55,000.*
Artemovsk, *t.*, Ukrainian S.S.R.; salt, coal, iron, mercury; p. (1959) *61,000.*
Arth, *t.*, Schwyz, Switzerland; starting point of rly. up the Rigi; p. (1957) *2,904.*
Arthur's Pass, pass running through the Southern Alps, S. Island, New Zealand, alt. 3,109 ft.
Arthur's Seat, famous hill, Edinburgh, Scot.; 822 ft.
Artois, *old div.*, France; now dept. Pas de Calais.
Aru, *Is.*, group, Indonesia, off coast New Guinea; pearl, tortoise-shell; a. 3,244 sq. m.; p. *18,139.*
Aruba, *I.*, Leeward Is., Neth. Antilles; oil refining, shipping; a. 73 sq. m.; p. (1957) *57,213.*
Arun, *R.*, Sussex, Eng.; flows into English Channel at Littlehampton; length 40 m.
Arundel, *mun. bor.*, *mkt. t.*, W. Sussex, Eng.; on the Arun; Arundel Castle, seat of Duke of Norfolk; p. (1961) *2,614.*
Aruppukkottai, *t.*, Madras, India, 35 m. S. of Madura; p. (1961) *50,200.*
Aruwimi, *R.*, Central Africa; trib. of Congo; route of Stanley's famous forest march in 1887; length 1,800 m.
Arve, *R.*, Haute-Savoie, France; falls into Rhône near Geneva; length 45 m.
Arvida, *t.*, S. Quebec, Canada; aluminium plant; nearby Shipshaw power development; p. (1961) *14,460.*
Arvika, *t.*, N. of L. Vänern, Sweden; agr. machin. and implements, pianos, organs; p. (1961) *15,778.*
As, *t.*, W. Bohemia, ČSSR.; 12 m. N.W. of Cheb; textile mnfs.; p. (1961) *9,640.*
Asaba, *t.*, S. Nigeria, W. Africa; former admin. ctr. of the Royal Niger Company, p. *7,500.*
Asahikawa, *t.*, Japan; rice-growing ctr.; p. (1950) *123,238.*
Asansol, *t.*, W. Bengal, India; rly. junction; coal-mng., iron, steel; p. (1961) *103,405.*
Asbury Park, *t.*, N.J., U.S.A.; resort; elec. prod., seafood, trucks; p. (1960) *17,366.*
Ascension I., part of Brit. col. St. Helena, 760 m. N.W.; Green Mtn., 2,817 ft.; nesting pl. of sooty tern; British space sta. projected; a. 34 sq. m.; p. (1962) *418.*
Aschaffenburg, *t.*, Bavaria, Germany; on R. Main; cas.; inds. paper, textiles, engin.; transhipment pt.; p. (1963) *55,000.*
Aschersleben, *t.*, Halle, E. Germany; potash and lignite mining, chemicals, textiles, engin., horticulture; p. (1963) *35,558.*
Ascoli Piceno, *cath. c.*, Central Italy; cap. of prov. of same name; p. (1961) *49,070.*
Ascot, *par.*, Berks, Eng.; famous racecourse at Ascot Heath.
Asenovgrad, *t.*, Bulgaria; S.E. of Plovdiv; p. (1956) *25,265.*
Ashanti, region within the independent state of Ghana; formerly powerful native state; timber, cocoa, gold-mines; cap. Kumasi; a. 24,379 sq. m.; p. (1960) *1,108,548.*
Ashbourne, *mkt. t.*, Derby, Eng.; near Dovedale; quarrying, milk processing, corsetry; p. (1961) *5,656.*
Ashburton, *urb. dist.*, Devon, Eng.; old mkt. t. S. gateway to Dartmoor; p. (1961) *2,715.*
Ashburton, *t.*, S. Island, New Zealand; ctr. of great wheat-growing dist.; p. (1961) *11,604.*
Ashburton, *R.*, West Australia; flows into Indian Ocean at Onslow; length 400 m.
Ashby-de-la-Zouch, *urb. dist.*, Leicester, Eng.; hosiery, open-cast mining, soap mftg.; ruined cas. in which Mary Queen of Scots was imprisoned; p. (1961) *7,425.*
Ashby Woulds, *urb. dist.*, Leicester, Eng.; coal and clay mining, pottery; p. (1961) *3,318.*
Ashdod, *pt.*, Israel; new modern deep-water pt. on Med. cst., 20 m. S. of Jaffa (closed 1965).
Asheboro, *t.*, N.C., U.S.A.; chemicals, lumber, furniture, hosiery; p. (1960) *9,449.*
Asheville, *c.*, *winter resort*, N. Carolina, U.S.A.; leather, textiles, furniture; p. (1960) *60,192.*
Ashford, *urb. dist.*, *mkt. t.*, Kent, Eng.; agr. implements, ironfounding; p. (1961) *27,962.*
Ashikaga, *t.*, Japan; weaving, cultural ctr.; p. (1947) *48,310.*
Ashington, *urb. dist.*, Northumberland, Eng.; coal; p. (1961) *27,294.*
Ashio, *t.*, Japan; 65 m. N. of Tokyo; copper; commerce; p. (1947) *20,997.*
Ashland, *c.*, Kentucky, U.S.A.; on R. Ohio; iron, steel, lumber, leather; p. (1960) *31,283.*
Ashland, *t.*, Penns., U.S.A.; coal-mining, knitwear, mine pumps; p. (1960) *5,237.*
Ashland, *t.*, Wisconsin, U.S.A.; iron, steel; p. (1960) *10,132.*
Ashtabulo, *t.*, Ohio, U.S.A.; near L. Erie; farm implements, leather; p. (1960) *24,559.*
Ashton-in-Makerfield, *urb. dist.*, Lancs., Eng.; near Wigan; coal; p. (1961) *19,262.*
Ashton-under-Lyne, *mun. bor.*, *mftg. t.*, Lancs., Eng.; nr. Manchester; iron and steel, coal-mining, textiles, light engin.; p. (1961) *50,165.*
Ashuapmuchuan, *L.*, Quebec, Canada.
Asia, *largest continent*, extends over nearly one-third of the land surface of the earth. Chief mtn. ranges: Himalayas, Kunlun, Tien Shan, Altai; Tibetan plateau; chief Rs.: Ob, Yang-tze-Kiang, Yenisei, Lena, Amur, Hwang-ho; deserts: Arabia, Thar, Takla Makan, Gobi; some very fertile valleys and plains. Climate very varied, extreme in N., monsoonal in S. and E. Gold, coal, oil, iron, manganese, antimony, tin. Principal countries, in Asia: Turkey in Asia, Israel, Jordan, Iran, Iraq, Afghanistan, India, Pakistan, Ceylon, Burma, China, Viet-Nam, Indonesia, Thailand, Malaysia, Korea, Japan and Soviet Asia. Industrialisation greatest in Japan, China, India, and Soviet Asia; a. *c.* 17,700,000 sq. m.; p. *c. 1,600,000,000* (half world's total).
Asiago, *t.*, Vicenza, Italy; straw hats; ste of Austro-Italian battle, 1916; p. *2,861.*
Asia Minor (Anatolia), W. portion of Asia, part of Asiatic Turkey; chief c. Izmir, important spt. of Levant.
Asinara, *I.*, Mediterranean Sea; off N.W. coast Sardinia; 11 m. long; the ancient I. of Hercules.
Asir, part of Saudi Arabia, S. Arabia; cst. region between Yemen and Hejaz.
Askeaton, *t.*, on estuary of R. Shannon, Limerick, Ireland.
Asmara, *cap.* former Italian colony of Eritrea, N.E. Africa; on rly. which connects Massawa and Agordat; p. (estd. 1958) *120,000.*
Asnières, *t.*, Seine, France; dyes, perfumery; regattas; p. (1962) *82,201.*
Asolo, *t.*, N.E. Italy; Roman remains.
Aspatria, *t.*, Cumberland, Eng.; dairying, etc.; p. (estd.) *3,000.*
Aspropotamos, *R.*, Greece; longest R. in the country; length 115 m.
Aspull, *urb. dist.*, Lancs, Eng.; near Wigan; coal, cotton; p. (1961) *6,753.*
Assab, on Red Sea, Ethiopia; oil refinery.
Assam, *st.*, India; Brahmaputra R. flows through it; extensive tea plantations; rice, cotton, coal; oil development; cap. Shilong; a. 47,091 sq. m.; p. (1961) *11,872,772.*
Assen, *t.*, cap. Drenthe, Netherlands; p. (1960) *28,918.*
Assens, *t.*, *I.* of Fyne, Denmark, on the Little Belt, p. (1960) *4,937.*
Assiniboine, *R.*, Manitoba, Canada; joins Red R. at Winnipeg; length 1,500 m.
Assisi, *t.*, Umbria, Central Italy; 15 m. S.E. of Perugia; birthplace of St. Francis; fine cath. and old cas.; p. *5,353.*
Assynt, *dist.*, *L.*, Sutherland, Scot., 7 m.; agr. and creameries; p. (1961) *831.*
Assyria, *heart of former empire*, N. plain of Mesopotamia (Iraq); drained by R. Tigris; now mainly pastoral farming a.; ruins of many ancient cas.; cap. Nineveh.
Astara, *spt.* on the Caspian, at Persian N.W. frontier; important trading ctr.
Asterabad, *t.*, N. Iran; on S.E. shore of Caspian Sea; p. *28,000.*
Asti, *t.*, Alessandria, Italy; fine cath.; wines; silk, motor cycles; p. (1961) *60,217.*
Astipalaia, *I.*, Grecian Archipelago.
Astorga, *t.*, Spain, nr. Leon; cath.; p. (1957) *9,916.*
Astoria, *t.*, Oregon, U.S.A.; salmon-canning; p. (1960) *11,239.*
Astoria, N.Y., U.S.A.; industl. and residtl.; part of Queen's *bor.*, New York City; p. *10,349.*
Astrakhan, *t.*, R.S.F.S.R.; on delta of R. Volga; univ.; fish, caviare, astrakhan wool, fruits, wheat, elec. power, engin.; p. (1960) *320,000.*

Astrolabe Bay, on N.E. coast of New Guinea; arm of the Pacific Ocean.

Asturias, *old prov.*, N. Spain; now Oviedo, on Bay of Biscay.

Asunción, *cap.*, Paraguay; on junction of Rs. Paraguay and Pilcomayo; cath.; tobacco, sugar, leather; p. (estd. 1960) *305,000*.

Aswan, *administrative div.*, Upper U.A.R., N.E. Africa; a. 337 sq. m.; p. (1960) *385,000*.

Aswan, *t.*, Upper U.A.R.; on Nile at 1st cataract, ancient name Syene; near famous ruins, temples, catacombs; tourism; p. (1960) *48,000*.

Aswan Dam, Aswan, Upper U.A.R.; built 1902 to control Nile flood in U.A.R.; High Dam under constr. to provide cheap electric power and irrigation of 2 million acres in Lower U.A.R.

Asyut (Assiut), *prov.*, Upper U.A.R.; cap. Asyut; a. 787 sq. m.; p. (1957) *1,213,000*

Asyut, *t.*, Upper U.A.R., N.E. Africa; pottery, ivory work; p. (1957) *121,000*.

Atacama, *prov.*, N. Chile; cap. Copiapo; rich in minerals, nitrates, borax, guano; a. 30,834 sq. m.; p. (1960) *104,266*.

Atacama Desert, Chile; arid coastal tract, rich in nitrates.

Atami, *t.*, Japan; wat. pl. on Sagami Sea; p. *14,477*.

Atar, *t.*, Mauritania, W. Africa; rly. terminus, chief inland town; p. (1954) *4,200*.

Atbara, *t.*, Sudan; at confluence of Atbara R. with Nile; rly. wkshps., cement; p. (estd. 1951) *36,100*.

Atbara R., or Black Nile, Ethiopia and Sudan; trib. of Nile; length 790 m.

Ath, *t.*, Hainaut, Belgium; sugar refining, furniture, chemicals, silk; p. (1962) *10,978*.

Athabaska, *R.*, Alberta, Saskatchewan, Canada; navigable by steamers, save at Grand Rapids, near mouth of Clearwater R.; length 740 m.

Athabaska, *L.*, Alberta, Saskatchewan, Canada; a. 3,085 sq. m.

Athelney, hill formerly encircled by marsh near Taunton, Somerset, Eng.; between the Rs. Tone and Parret; King Alfred's hiding-place.

Athenry, *mkt. t.*, Galway, Ireland; old Dominican monastery; p. (1951) *1,181*.

Athens, *cap.* Greece; most renowned c. in antiquity; ancient ctr. of Greek art and learning; Acropolis and many splendid temples; spinning, distilling, tanning, carpets; p. of greater Athens (inc. Piraeus) (1961) *1,850,000*, of c. (1961) *628,000*.

Athens, *t.*, Georgia, U.S.A.; univ.; cotton goods, lumber; p. (1960) *31,355*.

Athens, *t.*, Ohio U.S.A.; univ.; coal, light inds.; p. (1960) *16,470*.

Atherstone, *mkt. t.*, *rural dist.*, Warwick., Eng.; N. of Coventry; hats, coalmng., footwear, granite quarrying; p. (rural dist. 1961) *24,394*.

Atherton, *urb. dist.*, Lancs., Eng.; 13 m. N.W. Manchester; coal, cotton, light engin.; p. (1961) *19,755*.

Athis-Mons, *t.*, Seine-et-Oise, France; p. (1954) *14,120*.

Athlone, *urb. dist.*, *military sta.*, Westmeath, Ireland; on R. Shannon; p. (1961) *9,624*.

Atholl, *dist.*, N. Perth, Scot.; extensive deer forests and grouse moors; a. 450 sq. m.

Athos, *mtn.*, Greece; on promontory of Chalkidike, known as the "Holy Mountain" and the "Monks' Peninsula"; self-governing monastic community; cap. Karyai; p. (1951) *3,100*.

Athy, *urb. dist.*, Kildare, Ireland; p. (1961) *3,842*.

Atikokan, *sm. t.*, Ontario, Canada; on Canadian National Rly., 110 m. W. of Fort William; ctr. of Steep Rock iron-ore mines.

Atiquizaya, *t.*, Ahuachapán, Salvador, Central America; p. *5,901*.

Atlanta, *cap. largest c.*, Georgia, U.S.A.; univ.; cotton, paper, farm implements, printing, clothing; p. (1960) *487,455*.

Atlantic City, *summer resort*, N.J., U.S.A.; p. (1960) *59,544*.

Atlantic Ocean, the most important of the three great oceans, lies between the Old and New Worlds. It is 9,000 m. long and from 1,600 to 5,000 m. broad. Total a. (estimated) 33,000,000 sq. m. Greatest depth yet found, 30,246 ft. in the Puerto Rico Deep.

Atlántico, *dep.*, Colombia, S. America; cap. Barranquilla; a. 1,340 sq. m.; p. (estd. 1961) *612,170*.

Atlas, *great mtn. range*, N.W. Africa; extending 1,500 m. through Morocco and Algeria to Tunis. Highest point, Tizi-n-Tamjurt, 14,500 ft.

Atlit (Athlit), *t.*, Israel; S. of Haifa; site of Crusaders' pt.

Atmore, *t.*, Ala., U.S.A.; 35 m. N.E. of Mobile Bay; p. (1960) *8,173*.

Atoka, *t.*, Okla., U.S.A.; flour, lumber mills; p. (1960) *2,877*.

Atrato, *R.*, Colombia, S. America; flowing to G. of Darien, length 275 m.

Atrauli, *t.*, Uttar Pradesh, India; 16 m. from Aligarn; p. (1961) *17,936*.

Atrek, *R.*, Iran; enters Caspian Sea; length 250 m.

Atshan, *t.*, Fezzan, Libya, N. Africa; oil.

Attica, *dep.*, Greece; olives, grapes, figs; a. 1452 sq. m.; p. (1961) *2,057,994*.

Attica, *t.*, New York, U.S.A.; p. (1960) *2,758*.

Attleboro, *c.*, Bristol, S.E. Mass., U.S.A.; p. (1960) *27,118*.

Attock, *t.*, Pakistan; between Peshawar and Islamabad; oil wells.

Atzcapotzalco, *t.*, Fed. Dist., Mexico; oil ref.; petro-chemicals.

Aubagne, *t.*, Bouches-du-Rhône, France; bricks, tiles, corks, meat processing; p. (1954) *17,639*.

Aube, *dep.*, N.E. France; cereals, fruit, livestock; cap. Troyes; a. 2,326 sq. m.; p. (1962) *255,099*.

Aube, *R.* France; trib. Seine; length 1,255 m.

Aubervilliers, *t.*, Seine, France; industl.; p. (1962) *70,836*.

Aubrac, *mtns.*, Auvergne, France.

Auburn, *t.*, Ind., U.S.A.; comm. ctr. for agr. area; light engin.; p. (1960) *6,350*.

Auburn, *c.*, Maine, U.S.A.; footwear; p. (1960) *24,449*.

Auburn, *t.*, N.Y., U.S.A.; shoes, woollens, farm implements; p. (1960) *35,249*.

Auch, *t.*, *cap.*, Gers, France; cottons, woollens, poultry, wines; p. (1954) *16,382*.

Auchel, *t.*, Pas de Calais, France; coal; p. (1954) *14,825*.

Auchinleck, *par.*, Ayr., Scot.; coal; p. (1951) *6,808*.

Auchterarder, *burgh*, Scot.; 15 m. S.W. of Perth; health resort S. slopes of the vale of Strathearn; woollen inds.; p. (1961) *2,426*.

Auchterderran, *par.*, Fife., Scot.; coal; p. (1951) *17,599*.

Auchtermuchty, *burgh*, Fife., Scot.; at S. foot of Ochil Hills, 25 m. N.E. of Alloa; distilling, cotton spinning; p. (1961) *1,354*.

Auckland, *prov.*, N.I., New Zealand; farming, gold, Kauri gum, coal; a. 25,400 sq. m.; p. (1961) *996,281*.

Auckland, *spt.*, *c.*, N.I., New Zealand; lgst. *c.* in N.Z.; seat of government 1845–64; extensive tr. and shipping; univ.; sawmills, sugar refinery, shipbldg., glass; steelwks projected 25 m. S. of A., in Waikato iron sand a.; p. (1961) *448,218*, of c. *143,426*.

Auckland Is., uninhabited group in Southern Ocean; 200 m. off New Zealand, discovered by British in 1806.

Aude, *maritime dep.*, S.E. France; grain, fruit, wine; slate, iron; cap. Carcassonne; a. 2,448 sq. m.; p. (1962) *269,782*.

Audenshaw, *urb. dist.*, Lancs., Eng.; metals, leather, pharmaceutics; p. (1961) *12,112*.

Audincourt, *t.*, Doubs, France; forges, automobile and textile plants; p. (1954) *10,282*.

Audubon, *t.*, W. Iowa, U.S.A.; canneries; p. (1960) *2,928*.

Aue, *t.*, Karl-Marx-Stadt, E. Germany; nr. Zwickau; uranium-mining, metallurgy, textiles; p. (1963) *31,740*.

Auerbach, *t.*, Karl-Marx-Stadt, E. Germany; textiles; p. (1963) *19,082*.

Augsburg, *c.*, Bavaria, Germany; at confluence of Rs. Lech and Wertach; cath; theological institute; textiles, aircraft and diesel engines route ctr.; p. (1963) *210,500*.

Augusta, *t.*, Sicily, Italy; on sm. I. connected to E. cst.; good harbour used as naval base, fishing; lubricants; p. *25,437*.

Augusta, *spt.*, S.W. coast, W. Australia.

Augusta, *t.*, *cap.*, Me., U.S.A.; on Kennebec R.; footwear, cotton goods, paper; p. (1960) *21,680*.

Augusta, *c.*, Ga., U.S.A.; on Savannah R.; cotton, cotton-seed oil, chemicals, foundries; p. (1960) *70,626*.

Augustow, *t.*, Poland; on Suwalki canal; p. (1946) *8,338*.

Auja El, *t.*, Israel, S.W. Asia; on Egyptian frontier; p. *2,000*.

Aulnay-sous-Bois, *t.*, Seine-et-Oise, dep., France; p. (1962) *47,686*.

Aunjetitz, *t.*, ČSSR.; site of early Bronze Age culture.

Aurangabad, *t.*, Maharashtra, India; textiles; p. (1961) *87,579*.

Auray, or Alrac, *t.*, Morbihan, Brittany, France; oysters, dairy produce.

Aurès, *mtn. massif*, Algeria, N. Africa; Berber stronghold.

Aurignac, *commune*, Haute-Garonne, France; caves, paleolithic remains; tanneries.

Aurillac, *t.*, *cap.*, Cantal, France; industl.; p. (1954) *22,224*.

Aurora, *t.*, Col., U.S.A.; residtl. sub. 5 m. E. of Denver; p. (1960) *48,548*.

Aurora, *t.*, E. Ind., U.S.A.; lumber, mnfs. coffins, furniture; p. (1960) *4,119*.

Aurora, *rly. c.* Ill., U.S.A.; textiles, foundries; p. (1960) *63,715*.

Aurora, *t.*, Mo., U.S.A.; mining region; p. (1960) *4,683*

Au Sable, *R.*, New York, U.S.A.; flows from the Adirondack Mtns. to L. Champlain.

Au Sable, *R.*, Mich., U.S.A., emptying into L. Huron.

Aussig, *see* Usti.

Austin, *t.*, Minn., U.S.A.; food prods.; p. (1960) *27,908*.

Austin, *c.*, *cap.*, Texas, U.S.A.; on R. Colorado; st. univ.; farming ctr.; bricks, furniture; p. (1960) *186,545*.

Austral and Rapa Is., French group in Pacific Ocean; largest I. Rurutu; a. 115 sq. m.; p. (1962) *4,371*.

Australasia, div. of Oceania including Australia, Tasmania, New Zealand, New Guinea and neighbouring archipelagos.

Australia, Commonwealth of, largest I. in world; Cook took possession for Britain 1770; Commonwealth proclaimed 1901, federation of N.S.W., Victoria, Queensland, S. Australia, W. Australia and Tasmania; includes also federal cap. terr., N. Territory; cap. Canberra (administered separately). Mtns. in E.; most salient feature great interior plains, mainly arid; chief rivers: Murray, Darling, Swan; saline lakes. Climate: interior extremely hot and dry, cst. more moderate, N. coast tropical. Agr.: wheat, hay, cane-sugar, fruit; sheep, cattle, dairying; timber; minerals: gold, lead, silver, coal, copper; steel wks.; a. 2,974,581 sq. m.; p. (1964) *11,250,708*.

Australia, South, *st.* of the Australian Commonwealth, the "Desert State"; mainly undulating, interior forms part of central plateau of continent, mtns. in S. and S.E., 3,000 ft.; wheat crops, stock-raising, dairying, fruit, olives; lead, iron, uranium; exp. corn, wool, mutton; cap. Adelaide; a. 380,070 sq. m.; p. (1964) *1,044,662*.

Australia, Western, *st.* of the Australian Commonwealth, and the largest, occupying nearly a third of western part of continent; cap. Perth, on the Swan R.; wool, fruit, wheat, frozen meat; gold, bauxite, coal, high grade iron-ore, asbestos and ilmenite deposits; Kununurra Dam irrigation scheme for semi-arid northern regions; a. 975,920 sq. m.; p. (1964) *799,626*.

Australian Alps, *see* Alps, Australian.

Australian Antarctic territory, part of Antarctica; between 45° E. and 160° E.; inc. Oates Land, King George V Land, Wilkes Land, Queen Mary Land, Kaiser Wilhelm II Land, Princess Elizabeth Land, MacRobertson Land, Kemp Land, Enderby Land, MacDonald Is., together with the research stas. of Mawson, Davis, and Wilkes; a. (estd.) 2,472,000 sq. m.

Australian Bight, Great, large indentation on Australian S. coast between C. Catastrophe and C. Arid (850 m.)

Australian Capital Territory, area surrounding Canberra, seat of Fed. Govt. of Australia; predominantly pastoral; a. 939 sq. m.; p. (1964) *84,686*.

Austria, *rep.*, Europe; in 1938 forcibly incorporated in German Reich, liberated in 1945, and recovered its sovereignty and indep. 1955; mountainous, forested, drained by R. Danube; agr.; tourism; lignite, anthracite, iron, textiles, pianos, brewing; cap. Vienna; a. 32,393 sq. m.; p. (1961) *7,073,807*.

Austria, Lower, *st.*, Austria; cap. Vienna; a. (excluding Vienna) 7,098 sq. m.; p. (excluding Vienna) (1961) *1,374,012*.

Austria, Upper, *st.*, Austria; cap. Linz; a. 4,625 sq. m.; p. (1961) *1,131,623*.

Autlán de Navarro, *t.*, Mexico; S.W. Jalisco state; p. *10,915*.

Autun, *c.*, Saône-et-Loire, France; anc. Augustodunum; Roman remains; oil-shale refinery, leather, furniture, dyes, fertilisers; p. (1954) *14,399*.

Auvergne, old French prov. forming the present deps. of Puy-de-Dôme, Cantal and a small part of Haute-Loire.

Auvergne Mtns., *mtns.*, Central France; in N.W. of Central Plateau; highest peak, Mt. Dore, 6,188 ft.

Aux Cayes, *spt.*, Rep. of Haiti, W. Indies; on S. cst.; p. *25,000*.

Auxerre, *industl. c.*, *cap.*, Yonne, France; cath.; vines, bricks, iron and steel; p. (1954) *26,583*.

Auxonne, *fortfd. t.*, Côte d'Or, France; on R. Saône; mkt. gardening; p. (1954) *5,657*.

Ava, *c.*, Burma; on the Irrawaddy R.; former cap.; many pagodas, now ruins.

Avallon, *t.*, Yonne, France; on Cousin R.; ancient church; tourist ctr.; p. (1954) *5,497*.

Avebury (Abury), *par.*, *vil.*, Wilts., near Marlborough, Eng.; famous for its Megalithic remains.

Aveiro, *spt.*, *t.*, Portugal; wine-producing prov. of Beira Littoral; sardines, fruit; p. (1940) *11,247*.

Avellaneda, *industl. sub.* of Buenos Aires, Argentina; hides, wool; p. (1960) *170,000*.

Avellino, *t.*, *cap.*, Avellino prov., Italy; monastery; hazelnuts, linen, paper; p. (1961) *41,509*.

Averno, Alpine valley of Switzerland.

Aversa, *garrison t.* Italy; W. of Caserta; wine, hemp, soap and chemicals; p. (1961) *40,336*.

Aves (Bird Is.), group in the Caribbean Sea, W. Indies, belonging to Venezuela.

Avesnes, *t.*, Nord, France; 11th-century cas.; p. *4,576*.

Avesta, *t.*, Kopparberg, Sweden; on Dal R.; iron, aluminium and charcoal wks.; p. (1961) *10,880*.

Aveyron, *dep.*, France; on rim of Central Plateau, watered by Rs. Lot, Aveyron, Tarn; extensive forests; grain, dairying, sheep; coal; cap. Rodez; a. 3,385 sq. m.; p. (1962) *290,442*.

Aviemore, *t.*, Inverness, Scot.; on R. Spey, 12 m. S.W. of Grantown; rly. junction; tourist resort.

Avigliano, *t.*, Lucania, Italy; 8. m. N.W. of Potenza; marble; p. *14,333*.

Avignon, *ch. t.*, Vaucluse, S.E. France; residence of Popes 1309–78, and anti-Popes 1378–1417; wines, silk-worm eggs, chemicals, leather; p. (1962) *75,181*.

Avila, *t.*, *cap.*, Avila prov., Spain; univ., cath.; wool, pottery; p. (1957) *25,000*.

Aviles, *spt.*, Oviedo, Spain; exp. coal, lead, zinc, chemicals, fishing; p. (1957) *50,000*.

Avion, *t.*, Pas-de-Calais, France; coal-mining; p. (1954) *19,471*.

Avoca, *R.*, Ireland; drains Wicklow Mtns.

Avola, *t.*, Syracuse, Italy; almonds; p. (1936) *23,344*.

Avon, *R.*, Somerset, Eng.; enters Bristol Channel at Avonmouth; length 80 m.

Avon, *R.*, Warwick., Eng.; flows past Stratford to Severn at Tewkesbury.

Avon, *R.*, Wilts and Hants, Eng.; flows past Salisbury into English Channel at Christchurch; length 65 m.

Avonmouth, *spt.*, Gloucester, Eng.; outport of Bristol; at mouth of R. Avon; docks; seed crushing, petrol refinery.

Avon Plains, *agr. township*, Victoria, Australia; 175 m. N.W. of Melbourne.

Avranches, *t.*, Manche, France; typical Normandy mkt. t. dealing in cider and dairy produce; p. (1954) *8,004*.

Awaji, *I.* at entry of Inland Sea, Japan; a. 219 sq. m.; highest peak, Yurimbayama, 1,998 ft.

Awe, Loch, Argyll, Scot.; 8 m. W. of Inveraray, bordered by Ben Cruachan (16 sq. m.); salmon and trout fishing; hydro-elec. sta. at Cruachan under construction.

Axar, *fiord*, N. Iceland.

Axbridge, *rural dist.*, Somerset, Eng.; p. (1961) *30,761*.

Axe, *R.*, Somerset, Eng.; rising in Mendip Hills and flowing to Severn.

Axholme, I. of N.W. Lincs, Eng.; formed by Rs. Trent, Don and Idle, and comprising seven

parishes; rural dist. agr. and engin.; p. (estd. 1961) *14,110*.
Axminster, *rural dist.*, Devon, Eng.; brushes; flour and saw mills; carpet and press tool mftg.; p. (1961) *14,350*.
Axmouth, *t.*, E. Devon; nr. Beer and Seaton; fishing, holiday resort.
Ay, *t.*, Marne, France; Ay wine; p. (1954) *6,806*.
Ayacucho, *t.*, Peru; founded by Pizarro in 1539; univ.; cap. Ayacucho dept.; p. (1961) *22,000*.
Ayacucho, *dep.*, Peru, S. America; a. 18,185 sq. m.; p. (1961) *427,812*.
Ayamonte, *spt.* Spain; on Spanish–Portuguese frontier; p. (1957) *12,124*.
Ayaviri, *t.*, Puno, Peru; N.W. of L. Titicaca; p. [*6,586*.
Aydin, *t.*, Turkey; ancient Tralles; rly.; cotton, grapes, olives, magnesite, lignite and arsenic; p. (1960) *35,671*.
Aylesbury, *mun. bor.*, *co. t.*, Bucks, Eng.; mkt. t., dairying; p. (1961) *27,891*.
Aylesford, *t.*, Kent, Eng.; scene of battle between Britons and Saxons 445, death of Horsa; mkt. t., cement, paper mills; p. (1951) *3,644*.
Aylesham, *t.*, Kent, Eng.; N. of Dover; on Kent coalfield.
Aylsham, *mkt. t.*, Norfolk, Eng.; p. *2,646*.
Ayr, *lge. burgh, spt.*, Ayr., Scot.; on Firth of Clyde, 30 m. S.W. of Glasgow; Burns born near by, 1759; racecourse; carpets, engin., footwear; p. (1951) *43,011*.
Ayrshire, *co.*, S.W. Scot.; dairy produce, early potatoes; coal, iron, woollens, cottons; civil nuclear power-sta. at Hunterston; a. 1,132 sq. m.; p. (1961) *342,855*.
Ayre, Point of, northernmost point, Isle of Man.
Aysen, *prov.*, Chile; a. 34,348 sq. m.; p. (1957) *31,518*.
Ayutthaya, *t.*, Thailand; 42 m. N. of Bangkok; temples; former capital.
Azamgarh, *t.*, Uttar Pradesh, India; p. (1961) *32,391*
Azbest, *t.*, Sverdlovsk dist., U.S.S.R.; asbestos quarries; p. (1959) *60,000*.
Azerbaijan, *prov.*, N.W. Iran; W. of Caspian Sea; a. 41,000 sq. m.; ch. prod. wool.
Azerbaydzhan, Transcaucasia, constituent rep. of the U.S.S.R.; impt. oil industry; chemicals, farming, cattle, fishing; cap. Baku; a. 33,460 sq. m.; p. (1959) *3,700,000*.
Azogues, *t.*, cap. Canar prov., Ecuador; straw hats; p. (1950) *6,579*.
Azores, Portuguese group of islands in mid-Atlantic; abt. 900 m. W. of Lisbon; volcanic; fruit, wine; ch. seaports: Ponta Delgada on San Miguel I., Horta on Fayal I. and Angra do Heroismo on Terceira I.; a. 922 sq. m.; p. (1950) *318,686*.
Azov, *t.*, *spt.*, R.S.F.S.R., on R. Don; fisheries; p. [*27,500*.
Azov, *sea*, U.S.S.R.; joins Black Sea by Kerchenski Strait; fisheries, caviare.
Azpeitia, *t.*, N. Spain; nr. birthplace of St. Ignatius Loyola; mineral springs; p. (1957) *8,991*
Azuay, S. *prov.*, Ecuador, S. America; cap. Cuenca; Panama hats; a. 3,873 sq. m.; p. (1950) *243,920*.
Azul, *t.*, Buenos Aires, Argentina; cattle and mkt. ctr.; p. (1960) *45,000*.
Azusa, *t.*, *spt.*, Cal., U.S.A., exp. citrus fruit; p. (1960) *20,497*.

B

Baalbek, *c.*, Lebanon, S.W. Asia; old Heliopolis; ruins.
Baarn, *t.*, Netherlands; summer resort; p. (1948) *12,141*.
Bab-el-Mandeb, *strait* connecting Red Sea and Indian Ocean, 20 m. wide.
Babol, *spt.*, Iran, on Caspian Sea; fruits, cottons, silks; p. (1956) *36,242*.
Babushkin, *t.*, U.S.S.R.; residtl. and industl. sub. of Moscow; p. (1959) *112,000*.
Babuyan Is., group in Pac. Oc.; N. of Luzon in Philippines.
Babylon, *ancient cap.* of Babylonian Empire in Euphrates Valley about 60 m. S. of Baghdad, Iraq.
Bacacay, *t.*, Luzon, Philippines; hemp; p. (1948) [*26,504*.
Bacau, *t.*, E. Romania; on R. Moldava; oil, sawmilling, textiles; p. (estd. 1958) *60,000*.
Back R., in N.W. Terr., Canada; falls into Arctic Ocean; length 360 m.
Bacolod, *t.*, *cap.* Negros I., Philippines; tr. ctr., sugar; p. (1960) *127,000*.
Bacup, *mun. bor.*, *mftg. t.*, S.E. Lancs, Eng.; 20 m. Manchester; cotton, iron, brass, footwear; p. (1961) *17,295*.
Badagri, *t.*, W. of Lagos, Nigeria, W. Africa; on the Bight of Benin, formerly a great slave pt.
Badajoz, *prov.*, Spain; great reclamation scheme in progress; a. 8,349 sq. m.; p. (1959) *865,004*.
Badajoz, *fortfd. t.*, Badajoz prov., Spain; on Guardina R.; cath.; woollens, wax; p. (1959) *98,088*.
Badakshan, *prov.*, Afghanistan; drained by Oxus and trib.; salt, lapis lazuli; cap. Faizabad.
Badalona, *t.*, Barcelona prov., Spain; p. (1959) *87,665*.
Baden, *former Land*, W. Germany; consisting of the S. part of the former st. Baden; cap. Freiburg; agr., grain, tobacco, hops, vines, beet-sugar; a. 3,842 sq. m.; p. (1950) *1,338,629*.
Baden, *t.*, Switzerland; health resort, mineral springs; p. (1950) *11,595*.
Baden-Baden, *t.*, Baden–Württemberg, Germany; fashionable spa; p. (1963) *40,200*.
Baden-bei-Wien, *wat. pl.*, Austria; 14 m. S.W. of Vienna; p. (1961) *22,484*.
Badenoch, *dist.*, Inverness, Scot.; mountainous, drained by Spey; deer forest.
Badenweiler, *wat. pl.*, Baden, W. Germany; W. part of Black Forest.
Baden-Württemberg, *Land*, S.W. Germany; mountainous and afforested (Black Forest) with much mineral wealth; salt; cap. Stuttgart; a. 5,960 sq. m.; p. (1961) *7,759,000*.
Bad Lands, S. Dakota, U.S.A.; stretches of infertile badly eroded soil.
Badminton, *vil.*, Gloucester, Eng.; rly. junction.
Badrinath, *mtn.* and *t.*, Uttar Pradesh, India; pilgrim shrine of Vishnu.
Badulla, *t.*, Ceylon; tea; p. *13,387*.
Badwater, *salt pool*, California, U.S.A.; 280 ft. below sea-level, lowest point in N. America.
Baena, *t.*, Spain; olive oil; horse-breeding; p. (1957) *22,031*
Baeza, *t.*, S. Spain; ancient Moorish city; olives, wine; p. (1957) *16,895*
Baffin Bay, Canada; W. of Greenland, joined to the Atlantic by Davis Strait and to Arctic Oc. by Smith Sound; open 4 months a year.
Baffin I., Canada; a. 236,000 sq. m.; inhabited by scattered Eskimos; iron ore deposit.
Bagamoyo, *spt.*, *tr. ctr.*, Tanzania, E. Africa; p. *5,000*.
Bagé, *t.*, S. Brazil; tr. ctr.; p. (1960) *47,930*.
Bagenalstown, *t.*, Carlow, Ireland; milling, granite; p. (1956) *1,984*.
Baghdad, *prov.* or *liwa*, Iraq; between Persia and Syrian Desert; inc. some of the most fertile lands in the Tigris and Euphrates valleys; p. (1956) *912,409*.
Baghdad, *cap.*, Iraq; on R. Tigris; airport, caravan ctr. textiles, gum, bricks, tiles, metal inds.; p. (1960) *552,000*.
Bagheria, *t.*, Sicily, Italy; p. *19,000*.
Bagirmi, *dist.*, Central African Rep.; S. of L. Chad; cap. Messenya.
Bagnacavallo, *t.*, prov. Ravenna, Italy; p. *3,676*.
Bagnara, *t.*, prov. Reggio, Italy; wine, honey; p. (1936) *11,580*.
Bagnères de Bigorre, *t.*, Pyrenees, France; mineral springs; p. (1954) *11,044*.
Bagnes de Chable, *wat. pl.*, Valais, Switzerland.
Bagneux, *t.*, Seine, France; p. (1954) *13,774*.
Bagni di Lucca, *t.*, Italy; 13 m. N. of Lucca; warm springs; p. *14,000*.
Bagni de San Guiliano, *t.*, Italy, nr. Pisa; warm, radioactive springs; p. (1936) *21,894*.
Bagnolet, *t.*, Seine, France; sub. of Paris; famous for "plaster of Paris" from local gypsum; textiles; p. (1954) *26,779*.
Bagolino, *t.*, prov. Brescia, Italy; sulphur spring; p. *3,613*.
Bagshot, *rural dist.*, Surrey, Eng., adjoining heath of same name; historically old postal town, 26 m. S.W. of London; p. (1961) *16,744*.
Baguio, *summer cap.* of Philippine Is.; in mtn. prov.; p. *35,177*.
Bahamas, *Is.*, self-gov. Br. col., W. Indies; first land in New World sighted by Columbus, extending 780 m. from Florida to Turks Is.; collective cap. Nassau, New Providence; salt, tomatoes, crawfish, sponges, Bahama hemp; a. 4,404 sq. m.; p. (estd. 1965) *134,000*.

Bahawalpur, *div.*, West Pakistan; a. 15,918 sq. m.; p. (1961) *3,205,000.*
Bahia, *spt.*, Ecuador, S. America; p. *10,820.*
Bahia Blanca, *spt.*, Argentina; chief naval univ.; wool, wheat, maize; p. (1960) *150,000.*
Bahia de Caraquez, *spt.*, Ecuador, S. America; p. *10,499.*
Bahia Honda, *coaling sta.*, Cuba, W. Indies; W. of Havana.
Bahrein Is., sheikhdom group in Persian G.; famous pearl fisheries; oil-wells; cap. Manama; a. about 213 sq. m.; p. (1950) *109,650.*
Bahr El Benat Is., group in Persian G., off coast of Trucial Oman.
Bahr-el-Ghaza, *R.*, Sudan; trib. of White Nile R.
Bahr-el-Ghazal, *prov.*, Sudan, N.E. Africa; cap. Wau (*q.v.*); a. 77,820 sq. m.; p. (estd. 1951) *771,000.*
Baia, *see* **Salvador.**
Baia, *st.*, Brazil; cap. Salvador; cocoa, thorium; a. 217,670 sq. m.; p. (1960) *5,990,605.*
Baia, *historic vil.*, Campania, Italy; beautifully situated on Bay of Naples; celebrated Roman pleasure resort.
Baia-Mare, *t.*, Romania; on Somes R.; gold, silver, lead, zinc, chemicals, uranium; p. (1959) *40,000.*
Baie-St. Paul, *t.*, Quebec, Canada; summer resort; hunting, fishing; p. (1961) *4,674.*
Baii, *t.*, on oil pipe-line, Iraq.
Baikal, *L.*, Siberia, U.S.S.R.; fresh-water; 6th lgst. in the world; frozen Nov.–May; skirted by Trans-Siberian Rly.; sturgeon, salmon; 40 m. wide; a. 13,700 sq. m.
Baildon, *urb. dist.*, W.R. Yorks, Eng.; nr. Bradford; p. (1961) *12,147.*
Baile Atha Cliath, *see* **Dublin.**
Bailen, *t.*, Spain; lead, ore; p. (1957) *10,129.*
Bailleul, *t.*, Nord, France; lace, linen; p. (1954) *11,964.*
Baillieston, *t.*, Lanark, Scot.; coal-mining.
Baird, *t.*, Texas, U.S.A.; rly. junction; cotton, oil; p. *1,810.*
Bairnsdale, *t.*, Vic., Australia; on Mitchell R.; agr., pastoral, dairying; p. (1961) *7,418.*
Bakchisaray, *t.*, Crimea, U.S.S.R.; *old cap.* of Tartar Khans; p. (1956) *10,000.*
Baker I., Pacific Ocean.
Baker, *L.*, N.W. Terr., Canada.
Baker, *t.*, Ore., U.S.A.; gold, silver, lead, mineral springs; p. (1960) *9,986.*
Bakersfield, *c.*, S. Cal., U.S.A.; ctr. of oil-wells, refining; p. (1960) *56,848.*
Bakewell, *urb. dist.*, Derby, Eng.; tourist centre, Peak District; agr., mining, woollens; p. (1961) *3,603.*
Bakhchisarai, *t.*, Crimea, U.S.S.R.; leather, copper; p. *10,800.*
Bakony Wald, *mtns.*, forested, Hungary.
Baku, *cap.* Azerbaydzhan, S.S.R.; pt. of Caspian Sea; univ.; oil-wells; p. (1962) *1,067,000.*
Bala, *urb. dist.*, N. Wales; nr. Denbigh, Merioneth; light engin.; p. (1961) *1,603.*
Bala, *L.*, Merioneth, N. Wales; drained by the Dee.
Balaclava, *t.*, S. Australia; 67 m. from Adelaide; ctr. of agr. dist.; p. (1947) *1,290.*
Balashov, *t.*, Saratov area, R.S.F.S.R.; on Khoper R.; engin, aircraft plant; p. (1959) *64,000.*
Balasinor, former Gujarat st. now merged into Bombay st., India.
Balasore, *spt.*, Orissa, India; p. (1961) *33,931.*
Balaton, *L.*, lgst. in Hungary; 50 m. S.W. of Budapest; 50 m. long, 2–7 m. wide.
Balayan, *t.*, Luzon, Philippine Is.; at head of G. of Balayan; p. (1948) *18,305.*
Balboa, *dist.*, S.E. Canal Zone, Central America; p. (1960) *30,623*; *t.*, Pacific end of Panama Canal; p. (1960) *3,139.*
Balbriggan, *spt.*, Dublin, Ireland; hosiery; p. (1951) *2,920.*
Balclutha, *t.*, S.I., N.Z.; nr. Dunedin; p. (1961) [*3,928.*
Bald Head Peak, Victoria, alt. 4,625 ft.; highest point in Dividing Range, Australia.
Bald Mtn., peak in Front Range, Col., U.S.A.; alt. 12,000 ft.
Baldock, *urb. dist.*, Herts., Eng.; on N. edge of Chiltern Hills and Gr. N. Road; hosiery, malting, light engin.; p. (1961) *6,764.*
Baldwin, *t.*, N.Y., U.S.A.; on S. Long I.; fisheries; p. (1960) *30,204.*
Baldwin, *t.*, Penns., U.S.A.; p. (1960) *24,489.*
Baldwinsville, *t.*, N.Y., U.S.A.; agr., livestock natural gas; p. (1960) *5,985.*
Balearic Is., Spain; include Majorca, Minorca, Iviza, Formentera; *ch.t.* Palma; fruit, fish, pigs; tourist ctr.; a. 1,936 sq. m.; p. (1959) *441,842.*
Baleswar, *R.*, one of the chief distributaries of the Ganges to Bay of Bengal.
Bali, off Java, Indonesia; mainly engaged in agr.; famous native dancers; a. (inc. Lombok) 3,937 sq. m.; p. (1961) *1,782,529.*
Balikesir, Turkey; p. (1960) *61,012.*
Balikpapan, *t.*, Kalimantan, Indonesia; oil; p. (1961) *91,706.*
Baliuag, *t.*, Luzon, Philippine Is.; rice, bamboo hats, mkt.; p. (1948) *30,670.*
Balkan Mtns., Bulgaria; highest peak, 7,780 ft.; Shipka Pass.
Balkan Peninsula, the easternmost of the three great southern peninsulas of Europe, between the Adriatic and Ionian seas on the W., and the Black Sea, Sea of Marmara and the Ægean Sea on the E., with an area of, roughly, 200,000 sq. m.; includes Jugoslavia, Bulgaria, Albania, Greece; chief mtns.: Rhodope, Pindus, Balkan; ch. rivers: Danube, Maritza, Vardar; ch. lakes: Scutari, Okhrida.
Balkh, *dist.*, Afghanistan; between the Kabul and the Oxus; corresponding to the ancient Bactria, rival of Nineveh and Babylon.
Balkh, *t.*, Afghanistan; associated with Zoroaster, called the " Mother of Cities "; destroyed by Jenghis Khan in 1221; silk; p. *12,466.*
Balkhash, *L.*, U.S.S.R.; fresh water, nr. frontier of W. Mongolia receives the Ili R., but has no outlet, length 450 m., width 30–50 m.
Balkhash, *t.*, Kazakhstan S.S.R.; on N. shore of L.; copper, molybdenum; vermiculite discovered nearby; p. (1959) *53,000.*
Ballachulish, *vil.*, Argyll, Scot.; on S. shore of L. Leven, N.E. of Oban; tourism.
Ballaghadorreen, *t.*, Roscommon, Ireland; p. (1951) *1,359.*
Ballantrae, *par.*, Ayr., Scot.; fishing; p. (1951) *886.*
Ballapali, forest reserve, Madras, India.
Ballarat, *c.*, Victoria, Australia; 73 m. N.W. Melbourne, former gold-field dist.; farming ctr.; flour milling, wool; p. (1961) *54,913.*
Ballater, *burgh*, Aberdeen, Scot.; on R. Dee, 37 m. S.W. of Aberdeen; tourist resort, mineral wells; nr. the royal Highland residence of Balmoral; p. (1961) *1,132.*
Ballenas Bay, W. Coast, Lower California, Mexico.
Balleny Is., S. Ocean; volcanic isles.
Ballina, *urb. dist.*, *spt.*, Mayo, Ireland; agr. machin., flour mills; p. (1961) *6,028.*
Ballina, *t.*, N.S.W., Australia; 530 m. from Sydney at mouth of Richmond R.; p. *3,201.*
Ballinasloe, *urb. dist.*, Galway and Roscommon, Ireland; large cattle fair; p. (1961) *5,711.*
Ballinger, *t.*, Texas, U.S.A.; grain, cattle, cotton-seed oil, flour; p. (1960), *5,043.*
Ballinrobe, *rural dist.*, Mayo, Ireland; E. of L. Mask; p. (1961) *13,492.*
Ballon d'Alsace, *mtns.* (4,101 ft.), Vosges, France; highest peak Ballon de Guebwiller, 4,690 ft.
Ballston Spa, *wat. pl.*, Saratoga, N.Y., U.S.A., p. (1960) *4,991.*
Bally L., Roscommon, Ireland, nr. Castlereagh.
Ballycastle, *spt.*, *mkt. t.*, *urb. dist.*, Antrim, N. Ireland; abbey and cas. ruins; p. (1961) *2,643.*
Ballyclare, *urb. dist.*, Antrim, N. Ireland; paper, linen, dyeing; p. (1961) *4,441.*
Ballycottin Is., Ballycottin Bay, Cork, Ireland.
Ballymena, *mkt. t.*, *mun. bor.*, Antrim, N. Ireland; on R. Braid; linen and dyeing; p. (1961) *14,740.*
Ballymoney, *mkt. t.*, *urb. dist.*, Antrim, N. Ireland; 40 m. N.W. of Belfast; linen, dairying; p. (1961) *3,409.*
Ballyness Bay, Donegal, Ireland.
Ballyshannon, *rural dist.*, *spt.*, Donegal, Ireland; at mouth of R. Erne; salmon fishery; p. (1961) *5,305.*
Balmain, *t.*, N.S.W., Australia; industl. sub. of Sydney; foundries, chemicals, glass, ship-bldg., lumber; p. (1947) *28,268.*
Balmoral Cas., Aberdeen, Scot.; royal residence, on R. Dee, 8 m. W. of Ballater.
Balotra, *t.*, Rajasthan, India; p. (1961) *12,110.*
Balquhidder, *par.*, Perth, Scot.; p. (1951) *671.*
Balranald, *t.*, N.S.W., Australia; on R. Murrumbidgee, p. *1,249.*
Balsas, *R.*, Mexico; flows S. to Pacific Ocean through impt. sugar-cane growing valley of Morelos; length approx. 500 m.

Balta I., Shetland Is., Scot.
Baltic Is. (Fyn, Lolland, Nykobing, etc.); farming div. of Denmark; a. 5,123 sq. m.; p. *1,291,772.*
Baltic Sea, an arm of the Atlantic, opens into N. Sea by narrow channels between Denmark and Sweden; joined to White Sea and Arctic by White Sea Canal; surrounded by Sweden, Denmark, Germany, Finland and the Baltic Reps. of the U.S.S.R.; 900 m. long, greatest width 200 m., a. 160,000 sq. m.; partly frozen in winter.
Baltic–White Sea Canal, *see* Volga Baltic Waterway.
Baltimore, *c.*, *spt.*, Maryland, U.S.A.; nr. head of Chesapeake Bay; fine harbour; sugar refining, steel, radios, aircraft, clothing, machin., shipbldg., food canning; world's 1st nuclear-powered lighthouse; p. (1960) *939,024.*
Baluchistan, *reg.*, West Pakistan; S. of Afghanistan; largely desert and rugged barren mtns.; cap. Quetta; a. 52,900 sq. m.; cereals, potatoes, fruits, dates; p. (estd. 1951) *622,000.*
Baluchistan States, consisted of 4 states, Kalat, Las Bela, Kharan and Mekran, all of which acceded to and were incorporated in W. Pakistan, 1955.
Bam, *t.*, Iran; dates, henna; p. (1942) *13,938.*
Bamako, *c.*, Mali; p. (1957) *68,600.*
Bamangwato, *tr. dist.*, Botswana, S. Africa.
Bamberg, *c.* Bavaria, Germany; cath.; philosophical and theological institute; textiles, elec., leather and engin. inds.; p. (1963) *73,700.*
Bamberg, *t.*, S.C., U.S.A.; agr., lumbering, pine timber; p. (1960) *3,081.*
Bambuk or Bambouk, Mali; W. Africa; gold and iron dist.
Bamburgh, *t.*, Northumberland, Eng.; birthplace of Grace Darling, cas.
Bamian, *t.*, Afghanistan, N.W. of Kabul; rock-cut caves, colossal Buddhist statues.
Banam, *t.*, Cambodia; on Mekong R.; boat bldg., rice distilling; p. *28,000.*
Banana, *t.*, *pt.*, Congo, Africa; nr. mouth of Congo R.; p. *1,000.*
Banana I., Brazil; length 220 m., width 50 m.
Banana Is., sm. group nr. Sierra Leone.
Banat, *dist.*, Romania; N. of R. Danube and E. of R. Tisza; p. (estd. 1960) *1,230,000.*
Banbridge, *t. urb. dist.*, Down, N. Ireland; on Bann R.; linen; p. (1961) *6,115.*
Banbury, *mun. bor.*, *mkt. t.*, Oxford, Eng.; 80 m. from London; aluminium ind., furniture, printing, ladies wear; p. (1961) *20,996.*
Banchory, *burgh*, Kincardine, Scot.; on R. Dee, 17 m. S.W. of Aberdeen; p. (1961) *1,918.*
Banda, *t.*, Uttar Pradesh, India; cotton; p. (1961) *37,744.*
Banda Is., group in Moluccas, in Banda Sea, Indonesia; nutmegs and mace.
Bandar Abbas, *spt.*, Iran; dates, raisins, almonds, carpets; p. *10,000.*
Bandar Shah, *spt.* on Caspian Sea, N. Iran.
Bandar Shahpur, *spt.* Iran; on N. end Persian G.
Bandawe, *mission sta.* on L. Malawi, Africa.
Bandjarmasin, *t.*, Kalimantan, Indonesia; rubber; p. (1961) *214,096.*
Bandoeng or Bandung, *t.*, W. Java; quinine, rubber, chemicals; radio sta.; p. (1961) *973,000.*
Bandon, *mkt. t.*, Cork, Ireland; on Bandon R., distilling, tanning; p. (1961) *2,308.*
Banff, *burgh*, *cap.*, Banff, Scot.; on Moray Firth at mouth of R. Deveron; fisheries; tourism; p. (1961) *3,329.*
Banff, *co.*, Scot.; oats, barley, fisheries, distilling, woollen mnfs.; a. 630 sq. m.; p. (1961) *46,400.*
Bangalore, *c.*, Mysore st., India; former Brit. military sta. and administrative H.Q.; silks, cottons, carpets, aircraft; p. (1961) *905,134.*
Bangka (Banka), *I.*, between Sumatra and Kalimantan, Indonesia; tin; a. 4,611 sq. m.; p. (1930) *205,363.*
Bangkok (Krung Thep), *spt.*, *cap.*, Thailand; on Menam R.; 20 m. from the sea; royal palace, univ.; rice, tea, teak; p. (1963) *1,608,000.*
Bangor, *c.*, *mun. bor.*, Caernarvon, Wales; on S. shore of Menai Strait; cath., univ. coll.; slate, light engin.; p. (1961) *13,977.*
Bangor, *wat. pl.*, *mun. bor.*, Down, N. Ireland; on S. shore of Belfast Lough, 10 m. N.E. of Belfast; linen, fisheries; p. (1960) *23,865.*
Bangor, *pt.*, Maine, U.S.A.; on Penobscot R., lumber, boots, shoes, clothing, paper; p. (1960) *38,912.*
Bangor, *bor.*, E. Penns., U.S.A.; slate, agr., clothes; p. (1960) *5,766.*
Bangui, *cap.* of Ubangi-Shari terr., Central African Rep; on R. Ubangi; p. (1950) *41,100.*
Bangweulu, *L.*, Zambia; 150 m. long, 80 m. wide, contains 3 islands. Dr. Livingstone died at Illala, on S. shore of this L., in 1873.
Banias, *spt.*, Syria; terminus of oil pipe-line from Kirkuk, opened 1952.
Banjaluka, *t.*, Bosnia and Hercegovina, Jugoslavia; hot springs; tobacco; p. (1960) *45,000.*
Banka, *see* Bangka.
Banks I., Canada, Arctic Ocean; separated by Banks Strait from Melville I.
Banks Is., group of sm. Is. in S. Pacific; N.E. of New Hebrides.
Banks Peninsula, on E. coast of S.I., New Zealand.
Banks Strait, separating Furneaux Is. from Tasmania.
Bankura, *t.*, W. Bengal, India; on Hooghly R.; shellac, silk; p. (1961) *62,833.*
Bann, Upper and Lower R., N. Ireland; rises in co. Down, and flows through Lough Neagh to Atlantic nr. Coleraine; length 90 m.
Bannockburn, *vil.*, Stirling, Scot.; 3 m. S. of Stirling; Bruce's victory over Edward II, June 24th, 1314; coal, confectionery.
Bannu, *t.*, W. Pakistan; on Kurram R.; military sta.; p. *38,504.*
Banska Bystrica, *region*, Slovakia, ČSSR.; copper and silver mng., metal wks.; a. 3,564 sq. m.; p. (1961) *129,290.*
Banska Stiavnica, *t.*, ČSSR.; tr. ctr., gold, silver prod., lead, copper, zinc; p. (1947) (inc. Banska Bela) *11,870.*
Banstead, *urb. dist.*, Surrey, Eng.; p. (1961) *41,573.*
Bantam, *dist.*, W. Java; suffered severely from fever and volcanic eruption.
Bantry, *rural dist.* and *spt.*, Cork, Ireland; at head of Bantry Bay; fishing, farming; p. (1961) *7,814.*
Banwy, *R.*, Montgomery, Wales.
Banzyville, *t.*, Congo; on R. Uele; p. *1,000.*
Ba'quba, *t.*, Iraq; on Diyala R., 32 m. N.E. of Baghdad; agr., rly.; p. *10,000.*
Bar, *spt.*, Dalmatian cst. Jugoslavia; p. *5,500.*
Bar Harbor, *t.*, S.E. Me., U.S.A.; holiday resort; p. (1960) *2,444.* [*6,726.*
Baraboo, *t.*, Wis., U.S.A.; agr. tr. ctr.; p. (1960)
Baracaldo, *t.*, Biscay, Spain; ironwks.; p. *36,165.*
Baracoa, *spt.*, Cuba; bananas, coconuts; p. *10,395.*
Barada, *R.*, Syria; in plain of Damascus.
Barajas, *vil.*, Madrid, Spain; airport; p. *1,800.*
Baranovichi, *t.*, Byelorussian S.S.R.; 80 m. S.W. of Minsk; p. (1959) *58,000.*
Barauni, *t.*, N. Central Bihar, India; oil refining; oil pipelines to Gauhati, to Kanpur and from Haldia; p. (1961) *40,321.*
Barbacena, *t.*, E. Brazil; creameries; ceramics, glass; p. (1960) *41,931.*
Barbados, I. most easterly of W.I.; sugar, molasses, rum, cotton; cap. Bridgetown; a. 166 sq. m.; p. (estd. 1965) *242,000.*
Barbary, *region*, N. Africa; includes Morocco, Algeria, Tunis, Tripoli, Barka and Fezzan.
Barbary Coast, general name applied to Mediterranean cst. of N. Africa between Strait of Gibraltar and C. Bon.
Barbastro, *t.*, Huesca, Spain; on R. Cinca; p. (1957) *9,381.*
Barberton, *t.*, Transvaal, S. Africa; citrus fruits, gold, asbestos, magnesite, talc, cotton; p. (1960) *11,016* inc. *2,705* whites.
Barberton, *t.*, Ohio, U.S.A., S.S.W. of Akron; tyre mftg.; p. (1960) *33,805.*
Barbizon, *vil.*, nr. forest of Fontainebleau; haunt of painters.
Barbuda and Redonda, *Is.*, Leeward Is., W.I.; dependencies of Antigua; sea-island cotton; a. 63 sq. m.; p. *1,000.*
Barcaldine, *t.*, Queensland, Australia; p. (1947) *1,682.*
Barcellona, *t.*, Sicily, Italy; silks; p. *25,580.*
Barcelona, *prov.*, N.E. Spain; cap. Barcelona; a. 2,942 sq. m.; p. (1959) *2,735,802.*
Barcelona, *c.*, *spt.*, *cap.*, Barcelona prov., Spain; "Manchester of Spain"; cottons, paper, leather, glass, soap; exp. olives, wines, cork; p. (1959) *1,503,312.*
Barcelona, *t.*, N. Venezuela; *cap.* of Azoátegui st.; agr. tr.; browing; p. (1961) *44,773.*

Barcoo R., *see* Cooper's Creek. [9,175.
Bardejov, *t.*, ČSSR.; hot springs; p. (1961)
Bardera, *t.*, Somalia; head of navigation on Juba R.; p. *1,500.*
Bardsey, *I.*, Irish Sea; off coast of Wales, nr. N. point of Cardigan Bay; lighthouse.
Bareilly, *c.*, Uttar Pradesh, India; bamboo, furniture; p. (1961) *272,828.*
Barents Sea, part of Arctic Ocean E. of Spitzbergen to N. Cape; cod, haddock.
Barfurush, *see* Babul.
Bari, *spt.*, S. Italy; on Adriatic, 69 m. N.W. of Brindisi; cath.; olive oil, wines, fruit, soap; p. (1961) *311,268.*
Barinas, *t.*, cap. Barinas st., Venezuela; cattle, oil; p. (1961) *25,707.*
Barisal, *t.*, East Pakistan; nr. Tetulia at mouth of Ganges; river pt.; great damage and loss of lives due to cyclone 1965; p. (1961) *59,900.*
Barka, *dist.*, Libya, N. Africa.
Barking, *outer bor.*, E. London, Eng.; on R. Roding; inc. Dagenham; metal refining and smelting, insulation, cellulose; lge. power sta. and largest gaswks. in Europe; p. (1964) *178,645.*
Barkly Tableland, N. Terr., Australia.
Barkly West, *t.*, Cape Province, S. Africa; diamonds.
Barkul, *t.*, Shensi, W. China; p. (estd. 1947) *19,097.*
Barlad, *t.*, Romania, Moldavia; soap, textiles; p. (1948) *24,035.*
Bar-le-Duc, *t.*, *cap.*, Meuse, France; cotton, hosiery; p. (1954) *16,609.*
Barlee, *L.*, W. Australia.
Barletta, *t.*, *spt.*, Italy; wine; p. (1961) *68,035.*
Barlin, *t.*, Pas de Calais, France; coal-mines, lime, cement; p. (1954) *9,186.*
Barmouth, *t.*, *urb. dist.*, Merioneth, Wales; on cst. of Cardigan Bay; chemicals; p. (1961) *2,348.*
Barnack, *rural dist.*, Huntingdon and Peterborough, Eng.; p. (1961) *4,420.*
Barnard Castle, *mkt. t.*, *urb. dist.*, Durham, Eng.; health resort; woollens, penicillin; p. (1961) *4,969.*
Barnaul, *t.*, W. Siberia, R.S.F.S.R.; chemicals, engin., textiles, sawmilling; p. (1962) *347,000.*
Barnes, *see* Richmond upon Thames.
Barnesville, *t.*, Ga., U.S.A.; cotton mills; p. (1960) *4,919.*
Barnesville, *t.*, Ohio U.S.A.; coal, natural gas, glass, paper, evaporatde milk; p. (1960) *4,425.*
Barnet, *former urb. dist.*, Herts, Eng.; now outer bor., Greater London; comprising former bors. of Finchley and Hendon, and urb. dists. of Barnet, East Barnet and Friern Barnet; p. (1964) *318,051.*
Barneveld, *t.*, Gelderland, Netherlands; p. (1951) *20,058.*
Barnoldswick, *urb. dist.*, W.R. Yorks, Eng.; p. (1961) *10,267.* [p. *1,663.*
Barnsdall, *t.*, N. Okla., U.S.A.; oil, gas, agr.;
Barnsley, *mftg. t.*, *co. bor.*, W.R. Yorks, Eng.; coal, machin., plastics; p. (1961) *74,650.*
Barnstable, *t.*, Mass., U.S.A.; summer resort; fisheries; p. (1950) *10,480.*
Barnstaple, *mkt. t.*, *mun. bor.*, Devon, Eng.; on R. Taw; seaside resort; concrete, glove mkg.; p. (1961) *15,907.*
Baroda, *former st.*, India; now part of Gujarat st.; cereals, cotton, sugar, tobacco, opium; a. 2,961 sq. m.; p. (1961) *1,527,326.*
Baroda, *t.*, Gujarat, India; univ.; palaces, Hindu temples; p. (1961) *295,144.*
Barotseland, *prov.*, Zambia; savannah grasslands; livestock, grain, teak; a. 63,000 sq. m.; p. *c. 300,000.*
Barquisimeto, *t.*, Venezuela; sugar, coffee, cacao, cereals, cattle, copper, textiles; p. (1961) *196,557.*
Barra Is., southerly groups, Outer Hebrides, Scot.; a. 348 sq. m.; lighthouse on Barra Head; p. *2,250.*
Barraba, *t.*, Darling, N.S.W., Australia; pastoral; wool.
Barrage, *vil.*, U.A.R., N.E. Africa; on Nile, 35 m. N. of Cairo.
Barranca Bermeja, *t.*, Colombia, S. America; oil-field, oil-refining, paper mkg., petro-chemicals; p. (estd. 1959) *65,000.*
Barranqueras, *t.*, Chaco terr., N. Argentina; on Parana R.; exp. hardwoods, cotton.
Barranquilla, *pt.*, Colombia, S. America, on left bank nr. mouth of R. Magdalena; textiles, perfumes, saw mills, cement, pharmaceutics, river craft; p. (estd. 1962) *452,140.*
Barre, *c.*, Vt., U.S.A.; granite; p. (1960) *10,387.*
Barren I., volcano in Bay of Bengal.
Barren R., Ky. U.S.A.; length 120 m.
Barrhead, *mftg. burgh*, Renfrew, Scot.; 7 m. S.W. of Gasgow; iron and cotton; p. (1961) *14,422.*
Barrie, *c.*, Ontario, Canada; light inds., boat bldg.; p. (1956) *16,573.*
Barrier Ranges, *mtns.*, on boundary of S. Australia and N.S.W., Australia; alt. 2,000 ft.
Barrier Reef, Great, *coral reef*, Pac. Oc.; extending for 1,200 m., 10–150 m. from coast of Australia.
Barrington, *t.*, R.I., U.S.A.; shipbuilding, fish, residtl. resort; p. (1960) *13,826.*
Barron, *t.*, Wis., U.S.A.; dairy products, lumber; p. (1960) *2,338.*
Barrow, *C.*, Mackenzie, Canada.
Barrow Falls, nr. Keswick, Cumberland, Eng.
Barrowford, *urb. dist.*, Lancs., Eng.; p. (1961) *4,531.*
Barrow, R., Leinster, Ireland; rises in Slieve Bloom Mtns., and flows to Waterford Harbour.
Barrow-in-Furness, *spt. co. bor.*, N. Lancs, Eng.; iron and steel, paper, shipbldg., engin.; p. (1961) *64,824.*
Barrow-on-Soar, *rural dist.* and *t.*, Leicester, Eng.; p. (rural dist. 1961) *57,131.*
Barrow Point, most northerly headland in Alaska, N. America.
Barry, *mun. bor.*, Glamorgan, Wales; "outport" of Cardiff; coal, tin-plate, chemicals, plastics; p. (1961) *42,039.*
Barsac, *t.*, Gironde, France; Sauterne wine; p. (1954) *2,320.*
Barsi, *t.*, Maharashtra, India; cotton, oil-seeds; p. (1961) *50,389.*
Barstow, *t.*, Cal., U.S.A.; early silver mining and frontier town; p. (1960) *11,644.*
Bar-sur-Aube, *t.*, Aube, France; wine, brandy; furniture; p. (1954) *4,387.*
Bar-sur-Seine, *t.* Aube, France; p. (1954) *2,422.*
Barth, *spt.*, Rostock, E. Germany; shipyd. engin., furniture, sugar; p. (1963) *12,406.*
Bartholomew Bayou, *R.*, Ark., U.S.A., l. 275 m.
Bartin, *t.*, N. Turkey; p. (1960) *11,655.*
Bartlesville, *t.*, Okla., U.S.A.; oil refining, zinc smelting, metal prod., leather goods; p. (1960) *27,893.*
Barton-upon-Humber, *urb. dist.*, Lindsey, Lincs, Eng.; cycles, rope-making, bricks, tiles, chemical manure; p. (1961) *6,584.*
Bartow, *t.*, Fla., U.S.A.; phosphates, citrus canneries, cigar-mkg.; p. (1960) *12,849.*
Barvas, *par.*, Lewis, Scot.; p. *5,876.*
Basel, *can.*, Switzerland; divided into the half-cantons, Basel-Stadt, a. 14 sq. m., cap. Basel; p. (1961) *225,588*, and Baselland, a. 165 sq. m., cap. Liestal; farming, vines, forests; p. (1961) *148,282.*
Basel, *c.*, *cap.*, Basel, Switzerland; head of barge navigation on Rhine; chemicals, ribbons; p. (1961) *205,800.*
Bashee R., Cape Province, S. Africa.
Bashi I., gr. in Pac. Oc.; N. of Luzon in the Philippines.
Bashkir, *Rep.* R.S.F.S.R., U.S.S.R.; farming, gold, copper, coal, oil, engin., chemicals, textiles; cap. Ufa; p. (1959) *3,335,000.*
Basildon, *t.*, Essex, Eng.; in lower Thames valley, 8 m. S.E. of Brentwood; one of "New Towns" designated 1949 to relieve population congestion in London; incorporated S. part of Billericay urb. dist. and N. part of Thurrock urb. dist; gen. and elec. engin., cars, clothing, tobacco, photographic apparatus; p. (estd. 1965) *66,486.*
Basilicata, *dep.*, Italy; wheat, maize, vines, olive, oil; a. 3,855 sq. m.; p. (1961) *602,661.*
Basingstoke, *mftg. and mkt. t.*, *mun. bor.*, N. Hants Eng.; 50 m. W. London; vehicles, farm implements, pharmaceutics; p. (1961) *25,940.*
Basle, *see* Basel.
Basque Prov., Spain; comprising three provs., Alava, Guipuzcoa, Vizcaya, where Basque language is spoken and also N. of Pyrenees in France.
Basra, *prov.* or *liwa* on Euphrates, Iraq; 60 m. from the sea; p. (1956) *404,308.*
Basra, *t.*, *river pt.*, Iraq; dates; p. (1956) *159,355.*
Bass Rock, in Firth of Forth, opposite Tantallon Castle, E. Lothian, Scot.; gannetry.
Bass Strait, between Victoria and Tasmania; length about 200 m., breadth about 140 m.

Bassano, *t.*, Italy; on R. Brenia; vines, olives, majolica; p. *20,527.*
Bassein, *t.*, Burma; on mouth of Irrawaddy R., univ.; exp. rice; p. (1931) *45,662.*
Bassein, *R.*, Burma.
Bassenthwaite, *L.*, Cumberland, Eng.; length 4 m., breadth 1 m.; fishing.
Basses-Alpes, *frontier dep.*, S.E. France; olives, wines; cap. Digne; a. 2,697 sq. m.; p. (1954) *84,335.*
Basses-Pyrénées, *dep.*, France; cattle, sheep, forest; cap. Pau; a. 2,977 sq. m.; p. (1954) *85,067.*
Basse-Terre, *ch. t.*, Guadeloupe, Fr. W. Indies; p. *13,638.*
Basseterre, *cap.*, St. Kitts I. Leeward group; W.I.; p. (1957) *35,878.*
Båstad, *summer resort*, Sweden; international tennis; p. *2,300.*
Bastia, *t.*, *spt.*, Corsica, France; p. (1962) *50,880.*
Bastogne, *t.*, Belgium, nr. Luxembourg; p. (1962) *5,893.*
Bastrop, *t.*, N. La., U.S.A.; on Colorado R. mills; p. (1960) *15,193.*
Bastrop, *t.*, Texas, U.S.A.; on Colorado R.; lignite; p. (1960) *3,001.*
Basutoland, *terr.* self-gov. Brit. prot., S. Africa; indep. due 1966; at head of Orange R., and enclosed on S. by the Drakensberg Mtns.; mountainous plateau, purely native territory; univ. at Roma; mainly agr., maize, wool, mohair; cap. Maseru; a. 11,716 sq. m.; p. (estd. 1965) *733,000*
Bata, *ch. t.*, Spanish Guinea, W. Africa; p. *5,000.*
Bataan, *t.*, Philippine Is.
Batabanó, *t.*, Cuba; sponges; p. (1953) *5,075.*
Batangas, *prov.*, Philippine Is., oil refinining.
Batavia, *see* **Djakarta.**
Batavia, *c.*, N.Y., U.S.A.; farm implements; p. (1960) *18,210.*
Bataysk, *t.*, Rostov region, R.S.F.S.R.; rly. junction; grain and cattle, engin., p. (1959) *52,000.*
Batesar, *t.*, Agra dist., India; on the R. Jumna; comm. ctr.
Batesville, *t.*, Ark., U.S.A.; marble, manganese; p. (1960) *6,109.*
Batesville, *t.*, Ind., U.S.A.; furniture; p. (1960) *3,349.*
Bath, *t.*, Maine, U.S.A.; on R. Kennebec; p. (1960) *10,717.*
Bath, *c.*, *co. bor.*, Somerset, Eng.; Roman baths, hot springs, medicinal waters; fine Regency architecture; elect. engin., metals and limestone; p. (1961) *80,856.*
Bathgate, *burgh*, West Lothian, Scot.; 6 m. S. of Linlithgow; coal-mng., quarrying, metal, elec., hosiery, cars; p. (1961) *12,686.*
Bathurst, *I.*, off coast of N. Terr., Australia; 30 m. long.
Bathurst, *t.*, N.S.W., Australia; gold-mining; ctr. of pastoral, agr., fruit district; brewing, boots and shoes; p. (1961) *16,934.*
Bathurst, *sp.*, *cap.*, Gambia, W. Africa; at mouth of Gambia R.; airport; groundnuts; p. (estd. 1956) *28,820.*
Bathurst Is., N.W. Terr., Canada.
Batina, fertile coastal plain Muscat and Oman, Arabia; produces early-ripening dates famous for flavour.
Batley, *industl. t.*, *mun. bor.*, W.R. Yorks, Eng.; woollens, shoddy; p. (1961) *39,390.*
Batna, *commune*, Algeria; N. Africa; rly. to Biskra; p. *10,622.*
Baton Rouge, *cap.*, Louisiana, U.S.A.; on Mississippi R.; cotton seed, oil-refining; p. (1960) *152,491.*
Battambang, *prov.*, Cambodia; 180 m. N.E. of Pnom-Penh; p. (1962) *551,860.*
Battam I., Malay Arch.; 20 m. S. of Singapore.
Battersea, *see* **Wandsworth.**
Batticaloa, *t.*, *cap.*, E. Prov., Ceylon; p. *12,984.*
Battle, *t.*, *rural dist.*, Sussex, Eng.; battle of Hastings fought here 1066; p. (rural dist. 1961) *30,558.*
Battle Creek, *c.*, Michigan, U.S.A.; on Kalamazoo R.; engin., cereal prod.; p. (1960) *44,169.*
Battleford, N., *t.*, Canada; at junction of Battle R. with Saskatchewan R.; mixed farming; p. (1951) *7,489.*
Battle Harbour, nr. Strait of Belle I., Labrador.
Battle Mountain, *t.*, Nev., U.S.A.; copper-mines.
Batu Gajah, *t.*, Malaya; in valley Kinta R.; tin-mines; residtl.; p. (1947) *7,480.*
Batu, I., E. Indies, Indonesia.
Batumi, *t.*, *spt.*, Georgian S.S.R.; oil, engin., citrus fruits, tea; p. (1959) *82,000.*
Bauchi, *t.*, central Nigeria; ctr. of impt. tin-mining a.; p. *10,000.*
Baud, *t.*, Orissa, India; on R. Mahanadi.
Bauld, *C.*, northernmost part of Newfoundland, N. America.
Baures, *R.*, E. Bolivia; flowing from L. Guazamire to R. Guapore; length 300 m.
Bautzen, *t.*, Dresden, E. Germany; on R. Spree; textiles, engin., iron inds.; p. (1963) *42,431.*
Bauya, *t.*, Sierra Leone, W. Africa; rly. junction.
Bavaria, *Land*, Germany; hilly, forested; ch. rivers; Danube, Main, Isar, Inn; ch. inds.; agr., dairying, rye, oats, hops, sugar-beet, brewing, glass, sugar, toys, chemicals, jewellery; cap. Munich (*q.v.*); a. 27,112 sq. m.; p. (1961) *9,514,000.*
Bavarian Alps, *mtns.*, Germany.
Bawdwin, *t.*, Burma; wolfram, lead, zinc, silver, rubies.
Bawtry, *mkt. t.*, W.R. Yorks, Eng.; 8 m. S. of Doncaster; p. (1951) *1,460.*
Baxley, *t.*, S.E. Ga., U.S.A.; pecan nuts, tobacco; p. (1950) *3,234.*
Baxter Springs, *t.*, S.E. Kan., U.S.A.; lead- and zinc-mines; p. (1960) *4,498.*
Bayamon, *t.*, Puerto Rico, W. Indies; fruit, tobacco, sugar, coffee; p. (1960) *72,134.*
Baybay, *t.*, Leyte, Philippine Is.; impt. comm. pt.; p. (1948) *50,725.*
Bayburt, *t.*, Turkey, p. (1960) *11,968.*
Bay City, *mftg. t.*, Mich., U.S.A.; on Saginaw R., 108 m. N.W. of Detroit; fishing, chemicals, beet-sugar; p. (1960) *53,604.*
Bay City, *t.*, Texas, U.S.A.; sulphur, oil; p. (1960) *11,656.*
Bayeux, *t.*, Calvados, France; cath., museum, Bayeux tapestry; p. (1954) *10,077.*
Bay Is., group G. of Honduras, Central America; lgst., Ruatan; coconuts, bananas; p. (1961) *8,863.*
Bay of Islands, inlet and harbour on N.I., New Zealand.
Bayombong, *t.*, Philippine Is.; p. (1948) *14,079.*
Bayonne, *fortfd. t.*, Basses-Pyrénées, S.W. France; cath.; noted for fine hams, invention of bayonet; aircraft; p.(1962) *41,149.*
Bayonne, *t.*, N.J., U.S.A.; 6 m. from New York; chemicals, oil-refining; p. (1960) *74,215.*
Bayport, *t.*, Minn., U.S.A.; on St. Croix R.; state prison; p. (1960) *3,205.*
Bayreuth, *c.*, Bavaria, S. Germany; home of Wagner; famous for musical festivals in magnificent national theatre; textiles, porcelain, engin.; p. (1963) *61,700.*
Baytown, *t.*, S.E. Texas, U.S.A.; oil-wells, toluene factory; p. (1960) *28,159.*
Baza, *t.*, S. Spain; W. of Lorca; lead, iron, mercury, sugar; p. (1957) *23,450.*
Beachy Head, 575 ft. high, on Sussex cst., loftiest headland in S. Eng.
Beaconsfield, *t.*, Tasmania, Australia; on W. of estuary of Tamar R.; tin mining.
Beaconsfield, *urb. dist.*, Bucks., Eng.; residtl.; p. (1961) *10,019.*
Beaconsfield, *t.*, Cape Province, S. Africa; diamonds.
Bear I., Arctic Ocean; 130 m. S. of Spitzbergen.
Bear L., on border of Idaho and Utah, U.S.A.
Bear L., Great, N.W. Terr., Canada; outlet to Mackenzie R. through Great Bear R.; a. 14,000 sq. m.
Béarn, *old prov.* now Basses-Pyrénées, France.
Bearsden, *burgh*, Dunbarton, Scot.; p. (1961) *17,022.*
Beas (Bias), *R.*, Punjab, India; trib. of Sutlej R.; one of the " five rivers."
Beas de Segura, *t.*, Spain; wine, oil, fruits, flax; p. *14,953.*
Beatrice, Neb., U.S.A.; health resort on Big Blue R.; p. (1960) *12,132.*
Beattock, *pass*, S. Uplands, Scot.; gives access from valley of R. Clyde to R. Annan; used by main W. cst. rly. route from Carlisle to Glasgow and Edinburgh; alt. 1,014 ft.
Beaucaire, *t.*, Gard, France; noted fair; p. (1954) *10,197.*
Beauce, *natural division* (" *pays* "), Central France; low, level, plateau of limestone S.W.

of Paris and R. Seine; arid, few surface streams; thin layer of loam (limon) permits agr.; impt. wheat-growing area; population mainly grouped in lge. vils.
Beaufort, *t.*, S.C., U.S.A.; S.W. of Charleston; canning and shipping point for farming and fishing region; tourist ctr.; p. (1960) *6,298.*
Beaufort West, *t.*, Cape Province, S. Africa; sheep, karakul; p. (1960) *16,323* inc. *5,297* whites.
Beaujolais, France; wine-growing dist.
Beaulieu, *par.*, Hants, Eng.; on Beaulieu R.; yachting; p. *1,201.*
Beauly, *R.*, Inverness, Scot.; flows to Beauly Loch.
Beauly, *t.*, Inverness, Scot.; on Beauly R.; p. *890.*
Beaumaris, *mun. bor.*, *wat. pl.*, cap. Anglesey, N. Wales; on Menai Strait; cas., ruins; light engin.; p. (1961) *1,960.*
Beaumont, *c.*, E. Texas, U.S.A.; lumbering, petroleum; p. (1960) *119,175.*
Beaune, *t.*, Côte d'Or, France; wines, casks, farm implements; p. (1954) *13,175.*
Beausoleil, *t.*, Alpes-Maritime, France; p. (1954) *11,504.*
Beauvais, *t.*, *cap.*, Oise, France; cath.; Gobelin tapestry; p. (1954) *26,756.*
Beaver, *R.*, Penns., Ohio, U.S.A.; rises in Allegheny Plateau, flows N. towards L. Erie, turns S.E. into R. Ohio just below Pittsburgh; valley provides easiest route from Pittsburgh to L. Erie pts., contains many steel-mkg. ts., Youngstown, Newcastle, Warren; length 130 m.
Beaver Dam, *c.*, Wisconsin, U.S.A.; summer resort on L.; p. (1960) *13,118.*
Beaver Falls, *t.*, Penns., U.S.A.; machin., pottery, coal, natural gas; p. (1960) *16,240.*
Beaver Meadows, *bor.*, E. Penns., U.S.A.; anthracite, textiles; p. (1960) *1,392.*
Beawar, *t.*, Rajasthan, India; cotton; p. (1961) *53,931.*
Bebington, *mun. bor.*, Cheshire, Eng.; soap, chemicals, engin.; p. (1961) *52,202.*
Beccles, *mun. bor.*, Suffolk, Eng.; printing, engin., malting; p. (1961) *7,330.*
Béchar (Colom-Béchar), *t.*, N.W. Algeria; terminus of rly. through Oran dep.; p. (estd.) *25,000.*
Bechuanaland, *see* **Botswana.**
Beckenham, *former mun. bor.*, Kent, Eng., now inc. in Bromley outer London bor. (*q.v.*); p. (1961) *77,265.*
Beckley, *c.*, S.W. Va., U.S.A.; coal; p. (1960) *18,642.*
Beckum, *t.*, N. Rhine–Westphalia, Germany; cement, chalk, engin. wks.; p. (1963) *21,200.*
Bedale, *mkt. t.*, *rural dist.*, N.R. Yorks, Eng.; at N. end of Vale of York; tent mkg.; p. (rural dist. 1961) *8,215.*
Beddgelert, *par.*, Caernarvon, Wales; resort; slate.
Beddington and Wallington, *mun. bor.*, Surrey, Eng. nr. Croydon; p. (1961) *32,588.*
Bedford, *mun. bor.*, Beds, Eng.; on R. Ouse, 50 m. N. of London; general engin. inc. marine and elect., bricks, ironfounding, aero research; p. (1961) *63,317.*
Bedfordshire, S. Midland *co.*, Eng.; co. t. Bedford (*q.v.*); agr., mkt. gardening, brickmkg., cement, vehicles, engin.; a. 473 sq. m.; p. (1961) *380,704.*
Bedford, *t.*, Indiana, U.S.A.; p. (1960) *13,024.*
Bedford, *t.*, Ohio, U.S.A.; p. (1960) *15,223.*
Bedford Level, once over 400,000 acres of peat marsh in S. Fenland; first successful draining initiated by Earl of Bedford in 1634.
Bedlington, *urb. dist.*, Northumberland, Eng.; iron, coal; p. (1961) *29,373.*
Bedloe's I., or **Liberty I.**, N.Y. harbour, U.S.A.; on which statue of Liberty stands.
Bedminster, *t.*, Somerset, Eng.; sub. of Bristol.
Bedourie, *t.*, Queensland, Australia.
Bedrashem, *t.*, U.A.R., N.E. Africa; on R. Nile.
Bedwas and Machen, *urb. dist.*, Mon., Eng.; gas, coal and coke by-prods.; p. (1961) *10,231.*
Bedwellty, *urb. dist.*, Mon., Eng.; coal, iron, elec. goods, car upholstery; p. (1961) *27,336.*
Bedworth, *urb. dist.*, Warwick., Eng.; coal-mng., limestone quarrying, engin., textiles; p. (1961) *32,501.*
Bedzin, *t.*, S. Poland; coal, zinc, metals, chemicals, bricks, sugar-beet; p. (1960) *39,000.*
Beechworth, *t.*, Victoria, Australia; gold, pastoral and agr.
Beechy Point, *C.*, N.E. cst. Alaska, U.S.A.
Beemaning Mtn., highest peak Blue Mtns., N.S.W., Australia; alt. 4,100 ft.
Beenleigh, *t.*, Queensland, Australia; 24 m. S. Brisbane.
Beerberg, *highest mtn.*, Thüringer Wald, Germany; alt. 3,266 ft.
Beernem, *t.*, W. Flanders, Belgium; p. (1962) *5,829.*
Beersheba, *t.*, Israel; ctr. for development of the Negev; p. (1953) over *20,000.*
Beeskow, *t.*, Germany; on R. Spree.
Beeston and Stapleford, *urb. dist.*, Nottingham, Eng.; engin., drugs, telephones; p. (1961) *56,720.*
Beeville, *c.*, Texas, U.S.A.; mnfs. oilfield equipment; oil-wells; p. (1960) *13,811.*
Beg, *L.*, Antrim, N. Ireland.
Bega, *R.*, S. Hungary; canalised trib. to R. Tisza.
Bègles, *t.*, Gironde, France; mftg.; p. (1954) *23,176.*
Beheira, *prov.*, Lower U.A.R., N.E. Africa; in delta of Nile R.; cotton; a. 1,639 sq. m.; p. (1957) *1,493,000.*
Behistun, *t.*, Iraq; in ruins; monuments of Darius the Great.
Beilan, *t.*, *mtn. pass*, Syria-S.W. Asia; E. of G. of Iskenderun; ancient Amanus of "Syrian Gates."
Beilngries, *t.*, Bavaria, Germany; on Ludwig's canal.
Beilstein, *t.*, Germany; on R. Moselle.
Beira, *spt.*, *cap.*, prov. Manica and Sofala, Mozambique; airport; rly. runs inland to Salisbury (Rhodesia) and Blantyre (Malawi); exp. sugar, maize, cotton; oil pipeline to Umtali; p. (1960) *64,600* inc. *16,000* Europeans.
Beira Alta, *prov.*, Portugal; a. 3,682 sq. m.; p. (1950) *691,713.*
Beira Baixa, *prov.*, Portugal; a. 2,897 sq. m.; p. (1950) *355,806.*
Beira Litoral, *prov.*, Portugal; a. 2,908 sq. m.; p. (1950) *969,166.*
Beirut, *cap.* Lebanon, S.W. Asia; most impt. *spt.* Syria and Lebanon; ancient historic t., now busy shipping and mercantile ctr.; silk, wool, fruits; p. (estd 1960) *500,000.*
Beit el Faki, *t.*, Yemen, Arabia; coffee.
Beit Jala, *t.*, Jordan, S.W. Asia; p. (estd. 1946) *3,740.*
Beit Jibrin, *t.*, Israel, S.W. Asia; in Judæan Hills, 20 m. W.S.W. Jerusalem; p. *1,000.*
Beja, *dist.*, Portugal; pig-breeding dist.; olive oil, pottery; cath.; airfield under construction for training of German pilots; p. (1960) *283,152.*
Bejaia (Bougie), *spt.*, Algeria; impt. tr. ctr.; exp. wood, hides; oil pipe-line connection to Hassi-Messoud; p. (1954) *43,934.*
Bejar, *t.*, Spain; cloth; p. *12,875.*
Bekes, *t.*, Hungary; wheat; p. (1962) *24,100.*
Békéscsaba, *t.*, Hungary; milling; rly. junction; p. (1962) *50,664.*
Bela Crkva, *t.*, Serbia, Jugoslavia; p. (1959) *11,000.*
Belalcazar, *t.*, Spain; woollen mnfs.; p. *9,471.*
Belaya Tserkov, *t.*, N. Ukrainian S.S.R.; agr. and comm. ctr.; p. (1959) *71,000.*
Belbeis, *t.*, U.A.R., N.E. Africa; agr. ctr. on W. edge of cultivated Nile delta.
Belcher Is., two sm. groups in Hudson Bay, N.W. Terr., Canada.
Belding, *c.*, Mich., U.S.A.; silk mills; p. (1960) *4,887.*
Belem, *sub.* of Lisbon, Portugal; fine church, monastery.
Belém, *cap.*, Pará st., Brazil; cath., bishop's palace; arsenal, museum; coaling sta., rubber, rice, sugar; p. (1960) *402,170.*
Belen, *t.*, Catamarca, Argentina.
Bélep Arch., about 7 m. N.E. of New Caledonia.
Belfast, *spt.*, *co. bor.*, *cap.* N. Ireland; Antrim (and partly Down), at head of Belfast Lough; linen mnf., rope, tobacco, shipbldg., distilling, aircraft, patent glazing; oil refinery on E. side of harbour; univ.; Houses of Parliament, Stormont Cas.; p. (1961) *416,094.*
Belfast, *t.*, Maine, U.S.A.; p. (1960) *6,140.*
Belfodio, *t.*, Ethiopia; nr. border with Sudan; p. *1,000.*
Belford, *rural dist.*, Northumberland, Eng.; agr., whinstone quarrying; p. (1961) *4,994.*

Belfort, *fortress t.*, Belfort, France; between Jura and the Vosges; heavy inds., rly. wks., sm. cotton ind.; p. (1962) *51,280*.

Belfort, *dep.*, France; ch. t., Belfort; a. 235 sq. m.; p. (1962) *109,371*.

Belgaum, *t.*, Mysore, India; cotton; p. (1961) *126,727*.

Belgian Congo. *See* Congo.

Belgium, *cty.*, W. Europe; climate temperate; ch. rivers: Scheldt, Meuse; races: Flemish, Walloon; languages: Flemish, French; religion: Roman Catholic; ch. inds.: agr., cereals, sugar-beet, potatoes, cattle, pigs, horses; minerals: coal; mnfs.: iron and steel machin., engin., metals, shipbldg., textiles, brewing, distilling; exp. mnf. goods; communications: rail, road, canal; cap. Brussels; ch. port, Antwerp; univ. at Brussels, Ghent, Liége, Louvain; a. 11,755 sq. m.; p. (1962) *9,251,414*.

Belgorod, *t.*, Kursk, R.S.F.S.R.; chalk, slate, lumber, soap, leather, engin.; p. (1959) *71,000*.

Belgorod-Dnestrovski, *t.*, Ukraine, U.S.S.R.; mouth of Dniester R.; wine, wool, fruit; p. (1956) *21,600*.

Belgrade (Beograd), *c. cap.*, Serbia, Jugoslavia; at junc. of Save and Danube; univ.; mnfs. tobacco, woollens, aircraft; p. (1961) *594,000*.

Belhaven, *t.*, N.C., U.S.A.; on Pamlico Sound; fishing, lumbering; p. (1960) *2,386*.

Belitung or Billiton, *I.* Between Sumatra and Kalimantan, Indonesia; tin; a. 1,866 sq. m.; p. *102,375*.

Belize, *R.*, Brit. Honduras, Central America; 150 m. long; rises in N.E. Guatemala and flows E. into G. of Honduras at B.

Belize, *t.*, *cap.*, British Honduras, Central America; mahogany, dyewoods, bananas; almost devastated by hurricane 31 Oct. 1961; cap. to be moved to new site 50 m. further inland; p. (1960) *32,824*.

Bell, *I.*, Newfoundland, E. Canada; in Conception Bay, 20 m. N.W. of St. Johns; impt. Wabana iron-ore deposits outcrop on N.W. cst., smelted on Pictou coalfield, Nova Scotia; a. 12 sq. m.; p. of Wabana (1956) *7,873*.

Bell, *R.*, Quebec, Canada; flows N. into James Bay.

Bell, *t.*, Cal., U.S.A.; residtl c. 5 m. S. of Los Angeles; p. (1960) *19,371*.

Bell Rock, Scot.; famous rock and lighthouse 12 m. S.E. of Arbroath.

Bellagio, *t.*, Italy; on L. Como; resort.

Bellaire, *mftg. t.*, Ohio, U.S.A. on Ohio R.; coal, limestone, glass, enamelware; p. (1960) *11,502*.

Bellary, *fortfd. c.*, Mysore, India; cotton; p. (1961) *85,673*.

Belleek, *par.* and *vil.*, Fermanagh, N. Ireland; on Erne R.; china; p. *1,300*.

Bellefontaine, *t.*, Ohio, U.S.A.; agr. ctr., light mnfs.; holiday resort; p. (1960) *11,424*.

Bellefonte, *bor.*, Penns., U.S.A.; limestone quarries; p. (1960) *6,088*.

Belle Fourche, *t.*, S.D., U.S.A.; on Belle Fourche R.; beet sugar, flour, bricks, dairy produce; p. (1960) *4,087*.

Bellegarde, *fort* on frontier of France and Switzerland, near Geneva.

Belle Ile, *I.* off S. coast of Brittany, France.

Belle Isle Strait, N. America; between Newfoundland and Labrador, on N. shipping route to Canada from Europe.

Bellenden Ker Hills, *mtn. range*, N. Queensland, Australia.

Belleville, *c.*, Ontario, Canada; dairying, fruit; p. (1961) *30,655*.

Belleville, *t.*, Ill., U.S.A.; brewing, iron founding, shoes, flour; p. (1960) *37,264*.

Belleville, *t.*, N.J., U.S.A.; p. (1960) *35,005*.

Bellevue, *t.*, Ohio, U.S.A.; limestone, farm implements, car parts; p. (1960) *8,282*.

Bellevue, *t.*, Penns., U.S.A.; p. (1960) *11,412*.

Bellevue, *t.*, Queensland, Australia; goldfields.

Belley, *t.*, Ain, France; p. (1954) *5,470*.

Bellflower, *t.*, Cal., U.S.A.; p. (1960) *44,846*.

Bellingham, *rural dist.*, Hexham, Northumberland, Eng.; coal; p. (1961) *5,285*.

Bellingham, *t.*, *spt.*, Wash., U.S.A.; saw-mills, paper-mills, salmon canning; p. (1960) *34,688*.

Bellingshausen, *sea*, S. Antarctic; lying W. of Graham Land.

Bellinzona, *t.*, Switzerland; on R. Ticino; 14 m. N. of Lugano; three castles built on hills dominating t.; p. (1957) *12,060*.

Bellot Strait, channel on Arctic coast, N. America; separates Boothia and N. Somerset.

Bellows Falls, *t.*, Vt., U.S.A., on Connecticut, R.; paper, farm implements; p. (1960) *3,831*.

Belluno, *c.*, Venetia, N. Italy; fine cath.; silk; p. (1961) *31,224*.

Belluno, *prov.*, Venetia, N. Italy; a. 1,276 sq. m.; p. (1961) *205,700*.

Belmar, *t.*, N.J., U.S.A.; seaside resort, fishing; p. (1960) *5,190*.

Belmez, *t.*, Córdoba prov., S. Spain; on N. flank of Sierra Morena, 38 m. N.W. of Córdoba; ctr. of sm. coalfield; p. (1959) *9,672*.

Belmont, *t.*, Cape Province, S. Africa; 56 m. S. of Kimberley.

Belmont, *t.*, Mass., U.S.A.; p. (1960) *28,715*.

Belmont, *t.*, N.C., U.S.A.; p. (1960) *5,007*.

Belo Horizonte, *t.*, *cap.*, Minas Gerais st., Brazil; gold, iron, manganese; diamond-cutting; ctr. of agr. inds.; cotton; p. (1960) *693,328*.

Beloit, *c.*, Wisconsin, U.S.A.; on Rock R., diesel engines, farm implements; p. (1960) *32,846*.

Beloit, *c.*, Kan., U.S.A.; on Solomon R.; tr. ctr. for agr. region; p. (1960) *3,837*.

Beloretsk, *t.*, Bashkir A.S.S.R.; iron, metal inds.; p. (1959) *59,000*.

Belovo, *t.*, W. Siberia, R.S.F.S.R.; coal mng., zinc, engin.; p. (1959) *107,000*.

Beloyarsk, R.S.F.S.R.; atomic power sta. in Urals.

Belper, *urb. dist.*, Derby, Eng.; hosiery, textiles, paint, oil wks., iron foundries; p. (1961) *15,563*.

Belt, Great, *strait*, Denmark; separates Fyn I. from Själland I.; deep-water channel too winding for easy navigation; crossed by train ferry at its narrowest point (16 m.) between Nyborg and Korsor; approx. length 37 m.

Belt, Little, *strait*, Denmark; separates Fyn I. from Jutland; too shallow for large ships; bridged by road-railway bridge nr. Fredericia; approx. length 30 m.

Belterra, *dist.*, Para st., N.E. Brazil; on R. Tapajoz, 30 m. S. of confluence with R. Amazon at Santarem; experimental Ford rubber plantations; a. 950 sq. m.; p. (with Fordlandia) *12,000*.

Beltsy, *t.*, Moldavian S.S.R.; on trib. of Dniester R.; p. (1959) *67,000*.

Belturbet, *t.*, *urb. dist.*, Cavan, Ireland; on R. Erne; distilling; p. (1951) *1,152*.

Bembridge, *vil.*, I. of Wight, Eng.; resort, yachting; p. *1,975* (par.).

Bemfica, Angola, W. Africa; oilfields.

Bemidji, *t.*, Minn., U.S.A.; lumber, cement, bricks, woollen goods; resort; p. (1960) *9,958*.

Ben Alder, *mtn.*, Grampian Range, Scot.; nr. Loch Erich; alt. 3,757 ft.

Ben Arthur, *mtn.*, Argyll, Scot.; alt. 2,891 ft.

Ben Attow, *mtn.*, Ross and Inverness, Scot.; alt. 3,383 ft.

Ben Avon, *mtn.*, Aberdeen, Scot.; alt. 3,834 ft.

Ben Cruachan, *mtn.*, Argyll, Scot.; alt. 3,689 ft.

Ben Doran or Doireann, *mtn.*, Argyll, Scot.; alt. 3,523 ft.

Ben Hope, *mtn.*, Sutherland, Scot.; alt, 3,040 ft.

Ben Lawers, *mtn.*, Perth, Scot.; by Loch Tay; alt. 3,984 ft. [alt. 2,875 ft.

Ben Ledi, *mtn.*, Perth, Scot.; N.W. of Callander;

Ben Lomond, *mtn.*, Stirling, Scot.; E. side of L. Lomond; alt. 3,192 ft.

Ben Lomond, *mtn.*, New England range, N.S.W., Australia; alt. 5,000 ft. [5,010 ft.

Ben Lomond, *mtn.*, Tasmania, Australia; alt.

Ben Macdhui, *mtn.*, S.W. Aberdeen, Scot.; Cairngorm gr; second highest peak in Brit. Is.; alt. 4,296 ft.

Ben More, *mtn.*, S.W. Perth, Scot.; 10 m. W. of Loch Earn; alt. 3,843 ft.; also mtns. in Sutherland, the Hebrides and the I. of Mull.

Ben Nevis, *mtn.*, Inverness, Scot.; at Lochiel; highest peak in Brit. Isles, alt. 4,406 ft.

Ben Nevis, *mtn.*, Otago, New Zealand; alt. 9,125 ft.

Ben Nevis, *mtn.*, Cornwall, Tasmania, Australia; alt. 3,910 ft.

Ben Venue, *mtn.*, nr. Loch Katrine, Perth, Scot.; alt. 2,393 ft.

Ben Vorlich, *mtn.*, Perth, Scot.; alt. 3,224 ft.

Ben Wyvis, *mtn.*, Ross, Scot.; nr. Dingwall; alt. 3,429 ft.

Benalla, *t.*, *dist.*, Victoria, Australia; pastoral and agr.; p. (1961) *8,483*.

Benares, *see* Varanasi.

Benbecula I., Outer Hebrides, Inverness, Scot.; a. 36 sq. m. [Uist.
Benbecula Sound, passage between the I. and S.
Bendery, *t.*, Moldavian S.S.R.; textiles, p. (estd. 1961) *63,000*.
Bendigo, *c.*, Victoria, Australia; gold-mining dist., rich farming and wine-producing terr.; p. (1961) *40,309*.
Benevento, *prov.*, Italy; a. 819 sq. m., containing many Roman remains; p. (1961) *297,153*.
Benevento, *c.*, Italy; cath.; leather; p. (1961) *54,744*.
Benfleet, *urb. dist.*, Essex, Eng.; saw mills, joinery wks., light inds.; p. (1961) *32,395*.
Bengal, West, *st.*, India; a. 33.928 sq. m.; p. (1961) *34,926,279*; rice, oilseeds, sugar cane, tobacco, jute, silk, tea, coal, mesta, potatoes; served by 3 st. rlys.; Ganges alluvial plains and delta; ch. c. Calcutta which adjoins jute manuf. ctr. Howrah. (Former prov. of Bengal split 1947—W. Bengal to India, E. Bengal to Pakistan).
Bengal, Bay of, part of Indian Ocean washing E. shores of India and W. shores of the Indo-Chinese Peninsula; receives waters of Rs. Krishna, Ganges, Brahmaputra, Irrawaddy.
Benghazi, *spt.*, Libya, N. Africa; on the G. of Sidra; joint cap. with Tripoli; former starting-point for caravans to Egypt and the interior; cereals; p. (estd. 1954) *71,000*.
Bengore Head, *C.*, Antrim, N. coast Ireland; E. of Giant's Causeway.
Benguela, *c.*, Angola, S.W. Africa; rly. runs inland to Katanga prov., Congo and Zambia; beeswax, maize, cattle, sugar; p. (1960) *52,300* inc. *11,500* whites.
Benha, *t.*, U.A.R.; impt. mkt. t., rail and road ctr. in heart of cultivated a. of Nile delta.
Benholm, *par.*, Kincardine, Scot.; ancient cas.; p. (1951) *1,028*.
Beni, *dep.*, N.E. Bolivia, S. America; cap. Trinidad; a. 93,354 sq. m.; p. (1962) *161,800*.
Benicarlo, *spt.*, Valencia, Spain; on Mediterranean cst.; wines; p. (1957) *9,385*.
Benin, W. Africa; between Niger delta and Dahomey; traversed by Benin R.; former African kingdom and slaving ctr., now dist. incorporated in Nigeria; palm prod. and foodstuffs; famous African bronze ctr.; ch. t. Benin.
Benin, *t.*, Nigeria; W. Africa; cap. Mid-West region; palm oil, mahogany; p. (1953) *54,000*.
Benin, Bight of, part of G. of Guinea, W. Africa.
Beni Suef, *t.*, U.A.R.; on Nile, 60 m. S. of Cairo; carpets, cotton; p. (1960) *79,000*.
Benkulen, *spt.*, Sumatra, Indonesia; p. *13,418*.
Benmore, *C.*, Antrim, N.E. point of N. Ireland; alt. 636 ft.
Bennettsville, *t.*, S.C., U.S.A.; yarn, tyre linings, lumber; p. (1960) *6,963*.
Bennington, *t.*, Vt., U.S.A.; p. (1960) *8,023*.
Benoni, *t.*, Transvaal, S. Africa; engin.; p. (1960) *135,467* (inc. *41,305* whites).
Benrath, *t.*, Germany; on Rhine R.; R. pt. and industl. t.; chemicals, machin.; p. *25,929*.
Bensberg, *t.*, N. Rhine-Westphalia, Germany; 10 m. from Cologne; iron-mining, foundries; p. (1963) *33,400*.
Bensheim, *t.*, Hessen, Germany; ctr. of fruit and wine dist.; textiles, paper, metallurgy; p. (1963) *24,800*.
Bentang (Bintang), *t.*, Kalimantan, Indonesia.
Bentley with Arksey, *urb. dist.*, W.R. Yorks, Eng.; p. (1961) *22,952*.
Benton, *t.*, Ark., U.S.A.; p. (1960) *10,399*.
Benton, *t.*, Ill., U.S.A.; p. (1960) *7,023*.
Benton Harbor, *t.*, Mich., U.S.A.; midway along E. cst. L. Michigan; p. (1960) *19,136*.
Benue, *R.*, W. Africa; chief trib. of Niger.
Benwell, *t.*, Northumberland, Eng.; sub. of Newcastle.
Ben-y-Gloe, *mtn.*, Glen Tilt, Perth, Scot.; alt. 3,671 ft.
Beograd, *see* **Belgrade**.
Berat, *prefecture*, Albania; p. (estd.) *169,431*.
Berat, *c.*, Albania; p. (1945) *11,872*.
Berbera, *beach pt.*, Somalia, N.E. Africa; on G. of Aden; former cap. of Br. Somaliland Prot.; exp. gum, raisins, skins; p. in hot season about *15,000*, in cold season about *30,000*.
Berbice, *co.*, Guyana, S. America; bauxite; p. (1946) *96,623*.
Berchem, *commune*, Belgium; sub. of Antwerp; metals; p. (1962) *48,880*.
Berdichev (Ossipevsk), *t.*, Ukrainian S.S.R.; ctr. of sugar a.; engin., lt. inds.; p. (1959) *53,000*.
Berck-sur-Mer, *wat. pl.*, France, on Eng. Channel; p. (1954) *14,285*.
Berdyansk (Osipenko), *spt.*, Ukrainian S.S.R.; on Sea of Azov; a ctr. of the salt ind.; exp. grain, hemp, wool, agr. machin.; engin., oil refining; p. (1959) *65,000*.
Berea, *t.*, N. Ohio, U.S.A.; sandstone quarries, building blocks; p. (1960) *16,592*.
Bere Regis, *mkt. t.*, Dorset, Eng.
Berezina, *R.*, U.S.S.R.; trib. Dnieper; French disaster on the retreat from Moscow; length 350 m.
Berezniki, *t.*, R.S.F.S.R., salt, chemicals, paper; p. (1959) *106,000*.
Berga, *t.*, Spain; medieval cas.; p. (1957) *8,023*.
Bergama, *t.*, Turkey; ancient Pergamos, ruins; p. (1960) *21,797*.
Bergamo, *c.*, Lombardy, Italy; 34 m. N.E. Milan; fine cath. and academy; silk industry; p. (1961) *113,512*.
Bergedorf, *t.*, Germany; sub. of Hamburg; on R. Elbe; glass, leather; p. *19,962*.
Bergen, *spt.*, W. coast Norway; univ.; most impt. comm. pt. in kingdom; shipping, fishing; mftg. inds.; p. (1963) *116,555*.
Bergenfield, *t.*, N. J., U.S.A.; clothing, light mnfs., pianos; p. (1960) *27,203*.
Bergen-op-Zoom, *t.*, Netherlands; sugar-beet; p. (1960) *34,984*.
Bergerac, *t.*, Dordogne, France; on R. Dordogne; grain, wine; ancient Huguenot stronghold; p. (1954) *23,622*.
Bergisch-Gladbach, *t.*, N. Rhine-Westphalia, Germany; E. of Cologne; paper, metallurgy, textiles; p. (1963) *44,500*.
Bering I., most W. of the Aleutian Is., N. America.
Bering Sea, part of N. Pac. Oc. between Aleutian Is. and Bering Strait, upwards of 1,600 sq. m.; fishing.
Bering Strait, *narrow sea* which separates Asia from N. America; 36 m. wide at narrowest part.
Bering Current (Okhotsk Current, or Oyashio), *ocean current*, N. Pac. Oc.; flows through Bering Strait from Arctic, along E. cst. of Kamchatka and Japanese Is. Hokkaido, Honshu; relatively cold; moderate summer temperatures along cst. causes fogs.
Berja, *t.*, Almeria, Spain; wine and fruit; p. (1957) *11,011*.
Berkeley, *parish*, Gloucester, Eng.; nr. R. Severn, 2 m. S. of Sharpness; civil nuclear power-sta.; p. *1,116*.
Berkeley, *c.*, Cal., U.S.A.; univ.; p. (1960) *111,268*.
Berkeley Canal, Gloucester, Eng.; connects Sharpness on S. side Severn estuary with Gloucester; navigable only for small coasting vessels; opened 1827; length 15 m., depth 11 ft.
Berkhampstead (Berkhamsted), *urb. dist.*, Herts, Eng.; chemicals, wooden ware; p. (1961) *13,051*.
Berkley, *t.*, Mich., U.S.A.; sub. of Detroit; p. (1960) *23,275*.
Berkshire, *co.*, Eng.; downland including Inkpen Beacon, White Horse Hills, drained by Thames and tribs., Kennet, Cole, Pang; wooded; agr.; oats, dairying; biscuits; co. t. Reading; a. 725 sq. m.; p. (1961) *503,357*.
Berlin, *c.*, former cap. of Germany; on R. Spree; fourth c. on continent of Europe for population; at present under military control of U.S.A., Great Britain, France and U.S.S.R.; total a. 890 sq. km.; inds. include, elec. goods, optical and chemical prod., furniture, paper, foodstuffs, textiles, machin., publishing and printing; gr. route ctr. (each occupying force has 1 airfield); p. (1963) *3,241,896* (W. Berlin *2,176,600*; E. Berlin *1,065,296*.)
Berlin, *t.*, New Hampshire, U.S.A.; p. (1960) *17,821*.
Bermejo, *t.*, Tarija dep., Bolivia; oil.
Bermejo R., *trib.* R. Parana, Argentina.
Bermeo, *spt.*, Spain; nr. Bilbao, Bay of Biscay; fishing; p. (1957) *12,517*.
Bermondsey, *see* **Southwark**.
Bermuda, Brit. group coral islands (360 in number of which 20 are inhabited) N. Atlantic; about 600 miles E. of S. Carolina, U.S.A.; total area 21 sq. m.; Hamilton, on Long Island is the ch. t.; British and U.S. air and naval

stations; favourite winter resort for Americans; potatoes, onions, lily bulbs; bananas; p. (of gr.) (estd. 1965) *48,000*.
Bermudez, asphalt lake, Venezuela, S. America; a. 2 sq. m.
Bernard, Great St., one of the Alps in the S. of the Valais, Switzerland; highest point 11,116 ft.; height of mtn. pass between Italy and Switzerland, 8,120 ft.; famous hospice for travellers in monastery on mtn. Great St. Bernard road tunnel, *see* **K146**.
Bernard, Little St., one of Graian Alps, Savoy, S. of Mt. Blanc, France; pass traversed by Hannibal 218 B.C.
Bernay, *t.*, Eure, France; horse fair; dairying, clothing mftg., soap; p. (1954) *8,798*.
Bernburg, *t.*, Halle, E. Germany; cas.; chemicals, machin.; p. (1963) *44,738*.
Berne, *c.*, *cap.* can. Berne and *fed. cap.* Switzerland; on Aar R.; cath., univ.; textiles; p. (1961) *166,100*.
Berne, *can* Switzerland; fertile valleys, dairying; watches; tourist district; a. 2,657 sq. m.; p. (1961) *889,523*.
Bernese Oberland, Switzerland; Alpine region; ch. peaks; Finsteraarhorn, Jungfrau; resorts: Interlaken, Grindelwald; summer and winter ctrs.
Bernina, *pass* and *mtn.*, Switzerland; alt. 13,300 ft.
Beroun, *t.*, Bohemia, ČSSR.; textiles, sugar ref., cement, coal, iron, limestone; p. (1961) *15,597*.
Berry, *t.*, N.S.W., Australia; dairying.
Bertinoro, *t.*, Forli, Italy; famous wines.
Berwick, *maritime co.*, S.E. of Scot.; co. t. Duns; hilly; agr.: sheep, cattle; woollens, fishing, paper; a. 457 sq. m.; p. (1961) *22,441*.
Berwick-on-Tweed, *spt.*, *mun. bor.*, Northumberland, Eng.; fishing, light engin., tweeds, knitwear; p. (including Tweedmouth and Spittall) (1961) *12,166*.
Berwyn, *t.*, Ill., U.S.A.; p. (1960) *54,224*.
Berwyn Mtns., range mid-Wales; alt. of highest peak 2,716 ft.
Besançon, *t.*, Doubs, France; observatory; univ.; farm implements, textiles; watch- and clock-making; p. (1962) *101,729*.
Besikias, now **Besiktas,** *dist. and sub.*, Istanbul, Turkey; p. (1950) *63,611*.
Beskids, W. and E., *mtn. range*, Poland, Czechoslovakia, E. Europe; northern range of Carpathian mtn. system, seldom exceeds alt. 4,000 ft., many passes; forested; length 200 m.
Bessarabia, *terr.*, ceded to U.S.S.R. by Romania, 1940, and now part of Moldavian S.S.R.; agr. region.
Bessbrooke, *t.*, Armagh, N. Ireland; on Newry Canal; p. (1961) *3,084*.
Bessèges, *t.*, Gard, France; coal-mining, steel, silk; p. (1954) *5,823*.
Bessemer, *t.*, Ala., U.S.A.; iron and steel; p. (1960) *33,054*.
Bessemer, *t.*, Mich., U.S.A.; iron; p. (1960) *3,304*.
Besshi, *see* **Niihama.**
Besuki, *mountainous prov.* E. Java, Indonesia.
Betanzos, *t.*, Spain; wine; p. (1957) *10,824*.
Bethany, *vil.* on Mt. of Olives 2 m. Jerusalem, now Eizariya.
Bethany, *missionary sta.*, S.W. Africa; p. *544*.
Bethel, *anc. c.*, the modern Beitin, Jordan; 10 m. N. Jerusalem.
Bethel, *t.*, Cape Province, S. Africa; rich farming a.; p. (1960) *11,952* inc. *4,003* whites.
Bethesda, *t.*, Maryland, U.S.A.; p. (1960) *56,527*.
Bethesda, *urb. dist.*, Caernarvon, Wales; slate, light engin.; p. (1961) *4,151*.
Bethlehem, *t.*, Jordan; 5½ m. S.W. Jerusalem; birthplace of Christ; p. (1961) *15,777*.
Bethlehem, *t.*, Penns., U.S.A.; 50 m. N. of Philadelphia; iron-wks.; p. (1960) *75,408*.
Bethnal Green, *see* **Tower Hamlets.**
Bethphage, former vil. on Mt. of Olives, above Bethany, Israel, S.W. Asia.
Bethsaida, ancient vil. on W. side of Sea of Galilee, Israel, S.W. Asia.
Bethshemesh, *t.*, Israel, S.W. Asia; 24 m. W. of Jerusalem; archaeological site.
Béthune, *t.*, Pas de Calais, France; oil, salt, coal; p. (1954) *22,376*.
Bettendorf, *t.*, Iowa, U.S.A.; steel, oil burners; p. (1960) *11,534*
Betteshanger, *mining vil.*, Kent, Eng.; on N. flank of N. Downs, 4 m. W. of Deal; on Kent coalfield, coal despatched by overhead cable to Dover.
Betws-y-Coed, *urb. dist.*, Caernarvon, Wales; tourist and artists' resort; p. (1961) *778*.
Betul, *t.*, Madhya Pradesh, India; p. (1961) *19,860*.
Betwa, *R.*, of Bhopal, India, trib. of Jumna R.; length 360 m.
Beuel, *t.*, N. Rhine-Westphalia, Germany; on R. Rhine opposite Bonn; chemicals, furniture; p. (1963) *33,000*.
Beuthen, *see* **Bytom.**
Beuzeval, *t.*, Calvados, France; on Eng. Channel; seaside resort.
Beveland, *I.*, S. Netherlands; between the old Maas and Hollands Diep.
Beverley, *mkt. t.*, *mun. bor.*, E.R. Yorks, Eng.; fine minster; p. (1961) *16,024*.
Beverly, *c.*, Mass., U.S.A.; boots, shoes, machin.; p. (1960) *36,108*.
Beverly Hills, *t.*, California, U.S.A.; p. (1960) *30,817*.
Beverwyk, *t.*, nr. Haarlem, N. Holland, Netherlands; p. (1960) *35,398*.
Bewdley, *mun. bor.*, Worcester, Eng.; p. (1961) *5,033*.
Bexhill, *mun. bor.*, Sussex, Eng.; resort; p. (1961) [*28,926*.
Bexley, *former bor.* W. Kent; now outer bor., Greater London, Eng., inc. Chislehurst and Sidcup (N. of the A.20) Crayford and Erith; p. (1964) *209,937*.
Bexley, *t.*, Ohio. U.S.A.; p. (1960) *14,319*.
Beykoz, *t.*, Turkey; on Bosporus Strait; p. (estd. 1960) *40,000*.
Beyoglu, *div.* of Istanbul, Turkey; residtl. quarter of Europeans; p. (1945) *234,750*.
Beypazari, *t.* Turkey; 65 m. W. of Ankara; rice, fruit, cotton; p. (1960) *8,866*.
Beysehir, *L.*, Turkey; 25 m. long; alt. 7,068 ft.
Bezhitsa, *t.*, R.S.F.S.R.; fused with Bryansk (*q.v.*) in 1956.
Béziers, *t.*, Hérault, France; wines, brandy; chemicals; p. (1962) *75,541*.
Bezons, *sub.* of Paris, France; on Seine R.; light mnfs; p. (1954) *16,993*.
Bezwade, *see* Vijyavada.
Bhadravati, *t.*, Mysore, India; steel; p. (1961) *65,776*; of new town *41,281*.
Bhagalpur, *t.*, Patna, Bihar, India; rice, maize; p. (1961) *143,850*.
Bhamo, *t.*, Upper Burma; on R. Irrawaddy; ancient cap. of Shan State of Manmaw; teak; p. *8,611*.
Bhandara, *dist.*, Maharashtra, India, a. 3,582 sq. m.; rice, oilseeds, wheat, bamboo, tobacco; p. (1961) *1,268,286*.
Bhandara, *cap.* of Bhandara dist., Maharashtra, India; 30 m. E. of Nagpur; cotton cloth, brass mftg.; p. (1961) *27,710*.
Bharatpur, *t.*, Rajasthan, India; cloth; p. (1961) [*49,776*.
Bhatpara, *t.*, W. Bengal, India; on R. Hooghly; p. (1961) *147,630*.
Bhavnagar, *dist.*, Gujarat, India; a. 4,652 sq. m.; p. (1961) *1,119,435*.
Bhavnagar, *t.*, *spt.*, Gujarat, India; cotton, silk and gold embroidery; p. (1961) *176,473*.
Bhilai, Madhya Pradesh, India; steel plant; rails and rly. sleepers; p. (1961) of industl. t. *86,116*; of Durg *47,114*.
Bhim-Gora, sacred pool, place of Hindu pilgrimage, Uttar Pradesh, India.
Bhir, *dist.*, Maharashtra, India; a. 4,268 sq. m.; wheat, cotton, linseed, sugar; cap. Bhir, 190 m. E. of Bombay; p. (1961) *1,001,466*.
Bhiwani, *t.*, India; cottons; p. (1961) *58,194*.
Bhopal, *c.*, st. cap., Madhya Pradesh, India; p. (1961). *185,374*.
Bhuj, *ch. t.*, Kutch, Gujarat, Bombay, India; p. (1961) *38,953*.
Bhutan, *indep. st.*, E. Himalayas; cap. Punakha; ch. prod.: Indian corn, millet, lac, rice, cloth; valuable forests; a. (approx.) 18,000 sq. m.; first motor road link with India constr. 1960–2; p. scattered and nomadic, *c. 700,000*.
Bhuvaneshwar, *cap.*, Orissa, India; 18 m. from Cuttack; p. (1961) *38,211*.
Biafra, Bight of, W. Africa; bay lying E. of the G. of Guinea between the Niger and Cape Lopez.
Biala-Krakowska, *commune*, Krakow dep., Poland; agr., tr. ctr., cattle, textiles; p. *30,337*.
Bialogard, *c.*, N.W. Poland; formerly in Germany; industl. and transport ctr.; p. (1946) *12,211*.
Bialystok, *prov.*, E. Poland; cap. Bialystok; a. 9,021 sq. m.; p. (1961) *1,115,000*.
Bialystok, *t.*, Poland; *cap.* of Bialystok prov.;

nr. Grodno; engin., textiles, chemicals, saw-milling; p. (1960) *121,000*.
Biancavilla, *t.*, Sicily, Italy; oranges.
Biarritz, *t.*, Basses-Pyrénées, France; on Bay of Biscay; seaside resort; p. (1954) *22,922*.
Biba-El-Kubra, *t.*, U.A.R., N.E. Africa; on Nile; p. *1,000*.
Biberach, *t.*, Baden-Württemberg, Germany; on R. Riss; spa; wood, metal and engin. inds.; p. (1963) *23,100*.
Bibi Eibat, *locality*, Azerbaijan, U.S.S.R.; very rich oilfields.
Bicester, *urb. dist.*, Oxford, Eng.; rly. junction; lace; p. (1961) *5,513*.
Bida, *t.*, N. Nigeria, W. Africa; p. *10,000*.
Bidassoa, *R.*, on Spanish-French frontier.
Biddeford, *c.*, Maine, U.S.A.; cotton mnf.; resort; p. (1960) *19,255*.
Biddulph, *urb. dist.*, Stafford, Eng.; nr. Leek; coal mng., machin., textiles, furniture; p. (1961) *14,060*.
Bideford, *mun. bor.*, N. Devon, Eng.; on R. Torridge; ropes, sails, boat bldg., glove mkg.; p. (1961) *10,265*.
Biebrich, *t.*, Germany; on Rhine; dyes; p. *19,504*.
Biel (Bienne), *t.*, Berne, Switzerland; watches; p. (1961) *61,200*.
Bielawa, *t.*, Wroclaw prov., S.W. Poland; textiles; p. (1960) *28,000*.
Bielaya-Tserkov, *t.*, Ukraine, U.S.S.R.; on trib. of Dnieper R.; fairs, tr. in cattle, beer, grain; p. *54,000*.
Bielefeld, *t.*, Rhine-Westphalia, Germany; ch. ctr. of linen industry; machin., bicycles; p. (1963) *172,800*.
Biella, *t.*, Novara, Italy; textiles; p. (1961) *50,209*.
Bielsko-Biala, *t.*, Katowice prov., Poland; woollens, linen, metal, chem.; p. *76,000*.
Bien-hoa, *t.*, nr. Saigon, S. Viet-Nam; p. *5,000*.
Bienne, *L.*, N.E. Neuchâtel, Switzerland.
Bierley, *par.*, W. Riding, Yorks, Eng.; coal, iron; p. *16,000*.
Bies-Bosch, reclaimed fenland area between N. Brabant and S.W. Netherlands; sugar refining, dairying; a. 55 sq. m.; p. (1947) *1,517*.
Big Black, *R.*, trib. of Mississippi, U.S.A.
Big Bone Lick, *locality*, N. Ky., U.S.A.; E. of Ohio R.; deposit of fossil mammoth.
Biggar, *burgh*, Lanark, Scot.; in S. Uplands, 10 m. S.E. of Lanark; p. (1961) *1,403*.
Biggarsberg, *mtns.*, Natal, S. Africa; branch of the Drakensberg, highest point, Indumeni, 7,200 ft.
Biggleswade, *urb. dist.*, Beds, Eng.; in valley of R. Ouse, 9 m. S.E. of Bedford; ctr. of fruit-growing and mkt. gardening dist.; hydraulic machin. tools, hosiery, caravans; p. (1961) *8,047*.
ig Horn Mtns, Wyo. and Mont., U.S.A.; Rockies; highest alt., 12,000 ft.
ig Horn, *R.*, Wyo., U.S.A.; trib. of Yellow-stone R.
ihač, *t.*, Jugoslavia; on R. Una; p. (1959) *14,000*.
ihar, *state*, Indian Union; a. 67,196 sq. m.; cap. Patna (*q.v.*); ch. R., Ganges; agr.: rice, wheat, maize, sugar-cane, tobacco, oil-seeds; minerals: coal, iron, mica; ind.: iron and steel, oil refining at Barauni; p. (1961) *46,455,610*.
ihé, *dist.*, Angola (Port. W. Africa).
ihor Mtns., Romania.
isk, *c.*, Siberia, U.S.S.R.; p. (1959) *146,000*.
ijapur, *t.*, Mysore, India; cotton; ruins; p. (1961) *78,854*.
ijeljina, *t.*, Jugoslavia; p. (1959) *18,000*.
ijnore, *t.*, Uttar Pradesh, India; p. (1961) *33,610*.
ikaner, *t.*, Rajasthan, India; p. (1961) *150,634*.
ikini, *atoll*, Pacific Ocean; scene of atomic-bomb tests.
laspur, *t.*, Madhya Pradesh, India; silks, cottons; p. (1961) *86,706*.
lbao, *spt.*, N. Spain; cap. Basque prov. of Viscaya; formerly famous for rapier making; iron ore, smelting; p. (1959) *281,469*.
iecik, *t.*, Turkey; p. (1960) *7,535*.
lina, *c.*, Bohemia, CSSR.; wat. pl., mineral springs; p. (1961) *10,394*.
llabong, *R.*, N.S.W., Australia.
llericay, *mun. bor.*, Essex, Eng.; lost land and individuality to Basildon.
llinge and Winstanley, *urb. dist.*, Lancs, Eng.; coal bricks; p. (1961) *6,941*.
llingham, *t.*, *urb. dist.*, Durham, Eng.; on N. of Tees estuary; chemicals, shipbldg. and repairing, iron and steel, plastics, fertilisers; p. (1961) *32,130*.
Billings, *t.*, Montana, U.S.A.; cattle-raising, wool; p. (1960) *52,851*.
Billingsgate, London, Eng.; old river-gate and wharf, now chief fish mkt. of England.
Billiton (Belitung) I., Indonesia; tin.
Bilma, *oasis*, Niger, W. Africa; p. *1,000*.
Biloxi, *t.*, Miss., U.S.A.; fishing, tourist ctr., U.S. Air Force base; p. (1960) *44,053*.
Bilsen, *t.*, Belgium; mkt. ctr. for fruit growing area; p. (1962) *6,517*.
Bilston, *mun. bor.*, Stafford, Eng.; coal mng., iron, steel, non-ferrous castings; p. (1961) *33,077*.
Bima, *t.*, Sumbawa, Indonesia.
Binab, *t.*, Azerbaijan, Persia; nr. L. Urmia.
Binalbagan, *mun.*, Philippine Is.; sugar; p. (1948) *19,748*.
Binalonam, *t.*, Luzon, Philippine Is.; road ctr.; p. (1948) *23,260*.
Binan, *t.*, Luzon, Philippines; rice; p. (1948) *20,794*.
Binangonan, *t.*, Luzon, Philippine Is.; cement; p. (1948) *20,422*.
Binche, *t.*, Belgium; lace, clothing; p. (1962) *10,426*.
Bingara, *t.*, N.S.W., Australia; wool, wheat, cattle.
Bingen, *t.*, Rhineland Palatinate, Germany; on Rhine R.; at S. entrance to Rhine gorge; wine; beautiful scenery; p. (1963) *20,500*.
Bingerville, *spt.*, Ivory Coast, W. Africa.
Bingham, *rural dist.*; Notts., agr.; p. (1961) *25,145*.
Bingham Canyon, *t.*, N. Utah, U.S.A.; copper, silver, gold, lead; p. (1960) *1,516*.
Binghamton, N.Y., U.S.A.; on Susquehanna R.; boot factories; p. (1960) *75,941*.
Bingley, *urb. dist.*, *mkt. t.*, W.R. Yorks, Eng.; on R. Aire, 16 m. N.W. of Leeds; textiles, engin., agr.; p. (1961) *22,308*.
Bingol-dag, *mtns.*, Turkey; S. of Erzurum; highest peak 12,310 ft.
Bintang I., largest island of the Riouw Archipelago, Indonesia; bauxite.
Bio-Bio, *R.*, Chile; rises in Andes, flows N.W. to Pac. Oc. at Talcahuano; length 300 m.
Bio-Bio, *prov.*, Chile; cap. Los Angeles; a. 4,342 sq. m.; p. (1960) *179,984*.
Biratnagar, *t.*, S.E. Nepal, in the Terai; jute, sugar, cotton milling; p. (1961) *33,293*.
Birbhum, *dist.*, W. Bengal, India; cap. Suri; healthy climate; rice, sugar; mnfs. silk, cotton; a. 1,757 sq. m.; p. (1961) *1,446,158*.
Birchington, *t.*, Kent, Eng.
Birdsboro, *bor.*, Penns., U.S.A.; on Schuylkill R.; coal, steel; p. (1960) *3,025*.
Birdum, *t.*, N. Terr., Australia; on rly., 300 m. S. of Darwin; cattle.
Birjand, *t.*, Iran; p. *25,000*.
Birkenhead, *co. bor.*, Cheshire, Eng.; on R. Mersey, opp. Liverpool; docks, shipbldg., engin., clothing, metal, wood, glass; p. (1961) *141,683*.
Birket El Qarun, "Lake of the Horns," Fayum, Egypt, N.E. Africa.
Birmingham, *co. bor.*, Warwick, Eng.; industl. cap. Midlands, second lgst. c. Gt. Britain; famous for its metal mnfs.; motors and cycles, plastics; univ., cath., town hall; p. (1961) *1,105,651*.
Birmingham, *t.*, *cap.*, Ala., U.S.A.; coal, iron, limestone, steel, aircraft, chemicals, textiles; p. (1960), *340,889*.
Birmingham, *t.*, Mich., U.S.A.; p. (1960) *25,525*.
Birnam, *vil.*, Perth, Scot.; location of Birnam Wood—Macbeth; former royal forest.
Birni, *t.*, Dahomey, W. Africa; p. *1,000*.
Birobidzhan, *t.*, U.S.S.R.; admin. ctr.; lt. and wood inds.; p. (1959) *41,000*.
Birr, *mkt. t.*, *urb. dist.*, Offaly, Ireland; on Little Brosna R.; farming; observatory; p. (1961) *3,221*.
Bir Tlacsin, Libya, Africa; 120 m. S.W. Tripoli; oilfields.
Bisbee, *t.*, Arizona, U.S.A.; very rich copper deposits, gold, silver, lead; p. (1960) *9,850*.
Biscarosse, Landes, France; 45 m. S.W. Bordeaux; rocket and missile testing range projected.
Biscay, *see* **Vizcaya**.
Biscay, Bay of, stormy a. of the Atl. W. of France and N. of Spain, from Ushant to C. Ortegal; the Roman Sinus Aquitanicus; heavy seas.
Bisceglie, *t.*, *spt.*; Apulia, Italy; on E. cst. 22 m. N.W. of Bari; fishing; p. (1961) *41,451*.
Bischheim, *t.*, Bas-Rhin, France; N.W. sub.

of Strasbourg, furniture, porcelain; p. (1954) *11,430*.

Bischoff, Mt., *t.*, Tasmania, Australia: tin.

Bischofswerda, *t.*, Dresden, E. Germany; quarrying, glass and iron inds.; rly. ctr.; p. (1963) *11,285*.

Bishop, *t.*, Cal., U.S.A.; cattle, tungsten; p. (1960) *2,875*.

Bishop Auckland, *urb. dist.*, Durham, Eng.; contains palace of Bishop of Durham; coal, iron, light engin.; p. (1961) *35,276*.

Bishop Rock, *isolated rock, lighthouse*, Scilly Is., 36 m. S.W. of Land's End, Cornwall; recognised internationally as E. end of trans-Atlantic ocean crossing.

Bishop's Castle, *mun. bor.*, Salop, Eng.; p. (1961) *1,229*.

Bishop's Stortford, *mkt. t.*, *urb. dist.*, Herts., Eng.; on Stort R.; grain; p. (1961) *18,342*.

Bishop's Waltham, *par.*, Hants, Eng.; bricks.

Bishop Wearmouth, *t.*, pt. of Sunderland, Co. Durham.

Biskra, *t.*, Algeria, N. Africa; olives, dates; winter resort; p. *36,347*.

Bisley, *t.*, Gloucester, Eng.; nr. Stroud; source of R. Thames.

Bismarck, *cap. c.*, N. Dakota, U.S.A.; on Missouri R.; p. (1960) *27,670*.

Bismarck Arch., 3 large and several small islands off New Guinea, formerly German, now Australian Trust Terr.; total native p. (estd. 1962) *174,115*.

Bissagos Is., off W. Africa, Port Guinea; ch. t. Bolama.

Bissao, *t.*, *spt.*, Port Guinea; p. *5,000*.

Bistrita, *t.*, Romania; p. (1956) *20,292*.

Bitetto, *t.*, *sm. spt.*, Apulia, Italy; on E. cst. 5. m. N.W. of Bari; fishing; p. *5,991*.

Bitlis, *I.*, Turkey; p. (1945) *74,449*.

Bitlis, *t.*, Turkey; minerals, Armenian massacre; p. (1960) *16,562*.

Bitolj (Monastir), *t.*, Macedonia, Jugoslavia; many mosques, military H.Q., great tr. in corn, grain, flour, hides and woollen stuffs; tanning, carpets; p. (1959) *43,000*.

Bitonto, *t.*, Apulia, on E. cst. 7 m. N.W. of Bari; Italy; olive oil, wine; fine cath.; p. *29,731*.

Bitterfeld, *t.*, Halle, E. Germany; lignite mining; engin., chemicals; p. (1963) *30,900*.

Bitterfontein, *t.*, Cape Province, S. Africa.

Bitter Lakes, Isthmus of Suez, U.A.R., utilised by Suez Canal.

Bitterroot, *mtns.*, U.S.A.; range of the Rockies, highest point Ajax Mtn., 10,900 ft.; rly. tunnel 2 m. long.

Bitton, *t.*, Gloucester, Eng.; mining.

Biwa, *L.*, Japan; a. 180 sq. m.; 330 ft. above sea-level; 300 ft. deep; connected by canal with Osaka.

Biyala, *t.*, Gharbiya prov.; Lower U.A.R.; N.E. Africa; rice, millet, cotton; p. (1947) *17,731*.

Biysk, *t.*, W. Siberia, R.S.F.S.R.; engin., textiles; p. (1959) *146,000*.

Bizerta, *spt.*, Tunisia, N. Africa; the ancient Hippo Zaritus; fishing; oil refining; steelwks. projected; p. (1956) *46,681*.

Bizot, *commune*, N.E. Algeria; p. *10,845*.

Bjelovar, *t.*, Croatia, Jugoslavia; p. (1959) *12,000*.

Björnborg, *see* **Pori**.

Blaauw B. Mtns., Transvaal, S. Africa.

Blaavands Huk, Denmark; nr. Esbjerg.

Black Belt, *area* on coastlands of Miss. and Ala., U.S.A.; black soil prairie land, good for cotton.

Black Bluff, *mtn.*, N. Tasmania, Australia.

Blackburn, *co. bor.*, Lancs, Eng.; textiles, engin., light inds.; p. (1961) *106,114*.

Black Country, Eng., Midlands; formerly impt. iron-working and coal-mining district round the Birmingham area.

Blackdown Hills, Devon, Eng.

Black Forest (Schwarzwald), *mtns.*, Germany; resort, forests, a. 1,844 sq. m.; highest peak Feldberg, alt. 4,696 ft.

Black Gang Chine, picturesque ravine on S. Coast, Isle of Wight, Eng.

Black Hawk, *mining t.*, Rocky Mtns., Colorado, [U.S.A.

Black Head, *C.*, Galway Bay, Clare, Ireland.

Blackhead, *C.*, on N. entrance to Belfast Lough, N. Ireland; lighthouse.

Blackheath, *open common*, S.E. London, Eng.; a. 267 acres.

Black Hills, *mtns.*, between S.D. and Wyo., U.S.A.; highest, Horney Peak, alt. 7,240 ft.

Black Isle, *peninsula*, between Cromarty and Beauly Firths, Ross and Cromarty, Scot.; agr., fisheries, quarrying; a. 240 sq. m.

Black Lake, *t.*, S. Quebec, Canada; asbestos mines; p. (1961) *4,180*.

Blackley, *t.*, S.W. Lancs, Eng.; N. sub. of Manchester; dye wks.

Black Mountain, *t.*, N.C., U.S.A.; resort.

Black Mtns., range of Appalachians, U.S.A.; Mt. Mitchell, alt. 6,684 ft.

Black Mtns., *range*, Brecknock, S. Wales; highest peak, Brecknock Van, alt. 2,631 ft.

Blackpool, *co. bor.*, *seaside resort*, Lancs, Eng. on cst. of Fylde dist.; p. (1961) *152,133*.

Black Prairie, *region*, Texas, U.S.A.; extends 350 m. S.W. from Ouochita Mtns. to Austin; contains very fertile Black Waxy and Grande Prairie sub-regions devoted almost entirely to cotton growing; ch. ts., Dallas, Fort Worth, Austin; a. 30,000 sq. m.

Black River Falls, *t.*, Wis., U.S.A.; lumber, flour, dairying, poultry; p. (1960) *3,195*.

Blackrock, *t.*, Ireland; sub. 4 m. from Dublin.

Blackrod, *urb. dist.*, Lancs, Eng.; nr. Chorley; weaving; p. (1961) *3,609*.

Black Sea, *inland sea* between Russia and Turkey; 740 m. long, 390 m. broad; receives waters of Danube, Dnieper, Dniester, Don, Bug and other rivers; communicates with Mediterranean by Strait of Bosporus, Sea of Marmara and Dardanelles.

Blacksod Bay, coast of Mayo, Ireland.

Blackstone, *t.*, Mass., U.S.A.; textiles; p. (1950) *4,968*.

Blackstone, *t.*, Va., U.S.A.; tobacco mkt.; p (1960) *3,659*.

Black Volta, *R.*, Upper Volta and Ghana; rises in Futa Jallon Plateau, flows E., S. and E. into R. Volta; length, over 800 m.

Black Warrior, *R.*, Ala., U.S.A.; flows throug coalfields; navigable; water power.

Blackwater, *R.*, Hants and Essex, Eng.

Blackwater, *R.*, Ireland; three of this name.

Blackwater, *R.*, U.S.A. (Mont., Fla., and Va.).

Black Waxy, *see* **Black Prairie**.

Blackwell, *c.*, Okla., U.S.A.; gas, oil, wells, re fining, zinc smelting; meat packing; p (1960) *9,588*.

Blaenau Ffestiniog, *see* **Ffestiniog**.

Blaenavon, *t.*, *urb. dist.*, Monmouth, Eng. mining; p. (1961) *8,424*.

Blagoevgrad, *t.*, formerly Gorna Dzhumaya, ch. t Bulgarian Macedonia; p. (1956) *21,833*.

Blagoveshchensk, now **Blagoyevgrad**, *t.*, E. Siberia R.S.F.S.R. on R. Amur; wat. pl.; engin., saw milling; p. (1959) *94,000*.

Blair Atholl, *par.*, Perth, Scot.; tourist resort p. (1951) *1,868*.

Blairgowrie and Rattray, *burgh*, Perth, Scot. at foot of Scot. Highlands, 18 m. N.E. of Perth fruit; linen; agr. machin., canning inds.; p (1961) *5,168*.

Blairmore, *t.*, Alberta, W. Canada; on Canadia Pacific Rly., 160 m. S.W. of Medicine Hat, a approach to Crow's Nest Pass: coal-minin ctr. on Alberta Coalfield; p. (1961) *1,980*

Blairsville, *t.*, Penns., U.S.A.; p. (1960) *4,930*.

Blakely, *t.*, Ga., U.S.A.; peanuts, lumber, turpen tine; p. (1960) *3,580*.

Blanc-Mesnil (Le), *t.*, Seine-et-Oise, France; (1954) *25,363*.

Blanc, Mt., France; highest peak of Alps; al 15,782 ft.

Blanca Pk., Col., U.S.A.; alt. 14,390 ft.

Blanche Bay, on N.E. coast of New Britai Bismarck Arch.; inner part site of Rabaul.

Blanchester, *t.*, Ohio, U.S.A.; textiles, pump p. (1960) *2,944*.

Blanco, *t.*, Cape Province, S. Africa.

Blandford, or **Blandford Forum**, *mkt. t.*, *mun. bo* Dorset, Eng.; lime and stone, agr. implement p. (1961) *3,558*.

Blanes, *spt.*, Spain; N.E. of Barcelona; holida resort; p. (1957) *7,039*.

Blankenberge, *spt.*, N. Belgium; seaside resor p. (1962) *10,252*.

Blantyre-Limbe, *t.*, Malawi; in Shire Highland linked by rail to Beira; comm. ctr.; tobacc p. *33,000* (inc. *3,400* Europeans).

Blantyre, *par.*, Lanark, Scot.; birthplace of I Livingstone; aero engines; p. (1951) *17,766*.

Blarney, *vil.*, 4 m. N.W. Cork, Ireland; cas, a Blarney stone; woollen mftg.

Blaydon, *urb. dist.*, Durham, Eng.; coal-mining; p. (1961) *30,615.*
Blekinge, *co.*, Sweden; a. 1,173 sq. m.; p. (1961) *144,468.*
Blenheim, *t.*, S.I., New Zealand; fruit; p. (1961) *11,942.*
Bletchley, *urb. dist.*, Bucks, Eng.; rly. junction, bricks, brushes; p. (1961) *17,093.*
Blida, *t.*, Algeria, N. Africa; flour, citrus fruits; p. (1954) *67,000.*
Bloemfontein, *t.*, *cap.*, O.F.S., S. Africa; cattle ctr.; engin., glass, bricks, meat canning; p. (1960) *140,924* inc. *61,213* Whites.
Blois, *c.*, Loire-et-Cher, France; on Loire; 30 m. S.W. of Orleans; château; wines; p. (1954) *28,190.*
Blood R., Natal, S. Africa.
Bloody-Foreland, *C.*, Donegal, N.W. Ireland.
Bloomfield, *t.*, Ind., U.S.A.; p. (1960) *2,224.*
Bloomfield, *t.*, N.J., U.S.A.; p. (1960) *51,867.*
Bloomington, *t.*, Ill., U.S.A.; coal, motor cars; p. (1960) *36,271.*
Bloomington, *t.*, Ind., U.S.A.; wheat, corn, alfalfa; furniture, structural glass, radios; p. (1960) *31,357.*
Bloomsburg, *t.*, Penns., U.S.A.; iron; p. (1960) *10,655.*
Blorca, *t.*, Java, Indonesia; teak; p. *18,451.*
Bludenz, *t.*, Austria; cotton, watches; p. (1961) *11,127.*
Bluefield, *t.*, W. Va., U.S.A.; coal, iron, limestone, steel foundries, silica, lumber; p. (1960) *19,256.*
Bluefields, *R.* in Nicaragua, Central America.
Bluefields, *t.*, Nicaragua; on E. cst.; bananas, timber; p. (1960) *11,376.*
Blue Grass, *dist.*, Ky., U.S.A., area where blue grass abundant; horse breeding.
Blue Mountains, chain in N.S.W., Australia; highest peak, 4,100 ft.
Blue Mountains, *t.*, N.S.W., Australia; tourist centre; p. (1961) *28,070.*
Blue Mountains, Jamaica, W. Indies.
Blue Nile (Bahr-el-Azrek), *R.*, rising in tablelands of Ethiopia, joins the White Nile at Khartoum; its seasonal flooding provides the bulk of water for irrigation in Sudan and U.A.R.
Blue Nile, *prov.*, Sudan; a. 54,577 sq. m.; cap. Wad Medani (*q.v.*); p. (estd. 1951) *1,840,600.*
Blue Point, Long I., U.S.A.; oysters.
Blue Ridge Mtns., U.S.A.; most E. ridge of Appalachian Mtns. in Virginia and North Carolina.
Bluff Harbour, S.I., New Zealand; 18 m. from Invercargill; spt. for Southland prov.
Bluffton, *t.*, Ind., U.S.A.; farm implements, lumber; p. (1960) *6,238.*
Blumenau, *t.*, Brazil; butter, sugar; p. (1960) *46,591.*
Blumental, *t.*, Hanover, Germany; on R. Weser; industl.; p. *12,764.*
Blyth, *spt. mun. bor.*, Northumberland, Eng.; exp. coal; shipbldg.; p. (1961) *35,933.*
Blytheville, *t.*, Ark., U.S.A.; tr. ctr. for agr. region; p. (1960) *20,797.*
Blythswood, *t.*, Cape Province, S. Africa.
Bo, *t.*, Sierra Leone, W. Africa; second lgst. t. in dominion; gold; adm. hdqtrs.; p. (1963) of dist. *209,000.*
Bobadilla, *t.*, S. Spain; N. of Málaga.
Bobbili, *t.*, Andhra Pradesh, India; tr. ctr. in agr. a.; p. (1961) *25,592.*
Bobigny, *t.*, Seine, France; p. (1954) *18,521.*
Bobo-Dioulasso, *ch. t.*, Voltaic Rep., W. Africa, on rly. from Abidjan; road and comm. ctr., cotton, kapok, wax; p. *34,500.*
Bobrawa, *R.*, Lower Silesia; W. Poland; trib. of R. Oder; length 158 m.
Bobrek Karb, *t.*, Silesia, Poland; German before 1945; coal, coke, steel, ammonia; p. (1939) *22,095.*
Bobrinets, *t.*, Ukrainian S.S.R.; tobacco factories; p. *10,000.*
Bobruisk, *fortress, t.*, Byelorussian S.S.R., on R. Berezina; engin., sawmilling; p. (1959) *97,000.*
Bocas del Toro, *prov.*, Panama; cap. B. del T.; p. (1960) *32,600.*
Bochetta, La, *pass*, Liguria, Italy; used by main routes across Ligurian Apennines from Genoa to Lombardy Plain.
Bocholt, *t.*, N. Rhine-Westphalia, Germany; machin., textiles, elect. goods; p. (1963) *46,100.*
Bochum, *t.*, N. Rhine-Westphalia, Germany; 11 m. W. of Dortmund: ctr. of steel ind.; coal and iron, chemicals, foodstuffs; p. (1963) *361,100.*
Bockum-Hövel, *t.*, N. Rhine-Westphalia, Germany; N.W. of Hamm; coal-mining; p. (1963) *24,700.*
Bodaibo, *t.*, R.S.F.S.R.; N.E. of L. Baikal; gold, engin.; p. (1956) *14,600.*
Bodega Bay, Cal., U.S.A.; 20 m. W. of Santa Rosa; nuclear power sta.
Bodele, *area*, Chad, W. Africa; cotton, tobacco, forage grasses.
Boden, *t.*, Sweden; on Lulea R.; mil. ctr.; comm. ctr.; p. (1961) *13,719.*
Bodensee, *see* **Constance, L.**
Bodmin, *mun. bor., co. t.*, Cornwall, Eng.; on S.W. flank of Bodmin Moor; china clay, lt. engin.; p. (1961) *6,209.*
Bodmin Moor, *upland*, N.E. Cornwall, Eng.; granite quarries, kaolin; lower slopes cultivated, higher slopes used for sheep pastures; average alt. 1,000 ft., highest point, Brown Willy, alt. 1,375 ft.
Bodö, *spt.*, Norway; within Arctic Circle at entrance to Salten Fjord, fishing, woollen goods; p. (1961) *12,445.*
Boeleleng, *spt.*, Bali, Indonesia; rice; harbour unsafe during monsoon.
Boeotia, *prov.*, Greece; a. 1221 sq. m.; p. (1961) *114,474.*
Bogalusa, *t.*, La., U.S.A.; p. (1960) *21,423.*
Bognor Regis, *t.*, *urb. dist.*, Sussex, Eng.; seaside resort; p. (1961) *28,144.*
Bogor, *t.*, Java, Indonesia; p. (1961) *154,092.*
Bogotá, *cap.*, Columbia, S. America in E. Cordilleras, 9,000 ft. above sea level; cath., museum, univ.; textiles, cement and brick mkg., leather, glassware, tyres; p. (1962) *1,329,230.*
Bogovodsk, *see* **Noginsk.**
Bohemia, former W. prov. of Czechoslovakia; abolished 1948; plateau girdled by mountains; drained by R. Elbe; agr.: wheat, rye, hops, flax, sugar-beet; minerals: lignite, graphite; mnfs. textiles, sugar, pottery, machin., boots; p. inc. Moravia (1962) *9,566,753.*
Böhmerwald (Bohemian Forest) Mtns., forested range between Czechoslovakia and Bavaria; 150 m. long; highest points; Aber, alt. 4,848 ft., Rachelberg, alt. 4,743 ft.
Bohol, *I.*, Philippines; 1,492 sq. m.
Bohotle, *t.*, Somalia, Africa; p. *1,000.*
Boiro, *commune*, La Coruña, Spain; cattle, fishing, sardine canning; p. *11,668.*
Bois-Colombes, *t.*, Seine, France; p. (1954) *27,899.*
Boise City, *t.*, *cap.*, Idaho, U.S.A.; silver, hot springs; p. (1960) *34,481.*
Boise, *R.*, Idaho, U.S.A.
Bojador, *C.*, Rio de Oro, Africa.
Bokaro, *t.*, Bihar, India; 150 m. N.W. of Calcutta; steel plant projected 1964.
Bokn Fjord, Norway; N. of Stavanger, 35 m. long, 10–15 m. wide.
Boksburg, *t.*, Transvaal, S. Africa; gold, coal; p. (1960) *70,933* inc. *27,806* whites.
Bolama, *spt.*, Port. Guinea; p. *4,000.*
Bolan Pass, Baluchistan, Pakistan; pass from Pakistan to Afghanistan; summit 5,900 ft.
Bolbec, *t.*, Seine-Maritime, France; 12 m. E. of Le Havre; p. (1954) *11,716.*
Boldon, *urb. dist.*, Durham, Eng.; p. (1961) *25,218.*
Boleslawiec (Bunzlau), *t.*, Lower Silesia, Poland, German before 1945; on the Bobrawa R., pottery; p. (1960) *23,000.*
Bolgrad, *t.*, Ukrainian S.S.R.; corn; p. *10,000.*
Bolivar, *t.*, Argentina; p. (1947) *13,773.*
Bolivar, *dep.*, Colombia, S. America, cap. Cartagena; a. 22,981 sq. m.; p. (estd. 1959) *780,650.*
Bolivar, *prov.*, Ecuador, S. America; cap. Guarando; a. 1,150 sq. m.; p. (1950) *109,305.*
Bolivar, *st.*, Venezuela; ch. t., Cuidad Bolivar; a. 91,868 sq. m.; p. (1961) *213,543.*
Bolivia, *inland rep.*, S. America, bounded by Brazil, Paraguay, Argentina, Chile and Peru; cap. nominally Sucre, actual administrative H.Q. La Paz; plateau, mountains; Boliv. Andes; volcanoes; L. Titicaca, Poope, drained by tribs. of Amazon; climate varies with elevation; monkeys, jaguars; forests; savannahs; agr. in backward condition; rubber, quinine, cattle, hides; ch. exp. tin; petroleum; language Spanish; a. 514,155 sq. m.; p. (1962) *3,556,000.*
Bolkhov, *t.*, Ukrainian S.S.R. monastery; impt. inds.; p. *10,000.*
Bollington, *t.*, *urb. dist.*, Cheshire, Eng.; nr.

Macclesfield, cotton, calico printing and dye wks.; p. (1961) *5,642.*

Bolobo, *t.*, Congo, Africa, on R. Ubangi.

Bologna, *ancient c.*, Emilia, N. Italy; on N. flank of Apennines; impt. route ctr. commanding road (over Futa Pass) and rly. (through Apennine Tunnel) across Apennines to Florence; mnfs. sugar, macaroni, nuclear research ctr.; p. (1961) *441,143.*

Bologna, *prov.*, Italy; a. 1,465 sq. m.; p. (1961) *848,440.*

Bologoye, *t.*, R.S.F.S.R.; depot and impt. junction on the Leningrad and Moscow Rly.; p. *10,000.*

Bolonchen, *t.*, Campeche, Mexico.

Bololondron, *mun. t.*, Matanzas, W. Cuba; p. (estd.) (of mun.) *11,823* (of t.) *3,710.*

Bolsena, *L.*, Latium region, Italy; occupies lge. extinct volcanic crater in S. of Tuscan Hills; a. (approx.) 50 sq. m.

Bolshoya Volga, *t.*, R.S.F.S.R.; 80 m. N. of Moscow, at junct. of Volga and Moscow Volga Canal; Soviet Institute of Nuclear Studies.

Bolson de Mapimi, *t.*, Sierra Majada, Mexico.

Bolsover, *urb. dist.*, Derby, Eng.; limestone, coal, textiles; p. (1961) *11,770.*

Bolsward, *t.*, Netherlands; dairying, linseed, bricks; p. (1947) *7,389.*

Bolt Hd., *headland*, Devon, Eng.; alt. 430 ft.

Bolton, *co. bor.*, Lancs, Eng.; cotton, iron, coal, chemicals; p. (1961) *160,887.* [abbey.

Bolton, Abbey, W.R. Yorks, Eng.; famous ruined

Bolu, *t.*, Turkey; in ancient state of Bithynia; at Hija, S. of the t., are warm medicinal springs; p. (1960) *13,743.*

Bolus Head, *C.*, Kerry, Ireland.

Bolzano, *t.*, Venetia Tridentina, Italy; on R. Isarco at S. approach to Brenner Pass; resort; p. (1961) *89,070*

Boma, *t.*, Congo, Africa, p. *10,839.*

Bomarsund, *strait*, Ahvenanmaa Is., Gulf of Bothnia.

Bombay, *former st.*, India; divided into sts. of Maharashtra and Gujarat 1 May 1960.

Bombay, Greater, *spt.*, *cap.* Maharashtra, India; harbour, docks, rly. ctr.; univ.; greatest cotton ctr. in India; pt. handles nearly half of cty's foreign tr.; p. (1961) *4,152,056.*

Bomnak, *t.*, Chita Region, U.S.S.R.; on S. slopes of Stanovoi Mtns., in valley of R. Zeya; centre of alluvial gold workings.

Bonaca I., Honduras, Central America; in Caribbean Sea.

Bonaire I., Netherlands W. Indies; off N. cst. of Venezuela; goat rearing; scantily populated.

Bonavista Bay, Newfoundland, Canada.

Bonduku, *t.*, E. Ivory Cst., nr. Ghana; impt. trading sta.; p. (estd. 1949) *5,400.*

Bondy, *commune*, France; N.E. sub. of Paris; brewing, chemicals; p. (1954) *22,411.*

Bône, *see* **Annaba.**

Bo'ness, *spt.*, *burgh*, W. Lothian, Scot.; on Firth of Forth, 4 m. E. of Grangemouth; mng., quarrying, distilling, marine engin., iron-founding, fertilisers, chemicals; p. (1961) *10,194.* [*7,357.*

Bonham, *t.*, Texas, U.S.A.; cotton; p. (1960)

Bonhill, *par.*, Dunbarton, Scot.; dyeing; p. (1951) *16,338.*

Bonifacio, *spt.*, *fort.*, Corsica, France; opposite Sardinia, on Strait of Bonifacio; cork, olive-oil, oyster tr.; p. (1954) *2,157.*

Bonin Is., Pacific Ocean; 15 islands, volcanic; 600 m. S. of Tokyo.

Bonn, *t.*, federal cap. W. Germany; at confluence of Rs. Sieg and Rhine; univ.; seat of W. German parliament; birthplace of Beethoven; metal, paper and elect. goods; p. (1963) *143,700.*

Bonne Terre, *c.*, E. Mo., U.S.A.; lead mines; p. (1960) *3,219.*

Bonneville Dam, Ore., Wash., U.S.A.; across R. Columbia 40 m. above Portland (Ore.); provides irrigation to valleys in Columbia–Snake Plateau; lge. hydro-electric power-sta.; locks permit navigation from Portland up middle courses of Columbia and Snake Rs.

Bonneville Salt Flats, Utah, U.S.A.; remains of ancient lake; world automobile speed tests, 1937–47.

Bonny, *t.*, S. Nigeria, W. Africa; at mouth of R. Bonny, Bight of Biafra.

Bonnyrigg and Lasswade, *burgh*, Midlothi an Scot.; 7 m. S.E. of Edinburgh; paper, carpets; p. (1961) *6,331.*

Bonthe, *t.*, Sierra Leone, W. Africa; p. (1963) of dist. *80,000.*

Boom, *t.*, Antwerp, Belgium; bricks, tanning, brewing; p. (1962) *17,431.*

Boonah, *t.*, Queensland, Australia; dairying.

Boone, *t.*, Iowa, U.S.A.; coal; p. (1960) *12,468.*

Booneville, *c.*, W. Ark., U.S.A.; lumber and cotton mills; tuberculosis sanatorium; p. (1960) *2,690.*

Boonton, *t.*, N.J., U.S.A.; agr. and industl. ctr.; p. (1960) *7,981.*

Boothia, *peninsula* (a. 13,100 sq. m.) and G. on Arctic coast; Franklin dist. Canada.

Bootle, *co. bor.*, Lancs, Eng.; on E. side of entrance to Mersey estuary; shipping, engin., timber, flour; p. (1961) *82,829.*

Boppard, *t.*, Rhineland Palatinate, Germany; p. (1946) *7,189.*

Borås, *t.*, S. Sweden; on R. Wiske, nr. Göteborg; cotton spinning and weaving textiles, hosiery; p. (1961) *67,069.*

Bordeaux, *spt.*, Gironde, France; nr. mouth of R. Garonne; cath., univ.; exp. wines, liqueurs, sugar, potatoes, pit props; oil refining; p. (1962) *254,122.*

Bordentown, *c.*, N.J., U.S.A.; on Delaware R.; formerly impt. pt.; p. (1960) *4,974.*

Bordeyri, *t.*, Iceland; on Rumaflot inlet.

Bordighera, *t.*, Italy; Riviera winter resort; p. *5,462.*

Bordon, Hants, Eng.; military camp.

Boreham Wood, *t.*, Herts, Eng.; light engin., computors, film studios.

Borger, *c.*, N.W. Texas, U.S.A.; gas and petroleum; p. (1960) *20,911.*

Borgerhout, sub. of Antwerp, Belgium; candle and tobacco factories; p. (1962) *51,115.*

Borgo, San Donnino, *t.*, Italy; cath.; p. *17,154.*

Borgo, San Lorenzo, *t.*, Italy; olives and wine.

Borgosesia, *commune*, N.W. Italy; on Sesia R.; textiles; p. *13,716.*

Borgo Val di Taro, *commune*, N. Italy; lignite; p. *15,209.*

Borinage, *dist.* round Mons, Belgium; coal.

Borislav, *c.*, Ukrainian S.S.R., formerly Polish; oilfield, natural gas, engin.; p. (1956) *29,600*

Borisoglebsk, *t.*, R.S.F.S.R.; p. (1959) *54,000.*

Borisokova, *t.*, Kursk, U.S.S.R.; metals.

Borisov, *t.*, Byelorussian S.S.R.; scene of defeat of Napoleon, 1812; chemicals, saw mills, hardware; p. (1959) *59,000.*

Borispool, *t.*, Ukrainian S.S.R.; p. *25,000.*

Borlänge, *t.*, Sweden; iron, paper, engin. and chemical wks.; p. (1961) *26,685.*

Bormio, *vil.*, Lombardy, Italy; alpine resort; mineral springs; p. *1,910.*

Borna, *t.*, Leipzig, E. Germany; lignite, machin. p. (1963) *19,331.*

Bornem, *t.*, Antwerp, Belgium; chemicals, elec. goods; p. (1961) *9,896.*

Borneo, lgst. island Malay Arch.; a. 285,000 sq. m., length 830 m., breadth 600 m.; Kinibalu Range, alt. 13,700 ft.; forests, jungle, swamps; rice, sago, spices, coconuts, rubber, hardwood; politically divided into Indonesian Borneo (Kalimantan) and Sabah.

Borneo, N., part of Fed. of Malaysia, *see* **Sabah.**

Bornholm, Danish I., Baltic; a. 210 sq. m. agr.; fishing; porcelain, clay; cap. Rönne; p (1960) *48,373.*

Bornu, *cty.*, Nigeria, Africa; S.W. Lake Chad formerly a Negro kingdom, 51,000 sq. m. p. (estd.) *5,000,000.*

Boroboedoer, Java, Indonesia; gr. Buddhis temple, once ruined, now restored unde government care.

Boronga Is., in Bay of Bengal.

Borongan, *t.*, Philippine Is.; on cst., 36 m. E. c Catbalogan; coconut plantations; p. (estd. *21,340.*

Borovichi, *t.*, R.S.F.S.R.; on Msta R., 160 m S.E. of Leningrad; p. (estd.) *28,500.*

Borroloola, N. Terr., Australia; sheep.

Borromean Is., four sm. islets in L. Maggiore; incl Isola Bella, site of Stresa Conf., 1935.

Borrowdale, *valley*, Cumberland, Eng.; touris resort; blacklead mines.

Borthwick, *par.*, Midlothian, Scot.; with old cas. p. (1951) *3,163.*

Borzhom, *wat. pl.*, Georgian S.S.R.; hot minera springs; p. (1956) *15,600.*

Boscastle, *sm. spt.*, Cornwall, Eng.; resort pilchard fishing.

Bosham, *vil.*, Sussex, Eng.; 4 m. W. of Chichester; court of King Canute and Roman Emperor Vespasian; Saxon church; resort, yachting, fishing.

Boskoop, *commune*, Netherlands; flowering-shrub nurseries; p. (1947) *8,571*.

Bosnia and Hercegovino, *fed. unit*, Jugoslavia; formerly part of Austria; cap. Sarajevo; mountainous, forested, fertile valleys; agr.; tobacco, cereals, fruit; cattle, sheep pigs; a. 19,768 sq. m.; p. (1960) *3,377,000*.

Bosporus or Strait of Constantinople, between Black Sea and Sea of Marmara.

Bossier City, *t.*, La., U.S.A.; p. (1960) *32,776*.

Boston, *t.*, *mun. bor.*, *spt.*, Holland, Lincs, Eng.; on R. Witham, 4 m. from the Wash; shipping, agr. mkt., timber, fruit and vegetable canning; p. (1961) *24,903*.

Boston, *spt. c.*, *cap.* Mass., U.S.A.; univ., museum; fine harbour; 2nd Atlantic pt.; comm. fisheries; metal, leather, rubber and elec. goods, textiles, shoes; rly. ctr.; p. (1960) *697,197*.

Bosworth or Market Bosworth, *t.*, *rural dist.*, Leics., Eng.; battle between Richard III and Henry VII, 1485; p. (rural dist. 1961) *27,493*.

Botany Bay, N.S.W., Australia; on E. cst., 10 m. S. of Sydney; resort; first settled by British in 1787; old penal colony.

Bothnia, G. of, N. of Baltic; between Finland and Sweden, breadth about 100 m.

Bothwell, *par.*, Lanark, Scot.; coal, iron; p. (1951) *63,185*.

Botosani, *t.*, N. Moldavia, Romania; rich pastoral cty.; flour milling, tanning; p. (1956) *29,569*.

Botswana, Rep. of, *indep. sov. st.* within Brit. Commonwealth (Sept. 1966), S.W. Africa; stretches from Orange R. to Zambesi R., and merges W. into Kalahari desert; Bamangwato ch. tribe; cap. Gaberones; cattle-rearing; a. 222,000 sq. m.; p. (est. 1965) *548,000*.

Bottrop, *t.*, N. Rhine–Westphalia, Germany; N.W. of Essen; coal, coke, chemicals; p. (1963) *112,000*.

Botucatu, *t.*, Brazil; p. (1960) *33,878*.

Bouches-du-Rhône, *dep.*, S. France; cap. Marseilles; cereals, olives, vines; pottery, silk; a. 2,035 sq. m.; p. (1962) *1,248,355*.

Bougainville I., Solomon Is., Pac. Oc.; a. 4,100 sq. m.; p. (1959) *53,130*. [Australia.

Bougainville, *C.*, jutting into Timor Sea, W.

Bougie, *see* **Bejaia**.

Bouillon, *t.*, Ardennes, Belgium; p. (1962) *3,042*.

Boulder, *t.*, West Australia; gold-mining; p. (1947) *6,463*.

Boulder, *t.*, Col., U.S.A.; gold- and silver-mining dist.; univ.; p. (1960) *37,718*.

Boulder City, *t.*, Nevada, U.S.A.; nr. Great Boulder Dam, gr. engin. project; p. (1960) *4,059*.

Boulogne-Billancourt, S.W. sub. of Paris, France; p. (1962) *107,074*.

Boulogne-sur-Mer, *spt.*, Pas de Calais, France; resort; fishing; cement; chocolates; channel ferry; p. (1962) *50,036*.

Boundary, *t.*, Yukon, Canada.

Bound Brook, *bor.*, N.J., U.S.A.; paints, chemicals, asbestos, clothing; p. (1960) *10,263*.

Bountiful, *t.*, Utah, U.S.A.; mkt. gardens, fruit, especially cherries; irrigation necessary; p. (1960) *17,039*.

Bounty I., New Zealand, S. Pac. Oc.

Bourbon l'Archambault, *t.*, France.

Bourbonnais, *old prov.*, France.

Bourbonne-es-Bains, *t.*, France; mineral springs; p. *2,881*.

Bourg-en-Bresse, *t.*, *cap.*, Ain dep., France; copper goods, pottery; p. (1954) *26,699*.

Bourges, *t.*, *cap.*, Cher dep., France; cath.; brewing, cutlery, machin., aircraft; p. (1962) *63,479*.

Bourget, *L.*, Savoy, France.

Bourg-la-Reine, *t.*, Seine, France; p. (1954) *11,708*.

Bourg-Madame, *vil.*, France; on Franco-Spanish border; international bridge. [*6,488*.

Bourgoin, *t.*, Isère, France; industl.; p. (1946)

Bourke, *t.*, N.S.W., Australia; on R. Darling nr. head of intermittent navigation, terminus of rly. running inland from Sydney and Newcastle; collects wool from sheep farms and despatches by R. to Adelaide (S. Australia) and by rail to Sydney; p. (1947) *2,205*.

Bourne, *urb. dist.*, Kesteven, Lincs., Eng.; agr. machin., manures, malting, seed growing; B.R.M. car mftg.; p. (1961) *5,339*.

Bournemouth, *co. bor.*, Hants, Eng.; on S. cst., E. of Poole Harbour; seaside resort; p. (1961) *153,965*.

Bournville, *model industl. t.*, Warwick., Eng.; 4 m. S.W. of Birmingham; initiated by Mr. Geo. Cadbury; chocolate and cocoa wks.

Bourtange, *t.*, Netherlands; nr. German frontier.

Boussu, *commune*, Belgium; coal, industl.; p. (1962) *11,488*.

Bouvet I., uninhabited island in S. Atlantic belonging to Norway, a. about 22 sq. m.

Boves, *t.*, Sommes dep., France; S.E. Amiens.

Bovino, *t.*, Apulia Italy.

Bow, *par.*, E. London, Eng.; industl.; properly Stratford-at-Bow.

Bow, *R.*, Alberta, N.W. Canada; head of Saskatchewan R.

Bow Fell, Pennine range, W.R., Yorks, Eng.

Bowden, *urb. dist.*, Cheshire, Eng.; p. (1961) *4,478*.

Bowen, *spt.*, N. Queensland; on Port Denison, 725 m. N.W. of Brisbane; in fine pastoral country; p. (1948) *3,276*.

Bowes, *t.*, W.R., Yorks, Eng.; on R. Greta S.W. of Barnard Castle; mkt. t. for Stainmore dist. of Pennines.

Bowesdorp, *t.*, Cape Prov., S. Africa.

Bowie, *t.*, N. Texas, U.S.A.; oil, gas, coal, clay mining; p. (1960) *4,566*.

Bowland, Forest of, *hills*, Lancs, Eng.; millstone grit moors; many reservoirs supply water to industl. S. Lancs.

Bowling, *vil.*, Dumbarton, Scot.; on N. bank of R. Clyde, 10 m. N.W. of Glasgow; at W. entrance to Forth and Clyde Canal; large oil refinery.

Bowling Green, *t.*, Ky., U.S.A.; tr. ctr. for agr. a.; limestone; p. (1960) *28,338*. [*7,397*.

Bowmanville, *pt.* L. Ontario, Canada; p. (1961)

Bowness, *t.*, Westmorland, Eng.; on L. Windermere; tourist ctr.

Bowness, *par.*, Cumberland, Eng.; p. *1,050*.

Box Hill, nr. Dorking, Surrey, Eng.; E. of R. Mole gap through N. Downs; chalk; wooded, fine views.

Boyacá, *dep.*, Colombia, S. America; cap. Tunja; a. 24,928 sq. m.; p. (1962) *849,390*.

Boyle, *mkt. t.*, Roscommon, Ireland; on R. Boyle; dairying; p. (1951) *1,934*.

Boyne, *R.*, Leinster, Ireland; length 80 m.

Bozrah, *ancient c.*, S. Damascus, Syria, S.W. Asia; modern Busra; many arch. remains.

Bra, *t.*, Piedmont, Italy; 28 m. S. of Turin; p. *22,263*.

Brabant, *cent. prov.*, Belgium; fertile and wooded; many breweries; mnfs. linen, cloth, paper, lace; cap. Brussels (*q.v.*); a. 1,267 sq. m.; p. (1962) *2,011,842*.

Brabant, North, *prov.*, Netherlands; S. of Gelderland; N. half of former Duchy; cattle rearing; grain, hops, beetroot, etc.; cap. s'Hertogenbosch; a. 1920 sq. m.; p. (estd. 1960) *1,512,787*.

Brac, *I.*, Adriatic Sea, Jugoslavia.

Bracadale, *vil.* and *L.*, Skye, Scotland.

Brackley, *t.*, Northants, Eng.; p. (1961) *3,202*.

Bracknell, *t.*, Berkshire, Eng.; on Thames Valley terrace, 10 m. S. of Windsor; one of "New Towns" designated 1949 to relieve population congestion in London; extends N. and W. of old vil. of Bracknell; engin., sealing compounds, plastics; central weather forecast sta.; p. (estd. 1965) *25,448*.

Brackwede, *t.*, N. Rhine–Westphalia, Germany; S.W. of Bielefeld; iron and machin.; p. (1963) *26,300*.

Brad, *t.*, Romania, on R. Muresul; p. (1956) *9,963*.

Braddock, *t.*, Penns., U.S.A.; iron and steel; p. (1960) *12,337*.

Bradford, *t.*, Penns., U.S.A.; oil; p. (1960) *15,061*.

Bradford, *co. bor.*, *c.*, W.R. Yorks, Eng.; 9 m. W. of Leeds; ctr. wool-textile inds.; engin., and chemical inds.; p. (1961) *295,768*.

Bradford-on-Avon, *t.*, *urb. dist.*, Wilts, Eng.; on R. Avon on E. flank of Cotswolds; mnfs. rubber goods, elect. instruments; p. (1961) *5,757*.

Brading, *par.*, Isle of Wight, Eng.; commands gap through central chalk ridge.

Bradwell, *par.*, Essex, mouth of R. Blackwater; civil nuclear power-sta.; p. (1961) *1,116*.

Brady, *t.*, Texas, U.S.A.; p. (1960) *5,338*.

Braemar, *par.*, in the Grampians, Aberdeen, Scot.;

containing Balmoral estate; p. (1951 with Crathie) *1,291*.

Braeriach, *mtn.*, Scot.; Inverness and Aberdeen; alt. 4,248 ft.

Braga, *c. cap.*, Minho, Portugal, nr. Oporto; cath.; wine-growing dist.; steel; p. (1950) *32,624*.

Bragança, *dist.*, Tras-os-Montes, Portugal; silk; p. (1960) *238,588*.

Bragança, *t.*, Portugal; mediæval cas.; p. (1940) *6,977*.

Brahmaputra, *R.*, India, Tsangpo in Tibet; length 1,800 m.

Braich-y-Pwll, S.W. point of Caernarvon, Wales.

Braila, *t.*, Romania; on Danube, nr. Galati; grain ctr.; p. (1956) *102,491*.

Braintree, *t.*, Mass., U.S.A.; p. (1960) *31,069*.

Braintree and Bocking, *urb. dist.*, Essex, Eng.; on Blackwater; rayon mftg., metal windows, engin.; p. (1961) *20,600*.

Brakpan, *t.*, Transvaal, S. Africa; p. (1960) *78,788*.

Brampton, *par.*, Cumberland, Eng.; tweeds; p. (1951) *2,526*.

Brampton, *t.*, Ontario, Canada; flower growing ctr., tanning, timber; p. (1961) *18,467*.

Brancaster, *par.*, Norfolk, Eng.; p. *900*.

Branco, *C.*, Brazil, Pernambuco st.

Brandenburg, *see* **Neubrandenburg**.

Brandenburg, *t.*, Potsdam, E. Germany; on R. Havel; steel, tractors, bicycles, textiles, machin.; p. (1963) *89,243*.

Brandon, *c.*, Manitoba, Canada; p. (1961) *28,166*.

Brandon and Byshottles, *urb. dist.*, Durham, Eng.; coal-mining; p. (1961) *19,531*.

Brandywine Creek, *R.*, Penns, U.S.A.; Americans defeated by British, 1777.

Branford, *t.*, Conn., U.S.A.; light mnfs., fishing, oysters; resort; p. (1960) *16,567*.

Brantford, *c.*, Ontario, Canada; farm implements, cycles, bus and truck parts; p. (1961) *55,201*.

Brasilia, *new cap.*, Brazil, Goiás st.; inaugurated 21 April 1960; 600 m. N.W. Rio de Janeiro; designed for pop. 500,000; p. (1960) *141,742*.

Brasov, *t.*, Romania; at foot of Transylvanian Alps; cloth, leather; p. (1956) *123,834*.

Brass, *t.*, Nigeria, W. Africa; at mouth of Brass R.; trading settlement.

Bratislava, *t.*, ČSSR.; on R. Danube 30 m. below Vienna; univ.; 2 palaces; rly. ctr.; textiles, chemicals, engin., oil refining; linked to Mozyr', U.S.S.R. by "Friendship Oil Pipeline"; p. (1961) *242,091*.

Bratsk, *t.*, central Irkutsk Oblast, R.S.F.S.R. on Angara R., at mouth of Oka R., 115 m. N.N.E. of Tulun; ship repair yards, lumber, iron-ore, wood processing, chemicals; large hydro-electric sta.; p. (1959) *51,000*.

Brattleboro, *t.*, Vt., U.S.A.; p. (1960) *9,315*.

Brava, *spt.*, Somalia; p. *4,000*.

Bray, *urb. dist.*, Wicklow, Ireland; on Irish Sea cst., 11 m. S. of Dublin; popular wat. pl.; p. (1961) *11,680*.

Bray Head, point on E. cst. of Ireland, S. of Dublin.

Brazil, *rep.* S. America; length 2,600 m.; greatest breadth 2,690 m.; in S. Plateau bounded on E. by mtns., in N. Amazon; mainly tropical climate, temperate on plateaus; vast forests; ch. R Amazon and tribs.; agr.: coffee, maize, sugar-cane, cotton, rubber, fruits, hardwoods; cattle-raising; minerals: manganese, iron, gold, diamonds; mnfs.: textiles, brewing; religion R.C.; administered through 21 sts., fed. dist. and 3 terrs.; cap. Brasilia; a. 3,288,063 sq. m.; p. (estd. 1960) *70,528,625*.

Brazil, *t.*, Ind., U.S.A.; coal, clay, bricks, china; p. (1960) *8,853*.

Brazil Current, *ocean current*; flows S. along E. cst. of Brazil; relatively warm.

Brazos, *R.*, Texas, U.S.A.; length 950 m.

Brazzaville, *cap.*, Congo (ex French), Equat. Africa; connected by rly. with the Atlantic at Pointe-Noire; R. pt. under construction; airport; p. (1962) *135,632*.

Breadalbane, *mountainous dist.*, W. Perth, Scot.

Brechin, *par.*; Angus, Scot.; with ancient cath., on S. Esk; sail-cloth, linen, distilling, agr. machin., lt. engin.; p. (1961) *7,114*.

Breckenridge, *t.*, N. Texas, U.S.A.; oil, gas wells; exp. cattle, grain; p. (1960) *6,273*.

Breckland, *geographical region*, S.W. Norfolk, N.W. Suffolk, Eng.; chalk, overlain by sand, gives dry soils; much heathland; sm. fertile valleys cultivated, wheat, rye, sugar-beet; ch. ts. Brandon, Lakenheath; a. 200 sq. m.

Brecknock, *co.*, Wales; mountainous; rs. Wye, Usk; cereals, dairy produce; timber; coal, iron; a. 744 sq. m.; p. (1961) *55,544*.

Brecon, (Brecknock), *mun. bor.*, Wales; agr.; p. (1961) *5,797*.

Brecon Beacons, *mtns.*, S. Wales 5 m. S. of Brecon; highest peak, 2,910 ft.; National Park.

Breda, *ancient t.*, Netherlands; fortress; rayon, linen carpets, soap, brewing; p. (1960) *107,127*.

Bredbury and Romiley, *urb. dist.*, Cheshire, Eng.; iron, steel, paper; p. (1961) *21,613*.

Bregenz, *cap.*, Vorarlberg, Austria; at E. end of L. Constance; the Roman Brigantium; resort; p. (1961) *21,428*.

Breidha Fjord, large inlet, W. coast, Iceland.

Bremen, *t.*, *spt.*, cap. of *Land* Bremen, Germany; on R. Weser 40 m. from N. Sea; ocean liner, tr. and trans-shipment pt.; imports cotton, cereals, tobacco; inds.: cars, machin., textiles, tobacco, shipbldg., oil refining, steel mill; p. (1963) *577,900*.

Bremen, *Land*, W. Germany; cattle rearing, mkt. gardening; a. 156 sq. m.; p. (1961) *706,000*.

Bremerhaven, *spt.*, Germany; "outport" of Bremen at mouth of Weser R.; docks; impt. fish. pt., shipbldg.; p. (1963) *143,200*.

Bremersdorp, *see* **Manzini**.

Bremerton, *t.*, Wash., U.S.A.; on Puget Sound; naval dockyard; elec. equipment, machin.; p. (1960) *28,922*.

Brenham, *t.*, Texas, U.S.A.; oil, cotton, dairy produce; p. (1960) *7,740*.

Brenner Pass, Italy; famous pass leading from Italy into Austria, over Alps.

Brent, *outer bor.*, Greater London, Eng.; comprising the former mun. bors. of Wembley and Willesden; p. (1964) *295,678*.

Brentford and Chiswick, *former mun. bor.*, Middx., Eng. now inc. in Hounslow (*q.v.*); brewing, soap, coal gas, light engin.; p. (1961) *54,832*.

Brentwood, *urb. dist.*, *mkt. t.*, Essex, Eng.; films, agr. implements, steel-tubing; p. (1961) *49,242*.

Brentwood, *sub.* of St. Louis, Mo., U.S.A.; residtl.; p. (1960) *12,250*.

Brescia, *t.*, Italy; cath.; palace; silks, woollens, iron and steel; p. (1961) *174,116*.

Breslau, *see* **Wroclaw**.

Bressanone, *t.*, N.E. Italy; ceded to Italy 1919 by Austria; cath., health resort; p. *9,503*.

Bressay I., Shetland Is., Scotland.

Brest, *t.*, *spt.*, Finistère dep., N.W. France; naval sta., arsenal; fishing, ropes, soap; p. (1962) *142,901*.

Brest (Brest Litovsk), *t.*, Byelorussian S.S.R., on Polish frontier; Treaty of Brest Litovsk, March 1918; route ctr. and agr. mkt.; textiles; p. (1959) *73,000*.

Bretton Woods, N.H., U.S.A.; resort; site o U.S. monetary and financial conference, 1944.

Brevik, *t.*, *pt.*, Norway; p. (1961) *12,338*.

Brewer, *t.*, Me., U.S.A.; on Penobscot R.; woo pulp, paper, bricks; p. (1960) *9,009*.

Briançon, *t.*, France; p. (1954) *8,274*.

Bridgend, *urb. dist.*, *mkt. t.*, Glamorgan, S. Wales industl. trading estate; iron, coal, stone, paper p. (1961) *15,156*.

Bridge of Allan, *burgh*. Stirling, Scot.; 2 m. N of Stirling; mineral springs; glass; p. (1961 *3,312*.

Bridgeport, *t.*, Conn., U.S.A.; sewing machines typewriters, valves, hardware, machin., rubbe and elec. goods, chemicals, plastics; p. (1960 *156,748*.

Bridgeport, *t.*, Ohio, U.S.A.; on Ohio R.; glas tin, sheet metal, boat bldg.; p. (1960) *3,824*.

Bridgeport, *bor.*, Penns., U.S.A.; iron and stee woollens, quarrying; p. (1960) *5,306*.

Bridgeton, *t.*, N.J., U.S.A.; founded by Quakers glasswks., fruit; p. (1960) *20,966*. [frui

Bridgetown, *t.*, W. Australia; S. of Perth

Bridgetown, *t.*, Barbados, W.I.; deep wat harbour; p. (1957) *18,650*.

Bridgewater, *mftg. t.*, Mass., U.S.A.; nr. Boston p. (1960) *10,268*.

Bridgewater Canal, Manchester–Runcorn–Leigh crosses ship canal by means of Barton swi bridge, length 38 m.

Bridgnorth, *mun. bor., mkt. t.,* Salop, Eng.; cas.; carpets, radio equipment; p. (1961) *7,552.*
Bridgwater, *mun. bor., pt.,* Somerset, Eng.; on R. Parrett, 10 m. from Bristol Channel; bricks and tiles, engin., wire rope, fibre fabrics, cellophane; p. (1961) *25,582.*
Bridlington *mun. bor.,* E. Riding, Yorks, Eng.; on Bridlington Bay, S. of Flamborough Head; impt. fishing; seaside resort; p. (1961) *26,007.*
Bridport, *mun. bor., mkt. t.,* Dorset, Eng.; rope, line and twine, engin., concrete prods.; sm. seaside resort; p. (1961) *6,517.*
Brie, *natural division* ("*pays*"), Central France; low, level, plateau of limestones and clays, S.E. of Paris; loam (limon) cover and plentiful water supply encourage agr.; grains, sugar-beet, fruit, dairy cattle; densely populated.
Brieg, *see* **Brzeg.**
Briel, *fortfd. spt.,* R. Maas, S. Holland, Netherlands; on Voorn I.
Brienz, *t.,* Switzerland; resort; wood carving; on L. Brienz; p. *2,637.*
Brierfield, *urb. dist.,* Lancs, Eng.; cotton weaving; p. (1961) *6,958.*
Brierley Hill, *urb. dist.,* Staffs., Eng.; on R. Stour; cut glass, castable metal goods, fire-bricks, roofing and tilling; p. (1961) *56,377.*
Brigg, *mkt. t., urb. dist.,* Lindsey, Lincs, Eng.; ctr. of agr. dist. between Lincoln Heights and Wolds; sugar-beet, jam, seed crushing, hosiery; p. (1961) *4,906.*
Brigham, *t.,* Utah, U.S.A.; sugar-beet, peaches, canning, woollens; p. (1960) *11,728.*
Brighouse, *industl. t., mun. bor.,* W.R., Yorkshire, Eng.; on R. Calder, 3 m. S.E. of Halifax; textiles and engin.; p. (1961) *30,783.*
Brightlingsea, *urb. dist.,* Essex, Eng.; on R. Colne; oysters, boat bldg.; p. (1961) *4,801.*
Brighton, *co. bor.,* E. Sussex, Eng.; 50 m. S. of London; lge. seaside resort and residtl *t.*; univ.; light inds.; p. (1961) *162,757.*
Brindisi, *spt.,* Apulia, S. Italy; on Adriatic cst. sea and air connections to Middle East; cath.; cas.; wine, olive oil, silk, petrochemicals; p. (1961) *70,084.*
Brinkley, *t.,* Ark., U.S.A.; cotton, lumber; p. (1960) *4,636.*
Brioude, *t.,* Haute-Loire, France; tr. ctr. for agr. a.; p. (1954) *5,687.*
Brisbane, *t., pt., cap.,* Queensland, Australia; univ.; docks; meats, wool, hides and skins; p. (1961) *620,121.*
Bristol, *t.,* Conn., U.S.A.; foundries, ball bearings, clocks, bells; p. (1960) *45,499.*
Bristol, *c., co., co. bor., spt.,* Gloucester–Somerset border, Eng.; on R. Avon 9 m. from Bristol Channel; "outport" at Avonmouth; cath., univ.; docks; aircraft engin., tobacco, paint, printing and light inds.; p. (1961) *436,440.*
Bristol, *t.,* Penns., U.S.A.; cottons, woollens; p. (1960) *12,364.*
Bristol, *c.,* Va., U.S.A.; dairy produce, tobacco; (p. (1960) *17,144.*
Bristol, *t.,* R.I., U.S.A.; fish, textiles, rubber goods, shoes, wire, yacht wks., yachting; p. (1960) *14,570.*
Bristol, *t.,* Tenn., U.S.A.; rayon, paper, leather goods, furniture, mining equipment, transport ctr., especially for cattle; p. (1960) *17,582.*
Bristol Channel, arm of the Atlantic between S. cst. of Wales and Somerset and Devon; noted tidal bores.
British Antarctic Territory, *Brit. col.,* created 3 March 1962; consists of all land and Is. S. of lat. 60° S. and between 20° and 80° W. longitude; comprising Graham Land peninsula, S. Shetlands, S. Orkneys and smaller Is., excluding S. Georgia and S. Sandwich Is. *See* **K190.**
British Columbia, *prov.,* Canada; mountainous, largely forested; principal Rs.: Columbia, Fraser, Kootenay, Peace; climate: temperate, rainy on coast, drier interior; communications: rlys.; lumbering, farming, dairying and livestock; fruit growing, canning, salmon fisheries; minerals: coal, copper, gold, lead, silver, oil in N.E.; cap. Victoria; a. 355, 855 sq. m.; p. (1961) *1,629,082.*
British East Africa, formerly comprised Kenya, Tanganyika, Uganda, together with the islands of Zanzibar and Pemba. *See* under their respective headings.
British Guiana, *see* **Guyana.**
British Honduras, *self-gov. Br. col.,* Central America; heavy rainfall; tropical forests; mahogany, logwood, bananas; poor communications; cap. Belize; subject to tropical hurricanes; a. 8,866 sq. m.; p. (estd. 1965) *103,000.*
British Indian Ocean Terr., *Brit. col.,* created Nov. 1965; consists of the Chagos Archipelago (of which Diego Garcia is lgst. I.) 1200 m. N.E. of Mauritius, and Is. of Aldabra, Farquhar, and Desroches in the W. Indian Oc.; p. (1965) *1,400*; to provide defence facilities for U.K. and U.S. Govts.
British Is., *archipelago,* N.W. Europe, comprising 2 large islands: Great Britain, Ireland; and 5,000 small islands; a. 121,633 sq. m.
British Solomon Is., *prot.,* W. Pacific; coconuts, rubber, pineapples, bananas; a. 11,500 sq. m.; p. (estd.) *137,000.*
British Virgin Islands, *see* **Virgin Islands.**
British West Africa, formerly comprised Gambia, Sierra Leone, Gold Coast (Ghana), Nigeria, and parts of Togoland and Cameroons. *See* under their separate headings.
Briton Ferry, *t., pt.,* Glam., S. Wales; at mouth of R. Neath; steel wks., engin., ship-breaking.
Brittany, *prov.,* France; farming; fishing; a. 13,643 sq. m.; p. *3,000,000.*
Brittle, *L.,* Skye, Scot.
Brive, *t.,* Corrèze dep., France; vegetables, wines; truffles, straw; p. (1962) *43,683.*
Brixham, *urb. dist.,* S. Devon, Eng.; fishing; resort; p. (1961) *10,679.*
Brixton, *dist.,* S.W. London, Eng.
Brno, *t.,* ČSSR.; brewing, cloth, engin.; cath. univ.; p. (1961) *314,379.*
Broad Haven, *t.,* New Town planned on St. Brides Bay, Wales.
Broad Law, *mtn.,* Peebles, Scot.
Broads, The, Norfolk, Eng.; yachting, fishing and fowling centre.
Broadstairs, *urb. dist.,* Kent, Eng.; seaside resort; 3 m. N.E. of Ramsgate; p. (1961) *16,979.*
Broadway, *par.,* Worcester, Eng.; tourist ctr., Cotswolds; p. *1,860.*
Brocken, Harz Mtns., Germany; highest point [(3,745 ft.).
Brockport, *t.,* N.Y., U.S.A.; dairying, mkt. gardens; N.Y. St. Teachers' College; p. (1960) *5,256.*
Brockton, *c.,* Mass., U.S.A.; shoes, machin.; p. [(1960) *72,813.*
Brockville, *c.,* Ont., Canada; entry pt. on R. St. Lawrence; farm implements; marine engin.; p. (1961) *17,744.*
Brody, *t.,* Ukranian S.S.R.; oil, linked to Czechoslovakia by "Friendship Oil Pipeline".
Broken Hill, *c.,* N.S.W., Australia; silver, lead, zinc; ctr. wool-producing area; p. (1961) *31,268.*
Broken Hill, Zambia; comm. and mng. ctr., lead, zinc, vanadium; p. *30,000* (inc. *4,400* Europeans).
Bromberg, *see* **Bydgoszcz.**
Bromborough, *see* **Bebington and Bromborough.**
Bromley, *former mun. bor.,* Kent, Eng.; now outer bor., Greater London, inc. Beckenham, Chislehurst, and Sidcup (S. of the A.20) Orpington, Penge; p. (1964) *294,344.*
Bromsgrove, *urb. dist., old mkt. t.* Worcs., Eng.; 13 m. S.W. Birmingham; wrought ironwk., lt. engin.; p. (1961) *34,474.*
Bromyard, *urb. dist., mkt. t.,* Hereford, Eng.; hops, glove mkg., engin., floor-tiles; p. (1961) *1,681.*
Bron, *t.,* Rhône, France; p. (1954) *14,195.*
Bronx, one of the five boroughs of N.Y. City, U.S.A.; and connected by bridges with bor. of Manhattan; p. (1960) *1,424,815.*
Bron y Mor, *t.,* Cardigan Bay, Wales; new seaside [town.
Brookline, sub. of Boston, Mass., U.S.A.; resdtl.; p. (1960) *54,044.*
Brooklyn, *bor.,* N.Y. City, linked with Manhattan bor. by Brooklyn, Manhattan and Williamsburgh suspension bridges across East R.; and with Staten I. by Verrazano-Narrows bridge (longest in world); mainly residtl. with numerous mftg. and comm. interests; p. (1960) *2,627,319.*
Broom, *loch* on N.W. cst. of Ross and Cromarty, Scot.
Broome, *t.,* W. Australia; pearl fishing; p. *754.*
Brora, *t.,* Sutherland, Scot.; on E. cst., 12 m. N.E. of Dornoch Firth; ctr. of sm. coalfield; Harris Tweed ind.
Brotton, *t.,* N.R. Yorks, Eng., nr. Guisborough; iron and steel mftg.
Brough, *mkt. t.,* Westmorland, Eng.; in upper Vale of Eden, 4 m. N. of Kirkby-Stephen.
Broughshane, *vil.,* Antrim, N. Ireland.

Broughton, *par.*, Lancs, Eng.; iron- and copper-mines.
Brownhills, *urb. dist.*, Staffs, coal-mining; p. (1961) *26,392*.
Brownsville, *t.*, Texas, U.S.A.; livestock, sugar-cane; p. (1960) *48,040*.
Brown Willy, *mtn.*, Cornwall, Eng.; alt. 1,375 ft.
Brownwood, *t.*, Texas, U.S.A.; exp. cotton, grain, wool, poultry, dairy prod.; p. (1960) *16,974*.
Broxbourne, *t.*, Hertford, Eng.; on gravel terrace to W. of R. Lea about 20 m. N.E. of London; ctr. of very intensively cultivated district, mkt.-garden and glasshouse crops; light inds.; "dormitory" t. linked with London; p. (1961) *3,839*.
Bruay-en-Artois, *t.*, Pas de Calais, France; p. (1954) *31,923*.
Bruchsal, *t.*, Baden-Württemberg, Germany; tobacco, paper, machin.; p. (1963) *23,600*.
Bruck, *t.*, Austria; p. (1961) *16,087*.
Brue, *R.*, Somerset, Eng.
Bruges (Brugge), *t.*, *inland pt.*, Belgium; mkt.-hall with 13th-century belfry; univ.; impt. mkt. for grain, cattle, horses, engin., elec. goods; glass, textiles, lace; p. (1962) *52,463*.
Brühl, *t.*, N. Rhine-Westphalia, Germany; 8 m. S. of Cologne; cas.; lignite, iron, sugar refining; p. (1963) *37,200*.
Brunei, *Br. prot. st.*, N. Borneo; oilfields; cutch, rubber, sago; a. 2,226 sq. m.; p. (est. 1960) *83,877*.
Brünn, *see* **Brno**.
Brunsbüttelkoog, *t.*, mouth of Elbe, canal opposite Cuxhaven, Germany; p. (estd. 1954) *10,100*.
Brunswick (Braunschweig), *c.*, Lower Saxony, Germany; on R. Oker; medieval bldgs.; canning, tinplate mftg., optics, pianos, drugs, vehicles; p. (estd. 1954) *236,900*.
Brunswick, *t.*, Me., U.S.A.; p. (1960) *9,444*.
Brussels, *c.*, *cap.* Belgium; town hall, palace, parliament houses, univ., museum; mnfs., lace, carpets, silk, cottons, rayon; p. (1962) *1,453,581* inc. subs.; of c. *169,211*.
Bryan, *t.*, Texas, U.S.A.; mkt. ctr.; cotton gins, compresses; oil mills; p. (1960) *27,542*.
Bryansk, *t.*, R.S.F.S.R.; sawmilling, engin., textiles, chemicals, phosphates, steel; oil pipeline from Kuybyshev under constr.; p. (1959) *206,000*.
Brynmawr, *urb. dist.*, Brecon, Wales; iron, coal, steel, rubber goods; p. (1961) *6,471*.
Brzeg, (Brieg), *t.*, Silesia, Poland; German before 1945; on R. Oder; chemicals; p. (1960) *24,000*.
Bua, *t.*, Fiji Islands, Pacific.
Bucaramanga, *t.*, cap. Santander, Colombia; coffee; cigar and cigarette mkg.; p. (estd. 1962) *221,779*.
Buchan Ness, *C.*, nr. Peterhead, E. Scot.
Bucharest, *c.*, *cap.*, Romania; cath.; palace, univ.; textiles, grain, chemicals, pharmaceutics, oil refinery engin.; p. (1960) *1,291,000*.
Buckfast, S. Devon, Eng.; famous Abbey.
Buckfastleigh, *urb. dist.*, S. Devon, Eng.; wool, quarrying; p. (1961) *2,550*.
Buckhannon, *t.*, W. Va., U.S.A.; agr. and pastoral ctr.; coal, gas, lumber, leather; p. (1960) *6,386*.
Buckhaven, and Methil, *burgh*, Fife, Scot.; on N. side of Firth of Forth, 8 m. N.E. of Kirkcaldy; coal, oilsilk, brickmkg. inds; p. (1961) *21,104*.
Buckie, *burgh*, Banff, Scot.; boat- and yacht-bldg.; fisheries; p. (1961) *7,666*.
Buckingham, *co.*, England; wooded, beeches; includes Vale of Aylesbury; farming, dairy produce, ducks, sheep; mnfs., chairs, lace, paper; a. 749 sq. m.; p. (1961) *486,183*.
Buckingham, *mun. bor.*, Bucks, Eng.; on Ouse R.; agr. bricks; p. (1961) *4,377*.
Buckley, *urb. dist.*, Flint, Wales; small castings; (1961) *7,658*. [p. (1960) *12,276*.
Bucyrus, *t.*, Ohio, U.S.A.; machine-mnfs.;
Budafoc, *sub.* of Budapest, Hungary.
Budapest, *twin-cap.*, Hungary; Buda on right bank and Pest on left bank of Danube; parlt., univ.; steel, textiles, chemicals, engin., motor-buses, oil refining; mineral springs; p. (1962) *1,844,000*.
Budaun, *t.*, Uttar Pradesh, India; sugar-cane, rice; ruins; p. (1961) *58,770*.
Bude, *see* **Stratton and Bude**, Cornwall.
Budejovice, *t.*, ČSSR.; pencils, beet, porcelain, anthracite, domestic woodware; p. (1961) *63,949*.

Budge-Budge, *t.*, W. Bengal, India; hemp, rice; p. (1961) *39,824*. [p. (1961) *3,871*.
Budleigh Salterton, *urb. dist.*, E. Devon; resort;
Buena Park, *t.*, Cal., U.S.A.; citrus fruits, truck farms, oilfields; p. (1960) *46,401*.
Buenaventura, *spt.*, Colombia; lumber yards, tanning, fish canning; p. (estd. 1962) *60,220*.
Buenos Aires, *c.*, *cap.* Argentina; on R. La Plaat, fine buildings, lgst. c. in S. hemisphere; univ.; tr. ctr.; carpets, cloth, cigars, boots and shoes, iron-ore; p. (1960) *2,967,000*.
Buenos Aires, *prov.*, Argentina; a. 118,467 sq. m.; treeless plain; sheep and cattle; cereals, fruit, tobacco; p. (1960) *6,735,000*.
Buffalo, *c.*, *pt.*, N.Y., U.S.A.; on L. Erie; univ.; iron, steel, oil refining, aircraft, car parts, elec. goods, textiles, meat packing, brewing; p. (1960) *532,759*. [348 m.
Bug, *R.*, in Ukraine, flows into Black Sea; length
Bug, *R.*, Poland; trib. of Vistula R.; since 1939 frontier between Poland and Ukraine S.S.R.
Buga, *c.*, Colombia, S. America; tr. ctr. for sugar, coffee, cacao, rice, cotton; p. (estd. 1959) *75,220*.
Buganda, *prov.*, Uganda, E. Africa; located W. of L. Victoria largely at alt. between 4,500 and 6,000 ft.; intensive cultivation, cotton (ch. comm. crop), plantains, millets; cap. Kampala.
Bugisu, *dist.*, Uganda; coffee.
Bugulma, *t.*, Tatar A.S.S.R., R.S.F.S.R.; oil ctr.; p. (1959) *61,000*.
Builth Wells, *urb. dist.*, N. Brecknock, Wales; on upper course, R. Wye; medicinal springs; p. (1961) *1,602*.
Buitenzorg, *see* **Bogor**. [*12,796*.
Bujalance, *c.*, Spain; E. of Cordova; p. (1957)
Bukhara (Bokhara), *t.*, Uzbek S.S.R., U.S.S.R.; in Amu Darya valley at W. foot of Tien Shan; mkt. for cotton, sunflower seed, wheat grown in irrigated Bukhara Oasis; impt. tr. ctr. at W. terminus of ancient caravan route from China; linked by Trans-Caspian rly. to Krasnovodsk, by Turk-Sib. rly to Novo Sibivsk; natural gas nearby; pipeline to Urals; textiles; p. (1959) *69,000*. [*53,700*.
Bukittinggi, *t.*, Sumatra, Indonesia; p. (1957)
Bukoba, *t.*, *pt.*, Tanzania, E. Africa; located midway along W. shore of L. Victoria; exp. coffee, rice, plantains and other foodstuffs to L. pts. in Kenya and Uganda.
Bukovina, Northern, formerly Romania, ceded to U.S.S.R. in 1940; now part of Ukraine; a. about 6,000 sq. km.; ch. t. Chernovitsy; Carparthian Mtns., forested; farming, cereals; cattle.
Bulawayo, *t.*, Rhodesia; impt. rly. and indus. ctr.; airpt.; agr. mnfs.; p. (1962) *190,000* inc. *50,000* whites.
Buldan, *t.*, Turkey; p. (1960) *10,431*.
Bulgaria, *rep.*, Eastern Europe; mountainous; Balkan Mtns., R. Danube N. boundary; climate: hot summer, cold winter, milder in S.; heavy summer rainfall; 5 lge. dams; hydro-electric stas.; religion: Greek Orthodox; communications: main rail from Central Europe passes through to Istanbul; grain, wines, rose-oil, pigs, iron, manganese, copper, lead, zinc, pyrites, salt, chemicals, oil; a. 42,796 sq. m.; p. (1962) *8,000,000*.
Bulla, *t.*, Bourke, Victoria, Australia.
Bullawarra, *t.*, Queensland, Australia.
Bulli, *t.*, N.S.W. Australia; on E. cst., 40 m. S. o Sydney; impt. coal-mining ctr.
Bultfontein, *t.*, Cape Province, S. Africa; dia monds; p. (1960) *3,491* inc. *1,380* whites.
Bunbury, *t.*, *spt.*, W. Australia; on cst. 112 m. S of Fremantle; pt. and comm. ctr. of lge pastoral, agr., fruit growing and timber dist. lge. co-op. butter factory; p. (1961) *13,351*.
Buncrana, *urb. dist.*, Donegal, Ireland; salmon p. (1961) *2,960*.
Bundaberg, *t.*, Queensland, Australia; on Burnet R.; sugar factories, timber, dairying, mining p. (1961) *22,791*.
Bungay, *urb. dist.*, Suffolk, Eng.; on R. Waveney printing, malting; p. (1961) *3,581*.
Bunker Hill, Charlestown, now part of Bostor Mass., U.S.A.; battle between Americans an British, 1775.
Buntingford, *par.*, Herts, Eng.; on E. Anglia Heights, 10 m. N.W. of Bishop's Stortford; (1961) *1,559*.
Bunzlau, *see* **Boleslawiec**. [*50,00*
Buraida, *t.*, Nejd, Saudi Arabia; p. (estd

Burbank, *c.*, Cal., U.S.A.; airport, aeroplanes; p. (1960) *90,155.*

Burdur, *t.*, Turkey; p. (1960) *25,372.*

Bure, *R.*, Norfolk, Eng.

Burg, *t.*, Magdeburg, E. Germany; on Ihle Canal; leather goods, iron, furniture, machin.; p. (1963) *30,026.*

Burgas, *spt.*, Bulgaria; on Black Sea; copper, engin., chemicals, textiles; oil refining; pt. for oil tankers under construction; p. (1956) *72,795.*

Burgenland, *prov.*, Austria; a. 1,526 sq. m.; p. (1961) *271,001.*

Burgess Hill, *urb. dist.*, Sussex, Eng.; bricks, tiles; p. (1961) *13,990.*

Burghead, *burgh.*, Moray, Scot.; on Moray Firth, 7 m. N.W. of Elgin; fisheries; p. (1961) *1,346.*

Burgos, *c.*, Spain; cath.; hosiery, leather cloth; p. (1959) *87,520.*

Burgos, *prov.*, Old Castile, Spain; ch. t., Burgos; oil; a. 5,425 sq. m.; p. (1959) *401,891.*

Burgstädt, *t.*, Karl-Marx-Stadt, E. Germany; textiles, machin.; p. (1963) *17,167.*

Burgundy, *old prov.*, N.E. France; composed largely of upper valley of R. Saône; famous vineyards; strategic position on route leading between plateau of Vosges and Jura Mtns. from Rhône valley to Rhine valley.

Burhanpur, *t.*, Madhya Pradesh, India; ancient walled Mogul city; textiles, brocades; p. (1961) *82,090.*

Burlington, *t.*, S. Ont., Canada, on L. Ontario, N.E. of Hamilton; in fruit-growing a.; industl. development; tourism; p. (estd.) *47,000.*

Burlington, *c.*, Iowa, U.S.A.; on bluffs of Mississippi R.; machin., furniture; p. (1960) *32,430.*

Burlington, *pt.*, Vt., U.S.A.; E. side of L. Champlain; state univ.; timber; p. (1960) *35,531.*

Burma (Union of), *rep.* 1948; ch. mtns.: Arakan Yoma, Pegu Yoma; chief rivers: Irrawaddy, Salween; forested; agr.: rice, fruit, tobacco; timber, teak; minerals; petroleum, precious stones, rubies, sapphires; inds.: carving, lacquer; cap. Rangoon; a. 261,789 sq. m., p. (estd.) *21,526,824.*

Burnham, *par.*, nr. Maidenhead, Berks, Eng.; public woodland, "Burnham Beeches."

Burnham-on-sea, *t.*, *urb. dist.*, Somerset, Eng.; on Bridgwater Bay, 10 m. S. of Weston-super-Mare; resort; p. (1961) *9,850.*

Burnham-on-Crouch, *urb. dist.*, Essex, Eng.; yacht sailing, oysters, boat bldg.; p. (1961) *4,167.*

Burnie, *spt.*, Tasmania, Australia; pastoral and agr., paper pulp mftg.; p. (1961) *14,380.*

Burnley, *industl. t.*, *co. bor.*, Lancs, Eng.; cotton, weaving, coal; p. (1961) *80,588.*

Burntisland, *royal burgh*, East Fife, Scot.; on F. of Forth, nr. Kirkcaldy; shipbldg., aluminium inds.; p. (1961) *6,036.*

Burra, E. and W., two Shetland Is., Scot.

Burray, one of the Orkney Is., Scot.

Burriana, *t.*, *spt.*, Spain; oranges, wine; p. (1957) *17,697.*

Burrinjuck, *t.*, N.S.W. Australia; on Murrumbidgee R., N. of Canberra; site of impt. dam providing irrigation in Riverina dist.

Burry Port, *urb. dist.*, Carmarthen, Wales; p. (1961) *5,671.*

Bursa, *c.*, Turkey; 60 m. S. Istanbul; fruits, carpets, tapestry; cap. of Bithynia prior to the Christian Era, and later of the Ottoman Empire; p. (1960) *153,574.*

Burslem, *t.*, part of Stoke-on-Trent, Staffs.

Burton Latimer, *urb. dist.*, Northants., Eng.; p. (1961) *4,401.*

Burton-on-Trent, *industl. t.*, *co. bor.*, Staffs, Eng.; brewing, malting, rubber goods, engin., steel, footwear, chemicals; p. (1961) *50,766.*

Buru, *I.*, Indonesia; W. of Serang.

Burujird, *t.*, Iran; cotton, carpets; p. (1956) *49,228.*

Burundi, *indep. kingdom* (1 July 1962), formerly Urundi, part of U.N. trust terr. of Ruanda-Urundi under Belgian adm.; cap. Bujumbura; coffee; a. 10,747 sq. m.; p. (est. 1962) *2,213,000.*

Bury, *industl. t.*, *co. bor.*, S.E. Lancs.; on R. Irwell to S. of Rossendale Fells; cotton, textiles, engin., paper mkg.; p. (1961) *59,984.*

Bury St. Edmunds, *mun. bor.*, W. Suffolk; monastic remains; farm implements, brewing, sugar-beet processing; p. (1961) *21,144.*

Buryat, *rep.*, R.S.F.S.R., U.S.S.R.; lge. deposit of graphite; ch. t. Ulan Ude; a. 135,500 sq. m.; p. (1959) *671,000.*

Bushey, *t.*, *urb. dist.*, Herts., Eng.; p. (1961) *20,666.*

Bushire, *spt.*, Iran; on Persian G.; exp. carpets, hides, tobacco, fruit, nuts, drugs, cotton; p. *c.* *30,000.*

Buskerud, *co.*, Norway; a. 5,738 sq. m.; p. (1963) *170,441.*

Busto Arsizio, *t.*, Varese prov., N. Italy; 19 m. N.W. of Milan; cotton milling ctr., iron, steel, rayon, textile machin.; p. (1961) *64,367.*

Bute, *I.*, *co.*, Firth of Clyde, Scotland; 16 m. long and 3–5 m. broad; ch. t., Rothesay; a. 218 sq. m.; p. (1961) *15,129.*

Bute, Kyles of, *strait*, 6 m. between isle of Bute and Argyll.

Buton, *I.*, off coast of Sulawesi I., Indonesia.

Butt of Lewis, *promontory* with lighthouse; Lewis, Hebrides, Scot.

Butte, *c.*, Montana, U.S.A.; copper, lead, silver; p. (1960) *27,877.*

Buttermere, *vil.*, Cumberland, Eng.; tourist resort.

Buttermere, *L.*, Cumberland, Eng.; 1¼ m. long, ¾ m. wide.

Buxton, *mun. bor.*, Derby, Eng.; wat. p. nr. High Peak dist.; spa t.; p. (1961) *19,236.*

Buzau, *t.*, Romania; rly. ctr.; cath.; wheat, timber, petroleum; p. (1960) *75,569.*

Buzuluk, *t.*, R.S.F.S.R.; in Urals; engin.; ctr. of agr. a.; p. (1959) *55,000.*

Bydgoszcz (former German **Bromberg**), *t.*, Poland; on R. Brda; engin., textiles, chemicals, lignite; p. (1960) *231,000.*

Byelorussia (White Russia), *constituent rep.*, U.S.S.R.; cap. Minsk; a. 81,090 sq. m.; p. (1959) *8,060,000.*

Byron C., most easterly point of Australia, Pacific coast of N.S.W.

Bytom (Beuthen), *t.*, Upper Silesia, Poland; German before 1945; coal, zinc, lead and iron mining; iron inds.; p. (1960) *182,000.*

C

Cabo Juby, Spanish terr. on Atlantic coast, N. of Rio de Oro, N. Africa.

Cabot Strait, entrance of Gulf of St. Lawrence between C. Breton I. and Newfoundland.

Cabra, *t.*, Spain; 30 m. S.E. of Córdova; college; p. (1957) *22,174.*

Cabrera I., Balearic Is.; in Mediterranean, 9 m. S. of Majorca; a. 8 sq. m.; penal settlement.

Cáceres, *prov.*, W. Spain; pastoral; a. 7,705 sq. m.; p. (1959) *566,202.*

Cáceres, *t.*, Spain; largest bull-ring in Spain, ancient Castra Caecilia; p. (1957) *52,000.*

Cachan *t.*, Seine, France; p. (1954) *16,965.*

Cachar, *dist.*, Assam, India; tea-growing ctr.; a. 2,688 sq. m.; p. (1961) *1,378,476.*

Cachoeira, *t.*, nr. Salvador, Brazil; p. (1960) *39,470.*

Cadarache, *t.*, S. France; nr. Aix-en-Provence; nuclear research centre.

Cader Idris, *mtn.*, Merioneth, Wales; alt. 2,929 ft.

Cadillac, *t.*, Mich., U.S.A.; rubber tyres, wood and metal prod.; p. (1960) *10,112.*

Cadiz, *maritime prov.*, S. Spain; cap. Cadiz; a. 2,827 sq. m.; p. (1959) *811,581.*

Cadiz, *fortress t.*, *spt.*, Andalusia, S. Spain; sherry, cork, fruit, olive oil, tunny fish; naval base; univ.; one of most ancient ts. in Europe, built by Phoenicians, *c.* 1100 B.C.; p. (1959) *113,325.*

Caen, *c. cap.*, Calvados, France; fine church and abbey, tomb of William the Conqueror; univ.; iron ore, lace, gloves exported; scene of fierce fighting in Second World War, when it was severely damaged; p. (1962) *95,238.*

Caerleon, *urb. dist.*, Monmouth, Eng.; on R. Usk, 3 m. N.E. of Newport; Roman remains; agr. machin. tools, bricks; p. (1961) *4,184.*

Caernarvon, *t.*, *royal bor.*, *cap.*, Caernarvonshire, N. Wales; on S. shore of Menai Strait; cas. where first Prince of Wales (Edward II) was christened; slate, bricks, plastics; p. (1961) *8,998.*

Caernarvonshire, *mtnous. marit. co.*, N. Wales; slate and stone quarries, lead-mines; oats, barley, sheep, cattle; highest peak, Snowdon (3,560 ft.); a. 569 sq. m.; p. (1961) *121,194.*

Caerphilly, *t.*, *urb. dist.*, Glamorgan, S. Wales; cas.; coal, iron, light inds.; p. (1961) *36,008.*

Caesarea, *t.*, on coast of Israel; once the official residence of the Herods and Roman Governors of Palestine.

Caesarea Mazaca, Turkey; once residence of Kings of Cappadocia; now tr. ctr.

Caeté, *t.*, Minas Geraes st., Brazil; at foot of Serra do Espinhaço, 50 m. E. of Belo Horizonte; lge. iron and steel wks.

Cagayan, *prov.*, Luzon, Philippine Is.; p. (estd.) *320,000*.
Cagliari, Italian *prov.*, comprising S. half of Sardinia; a. 5,179 sq. m.; p. (1961) *733,489*.
Cagliari, *spt.*, *cap.* Sardinia, on S. cst.; cath. and univ.; exp. lead, zinc; p. (1961) *181,499*.
Cagnes-sur-Mer, *t.*, Alpes-Maritimes dep., France; Riviera resort; p. (1954) *11,066*.
Caha, *mtns.*, on boundary of Cork and Kerry, Ireland; cas.; highest point 2,249 ft.
Caher, *t.*, Tipperary, Ireland; on R. Suir; ancient cas. and abbey; p. (1951) *1,589*.
Cahirciveen, *t.*, Kerry, Ireland; p. (1951) *1,687*.
Cahors, *t.*, *cap.*, Lot, France; cath.; distilleries, shoe factories; p. (1954) *15,384*.
Caibarien, *t.*, Cuba; sugar pt.; p. (1953) *22,657*.
Caicos Is., *see* **Turks and Caicos Is.**
Cairngorm, *mtn.*, Inverness and Banff, Scot.; alt. 4,084 ft.; national nature reserve.
Cairns, *spt.*, Queensland, Australia; on Trinity Bay; fine sugar, tropical fruit growing, dairying, mining; p. (1961) *25,358*.
Cairntoul, *mtn.*, Inverness and Aberdeen, Scot.; [alt. 4,241 ft.
Cairo, *c.*, *cap.* U.A.R.; on R. bank of Nile at head of Nile delta; univ.; tourist ctr.; mnfs. cotton, paper, silk; p. (1960) *3,346,000*.
Cairo, Ill., U.S.A.; confluence of Mississippi and Ohio; extensive traffic; p. (1960) *9,348*.
Caister, *vil.*, N. of Yarmouth, Norfolk, Eng.; ruined cas.; holiday resort.
Caithness, *co.*, Scot.; most N. part of mainland; flat, with much moorland; herring fishery; poor agr.; quarrying; ch. ts. Wick, Thurso; a. 686 sq. m.; p. (1961) *27,345*.
Caivano, *industl. t.*, Italy; N.E. of Naples.
Cajalco Reservoir, S. Cal., U.S.A.; hill-top location nr. Riverside, 55 m. S.E. of Los Angeles; stores water brought 242 m. by aqueduct from Parker Res. on R. Colorado, for distribution throughout Los Angeles plain.
Cajamarca, *dep.* N. Peru; mining and agr.; a. 12,538 sq. m.; p. (1961) *543,090*.
Cajamarca, *t.*, *cap.*, Cajamarca prov., Peru; mng. ctr., dairying, cloth, leather, straw hats; thermal springs; p. (1961) *37,000*.
Calabar, *spt.*, S.E. Nigeria, W. Africa; exp. palm oil, kernels, rubber, ivory; p. *16,653*.
Calabozo, *t.*, N. Venezuela, S. America; cattle, agr., tr. ctr.; p. *7,123*.
Calabria, *region*, extreme S.W. Italy; mountainous and fertile; highest point Mt. Pollino 7,325 ft.; ch. R. Crati; cereals, wine, olives, fruit; copper, marble; tunny fish; a. 5,830 sq. m.; p. (1961) *2,045,215*.
Calafat, *t.*, Romania; on Bulgarian frontier, opp. Vidin; p. (1956) *8,069*.
Calahorra, *t.*, Logrono, Spain; cath.; pimentoes, wine; on R. Ebro; p. (1957) *13,524*.
Calais, *spt.*, Pas de Calais, N.E. France; cross-channel ferry pt. opposite to and 21 m. distant from Dover; lace, fishing; p. (1962) *70,707*.
Calama, *oasis*, Antofagasta prov., N. Chile; in Atacama desert at foot of Andean Cordillera, 130 m. N.E. of Antofagasta on main rly. to La Paz; water from R. Loa supplies Antofagasta and used for irrigation locally.
Calama, *t.*, alt. 7,430 ft.; explosives; p. (1960) [*20,000*.
Calamar, *t.*, Bolivar dep., Colombia; on R. Magdalena 60 m. from mouth, connected by rail to Cartagena; handles traffic between Cartagena and Magdalena valley; p. (estd. 1959) *21,000*.
Calamianes Is., Philippine Is.; between Mindoro and Palawan Is. [p. *11,285*.
Calañas, *commune*, S. Spain; pyrites, olives;
Calarasi, *t.*, S.E. Romania; on the Danube; comm. ctr.; p. (1956) *25,555*.
Calasiao, *t.*, Luzon, Philippines; hats; p. (1948) [*23,269*.
Calatafimi, *commune*, Sicily; Garibaldi defeated Neapolitans, May 1860; p. *11,484*.
Calatayud, *t.*, Spain; 55 m. S.W. Saragossa; cas.; weapons; flour milling; p. (1957) *18,762*.
Calbayog, *t.*, Samar, Philippine Is.; hemp trade, fisheries; p. (1948) *79,503*.
Calbe, *t.*, Magdeburg, E. Germany; on R. Saale; iron smelting, lignite mng., machin., chemicals; p. (1963) *16,859*.
Calcutta, *c.*, *spt.*, W. Bengal, India; on R. Hooghli; vast tr. from Ganges plain; univ.; jute-mills; exp. jute, cotton, sugar-cane, rice, tea, silk, coal; p. (1961) corporation a. *2,927,289*; metropolitan a. *5,500,195*.
Caldas, *dep.*, Colombia, S. America; cap. Manizales; a. 5,160 sq. m.; p. (1962) *1,399,590*.
Calder, *t.*, S.W. Midlothian; shale mines, oilwks.; p. *3,200*.
Calder, *R.*, Lancs, Eng.; joins the Ribble.
Calder, *R.*, W.R. Yorks, Eng.; trib. of Aire R.
Calder Hall, Cumberland; first full-scale nuclear power sta. in world (1956) owned and operated by U.K. Atomic Energy Authority; electricity and plutonium prod.
Caldwell, *t.*, Idaho, U.S.A.; p. (1960) *12,230*.
Caldy I., off Pembroke coast, Wales; lighthouse; Trappist monastery.
Caledonian Canal, from Moray Firth to Loch Linnhe, Scot., connecting North Sea with Atlantic; 62½ m. long; opened in 1822.
Calf of Man, *sm. I.*, S.W. I. of Man, Eng.; a. 620 acres.
Calgary, *ch. t.*, Alberta, Canada; ctr. of ranching country; lumber-mills, tanneries, oil refining; p. (1961) *279,062*.
Cali, *t.*, *cap.*, Valle del Cauca, Colombia; on Cauca R.; comm. ctr.; in rich agr. a.; coal mined nearby; textiles, tyres, paper, plastics; p. (estd. 1962) *693,120*.
Calicut, *spt.*, *mftg. t.*, Kerala, India; exp. coffee, spices; p. (1961) *192,521*.
California, most impt. of Pacific States, U.S.A.; mountainous and forested but fertile valleys; salubrious climate; rich in minerals, oil, natural gas, gold, silver, copper, steel; oil refining; films; fruit; cap. Sacramento; ch. pt. San Francisco, lgst. c. Los Angeles; has 279 incorporated cities; a. 158,693 sq. m.; p. (1964) *18,084,000*.
California Current, E. Pac. Oc.; flows N. to S. along cst. of Ore., and Cal., U.S.A.; relatively cold water; reduces summer temp. and causes fog in cst. a. especially nr. San Francisco.
California, G. of, Mexico; 700 m.l.; inlet of Pac. Oc.
California, Lower, *terr.*, Mexico; between Gulf of C. and Pacific; cap. La Paz; chiefly a sterile region; some mineral wealth; a. 55,654 sq. m.; p. (1950) *287,366*.
Calimere Point, most S. point of Coromandel [Coast, India.
Calistoga, *t.*, Cal., U.S.A.; tr. ctr., wine, grapes; hot springs; p. (1960) *1,514*.
Callan, *rural dist.*, *mkt. t.*, Kilkenny, Ireland; on the King's R.; p. (1961) *5,963*.
Callander, *mkt. t.*, *burgh*, Perth, Scot.; on R. Teith, 15 m. N.W. of Stirling; "the gate of the Highlands," tourist resort; p. (1961) *1,654*.
Callao, *dep.*, Peru; cap. C.; a. 14 sq. m.; p. (1961) *213,206*.
Callao, *t.*, *spt.*, cap. Callao dep., Peru; linked by rly. to Lima; exp. sugar, cotton; p. (estd. 1963) *214,186*.
Calne, *mkt. t.*, *mun. bor.*, Wilts, Eng.; on Marlan R.; dairying, food processing; p. (1961) *6,559*.
Calonne-Ricouart, *commune*, Pas-de-Calais dep., France; coal; p. (1954) *10,897*.
Calota, gold-field dist., Colombia, S. America.
Calstock, *t.*, E. Cornwall, Eng.; on Tamar estuary.
Caltagirone, *c.*, Catania, Sicily; cath.; local mkt.; p. (1961) *44,212*.
Caltanissetta, *t.*, *cap.*, Caltanissetta prov., Sicily, Italy; cath.; sulphur; p. (1961) *62,115*.
Caluire-et-Clare, *t.*, Rhône, France, on Saône R.; coal; p. (1954) *19,886*.
Calumet, *t.*, Mich., U.S.A.; on peninsula in L. Superior; copper-mining; p. (1960) 1,139.
Calvados, *dep.*, N.W. France; cap. Caen; livestock, dairying, fisheries, textiles, liqueur brandy; a. 2,197 sq. m.; p. (1962) *480,686*.
Calvi, *spt.*, N.W. cst., Corsica; fishing; p. *2,035*.
Calvinia, *t.*, Cape Province, S. Africa; p. *3,627*.
Cam, *R.*, Cambridge, Eng.; trib. of Ouse; length 40 m.
Camagüey, *prov.*, Cuba, W. Indies; a. 10,169 sq. [m.; p. (1953) *618,258*.
Camagüey, *t.*, *cap.*, Camagüey, Central Cuba; p. (1953) *110,388*.
Camagüey, *t.*, Peru; sugar-cane; p. (1953) *110,388*.
Camajore, *t.*, Central Italy; foot of Apuan Alps, in prov. of Lucca; old church.
Camargue, *delta dist.*, Bouches-du-Rhône, France; at mouth of R. Rhône; famous col. of flamingoes; a. 300 sq. m.
Camarihes Norte, *prov.*, Luzon, Philippine Is.; mtns. and fertile land; agr., minerals; cap. Daet; a. 829 sq. m.; p. *98,324*.
Camas, *t.*, Wash., U.S.A.; agr., pulp, paper, fruit canning; p. (1960) *5,666*.
Cambay, G., separates Kathiawar peninsula from Gujerat st., India.
Camberwell, *see* **Southwark**.

Cambodia, *ind. st.*, formerly within the French Union, contains the great Tonle Sap L.; cap. Phnom-Penh on Mekong R.; agr., rice, rubber, maize, pepper, livestock, kapok, fisheries, car assembly, cigarette mkg.; a. 46,880 sq. m.; p. (1962) *5,748,842*.

Cambodia, C., extreme S. of Cambodia, Indo-China.

Camborne, *t.*, Cornwall, Eng.; 11 m. S.W. Truro; old tin- and copper-mines; engin., radio-television assembly, textiles and chemicals; p. (Camborne–Redruth urb. dist.) (1961) *36,090*.

Cambrai, *t.*, Nord dep., France; on Schelde R.; linen, brewing, soap; p. (1954) *29,567*.

Cambridge and Isle of Ely, *co.*, Eng.; Rs. Ouse, Nen, Cam; wheat, oats, potatoes, fruit, dairying, light engin., light indus.; p. (estd. 1965) *290,390*.

Cambridge, *mun. bor.*, *univ. c.*, *co. t.*, Cambridge, Eng.; on Cam R.; famous univ. with residtl. colleges; radio, scientific instruments, asphalt, boat bldg.; p. (1961) *95,358*.

Cambridge, *t.*, Md., U.S.A.; oysters; p. (1960) *12,239*.

Cambridge, *c.*, Mass., U.S.A., 3 m. from Boston; seat of Harvard Univ.; mnftg.; impt. research ctr.; p. (1960) *107,716*.

Cambridge, *t.*, Ohio, U.S.A.; coal, iron, clay, oil; glassware, pottery; p. (1960) *14,562*.

Cambuslang, *par.*, Lanark, Scot.; turkey red dye-works, hosiery, engin, plate mill; on Clyde R.; p. (1951) *26,861*.

Camden, *inner bor.*, N. London, Eng.; incorporating former bors. of Hampstead, Holborn and St. Pancras; p. (1964) *245,776*.

Camden, *mftg. and residtl. c.* N.J., U.S.A.; on Delaware R., suburban and opposite Philadelphia; iron foundries, chemicals, glass, wireless sets, shipbldg.; p. (1960) *117,159*.

Camden Town, *industl. and residtl. dist.*, London, Eng.; N.E. of Regent's Park.

Camel, *R.*, E. Cornwall, Eng.; length 30 m.

Camerino, *c.*, Macerata, Central Italy, in Apennines; the ancient Camerium annexed to Papal States in 16th century; univ. cath.

Cameron, *c.*, Texas, U.S.A.; p. (1960) *5,640*.

Cameron Bay, *t.*, N.W. Terr., Canada; by Gr. Bear Lake; radium.

Cameroons, British (North and South), former U.N. trust terrs. under British adm. (Northern part achieved independence as part of Nigeria (Sardauna prov.), and Southern part as part of Cameroun (Western prov.) (1961); a. 34,081 sq. m.; p. (estd. 1960) *1,621,000*.

Cameroun, Fed. Rep. of, *ind. sovereign st.* (Jan. 1960); comprises Eastern Cameroun (former U.N. trust terr. under French adm.) and Western Cameroun (former U.N. trust terr. under British adm.). Fed. cap. Yaoundé; timber, cocoa, palm kernels, palm oil, groundnuts, bananas, coffee; a. 143,500 sq. m.; p. (1961) *4,907,000*.

Camiguin, *I.*, Philippines; in Mindanao Sea; mtns.; sugar, rice, tobacco; a. 96 sq. m.; p. (1948) *60,099*.

Campagna, Italy; malarial coastal plain round Rome; now being drained; new commune of Latina founded 1932.

Campanha, *t.*, Minas Geraes, Brazil; industl.

Campania, *region*, S. Italy; ch. t. Naples; a. 5,250 sq. m.; p. (1961) *4,756,094*.

Campaspe, *R.*, Victoria, Australia; rises in Grampian Mtns., flows N. into R. Murray at Echuca; supplies water for irrigated area between Rochester and Echuca; length, 140 m.

Campbellton, *t.*, *spt.*, New Brunswick, Canada; lumbering, fishing; (1961) *9,873*.

Campbelltown, *t.*, N.S.W., Australia; p. (1961) [*18,649*.

Campbeltown, *burgh*, *spt.*, Argyll, Scot.; on Firth of Clyde cst. of peninsula of Kintyre; distilling, fishing; p. (1961) *6,525*.

Campeche, *st.*, Yucatan, Mexico; hot, flat and unhealthy; rice, cotton, logwood, chicle, sisal; a. 19,670 sq. m.; p. (1960) *168,219*.

Campeche, *cap. t. of st.*, *spt.*, Mexico; on G. of Mexico; exp. logwood, sisal, hemp; p. (1960) *31,272*.

Camperdown, *t.*, Victoria, Australia; dairying [dist.; p. *3,029*.

Camperdown, *vil.* on dunes, N. Holland, Netherlands; battle 1797.

Campinas, *t.*, Brazil; 55 m. N. of São Paulo; coffee; machin.; rubber gds.: p. (1960) *179,797*.

Campine or **Kempenland**, *dist.*, provs. Limburg and Antwerp, Belgium; coalfield.

Campo Belo, *t.*, Minas Geraes st., Brazil; 200 m. by rail N.E. of Guanabara; impt. cattle ctr.

Campobasso, *prov.*, Abruzzi and Molise, Italy; among the Apennines; a. 1,692 sq. m.; p. (1961) *332,121*.

Campobasso, *fortfd. t.*, 50 m. N.E. Naples, Italy; famous for cutlery and arms; p. (1961) *34,314*.

Campobello di Licata, *t.*, Sicily; sulphur-mines.

Campobello di Massara, *t.*, Sicily; quarrying.

Campos, *c.*, Rio de Janeiro, Brazil; coffee, sugar, alcohol distilling; p. (1960) *90,601*.

Campsie Fells, *range of hills*, Stirling, Scot.; highest point, 1,894 ft.

Campulung, *t.*, Muscel, Romania; N.W. of Bucharest; summer resort; p. (1948) *18,174*.

Canada, Dominion of, N. America; dominion founded 1867, and now inc. all Brit. N. American Federation of ten provinces; Nova Scotia, New Brunswick, Prince Edward I., Quebec, Ontario, Manitoba, Saskatchewan, Alberta, Brit. Columbia, Newfoundland with Labrador, and the terr. of Yukon and N.W. Territories (Franklin, Keewatin, Mackenzie); cap. Ottawa; Great Lakes; Rocky Mtns.; Great Plains; St. Lawrence, Saskatchewan, and Mackenzie Rs.; Trans-Canada Highway 4860 m. long runs from St. John's (Newfoundland) to Victoria (B.C.) opened 3 Sept. 1962; extreme climate, Pacific seaboard mild; conniferous forest belt except for Central grass-lands, tundra in N.; agr.: wheat, oats, dairying; pulp, paper; coal, gold, copper, nickel, zinc, lead, radium, uranium; oil, natural gas; fisheries; furs; hydro-electric power; impt. mnfs.; a. 3,851,809 sq. m.; p. (1961) *18,928,000*

Canada Dam, Bihar, Indian Union; on R. Mayurakshi, 160 m. from Calcutta.

Canadian Coast Range, *mtns.*, B.C., W. Canada; extend N.W. to S.E. along cst.; penetrated by deep inlets (fjords) with very little cst. plain; drained by short, swift Rs., crossed only by R. Skeena in N., R. Fraser in S., which give access to interior; marked climatic barrier, to W. equable climate with heavy all-year rain, to E. more extreme semi-arid climate, especially on valley floors.

Canadian R., trib. (flowing from New Mexico) of Arkansas R., U.S.A.; length 900 m.

Canal du Centre, *canal*, Saône-et-Loire dep., France; links Rhône–Saône valley at Chalon-sur-Saône with R. Loire at Digoin; serves Le Creusot Coalfield; length 60 m.

Canal Zone, Panama; strip of land leased to U.S.A. for Panama Canal; a. 648 sq. m. (276 sq. m. water); p. (1960) *42,122*.

Cananea, *t.*, Mexico; cattle, copper, silver, lead, zinc; p. *11,006*.

Cañar, *prov.*, Ecuador; cap. Azoques; Inca remains; agr., Panama hats; a. 1,521 sq. m.; p. (estd. 1962) *112,618*.

Canaries Current, *ocean current*; flows S. along N.W. cst. of Africa from Casablanca to C. Verde; relatively cold and has very marked cooling effect on Saharan coastlands.

Canary Is., or **Canaries**, N. Atl. Oc.; group of 7 Is. belonging to Spain, 60 m. off cst. Africa and 700 m. S. of Gibraltar; compr. Tenerife I., the lgst. (cap. Santa Cruz), Gran Canaria (cap. Las Palmas), Palma, Gomera, Hierro, Fuerteventura, Lanzarote; tropical produce; ch. exp., bananas, oranges, tomatoes, vegetables and tobacco; wine, cochineal; a. 4,685 sq. m.; p. (1962) *967,177*.

Canastota, *t.*, N.Y., U.S.A.; engin., furniture, plastics; p. (1960) *4,896*.

Canberra, Australian Capital Territory, Australia; in Gr. Dividing Range (alt. *c.* 6,000 ft.) 200 m. S.W. of Sydney; *seat of govt.* of Commonwealth; univ.; 911 sq. m.; p. (of t. 1963) *65,000*.

Cancale, *t.*, Ille-et-Vilaine dep., N. France; St. Michael's Bay; oysters; p. (1954) *5,463*.

Candia (Herakleion), *c.*, Crete; midway along N. cst.; olive oil, raisins; p. (1961) *64,492*.

Candon, *t.*, Luzon, Philippines; p. (1948) *22,362*.

Canea, *see* **Khania**.

Canelones, *dep.*, Uruguay; wine; a. 1,834 sq. m.; p. (1953) *201,359*.

Cañete, *sm. spt.*, Lima dep., Peru, S. America; 75 m. S.E. of Callao; exp. cotton grown under irrigation in Canete valley.

Cangas de Onis, *commune*, Spain; agr., cattle; coal, copper, tanning; p. (1957) *10,713*.

Cangas de Tineo, *t.*, Oviedo, Spain; nr. N. cst., 35 m. E. of Oviedo; woollens, linens; p. (1957) *21,500*.

Canicattì, *t.*, Sicily; sulphur; in fruit-growing dist.; p. *27,860*.

Canna, *sm. I.*, Hebrides, Scot.; basaltic pillars.

Cannanore, *t.*, Kerala, India; exp. timber, coconuts; p. (1961) *48,960*. [*11,601*.

Cannet (Le), *t.*, Alpes-Maritime, France; p. (1954)

Cannes, *spt.*, dep. Alpes-Maritimes, France; 20 m. S.W. Nice; famous winter resort; perfumes; p. (1962) *59,173*.

Cannock and Hednesford, *urb. dist.*, Staffs, Eng., on S.W. flank of Cannock Chase, 7 m. N.E. of Wolverhampton; coal-mng., engin., bricks, tiles, tools, elec. goods, car parts; p. (1961) *42,186*.

Canonsburg, *bor.*, Penns., U.S.A.; coal, gas, oil; p. (1960) *11,877*. [Serapis.

Canopus, *anc. c.*, Lower U.A.R.; gr. temple to

Canosa, *t.* Apulia, S. Italy; cath.; the Roman Canusium; ctr. of olive-growing dist.; p. *27,341*.

Cantabrians, *mtns.*, N. Spain, from Pyrenees to Cape Finisterre, hgst. pk. Peña Vieja (8,736 ft.).

Cantal, *mountainous dep.*, Central France; mineral springs, grain, dairying; coal, marble; cap. Aurillac; a. 2,229 sq. m.; p. (1962) *172,977*.

Canterbury, *c.*, *co. bor.*, Kent, Eng.; at foot of N. Downs on R. Stour; famous cath. founded A.D. 597 by St. Augustine; shrine of the murdered Thomas à Becket, a place of pilgrimage for centuries; univ.; fruit growing, tanning; p. (1961) *30,376*.

Canterbury, *prov.*, S.I., N.Z.; cap. Christchurch; a. 13,940 sq. m.; p. (1961) *339,883*.

Canterbury Plains, rich grazing and wheat-growing dist. S.I., N.Z.; along E. cst., famous for "Canterbury Lamb"; ch. t. Canterbury; ch. pt. Lyttelton.

Can Tho, *t.*, S. Vietnam; on Mekong R.; rice, fish; tr. ctr.; p. *27,000*.

Canton (Guangzhou) *ch. c.*, Kwantung, S. China; on bank of Chu-kiang (Pearl R.); former treaty pt; impt. tr. ctr.; thermal power stas;. p. (1957) *1,840,000*.

Canton, *t.*, Ill., U.S.A.; mnfs.; p. (1960) *13,588*.

Canton, *industl. and agr. c.*, Ohio, U.S.A.; coal, farm machin., engin.; p. (1960) *113,631*.

Canton R., *see* **Chukiang**.

Canvey I., *urb. dist.*, Essex; fronting the Thames; bungalow resort; radio components, bookbinding, iron and wire wk., oil storage; liquid gas terminal; p. (1961) *15,605*.

Cap-de-la-Madeleine, *t.*, Que., Canada; p. (1961) *26,925*.

Cap Haitien, *spt.*, Rep. of Haiti; on N. cst.; bombarded by British 1865; p. (1961) *24,959*.

Capannori, *t.*, Lucca, Italy; silk ind.; p. *39,527*.

Cape Breton I., Nova Scotia, E. Canada; farming, timber, fishing; ch. t. Sydney; a. 3,120 sq. m.

Cape Chidley, *I.* off N. point of Labrador.

Cape Coast, *t.*, Ghana; on cst. 60 m. S.W. of Accra; palm oil; p. (1960) *41,143*.

Cape Giradeau, *t.*, Mo., U.S.A.; p. (1960) *47,924*.

Cape Kennedy, E. Fla., U.S.A., on Atl. Oc., seaward extremity of barrier is. sheltering Bahama R. Lagoon; mil. base for testing missiles.

C. of Good Hope, S. Africa; famous headland, S. of Cape Town, 1,000 ft. high.

Cape Province (formerly **Cape of Good Hope Colony**), *prov.*, Rep. of S. Africa; physical features; Drakensberg Mtns., Orange and Caledon R., Gr. Karroo, Lit. Karroo; scanty rain except S. and E. cst.; sheep raising; wheat, citrus fruits, grapes, tobacco; fisheries; diamond and copper mng. in Namaqualand; automobile assembly, textiles, food canning; includes Transkeian terrs. in east.; a. 278,465 sq. m.; p. (1960) *5,362,853* incl. *1,003,207* whites.

Cape Town, *c.*, *spt.*, cap. of Cape Province, and legislative cap. of Rep. of S. Africa; on Table Bay, 30 m. N. of C. of Good Hope; communication by rail direct with Rhodesia, Transvaal, Orange and Natal; docks; cath.; univ.; exp. wool, gold, diamonds; p. (1960) *745,942* (inc. *286,418* Whites).

C. Verde Islands, Portuguese Is., in Atlantic, 350 m. W. of C. Verde, Africa; divided into two groups, Barlavento (Windward) and Sotavento (Leeward); 15 Is. and islets; a. 1,557 sq. m.; agr., sugar, and fruit-growing; cap. Praia; São Vicente coaling sta for all navigation to S. America; p. (1960) *180,000*.

Capernaum (Tell Hum), *ruins*, in time of Christ impt. place in Palestine, on the N. shore of the L. of Galilee.

Capis, *prov.*, Panay, Philippines, mnfs.; p. *466,000*.

Capo d'Istria, *see* **Koper**.

Cappoquin, *t.*, Waterford, R.o.I. on Blackwater R.

Capraja, Italian I. in the Mediterranean, 16 m. E. Corsica; anciently called Capraria.

Caprera, Italian I. off N.E. Sardinia, where Garibaldi lived.

Caprese, *commune*, Tuscany, Italy; birthplace of Michelangelo; p. *3,195*.

Capri, *I.* and *t.*, in Bay of Naples; tourist resort; residence of Augustus and Tiberius; the ancient Caprae; famous Blue Grotto; fine wines; p. (*t.*) *4,500*; (*I.*) *8,050*.

Capua, *ancient fort. c.*, Campania, Italy; 20 m. N. of Naples; founded by the Etruscans, came under Roman rule, sacked by the Saracens; modern t. 2 m. N. of site of ancient Casilinum; fireworks-mkg.; cath.; p. *14,375*.

Carácas, *cap.*, Venezuela; 8 m. inland from its pt., La Guaira; alt. about 3,000 ft.; cath.; univ.; coffee, cacao, textiles, soaps, detergents, steel, car assembly; underground rly. projected; p. (1961) *739,255*.

Caravaca, *t.*, Murcia, Spain; iron, tanning; p. (1957) *21,700*. [(1957) *20,965*.

Carballo, *t.*, Corunna, Spain; industl.; fishing; p.

Carbon County, N. Utah, U.S.A.; contains immense reserves of good coking coal suitable for blast furnaces; not yet developed.

Carbondale, *t.*, Penns., U.S.A.; anthracite; p. (1960) *13,595*.

Carbonia, *t.*, Sardinia; built 1937–38 nr. lignite and barite area; p. *12,000*.

Carcagente, *t.*, W. of Cullera, Valencia, Spain; oranges; p. (1955) *18,002*.

Carcar, *t.*, Cebu, Philippine Is.; sugar ind.; p. (1948) *32,818*.

Carcassonne, *t.*, Aude, France; on Aude R.; historic citadel guarding impt. routeway from Aquitaine to Rhône valley; farm implements; wines, cloth; p. (1962) *43,709*.

Carchi, *prov.*, Ecuador; cap. Tulcan; a. 1,495 sq. m.; p. (1962) *93,824*.

Cardamon Hills, Travancore, S. India; forms extreme S.W. edge of Deccan plateau; drained W. by R. Periyan, E. by R. Vaigai; rainfall less seasonal than over most of India; "China" tea plantations on middle slopes; rise to over 8,000 ft. alt.

Cardenas, *t.*, Matanzas, Cuba; sugar, rice, rum; p. (1953) *47,750*.

Cardiff, *cap. c.*, *spt.*, *co. bor.*, Glamorgan, Wales; univ.; docks, coal, iron, steel, engin., elect. goods, brewing, paper; p. (1961) *256,270*.

Cardigan, *mun. bor.*, *co. t.*, Cardigan, S. Wales; on Teifi R.; p. (1961) *3,780*. [N. and S.

Cardigan Bay, *lge. bay*, W. Wales, 70 m. extent

Cardiganshire, *maritime co.*, S. Wales; mountainous; mainly agr., mines and quarries; a. 692 sq. m.; p. (1961) *53,564*.

Cardón, *t.*, N. Venezuela, Paraguaná peninsula; oil refining.

Cardross, *industl. vil.*, Dunbarton, Scot.; on R. Clyde; Robert Bruce d. 1329 in Cardross Castle.

Cardwell, *t.*, Queensland, Australia; harbour; gold-mining dist. [(1960) *3,722*.

Carey, *t.*, Ohio, U.S.A.; mkt. gardening; p.

Cargenbridge, *t.*, Kirkcudbright, Scot.; chemicals, plastics.

Caribbean Sea, between W. Indies and Central and S. America; a. 7,500 sq. m.

Caribou Range, *mtns.*, B.C., W. Canada; mass of ancient crystalline rocks inside the gr. bend of R. Frazer; widespread occurrence of lode and alluvial gold; mainly above 5,000 ft.

Caribou, *t.*, Maine, U.S.A.; p. (1960) *8,305*.

Caribrod, *t.*, Jugoslavia; on Nisava R.; p. *4,000*.

Carimata I., off S.W. Borneo, Indonesia.

Carinthia, *prov.*, Austria; cap. Klagenfurt; mtnous.; mineral springs; rye, oats; lead iron; a. 3,681 sq. m.; p. (1961) *495,226*.

Carisbrooke, *t.*, I. of Wight, Eng.; cas. prison o Charles I (1647–8); p. (1951) *5,232*.

Carlingford, *t.*, *spt.*, Louth, Ireland; on Carlingford Bay; oysters.

Carlingford, Lough, *inlet* of sea between Down and Louth, Ireland.

Carlinville, *t.*, Ill., U.S.A.; bricks and tiles, agr machin.; p. (1960) *5,440*.

Carlisle, *c.*, *co. bor.*, Cumberland, Eng.; on Eden R.; 8 m. from Solway Firth; impt. rout ctr.; ancient cas. and cath.; textiles, biscuits metal boxes; p. (1961) *71,112*.

Carlisle, *bor.*, Penns., U.S.A.; boots and shoes; p. (1960) *16,623.*
Carlow, *co.*, Leinster, Ireland; co. t., Carlow; a. 346 sq. m.; p. (1961) *33,345.*
Carlow, *t.*, Ireland; brewing, milling, sugar, footwear; p. (1961) *7,707.*
Carlsbad, *see* **Karlovy Vary.**
Carlsbad, *t.*, N.M., U.S.A.; p. (1960) *25,541.*
Carlsbad Cavern, N.M., U.S.A.; gr. cave in limestone through which flows R. Pecos; stalactites, stalagmites; tourist attraction; length 4,000 ft., width 600 ft., height of roof 300 ft.
Carlsruhe, *see* **Karlsruhe.**
Carlstadt, *bor.*, N.J., U.S.A.; brass, marble; p. (1960) *6,042.*
Carlton, *urb. dist.*, Notts, Eng.; 2 m. N.E. of Nottingham; lace, hosiery; p. (1961) *38,790.*
Carluke, *t., par.*, Lanark, Scot.; engin., mng., fruit growing and preserving; p. (1951) *11,415.*
Carmagnola, *mftg. t.*, N. Italy; on Melba R.; p. *12,241.*
Carmarthen, *mun. bor., co. t.*, Carmarthenshire, Wales; on Towy R.; anthracite, limestone quarrying; p. (1961) *13,249.*
Carmarthen Bay, Carmarthen, Wales; 18 m. across.
Carmarthenshire, *co.*, S. Wales; co. t., Carmarthen; mountainous; mining; mainly pastoral land; a. 920 sq. m.; p. (1961) *167,736.*
Carmaux, *t.*, Tarn, France; glass mftg.; p. (1954) *11,485.*
Carmel, Mt., Israel; alt. 1,932 ft.
Carmen de Bolivar, *spt.*, Campeche Bay, Mexico.
Carmiel *c.*, N. Israel; new t. built between Acre and Safad, in the Galilean hills; planned for p. *50,000.*
Carmona, *t.*, Spain; olives, wine, fruit; p. (1957) *27,115.*
Carnac, *vil.*, Morbihan, N.W. France; S.E. of Lorient; prehistoric stone monuments and circles.
Carnarvon, *t.*, W. Australia; on R. Gascoyne; p. *845.*
Carnatic, *region*, S.E. India, between E. Ghats and Coromandel cst. where earliest European settlements were established.
Carnegie, *bor.*, Penns., U.S.A.; steel, iron; p. (1960) *11,887.*
Carnegie, *L.*, W. Australia.
Carnew, *vil.*, Wicklow, Ireland; granite, slate.
Carnforth, *t., urb. dist.*, Lancs, Eng.; rly. ctr.; p. (1961) *4,113.*
Carnoustie, *burgh*, Angus, Scot., on N. Sea; 6 m. S.W. of Arbroath; resort; p. (1961) *5,511.*
Carnsore Point, S. Wexford, Ireland.
Carntogher Mtns., *range of mtns.*, Londonderry, N. Ireland.
Carnwath, *vil.*, Lanark, Scot.; coal, shale, iron.
Caro, *t.*, Mich., U.S.A.; sugar-beet refining; p. (1960) *3,534.*
Carolina, *see* **N. and S. Carolina.**
Caroline Is., *archipelago* in W. Pac. Oc.; 549 in number, lying between the Philippines and the Marshall Gr., former Japanese mandate now part of U.S. Pac. Trust Terr.; ch. exp. copra.
Caroni R., Venezuela, S. America; hydro-elec. complex at confluence Orinoco R. under constr.
Carpathian Mtns., *range* separating Czechoslovakia and Hungary from Galicia, and Transylvania from Moldavia, 805 m. long; highest point, Tatra 8,740 ft.
Carpentaria, G. of, North Australia; between C. Arnhem and C. York.
Carpentras, *c.*, Vaucluse, France; on R. Auzon; many antiquities; p. (1954) *15,076.*
Carpi, *industl. t.*, Modena, Central Italy; cath.; p. (1961) *45,208.*
Carrantuohill Mtn., Kerry, Ireland; loftiest in Magillicuddy's Reeks and all Ireland, alt. 3,414 ft.
Carrara, *t.*, Massa-e-Carrara, Central Italy; famed for white marble; p. (1961) *64,901.*
Carrickfergus, *spt., mun. bor.*, Antrim, N. Ireland; on N. shore of Belfast Lough; salt mines, textiles, nylon fibres; p. (1961) *10,211.*
Carrickmacross, *mkt. t., urb. dist.*, Monaghan, Ireland; hand made lace; p. (1961) *1,940.*
Carrick-on-Shannon, *co. t., rural dist.*, Leitrim, Ireland; p. (of dist.) (1961) *6,962.*
Carrick-on-Suir, *mkt. t., urb. dist.*, Tipperary, Ireland; coal, timber; p. (1961) *4,667.*
Carrizal-Bajo, *t.*, Atacama prov., Chile; port for Carrizal-Alto, 25 m. E. [*10,973.*
Carrollton, *t.*, Ga., U.S.A.; textiles; p. (1960)
Carron, *vil.*, Stirling, Scot.; nr. Falkirk; famous ironwks.
Carron, Loch, *inlet*, W. cst., Ross and Cromarty, Scot.; followed by rly. from Dingwall to Kyle and Lochalsh.
Carse of Gowrie, Perth, Scot.; fertile cstl. dist. between Perth and Dundee, S. of Sidlaw Hills; sm. fruits, especially raspberries.
Carshalton, *see* **Sutton.**
Carson City, *st. cap.*, Nevada, U.S.A.; silver- and gold-mining dist.; p. (1960) *5,163.*
Carstairs, *vil.*, Lanark, Scot.; N.E. of Lanark t.
Cartagena, *spt., cap.*, dep. Bolivar, Colombia, S. America; shares with Barranquilla tr. brought down Magdalena R.; platinum, coffee, chemicals, textiles, fertilisers; oil pipe terminal; p. (estd. 1962) *185,160.*
Cartagena, *spt.*, Murcia, E. Spain; fine wharves and harbour; naval arsenal; cath.; shipbldg., metal-wkg.; p. (1959) *123,301.*
Cartago, *t.*, Cauca, Colombia, S. America; coffee, tobacco, cattle; p. (estd. 1959) *64,830.*
Cartago, *prov.*, Costa Rica, Central America; cap. C.; coffee, fruits; p. (1963) *154,500.*
Carteret, *bor.*, N.J., U.S.A.; metal and oil refining, chemicals, tobacco; p. (1960) *20,502.*
Carter Fell, *mtn.*, Northumberland, Eng., 1,815 ft.
Carterton, *bor.*, Wellington, N.I., New Zealand; p. (1961) *3,077.*
Carthage, *c.*, N.E. Tunis, N. Africa; with ruins of ancient Carthage, destroyed by the Romans 146 B.C.
Carthage, *t.*, Mo., U.S.A.; coal; p. (1960) *11,264.*
Cartmel, *par.*, Lancs, Eng.; near Ulverston.
Carupano, *spt.*, Venezuela, S. America; exp. coffee, cacao; airport; p. (1961) *30,000.*
Carvine, *t.*, Pas-de-Calais, France; p. (1954) *15,780.*
Casablanca, autonomous *c.*, Morocco, N. Africa; motor plant; p. (1960) *965,277.*
Casablanca, *t.*, Valparaiso, Chile.
Casa Branca, *t.*, S.E. of Lisbon, Portugal.
Casale, *t.*, Piedmont, Italy; cath.; cement; p. (1961) *40,827.*
Casalmaggiore, *t.*, Italy; on R. Po, near Parma; [p. *15,012.*
Casas Grandes, *t.*, N.W. Chihuahua st., Mexico; Aztec ruins; p. *2,000.*
Cascade Range, N. America; extends N. and S. through Brit. Columbia, Washington and Oregon between Rocky Mtns. and Pacific cst. Highest peak, Mt. Rainier, 14,408 ft.
Cascade Tunnel, longest rly. tunnel in N. America, Wash., U.S.A.; carries trunk rly. from Spokane to Seattle through Cascade Mtns.; length 7¾ m.
Cascina, *t.*, Pisa, Italy; on R. Arno; silk mnfs.
Caserta, *t.*, Italy; on N. edge of Plain of Naples; royal palace; cath.; silks; p. (1961) *50,810.*
Cashel, *c., urb. dist.*, Tipperary, Ireland; cath. (ruined) on Rock of Cashel; p. (1961) *2,679.*
Casino, *t.*, N.S.W., Australia; p. (1961) *8,090.*
Casiquiare, *R.*, Venezuela, joins Orinoco to the Rio Negro, a trib. of the Amazon.
Caspe, *t.*, Spain; on R. Guadalupe; p. *9,033.*
Casper, *t.*, Wyo., U.S.A.; petroleum; p. (1960) *38,930.*
Caspian Sea, U.S.S.R.; 760 m. long, 270 m. wide, 170,000 sq. m., between Asia and Europe; lgst. inland sea in the world; surface 85 ft. below ocean; fisheries; pts.: Astrakhan, Baku, Derbent.
Casquets, *dangerous rocks*, 7 m. W. of Alderney, Channel Is; lighthouse.
Cassaba (Kassaba), *see* **Turgutlu.**
Cassel, *t.*, *see* **Kassel.**
Cassilis, *t.*, N.S.W., Australia; 115 m. N.W. of Newcastle in impt. gap in Gr. Dividing Range between Hunter and Liverpool Ranges, giving access from Newcastle to interior.
Cassino, *t.*, Campania, Italy; formerly San Germano; the ancient Casinum nr. famous monastery.
Castelbuono, *t.*, Sicily; mineral springs.
Castelfiorentino, *t.*, Tuscany, nr. Florence, Italy.
Castelfranco, *t.*, Bologna, Italy; p. *2,925.*
Castelfranco, *t.*, Treviso, Italy; fine church and paintings; silk; p. *4,240.*
Castellamare, *dockyard t.*, Italy; on Bay of Naples at foot of Vesuvius; mineral springs; wat. pl.; p. (1961) *64.618.*
Castellamare del Golfo, *spt.*, N.W. Sicily; wat. pl., tuna fishing; p. *18,032.*
Castellón de la Plana, *prov.*, Spain; on Mediterranean, part of ancient Valencia, mainly mtns.a., 2,579 sq. m.; cap. Castellon; p. (1959) *334,472.*

Castellon de la Plana, *t.*, Spain; porcelain, oranges, carob-wood, onions, wines; p. (1959) *57,780.*

Castelnaudary, *t.*, Aude, France, on Languedoc canal, burned by Black Prince, 1355; p. (1954) *8,760.*

Castelo Branco, *c.*, Portugal; *cap.* of dist. same name; p. of dist. (1960) *325,800.*

Castelvetrano, *t.*, Sicily, Italy; industl.; wine; p. *24,746.*

Castiglione, *t.*, Sicily, Italy; near Catania; sulphur refining.

Castiglione Fiorentino, *t.*, Italy; nr. Arezzo; sericulture.

Castile, formerly a kingdom of Spain; now div. into Old and New Castile.

Castine, *t.*, Me., U.S.A.; on Penobscot Bay; resort; fishing.

Castlebar, *urb. dist.*, *cap.*, Mayo, Ireland; "Race of Castlebar" battle fought here in 1798 Rebellion; bacon curing, hat-mkg.; p. (1961) *5,482.*

Castleblayney, *urb. dist.*, Monaghan, Ireland; nr. Dundalk; p. (1961) *2,125.*

Castle Cary, *mkt. t.*, Somerset, Eng.; N.E. of Yeovil: dairying and flax growing; p. (1951) *1,664.*

Castlecary, *vil.*, Stirlingshire, Scot.; sta. on Roman wall; silica, fire-clay deposits.

Castlecomer, *rural dist.*, N. Kilkenny, Ireland; p. (1961) *7,328.*

Castle Donington, *t.*, *rural dist.*, Leics. Eng.; p. (of dist. 1961) *9,809.*

Castle Douglas, *burgh*, Kirkcudbright, Scot.; 15 m. S.W. of Dumfries; cattle fairs; p. (1961) *3,253.*

Castleford, *mun. bor.*, W.R. Yorks, Eng.; 10 m. S.E. of Leeds at confluence of Rs. Aire and Calder; coal-mng., chemical, glass and clothing mnfs., flour-milling, brick-mkg.; p. (1961) *40,345.*

Castleisland, *t.*, Kerry, Ireland; agr. ctr.; p. (1951) *1,491.*

Castlemaine, *t.*, Victoria, Australia; at foot of Gr. Dividing Range, 25 m. S. of Bendigo; fruit, wine; p. (1961) *7,216.*

Castlerea, *rural dist.*, Roscommon, Ireland; p. (of dist.) (1961) *18,337.*

Castletown, *t.*, Isle of Man; former cap.; p. (1956) *1,755.*

Castletown Berehaven, *spt.*, Cork, Ireland; on Bantry Bay.

Castres, *t.*, Tarn, France; on R. Agoût; former Huguenot stronghold; cath.; woollens, soap, earthenware; p. (1962) *40,005.*

Castries, *cap.*, *spt.*, St. Lucia, Windward Is.; W.I., greatly damaged by fire June 1948; fine harbour; p. (1957) *25,000.*

Castro del Río, *t.*, Andalusia, Spain; on R. Guadjo; industl.; p. (1957) *14,126.*

Castrogiovanni, *see* **Enna.**

Castrop-Rauxel or **Kastrop Rauxel,** *t.*, N. Rhine-Westphalia, Germany; industl.; coal, cement, tar prod., tiles, brandy; p. (1963) *88,500.*

Castro Urdiales, *spt.*, Santander, N. Spain; sardines, iron ore; p. (1957) *11,646.*

Castrovillari, *hill t.*, S. Italy; built on cliff above R. Coscile; mkt. ctr. for local cereals, wine, oil and silkworms; p. (estd.) *10,000.*

Cat I. (or **Guanahani**), Bahamas, W. Indies; a. 340 sq. m.; p. (1953) *3,201.*

Catacaos, *t.*, Piura dep., Peru; Panama hats.

Catalonia, *old prov.*, N.E. Spain; mountainous; wooded; cereals; mnfs.: cottons, woollens, silks; rich in minerals; cap. Barcelona; nuclear power sta. projected; a. 12,427 sq. m.; p. (1957) *3,240,000.*

Catamarca, *prov.*, N.W. Argentina; cap. C.; farming; gold, silver, copper mng.; a. 40,942 sq. m.; p. (1960) *172,000.*

Catamarca, *t.*, *cap.*, Catamarca prov., N.W. Argentina; located in Andean foot-hills 80 m. S. of Tucuman; ctr. of irrigated oasis producing vines, apricots, cherries, cotton; thermal springs; p. (1960) 29,000.

Catanduanes, *I.*, off Luzon, Philippines; hilly, fertile; rice, corn, cotton, hemp, coconuts; a. 552 sq. m.; p. *63,530.*

Catania, *prov.*, Sicily; ch. t., Catania; a. 1907 sq. m.; p. (1961) *884,447.*

Catania, *c.*, Sicily; on E. cst. at foot of Mt. Etna; city several times rebuilt in consequence of earthquakes; cath.; univ.; textiles, dyeing; p. (1961) *361,466.*

Catanzaro, *c.*, S. Italy; univ.; silks, velvets; p. (1961) *72,723.*

Catasauqua, *bor.*, Penns., U.S.A.; industl.; flour, cement, textiles; p. (1960) *5,062.*

Catastrophe, C., S. extremity of Eyre Peninsula, S. Australia.

Catawba, *R.*, N.C., U.S.A.; rising in Blue Ridge Range; length 300 m.

Caterham and Warlingham, *urb. dist.*, Surrey, Eng.; on N. Downs; residtl.; p. (1961) *34,808.*

Cathay, ancient name for China and E. Tartary.

Catoche, C., N.E. point of Yucatan, Mexico.

Catrine, *t.*, Ayr, Scot.; mftg.

Catskill Mtns., N.Y., U.S.A.; gr. in Appalachians, W. of Hudson R.; holiday resort.

Cauca, *I.*, Colombia; trib. of Magdalena; length 600 m.

Cauca, *dep.* Colombia Rep.; cap. Popayán; a. 11,657 sq. m.; p. (1962) *529,040.*

Caucasia, region between Black Sea and Caspian, divided by Caucasus Mtns. into N. or Cis-Caucasia and Trans-Caucasia.

Caucasus, *lofty mtn. range* between Caspian and Black Sea; highest summits Mt. Elbruz (18,463 ft.) and Kasbek (16,546 ft.); length of system about 950 m., greatest width 120 m.; many lofty passages and lge. glaciers.

Caudebec, *ancient t.*, Seine-Maritime, France; p. (1954) *9,429.*

Cauderan, *commune*, Gironde, France; sub. of Bordeaux; p. (1954) *26,548.*

Caudete, *t.*, Albacete, Spain; p. (1957) *7,862.*

Caudry, *t.*, Nord, France; lace and tulle; p. (1954) *12,173.*

Cauquenes, *t.*, Chile; cap. of Maule prov.; p. *12,987.*

Causses, Les, *limestone plateau*, Aveyron, Tarn deps., S. France; on S.W. flank of Central Plateau; caverns, gorges of Rs. Lot and Tarn; sheep provide milk for Roquefort cheese; alt. 3,000–6,000 ft.

Cauterets, *vil.*, dep. Hautes-Pyrénées, France; mineral springs.

Cautin, *prov.*, S. Chile; cap. Temuco; a. 6,705 sq. m.; p. (1960) *475,121.*

Cauvery, *R.*, S. India; rises in the W. Ghats, flows into Bay of Bengal through Mysore and Madras; length 400 m.

Cava or **La Cava,** *t.*, Salerno, Italy; summer resort; textiles; p. (1961) *42,235.*

Cavaillon, *commune*, Vaucluse, France; cath.; p. (1954) *14,831.*

Cavan, *inland co.*, Ulster, Ireland; a. 746 sq. m.; agr.; distilling; p. (1961) *56,597.*

Cavan, *urb. dist.*, *co. t.*, Cavan, Ireland; 72 m. S.W. Belfast; p. (1961) *3,207.*

Cavarzere, *t.*, Venice, N. Italy; on R. Adige; industl.; p. *22,821.*

Cavite, *spt.*, Luzon, Philippines; p. (1948) *35,052.*

Cavour Canal, *irrigation canal*, Piedmont and Lombardy regions, N. Italy; links R. Po nr. Chivassa with R. Ticino 10 m. N.E. of Novara; provides water for 250,000 acres of rice-fields and meadow-land; length 80 m.

Cawnpore (Kanpur), *cap.*, Cawnpore dist., Uttar Pradesh, India; on the Ganges; 130 m. N.W. of Allahabad; grain, cotton, woollens, aircraft mftg.; p. (1961) *947,793.*

Caxias, *t.*, Maranhão, Brazil; on Itapecuru R.; cotton, rice; p. (1960) *60,607.*

Cayambe, *mtn.*, Andes, Ecuador; alt. 19,535 ft.

Cayenne, *spt.*, *cap.*, Fr. Guiana, S. America; famous for pepper; p. (1959) *13,346.*

Cayey, *t.*, S.E. Puerto Rico; tobacco, coffee, sugar; p. *5,622.*

Cayman Is., West Indies, a. 100 sq. m.; p. (estd. 1965) *8,853*; consists of Grand Cayman, cap. Georgetown; Little Cayman; and Cayman Brac.; turtle and shark fishing.

Cazalla de la Sierra, S.W. Spain; iron and lead; aniseed; p. (1957) *11,347.*

Ceará, *st.*, N. Brazil; sugar, cotton, coffee, rubber; cap. Fortaleza; a. 59,168 sq. m.; p. (1960) *3,337,856.*

Ceará, *see* **Fortaleza.**

Cebu, *I.*, Philippines; mountainous, forested; coal; a. 1,707 sq. m.; p. *1,183,000.*

Cebu, *ch. t.*, Cebu I., Philippines; exp. copra, tobacco, sugar; p. (1960) *251,000.*

Cedar or **Red Cedar,** *R.*, Iowa, U.S.A.; trib. of Mississippi R., length 400 m.

Cedar Falls, *t.*, Iowa, U.S.A.; p. (1960) *21,195.*

Cedar Mountain, *hill*, Va., U.S.A.; here Stonewall Jackson defeated Banks 1862.

Cedar Rapids, *c.*, Iowa, U.S.A.; rly. ctr.; farm machin., lumber; p. (1960) *92,035*.
Cedartown, *t.*, Ga., U.S.A.; textiles, rubber tyres; cottonseed oil; p. (1960) *9,340*.
Cedros, *I.*, off W. coast, Lower Cal., Mexico.
Ceduna, *spt.*, S. Australia; 250 m. W. of Pt. Augusta; p. *499*.
Cefalu, *spt.*, Palermo, N. Sicily; sardine fishing; p. *10,625*.
Ceglie, *c.*, Lecce, S. Italy; olive oil, building stone; p. *20 707*.
Cehegin, *t.*, Murcia, Spain; on R. Quipar; p. (1957) *15,830*.
Celaya, *t.*, Guanajuato, Mexico; silver, carpets; p. *50,000*.
Celebes, see **Sulawesi**.
Celina, *t.*, W. Ohio, U.S.A.; resort; furniture, canning; p. (1960) *7,659*.
Celje, *t.*, Slovenia, Jugoslavia; lignite, zinc smelting; p. (1960) *29,000*.
Celle, *t.*, Lower Saxony, Germany; on R. Aller; former residence of the Dukes of Brunswick-Lüneberg; cas.; metal, leather, paints, textiles, oil; p. (1963) *59,000*.
Cenis, Mont, *see* **Mont Cenis**.
Cento, *t.*, Ferrara, Italy; industl.; p. *4,942*.
Central African Republic, *ind. sov. st. within French Community*, Equatorial Africa; cap. Bangui; a. 190,000 sq. m.; p. (1961) *1,227,000*.
Central America, between Mexico and S. America, from the Isthmus of Tehuantepec to that of Panama; includes Guatemala, Honduras, Nicaragua, Salvador, Costa Rica, Panama, Brit. Honduras; tropical climate; forests, savannahs.
Central Asia, usually applied to regions between 30° and 40° N. lat. and 55° and 85° E. long.; Russian C.A. is the land between China and Afghanistan and the Caspian, now consisting of various Soviet Reps.
Central Falls, *c.*, Rhode Is., U.S.A.; nr. Pawtucket; cotton goods; p. (1960) *19,858*.
Central Greece and Euboea, *geographical div.*, Greece; contains the cap. Athens; a. 9,704 sq. m.; p. (1961) *2,823,658*.
Central Provinces, *see* **Madhya Pradesh**.
Centralia, *t.*, Ill., U.S.A.; p. (1960) *13,904*.
Centuripe, *commune*, Enna, Sicily; sulphur, marble; p. *10,802*.
Cephalonia, *see* **Kephallenia**.
Ceram (Serang), *I.*, Moluccas, Indonesia; a. 6,621 sq. m.; tobacco, sago; p. *83,000*.
Ceres, *t.*, Cape Province, S. Africa; on R. Hex; health resort; p. (1960) *6,173*.
Cerignola, *t.*, Foggia, Italy; Spanish victory over French 1503; p. (1961) *49,287*.
Cerigo, *see* **Kythera**.
Cernauti, *see* **Chernovtsy**.
Cernavoda, *t.*, Dobrogea, Romania; on R. Danube, 70 m. S. of Braila; p. (1956) *8,802*.
Cerro de Pasco, *t.*, dep. Junin, Peru; silver, coal, lead; copper smelting; large vanadium mines W. of t.; p. (1961) *19,354*.
Cerro Rico, *mtn.*, Bolivia; in Andes, W. of Potosi; alt. 15,680 ft.; v. rich silver, tin, tungsten ores.
Certaldo, *commune*, Firenze, Italy; anc. cas.; home of Boccaccio; p. *12,094*.
Cesena, *old industl. t.*, Forli, Italy; cath.; antiquities; sulphur-mines, wines; p. (1961) *79,704*.
Ceská Lipa, *t.*, ČSSR.; on R. Ploucnice N. o Prague; industl.; p. (1961) *14,038*.
Ceská Trebová, *old t.*, ČSSR.; W. of Pardubice; engin., textiles; p. (1961) *13,031*.
Ceské Budejovice, *t.*, ČSSR.; on R. Vltava 80 m. S. of Prague; pencils, porcelain, brewing, anthracite; p. (1961) *63,949*.
Cesky Tesin, (Teschen), Silesia, ČSSR., (divided between Poland and Czechoslovakia); coal and ironwks.; p. (1961) *15,508*.
Cessnock, *t.*, N.S.W., Australia; coal-mining; dairying and farming; p. *35,270*.
Cette, *see* **Sète**.
Ceuta, *spt.*, Morocco; opposite to and 16 m. from Gibraltar; cath.; the ancient Abyia, one of the Pillars of Hercules; p. (1950) *59,936*.
Cévennes, *mtns.*, S. France; separating basins of Rhône, Loire and Tarn; highest point Mt. Mézenc, alt. 5,794 ft.
Ceylon, *I.*, *indep. sov. st.* within Br. Commonwealth (1948); in Indian Ocean, S.E. of India; fertile plains, mountainous interior; principal prod.: rice, rubber, tea, coconuts, fruits and spices; cap. and ch. spt. Colombo; a. 25,332 sq. m., p. (1963) *10,644,809*.
Chacaburo, *t.*, E. Argentina; agr. ctr.; p. *15,000*.
Chachapoyas, *t.*, cap. of Amazonas dep., N. Peru; agr., forest prod.; p. (1946) *5,494*.
Chaco, *terr.*, N. of Argentina; part of Gran Chaco; farming and prairie land; cap. Resistencia; a. 38,468 sq. m.; p. (1960) *535,000*.
Chad, *L.*, lge sheet of water of N. Central Africa; a. 50,000 sq. m. when in flood, varies in extent with season, and is drying up, shallow, many Is., lies between the wooded region of the Sudan and the steppes leading to the Sahara desert.
Chad, *ind. sov. st. within French Community*, Equatorial Africa; cap. Fort Lamy; a. 495,000 sq. m.; p. (1961) *2,675,000*.
Chadderton, *urb. dist.*, Lancs, Eng.; cotton and chemical mftg.; p. (1961) *32,494*.
Chagford, *par.*, Devon, Eng.; stone circles.
Chagos, Is., Indian Ocean; administered from Mauritius; fine harbour in Diego Garcia.
Chagres, *spt.*, Panama, S. America; on N. side of Isthmus of Panama; p. *1,300*.
Chaguaramas, Trinidad, W.I., part of naval base leased to U.S.A. since 1941.
Chalcidice, *see* **Khalkidhiki**.
Chalcis, *t.*, Eubœa, Greece; p. (1961) *24,745*.
Chaleur Bay, Canada; between N. Brunswick and Gaspé Peninsula, Quebec.
Chalfont St. Giles, *vil.*, Bucks., Eng.; residtl.; p. *2,100*.
Chalon-sur-Saône, *ancient industl. c.*, Saône-et-Loire, E. France; glass ,iron; p. (1962) *45,993*.
Chalons-sur-Marne, *c.*, Marne, N.E. France; 20 m. E. of Epernay; cath.; military ctr.; brewery ind.; p. (1962) *45,348*.
Chamalières, *t.*, Puy-de-Dôme, France; p. (1954) *11,473*.
Chaman, *t.*, Baluchistan, Pakistan; on Afghan frontier; terminus of rly. through Quetta.
Chamba, *t.*, Himachal Pradesh, India; 100 m. N.E. of Amritsar; p. (1961) *8,609*.
Chambal, *R.*, trib. of R. Jumna rising in Vindhya hills; length 650 m.
Chambersburg, *bor.*, Penns., U.S.A.; foundries, brewing; p. (1960) *17,670*.
Chambéry, *t.*, *cap.*, Savoie, S.E. France; silk, leather; p. (1962) *47,447*.
Chambolle-Musigny, *commune*, Côte d'Or, France; wines.
Chambon-Feugerolles, *t.*, Loire, France; coal, iron, steel mftg.; p. (1954) *17,695*.
Chamonix, *t.*, Haute-Savoie, France; at foot of Mont Blanc, in valley of R. Arve; winter sports ctr.; road tunnel links to Aosta; p. (1954) *5,699*.
Champagne, *old prov.*, N.E. France; famous for its wine; wheat, sheep, impt. tr. fairs in Middle Ages.
Champagne Humide, *natural division* ("*pays*"), Central France; clay vale, runs 100 m. N.E. from Auxerre to Bar-le-Duc; drained by Seine, Aube, Marne, Aisne and many tribs.; heavily wooded, marshy; where cleared and drained, grain cultivation.
Champagne Pouilleuse, *natural division* ("*pays*"), Central France; barren chalk plateau, extends 80 m. N.E. from Sens to Reims; drained by Aisne, Vesle, Seine, Aube, Marne; dusty downland pastures; sheep; vine growing on S.-facing valley sides and S.E.-facing escarpment of Falaise de l'Ile de France favours production of Champagne wines, ch. producing ctrs.: Châlons-sur-Marne, Reims, Epernay.
Champaign, *t.*, Ill., U.S.A.; foundries; p. (1960) *49,583*.
Champerico, *spt.*, S.W. Guatemala; coffee; p. *2,000*.
Champigny-sur-Marne, *t.*, Seine, France; embroidery; piano keys; p. (1962) *57,925*.
Champlain, *L.*, U.S.A.; N. frontier of N.Y., state; discharges by Richelieu R. into St. Lawrence; flanked by trunk route from New York to Montreal; a. 600 sq. m.
Champlain Canal, N.Y., U.S.A.; follows gap between Adirondack Mtns. and Green Mtns. occupied by Hudson R.; links Albany with *L.* Champlain and allows through barge traffic between New York and St. Lawrence valley.
Chanaral, *spt.*, N. Atacama, Chile; lies in gold and copper mng. ctr.; p. (1960) *21,098*.
Chancelade, *commune*, Dordogne, France; arch. type-site of Chancelade culture (late paleolithic).

Chanda, *t.*, Nagpur, Maharashtra, India; ancient temples; p. (1961) *51,484*.

Chanda, *dist.*, Maharashtra, India; teak forests, coal, iron; a. 9,200 sq. m.; p. (1961) *1,238,070*.

Chandausi, *t.*, Uttar Pradesh, India; cotton, hemp; rly. ctr.; p. (1961) *48,557*.

Chandernagore, *t.*, W. Bengal, India; on Hooghly R.; French 1816–1949; cotton; p. (1961) *67,105*.

Chandigarh, new cap. E. Punjab, India; situated on plateau at foot of Himalaya, S.W. of Simla; built 1951–3 by Le Corbusier; univ.; p. (1961) *89,321*.

Changchow (Changzhou), *c.*, Kiangsu, China; in Yangtze Kiang valley, on Grand Canal 70 m. S.E. of Nanking; mkt. for intensively cultivated dist.; silk; p. (1953) *297,000*.

Changchun, *c.*, Kirin, China; rly. ctr.; p. (1953) *855,000*.

Changnacheri, *t.*, Kerala, S. India; tea, cotton spinning, silk; p. (1961) *42,376*.

Changpai Shan, *mtns.*, form bdy. between China and N. Korea; drained by Rs. Yalu, Ertao, Tumen; highest point, Peiktusan, alt. 8,005 ft.

Changsha, *c.*, *cap.*, Hunan prov., China; tea, rice, antimony; p. (1953) *651,000*.

Changshu, *c.*, Kiangsu, China; in Yangtze Kiang valley 65 m. N.W. of Shanghai; mkt. for local agr. produce; p. (1953) *101,000*.

Channel Islands, *gr.* of self-governing Is. belonging to the British Crown off N.W. cst. France, of which the lgst. are Jersey, Guernsey, Alderney and Sark; part of the old Duchy of Normandy; vegetables, flowers, fruit, granite; two famous breeds of dairy cattle; tourist resort; German occupation, 1940–45; ch. t. St. Helier, Jersey; total a. 75 sq. m.; p. (1961) *110,503*.

Chantaburi, *t.*, *spt.*, Thailand, rubies and other precious stones.

Chantada, *commune*, N.W. Spain; cattle, leather, soap, bricks, linen; p. (1957) *14,467*.

Chantilly, *t.*, Oise, France; famous race-course; p. (1946) *5,105*.

Chanute, *mkt. t.*, Kan., U.S.A.; oil, gas; refineries, cement; p. (1960) *10,849*.

Chaochow (Chaozhou), *c.*, Kwangtung, S. China; on Han R. 20 m. N. of Swatow; ctr. of cultivated plain; rice, sugar, tea; linked to Swatow by rly.; p. (1953) *101,000*.

Chapada Diamantina, *t.*, Matoo Grosso, Brazil; diamond dist. [1,300 sq. m.

Chapala, *L.*, Mexico; chiefly in Jalisco st.; a.

Chapayev, *see* **Gurev.**

Chapayevsk, *t.* Kuibyshev Region, R.S F.S.R.; chemicals, agr. machin.; p. (1959) *83,000*.

Chapelcross, nr. Annan, Dumfriesshire, Scot.; nuclear reactor sta.; power and plutonium prod.

Chapel-en-le-Frith, *mkt. t.*, *rural dist.*, Derby, Eng.; p. (1961 rural dist.) *18,366*.

Chapelizod, *sub.* of Dublin, Ireland; on R. Liffey.

Chapra, *t.*, Bihar; on Ganges R.; ctr. of saltpetre and indigo tr.; p. (1961) *75,580*.

Chard, *mun. bor.*, Somerset, Eng.; lace, iron, engin., shirt and cotton mftg.; p. (1961) *5,778*.

Chardzhou, *t.*, Turkmen S.S.R.; on the Central Asia Rly.; textiles, chemicals; p. (1959) *66,000*.

Charente, *dep.*, W. France; cap. Angoulême; ctr. of distilling tr., cognac; a. 2,305 sq. m.; p. (1962) *327,658*.

Charente, R., W. France; flows into Bay of Biscay below Rochefort.

Charente-Maritime, *dep.*, S.W. France; cap. La Rochelle; wine, wheat; oysters, pilchards; a. 2,791 sq. m.; p. (1962) *470,897*.

Charenton-le-Pont, *commune*, Seine dep., France; N.E. sub. of Paris; boats, pottery, rubber; p. (1954) *22,079*.

Charleroi, *t.*, Hainaut, Belgium; on R. Sambre; coal-mng.; glass; p. (1962) *26,056*.

Charleroi, *t.*, Penns., U.S.A.; steel glass; p. (1960) *8,148*. [(1960) *9,964*.

Charles City, *c.*, Iowa, U.S.A.; on Cedar R.; p.

Charleston, *t.*, Ill., U.S.A.; dairy produce, flour, shoes; p. (1960) *10.505*.

Charleston, *c. spt.*, S. Carolina, U.S.A.; lumber, metal, concrete, fertilisers, chemicals, plastics, cigars, fabrics; p. (1960) *60,182*.

Charleston, *t.*, *cap.*, W. Virginia, U.S.A.; on Kanawha R.; in bituminous coal dist.; chemicals, glass, tools, oil, natural gas, lumber, coal processing; p. (1960) *85,796*.

Charlestown, *ch. t.*, Nevis I., Leeward Group; p. (1957) *15,446*.

Charleville, *see* **Rathluirc.**

Charleville, *t.*, Ardennes dep., N.E. France; on Meuse R. opposite Mézières; iron, bricks; p. (1954) *22,536*.

Charleville, *t.*, Queensland, Australia; on Warrego R., 400 m. W. of Brisbane; pastoral dist.; p. (1947) *3,548*.

Charlevoix, *pt.*, *t.*, L. Michigan, U.S.A.; p. (1960) *2,751*.

Charlotte, *c.*, N.C., U.S.A.; key rly. junction; machin., chemicals, textiles; p. (1960) *201,564*.

Charlotte, *t.*, S. Mich., U.S.A.; furniture, car parts; p. (1960) *7,657*.

Charlottenburg, *t.*, Germany; on R. Spree; sub. of Berlin; palace; china, beer, machin.

Charlottesville, *t.*, Va., U.S.A.; on Rivanna R.; univ.; Monticello—home of Thomas Jefferson; p. (1960) *29,427*.

Charlottetown, *spt.*, *cap.*, Prince Edward I., Canada; Parliament buildings; iron foundry, shipyards, fisheries; p. (1961) *18,318*.

Charlton Kings, *urb. dist.*, Gloucester, Eng.; at foot of Cotswolds nr. Cheltenham; p. (1961) *7,744*.

Charnwood Forest, *upland district*, Leicester, Eng.; to W. of Soar valley, 12 m. N.W. of Leicester; composed of ancient rocks; stone-crushing; largely forests; used for recreation by industl. ts. of E. Midlands; alt. 600–900 ft.

Charters Towers, *t.*, N. Queensland, Australia; 925 m. by rail from Brisbane; p. (1961) *7,621*.

Chartres, *c.*, *cap.*, dep. Eure-et-Loir, France; fine Gothic cath.; milling, brewing, distilling; p. (1954) *28,750*.

Chartreuse, La Grande, France, famous monastery near Grenoble.

Châteaubriant, *t.*, Loire-Inférieure, France; rly. ctr.; p. (1946) *7,965*.

Château Thierry, *t.*, Aisne, France; on R. Marne; p. (1946) *7,283*.

Châteauroux, *t.*, Indre, France; 60 m. S.E. of Tours on R. Indre; woollens, machin.; p. (1962) *46,772*.

Châtelet, *t.*, Hainaut, Belgium; on R. Sambre; coal, pottery; p. (1962) *15,483*.

Châtelineau, *t.*, Hainaut, Belgium; p. (1962) *20,095*.

Châtellerault, *t.*, Vienne, France; 40 m. S. of Tours; cutlery, small arms; p. (1954) *23,583*.

Châtenay-Malabry, *t.*, Seine, France; p. (1954) *14,269*.

Chatham, *mun. bor.*, *dockyard*, (*former naval arsenal*), Kent, Eng.; on estuary of R. Medway; light inds.; p. (1961) *48,989*.

Chatham, *t.*, *spt.*, New Brunswick, Canada; lumbering, fish exporting; p. (1961) *7,109*.

Chatham, *c.*, Ontario, Canada; farming, fruit, machin., canned vegetables; p. (1961) *29,826*.

Chatham, Is., New Zealand dependency; a. 372 sq. m.; lgst. I., Wharekauri; (1961) *487*.

Châtillon-sur-Seine, *t.*, Côte d'Or, France; on R. Seine, 45 m. S.E. of Troyes; p. (1954) *12,526*.

Chatou, *t.*, Seine-et-Oise, France; p. (1954) *15,338*.

Chatsworth, *par.*, Derby, Eng.; on R. Derwent; seat of Duke of Devonshire.

Chattanooga, *c.*, Tenn., U.S.A.; on Tennessee R.; univ.; rly. ctr.; cottons; iron, steel, chemicals, paper, metals; p. (1960) *130,009*.

Chatteris, *urb. dist.*, Cambridge and Isle of Ely, Eng.; mkt. t.; p. (1961) *5,490*.

Chaudière Falls, on Ottawa R., above Ottawa, Canada; hydro-electric power-sta.

Chaumont, *t.*, Haute-Marne, France; gloves, leather; p. (1954) *19,346*.

Chauny, *t.*, Aisne, France; on R. Oise; chemicals, glass; p. (1954) *10,544*.

Chautauqua, *L.*, N.Y. st., U.S.A.; summer resort.

Chaux-de-Fonds, La, *t.*, *can.*, Neuchâtel, Switzerland; ctr. of watchmkg. ind.; p. (1957) *33,300*.

Chaves, *commune*, N. Portugal; cath.; hot salt springs; linen, silk; p. *6,482*.

Chaville, *t.*, Seine-et-Oise, France, p. (1954) *14,508*.

Cheadle, *rural dist.*, Staffs, Eng.; coal pits, metal mnfs.; p. (1961) *38,153*.

Cheadle and Gatley, *urb. dist.*, Cheshire, Eng.; textile finishing and bleaching; p. (1961) *45,599*.

Cheb, *t.*, ČSSR.; nr. Bavarian frontier; industl. ctr.; motor cycles, machin., textiles; p. (1961) *20,590*.

Cheboksary, *t.*, cap. R.S.F.S.R.; textiles, hydro-elec., engin., wood-working; p. (1959) *104,000*.

Cheboygan, *t.*, Mich., U.S.A.; on L. Huron; sawmills; p. (1960) *5,859*.

Cheddar, *vil.*, Somerset, Eng.; famous limestone caves in Mendips; cheese, strawberries.

Cheduba I., Bay of Bengal, Burma; fertile, well-wooded; a. 240 sq. m.

Chefoo (Yantai), *c.*, *former treaty pt.*, Shantung, China; on N. cst. of peninsula; p. (1953) *116,000*.

Chekiang (Zhijiang), *maritime prov.*, S.E. China; cap. Hangchow; exp. silk, cotton, etc.; a. 39,486 sq. m.; p. (1953) *22,865,747*.

Cheling Pass, on bdy. between Kwangtung, Hunan, S. China; historic route across Nanling mtns., now followed by Hankow to Canton trunk rly.; alt. 984 ft.

Chelles, *t.*, Seine-et-Marne, France; p. (1954) *19,539*.

Chelm, *t.*, E. Poland; nr. Lublin; cath.; 1944 Manifesto of Poland's Liberation issued here; p. (1960) *31,000*.

Chelmer, *R.*, Essex, Eng.; joins R. Blackwater at Maldon.

Chelmno (Kulm), *t.*, Pomerania, Poland; on R. Vistula; ancient wells; large oil mills, engin., impt. tr.; p. (1946) *11,634*.

Chelmsford, *co. t.*, *mun. bor.*, Essex, Eng.; 30 m. N.E. London; cath.; agr. mkt.; radio, elec. engin., brewing; p. (1961) *49,908*.

Chelmza (Kulmsee), *t.*, Pomerania, Poland; N. of Torun; p. (1946) *10,764*.

Chelsea, *see* **Kensington and Chelsea.**

Chelsea, *t.*, Mass., U.S.A.; rubber goods, shoes, paper; p. (1960) *33,749*.

Cheltenham, *t.*, *mun. bor.*, Gloucester, Eng.; spa; educational ctr.; aircraft mftg. and repair, precision instruments; p. (1961) *71,968*.

Chelyabinsk, *t.*, R.S.F.S.R.; on Mijas R. W. Siberian lowlands; metallurgy and machin.; pipeline to natural gas field Gazli opened Nov. 1963; p. (1962) *751,000*.

Chelyuskin C., most N. point of Asia.

Chemnitz, *see* **Karl-Marx-Stadt.**

Chemulpo, *see* **Inchon.**

Chenab, *R.*, W. Punjab, Pakistan; one of "five rivers" of Punjab; rises in Himalayas, flows S.W. into R. Sutlej; dams at Merala and Khanki provide water for Upper and Lower Chenab Irrigation Canal Systems; length approx. 900 m.

Chengchow (Zhengzhou), *c.*, *cap.* Honan prov., China; 15 m. S. of Hwang-Ho, where it emerges on to N. China Plain; impt. route ctr. and rly. junction where Peking to Hankow rly. crosses Sian to Tunghai rly.; p. (1953) *595,000*.

Chengtu (Chengdu), *c.*, *cap.* Szechwan prov., China; silk, rice; p. (1957) *1,107,000*.

Chepstow, *mkt. t.*, *urb. dist.*, Monmouth, Eng.; on R. Wye 2 m. above confluence with R. Severn; fine ruined cas.; light engin., brush mkg., asphalt, limestone; p. (1961) *6,041*.

Chequers, *seat*, Bucks, Eng.; official residence of Prime Minister.

Cher, *central dep.*, France; cap. Bourges; grain, wines, iron, porcelain; a. 2,819 sq. m.; p. (1962) *293,514*.

Cher, *R.*, France, trib. of R. Loire, flowing from Auvergne Mtns.

Cherbourg, *spt.*, Manche, France; N. cst. of Contentin Peninsula; opposite to and 80 m. dist. from Portsmouth; naval arsenal, ship-bldg.; ropes, fishing; p. (1962) *40,018*.

Cheremkhovo, *t.*, R.S.F.S.R.; N W. of Irkutsk; coal, engin., chemicals; p. (1959) *123,000*.

Cherepovets, *c.*, R.S.F.S.R.; steel, engin., saw-mills; p. (1959) *92,000*.

Cheribon, *spt.*, Java, Indonesia; N. cst., 120 m. E. of Jakarta; rice, tea, coffee; p. *54,079*.

Cherkassy, *t.*, Ukrainian S.S.R.; nr. Kiev, on Dnieper R.; sugar, engin.; p. (1959) *83,000*.

Chernigov, *t.*, Ukrainian S.S.R.; on Desna R.; caths.; univ.; flour, textiles, chemicals; p. (1959) *89,000*.

Chernogorsk, *t.*, R.S.F.S.R.; 10 m. N. of Abakan; ctr. of Minusinsk coal-mng. basin; p. (1959) *51,000*.

Chernovtsy, *t.*, Ukrainian S.S.R.; univ.; Greek cath.; wheat, dairy produce, textiles, engin., chemicals; p. (1959) *145,000*.

Chernyakovsk (Insterburg), *t.*, Lithuanian S.S.R.; chemicals, textiles; p. (1959) approx. *50,000*.

Cherokee, *t.*, Iowa, U.S.A.; p. (1960) *7,724*.

Cherrapunji, *t.*, Assam, India; in Khasi Hills; reputed wettest place in world, av. annual rainfall 500 in.

Chertsey, *urb. dist.*, Surrey, Eng.; on S. bank of R. Thames, 4 m. below Staines; residtl.; aircraft components, cement; p. (1961) *40,376*.

Cherwell, *R.*, trib. of Thames, nr. Oxford; length 30 m.

Chesapeake Bay, *inlet* on Atlantic coast, U.S.A.; extending 200 m. from mouth of Susquehanna R. to C. Charles; shellfish ind.; bridge-tunnel (opened 1964) spans entrance to Bay.

Chesham, *residtl. t.*, *urb. dist.*, Bucks, Eng.; in heart of Chiltern Hills; printing, textiles, light engin.; p. (1961) *16,236*.

Cheshire, *co.*, Eng.; cap. Chester; plain; Rs. Mersey and Dee; dairying, mkt. gardening; salt, coal; mnfs.; textiles, chemicals, ship-bldg.; a. 1,056 sq. m.; p. (1961) *1,367,860*.

Cheshire, *t.*, Conn., U.S.A.; agr., formerly copper and barytes mined; p. (1960) *12,981*.

Cheshunt, *urb. dist.*, Herts, Eng.; in Lea valley, 7 m. S. of Hertford; bricks, mkt. gardening, horticulture; p. (1961) *35,371*.

Chesil Bank, Dorset, Eng.; shingle ridge from Portland to Bridport.

Chester, *c.*, *co. bor.*, Cheshire, Eng.; at head of estuary of R. Dee; cath., ancient walls and old timbered houses; engin., metal goods; p. (1961) *59,283*.

Chester, *t.*, S.C., U.S.A.; cotton mnfs.; flour; granite; p. (1960) *6,906*.

Chester, *t.*, Penns., U.S.A.; large inds., textiles; p. (1960) *63,658*.

Chesterfield, *mkt. t.*, *mun. bor.*, colly. dist., Derby, Eng.; on Rother R.; 8 m. S. of Sheffield; iron, steel, engin., coal-mng., glass, elec. lamps, galvanised goods, chemicals; p. (1961) *67,833*.

Chesterfield Inlet, arm of Hudson Bay, Canada; 250 m. by 25 m.

Chesterfield Is., *dep.*, New Caledonia, Pac. Oc.; French; about 342 m. W. of N.C.

Chester-le-Street, *urb. dist.*, Durham, Eng.; clothing, confectionery; p. (1961) *18,948*.

Chesterton, *sub.* of Cambridge, Eng.; p. *35,950*.

Cheviot, *t.*, S.W. Ohio, U.S.A.; clothes, leather goods; flour; p. (1960) *10,701*.

Cheviot Hills, between Scot. and Northumberland, Britain; highest point The Cheviot, 2,676 ft.

Cheyenne, *R.*, S.D., U.S.A.; trib. of Missouri; length 500 m.

Cheyenne, *cap.*, Wyo., U.S.A.; cattle-ranching dist.; rly. ctr.; p. (1960) *43,505*.

Chiana, Val de, *valley*, central Italy; longitudinal depression separating Tuscan Hills from Central Apennines; occupied by upper course of R. Arno, middle course of R. Tiber; followed by main route from Florence to Rome.

Chiangmai, *prov.*, N.W. Thailand; cap. Chiangmai; a. 8,839 sq. m.; p. (estd.) *544,000*.

Chiangmai, *t.*, Chiangmai prov., N.W. Thailand; on Ping R.; tr. ctr., teak; p. *50,000*.

Chiapas, *Pacific st.*, Mexico; cap. Tuxtla-Gutierrez; mountainous, forested; coffee, tobacco, sugar and cocoa, cattle; a. 28,729 sq. m.; p. (1960) *1,210,870*.

Chiatura, *t.*, Georgian S.S.R.; manganese; p. (1956) *19,200*.

Chiavari, *t.*, Liguria, Italy; on the Riviera; shrine of the Madonna; p. *17,586*.

Chiba, *cap.* of Chiba prefecture, Japan; on E. Tokyo Bay; impt. tr. ctr.; giant shipyard; p. (1962) *267,000*.

Chicago, *c.*, Ill., U.S.A.; at S.W. corner of L. Michigan; second c. in America; immense tr. by rail and Great Lakes, flourishing univ.; grain mkt., pork, beef canning, agr. implements, iron and steel, machin., clothing, furs, electronic equipment, metals, chemicals, petrol, coal; p. (1960) *3,550,404*.

Chichester, *c.*, *mun. bor.*, W. Sussex, Eng.; on S. cst. plain, 11 m. W. of Arundel; fine cath.; agr.; p. (1961) *20,118*.

Chickamauga Creek, U.S.A.; branch of the Tennessee R. above Chattanooga; Civil War battles; site of National Park.

Chickasha, *t.*, Okla., U.S.A.; maize, cotton; p. (1960) *14,866*.

Chiclana, *mftg. t.*, Spain; nr. Cadiz; p. (1957) *18,262*.

Chiclayo, *ch. t.*, Lambayeque dep., Peru; rice, sugar, wheat, coffee; p. (1961) *54,400*.

Chico, *t.*, N. Cal., U.S.A.; food processing, lumber, cement; p. (1960) *14,757*.

Chicopee, *t.*, Mass., U.S.A.; on Connecticut R.; hardware, carpets, cars; p. (1960) *61,553.*
Chicoutimi, *t.*, Quebec, Canada; on Chicoutimi R.; hydro-elec. power-sta.; lumber, pulp, paper; p. (1961) *31,657.*
Chidambaram, *t.*, Madras, India; nr. Cuddalore; p. (1961) *40,694.*
Chidley C., most N. point of Labrador, Hudson Strait, Canada.
Chiem, *L.*, large lake nr. Munich, Germany, 1,500 ft. above sea-level.
Chieri, *t.*, Piedmont, Italy; nr. Turin; was mediæval republic; Gothic church; silks, cottons; p. *14,747.* [*347,824.*
Chieti, *prov.*, S. Italy; a. 1,142 sq. m.; p. (1961)
Chieti, *t. cap.*, prov. Chieti, S. Italy; the ancient Teate Marrucinorum; p. (1961) *48,011.*
Chigirik, *t.*, Uzbek S.S.R.; new town being built (1963), 21 m. S. of Tashkent.
Chignecto Bay, inlet of Bay of Fundy, Canada.
Chigwell, *urb dist.*, Essex, Eng.; on borders of Epping Forest; Hainault Estate, now incorporated in Redbridge, Greater London; residtl.; p. (1961) *61,021.*
Chihli, *see* **Hopei.**
Chihli, G. of, *see* **Pohai, Gulf of.**
Chihuahua, *st.*, Mexico; adjoining the U.S.A.; mining, stock-raising and agr.; a. 94,822 sq. m.; p. (1960) *1,226,793.*
Chihuahua, *c.*, *cap.*, Chihuahua st., Mexico; fine cath.; on Mexican Central Rly.; silver, cottons, woollens; p. (1960) *150,430.*
Chikuho, *t.*, N. Kyushu, Japan; largest coal-mines in the country.
Chilcoot, *R.*, *pass*, Alaska, leading into Yukon Valley.
Chile, *rep.*, S. America, independent of Spain since 1818; Pacific coastal strip rising sharply to Andes; Atacama Desert in N., fertile valleys in ctr., heavy rains in S.; Spanish language; Roman Catholic; forested in S.; dairying, sheep, wool; gr. nitrate output, copper, iron ore, coal, iodine, paper, petroleum; cap. Santiago; ch. pt. Valparaiso; length 2,660 m., breadth 69–270 m., a. 285,133 sq. m.; p. (1962) *8,074,561.*
Chilka, *L.*, *inlet*, E. coast, Orissa, India.
Chillán, *c.*, *cap.* Nuble prov., Chile; destroyed 1939 by one of world's worst recorded earthquakes; since rebuilt; agr. and comm. ctr.; p. (1961) *82,947.*
Chillicothe, *t.*, Mo., U.S.A.; p. (1960) *9,236.*
Chillicothe, *c.*, Ohio, U.S.A.; on Scioto R., mftg.; furniture, leather; p. (1960) *24,957.*
Chilliwack, *t.*, B.C., Canada; on Fraser R.; dairy produce, fruit, lumber; p. (1961) *8,259.*
Chiloé, *I.* and *S. prov.* Chile; cap. San Carlos, suffered earthquakes 1939 and 1960; ch. pt. Ancúd destroyed 1960; a. 9,058 sq. m.; p. (1960) *98,662.*
Chilpaneingo, *c.*, *cap.*, Guerrero st., Mexico; (1960) *12,673.*
Chiltern Hills, *chalk hills*, Oxon., Bucks., Beds, and Herts., Eng.; highest point 904 ft. nr. Wendover.
Chimborazo, *mtn.*, Ecuador, Andes; extinct volcano, alt. 20,610 ft.
Chimborazo, *prov.*, Ecuador; cap. Riobamba; a. 2,089 sq. m.; p. (estd. 1962) *279,607.*
Chimbote, *spt.* Peru; steel, iron-ore, coal; tinned fish, fish-meal; p. (1961) *90,000.*
Chimkent, *t.*, Kazakh S.S.R.; chemicals, engin. textiles, lead smelting; p. (1959) *153,000.*
China, People's Republic of, Asia, consists of 27 provs. (inc. Taiwan, the aut. regions of Kwangsi Chuang, Ningsia, Inner Mongolia, Sinkiang, Tsinghai, and Tibet). Total a. 3,643,000 sq. m.; mountainous in N. and W., fertile valleys and plains in E.; Rs.: Hwang-ho, Yangtze, Si-kiang; climate, extreme in N.; monsoon in S.; wheat, barley, maize, millet in N.; rice (staple food), sugar in S.; cotton, tea, hemp, jute, flax; livestock; cotton, woollen and silk mnfs.; flour- and rice-milling; great mineral wealth; coal, iron, tin, antimony, wolfram, bismuth, molybdenum; rural electrification; p. (estd. 1965) *730,000,000.*
China Sea, part of W. Pacific between Korea and Philippines; divided by the narrow Formosa Strait into two areas; N. China Sea, including Yellow Sea, and S. China Sea.
Chinandega, *t.*, Nicaragua, Central America; cotton, sugar, bananas; iron wks.; p. (1960) *19,025.*
Chincha Is., gr. off cst. of Peru; p. (of ch. t.) *14,763.*
Chinchilla, *t.*, Albacete prov., Central Spain; p. (1957) *7,621.*
Chinchow (Jinzhou), *c.*, Liaoning prov., China; cement, glass, bricks, tiles, paper and wood pulp, oil; p. (1953) *352,000.*
Chincoteague, *t.*, and *I.*, E. Va., U.S.A.; fisheries, poultry; p. (1960) *2,131.*
Chindwin, *R.*, Burma; ch. trib. of Irrawaddy; rising in Patkoi Hills, navigable in rainy season.
Chindwin, Upper and Lower, *provs.*, Burma; fertile plains and extensive teak forests, rice.
Chingford, *see* **Waltham Forest.**
Chingleput, *t.*, India; S. of Madras; cotton weaving, salt mnfs.; p. (1961) *25,977.*
Chinju or Shinshu, *t.*, S. Korea; cotton; p. *30,269.*
Chinkiang (Zhenjiang), *c.*, Kiangsu, China; former treaty pt. Yangtse-kiang, 48 m. below Nanking; tr. ctr.; p. (1953) *201,000.*
Chinkolobwe, *mines*, Congo; uranium.
Chinon, *t.*, Indre-et-Loire, Central France; on R. Vienne, industl.; ruined cas., once a royal residency; nuclear power sta.; p. (1954) *6,743.*
Chinquinquira, *t.*, Boyaca, Colombia; pilgrimage ctr.; comm. ctr.; coffee, cattle; p. (estd. 1959) *24,150.*
Chinwangtao (Qinhuangdao), *c.*, *spt.*, *former treaty pt.*, Hopeh, N. China; on Yellow Sea cst., 150 m. N.E. of Tientsin; only good natural harbour on N. China cst.; exp. coal from Kailan mines; p. (1953) *187,000.*
Chioggia, *spt.*, *cath. c.*, N. Italy; on I. in G. of Venice; fishing; p. (1961) *47,151.*
Chios, *see* **Khios.**
Chippenham, *t.*, *mun. bor.*, Wilts, Eng.; mkt. t. on R. Avon; rly. signal and brake equipment, bacon curing, tanning; p. (1961) *17,525.*
Chippewa Falls, *c.*, Wis., U.S.A.; flour, lumber; p. (1960) *11,708.*
Chipping Campden, *vil.*, Gloucester, Eng.; in Cotswold Hills, on R. Stour; formerly impt. for woollens.
Chipping Norton, *mun. bor.*, *mkt. t.*, Oxford, Eng., nr. Banbury; p. (1961) *4,241.*
Chipping Sodbury, *mkt. t.*, Gloucester, Eng.; 8 m. N.E. of Bristol.
Chirchik, *t.*, Uzbekistan S.S.R.; 20 m. N.E. of Tashkent; engin., chemicals; hydro-elec. stas.; p. (1959) *65,000.* [*188,350.*
Chiriqui, *prov.*, Panama; cap. David; p. (1960)
Chirk, *t.*, Denbigh, Wales; on R. Clerlog, S. of Wrexham; slate, coal.
Chisinau, *see* **Kishinev.**
Chislehurst and Sidcup, *see* **Bexley and Bromley.**
Chistyakovo, *see* **Thorez.**
Chita, *t.*, *rly. junct.* Siberia, R.S.F.S.R.; on upper Amur R., 400 m. E. of L. Baikal; coal, engin., chemicals, sawmilling; p. (1959) *171,000.*
Chitral, *t.*, N.W. Frontier Prov., Pakistan; on the Kashkar R.; p. *1,000.*
Chitral, *st.*, Pakistan; N.W. Frontier Provs.
Chittagong, *dist.*, East Pakistan; ch. t., Chittagong; p. (estd. 1951) *11,783,000.*
Chittagong, *c.*, *spt.*, East Pakistan; on E. cst. of Bay of Bengal; exp. jute, tea; oil refinery under construction; suffered severe damage by cyclone May 1963; p. (1961) *364,205.*
Chittaranjan, *t.*, W. Bengal, India; new t. on Barakhar R., in steel ctr., of Asasol and Tatanagan; rly. locomotive wks.; p. (1961) *28,957.*
Chobrum, *see* **Godwin-Austen Mt.** [180 m.
Choctawhatchee, *R.*, Ala. and Fla., U.S.A.; length
Choisy-le-Roi, *t.*, Seine, France; cloth factories; p. (1962) *41,269.*
Cholet, *t.*, Maine-et-Loire, France; cotton, linen, flannel mnfs.; p. (1954) *29,358.*
Cholon, *t.*, S. Viet-Nam; 10 m. S.W. of Saigon; rice; p. (estd. 1948) *480,000.*
Cholula, *ancient c.* of Puebla, prov., Mexico; Aztec temple, pyramid of Cholula, and other remains.
Chomutov, *mftg. t.*, ČSSR.; p. (1961) *33,152.*
Chonos Archipelago, Chile, about 120 in number, on W. coast of Patagonia.
Chooz, *t.*, Ardennes, France; pressurized water reactor projected 1963.
Chorley, *industl. t.*, *mun. bor.*, N. Lancs, Eng.; on W. flank of Rossendale Fells, 7 m. S.E. of Preston; cotton, engin.; p. (1961) *31,262.*
Chorley Wood, *urb. dist.*, Herts, Eng.; p. (1961) *6,964.*
Chorrilos Pass, **Argentina**; in E. cordillera of Andes at alt. 14,655 ft.; used by rly. from Tucuman to Antofagasta.

Chorzow (**Królewska Huta**), *t.*, Upper Silesia, Poland; coal, iron and steel, chemicals, engin.; p. (1960) *147,000.*
Choukoutien, *vil.*, Hopeh prov., N.E. China; site of discovery of bones of extinct Pekin man.
Chowtsun, *t.*, *former treaty pt.*, Shantung, N.E. China; silk; rly.; p. *46,200.*
Christchurch, *t.*, *mun. bor.*, Hants, Eng.; on S. cst. 5 m. E. of Bournemouth; holiday resort, aircraft, light inds.; p. (1961) *26,498.*
Christchurch, *cap.*, Canterbury, S.I., N.Z.; univ.; cath., mus.; comm. ctr. of lamb, wool and grain prov.; airpt.; p. (1961) *220,322*, of c. *151,333.*
Christiansand, *see* Kristiansand.
Christianshaab, Danish settlement on Disco Bay, W. Greenland; meteorological sta.
Christianstad, *see* Kristianstad.
Christiansund, *see* Kristiansund.
Christmas I., in Indian Oc., Australian terr. since Oct. 1, 1958; a. 62 sq. m., healthy climate, phosphate deposits; p. (1960) *3,099.*
Christmas I., lge. coral atoll in Pacific, one of Line Is.; discovered by Cook 1777; 100 m. in circum; U.K. nuclear test site, 1957–64.
Chrudim, *t.*, ČSSR.; horse mkt., mnfs.; p. (1961) *15,514.*
Chrzanow, *commune*, S. Poland; 27 m. from Krakow: coal, locomotives, leather, bricks; p. (1960) *21,000.*
Chu, *R.*, Kazakh S.S.R., U.S.S.R.; rises in Tien Shan, flows N.W. for 500 m. into inland drainage basin; Chumysh Dam provides hydro-electricity and water for intensive cultivation under irrigation of cotton, sugar-beet, citrus fruits.
Chuanchow (**Quanzhou**), *c.*, Fukien prov.; China; rice, wheat, sugar cane; p. (1953) *108,000.*
Chuchow (**Zhuzhou**), *c.*, Hunan prov., China; p. (1953) *127,000.*
Chu Kiang (**Canton R. or Pearl R.**), Kwangtung, S. China; one of most impt. waterways of China; fertile delta known as "land of fish, rice and fruit"; around Canton network of elec. drainage and irrigation stas., built since 1959.
Chubut, *prov.*, Argentine; cap. Rawson; a. 87,152 sq. m.; agr.; p. (1960) *142,000.*
Chudleigh, *mkt. t.*, Devon, Eng.; on R. Teign; stone quarrying; p. (1951) *1,944.*
Chudskoye, *L.*, between R.S.F.S.R. and Estonia S.S.R.; 70 m. long.
Chula Vista, *t.*, Cal., U.S.A.; agr., aircraft; p. (1960) *42,034.*
Chulucanas, *t.*, Piura dep., Peru; p. (1940) *12,622.*
Chungking (**Zhongqing**), *t.*, *former treaty pt.*, Szechwan, China; on Yangtze-Kiang; comm. ctr., S.W. China; exp. silk, soya-beans, sugar; p. (1957) *2,121,000.*
Chuquibamba, *t.*, Peru; nr. Arequipa; p. *2,480.*
Chuquibamba Mtns. (alt. 21,000 ft.), Peru.
Chuquicamata, *part* of Calama *commune*, N. Chile; lgst. copper-mines in the world; p. (1960) *30,476.*
Chuquisaca, *dep.*, Bolivia; cap. Sucre; a. 36,132 sq. m.; p. (1962) *307,600.*
Chur (**Coire**), *t.*, *cap.* Grisons can., Switzerland; Upper Rhine Valley; cath. and hist. bldgs.; p. (1950) *19,256.*
Church, *urb. dist.*, *sub.* Accrington, Lancs, Eng.; cotton weaving and engin.; p. (1961) *5,880.*
Church Stretton, *urb. dist.*, Salop, Eng.; p. (1961) *2,712.*
Churchill, *R.*, Canada; enters Hudson Bay at Churchill; 925 m.; fine harbour.
Churchill, *t.*, Manitoba, Canada; terminus of Hudson Bay rly.; summer wheat route from prairie provs.
Chusan I., off E. cst. of China; cap. Tinghai; tea, rice.
Chusovoy, *t.*, R.S.F.S.R.; in Urals; iron and steel; p. (1959) *60,000.*
Chuvash, *rep.*, A.S.S.R., U.S.S.R.; a. 7,107 sq. m.; p. (1959) *1,098,000.*
Cibao, *lowland area*, Dominican Republic, Central America; extends along N. side of Cordillera de Cibao for approx. 100 m.; cacao, tobacco, maize; densely populated, ch. t. Santiago.
Cicero, *t.*, Ill., U.S.A.; p. (1960) *69,130.*
Ciechanów, *t.*, Poland; 49 m. N.W. of Warsaw; agr. inds.; p. (1960) *20,000.*
Cienaga, *spt.*, N. Colombia; exp. cotton, bananas, cacao; p. (estd. 1962) *69,900.*
Cienfuegos, *t.*, *spt.*, Cuba; sugar, tobacco; p. (1953) *57,991.*
Cieszyn, *t.*, Katowice, Poland; p. (1960) *23,000.*
Cieza, *t.*, Murcia, Spain; in fertile raisin and orange-growing dist.; p. (1957) *23,328.*
Cilicia, *ancient prov.*, S.E. Anatolia, Turkey.
Cincinnati, *c.*, Ohio, U.S.A.; on Ohio R.; "the Queen City"; univ.; pork-packing, machin., tools, soap, electrotypes, seed processing, chemicals; p. (1960) *502,550.*
Cinderford, *lge. vil.*, Gloucester, Eng.; in Forest of Dean, 12 m. S.W. of Gloucester; ch. mining ctr. on sm. F. of D. coalfield.
Cinque Ports, five ancient English pts. on cst. of Kent and Sussex; Sandwich, Dover, Hythe, Romney and Hastings.
Cinto, *mtn.* Corsica.
Cintra, *see* Sintra.
Circleville, *t.*, Ohio, U.S.A.; agr. ctr., maize: wheat; p. (1960) *11,059.*
Cirencester, *t.*, *urb. dist.*, Gloucester, Eng.; the Roman Corineum; p. (1961) *11,836.*
Citlaltépetl, (Aztec name for **Orizaba**), *mtn.*, volcanic peak, Veracruz st., Mexico, highest point in Mexico; 18,701 ft.
Cittadella, *t.*, Venetia, Italy; nr. Padua; mediæval walls and towers; p. *12,679.*
Cittanova, *t.*, Reggio, Italy; built on ruins of Casalnuovo; olive-oil ind.
Citta Vecchia, *c.*, Central Malta; former cap.
Ciudad Bolivar, *spt.*, Bolivar st., Venezuela; on R. Orinoco; (formerly called Angostura); great comm. ctr.; coffee; cattle; p. (1961) *56,032.*
Ciudad Juarez, *t.*, Mexico; p. (1960) *261,683.*
Ciudad Madero, *t.*, Mexico; styrene and detergent plants.
Ciudad Real, *prov.*, S. Central Spain; grazing grounds, forest and quicksilver mines; cap. Ciudad Real; a. 7,622 sq. m.; p. (1959) *583,930.*
Ciudad Rodrigo, *c.*, Salamanca, Spain; captured by French 1707 and 1710, by the English 1706, stormed by Wellington in 1812; fine cath.; p. (1957) *12,600.*
Ciudad Trujillo, *see* Santo Domingo.
Civitavecchia, *spt.*, Latium, Italy; on W. cst., 30 m. N. of mouth of R. Tiber; sulphur springs; p. *34,400.*
Clackmannan, *smallest co.*, Scot.; flat in Carse, and hilly elsewhere; co. t. Alloa; coal, textiles (esp. woollens), metal work, brewing, distilling, agr.; a. 54½ sq. m.; p. (1961) *41,391.*
Clacton-on-Sea, *t.*, *urb. dist.*, Essex, Eng.; on E. cst., 12 m. S.E. of Colchester; seaside resort; light inds.; residtl.; p. (1961) *27,572.*
Clairton, *t.*, S.W. Penns., U.S.A.; coal, iron, steel, chemicals; p. (1960) *18,389.*
Clairvaux, *vil.*, Aube, France; famous Cistercian Abbey.
Clamart, *t.*, Seine, France; p. (1962) *48,290.*
Clanwilliam, *t.*, Cape Province, Rep. of S. Africa, on Oliphant R.; p. *1,468.*
Clare, *co.*, Munster, Ireland; co. t. Ennis; oats, potatoes; sheep, cattle; oysters, salmon; a. 1,294 sq. m.; p. (1961) *73,710.*
Clare, *t.*, S. Australia; on W. flank of Flinders Mtns., 70 m. N.E. of Adelaide; ctr. of wine-producing dist.
Clare I., Clew Bay, Mayo, Ireland.
Clarence Strait, between Melville I. and P. Darwin, N. Terr., Australia.
Clarence, *R.*, N.S.W., Australia; length 240 m.
Clarksburg, *t.*, W. Virginia, U.S.A., machin., glass, pottery; p. (1960) *28,112.*
Clarksdale, *t.*, Miss., U.S.A.; p. (1960) *21,105.*
Clarksville, *t.*, Tenn., U.S.A.; on Cumberland R.; tobacco mkt.; p. (1960) *22,021.*
Claustal-Zellerfeld, *t.*, Lower Saxony, Hanover, Germany; iron, lead, copper, silver, zinc; tourist ctr.; p. (estd. 1954) *17,200.*
Clawson, *t.*, Mich., U.S.A.; p. (1960) *14,795.*
Clay Cross, *urb. dist.*, Derby, Eng.; coal and iron; p. (1961) *9,173.*
Clayton-le-Moors, *urb. dist.*, Lancs, Eng.; nr. Blackburn; textile machin., cotton and blanket weaving, bristles, soap; p. (1961) *6,421.*
Clear, Alaska; site of American ballistic missile early warning station.
Clear, C. (southernmost point of Ireland), Clear I., [off S.W. cst.
Clearwater, *t.*, Fla., U.S.A.; citrus fruit, flowers, fish; resort; p. (1960) *34,653.*
Cleator Moor, *colly. t.*, Cumberland, Eng.; p. *8,291.*
Cleburne, *t.*, Texas, U.S.A.; rly wks., flour; p. (1960) *15,381.*

Cleckheaton, *mftg. t.*, Yorks, Eng.; nr. Bradford; woollens, blankets.
Clee Hills, Salop, Eng.; between Rs. Severn and Teme; alt. 1,800 ft.
Cleethorpes, *t.*, *mun. bor.*, Lindsey, Lincs, Eng.; on E. cst. 3 m. S. of Grimsby; resort; p. (1961) *32,705*.
Clent, *hills*, N.E. Worcester, Eng.; about 10 m. S.W. of Birmingham, on S. edge of S. Staffordshire coalfield, overlooking valley of R. Stour; well wooded; used for recreation by industl. ts. around Birmingham; maximum alt. 1,036 ft.
Clerkenwell, *industl. dist.*, London, Eng.; immediately N. of the City.
Clermont-Ferrand, *t.*, Puy-de-Dôme, France; fine Gothic cath.; former cap. of Auvergne; rubber; chemicals; food ind.; p. (1962) *134,263*.
Clevedon, *urb. dist.*, Somerset, Eng.; at mouth of R. Severn; seaside resort; quarrying, bricks, footwear; p. (1961) *10,642*.
Cleveland, *hilly agr. dist.*, N.R. Yorks, Eng.; between R. Tees and Whitby.
Cleveland, *c.*, *port*, Ohio, U.S.A.; on L. Erie; rly. ctr.; steamboat mnfs.; machin., iron foundries, lumber, coal, oil-refining, meat canning, steel, metals, aircraft, refrigerators, chemicals; p. (1960) *876,050*.
Clew Bay, Mayo, Ireland; 10 m. by 7 m.
Clichy, *t.*, Seine, France; p. (1962) *56,495*.
Clifton, *sub.*, Bristol, Eng.; on R. Avon; mineral springs; famous suspension bridge.
Clifton, *t.*, New Jersey, U.S.A.; nr. Passaic; p. (1960) *82,084*.
Clinton, *c.*, Iowa, U.S.A.; on Mississippi R.; iron and steel; p. (1960) *33,589*.
Clinton, *t.*, Mass., U.S.A.; on Nashua R.; machin., carpets; p. (1960) *12,848*.
Clinton Golden Lake, *L.*, Mackenzie, N.W. Terr., Canada.
Clitheroe, *t.*, *mun. bor.*, Lancs, Eng.; on R. Ribble; cotton weaving, limestone quarrying; p. (1961) *12,147*.
Clonakilty, *urb. dist.*, Cork, Ireland; nr. Bandon; corn, farming; p. (1961) *2,417*.
Cloncurry, *t.*, Queensland, Australia; in pastoral and lge. copper-producing dist. S. of the G. of Carpentaria; p. (1948) *1,584*.
Clones, *mkt. t.*, *urb. dist.*, nr. Dundalk, Monaghan, Ireland; rly. ctr.; p. (1961) *2,107*.
Clonfert, *c.*, Galway, Ireland; famous monastery with seven altars.
Clonmel, *urb. dist.*, Tipperary, Ireland; on R. Suir; agr. ctr.; fairs; cider, footwear; p. (1961) *10,617*.
Clovelly, *par.*, Devon, Eng.; seaside resort, picturesque fishing vil.
Clovis, *t.*, N.M., U.S.A.; rly. junction, tr. ctr., wheat, cattle; p. (1960) *23,713*.
Cloyne, *mkt. t.*, nr. Middleton, Cork, Ireland.
Cluj, *c.*, Romania; textiles, uranium, engin.; p. (1959) *162,000*.
Clunes, *gold-mining t.*, Victoria, Australia, nr. Ballarat.
Clutha R., S.I., New Zealand.
Clwyd, *R.*, Denbigh, N. Wales; flows into Irish Sea at Rhyl; length 30 m.
Clydach, *t.*, Glamorgan, Wales; on R. Tawe, 5 m. N.E. of Swansea; steel wks., nickel refineries.
Clyde, *R.*, Lanark, S.W. Scot.; navigable to Glasgow; greatest shipbldg. ctr. in world; length 96 m.; twin-road tunnel under R. in Glasgow (Whiteinch–Linthouse) completed 1963.
Clyde, Firth of, Scot.
Clydebank, *burgh*, Dunbarton, Scot.; on the Clyde adjoining Glasgow; shipbldg., sewing machin., tyres, biscuits; p. (1961) *49,654*.
Clydesdale, *valley* of R. Clyde, S.W. Scot., agr.; fine horses.
Coachella Valley, Cal., U.S.A.; part of old bottom of G. of Cal. which lies N.W. of Stalon Sea; arid; dates and citrus fruits under irrigation from Imperial Valley irrigation system.
Coahuila, *st.*, Mexico; cap. Saltillo; maize, cotton; silver, copper, coal, gold; a. 55,062 sq. m.; p. (1960) *907,734*.
Coalbrookdale, *vil.*, Salop, Eng.; old coal- and iron-mines.
Coalville, *t.*, *urb. dist.*, Leics, Eng.; nr. Ashby-de-la-Zouch; coal-mining, engin., elastic webbing; p. (1961) *26,159*.
Coanza, R., Angola; length 660 m.
Coast Range, *mtns.*, U.S.A.; along Pacific cst.
Coatbridge, *burgh*, Lanark, Scot.; 10 m. E. of Glasgow; coal, iron and steel, prefabricated houses, tubes, engin.; p. (1961) *53,946*.
Coatesville, *t.*, Penns., U.S.A.; iron, steel, brass, textiles; p. (1960) *12,971*.
Coats I., S. of Southampton I., Hudson Bay, Canada.
Coatzacoalcos (Puerto México), *spt.*, Mexico; on G. of Campeche; oil refinery; chemicals; p. *13,740*.
Cobalt, *t.*, Ontario, Canada; silver, cobalt, arsenic, nickel; p. (1961) *2,209*.
Coban, *t.*, Guatemala, Central America; coffee and Peruvian bark tr.; p. (estd. 1960) *42,300*.
Cobar, *t.*, N.S.W., Australia; copper; p. (1947) *2,044*.
Cobh (Queenstown), *spt.*, *urb. dist.*, Cork, Ireland; fine harbour and docks; p. (1961) *5,266*.
Cobija, *cap.* of Pando dep., N.W. Bolivia; rubber; p. (1962) *2,537*.
Cobourg, *t.*, Ontario, Canada; on L. Ontario; dairying, fruit, woollens; p. (1961) *10,646*.
Coburg, *t.*, Bavaria, Germany; old cas.; wickerwork, furniture, metal, machines, toy inds.; p. (1963) *43,100*.
Cochabamba, *dep.*, Bolivia; a. 25,288 sq. m.; p. (1962) *550,300*.
Cochabamba, *t.*, *cap.*, dep. Cochabamba, Bolivia; cath.; oil refining, shoes, rubber tyres, fruit, canning; modern milk plant; hydro-elec. plant projected; p. (1962) *92,008*.
Cochin, *spt.*, Kerala, India; Malabar cst.; exp. coconut oil, tea; oil refining; p. (1961) *35,076*.
Cochin China, name formerly applied to the whole E. part of Indo-China, now limited to S.E. of the peninsula; since 1946 within S. Viet-Nam; rice, silk, coffee, rubber, maize, cotton; cap. Saigon; a. 26,476 sq. m.; p. *5,600,000*.
Cockburn Land, N. of Baffin I., Arctic Canada.
Cockenzie and Port Seton, *burgh*, East Lothian, Scot.; on Firth of Forth, 9 m. E. of Edinburgh; p. (1961) *3,462*.
Cockermouth, *t.*, *urb. dist.*, Cumberland, Eng.; coal, agr., shoe mfg.; p. (1961) *5,823*.
Cocle, *prov.*, Panama, Central America; cap. Penonomé; p. (1960) *93,156*.
Cocos or Keeling Is., *2 coral atolls*, Indian Ocean; since 1955 terr. of Australia; ch. prod. coconuts; strategic psn. S.E. of Ceylon, 530 m. W. of Christmas I., N.E. of Mauritius; radio and cable sta.; civil aviation marine base; German raider beached and destroyed on N. Keeling I. in 1914; a. 5 sq. m.; p. (estd. 1960) *607*.
Cod, C., S.E. point of Mass. Bay, U.S.A.; summer resort; fishing boat bldg.; p. (estd. 1960) *55,000*.
Coesfeld, *t.*, N. Rhine–Westphalia, Germany; textiles, machin.; p. (1963) *20,700*.
Coeur d'Alene, *t.*, Idaho, U.S.A.; lead, silver, lumber; p. (1960) *14,291*.
Coffeyville, *t.*, Kan., U.S.A.; p. (1950) *17,133*.
Coggeshall, *par.*, Essex, Eng.; on Blackwater R.; silk; isinglass; p. (1961) *3,027*.
Cognac, *t.*, Charente, France; cognac, bottles; p. (1954) *19,026*.
Cohoes, *c.*, N.Y., U.S.A.; on Hudson R.; hosiery, paper, foundries; p. (1960) *20,129*.
Coimbatore, *t.*, Madras, India; coffee, sugar, cotton spinning; p. (1961) *286,305*.
Coimbra, *c.*, *cap.*, Beira Litoral prov., Portugal; cath., univ.; wine-growing, earthenware mnfs.; p. (1950) *98,883*.
Coin, *commune* Malaga, Spain; soap, paper, textiles, oil, wine, marble; p. (1957) *20,000*.
Cojutepeque, *t.*, El Salvador, Central America; cigars; rice, sugar, coffee in a.; p. (1960) *18,536*.
Colac, *t.*, Victoria, Australia; nr. Melbourne; farming and dairying dist.; p. (1961) *9,255*.
Colchagua, *prov.*, Chile; cap. San Fernando; stock raising; a. 3,422 sq. m.; p. (1961) *181,593*.
Colchester, *mun. bor.*, Essex, Eng.; on R. Colne; univ.; light inds., engin., oyster fisheries; p. (1961) *65,080*.
Cold Harbour, *vil.*, Va., U.S.A.; battles between Grant and Lee, 1864.
Coldstream, *burgh.*, Berwick, Scot.; on R. Tweed; agr. engin., and knitwear; p. (1961) *1,227*.
Coldwater, *t.*, Mich., U.S.A.; engin.; flour, cement, leather goods; p. (1960) *8,880*.
Coleford, *t.*, Gloucester, Eng.; in Forest of Dean; ctr. of sm. coal-mining dist.; p. *2,800*.

Colenso, *t.*, Natal, S. Africa; on R. Tugela; battle 1899; p. *2,145.*

Coleraine, *urb. dist., spt.*, Londonderry, N. Ireland; on R. Bann, 4 m. from sea; linen, acrilan mftg., distilling; p. (1961) *11,912.*

Coleshill, *t.*, Warwick, Eng.; lurgi gasification plant projected; p. *3,177.*

Colima, *volcano* (30 m. N.E. of c.), Mexico, alt. 12,685 ft.

Colima, *st.* Mexico; on Pacific cst.; cap. Colima; a. 2,009 sq. m.; p. (1960) *164,450.*

Colima, *c.*, Mexico; on Colima R. in fertile valley; p. (estd.) *25,000.*

Coll, *I.*, off coast of Mull, Argyll, Scot.; agr., lobster fishing ind.

Colle di Val d'Elsa, *commune*, Siena, Italy; cath.; metal mftg.; p. *11,052.*

Collie, *t.* Western Australia; p. (1961) *7,545.*

Collingswood, *t.*, N.J., U.S.A.; p. (1960) *17,370.*

Collingwood, *t.*, Ontario, Canada; on L. Huron; shipbldg., steel; p. (1961) *8,385.*

Collinsville, *t.*, Ill., U.S.A.; coal, zinc smelting, canning; women's clothes; p. (1960) *14,217.*

Colmar, *t.*, cap. Haut-Rhin dep., France; vines, textiles, rayon, brewing; p. (1962) *54,264.*

Colne, *t.*, *mun. bor.*, E. Lancs, Eng.; cotton mnfs.; p. (1961) *19,410.*

Colne, *R.*, Essex, Eng.; oysters.

Colne Valley, *urb. dist.*, W.R. Yorks; woollens; p. (1961) *21,309.*

Cologne, (Köln), *c.*, *Land* N. Rhine–Westphalia, Germany; on R. Rhine at N. end of Rhine gorge; cath.; univ.; eau-de-Cologne, electrotechnical ind., machin., metallurgy, paper, wood, chemicals, cars, oil refining, textiles; impt. R. pt. and route ctr.; p. (1963) *832,400.*

Colomb-Béchar, *see* Béchar.

Colombes, *t.*, Seine, France; mftg. sub. of Paris; p. (1962) *77,090.*

Colombia, *rep.*, S. America, mountainous in W. (Cordilleras), swampy, llanos in E.; climate mainly tropical. Rs.: Magdalena, Canea and tribs. of Amazon; Spanish language; Roman Catholic; coffee, tobacco, cocoa, cattle; gold, platinum, oil, emeralds; oilfield in Amazon a.; cap. Bogotá; a. 439,997 sq. m.; p. (estd. 1963) *16,525,000.*

Colombo, *cap.*, *pt*, Ceylon; exp. tea, rubber, coconuts; p. (1963) *510,947.*

Colón, *c.*, Panama, Central America; at Atlantic end of Panama Canal; comm. ctr., oil refining nearby; p. (1960) *59,598.*

Colonia, *dep.* Uruguay; cap. Colonia; a. 2,193 sq. m.; p. (1953) *135,038.*

Colonsay, *I.*, Inner Hebrides, Scot.; 8 m. long; ecclesiastical antiquities; p. (inc. Oronsay) *238.*

Colorado, *st.*, U.S.A.; in Rocky Mtns.; agr. with irrigation; pastoral; gold, copper, silver, coal, petroleum, uranium; cap. Denver (*q.v.*); a. 104,247 sq. m; p. (1960) *1,753,947.*

Colorado, *R.*, W. of N. America, formed by union of Grand and Green Rs. (2,000 m. long, navigable for 600 m.), with cañon (6,000 ft. deep).

Colorado, *R.*, Texas, U.S.A.; length 900 m.

Colorado, *R.*, flows into Blanca Bay, Argentina.

Colorado Springs, *wat. pl.*, *health resort*, Col., U.S.A.; 64 m. S. Denver; smelting; p. (1960) *70,194.*

Colton, *t.*, S.E. Cal., U.S.A.; fruit and vegetable canning; mkt. gardening; p. (1960) *18,666.*

Columbia, *c.*, Mo., U.S.A.; st. univ.; flour, lumber; p. (1960) *36,650.*

Columbia, *t.*, Penns., U.S.A.; mnfs.; p., (1960) *12,075.*

Columbia, *cap.*, S.C., U.S.A.; burned 1865; univ.; cotton mills; ironwks.; p. (1960) *97,433.*

Columbia, *t.*, Tenn., U.S.A.; mftg.; livestock mkt.; p. (1960) *17,624.*

Columbia, *R.*, on Pacific slope of N. America; rises in Brit. Columbia, flows through Wash., U.S.A.; salmon fishing; length 1,400 m.

Columbia, Dist. of, U.S.A.; on left bank of Potomac R.; contains Washington, the federal cap. of U.S.A.; a. 69 sq. m.; p. (1960) *763,956.*

Columbia, Mt., Alberta, Canada (alt. 12,294 ft.).

Columbus, *st. cap.*, Ohio, U.S.A.; rly. ctr.; st. univ.; machin., paper, aircraft machin., chemicals; p. (1960) *471,316.*

Columbus, *t.*, Ga., U.S.A.; cotton goods, machin.; p. (1960) *116,779.*

Columbus, *t.* Ind., U.S.A.; engin.; leather goods; p. (1960) *20,778.*

Columbus, *t.*, Miss., U.S.A.; cotton, dairying; p. (1960) *24,771.*

Colwyn Bay, *t.*, *mun. bor.*, on cst., 6 m. E. of Llandudno; Denbigh, N. Wales; seaside resort; diamond tools; p. (1961) *23,090.*

Comacchio, *c.*, Italy; nr. the Adriatic, 20 m. N. Ravenna; p. *12,609.*

Comayagua, *c.*, Honduras Rep., Central America; cath.; univ.; p. (1961) *5,192.*

Combe Capelle, *rock shelter*, nr. Dordogne, France; discovery of race type of Aurignacian period, 1909.

Combe Martin, *vil.*, Devon, Eng.; 5 m. E. of Ilfracombe; popular seaside resort; p. (1951) *1,920.*

Comber, *t.*, Down, N. Ireland; distilleries, linen; p. (1961) *3,980.*

Comiso, *t.*, Sicily, Italy; medicinal spring, porcelain mnfs.; p. *29,555.*

Commentary, *t.*, Allier, France; nr. Moulins; mining; p. (1954) *9,259.*

Como, *c.*, N. Italy; at foot of Alps, on L. Como; silk ind.; oranges, olives; p. (1961) *82,070.*

Como, *L.*, N. Italy (35 m. long), tourist resort.

Comodoro Rivadavia, *spt.*, Chubut prov. Argentina; on San Jorge Gulf, 550 m. S.W. of Bahia Blanca; military zone; ch. source of oil in Argentine; p. (1960) *40,000.*

Comorin, C., most S. point of India.

Comoro Is., unit of French Community with full intern. aut., Mozambique channel, midway between Africa and Malagasy; cap. Dzaoudzi on Mayotte I.; total a. about 838 sq. m.; turtle fishing; vanilla, copra, sisal, timber, perfume plants; p. (1958) *183,133.*

Compiègne, *t.*, Oise, France; sugar-mills, rope; Armistice signed between Allies and Germany 1918; French surrendered to Hitler in 1940; p. (1954) *22,325.*

Compton, *t.*, Cal., U.S.A.; heavy engin., glass, oil refining; p. (1960) *71,812.*

Conakry, *cap.*, Guinea; experimental fruit gardens; airfields; p. (1957) *49,200.*

Concarneau, *t.*, Finistère, France; on I. nr. Quimper; salted fish and preserve tr.; p. (1954) *10,341.*

Concepción, *prov.*, Chile; cap. Concepción; Lota-Coronel coalfield, lgst in Chile; a. 2,201 sq. m.; p. (1961) *535,633.*

Concepción, *c.* prov. cap., Chile; shipping ctr. through its pt. Talcahuano; univ.; comm. and cultural t.; severe earthquakes 1939 and 1960; p. (1961) *186,700.*

Concepción, *t.*, Paraguay; trade ctr.; p. (estd. 1960) *34,000.*

Concepción C., on cst. of California, U.S.A.

Conception Bay, Newfoundland, Canada; N.W. of St. Johns.

Conchos, *R.*, Chihuahua prov., Mexico, Central America; flows N.E. from Sierra Tarahumare to Rio Grande; cotton under irrigation in upper valley.

Concón, *t.*, Chile; on N.E. point of Valparaiso Bay; oil refining.

Concord, *t.*, Mass., U.S.A.; literary ctr.; textiles; p. (1960) *12,275.*

Concord, *t.*, N.C., U.S.A.; cotton, textiles; p. (1960) *17,799.*

Concord, *t.*, *cap.*, N.H., U.S.A.; on Merrimore R.; granite, machin., textiles; p. (1960) *28,991.*

Concordia, *t.*, Argentina; on Uruguay R.; p. (1960) *56,000.*

Condamine, *R.*, Queensland, Australia; trib. of R. Darling.

Conegliano, *commune*, N. Italy; silks, wines, light mftg.; p. *15,434.*

Coney I., *t.*, N.Y., U.S.A.; on Long I., 5 m. long, comprises Manhattan Beach, Brighton Beach, W. Brighton and W. End; seaside resort.

Congleton, *t.*, *mun. bor.*, E. Cheshire, Eng.; on S.W. margin of Pennines; agr., salt, clothing, textiles; p. (1961) *16,802.*

Congo, Rep. of the, *ind. sov. st. within French Community*, Equatorial Africa; cap. Brazzaville; a. 132,000 sq. m.; p. (1962) *864,684.*

Congo, Rep. of the, *ind. sov. st.* (ex-Belgian); Central Africa; climate: uniformly hot, heavy rains; tropical forests; agr., palm oil, cotton, rice, copal, coffee, ivory, rubber; minerals: copper, gold, diamonds, tin, uranium; communications mainly river, some rail; cap. Leopoldville; ch. ts. Boma, Stanleyville, Elisabethville; a. 905,400 sq. m.; p. (1961) *14,150,000.*

Congo, *R.*, greatest R. in Africa, numerous tribs.; estd. length 3,000 m.; drains 1,500,000 sq. m., navigable from sea to Matadi for ocean steamers, from Matadi to Stanley Pool interrupted by rapids and falls, again navigable to Stanley Falls; estuary, 7–10 m. wide.

Conisborough, *t.*, *urb. dist.*, W.R., Eng.; limestone, bricks, tiles; p. (1961) *17,596*.
Coniston, *t.*, Ontario, Canada; on rly. 8 m. E. of Sudbury; nickel smelting; town built by and for nickel-mining company.
Coniston Old Man, *mtn.*, nr. L. Coniston, Lancs, Eng. (alt. 2,575 ft.).
Coniston Water, *L.*, N. Lancs, Eng.; length 5¼ m.; tourist resort.
Conjeeveram (**Kancheepuram**), *t.*, Madras, S. India; pilgrimage ctr.; silk, cotton, weaving; p. (1961) *92,714*.
Connacht, *prov.*, Ireland; (includes cos. Galway, Mayo, Sligo, Leitrim, Roscommon); a kingdom till reign of Henry I; mountainous in W.; farming, fishing; a. 6,863 sq. m.; p. (1961) *419,221*.
Connah's Quay, *urb. dist.*, Flint, Wales; p. [(1961) *8,355*.
Connaught, *see* Connacht.
Connaught Tunnel (Can. Pac. Rly.), B.C., Canada; longest in N. America (5 m.), 5,000 ft. under Mt. Sir Donald (Selkirk Mtns.).
Connecticut, *st.*, New England, U.S.A.; cereals, tobacco, dairying; fishing; watches and clocks, firearms, aircraft, engin., copper, brass, machin.; cap. Hartford; lgst. c. New Haven; a. 5,009 sq. m.; p. (1960) *2,535,234*.
Connecticut, *R.*, flows S. to Long I. Sound, U.S.A.; length 450 m.
Connellsville, *t.*, Penns., U.S.A.; coke, machin., motor cars; p. (1960) *12,814*.
Connemara, *mtns.*, *dist.*, W. of Ireland, Galway; many lakes and bogs; tourist resort.
Conowingo Dam, Penns., U.S.A.; situated on lower Susquehanna R.; hydro-electric power-sta. supplies power to inds. in Philadelphia.
Conroe, *t.*, Texas, U.S.A.; oil, timber; p. (1960) *9,192*.
Consett, *urb. dist.*, Durham, Eng.; on edge of Pennines, 10 m. S.W. of Newcastle; iron, steel, coke, coal; p. (1961) *38,927*.
Conshohocken, *bor.*, Penns., U.S.A.; iron, steel, surgical instruments, textiles; p. (1960) *10,259*.
Constance (**Konstanz**), *c.*, Baden-Württemberg, Germany; on L. Constance; cath.; textiles, machin., chemicals, elect. inds.; route ctr.; p. (1963) *55,100*.
Constance, L., or **Bodensee**, between Switzerland and Germany; 45 m. long, 9 m. broad; a. 207 sq. m.; R. Rhine flows through.
Constanta, *spt.*, Romania; on the Black Sea; exp. petroleum, wheat; p. (1959) *110,000*.
Constantina, *t.*, Andalusia, Spain; p. (1957) *14,619*.
Constantine, *dep.*, N. Algeria; cap. Constantine; p. (1960) *1,411,000*.
Constantine, *t.*, N. Algeria; wheat, woollens, leather; stands 2,130 ft. high upon a rock; p. (1960) *223,000*.
Constantinople, *see* **Istanbul**.
Conversano, *c.*, Bari, S. Italy; cath.; olives, citrus fruits; mnfs.
Conway, *t.*, S.C., U.S.A.; river pt.; cotton, tobacco, lumber; p. (1960) *8,563*.
Conway, *mun. bor.*, *spt.*, Caernarvon, N. Wales; at mouth of R. Conway; sm. seaside resort; cas.; quarrying, light engin.; p. (1961) *11,392*.
Cooch Behar, *dist.*, W. Bengal, India; a. 1,289 sq. m.; rice, jute, tobacco; p. (1961) *1,019,806*.
Cooch Behar, *t.*, Cooch Behar, India; on Torsha R.; suffered severely from earthquake 1897; p. (1961) *41,922*.
Cook, *mtn.*, alt. 12,349 ft.; highest point in S. Alps, New Zealand.
Cook Inlet, S. cst., Alaska; U.S.A. (200 m. long).
Cook Is., British group (Rarotonga, lgst.) in S. Pacific, annexed to New Zealand, 1901; internal self govt. 1965; bananas, oranges, copra; p. (1959) *17,654*.
Cook Strait, *channel* between N. and S. Is. of N.Z.; 15–18 m. wide; undersea cable completed 1965.
Cookham, *t.*, *rural dist.*, Berks., Eng.; on R. Thames nr. Maidenhead; p. (rural dist. 1961) *17,169*.
Cookstown, *mkt. t.*, *urb. dist.*, Tyrone, Ireland; linen; p. (1961) *4,964*.
Cooktown, *spt.*, Queensland, Australia; at mouth of Endeavour R.; pearl fishery and mining dist.
Coolac, *t.*, southern New South Wales; cattle.
Coolgardie, *gold mining t.*, W. Australia; p. *650*.
Coolin Mtns., *see* **Cuillin Hills**.
Coonoor, *t.*, Madras, India; sanatorium 6,000 ft. above sea-level; p. (1961) *30,690*.
Coopers Creek (**Barcoo**), *R.*, Central Australia; rises in Warrego Range, Gr. Dividing Range, flows S.W. into marshes of L. Eyre; flow is intermittent and seasonal, but provides water for livestock in this semi-arid region; length approx. 900 m.
Coorg, *former st.*, now inc. in Mysore, India; mountainous, forests; coffee, rice, rubber, tea; cap. Mercara; a. 1,587 sq. m.; p. (1961) *322,829*.
Coorong, The, S. Australia; lagoon and long tongue of land on cst.
Coosa, *R.*, Ala., U.S.A.; length 350 m.
Cootamundra, *t.*, N.S.W., Australia; agr. and mftg.; p. (1947) *5,252*.
Cootehill, *mkt. t.*, *urb. dist.*, Cavan, Ireland; Bellamont forest; p. (1951) *1,489*.
Copeland Is., gr. off N.W. coast of Down, N. Ireland, at entrance to Belfast Lough.
Copenhagen, *ch. spt.*, *cap.*, Denmark; on E. cst. of Själland I.; royal palace, univ., library; naval sta.; steel, metal, textiles, clothing, breweries; airport; p. (1960) *721,381*.
Copiapo, *cap.*, Atacama prov., Chile; impt. copper and iron mng. ctr.; p. (1960) *37,224*.
Copparo, *commune*, Ferrara, N. Italy; drained agr. land, in R. Po delta; p. *23,777*.
Coppercliff, *t.*, E. Ontario, Canada; mining, nickel-copper smelting; p. (1961) *3,600*.
Coppermine, *R.*, N.W. Terr., Canada; flows N. into Arctic Ocean; length 300 m.
Coquet I., off cst. Northumberland, Eng.
Coquilhatville, *t.*, Congo; at confluence of Rs. Congo and Ruki; p. *10,435*.
Coquimbo, *prov.*, Chile, on Argentine border; copper-mining dist.; cap. La Serena; a. 15,397 sq. m.; p. (1960) *393,664*.
Coquimbo, *spt.*, Chile; prin. exps. iron, copper, and manganese ores; p. (1962) *52,250*.
Coracora, *t.*, S. Peru; mining; pt. Chala; p. *8,000*.
Coral Sea, Pacific Ocean, extending from the New Hebrides to Australia.
Coraopolis, *bor.*, S.W. Penns., U.S.A.; iron, steel, glass; p. (1960) *9,643*.
Corato, *t.*, Apulia, Italy; farming ctr., olive oil, wine; p. *44,139*.
Corbeil-Essonnes, *t.*, Seine-et-Oise, France; on R. Seine, 12 m. S.E. of Paris; flour mills, printing, paper; p. (1954) *22,891*.
Corbridge, *t.*, Northumberland, Eng.; on R. Tyne, nr. Hexham; p. *2,415*.
Corby, *t.*, Northants, Eng.; 7 m. N. of Kettering; steel wks.; one of "New Towns," designated 1950; steel wks., shoes, clothing, lamps; p. (estd. 1965) *44,745*.
Cordeli, *t.*, S.W. Ga., U.S.A.; tr. ctr.; peanuts, cotton mills, sawmills; p. (1960) *10,609*.
Córdoba, *agr. prov.*, Argentina; cap. Córdoba; a. 65,195 sq. m.; p. (1960) *1,760,000*.
Córdoba, *c.*, Argentina; univ.; wheat, flour, wool, shoes; car and aircraft prod.; p. (1960) *600,000*.
Córdoba, *dep.*, Colombia, S. America; cap. Monteria; p. (estd. 1959) *377,690*.
Córdoba, *t.*, Veracruz, Mexico; cottons, woollens, coffee; p. (1960) *32,883*.
Córdova, *prov.*, Andalusia, Spain; cap. Córdova; agr., olives, vines, livestock; a. 5,299 sq. m.; p. (1959) *805,150*.
Córdova, *t.*, Andalusia, Spain; cap. of C. prov.; on Guadalquivir R.; cath.—formerly a sacred mosque of Mohammedans; textiles, leather, distilling; p. (1959) *188,161*.
Corentyne, *R.*, forms bdy. between Brit. and Netherland Guiana; length 400 m.
Corfe Castle, *par.*, Dorset, Eng.; cas. ruins; mkt., potter's clay.
Corfu, *see* **Kerkyra**.
Corigliano, *t.*, S. Italy; 4 m. from E. cst. of Calabria; agr.; p. *15,926*.
Coringa, *t.*, Madras, India; at mouth of Godavari R.
Corinth, Isthmus of, divides the Saronic G. from G. of Corinth, Greece; cut across by Ship Canal.
Corinth Canal, *ship canal*, S. Greece; traverses Isthmus of Corinth, links G. of Corinth and Ionian Sea with Saronic G. and Ægean Sea; opened 1893; length 3¼ m., depth 26 ft.
Corinthia, *prov.*, Greece; p. (1961) *112,491*.
Corinto (**Corinth**), *c.*, Greece; at W. end of Isth. of Corinth; occupies a site 3 m. distant from

the ancient classic c. destroyed by earthquake. 1858; currants, olive oil, silk; p. (1961) *15,892*.
Corinto, *ch. spt.*, N.W. Nicaragua; exp. hides, sugar, coffee; p. (1960) *7,096*.
Cork, *co.*, S. Ireland; lgst. and most S.; mtns.; dairying, brewing, agr., fisheries; cap. Cork; a. 2,890 sq. m.; p. (1961) *330,106*.
Cork, *spt., co. bor.*, Cork, Ireland; at mouth of R. Lee; woollens, butter, cattle, brewing, cars, rubber; p. (1961) *77,860*.
Cork Harbour, pt. of call (Cobh) for Atlantic steamers.
Corleone, *t.*, Palermo, Sicily, Italy; mineral [springs; p. *13,704*.
Corlu, *t.*, Turkey in Europe; grain mkt.: p. (1960) *21,956*. [(1954) *10,638*.
Cormeilles-en-Parisis, Seine-et-Oise, France; p.
Corner Brook, *c.*, W. Newfoundland; gd. harbour; pulp, paper; p. of E. and W. (1961) *25,185*.
Corning, *t.*, N.Y., U.S.A.; dairying, tobacco; p. (1960) *17,085*.
Cornwall, *co.*, S.W. Eng.; mkt. gardening, oats, cattle, fishing, minerals, kaolin, granite, tin, lt. engin.; extreme point Land's End; co. to. Bodmin; a. 1,357 sq. m.; p. (1961) *341,746*.
Cornwall, *c.*, Ontario, Canada; on St. Lawrence R.; H.Q. of Seaway Authority; textiles, pulp, paper, flour; p. (1961) *43,639*.
Cornwallis Is., Arctic Ocean, Brit. N. America.
Coro, *t.*, Venezuela; agr.; p. (1950) *28,307*.
Corocoro, *sm. t.*, La Paz dep., Bolivia; at alt. 13,000 ft. in Central Andes, 50 m. S. of La Paz; impt. copper-mining ctr.; p. (1946) *4,500*.
Coromandel Cst., cst. of S.E. Madras, India.
Coronado, Cal., U.S.A.; fashionable seaside resort; p. (1960) *18,039*.
Coronation Gulf, arm of Arctic Ocean; extreme point N. Canada; discovered by Franklin.
Coronel, *spt.*, Chile; p. *28,027*.
Coronel Oviedo, *t.*, Paraguay; p. (1945) *33,098*.
Corowa, *t.*, N.S.W., Australia; on R. Murray, 40 m. downstream from Albury; collecting ctr. for Riverina dist., vines, fruit, wheat, red-gum timber; valuable new coal deposits.
Corpus Christi, *c.*, Texas, U.S.A.; cotton; p. (1960) *167,690*.
Corrèze, *mtnous. dep.*, S. Central France; cap. Tulle; cereals, wines, cattle, timber, coal, granite, iron; a. 2,272 sq. m.; p. (1962) *237,926*.
Corrib, Lough, *L.*, Galway and Mayo, R.o.I.; a. 68 sq. m.; R. Corrib flows from it into Atl.
Corrientes, *prov.*, Argentina; cap. Corrientes; a. 34,325 sq. m.; p. (1960) *543,000*.
Corrientes, *t.*, Argentina; on Parana R.; univ.; cattle, sugar, rice, cotton; p. (1960) *104,000*.
Corrientes, C., Mozambique, Port. E. Africa.
Corry, *t.*, Penns., U.S.A.; oil, engin., metal wks., furniture; p. (1960) *7,744*.
Corsham, *mkt. t.*, Wilts, Eng.
Corsica (Corse), French I. and dep. in Mediterranean; forested, mtns.; agr., olives, lemons, chestnuts, vine growing; cap. Ajaccio; a. 3,367 sq. m.; p. (1962) *275,465*, excluding Bastia.
Corsicana, *t.*, Texas, U.S.A.; p. (1960) *20,344*.
Corso, C., N. point of Corsica.
Cortland, *t.*, N.Y., U.S.A.; stoves, wine; p. (1960) *19,181*.
Cortona, *t.*, Tuscany, Italy; nr. Perugia; silk factories; p. *30,222*.
Coruh, *prov.*, N.E. Turkey, a. 3,408 sq. m.; p. (1960) *193,684*, *spt.*, the *cap.* p. *13,861*.
Corum, *prov.*, N. Central Turkey in Asia, a. 4,339 sq. m.; p. (1950) *342,290*, *t.* its *cap.* p. (1960) *34,629*.
Corumba, *port*, Mata Grosso, Brazil; on R. Paraguay; p. (1960) *36,744*.
Coruña, *prov.*, N.W. Spain; cap. La Coruña (Corunna); a. 3,051 sq. m.; p. (1950) *955,772*.
Corunna, *see* **La Coruña**.
Corvallis, Ore., U.S.A.; rich farming section, canning, lumber; p. (1960) *20,669*.
Coryton, *t.*, Essex, Eng.; on Thames, oil refining.
Coseley, *t.*, Staffs., Eng.; W. edge of Black Country; heavy iron steel wks.; p. (1961) *39,557*.
Cosenza, *c.*, S. Italy; ctr. for figs, oranges, olive oil, wine, silk; cath., cas.; p. (1961) *77,590*.
Cosenza, *prov.*, Calabria, Italy; a. 2,566 sq. m.; p. (1951) *685,572*.
Coshocton, *t.*, Ohio, U.S.A.; coal, gas, oil; pottery, enamelware; p. (1960) *13,106*.
Cosne, *t.*, Nièvre, France; on R. Loire; pottery.
Costa Brava, *reg.*, Catalonia, Spain; tourism.
Costa del Sol, *reg.*, Malaga cst., Spain; tourism.
Costa Rica, *rep.*, Central America; cap. San José volcanic mtns.; agr., coffee, bananas, rubber, gold; a. 19,656 sq. m.; p. (1963) *1,325,155*.
Côte d'Or Mtns., N.E. part of Central Massif; max. alt. 1,968 ft.
Côte d'Or, *dep.*, E. France; traversed by R. Saône; cap. Dijon; wines, live-stock, iron and steel; a. 3,391 sq. m.; p. (1962) *387,869*.
Cotentin, *peninsula*, N. France; 50 m. long; Cherbourg, at its extremity, 80 m. from Portsmouth.
Côtes-du-Nord, *agr. dep.*, Brittany, W. France; cap. St. Brieuc; wheat, flax, iron, slate, fishing, linen-mkg.; a. 2,787 sq. m.; p. (1962) *501,923*.
Cotopaxi, *vol.*, (alt. 19,613 ft.) in the Andes of Ecuador, nr. Quito; loftiest active volcano in the world; recent eruptions have caused great damage to Ecuador.
Cotopaxi, *prov.*, Ecuador, S. America; cap. Latacunga; a. 2,595 sq. m.; p. (estd. 1962) *193,929*.
Cotrone, *spt.*, Catanzaro, S. Italy; good tr. in wine, olive oil, etc.; p. *21,496*.
Cotswold Hills, W. Eng., between Lower Severn and Upper Thames; highest point, Cleeve Cloud, 1,031 ft.; fine sheep pastures.
Cottbus, *t.*, Cottbus, Germany; on R. Spree; textiles, metallurgy; rly. ctr.; p. (1963) *71,390*.
Coudekerque-Branche, S. E. sub. of Dunkerque, Nord dep., France; tar and lubricant refinery, textiles; p. (1954) *15,334*.
Coueron, *t.*, Loire Atlantique, France; p. (1954) [*11,092*.
Coulsdon and Purley, *former urb. dist.*, Surrey, Eng., now inc. in Croydon outer bor. Greater London; in dry valley of N. Downs, 4 m. S. of Croydon; residtl.; chalk quarries; p. (1961) *74,738*.
Council Bluffs, *c.*, Iowa, U.S.A.; on Missouri R.; rly. ctr., farm implements, paper, machin.; p. (1960) *54,361*.
Coupar Angus, *mkt. burgh*, Perth, Scot.; in Strathmore, 16 m. S.W. of Forfar; p. (1961) *2,049*.
Courbevoie, *t.*, industl. sub. of Paris, France; on R. Seine; p. (1962) *59,941*.
Courcelles, *t.*, Hainaut, Belgium; coal, linen, factories; p. (1962) *17,331*.
Courneuve (La), *t.*, Seine, France; p. (1954) *18,349*.
Courtrai, *see* **Kortrijk**.
Cove and Kilcreggan, *burgh*, Dunbarton, Scot.; at junction of Loch Long and R. Clyde; p. (1961) *877*.
Coventry, *mftg. c., co. bor.*, N. Warwick, Eng.; 18 m. E.S.E. of Birmingham; ctr. of cycle, motor-cycle, motor-car ind.; aircraft, tools; chemicals; projectiles, textiles; cath.; univ.; p. (1961) *305,060*.
Covilha, *t.*, Beira Baixa, Portugal; cloth factories; [p. *19,213*.
Covington, *industl. c.*, Ky., U.S.A.; on R. Ohio, opp. Cincinnati; machin., leather, furniture; p. (1960) *60,376*.
Covington, *t.*, Va., U.S.A.; X-ray equipment, paper, rayon, textiles; p. (1960) *11,062*.
Cowbridge, *mun. bor.*, Glamorgan, S. Wales; nr. Cardiff; p. (1961) *1,065*.
Cowdenbeath, *burgh*, Fife, Scot.; 5 m. N.E. of Dunfermline; coal; p. (1961) *11,918*.
Cowes, *t., urb. dist.*, I. of Wight, Eng.; on both sides of estuary of R. Medina; home of the Royal Yacht Squadron; regattas and yacht bldg.; aircraft, p. (1961) *16,974*.
Cowley, *sub.*, Oxford, Oxfordshire, Eng.; 3 m. S.E. of Oxford; mnfs. motor vehicles.
Cowpen, *t.*, Northumberland, Eng.; nr. Morpeth; coal.
Cowra, *t.*, N.S.W., Australia; famous wheat dist. and site of st. experimental farm; p. (1958) *6,150*.
Cozenza, *t., cap.*, prov. Cozenza, Italy; iron and steel; p. *40,032*.
Cozumel I., E. of Yucatan Peninsula; Mexico.
Craców, *see* **Kraków**.
Cradle, Mt., *mtn.*, Tasmania, alt. 5,069 ft.
Cradock, *t.*, Cape Province; wool tr.; p. (1960) *19,476* inc. *5,200* whites.
Crail, *burgh*, Fife, Scot.; p. (1961) *1,066*.
Craiova, *cap.*, Oltenia, Romania; p. (1958) *106,000*.
Cramlington, *t.*, Northumberland, Eng; 8 m. N. of Newcastle; "New Town" designated 1964 (local authorities and private enterprise); proposed p. *48,000*.
Cranbrook, *rural dist., mkt. t.*, Kent, Eng.; hops and grain; p. (rural dist. 1961) *14,158*.

Cranford, *t.*, N.J., U.S.A.; iron, chemicals; p. (1960) *26,424*. [*66,766*.
Cranston, *c.*, Rhode I., U.S.A.: mnfs.; p. (1960)
Crater L., Ore., U.S.A.; in National Park, is a gr. body of water 2,000 ft. deep and 6 m. across, set in a crater of an extinct gigantic volcano, 8,000 ft. high.
Crathie and Braemar, *pars.*, Aberdeenshire, Scot.; adjoining Balmoral Cas. and Abergeldie Cas. estates; p. (1951) *1,291*.
Crato, *t.*, Ceara st., Brazil; at foot of Chapados de Araripe, approx. 300 m. by rail S. of Fortaleza; ctr. of irrigated area producing cotton, sugar, rice; p. (1960) *27,649*.
Crau, La, *region*, Bouches-du-Rhône dep., S.E. France; dry, pebbly area E. of Rhône delta; winter pasture for sheep.
Craven, *dist.*, Central Pennines, Eng.; relatively low limestone plateau, alt. mainly below 800 ft. except where capped by grits in N. Craven; typical limestone features, caves, stalactites and stalagmites, steep-sided valleys (dales); drained by R. Ribble to S.W., R. Aire to S.E.; largely moorland, sheep rearing in valleys, rearing of cattle for fattening elsewhere, cultivation of root and fodder crops; R. valleys give the only easy routes across Central Pennines, Leeds to Preston, Leeds to Carlisle; ch. mkt. ts. and route ctrs., Skipton, Settle.
Crawfordsville, *t.*, Ind., U.S.A.; p. (1960) *14,231*.
Crawley, *t.*, Sussex, Eng.; on N.W. flank of the Weald 9 m. S. of Reigate; one of "New Towns" designated 1947 to relieve population congestion in London; extends from vil. of Crawley N. towards Horley; engin., pharmaceutics, metal, leather, wooden goods; p. (estd. 1965) *60,717*.
Crayford, *former urb. dist.*, Kent, Eng.; now inc. in Bexley, Greater London; engin., fabric printing, oil and resin ref. [*4,422*.
Crediton, *mkt. t., urb. dist.*, Devon, Eng.; p. (1961)
Creil, *t.*, Oise, France; on R. Oise, 30 m. N. of Paris; machin. mnf.; p. (1954) *13,500*.
Crema, *commune*, Cremona, N. Italy; cath.; wine, silk, linen, lace, hats; p. *25,163*.
Cremona, *c.*, N. Italy; on R. Po; silk, cotton, stringed instruments; birthplace of Stradivari; p. (1961) *74,242*.
Crete, *I.*, E. Mediterranean; 60 m. from Greek mainland; cap. Khania (Canea), Heraklion (Candia) lgst. c.; incorporated into Greece after Balkan Wars (1913); exp. fruit, oil, etc.; a. 3,235 sq. m.; p. (1961) *483,258*.
Créteil, *t.*, Seine, France; p. (1954) *13,793*.
Creus, C., juts out into Mediterranean Sea, Spain, nr. French border.
Creuse, *dep.*, Central France; agr., etc.; cap. Gueret; a. 2,164 sq. m.; p. (1962) *163,515*.
Creusot, Le, *t.*, Saône-et-Loire, France; lge. ordnance works; p. (1954) *28,663*.
Creutzwald-la-Croix, *t.*, Moselle dep., N.E. France; coal, iron foundries; p. (1954) *10,183*.
Crevillente, *t.*, Spain; wine, wheat and fruit; p. (1957) *12,636*.
Crewe, *t., mun. bor.*, Cheshire, Eng.; 20 m. S.E. of Chester; lge. rly. wks.; impt. rly. junction; aircraft and refrigerator wks., clothing, engin., motor vehicles; p. (1961) *53,394*.
Crewkerne, *mkt. t., urb. dist.*, Somerset, Eng.; 8 m. S.W. of Yeovil; sailcloth, twine, webbing, gloves, concrete prod.; p. (1961) *4,215*.
Criccieth, *t., urb. dist.*, Caernarvon, N. Wales; on N. shore of Cardigan Bay; sm. seaside resort; p. (1961) *1,671*.
Crickhowell, *rural dist., mkt. t.*, Brecon, S. Wales; on R. Usk; paper; p. (rural dist. 1961) *7,483*.
Cricklade, *t., rural dist.*, N. Wilts., Eng.; on R. Thames, 8 m. N.W. of Swindon; p. (rural dist. 1961) *17,869*.
Crieff, *burgh, summer resort*, Perth, Scot.; on R. Earn, 15 m. W. of Perth; egg hatchery, preserve wks.; p. (1961) *5,773*.
Crimea Peninsula, jutting into Black Sea, U.S.S.R.; wheat, tobacco, fruit; campaign 1854–55 between Russia and the Allied Force of Turkey, Britain, France and Sardinia was chiefly fought out here (Alma, Balaclava and Sevastopol).
Crimmitschau, *t.*, Karl-Marx-Stadt, E. Germany, nr. Zwickau; woollen-cloth, machin.; p. (1963) *30,891*.
Crinan Canal, across peninsula of Kintyre, S.W. Scot.; connecting Loch Gilp with the Atlantic; length 6 m.
Cristóbal, *dist.*, Panama Canal Zone, Central America; adjoins Colón at N. entrance to Canal; p. (1960) *11,499*; of t. (1960) *817*.
Croaghpatrick, *mtns.*, Mayo, Ireland, 2,510 ft.
Croatia, *fed. unit*, Jugoslavia; formerly part of Austria; mtns.; cereals, potatoes, tobacco, timber, pigs, sheep, cattle; cap. Zagreb; a. 16,418 sq. m.; p. (estd. 1960) *4,207,000*.
Crockett, *t.*, E. Texas, U.S.A.; lumber, cotton-seed oil, pecan nuts; p. (1960) *5,356*.
Crocodile R., *see* **Limpopo.**
Croix, *t.*, Nord, France; p. (1954) *18,702*.
Cromarty, *burgh*, Ross and Cromarty, Scot.; off N.E. cst. of Black Isle; p. (1961) *605*.
Cromer, *t., urb. dist.*, Norfolk, Eng.; on N. cst. of E. Anglia; seaside resort; p. (1961) *4,895*.
Crompton, *mftg. t., urb. dist.*, Lancs, Eng.; 2 m. S. of Rochdale; cotton, engin., elec. lamps; p. (1961) *12,707*.
Cronenberg, *t.*, Rhineland, Germany; iron, silk weaving; p. *14,051*.
Crooked I., Bahama Is., W. Indies; p. (1953) *836*.
Crosby or Great Crosby, *mun. bor.*, S. Lancs., Eng.; on Liverpool Bay, 3 m. N. of Bootle; residtl.; seaside resort; p. (1961) *59,707*.
Cross, *R.*, S.E. Nigeria; rises in Cameroon Highlands, flows W. and S. into G. of Guinea at Calabar; useful inland waterway; length approx. 400 m.
Cross Fell, *mtn.*, Cumberland, Eng.; on E. border of co.; alt. 2,930 ft.
Crow Head, *C.*, Kerry, Ireland.
Crowley, *t.*, S. La., U.S.A.; rice mills, rice experiment sta.; p. (1960) *15,617*.
Crows Nest Pass, B.C., Alberta, Canada; southernmost pass across Canadian Rocky Mtns.; used by rly. from Medicine Hat to Spokane (U.S.A.); alt. summit 4,459 ft.
Croydon, *residtl. t., former co. bor.*, Surrey, Eng., now outer bor. Greater London; inc. Coulsdon and Purley; lt. inds.; fmr. airpt. (closed 1959); p. (1964) *327,125*.
Crozet Is., mountainous uninhabited group in S. Indian Ocean; French.
Cruzeiro, *t.*, S. Brazil, on trib. of Uruguay R.; coffee, tobacco; p. (1960) *27,005*.
Csongrad, *mkt. t., agr. dist.*, Hungary; at junction of Rs. Theiss and Koros; p. (1962) *20,399*.
Cuba, *I.*, W. Indies; taken from Spain by the U.S.A., but later constituted an independent rep.; climate, insular tropical, plentiful rainfall; tropical forest; agr., sugar-cane, tobacco, maize, fruits, mahogany and cedar, hardwoods, iron, copper, rayon, cement; cap. Havana; a. 44,206 sq. m.; p. (1953) *5,829,029*.
Cubango, *R.*, S. Africa, enters L. Ngami.
Cuckfield, *mkt. t., urb. dist.*, Sussex, Eng.; p. (1961) *20,113*.
Cuckmere, *R.*, Sussex, Eng.; rises in High Weald and flows S. into English Channel 4 m. W. of Beachy Head; passes through S. Downs in very beautiful gap; length 23 m.
Cucuta, *t.*, cap. Santander del Norte, Colombia, S. America; coffee, tobacco, cattle; p. (estd. 1959) *131,410*.
Cudahy, *t.*, Wis., U.S.A.; p. (1960) *17,975*.
Cuddalore, *spt.*, Madras, India; nr. Pondicherry; exp. oil-seeds, cottons; p. (1961) *79,168*.
Cuddapah, *t.*, Andhra Pradesh, India; cotton, cloth factories, millet, rice; p. (1961) *49,027*.
Cudillero, *commune*, Oviedo, N.W. Spain; manganese; p. *10,630*. [*9,042*.
Cudworth, *urb. dist.*, W.R. Yorks, Eng.; p. (1961)
Cue, *t.*, W. Australia; goldfields.
Cuenca, *c.*, Cuenca, Spain; on R. Jucar; p. (1949) *25,215*.
Cuenca, *agr. and mining prov.*, Central Spain; furniture, leather, paper; a. 6,588 sq. m.; p. (1959) *326,753*.
Cuenca, *cap.*, Azuay, Ecuador; univ.; cath.; sugar, tyres, flour mills; p. (1962) *63,000*.
Cuernavaca, *cap.*, Morelos St., Mexico; ancient Indian t. captured by Cortes; p. *30,567*.
Cuesmes, *coal mng. t.*, adjoining Mons, Belgium; p. (1962) *10,799*.
Cuiabá, *c., cap.*, Mato Grosso, Brazil; ctr. pastoral a.; gold and diamonds produced; galena deposit nearby; p. (1960) *57,860*.
Cuidadela, *t.*, Balearic Is., Spain; W. cst. of Minorca; cath.; ancient ruins; cheese mnfs.; p. *10,716*.
Cuillin Hills, I. of Skye, Scot.; highest peak Sgurr Alasdair; alt. 3,251 ft.

Culebra, *valley and mtns.*, N. New Mexico.
Culebra, *spt. and I.*, Puerto Rico; W. Indies.
Culgoa, *R.*, trib. of Darling R., Queensland and N.S.W., Australia.
Culiacau, *cap.*, Sinaloa, Mexico; p. (1950) *144,550.*
Cullen, *burgh*, Banff, Scot.; between Buckie and Portsoy; p. (1961) *1,327.*
Cullera, *spt.*, Valencia, Spain; on R. Jucar; p. (1957) *14,831.*
Cullinan, *t.*, Transvaal, S. Africa; ctr. of diamond-mining ind.
Culloden Moor, 6 m. E. of Inverness, Scot.; defeat of Bonnie Prince Charlie, 1746.
Cullompton (Cullumpton), *mkt. t.*, Devon, Eng.; paper, mftg., leather; p. *2,737.* [*514.*
Culross, *burgh*, F. of Forth, Fife, Scot.; p. (1961)
Culver City, Cal., U.S.A.; large motion-picture plant; p. (1960) *32,163.*
Cumaná, *spt., c.*, Sucre. Venezuela; coffee, cacao; sardine canning; airport; p. (1961) *73,400.*
Cumaná, *G.*, N. cst., Venezuela.
Cumberland, *co.*, Eng.; S.E. part of Lake Dist., ch. mtns.; Scafell, Helvellyn, Skiddaw; ch. Ls.: Ullswater, Derwentwater, Thirlmere; oats, sheep rearing, dairying, fishing, coal, iron ore, iron and steel, shipbldg.; a. 1,516 sq. m.; p. (1961) *294,162.*
Cumberland, *industl. t.*, Md., U.S.A.; on Potomac R.; iron and steel; p. (1960) *33,450.*
Cumberland, *t.*, R.I., U.S.A.; iron, cotton, silk, granite; p. (1960) *18,763.*
Cumberland, *R.*, Ky., U.S.A.; trib. of Ohio; length 700 m.
Cumberland Gap, Ky., U.S.A.; ch. break in high E. wall of Cumberland Plateau; gives access from upper Tennessee valley to Cumberland and Ohio valleys; very impt. routeway in colonisation of Ky.
Cumberland Is., off coast of Queensland, Australia.
Cumberland Plateau, *mtn. region*, Ky., Tenn., Ala., U.S.A.; forms S.W. zone of Appalachian mtn. system terminating abruptly towards Tennessee valley to E., Cumberland valley to W.; drained W. by tribs. of Cumberland and Ohio Rs.; composed of horizontal sandstones overlying coal; thinly populated by backward farming communities except where mining ts. occur in valleys cut down to coal; mainly between 1,200 and 3,000 ft.
Cumbernauld, Dunbarton, Scot.; designated "New Town" 1955; to accommodate 50,000 "overspill" from Glasgow; adding machines; p. (estd. 1965) *16,448.*
Cumbrae, *Is.*, in F. of Clyde, off cst. of Ayr, Scot.
Cumbrian Mtns., Lake District, Cumberland, Westmorland and Lancashire, Eng.
Cumnock and Holmhead, *sm. burgh, mng. dist.*, Ayr, Scot.; p. (1961) *5,403.*
Cundinamarca, *dep.*, Colombia, S. America; contains the fed. cap. Bogotá; a. 9,106 sq. m.; p. (1962) *2,121,680.*
Cunene, see **Kunene, R.** [*529,968.*
Cuneo, *prov.*, Italy; a. 2,870 sq. m.; p. (1961)
Cuneo, *cap.*, Cuneo prov., Italy; cath.; cotton, paper; p. (1961) *45,709.*
Cunnamulla, *t.*, Queensland, Australia; on Warrego R.; p. *2,189.*
Cupar, *burgh*, Fife, Scot.; on R. Eden, W. of St. Andrews; linen mkg.; sugar beet; p. (1961) *5,495.*
Curaçao I. (Netherlands Antilles), in the Caribbean, off N. cst. of Venezuela; oil refining, phosphates, salt, aloes, resin, hides, skins; a. 210 sq. m.; p. (1963) *127,164.*
Curanilahua, *commune*, Aranco, Chile; coal-mining; p. *13,026.*
Curepipe, *t.*, Central Mauritius; health resort; p. (1962) *35,275.* [*116,391.*
Curico, *prov.*, Chile; a. 2.214 sq. m.; p. (1961)
Curico, *t.*, Chile; agr. and comn. ctr.; flour milling, brewing, wines; p. (1961) *82,600.*
Curitiba, *cap.*, Paraná st., Brazil; univ.; coffee, matches, porcelain, yerba maté; p. (1960) *361,309.*
Curtea de Arges, *t.*, Romania; on S. slopes of the Transylvanian Alps; p. (1956) *10,764.*
Curwensville, *bor.*, Penns., U.S.A.; firebrick, leather, clay, clothing; p. (1950) *3,332.*
Curzola or Korcula, I., *t.*, Dalmatia, Jugoslavia; in the Adriatic; fishing, seafaring, agr.
Cushing, *t.*, Okla., U.S.A.; oil, gas, refineries, industl. ctr.; p. (1960) *8,619.*
Cuttack, *t.*, Orissa st., India; on Mahanadi R.; long famous for gold and silver filigree work; p. (1961) *146,308.*
Cuxhaven, *spt.*, Lower Saxony, Germany; outport of Hamburg at the mouth of R. Elbe; fine harbour, docks, fishing; p. (1963) *44,900.*
Cuyahoga, *R.*, in N. Ohio, U.S.A., flowing into L. Erie at Cleveland; length 85 m.
Cuyahoga Falls, *t.*, Ohio, U.S.A.; p. (1960) *47,922.*
Cuyapo, *mun.*, Luzon, Philippines; rice, sugar, tobacco, hemp; p. *24,570.*
Cuyuri, *R.*, Venezuela, enters sea Brit. Guiana.
Cuzco, *ancient t.*, Peru; in the Andes at alt. 11,400 ft. in valley of Urubamba R.; once cap. of the Incas; temple and fortress; besieged and sacked by Manco Inca in 1536; cath.; cottons, woollens; p. (1961) *68,000.*
Cuzco, *dep.*, Peru; a. 55,716 sq. m.; p. (1961) *590,958.*
Cwmamman, *urb. dist.*, Carmarthen, Wales; on R. Loughor, 12 m. N.E. of Llanelly; p. (1961) *4,272.*
Cwmbran, *t.*, Monmouth, Eng.; in valley of Avon-Lwyd, 5 m. N. of Newport; one of "New Towns" designated 1949 comprises bulk of Cwmbran urb. dist. and extends N. towards Pontypool; iron, motor accessories, wire, elec. goods, bricks, tiles, pipes; p. (estd. 1965) *35,860.*
Cyclades, group of about 220 Is. Grecian arch.; ch. t. Hermopolis (Syros); a. 1,023 sq. m.; p. (1961) *99,931.*
Cyprus, Republic of, *I.*, indep. Commonwealth nation, E. Mediterranean; 40 m. from Anatolia, 60 m. from Syria; cap. Nicosia; salt, iron, copper, agr., sponge fishing; a. 3,572 sq. m.; p. (1960) *577,639.*
Cyrenaica, *see* **Libya.**
Czechoslovak Socialist Republic (ČSSR.), Central Europe; country divided into 11 regions; mtns.; former provs. of Bohemia, Moravia, Slovakia of geographical significance only; fertile valleys; agr.: potatoes, sugar-beet, cereals, hops, lumbering; coal, iron, granite, beer distilling, sugar, textiles, glass, stoneware, machin., chemicals; cap. Praha (Prague); a. 49,381 sq. m.; p. (1961) *13,741,770.*
Czeladz, *t.*, S.W. Poland; coal; p. (1960) *30,000.*
Czernowitz, *see* **Chernovtsy.**
Czestochowa, *c.*, Katowice prov., S. Poland; on Warta R.; old pilgrimage monastery; rly. and industl. ctr.; iron and steel, textiles; p. (1960) *164,000.*
Czirknitzer (Zirknitzer), *L.*, with I. in Carniola, Jugoslavia, S. of Ljubljana, 6 m. long; extraordinary variations in depth.

D

Daanbantayan, *mun.*, N. Cebu, Philippine Is.; rice, sugar; p. *24,198.*
Dabhoi, *t.*, Gujarat, India; architectural remains; p. (1961) *30,841.*
Dabrowa, *t.*, Poland; 38 m. N.W. of Kraków; coal, zinc, iron ore; p. (1960) *56,000.*
Dacca, *ch. c.*, E. Pakistan; univ.; on Buriganga R., old channel of Ganges; jute, muslin; medical radioisotope ctr.; p. (1961) *556,712.*
Dachau, *t.*, Bavaria, Germany; paper, elec. goods, brewing; p. (1963) *30,000.*
Dachstein, *mtn.*, Salzkammergut, Austria; alt. 9,830 ft.
Dade City, *t.*, Fla., U.S.A.; ctr. of mkt. gardening and citrus region; kaolin; p. (1960) *4,759.*
Dagenham, *former mun. bor.*, Essex, Eng.; on N. bank of R. Thames, 10 m. E. of London; now inc. in Barking outer London bor. (except N. Chadwell Heath Ward inc. in Redbridge); motor cars, drugs, chemicals; p. (1961) *108,363.*
Dagestan, Caucasian prov. of R.S.F.S.R., U.S.S.R.; one of the most mountainous dists. in the world; cap. Makhachkala; cotton, orchards and vineyards; machin., engin, oil; a. 19,400 sq. m.; p. (1959) *1,063,000.* [Finland.
Dago (Hiiumaa), *I.*, Estonia, at entrance G. of
Dagupan, *t.*, Pangasiman, Luzon, Philippines; on Lingayen Bay; p. (1948) *43,838.*
Dahlak Archipelago, gr. of Is. in Red Sea, nr. Massawa; pearl fishing.
Dahomey, *ind. sov. st. within French Community*, W. Africa; forests, palm-oil; cap. Porto Novo; a. 44,000 sq. m.; p. (1961) 1,934,000.
Daimiel, *mkt. t.*, Ciudad Real, Spain; cheeses, oil, wine; p. (1957) *20,204.*

Dairen, *see* Talien.

Dakar, *spt., air and naval base*, Senegal, W. Africa, S.E. of Cape Verde behind Gorée I., impt. adm. ctr.; airpt. for S. America; groundnuts; p. (1960) *383,000*.

Dakhla, *oasis*, Libyan Desert, U.A.R.; 170 m. S.W. of Asyut; dates, olives; stage on caravan route from Cyrenaica to Upper U.A.R.

Dakota, *R.*, trib. of Missouri R., U.S.A.

Dakovica, *t.*, Jugoslavia; 80 m. E. of Cetinje; p. (1959) *20,000*.

Dalälven, *R.*, S. Central Sweden; length 325 m.

Dalaguete, *t.*, Cebu, Philippines; sugar, maize; p. *30,000*.

Dalat, *t.*, S. Viet-Nam; 140 m. N.E. Saigon; nuclear reactor (1963).

Dalbeattie, *burgh*, Kircudbright, Scot.; granite, dairy prod. gloves; p. (1961) *3,104*.

Dalby, *t.*, Queensland, Australia; pastoral, agr., dairying, cotton, timber; p. (1961) *7,394*.

Dalgety, *t.*, on Fife cst., Scotland; New t. proposed p. *10,000*.

Dalhousie, *health resort*, Chamba, Himachal Pradesh, India; 7,687 ft. above sea-level.

Dalhousie, *spt.*, N.B., Canada; lumber, lobsters, salmon; resort; p. (1961) *5,856*.

Dalkeith, *burgh*, Midlothian, Scot.; 6 m. S.E. of Edinburgh; coal; ironwks.; p. (1961) *8,864*.

Dalkey, *t.*, Dublin, Ireland; on E. cst.; 4 m. N. of Wicklow border; seaside resort; residtl.; p. (1956) *5,526*.

Dallas, *c.*, Texas, U.S.A.; in cotton and grain-growing region; machin., aeroplanes; p. (1960) *679,684*.

Dalmatia, *dist.*, N.E. Adriatic cst., Jugoslavia; limestone (Karst) plateau; olive oil, wine; a. 4,916 sq. m.; p. *622,000*.

Dalton, *t.*, N. Ga., U.S.A.; cotton and sawmills; p. (1960) *17,868*.

Daltonganj, *t.*, Bihar, India; on R. Koël; shellac, cement; p. (1961) *25,270*.

Dalton-in-Furness, *t., urb. dist.*, N. Lancs, Eng.; limestone quarrying, woollens, felt mftg.; abbey ruins; p. (1961) *10,317*.

Daly, *R.*, N. Terr., Australia; flowing into Anson [Bay.

Daly City, *t.*, Cal., U.S.A.; residtl., absorbed former t. of Colma.

Daman, or **Damão**, *spt.*, India; 100 m. N. of Bombay; fishing, ship-bldg., cotton; p. *60,000*.

Damanhur, *t.*, U.A.R.; on E. margin of Nile delta, 25 m. S.E. of Alexandria; mkt. for local agr. produce; p. (1960) *126,000*.

Damaraland, formerly part of German S.W. Africa now administered by Union of S. Africa; only pt., Walvis Bay; cattle rearing.

Damascus (Arabic Esh-Sham), *cap.*, Syria; 57 m. S.E. of its pt. Beirut; claims to be oldest continuously inhabited c. in world; metal-wk., glass, cement; p. (1961) *507,503*.

Dambovitta, *R.*, Romania; rises in Mt. Omul (Transylvanian Alps), flows S. through Bucharest to R. Danube; flows through impt. oilfields; length 150 m.

Damghan, *t.*, Iran; nr. Caspian Sea; p. *16,500*.

Damietta, *t.*, Nile Delta, U.A.R.; cotton; p. (1960) *72,000*.

Damoh, *t.*, N. Madhya Pradesh, India; agr. ctr. and mkt.; p. (1961) *44,678*.

Dampier, *spt.*, W. Australia; mouth of Fitzroy R.

Dampier Archipelago, *gr. of sm. Is.*, off N.W. Australia.

Dampier Strait, *channel* between N.W. of New Guinea and Waigeu I.

Dampier Strait, Bismarck archipelago, between Umboi and New Britain.

Dampremy, *commune*, Hainaut, Belgium; coal; p. (1962) *10,012*.

Danakil or Dankali Country, Eritrea; cst. land between Red Sea and Ethiopia (Abyssinia).

Danao, *t.*, Cebu, Philippines; rice and sugar dist.; p. (1948) *26,461*.

Danbury, *t.*, Conn., U.S.A.; hat-mkg. ind. since 1780; p. (1960) *22,928*.

Dandenong, *t.*, Victoria, Australia; dairy and mkt.-gardening ctr.; veg. dehydration; p. *6,000*.

Dannemora, *t.*, Sweden; 25 m. N.E. of Uppsala; iron ore worked since 1579; p. *1,062*.

Dannevirke, *t.*, N.I., N.Z.; p. (1961) *5,517*.

Dansalan, *chartered c.*, cap. of Lanao prov., Philippine Is.; resort; p. (1948) *19,657*.

Danube, *R.*, second longest R. in Europe; rises in Black Forest, Germany, and flows E. into Black Sea; navigation for steamers from Ulm to the sea; Vienna, Budapest, Belgrade and other large cs. on its banks; length 1,750 m.

Danvers, *t.*, Mass., U.S.A.; p. (1960) *21,926*.

Danville, *c.*, Ill., U.S.A.; coal; p. (1960) *41,856*.

Danville, *t.*, Ky., U.S.A.; mkt. for tobacco, hemp; horses; p. (1960) *9,010*.

Danville, *c.*, Va.: cotton, tobacco; p. (1960) *46,577*.

Danzig, *see* Gdansk.

Darbhanga, *t.*, Bihar, India; rice, oil-seeds, grain, sugar; p. (1961) *103,016*.

Dardanelles, *strait* between Europe and Turkey, connecting Ægean Sea with Sea of Marmara; (the ancient Hellespont), 40 m. long.

Dar-es-Salaam, *spt., cap.*, Tanzania, E. Africa; univ. coll.; textile mill projected; oil refinery under construction; p. (1957) *128,732*. incl. *4,478* Europeans *93,363* Africans.

Darfield, *urb. dist.*, W.R. Yorks, Eng.; p. (1961) *6,881*.

Darfur, *prov.*, Sudan, N.E. Africa; between Kordofan and Wadai; inhabited by Arabs and Negroes; cap. El Fasher; a. 138,150 sq. m.; p. (1947) *882,800*.

Darien, *region*, Panama; tortoiseshell, pearls, gold; p. (1960) *19,715*.

Darjeeling, *hill t.*, West Bengal, India; tea, quinine; has suffered from earthquake and landslips; p. (1961) *40,651*.

Darlaston, *urb. dist.*, Staffs, Eng.; nuts, bolts, fabricated steel mnfs., drop forgings, car components, pot and tile mkg.; p. (1961) *21,732*.

Darling, *R.*, N.S.W., Australia; rises in Gr. Dividing Range, flows S.W. into Murray R. at Wentworth; length 1,702 m.

Darling Downs, *plateau*, S.E. Queensland, Australia; grazing cty.; ch. t. Toowomba.

Darling Range, *mtns.*; granite range; gt. grazing cty. of W. Australia; parallel with cst., highest peak, 3,500 ft.

Darlington, *t., co. bor.*, Durham, Eng.; locomotive, wagon and bridge bldg., woollen yarn mnf.; engin.; p. (1961) *84,162*.

Darmstadt, *t.*, Hessen, Germany; on Darm R.; cas.; metallurgy, paper, machin., radio, chemicals, plastics; p. (1963) *139,600*.

Dart, *R.*, Devon, Eng.; rises in Dartmoor, flows S. into English Channel at Dartmouth; l. 46 m.

Dartford, *mkt. t., mun. bor.*, Kent, Eng.; nr. S. cst. of Thames estuary 15 m. E. of London; Dartford–Purfleet road tunnel (1963); engin., chemicals, quarrying, paper; p. (1961) *45,643*.

Dartmoor, *high stony plateau*, S.W. Devon, Eng.; granite; kaolin; sheep and ponies; a. 220 sq m.; highest point, High Willhays, 2,039 ft.

Dartmouth, *spt., mun. bor.*, S. Devon, Eng.; on W. of estuary of R. Dart; Royal Naval College; shipbldg.; p. (1961) *5,757*.

Dartmouth, *t.*, Nova Scotia; p. (1961) *46,966*.

Dartmouth, *t.*, Mass., U.S.A.; p. (1960) *14,464*.

Dartmouth, *pt.*, Richmond Bay, Prince Edward I., Canada. [coal; p. (1961) *14,111*

Darton, *urb. dist.*, W.R. York., Eng.; nr. Barnsley

Darvel, *burgh*, Ayr, Scot.; on R. Irvine, 8 m. E Kilmarnock; curtains, carpet; p. (1961) *3,255*

Darwen, *t., mun. bor.*, N.E. Lancs, Eng.; o flank of Rossendale Fells, 3 m. S. of Blackburn cottons, tile and glaze brick, paint and paper mftg.; p. (1961) *29,452*.

Darwin, *t., spt.*, N. Terr., Australia; landing plac of world airlines—England to Australia; p (1961) *12,480*.

Dashava, settlement in Lvov Oblast, W. Ukraine U.S.S.R.; ctr. of rich natural gas field and start ing point of gas pipe-line to Kiev and Moscow built after 2nd. World War.

Datia, *t.*, Madhya-Pradesh, India; stone-walled palaces; p. (1961) *29,430*.

Datteln, *t.*, N. Rhine–Westphalia, Germany; coa leather, iron; p. (1963) *31,200*.

Daugavpils, *t.*, Latvian S.S.R., on Dvina R.; tex tiles, engin., rly. repair wks.; p. (1959) *65,00*

Daura, *t.*, nr. Baghdad, Iraq; oil refining.

Davão, *t.*, Mindanao, Philippines; p. (196 *225,712*.

Davenport, *c.*, Iowa, U.S.A.; at foot of Rock I rapids; on Mississippi R.; flour mills; p (1960) *88,981*.

Daventry, *t., mun. bor.*, Northampton, England 9 m. S.E. of Rugby; boot-mkg., light engin wireless-transmission sta.; p. (1961) *5,846*.

David, *t.*, cap. Chiriqui prov., Panama; timbe coffee, cacao, sugar; p. (1960) *22,924*.

Davis Strait, *channel* between Greenland ar

Baffin Land, N.W. Terr., Canada; connects Atlantic with Baffin Bay.

Davos-Platz, *Alpine winter resort*, Grisons, Switzerland; alt. 4,845 ft.; p. *9,259*.

Dawley, *t.*, *urb. dist.*, Shropshire, Eng.; on S.E. flank of The Wrekin; ironwks., pipe, cement, roadstone, asphalt and brick wks., engin.; "New Town" designated 1963; p. (estd. 1965) *21,500*.

Dawlish, *t.*, *urb. dist.*, S. Devon, Eng.; on S. cst. between estuaries of Rs. Exe and Teign; seaside resort; p. (1961) *7,807*.

Dawson, *t.*, Yukon Terr., Canada; on Yukon R., nr. the Klondyke goldfields; p. (1961) *846*.

Dax, *t.*, Landes, S.W. France; on Adour R.; hot sulphur spring; horse mart; p. (1954) *14,557*.

Daylesford, *t.*, Victoria, Australia; 75 m. from Melbourne; resort, gold-mng, wheat; p. *3,100*.

Dayton, *c.*, Ohio, U.S.A.; on Great Miami R.; univ.; aeroplanes, elec. machin., rubber goods; p. (1960) *262,332*.

Daytona Beach, *t.*, Fla., U.S.A.; resort, tr. and shipping, ctr.; p. (1960) *37,395*.

De Aar, *t.*, *rly. junction*, Cape Province, S. Africa; 500 m. from Cape Town; rlys. from N.W. (Luderitz, Walvis Bay) and S.E. (Pt. Elizabeth, E. London) join Cape Town to Johannesburg trunk rly.; p. *9,137*.

Dead Sea, *salt-water L.* between Israel and Jordan; surface 1,286 ft. below level of the Mediterranean; a. 340 sq. m., length 47½ m., greatest width 9½ m., greatest depth 1,309 ft.; receives waters of Jordan; high mineral content.

Deal, *mun. bor.*, *ancient spt.*, E. Kent, Eng.; on S.E. cst. 7 m. N.E. of Dover; opposite Goodwin Sands; seaside resort; Julius Cæsar is said to have first landed nr.; p. (1961) *24,791*.

Dean, Forest of, Gloucester, Eng.; between Wye and Severn Rs.; coal-mining.

Dearborn, *t.*, Mich., U.S.A.; p. (1960) *112,007*.

Dearne, *urb. dist.*, W.R. Yorks, Eng.; p. (1961) *26,453*.

Death Valley, *depression*, Cal., U.S.A.; in Mohave Desert, 150 m. N.E. of Los Angeles; completely arid; floor covered with saline deposits; tourist attraction; depth of valley floor 276 ft. below sea-level.

Debar, *t.*, Jugoslavia; nr. Drin R.; tr. ctr., cattle breeding, sulphur springs; p. *6,913*.

Debra Markos, *cap.*, Gojjam prov., Ethiopia; p. approx. *5,000*.

Debrecen, *t.*, Hungary; 114 m. E. of Budapest; univ.; ctr. of pastoral dist.; fairs; pharmaceutics, medical instruments; p. (1962) *134,000*.

Decatur, *t.*, Ala., U.S.A.; steel, textiles; p. (1960) *29,217*.

Decatur, *t.*, Ga., U.S.A., p. (1960) *22,026*.

Decatur, *c.*, Ill., U.S.A.; mnfs., coal; p. (1960) *78,004*.

Decazeville, *t.*, Aveyron, S. France; coalmine (due for closure); p. (1954) *11,510*.

Deccan, The, gr. upland of S. India, bounded by the Narbada and Kistna Rs.

Dedham, *t.*, Mass., U.S.A.; p. (1960) *23,869*.

Dee, *R.*, N. Wales and Cheshire; length 90 m.

Dee, *R.*, Aberdeen and Kincardine, Scot.; length 87 m.

Dee, *R.*, Kirkcudbright, Scot.; length 38 m.

Dee, *R.*, Louth, Ireland; flowing to Dundalk Bay; length 20 m.

Defiance, *t.*, N.W. Ohio, U.S.A.; light mftg., tr. and agr. ctr.; p. (1960) *14,553*.

De Funiak Springs, *t.*, Fla., U.S.A.; in agr. region; turpentine; p. (1960) *5,282*.

ehiwala (Mt. Lavinia), *t.*, Ceylon; p. (1963) *111,013*. [*156,341*.

ehra Dun, *t.*, Uttar Pradesh, India; p. (1961)

eir-ez-Zor, *t.*, Syria; on Euphrates R.; on motor route between Damascus and Baghdad; p. (1961) *59,757*.

ej, *t.*, on Szamos R., Romania; lge. distillery; p. (1956) *19,281*.

elabole, *vil.*, Cornwall, Eng.; on N.W. flank of Bodmin Moor; lge. slate quarries.

elagoa Bay, *natural harbour*, Mozambique; Port E. Africa; ch. pt. Lourenço Marques.

elaware, *Atlantic st.*, U.S.A.; agr., lumber, fertilisers, minerals, leather, chemicals, machin.; cap. Dover; ch. pt. Wilmington; a. 2,057 sq. m.; p. (1960) *446,292*.

elaware, *R.*, flows from New York State along the Pennsylvania border, through New Jersey to Delaware Bay; length 350 m.

Delaware Bay, *inlet*, Atlantic cst., U.S.A.; drowned estuary of R. Delaware, extends 80 m. inland from C. May into heart of highly industl. a. of Philadelphia.

Delaware, *c.*, Ohio, U.S.A.; p. (1960) *13,282*.

Delft, *ancient t.*, *pt.*, S. Holland, Netherlands; on Schie R. nr. Rotterdam; butter and cheese mart; earthenware mnfs., tool mftg., precision instruments; p. (1960) *73,323*.

Delftshaven, *t.*, on Maas R., Netherlands; sub. of Rotterdam; p. (1947) *8,396*.

Delhi, *union terr.*, India; hot and arid region between Indus valley and alluvial plain of Ganges; irrigation to support agr.; New Delhi (*q.v.*) and Old Delhi chief ctrs.; a. 578 sq. m.; p. (1961) *2,359,408*.

Delitzsch, *t.*, Leipzig, E. Germany; 16 m. E. of Halle; sugar, chemicals; p. (1963) *23,614*.

Delmenhorst, *t.*, Lower Saxony, Germany; nr. Bremen; jute, woollens, linoleum, foodstuffs; p. (1963) *59,300*.

Delphi, N. of Chalcis, in Eubœa, Greece; famous for Delphic oracle on Mt. Parnassus.

Del Rio, *spt.*, Texas, U.S.A.; mkt. for agr a., grapes; exp. wool, sheep; p. (1960) *18,612*.

Demavend, *mtn.*, 17,604 ft.; highest peak, Elburz Mtns., N. Persia, extinct volcano.

Demerara, *co.*, Guyana; between Essequibo and Demerara Rs.; exp. sugar, molasses, rum; p. (1946) *220,639*.

Demirhissar, *t.*, Macedonia, Greece; under Turkish rule; p. *12,359*.

Demirkapu, "The Iron Gate," rocky defile, through which the Danube rushes, in the Transylvanian Alps.

Demmin, *t.*, Neubrandenburg, E. Germany; sugar ind.; p. (1963) *16,735*.

Demonte, *fortfd. t.*, Italy; on Stora R.; lead-mines; p. *3,350*.

Denain, *t.*, Nord, N. France; nr. Douai; coal; p. (1954) *27,449*.

Denbigh, *co.*, Wales; sheep, dairying, coal, slate, quarrying; a. 669 sq. m.; p. (1961) *173,843*.

Denbigh, *mun. bor.*, *co. t.*, Denbigh, N. Wales; dairying, slate; in Vale of Clwyd, 10 m. S. of Rhyl; p. (1961) *8,044*.

Denby Dale, *urb. dist.*, W.R. Yorks, Eng.; 8 m. W. of Barnsley; coal-mining, woollen textiles; p. (1961) *9,304*.

Dendermonde or Termonde, *t.*, E. Flanders, Belgium; nr. Ghent; p. (1962) *9,740*.

Denham, *vil.*, Bucks., Eng.; 1 m. E. of Gerrards Cross; impt. ctr. of film industry; residtl.

Den Helder, *see* Helder.

Denholme, *t.*, *urb. dist.*, W.R. Yorks, Eng.; nr. Bradford; dairying, textiles; p. (1961) *2,596*.

Denia, *spt.*, Spain; 45 m. N.E. of Alicante; oranges, raisins, grapes, onions; toy mkg.; p. (1957) *11,859*.

Deniliquin, *t.*, Riverina, N.S.W., Australia; on Edward R.; sheep ctr.; p. *3,196*.

Denison, *t.*, Iowa, U.S.A.; ctr. of agr. region; p. (1960) *4,930*.

Denison, *c.*, Texas, U.S.A.; on Red R.; cotton, lumber; p. (1960) *22,748*.

Denizli, *t.*, Anatolia, Turkey; 47 m. S.W. of Izmir; gardens—"the Damascus of Anatolia"; nr. site of Laodicea; p. (1960) *49,042*.

Denmark, *kingdom*, N.W. Europe; consisting of peninsula of Jutland and islands in Baltic; agr. and associated inds.; coastal fisheries; shipbldg., diesel engines; cap. Copenhagen; a. 16,576 sq. m.; p. (1960) *4,585,256*.

Denny and Dunipace, *burgh*, Stirling, Scot.; 6 m. W. of Falkirk; steel castings, precast concrete; p. (1961) *7,761*.

Dent Blanche, *mtn.*, in Pennine Alps, S. Switzerland; height 14,318 ft.

Dent du Midi, *mtn.*, Valais Alps, Switzerland; alt. 10,778 ft.

Denton, *urb. dist.*, Lancs, Eng.; nr. Manchester; felt-hat mkg.; p. (1961) *31,086*.

D'Entrecasteaux Is., gr. off S.E. New Guinea, administered by Australia.

D'Entrecasteaux Point, *C.*, S.W. extremity of Australia.

Denver, *c.*, *cap.*, Col., U.S.A.; on the E. slope of Rocky Mtns., on South Platte R.; univ.; oil, electronic equipment, mng. machin., livestock, canning; tourism; p. (1960) *493,887*.

Deoband, *t.*, Uttar Pradesh, India; nr. Meerut; p. (1961) *29,980*.

Deogarh, *t.*, Santal Pargans dist., Bihar, India;

numerous temples, place of pilgrimage; p. (1961) *30,813*.
Deori, *t.*, Madhya Pradesh, India; nr. Sagar; p. (1961) *9,383*.
De Pere, *t.*, Wis., U.S.A.; agr. ctr.; mftg.; boots, paper, chemicals, bricks; p. (1960) *10,045*.
Deptford, *see* **Lewisham.**
De Quincy, *t.*, La., U.S.A.; oil, gas, lumber, rice, sugar; p. (1960) *3,928*.
Dera Ghazi Khan, *cap.*, West Punjab, Pakistan; W. side of R. Indus; silk, brass, ivory goods, handsome mosques; p. *25,000*.
Dera Ismail Kahn, *div.*, W. Pakistan; p. (1961) *2,085,000*.
Dera Ismail Khan, *t.*, W. Pakistan; on Indus R.; adm. ctr., caravan ctr.; p. (1961) *46,100*.
Derbent, *t., spt.*, R.S.F.S.R.; on W. side of Caspian Sea; textiles, petrol; p. (1956) *41,800*.
Derby, *co. bor., co. t.*, Derbyshire, Eng.; on R. Derwent; rly. wks., pottery, aircraft engine mnf. and repair, vehicles, textiles; natural gas beneath Calow vil.; p. (1961) *132,325*.
Derby, *t.* Conn., U.S.A.; rubber, metal, hardware mftg.; p. (1960) *12,132*.
Derby, *sm. spt.*, W. Australia; on natural harbour of King Sound on N.W. cst. of Australia; hinterland little developed but potential gold and cattle-ranching within a. of artesian basin.
Derbyshire, *co.*, Eng.; hilly and rich in minerals; lge. part of N. and W. scheduled as Nat. Park; E. part highly industl.; *co. t.*, Derby; a. 1,041 sq. m.; p. (1961) *877,548*.
Dereham, East, *t., urb. dist.*, Norfolk, Eng.; 14 m. W. Norwich; agr. implements; p. (1961) *7,197*.
Derg, Lough, in basin of R. Shannon, Ireland, separating Galway and Clare from Tipperary.
Derg, *L.*, Donegal, with cave on I. much visited by R.C. pilgrims and known as "St. Patrick's Purgatory."
Derna, *spt.*, Libya, N. Africa; p. (estd. 1951) *15,600*.
Derry, *t.*, N.H., U.S.A.; boots, shoes; p. (1960) *6,987*.
Derwent, *R.*, Cumberland, Eng.; length 33 m.
Derwent, *R.*, Derby, Eng.; length 60 m.
Derwent, *R.*, Yorks, Eng.; length 57 m.
Derwent, *R.*, trib. of the Tyne R., Eng.; length 30 m.
Derwent, *lgst. R.*, Tasmania; flowing to Storm Bay; length 30 m.
Derwentwater, *L.*, Cumberland, Eng., nr. Keswick; 3 m. long.
Desaguadero, *R.*, Bolivia, S. America; outlet of [L. Titicaca.
Desaguadero, *plateau*, S. Peru and W. Bolivia between the Andes ranges, the second highest in the world.
Desborough, *t., urb. dist.*, Northants, Eng.; boot and shoe mnfs., iron; p. (1961) *4,555*.
Désirade, *I.*, Fr. W. Indies; nr. Guadeloupe; a. 10 sq. m.; p. *1,581*.
Des Moines, *R.*, Iowa, U.S.A.; trib. of Mississippi rising in Minnesota; length 550 m.
Des Moines, *c., cap.* Iowa State, U.S.A.; rly. and mftg. ctr.; p. (1960) *208,982*.
Des Plaines, *t.*, Ill., U.S.A.; p. (1960) *34,886*.
Desna, *R.*, trib. of Dnieper R., U.S.S.R.; length 550 m.
Despoto Dagh, *mtn. range*, Balkans; alt. 7,800 ft.
Dessau, *t.*, Halle, E. Germany; at confluence of Mulde and Elbe Rs.; cas.; machin., rly. carriages, paper, sugar, chemicals; route ctr.; p. (1963) *95,730*.
Detmold, *t.*, N. Rhine–Westphalia, Germany; cas.; paints, wood inds.; p. (1963) *30,600*.
Detroit, *ch. c., pt.*, Mich., U.S.A.; busy comm. and industl. ctr.; univ.; gt. grain mart; and ctr. of the "Ford" motor-car wks., aeroplanes, military tanks, synthetic diamonds, pharmaceutics, tools, chemicals, steel; lgst. exporting t. on Great Lakes; p. (1960) *1,670,144*.
Detroit, *R.*, channel between L. St. Clair and L. Erie (25 m.), separates st. of Michigan from Ontario, Canada; carries more shipping than any other inland waterway in the world; navigable for eight months in the year.
Deurne, *t.*, Belgium; nr. Antwerp; p. (1962) *69,498*.
Deventer, *c., old Hanse t.*, Overyssel, Netherlands; on R. Yssel, 15 m. S.E. of Zwolle; carpets; p. (1960) *55,797*.
Deveron, *R.*, Aberdeen and Banff, Scot.; flows into Moray Firth; length 61 m.
Devizes, *mkt. t., mun. bor.*, N. Wilts, Eng.; on Kennet Avon Canal at N. foot of Marlborough Downs; tobacco and snuff, bricks, tiles, bacon curing; p. (1961) *8,497*.
Devon, *R.*, trib. of Forth, Scot.; length 34 m.
Devonport, *fortfd. spt.*, S. Devon, Eng.; adjoins Plymouth on Tamar estuary; royal dockyards and naval sta.; road bridge to Saltash across Tamar; p. included with Plymouth.
Devonport, *spt.*, Tasmania, Australia; 82 m. from Launceston; agr. dist.; p. (1961) *13,053*.
Devonport, *suburban bor.*, Auckland, N.Z.; naval base and dockyard; p. (1961) *10,949*.
Devonshire, *maritime co.*, S.W. Eng.; between English and Bristol Channels; famous for cream and cider; ch. ts. Exeter and Plymouth; a. 2,611 sq. m.; p. (1961) *822,906*.
Dewsbury, *t., co. bor.*, W.R. Yorks, Eng.; on R. Calder, 8 m. from Leeds; heavy woollens, coal-mining, dyewks.; p. (1961) *52,942*.
Dexter, *t.*, Mo., U.S.A.; cotton, flour, poultry; p. (1960) *5,519*.
Dez Dam, Iran, over Dez R., Khurzistan prov., opened 16 Mar. 1963.
Dhahran, *spt.*, Saudi-Arabia; oil.
Dhanushkodi, *t.*, Madras, India; on I. Palk Strait; ferry pt. for passenger traffic from India to Ceylon.
Dhar, *t.*, Madhya Pradesh, India; cultural and tr. ctr.; p. (1961) *28,325*.
Dharmsala, *hill sta.*, E. Punjab, India; 100 m. N.E. of Amritsar; sanatorium; alt. 6,000 ft.; imposing mtn. scenery; p. (1961) *10,255*.
Dharwar, *t.*, Mysore, India; 70 m. E. of Goa, Carnatic; univ.; cotton mnf.; p. (1961) *77,163*.
Dhaulagiri, *mtn.*, Himalayas, Nepal; alt. 26,810 ft.
Dhekelia, Cyprus; Brit. sovereign a. within Rep.; p. (1960) *3,602*.
Dhofar, *fertile prov.*, Muscat and Oman, Arabia; sugar-cane, cattle; ch.t.Salalah; ch.pt.Murbat.
Dholpur, *t.*, Rajasthan, India; p. (1961) *27,412*.
Dhrangadhra, Saurashtra, India; 75 m. W. of Ahmedabad; chemicals, salt, cotton, bldg. stone, brass vessels, pottery; p. (1961) *32,197*.
Dhulia, *t.*, Khandesh dist., Maharashtra, India; cotton ind., p. (1961) *98,893*.
Diamante, *t.*, E. Argentina; on Paraná R.; grain, cattle; p. *11,518*.
Diamante, *R.*, Mendoza prov., Argentina; rises in Andes, flows E. to R. Salado; irrigates oasis of San Rafael; length 200 m.
Diamantina, *t.*, Minas Gerais, Brazil; ctr. of diamond dist.; p. (1960) *52,170*.
Diber, *prefecture*, Albania; p. (estd.) *83,491*.
Dibrugarh, *t.*, Assam, India; terminus of rail and river communications along Brahmaputra from Calcutta; coal, tea; p. (1961) *58,480*.
Dickson I., Kara Sea, Arctic Ocean, U.S.S.R.
Didymoteikhon, *t.*, Thrace, Greece; on R. Maritza; p. *10,150*.
Diego Garcia, *I.*, Brit. Indian Oc. Terr.; coaling sta.; 12½ m. long, 6¼ m. wide; ch. exp. coconut oil, tortoise-shell; p. (1962) *660*.
Diego Suarez, *t.*, *Bay*, extreme N. of Malagasy meat preserving; p. (1957) *38,212*.
Dieppe, *cross-Channel pt.*, Seine-Maritime, France 35 m. N. of Rouen; fisheries, shipbldg., machin. p. (1954) *26,427*.
Differdange, *t.*, S.W. Luxembourg; iron ore cattle; p. (1958) *17,946*.
Digboi, N.E. Assam, India; oil fields and refinery p. (1961) *35,028*.
Digne, *t.*, Basses-Alpes, France; nr. Aix; cath. p. (1954) *10,436*.
Dijon, *t.*, Côte-d'Or, E. France; the Roman *Divonense castrum*; cath.; bathing; casino gt. wine tr., tobacco, brewery, textiles; p. (1962) *141,104*.
Diksmuide, *t.*, W. Flanders, Belgium; on Yser R. p (1962) *3,867*.
Dillingen, *t.*, Bavaria, Germany; on R. Danube 20 m. downstream from Ulm; p. *6,500*.
Dilolo, *L.*, Angola; nr. source of Zambesi R.
Dimitrovgrad, *t.*, Bulgaria; founded 1947; fertilisers, chemicals, super phosphate plant, iron thermo-electric sta.; p. (1956) *34,162*.
Dimitrovo, *t.*, Bulgaria, formerly Pernik; steel blast furnaces; p. (1956) *59,721*.
Dinan, *t.*, Côtes-du-Nord, France; nr. St. Brieux medieval houses and ramparts; mineral water p. (1954) *13,844*.
Dinant, *fortfd. t.*, Namur, Belgium; on R. Meuse brass, copperware, summer resort; p. (196[illegible] *6,808*.

Dinapore, *military t.*, Bihar, India; on Ganges R., nr. Patna; p. (1961) *70,766*.
Dinard, *hol. res.*, Ille-et-Vilaine, France; opposite St. Malo; ch. wat. pl. of Brittany; p. *8,540*.
Dinaric Alps, *mtn. range*, Jugoslavia; highest peak, Dinara, alt. 6,007 ft.
Dindigul, *t.*, Madras, India; 25 m. S. of Trichinopoly; cigars, tobacco; p. (1961) *92,947*.
Dingras, *mun.*, Luzon, Philippine Is.; rice, hemp, tobacco; p. *22,434*.
Dingwall, *burgh*, Ross and Cromarty, Scot.; at head of Cromarty Firth; rly. junction; livestock mkt. ctr.; distilling, hand-loom weaving; p. (1961) *3,752*.
Dinslaken, *t.*, N. Rhine-Westphalia, Germany, N. of Duisburg; coal, steel, iron, footwear, timber; p. (1963) *46,400*.
Diomede Is., two barren granitic islets in Behring Strait between Alaska and Siberia; accepted bdy. between Soviet and U.S. territory.
Diosgyör, *mkt. t.*, N. Hungary; linked to Miskolcz in 1945 (*q.v.*).
Diourbel, *t.*, Senegal, W. Africa; hides, groundnuts; p. *18,006*.
Diredawa, *t.*, Ethiopia; 25 m. N. of Harar, rly. wks.; p. (estd. 1960) *40,000*.
Dirk Hartog I., off Shark Bay, W. Australia.
Disko I., off W. cst. of Greenland in Baffin Bay; contains harbour of Godhavn, cap. N. Greenland; rendezvous for whalers; a. 3,200 sq. m.
Dismal Swamp, *morass*, S. Virginia and N. Carolina, U.S.A.; contains L. Drummond and extends 30–40 m. S. from nr Norfolk.
Diss, *mkt. t., urb. dist.*, Norfolk, Eng.; on R. Waveney 28 m. S.W. of Norwich; agr. implements; p. (1961) *3,682*.
Ditchling Beacon, nr. Brighton, Sussex, Eng.; alt. 813 ft.
Dittersbach, *commune*, S.W. Poland; coal, drugs; [p. *14,916*.
Diu, *spt., I.*, off S. coast of Bombay, India; oil nearby at Kayakoy; a. 20 sq. m.; p. *13,600*.
Divion, *commune*, Pas de Calais, France; coal; p. (1954) *11,187*.
Divnogorsk, *t.*, R.S.F.S.R.; 25 m. W. of Krasnoyarsk on R. Yenisei; dam builders' t.; p. (1963) *25,000*.
Dixon Entrance, *channel* between Queen Charlotte I. and Alaska, Brit. Columbia, Canada.
Diyarbakir, *t.*, Anatolia, Turkey; on Tigris R.; head of navigation; ancient Amida, old walls, gates, citadel; morocco leather, filigree work; p. (1960) *80,645*.
Dizful, *t.*, Persia; 32 m. N.W. of Shushtar; indigo; p. (1956) *52,153*.
Djakarta (Batavia), *t.*, cap., Java, Indonesia; comm. ctr.; textiles; p. (1961) *2,973,052*.
Djambi, *dist.* and *t.*, Sumatra, Indonesia; on E. cst. plain 100 m. N.W. of Palembang; productive oil-field; a. (dist.) 17,345 sq. m.; p. (1961) of dist. *744,381* of t. *113,080*.
Djapara-Rembang, *prov.*, N.E. Java; petroleum, sugar, rice; a. 2,339 sq. m.; p. *1,885,548*.
Dneprodzerzhinsk, *t.*, Ukrainian S.S.R.; W. of Dnepropetrovsk on Dnieper R.; iron and steel, engin., chemicals; hydro-elec. sta. nearby; p. (1959) *194,000*.
Dneprograd, *t.*, Ukrainian S.S.R.; new residtl. t. on S. shore of Kakhorka reservoir (1963).
Dnepropetrovsk, *t.*, Ukrainian S.S.R.; on Dnieper R.; univ.; coal, iron, steel, manganese, engin., chemicals, sawmilling, tyres; p. (1962) *722,000*.
Dneprostroy, *see* **Zaporozhe.**
Dnieper, *R.*, S.E. Europe; rises in U.S.S.R., flows into the Black Sea; connected by canals with Baltic, etc.; the Dneprostroy dam, a barrage erected across the R. at Kichkas by the Soviet Government, feeds the lgst. power-sta. in the world; length 1,400 m.
Dniester, *R.*, S.E. Europe; rises in Carpathians and flows into the Black Sea; length 700 m.
Doab, *dist.*, between "two rivers" Jumna and Ganges, Uttar Pradesh, India.
Döbeln, *t.*, Leipzig, E. Germany; machin., metallurgy, wood, cigar and sugar inds.; p. (1963) *29,327*.
Dobrich, *t.*, *see* Tolbukhin.
Dobruja, *dist.*, E. Romania; a. 6,102 sq. m., ch. pt. Constanta, traversed by ancient wall of Trajan; p. (1948) *503,217*.
Dobsina, *t.*, ČSSR.; cave containing ice-field of 2 acres; asbestos, iron ore; p. *5,300*.
Doce, *R.*, Brazil; flows to Atlantic; length 400 m.
Dodecanese, *gr.* of 12 Greek Is. in Ægean Sea, to S. of Greek Archipelago; Italian 1912–46; a. 1,055 sq. m.; p. (1961) *122,346*.
Dodge City, *t.*, Kan., U.S.A.; p. (1960) *13,520*.
Dodoma, *mkt. t.*, Tanzania, E. Africa; 250 m. W. of Dar-es-Salaam on central Tanganyika rly. from Dar-es-Salaam to Kigoma; also on main N. to S. motor road.
Dodworth, *urb. dist.*, W.R. Yorks, Eng.; nr. Barnsley; coal; p. (1961) *4,139*.
Dogger Bank, *sandbank* in N. Sea, between England and Denmark; depth varies from 6 to 20 fathoms; valuable fishing ground; action between British fleet under Beatty and German fleet under Hipper; *Blücher* sunk Jan. 1915.
Dogs, I. of, *riverside dist.*, formed by bend in the R. Thames off Greenwich, London, Eng.; Millwall docks and shipbldg. yards.
Dokai Bay, *inlet*, N. Kyushu, Japan; landlocked bay on S. side of Shimonoseki Straits; flanked by highly industl. zone inc. Yawata, Wakamatsu, Tobata cs.; requires constant dredging; length 4 m., width ½–1½ m.
Dokkum, *t.*, Friesland, Netherlands; p. *5,073*.
Dôle, *t.*, Jura, E. France; on R. Doubs, nr. Dijon; ancient cap. of Franche-Comté, ceded to France in 1678; birthplace of Pasteur; p. (1954) *22,022*.
Dolgarrog, *sm. t.*, N.E. Caernarvon, Wales; on R. Conway; aluminium, milling; p. (1951) *572*.
Dolgelly, *urb. dist., ch. t.*, Merioneth, N. Wales; agr., quarrying, timber; p. (1961) *2,267*.
Dollar, *burgh*, Clackmannan, Scot.; at foot of Ochil Hills, 6 m. N.E. of Alloa; noted for its academy founded in 1818 by Capt. John Mcnab; p. (1961) *1,955*.
Dollar Law, *mtn.*, nr. Peebles, Scot.; alt. 2,680 ft.
Dolomites, *gr. of limestone mtns.*, S. Tyrolese Alps, N.E. Italy; tourist district; peaks assume fantastic forms; principal peak, Marmolata 11,000 ft.
Dolon-Nor, *t.*, Mongolia, China; Buddhist temples; brass idols; p. *30,000*.
Dom, *mtn.*, Valais, Switzerland; alt. 14,942 ft.
Dominica, *Brit. col.*, Windward Is., W.I.; lime-juice, sugar, cacao, fruits, spices; extremely beautiful; cap. Roseau; a. 305 sq. m.; p. (estd. 1965) *64,000*.
Dominican Rep, indep. Spanish-speaking E. part of I. of Hispaniola, Antilles; cap. Santo Domingo; sugar, coffee, cacao, bananas, tobacco, bauxite, iron ore, cement; a. 19,332 sq. m.; p. (1961) *3,013,525*.
Domodossola, *frontier t.*, Piedmont, N. Italy, nr. Simplon; tourist ctr.; p. *10,350*.
Don, *R.*, Aberdeen, Scot.; flows into N. Sea; salmon; length 82 m.
Don, *R.*, W.R. Yorks, Eng.; trib. of R. Ouse, [length 70 m.
Don, *R.*, Maine-et-Loire, France; length 40 m.
Don, *lge. R.*, W. Russia; falls into Sea of Azov below Rostov; navigable to Voronezh; access to the Volga by the Don–Volga Canal.
Donaghadee, *spt., urb. dis.*, Down, N. Ireland; nearest point to Scot.; flax; p. (1961) *3,226*.
Donaueschingen, *t.*, Baden-Württemberg, Germany; at confluence of Rs. Brigach and Breg forming R. Danube; cas.; textiles; p. (estd. 1954) *8,900*.
Donawitz, *commune*, Styria prov., Austria; lignite, iron and steel; p. *17,623*.
Donbas, *industl. region*, Ukraine, U.S.S.R.; in valleys of Rs. Donetz and lower Dnieper; about 9,000 sq. m.; produces 60% Russia's coal; adjoins Krivoi Rog ironfields; many lge. industl. ts.
Don Benito, *t.*, Badajoz, Spain; tr. in wheat, [wine, fruit; p. *21,095*.
Doncaster, *t., co. bor.*, W.R. Yorks, Eng., on Don R. 17 m. N.E. of Sheffield; rly. wks. mnfs. nylon; racecourse; p. (1961) *86,402*.
Donchery, *ancient t.*, Ardennes, France, on R. Meuse, nr. Sedan; scene of gr. battle 1870.
Donegal (Tirconnail), *co.*, N.W. Ireland; ch. t. Donegal, a. 1,865 sq. m.; p. (1961) *113,815*.
Donegal, *spt., cap.*, Co. Donegal, Ireland; on W. cst. of Donegal Bay; homespun tweeds, carpets; p. (1951) *1,131*.
Donets, *R.*, Ukraine S.S.R., U.S.S.R.; rises in uplands of central Russia, flows S.E. 400 m. into R. Don; crosses impt. Donets coalfield. *See* **Donbas.**
Donetsk (Stalino), *t.*, Ukraine S.S.R.; coal, iron, steel, engin., chemicals; p. (1962) *760,000*.
Dongola, New, *t.*, Sudan; left bank of R. Nile above 3rd Cataract; replaced Old D., now in ruins; p. *5,000*.

Donna, *t.*, S. Texas, U.S.A.; sugar refining, fruit and vegetables; p. (1960) *7,522*.
Donnybrook, *t.*, W. Australia; S. of Perth; fruit.
Donzère-Mondragon, Provence, France; site of gr. barrage on Rhône supplying hydro-elec. power, completed 1952.
Doon, *R.*, Ayr, Scot.; flows from Loch Doon to Firth of Clyde; length 26 m.
Dora Baltea, *R.*, N. Italy; rises in Mt. Blanc, flows E. and S. through Val d'Aosta to R. Po at Chivasso; impt. routeway from N. Italy to Switzerland (through Gr. St. Bernard Pass) and France (through Little St. Bernard Pass); length 95 m.
Dora Riparia, *R.*, Italy; trib. of R. Po, flowing from Cottian Alps past Turin; length 60 m.
Dorchester, *mun. bor. co. t.* Dorset, Eng.; on R. Frome; Roman remains; lime, agr., engin., tent mkg.; p. (1961) *12,266*.
Dorchester, *pt. of entry*, N.B., Canada; on Penticodiac R.; p. *1,000*.
Dordogne, *dep.*, S.W. France; a. 3,550 sq. m.; cap. Périgueux; p. (1962) *375,455*.
Dordogne, *R.*, France; joins Garonne to form the Gironde; length 290 m.
Dordrecht, *t.*, nr. Rotterdam, Netherlands, on R. Maas; timber, shipbldg., seaplanes; p. (1960) *81,909*.
Dorking, *mkt. t.*, *urb. dist.*, Surrey, Eng.; on R. Mole to S. of gap through N. Downs; residtl.; light inds.; p. (1961) *22,594*.
Dornoch, *burgh*, Sutherland, Scot.; on N. side of Dornoch Firth; health resort; p. (1961) *933*.
Dorohoi, *t.*, Moldavia, Romania; 33 m. S.E. of Chernovtsy; gr. annual fair; p. (1956) *14,771*.
Dorp, *t.*, Germany; on R. Wupper, nr. Cologne; mnfs.; p. *14,000*.
Dorset, *co.*, S. Eng.; mainly agr.; sheep; Purbeck marble, Portland stone; co. t. Dorchester; a. 988 sq. m.; p. (1961) *309,176*.
Dorset Heights, *hills*, extend E. to W. across Central Dorset, Eng.; chalk, smooth slopes, few streams; short, dry, grass; pastoral farming, sheep; some cultivation where soil is deep enough; rise to 800–900 ft.
Dorsten, *t.*, N. Rhine–Westphalia, Germany; on R. Lippe; coal, iron, elec., chemical inds.; p. (1963) *37,600*.
Dortmund, *t.*, N. Rhine–Westphalia, Germany; impt. Ruhr comm. ctr.; coal, iron, steel, machin., brewing; p. (1963) *650,900*.
Dortmund–Ems Canal, N. Rhine–Westphalia, Germany; links Dortmund on Ruhr Coalfield with R. Ems 5 m. above Lingen; impt. coal, iron-ore traffic; length 90 m.
Dorval, *t.*, Quebec, Canada; p. (1961) *18,592*.
Dothan, *t.*, Ala., U.S.A.; p. (1960) *31,440*.
Douai, *t.*, Nord, France; nr. Lille on Scarpe R.; coal, iron and engin. wks.; bell founding, arsenal; p. (1962) *50,104*.
Douarnenez, *spt.*, Finistère, N.W. France; on D. Bay; sardine fisheries; p. (1954) *20,089*.
Doubs, *dep.*, E. France; traversed by the Jura range and the R. Doubs; chiefly agr.; watch-mkg. ind.; cap. Besançon; a. 2,052 sq. m.; p. (1962) *384,881*.
Douglas, *cap.*, I. of Man; 75 m. W. of Liverpool, Eng.; seaside resort; p. (1956) *20,361*.
Douglas Point, on shore of L. Huron, Ont., Canada; nuclear power sta.
Dounreay, Caithness, Scot.; fast-breeder nuclear reactor.
Douro, *R.*, Portugal and Spain; enters Atlantic below Oporto; known as Duero R. in Spain; length 485 m.
Douro Littoral, *prov.*, Portugal; textiles, wine, fruit, cattle; cap. Oporto; a. 1,314 sq. m.; p. (1950) *1,237,170*.
Dove, *R.*, Derby and Staffs, Eng.; trib. of Trent; flows through beautiful dales; length 45 m.
Dover, *spt.*, *mun. bor.*, Kent, Eng.; one of old Cinque pts.; nearest spt. to France, the Strait of D. being only 21 m. wide; chief pt. for passenger and mail traffic with Continent; p. (1961) *35,248*.
Dover, *cap.*, Del., U.S.A.; p. (1960) *7,250*.
Dover, *t.*, N.H., U.S.A.; p. (1960) *19,131*.
Dover, *t.*, N.J., U.S.A.; iron, munitions, explosives; knitwear, silk; p. (1960) *13,034*.
Dovercourt, *sub.*, Harwich, Essex, Eng.; seaside resort.
Dowlais, *mining dist.*, Merthyr Tydfil, S. Wales; fertilisers, nylon.
Down, *maritime co.*, N. Ireland; agr. and fisheries; industl. round Belfast; cap. Downpatrick; a. 957 sq. m.; p. (1961) *267,013*.
Downers Grove, *t.*, N.E. Ill., U.S.A.; dairy produce; tools, furniture; p. (1960) *21,194*.
Downey, *t.*, Cal., U.S.A.; agr.; aircraft, cement, asbestos prod., machin., soap.; p. (1960) *82,505*.
Downham Market, *t.*, *urb. dist.*, Norfolk, Eng.; on R. Ouse; flour-milling, malting, sheet-metal wks.; p. (1961). *2,650*
Downpatrick, *urb. dist.*, *co. t.*, Down, N. Ireland; on R. Quoile; linen; p. (1961) *4,219*.
Downs, *roadstead*, natural harbour of refuge for shipping between Kent coast and Goodwin Sands in the English Channel.
Downs, North and South, two chiefly pastoral broad chalk ridges in S.E. Eng.; N. Downs ending at Dover, and S. Downs at Beachy Head and enclosing the Weald; fine grazing ground for sheep.
Downton, *t.*, S. Wilts, Eng.; nr. Salisbury; on R. Avon; agr. college.
Drachenfels, *mtn. peak* on the Rhine, the steepest of the Siebengebirge range, nr. Königswinter; alt. 1,065 ft.; ascended by light rly.; famous cave of legendary dragon.
Draguignan, *cap.*, Var. dep., S.E. France; nr. Toulon; p. (1954) *13,402*.
Drakensberg, *mtn. chain* between Natal and Orange Free State, S. Africa; extending 500 m. from Gt. Fish R. to Olifants R.; highest peak Mont-aux-Sources 10,763 ft.; rly. crosses range by Van Reenen Pass.
Drama, *pref.* Macedonia, Greece; cap. Drama; p. (1961) *120,936*.
Drammen, *spt.*, Norway; nr. Oslo, on the Drammen R.; shipyard; exp. timber, wood-pulp, paper; p. (estd. 1960) *31,000*.
Drancy, *t.*, Seine, France; p. (1962) *65,940*.
Drava, *R.*, Jugoslavia; trib. of Danube, flows from the Tyrol across Carinthia and Styria, joining D. nr. t. of Osijek; length 450 m.
Drenthe, *E. prov.*, Netherlands; on German frontier; cap. Assen; a. 1,028 sq. m.; p. (estd. 1959) *311,196*.
Dresden, *t.*, Dresden, E. Germany; on R. Elbe 50 m. E. of Leipzig; fine art collections; cigarette, engin., chem., brewing, gen. inds., optical and photographic apparatus, porcelain, glass, impt. route ctr.; p. (1963) *499,014*.
Dreux, *t.*, Eure-et-Loir, France; nr. Chartres; hardware, heavy iron mnfs.; p. (1954) *16,818*.
Driffield, *urb. dist.*, E.R. Yorks, Eng.; on Yorks. Wolds 13 m. N. of Beverley; oil-cake wks.; p. (1961) *6,890*.
Drina, *R.*, trib. Sava, Jugoslavia, separating Serbia from Bosnia; length 300 m.
Dröbak, *spt.*, S.E. Norway; winter pt. for Oslo; summer resort; p. (1961) *2,735*.
Drogheda, *spt.*, Louth, Ireland; considerable tr. in agr. produce, salmon, etc.; stormed by Cromwell in 1649; p. (1961) *17,071*.
Drogobych, *t.*, Ukrainian S.S.R.; petroleum, engin.; p. (1959) *42,000*.
Drohobycz, *t.*, Ukraine, U.S.S.R.; 40 m. S.W. of Lwow; ctr. of lge. oilfields, refineries; p. *32,622*.
Droitwich, *t.*, *mun. bor.*, Worcester, Eng.; brine baths, salt wks., wireless-transmission sta.; light inds.; p. (1961) *7,975*.
Drôme, *dep.*, S.E. France; traversed by Alps and watered by Rs. Rhône, Drôme and Isère; cap. Valence; agr., forestry, sericulture, textile ind.; a. 2,533 sq. m.; p. (1962) *304,227*.
Dromore, *mkt. t.*, *urb. dist.*, Down, N. Ireland; on Lagan R.; linen; p. (1961) *2,125*.
Dronfield, *t.*, *urb. dist.*, Derby, Eng.; between Chesterfield and Sheffield; iron, coal, edged tools, engin. and agr. implements; p. (1961) *11,294*.
Droylsden, *urb. dist.*, Lancs., Eng.; sub. of Manchester; cotton spinning; chemicals; p. (1961) *25,457*.
Drummondville, *t.*, Quebec, Canada; 45 m. N.E. of Montreal; woollens; p. (1961) *27,909*.
Drummoyne, *c.*, N.S.W., Australia; sub. of Sydney, on Parramatta R.; p. *29,214*.
Drumochter Pass, Grampian Mtns., Scot.; carries main Perth to Inverness rly. from Glen Garry into valley of R. Spey; highest alt. reached by any main rly. in Gr. Britain, 1,484 ft.

Duala, *spt.*, Cameroun Rep., W. Africa; rly. to Yaoundé; p. *18,000.*
Dubbo, *t.*, N.S.W., Australia; on Macquarie R., 180 m. N.W. of Sydney; in extensive pastoral and agr. dist.; p. (1961) *14,130.*
Dublin, *co.*, Ireland; co. t. Dublin; a. (inc. c. of Dublin) 356 sq. m.; p. (1961) *716,156.*
Dublin (Baile Atha Cliath), *co. bor.*, *cap.* Rep. of Ireland; at mouth of R. Liffey; cath., univ., cas.; spirit and chemical produce, stout, glass, etc.; p. (1961) *535,488.*
Dubois, *c.*, Penns., U.S.A.; 75 m. N.E. of Pittsburgh; coal; p. (1960) *10,667.*
Dubrovnik (Ragusa), *c.*, W. coast of Jugoslavia; oil, silk, leather inds.; p. (1960) *21,000.*
Dubuque, *c.*, Iowa, U.S.A., on Mississippi R.; clothing, carriage wks.; p. (1960) *56,606.*
Duchov, *t.*, N.W. Bohemia, ČSSR.; 5 m. S.W. of Teplice; glass, pottery; p. *15,000.* [nickel.
Dudinka, Arctic *spt.* on R. Yenisei, R.S.F.S.R.;
Dudley, *t.*, *co. bor.*, Worcester, Eng.; 8 m. N.W. Birmingham; engin., clothing, leather goods, firebricks, chains, cables; p. (1961) *61,748.*
Dudweiler, *t.*, nr. Saarbrücken, Saarland; coal-mines and ironwks.; p. (1963) *29,700.*
Dueñas, *mun.*, Panay, Philippine Is.; rice, hemp; p. *16,310.*
Duffel, *commune*, Antwerp, Belgium; foundries, distilleries, paper, coarse woollen cloth; p. (1962) *13,365.*
Duisburg, *t.*, *R. pt.*, N. Rhine–Westphalia, Germany; on E. bank of R. Rhine at confluence with R. Ruhr, 10 m. N. of Düsseldorf; extensive iron and steel inds., machin., textiles, chemicals, impt. route and R. tr. ctr.; p. (1963) *501,100.*
Dukeries, *dist.*, Sherwood Forest, Notts, Eng.; so called from ducal mansions in dist.
Dukinfield, *t.*, *mun. bor.*, Cheshire, Eng.; 6 m. S.E. of Manchester; textiles, engin., rope and twine; p. (1961) *17,318.*
Dukla, *pass*, Carpathian Mtns., Central Europe; easy route N. from Hungarian Plain to Poland; alt. 1,650 ft.
Dulag, *mun.*, Leyte I., Philippine Is.; hemp, rice, cotton, sugar; p. *28,693.*
Dulcigno (Ulcinj), *ancient c.*, Montenegro, Jugoslavia; tobacco, olive oil; p. *5,000.*
Dülken, *t.*, N. Rhine–Westphalia, Germany; nr. Krefeld. machin., textiles, leather goods; p. (1963) *21,300.*
Duluth, *pt.*, Minn., U.S.A.; at W. end of L. Superior; gr. tr. in grain, timber and iron ore; p. (1960) *106,884.*
Dumaguete, *spt.*, Negros, Philippines; on Tañon Strait; p. *16,636.*
Dumbarton, *burgh.*, *co. t.*, Dunbarton, Scot.; on N. bank of R. Clyde, 12 m. below Glasgow; shipbldg, valve and tube-mkg., iron and brass-ware; p. (1961) *26,335.*
Dum-Dum, South, *t.*, W. Bengal, India; ammunition; p. (1961) *111,284.*
Dumfries, *maritime co.*, S. Scot.; on Solway Firth; N. parts mtns., much of the remainder pastoral; lead ore, coal, sandstone; a. 1,068 sq. m.; p. (1961) *88,423.*
Dumfries, *co. burgh*, Dumfries, Scot.; on R. Nith, 10 m. from Solway Firth; p. (1961) *27,275.*
Dunaujváros, *t.*, Hungary; New Town built from vil. of Dunapentele; paper inds., engin.; p. (1962) *34,998.*
Dunbar, *spt.*, *burgh*, E. Lothian, Scot.; 25 m. E. of Edinburgh; potatoes; p. (1961) *4,003.*
Dunbarton, *co.*, W. Scot;. agr., stock-raising, shipbldg., chemicals, dyeing, paper-mkg., mining, quarrying, lt. engin.; a. 246 sq. m.; p. (1961) *184,546.*
Dunblane, *mkt. burgh*, Perth, Scot.; on Allan Water, 5 m. from Stirling; ancient cath.; woollen ind., light engin.; p. (1961) *2,922.*
Duncan, *c.*, Okla., U.S.A.; oil; oilwell machin.; asphalt, cottonseed oil; p. (1960) *20,009.*
Duncan Bay, *t.*, Vancouver I., B.C.; newsprint.
Duncansby Head, *promontory*, Caithness, N.E. Scot.
Dundalk, *spt.*, *urb. dist.*, *cap.*, Louth, Ireland; impt. rly. ctr.; engin., footwear, tobacco, brewing; p. (1961) *19,706.*
Dundas, *t.*, N.S.W., Australia; p. *6,017.*
Dundas, *t.*, Ontario, Canada; at W. end of L. Ontario; leather, paper; p. (1961) *12,912.*
Dundee, *c.*, *spt.*, Angus, Scot.; on Firth of Tay, 50 m. N. Edinburgh; jute, preserves, shipbldg., textile machin., cash registers, adding machin., linoleum, oil refining; univ. to be inaugurated 1966; p. (1961) *182,959.*
Dundee, *t.*, N. Natal, S. Africa; coal; p. *7,073.*
Dundonald, *vil.*, coast of Ayr, 5 m. S.W. of Kilmarnock; coal; p. (par.) *18,400.*
Dunedin, *cap.*, Otago, S.I., N.Z.; named after the old name of Edinburgh; univ.; wool and dairy produce; p. (1961) *105,053* of c. *73,226.*
Dunfermline, *burgh*, Fife, Scot.; at foot of Leven Hills, 14 m. E. of Alloa; damask linen tr., rubber; p. (inc. Rosyth) (1961) *47,159.*
Dungannon, *t.*, Tyrone, N. Ireland; linen; p. (1961) *6,494.*
Dungarvan, *spt.*, *urb. dist.*, Waterford, Ireland; brewing, woollens; p. (1961) *5,188.*
Dungeness, *headland of shingle*, Kent, Eng.; 10 m. S.E. of Rye; civil nuclear power-sta. (1964); a second to be built; linked by power cable to France 1961.
Dunkeld, *t.*, *par.*, Perth, Scot.; on R. Tay at entrance to Strathmore; cath.; tourist resort; p. (1951) *833.*
Dunkirk or Dunkerque, *spt.*, Nord, France; strong fort; gd. harbour and tr.; fisheries, shipbldg., oil refining; steel mill; scene of evacuation of B.E.F. 1940; p. (1954) *21,136.*
Dunkirk, *pt.*, N.Y., U.S.A.; on L. Erie; p. (1960) *18,205.*
Dun Laoghaire (Kingstown), *spt.*, *co. bor.*, Dublin, Ireland; mail packet sta., fishing; p. (1961) *47,803.* [Kerry, Ireland.
Dunloe, Gap of, *mtn. pass*, nr. L. of Killarney,
Dunmanway, *t.*, Cork, Ireland; on R. Brandon; tweeds, blankets; p. (1951) *1,439.*
Dunmore, *t.*, Penns., U.S.A.; nr. Scranton; anthracite; p. (1960) *18,917.*
Dunmow, Gr., *mkt. t.*, Essex, Eng.; on R. Chelmer; 10 m. N.W. of Chelmsford; p. (par.) (1961) *3,827.*
Dunmow, Little, *vil.*, 2 m. E. of Gr. Dunmow; "Dunmow Flitch" trial here annually; p. (1961) *359.*
Dunnet Head, *promontory*, Caithness, N.E. Scot.
Dunnottar, *par.*, Kincardine, Scot.; nr. Stonehaven; ruined cas.; p. (1951) *1,514.*
Dunoon, *burgh*, *wat. pl.*, Argyll, Scot.; on N. side of Firth of Clyde, nearly op. Greenock, ancient cas.; holiday resort; p. (1961) *9,211.*
Duns, *burgh*, Berwick, Scot.; agr. and allied inds.; p. (1961) *1,838.*
Dunsinane, *hill*, Sidlaws, Scot.; nr. Perth; alt. 1,012 ft.; referred to by Shakespeare in "Macbeth."
Dunsmuir, *t.*, N. Cal., U.S.A.; summer resort; hunting, fishing; p. (1960) *2,873.*
Dunstable, *t.*, *mun. bor.*, Beds, Eng.; on N. edge of Chiltern Hills, 4 m. W. of Luton; motor vehicles, sparking-plugs, car components, engin., cement, rubber and plastic goods; p. (1961) *25,618.*
Duque de Caxias, *t.*, Rio de Janeiro st., Brazil; oil refining; p. (1960) *173,077.*
Duquesne, *c.*, Penns., U.S.A.; 9 m. S.E. of Pittsburgh; steelwks.; p. (1960) *15,019.*
Du Quoin, *c.*, Ill., U.S.A.; meat packing, flour, leather goods, shoes; p. (1960) *6,558.*
Durance, *R.*, S.E. France; trib. of Rhône; rapid current; length 217 m.
Durango, *inland st.*, N.W. Mexico; mining, agr., stock-raising; a. 42,272 sq. m.; p. (1960) *760,836.*
Durango, *cap.*, D. state, Mexico; cath.; silver, gold, copper, iron-ore; p. (1960) *70,000.*
Durant, *c.*, S. Okla., U.S.A.; cotton gins and compresses, cottonseed oil; p. (1960) *10,467.*
Durban, *spt.*, Natal, Rep. of S. Africa; ch. comm. t. in S.E. Africa; maize, wool, hides, oil and sugar refining, chemicals, textiles, engin.; p. (1960) *655,370* (inc. *194,276* Whites).
Düren, *t.*, N. Rhine–Westphalia, Germany; on R. Ruhr, 23 m. S.W. of Cologne; textiles, leather, machin., rly ctr.; p. (1963) *52,600.*
Durgapur, *t.*, W. Bengal; steel plant, coke oven plant; p. (1961) *41,696.*
Durham, *cath. c.*, *mun. bor.*, *co. t.*, Durham, N.E. Eng.; univ.; carpet, organ, confectionery mftg.; p. (1961) *20,484.*
Durham Co., N.E. Eng.; fertile valleys, moorland; coal, limestone; cattle; shipbldg., iron, steel, chemicals; a. 1,015 sq. m.; p. (1961) *1,517,039.*
Durham, *c.*, N.C., U.S.A.; tobacco factories; p. (1960) *78,302.*
Durlach, *t.*, Baden-Württemberg, Germany;

2½ m. E. Karlsruhe; cas.; cycles, machin.; p. (estd. 1954) *25,000*.

Dürrës (Durazzo), *spt.* Albania, on Adriatic; pt. for Tirana; tobacco ind.; p. (1960) *32,000*.

Dursley, *t.*, Glos., Eng.; 13 m. S. by W. of Gloucester; engin. inds., agr. mach.; p. *5,355*.

Duryea, *bor.*, Penns., U.S.A.; anthracite; silk; p. (1960) *5,626*.

Dushanbe (former **Stalinabad**), *t.* cap. Tadzhik S.S.R.; univ.; engin., textiles; p. (1962) *260,000*.

Düsseldorf, *cap.*, N. Rhine-Westphalia, Germany; on R. Rhine, 20 m. N. of Cologne; admin. and cultural ctr., art and medical academies; iron, steel, machin., soap, cars, paper, chemical inds.: impt. trans-shipment pt.; p. (1963) *704,000*.

Dust Bowl, *region*, U.S.A.; name applied to Great Plains on E. flank of Rocky Mtns.; subject to severe soil erosion by wind, particularly in drought years (1933, 1936) due to destruction of natural vegetation by excessive ploughing.

Dutch Guiana, *see* **Surinam**.

Dutch Harbour, *t.*, Unalaska I., Aleutian gr., N. Pac. Oc.; strategic American naval base.

Dvina, *R.*, (N.) flows to White Sea at Arkhangelsk, and is formed by the junction of the Rs. Sukhona and Vychgeda, U.S.S.R.; connected by canal with Neva and Volga; length 1,000 m.

Dvina, *R.*, Latvia, U.S.S.R.; rises near sources of Volga and Dnieper, flows to G. of Riga; l. 65 m.

Dysart, *spt.*, *mun. bor.*, Fife, on F. of Forth, Scot.; linen, coal; p. *9,068*.

Dzaudzhikau, *see* **Ordzhonikidze**.

Dzerzhinsk, *industl. t.*, R.S.F.S.R.; W. of Gorki; chemicals (fertilisers, explosives); p. (1959) *163,000*.

Dzhalil, *t.*, R.S.F.S.R.; new t. 30 m. N.E. of Almetyevsk to serve new A. oilfield.

Dzhambul, *t.*, Kazakhstan S.S.R.; on R. Talis and Turksib rly.; chemicals; p. (1959) *67,000*.

Dzhezkazgan, *t.*, Kazakh S.S.R.; 350 m. W. of L. Balkhash; copper-mines; manganese ore near-by; p. (1956) *29,100*.

Dzierzoniow, *t.*, S.W. Poland, formerly Germany; ceded to Poland at Potsdam conference; textiles, machin.; cattle, grain mkt.; p. (1960) *27,000*.

Dzungaria, *broad trench* leading to the Mongolian plateau from the lowlands round L. Balkhash; formerly independent state.

E

Eagle Grove, *c.*, N. Iowa, U.S.A.; gypsum, agr.; p. (1960) *4,381*.

Ealing, *outer bor.*, Greater London; comprising former bors. of Acton, Ealing and Southall; p. (1964) *299,762*.

Earby, *urb. dist.*, W.R. Yorks, Eng.; cotton, plastic, cloths, agr. machin.; p. (1961) *4,983*.

Earlestown, *mftg. t.*, S. Lancs., Eng.; included in Newton le Willows urb. dist.; engin., glass.

Earn, *R.*, Perth, Scot.; issues from Loch Earn (6½ m. long) and flows into the Tay R.; length 46 m.

Earnslaw, *mtns.*, S. I., N.Z.; highest peak, 9,165 ft.

Easdale, *I.*, off W. Argyll, Scot.; nr. Oban; slate quarries.

Easingwold, *t.*, N.R. Yorks, Eng.; rope, steel, agr. ctr.; p. *2,043*.

East C., extreme N.E. point of Asia.

East C., extreme E. point of New Zealand, named by Capt. Cook on his first voyage in 1769.

East Anglia, *dist.*, comprising Norfolk and Suffolk, Eng.; former Anglo-Saxon kingdom.

East Anglian Heights, *hills*, extend S.W. to N.E. across N.E. Hertfordshire, N. Essex and S.W. Suffolk, Eng.; chalk overlain by glacial clays and sands; smooth, rolling surface; region of lge. farms and lge. fields, mixed farms mainly grain; rarely exceed 600 ft. alt.

East Barnet, *former urb. dist.*, Herts, Eng., now inc. in Barnet outer bor., Greater London (*q.v.*); residtl.; p. (1961) *40,641*.

East Bengal, E. *div.* of Pakistan; includes part of former Bengal Presidency; rice, jute, cotton; a. 5,091 sq. m.; p. (estd. 1951) *42,119,000*.

East Bridgewater, *t.*, Mass., U.S.A.; nr. Boston, p. (1960) *6,127*.

East Chicago, *c.*, Ind., U.S.A.; L. Michigan; iron and steel wks., oil refining; p. (1960) *57,669*.

East Cleveland, *t.*, Ohio, U.S.A.; residtl.; p. (1960) *37,991*.

East Greenwich, *t.*, Rhode I., U.S.A.; light mftg.; shellfish; summer resort; p. (1960) *6,100*.

East Grinstead, *t.*, *urb. dist.*, E. Sussex, Eng.; in ctr. of the Weald, 9 m. W. of Tunbridge Wells; agr. mkt.; famous hospital for plastic surgery; p. (1961) *15,421*.

East Ham, *former co. bor.*, Essex, Eng.; mftg. sub. E. of London, docks; chemicals; now inc. in Newham bor., Greater London.

East Indies (Malay Archipelago), gr. of Is. between Asia and Australia, inc. Borneo, Sulawesi, New Guinea, Sumatra, Java, Bali, Timor (see under **Kalimantan** and **Indonesia**); sugar, coffee, spices, fruits, rubber, tobacco, sago, tapioca, canes.

East Kilbride, *t.*, N. Lanark, Scot., 7 m. S.S.E. of Glasgow; designated "New Town" 1947; lge. agr. machin., aero engines, engin., elec. goods; knitwear, clothing; p. (estd. 1965) *45,933*.

East Liverpool, *c.*, Ohio, U.S.A.; pottery mnfs.; p. (1960) *22,306*.

East London, *spt.*, C. Prov., S. Africa; at mouth of Buffalo R.; holiday resort; trading ctr.; inds. inc. car assembly, textiles, engin.; p. (1960) *114,584* (inc. *48,725* Whites).

East Lothian (Haddington), *co.*, S.E. Scot.; cereals, potatoes, sheep, coal; *co. t.*, Haddington, a. 267 sq. m.; p. (1961) *52,653*.

East Main R., Labrador, Newfoundland, Canada; flowing into James Bay.

East Moline, *t.*, Ill., U.S.A.; p. (1960) *16,732*.

East Orange, *t.*, N.J., U.S.A.; residtl. sub., New York; p. (1960) *77,259*.

East Pakistan, *prov.*, Pakistan; comprises E. terrs. of prov. of Bengal and former Assam dist. of Sylhet; divided into 3 divs. and 17 dists.; cap. Dacca; a. 54,501 sq. m.; p. (1961) *50,844,000*.

East Palestine, *t.*, Ohio, U.S.A.; clay, coal, oil, pottery; p. (1960) *5,232*.

East Providence, *t.*, Rhode I., U.S.A.; p. (1960) *41,955*.

East Retford, *mun. bor.*, Notts, Eng.; on R. Idle, 6 m. E. of Worksop; rubber, wire ropes, engin.; p. (1961) *17,788*.

East Riding, Yorkshire, *see* **Yorkshire, East Riding**.

East River, *tidal strait* about 16 m. long and from 600 to 4,000 ft. wide; the R. separates the bors. of Manhattan and Bronx from the bors. of Queens and Brooklyn.

East St. Louis, *c.*, *R. pt.*, Ill., U.S.A.; on Mississippi R.; large stockyards; meat packing; p. (1960) *81,712*.

East Stonehouse, *t.*, Devon, Eng.; adjoining Plymouth and Devonport.

Eastbourne, *t.*, *co. bor.*, E. Sussex, Eng.; on S. cst. to E. of Beachy Head; seaside resort; p. (1961) *60,897*.

Easter I., E. Pac. Oc., W. of Chile; stone images, ruins; p. *250*.

Eastern Province, Zambia; groundnuts, maize, tobacco; prov. ctr. Fort Jameson; a. 22,350 sq. m.; p. (estd. 1963) *450,000*.

Eastham, *vil.*, Cheshire, Eng.; on S. of Mersey estuary, nr. entrance to Manchester Ship Canal.

Easthampton, *t.*, Mass., U.S.A.; p. (1950) *10,694*.

Eastleigh, *t.*, *mun. bor.*, Hants, Eng.; locomotives; p. (1961) *36,577*.

Easton, *t.*, Mass., U.S.A.; p. (1960) *9,069*.

Easton, *c.*, Penns., U.S.A.; on Delaware R.; rly. ctr., coal, steel, machin., furniture; p. (1960) *31,955*.

Eastview, *t.*, Ontario, Canada; p. (1961) *24,555*.

Eastwood, *t.*, *urb. dist.*, Notts, Eng.; coal; p. (1961) *10,585*.

Eau Claire, *c.*, Wis., U.S.A.; on Chippewa R.; timber, paper, furniture; p. (1960) *37,987*.

Eaux Bonnes, Les, *wat. pl.*, Pyrenees, S. France.

Eaux Chaudes, *wat. pl.*, Pyrenees, S. France.

Ebal, Mt., Israel; opposite Gerizim; alt. 2,986 ft.

Ebbw Vale, *t.*, *urb. dist.*, Monmouth, Eng.; 17 m. N.W. of Newport; coal, iron, steel, tinplate, bricks, pipes, precast concrete; p. (1961) *28,631*.

Eberswalde, *t.*, Frankfurt, E. Germany; N.E. of Berlin; iron, wood and cardboard wks.; p. (1963) *32,906*.

Ebingen, *c.*, Württemberg, Germany; knitwear, velvet, precision tools; p. (1963) *21,400*.

Eboil or Evoli, *t.*, Campagna, Italy; E. of Salerno; p. *13,275*.

Ebro, *R.*, N.E. Spain; flows to Mediterranean from Cantabrian Mtns.; length 440 m.

Ebury, *R.*, Monmouth, Eng.; trib. of Usk R.

Eccles, *mun. bor.*, Lancs, Eng.; 4 m. W. of Manchester; iron and steel, cotton, textiles, leather, chemicals, coal-mining; p. (1961) *43,184*.

Ecclesfield, *t.*, W.R. Yorks, Eng.; N. of Sheffield; cutlery.

Eccleshall, *mkt. t.*, Staffs, Eng.; 6 m. N.W. of Stafford; p. *3,630*.
Echague, *t.*, Philippine Is.; tobacco ctr.
Echternach, *t.*, Luxembourg; famous abbey; Whitsun dancing-procession.
Echuca, *t.*, Victoria, Australia; on R. Murray; 50 m. N.E. of Bendigo; rly. ctr.; irrigation wks.; wine, sheep; p. (1951) *6,000*.
Ecija, *t.*, Seville, Spain; olive oil, wine, pottery; the Roman Astigi; p. *34,944*.
Eck, Loch, *L.*, Argyll, Scot.; 6 m. long.
Eckernförde, *spt.*, Schleswig-Holstein, Germany; on Baltic N.W. of Kiel; fishing; resort; p. (1963) *20,400*.
Eckington, *t.* Derby, Eng.; S.E of Sheffield; coal, agr. implements; p. *14,614*.
Ecorse, *t.*, Mich., U.S.A.; p. (1960) *17,328*.
Ecuador, *rep.*, S. America; on Equatorial Pacific cst.; Andes mtns.; Chimborazo, 20,600 ft.; climate: lowlands tropical, uplands cool and dry; race chiefly Indian speaking the Quechua language; poor communications; cocoa, sugar, coffee, cereals, fruits, gold, copper, silver, Panama hats; cap. Quito; a. 106,508 sq. m.; p. (1962) *4,650,000*.
Edam *t.*, Holland, Netherlands; coast of Zuider Zee; cheese, tool mftg.; p. *8,295*.
Eday, *I.*, Orkney Is., Scot.; the Ocelli of Ptolemy.
Ed Damar, *cap.*, Northern Prov., Sudan; p. (estd. 1949) *8,000*.
Eddystone, *rock with lighthouse*, Eng. Channel; 15 m. S.W. of Plymouth.
Ede, *commune*, E. Netherlands; livestock; p. (1960) *55,785*.
Ede, *t.*, W. Prov., Nigeria; p. *57,500*.
Eden, *R.*, Westmorland, Eng.; rises in Pennines, flows N.W. to Solway Firth below Carlisle; length 65 m.
Eden, *t.*, N.S.W., Australia; on Tasman Sea; p *661*.
Edenton, *t.*, N.C., U.S.A.; groundnuts, cotton, herring fisheries; p. (1960) *4,458*.
Edessa (Edhessa), *t.*, *cap.*, Pella prefecture, Macedonia, Greece; p. (1961) *15,534*.
Edfu, *see* **Idfu.**
Edgbaston, *residtl. dist.*, Birmingham, Eng.
Edgehill, *ridge*, 15 m. S. Warwick, Eng.; first battle in Civil War, 1642.
Edgewater, *t.*, N.J., U.S.A.; sub., connected by ferry with New York; p. (1960) *4,113*.
Edgware, *t.*, Middlesex, Eng.; N. sub. of London; residtl.; p. (1961) *20,127*.
Edina, *t.*, Minn., U.S.A.; p. (1960) *28,501*.
Edinburgh, *c.*, Midlothian; cap. Scot.; royal burgh on F. of Forth; univ., cas.; palace (Holyrood); printing, publishing, brewing; Edinburgh Festival in August; Leith, with docks is joined to E.; p. (1961) *468,378*.
Edirne, *c.*, Turkey; on left bank of the Marica R.; greatly developed by Hadrian 125; residence of the Sultans 1366–1453; wine, tobacco, silk, perfume; p. (1960) *31,865*.
Edjelé, *t.*, nr. Tripoli, Algeria, Africa; oilfields.
Edmonton, *c.*, cap. Alberta, Canada; fast-growing c. (46 sq. m.) on both sides of N. Saskatchewan R.; high-level bridge links Strathcona; immense war-time activity ("invasion"), now major Canadian military ctr.; univ.; international air ctr.; oilfields and farming; oil and chemical inds.; p. (1961) *337,568*.
Edmonton, *former mun. bor.*, Middlx., Eng.; now inc. in Enfield outer bor., Greater London (*q.v.*); residtl.; light inds.; p. (1961) *91,956*.
Edremit, *t.*, Balikesir, N.W. Turkey; cereals, opium; silverwk.; p. (1960) *22,246*.
Edward, *L.*, on frontier of Uganda and the Congo (ex-Belgian), one of the sources of R. Nile; alt. 3,000 ft., length 44 m., breadth 32 m.
Edwardsville, *t.*, Ill., U.S.A.; p. (1960) *9,996*.
Eekloo, *t.*, E. Flanders, Belgium; textiles; p. (1962) *18,571*.
Eger, *c.*, Hungary; wine, soap; cath.; p. (1962) *35,832*.
Egersund, *spt.*, S. cst., Norway; pottery, china, engin.; fishing; p. (1946) *3,419*.
Eggan, *R. pt.*, Ilorin, Nigeria; p. *10,000*.
Egham, *urb. dist.*, Surrey, Eng.; on R. Thames, nr. Staines; contains field of Runnymede, where King John signed Magna Carta; residtl.; p. (1961) *30,553*.
Egmont, *mtn.*, N.I., N.Z.; volcanic; alt. 8,200 ft.
Egremont, *mkt. t.*, Cumberland, Eng.; 10 m. S. of Whitehaven; limestone, iron ore; p. *16,727*.
Egypt, *see* **United Arab Republic.**
Ehen, *R.*, Cumberland, Eng.; issues from Ennerdale Water to Irish Sea; length 12 m.
Ehrenbreitstein, *t.*, *fort.*, Germany; on R. Rhine opposite Koblenz.
Eibar, *c.*, Guipuzcoa, N. Spain; iron, steel mftg., ordnance wks.; p. (1957) *16,318*.
Eibenstock, *t.*, Saxony, Germany; p. *7,760*.
Eider, *R.*, Germany; connected with Kiel canal; length 90 m.
Eifel, *plateau of ancient rocks*, W. Germany; lies N. of R. Moselle, terminates in steep slope forming W. edge of Rhine gorge between Koblenz and Bonn; drained by Kyll, Ahr, Rur; formerly cultivated, now largely woodland and moorland; farming in valleys; rises to just over 2,000 ft.
Eiger, *mtn.*, one of the highest peaks of the Bernese Oberland, Switzerland; alt. 13,042 ft.
Eigg, *I.*, Inner Hebrides, Scot.; 15 m. S.W. of Mallaig; basaltic rocks on cst.; rises to 1,289 ft.
Eilat, *new spt.*, Negev, Israel; on Gulf of Akaba; oil; copper at Timna; p. (estd. 1953) *400*.
Eildon Hills, Roxburgh, Scot.; S. of Melrose; highest point 1,385 ft.
Eilenburg, *t.*, Leipzig, E. Germany; rly. junction; machin., chemicals; p. (1963) *21,050*.
Eindoven, *t.*, N. Brabant, Netherlands; tobacco, textile, elec. and radio goods, machin.; p. (1960) *166,032*.
Einsiedeln, *t.*, Schwyz, Switzerland; monastery, pilgrim ctr.
Eire, *see* **Ireland, Republic of.**
Eisenach, *t.*, Erfurt, E. Germany; on R. Hörsel, at foot of Thuringian forest; ctr. of Werra potash field; cars, machin., textiles; birthplace of J. S. Bach; p. (1963) *47,854*.
Eisenberg, *t.*, Gera, E. Germany; pianos, porcelain, cement, machin.; p. (1963) *13,666*.
Eisenerz Alps, *mtn. range*, Austria; most northerly range of Alps, overlooking Danube valley between Linz and Vienna; impt. iron-ore deposits; alt. from 6,000 to 9,000 ft.
Eisenhuttenstadt, *t.*, Frankfurt, E. Germany; iron smelting; p. (1963) *35,671*.
Eisleben, *t.*, Halle, E. Germany; birthplace of Luther; machin., copper- and silver-mining ctr.; p. (1963) *33,589*.
Ekibastuz, *t.*, Kazakhstan S.S.R.; 75 m. S.W. of Pavlodar; ctr. of rapidly developing mng. a. coal, gold, metals; coal-fed generating plant projected, to supply power to European Russia; p. (1956) *15,000*.
El Alamein, *vil.*, U.A.R.; in Libyan Desert 60 m. S.W. of Alexandria, scene of gr. Allied victory, Second World War.
El Callao, *t.*, Bolivar, st., Venezuela; in ctr. of Guiana Highlands, 125 m. S.E. of Ciudad Bolivar; ctr. of impt. gold-mining region.
El Centro, Cal., U.S.A.; rich agr. a. reclaimed from the desert; p. (1960) *16,811*.
El Dorado, *t.*, Ark., U.S.A.; oil; p. (1960) *25,292*.
El Dorado, *t.*, Kan., U.S.A.; p. (1960) *12,523*.
El Faiyûm or El Fayum, *oasis t.*, *cap.* of Faiyûm prov., U.A.R.; nr. L. Moeris; predynastic arch. finds; lgst. cultivated a. of U.A.R. outside Nile flood plain; uranium; p. (1960) *102,000*.
El Fasher, *cap.*, Darfur Prov., Sudan; p. (estd. 1961) *28,462*.
El Hasa, *dist.*, Saudi Arabia; on Persian Gulf, ch. t. Hofuf.
El Jadida (Mazagan), *spt.*, Morocco; grain and wool tr.; p. (1960) *40,302*.
El Khârga, *oasis*, Libyan desert, U.A.R.; 85 m. S.W. of Asyut; p. *5,000*.
El Misti, *volcano*, Peru, S. America; N.E. of Arequipa; alt. 19,170 ft.
El Obeid, *cap.*, Kordofan, Sudan; 200 m. S.W. of Khartoum; ivory, gums, ostrich feathers; p. (estd. 1961) *56,970*.
El Oro, *prov.*, Ecuador; cap. Machala; a. 2,238 sq. m.; p. (estd. 1962) *162,591*.
El Paso, *c.*, Texas, U.S.A.; on Rio Grande; natural gas distribution, ore refining; p. (1960) *276,687*.
El Quantara (El Kantara), *t.*, U.A.R.; on E. bank of Suez Canal, 21 m. S. of Pt. Said; terminus of Palestine Rly. system; linked by ferry across canal (and temporary swing bridge) to El Quantara (W.) on Egyptian Rly. systems.
El Salvador, *see* **Salvador.**
El Teniente, *t.*, central Chile; copper-mines; p. *11,761*.

Elan, *R.*, Radnor, Wales; rises on S.E. sides of Plynlimon, flows S.E. then N.E. into R. Wye at Rhayader; lower valley contains series of 4 lge. reservoirs, length 4 m., capacity 10,000 million gall.; ch. source of water for Birmingham.
Elâzig, *t.*, E. Turkey; dam and hydro-elec. project planned at Keban, 30 m. to N.W. at confluence of E. and W. branches of Euphrates; p. (1960) *60,438*.
Elba, *I.*, off Tuscan cst., Italy; iron ore, wine, marble, salt; Napoleon's first exile here; ch. t. Porto Ferrajo; a. 140 sq. m.; p. (1960) *26,000*.
Elbasan, *prefecture*, Albania; cap. Elbasan; p. (1958) *430,000*.
Elbe, *R.*, Czechoslovakia, Germany; the Roman "Albis"; rises in Bohemia and flows into N. Sea at Cuxhaven, 65 m. below Hamburg; navigable for 500 m. of total length 725 m.
Elbert, *mtn.*, Col., U.S.A.; alt. 14,420 ft.
Elbeuf, *t.*, Seine-Maritime, France; woollens; p. (1954) *17,293*.
Elblag (Elbing), *spt.*, E. Prussia, Poland; German before 1945; shipbldg., machin., vehicles; p. (1960) *77,000*.
Elbruz Mt., Caucasus, highest in Europe (18,480 ft.), over-topping Mont Blanc by 2,698 ft.
Elburz, *mtn. range*, N. Iran; bordering on Caspian Sea; highest peak, Demavend, 18,500 ft.
Elche, *t.*, Alicante, Spain; 15 m. S.W. of Alicante; palm groves; oil, soap; p. (1959) *72,706*.
Eldorado, *radium mine*, N.W. Terr., N. Canada; situated on E. shore of Gr. Bear Lake nr. Arctic Circle; produces 40% of world's radium, sent to Pt. Hope, Ontario, for refining.
Electra, *t.*, N. Texas, U.S.A.; oil; drilling tools and equipment; p. (1960) *4,759*.
Elektrenai, *t.*, Lithuanian S.S.R.; new township nr. Vievis, at site of thermal power sta.
Elektrostal, *t.*, R.S.F.S.R.; 35 m. E. of Moscow; steel, engin.; p. (1959) *97,000*.
Elephant Butte Dam, N.M., U.S.A.; on Rio Grande, 125 m. above El Paso; built to control flood water; lake, a. 60 sq. m., supplies irrigation water to 780 sq. m. in N.M. and Texas, water also supplied to Mexico.
Elephanta, *I.*, Bombay Harbour, India; cave sculptures.
Elephantine, *I.*, in Nile, Upper U.A.R.; site of nilometer.
Eleuthera, *I.*, Bahamas, T.W.I.; p. (1953) *6,070*.
Elgin, *t.*, Ill., U.S.A.; watches, elec. goods, machin. chemicals, wood prod.; p. (1960) *49,447*.
Elgin, *co. t.*, *burgh*, Moray, Scot.; ancient ruined cath.; woollens; p. (1961) *11,971*.
Elgon Mt., *extinct volcano*, on bdy. of Kenya and Uganda; 40 m. in diam.; alt. 14,100 ft.; cave dwellings on slopes.
Elie and Earlsferry, *burgh*, Fife, Scot.; summer resort; p. (1961) *1,128*.
Elisabethville, *t.*, Katanga, Congo; copper-mining ctr.; p. (1959) *183,808* inc. *13,808* whites.
Elizabeth, *mftg. t.*, N.J., U.S.A.; univ.; sewing machines, iron, oil-ref.; p. (1960) *107,698*.
Elizabeth, satellite t. of Adelaide, S. Australia.
Elizabeth, *t.*, N.C., U.S.A.; timber ind.; p. (1960) 14,062.
Elizabethton, *t.*, Tenn., U.S.A.; manganese; rayon; p. (1960) *10,896*.
Elkhart, *t.*, Ind., U.S.A.; E. of Chicago; paper, machin.; p. (1960) *40,274*.
Elk Mtns., *lofty range*, W. Col., U.S.A.; highest point Castle Peak, alt. 14,115 ft.
Elland, *t.*, *urb. dist.*, W.R. Yorks, Eng.; on R. Calder, 3 m. S.E. of Halifax; woollens; p. (1961) *18,353*.
Ellesmere, *t.*, *urb. dist.*, Shropshire, Eng.; 8 m. N.W. of Wem; mkt., agr.; p. (1961) *2,254*.
Ellesmere, *agr. dist.*, S.I., N.Z.; on Canterbury Plain nr. Christchurch.
Ellesmere I., lge. I. extreme north of Arctic Canada; barren, uninhabited; a. 41,000 sq. m.
Ellesmere Port, *t.*, *mun. bor.*, N.W. Cheshire, Eng.; on Manchester Ship Canal and 9 m. S.S.E. of Liverpool; impt. petrol docks and refinery; metal mftg., paper, engin.; p. (1961) *44,714*.
Ellichpur, *t.*, Berar, Madhya Pradesh, India; cotton tr.; p. *24,000*. [p. *25,000*.
Elliot Lake, *t.*, N. Ontario; ctr. of uranium mines;
Ellis I., New York harbour, U.S.A.; served as ch. immigration ctr., 1892–1943.
Ellon, *burgh*, Aberdeen, Scot.; on R. Ythan; p. (1961) *1,456*.
Ellwood, *t.*, Penns., U.S.A.; p. (1960) *12,413*.
Elmhurst, *t.*, Ill., U.S.A.; p. (1960) *36,991*.
Elmina, *t.*, Ghana, W. Africa; fortress; tr. in palm oil, ivory, gold; p. *15,200*.
Elmira, *mftg. t.*, N.Y., U.S.A.; rly. goods, farm implements; burial place of Mark Twain; p. (1960) *46,517*.
Elmshorn, *t.*, Germany; N.W. of Hamburg; p. (1963) *35,400*.
Elsinore (Helsingör), *t.*, *spt.*, Denmark; shipbldg.; p. (1960) *26,658*.
Elstree, *t.*, Herts., Eng.; 4 m. W. of Barnet; residential; films, light engin., silk hosiery; p. (1961) *24,782*.
Eltham, *residtl. dist.*, Kent, Eng.; S. sub. of London.
Eluru, *t.*, Andra Pradesh, India; cotton; carpets, hosiery, oil; p. (1961) *108,321*.
Elvas, *c.* (*fortfd.*), Portugal; on Guadiana R.; plums, olives; p. *13,615*.
Elwood, *industl. t.*, Ind., U.S.A.; on Duck Creek; grain, tinplate; p. (1960) *11,793*.
Ely, *c.*, Cambridge and I. of Ely, Eng.; on S. fringe of the Fens; mkt., cath.; agr. ctr. (fruit, roots); p. (1961) *9,815*.
Ely, I. of, *see* **Cambridge and Isle of Ely**.
Elyria, *t.*, Ohio, U.S.A.; mftg.; p. (1960) *43,782*.
Emba, R., Kazakh S.S.R.; rises in S. end of Ural Mtns., flows S.W. to Caspian Sea; crosses productive Ural–Emba oilfield.
Emden, *spt.*, Lower Saxony, Germany; nr. mouth of R. Ems; freighting, shipbldg., cars; fishing prod., imports iron ore, corn; exp. coal and iron from Ruhr; p. (1963) *46,100*.
Emilia-Romagna, *region*, N. Italy; S. of Po R.; agr. (grain, wine, fruits); a. 8,542 sq. m.; p. (1961) *3,646,507*.
Emmaus, *bor.*, Penns., U.S.A.; textiles, rubber prod.; p. (1960) *10,262*.
Emmaville, *t.*, N.S.W., Australia; mining.
Emmen, *t.*, Drenthe, Netherlands; 30 m. S.E. of Groningen; p. (1960) *66,000*.
Empedrado, *t.*, Argentina; oranges, rice in a.; p. (1960) *21,000*.
Empoli, *t.*, Florence, Italy; textile mnfs., straw plaiting, leather goods, pottery; p. *21,000*.
Emporia, *t.*, Kan., U.S.A.; stock-raising; p. (1960) *18,190*. [p. *7,070*.
Ems, *t.*, Germany; on Lahn R.; spa, silver, lead;
Ems, *R.*, N. Germany; rises in Teutoberger Wald, flows N. to N. Sea at Emden; length 205 m.
Emscher, *R.*, W. Germany; rises in Sauerland, flows W. through heart of Ruhr coalfield to enter R. Rhine at Hamborn; canalised for most of its course; length 55 m.
Emsdetten, *t.*, Germany; on R. Ems; textiles; p. (1963) *26,000*.
Encarnación, *pt.*, *cap.*, Ipatua dep., S.E. Paraguay; on Paraná R.; exp. timber, maté, tobacco, cotton, hides; p. (estd. 1960) *35,000*.
Encounter Bay, S. Australia, receives Murray R.
Enderby Land, *terr.*, Antarctica; S. of C. of Good Hope.
Endicott, *t.*, N.Y., U.S.A.; shoe mftg.; p. (1960) *18,775*.
Endrick, *R.*, Stirling, Scot.; flows to Loch Lomond; length 29 m.
Enez, *t.*, S. Turkey-in-Europe; nr. Gallipoli; p. (1960) *1,485*.
Enfield, *former mun. bor.*; Middlesex Eng.; now outer bor. Greater London; comprising former bors. of Edmonton, Enfield and Southgate; p. (1964) *273,637*.
Engadine, Switzerland; upper valley of Inn R.; health resort; chief t. St. Moritz.
Engaño, *c.*, S. extremity of Luzon, Philippine Is.
Engelberg, *t.*, Unterwalden, Switzerland; tourists; old monastery; p. *2,409*.
Engels, *t.*, R.S.F.S.R.; on Volgar R. opposite Saratov; textiles, chemicals, petroleum refining; p. (1959) *90,000*.
Enghien-les-Bains, *t.*, Seine-et-Oise, France; p. (1954) *12,062*.
England (with Wales), forms S. and lgst. div. Gr. Britain; length 420 m., greatest breadth 360 m.; ch. mtns.: Cheviot Hills, Pennine Chain, Cumbrian Gr., Cambrian Mtns., Dartmoor, Exmoor; ch. Rs.: Thames, Severn, Trent, Mersey, Gr. Ouse, Yorkshire Ouse; climate: temperate maritime; vegetation: woods, moor, heath, grassland; ch. inds.: agr.: arable, pastoral, dairying; ch. crops: wheat, barley, oats, sugar-beet, potatoes, hops, fruit.

livestock; cod, haddock; coal, iron; iron and steel mnfs., machinery, machine tools, engin. prods., road vehicles and aircraft, ships, textiles, pottery; good road and rail comm.; cap. London; a. 50,875 sq. m.; p. (1961) *46,071,604*.
Englewood, *t.*, N.J., U.S.A.; p. (1960) *26,057*.
English Channel (La Manche), *narrow sea* separating England from France; extends from Strait of Dover to Land's End in Cornwall; length 300 m., greatest width 155 m.
Enham-Alamein, Hants.; rehabilitation ctr. for disabled ex-service men; 2½ m. N. of Andover; light inds.
Enid, *t.*, Okla., U.S.A.; ironwks., farm implements; p. (1960) *38,859*.
Enkhuizen, *t.*, *spt.*, Netherlands; on W. cst. Zuider Zee; p. *9,634*.
Enna (Castrogiovanni), *t.*, Sicily; rock salt, sulphur-mines; famous for its connection with the Proserpine legend; p. (1961) *28,145*.
En Nahud, *t.*, central Sudan; tr. in cattle, ivory, cotton, ostrich feathers; p. *19,300*.
Ennepetal, *t.*, N. Rhine–Westphalia, Germany; on R. Ennepe; t. created 1949 with merging of Milspe and Voerde; iron, machin.; p. (1963) *32,000*.
Ennerdale Water, *L.*, Cumberland, Eng.
Ennis, *mkt. t.*, *urb. dist.*, Clare, Ireland; farming, flour; p. (1961) *5,678*.
Enniscorthy, *mkt. t.*, *urb. dist.*, Wexford, Ireland; brewing, tanning; p. (1961) *5,756*.
Enniskillen, *co. t.*, *mun. bor.*, Fermanagh, N. Ireland; brewing, nylon mftg.; p. (1961) *7,438*.
Enns, *R.*, Austria; S. trib. of Danube; 112 m. l.
Enschede, *t.*, Overyssel, Netherlands; cotton-spinning, weaving, textile mach., engin.; p. (1960) *123,799*.
Entebbe, *t.* Uganda, E. Africa; on L. Victoria; univ.; cotton ginning; p. (estd.) *11,000*.
Enterprise, *c.*, Ala., U.S.A.; peanuts; p. (1960) *11,410*.
Entre Rios, *prov.*, Argentina; between Paraná and Uruguay Rs.; wheat, linseed, livestock; cap. Paraná; a. 29,427 sq. m.; p. (1960) *804,000*.
Entrocamiente, *t.*, Central Portugal, on Tagus R.
Enugu, *cap.* E. prov., Nigeria; coal; p. (1953) *63,000*.
Epernay, *t.*, Marne, France; champagne; p. (1954) *21,222*.
Ephesus, *ruined c.*, Turkey, S. of Izmir.
Ephrata, *t.*, S.E. Penns., U.S.A.; cattle rearing, printing; p. (1960) *7,688*.
Epinal, *cap.*, Vosges dep., France; on Moselle R.; cotton, printing; p. (1954) *28,688*.
Epirus, *dist.*, N.W. Greece; a. 3,688 sq. m.; p. (1961) *352,604*.
Epping, *t.*, *urb. dist.*, Essex, Eng.; mkt. gardening, dairying; p. (1961) *10,001*.
Epping, *forest*, Essex, Eng.
Epsom and Ewell, *mun. bor.*, Surrey, Eng.; 18 m. S.W. of London; residtl., racecourse; drain pipes, brick tiles; p. (1961) *71,177*.
Equatoria, *prov.*, Sudan; a. 76,995 sq. m.; cap. Juba; p. (estd. 1951) *632,900*.
Erandio, *t.*, N. sub. of Bilbao, Spain; iron ore, paper, tobacco, wine; p. *11,268*.
Erebus, *mtn.*, active volcano, Victoria Land, Antarctica.
Ereğli, *spt.*, Black Sea, Turkey; rly. to Zonguldak coal-mines; steel wks.; p. (1960) *8,815*.
Erfurt, *c.*, *cap.*, Erfurt, E. Germany; cath., ctr. of mkt. gardening and seed-growing dist., textiles, machin., foodstuffs, footwear, radios, heavy engin.; p. (1963) *189,817*.
Ericht, *loch*, Perth, Inverness, Scot.; in central Grampians; 15½ m. long; hydro-elec. scheme.
Erie, *lake*, N. America; separating Canada from U.S.A.; a. 9,940 sq. m.; 241 m. long, 57 m. broad.
Erie, *industl. c.*, *lake pt.*, Penns., U.S.A.; iron and steel ind., engin.; p. (1960) *138,440*.
Erie Canal, *see* New York State Barge Canal.
Eriskay, I., Outer Hebrides, Scot.
Erith, *former mun. bor.*, Kent, Eng.; on S. bank of Thames estuary 5 m. below London; engin., oil refining, cables, plastics, paints and varnishes, timber, concrete prods.; p. (1961) *45,043*; now inc. in Bexley bor., Greater London.
Eritrea, *prov.*, Ethiopia; fed. within Ethiopia 1952; former Italian col., N.E. Africa; tobacco, cereals, pearl fishing; cap. Asmara, a. *45,754* sq. m.; p. (estd. 1960) *1,000,000*.
Erivan, *cap.* Armenian S.S.R., U.S.S.R.; situated in deep valley in Caucasus Mtns.; woollen mnfs., fruit canning, machine tools; p. (1939) *200,000*.
Erlangen, *t.*, Bavaria, Germany; univ.; textiles, elec. and precision engin., gloves; p. (1963) *73,200*.
Ernakulam, *t.*, Kerala, India; cotton, coffee, hides; p. (1961) *117,253*.
Erne, *R.*, (72 m.) and *L.*, N. Ireland, flows to Donegal Bay.
Erode, *t.*, S. Madras, India; cotton; p. (1961) [*73,762*.
Erzgebirge (Ore Mns.), *mtn. range*, Germany; highest peak, 4,122 ft.
Erzurum, *t.*, Turkey; agr. ctr. on fertile plateau 6,200 ft. a.s.l.; formerly of gr. strategic impt.; p. (1960) *91,196*.
Esbjerg, *spt.*, Denmark; W. cst. of Jutland; export harbour on N. Sea cst.; exp. agr. prod.; fishing; airport; p. (1960) *55,171*.
Escalante, *t.*, Philippine Is.; p. *28,934*.
Escanaba, *t.*, Mich., U.S.A.; iron, shipping, lumber, chemicals; p. (1960) *15,391*.
Escatrón, *t.*, Spain; on Elbro R.
Esch-sur-Alzette, *t.*, Luxembourg; mining ctr.; p. (1958) *28,832*.
Eschwege, *t.*, Hessen, Germany; cas.; machin., textiles, leather, cigars, chemicals; p. (1963) *24,000*.
Eschweiler, *t.*, N. Rhine–Westphalia, Germany; N.W. of Aachen; lignite mng., steel, iron, metallurgy, leather, textiles; p. (1963) *40,000*.
Escondido, *t.*, Cal., U.S.A.; p. (1960) *16,377*.
Escoublac-La-Baule, *t.*, Loire-Atlantique, France; p. (1954) *13,166*.
Esdraelon, *plain*, Israel; S.W. Asia; between Carmel and Gilboa Mtns.
Esher, *urb. dist.*, Surrey, Eng.; on R. Mole, residtl.; Sandown Park racecourse; p. (1961) *60,586*.
Eshowe, *health resort*, Natal, S. Africa; 40 m. from Tugela R.; p. (1960) *4,919* inc. *1,945* whites.
Esk, *R.*, Dumfries, Scot., rises in S. Uplands, flows S. into Solway Firth; length 50 m.
Esk, *R.*, N.R. Yorks, Eng.; rises in Cleveland Hills, flows E. into N. Sea at Whitby; length 28 m.
Eskilstuna, *t.*, Sweden; on R. of same name; iron, steel, machin.; p. (1961) *59,072*.
Eskisehir, *t.*, Turkey; W. of Ankara, anc. Dorylaeum; rly. ctr.; meerschaum; p. (1960) *153,190*.
Esmeralda, *t.*, Venezuela, S. America; on Orinoco R.
Esmeraldas, *prov.*, Ecuador, S. America; cap. E. on R. of same name; cacao, tobacco; a. 5,464 sq. m.; p. (estd. 1962) *124,742*.
Esmeraldas, *pt.*, Ecuador; bananas, timber, tobacco, cacao, rubber; gold mines nearby; p. (1962) *13,169*.
Esperanza, *old t.*, Santa Clara, Cuba; guava jelly; p. *18,091*.
Espirito Santo, *maritime st.*, Brazil; sugar, cotton, coffee, fruits, forests, thorium; cap. Vitória; a. 15,785 sq. m.; p. (1960) *1,188,665*.
Essaouira (Mogador) *spt.*, Morocco, N. Africa; cereals, almonds, gum-arabic, crude oil; p. (1960) *26,392*
Essen, *t.*, N. Rhine–Westphalia, Germany; ch. t., in W. Ruhr; coal-mng., steel (Krupp), elec. and light engin.; p. (1963) *729,400*.
Essendon, *sub.*, Melbourne, Victoria, Australia; racecourse, air-port; p. (1958) *60,736*.
Essentuki, *t.*, Stavropol, U.S.S.R.; light mnfs., medicinal springs; p. *23,000*.
Essequibo, *R.*, Guyana; length 620 m.
Essex, *co.*, Eng.; bounded on S. by Thames, on E. by North Sea; co. t. Chelmsford; lies mainly on London Clay and chalk; agr.: wheat, barley, sugar-beet; market gd.; S.W. part of Greater London with manf. subs.; motor wks. at Dagenham; oil refs. at Shell Haven; civil nuclear power-stn. at Bradwell; univ. at Colchester; a. 1,528 sq. m.; p. (1961) *2,288,058*.
Esslingen, *t.*, Baden-Württemberg, Germany; on R. Neckar; mach. and rly. shops; textiles, chemicals, leather goods; Liebfrauen church (1440); p. (1963) *83,900*.
Este, *t.*, N.E. Italy; ancient fortress; iron, pottery, chemicals; p. *14,438*.
Esteli, *dep.*, W. Nicaragua; a. 772 sq. m.; p. [*53,872*.
Estepona, *spt.*, Malaga, Spain; wine, olives, citrus fruit, sardines; p. (1957) *12,913*.
Estevan, *t.*, Saskatchewan, Canada; 110 m. S.E. of Regina; coal; p. (1961) *7,728*.
Eston, *t.*, *urb. dist.*, N.R. Yorks, Eng.; 3 m. E. of Middlesbrough; iron and steel, shipbldg. and repairing; p. (1961) *37,160*.

Estonia, *constituent rep.*, U.S.S.R.; formerly independent st.; climate: severe winter, mild summer, moderate rainfall; farming and dairying, textiles, matches, leather; a. 17,610 sq. m.; cap. Tallin; p. (1959) *1,196,000*.
Estoril, watering-place and thermal spa, Portugal; N. side of Tagus estuary.
Estrela, Serra da, *mtn. range*, Portugal; highest peak 7,524 ft.
Estremadura, *prov.*, Portugal; cap. Lisbon; a. 2,064 sq. m.; p. (1950) *1,595,067*.
Esztergom, *t.*, Hungary; weaving; mineral springs; cath.; p. (1962) *23,716*.
Etampes, *t.*, Seine-et-Oise; France; 30 m. S. of Paris; commerce; p. (1954) *11,890*.
Etang de Berre, *lagoon*, Bouches-du-Rhône, S.E. France; lies E. of Rhône delta, separated from Gulf of Lions by low Chaîne de l'Estaque; traversed by Rhône–Marseille Canal; salt pans; oil refineries in a.; approx. a. 100 sq. m.
Etaples, *t.*, Pas de Calais, France; seaside resort; p. *6,534*.
Etawney, *L.*, Manitoba, Canada.
Ethiopia (Abyssinia), *indep. sovereign st.*, Africa; under Italian domination 1936–41; federated with Eritrea 1952; tableland with average height 3,000 ft. intersected deep valleys; Samen Mtns. 15,000 ft.; summer rains; pastoral, farming, coffee; cap. Addis Ababa. a. 400,000 sq. m.; p. (1961) *21,800,000*.
Etna, *volcano*, N.E. Sicily, Italy; recent eruptions have raised height from 10,768 ft. to 11,121 ft.
Etna, *t.*, Penns., U.S.A.; p. (1960) *5,519*.
Eton, *t.*, *urb. dist.*, Bucks, Eng.; on N. bank of R. Thames opposite Windsor; famous public school, founded by Henry VI, p. (1961) *3,901*.
Etowah, *R.*, Ga., U.S.A.; trib. of Coosa R.
Etruria, *t.*, Staffs, Eng.: potteries, ironwks.
Ettelbrück, *t.*, Luxembourg; p. *4,373*.
Etterbeek, *commune*, sub. Brussels, Belgium; carpets, brewing; p. (1962) *53,091*.
Ettrick, *R.*, Selkirk, Scot.; length 32 m.
Eucla, *t.*, W. Australia; close to bdy. of S. Australia on Transcontinental rly.; artesian wells.
Euclid, *t.*, Ohio, U.S.A.; p. (1960) *62,998*.
Eucombene Dam and L., N.S.W., Australia, will hold eight times as much water as Sydney Harbour when completed.
Eugene, *t.*, Ore., U.S.A.; univ.; ironwks.; p. (1960) *50,977*.
Eunice, *t.*, La., U.S.A.; cotton, rice; p. (1960) *11,326*.
Euphrates, *lgst. R.* in S.W. Asia; rises in Armenian uplands and joined by the Tigris, enters Persian G. at Shatt-et-Arab; length 1,780 m.
Eure, *dep.*, Normandy, France; agr., fruit, livestock, textiles; cap. Evreux; a. 2,331 sq. m.; p. (1962) *361,904*.
Eure-et-Loir, *dep.*, N. France; flour, textiles, iron, paper; cap. Chartres; a. 2,291 sq. m.; p. (1962) *277,546*.
Eureka, *c.*, Cal., U.S.A.; timber; p. (1960) *28,137*.
Europe, *continent*; a. 3,900,000 sq. m.; greatest length N. to S. 2,400 m., breadth E. to W. 3,000 m.; ch. mtns.: Alps, Pyrenees, Carpathians, Balkans, Apennines, Sierra Nevada, Urals, Caucasus; ch. Rs.: Volga, Danube, Rhine, Dnieper, Ural, Don; ch. lakes; Ladoga, Onega, Peipus, Vänern, Vättern; climate: Arctic border, long cold winter, short cool summer, snow; W. seaboard, cool summer, mild winter, abundant rainfall; Continental, warm summer, cold winter; Mediterranean, hot dry summers, warm wet winters; vegetation: N. tundra; Scandinavia and N. Russia, coniferous forests; European plain, woodlands; Mediterranean, drought-resisting evergreens; S. Russia, steppe; Caspian shores, desert; ch. inds.: agr., cereals, fruits, sugar-beet, potatoes, flax, hemp; pastoral, cattle-rearing, dairying, fishing; forestry; wood pulp, paper; mining, iron, coal, petroleum; hydro-elec. power; mountainous regions. Politically divided into reps., kingdoms, principalities and a grand duchy; p. (est.) *533,000,000*.
Europort, *t.*, nr. Rotterdam, Netherlands; new Common Market pt., capable of handling 100,000-ton oil-tankers.
Euros, *prefecture*, Thrace, Greece; cap. Alexandroupolis; p. (1961) *157,901*.
Euskirchen, *t.*, N. Rhine–Westphalia, Germany; W. of Bonn; cloth, glass, wood, paper wks.; p. (1963) *21,000*.
Evanston, *t.*, Ill., U.S.A.; on L. Michigan; sub. of Chicago, seat of N.W. Univ.; p. (1960) *79,283*.
Evanston, *t.*, Wyo., U.S.A.; coal, oil, iron; dairying, agr.; p. (1960) *4,901*.
Evans Strait, divides Southampton Land from Coats I., Hudson Bay, Canada.
Evansville, *mftg. c.*, Ind., U.S.A.; on Ohio R.; hardwood tr., coal, farm implements; p. (1960) *141,543*.
Everest, Mt. (Chomolungma = Goddess Mother of the Earth), Himalaya, on frontier of Nepal and Tibet; alt. 29,028 ft.; highest mtn. in the world; Hillary and Tenzing first to reach summit in 1953.
Everett, *mftg. t.*, Mass., U.S.A., nr. Boston; iron and steel; p. (1960) *43,544*.
Everett, *t.*, Wash., U.S.A.; timber, salmon, fruit; p. (1960) *40,304*.
Everglades, Fla., U.S.A.; extensive marshes.
Evesham, *mkt. t.*, *mun. bor.*, Worcester, Eng.; on R. Avon, in Vale of Evesham, 15 m. S.E. of Worcester; fruit ctr.; p. (1961) *12,608*.
Evora, *cap.*, Alto Alemtejo prov., Portugal; iron, cork; famous for its mules; p. *27,038*.
Evreux, *t.*, *cap.*, Eure, France; iron, glass, textiles; p. (1962) *40,158*.
Evvoia (Euboea), *Greek I.*, Ægean Sea; 115 m. long; wheat, olive oil, wine; cap. Khalkis; p. (1951) *163,720*.
Ewell, *t.*, Surrey, Eng.; residtl.; pottery.
Ewing, *t.*, N.J., U.S.A.; p. (1960) *26,628*.
Exe, *R.*, Somerset and Devon, rises on Exmoor, flows S. to English Channel at Exmouth; length 44 m.
Exeter, *c.*, co. bor., co. t., mkt. t., Devon, Eng.; E. of Dartmoor on R. Exe 8 m. from the sea; univ.; cath.; aircraft components, leather goods; p. (1961) *80,215*.
Exeter, *bor.*, Penns., U.S.A.; coal, timber; p. (1950) *5,130*.
Exmoor, *moorland tract*, Somerset, Devon, Eng.; highest point, Dunkery Beacon, 1,707 ft.
Exmouth, *t.*, *urb. dist.*, Devon, Eng.; on E. side of estuary of R. Exe; holiday resort; p. (1961) *19,740*.
Exploits, *R.*, Newfoundland, Canada; length 150 m.
Extremadura, *old prov.*, S.W. Spain; largely plateau, alt. 1,500–3,000 ft.; heathy moorland; sheep; less arid conditions than in remainder of central Spain allow olives, vines, cereals; irrigation in valleys of Tagus, Guadiana; gov. project to develop a. in progress.
Exuma, *gr. sm. Is.*, Bahamas, W.I.; p. (1953) *2,919*.
Eye, *mkt. t.*, *mun. bor.*, Suffolk, Eng.; 18 m. N. of Ipswich; anc. church; p. (1961) *1,580*.
Eyemouth, *burgh*, Berwick, Scot.; on E. cst., 9 m. N. of Berwick; fishing; p. (1961) *2,160*.
Eyre, *L.* (*salt*), N. part of S. Australia; a. 4,000 sq. m., 38 ft. below sea-level; practically dried up.
Eyre Peninsula, S. Australia; between G. of St. Vincent and Spencer G.
Eyzies, Les, *commune*, Dordogne dep., France; caves, arch. interests, Paleolithic paintings, Cromagnon type site.

F

Faaborg, *spt.*, Fyn I., Denmark; p. (1960) *5,135*.
Fabriano, *mftg. t.*, Marches, Italy; 30 m. S.W. of Ancona; fine cath.; paper; p. *26,625*.
Fabrizia, *t.*, nr. Monteleone, Italy; p. *4,150*.
Facone, *sacred L.*, Honshu, Japan; 57 m. from Tokyo.
Faenza, *t.*, Ravenna, Italy; at foot of Apennines, 15 m. S.W. of Ravenna; pottery (faience), silk; p. (1961) *51,085*.
Fagersta, *t.*, Vastmanland, Sweden; iron, steel smelting; p. (1961) *15,527*.
Failsworth, *t.*, *urb. dist.*, Lancs, Eng.; N.E. of Manchester; textiles, elec. goods; p. (1961) *19,805*.
Fair I., midway between Shetland and Orkney, Scot.; bird sanctuary; famous for brightly patterned, hand-knitted articles.
Fairbanks, *t.*, Alaska, U.S.A.; p. (1960) *13,311*.
Fairfield, *t.*, Ala., U.S.A.; p. (1960) *15,816*.
Fairhaven, *t.*, Mass., U.S.A.; p. (1960) *14,233*.
Fairhead, *C.*, N.W. Antrim, N. Ireland.
Fair Lawn, *t.*, N.J., U.S.A.; p. (1960) *26,628*.
Fairmont, *t.*, W. Va., U.S.A.; p. (1960) *27,477*.
Fairweather, *mtn.*, Alaska, N. America; alt. 14,872 ft.

Faiyum, *see* **El Faiyum.**
Faizabad, *ch. t.*, Badakhshan, N.E. Afghanistan.
Fakenham, *t.*, Norfolk, Eng.; on R. Wensum.
Fal, *R.*, Cornwall, Eng.; flows to the English Channel; length 23 m.
Falaise, *t.*, Calvados, France; birthplace of William the Conqueror; scene of rout of a German Army, 1944; p. 5,715.
Falaise de l'Ile de France, *low S.E.-facing escarpment*, 50 m. S.E. and E. of Paris, France; overlooks "pays" of Champagne Pouilleuse; ch. vine-growing dist. for champagne-wine ind. of Rheims, Epernay.
Falcón, *st.*, Venezuela; bordering Caribbean Sea; cap. Coro; p. (1961) *340,450*.
Falkirk, *burgh*, Stirling, Scot.; 10 m. S.E. of Stirling; foundries, bricks, chemical, aluminium wks., concrete, timber yards; battles 1298 and 1746; p. (1961) *38,043*.
Falkland, *burgh*, Fife, Scot.; 3 m. S. of Auchtermuchty; mkt.; p. (1961) *1,032*.
Falkland Is., *Brit. Crown col.*, S. Atlantic, comprises E. and W. Falkland and adjacent Is.; sheep rearing (for wool); cap. Stanley on E. Falkland I.; a. 4,700 sq. m.; p. (1962) *2,172*.
Falkland Is. Dependencies, comprise S. Georgia (ctr. of whaling ind.) and S. Sandwich Is. (S. Shetland, S. Orkney Is., and Graham's Land were constituted a separate col. in 1962 and now form British Antarctic Territory (*q.v.*)). *See* **K190.**
Fall River *industl. c.*, Mass., U.S.A.; cottons, dyeing, brewing, iron; p. (1960) *99,942*.
Falmouth, *spt., mun. bor.*, Cornwall, Eng.; on W. side of estuary of R. Fal, 10 m. S. of Truro; fine sheltered harbourage; seaside resort; fisheries, ship repairing, mng., quarrying, lt. engin.; p. (1961) *15,427*.
False Bay, *inlet* on E. side of C. of Good Hope peninsula.
Falster, *I.* in the Baltic, Denmark; cap. Nyköbing; p. (1960) *46,662*. [*13,305*.
Falticeni, *t.*, N.E. Romania; timber; p. (1956)
Falun, *t.*, Kopparberg, Sweden; iron, paper, pyrites, zinc and lead ore; p. (1961) *18,813*.
Famagusta, *t., spt.*, Cyprus; on E. cst., 2½ m. S. of ruins of ancient Salamis; p. (1960) *34,774*.
Famatina, *t.*, La Rioja prov., Argentina; in foothills of Andes, 360 m. N.W. of Cordoba; copper-mines.
Fannich, *loch*, Ross, Scot.; (6½ m. long), drains to Cromarty F.
Fanning, *Brit. I.*, Gilbert and Ellice Is. col.; N. Pac. Oc.; a. 15 sq. m.; guano, mother-of-pearl; p. *196*.
Fano, *t.*, Italy; on Adriatic cst., N. of Ancona; resort; p. (1961) *41,033*.
Fanö, I., Denmark; off W. cst. of Jutland, opposite Esbjerg; a. 20 sq. m.; p. (1960) *2,675*.
Farafra, *oasis*, Libyan Desert, U.A.R.; 200 m. W. of Asyut; dates; stage on caravan route from Cyrenaica to Upper U.A.R.
Farciennes, *commune*, S.W. Belgium; coal, mftg.; p. (1962) *11,359*.
Fareham, *t., urb. dist.*, Hants., Eng.; at N.W. corner of Portsmouth Harbour; sm. boats, ceramics; p. (1961) *58,277*.
Farewell, *C.*, southernmost tip of Greenland.
Farewell, *C.*, most northerly point S.I., N.Z.
Fargo, *c.*, N.D., U.S.A.; on Red R.; grain, farm-machin.; p. (1960) *46,662*.
Faribalut, *t.*, Minn., U.S.A.; flour, factories; p. (1960) *16,928*.
Faridpur, *t.*, E. Bengal, Pakistan; cloth, carpets; p. (1961) *28,300*.
Faringdon, *mkt. t.*, Berks, Eng.; on N. edge of Vale of White Horse; p. *11,450*.
Farmington, *t.*, N.M., U.S.A.; p. (1960) *23,786*.
Farmington, *t.*, N. Conn., U.S.A.; residtl. and industl.; p. (1960) *10,798*.
Farnborough, *t., urb. dist.*, Hants, Eng.; 3 m. N. of Aldershot military camp; Royal Aircraft Establishment; p. (1961) *31,437*.
Farne Is., off Northumberland cst., Eng.; a. 80 acres; since 1923 bird sanctuaries.
Farnham, *mkt. t., urb. dist.*, Surrey, Eng.; at N. Foot of N. Downs, 10 m. W. of Guildford; pottery, engin., coach mkg.; p. (1961) *26,927*.
Farnworth, *mftg. t., mun. bor.*, Lancs, Eng., nr. Bolton, cotton mnfs.; p. (1961) *27,474*.
Faro, *spt., cap.*, Algarve prov., Portugal; wine, fruit, cork; p. (1950) *33,903*.
Faro, *C.*, N. point of Sicily, nearest to Italy.

Faroe Is., 200 m. N.W. of the Shetlands, Scot.; cap. Thörshavn (Strömö I.); Danish possession; fishing, agr.; a. 540 sq. m.; p. (1960) *34,596*.
Farrell, *t.*, Penns., U.S.A.; p. (1960) *13,793*.
Farrukhabad, *t.*, Uttar Pradesh, India; on Ganges R.; gold, lace, brass wk.; p. (1961) *94,591*.
Fars, *S.W. prov.*, Iran; on the Persian G.; cap. Shiraz.
Fasa, *t.*, Fars Prov., Iran; silk, wool; p. *10,000*.
Fasano, *t.*, Bari, Italy; industl.; p. over *20,000*.
Fastnet, *lighthouse* in Atlantic, 4½ m. S.W. C. Clear, Irish cst.
Fatehpur, *t.*, Uttar Pradesh, India; hides, grain; p. (1961) *28,323*.
Fatshan (Foshan), *c.*, Kwangtung, China; S.W. of Canton; iron and steel, textiles; p. (1953) *123,000*.
Faucilles, Les Monts, *range of hills*, connecting Vosges and Langres plateau, E. France; highest point about 1,600 ft.
Favara, *t.*, Sicily, Italy; sulphur, marble; p. *21,500*.
Faversham, *old mkt. t., mun. bor.*, Kent, Eng.; 10 m. W. Canterbury; fruit, hops, bricks, brushes, engin.; p. (1961) *12,983*.
Fawley, *t.*, Hants, Eng.; on W. shore of Southampton Water, 2 m. N.W. of Calshot; oil refining; p. (1951) *6,515*.
Fayal I., Azores; orange growing; cap. Horta.
Fayetteville, *t.*, Ark., U.S.A.; univ.; rly. and tr. ctr., agr. implements, resort; p. (1960) *20,274*.
Fayetteville, *t.*, N.C., U.S.A.; p. (1960) *47,106*.
Fear, *C.*, point of the N. Carolina cst. U.S.A.
Feather, *R.*, Cal., U.S.A.; trib. of Sacramento R.
Featherstone, *t., urb. dist.*, W.R. Yorks, Eng.; coal; p. (1961) *14,633*.
Fécamp, *sm. spt., wat. pl.*, Seine-Maritime, France; 12th cent. abbey; fishing; p. (1954) *18,201*.
Fedchenko, *glacier*, lgst in U.S.S.R.; in Pamir-Altai mtns of central Asia; 50 m.l.
Federal Dist., *st.*, Mexico; a. 431 sq. m.; p. (1960) *4,871,000*.
Fehmarn, *I.*, in W. Baltic Sea; pastureland; belongs to Schleswig-Holstein, Germany; a. 72 sq. m.; p. *12,000*.
Feilding, *t.*, Wellington, N.Z.; p. (1951) *5,810*.
Feldberg, *mtn. peak*, Black Forest, Germany; alt. 4,900 ft.
Feldkirch, *t.*, Vorarlberg, Austria; on Swiss frontier; p. (1961) *17,343*.
Felixstowe, *t., urb. dist.*, E. Suffolk, Eng.; 12 m. S.E. Ipswich; seaside resort, fertilisers; dock development; p. (1961) *17,254*.
Felling, *urb. dist.*, Durham, Eng.; Tyneside mftg. and colly. dist.; p. (1961) *35,602*.
Feltham, *see* **Hounslow.**
Feltre, *t.*, Venetia, Italy; cath.; silk, wine; p. *19,000*.
Fenny Stratford, *mkt. t.*, Bucks, Eng.; 2 m. E. of Bletchley; straw-plaiting; p. *4,300*.
Fens, The, *low-lying dist.* round Wash; protected by high embankments against flooding by spring tides; includes parts of 6 English cos.
Fenton, *t.*, Staffs, Eng.; nr. Stoke-on-Trent; earthenware wks.
Feodosiya, *spt.*, Crimea, U.S.S.R.; harbour; tobacco, hosiery; p. (1956) *42,600*.
Ferbane, *vil.*, Co. Offaly, Ireland; milled peat elec. generating sta.
Ferentino, *t.*, prov. Rome, Italy; wine, olive oil; cath.; p. *14,625*.
Ferghana, *region*, Uzbek S.S.R., U.S.S.R.; deep basin at W. end of Tien Shan Mtns.; drained W. by R. Syr Darya; semi-arid but extensive irrigation system allows intensive cultivation of cotton, citrus fruits, silk, rice; ch. ts., Kokand, Namangan.
Ferghana, *t.*, Uzbekistan S.S.R.; hydro-elec., petroleum refining, textiles; deposits of ozocerite located nearby; p. (1959) *80,000*.
Fergus Falls, *t.*, Minn., U.S.A.; flour, dairy produce; p. (1960) *13,733*.
Fermanagh, *inland co.*, N. Ireland; bisected by R. Erne and lakes; cap. Enniskillen; stock-raising, dairying, stone; a. 714 sq. m.; p. (1961) *51,613*.
Fermo, *c.*, Ascoli, Italy; p. *25,000*.
Fermoy, *t.*, Cork, Ireland; on R. Blackwater; p. (1961) *3,241*.
Fernando de Noronha, *st.*, consisting of Is. off E. cst. Brazil; penal sta; p. (1960) *1,389*.
Fernando Po, *I.*, Span. overseas prov. (aut. status) W. Africa; in Bight of Biafra; mtnous; coffee,

cocoa, timber; a. 1,000 sq. m.; cap. Santa Isabel; p. (1963) *80,000*.

Ferndale, *t.*, Mich., U.S.A.; p. (1960) *31,347*.

Fernie, *t.*, Brit. Columbia, Canada; in Rockies, nr. Crows Nest Pass; coal. [*97,932*.

Ferozepore, *t.*, Punjab, India; wheat; p. (1961)

Ferrara, *prov.*, N. Italy; cap. Ferrara; a. 1,019 sq. m.; p. (1961) *398,663*.

Ferrara, *fortfd. c.*, N. Italy; nr. head of delta of R. Po; cath., univ.; mnfs. silk, hemp, wine; mkt. for fertile plain; oil refinery nearby; petrochemicals; p. (1961) *151,145*.

Ferro, *most S.W. I.*, Canary Is.; a. 106 sq. m.; was chosen by Fr. scientists (1630) as first meridian; cap. Valverde.

Ferrol, *spt.*, *naval arsenal*, Spain; on N.W. cst. nr. Corunna; p. (1950) *77,030*.

Ferryhill, *vil.*, Durham, Eng.; 5 m. S. of Durham, in gap through limestone ridge which separates Wear valley from Tees valley; commands main N. to S. route along lowland E. of Pennines.

Fertile Crescent, an arc of fertile land from the Mediterranean Sea, N. of the Arabian Desert, to Persian Gulf; home of some very early civilisations and migrations.

Festiniog, *see* **Ffestiniog**.

Fethiye, *spt.*, Turkey; opp. Rhodes; p. (1960) *7,652*.

Fetlar I., Shetland Is., Scot.; 6½ m. long by 2¾ m. wide.

Feuerbach, *industl. c.*, Baden–Württemberg, Germany; N.W. sub. of Stuttgart; sandstone; p. (1963) *27,000*.

Fez, *c.*, Morocco, N. Africa; lies inland 100 m. E. of Rabat; one of the sacred cities of Islam; univ. attached to mosque (one of lgst. in Africa); impt. comm. ctr.; p. (1960) *216,133*.

Fezzan, *prov.*, Libya, N. Africa; numerous wells and inhabited oases.

Ffestiniog (Festiniog), *urb. dist.*, Merioneth, N. Wales; at head of Vale of Ffestiniog 9 m. E. of Portmadoc; contains vils. of Ffestiniog and Blaenau Ffestiniog; impt. slate quarries; world's lgst pumped-storage hydroelec. sta. (1963); cement; p. (1961) *6,677*.

Fianarantsoa, *t.*, Malagasy; p. (1957) *34,845*.

Fichtelgebirge (Fir Mtns.), *mtn. range*, N.E. Bavaria, Germany; highest peak, Schneeberg; alt. 3,454 ft.

Fife, *peninsula*, *co.*, E. Scot.; between the F. of Tay and Forth; *co. t.* Cupar; a. 492 sq. m.; p. (1961) *320,541*.

Fife Ness, extreme E. point, Fife, Scot.

Figuéira da Foz, *t.*, Portugal; resort at mouth of R. Mondego; corn, wine; p. *10,229*.

Figuéras, *fortfd. t.*, Gerona, Spain; nr. French frontier; glass, cork, leather; p. (1957) *16,589*.

Fiji, *archipelago of* 322 coral Is. (106 inhabited) in S. Pac.; Brit. Crown Col.; forests, bananas, coconuts, sugar-cane; cap. Suva on Viti Levu I.; a. 7,083 sq. m.; p. (estd. 1965) *449,000*.

Filey, *t.*, *urb. dist.*, E.R. Yorks, Eng.; on E. cst. 5 m. S.E. of Scarborough; seaside resort; p. (1961) *4,705*.

Filton, Bristol, Somerset; aircraft wks.

Finchley, *former mun. bor.*, Middx., Eng., now inc. in Barnet outer bor., Greater London, (*q.v.*); residtl.; p. (1961) *69,370*.

Findhorn, *fishing vil.*, Moray, Scot.; resort.

Findlay, *mftg. t.*, Ohio, U.S.A.; on Blanchard R.; p. (1960) *30,344*.

Findochty, *sm. burgh.*, Banff, Scot.; p. (1961) *1,331*.

Findon or Finnan, *fishing vil.*, Kincardine, Scot.

Fingal's Cave, Staffa I., Inner Hebrides, W. Scot.; basaltic columns.

Finistère, *dep.*, N.W. France; cap. Quimper; cereals fruit, livestock; coal, granite; fishing; a. 2,730 sq. m., p. (1962) *749,558*.

Finisterre, *C.*, extreme N.W. point of Spain.

Finland, *rep.*, Europe, low-lying tableland, glaciated, innumerable lakes; forested; oats, rye, barley, potatoes; timber, wood-pulp, textiles; iron mining; official languages, Finnish and Swedish (Swedish names mainly as alternatives on W. cst.); mainly agr.; cap. Helsinki; a. 117,975 sq. m.; p. (1961) *4,446,222*.

Finland, G. of, E. arm of Baltic Sea, 250 m. l.

Finnart, Dunbartonshire, Scot.; oil terminal situated in Loch Long, N.W. Glasgow; pipeline to Grangemouth.

Finnmark, *most northerly co.*, Norway; inhabited by Lapps; whale fisheries; lge. copper deposits discovered nr. Reppan fjord; a. 18,581 sq. m.; p. (1963) *73,229*.

Finsbury, *see* **Islington**.

Finsteraarhorn, *mtn.*, Switzerland, (14,023 ft.) highest peak in Bernese Oberland.

Finsterwalde, *t.*, Cottbus, E. Germany; textiles, furniture, metallurgy, glass; p. (1963) *21,117*.

Fir Mountains, *see* **Fichtelgebirge**.

Firenze, *see* **Florence**.

Firminy, *mftg. t.*, Loire, France; S.E. of St. Etienne; p. (1954) *21,161*.

Fishguard and Goodwick, *spt.*, *urb. dist.*, N. Pembroke, Wales; on S. of Cardigan Bay; steamer connection to Cork and Rosslare (Ireland); p. (1961) *4,898*.

Fitchburg, *c.*, Mass., U.S.A.; woollens, paper, machin.; p. (1960) *43,021*.

Fitzroy, *R.*, W. Australia; flows into King Sound.

Fiume, *see* **Rijeka**. [p. *17,550*.

Fivizzano, *t.*, Tuscany, Italy; mineral springs;

Flagstaff, *t.*, Arizona, U.S.A.; seat of Lowell Univ.; p. (1960) *18,214*.

Flamborough Head, *C.*, Yorks cst., Eng.; chalk cliffs, alt. 500 ft.; lighthouse.

Fläming, *heathland*, Potsdam, E. Germany; occupies low sandy ridge, alt. below 800 ft., 50 m. S.W. of Berlin; heathland, coniferous woodland; former military training a.

Flanders, *dist.*, Belgium. divided into two provs. of W. (1,248 sq. m., p. (1962) *1,075,949*) and E. (1,147 sq. m., p. (1962) *1,276,803*; caps. Bruges and Ghent.

Flat River, *c.*, Mo., U.S.A.; lead mines; p. (1960) *4,515*.

Flattery Cape, on Pacific cst., Wash., U.S.A.

Flèche, La, *t.*, Sarthe, France; nr. Le Mans; p. (1954) *11,275*.

Fleet, *t.*, *urb. dist.*, Hants, Eng.; 4 m. N.W. of Aldershot; p. (1961) *13,672*.

Fleetwood, *spt.*, *mun. bor.*, Lancs., Eng.; at mouth of Wyre; fishing; lge. chemical plant projected nearby; p. (1961) *27,760*.

Flémalle, 2 *communes*, Liége prov., Belgium; glass; p. (1962) *13,857*.

Flensburg, *spt.*, Schleswig-Holstein, Germany; on Baltic cst.; coal; shipbldg., machin., iron, chemicals, fishing; p. (1963) *97,000*

Flevosted, *t.*, Netherlands; administrative ctr. of new S.E. Polder.

Flinders, *R.*, Queensland, Australia; flowing to G. of Carpentaria.

Flinders Range, *mtns.*, S. Australia; extend 250 m. N.E. from head of Spencer G.; alt. 3,900 ft.

Flin Flon, *t.*, Manitoba, Canada; 90 m. by rly. N. of The Pas; ctr. of gold-mining a.; p. (1961) *11,104*.

Flint, *co.*, Wales; stock-raising; coal, iron, textiles chemicals; a. 257 sq. m.; p. (1961) *149,888*.

Flint, *c.*, Mich., U.S.A.; motor cars, lumber, woollens, aeroplane engines; p. (1960) *196,940*

Flint, *mun. bor.*, *co. t.*, Flint, Wales; viscos textile yarn, pulp; p. (1961) *13,690*.

Flint I., (Brit.), Pac. Oc.; uninhabited.

Flodden, *vil.*, Northumberland, Eng.; on R. Till famous battle 1513, James IV of Scotlan defeated by the Earl of Surrey.

Flora, *c.*, Sogn og Fjordane, Norway; new 85 m. N. of Bergen; p. (1965) *7,700*.

Florange, *t.*, Moselle, France; p. (1954) *12,039*.

Florence (Firenze), *c.*, Tuscany, Italy; on R Arno; leather-work; famous for art treasures cath. and churches; ruled by Medici 1421–1737 birthplace of Dante and Michelangelo; p. (1961 *438,138*.

Florence, *c.*, N.W. Ala., U.S.A.; iron, textiles lumber, food; airport; p. (1960) *31,649*.

Florence, *t.*, S.C., U.S.A.; p. (1960) *24,722*.

Flores, *I.*, most north-westerly of the Azore gr.; Portuguese; cap. Santa Cruz; French set up ballistic missiles tracking sta.

Flores, *I.*, Indonesia; divided between Indonesi and Portugal; mountainous, volcanic, densel forested; a. 8,870 sq. m.; p. *500,000*.

Flores, *dep.*, Uruguay; cap. Trinidad; a. 1,74 sq. m.; p. (1953) *35,565*. [nesi

Flores Sea, between Sulawesi and Flores, Ind

Florianopolis, *spt.*, cap. Santa Catarina st., Brazi cst tr.; p. (1960) *98,520*.

Florida, *st.*, U.S.A.; between Atlantic and of Mexico; resort a.; tourism; lumber, pape minerals; fruit, vegetables, sugar, cotto cattle raising; cap. Tallahassee; a. 58,560 s m.; p. (1960) *4,951,560*.

Florida, *dep.*, Uruguay; cap. Florida; a. 4,673 s m.; p. (1953) *106,284*.

Floridabanca, *t.*, Luzon, Philippine Is.; sugar, rice; p. *17,521*.

Florida Strait, between Florida and Bahama Is.; course of " Gulf Stream " from Gulf of Mexico.

Florina, *see* **Phlorina**.

Flume, The, picturesque gorge, Franconia Mtns., N.H., U.S.A.

Flushing, *spt.*, *wat. pl.*; Walcheren I., Netherlands; steam-packet sta.; p. (1951) *24,048*.

Flushing Meadow, *t.*, Flushing Bay, Long Island, N.Y., U.S.A.; U.N.O. meeting place.

Fly, *R.*, New Guinea; flows S.E. to G. of Papua.

Fochabers, *vil.*, Moray, Scot.; nr. mouth of Spey; tourist resort; food canning ind.

Focsani, *t.*, Putna dist., Romania; on R. Milkov; soap, petroleum (1956) *28,244*.

Foggia, *prov.*, Apulia, S. Italy; a. 2,683 sq. m.; p. (1961) *632,332*.

Foggia, *t.*, S. Italy, Apulia; cath.; industl.; p. (1961) *117,485*.

Fogo, *I.*, Atl. Oc.; in Cape Verde gr.; volcanic.

Folda Fjord, W. coast, Norway.

Foligno, *t.*, Perugia, Italy; remarkable grotto; numerous factories; p. (1961) *48,069*.

Folkestone, *spt.*, *mun. bor.*, Kent, Eng.; seaside resort, pt. for Folkestone–Boulogne route to France 29 m.; p. (1961) *44,129*.

Fond du Lac, *mftg. t.*, Winnebago Lake, Wis., U.S.A.; cath.; p. (1960) *32,719*.

Fonsagrada, *industl. t.*, Lugo, Spain; p. (1957) *13,925*.

Fonseca Bay, *inlet* on Pacific cst. of C. America, bordering on Nicaragua; U.S.A. naval base; (U.S.A. have acquired the option for a canal route through Nicaragua).

Fontainebleau, *t.*, Seine-et-Marne, France; on R. Seine, 35 m. S.E. of Paris; magnificent forest (a. 42,500 acres) and palace; porcelain; Ecole d'Artillerie; p. (1954) *19,915*.

Fontenay-le-Comte, *industl. t.*, Vendée, France; p. (1954) *9,519*.

ontenay-sous-Bois, *t.*, Seine, France; sub. of Paris; p. (1954) *36,739*.

ontenoy, *vil.*, Belgium; nr. Tournai; battle, 1745; Marshall Saxe defeated the Allies under Duke of Cumberland; p. (1962) *639*.

ontevrault, *t.*, dep. Maine-et-Loire, France.

oochow (Fuzhou), *c.*, Fukien, China; former treaty pt.; gr. tea-exporting ctr.; p. (1953) *553,000*.

oots Cray, *sm. t.*, Kent, Eng.; paper-mills.

orbach, *t.*, Moselle, France; p. (1954) *21,591*.

orbes, *t.*, N.S.W., Australia; p. (1958) *6,730*.

ordingbridge, *mkt. t.*, Hants, Eng.; on R. Avon, sail-cloth; p. *3,394*.

ordlandia, *t.*, Para, N.E. Brazil; on Tapajoz R.; one of the Ford rubber plantations.

oreland, N. and S., two headlands, on E. cst. of Kent, Eng.; lighthouse.

orest Hill, *t.*, Ontario, Canada; p. (1961) *20,489*.

orest Hills, *residtl. a.*, part of Queen's bor., N.Y., U.S.A.; on Long I.; p. *21,400*.

orest Park, *t.*, Georgia, U.S.A.; p. (1961) *14,201*.

orfar, *burgh*, Angus, Scot.; in Strathmore, 17 m. S.W. of Montrose; linen, jute; p. (1961) *10,252*.

orli, *ancient c.*, Emilia Italy; silk factories, ironwks.; felt; p. (1961) *91,146*.

ormby, *t.*, *urb. dist.*, Lancs, Eng.; on W. cst., 6 m. S.W. of Southport; p. (1961) *11,730*.

ormentera, *I.*, Balearic Is., S. of Ibiza; 13 m. long; cereals, wine, tunny fishing; p. (1957) *2,657*.

ormia, *t.*, Caserta, Italy; the ancient Formiæ.

ormigine, *t.*, Modena prov., N. Italy; silk, leather; p. *10,985*.

ormosa, *see* **Taiwan**.

ormosa, *prov.*, N. Argentina; bordering on Paraguay; timber; cap. Formosa; a. 27,825 sq. m.; p. (1960) *178,000*.

rnaes, *c.*, extreme E. point of Jutland.

rres, *burgh*, Moray, Scot.; nr. mouth of R. Findhorn, 25 m. E. of Inverness; distilling, oat and woollen mills; p. (1961) *4,780*.

rst, *t.*, Cottbus, E. Germany; on R. Neisse; E. section of t. Polish since 1945; textiles; p. (1963) *28,981*.

rt Augustus, *vil.*, Inverness, Scot.; at S.W. end of Loch Ness; on Caledonian Canal; Fort now Abbey.

rt Collins, *c.*, Col., U.S.A.; ctr. of rich farming a.; grain, sugarbeet, livestock; site of Colorado State Univ.; p. (1960) *25,027*.

Fort de France (formerly **Fort Royal**), *cap.*, Martinique, W. Indies; has a land-locked harbour of some 16 sq. m.; exp. rum, sugar; p. (estd. 1960) *60,648*.

Fort Dodge, *t.*, Iowa, U.S.A.; on Des Moines R., in rich agr. cty.; grain, pottery, coal; p. (1960) *28,399*.

Fort Frances, *t.*, Ontario, Canada; pulp, lumbering; p. (1961) *9,481*.

Fort George, *R.*, Labrador, Canada; flowing into James Bay.

Fort Jameson, *t.*, Eastern Prov., Zambia; cotton.

Fort Lamy, *t.*, *cap.*, Chad, Africa; p. *18,465*.

Fort Landerdale, *t.*, Fla., U.S.A.; prefab. bldg. mftg., concrete prod., fertilisers; p. (1960) *83,648*.

Fort Madison, *c.*, Iowa, U.S.A.; meat packing; p. (1960) *15,247*.

Fort Monroe, Va., U.S.A.; at mouth of James R.; p. *2,000*.

Fort Myers, *t.*, Fla., U.S.A.; p. (1960) *22,523*.

Fort Pierce, *t.*, Fla., U.S.A.; p. (1960) *25,256*.

Fort St. John, *t.*, B.C., Canada; on Peace R.; oilfield; p. (1961) *3,619*

Fort Scott, *t.*, Kan., U.S.A.; maize, wheat, cattle; p. (1960) *9,410*.

Fort Smith, *c.*, Ark., U.S.A.; on Arkansas R.; rly. ctr., cotton, maize, wagons, furniture; p. (1960) *52,991*.

Fort Victoria, *t.*, Rhodesia; agr. and mining ctr., cattle; historic ruins in Zimbabwe Nat. Park; p. (1958) *10,700* (incl. *1,700* Europeans).

Fort Wayne, *c.*, Ind., U.S.A.; rly.-carriage bldg. and machine shops; p. (1960) *161,776*.

Fort William, *c.*, Ontario, Canada; on L. Superior; grain pt.; p. (1961) *45,214*.

Fort William, *burgh*, Inverness, Scot.; nr. head of Loch Linnhe, at base of Ben Nevis; aluminium factory; pulp- and paper-mill projected at Corpach; p. (1961) *2,715*.

Fort Worth, *c.*, Texas, U.S.A.; rly. and comm. ctr. on Trinity R.; livestock and grain mkt.; petroleum, meat packing, aeroplanes, oilfield equipment; site of Texas Christian Univ.; p. (1960) *356,268*.

Fort Yukon, Alaska, U.S.A.; trading sta. on Yukon R.; p. *274*.

Fortaleza, *cap.*, Ceará st., Brazil; exp. sugar, rubber, cotton, carnauba wax; p. (1960) *514,818*.

Fortescue, *R.*, W. Australia.

Forth, *R.*, Scot.; rises on Ben Lomond, and flows E. into F. of Forth nr. Alloa; length 65 m.

Forth Bridge, *rly. bridge*, Scot.; spans F. of Forth between N. and S. Queensferry; length $1\frac{1}{2}$ m. Forth road bridge (suspension) just upstream opened 1964.

Forth, Firth of, *lge. inlet*, E. cst. of Scot.; submerged estuary of R. Forth; navigable by lge. vessels for 40 m. inland to Grangemouth; other pts., Leith, Rosyth (naval), Bo'ness; length (to Alloa) 50 m., width varies from 1 to 13 m.

Forth and Clyde Canal, Scot.; links F. of Forth at Grangemouth, and F. of Clyde at Glasgow; length 38 m.

Fortrose, *t.*, *burgh*, Ross and Cromarty, Scot.; on S. cst. of Black Isle, on Moray Firth; p. (1961) *902*.

Fortune Bay, *inlet*, S. cst. of Newfoundland, [Canada.

Fossano, *t.*, Italy; nr. Turin; cath.; paper, silk; p. *21,850*.

Fostoria, *t.*, Ohio, U.S.A.; glass, quarries, stockyards; p. (1960) *15,732*.

Fotheringhay, *vil.*, on R. Nene, Northampton, Eng.; Mary Queen of Scots beheaded in F. Castle, 1587.

Fougères, *t.*, Ille-et-Vilaine, France; cas.; p. (1954) *23,151*.

Fougerolles, *t.*, Haute-Saône, France.

Foula, I., Shetland Is., Scot.; westward of main gr.

Foulness Island, Essex, Eng.

Foulweather, *C.*, Ore., U.S.A.

Fountains Abbey, fine ruin, Cistercian, founded 1132, W.R. Yorks, Eng.; nr. Ripon.

Fourchambault, *t.*, Nièvre, France; on R. Loire; p. *4,817*.

Fourmies, *t.*, Nord, France; nr. Valenciennes; p. (1954) *13,414*.

Foveaux Strait, N.Z.; separates S.I. from Stewart I.

Fowey, *spt.*, *mun. bor.*, Cornwall, Eng.; on W. of Fowey estuary, 22 m. W. of Plymouth; seaside resort, fishing; exp. kaolin; p. (1961) *2,237*.

Fox Is., one of the Aleutian Is. gr.
Foxe Basin and Channel, to N. of Hudson Bay, between Baffin I. and Southampton I.
Foxe Peninsula, Baffin I., Franklin, Canada.
Foyers, *falls*, Inverness, Scot.; E. of Loch Ness, nr. Fort Augustus; aluminium wks., hydro-elec. scheme.
Foyle, Lough, estuary of Foyle R., between Donegal and Londonderry, N. Ireland.
Foynes, *spt.* and *airport*, Ireland; on S. shore of Shannon estuary 20 m. S.W. of Limerick; imports coal, petroleum; impt. refuelling base on trans-Atlantic air services (mainly American) from U.S.A. to Europe.
Framingham, *industl. t.*, Mass., U.S.A.; 10 m. W. of Boston; p. (1960) *44,526*.
Framlingham, *mkt. t.*, E. Suffolk, Eng.; 15 m. N.E. of Ipswich.
Franca, *c.*, São Paulo st., Brazil; 160 m. N. of Campinas; p. (1960) *47,244*.
Francavilla, *t.*, Lecce, Italy; wine, oil, leather; p. *21,375*.
France, *rep.* (*former monarchy and empire*), W. Europe, bounded N. by Belgium and English Channel, W. by the Bay of Biscay, S. by the Pyrenees and the Mediterranean, E. by Italy, Switzerland and Germany. Greatest length about 600 m., greatest breadth 540 m.; a. 212,600 sq. m., or 3½ times size of England and Wales; F. is divided into 90 metropolitan deps.; ch. ts. are Paris (the cap., the fifth lgst. c. in Europe), Bordeaux, Marseilles, Lyons, Lille, Nice and Toulouse: 19 univs.; ch. mtns.: Cevennes, Jura, Vosges, Pyrenees; ch. Rs.: Seine, Loire, Rhône, Garonne; climate, temperate; agr.: wheat, oats, potatoes, sugar-beet, vine, fruits, silk, cattle, sheep, dairying; minerals: coal, iron, bauxite, potash; mnfs.: iron and steel, machin., textiles; communications excellent; p. of the Rep. (1965) *48,492,700*. The French Community was set up in 1959 as successor to the French Union.
Franceville, *t.*, Gabon, Equatorial Africa; on R. Ogowe; manganese mines opened 1962.
Francisco Morazán, *dep.* central Honduras; a. 3,870 sq. m.; p. (1961) *284,540*.
Francis Lake, *L.*, Yukon, Canada.
Francistown, *gold-mining t.*, Botswana, Africa; p. *10,000*.
Frankental, *t.*, Rhineland Palatinate, Germany; N.W. of Mannheim; engin., farm implements, metallurgy, cork; p. (1963) *35,800*.
Frankfort, *t.*, Ky., U.S.A.; mining, horse-breeding; p. (1960) *18,365*.
Frankfort, *t.*, Ind., U.S.A.; p. (1960) *15,302*.
Frankfurt-on-Main, *c.*, Hessen, W. Germany; restored cath.; univ.; birthplace of Goethe; machin., cars, chemicals, publishing, elec. engin., transhipment pt., impt. airfield; p. (1963) *694,200*.
Frankfurt-on-Oder, *t.*, Framfurt, E. Germany; 50 m. from Berlin; gr. route ctr.; machin., iron; E. section of t. Polish since 1945; p. (1963) *58,339*.
Frankischer (Franconian) Jura, *plateau with steep N.-facing edge*, S.W. Germany; runs 80 m. S.W. from Fichtel Gebirge (Fir Mtns.), highest elevation just exceeds 3,000 ft.; drained by Regnitz Altmühl; slate quarrying; vine, maize in sheltered valleys.
Franklin, *t.*, N.H., U.S.A.; p. (1960) *6,742*.
Franklin, *bor.*, N.J., U.S.A.; ctr. of U.S. zinc ind.; p. (1960) *3,624*.
Franklin, *c.*, Penns., U.S.A.; petroleum, oil-well tools, rolling stock; p. (1960) *9,586*.
Franklin, *t.*, Tasmania, Australia; 20 m. from Hobart; principal fruit-growing dist. in island.
Franklin, *dist.*, N.W. Terr., Canada; comprising the Is. of Arctic Canada from Banks I. to Baffin I., including Boothia Peninsula and Melville Peninsula; sparsely populated; furs; a. 554,032 sq. m.
Frantiskové Lázne (Franzenbad), *t.*, *wat. pl.*, ČSSR.
Franz Josef Land, U.S.S.R., *archipelago* in Arctic Ocean; N. of Novaya Zemlya; a. 7,050 sq. m.; mainly ice-covered.
Frascati, *t.*, Italy; 12 m. S.E. of Rome; summer resort; famous villas and arch. remains; nuclear research ctr.; p. *11,425*.
Fraser, *R.*, B.C., Canada; rises at 6,000 ft. on W. slopes Rocky Mtns.; famous salmon fisheries; lenth 850 m.
Fraserburg, *agr. t.*, Cape Province, S. Africa; supply sta. for stock-raisers between Calvinia and Carnarvon.
Fraserburgh, *cst. burgh*, N.E. Aberdeen, Scot.; extreme N.E. of Buchan peninsula; impt. herring fishery; granite; p. (1961) *10,462*.
Fraserville, *t.*, Quebec, Canada; on St. Lawrence R.
Fratta Maggiore, *t.*, Italy; 6 m. from Naples; p. *18,100*. [cotton; p. (1957) *10,048*.
Frauenfeld, *cap.*, Thurgau, Switzerland; cas.;
Fray Bentos, *t.*, *cap.*, Río Negro, Uruguay; on R. Uruguay 50 m. from its mouth; meat canning and salting, meat extracts; p. (1963) *14,000*.
Frechen, *t.*, N. Rhine-Westphalia, Germany; W. of Cologne; lignite, pottery; p. (1963) *28,000*.
Fredericia, *spt.*, *t.*, Veile, Jutland, Denmark; traffic ctr., barracks; new bridge over Little Belt; textiles, silver and plates wks., art. fertilisers; oil refinery projected; p. (1960) *29,870*.
Frederick, *c.*, Md., U.S.A.; canning, tanning; p. (1960) *21,744*.
Fredericksburg, *t.*, Va., U.S.A.; scene of severe Federal rebuff, Civil War; p. (1960) *13,639*.
Fredericton, *t.*, *cap.*, N.B., Canada; on St. John R.; univ., cath.; lumbering; p. (1961) *19,683*.
Frederiksberg, *sub.*, Copenhagen, Denmark; p. (1960) *114,285*.
Frederikshaab, *sm. spt.* on W. cst. of Greenland.
Frederikshavn, *spt.*, *fishing t.*, N. cst. of Jutland; iron wks., canneries; p. (1960) *22,522*.
Frederikstad, *t.*, Norway; at mouth of Glommen R.; tr. ctr.; pulp, paper, electrotechnical inds., shipbldg., whale oil refining; p. (1960) *13,746*.
Fredonia, *t.*, N.Y., U.S.A.; p. (1960) *8,477*.
Freehold, *t.*, N.J., U.S.A.; p. (1960) *9,140*.
Free Port, *mftg. t.*, Ill., U.S.A., on the Pecatonica R.; p. (1960) *26,628*. [(1960) *34,419*.
Free Port, *t.*, Long Island, N.Y.; U.S.A.; p.
Freeport, *spt.*, Texas; sulphur, chemicals, magnesium from sea; p. (1960) *11,619*.
Freetown, *cap.*, Sierra Leone, W. Africa; univ.; coaling sta.; exp. palm oil; diesel power plant; p. (1963) *128,000*.
Fregenal de la Sierra, *t.*, Spain; nr. Badajoz; p. (1957) *11,716*.
Freiberg, *c.*, Karl-Marx-Stadt, Germany; cath.; cas.; metallurgy, textiles, glass, porcelain; p. (1963) *48,062*.
Freiburg (Fribourg), *can.*, Switzerland; much forest and unproductive land; a. 645 sq. m.; p. (1961) *159,194*.
Freiburg, *cap.*, Freiburg, Switzerland; between Berne and Lausanne; fine viaduct and bridges; univ.; machin., chocolate; p. (1957) *29,005*.
Freiburg, *t.*, Baden-Württemberg, Germany; in Black Forest; cath., univ.; textiles, paper, metallurgy; p. (1963) *150,400*.
Freising, *c.*, Bavaria, Germany; cath.; agr machin., textiles, brewing; p. (1963) *28,800*.
Freital, *t.*, Dresden, E. Germany; coal-mining iron, leather, glass, uranium ore processing p. (1963) *35,805*.
Fréjus, *cst. t.*, Var, France; p. (1954) *13,452*.
Fréjus, Col de, the Alpine pass under which the Mont Cenis tunnel runs.
Fremantle, *spt.*, W. Australia; at mouth of Swan R., 12 m. S.W. from Perth, principal pt. of commerce in W. Australia and first Australian pt. of call for mail steamers; p. (1947) *27,926*.
Fremont, *t.*, Cal., U.S.A.; p. (1960) *43,790*.
Fremont, *t.*, Nebraska, U.S.A.; on Platte R.; 33 m from Omaha; flourmills, canneries; p. (1960 *19,698*.
Fremont, *c.*, Ohio, U.S.A.; on Sandusky R. petroleum field; p. (1960) *17,573*.
Fremont's Peak, highest peak of Wind River Range, Wyoming St., U.S.A.; alt. 13,570 ft.
French Equatorial Africa, formerly comprised the French African cols. Gabon (cap. Libreville) Middle Congo (cap. Brazzaville), Ubangi-Shari (cap. Bangui), and Chad (cap. Fort Lamy) timber, ivory; a. 953,740 sq. m.; p. (1957 *4,879,000*. These sts. are now indep. within Fr. Community. *See* under separate headings Gabon, Congo, Central African Rep., Chad.
French Guiana, *col.*, S. America; forests; cocoa gold, phosphates; poor communications; cap Cayenne; a. 34,740 sq. m.; p. (1961) *33,000*.
French, *R.*, Ontario, Canada; the outlet of L Nipissing into L. Huron.
French Somaliland, *see* **Somaliland, French.**
French Soudan. *See* **Mali.**
French West Africa, comprised former French col of Dahomey, Ivory Coast, Mauritania, Nige

French Guinea, Upper Volta, Senegal, French Soudan.

Freshwater, *sm. t.*, *bathing resort*, I. of Wight, Eng.; at W. end of I., 8 m. W. of Newport.

Fresnillo, *t.*, Zacatecas St., Mexico; p. *25,000*.

Fresno, *c.*, Cal., U.S.A.; ctr. of impt. irrigated fruit-growing dist.; dairying, copper, petroleum; p. (1960) *133,929*.

Friedrichshafen, *t.*, *L. pt.*, Germany; on L. Constance; machin., boat bldg., motors; p. (1963) *39,300*.

Friedrichstal, *t.*, Saar; coal-mining, steel wks.; p. (estd. 1954) *16,400*.

Friendly Is. (Tonga), Pac. Oc.; 400 miles S.E. Fiji; independent Polynesian kingdom under Brit. protection; mild and healthy climate; ch. I., Tongatapu; cap. Nukualofa in Tongatapu; copra, bananas; a. 270 sq. m.; p. (estd.) *71,000*

Friern Barnet, *former urb. dist.*, Middx., Eng.; now inc. in Barnet outer bor., Greater London (*q.v.*); residtl.; p. (1961) *28,813*.

Friesland, *prov.*, Netherlands; cap. Leeuwarden; dairying, horses, cattle; natural gas on Ameland I.; a. 1,325 sq. m.; p. (estd. 1959) *478,206*.

Frimley and Camberley, *urb. dist.*, Surrey, Eng.; 3 m. N. of Farnborough (Hants); light engin., plastics; p. (1961) *30,342*.

Frinton and Walton, *urb. dist.*, Essex, Eng.; on E. cst., 5 m. N.E. of Clacton; seaside resort; p. (1961) *9,576*.

Friol, *commune*, Lugo, N.W. Spain; leather, linen; p. *10,667*.

Frisches Haff, *shallow freshwater lagoon*, Baltic cst. of Poland; 53 m. long, 4–11 m. broad.

Frische Nehrung, *sandspit*, G. of Gdansk, Baltic Sea; astride bdy. between Poland, U.S.S.R.; almost separates Frisches Haff (Zalew Wislany) from G. of Gdansk; length 36 m.

Frisian Islands, *chain of Is.* stretching from Zuyder Zee and N. to Jutland, along the csts. of the Netherlands and N. Germany; ch. Is. are Texel, Vlieland and Ameland.

Friuli-Venezia Giulia, *aut. reg.* (created 1963), N.E. Italy; comprising 3 provs. Udine (p. *800,000*), Gorizia (p. *140,000*), and Trieste (p. *300,000*); cap. Trieste.

Frobisher Bay, *inlet* in S. Baffin I., N. Canada, extending 200 m. between Cumberland Sound and Hudson Strait.

Frodingham, *t.*, Lincoln, Eng.; on W. flank of limestone ridge, Lincoln Edge; impt. iron-ore open-cast mines; mnfs. iron and steel; p. (1961) *67,257* (with Scunthorpe).

Frodsham, *mkt. t.*, Cheshire, Eng.; 10 m. N.E. Chester; chemicals.

Frome, *mkt. t.*, *urb. dist.*, Somerset, Eng.; on R. Frome, 11 m. S. of Bath; woollens, printing, brewing, iron, metal and plastic wks.; p. (1961) *11,440*.

Frontignan, *t.*, Herault, S. France; oil refining; oil pipeline under sea from Sète.

Frosinone, *industl. t.*, Lazio, Italy; on R. Cosa; p. (1961) *30,796*.

Froward, *C.*, Magallanes prov., Southern Chile.

Frunze, *cap.*, Kirgiz S.S.R.; univ.; meat packing, engin., textiles; p. (1962) *312,000*.

Fthiotis and Focis, *pref.*, Greece; cap. Lamia; p. (1951) *199,794*.

Fucino, *L.* (*now drained*), Aquila, Central Italy; old volcanic crater.

Fuente-Alamo, *industl. t.*, S.E. Spain; 18 m. S. from Murcia; p. *9,270*.

Fuente de Cantos, *industl. t.*, Badajoz, Spain; p. (1957) *10,027*.

Fuente-Ovejuna, *t.*, Cordoba, Spain; ctr. of lead-mining dist., honey prod.; p. (1957) *17,000*.

Fuerteventura, *I.*, Canary gr.; a. 663 sq. m.; p. (1962) *18,333*.

Fujiyama, extinct volcano, Japan, 60 m. S.W. of Tokyo; pilgrim resort; alt. 12,395 ft.

Fukien (Fujian) *prov.*, China; cap. Foochow (Fuzhou); tea, rice, cotton, sugar, tobacco; paper, coal, gold, silver; a. 45,845 sq. m.; p. (1953) *13,142,721*. [*125,304*.

Fukui, *t.*, Honshu, Japan; silk, paper; p. (1955)

Fukuoka, *t.*, Kyushu, Japan; silk-weaving; p. (1962) *647,000*. [*140,603*.

Fukuyama, *t.*, S. Hokkaido, Japan; p. (1960)

Fulda, *c.*, Hessen, Germany; nr. Cassel; on R. Fulda; palace, abbey; textiles, metallurgy, rubber; route ctr.; p. (1963) *44,900*.

Fulda, *R.*, Central Germany; with the Werra forms the R. Weser.

Fulham, *see* **Hammersmith**.

Fullerton, *t.*, Cal., U.S.A.; p. (1950) *56,180*.

Fulton, *t.*, Mo., U.S.A.; firebrick and shoe factories; p. (1960) *11,131*.

Fulton, *c.*, N.Y., U.S.A.; woollens, cutlery, paper; p. (1960) *14,261*.

Fulwood, *urb. dist.*, Lancs, Eng.; 2 m. N.E. of Preston; p. (1961) *15,966*.

Funchal, *t.*, *spt.*, *cap.*, Madeira; winter resort; wine; p. (1960) *95,765*.

Fundy, Bay of, *inlet* between Nova Scotia and New Brunswick, Canada.

Furneaux, *Is.*, gr. in Bass Strait, belonging to Tasmania.

Furnes (Veurne), *industl. t.*, Belgium; nr. Bruges; p. (1962) *7,315*.

Furness, *dist.*, N.W. Lancs, Eng.; between Morecambe Bay and the Irish Sea; haematite iron ore.

Fürstenwalde, *industl. t.*, Frankfurt, E. Germany; on R. Spree; metallurgy, leather; p. (1963) *31,881*.

Fürth, *t.*, Bavaria, Germany; nr. Nürnberg; furniture mftg., toys, metallurgy, glass, paper, radio, footwear; p. (1963) *98,300*.

Fusan, *see* **Pusan**.

Fushiki, *t.*, *spt.*, Honshu, Japan; on Toyama Bay to E. of Noto Peninsula; lge. coastwise tr. in rice from Koga and Toyama plains; exp. chemicals, lumber, metals; imports metals, coal, bean-cake, flax.

Fushun, *c.*, Liaoning, N. China; at foot of Changpai Shan, 22 m. S.E. of Mukden; most impt. coal-mines in Far East; possesses world's thickest bituminous coal seam (417 ft.) worked by deep and open-cast mines; p. (1953) *679,000*. [*29,700*.

Fushimi, *c.*, Honshu, Japan; sub. of Kyoto; p.

Fusin (Fuxin), *c.*, Liaoning prov., China; coal mng.; agr.; p. (1953) *105, 000*.

Futa, La, *pass*, Tusco-Emilian Apennines, N. Italy; used by main road from Bologna to Florence; alt. 2,962 ft.

Futa Jalon, *upland dist.*, mostly in Guinea, W. Africa, with outliers in Liberia and Sierra Leone.

Futuna and Alofi, *Is.*, S. of Wallis Is., dependency of Fr. col. of New Caledonia; p. about *2,000*.

Fylde, *rural dist.*, *geographical sub-region*, W. Lancs., Eng.; extends along W. cst. between estuaries of Ribble and Wyre; low, flat plain behind coastal sand dunes, covered by fertile glacial deposits; cultivated where drained, grain, vegetables; impt. pig and poultry rearing dist.; ch. t., Blackpool, famous holiday resort; p. (rural dist., 1961) *16,928*.

Fylingdales, ballistic missile early warning station on Yorkshire moors.

Fyn, *I.*, Denmark; in the Baltic Sea; a. 1,320 sq. m.; cap. Odense; p. (1960) *376,872*.

Fyne, *loch* on Argyll cst. W. Scot.; an arm of F. of Clyde; length 40 m.

Fyzabad, *t.*, Uttar Pradesh, India; sugar; p. (1961) *88,296*.

G

Gabes, *spt.*, Tunisia, on G. of Gabes, 200 m. S. of Tunis; dates, henna, wool; p. (1961) *24,400*.

Gaberones, *cap.*, Botswana, S.W. Africa; p. (estd. 1965) *12,000*.

Gabon, *ind. sovereign st.*, within Fr. Community, Equatorial Africa; cap. Libreville; ivory, ebony, palm-oil; a. 103,000 sq. m.; p. (1961) *440,000*.

Gadag-Betgeri, *t.*, Mysore, India; cotton and silk weaving; p. (1961) *76,614*.

Gadsen, *industl.*, *c.*, Ala., U.S.A.; cotton, cars, coal, iron, steel; p. (1960) *58,088*.

Gaeta, *spt.*, *fort*, Caserta, Italy; 40 m. N.W. of Naples; the ancient Caietae Portus; cath.; p. *22,882*.

Gaffney, *t.*, S.C., U.S.A.; limestone, textiles; p. (1960) *10,435*.

Gafsa, *t.*, Tunisia; phosphates; p. (1961) *24,300*.

Gagny, *commune*, Seine-et-Oise, France; light inds.; p. (1954) *17,255*.

Gaillac, *t.*, Tarn, France; wines; p. (1954) *8,356*.

Gaillard Cut, *excavated channel*, Panama Canal Zone; carries Panama Canal through Culebra Mtn. from L. Gatun to Pac. Oc.; length 7 m.

Gainesville, *t.*, Fla., U.S.A.; p. (1960) *29,701*.

Gainesville, *t.*, Ga., U.S.A.; p. (1960) *16,523*.

Gainesville, *t.*, Texas, U.S.A.; p. (1960) *13,093*.

Gainsborough, *mkt. t., urb. dist.*, Lincs., Eng.; on R. Trent, 15 m. N.W. of Lincoln; shipping, agr. implements, engin., milling, malting, timber; p. (1961) *17,276.* [broad.

Gairdner, *L.*, S. Australia; 130 m. long, 23 m.

Galápagos, *volcanic Is.*, Pac. Oc.; 600 m. W. Ecuador; consists of 12 lge. and several 100 sm. Is.; only 5 inhabited; administered by Ecuador; peculiar fauna and flora; guano; a. 2,868 sq. m.; p. (1962) *2,412.*

Galashiels, *burgh*, Selkirk, Scot.; on Gala Water, 2 m. above confluence with R. Tweed; tweeds, woollens; p. (1961) *12,374.*

Galati, *Black Sea pt.*, Romania, on Danube R.; naval base; engin., steel; p. (1959) *101,000.*

Galatina, *t.*, Apulia, Italy; p. *20,300.*

Galena, *t.*, Ill., U.S.A.; lead, zinc, marble, granite; p. (1960) *4,410.*

Galesburg, *t.*, Ill., U.S.A.; engin.; p. (1960) *37,243.*

Galicia, *former Austrian prov.*, Polish 1918–39, since 1939 E. part transferred to Ukrainian S.S.R. and W. remaining Polish (provs. Kraków and Rzeszów).

Galicia, *old prov.*, N.W. Spain; now forming provs. of La Coruña, Lugo, Orense and Pontevedra; mountainous; dairying; mining, lead, copper, iron; p. (1957) *2,600,000.*

Galilee, *N. div.* of Palestine in Roman period, containing Capernaum, Nazareth.

Galilee, Sea of (Lake Tiberias), also known as L. Gennesaret; 13 m. l., 6 m. wide, 150 ft. deep, 680 ft. below level of Med.; Israel plans to draw water from L. to irrigate Negev.

Galion, *t.*, Ohio, U.S.A.; mftg.; rly. ctr.; p. (1960) *12,650.*

Galla and Sidamo, *prov.*, Ethiopia.

Galle, *spt.*, Ceylon; on S.W. cst.; extensive tr. in tea, coconut oil; p. (1963) *64,942.*

Galleana, *mkt. t.*, Leon Prov., Mexico; at foot of Sierra Madre Oriental, 120 m. S. of Monterrey; focus of tr. between tropical lowlands and high plateau.

Gallego, *R.*, N.E. Spain; rises in Pyrenees, flows S. to R. Ebro at Zaragoza; R. provides water for irrigation around Zaragoza; valley used by main rly. across Pyrenees from Pau (France) to Zaragoza; length 110 m.

Gallegos, *t., cap.*, Santa Cruz terr., Argentina; p. *7,003.* [p. *12,200.*

Gallipoli, *spt.*, Italy; on E. shore G. of Taranto;

Gallipoli, *see* Gelibolu.

Gallipolis, *t.*, Ohio U.S.A.; p. (1950) *7 871.*

Gällivare, *dist.*, N. Sweden; inside Arctic Circle, 120 m. N.W. of Lulea; iron ore; p. *26,200.*

Galloway, *dist.*, S.W. Scot.; inc. the cos. of Wigtown and Kirkcudbright.

Galloway, Mull of, extreme S.W. point of Scot.

Gallup, *t.*, N.M., U.S.A.; coal, wool, sheep, cattle rearing; p. (1960) *14,089.*

Galston, *burgh*, Ayr, Scot.; on R. Irvine, nr. Kilmarnock; hosiery, lace; p. (1961) *4,023.*

Galt, *t.*, Ontario, Canada; mnfs.; p. (1961) *27,830.*

Galty Mtns., Tipperary, Ireland; alt. 3,000 ft.

Galveston, *c., spt.*, Texas, U.S.A.; on I. in G. of Mexico; gr. cotton pt.; mills, foundries; p. (1960) *67,175.*

Galway, *co.*, Galway Bay, Connacht, Ireland; fishery, cattle, marble quarrying; a. 2,452 sq. m.; p. (1961) *149,800.*

Galway, *t., cap.*, Galway, Ireland; p. (1961) *21,989.*

Gambela, *tr. sta.*, leased to Sudan by Ethiopia.

Gambia, *indep. sov. st.* within Brit. Commonwealth (1965), W. Africa; narrow terr., average 20 m. wide, extends 200 m. inland astride R. Gambia; hot all year, summer rain; savannah grassland; ground-nuts, palm-kernals, beeswax, hides; cap. Bathurst; a. 4,003 sq. m.; p. (estd. 1964) *315,999.*

Gambia, *R.*, Fr. W. Africa and Gambia, rises in Futa Jallon Plateau, flows N. and W. into Atl. Oc. at Bathurst; forms main means of communication through Gambia.

Gander, *airport*, Newfoundland, Canada; p. (1961) *5,725.*

Gandhinagar, *new cap.*, Gujarat, India; on Sabarmati R. 13 m. N. of Ahmedabad; under construction; planned initial p. *75,000* rising to *200,000.*

Gandia, *t. spt.*, Valencia, Spain; fruit exp.; silk spinning p. (1957) *20,160.*

Ganges, *gr. sacred R.*, India; rises in Himalayas and flows to Bay of Bengal, by several delta mouths, on one of which stands Calcutta. Delta very fertile and densely populated. Navigable for lge. ships from Allahabad; length 1,500 m.

Gangtok, *t.*, cap. Sikkim, E. Himalayas; trade ctr., carpets.

Ganjam, *dist.*, Orissa, India; a. 4,324 sq. m.; p. (1961) *1,872,530.*

Gap, *c.*, Hautes Alpes, S.E. France; silk and other textiles; p. (1954) *12,317.*

Gard, *Mediterranean dep.*, France; cap., Nîmes; vines, olives, sericulture; a. 2,270 sq. m.; p. (1962) *435,482.*

Garda, *L.*, between Lombardy and Venezia, Italy; a. 143 sq. m.; greatest depth, 1,135 ft.

Garden City, *t.*, Mich., U.S.A.; p. (1960) *38,017.*

Garden City, *t.*, N.Y., U.S.A.; p. (1960) *23,948.*

Garden Grove, *t.*, Cal., U.S.A.; p. (1960) *84,238.*

Gardena, *t.*, S.W. Cal., U.S.A.; mkt.-gardening; p. (1960) *35,943.*

Gardiner, *t.*, Me., U.S.A.; p. (1960) *6,897.*

Gardner, *t.*, Mass., U.S.A.; chair mftg.; p. (1960) *19,038.*

Garfield, *t.*, N.J., U.S.A., p. (1960) *29,253.*

Garfield Heights, *t.*, Ohio, U.S.A.; iron, steel, oil refineries, abrasives; p. (1960) *38,455.*

Garforth, *urb. dist.*, W.R. Yorks, Eng.; p. (1961) *14,641*

Garigliano, Italy; nuclear power plant projected.

Garland, *t.*, Texas, U.S.A.; p. *38,501.*

Garmisch-Partenkirchen, *t.*, Bavaria, Germany; winter sports; p. (1963) *26,600.*

Garo Hills, *mountainous dist.*, Assam, India; a. 3,119 sq. m.; dense forests; p. (1961) *307,228.*

Garonne, *R.*, S.W. France; rises at foot of Mt. Maladetta (Pyrenees), and enters the Gironde estuary 20 m. below Bordeaux; length 350 m.

Garonne, Haute, *dep.*, S. France; a. 2,458 sq. m.; p. (1962) *594,633.*

Garrigue, *region*, Languedoc, S. France; low limestone hills, run N.E. to S.W., W. of Rhône delta; semi-arid; scanty vegetation; winter pasture for sheep, olives; Montpellier, Nîmes located on S. flank.

Garston, *spt.*, Mersey estuary, Lancs, Eng.; docks; p. *28,000.*

Garut, *t.*, W. Java, Indonesia; mtn. resort; p. *24,219.*

Gary, *c.*, Ind., U.S.A.; at S. end of L. Michigan; steel, tin-plate, cement, soap, chemicals, oil refining; p. (1960) *178,321.*

Gascony, *ancient prov., duchy*, S.W. France.

Gaspé, *peninsula*, Quebec, Canada; on S. side of St. Lawrence.

Gastein, *t.*, Salzburg, Austria; mineral springs.

Gastonia, *c.*, N.C., U.S.A.; p. (1960) *37,276.*

Gateshead, *t., co. bor.*, Durham, Eng.; on R. Tyne, opposite Newcastle; engin.; p. (1961) *103,232.*

Gatesville, *t.*, Texas, U.S.A.; cotton processing; p. (1960) *4,626.*

Gatineau, *R.*, Canada; trib. of Ottawa R., which it joins nr. Ottawa; length 300 m.

Gatooma, *t.*, Rhodesia; farming, mining and cotton mnfs., gold, mineral deposits; p. (1958) *10,000* (incl. *2,000* Europeans).

Gatun, *artificial L.*, Panama Canal Zone, Central America; passed through by Panama Canal; alt. 40 ft. above Caribbean Sea; a. 250 sq. m.

Gatwick, Surrey–Sussex border; 25 m. S. London; 1st airport in world where trunk road, main rly. line and air facilities combined in one unit.

Gauhati, *t.*, Assam, India; univ.; silk, cotton, lace oil refinery; oil pipeline from Barauni; p. (1961) *100,702.*

Gauri-Sankar, *mtn.* in Himalayas; 35 m. W. of Mt. Everest; alt. 23,440 ft.

Gävle, *spt.*, Sweden; timber, textiles, steel, porcelain; p. (1961) *54,768.*

Gävleborg, *co.*, Sweden; ch. t., Gävle; a. 7,61 sq. m.; p. (1961) *293,070.*

Gawler, *t.*, S. Australia; iron foundries; p. *4,427*

Gaya, *t.*, Bihar, India; famous Buddhist pilgrim ctr.; cottons, silks; p. (1961) *151,105.*

Gayyarah, Mosul, Iraq; bitumen refinery.

Gaza, *spt.*, U.A.R.; exp. cereals, wool; p. c *100,000.*

Gaziantep, *t.*, Turkey; S.W. of Malatya; p (1960) *125,498.*

Gazli, Uzbekistan S.S.R.; 60 m. N.W. of Bukhara; natural gas field discovered mid-1950's pipeline to Chelyabinsk opened Nov. 1963.

Gdansk *prov.* (*voivodship*), Poland; ch. t. Gdansk (Danzig); a. 4,290 sq. m.; p. (1961) *1,261,00*

Gdansk (Danzig), *spt.*, Poland; on R. Vistula impt. Baltic pt.; Prussian, 1814–1919; free cit under Treaty of Versailles; annexed to Germany, 1939; restored to Poland, 1945; industr. and comm. ctr.; shipbldg., machin., chemicals, metals; p. (1960) *286,000*.

Gdynia, *spt.*, Poland; built by Poland as pt. after 1924 when Danzig was a free city; impt. comm. pt.; rly. ctr.; metal, machin., food inds.; p. (1960) *148,000*.

Géant, Aiguille du, *mtn.* in Savoy Alps, France; alt. 13,170 ft.; nearby Col du Géant, pass from Chamonix to Italy, alt. 11,145 ft.

Geel, *t.*, Belgium; 30 m. E. of Antwerp; nuclear power plant projected.

Geelong, *spt.*, Port Phillip, Victoria, Australia; fine harbour; tr. in flour, wool; oil refining; aluminium; p. (1961) *91,666*.

Geislingen, *t.*, Württemberg, Germany; p. (1963) *25,800*.

Gela, *t.*, S. Sicily, Italy; in cotton growing a.; p. (1961) *54,774*.

Gelderland, *prov.*, Netherlands; S.E. of Zuider Zee; a. 1,939 sq. m.; cap. Arnhem; cereals, tobacco; cattle rearing; p. (estd. 1959) *1,270,173*.

Gelibolu, (Gallipoli), *t.* and *peninsula* on the Dardanelles, Turkey; vines, sericulture; scene of unsuccessful landing by British and Anzac troops 1915; p. (1960) *12,956*.

Gelligaer, *t.*, *urb. dist.*, Glamorgan, Wales; 4 m. N.E. of Pontypridd; mining; p. rural dist. (1961) *34,572*.

Gelsenkirchen, *t.*, N. Rhine–Westphalia, Germany; nr. Dortmund; collys., ironwks., glass, chemicals, oil refining; p. (1963) *380,600*.

Gemmi, *mtn. pass* across Swiss Alps, Valais to Berne; alt. 7,600 ft.

General Pico, *t.*, S. central Argentina; grain, cattle; p. *14,500*.

Geneva, *c.*, *cap. can.* Geneva, Switzerland; at W. end of L. Geneva, R. Rhone flows through c.; cath., univ.; former H.Q. of League of Nations, H.Q. of I.L.O., W.H.O., I.T.U., International Red Cross; watch-mkg., jewellery, elec. goods, chocolate; tourist resort; p. (1961) *179,400*.

Geneva, *can.*, Switzerland; a. 109 sq. m.; p. (1961) *259,234*.

Geneva, *L.*, S.W. corner of Switzerland; length 40 m., greatest breadth 8½ m.; a. 108 sq. m.

Geneva, *t.*, Ill., U.S.A.; foundries, car parts; livestock; p. (1960) *7,646*.

Geneva, *t.*, N.Y., U.S.A.; engin.; p. (1960) *17,286*.

Génissiat, France; site of gr. barrage and hydro-elec. power sta. on Rhône below Geneva; completed 1950.

Genk, *t.*, Limburg, Belgium; stainless steel wks.; p. (1962) *49,483*.

Gennevilliers, *t.*, Seine, France; p. (1962) *42,611*.

Genoa, *maritime prov.*, Liguria, N. Italy; a. 1,582 sq. m.; p. (1961) *1,044,633*.

Genoa (Genova), *spt.*, *comm. c.*, on G. of Genoa; fine palaces, cath., univ.; shipbldg., engin., tanning, sugar, textiles; p. (1961) *775,106*.

Gentilly, *t.*, Seine, France; p. (1954) *17,497*.

George, *t.*, Cape Province, S. Africa; footwear, sawmilling, hops; p. (1960) *14,505* inc. *8,635* whites.

Georgetown, *cap.*, Guyana, S. America; on Demerara R.; exp. sugar, cocoa, coffee, timber, gold, diamonds, bauxite; p. (1962) *98,350*.

Georgetown, *t.*, S.C., U.S.A.; fish, lumber, cotton; p. (1960) *12,261*.

Georgetown, *t.*, Washington D.C., U.S.A.; on R. Potomac; univ., cath.

Georgetown, *c.*, *spt.*, Penang, Malaya; p. *189,068*.

Georgia, *st.*, U.S.A.; on Atlantic cst.; forested, agr.: cotton, tobacco, corn, peanuts, fruit; textiles, lumber, chemicals, steel,; chief ts.; Atlanta (cap.) and Savannah: a. 58,876 sq. m.; p. (1960) *3,943,116*.

Georgia, *constituent rep.*, U.S.S.R.; maize, tobacco, wheat; engin., metallurgy, manganese mng., oil, cap. Tbilisi; a. 37,570 sq. m.; p. (1959) *4,049,000*.

Georgian Bay, *lge. inlet*, Ontario, Canada; E. shore of L. Huron; many impt. lake pts. (Owen Sound, Parry Sound) where Prairie wheat is transhipped to rly. for despatch to Montreal; a. approx. 4,500 sq. m.

Gera, *t.*, Gera, E. Germany; lignite, woollens, printing; p. (1963) *104,198*.

Geraldton, *spt.*, W. Australia; 306 m. from Perth; in agr. and pastoral dist.; exp. gold, copper, wool; p. (1961) *10,878*.

Germany, after defeat in Second World War divided into E. and W. Germany. W. Germany is Federal st. (declared sovereign May 5, 1955) of 9 Länder, Schleswig-Holstein, Hamburg, Lower Saxony, Bremen, North Rhine–Westphalia, Hesse, Rhineland, Palatinate, Baden–Württemberg, and Bavaria. Previously divided into British, American, and French zones; a. 94,716 sq. m.; admin. ctr. Bonn; Saar incorporated, 1956; a. 991 sq. m.; p. (1963) *58,587,500* inc. Saar, and W. Berlin; E. Germany comprises 14 dists., Rostock, Schwerin, Neubrandenburg, Magdeburg, Potsdam, Frankfurt, Erfurt, Halle, Leipzig, Cottbus, Suhl, Gera, Karl-Marx-Stadt, Dresden. Previously the Soviet zone, became sovereign st., March 25, 1954; a. 41,571 sq. m.; p. (1961) *17,181,083*. Berlin under four-Power control; ch. German inds.: agr.: rye, oats, wheat, potatoes, sugar-beet, wines; pastoral; cattle, pigs, sheep; forests, timber; minerals; coal, lignite, iron, potash, copper, zinc, salt; mnfs., machine., shpbldg., textiles, chemicals, dyes, printing, etc.; commerce; communications very good.

Germiston, *t.*, Transvaal, S. Africa; nr. Johannesburg; gold mng.; rly. wkshps., engin., machin., chemicals; p. (1960) *204,605* (inc. *84,419* Whites).

Gerona, *maritime prov.*, N.E. Spain; cap. G.; textiles, coal, paper; a. 2,264 sq. m.; p. (1959) *345,320*.

Gerona, *mun.*, Luzon, Philippine Is.; rice, sugar, pineapples; p. *20,892*.

Gerrard's Cross, *t.*, S.E. Bucks, Eng.; 9 m. E. of High Wycombe; residtl.; projected nuclear power sta. for aircraft; p. (1951) *2,942*.

Gers, *dep.*, S.W. France; cap. Auch; grain, vines, brandy; a. 2,429 sq. m.; p. (1962) *182,264*.

Gers, *R.*, rising in the Pyrenees, flows to the Garonne; length 75 m.

Gettysburg, *t.*, Penns., U.S.A.; Federal victory 1863; granite; p. (1960) *7,960*.

Gevelsberg, *c.*, Westphalia, Germany; iron stoves; p. (1963) *32,100*.

Geyser Springs, *summer resort*, Cal., U.S.A.; 90 m. N.W. of San Francisco.

Gezira, *dist.*, Sudan, N.E. Africa; situated between Blue and White Niles above confluence at Khartoum; approx 4,700 sq. m. capable of irrigation by water drawn from Blue Nile at Sennar Dam; large-scale growing of high-quality cotton; total a. approx. 7,800 sq. m.

Ghadames, *oasis*, Sahara Desert, Libya; N. Africa; at point where terr. of Tunis, Algeria, Libya converge 300 m. S.W. of Tripoli; impt. focus of caravan routes.

Ghana, Rep. of, W. Africa; sovereign and ind. st. within British Commonwealth since 6 March 1957; member of Union of African States; agr.; cocoa, palm-oil, ground-nuts; mahogany, manganese, gold, diamonds; cap. Accra; total a. 91,843 sq. m.; p. (1961) *6,691,000*.

Ghardaia, *terr.*, S. Algeria, N. Africa; caravan tr.; dates; p. *166,366*.

Ghats, E. and W., *two mtn. ranges* bordering the triangular upland of S. India, the Deccan; alt. of ch. summits, 4,700–7,000 ft.

Ghazipur, *t.*, N. India; on Ganges R., E. of Varanasi; agr. school; p. (1961) *37,147*.

Ghazni, *fortfd. mtn. t.*, Afghanistan; 78 m. S.W. of Kabul; gr. tr. ctr.; cap. of the Empire of Mahmud, c. A.D. 1000; p. *10,500*.

Ghent, *c.*, Belgium; cap. of E. Flanders, on R. Scheldt; cath. univ.; extensive cotton, woollen, sugar inds.; plastics, photographic materials; p. (1962) *156,499*.

Ghernigap, *t.*, Victoria, Australia; 55 m. from Melbourne; p. *4,500*.

Giant's Causeway, *famous basaltic columns*, on promontory of N. cst. of Antrim, Ireland.

Giarre, *t.*, Sicily, Italy; nr. Mt. Etna; industl.; p. *20,050*.

Gibare, *t.*, Oriente prov., Cuba, W. Indies; exp. bananas; p. *8,045*.

Gibraltar, *Brit. fortress and naval base* of gr. strategic importance, W. end of Mediterranean; on rocky peninsula (1,396 ft.), extreme S. of Spain; captured by British in 1704; a. 2¼ sq. m.; civilian p. (estd. 1965) *24,386*.

Gibraltar, Strait of, connects Atlantic and Mediterranean; its narrowest breadth is 9 m.

Gibson Desert, centre of W. Australia.

Giessen, *t.*, Hesse, Germany; on R. Lahn; univ.; tobacco, engin., textiles; p. (1963) *69,800*.

Gifu, *t.*, Central Honshu, Japan; silk; paper; p. (1960) *304,000*.
Gigha, *I.*, Argyll, Scot.; off W. cst.; 6 m. long, 2 m. wide; p. (with Cara) *243*.
Gijón, *spt.*, Oviedo, Spain; on Bay of Biscay; fine harbour; tobacco, petroleum, coal, earthenware; p. (1959) *121,692*.
Gila, *R.*, New Mexico and Arizona, U.S.A.; trib. of Rio Colorado; water used for irrigation in Imperial Valley; length 650 m.
Gilan, *prov.*, N. Iran; on S.W. shore Caspian Sea; a. 4,673 sq. m.; cap. Resht.
Gilbert and Ellice Islands Colony, *gr. of Is.* (Brit.), Micronesia, Pac. Oc.; ch. crops: pandanas fruit and coconuts; exp. phosphates and copra; a. 369 sq. m.; p. (estd.) *50,000*.
Gilgit, *cap.*, G. extreme N.W. dist. of Kashmir.
Gilgit, *R.*, of the Punjab rising in Chitral, trib. of the Indus, flowing along the Gilgit valley into Kashmir.
Gill, Lough, *L.*, on borders of cos. Sligo and Leitrim, Ireland.
Gillespie, *t.*, Ill., U.S.A.; coal; p. (1960) *3,569*.
Gillingham, *t.*, *mun. bor.*, Kent, Eng.; 2 m. E. of Chatham; cherry orchards, cement, light inds.; p. (1961) *72,611*.
Gilly, *t.*, Hainaut, Belgium, nr. Charleroi; coal; p. (1962) *23,878*.
Gilolo I., *see* **Halmahera I.**
Gilp Loch, Argyll, Scot.; inlet of Loch Fyne, at head of Crinan Canal.
Gioja del Colle, *c.*, Bari, S. Italy; olive oil, wine, wool; p. *24,000*.
Giovinazzo, *spt.*, S. Italy; on the Adriatic, N. of Bari; p. *12,150*.
Gippsland, *dist.*, S.E. Victoria, Australia; a. 13,900 sq. m.; mountainous; farming, grazing; coal.
Girardot, *t.*, Colombia, S. America; impt. R. pt. and airport on upper course of R. Magdalena, 685 m. upstream from Caribbean Sea; linked by rly. (70 m.) to Bogotá; coffee, hides, ceramics; p. (estd. 1959) *50,000*.
Giresun, *spt.*, Black Sea, Turkey, W. of Trabzon; p. (1960) *19,946*.
Girga, *t.*, Upper U.A.R.; on R. Nile; p. *1,000*.
Girga, *admin. div.*, Upper U.A.R., N.E. Africa; a. 595 sq. m.; p. (1960) *1,574,000*.
Girgenti, (same as Agrigento, *q.v.*), *t.*, S. Sicily, Italy; famous for its Greek temples.
Girishk, *t.*, Afghanistan; on Helmand R.; ctr. of agr. dist.
Gironde, *dep.*, France; vineyards, grain, fruit, wines; cap. Bordeaux; a. 4,140 sq. m.; p. (1962) *935,448*.
Gironde, *R.*, *estuary*, S.W. France; formed by junction of Rs. Garonne and Dordogne; navigable to Pauillac.
Girton *par.*, nr. Cambridge, Eng.; women's college.
Girvan, *burgh*, Ayr, Scot.; on F. of Clyde, 18 m. S.W. of Ayr; summer resort; p. (1961) *6,159*.
Gisborne, *spt.*, N.I., N.Z.; on Poverty Bay, 60 m. N.E. of Napier; freezing-wks.; p. (1961) *25,064*.
Gisburn, *t.*, W.R. Yorks; on R. Ribble, nr. Clitheroe.
Giugliano, *t.*, Italy; N.W. of Naples; mnfs.; p. *20,500*.
Giulianova, *t.*, Teramo, Italy; fruit, grain; p. *20,000*.
Giurgiu, *pt.*, Romania; on R. Danube; opposite Ruse; good tr.; timber; p. (1956) *32,617*.
Givet, *t.*, Ardennes, N.E. France; on R. Meuse; tanneries; p. *6,000*.
Givors, *t.*, Rhône dep., France; on Rhône R., 10 m. S. of Lyons; mnfs.; p. (1954) *14,242*.
Giza, *admin div.*, U.A.R.; cap. Giza; a. 392 sq. m.; p. (1960) *1,337,000*.
Giza, *t.*, Lower U.A.R.; on the Nile, 3 m. S.W. of Cairo; nr. pyramids of Khafra (Chephren), Khufu (Cheops) and Men-ka-va; also the Sphinx; contains Museum of Egyptian antiquities; film ind.; p. (1960) *250,000*.
Gjinokastër (Argyrocastro), *prefecture*, Albania; cap. G.; p. (estd.) *159,695*.
Gjövik, *t.*, S. Norway; on L. Mjosa; furniture, footwear, light inds.; p. (1961) *7,738*.
Gjuhëzës, C. (Glossa C.), Albania, Strait of Otranto.
Glace Bay, *t.*, Nova Scotia, Canada; coal; p. (1961) *24,186*.
Gladbeck, *t.*, N. Rhine–Westphalia, Germany; N. of Essen; coal-mining, chemicals, rly. junction; p. (1963) *83,700*.
Gladewater, *t.* N.E. Texas, U.S.A.; oil, lumber; p. (1960) *5,742*.
Gladstone, *t.*, Queensland, Australia; alumina plant under construction; p. (1961) *7,182*.
Gladstone, *t.*, S. Mich., U.S.A.; harbour; mnfs. sports equipment; p. (1960) *5,267*.
Glamorgan, *co.*, S. Wales; immense coal and iron deposits; copper and tin smelting; machin.; chemicals; co. t. Cardiff; a. 813 sq. m.; p. (1961) *1,227,828*.
Glamorgan, Vale of, *see* **Gwent, Plain of.**
Glarus, *can.*, Switzerland; E. of Schwyz; a. 264 sq. m.; sheep, cheese, cottons; p. (1961) *40,148*.
Glarus, *c.*, *cap.*, can. G., Switzerland; on R. Linth, nr. Weesen; p. (1957) *5,724*.
Glasgow, *c. burgh*, Lanark, Scot.; on R. Clyde; third lgst. c. in Gr. Britain; many thriving mnfs.; shipbldg., heavy and light engin., printing; ctr. of great industrial belt; univ. and famous cath.; p. (1961) *1,054,913*.
Glasport, *bor.*, Penns., U.S.A.; tools, steel, hoops, glass; p. (1960) *8,418*.
Glastonbury, *t.*, *mun. bor.*, Somerset, Eng.; at foot of Mendip Hills, 5 m. S.W. of Wells; noted 8th-century abbey with legend of thorn planted by Joseph of Arimathea, also adjacent to Avalon, burial I. of King Arthur; gloves, sheepskin rug and slipper mnfs.; p. (1961) *5,796*.
Glatz, *see* **Kladzko.**
Glauchau, *t.*, Karl-Marx-Stadt, E. Germany; on R. Mulde; woollens, calicoes, dyes, machin.; p. (1963) *33,370*.
Glazov, *t.*, R.S.F.S.R., in Urals; saw-milling, metal inds.; p. (1959) *59,000*.
Gleiwitz, *see* **Gliwice.**
Glen, The, beautiful valley and resort in White Mountain dist. of New Hampshire, U.S.A.
Glen Affric, Inverness, Scot.; drained E. to Moray Firth; hydro-elec. scheme.
Glen Garry, Inverness, Scot.; used by Perth to Inverness rly. on S. approach to Drumochter Pass.
Glen Innes, *hill t.*, N.S.W., Australia; alt. 3,518 ft.; pastoral and agr dist.; p. *5,462*.
Glen More. Scottish valley traversed by Caledonian canal, from Fort William to Inverness; cattle-ranching being attempted.
Glen Roy, Inverness, Scot.; 15 m. N.E. of Fort William; remarkable terraces, remains of series of glacial lakes.
Glen Spean, Inverness, Scot.; used by Glasgow to Fort William rly.
Glencoe, Argyll, Scot.; S.E. of Ballachulish; scene of massacre of MacDonalds, 1692.
Glendale, *t.*, Cal., U.S.A.; p. (1960) *119,442*.
Glendalough, *valley*, Wicklow, Ireland; scenic beauty; ecclesiastical ruins; tourists.
Glendora, *t.*, Cal., U.S.A.; p. (1960) *20,752*.
Glenelg, *R.*, S.W. Victoria, Australia; length 200 m.
Glenelg, *t.*, S. Australia; on Holdfast Bay, nr. Adelaide.
Glenluce, *vil.*, Wigtown, Scot.; at head of Luce Bay; p. *806*.
Glenolden, *bor.*, Penns., U.S.A.; surgical instruments; p. (1960) *7,249*.
Glenrothes, *t.*, Fifeshire, Scot.; one of the "New Towns" designated 1948; coal, transistor factory, mng. machin.; p. (estd. 1965) *17,443*.
Glens Falls, *t.*, N.Y., U.S.A.; on Hudson R.; lime kilns and many mnfs.; lumber, paper; p. (1960) *18,580*.
Glenside, *t.*, S.E. Penns., U.S.A.; mnfs. rubber and wood prod.; paints, toys; p. (1950) *9,654*.
Glittertind, *mtn.*, Opland co., S. Norway; highest peak in Scandinavia; alt. 8,140 ft.
Gliwice, (Gleiwitz), *t.*, Upper Silesia, Poland German before 1945; nr. Katowice; chemicals iron and steel; p. (1960) *135,000*.
Globe, *t.*, Ariz., U.S.A.; copper, manganese, gold silver, vanadium, tungsten mining; p. (1960) *6,141*.
Glogów (Glogau), *c.*, Poland, German before 1945 on R. Odra; cath.; sugar, wood, iron inds. rly. junction; p. (1946) *1,681*.
Glommen R., Norway; lgst. Norwegian R., flow S. in Skaggerak.
Glossa, C. (*see* **Gjiuhëzës, C.**), *strait*, Otranto Albania.
Glossop, *mkt. t.*, *mun. bor.*, Derby, Eng.; at W foot of Pennines, 12 m. S.E. of Manchester cotton, paper, food canning; p. (1961) *17,490*.

Gloucester, *co.*, W. of Eng.; fertile valleys, Cotswold Hills; dairying, cheese, sheep, coal machin., textiles, glass, broadcloth; a. 1,257 sq. m.; p. (1961) *1,000,493.*
Gloucester, *cath. c., co. bor.*, on R. Severn; aircraft mftg. and repair, wagon wks., engin., matches, nylon; p. (1961) *69,687.*
Gloucester, *t.*, Mass., U.S.A.; fishing; granite; p. (1960) *25,789.* [*21,741.*
Gloversville, *c.*, N.Y., U.S.A.; gloves; p. (1960)
Glyder Fach, *mtn.*, Caernarvonsh., N. Wales; alt. 3,262 ft. [3,279 ft.
Glyder Fawr, *mtn.*, Caernarvonsh., N. Wales; alt.
Glyncorrwg, *urb. dist.*, Glamorgan, Wales; 4 m. N. of Maesteg; coal, iron; p. (1961) *9,902.*
Gmünd, *t.*, Austria, on Czechoslovakian border.
Gmünd, *t.*, Baden-Württemberg, Germany; on R. Rems, nr. Stuttgart; clocks, metallurgy, glass, costume jewellery; p. (estd. 1954) *34,100.*
Gniezno (Gnesen), *mftg. t.*, Poland; E. of Poznan; cath.; linen; p. (1960) *44,000.*
Gôa, Daman and Diu, Union Terr. of, India, former Port. India; iron pyrites, manganese, cocunuts, fish, spices, cashew nuts, salt, copra; p. (1960) *626,978.*
Goajira, *peninsula* on G. of Maracaibo, N. cst. of S. America; crossed by bdy. of Venezuela and Colombia.
Goalunda, *pt.*, Pakistan; at junction of Rs. Ganges and Brahmaputra. [2,866 ft.
Goat Fell, *mtn.*, I. of Arran, Bute, Scot.; alt.
Gobi, steppes and stony or sandy desert in Central Asia; divided into two principal divs.; Shamo in Central Mongolia, and the basins of the Tarim, E. Turkestan; length about 1,500 m. (E. to W.), breadth 500–700 m.; average elevation 4,000 ft.; crossed by Kalgan–Ulan Bator highway.
Godalming, *t., mun. bor.*, Surrey, Eng.; 4 m. S.W. of Guildford; 1st public supply of elec. 1881; tanning, timber yards, corn mills, knitwear; Charterhouse School; p. (1961) *15,771.*
Godavari, *R.*, India; flows E. across Deccan to Bay of Bengal; forms large delta; length 900 m.
Goderich, *pt.*, Ont., Canada; on S.E. cst. L. Huron; transh. wheat from prairies; p. (1961) *6,411.*
Godesberg, Bad, N. Rhine–Westphalia, Germany; nr. Bonn; famous Spa; chalybeate springs; p. (estd. 1954) *46,700.*
Godhavn, Danish settlement, Disco I., W. of Greenland; whaling; scientific sta.
Godhra, *t.*, Gujarat, India; timber tr.; tanneries; p. (1961) *52,167.*
Godmanchester, *sm. t., mun. bor.*, Hunts, Eng.; on R. Ouse; clothing, printing; p. (1961) *8,812.*
Godstone, *vil., rural dist.*, Surrey, Eng.; nr. Reigate; p. (1961) rural dist. *40,068.*
Godthaab, *t.*, Greenland; first Danish col. 1721; p. (1960) *4,306.*
Godwin Austen (K²), Mt., Himalaya, second highest in the world; alt. 28,250 ft. Summit reached by Prof. Desio in July 1954. Mt. named Chobrum. [(1961) *5,472.*
Gogo, *spt.*, Gujarat, India; on G. of Cambay; p.
Gogra, *sacred R.*, India; rising in Tibet, trib. of Ganges; length 600 m.
Goiânia, *cap.*, Goiás State, Brazil; p. (1960) *153,505*
Goiás, *st.*, Central Brazil; mountainous, forested; stock raising; tobacco; gold, diamonds; cap. Goiânia, on Vermelho R.; a. 240,334 sq. m.; p. (1960) *1,954,862.*
Golborne, *t., urb. dist.*, Lancs, Eng.; man-made fibres; p. (1961) *21,277.*
Golconda, *fort and ruined c.*, nr. Hyderabad, S. India; famous for diamonds in former days and mausoleums of ancient kings.
Gold Coast, *see* **Ghana.** [*7,118.*
Golden, *c.*, Col., U.S.A.; nr. Denver; p. (1960)
Golden Gate, entrance of Bay of San Francisco, California, U.S.A.; famed Golden Gate Bridge, opened 1937.
Golden Horn, *peninsula* on the Bosporus, forming the harbour of Istanbul.
Golden Vale, *dist.*, Limerick, Tipperary, Ireland; lies between Slieve Bloom Mtns. and Galtee Mtns., drained W. to Shannon and E. to Suir; rich farming a., beef and dairy cattle, pigs.
Golden Valley, *t.*, Minn., U.S.A.; p. (1960) *14,559.*
Goldsboro, *t.*, N.C., U.S.A.; on Neuse R.; cotton, tobacco; p. (1960) *28,873.*
Golspie, *co.t.*, Sutherland, Scot.; fishing pt.
Gomal Pass, from Afghanistan to W. Punjab, Pakistan, over Sulaiman mtns.
Gomel, *t.*, Byelorussia S.S.R.; on R. Sozh; engin., chemicals, clothing inds.; p. (1959) *166,000.*
Gomera, *I.*, Canaries; 13 m. S.W. Tenerife; cap. San Sebastian; p. (1962) *30,747.*
Gometray I., Hebrides, included in co. Argyll, Scot.; fishing, sta., and harbour.
Gonaives, *spt.*, Haiti, W. Indies; on W. cst.; p. *21,000.*
Gonda, *t.*, Uttar Pradesh, India; p. (1961) *43,496.*
Gondar, *t.*, Amhara prov., Ethiopia; p. *22,000.*
Gonzaga, *t.*, Mantua, N. Italy; p. *9,950.*
Good Hope, *t.*, N.W. Terr., Canada; on Mackenzie R.
Good Hope, C. of, *see* **C. of Good Hope.**
Goodenough Bay, *inlet*, N. coast of Papua, New Guinea, E. Indies.
Goodwick, *see* **Fishguard and Goodwick.**
Goodwin Sands, *dangerous sand-banks* off E. cst. of Kent, Eng.; shielding the Down roadstead.
Goole, *t. mun. bor.*, W.R. Yorks, Eng.; second pt. to Hull on Humber est.; iron, shipbldg., flour milling, fertilisers, alum and dextrine mftg.; p. (1961) *18,875.*
Goose Bay, *t.*, Labrador, Canada; on Hamilton R.
Göppingen, *t.*, Baden–Württemberg, Germany; between Ulm and Stuttgart; machin., iron, wood, chemicals; p. (1963) *48,600.*
Gorakhpur, *t.*, Uttar Pradesh, India; on the Rapti R., 100 m. N. of Varanasi; grain, timber; Govt. agr. school; p. (1961) *180,255.*
Gordon, *t.*, Victoria, Australia; mining and agr. dist.
Gordon Bennett, *mtn.*, in Ruwenzori range, Central Africa; nr. L. Albert Nyanza; alt. 16,000 ft.
Gore, *t.*, Southland, S.I., N.Z.; p. (1961) *7,270.*
Gorgonzola, *t.*, N. Italy; 12 m. N.E. of Milan, famous for its cheese; p. *5,725.*
Gori, *t.*, Georgia, U.S.S.R.; grain, timber; p. (1961) *33,100.*
Gorinchem, *t.*, S. Holland, Netherlands; p. *14,433.*
Goring, *t.*, on R. Thames, Oxford, Eng.; p. *1,989.*
Gorki (formerly **Nizhni-Novgorod**), *t.*, R.S.F.S.R.; at confluence of Rs. Oka and Volga; gr. comm. ctr.; engin., chemicals, petroleum refining, steel, textiles, cars, glass; p. (1962) *1,025,000.*
Gorkum or Gorcum, *t.*, Netherlands; nr. Rotterdam on the Merewede Canal.
Gorleston, Norfolk, Eng.; at mouth of R. Yare; seaside resort; inc. in co. bor. of Gt. Yarmouth.
Gorlitz, *t.*, Dresden, E. Germany; on W. Neisse R.; iron, wood, metallurgy, machin.; p. (1963) *89,578.*
Gorlovka, *t.*, Ukrainian S.S.R.; in Donets Basin; coal, chemicals, engin.; oil pipeline connects with Groznyy oilfields; p. (1962) *309,000.*
Gorno-Altaysk, *t.*, R.S.F.S.R.; 60 m. S.E. of Biysk, nr. Chuya highway to Mongolia; p. (1959) *27,000.*
Gorseinon, *vil.*, Glamorgan, S. Wales; nr. Loughour estuary, 4 m. N.W. of Swansea; steel-wks., zinc refineries.
Gort, *rural dist.*, Galway, Ireland; p. (1961) *8,187.*
Gorizia (Görz), *c.*, cap. Gorizia prov., N.E. Italy, cas.; agr. mkt., fruit, wine; cotton mills, textile mach.; p. (1961) *41,854.*
Göschenen, *vil.*, Switzerland; at W. end of St. Gotthard tunnel.
Gosford, *t.*, N.S.W., Australia: 50 m. N. of Sydney; p. (1961) *7,315.*
Gosforth, *t., urb. dist.*, sub. to Newcastle-on-Tyne, Eng.; coal; p. (1961) *27,072.*
Goshen, *c.*, Ind., U.S.A.; p. (1960) *13,718.*
Goslar, *t.*, Lower Saxony, Germany; at foot of Harz Mtns.; clothing mnfs., wood inds.; rly. junction; p. (1963) *41,000*
Gosport, *mun. bor., spt., Naval depot*, Hants, Eng.; W. side of Portsmouth harbour; shipbldg., engin.; p. (1961) *62,436.*
Gossau, *t.*, St. Gallen, Switzerland; embroidery, lace; p. *7,914.*
Göta, *R.*, Sweden; flows from L. Vänern to the Kattegat; also canal connecting L. Vänern with the Baltic; the G. Canal provides a popular tourist trip from Stockholm to Göteborg.
Götaland, southernmost of 3 old provs. of Sweden; a. 39,000 sq. m.; name used only in weather forecasts.
Göteborg and Bohus, *prov.*, Sweden; on cst. of Kattegat; a. 1,989 sq. m.; p. (1961) *624,762.*
Göteborg, *c., cap.*, Göteborg and Bohus, Sweden; at mouth of R. Göta; second c. in Sweden for commerce and ind.; shipbldg.; p. (1960) *404,758.*
Gotha, *t.*, Erfurt, E. Germany; iron, machin.,

porcelain, printing, cartography; p. (1963) *56,611*.
Gotland I., *fertile Swedish I.* in the Baltic; cap. Visby; a. 1,225 sq. m.; p. (1961) *54,322*.
Gottesberg, *t.*, S.W. Poland; coal, mftg.; assigned to Poland at Potsdam conference; p. *8,000*.
Göttingen, *t.*, Lower Saxony, Germany; univ.; scientific instruments, pharmaceutics, film studios; p. (1963) *82,600*.
Gottwaldov (Zlin), *industl. t.*, ČSSR.; 40 m. E. of Brno; footwear, leather and domestic woodware inds.; p. (1961) *54,189*.
Gouda, *t.*, Netherlands; on R. Yssel 11 m. from Rotterdam; famous cheese; p. (1960) *43,118*.
Gough I., Atl. Oc. dependency of St. Helena; breeding ground of the great shearwater.
Goulburn, *t.*, N.S.W., Australia; commands route across Gr. Dividing Range; in agr. dist. 134 m. W. of Sydney; mnfs.; p. (1961) *20,550*.
Goulburn R., Victoria, Australia.
Gourock, *burgh*, Renfrew, Scot.; on Firth of Clyde, 2 m. W. of Greenock; p. (1961) *9,609*.
Gouverneur, *t.*, N. N.Y., U.S.A.; mines talc, lead, zinc; mnfs. wood pulp, silk; p. (1960) *4,946*.
Govan, *par.*, Lanark, Scot.; on the Clyde, part of Glasgow; shipbldg.; p. (1951) *312,911*.
Governor's I., *fort*, Boston Harbour; also fortfd. islet in harbour of N.Y., U.S.A.
Govindpura, *t.*, Madhya Pradesh, India; nr. Bhopal; heavy elec. goods; p (1961) *20,747*.
Gower, *peninsula*, W. Glamorgan, Wales.
Gowerton, *vil.*, Glamorgan, S. Wales; S. cst. of Loughour estuary, 4 m. W. of Swansea; new steel-wks.
Gowrie, Carse of, fertile tract N. side Firth of Tay, Scot.; includes Dundee, Kinnoul, Perth.
Goya, *t.*, Argentina; on R. Paraná; cattle; p. (1960) *40,000*.
Goyanna, *comm. t.*, Brazil; 40 m. N. of Recife.
Gozo, *Br. I.* in Mediterranean, nr. Malta; the ancient Gaulos; surrounded by perpendicular cliffs; a. 26 sq. m.; p. *27,612*.
Graaff-Reinet, *t.*, Cape Province, S. Africa; fruit growing, wool; p. (1960) *16,703* inc. *5,565* whites.
Graciosa, *I.*, Azores gr., N.W. of Terceira.
Grado, *commune*, Oviedo, N.W. Spain; iron foundries; p .(1957) *17,885*.
Grado-Aquileia, N. Adriatic, prov. Gorizia, Italy; pleasure resort and former Roman spt.; rich in early Christian mosaics and other antiquities; p. (est.) *3,000*.
Graengesberg, *dist.*, Kopparberg co., Sweden; on S. fringe of Scandinavian mtns.; iron ore deposits.
Grafton, *t.* N.S.W., Australia; on Clarence R.; p. (1961) *15,533*.
Graham, *t.*, N. Texas, U.S.A.; oil refining, flour milling; p. (1960) *8,505*.
Graham I., the lgst. of the Queen Charlotte gr. in the Pacific; off cst. of Brit. Columbia.
Graham Land, Falkland Is. Dependencies, Antarctica; mtnous, icebound; discovered 1832.
Grahamstown, *c.*, Cape Province, S. Africa; univ.; cath.; p. (1960) *32,611* inc. *10,668* Europeans.
Graian Alps, *mtns.* between Savoy and Piedmont; highest point Gran Paradiso; alt. 13,320 ft.
Grain Coast, general name formerly applied to cst. of Liberia, W. Africa; "grain" refers to pepper, spices, etc.
Grammichele, *t.*, E. Sicily, Italy; 23 m. S.W. of Catania; marble; p. *14,014*.
Grammont, *t.*, E. Flanders, Belgium; nr. Ghent, on Dender R.; mftg; p. (1962) *9,585*.
Grampians, *highest mtns.* of Scot.; highest point Ben Nevis; alt. 4,406 ft.; includes Cairngorms, high granitic mtns.
Granada, *prov.*, S. Spain; traversed by Sierra Nevada; wheat, olives, textiles, liqueurs, paper; a. 4,838 sq. m.; p. (1959) *779,434*.
Granada, *ancient c.*, Granada, S. Spain; at foot of Sierra Nevada; formerly cap. of the Moorish Kingdom of G., now cap. of fertile maritime prov.; famous 14th-century Alhambra; p. (1959) *145,169*.
Granada, *c.*, Nicaragua, Central America; distilling, soap, furniture; p. *38,918*.
Granby, *c.*, Quebec, Canada; on Yamaska R.; sawmills, leather; p. (1961) *31,463*.
Gran Chaco, *extensive dist.*, N. Argentina and Paraguay; flat with lge. areas of forest; quebracho.
Grand Bank, *submarine plateau*, extending S.E. from Newfoundland, Canada; a. 500,000 sq. m.; impt. cod fisheries.
Grand Bassam, *t.*, *spt.*, Ivory Cst., W. Africa; exp. bananas, palm-kernels; p. *5,743*.
Grand Bahama, one of the Bahama Is., W. Indies; p. (1953) *4,095*.
Grand Canal, *canal*, N. China; about 1,000 m. long from Tientsin to Hangchow; built between A.D. 605–18 and 1282–92; now silted up and cst. or rail transport more impt.
Grand Canal, main water thoroughfare through Venice, Italy. [(1962) *404,581*.
Grand Canary, *I.*, Canaries; cap. Las Palmas; p.
Grand Canyon, Arizona, U.S.A.; narrow gorge, 3,000 to over 5,000 ft. deep of Colorado R.
Grand Cayman I., T.W.I.; a. 85 sq. m.; coconuts; cap. Georgetown; p. (estd. 1957) *6,636*.
Grand Combin, *mtn.* in the Alps, N. of Aosta, Italy; alt. 14,141 ft. [*14,565*.
Grand-Comme (La), *t.*, Gard, France; p. (1954)
Grand Coulée Dam, Wash., U.S.A.; across R. Columbia 110 m. below Spokane; world's lgst. dam; reservoir formed 151 m. long, a. 130 sq. m. supplies irrigation water to 1,900 sq. m. between Rs. Columbia and Snake; hydro-elec. power sta. when complete will generate 2,700,000 h.p.
Grande Chartreuse, La, *monastery*, Isère, France; 15 m. N. of Grenoble; famous for its liqueur.
Grande Prairie, *t.*, Alberta, Canada; wheat; p. *2,267*.
Grand Forks, *t.*, N.D., U.S.A.; on Red R.; in wheat region; p. (1960) *34,451*.
Grand Island, *c.*, Nebraska, U.S.A.; cattle and grain t.; p. (1960) *25,742*.
Grand Junction, *t.*, Col., U.S.A.; p. (1960) *18,694*
Grand Lake, *lgst. L.*, Newfoundland; a. about 200 sq. m.
Grand Lahou, *t.*. Ivory Cst., W. Africa; p. *1,000*.
Grand' Mère, *t.*, Quebec, Canada; pulp and paper mills; p. (1961) *15,806*.
Grand Prairie, *see* **Black Prairie**.
Grand Rapids, *c.*, Mich., U.S.A.; on Grand R. furniture mkg., car and aircraft parts, chemicals paper; p. (1960) *177,313*.
Grand R., Mich., U.S.A.; enters L. Mich. a Grand Haven, navigable to Grand Rapids length 250 m.
Grand R., W. Colorado and E. Utah, U.S.A. trib. of the Colorado R.; length 350 m.
Grand Turk I., *seat of government*, Turks an Caicos Is.; p. *1,693*.
Grange, *t.*, *urb. dist.*, N. Lancs, Eng., on N. cst of Morecambe Bay; sm. summer resort; p (1961) *3,117*.
Grangemouth, *burgh*, Stirling, Scot.; on F. o Forth, 20 m. W. of Leith; shipbldg. and repair marine engin., oil refining, petroleum prods chemicals, pharmaceutics; electronics and ele ind; oil pipeline to Finnart; p. (1961) *18,860*.
Granite City, Ill., U.S.A.; p. (1960) *40,073*.
Gran Sasso d'Italia, *rugged limestone highland* Abruzzi, Central Italy; highest part c Apennines, Monte Corno alt. 9,584 ft.; winte sports ctr., Aquila.
Grantham, *t.*, *mun. bor.*, Lincoln, Eng.; o Witham R.; tanning, agr. machin., engin brewing, malting, basket mkg.; p. (1961) *25,03*
Grant Land, *region*, N. of Ellesmere I., Arct Canada.
Grantown-on-Spey, *burgh*, Moray, Scot.; on I Spey; health resort; p. (1961) *1,581*.
Grants Pass, *t.*, S.W. Ore., U.S.A.; fruit growing lumber, mining, fishing; p. (1960) *10,118*.
Granville, *spt.*, *wat. pl.*, Manche, France; at mou of the Bosq; fisheries; p. (1954) *10,368*.
Granville, *sub.*, Sydney, N.S.W., Australia; *19,717*.
Grasmere, *vil.*, Westmorland, Eng.; at head Grasmere L.; home of Wordsworth.
Grasse, *t.*, *health resort*, Alpes-Maritimes, S. France; perfumes; p. (1954) *22,187*.
Graubünden (Grisons), *can.*, Switzerland; ca Chur; a. 2,746 sq. m.; p. (1961) *147,458*.
Graudenz, *see* **Grudziadz**.
's-Gravenhage, *see* **Hague**.
Graves, Pointe de, N. point of Médoc Peninsu France; in famous wine dist.
Gravesend, *spt.*, *mun. bor.*, Kent, Eng.; S. bank Thames facing Tilbury; shipping, paper, ment, rubber tyres, engin.; p. (1961) *51,388*.
Gravina, *industl. c.*, Apulia, Italy; p. *20,775*.
Gray's Peak, Rocky Mtns., Col., U.S.A.; a 14,341 ft.
Grays Thurrock, *urb. dist.*, Essex, Eng.; on t

Thames, nr. Tilbury Fort; oil refining, metal refining, cement, paper board, margarine, soap mftg.; p. (1961) *114,263.*

Graz, *t.*, Austria; on R. Mur; machin., iron and steel, rly. wks.; p. (1961) *237,080.*

Great Altai, *range of mtns.*, lying mainly in outer Mongolia but also in Western Siberia.

Great Atlas, *mtns.*, N.W. Africa; alt. 7,000 ft.

Great Australian Basin, *artesian basin*, Australia; underlies plains of S.W. Queensland, N.W. New South Wales, N.E. of S. Australia; water supply used on sheep-farms, cattle-ranches, in a. from Normanton in N. to Renmark in S., Oodnadatta in W. to Roma in E.; a. 570,000 sq. m.

Great Australian Bight, *wide inlet*, S. of Australia, between C. Arid and Port Whidbey; 850 m.

Great Barrier Reef, *coral reef barrier*, off N.E. cst. of Australia; 1,000 m. long, 75–100 m. from cst.

Great Basin, *high plateau region* between the Wasatch and Sierra Nevada Mtns., U.S.A., inc. most of Nev., parts of Utah, Cal., Idaho, Ore., Wyo.; inland drainage ctr. Great Salt Lake; a. 210,000 sq. m.; much desert; sparse p.

Great Bear Lake, on the Arctic Circle, in N.W. Terr., Canada, over 150 m. long; a. 14,000 sq. m.; outlet through Great Bear R. to Mackenzie R.

Great Belt, *strait*, separating I. of Fyn from Zealand, Denmark.

Great Britain, *see* **England, Scotland, Wales, British Isles.**

Great Dividing Range, *mtn. system*, E. Australia; extends, under different local names, from Queensland to Victoria and separates E. cst. plains from interior; reaches max. alt. in Mt. Koskiusko (7,328 ft.), in Australian Alps, on bdy. between Victoria and New South Wales.

Great Falls, *t.*, Mont., U.S.A.; on Missouri R.; wool; gold, silver; lead and copper smelting; p. (1960) *55,357.*

Great Fish R., Cape Province, S. Africa.

Great Fisher Bank, *submarine sandbank* in N. Sea; 200 m. E. of Aberdeen, 100 m. S.W. of Stavanger; valuable fishing-ground; depth of water, from 25 to 40 fathoms.

Great Gable, *mtn.*, Cumberland, Eng.; alt. 2,949 ft.

Great Harwood, *t.*, *urb. dist.*, Lancs, Eng.; 5 m. N.E. of Blackburn; cotton weaving, textiles, engin.; p. (1961) *10,718.*

Great Inagua, *I.*, one of the Bahama Is., W. Indies; p. (1953) *999.*

Great Karroo, Cape Province, S. Africa; high plateau; ostrich farming.

Great Lakes, N. America; comprising 5 fresh-water Ls.: Superior, Michigan, Huron, Erie, Ontario; frozen 4 to 5 months in winter; enormous L. traffic in cereals, iron, coal, etc.; a. 96,000 sq. m. *See* **St. Lawrence Seaway.**

Great Makarikari, Botswana, South Africa; salt pan.

Great Namaqualand, S. region of S.W. Africa.

Great Ormes Head, *promontory*, N. Wales; nr. Llandudno.

Great Plains, *lowland area* of central N. America, extending E. from Rocky Mtns. and S. from Mackenzie to S. Texas.

Great St. Bernard, *pass*, Switzerland; 8,120 ft. over Pennine Alps. *See* **K146.**

Great Salt Lake, Utah, U.S.A.; in the Great Basin plateau of N. America; 90 m. long; a. over 2,000 sq. m.; alt. 4,218 ft.; receives Bear, Jordan and Beaver Rs.; no outlet.

Great Sandy Desert, N. part, W. Australia.

Great Slave Lake, N.W. Terr., Canada; length 300 m.; greatest breadth 50 m., outlet Mackenzie R.

Great Slave R., Canada, flowing between L. Athabaska and the Great Slave L.

Great Smoky Mtns., Tenn., U.S.A.; with Blue Ridge Mtns. form E. Zone of Appalachian Mtn. system; rise to alt. over 6,000 ft.; largely preserved as National Park.

Great Victoria Desert, W. and S. Australia, lies north of Nullarbor Plain.

Great Yarmouth, *see* **Yarmouth, Great.**

Greater Antilles Is., W. Indies.

Greece, *kingdom*, S. part of Balkan Peninsula, bounded on N. by Albania, Jugoslavia and Bulgaria, on W. and S. by the Mediterranean, and on the E. by the Ægean Sea, and inc. Is. in the Mediterranean, Ægean and Ionian Seas; cap. Athens; agr.: cereals, tobacco, currants, vines, fruit; sheep, goats, cattle; minerals: iron, lead, magnesite, lignite; mnfs.: olive oil, wine, textiles, chemicals, shipyds., oil refining; a. 51,182 sq. m.; p. (1961) *8,388,553.*

Greeley, *t.*, Col., U.S.A.; nr. Denver, site of st. college of education; lumber, flour; p. (1960) *26,314.*

Green Bay, *c.*, Wis., U.S.A.; tr. in timber, flour, etc., paper, coal; p. (1960) *62,888.*

Greenfield, *t.*, Mass., U.S.A.; p. (1960) *14,389.*

Greenford, *sub.* of London, W. Middx., Eng.; p. (1961) *39,742.*

Greenhithe, Thames-side, nr. Dartford, Kent, Eng.

Greenland, *I.*, between Arctic Ocean and Baffin Bay; lofty ice-capped plateau; peopled by coastal settlements of Eskimos; whale oil, seal skins; some coal, lead, zinc; U.S. base at Thule; part of Danish kingdom; cap. Godthaab; a. 840,000 sq. m., of which 708,000 sq. m. are under a permanent ice-cap; p. (estd. 1960) *33,113.*

Greenlaw, *t.*, Berwick, Scot.

Green Mtns., Vermont section of Appalachian mtns.; highest peak, alt. 4,430 ft.

Greenock, *burgh*, Renfrew, Scot.; on S. shore of Firth of Clyde, 20 m. W. of Glasgow; shipbldg., sugar-refining, woollens, chemicals, aluminium casting, tin plate inds.; p. (1961) *74,578.*

Greenore, *cape*, Louth, Ireland; separating Dundalk Bay from Carlingford, Lough.

Green R., trib. of Grand R., Utah, U.S.A.; length 750 m.

Greensboro', *c.*, N.C., U.S.A.; cotton, tobacco; p. (1960) *119,574.*

Greensburg, *t.*, Penns., U.S.A.; iron and glass factories; p. (1960) *17,383.*

Greenville, *t.*, Miss., U.S.A.; on Miss. R.; cotton tr.; p. (1960) *41,502.*

Greenville, *c.*, S.C., U.S.A.; in the cotton belt; p. (1960) *66,188.*

Greenville, Texas, U.S.A.; cotton, rayon, shipping; p. (1960) *19,087.*

Greenwich, *inner bor.*, London, Eng.; inc. most of former bor. of Woolwich on S. bank of R. Thames; famous for its Hospital, Observatory (now moved to Herstmonceux) and R.N. College; longitudes conventionally calculated Greenwich meridian either E. or W.; p. (1964) *230,082.*

Greenwood, *t.*, Miss., U.S.A.; p. (1960) *20,436.*

Greenwood, *t.*, S.C., U.S.A.; p. (1960) *16,644.*

Greifswald, *spt.*, Rostock, E. Germany; on Baltic inlet; shipbldg., textiles, wood inds.; p. (1963) *47,563.*

Greiz, *t.*, Gera, E. Germany; paper, textiles, chemicals; p. (1963) *38,470.*

Grenaa, *t.*, Randers, Jutland, Denmark; textiles, furniture, engin.; p. (1960) *9,088.*

Grenada, *I.*, W.I.; cap. St. George's; fruit, cocoa, spices; a. 133 sq. m.; p. (estd. 1965) *93,000.*

Grenadines, *Brit. gr. of sm. Is.*, between Grenada and St. Vincent, Windward Is.; sea-island cotton; p. (1960) *6,433.*

Grenoble, *fortfd. c.*, Isère, S.E. France; on R. Isère; 60 m. from Lyons; gloves, buttons, machin., liqueurs, cement; joint Franco-German nuclear research reactor; p. (1962) *162,764.*

Gretna, *t.*, La., U.S.A.; on the Mississippi R.; p. (1960) *21,967.*

Gretna Green, *vil.*, Dumfriesshire, Scot., on Eng. border; famous as place of runaway marriages, 1754–1856.

Grey Range, *mtns.*, S.W. Queensland, Australia; extends S.W. from Gr. Dividing Range towards Flinders Range and Spencer G.; forms divide between streams draining E. to R. Darling and those draining W. to L. Eyre.

Greymouth, *spt.*, S.I., N.Z.; on W. cst. at mouth of Grey R.; ch. t. prov. of Westland; coal; p. (1961) *8,877.*

Greytown, *see* **San Juan del Norte.**

Griffin, *c.*, Ga., U.S.A.; cotton factories and tr.; p. (1960) *21,735.*

Grim, *C.*, N.W. Tasmania.

Grimaldi, *caves*, N.W. Italy; remains of prehistoric man, late Paleolithic, found there.

Grimsby, *spt.*, *co. bor.*, Lincoln, Eng.; on S. bank of R. Humber; fishing, shipbldg., fertilisers, chemicals, engin., paper mkg., tanning and cod liver oil, acrylic fibre; p. (1961) *96,665.*

Grimsel Pass, Bernese Alps, Switzerland; alt. 7,100 ft.

Grindelwald, *vil.*, Bernese Oberland, Switzerland; tourist ctr.

Griqualand East, *dist.*, Cape Province, S. Africa;

pastures, wool; ch. t. Kokstad; a. 6,602 sq. m.; p. *265,000.*

Griqualand W., *dist.*, Cape Province, S. Africa; diamonds; ch. t., Kimberley; a. 15,197 sq. m.; p. *160,793.*

Gris-Nez, *C.*, N.E. France; nearest point on French cst. to Dover.

Grisons (Graubünden), *can.*, Switzerland; one-half only productive, many glaciers, contains the mtn. health resorts of Davos-Platz (alt. 5,115 ft.), St. Moritz (alt. 6,089 ft.), Arosa (alt. 6,108 ft.); a. 2,746 sq. m.; p. (1960) *145,600.*

Grivegnee, *t.*, Belgium; nr. Liége; ironwks.; p. (1962) *23,340.*

Grodno, *t.*, W. Byelorussia (Polish until 1939); agr.; engin., textiles, chemicals; p. (1959) *72,000.*

Grodzisk Mazowiecki, *commune*, Poland; 12 m. S.W. of Warsaw; p. *18,737.*

Gronau, *t.*, N. Rhine-Westphalia, Germany; nr. Dutch frontier; textiles, rly. junction; p. (1963) *26,000.*

Grong, *spt.*, Norway, on Falda Fjord; p. (1961) *2,052.*

Groningen, *t.*, *cap.*, Groningen, Netherlands; woollens, glucose, shipbldg.; p. (1960) *144,485.*

Groningen, *prov.*, N.E. Netherlands; agr. and dairying; natural gas deposits at Slochteren; a. 883 sq. m.; p. (estd. 1959) *474,657.*

Groote Eylandt, *I.*, G. of Carpentaria; off cst. of N. Terr., Australia.

Grootfontein, *t.*, S.W. Africa; copper- and lead-mining; world's lgst. known meteorite on nearby farm; p. (1960) *3,722* inc. *1,195* whites.

Grosseto, *prov.*, central Italy; ch. t. Grosseto, a. 1,735 sq. m.; p. (1963) *216,704.*

Grosseto, *t*, *cap.* Grosseto Prov., Central Italy; p. (1961) *51,004.*

Groton, *industl. t.*, Conn., U.S.A.; opp. New London at mouth of Thames R.; p. (1960) *10,111.*

Grottaglie, *t.*, Lecce, Apulia, Italy; nr. Brindisi; white glaze pottery; p. *14,850.*

Grove City, *bor.*, Penns., U.S.A.; engines, carriages; p. (1960) *8,368.*

Grozny, *t.*, N. Caucasia, R.S.F.S.R.; on R. Terek; naphtha wells, refinery, engin.; starting point of oil pipelines to Makhachkala Tuapse and Gorlovka; p. (1962) *280,000.*

Grudziadz (Graudenz), *t.*, on R. Vistula, Polish Pomerania; sawmilling; p. (1960) *65,000.*

Grünberg, *see* **Zielona Gora.**

Gruyère, *dist.*, can. Fribourg, Switzerland; cheese.

Gstaad, *fashionable summer and winter res.*, Bernese Oberland, Switzerland.

Guadalajara, *c.*, Mexico; cap. of Jalisco st.; cotton and wool mnfs.; cath.; p. (1960) *736,800.*

Guadalajara, *prov.*, Spain; agr. and salt mines; a. 4,709 sq. m.; p. (1959) *195,637.*

Guadalajara, *mftg. t.*, G. prov., Spain; woollens, leather; p. (1957) *15,700.*

Guadalaviar, *R.*, E. Spain; flows into Mediterranean, nr. Valencia; length 130 m.

Guadalcanal, *I.*, Brit. Solomon Is., Pac. Oc.

Guadalquivir, *R.*, Spain; flows through Andalusia to Atlantic; length 375 m.

Guadalupe Hidalgo, *t.*, Mexico; treaty signed 1848 ending Mexican-U.S. war; p. (estd.) *29,000.*

Guadeloupe and Dependencies, Leeward gr.; a. 722 sq. m.; sugar produce; ch. pt. Pointe à Pitre; p. (1961) *282,000.* French Overseas Dept.; Leeward gr. consists of Guadaloupe (p. *113,412*, ch. t. Basse-Terre), Grande Terre p. (*113,545*, ch. t. Pointe à Pitre); united a. of Is., 583 sq. m.; and 5 smaller Is., Marie Golante, Désirade, St. Barthelemy and St. Martin (total p. *304,000*) still inhabited by white descendants of French emigrants of 300 years ago; mountainous; rum, sugar, coffee, bananas.

Guadiana, *R.*, forms part of Spanish and Portuguese frontier; flows into Bay of Cadiz; length 510 m.; Extremadura valley reclamation scheme in progress.

Guadiana del Caudillo, *new t.*, nr. Badajoz, Spain; linen, hemp goods, cattle foods.

Guadix, *c.*, Granada, S. Spain; cath.; hats, hemp, brandy, pottery, mats, carpets; p. (1957) *30,088.*

Guaira, La, *spt.*, Venezuela; motor road to Carácas; exp. hides, cocoa, coffee; p. (1961) 20,275.

Gualdo Tadino, *commune*, central Italy; cath.; pottery; p. *12,791.*

Gualeguaychu, *t.*, Entre Rios, Argentina; cattle and agr. ctr.; p. (1960) *43,000.*

Guam, *I.*, most S. and lgst. of Marianas Archipelago, N. Pacific; naval sta. of the U.S.A.; Polaris submarine base at Apra harbour; ch. t. Agaña and spt. is Piti; maize, sweet potatoes, bananas; a. 209 sq. m.; p. (1960) *67,044.*

Guanabacoa, *industl. t.*, nr. Havana, Cuba; p. *21,999.*

Guanabara, *st.*, Brazil; formerly fed. dist. of Rio de Janeiro; *q.v.* p. (1963) *141,523.*

Guanacasta, *prov.*, Costa Rica, Central America;

Guanajuato, *st.*, Central Mexico; very fertile, productive and prosperous; a. 11,804 sq. m.; p. (1960) *1,735,490.*

Guanajuato, *ch. t.*, G. st., Mexico; 250 m. from Mexico c.; cotton, silver, lead; p. (1960) *23,379.*

Guanta, *spt.*, Anzoategui st., Venezuela, S. America; on Caribbean Sea, linked by road to Barcelona (10 m.); exp. oil.

Guantanamo, *t.*, Cuba; sugar, coffee, bananas, cacao; p. (1953) *64,671.*

Guapore, *R.*, Brazil, S. America; joins the Mamore; length 900 m.

Guarda, *t.*, Portugal; alt. over 3,000 ft.; p. *9,766.*

Guarda, *wine-growing dist.*, Portugal; between Rs. Tagus and Douro; a. 2,126 sq. m.; p. (1950) *307,003.*

Guardafui, *C.*, most E. point of Africa.

Guastalla, *commune*, N. Italy; spun silk, leather, cheese; p. *13,732.*

Guatemala, *republican st.*, Central America; adjoins Mexico, Br. Honduras and El Salvador, coffee, bananas, chicle; lead, zinc, and cadmium mined in sm. quantities; a. 45,452 sq. m.; p. (estd. 1960) *3,950,000.*

Guatemala City, *cap. c.*, Guatemala; cath.; univ.; minerals: gold, silver, copper, lead; p. (estd. 1960) *407,000.*

Guayaquil, *ch. pt.*, Ecuador, S. America; on Guayas R., 30 m. above its entrance into the Bay of Guayaquil; devastated by fire in 1896 and 1899; univ.; cath.; sawmills, foundries, machin., brewing; p. (1963) *506,000.*

Guayas, *prov.*, Ecuador; cap. Guayaquil; a. 8,331 sq. m.; p. (1960) *825,600.*

Guaynabo, *t.*, Puerto Rico W.I.; p. (1960) *40,257.*

Gubat, *mun.*, Luzon, Philippine Is.; hemp, coconuts, sugar-cane region; p. *22,880.*

Gubbio, *t.*, Perugia, Italy; lustre ware; p. *30,850.*

Gubin (Guben), *t.*, Brandenburg, Poland; W. sector of t. still German; on R. Neisse; textiles, machin., leather, synthetic fibre; p. (estd. 1939) *45,800.*

Gudbrandsdal, *gr. valley*, S. Norway; leads S.E. from Dovre Fjeld towards Oslo; drained by R. Logan; used by main road Oslo to Trondheim; provides relatively lge. a. of cultivable land; hay, oats, barley, dairy cattle.

Gudiyatam, *t.*, Madras India; p. (1961) *50,384.*

Guebwiller, *t.*, Haut-Rhin, France; cottons; p. (1954) *10,414.*

Guelders (Gelderland), *prov.*, Netherlands; cap. Arnhem; a. 1939 sq. m.; p. (1947) *1,039,025.*

Guelph, *c.*, Ontario, Canada; cloth, yarn, pottery, agr. and veterinary colleges; p. (1961) *39,838.*

Guernsey, Channel Is., between cst. of France and England; tomatoes, grapes (under glass), flowers, cattle; tourist res.; t. and ch. spt. St Peter Port; a. 15,654 acres; p. (1961) (inc Herm and Jethou) *45,126.*

Guerrero, *Pacific st.*, Mexico; cereals, cotton coffee, tobacco; cap. Chilpancingo; ch. pt Acapulco; a. 24,885 sq. m.; p. (1960) *1,186,716*

Guiana, *region*, S. America; a. 179,000 sq. m. comprises Guyana and Fr. Guiana and Surinam

Guiana Highland, *plateau*, S. America; extend approx. 900 m. from E. to W. across S. parts o Venezuela, Guyana, Surinam, Fr. Guiana; stee sides, rounded tops approx. 3,000 ft. alt. bu rises to 8,635 ft. in Mt. Roraima; chiefly com posed crystalline rocks rich in minerals.

Guienne, *old French prov.*, separated by R. Garonn from Gascony.

Guildford, *c.*, *co. t.*, *mun. bor.*, Surrey, Eng.; 3 m. S.W. London; on gap cut by R. We through N. Downs; cath.; vehicles, agr. imple ments, light inds.; residtl.; p. (1961) *53,977.*

Guinea, *ind. rep.* (Oct. 1958), formerly Fr. Guinea member of Union of African States; iron-ore bauxite, diamonds, groundnuts, palm oil; cap Conakry; a. 94,900 sq. m.; p. (1961) *3,000,00*

Guinea, general name for W. African coastland round the greatest bend of G. of G. from th Gambia to the Congo.

Guinea, Portuguese. *See* **Portuguese Guinea.**

Guinea, Spanish. *See* **Spanish Guinea.**

Guinea Current, *ocean current*, flows W. to I

along Guinea Cst., diverted away from cst. in Bight of Benin by C. Three Points.

Güines, *t.*, Havana, Cuba, W. Indies; sugar; p. *22,669*.

Guinobatan, *mun.*, Luzon, Philippine Is.; hemp; lime deposits; p. *26,419*.

Guipuzcoa, *Basque prov.*, Spain; mftg., minerals, agr.; cap. San Sebastian; tourism; a. 728 sq. m.; p. (1959) *455,388*.

Guisborough, *t.*, *urb. dist.*, N.R. Yorks, Eng.; in Cleveland iron-mng.; a. S.E. of Middlesbrough; steel, sawmilling, clothing; p. (1961) *12,079*.

Gujarat, *st.*, India; formerly part of Bombay st.; cap. temporarily Ahmedabad; new cap. Gandhinager, 13 m. N. of A. under construction 1965; oil development in Cambay area; fertiliser plant projected; a. 72,245 sq. m.; p. (1961) *20,633,350*.

Gujranwala, *c.*, W. Pakistan; N. of Lahore; power plant projected; p. (1951) *120,860*.

Gujrat, *t.*, W. Pakistan; on Chenab R.; pottery and furniture; p. (1941) *22,000*. [*53,000*.

Gukhovo, *t.*, N. Caucasus, R.S.F.S.R.; p. (1959)

Gulbarga, *t.*, Gulbarga dist., Mysore, India; oil, cotton, flour, paint; p. (1961) *97,069*.

Gulf Basin, W. Australia; artesian well basin.

Gulfport, *t.*, Miss., U.S.A.; p. (1960) *30,204*.

Gulf Stream, current of the Atlantic, issuing from Gulf of Mexico by Florida Strait.

Gulf Stream Drift, *see* **North Atlantic Drift.**

Gummersbach, *t.*, N. Rhine–Westphalia, Germany; textiles, leather, metallurgy, paper, machin.; p. (1963) *32,400*.

Gumti, *R.*, trib. of Ganges, India; flows past Lucknow. [p. (1961) *187,122*.

Guntur, *t.*, Andhra Pradesh, India; cotton mftg.;

Gurgan (Asterabad), *t.*, N. Persia; nr. S.E. end of Caspian Sea; carpets, cotton, rice.

Guryev, *t.*, Kazakh S.S.R.; on mouth of R. Ural, entrance to Caspian Sea; petrol refining, engin.; oil pipeline to Orsk; p. (1959) *78,000*.

Gus-Khrustalnyy, *t.*, R.S.F.S.R., 40 m. S. of Vladimir; impt. ctr. of glass ind.; p. (1959) *53,000*.

Güstrow, *t.*, Schwerin, E. Germany; S. of Rostock; cas.; steel and wood inds.; rly. junction; p. (1963) *38,897*.

Gütersloh, *t.*, N. Rhine–Westphalia, Germany; nr. Bielefeld; silk and cotton inds.; famous for its Pumpernickel (Westphalian rye bread); machin., furniture, publishing, metallurgy; p. (1963) *53,300*.

Guyana, *indep. sov. st.* within Brit. Commonwealth (1966), S. America; flat, swampy cst., interior highlands; climate, very hot, heavy rainfall along cst.; tropical forests; agr.: sugar, rice, coffee; cattle; hardwoods; minerals: bauxite, diamonds, gold, manganese; poor communications; cap. Georgetown; a. 83,000 sq. m.; p. (estd. 1965) *650,000*; option of becoming rep. after beginning of 1969.

Guthrie, *t.*, Okla., U.S.A.; p. (1960) *9,502*.

Gwadar, *t.*, W. Pakistan; p. *15,000*.

Gwalior, *dist.*, Madhya Pradesh, India; a. 2,002 sq. m.; p. (1961) *657,876*.

Gwalior, *t.*, Madhya Pradesh, India, formerly Lashkar, 76 m. S. of Agra; cotton spinning, muslin, carpets, cereals, sugar-cane; bauxite; p. (1961) *300,587* inc. Morar. [Pakistan.

Gwatar, *spt.* on G. of Oman, Persia; by border of

Gwelo, *t.*, Rhodesia; impt. indust. ctr.; p. (1961) *37,590* inc. *8,590* Europeans.

Gwent, Plain of (Vale of Glamorgan), *lowland dist.*, Glamorgan, S. Wales; lies S. of moorland of S. Wales Coalfield, extends E. into Monmouth; fertile soils; mixed farming except in industl. areas of Cardiff, Barry.

Gympie, *t.*, Queensland, Australia; on Mary R., 106 m. from Brisbane; former goldfield; now dairying and pastoral dist., with extensive banana plantations; p. (1961) *11,082*.

Györ, *c.*, Hungary; at junction of R. Raab with arm of R. Danube; cath.; horses, textiles, chemicals, engin.; p. (1962) *72,319*.

Gytheon, *spt.*, Peloponnese, Greece; on G. of Laconia; p. (1951) *6,902*.

H

Haarlem, *t.*, *cap.*, N. Holland, Netherlands; textiles, printing, brewing, bulb growing; p. (1960) *169,215*.

Habab, *dist.*, W. coast Red Sea, Ethiopia.

Hachioji, *c.*, Honshu, Japan; weaving, silk–cotton mixtures; p. (1947) *73,494*.

Hackensack, *t.*, N.J., U.S.A.; iron foundries, silk, jewellery, paper; p. (1960) *30,521*.

Hackney, *inner bor.*, N.E. London, Eng.; incorporates former bors. of Shoreditch and Stoke Newington; furniture, clothing, footwear; p. (1964) *257,301*.

Haddington, *burgh, cap.*, E. Lothian, Scot.; on R. Tyne 16 m. E. of Edinburgh; woollen mnf.; grain mkt., corn mills, lt. engin., hosiery; p. (1961) *5,506*.

Haderslev, *t.*, Denmark; tobacco, clothing, knitted goods p. (1960) *19,735*.

Hadhramaut, *dist.* Arabia; E. of Aden Protectorate; subject to loose British control; fertile coastal valley; frankincense, aloes, tobacco, shawls, carpets; p. *150,000* (estd.).

Hadsund, *t.*, Jutland, Denmark; p. (1960) *3,424*.

Hafnarfjördur, *t.*, S. of Reykjavik, Iceland; p. (1962) *7,490*.

Hagen, *t.*, N. Rhine–Westphalia, Germany, N.E. of Wuppertal; iron, steel, chemicals, textiles, paper; p. (1963) *198,800*.

Hagenau, *t.*, Bas-Rhin, France; textiles, porcelain, soap, beer; p. (1954) *19,531*.

Hagerstown, *c.*, Md., U.S.A.; machin., furniture, chemicals; p. (1960) *36,660*.

Hagonoy, *mun.*, Luzon, Philippine Is.; maize, rice, sugar; p. *29,734*.

Hague, C. de La, Cotentin Peninsula, France; French fleet defeated by British 1692.

Hague, The, or 's-Gravenhage or Den Haag, *t.*, S. Holland, Netherlands; seat of government; permanent court of international justice; adm. ctr.; urban inds., mach. and metal wares; engin., printing; p. (1960) *606,110*.

Haifa, *ch. spt.*, Israel; on Bay of Acre at foot of Mt. Carmel; terminus of Iraq oil pipeline; inds., inc. oil refining, car assembly, steel, chemical wks, petro-chemicals; Technion univ.; p. (estd. 1951) *190,000*.

Hail, *t.*, Nejd, Saudi Arabia; p. over *10,000*.

Hailsham, *mkt. t.*, *rural dist.*, Sussex, Eng.; 5 m. N. of Eastbourne; mats, rope and twine; p. (rural dist. 1961) *42,372*.

Hainan, *I.*, S. coast of China; ch. t. Kiungchow; densely wooded, camphor, mahogany, rosewood; a. 13,974 sq. m.

Hainaut, *prov.*, Belgium, adjoining N.E. border of France; industl. and agr.; coal- and iron-mines; a. 1,436 sq. m.; p. (1962) *1,249,536*.

Hainburg, *t.*, Austria; on R. Danube; tobacco; Roman remains; p. (1961) *6,437*.

Haine, *R.*, Belgium, and Nord, France; trib. of R. Scheldt; length 40 m.

Haiphong, *t.*, *ch. port*, N. Viet-Nam; thriving tr.; cotton, thread, soap; p. (1960) *369,000*.

Haiti, *rep.* (the " Black Republic "), W. Indies; consists of W. portion of I. of Hispaniola; cap. Port au Prince; language French; coffee, sisal, sugar, textiles, soap, cement, rum; a. 10,204 sq. m.; p. (estd. 1964) *4,000,000*.

Hakodate, *spt.*, Hokkaido, Japan; fishing ctr., sulphur, dried fish, timber; p. (1962) *253,000*.

Hal, *t.*, central Belgium; flax; p. (1962) *19,508*.

Halberstadt, *c.*, Magdeburg, E. Germany; cath.; metallurgy, rubber inds., engin.; rly. junction; p. (1963) *46,355*.

Halden, *t.*, S.E. Norway; wood-pulp, paper, footwear, cotton spinning; nuclear research reactor; p. *9,973*.

Haldensleben, *t.*, Magdeburg, E. Germany; N.W. of Magdeburg; leather, stoneware; p. (1963) *21,254*.

Haldia, *pt.*, W. Bengal, India; nr. mouth of R. Hooghli; satellite pt. for Calcutta due for completion 1967, to handle coal, ore, grain; oil pipeline to Barauni.

Halesowen, *industl. t.*, *mun. bor.*, S.W. of Birmingham, Worc., Eng.; coal, weldless tubes, elec. gds., stainless steel forgings, engin.; p. (1961) *44,160*.

Halesworth, *t.*, *urb. dist.*, E. Suffolk, Eng.; on R. Blyth, 7 m. S. of Beccles; farming, corn mills, malting, engin.; p. (1961) *2,252*.

Halifax, *spt.*, *cap.*, Nova Scotia, Canada; gr. tr.; univ.; naval sta. and dockyard, open in winter; machin., iron foundries, boots and shoes, oil refining; p. (1961) *183,946*.

Halifax, *t.*, *co. bor.*, W.R. Yorks, Eng.; in valley of R. Calder, 7 m. S.W. of Bradford; carpets, textiles and machine tools; p. (1961) *96,073*.

Hall Peninsula, S.E. Baffin Land, Canada; between Cumberland Sound and Frobisher Bay.

Hallamshire, S., *dist.*, W.R. Yorks, Eng.; inc. Sheffield and Ecclesfield. [*170,060.*

Halland, *co.*, Sweden: a. 1,901 sq. m.; p. (1961)

Halle, *t.*, Halle, E. Germany; on R. Saale: univ.; lignite, potash, engin., chemicals; p. (1963) *278,729.*

Hallein, *t.*, Salzburg, Austria; on Austro-German frontier, 13 m. S. of Salzburg; impt. salt-mines; p. (1961) *13,329.*

Halliwell, *t.*, Lancs, Eng.; nr. Bolton; cotton.

Hallstatt, *vil.*, Upper Austria; early Iron Age culture type site.

Halluin, *frontier industl. t.*, Nord, France; on R. Lys; p. (1954) *13,345.*

Halmahera, *I.*, Indonesia; mountainous, active volcanoes, tropical forests; spices, pearl fisheries; grows sago and rice; a. 6,648 sq. m.

Halmstad, *spt.*, Kattegat, Sweden; iron and steel wks., machin. engin., cycles, textiles, leather, jute, wood-pulp; p. (1961) *39,032.*

Hals, *t.*, Jutland, Denmark; on Lim Fjord; p. (1960) *1,563.*

Hälsingborg, *see* **Helsingborg.**

Halstead, *t.*, *urb. dist.*, Essex, Eng.; on R. Colne, 12 m. N.W. of Colchester; rayon weaving, farming; p. (1961) *6,465.*

Haltemprice, *t.*, *urb. dist.*, E. Riding, Yorks, Eng.; p. (1961) *42,388.*

Haltom City, *t.*, Texas, U.S.A.; p. (1960) *23,133.*

Haltwhistle, *mkt. t.*, *rural dist.*, Northumberland, Eng.; on R. Tyne; coal, paint wks., agr.; p. (rural dist. 1961) *6,884.*

Ham, *t.*, Somme dep., N. France; on R. Somme, nr. Amiens; old cas.; p. (1954) *3,598.*

Hama, *c.*, Upper Syria; on R. Orontes; the ancient Hamath, cap. of a kingdom in times of Kings David and Solomon; cement wks.; p. (1961) *116,362.*

Hamadan, *c.*, Iran; the ancient Ecbatana; carpet mftg.; shellac; p. (1956) *100,029.*

Hamamatsu, *t.*, S. Honshu, Japan; on cst. plain 60 m. S.E. of Nagoya; ctr. of impt. cotton-mftg. region; textiles, dyeing, musical instruments, motor cycles; p. (1960) *333,000.*

Hamar, *t.*, Norway; on L. Mjösa; ctr. of rich agr. dist.; tr. and mftg. inds.; p. (estd. 1960) *13,000.*

Hamburg, *Land*, W. Germany; cap. Hamburg; a. 299 sq. m.

Hamburg, *gr. spt.*, *industl. and comm. t.*, *Land* Hamburg, N. Germany; astride R. Elbe, 85 m. upstream from N. Sea; second lgst. German t., and ch. pt.; univ. and hydrographic institute; handles vast tr., inc. liner traffic and barge traffic down Elbe from Saxony and Bohemia (Czechoslovakia), also much trans-shipment of goods; imports, fuel, raw materials for inds., foodstuffs; exp., textiles, leather goods, chemicals, light-engin. prod.; inds. shipbldg., fishing, food processing, leather, brewing, tobacco, textiles, rubber, oil, wood; also impt. airport; severe flooding caused by gales, Feb. 1962; p. (1963) *1,851,200.*

Hamburg, *t.*, N.Y., U.S.A.; optical goods; mkt. gardening; p. (1960) *9,145.*

Hamburg, *bor.*, S.E. Penns., U.S.A.; coal, mnfs.; p. (1950) *3,805.*

Hame (Tavastehus), *dep.*, Finland; a. 7,118 sq. m.; p. (1961) *580,765.*

Hamelin (Hameln), *t.*, Lower Saxony, Germany; on R. Weser; iron, textiles; legend of " The Pied Piper "; p. (1963) *49,500.*

Hamilton, *cap.* Bermudas (on largest I.); p. (estd. 1957) *3,000.* [*9,483.*

Hamilton, *t.*, W. Victoria, Australia; p. (1961)

Hamilton, *c.* and *L. pt.*, S.E. Ontario, Canada; at W. end of L. Ontario; varied metallurgical mnfs. and has been called the " Birmingham " and " Manchester " of Canada; fruit ctr.; univ.; p. (1961) *395,189.*

Hamilton, *c.*, N.Z.; univ.; p. (1961) *50,433.*

Hamilton, *burgh*, Lanark, Scot.; in Clyde valley, 10 m. S.E. of Glasgow; elec. goods, iron and steel foundries, carpet mftg., cotton, woollen and knit-wear goods; p. (1961) *41,928.*

Hamilton, *c.*, Ohio, U.S.A.; on the Gr. Maine R., thriving ind. and tr.; p. (1960) *72,354.*

Hamilton, *R.*, flows into H. Inlet, cst. of Labrador, Canada; magnificent waterfall, Grand Falls.

Hamlet, *t.*, N.C., U.S.A.; rly. ctr. in peach- and tobacco-growing region; p. (1950) *5,061.*

Hamm, *t.*, N. Rhine–Westphalia, Germany; on R. Lippe, nr. Dortmund; rly. marshalling yards, iron inds.; p. (1963) *71,300.*

Hamme, *t.*, E. Flanders, Belgium; rope, linen and lace factories; p. (1962) *16,880.*

Hammerfest, *spt.*, Norway; world's most northerly t.; fishing; p. (1961) *5,604.*

Hammersmith, *Thames-side inner bor.*, London, Eng.; inc. former bor. of Fulham; industl., residtl.; elec. and car accessories, synthetic rubber; p. (1964) *222,059.*

Hammond, c., Ind., U.S.A.; ironwks., pork packing; p. (1960) *111,698.*

Hammond, *t.*, La., U.S.A.; strawberry culture; p. (1960) *10,563.*

Hamoaze, estuary of R. Tamar, Plymouth, Eng.

Hampshire, *co.*, Eng.; ch. town Southampton; farming; shipbldg., brewing, tanning; a. 1,503 sq. m.; p. (1961) *1,336,084.*

Hampstead, *see* **Camden.**

Hampton, *Thames-side t.*, inc. in Richmond upon Thames, outer London bor., Eng.; Hampton Court Palace in the par.; Hampton Wick is a mile E. of H. Court.

Hampton, *t.*, S.E. Va., U.S.A.; oldest English community in the U.S.; fishing, oyster and crab packing; p. (1960) *89,258.*

Hamtramck, *t.*, Mich., U.S.A.; p. (1960) *34,137.*

Han Kiang, *R.*, Hupeh, China; rises in E. edge of Tibet plateau, flows S.E. between Tsinling Shan and Tapa Shan into Yangtze-Kiang at Hankow; upper course crosses fertile Nancheng valley, length 60 m., width 12 m.; lower course interrupted by many deep gorges, especially below Ankang; ch. trib. of Yangtze-Kiang, length over 1,000 m.

Hanau, *t.*, Hessen, Germany, on R. Main; rubber and non-ferrous metals inds., jewellery; p. (1963) *48,500.*

Hancock, *t.*, Mich., U.S.A.; copper-mines; iron and brass mnfs.; p. (1960) *5,022.*

Hangchow (Hangzhou), *c.*, *cap.*, Chekiang, China; head of H. Bay; former treaty pt.; extensive tr.; ctr. of silk-weaving ind.; p. (1953) *697,000.*

Hanko, *t.*, on S. point, Finland; p. (1961) *8,178.*

Hankow, *c.*, *former treaty pt.*, Hupeh, China; 700 m. from mouth of Yangtze-Kiang; great tea mart, also lge. tr. in opium, raw silk, cotton, etc., iron and steel wks., textiles, flour. *See also* **Wuhan.**

Hanley, *industl. t.* (now inc. in co. bor. of Stoke-on-Trent), Staffs, Eng.; pottery, china.

Hannibal, *c.*, Mo, U.S.A.; on R. Mississippi; timber and wagon bldg.; p. (1960) *20,028.*

Hanoi, *c.*, *cap.*, N. Viet-Nam; ancient " Ke-Sho " or " great market " on the Red R.; old Annamese fort, now modern comm. ctr.; univ.; cotton, silks, tobacco, pottery; p. (1960) *644,000.*

Hanover, *t.*, *cap.*, Lower Saxony, Germany; W. of Brunswick; iron, textiles, machin., paper, biscuits, cigarettes, cars, rubber processing, chemicals; gr. route ctr.; p. (1963) *571,300.*

Hanover, *bor.*, Penns., U.S.A.; mnfs. shoes, jute, wire cloth; p. (1960) *15,538.* [*24,991.*

Hanwell, *t.*, Middlx., Eng.; on R. Brent; p. (1961)

Hanyang, *industl. c.*, China; opp. Hankow, on Yangtze-kiang; lge. iron wks. *See also* **Wuhan.**

Haparanda, *spt.*, N. Sweden; salmon fishing; exp., timber, and prod. of the Lapps; p. (1961) *3,394.*

Hapur, *t.*, W. Uttar Pradesh, India; tr. in sugar, timber, cotton, brassware; p. (1961) *55,248.*

Harar, *cap.* Harar prov., Ethiopia; hides and skins, ivory, cattle; p. approx. *25,000.*

Harbin, *c.*, Heilungkiang, China; former treaty pt.; rly. junction; soya-beans, flour, tanning, distilling; p. (1953) *1,163,000.*

Harbour Grace, *t.*, *pt.*, Conception Bay, Newfoundland, Canada; p. (1961) *2,650.*

Harburg, *spt.*, Hanover, Germany; on R. Elbe, nr. Hamburg; linseed-crushing, india-rubber ind., etc.

Hardanger Fjord, W. cst. Norway; 75 m. long.

Hardt Mtns., W. Germany; northward continuation of Vosges on W. of Rhine rift valley; formerly forested, now lgely cleared for pasture; highest points reach just over 2,000 ft.

Hardwar, *t.*, Uttar Pradesh, India; on R. Ganges; gr. annual fair and pilgrimage; p. (1961) *58,513.*

Harelbeke, *t.*, N.W. Belgium; tobacco; p. (1962) *16,998.*

Harfleur, *t.*, *spt.*, Calvados, France; potteries, distilling, chemicals; p. *5,080.*

Haringey, *outer bor.*, Greater London, Eng.; comprising former bors. of Hornsey, Tottenham and Wood Green; p. (1964) *258,908.*

Hari-Rud, *R.*, N. Afghanistan and Iran; the ancient "Arius"; length 650 m.
Harlech, *t.*, Merioneth, Wales; on Cardigan Bay, 10 m. N. of Barmouth; famous cas.; farming.
Harlem, *R.*, N.Y., U.S.A.; and Spuyten Duyvil Creek together form a waterway *c.* 8 m. long, extending from the East R. to Hudson R., and separates the bors. Manhattan and Bronx.
Harlingen, *spt.*, Friesland, Netherlands; margarine, mixed farming, fish; p. *10,400.*
Harlow, *t.*, Essex, Eng.; in valley of R. Stort, 22 m. N.E. of London: one of "New Towns" designated 1947; spreads S.W. from nucleus of old mkt. t. of Harlow; engin., glass, furniture mkg., metallurgy; p. (estd. 1965) *68,736.*
Härnosand, *t.*, Sweden; on G. of Bothnia; engin., saw-mills, pulp; p. (1961) *17,163.*
Harpenden, *t., urb. dist.*, Herts, Eng.; in Chiltern Hills, 5 m. N. of St. Albans; Rothamsted agr. experimental sta.; rubber, hosiery, basket mftg., engin.; p. (1961) *18,307.*
Harringay, *see* **Haringey.**
Harris, *par.*, Lewis I., Outer Hebrides, Scot.; inc. several sm. islets; tweeds, fishing; p. *4,467.*
Harrisburg, *c., cap.*, Penns., U.S.A.; iron, steel factories, machin., cigarettes, cotton goods; p. (1960) *79,697.*
Harrisburg, *t.*, Ill., U.S.A.; p. (1960) *9,171.*
Harrison or East Newark, *industl. t.*, N.J., U.S.A.; p. (1960) *11,743.*
Harrogate, *t., mun. bor., spa*, W.R. Yorks, Eng.; in valley of R. Nidd, 14 m. N. of Leeds; numerous chalybeate springs; p. (1961) *56,332.*
Harrow, *outer bor.*, Greater London, Eng.; famous public school; camera mftg.; p. (1961) *209,080.*
Harsova, *t.*, Romania; on R. Danube, N. of Cernovada; p. *3,762.*
Harstad, *ch. t.*, Lofoten Is., N.W. Norway; herring ind., woollen goods; p. *4,283.*
Hart Fells, *mtn.*, between Peebles and Dumfries, Scot.; alt. 2,651 ft.
Hartebeestpoort Dam, Transvaal, Rep. of S. Africa; on R. Crocodile (Limpopo), 25 m. W. of Pretoria; supplies water for cultivation, under irrigation, of cotton, maize. tobacco.
Hartford, *cap.*, Conn., U.S.A.; lge. comm. ctr., seat of Trinity College; small arms, typewriters, elec. machin., aircraft engin., ceramics, plastics; p. (1960) *162,178.*
Hartford City, Ind., U.S.A.; p. (1960) *8,053.*
Hartland Point, Barnstaple Bay, N. Devon. Eng.
Hartlepool, *spt., mun. bor.*, Durham, Eng.; on E. cst., 2 m. N. of W. Hartlepool; fishing; p. (1961) *17,674.*
Hartlepool, W., *spt., co. bor.*, Durham, Eng.; on E. cst., 3 m. N. of estuary of R. Tees; iron inds., shipbldg., light inds., timber; p. (1961) *77,073.*
Hartsville, *t.*, S.C., U.S.A.; cotton, rayon, silk, textiles; p. (1960) *6,392.*
Harvey, *t.*, N.E. Ill., U.S.A.; rolling stock, diesel engines, heavy machin.; p. (1960) *29,071.*
Harwell, *vil.*, Berkshire, Eng.; 12 m. S. of Oxford; Atomic Energy Research Estab.; nuclear power research and prod. of radioisotopes.
Harwich, *spt., mun. bor.*, Essex, Eng.; on S. cst. of estuary of R. Stour; packet sta. for Belgium, Netherlands, Denmark; docks, naval base, fisheries, light inds.; p. (1961) *13,699.*
Harz Mtns., *range* in Hanover and Brunswick, Germany; highest peak the Brocken; 1,142 m. forested slopes rich in minerals; length 57 m.
Haslemere, *mkt. t., urb. dist.*, Surrey, Eng.; 13 m. S.W. of Guildford, on hills of Hindhead and Blackdown; residtl.; lt. inds.; p. (1961) *12,528.*
Haslingden, *t., mun. bor.*, Lancs, Eng.; on Rossendale Fells, 3 m. S. of Accrington; cotton, stone quarrying, engin.; p. (1961) *14,370.*
Hasselt, *t.*, prov. Limbourg, Belgium; gin distilleries; p. (1962) *37,198.*
Hassi Messoud, *t.*, Algeria, Africa; lge. oilfield; 24 inch pipe-line to Bejaia.
Hassi R'Mel, *t.*, Algeria, Africa; natural gas.
Hastings, *t., co. bor.*, E. Sussex, Eng.; on S. cst., midway between Beachy Head and Dungeness; seaside resort; one of the Cinque Ports; p. (1961) *66,346.*
Hastings, *t.*, N.I., N.Z.; on Hawke's Bay, nr. Napier; p. (1961) *32,479.*
Hastings, *t.*, Nebraska, U.S.A.; p. (1960) *21,412.*
Hastings-on-Hudson, *t.*, N.Y., U.S.A.; residtl.; mnfs. copper chemicals; p. (1960) *8,979.*
Hatay (formerly Sanjak of Alexandretta), ceded to Turkey by France 1939; p. (1960) *441,209.*
Hatfield, *t.*, Herts, Eng.; on Great North Road, 19 m. N. of London; one of "New Towns" designated 1948 growing around old t. of Bishops Hatfield; light engin., aircraft; p. (estd. 1965) *23,635.*
Hathras, *t.*, Aligarh dist., W. Uttar Pradesh, India; sugar, cotton, carved work; p. (1961) *64,045.*
Hatteras, *C.*, N.C., U.S.A.; stormy region.
Hattiesburg, *t.*, Miss., U.S.A.; p. (1960) *34,989.*
Hattingen, *t.*, N. Rhine–Westphalia, Germany; S.E. of Essen; machin., textiles; p. (1963) *30,700.*
Hatvan, *mkt. t.*, Hungary; E. of Budapest; p. [(1962) *20,080.*
Haubourdin, *t.*, Nord, France; nr. Lille; p. (1954) *12,095.*
Haugesund, *spt.*, S. Norway; on S.W. coast, 35 m. N. of Stavanger; ch. ctr. of herring fishery; canning inds.; p. (estd. 1960) *20,000.*
Hauraki, *G.*, E. cst. N.I., N.Z.
Hautmont, *t.*, Nord, France; p. (1954) *15,978.*
Haut-Rhin, *see* **Rhin-Haut.**
Haute-Garonne, *see* **Garonne-Haute.**
Haute-Loire, *see* **Loire-Haute.**
Haute-Marne, *see* **Marne-Haute.**
Haute-Saône, *see* **Saône-Haute.**
Haute-Savoie, *see* **Savoie-Haute.**
Haute-Vienne, *see* **Vienne-Haute.**
Hautes-Pyrénées, *see* **Pyrénées, Hautes.**
Havana, *prov.*, Cuba; cap. H.; lge. exp. tr.; a. 3,173 sq. m.; p. (1953) *1,538,803.*
Havana, *spt., cap.*, Cuba; ch. c. of the W. Indies; cigars, tobacco, sugar, rum, coffee, woollens, straw hats, iron-ore; oil refining on outskirts of t.; p. (estd. 1960) *788,000.*
Havant and Waterloo, *urb. dist.*, Hants, Eng.; at foot of Portsdown Hill, 6 m. N.E. of Portsmouth; malting, brewing, tanning; p. (1961) *74,564.*
Havel, *R.*, Germany; flowing to R. Elbe (221 m.).
Haverfordwest, *co. t., mun. bor.*, Pembrokeshire, Wales; 6 m. N.E. of Milford Haven; agr. mkt.; Norman cas.; p. (1961) *8,872.* [*5,446.*
Haverhill, *t., urb. dist.*, Suffolk, E. Eng.; p. (1961)
Haverhill, *t.*, Mass. U.S.A.; boot factories; p. (1960) *46,346.*
Havering, *outer bor.*, E. London, Eng.; inc. Hornchurch and Romford (*q.v.*); p. (1964) *242,706.*
Haverstraw, *t.*, N.Y., U.S.A.; brick-mkg.; p. (1960) *5,771.*
Havre, Le, *spt.*, Seine-Maritime, France; on English Channel at mouth of R. Seine; fine boulevards; ship-bldg., engin., chemicals, ropes, cottons, oil refining; p. (1962) *184,133.*
Havre de Grace, *t.*, Md., U.S.A.; resort; duck shooting; p. (1950) *7,809.*
Hawaii, *I.*, lgst. and most attractive of the Hawaiian gr.; mountainous, highest peak Mauna Kea, alt. 13,820 ft.; Mauna Loa has lgst. active volcano in the world extending about 60 m. and over 13,600 ft., whilst Maiua Haleakala has lgst. pit crater; forested, cane sugar, pineapples, tourism, livestock, fishing, steel mill; oil refinery projected in Honolulu; a. 4,016 sq. m.; p. (1960) *61,332.*
Hawaiian Is. (Sandwich Is.), Pac. Oc., *st.*, U.S.A. 1959); a. 6,423-sq. m.; cap. Honolulu; p. (1960) *632,772.*
Hawarden, *t., rural dist.*, Flint, N. Wales; steel plant; p. (rural dist. 1961) *36,290.*
Hawash, *R.*, Ethiopia, flows E. of Shoa frontier; length 500 m.
Hawera, *t.*, N.I., N.Z.; p. (1961) *7,537.*
Hawes Water, *L.*, Westmorland, Eng. (2½ m.).
Hawick, *burgh*, Roxburgh, Scot.; on R. Teviot, 18 m. S.W of Kelso; hosiery, tweed and woollens; p. (1961) *16,204.*
Hawke's Bay, *prov. dist.*, N.I., N.Z.; on E. cst.; cap. Napier; a. 4,260 sq. m.; p. (1961) *114,516.*
Hawkesbury, *R.*, N.S.W., Australia; length 330 m.
Hawkesbury, *t.*, Ontario, Canada; p. (1956) *7,874.*
Haworth, *t.*, W.R. Yorks, Eng.; nr. Keighley; home of the Brontës.
Hawthorne, *t.*, S.W. Cal., U.S.A.; residtl.; in gas- and oil-producing area; p. (1960) *33,035.*
Hawthorne, *bor.*, N.J., U.S.A.; paint, glass textiles, dyewks.; p. (1960) *17,735.*
Hay, *R.*, Alberta, Canada; flows into G. Slave Lake. [p. (1961) *1,321.*
Hay, *urb. dist.*, Brecknock, Wales; on R. Wye;
Hay, *t.*, N.S.W., Australia; situated on R. Murrumbidgee on N. edge of Riverina dist.; collecting ctr. for fruit and wheat grown under

irrigation, for despatch by rail E. to Narandera and Sydney, or by river W. to Adelaide.
Hayange, *t.*, Moselle, France; ironwks.; p. (1954) *11,060.*
Hayden, *Mt.*, or Grand Teton peak, Rockies, Wyo., U.S.A.; alt. 13,600 ft.
Haydock, *t.*, *urb. dist.*, Lancs, Eng.; coal-mining; p. (1961) *12,070.*
Hayes and Harlington, *former urb. dist.*, Middx., Eng.; now inc. in Hillingdon outer bor., Greater London (*q.v.*); residtl.; elec. goods, gramophones, aeroplane mftg.; p. (1961) *67,912.*
Hayle, *t.*, Cornwall, Eng.; nr. St. Ives; engin.; p. *5,800.*
Hayling Island, *resort*, Hants, Eng.; E. of Portsmouth.
Haystack, *summit* of the Adirondacks, Vt., U.S.A.; alt. 4,919 ft.
Hayward, *t.*, Cal., U.S.A.; p. (1960) *72,700.*
Hayward's Heath, *mkt. t.*, Sussex, Eng.; nr. Cuckfield; cattle mkt.; p. *5,400.*
Hazard, *t.*, Ky., U.S.A.; gas, coal, sawmills, steel mills; p. (1960) *5,958.*
Hazaribagh, *t.*, Bihar, India; coal, mica; p. (1961) *[40,958.*
Hazebrouck, *t.*, France, Nord; rly. ctr., textiles, grain, livestock; p. (1954) *15,525.*
Hazel Grove and Bramhall, *urb. dist.*, Cheshire, Eng.; p. (1961) *30,399.*
Hazleton, *c.*, Penns., U.S.A.; anthracite region; coal, iron, textiles, iron and steel mnfs.; p. (1960) *32,056.*
Headingley, *sub.*, Leeds, Yorks, Eng.; mainly [residtl.
Healdtown, *mission sta.*, nr. Fort Beaufort, Cape Province, S. Africa.
Heanor, *t.*, *urb. dist.*, Derby, Eng.; 7 m. N.E. of Derby; coal, hosiery, rly. wagons, pottery, prefabricated timber bldgs. mftg.; p. (1961) *23,867.*
Heard, *I.*, S. Indian Ocean; 280 m. S.E. of Kerguelen I.; Australian possession.
Heathrow, *vil.*, Middx, Eng.; on W. margin of built-up area of London; site of London Airport; arterial road link with London.
Heaton Norris, *industl. t.*, Lancs, Eng.; on R. Mersey; p. *11,000.*
Hebburn, *t.*, *urb. dist.*, Durham, Eng.; on R. Tyne, 4 m. below Gateshead; shipbldg., engin., and colliery inds.; p. (1961) *25,042.*
Hebden Royd, *urb. dist.*, W.R. Yorks, Eng.; cotton factories, dyewks., heavy engin.; p. (1961) *9,409.*
Hebrides or Western Is., Scot., grouped as Outer and Inner Hebrides; ch. t. Stornoway, Lewis; a. 2,850 sq. m.
Hebron, *t.*, Jordan; 16 m. S.W. of Jerusalem; p. (1961) *37,911.*
Heckmondwike, *t.*, *urb. dist.*, W.R. Yorks, Eng.; p. (1961) *8,420.*
Hedmark, *co.*, Norway; on Swedish border; a. 10,621 sq. m.; p. (1963) *177,730.*
Hedon, *mun. bor.*, E.R. Yorks, Eng.; p. (1961) *2,338.*
Heerenveen, *commune*, Friesland prov., N. Netherlands; livestock; p. (1960) *25,844.*
Heide, *t.*, Schleswig-Holstein, Germany; ctr. of petroleum dist.; machin., food preserving; p. (1963) *20,100.*
Heidelberg, *famous univ. t.*, Baden-Württemberg, Germany; on R. Neckar, nr. Mannheim; cas.; tobacco, wood, leather, rly. carriages; rly. junction; nylon plant projected; p. (1963) *126,500.*
Heidenheim, *t.*, Baden-Württemberg, Germany; N.E. of Ulm; textiles, machin., metallurgy, furniture; p. (1963) *50,000.*
Heilbronn, *t.*, *r. pt.*, Baden-Württemberg, Germany; engin., vehicles, foodstuffs; p. (1963) *92,400.*
Heilungkiang (Heilungjiang), *prov.*, N. China; a. *c.* 180,000 sq. m.; tractor farming, lumbering; coal, gold; cap. Harbin; p. (1953) *11,897,309.*
Hejaz, *region*, Saudi Arabia; mainly desert; very poor communications; ch. t. Mecca; a. 150,000 sq. m.; p. *1,000,000* (estimated).
Hekla, *volcano*, Iceland; alt. 5,095 ft.
Helder (Den Helder), *t.*, N. Holland, Netherlands; on cst. of Holland, 50 m. N. of Amsterdam, and connected by Helder Canal; arsenal and garrison; p. (1960) *48,569.*
Helena, *t.*, Ark., U.S.A.; on Mississippi R.; shipping ctr. for cotton; p. (1960) *11,500.*
Helena, *cap.*, Mont., U.S.A.; gold, silver, iron, smelting; p. (1960) *20,227.*
Helensburgh, *residtl. burgh*, Dunbarton, Scot.; on N. side of Firth of Clyde at entrance to Gare Loch; metal goods; p. (1961) *9,605.*
Heletz, Negev, Israel; oilwells.
Heligoland, *German I.*, N. Sea, off mouth of Elbe; formerly British.
Helikon, *mtn.*, Greece; between G. of Corinth and L. Kopais; alt. 5,736 ft.
Hell Gate R., Mont., U.S.A.; trib. of Bitter Root R.
Hellendoorn, *commune*, E. Netherlands; textiles; p. *13,721.*
Hellespont, *see* **Dardanelles.**
Hellin, *t.*, Albacete, Spain; sulphur-mines; p. (1957) *30,026.*
Helmond, *t.*, N. Brabant, Netherlands; on the Bois-le-Duc Canal; textiles; p. (1960) *43,056.*
Helmstedt, *t.*, Lower Saxony, Germany; E. of Brunswick; coal and potassium mining, textiles, machin.; p. (1963) *29,100.*
Helmund, *R.*, Afghanistan; falls into L. Hamun; length 650 m.
Helsingborg or Hälsingborg, *spt.*, Sweden; on the Sound, opposite Helsingör, Denmark; shipyd., engin., textiles, rubber goods, chemicals; p. (1961) *76,574.*
Helsingör, *t.*, Själland, Denmark; shipyds, textiles, rubber boots; p. (1960) *26,658.*
Helsinki (Helsingfors), *spt.*, *cap.* Finland; on G. of Finland, harbour ice-bound Jan. to April except for channel opened by ice-breaker; univ.; timber prod., textiles, carpets, etc.; p. (1961) *457,121.*
Helston, *mkt. t.*, *mun. bor.*, Cornwall, Eng.; on R. Cober, 8 m. W. of Falmouth; tourist ctr.; famous for its festival of the Furry or Floral Dance (8 May); p. (1961) *7,085.*
Helvellyn, *mtn.*, Cumberland, Eng.; 9 m. S.E. Keswick; alt. 3,118 ft.
Hemel Hempstead, *t.*, Herts, Eng.; on S. slopes of Chilterns, 9 m. N. of Watford; one of "New Towns" designated 1947; consists of bulk of mun. bor. of Hemel Hempstead with new growth to E. and S.E.; mun. bor. exists as separate entity; scientific glass, elec. engin., cars; p. (estd. 1965) *66,440.*
Hempstead, *t.*, Long I., N.Y., U.S.A.; p. (1960) *34,641.*
Hemsworth, *urb. dist.*, W.R. Yorks, Eng.; 6 m. S.E. of Wakefield; p. (1961) *14,401.*
Henderson, *c.*, Ky., U.S.A.; tobacco, cotton, coal; p. (1960) *16,892.*
Henderson, *t.*, N.C., U.S.A.; cotton, tobacco, mkt. and mnfs.; p. (1950) *10,996.*
Hendon, *former mun. bor.*, Middx., Eng.; now inc. in Barnet outer bor. Greater London, (*q.v.*); many light inds.; p. (1961) *151,843.*
Hengyang, *c.*, Hunan, China; on Siang Kiang in foot-hills to S. of Yangtze plain; nr. impt. lead- and zinc-mng. dist.; p. (1953) *235,000.*
Hénin-Liétard, *t.*, Pas-de-Calais, France; p. (1954) *23,673.*
Henley-on-Thames, *mun. bor.*, Oxford, Eng.; 5 m. N.E. of Reading; mkt. gardening, brewing; p. (1961) *9,131.*
Hennebont, *t.*, Morbihan, France; on R. Blavet; p. (1954) *11,279.*
Henrietta Maria, *C.*, Ontario, Canada; on Hudson Bay.
Henry, *C.*, Va., U.S.A.; at S. entrance to Chesapeake Bay.
Hensbarrow, *upland a.*, Cornwall, Eng.; granite; impt. kaolin-mining dist., kaolin exported by sea from Par, Fowey; rises to over 1,000 ft.; a. 30 sq. m.
Henzada, *t.*, Burma, on R. Irrawaddy; p. *28,542.*
Herat, *cap. c.* of prov. same name, Afghanistan; on Hari Rud; strongly fortified; has been called "the key of India"; crude petroleum and chrome ore in a.; p. (1948) (of prov.) *1,142,343*; (of t.) (1964) *62,000.*
Hérault, *dep.*, S. France; wines, fruit, olives, cheese, sheep-rearing; cap. Montpellier; a. 2,402 sq. m.; p. (1962) *516,658.*
Herberton, *t.*, E. Queensland, Australia; on Atherton Plateau, Gr. Dividing Range, 45 m. S.W. of Cairns to which it is linked by rail; tin-mining.
Herculaneum, *buried c.*, Italy; 7 m. E.S.E. Naples; re-discovered in 1709.
Hercules, *t.*, Transvaal, S. Africa; sub. of Pretoria; p. *16,119.*
Heredia, *prov.*, Costa Rica, Central America; cap. Heredia; p. (1963) *83,878.*
Hereford, *co.*, Eng.; on Welsh border; fertile

fruit, cereals, hops cattle, sheep, cider, salmon, limestone; a. 842 sq. m.; p. (1961) *130,919*.
Hereford, *c., mun. bor., co. t.*, Hereford, Eng.; on R. Wye, in ctr. of plain of Hereford; cath.; steel for turbines and aircraft rockets, tiles, engin., timber, cider and preserves; p. (1961) *40,431*.
Herenthals, *commune*, N. Belgium; mftg; p. (1962) *17,697*.
Herford, *t.*, N. Rhine–Westphalia, Germany; on R. Werra; cotton, flax, furniture, cigars, confectionery, metallurgy; p. (1963) *55,700*.
Herisau, *t., cap. can.* Appenzell Ausser–Rhoden, Switzerland; muslin mftg., embroidery, dyeing; p. (1957) *13,407*.
Herkimer, *t.*, N.Y., U.S.A.; dairy ctr.; p. (1960) *9,396*.
Herm, *sm. I.* of Channel Is., English Channel; 4 m. N.W. Sark and N.E. of Guernsey; remarkable shell-beach; a. 320 acres; p. *90*.
Hermon, *mtn.*, Syria; in Anti-Lebanon mtns.; alt. 9,385 ft.
Hermosillo, *t., cap.*, Sonora, Mexico; on Sonora R; univ.; impt. tr.; distilling, silver; p. (1960) *50,000*.
Hermoupolis, *spt., cap.*, Cyclades, Greece; p. (1961) *14,402*.
Herne, *t.*, N. Rhine–Westphalia, Germany; nr. Dortmund; coal, iron, machin., chemicals; p. (1963) *111,200*.
Herne Bay, *t., urb. dist.*, Kent, Eng.; on cst., 62 m. from London; p. (1961) *21,273*.
Herning, *t.*, Jutland, Denmark; knitting ind.; p. (1960) *24,790*.
Herrera, *prov.*, Panama, cap. Chitré; p. (1960) *61,672*.
Hersfeld, *c.*, Hessen, Germany; textiles; machin., wood, iron, leather, mineral baths; p. (estd. 1954) *22,800*.
Herstal, *t.*, Belgium; nr. Liége; repeating rifle wks., aero-engines; p. (1962) *29,698*.
Herstmonceux, *vil.*, nr. Hastings, Sussex, Eng.; cas.; site of Royal Greenwich Observatory.
Herten, *t.*, N. Rhine–Westphalia, Germany; coal, machin.; p. (1963) *52,300*.
Hertford, *co.*, Eng.; undulating parks, woods, wheat, fruit; light inds., elec. engin., pharmaceutics; a. 632 sq. m.; p. (1961) *832,901*.
Hertford, *co. t., mun. bor.*, Hertford, Eng.; on R. Lea, 20 m. N. of London; pharmaceutics, flour milling, rolling stock, diesels, brewing; p. (1961) *15,734*.
'sHertogenbosch, *t.*, Netherlands; on R. Maas; cap. of N. Brabant prov.; p. (1960) *71,286*.
Hessen, *Land*, Germany; a. 7,931 sq. m.; cap. Wiesbaden; p. (1961) *4,814,000*.
Hessen Nassau, *former Prussian prov.*, Germany; a. 6,472 sq. m.; cap. Cassel; forested, cereals, tobacco, flax, potatoes, mineral springs, iron, coal, copper.
Heston and Isleworth, *see* **Hounslow.**
Hetch Hetchy Dam, Cal., U.S.A.; on R. Tuolumne 100 m. upstream from St. Joaquin R.; ch. source of irrigation for middle St. Joaquin valley; supplies water and hydro-elec. to San Francisco; height 430 ft., capacity 1,466,000 million gallons.
Hetton, *t., urb. dist.*, Durham, Eng.; 5 m. N.E. of Durham; coal; p. (1961) *17,463*.
Héverlé, *commune*, central Belgium; mkt. gardens; p. (1962) *16,495*.
Hex, *R.*, Cape Province, Rep. of S. Africa; rises in Lange Berge, flows S.W. to Gr. Berg R. at Worcester; valley gives access to Gr. Karroo and Central African tableland, is used by trunk rly. from Cape Town to Johannesburg.
Hexham, *mkt. t., urb. dist.*, Northumberland, Eng.; on R. Tyne, 20 m. W. of Newcastle; p. (1961) *9,897*.
Heysham, *see* **Morecambe and Heysham.**
Heywood, *t., mun. bor.*, Lancs, Eng.; 3 m. E. Bury; coal, cotton, chemicals; p. (1961) *24,053*.
Hiawassee, *R.*, Tenn., U.S.A.; trib. Tenn. R.
Hibbing, *t.*, Minn., U.S.A.; iron ore; p. (1960) *17,731*.
Hickory, *t.*, N.C., U.S.A.; p. (1960) *19,328*.
Hidalgo, *st.*, Mexico; cap. Pachuca; mng., coffee, sugar, tobacco; a. 8,057 sq. m.; p. (1960) *994,598*.
High Point, *c.*, N.C., U.S.A.; textiles; p. (1960) *62,063*.
High Wycombe, *t., mun. bor.*, Bucks, Eng.; 15 m N.W. of Windsor; furniture, paper mkg.; freeze dry egg processing; p. (1961) *50,301*.
Higham Ferrers, *mkt. t., mun. bor.*, Northants, Eng.; 3 m. E. of Wellingborough; footwear and leather dressing; p. (1961) *3,756*.
Highgate, *residtl. dist.*, London, Eng.; on hill N. of Camden bor.; p. (1961) *15,580*.
Highland, Park, *t.*, Mich., U.S.A.; motor cars; p. (1960) *38,064*.
Highland Park, *bor.*, N.I., U.S.A.; non-metallic sta. of U.S. Bureau of Mines; p. (1960) *11,049*.
Hilden, *t.*, N. Rhine–Westphalia, Germany; S.E. of Düsseldorf; textiles, iron, chemicals; p. (1963) *39,900*.
Hildesheim, *c.*, Lower Saxony, Germany; at foot of Harz Mtns.; cath.; machin., farm implements, textiles, ceramics; p. (1963) *98,800*.
Hilla, *liwa*, Iraq; on R. Euphrates; nr. ancient Babylon; p. (1956) *274,567*.
Hilleröd, *t.*, N.E. Själland, Denmark; agr. implements; p. (1960) *11,605*.
Hillingdon, *outer bor.*, Greater London, Eng.; comprising former urb. dists. of Hayes and Harlington, Ruislip and Northwood, Yiewsley and W. Drayton and mun. bor. of Uxbridge; p. (1964) *227,913*.
Hillside, *t.*, N.J., U.S.A.; engines; speed boats; drugs; lumber; p. (1960) *22,304*.
Hilo, *c.*, Hawaii; nr. lgst. active volcano in the world, Mauna Loa; alt. 13,600 ft.
Hilversum, *t.*, Netherlands; nr. Utrecht; floorcloth factories, wireless equipment; broadcasting sta.; p. (1960) *101,238*.
Himachal Pradesh, *Union terr.*, India; a. 10,885 sq. m.; cap. Simla; p. (1961) *1,351,144*.
Himalayas, *vast chain of mtns.* along N. border of India; 1,600 m. long; highest peak, Mt. Everest, 29,028 ft.
Himeji, *industl. t.*, S. Honshu, Japan; on shore of Inland Sea, 30 m. W. of Kobe; iron and steel ind., heavy engin.; p. (1960) *329,000*.
Hinckley, *mkt. t., urb. dist.*, on border of Leicester and Warwick, Eng.; hosiery, boots, carboard boxes, dye wks., engin.; p. (1961) *41,573*.
Hindenburg, *see* **Zabrze.**
Hindhead, *hilly common and health resort*, Surrey, nr. Haslemere, Eng.
Hindiya Barrage, *dam*, Iraq; across R. Euphrates, 30 m. above Hilla; provides flood control and irrigation in a. between Shatt el Hilla and R. Euphrates.
Hindley, *t., urb. dist.*, Lancs, Eng.; 2 m. S.E. of Wigan; cotton, paint, knitwear, asbestos; p. (1961) *19,395*.
Hindu Kush, *mtn. range*, mainly in N.E. Afghanistan; highest peak Tirich Mir (25,426 ft.) in Chitral dist., W. Pakistan; Salang tunnel (opened 1964) with 2-lane motor highway cuts H.K. at height of 11,000 ft., runs 800 ft. below mtn. top, 1½ m.
Hindustan, former name of part of N. India between Himalayas and Vindhya ranges.
Hinkley Point, Somerset, Eng.; civil nuclear power-sta.
Hinojosa del Duque, *commune*, S. Spain; copper; agr.; textiles; p. (1957) *15,629*.
Hirado, *I.*, off W. cst. Japan; nr. Sasebo; famous for blue and white porcelain.
Hirfanli Dam, project on R. Kizilirmak 90 m. S.E. Ankara, Turkey, 1961. [*51,948*.
Hirosaki, *t.*, Honshu, Japan; lacquer ware; p.
Hiroshima, *spt., c.*, central Honshu, Japan; close to the "Island of Light" with its famous Shinto temple; first city to be destroyed by atomic bomb (6 Aug. 1945); now rebuilt; p. (1960) *431,000*.
Hirschberg, *see* **Jelenia Gora.**
Hispaniola, Greater Antilles, W. Indies; *lge. I.*, divided between the Haiti and Dominican Reps; a. 29,536 sq. m.
Hispar, *glacier*, Karakoram mtns., length 38 m.
Hitchin, *mkt. t., urb. dist.*, Herts, Eng.; in gap through Chiltern Hills, 35 m. N. of London; light engin., tanning, chemicals, distilling; p. (1961) *24,243*. [185 sq. m.
Hjälmaren Lake, Sweden; S.W. of L. Malar; a.
Hjorring, *t.*, Jutland, N. Denmark; biscuit and clothing wks.; p. (1960) *15,038*.
Hlaing (Rangoon), *R.*, Burma; flows to G. of Martaban.
Hobart, *spt., cap.*, Tasmania, Australia; on R. Derwent; univ.; gr. fruit exp.; since, cadmium, superphosphates; p. (1961) *115,887*.
Hobbs, *t.*, N.M., U.S.A.; oilwell area; supply ctr.; p. (1960) *26,275*.

Hoboken, *t.*, Antwerp, Belgium; shipbldg.; refractory metals; p. (estd. 1957) *30,552.*
Hoboken, *c.*, N.J., U.S.A.; lge. ocean commerce; p. (1960) *48,441.*
Hobro, *spt.*, Jutland, Denmark; at W. end of Mariager Fjord; cattle feed factory; p. (1960) *8,208.* [*15,791.*
Höchst, *t.*, Hessen; Germany; on R. Main; p.
Hochstetter, *mtn.*, S.I., N.Z.; in Southern Alps; alt. 11,200 ft.
Hoddesdon, *t.*, *urb. dist.*, Herts, Eng.; in Lea valley, 4 m. S. of Ware; nursery trade, tomatoes, etc.; p. (1961) *17,908.*
Hodeida, *spt.*, Yemen, Arabia; on Red Sea; naval base; p. *50,000.*
Hodmezovarsarhely, *t.*, S.E. Hungary; wheat, fruit, tobacco, cattle; p. (1962) *53,228.*
Hof, *t.*, Bavaria, Germany; on R. Saale; textiles, iron, machin., porcelain, glass, brewing; p. (1963) *56,200.*
Hofei (Hefei), *c.*, *cap.* Anhwei prov., China; rice growing a.; cotton and silk; p. (1953) *184,000.*
Hofman, *mtn. peak* of the Sierra Nevada, California; alt. 8,108 ft. [*100,000.*
Hofuf, *t.*, Hasa, Saudi Arabia; p. (estd. 1956)
Hog's Back, Surrey, Eng.; chalk ridge; alt. 505 ft.
Hohe Tauern, *Alpine range*, Tyrol, Austria; rugged crystalline rocks; highest point, Grau Glockner, alt. 12,461 ft.
Hohenlimburg, *t.*, N. Rhine–Westphalia, Germany; nr. Dortmund; cas.; textiles, iron, steel; p. (1963) *26,800.*
Hohenstein-Ernstal *t.*, Karl-Marx-Stadt, E. Germany; textiles, metal goods; p. (1963) *17,136.*
Hohenzollern, *former prov.*, Germany; Upper Danube; a. 441 sq. m.
Hoihow (Haikou), *c.*, Kwangtung prov., China; comm. ctr.; p. (1953) *135,000.*
Hokitika, *t.*, S.I., N.Z.; on W. cst., 20 m. S. of Greymouth; p. (1961) *3,005.*
Hokkaido, *lge. I.*, Japan, N. of Honshu; a. 34,276 sq. m.; p. (1962) *5,000,000.*
Holbaek, *t.*, Sjaelland, Denmark; W. of Copenhagen; engin. and motor wks.; p. (1960) *15,475.*
Holbeach, *mkt. t.*, S. Lincoln, Eng.; in Fens, 7 m. E. of Spalding; agr., brewing; p. (1948) *5,382.*
Holborn, *see* Camden.
Holderness, *div.*, E.R. Yorks, Eng.; between R. Humber and N. Sea; agr. and pastoral.
Holguin, *t.*, E. Cuba, W. Indies; exp. cattle, maize, tobacco, hardwoods; p. *171,997.*
Holland, *see* Netherlands.
Holland, Parts of, *admin. div.* of Lincoln, Eng.; adjoining the Wash; ch. ts. Boston, Spalding; a. 419 sq. m.; p. (1961) *103,327.*
Holland, *t.*, Mich., U.S.A.; p. (1960) *24,777.*
Holland, N., *prov.*, Netherlands; a. 1,051 sq. m.; p. (1959) *2,054,509.*
Holland, S., *prov.*, Netherlands; a. 1,130 sq. m.; p. (1959) *2,697,894.*
Hollandia, *see* Kota Baru.
Holidaysburg, *bor.*, Penns., U.S.A.; coal, iron ore, limestone; foundries, machine shops; p. (1960) *6,475.*
Holloway, N. dist., Islington bor., London, Eng.
Hollywood, sub. Los Angeles, Cal., U.S.A.; ctr. of film industry.
Holmesdale, Vale of, *geographical sub-region*, Kent, E. Surrey, Eng.; extends along foot of N. Downs escarpment E. from Dorking; drained by Rs. Mole, Darent, Medway, Len, Stour; heavy clay soils; woodland or rich meadowland; dairy farming; some cultivation along N. and S. fringe; ch. ts., Dorking, Reigate, Sevenoaks, Maidstone, Ashford have grown up on gaps through hills to N. and S. of the Vale; length 60 m., average width 1 m.
Holmfirth, *t.*, *urb. dist.*, W.R. Yorks, Eng.; 5 m. S. of Huddersfield; textiles, engin.; p. (1961) *18,391.* [p. *15,915.*
Holroyd, *t.*, N.S.W., Australia; sub. of Sydney,
Holstein, former Danish Duchy, now inc. in Schleswig-Holstein *Land* of Germany.
Holston, *R.*, U.S.A.; head of Tenn. R.; flows through Va. and Tenn.; length 300 m.
Holsworthy, *rural dist.*, *mkt. t.*, N. Devon, Eng.; p. (1961) rural dist. *5,795*; t. *1,619.*
Holt, *t.*, Denbigh, Wales; on R. Dee, 7 m. S. of Chester. [Sheringham.
Holt, *mkt. t.*, N. Norfolk, Eng.; 5. m. S.W. of
Holyhead, *spt.*, *urb. dist.*, Anglesey, Wales; on Holyhead I.; mail packet sta. for Ireland; light engin., woodwkg., clocks; I. is 7½ m. long, width ½ m. to 4 m.; p. (1961) *10,408.*
Holy I., off cst. of Anglesey, Wales.
Holy I., Scot., in F. of Clyde, nr. I. of Arran.
Holy I. (Lindisfarne), off cst. of Northumberland, Eng.
Holyoke, *c.*, Mass., U.S.A.; impt. mftg. ctr., paper, machin.; on Connecticut R.; seat of Mount Holyoke College for women; p. (1960) *52,689.*
Holytown, *t.*, Lanark, Scot.; nr. Glasgow; coal, steel; p. *20,669.*
Holywell, *mkt. t.*, *urb. dist.*, Flint, N. Wales; woollen, rayon and paper inds.; p. (1961) *8,459.*
Holywood, *spt.*, *urb. dist.*, Down, N. Ireland; on S. shore of Belfast Lough; seaside resort; p. (1961) *8,060.*
Holzminden, *t.*, Lower Saxony, Germany; on R. Weser; chemicals, machin., lumber; p. (1963) *22,900.*
Homberg, *t.*, N. Rhine–Westphalia, Germany; on R. Rhine opposite Duisburg; coal-mining, machin., chemicals; p. (estd. 1954) *32,200.*
Homburg, *t.*, Hessen, Germany; spa, cas.; iron, machin., dyes, leatherwk.; p. (1963) *35,500.*
Homburg, *t.*, Saar; univ.; iron, wood, glass, brewing; p. (1963) *31,000.*
Home Counties, term applied to the counties adjoining London, *i.e.*, Middlesex, Surrey, Essex, and Kent; sometimes Hertfordshire, Buckinghamshire, and Berkshire are included, and occasionally Sussex.
Homestead, *bor.*, Penns., U.S.A.; ironwks.; p. (1960) *7,562.*
Homs, *t.*, W. Syria; on R. Orontes; ancient Emesa; silk, textiles, cement; p. (1961) *164,362.*
Honan (Henan), *fertile prov.*, N.E. China; traversed by Yellow R.; cap. Kaifeng; cereals, coal; a. 64,545 sq. m.; p. (estd. 1957) *48,670,000.*
Honda, *t.*, Tolima dep., Colombia; coffee; p. (estd. 1959) *21,000.*
Honduras, *rep.*, Central America; mtnous.; bananas, coconuts, coffee, hardwoods; panama hat mkg.; silver and lead mng.; cap. Tegucigalpa; a. 43,227 sq. m.; p. (1961) *1,883,360.*
Honduras, British, *see* British Honduras.
Honesdale, *bor.*, Penns., U.S.A.; coal, textiles, shoes, glass; p. (1960) *5,569.*
Honfleur, *spt.*, Caen, France; fine harbour; p. (1954) *8,661.*
Hong Kong, *Brit. I.* and *Crown Col.*, China; at mouth of R. Canton; inc. peninsula of Kowloon and Is.; cap. c. Victoria; total a. 398 sq. m.; univ.; military and sm. naval base; engin., textiles (50 per cent of total exports), shipbldg.; p. (estd. 1965) *3,692,000.*
Honiton, *mkt t.*, *mun. bor.*, E. Devon, Eng.; on R. Otter, 16 m. E. of Exeter; trout fishing; p. (1961) *4,724.*
Honolulu, *c.*, *cap.*, Hawaiian Is.; on the I. of Oahu; gd. harbour, fruit, canning, sugar; p. (1960) *294,179.*
Honshu, *lgst. I.* of Japan; oil; a. 88,919 sq. m.
Hood Mt., highest peak Cascade range, Ore., U.S.A.; alt. 11,225 ft.
Hoogeven, *t.*, Drenthe, Netherlands; p. (1960) *25,192.*
Hooghli or Hughli, *R.*, W. branch of R. Ganges, India; flows into Bay of Bengal; Calcutta on its banks.
Hook of Holland, *spt.*, Netherlands; packet sta. with steamer connections to Harwich, Eng.
Hooker Mt., Rockies, Brit. Columbia, Canada.
Hoole, *t.*, *urb. dist.*, Cheshire, Eng.; 2 m. N.E. of Chester; mnfs.; p. (1951) *9,054.*
Hoopstad, *t.*, Orange Free State, S. Africa; on Vet R.
Hoorn, *old fishing t.*, N. Holland, Netherlands; on Ysselmeer, 20 m. N. of Amsterdam; cheese and cattle mkts.; birthplace Tasman, discoverer of Tasmania and New Zealand, founder of Batavia; p. (1948) *12,770.*
Hoosack, *mtns.*, part of Green Mtn. range, Mass. U.S.A.
Hoosick Falls, *t.*, N.Y., U.S.A.; paper, elec goods; agr. implements; p. (1960) *4,023.*
Hopedale, *t.*, Labrador cst., Newfoundland Canada.
Hopeh (Hebei), *prov.*, N.E. China; cap. Tientsin cereals, cotton, iron ore; a. *c.* 75,000 sq. m.; p. (estd. 1957) *44,720,000.*
Hopetown, *t.*, Cape Province, S. Africa; on Orange R.; p. (1960) *2,631.*

Hopewell, *t.*, Va., U.S.A.; synthetic textiles, chemicals, pottery; p. (1960) *17,895.*
Hopkinsville, *c.*, Ky., U.S.A.; p. (1960) *19,465.*
Hoquiam, *spt.*, Wash., U.S.A.; lumber, salmon, tuna fishing, oysters, canning; p. (1960) *10,762.*
Hor Mt., Arabia Petrea between Dead S. and G. of Akaba; alt. 4,360 ft.
Horbury, *urb. dist.*, W.R. Yorks, Eng.; nr. Wakefield; p (1961) *8,642.*
Hordaland, *dist.*, Norway; a. 6,043 sq. m.; ch. t. Bergen; p. (1963) *230,937.*
Horde, *t.*, Germany; nr. Dortmund; coal, iron, steel; p. *35,000.*
Horeb, *mtn.*, Arabia (*see* **Sinai**).
Horley, *sm. t.*, Surrey, Eng.; on R. Mole, 7 m. S.E. of Dorking.
Hormuz, *I.*, off S. cst. of Iran and nr. Qishm I.; in Hormuz Strait.
Horn, C., most S. point of S. America; noted for severe gales encountered there.
Horn (North C.), N. point of Iceland.
Horncastle, *mkt. t.*, *urb. dist.*, Lindsey, Lincoln, Eng.; at confluence of Rs. Bain and Waring at foot of Lincoln Wolds; impt. cattle fairs, malting, corn, horse fairs; p. (1961) *3,768.*
Hornchurch, *former urb. dist.*, Essex, Eng.; nr. Romford; residtl.; general engin.; now inc. in Havering bor., Greater London; p. (1961) *131,014.*
Hornell, *c.*, N.Y., U.S.A.; rly. car wks.; p. (1960). [*13,907.*
Hornsea, *t.*, *urb. dist.*, E.R. Yorks, Eng.; on E. cst.. 13 m. N.E. of Hull; seaside resort; p. (1961) *5,949.*
Hornsey, *see* **Haringey.**
Horsens, *spt.*, Jutland, Denmark; brewing, diesel engines, weaving, elec. goods; p. (1960) *37,261.*
Horsforth, *t.*, *urb. dist.*, W.R. Yorks, Eng.; in Aire valley 4 m. N.W. of Leeds; cloth, tanning, light engin.; p. (1961) *15,351.*
Horsham, *t.*, *urb. dist.*, W. Sussex, Eng.; on R. Arun at W. end of forested dist. of the High Weald; agr., timber, engin., and chemicals; p. (1961) *21,155.*
Horsham, *t.*, Victoria, Australia; on R. Wimmera; pastoral, dairying and agr. dist.; p. (1961) *9,243.*
Horta, *ch. spt.*, Fayal I., Azores, Atl. Oc.; cap. of dist.; fruit, wine, winter resort; p. of dist. (1960) *49,735.*
Horten, *spt.*, Norway; nr. Oslo; naval base; shipbldg., mftg. inds.; p. (1960) *13,289.*
Horton, *R.*, N.W. Terr., Canada; flows into Arctic Ocean.
Horwich, *t.*, *urb. dist.*, S. Lancs, Eng.; on W. edge of Rossendale Fells, 4 m. N.W. of Bolton; bleaching and cotton spinning, calico printing, paper, coal, stone; p. (1961) *16,067.*
Hoshangabad, *t.*, Madhya Pradesh, India; on Narbada R.; p. (1961) *19,284.*
Hoshiarpur, *t.*, Punjab, India; lacquer wks., inlaid goods; p. (1961) *50,739.*
Hospitalet, *t.*, Spain; p. (1959) *111,013.*
Hot Springs, *c.*, Ark., U.S.A.; health resort; p. (1960) *28,337.*
Houdeng-Goegnies, *commune*, S.W. Belgium; coal, smelting, glasswks.; p. (1962) *8,769.*
Houghton-le-Spring, *t.*, *urb. dist.*, Durham, Eng.; 5 m. S.W. of Sunderland; coal; p. (1961) *31,049.*
Houilles, *t.*, Seine-et-Oise, France; p. (1954) *22,974.*
Hounslow, *outer bor.*, Greater London, Eng.; inc. former bors. of Brentford and Chiswick, Heston and Isleworth, Feltham and Hounslow; p. (1964) *208,770.*
Housatonic, *R.*, Conn. and Mass., U.S.A.; empties into Long Island Sound; length 150 m.
Houston, *c.*, *spt.*, Texas, U.S.A.; on Buffalo Bay; rly. ctr., canal to est., oil refineries, machin.; meat pkg., steel, chemicals, cotton; p. (1960) *938,219.*
Houston Ship Canal, Texas, U.S.A.; links Houston to head of shallow Galveston Bay and continues through bay to deep water; provides site for heavy inds., cement, paper, fertilisers, oil-refining, etc.; opened 1915; total length 45 m.
Hove, *t.*, *mun. bor.*, E. Sussex, Eng.; on S. cst., continuous with Brighton; residtl; holiday resort; p. (1961) *72,843.*
Howe, *C.*, Victoria; S.E. extremity of Australia.
Howell, *t.*, S.E. Mich., U.S.A.; dairy prod.; p. (1960) *4,861.*
Howrah, *c.*, W. Bengal, India; faces Calcutta across Hooghli R.; jute, cotton, shipbldg.; p. (1961) t. *512,598*, dist. *2,038,477.*
Howth, *hill*, nr. Dublin; alt. 563 ft.
Hoy, *I.*, Orkneys, Scot.
Hoylake, *t.*, *urb. dist.*, Cheshire, Eng.; on N. cst. of Wirral peninsula; residtl.; p. (1961) *32,268.*
Hoyland Nether, *urb. dist.*, W.R. Yorks, Eng.; p. (1961) *15,707.*
Hradec Králové, *t.*, ČSSR.; p. (1961) *55,147.*
Hron, *R.*, ČSSR.; trib. of R. Danube.
Huacho, *spt.*, Peru, S. America; pt. for cotton and sugar, cottonseed oil; p. (1963) *27,219.*
Huancavelica, *dep.*, Central Peru; a. 8,297 sq. m.; cap. H.; p. (1961) *298,892.*
Huancayo, *cap.*, Junin, Peru; woollen mills, artificial silk; p. (1961) *20,000.*
Huanuco, *dep.*, Central Peru; a. 15,426 sq. m.; ch. t. Huanco; p. (1961) *339,888.*
Huaras, *ch. t.*, Ancash, Peru; mineral springs, copper, silver, coal; p. (1961) *11,628.*
Huasco, *spt.*, Atacama, Chile; exp. copper, silver, gold, cattle; p. *2,311.*
Hubli, *t.*, Mysore, India; E. of Goa; cotton, silk-weaving; p. (1961) *171,326.*
Hucknall, *industl. t.*, *urb. dist.*, Nottingham, Eng.; 5 m. N. of Nottingham; hosiery, coal; p. (1961) *23,246.*
Huddersfield, *mftg. t.*, *co. bor.*, W.R. Yorks, Eng.; on edge of Pennines, 10 m. S. of Bradford; wool, textiles, chemicals, engin.; p. (1961) *130,302.*
Hudiksvall, *spt.*, Sweden; on inlet of G. of Bothnia; salting and engin. wks., sawmills; p. (1961) *11,979.*
Hudson, *t.*, N.Y., U.S.A.; cement, textiles, machin.; p. (1960) *11,075.*
Hudson, *R.*, N.Y., U.S.A.; flows from the Adirondacks to New York Harbour; with valley of Mohawk R. makes gr. highway of tr. between Gr. Lakes and New York; length 350 m.
Hudson Bay, *inland sea*, Canada; communicating by Hudson's Strait (400 m. long) with Davis Strait; salmon, cod; a. 540,000 sq. m.
Hué, *c.*, S. Viet-Nam; nr. mth. of Hué R.; royal palace; glass factories; impt. tr.; p. (1960) *103,870.*
Huelva, *maritime prov.*, S.W. Spain; copper-mining, vine and olive growing, stock-raising, fisheries, brandy distillery, etc.; a. 3,906 sq. m.; p. (1959) *403,090.*
Huelva, *spt.*, cap. Huelva, Spain; on G. of Cadiz; oil refinery projected; p. (1959) *76,845.*
Huercal Overa, *t.*, Almeria, S.E. Spain; silver-, lead- and copper-mining; p. (1957) *13,968.*
Huesca, *frontier prov.*, N.E. Spain; mtnous.; forested; a. 5,849 sq. m.; p. (1959) *242,332.*
Huesca, *t.*, *cap.*, Huesca prov., Spain; on R. Isuela; cath.; gr. wine and timber tr. with France, pottery, leather, cereals; p. (1957) *25,500.*
Hugh Town, *cap.*, St. Mary's I. Scilly Isles.
Huhehot, *c.*, Inner Mongolia; China; p. (1953) *148,000.*
Huila, *dep.*, Colombia, S. America; a. 7,990 sq. m.; cap. Neiva; p. (estd. 1959) *353,090.*
Huizen, *commune*, W. Netherlands; radio sta.; fishing; p. *7,500.*
Hulan, *t.*, N. China; 20 m. N. of Harbin; tr. ctr.; on Harbin-Aigun rly.
Hull or Kingston-upon-Hull, *spt.*, *co. bor.*, E.R. Yorks, Eng.; third pt. of U.K.; at influx of R. Hull, in estuary of the Humber; univ.; impt. mnfs. and gr. shipping tr.; docks, fishing, ship repairing, rope, machin., chemicals, tanning, veg. oils, flour milling, seed crushing, paint, cement; p. (1961) *303,268.*
Hull, *c.*, Quebec, Canada; faces Ottawa across R. Ottawa; sawmills, paper; p. (1961) *56,929.*
Humber, *estuary* of Rs. Ouse and Trent, separating Yorks and Lincoln, Eng.; fine waterway; 1–7 m. wide, length 38 m.
Humboldt Bay, *inlet*, Cal., U.S.A.; nuclear experimental breeder reactor.
Humboldt, *mtn. range*, E. Nevada, U.S.A.
Humboldt Current, *see* **Peru Current.**
Hume Reservoir, *artificial lake*, N.S.W., Australia; formed by dam where R. Murray leaves Gr. Dividing Range, just below confluence with R. Mitta Mitta; supplies water for irrigation in upper Riverina dist.; approx. capacity 4,000 million cu. ft.
Hunan, *inland prov.*, China; coal, zinc, tea, wheat, rice, tung oil; cap. Changsha; a. 79,378 sq. m.; p. (1953) *33,226,954.*
Hungary, *rep.*, Central Europe; ch. physical features; central plain of treeless steppes; R. Danube, R. Tisza, Carpathian mtns., L.

Balaton; hot and dry summer, rainfall moderate; race, Magyar; agr., wheat, maize, potatoes, sugar-beet, horse-breeding, cattle, sheep, pigs; coal, lignite, bauxite; milling, brewing, sugar; communications good; cap. Budapest; a. 35,912 sq. m.; p. (1960) *9,977,870*.
Hungerford, *mkt. t., rural dist.*, Berks, Eng.; on R. Kennet, p. (rural dist. 1951) *9,411*.
Hunmanby, *t.*, E.R. Yorks, Eng.; S. of Scarborough; bricks and tiles.
Hunsrück, *mtn. a.*, Rhineland-Palatinate, Germany; highest point, 2,677 ft.
Hunstanton, *urb. dist.*, Norfolk, Eng.; S.E. shore of Wash; seaside resort; p. (1961) *4,843*.
Hunter, *R.*, N.S.W., Australia; rises in Liverpool Range, Gr. Dividing Range, flows S. and E. into Tasman Sea at Newcastle; valley of Hunter and ch. trib. Goulburn lead from Newcastle up to Cassilis Gate through Gr. Dividing Range to interior; length, approx. 250 m.
Hunterston, Ayrshire, Scot.; civil nuclear power station.
Huntingdon and Peterborough, *inland co.*, Eng; mkt. gardening, fruit-growing, agr.; p. (estd. 1965) *170,180*.
Huntingdon, *co. t., mun. bor.*, Hunts, Eng.; on R. Ouse, 6 m. above St. Ives; birthplace of Oliver Cromwell; canning, engin., processed rubber, confectionery; p. (1961) *8,812*.
Huntington, *t.*, Ind., U.S.A.; on Little R.; rly. and wool wks.; p. (1960) *16,185*.
Huntington, *c.*, W. Va., U.S.A.; on Ohio R.; machine wks., lumbering; p. (1960) *83,627*.
Huntly, *mkt. burgh*, Aberdeen, Scot.; at confluence of Rs. Bogie and Deveron; farming, woollens; p. (1961) *3,952*.
Huntly, *t.*, N.I., N.Z.; on Waikato R.; 65 m. S. of Auckland; coal; p. (1961) *4,617*.
Huntsville, *t.*, Ala., U.S.A.; cotton-mills; p. (1960) *72,365*.
Huon, *I.*, 170 m. N. of and *dep.* of New Caledonia, Pacific; very barren group.
Hupeh (Hubei), *prov.*, China; N. of the Yangtze-Kiang; cap Wuhan; tea, cotton, wheat, coal, paper; a. 71,955 sq. m.; p. (1953) *27,789,693*.
Hurlford and Crookedholme, *ts.*, Ayr, Scot.; nr. Kilmarnock; iron, fireclay, worsteds, coal-mng.
Huron, *L.*, between Canada and U.S.A.; one of the Gr. Lakes of the St. Lawrence basin; a. 23,610 sq. m.; 280 m. long.
Huron, *t.*, S.D., U.S.A.; meat prod.; p. (1960) *14,180*.
Hurstville, *sub.*, S. of Sydney, N.S.W., Australia; p. *22,667*.
Hürth, *t.*, N. Rhine–Westphalia, Germany; S.W. of Cologne; lignite-mining, machin., chemicals; impt. elec. power sta.; p. (1963) *47,500*.
Husi, *mftg. t.*, Romania; tobacco, wine; p. (1956) *18,155*.
Huskvarna, *t.*, Sweden; S. extremity of L. Vättern; lt. inds.; p. (1961) *13,763*.
Husum, *spt.*, Schleswig-Holstein, Germany; rly. junction; p. (1963) *24,600*.
Hutchinson, *c.*, Kan., U.S.A.; p. (1960) *37,574*.
Hutt, *urb. a.*, N.I., N.Z.; p. (1961) *98,991*.
Huy, *t.*, Belgium; on R. Meuse; nr. Liége; vine-growing dist.; p. (1962) *13,493*.
Huyton with Roby, *urb. dist.*, Lancs, Eng.; sub. of Liverpool; p. (1961) *63,041*.
Hwai Ho (Huai Ho), *R.*, N. China; rises in Tungpeh Shan, flows E. between N. China plain and lower Yangtze; subject to disastrous floods and changes of course; since 1950 flood control and irrigation canal to sea.
Hwainan (Huainan), *c.*, Anhwei prov., China; impt. coalfield; p. (1953) *287,000*.
Hwang Hai (Yellow Sea), arm of the Pac. Oc. between Korea and China; branches into the Gs. of Pohai and Liaotung; greatest width 400 m., length 600 m.
Hwang Ho (Yellow R.), China; rises nr. source of Yangtze-Kiang, Tibet, flows through N.W. China into G. of Pohai; l. 2,600 m.
Hwangshih (Huangshi), *c.*, Hupeh prov., China; cement and lime wks.; p. (1953) *111,000*.
Hyde, *industl. mkt. t., mun. bor.*, Cheshire, Eng.; on R. Tame, 5 m. S.E. of Manchester; textiles, clothing, engin., leathercloth, rubber, paper prod.; p. (1961) *31,710*.
Hyderabad, *dist.*, Andhra Pradesh, India; rice, cotton, wheat; a. 1,957 sq. m.; p. (1961) *2,062,995*.
Hyderabad, *ch. t.*, of Andhra Pradesh, India; on R. Musi; walled t. and impt. comm. ctr.; univ.; p. (1961) *1,251,119*.
Hyderabad, *t.*, W. Pakistan; on R. Indus; arsenal; univ.; silks, gold and silver wk., pottery, cement; heavy elec. plant; p. (1961) *434,537*.
Hyderabad, *dist.*, W. Pakistan; p. (1961) *2,342,000*.
Hydra, *I.*, Greece; off Morea: a. 26 sq. m.; p. *3,693*.
Hyères, *winter health resort*, Var, France; vines, oranges, flowers, fruit; p. (1954) *29,061*.
Hyères, Iles d', *sm. archipelago of Is.*, off French Riviera cst.
Hythe, nr. Southampton, Hants., Eng.; synthetic rubber plant.
Hythe, *t., mun. bor.*, Kent, Eng.; on S. cst., 3 m. W. of Folkestone; one of the Cinque Ports; Royal school of musketry; p. (1961) *10,026*.

I

Iasi, *see* Jassy.
Iba, *spt., mun.*, cap. of Zambales prov., Luzon, Philippine Is.; uranium, lumbering; p. *8,299*.
Ibadan, *t.*, cap. Western prov., Nigeria; 60 m. N. of Lagos; silk, tobacco, cotton; univ.; p. *600,000*.
Ibagué, *cap.*, Tolima, Colombia, S. America; cotton, tobacco, sugar, leather gds.; p, (estd. 1959) *133,380*.
Ibarra, *t.*, Ecuador, S. America; at foot of Volcano of Imbabura; p. (1962) *14,031*.
Iberian Peninsula, S.W. peninsula of Europe; containing sts. of Spain and Portugal; derived from the Iberian people who lived along the R. Ebro (Iberus); a. 229,054 sq. m.; p. *35,470,953*.
Iberville, *t.*, Quebec, Canada; lt. engin.; p. (1961) *7,588*.
Ibicui, *t.*, S. Paraguay; iron ore; p. *14,350*.
Ica, *cst. dep.*, Peru; cap. Ica; a. 9,796 sq. m.; p. (1961) *243,617*.
Iceland, *I.*, N. Atl. Oc.; 130 m. E. Greenland; independent rep.; barren and mtnous., with ice-covered plateaus and volcanoes; glacier fields cover 5,000 sq. m.; highest peak, Oraëfa Jökull, alt. 6,950 ft.; main ind. fishing; cap. Reykjavik; a. 39,709 sq. m.; p. (1962) *183, 478*.
Ichang, *pt.*, Hupeh, China; on Yangtze-Kiang; cotton, rice, oil; large tr.; p. *107,940*.
Ichinomiya, *t.*, S.E. Honshu, Japan; ancient Shinto shrine; textiles, pottery; p. (1960) *182,984*.
Ichow, *c.*, Shantung, China; at foot of Shantung highlands, 80 m. N.E. of Tungshan (Suchow); silk ind.; p. (estd.) *100,000*.
Icknield Way, *ancient highway* in S. Eng.; from nr. Bury St. Edmunds, through Wantage to Cirencester and Gloucester.
Icod, *commune*, N.W. Tenerife, Canary Is.; agr., silk; p. *13,263*.
Ida, *mtn.*, Central Crete, Greece; famous in Greek mythology; 8,058 ft.
Idaho, *mtn. st.*, U.S.A.; part of Rocky Mtns. in st.; rich mineral region; cap. Boise City; a. 83,557 sq. m.; p. (1960) *622,856*.
Idaho Falls, *t.*, Idaho, U.S.A.; food processing, lumbering; silver, lead, and gold mines near by; nuclear experimental breeder reactor; p. (1960) *33,161*.
Idar-Obestein, *t.*, Rhineland-Palatinate, Germany; gem cutting, jewellery; p. (1963) *30,400*.
Idle, *mftg. t.*, W.R. Yorks, Eng.; in Aire valley, 3 m. N. of Bradford; woollens, motor cars; p. *7,900*.
Idle, *R.*, Notts, Eng.; trib. to R. Trent.
Idrija, *t.*, N.W. Jugoslavia; ancient cas.; mercury mines; cinnabar; p. *10,317*.
Ifni, *Span. overseas prov.*, enclave S. Morocco; cap Sidi Ifni; a. 700 sq. m.; p. (1963) *54,000*.
Igarka, *sm. t.*, Siberia, R.S.F.S.R.; on R. Yenesei 400 m. from its mouth; graphite plant, nickel mines, lumber-mills; p. (1956) *15,200*.
Iglesias, *t.*, Sardinia, Italy; N.W. of Cagliara cath.; p. *23,575*.
Igualada, *t.*, Barcelona, Spain; leather, textiles ctr. of wine-producing dist.; p. (1957) *16,945*.
Iguassu, *R.* S. Brazil; famous falls.
Iisalmi, *t.*, Finland; E. of Kokkola; p. (1961 [6,136
Ijmuiden, *t.*, W. Netherlands; on cst. at mouth o N. Sea Canal; fishing; gasification plant, steel mill; p. (1960) *112,556*.
Ijsselmeer (Lake Ijssel), Netherlands; shallow expanse of water, formerly Zuider Zee; sepa

rated from N. Sea by Wierengen–Friesland Barrage (length 19 m.) constructed 1932; active land reclamation in progress, lgst. a. being Northeast Polder (185 sq. m.); chief c. on inlet (Ij) is Amsterdam; when reclamation complete, water a. will be reduced to 408 sq. m.
Ilagan, *cap.*, Isabela prov., Luzon, Philippines; tobacco; p. *23,000*. [Yeovil.
Ilchester, *t.*, Somerset, Eng.; on R. Yeo; N.W. of
Iletsk, *t.*, Kazakh. S.S.R., on R. Ilek, trib. of R. Ural; S. of Chkalov; rock salt; p. *13,010*.
Ilford, *former mun. bor.*, Essex, Eng.; E. sub. of London on R. Roding; bordering on Hainault Forest, now inc. in Redbridge Outer London bor. (*q.v.*); paper-mills, elec. and radio equipment, films and photoplate wks.; p. (1961) *178,024*.
Ilfracombe, *t.*, *urb. dist.*, N. Devon, Eng.; on cst. of Bristol Channel; seaside resort; p. (1961) *8,701*.
Ilhavo, *spt.*, Beira Litoral, Portugal; glass, porcelain, fisheries; p. *16,335*.
Ilhéus, *spt.*, Baia, Brazil; exp. cacao, timber; p. (1960) *46,000*.
Ili, *R.*, Central Asia; rises in Tien Shan and flows into L. Balkhash; length 850 m.
Ilia (Elis), *prefecture*, S. Greece; cap. Pyrgos; p. (1951) *188,274*.
Ilion, *t.*, N.Y., U.S.A.; firearms; office equipment; p. (1960) *10,199*.
Ilkeston, *t.*, *mun. bor.*, Derby, Eng.; 7½ m. W. of Nottingham; coal, iron, engin., locknit fabrics, needles, plastics; p. (1961) *34,672*.
Ilkley, *t.*, *urb. dist.*, *spa*, W.R. Yorks, Eng.; on R. Wharfe 15 m. N.W. of Leeds; local mkt.; p. (1961) *18,519*.
Ill, *R.*, E. France; rises in Jura Mtns., flows N. through Mulhouse, Colmar, Strasbourg, enters Rhine 12 m. below Strasbourg; length 135 m.
Illawara, *dist.*, N.S.W., Australia; forming belt of land between S. tableland and cst.; very fertile; dairy farming; coal seams; ch. ts., Kiama, Wollongong, Bulli, Geringong.
Ille-et-Vilaine, *dep.*, N.W. France; on English Channel; a. 2,699 sq. m.; agr.; cap. Rennes; p. (1962) *614,268*.
Illimani, Mt., nr. La Paz, Bolivia; 21,184 ft.
Illinois, *st.*, U.S.A.; named after its principal R.; a large trib. (360 m.) of Mississippi R.; cap. Springfield; lgst. t. Chicago; iron and steel, coal and oil; agr.; a. 56,400 sq. m.; p. (1960) *10,081,158*.
Illogan, *vil.*, Cornwall, Eng.; N.W. of Redruth; tin, copper; p. (par.) *8,300*.
Illyria, *region*, mainly Jugoslavia, stretching along Adriatic Sea from Trieste in N. to Albania in the S. and inland as far as Rs. Danube and Morava. [fisheries.
Ilmen, *L.*, S. of Novgorod, Russia; a. 360 sq. m.;
Ilmenau, *t.*, Suhl, E. Germany; at N. base of Thüringer Wald, S.S.E. of Gotha; porcelain, toys, glass; p. (1963) *19,115*.
Ilminster, *t.*, *urb. dist.*, Somerset, Eng.; 10 m. S.E. of Taunton; cutstone, concrete, collars, radio valves; p. (1961) *2,784*.
Ilobasco, *c.*, Salvador, Central America; cattle, coffee, sugar, indigo; p. *21,225*.
Iloilo, *cap.*, prov of Iloilo, Panay, Philippines; coconut oil; p. (1960) *151,266*.
Ilorin, *t.*, N. Nigeria, W. Africa; on Lagos–Kano rly.; agr. and caravan ctr.; govt. sugar growing scheme at Bacita; p. *54,686*.
Ilsley, *t.*, Berks, Eng.; 11 m. S. of Abingdon; sheep mkts. and fair. [of Sydney.
Iluka, *spt.*, N.S.W., Australia; on Clarence R., N.
Imabari, *t.*, *spt.*, N.W. Shikoku, Japan; on shore of Inland Sea; mnfs. cotton textiles, paper, canned fruits; p. (1960) *100,082*.
Imbabura, *prov.*, Ecuador; a. 2,414 sq. m.; cap. Ibarra; p. (1960) *182,700*.
Imbros, *Turkish I.*, Ægean Sea; fertile fruit-growing dist.
Immingham, *pt.*, Lindsey, Lincoln, Eng.; on S. cst. of Humber, 8 m. N.W. of Grimsby; lge. docks; new dry dock; chemicals, engin..
Imola, *t.*, Italy; S.E. of Bologna; cath.; glass, pottery; p. (1961) *51,289*.
Imperial Valley, S. Cal., U.S.A.; extends 30 m. S.E. from Salton Sea to Mexican bdy.; mainly below sea-level; hot, arid climate; cotton, dates, wheat under irrigation; water brought from Colorado R. by Imperial Canal (Laguna Dam) and All-American Canal (Imperial Dam) nr. Yuma; total irrigated a. (1938) 700 sq. m.
Imphal, *ch. t.*, Manipur, India; p. (1961) *67,717*.
Inari L., *extensive L.*, Lappi, Finland; outlet into Barents Sea; a. 685 sq. m.
Inca, *t.*, I. of Majorca, Spain; p. (1957) *12,522*.
Ince-in-Makerfield, *urb. dist.*, Lancs., Eng.; nr. Wigan; coal, cotton, engin., wagon-bldg.; p. (1961) *18,027*.
Inchgarvie, *islet*, F. of Forth, Scot.; forms central support of the Forth rail bridge.
Inchkeith, *fortfd. I.*, F. of Forth, Fife, Scot.
Inchon, *spt.*, S. Korea; on W. cst.; exp. soya beans, rice; p. (1962) *430,000*.
Indan, *mun.*, Luzon, Philippine Is.; rice; p. *11,240*.
Independence, *t.*, Mo., U.S.A.; on prairie, S. of Missouri R.; p. (1960) *62,328*.
Independence, *t.*, Iowa, U.S.A.; p. (1960) *7,069*.
Independence, *t.*, Kan., U.S.A.; p. (1960) *11,222*.
India, *peninsula subcontinent*, Asia; now subdivided into the Dominion of the Union of India, the Dominion of Pakistan, the Dominion of Ceylon; ch. mtns.: Himalayas (Everest 29,028 ft.), E. and W. Ghats, Sulaimain range, Hindu Kush, Karakoram; Ganges Plain, Thar desert; ch. Rs.: Indus, Ganges, Brahmaputra; climate: monsoonal; vegetation: dense forests in region of high rainfall; sal, teak; elsewhere savannah or jungle, bamboo; coconuts on cst.; variety of races; inds.: agr., rice, wheat, millet, sugar-cane, cotton, jute, tea, rubber, linseed, cattle, sheep, goats; forests, timber; minerals: coal, petroleum, manganese, lead, gold, silver; mnfs.: cottons, jute, milling, engin., machin., brass, carpets; communications: good rail and sea; total a. 1,606,742 sq. m.; total p. (1961) approx. *542,851,695*.
India, Republic of (Indian Union), *indep. sov. st.* within Br. Commonwealth (1947), consists of 16 states and 9 centrally adm. terrs.; cap. New Delhi; mainly agr.; prin. expts. tea, cottons, fabrics, raw cotton, leather, fruits, nuts, iron and other metal ores; a. 1,178,995 sq. m.; p. (1961) *439,235,082*.
India, French, possessions of France in India were the four settlements, Karikal, Mahé, Pondicherry, and Yanaon; now integrated in India.
India, Portuguese, consisted of Goa, Angediva São Jorge and Morcegos Is., on Malabar cst.; Daman (*Port.* Damão), Dadarā and Nagar-Aveli on G. of Cambay, and Diu with Gogola and Simbor on S. cst. of Bombay; became part of India 14 March 1962, known as Union Terr. of Goa, Daman and Diu. [Inlet, Canada.
Indian Harbour, Labrador cst., nr. Hamilton
Indian Ocean extends from S. of Asia and E. of Africa to the C. of Good Hope and C. Leeuwin in Australia, separated from the Pacific by the Malay Archipelago and Australia; a. 29,340,000 sq. m.
Indian Territory, since 1907 part of the st. of Okla., U.S.A.; Indian reservations have an a. of 5 sq. m.
Indiana, *st.*, between Kentucky and Michigan, Illinois and Ohio, U.S.A.; agr., coal, limestone, clay, petroleum, cement, glass; cap. Indianapolis; a. 36,291 sq. m.; p. (1960) *4,662,498*.
Indianapolis, *cap.*, Ind., U.S.A.; on White R.; impt. rly. ctr.; meat packing, jet engines, aircraft parts, chemicals, pharmaceutics; p. (1960) *476,258*.
Indigirka R., Yakut, U.S.S.R.; flows into Laptev Sea; length 1,100 m.
Indo-China, S.E. Asia; federation in French Union until end of hostilities July 1954. Consisted of the three sts. of Viet-Nam, Cambodia and Laos.
Indonesia, Republic of, S.E. Asia (comprising Java, Sumatra, Kalimantan, Sulawesi, West Irian, 15 minor Is., thousands of smaller ones); climate: tropical, abundant rainfall; equatorial forest; race: Malay; agr.: rice, maize, sweet potatoes, sugar-cane, coffee, tea, tobacoo, oil palms, cinchona, spices, rubber; petroleum, tin, coal, bauxite; mineral wealth; cap. Djakarta (Batavia); p. (1961) *97,085,348*.
Indore, *t.*, Madhya Pradesh, Indian Union; in valley of R. Narbada; cotton-mills; p. (1961) *394,941*.
Indre, *dep.*, Central France; agr. and industl.; cap. Châteauroux; a. 2,666 sq. m.; p. (1962) *251,432*.

Indre-et-Loire, *dep.*, Central France; to the N.W. of Indre; agr., vines, silk factories; cap. Tours; a. 2,377 sq. m.; p. (1962) *395,210*.

Indus, *R.*, W. Pakistan; rises in Tibet, and flows through Kashmir, Punjab, Sind, to the Arabian Sea; length 1,800 m.

Inebolu, *spt.*, Anatolia, Turkey; on cst. of Black Sea; tr. in mohair and wool; p. (1960) *5,886*.

Infanta, *mun.*, Luzon, Philippine Is.; p. *20,331*.

Ingersoll, *t.*, Ontario, Canada; N.E. of Hamilton; p. (1961) *6,874*.

Ingleborough, *mtn.*, near Settle, Yorks, Eng.; limestone; underground caves, stalactites, stalagmites; alt. 2,373 ft.

Inglewood, *c.*, S.W. Cal., U.S.A.; chinchilla farms; furniture; light engin.; p. (1960) *63,390*.

Ingolstadt, *t.*, Bavaria, Germany; on Danube, nr. Munich; cas.; machin., cars, tobacco, oil refining; p. (1963) *64,600*.

Inhambane, *spt.*, Mozambique; sugar, copra, oil-seeds, bricks, soap, tiles; p. (1960) *67,265*.

Inishmore, *lgst. of Aran Is.*, Galway, Ireland; 30 m. S.W. of Galway; fishing; p. *1,800*.

Inkerman, *t.*, Crimea, U.S.S.R.; nr. E. extremity of Sevastopol harbour; battle 1854.

Inkpen Beacon, *hill*, Berks., Eng.; W. end of N. Downs, 7 m. S.W. of Newbury; highest point reached by chalk hills in Eng.; alt. 975 ft.

Inkster, *t.*, S.E. Mich., U.S.A.; residtl.; p. (1960) *39,097*.

Inland Sea, Japan; length 250 m., breadth 10–40 m.; ch. spts.: Hiroshima, Okayama, Kobe.

Inn, *R.*, traversing Switzerland, the Austrian Tyrol and Bavaria; enters R. Danube at Passau; the ancient Œnus; length 320 m.

Innerleithen, *burgh and health resort*, Peebles, Scot.; on R. Tweed, 5 m. S.E. of Peebles; woollen cloth and knitwear; p. (1961) *2,299*.

Inner Mongolia, *aut. region*, N. China; stretches along S. border of Mongolian People's Rep.; cap. Huhehot; p. (1957) *9,200,000*.

Innisfail, *t.*, Queensland, Australia; ch. sugar-producing ctr. of Australia; p. *4,000*.

Innsbruck, *cap.*, the Tyrol, Austria; on R. Inn; commands N. approach to Brenner Pass; univ.; military stronghold; p. (1961) *100,695*.

Inowroclaw, *t.*, N. Poland; nr. Bydgoszcz; rock-salt, iron pyrites; agr. prod.; p. (1960) *47,000*.

Insein, *dist.*, Lower Burma; a. 1,914 sq. m.; p. *331,145*; *cap.* I.; p. *20,487*.

Insterburg, *see* **Tchernjachowsk.**

Interlaken, *t.*, Bernese Oberland, Berne, Switzerland; on R. Aar, between Ls. Thun and Brienz; tourist resort; p. (1957) *4,368*.

Inuvik, *t.*, Canadian Arctic; built above the permanent frost.

Inveraray, *burgh*, Argyll, Scot.; nr. head of Loch Fyne; herring fishing; p. (1961) *501*.

Inverbervie, *burgh*, Kincardine, Scot.; on E. cst., 8 m. S. of Stonehaven; linen, rayon inds.; p. (1961) *921*.

Invercargill, *c.*, S.I., N.Z.; on S.E. cst.; sawmills, freezing wks.; aluminium smelter; served by Bluff Harb.; p. (1961) *41,087*.

Inverell, *t.*, N.S.W., Australia; 383 m. N. of Sydney; p. (1961) *8,202*.

Invergordon, *burgh, spt.*, Ross and Cromarty, Scot.; on N. side of Cromarty Firth, 12 m. N.E. of Dingwall; naval pt.; p. (1961) *1,640*.

Inverkeithing, *burgh*, Fife, Scot.; on F. of Forth, nr. Dunfermline; shipbreaking, paper mkg., quarrying; p. (1961) *4,069*.

Inverkip, *par., vil.*, Renfrew, Scot.; 6 m. S.W. of Greenock; par. contains Gourock; wat. pl.; p. (1951) *17,288*.

Inverness, *co.*, Scot.; mountainous and well wooded; rising to Ben Nevis 4,406 ft.; Caledonian Canal crosses co.; little cultivation; deer forests and grouse moors, fishing, sheep breeding, distilleries; hydroelec. schemes at Foyers, Glen Cannich, and Lochaber; a. 4,351 aq. m.; p. (1961) *83,425*.

Inverness, *burgh, co. t.*, Inverness, Scot.; on Moray Firth nr. N.E. end of Caledonian Canal; distilleries, light engin., tweeds; fisheries and agr.; p. (1961) *29,773*.

Inverurie, *burgh*, Aberdeen, Scot.; on R. Don, 14 m. N.W. of Aberdeen; rly. ctr., wool fair; tourism; p. (1961) *5,152*.

Investigator I., off cst. of Eyre Peninsula, S. Australia.

Inyokern, *t.*, E. Cal., U.S.A.; naval ordnance research sta.; p. (1960) *11,684*.

Ioannina (Janina), *prefecture*, Epirus, Greece; ch. t. Ioannina; p. (1961) *154,201*.

Ioannina (Janina), *t.*, Epirus, Greece; nr. Albanian frontier; embroidery; p. (1961) *34,997*.

Iona, *I.*, off cst. of Mull, Argyll, Scot.; early Scottish Christian ctr.; restored abbey; St. Columba's burial place; ancient burial place of Scottish kings.

Ionian Is., gr. in Mediterranean, belonging to Greece, formerly under British protection; comprising Kerkyra, (Corfu), Kephallenia, Zákynthos, Levkás, Ithake, Paxos and Kytherá; suffered from severe earthquakes in Aug. 1953; total a. 752 sq. m.; p. (1961) *212,573*.

Ionian Sea, Mediterranean; between Greece on E; Italy and Sicily on W.

Iowa, *st.*, U.S.A.; prairie cty; over 1,000 ft. above sea-level; watered by Mississippi and Missouri; farming, dairying, maize, wheat, oats, potatoes; coal; cars, chemicals; cap. Des Moines; a 56,290 sq. m.; p. (1960) *2,757,537*.

Iowa City, Iowa, U.S.A.; farming, stockbreeding; p. (1960) *33,443*.

Ipin (Yibin), *c.*, Szechwan prov., China; cereals, match mfg.; p. (1953) *176,000*.

Ipoh, *t.*, Perak, Malaya; tin; p. *80,874*.

Ipswich, *co. t., co. bor.*, Suffolk, Eng.; at head of estuary of R. Orwell; agr. implements, brewing, clothing, printing; p. (1961) *117,325*.

Ipswich, *c.*, S.E. Queensland, Australia; coal, woollens; p. (1961) *48,668*.

Iquique, *c.*, N. Chile, a pt. on Pacific; exports nitrates and iodine from Atacama desert; fish canning; p. (1960) *53,800*.

Iquitos, *ch. t.*, Loreto, Peru; shipyards, docks; rubber, cotton, saw-mills, oil refining; p. (1961) *54,300*.

Iraklion (Heraklion), *prefecture*, Crete; cap. Iraklion; p. (1961) *207,437*.

Iraklion (Candia), *cap.*, Crete; central position on N. cst. at foot of terraced hill slopes; wine, olive oil, fishing; p. (1961) *63,458*.

Iran, *see* Persia.

Irapuata, *c.*, central Mexico; agr. ctr.; p. *60,000*.

Iraq, *rep.* (since July 1958), S.W. Asia; approx. co-extensive with ancient Mesopotamia; ch. Rs.; Tigris, Euphrates; climate, hot, rainless in summer, cool in winter, scanty rainfall; races: Arabs, Kurds; language Arabic; ch. crops: dates, wheat, maize, barley, beans, cotton; impt. oilfields; communications: rail, Mosul–Baghdad–Persian G; cap. Baghdad; dam and power sta. on Euphrates projected. a. 116,600 sq. m.; p. (1957) *6,538,109*.

Irbit, *t.*, Sverdlovsk region, U.S.S.R.; engin., motor cycles, wood-wkgs., pharmaceutics; mkt., famous fair; p. (1956) *41,200*.

Ireland, 2nd. lgst. I., Brit. Is.; ch. physical features: L. Neagh in N.E., Rs. Shannon, Boyne, Blackwater, Barrow, Nore, Suir, Liffey; ch. mtn. groups—all near cst.—Mourne Mtns., Wicklow Mtns., Mtns. of Kerry; peat bogs over considerable areas, large areas grassland; climate, mild and damp; vegetation, chiefly meadowland; communications, rail and canal; a. 32,531 sq. m.; greatest length 280 m., width 180 m.; p. (1961) *4,321,411*.

Ireland, Republic of (Eire), *sov. ind. st.* covering 26 of the 32 cos. of Ireland inc. the 3 provs. of Leinster, Munster and Connaught (Connacht) together with 3 of the cos. (Cavan, Monaghan and Donegal), of the former. prov. of Ulster. Ceased to be member of Brit. Commonwealth in 1949; agr.: potatoes, turnips and other root crops, oats, barley, hay, cattle, sheep, pigs, horses; fisheries; mnfs.: grain milling, flour, dairy produce, bacon, brewing, tobacco, clothing, etc.; religion, R.C.; cap. Dublin; a. 26,600 sq. m.; p. (1961) *2,814,703*.

Iriga, *mun.*, Luzon, Philippine Is.; hemp, copra, agr.; p. *30,005*.

Irish Sea, Brit. Is.; between Gr. Britain and Ireland, connecting N. and S. with Atl. Oc.; 200 m. long; 50–140 m. wide; greatest depth 140 fathoms; a. 7,000 sq. m.

Irkutsk, *t.*, R.S.F.S.R.; on R. Angara; on Trans-Siberian Rly.; univ.; engin., sawmilling, petroleum refining, chemicals; hydro-elec. power stn.; p. (1962) *385,000*.

Irlam, *t., urb. dist.*, Lancs, Eng.; steel, engin., tar, soap, glycerine, margarine; p. (1961) *15,365*.

Iron Country, Utah, U.S.A.; vast reserves of iron ore; undeveloped due to inaccessibility.

Iron Gate, Romania; famous rapids in R. Danube; Romanian-Yugoslavian hydro-elect. and navigation project, 1964–71.

Iron Knob, *t.*, S. Australia; S.W. of Port Augusta; iron ore.

Iron Mountain, *t.*, Mich., U.S.A.; former iron mining ctr.; p. (1960) *9,299.*

Ironton, *c.*, Ohio, U.S.A.; machin.; coal, iron, fireclay; p. (1960) *15,745.*

Ironwood, *t.*, Mich., U.S.A.; iron-mining, lumbering; p. (1950) *11,466.*

Irrawaddy, *R.*, Burma; flows S. to Bay of Bengal; navigable for lge. steamers 900 m.; irrigation wks.; length 1,300 m.

Irthlingborough, *t.*, *urb. dist.*, Northants., Eng.; p. (1961) *5,125.*

Irtysh, *R.*, Siberia, U.S.S.R.; trib. of R. Ob; two-thirds navigable; crossed by Trans-Siberian Rly. at Omsk; length 2,500 m.

Irun, *t.*, N.E. frontier, Spain; nr. San Sebastian; tanning and brandy distillery; paper mills, iron; Roman remains; p. (1957) *19,956.*

Irvine, *burgh, spt.*, Ayr, Scot.; nr. mouth of R. Irvine, 7 m. W. of Kilmarnock; hosiery, lt. engin., bottle, chemical wks.; p. (1961) *16,910.*

Irvington, *t.*, N.J., U.S.A.; p. (1960) *59,379.*

Irvington, *t.*, N.Y., U.S.A.; residtl.; light engin.; p. (1960) *5,494.*

Irwell, *R.*, S. Lancs, Eng.; flows past Manchester to the Mersey; length 30 m.

Isarco, *R.*, N. Italy; rises nr. Brenner Pass, flows S. into R. Adige at Bolzano; used by main rail and road routes from N. Italy to Austria; length 50 m.

Ischia, *I.*, in G. of Naples, Italy; saline baths; cap. I.; a. 26 sq. m.; p. *30,000.*

Ischl, *t.*, Austria; wat. pl., saline baths; p. (1961) *12,703.*

Isdud (Ashdod), *ancient Philistine c.*, Israel; 20 m. S. of Jaffa.

Ise Bay, *inlet*, S. Honshu, Japan; flanked by ch. textile mftg. a. of Japan with 5 million people ctred on Nagoya; length 40 m., width 15–20 m.

Iselle, *t.*, N.W. Italy; S. terminal of Simplon Pass and tunnel.

Isère, *dep.*, S.E. France; drained by Rs. Isère and Rhône; cap. Grenoble; mtnous.; cereals; wine, butter cheese; iron, coal, lead, silver, copper; gloves, silks; a. 3,178 sq. m.; p. (1962) *729,789.*

Isère, R., S.E. France; rises in W. Alps (Grande Sassière), flows W. into R. Rhône nr. Valence; used to generate hydro-elec.; used, with trib. R. Arc, by main rly. from France to N. Italy through Mt. Cenis (Fréjus) Tunnel.

Iserlohn, *t.*, N. Rhine-Westphalia, Germany; iron, steel, metalwks.; needles; p. (1963) *56,300.*

Iseyin, *t.*, W. Prov., Nigeria, W. Africa; p. (1946) *48,470.*

Isfahan (ancient Aspadana), *prov.*, Iran; cap. I., former cap. of Persia, on R. Zaindeh; carpet mftg.; woollen and cotton cloth and yarns mftg.; matches; p. (1960) *280,000.*

Ishikari, *t.*, Hokkaido, Japan; on cst. of Otaru Bay, 10 m. N. of Sapporo; ctr. of second lgst. coalfield in Japan; sm. petroleum production.

Ishimbay, *t.*, Bashkir A.S.S.R., R.S.F.S.R.; on R. Belaya; ctr. of Ishimbay oilfields; p. (1956) *44,400.*

Ishpeming, *c.*, Mich., U.S.A.; machin., gold, silver, iron, marble; p. (1960) *8,857.*

Isis, *R.*, head stream of R. Thames, Eng.; so named until its confluence with Thames at Dorchester, Oxfordshire.

Iskenderun, *spt.* Hatay, Turkey; pt. and rly. terminus; oil; fertilisers; p. (1960) *63,736.*

Isla, *R.*, Perth and Forfar, Scot.; trib. of R. Tay; length 40 m.

Islamabad, *cap.*, Pakistan; outside Rawalpindi below Himalayas.

Islay, *I.*, Inner Hebrides; Argyll, Scot.; 13 m. W. Kintyre; a. 235 sq. m.; farming, dairying, distilleries.

Isle of Grain, *rural a.*, Kent; flat promontory once separated from mainland by a tidal estuary; lge. oil refinery.

Isle Royale, *I.*, in L. Superior, Mich., U.S.A.; length 40 m.

Isleworth, *see* **Hounslow.**

Islington, *inner bor.*, London, Eng.; N. of City; incorporates former bor. of Finsbury; industl. and residtl.; p. (1964) *261,822.*

Ismailia, *t.*, U.A.R., at mid-point of Suez Canal on L. Timsah, 45 m. N.N.W. of Suez; has rail connections with Cairo, Suez and Port Said; p. (1960) *25,194.*

Isna (Esneh), *t.*, Upper U.A.R.; caravan ctr.; barrage; p. (1947) *18,458.*

Isonzo, *R.*, Illyria, Italy; flows into Adriatic Sea.

Isparta, *t.*, Turkey; N. of Antalya; p. (1960) *36,201.*

Ispra, *t.*, Varese, Italy, nr. L. Maggiore; nuclear research ctr.

Israel, *indep. Jewish rep.*, since 1948; part of former Palestine mandate; cap. Jerusalem, impt. ts. Tel Aviv, Haifa; mainly agr.: grains, vegs., olives, citrus-fruit prod.; processed foods, textiles, wearing apparel, pharmaceuticals; little mineral wealth except for potash and other chemicals from Sea of Galilee and Dead Sea; a. 8,050 sq. m.; p. (1964) *2,525,600.*

Issoire, *commune*, Puy-de-Dôme, France; old church; p. (1954) *8,541.*

Issoudun, *t.*, Indre, France; leather, parchment, woollens, farm implements; p. (1954) *12,945.*

Issy, *t.*, France; on R. Seine; sub. of Paris; p. (1962) *53,298.*

Issyk-kul, *L.*, Kirgizia, U.S.S.R.; alt. 4,476 ft.; a. 250 sq. m.; drained by R. Chu.

Istanbul (Constantinople), *ch. spt.*, former cap., Turkey; on Golden Horn pen. on European cst. at entry of Bosporus into Sea of Marmara; div. into old "Stamboul" on S. side and dists. of Galata and Beyoglu (Pera) on N.; the ancient Byzantium; magnificent mosque of Sta Sophia; light inds.; p. (1960) *1,459,528.*

Istria, *peninsula*, N. Adriatic Sea; formerly Italian, now divided between Jugoslavia and Italy; agr., olives, vines, oranges, maize; rural p. mainly Slavs, ts. mainly Italian.

Ita, *c.*, S. Paraguay; cattle, agr.; leather; p. *16,892.*

Itabira, *t.*, Minas Geraes st., Brazil; on Brazilian Plateau, 60 m. N.E. of Belo Horizonte; lgst. deposits of iron ore in Brazil.

Itabuna, *c.*, E. Brazil; coffee, tobacco; p. (1960) *54,268.*

Itajai, *t.*, at mouth of Itajai R., S. Brazil; exp. lumber, tobacco, starch, sassafras oil; p. (1960) *55,000.*

Italy, *rep.*, S. Europe; peninsula 750 m. long and 100–120 m. broad; many Is. (ch. Sardinia, Sicily); mtns. in N. (Alps) and in ctr. and S. (Apennines); ch. R. Po; climate, Mediterranean; wheat and other cereals; vines, olives, fruit; cattle, sheep; sulphur, iron and iron pyrites, mercury, lead, zinc; Carrara marble; hydro-elec. power, natural gas; mnfs.: cottons, silks, sugar, glass, furniture, olive oil; gen. engin., cars; fisheries; cap. Rome; a. 116,235 sq. m.; p. (1961) *50,463,762.*

Itasca, *L.*, a source of Mississippi R., Minn., U.S.A.; alt. 1,575 ft.

Itatiaia, *mtn.*, highest mtn. in Brazil; 9,255 ft.

Itaugua, *t.*, S.W. Paraguay; lace mkg.; p. *11,300.*

Itchen, *R.*, Hants, Eng.; flows to Southampton Water; length 25 m.

Ithaca, *t.*, N.Y., U.S.A.; on Cayuga L.; seat of Cornell Univ.; elec. clocks; p. (1960) *28,799.*

Ithake, *one of the Ionian Is.*, Greece; a. 37 sq. m.; ch. t. Ithake; severe earthquake, 1953.

Itzehoe, *t.*, Schleswig-Holstein, Germany; on Stor R.; wood, cement, machin.; p. (1963) *36,900.*

Ivano-Frankovsk, *t.*, Ukrainian S.S.R.; oil; p. (1959) *66,000.*

Ivanovo, *t.*, R.S.F.S.R.; N.E. of Moscow; textiles, iron and chemical wks.; peat-fed power stas.; p. (1962) *360,000.*

Ivigtut, *Danish sttlement*, S.W. Greenland; cryolite.

Iviza, *I.*, Balearic gr. in the W. Mediterranean; Spanish; cath., fortress.

Ivory Coast, *ind. sov. st.*, within French Community, W. Africa; climate, tropical; maize, coffee, rubber, mahogany; dense forests; cap. Abidjan; a. 124,000 sq. m.; p. (1961) *3,300,000.*

Ivrea, *t.*, Italy; on the Dora Baltea, nr. Turin; silks, cotton mnfs.; p. *14,473.*

Ivry-sur-Seine, *t.*, France; on R. Seine, sub. of Paris; organs, chemicals, iron and steel; p. (1962) *53,646.*

Iwamizawa, *t.*, W. Hokkaido, Japan; rly. junction; coalfield; p. (1960) *60,650.*

Iwanai, *spt.*, S.W. Hokkaido, Japan; copper, coal, sulphur; fisheries; p. (1947) *20,394.*

Iwo, *t.*, Nigeria, W. Africa; nr. Ibadan; p. (1953) *100,000.*

Ixmiquilpan, *t.*, Hidalgo st., Mexico; silver; p. *1,543.*

Izegem, *commune*, N.W. Belgium; linen, tobacco; p. (1962) *17,157.*

Izhevsk, *t.*, R.S.F.S.R.; steel, engin.; p. (1962) *322,000.*

Izieux, *t.*, Loire, France; nr. St. Etienne.
Izmail, *former prov.* of Bessarabia, Romania; ceded to U.S.S.R. in 1940, and now part of Ukrainian S.S.R.
Izmail, *t.*, Ukrainian S.S.R.; on R. Danube; food inds.; p. (1956) *43,400.*
Izmir (Smyrna), *c.*, Turkey; at head of G. of Smyrna, Anatolia; exp. figs, raisins, tobacco, carpets, rugs; anc. and historic c.; ch. comm. ctr. of the Levant; p. (1960) *370,923.*
Izmit, *t.*, Turkey; E. end of Sea of Marmara; cereals, tobacco, oil refinery and polythene plant under construction; p. (1960) *73,705.*
Izúcar, *t.*, Puebla, Mexico; nr. Popocatepetl; p. *7,065.*

J

Jabbok, *R.*, Syria, trib. of R. Jordan; length 45 m.
Jablonec, *t.*, ČSSR.; on R. Neisse; artificial jewellery; p. (1961) *27,266.*
Jaboatoa, *c.*, E. Brazil; sub. of Recife; p. (1960) *33,963.*
Jaca, *fortfd. t.*, N. Spain; at foot of Pyrenees; p. [(1957) *9,035.*
Jachymov, *t.*, ČSSR.; spa; uranium-mines, pitchblende, lead, silver, nickel, cobalt; p. *6,806.*
Jackson, *c.*, Mich., U.S.A.; on Grand R.; locomotives, motor-car accessories; p. (1960) *50,720.*
Jackson, *t.*, cap. Miss., U.S.A.; cotton tr.; p. (1960) *144,422.*
Jackson, *t.*, Tenn., U.S.A.; univ.; cotton, cottonseed oil, engines, sewing-machines; p. (1960) *33,849.*
Jackson, *t.*, Ohio, U.S.A.; foundries, gas wells; p. (1960) *6,980.*
Jacksonville, *t.*, Ark., U.S.A.; p. (1960) *14,488.*
Jacksonville, *c.*, *pt.* Fla., U.S.A.; univ.; on St. John's R.; chemicals, shipbldg. and repair, printing, lumber, cigar mftg.; p. (1960) *201,030.*
Jacksonville, *t.*, Texas, U.S.A.; rly., ctr.; fruit, vegetables, cotton; p. (1960) *9,540.*
Jacksonville, *c.*, Ill., U.S.A.; woollens, rly. wks.; p. (1960) *21,690.*
Jacobabad, *frontier sta.*, Sind, Pakistan; one of hottest places in the Indian sub-continent; p. (1961) *35,200.*
Jacobina, *t.*, Baia, Brazil; on R. Itapicura; p. *4,389.*
Jacobsdal, *t.*, Orange Free State, S. Africa; on Riet R.
Jacobstadt, *see* **Yekabpils.**
Jacques-Cartier, *R.*, Quebec, Canada; trib. of St. Lawrence.
Jacques-Cartier, *t.*, Quebec, Canada; p. (1961) *40,807.*
Jacuhy, *R.*, S. Brazil; rises in S. edge of Brazilian Plateau, enters Atl. Oc., through lagoon, Lagoa dos Patos; length 350 m.
Jade, or Jahde, *estuary*, N. Sea, Germany; fine harbour and entrance to pt. of Wilhelmshaven.
Jaen, *prov.*, S. Spain; mines, wine, garden produce, leather, weaving; a. 5,209 sq. m.; p. (1959) *773,563.*
Jaen, *t.*, *cap.*, Jaen, S. Spain; N. of Granada; p. (1959) *60,395.*
Jaffa–Tel Aviv, *t.*, Israel; orange-growing dist.; p. (estd. 1956) *364,000.*
Jaffna, *t.*, *spt.*, N. Ceylon; p. (1963) *94,248.*
Jagdalpur, *t.*, Madhya Pradesh, India; p. (1961) *20,412.*
Jagersfontein, *t.*, O.F.S., S. Africa; most impt. diamond mine; p. (1960) *3,885* inc. *785* whites.
Jahrom, *t.*, Fars, Iran; tobacco, dates; p. *15,000.*
Jakarta, *see* **Djakarta.**
Jaipur, *cap. c.*, Rajasthan, India; comm. ctr.; univ.; p. (1961) *403,444.*
Jalalabad, *t.*, S. of Kabul R., Afghanistan; cane sugar; p. (estd. 1964) *44,000.*
Jalapa, *dep.*, S.E. Guatemala; maize, beans; cap. Jalapa; a. 797 sq. m.; p. (1964) *97,996.*
Jalapa, *cap.*, Veracruz st., Mexico; p. (1960) *60,000.*
Jalgaon, *t.*, *dist.*, Maharashtra, India; cotton, linseed; p. (1961) of t. *80,351*; of dist. *1,765,047.*
Jalisco, *Pacific st.*, Mexico; well timbered, agr., mining; cap. Guadalajara; a. 31,149 sq. m.; p. (1960) *2,443,261.*
Jallieu, *commune*, Isère, S.E. France; light mnfs.; p. (1954) *5,241.*
Jalna, *t.*, Maharashtra, India; E. of Aurangabad; p. (1961) *67,158.*
Jalon, *R.*, Spain; rises in Iberian Mtns., flows N.E. into R. Ebro nr. Zaragoza; valley forms main rly., road route from Madrid to Ebro Valley.
Jaluit, *I.*, Marshall Is., Pa., Oc.
Jamaica, *I.*, *indep. sov. st.* within Br. Commonwealth (1962); W.I., divided into three cos., Middlesex, Surrey and Cornwall; mountainous, highest peak (in Blue Mtns.) 7,420 ft.; cap. Kingston; univ.; bauxite, alumina, sugar, rum, coffee, bananas, cocoa; a. 4,411 sq. m.; p. (estd. 1964) *1,635,000.*
Jamalpur, *t.*, N.E. Bihar, Indian Union; p. (1961) [*57,039.*
Jambes, *commune*, S. Belgium; sub. of Namur; glass, engin.; p. (1962) *13,426.*
James (or Powhattan), *R.*, Va., U.S.A.; flows from Blue Ridge to Chesapeake Bay; length 450 m.
James Bay, S. part of Hudson Bay, Canada; length about 1,250 m.
James W. Ellsworth Land, Antarctica; claimed by U.S.A.
Jamestown, *c.*, N.D., U.S.A.; cattle; food processing; p. (1960) *15,163.*
Jamestown, *spt.*, *cap.*, St. Helena I.; flax; p. (1961) *1,700.*
Jamestown, *c.*, N.Y., U.S.A.; summer resort and mftg.; p. (1960) *41,818.*
Jamestown, *t.*, *dist.*, Va., U.S.A.; nr. mouth of James R., where first English permanent settlement was founded 1607.
Jammer Bay, *bay*, W. cst. of Vendsyssel, Jutland, Denmark.
Jammu and Kashmir, *st.*, N.W. India and N.E. Pakistan; divided along cease-fire line; traversed by ranges of the Himalayas; in Jhelum valley is the celebrated vale of Kashmir, producing abundant crops of wheat and rice; cap. Srinagar; winter cap. Jammu; a. 92,780 sq. m.; p. (1961) *3,560,976.*
Jamshedpur, *t.*, Bihar, India; W. of Calcutta; Tata iron and steel wks.; p. (1961) *328,044.*
Jämtland, *co.*, Sweden; a. 19,967 sq. m.; p. (estd. 1963) *134,200.*
Janesville, *t.*, Wis., U.S.A.; in agr. region; textiles, machin.; p. (1960) *35,164.*
Janina, *see* **Ioannina.**
Janiuay, *t.*, Panay, Philippines; fine woven fabrics.
Jan Mayen I., between Spitzbergen and Iceland, Arctic Ocean; belongs to Norway; seal and whale fisheries; government weather-forecast sta.; a. about 144 sq. m.
Japan, *cty.*, E. Asia; ch. Is. Shikoku, Hokkaido, Honshu, Kyushu; mountainous, largely volcanic, 18 active volcanoes; subject to disastrous earthquakes; only one-tenth of total surface is agr. land; climate varies according to latitude, in N. temperate, in S. sub-tropical, warm summers, abundant rainfall; vegetation, broad-leaved forest and meadows, coniferous forest; fine harbours, good communications; ch. inds.; agr., rice, cereals, mulberry and silk, tobacco, cotton, tea; coal, iron, copper; lumber; fisheries; textiles, silks, cottons, woollens; shipbldg., engin., machin., paper; oil from Honshu; cap. Tokyo; a. 182,700 sq. m.; p. (1962) *95,180,000.*
Japan, Sea of, portion of Pac. Oc. between Korea, U.S.S.R. and Japan.
Japan Current, *see* **Kuroshio.**
Jappen I., Geelvink Bay, New Guinea, Indonesia.
Japura, *R.*, Colombia, Brazil, S. America; rising in the Andes of Colombia, and flowing through Brazil to R. Amazon; length 1,300 m.
Jarocin, *t.*, Poland; S. of Poznan; p. *11,818.*
Jaroslaw, *mftg. t.*, Rzeszow, Poland; on R. San; garrison; p. (1960) *26,000.*
Jarrahi, *R.*, S.W. Iran; flows into Persian G.
Jarrow, *t.*, *mun. bor.*, Durham, Eng.; on S. bank of R. Tyne, 7 m. below Gateshead; ship repairing and engin.; steel and tube wks.; oil storage; birthplace of Venerable Bede: diecastings and knitting wool mkg. at Bede Trading Estate; p. (1961) *28,752.*
Jaslow, *commune*, Rzeszow, Poland; oil wells; p. *12,000.*
Jasper, *t.*, E. Texas, U.S.A.; cattle, agr., lumber; p. (1960) *4,880.*
Jasper Place, *t.*, Alberta, Canada; p. (1961) *30,530.*
Jassy (Lasi), *t.*, Romania; former cap. Moldavia; in vineyard dist.; textiles, chemicals; p. (1959) *122,000.*
Jászbereny, *t.*, Hungary; on R. Zagyva; engin.; p. (1962) *30,454.*

Jativa, *t.*, Valencia, Spain; wine, oil, fruit; p. (1957) *18,092.*
Jau, *c.*, São Paulo st., S.E. Brazil; coffee; p. *18,655.*
Jauf, *t.*, Nejd, Saudi Arabia; p. exceeds 10,000.
Jauja, *t.*, Junin, Central Peru; E. of Lima; p. *8,276.*
Jaunpur, *t.*, Uttar Pradesh, India; on R. Gumti; perfumes; p. (1961) *61,851.*
Java, *ch. I.*, Indonesia; mtns. (many volcanic); loftiest peak, 12,057 ft.; agr., rubber, tobacco, sugar, coffee, tea; oil palms, cinchona, spices; coal, tin, gold, silver; teak forests; petroleum; densely populated; cap. Djakarta; a. 50,390 sq. m.; p. (inc. Madura) (1961) *63,059,575.*
Javari (Yavari), *R.*, forms bdy. between Peru and Brazil; trib. of R. Amazon.
Java Sea, part of the Pac. Oc. between N. cst. Java, Borneo and Sumatra.
Jawor (Jauer), *t.*, Lower Silesia, Poland; p. *12,114.*
Jaworzno, *industl. t.*, Poland; nr. Cracow; coal; p. (1960) *53,000.*
Jaxartes R., *see* Syr Darya.
Jayuya, *mun.*, central Puerto Rico, W. Indies; sugar, tobacco, cotton; p. *14,589.*
Jeanerette, *t.*, S. La., U.S.A.; sugar, pecan nuts, rice; p. (1960) *5,568.*
Jeanette, *bor.*, Penns., U.S.A.; natural-gas region; p. (1960) *16,565.*
Jebba, *t.*, Nigeria, W. Africa; on R. Niger.
Jebel Aulia, *vil.*, Sudan; S. of Khartoum; proposed site for dam across White Nile R.
Jebel ed Druz, *terr.*, S.E of Hauran, Syria; ch. t. Es Suweida.
Jebel-Hauran, high tableland of Syria; alt. 6,000 ft.
Jebel Serbal, *mtn.*, Sinai peninsula, U.A.R.; alt. 6,760 ft.
Jebl-us-Siraj, *t.*, Afghanistan; cement wks.
Jedburgh, *burgh*, Roxburgh, Scot.; on R. Jed, 12 m. S.W. of Kelso; abbey ruins, tweeds, woollens, rayon; p. (1961) *3,647.*
Jefferson, *t.*, Texas, U.S.A.; near oilfield; cattle, grain; p. (1960) *3,082.*
Jefferson City, *cap.*, Mo., U.S.A.; on R. Missouri, 100 m. W. of St. Louis; shoes, tiles, farm implements; p. (1960) *28,228.*
Jeffersonville, *mftg.*, Ind., U.S.A.; on Ohio R.; p. (1960) *19,522.*
Jehol, former *prov.*, China; divided 1955 among Hopei and Liaoning provinces and Inner Mongolian Region; p. (1953) *5,160,822.*
Jelenia Góra (Hirschberg), *t.*, Lower Silesia, Poland, German before 1945; spa, rly. junction; p. (1960) *50,000.*
Jelep-la, *high pass*, leading from Sikkim, N. India, to Tibet; alt. 14,390 ft.
Jelgava (Mitau), *t.*, Latvia U.S.S.R.; on R. Aa; textiles, sugar; p. (1956) *31,600.*
Jemappes, *industl. t.*, Hainaut, Belgium; on the Halne R.; coal, iron; French victory over Austria 1792; p. (1962) *12,950.*
Jena, *t.*, Gera, E. Germany; on R. Saale; univ.; observatory; glass, books, pianos, optical mftg. (Zeiss); p. (1963) *83,451.*
Jenkins, *t.*, Ky., U.S.A.; on coalfield; p. (1960) *3,202.*
Jenkintown, *bor.*, Penns., U.S.A.; residtl.; p. (1960) *5,017.*
Jennings, *t.*, La., U.S.A.; agr.; oil wells; p. (1960) *11,887.*
Jenolan Caves, N.S.W., Australia; in Blue Mtns., 20 m. S.W. of Katoomba; lge. natural caves in limestone, stalactites, stalagmites.
Jeremie, *spt.*, S.W. Haiti; p. *6,000.*
Jerez de la Frontera, *t.*, Andalusia, Spain; 14 m. N.E. of Cadiz; sherry; p. (1959) *127,194.*
Jerez de los Caballeros, *commune*, S.W. Spain; marble, cork, tr. ctr. for agr. region; p. *16,154.*
Jericho, *vil.*, Jordan Valley, Jordan; estd. through recent excavations as oldest t. in the world (6000 B.C.); p. (1961) *10,284.*
Jersey, *I.*, lgst. of Channel Is., 13 m. W. of Fr. cst; potatoes, tomatoes, cauliflowers, flowers, fruit, cattle; tourist resort; t. St. Helier; a. 45 sq. m.; p. (1961) *63,345.*
Jersey City, *spt.*, N.J., U.S.A.; opp. New York on Hudson R.; canning, iron, steel, tobacco, chemicals; rly. ctr.; p. (1960) *276,101.*
Jerusalem, *c.*, Holy Land; 2,660 ft. above sea-level, between Dead Sea and Mediterranean; the "Holy City" of the Jews and sacred c. of Christians and Mohammedans; since 1950 c. divided between Israel and Jordan; cap. of Israel; "Old City" in Jordan and considered 2nd. cap. of Jordan; Hebrew univ.; varied inds.; Israel Museum; p. (estd. 1960 Israel) *164,000*; (1961 Jordan) *60,337.*
Jervis Bay, *Commonwealth terr.*, acquired as site for port for Canberra by Federal Government of Australia 1909; a. 28 sq. m.; p. *360.*
Jesi, *t.*, Ancona, Italy; cath.; p. *23,600.*
Jesselton, *impt. spt.*, cap. Sabah, Malaysia; on W. cst.; rubber; p. (1960) *21,719.*
Jhansi, *t.*, Uttar Pradesh, India; p. (1961) *169,712.*
Jhelum, *R.*, W. Punjab, Pakistan; most W. of the five Rs. of the Punjab; flows from Kashmir to join the Chenab.
Jibuti (Djibouti), *pt.* on G. of Aden, cap. French Somaliland; rly. link with Addis Ababa; impt. transit trade; p. (1960) *40,000.*
Jičín, *t.*, N.E. Bohemia, ČSSR.; mkt.; p. (1961) *12,970.*
Jidda, *spt.*, *t.*, Hejaz, nr. Mecca, Saudi Arabia; steel mill projected; p. (estd.) *150,000.*
Jihlava, *t.*, Moravia, ČSSR.; timber, grain, textiles; p. (1961) *34,744.*
Jimena de la Frontera, *t.*, Spain; nr. Cadiz; p. *10,123.*
Jimma, *t.*, *prov.*, Ethiopia; ch. prod. Jimma coffee; connected by road with Addis Ababa.
Jinja, *t.*, Uganda, E. Africa; on N. shore of L. Victoria where R. Nile drains from L. over Ripon Falls; hydro-elec. power scheme; cotton mnfs., copper smelting, flour and maize milling; brewing; rly. to Kampala; p. (1960) *29,741.*
Jinotega, *t.*, Nicaragua; coffee; p. (1961) *50,325.*
Joao Pessóa, *cap.*, Paraíba st., Brazil; sugar, cotton, mandioca, sisal; p. (1960) *155,117.*
Joban, *dist.*, N.E. Honshu, Japan; third lgst. coalfield in Japan; ch. t. Fukushima.
Joda, Orissa, India; ferromanganese plant.
Jodhpur, *t.*, Rajasthan, Indian Union; p. (1961) *224,760.*
Joënsuu, *t.*, on chain of Ls., S.E. Finland; p. (1961) *28,760.*
Joeuf, *t.*, Meurthe-et-Moselle, France; p. (1954) *11,034.*
Jogjakarta, *c.*, Java; 40 m. S. of Semarang; connected with Jakarta by rail; citadel, with palace; p. (1961) *313,000.*
Johanna, *I.*, of the Comoro gr. in Mozambique Channel; p. *12,870.*
Johannesburg, *c.*, Transvaal, S. Africa; univ.; gold-mining ctr. of Witwatersrand; diamond cutting, engin., textiles, chemicals; p. (1960) *1,110,905* (inc. *398,517* whites).
John o' Groat's House, *place* nr. Duncansby Head, Caithness, Scot.
Johnsonburg, *bor.*, Penns., U.S.A.; chemicals, paper, iron and steel; p. (1950) *4,567.*
Johnson City, *t.*, N.Y., U.S.A.; leather, chemicals, paper; p. (1960) *19,118.*
Johnson City, N.E. Tenn., U.S.A.; mkt., iron, textiles; p. (1960) *29,892.*
Johnston, *t.*, Providence, Rhode I., U.S.A.; p. (1960) *16,898.*
Johnstone, *mftg. burgh*, Renfrew, Scot.; on R. Black Cart, nr. Paisley; iron, brass, machine tools, textile ind.; p. (1961) *18,369.*
Johnstown, *t.*, N.Y., U.S.A.; glove mftg.; p. (1960) *10,390.*
Johnstown, *c.*, Penns., U.S.A.; on Connemaugh R.; immense steel wks.; p. (1960) *53,949.*
Johore, *st.*, Malaysia, at S. end of Malaya; forested; rubber, rice, copra, tin, iron, bauxite; a. 7,330 sq. m.; p. (1961) *1,084,351.*
Johore Bharu, *t.*, cap. Johore, Malaya; across the Strait from Singapore; p. (1957) *126,099.*
Joinville, *t.*, Santa Catarina, Brazil; exp. timber, matté tea; textiles, machin., car parts, plastics; p. (1960) *45,500.*
Jökulsa, *R.*, flowing into Axar Fjord, Iceland.
Joliet, *t.*, Ill., U.S.A.; rly. and mftg. ctr.; p. (1960) *66,780.*
Joliette, *t.*, Quebec, Canada; woollens, paper, tobacco; p. (1961) *18,088.*
Jonesborough, *t.*, Ark., U.S.A.; p. (1960) *21,418.*
Jönköping, *co.*, Sweden; cap. Jönköping; a. 4,447 sq. m.; p. (1961) *285,271.*
Jönköping, *t.*, cap. Jönköping, Sweden; paper, matches, textiles, footwear; p. (1961) *50,652.*

Jonquière, *t.*, S. Quebec, Canada; lumber, rly. shops; p. (1961) *28,588.*
Joplin, *t.*, Mo., U.S.A.; lead-mng; p. (1960) *38,958.*
Jordan, *kingdom*, bounded by Israel, Syria, Saudi Arabia and Iraq; agr. but lge. areas of desert; phosphate deposits and potash; cap. Amman; a. 34,750 sq. m.; p. (1961) *1,752,095.*
Jordan, *R.*, famous in Bible history; flowing S. from Anti-Lebanon along a sinuous course, mostly below sea-level to the Dead Sea, its rapidity and variant depth render it unnavigable, and no t. of any importance has ever been built on its banks; length 120 m.
Jorullo, *volcano*, Michoacan st., Mexico; alt. 4,265 ft.
Jos, *t.*, central Nigeria; on Bauchi Plateau, 60 m. S.W. of Bauchi; impt. tin-mines; on branch line linking with E. Nigerian rly. system to Pt. Harcourt.
Jotunheimen, *mtn. region*, central Norway; Goldhopiggen, alt. 8,097 ft., Glittertind, alt. 8,048 ft.
Joyce's Country, *mtnous. dist.*, Galway, Ireland.
Juan de Fuca Strait, between Vancouver I. and Washington st., U.S.A.
Juan Fernandez, *rocky I.*, S. Pac. Oc.; belonging to Chile; a. 38 sq. m.; famous for Alex. Selkirk (Robinson Crusoe), 1704–9.
Juba, *R.*, E. Africa; flows to Indian Ocean, nr. the Equator.
Juba, *cap.*, Equatorial Prov., Sudan; p. *10,000.*
Jubbulpore, *t.*, Madhya Pradesh, India; carpets, cottons; oil mills, ordnance wks.; p. (1961) *367,215.*
Juby, *C.*, Rio de Oro., N.W. Africa.
Jucar, *R.*, E. Spain; rises in Serrania de Cuenca, flows S.E. to G. of Valencia, Mediterranean Sea; length 250 m.
Juchitan, *t.*, S.E. Mexico; mkt. for rich agr. region; p. (1950) *14,550.*
Judaea, *div.* of Palestine in the Roman period.
Judenburg, *t.*, Styria, Austria; on R. Mur; p. (1961) *9,869.*
Juggernaut, *see* **Puri.**
Jugoslavia, *Federal People's Rep.*, comprising former terrs. of Serbia, Montenegro, Croatia, Dalmatia, Bosnia, Herzegovina and Slavonia; farming, wheat, maize, barley, rye, oats, fruits, plums; sheep, cattle, pigs, goats; timber, coal, iron, copper, lead, cement, chromium, salt, bauxite; cap. Belgrade; a. 98,386 sq. m.; p. (1960) *18,643,000.*
Juiz de Fora, *mftg. t.*, E. Brazil: textiles, lumber, brewing, sugar refining; p. (1960) *124,979.*
Jujuy, *prov.*, Argentina; cap. San Salvador de Jujuy; a. 16,859 sq. m.; p. (1960) *240,000.*
Julian Alps, *mtn. range*, Venetia, Carinthia, Carniola and Croatia; highest peak, Triglav, 9,394 ft.
Julianehaab, sta., Greenland; N.W. of C. Farewell.
Jülich, *t.*, Germany; nr. Aachen; "pebble bed" nuclear reactor projected.
Jullundur, *t.*, Punjab, India; cotton and silk mnfs.; p. (1961) *222,569.*
Jumet, *t.*, Belgium; nr. Charleroi; mftg. and mining; p. (1962) *28,653.*
Jumilla, *t.*, Murcia, Spain; exp. fabrics; p. (1957) *20,851.*
Jumna, *R.*, N. India; ch. trib. of R. Ganges; rises in the Himalayas and flows past Delhi and Agra to Allahabad; length 860 m.
Junction City, Kan., U.S.A.; p. (1960) *18,700.*
Jundiai, *t.*, S.E. Brazil; rly. junction; textiles, steel; p. (1960) *79,536.*
Juneau, *c.*, cap., Alaska, U.S.A.; at foot of Chilkoot mtns.; lumbering; fisheries; gold settlement (1881); p. (1960) *6,797.*
Jungfrau, *peak*, Bernese Oberland, Switzerland; height 13,642 ft.; electric rly. from Kleine Scheidegg to Jungfraujoch.
Juniata, *R.*, Penns., U.S.A.; flows to the Susquehanna at Petersburg.
Junin, *inland dep.*, Peru; traversed by the Andes; copper, silver, lead; ch. t. Huancayo; a. 22,814 sq. m.; p. (1961) *507,908.*
Jura, *mtns.*, Switzerland and France; highest peak Crête de la Neige; alt. 5,654 ft.; length 180 m., width up to 30 m.
Jura, *dep.*, E. France; named from the mtns.; many vineyards; forests, cereals, watches, toys; a. 1,951 sq. m.; p. (1962) *225,682.*
Jura, *I.*, Argyll, Scot.; off W. cst.; a. 146 sq. m.
Jurua R., trib. of R. Amazon.
Juticalpa, *t.*, Honduras, C. America; cattle, cereals, sugar; p. (1961) *3,836.*
Jutland, *peninsula*, Denmark; intensive agr. and poultry farming; a. 11,411 sq. m.; p. (1960) *2,018,168.*
Jyväskylä, *t.*, central Finland; mkt.; pulp and paper; p. (1961) *39,916.*

K

K², *see* **Godwin-Austen, Mt.**
Kabankalan, *mun.*, Negros Occidental, Philippine Is.; agr.; p. *29,315.*
Kabansk, *t.*, E. Siberia, U.S.S.R.; nr. L. Baikal; agr. and industl.
Kabarda-Balkar, A.S.S.R., Transcaucasia, U.S.S.R.; non-ferrous metals, gold, platinum, iron ore, coal, arsenic; a. 4,800 sq. m.; p. (1959) *420,000.*
Kabinda, *t.*, Angola, W. Africa; on W. cst., 30 m. N. of Congo estuary; p. *1,000.*
Kabul, *c.*, *cap.*, Afghanistan; on R. Kabul, S. of the Hindu Kush; 6,900 ft. above sea level; univ.; excellent climate; p. (estd. 1964) *400,000.*
Kabul, *R.*, flowing through Afghanistan to the R. Indus at Peshawar, Pakistan; length 270 m.
Kachin State, *div.*, Burma; comprising former Myitkyina and Bhamo dists; 29,500 sq. m.
Kadina, *t.*, S. Australia; 6 m. E. of Wallaroo; comm. ctr.; ctr. of mixed farming area.
Kadiyevka, *t.*, Ukrainian S.S.R.; coal, iron and steel, synthetic rubber; p. (1959) *180,000.*
Kaduna, *t.*, N. Nigeria; cap. of Northern Provs.; impt. rly. junction with main rlys. to Lagos, Pt. Harcourt; p. *10,000.*
Kaffraria, *extensive dist.*, Cape Province, S. Africa; comprising Griqualand E., Tembuland, Transkei, and Pondoland.
Kafue, *R.*, Zambia; famous gorge.
Kagoshima, *spt.*, at S. end of Kyushu I., Japan; p. (1960) *296,000.*
Kahoolawe, *I.*, Hawaiian Is.; a. 45 sq. m.; uninhabited.
Kai Islands, *Is.*, Indonesia; between New Guinea and Timor; timber; a. 680 sq. m.; p. *51,000.*
Kaiapoi, *t.*, S.I., N.Z.; on the Waimakariri R., 14 m by rail from Christchurch; woollens; p. (1961) *3,109.*
Kaieteur Falls, Guyana, S. America; located where R. Potaro leaves Guiana Highlands; among world's highest falls (741 ft.).
Kaifeng, *c.*, *cap.*, Honan, China; on Hwang-Ho R.; one of the most ancient cities in China; cottons; p. (1953) *299,000.*
Kaikoura, *t.*, S.I., N.Z.; on E. cst., 80 m. N.E. of Lyttelton; in this region are the Kaikoura ranges, in which the highest peaks are Tapuaenuku (9,465 ft.) and Alarm (9,400 ft.).
Kaiping, *t.*, Hopeh, N. China; 80 m. N.E. of Tientsin; second lgst. coal-mining a. (Kailan mines) in China; coal exported through Chinwangtao.
Kairouan, *holy c.* of the Moslems, Tunisia N. Africa; 80 m. S.S.E. of Tunis; founded *c.* A.D. 670; mosque; p. (1961) *34,000.*
Kaiserslautern, *t.*, Rhineland Palatinate, Germany; nr. Mannheim; iron, textiles, machin., tobacco, wood; p. (1963) *86,900.*
Kaiser Wilhelm's Land, *Australian Dependency*, Antarctica.
Kaishu, *cap.* of Kokai prov., W. Korea; p. *29,688.*
Kajaani, *t.*, on Oulu L., Finland; p. (1961) *14,683.*
Kakamega, *t.*, Kenya, E. Africa; 30 m. N. of Kisumu; ctr. of gold-mining dist.
Kakhovka, *t.*, Ukrainian S.S.R.; on R. Dnieper; hydro-elec. sta.; p. (1956) *19,200.*
Kakinada, *t.*, *spt.*, Andhra Pradesh, India; cotton, oil seeds; p. (1961) *122,865.*
Kalafat, *t.*, Romania; on R. Danube, opposite Vidin.
Kalahari Desert, *gr. infertile tract* of S. Central Africa, between the R. Orange and the Zambesi; mainly in Botswana; alt. 3,700 ft.; a. 20,000 sq. m.; inhabited chiefly by Bushmen.
Kalamata, *t.*, Peloponnese, Greece; nr. Sparta; silk ind., figs, currants, olive oil exp.; p. (1961) *38,211.*
Kalamazoo, *c.*, Mich., U.S.A.; rly. ctr., engin.; college; p. (1960) *82,089.*
Kalat, *div.*, W. Pakistan; a. 53,995 sq. m.; p. (1961) *589,000.*

Kalgan (Zhangjiakou), *c.*, Hopeh prov., China; nr. Gt. Wall 110 m. N.W. of Peking; tea, wool, hides; p. (1953) *229,000.*
Kalgoorlie, *t.*, W. Australia; on transcontinental rly. route 350 m. E. of Perth; semi-desert conditions; gold-mng. a.; p. (1961) *21,770.*
Kalimantan (Indonesian Borneo); oil, rubber, rice, hardwood; a. 208,286 sq. m.; quartzites discovered in S.E.; p. (1961) *4,101,475.*
Kalinin, *t.*, R.S.F.S.R.; on trib. of R. Volga; cath.; engin., textiles, chemicals; p. (1962) *286,000.*
Kaliningrad, *prov.*, R.S.F.S.R., U.S.S.R.; cap. K., oil discovered in a.
Kaliningrad (formerly **Königsberg**), *t.*, formerly E. Prussia, now U.S.S.R.; on R. Pregel; cath.; fine bldgs; shipbldg., machin., wood-pulp, chemicals, sugar-beet; tea ctr.; p. (1959) *202,000.*
Kalisz, *t.*, Poland; on R. Prosna; industl. ctr., textiles; one of oldest Polish ts., mentioned in 2nd century A.D. by Ptolemy; p. (1960) *70,000.*
Kalmar, *co.*, S. Sweden; cap. Kalmar; a. 4,485 sq. m.; p. (1961) *235,770.*
Kalmar, *spt.*, Sweden; on E. cst.; matches, shipbldg., food inds.; p. (1961) *30,839.*
Kalna, *vil.*, on Mt. Trara Planina, Yugoslavia; uranium mine and plant; nuclear power sta.
Kalocsa, *t.*, Hungary; on R. Danube; cath., palace; wine; p. (1962) *13,786.*
Kaluga, *t.*, R.S.F.S.R.; on R. Oka; chemicals, engin., hydro-elec.; p. (1959) *133,000.*
Kalyan, *spt.*, Thana, Maharashtra, India; p. (1961) *73,482.*
Kama, *R.*, U.S.S.R.; trib. of R. Volga, which it joins S. of Kazan; length 1,400 m.
Kamaishi, *t.*, *spt.*, N.E. Honshu, Japan; serves Kamaishi–Sennin iron-ore field, lgst. worked deposits and reserves in Japan; impt. iron and steel ind.; p. (1947) *26,200.*
Kamaran I., Red Sea; under Aden admin.; quarantine sta. for pilgrims travelling to Mecca from the E.; a 22 sq. m.; p. about *2,200.*
Kamchatka, *peninsula*, E. Siberia, U.S.S.R.; mtns. with volcanoes (Klyuchevsk, alt. 16,512 ft.); mineral wealth, fisheries on cst., climate cold, wet and foggy; cap. Petropavlovsk.
Kamenets Podolski, *t.*, Ukrainian S.S.R.; brewing, tobacco; p. (1956) *33,000.*
Kamensk-Shakhtinskiy, *t.*, R.S.F.S.R.; on R. Severskiy Donets; coal-mng., engin., artificial fibres; p. (1959) *58,500.*
Kamensk Uralsk, *t.*, R.S.F.S.R.; aluminium, iron, steel, engin.; p. (1959) *141,000.*
Kamet, *mtn.*, N. Garhwal dist., Himalayas; alt. 25,477 ft.; until 1953 (Everest) highest mtn. climbed (Smythe, 1931).
Kamloops, *c.*, B.C., Canada; on Thompson R.; formerly Fort Thompson; in "Wild West" area; on transcontinental rlys.; supply ctr. for mining and grazing dist.; p. (1961) *10,076.*
Kampala, *cap.*, Uganda, E. Africa; univ. coll.; ch. comm. ctr.; lt. inds.; p. (1959) *46,780.*
Kampar, *t.*, Perak, Malaysia; p. *17,449.*
Kampen, *t.*, Overyssel, Netherlands; on R. Yssel; p. (1960) *26,668.*
Kamp-Lintfort, *t.*, N. Rhine–Westphalia, Germany; Cistercian abbey; coal-mng.; p. (1963) *35,900.*
Kampot, *prov.*; Cambodia; pepper; p. (1962) *337,879.*
Kamyshin, *mftg. t.*, R.S.F.S.R.; on R. Volga; textiles; mkt. gardening, grain; p. (1959) *55,000.*
Kan, *R.*, S. China; rises in Nan Shan, flows N. into L. Poyang; valley provides route for main road from Kiangsi prov. to Kwangtung prov. over Meiling Pass.
Kanawha, *R.*, W. Va., U.S.A.; rises in Allegheny Mtns., flows S.W. to Hinton, then turns N.W. across Allegheny Plateau into R. Ohio; lower course runs through ch. mining a. of W. Va. coalfield nr. Charleston; length 350 m. approx.
Kanazawa, *t.*, Kaga, Honshu, Japan; silks and pottery; p. (1960) *299,000.*
Kanchenjunga, *mtn.*, on Nepal–Sikkim bdy., N.E. India; 3rd highest mtn. in world; alt. 28, 146 ft.
Kandahar, *prov.*, S. Afghanistan; mountainous; cap. K.; p. (1948) *1,063,496.*
Kandahar, *c.*, former cap., Afghanistan; alt. 3,400 ft.; 370 m. from Herat; linked by road to Kushka (Turkmenia) via Herat; p. (estd. 1964) *115,000.*
Kandy, *t.*, Ceylon; in ctr. of I., 75 m. from Colombo at alt. 3,000 ft.; resort in hot season; tea and cocoa; p. (1963) *67,768.*
Kane, *bor.*, Penns., U.S.A.; natural-gas region; p. (1960) *5,380.*
Kangaroo I., S. Australia; eucalyptus.
Kankakee, *t.*, Ill., U.S.A.; farm implements; machin.; p. (1960) *27,666.*
Kannopolis, *t.*, N.C., U.S.A.; textiles; p. (1950) *28,448.*
Kano, *c.*, N. Nigeria, W. Africa; gr. emporium for the whole Sudan region; impt. airport and rly. terminus; p. (1953) *130,000.*
Kansas, *st.*, U.S.A.; called the "Sunflower State"; prairie; farming, maize, wheat; cattle, dairying, pigs; coal, petroleum, natural gas, lead, meat-packing, flour-milling, aircraft, chemicals, machin.; cap. Topeka; a. 82,276 sq. m.; p. (1960) *2,178,611.*
Kansas City, Mo., U.S.A.; on right bank of R. Missouri; univ.; gr. livestock mart., car and aircraft assembly, steel, metal; meat pkg., food processing; p. (1960) *475,539*, adjoins Kansas City, Kansas; p. (1960) *121,901.*
Kansk, *t.*, R.S.F.S.R., on Trans-Siberian Rly.; ctr. of industl. a.; textiles, wood-working; p. (1959) *74,000.*
Kansu (Gansu), *prov.*, N. China; bordering Inner Mongolia; cap. Lanchow; wheat, cotton, tobacco; livestock; mineral resources; a. 151,161 sq. m.; p. (1953) *12,928,102.*
Kant, *t.*, Kirgiz S.S.R.; 12 m. E. of Frunze; to be expanded to industl. c.; proposed p. *100,000.*
Kaohsiung, *spt.*, Taiwan; on S.W. cst.; exp. rice. sugar; oil refining; p. (1962) *276,000.*
Kapfenberg, *commune*, Austria; iron, chemicals, paper; resort; p. (1961) *23,859.*
Kaposvar, *t.*, Hungary; textiles; p. (1962) *45,054.*
Kara-Bogaz, *lge. G.* on E. cst. of Caspian Sea, Turkmen S.S.R.; very high salinity, impt. deposits of Glauber's salt used in local chemical ind.; a. 7,000 sq. m.
Karabuk, *t.*, Turkey; N. of Ankara; steel wks.; p. (1960) *31,440.*
Karachi, Fed. Terr. of, *div.*, W. Pakistan, on the Indus delta; univ.; spt., air ctr.; oil ref. under construction; industl. gases; a. 8,400 sq. m.; p. (1961) *2,153,000.*
Karaganda, *t.*, Kazakh S.S.R.; town built on impt. coalfield; engin.; p. (1962) *459,000.*
Karakorum Mtns., Kashmir, India; on border with China; hgst peak Godwin-Austen.
Kara-Kum, *sand desert*, Turkmen S.S.R.; canal 510 m. long across desert completed 1962.
Kara Sea, Arctic Ocean; E. of Novaya Zemlya; navigation open July–Sept.
Karbala, *t.*, Iraq; N.W. of Hilla; ctr. of pilgrimage; sacred c. of Shiites; p. (1961) *219,015.*
Karcag, *t.*, E. Hungary; tortoiseshell goods; p. (1962) *25,787.*
Karelia A.S.S.R., U.S.S.R., incorporated into R.S.F.S.R. July '56; cap. Petrozavodsk; rich in timber, minerals, precious metals; a. 69,720 sq. m.; p. (1959) *649,000.*
Karen State, *see* **Kawthoolei.**
Kariba Dam, in Kariba gorge of Zambezi R., on Rhodesia–Zambia border; operated jointly by the two govts.; one of lgst dams in world with vast artificial lake supplying hydroelec. power to Rhodesia, Malawi, and the Copperbelt of Zambia; completed 1960.
Karikal, *former Fr. prov.*, united with India 1954; on E. cst.; p. (1961) *22,252.*
Karkonosze (Riesengebirge), *mtn. range*, between Polish Silesia and Bohemia; highest peak Sniezka (Schneekoppe), 5,275 ft.
Karl-Marx-Stadt, *t.*, Karl-Marx-Stadt, E. Germany; cottons, woollens, machin., cars, furniture, chemicals, engin.; p. (1963) *288,597.*
Karlovac, *t.*, Croatia, Jugoslavia; S.W. of Zagreb; chemicals; p. (1959) *30,000.*
Karlovy Vary, *t.*, *wat. pl.*, ČSSR.; on R. Ohre; health resort; porcelain; p. (1961) *42,819.*
Karlshamn, *t.*, Sweden; oil refining, demagnetising sta.; p. (1961) *11,657.*
Karlskoga, *mkt. t.*, Sweden; E. of L. Vänern; armaments, iron and steel; p. (1961) *35,606.*
Karlskrona, *ch. naval sta.*, Sweden; on the S. cst.; lighting fixtures, china; p. (1961) *32,977.*
Karlsruhe, *t.*, Baden-Württemberg, Germany; chemicals, engin., elec., tobacco ind, oil refining; rly. junction; outport on Rhine; nuclear reactor projected (1957); oil pipeline to Lavera, nr. Marseilles, opened 1963; p. (1963) *249,500.*
Karlstad, *t.*, Sweden; on N. shore L. Vänern; ironwks. hy. engin., machin.; p. (1961) *43,064.*

Karnak, *vil.* Upper U.A.R.; on Nile, the site of ancient Thebes; ruined temples.
Karpathos, *I.*, Dodecanese, Greece; Mediterranean Sea; between Rhodes and Crete, p. *8,747.*
Karroos, **Gr.** and **Little**, extensive treeless plateau between mtn. ranges covered by scrub, C. of Good Hope, S. Africa.
Kars, *c.*, Turkey; woollens, carpets; p. (1960) *32,046.* [(1961) *46,842.*
Karvina, *t.*, ČSSR.; coal, iron, chemicals; p.
Kasai, *R.*, Angola and Congo, Central Africa; rises in Bihé Plateau (Angola) and flows over 1,200 m. into R. Congo 120 m. above Leopoldville; navigable from R. Congo upstream to Pt. Francqui, where connection made with Katanga rly.
Kasanlik, *t.*, Central Bulgaria: captured from Turks at surrender of Sipka Pass 1878; famous for attar of roses; p. (1956) *30,934.*
Kashan, *prov.*, Iran; between Isfahan and Qum; cap. c. K.; carpets; p. (prov.) 1,000,000; p. (c.) (1956) *45,998.*
Kashgar, *R.*, E. Turkestan; flowing 500 m. to the R. Yarkand.
Kashing, *t.*, N. Chekiang, E. China; on Grand Canal; mkt. and tr. ctr.; p. *c. 86,000.*
Kashmir, *see* **Jammu and Kashmir.**
Kassala, *prov.*, Sudan; a. 134,450 sq. m.; p. (estd. 1951) *788,200.*
Kassel, *t.*, Hessen, Germany; on R. Fulda; cas.; iron, machin., cars, wood; route ctr.; p. (1963) *211,800.*
Kastamonu, *t.*, Karasu, Turkey; cap. of Turkish I. same name; great comm. ctr.; fruit, cotton, mohair; p. (1960) *19,450.* [*10,162.*
Kastoria, *t.*, N. Greece; E. of Vérroia; p. (1961)
Katahain, *mtn.*, N. of Bangor, Maine, U.S.A.; alt. 5,385 ft.
Katanga, *former prov.*, Congo; now divided into 3 provs.: N. Katanga, E. Katanga, and Lualaba; copper, radium, uranium; cattle; a. 180,000 sq. m.; p. *1,178,029.*
Katmandu, *cap.*, Nepal; on Vishnumati R., 75 m. from Indian frontier; highway to Kodari opened 1964; hydro-elec. sta. nearing completion 1965; p. (1961) *195,260.*
Kathiawar, *peninsula*, Gujarat, India.
Katoomba, *see* **Blue Mountains.**
Katowice, *industl. c., cap.*, Upper Silesia, Poland; ironwks., coal-mines; p. (1960) *269,000.*
Katrine, Loch, S.W. Perth, Scot.; on R. Teith, 8 m. long; principal source of Glasgow water supply; beautiful scenery.
Kattegat, arm of North Sea linked with Baltic; separates Denmark (Jutland) from Sweden; 40–70 m. wide. [*28,176.*
Kauai, *I.*, Hawaiian Is.; a. 555 sq. m.; p. (1960)
Kaunas (Kovno), *t.*, Lithuanian S.S.R.; on R. Niemen; old-time cap.; univ.; metal goods, chemicals, textiles; hydro-elec. sta. under construction; p. (1959) *214,000.*
Kavalla, *prefecture*, Macedonia, Greece; ch. t. Kavalla; p. (1961) *140,445.*
Kavalla, *t.*, Kavalla, Greece; on Bay of Kavalla; gr. tobacco-preparing and exp. ctr.; p. (1961) *44,517.*
Kawasaki, *c.*, Honshu, Japan; S. sub. of Tokyo; pilgrims; engin.; steel plate, petro-chemicals, synthetic resins, rubber; p. (1960) *633,000.*
Kawerau, *t.*, N.I., N.Z.; pulp and paper mill; p. (1961) *4,413.*
Kawthoolei, *div.*, Burma; former Karen st. extended to include areas in Tenasserim and Irrawaddy, inhabited by Karens. [*19,000.*
Kayes, *t.*, Mali, W. Africa; on Senegal R.; p.
Kayseri, *t.*, Turkey; S.E. of Ankara; p. (1960) *102,795.*
Kazakhstan, *constituent rep.*, U.S.S.R.; cap. Alma-Ata; steppe with stock-raising; lge. desert areas, being made fertile by irrigation; grain in N.; coal at Karaganda; minerals, oil; a. 1,072,797 sq. m.; p. (1959) *9,301,000.*
Kazan, *t.*, R.S.F.S.R.; impt. tr. ctr. for E. U.S.S.R., Turkestan, Bokhara and Iran; cath., univ.; engin., chemicals, synthetic rubber, textiles, oil refining, paper; natural gas pipeline to Minnibayevo (Tatar A.S.S.R.); p. (1962) *711,000.*
Kazan Retto (Volcano Is.), *gr. of Is.*, Pac. Oc.; S. of Ogasawara Is. and of Japan.
Kazerun, *t.*, S.W. Iran; oranges, cotton, opium; p. (1956) *30,659.* [*17,417.*
Kazincbarcika, *t.*, Hungary; chemicals; p. (1962)
Kazvin, *t.*, Navistain, Iran; good transit tr.; p. (estd. 1950) *80,000.*

Keady, *t., urb. dist.*, Armagh, N. Ireland; 10 m. S. of Armagh; p. (1961) *1,638.*
Kearny, *t.*, N.J., U.S.A.; mnfs.; p. (1960) *37,472.*
Kearsley, *urb. dist.*, Lancs, Eng.; chemicals and paper, cotton; p. (1961) *10,302.*
Kecskemet, *industl. t.*, Hungary; nr. Budapest; p. (1962) *68,327.*
Kedah, *st.*, Malaysia, N.W. Malaya; rice, rubber, coconuts; a. 3,660 sq. m.; cap. Alor Star; p. (1961) *794,086.*
Kedzierzyn, *t.*, Opole, Poland; p. (1960) *20,000.*
Keeling Is., *see* **Cocos Is.**
Keen, *mtn.*, nr. Ballater, Forfar and Aberdeen, Scot.; alt. 3,077 ft.
Keene, *c.*, N.H., U.S.A.; mnfs.; p. (1960) *17,562.*
Keeper, *mtn.*, Tipperary, Ireland; alt. 2,265 ft.
Keewatin, *dist.*, N.W. Terr., Canada; chiefly "barren lands"; a. 228,160 sq. m.
Kei (Kai) Is., *gr.* off cst. of W. Irian, Indonesia, in Banda Sea; densely forested; p. *50,648.*
Keighley, *t., mun. bor.*, W.R. Yorks., Eng.; in Aire valley, 15 m. N.W. of Leeds; engin., textiles; p. (1961) *55,852.*
Keith, *burgh*, Banff, Scot.; on Isla R.; mftg. inds.; in agr. dist.; p. (1961) *4,208.*
Kelantan, *st.*, Malaysia; N.E. Malaya; rice, coconuts, rubber; a. 5,720 sq. m.; cap. Kota Bharu; p. (1961) *579,246.* [(1960) *5,061.*
Kellogg, *c.*, N.E. Idaho, U.S.A.; lead-mines; p.
Kells, *mkt. t., urb. dist.*, Meath, Ireland; on R. Blackwater; p. (1961) *2,193.*
Kelowna, *t.*, B.C., Canada; p. (1961) *13,188.*
Kelso, *burgh*, Roxburgh, Scot.; at confluence of Rs. Teviot and Tweed; p. (1961) *3,964.*
Kelvin, *R.*, Scotland, flows S.W. to Clyde at Partick; length 21 m.
Kemerovo, *t.*, R.S.F.S.R.; S.E. of Tomsk; iron, chemicals, coal, textiles; p. (1962) *305,000.*
Kemi (Kymmene), *dep.*, Finland; a. 3,537 sq. m.; cap. K.; p. (1958) *329,757.*
Kempsey, *t.*, N.S.W., Australia; p. (1961) *7,999.*
Kempston, *urb. dist.*, Bedford, Eng.; on R. Ouse, 3 m. S.W. of Bedford; p. (1961) *9,173.*
Kempten, *t.*, Bavaria, Germany; nr. L. Constance; Benedictine Abbey; textiles, furniture, paper; rly. junction; p. (1963) *44,500.*
Ken, *R.*, N. India, flows to the Jumna; length 230 m.
Kena, *see* **Qena.**
Kendal, *mkt. t., mun. bor.*, Westmorland, Eng.; on R. Kent; engin., footwear, woollens; p. (1961) *18,595.*
Kenilworth, *mkt. t., urb. dist.*, Warwick, Eng.; 4 m. S.W. of Coventry; ruined cas.; lt. engin., agr. repair wk.; p. (1961) *14,427.*
Kenitra. *See* **Mina Hassan Tani.** [*6,982.*
Kenmare, *rurl dist., t.*, Kerry, Ireland; p. (1961)
Kenmore, *t.*, N.Y., U.S.A.; p. (1960) *21,261.*
Kennebec, *R.*, Maine, U.S.A.; flows to Atlantic; length 200 m.
Kennet, *R.*, Wilts and Berks, Eng.; trib. of R. Thames; followed by main rly. London to W. of England; length 44 m.
Kenosha, *c.*, Wis., U.S.A., on W. shore of L. Michigan; mnfs.; p. (1960) *67,899.*
Kensal Green, *dist.*, Middx, Eng.; sub. N.W. London.
Kensington and Chelsea, Royal Borough of, *inner bor.*, W. London, Eng.; mainly residtl.; contains K. Palace and Gardens; p. (1964) *217,976.*
Kent, *maritime co.*, S.E. Eng.; agr., stock-raising, hops and cherries; co. t. Maidstone; a. 1,525 sq. m.; p. (1961) *1,701,083.*
Kenton, *t.*, Ohio, U.S.A.; onions; quarries, foundries; novelty mnfs.; p. (1960) *8,747.*
Kent's Cavern, *cave*, nr. Torquay, Devon, Eng.; 650 ft. long.
Kentucky, *E. central st.*, Mississippi basin, U.S.A.; agr., coal, fluorspar, petroleum, natural gas; tobacco, chemicals, machin., metal, steel, hemp, asphalt; tobacco, hay, corn; cattle and horse raising; cap. Frankfort; lgst. c. Louisville, at falls of Ohio R.; a. 40,395 sq. m.; p. (1960) *3,038,156.*
Kentucky, *R.*, U.S.A.; flows from Cumberland Mtns. to the Ohio R.; length 350 m.
Kenya, Rep. of, *indep. sov. st.* within Brit. Commonwealth (1963), E. Africa; cst. strip flat, interior elevated; climate varies according to elevation; vegetation, tropical; forests on cstal. belt, semi-desert and grasslands on uplands; races, Bantu Negroes, Indians and Arabs; agr., maize, sugar, coconuts, sisal, cotton, coffee, pyrethrum; cattle, sheep; bamboo, pencil

cedar, hardwoods; gold; oil refining at Changamwe; cap. Nairobi; a. 224,960 sq. m.; p. (estd. 1964) *8,676,000.*
Kenya, Mt., *volcanic pk.,* Kenya; 17,040 ft.
Keokuk, *industl., c.,* S.E. Iowa, U.S.A.; on Mississippi at foot of Des Moines rapids; p. (1960) *16,316.* ([1961) *62,090.*
Keos (Chios), Ægean Is., Greece; cap. Keos; p.
Kephallenia (Cephalonia), one of the Ionian Is., Greece; currants, olive oil; cap. Argostolion; devastated by earthquake 1953; a. 315 sq. m.; p. (1961) *46,302.*
Kerala, *st.,* India; cap. Trivandrum; plantations producing rubber, tea, pepper; zircon; a. 15,002 sq. m.; p. (1961) *16,903,715.*
Kerch, *spt.,* Ukrainian S.S.R.; iron and steel, shipbldg.; fisheries; p. (1959) *99,000.*
Kergulen, *French archipelago,* dependency of Madagascar, S. of Indian Ocean; whaling and fishing sta.; a. 1,400 sq. m.
Kérkyra (Corfu), most N. of Ionian Is., Greece; a. 274 sq. m.; mtnous.; p. (1961) *101,555.*
Kérkyra, *spt., cap.,* Kérkyra I., Greece; wine, fruits, olives; p. (1961) *26 991.*
Kermadec Is., S. Pac. Oc., gr. belonging to New Zealand, 600 m. N.N.E. of New Zealand; a. 13 sq. m.; meteorological sta. on Sunday I. (lgst. of gr.); p. (1961) *10.*
Kerman, *prov.,* Iran; on Persian G.; cap. Kerman; carpet mftg.; p. (1956) *62,175.*
Kermanshah, *c.,* cap. Kermanshah prov., Persia; S. of Kurdistan; wool; p. (1956) *125,181.*
Kern, *L.,* S. Cal., U.S.A.; once ctr. of inland drainage in S. of Central Californian Valley, 20 m. W. of Bakersfield; now permanently dry; feeding rs. diverted for irrigation.
Kerrville, *t.,* Texas, U.S.A.; cattle, cotton, mkt., resort; p. (1960) *8,901.*
Kerry, *maritime co.,* Munster, Ireland; a. 1,816 sq. m.; cap. Tralee; p. (1961) *116,405.*
Keski Suomen, *dep.* Finland; p. (1961) *245,014.*
Kesteven, *administrative div.,* Lincoln, Eng.; ch. ts. Grantham, Stamford and Sleaford; a. 724 sq. m.; p. (1961) *49,946.*
Keswick, *mkt. t., urb. dist.,* Cumberland, Eng.; on Greta R.; at N. end of L. Derwentwater; tourist ctr.; pencils; p. (1961) *4,752.*
Ketchikan, *t.,* Alaska, U.S.A.; halibut, salmon; pulp, lead, zinc; p. (1960) *6,483.*
Kettering, *mkt. t., mun. bor.,* Northants, Eng.; nr. Wellingborough; iron, steel, boots, shoes; p. (1961) *38,631.*
Kettering, *t.,* Ohio, U.S.A.; p. (1960) *54,462.*
Kew, *sub.* London, Surrey, Eng.; on R. Thames opp. Brentford; contains Kew Gardens. (Kew Observatory is in Old Deer Park, Richmond.)
Kewanee, *t.,* N.W. Ill., U.S.A.; agr.; coal, engin.; p. (1960) *16,324.* [*15,144.*
Keynsham, *t., urb. dist.,* Somerset, Eng.; p. (1961)
Key West, *c.,* Fla., U.S.A.; on sm. I. same name about 100 m. from the mainland; naval sta., and cigar factories; nearest U.S.A. pt. to the Panama Canal; p. (1960) *33,956.*
Khabarovsk, *t.,* R S.F.S.R.; on Amur R.; cath.; oil refining, aircraft engin., sawmilling; oil pipeline connects with oilfields in N. Sakhalin; p. (1962) *363,000.*
Khairpur, *div.,* W. Pakistan; a. 6,050 sq. m.; p. (1961) *2,586,000.*
Khalkidhiki (Chalcidice), *prefecture,* Macedonia, Greece; cap. Poliyicos; p. (1961) *79,838.*
Khamgaon, *t.,* Maharashtra, India; cotton; p. (1961) *44,432.* [refinery; p. *5,000.*
Khanaqin, *t.,* Iraq; nr. E. frontier; oil-fields,
Khandwa, *t.,* Madhya Pradesh, India; S. of Indore; cotton, oil-pressing; p. (1961) *63,505.*
Khania (Canea), *prefecture* I. of Crete; cap. Khania; p. (1961) *130,898.*
Khania (Canea), *cap.* Crete; in sheltered bay on N.W. cst.; p. (1961) *38,467.*
Khanka Lake, *L.,* on Manchurian border, U.S.S.R.
Kharan, *dist.,* W. Pakistan; a. 18,508 sq. m.; p. (estd. 1951) *54,000.*
Kharkov, *c.,* Ukrainian S.S R.; on R. Donets; univ., cath.; rly. ctr., farm implements, engin., paper, chemicals; p. (1962) *990,000.*
Khartoum, *prov.,* Sudan; a. 5,700 sq. m.; p. with Omdurman (1956) *275,000.*
Khartoum, *cap.* Sudan; at confluence of White and Blue Niles; univ.; ivory, gum, ostrich feathers, brewing; p. (estd. 1956) *87,000.*
Khartoum North, *t.,* Sudan; lge. textile mill; p. (1961) *39,081.*
Khashm el Girba, *t.,* Sudan; new t. on Atbara R., between Khartoum and Ethiopian border; for p. of Wadi Halfa which will be inundated by Aswan Lake.
Khasi Hills, Assam, N.E. India; form abrupt S. edge to middle Brahmaputra valley; very heavy monsoon rains on S.-facing slopes; lower slopes forested; middle slopes constitute impt. tea-growing region; rise to over 6,000 ft.
Khaskovo, *t.,* Bulgaria; woollens, carpets, silk, tobacco; p. *27,294.*
Kherson, *t.,* Ukrainian S.S R.; 10 m. up R. Dnieper from Black Sea; grain, oil refining, engin., textiles, shipbldg; p. (1959) *157,000.*
Khingan, Gr. and Little, *mtn. ranges,* Mongolia and Manchuria; separating the plateau from the plains.
Khios, *I.,* Ægean Is., Greece; wines, figs, fruits, marble; cap. Khios; p. (1961) *62,090.*
Khiva, *originally vassal st.* of Russia; now part of Uzbekistan, U.S.S.R.
Khiva, *t.,* Uzbekistan, U.S.S.R.; silks, cottons, carpets; p. (estd.) *25,000.*
Khmelnitskiy (Proskurov), *t.,* Ukrainian S.S.R.; on R. Bug; machin. tools, textiles, food inds.; p. (1959) *62,000.*
Khor Abdulla, Iraq; deep water oil loading island terminal inaugurated 1963.
Khorramshahr, *spt.,* S.W. Iran; leading pt. on Persian G.; exports dates; p. (1956) *43,840.*
Khotin, *c.,* Ukrainian S.S.R., in Bessarabia, on Dniester R.; food processing plants; p. (estd.) *10,000.*
Khovu-Aksy, *t.,* Tuva A.S.S.R.; on R. Elegest, 50 m. S.W. of Kyzyl; new town 1956; cobalt deposit being developed.
Khurasan, *prov.,* Iran; W. of Afghanistan; ch. prod. wool; cap. Meshed; p. (estd. 1956) *1,300,000.* [p. (1961) *41,491.*
Khurja, *t.,* Uttar Pradesh, India; cotton, pottery;
Khyber, *difficult mtn. pass,* between W. Punjab, Pakistan and Afghanistan; followed by route from Peshawar to Kabul, traversed by Alexander the Great and by two British expeditions.
Kiama, *t.,* N.S.W., Australia; agr.; coal; artificial harbour; p. (1947) *2,426.*
Kiamusze (Jiamusi) *c.,* Heilungkiang prov., China; p. (1953) *146,000.*
Kiang-si (Jiangxi), *inland prov.,* China; S. of the Yangtze-Kiang; cap. Nanchang; rice, wheat, tea, silk, cotton; a. 66,600 sq. m.; p. (1953) *16,772,865.*
Kiangsu (Jiangsu), *maritime prov.,* China; exp. much silk; a. 42,085 sq. m.; cap. Chinkiang; p. (1953) *41,252,192.* [Peninsula, China.
Kiaochow Bay, *inlet* on S. side of Shantung
Kicking Horse Pass, *mtn. pass,* over Rocky Mtns., B.C., Canada; used by Canadian Pac. Rly.
Kidderminster, *t., mun. bor.,* Worcester, Eng.; on R. Stour 4 m. above its confluence with R. Severn; carpets, engin., sugar-beet refining, textile machin., elec. vehicles, drop forgings; p. (1961) *40,822.*
Kidsgrove, *mfig. t., urb. dist.,* "Potteries," Staffs., Eng.; 3 m. N.W. of Stoke-on-Trent; chemicals, metal wks., rayon, silk and nylon spinning, precast concrete, ceramics; p. (1961) *19,726.*
Kidwelly, *mun. bor.,* Carmarthen, Wales; on cst., 7 m. N.W. of Llanelly; coal; p. (1961) *2,879.*
Kiel, *spt.,* cap. Schleswig-Holstein, Germany; univ.; Baltic naval pt.; shipbldg. and allied inds., elec. goods, textiles, fishing; p. (1963) *270,800.*
Kiel Canal (Kaiser-Wilhelm-Kanal), Germany; 61 m. long, connects N. Sea with the Baltic; opened in 1895, reconstructed 1914.
Kielce, *co.,* Central Poland; minerals, agr.; cap. K.; a. 17,000 sq. m.; p. (1961) *1,857,000.*
Kielce, *t.,* Central Poland; tr. ctr., metal inds., sawmills, glass and food processing factories; dates from 12th cent.; p. (1960) *89,000.*
Kiev, *c., cap.,* Ukraine, U.S.S.R.; on R. Dnieper; once cap. of Muscovite Empire; cath.; univ.; machin., grain, in a. of rich mineral deposits, engin.; natural gas pipeline runs from Dashava; p. (1962) *1,208,000.*
Kigoma, *impt. tr. t.,* Tanzania, Africa; W. terminus of the Central Rly. on L. Tanganyika; p. (1957) *3,970.*
Kikinda, *t.,* Vojvodina, Jugoslavia; p. (1959) *31,000.*
Kilauea, *volcano,* Hawaii; lgst. active crater in the world; 2 m. diameter; alt. 4,088 ft.

Kilbarchan, *par.*, Renfrew, Scot.; S.W. of Glasgow; textiles; p. (1951) *8,193*.
Kilbride, W., *par.*, Ayr, Scot.; nr. Ardrossan; (1951) *4,243*.
Kilburn, *sub.*, N.W. London, Eng; p. (1961) *12,759*.
Kildare, *inland co.*, Leinster, Ireland; a. 654 sq. m.; p. (1961) *64,346*.
Kildare, *mkt. t., cap.*, Kildare, Ireland; cath.; close by is the famous racecourse, the Curragh of Kildare; p. (1951) *2,286*.
Kilimanjaro, *volcanic mtn.*, Tanzania, E. Africa; highest peak in the continent; alt. 19,321 ft.
Kilindini, *spt.*, Kenya; adjoins Mombasa; the finest harbour on E. cst. of Africa.
Kilkenny, *inland co.*, Leinster, Ireland; cap. Kilkenny; pastoral farming, coal, black marble; a. 796 sq. m.; p. (1961) *61,670*.
Kilkenny, *t.*, cap. Kilkenny, Ireland; on R. Nore; local mkt.; p. (1961) *10,155*.
Kilkieran Bay, *lge. intricate indentation*, Galway, Ireland.
Kilkis, *prefecture*, Macedonia, Greece; cap. Kilkis; p. (1961) *102,847*.
Killarney, *t., urb. dist.*, Kerry, Ireland; local mkt. and tourist ctr.; p. (1961) *6,824*.
Killarney, Is. of, Lower, Middle and Upper, celebrated for their beauty; tourist resorts.
Killiecrankie, Pass of, Scot.; on R. Garry; at S. approach to Drumochter Pass; used by main rly. Perth to Inverness.
Kill van Kull, channel between N.J. and Staten I., N.Y., c., U.S.A.
Killybegs, *t.*, Donegal, Ireland; on Donegal Bay.
Killyleagh, *t.*, on Stangford L., Down, N. Ireland; p. (1961) *1,876*.
Kilmacolm, *par.*, Renfrew, Scot.; on Gryfe Water; p. (1951) *4,651*
Kilmarnock, *rly. ctr., lge. burgh*, Ayr, Scot.; on R. Irvine, 11 m. N.E. of Ayr; carpet factories, textile and ironwks.; p. (1961) *47,509*.
Kilmore, *t.*, Victoria, Australia; 30 m. N. of Melbourne; in impt. gap between Grampian Mtns. and Australian Alps.
Kilo-Moto, *goldfield*, Congo, Central Africa; in N.E. of st., 50 m. W. of L. Albert; linked by motor road to R. Congo (Stanleyville) and L. Albert (Kasenyi).
Kilpatrick, New, *par.*, Dunbarton, Scot.; on left bank of R. Clyde; p. (1951) *54,931*.
Kilpatrick, Old, *par.*, Dunbarton, Scot.; on bank of R. Clyde, 9 m. N.W. of Glasgow; lowest ferry across Clyde; p. (1951) *49,248*.
Kilrenny and Anstruther, *burgh*, Fife, Scot.; at entrance to Firth of Forth; fishing, hosiery, oilskin mnfs.; p. (1961) *2,888*.
Kilrush, *spt., urb. dist.*, S.W. Clare, Ireland; on R. Shannon; p. (1961) *2,861*.
Kilsyth, *burgh*, Stirling, Scot.; at S. foot of Campsie Fells, 10 m. W. of Falkirk; whinstone quarries, coal-mining; p. (1961) *9,831*.
Kilwinning, *burgh*, N. Ayr, Scot.; 5 m. E. of Ardrossan; p. (1961) *7,287*.
Kimberley, *c.*, Cape Province, S. Africa; 20 m. from R. Vaal; diamond-mng. dist.; asbestos, manganese, iron, cement, engin.; p. (1960) *91,816* inc. *27,460* Europeans.
Kimberley, *goldfield dist.*, W. Australia.
Kimberly, *t.*, B.C., Canada; on R. Kootenay in valley between Selkirk Range and Rocky Mtns.; site of Sullivan Mine; lg. lead- zinc mine; ores smelted at Trail; p. (1956) *5,730*.
Kincardine, *maritime co.*, E. Scot., between Angus and Aberdeen; agr. and fishing; co. t. Stonehaven; a. 383 sq. m.; p. (1961) *48,810*.
Kinder Scout, *mtn.*, N. Derby, Eng.; highest point of the Peak dist.; alt. 2,088 ft.
Kindu, *t.*, Congo, Central Africa; on R. Congo; p. *10,628*.
Kineshna, *t.*, U.S.S.R.; N.W. of Gorki; pt. for Ivanovo industl. a.; textiles; p. (1959) *84,000*.
Kineton, *mkt. t.*, Warwick, Eng.; nr. Stratford-on-Avon.
King George's Sound, W. Australia; nr. Albany; fine harbour and bay.
Kinghorn, *burgh*, Fife, Scot.; on Firth of Forth, 3 m. S. of Kirkcaldy; p. (1961) *2,112*.
Kingsbridge, *mkt. t., urb. dist.*, S. Devon, Eng.; at head of Kingsbridge estuary, 10 m. S.W. of Dartmouth; p. (1961) *3,283*.
Kingsclere and Whitchurch, *mkt. t., rural dist.*, N. Hants, Eng.; on R. Test, 10 m. S.W. of Basingstoke; p. (rural dist. 1961) *23,264*.
Kings Langley, *t.*, Herts, Eng.; 5 m. N. of Watford; paper, light engin.; p. (1961) *4,255*.
King's Lynn, *spt., mun. bor.*, Norfolk, Eng.; on R. Ouse, 3 m. above its mouth; fishing, agr. machin., canning, chemical fertilisers, shoes; p. (1961) *27,554*.
King's Norton (with Northfield), *industl. t.*, Worcester, Eng.
King's River, Cal., U.S.A.; flows from Sierra Nevada to L. Tulare.
Kingsport, *t.*, N.E. Tenn., U.S.A.; varied mnfs.; p. (1960) *26,314*.
Kingston, *c.*, Ont., Canada; E. end of L. Ontario; cap. of United Canada, 1841–4; univ., military college; lge inds; p. (1961) *53,926*.
Kingston, *cap.*, Jamaica, W. Indies; oil refining; p. (estd. 1962) *180,000*.
Kingston, *t.*, N.Y., U.S.A.; tobacco mftg.; p. (1960) *29,260*.
Kingston, *t.*, Penns., U.S.A.; p. (1960) *20,261*.
Kingston-upon-Hull, *see* **Hull.**
Kingston-upon-Thames, *former co. t., mun. bor.*, Surrey, Eng.; now **The Royal Borough of Kingston-upon-Thames,** *outer bor.*, Greater London; inc. bors. of Malden and Coombe and Surbiton; residtl.; with Royal Park; aircraft parts; p. (1964) *145,977*.
Kingstown, *see* **Dun Laoghaire.**
Kingstown, *spt., cap.*, St. Vincent, W.I.; cath., botanic gardens; p. (1956) *6,500*.
Kingsville, *t.*, Texas, U.S.A.; in ranching area; agr., light inds.; p. (1960) *25,297*.
Kingswood, *urb. dist.*, Gloucester, Eng.; nr. Bristol: elec. vehicles, motor cycles, boots, brushes, tools; p. (1961) *25,419*.
Kington, *mkt. t., urb. dist.*, N.W. Hereford, Eng.; 12 m. W. of Leominster; p. (1961) *1,861*.
Kingussie, *burgh*, Inverness, Scot.; between Cairngorm Mtns. and Monadhliath Mtns., on R. Spey; summer resort; p. (1961) *1,079*.
King William I., off Boothia peninsula in Arctic Ocean, Canada.
King William's Town, *t.*, Cape Prov., S. Africa; on Buffalo R.; industl. ctr.; p. (1960) *14,328* inc. *6,873* whites.
Kinhwa, *c.*, Chekiang, China; in fertile, intensively cultivated basin, 85 m. S.W. of Hangchow p. (estd. 1947) *211,140*.
Kinibalu, *mtn.*, Sabah; alt. 13,455 ft.
Kinlochleven, *vil.*, Argyll, Scot.; at head of Loch Leven; hydro-elec. power sta., aluminium smelting; p. *3,757*.
Kinnaird Head, *promontory*, nr. Fraserburgh, on N.E. Aberdeen cst., Scot.
Kinross, *sm. inland co.*, Scot.; between Fife and Perth; hilly; oats, potatoes, sheep, cattle; a. 78 sq. m.; p. (1961) *6,704*.
Kinross, *co. burgh*, Kinross, Scot.; on Loch Leven, 16 m. N.E. of Alloa; coal, linen mnfs.; p. (1961) *2,365*.
Kinsale, *spt., urb. dist.*, on K. Harbour, Cork, Ireland; p. (urb. dist. 1961) *7,993*.
Kinta Valley, S.E. Perak, Malaya; very impt. deposits of alluvial tin.
Kintyre, *peninsula*, Argyll, Scot.; length 40 m., greatest breadth 11 m.; S. point the Mull of Kintyre.
Kioga, *L.*, Uganda, E. Africa; on R. Nile midway between L. Victoria and L. Albert; very shallow, fringed with marsh; land reclamation.
Kiölen or Kjölen, *mtn. range*, Scandinavia; highest point Mt. Sulitelma; alt. 6,150 ft.
Kirgiz Steppes, *gr. plains and uplands*, Kirghizia S.S.R., U.S.S.R.; N. of the Caspian and Aral Seas, inhabited by the wandering Mongolian Tatar race numbering nearly *3,000,000*.
Kirghizia, *constituent rep.*, U.S.S.R.; S.W. of Siberia; livestock breeding, mineral resources; a. 75,900 sq. m.; cap. Frunze; p. (1959) *2,063,000*.
Kirin (Jilin), *prov.*, China; S. of the Sungari R. and N. of Korea and the Liaotung Peninsula; fertile; soyabeans; timber; good rly. services; cap. Kirin, a. 34,616 sq. m.; p. (1953) *11,290,073*.
Kirin (Jilin), *c., cap.*, Kirin, N.E. China; on Sungari R. at outlet of Sungari reservoir; impt. position on rly. from Changchun to coastal ports, p. (1953) *435,000*.
Kirkburton, *urb. dist.*, W.R. Yorks, Eng.; S.E. of Huddersfield; woollens; p. (1961) *18,066*.
Kirkby, *urb. dist.*, Lancs., Eng.; p. (1961) *52,207*.
Kirkby in Ashfield, *t., urb. dist.*, Notts, Eng.; 10 m. N.W. of Nottingham; coal; p. (1901) *21,690*.

Kirkby Moorside, *mkt. t.*, *rural dist.*, N.R. Yorks, Eng.; sailplanes, gliders; p. (1961) *4,402*.
Kirkcaldy, *spt. t.*, *burgh*, Fife, Scot.; on N. side of F. of Forth; shipping; linoleum, potteries, linen bleaching, engin.; p. (1961) *52,371*.
Kirkcudbright, *maritime co.*, S.W. Scot.; abutting on Irish Sea and Solway Firth; chiefly agr.; a. 909 sq. m.; p. (1961) *28,877*.
Kirkcudbright, *co. burgh*, Kirkcudbright, Scot.; on Kirkcudbright Bay, Solway Firth, 25 m. S.W. of Dumfries; agr., hosiery; p. (1961) *2,448*.
Kirkenes, *t.*, Finnmark, N. Norway; on S. arm of Varanger Fjord, nr. Norway–U.S.S.R. bdy.; iron-ore mines.
Kirkham, *t.*, *urb. dist.*, Lancs., Eng.; cotton weaving; p. (1961) *4,760*.
Kirkintilloch, *burgh*, Dunbarton, Scot.; on Forth and Clyde Canal; iron, coal-mng; p. (1961) *18,257*.
Kirkland Lake, *t.*, Ontario, Canada; on rly. nr. Quebec–Ontario bdy., 45 m. N. of Cobalt; ctr. of impt. gold-mng. dist.; p. (estd. 1956) *19,000*.
Kirkstone Pass, *mtn. pass*, Westmorland, Eng.; used by main road between Ullswater and Windermere Lakes.
Kirksville, *industl. t.*, Mo., U.S.A.; p.(1960) *13,123*.
Kirkuk, *t.*, Iraq; mart for Arab horses; lge. oilfield with pipelines to Tripoli, Haifa and Banias; p. (1956) *89,917*.
Kirkwall, *burgh*, Pomona I., Orkneys, Scot.; off the N.E. Scottish cst.; p. (1961) *4,315*.
Kirkwood, *sub.*, St. Louis, Mo., U.S.A.; p. (1960) *29,421*.
Kirov, *t.*, R.S.F.S.R.; on trans-Siberian Rly.; engin., sawmilling, chemicals, leather inds.; p. (1962) *277,000*.
Kirovabad, *t.*, W. Azerbaydzhan S.S.R.; copper, manganese mines; textiles, petroleum, aluminium plant under construction; p. (1959) *116,000*.
Kirovgrad, *t.*, Urals; copper; p. (1954) *50,000*.
Kirovograd, *t.*, Ukrainian S.S.R.; engin.; p. (1959) *127,000*.
Kirovsk, *t.*, R.S.F.S.R.; on Kola peninsula; apatite, nephelite, chemicals; p. (1954) *50,000*.
Kirriemuir, *burgh*, Angus, Scot.; on N. margin of Strathmore, 5 m. W. of Forfar; jute weaving, oat milling; p. (1961) *3,485*.
Kiruna, *t.*, N. Sweden; inside Arctic Circle, N.W. of Lulea; linked by rly. to Narvik (Norway); impt. deposits of iron ore; p. (1961) *26,804*.
Kiselevsk, *t.*, W. Siberia, R.S.F.S.R.; coalmng., engin.; p. (1959) *130,000*.
Kishinev, *cap.* Moldavian S.S.R., U.S.S.R.; univ.; agr., engin.; vineyards; p. (1963) *254,000*.
Kislovodsk, *t.*, R.S.F.S.R.; spa; p. (1959) *79,000*.
Kissimee R., Fla., U.S.A., flows to L. Okeechobee; length 90 m.
Kistna, *R.*, S. India; rises in W. Ghats, flows E. across Deccan plateau into Bay of Bengal; lower valley and delta under intensive rice cultivation; densely populated; length 850 m.
Kisumu, *spt.*, *cap.*, Nyanza prov., Kenya, E. Africa; at head of Kavirondo G. on L. Victoria; original W. terminus of rly. from Mombasa; still handles bulk of cotton from Buganda and coffee from N. Tanzania for transhipment E. by rail; p. (1962) *23,200*.
Kitakyushu City, *c.*, N. Kyushu, Japan; one of Japan's largest municipalities on merging (1963) of ts. Moji, Kokura, Tobata, Yawata and Wakamatsu; sixth c. to enjoy special aut. rights; p. (1963) *1,050,000*.
Kitchener, *c.*, Ontario, Canada; agr. machin., tyres, hardware, p. (1961) *74,485*.
Kittatinny Mtns. or **Blue Mtns.**, *range* in Penns. and N.J., U.S.A.; a continuation of the Appalachian system.
Kitwe, *t.*, Zambia; contiguous to mine township of Nkana, ctr. of copperbelt; p. (incl. Nkana) (1960) *92,390* (incl. *12,390* Europeans).
Kiukiang, *c.*, *former treaty pt.*, Kiangsi, China; Yangtze-Kiang; p. (1948) *180,897*.
Kiungchow, *c.*, *cap.*, Hainan Is., China; on N. cst.; former treaty pt.
Kivu, *L.*, Central Africa; N. of L. Tanganyika by which it is joined by Russisi R.; length 55 m.; a. 1 100 sq. m.
Kizel, *t.*, R.S.F.S.R., in Urals; ctr. of coal mng. a.; mng. equipment; p. (1959) *60,000*.
Kizilirmak (or Red River), the lgst. R. of Turkey in Asia; rises in Kisil Dagh, flows to Black Sea via Sivas; l. 600 m.
Kladno, *mng. t.*, ČSSR.; 10 m. N.W. of Prague; coal, iron, steel, engin.; p. (1961) *49,561*.
Klagenfurt, *t.*, *cap.*, Carinthia, Austria; white-lead, tobacco and silk factories; p. (1961) *69,218*.
Klaipeda (Memel), *spt.*, Lithuanian S.S.R.; nr. N. extremity Kurisches Haff; exp. timber, textiles, chemicals, paper; p. (1959) *89,000*.
Klamath, *L.*, Cal. and Ore., U.S.A., discharges by K. R. (275 m.) to Pacific.
Klamath Falls, *t.*, Ore., U.S.A.; p. (1960) *16,949*.
Klamono, *t.*, New Guinea, nr. Klasafet R.; oil pipe-line to Sorong harbour.
Klang, *t.*, Selangor, Malaya; designated future st. cap.; coffee, rubber; p. *33,506*.
Klatovy, *t.*, S.W. Bohemia, ČSSR.; mkt.; rose-growing a., textiles; p. (1961) *14,004*.
Klerksdorp, *t.*, S. Transvaal, S. Africa; gold, diamonds; p. (1962) *48,500* inc. *22,000* whites.
Kleve, *t.*, N. Rhine–Westphalia, Germany; nr. Netherlands frontier; foodstuffs, leather, machin., tobacco; p. (1963) *22,100*.
Klin, *t.*, R.S.F.S.R., 45 m. from Moscow: glass, textiles: p. (1959) *53,000*.
Klondyke, *R.*, Yukon, Canada; small trib. of Yukon in gold-mine region.
Klodzko (Glatz), *t.*, Lower Silesia, Poland, German before 1945; on R. Nisa (Neisse); rly. junction; p. (1960) *23,000*.
Knaresborough, *mkt. t.*, *urb. dist.*, W.R. Yorks., Eng.; 3 m. N.E. of Harrogate; p. (1961) *9,311*.
Knighton, *mkt. t.*, *urb. dist.*, Radnor, Wales; on R. Teme; p. (1961) *1,817*.
Knockmealdown Mtns., cos. Waterford and Tipperary, Ireland; highest point 2,609 ft.
Knossos, *ruined c.*, *cap.* of ancient Crete; S.E. of Candia; ctr. of Cretan Bronze Age culture, c. 1800 B.C.
Knottingley, *t.*, *urb. dist.*, W.R. Yorks, Eng.; on R. Aire, 12 m. S.E. of Leeds; engin., glass, tar distilling, chemicals, shipbldg.; p. (1961) *11,153*.
Knoxville, *c.*, Tenn., U.S.A.; univ.; textiles; marble, plastics, chemicals, aluminium; agr. tobacco; p. (1960) *111,827*.
Knutsford, *mkt. t.*, *urb. dist.*, Cheshire, Eng.; 6 m. N.E. of Northwich; p. (1961) *9,389*.
Kobe, *t.*, *spt.*, Honshu, Japan: at E. end of Inland Sea; shipbldg., silk-weaving; gr. tr.; p. (1962) *1,162,000*.
Koblenz (Coblenz), *t.*, Rhineland Palatinate, Germany; at confluence of Rs. Rhine and Moselle; fine buildings, wine, paper, machin., leather, ceramics; p. (1963) *101,200*.
Kocaeli, *prov.*, Turkey; on G. of Sea of Marmara.
Kodiak I., N. Pac. Oc.; the lgst. I. of W. Alaska; (90 m. long); fur-trading, extensive salmon fishing, canning; ch. settlement St. Paul, on Chiniak R.; suffered earthquake damage 28 Mar. 1964; p. (1960) *2,628*.
Kofu, *c.*, Honshu, Japan; silk, vegetables, grapes; p. (1960) *160,963*.
Kohat, *t.*, N.W. Pakistan; on trib. of Indus; military t.; p. (1961) *49,800*.
Koh-I-Baba Mtns., Afghanistan, spur of the Hindu Kush; highest point 17,640 ft.
Kohima, *dist.*, Nagaland, India; a. 2,374 sq. m.; p. (1961) *108,924*.
Kokand, *t.*, Uzbek S.S.R.; textiles, hemicals, engin.; p. (1959) *105,000*.
Kokiu (Gejiu), *c.*, Yunnan prov., China; tin-mng.; p. (1953) *160,000*.
Kokkola (Gamla Karleby), *t.*, Finland; on cst. G. of Bothnia; p. (1961) *16,153*.
Kokomo, *c.*, Ind., U.S.A.; on Wild Cat R.; steel, glass, agr. region; p. (1960) *47,197*.
Koko-Nor, *salt L.*, Tsinghai prov., China; a. 2,040 sq. m.; no outlet.
Kokura, *c.*, N. Kyushu, Japan: 40 m. N.E. of Fukuoka; steel, chemicals, porcelain ware, textiles, p. (1960) *286,000*.
Kola, *peninsula*, R.S.F.S.R.; extension of Lapland.
Kola, *t.*, R.S.F.S.R.; nr. Murmansk, on Kola Peninsular.
Kolar Gold Fields, Mysore, India; p. (1961) [*146,811*.
Kolding, *mkt. t.*, Vejle, Denmark; good harbour; engin., lt. inds.; p. (1960) *35,101*.
Kolguev, *I.*, Arctic Oc.: at entrance of Cheshsk G., N.E. of Arkhangelsk.
Kolhapur, *t.*, Maharashtra, India; bauxite; p. [(1961) *187,442*.
Kolo, *t.*, Poland; on I. of the Warta; pottery.
Kolobrzeg (Kolberg), *c.*, *spt.* W. Pomerania, Poland, German before 1945; cath.; resort; fishing; p. (1939) *36,616*; (1946) *2,816*.
Kolomna, *t.*, R.S.F.S.R., 72 m. S.E. of Moscow; engin., locomotives, machin.; p. (1959) *100,000*.
Kolyma R., flows into E. Siberian Sea, R.S.F.S.R.

Komárno, *industl. t.*, ČSSR.; on R. Danube; textiles; p. (1961) *24,009*. [p. (1962) *25,832*.
Komlo, *t.*, Hungary; new mng. t.; coking coal;
Komotene, *cap.*, Rhodope, Thrace, Greece; p. (1961) *28,335*.
Komsomolsk, *c.*, R.S.F.S.R.; built by volunteer youth labour, after 1932; heavy industl. development; oil refining; pipeline connects with oilfield in N. Sakhalin; p. (1959) *177,000*.
Komsomoloskiy, *c.*, Mordvinian A.S.S.R.; under construction 1963 on site of present workers' settlement; planned p. *50,000*.
Konigshütte, *see* Chorzow.
Konotop, *t.*, Ukrainian S.S.R.; rly. junct. on Moscow–Kiev line; engin., metals; p. (1959) *53,000*.
Konstantinovka, *industl. t.*, Ukraine, S.S.R. U.S.S.R.; in heart of Donbas industl. region, 38 m. N. of Donetsk; heavy engin., iron and steel, zinc smelting; p. (1959) *89,000*.
Konya, *I.*, Turkey; well wooded; opium; ch. t. K. (the ancient Iconium); impt. tr.; p. (1960) *122,704*.
Kootenay R. (Flat Bow R.), trib. of the Columbia R. flowing in Mont., U.S.A., and B.C.; length 450 m.
Koper (Capo d'Istria), *spt.*, Jugoslavia; cath., old fort; Austro-Italian disputes over ownership since very early days; p. (1960) *10,100*.
Kopeysk, *t.*, R.S.F.S.R.; in Urals; lignite mng., agr. and mng. machin.; p. (1959) *160,000*.
Köping, *t.*, Sweden; W. of L. Malaren; iron ore and minerals; p. (1961) *17,692*.
Kopparberg, *co.*, Sweden; a. 11,649 sq. m.; p. (1961) *285,862*. [1962.
Korangi, *t.*, W. Pakistan; oil refinery opened Nov.
Korce (Koritza), *t.*, S.E. Albania; sugar refining, brewing; p. (1960) *34,000*.
Kordofan, *prov.*, Sudan, Africa; a. 146,930 sq. m.; cap. El-Obeid; p. (estd. 1951) *1,671,600*.
Korea, *rep.*, *peninsula*, E. Asia; extending between Yellow Sea and Sea of Japan; annexed by Japan in 1910; after Second World War separated into 2 zones along 38th parallel, N. under Russian influence, the S. under American. **Korea, N.**; a. 46,814 sq. m.; mainly agr.; iron ore, steel ingots, oilwells; ch. t. Pyongyang; p. *8,229,000*. **Korea, S.**; a. 38,452 sq. m.; mainly agr.; tungsten, salt; oil refining at Ulsan; cap. Seoul; p. (1960) *24,994,117*.
Korkino, *t.*, R.S.F.S.R.; in Urals; coal mng.; p. (1959) *85,000*.
Korsör, *spt.*, Sjaelland I., Denmark; fine harbour; glass wks.; p. (1960) *14,276*.
Kortrijk (Courtrai), *t.*, W. Flanders, Belgium; 25 m. S.W. of Ghent; linen, lace; p. (1962) *43,894*.
Korumburra, *t.*, Victoria, Australia; dairy farming.
Kos (Cos), *I.*, Dodecanese Is., Greece; ch. t., Kos; p. (1940) *20,982*.
Kosciusko, *peak*, Australian Alps, N.S.W., Australia; highest peak in Gr. Dividing Range; alt. 7,328 ft.
Kosi, *barrage*, Bhimnagar, nr. Nepalese–Indian frontier and few m. below foothills of Himalayas, inaugurated 1965; hydroelec. plant. projected.
Kosiče, *c.*, ČSSR.; Gothic cath.; univ.; magnesite, chemicals, textiles, sheet steel; p. (1962) *79,581*.
Koslin, *see* Koszalin. [*950,000*.
Kosova-Metohija, *aut. reg.*, Yugoslavia; p. (1959)
Kostroma, *c.*, R.S.F.S.R.; at confluence of Rs. Volga and Kastromo; textiles, engin.; p. (1959) *171,000*.
Kostrzyn (Küstrin), *t.*, Brandenburg, Poland; machin., wood ind.; rly. junction; p. (1939) *23,711*; (1946) *634*.
Koszalin (Koslin), *t.*, Poland; N.E. of Szczecin; paper mftg., engin., textiles; p. (1960) *44,000*.
Kota Baru (formerly **Hollandia**), *cap.*, West Irian, Indonesia. [muslins; p. (1961) *120,345*.
Kotah, *t.*, Rajasthan, India; on R. Chambal;
Köthen, *t.*, Halle, E. Germany; N. of Halle; cas.; metallurgy, sugar, machin., chemicals; rly. junction; p. (1963) *38,778*.
Kotka, *spt.*, on Gulf of Finland; wood pulp; p. (1961) *30,780*.
Kotri, *t.*, W. Pakistan; on R. Indus, opposite Hyderabad; barrage 4½ m. N. of the t., started to help irrigate Sind; p. *7,617*.
Kottayam, *t.*, Kerala, India; p. (1961) *52,685*.
Koulikoro, *t.*, Mali, W. Africa; on upper course of R. Niger; mkt. for ground-nuts, gum-arabic, sisal; linked by R. to Timbuktu and Gao; rly. terminus, 760 m. from Dakar.
Kovrov, *t.*, R.S.F.S.R.; on Gorki rly. line and R. Klyazma; impt. agr. exp. ctr.; engin., textiles; p. (1959) *100,000*.
Kowloon, *spt.*, S.E. China; on mainland opp. Hong Kong I.; tr. ctr.; p. (1961) *726,976*.
Koyali, *nr.* Baroda, Gujarat, India; oil refinery projected.
Kozani, *prefecture*, Macedonia, Greece; cap. Kozani; p. (1961) *190,607*.
Kragerö, *spt.*, Telemark, Norway; exp. ice, timber, wood-pulp, etc.; p. (1961) *4,329*.
Kragujevac, *t.*, central Serbia, Jugoslavia; cath., college, arsenal, garrison; p. (1960) *46,000*.
Kra, Isthmus of, between G. of Siam and Indian Oc.; connects Malaya with Asian mainland.
Krakatao, *volcanic I.*, Strait of Sunda, Indonesia; greater part destroyed by eruption, 1883.
Kraków, *prov.*, Poland; cap. Kraków; a. 6,367 sq. m.; p. (1961) *2,040,000*.
Kraków, *t.*, Poland; machin., chemicals, farm implements; univ.; p. (1961) *490,000*.
Kramatorsk, *c.*, E. Ukraine, U.S.S.R.; heavy engin., metallurgy; p. (1959) *115,000*.
Kraslice, *t.*, ČSSR.; nr. German border; p. *13,558*.
Krasnodar, *t.*, R.S.F.S.R.; on R. Kuban; oil refining, engin., textiles; p. (1962) *354,000*.
Krasnoturinsk, *t.*, R.S.F.S.R.; in Urals, 6 m. N.W. of Serov; aluminium, coal; p. (1959) *62,000*.
Krasnovodsk, *t.*, Turkmen S.S.R.; oil refining, engin.; p. (1956) *38,000*.
Krasnoyarsk, *t.*, R.S.F.S.R.; on Trans-Siberian Rly. at crossing of R. Yenesei; oil refining, engin., synthetic rubber; copper deposits nearby; polyester fibre plant projected; chemical plants; iron ore deposits to be developed; p. (1962) *465,000*.
Krasnyy Luch, *t.*, Ukrainian S.S.R.; coal mng.; Shterovka power sta. nearby; p. (1959) *94,000*.
Krefeld, *t.*, N. Rhine–Westphalia, Germany; ctr. of German silk ind.; steel, machin., chemicals, soap; rly. junction; p. (1963) *216,900*.
Kremenchug, *t.*, Ukrainian S.S.R.; on R. Dnieper; timber, engin., textiles; hydro-elec. sta.; p. (1959) *86,000*.
Krems, *industl. t.*, Austria; on R. Danube; vinegar, white lead; p. (1961) *21,046*.
Kreuznach, *t.*, N. Rhine–Westphalia, Germany; on R. Nahe; metallurgy, leather, optical and chemical inds.; viticulture; mineral baths; p. (estd. 1954) *31,800*.
Kristiansand, *spt.*, Norway; 160 m. S.W. of Oslo; cath.; tr., inds., shipping; p. (1960) *27,748*.
Kristianstad, *co.*, Sweden; a. 2,485 sq. m.; p. (1961) *256,475*.
Kristianstad, *t.*, Sweden; 10 m. from the Baltic; clothing, machin.; p. (1961) *25,813*.
Kristiansund, *spt.*, W. cst. Norway; exp. dried fish; p. (1960) *17,105*.
Kristinehamn, *L.*, *pt.*, Sweden; on L. Vänern; egin., machin.; p. (1961) *21,547*.
Krivoi Rog, *t.*, Ukrainian S.S.R.; on R. Ingulats; rich coal and iron dist.; p. (1962) *448,000*.
Krkonose (Riesengebirge), range between Polish Silesia and Bohemia; highest peak Snežka (Schneekoppe) 5,275 ft.
Kroměřiz, *t.*, Moravia, ČSSR.; mnfs., engin.; p. (1961) *20,583*. [(1961) *158,977*.
Kronoberg, *co.*, Sweden; a. 3,828 sq. m.; p.
Kronstadt, *spt.* (*strongly fortfd.*), on I. in G. of Finland; Baltic pt. and naval sta., R.S.F.S R.; scene of naval mutiny which precipitated the Russian Revolution; p. (1954) *50,000*.
Kroonstad, *t.*, O.F.S., S. Africa; on R. Valseh; agr. and rly. ctr.; engin., milling; p. (1960) *42,438* inc. *13,068* whites.
Kropotkin, *t.*, E. Krasnodar terr., R.S.F.S.R.; grain; engin.; p. (1959), *54,000*.
Krugersdorp, *t.*, Transvaal, S. Africa; named after President Kruger; gold-mining, uranium, manganese; p. (1960) *89,493* inc. *30,241* whites.
Krumlov, *t.*, Bohemia, ČSSR.; on N. slopes of Böhmer Wald; graphite-mines; p. (1961) *8,931*.
Krusevac, *t.*, Jugoslavia; mkt.; munitions; p. (1959) *25,000*.
Kuala Lumpur, *t.*, S.W. Malaya; triple cap. of (*a*) Selangor, (*b*) Malaya, (*c*) Fed. of Malaysia; univ.; p. (1959) *477,238*.
Kuban, *region* of R.S.F.S.R., U.S.S.R.; produces wheat, maize, sunflowers; stock-raising.
Kubango (Okovango), *R.*, flows from Angola into L. Ngami, Botswana.

Kuching, *cap.*, Sarawak, Malaysia; gold discovered nearby at Bau; p. (1960) *50,579.*
Kuchinoerabu, *I.*, Japan; S. of Kyushu; mtns.
Kuçovë, nr. Berat, Albania; oil prod. and refining; pipe-line connects to Vlonë.
Kudamatsu, *c.*, S.W. Honshu, Japan; oil-refining; p. (1947) *34,045.*
Kufra, *oasis*, Libya.
Kuibyshev, *t.*, R.S.F.S.R.; on R. Volga; at head of central Asian and Siberian rlys.; comm. ctr.; engin., sulphur, paper, oil refining; p. (1962) *882,000.*
Kuldja (Yining), *c.*, Sinkiang, China; iron, coal mines; p. (1953) *108,000.*
Kulmbach, *t.*, Bavaria, Germany; textiles, cars, brewing; p. (1963) *23,100.*
Kumamoto, *spt.*, W. Kyushu, Japan; p. (1960) *374,000.*
Kumasi, *ch. t.*, Ashanti, Ghana; univ.; aerodrome; p. (1960) *190,323.*
Kumbakonam, *t.*, *sacred c.*, Madras, India; Cauvery delta; silks, cottons; p. (1961) *92,581.*
Kumta, *t.*, Mysore, India; on sea cst.; sandalwood; carving; p. (1961) *16,223.*
Kunene (Cunene), *R.*, S.W. Africa; forming bdy. between Angola and Brit. S.W. Africa, and mainly in Portuguese terr.; length 700 m.
Kungur, *t.*, R.S.F.S.R., S.E. Perm.; agr.; leather; kaolin; oil ind. equip.; p. (1959) *65,000.*
Kun Lun (Kwen Lun), *mtns.*, Tibet; extend 1,800 m. E. from Pamirs along N. edge of high plateau of Tibet; drained N. into inland drainage basin of Lop Nor; alt. frequently exceeds 18,000 ft.
Kunming, *c.*, Yunnan, China; univ.; comm. ctr.; industl.; p. (1953) *699,000.*
Kununurra Dam, Ord R., W. Australia; opened 1963; to irrigate 200,000 acres of semi-arid land for cotton, rice, and cattle.
Kuopio, *dep.*, Finland; p. (1961) *270,504.*
Kuopio, *t.*, Finland; on L. Kalki; p. (1961) *44,740.*
Kur, *R.*, Transcaucasia, U.S.S.R.; flows to Caspian S.; length 520 m.
Kurdistan (Country of the Kurds), includes parts of E. Turkey, Soviet Armenia, N.E. Iraq, and N.W. Iran.
Kure, *c.*, S.W. Honshu, Japan; spt. and naval base; engin.; p. (1960) *210,027.*
Kurgan, *t.*, R.S.F.S.R.; on the Trans-Siberian Rly. nr. Tobolsk; tr. in cattle and foodstuffs, agr. engin.; p. (1959) *145,000.*
Kuria Muria Is., part of Brit. col. of Aden off S. Arabia, consisting of 5 islands.
Kuril Is., *chain of sm. Is.*, N. Pacific, U.S.S.R.; extending from Kamchatka to Hokkaido; mainly mtns.
Kurisches Haff (Kurštu Martos), *shallow lagoon*, Baltic cst. of Lithuanian S.S.R., U.S.S.R.; receives water of R. Niemen; narrow entrance to Baltic Sea at N. end of lagoon commanded by pt. of Klaipeda (Memel); length, 60 m., maximum width, 20 m.
Kurische Nehrung, *sandspit*, Baltic Sea; almost cuts off Kurisches Haff from Baltic Sea; length, 55 m.
Kurnell, *t.*, Australia; oil refining.
Kuroshio (Japan Current), *ocean current*, flows N.E. along Pacific cst. of Kyushu, Shikoku and S. Honshu, relatively warm water, exerts slight warming influence on this cst. in winter.
Kursk, *region*, adj. N. Ukraine, R.S.F.S.R.
Kursk, *t.*, R.S.F.S.R.; in fruit-growing dist., gr. annual fair; engin., textiles, synthetic rubber; p. (1959) *203,000.*
Kustanay, *t.*, Kazakh S.S.R.; on R. Tobol; light inds.; p. (1959) *86,000.*
Kustendil, *t.*, Bulgaria; on trib. of R. Struma; fruit-growing dist; p. (1956) *25,025.*
Kütahya, *t.*, W. Central Turkey; agr. market ctr., ceramics; p. (1960) *39,857.*
utaisi, *c.*, Georgian S.S.R.; on R. Rion; chemicals, textiles, barium, engin., p. (1959) *128,000.*
utaradja, *t.*, N. Sumatra, Indonesia; p. (1958) *20,976.*
utch, *peninsula*, N.W. cst., India, Gujarat st., suffered much in famine 1899–1900 also from plague; silver filigree work; p. (1961) *696,440.*
utch, Rann of, *desert region* covered with salt, but flooded during monsoons.
utchan, *t.*, S.W. Hokkaido, Japan; 45 m. N.W. of Muroran; ctr. of second lgst. iron-ore field in Japan; ore smelted at Muroran.
utno, *t.*, Lodz, Poland; p. (1960) *26,000.*

Kuwait, *indep. sov. st.*, Arabia; on N.W. cst. of Persian G.; sand, bricks; impt. oil wells, petrochem. ind. projected; p. (1961) *321,000.*
Kuzbas (Kuznetsk Basin), *industl. reg*, Siberia, U.S.S.R.; lies S. of Trans-Siberian Rly. in upper valleys of Rs. Ob and Tom; second lgst. coal output in U.S.S.R., iron and steel mftg., heavy metallurgical ind.; ch. ts., Novosibirsk, Novokuznetsk, Kemerovo, Leninsk-Kuznetsky.
Kwangchow, *spt.*, Kwantung, China; on S. cst. opposite Hainan I.
Kwangsi Chuang (Guang Zhuang), *aut. reg.*, China; cap. Nanning; sugar, tobacco, rice, indigo, silk; a. 85,452 sq. m.; p. (1953) *19,560,822.*
Kwangtung (Guangdong), *prov.*, China; cap. Canton; rice, tea, sugar, silk; a. 85,447 sq. m.; p. (1953) *34,770,059.*
Kwanto Plain, S.E. Honshu, Japan; lgst. a. of continuous lowland in Japan, extends 80 m. inland from Tokyo; composed of: (1) low, badly-drained alluvial plain devoted to intensive rice cultivation; (2) higher, drier terraces under mulberry, vegetables, tea, tobacco; very dense rural p., especially on lower ground; lge. number of urban ctrs., inc. Tokyo, Yokohama; a. 5,000 sq. m.
Kwanza (Cuanza), *R.*, Angola, W. Africa; rises in Bihé and flows to Atlantic; length 700 m.
Kweichow (Guizhou), *prov.*, S.W. China; cap. Kweiyang; cereals, silk, timber, gold, silver, mercury; a. 68,139 sq. m.; p. (1953) *15,037,310.*
Kweilin (Guilin), *c.*, Kwangai Chuang, China; univ.; textiles, sugar refining, timber; p. (1953) *145,000.*
Kweiyang (Guiyang), *c.*, Kweichow prov., China; univ.; comm. and industl. ctr.; p. (1953) *271,000.*
Kwidzyn (Marienwerder), *c.*, Poland, German before 1945; cath.; cas.; p. (1960) *20,000.*
Kwinana, *t.*, W. Australia; 12 m. from Fremantle on shores of Cockburn Sound; recent oil refinery and steel plant.
Kyle of Lochalsh, *vil.*, *sm. spt.*, Ross and Cromarty, Scot.; at entrance to Loch Alsh, facing S. end of I. of Skye; terminus of rly. across Highlands from Dingwall; ch. pt. for steamers to N.W. cst., I. of Skye, Outer Hebrides; p. (1951) *1,525.*
Kyles of Bute, *sound*, between Argyll cst. and N. Bute, Scot.
Kymore, *t.*, Madhya Pradesh, India; nr. Katni; cement wks.; p. (1961) *12,319.*
Kyoto, *c.*, *cap.* Kyoto *prefecture*, Honshu, Japan; univ., temples; former cap. of Japan; p. (1962) *1,306,000.*
Kyrenia, *t.*, Cyprus; on N. cst.; p. (1960) *3,498.*
Kythera (Cerigo), *I.*, S. of Peloponnesos, Greece; a. 107 sq. m.
Kyushu, one of the lge. Is. of Japan; W. of Shikoku; mtns.; rice, wheat, tea, hemp, coal, copper; ch. t. Nagasaki; a. 16,247 sq. m.
Kzyl Orda, *R.*, Kazakh S.S.R.; large dam being constructed to irrigate rice plantations.

L

La Ceiba, *spt.*, Honduras; on Atlantic cst.; exp. bananas; p. (1961) *24,868.*
La Coruña, *prov.*, N.W. Spain; cap. La Coruña; oil refinery; a. 3,051 sq. m.; p. (1959) *1,010,695.*
La Coruña, *spt.*, cap. La Coruña prov., N.W. Spain; fishing; import. tr.; p. (1959) *161,772.*
La Crosse, *t.*, W. Wis., U.S.A.; mkt., agr.; light mnfs.; rubber; p. (1960) *47,575.*
La Estrada, *c.*, N.W. Spain; mineral springs; agr., cattle; p. *27,240.*
La Grange, *t.*, Ga., U.S.A.; p. (1960) *23,632.*
La Grange, *t.*, Ill., U.S.A.; p. (1960) *15,285.*
La Guaira, *see* **Guaira, La.**
La Hague, *see* **Hague.**
La Libertad, *dep.*, Peru; a. 10,206 sq. m.; ch. t. Trujillo; p. (1961) *586,681.*
La Linia, *t.*, Spain, nr. Gibraltar; vegetables, fruit; p. (1959) *61,119.*
La Madeleine, *t.*, Nord, France; p. (1954) *22,831.*
La Mancha, *see* **Mancha, La.**
La Pampa, *terr.*, Argentina; a. 55,669 sq. m.; cap. Santa Rosa; p. (1960) *158,000.*
La Paz, *dep.*, Bolivia; traversed by the Andes; cap. La Paz; cocoa, coffee, rubber, minerals; a. 40,686 sq. m.; p. (1962) *1,140,300.*
La Paz, *t.*, Bolivia, seat of govt., Sucre is legal

cap.; impt. comm. ctr.; copper, alpaca wool, cinchona, textiles; p. (1960) *347,394.*

La Plata, *c., spt.,* Argentina; cap. Buenos Aires prov.; univ.; refrigerated meat prods.; oil refining; p. (1960) *340,000.*

La Plata, Rio de (R. Plate), *lge. estuary,* between Argentina, Uruguay, S. America; receives water of Rs. Parana, Uruguay; cst. provides sites for lge. spts. Buenos Aires, La Plata, Montevideo; length 200 m., max. width 50 m.

La Porte, *t.,* Ind., U.S.A.; flour, iron and steel, woollens; p. (1960) *21,157.*

La Puebla, *t.,* Majorca, Balearic Is.; p. *10,147.*

La Rioja, *prov.,* Argentina; a. 33,394 sq. m.; cap. La R.; p. (1960) *128,000.*

La Rochelle, *t., spt., cap.,* Charante-Maritime, France; locomotives, glass, sugar, fish; cath.; p. (1962) *68,445.*

La Salle, *c.,* Ill., U.S.A.; coal; p. (1960) *11,897.*

La Salle, *t.,* Quebec, Canada; p. (1961) *30,904.*

La Serena, *cap.* Coquimbo prov., Chile; cath.; p. (1962) *61,500.*

La Skhirra, *pt.,* on G. of Gabes, Tunisia; oil; pipe-line to Edjelé under construction.

La Tuque, *t.,* S. Quebec, Canada; R. pt.; lumbering; resort; p. (1961) *13,023.*

La Unión, *t.,* Spain; nr. Cartagena; iron, manganese, sulphur; p. (1957) *10,131.*

Laaland, *I.,* Danish, Baltic Sea; a. 462 sq. m.; forests; cap. Maribo.

Labe, *R., see* **Elbe.**

Labrador, *peninsula,* Newfoundland, Canada; sterile, climate severe, fisheries; cap. Battle Harbour; a. 110,000 sq. m.

Labuan, *I.,* Sabah, Malaysia; rubber, rice, coconuts; cap. Victoria; a. 35 sq. m.; p. (1960) *14,904.*

Laccadive, *Is.,* Arabian Sea; about 200 m. off Malabar cst. joined with Minicoy and Amindivi Is. to form Union Territory, India; coir, coconuts; p. of Territory (1961) *24,108.*

Lachine, *t.,* Quebec, Canada; at head of L. rapids; summer resort, timber, bridge-bldg., wire, rope; p. (1961) *38,630.*

Lachine Canals, Quebec, E. Canada; skirt Lachine Rapids on St. Lawrence R. immediately above Montreal; give access to Montreal from Gr. Lakes for steamers of 14 ft. draught; length 9 m.

Lachlan, *R.,* N.S.W., Australia; trib. R. Murrumbidgee; length 700 m.

Lackawanna, *t.,* N.Y., U.S.A.; on L. Erie; iron and steel; p. (1960) *29,564.*

Laconia, div. of Peloponnesus, Greece; cap. Sparta; p. (1961) *118,449.*

Laconia, *G.,* S. Peloponnesus, Greece.

Laconia, *c.,* N.H., U.S.A.; hosiery, rly. wks.; p. (1960) *15,288.*

Lacq, *t.,* S.W. Aquitaine, France; 15 m. N.W. Paris; oil, natural gas, sulphur. [monastery.

Lacroma, *I.,* Jugoslavia; holiday resort, château,

Lacrosse, *c.,* Wis., U.S.A.; rly. ctr., flour, timber; p. (1960) *47,575.*

Ladakh, *dist.,* of the Upper Indus, bordering Tibet; ch. t. Leh; p. (1961) *88,651.*

Ladoga, *L.,* nr. Leningrad, U.S.S.R. (lgst. in Europe); a. 7,100 sq. m.; drained to G. of Finland by R. Neva.

Ladrones, *see* **Marianas Is.**

Ladybank, *burgh,* Fife, Scot.; 5 m. S.W. of Cupar; rly. wks., malt, linen; p. (1961) *1,207.*

Ladysmith, *t.,* Natal, S. Africa; rly. wks., coal, cotton mills; besieged by Boers 1899–1900; p. (1960) *22,997* inc. *7,260* Europeans.

Lafayette, *c.,* Ind., U.S.A.; univ.; timber, farm implements; p. (1960) *42,330.*

Lafayette, *t.,* La., U.S.A.; timber, cottonseed oil; p. (1960) *40,400.* [alt. 5,259 ft.

Lafayette, *peak,* White mtns. range, N.H., U.S.A.;

Lagan, *R.,* N. Ireland; flows into Belfast Lough; length 35 m.

Lagoa dos Patos, *L.,* Brazil; drained by Rio Grande do Sul; length 140 m.

Lagoa Mirim, *L.,* on bdy. between Brazil and Uruguay; drains N.; length 110 m.

Lagos, *spt., cap.,* Nigeria; good natural harbour; univ.; exp. palm oil and kernels, cocoa, groundnuts, hides; imports machin., cotton piece goods; rly. wks.; p. (1963) *675,352.*

Laguna, *dist.,* Durango st. Mexico; former L. bed irrigated by R. Nazas and Aguanaval; ch. cotton-growing region in Mexico; ch. t., Torréon; a. 100,000 sq. m.

Laguna Dam, *see* **Imperial Valley.**

Laguna de Terminos, *inlet,* Campeche, Mexico; 70 m. by 40 m.

Laguna Madre, *lagoon,* Texas, U.S.A.; 110 m. by 14 m.

Lahn, *R.,* Germany; enters R. Rhine at Koblenz; length 135 m.

Lahore, *div.,* W. Pakistan; ch. t. Lahore; p. (estd. 1951) *5,340,000.*

Lahore, *ch. c.,* W. Pakistan; univ., cath., temples, mosques; textiles, pottery, carpets, industl. gases; atomic research ctr.; p. (1961) *1,296,477.*

Lahr, *t.,* Baden-Württemberg, Germany; at W. edge of Black Forest; tobacco, cardboard, leather, precision mechanics; p. (1963) *22,800.*

Lahti, *t.,* S. Finland; p. (1961) *67,144.*

Laibach, *see* **Ljubljana.**

Lake Charles, *t.,* La., U.S.A.; oil, rice, timber; holiday resort; p. (1960) *63,392.*

Lake District, *mountainous dist.,* Cumberland and Westmorland, Eng.; tourist resort, beautiful scenery, inc. Ls. Windermere, Ullswater, Derwentwater, etc.

Lake Forest, *t.,* Ill., U.S.A.; on L. Michigan; p. (1960) *10,687.*

Lake of the Woods, *L.,* E. of Winnipeg, Ontario, Canada; on bdy. between Canada and U.S.A.

Lake Success, *vil.,* N.Y., U.S.A.; temporary H.Q. of U.N.O. since 1946; p. (1960) *2,954.*

Lakeland, *t.,* Fla., U.S.A.; agr., fruit ctr., phosphates; holiday resort; p. (1960) *41,350.*

Lakeview, *t.,* Ont., Canada; thermal elec. power plant projected; to be lgst. in world.

Lakeview, Ore., U.S.A., uranium mill; p. *3,262.*

Lakewood, *t.,* N.J., U.S.A.; winter resort; p. (1960) *13,004.*

Lakewood, *t.,* Ohio, U.S.A.; sub. of Cleveland; grapes; p. (1960) *66,145.*

Lalin, *t.,* N.W. Spain; agr. ctr., paper, tanning; p. *18,620.*

Lambay, *I.,* off cst. Dublin co., Ireland.

Lambayeque, *dep.,* N. Peru; sugar, cotton, tobacco; cap. Chiclayo; a. 4,613 sq. m.; p. (1961) *363,297.*

Lambersart, *commune,* Nord, France; sub. Lille; spinning; p. (1954) *19,092.*

Lambeth, *inner bor.,* London, Eng.; inc. part o former bor. of Wandsworth (Clapham an Streatham); L. Palace, residence of Arch bishop of Canterbury; p. (1964) *340,762.*

Lambezellec, *t.,* Finistère, France; tr. ctr.; p (1946) *19,227.*

Lambourn, *par.,* Berks, Eng.; agr.; trainin stables; p. *2,316.*

Lamesa, *t.,* N.W. Texas, U.S.A.; cotton, maize cattle; p. (1960) *12,438.*

Lamia, *cap.,* Phthiotis prefecture, Greece; p (1961) *21,509.*

Lammermuir Hills, E. Lothian, Scot.; highes peak Lammer Law, alt. 1,733 ft.

Lampedusa, *I.,* Mediterranean; S. of Malta.

Lampeter, *mkt. t.,* mun. bor., Cardigan, S. Wales on R. Teifi; St. David's College; p. (1961 *1,853.*

Lampong, *dist.* at S. extremity Sumatra, In donesia; a. 11,113 sq. m.; p. (1930) *361,563.*

Lamu, I., off cst. of Kenya; p. *3,576* (non-African)

Lanai, one of the Hawaiian Is.; fruit, suga cotton, livestock; a. 141 sq. m.; p. *3,360.*

Lanark, *co.,* Scot.; coal, iron, steel, textiles; c t. Lanark; a. 897 sq. m.; p. (1961) *1,626,317*

Lanark, *burgh, co. t.,* Lanark, Scot.; in Clyd valley 22 m. S.E. of Glasgow; hosiery, chenill fabrics, tanning; p. (1961) *8,436.*

Lancashire, *mftg. dist., industl. co.,* N.W. Eng. Liverpool most impt. spt.; Manchester g comm. ctr.; Preston adm. hdqrs.; mnfs. in textiles, engin. prod., chemicals, foodstuff coal-mining; co. t. Lancaster; a. 1,875 sq. m p. (1961) *5,131,646.*

Lancaster, *mun. bor., co. t.,* Lancs, Eng.; 6 n up R. Lune; cas.; univ.; linoleum, cotto artificial silk inds.; p. (1961) *48,887.*

Lancaster, *t.,* Ohio, U.S.A.; in natural-gas regio agr.; flour, machin., glass; p. (1960) *29,916.*

Lancaster, *bor.,* Penns., U.S.A.; agr. ctr.; mn light and heavy iron and steel prod.; p. (196 *61,055.* [wid

Lancaster, *sound,* N.W. Terrs., Canada; 50

Lanchow (Lanzhou), *c., cap.,* Kansu, China; on Hwang-Ho; silk, tobacco, grain, tea-tr. ct p. (1953) *397,000.*

Lanciano, *t.*, Abruzzi e Molise, Italy; wine, fruit, oil, silk, linen; p. *22,450*.
Lancing, *vil.*, Sussex, Eng.; on S. cst., 2 m. E. of Worthing; seaside resort; college; light inds.; p. *13,000*.
Landau, *t.*, Rhineland-Palatinate, Germany; on R. Queich; cigar mftg., wine, iron ind.; here the carriages called Landaus were first made; p. (1963) *30,000*
Landes, *dep.*, S.W. France; on Atlantic cst.; agr., vineyards, resin; cap. Mont-de-Marson; a. 3,604 sq. m.; p. (1962) *260,495*.
Landes, Les, *coastal sub-region*, Aquitaine, S.W. France; fringes Bay of Biscay from Pointe de Grave to Biarritz; coastal sand dunes and lagoons backed by low, flat plain of alternate sandy tracts and marsh; reclaimed by drainage and afforestation, now over half a. covered by pine forests; turpentine, timber; oilfield; length 150 m., maximum width of dune belt 7 m., of plain 40 m.
Landrecies, *t.*, Nord, France; on R. Sambre.
Land's End, extreme S.W. point of Eng. on Cornish cst.
Landshut, *t.*, Bavaria, Germany; on R. Isar; cas.; elec. inds., glass, metallurgy, textiles, coal; rly. junction; p. (1963) *50,600*.
Landskrona, *spt.*, Sweden; shipping and tr. ctr.; hy. machin., lt. inds.; p. (1961) *28,826*.
Lanett, *t.*, E. Ala., U.S.A.; textiles; p. (1960) *7,674*.
Langanes, *C.*, N.E. cst., Iceland.
Langebergen, *mtns.*, Cape Province, Rep. of S. Africa; extend 150 m. E. to W. parallel to S. cst. of Africa; form barrier to access from cst. plain to Little Karroo, broken across by valley of R. Gouritz; max. alt. exceeds 4,500 ft.
Langefjell, *mtn. gr.*, Romsdal, Norway; highest peak 8,101 ft.
Langeland, *I.*, Gr. Belt, Denmark; a. 111 sq. m.; p. (1960) *18,692*.
Langholm, *mkt. burgh*, Dumfries, Scot.; on R. Esk; 18 m. N. of Carlisle; woollen mills, tanning; p. (1961) *2,369*.
Langley, *industl. dist.*, nr. Birmingham, Worcs., [Eng.
Langnau, *t.*, Switzerland; ch. t. of the Emmental; p. *8,300*.
Langreo, *t.*, Asturias, Spain; hilly, agr. and fruit-growing dist., colly. and iron-wks.; p. (1959) *64,347*.
Langres, *fortfd. t.*, Haute-Marne, France; the ancient Andematunnum; cath.; grain, livestock, cutlery, wine; p. (1954) *8,300*.
Languedoc, *prov.*, S. France; wine.
Languedoc, *canal*, S. France; unites Mediterranean with R. Garonne at Toulouse, France.
Lannemazan, *sub-region*, Aquitaine, S.W. France; belt 50 m. wide stretches over 100 m. along foot of Pyrenees W. of Toulouse; consists of immense deltas of glacial gravel deeply cut by tribs. of Rs. Garonne and Adour; valleys liable to severe floods in summer, intervening plateau dry, bare; scantily populated.
Lansdowne, *t.*, *sub.*, Philadelphia, S.E. Penns., U.S.A.; p. (1960) *12,612*.
Lansford, *bor.*, Penns., U.S.A.; p. (1950) *1,487*.
Lansing, *cap.*, Mich., U.S.A.; tr., mnfs. iron goods; cars; chemicals; p. (1960) *107,807*.
Lanzarote, *I.*, Canary Is.; volcanic. mountainous; grapes, cochineal; cap. Arrecife; p. (1962) *36,519*.
Laoag, *t.*, N. Luzon I., Philippines; cereals, tobacco, cotton, sugar; p. *40,800*.
Laoighis or **Leix Co.**, Leinster, Ireland; mtns. and bog; inland pasture and tillage; cap. Port Laoighise (Maryborough); a. 664 sq. m.; p. (1961) *45,062*.
Laon, *cap.*, Aisne, France; fort, cath.; metal, linen mftg.; p. (1954) *21,931*.
Laos, *kingdom*, former associate st. of Fr. Union; mtnous. and densely forested; a. 89,320 sq. m.; main religion Buddhism; cereals, sugar, cotton, cattle, some minerals but only tin mined in sm. quantities; modern saw and rice mills; admin. cap. Vientiane; p. (estd. 1962) *2,200,000*.
Lapeer, *t.*, E. Mich., U.S.A.; wooden prod.; p. (1960) *6,160*.
Lapland, *terr.*, N. Europe, in Norway, Sweden, Finland and U.S.S.R., extending from the Norwegian cst. to the White Sea; mainly mtn. and moorland, with many lakes; a. 130,000 sq. m.; p. *100,000*.
Lappi (Lappland), *dep.*, N. Finland; a. 36,308 sq. m.; p. (1961) *205,113*.
Laptev Sea (**Nordenskiöld Sea**), *inlet* of Arctic Ocean; between Severnaya Zemlya and N. Siberian Is., R.S.F.S.R.
Larache, *spt.*, Morocco; on Atl. cst. 40 m. S. of Tangier; cork; p. (1960) *30,763*.
Laramie, *c.*, Wyo., U.S.A.; univ., cattle; p. (1960) *17,520*.
Larbert, *par.*, Stirling, Scot.; brass and copper wares, chemicals, confectionery; p. *13,763*.
Laredo, *c.*, Texas, U.S.A.; frontier c. on Rio Grande; iron, steel, oil, bricks, hides, wool; p. (1960) *60,678*.
Largo, *par.*, Fife, Scot.; fishing, holiday resort; p. (1951) *2,499*.
Largs, *burgh*, Ayr, Scot.; on F. of Clyde opposite Is. of Bute and Cumbrae; seaside resort, fishing, weaving; battle 1263; p. (1961) *9,100*.
Larissa, *prefecture*, Thessaly, Greece; cap. Larissa; p. (1961) *237,683*.
Larissa, *t.*, Thessaly, Greece; silk, cotton goods; p. (1961) *55,391*.
Laristan, *prov.*, S. Iran; on Persian G.; mainly mtns., camels, silk; cap. Lar.
Lark, *R.*, Cambridge, Eng.; trib. of R. Ouse; length 26 m.
Larkhall, *t.*, Lanark, Scot.; Industl. Estate; foundry, hosiery, silk dye wks.; p. *14,055*.
Larnaka, *spt.*, Cyprus; the ancient Citium; grain, cotton, fruit; p. (1960) *19,824*.
Larne, *spt.*, *mun. bor.*, Antrim, N. Ireland; at entrance to Larne Lough, 18 m. N. of Belfast; salt deposits; linen, flour; seaside resort; p. (1961) *16,341*.
Larvik, *spt.*, Norway; S.W. of Oslo; seaside resort; engin., pulp, stone; p. (1961) *10,479*.
Las Bela, *dist.*, Baluchistan, Pakistan; a. 7,132 sq. m.; p. (estd. 1951) *76,000*.
Las Cruces, *t.*, N.M., U.S.A.; agr. with irrigation; lead, fluorspar mining; p. (1960) *29,367*.
Las Palmas, *Spanish prov.*, Canary Is.; comprising Gran Canaria, Lanzarote, Fuerteventura and smaller Is.; bananas, potatoes, tomatoes, fishing; a. 1,565 sq. m.; p. (1962) *459,433*.
Las Palmas, *t.*, Gran Canaria, Canary Is.; cap. of Las Palmas prov.; p. (1962) *182,217*.
Las Tres Marias, *Is.*, off W. cst. Mexico.
Las Vegas, *t.*, Nevada, U.S.A.; resort; p. (1960) *64,405*.
Las Vegas, *t.*, N. Mexico, U.S.A.; E. of Santa Fé; p. (1960) *6,028*.
Las Villas, *prov.*, Cuba; a. 8,264 sq. m.; p. (1953) *1,030,162*.
Lashio, *t.*, Burma; on R. Salween; end of the Burma Road to China; p. *4,638*.
Lashkar, *see* **Gwalior**.
Lasithi, *prefecture*, Crete; cap. Ayios Nikolaos; p. (1961) *73,843*.
Lasswade, *see* **Bonnyrigg and Lasswade**.
Latacunga, *cap.*, Cotopaxi prov., Ecuador; tr. ctr., paper, malt; p. (1960) *29,423*.
Latakia, *spt.*, Syria; tobacco, olive oil, sponges; p. (1961) *68,498*.
Latin America, the Spanish-, Portuguese- and French-speaking countries of N. America, S. America, Central America and the West Indies, incl. the reps. of Argentina, Bolivia, Brazil, Chile, Colombia, Costa Rica, Cuba, Dominican Republic, Ecuador, El Salvador, Guatemala, Haiti, Honduras, Mexico, Nicaragua, Panama, Paraguay, Peru, Uruguay and Venezuela; sometimes Puerto Rico, French West Indies, and other Is. of the West Indies are included, and occasionally Brit. Honduras, Guyana, French Guiana, and Surinam.
Latina, *see* **Littoria**.
Latium, *see* **Lazio**.
Latrobe, *t.*, Tasmania, Australia; on N. cst.
Latrobe, *t.*, S.E. Penns., U.S.A.; p. (1960) *11,932*.
Latronico, *t.*, Potenza, Italy; p. *5,175*.
Latvia, *constituent S.S. rep.*, U.S.S.R., on the Baltic Sea; former independent st.; mainly agr.; cap. Riga; principal spts. Ventspils, Liepaya; a. 24,800 sq. km.; p. (1959) *2,094,000*.
Lauenburg, *see* **Lebork**.
Launceston, *t.*, *mun. bor.*, Cornwall, Eng.; agr. mkt.; mng., quarrying, lt. engin.; p. (1961) *4,518*.
Launceston, *c.*, Tasmania, Australia; wool, textiles, fruit; p. (1961) *56,837*.
Laurel, *t.*, Miss., U.S.A.; p. (1960) *27,889*.
Laurens, *t.*, S.C., U.S.A.; cotton, glass; p. (1960) *9,598*.

Laurentide, *escarpment* of Laurentian plateau, E. Canada.
Laurium, *hills, dist.*, Greece; silver and lead.
Laurium (formerly **Calumet**), *vil.*, Mich., U.S.A.; copper; p. (1950) *3,211.*
Lausanne, *cap.*, Vaud, Switzerland; nr. L. Geneva; cath., univ.; rly. junction, iron, chocolate, paper; p. (1961) *130,500.*
Lauterbrunnen, *vil.*, Bern can., Switzerland; highest and most famous of its waterfalls (Staubbach 980 ft.); tourist ctr.; p. *2,958.*
Lautoka, *spt.*, Viti Levu, Fiji Is.; sugar ctr.
Lauven, *R.*, Norway; length 200 m.
Lavagna, *t.*, Genoa, Italy; shipbldg., marble; p. *8,100.*
Laval, *t., cap.*, Mayenne, France; cotton, paper, machin., marble; cas.; p. (1962) *43,196.*
Lavera, *pt.*, nr. Marseilles, commencement of 470 m. pipeline to Karlsruhe, W. Germany, operated April 1963.
Laverton, *t.*, W. Australia; 200 m. N. Kalgoorlie.
Lawndale, *t.*, Cal., U.S.A.; p. (1960) *21,740.*
Lawrence, *c.*, Kan., U.S.A.; st. univ., paper, machin.; p. (1960) *32,858.*
Lawrence, *c.*, Mass., U.S.A.; on Merrimac R., N.W. of Boston; textiles paper, footwear, engin.; p. (1960) *70,933.*
Lawrenceburg, *t.*, Tenn., U.S.A.; textiles, cheese, phosphates; p. (1950) *5,442.*
Lawton, *t.*, Okla., U.S.A.; p. (1959) *61,697.*
Laxey, *vil.*, I. of Man; lead-mining.
Lazio, *region*, Italy; a. 6,634 sq. m.; p. inc. Vatican City and Rome; p. (1961) *3,922,783.*
Le Bouscat, *t.*, Gironde, France; p. (1954) *19,558.*
Le Havre, *see* **Havre, Le.**
Le Maire, *strait*, between Staten I. and Tierra del Fuego, S. America.
Le Mans, *cap.*, Sarthe, France; cath.; linen, ironmongery, chemicals, motor cars, aeroplanes; motor-racing; p. (1962) *136,083.*
Le Puy, *t.*, Haute-Loire, France; p. (1954) *23,453.*
Lea, *R.*, Eng.; rises in Chiltern Hills nr. Luton, flows E. and S. into R. Thames; length 46 m.
Lead, *t.*, S.D., U.S.A.; gold, mnfs. jewellery, mng. equipment; resort; p. (1960) *6,211.*
Leader Water, *R.*, Scot.; trib. of R. Tweed, which it joins nr. Melrose; length 21 m.
Leadgate, *t.*, Durham, Eng.; 2 m. N.E. of Consett; coal, mftg.
Leadhills, *mng. vil.*, S.W. Lanark, Scot.; lead.
Leadville, *c.*, Col., U.S.A.; in Arkansas valley; mining ctr.; p. (1960) *4,008.*
Leaf, *R.*, flowing into Ungava Bay, Labrador, Canada.
Leam, *R.*, Warwick, Eng.; trib. of R. Avon; length, 25 m.
Leamington, *t.*, Ont., Canada; tobacco, canned vegetables; p. (1961) *9,030.*
Leamington (Royal Leamington Spa), *t., mun. bor.*, Warwick, Eng.; on R. Leam, 24 m. S.E. of Birmingham; fashionable spa; gen. (engin.) inds.; p. (1961) *43,236.*
Leaside, *t.*, Ontario, Canada; p. (1961) *18,579.*
Leatherhead, *t., urb. dist.*, Surrey, Eng.; on R. Mole to N. of gap through N. Downs; boiler mftg., engin.; p. (1961) *35,554.*
Leavenworth, *c.*, Kan., U.S.A.; on Missouri; rly. ctr. and military post, furniture, machin., bricks, coal; p. (1960) *22,052.*
Lebanon, *rep.*, S.W. Asia; mountainous; mainly agr.; textiles, garments, wooden, metal goods; cap. Beirut; a. 3,400 sq. m.; p. (estd. 1953) *1,300,000.*
Lebanon, *mtn. range*, Lebanon st. and N. Israel; highest peaks Dahr-el-Khadeb (10,052 ft.) and Timarum (10,539 ft.).
Lebanon, *t.*, Penns., U.S.A.; coal, iron, steel, mnfs.; rubber, food, tobacco; p. (1960) *30,045.*
Lebork (former German **Lauenburg**), *t.*, Poland; p. (1960) *21,000.*
Lebu, *spt., cap.*, Arauco prov., Chile; coal; p. (1961) *12,560.*
Lecce, *t.*, Apulia, Italy; cas.; p. (1961) *74,123.*
Lecco, *t.*, Italy; on L. Como; silk, cotton, copper, iron; p. (1961) *48,230.*
Lech, *R.*, Germany; trib. of Danube; 177 m.
Leczyca, *t.*, Poland; p. *20,996.*
Ledbury, *t., urb. dist.*, Hereford, Eng.; at W. foot of Malvern Hills; mkt., fruit preserving, tanning; p. (1961) *3,632.*
Ledeberg, *t.*, Belgium; nr. Ghent; industl.; p. (1962) *11,127.*

Lee, *R.*, Cork, Ireland; flows past Cork c. to Cork harbour; length 50 m.
Lee-on-Solent, *t.*, Hants, Eng.; on Southampton Water; p. *4,000.*
Leeds, *co. bor.*, W.R. Yorks, Eng.; on R. Aire; at E. margin of Pennines; univ.; lge. clothing ind., varied engin. mnfs., furniture, tanning; p. (1961) *510,597.*
Leek, *mkt. t., urb. dist.*, Staffs, Eng.; 11 m. N.E. of Stoke-on-Trent; silk mnfs.; p. (1961) *19,173.*
Leer, *pt.*, Lower Saxony, Germany; nr. confluence of Leda and Ems; iron, machin., textiles; harbour and route ctr.; p. (1963) *20,200.*
Lees, *urb. dist.*, Lancs, Eng.; cotton; p. (1961) *3,729.*
Leeston, *t.*, S.I., N.Z.; on Canterbury Plain, nr. Christchurch; agr. ctr.; p. (1951) *738.*
Leete's I., Conn., U.S.A.; on Long I. sound.
Leeuwarden, *prov. cap.*, Friesland, Netherlands; agr.; iron, metal goods, bicycles; p. (1960) *82,649.*
Leeuwin, *C.*, S.W. point of Australia.
Leeward Is., W.I.; inc. Antigua, Barbuda, Redonda, Montserrat, Virgin Is., St. Kitts, Nevis, Anguilla, Sombrero; ch. prod., sugar, fruit; Is. cap. St. John's, Antigua; total a. 423 sq. m.; p. (1952) *119,700.*
Leeward Is. (Dutch), part of Neth. Antilles, consisting of St. Maarten (a. 34 sq. m.; p. *1,697*), St. Eustatius (a. 31 sq. m.; p. *945*), Saba (a. 9 sq. m.; p. *1,150*).
Leeward Is. (French), E. Pacific, inc. Huahiné Raiatéa, Tahaa, Bora-Bora-Maupiti; p. (1962) *16,177.*
Leghorn or Livorno, *prov.*, Italy; a. 133 sq. m.; p. (1961) *313,599.*
Leghorn or Livorno, *spt., prov. cap.*, Italy; on W. cst., 10 m. S. of mouth of R. Arno; shipbldg., glass, wire, olive oil, hats, marble; p (1961) *159,973.*
Legionowa, *t.*, Warsaw, Poland; new town (1951); p. (1960) *20,000.*
Legnago, *t.*, Lombardy, Italy; on R. Adige; fort, sugar, cereals; p. *20,175.*
Legnano, *t.* Lombardy, Italy; N.W. of Milan; cotton, silk, machin.; p. (1961) *42,460.*
Leh, *ch. t.*, Ladakh, Kashmir, India; on R. Indus; caravan ctr; p. (1961) *3,720.*
Lehigh, *R.*, Penns., U.S.A.; trib. of Delaware R.; length 120 m.
Lehighton, *bor.*, Penns., U.S.A.; anthracite; p. (1960) *6,318.*
Leicester, *co. t., co. bor.*, Leics., Eng.; on R. Soar; univ.; footwear, hosiery, knitwear, engin., and elec. goods, chemicals; p. (1961) *273,298.*
Leicestershire, *co.*, Eng.; mainly agr.; co. t. Leicester; a. 832 sq. m.; p. (1961) *682,196.*
Leichhardt, W., *sub.* of Sydney, N.S.W., Australia; p. *31,500.*
Leiden (Leyden), *t.*, S. Holland, Neth.; printing, textiles, medical apparatus; univ.; p. (1960) *96,440.*
Leigh, *t., mun. bor.*, S.W. Lancs, Eng.; 5 m. S.E. of Wigan; mkt.; coal-mining; silks, cottons, brass, iron; p. (1961) *46,153.*
Leigh-on-Sea, *t.*, Essex, Eng.; on N. cst. of Thames estuary, 2 m. W. of Southend; holiday resort, fishing; p. (1961) *10,059.*
Leigh's L., Wyo., U.S.A.; links with Snake R.
Leighton Buzzard, *t., urb. dist.*, Bedford, Eng. at N.E. end of Vale of Aylesbury; tiles, engin. sand quarrying; p. (1961) *11,649.*
Leine, *R.*, N.W. Germany; trib. of R. Aller length 130 m.
Leinster, *S.E. prov.*, Ireland; a. 7,620 sq. m.; agr.; p. (1961) *1,329,625.*
Leipzig, *c.*, Leipzig, E. Germany; at junction of Rs. Pleisse, Elster and Parthe; univ., cath. comm., publishing, metal, textile, chemical steel, paper, machin. and elec. inds., vehicles birthplace of Wagner; p. (1963) *588,135.*
Leiston-cum-Sizewell, *t., urb. dist.*, E. Suffolk Eng.; on cst., 4 m. E. of Saxmundham; agr implements; p. (1961) *4,119.*
Leith, *spt.*, Midlothian, Scot.; Edinburgh sub. shipbldg., timber, whisky; p. *81,618.*
Leith Hill, Surrey, Eng.; nr. Dorking; alt. 993 ft
Leitmeritz, *see* **Litoměřice.**
Leitrim, *co.*, Connacht, Ireland; agr.; cap Carrick-on-Shannon; a. 613 sq. m.; p. (1961) *33,468.*
Leix, *co.*, see **Laoighis.**
Leixões, *spt.*, Portugal; at mouth of R. Douro.

Lek (**Neder Rijn**), *R.*, Netherlands; more northerly of two branches by which Rhine enters N. Sea; leaves main R. 16 m. above Arnhem, flows through Rotterdam, enters N. Sea by three mouths; length 110 m.
Leland, *t.*, Miss., U.S.A.; cotton, vegetables, nuts; p. (1960) *6,295.*
Lema, *Is.*, Sea of Hong Kong in China Sea.
Lemgo, *t.*, N. Rhine-Westphalia, Germany; E. of Bielefeld; furniture and textiles; p. (1963) *21,700.*
Lemnos, *I.* (Greek), Ægean Sea; 20 m. long; fertile valleys; tobacco, fruit, sheep, goats; cap. Kastron; p. *4,000.*
Lemvig, *spt.*, Jutland, Denmark; fishing, agr. machin.; p. (1960) *5,783.*
Lena, *gr. R.*, Siberia, R.S.F.S.R.; rising in mtns. W. of Lake Baikal and flowing N. to the Arctic Ocean; length 2,800 m.
Lena, *commune*, N.W. Spain; iron, coal, mercury; meat packing; p. *15,532.*
Lenin Dam (**Dnieper Dam**), *see* **Zaporozhe.**
Leninabad, *t.*, Tadzhik S.S.R.; on R. Syr Darya, S. of Tashkent; cottons, silks, fruit-preserving; hydro-elec. sta.; p. (1959) *77,000.*
Leninakan, *t.*, Armenian S.S.R.; silk, textiles, engin., p. (1959) *108,000.*
Leningrad, *c.*, R.S.F.S.R.; at mouth of R. Neva; cath., palaces, univs.; engin., oil ref., chemicals, textiles, synthetic rubber, steel, paper; founded by Peter the Gr. as St. Petersburg; p. (1962) *3,498,000.*
Leninogorsk, *t.*, Kazakh S.S.R.; lead, zinc, silver, copper, gold; p. (1959) *67,000.*
Leninsk-Kuznetski (**Charjui**), *t.*, R.S.F.S.R.; heavy engin., power-sta., coal, gold; p. (1959) *132,000.*
Lenkoran, *spt.*, Azerbaydzhan S.S.R.; on Caspian Sea; ctr. of rice, citrous fruits, tea a.; p. (1956) *30,800.*
Lennox, *ancient Scottish div.*, comprising Dunbarton, parts of Stirling, Perth and Renfrew.
Lennox Hills, *mtn. range*, between Dunbarton and Stirling, Scot.
Lennoxtown, *t.*, Stirling, Scot.; coal-mining, bleaching, print and alum wks.; p. *2,590.*
Lennoxville, *t.*, Quebec, Canada; on St. Francis R.; univ.; p. *1,927.*
Lenoir, *t.*, N.C., U.S.A.; cotton, lumber; tourist resort; p. (1950) *7,888.*
Lens, *t.*, Pas de Calais, France; on canal of same name; ironwks., soap, sugar; p. (1962) *42,733.*
Lentini or **Leontini,** *t.*, Sicily, Italy; on plain of Catania; cereal, oil, wine; p. *23,150.*
Leoben, *old mining t.*, Styria, Austria; walls and tower; p. (1961) *36,257.*
Leominster, *t.*, *mun. bor.*, Hereford, Eng.; 13 m. N. of Hereford; rly. junction, mkt., cider, cattle, agr. tools, glove mkg.; p. (1961) *6,403.*
Leominster, *c.*, Mass., U.S.A.; wood prod., light mnfs.; p. (1960) *27,929.*
León, *t.*, Nicaragua; cath., univ.; footwear, textiles; p. (1960) *46,000.*
León, *t.*, Mexico; textiles, leather, gold, silver; p. (1960) *209,469.*
León, *prov.*, Spain; agr., livestock, coal, iron; cap. León; a. 5,937 sq. m.; p. (1959) *591,231.*
Leonforte, *t.*, Sicily, Italy; sulphur-mines, cattle, oil, wine; p. *19,400.*
Leonidion, *t.*, Greece; on G. of Nauplia; p. *3,452.*
Leonora, *sm. t.*, W. Australia; 140 m. N. of Kalgoorlie; gold-mines.
Léopoldville, *cap.*, Congo; above the cataracts on R. Congo; founded by Stanley; p. (1960) *390,000.*
Lercara, *t.*, Sicily, Italy; macaroni mftg., sulphur-mines; p. *11,000.*
Lerici, *coastal t.*, Italy; nr. Spezia; macaroni mftg.; old cas.
Lérida, *prov.*, Spain; wine, olive oil, livestock, wool, timber; a. 4,656 sq. m.; p. (1959) *334,807.*
Lérida, *t.*, *cap.* of L. prov., Spain; on R. Segre; 2 caths.; textiles, leather, glass; p. (1959) *59,040.*
Lerins, *Is.* (French), in Mediterranean; nr. Cannes.
Leros, *Is.*, Dodecanese, Greece.
Lerwick, *cap.*, Shetland Is., Scot.; on Mainland; fishing; p. (1961) *5,906.*
Les Baux, *commune*, Bouches-du-Rhône, France; bauxite first discovered here; not impt. now.
Les Causses, *see* **Causses, Les.**
Les Landes, *see* **Landes, Les.**
Les Lilas, *commune*, Seine, France; glass, chemicals, metallurgy; p. (1954) *18,590.*
Les Sables d'Olonne, *commune*, Vendée, France; shipbldg.; fish. canning; p. (1954) *17,761.*
Lesbos, *see* **Mytilene I.**
Leskovac, *t.*, Serbia, Jugoslavia; on R. Morava; hemp, flax, tobacco; p. (1959) *29,000.*
Leslie, *burgh*, Fife, Scot.; 7 m. N. of Kirkcaldy; paper, flax, bleaching; p. (1961) *3,421.*
Lesser Antilles, *see* **Antilles.**
Lesser Slave, *L.*, Central Alberta, Canada.
Lesvos (**Lesbos**), *Greek prefecture* and *I.* in Ægean Sea; cap. Mitilini (Mytilene); p. (1961) *140,144.*
Leszno, *commune*, W. Poland; engin., distilling, tobacco; p. *20,881.*
Letchworth (**Garden City**), *t.*, *urb. dist.*, Herts, Eng.; at foot of Chiltern Hills, 2 m. N.E. of Hitchin; model residtl. and industl. t.; all types of engin., office equipment; p. (1961) *25,515.*
Lethbridge, *t.*, Alberta, Canada; coal, oil; p. (1961) *35,454.*
Letterkenny, *t.*, Donegal, Ireland; on Lough Swilly; tourist ctr., flax; p. (1961) *4,329.*
Leucadia, *see* **Levkas.**
Levanger, *spt.*, Norway; at N. end of Trondheim Fjord; p. (1961) *1,711.*
Levant, French and Italian name for E. cst. of Mediterranean.
Leven, *burgh*, Fife, Scot.; on N. side of F. of Forth, 10 m. N.E. of Kirkcaldy; linen, coal; p. (1961) *8,872.*
Leven, *L.*, Kinross, Scot.; associated with escape of Mary Queen of Scots from Castle I., 1568.
Leven, *salt-water L.*, Argyll, Inverness, Scot.
Levenshulme, *industl. t.*, Lancs, Eng.; sub. of Manchester.
Leverkusen, *t.*, N., Rhine-Westphalia, Germany; on R. Rhine, N. of Cologne; iron, machin., textiles, chemicals; p. (1963) *99,300.*
Levin, *t.*, N.I., N.Z.; p. (1961) *7,940.*
Levis, *t.*, Quebec, Canada; on St. Lawrence R., opposite Quebec; rly. terminus, landing place for Transatlantic passengers; p. (1961) *15,112.*
Levkas (**Santa Maura**), Ionian Is., Greece; ch. t. and spt., L.; mtns.; grapes, currants; a. 110 sq. m.; p. (1961) *28,969* of t. *6,552.*
Levoča, *t.*, ČSSR.; N.W. of Kosice; industl.; p. (1961) *13,768.*
Lewes, *co. t.*, *mun. bor.*, E. Sussex, Eng.; on R. Ouse at N. entrance to gap through S. Downs; mkt., agr. ctr.; old buildings, iron wks.; p. (1961) *13,637.*
Lewis, *I.*, Outer Hebrides, Scot.; fishing, tweeds; ch. t. Stornoway; a. 770 sq. m.; p. *31,687.*
Lewisham, *inner bor.*, London, Eng.; inc. former bor. of Deptford; residtl.; industl.; p. (1964) *289,857.*
Lewiston, *t.*, Idaho, U.S.A.; gold, silver, lead; agr., lumber; p. (1960) *12,691.*
Lewiston, *c.*, Maine, U.S.A.; textiles, machin., timber; p. (1960), *40,804.*
Lexington, *c.* Ky., U.S.A.; univ.; tobacco, horse-rearing; p. (1960) *62,810.*
Lexington, *t.*, Mass., U.S.A.; nr. Boston; mftg.; first battle in American War of Independence, 1775; p. (1960) *27,961.*
Leyburn, *t.*, N.R. Yorks, Eng.; in lower Wensleydale; mkt.; lead, lime; p. *1,440.*
Leyden, *see* **Leiden.**
Leyland, *t.*, *urb. dist.*, Lancs, Eng.; 5 m. S. of Preston; motors, cotton, paint and varnish, rubber goods; p. (1961) *19,241.*
Leyre, *R.*, S.W. France; length 40 m.
Leyte, *I.*, Philippines; a. 2,785 sq. m.; p. *727,600.*
Leytha (**Leitha**), *R.*, Austria; flowing to the Danube below Vienna.
Leyton, *see* **Waltham Forest.**
Leytonstone, part of Waltham Forest, Eng.; p. (1961) *12,254.*
Lhasa (**Lasa**), *c.*, *cap.*, Tibet, China; "forbidden" c.; Buddhist ctr., temple, monasteries, shrines; caravan tr. in carpets, silk, lace, gold, tea; p. (1953) *50,000.*
Liao-ho, *R.*, Liaoning, N.E. China, flows into G. of Liaotung, Yellow Sea; navigable for last 400 m. of course; length approx. 1,000 m.
Liaoning, *prov.*, N.E. China; incl. lower course and delta of Liao-ho; extremely fertile; gr. mineral resources; cap. Mukden; p. (1953) *18,545,147.*
Liaotung, *peninsula*, N.E. China; nr. G. of same name.
Liaoyang, *c.*, Liaoning, N.E. China; in fertile valley of Liao-ho; 35 m. S.W. of Mukden;

battle in Russo-Japanese war, 1904; p. (1953) *102,000*.
Liaoyuan, *c.*, Kirin, China; p. (1953) *120,000*.
Liberal, *t.*, S.W. Kan., U.S.A.; natural gas, flour, machin.; p. (1960) *13,813*.
Liberec, *t.*, ČSSR.; on R. Neisse; univ.; textiles, chemicals, tr. ctr.; p. (1962) *65,267*.
Liberia, *rep.*, W. Africa; coffee, palm oil, ivory, sugar; cap. Monrovia; a. 43,000 sq. m.; p. (1961) *1,250,000*.
Libmanan, *mun.*, Luzon, Philippine Is.; hemp, rice; p. *23,000*.
Libourne, *t.*, Gironde, France; on R. Dordogne; vineyards, brandy, sugar, woollens; p. (1954) *19,474*.
Libreville, *c.*, *cap.* Gabon; pt. on G. of Guinea; exp. tropical hardwoods, rubber, cacao; p. *c. 31,000*.
Libya, *indep. sov. st.* (1951), formerly Italian col., adm. after Second World War by Britain and France, N. Africa; cap. Beida; some agr., fruits, fishing, oil; a. 679,400 sq. m.; p. (1961) *1,195,000*.
Libyan Desert, part of the Sahara, Africa.
Lichfield, *c.*, *mun. bor.*, Staffs, Eng.; 7 m. N.W. of Tamworth; cath.; agr. and light inds.; p. (1961) *14,077*.
Lichtenstein, *t.*, Karl-Marx-Stadt, E. Germany; textiles; p. (1963) *13,978*.
Lick Observatory, on Mt. Hamilton, Cal., U.S.A.
Lickey Hills, Worcester, Eng.; 4 m. S.W. of Birmingham; sm. I. of ancient rocks; largely wooded; rise to 956 ft.
Licking, *R.*, Ky., U.S.A.; trib. of Ohio R.; length 220 m.
Licosa, *C.*, Italy; S. side of G. of Salerno.
Liddel, *R.*, Roxburgh, Dumfries, Scot.; trib. of R. Esk.; valley used by "Waverley Route" rly. from Carlisle to Edinburgh.
Lidköping, *t.*, Sweden; on L. Vänern; iron, porcelain inds.; p. (1961) *16,853*.
Liechtenstein, *sm. principality*, Europe; between Austria and Switzerland; agr., cattle, cotton weaving and spinning, leather goods; cap. Vaduz; a. 62 sq. m.; p. (1955) *14,757*.
Liége, *prov.*, Belgium; minerals; cap. Liége; a. 1,525 sq. m.; p. (1962) *1,007,516*.
Liége (Luik), *c.*, *prov. cap.*, Belgium; at junction of Rs. Meuse and Ourthe; cath., univ.; textiles, machin., coal, iron, glassware, fire-arms; p. (1962) *153,133*.
Lier, *t.*, Belgium; textiles, mnfs.; p. (1962) *28,887*.
Liepaja, *spt.*, Latvian S.S.R.; fishing inds.; engin, steel, chemicals; p. (1959) *71,000*.
Liestal, *cap.* of the half-can. Baselland, Switzerland; p. *7,211*.
Liévin, *mftg. t.*, Pas-de-Calais, France; adjoining Lens; coal-mining; p. (1954) *31,808*.
Liévres, *R.*, Quebec, Canada; trib. of St. Lawrence R.
Liffey, *R.*, Ireland; flows from Wicklow to Dublin Bay; length 50 m.
Lifu, *I.* (French); Loyalty Is., Pacific.
Ligao, *t.*, Luzon, Philippine Is.; sugar, rice.
Lignice (Liegnitz), *t.*, Silesia, Poland; German before 1945; cas.; foodstuffs, textiles, rly. junction; p. (1960) *64,000*.
Liguria, *region*, N.W. Italy; inc. provs. of Genoa and Porto Maurizio; a. 2,089 sq. m.; p. (1961) *1,717,630*.
Ligurian Sea, Mediterranean; N. of Corsica.
Lika, *R.*, Jugoslavia; partly underground; length 30 m.
Lille, *cap.*, Nord, France; on R. Deule; univ.; linens, cottons, rayons, iron, sugar, chemicals; p. (1962) *199,033*.
Lillehammer, *t.*, Norway; in R. Lagen valley; tourist ctr.; agr., lumbering; p. (1961) *6,153*.
Lilongwe, *t.*, cap., Central Prov. Malawi; new cap. under construction.
Lim Fjord, *shallow strait*, Jutland, Denmark; connects N. Sea with Kattegat; length 100 m.
Lima, *dep.*, Peru; a. 15,048 sq. m.; p. (1961) *2,321,198*.
Lima, *cap.*, Peru; univ.; comm. ctr., textiles, leather, furniture, iron-ore; spt. Callao; p. (1963) *1,960,000*.
Lima, *c.*, Ohio, U.S.A.; on Ottawa R.; rly. wks., oil, car bodies, refrigerators; p. (1960) *51,037*.
Limassol, *spt.*, Cyprus; wine, grapes, raisins; p. (estd. 1959) *37,000*.
Limavady, *t.*, *urb. dist.*, Londonderry, N. Ireland; mkt.; linen; p. (1961) *4,324*.
Limbach, *t.*, Karl-Marx-Stadt, E. Germany; hosiery, textiles, machines; p. (1963) *26,287*.
Limbe, *t.*, Malawi, Africa; merged with Blantyre (*q.v.*); elec. and power plants; p. *7,140*.
Limburg, *prov.*, Belgium; agr., livestock, gin, sugar-beet, mftg.; cap. Hasselt; a. 930 sq. m.; p. (1962) *586,279*.
Limburg, *prov.*, Neth.; drained by R. Maas (Meuse); cap. Maastricht; agr., cattle, coal, iron; a. 846 sq. m.; p. (estd. 1959) *882,386*.
Limburg, *c.*, Hessen, Germany; on R. Lahn; cath.; iron, machin., glass, paper; rly. junction; p. (estd. 1954) *15,800*.
Limehouse, *par.*, Tower Hamlets, E. London, Eng.; on R. Thames; p. (1961) *7,582*.
Limeira, *t.*, Sao Paulo, Brazil; ctr. of orange cultivation; hats, matches; p. (1960) *54,000*.
Limerick, *co.*, Munster, Ireland; agr., livestock, fishing; a. 1,1064 sq. m.; p. (1961) *133,025*.
Limerick, *co. bor.*, *spt.*, *cap.*, Limerick, Ireland; at head of Shannon estuary; bacon, tanning, shipbldg.; p. (1961) *50,497*.
Limmat, *R.*, Switzerland; trib. of R. Aar; flows through c. of Zurich; length 80 m.
Limoges, *ch. t.*, Haute-Vienne France; porcelain, kaolin paste; p (1962) *120,596*.
Limón, *prov.*, Costa Rica, Central America; p. (1963) *68,263*.
Limón, *prov. cap.*, *spt.*, Costa Rica, Central America; comm. ctr.; p. (1963) *22,505*.
Limousin, *old prov.*, and *natural division* ("pays"), Central France; located W. of Auvergne; plateau, average alt. 1,000 ft., composed of old crystalline rocks; exposed, damp climate; rich pasture favours raising of dairy cattle, horses; kaolin deposits; ch. t., Limoges.
Limpopo, or Crocodile R., S. Africa.
Linares, *prov.*, Chile; a. 3,790 sq. m.; cap. L.; p. (1961) *190,350*.
Linares, *t.*, Chile; wine, fruit, cereals, vegetables; p. (1961) *51,481*.
Linares, *t.*, Spain; lead-mining and mftg.; p. (1959) *58,327*.
Lincoln, *agr. co.*, Eng.; a. 2,665 sq. m.; divided into 3 administrative dists.; Holland, p. (1961) *103,388*; Kesteven, p. (1961) *135,317*; Lindsey, engin., agr. machin.; p. (1961) *504,678*.
Lincoln, *c.*, *co. bor.*, *co. t.*, Lincoln, Eng.; on R. Witham in gap through Lincoln Edge; cath.; heavy engin., iron foundries, bricks, lime, seed milling, malting; p. (1961) *77,065*.
Lincoln, *c.*, Ill., U.S.A.; coal, agr.; pottery; p. (1960) *16,890*.
Lincoln, *cap.*, Nebraska, U.S.A.; rly. ctr., flour; agr. machin., watches, cars, chemicals, rubber goods; p. (1960) *128,521*.
Lincoln, *t.*, R.I., U.S.A.; limestone, textiles; p. (1960) *13,545*.
Lincoln Edge, *hill ridge*, Lincoln, Eng.; runs N. from Ancaster through Lincoln to Humber; narrow ridge with steep scarp slope to W., broken across by R. Witham at Lincoln; composed of limestone, little surface drainage; iron-ore deposits worked in N. nr. Scunthorpe; sheep, barley; rarely exceeds 300 ft. alt.
Lincoln Park, *sub.* of Detroit, Mich., U.S.A.; residtl.; p. (1960) *53,933*.
Lincoln Wolds, *low plateau*, Lindsey, Lincoln, Eng.; runs N. 45 m. from Wash to Humber; chalk covered with glacial deposits; mixed farming, grains, roots, sheep; lge. farm units; scantily populated; rise to approx. 450 ft.
Lindau, *t.*, Bavaria, Germany; situated on I. in L. Constance; foodstuffs, machin., elec. goods; route ctr.; p. (1963) *25,500*.
Linden, *t.*, N.J., U.S.A.; p. (1960) *39,931*.
Lindsey, *N. div.*, Lincoln, Eng.; ch. ts. Lincoln, Grimsby; a. 1,520 sq. m.; p. (1961) *504,678*.
Lingen, *t.*, Lower Saxony, Germany; on Dortmund–Ems Canal; oil refining, textiles, cheese, cellulose; route ctr.; p. (1963) *25,400*.
Linköping, *t.*, S.E. Sweden; hy. engin., aero-engin., pianos, furniture; p. (1961) *65,237*.
Linlithgow, *burgh*, *co. t.*, W. Lothian, Scot.; 15 m. W. of Edinburgh; paper, glue, chemicals, distilling, brewing; p. (1961) *4,327*.
Linnhe, *L.*, Argyll, Scot.; 21 m. long; entrance to Caledonian canal.
Linosa, *I.* (Italian), Mediterranean, W. of Malta.
Linslade, *t.*, *urb. dist.*, Bucks, Eng.; 1 m. N.W. of Leighton Buzzard; p. (1961) *4,127*.

Linwood, *t.*, N.E. Renfrew, Scotland; 3 m. W. of Paisley; cars.
Linz, *c.*, *cap.*, Upper Austria; on Danube; boats, brewing, printing, iron, steel, textiles; cath.; p. (1961) *195,978*.
Lions, G. of, Mediterranean, S. France.
Lipa, *t.*, Luzon, Philippine Is.; sugar, tobacco, cocoa, maize; p. *45,175*.
Lipari Is., Italy; volcanic, Stromboli 3,155 ft.; a. 45 sq. m.; olives, grapes, wine, sulphur; lgst. I. and cap. L.; p. *19,500*.
Lipetsk, *industl t.*, R.S.F.S.R.; on the R. Voronezh; iron, engin., ferro-alloys; p. (1959) *156,000*.
Lippe, *R.* Germany; trib. of Rhine; length 110 m.
Lippstadt, *t.*, N. Rhine–Westphalia, Germany; on R. Lippe; metallurgy, textiles, rly. ctr.; p. (1963) *38,500*.
Liri, *R.*, Central Italy; rises in Alban Hills, flows S.E. to Cassino and then S.W. to G. of Gaeta; valley followed by main road from Rome to Naples; length 105 m.
Lisbon, *spt.*, *cap.*, Portugal; on R. Tagus; cas., cath.; univ.; cotton, silk, gold, silver, chemicals; p. (1960) *818,000*.
Lisburn, *t.*, *urb. dist.*, Antrim, N. Ireland; on R. Lagan, 6 m. S.W. of Belfast; linen mftg.; p. (1961) *17,691*.
Lisieux, *t.*, Calvados, France; cath.; flannel, dairying, footwear, machin.; p. (1954) *15,342*.
Liskeard, *mkt. t.*, *mun. bor.*, Cornwall, Eng.; on R. Looe at S. edge of Bodmin Moor; mining, tanning, chemicals; p. (1961) *4,490*.
Lisle, *t.*, Tasmania; gold.
Lismore, *mkt. t.*, *rural dist.*, on R. Blackwater, Waterford, Ireland; p. (1961) *8,027*.
Lismore, Scot., *I.*, 12 m. long in Loch Linnhe near Oban; p. *200*.
Lismore, *t.*, N.S.W., Australia; dairying, sugar-refining, maize, potatoes; p. (1961) *18,927*.
Lissa, *I.*, Jugoslavia; wine.
Listowel, *urb. dist.*, Kerry, Ireland; on R. Feale; cas. ruins; p. (1961) *2,858*.
Litchfield, *c.*, Ill., U.S.A.; natural gas, oil; p. (1960) *7,330*.
Litherland, *urb. dist.*, Lancs, Eng.; N. sub. of Liverpool; tanning, rubber processing, tar distilling, tin smelting; p. (1961) *24,872*.
Lithgow, *t.*, N.S.W., Australia; coal-mining, ironwks., potteries; p. (1961) *14,222*.
Lithuania, *constituent rep.*, U.S.S.R.; former independent st.; agr., livestock, timber; cap. Vilnius; a. 31,600 sq. m.; p. (1959) *2,713,000*.
Litomerice, *t.*, ČSSR.; on R. Elbe; brewing, agr. ctr.; p. (1961) *16,884*.
Little Bahama, one of the Bahama Is., W.I.
Little Belt, *strait*, separating Jutland from I. of Fyn, Denmark.
Little Cayman, *I.*, *see* **Cayman Is.**
Little Colorado, *R.*, Arizona, U.S.A.; trib. of Colorado R.
Little Falls, *c.*, Minn., U.S.A.; on R. Mississippi; timber; p. (1960) *7,551*.
Little Falls, *t.*, N.Y., U.S.A.; on Mohawk R.; paper, leather, bicycles, knitted goods; p. (1960) *8,935*.
Little Lever, *urb. dist.*, Lancs, Eng.; residtl. and industl.; p. (1961) *5,088*.
Little Rock, *c.*, Ark., U.S.A.; on Arkansas R.; oil, cotton-seed cakes, cotton, machin., and many diversified inds.; livestock; p. (1960) *107,813*.
Little Sioux, *R.*, Iowa, U.S.A.; trib. of Missouri; length 300 m.
Littleborough, *t.*, *urb. dist.*, Lancs, Eng.; 3 m. N.E. of Rochdale; cotton, woollens, dyeing; p. (1961) *10,514*.
Littlehampton, *t.*, *urb. dist.*, W. Sussex, Eng.; on S. cst. at mouth of R. Arun; holiday resort, sm. spt.; p. (1961) *15,647*.
Littleport, *mkt. t.*, Cambs, Eng.; N. of Ely; agr.; p. (par.) *4,709*.
Littleton, *t.*, N.H., U.S.A.; mftg.; p. (1960) *3,355*.
Littoria (Latina), *t.*, Lazio, Italy; in ctr. of reclaimed area of Pontine Marshes, 38 m. S.E. of Rome; mkt. ctr., on which planned road system converges; built since 1932; nuclear power sta. nearby; p. (1961) *48,395*.
Liverpool, *c.*, *spt.*, *co. bor.*, Lancs, Eng.; 2nd lgst. pt. in Gr. Britain, on N. bank at entrance to Mersey estuary; shipping and shipbldg.; elec. mnfs. and engin., flour milling, sugar refining, tobacco, seed and rubber processing; cath., univ.; p. (1961) *747,490*.
Liverpool, *t.*, N.S.W., Australia; poultry farming, dairying, mkt. gardening; p. (1947) *12,642*.
Liversedge, *t.*, W.R. Yorks, Eng.; woollens, chemicals, machin.; p. *15,000*.
Livingston, *t.*, Mont., U.S.A.; industl.; p. (1960) *8,229*.
Livingston, "new town" (designated 1962), on bdy. of W. Lothian and Midlothian, Scot.; p. (estd. 1965) *2,228*.
Livingstone Falls, cataracts on R. Congo, Africa.
Livingstone, *t.*, Zambia; on Zambesi R. where the rly. bridges the r., stands at 3,000 ft.; former cap.; impt. saw-mills ctr.; p. (1962) *31,560* inc. *4,000* Europeans.
Livingstone, *mtns.*, Tanzania, highest point, 9,600 ft.
Livorno, *see* **Leghorn.**
Livry-Gargain, *t.*, Seine-et-Oise, France; p. (1954) [*25,322*.
Lizard, The, *C.*, Cornwall, Eng.; S. point of Eng.
Ljubljana, *cap.*, Slovenia, Jugoslavia; on Laibach R.; textiles, chemicals, bell mftg, engin.; p. (1960) *155,000*.
Llanberis, *t.*, Caernarvon, Wales; tourist ctr. at base of Snowdon; p. *2,370*.
Llanberis, *pass*, Caernarvon, N. Wales; between mtns. Snowdon and Clyder Fawr; road carries heavy tourist traffic; summit alt. 1,168 ft.
Llandaff, *c.*, Glamorgan, S. Wales; part of Cardiff; cath.; p. *13,227*.
Llandarcy, *vil.*, Glamorgan, S. Wales; on cst. Swansea Bay, Bristol Channel; lge. oil-refinery; pipe-line to Angle Bay, Pembroke.
Llandilo, *t.*, *urb. dist.*, E. Carmarthen, Wales; on R. Towy, 10 m. E. of Carmarthen; agr. mkt.; p. (1961) *1,906*.
Llandovery, *t.*, *mun. bor.*, N.E. Carmarthen, Wales; on R. Towy, 11 m. N.E. of Llandilo; agr., forestry; fertilisers, cattlefood, bricks, tourist ctr.; p. (1961) *1,896*.
Llandrindod Wells, *t.*, *urb. dist.*, mid-Radnor, Wales; medicinal waters; p. (1961) *3,248*.
Llandudno, *t.*, *urb. dist.*, Caernarvon, Wales; between Gr. and Little Orme's Head; resort; elec. domestic goods; p. (1961) *17,852*.
Llandysul, *t.*, S. Cardigan, Wales, on R. Teifi; woollen milling; p. (1951) *2,590*.
Llanelly, *spt.*, *mun. bor.*, Carmarthen, Wales; on N. cst. of Loughor estuary; coal-mng., steel and tin-plate wks., mng. machin.; p. (1961) *29,994*.
Llanera, *commune*, N.W. Spain; horticulture; coal; p. *11,424*.
Llanfairfechan, *t.*, N. Caernarvon, Wales; under Penmaenmawr Mt.; seaside resort; granite quarrying; p. (1961) *2,861*.
Llanfair Caereinion, *t.*, Montgomery, Wales; mkt., flannel; p. *1,665*.
Llanfyllin, *t.*, *mun. bor.*, Montgomery, Wales; 11 m. S.W. of Oswestry; brewing, malting; Roman remains; p. (1961) *1,251*.
Llangefni, *t.*, *urb. dist.*, Anglesey, Wales; in ctr. of the I.; mkt. and agr. t.; p. (1961) *3,209*.
Llangollen, *t.*, *urb. dist.*, Denbigh, Wales; on R. Dee; mkt., tourist ctr., flannel mftg., light engin., slate quarrying; p. (1961) *3,050*.
Llanidloes, *t.*, *mun. bor.*, Montgomery, Wales; on R. Severn; leather, ironfoundry, engin. wks.; p. (1961) *2,375*.
Llanos, *lowland region*, Venezuela and Colombia, S. America; drained by R. Orinoco and tribs.; high temperatures throughout year, but rain chiefly in summer; ch. vegetation, coarse grass which withers during dry season (Dec. to May); little developed, some cattle-rearing.
Llanos de Urgel, *upland region*, Lérida, N.E. Spain; semi-arid; formerly steppe-land, now irrigated by R. Segre; vine, olive, maize, tobacco.
Llanquihue, *prov.*, Chile; a. 7,005 sq. m.; p. [(1960) *182,181*.
Llanrwst, *t.*, *urb. dist.*, Denbigh, Wales; on R. Conway; 10 m. S. of Conway; mkt., tourist ctr.; p. (1961) *2,571*.
Llanstephan, *vil.*, Carmarthen, Wales; cas.
Llantrisant, *rural dist.*, Glamorgan, Wales; iron, coal, quarrying; p. (rural dist. 1961) *27,125*.
Llanwrtyd Wells, *t.*, *urb. dist.*, Brecknock, Wales; iron, farming; p. (1961) *536*.
Lleyn, *peninsula*, *rural dist.*, Caernarvon, N. Wales; extends W. from Snowdonia to Bardsey I., separates Cardigan Bay from Caernarvon Bay; crystalline rocks form hills in E., otherwise low, undulating; pastoral farming, sheep, cattle; settlements mainly on cst., fishing vils. and sm. seaside resorts; ch. t.,

Pwllheli; a. 180 sq. m.; p. rural dist. (1961) *16,521.* [*24,903.*
Llwchwr, *urb. dist.*, Glam., S. Wales; p. (1961)
Loa, *R.*, N. Chile.
Loango, *spt.*, Congo (ex-French), Eq. Africa; N. of mouth of R. Congo; rubber, palm-oil exp.
Loanhead, *burgh*, Midlothian, Scot.; 5 m. S.E. of Edinburgh; coal, iron ore, engin.; p. (1961) *5,023.*
Löbau, *industl. t.* Dresden, E. Germany; p. (1963) *16,805.*
Lobaye, *R.*, Congo rep., Eq. Africa.
Lobito, *spt.*, Angola, Africa; N. of Benguela; exp. copper, maize; rly. terminus; p. (1960) *79,600* (inc. *15,000* whites).
Lobitos, *t.*, Piura dep., Peru; on cst. 20 m. N. of Talara; oil-wells.
Locarno, *t.*, Switzerland; on L. Maggiore; tourist ctr.; L. treaty 1925; p. *5,500.*
Lochaber, *mountainous dist.*, S. Inverness, Scot.; contains Ben Nevis.
Lochalsh, *see* **Kyle of Lochalsh.**
Lochgelly, *burgh*, Fife, Scot.; nr. Dunfermline; coal-mining; p. (1961) *9,114.*
Lochgilphead, *co. t.*, Argyll, Scot.; on arm of Loch Fyne; at E. entrance to Crinan Canal; tourist ctr.; p. (1961) *1,208.*
Lochmaben, *burgh*, Dumfries, Scot.; in Annandale, 7 m. N.E. of Dumfries; p. (1961) *1,279.*
Lochy, Loch, Inverness, Scot.; used by Caledonian Canal; 10 m. long; R. Lochy flows 8 m. to Fort William from S. end of the loch.
Lockerbie, *burgh*, Dumfries, Scot.; in Annandale 10 m. E. of Dumfries; sheep mkt.; p. (1961) *2,826.*
Lockhart, *t.*, Texas, U.S.A.; cotton, petroleum, agr.; p. (1960) *6,084.*
Lock Haven, *c.*, Penns., U.S.A.; on Susquehanna R.; timber; p. (1960) *11,748.* [*7,560.*
Lockport, *t.*, Ill., U.S.A.; rly. ctr.; p. (1960)
Lockport, *c.*, N.Y., U.S.A.; on Erie canal; machin., paper pulp, fruit; p. (1960) *26,443.*
Loddon, *R.*, Victoria, Australia; rises in Grampian Mtns., flows N. into R. Murray at Swan Hill; water used for irrigation in N. Victoria; length approx. 200 m. [p. (1954) *6,426.*
Lodève, *t.*, Hérault, France; cloth mftg.; cath.;
Lodi, *c.*, Italy; on R. Adda; cheese, majolica ware; cath.; p. *29,000.*
Lodi, *t.*, Cal., U.S.A.; in San Joaquin valley; agr., especially grapes; packing plants; p. (1960) *22,229.*
Lodi, *t.*, N.J., U.S.A.; p. (1960) *23,502.*
Lodore, *waterfall*, nr. Keswick, Cumberland, Eng.
Lodz, *prov.*, Central Poland; a. 7,904 sq. m.; p. (1961) *1,632,000.*
Lodz, *t.*, central Poland; the "Manchester of Poland"; textiles, paper, engin.; p. (1961) *723,000.*
Lofoten Is., *storm-swept gr.*, off N.W. cst. Norway; stretching 175 m.; mainly mtns.; cod and herring fishing.
Loftus, *t.*, *urb. dist.*, N.R. Yorks, Eng.; on N.E. flank of Cleveland Hills; stone, iron and steel; p. (1961) *8,111.*
Logan, *c.*, Utah, U.S.A.; p. (1960) *18,731.*
Logan, *t.*, Ohio, U.S.A.; coal, natural gas, oil; leather, wool mnfs.; p. (1960) *6,417.*
Logan, *mtn.*, S.E. Yukon, Canada; alt. 19,850 ft.
Logansport, *c.*, Ind., U.S.A.; on Wabash and Erie canal; timber, fruit, grain, machin., woollens; p. (1960) *21,106.*
Logroño, *prov.*, N. Spain, cap. Logroño; a. 1,946 sq. m.; p. (1959) *232,386.*
Logroño, *c.*, N. Spain, ctr. of wine growing a.; comm. and agr. mkt. t.; p. (1957) *55,465.*
Loir, *R.*, France; trib. of R. Sarthe; length 150 m.
Loire, *R.*, France; lgst. in cty., flows from Cévennes Mtns. to Atlantic; length 625 m.
Loire, *dep.*, France; agr. (potatoes vineyards), mining, mftg.; cap. St. Etienne; a. 1,853 sq. m.; p. (1962) *696,348.*
Loire, Atlantique, *dep.*, W. France; cap. Nantes; a. 2,695 sq. m.; p. (1962) *803,372.*
Loire, Haute, *dep.*, France; cap. Le Puy; a. 1,930 sq. m.; p. (1962) *211,036.*
Loiret, *dep.*, France; agr., vineyards, distilling, mftg.; cap. Orléans; a. 2,630 sq. m.; p. (1962) *389,854.*
Loir-et-Cher, *dep.*, Central France; cap. Blois; a. 2,479 sq. m.; p. (1962) *250,741.*
Loja, *prov.*, Ecuador; cap. Loja; a. 3,705 sq. m.; p. (estd. 1962) *285,351.*
Lokeren, *t.*, Belgium; textiles, chemicals, tobacco; p. (1962) *25,975.*
Lokoja, *t.*, Nigeria; at confluence of Rs. Niger and Benue; military sta.; importance decreased since rlys. opened; p. *2,122.*
Lolland, *I.*, Danish, Baltic Sea; a. 462 sq. m.; forests; cap. Maribo; p. (1960) *83,170.*
Lombardy, *region*, N. Italy; in R. Po Valley; a. 9,190 sq. m.; p. (1961) *7,390,492.*
Lombardy, Plain of, N. Italy; extensive lowland flanked by Alps, Apennines, Adriatic Sea; built up by alluvium from R. Po, its tribs. and R. Adige; zone bounding main Rs. liable to floods, elsewhere irrigation necessary on account of hot summers; intensively cultivated, rice, maize, flax, clover, lucerne, wheat, apples, dairy cattle, mulberry; densely populated; many industl. ts., Milan, Novara, Pavia, etc.; length 250 m., width from 50 to 120 m.
Lombok, one of the lesser Sunda Is., Indonesia, Malay Archipelago; mtns., peak of Lombok 11,810 ft., volcanic; Wallace's Line passes between Lombok and Bali; ch. t. Mataram; p. *701,298.*
Lomé, *spt.*, *cap.*, Togo, W. Africa; on G. of Guinea; exp. cacao, cotton, palm prods.; phosphates; p. (estd. 1964) *80,000.*
Lomme, *commune*, Nord, France; spinning, hats; p. (1954) *23,488.*
Lomond, *L.*, between Dunbarton and Stirling cos., Scot.; contains 30 Is.; lgst. loch in Scot.; length 20 m.; a. 27 sq. m.
Lomond Hills, Kinross and Fife, Scot.; alt. 1,713 ft. and 1,471 ft.
Lomza, *t.*, Poland; on Narew R.; grain, timber; p. (1960) *20,000.*
London, *cap. c.*, *spt.*, Eng.; on R. Thames; inc. 12 inner and 20 outer bors.; tourist ctr., lge. tr., gr. fin., industl. and cult. ctr.; univ.; many historic bldgs.; p. (1964) *7,998,417* (Greater London); (1961) *4,767* (c.).
London, *t.*, Ontario, Canada; on R. Thames, 65 m. W. of Hamilton; industl. ctr.; univ.; p. (1961) *181,283.*
Londonderry, *co.*, N. Ireland; a. 816 sq. m.; p. (excl. co. bor.) (1961) *111,565.*
Londonderry (or Derry), *co. bor.*, N. Ireland; on left bank of R. Foyle, 4 m. upstream from Lough Foyle; shirt mftg.; p. (1961) *53,744.*
Londonderry, *C.*, jutting into Timor Sea, W. Australia.
Long Beach, *c.*, Cal., U.S.A.; tourism; petrol, shipbldg., fishing, canning, aircraft, chemicals; p. (1960) *344,168.*
Long Beach, *t.*, Long I., N.Y., U.S.A.; holiday resort; p. (1960) *26,473.*
Longbenton, *t.*, *urb. dist.*, Northumberland, Eng.; 3 m. N.E. of Newcastle; coal-mng.; p. (1961) *44,633.*
Long Branch, *c.*, N.J., U.S.A.; seaside resort; p. (1960) *26,228.*
Long Eaton, *t.*, *urb. dist.*, Derby, Eng.; on R. Trent, 5 m. S.W. of Nottingham; rly. wks., lace mftg., elec. cables, flexible tubing, hosiery; p. (1961) *30,464.*
Longford, *co.*, Leinster, Ireland; peat bogs; dairy farming; a. 421 sq. m.; p. (1961) *30,642.*
Longford, *co. t.*, Longford, Ireland; agr. ctr.; p. (1961) *3,558.*
Long Forties Bank, *submarine sandbank*, N. Sea; 80 m. E. of Aberdeen; valuable fishing-grounds; depth of water, from 25 to 40 fathoms.
Long I., part of N.Y., U.S.A.; separated from mainland by East R.; contains Queens and Brooklyn, bors. of New York City; mkt. gardening, fisheries, oysters, holiday resorts; a. 1,682 sq. m.
Long I., Bahamas Is., W.I.; p. (1953) *3,755.*
Long I. City, part of Queen's bor., N.Y., U.S.A.; industl. ctr.; food, engin., leather.
Long, Loch, *arm of sea*, between Dunbarton and Argyll, Scot.; length 17 m.
Longmeadow, *t.*, S.W. Mass., U.S.A.; residtl.; p. (1960) *10,547.*
Longreach, *t.*, Queensland, Australia; in ctr. of Gr. Australian (artesian) basin, 400 m. W. of Rockhampton; where rly. from cst. crosses R. Thompson; collecting and forwarding ctr. for cattle and wool.
Longridge, *t.*, *urb. dist.*, Lancs, Eng.; 6 m. N.E. of Preston; cotton, nails; p. (1961) *4,677.*
Long's Peak, *mtn.*, Col., U.S.A.; alt. 14,271 ft.

Longtown, *mkt. t.*, Cumberland, Eng.; on R. Esk; agr.; p. *6,676.*
Longueuil, *t.*, Quebec, Canada; p. (1961) *24,131.*
Longview, *t.*, Texas, U.S.A.; p. (1960) *40,050.*
Longview, *t.*, Wash., U.S.A.; p. (1960) *23,349.*
Longwy, *t.*, Meurthe-et-Moselle, France; fortfd.; iron, porcelain; p. (1954) *16,578.*
Long Xuyon, *mkt. t.*, S. Vietnam; p. *148,000.*
Lons-le-Saunier, *cap.*, Jura, France; salt springs; wine, agr.; livestock; p. (1954) *15,030.*
Looe, *t., sm. spt., urb. dist.*, Cornwall, Eng.; on both sides of Looe estuary, 10 m. W. of Plymouth Sound; fishing and fish-canning; holiday resort; p. (1961) *3,878.*
Lookland, *t.*, S.W. Ohio, U.S.A.; chemicals, paper, light mnfs.; p. (1960) *5,292.*
Loos, *t.*, Pas-de-Calais, France; coal-mining; p. (1954) *14,882.*
Lop Nor, *marsh*, Sinkiang, W. China; in Tarim Basin at foot of Altyn Tagh; ctr. of inland drainage, receives water from R. Tarim; almost uninhabited.
Lorain, *c.*, Ohio, U.S.A.; on L. Erie; shipbldg., steelwks., fisheries; p. (1960) *68,932.*
Lorca, *t.*, Murcia, Spain; agr. prod., woollens, chemicals; bishop's palace; p. (1959) *61,657.*
Lord Howe I., Australian I., S. Pac. Oc., length 7 m., width 1½ m.; *c.* 436 m. N.E. of Sydney; palm seed ind.; p. (1958) *223.*
Lorena, *c.*, S.E. Brazil; cotton, coffee; p. *10,262.*
Loreto, *t.*, Ancona, Italy; pilgrim ctr.; p. *6,700.*
Loreto, *dep.*, Peru; rubber; cap. Iquitos; a. 119,270 sq. m.; p. (1961) *330,335.*
Lorient, *spt.*, Morbihan, France; on Bay of Biscay; govt. dockyds. and arsenal; fishing; p. (1962) *63,924.*
Lörrach, *t.*, Baden-Württemberg, Germany; N.E. of Basle; textiles, tobacco, chocolate mnfs., machin.; p. (1963) *31,200.*
Lorraine, *prov.*, France; agr., wine, iron.
Los Angeles, *c.*, S. Cal., U.S.A.; ch. comm. ctr. on W. cst.; winter resort, fruit, clothing, steel, oil refining, aircraft mftg., car assembly; machin., chemicals; film ctr.; p. (1960) *2,479,015.*
Los Angeles, *cap. c.*, Bio Bio, Chile; wine, fruit, timber; p. (1960) *79,000.*
Losinj, *I.*, Jugoslavia; summer resort, tr.
Los Rios, *prov.*, Ecuador, S. America; a. 2,295 sq. m.; cap. Babahoyo; p. (estd. 1962) *244,651.*
Los Santos, *prov.*, Panama, Central America; cap. Las Tablas; p. (1960) *70,554.*
Lossiemouth, *burgh*, Moray, Scot.; on Moray F., 5 m. N. of Elgin; fishing; p. (1961) *5 855.*
Lostwithiel, *t., mun. bor.*, Cornwall, Eng.; at head of Fowey estuary; mkt., angling; p. (1961) *1,954.*
Lot, *R.*, S. France; trib. of Garonne R.; length 272 m.
Lot, *dep.*, S.W. France; livestock, wine, cereals, coal, iron; a. 2,018 sq. m.; cap. Cahors; p. (1962) *149,929.*
Lota, *pt.*, Chile; coal-mng. ctr.; ceramics; p. [(1961) *51,679.*
Lot-et-Garonne, *dep.*, S.W. France; agr. (cereals, vines, fruit); cap. Agen; a. 2,079 sq. m.; p. (1962) *275,028.*
Lothians, *Scottish dist.*, S. of F. of Forth, cos. Mid Lothian, W. Lothian and E. Lothian.
Lötschental, *picturesque valley*, can. Valais, Switzerland; reached from Goppenstein on Lötschberg rly.; leads to Langgletscher; ch. vil., Kippel.
Loughborough, *t., mun. bor.*, Leicester, Eng.; on R. Soar 10 m. N. of Leicester; engin., elec. gds., chemicals, textiles; college; p. (1961) *38,621.*
Loughor, *R.*, Glamorgan, S. Wales; rises in Black Mtns., flows S.W. into Bristol Channel; lower valley submerged to form estuary, length 8 m., width 4 m., around which cluster steel-wks. and zinc refineries of Llanelly, Bynea, Gorseinon, Gowerton, etc.
Loughton, *t.*, Essex, Eng.; on border of Epping Forest; residtl.; p. (1961) *33,864.*
Louisiana, *st.*, U.S.A.; agr., tobacco, cotton, sugar, timber, minerals and mftg., oil, gas; cap. Baton Rouge; ch. spt. New Orleans; a. 48,523 sq. m.; p. (1960) *3,257,022.*
Louisville, *c.*, Ky., U.S.A.; on Ohio R.; univ.; lgst. tobacco mkt. in world; chemicals, paints, cars, machin., elec. goods, synthetic rubber; p. (1960) *390,639.*
Loulé, *t.*, Portugal; esparto-grass ctr.; porcelain, [leather; p. *23,000.*
Lourdes, *t.*, France; on R. Pau; great pilgrim ctr.; slate, marble; p. (1954) *15,829.*
Lourenço Marques, *cap., spt.*, Mozambique, Port. E. Africa; rly. terminus, coaling-sta., oil refining; p. (1961) *183,798* inc. *62.000* Europeans.
Louth, *t., mun. bor.*, Lindsey, Lincoln, Eng.; on E. edge of Lincoln Wolds; abbey ruins; cattle mkt., farm implements, rope mkg., lime, malting, canning; p. (1961) *11,556.*
Louth, *maritime co.*, Leinster, Ireland; mtns., bog and barren land; salmon fishing; cap. Dundalk; a. 316 sq. m.; p. (1961) *67,284.*
Louvain, *t.*, Belgium; univ.; lace, brewing, tobacco mftg.; p. (1962) *32,474.*
Louviers, *t.*, Eure, France; on R. Eure; cloth mftg.; p. (1954) *10,746.*
Loveland, *t.*, N. Col. U.S.A.; beet-sugar refined, vegetables, fruit canning; p. (1960) *9,734.*
Low Archipelago, *see* **Tuamotu Is.**
Low Countries. Name applied to Belgium and The Netherlands. *See under separate headings.*
Lowell, *c.*, Mass., U.S.A.; at junction of Merrimac and Concord Rs.; 30 m. N. of Boston; textiles, machin., chemicals, carpets; James Whistler, the artist, born here; p. (1960) *92,107.*
Lower Austria, *prov.*, Austria; industl., agr.; ch. t. Vienna; a. 7,098 sq. m.; p. (1961) *1,374,012.*
Lower Hutt, *c.*, N.I., New Zealand; p. (1961) *53,010.*
Lower Saxony, *Land*, Germany; a. 18,226 sq. m. [p. (1961) *6,641,000.*
Lowestoft, *spt., mun. bor.*, Suffolk, Eng.; on E. Anglian cst. 9 m. S. of Gr. Yarmouth; holiday resort, fishing ctr., boat bldg., engin., vehicle mftg.; p. (1961) *45,687.*
Lowther Hills, *mtns.*, between Dumfries and Lanark, Scot.; highest point 2,403 ft.
Loyalty Is., S. Pac. Oc.; included in French administration of New Caledonia; copra; lgst. Is., Maré, Lifou, Uvéa; a. about 800 sq. m.
Loyang, *c.*, Honan prov., China; industl.; p. (1958) *500,000.*
Lozère, *dep.*, S.E. France; traversed by Cévennes Mtns.; agr., silkworm-rearing, stock-raising; cap. Mende; a. 1,996 sq. m.; p. (1962) *81,868.*
Lualaba, *R.*, Congo, Central Africa; rises nr. Elisabethville in Katanga prov., flows N. approx. 500 m. to Kikondja, where joined by R. Lufira to form R. Congo; name also applied to main stream of R. Congo as far downstream as Ponthierville.
Luanda, *cap., pt.*, Angola; oil refining; hydro-elec. wks; p. (1962) *220,000* inc. *55,000* whites.
Luang Prabang, *c.*, Laos, on Mekong R.; silk, ivory, rubber; pagoda; p. *25,000.*
Lubbock, *c.*, N. Texas, U.S.A.; p. (1960) *128,691.*
Lübeck, *c., spt.*, cap. Schleswig-Holstein, Germany; on R. Trave; cath.; shipbldg., machin., chemicals, textiles, iron, foodstuffs; pt. and rly. junction; p. (1963) *236,000.*
Lublin, *prov.* E. Poland; agr.; a. 10,834 sq. in. p. (1961) *1,842,000.*
Lublin, *t., prov. cap.*, Poland; textiles, engin., agr. tr.; cath., 2 univs.; p. (1960) *181,000.*
Lubnaig, *Loch*, Perth, Scot.; drains to R. Teith by the R. Leny.
Lubny, *t.*, Ukrainian S.S.R.; on rly. E. of Kiev; [engin., chemicals; p. *23,332.*
Lucca, *c., cap.* Lucca, Tuscany, Italy; nr. Pisa; cath., churches; jute mftg., tobacco, silk, cotton, and oil-refining inds.; p. (1961) *85,940.*
Lucena, *t.*, Córdoba, Spain; olive oil, ceramics, gilt metals; p. (1957) *35,830.*
Lucena, *commune*, S. Spain; metallurgy; leather, pottery, linen; horse-breeding; p. *32,687.*
Lucenec, *t.*, ČSSR.; on Hungarian border; magnesite, textiles, sawmilling; p. (1961) *16,102.*
Lucera, *t.*, Apulia, Italy; 8 m. W. of Foggia; cas., cath.; silk mftg.; p. *17,000.*
Lucerne (Luzern), *can.*, Switzerland; agr., pastoral, vineyards; cap. Lucerne; a. 576 sq. m.; p. (1961) *253,446.*
Lucerne (Luzern), *t., cap.*, Lucerne can., Switzerland; at W. end of L. Lucerne, 45 m. E. of Berne; light inds.; impt. tourist ctr.; p. (1961) *70,600*
Lucerne, *L.*, Switzerland; also known as Lake of the Four Cantons; length 23 m.
Luchow (Luzhou), *c.*, Szechwan, China; coal, iron, kaolin; p. (1953) *289,000.*
Luckenwalde, *t.*, Potsdam, E. Germany; on R. Nuthe; textiles, footwear, machin., wood and metals, chemicals; p. (1963) *28,741.*
Lucknow, *c.*, cap. Uttar Pradesh India; on R. Gumti; rly. ctr., muslin embroidery, brocade mftg.; famous defence of L. in Indian Mutiny 1857; univ.; p. (1961) *655,673.*

Lüdenscheid, *t.*, N. Rhine–Westphalia, Germany; S.E. of Barmen; hardware; p. (1963) *58,500*.

Lüderitz, *t.*, S.W. Africa; on cst. of Kalahari desert; linked by rly. to S. African rly. system at De Aar; diamonds; p. (1960) *3,604*.

Ludhiana, *t.*, Punjab, India; nr. R. Sutlej, W. of Simla; p. (1961) *244,032*.

Ludington, *t.*, Mich., U.S.A.; on Lake M.; woodwkg.; p. (1960) *9,421*.

Ludlow, *mkt. t., mun. bor.*, Salop, Eng.; at foot of Clee Hills on R. Teme; agr. mkt., agr. implements, oil pressure appliances, meters, gauges; p. (1961) *6,774*.

Ludvika, *t.*, Sweden; elec. goods; p. (1961) *12,253*.

Ludwigsburg, *t.*, Baden-Württemberg, Germany; N. of Stuttgart; cas.; textiles, foodstuffs, machin., toys; p. (1963) *75,500*.

Ludwig's Canal, Germany; unites Rs. Danube and Main; length 110 m.

Ludwigshafen, *t.*, Rhine-Palatinate, Germany; on R. Rhine, opposite Mannheim; chemicals, marine diesel engines, metallurgy, glass; R. pt. and rly. junction; p. (1963) *171,500*.

Lufkin, *c.*, Texas, U.S.A.; lumber, engin.; food prod.; p. (1960) *17,641*.

Lug, *R.*, trib. of R. Wye, Hereford, Eng.

Lugano, *t.*, Ticino, Switzerland; on L. Lugano; tourist ctr., silk, paper; p. (1957) *19,112*.

Lugano, *L.*, Italy–Switzerland; length 16 m.

Lugansk, *industl. t.*, Ukraine S.S.R.; S. of R. Donets in Donbas region; impt. rly. eng. factories; textiles; p. (1962) *306,000*.

Lugnaquilla, *mtn.*, Wicklow, Ireland; highest point in Wicklow Mtns., alt. 3,039 ft.

Lugo, *prov.*, N.W. Spain; fisheries, leather; cap. Lugo; a. 3,815 sq. m.; p. (1959) *500,648*.

Lugo, *t., prov. cap.*, Spain; on R. Minho; tanning, textiles; p. (1959) *50,137*.

Luichow (Luizhou), *c.*, Kwangsi Chuang, China; comm. ctr.; p. (1953) *159,000*.

Lukuga, intermittent outlet of L. Tanganyika, Africa, linking with R. Congo.

Luleå, *spt.*, N. Sweden; on Lule R. at head of G. of Bothnia; iron ore, timber, engin.; p. (1961) *65,237*.

Lulworth Cove, *sm. inlet*, Dorset, Eng.; on S. cst., 9 m. E. of Weymouth; formed by sea breaching hard coastal rocks and eroding softer rocks behind; tourists.

Lumbira, *t.*, on N. shore of L. Nyasa, Tanzania.

Lund, *t.*, Sweden; nr. Malmö; univ.; packaging ind.; steam boilers; p. (1961) *40,380*.

Lundy I., Bristol Channel; 12 m. N.W. of Hartland Point, N. Devon, Eng.; 2½ m. long by 1 m. wide.

Lune, *R.*, Lancs and Westmorland, Eng.; flows 45 m. to Irish Sea.

Lüneburg, *t.*, Lower Saxony, Germany; S.E. of Hamburg, on Ilmenau R.; chemicals, wood, iron, paper; rly. junct.; p. (1963) *60,900*.

Lünen, *t.*, N. Rhine–Westphalia, Germany; N.E. of Dortmund; coal, metallurgy, glass, wood; R. pt. and rly. ctr.; p. (1963) *72,200*.

Lunéville, *t.*, Meurthe-et-Moselle, France; S.E. of Nancy, on R. Meurthe; cottons, woollens, hosiery, porcelain; p. (1954) *22,690*.

Lungchow, *t.*, Kwangsi, China; nr. Vietnam frontier; military sta.; p. *13,600*.

Lungi, *t.*, Sierra Leone, W. Africa; nr. Freetown; only civil airport in st.

Lupata Gorge, Mozambique, Port. E. Africa; narrow pass occupied by R. Zambesi.

Lurgan, *t., mun. bor.*, Armagh, N. Ireland; textiles, tobacco mftg.; p. (1961) *17,873*.

Luristan, *prov.*, W. Iran; grain, carpets.

Lusaka, *c., cap.*, Zambia; p. (estd. 1958) *61,000* Africans, *12,500* Europeans, *1,500* others.

Lushun, *see* **Port Arthur.**

Luta, *special mun.*, S. Liaoning prov., China: comprising Port Arthur Naval Base District and the pts. of Port Arthur and Talien (Dairen).

Luton, *t., co. bor.*, Beds,. Eng.; in Chiltern Hills nr. source of R. Lea; motor vehicles, engin., hat mkg., aircraft, gear instruments, chemicals; p. (1961) *131,505*.

Lutong, *pt.*, N. Sarawak, Malaysia; oil refining.

Lutsk, *t.*, Ukrainian S.S.R.; comm. ctr., mnfs.; p. (1959) *49,000*.

Luxembourg, *prov.*, S.E. Belgium; on French border; wooded and hilly; a. 1,705 sq. m.; cap. Arlon; p. (1962) *216,975*.

Luxembourg, *grand duchy*, Europe; on borders of France, Germany, Belgium; upland, much over 1,000 ft.; very impt. deposits of iron ore; cap. Luxembourg; a. 999 sq. m.; p. (1958) *317,853*.

Luxembourg, *t., cap.*, Luxembourg; in S. of Grand Duchy; iron and steel, heavy engin., leather, paper inds.; p. (1958) *70,158*.

Luxor, *vil.*, Upper U.A.R.; on E. bank of R. Nile; site of Thebes; ruined temples; p. *5,000*.

Luzerne, *bor.*, Penns., U.S.A.; on Susquehanna R.; p. (1950) *6,176*.

Luzon, *I.*, lgst. in Philippines; mtns.; cotton, coffee, sugar, cereals, coal, copper; cap. Manila; a. 40,420 sq. m.; p. *4,000,000*.

Lvov, (Pol. Lwów, Ger. Lemberg), *c.*, Ukraine, U.S.S.R.; ceded by Poland 1939; univ., 3 caths.; engin., textiles, chemicals, oil-refining, sawmilling; p. (1962) *447,000*.

Lyallpur, *t.*, W. Punjab, Pakistan; univ.; cotton, chemicals, fertilisers; p. (1961) *425,200*.

Lydd, *mkt. t., mun. bor.*, Kent, Eng.; on Romney Marsh, 4 m. S.W. of New Romney; "lyddite" shells, concrete; airport; p. (1961) *2,685*.

Lydda, *t.*, Israel; rly. junction, airport; p. (1946) *20,000*.

Lydenburg, *t.*, Transvaal, S. Africa; gold, cotton, wheat, sheep; p. (1960) *7,393* inc. *3,306* whites.

Lydford, *par.* and *vil.*, Devon, Eng.; old stannary ctr. for Devon; p. *2,200*.

Lydney, *par.*, Gloucester, Eng.; in Forest of Dean; iron, coal; p. *4,158*.

Lyell, *mtn.*, Stanley Range, N.S.W., Australia; [alt. 2,000 ft.

Lyell, *mtn.*, Cal., U.S.A.; in Sierra Nevada; alt. 13,190 ft.

Lyme Regis, *spt., mun. bor.*, Dorset, Eng.; on bdy. between Devon and Dorset; holiday resort, p. (1961) *3,533*.

Lymington, *t., mun. bor.*, Hants, Eng.; on The Solent at mouth of R. Beaulieu; small spt., yachting; p. (1961) *28,642*.

Lymm, *t., urb. dist.*, Cheshire, Eng.; 5 m. W. of Altrincham; salt mftg.; mainly residtl.; p. (1961) *7,330*.

Lynbrook, *t.*, Long I., N.Y., U.S.A.; p. (1960) [*19,881*.

Lynchburg, *c.*, Va., U.S.A.; footwear, agr. implements, tobacco; p. (1960) *54,790*.

Lyndhurst, *t.*, N.J., U.S.A.; synthetic perfumery; p. (1960) *21,867*.

Lynher, *R.*, Cornwall, Eng.; length 26 m.

Lynn, *spt.*, Mass., U.S.A.; footwear, elec. appliances; p. (1960) *944,78*.

Lynn Canal, *fiord*, Alaska, U.S.A.; continuation of Chatham strait.

Lynton, *t., urb. dist.*, N. Devon, Eng.; 17 m. W. of Minehead on Bristol Channel; seaside tourist ctr. of Exmoor; p. (1961) *1,918*.

Lynwood, *t.*, S.W. Cal., U.S.A.; engin.; p. (1960) [*31,614*.

Lyon, *c.*, Iowa, U.S.A., on Mississippi R.; p. (1960) *14,468*.

Lyon, *R.*, Perth, Scot.; trib. of R. Tay; length [38 m.

Lyonnais, *mtns.*, France; W. of Lyons.

Lyons, *c. cap.*, Rhône dep., France; at confluence of Rs. Saône and Rhône; comm. ctr., silk, rayon, chemicals, engin.; heavy lorries; univ.; oil refinery nearby; world ctr. for cancer research; p. (1962) *535,784*.

Lys, *R.*, Belgium and France, trib. of R. Scheldt; length 100 m.

Lysterfiord, N.E. arm of the Sogne fiord, Norway; length 25 m.

Lytham St. Annes, *t., mun. bor.*, N. Lancs, Eng.; on N. cst. of Ribble estuary, 4. m. S. of Blackpool; holiday ctr., shipbldg.; p. (1961) *36,222*.

Lyttelton, *spt.*, S.I., N.Z.; on N. cst. of Banks Peninsula; ch. pt. of Canterbury Plain; exp. mutton, wool, wheat; p. (1961) *3,403*.

M

Ma'an, *t.*, S. Jordan, term. of rly. through Amman to Beirut; restoration of Hijaz rail line to Medina (1964–7); p. (1961) *6,899*.

Maas, *R.*, Dutch name for the R. Meuse after it has entered the Neth.

Maasin, *mun.*, S.W. Leyte, Philippine Is.; cst. tr.; hemp; p. *29,264*.

Maastricht, *t., cap.*, Limburg, Neth.; on R. Meuse; pottery, glass, textiles, brewing; p. (1960) *90,202*.

Mablethorpe and Sutton, *t., urb. dist.*, Lindsey, Lincs, Eng.; on E. cst., 15 m. N. of Skegness; holiday resort; p. (1961) *5,389*.

Macao, *Port. terr.*, S. China; consists of peninsula and 2 sm. Is. (Taipa and Colôane) to S. of estuary of Canton R.; a. 6 sq. m.; p. (1950) *187,772* (inc. *2,719* Europeans).

Macao, *c.*, Macao terr., S. China; occupies peninsula section of the terr.; impt. fisheries; p. (1950) *166,544*.

Macapá, *cap.*, Amapa st., Brazil; at mouth of R. Amazon; p. (1960) *46,905*.

Macassar, *ch. t.*, *pt.*, Sulawesi, *see* Makasar.

Macassar, *strait*, Indonesia, *see* Makasar.

Macau, *spt.*, Rio Grande do Norte, Brazil; p. *6,656*.

Macclesfield, *t.*, *mun. bor.*, Cheshire, Eng.; at foot of Pennines, 10 m. S. of Stockport; on R. Bollin; mkt., textiles, clothing, paper prods., engin.; p. (1961) *37,578*.

Macdonald Is., *terr.* of Australia, Antarctica.

Macdonnell Range, *mtns.*, Northern Terr., Australia; highest part of desert tableland, centrally situated within the continent; some gold and mica mines, but development hampered by aridity and isolation; highest alt. 4,482 ft.

Macduff, *spt. burgh*, Banff, Scot.; 2 m. E. of Banff; fishing; p. (1961) *3,479*.

Macedonia, *dist.*, Greece; cereals tobacco, fruit, opium, fishing; p. (1961) *1,890,654*.

Macedonia, *fed. unit*, Jugoslavia; cap. Skopje; a. 10,598 sq. m.; p. (1960) *1,387,000*.

Maceió, *spt.*, *cap.*, Alagoas st., Brazil; cotton, sugar, tobacco, soap, sawmills, distilleries; p. (1960) *170,134*.

Macequece, *t.*. Manica dist., Mozambique; p. *9,284*.

Macequece, *t.*, Manica dist., Mozambique; p. *9,284*.

Macerata, *prov. cap.*, Italy; cath., univ.; terra-cotta, glass, chemicals; p. (1961) *37,464*.

Macgillicuddy's Reeks, *mtns.*, Kerry, Ireland; highest peak, Carrantuohill, alt. 3,414 ft.

Machala, *t.*, S.W. Ecuador; cocoa, coffee, leather, gold; p. (1962) *22,730*.

Machynlleth, *t.*, *urb. dist.*, Montgomery, Wales, on R. Dovey; tourist ctr., clothing mftg.; p. (1961) *1,903*.

Macintyre, *R.*, N.S.W., Australia; forms border between Queensland and N.S.W.; trib. of R. Darling; length 350 m.

Mackay, *spt.*, Queensland, Australia; on R. Pioneer; gold, sugar, dairying and banana ctr.; p. (1961) *16,795*.

Mackenzie, *township*, Guyana; bauxite; p. approx. *15,000* mostly Negro.

Mackenzie, *dist.*, N.W. Terrs., Canada; a. 527,490 sq. m.; forests and tundra; oil, radium, uranium; furs and timber.

Mackenzie, *R.*, N.W. Terrs., Canada; rises in Rocky Mtns. as Athabaska R. and flows into L. Athabaska, leaves as Slave R. and thence into Gr. Slave L., which it leaves as M. R. into Beaufort Sea; length 2,350 m.

Mackinac Sound, connects Ls. Michigan and Huron, N. America.

Mackinney, *c.*, N.E. Texas, U.S.A.; cotton ctr.; (1960) *13,763*.

Macmillan, *R.*, N.W. Terrs., Canada; trib. of Yukon R.

Macnean, *L.*, cos. Leitrim and Fermanagh, Ireland.

Macomb, *c.*, Ill., U.S.A.; industl.; p. (1960) *12,135*

Mâcon, *t.*, *cap.*, Saône-et-Loire, France; on R. Saône; ruined cath.; agr. implements, wines, copper; rope, p. (1954) *22,393*.

Macon, *c.*, Ga., U.S.A.; on Ocmulgee R.; univ.; rly. junction, ironwks., cotton mftg.; p. (1960) *69,764*.

Macon, *t.*, E. Miss., U.S.A.; cotton, dairying, lumbering; p. (1960) *2,432*.

Macquarie, I., *Australian I.*, S. Pacific; 900 m. S.E. of Tasmania, Australia; 21 m. long, 2 m. wide; uninhabited except for meteorological and research base.

Macquarie, *R.*, N.S.W., Australia; trib. of R. Darling; length 350 m.

Macroom, *t.*, Cork, Ireland; on R. Sullane; agr. tr., fishing; p. (1961) *2,169*.

Mactan, *I.*, off Cebu, Philippine Is.; mangroves, coconuts; a. 24 sq. m.; p. *40,103*.

Madagascan Republic, *see* Malagasy.

Madang, *t.*, Papua–New Guinea; copra ctr.; p. *500*.

Madawaska, *t.*, Me., U.S.A.; spt.; lumber, pulp, paper-mills; p. (1960) *4,035*.

Madawaska, *R.*, Ontario, Canada; trib. of Ottawa R.; length 230 m.

Maddalena, *I.*, off N.E. cst. of Sardinia, Italy.

Maddaloni, *t.*, Naples, Italy; p. *21,975*.

Madeira, *Portuguese I.*, Atl. Oc.; wine, sugar, fruits; holiday resort; cap. Funchal; a. 315 sq. m.; p. (1950) *269,179*.

Madeira, *R.*, Brazil; trib. of R. Amazon; together with Mamoré R.; l. 2,000 m.

Madeley, *t.*, Salop, Eng.; on R. Severn; mkt., coal- and iron-mining; p. *7,300*.

Madera, *t.*, central Cal., U.S.A.; agr., lumber, wines; p. (1960) *14,430*.

Madhya Bharat, formerly a st., absorbed by Madhya Pradesh, 1 Nov. 1956.

Madhya Pradesh, *st.*, Indian Union; absorbed the sts. of Bhopal, Uindhya Pradesh, and Madhya Bharat 1 Nov. 1956; rice, jute, pulses, oilseeds, cotton; forests; manganese, coal, marble, limestone; cotton textiles; cap. Bhopal; a. *171,217* sq. m.; p. (1961) *32,372,408*.

Madinet El Faiyûm, *see* El Faiyûn.

Madison, *c.*, Ind., U.S.A.; on Ohio R.; mftg.; p. (1960) *10,097*.

Madison, *t.*, Ill., U.S.A.: heavy engin. wks.; [p. (1960) *6,861*.

Madison, *cap.*, Wis., U.S.A.; univ.; agr. tools, machin., footwear; p. (1960) *126,706*.

Madison Heights, *t.*, Mich., U.S.A.; p. (1960) *33,343*.

Madisonville, *t.*, Ky., U.S.A.; p. (1960) *13,110*.

Madras, *st.*, India; rice, millet, oilseeds, cotton, indigo, spices, tobacco, tea; ch. ts. Madras, Madurai, Tiruchirapalli; a. 50,331 sq. m.; p. (1961) *33,686,953*.

Madras, *c.*, *spt.*, *cap.*, Madras, S. India; on S.E. (Coromandel) cst.; cath., univ.; comm. ctr., cottons, tanning, brewing, potteries; oil refinery projected; p. (1961) *1,729,141*.

Madre de Dios, *dep.*, E. Peru; ch. t. Maldonado; forested; gold, silver; a. 58,827 sq. m.; p. (1961) *13,437*.

Madre de Dios, *R.*, Bolivia; trib. of R. Madeira; rises in Peru.

Madrid, *cap.*, Spain; on R. Manzanares; univ., cath., palace; Prado; gold and silver work; leather goods; chemicals, furniture mftg.; p. (1959) *1,975,666*.

Madrid, *prov.*, Spain; agr., freestone, granite, gypsum quarried; a. 3,089 sq. m.; cap. M.; p. (1959) *2,300,791*.

Madura, *I.*, Indonesia; off N.E. of Java; cereals, coconuts, fishing, cattle rearing, salt; a. 1,770 sq. m.; p. (1930) *1,962,462*.

Madurai, *c.*, Madras, India; univ.; coffee, muslin, brasswk., wood carving; p. (1961) *424,810*.

Maebashi, *c.*, Honshu, Japan; mulberry trees, silk production; p. (1955) *171,265*.

Maelstrom, *whirlpool*, N.W. cst., Norway.

Maentwrog, *vil.*, Merioneth, N. Wales; in Vale of Festiniog, 2 m. E. of Festiniog; ch. hydro-elec. power-sta. in N. Wales.

Maesteg, *t.*, *urb. dist.*, Glamorgan, Wales; dorm. t. for steel wks. at Pt. Talbot; coal-mining, cosmetics; p. (1961) *21,652*.

Mafeking, *t.*, C. Prov., S. Africa; famous siege, 1899–1900; p. (1960) *8,279* inc. *4,159* whites.

Magadan, *spt.* R.S.F.S.R.; on N. side of Sea of Okhotsk; engin.; p. (1959) *62,000*.

Magallanes, *prov.*, Chile; sheep-rearing; cap. Punta Arenas; fox breeding; petroleum; a. 52,271 sq. m.; p. (1960) *73,037*.

Magdalen, Is., G. of St. Lawrence, Canada.

Magdalena, *dep.*, Colombia; coffee, cotton, rubber; cap. Santa Marta; a. 20,813 sq. m.; p. (estd. 1961) *500,640*.

Magdalena, *R.*, Colombia; length 1,000 m.

Magdeburg, *c.*, Magdeburg, E. Germany; on R. Elbe; cath.; beet-sugar, chemicals, iron, steel, mng. machin., heavy engin.; route ctr. and R. pt.; p. (1963) *267,733*

Magelang, *t.*, Java, Indonesia; tr. ctr.; p. (1961) *96,454*.

Magellan, *strait*, between Tierra del Fuego and Chile, S. America.

Magenta, *t.*, N. Italy; nr. Milan; silk, matches; p. *12,650*.

Magenwil, Aargau, Switzerland; oil refinery projected.

Maggiore, *L.*, N. Italy–Switzerland; a. 82 sq. m.; contains Borromean Is.; tourist resort.

Maghreb, collective name given to Arabic speaking countries bordering Mediterranean in N. Africa (Morocco to Libya).

Magnet Mtn., S. Urals, R.S.F.S.R.; very rich deposit of magnetite iron ore; smelted at Magnitogorsk, and in Kuzbas region.

Magnitogorsk, *t.*, R.S.F.S.R.; at S. end of Ural Mtns.; iron, steel, engin., iron ore, chemicals; term. of oil pipeline from Shkapovo in Bashkiria; p. (1962) *333,000*. [p. (1961) *13,139*.

Magog, *t.*, S. Quebec, Canada; textiles, mnfs.;

Mahad Al-Dhahab, *t.*, Hejaz, Saudi-Arabia; between Mecca and Medina; gold-mining.

Mahalla El Kubra, *t.*, Lower U.A.R.; p. (1960) *63,000*.

Mahanadi, *R.*, India; flows from Orissa to Bay of Bengal; length 520 m. [p. (1960) *8,536*.

Mahanoy City, *t.*, Penns., U.S.A.; anthracite;

Maharashtra, *st.*, India; ch. ts.: Greater Bombay (cap.), Poona, Nagpur, Sholapur, Kolhapur, Amravati, Nasik, Malegaon, Nagar, Akola, Ulhasuagar, Thana; a. 118,717 sq. m.; p. (1961) *39,553,718*.

Mahé, *former Fr. prov.*, S. India; united with India 1954; cap. Mahé. [cheese; p. *18,220*.

Mahon, *spt. cap.*, Minorca, Balearic Is., Spain;

Maidenhead, *t.*, *mun. bor.*, Berks, Eng.; on R. Thames, 9 m. above Windsor; light engin., printing, jam mkg.; p. (1961) *35,374*.

Maidens, The, *gr. of dangerous rocks*, nr. Larne, off Antrim cst., N. Ireland.

Maidstone, *co. t.*, *mun. bor.*, Kent, Eng.; on R. Medway; hops, fruit ctr.; brewing, paper, agr. tools, confectionery; p. (1961) *59,761*.

Maikop, *t.*, Adygeysk, U.S.S.R.; oil-refineries; woodwkg., food inds.; p. (1959) *82,000*.

Main, *R.*, Germany; trib. of R. Rhine; l. 304 m.

Main, *Hudson Bay Co's.* fort, at mouth E. Main R., Labrador, Canada.

Maine, *st.*, New England, U.S.A.; mtns., with much forest; potatoes, paper pulp, metals, woollens, shoes, processed foods; cap. Augusta; ch. spt. Portland; a. 33,215 sq. m.; p. (1960) *969,265*.

Maine, *R.*, France; formed by junction of Sarthe and Mayenne, flows 7 m. to R. Loire at Angers.

Maine-et-Loire, *dep.*, France; agr., vineyards; cap. Angers; a. 2,811 sq. m.; p. (1962) *556,272*.

Mainland. (1) *I.*, lgst. of Shetlands, Scot. (2) *I.*, lgst. of Orkneys, *see* **Pomona**.

Mainz, *c.*, *cap.* Rhineland-Palatinate, Germany; at confluence of Rs. Rhine and Main; R. pt; cath., univ., cas.; cement, engin., optical glass, food processing; p. (1963) *139,400*.

Maison-Carrée, *commune*, N. Algeria; 5 m. E. of Algiers; airport; p. *24,341*.

Maisons-Alfort, *t.*, Seine, France; p. (1962) *51,689*.

Maisons-Laffitte, *t.*, Seine-et-Oise, France; p. (1954) *15,481*.

Maitland West, *t.*, N.S.W., Australia; on R. Hunter, nr. Newcastle; agr., pastoral ctr., coal-mining; p. (1961) *27,344*.

Maizuru, *c.*, *spt.*, Honshu, Japan; naval base; sheet glass; p. (1960) *99,615*.

Majorca *or* **Mallorca**, *see* **Balearic Is.**

Majunga, *spt.*, Malagasy; on N.W. cst., at mouth of R. Ikopa; p. (1957) *50,356*. [*384,000*.

Makasar, *ch. t.*, *pt.*, Sulawesi, Indonesia; p. (1961)

Makasar, *strait*, Indonesia; separates Kalimantan from Sulawesi; 240 m. wide.

Makeyevka, *t.*, Ukrainian S.S.R.; iron and steel, engin. coal; p. (1962) *381,000*.

Makhachkala, *spt.*, R.S.F.S.R.; oil-refining, chemicals, textiles, engin.; p. (1959) *119,000*.

Makó, *t.*, Hungary; agr.; flour milling; p. (1962) *29,541*.

Makran, *reg.*, W. Pakistan–Iran; a. 26,000 sq. m.; p. (estd. 1951) *143,000*.

Makurdi, *t.*, Nigeria, W. Africa; on R. Benue, 150 m. upstream from confluence with R. Niger at Lokoja; mkt. for palm prod., ground-nuts; site of rly. bridge across R. Benue on E. main rly. from Pt. Harcourt to Kaduna.

Makwar, *vil.*, Sudan, N.E. Africa; on R. Blue Nile, 200 m. upstream from Khartoum; site of Sennar Dam.

Malabar Coast, India; name applied to W. cst. of India from Goa to southern tip of peninsula at Cape Comorin; sand dunes backed by lagoons; coastlands intensively cultivated, rice, spices, rubber, coconuts; ch. pt. Cochin.

Malacca, *st.*, Malaysia, S.W. Malaya; originally part of Brit. Straits Settlements (*q.v.*); cap. M.; a. 640 sq. m.; p. (1961) *341,319*. [Peninsula.

Malacca, *strait*, separates Sumatra from Malay.

Maladetta, with **Pic d' Anéto**, highest point in the Pyrenees; alt. 11,174 ft.

Málaga, *Mediterranean prov.*, S. Spain; agr., exp. wine, fruits, olive oil; a. 2,813 sq. m.; p. (1959) *772,517*.

Málaga, *spt.*, *cap.* Málaga, Spain; cotton, sugar, leather; p. (1959) *283,444*.

Malagasy Republic, *I.*, *indep. sov. st.*, E. African cst.; within Fr. Community; cap. Tananarive; ch. spt. Tamatave; a. 227,800 sq. m.; p. (1961) *5,487,000*.

Malakal, *cap.*, Upper Nile, Sudan; p. (1956) *9,680*.

Malakoff, *t.*, S.W. Paris, France; residtl.; p. (1954) *28,876*.

Malang, *t.*, Java, Indonesia; p. (1961) *342,000*.

Mälar, L., S.E. Sweden; connected with the Baltic by Södertelge canal, has 1,260 Is.; length 80 m.; a. 477 sq. m. [(1960) *84,162*.

Malatya, *t.*, central Turkey; fruit, opium; p.

Malawi, Rep. of, *indep. sov. st.* within Brit. Commonwealth (1964), Central Africa; along W. cst. L. Malawi; hot wet summers, cool dry winters; savannah vegetation, subtropical forest; tea, tobacco, groundnuts, cotton, coffee, ivory; cap. Lilongwe; a. 47,747 sq. m.; p. (estd. 1964) *3,000,000*.

Malawi, *L.*, Central Africa, southward extension of the Great Rift Valley; 1,500 ft. above sea-level; length 350 m., breadth 40 m.; drains by R. Shire into R. Zambesi.

Malay Archipelago, *lge. gr. of tropical Is.* extending 4,800 m. from the Nicobar Is. in Bay of Bengal to the Solomon Is. in the Pacific; inc. Sumatra, Java, Borneo, Celebes, Philippines, New Guinea, Bismarck Archipelago.

Malaya, *st.*, Malaysia, former federation of 9 Malay sts. and Penang and Malacca; joined with Singapore (seceded 1965), Sarawak and Sabah to form Malaysian Fed. (Sept. 1963); rubber, tin, iron ore, palm oil and kernels, coconut oil, copra; fed. cap. Kuala Lumpur; a. 50,840 sq. m.; p. (1960) *7,017,533*.

Malaysia, Federation of, *indep. fed.* of 13 sts. within Brit. Commonwealth comprising 11 sts. of Malaya, Sabah (formerly Brit. N. Borneo), and Sarawak; plantation inds., mineral wealth; fed. cap. Kuala Lumpur; a. 127,298 sq. m.; p. (estd.) *8,416,345*.

Malbork (Marienburg), *t.*, Poland, German before 1945; on R. Nogat; cas.; rly. junction; p. (1960) *25,000*.

Malden, *c.*, Mass., U.S.A.; mftg. sub. of Boston; rubber gds., hosiery furniture; p. (1960) *57,676*.

Malden I., (Brit.) in Pac. Oc.; a. 35 sq. m.; guano, uninhabited.

Malden and Coombe, *former mun. bor.*, Surrey, Eng.; now inc. in *Royal Borough* of Kingston-upon-Thames; light inds.; p. (1961) *46,587*.

Maldive Is., *indep. sultanate* (1965), 2,000 low-lying coral Is., under Brit. prot. 1887–1965; 400 m. S. W. of Ceylon, about 215 of which are inhabited; cap. Malé; Britain retains facilities on Addu Atoll (incl. airfield on Gan I.) until 1986; coconuts, millet, fruit, fishing, coir and lacemkg.; p. (estd.) *90,000*.

Maldon, *t.*, *mun. bor.*, Essex, Eng.; at head of Blackwater estuary; agr. machin., steel window-frames, flour milling; p. (1961) *10,507*.

Maldonado, *dep.*, Uruguay; a. 1,587 sq. m.; p. (1953) *67 933*.

Malham Cove, W. Riding, Yorks, Eng.; in Craven dist. of N. Pennines, 10 m. N.W. of Skipton; semi-circular amphitheatre surrounded by limestone cliffs from base of which emerges R. Aire.

Malin Head, Donegal, Ireland; most N. point.

Mali, Republic of, *ind. sovereign st.*, W. Africa; millet, sorghum, rice, maize, groundnuts, cotton; cap. Bamako; a. 460,200 sq. m.; p. (1961) *4,100,000*. [p. *15,089*.

Malinao, *mun.*, Luzon, Philippine Is.; hemp;

Malines (Mechelen), *c.*, Belgium; on R. Dyle; cath.; rly. ctr., furniture, textiles, leather, car assembly, detergents, paint; p. (1962) *64,847*.

Malita, *t.*, Mindanao, Philippines; p. *30,755*.

Mallaig, *vil.*, S.W. Inverness, Scot.; on Sound of Sleat; rly. terminus; fish; p. *1,000*.

Malleco, *prov.*, S. Chile; cap. Angol; a. 5,511 sq. m.; p. (1960) *207,477*.

Malling, *t.*, *rural dist.*, Kent, Eng.; 3 m. W. of Maidstone; mkt., fruit ctr., chemicals; p. (rural dist. 1961) *40,680*.

Mallow, *mkt. t.*, Cork, Ireland; on R. Blackwater; agr., fishing, flour mills, tanneries, condensed milk, dehydrated foods; p. (1961) *5,520*.

Malmédy, *t.*, Belgium; transferred to Belgium from Germany after the First World War; tanning, dyeing, paper-wks.; p. (1962) *6,387*.
Malmesbury, *t.*, *mun. bor.*, Wilts, Eng.; on R. Avon, 8 m. N. of Chippenham; mkt.; abbey; elec. eng. ind.; p. (1961) *2,606*.
Malmesbury, *t.*, Victoria, Australia; on R. Campaspe, 20 m. S.E. of Bendigo; dam across R. provides water for domestic and mining purposes to Bendigo.
Malmesbury, *t.*, S.W. Cape Prov., S. Africa; mineral springs; p. *5,731*.
Malmö, *spt.*, S. Sweden; on The Sound; shipbldg., textiles, cement; p. (1961) *229,388*.
Malmöhus, *co.*, Sweden; a. 1,872 sq. m.; p. (1961) *625,667*.
Malo-les-Bains, *sub.* of Dunkerque, Nord, France; seaside resort; p. (1954) *12,101*.
Malone, *t.*, N.Y., U.S.A.; iron-mining; p. (1960) [*8,737*.
Malta, *I.*, *indep. sov. st.* within Brit. Commonwealth (1964); in Mediterranean, 60 m. S. of Sicily; cap. Valetta; received George Cross for heroism in Second World War; deep water quay; dry docks; no raw materials; a. (inc. Gozo and Comino) 122 sq. m.; p. (estd. 1962) *329,285*.
Maltby, *urb. dist.*, W. Riding, Yorks, Eng.; p. (1961) *13,691*.
Malton, *mkt. t.*, *urb. dist.*, N.R. Yorks, Eng.; on R. Derwent, in S.W. of Vale of Pickering; brewing, ironwks.; p. (1961) *4,430*.
Maluti, *mtn. range*, Basutoland, S. Africa; highest peak Machacha, alt. 10,990 ft.
Malvern or Great Malvern, *t.*, *urb. dist.*, Worcester, Eng.; at E. foot of Malvern Hills; spa; annual dramatic festival; stone quarrying, agr. machin., motor-cars, electronics wks., plastics; p. (1961) *24,373*.
Malvern Hills, *narrow ridge* forming bdy. between Worcester and Hereford, Eng.; rises very abruptly from Severn Valley to over 1,000 ft. between Malvern and Bromsberrow; moorland, woodland on lower slopes; length 8 m., width, under 1 m., maximum alt., 1,395 ft.
Malverne, *t.*, N.Y., U.S.A., on Long I.; residtl. sub. of New York; p. (1960) *9,968*.
Mamaroneck, *t.*, N.Y., U.S.A.; textiles, mnfs. oils; p. (1960) *17,673*.
Mammola, *t.*, Reggio, S. Italy; p. *9,925*.
Mammoth Caves, Ky., U.S.A.; Green R.; stalactite formations in avenues aggregating 150 m. long.
Mamore or Rio Grande, *R.*, Bolivia; trib. of R. Beni; length 500 m.
Mam Soul, *mtn.*, Ross and Inverness, Scot.; alt. 3,862 ft.
Man, I. of, in Irish Sea; 30 m. from England (Cumberland), and N. Ireland (Down), 20 m. from Scotland (Wigtown); tourist ctr.; agr., sheep, lead, zinc; ch. t. Douglas; old cap. Castletown; administered according to own laws; a. 227 sq. m.; p. (1961) *48,151*.
Mana, *R.*, Fr. Guiana, S. America; 175 m.
Manabi, *prov.*, Ecuador; on W. slope of the Andes; cap. Puertoviejo; cacao, sugar; a. 7,891 sq. m.; p. (estd. 1962) *614,803*.
Manacor, *t.*, Majorca, Spain; 30 m. from Palma; artificial pearls, wine; 7 m. from its spt. Porto Cristo; stalactite caves of Drach and Hams; p. (1957) *18,956*.
Managua, *cap.*, Nicaragua; nr. Lake M.; univ., palace; coffee, cotton; p. (1960) *207,000*.
Manama, *cap.*, Bahrein, Is., Persian Gulf; p. (1950) *39,648*.
Mananjary, *t.*, E. Malagasy, sugar, coffee; p. *5,000*.
Manaqil Canal, fed by waters from Blue Nile released through Semnar dam; helps cultivate 600,000 acres of Gezira desert.
Manar, *G.*, with Palk Strait separates India from Ceylon.
Manasarowar, *sacred L.*, Tibet.
Manatee, *t.*, Fla., U.S.A.; lumber, fruit and vegetable canning; p. (1950) *3,582*.
Manáus (Manaos), *t.*, *cap.*, Amazonas, Brazil; at confluence of R. Negro with R. Amazon; univ.; rubber tr.; p. (1960) *175,343*.
Mancha, La, *plain*, Cuidad-Real prov., S. Spain; in shallow depression on central plateau, average alt. between 1,500 and 3,000 ft., drained by headstreams of R. Guadiana; semi-arid climate with hot summers, cold winters; widespread salt deposits; Merino sheep, esparto grass; Spain's lgst. grape-growing region.
Manche, *maritime dep.*, N.W. France; on English Channel; agr. and dairying; cap. Saint Lo; ch. port Cherbourg; a. 2,475 sq. m.; p. (1962) *446,878*.
Manchester, *c.*, *spt.*, *co. bor.*, S. Lancs, Eng.; on R. Irwell (which separates it from Salford); inland terminus of Manchester Ship Canal; ctr. of cotton tr. and ind.; also engin. heavy, light and elec., and aircraft, paper, foodstuffs; univ.; gr. comm., cultural and recreational cap. of N.W. England; p. (1961) *661,041*.
Manchester, *t.*, E. Iowa, U.S.A.; tr. ctr.; flour milling; woollen goods; p. (1960) *4,402*.
Manchester, *c.*, N.H., U.S.A.; at Amoskeag Falls, on the Merrimac R.; textiles, footwear, machin.; p. (1960) *88,282*.
Manchester, *t.*, Conn., U.S.A.; textiles (silk); p. (1960) *41,906*.
Manchester Ship Canal, *ship canal*, S. Lancs, Ches., Eng.; joining Manchester to Mersey estuary at Eastham; can be used by ocean steamers; length 35½ m.
Manchuria, *former Chinese outer terr.*, no longer exists as administrative unit, comprised nine provs.—Liaoning, Kirin, Heilungkiang, Liaopeh, Nunkiang, Hsingan, Sunkiang, Hokiang and Antung; mountainous, N.W. and E.; drained to N. by Sungari and S. by Liao Rs.; forested; soya-beans, wheat, coal, iron, gold, silver.
Mandal, *t.*, Norway; steel, hempropes; p. (1961) *5,156*.
Mandalay, *c.*, Upper Burma; on the R. Irrawaddy, 400 m. N. of Rangoon; formerly cap. of kingdom; silk, old carved wooden palace and many pagodas; p. (1955) *182,367*.
Mandaue, *t.*, Cebu, Philippines; rice.
Manduria, *t.*, Italy; tr. ctr.; p. *17,675*.
Mandvi, *spt.*, Kutch, India; p. (1961) *26,609*.
Manfalut, *t.*, Upper Egypt; on R. Nile; p. *5,000*.
Manfredonia, *spt.*, Foggia, Italy; cath.; cereals, fruit; p. *18,600*.
Mangaldan, *t.*, Luzon, Philippines; rice.
Mangalore, *spt.*, Mysore, India; exp. coffee, coconuts, rice, spices; p. (1961) *142,669*.
Mangere, N.I., N.Z., 13 m. S. of Auckland; international airport (opened 1965).
Mangerton, *mtn.*, Kerry, Ireland.
Mangotsfield, *urb. dist.*, Gloucester, Eng.; p. (1961) *24,092*.
Manhattan, I., N.Y., U.S.A.; at mouth of Hudson R.; a. 22 sq. m., forms major part of bor. of Manhattan (p. (1960) *1,698,281*) of N.Y. City.
Manica and Sofala, *prov.*, Mozambique; comprises dists. of Beira and Tete; cap. Beira; p. (1962) *779,462*.
Manicouagan, *R.*, Canada; flows S. from Quebec prov. to St. Lawrence, S.W. of Baie Comeau where there is dam and hydroelec. plant; length 300 m.
Manihiki, Cook Is., N.Z.; p. *454*.
Manila, *c.*, cap. Philippines, S.W. Luzon; ch. pt. of Is.; univ., cath.; general tr.; p. (1960) *1,138,611*.
Manipur, Union Terr., India; rice, cotton, fruits; cap. Imphal; a. 8,628 sq. m.; p. (1961) *780,037*.
Manisa, *t.*, Turkey; comm. ctr., cotton, silk; p. (1960) *59,223*.
Manistee, *c.*, Mich., U.S.A.; on L. Michigan; timber, salt, fruit; p. (1960) *8,324*.
Manistique, *t.*, Mich., U.S.A.; on M. R.; p. (1960) *4,875*.
Manitoba, *prov.*, Canada; wheat, minerals, furs, oil; cap. Winnipeg; a. 246,512 sq. m.; p. (1961) *921,686*.
Manitowoc, *c.*, Wis., U.S.A.; on L. Michigan; shipbldg., iron, aluminium goods, flour; p. (1960) *32,275*.
Manizales, *cap.*, Caldas, Colombia; coffee, textiles, leather gds., chemicals; p. (estd. 1962) *176,080*.
Manjil Dam, Iran; over Sefid Rud R., Gilan prov., N.W. Teheran; 352 ft. high.
Mankato, *c.*, Minn., U.S.A.; agr. tools, flour, brewing; p. (1960) *23,747*.
Mannheim, *t.*, Baden-Württemberg, Germany; gr. R. pt. at confluence of Rs. Neckar and Rhine; cas.; machin., vehicles, cellulose, steel, elec., foodstuffs, tobacco, wood, textiles, chemicals; p. (1963) *321,100*.
Manningtree, *par.*, Essex, Eng.; head of Stour estuary; fishing, yachting; p. (1961) *524*.
Manorhamilton, *t.*, Leitrim, Ireland; rly. wks.; p. *1,012*.
Manresa, *t.*, Spain; textiles, paper, chemicals, [ironwks.; p. (1957) *40,452*.

Mans, Le, *see* **Le Mans.** [Coats I.

Mansel I., Hudson Bay, Canada; S.E. of

Mansfield, *t., mun. bor.*, Notts, Eng.; on E. flank of Pennines, 12 m. N. of Nottingham; iron, coal, hosiery, footwear mftg., sand-quarrying, metal box wks., lace, cotton, lt. engin.; p. (1961) *53,222.*

Mansfield, *t.*, Mass., U.S.A.; textiles, engin.; confectionery; p. (1960) *4,674.*

Mansfield, *c.*, Ohio, U.S.A.; machin., farm tools, paper, rubber goods; p. (1960) *47,325.*

Mansfield Woodhouse, *t., urb. dist.*, Notts, Eng.; 2 m. N. of Mansfield; stone quarries; Roman remains; p. (1961) *20,137.*

Mansura, *t.*, Lower U.A.R.; cotton mftg.; p. (1960) *152,000.*

Manta, *t.*, Ecuador; coffee, panama hats,: p. (1962) *19,228.*

Mantanzas, *t.*, Venezuela; on S. bank of R. Orinoco; steel wks.

Mantes-la-Jolie, *t.*, Seine-et-Oise, France; on R. Seine; cath., agr. prod., hosiery, musical instruments; p. (1954) *15,155.*

Mantiqueira, *mtn. range*, Brazil; N.W. of Rio de Janeiro; highest peak Itatiaia 9,255 ft.

Mantua, *prov.*, Italy; a. 903 sq. m.; p. (1961) *382,515.*

Mantua, *t.*, N. Italy; on R. Mincio; ironwks.; p. (1961) *61,580.*

Manukau Harbour, N.I., N.Z.; *lge. shallow inlet* on W. cst. of Auckland Peninsula which is here less than 6 m. wide; provides additional harbour facilities for spt. of Auckland but shallow water limits usefulness; mainly used for recreational sailing.

Manych, *R.*, U.S.S.R.; trib. of R. Don; length 300 m.; canal is being built through R. to the Caspian to provide through connection with Black Sea.

Manzala (Menzala), *lagoon*, Mediterranean cst., Egypt, N.E. Africa; extends E. from Damietta mouth of Nile to Pt. Said; fringed by salt marsh; a. 800 sq. m.

Manzanares, *R.*, Spain; trib. of R. Jarama.

Manzanares, *t.*, Spain; 30 m. E. of Ciudad Real; soap, bricks, pottery mftg., agr. prod.; p. (1957) *18,204.* [*42,252.*

Manzanillo, *spt.*, Cuba; sugar, rice; p. (1960)

Manzanillo, *spt.*, Colima, Mexico; Mexico's chief inlet and outlet on Pac. Oc.; p. (1961) *13,030.*

Manzini, (Bremersdorf), *t.*, Swaziland, S. Africa.

Mar, *ancient dist.*, Aberdeen, Scot.; between Rs. Don and Dee.

Maracaibo, *spt., cap.*, Zulia st., Venezuela; on W. of narrow entrance to L. Maracaibo; univ.; oil, coffee, cocoa, and hide exp.; shipbldg.; p. (1961) *432,902.*

Maracaibo, *G.*, and *L.*, Zulia st., Venezuela, S. America; brackish lake, 120 m. long, 60 m. wide; oil-wells on fringes and drilled into lake floor.

Maracay, *t.*, W. Venezuela; mftg. and military ctr.; p. (1961) *134,120.* [(1956) *36,556.*

Maragheh, *t.*, Iran; on N. end of L. Urmia; p.

Marajó, *I.*, at mouth of the Rs. Amazon and Pará, Brazil; a. 173 sq. m.

Maralinga, S. Australia; 200 m. N.E. Eucla; joint U.K.–Australian atomic testing ground; first weapon exploded here 27 Sept. 1956.

Maranhão, *st.*, N.E. Brazil; rice, cotton, sugar, tobacco, coffee, cattle, gold, copper; cap. São Luiz; a. 129,271 sq. m.; p. (1960) *2,492,139.*

Marañon, *R.*, *see* **Amazon, R.**

Marans, *t.*, Charente-Maritime, France; industl.; p. (1954) *3,711.*

Maras, *t.*, S. central Turkey; tr. in Kurdish carpets; p. (1960) *54,646.*

Marathon, *plain*, Greece; battle between Greeks and Persians 490 B.C.

Marazion, *mkt. t.*, Cornwall, Eng.; on Mount's Bay; pilchard fisheries; p. *1,100.*

Marbella, *spt.*, Malaga, Spain; cas.; iron mines; oranges, sugar cane, cotton; p. (1957) *9,921.*

Marble, *I.*, Keewatin, N.W. Terrs., Canada.

Marble Bar, *t.*, W. Australia; located 85 m. inland by rail from Pt. Hedland; ctr. of Pilbara goldfields.

Marblehead, *spt.*, Mass., U.S.A.; holiday resort, footwear; p. (1960) *18,521.*

Marburg, *t.*, Hessen, Germany; univ., cas.; instruments, pharmaceuticals, wall-paper mftg.; p. (1963) *47,800.* [*10,475.*

Marcaria, *t.*, Italy; on R. Oglio; industl.; p.

March, *mkt. t., urb. dist.*, I. of Ely, Eng.; in Fens, 12 m. N.W. of Ely; impt. rly. junction; mkt., farm tools; p. (1961) *13,119.*

Marchena, *t.*, Spain; on R. Guadalquivir; mftg.; p. (1957) *20,326.*

Marches, The, *region*, central Italy; extending from eastern slopes of Apennines to Adriatic cst.; embracing provs. of Macerata, Ascoli-Piceno, Acona, and Pesaro e Urbino; maize, wine, tobacco, silk, paper; a. 3,744 sq. m.; p. (1961) *1,347,234.*

Marchienne-au-Pont, *t.*, Belgium; on R. Sambre; tr. ctr.; p. (1962) *19,870.*

Marcq-en-Barœul, *commune*, sub. Lille, Nord, France; textiles, foundries; p. (1954) *24,564.*

Marcus Hook, *t.*, Del., U.S.A.; on right bank of R. Del. 15 m. below Philadelphia.

Mar del Plata, *t.*, Argentina; on C. Corrientes; seaside resort; p. (1960) *300,000.*

Mardin, *t.*, Turkey; agr., textiles; p. (1960) *27,390.*

Maree, *L.*, Ross and Cromarty, Scot.; length 12½ m., breadth 2½ m.; contains many Is.

Mareotis or Birket-et-Mariut, *L.*, Lower Egypt; separated from Mediterranean by ridge of sand on which stands Alexandria; length 50 m., width 20 m.

Margam, *t.* in Pt. Talbot mun. bor., W. central Glamorgan, S. Wales; on cst. of Swansea Bay; lge. new steel-wks., lgst. steel-rolling mill in Europe; p. (estd. 1955) *18,300.*

Margarita, *I.*, Venezuela; in the Caribbean S.; pearl fisheries, fishing, fibre wks.; cap. Asuncion, a. 450 sq. m.; p. (1961) *87,500.*

Margate, *t., mun. bor.*, Kent, Eng.; W. of N. Foreland, in the Isle of Thanet; seaside resort; p. (1961) *45,708.*

Margelan, *t.*, E. Uzbek S.S.R.; agr. ctr., tr. especially cotton and silk; p. (1959) *68,000.*

Mari, *autonomous Soviet Socialist rep.*, U.S.S.R.; cap. Ioshkar Ola; p. (1959) *647,000.*

Mariana, *t.*, Minas Gerais, Brazil; tr. ctr;. gold mng.; p. (1960) *34,500.*

Mariana Is., *chain of 15 Is.*, N. Pacific; U.S. Pac. Trust Terr.; a. 450 sq. m.; admin. ctr., Saipan; p. (1935) *39,728* Japanese, *4,297* natives.

Marianské Lázne (Marienbad), *t.*, ČSSR.; spa; antimony; p. (1961) *12,597.*

Maribor, *t.*, Slovenia, Jugoslavia; fruit ctr., leather goods, wine, rly. wks.; p. (1960) *84,000.*

Marie Galante, *I.*, Lesser Antilles gr.; Fr. possession; sugar-cane; p. (1960) *16,037.*

Marienburg, *see* **Malbork.**

Marienwerder, *see* **Kwidzyn.**

Marietta, *t.*, Ohio, U.S.A.; at confluence of Muskingum R. with Ohio R.; timber, ironwks., coal, oil, natural gas; p. (1960) *16,847.*

Marigliano, *t.*, Campagna, Italy; p. *14,155.*

Mariinsk Canal, *see* **Volga Baltic Waterway.**

Marin, *spt.*, N.W. Spain; fishing; textiles; naval school; p. (1957) *17,592.*

Marinette, *t.*, Wis., U.S.A.; on L. Michigan; paper, pulp, timber; p. (1960) *13,329.*

Marino, *t.*, Sicily, Italy; p. *6,625.*

Marion, *c.*, Ind., U.S.A.; natural gas, iron, paper, glass, wireless sets; p. (1960) *37,854.*

Marion, *t.*, Ohio, U.S.A.; agr. implements, steam shovels, tractors; p. (1960) *37,079.*

Marion, *c.*, S. Ill., U.S.A.; fruit; coal; engin.; p. (1960) *11,274.*

Maritime Alps, *mtn. ranges*, S. France–Italy.

Maritime Provinces, embraces Canadian provs. of Nova Scotia, New Brunswick, Pr. Edward I.

Maritsa, *R.*, Bulgaria and Greece; length 260 m.

Maritzburg, *see* **Pietermaritzburg.**

Mariupol, *see* **Zhdanov.**

Marken, *I.*, nr. Amsterdam, Netherlands tourist ctr.

Market Deeping, *t.*, Lincoln, Eng.; on R. Welland brewing, rope; p. *876.*

Market Drayton, *t., urb. dist.*, Salop, Eng.; on R Tern 5 m. S. of Newcastle-under-Lyme; agr implements, nylon mftg.; p. (1961) *5,853.*

Market Harborough, *t., urb. dist.*, Leicester, Eng. on R. Welland, 8 m. N.W. of Kettering elec. engin., foodstuffs, corsetry; p. (1961 *11,556.*

Market Rasen, *t., urb. dist.*, Lindsey, Lincoln Eng.; 14 m. N.E. of Lincoln; agr. ctr.; p (1961) *2,257.*

Market Weighton, *t.*, E.R. Yorks, Eng.; malting, iron; p. *1,735*.

Markinch, *burgh*, Fife, Scot.; 8 m. N. of Kirkcaldy; paper mftg., whisky blending and bottling; p. (1961) *2,446*.

Marl, *t.*, N. Rhine–Westphalia, Germany; in the Ruhr; coal-mining and chemicals; p. (1963) *73,300*.

Marlboro, *c.*, Mass., U.S.A.; boot mftg.; p. (1960) *18,819*.

Marlborough, *t.*, *mun. bor.*, Wilts, Eng.; on R. Kennet in heart of Marlborough Downs; agr., tanning, brewing; public school; p. (1961) *4,843*.

Marlborough, *prov. dist.*, S.I., N.Z.; pastoral; a. 4,220 sq. m.; cap. Blenheim; p. (1961) *27,740*.

Marlborough Downs, *hills*, Wilts, Eng.; chalk; highest point, Milk Hill, 976 ft.

Marlin, *t.*, Texas, U.S.A.; hot artesian water; oil; cotton; dairying; p. (1950) *7,099*.

Marlow, *t.*, *urb. dist.*, Bucks, Eng.; on R. Thames; mkt., tourist ctr.; brewing and chair mkg.; p. (1961) *8,704*.

Marmande, *t.*, Lot-et-Garonne, France; on R. Garonne; brandy, liqueur, woollens, iron; p. (1954) *12,368*.

Marmara, *sea*, separates Europe from Anatolia.

Marmolata, highest point of Dolomite Alps, S. Tyrol, Italy; alt. 11,045 ft.

Marne, *R.*, Central France; rises in Plateau de Langres, flows N.W. and W. across Champagne Humide, Champagne Pouilleuse and Beauce, joins R. Seine just above Paris; with Marne–Rhine and Marne–Saône Canals it forms impt. inland waterway linking Seine with Rhine and Rhône valleys; length (approx.) 325 m.

Marne, *dep.*, N.E. France; agr., wines, textiles, minerals; cap. Chalons-sur-Marne; a. 3,168 sq. m.; p. (1962) *442,195*.

Marne, Haute, *dep.*, France; a. 2,420 sq. m.; cap. Chaumont; p. (1962) *208,446*.

Maros, *R.*, Hungary; trib. of R. Theiss; length 400 m.

Marple, *t.*, *urb. dist.*, Cheshire, Eng.; 3 m. E. of Stockport; textiles; p. (1961) *16,812*.

Marquesas, *I. gr.* (Fr.), Pac. Oc.; a. 480 sq. m.; lgst. Is. Nukuhiva and Hivaoa; bananas, sugar-cane, copra; p. (1962) *4,837*.

Marquette, *c.*, Mich., U.S.A.; on L. Superior; iron-ore deposits, timber, rly. wks.; p. (1960) *19,824*.

Marradi, *t.*, Italy; p. *8,275*.

Marrakesh, *c.*, Morocco; tourist ctr., leather goods; p. (1960) *243,134*.

Marree, *sm. t.*, S. Australia; on rly. from Pt. Augusta to Alice Springs; terminus of overland stock route from Queensland.

Marsa el-Brega, *new pt.*, Gulf of Sirte, Libya; oil pipeline from Zelten; one projected from Raguba oilfield; refinery projected.

Marsala, *spt.*, Sicily, Italy; wine ctr.; p. (1961) *81,327*.

Marseilles, *t.*, N. Ill., U.S.A.; paper, bricks; p. [(1960) *4,347*.

Marseilles, *c.*, *spt.*, cap. Bouches-du-Rhône, S. France; cath., univ., palace; comm. pt., coal, iron, bauxite, marine engin., aircraft, glass, agr. prod., wines, oil refining; oil pipeline to Karlsruhe (1963); p. (1962) *783,738*.

Marshall, *c.*, Mo., U.S.A.; p. (1960) *9,572*.

Marshall, *c.*, Texas, U.S.A.; rly. wks., canning, foundries; p. (1960) *23,846*.

Marshall, *spt.*, W. Liberia, W. Africa; exp. rubber; p. *1,000*.

Marshall, *I. gr.*, N. Pac. Oc.; U.S. Pac. Trust Terr., formerly Japanese mandate; total a. 150 sq. m.; sugar-cane, copra; ch. I. Jaluit; p. (1958) *13,928*.

Marshalltown, *t.*, Iowa, U.S.A.; on I. R.; iron, steel, machin., food canning; p. (1960) *22,521*.

Marshfield, *spt.*, Ore., U.S.A.; fishing, lumber, mining; p. (1950) *5,218*.

Marshfield, *t.*, Wis., U.S.A.; mgtg. ctr. in timber region; p. (1960) *14,153*.

Martaban, *t.*, Burma; on R. Salween.

Martha's Vineyard, *I.*, Mass., U.S.A.; holiday resort, ch. ts. Vineyard Haven, Oak Bluffs, Edgartown; 21 m. long.

Marti, *t.*, Cuba; sugar, sisal; p. *5,060*.

Martigny, *t.*, Valais, Switzerland; peaches, tourist resort; linked by road tunnel to Aosta, Italy; p. (1957) *6,572*.

Martigues, *t.*, Bouches-du-Rhône, France; nr. Marseilles; p. (1954) *15,150*.

Martinao, *t.*, Italy; industl., tr. ctr.; p. *38,325*.

Martinez, *c.*, W. Cal., U.S.A.; industl., oil refineries, copper smelting; p. (1960) *9,604*.

Martinique, *I.*, (Fr.) W. Indies; cap. Fort-de-France; sugar, rum; a. 385 sq. m.; p. (1961) *291,000*.

Martinsburg, *c.*, W. Va., U.S.A.; in Shenandoah valley; rly. wks., cider, textiles; p. (1960) *15,179*.

Martin's Ferry, *t.*, Ohio, U.S.A.; on O. R., iron and steel mftg., coal-mining; p. (1960) *11,919*.

Marton, *t.*, N.I., N.Z., p. *2,810*.

Martos, *t.*, Andalusia, Spain; agr. ctr., wines, sulphur springs; p. (1957) *30,404*.

Mary, *t.*, Turkmen. S.S.R.; cereals, fruit, textiles; p. (1959) *48,000*.

Maryborough, *t.*, Queensland, Australia; fruit ctr.; gold, coal, timber, sugar; p. (1961) *19,136*.

Maryborough, *t.*, Victoria, Australia; rly. ctr.; agr., pastoral; gold; p. (1961) *7,237*.

Maryborough, *see* **Port Laoighise, Ireland.**

Mary Kathleen, *t.*, Queensland, Australia; new t., nr. uranium field in Cloncurry a.

Maryland, *st.*, U.S.A.; steel, copper, smelting and refining, coal, asbestos, potash, salts, aircraft, chemicals; agr., livestock; cap. Annapolis; lgst. c. Baltimore; a. 10,577 sq. m.; p. (1960) *3,038,156*.

Maryport, *mkt. t.*, *urb. dist.*, Cumberland, Eng.; on the Irish Sea; coal, iron, plastics, footwear; p. (1961) *12,334*.

Marysville, *t.*, Cal., U.S.A.; fruit; p. (1960) *9,553*.

Marysville, *t.*, Kan., U.S.A.; rly. ctr. in rich agr. region; p. (1960) *4,143*.

Marysville, *t.*, Ohio, U.S.A.; mkt., grass seed, livestock; p. (1960) *4,952*.

Maryville, *c.*, E. Tenn., U.S.A.; lumber; clothes; quarries; p. (1960) *10,348*.

Masai Land, *dist.*, S. Kenya, Africa.

Masaya, *cap. c.* of M. dep. S.W. Nicaragua; agr., tobacco; p. (1959) *99,573*.

Masbate, *I.*, Philippines; a. 1,262 sq. m.; p. *108,800*.

Mascara, *t.*, Algeria; wine, oil, cereals; p. (1948) *35,078*.

Mascarene Is., collective name of Mauritius, Rodriguez and Réunion, in Indian Ocean.

Masham, *t.*, N.R. Yorks, Eng.; on R. Ure; 9 m. N.W. of Ripon; mkt., sheep fair; p. *1,702*.

Mashonaland, *prov.* Rhodesia; tobacco and maize cultivation.

Masira, I., off est. of Oman, Arabia.

Mask, *L.*, Mayo and Galway, Ireland; length 12 m., width 2–4 m.

Mason City, *t.*, Iowa, U.S.A.; on the Sheel Rock R.; cement, bricks, sugar-beet; p. (1960) *30,642*.

Massa or Massa Carrara, *t.*, Italy; olive oil, paper, tobacco, marble; p. (1961) *55,831*.

Massachusetts, *st.*, New England, U.S.A.; fisheries, agr., textiles, footwear, iron and steel goods, elec. machin., rubber goods, leather, paper, wood pulp; cap. Boston; a. 8,257 sq. m.; p. (1960) *5,148,578*.

Massafra, *t.*, Italy; industl.; p. *12,275*.

Massarosa, *commune*, Tuscany, Italy; agr.; p. *12,546*.

Massawa, *spt.*, Eritrea; pt. for Ethiopia; pearl fishing; p. *17,169*.

Massena, *t.*, N.Y., U.S.A.; p. (1960) *15,478*.

Messenya, *t.*, Central African Rep., nr. L. Chad; cap. of Bagirmi.

Massillon, *c.*, Ohio, U.S.A.; coal, machin., glass, aluminium ware; p. (1960) *31,236*.

Masterton, *t.*, N.I., N.Z.; p. (1961) *15,121*.

Masulipatam, (Bandar), *spt.*, Kistna dist., Andhra Pradesh, India; on the Coromandel cst.; cotton mftg., rice; p. (1961) *101,417*.

Matabeleland, *dist.*, Rhodesia; cereals, sugar, cotton, gold.

Matadi, *pt.*, Congo; nr. mouth of R. Congo; p. [*23,000*.

Matagalpa, *t.*, Nicaragua; coffee, cattle; gold mng. in a.; p. (1961) *14,000*.

Matale, *t.*, Ceylon; Buddhist monastery; p. (1941) *14,090*.

Matamoros, *t.*, Mexico, on Rio Grande; livestock tr. ctr.; p. (1960) *93,334*.

Matanzas, *prov.*, Cuba; sugar, tobacco, rice; a. 3,259 sq. m.; p. (1953) *395,780*.

Matanzas, *spt.*, *prov. cap.*, Cuba; exp. sugar, cigars; rayon plant; p. (1953) *63,916*.

Matapan, *C.*, W. side of G. of Laconia, Greece.

Matara, *spt.*, S. Ceylon; p. *22,908*.

Mataro, *spt.*, Spain; nr. Barcelona; fisheries, textiles, chemicals, paper; p. (1957) *31,642*.

Matera, *t.*, Italy; N.W. of Taranto; tr. ctr., leather, oil; p. (1961) *38,233.*
Matlock, *t., urb. dist.*, Derby, Eng.; on R. Derwent; 15 m. N. of Derby; health resort, tourist ctr., quarrying, light inds.; p. (1961) *18,486.*
Mato Grosso, *st.*, Brazil; cap. Cuiaba; a. 487,482 sq. m.; p. (1960) *910,262.*
Mato Grosso, *plateau*, Mato Grosso st., Brazil; average alt. 3,000 ft., acts as divide between Amazon and Parona–Paraguay R. systems; reserves of gold, diamonds, manganese but largely undeveloped.
Matrah, *t.*, Muscat and Oman, Arabia; tr. route ctr.; p. *8,500.*
Matsue, *t.*, Honshu, Japan; p. (1960) *106,476.*
Matsumoto, *t.*, Japan; silkworm tr.; p. (1960) *148,710.*
Matsuyama, *t.*, Japan; p. (1962) *268,000.*
Matterhorn, German name for (Fr.) Mt. Cervin, (It.) Monte Cervino; Pennine Alps, Switzerland; alt. 14,678 ft, (*see* Zermatt).
Mattoon, *c.*, Ill., U.S.A.; ironwks., flour, bricks, agr. tr.; p. (1960) *19,088.*
Maturin, *t.*, Venezuela; comm. ctr.; airport; p. (1961) *53,445.*
Matyásföld, *sub.* Budapest, Hungary; lge bus wks., refrigerator vans.
Matzen, *vil.*, E. Lower Austria; 4m. N. of Gänserndorf; oil.
Mauban, *spt.*, Luzon, Philippine Is.; p. *14,832.*
Maubeuge, *t.*, Nord, France; metal, glasswks.; p. (1954) *24,215.*
Mauch Chunk, *bor.*, E. Penns., U.S.A.; coal, carnotite, clothing; p. (1950) *2,959.*
Mauchline, *par.*, Ayr, Scot.; associated with Robert Burns; p. *4,000.* [*42,576.*
Maui, *I.*, Hawaiian Is.; a. 728 sq. m.; p. (1960)
Maule, *prov.*, Chile; a. 2,172 sq. m.; p. (1961) *93,942.*
Maumee, *R.*, Ind., U.S.A.; flows to L. Erie; length 180 m.
Mauna Kea, *volcano*, Hawaii; alt. 13,823 ft.
Mauna Loa, *volcano*, Hawaii; alt. 13,675 ft.
Mauritania, Islamic Republic of, *ind. sov. st.* within French Community, W. Africa; livestock, gum, salt; cap. Nouakchott; a. 430,000 sq. m.; p. (1961) *727,000.*
Mauritius, *I., Brit. col.* Indian Ocean; 500 m. E. of Malagasy; independence due 1966; sugar, rum; cap. Port Louis; a. 720 sq. m.; p. (estd. 1965) *741,000.*
Mawddach, *R., estuary*, Merioneth, Wales; 19 m.
Mawson, Australian national research base, Antarctica.
Maxwelltown, *t.*, Dumfries, Scot.; on R. Nith; textiles, timber.
May, *I.*, Firth of Forth, Fife, Scot.
Mayaguana I., Bahamas, W. Indies; p. (1953) *615.*
Mayagüez, *c., spt.*, Puerto Rico; sugar, coffee, tobacco; p. (1960) *50,808.*
Maybole, *burgh*, Ayr, Scot.; 8 m. S. of Ayr; footwear, agr. implements; p. (1961) *4,677.*
Mayen, *c.*, Rhine prov., Germany; mftg., brewing; leather; quarries; p. *14,327.*
Mayenne, *dep.*, N.W. France; pastoral and agr.; cap. Laval; a. 1,987 sq. m.; p. (1962) *250,030.*
Mayenne, *R.*, France; trib. of R. Sarthe; 125 m.
Mayfield, *t.*, S.W. Ky., U.S.A.; tobacco; dairy prod.; clothing; p. (1960) *10,762.*
Mayo, *maritime co.*, Connacht, Ireland; broken cst., much barren mtn. land, many large lakes; agr., fishery; co. t. Castlebar, a. 2,126 sq. m.; p. (1961) *123,180.*
Mayotte, *ch. I.*, Fr. col., Comoro Archipelago, Mozambique Channel; sugar-cane, vanilla, cacao, a. 140 sq. m.; p. *18,000.*
Maywood, *t.*, Ill., U.S.A.; adjoining Chicago; residtl., some mnfs.; p. (1960) *27,330.*
Mazagan, *see* **El Jadida.**
Mazamet, *t.*, Tarn, France; tanning, leather wks.; p. (1954) *17,070.*
Mazanderan, *prov.*, N. Iran, on Caspian Sea; wool, tobacco; a. 10,460 sq. m.; p. *200,000.*
Mazar, *t.*, Afghanistan; 200 m. N. of Kabul; chemical fertilisers from natural gas and thermal elec. plant projected; p. (estd. 1964) *40,000.*
Mazarron, *t.*, Murcia, Spain; metal wks., flour, soap; p. (1957) *15,225.*
Mazatenango, *t.*, S.W. Guatemala; coffee, cacao, sugar, fruit; p. (1960) *26,120.*
Mazatepec, *t.*, Puebla, Mexico; hydro-elec. plant.
Mazatlán, *spt.*, W. cst. Mexico; hides, minerals, fruit; oil ref nery being built; p. (1960) *50,000.*
Mazingarbe, *t.*, Pas-de-Calais, France; p. (1954) *10,311.* [prod.; p. *24,250.*
Mazzara, *t.*, Sicily, Italy; cath., ruined cas.; agr.
Mazzarino, *t.*, Sicily, Italy; mftg.; p. *21,580.*
M'babane, *t.*, Swaziland; alt. 3,800 ft.; administrative ctr.; European p. (1960) *1,092.*
M'Bao, Senegal, W. Africa; 11 m. from Dakar; oil refinery.
M'Bega, Equatorial Africa; oilfields.
McAlester, *t.*, Okla., U.S.A.; coal-mining ctr., rly. wks.; p. (1950) *17,878.*
McClintock Channel, *strait*, between Prince of Wales's land and Victoria I., Arctic Canada.
McComb, *t.*, Miss., U.S.A.; p. (1960) *12,020.*
McKeesport, *c.*, Penns., U.S.A., on Monongahela R.; coal, iron and steel; p. (1960) *45,489.*
McKees Rocks, *t.*, Penns., U.S.A.; on Ohio R.; iron, glass; p. (1960) *13,185.*
M'Clure, *strait*, between Banks I. and Melville I., Canada.
McPherson, *t.*, Yukon, Canada; on Peel R.
McPherson, *t.*, Kan., U.S.A.; in oil-field region; refining plants; p. (1950) *8,689.*
Mead, *L.*, Cal., U.S.A.; on R. Colorado behind Boulder (Hoover) Dam; world's lgst. reservoir; stores water for irrigation in Imperial Valley and Yuma dist.; length 115 m.
Meadville, *c.*, Penns., U.S.A.; on French Creek; univ.; rly. wks., rayon yarn; p. (1960) *16,671.*
Mealfuarvonie, *mtn.*, on side of L. Ness, Scot.; alt. 2,284 ft.
Meath, *maritime co.*, Leinster, Ireland; pastoral; co. t., Trim; a. 906 sq. m.; p. (1961) *65,106.*
Meathus Truim, *see* **Edgeworthstown.**
Meaux, *t.*, Seine-et-Marne, France; on R. Marne; cath.; dairying; p. (1954) *16,767.*
Mecca, *holy c.*, Saudi Arabia; Mohammedan pilgrim ctr.; p. (estd.) *200,000.*
Mechanicsburg, *bor.*, S. Penns., U.S.A.; steel; clothes; p. (1950) *6,786.*
Mechelen, *see* **Malines.**
Mecklenburg, former *Land*, Soviet Zone, Germany; bordering on Baltic Sea; abolished as admin. unit, 1952; Schwerin was the cap.; a. 8,856 sq. m.
Medan, *cap.*, E. Sumatra, Indonesia; rubber, tobacco; p. (1961) *479,000.*
Medellin, *c.*, Colombia, S. America; univ.; textiles, tobacco, coffee, cement, glass, steel; hydroelec. plant; p. (estd. 1962) *690,710.*
Medford, *t.*, Mass., U.S.A.; sub. of Boston; residtl.; chemicals, machin., textiles; p. (1960) *64,971.* [leather; p. *14,903.*
Medicina, *commune*, N. Italy; textiles, agr.;
Medicine Bow, *mtns.*, Col. and Wyo., U.S.A.
Medicine Hat, *t.*, Alberta, Canada; on S. Saskatchewan R.; rly. junction; coal, natural gas, flour; p. (1961) *24,484.*
Medina, *t.*, W. Australia; oil refinery.
Medina, *t.*, N. Ohio, U.S.A.; bees, honey, beeswax; p. (1960) *8,235.*
Medina, *c.*, Saudi Arabia; tomb of Mohammed; rail line to Ma'an being restored (1964–7); harbour at Yenbo (Yanbu); fruit, dates; p. (estd.) *50,000.* [*14,889.*
Medinia-Sidonia, *t.*, Spain; agr. prod.; p. (1957)
Mediterranean, *gr. inland sea*, almost tideless, dividing Europe from Africa; and communicating with the Atlantic by the Strait of Gibraltar and Black Sea by the Dardanelles, Sea of Marmara and Bosporus, E. part touches Asia in the Levant; total length W. to E. 2,200 m.; greatest width of sea proper about 700 m.; water a. 900,000 sq. m.; greatest depth 14,695 ft.; ch. Is.: Corsica, Sardinia, Sicily, Crete, Cyprus, and the Balearic, Lipari, Maltese, Ionian grs., also Grecian Archipelago.
Médoc, *old dist.*, Gironde, France, extending for about 48 m. along Garonne R.; noted for wines.
Medveditsa, *R.*, U.S.S.R.; trib. of R. Don; length 330 m.
Medway, *R.*, Kent, Eng.; length 70 m.; Medway Bridge (part of London–Dover motorway) completed 1962.
Meekatharra, *t.*, Murchison goldfields, W. Australia.
Meerane, *t.*, Karl-Marx-Stadt, E. Germany; textiles, machin., chemicals; p. (1963) *24,170.*
Meerut, *c.*, Uttar Pradesh, India; scene of outbreak of Indian Mutiny, 1857; p. (1961) *283,997.*
Megara, *t.*, Greece; p. (1951) *14,118.*
Mehsana, *t.*, Gujarat, India; rice, cotton, toabcco; p. (1961) *32,577.*
Meiktila, *dist.*, Upper Burma; teak forests; cap. M.; p. (of t.) *8,830.*

Meiling Pass, on bdy. between Kwangtung, Kiangsi, S. China; provides historic routeway across Nanling mtns., followed by old imperial highway from Nanking to Canton; alt. approx. 1,000 ft.
Meiningen, *t.*, Suhl, E. Germany; on R. Werra; cas.; machin., chemicals; p. (1963) *24,379*.
Meiringen, *t.*, Switzerland; nr. to Aar Gorge; resort; p. *3,285*.
Meissen, *c.*, Dresden, E. Germany; on R. Elbe; cath.; famous porcelain wks., textiles, iron, furniture, elec. machine.; p. (1963) *47,676*.
Meknès, *c.*, Morocco, N. Africa; one of the caps. of M.; agr. ctr., olives; p. (1960) *175,943*.
Mekong, *R.*, S.E. Asia; rises in Tibet and separates Laos and Siam; length 2,800 m.
Melanesia, *chain of I. grs.*, S. Pacific; New Britain, Solomon, Santa Cruz, New Hebrides, New Caledonia, Loyalty and other archipelagos.
Melbourne, *spt. cap.*, Victoria, Australia; at mouth of Yarra R.; univ., caths.; cattle, sheep, fish and rabbit mkts.; p. (1961) *1,907,366*.
Meld, *t.*, Potenza, Italy; cath.; p. *14,300*.
Melilla, *spt.*, Morocco, N. Africa; exp. iron ore; convict settlement; p. (1950) *85,010*.
Melipilla, *t.*, central Chile; agr., dairy prod.; p. (1940) *9,316*.
Melitopol, *t.*, Ukrainian S.S.R.; engin.; ctr. of rich fruit growing a.; p. (1959) *95,000*.
Melksham, *t.*, *urb. dist.*, Wilts, Eng.; on R. Avon, 5 m. N.E. of Bradford-on-Avon; rubber wks., heavy engin., flour mills, creameries, rope and matting; p. (1961) *8,279*.
Mělnik, *t.*, ČSSR.; p. (1961) *13,100*.
Melrose, *burgh*, Roxburgh, Scot.; on R. Tweed; 4 m. E. of Galashiels; ruined abbey, dist. ass. with Sir Walter Scott; p. (1961) *2,133*.
Meltham, *t.*, *urb. dist.*, W.R. Yorks, Eng.; 4 m. S.W. of Huddersfield; woollen textiles; p. (1961) *5,413*.
Melton Mowbray, *t.*, *urb. dist.*, Leicester, Eng.; on Lincoln Heights, 15 m. N.E. of Leicester; mkt., hunting dist.; famous pork pies; footwear, wool spinning mills; p. (1961) *15,913*.
Melun, *t.*, cap. Seine-et-Marne, France; on R. Seine; agr. tools and prod.; p. (1954) *20,219*.
Melville I., off N. cst., Arnhem Land, Australia.
Melville I., N.W. Terrs., Arctic Canada.
Memaliaj, *t.*, Albania; new mng. t. on banks of R. Vjosa.
Memmingen, *t.*, Bavaria, Germany; rly. junction; machin., textiles; p. (1963) *31,300*.
Memphis, *ancient c.*, Egypt; on R. Nile; 10 m. S. of Cairo; near by are Sakkara ruins.
Memphis, *c.*, Tenn., U.S.A.; on R. Mississippi; rly. ctr., timber, cotton seed, ironwks., oil; textiles, chemicals; p. (1960) *497,524*.
Mena, *t.*, W. Ark., U.S.A.; lumber, bricks, cotton, flour; tourist resort; p. (1960) *4,388*.
Menado, *t.*, Sulawesi, Indonesia; p. (1961) *129,912*.
Menai Bridge, *urb. dist.*, Anglesey, Wales; p. (1961) *2,337*.
Menai Strait, separates Isle of Anglesey from Caernarvon, Wales; crossed by Britannia rly. and Menai suspension bridges; 14 m. long, ½ m. to 2 m. wide.
Menam, *R.*, W. Thailand, length 750 m.
Menasha, *t.*, Wis., U.S.A.; on L. Winnebago; mnfs.; p. (1960) *14,647*.
Mende, *t.*, cap. Lozère, France; on R. Lot; serge mftg.; p. (1954) *7,752*.
Menden, *t.*, N. Rhine–Westphalia, Germany; metallurgy, elec. prod.; p. (1963) *28,400*.
Menderes, *R.*, Anatolia, Turkey; length 200 m.
Mendip Hills, Somerset, Eng.; limestone range containing many karst features inc. Cheddar Gorge and Wookey Hole; length 20 m.; highest point 1,067 ft.
Mendota, *c.*, Ill., U.S.A.; nr. Chicago, mftg.; p. [(1960) *6,154*.
Mendoza, *prov.*, W. Argentina; alfalfa, vines, olives, fruit, peppermint; cap. Mendoza; a. 57,445 sq. m.; p. (1960) *826,000*.
Mendoza, *t.*, cap. Mendoza prov., Argentina; on Transandine Rly.; wine-producing dist.; petroleum; p. (1960) of c. *110,000* greater M. *250,000*.
Menen, *t.*, W. Flanders, Belgium; tobacco tr., textiles, rubber gds., soap; p. (1962) *22,520*.
Menfi, *t.*, Sicily, Italy; industl.; p. *10,225*.
Mengtsz, *c.*, Yunnan, China; ruined in Tai-ping rebellion; tin, cotton ginning ctr.; p. *193,004*.
Menominee, Mich., U.S.A.; on M. R.; industl. ctr. for lumber, sugar beets, dairy prod.; p. (1960) *11,289*.
Menomonie, *c.*, Wis., U.S.A.; on Red Cedar R.; farm ctr. and dairy prod.; p. (1960) *18,276*.
Menteith, L., of, S.W. Perth, Scot.; between Rs. Forth and Teith; a. 2½ sq. m.
Mentone, *t.*, Alpes-Maritimes, S. France; on Mediterranean cst.; health resort, olive oil, wines, perfumes; p. (1954) *17,109*.
Meppel, *t.*, Neth.; nr. Zuider Zee, shipbldg.; p. *12,133*.
Merano, *t.*, Tyrol. N. Italy; health resort; p. *30,350*.
Merced, *t.*, Cal., U.S.A.; p. (1960) *20,068*.
Mercedes, *cap.*, Soriano dep., Uruguay; livestock ctr.; resort; p. (1963) *34,000*.
Mercedes, *t.* S. Texas, U.S.A.; cotton, oil, fruit; veg. canning; p. (1960) *10,943*.
Merchantville, *bor.*, N.J., U.S.A.; paper, lead mnfs.; p. (1960) *4,075*.
Mergui, *archipelago*, Burma; teak, rice, pearl fishing.
Mergui, *t.*, Tenasserim, Lower Burma; on Bay of Bengal; pearl fishing; p. *20,405*.
Mérida, *t.*, Badajoz, Spain; on R. Guadiana; agr. dist., textiles; p. *28,886*.
Mérida, *cap.*, Yucatán, Mexico; univ.; sisal-hemp, ropes, cigars, brandy; p. (1960) *170,834*.
Mérida, *t.*, cap. Mérida st., Venezuelan Andes; univ., cath; tourist ctr.; world's highest cable rly. to Espejo peak (15,380 ft.); p. (1961) *40,404*.
Meriden, *c.*, Conn., U.S.A.; hardware mftg.; p. (1960) *51,850*.
Meridian, *t.*, Miss., U.S.A.; in cotton-growing region; p. (1960) *49,374*.
Mérignac, *commune*, Gironde dep., S.W. France; cattle mkt.; p. (1954) *23,050*.
Merioneth, *maritime co.*, N. Wales; pastoral and mining; nuclear power-sta. at Trawsfynydd; co. t., Dolgellau; a. 600 sq. m.; p. (1961) *39,007*.
Meriti, *c.*, S.E. Brazil; 10 m. N. Rio de Janeiro; p. (1947) *38,645*.
Merom, Waters of, *L.*, modern Hule L., Upper Galilee, Israel.
Merrick, *mtn.*, Kirkcudbright, Scot.; highest peak in S. Uplands of Scot.; alt. 2,764 ft.
Merill, *t.*, N. Wis., U.S.A.; wooden goods, paper, knitwear; p. (1960) *9,451*.
Merrimac, *R.*, N.H. and Mass., U.S.A.
Merse, *geographical sub-region*, S.E. Scot.; comprises lower valleys of Rs. Tweed and Teviot below Melrose and Hawick; glacial deposits form low hillocks *en échelon*, which largely influence the pattern of streams, roads, settlements, etc.; most favoured part of Scot. for crop growing, wheat, barley, root crops (for feeding to cattle, sheep); ch. ts. Hawick, Kelso, Berwick-on-Tweed (Eng.); a. approx. 220 sq. m.
Mersea, *I.*, at mouth of R. Colne, Essex, Eng.; oysters; holiday resort; length 5 m., width 2 m.
Merseburg, *c.*, Halle, E. Germany; on R. Saale; cath., cas.; paper, machin., tobacco, chemicals; p. (1963) *52,545*.
Mersey, *R.*, between Lancs and Cheshire, Eng.; enters Irish Sea by fine estuary at Liverpool; length 68 m.
Merseyside, *lge. conurbation*, S.W. Lancs and N. Cheshire, Eng.; comprises: (1) spt. and industl. a. either side of lower Mersey estuary; (2) residtl. a. of W. Wirral Peninsula; a. 150 sq. m.; p. (1961) *1,385,702*. *See also under* **Bebington, Birkenhead, Bootle, Crosby, Ellesmere Pt., Hoylake, Huyton, Litherland, Liverpool, Neston, Wallasey, Wirral.**
Mersey Tunnel, biggest underwater tunnel in world, linking Liverpool and Birkenhead; opened 1934; main tunnel 2 m. l., with branch bores, 3 m.; second tunnel (two-way) planned.
Mersin, *spt.*, Turkey; oil refining; textiles, fruit, cereals, timber; p. (1960) *68,574*.
Merthyr Tydfil, *t.*, *co. bor.*, Glamorgan, S. Wales; in narrow valley of R. Taff, 22 m. N.W. of Cardiff; hosiery, aircraft, bricks, elec. domestic goods; p. (1961) *59,008*.
Merton, *outer bor.*, Greater London, Eng.; inc. former bors. of Mitcham, Wimbledon, and Merton and Morden; p. (1964) *188,621*.
Meru, *mtn.*, Tanzania, E. Africa; extinct volcano overlooking E. arm of Gr. Rift valley; coffee plantations at alt. 5,000–6,000 ft., some rubber below 4,000 ft.; alt. summit 14,953 ft.
Merv, *see* **Mary.**
Mesa, *t.*, Arizona, U.S.A.; agr. and cotton ginning ctr.; helicopter mftg.; p. (1960) *33,772*.

Mesabi Range, *hills*, N.E. Minn., U.S.A.; about
100 m. long, alt. 200–500 ft.; vast iron-ore
deposits.

Mesagna, *t.*, S. Italy; mnfs.; p. *17,300*.

Meshed, *c.*, Khurasan, Iran; nr. Kashaf Rud
R.; tr., pilgrim ctr.; silks, carpets; p. (1960)
266,000.

Mesopotamia, *see* **Iraq.**

Messina, *c., spt.*, Sicily, Italy; opposite Reggio;
univ.; exp. fruit, wine, silk, oil; silk mnf.;
p. (1961) *251,423*.

Messina, *strait*, between Sicily and Italian mainland; length 22 m. minimum width 3 m.

Messinia, *prefecture*, Peloponnese, Greece; cap.
Kalamai; p. *210,728*.

Mesta, *R.*, Bulgaria, Greece; rises in Rhodope
Mtns., flows S.E. into Ægean Sea 15 m. E. of
Kaválla; valley famous for tobacco; known in
Greece as Nestos; approx. length 175 m.

Mestre, *t.*, Italy; on lagoon at landward end of
causeway linking Venice to mainland; p. *11,750*.

Mesurado, *R.*, Liberia, Africa; 300 m. long.

Meta, *R.*, Colombia and Venezuela; navigable for
400 m.; trib. of R. Orinoco; length 750 m.

Metemma, *t.*, Sudan; opposite Shendi, on R. Nile.

Methil, *t.*, Fife, Scot.; on F. of Forth; united
with Buckhaven.

Methuen, *t.*, Mass., U.S.A.; textiles, footwear;
p. (1960) *28,114*. [(1960) *7,339*.

Metropolis, *c.*, Ill., U.S.A.; on R. Ohio; p.

Mettmann, *t.*, N. Rhine–Westphalia, Germany;
nr. Düsseldorf; iron, machin.; p. (1963) *25,800*.

Metuchen, *bor.*, N.J., U.S.A.; residtl., chemicals,
needles, rubber; p. (1960) *14,041*.

Metz, *c.*, cap. Moselle, France; on R. Moselle 25 m.
N. of Nancy; cath.; wines, leather goods,
preserved fruits; p. (1962) *109,678*.

Meudon, *t.*, Seine-et-Oise, France; nr. Versailles;
observatory; glass, linen, ammunition; p.
(1954) *24,729*.

Meurthe, *R.*, France; length 70 m.

Meurthe-et-Moselle, *dep.*, E. France; agr.,
vineyards, mining; cap. Nancy; a. 2,037 sq.
m.; p. (1962) *678,078*.

Meuse, *dep.*, N.E. France; livestock, mining,
wine; cap. Bar-le-Duc; a. 2,408 sq. m.; p.
(1962) *215,985*.

Meuse (Maas,) *R.*, France; rises in Haute-Marne,
flows past Verdun into Belgium past Namur
and Liége into the Netherlands and joins the
Waal, left arm of the Rhine; length 570 m.

Mevagissey, *vil.*, Cornwall, Eng.; fishing and fish
canning; tourist resort; p. *1,739*.

Mexborough, *t., urb. dist.*, W.R. Yorks, Eng.;
on R. Don, 10 m. above Doncaster; potteries,
iron; p. (1961) *17,095*. [500 m.

Mexcala, *R.*, S. Mexico; flows into Pacific; length

Mexia, *t.*, Texas, U.S.A.; rly. ctr.; cotton, oil,
engin.; p. (1960) *6,121*.

Mexicali, *cap.*, N. Terr., Lower California, Mexico;
p. (1960) *174,540*.

Mexico, *fed. rep.*, S. of N. America; contains
much forest, fertile land and mtn. dists.;
rich in minerals, silver, copper, arsenic, oil,
zinc, lead; stock-raising and agr. are the ch.
occupations in the N States; cap. Mexico City;
a. 761,600 sq. m.; p. (1960) *34,923,129*.

Mexico City, *cap. c.*, Mexico; in plain, alt. 7,460 ft.
above sea-level; many noteworthy bldgs.; extensive tr. and inds.; p. (1960) *2,832,133*.

Mexico, *st.*, Mexico; a. 8,267 sq. m.; cap. Toluca;
p. (1960) *1,897,851*.

Mexico, *c.*, Mo., U.S.A.; firebrick and shoe
factories; p. (1960) *12,889*.

Mexico, G. of, *lge. inlet* of the Atlantic (1,000 m.
E. to W. by 800 m. N. to S.) lying S. of U.S.A.
and E. of Mexico. Communicates by Florida
Strait with the Atlantic and by Channel of
Yucatán with the Caribbean Sea.

Meycauayan, *mun.*, Luzon, Philippines; rice,
sugar, maize; p. *16,082*.

Mezhdurechensk, *t.*, R.S.F.S.R.; W. Siberia, on R.
Tom'; new coalmng. ctr.; p. (1959) *55,000*.

Mézières, *t.*, Ardennes, France; on R. Meuse;
nails, hardware, type-founding; p. (1954)
11,073.

Mezökovesd, *t.*, Hungary; industl.; p. (1962)
18,640.

Mezötur, *t.*, Hungary; mkt., flour, pottery; p.
(1962) *23,329*.

Mhow, *t.*, Madhya Pradesh, India; cotton; p.
(1961) *48,032*.

Miagao, *t.*, Panay, Philippines; tr. ctr., mnfs.

Miami, *c.*, Fla., U.S.A.; winter resort, fruits,
fishing; chemicals, paper, fabricated metals; p.
(1960) *291,688*.

Miami, *t.*, Okla., U.S.A.; tr. ctr., agr., cattle;
packing, mining; p. (1960) *12,869*.

Miamisburg, *t.*, Ohio, U.S.A.; p. (1960) *9,893*.

Miani, *t.* N.W. Punjab, Pakistan; salt; p. about
6,000. [(1951) *550,000*.

Mianwali, *dist.*, W. Punjab, Pakistan; p. (estd.

Michigan, *st.*, U.S.A.; in valley of Gr. Lakes;
industl.; cars, iron and steel goods, petroleum,
minerals; some agr.; cap. Lansing; a. 58,216
sq. m.; p. (1960) *7,823,194*.

Michigan, *L.*, N. America; in basin of St. Lawrence R., enclosed by two peninsulas of the
St. of M. and by Wis., Ill. and Ind.; a. 23,900
sq. m.; discharges by Straits of Mackinac to
L. Huron.

Michigan City, *t.*, Ind., U.S.A.; on L. M.; rly.
wks., furniture, hosiery; (1960) *36,653*.

Michipicoten, *R.*, Ontario, Canada; flows 125 m.
to L. Superior.

Michoacan, *st.*, Mexico; on the Pacific; mtnous.
and rich in minerals; cap. Morelia; a. 23,200
sq. m.; p. (1960) *1,851,876*.

Michurinsk, *t.*, R.S.F.S.R.; N.W. of Tambov;
engin., textiles, food inds.; agr. exp. ctr.; p.
(1959) *80,000*.

Micronesia, *grs. of sm. Is.*, S. Pacific; includes
Carolines, Marianas (Ladrones), Marshall,
Pelews, etc.

Middelburg, *t.*, cap. Zeeland, Neth.; on Walcheren
I. nr. Flushing; margarine, timber; p. (1951)
21,417.

Middelburg, *t.*, Transvaal, S. Africa; coal, iron,
copper, cobalt; p. (1960) *12,907* inc. *4,886* Europeans.

Middelfart, *t.*, Fyn, Denmark; off Fredericia;
p. (1960) *8,801*. [*6,003*.

Middleboro, *t.*, Mass., U.S.A.; agr. ctr.; p. (1960)

Middle Congo, fmr. Fr. col. *See* **Congo, Rep. of.**

Middlesboro, *t.*, Ky., U.S.A.; p. (1960) *12,607*.

Middlesbrough, *spt., co. bor.*, Cleveland dist., N.R.
Yorks, Eng.; on S. side of Tees estuary; impt.
iron and steel ind., heavy engin., shipbldg. and
coal exp.; oil refinery projected; p. (1961)
157,308.

Middlesex, *former co.*, S.E. Eng.; N. of R. Thames;
completely absorbed in Greater London 1964;
a. 232 sq. m.; p. (1961) *2,230,093*.

Middleton, *mkt. t.*, Durham, Eng.; civil airport
projected; on R. Tees.

Middleton, *t., mun. bor.*, S.E. Lancs, Eng.; mkt.;
textiles, engin., chemicals; p. (1961) *56,674*.

Middletown, *c.*, Conn., U.S.A.; on C. R.; univ.;
p. (1960) *33,250*.

Middletown, *c.*, N.Y., U.S.A.; on Walkill R.;
ironwks.; p. (1960) *23,475*.

Middletown, *c.*, Ohio, U.S.A.; in Miami and Erie
canal; p. (1960) *42,115*.

Middletown, *bor.*, Penns., U.S.A.; on Susquehanna R.; p. (1960) *11,182*.

Middlewich, *t., urb. dist.*, Cheshire, Eng.; on Rs.
Dane, Wheelock, and Croco, 5 m. N. of Crewe;
salt, chemicals, silk, clothing; p. (1961) *6,833*.

Midhurst, *t.*, Sussex, Eng.; on R. Rother; mkt.,
agr. ctr.; brick, timber, lime wks.; p. *1,812*.

Midland, *t.*, Mich., U.S.A.; chemicals, salt, oil; p.
(1960) *27,779*.

Midland, *t.*, Texas, U.S.A.; oilfield ctr., cotton
ginning, natural gas; p. (1960) *62,625*.

Midland Junction, *t.*, W. Australia.

Midleton, *urb. dist.*, Cork, Ireland; mkt.; p. (1961)
2,770.

Midlothian, *co.*, Scot.; dairying, coal-mining,
paper, brewing, fishing; a. 362 sq. m.; p.
(1961) *580,332*.

Midnapore, *t.*, W. Bengal, India; silkworm tr.; p.
(1961) *59,532*.

Midway, *Is.*, Pac. Oc.; calling-place on air-
routes between San Francisco and Asia, midway between Asia and U.S.A. (to which it
belongs).

Miechowice, *t.*, S.W. Poland; coal, iron foundries;
p. *14,608*.

Miedzyrzecz (Meseritz), *t.*, E. Poland; agr.,
leather; p. *16,837*.

Mieres, *t.*, Spain; on R. Leno, nr. Oviedo;
minerals, agr. prod.; p. (1959) *69,623*.

Mihoro, Gifu, Japan; power plant under construc
tion.

Mikkeli (St. Michel), *dep.*, Finland; a. 6,750 sq. m.
p. (1961) *234,629*.

Milan, *c.*, N. Italy; on R. Olona; cath., univ.; textiles, machin., motors, chemicals, porcelain; cultural, comm. and industrl. ctr.; p. (1961) *1,580,978.*
Milas, *t.*, S.W. Turkey in Asia; agr., fruit; carpets; p. (1960) *11,676.*
Mildenhall, *t.*, W. Suffolk, Eng.; on R. Lark, 10 m. N.W. of Bury St. Edmunds; mkt., flour; p. *3,235.*
Mildura, *c.*, Victoria, Australia; on R. Murray; irrigation ctr., fruit; p. (1961) *12,273.*
Miles City, *c.*, Mont., U.S.A.; on Yellowstone R.; cattle; p. (1960) *9,665.*
Milford, *t.*, Conn., U.S.A.; residtl., resort; fish; light engin.; p. (1960) *41,662.*
Milford, *t.*, Mass., U.S.A.; boot mnfs.; p. (1960) *13,722.*
Milford Haven, *spt.*, *urb. dist.*, Milford Haven, Pembroke, Wales; major oil pt., providing access and anchorage for 100,000-ton oil tankers; refinery, fishing, trawlers built and repaired, net mkg., beryllium; p. (1961) *12,802.*
Milford Sound, *inlet*, at S. extremity of S.I. N.Z., tourist restort; noted for grandeur of scenery, and rare birds.
Milianah, *t.*, Algeria; tr. ctr.; p. *5,000.*
Militello, *t.*, Sicily, Italy; agr., interests; p. *10,770.*
Milk, *R.*, Mont., U.S.A.; trib. of Missouri R.; length 500 m.
Millau, *t.*, Aveyron, France; on R. Tarn; glove mnfs.; p. (1954) *19,209.*
Millbrook, *t.*, Hants, Eng.; at mouth of R. Test, nr. Southampton.
Millersburg, *bor.*, Penns., U.S.A.; machin., shoes; p. (1950) *2,861.*
Millinocket, *t.*, Me., U.S.A.; paper; p. (1960) [*7,318.*
Millom, *t.*, Cumberland, Eng.; on N.W. cst. of Duddon estuary; iron-ore mining, ironwks.; p. *8,708.*
Millport, *burgh*, Bute, Scot.; on Gr. Cumbrae I., in F. of Clyde; resort; cath.; quarries; p. (1961) *1,592.*
Millville, *c.*, N.J., U.S.A.; on Maurice R.; glass, iron, cotton; p. (1960) *19,096.*
Milngavie, *burgh*, Dunbarton, Scot.; 5 m. N.W. of Glasgow; textiles; p. (1961) *8,894.*
Milnrow, *t.*, *urb. dist.*, S.E. Lancs, Eng.; sub. of Rochdale; cotton and waste spinning, engin., brick mkg., paper and tube mftg.; p. (1961) *7,819.*
Milos, *I.*, Cyclades, Greece; volcanic; length 13 m.; fruits, gypsum, sulphur; famous statue of Venus found here in 1820.
Milspe, *commune*, Westphalia, Germany; ironwks.; p. *11,291.*
Milstin, *peak*, Atlas Mtns., Morocco, N. Africa; alt. 11,400 ft.
Milton, *t.*, Mass., U.S.A.; sub. of Boston; p. (1960) *26,375.*
Milton, *t.*, Penns., U.S.A.; on Susquehanna R.; ironwks.; p. (1960) *7,972.*
Milverton, *t.*, Somerset, Eng.; 6 m. W. of Taunton; [mkt.
Milwaukee, *c.*, Wis., U.S.A.; on L. Michigan, 70 m. N. of Chicago; univ.; rly. ctr., cars, meat canning, agr. tools, machin., iron and steel castings, generators; dairying; p. (1960) *741,324.*
Mimico, *t.*, Ontario, Canada; p. (1961) *18,212.*
Minab, *t.*, Iran; orchards; p. about *10,000.*
Mina Hassan Tani (Kenitra), *t.*, Morocco; 18 m. N. of Rabat; developed since 1912; exp. grain; p. (1960) *86,775.*
Minas Basin, *E. arm*, Bay of Fundy, Nova Scotia, Canada.
Minas Gerais, *st.*, Brazil; extensive mining, diamonds, gold, iron, manganese, aluminium, cotton, coffee, agr.; cap. Belo Horizonte; a. 224,701 sq. m.; p. (1960) *9,798,880.*
Minas Novas, *t.*, Minas Gerais, Brazil.
Minatitlán, *t.*, E. Mexico; petroleum refineries; petrochemicals; p. (1940) *18,539.*
Minch, The, *channel* between the Outer and Inner Hebrides; 24 m. to 40 m. wide.
Minchinhampton, *t.*, Gloucester, Eng.; in Cotswold Hills, 4 m. S.E. of Stroud; mkt., woollens, brewing; p. *3,500.*
Mincio, *R.*, Italy; trib. of R. Po; drains L. Garda; length 38 m.
Mindanao, 2nd lgst. I. of Philippines; pineapples, hemp, coconuts, coffee; iron, gold, coal, copper; ch. ts. Zamboanga, Davao; off N.E. cst. is Mindanao Deep (*c.* 35,000 ft.), one of greatest known ocean depths; a. 36,536 sq. m.; p. *2,356,700.*
Minden, *c.*, N. Rhine–Westphalia, Germany; on R. Weser at crossing of Mittelland Canal; cath.; glass, tobacco, metal, wood, leather, meat prod.; p. (1963) *48,900.*
Minden, *t.*, La., U.S.A.; exp. cotton; petroleum, natural gas; p. (1960) *12,785.*
Mindoro, *I.*, Philippines, S. of Luzon; a. 3,759 sq. m.; p. *100,000.*
Minehead, *t.*, *urb. dist.*, Somerset, Eng.; at N. foot of Exmoor, on Bristol Channel cst.; mkt., holiday resort; p. (1961) *7,674.*
Mineo, *t.*, Sicily, Italy; mftg.; p. *11,400.*
Mineola, *t.*, N.Y., U.S.A.; sub. N.Y. c.; glass, packing; p. (1960) *20,519.*
Minersville, *bor.*, Penns., U.S.A.; on Schuylkill R.; p. (1960) *6,606.*
Minervino, *t.*, S. Italy; industl.; p. *18,375.*
Minho, *prov.*, N. Portugal; fruit-growing, cattle, textiles; a. 1,889 sq. m.; p. (1950) *815,909.*
Minho, *R.*, separates Portugal from Spain in N.W.; length 170 m.
Minia, *t.*, U.A.R.; on R. Nile; cotton, tr. ctr; p. (1960) *94,000.*
Minicoy Is., Arabian Sea, joined with Laccadive and Amindivi Is. to form *Union terr.* (India).
Minneapolis, *c.*, Minn., U.S.A.; on Mississippi R., at Falls of St. Anthony; univ.; flour, timber, agr. machin., linseed oil; chemicals, textiles, paper; p. (1960) *482,827.*
Minnesota, *st.*, U.S.A.; iron-ore, agr., flour, timber, meat; cap. St. Paul; a. 84,068 sq. m.; p. (1960) *3,413,864.*
Minnick, Water of, *R.*, Ayr and Kirkcudbright, Scot.; trib. of R. Cree; length 15 m.
Minorca (Menorca), Spanish I., Balearic Is., Mediterranean Sea; fruits, olives, cereals, cattle, minerals; cap. Mahón; a. 283 sq. m.; p. (1957) *42,478.*
Minot, *t.*, N.D., U.S.A.; p. (1960) *30,604.*
Minsk, *cap.*, Byelorussian S.S.R.; univ.; engin., textiles, elec. power; p. (1962) *599,000.*
Minya Konka, *mtn.*, Szechwan, China; at E. end of Plateau of Tibet; highest mtn. in China; alt. approx. 23,000 ft.
Miosnavo, *L.*, Norway; length 24 m.
Miquelon, *I.*, French, off S. cst. Newfoundland, Canada; fisheries.
Mira, *t.*, Italy; on Brenta Morta; p. *19,600.*
Miranda, *st.*, N. Venezuela; pastoral and agr.; cap. Los Teques; p. (1961) *492,349.*
Miranda, *t.*, N.E. Spain; on R. Ebro; p. (1957) *18,094.*
Mirandola, *t.*, Modena, Italy; p. *20,875.*
Mirano, *t.*, N. Italy; p. *14,600.*
Mirfield, *urb. dist.*, W.R. Yorks, Eng.; on R. Calder, 3 m. S.W. of Dewsbury; woollens; p. (1961) *12,289.*
Miri, *t.*, Sarawak; oil ctr.; p. (1960) *13,350.*
Mirim, *L.*, Brazil and Uruguay; 115 m. long, 20 m. wide.
Mirzapur, *t.*, Uttar Pradesh, India; on R. Ganges; carpets, brassware; p. (1961) *100,097.*
Misburg, *vil.*, Lower Saxony, Germany; on Weser–Elbe Canal, 5 m. E. of Hanover; oil refining; p. (estd.) *8,830.*
Mishawaka, *c.*, Ind., U.S.A.; on St. Joseph R.; agr. implements; p. (1960) *33,361.*
Misilmeri, *t.*, Sicily, Italy; p. *11,420.*
Misiones, *terr.*, Argentina; farming and stock-raising; cap. Posadas; a. 11,749 sq. m.; p. (1960) *391,000.*
Miskolcz, *t.*, Hungary; univ.; flour, leather, porcelain, textiles, iron and steel; p. (1962) *151,000.*
Misoöl, *I.*, N. of Ceram, Indonesia.
Mission, *t.*, S. Texas, U.S.A.; fruit, cotton, vegetables; engin.; p. (1960) *14,081.*
Mississinewa, *R.*, Ind., U.S.A.; trib. of Wabash R.; length 140 m.
Mississippi, *st.*, U.S.A.; cotton, sweet potatoes, pecan nuts, rice, sugar cane, sorghum cane; cable; petroleum, natural gas, chemicals, shipbldg.; cap. Jackson; a. *47,716* sq. m.; p. (1960) *2,178,101.*
Mississippi, *R.*, Canada; trib. of Ottawa R.; length 100 m.
Mississippi, *R.*, U.S.A.; length c. 2,350 m. (Mississippi–Missouri–Red Rock, c. 3,860 m.).
Missolonghi, *c.*, *spt.*, *cap.*, Aetolia and Acarnania, Greece; currants; p. (1961) *11,266.*

Missoula, *c.*, Mont., U.S.A.; on Klark R.; univ.; rly. wks., agr., fruit, oil ref.; p. (1960) *27,090.*
Missouri, *st.*, U.S.A.; livestock, maize, coal, iron, tobacco; cap. Jefferson City; ch. t. St. Louis; a. 69,674 sq. m.; p. (1960) *4,319,813.*
Missouri, *R.*, U.S.A.; trib. of Mississippi R.; length (including the Madison) *3,047* m., navigable 2,400 m.
Missouri Coteau, *hill ridge*, N. America; runs N.W. to S.E. across prairies of Saskatchewan (Canada), N. and S. Dakota (U.S.A.); rises abruptly from 1,600 to 2,000 ft.
Missouri, Little, *R.*, U.S.A.; trib. of M. R.; length 450 m.
Mistassini, *L.*, Quebec, Canada; 100 m. long.
Misterbianco, *commune*, E. Sicily; lava, sulphur; agr.; p. *11,387.*
Mistretta, *t.*, Sicily, Italy; mnfs.; p. *10,800.*
Misurata, *t.*, Tripolitania, Libya, N. Africa; on cst. of Mediterranean, 110 m. E. of Tripoli; mkt. for local agr. produce; fishing; p. (1954) *66,735.*
Mitau, *see* **Jelgava.**
Mitcham, *former mun. bor.*, Surrey, Eng.; now inc. in Merton outer London bor.(*q.v.*); paint, calico printing, elec. engin.; p. (1961) *63,653.*
Mitchell, *dist.*, N.S.W., Australia; silver mining.
Mitchell, *R.*, Queensland, Australia; flows into G. of Carpentaria.
Mitchell, *t.*, Ind., U.S.A.; cement; p. (1960) *3,552.*
Mitchell, *t.*, S. Dakota, U.S.A.; univ.; farming; p. (1960) *12,555.*
Mitchell, *mtn. pk.*, Black Mtns., N. Carolina, U.S.A.; alt. 6,684 ft.; also called the "Black Dome."
Mitchelstown, *t.*, Cork, Ireland; nr. Fermoy; [p. (1951) *2,148.*
Mitidja, *plain*, Algeria, N. Africa; borders Mediterranean 25 m. E. and W. of Algiers; intensive cultivation of vine; ch. ts. Algiers, Blida.
Mitrovica, *t.*, Jugoslavia; on R. Sava; livestock, mkt.; p. (1959) *22,000.*
Mittelland Canal, *inland waterway system*, N. Germany; system of canals and canalised Rs.; links Dortmund–Ems Canal nr. Rheine through Minden, Hanover, Magdeburg, Berlin to R. Oder at Frankfurt-on-Oder; makes use of natural E.–W. troughs across the N. German Plain.
Mittweida, *t.*, Karl-Marx-Stadt, E. Germany; metallurgy, textiles; p. (1963) *20,592.*
Miyako, *spt.*, Japan; p. *32,879.*
Mizen Head, *C.*, S. Ireland; W. of C. Clear.
Mjösa, *lgst. L.*, Norway; 55 m. long.
Mlada Boleslav (Jungbunzlau), *t.*, Bohemia, ČSSR.; religious ctr., chemicals; p. (1961) *25,694.*
Mlawa, *t.*, Warsaw, Poland; tanning, grain, agr. implements; p. *14,000.*
Mljet, *I.*, Adriatic Sea; part of Jugoslavia.
Moanda, Leopoldville, Congo; oil refinery.
Moate, *t.*, W. Meath Ireland; p. (1951) *1,274.*
Moberly, *c.*, Mo., U.S.A.; rly. wks., grain, iron, hosiery, footwear; p. (1960) *13,170.*
Mobile, *c.*, *spt.*, Ala., U.S.A.; on R. M.; shipbldg., cotton exp.; p. (1960) *202,779.*
Mocha, *fortfd. spt.* Yemen, Arabia; on Red Sea; coffee; p. *5,000.*
Modane, *t.*, S.E. Savoie, France; commands routes via Mont Cenis Pass and tunnel; p. (1954) *4,064.*
Modder, *R.*, C. Prov., S. Africa; trib. of Orange R.
Modena, *t.*, *prov. cap.*, Italy; cath., univ.; textiles, fruit, grain, leather; p. (1961) *139,496.*
Modesto, *t.*, Cal., U.S.A.; fruit, vegetables; p. (1960) *36,585.*
Modica, *t.*, Sicily, Italy; cheese, macaroni, grain, wines; p. (1961) *44,050.*
Modjokerto, *t.*, E. Java, Indonesia; sugar; fossil man discovered 1934; p. *23,600.*
Mödling, *t.*, Austria; on R. Brühl, metalwks., sulphur-baths; p. (1961) *17,274.*
Moers, *t.*, N. Rhine–Westphalia, Germany; N.E. of Krefeld; cas.; coal-mining, metal ind.; p. (estd. 1954) *36,300.*
Moffat, *burgh*, Dumfries, Scot.; in Annandale, 15 m. N.W. of Lockerbie; health resort; p. (1961) *1,917.*
Moffat Tunnel, Col., U.S.A.; carries trunk rly. from Chicago to San Francisco under Rocky Mtns. between Denver and Salt Lake City; length 6¼ m.
Mogadishu, *cap.*, Somalia, N.E. Africa; fish canning, hides; p. (1958) *86,643.*
Mogador, *see* **Essaouira.**
Mogilev, *c.*, Byelorussian S.S.R.; on R. Dnieper; engin., textiles, chemicals; p. (1959) *121,000.*
Mogilev Podolski, *t.*, Ukrainian S.S.R.; on Dniester R.; tr., flour, sugar refining; p. (1939) *22,271.*
Mohác, *t.*, Hungary; on R. Danube; R. pt.; flour, brewing; p. (1962) *18,100.*
Mohammedia, *t.*, Morocco, N. Africa; oil refining; p. (1960) *35,010.*
Mohawk, *R.*, N.Y., U.S.A.; trib. of Hudson R.; followed by impt. road, rly. and canal routes across Appalachian Mtns.; length 175 m.
Moidart, *L.*, *cst. dist.*, S.W. Inverness, Scot.
Moisie, *R.*, Labrador, Canada, flows S. into G. of St. Lawrence.
Moissac, *t.*, France; on R. Tarn; abbey; p. *7,435.*
Mojave, *desert*, Cal., U.S.A.
Moji, *spt.*, Kyushu, Japan; now part of Kitakyushu City newly formed 1963 (*q.v.*); exp. coal, cement, timber, sugar, cotton, thread; p. (1960) *152,081.*
Mokau, *R.*, S.I., N.Z.
Mokpo, *spt.*, W. cst. S. Korea; ctr. of food-processing and cotton-ginning; p. (1955) *113,492.*
Mol, *t.*, N.E. Belgium; nuclear energy research ctr.; p. (1962) *25,404.*
Mola di Bari, *spt.*, Apulia, Italy; grain, livestock, olives, wine; p. *18,775.*
Mola di Gaeta, *t.*, Italy; p. *15,950.*
Mold, *co. t.*, *urb. dist.*, Flint, N. Wales; on R. Alyn; chemicals, roadstone; p. (1961) *6,857.*
Moldau, *see* **Vltava.**
Moldavian S.S.R., *const. rep.*, U.S.S.R.; viniculture, fruit-growing, mkt. gard.; cap. Kishinev; a. 13,200 sq. m.; p. (1959) *2,880,000.*
Moldavia, *prov.* Romania; a. 14,660 sq. m.; wine; ch. t. Jassy; p. *2,850,068.*
Mole, *R.*, Surrey, Eng.; rises in central Weald, flows N. into R. Thames nr. Molesey; cuts impt. gap through N. Downs between Dorking and Leatherhead; length approx. 50 m.
Molenbeek-Saint-Jean, *t.*, Belgium; nr. Brussels; large mftg. ctr.; p. (1962) *63,488.*
Molesey, E. and W. *t.*, Surrey, Eng.; at junction of Rs. Mole and Thames; residtl.; p. *8,500.*
Molfetta, *spt.*, Apulia, Italy; olive oil, macaroni, wine; p. (1961) *61,684.*
Molina de Segura, *commune*, S.E. Spain; tinned food and jams; salt wks; p. (1957) *14,683.*
Moline, *c.*, Ill., U.S.A.; on Mississippi R.; agr. implements, ironwks., flour; p. (1960) *42,705.*
Mollendo, *spt.*, Peru; bricks, fishing; p. (1961) *18,000.*
Mölndal, *c.*, S.W. Sweden; paper, textiles; margarine; p. (1961) *26,502.*
Molokai, *I.*, Hawaiian Is.; a. 260 sq. m.; p. *5,258.*
Molotov, *see* **Perm.**
Molsheim, *t.*, Bas-Rhin, France; W. of Strasbourg; sword and bayonet mkg.
Molucca or Spice Is., Indonesia; between Sulawesi and West Irian; spices, sago, timber, pearls, rice, copra; ch. t. Ternate; a. 191,681 sq. m.; p. (1961) *789,534.*
Mombasa, *spt.*, Kenya; ch. harbour, Killindini; rly. terminus; oil refinery; exp. tropical produce (ivory, hides, rubber, etc.); p. (1962) *178,400.*
Mön, *I.*, off cst. of Själland, Denmark; a. 90 sq. m.; cap. Stege; p. (1960) *13,107.*
Mona Passage, *strait*, Caribbean Sea; separates Hispaniola from Puerto Rico.
Monaca, *bor.*, Penns., U.S.A.; glass, light engin.; p. (1960) *8,394.*
Monaco, *principality*, S. France; divided into 3 sections, Monaco Ville, La Condamine and Monte Carlo (famous Casino); tourism; olive oil, perfumes; a. 8 sq. m.; p. (1961) *20,441.*
Monadhliath Mtns., Inverness, Scot.; on W. side Strathspey; highest peak Carn Mairg, 3,087 ft.
Monaghan, *inland co.*, Ireland; mainly pastoral and agr.; a. 500 sq. m.; p. (1961) *47,077.*
Monaghan, *co. t.*, Monaghan, Ireland; on the Ulster Canal; cath.; p. (1961) *4,010.*
Monaro, *mtn. plateau*, N.S.W., Australia; a 8,335 sq. m.
Monastir, *see* **Bitolj.**
Moncaleiri, *commune*, Piedmont, N.W. Italy; on R. Po; industl.; p. *21,181.*
Mönch or "The Monk", *mtn.*, Bernese Alps Switzerland; alt. 13,468 ft.
Mönchen-Gladbach, *t.*, *Land*, North Rhine Westphalia, Germany; 16 m. W. of Düsseldorf rly. ctr., cotton and wool; p. (1963) *153,400.*

Monchique, *t.*, Algarve, Portugal; spa; wine, oil, chestnuts; p. *10,000.*
Monclova, *t.*, N.E. Mexico; coffee; copper, silver, zinc, lead-mines; p. (1941) *7,181.*
Moncton, *t.*, N.B., Canada; rly. ctr., textiles; oil near by; p. (1961) *43,840.*
Mondego, *R.*, Portugal; length 130 m.
Mondovi, *t.*, Cuneo, Italy; porcelain, paper, silk; p. *20,900.*
Monessen, *t.*, Penns., U.S.A.; steel, tinplate, wire; p. (1960) *18,428.*
Monfalcone, *commune*, N.E. Italy; chemicals, shipbldg., cotton mills; p. (1948) *19,634*
Monferrato, *low hills*, Piedmont, N. Italy; S. and S.E. of Turin between valleys of R. Po and R. Tanaro; celebrated vineyards, produce Asti Spumante wines; alt. never exceeds 1,500 ft.
Monforte, *t.*, Galicia, Spain; soap, linen; p. (1957) *21,682.*
Monghyr, *dist.*, Bihar, India; a. 3,975 sq. m.; agr., mica; p. (1961) *3,387,082.*
Mongol-Buryat, A.S.S.R., U.S.S.R.; E. of L. Baikal; cattle breeding.
Mongolia, *vast elevated plateau*, in heart of Asia between China and U.S.S.R. *See* **Mongolian People's Republic and Inner Mongolia.**
Mongolia, Inner, *see* **Inner Mongolia.**
Mongolian People's Republic (Outer Mongolia), *indep. st.*, Asia; bordered by China on W., S. and E. and by U.S.S.R. on N.; mainly plateau 5,000–10,000 ft. with Altai mtns. in N.W. and Gobi Desert in S.; watered by numerous Rs.; many Ls.; cap. Ulan Bator; livestock, wool, hides, skins; gold, coal; close links with U.S.S.R.; a. estd. 1,750,000 sq. m.; p. estd. *3,000,000–5,000,000.*
Monmouth, *co.*, Eng.; coal, iron, steel, agr.; a. 546 sq. m.; p. (1961) *443,689.*
Monmouth, *co. t.*, *mun. bor.*, Monmouth, Eng.; at confluence of Rs. Wye and Monnow; mkt. ctr.; tinplate, timber, crushed limestone, wrought ironwk.; p. (1961) *5,505.*
Monmouth, *t.*, Ill., U.S.A.; mnfs., coal; p. (1960) *10,372.*
Monnow, *R.*, Monmouth and Hereford, Eng.; trib. of R. Wye; length 28 m.
Monongahela, *R.*, W. Va., U.S.A.; joins Allegheny R. at Pittsburgh to form Ohio R.
Monongahela City, Penns., U.S.A.; mining, natural gas; p. (1960) *8,388.*
Monopoli, *spt.*, Apulia, Italy; oil, wine, fruit, flour tr.; p. *26,725.* [p. *18,625.*
Monreale, *t.*, Sicily, Italy; cath.; fruit, almonds;
Monroe, *c.*, La., U.S.A.; cotton ctr., natural gas, paper, printing ink; p. (1960) *52,219.*
Monroe, *t.*, Mich., U.S.A.; paper, machin.; p. (1960) *22,968.*
Monroe, *t.*, N.C., U.S.A.; marble quarries; mftg.; p. (1960) *10,882.*
Monrovia, *cap.*, *spt.*, Liberia, Africa; at mouth of R. St. Paul; exp. rubber, palm oil; p. *18,000.*
Mons, *t.*, Belgium; on R. Trouville; cath.; rly. junction; coal, cotton, rayon, iron, engin., glass, brewing, radios, aluminium ware; p. (1962) *27,062.*
Monselice, *t.*, Italy; mnfs.; p. *4,143*
Monserrat or Montserrat, *mtn.*, Spain; alt. 4,000 ft.
Monsummano, *t.*, Italy; N.W. of Florence; health resort; some mnfs.; p. *9,125.*
Montagnana, *t.*, Italy; p. *12,100.*
Mont Blanc, *mtn.*, Alps; on confines of Italy and France; alt. 15,782 ft.; longest road tunnel in world (opened to traffic 1965) linking Courmayeur (Italy) and Chamonix (France), length 7½ m.
Mont Cenis Pass, W. Alps; on bdy. between France and Italy; approached from W. by Isère–Arc valleys, from E. by Dora Riparia; alt. 6,876 ft.
Mont Cenis Tunnel, W. Alps; on bdy. between France and Italy; carries main rly. from Lyons to Turin under Col de Fréjus; approached from W. by Isère–Arc valleys, from E. by Dora Riparia; opened 1871; length 7½ m.
Mont-d'Or, *mtns.*, France; highest peak, 6,188 ft.
Mont Genèvre, *mtn.*, Cottian Alps, France; alt. 6,100 ft. [power project.
Mont St. Michel, *I.*, N. France; tourist ctr; tidal
Montalcino, *t.*, Italy; industl.; p. *9,925.*
Montana, *st.*, U.S.A.; cap. Helena; Rocky Mtns.; copper, silver, gold, lead; pastoral, agr.; a. 147,138 sq. m.; p. (1960) *674,767.*
Montargis, *t.*, Loiret, France; hosiery, chemicals, rubber; p. (1954) *15,117.*
Montauban, *t.*, Tarn-et-Garonne, France; on R. Tarn; cath.; silk, agr. produce, wines; p. (1962) *43,401.*
Montbéliard, *t.*, Doubs, France; S. of Belfort; watch, textiles, mnfs., agr. tr.; p. (1954) *17,023.*
Montceau-les-Mines, *t.*, Saône-et-Loire, France; coal, textiles, metal-working; p. (1954) *28,308.*
Montclair, *t.*, N.J., U.S.A.; residtl. suburb of New York; paper goods mnfs.; p. (1960) *43,129.*
Mont-de-Marsan, *t.*, Landes, France; p. (1954) *17,120.*
Monte Bello Is., *gr.*, off N.W. cst., Australia, about 85 m. N. of pt. of Onslow; first British atomic weapon exploded here 3 Oct. 1952.
Monte Carlo, *t.*, Monaco; tourist resort, casino; p. (1961) *9,516.* [alt. 9,583 ft.
Monte Corno, *mtn.*, Italy; in Central Apennines;
Monte Gargano, *peninsula*, S. Italy; projects into Adriatic Sea nr. plain of Foggia; formed by limestone plateau, alt. over 3,000 ft.; pasture on upper slopes, woodland on lower slopes; a. approx. 400 sq. m. [p. *5,575.*
Monte Maggiore, *t.*, Sicily, Italy; agr. interests;
Monte Perdu, *mtn.*, Pyrenees, Spain; alt. 10,997 ft.
Monte Rosa, *gr.*, Pennine Alps, on border of Italy and Switzerland; highest peak 15,203 ft.
Monte Rotondo, *highest mtn.*, Corsica; alt. 9,071 ft.
Monte Sant-Angelo, *t.*, Italy; pilgrim ctr.; p. *24,550.*
Monte Viso, *mtn.*, Cottian Alps, Italy; alt. 12,605 ft.
Montecatini, *t.*, Italy; nr. Volterra; p. *9,125.*
Montecristi, *t.*, W. Ecuador; Panama hats; copra mkt.; p. (estd. 1962) *4,000.*
Montefrío, *t.*, Spain; W. of Granada; cas.; alcohol, soap, cotton mnfs.; p. *12,000.*
Montégnée, *commune*, Liége prov., E. Belgium; mftg. sub. Liége; p. (1962) *11,503.*
Montego Bay, *spt.*, Jamaica; famous for its beauty; p. (1947) *11,547.*
Monteleone di Calabria, *t.*, Italy; cas.; p. *15,675.*
Montélimar, *t.*, Drôme, France; nr. R. Rhône; bricks, tiles, "nougat," coal-mining; p. (1954) *16,632.*
Montenegro, *dist.*, Jugoslavia; agr., pastoral; cap. Cetinje; a. 13,837 sq. m.; p. (1960) *489,000.*
Montereau-faut-Yonne, *t.*, Seine-et-Marne, France; on R. Seine; agr. tools, footwear, brick mftg.; p. (1954) *10,119.*
Monterey, *c.*, Cal., S. of San Francisco; resort of artists and writers; impt. sardine indus., fruit, and veg. canneries; p. (1960) *22,618.*
Monteria, *t.*, cap. Cordoba, Colombia, S. America; tobacco, cacao, cotton, sugar; p. (1959) *96,150.*
Monterrey, *t.*, *cap.*, Nuevo León, Mexico; cath.; textiles, brewing, ironwks., minerals; thermo-elec. plant; sheet metal; p. (1960) *596,993.*
Montespertoli, *mkt. t.*, Italy; S.W. Florence; p. *11,850.* [p. *15,300.*
Montevarchi, *t.*, Italy; on R. Arno; industl.;
Montevideo, *spt.*, *cap.*, Uruguay; on N. cst. of La Plata estuary; univ.; livestock prod. mnfs. and exp.; p. (estd. 1956) *922,885.*
Montezuma, *t.*, Ga., U.S.A.; mkt. for winter mkt. garden produce, cottonseed oil; p. (1950) *2,921.*
Montgomery, *co.*, N.E. Wales; cap. Montgomery; a. 797 sq. m.; p. (1961) *44,228.*
Montgomery, *co. t.*, *mun. bor.*, Montgomery, N.E. Wales; in upper Severn valley, 8 m. N.E. of Newtown; agr. mkt.; p. (1961) *970.*
Montgomery, *c.*, *cap.*, Ala., U.S.A.; cotton, timber, fertilisers; comm. ctr.; rly. wks.; p. (1960) *134,393.*
Montgomery, *t.*, W. Punjab, Pakistan; livestock; leather, cotton; p. (1961) *25,100.*
Montichiari, *commune*, Lombardy, N. Italy; mftg.; p. *11,650.*
Montignies-sur-Sambre, *t.*, Belgium; coal, iron-wks.; p. (1962) *24,092.*
Montigny-lès-Metz, *commune*, Moselle, France; residtl. sub. Metz; botanic gardens; p. (1954) *19,271.*
Montilla, *commune*, S. Spain; agr., wines; textiles, pottery, soap; p. (1957) *24,002.*
Montluçon, *t.*, Allier, France; on R. Cher; agr. ctr.; machin., cutlery, chemicals, mirrors; p. (1962) *58,855.* [*14,094.*
Montmorency, *t.*, Seine-et-Oise, France; p. (1954)
Montoro, *c.*, S.W. Spain; on R. Guadalquivir; agr. prod., olive oil; p. (1957) *15,396.*
Montpelier, *c.*, cap. Vt., U.S.A., on Winooski R.; varied inds.; p. *8,000.*
Montpellier, *t.*, cap. Hérault, France; univ., wines, fruit, silk, chemicals, agr.; p. (1962) *123,367.*

Montreal, *c.*, *spt.*, Quebec, Canada; at confluence of Ottawa and St. Lawrence Rs.; caths., univ.; rly. ctr.; brewing, tobacco, footwear, oil refining; comm. ctr.; lgst. c. and spt. in Canada; p. (1961) *2,109,509*.

Montreuil-sous-Bois, *t.*, Seine, France; mnfs., fruit; p. (1962) *92,316*.

Montreux, *t.*, Switzerland; on L. Geneva; health resort; p. *19,000*.

Montrose, *spt.*, *burgh*, Angus, Scot.; on E. cst. at mouth of S. Esk R.; chemicals, and rope wks., linen, fisheries; p. (1961), *10,702*.

Montrouge, *t.*, Seine, France; paper, perfumes, precision tools; p. (1962) *45,324*.

Montserrat, *I.*, Leeward Is., W.I.; limes, fruits, carrots and onions; ch. t. Plymouth; a. 32 sq. m.; p. (estd. 1965) *13,000*.

Montville, *t.*, S.E. Conn., U.S.A.; paper, textiles; p. (1960) *1,060*.

Monza, *t.*, Lombardy, Italy; cath.; comm., textiles, leather, hats; p. (1961) *84,445*.

Moonie, *t.*, Queensland, Australia; 200 m. W. of Brisbane; oilfields; pipeline to Lytton, at mouth of Brisbane R.

Moonta, *t.*, S. Australia; on E. side of Spencer's G., 70 m. S. of Pt. Pirie; once impt. copper-mines, now declining.

Moorea, *one of the ch. Is.*, the Society gr., Pac. Oc.; a. 50 sq. m.; p. (1962) *4,147*.

Moorfoot Hills, *range*, Peebles and Midlothian, Scot.; alt. 2,136 ft.

Moorhead, *t.*, W. Minn., U.S.A.; potatoes, dairying, poultry; p. (1960) *22,934*. [Bay.

Moose R., Ontario, Canada; flows to James

Moosehead, *L.*, Me., U.S.A.; source of Kennebec R.; 35 m. long, 10 m. wide.

Moose Jaw, *c.*, Saskatchewan, Canada; rly. junction; agr. ctr.; agr. implements, oil refining; p. (1961) *33,206*.

Moquegua, *dep.*, S. Peru; cotton, maize, fruit; cap. M.; a. 5,549 sq. m.; p. (1961) *51,315*.

Moquegua, *t.*, Peru; wines; p. (1961) *3,885*.

Mora, *t.*, Spain; industl.; p. (1957) *10,844*.

Morar, *c.*, Gwalior, Madhya Pradesh, India; p. inc. Gwalior (*q.v.*).

Moratalla, *t.*, Spain; N.W. of Murcia; cloth, alcohol, wines; p. *14,536*.

Moratuwa, *t.*, Ceylon; p. (1946) *50,700*.

Morava, *R.*, Czechoslovakia and Austria; trib. of R. Danube; length 212 m.

Morava, *R.*, Jugoslavia; rises in Crna Gora (S. of Dinaric Alps), flows N. into R. Danube 50 m. below Belgrade; valley used by trunk rly. from Belgrade to Thessaloniki (Salonika) and Athens, Sofia and Istanbul (Constantinople); length approx. 350 m.

Moravia, *old prov.*, Czechoslovakia; agr., forestry, coal, textiles; p. inc. Bohemia (1962) *9,566,753*.

Moray, *co.*, N.E. Scot.; cereals, fisheries, distilling, woollens; co. burgh, Elgin; a. 482 sq. m.; p. (1961) *49,156*.

Moray Firth, *arm* of N. Sea; on Scottish E. cst., between Ross and Cromarty, and Nairn, Moray cos.

Morbihan, *dep.*, France; on Bay of Biscay; agr. (apples), mining, fishing; cap. Vannes; a. 2,739 sq. m.; p. (1962) *530,833*.

Morceux, *t.*, Landes, France; p. (1954) *3,013*.

Mordov A.S.S.R., U.S.S.R.; between Rs. Oka and Volga; agr.; a. 9,843 sq. m.; p. (1959) *1,000,000*.

Morea, *see* **Peloponnisos**.

Morecambe and Heysham, *t.*, *mun. bor.*, N. Lancs, Eng.; on S. shore of Morecambe Bay; Morecambe, holiday resort; Heysham, port for N. Ireland and oil refinery; p. (1961) *40,950*.

Moree, *t.*, N.S.W., Australia; in agr. and grazing region; mkt.; p. (1947) *4,361*.

Morelia, *c.*, *cap.*, Michostán, Mexico; cath.; textiles, sugar; p. (1960) *100,828*.

Morelos, *inland st.*, Mexico: mtns., forested; cap. Cuernavaca; a. 1,916 sq. m.; p. (1960) *386,264*. [(1963) *214,879*.

Möre Og Romsdal, *dist.*, Norway; a. 5,812 sq. m.;

Moret-sur-Loing (Moret les Sablons), *t.*, 40 m. S. of Paris on picturesque R. Loing.

Morez, *t.*, S.E. Jura, France; precision instruments, optical equipment, winter sports.

Morgan, *t.*, *R. pt.*, S. Australia; on R. Murray, where it suddenly turns S. approx. 150 m. from its mouth; handles transhipment of Murray and Darling R. traffic to rail for despatch to Adelaide.

Morgantown, *t.*, W. Va., U.S.A.; coal, oil, gas fields; chemicals, heavy ind.; p. (1960) *22,487*.

Morioka, *c.*, N. Honshu, Japan; textiles, ironwks.; p. (1955) *142,875*.

Morlaix, *spt.*, Finistère, France; tobacco, paper, brewing, agr.; p. (1954) *15,037*.

Morley, *t.*, *mun. bor.*, W.R. Yorks, Eng.; 3 m. S.W. of Leeds; woollens, coal-mining, stone quarrying, tanning; p. (1961) *40,322*.

Morocco, *ind. sovereign st.*, since March 1956 (formerly French and Spanish prots.) N.W. Africa; cap. Rabat; chief ts. Casablanca, Marrakesh, Tangier, Fez, Meknès, Tetuan, Oujda, Safi, Mina Hassan Tani; agr., forest, and animal prod.; fruits; phosphates, manganese, iron ore, lead, zinc; coal, petroleum, sugar refining; a. 171,000 sq. m.; p. (1961) *11,626,000*.

Morogoro, *t.*, Tanzania, E. Africa; on E. edge of Central African plateau, alt. approx. 3,000 ft., 110 m. by rail W. of Dar-es-Salaam; ctr. of sisal- and cotton-growing a.

Morón de la Frontera, *commune*, S.W. Spain; olives; iron ore; marble; p. (1957) *30,137*.

Morotai I., N. of Molucca, Indonesia.

Morpeth, *mun. bor.*, Northumberland, Eng.; nr. Newcastle; coal-mining, iron; p. (1961) *12,430*.

Morrinsville, *t.*, N.I. N.Z.; agr. ctr.; p. (1961) *4,111*.

Morriston, *vil.*, Glamorgan, S. Wales; on R. Tawe, 2 m. N.E. of Swansea; zinc smelting and refining steel. [p. (1960) *17,712*.

Morristown, *t.*, N.J., U.S.A.; holiday ctr., fruit;

Morrisville, *bor.*, Penns., U.S.A.; on Delaware R.; rubber prod.; p. (1960) *7,790*.

Morro Velho, *mng-dist.*, Minas Geraes, Brazil; in Serra do Espinhaco, 10 m. S. of Belo Horizonte; deep rich gold-mines; ch. t. Nova Lima.

Mors, *I.*, N. Jutland, Denmark; a. 138 sq. m.; p. (1960) *26,766*.

Mortlake, *t.*, Surrey, Eng.; on R. Thames; residtl. sub. of London; cement, pottery.

Morven, *mtn.*, Aberdeen, Scot.; nr Ballater; alt. 2,862 ft.

Morven, *mtn.*, Caithness, Scot.; nr. Berriedale; alt. 2,313 ft.

Moscow, *c.*, R.S.F.S.R.; *cap.*, U.S.S.R.; on R. Moskva; caths., univ., Kremlin, palaces; leading cultural, political and comm. ctr.; textiles, steel, engin., oil refining, chemicals; p. (1964) *6,388,000*; Greater M. (1962) *7,208,000*.

Moscow Sea (Ucha Reservoir), *artificial L.*, R.S.F.S.R.; created behind dam on R. Volga at Ivankovo; supplies water to Moscow, maintains level on Moscow–Volga Canal, and supplies water to 8 hydro-elec. power-stas.; a. 127 sq. m.

Moscow–Volga Canal, R.S.F.S.R.; links R. Volga at Ivankovo with Khimki suburb of Moscow forms part of Leningrad–Moscow inland waterway; opened 1937; length 80 m.

Moselle, *dep.*, N.E. France; cap. Metz; a. 2,40 sq. m.; p. (1962) *919,412*.

Moselle, *R.*, France and Germany; trib. of R Rhine; length 328 m.; canalised betwee Thionville and Coblenz (168 m.).

Moshi, *t.*, Tanzania, E. Africa; on S.E. flank c Mt. Kilimanjaro; ctr. of coffee-growing dist. a alt. approx. 5,500 ft.; despatches coffee by ra to Tanga or Mombasa. [249 m

Moskva, *R.*, U.S.S.R.; trib. of R. Oka; lengt

Moss, *spt.*, Norway; pulp, paper, machin., texti inds.; p. (1960) *20,461*.

Mossamedes, *spt.*, Angola, Africa; exp. rubber fishing, fertilisers; p. *8,977*.

Mossel Bay, *spt.*, C. Prov., S. Africa; oyster whaling; wool, cereals; p. (1960) *12,178* in *4,333* whites.

Mossend, *t.*, Lanark, Scot.; nr. Glasgow; iron an steel; p. *6,000*.

Mossgiel, *t.*, S.I., N.Z.; woollens; p. (1961) *6,46*

Mossley, *mun. bor.*, Lancs, Eng.; 3 m. E. c Oldham; mkt. t., textiles, iron and steel; (1961) *9,795*. [*44,49*

Most, *t.*, CSSR.; lignite, chemicals; p. (1961

Mostaganem, *t.*, Algeria; vineyards, flour, leathe p. (1948) *53,464*.

Mostar, *t.*, Herzegovina, Jugoslavia; on I Naretva; bauxite, lignite, aluminium plant; (1960) *43,000*.

Mosul, *t.*, Iraq; on R. Tigris; comm. ctr., imp during crusades; agr. prod., livestock, textile p. (1960) *341,000*.

Motala, *t.*, on L. Vättern, Sweden; radio sta.; e gin., woollen goods; p. (1961) *27,148*.

Motherwell and Wishaw, *burgh*, Lanark, Scot.; in Clyde valley, 15 m. S.E. of Glasgow; coal, iron, steel, machin., engin., silk, nylon; p. (1961) *72,799.* [p. (1957) *23,420.*

Motril, *spt.*, Spain; minerals, cotton, sugar, fruits;

Mottarone, Monte, *mtn.*, Italy, between L. Maggiore and L. Orta; alt. 4,892 ft. [*3,310.*

Motueka, *t.*, S.I., N.Z.; fruit, tobacco; p. (1961)

Moulins, *t.*, cap. Allier, France; on R. Allier; cath., ruined château; timber wks., brewing; p. (1954) *24,437.*

Moulmein, *spt.*, Burma on R. Salween; rice, timber; p. (1955) *101,720.*

Moundsville, *c.*, W. Va., U.S.A.; on Ohio R.; coal, glass, zinc; p. (1960) *15,163.*

Mount Adams, *peak*, White Mtns., N.H., U.S.A.; alt. 5,679 ft. [fruit.

Mount Barker, *t.*, extreme S.W. of W. Australia;

Mount Carmel, *bor.*, Penns., U.S.A.; on Wabash R.; coal-mng., clothing mftg.; p. (1960) *10,760.*

Mount Clemens, *t.*, Mich., U.S.A.; on Clinton R.; mineral springs; p. (1960) *21,016.*

Mount Desert, *I.*, Me., U.S.A.; a. 100 sq. m.; mtns.; summer resort.

Mount Gambier, *t.*, S. Australia; pastoral, agr. ctr.; p. (1961) *15,354.*

Mount Holly, *t.*, N.J., U.S.A.; textiles, clothes, leather; p. (1960) *13,271.*

Mount Isa, *t.*, W. Queensland, Australia; in Selwyn Range 80 m. W. of Cloncurry, linked by rly. through Cloncurry to E. cst. at Townsville; silver–lead mines; p. (1961) *13,315.*

Mount Kennedy, *mtn.*, Yukon, 3 m. E. of Mt. Hubbard on Alaskan border; alt. 14,000 ft.

Mount Lofty Range, *mtn. range*, S. Australia; lies immediately E. of Adelaide approx. 5 m. from St. Vincent G.; forms barrier to routes leaving Adelaide N.E. and E.; lower slopes support vineyards and outer suburbs of Adelaide; rises to over 3,000 ft.

Mount Pleasant, *t.*, Mich., U.S.A.; oil, lumber, sugar-beet, dairy prod.; p. (1960) *14,875.*

Mount Prospect, *t.*, Ill., U.S.A.; p. (1960) *18,906.*

Mount Vernon, *c.*, Ill., U.S.A.; timber, flour, woollens, coal; p. (1960) *15,566.*

Mount Vernon, *c.*, N.Y., U.S.A., on Bronx R.; sub. of N.Y.; residtl.; p. (1960) *76,010.* Takes its name from George Washington's house on the Potomac, in Virginia, 15 m. S. of Washington, D.C.

Mount Vernon, *c.*, Ohio, U.S.A.; on Kokosing R.; timber goods, mnfs.; p. (1960) *13,284.*

Mountain Ash, *urb. dist.*, Glamorgan, Wales; in narrow valley 3 m. S.E. of Aberdare; coal; p. (1961) *29,590.*

Mountain Province, *prov.*, N. Luzon, Philippines; rice, metal working; a. 5,458 sq. m.; p. *296,874.*

Mountain View, *t.*, Cal., U.S.A.; p. (1960) *30,889.*

Mountmellick, *t.*, *rural dist.*, Laoighis, Ireland; mkt., tanning, malting; p. (rural dist. 1961) *22,596.*

Mount's Bay, *inlet*, S. cst. Cornwall, Eng.; 20 m. wide; fishery grounds.

Mourenx, *t.*, S.W. Aquitaine, France; nr. Lacq; new town in oil dist. [2,796 ft.

Mourne Mtns., Down, N. Ireland; highest peak,

Mouscron, *t.*, Belgium; cotton- and wool-weaving; p. (1962) *36,595.*

Mouse or Souris, *R.* Canada and U.S.A.; trib. of Assiniboine R.; length 500 m.

Moy, *R.*, Mayo and Sligo, Ireland; length 35 m.

Moyeuvre-Grande, *t.*, Moselle, France; p. (1954) *10,707.*

Mozambique, *Portuguese col.*, E. Africa; sugar, oil-nuts, cotton, maize; oil refining, cement; cap. Lourenço Marques; a. 302,327 sq. m.; p. (1962) *6,592,988.*

Mozambique Channel, *strait*, Indian Ocean; separates Malagasy from mainland of Africa; length 1,000 m., width from 250 to 600 m.

Mozambique Current, *ocean current*, flows N. to S. along E. cst. of Mozambique and Natal, E. Africa; relatively warm water.

Mozdok, *t.*, R.S.F.S.R.; on Rostov–Baku rly.; oil pipe-lines; p. *14,008.*

Much Wenlock, *see* **Wenlock.**

Muck, *I.*, Inner Hebrides, Scot.; S. of Eigg.

Mühlhausen, *t.*, Erfurt, E. Germany; on R. Unstrut; textiles, machin., tobacco; p. (1963) *45,362.*

Muizenberg, *t.*, S.W. Cape Prov., S. Africa; tourist resort; p. *10,000.*

Mukachevo (Munkács), *t.*, Ukrainian S.S.R.; furniture, textiles, tobacco; p. (1956) *44,000.*

Mukden (Shenyang), *c.*, *cap.*, Liaoning, N.E. China; on Hun-Ho in narrowest part of lowland with hilly country on both sides; impt. rly. junction with main routes N. to Harbin and Trans-Siberian Rly., S. to Peking, Luta and into Korea; gr. comm. and political ctr.; p. (1956) *2,290,000.*

Mula, *t.*, Spain; tr. ctr.; p. (1957) *15,127.*

Mulde, *R.*, Germany; trib. of R. Elbe; length 130 m.

Mulhacén, *mtn.*, Sierra Nevada range, Spain; alt. 11,420 ft. (highest peak Europe, outside Alps).

Mülheim-an-der-Ruhr, *t.*, N. Rhine–Westphalia, Germany; on R. Ruhr; cas.; coal-mining, iron, steel, tobacco, engin., elec., oil refining; airport; p. (1963) *189,900.*

Mulhouse, *t.*, Haut-Rhin, France; textiles, chemicals, machin.; p. (1962) *110,735.*

Mull, *I.*, Argyll, Scot., included in Hebrides; a. 357 sq. m.; granite, pastoral farming; ch. t. Tobermory.

Mull of Galloway, S. point of Wigtown, Scot.

Mullet, The, *peninsula*, W. cst. Mayo, Ireland.

Mullingar, *co. t.*, Westmeath, Ireland; on Brosna R.; mkt., agr. ctr., tanning; p. (1961) *5,894.*

Multan, *div.*, W. Punjab, Pakistan; ch. t., Multan; p. (1961) *6,953,000.*

Multan, *t.*, W. Punjab, Pakistan; on R. Chenab; carpets, silks, pottery; steel plant; thermal sta.; natural gas pipeline to Lyallpur; p. (1961) *358,000.*

Mumbles, *holiday resort*, residtl. dist., Glamorgan, S. Wales; within Swansea bor.; p. *10,000.*

Muncie, *t.*, Ind., U.S.A.; on White R.; iron, steel, glass and paper; p. (1960) *68,603.*

Münden, *t.*, Germany; on R. Weser; picturesque medieval t., cas.; leather and rubber goods tobacco fact.; p. *22,000.*

Munhall, *t.*, Penns., U.S.A.; p. (1960) *17,312.*

Munich (München), *c.*, cap. Bavaria, Germany; on R. Isar; univ., cath., palace, museum, "English Garden"; comm. ctr.; scientific instruments; machin., brewing, textiles, tobacco, chemicals, elec. engin.; film studios; route ctr.; p. (1963) *157,300.*

Münster, *c.*, N. Rhine–Westphalia, Germany; cath., univ., cas.; leather, metal machin., rly. junction; p. (1963) *189,700.*

Munster, *prov.*, S.W. Ireland; includes cos. Waterford, Kerry, Cork, Limerick, Clare, Tipperary; a. 9,475 sq. m.; p. (1961) *848,368.*

Muonio, *R.*, part of boundary between Finland and Sweden; flows into G. of Bothnia.

Mur, *R.*, Austria; trib. of R. Drava; length 250 m. [Canada.

Murchinson, *C.*, Hall Peninsula, Baffin I.,

Murchison, *R.*, W. Australia; length 800 m.

Murchison, *peak*, Rocky Mtns., B.C., Canada; alt. 13,500 ft.

Murchison Falls, on Victoria Nile, Uganda.

Murcia, *prov.*, S.E. Spain; former kingdom; minerals, cereals, fruit; cap. Murcia; a. 4,369 sq. m.; p. (1959) *808,610.*

Murcia, *c.*, *cap.*, Murcia, Spain; on R. Segura; cath., univ.; silk, glass, hats, gloves; p. (1960) *250,000.*

Murfreesboro, *t.*, Tenn., U.S.A.; p. (1960) *18,991.*

Murg, *R.*, Germany; trib. of R. Rhine; length 40 m.

Murgab or Murghab, *R.*, Afghanistan; flows 250 m. to desert swamps.

Murmansk, *spt.*, R.S.F.S.R., U.S.S.R.; on Kola-peninsula; ice-free throughout year; engin., elec. power; fishing, shipbldg.; p. (1963) *254,000.* [engin.; p. (1959) *73,000.*

Muron, *t.*, R.S.F.S.R.; mkt. gardening; textiles,

Muroran, *t.*, Hokkaido, Japan; on W. cst.; p. (1960) *145,679.*

Muros, *commune*, N.W. Spain; agr., flour, soap, textiles; fishing; p. (1957) *11,155.*

Murphysboro, *c.*, Ill., U.S.A.; on Big Muddy R.; p. (1960) *8,673.*

Murray, *R.*, separates N.S.W. and Victoria, Australia; lgst. R. in continent, length 1,600 m.

Murray, R., dist., N.E. Victoria, Australia.

Murray, *t.*, N. Utah, U.S.A.; sub. Salt Lake City; lead smelting; p. (1960) *16,806.*

Murrumbidgee, *R.*, N.S.W., Australia; trib. of R. Murray; length 1,350 m.

Murshidabad, *t.*, W. Bengal, India; silk, weaving,

ivory carving, gold and silver embroidery; p. (1961) *16,990*.

Murupara, *t.*, N.I., N.Z.; in Kaingaroa Forest a.; timber inds.; p. (1961) *1,560*.

Murwillumbah, *t.*, N.S.W., Australia; dairying, fruit, timber.

Murzuk, *t.*, Libya, N. Africa; in Fezzan Oasis; tr. ctr.; p. *1,000*.

Mus, *t.*, Turkey; W. of L. Van; p. (1960) *12,015*.

Musa Jebel, *mtn.*, Egypt; alt. 7,375 ft.; identified with the Biblical Sinai.

Muscat and Oman, *sultanate*, Arabia; agr., fruit (dates); cap. Muscat; a. 82,000 sq. m.; p. *550,000*.

Muscat, *t.*, *cap.*, Muscat and Oman, Arabia; on S. cst. of G. of Oman; sm. tr.; pearl fisheries; p. *5,500*.

Muscatine, *c.*, Iowa, U.S.A.; on Mississippi R.; meat packing, timber ind.; p. (1960) *20,997*.

Muscle Shoals, *rapids*, in Tennessee R., U.S.A.; site of Wilson dam.

Musgrave Range, *mtns.*, on bdy. between S. Australia and N. Terr., Australia; isolated highland in ctr. of continent; arid; rise to over 3,000 ft.

Muskegon, *c.*, Mich., U.S.A.; engin., motor cars, accessories, aeroplane engines; p. (1960) *46,485*.

Muskingum, *R.*, Ohio, U.S.A.; trib. of Ohio R.; length 240 m.

Muskogee, *t.*, Okla., U.S.A.; rly. wks., oil refining, cotton, flour; p. (1960) *38,059*.

Musselburgh, *anc. burgh*, Midlothian, Scot.; on S. side of Firth of Forth at mouth of R. Esk; wire, cables, nets, twine; paper mkg.; golf course; hist. bldgs; now virtually sub. of Edinburgh; p. (1961) *17,273*.

Mussel Shell, *R.*, Mont., U.S.A., trib. of Missouri R.

Mussomeli, *t.*, Sicily; agr. interests; p. *12,500*.

Mutankiang (Mudanjiang), *c.*, Heilungkiang prov., China; pulp, paper, machin., flour milling; p. (1953) *151,000*.

Muttra or Mathura, *t.*, Uttar Pradesh, India; on R. Jumna; Hindu ctr.; p. (1961) *125,258*.

Muz Tagh, *mtn. pass*, Karakoram Mtns., E. Turkestan; alt. 18,980 ft.

Muzaffarpur, *t.*, Bihar, India; univ.; p. (1961) *109,048*.

Muzo, *mun.*, central Colombia; emerald-mining; p. (1959) *5,000*.

Mwanza, *t.*, N. Tanzania, E. Africa; pt. on L. Victoria; rly. terminus; p. *6,000*.

Mweelrea, *mtn.*, Mayo, Ireland; alt. 2,688 ft.

Mweru, *L.*, between Congo and N. Rhodesia; a. 2,700 sq. m.

Myaungmya, *dist.*, Lower Burma; ch. t. Patanawa; p. *7,773*.

Mycenae, *ancient c.*, Greece; ruined.

Mykonos, *I.*, N. Cyclades, Greece; p. *4,188*.

Mymensingh, *t.*, Bengal, Pakistan; rice, jute; p. (1961) *53,200*.

Mynyddislwyn, *t.*, *urb. dist.*, Monmouth, Eng.; in narrow valley of W. Ebbw R., 7 m. N.W. of Newport; coal-mng., elec. goods, kerb- and flagstones; p. (1961) *15,433*.

Mynydd-Mawr, *mtn.*, N. Wales; alt. 2,293 ft.

Myslowice, *t.*, Poland; nr. Katowice; rly. junction, coal, flax mills, bricks; p. (1960) *40,000*.

Mysore, *st.*, S. India; hydro. elec. power; gold, iron and steel, manganese; coffee, tea, cotton; cap. Bangalore; a. 74,210 sq. m.; p. (1961) *23,586,772*.

Mysore, *t.*, Mysore, India; univ.; carpets, comm. ctr.; p. (1961) *253,524*.

Mytishchi, *t.*, R.S.F.S.R., 12 m. N.E. Moscow; lorries, coaches; p. (1959) *99,000*.

Mytilene (Lesbos), *I.*, Greece, in Aegean Sea; highest point 3,080 ft.; olives, figs, lemons, oranges, grapes; antimony and marbles; ch. t. Mytilene; a. 618 sq. m.; p. (1951) *154,683*.

Mytilene, *cap.*, *spt.*, M.I., Greece; p. (1951) *27,125*.

Mzombe, *R.*, Kenya; trib. of Ruaha R.; length 110 m. [length 80 m.

Mzymta, *R.*, U.S.S.R.; flows to Black Sea;

N

Naab, *R.*, Bavaria, Germany; joins R. Danube nr. Ratisbon; length 90 m.

Naarden, *t.*, N. Holland, Neth.; nr. Amsterdam; destroyed by Spaniards 1572.

Naas, *mkt. t.*, *cap.*, Kildare, Ireland; former cap. Leinster; p. (1961) *4,021*.

Nabeul, *t.*, Tunisia, N. Africa; winter resort; p. *15,000*.

Nabi Saleh, *I.*, forming part of st. of Bahrein, Arabia; about 2 m. in circumference.

Nablus, *c.*, Jordan; N. of Jerusalem; nr. Old Testament c. of Shechem (Sichem, Sychem), the first Palestinian site mentioned in Genesis; Jacob's Well and Mt. Gerizim adjacent; p. (1961) *45,658*.

Nachod, *t.*, ČSSR.; on R. Mettaj at entrance to Lewin Nachod Pass; Prussian victory over Austrians 1866; cotton spinning, dyeing; p. (1961) *17,848*. [mftg.; p. (1960) *12,674*.

Nacogdoches, *t.*, Texas, U.S.A.; lignite; mkt.;

Naestved, *mkt. t.*, Själland, Denmark; paper, iron, footwear; p. (1960) *19,617*.

Nagaland, *st.*, India (1963); incorporates Naga Hills and Tuengsang; tribal a., formerly parts of Assam; adm. ctr. Kohima; a. 6,366 sq. m.; p. (1961) *369,000*.

Nagano, *c.*, central Honshu, Japan; on R. Sinanogawa, 100 m. S.W. of Niigata; silk mftg., reed organs; p. (1955) *152,547*.

Nagaoka, *t.*, N.W. Honshu, Japan; lge. oil production ctr.; p. (1960) *148,254*.

Nagapattinam, *t.*, Madras, India; at mouth of R. Vettar; rly. terminus; cotton, tobacco, groundnuts; p. (1961) *59,063*.

Nagasaki, *c.*, *spt.*, Kyushu, Japan; engin., shipbldg., enamelled and lacquer ware; 2nd c. to be destroyed by atomic bomb in Second World War; since rebuilt; p. (1960) *344,000*.

Nagh Hamadi (Nag' Hammâdi), *t.*, Upper U.A.R., N. Africa; on R. Nile 160 m. above Asyût; site of barrage (opened 1930) to regulate Nile flood and ensure irrigation of Girga prov.; barrage carries Cairo–Shellal rly. across Nile; junction for light rly. to Kharga Oasis.

Nagina, *t.*, Uttar Pradesh, India; sugar; p. (1961) *30,427*.

Nagoya, *t.*, Owari, Honshu, Japan; thriving cap., gr. tr., ch. ceramic ind. ctr., also cotton and silk factories; p. (1962) *1,689,000*.

Nagpur, *t.*, Maharashtra, India; univ.; Hindu temples; salt, grain, cotton; p. (1961) *643,659*.

Nagy Banya, *mining t.*, Romania; gold, silver, lead.

Nagy Becskerek, *industl. t.*, Jugoslavia; on R. Bega.

Nagyenyed, *t.*, Transylvania, Romania; on R. Maros; wood carving, educational ctr., famous for wine in Middle Ages. [p. (1962) *34,491*.

Nagykanizsa, *t.*, Hungary; distilling, milling;

Nagykikinda, *t.*, Torontál, Jugoslavia; flour and fruit ctr. [*25,250*.

Nagykörös, *industl. t.*, Hungary; wine; p. (1962)

Naha, *spt.*, Ryuku Is., Japan; U.S.A. control; mkt., textiles; U.S.A. air base; p. (1950) *44,779*.

Nahe, *R.*, Germany, flows 69 m. to R. Rhine, nr. Bingen. [(1961) *8,877*

Nahorkatiya, N.E. Assam, India; oil-fields; p.

Nailsworth, *t.*, *urb. dist.*, Gloucester, Eng.; in Cotswold Hills, 4 m. S. of Stroud; woollens; p. (1961) *3,614*. [Labrador

Nain, *settlement Moravian Brethren*, E. cst

Nairn, *mar. co.*, Scot., on Moray F. between Moray and Inverness; much moorland; farming quarries, fishing; a. 200 sq. m.; p. (1961) *8,421*

Nairn, *burgh*, Nairn, Scot.; on S. side of Moray Firth 13 m. N.E. of Inverness; resort, bricks road metal, chips, kerbs; p. (1961) *4,899*.

Nairobi, *c.*, *cap.*, Kenya, E. Africa; 327 m. from Mombasa; univ.; Uganda Rly. ctr.; lt. inds. big-game shooting; p. (1962) *266,700*.

Naivasha, *L.*, Kenya; located on floor of Gr African Rift Valley; alt. 6,000 ft.

Najibabad, *t.*, Uttar Pradesh, India; tr. in timber sugar, metal mnfs.; p. (1961) *34,310*.

Nakhichevan, *t.*, Azerbaydzhan S.S.R.; salt mine in a.; food and wine inds.; p. (1959) *25,000*.

Nakhodka, *t.*, R.S.F.S.R.; pt. on Sea of Japan 45 m. E. of Vladivostok; pt. of call for foreig ships; new town 1950; p. (1959) *63,000*.

Nakhon Ratchasima, *t.*, Thailand; copper mkt. p. *12,000*

Nakuru, *t.*, Kenya rift valley (6,024 ft.), E. Africa protected bird sanctuary (flamingoes) on L Nakuru; p. (1962) *37,900*.

Nakshov, *spt.*, Laaland I., Denmark; suga refining; p. (1960) *16,639*. [*87,000*

Nalchik, *t.*, R.S.F.S.R.; N. Caucasus; p. (1959

Namaqualand, *region*, south west cst. of Africa divided by Orange R. into Great N. in S.W Africa, and Little N. in Cape Province, Rep o S. Africa; semi-arid; a. 100,000 sq. m.; coppe diamonds.

Namangan, *industl. t.*, Uzbekistan, S.S.R.; on the Syr Daria; textiles, leather; p. (1959) *122,000*.

Nam Dinh, *impt. tr. t.*, N. Vietnam, nr. mouth of Red R.; p. *25,000*.

Namoi, *R.*, in N.S.W., Australia; trib. of Darling R.; 270 m.

Nampula, *ch. t.*, Mozambique, Port. E. Africa; p. *5,000*.

Namsos, *spt.*, central Norway; on Folda Fjord lumber, fish canning; textiles; copper; p. (1961) *5,269*.

Namur, *prov.*, Belgium; bordering on France; collieries, iron ore, woodland; a. 1,413 sq. m.; p. (1962) *370,870*.

Namur, *fortfd. c.*, Belgium; at confluence of Meuse and Sambre Rs.; p. (1962) *32,396*.

Nanaimo, *t.*, B.C., Canada; coal, timber, brewing; p. (1961) *14,135*.

Nanchang, *c.*, Kiangsi, China; on Kan-Kiang; tea, rice, cotton; p. (1963) *398,000*.

Nanchung (Nanchong), *c.*, Szechwan, China; agr. tr. ctr.; p. (1953) *165,000*.

Nancy, *ch. t.*, Meurthe-et-Moselle, France; old cap. Lorraine; gr. industl. activity, cottons, woollens, chemicals, embroidery; p. (1962) *133,532*

Nanda Devi, *mtn.*, Uttar Pradesh, India; alt. 25,645 ft.; first climbed by British team, 1936.

Nanded, *t.*, Maharashtra, India; on R. Godovari; muslins and tr. ctr.; p. (1961) *81,087*.

Nanga Parbat, *mtn.*, N.W. Kashmir, India, in W. Himalayas; alt. 26,660 ft.

Nanking (Nanjing), *gr. c.*, Kiangsu, China; on Yangtze-kiang; cap. during Kuomintang régime, 1928–49; famous seat of learning; cotton cloth, silk, ink; contains tombs of founders of the Ming dynasty; p. (estd. 1952) *1,020,000*.

Nanling (Nanshan), *mtns.*, S. China; form divide between Rs. flowing N. to Yangtze-kiang and S. to Si-kiang; crossed by historic Cheling and Meiling Passes; alt. mainly below 6,000 ft.

Nanning, *cap., former treaty pt.*, Kwangsi, China; on the Yu-kiang; ch. mkt. on S. frontier; p. (1953) *195,000*.

Nan Shan, *mtns.*, Central China; between Yangtze-kiang basin and that of the Si-kiang.

Nanterre, *t.*, Seine, France; nr. Paris; noted for cakes; aluminium mftg.; p. (1962) *83,528*.

Nantes, *t.*, cap. Loire-Atlantique, France; on R. Loire; univ.; locomotives, biscuit mftg., wood pulp, bell foundries, machine wks., chemicals, sugar, oil, textiles, stained glass, nursery gardens; p. (1962) *246,227*.

Nanticoke, *t.*, Penns., U.S.A.; on Susquehanna R.; anthracite, canning; p. (1960) *15,601*.

Nantucket, *I.*, Mass., U.S.A.; official W. end of trans-Atlantic sea-crossing; summer resort; fishing; p. (1960) *2,804*.

Nantung (Nantong), *c.*, Kiangsu, China; on N. bank of Yangtze-kiang estuary 20 m. N.W. of Hai-men; p. (1953) *260,000*.

Nantwich, *mkt. t.*, *urb. dist.*, Cheshire, Eng.; on R. Weaver, 3 m. S.W. of Crewe; brine baths, fox-hunting ctr.; clothing, food prodn.; p. (1961) *10,454*.

Nantyglo and Blaina, *urb. dist.*, Monmouth, Eng.; in narrow valley 2 m. N. of Abertillery; coal, iron, footwear, rubber prods.; p. (1961) *10,950*.

Nao, *C.*, E. cst. Spain; opposite Balearic Is.

Napier, *c.*, *cap.*, Hawke's Bay, N.I. N.Z.; fine esplanade, suffered great damage by earthquake 1931, rebuilt by 1933; exp. frozen meat; p. (1961) *32,767*.

Naples, (Napoli), *c.*, *spt.*, Campania, S. Italy; on Bay of N., at foot of Vesuvius, opposite site of ancient Pompeii; sanctuary of Madonna di Pompeii; grotto of Pozzuoli, Castel del Ovo, grand cath.; votive church of San Francesco di Paola; monastery of San Martino; subject to earthquakes and volcanic eruptions; impt. shipping; mnfs.; macaroni, vermicelli, wine, olive-oil, shipbldg.; p. (1961) *1,179,608*.

Napo, *R.*, Ecuador; trib. of Amazon; length 800 m.

Napoleon, *t.*, N.W. Ohio, U.S.A.; light mnfs.; p. (1960) *6,739*.

Nara, *t.*, Honshu, Japan; S. of Kyoto; shrines and temples, colossal image of Buddha; old cap. of Japan; p. (1955) *115,674*.

Narbada or Nerbudda, *R.*, India; flowing from Rewa to the G. of Cambay, in the Arabian Sea; length 800 m.

Narbeth, *mkt. t.*, *urb. dist.*, Pembroke, Wales; nr. head of Milford Haven; p. (1961) *960*.

Narbonne, *t.*, Aude, France; wines, sulphur, tiles; p. (1954) *32,060*.

Nardo, *t.*, Lecce, Italy; textiles; p. *20,558*.

Narenta, *R.*, Jugoslavia; flowing 140 m. to Adriatic.

Narew, *R.*, Poland; flows to R. Bug, nr. Warsaw; length 200 m.

Narino, *dep.*, Colombia, S. America; a. 11,545 sq. m.; cap. Pasto; p. (estd. 1959) *628,840*.

Narni, *t.*, Perugia, Italy; linoleum.

Narrabri, *t.*, N.S.W., Australia; 300 m. N. of Sydney; observatory with stellar interferometer (1964); p. (1947) *3,328*.

Narragansett Bay, *inlet* of the Atlantic off cst. of Rhode I., U.S.A.

Narrandera, *t.*, New South Wales, Australia; on R. Murrumbidgee on N. margin of Riverina dist.; collecting ctr. for wool, mutton, wheat and fruits produced in irrigated a. fringing Murrumbidgee from Narrandera to Hay.

Narrogin, *t.*, W. Australia; p. (1957) *4,201*.

Narva, *t.*, Estonian S.S.R.; founded in 1223 by the Danes; cath.; textile factories, engin.; hydro-elec.; p. (1956) *21,000*.

Narvik, *t.*, N.W. Norway; opposite Lofoten Is.; ice-free throughout year, linked by rly. to impt. iron-ore fields in N. Sweden; exp. iron ore; p. (1946) *10,233*.

Nashua, *c.*, N.H., U.S.A.; cotton, paper, carpets, ironwks.; p. (1960) *39,096*.

Nashville, *c.*, *cap.*, Tenn., U.S.A.; on Cumberland R.; river pt., rly. ctr; fine capitol and other public bldgs.; impt. comm. and educat. ctr.; univs. and colleges; cellophane, rayon, food and tobacco prods., shoes, printing and publishing; p. (1960) *170,874*.

Nasik, *t.*, Maharashtra, India; on R. Godavari; Hindu pilgrim ctr.; metal work, cotton weaving; p. (1961) *131,103*.

Nasirabad, *t.*, Ajmer dist., Rajasthan, India; p. (1961) *24,148*.

Naso, *t.*, nr. Messina, Sicily; industl.; p. *8,000*.

Nassau, *I.*, Cook Is., S. Pac. Oc.; New Zealand terr.; uninhabited.

Nassau, *t.*, cap. Bahamas, W. Indies; all impt. Is. of the Bahamas connected with N. by radio telegraphy; resort; pearls, sponges, fruit; p. (1943) *29,391*.

Nasser City, rural development at Kom Ombo, N. of Aswan, to resettle 50,000 Nubians before the formation of the artificial L. behind the High Dam. [p. *18,400*.

Nässjö, *t.*, S. Sweden; rly ctr.; furniture, textiles;

Natal, *cap.*, Rio Grande do Norte, Brazil; sugar, cotton, salt, carnauba wax, hides; p. (1960) *162,537*.

Natal, *prov.*, Rep. of S. Africa; sub-tropical coastal climate; sugar-cane, tea, cereals; minerals (especially coal); oil discovered at Dannhauser; cap. Pietermaritzburg; a. 33,578 sq. m.; p. (1961) *2,979,920*.

Natanz, *prov.*, Iran; in hill cty. between Kashan and Isfahan; pears and other fruits.

Natchez, *c.*, Miss., U.S.A; in rich cotton-growing dist.; p. (1960) *23,791*.

Natchitoches, *t.*, La., U.S.A.; on Red R.; p. (1960) *13,924*. [*28,831*.

Natick, *t.*, Mass., U.S.A.; boots, shoes; p. (1960)

Natick, *t.*, R.I., U.S.A.; cotton, light mnfs.; p. *3,660*.

Naturaliste, C., N.E. Tasmania.

Naturaliste, C., S. of Geographe Bay, W. Australia.

Naucratis, *ancient c.*, between Cairo and Alexandria; excavated by Flinders Petrie and Gardiner.

Naugatuck, *industl. t.*, Conn., U.S.A.; mnfs. rubber, iron castings; p. (1960) *19,511*.

Naumburg, *c.*, Halle, E. Germany; at confluence of Rs. Unstrut and Saale; annual Hussite feast; cath.; textiles, leather, toys, chemicals; p. (1963) *37,905*.

Nauplia, *see* **Navplion.**

Nauru, *I.*, S. Pac. Oc.; 26 m. S. of Equator; administered jointly by Gr. Britain, Australia and New Zealand; phosphate ind.; a. 8 sq. m.; p. (1960) *4,613*. [Ucayali.

Nauta, *t.*, Peru; on confluence of Rs. Marañon and

Navan (An Uamh), *urb. dist.*, Meath, Ireland; p. (1961) *3,996*.

Navanagar, *see* **Bhavnagar.**

Navarino or Neocastro, *spt.*, Greece; on W. cst. Morea; Turkish–Egyptian fleet destroyed in the harbour by allied English, French and Russians in 1827.

Navarra, *prov., old kingdom*, N. Spain; bounded by the Pyrenees; cap. Pamplona; grain, fruits, olives, wines, cattle-rearing, copper, silver, lead; a. 4,055 sq. m.; p. (1959) *399,038*.

Navasota, *t.*, E. Texas, U.S.A.; mkt., cotton processing mills; p. (1960) *4,937*.

Navplion, *t.*, Peloponnesos, Greece; on G. of Navplion; p. (1961) *8,918*.

Navsari, *t.*, Gujarat, India; cotton, leather, metalwork; p. (1961) *51,400*.

Naxos, *I.*, Greece; lgst. of the Cyclades; a. 164 sq. m.; famous for wine and fruit.

Nayarit, *st.*, Mexico; a. 10,444 sq. m.; cap. Tepia; p. (1960) *389,929*.

Nazare, *t.*, Brazil; p. *13,482*.

Nazareth, *t.*, Israel; 21 m. S.E. Acre; associations with early life of Christ; p. (1963) *26,400*.

Naze, The, *c.*, S. point of Norway.

Nazilli, *t.*, S.W. Turkey; on R. Menderes; agr., esp. olives; p. (1960) *36,601*.

Ndola, *t.*, Zambia, Central Africa; nr. bdy. with Katanga prov., Congo, 110 m. by rail N. of Broken Hill; ctr. of rich copper-mng. a. less impt. lead- and zinc-mng; minerals despatched by rail E. to Beira and W. to Lobito Bay; p. (1960) *85,700* inc. *10,400* Europeans.

Neagh, Lough, *L.*, N. Ireland; lgst. in British Is.; a. 153 sq. m.; drained by R. Bann.

Neath, *t.*, *mun. bor.*, Glamorgan, Wales; 6 m. up R. Neath from Swansea Bay; coal, aluminium inds., oil ref.; p. (1961) *30,884*.

Nebit-Dag, *t.*, Turkmen S.S.R.; 95 m. S.E. of Krasnovodsk; ctr. of oil and ozokerite a.; p. (1956) *30,400*.

Nebraska, *st.*, U.S.A.; mainly prairie; cap. Lincoln; farming, meat-packing, oats, wheat, maize, hay, potatoes, sugar-beet, apples, wool, livestock, petroleum, cement, mng., minerals; a. 77,227 sq. m.; p. (1960) *1,411,330*.

Nebraska, *R.*, trib. of Missouri R., U.S.A.

Neckar, *R.*, Germany; rising between the Swabian Jura, nr. Schwenningen, and the Black Forest; through Württemberg–Baden to the Rhine at Mannheim; length 240 m.

Neder Rijn, *see* **Lek**.

Needham, *t.*, Mass., U.S.A.; nr. Boston; mnfs.; p. (1960) *25,793*. [p. *1,349*

Needham Market, *t.*, Suffolk, Eng.; on R. Gipping;

Needles, *gr. of rocks*, jutting out at W. extrem. I. of Wight, Eng. [*36,287*.

Neemuch, *t.*, Madhya Pradesh, India; p. (1961)

Neenah, *c.*, Wis., U.S.A.; timber yards, flour and paper mills; summer resort; p. (1960) *18,057*.

Neftyne Kamni, *t.*, built on piles over Caspian Sea for Russian oil workers.

Negapatam, *see* Nagapattinam.

Negev, *reg.*, S. Israel, pioneering area.

Negoiul, *mtn.*, Transylvanian Romania: 8,346 ft.

Negombo, *spt.*, *urb. dist.* N.W. prov., Ceylon: native work in metal, leather; p. (1963) *47,028*.

Negotin, *t.*, E. Jugoslavia; on Romanian border; p. *6,633*.

Negril Beach, Jamaica; 25 m. W. of Montego Bay; new resort to further Jamaica's tourist tr.

Negri Sembilan, *st.*, Malaysia; S.W. Malaya; a. 2,580 sq. m.; cap. Seremban; p. (1961) *430,227*.

Negritos, *t.*, Piura dep., Peru; on cst., 15 m. S. of Talara; impt. oil-field.

Negro, Rio, *prov.*, Argentina; a. 77,610 sq. m.; cap. Viedma; p. (estd. 1960) *204,200*.

Negro Rio, *R.*, Argentina; flows into G. of St. Mathias.

Negro, Rio, Brazil, Colombia, S. America; one of the ch. tribs. of R. Amazon; rises in Colombia, joins the Amazon in N. Brazil.

Negros, *I.*, Philippines; S. of Mindanao; a. 4,905 sq. m.; p. *1,250,000*.

Nehbandan Range, *mtns.*, E. Persia.

Neheim-Hüsten, *t.*, N. Rhine–Westphalia, Germany; at confluence of Rs. Möhne and Ruhr; lamps, metals, chemicals; p. (1963) *34,700*.

Neikiang (Neijiang), *c.*, Szechwan prov., China; agr. ctr.; p. (1953) *190,000*.

Neilston, *par.*, nr. Glasgow, Renfrew, Scot.; bleachfields, cotton, coal.

Neisse or Nisa, *R.*, tribs. of R. Oder, (1) Western Neisse, now frontier between Poland and Germany to Czechoslovak frontier, (2) Eastern Neisse in E. Silesia.

Neiva, *t.*, Colombia, S. America; on R. Magdalena; cattle, coffee, panama hats; p. (estd. 1959) *71,170*.

Nejd, *dist.*, Central Arabia; with Hejaz, forms kingdom of Saudi Arabia; mainly desert; impt. oil wells, horses, camels, dates, various fruits; cap. Riyadh; p. *4,000,000* (estimated).

Nellore, *t.*, Andhra Pradesh, India; dyeing; rice; p. (1961) 106,797.

Nelson, *mftg. t.*, *mun. bor.*, Lancs, Eng.; on N. flank of Rossendale 3 m. N.E. of Burnley; cotton, rayon, iron and brick wks., light engin.; p. (1961) *31,950*.

Nelson, *prov.*, S.I. N.Z.; cap. Nelson; a. 10,870 sq. m.; p. (1961) *74,281*.

Nelson, *t.*, S.I. N.Z.; nr. head of Tasman Bay; fruit packing, timber, cath.; p. (1961) *25,310*.

Nelson, *R.*, Canada; drains L. Winnipeg to Hudson Bay; length (with its gr. trib. the Saskatchewan) 1,450 m.

Nemunas, *R.*, U.S.S.R.; flowing to the Kurisches Haff, S.E. Kaliningrad; length 50 m.

Nenagh, *mkt. t.*, *urb. dist.*, Tipperary, N. Riding, Ireland; p. (1961) *4,317*.

Nene, *R.*, Northants, Eng., rises nr. Naseby and flows 90 m. to the Wash, 3 m. N. of Sutton Bridge.

Neosho, *R.*, Kan., U.S.A.; trib. of Arkansas R.; length 450 m.

Neosho, *t.*, S.W. Mo., U.S.A.; mkt., lumber, agr., lead-mining; p. (1960) *7,452*.

Nepal, *ind. kingdom*, Himalayas; bounded on N. by Tibet, on E. by Sikkim, on S. and W. by India; exp. cattle, hides and skins, opium and other drugs, timber; cigarette and sugar factories at Janakpur and Brijung; cap. Katmandu; a. 54,362 sq. m.; p. (1961) *9,407,127*.

Nepalgant, *t.*, S.W. Nepal; in the Terai; tr. ctr.; cereals, oilseeds, hides; p. (1961) *15,817*.

Nephin, *mtn.*, Mayo, Ireland; alt, 2,646 ft.

Nepanagar, *t.*, E. Nimar, Madhya Pradesh, India; India's only newsprint plant; p. (1961) *8,780*.

Nerbudda, *see* **Narbada**.

Nerchinsk, *t.*, R.S.F.S.R.; on Nertcha R., S.E. Siberia; gold, non-ferrous metals; p. (1956) *11,600*.

Ness, Loch, *L.*, Inverness, Scot.; occupies N.E. end of Glenmore; forms link in Caledonian Canal; very deep; 22½ m. long.

Neston, *t.*, *urb. dist.*, Cheshire, Eng.; on N. side of Dee estuary; residtl.; p. (1961) *11,836*.

Nestos, *R.*, *see* **Mesta**.

Nesvizh, *t.*, W. Byelorussia, U.S.S.R.; p. *10,000*.

Netherlands, *kingdom*, W. Europe; divided into 11 provinces; bounded by the N. Sea, Germany, and Belgium; ch. cs.: Amsterdam (cap.), Rotterdam (ch. pt.), The Hague (seat of Government), Utrecht, Haarlem, Groningen; country low-lying, cst. protected by dykes; fertile and productive; agr., butter- and cheese-mkg., mkt. gardening, distilling and various mnfs., shipbldg., machin., tobacco, sugar, diamond-cutting, commerce; a. 12,868 sq. m.; p. (estd. 1959) *11,417,254*.

Netherlands Antilles (Curaçao), grs. of Is. Caribbean Sea; off N. cst. of Venezuela; consist of the Neth. Windward Is. and the Neth. Leeward Is.; a. 403 sq. m.; cap Willemstad; p. (1963) *196,100*.

Netze, *see* **Notec**.

Neubrandenburg, *dist.* E. Germany; mng. an agr.; p. (1963) *650,877*.

Neubrandenburg, *t.*, Neubrandenburg, E. Germany heavily bombed during Second World War fibreglass, machin., chemicals; p. (1963 *38,762*.

Neuchâtel, *can.*, Switzerland; mountainous dist Jura Mtns.; cattle, cheese, chocolate, watches cutlery, cottons, hosiery; a. 309 sq. m.; p (1961) *147,633*.

Neuchâtel, *t.*, *cap.*, Neuchâtel, Switzerland; o N.W. shore of Lake N.; watchmkg., jewellery condensed milk; oil refinery projected nearby p. (1941) *23,799*.

Neuchâtel, *L.*, Switzerland; at S.E. foot of Jur Mtns. at the W. end of the central Swis plateau; drains N.E. to R. Aar; length 36 m. width 3–5 m.

Neugersdorf, *t.*, Dresden, E. Germany; ironwks textiles; p. (1963) *12,083*.

Neuhausen, *commune*, N. Switzerland; aluminiur wks.; p. (1941) *6,355*.

Neuilly-sur-Seine, *sub.*, W. of Paris, France fine bridge and cas.; p. (1902) *73,315*.

Neumünster, *t.*, Schleswig-Holstein, Germany; N. of Hamburg; tanning, cloth, machin., chemicals; p. (1963) *75,000.*
Neunkirchen, *t.*, Saar, Germany; iron, coal; p. (1963) *46,100.*
Neuquén, *prov.*, Argentina; agr. and stock-raising; a. 37,245 sq. m.; cap. Neuquén; p. (1960) *111,000.*
Neuquen, *t.*, cap. Neuquen Prov., Argentina; fruit farming; p. (1960) *17,500.*
Neu-Ruppin, *t.*, Potsdam, Germany; on L. Ruppin; fire extinguishers, chemicals; p. (1963) *22,102.*
Neusalz, *see* **Nowa Sól.**
Neusandetz, *see* **Nowy Sacz.**
Neusatz (Novi Sad), *t.*, Jugoslavia; on R. Danube; formerly a royal free c.; almost destroyed by the Austrians in 1849; literary and comm. ctr.; coal; p. (estd. 1959) *97,000.*
Neuse, *R.*, N.C., U.S.A.; flows to Pamlico Sound; length 300 m.
Neuss, *c.*, N. Rhine–Westphalia, Germany; mnfs. iron goods, textiles, paper; rly. junction; p. (1963) *101,400.*
Neustadt, *see* **Wiener-Neustadt.**
Neustadt, *t.*, Rhineland-Palatinate, Germany; on R. Haardt; metal, paper, textiles; p. (1963) *30,800.*
Neustrelitz, *t.*, Neubrandenburg, E. Germany; machin.; p. (1963) *28,334.*
Neutitischeim, *see* **Novy Jičin.**
Neutra, *see* **Nitra.**
Neuwied, *t.*, Rhineland-Palatinate, Germany; on R. Rhine; cas.; ironwk., wood, pumice stone; p. (1963) *26,600.*
Neva, *R.*, R.S.F.S.R.; drains L. Ladoga S.W. via Leningrad to G. of Finland; 40 m. long.
Nevada, *mtn. st.*, U.S.A.; between Utah, Oregon and Idaho, and bounded S. and W. by California; mining: gold, silver, copper, tungsten, gypsum, iron, lead; livestock, agr., timber; tourism; cap. Carson City; a. 110,540 sq. m.; p. (1960) *285,278.*
Nevada, *c.*, Mo., U.S.A.; zinc-mining and smelting; p. (1960) *8,416.*
Nevers, *c.*, cap. Nièvre, France; on R. Loire; cath.; the Roman Noviodunum; porcelain and faience industry; iron goods; farm implements; aircraft; p. (1962) *41,051.*
Neves, *t.*, S.E. Brazil; sugar, coffee; p. (1960) *85,741.*
Nevis, *I.*, Leeward Is., W.I.; ch. prod. cotton; ch. t. Charlestown; a. 50 sq. m.; p. *11,383.*
Nevis, Loch, *arm of sea*, off cst. of Inverness, Scot.; 14 m. long.
New Albany, *c.*, Ind., U.S.A.; on R. Ohio; glass, furniture, leather, iron and steel, car bodies; p. (1960) *37,812.*
New Amsterdam, *t.*, Guyana; on Berbice R.; p. (1962) *15,000.*
New Amsterdam, *t.*, Manhattan I., U.S.A., taken by English from Dutch, 1664, and renamed New York.
New Antwerp, *t.*, on Congo R., Congo.
New Bedford, *c.*, *spt.*, Mass., U.S.A.; on estuary of R. Acushnet; whale-fishery ctr.; mnfs. cottons, cordage, glass, shoes; p. (1960) *102,477.*
New Bern, N.C., U.S.A.; tr. in timber, tobacco, cotton; p. (1960) *15,717.*
New Braunfels, *c.*, Texas, U.S.A.; cotton goods, leather; lime; beauty spot; p. (1960) *15,631.*
New Brighton, *t.*, Cheshire, Eng.; at entrance to Mersey estuary; residtl.; resort.
New Brighton, *t.*, N.Y., U.S.A., on Staten Is.; warehouses and factories.
New Brighton, *bor.*, Penns., U.S.A.; coal-mining; p. (1960), *8,397.*
New Brighton, *t.*, S.I., *seaside resort*, nr. Christchurch, New Zealand; p. (1961) *10,219.*
New Britain, *lgst. I.*, Bismarck Archipelago, Papua–New Guinea; a. (with adjacent Is.) 14,600 sq. m.; p. (1957) *100,375* (inc. approx. *3,856* non-indigenous).
New Britain, *c.*, Conn., U.S.A.; iron and brass mnfs.; p. (1960) *82,201.*
New Brunswick, *prov.*, Canada; forest-clad, mtns., many Ls.; lumber, pulp, paper, agr., fishing, canning; lead, zinc, barytes, natural gas; mnfs.; cap. Federiction; combined road and rail tunnel, bridge and causeway link with Prince Edward I. projected (1966–70); a. 27,985 sq. m.; p. (1961) *597,936.*
New Brunswick, *c.*, N.J., U.S.A.; on Raritan R.; chemicals, motor lorries, motor parts, leather, hosiery and hardware; p. (1960) *40,139.*
New Caledonia, *I.*, *Fr. Col.*, S. Pacific; coffee, copra, chrome ore, nickel, iron, manganese; cap. Nouméa; a. 8,548 sq. m.; p. (1962) *75,000.*
New Castle, *t.*, Ind., U.S.A.; steel mnfs., motor parts; p. (1960) *20,349.*
New Castle, *t.*, Penns., U.S.A.; tinplate, glass, steel wire, iron, coal; p. (1960) *44,700.*
New Cumberland, *bor.*, Penns., U.S.A.; tobacco, clothes; p. (1960) *9,257.*
New Delhi, *c.*, cap. India; on Jumna R.; adm. and trade ctr.; textile mills, printing, light inds.; univ.; government house; adjoining is **Old Delhi**, anc. cap. of Mogul empire; p. *260,272* (incl. Old Delhi, *292,429*).
New Dongola or **Maraka,** *t.*, Nubia, Sudan; on R. Nile; p. *10,000.*
New England, the six N.E. Atlantic sts. of U.S.A.: Me., N.H., Vt., Mass., R.I., Conn.
New Forest, *woodland region*, Hants, Eng.; a. 93, 000 acres; ch. t. Lyndhurst.
New Forest, *rural dist.*, Hants, Eng.; p. (1961) *57,451.*
New Galloway, *burgh*, Kirkcudbright, Scot.; on R. Dee; p. (1961) *327.*
New Glasgow, *spt.*, Nova Scotia, Canada; p. (1961) *9,782.*
New Granada, former name of the United States of Colombia, S. America.
New Guinea (Australian), *see* **Papua–New Guinea.**
New Guinea, West, *see* **West Irian.**
New Hampshire, *st.*, New England, U.S.A., touching the Canadian border; forested and mountainous; agr. and fruit-growing extensively pursued; paper and forest products, textiles, shoes; granite; cap. Concord; ch. spt. Portsmouth; principal mftg. ctr. Manchester; a. 9,304 sq. m.; p. (1960) *606,921.*
New Haven, *c.*, *pt.*, Conn., U.S.A.; on New Haven Harbour, inlet of Long I. Sound; Yale Univ.; firearms, clocks, hardware, radiators, rubber goods; meat-packing; p. (1960) *152,048.*
New Hebrides Condominium, *I.*, Pac. Oc.; roughly 500 m. W. of Fiji and 250 m. N.E. of New Caledonia; administered jointly by France and Britain; 3 active volcanoes, on Tanna, Ambrym and Lopevi; earth tremors frequent; copra, cotton, cocoa; a. 5,700 sq. m.; p. (estd.) *66,000.*
New Holland, *ferry, rly. sta.*, on R. Humber, [Lincoln, Eng.
New Hunstanton, *see* **Hunstanton.**
New Iberia, *sm. pt.*, La., U.S.A.; fishing, sugar, cotton, rice; timber tr.; p. (1960) *29,062.*
New Ireland, *I.*, Bismarck Archipelago, Papua–New Guinea; a. (with adjacent Is.) 3,800 sq. m.; p. (1957) *36,512* (native), (1954) *713* (non-indigenous).
New Jersey, *Atlantic st.*, U.S.A.; adjoining New York; mixed farming, petroleum-refining, smelting, chemicals, sanitary ware, motor vehicles; glass sand, zinc, iron ore, clay; cap. Trenton; ch. cs.; Newark and Jersey City; a. 7,836 sq. m.; p. (1960) *6,066,782.*
New Kensington, *t.*, Penns., U.S.A.; aluminium ind.; p. (1960) *23,485.*
New Lexington, *t.*, Ohio, U.S.A.; coal, oil and natural gas; p. (1960) *4,514.*
New London, *c.*, *pt.*, Conn., U.S.A.; at mouth of R. Thames; fine harbour; fishing, engin., machin., silk and woollen factories; p. (1960) *34,182.*
New Mexico, *st.*, U.S.A.; N. of the Mexican Rep., and S. of Colorado st.; traversed by the Rocky Mtns.; uranium, potash salts, pumice, beryllium, copper, petroleum; agr.: cereals, fruit, vegetables, cotton, livestock; cap. Santa Fé; a. 121,666 sq. m.; p. (1960) *951,023.*
New Milford, *t.*, Milford Haven, Pembroke, Wales.
New Milford, *t.*, N.W. Conn., U.S.A.; dairy prods., tobacco, foundries, textiles, chemicals; p. (1960) *3,023.*
New Mills, *industl. t.*, *urb. dist.*, Derby, Eng.; at W. foot of Pennines 6 m. S.E. of Stockport; textile printing, bleaching and dyeing, rayon, paper, emery and glass-cloth mftg., iron and brass mnfs.; p. (1961) *8,510.*
New Norfolk, *t.*, Tasmania, Australia; fruit-growing; p. (1947) *7,921.*
New Orleans, *c.*, *spt.*, La., U.S.A.; on delta of Mississippi R.; the gr. cotton mart of America, and a busy comm. and mftg. ctr.; univ., cult. tr.; p. (1960) *627,525.*

New Philadelphia, *c.*, Ohio, U.S.A.; impt. rly. and canal ctr.; p. (1960) *14,241.*

New Plymouth, *spt., cap.*, Taranaki, N.I., N.Z.; on W. cst. at N. foot of Mt. Egmont; sm. oil deposits; ctr. of dairy-farming dist.; p. (1961) *32,374.*

New Providence, *I.*, Bahama Is., W. Indies; contains cap., Nassau; p. (1953) *46,125.*

New Quay, *t., urb. dist.*, Cardigan, Wales; on cst. of Cardigan Bay, 18 m. S.W. of Aberystwyth; p. (1961) *951.*

New Radnor, *rural dist., co. t.*, Radnor, Wales; on slope of Radnor Forest, 6 m. S.W. of Presteign; p. (of dist. 1961) *2,050.*

New River, *artificial aqueduct*, Herts to Islington, London, Eng.; length 36 m.

New Rochelle, *c.*, N.Y., U.S.A.; on Long I. Sound; residtl.; p. (1960) *76,812.*

New Romney, *t mun. bor.*, Kent, Eng.; nr. S. cst. to E. of Dungeness; one of the Cinque Ports, in the rich agr. dist. Romney Marsh; old harbour silted up by shingle, and now a mile from sea; p. (1961) *2,556.*

New Ross, *mkt. t., urb. dist.*, Wexford, Ireland; brewing and malting; p. (1961) *4,494.*

New Siberian Is., off Arctic cst., U.S.S.R.

New South Wales, *st.*, S.E. Australia; much mineral wealth in tablelands and mtns.; silver, lead, coal, zinc, iron and steel; agr., corn, potatoes, fruit-growing, sheep, wool, cattle, meat: cap. Sydney; a. 309,433 sq. m. (exclusive of Capital Terr. of Canberra); p. (1964) *4,158,926.*

New Waterway (Nieuwe Waterweg), *ship canal*, S. Holland, Neth.; connects R. Lek 7 m. below Rotterdam with N. Sea cst. at Hook of Holland; length 11 m.

New Westminster, *t.*, B.C., Canada; at mouth of R. Fraser; former cap. col.; exp. timber, canned salmon; p. (1961) *33,654.*

New York, *st.*, U.S.A.; one of the original sts.; touching Canada on the N., and reaching the Atlantic on the S.; known as the "Empire State"; inc. Long I. and Staten I.; mixed agr., Portland cement, iron ore, stone, sand and gravel, zinc, petroleum, gypsum, titanium concentrate, steel; Albany is the state cap. a. 49,576 sq. m.; p. (1964) *17,915,000.*

New York, *c., spt.*, N.Y., U.S.A.; ch. comm. ctr. of U.S.A. and W. hemisphere; originally founded by Dutch settlers as New Amsterdam on Manhattan I.; gr. portion situated on Long I.; fine parks and bridges, skyscrapers, gd. harbour; world's longest bridge (Verrazano) spans mouth of N.Y. harbour opened 1964; univ.; ch. inds.; cloth textiles, printing and publishing, iron and steel work, machin., sugar-refining, meat packing, chemicals, leather; p. (1960) *7,781,984.*

New York State Barge Canal (Erie Canal), N.Y. st., U.S.A.; links Tonawanda on Niagara R. with Hudson R. via the Mohawk gap through Appalachian Mtns.; provides through water route from N.Y. to Gr. Lakes; opened as Erie Canal 1825, improved 1918; length 339 m. (with branches 525 m.), depth 12 ft.

New Zealand, *Brit. Dominion*, S. Pac. Oc.; E. of S.E. Australia and Tasmania, just over 1,200 m. from Sydney, N.S.W.; it consists of two main Is., N.I. and S.I. (a. 102,375 sq. m.), Stewart I. (670 sq. m.), Chatham Is. (372 sq. m.), Cook I. and several smaller Is.; the Is. are mountainous and contain numerous Ls., thermal springs and geysers; the scenery being varied and beautiful, and the climate everywhere healthy; there are active and dormant volcanoes in N.I.; cap. Wellington; principal exp.; wool, butter, frozen meat, cheese, hides, skins and pelts; p. (1961) *2,414,064* inc. *165,006* Maoris.

Newark, *t.*, Del., U.S.A.; univ.; p. (1960) *11,404.*

Newark, *mkt. t., mun. bor.*, Notts, Eng.; on R. Trent 17 m. N.E. of Nottingham; ball bearings, brewing and malting; p. (1961) *24,610.*

Newark, *c.*, N.J., U.S.A.; meat packing, printing, elec. goods, paints, chemicals, cars, aircraft, leather; p. (1960) *405,220.*

Newark, *c.*, Ohio, U.S.A.; on R. Licking; rly. carriage wks., mnfs.; p. (1960) *41,790.*

Newark, *t.*, N.Y., U.S.A.; horticulture, glass, light mnfs.; p. (1960) *12,868.*

Newberry, *t.*, S.C., U.S.A.; cotton prod., dairying; lumbering; p. (1950) *7,546.*

Newbiggin-by-the-Sea, *t., urb. dist.*, on E. cst., 4 m. N. of Blyth; sm. seaside resort; coal-mining; Northumberland; Eng.; p. (1961) *10,066.*

Newburgh, *burgh*, Fife, Scot.; on S. side of Firth of Tay, 8 m. E. of Perth; p. (1961) *2,079.*

Newburgh, *c.*, N.Y., U.S.A.; on Hudson R.; clothing and machin. mftg.; p. (1960) *30,979.*

Newburn, *t., urb. dist.*, Northumberland, on R. Tyne, 3 m. W. of Newcastle; Eng.; pure graphite for nuclear reactors; p. (1961) *27,879.*

Newbury, *mkt. t., mun. bor.*, Berks, Eng.; on R. Kennet, 17 m. S.W. of Reading; engin., furniture, paper, cardboard boxmaking; p. (1961) *20,386.*

Newburyport, *c., spt.*, Mass., U.S.A.; on Merrimac R.; boot and shoe factories, comm. and fisheries; p. (1960) *14,004.*

Newcastle, *spt., urb. dist.*, on Dundrum Bay; Down, N. Ireland; p. (1951) *3,076.*

Newcastle, *t.*, W. Natal, S. Africa; coal, iron, steel, wood, grain, hemp; p. (1960) *17,539* inc. *3,212* whites.

Newcastle, Greater, *c.*, N.S.W., Australia; at mouth of R. Hunter; 2nd c. of st.; gr. coal depot of S. hemisphere and leading provincial industl. ctr. of Commonwealth; iron and steel, engin., shipbldg.; p. (1961) *208,905.*

Newcastle Emlyn, *urb. dist.*, Carmarthen, Wales; on R. Teifi; p. (1961) *648.*

Newcastle-under-Lyme, *t., mun. bor.*, Staffs, Eng.; 2 m. W. of Stoke-on-Trent, on Lyme Brook; iron and steel, mining and quarrying, textiles and non-ferrous metals, bricks, tiles; p. (1961) *76,433.*

Newcastle upon Tyne, *c., spt., co. bor.*, Northumberland, Eng.; on N. bank of R. Tyne, 10 m. from the N. Sea; connected by bridges with Gateshead, Durham; great shipbldg. and colly. pt.; univ., cath., many fine public bldgs.; coal-mining, heavy engin., iron and steel, heavy chemicals; p. (1961) *269,389.*

Newcomerstown, *t.*, E. Ohio, U.S.A.; coal, steel, tinplate, bricks; p. (1960) *4,273.*

Newent, *mkt. t., rural dist.*, Gloucester, Eng.; 8 m. S. of Ledbury; p. (rural dist. 1961) *8,724.*

Newfoundland, *I.*, prov. Canada; E. of the G. of St. Lawrence; in E. low, in W. rugged mtns., many Ls.; coniferous forest; fishing, cod, salmon, halibut, lobster, seal; lumber, wood-pulp, paper; iron ore, lead, zinc, copper, asbestos; hydro-elec. power; climate is severe; cap. St. John's; Viking village recently discovered at L'Anse-aux-Meadows at N. tip of I. a. *156,185* sq. m.; p. (1961) *457,853.*

Newham, *outer bor.* Greater London, Eng.; comprising the former co. bors. of East and West Ham, part of Barking, (W. of Barking Creek), Woolwich (N. of the Thames); p. (1964) *264,545.*

Newhaven, *spt., urb. dist.*, E. Sussex, Eng.; on S. cst. at mouth of R. Ouse, 9 m. E. of Brighton; the passenger pt. for Dieppe; boat bldg. and light inds.; p. (1961) *8,325.*

Newlyn, *picturesque vil.*, Cornwall, Eng.; on Mount's Bay, 1 m. W. of Penzance; fishing and fish canning; p. *3,902.*

Newmarket, *t., urb. dist.*, Suffolk, Eng.; at foot of E. Anglian Heights, 11 m. N.E. of Cambridge; horse-racing ctr.; famous Heath (partly in Cambridgeshire); mkt. gardening, agr. and agr engin.; p. (1961) *11,207.*

Newmarket, *t.*, S.E. Ont., Canada; leather mnfs. [p. (1961) *8,932*

Newmilns and Greenholm, *burgh*, Ayr, Scot.; on R. Irvine, 12 m. E. of Kilmarnock; muslin and lace curtain mnf.; p. (1961) *3,541.*

Newport, *t., mun. bor., cap. of I.*, I. of Wight, Eng. on R. Medina, in gap through central Chalk ridge; mkt.; brewing, joinery and coach wks. bait mnfs.; p. (1961) *19,482.*

Newport, *t., co. bor.*, Monmouth, Eng.; on R. Usk 5 m. from its mouth; shipbldg., engin., iron and steel, aluminium, coal, paper-board, confectionery, chemicals, plastics; p. (1961) *108,107*

Newport, *mkt. t., urb. dist.*, Salop, Eng.; 8 m. N.E of Wellington; p. (1961) *4,370.*

Newport, *burgh*, Fife, Scot.; on S. side of Firth of Tay, opp. Dundee; p. (1961) *3,326.*

Newport, *c.*, Ky., U.S.A.; on Ohio R.; a. residtl sub. of Cincinnati, with impt. local inds.; p (1960) *30,070.*

Newport, *c.*, R.I., U.S.A.; on Narragansett Bay seaside resort; permanent p. (1960) *47,049.*

Newport News, *c., spt.*, Va., U.S.A.; on north shore of estuary of James R. on Hampton Roads; lge. harbour; shipbldg.; outlet for Virginian tobacco and Appalachian coal; p (1960) *113,662.*

Newport Pagnell, *mkt. t., urb. dist.*, Bucks, Eng.; on R. Ouse, 11 m. S.W. of Bedford; p. (1961) *4,722*.
Newquay, *t., urb. dist.*, Cornwall, Eng.; on N. Cornish cst.; seaside resort; p. (1961) *11,877*.
Newry, *t., urb. dist.*, Down, N. Ireland; at head of Carlingford Lough; machin., rope, brewing, granite; p. (1961) *12,450*.
Newton, *c.*, Kan., U.S.A.; silks, worsted; p. (1960) *14,877*.
Newton, *c.*, Mass., U.S.A.; on R. Charles; mnfs.; p. (1960) *92,384*.
Newtonabbey, *urb. dist.*, Antrim, N. Ireland; p. (1961) *37,440*.
Newton Abbot, *mkt. t., urb. dist.*, Devon, Eng.; at head of Teign estuary; rly. junction; pottery, lt. engin.; p. (1961) *18,066*.
Newton Aycliffe, *t.*, Durham, Eng.; 6 m. N.W. of Darilngton; one of "New Towns" designated 1947; engin. prod., textiles, plastics, paints; p. (estd. 1965) *16,040*.
Newton-le-Willows, *t., urb. dist.*, Lancs, Eng.; wagon repair and locomotive wks., paper, textiles; p. (1961) *21,761*.
Newton-Stewart, *burgh*, Wigtown, Scot.; on R. Cree, 5 m. N. of Wigtown; wool, creameries and agr. inds.; p. (1961) *1,980*.
Newtown, *c.*, N.S.W., Australia; S. sub. Sydney; ironwks., paint; p. (1947) *25,293*.
Newtown and Llanllwchaiarn, *mkt. t., urb. dist.*, Montgomery, Wales; on R. Severn, 8 m. S.W. of Montgomery; precision instruments, machin. tools; p. (1961) *5,512*.
Newtownards, *spt., mkt. industl. t., mun. bor.*, Down, N. Ireland; 7 m. E. of Belfast; muslin, linen; p. (1961) *13,090*.
Neyland, *t., urb. dist.*, Pembroke, Wales; on Milford Haven; rly. terminus; p. (1961) *2,149*.
Nezhin, *t.*, Ukrainian S.S.R.; rly. junction on Kiev–Moscow line; p. (1954) *50,000*.
Ngami, *L.*, Botswana, S. W. Africa; swamp, the remnant of a much larger L. [alt. 7,515 ft.
Ngauruhoe, *mtn.*, N.I., N.Z.; an active volcano;
Niagara, *R.*, forming part of boundary between Canada and U.S.A.; flows from L. Erie to L. Ontario; has rapids and the famous falls (167 ft.); gr. hydro-elec. power-sta.; length 35 m.
Niagara Falls, *t.*, Ontario, Canada; opp. the falls; carborundum, canning, silverware, castings; p. (1961) *22,351*.
Niagara Falls, *c.*, N.Y., U.S.A.; extending along the summit of cliff for 3 miles; paper, flour, aluminium; p. (1960) *102,394*.
Niamey, *t.*, Niger rep., W. Africa; one of the termini (the other is Zinder) of the trans-Sahara motor routes; p. *18,100*.
Nias, *I.*, W. of Sumatra, Indonesia; 95 m. long.
Niassa, *prov.*, Mozambique, Port. E. Africa; ch. t. Nampula; p. (1962) *276,795*.
Nicaragua, *rep.*, Central America; tropical forest; heavy rain in summer; uniformly hot; coffee, cocoa, sugar, bananas; gold and silver; cap. Managua; a. 57,145 sq. m.; p. (1960) *1,500,000*.
Nicastro, *mftg. t.*, Calabria, Italy; W. of the Apennines; olives, wine; p. *24,869*.
Nice, *c., spt., cap.*, Alpes Maritimes, France; on Mediterranean cst., at the foot of the Alps; beautiful climate and surroundings; joins ancient t. of Cimiez; ceded to France in 1860 by Sardinia; winter health resort; fruit and flower exp., perfume mftg.; p. (1962) *294,976*.
Nicobar Is., *see* **Andaman and Nicobar Is.**
Nicosia, *c., cap.*, Cyprus; the ancient Ledra; fortified, mosques; hand weaving; cap. of admin. dist. same name; p. (1960) *95,515*.
Nicoya, G. of, *inlet*, Costa Rica.
Nictheroy, *see* Niteroi.
Nidd, *R.*, trib. of R. Ouse, W.R. Yorks, Eng.
Nidwalden, *can.*, Switzerland; a. 106 sq. m.; p. (1961) *22,188*.
Niederhernsdorf, *t.*, S.W. Poland; formerly Germany; coal, explosives; p. *11,706*.
Niederwald, *hill*, opposite Bingen-on-the-Rhine, Germany; national monument commemorating German triumph over France 1870–71, and formation of the G. Empire.
Niemen or **Memel**, *R.*, Poland and U.S.S.R.; flowing to the Kurisches Haff; length 500 m.
Nienburg, *t.*, Lower Saxony, Germany; on R. Weser; glass, metal, wood, chemicals; p. (1963) *23,300*.
Nieuwveld Range, *mtns.*, C. of Gd. Hope, Union of S. Africa; part of S. terminal escarpment of African tableland; overlooks Gr. Karroo to its S.; forms impenetrable barrier to routes; mainly over 5,000 ft., max. alt. 6,276 ft.
Nièvre, *central dep.*, France; traversed by Morvan Mtns.; forests, livestock, coal, iron, steel; cap. Nevers; a. 2,659 sq. m.; p. (1962) *245,921*.
Nigde, *t.*, Turkey; p. (1960) *18,010*.
Nigel, *t.*, Transvaal, S. Africa; gold mng.; industl.; p. (1960) *33,896* inc. *7,880* whites.
Niger, *gr. R.*, W. Africa; rises nr. sea in outer mtn. zone of W. Africa, as R. Tembi, and sweeps round by Timbuktu to a delta in the G. of Guinea, on a circuitous course of 2,600 m., receiving its gr. trib. the R. Benue, about 250 m. from the mouth; navigable for 1,000 m.
Niger, *indep. sovereign st.*, W. Africa; millet, groundnuts, rice; sheep, goats; cap. Niamey; a. 494,000 sq. m.; p. (1961) *2,870,000*.
Niger Dam, Nigeria; at Kainji I.; dam projected 1964.
Nigeria, Republic of, *indep. sovereign st.*, within Br. Commonwealth (Oct. 1, 1960), West Africa; occupying lower basin of R. Niger, with region adj. up to Lake Chad; cap. Lagos. Terr. divs.: Northern (cap. Kaduna), Eastern (cap. Enugu), Western (cap. Ibadan); Mid-Western (cap. Benin). N. Cameroons became ind. as part of Nigeria, Feb. 1961; groundnuts, cotton, hides and skins, timber, palm-oil, cocoa, tyres, brewing; natural gas pipeline from fields at Owaza to Aba, E. Nigeria; total a. 356,669 sq. m.; p. (1963) *55,600,000*.
Nightingale, *I.*, most S. of Tristan da Cunha gr., [S. Atlantic.
Niigata, *c., port*, Honshu, Japan; coal, petroleum; gas pipeline to Tokyo under constr.; p. (1960) *315,000*.
Niihama, *c.*, N. Shikoku, Japan; on cst. of Inland Sea 20 m. S.E. of Imabari; refines copper obtained from Besshi Mines 12 m. to the S.; petrochemicals; p. (1947) *42,392*.
Niitakayama, *mtn.*, Taiwan I., China; highest mtn. of Niitaka Chain; alt. 12,939 ft.
Nijar, *t.*, Almeria, Spain; fruit, nuts, grain; textiles, porcelain; lead, manganese, iron ore; p. *10,107*.
Nijmegen, *fortfd. t.*, E. Neth.; on R. Waal, nr. Arnhem; univ.; mnfs. ale, Prussian blue, cigars, pottery, metal-work; p. (1960) *129,576*.
Nijni-Novgorod, *see* **Gorki**.
Nikaria, *I.*, Dodecanese Archipelago, Greece.
Nikko, *t.*, Honshu, Japan; famous temples and shrines; beautiful tourist resort; p. *8,000*.
Nikolayev, *fortfd. t.*, Ukrainian S.S.R.; nr. Kherson, at head of estuary R. Bug; 2nd lgst. shipbldg. ctr. in U.S.S.R.; engin., petroleum refining; p. (1962) *258,000*.
Nikolayevsk, *t., pt.*, R.S.F.S.R.; on R. Amur; iron ore, engin., oil refining; p. (1954) *50,000*.
Nikopol, *t.*, Ukrainian S.S.R.; on R. Dnieper; manganese prod.; engin., steel; p. (1959) *81,000*.
Nikšic, *t.*, Montenegro, Jugoslavia; N. of Cetinje; p. (1960) *16,000*.
Nile, *the longest R.* in the world (*see* **White Nile** (Bahr-el-Abiad) and **Blue Nile** (Bahr-el-Azrek)); flows through a longer stretch of basin (over 2,450 m. in a direct line) than any other R. in the world, and along all its windings measures 4,145 m.; on Upper Nile navigation is hindered by sudd (floating vegetation); R. rises April, overflows Sept.; formerly cultivation entirely dependent on annual floods, but now assisted by dams, at Asyût, Aswan, Sennar, for regulating flow and navigation; first stage of Aswan High Dam completed 1964 when Nile waters were diverted.
Niles, *t.*, Ohio, U.S.A.; p. (1960) *19,545*.
Nilgiri Hills, Madras, S. India.
Nîmes, *t.*, Gard, France; Roman antiquities, educational institutions; silk, cottons, carpets, machin., wine tr.; p. (1954) *89,130*.
Nineveh, *celebrated ancient c.*, Iraq, stood on E. bank of upper R. Tigris, opp. modern Mosul.
Ningan, *t.*, E. Manchuria; mkt., tobacco, millet, maize; p. *30,000*.
Ningpo (Ningbo), *c., spt.*, Chekiang, China; 100 m. from Shanghai; leading fishing pt., comm. and mnf. ctr. p. (1953) *238,000*.
Ningsia, *aut. reg.*, N.W. China; bounded on N. by Inner Mongolia; cap. Yinchwan; p. (estd. 1957) *1,810,000*.
Ninh Binh, *t.*, N. Viet-Nam; p. *25,000*.
Ninove, *t.*, Belgium; on R. Dender; industl.; p. (1962) *11,898*.
Niobrara, *R.*, U.S.A.; trib. of Missouri R.; flows from Wyoming to Nebraska; length 450 m.

Niort, *t.*, Deux-Sèvres, France; noted for its mkt. gardens, and leather mnf. (gloves); p. (1954) *33,167*.

Nipigon, *L.*, in Thunder Bay dist., Ontario, Canada; 70 m. long, 50 m. wide, 1,000 Is.; discharges by N. R. to Lake Superior; 30 m.

Nipissing, *L.*, Ontario, Canada; 50 m. long, 35 m. wide.

Niriz, *t.*, Fars prov., S.W. Iran; on old caravan route from Kerman to Shiraz; p. *9,000*.

Niš, *t.*, Jugoslavia; on R. Nishava; p. (1960) *75,000*.

Nisa R., *see* **Neisse R.**

Nišava, *R.*, Jugoslavia; rises in Stara Planina, flows N.W. into R. Morava nr. Nis; valley used by trunk rly. from Belgrade to Sofia and Istanbul (Constantinople); length over 100 m.

Niscenic, *commune*, Caltanissetta prov., Sicily; sulphur, agr.; p. *20,281*.

Nishapur, *prov.*, N. Khurasan, Iran; grows grain, cotton; and contains famous turquoise mines; cap. N., c. with good fruit tr.; mosque with tombs of Omar Khayyám.

Nishinomiya, *c.*, S. Honshu, Japan; brewing, vegetable oils; p. (1962) *288,000*.

Niterói, *t.*, *cap.*, Rio de Janeiro st., Brazil; soap, textiles; p. (1960) *245,467*.

Nith, *R.*, S.W. Scot.; flows to Solway Firth, S. of Dumfries; followed by main rly. from Carlisle to Kilmarnock and Glasgow; length 71 m.

Nitra (Neutra), *R.*, ČSSR.; trib. of R. Waag; length 100 m.

Nitra, *t.*, ČSSR.; on R. Nitra; p. (1961) *34,242*.

Niue or Savage I., Pac. Oc.; one of Cook Is., but under separate admin.; belongs to New Zealand; ch. pt. Alofi; copra, plaited basketware, sweet potatoes; a. 100 sq. m.; p. (1959) *4,781*.

Nivelles, *t.*, Brabant, Belgium; rly. wkshps., paper; p. (1962) *14,483*.

Nivernais, *old prov.*, France, now forming Nièvre prov. and part of Cher.

Nizampatam, *t.*, *spt.*, Madras, India; formerly called Pettipollee after the neighbouring village of Pedapalle; first trg. estab. made by the Brit. in the Madras presidency in 1611.

Nizheudinsk, *t.*, W. Irkutsk, R.S.F.S.R.; new mftg. t.; p. *10,342*.

Nizhniy Tagil, *t.*, R.S.F.S.R.; in Ural mtns.; iron ore, iron and steel, railway cars, engin., chemicals; p. (1962) *359,000*.

Njole, *t.*, Congo Rep., Equatorial Africa; on R. [Ogowe

No, *L.*, Bahr-el-Ghazal prov., Sudan, N.E. Africa; vast swamp a. 350 m. S.W. of Khartoum receiving Rs. Bahr-el-Jebel and Bahr-el-Ghazal (to form White Nile); flow of water blocked by papyrus reed and floating weed (sudd); gr. loss of water by evaporation.

Noakhali, *dist.*, and *t.*, Chittagong div., Pakistan; p. (of t.) *13,063*.

Nobi Plain, S. Honshu, Japan; located at head of Ise Bay; composed of: (1) low, badly drained alluvial plain on W. under intensive rice cultivation, (2) higher, drier, terraces on E. under mulberry, vegetables, pine-woods; very dense urban and rural p.; ch. textiles and pottery mftg. a. in Japan; inc. cities Nagoya, Gifu, Yokkaichi; a. 720 sq. m.

Noblesville, *t.*, Ind., U.S.A.; agr., horse breeding; p. (1960) *7,664*.

Nocera Inferiore, *t.*, Italy; nr. Naples; the ancient Nuceria Alfaterna; p. (1961) *43,050*.

Nogent-sur-Marne, *t.*, Seine, France; S.E. sub. Paris; chemicals, knives; p. (1954) *23,581*.

Noginsk, *t.*, R.S.F.S.R.; nr. Moscow; textiles, metals; natural gas pipeline from Central Asia projected; p. (1959) *93,000*.

Noisy-le-Sec, *t.*, Seine, France; p. (1954) *22,337*.

Nola, *t.*, Italy; at foot of Vesuvius, 12 m. N.E. of Naples; was an ancient c. of Campania, noted for its vases; p. *20,253*.

Nome, *cst. t.*, Alaska, U.S.A.; gold; (1960) *2,316*.

Noordoostelijke Polder, land reclaimed from Zuider Zee, Neth., 1942, not yet included in any prov.; a. 185 sq. m.; p. (1960) *28,176*.

Noordwijk, *resort*, W. cst., Neth.; p. (1950) *16,686*.

Noranda, *t.*, Quebec, Canada; 12 m N.E. of Rouyn; goldmines; p. (1961) *11,477*.

Norcia, *t.*, Italy; old walls, cath.; famous for pork and terra-cotta.

Nord, *N. dep.*, France; on Belgian frontier and N. Sea; flourishing agr., mining, iron and coal, textile and chemical mnfs.; cap. Lille; a. 2,229 sq. m.; p. (1962) *2,293,112*.

Nordenham, *pt.*, Lower Saxony, Germany; on Lower Weser; cables, textiles, metals, shipbldg., fishing pt.; p. (1963) *27,100*.

Norderney, *I.*, Frisian Is., Germany; resort.

Nordhausen, *c.*, Erfurt, E. Germany; in Harz Mtns.; cath.; engin., agr. machin., clothing inds.; rly. junction; p. (1963) *41,401*.

Nordhorn, *t.*, Lower Saxony, Germany; nr. Neth. frontier; textiles; p. (1963) *40,200*.

Nordkapp or **N. Cape**, *most N. point*, Europe; on Magerö I., Norway.

Nordkyn, *most N. point*, with N. Cape, of the European mainland, Norway, opposite N. Cape.

Nordland, *co.*, Norway; a. 14,728 sq. m.; p. (1963) *240,314*.

Nordlingen, *t.*, Bavaria, Germany; carpet factories; p. *8,800*.

Nore, The, *sandbank*, *lightship*, Thames estuary, Eng.

Nore, *R.*, Ireland; trib. of R. Barrow; length 70 m.

Norfolk, *co.*, E. Eng.; noted for shallow lake expanses known as the Broads, popular yachting region; farming, corn, potatoes, cattle, fisheries (Yarmouth), brewing, boots, mustard, farm machin.; cap. Norwich; a. 2,055 sq. m.; p. (1961) *561,980*.

Norfolk, *c.*, Nebraska, U.S.A.; on Elkhorn R.; in farming country; p. (1960) *13,111*.

Norfolk, *c.*, Va., U.S.A.; impt. naval sta.; spt.; shipbldg. and repair, car assembly, food processing, lumber, fertilisers; p. (1960) *305,872*.

Norfolk I., *fertile Australian I.*, Pac. Oc.; 800 m. E. of N.S.W. partial autonomy 1957; formerly a penal settlement; discovered by Captain Cook, 10 Oct. 1774; bean seed, whaling; a. 13 sq. m.; p. (1959) *1,048*.

Noric Alps, *mountainous region*, Styria, S. Austria.

Norilsk, *t.*, E. Siberia, R.S.F.S.R.; most N. t. in Russia; coal mng., uranium, nickel, copper; natural gas pipeline from W. Siberia; p. (1959) *108,000*.

Normal, *t.*, Ill., U.S.A.; mkt. gardening, fruit, plants; univ.; p. (1960) *13,357*.

Norman, *t.*, Okla., U.S.A.; oil-field; cotton processing; agr.; univ. of Okla.; p. (1960) *33,412*.

Norman Wells, *t.*, N.W. Terr., Canada; at confluence of R. Mackenzie and G. Bear R., 70 m. W. of G. Bear L.; ctr. of rich oil-field.

Normandy, *old French prov.*, on Eng. Channel; mainly agr.; now divided into deps. Manche, Calvados, Eure, Seine-Maritime and part of Orne; Rouen was cap.; the Roman Lugdunensis; later a powerful Dukedom; conquered England, 1066.

Normanton, *t.*, *urb. dist.*, W.R. Yorks, Eng.; on R. Calder 2 m. E. of Wakefield; coal-mining, rly. wks.; p. (1961) *18,307*.

Norrbotten, *co.*, N. Sweden; a. 40,754 sq. m.; cap. Piteå; p. (1961) *261,672*.

Norris Dam, Tenn., U.S.A.; across R. Clinch at confluence with R. Tenn., N.W. of Knoxville; lgst. dam Tenn. Valley Authority (TVA); built for flood control and hydro-elec.

Norristown, *bor.*, Penns., U.S.A.; textiles, hosiery, carpets; p. (1960) *38,925*.

Norrköping, *pt.*, *t.*, Sweden; N.E. of Linköping; textiles, margarine, paper; agr. machin.; ocean-going shipping through Lindö Canal; p. (1960) *91,661*.

Norte de Santander, *dep.*, Colombia, S. America; a. 8,295 sq. m.; cap. Cucuta; p. (estd. 1959) *412,440*.

North Adams, *c.*, Mass., U.S.A.; on R. Hoosac; textiles, boots, and shoes; p. (1960) *19,905*.

North America, *northern continent*, comprising Mexico, Central America, West Indies, U.S.A., Canada, Greenland; cst. much indented; on W. high chain of mtns., lower range in E., and central plain. Climate varies considerably owing to wide range of latitude and altitude; great extremes of temperature; abundant rainfall on E. cst. and N. of W. cst.; S. of W. cst. Mediterranean; Mexico, sub-tropical and tropical. Vegetation diverse, varying with alt., latitude and climate; coniferous forest in N.; originally deciduous forests from E. cst. to approx. 100° W., then grassland to mtn. vegetation of W. range; semi-desert in S.W.; tropical forests Central America. Prairies once home of bison. Agr.: temperate and tropical prod., cereals, cotton, tobacco, sugar-beet, potatoes, etc.; lumbering; rich in minerals, coal, petroleum, iron, manganese, etc. Gen inds., comm., shipbldg. Formerly inhabited by Red Indians; now mainly occupied by White races, with many negroes in S.; a. 8,700,000 sq. m.; p. *185,000,000* (estimated).

North Atlantic Drift, drift of surface waters of Atl. Oc. N.E. from Gulf Stream towards Europe; relatively warm; supplies prevailing S.W. winds with warmth and moisture to modify climate of Brit. Is. and countries on N.W. margin of European Continent. *See* **Gulf Stream**, Gen. Inf.

North Attleboro, *t.*, Mass., U.S.A.; jewellery mnfs.; p. (1960) *14,704*.

North Bay, *c.*, Ontario, Canada; p. (1961) *23,781*.

North Berwick, *burgh*, E. Lothian, Scot.; on S. of F. of Forth, 20 m. E .of Edinburgh; seaside resort; golf course; p. (1961) *4,161*.

North Brabant, *prov.*, Neth.; cap. s'Hertogenbosch; a. 1,920 sq. m.; p. (estd. 1959) *1,484,671*.

North Braddock, *t.*, Penns., U.S.A.; p. (1960) *13,204*.

North Cape, *see* **Nordkapp**.

North Cape, *most northerly point*, N.I., N.Z.

North Carolina, *S. Atlantic st.*, U.S.A., E. of Tennessee and S. of Virginia; agr., maize, cotton-growing and mftg., tobacco culture and mftg., timber, scrap mica, textiles; cap. Raleigh; ch. pt., Wilmington; a. 52,712 sq. m.; p. (1960) *4,556,155*.

North Channel, Brit. Is.; gives access from Atl. Oc. to Irish Sea between S.W. Scotland (Galloway) and N.E. Ireland (Antrim); length 60 m.; narrowest width 15 m.

North Chicago, *t.* Ill., U.S.A.; chemicals, metallurgy, elec. goods; p. (1960) *20,517*.

North Crimean Canal, *canal*, U.S.S.R.; linking R. Dnieper with Black Sea and Sea of Azov, crossing steppes of S. Ukraine and the Crimea, terminating at Kerch; 1st section (77 m. long) opened Oct. 1963; when completed will be 220 m. long, 125 m. of which will be navigable.

North Dakota, *N.W. st.*, U.S.A.; mainly rolling prairie; agr., wheat, maize, oats, barley, flax, cattle, horses, sheep; coal, petroleum; cap. Bismarck; a. 70,665 sq. m.; p. (1960) *632,446*.

North Downs, range of low chalk hills across S. Eng., forming cliffs at Dover; alt. about 800 ft.

North Eastern New Guinea, part of New Guinea under Australian administration as Trusteeship terr. under United Nations; a. 69,700 sq. m.

North East Passage, along N. cst. Europe and Asia between Atlantic and Pacific. *See* Gen. Inf.

North Holland, *prov.*, Neth.; a. 1,051 sq. m.; cap. Haarlem; natural gas in Schermer Polder nr. Alkmaar; p. (1959) *2,054,509*.

North Island, *lge I.*, New Zealand; dairy prod.; lge. clay deposits at Matauri Bay; processing at Kaco; a. 44,281 sq. m.; p. (1961) *1,684,139* inc. *158,086* Maoris.

North Little Rock, *t.*, Ark., U.S.A.; p. (1960) *58,032*.

North Osetian, A.S.S.R., U.S.S.R.; a. 3,100 sq. m.; cereals, livestock, petroleum; p. (1959) *449,000*.

North Platte, *c.*, Nebraska, U.S.A., on N. Platte R.; in irrigated reg. of the Great Plains; grain, livestock, processed meat; p. (1960) *17,184*.

North Platte, *R.*, rises N. Colorado, flows 680 m. through Wyoming, across W. Nebraska to join S. Platte at c. of North Platte; extensive power and irrigation developments.

North Providence, *see* **Nassau**.

North Rhine-Westphalia, *Land*, Germany; a. 13,153 sq. m.; p. (1961) *15,902,000*.

North River, Kwangtung, S. China; rises in Nan Ling mtns., flows S. into Canton delta; length 300 m.

North Sea, arm of the Atlantic, E. of Gr. Brit., W. of Norway, Sweden and N. Germany, and N. of Holland, Belgium and France; length 600 m., width 400 m.; good fisheries.

North Sea Canal, *ship canal*, N. Holland, Neth.; connects Amsterdam to N. Sea at Ijmuiden; depth 46 ft., length 16 m.

North Shields, *mkt. t.*, Northumberland, Eng.; Tyne pt. and part of the borough Tynemouth; marine engines, chain cables, anchors, rope.

North Sydney, *spt.*, C. Breton I., Nova Scotia; Canada; docks, coal; p. (1961) *8,657*.

North Tonawanda, *c.*, N.Y., U.S.A.; on Niagara R.; mnfs.; p. (1960) *34,757*.

North Walsham, *mkt. t.*, *urb. dist.*, Norfolk, Eng.; 13 m. N.E. of Norwich; p. (1961) *5,010*.

North-West Frontier Province, *former prov.* (dissolved 1955), now incl. in Peshawar div., W. Pakistan; mtnous, fertile valleys; bounded by Hindu Kush and Afghanistan on N., and on S. by Baluchistan and Punjab; ch. c., Peshawar; wheat, barley, sugar cane, tobacco, cotton; iron, copper, marble quarrying; irrigation wks.; a. 14,263 sq. m.; p. (estd. 1951) *3,239,000*.

North-West Passage, between Atl. and Pac. along Arctic cst. of Canada. *See* Gen. Inf.

North-West Staging Route, a daisy chain of airfields built during last war linking Edmonton, Alberta, with Whitehorse, Yukon.

North-West Territories, Canada; the N.W. region of Canada between the Yukon on the W., Hudson Bay on the E., and B.C., Alberta, Saskatchewan and Manitoba on the S.; divided into 3 dists., Franklin, Mackenzie and Keewatin; gold- and silver-mng., petroleum, furs, fisheries; a. 1,304,903 sq. m.; p. (1961) *22,998*.

North York. Moors, *limestone plateau*, N.R., Yorkshire; lies S. of estuary of R. Tees; drained N. to R. Tees, S. to R. Derwent and to N. Sea by R. Esk; heather moorland; some pastoral farming on lower slopes; impt. iron-ore quarrying along N. edge in Cleveland dist.; alt. varies from 1,000 to 1,500 ft.

Northallerton, *t.*, *urb. dist.*, N.R. Yorks, Eng.; in broad gap between Cleveland Hills and Pennines; dairy farming and agr. dist.; car and agr. engin., leather; p. (1961) *6,720*.

Northam, *t.*, W. Australia; on R. Avon, 66 m. from Perth, Australia; p. (1961) *7,192*.

Northampton, *S. Midland co.*, Eng.; chiefly agr.; iron, mining and mftg.; footwear, lace, leather, flax, light engin.; co. t., Northampton; a. 998 sq. m.; p. (1961) *398,132*.

Northampton, *t.*, *co. bor.*, Northampton, Eng.; on R. Nene; footwear mftg., leather goods, light engin.; p. (1961) *105,361*.

Northampton, *c.*, Mass., U.S.A.; textiles, paper; univ.; p. (1960) *30,058*.

Northampton, *t.*, Penns., U.S.A.; cement; beer; clothes; quarrying; p. (1960) *8,866*.

Northbridge, *industl. t.*, Mass., U.S.A.; p. (1950) *10,476*.

Northcote, *t.*, Victoria, Australia; N. sub. Melbourne; mnfs.; p. (1947) *42,713*.

Northern Ireland, consists of the administrative cos. of Antrim, Armagh, Down, Fermanagh, Londonderry and Tyrone, and administrative bors. of Belfast and Londonderry. Has its own parliament and executive Government under a Governor appointed by the Crown. Returns 12 members to British House of Commons; agr., oats, potatoes, etc., flax, fruit, hay, chalk, granite, etc., linen, shipbldg.; new inds. being established; cap. Belfast; a. 5,238 sq. m.; p. (1961) *1,425,462*.

Northern Rhodesia, *see* **Zambia**.

Northern Territories, Ghana, West Africa; lies N. of latitude 8° N.; ch. t. Tamale; incl. Togoland a. 41,063 sq. m.; p. (1948) *1,076,696*.

Northern Territory, a large tract of land N. of S. Australia; stock-raising, copper, gold, uranium, manganese, salt, bauxite; silver, mica, tin, tungsten; rice at Humpty Doo, 30 m. S. of Darwin; a. 523,620 sq. m.; ch. t. Darwin; p. (1964) *30,946*.

Northfield, *c.*, S. Minn., U.S.A.; agr., dairying; p. [(1960) *8,707*.

Northfleet, *t.*, *urb. dist.*, Kent, Eng.; on S. bank of R. Thames, adjoining Gravesend; cement, paper, rubber, tyres, cables; p. (1961) *22,084*.

Northumberland, *N. maritime co.*, Eng.; on border of Scot.; pastoral, mining, coal and lead, mftg.; chemicals, glass, engin., and shipbldg. on Tyneside; cap. Newcastle-upon-Tyne; a. 2,019 sq. m.; p. (1961) *818,988*.

Northumberland Straits, separates Prince Edward I. from Nova Scotia and New Brunswick; 9 m. combined road and rail tunnel, bridge and causeway to link provs. projected.

Northwich, *mkt. t.*, *urb. dist.*, Cheshire, Eng.; on R. Weaver, 10 m. S.E. of Runcorn; chemicals, salt, engin.; p. (1961) *19,374*.

Norton, *t.*, S.W. Va., U.S.A.; coal, mftg.; p. (1950) *4,315*.

Norton, *t.*, *urb. dist.*, E.R. Yorks, Eng.; on R. Derwent opposite Malton; p. (1961) *4,773*.

Norton Sound, *inlet*, W. cst. Alaska, Behring Sea; 200 m. long.

Norwalk, *t.*, Conn., U.S.A.; on Long I. Sound; good harbour, oysters, iron foundries, clothing; p. (1960) *67,775*.

Norwalk, *t.*, Cal., U.S.A.; oil refining; p. (1960) [*88,739*.

Norwalk, *bor.*, Ohio, U.S.A.; mftg. ctr. of farming dist.; p. (1960) *12,900*.

Norway, *kingdom*, N. Europe; fjord cst., mtnous; climate influenced by prevailing winds, heavy rain and snowfall cstal regions; barley, forest prod., aluminium, pyrites; fisheries; hydro-elec. power; cap. Oslo; a. 124,556 sq. m.; p. (1963) *3,654,030*.

Norwich, *c.*, *co. bor.*, *co. t.*, Norfolk, Eng.; on R. Wensum just above confluence with R. Yare; univ.; cath., old cas., cult. ctr., agr. ctr.; boots, shoes, textiles, gen. inds.; p. (1961) *119,904*.

Norwich, *c.*, Conn., U.S.A.; firearms, cutlery and machin., textiles; p. (1960) *38,506*.

Norwood, S., *sub. div.*, Lambeth, Surrey, Eng.; mainly residtl.

Norwood, Ohio, U.S.A.; *sub.*, Cincinnati; p. [(1960) *34,580*.

Norwood, *t.*, Mass., U.S.A.: p. (1960) *24,898*.

Nossi Bé, *Is.*, Indian Ocean; off W. cst of. Malagasy; a. 130 sq. m.; rice, coffee, tobacco.

Notec (Netze), *R.*, Poland; trib. R. Warta; 140 m.

Noto, *c.*, Sicily; W. of Syracuse; cath.; wine, olive oil, mnfs.; p. *32,575*.

Notodden, *t.*, S. Norway; hydro-elec. power; iron smelting; nitrates; p. (1961) *7,383*.

Notre Dame Bay, N. cst., Newfoundland, Canada.

Nottingham, *midland co.*, Eng.; wheat, oats, barley, cattle, coal, oil; co. t. Nottingham; a. 844 sq. m.; p. (1961) *902,966*.

Nottingham, *c.*, *co. bor.*, *co. t.*, Nottingham, Eng.; on R. Trent, at S.E. end of Pennines; ctr. of English lace ind.; univ., R.C. cath., fine buildings, cas., museum, gr. mkt. square; hosiery, engin., pharmaceutical ind., chemicals, cycles; p. (1961) *311,645*.

Nouakchott, *cap.*, Mauritania, W. Africa.

Nouméa or **Port de France**, *cap.*, New Caledonia; p. (1962) *35,000*.

Nova Lima, *t.*, Minas Gerais st., Brazil; in Serra do Espinhaço, 10 m. S. of Belo Horizonte; adjacent to impt. gold-mines of Morro Velho; p. (1960) *21,135*.

Nova Lisboa (Huambo), *t.*, Angola, Africa; E. of Benguela; rly. repair shops; p. (1960) *60,800* (inc. *14,000* whites).

Novara, *Alpine prov.*, N. Italy; a. 2,548 sq. m.; p. *458,905*.

Novara, *mftg. t.*, nr. Milan; p (1961) *86,190*.

Nova Scotia, *maritime prov.*, Canada; mainly fertile uplands and rich valleys, but with mtns. along the cst. nr. Bay of Fundy; agr., fruit, livestock, dairying, much mineral wealth, coal and gypsum, and very valuable fisheries; cap. Halifax; a. 21,068 sq. m.; p. (1961) *737,007*.

Nova Zembla (Novaya Zemlya), *lge. Is.*, Arctic Ocean, U.S.S.R.; furs, walrus, whale, seal fisheries, lead, zinc and copper; nuclear testing a.

Nove Zamky, *t.*, Slovakia, ČSSR.; mkt. and mftg.; p. (1961) *22,041*.

Novgorod, *t.*, R.S.F.S.R.; sawmills, engin., p. (1959) *61,000*.

Novi Ligure, *t.*, Alessandria, Italy; nr. Genoa; noted for silk mftg.; p. *21,575*.

Novi Pazar, *t.*, Serbia, Jugoslavia; on R. Rashka; p. (1959) *17,000*.

Novi Sad (Neusatz), *t.*, Jugoslavia; on R. Danube; opposite Petrovaradin; formerly royal free c., almost destroyed by Austrians 1849; tr. in fruit, wine, vegetables, corn; p. (1959) *97,000*.

Novocherkask, *t.*, R.S.F.S.R.; 20 m. N.E. of Rostov; engin., chemicals; p. (1959) *94,000*.

Novokuybyshevsk, *t.*, R.S.F.S.R.; Volga region; lge. oil processing plant; p. (1959) *63,000*.

Novokuznetsk (Stalinsk) *t.*, R.S.F.S.R.; Kuznets; coal, iron, steel, engin., chemicals, aluminium; p. (1962) *410,000*.

Novomoskovsk (Stalinogorsk), *t.*, R.S.F.S.R.; on R. Don; lignite, fertilisers, chemicals; p. (1959) *107,000*.

Novorossiisk, *spt.*, R.S.F.S.R.; on N.E. cst. of Black Sea; engin., textiles; lgst. cement producer in U.S.S.R.; p. (1959) *93,000*.

Novoshakhtinsk, *t.*, R.S.F.S.R.; on Rostov–Kharkov highway; coalmng., chemicals; p. (1959) *104,000*.

Novosibirsk, *t.*, R.S.F.S.R.; on R. Ob; hydro-elec., steel, tin smelting, engin., textiles, chemicals, sawmiilng; p. (1962) *985,000*.

Novo Troitsk, *t.*, R.S.F.S.R.; in Urals, 11 m. S.W. of Orsk; cement, iron and steel; p. (1959) *57,000*.

Novovoronezh, U.S.S.R., on R. Don; nuclear power sta.

Nòvý Jičín (Neutitschein), *t.*, Moravia, ČSSR.; farm machin. and engin.; p. (1961) *16,560*.

Nowa Huta, *t.*, Poland; S.E. Kraków, on R. Vistula; newly developed metallurgical ctr.; p. (1954) *50,000*.

Nowa Sól (Neusalz), *t.*, Lower Silesia, Poland; on R. Oder; chemicals; p. *13,474*.

Nowata, *t.*, N.E. Okla., U.S.A.; agr., natural gas, oil-field gear; p. (1950) *3,965*.

Nowawes, *c.*, Brandenburg, Germany; textiles, engin., chemicals; p. *26,975*.

Nowra, *t.*, N.S.W., Australia; on E. cst. at mouth of Shoalhaven R.; collecting ctr. for agr. and pastoral prod. of coastal plain; at S. terminus of rly. along E. cst. of Australia.

Nowy Sacz, *industl. t.*, Krakow, S. Poland; on R. Dunajec; lignite; p. *23,000*.

Nsanje (Port Herald), *t.*, Malawi, Africa; pt. on Shire R.

Nubia, *region*, Africa, extending on both sides of Nile from Aswan, U.A.R., southwards to Khartoum, Sudan.

Nubian Desert, Sudan, N.E. Africa; between R. Nile and Red Sea; alt. 1,200–9,000 ft.; a. approx. 90,000 sq. m.

Nuble, *prov.*, Chile; bordering on Argentina; a. 5,484 sq. m.; cap. Chillan; p. (1961) *327,105*.

Nueces, *R.*, Texas, U.S.A.; flows to G. of Mexico; length 400 m. [p. (1961) *89,492*.

Nueva Esparta, *st.*, Venezuela; cap. La Asuncion;

Nuevo Laredo, *c.*, E. Mexico; agr., cotton, maize, cattle rearing; p. (1960) *107,473*.

Nuevo León, *st.*, Mexico; agr. and stock raising, sugar; cap. Monterrey; a. 25,134 sq. m.; p. (1960) *1,078,848*.

Nukualofa, *cap.* of Polynesian kingdom of Tonga.

Nukus, *t.*, Uzbek S.S.R.; in Khorezm oasis; p. (1959) *39,000*.

Nullarbor Plain, S. Australia; low, level, limestone plateau fringing Gr. Australian Bight; arid; treeless, salt-bush scrub; crossed by Trans-continental Rly. between Naretha (W. Australia) and Ooldea; rly. is dead straight, dead level for over 300 m.

Nun, *ch. mouth* of R. Niger, Africa.

Nun, *R.*, Inner Mongolia, Heilungkiang, N. China; trib. of Sungari; length 500 m.

Nun, *R.*, on S. frontier of Morocco, N. Africa; with t. thereon; length 130 m.

Nuneaton, *mkt. t.*, *mun. bor.*, Warwick, Eng.; on R. Anker, 18 m. E. of Birmingham; coal-mining, quarrying, textiles, engin., lt. inds.; p. (1961) *56,598*.

Nuremberg (Nürnberg), *t.*, Bavaria, Germany; cas., museum, cultural academy and many historic bldgs.; elec. mnfs., machin., heavy vehicles, toys, pencils and crayons; rly. junction; p. (1963) *466,100*.

Nusa Tenggara, *Is.*, Indonesia; p. (1961) *3,775,127* inc. Bali *5,557,656*.

Nutley, *t.*, N.J., U.S.A.; p. (1960) *29,513*.

Nyasa, *L.*, *see* **Malawi, L.**

Nyasaland, *see* **Malawi.**

Nyborg, *t.*, Denmark; on Fyn I.; p. (1960) *11,667*.

Nyeri, *t.*, Kenya; p. (1962) *7,400*.

Nyiregyhháza, *mftg. t.*, Hungary; wine, farming; implements; p. (estd. 1957) *55,000*.

Nykobing, spt., Falster I.,Denmark; light engin., food-packing, margarine, sugar-refining, tobacco ind.; p. (1960) *17,850*.

Nyköping, *spt.*, Sweden; at head of inlet on cst., comm. and industr.; cars; p. (1961) *24,250*.

Nystad (Uusikapunki), *spt.*, Abo-Björneborg, Finland; on G. of Bothnia; p. (1961) *4,544*.

O

Oadby, *urb. dist.*, Leics, Eng.; 3 m. S.E. of Leic.; boots and shoes; p. (1961) *12,266*.

Oahu, *I.*, Hawaiian Is., Pac. Oc.; sugar, pineapples; tourist tr.: cap. Honolulu; a. 604 sq. m.; p. (1960) *500,409*.

Oak Park Village, *t.*, Ill., U.S.A.; now included in Chicago; p. (1960) *61,093*.

Oakengates, *t.*, urb. dist., Salop, Eng.; 15 m. N.W. of Wolverhampton; iron and steel, pre-cast concrete, engin.; p. (1961) *12,158*.

Oakham, *co. t., urb. dist.*, Rutland, Eng.; 9 m. S.E. of Melton Mowbray; mkt.; hosiery; p. (1961) *4,571*.
Oakland, *c.*, Cal., U.S.A.; on San Francisco Bay; residtl. sub.; cars, shipbldg., fruit canning, elec. machin., clothing, tanneries, chemicals; p. (1960) *367,548*.
Oamaru, *bor., spt.*, S.I., N.Z.; wool, frozen meat; p. (1961) *12,401*.
Oaxaca, *st.*, Pacific cst., Mexico; cereals, rubber, coffee, mining; cap. Oaxaca; a. 36,371 sq. m.; p. (1960) *1,727,266*.
Oaxaca, *c., cap.*, Oaxaca st., Mexico; alt. 4,800 ft.; ctr. of cochineal tr.; table linen weaving, wool zarapes; coffee; silver, gold; cattle; p. (1960) *60,000*.
Ob, *G.*, U.S.S.R.; inlet of Arctic Oc.; length 600 m.
Ob, *R.*, W. Siberia, U.S.S.R.; flows from the Altai Mtns. to the G. of Ob; length (with trib. R. Irtish) 2,600 m.
Oban, *spt., burgh*, Argyll, Scot.; on F. of Lorne; summer resort of Highland tourists; terminus of rly. from Stirling; ctr. for local shipping; woollens, tartans; p. (1961) *6,859*.
Oberlahnstein, *t.*, Germany; at junction of Rs. Rhine and Lahn; cas., ancient walls; mng.
Oberammergau, *vil.*, Upper Bavaria, Germany; scene of decennial Passion Play; p. *1,500*.
Oberhausen, *t.*, N. Rhine-Westphalia, Germany; nr. Duisburg; cas.; coal, iron, steel, zinc, chemicals, rly. junction; p. (1963) *259,800*.
Obi I., *sm. I.*, between Halmahera and Serang, Indonesia.
Obidos, *t., R. pt.*, Brazil; 500 m. up R. Amazon; cacao, cotton; p. (1960) *3,500*.
Obihiro, *t.*, Hokkaido, Japan; p. (1947) *36,555*.
Obninsk, *t.*, R.S.F.S.R.; 60 m. S.W. of Moscow; atomic power sta.
Obok, *spt.*, Fr. Somaliland, N.E. Africa; in the Red Sea; coaling sta.; p. *1,000*.
Obuasi, *t.*, Ghana, W. Africa; p. (1960) *23,000*.
Obwalden, *can.*, Switzerland; a. 190 sq. m.; p. (1961) *23,135*.
Ocaña, *ancient t.*, Toledo, Spain; on Ocaña plateau; cas.; pottery, wine; p. (1957) *6,840*.
Ocaña, *t.*, Magdalena st., Colombia; coffee, hides; p. (estd. 1959) *21,200*.
Ocean I., Brit. col., Gilbert and Ellice Is., Pac. Oc.; high-grade phosphate; p. (1956) *2,446*.
Oceania, name given to the Is. of the Pacific; comprising Australasia, Polynesia, Melanesia, Micronesia; copra, sugar, fruit, timber; pearl fishing; gold, minerals, phosphates; a. 3,201,000 sq. m.; p. approx. *11,000,000*.
Ochil Hills, Scottish range reaching from the F. of Tay to nr. Stirling; highest peak, Ben Cleugh, 2,363 ft.
Ockmulgee, *R.*, Ga., U.S.A.; trib. of Altamaha R.; length 280 m.
Oconee, *R.*, Ga., U.S.A.; joins the Ockmulgee; length 250 m.
Odawara, *t.*, Japan; nr. Tokyo; gr. tr.; p. *51,838*.
Odda, *t.*, S. Norway; on Haugesund; electro-chem. and metallurgic inds.; p. (1961) *7,383*.
Odemiš, *t.*, Asiatic Turkey; N.E. of Aydin; tobacco, cereals, silk, cotton, flax, olives, raisins, figs; minerals; p. (1960) *28,525*.
Odendaalsrust, *t.*, O.F.S., S. Africa; gold ctr.; p. (1960) *15,047* inc. *6,070* whites.
Odense, *co.*, Denmark; now includes all N.W. Fyn; a. 699 sq. m.; p. (1960) *264,745*.
Odense, *spt.*, cap. of Fyn, Denmark; ancient c. said to have been founded by Odin; birthplace of Hans Andersen; elec. motors, shipyd., engin., textiles, footwear; p. (1960) *111,145*.
Odenwald, *mtns.*, Hessen, Germany; wooded; highest point Katzenbuckel, 2,057 ft.
Oder or Odra, *R.*, Central Europe; flowing from Moravia to Baltic through Polish Silesia, forming (since 1945) frontier between Poland and Germany, flows past Wroclaw (Breslau), Frankfurt and Szczecin (Stettin); length 560 m.
Odessa, *t.*, Texas, U.S.A.; impt. oil ctr., chemicals, foundry prod.; p. (1960) *80,338*.
Odessa, *spt.*, Ukrainain S.S.R.; on Black Sea; cath., univ.; gr. grain exp.; engin., oil-refining, chemicals; ice-bound for a few weeks in winter; bombarded by English and French 1845; p. (1962) *703,000*.
Offaly, *co.* (late King's co.), prov. Leinster, Ireland; much marshy land (inc. Bog of Allen), barren uplands (Slieve Bloom and other mtns.); fertilising factory for ammonium nitrate from peat in Blackwater Bog; ch. t. Tullamore; a. 772 sq. m.; p. (1961) *51,532*.
Offenbach, *t.*, Hessen, Germany; on R. Main; cas., leather museum; machin., chemicals, leather goods, metals; p. (1963) *118,000*.
Offenburg, *t.*, Baden-Württemberg, Germany; on R. Kinzig; textiles, glass, rly. junction; p. (1963) *28,600*.
Ogbomosho, *t.*, Nigeria; p. (1953) *140,000*.
Ogden, *c.*, Utah, U.S.A.; nr. the Great Salt L.; rly. ctr.; beet sugar, meat packing, flour milling; p. (1960) *70,197*.
Ogdensburg, *c., pt.*, N.Y., U.S.A.; on St. Lawrence R., opp. Prescott; gd. tr.; p. (1960) *16,122*
Ogeechee, *R.*, Ga., U.S.A.; flows to Atlantic, S. of Savannah; length 200 m.
Oglio, *R.*, Italy; traverses L. Iseo; flows to the Po; length 135 m.
Ogmore and Garw, *t., urb. dist.*, Glamorgan, Wales; in narrow valley, 6 m. N. of Bridgend; industl.; p. (1961) *20,955*.
Ogowe, *R.*, Gaboon, Africa; length 750 m.
Ohau, *L.*, Mt. Cook dist., S.I., N.Z.; fed by glaciers; 12 m. by 22 m.; hydroelec. plant projected.
O'Higgins, *prov.*, Chile; a. 2,745 sq. m.; p. (1961) *292,296*.
Ohio, *R.*, U.S.A.; trib. of Mississippi R.; formed in Penns., by the junction of the Monongahela and Allegheny Rs. at Pittsburgh, thence navigable for 975 m. to Cairo in Kentucky, 1,200 m. from the mouth of the Mississippi R.
Ohio, *st.*, U.S.A.; drained by Ohio R. and tribs.; gr. agr. and industl. region; maize, wheat, oats, cattle; lime, sand and gravel, salt, coal, petroleum, gas, iron and steel wks., machin., timber; cap. Columbus; lgst. cs. Cleveland and Cincinnati; a. 41,122 sq. m.; p. (1960) *9,706,397*.
Ohre (Eger), *R.*, Bohemia, Czechoslovakia; rises in Fichtelgebirge, flows N.E. into Labe (Elbe) at Litoměrice; flows through several sm. lignite fields, spas of Karlovy Vary (Karlsbad); length 140 m.
Ohrid, *t.*, S. Jugoslavia; nr. Albanian border; p. (1959) *15,000*.
Oich, Loch, *L.*, Great Glen, Inverness, Scot.; 6 m. long, 1 m. wide.
Oil City, Penns., U.S.A.; on Allegheny R.; oil, machin.; p. (1960) *17,692*.
Oise, *dep.*, N. France; traversed by R. Oise; forests, cereals, fruits, iron, textiles; cap. Beauvais; a. 2,272 sq. m.; p. (1962) *481,289*.
Oise, *R.*, trib. of R. Seine, France; canalised, navigable to Chauny; length 186 m.
Oita, *spt.*, Japan; exp. coal; cattle; p. (1955) *112,429*.
Ojos del Salado, *mtn.*, N.W. Argentina; alt. 22,572 ft.
Oka, *R.*, U.S.S.R.; trib. of R. Volga at Gorki; length 929 m.
Oka, *R.*, Siberia, U.S.S.R.; trib. of R. Angora; length 500 m.
Okanagan, *R.* and *L.*, B.C., Canada; fruit-growing dist.
Okasaki, *t.*, Honshu, Japan; nr. G. of Ovari; industl.
Okayama, *t.*, Honshu, Japan; exp. paper, minerals, firebricks; shipbldg.; rly. ctr.; cattle rearing; p. (1962) *289,000*.
Okehampton, *mkt. t., mun. bor.*, Devon, Eng.; on N. flank of Dartmoor; stone; p. (1961) *3,833*.
Okha, *spt.*, E. cst. Sakhalin I., R.S.F.S.R.; exp. petroleum; p. (1954) *50,000*.
Okhotsk, Sea of, N.E. Asia; 1,000 m. by 500 m.; enclosed by the Siberian mainland, Kamchatka, the Kurils and Sakhalin I.
Oki Is., off cst. of Honshu, Japan; a. 135 sq. m.
Okinawa, *I.*, Ryuku Is., Japan, under U.S. control; lgst. and most impt. of Ryuku Is., cap. Naha; 2 lgst. U.S. air bases Kadena and Naha; a. 579 sq. m.; p. (1956) *665,315*.
Oklahoma, *st.*, U.S.A.; prairie, plains and mtns.; cereals, cotton, stock-raising, petroleum, gas, zinc, coal, gypsum, lead; ch. ind. petroleum refining; cap. Oklahoma City; a. 69,919 sq. m.; p. (1960) *2,328,284*.
Oklahoma, *c.*, Okla., U.S.A.; univ.; oil and by-prod., oil processing, field machin., iron, steel, flour mills, meat pkg.; p. (1960) *324,253*.
Okmulgee, *t.*, Okla., U.S.A.; p. (1960) *15,951*.
Oktyabrsky, *t.*, Bashkir., A.S.S.R.; on R. Ik; in new oil-mng. dist., the "New Baku"; p. (1959) *65,000*.

Öland, I., Baltic Sea; off E. cst. Sweden; separated from mainland by Kalmar Sound; a. 533 sq. m.; ch. t. Borgholm, a seaside resort.
Old Castile, *historical div.*, Spain; now divided into Santander, Soria, Segovia, Logrono, Avila, Valladolid, Palencia and Burgos provs.
Old Fletton, *urb. dist.*, Hunts, Eng.; on R. Nene opposite Peterborough; bricks, gen. and elec. engin., beet sugar, fruit and vegetable canning, tar distilling; p. (1961) *11,678.*
Old Forge, *bor.*, Penns., U.S.A.; anthracite coal; p. (1960) *8,928.*
Old Kilpatrick, *see* Kilpatrick, Old.
Oldbury, *mun. bor.*, Worcs., Eng.; nr. Birmingham; iron, steel, chemical, brick, glass inds.; p. (1961) *53,935.*
Oldbury-on-Severn, Glos., Eng.; nuclear power sta. under construction.
Oldenburg, *t.*, Lower Saxony, Germany; on R. Hunte; grand-ducal palace; impt. horse fair; food processing, lt. inds.; rly. junction; natural gas nr. to cst.; p. (1963) *126,200.*
Oldham, *mftg. t., co. bor.*, Lancs, Eng.; on R. Medlock, 4 m. N.E. of Manchester; cotton, textile, and machin. mftg.; p. (1961) *115,426.*
Oldmeldrum, *burgh*, Aberdeen, Scot.; 4 m. N.E. of Inverurie; p. (1961) *1,083.*
Olean, *t.*, N.Y., U.S.A.; on Allegheny R.; oil region; p. (1960) *21,868.*
Olenek, *R.*, Ukrainian S.S.R.; flows W. of the Lena, into Laptev Sea, Arctic Ocean; length 800 m.
Oléron, Ile d', *I.*, Bay of Biscay; lies off estuary of R. Charente, Aquitaine, France; vine, oysters, salt; length 18 m., maximum width 7 m.
Olga, *spt.*, R.S.F.S.R.; on cst. of Japan Sea; iron ore; p. *1,000.*
Olhão, *t.*, Faro, Portugal; fisheries; p. *13,627.*
Olifant, *R.*, Transvaal, S. Africa; trib. of Limpopo.
Olinda, *c.*, Pernambuco st., Brazil; seaside resort; phosphates; p. (1960) *100,545.*
Oliobiri, S. Nigeria; oilfields; pipe-line to Pt. Harcourt, 80 m. W.
Oliva, *t.*, Valencia, Spain; nr. Alicante; wine dist., ducal palace; p. (1957) *13,343.*
Olivenza, *t.*, Spain; nr. Portuguese frontier; p. (1957) *13,834.*
Olivos, *sub.* Buenos Aires, Argentina, S. America; p. (estd. 1960) *160,000.*
Olkhon, I., L. Baykal, R.S.F.S.R.; manganese.
Olmutz, *see* Olomouc.
Olney, *t.*, N. Bucks, Eng.; 11 m. S.E. Northampton; boots, shoes, lace; dairying; p. *2,651.*
Olomouc (Olmütz), *c.*, ČSSR.; formerly one of the ch. fortresses of Austria; cath., univ.; iron and steel engin., textiles; p. (1962) *70,116.*
Oloron, *t.*, Basses-Pyrénées, France; on Gave d'Oloron; cath.; p. (1954) *11,407.*
Olsnitz, *t.*, Saxony, Germany; on Weisse Elster; carpet mnfs.
Olsztyn (Allenstein), *t.*, N.W. Poland (formerly E. Prussia); on R. Alle, 100 m. N. of Warsaw; cas.; machin., wood inds.; p. (1960) *68,000.*
Olt, *R.*, Romania; joins R. Danube at Nikopol.
Olten, *t.*, Switzerland; on R. Aare; rly. junction; motor, cement, machin. wks.; p. (1957) *16,485.*
Oltenita, *t.*, Romania; on R. Danube, nr. Bulgarian border; p. (1956) *14,111.*
Olvarria, *t.*, E. Argentina; 200 m. S.W. Buenos Aires; rly. ctr.; p. *24,326.*
Olvera, *t.*, Spain; nr. Cadiz; on R. Guadalete; p. (1957) *10,232.*
Olympia, *plain*, Peloponnesus, Greece, on R. Ellis where the Olympic Games were held.
Olympia, *cap.*, Washington st., U.S.A.; timber, machin., farm prod.; p. (1960) *18,273.*
Olympus, *mtn.*, Thessaly, Greece; W. of G. of Thessalonika; alt. 9,753 ft.; home of ancient Greek Gods.
Olympus, *mtn.*, Turkey; nr. Troy.
Olympus, Mt., Wash., U.S.A.; alt. 8,150 ft.
Om, *R.*, Siberia, R.S.F.S.R.; trib. of R. Irtish; length 330 m.
Omagh, *t., urb. dist.*, Tyrone, N. Ireland; on R. Strule 28 m. S. of Londonderry; corn, tanning; shirt factories; tourist ctr.; p. (1961) *8,109.*
Omaha, *c.*, Nebraska, U.S.A.; on Missouri R.; gr. tr., ctr., one of the lgst. livestock and meat-packing ctrs. in the U.S., gold and silver smelting and refining, steel fabrication, industl. alcohol prod.; p. (1960) *301,598.*
Oman, *see* Muscat and Oman.
Oman, G. of, Arabian Sea; connected through strait of Hormuz to Persian G.; length 300 m., width 130 m.
Omaruru, *t.*, S.W. Africa; creamery, aerodrome; p. (1960) *2,689* inc. *743* whites.
Ombai Is., Indonesia; N. of Timor.
Omdurman, *c.*, Sudan on R. Nile, opp. Khartoum; built by the Mahdi; old Dervish cap.; here Kitchener defeated the Dervishes, 1898; tr. in ivory, gum arabic, cattle, camels; p. (estd. 1956) *130,000.*
Ometepe, *I.*, L. Nicaragua, Central America, with volcano; alt. 5,747 ft.
Omine, *t.*, Japan; anthracite coal-mines.
Omsk, *t.*, W. Siberia, R.S.F.S.R.; on the R. Irtish; on Trans-Siberian Rly., caravan ctr.; cath.; engin., chemicals, textiles, oil refining; p. (1962) *650,000.*
Omuta, *t.*, Kyushu, Japan; coal; p. (1950) *191,978.*
Onahama, *pt.*, N.E. Japan; copper refinery under construction.
Onate, *t.*, Guipuzcoa, Spain; nr. Bilbao; industl; p. (1957) *7,225.*
Onega, *L.*, R.S.F.S.R.; 85 m. from L. Ladoga; a. 3,765 sq. m.; connection with R. Volga by canal.
Onega, *R.*, R.S.F.S.R.; flows to G. of Onega; length 400 m.
Oneglia, *spt.*, Italy; on G. of Genoa, nr. Nice, Italy; olive-oil tr.
Onehunga, *spt., bor.*, N.I., N.Z.; nr. Auckland; p. (1961) *16,375.*
Oneida, *L.*, N.Y., U.S.A.; nr. Syracuse; 20 m. by 6 m.; discharges via Oneida R. to Seneca R.
Oneonta, *t.*, N.Y., U.S.A.; on Susquehanna R.; rly. wagon wks.; p. (1960) *13,412.*
Onomichi, *t.*, Honshu, Japan; p. (1947) *48,726.*
Onstwedde, *t.*, Groningen, Neth.; mnfs.; p. (1951) *21,853.*
Ontario, *L.*, N. America; smallest of the Gr. Lakes of the St. Lawrence basin, separating the Canadian prov. of O. from N.Y., U.S.A.; a. 7,500 sq. m.; depth 740 ft.
Ontario, *prov.*, Canada; formerly called Upper Canada; St. Lawrence and Ottawa Rs., Gr. Lakes; extreme climate, milder in peninsula in S.; coniferous forest; good communications; hydro-elec. power; nuclear power sta. at Chalk R.; wheat, oats, fruit, dairying, cattle, lumbering, gold, silver, copper, lead, uranium, nickel, oil, farm implements, rly. rolling stock, motor vehicles, machin., textiles, furs, wood pulp, newsprint, cap. Toronto; contains Ottawa; a. 412,582 sq. m.; p. (1961) *6,236,092.*
Onteniente, *t.*, Valencia, Spain; on R. Clariano; woollen gds., paper mills; p. (1957) *14,689.*
Oodnadatta, *t.*, S. Australia; on uncompleted N. to S. trans-continental rly.; p. *100.*
O'okiep, *t.*, Cape Province, S. Africa; copper-mining dist.; p. (with neighbouring villages—whites and non-whites) *5,000.*
Oosterhout, *t.*, N. Brabant, Netherlands; nr. Breda; mnfs.; p. (1960) *24,831.*
Ootacamund, *t.*, Madras, India; ch. t. in Nilgiri Hills; summer headquarters of Madras Govt.; sanatorium; p. (1961) *50,140.*
Opala, *t.*, Congo; on Lomami R.; palm-nuts, gum copal.
Opalton, *t.*, Queensland, Australia; opals.
Opatija, (former It. Abbazia), *t.*, Jugoslavia, tourist resort known as the "Nice" of the Adriatic.
Opava, (former Troppau), *t.*, ČSSR.; textiles, paper, sugar; p. (1961) *42,523.*
Ophir, *dist.*, N.S.W., Australia; nr. Bathurst; gold.
Ophir, *mtn.*, S. Malaya, alt. 4,186 ft.
Ophir, *mining t.*, S.I., N.Z.; nr. Dunedin.
Opladen, *t.*, N. Rhine-Westphalia, Germany; on R. Wupper; metals, textiles, chemicals; p. (1963) *36,300.*
Opobo, *spt.*, Nigeria; exp. palm-oil and kernels.
Opole (Oppeln), *t.*, Upper Silesia, Poland, German before 1945; on R. Oder; former cap. of principality; remains of palace; seat of administration Upper Silesia; engin.; p. (1960) *61,000.*
Oporto, *spt.*, Portugal; on R. Douro; second c. in Portugal; comm.; royal palace of Torre de Marca; cath.; univ.; ctr. of port-wine tr., sardine fisheries, cottons, woollens, silks, distilling, sugar refineries; fruit; p. (1960) *310,000.*
Opotiki, *t.*, N.I., N.Z.; ctr. of maize dist.; p. (1961) *2,559.*
Oppeln, *see* Opole.

Oppland, *co.*, Norway; a. 9,608 sq. m.; p. (1963) *166,823.*

Oradea, (former **Nagyvarad**), *t.*, Romania; nr. Hungarian border; rly. junction, farming, pottery, engin.; p. (1959) *105,000.*

Öraefa Jokull, *highest mtn.*, Iceland; alt. 6,409 ft.

Oran, *dep.*, N. Algeria; p. (1948) *1,990,729.*

Oran, *spt.*, Algeria; cath.; mosque; tr. in wines, wool, cereals, cattle, sheep, hides; French naval and military sta.; p. (1960) *393,000.*

Orange, *t.*, N.S.W., Australia; fruit growing, gold, copper, silver; p. (1961) *18,952.*

Orange, *ancient t.*, Vaucluse, France; silks, sugar, fruit; p. (1954) *17,473.*

Orange, *t.*, Mass., U.S.A.; p. (1960) *3,689.*

Orange, *c.*, N.J., U.S.A.; adj. Newark; calculating machines, radio, textiles, drugs; p. (1960) *35,789.*

Orange, *C.*, N. Brazil, S. America.

Orange, *R.*, Cape Province, S. Africa; flows from Basutoland to the Atlantic; part forms S. bdy. between Cape Province and Orange Free State; length 1,300 m.

Orange Free State, *prov.*, Rep. of S. Africa; plateau land, Drakensberg to N.E., Rs. Orange, Vaal and Caledon; sheep, cattle, horses, wheat, maize, fruit, tobacco, coal, diamonds; cap. Bloemfontein; a. 49,647 sq. m.; p. (1960) *1,386,547* (inc. *276,745* whites).

Oranienburg, *t.*, Potsdam, E. Germany, on R. Havel; industl.; chemicals, metals, machin.; p. (1963) *21,075.*

Oras, *t.*, Samar, Philippines; p. *20,962.*

Orastie, *t.*, Romania; on R. Muresul; p. (1956) *10,488.*

Orbetello, *t.*, Tuscany, Italy; cath.; p. *10,631.*

Ord of Caithness, *hill, headland*, nr. Helmsdale, Scot.; alt. 1,200 ft.

Ordos, *desert region*, Inner Mongolia; lies S. and E. of Yellow R.; pastoral nomads; mean alt. 3,300 ft.

Ordu, *spt.*, Turkey; on N. cst.; gd. tr.; exp. manganese; p. (1960) *20,171.*

Ordzhonikidze, *t.*, Caucasia, R.S.F.S.R.; on R. Terek; hydro-elec., lead, silver and zinc smelting; natural gas pipeline to Tbilisi; p. (1959) *164,000.*

Ore Mtns., *see* **Erzgebirge.**

Örebro, *co.*, Sweden; timber, machin., matches; cap. Örebro; a. 3,650 sq. m.; p. (1961) *262,239.*

Örebro, *t.*, *cap.*, Örebro, Sweden; footwear, textiles, paper; p. (1961) *75,434.*

Oregon, *Pacific st.*, U.S.A.; Cascade, Cst. and Blue Mtns.; Colombia R. and tribs.; L., valleys; rainy cst., drier interior (agr with irrigation); cereals, sugar-beet, fruit, cattle, gold, silver, copper, coal, uranium; fisheries, canning, meat-packing, timber, milling; cap. Salem; a. 96,891 sq. m.; p. (1960) *1,768,687.*

Oregon City, Ore., U.S.A.; on Willamette R. at the falls; p. (1950) *7,682.*

Orekhovo-Zuyevo, R.S.F.S.R.; E. of Moscow, on R. Klyazma; cottons, woollens, silk, linen and knitted goods; p. (1959) *108,000.*

Orel, *t.*, R.S.F.S.R.; on R. Oka; univ.; iron, engin.; p. (1959) *152,000.*

Orenburg, *c.*, R.S.F.S.R.; on Ural R.; engin., leather, silk; p. (1962) *288,000.*

Orense, *inland prov.*, N.W. Spain; timber and fruit-growing, agr.; cap. Orense; a. 2,694 sq. m.; p. (1959) *468,242.*

Orense, *t.*, cap. Orense, Spain; on R. Minho; flour, leather, iron; p. (1959) *64,747.*

Ore Sound, *str.*, between Sjaelland and S. Sweden; freezes occasionally.

Orford Ness, *cst. prom.*, Suffolk, Eng.; 2½ m. long.

Oriente, *prov.*, Cuba; a. 14,128 sq. m.; p. (1953) *1,797,606.*

Oriente, *terr.*, S. America; in dispute between Peru and Ecuador; situated E. of Andes, between R. Putumayo and R. Marañon; mainly dense forest, reputedly rich in minerals.

Orihuela, *t.*, Alicante, Spain; on R. Segura; leather, silks, textiles, wine, cereals, fruit; p. (1957) *44,979.*

Orillia, *t.*, Ont., Canada; wood-working, metal; p. (1961) *15,345.*

Orinoco, *R.*, Venezuela; rises Parima mtns., flows circuitously to Atlantic opposite Trinidad; its trib., the Cassiquiare, connects it with the Rio Negro and the Amazon; length 1,480 m.

Orissa, *st.*, India; agr. with few ts.; Hirakud dam across Mahanadi R.; Paradeep being devel. as pt.; rice; cap. Bhuvaneshwar; a. 60,164 sq. m.; p. (1961) *17,548,846.*

Orizaba, *t.*, Veracruz, Mexico; textiles, paper mills, breweries; p. (1960) *70,000.*

Orizaba, *mtn.*, Veracruz, Mexico; volcanic; called Citlatépetl in Aztec times; alt. 18,701 ft.

Orkney, *co.*, Scot.; a gr. of 68 Is. in the N. Sea, 29 being inhabited; principal Is. Pomona, Sanday, Westray; antiquarian remains, stone circles; farming, fishing; cap. Kirkwall; total a. about 360 sq. m.; p. (1961) *18,743.*

Orlando, *c.*, Fla., U.S.A.; winter resort; citrus fruit; industl.; p. (1960) *88,135.*

Orléanais, *old prov.*, France, corresponding mainly to deps. Loire-et-Cher, Eure-et-Loire Loiret.

Orléans, *c.*, Loiret, France; on R. Loire; cap. of Orléanais; cath.; univ.; gr. tr. in wine, brandy, wool, blankets, etc.; farm implements; statue of Joan of Arc; p. (1962) *88,105.*

Orleans, I. of, Quebec, Canada; in St. Lawrence R., nr. Quebec; a. 70 sq. m.

Ormes Head, Great and Little, promontories on cst. Caernarvon, N. Wales.

Ormos, *t.*, Philippines.

Ormskirk, *t.*, *urb. dist.*, Lancs., Eng.; 14 m. N.E. of Liverpool; light engin., clothing, timber, agr.; p. (1961) *21,815.*

Orne, *dep.*, Normandy, France; agr., dairying, stock-keeping, fruit-growing, cider, mineral springs, iron; cap. Alençon; a. 2,372 sq. m.; p. (1962) *280,549.*

Örnsköldsvik, *t.*, Sweden; on G. of Bothnia; industl. ctr.; p. *8,400.*

Oronsay, *sm. I.*, S. Colonsay, Argyll, Scot.

Orontes, *R.*, Lebanon, Syria, Turkey; rises in Lebanon Mtns., flows N. in deep trench between Lebanon and Anti-Lebanon Mtns. to Plain of Antioch (Antakya), then turns W. and breaks through mtns. to Mediterranean Sea; upper valley above Hama forms cultivated belt, width 10 m., used by Aleppo–Beirut rly.; middle valley is marshy; lower valley and Plain of Antioch intensively cultivated, mulberry, citrus and hard fruits, grain; length over 400 m.

Oroquieta, *t.*, Mindanao, Philippines; p. *26,640.*

Orosháza, *mkt. t.*, S.E. Hungary; in agr. and pig-keeping dist.; p. (1962) *31,867.*

Orotava, *t.*, Tenerife, Canary Is.

Oroya, *t.*, Peru, S. America; copper smelting; lead refining; p. (1961) *15,000.*

Orpington, *see* **Bromley.**

Orrell, *t.*, *urb. dist.*, Lancs., Eng.; W. of Wigan; p. (1961) *10,663.*

Orsha, *t.*, Byelorussian S.S.R.; on R. Dnieper; textiles, metal workings; p. (1959) *64,000.*

Orsk, *t.*, R.S.F.S.R.; on R. Ural; growing industl. t. of the Ural industl. reg.; iron and steel, locomotives, iron–chrome–nickel ores; term. of oil pipeline; p. (1959) *176,000.*

Orsova, *mkt. t.*, Romania; on R. Danube, nr. the Iron Gates Pass; oil-refining; p. (1965) *6,527.*

Orta, *L.*, Italy; W. of Lago Maggiore; a. 7 sq. m.

Orta, *t.*, Foggia prov., Italy; on shore of L. Orta.

Ortegal, *C.*, N. cst. Spain.

Orthez, *t.*, Basses-Pyrénées, France; scene of Wellington's victory over Soult (1814); leather, hams, chocolate; p. (1954) *6,713.*

Ortona, *t.*, Abruzzi Molise, Italy; cap. of ancient Frentani; on Adriatic; cath.; wines; p. *19,104.*

Oruro, *dep.*, Bolivia; a. 20,657 sq. m.; cap. Oruro; p. (1962) *265,400* (large proportion Indians).

Oruro, *t.*, Bolivia; alt. 12,160 ft.; gold, silver, copper, tin; p. (1962) *86,985.*

Orvieto, *t.*, Umbria, Italy; on R. Paglia; cath., Etruscan antiquities; wines, olive oil, cereals; pottery, lace; p. *20,352.*

Orwell, *R.*, Suffolk, Eng.; estuary of R. Gipping; runs from Ipswich to Harwich.

Osaka, *lge. spt.*, *c.*, *comm. ctr.*, Honshu I., Japan; gr. tr.; silk, cotton, rayon cloth, tea, iron, glass, shipbldg., sugar-refining, arsenal; Shinto and Buddhist temples; p. (1962) *3,148,000.*

Oschersleben, *t.*, Magdeburg, E. Germany; sugar, chemicals, engin.; p. (1963) *19,128.*

Ösel I. (Saaremaa), Baltic, Estonian S.S.R.; ch. t. Kuressare.

Osh, *t.*, Kirghiz, S.S.R.; silk, food inds.; p. (1959) *65,000.*

Oshawa, *c.*, Ontario, Canada; motors; p. (estd. 1965) *69,000.*

Oshima, *I.*, Tokyo Bay, Japan; lgst and most northerly of Izu-shichito gr.; site of volcanic Mt. Mihara (2,477 ft.).
Oshkosh, *c.*, Wis., U.S.A.; on Fox R.; meat pkg., farming, flour, motors; p. (1960) *45,110.*
Oshogbo, *t.*, Nigeria; p. (1953) *123,000.*
Osijek (Esseg), *t.*, Croatia, Jugoslavia; nr. Hungarian front.; cottons, silks, beet-sugar, glass, oil refining; p. (1959) *75,000.*
Osinniki, *t.*, R.S.F.S.R.; W. Siberia; new ctr. of coal mng.; thermal power sta.; p. (1959) *68,000.*
Osipenko, *see* **Berdyansk.**
Oskaloosa, *t.*, Iowa, U.S.A.; in agr. and colly. region; p. (1960) *11,053.*
Oskarshamn, *spt.*, Sweden; on Kalmar Sound; seldom icebound; shipbldg.; p. *12,900.*
Oslo (formerly **Christiania**), *c.*, *cap.*, *ch. spt.*, Norway; on fjord of same name; cath., univ.; woollens, cottons, condensed milk, paper; exp. timber, fish, matches; p. (1963) *482,495.*
Osnabrück, *c.*, N. Rhine–Westphalia, Germany; cath., cas.; textiles, machin., tobacco, metals, engin.; rly. junction; p. (1963) *141,000.*
Osorno, *t.*, Chile; agr. ctr.; in beautiful, forested cty.; Germanic atmosphere; p. (estd.) *93,686.*
Osorno, *mtn.*, Chile; volcanic peak, 8,790 ft.
Osorno, *prov.*, S. Chile; p. (1960) *160,156.*
Ossa (Kissavos), *mtn.*, Thessaly; N. of Vale of Tempe and Olympus; alt. 6,194 ft.
Ossett, *mun. bor.*, W.R. Yorks, Eng.; 3 m. W of Wakefield; woollens, coal-mining, engin.; p. (1961) *14,729.*
Ossining, *t.* N.Y., U.S.A.; on Hudson R.; famous "Sing-Sing" prison; p. (1960) *18,662.*
Ostend, *spt.*, Belgium; passenger route between Britain and continent of Europe; popular resort; casino, fisheries, shipbldg., textiles, tobacco; p. (1962) *56,811.*
Östergötland, *co.*, Sweden; on Baltic cst.; a. 4,266 sq. m.; cap. Linköping; p. (1961) *357,693.*
Östersund, *t.*, Jämtland, Sweden; on Stor L.; mil. ctr.; rly. wkshps., bricks; p. (1961) *24,866.*
Östfold, *dist.*, Norway; a. 1,613 sq. m.; p. (1963) *206,073.*
Ostia, *ancient pt.*, Italy; at mouth of R. Tiber; marshy situation; arch. remains, cath.; p. *4,000.*
Östra Kvarken, *channel*, Gulf of Bothnia, between Sweden and Finland.
Ostrava, *t.*, ČSSR.; univ.; coal, iron, steel, chemicals, oil-refining; p. (1962) *234,671.*
Ostrog, *t.*, on Horýn R., W. part of Ukrainian S.S.R. (Volhynia), U.S.S.R.
Ostrogochsk, *t.*, R.S.F.S.R.; nr. R. Don; tallow and cattle tr., tanneries; p. *10,000.*
Ostrow, *t.*, Poznan, Poland; agr. machin.; perfume; p. (1960) *42,000.*
Ostrowiec (Ostrovets), *t.*, Kielce, Poland; on trib. Oder; lignite, iron ore, iron; cattle mkt.; p. (1960) *38,000.*
Ostuni, *t.*, Leece, Italy; mnfs. and tr.; p. *27,602*
Osuna, *t.*, Seville, Spain; p. (1957) *23,250.*
Oswaldtwistle, *t.*, *urb. dist.*, Lancs, Eng.; at N. foot of Rossendale Fells, 3 m. E. of Blackburn; cotton weaving, spinning and dyeing; chemicals; p. (1961) *11,915.*
Oswego, *c.*, N.Y., U.S.A.; on L. Ontario; taken by Montcalm 1756, and the British 1814; water-power; hosiery, matches, textiles, engines; p. (1960) *22,155.*
Oswestry, *mkt. t.*, *mun. bor.*, Salop, Eng.; at foot of Welsh mtns., 18 m. N.W. of Shrewsbury; cas.; rly. engine wks.; p. (1961) *11,193.*
Oswiecim, *t.*, Krakow, Poland; p. (1960) *31,000.*
Otago, *dist.*, S.I., N.Z.; mtnous., afforested, rich in gold; farming, sheep, fruit; cap. Dunedin (*q.v.*); a. 25,220 sq. m.; p. (1961) inc. Southland *270,067.*
Otago Harbour, Otago dist., S.I., N.Z.; Dunedin and Port Chalmers are ports on this harbour.
Otanmäki, Finland; rich deposit of magnetite-ilmenite ore found 1953.
Otaru, *spt.*, Hokkaido, Japan; herring fisheries; coal-mining, lumbering; p. (1950) *178,330.*
Otira Tunnel, S.I., N.Z.; carries rly. from Christchurch to Greymouth through S. Alps nr. Arthur's Pass; length 5¼ m.
Otley, *t.*, *urb. dist.*, W.R. Yorks, Eng.; on R. Wharfe, 10 m. N.W. of Leeds; printing, machin., wool, paper mkg., leather, furnishings; p. (1961) *11,930.*
Otranto, *fishing t.*, S. Italy; on Strait O.; cas.; submarine cable sta.; once a flourishing c.; cath., fine mosaic pavement; p. *2,950.*
Otsu, 2 *ts.*, Hokkaido, Japan; busy tr.; p. (1955) *107,498.*
Ottawa, *c.*, Ontario, Canada; cap. of Dominion of Canada; on R. Ottawa, 100 m. W. of Montreal; univ., caths., parliament bldgs.; hydro-elec. power, lumbering, sawmills, paper, flour, leather, matches, machin., ironware; p. (1961) *429,750.*
Ottawa, *R.*, Canada; trib. of St. Lawrence, forming boundary between Ontario and Quebec; length 625 m.
Ottawa, *t.*, Ill., U.S.A.; at mouth of Fox R.; grain, glass; p. (1960) *19,408.*
Ottawa, *t.*, Kan., U.S.A.; on Osago R.; rly. wks.; p. (1960) *10,673.*
Ottery St. Mary, *mkt. t.*, *urb. dist.*, Devon, Eng.; 10 m. E. of Exeter; silk, rope, brushes; birthplace of S. T. Coleridge; p. (1961) *4,121.*
Ottoshoop, *t.*, Transvaal, S. Africa; gold, fluorspar.
Ottumwa, *c.*, Iowa, U.S.A.; on Des Moines R.; in midst of great coalfield and agr. dist.; iron and steel, meat packing; p. (1960) *33,871.*
Otway, *hills*, S.W. Victoria, Australia; sheep.
Otwock, *t.*, Warsaw, Poland; p. (1960) *36,000.*
Ouachita or Washita, *R.*, Arkansas, U.S.A.; trib. of Red R.; length 550 m.
Oudenaarde (Audenarde), *t.*, Belgium; town hall; Allies defeated French 1708; textiles; p. (1962) *6,906.*
Oudtshoorn, *t.*, Cape Province, S. Africa; on Olifants R.; ostrich farms, tobacco, fruit; p. (1960) *22,186* inc. *8,921* whites.
Oued Gueterini, *t.*, Algeria, 70 m. S.E. Algiers, oil.
Ougadougou, *t.*, *cap*, Voltaic Rep., W. Africa; p. *18,000.*
Ougnter, L., *lough*, Cavan, Ireland.
Oughterard, *t.*, Galway, Ireland; marble quarries, farming, fishing; p. (1951) *498.*
Oujda, *t.*, Morocco; phosphate dist.; p. (1960) *128,645.*
Oullins, *t.*, dep. Rhône, France; nr. Lyons; locomotive repair shops; textiles, glass, leather; p. (1954) *19,224.*
Oulton Broad, *L.*, Suffolk, Eng.; nr. Lowestoft.
Oulu (Uleåborg), *co.*, N. Finland; partly forest and partly agr.; cap. Oulu; a. 21,887 sq. m.; p. (1961) *406,992.*
Oulu (Ouleåborg), *t.*, *cap.*, Oulu, Finland; on G. of Bothnia (Baltic Sea) at mouth of R. Oulu; lumbering; p. (1961) *59,163.*
Oulu, *L.*, Finland; 40 m. long.
Oundle, *mkt. t.*, *urb. dist.*, Northants, Eng.; on R. Nene, 7 m. S.W. of Peterborough; public school; p. (1961) *2,546.*
Ouro Preto, *t.*, Brazil; former cap. of Minas Gerais st.; iron, manganese, gold; textiles; p. (1960) *31,400.*
Ourthe, *R.*, Belgium; trib. of R. Meuse; l. 90 m.
Ouse or Great Ouse, *R.*, Norfolk, Eng.; flows N.E. to the Wash; length 156 m.
Ouse, *R.*, Yorks, Eng.; formed by Rs. Swale and Ure, flows to Humber estuary; length 130 m.
Ouse, *R.*, Sussex, Eng.; flows to English Channel at Newhaven; length 30 m.
Outremont, *t.*, Quebec, Canada; p. (1961) *30,753.*
Ovalle, *t.*, Coquimbo prov., Chile; fruit, wool; manganese, mng.; p. (1960) *46,553.*
Ovar, *t.*, Beira Litoral, Portugal; on Avera lagoon; onions and other vegetables, sardines, wine, wheat; p. *12,729.*
Overijssel, *prov.*, Neth.; bordering on Zuider Zee; dairying, fishing, cottons; a. 1,299 sq. m.; p. (estd. 1959) *770,848.*
Overton, *t.*, *rural dist.*, Flint, N. Wales; 5 m. S.E. of Wrexham; p. (rural dist. 1951) *6,760.*
Oviedo, *maritime prov.*, N. Spain; agr., fruit, sardine. and other fisheries; cap. O.; a. 4,204 sq. m.; p. (1959) *995,233.*
Oviedo, *t.*, *cap.*, Oviedo, Spain; on R. Nalon; Gothic cath., univ.; coal; textiles, leather matches; gr. mkt.; p. (1959) *128,766.*
Owatonna, *t.*, Minn., U.S.A.; p. (1960) *13,409.*
Owen Falls Dam, Uganda; inaugurated 1 Apr 1954; converts L. Victoria into reservoir fo irrigation of U.A.R. and Sudan; also to suppl Uganda industries with hydro-elec. power.
Owen Sound, *t.*, *L. pt.*, Ontario, Canada; on S.W cst. of Georgian Bay, L. Huron; E. terminu of lgst. wheat-carrying L. steamers; linked b

rly. to Toronto (125 m.) and Montreal; p. (1961) *17,421*.

Owen Stanley, *range*, Papua, New Guinea; highest peak Mt. Victoria; alt. 13,121 ft.

Owens, L., S. Cal., U.S.A.; on E. flank of Sierra Nevada 20 m. S.E. of Mt. Whitney; water taken by 225-m.-long aqueduct to Los Angeles; a. 120 sq. m.

Owensboro', *t.*, Ky., U.S.A.; petroleum, farming, stock-raising, tobacco; p. (1960) *42,471*.

Owosso, *c.*, Mich., U.S.A.; on Shiawassee R.; timber tr.; p. (1960) *17,006*.

Owyhee, *R.*, Ore., U.S.A.; trib. of Snake R.; length 350 m.

Oxelösund, Sweden; on Baltic cst., S. of Stockholm; steelwks., tarcoke, glass; p. (1961) *10,007*.

Oxford, *co.*, S. Midlands, Eng.; mainly agr.; cereals, paper, gloves, blankets, agr. implements, motor cars; cap. O.; a. 749 sq. m.; p. (1961) *309,458*.

Oxford, *mun. bor.*, *univ. c.*, *co. t.*, Oxford, Eng.; between Thames and its trib. Cherwell, 63. m. from London by rail; famous univ. with residtl. colleges, printing, steel wks., motor wks. at Cowley; p. (1961) *106,124*.

Oxnard, *t.*, Cal., U.S.A.; citrus fruits, sugar beet, oil refining; p. (1960) *40,265*.

Oxus R., *see* **Amu Darya**.

Oyashio, *see* **Bering Current**.

Oyo, *t.*, Nigeria; p. (1953) *72,000*.

Oyster Bay, *t.*, *cst. resort*, N.Y., U.S.A.; on Long I.; home of Theodore Roosevelt; p. (1950) *5,215*.

Ozark Mtns., Okla. and Ark., U.S.A.; lead, zinc; ch. *t.* Joplin.

Ozd, *t.*, Hungary; p. (1962) *35,959*.

Ozieri, *t.*, Sardinia, Italy; p. *10,541*.

P

Paarl, *t.*, Cape Province, S. Africa; summer resort; wines, fruit, tobacco; flour, saw and textile mills; p. (1960) *41,540*,(inc. *14,128* whites).

Pabianice, *t.*, Poland; nr. Lodz; textiles, farming implements, paper; p. (1960) *56,000*.

Pabna, *t.*, Bengal, E. Pakistan; oil, carpets; p. (1961) *40,700*.

Pacasmayo, *spt.*, Peru, S. America; exp. rice, sugar, cotton, cacao, hides, copper, lead, zinc, silver; p. (1961) *6,000*.

Pachitea, *R.*, Peru, S. America; rises in Andes, flows N. to R. Ucayali; sm. German immigrant colonies in upper valley; length 320 m.

Pachmarhi, Madhya Pradesh, India; summer cap., tourist ctr.; p. (1961) *6,142*.

?achuca, *cap.*, Hidalgo st., Mexico; silver; p. (1960) *70,000*.

?acific Ocean; a. 68,000,000 sq. m.; lgst. ocean in the world; extends from W. cst. of America to E. cst. of Asia and Australia and the S. Ocean in the S.; enters Arctic Ocean via Bering Strait; greatest length N. to S. 8,000 m.; breadth, 10,000 m.; mean depth 12,560 ft., greatest depth 37,800 ft. in the Marianas Trench (1960 dive).

'adang, *spt.*, Sumatra, Indonesia; coffee, spices, rubber, tobacco, copra; p. (1961) *143,699*.

'addington, *see* **Westminster, City of**.

'aderborn, *c.*, N. Rhine–Westphalia, Germany; cath., other historic bldgs.; foodstuffs, textiles, metals; p. (1963) *56,600*.

'adiham, *urb. dist.*, Lancs, Eng.; at N. foot of Rossendale Fells, 4 m. S.W. of Nelson; textiles; p. (1961) *9,893*.

'adstow, *t.*, *spt.*, *urb. dist.*, Cornwall, Eng.; on W. side of Camel estuary 4 m. N.W. of Wadebridge; light inds.; sm. seaside resort; p. (1961) *2,676*.

adua, *t.*, Italy; cath., arcades, ancient bridges; machin., chemicals, silks, cloth, distilling; p. (1961) *198,403*.

aducah, *c.*, Ky., U.S.A.; on Ohio R.; saw-mills, tobacco, railway wks.; p. (1960) *34,479*.

aeroa, *bor.*, N.I., N.Z.; p. (1961) *2,896*.

ag, *I.* and *spt.*, Jugoslavia; timber, salt; cath.; p. (of I.) *4,349*.

agan, *t.*, Burma; ruins; lacquer work.

ago-Pago, *spt.*, Samoan Is., Pac. Oc.; U.S. naval sta.; p. (1950) *1,586*.

ahang, *st.*, Malaysia; central Malaya; cap. Kuala Lipis; forested; a. 13,280 sq. m.; p. (1961) *359,739*.

ahiatua, *bor.*, N.I., N.Z.; dairying; p. (1961) *2,577*.

Pahlevi, *t.*, Iran; nr. Resht, on Caspian Sea; rice, hides, skins, fruit; p. (estd. 1949) *48,000*.

Pai, *R.*, Hopeh, China; unites with Yungting R. Huto R., and flows to G. of Chihli; length 300 m.

Paignton, *t.*, *urb. dist.*, S. Devon, Eng.; on Tor Bay; resort; farming, cider; p. (1961) *30,289*.

Paimpol, *fishing pt.*, Côtes du Nord, N.W. France; on N. cst. of Brittany, 20 m. N.W. of St. Brieuc; lobster fishing; p. *2,795*.

Painted Desert, area of bare, multi-coloured rocks, Arizona, U.S.A.

Paisley, *burgh*, Renfrew, Scot.; 5 m. W. of Glasgow; ancient abbey; thread and rope spinning, shipbldg., chemicals, engin., preserves, car bodies; p. (1961) *95,753*.

Paita, *pt.*, Peru, S. America; exp. cotton, wool, flax, panama hats; lge. whaling sta. to S.; p. (1961) *6,958*.

Pakhoi, *former treaty pt.*, Kwangtung prov., China; indigo, groundnuts, hides, leather, sugar, fish; p. (1931) *36,000*.

Pakistan, Islamic Republic of, *indep. sov. st.* within Br. Commonwealth (1947), forming part of sub-continent of India; consists of 3 provs.: West Pakistan (cap. Lahore), East Pakistan (cap. Dacca) and Fed. Terr. of Karachi; prin. expts. raw jute, cotton, hides and skins, oilseeds, tea; cap. Islamabad; a. 365,529 sq. m.; p. (1961) *93,831,982*.

Paknampoh, *t.*, Thailand; on R. Meinam, at upper limit of steam navigation.

Pakokku, *t.*, Burma; comm. ctr.; sugar, rice, tobacco, oil-fields, teak; p. *23,115*.

Palagruz, *I.*, Adriatic Sea; formerly Italian; ceded to Jugoslavia by peace treaty 1947.

Palanpur, *t.*, Gujarat, India; p. (1961) *29,139*.

Palatinate, *see* **Rhineland Palatinate, Germany**.

Palau Is., *group of Is.*, in Pac. Oc.; p. (1958) *8,845*.

Palawan, *I.*, Philippines; coffee, resin, timber; a. 4,550 sq. m.; p. *107,000*.

Palayamcottai, *t.*, Madras, India; rice, coffee, cotton, tobacco; p. (1961) *51,002*.

Palembang, *t.* Sumatra, Indonesia; cap. P. residtl.; cotton, rubber, coffee; p. (1961) *475,000*.

Palencia, *inland prov.*, Old Castile, Spain; partly fertile plain, partly wooded and mntainous; cap., Palencia; a. 3,093 sq. m.; p. (1959) *239,041*.

Palencia, *t.*, *cap.*, Palencia, Spain; N. of Valladolid; ctr. of rich wheat-growing dist.; iron-founding and weaving; p. (1957) *50,000*.

Palermo, *spt.*, Sicily, Italy; cath., univ.; machin., chemicals, wines, fruit, tobacco; p. (1961) *587,063*.

Palestine or **The Holy Land**, historic region, bounded by Syria and Lebanon on the N., Jordan on the E., the Egyptian prov. of Sinai on the S., and the Mediterranean on the W.; a. when under British mandate 10,429 sq. m.; p. (estd. 1948) *782,000*. *See* **Israel**.

Palestine, *t.*, Texas, U.S.A.; agr. and forest region; p. (1960) *13,974*.

Palghat, *t.*, Kerala, India; p. (1961) *77,620*.

Palitana, *t.*, Gujarat, India; a. c. of Jain temples inhabited by priests and their servants; p. (1961) *24,581*.

Palk Strait, India; separating India from [Ceylon.

Palm Beach, *t.*, Fla., U.S.A.; Atl. coastal resort.

Palm Beach, *t.*, N.S.W., Australia; N. of Sydney; tourist resort.

Palma, *spt.*, Majorca I., Spain; cath., palaces; wine, fruit, silk; cap. Balearic Is.; p. (1959) *149,921*.

Palmarola I., Pontine Is., Italy; vineyards.

Palmerston North, *c.*, N.I., N.Z.; dairying, sheep; univ; rly. junction; p. (1961) *43,164*.

Palmira, *t.*, Colombia; tobacco, coffee, rice, cocoa, sugar, grain; p. (estd. 1959) *124,000*.

Palmyra (ancient **Tadmor**), *c.*, in Syrian desert, 120 m. N.E. of Damascus; extensive ruins; p. *10,000*.

Palmyra Is., Pac. Oc., U.S.A.; coral islets; [coconuts; p. *32*.

Palni Hills, *range*, between E. and W. Ghats, S. Deccan, India; highest peak 7,050 ft.

Palos, *spt.*, Huelva, S. Spain; on Rio Tinto; starting point for Columbus in 1492.

Palos, C. de., Mediterranean, S.E. cst. of Spain.

Palua, *pt.*, Venezuela; pt. of shipment for iron mines at El Pao; nearby Caroni hydro-elec. plant built to serve steel wks. and aluminium plant.

Pamiers, *t.*, Ariège, France; elec. steel furnaces; wine; leather; p. (1954) *12,822*.

Pamir Mtns., *high mtn. plateau* ("roof of the world"), Tadzik S.S.R., Central Asia; Mt. Communism (24,590 ft.) climbed by Russo-British team 1962.

Pamlico Sound, *lge. lagoon*, on E. cst. of N.C., U.S.A.; length 75 m., width 25 m.

Pampa, La, *terr.*, Central Argentina; stock-rearing; cap. Santa Rosa; a. 55,669 sq. m.; p. (1947) *166,929*.

Pampas, Argentina; vast plains stretching from the Rio Negro on the S. to the Gran Chaco in the N., and E. from the Andes to the Atlantic; woodless, level country; rich pastures in E., supporting countless numbers of sheep and cattle, W. mostly barren.

Pamplona, *t.*, Colombia; coal, gold, coffee, cocoa, wheat, brewing, textiles; p. (estd. 1959) *22,800*.

Pamplona, *t.*, Spain; cath., fortress, univ.; textiles, leather, paper, flour, soap, earthenware; p. (1959) *88,410*.

Panagyurište, *t.*, Bulgaria; p. (1956) *14,000*.

Panama, *rep.*, Central America; mountainous; climate hot throughout year, abundant rains; languages Spanish; religion R.C.; communications poor; cattle-raising, farming; pearls, bananas, cocoa, coconuts, rubber, sugar, coffee, timber, shrimps; cap. Panama City; a. 28,575 sq. m.; p. (1963) *1,100,000*.

Panama, *canal zone*, Panama; strip of land 47 m. long by 10 m. wide, extending 5 m. on either side Panama Canal, under U.S. jurisdiction; p. (1960) *41,683* (inc. Forces personnel).

Panama Canal, Canal Zone, Panama; length 51 m. ranging in width from 300 to 1,000 ft., minimum depth 41 ft.; time of transit through canal 7–8 hours; canal starts at Cristobal (Atlantic), to Gatun locks, through Gatun Lake, Culebra cut, Pedro Miguel locks, Miraflores locks to Balboa (Pacific). *See also* **L 89**.

Panama City, *c.*, *spt.*, cap. Panama; harbour at S. entrance to Canal; cath.; oil refining, steel rolling mill, cement plant, lt. inds.; p. (1960) *369,280*.

Panaria, *I.*, Lipari Is., Italy; a. 1 sq. m.; hot springs, vineyards, olives; p. (1960) *1,400*.

Panarukan, *spt.*, Java, Indonesia; exp. tobacco, sugar; p. *7,455*.

Panay, *I.*, Philippines; between Negros I. and Mindoro I.; a. 4,446 sq. m.; cotton, rice, sugar, coffee; p. *1,520,143*.

Pancevo, *t.*, Voivodina, Jugoslavia; wheat, maize, timber, glass, textiles, ironwks.; p. (1959) *40,000*.

Panchet Hill Dam and power sta. Bihar, India; on R. Damodar.

Pandharpur, *t.*, Maharashtra, India; on R. Bhima; temple, pilgrimages; p. (1961) *45,421*.

Pando, *dep.*, Bolivia; p. *18,600*; cap. Cobija; p. (1962) *24,400*.

Panevežys, *t.*, Lithuanian S.S.R.; textiles; p. (1954) *60,000*.

Pangalanes Canal (Canal Des Pangalanes), Malagasy; follows E. cst. from Farafangana to Tamatave, through series of lagoons; 300 m.

Pangani, *spt.*, Tanzania, E. Africa; copra, sisal hemp, maize; p. *3,000*.

Pangkalanbrandan, *spt.*, Sumatra, Indonesia; oil-refining and exp.

Panipat, *t.*, E. Punjab, India; silver and brass, cotton goods, blankets, carpets, pottery; p. (1961) *67,026*.

Panjsher Valley, Afghanistan; silver-mines, unexploited; mica-mine. [p. *8,000*.

Pantar I., Lesser Sunda Is., Indonesia; mtns.;

Pantelleria, *volcanic I.*, Mediterranean, Italy; midway between W. Sicily and Tunisia; a. 58 sq. m.; ch. t. P. on N.W. cst.; figs, raisins, vines, capers, cereals; fishing; p. *10,000*.

Pantin, *sub.*, Paris, France; glasswork, sugar ref., tobacco factories, chemicals, leather, tallow; p. (1962) *46,401*.

Paoki (Baoji), *c.*, Shensi prov., China; cotton weaving; millet, wheat; p. (1953) *130,000*.

Paola, *cst. t.*, Calabria, Italy; oil and wine tr.; p. *13,625*.

Paoting (Baoding), *c.*, Hopeh prov., China; on the Yungting R.; gr. tr.; p. (1953) *197,000*.

Paotow (Baotou), *c.*, Inner Mongolia; on left bank of Yellow R., on road and rly. routes to E. China; airfield; terminus of caravan routes through Gobi desert and Tarim basin to Turkestan; gr. tr. and industl. ctr.; steelwks.; p. (1958) *650,000*.

Papeete, *t.*, *pt.*, Tahiti I. Pac. Oc.; cap. Tahiti and of French Settlements in Oceania; exp. copra, vanilla, phosphates and mother-of-pearl; p. (1962) *19,903*.

Paphos, *administrative dist.*, Cyprus; ancient c., ruins; serious earthquake 1953; p. (1960) of dist. *58,159*, of t. *9,083*.

Papua–New Guinea, *terr.*, Eastern New Guinea; administered by Australia; adm. H.Q. Port Moresby (cap. of Papua); gold, copra, rubber, timber; Sirinumu Dam (*q.v.*) opened 1963; total a. 183,540 sq. m.; p. (1960) *1,972,000*.

Pará, *st.*, Brazil; densely forested; rubber, fruits, cacao, Brazil nuts; cap. Bélem; a. 464,780 sq. m.; p. (1960) *1,550,935*.

Pará, *spt.*, Brazil, *see* **Bélem**.

Paraguay, *rep.*, S. America; undulating cty., swamps, forests; Rs., Paraguay, Pilcomayo, Paraná; climate, hot summers, warm winters, moderate rainfall; religion, R.C.; communications poor; fertile; cattle, yerba maté, oranges, sugar, maize, cotton, tobacco, lumber, quebracho extract; iron, manganese, copper; meat packing; cap. Asunción; a. 157,006 sq. m.; p. (estd. 1962) *1,850,000*.

Paraguay, *R.*, S. America; rises in plateau of Mato Grosso, flows S. and joins R. Paraná nr. Corrientes; forms bdy. between Brazil and Bolivia, Brazil and Paraguay; approx. length 1,200 m.

Paráiba, *st.*, Brazil; cotton, cocoa, sugar, rubber, tobacco; cap. João Pessóa; a. 21,730 sq. m.; p. (1960) *2,018,023*.

Paráiba, *R.*, Brazil; flows to Atlantic in st. of P.; length 200 m.

Paráiba, *R.*, S. Brazil; rising in São Paulo st., and flowing between Rio de Janeiro and Minas Gerais to the Atlantic N.E. of Rio de J.; length 658 m.

Paramaribo, *spt.*, *cap.*, Neth. Guiana; (Surinam); on R. Surinam; ch. exp., bauxite, timber, rubber, rice, fruit; p. (1959) *113,478*.

Paraná, *cap.*, Entre Rios prov., Argentina; pt. for grain, cattle, sheep; road tunnel to Santa Fé under construction; p. (1960) *109,600*.

Paraná, *st.*, Brazil; extensively forested; cap. Curitiba; a. 77,717 sq. m.; p. (1960) *4,277,763*.

Paraná, *R.*, Brazil; formed by junction of Rs. Rio Grande and Parnaiba; flows W. between Paraguay and Argentina; flows into Rio de la Plata; navigable to Brazil frontier nr. Iguassú Falls; length 2,000 m.

Paranaguá, *spt.*, Paraná st., Brazil; ch. pt. for Paraná; in lagoon harbour; exp. maté, timber, bananas, iron ore; p. (1960) *27,728*.

Pardubice, *t.*, ČSSR.; univ.; saw-milling; brewing, distilling; p. (1961) *52,655*.

Parentis, *t.*, Landes, France; nr. L. Biscarosse, 40 m. S.S.W. Bordeaux; oil; lignite mined nearby. [remains.

Parenzo, *spt.*, Italy; cath.; fishing; Roman

Pariñas, *C.*, Peru, S. America.

Paris, *c.*, *cap.*, France, on R. Seine, 110 m. from mth.; cultural ctr.; 12 boulevards radiate from Arc de Triomphe; Notre Dame, Louvre Tuileries, Palais Royal; oldest bridge Pont Neuf (1578–1604); royal forests and palaces nearby, *e.g.*, Fontainebleau, Rambouillet Chantilly; univ. (founded 12th cent.); German siege 1870–71; German occupation 1940–45 luxury inds., publishing, furniture, food clothing; heavy inds. in northern subs.; p (1962) *2,811,171*.

Paris, *t.*, Texas, U.S.A.; cotton, fruit, canne goods; p. (1960) *20,977*.

Parkersburg, *c.*, W. Va., U.S.A.; on Ohio R. iron- and steel-wks., oil and natural gas coal, glassware, rayon, porcelain; p. (1960 *44,797*.

Parkes, *t.*, N.S.W., Australia; p. (1961) *8,228*.

Parma, *prov.*, Emilia, Italy; a. 1,258 sq. m. p. (1961) *381,624*.

Parma, *t.*, N. Italy; between the Apennines and th R. Po; univ., cath.; flourishing tr.; foo processing, wine, cheese; precision instruments agr. machin., footwear, felt hats; p. (1961 *140,844*.

Parnaiba, *R.*, rises in Brazil, flows into N. Atlanti Ocean, forms bdy. between Maranhão an Piaui; length 750 m. [(1960) *39,95*

Parnaiba, *spt.*, Piaui, Brazil; cotton, cattle;

Parnassos, *mtn. ridge*, Greece; 83 m. N.W. Athens, nr. the ancient Delphi, the moder

Liakhura; highest summit, Licoreia, alt. 8,068 ft.
Parnu, *t.*, Estonian S.S.R.; on G. of Riga; resort; flax, timber, wood pulp, woollens; p. (1956) *33,600.*
Páros, *I.*, Grecian Archipelago; W. of Naxos; a. 63 sq. m.; cap. P.
Parramatta, *mun.*, N.S.W., Australia; pt. near head of Parramatta R. (spanned by lgst concrete bridge in world) in met. a. of Sydney; expts woollen and leather goods; p. (1954) *76,100.*
Parrett, *R.*, Somerset, Eng.; flows to Bristol Channel, nr. Bridgwater; length 35 m.
Parry (Mauke), *I.*, Pac. Oc.; part Cook Is., N.Z.; p. *773.* [(1961) *6,004.*
Parry Sound, *t.*, Ont., Canada; lumbering; p.
Parsons, *t.*, Kan., U.S.A.; coal, natural gas, machin.; p. (1960) *13,929.*
Partinico, *t.*, Sicily, Italy; silk; p. *22,080.*
Pasadena, *c.*, Cal., U.S.A.; N. of Los Angeles; in fruit-growing region, base of San Gabriel Mtns.; 200-in. telescope on Mt. Palomar; famous for its carnival; p. (1960) *116,401.*
Pasco, *t.*, Wash., U.S.A.; on Snake R.; p. (1960) *14,522.*
Pasco, *see* **Cerro de Pasco.**
Pas-de-Calais, *dep.*, N. France; coal, iron; farming, sugar distilling, paper, pottery; cap. Arras; a. 2,606 sq. m.; p. (1962) *1,366,282.*
Pasig, *t.*, Luzon, Philippines; comm. ctr. of the L. region; p. *29,170.*
Pasir Mas, *t.*, Kelantan, Malaysia; rly. junction.
Passage West, *urb. dist.*, *spt.*, Cork, Ireland; shipping, fishing; p. (1951) *2,658.*
Passaic, *c.*, N.J., U.S.A.; silk, chemicals, dyes, rubber goods, mill machin., springs, steel cabinets, tin cans; p. (1960) *53,963.*
Passaic, *R.*, N.J., U.S.A.; flows 100 m. to Newark Bay.
Passau, *t.*, Germany, at confluence of Rs. Danube, Inn and Ilz; near Austrian frontier; transshipment base, inds. inc. leather, porcelain, tobacco and brewing; p. (1963) *31,200.*
Passchendaele, *t.*, Belgium; impt. strategic point in First World War; p. (1962) *3,115.*
Passero I., Mediterranean Sea; off S.E. cst. of Sicily, Italy.
Pasto, *t.*, *cap.*, Narino dep., Colombia; on flank of Pasto volcano; univ.; gold near by; p. (estd. 1959) *110,790.*
Pasuruan, *spt.*, Java, Indonesia; exp. sugar, tapioca; p. *36,973.*
Patagonia, Argentina; extensive region, E. of Andes; elevated plateau, arid, sterile; principal Rs., Colorado, Rio Negro and Chubut; oil and minerals, unworked; lge. tracts of grazing for sheep, horses and cattle.
Patan, Gujarat, India; swords, silk and cotton goods; p. (1961) *50,264.*
Patan, *valley t.*, Nepal; p. (1961) *135,230.*
Patani, *spt.*, Thailand; tin exp., fishing; p. *109,252.*
Paterno, *t.*, Sicily, Italy; N.W. of Catania; mineral springs, wines; p. (1961) *42,935.*
Pater Noster Is., Indonesia; coconuts.
Paterson, *c.*, N.J., U.S.A.; principal ctr. silk mftg.; aeroplane engines; textiles; machin.; p. (1960) *143,663.*
Pathankot, *t.*, E. Punjab, India; fruit preserving; p. (1961) *46,330.*
Patia R., Colombia; gold, platinum found.
Patiala and East Punjab States (Pepsu), India. *See* **Punjab.**
Patiala, *t.*, Punjab, India; iron and steel mftg.; flour; p. (1961) *125,234.*
Patino Mines, *see* **Uncia.**
Patkai, *hills*, India; Chaukan; alt. 9,020 ft.
Patmos, *I.*, one of the Dodecanese, Aegean Sea; a. 13 sq. m.; p. (estd.) *3,000.* (According to Rev. 1. 9. the exiled St. John wrote the Revelation here.)
Patna, *cap.*, Bihar, India; univ.; rice, indigo, cotton, salt.; p. (1961) *364,594.*
Patras, *spt.* " Peloponnese ", Greece; citadel and cas.; currants, raisins, figs, olives, wine, skins, etc.; p. (1961) *95,364.*
Patricroft, *industl. t.*, nr. Manchester, Lancs, Eng.
Pau, *t.*, Basses Pyrénées, France; on Gave du Pau; cas.; health resort; linen, chocolate, hams, wine; p. (1954) *48,320.*
Paulis, *t.*, N.E. Congo; admin. offices; cotton ginneries; rly. repair shops; p. *4,399.*
Paulo Affonso, *falls*, São Francisco R., Brazil; 260 ft.; Tres Marias dam and power sta. inaugurated 1960.
Pavia, *t.*, Italy; cath., univ.; walled city; battle site 1525; olives, silk, wine; Parmesan cheese; oil refining at Spineto; p. (1961) *73,503.*
Pavlodar, *pt.*, Kazakh, S.S.R.; on R. Irtysh; chemicals, sulphates, agr. machin., locomotives, aluminium, oil processing; p. (1959) *90,000.*
Pavlovo, *t.*, R.S.F.S.R.; on R. Oka; iron and steel, engin.; p. (1956) *42,600.*
Pawtucket, *c.*, R.I., U.S.A.; on P. R. used for water-power, woollen, cotton and silk goods; machin.; chemicals; first cotton-spinning factory established in the U.S.A. 1790; p. (1960) *81,001.*
Paysandu, *dep.*, Uruguay; p. (1953) *92,417.*
Paysandu, *t.*, Uruguay; meat, cattle, sheep, wool; footwear, soap; p. (estd. 1956) *60,000.*
Pazardzhik, *t.*, Bulgaria; on main rly. line to Istanbul; p. (1956) *39,499.*
Paz de Rio, *t.*, Boyaca, Colombia; steel; iron ore, coal, limestone nearby; hydro-elec. sta. projected.
Peace, *R.*, Canada; rises in Rocky Mtns., and flows to L. Athabaska; length 1,000 m.
Peak, The, *Pennine hill dist.*, mid-Eng.; extending from Chesterfield to Buxton, and Ashbourne to Glossop; mainly composed of limestone with typical Karst features; tourists; highest point Kinder Scout, alt. 2,080 ft.
Pearl, *R.*, *see* **Chu Kiang.**
Pearl Harbour, *spt.*, Oahu I., Hawaiian Is., U.S. Naval base. Attacked by Japanese on 7 Dec. 1941.
Peary Land, Greenland.
Peč, *t.*, Jugoslavia; nr. Albanian border; tobacco, fruit; p. (1959) *25,000.*
Pechelbronn, Alsace, France; oilfields.
Pechenga (Petsamo), *spt.*, R.S.F.S.R., U.S.S.R.; on left bank of R. Petsamon 10 m. upstream from Barents Sea; formerly Finnish, ceded to U.S.S.R. Sept. 1944; ice-free throughout year, thanks to influence of N. Atlantic Drift; exp. nickel, timber, cobalt.
Pechora, *R.*, flowing into Arctic Ocean, R.S.F.S.R. 1,000 m. long, 700 m. navigable.
Pecos, *R.*, N.M. and Texas, U.S.A.; trib. of Rio Grande; length 764 m.
Pécs, *t.*, Hungary; cath., univ., airport; coal, chemicals, majolica; p. (1960) *114,625.*
Peebles, *bor.*, *co. t.*, Peebles, Scot.; on upper course of R. Tweed; hydro, woollen cloth, knitwear; p. (1961) *5,545.*
Peebles, *co.*, Scot.; hilly, Broad Law, 2,754 ft.; sheep, woollen cloth, knitwear; a. 346 sq. m.; p. (1961) *14,117.*
Peekshill, *t.*, N.Y., U.S.A.; on Hudson R.; ironwks.; p. (1960) *18,737.*
Peel, *t.*, I. of Man, Eng.; midway along W. cst.; cas., cath., ruins; resort; fisheries; p. *2,612.*
Peel Fell, *mtn.*, Northumberland, Eng.; 1,964 ft.
Pegasus, *Bay*, S.I., N.Z.
Pegu, *dist.*, Lower Burma; annexed by Brit. 1852; teak forests; p. *2,961,249.*
Pegu, *t.*, Burma; founded in A.D. 573; pagoda 320 ft. high, temple; rice; bronze statuettes mnfd.; p. *21,712.*
Pegu Yoma, *mtns.*, Burma; separate valleys of Rs. Irrawadi and Sittang.
Pei Kiang, *see* **North River.**
Peine, *t.*, Lower Saxony, Germany; N.W. of Brunswick; iron, furniture, textiles; p. (1963) *30,300.*
Peipus, *see* **Chudskoye.**
Peiraieus, *spt.*, Greece; pt. of Athens; principal pt. of Greece; arsenal; wines, brandy, currants, vinegar; marble; machin.; p. (1961) *1,853,000* inc. Athens.
Pekalongan, *t.*, N. cst. Java, Indonesia; exp. sugar, rubber; p. (1961) *102,380.*
Pekan, *t.*, Pahang, Malaya; p. *5,000.*
Pekin, *t.*, Ill., U.S.A.; cereal prods., distilling, leather, metal goods; p. (1960) *28,146.*
Peking (Beijing), *c.*, *cap.*, China; cultural ctr. and c. of gr. arch. beauty; for hundreds of years seat of the Chinese emperors (Mongol, Ming and Manchu régimes); surrounded by 22 m. of towering walls broken by 16 gates; p. (estd. 1958) *5,420,000.*
Pelée, *mtn.*, Martinique; active volcano, devastated town of St. Pierre 1902, loss of over 30,000 lives, later eruption caused further 2,000 deaths; alt. 4,400 ft.

Pelew Is., Caroline Is., Pac. Oc.; coral, primitive agr.; bauxite; p. *12,798.*

Pella, *prefecture*, Macedonia, Greece; cap. Edessa; p. (1961) *133,128.*

Pelly, *R.*, trib. of R. Yukon, N.W. Terr., Canada.

Peloponnesos, *peninsula*, S. part of Greece, separated from mainland proper by G. of Corinth; a. 8,356 sq. m.; p. (1961) *1,096,390.*

Pelotas, *t.*, Rio Grande do Sul, S. Brazil; at S. end of Lagõa dos Patos; tr. in sheep, cattle from interiors; mnfs. woollens, leather, wine; p. (1960) *121,280.*

Pelvoux, *mtn.*, France; between Isère and Hautes Alpes; alt. 12,920 ft.

Pemba, *I.*, part of indep. st. of Zanzibar; E. Africa; a. 380 sq. m.; cloves and copra, coconuts, exp. mangrove bark for tannin; p. (1958) *133,858.*

Pembroke, *t.*, Ont., Canada; lumbering; p. (1961) *16,791.*

Pembroke, *mtn.*, S.I., N.Z.

Pembroke, *co.*, Wales; fertile; stock-raising, steel, fishing, shipbldg.; a. 617 sq. m.; p. (1961) *93,980.*

Pembroke, *mkt. t.*, *mun. bor.*, Pembroke, Wales; on S. side of Milford Haven; cas., ruins of Monkton Priory; naval dockyard, light engin., metal ind., woollens; p. (1961) *12,737.*

Pembroke Dock, Pembroke, Wales.

Penang, *I.*, *st.* Malaysia; N.W. Malaya; cap. Georgetown, pt. for N. Malaya handling rubber and tin; the first Brit. Straits Settlement (*q.v.*); a. 400 sq. m.; p. (1961) *651,899.*

Penarth, *urb. dist.*, Glamorgan, Wales; on Severn estuary 2 m. S. of Cardiff; ship repairing, wood, cement, bricks; p. (1961) *20,897.*

Pendleton, *t.*, Ore., U.S.A.; p. (1960) *14,434.*

Penedo, *t.*, Brazil tr. ctr.; p. *12,651.*

Penge, *see* **Bromley.**

Pengpu (Bengbu), *c.*, Anhwei, China; on Hwai Ho 105 m. N.W. of Nanking; on Tientsin–Nanking rly.; p. (1953) *253,000.*

Penicuik, *burgh*, Midlothian, Scot.; on N. R. Esk, 7 m. S. of Edinburgh; paper, iron; p. (1961) *5,824.*

Penistone, *mkt. t.*, *urb. dist.*, W.R. Yorks., Eng.; on R. Don, 10 m. N.W. of Sheffield; steel; p. (1961) *7,071.*

Penki (Benqi), *c.*, Liaoning prov., China; metallurgical ctr.; p. (1953) *449,000.*

Penmaenmawr, *t.*, *urb. dist.*, Caernarvon, Wales; on N. cst. 4 m. W. of Conway; seaside resort; p. (1961) *3,754.*

Pennine Alps, Switzerland; division of Alpine system; ch. peaks; Matterhorn (14,782 ft.), Weisshorn (14,804 ft.). Mischabelhörner (14,942 ft.); includes Zermatt; winter sports.

Pennine Range, *mtn. range*, running N. to S. from Cheviot Hills to Derby, Eng.; length 140 m.

Pennsylvania, *st.*, U.S.A.; originally proprietary colony of Penn family, and later one of the 13 original sts. in the Union; traversed N.E. to S.W. by Appalachians; ch. Rs.: Delaware, Susquehanna, Allegheny and Monongahela; iron and steel, coal (bituminous and anthracite), natural gas, petroleum; maize, wheat, oats, rye; textiles, machin., motor cars, tobacco; cap. Harrisburg; ch. ts.: Pittsburgh, Philadelphia; a. 45,333 sq. m.; p. (1960) *11,319,366.*

Penrhyn, *dist.*, Caernarvon, Wales; nr. Bethesda; slate quarries.

Penrith, *mkt. t.*, *urb. dist.*, Cumberland, Eng.; at N. foot of Shap Fell, 18 m. S.E. of Carlisle; ruined cas.; agr. mkt.; agr. implements, egg-packing sta.; tourist ctr.; p. (1961) *10,931.*

Penryn, *t.*, *mun. bor.*, Cornwall, Eng.; on estuary of R. Fal, 2 m. N.W. of Falmouth; fishing; granite quarries; p. (1961) *4,448.*

Pensacola, *spt.*, Fla., U.S.A.; safest land-locked harbour in G. of Mexico; naval sta.; fish, naval requisites, wool, hides, cotton and lumber mills; p. (1960) *56,752.*

Penticton, *t.*, B.C., Canada; fruit farming, canning; p. (1961) *13,859.*

Pentire Point, headland, Cornwall, Eng.

Pentland Firth, strait between Orkney and the Caithness cst., N. Scot.

Pentland Hills, *range*, Scot.; running from Lanark–Edinburgh–Peebles; highest point Scald Law, 1,896 ft.

Pentland Skerries, *small Is.*, Pentland Firth, Scot.

Penybont, *rural dist.*, Glamorgan, Wales; coal-mining; p. (1961) *41,992.*

Pen-y-Ghent, peak in Pennine Range, W.R. Yorks, Eng.; 2,231 ft.

Penza, *t.*, R.S.F.S.R.; between Penza and Kuibyshev; grain, sawmills, paper, soap and candles, engin.; "Druzhba" oil pipeline from Mozyr; p. (1962) *286,000.*

Penzance, *t.*, *mun. bor.*, Cornwall, Eng.; on Mounts Bay; seaside resort, good harbour; pilchard fishing, copper, tin, and china clay, textiles, lt. engin.; p. (1961) *19,433.*

Peoria, *c.*, Ill., U.S.A.; river pt.; farming implements, grain; distilling, brewing, mng.; p. (1960) *103,162.*

Perak, *st.*, Malaysia; N.W. Malaya; cap. Ipoh; tin; a. 8,030 sq. m.; p. (1961) *1,404,952.*

Pereira, *t.*, Caldas, Colombia; cath.; coffee, brewing, thread mkg.; p. (estd. 1959) *183,730.*

Perekop, Isthmus of, connects Crimea with Ukraine, and rail focus in ctr. of maize-growing a.

Pergamino, *t.*, Buenos Aires prov., Argentina; on Pampas 60 m. S. of Rosario; impt. road and rail focus in ctr. of maize-growing a.

Périgueux, *t.*, *cap.*, Dordogne, France; on R. L'Isle; cath.; china, iron, woollens, figs, truffles; pâté de foie gras; marshalling yards; rly. repair shops; p. (1962) *41,134.*

Perim, *I.*, located in straits of Bab el Mandeb at entrance to Red Sea; part of Brit. col. of Aden; a. 5 sq. m.; p. (1946) *360*

Perlis, *st.*, Malaysia; N. Malaya; cap. Kangar; rice, tin, coconuts; a. 310 sq. m.; p. (1961) *102,726.*

Perm, *formerly* **Molotov**, *t.*, R.S.F.S.R.; on R. Kama, N.W. of Sverdlovsk; hydro-elec., oil, textiles, engin., chemicals, copper; p. (1962) *701,000.*

Pernambuco, *st.*, Brazil; sugar, fruits; mntnous interior, cst. fertile; cotton, coffee; cap. Recife; a. 37,458 sq. m.; p. (1960) *4,136,900.*

Pernis, *t.*, opp. Rotterdam, Netherlands; lge oil refinery; oil pipeline to Wesserling (nr. Cologne).

Perovo, *t.*, R.S.F.S.R.; nr. Moscow; engin., chemicals, agr. research institutes; p. (1959) *143,000.*

Perpignan, *fortfd. t.*, Pyrénées-Orientales, France; cath.; wine, brandy, silk, wool; p. (1962) *86,156.*

Perreux-sur-Marne, *t.*, Seine, France; p. (1954) *26,745.*

Persepolis, *ruins*, ancient cap. of Persia.

Pershore, *mkt. t.*, *rural dist.*, Worcs, Eng.; on R. Avon, 8 m. S.E. of Worcester; abbey church; preserves, machin.; p. (1961) *17,599.*

Persia (Iran), *kingdom*, Asia; tableland 6,000–8,000 ft., ch. range Elburz Mtns.; Demavend 18,500 ft.; Rs. unimportant; ctr. barren, N. cst. fertile; climate, summer, days very hot, nights cool, winters warm; religion Islam; poor communications; major earthquake affected N.W. a. 1 Sept. 1962; dates, rice and other cereals, cotton, tobacco, wool, carpets, impt. oilfields, cap. Tehran; a. 628,000 sq. m.; p. (1956) *18,944,821.*

Persian G., Asia; a. 80,000 sq. m.; inland sea between Arabia and Iran; shores barren.

Perth, *co.*, Scot.; Trossachs and P. of Killiecrankie; noted for beautiful scenery; crossed by Grampians in N. and W.; ch. peaks, Ben More, Ben Lowers, Schiehallion; ch. Rs.: Tay with tribs. Isla, Garry, Tummel, Sarn; pastoral; fruit; distilling; textiles; a. 2,493 sq. m.; p (1961) *127,018.*

Perth, *burgh*, Perth, Scot.; on R. Tay, in gap between Sidlaw and Ochil Hills; cap. of Scot till assassination of James I in 1437; near by is Scone Palace; cath.; linen, winceyettes brewing, rope, dyeing; p. (1961) *41,199.*

Perth, *t.*, cap. W. Australia; 12 m. above pt. o Fremantle; univ., observatory. race-courses p. (1961) inc. suburbs *419,755.*

Perth Amboy, *spt.*, N.J., U.S.A.; terracotta wks. shipyards and dry docks; p. (1960) *38,007.*

Peru, *rep.*, S. America; traversed N. to S. by th Andes, attaining 22,000 ft.; ch. Rs., Marañon Ucayali; in S.E., L. Titicaca (12,450 ft.) lgst. L in S. America; climate, eastern, very hot drenching rains, central or mountain zone, su intensely hot, but shade temperatures low; W and Pacific cst., heat not excessive, scanty rain fall; religion R.C.; poor communications sugar, cotton, coffee, wool, hides, timber, cocoa wheat, tobacco, petroleum, silver, copper; cap Lima; a. 482,258 sq. m.; p. (1961) *10,016,23* excl. nomadic Indians and Mestizo inhabitant estd. *11,000,000.*

Peru (Humboldt), Current, *ocean current*, S. Pac. Oc.; flows N. along cst. of N. Chile and Peru; relatively cold water causes lower air temperatures and produces cloud and fog.
Perugia, *spt.*, Umbria, Italy; on R. Tiber; univ., observatory; woollens, silks, lace; foodstuffs, furniture, pottery, chemicals, agr. machin.; p. (1961) *109,596*.
Pervouralsk, *t.*, R.S.F.S.R.; in Urals, 25 m. W. of Sverdlovsk; pipe rolling mill; p. (1959) *90,000*.
Pesaro, *Adriatic spt.*, Italy; N.W. of Ancona; resort; figs, wines, oil, silks; majolica ware; sulphur; sugar-refining; p. (1961) *65,601*.
Pescadores Is., *group of Is.*, 30 m. W. of Formosa; total a. about 51 sq. m.; since 1945 Chinese, formerly Japanese.
Pescara, *t.*, Italy; at estuary of R. Aterno, E. cst.; olive oil, soap, pasta, pottery; fishing; p. (1961) *87,076*.
Peshawar, *t.*, W. Pakistan; on rly. to Khyber Pass commanding route Afghanistan–India; military sta.; univ.; coal, fruit, sugar; cottons, ambroidery, wood carving, copper ware, boat bldg., marble; p. (1961) *218,691*.
Peshawar, *div.*, W. Pakistan; p. (1961) *5,088,000*.
Pesquilerto, *R.*, trib. of Rio Grande del Norte, Mexico.
Pessac, *t.*, Gironde, France; grid transf. sta.; wines; p. (1954) *19,226*.
Pest, *c.*, Hungary; on left bank of R. Danube, opposite Buda, and connected therewith by suspension bridge, the two cs. forming the Hungarian cap. of Buda-Pest (*see* **Budapest**).
Petah Tiqva, *t.*, Israel; agr. ctr.; oranges; textiles, chemicals, metal goods, tanning; p. (1960) *62,700*.
Peter I., *uninhabited I.*, Antarctic Ocean; belonging to Norway; a. about 94 sq. m.
Peterborough., *t.*, Ont., Canada; flour milling, elec. machin., trailers, agr. equipment, plastics, textiles, paper; p. (1961) *47,185*.
Peterborough, Soke of, *see* **Huntingdon and Peterborough.**
Peterborough, *c.*, *mun. bor.*, Huntingdon and Peterborough, Eng.; on R. Nene at the margin of The Fens; cath.; rly. ctr.; engin., bricks, paper, milling; p. (1961) *62,031*.
Peterhead, *spt., burgh*, E. Aberdeen, Scot.; on E. cst., 27 m. N.E. of Aberdeen; herring fisheries, tweed, lt. engin.; p. (1961) *12,497*.
Peterlee, *t.*, Durham, Eng.; on plateau of E. Durham, 11 m. E. of Durham; one of "New Towns" designated 1948; ctr. of coal-mng. dist.; mohair and worsted spinning; clothing and wood-wool mftg.; p. (estd. 1965) *17,963*.
Petermann Peak, Greenland; alt. 9,175 ft.
Petersburg, *t.*, Alaska, U.S.A.; p. (1960) *1,502*.
Petersburg, *c.*, Va., U.S.A.; tobacco, meat-canning, cotton; optical goods; p. (1960) *36,750*.
Petersfield, *t.*, *urb. dist.*, Hants, Eng.; on R. Rother, 12 m. N.W. of Chichester; college; malting, brewing; p. (1961) *7,379*.
Petit Morin, *R.*, France; trib. of R. Marne.
Petra, *ancient t.*, Jordan; temples, rock tombs and Roman ruins.
Petra, *t.*, Majorca, Spain; birthplace of founder of San Francisco.
Petropavlovsk, *spt.*, Kamchatka Pen., U.S.S.R.; fishing; p. (1959) *86,000*.
Petropavlovsk, *t.*, Kazakh. S.S.R.; on R. Ishim; flour, leather, meat canneries; furs, engin.; p. (1959) *131,000*.
Petropolis, *t.*, Rio de Janeiro, Brazil; health resort, 2,300 ft. above sea-level; p. (1960) *93,849*.
Petrosani, *t.*, Romania; S. of Deva; coal; p. (1956) *23,052*.
Petrovgrad, *t.*, N.W. Jugoslavia; p. *32,838*.
Petrovsk, *t.*, S.E. Siberia, R.S.F.S.R.; iron and steel, non-ferrous metallurgy; p. (1954) *50,000*.
Petrozavodsk, *t.*, R.S.F.S.R.; L. Onega; univ.; mica, paper, engin.; p. (1959) *135,000*.
Petsamo, *see* **Pechenga.**
Petten, *t.*, Netherlands; 30m. N.W. of Amsterdam, on cst.; atomic research ctr.
Petworth, *mkt. t.*, *rural dist.*, W. Sussex, Eng.; in Rother valley, 12 m. N.E. of Chichester; building stone; p. (rural dist. 1961) *9,463*.
Pevensey Levels, *marshy area*, E. Sussex, Eng.; lie behind coastal sand-bars between Eastbourne and Bexhill, extend 5 m. inland to Hailsham; now largely drained, cattle pastures; a. 24 sq. m.
Pewsey, *vil.*, *rur. dist.*, Wilts, Eng.; in Vale of Pewsey, 7 m. E. of Devizes; farming, iron, bricks, tiles; p. (rural dist. 1961) *16,971*.
Pforzheim, *t.*, Baden-Württemberg, Germany; S.E. of Karlsruhe; gold, silver, metal wks. jewellery; p. (1963) *86,100*
Phan Rang, ctr. of irrigation scheme, S. Viet-Nam. [fish; p. *5,000*.
Phan Thiet, *spt.*, S. Viet-Nam; exp. dried and salt
Pharsala, *c.*, Thessaly, Greece; S. of Larissa; Cæsar's triumphs over Pompey.
Philadelphia, *c.*, *pt.*, Penns., U.S.A.; univ., R.C. cath., masonic temple; mint, academy of fine arts; shipbldg., locomotives, machin., surgical instruments, carpets, woollens, cottons, worsteds; sugar, and petroleum refining; ctr. of War of Independence, from 1790 to 1809; fed. cap. founded by Wm. Penn 1682; p. (1960) *2,002,512*.
Philae, *I.*, Upper U.A.R.; in Nile above Aswan Dam; temples dating from late Egyptian and classical times incl. famous temple to Isis; submerged by dam waters.
Philippeville, *t.*, *spt.*, Algeria; wine, sheep, cattle, cereals, cork, cigarettes, mineral water, macaroni, fish canning; p. (1954) *70,000*. [*1,554*.
Philippeville, *t.*, Namur, S. Belgium; p. (1962)
Philippine Is., *rep.*, Asia; comprising over 7,000 Is., lgst. being Luzon, Mindanao, Mindoro and Palawan; mountainous, many volcanoes, highest Apo, 10,312 ft.; coal, iron, copper, gold; dye-woods, rice, maize, tobacco, coffee, cotton, Manila hemp; coconuts, cigars, pearl fisheries; cap. Quezon City; p. (1960) *27,087,685*.
Philippopolis, *see* **Plovdiv.**
Philipstown, *see* **Daingean.**
Phillipsburg, *c.*, N.J., U.S.A.; on Delaware R.; water-power, machin., rly. wks.; silk and pulp; p. (1960) *18,502*.
Phitsanulok, *t.*, central Thailand; temples; weaving; p. *25,000*.
Phlorina (Florina), *pref.*, Greece; occupied by Bulgaria, April 1941, restored to Greece by peace treaty of 1947; cap. Phlorina; p. (1961) *67,238*.
Phlorina (Florina), *t.*, Phlorina, Greece; in basin at alt. 3,000 ft., 10 m. from Jugoslav border, 15 m. from Albanian border, purely agr. interests; p. (1961) *11,933*.
Phnom-Penh, *t.*, *R. pt.*, cap. Cambodia, on Mekong R.; univ., airpt., rice, cotton; p. (1962) *403,000*.
Phoenix, *c.*, Arizona, U.S.A.; winter resort; iron, steel, aircraft, electronics, clothing; p. (1960) *439,170*.
Phoenix Group, *Is.*, Pac. Oc.; part of Gilbert and Ellice I. colony; a. 16 sq. m.; U.S. now have some rights over Canton and Enderbury; Canton used as international airport; p. (1956) *1,257*.
Phthiotis, *pref.*, Greece; cap. Lamia; p. (1961) *159,373*.
Piacenza, *prov.*, Emilia, Italy; a. 965 sq. m.; p. (1961) *282,813*
Piacenza, *t.*, Italy; cath., palaces, arsenal; motor cars, chemicals, cement; p. (1961) *87,930*.
Pianosa I., Italy; penal settlement; cereals, vineyards, olives; p. *1,000*.
Pias, *t.*, Alentejo Baixo, S. Portugal; E. of Beja.
Piatra, *t.*, Moldavia, Romania; timber, pharmaceuticals, soap; p. (1956) *32,648*.
Piaui, *st.*, Brazil; cattle, cotton, sugar, tobacco, rubber; silver, iron and lead; a. 96,262 sq. m.; cap. Teresina; p. (1960) *123,368*.
Piave, *R.*, N.E. Italy; flows to Adriatic; length 125 m.
Piazza Armerina, Sicily, Italy; oil, wines and nuts; remarkable Roman mosaics (recently discovered); p. *28,420*.
Pibor, *t.*, S.E., Sudan; p. *1,000*.
Picardy, *old prov.*, France; which included all the Somme dep. and parts of Pas de Calais, Aisne and Oise; old battle sites, Agincourt and Crécy.
Pichincha, *prov.*, Ecuador; cap. Quito—the cap. of Ecuador; a. 6,218 sq. m.; p. (1950) *386,520*.
Pickering, *mkt. t.*, *urb. dist.*, N.R. Yorks, Eng.; on N. margin of Vale of Pickering, 6 m. N. of Malton; church with murals; iron, bricks; p. (1961) *4,193*.
Pickering, Vale of, E.R. Yorks, Eng.; wide, flat-floored vale, once occupied by glacial lake; bounded to N. by N. York Moors, to S. by York Wolds; drained W. by R. Derwent, which

leaves Vale through Kirkham gap; alluvial soils, marshy in ctr.; crop-farming along margins, grain, fodder crops; cattle grazing on damper meadows in ctr.; ch. ts. Pickering, Malton, Helmsley.

Pico da Bandeira, *mtn.*, Brazil; alt. 9,462 ft.

Picton, *t.*, S.I., N.Z.; freezing wks.; tourist and fishing ctr.; p. (1961) *2,320*.

Pidurutalagala, *mtn.*, Ceylon; alt. 8,295 ft.; highest peak in Ceylon.

Piedmont, *region*, N. Italy; rice, wheat, vines, fruits; silk, cottons, woollens; a. 9,813 sq. m.; p. (1961) *3,889,962*.

Piedras Negras, *frontier t.*, Mexico; cattle mkt., coal, silver, zinc and copper; p. *15,663*.

Pierre, *t.*, *cap.*, S.D., U.S.A.; on Missouri R.; p. (1960) *10,088*.

Pietermaritzburg, *t.*, *cap.*, Natal, S. Africa; 30 m. N.W. of Durban; named after Piet Retief and Gerhardus Maritz, two Boer leaders; lt. inds.; tanning; iron-ore mng. in a.; p. (1960) *95,124* inc. *39,472* Europeans.

Pietersburg, *t.*, Transvaal, S. Africa; gold, asbestos, tin; cereals, tobacco, cotton, oranges, lemons; p. (1962) *28,000* inc. *11,000* whites.

Piet Retief, *t.*, Transvaal, S. Africa; tobacco, fruit, mealies, wattle gr. in dist.; p. (1960) *8,604* inc. *2,745* whites.

Pikes Peak, *mtn.*, Col., U.S.A.; alt. 14,109 ft.

Pila (Schneidemühl), *t.*, N.W. Poland (since 1945); formerly in Prussian prov. of Pomerania; trade ctr., lignite mines nearby; p. (1960) *34,000*.

Pilar, *t.*, Paraguay; cotton, timber, hides, oranges; p. (estd. 1960) *10,000*.

Pilatus, *mtn.*, Switzerland; alt. 6,988 ft.

Pilawa (Pilau), *t.*, *spt.*, R.S.F.S.R.; shipbldg., fishing.

Pilbarra, *dist.*, W. Australia; metal ores inc. gold, copper, tin; ch. mining ctr., Marble Bar.

Pilcomayo, *R.*, rising in S. Bolivia, and flowing through the Gran Chaco, separates W. Paraguay from Argentina; trib. of the Paraguay; length 1,400 m.

Pilibhit, *t.*, Uttar Pradesh, India; rice, pepper, sugar; p. (1961) *57,527*.

Pilion, *celebrated mtn.*, S. of Mt. Ossa, Thessaly, Greece; alt. 5,310 ft.

Pillon Pass, Switzerland; alt. 5,092 ft.

Pimlico, *dist.*, Westminster, London, Eng.

Pinar del Rio, *prov.*, W. Cuba, W. Indies; tobacco, asphalt; a. 5,211 sq. m.; p. (1953) *448,422*.

Pinar del Rio, *t.*, Cuba, W. Indies; tobacco; p. (1953) *38,885*.

Pinawa, *t.*, Manitoba, Canada; 55 N.E. of Winnipeg; nuclear research; p. (1965) *8,000*.

Pind Dadan Khan, *t.*, W. Pakistan; coal; p. *11,445*.

Pindus, *mtn. chain*, between Thessaly and Albania, Greece; highest peak 8,050 ft.

Pine Bluff, *c.*, Ark., U.S.A.; cotton, motor-cars; p. (1960) *44,037*.

Pine Creek, *t.*, Arnhem Land, N. Terr., Australia; gold; p. *115*.

Pinerolo, *t.*, Italy; S.W. of Turin; cath.; silk, cotton, woollens; p. *22,890*.

Pines, Is. of, *dependency* of Fr. col. New Caledonia; a. 58 sq. m.; convict settlement.

Pinetown, *t.*, Natal; residtl., industl.; p. (1960) *12,799* inc. *6,965* Europeans.

Pinios R., Greece; flows into G. of Thessaloniki.

Pinjarra, *t.*, W. Australia; rly. junction; timber and stock-raising dist.

Pinneberg, *t.*, Schleswig-Holstein, Germany; N.W. of Hamburg; rose cultivation, metals, leather; p. (1963) *29,900*

Pinos I. (I. of Pines), Caribbean Sea; S. of Cuba; a. 1,180 sq. m.

Pinsk, *t.*, Byelorussia, U.S.S.R.; paper, woodworking inds.; p. (1956) *36,500*.

Piombino, *t.*, Italy; port for Elba I.; steel wks.; p. *26,238*.

Piotrkow, *industl. t.*, Poland; S. of Lodz; p. (1960) *53,000*.

Pique, *t.*, Ohio, U.S.A.; N. of Dayton; ironwks., woollens; nuclear reactor; p. (1960) *19,219*.

Piraeus, *see* Peiraieus.

Piran, *spt.*, Istria, Jugoslavia; salt, wines, olives; p. *14,875*.

Piracicaba, *t.*, São Paulo, Brazil; sugar, cattle, coffee, oranges; p. (1960) *80,670*.

Pirmasens, *t.*, Rhineland–Palatinate, Germany; S.W. of Mannheim; footwear, leather goods; p. (1963) *53,100*.

Pirna, *t.*, Dresden, E. Germany; on R. Elbe; textiles, paper, glass; p. (1969) *41,076*.

Pirot, *t.*, Jugoslavia; nr. Bulgarian border; Jugoslavia; p. *13,033*. [*365,882*.

Pisa, *prov.*, Italy; a. 1,180 sq. m.; p. (1961)

Pisa, *c.*, Italy; at head of Arno delta, 12 m. N.E. of Leghorn; famous leaning tower, cath., univ.; mineral baths, cotton, silk; p. (1961) *91,108*.

Pisco, *spt.*, Peru, S. America; cotton; lead, zinc; whaling; p. (1961) *17,000*.

Pisco, *dep.*, Peru, S. America; p. (1961) *123,917*.

Pisek, *t.*, ČSSR.; brewing, iron foundries, textiles; p. (1961) *19,542*.

Pistoia, *t.*, Tuscany, Italy; on Arno plain, N.W. of Florence; iron and steel goods, silk, macaroni; p. (1961) *82,401*.

Pitcairn I., E. Pacific; British col.; incs. Henderson, Ducie, and Oeno Is.; sweet potatoes, bananas, oranges, coconuts; a. 2 sq. m.; p. (1965) *186*, mostly descendants of the mutineers of the *Bounty*.

Pitch Lake, Trinidad I., W.I.; located in the S. of the I., 10 m. S.W. of San Fernando; natural deposit of asphalt; tourism; a. 212 acres.

Pitea, *spt.*, N. Sweden; on G. of Bothnia; saw mills; p. (1961) *7,426*.

Pitesti, *t.*, Romania; on Arges R.; petroleum, fruit, grain; p. (1959) *42,000*.

Pitlochry, *burgh*, Perth, Scot.; on R. Tummel, 4 m. S. of Pass of Killiecrankie; summer resort; distilleries, hydros; p. (1961) *2,051*.

Pittenweem, *burgh*, Fife, Scot.; at entrance to Firth of Forth; fisheries; p. (1961) *1,576*.

Pittsburgh, *c.*, Penns., U.S.A.; univ.; R.C. cath., coll., Carnegie Library and Institute; port on Ohio R.; ctr. of richest American coalfield; natural gas, petroleum, iron and steel, machin., metal goods, meat packing, glass, aluminium, chemicals; p. (1960) *604,332*.

Pittsfield, *c.*, Mass., U.S.A.; textiles, paper, plastics, elec. machin., hol. resort; p. (1960), *57,879*.

Pittston, *t.*, Penns., U.S.A.; anthracite, coal, machin.; p. (1960) *12,407*. [*716,837*.

Piura, *N. dep.*, Peru; a. 15,190 sq. m.; p. (1961)

Piura, *t.*, Peru; p. (1961) *32,100*.

Pladju, *t.*, S. Sumatra, Indonesia; oil refining; linked by pipe-line with Tempino and Bejubang.

Plainfield, *c.*, N.J., U.S.A.; sub. New York City; printing, motor lorries, machin., chemicals, hosiery; p. (1960) *45,330*.

Plaistow, *dist.*, E. London, Eng.; p. (1961) *10,424*.

Planitz, *t.*, Saxony, Germany; S.W. of Zwickau; textiles, tobacco; p. (estd. 1954) *25,100*.

Plate R., or Rio de la Plata, estuary of the Rs. Paraná and Uruguay flowing to the Atlantic between Argentina and Uruguay, length 170 m.; width at head 25 m., at mouth 138 m.

Plattsburg, N.Y., U.S.A.; pt. of L. Champlain; tourist ctr.; military post; p. (1960) *20,172*.

Plauen, *t.*, Karl-Marx-Stadt, E. Germany; textiles, machin., cable, leather, paper, radios; rly junction; p. (1963) *79,111*.

Plenty, Bay of, N.I., N.Z.; on E. cst.; 130 m. wide.

Plettenberg, *t.*, N. Rhine–Westphalia, Germany; on R. Lenne; iron wks.; p. (1963) *29,000*.

Pleven, *fortfd. t.*, Bulgaria; many mosques; famous siege 1877; woollens, silks, wines; p (1956) *57,758*.

Plock, *t.*, Poland; on R. Vistula, nr. Warsaw agr.; oil refinery and petrochemical plant unde construction nearby; p. (1960) *42,000*.

Ploesti, *t.* Prahova dist., Romania; petroleum engin.; p. (1959) *124,000*.

Plonsk, *c.*, Poland; N.W. of Warsaw; grain sugar-beet; p. *7,866*.

Plovdiv (Philippopolis), *c.*, Bulgaria; on R Marica; univ., Greek cath.; wheat, fruit, silks woollens, tobacco, leather, attar of roses; p (1956) *162,518*.

Plumstead, *dist.*, S.E. London, Eng.

Plymouth, *c.*, *spt.*, *co. bor.*, S. Devon, Eng.; on Plymouth Sound; comprises the "three towns" of Plymouth, Devonport and Stonehouse; R.C. cath., guildhall, museum; shipbldg.; seaside resort; fishing and fish canning, light inds. p. (1961) *204,279*.

Plymouth, *spt.*, Mass., U.S.A.; Pilgrim Hal Pilgrim Fathers landed in 1620 from *Mayflower* established first English colony; textile cordage, machin., cottons, woollens; p. (195 *10,540*. [*2,50*

Plymouth, *ch. t.*, Montserrat I., T.W.I.; p. (195

Plymouth, *t.*, Penns., U.S.A.; coal; p. (1960) *10,401*.
Plynlimmon, *mtn.*, Montgomery and Cardigan, Wales; alt. 2,469 ft.
Pizeň (Pilsen), *t.*, ČSSR.; coal, iron ore, steel, engin, chemicals; p. (1961) *137,763*.
Po, *R.*, Italy; flows from Monte Viso, through Piedmont and Lombardy to the Adriatic; length, 340 m.; natural gas deposits Po valley.
Pocatello, *t.*, Idaho, U.S.A.; rly. wks.; livestock; cheese; p. (1960) *28,534*.
Pocklington, *mkt. t.*, *rural dist.*, E.R. Yorks, Eng.; at foot of York Wolds, 12 m. E. of York; milling, malting, bricks, tiles, agr.; p. (rural dist. 1961) *13,933*.
Podolsk, *t.*, R.S.F.S.R.; S. of Moscow; engin., tin smelting, cement; p. (1959) *124,000*.
Podrinye, *dist.*, W. Serbia, Jugoslavia; antimony.
Pohai (Chihli), G. of, N. China; together with G. of Liaotung forms shallow expanse of water almost cut off from Yellow Sea by Liaotung and Shantung peninsulas; receives water and silt of Hwang Ho; a. approx. 15,000 sq. m.
Pohjois Karjalan, *dep.*, Finland; p. (1961) *207,742*.
Point Clairette, Equatorial Africa; oilfield.
Point-à-Pierre, Trinidad; oil refinery; natural gas pipeline from Forest Reserve field.
Pointe-à-Pitre, *ch. t.*, Grande Terre I., Guadeloupe, Lesser Antilles; p. (1960) *26,160*.
Point-Claire, *t.*, Quebec, Canada; p. (1961) *22,709*.
Pointe-des-Galets, *ch. pt.*, Ile de la Réunion, Indian Ocean (Fr.).
Pointe-Noire, *impt. spt.*, Congo Rep. (ex-French), Equatorial Africa; aerodrome; copper ore, potash, timber, groundnuts; p. (1962) *54,643*.
Point Fortin, Trinidad; oil field and refinery.
Poitiers, *t.*, Vienne, France; univ.; Black Prince defeated French (1356); brewing, hosiery, cloth; p. (1962) *62,222*.
Pola, *see* Pula.
Poland, *rep.*, Europe; bounded by Germany, the Baltic Sea, Russia, and Czechoslovakia; largely lowland, rising from Baltic to Carpathians on S. border; ch. Rs.; Vistula and tribs.; climate: hot summers, very cold winters, moderate rainfall; good communications; agr.: cereals, potatoes, sugar-beet, forests, cattle, sheep, horses, pigs; minerals: coal, iron, steel, petroleum, natural gas, potash; cap. Warsaw; a. 121,131 sq. m.; p. (1962) *30,323,900*.
Pollokshields, *S.W. sub.*, Glasgow, Scot.; industl. and residtl.
Polotsk, *t.*, Byelorussian S.S.R.; cath.; gasoline prod., oil refining; oil pipeline to Latvian pt. of Ventspils; p. (1965) *38,100*.
Polotskiy, *t.*, Byelorussian S.S.R.; 8 m. W. of Polotsk; new oil workers' t. 1963.
Poltava, *industl. t.*, Ukrainian S.S.R.; horses, cattle, grain, engin., textiles; p. (1959) *141,000*.
Polynesia, *sub-div.*, Oceania; I. groups in Pacific within 30° N. and S. of the equator; between 135° E. and W. longitude.
Pomerania, *former prov.*, N. Germany; in post-war redivision part E. of R. Oder to Poland; part W. of R. Oder incorporated in *Land* Mecklenburg, E. Germany; farming, shipbldg. fishing.
Pomona or Mainland, lgst. of the Orkney Is., Scot. Kirkwall (cap.) and Stromness on I.
Pomona, *c.*, Cal., U.S.A.; fruit-culture; p. (1960) *67,157*.
Pomorze, *prov.*, Poland; cap. Bydgoszcz; a. 8,012 sq. m.
Pompeii, *ruined c.*, Italy; stood 13 m. S.E. of Naples, at foot of Vesuvius; destroyed A.D. 79 by volcanic eruption, site re-discovered in 1748; many most interesting excavations; also modern c. near by; fine church with famous collection of silver and gold plate.
Ponape I., Caroline Is., Pac. Oc.; copra, ivory, nuts, starch, bauxite; a. 134 sq. m.; p. (1958) *14,335*.
Ponca City, *t.*, Okla., U.S.A.; p. (1960) *24,411*.
Ponce, *c.*, Puerto Rico, W. Indies; coffee, sugar, rum; p. (1960) *114,965*.
Pondicherry, *cap.*, former Fr. Settlements in India; united with India 1954; cotton, rice; a. of dist. 185 sq. m.; p. (1961) *369,079*; of c. *40,421*.
Pont-à-Mousson, *t.*, Meurthe-et-Moselle, France; R. Moselle; ironwks., paper, velvet, cement wks.; p. (1954) *11,416*.
Ponta Delgada, *ch. t.*, *spt.*, San Miguel I., Azores; p. (1950) *22,706*.
Ponta Grossa, *t.*, Paraná, Brazil; rly. junction; maté, rice, timber, tobacco, bananas, cattle, jerked beef; p. (1960) *77,803*.
Pontardawe, *vil.*, Glamorgan, S. Wales; on R. Tawe, 9 m. N.E. of Swansea; zinc smelting and refining, steel wks.
Pontchartrain, Lake, *shallow lake*, lower Mississippi flood plain, U.S.A., connected by canal to New Orleans which lies 6 m. to the south, and by deltaic channels to the gulf of Mexico.
Pontefract, *t.*, *mun. bor.*, W.R. Yorks, Eng.; 7 m. E. of Wakefield; cas. ruins; coal, furniture, confectionery; p. (1961) *27,114*.
Pontevedra, *prov.*, Spain, on Atl. cst., bordering Portugal; agr., livestock, fisheries; cap. Pontevedra; a. 1,695 sq. m.; p. (1959) *736,069*.
Pontevedra, *spt.*, cap. Pontevedra prov.; Spain; fishing; p. (1949) *46,168*.
Ponthierville, *t.*, Congo, Africa; nr. Stanley Falls, Congo R.; p. *1,000*.
Pontiac, *c.*, Mich., U.S.A.; on Clinton R.; fishing and shooting, motor cars, rubber goods, machin., varnish; p. (1960) *82,233*.
Pontianak, *t.*, *cap.*, Kalimantan, Indonesia; exp. rubber, copra; p. (1961) *150,220*.
Pontine Is., off W. cst. of Italy; in Tyrrhenian Sea; a. 4½ sq. m.; p. *6,000*.
Pontine Marshes, *region*, Latium, S. Italy; coastal zone S.E. of Rome extending from Velletri to Terracina; formerly highly malarial fens, largely drained and colonised 1930–35; 3,200 new farms, 4 new ts.; ch. t. Littoria; a. *c.* 250 sq. m.
Pontresina, *t.*, Grisons, Switzerland; E. of St. Moritz; tourist resort.
Pont-y-mister, *vil.*, Monmouth, Eng.; in valley of R. Ebbw, 6 m. N.W. of Newport; lge. steel-wks., zinc refineries.
Pontypool, *t.*, *urb. dist.*, Monmouth, Eng.; coal, iron, steel, glass, bricks, tin galvanising, nylon at Manhilad; p. (1961) *39,879*.
Pontypridd, *t.*, *urb. dist.*, Glamorgan, Wales; on R. Taff, 12 m. N.W. of Cardiff; coal, iron; p. (1961) *35,536*.
Ponza I., Pontine Is., Italy; wine, wheat, flax; fishing; bentonite-mining; a. 3 sq. m.
Poole, *mkt. t.*, *spt.*, *mun. bor.*, E. Dorset, Eng.; on Poole Harbour, 4 m. W. of Bournemouth; seaplane base; yachting; marine engin., tent mkg., bricks, chemicals; p. (1961) *88,088*.
Poona, *t.*, Maharashtra, India; univ.; cotton, sugar, rice; p. (1961) *737,426*.
Poopo, *L.*, Oruro dep., Bolivia; S. America; situated in Andes at alt. 12,120 ft.; very shallow; fed from L. Titicaca by R. Desaguadero, which flows over saline beds; no outlet, therefore salt-water; max. length 50 m., width 30 m.
Popayan, *cap.*, Cauca Dep., Columbia; cath., univ.; gold, silver, platinum, copper near by; p. (estd. 1959) *57,770*.
Poperinghe, *t.*, W. Flanders, Belgium,; woollens linens, hops; p. (1962) *12,409*.
Poplar, *see* Tower Hamlets.
Popocatepetl, *volcano*, nr. Pueble, Mexico; alt. 17,887 ft.
Porbandor, *spt.*, Gujarat, India; cement, silk, cotton; imports coal, dates, timber, machin., petroleum; birthplace of Mahatma Gandhi; p. (1961) *75,081*.
Porcupine Hills, *t.*, Ont., Canada; on rly. 40 m. S. of Cochrane; ctr. of impt. gold-mng dist.
Pordenone, *t.*, Italy; cath.; cottons, silks, pottery; p. *82,506*.
Pori (Björneborg), *spt.*, S. Finland; at mouth of R. Kokemäen; copper refinery, rolling mills, match, paper and pulp wks.; p. (1961) *54,230*.
Porjus, *t.*, Norrbotten, N. Sweden; on R. Lulea, where it leaves Stora Lulevatten; impt. hydro-elec. power-sta. supplies power to iron-ore mining dists. of Gällivare and Kiruna, also to Narvik rly.
Porrentruy, *t.*, Berne, Switzerland; watches; p. *6,121*.
Porsgrunn, *spt.*, Norway; timber, shipping, engin., porcelain, explosives; p. (1961) *10,604*.
Port Alfred, *pt.*, Canada; Upper St. Lawrence R.; imports bauxite for smelting at Arvida (lgst. smelter in world, 1959).
Port Alfred, *t.*, Cape Province, S. Africa; resort; p. (1960) *6,171* (inc. *1,112* whites).
Port Amelia, *spt.*, Mozambique; sisal, coconuts, cotton, maize, groundnuts; p. (1960) *55,902*.
Port Antonio, *t.*, Jamaica, W. Indies; p. *5,482*.
Port Arthur, *c.*, S.W. Liaoning prov., China; naval base at entrance to Pohai R.; p. (estd.) *200,000*. *See* Luta.

Port Arthur, *L. pt.*, Ontario, Canada; on N.W. cst. of L. Superior; lumbering, mining, grain milling, exp. ctr.; p. (1961) *45,276.*
Port Arthur, *t.*, Texas, U.S.A.; p. (1960) *66,676.*
Port Arzew, *pt.*, Algeria; World's 1st comm. plant to liquefy natural gas for exp. opened 1964; oil pipeline from Haoud el Hamra projected.
Port au Prince, *spt.*, Haiti, W. Indies; coffee, cacao; p. (estd. 1964) *200,000.*
Port Augusta, *t., spt.*, S. Australia; at head of Spencer G.; fine harbour; salt field; exp. wheat, fruit; p. (1961) *9,705.*
Port Blair, *spt. cap.*, Andaman and Nicobar Is. p. (estd.) *16,000.*
Port Chalmers, *t., bor.*, S.I., N.Z.; docks, shipyards; p. (1961) *3,120.*
Port Chester, *t.*, N.Y., U.S.A.; on Long I. Sound; summer resort, cottons and woollens; p. (1960) *24,960.*
Port Colborne, *t.*, Ont., Canada; port on L. Erie; iron smelting; nickel, copper refining; p. (1961) *14,886.*
Port Elizabeth, *spt.*, Cape Province, S. Africa; on Algoa Bay; exp. skins, wool, ostrich feathers, mohair; foundries, soap, chemicals, car assembly, food preservation, sawmills; p. (1960) *270,815* (inc. *94,085* whites).
Port Erin, *vil.*, I. of Man, Eng.; on S.E. cst.; seaside resort, fisheries.
Port Essington, *N. point*, of Coburg Peninsula, N. Terr., Australia.
Port Francqui, *t.*, Congo; present terminus of Congo rly. on Kasai R.; p. *5,000.*
Port Fuad, *t.*, U.A.R.; N. entrance to Suez Canal; p. *1,000.*
Port Gentil, *spt.*, Gabon, Eq. Africa; exp. palm oil, mahogany, ebony; sawmills, fishing; oil refinery under construction; p. *5,000.*
Port Glasgow, *burgh, spt.*, Renfrew, Scot.; on S. bank of R. Clyde, 17 m. below Glasgow; shipbldg. and repairing, textiles, rope, canvas mftg.; p. (1961) *22,551.*
Port Harcourt, *spt.*, Nigeria; 30 m. from sea on E. branch of Niger delta; terminus of E. Nigerian rly. system; tin, palm oil, groundnuts; bitumen plant, tyres; oil refining; p. (1953) *72,000.*
Port Hedland, *sm. spt.*, W. Australia; on N.W. cst. 285 m. S.W. of Broome; exp. gold and other metals from Pilbarra gold-field; imports food and machin.; linked to Marble Bar by narrow-gauge rly.
Port Herald, *see* **Nsanje.**
Port Hope, *t.*, Ont., Canada; midway along N. shore of L. Ontario, fruit, dairying, radium refining; p. (1961) *8,091.*
Port Hunter, N.S.W., Australia; port for Newcastle.
Port Huron, *t.*, Mich., U.S.A.; on L. Huron; summer resort, mineral springs, dry docks, grain elevators; motor-car parts; p. (1960) *36,084.*
Port Jackson, N.S.W., Australia; *natural harbour* for Sydney.
Port Kembla, *spt.*, N.S.W., Australia; S. of Wollongong; iron and steel wks., gold refining, textiles.
Port Laoighise, *mkt. t.*, Laoighis, Ireland; cornmills; p. (1961) *3,133.*
Port Lincoln, *spt.*, S. Australia; exp. wheat, frozen meat, tallow, wool; p. (1961) *7,651.*
Port Louis, *cap.*, Mauritius, Indian Ocean; ch. comm. ctr. of col.; p. (1962) *89,096.*
Port Lyautey (Kenitra), *see* **Mina Hassan Tani.**
Port Macquarie, *t.*, N.S.W., Australia; on Hastings R.; p. (1947) *2,906.*
Port Mahon, *see* **Mahon.**
Port Moody, *terminus*, Canadian Pacific Rly., Vancouver, Brit. Columbia; p. *1,512.*
Port Moresby, *spt., ch. t.*, Papua, New Guinea; promising copper deposits; exp. copra, sandalwood, coffee, rubber, shell; p. *2,503.*
Port Natal, *see* **Durban.**
Port Nelson, *spt.*, Manitoba, Canada; on cst. of Hudson Bay at mouth of R. Nelson; linked by rly. to trans-continental systems via The Pas; exp. wheat, minerals; closed by ice for 7 months each year.
Port Nolloth, *spt.*, Cape Province, Rep. of S. Africa; pt. serving copper- and diamond-mining dists.
Port of Spain, *cap.*, Trinidad, W.I.; cocoa, sugar, asphalt; natural gas pipeline from Penal; p. (estd. 1963) *94,000.*
Port Phillip, *lge. inlet*, Victoria, Australia; land locked bay, with Melbourne on N., Geelong on W.
Port Pirie, *spt.*, S. Australia; smelting ores, gold refining; exp. wheat, minerals; p. (1961) *14,190.*
Port Radium, *t.*, N.W. Terr., Canada; on Gr. Bear L.; pitchblende deposits; p. *300.*
Port Royal, *t.*, Jamaica, West Indies; nr. Kingston; dock-yard.
Port Said, *spt.*, U.A.R.; N. end Suez Canal; coaling sta.; p. (1960) *246,000.*
Port St. Mary, *vil.*, I. of Man, Eng.; on S.E. cst.; resort; fisheries, boat-bldg.
Port Shepstone, *t.*, Natal, S. Africa; sugar, bark, fibre, maize, fruit, dairying, poultry; cement; p. (1960) *4,238* inc. *1,775* whites.
Port Sudan, *spt.*, Sudan; 30 m. N. of Suakin; linked by rail to Atbara and Khartoum; oil refinery being built; p. (1960) *51,790.*
Port Sunlight, Cheshire, Eng.; modern garden village founded 1888 by Lord Leverhulme for the employees of Lever Brothers' Port Sunlight factories; p. *6,000.*
Port Swettenham, *spt.*, Selangor, Malaysia; exp. tin, rubber, copra, pineapples; p. *11,300.*
Port Talbot, *t., mun. bor.*, Glamorgan, S. Wales; on E. side of Swansea Bay; impt. iron and steel ind., copper, coal; p. (1961) *50,223.*
Port Taufiq, *spt.*, U.A.R.; S. end of the Suez canal; p. *1,000.*
Port Vendres, *spt.*, Pyrénées-Orientales, France; nr. Perpignan; p. (1954) *4,180.*
Portadown, *t., mun. bor.*, Armagh, N. Ireland; on R. Bann, 25 m. S.W. of Belfast; linen, lace, farming; p. (1961) *18,605.*
Portaferry, *spt.*, Down, N. Ireland; shipping, fisheries; p. (1961) *1,406.*
Portage, *t.*, Wis., U.S.A.; iron; p. (1960) *7,822.*
Portage la Prairie, *spt.*, Manitoba, Canada; grain exp.; p. (1961) *12,388.*
Portalegre, *t.*, Portugal; cath.; mkt.; p. (1940) *12,046.*
Portarlington, *t.*, Offaly, Ireland; farming; first place to have elec. power-sta. using local peat fuel; p. (1951) *2,246.*
Portbou, *t.*, on Fr. side of Franco–Spanish border, opposite Rosas on Mediterranean cst.
Porthcawl, *t., urb. dist.*, Glam., Wales; on cst. 10 m. S.E. of Pt. Talbot; resort; p. (1961) *11,082.*
Portici, *spt.*, Campania, S. Italy; on Bay of Naples 5 m. S.E. of Naples; dockland sub. of Naples; p. (1961) *50,373.*
Portishead, *t., urb. dist.*, Somerset, Eng.; on Severn estuary 3 m. S.W. of Avonmouth; shipping; p. (1961) *6,440.*
Portknockie, *burgh*, Banff, Scot.; on N. Buchan cst., 5 m. E. of Buckie; sm. fishing pt.; p. (1961) *1,245.*
Portland, *urb. dist.*, Dorset, Eng.; 4 m. S. of Weymouth on sheltered N.E. side of I. of Portland; lge. artificial harbour; p. (1961) *11,542.*
Portland, *t., spt.*, Me., U.S.A.; comm. cap. of Me.; lge. fisheries; paper, pulp, lumber, processed food, clothing; p. (1960) *72,566.*
Portland, *c.*, Ore., U.S.A.; gr. wheat and wool tr.; flour milling, shipbldg., fishing and canning, aluminium, lumber; p. (1960) *372,676.*
Portland Canal, *fjord*, N.W. cst. of America, forming boundary between Alaska and B.C.
Portland, I. of, *peninsula*, Dorset, Eng.; limestone mass, linked to mainland by shingle spit, Chesil Bank, terminates S. in Portland Bill; naval base, prison, Borstal inst.; limestone quarrying; masonry wks.
Portmadoc, *spt., urb. dist.*, Caernarvon, Wales; on Tremadoc Bay; linked by light rly. to Ffestiniog; copper and slate exp.; p. (1961) *3,419.*
Porto, *see* **Oporto.**
Porto Alegre, *c., cap.*, Rio Grande do Sul st., Brazil; exp. lard, preserved meats, rice, timber, tobacco; textiles, chemicals, furniture, brewing, metallurgy; p. (1960) *641,173.*
Porto Empedocle, *spt.*, Sicily, Italy; sulphur refining, flour, furniture, lime, gypsum; p. *14,764.*
Porto Marghera, *spt.*, Venezia, N. Italy; extends along cst. S. from landward end of the causeway linking Venice to the mainland; the modern pt of Venice, reached by ship canal dredged through shallow lagoon; oil-refineries.

Porto Novo, *t., cap.,* Dahomey, W. Africa; nr. Bight of Benin; p. (1960) *31,500.*
Porto Vecchio, *t.,* Corsica; on E. cst.; p. *5,304.*
Porto Velho, *cap.,* Rondonia st., Brazil; p. (1960) *51,049.*
Portobello, *resort,* Midlothian, Scot.; on Firth of Forth, 3 m. E. of Edinburgh; bricks, pottery, paper.
Porto Torres, *spt.,* Sardinia, Italy; exp. iron ore; p. *7,251.*
Portree, *t., par.,* I. of Skye, Scot.; on sound of Raasay; fishing, small tweed mill; p. *2,120.*
Portrush, *spt., urb. dist.,* Antrim, N. Ireland; on N. cst. 5 m. N. of Coleraine; p. (1961) *4,263.*
Portsdown Hill, *chalk ridge,* Hants, Eng.; extends E. to W. behind Portsmouth from Havant to Fareham; water-storage reservoirs supply Portsmouth; lined with early 19th-century fortifications for defence of Portsmouth; length 6 m., alt. 400 ft.
Portsea Is., *fortfd. I.,* between Portsmouth and Langston Harbours.
Portslade-by-Sea, *urb. dist.,* E. Sussex, Eng.; 1 m. W. of Hove; p. (1961) *15,750.*
Portsmouth, *c., co. bor., naval pt.,* Hants, Eng.; opposite I. of Wight; has lgst. naval establishment in the world; Portsmouth is the garrison t.; Portsea has the naval dockyards, Landport is residtl., and Southsea is a popular wat. pl. within the bor. a.; across the harbour is Gosport; aircraft, light engin.; p. (1961) *215,198.*
Portsmouth, *t.,* N.H., U.S.A.; summer resort, naval dockyard, cotton; the 1905 Peace Treaty between Japan and Russia was negotiated here; p. (1960) *25,833.*
Portsmouth, *c.,* Ohio, U.S.A.; iron and steel goods, aircraft, boots, shoes, bricks; p. (1960) *33,637.*
Portsmouth, *spt.,* Va., U.S.A.; naval dockyard; farm produce, cotton, rly. wks.; p. (1960) *114,775.*
Portsoy, *spt., burgh,* Banff, Scot.; on N. Buchan cst., 5 m. W. of Banff; fisheries, meal milling; p. (1961) *1,690.*
Portugal, *rep.,* Iberian peninsula, S.W. Europe; interior mountainous, with wide, fertile valleys; mild winter, hot summers; agr.: cereals, fruit, etc.; livestock; cork, pine and other timbers; copper; fisheries; textiles, pottery, tanning, wine, olive oil; cap. Lisbon; a. 35,404 sq. m.; p. (1963) *8,889,000* (inc. Azores and Madeira).
Portugalete, *spt.,* Biscay prov., Spain; nr. Bilbao; p. (1957) *12,211.*
Portuguesa, *st.,* Venezuela; cap. Guanare; p. (1961) *203,707.*
Portuguesa, *R.,* Venezuela, trib. of R. Apure; length 200 m.
Portuguese East Africa, *see* **Mozambique.**
Portuguese Guinea, Portuguese col., W. Africa; on Atlantic cst.; cap. Bissau; palm nuts, groundnuts, rubber, wax; a. 13,900 sq. m.; p. (estd. 1960) *510,000.*
Portuguese Timor, *col.,* E. Indies; mtns.; copra, coffee, cocoa beans, maize, rice, hides, wax, timber; cap. Deli; a. 7,330 sq. m.; p. (1950) *442,378.*
Portuguese West Africa, *see* **Angola.**
Porvenir, *spt.,* Chile; chief t. Tierra del Fuego; wool; p. mainly Jugoslav.
Porvoo, *spt.,* Finland; engin. forest inds.; p. (1961) *11,869.*
Porz, *t.,* N. Rhine-Westphalia, Germany; on R. Rhine, S.E. of Cologne; glass, metals, paper; p. (1963) *51,000.*
Posadas, *t.,* Spain; on R. Guadalquivir, nr. Cordova; p. (1957) *7,491.*
Posados, *cap.,* Misiones Terr., Argentina; on Alto Paraná R., on border of Paraguay; yerba-maté, tobacco; p. (1960) *44,000.*
Posen, *see* **Poznan.**
Pössneck, *t.,* Gera, E. Germany; S.E. of Weimar; porcelain, textiles, leather; p. (1963) *19,455.*
Postillon Is., Lesser Sunda Is., Indonesia; coconuts.
Potchefstroom, *t.,* Transvaal, S. Africa; on the Mooi R.; univ.; agr.; malt, timber, engin.; p. (1962) *44,000* inc. *21,000* whites.
Potenza, *t.,* Italy, cap. of prov. Potenza; situated on hill above R. Basento 2,700 ft. above sea-level; agr. and ind. ctr.; p. (1961) *42,659.*
Potgietersrust, *t.,* Transvaal, S. Africa; agr. ctr.; cattle; citrus fruits; p. (1961) *11,000* (inc. *5,400* whites).
Poti, *spt.,* Georgian S.S.R.; manganese, saw-mills, engin.; p. (1956) *42,500.*
Potomac, *R.,* U.S.A.; dividing Virginia from Maryland; flowing past Washington to Chesapeake Bay; length 400 m.
Potosi, *dep.,* Bolivia, adjoining Chile and Argentina; famous for silver- and tin-mines; cap. Potosi; a. 45,031 sq. m.; p. (1962) *619,600.*
Potosi, *c.,* Bolivia; on slope of Cerro Gordo de Potosi, 13,350 ft. above sea-level; tin, silver, copper, lead; p. (1962) *55,233.*
Potsdam, *cap.,* Potsdam, E. Germany; lies on R. Havel 18 m. S.E. of Berlin; beautiful parks and gardens, and many palaces, inc. former Imperial residence; scene of conference between Allies on boundary questions, 1945; motor and locomotive wks., engin.; p. (1963) *115,093.*
Potteries, The, *dist.,* N. Staffs, Eng.; ctr. of earthenware ind., comprising ts. Burslem, Hanley, Fenton, Tunstall, Stoke, and Longton.
Potters Bar, *t., urb. dist.,* Herts., Eng.; residtl.; p. (1961) *23,376.*
Pottsdown, *t.,* Penns., U.S.A.; iron and steel, farm implements, silk; p. (1960) *26,144.*
Pottsville, *c.,* Penns., U.S.A.; iron and steel, rly. wks.; p. (1960) *21,659.*
Poughkeepsie, *c.,* N.Y., U.S.A.; on Hudson R.; clothing and iron factories; agr. implements; oil clarifiers; p. (1960) *38,330.*
Poulton-le-Fylde, *urb. dist.,* Lancs, Eng.; 4 m. N.E. of Blackpool; farming; p. (1961) *12,767.*
Povenets, *t.,* R.S.F.S.R.; on L. Onega; cellulose, paper; p. *2,000.*
Powis, Vale of, Montgomery, Wales; runs 12 m. N.E. from Montgomery between Welsh Mtns. and Long Mtn.; drained by R. Severn; cattle-rearing; ch. t. Welshpool; av. width 2 m.
Foyang Hu, *lge. L.,* Kiangsi, China; on S. margin of Yangtze-Kiang plain; receives water of Kan Kiang and tribs., drains N. into Yangtze-Kiang; surrounded by flat, intensively cultivated land, rice, sugar, mulberry; size varies greatly with season, max. a. (in late summer) 1,800 sq. m.
Poznan, *prov.,* W. Poland; stock-raising, mining, mnfs. inc. locomotives; a. 15,152 sq. m.; p. (1961) *2,046,000.*
Poznan, *t., cap. of prov., oldest cap. of* Poland; on R. Warta; cath., univ.; engin., iron founding, chemicals; p. (1961) *418,000.*
Pozoblanco, *t.,* Spain; cattle fairs, lead-mines; p. (1957) *14,703.*
Pozzuoli, *t.,* Italy; 2 m. W. of Naples; ancient Puteoli; mineral baths, ordnance wks.; notable Roman ruins; p. (1961) *51,308.*
Praded (Altvater), *Mtns.,* ČSSR.
Praest, *t.,* Själland, Denmark; on Fakse fjord; p. (1960) *1,528.*
Prague (Praha), *reg. c., cap.,* ČSSR.; picturesque ancient c. on R. Vitava; univ., founded in 1348; extensive mnfs.; machin., sugar, leather, milling, chemicals; p. (1961) *1,003,341.*
Prahova, *R.,* Walachia, Romania; rises in Transylvanian Alps, flows S. through impt. Ploesti oilfield into R. Ialomita; length approx. 110 m.
Prato, *t.,* Italy; 8 m. N.W. of Florence; cath., medieval cas. and fortifications; straw plaiting, cottons, woollens, machin.; p. (1961) *111,285.*
Prebalkhash (Balkhash), *t.,* Kazakh. S.S.R.; copper; p. (1954) *50,000.*
Predeal Pass, Romania; carries main road and rly. across Transylvanian Alps from Bucharest to Brasov; alt. over 4,000 ft.
Preesall, *urb. dist.,* Lancs, Eng.; N. of Blackpool; p. (1961) *2,356.*
Pregel, *R.,* Poland; flows to Frisches Haff, nr. Kaliningrad; length 125 m.
Prenzlau, *t.,* Neubrandenburg, E. Germany; p. (1963) *19,955.*
Prerov, *t.,* ČSSR.; S.E. of Olomouc; hardware, textiles; p. (1961) *30,511.*
Prescelli Myndd, *mtns.,* N.E. Pembroke, Wales.
Prescot, *mftg. t., urb. dist.* S.W. Lancs, Eng.; 4 m. S.W. of St. Helens; mkt., elec. cable ind.; p. (1961) *13,077.*
Prescott, *pt.,* Ontario, Canada; on R. St. Lawrence; p. (1961) *5,366.*
Presidio St. Vicente, *t.,* N.M., U.S.A.; on Rio Grande del Norte.

Prešov, *t.*, ČSSR.; linen mnfs.; p. (1961) *35,121.*
Prestatyn, *t.*, *urb. dist.*, Flint, Wales; on N. cst., 3 m. E. of Rhyl; seaside resort; p. (1961) *10,771.*
Prestea, *t.*, Ghana; gold-mining region.
Presteign, *mkt. t.*, *urb. dist.*, Radnor, Wales; on R. Lugg, 10 m. N.W. of Leominster; p. (1961) *1,190.*
Preston, *t.*, Ont., Canada; furniture; p. (1961) *11,577.*
Preston, *t.*, *pt.*, *co. bor.*, Lancs, Eng.; on R. Ribble; textiles, engin., aircraft wks.; p. (1961) *113,208*
Prestonpans, *burgh*, E. Lothian, Scot.; on S. side of Firth of Forth, 9 m. E. of Edinburgh; "Bonnie Prince Charlie" defeated British here in 1745; bricks, soap, brewing; p. (1961) *3,104.*
Prestwich, *industl. t.*, *mun. bor.*, Lancs, Eng.; in valley of R. Irwell, 3 m. N.W. of Manchester; cotton bleaching and dyeing, soap, furnishings; p. (1961) *34,191.*
Prestwick, *burgh*, Ayr, Scot.; on Firth of Clyde, 3 m. N. of Ayr; impt. golfing ctr. and trans-Atlantic airport; resort; p. (1961) *12,564.*
Pretoria, *admin. cap.*, Transvaal, Rep. of S. Africa; fine admin. bldgs., univ.; impt. tr. ctr.; inds. inc. engin., chemicals, iron and steel; p. (1960) *422,590* inc. *207,202* whites.
Préveza, *prefecture*, Greece; cap. Préveza; p. (1961) *62,387.*
Préveza, *fortfd. t.*, Préveza, Greece; on G. of Arta; gd. shipping tr.; p. (1961) *11,172.*
Pribalkhash, *see* Balkhash.
Pribram, *t.*, Bohemia, ČSSR.; lead-, silver-mng, zinc, barium, antimony; p. (1961) *25,729.*
Prichard, *t.*, Ala., U.S.A.; meat packing, canning, fertilisers, wood and paper prod.; p. (1960) *47,371.*
Prieska, *t.*, Cape Prov., S. Africa; on Orange R.; sheep, cattle, horses; blue asbestos; p. (1960) *6,464* (inc. *1,738* whites).
Prijedor, *t.*, Croatia, Jugoslavia; on E. flank of Dinaric Alps, 65 m. S.E. of Zagreb; iron-ore mines.
Prilep, *t.*, Macedonia, Jugoslavia; p. (1959) *36,000.*
Prince Albert, *t.*, Saskatchewan, Canada; lumbering, furs; p. (1961) *24,168.*
Prince Albert Peninsula, *dist.*, Victoria I., Arctic Canada.
Prince Albert Sound, *inlet*, Victoria I., Arctic Canada.
Prince Edward I., *prov.*, Canada; dairying, fishing, agr.; bridge-tunnel link with New Brunswick projected; cap. Charlottetown; a. 2,184 sq. m.; p. (1961) *104,629.*
Prince George, *t.*, B.C., Canada; p. (1961) *13,877.*
Prince of Wales I., off cst. of C. York Peninsula, Queensland, Australia.
Prince of Wales, *C.*, Bering Strait, Alaska.
Prince Rupert, *c.*, B.C., Canada; Pacific pt. of Canadian National Rly.; p. (1961) *11,987.*
Princes Risborough, *mkt. t.*, Bucks, Eng.; at N. foot of Chiltern Hills, in gap used by main rly.; chairs, brewing; p. *2,438.*
Princeton, *bor.*, N.J., U.S.A.; seat of Princeton Univ.; p. (1960) *11,890.* [son.
Princetown, *vil.*, Devon, Eng.; nr. Dartmoor pri-
Principe and S. Tomé, *Portuguese Is.*, G. of Guinea, Africa; products, cacao, coffee, coconuts, etc.; a. 372 sq. m.; p. (1960) *63,485.*
Pripet (Pripyat), *R.*, Byelorussian S.S.R.; trib. of R. Dnieper; length 350 m.
Pripet Marshes, Byelorussian S.S.R.; a. 30,000 sq. m.; greater part reclaimed.
Priština, *t.*, *cap.*, Kosmet, Jugoslavia; on R. Sitnic; many mosques; sugar and coffee; p. (1959) *32,000.*
Progreso, *spt.*, Yucatan, Mexico; sisal; warehousing; p. (1960) *14,000.*
Prokopevsk, *t.*, S.W. Siberia, R.S.F.S.R.; nr. Novokuznetsk; metallurgy, coal; p. (1962) *292,000.*
Prome, *t.*, Burma; on R. Irrawaddy; silk, rice, cotton, tobacco; p. *28,295.*
Proskurov, *see* Khmelnitskiy. [m.
Prosna, *R.*, Poland; trib. of R. Warta; length 120
Prostějov, *t.*, CSSR.; match-mkg., brewing, malt and sugar; geese-breeding; p. (1961) *35,519.*
Provence, *old maritime prov.*, S.E. France; now deps. Var, Basses-Alpes, Bouches-du-Rhône, and part of Vaucluse.
Providence, *c.*, R.I., U.S.A.; at head of Narragansett Bay; univ.; jewellery, textiles, silverware, rubber goods, machin., oil, coal; p. (1960) *207,498.*
Provo, *c.*, Utah, U.S.A.; at base of Wasatch mtns., nr. shore of Utah Lake; flour, bricks, blast furnaces; p. (1960) *36,047.*
Prudhoe, *urb. dist.*, Northumberland, Eng.; coal; p. (1961) *9,959.*
Prussia, *old st.*, former kingdom, Germany; cap. Berlin; E. Prussia partitioned between Russia and Poland.
Pruszkow, *t.*, Poland; nr. Warsaw; elec. plant; engin; p. (1960) *37,000.*
Prut, *R.*, flows between Romania and Bessarabia from the Carpathian Mtns. to the Black Sea; length 360 m.
Przemysl, *frontier t.*, Poland; on bdy. between Poland and Ukrainian S.S.R.; timber, leather, corn, chemicals; p. (1960) *46,000.*
Psel, *R.*, U.S.S.R.; flows to the R. Dnieper at Kremenchug; length 300 m.
Pskov, *t.*, R.S.F.S.R., U.S.S.R.; on R. Velykaya; flax tr., leather, sawmills, flour mills, cordage; p. (1959) *81,000.*
Pucalpa, *R. pt.*, Peru; on R. Ucayali; sawmills, rosewood oil; p. (1961) *20,000.*
Pudsey, *t.*, *mun. bor.*, W.R. Yorks, Eng.; between Leeds and Bradford; mnfs., woollens; p. (1961) *34,825.* [*50,488.*
Pudukkottai, *t.*, Madras, S. India; p. (1961)
Puebla, *st.*, Mexico; agr.; coffee and sugar growing; a. 13,124 sq. m.; p. (1960) *1,973,837.*
Puebla, *c.*, Mexico; one of the oldest and most impt. cs.; alt. 7,137 ft.; cath.; cottons, onyx, glazed tiles; p. (1960) *289,049.*
Pueblo, *c.*, Col., U.S.A.; on R. Arkansas; coal; iron- and steel-wks.; copper, gold and silver smelted; p. (1960) *91,181.*
Puenteareás, *t.*, Spain; nr. Vigo; vine growing, porcelain; p. (1957) *14,987.*
Puente Genil, *t.*, Córdoba, Spain; olive oil, quince pulp; p. (1957) *30,465.*
Puerto Barrios, *pt.*, Guatamala; rly. term.; oil refining; p. (estd. 1960) *30,980.*
Puerto Berrio, *R. pt.*, Colombia; on R. Magdalena; serves Medellin; p. (estd. 1959) *12,500.*
Puerto Cabello, *spt.*, Venezuela; on the Caribbean S., nr. Valencia; lge. exp.; asbestos, vegetable oils, soap, candles; p. (1961) *48,000.*
Puerto Colombia, *t.*, Colombia; resort; former ocean pt. for Barranquilla; p. (1947) *4,896.*
Puerto Cortes, *spt.*, Honduras rep., Central America; p. (1961) *17,412.*
Puerto de Santa Maria, *spt.*, Cadiz, Spain; wine, glass; p. (1957) *28,300.*
Puerto la Cruz, *t.*, Venezuela; 10 m. from Barcelona; oil refining; p. (1961) *45,000.*
Puerto Limon, Costa Rica; oil refinery under construction.
Puerto Mèxico, *see* Coatzacoalcos.
Puerto Montt, *spt.*, Chile; in sheep-farming dist.; S. term. of rlys.; devastated by earthquake, May 1960; lumber, cattle, potatoes; p. (1961) *45,400.*
Puerto Natales, *spt.*, Chile; wool, frozen meat; p. (1961) *11,705.*
Puerto Ordaz. *See* Santo Tomé de la Guayana.
Puerto Plata, *t.*, Dominican rep. Central America; p. (1960) *26,139.*
Puerto Real, *spt.*, Andalusia, Spain; summer resort; wine and oil tr.; p. (1957) *13,061.*
Puerto Rico, *W. Indian I.*, Greater Antilles; ceded by Spain to U.S.A. in 1898 (since 1952 free cmwlth. ass. with U.S.A.); nuclear reactor at Punta Higuera; sugar, tobacco, rum, textiles, iron ore, salt, marble, white clay; cap. San Juan; a. 3,423 sq. m.; p. (1960) *2,349,544* mainly natives of mixed Spanish and aboriginal descent.
Puerto Salinas, *spt.*, Venezuela; oil-transhipment.
Puerto Saurez, *R. pt.*, Bolivia; on R. Paraguay; collecting ctr. for rubber, coffee, Brazil nuts.
Puerto Varas, *t.*, Chile; tourist ctr. in Chilean "Switzerland"; p. (1961) *26,615.*
Puget Sound, Washington, U.S.A.
Puket, *t.*, ch. Thailand pt. on Malay Peninsula; tin-mines; p. *30,000.*
Pula, *spt.*, Croatia, Jugoslavia; arsenal, naval base; cement; ship-breaking; footwear, tar, flour, tobacco, fishing; p. (1959) *35,000.*
Pulacayo, *t.*, Bolivia; alt. 13,600 ft.; silver-mines; p. *8,000.*
Pulo Tantalam, strip of land connecting Burma with Malay Peninsula, Thailand.
Pulo Wai I., Sumatra, Indonesia; hilly, forests; ch. pt. Sabang.

Pultusk, *t.*, Poland; on R. Narew; copper-wks., woollens, hosiery; p. *8,787.*
Pumpherston, *vil.*, nr. Edinburgh, Scot.; oil refining.
Puna, bleak, uninhabited plateau of Peru and Bolivia; alt. 12,000–18,000 ft.
Punjab, *geographical region*, comprising N.W. of Indus plains, Indian sub-continent; extensive irrigation from the "five rivers"—Jhelum, Chenab, Ravi, Bias, Sutlej; cotton, sugar, cereals; now divided politically between India and Pakistan.
Punjab (East), *st.*, India, incorporating Himachal Pradesh and Pepsu, 1 Nov. 1956; cap. Chandigarh; a. 47,205 sq. m.; p. (1961) *20,306,812.*
Puno, *dep.*, Peru, S. America; p. (1961) *687,077.*
Puno, *t.*, Peru; p. (1961) *15,880.*
Punta Arenas, *t.*, *free pt.*, Magallanes prov., Chile; most S. c. in the world; mutton, wool; whaling; coal near by; p. (1961) *46,872.*
Puntarenas, *prov.*, Costa Rica; p. (1963) *155,599.*
Puntarenas, *spt.*, Costa Rica, Central America; one of the ch. comm. pts. of the country, stands on Gulf of Nicoya; p. (1963) *33,878.*
Purbeck, I. of, *dist.*, Dorset, Eng.; Corfe cas. in ctr.; limestone (Purbeck "marble") quarries.
Puri, *dist.*, Orissa, India; cap. P. famous for its temple and festival of the god Vishnu and his monster car, Juggernaut; p. (1961) *1,865,439.*
Purley, *former urb. dist.*, Surrey, Eng.; now inc. in Croydon outer bor. Greater London.
Purnea, *t.*, Bihar, Indian Union; tobacco; p. (1961) *40,602.*
Pursat, *mkt. t.*, Cambodia, Indo-China; between Pnompenh and Thailand frontier; p. *96,000.*
Purús, *R.*, Peru; trib. of R. Amazon; length 1,400 m.
Pusan (Fusan), *pt.*, S. Korea; on S.E. cst.; formerly ch. pt. for tr. with Japan mainland; silk, hides, rice; p. (1962) *1,271,000.*
Puteaux, *sub.*, Paris, France; woollens, dyes; p. (1954) *41,097.*
Putney, *S.W. residtl. and industl. Thames-side sub.*, London, Eng.
Putrid Sea, *see* **Sivash.**
Puttalam, *t.*, Ceylon; on W. cst.; pearl oysters, salt; p. *7,792.*
Putumayo, *R.*, Ecuador; trib. of R. Amazon; length 700 m.
Puy-de-Dôme, *peak*, Auvergne Mtns., France; alt. 4,806 ft.
Puy-de-Dôme, *dep.*, France; drained by R. Allier; generally mountainous; agr., vineyards; coal, silver, lead; cap. Clermont-Ferrand; a. 3,090 sq. m.; p. (1962) *508,928.*
Puy, Le, *cap.*, Haute-Loire, France; lace-mkg.; p. (1954) *23,453.*
Puymorens Tunnel, Pyrenees, on bdy. between France and Spain; carries main rly. between Toulouse and Barcelona.
Pwllheli, *spt.*, *mun. bor.*, Caernarvon, N. Wales; on S. cst. of Lleyn peninsula; seaside resort; inshore fishing, boat bldg.; p. (1961) *3,642.*
Pyatigorsk, *t.*, Caucasus, R.S.F.S.R.; spa, sulphur springs; engin., radio equip.; p. (1959) *69,000.*
Pyinmana, *t.*, Burma; rly. junction; p. *17,656.*
Pyongyang, *cap. c.*, N. Korea; located 40 m. up Taedong R.; coal and iron ore deposits; p. (1960) *940,000.*
Pyrenees, *range of mtns.*, S.W. Europe; dividing France from Iberian Peninsula; 270 m. long; highest peak Pic d'Anéto, or Maladetta, 11,174 ft.
Pyrénées, Basses, *dep.*, S.W. France; mainly agr. and livestock rearing; cap. Pau; a. 2,978 sq. m.; p. (1962) *466,038.*
Pyrénées, Hautes, *dep.*, S. France; agr., vines, nuts, livestock, marble quarries; cap. Tarbes; a. 1,750 sq. m.; p. (1962) *211,433.*
Pyrénées-Orientales, *dep.*, S. France; on Mediterranean; wheat, wine, silk-worm culture, stock-rearing; cap. Perpignan; a. 1, 599 sq. m.; p. (1962) *251,231.*
Pyrgos, *t.*, Elis, Greece; prov. Elis, nr. Patras; has suffered from earthquakes; p. (1961) *20,558.*

Q

Qaiyara, Al, *t.*, Iraq; route ctr.; oil resources undeveloped.
Qalqiliya, *vil.*, Jordan; rly. junction.
Qalyub, *t.*, U.A.R.; rly. junction; p. *5,000.*
Qalyûbîya, *administrative div.*, Egypt; a. 364 sq. m.; p. (1947) *690,156.*
Qara Dagh, *t.*, Iraq; gum.
Qarun (Karum), *see* **Birket el Qarun.**
Qasr el Azraq, *t.*, Jordan; oasis; rice.
Qasvin, *c.*, Iran; p. (1956) *66,386.*
Qatar, *sheikdom*, Arabia; includes Q. Peninsula, Persian G.; under British protection; oil-mining; a. 4,000 sq. m.; p. (1962) *55,000.*
Qatif, *fortfd. t.*, El Hasa, Saudi Arabia.
Qatlava Depression, N. Egypt; a. 7,000 sq. m.
Qena, *t.*, Egypt; on R. Nile; water jars and bottles; p. (1960) *58,000.*
Qishm, *I.*, part of Prot. of South Arabia (Aden); off S. cst. of Iran, at entrance of Persian G.; hilly; cereals, vegs., fruit, salt; p. *15,000.*
Qisil-Qum, *desert region*, central Asia; covering dried-up a. of extended Pleistocene Aral Sea.
Qizan, *spt.*, Saudi Arabia; cereals, pearl-fishing, salt.
Quantock Hills, Somerset, Eng.; S. of Bridgwater Bay; highest pt., 1,262 ft., officially designated (1957) as a place of "outstanding natural beauty."
Quaregnon, *t.*, Hainaut prov., Belgium; Mons colly. dist.; ironwks. and tobacco factories; p. (1962) *18,068.*
Quarnero, *G.*, Adriatic Sea; between Croatian cst. and Istria.
Quarto, G. of, *arm*, G. of Cagliari, Sardinia.
Quathlamba Mtns., *see* **Drakensberg.**
Quatre Bras, *nr.* Waterloo, S. Brabant, Belgium.
Queanbeyan, *t.*, N.S.W., Australia; pastoral, dairying and mixed farming dist.; gold, silver, copper; p. (1961) *9,445.*
Quebec, *prov.*, Canada; pulp, paper, textiles; metal smelting, chemicals; agr., forestry, mng., elec. power; cap. Quebec, lgst. c. Montreal; a. 594,860 sq. m.; p. (1961) *5,259,211.*
Quebec, *c. cap.*, Quebec, Canada; on St. Lawrence R.; univ.; fine harbour, handsome gov. bldgs.; furs, textiles, leather, paper; p. (1961) *357, 568.*
Quebec-Labrador Trough, Canada; geological formation extending through central Quebec prov. to Ungava Bay, Hudson Strait; immense reserves of iron-ore (locally "red gold").
Quedlinburg, *c.*, Halle, E. Germany; at foot of Hartz Mtns.; cas., cath.; cheese; aniline dyes, metals, engin.; p. (1963) *31,251.*
Queen Alexandria Ra., Antarctica; highest pk., Mt. Kirkpatrick, 14,600 ft.
Queenborough, *t.*, *mun. bor.*, Kent, Eng.; on R. Swale, I. of Sheppey; chemicals, glass, pottery, glue, iron; p. (1961) *3,044.*
Queen Carola Harbour, W. cst. Buka Is., Solomon Is., Pac. Oc.
Queen Charlotte's Is., *group*, N. of Vancouver I., off cst. of Brit. Columbia; ch. Is.: Graham I., Moresby I.; valuable halibut fishing ind.
Queen Charlotte Sound, *strait* separating Vancouver I. from Brit. Columbia mainland, a continuation of Johnstone Strait.
Queen Maud Land, Antarctica; claimed by Norway; ice crystal mtns., 10,000 ft. high for 100 m. along cst.
Queens, *bor.*, N.Y. City, U.S.A.; p. (1960) *1,809,578.*
Queenscliff, *t.*, Victoria, Australia; on Pt. Phillip Bay; resort; p. *1,969.*
Queensferry, *burgh*, W. Lothian, Scot.; on S. side of Firth of Forth, 8 m. N.W. of Edinburgh; S. end of Forth Bridge and ferry across Firth; whisky; tourism; p. (1961) *2,929.*
Queensferry N., *vil.*, Fife, Scotland.
Queensland, *st.*, N.E. Australia; great grassy plains and cst. highlands; agr.: maize, wheat, sugar-cane, cotton, pineapples, bananas; dairying; cattle, sheep, wool; timber; coal, copper, gold, uranium; cap. Brisbane; a. 670,500 sq. m.; p. (1964) *1,595,057.*
Queenstown, *see* **Cobh.**
Queenstown, *t.*, Cape Province, S. Africa; in the Great Kei R. valley; prosperous agr. region; p. (1960) *33,126* (inc. *9,743* whites).
Queenstown, *t.*, Tasmania, Australia; p. *3,400.*
Quelimane, *pt.*, Port. E. Africa; rly. term.; rubber, almonds, copra, coffee, cotton, sisal, tea, tobacco, sugar, wax, ivory; p. (1960) *156,887.*
Quelpart (Cheju Do), *I.*, Yellow Sea; 60 m. S. of Korea (40 m. by 17 m.) belonging to S. Korea; agr. and pearl-fishing.
Quemoy, *gr. of Is.*, off Chinese mainland near Amoy, held by Nationalist forces; p. (estd.) *50,000* (plus garrison of *40,000*).

Que Que, *t.*, Rhodesia; alt. 3,979 ft.; gold-mining, farming, ranching dist. ctr.; iron and steel; tobacco, vegs., citrus fruit; p. (1958) *11,200* (incl. *2,200* Europeans).
Quequen, *t.*, E. Argentina; seaside resort.
Querétaro, *st.*, central Mexico; agr.; minerals, famous for opals; a. 4,432 sq. m.; p. (1960) *355,045*.
Querétaro, cap. Q., Mexico; at alt. 6,346 ft., cotton mills; an Aztec c., Emperor Maximilian executed here (1867); p. (1960) *60,000*.
Querimba Is., off Mozambique.
Quesnel, *t.*, B.C., Canada; on R. Frazer, 360 m. N. of Vancouver; impt. alluvial gold workings.
Quetta, *t.*, W. Pakistan; at end of Bolan Pass, on road to Kandahar; tr. and military ctr.; thermal sta. under construction; p. (1961) *106,633*.
Quetta, *div.*, W. Pakistan; coloured marble in the Chagai a.; p. (1961) *585,000*.
Quezaltenango, *c.*, Guatemala, Central America; on slopes of Cerro Quemado volcano; ctr. of tr. for W. part of the rep.; textiles; p. *50,750*.
Quezon City, *cap.*, Philippines; N. E. of Manila; nuclear reactor; p. (1960) *398,000*.
Quibdo, *t.*, Colombia, S. America; on R. Atrato; p. (estd. 1959) *41,350*.
Quiberon, *t.*, Morbihan, France; on Quiberon Bay, nr. Lorient; p. *3,556*.
Quibor, *t.*, Venezuela; 40 m. S.S.W. Barquisimeto; blankets from local wool.
Quicamao, *t.*, st. Rio de Janeiro, Brazil; nr. Camos; industl.
Quilimane, *see* **Quelimane**.
Quillota, *comm. t.*, Valparaiso, Chile; nr. Santiago; p. *17,232*.
Quilmes, *industl. sub.*, Buenos Aires, Argentina; brewing, textiles, ironware, glass; Eng. public school; p. (estd. 1960) *120,000*.
Quilon, *t.*, Kerala, India; on Malabar cst., gd. tr.; coconuts, pepper, timber; p. (1961) *91,018*.
Quilpie, *t.*, Queensland, Australia; rly. connects interior with Brisbane.
Quimper, *fortfd. t.*, Finistère, France; nr. Brest; pilchards, pottery, paper, leather, brewing; p. (1962) *50,670*.
Quimperlé, *t.*, Finistère, France; 34 m. E.N.E. Quimper; industl.; p. (1954) *10,030*.
Quincy, *t.*, Ill., U.S.A.; milling, tobacco, ironware, machin.; p. (1960) *43,793*.
Quincy, *c.*, Mass., U.S.A.; granite, foundries, shipbldg.; p. (1960) *87,409*.
Quindio, *pass*, Columbia; provides impt. routeway through Cordillera Central; 11,099 ft.
Qui Nhon, *t.*, S. Viet-Nam; rice, coconut oil, copra, dried fish, groundnuts; p. *10,000*.
Quintana Roo, *terr.*, Mexico; cap. Chetumal; a. 19,438 sq. m.; p. (1960) *50,169*.
Quintero, *t.*, Chile; naval air sta.; copper refining.
Quintin, *t.*, dep Côtes-du-Nord, France; nr. St. Brieuc.
Quinto, *R.*, Argentina; flows S.E. from the Sierra de San Luis and becomes lost in a morass; length 250 m.
Quiringua, *ruined ancient t.*, nr. Isabel, Guatemala, Central America; on R. Mohtagua.
Quistello, *t.*, Mantua, Italy; on R. Secchia; p. *9,450*.
Quito, *c.*, *cap.*, Ecuador; in the Andes, 15 m. S. of the Equator; alt. 9,402 ft.; textiles, shoes, soap, pharmaceutics, brewing; p. (1963) *368,000*.
Qum, *c.*, Iran; pilgrim ctr.; mkt.; carpets, porcelain, cotton; p. (1956) *96,463*.
Quorndon, or **Quorn**, *sm. t.*, Leicester, Eng.; on R. Soar, 3 m. S. of Loughborough; ctr. of fox-hunting dist.
Quorra, *R.*, Africa; one of the names given to the R. Niger; below Timbuktu.
Quseir, *t.*, U.A.R.; on Red Sea cst.; caravan tr. ctr.; uranium; p. *1,000*.
Quyquyo, *t.*, S. Paraguay; copper, manganese; p. *6,590*.

R

Raab, *see* **Györ**.
Raalte, *t.*, Overyssel, Neth.; nr. Zwolle; industl.; p. *10,882*.
Raasay, *I.*, E. of Skye, Inverness, Scot.; 13 m. long, 3½ m. wide.
Rab I., at head of Adriatic, Jugoslavia; marble. silk mnfs.; resort; a. 74 sq. m.; p. *6,354*.
Rabat or **New Salle**, *c.*, *spt.*, Morocco; at mouth of Bu Regreg; cath., univ.; leather and carpet mnfs.; p. (1960) *227,445*.
Rabaul, *spt.*, New Britain, Papua-New Guinea; copra ctr.; p. *4,500*.
Rabot, *t.*, Malta; on Gozo I.
Racalmuto, *t.*, Girgenti, Sicily; agr.; p. *13,825*.
Race, *C.*, S.E. Newfoundland, Canada.
Racibórz (Ratibor), *t.*, Upper Silesia, Poland; German before 1945; on R. Oder; textiles, metals, wood, engin.; p. (1960) *32,000*.
Racine, *c.*, Wis., U.S.A.; on L. Michigan, 10 m., S. of Milwaukee; motor cars, farm implements; p. (1960) *89,144*.
Radauti, *t.*, Bukovina, Romania; paper, glass, engin.; p. (1956) *15,949*.
Radcliffe, *mun. bor.*, Lancs, Eng.; nr. Manchester; paper-mkg., cotton weaving, engin.; p. (1961) *26,720*.
Radebeul, *t.*, Dresden, E. Germany; on R. Elbe; machin.; p. (1963) *40,177*.
Radford, *t.*, Va., U.S.A.; iron smelting, lumbering; p. (1960) *9,371*.
Radnorshire, *inland co.*, S. Wales; oats, wheat; sheep rearing, breeding Welsh ponies, mineral springs; cap. Presteign; a. 471 sq. m.; p. (1961) *18,431*.
Radom, *industl. t.*, Kielce, Poland; nr. Warsaw; engin.; p. (1960) *130,000*.
Radomsko, *t.*, Poland; S. of Lodz; p. (1960) *27,000*.
Radomsyl, *t.*, Ukrainian S.S.R.; textiles.
Radstock (Norton Radstock), *t.*, *urb. dist.*, Somerset, Eng.; 10 m. S.E. of Bristol; collieries; p. (1961) *12,782*.
Radzionkow, *t.*, Katowice, Poland; New Town (1951) p. (1960) *24,000*.
Rafah, *t.*, U.A.R., on Israel bdy.
Raffadali, *t.*, Girgenti, Sicily, Italy; agr.; p. *10,825*.
Ragaz, Bad, *t.*, *resort*, St. Gall, Switzerland; on R. Tamina; hot springs; ancient Abbey of Pfäfers, 2,697 ft. above sea-level.
Ragusa, *c.*, Syracuse, Italy; cheese factories; oil; p. (1961) *55,274*.
Ragusa, *see* **Dubrovnik**.
Rahad, *R.*, Sudan; trib. of Blue Nile.
Rahmánfya, El, *t.*, Lower U.A.R.; nr. Rosetta; on R. Nile.
Rahway, *c.*, N.J., U.S.A.; on R. Rahway; residtl. for New York business men; p. (1960) *27,699*.
Raiatéa, *I.*, Society Is., Pac. Oc.; lgst. of Fr. Leeward gr. 130 m. N.W. Tahiti; p. (1962) *6,210*.
Raichur, *t.*, Mysore, India; pottery; p. (1961) *63,329*.
Raigarh, *t.*, cap. Raigarh *dist.*, Madhya Pradesh, India; silk mnfs.; rice; p. (1961) *36,933*.
Rainford, *urb. dist.*, Lancs, Eng.; nr. St. Helens; coal; p. (1961) *5,385*.
Rainier, *mtn.*, Washington, U.S.A.; 14,530 ft.
Rainton, E. and W., *colly. dists.*, nr. Durham, Eng.
Rainy, *L.*, on border of Canada and Minn., U.S.A., drained by Rainy R. to Lake of the Woods.
Raipur, *t.*, Madhya Pradesh, India; p. (1961) *139,792*.
Raismes, *t.*, Nord, France; nr. Valenciennes; lace ind.; p. (1954) *14,577*.
Rajahmundry, *t.*, Andhra Pradesh, India; on the delta of the Godivari R.; p. (1961) *130,030*.
Rajasthan, *st.*, India; farming, millet, cotton, pulses, textiles, ivory; ch. towns, Jaipur, (cap.), Udaipur, Alwar, Jodhpur; section of canal scheme inaugurated 1961 at Hanumangarh, 200 m. N.W. of New Delhi; nuclear power sta. projected; a. 132,077 sq. m.; p. (1961) *20,155,602*.
Rajkot, *t.*, Gujarat, India; p. (1961) *194,510*.
Rajshahi, *t.*, Rajshahi dist., E. Pakistan; on R. Ganges; univ.; silk inds.
Raki-Ura I., *see* **Stewart I.**
Rakka, *t.*, Nigeria, W. Africa; on Lower Niger R.
Rakos Palota, *sub.* Budapest, Hungary.
Rakovnik, *t.*, Bohemia, ČSSR.; mkt., mining; p. (1961) *11,979*.
Raleigh, *c.*, N.C. U.S.A.; educational ctr.; rly. wks., cotton-mills; p. (1960) *93,931*.
Ralick, *chain of Is.*, Marshall gr., Pac. Oc.; parallel with Ratack chain.
Ramacca, *commune*, E. Sicily; marble; linen; agr.; p. *12,521*.
Rambervilliers, *t.*, Vosges, France; nr. Nancy; p. (1954) *6,257*.

Rambouillet, *t.*, Seine-et-Oise, France; nr. Versailles; ancient château; p. (1954) *8,923*.

Rameswaram, *t.*, S. India; on Rameswaram I., Palk Strait; contains a great Dravidian temple, one of the Hindu holy places of pilgrimage; p. (1961) *6,801*.

Ramgunga, *R.*, India; trib. of R. Ganges, which it joins nr. Cawnpore; length 300 m.

Ramle, *t.*, Israel; S. of Lydda; p. (1946) *16,380*.

Ramleh, *t.*, U.A.R.; E. of Alexandria; p. *52,000*.

Ramme, *t.*, Ringkjobing, Jutland, Denmark.

Ramnad, *t.*, Madras, India; on peninsula projecting towards Rameswaram I.

Râmnicu-Sârat, *t.*, Romania; scene of several battles; petroleum; p. *19,267*.

Râmnicu-Vâlcea, *c.*, Romania; on R. Olt; cath., monasteries; salt-mining; hot springs; p. *15,162*.

Rampur, *t.*, Uttar Pradesh, India; N.W. of Bareilly; damask, sugar, pottery; p. (1961) *135,407*.

Ramree I., Bay of Bengal, Indian Ocean; off cst. Arakan, Lower Burma; 50 m. long.

Ramsbottom, *t.*, *urb. dist.*, Lancs, Eng.; on R. Irwell, 4 m. N. of Bury; cottons, bleaching, dyeing, engin., paper mftg., p. (1961) *13,813*.

Ramsey, *mkt. t.*, *urb. dist.*, Hunts, Eng.; on edge of The Fens, 7 m. N. of St. Ives; engin., agr.; p. (1961) *5,697*.

Ramsey, *t.*, *spt.*, I. of Man; on N.E. cst.; holiday resort; p. (1956) *4,621*.

Ramsey, *residtl. bor.*, N.J., U.S.A.; ctr. of dairying region; p. (1960) *9,527*.

Ramsey I., off cst. of Pembroke, Wales.

Ramsgate, *t.*, *mun. bor.*, Kent, Eng.; on S. cst. of I. of Thanet; seaside resort; p. (1961) *36,906*.

Rana Pratap Sagar, Rajasthan, India; nuclear power sta. projected.

Rancagua, *c.*, Colchagua prov., Chile; agr. tractors; p. (1961) *61,832*.

Rance, *R.*, Brittany, France; world's first major tidal hydro-elec. sta. projected.

Ranchi, *hot-weather seat of govt.*, Bihar, India; technical institute; rice, tea, shellac; p. (1961) *140,253*.

Rand, *gold-mining dist.*, Transvaal, S. Africa (*see* Witwatersrand).

Randazzo, *t.*, Catania, Sicily; on S. slopes of Mt. Etna; 2,474 ft. above sea-level; p. *16,325*.

Randers, *t.*, Denmark; medieval monastery; machin., foundries; exp. dairy produce; p. (1960) *42,238*. [*10,000*.

Ranenburg, *t.*, U.S.S.R.; on R. Voronezh; p.

Rangiora, *t.*, S.I., N.Z.; 20 m. N.W. of Christchurch; ctr. of lge. agr. dist.; p. (1961) *3,540*.

Rangitaiki R., N.I., N.Z.; flows N. into Bay of Plenty.

Rangoon, *c.*, *cap.*, Burma; on E. arm of Irrawaddy delta; 2 caths., many mosques, temples and pagodas; gr. tr., and many impt. mnfs.; rice, oil, lumber; ivory and wood carving; textiles; p. (1955) *737,079*.

Rangpur, *t.*, E. Pakistan; on R. Ghaghat; jute; p. (1961) *40,600*.

Raniganj, *t.*, W. Bengal, India; iron, coal-mines; p. (1961) *30,113*.

Rani-Nur, *famous rock-cave*, Khandgiri Hill, Puri dist., Orissa, India.

Rannoch, *Loch*, Perth, Scot.; 9 m. long, 1 m. wide; drained to R. Tay.

Rapallo, *t.*, *wat. pl.*, Liguria, N.W. Italy; on G. of Genoa, 22 m. E. of Genoa; most celebrated resort on Italian Riviera di Levante; p. (1946) *14,675*.

Rapanui or **Easter I.**, *I.*, Pac. Oc.; W. of Chile.

Raphoe, *par.*, co. Donegal, Ireland; cath.; mkt.; woollens, esp. tweeds; p. *2,600*.

Rapid City, *t.*, S.D., U.S.A.; p. (1960) *42,399*.

Rappollsweiler, *t.*, Bas Rhin, France; nr. Selestat; walled; known as "the pipers' town."

Ragqa, *t.*, Syria; on R. Euphrates; p. *2,000*.

Raritan, *t.*, N.J., U.S.A.; p. (1960) *15,334*.

Rarotonga, *volcanic I.*, Pac. Oc.; cap. of Cook Is.; fruit canning; ch. t. and pt. Avarua; p. *7,368*.

Ras-al-Had, *C.*, E. extremity Arabia.

Ras-al-Khaima, *t.*, on Persian G., st. of Bahrain, Arabia.

Rasgrad, *t.*, Bulgaria; nr. Ruschuk, on R. Ak-Lom.

Ras Lanuf, *oil terminal*, on G. of Sidra, Libya; pipeline from Hofra oilfield.

Ras Mohammed, *S. point*, Sinai Peninsula.

Ras Tannura, *spt.*, Nejd, Saudi Arabia; lge. oil-refinery.

Rashin, *t.*, N. Korea; nr. U.S.S.R. frontier.

Rasskazovo, *t.*, Tambov reg., U.S.S.R.; ironwks.; wheat; p. *25,168*.

Rastrick, *industl. t.*, W.R. Yorks, Eng.; on R. Calder, nr. Halifax.

Rat Is., *group of Is.*, Aleutian Archipelago.

Ratack, *chain of Is.*, Marshall Gr., Pac. Oc., parallel with Ralick chain.

Rathenow, *t.*, Potsdam, E. Germany; on R. Havel; optical glass; p. (1963) *29,491*.

Rathkeale, *mkt. t.*, *rural dist.*, Ireland; nr. Limerick; p. (rural dist. 1961) *11,726*.

Rathlin, *I.*, off Fair Head, N. Antrim, N. Ireland; 5 m. by 1 m.

Rathven, *par.*, Banff, Scot.; farming, sandstone, limestone, slate; p. *15,404*.

Ratibor, *see* Raciborz.

Ratingen, *t.*, N. Rhine–Westphalia, Germany; N.E. of Düsseldorf; textiles, machin., glass; p. (1963) *37,200*.

Ratisbon, *see* Regensburg.

Ratnagiri, *pt.*, Maharashtra, India; all weather pt.; p. (1961) *31,091*.

Ratnapura, *t.*, Ceylon; graphite; p. *12,441*.

Rattray Head, Aberdeen, Scot.

Rauma, *spt.*, Finland; on G. of Bothnia; p. (1961) *21,567*.

Raunds, *t.*, *urb. dist.*, Northants, Eng.; 5 m. N.E. of Wellingborough; p. (1961) *4,593*.

Rava Ruskaya, *t.*, Ukrainian S.S.R.; oil processing; quarrying; lignite; p. *12,000*.

Ravenglass, *t.*, Cumberland, Eng.; nr. mouth of R. Esk.

Ravenna, *region*, Emilia, Italy; a. 715 sq. m.; p. (1961) *328,969*.

Ravenna, *c.*, Emilia, N. Italy; on marshy plain, nr. the Adriatic, 45 m. E. of Bologna; cath., archiepiscopal palace, famous mosaics; agr. mkt. and ctr. for sugar-beet and beet sugar; sericulture; p. (1961) *115,205*.

Ravenna, *t.*, N.E. Ohio, U.S.A.; engin., rubber; p. (1960) *10,918*.

Ravensburg, *t.*, Baden-Württemberg, Germany; nr. Konstanz; p. (1963) *31,800*.

Ravenscraig, *t.*, nr. Motherwell, Lanark., Scot.; hot strip steelmill; cold reduction mill at Gartcosh 8 m. away. [Dewsbury.

Ravensthorpe, *industl. t.*, W.R. Yorks, Eng.; nr.

Ravi, *R.*, Punjab, India; trib. of the Chenab; used for irrigation; length 450 m.

Rawalpindi, *div.*, W. Pakistan; between Lahore and Peshawar; p. (1961) *3,879,000*.

Rawalpindi, *t.*, Pakistan; on R. Leh, W. Pakistan; fortfd.; admin., comm. and rly. ctr.; rly. wks., brewing, foundries, oil refining, industl. gases; p. (1961) *340,175*.

Rawlins, *t.*, S. Wyo., U.S.A.; mkt., coal, oilfields, ranching; p. (1950) *7,415*.

Rawmarsh, *t.*, *urb. dist.*, W.R. Yorks, Eng.; 2 m. N.E. of Rotherham; engin.; p. (1961) *19,603*.

Rawson, *spt.*, *cap.*, Chubut terr., Argentina; S. of Valdes Peninsula; fish, fruit, livestock; p. *2,500*.

Rawson, *industl. t.*, nr. Leeds, Yorks, Eng.

Rawtenstall, *t.*, *mun. bor.*, Lancs, Eng.; on R. Irwell in ctr. of Rossendale Fells; cotton weaving; p. (1961) *23,869*.

Ray, *C.*, S.W. Newfoundland, Canada; beginning of Long Range, of which the highest peak is 2,673 ft.

Rayleigh, *t.*, *urb. dist.*, Essex, Eng.; 5 m. N.W. of Southend; light inds.; p. (1961) *19,044*.

Raynham, *t.*, S.E. Mass., U.S.A.; mkt. ctr. for agr. products, poultry, eggs; p. *2,141*.

Razeim, *L.*, Dobrodea, Romania; 25 m. long.

Ré or **Rhe**, *I.*, W. cst. Charente-Inférieure, France; opp. a. Rochelle; salt mftg.; ch. t. St. Martin.

Reading, *t.*, *co. bor.*, Berks, Eng.; at confluence of Rs. Thames and Kennet; univ.; biscuits, engin., brewing, seed-growing and mkt. gardening, tin-box mftg., printing; p. (1961) *119,870*.

Reading, *t.*, Mass., U.S.A.; nr. Boston; p. (1960) *19,259*.

Reading, *c.*, Penns., U.S.A.; on Schuylkill R.; ironwks.; p. (1960) *98,177*.

Recanati, *t.*, Macerata, Italy; industl.; p. *16,325*.

Recife, *spt.*, *cap.*, Pernambuco, Brazil; univ.; exports sugar, cotton, coffee; called the Brazilian Venice; fine natural harbour; p. (1960) *788,580*.

Recklinghausen, *t.*, N. Rhine–Westphalia, W. Germany; nr. Dortmund; collieries, iron, machin., textiles, chemicals; p. (1963) *130,100*.

Recôncavo, *dist.*, Bahia st., N.E. Brazil; surrounds bay at mouth of R. Paraguassu; intensive cultivation of sugar-cane, cotton, tobacco, rice, by Negro farmers; ch. ts. São Salvador, Cachoeira.
Red Basin, *see* Szechwan.
Red Bay, Antrim, N. Ireland.
Red Deer R., trib. of Saskatchewan, R., Alberta, Canada.
Red Lake, *t.*, Ontario, Canada; nr. L. Winnipeg; [gold.
Red R. (China), *see* Song-koi.
Red R., U.S.A.; trib. Mississippi, flows from New Mexico through the Staked Plain; length, 1,600 m.
Red R. of the North, U.S.A.; rises in Minnesota and flows N., separating N. Dakota and Minnesota, U.S.A., and thence into Manitoba, Canada, to join Assiniboine R.; length 650 m.
Red Sea, *arm of the sea* separating Arabia from Africa; connects with the Indian Ocean by the Straits of Bab-el-Mandeb; length 1,400 m., greatest width 230 m.
Red Wing, *c.*, Minn., U.S.A.; on the Mississippi R., at head of L. Pepin; flour mills, grain tr.; p. (1960) *10,528*.
Redbank, *t.*, N.J., U.S.A.; summer resort, fishing, mkt. gardens, light mnfs.; p. (1960) *12,482*.
Redbridge, *outer bor.*, E. London, Eng.; incorporating former bors. of Ilford, Wanstead and Woodford, Chigwell (Hainalt Estate), Dagenham (N. Chadwell Heath ward); mainly residtl.; p. (1964) *248,569*.
Redcar, *t.*, *mun. bor.*, N.R. Yorks, Eng.; on E. cst., nr. mouth of R. Tees; seaside resort; steel wks., engin., slag bricks, toys; p. (1961) *31,460*.
Redcliffe, *t.*, Queensland, Australia; p. (1957) [*16,200*.
Redding, *c.*, N. Cal., U.S.A.; lumber, mining, agr.; tourists; p. (1960) *12,773*.
Redditch, *t.*, *urb. dist.*, Worcester, Eng.; 12 m. S. of Birmingham; needles, fish tackle, cycles, springs, aluminium alloys, chromium and cadmium plating; designated "New Town" 1964; p. (estd. 1965) *29,000*.
Rede, *R.*, Northumberland, Eng.; trib. of R. Tyne.
Redhill, *t.*, Surrey, Eng.; at foot of N. Downs, adjoining Reigate; residt.; refractory sands.
Redlands, *t.*, Cal., U.S.A.; p. (1960) *26,829*.
Redonda, *I.*, Leeward group, Caribbean Sea; between Montserrat and Nevis.
Redondela, *t.*, Pontevedra, Spain; on Vigo estuary; old feudal castles; p. (1957) *17,024*.
Redruth, *t.*, part of Camborne–Redruth urb. dist., Cornwall, Eng.; tin-mine dist., chemicals, engin., textiles; p. (1961) (with Camborne) *36,090*.
Redwood City, *c.*, W. Cal., U.S.A.; shipbldg., saltwks.; exp. sequoia; p. (1960) *46,290*.
Ree, Lough, *L.*, Ireland; between Roscommon, Longford and Westmeath, an extension of R. Shannon; 17 m. long.
Regello, *t.*, Val d'Arno, Italy; nr. Florence; p. *14,250*.
Regensburg (Ratisbon), *c.*, Bavaria, Germany; N.E. of Munich on R. Danube; cath.; brewing, machin., wood, chemicals; p. (1963) *125,300*.
Reggane, Central Sahara, Algeria; Fr. atomic testing ground.
Reggio di Calabria, *t.*, Calabria, Italy; on Strait of Messina; cath.; perfumes, silks, terracotta; train ferry to Messina (Sicily); has suffered from earthquakes; p. (1961) *150,334*.
Reggio nell' Emilia, *c.*, *cap.*, Emilia–Romagna, N. Italy; at N. foot of Apennines, 40 m. N.W. of Bologna; locomotives, aircraft; fine church of the Madonna della Ghiara; sericulture, cheese-mkg.; p. (1961) *116,515*.
Regina, *t.*, *cap.*, Saskatchewan, Canada; foundries, oil-wks., sawmills; helium gas exp.; p. (1961) *112,141*.
Region Oriental, Ecuador; a. 219,095 sq. m.; p. *295,200*; consists of provs.—Napo Pastaza and Santiago Zamora; about 110,000 sq. m. of region inhabited.
Regla, *t.*, Cuba, W. Indies; nr. Havana; p. *23,037*.
Rehoboth, *t.*, S.W Africa; salt. mining, cattle; p. *9,727*.
Rehovoth, Israel; agr. (citrus) and scientific ctr.; [p. *c. 10,500*.
Reichenbach, *t.*, Karl-Marx-Stadt, E. Germany; paper, metals; p. (1963) *29,189*.
Reichenberg, *see* Liberec.
Reidsville, *t.*, N.C., U.S.A.; tobacco mkt., mnfs., textiles, turpentine; p. (1960) *14,267*.
Reigate, *mkt. t.*, *mun. bor.*, Surrey, Eng.; at foot of N. Downs, 5 m. E. of Dorking; residtl.; fuller's earth, freestone; p. (1961) *53,710*.
Reims, *t.*, Marne, France; on R. Vesle; famous Gothic cath.; univ.; champagne ctr., cloth factories, woollen inds. and tr., dye wks.; p. (1962) *138,576*.
Reindeer L., Saskatchewan, Canada.
Rembang, *t.*, Java; oil, teak, rubber; p. *13,791*.
Remscheid, *t.*, N. Rhine–Westphalia, Germany; nr. Düsseldorf: cutlery, machin., textiles; p. (1963) *128,600*.
Renaix (Ronse), *t.*, Belgium; nr. Ghent; linen, woollens; dyeing, bleaching; p. (1962) *25,122*.
Rendsburg, *t.*, Schleswig-Holstein, Germany; on N. Sea–Baltic Canal; metals, elec. goods, shipbldg.; p. (1963) *35,100*.
Renfrew, *maritime co.*, W. Scot.; S. of R. Clyde; agr., mftg., and comm., coal, iron, shipbldg., machin., printing; ch. industl. ctrs. Paisley and Greenock; a. 245 sq. m.; p. (1961) *338,815*.
Renfrew, *co. t.*, *burgh*, Renfrew, Scot.; nr. R. Clyde, 5 m. W. of Glasgow; p. (1961) *17,946*.
Renfrew, *t.*, Ontario, Canada; p. (1961) *8,935*.
Renmark, *t.*, S. Australia; on Murray R.; ctr. of irrigated fruit-growing dist.; p. *1,914*.
Rennes, *c.*, *cap.*, Ille-et-Vilaine, France; 40 m. S. of St. Malo; univ.; dairying and agr. dist.; farm implements, sail-cloth, oil refining; p. (1962) *157,692*.
Reno, *lgst. c.*, Nevada, U.S.A.; seat of Univ. of Nevada; st. agr. college; famous for easy divorce procedure; p. (1960) *51,470*.
Rensselaer, *t.*, N.Y., U.S.A.; on R. Hudson facing Albany; p. (1960) *10,506*.
Repton, *rural dist.*, Derbyshire, Eng.; agr., clay, coal-mining, sanitary ware; p. *29,780*.
Republican Fork or Pawnee, *R.*, trib. of Kansas R., Col., U.S.A.; length 550 m.
Repulse Bay, on S. side of Melville Peninsula, N. Canada.
Requeña, *t.*, Valencia, Spain; sulphur springs of Fuentepodida; p. (1957) *20,253*.
Resht, *t.*, *cap.*, Gilan, Iran; nr. Caspian Sea; sericulture, rice; p. (1956) *109,493*.
Resina, *t.*, S. Italy; on Bay of Naples at W. foot of Vesuvius; p. (1961) *45,148*.
Resistencia, *t.*, *cap.*, Chaco, Argentina; cotton, quebracho, cattle; p. (1960) *94,000*.
Resolution, *t.*, N.W. Terr., Canada; on S. shore of Gr. Slave L.
Resolution I., off S.W. cst. of S.I., New Zealand.
Resolution Is. (Brit.), N. of Labrador, at entrance Hudson Strait, Franklin, Canada.
Resolven, *t.*, N. Glamorgan, Wales, on R. Neath 6 m. N.E. of Neath; aluminium; p. (1951) *4,353*.
Retalhulen, *t.*, *cap.*, R. dep., Guatemala, Central America; coffee, sugar; p. (1960) *29,361*.
Retford, E., *see* East Retford.
Rethymnon, *prefecture*, I. of Crete; cap. Rethymnon; p. (1961) *69,843*.
Rethymnon, *cap.*, Rethymnon, Crete; p. (1961) *14,999*.
Réunion, Ile de la (formerly Bourbon), *Fr. I.*, Indian Ocean; between Mauritius and Madagascar; sugar growing; cap. St. Denis; a. 970 sq. m.; p. (1961) *347,000*.
Reus, *t.*, Tarragona, Spain; textiles, leather, soap; p. (1957) *35,950*.
Reuss, R., Switzerland; flows N. from the St. Gotthard Pass through L. Lucerne, joining Aar R. near Brugg; length 98 m.
Reutlingen, *t.*, Baden-Württemberg, Germany; S. of Stuttgart; textiles, metals, machin., leather; p. (1963) *70,600*.
Reval, *see* Tallin.
Revda, *t.*, R.S.F.S.R.; in Urals, 29 m. W. of Sverdlovsk; iron, copper, chemicals; p. (1959) *55,000*.
Revere, *t.*, Mass., U.S.A.; sub. of Boston; resort; p. (1960) *40,080*.
Revilla Gigedo Is., *gr. of Is.*, belonging to Mexico, Pac. Oc.; ch. Is., Socorro, San Benito.
Rewa, *t.*, Madhya Pradesh, India; rice, coal; p. (1961) *43,065*.
Rewari, *t.*, Punjab, India; S.W. of Delhi; turban and brass-ware mnfs.; p. (1961) *36,994*.
Reykjavik, *c.*, *cap.*, Iceland; on S.W. cst.; univ., cath.; exp. fish, skins, wool; p. (1962) *74,978*.
Rezé, *t.*, Loire Atlantique, France; p. (1954) *19,000*.
Rhayader, *rural dist.*, Radnorshire, N. Wales; stock and sheep raising; p. (estd. 1955) *4,700*.
Rheine, *t.*, N. Rhine–Westphalia, Germany; on R. Ems; textiles, machin.; p. (1963) *46,400*.

Rheinhausen, *t.*, N. Rhine–Westphalia, Germany; on R. Rhine; S. of Duisburg; coal-mining, iron, textiles; p. (1963) *70,500.*
Rheinkamp (Repelen-Baerl before 1950), *t.*, N. Rhine–Westphalia, Germany; on R. Rhine, N.W. of Duisberg; coal-mng.; p. (1963) *38,900.*
Rheydt, *t.*, N. Rhine–Westphalia, Germany; W. of Düsseldorf; textiles, machin., rly. junction; p. (1963) *96,000.*
Rhin (Bas), *dep.*, N.E. France; cap. Strasbourg; a. 1,848 sq. m.; p. (1962) *770,150.*
Rhin (Haut), *dep.*, N.E. France; cap. Colmar; a. 1,354 sq. m.; p. (1962) *547,920.*
Rhine, *R.*, rises in Switzerland, can. Grisons, passes through L. Constance, skirts Baden, traverses Hesse, Rhineland, and the Neth., flowing to N. Sea by two arms, Oude Rijn and the Waal (the latter discharging finally by the Maas); famous for its beauty, especially between Bonn and Bingen; ch. falls at Schaffhausen; once a natural barrier between E. and W. Europe, the Rhine is now spanned by 30 rly. bridges, and its navigation declared free in 1868; length 800 m.
Rhineland Palatinate (Rheinland-Pfalz), *Land*, Germany; a. 7,665 sq. m.; cap. Mainz; p. (1961) *3,417,000.*
Rhinns (Rins), *peninsula*, on W. cst. Islay I., Inner Hebrides, Scot.; lighthouse.
Rhio-Lingga Archipelago, *gr. of Is.*, Indonesia; mainly in Malacca Strait; a. 12,235 sq. m.
Rhode Island, *st.*, New England, U.S.A.; washed by the Atlantic, and surrounded by Massachusetts and Connecticut; divided by Narragansett Bay, with many islands, lgst. being that from which the st. takes its name; jewellery, silverware, textiles, rubber, granite; agr., fisheries; cap. Providence; a. 1,214 sq. m.; p. (1960) *859,488.*
Rhodes (Rhodos), *I.*, Dodecanese Is.; off S.W. cst., Anatolia, belonging to Greece; cap. R.; figs, oranges, grapes; p. (1940) *61,791.*
Rhodes, *t.*, *cap.*, I. of Rhodes, Greece; on N.E. cst.; p. (1951) *24,186.*
Rhodesia, *self gov. Brit. col.* central Africa; tobacco, maize, fruit, cattle; gold, coal, asbestos, chrome ore; cap. Salisbury; a. 150,333 sq. m.; p. (estd. 1964) *4,210,000.*
Rhodope Mtns., *range*, S. Bulgaria; rise to 10,200 ft.
Rhodopi, *prefecture*, Thrace, Greece; cap. Komotini; p. (1961) *109,194.*
Rhöngebirge, *mtn. gr.*, Thuringia, Germany; highest peak 3,100 ft.
Rhondda, *t.*, *urb. dist.*, Glamorgan, Wales; in narrow Rhondda valley, 7 m. N.W. of Pontypridd; coal-mining; p. (1961) *100,314.*
Rhône, *R.*, Switzerland and France; rising in the Rhône glacier of the St. Gotthard mtn. gr., and flowing through the L. of Geneva and E. France to the G. of Lyons in the Mediterranean; length 507 m.; power stas. at Sion and Geneva; canals, dams, locks and power stas. form part of French Rhône Valley project (1937–72).
Rhône, *dep.*, S.E. France; drained by R. Rhône, and its trib. R. Saône, which unite at Lyons; agr., grain, potatoes, wine; vine-growing, many mnfs., silks, textiles; cap. Lyons; a. 1,104 sq. m.; p. (1962) *1,116,664.*
Rhyl, *t.*, *urb. dist.*, Flint, N. Wales; between Bangor and Chester, at entrance Vale of Clwyd; resort; furniture mkg.; p. (1961) *21,825.*
Rhymney, *t.*, *urb. dist.*, Monmouth, Eng.; on R. Rhymney, 4 m. E. of Merthyr Tydfil; mining; p. (1961) *8,859.*
Rialto, *I.* and *dist.* on Grand Canal, Venice; ctr. of comm.
Ribadesella, *spt.*, Spain; W. of Santander; iron mines; p. (1957) *7,692.*
Ribatejo, *prov.*, Portugal; a. 2,794 sq. m.; p. (1950) *459,853.*
Ribe, *mkt. t.*, Jutland, S. Denmark; on W. cst.; iron wks.; p. (1960) *7,809.*
Ribble, *R.*, Yorks and Lancs, Eng.; followed by main rly. route Leeds to Carlisle; length 75 m.
Ribeira, *t.*, Galicia, Spain; on peninsula of Arosa estuary; agr., cattle-rearing, fishing.
Ribeirão Preto, *c.*, S.E. Brazil; mkt. in rich agr. a. esp. coffee, cotton, sugar; p. (1960) *116,153.*
Riberalta, *R. pt.*, Colonia Terr., Bolivia, S. America; on R. Beni above rapids which limit navigation to upper course; collecting ctr. for wild rubber.
Richborough, *pt.*, Kent, Eng.; at mouth of R. Stour; pt. was derelict but now being developed as a private pt.; chemicals, antibiotics.
Richelieu or Chambly, *R.*, Quebec, Canada; flows from L. Champlain to the St. Lawrence R. at L. St. Peter; length 80 m.
Richmond-upon-Thames, *outer bor.*, Greater London, Eng.; inc. former bors. of Barnes, Richmond and Twickenham; industl. and residtl.; beautiful park and riverside scenery; p. (1964) *181,581.*
Richmond, *t.*, *mun. bor.*, N.R. Yorks, Eng.; at E. foot of Pennines on R. Swale; p. (1961) *5,764.*
Richmond, *t.*, Cal., U.S.A.; oil refining; p. (1960) *71,854.*
Richmond, *c.*, Ind., U.S.A.; on R. Whitewater; mnfs.; p. (1960) *44,149.*
Richmond, *c.*, Ky., U.S.A.; in tobacco-growing and horse-rearing region; p. (1960) *12,168.*
Richmond, one of the five bors. of New York City, U.S.A.; p. (1957) *210,146.*
Richmond, *c.*, *cap.*, Va., U.S.A.; on falls on R. James; gr. tobacco mftg. ctr. and mart; chemicals, iron and steel, lumber; p. (1960) *219,958.*
Rickmansworth, *mkt. t.*, *urb. dist.*, Herts, Eng.; at confluence of Rs. Colne and Chess, 3 m. S.W. of Watford; paper, brewing; residtl.; p. (1961) *28,442.*
Rideau Canal, Canada; from Ottawa R., to Kingston on L. Ontario; length 132 m.
Ridgefield, *t.*, N.J., U.S.A.; p. (1960) *10,788.*
Ridgewood, *t.*, N.J., U.S.A.; p. (1960) *25,391.*
Riesa, *t.*, Dresden, E. Germany; on R. Elbe, nr. Meissen; steel wks., sawmills; p. (1963) *38,929.*
Riesengebirge, *mtns.*, Germany; (Czech Krkonose, Polish Karkonesze).
Riesi, *t.*, Sicily, Italy; industl.; p. *20,200.*
Rieti, *t.*, Perugia, Italy; an ancient Sabine t. in famous fertile dist.; mnfs.; p. (1961) *34,580.*
Riff (Er Rif), *mtns.*, Morocco, N.W. Africa; extend E. along N. African cst. for 200 m. from Straits of Gibraltar; inaccessible and economically unattractive, terr. of semi-nomadic tribes; rises to over 7,000 ft. in many places.
Riga, *cap.*, Latvian S.S.R.; at head of G. of Riga; gr. industl. activity; machin., glass, paper, cottons; rly. and shipbldg., exp. wheat, flax, hemp, dairy produce; p. (1962) *620,000.*
Rigi, *mtn.*, nr. L. Lucerne, Switzerland; alt 5,905 ft.
Rijeka-Susak, *t.*, Jugoslavia; formerly Fiume; belonged to Austria-Hungary before First World War, then to Italy; ceded to Jugoslavia by Italy after Second World War; rival pt. to Trieste; petrol refining, tobacco, chemicals, hydro-elec., shipbldg.; p. (1959) *87,000.*
Rimac, *R.*, Lima dep., Peru; S. America; rises in W. cordillera of Andes and flows W. to Pac. Oc.; provides water for irrigation and for c. of Lima; length 75 m.
Rimini, *t.*, Emilia, Italy; on the Adriatic cst.; mineral springs, sea-bathing, thriving inds.; p. (1961) *92,912.*
Rimnic, *t.*, Romania; on R. Rimnic, nr. Bucharest; industl.
Rimouski, *t.*, Quebec, Canada; on S. bank St. Lawrence R.; lumber; tourists; p. (1961) *17,739.*
Ringerike, *c.*, Buskerud, Norway; new c. 25 m. N.W. of Oslo and inc. former t. of Hönefoss; p. (1965) *27,900.*
Ringköbing Fjord, *inlet*, W. cst. Jutland, Denmark.
Ringwood and Fordingbridge, *mkt. t.*, *rural dist.*, Hants, Eng.; on R. Avon, nr. Christchurch; p. (rural dist. 1951) *23,908.*
Rio Branco, *R.*, Brazil; prov. Baia, trib. of Rio Grande; length 120 m.
Rio Branco, *R.*, N. Brazil; flowing to Rio Negro; length 370 m.
Rio Branco, *t.*, cap. of Acre st., Brazil; p. (1960) *47,882.*
Rio Branco, *terr.*, Brazil; cap. Boa Vista; a. *82,749* sq. m.; p. (1960) *29,489.*
Rio Cuarto, *t.*, Cordoba prov., Argentina; agr. ctr.; p. (1960) *70,000.*
Rio das Mortes, *R.*, Brazil; trib. of the Araguay; length 500 m.
Rio de Janeiro, *maritime st.*, Brazil; a. 16,443 sq. m.; coffee plantations, sugar, cotton, tobacco; thorium; cap. Niterói; p. (1960) *3,402,728.*
Rio de Janeiro, *c.*, *spt.*, former fed. cap. Brazil; on Bay of Rio de Janeiro; many fine bdgs., flourishing tr. and inds.; rly. wks.; shipyards; mnfs. iron, steel, cement, textiles, sugar, tyres, pharmaceutics, china, sheet glass; p. (1960) *3,307,163.*

Rio de la Plata, *see* **Plate R.**
Rio de Oro, *prov.*, Spanish Sahara; a. 70,000 sq. m.
Rio de San Juan, *R.*, Utah, New Mexico and Colorado, U.S.A.; length 350 m.
Rio Dulce, *R.*, Santiago st., Argentina; length [400 m.
Rio Grande, *headstream* of the R. Paraná, Brazil.
Rio Grande City, *t.*, S. Texas, U.S.A.; on Rio Grande R.; mkt., agr., oil, natural gas; p. (1960) *5,835.*
Rio Grande de Santiago, *R.*, Mexico; flows into the [Pacific.
Rio Grande del Norte, *R.*, flows from st. of Colorado through New Mexico to the G. of Mexico; forms bdy. between Texas, U.S.A. and Mexico; length 1,800 m.
Rio Grande do Norte, *st.*, Brazil; sugar, cotton, cattle-rearing; cap. Natal; a. 20,482 sq. m.; p. (1960) *1,157,258.*
Rio Grande do Sul, *st.*, S. Brazil; cap. Porto Alegre; a. 109,067 sq. m.; p. (1960) *5,448,823.*
Rio Grande do Sul, *spt.*, Brazil; textiles, oil refining; cattle, agr.; p. *45,000.*
Rio Muni, *Span. overseas prov.* (aut. status granted 1963), W. Africa, on cst. between Cameroun and Congo; with Fernando Po and other Is. forms col. of Span. Guinea; ch. t. Bata; cacao, palm oil, coffee; a. 10,000 sq. m.; p. (1963) *200,000.*
Rio Negro, *R.*, Argentina; rises in the Andes, and flows through the terr. of Rio Negro to the Atlantic; length 650 m.
Rio Negro, *prov.*, Argentina; S. of Pampa; cap. Viedma; cattle-rearing region; a. 77,610 sq. m.; p. (1960) *193,000.*
Rio Negro, *R.*, S. America; rises in Colombia, and flows through N. Brazil to the Amazon; length 1,350 m.
Rio Negro, *dep.*, Uruguay; cap. Fray Bentos; a. 3,269 sq. m.; p. (1953) *51,954.*
Rio Piedras, *t.*, Puerto Rico, W. Indies; univ.; merged with San Juan 1951.
Rio Salada, *R.*, Argentina; rises in the Andes, and flows S.E. to R. Paraná, at Buenos Aires; length 1,000 m.
Rio Tinto, *t.*, Spain; at W. end of Sierra Morena, 40 m. N.E. of Huelva; lead- and copper-mines; p. (1957) *10,000.*
Riobamba, *c.*, Chimborazo, Ecuador; on R. St. Juan; woollens, cotton gds., cement, ceramics; Inca palace ruins; p. (estd. 1960) *35,099.*
Rioja, *region*, N. Spain, Upper Ebro; famous for wines, orange groves; ch. ctr. Logroño.
Rioja, La, *prov.*, Argentina; gold- and copper-mines; cap. La Rioja; a. 33,394 sq. m.; p. (1960) *128,000.*
Riom, *t.*, Puy-de-Dôme, France; nr. Clermont Ferrand; p. (1954) *12,664.*
Rion, *R.*, Georgian S.S.R.; flows from Caucasus to Black Sea; lower half navig.; hydro-elec. sta. at Kutais. (In Greek mythology the R. Phasis of the Argonauts.)
Rionero, *t.*, Potenza prov., S. Italy; nr. Melfi; industl.; p. *12,025.*
Ripley, *mkt. t., urb. dist.*, Derby, Eng.; 7 m. N.E. of Derby; coal, iron, heavy engin., bricks, agr. implements; p. (1961) *17,601.*
Ripley, *t.*, W. Tenn., U.S.A.; lumbering; veneer; cottonseed processing; p. (1960) *3,782.*
Ripon, *c., mun. bor.*, W.R. Yorks, Eng.; on R. Ure; fine cath.; paint and varnish, prefabricated concrete structures; p. (1961) *10,490.*
Ripon, *t.*, Wis., U.S.A., on Green L., p. (1950) *5,619.*
Ripon Falls, *see* **Jinja.**
Riposto, *t.*, Sicily, Italy; on E. cst. nr. Taormina; wine export; p. *10,725.*
Ripponden, *urb. dist.*, W.R. Yorks, Eng.; nr. Halifax; p. (1961) *5,765.*
Risca, *t., urb. dist.*, Monmouth, Eng.; on R. Ebbw, 5 m. N.W. of Newport; coal, iron and steel, bricks, tiles, plastics; p. (1961) *14,008.*
Rishton, *t., urb. dist.*, Lancs, Eng.; at N. foot of Rossendale Fells, 4 m. N.E. of Blackburn; p. (1961) *5,431.*
Risley, nr. Warrington, Lancs., Eng.; headquarters of Engineering Group of U.K. Atomic Energy Authority; site of Manchester's New t.; proposed p. *50,000.*
Riva, *t.*, Trentino, Italy; battle zone in First World War, Nov.–Dec. 1915; p. *12,950.*
Rivas, *spt.*, Nicaragua, Central America; p. (1960) *19,159.*
Rive-de-Gier, *t.*, Loire, France; on R. Gier, nr. Lyons; mining ctr.; p. (1954) *15,118.*
Rivera, *dep.*, Uruguay; cap. Rivera; a. 3,793 sq. m.; p. (1953) *91,740.*
Riverina, *pastoral cty.*, N.S.W., Australia; between Lachlan-Murrumbidgee and Murray Rs.; sheep, agr. with irrigation; gold, coal; ch. ts., Wagga Wagga, Albury; a. 26,600 sq. m.; p. *71,000.*
River Rouge, *t.*, Mich., U.S.A.; p. (1960) *18,147.*
Riversdale, *dist.*, *W. prov.*, Cape Prov. S. Africa; a. 2,462 sq. m.
Riverside, *t.*, Cal., U.S.A.; p. (1960) *84,332.*
Riverside, *t.*, N.J., U.S.A.; p. (1960) *8,474.*
Riverside, *t.*, Ontario, Canada; p. (1961) *18,089.*
Riviera, the belt of cst. between the mtns. of the shore of the G. of Genoa, N. Italy, from Spezia to Nice; picturesque scenery, sheltered, mild climate; fashionable health resort.
Riyadh, *t.*, Nejd, Saudi Arabia; p. (estd.) *300,000.*
Rizal, *prov., t.*, central Luzon, Philippine Is.; chiefly agr. a.; a. 791 sq. m.; p. of t. (1960) *132,673.*
Rize, *t.*, Turkey; nr. Trabzon, on Black Sea; in I. of same name; p. (1960) *22,261.*
Rjukan, *t.*, Telemark, S. Norway; 35 m. N.W. of Notodden, impt. nitrate factories; p. (1961) *5,637.*
Road Town, *spt. cap.*, Tortola and Virgin Is.; p. [(1960) *900.*
Roanne, *t.*, Loire, France; nr. St. Etienne; textile, cottons, woollens, silk; p. (1962) *53,203.*
Roanoke, *I.*, off cst. N.C., U.S.A.; 13 m. long.
Roanoke, *R.*, Va., and N.C., U.S.A.; flows into Albemarle Sound; length 230 m.
Roanoke, *t.*, Ala. U.S.A.; cotton mnfs., clothes; p. (1960) *5,288.*
Roanoke, *c.*, S.W. Va., U.S.A.; on R. R.; iron-wks.; p. (1960) *97,110.*
Roatan Is., Honduras, in G. of H.
Robin Hood's Bay, *picturesque inlet with fishing vil. on cst.*, N.R. Yorks, Eng.; nr. Whitby.
Robson, Mt., Alberta, Canada, 12,972 ft.
Roca, C. da, most W. point of estuary of R. Tagus Portugal.
Roch, *R.*, Lancs, Eng.; rises in E. of Rossendale Fells, central Pennines, flows S.W. into R. Irwell nr. Bury; with R. Calder provides relatively easy route across Pennines from Leeds to Manchester; used by rail, road, canal; length approx. 20 m.
Rocha, *dep.*, Uruguay; a. 4,280 sq. m.; cap. Rocha; p. (1953) *86,334.*
Rochdale, *t., co. bor.*, Lancs, Eng.; at S. foot of Rossendale Fells, on R. Roch; textiles, textile engin., rayon spinning, elec. engin.; co-operative movement started here, 1844; p. (1961) *85,785.*
Rochefort, *t.*, S. Belgium; p. (1962) *3,996.*
Rochefort, *fortfd. pt.*, Charente-Maritime, France; with arsenal and sm. cst. tr.; famous cheese; p. (1954) *30,858.*
Rochelle, La, *fortfd. spt., cap.*, Charente-Maritime, France; on Bay of Biscay; shipbldg., chemical wks., fisheries; p. (1954) *58,799.*
Roches Point, E. side of Cork harbour, Co. Cork, Ireland.
Rochester, *c., mun. bor.*, Kent, Eng.; on R. Medway, adjoining Chatham; cath., cas.; aeronautical, elec. and mechanical engin., paint, varnish; p. (1961) *50,121.*
Rochester, *c.*, Minn., U.S.A.; in grain-growing dist.; p. (1960) *40,663.*
Rochester, *t.*, N.H., U.S.A.; on Salmon Falls and Cocheco Rs.; boot factories; p. (1960) *15,927.*
Rochester, *c.*, N.Y., U.S.A.; on Genesee R.; univ.; hydro-elec. power; cameras, films, optical instruments, thermometers, electronic equipment; p. (1960) *318,611.*
Roche-sur-Yon, La, *t.*, Vendée, France; on R. Yon; cas.; called formerly Bourbon Napoleonville; p. (1954) *19,576.*
Rochford, *t., rural dist.*, Essex, Eng.; 3 m. N. of Southend; timber wharves, boat bldg., brick mkg.; p. (rural dist. 1961) *30,306.*
Rockall, *sm. I.*, N. Atl. Oc.; lies 200 m. W. of Outer Hebrides; forms highest part of submarine bank which forms good fishing-ground; uninhabited. Annexed by Britain, 1955.
Rockall Deep, *submarine trench*, N. Atl. Oc.; between N.W. Ireland and Rockall I.; depth exceeds 1,600 fathoms.
Rockaway, *bor.*, N.J., U.S.A.; iron founding and products; textiles, leather; p. (1960) *5,413.*
Rockaway Beach, *summer resort*, on sandbar of

Long I.; now incorporated with Queens, one of the 5 bors. of New York City, U.S.A.
Rockford, *c.*, Ill., U.S.A.; machin. and furniture mftg.; p. (1960) *126,706*.
Rockhampton, *c.*, Queensland, Australia; on R. Fitzroy; comm. cap. of Central Queensland. Has lgst. meat-preserving wks. in Commonwealth; mining; p. (1961) *44,102*.
Rock Hill, *c.* S.C., U.S.A.; industl.; p. (1960) *29,404*.
Rockingham, *t.*, N.C., U.S.A.; cotton mnfs., paper, lumbering, peaches; p. (1950) *3,356*.
Rock Island, *c.*, Ill., U.S.A.; on R. Mississippi; lumbering, flour mills, glass, farm implements; elec. equipment; p. (1960) *51,863*.
Rockland, *c.*, *spt.*, Ma., U.S.A.; on Penobscot Bay; shipbldg., granite quarrying; p. (1950) *9,234*.
Rockland, *t.*, Mass., U.S.A.; shoemkg., engin.; p. (1960) *13,080*.
Rock River, Wis., U.S.A.; trib. of the Mississippi; length 375 m.
Rockville, *c.*, Conn., U.S.A.; on Hockanum R.; silks, woollens; p. (1960) *9,478*.
Rocky Mount, *t.*, N.C., U.S.A.; p. (1960) *32,147*.
Rocky Mountains, *extensive chain*, N. America; extending along the W. portions of Canada and the U.S.A. from Alaska to Mexico; the highest accurately measured point in the U.S.A. system is Mt. Massive (14,418 ft.); other high peaks are Mt. Elbert (14,431 ft.), Blanca Peak (14,390 ft.), Mt. Harvard (14,399 ft.), La Plata Peak (14,340 ft.), and Mt. Uncompahgre (14,306 ft.), Mt. St. Elias, in Alaska, is computed to be 18,008 ft. high, and was long held to be the highest peak in N. America, but is now known to be surpassed by the adjacent Mt. Logan (19,850 ft.) and by Mt. Orizaba (18,701 ft.) in Mexico.
Rodas, *mun.*, Cuba; sugar; p. *21,288*.
Rödby, *t.*, Denmark; on S. cst. of Lolland; p. (1960) *3,551*.
Rodewisch, *t.*, Karl-Marx-Stadt, E. Germany; engin., textiles; p. (1963) *12,458*.
Rodez, *t.*, *cap.*, Aveyron, France; on R. Aveyron; cath.; woollens; p. (1954) *20,383*.
Rodosto, *see* **Tekirdag.**
Rodriguez, *I.*, British dependency of Mauritius, Indian Ocean; 350 m. N.E. of Mauritius; principal exp., cattle, beans, salt, fish and goats; 42 sq. m.; p. (1962) *18,300*.
Roebling, *t.*, N.J., U.S.A.; established by steel-cable mkg. company; p. (1960) *3,272*.
Roebourne, *spt.*, N.West cst. of W. Australia; iron-ore deposits.
Roermond, *t.*, Limburg, Neth.; on R. Maas; minster; paper, beer, cloth; p. (1960) *34,192*.
Roeselare, *t.*, W. Flanders, Belgium; on R. Lys, nr. Courtrai, cotton, linen, lace; p. (1962) *35,662*.
Roes Welcome, channel between Southampton I. and N.W. Terr. Canada.
Rogaland, *co.*, Norway; a. 3,546 sq. m.; p. (1963) [*244,103*.
Rogers, *t.*, Ark., U.S.A.; fruit, vegs.; tourists; p. (1960) *5,700*.
Rogerstone, *t.*, S. Monmouth, Eng., on R. Ebbw 3 m. W. of Newport; aluminium; p. (1951) *4,453*.
Rohtak, *t.*, Punjab, India; mkt., cotton textiles; fortifications; p. (1961) *88,193*.
Rokko, *C.*, Honshu, Japan; jutting into Sea of [Japan.
Rolphton, Ontario, Canada; nuclear power plant.
Roma, *t.*, Queensland, Australia; in agr. dist. nr. Mt. Horrible; natural gas; p. (1947) *3,880*.
Roman, *t.*, Romania; on R. Moldava; cath.; p. (1956) *27,948*.
Romania, *rep.*, E. Europe; bounded by U.S.S.R., Hungary, Jugoslavia and Bulgaria, consisting of provs. of Oltena, Muntenia (Wallachia), Dobrogea (Dobruja), Moldova (Moldavia), S. Bucovina, Transylvania, Banat, Crisana and Maramures; plain drained by Danube and tribs. Prut, Siret, Dambovita, Oit Jiu; except Transylvania, mountainous, Carpathians, Transylvanian Alps; very warm summers, severe winters, rainfall moderate, chiefly in summer; agr., maize, wheat, barley, oats; sheep, cattle, pigs, horses; forests, timber; minerals, petroleum, natural gas, lignite, copper, salt; flour-milling, brewing, distilling, oil-refining; cap. Bucharest; a. 91,671 sq. m.; p. (1956) *17,489,794*.
Romans, *t.*, Drôme, France; on R. Isère; formerly seat of ancient abbey; p. (1954) *22,559*.
Romblon Is., *prov.*, of Philippine Is.; low, fertile; ch. crops, abaca and copra; gold, marble; a. 512 sq. m.; p. *99,367*.
Rome, *c.*, *cap.*, Italy; on R. Tiber, 15 m. from the sea; one of the most famous cities in the world; ctr. of the Roman Catholic Church and former cap. of the greatest st. in the ancient world; situated on the original "seven hills" of the old Roman metropolis, and in the valleys between, along the R.; contains the celebrated cath. ch. of St. Peter, in the Vatican City, many historical monuments, a univ. and several institutions devoted to art and learning; created cap. of mod. United Italy in 1871; mnfs. and tr.; p. (1961) *2,160,773*.
Rome, *c.*, Ga., U.S.A.; on Coosa R.; in cotton region; p. (1960) *32,226*.
Rome, *c.*, N.Y., U.S.A.; on the Mohawk R.; dairying ctr.; p. (1960) *51,646*.
Romford, *former mkt. t.*, *mun. bor.*, Essex, Eng.; 12 m. E. of London; now inc. in Havering bor. Greater London; brewing, light inds.; p. (1961) *114,584*.
Romilly-sur-Seine, *t.*, Aube, France; nr. Troyes; textile factories; p. (1954) *13,731*.
Romney, *see* **New Romney.**
Romney Marsh, *coastal marsh*, Kent, Eng.; formed by blocking of R. Rother by shingle spit of Dungeness which extends from Rye to Hythe; now largely drained; pastures for special Romney Marsh breed of sheep; a. 50 sq. m.
Romsdal, Möre Og, *dist.* Norway; cap. Molde; a. 5,812 sq. m.; p. (1961) *212,020*.
Romsey, mun. bor., Hants.; Eng.; on R. Test, 8½ m. N.W. of Southampton; mkt. ctr.; p. (1961) *6,229*; rural dist. with Stockbridge (1961) *21,615*.
Ronaldshay, N. and S., Is. of the Orkneys.
Roncesvalles, *mtn. pass.*, in the Pyrenees, Spain; 20 m. N.E. of Pamplona, Navarra; Charlemagne's army under Roland, who was slain, defeated here, 778.
Ronda, *t.*, Malaga, Spain; ancient Moorish t. 42 m. N. of Gibraltar; mnfs. chocolate, leather, fruit, wines; p. (1957) *30,962*.
Rondonia *st.*, Brazil; on Bolivian border; cap. Porto Velho; p. (1960) *70,783*.
Rongotai, Wellington, N.Z.; international airport.
Rönne, *t.*, Denmark; on W. cst. of Bornholm; granite; p. (estd.) *13,000*.
Ronse, *see* **Renaix.**
Roodepoort-Maraisburg, *t.*, Transvaal, S. Africa; mng. and industl.; p. (1960) *94,740* (inc. *40,711* whites).
Rooppur, nr. Ishurdi, East Pakistan; nuclear power plant projected 1964.
Roorkee, *t.*, Uttar Pradesh, India; univ.; p. (1961) *45,801*.
Roosevelt, *R.*, trib. of Madeira R., Brazil.
Roosevelt Dam, Arizona, U.S.A.; on R. Salt 130 m. above Phoenix on edge of Colorado Plateau; supplies irrigation for cultivation of 360 sq. m. in lower valley of R. Salt and upper valley of R. Gila; hydro-elec. power-sta.
Roper R., N.E. Northern Terr., Australia; navigable for about 90 m. inland.
Roquefort-sur-Soulzon, *t.*, S.E. Aveyron, France; caves in limestone cliffs used for ripening cheese.
Roraima, *mtn.*, Guyana, Venezuela bdy.; alt. 9,000 ft.
Rorschach, *t.*, Switzerland; lace; p. (1957) *11,325*.
Rosa Monte, highest pk., Pennine Alps, Italy; alt. 15,217 ft.
Rosario, *t.*, Santa Fé, Argentina; on R. Paraná; rly. terminus; univ.; chemicals, metals, leather, bricks, milling; p. (1960) *760,000*.
Rosas, *t.*, Spain; on Franco-Spanish border, opp. Portbou on the Mediterranean cst; fishing pt.; p. (1957) *2,720*.
Roscommon, *inland co.*, Connaught, Ireland; a. 949 sq. m.; p. (1961) *59,215*.
Roscrea, *mkt. t.*, Tipperary and Offaly, Ireland; on Little Brosna R.; p. (1961) *3,372*
Roseau, *t.*, Dominica, Windward Is.; p. (1957) *13,500*.
Roseburg, *t.*, S.W. Ore., U.S.A.; roses, fruit, poultry; canning, sawmills; p. (1950) *8,390*.
Roselle, *t.*, N.J., U.S.A.; p. (1960) *21,032*.
Rosendaal, *t.*, S.W. Neth.; nr. Arnhem; p. (1960) *38,186*.
Rosendal-Nispen, *industl. t.*, N. Brabant, Neth.; [nr. Breda.
Rosenheim, *t.*, Bavaria, Germany; on R. Inn, 35 m. S.E. of Munich; sulphur springs; impt. brine wks., machin., wood, iron, textiles, brewing; rly. junction; p. (1963) *32,000*.

Rosetta (Rashid), *t.*, Lower U.A.R.; on W. distributary of R. Nile, 43 m. N.E. Alexandria; p. (1947) *28,698*. [p. (1960) *13,421*.
Roseville, *t.*, E. Cal., U.S.A.; exp. fruit, wines;
Roskilde, *mkt. t.*, Denmark; 20 m. W. of Copenhagen; fine cath. containing tombs of Kings and Queens of D.; royal palace; dairy prod.; leather; p. (1960) *31,928*.
Ross, *mkt. t., urb. dist.*, Hereford, Eng.; on R. Wye, cider; p. (1961) *5,643*.
Ross and Cromarty, *cst. and Highland co.*, Scot.; total a. 3,202 sq. m.; ch. t. Dingwall; p. (1961) *57,607*.
Ross Dependency, Antarctica, N.Z.; p. (1961) *198*.
Ross I., Victoria Land, Antarctica.
Ross Sea, *sea* extending to 85° S. in the Antarctic.
Rossan Pt., *headland*, N. side of Donegal Bay, Ireland.
Rossano, *c.*, Cosenza, S. Italy; nr. G. of Taranto; old t. under the Byzantium Empire; alabaster and marble quarries; silk, olive oil; p. *17,425*.
Rossendale Fells (Rossendale Forest), *upland region*, S.E. Lancs, Eng.; forms W. extension of Pennines between Mersey and Ribble valleys; composed of hard, impervious millstone grit; covered by boggy moorland; many reservoirs store soft water for cotton-spinning ts. along S. edge (Bolton, Bury, Rochdale), cotton-weaving ts. along N. edge (Blackburn, Accrington, Burnley) and sm. industl. ts. in Irwell valley within Rossendale; alt. mainly above 1,200 ft.
Rosslare, *spt.*, Wexford, Ireland; on extreme S.E. of Ireland; steamer connections to Fishguard (Wales).
Rostock, *spt.*, Rostock, E. Germany; nr. mouth of R. Warnow; univ.; shipbldg., ship repair ind., fisheries; deep-water harbour; p. (1964) *170,000*.
Rostov, *t., pt.*, R.S.F.S.R.; on R. Don, 10 m. up from Sea of Azov (Black Sea); a gr. grain mart and comm. and industl. ctr.; engin., elec. power, paper; p. (1962) *662,000*.
Roswell, *t.*, N.M., U.S.A.; p. (1960) *39,593*.
Rosyth, *t.*, Fife, Scot.; naval dockyard.
Rothamsted, *hamlet*, Herts, Eng.; in Chiltern Hills, 1 m. S. of Harpenden; lge. agr. experimental sta.
Rother, *R.*, Sussex and Kent, Eng.; rises in the Weald, flows S.E. into English Channel at Rye; length 31 m.
Rother, *R.*, Hants and Sussex, Eng.; trib. of R. Arun; length 24 m.
Rother, *R.*, Derby and Yorks, Eng.; flows to R. Don at Rotherham; length 21 m.
Rotherham, *t., co. bor.*, W.R. Yorks; on R. Don, 4 m. N.E. of Sheffield; iron, steel, coal, glass; p. (1961) *85,346*.
Rotherhithe, *S.E. Thames-side-dist.*, London, Eng.
Rothes, *burgh*, Moray, Scot.; on R. Spey, 12 m. S.E of Elgin; p. (1961) *1,105*.
Rothesay, *burgh*, Bute, Scot.; on E. cst. of I. of Bute in Firth of Clyde; tourism; p. (1961) *7,656*.
Rothwell, *t., urb. dist.*, Northants, Eng.; 3 m. N.W. of Kettering; boots, shoes; p. (1961) *4,766*.
Rothwell, *t., urb. dist.*, W.R. Yorks, Eng.; on R. Aire, 3 m. S.E. of Leeds; mining; chemicals, bricks, tiles, copper tubes, stone and sand quarrying; p. (1961) *25,360*.
Rotondo, *mtn.*, Corsica, France.
Rotorua, *t.*, N.I., N.Z.; health resort; hot springs; p. (1961) *25,074*.
Rotterdam, *spt., wealthy comm. c.*, Neth.; on R. Maas; linked to N. Sea at Hook of Holland by "New Waterway" ship canal; Europe's lgst. pt., second in world; breweries, sugar-ref., oil-ref., shipbldg., chemicals, clocks; p. (1960) *729,852*.
Rotti, *I.* (50 m. by 20 m.) off cst. of Timor, Malay Archipelago, Indonesia; p. *59,221*.
Roubaix, *t.*, Nord, France; nr. Lille; on the Roubaix canal 1 m. from the Belgian frontier; woollen mnfs., grape and tomato forcing; gr. tr., many educational institutions and fine bldgs.; p. (1962) *113,163*.
Rouen, *c.*, Seine-Maritime, France; over 50 m. up R. Seine; extensive cotton and woollen factories, magnificent cath. and church; silks, machin., shipbldg.; badly damaged Second World War; p. (1962) *123,474*.
Roulers, *see* **Roeselare.**
Roumania, *see* **Romania.**
Rourkela, *t.*, Orissa, India; steel, tinplate, iron; p. (1961) *90,287*.
Rousay, Orkney Is., Scotland.
Roussillon, *old prov.*, S. France; lies in depression at E. end of Pyrenees, in dep. of Pyrénées Orientales; largely irrigated by many sm. streams; olive, vine, wheat.
Rouyn, *mining t.*, Quebec, Canada; at end of L. Abitibi; gold, copper, zinc; p. (1961) *18,716*.
Rovereto, *c.*, S. Tyrol, Italy; on R. Adige; silk, leather, paper, cottons; p. *20,575*.
Rovigo, *prov.*, Venetia, Italy; cap. Rovigo; a. 684 sq. m.; p. (1961) *270,983*.
Rovigo, *t., cap.*, Rovigo prov., Italy; on R. Adige, 20 m. S. of Padua; agr. mkt.; p. (1961) *45,271*.
Rovno, *t.*, Ukrainian S.S.R.; 110 m. N.E. of Lvov; comm. ctr.; p. (1959) *57,000*.
Rowley Regis, *industl. t., mun. bor.*, Staffs, Eng.; adjoins Dudley; p. (1961) *48,166*.
Roxboro', *t.*, N.C., U.S.A.; cotton, tobacco, mnfs.; p. (1950) *4,321*.
Roxburgh, *inland co.*, S. Scot.; stretching halfway along the Eng. border; hilly; sheep-rearing; woollens, tweed; cap. Jedburgh; a. 670 sq. m.; p. (1961) *43,171*.
Royal Leamington Spa, *see* **Leamington.**
Royal Oak, *t.*, Mich., U.S.A.; p. (1960) *80,612*.
Royan, *t.*, Charente-Maritime, France; S. of Rochelle; fishery, tr., industl.; p. (1954) *12,289*.
Royersford, *bor.*, S.E. Penns., U.S.A.; light iron and steel mnfs.; glass; p. (1950) *3,862*.
Royston, *mkt. t., urb. dist.*, Herts, Eng.; at N. foot of E. Anglian Heights, 7 m. N.E. of Baldock; p. (1961) *6,166*.
Royston, *urb. dist.*, W.R. Yorks, Eng.; coal-mining; p. (1961) *8,490*.
Royton, *t., urb. dist.*, Lancs, Eng.; 4 m. N.E. of Manchester; cotton spinning; p. (1961) *14,476*.
Roznava, *t.*, ČSSR.; W. of Košice; antimony; p. (1961) *10,227*.
Ruabon, *par.*, Denbigh, N. Wales; on Salop border; coal, iron, tile wks., chemicals; p. *3,333*.
Ruanda-Urundi, *see* **Rwanda** and **Burundi.**
Ruapehu, *highest mtn.*, N.I., N.Z.; volcanic peak at S. extremity of central volcanic dist.; alt. 9,175 ft.
Rubicon, *R.* of Central Italy, flowing to the Adriatic, crossed by Julius Cæsar and his armies in 49 B.C. Has been identified with the Fiumicino or the Uso. There *is* a R. Rubicon (It. Rubico) a few m. N. of Rimini and S. of Cervia.
Rubtsovsk, *t.*, W. Siberia, R.S.F.S.R.; agr. engin.; p. (1959) *111,000*.
Ruby Mines, *dist.*, Mandalay, Upper Burma; hilly region of the Shan plateau, rich in precious stones; H.Q. t. Mogôk, in ctr. of the mining dist.
Ruda Slaska, *t.*, Katowice, Poland; industl; p. (1960) inc. Nowy Bytom *131,000*.
Rudnyy, *t.*, Kazakh S.S.R.; new town 30 m. S.W. of Kustanay; iron ore mining and dressing plant supplying Magnitogorsk; p. (1958) *c. 40,000*
Rudolf, *L.*, Kenya, E. Africa; N.E. of L. Victoria; a. 3,500 sq. m.
Rudolph I., N. of Franz Josef Land, Arctic Ocean; Russian naval base; met. sta.
Rudolstadt, *t.*, Gera, E. Germany; on R. Saale; cas.; porcelain, metals; p. (1963) *28,474*.
Rueil Malmaison, *t.*, Seine-et-Oise, France; nr. Paris; p. (1962) *56,024*.
Rufiji, *R.*, Tanzania; E. Africa; flows to the Indian Ocean; length 450 m.
Rugby, *mkt. t., mun. bor.*, Warwick, Eng.; on R. Avon, 11 m. E. of Coventry; famous Public school; elec. and gen. engin., motor and aircraft patterns; p. (1961) *51,651*.
Rugeley, *mkt. t., urb. dist.*, Staffs, Eng.; on R. Trent, 9 m. S.E. of Stafford; coal, iron, tanning; p. (1961) *13,012*.
Ruhr, *industl. dist.*, W. Germany; lies to E. of R. Rhine, on either side of R. Ruhr; rich coalfield; impt. iron and steel, heavy engin. inds. based on local coal and iron ore from Luxembourg, Spain, Sweden; water communications to N. Sea along R. Rhine and Dortmund–Ems Canal; ch. ts. Essen, Duisburg, Düsseldorf, Dortmund, Bochum.
Ruislip-Northwood, *former urb. dist.*, Middlesex, Eng.; now inc. in Hillingdon bor. Greater London (*q.v.*); residtl.; p. (1961) *72,791*.
Rukwa, *L.*, E. Africa; between L. Tanganyika and L. Malawi in the rift valley; 30 m. by 12 m.; a. increasing.
Rum, *I.*, Inner Hebrides, Argyll, Scot.; 8½ m. by 8 m.
Rumaila, Iraq; oilfield; pipe-line links to the Zubair–Fao system.

Rumania, *see* Romania.
Rum Jungle, N. Terr., Australia; 70 m. S.E. of Darwin; copper deposits.
Runcorn, *industl. t., urb. dist.*, Cheshire, Eng.; on S. side of Mersey estuary; new Runcorn–Widnes bridge over Mersey and Manchester Ship canal opened 1961 (lgst. span arch in Europe); designated "New Town" 1964; p. (estd. 1965) *28,500*.
Rupert, *R.*, Canada; flows from L. Mistassini to James Bay; length 300 m.
Ruse, *t.*, Bulgaria; on R. Danube, opp. Giurgiu in Romania; univ., arsenal, barracks; beer, sugar, tobacco; p. (1956) *53,523*.
Rushden, *t., urb. dist.*, Northants, Eng.; 3 m. E. of Wellingborough; shoes; p. (1961) *17,370*.
Rusholme, *t.*, E. of Manchester, S.E. Lancs, Eng.; industl. and residtl.
Russell *t.*, Kan., U.S.A.; mkt. in agr. and cattle region, oil and gas fields; p. (1960) *6,113*.
Rüsselsheim, *t.*, Hessen, Germany; on R. Main, E. of Mainz; car mftg. (Opel); p. (1963) *44,100*.
Russian Soviet Federal Socialist Republic (R.S.F.S.R.) *ch. constituent rep.*, U.S.S.R.; ch. inds.: wheat, rye, oats, barley, potatoes, sugar-beet, fruits, sunflower, cotton, hemp, tobacco; sheep, cattle, dairying, pigs, horses; lumbering, timber, wood-pulp; coal, petroleum, iron, manganese, etc.; machin., textiles, oil-refining, cement, bricks; a. 6,310,594 sq. m.; cap. Moscow; p. (1959) *117,494,000*.
Rustavi, *t.*, Georgian S.S.R., new *t.* 20 m. S.E. Tbilisi; metallurgical plant; p. (1959) *62,000*.
Rustenburg, *t.*, Transvaal, Rep. of S. Africa; on N.W. edge of High Veld, 60 m. W. of Pretoria; local mkt. for agr. produce, sorghum, maize, cotton; p. (1960) *20,866* (inc. *10,648* whites).
Rutbah, *t.*, Iraq; on oil pipe-line from Iraq to Haifa.
Rute, *t.*, Cordova, Spain; nr. Lucerna; industl.; p. *18,903*.
Ruthenia, *dist.*, U.S.S.R.; formerly part of Romania, ceded to U.S.S.R. in 1945, now part of Ukrainian S.S.R.
Rutherford, *t.*, N.J., U.S.A.; p. (1960) *20,473*.
Rutherfordton, *t.*, N.C., U.S.A.; gold, lumber, textiles; agr.; p. (1950) *3,146*.
Rutherglen, *burgh*, Lanark, Scot.; on R. Clyde, S.E. of Glasgow; industl., chemicals, tubes, paper, wire ropes, bolts, chenilles, webbing; p. (1961) *25,067*.
Ruthin, *t., mun. bor.*, Denbigh, Wales; Vale of Clwyd, 8 m. S.E. of Denbigh; p. (1961) *3,502*.
Rutigliano, *t.*, Bari, Italy; agr.; p. *10,650*.
Rutland, *midland co.*, Eng.; smallest in cty.; agr. farming, livestock; cheese, stone, iron; a. 152 sq. m.; cap. Oakham; p. (1961) *23,956*.
Rutland, *c.*, Vt., U.S.A.; marble quarries, machin. and furniture; p. (1960) *18,353*.
Ruvo, *t.*, Bari, Italy; cath.; olive-oil presses; p. *25,225*.
Ruwenzori, Mt., on bdy. between Uganda and Congo, Central Africa; overlooks W. arm of Gr. African Rift Valley midway between L. Albert and L. Edward; lower slopes covered in equatorial rain forest, coffee plantations on middle slopes above 5,000 ft.; alt. 16,790 ft.
Rwanda, *indep. rep.*, (1 July 1962), formerly kingdom of Ruanda, part of U.N. trust terr. of Ruanda-Urundi under Belgian adm.; coffee; cap. Kigali; a. 10,169 sq. m.; p. (estd. 1962) *2,634,000*.
Ryan Loch, *arm of sea*, on cst. Wigtown, Scot.; 8 m. by 2 m.
Ryazan, *t.*, R.S.F.S.R.; S.E. of Moscow; distilling, leather, engin.; p. (1962) *252,000*.
Rybinsk, *t., R. pt.*, R.S.F.S.R.; on R. Volga; engin. textiles, hydro-elec.; p. (1959) *181,000*.
Rybinsk Sea (Rybinsk Reservoir), R.S.F.S.R.; artificial L.; created behind dams on R. Volga and R. Sheksna at Rybinsk; part of scheme to regulate flow of R. Volga and to incorporate it in a vast inland waterway system; opened 1945; approx. a. 1,500 sq. m.
Rybnik, *t.*, S.W. Poland; engin., brewing, furniture-mkg.; p. (1960) *34,000*.
Rydal Water, *L.*, nr. Ambleside, Westmorland, Eng.; vil. adjacent contains Rydal Mount, where Wordsworth lived.
Ryde, *t., mun. bor.*, I. of Wight, Eng.; on N.E. cst.; yachting ctr. and seaside resort; boat and yacht bldg.; steamer connection across Spithead to Portsmouth; p. (1961) *19,796*.
Rye, *t., mun. bor.*, *Cinque Pt.*, E. Sussex, Eng.; at mouth of R. Rother to W. of Dungeness; shipbldg. and fishing; p. (1961) *4,429*.
Ryton, *t., urb. dist.*, Durham, Eng.; on R. Tyne W. of Newcastle; ironwks.; p. (1961) *13,485*.
Ryuku Archipelago, gr. of 89 Is., S. of Kyushu, Japan; under U.S.A. control since end of war; self govt. 1962; total a. 921 sq. m.; consisting of Okinawa, Amami, Tokra and others; ch. t. Naha on Okinawa; p. (1956) *807,400*.
Rzeszow, *prov.*, S.E. Poland; a. 7,110 sq. m.; agr.; p. (1961) *1,625,000*.
Rzeszow, *t.*, S.E. Poland; industl. development since 1950; p. (1960) *62,000*.
Rzhev, *t.*, R.S.F.S.R.; on R. Volga; industl. and comm. engin.; p. (1956) *42,000*.

S

Saale, *R.*, Halle and Gera, Germany; trib. of R. Elbe; length 225 m.
Saalfeld, *t.*, Gera, E. Germany; on R. Saale; famous cas. and grottos; machin., chocolate mftg.; p. (1963) *29,635*.
Saane, *R.*, Switzerland; flows to R. Aar, nr. Berne; length 65 m.
Saar, *R.*, Lorraine, Saarland, Palatinate; rises in the Vosges and flows N.W. to R. Moselle, nr. Trier; length 153 m.
Saar, *st.*, W. Europe; in valley of Saar; administered by League of Nations 1919–35 and returned to Germany after plebiscite; economic attachment of Saar to France agreed upon by Allied powers after Second World War; reunited politically with German Federal Republic 1 Jan. 1957 as a *Land*. Impt. coalfields, iron; ch. t. Saarbrucken; p. (1961) *1,072,000*.
Saarbrücken, *cap.*, Saarland, on R. Saar, opposite sister t. of Sanct. Johann; cas.; rich coalfield; iron and steel wks., textiles, leather, paper; p. (1963) *133,100*.
Saarebourg, *t.*, Moselle, France; on R. Saar, 30 m. N.W. of Strasbourg; mnfs. gloves, watch springs; p. (1954) *10,439*.
Saare Maa (Ösel), *I.*, Baltic Sea; at entrance to G. of Riga, Estonian S.S.R., U.S.S.R.; consists of low plateau, bleak and barren; ch. t., Kuresaare; a. approx. 900 sq. m.
Saarlouis, *t.*, Saarland, Germany; on R. Saar; coal-mng., wood, metals; p. (1963) *36,800*.
Saba, *I.*, Neth., Antilles, W. Indies; a. 4 sq. m.; p. (1948) *1,150*.
Sabac, *t.*, Jugoslavia; on R. Sava; old cas.; fruit, cattle, pigs, coal, zinc; p. (1959) *22,000*.
Sabadell, *t.*, Spain; N.W. of Barcelona; linen and cloth mills, flour, paper, distilling, iron founding; p. (1959) *86,417*.
Sabah, *formerly* N. Borneo; *st.* Malaysian Fed.; tropical climate but equable, heavy rainfall; largely forested; hardwoods, rubber, tobacco, copra, cutch, hemp; cap. Jesselton; a. 29,387 sq. m.; p. (1960) *454,421*.
Sabang, *spt.*, Sumatra, Indonesia; bunkering sta.; p. *6,855*.
Sabara, *t.*, Minas Gerais, Brazil; iron and steel; p. (1960) *16,800*.
Sabine, *R.*, Texas and La., U.S.A.; flows through S. Lake (an expansion of the R. 18 m. long) to Gulf of Mexico; length 500 m.
Sable Cape, *S. point*, Fla., U.S.A.
Sable I., off S.E. cst., Nova Scotia; 45 m. long.
Saco, *c.*, Me., U.S A.; cotton mnfs.; p. (1960) *10,515*.
Saco, *R.*, U.S.A.; flows from White Mtns. in New Hampshire to Saco B., Mne.; 160 m. long.
Sacramento, *c., cap.*, Cal., U.S.A.; on the R. Sacramento; Capitol and R.C. cath.; rail wkshps., smelting, meat and fruit packing, flour, lumber, metal prods., rocket and missiles ind.; p. (1960) *191,667*.
Sacramento, *R.*, Cal., U.S.A.; flows to San Francisco Bay; length 500 m.
Sadani, *spt.*, Tanzania, E. Africa; at mouth of R. Wami; p. *2,000*.
Saddleback (Blencathara), *mtn.*, Cumberland, Eng.; nr. Keswick; alt. 2,847 ft.
Saddleworth, *t., urb. dist.*, W.R. Yorks, Eng.; in Pennines, 5 m. N.E. of Oldham; woollen, paper mkg., engin.; p. (1961) *17,010*.
Sado, *I.*, off cst. of Honshu, Japan; gold and silver mines; rice, fishing; a. 331 sq. m.
Sadon, *t.*, R.S.F.S.R.; zinc. lead, lead smelting.
Safad, *t.*, N. of Sea of Galilee, Israel; p. *11,300*.

Saffron Walden, *mkt. t.*, *mun. bor.*, Essex, Eng.; on E. Anglian Heights 12 m. N. of Bishops Stortford; agr., hort. and engin.; p. (1961) *7,817.*

Safi, *spt.*, W. cst. Morocco; resort; poor harbour, gr. grain and wool tr.; lge. phosphate plant; fishing; p. (1960) *81,072.*

Saga, *t.*, Kyushu, Japan; coal-mining, fishing; p. (1955) *126,432.*

Sagaing, *div.*, Upper Burma; mtn. ridges, fertile plains; rice, wheat, peas, cotton; a. 50,086 sq. m.; p. *2,322,675.*

Sagaing, *t.*, Upper Burma; on R. Irrawaddy; pagodas; groundnuts, cotton, millets, tobacco, cattle; p. *14,127.*

Sagan, *see* **Zagan.**

Saganoseki, *sm. t.*, N.E. Kyushu, Japan; on Bungo Strait, 15 m. E. of Oita; impt. gold-, copper-, silver-mines. [*104,676.*

Sagar, *t.*, Madhya Pradesh, India; univ.; p. (1961)

Sagastyr, *I.*, at mouth of R. Lena, R.S.F.S.R.

Saginaw, *c.*, Mich., U.S.A.; on R. Saginaw; in agr. and timber region; machin., railwks., beet-sugar; p. (1960) *98,265.*

Sagua la Grande, *t.*, Cuba; on R. of same name; machin., chemicals, bricks, tiles, salt; p. (1953) *26,187.*

Saguenay, *R.*, Quebec, Canada; length from L. St. John to St. Lawrence R. about 100 m.; of gr. depth, beautiful scenery; hydro-elec. power developed.

Sagunto, *t.*, Spain; nr. Valencia; p. (1957) *26,932.*

Sahara, the gr. N. African desert between the Sudan and the Barbary sts., extending from the Atlantic to the Nile, inc. Tripoli and Fezzan; a. 3,500,000 sq. m.; the E. portion is known as the Libyan desert, that part E. of the R. Nile, being often called the Nubian Desert; numerous oases with ts. and tr. ctrs.; oil pipe lines to Algerian and Tunisian csts.; p. (estd. *2,500,000*), nomadic Arab and Berber tribes.

Saharan Atlas, S. range of Atlas mtns. in Algeria; ch. pks., J. Aures, 7,644 ft., J. Aissa, 7,350 ft., J. Ksel, 6,594 ft.

Saharan Oases, *terr.*, S. Algeria; p. *39,575.*

Saharanpur, *c.*, Uttar Pradesh, India; rly. wks., wood carving; furniture, paper, tobacco, mnfs.; p. (1961) *185,213.* [(1961) *31,409.*

Sahibganj, *t.*, Bihar, India; on R. Ganges; p.

Saida, *see* **Sidon.**

Saidabad or **Sirdjan**, *t.*, Laristan, Iran; S.W. of Kerman, nr. Kuh-i-Lalehzar mtn.; p. *10,000.*

Saigon, *c.*, *spt.*, S. Viet-Nam; on R. Saigon, to E. of Mekong delta, 60 m. from sea; lge. comm. ctr.; cath., citadel, arsenal and naval yd.; spices, rice; p. (1958) *1,799,175* (with Cholon).

Saimaa, *L.*, Finland; N. of Viborg; a. 150 sq. m.; outlet into L. Ladoga.

St. Abb's Head, *rocky promontory*, Berwick, Scot.

St. Agnes Head, Cornwall, Eng.

St. Albans, *c.*, *mun. bor.*, Herts, Eng.; on N. margin of Vale of St. Albans, 20 m. N.W. of London; faces remains of Roman Verulamium across R. Ver; light inds., electronics, instrument mkg.; cath.; residtl.; p. (1961) *50,293.*

St. Albans, *t.*, Vt., U.S.A.; dairy farming; p. (1960) *8,806.* [industl.; p. (1954) *10,765.*

St. Amand, *t.*, Cher., France; on R. Cher;

St. Andrews, *burgh*, Fife, Scot.; on N.E. cst. of Fife; seaside resort; univ.; famous golf course; p. (1961) *9,888.*

St. Anne, *t.*, Alderney, Channel Is.; church designed by Sir George Gilbert Scott.

St. Anthony, *waterfalls*, on R. Mississippi; U.S.A. predominant factor in site of Minneapolis (Minn.).

St. Arnaud, *t.*, Victoria, Australia; p. *2,900.*

St. Asaph, *c.*, *rural dist.*, Flint, N. Wales; on R. Clwyd, 4 m. N. of Denbigh; cath.; optical glass mkg.; p. (rural dist. 1961) *9,478.*

St. Augustine, *t.*, Fla., U.S.A.; resort; p. (1960) *14,734.*

St. Austell, *mkt. t.*, *urb. dist.*, Cornwall, Eng.; on S. flank of Hensbarrow, 14 m. N.E. of Truro; holiday resort; china clay, stone quarrying, engin., wood and cork; p. (1961) *25,027.*

St. Barthélemy, *French I.*, W. Indies; dependency of Guadeloupe; p. (1960) *2,079.*

St. Bees Head, *promontory*, 2½ m. N.W. of St. Bees, Cumberland, Eng.; freestone quarries, tin.

St. Benoit, *t.*, Ile de la Réunion, Indian Ocean; connected by rail with ch. port, Pointe-des-Galets.

St. Bernard Pass, Great, on Italian–Swiss bdy., W. Alps; carries main road from W. Switzerland to Plain of Lombardy; approached from N. by trib. of upper Rhône, from S. by Val d'Aosta; 8,120 ft. above sea level. The Great St. Bernard road tunnel (3½ m.) constr. 1958–62 links Cantine de Proz (Valais can., Switzerland) and St. Rhémy (Italy); under tunnel will run projected 260 m. pipeline from Genoa to Aigle.

St. Bernard Pass, Little, on French–Italian bdy., W. Alps.; links Isère valley with Val d'Aosta; alt. approx. 5,000 ft.

St. Boniface, *t.*, Manitoba, Canada; sub. of Winnipeg; p. (1961) *37,600.*

St. Bride's Bay, Pembroke, Wales.

St. Brieuc, *t.*, Côtes-du-Nord, France; college, cath.; ironwks., textiles, timber and cst. tr.; p. (1962) *47,307.*

St. Buryan, *par.*, Cornwall, Eng.; lobster and crab fishing; p. *1,132.*

St. Catharines, *c.*, Ont., Canada; on Welland Canal; mkt. for Niagara fruit-growing reg.; agr. implement wks., timber mills, flour mills, tanneries and varied inds.; (1961) *48,472.*

St. Chamond, *t.*, Loire, France; nr. St. Etienne; silk, ribbons, rayon; rly. wks.; coal-mining; p. (1954) *15,580.*

St. Charles, *c.*, Mo., U.S.A.; nr. St. Louis; tobacco and flour; p. (1960) *21,189.*

St. Clair, *L.*, Canada–U.S.A.; part of link between L. Huron and L. Erie.

St. Clair, *R.*, N. America; flows from L. Huron through L. of St. Clair into L. Erie; forms bdy. between Michigan (U.S.A.) and Ontario (Canada); impt. link in Gr. Lakes waterway; length 85 m., depth dredged to 20 ft.

St. Clair Shores, *t.*, Mich., U.S.A.; residtl. sub. of Detroit; p. (1960) *76,657.*

St. Claude, *t.*, Jura, France; at confluence of Rs. Tacon and Bienne; cath.; fancy shell, horn and ivory mnfs.; p. (1954) *11,301.*

St. Cloud, *t.*, Seine-et-Oise, France; 6 m. from ctr. of Paris; fine park, château; residtl.; porcelain; p. (1954) *20,671.*

St. Cloud, *t.*, Minn., U.S.A.; on R. Mississippi; timber yds., dairying, farming; p. (1960) *33,815.*

St. Croix, *I.*, Virgin Is., gr., U.S.A.; ch. inds. sugar cultivation, stock raising, vegetable growing, rum mnf.; a. 82 sq. m.; p. (1950) *12,096.*

St. Croix, *R.*, Wis., U.S.A.; trib. of the Mississippi; length 200 m.

St. Davids, *c.*, Pembroke, Wales; 15 m. S.W. of Fishguard; cath., ruins of Bishop's Palace; p. *1,595.*

St. Davids Head, *prom.*, on cst. of Pembroke, Wales.

St. Denis, *t.*, *N. sub.*, Paris, France; industl. and residtl.; abbey, burial pl. of Kings of France; chemicals, machin., spirits, soap; p. (1962) *95,072.*

St. Denis, *spt.*, *cap.*, Ile de la Réunion (French), Indian Ocean; p. (1960) *41,863.*

St. Dié, *t.*, Vosges, France; on R. Meurthe; cath.; iron, copper, machin., hosiery; p. (1954) *20,952.*

St. Dizier, *t.*, Haute-Marne, France; on R. Marne; iron, steel, copper, boats; p. (1954) *25,515.*

St. Elias, *mtn.*, Alaska, U.S.A.; alt. 18,024 ft.

St. Etienne, *t.*, *cap.*, Loire, France; nr. Lyons; ribbon-weaving, boot-lace, silk, velvet, engin., armaments, motor-cycles, cycles, chemicals, and iron mftg. ctr., in coal-field dist.; p. (1962) *203,633.*

St. Eustatius, one of the Neth. Antilles, W. Indies; a. 31 sq. m.; p. (1963) *1,103.*

St. Francis R., Quebec, Canada; hydro-elec. power.

St. Francis, *R.*, Mo., U.S.A.; trib. of R. Mississippi; forms bdy. of Ark.; length 450 m.

St. Gall (St. Gallen), *can.*, Switzerland; mountainous; forest; vineyards; cattle raising; cotton spinning, lace; cap. St. G.; a. 777 sq. m.; p. (1961) *339,489.*

St. Gall, *t.*, Switzerland; on R. Steinach; cath.; cottons and embroidery; p. (1961) *76,700.*

St. George, *bay*, W. cst. Newfoundland, Canada.

St. George, *I.*, Grenada Is., Brit. W. Indies; wireless sta.

St. George, *spt.*, N.B., Canada; various granites quarried; p. *1,169.*

St. George's Channel, Brit. Isles; part of Irish Sea separating Wales from Ireland.

St. George's I., Fla., U.S.A.

St. Germain, *t.* Seine-et-Oise, France; on R.

Seine; former royal château; cottons, woollens; p. (1954) *29,429*.
St. Germans, *mkt. t., rural dist.*, Cornwall, Eng.; 4 m. W. of Saltash; p. (rural dist. 1961) *14,775*.
Saint Gotthard, *mtn. gr.*, Alps, S. central Switzerland, crossed by St. Gotthard Pass (6,935 ft.). St. Gotthard Rly. passes through St. Gotthard tunnel (9¼ m., max. alt. 3,786 ft.). Road tunnel (6½ m.) under pass Göschenen to Airolo projected; motorways linking pass with Zurich, Basle and Lugano being built.
St. Gowan's Head, *promontory*, Pembroke, Wales.
St. Helena, *I., Brit. col.*, Atl. Oc.; 1,200 m. from W. cst. Africa; spt. and only t. Jamestown; Napoleon imprisoned 1815–21, and Boer captives 1900; famous for its wirebird, species of plover peculiar to I.; a. 47 sq. m.; p. (estd. 1965) *4,526*.
St. Helens, *t., co. bor.*, Lancs, Eng.; 12 m. E. of Liverpool; connected by canal with R. Mersey; coal, iron, alkali; copper smelting, glass, fibreglass, plastics; p. (1961) *108,348*.
St. Helier, *spt.*, Jersey, Channel Is.; p. *26,484*.
St. Hyacinthe, *c., spt.*, Quebec, Canada; on Yamaska R.; cath.; farm machin., woollens, leather; p. (1961) *22,354*.
St. Ives, *t., mun. bor.*, Cornwall, Eng.; at entrance to St. Ives Bay; fishing, holiday resort; p. (1961) *9,337*.
St. Ives, *mkt. t., mun. bor.*, Huntingdon, Eng.; on R. Ouse, 4 m. E. of Huntingdon; timber, gravel, concrete prod., engin., canning, agr. machin.; p. (1961) *4,076*.
St. James, *t.*, Man., Canada; p. (1961) *33,977*.
St. Jean, *t.*, Quebec, Canada; rly. junction; porcelain, pottery, tiles; p. (1961) *26,988*.
St. Jérôme, *t.*, Quebec, Canada; pulp, paper, knitted goods, woollens, rubber goods, cement, bricks; p. (1961) *24,546*.
St. John, *c., spt.*, N.B., Canada; cottons, woollens, machin., paper, lumbering, sugar refinery; fisheries; corn tr.; p. (1961) *95,563*.
St. John, *I.*, U.S. Virgin Is. gr.; a. 19 sq. m.; ch. inds. charcoal, stock-raising, tourists; was noted for bay leaf oil, but ind. now dormant.
St. John, *L.*, Quebec, Canada; on Saguenay R.
St. John, *R.*, N.B., Canada; flows to Bay of Fundy; length 450 m.
St. John, *t., cap.*, Antigua, W. Indies; p. (1957) [*12,000*.
St. John's Point, *C.*, Down, Northern Ireland; forming N. side of Dundrum Bay.
St. Johns R., Fla., U.S.A.; flows to Atlantic; length 350 m.
St. John's, *spt., c., cap.*, Newfoundland, Canada; on E. cst.; first Eng. settlement in America; univ.; gr. tr. in fish, cod, oil, etc.; p. (1961) *90,838*.
St. John's Wood, *residtl. dist.*, N.W. London, Eng.; contains Lord's Cricket Ground.
St. Joseph, *t.*, Mich., U.S.A.; on L. Mich.; resort; industl.; p. (1960) *11,755*.
St. Joseph, *c.*, Mo., U.S.A., on M. R.; rly. ctr.; meat packing, clothing, farm implements; p. (1960) *79,673*.
St. Joseph d'Alma, *t.*, Quebec, Canada; pulp, [paper; p. *6,449*.
St. Joseph Lake, Ontario, Canada.
St. Junien, *t.*, Haute Vienne, France; on R. Vienne; fine churches, shrine; gloves, leather; porcelain wks.; p. (1954) *10,618*.
St. Just, *t., urb. dist.*, Cornwall, Eng.; nr. Lands End, 6 m. W. of Penzance; dairying; tin-mining; p. (1961) *3,636*.
St. Kilda, *rocky I.*, most W. of the Hebrides, Scot.; 3 m. long. In 1930 the 36 inhabitants were removed to mainland; now bird sanctuary, famous for its wren, a sub-species.
St. Kilda, *wat. pl.*, Victoria, Australia; nr. Melbourne; p. *26,000*.
St. Kitts-Nevis, *I.*, Leeward gr., W.I.; sugar, sea island cotton, molasses; a. (inc. Anguilla) 138 sq. m.; cap. Basse-Terre; p. (estd. 1965) *59,000*.
St. Laurent, *t.*, Quebec, Canada; p. (1961) *49,805*.
St. Laurent du Maroni, *t.*, Fr. Guiana; penal admin. ctr.; p. *2,000*.
St. Lawrence, *G.* of, Canada; arm of Atlantic, partly enclosed by Newfoundland and Nova Scotia; impt. fisheries.
St. Lawrence I., Alaska, U.S.A.; in Bering Sea; 100 m. long.
St. Lawrence, *gr. R.*, of N. America; length from the source of its headstream, the St. Louis, 2,100 m.; forms the outlet of the great lakes (Superior, Michigan, Huron, Erie and Ontario) and the bdy. between the st. of N.Y., U.S.A., and Ontario, Canada; ch. tribs.: Ottawa, Richelieu, St. Maurice, Saguenay.
St. Lawrence Seaway, N. America; joint Canada–U.S.A. project links head of the Gr. Lakes with Atl. Oc., providing channel 27 ft. min. depth enabling lge. ocean-going vessels to reach American continent; provides major source of hydro-electric power to industl. areas; opened 1959.
St. Lawrence Ship Canal, Canada. Channel deepened to provide safe navigation for ocean-going vessels from deep water to Montreal; depth 35 ft. at low water; links St. Lawrence Seaway at Montreal.
St. Leonards, *t.*, Sussex, Eng.; W. of Hastings; seaside resort.
St. Lô, *t.*, Manche, France; on R. Vire; cath.; cloth mnfs.; p. (1954) *11,778*.
St. Louis, *t.*, Senegal, W. Africa; at mouth of R. Senegal; cath., pal.; rly. and road ctr.; airport; exp. oilseeds and skins; p. (1948) *51,000*.
St. Louis, *t.*, Ile de la Réunion, Indian Ocean; p. (1960) *25,220*.
St. Louis, *c.*, Mo., U.S.A.; on R. Mississippi 10 m. below confluence of Rs. Miss. and Mo.; two univs., impt. rly. and river junction; mkt. for furs, livestock, grain, farm prod.; banking and fin. ctr.; varied mnfs.; mach., cars, aircraft, leather goods, beer, chemicals; p. (1960) *750,026*.
St. Louis Park, *t.*, Minn., U.S.A.; tools, dental supplies; p. (1960) *43,310*.
St. Lucia Bay, *inlet* of the Indian Oc. at mouth of R. Umvolozi, S. of St. Lucia L., Natal, S. Africa.
St. Lucia I., *Brit. col.*, Windward Is., W.I.; exp. sugar, cocoa, lime juice, etc.; coaling sta.; a. 238 sq. m.; cap. Castries; p. (estd. 1965) *94,000*.
St. Malo, *fortfd. spt.*, Ille-et-Vilaine, France; cas. and church (formerly a cath.); agr. prod., shipping, fishing, and tourist inds.; p. (estd. 1954) *14,339*.
St. Maria di Leuca, *C.*, S. Italy.
St. Marie, *C.*, S. point of Malagasy.
St. Martin, *French I.*, W. Indies; dependency of Guadeloupe; p. (1946) *6,786*.
St. Martin, *I.*, Neth. Antilles, W. Indies; a. 13 sq. m.; p. (1948) *1,697*.
St. Marylebone, *see* **Westminster, City of.**
St. Mary's I., Scilly Is., Brit. Isles.
St. Matthew I., Alaska; U.S.A.; in Bering Sea.
St. Maur-des-Fosses, *sub.*, Paris, Seine, France; garden city; p. (1962) *70,681*.
St. Maurice, *vil.*, Valais, Switzerland; nr. Martigny; 6th-century abbey; once a leading Burgundian t.; p. *2,699*.
St. Maurice, *R.*, Quebec, Canada; trib. of St Lawrence R.; hydro-elec. power developed; length 400 m.
St. Mawes, *vil.*, Cornwall, Eng.; on E. cst. of estuary of R. Fal; holiday resort, fishing.
St. Michael's Mt., *castled rock*, Cornwall, Eng.; the ancient Ictis; alt. 230 ft.
St. Michel, *t.*, Que., Canada; p. (1956) *24,540*.
St. Mihiel, *t.*, Meuse, France; on R. Meuse, nr. Bar-le-Duc; industl.; Benedictine abbey; lace; p. (1946) *4,581*.
St. Monance, *burgh*, Fife, Scot.; p. (1961) *1,406*.
St. Moritz, *picturesque t., health resort*, Switzerland; in the Upper Engadine; winter sports; alt. 6,090 ft.; spa; p. *4,000*.
St. Nazaire, *t.*, Loire-Atlantique, France; at mouth of R. Loire, nr. Nantes; docks and shipping; steelwks., aircraft; exp. wine, sardines, silk, oil refining; p. (1962) *59,181*.
St. Neots, *mkt. t., urb. dist.*, Hunts, Eng.; on R. Ouse, 10 m. N.E. of Bedford; shoes, brewing, milling, paper mkg., sports equipment, plastics; (1961) *5,570*.
St. Niklaas, *mftg. t.*, E. Flanders, Belgium; nr. Antwerp; cottons, woollens, lace, rayon, carpets; p. (1962) *48,019*.
St. Ninians, *par.*, Stirling, Scot.; woollens, nails; p. *14,662*.
St. Omer, *t.*, Pas-de-Calais, France; cath., abbey ruins; brewing, distilleries, soap, linen; p. (1954) *19,280*.
St. Ouen, *t., sub.*, Paris, France; on R. Seine; light inds., copper, aluminium goods, furniture, gloves; power sta.; p. (1962) *52,103*.
St. Pancras, *see* **Camden.**
St. Paul, *c., cap.*, Minn., U.S.A.; faces Minneapolis across the R. Mississippi; cath.; univ.; meat-packing, foundries, cars, electronics, industl. abrasives; p. (1960) *313,411*.

St. Paul, *spt.*, Ile de la Réunion (French), Indian Ocean; p. (1960) *28,681*.
St. Paul, *R.*, Liberia; flows to the Atlantic nr. Monrovia; length 300 m.
St. Paul de Loanda, *t.*, Angola; exp. rubber, ivory, palm oil, coffee, coconuts, rum.
St. Peter, *L.*, Canada; expansion of St. Lawrence R. above Three Rivers; 20 m. by 9 m.
St. Peter Port, *seaport, cap.*, Guernsey, Channel Is.; wat. pl.; fruit, flowers, vegetables; p. *15,706*.
St. Petersburg, *c.*, Fla., U.S.A.; resort; p. (1960) *181,298*.
St. Pierre, *t.*, Martinique I., Fr. W. Indies; ch. t. in Fr. W. Indies; completely destroyed by eruption of Mt. Pelée, 1902.
St. Pierre and Miquelon, *French terr.*, consisting of 8 sm. Is. off S. cst. of Newfoundland; a. of St. Pierre gr., 10 sq. m.; a. of Miquelon gr., 83 sq. m.; ch. t. St. Pierre, fisheries; p. of St. P. and M. (1958) *4,904*.
St. Pierre-des-Corps, *t.*, Indre-et-Loire, France; p. (1954) *10,656*.
St. Pierre, *t.*, Réunion, Indian Ocean; p. (1960) *27,573*.
St. Pölten, *t.*, Lower Austria; nr. Vienna; cotton spinning and hardware mftg.; p. (1961) *40,112*.
St. Quentin, *t.*, Aisne, France; on R. Somme; lace, tulle, woollens, chemicals, ironwks.; p. (1962) *62,579*.
St Raphaël, *t.*, Var. France; p. (1954) *10,177*.
St. Rémy, *t.*, Bouches-du-Rhône, France; Roman antiquities.
St. Savine, *t.*, Aube, France; p. (1954) *10,947*.
St. Servan, *spt.*, Ille-et-Vilaine, France; opp. St. Malo; p. (1954) *13,763*.
St. Thomas I., *see* São Tomé.
St. Thomas, *I.*, Virgin Is. gr., Atl. Oc.; belongs to U.S.A.; rum and bay rum, sugar, truck-farming, cattle, deep-sea fishing; bunkering of ships, handicrafts, tourism; a. 32 sq. m.; p. (1950) *14,559* (with St. John).
St. Thomas, *t.*, Ontario, Canada; rly. wkshps., flour, flax; p. (1961) *22,469*.
St. Trond, *t.*, Limbourg, Belgium; brewing, distilling; p. (1962) *20,976*.
St. Valéry-sur-Somme, *spt.*, Somme, France; resort of pilgrims; here William the Conqueror embarked for Eng. 1066; fishing; p. *3,071*.
St. Vincent, *C.*, S.W. Portugal; Spanish fleet defeated by British 1797.
St. Vincent, Gulf of, *lge. inlet*, S. Australia; penetrates 100 m. inland, max. width 35 m.; Pt. Adelaide located on E. side.
St. Vincent, *I.*, Brit. col., W.I.; one of Windward gr.; sugar, arrowroot, cotton, peanuts; cap. Kingstown; a. 150 sq. m.; p. (estd. 1965) *85,000*.
Sainte Agathe des Monts, *t.*, Quebec, Canada; tourist resort; p. (1961) *5,725*
Sainte Croix, Virgin Is., W. Indies; former possession of Denmark, now U.S.A.
Saintes, *t.*, Charente-Maritime, France; cath.; Roman antiquities; suffered in Huguenot wars; agr. implements; earthenware; p. (1954) *23,768*.
Saipan I., Marianas, Pac. Oc., U.S.A. trusteeship; sugar, coffee, fruit; a. 71 sq. m.; p. (1958) *7,250*.
Sakai, *spt.*, Japan; local import ctr.; iron machin., vinyl pipe plant; p. (1960) *340,000*.
Sakania, *t.*, Congo; frontier sta. on rly. between Elizabethville and N. Rhodesia; p. *25,095*.
Sakata, *t.*, Honshu, Japan; p. *46,447*.
Sakhalin, *I.*, off E. cst. Asia; S. half ceded by Japan to U.S.S.R., 1945; a. about 13,930 sq. m.; herring fisheries, coal, naphtha, alluvial gold, oil, timber, natural gas; oil pipeline connects to Komsomolsk and Khabarovsk refineries; p. (1959) *651,000* inc. Kurile Is.
Sakishima, *Is.*, E. of Formosa.
Sakmara, *R.*, R.S.F.S.R.; rises in Ural Mtns., trib. of R. Ural; length 350 m.
Sala, *t.*, Västmanland, Sweden; silver-mine worked for over 400 years, now to limited extent; lime, bricks; p. (1961) *11,015*.
Saladillo, *R.*, N. Argentina; upper course of R. Dulce.
Salado Rio, *R.*, Argentina; trib. of the R. Paranà; length 1,000 m.
Salado, Río, *R.*, Mexico; trib. of Rio Grande del Norte.
Salaga, *t.*, Ghana, W. Africa; impt. tr.; p. *1,000*.
Salamanca, *t.*, Guanajuato st., Mexico; oil refining; ammonia plant; p. *11,985*.
Salamanca, *prov.*, Leon, W. Spain; cap. Salamanca; a. 4,756 sq. m.; p. (1959) *422,114*.
Salamanca, *t.*, *cap.*, Salamanca prov., Spain; on R. Tormes; oldest Spanish univ., 2 caths., many convents; p. (1959) *88,316*.
Salamaua, *t.*, *pt.*, New Guinea, Australian Trust. Terr.; gold.
Salamis, *I.*, Greece; opposite harbour of Athens; famous naval battle, 480 B.C.
Salamis, *spt.*, Greece; naval base; p. *17,312*.
Salar de Uyumi, windswept, dry, salt flat, S.W. Bolivia.
Salavat, *t.*, R.S.F.S.R.; in Bashkiria, 90 m. S. of Ufa; ctr. of oilfield; glass factory; became t. in 1954; p. (1959) *60,000*.
Salayer Is., *gr.*, S. of Celebes, Indonesia; a. of lgst., 180 sq. m.
Sala-y-Gomez I., Pac. Oc.; Chilean; uninhabited.
Salcombe, *t.*, *urb. dist.*, S. Devon, Eng.; 4 m. S. of Kingsbridge; resort; fishing; p. (1961) *2,558*.
Saldanha B., *inlet* on W. cst. C. of Good Hope, S. Africa; whaling, fishing; granite, quarrying; length 17 m.
Sale, *t.*, *mun. bor.*, Cheshire, Eng.; on R. Mersey, 2 m. S. of Stretford; p. (1961) *51,317*.
Sale, *t.*, Victoria, Australia; 128 m. from Melbourne; ctr. of lge. agr. and pastoral dist.; p. (1961) *7,897*.
Salé or Salch, *spt*, Fez, Morocco; formerly pirate headquarters; p. (1960) *75,799*.
Salekhard, *t.*, *R. pt.*, N.W. Siberia, R.S.F.S.R.; on R. Ob; fisheries, collecting ctr. for furs; exp. timber; p. (1956) *16,000*.
Salem, *t.*, Madras, India; carpets, weaving, farming ctr.; p. (1961) *249,145*.
Salem, *c.*, Mass., U.S.A.; 15 m. from Boston; cottons, lumber products, leather goods, machin. wireless valves; p. (1960) *39,211*.
Salem, *t.*, N.J., U.S.A.; in fruit-growing dist.; p. (1960) *8,941*.
Salem, *c.*, Ohio, U.S.A.; steel; p. (1960) *13,854*.
Salem, *c.*, *cap.*, Ore., U.S.A.; on Williamette R.; univ.; fruit-packing, flour milling and canning; p. (1960) *49,142*.
Salemi, *t.*, Sicily, Italy; the ancient Halicyæ; p. *19,100*.
Salerno, *spt.*, Campania, Italy; on G. of Salerno, 30 m. S.E. of Naples; cottons, silks, printing, leather; vine-growing dist.; p. (1961) *118,171*.
Salford, *c.*, *co. bor.*, Lancs, Eng.; on R. Irwell, adjoining Manchester; engin., clothing mftg.; p. (1961) *154,963*.
Salima, *t.*, Malawi, S. Africa; alt. 1,672 ft.; term. of rly. from Beira on L. Malawi.
Salina, *c.*, Kan., U.S.A.; on Smoky Hill R.; univ.; flour milling, cattle mkt., farm implements; p. (1960) *43,202*.
Salina, *I.*, Lipari Is., Italy; in the Mediterranean, 6 m. long; 2 volcanic cones.
Salina Cruz, *t.*, *spt.*, Oaxaca, Mexico; terminal pt. of Tehuantepec rly.; shallow harbour; dye-woods, coffee, hemp, hides and skins; p. *8,243*.
Salinas, *t.*, Ecuador; cable sta.; holiday resort; 118 m. from Guayaquil.
Salinas, *R.*, Cal., U.S.A.; rises in U.S. Coast Range, flows N.W. into Bay of Monterey, Pac. Oc.; fertile valley floor irrigated to produce hard and stone fruits, mkt.-garden produce (especially lettuce), alfalfa; length, 140 m.
Salinas-Grandes, *gr. marsh a.*, Argentina; N. of Córdoba.
Salisbury, *cath. c.*, *mun. bor.*, Wilts, Eng.; at S. foot of Salisbury Plain at confluence of Rs. Avon and Wily; cath., pure Early English with tallest spire in Eng. (404 ft.); mkt. t.; eng. inds.; p. (1961) *35,471*.
Salisbury, *c.*, *cap.* Rhodesia; airways ctr.; univ.; ctr. gold mng. a.; inds. inc. fertilisers, tobacco, machin.; p. (1958) *257,000* (inc. *82,000* Europeans).
Salisbury, *t.*, Md., U.S.A.; iron and steel goods, woodwork, canning; p. (1960) *16,302*.
Salisbury, *t.*, N.C., U.S.A.; cotton, grain, timber, textiles, refrigerators; p. (1960) *21,297*.
Salisbury Plain, Wilts Eng.; undulating upland N. of Salisbury; Stonehenge; army training-ground.
Sallaumines, *t.*, Pas-de-Calais, France; p. (1954) *14,541*.
Salmon, *R.*, Idaho, U.S.A.; trib. of Snake R.; length 450 m.
Salon, *t.*, Bouches-du-Rhône, France; on Canal de Craponne; soap and oil wks.; p. (1954) *17,597*.
Salpau Selka, Finland; most southerly gravel ridge; forested; winter sports.
Salsette I., N. of Bombay, India; a. 241 sq. m.; connected by bridge and causeway with Bombay; cave antiquities and temples.

Salt, *R.*, Arizona, U.S.A.; rises in Colorado Plateau, flows W. into Gila R. 20 m. below Phoenix; length 240 m. *See also* **Roosevelt Dam.**
Salt Fork, *R.*, Okla., U.S.A.; trib. of Arkansas R.
Salt Lake City, *c.*, *cap.*, Utah, U.S.A.; nr. Gr. Salt Lake, H.Q. of Mormonism; temple and univ.; mng.; agr.; steel, oil, textiles, meat pkg.; livestock; p. (1960) *189,454.*
Salta, *N. prov.*, Argentina; sugar, vines, oranges, oil; cap. Salta; a. 62,511 sq. m.; p. (1960) *413,000.*
Salta, *c.*, Argentina; on R. Salta; sugar, vines, oranges, tobacco, oil, minerals; cath., college; p. (1960) *120,000.*
Saltash, *mkt. t.*, *mun. bor.*, Cornwall, Eng.; on W. side of Tamar estuary; lowest bridge (rly.) and road bridge to Devonport across Tamar; farming, fishing, malting; p. (1961) *7,420.*
Saltburn, *t.*, *urb. dist.* (with **Marske**), N.R. Yorks, Eng.; on E. cst. 3 m. S.E. of Redcar; seaside resort; p. (1961) *12,482.*
Saltcoats, *sm. burgh*, Ayr, Scot.; on Firth of Clyde, 2 m. S. of Ardrossan; chemicals, shipyards and rly. sheds; p. (1961) *14,187.*
Saltillo, *cap.*, Coahuila st., Mexico; cottons, flour, woollens, cereals, gold, silver, lead, copper, iron, zinc, coal; p. (1960) *99,101.*
Saltney, *t.*, Flint, Wales; on R. Dee, 2 m. S.W. of Chester; oil and fat refining; p. (1951) *2,642.*
Salto, *dept.*, Uruguay; cap. Salto; a. 4,865 sq. m.; [p. (1953) *108,030.*
Salto, *cap.*, S. dep., Uruguay; leather, salted meats, sugar cane and beet; p. (estd. 1956) *60,000.*
Salton Sea, *L.*, S. Cal., U.S.A.; 263 ft. below sea-level in depression which extends N.W. from head of G. of Cal.; ctr. of inland drainage; a. 270 sq. m. *See also* **Imperial Valley.**
Salton Sink, Cal., U.S.A.; inland depression 287 ft. below sea-level.
Saluggia, *t.*, Piedmont; N. Italy; nuclear reactor.
Saluzzo, *t.*, Italy; nr. Cunei; cath., cas.; leather, silks, hats; p. *17,000.*
Salvador, El, *rep.*, Central America; on Pacific cst.; very hot, abundant summer rain but dry winter; coffee, sugar, rubber, tobacco, gold, silver, iron, mercury, ginned cotton; h.e.p. sta. at Guayabo Rapids; smallest and most densely populated of Central American States; cap. San Salvador; a. 13,173 sq. m.; p. (1961) *2,510,278.*
Salvador, *spt.*, Baia, Brazil; coffee, cocoa, tobacco, hides, castor seed, sisal; oil field and refinery at Matanipe; p. (1960) *655,735.*
Salween, *R.*, Burma; rises in Tibet, flows S. to G. of Martaban; many rapids; length 1,800 m.
Salzach, *R.*, Austria; trib. of R. Inn; length 130 m.
Salzburg, *prov.*, Austria, adjoining Bavaria and the Tyrol; on N. slope of E. Alps; many L., thermal springs; much mineral wealth; cap. Salzburg; a. 2,762 sq. m.; p. (1961) *347,292.*
Salzburg, *c.*, Austria; on R. Salzach; cath., cas.; birthplace of Mozart; tourist resort; salt, dairying, musical instruments; annual musical festival; p. (1961) *108,114.*
Salzgitter, *t.*, Lower Saxony, Germany; S.W. of Brunswick; steel, engin., wagon bldg., fertilisers; p. (1963) *113,200.*
Salzkammergut, *lake dist.*, Upper Austria; salt-mines.
Salzwedel, *t.*, Magdeburg, E. Germany; on R. Jeetze; chemicals, sugar, metals; p. (1963) *20,567.*
Samakh, *t.*, Israel; on Sea of Galilee; rly. junction.
Samar, *I.*, Philippines; S. of Luzon; 147 m. long, 50 m. wide; a. 5,050 sq. m.; p. *550,000.*
Samara, *see* **Kuibyshev.**
Samaria, *ancient c.*, Jordan, now **Sabastye.**
Samarinda, *t.*, Borneo, Indonesia; on E. cst.; p. *11,046.*
Samarkand, *c.*, Uzbek S.S.R.; E. of Bukhara; mosques and ancient ruins; univ.; textiles, engin.; p. (1959) *195,000.*
Samarra, *t.*, Iraq; on R. Tigris; Moslem holy c.; p. *8,000.*
Samawa, *t.*, Iraq; on R. Euphrates; cereals, carpets; p. *10,000.*
Sambalpur, *t.*, Orissa, India; on R. Mahanadi; ruined fort, old temples; cottons, silks; p. (1961) *38,915.*
Sambar, *C.*, S.W. Kalimantan, Indonesia.
Sambhal, *t.*, Uttar Pradesh, India; p. (1961) *68,940.*
Sambhar, *t.*, Rajasthan, India; p. (1961) *14,139.*
Sambre, *R.*, Belgium and N.E. France; trib. R. Meuse at Namur; length 110 m.
Samburu, *t.*, Kenya; rly. sta.
Samnan, *t.*, Iran; iron, sulphur ores, petroleum.
Samoa, Western, *ind. sov. st.* since Jan. 1962; not a member of Brit. Commonwealth but treated under N.Z. law as such; *gr.* of 9 Pacific Is. in Pac. Oc.; lgst., Savaii (a. 700 sq. m.); exp. copra, cacao beans, bananas; p. (estd.) *109,000.*
Samoa Is., Samoan gr. Pac. Oc.; E. of 171° long., W. of Greenwich; belong to U.S.A.; a. 76 sq. m.; lgst. I. Tutuila; ch. pt. Pago Pago; American naval sta.; p. (1960) *20,051.*
Samokov, *t.*, Bulgaria; S. of Sofia; industl.; p. (1956) *16,748.*
Samos, *I.*, Ægean Sea; Greek terr.; off W. cst. Anatolia; fine wine, silk, tobacco, cotton; cap. Vathéos; a. 180 sq. m.; p. (1961) *52,034.*
Samothrake, *rugged I.*, Ægean Sea; alt. 5,248 ft.; the "Thracian Samos"; sulphur springs, sponges; a. 71 sq. m.; p. mainly Greeks.
Samshui, *t.*, *former treaty pt.*, Kwangtung, China; good tr. with Hong Kong; p. (1931) *9,160.*
Samsö, *I.*, Kattegat, Denmark; a. 42 sq. m.; p. (1960) *6,429.*
Samsun, *spt.*, Trabzon, Turkey; on Black Sea cst.; exp. tobacco, grain, timber, wax, wool, skins, copper goods, antimony; p. (1960) *87,311.*
San, *R.*, S.E. Poland; trib. of R. Vistula, bdy. between Poland and Ukraine.
San Ambrosia, *I.*, off cst. Chile.
San Angelo, *t.*, Texas, U.S.A.; on R. Concho; cattle, wool, mohair mkt.; dairy produce, petroleum, machine-shop prod.; p. (1960) *58,815.*
San Antonio, *sm. coastal t.*, Angola, Africa; at mouth of R. Congo; serves as occasional pt. of embarkation for travellers from lower regions of Congo (ex-Belgian).
San Antonio, *spt.*, Chile; nearest pt. for Santiago; holiday resort; exp. copper; p. (1961) *64,722.*
San Antonio, *c.*, *winter resort*, Texas, U.S.A.; at mouth of San Pedro R.; cath., fort., arsenal, univ.; producing, refining and mnftg. oil prod. and equipment, textiles, machin; meat pkg., food processing; p. (1960) *587,718.*
San Antonio, *C.*, most westerly point of Cuba.
San Benito, *spt.*, G. of Tehuantepec, Mexico.
San Bernardino, *t.*, Paraguay; holiday resort.
San Bernardino, *c.*, Cal., U.S.A.; railroad ctr.; citrus-fruit packing and shipping ctr.; p. (1960) *91,922.*
San Carlos, *t.*, Luzon, Philippines; p. (1960) [*124,756.*
San Carlos de Bariloche, *t.*, Argentina; on S. shore of L. Nahuel Huapi; tourist ctr.; p. (1960) *18,000.*
San Casciano, *t.*, Italy; nr. Florence; industl.; p. *14,325.*
San Cataldo, *t.*, Sicily; Italy; good tr.; p. *22,700.*
San Cristóbal, (formerly **Cuidal Real**), *t.*, Chiapas, Mexico; cath.; textiles; p. (1940) *11,768.*
San Cristóbal, *c.*, *cap.*, Táchira st., Venezuela; cath.; cement; wireless sta.; p. (1961) *96,102.*
San Diego, *t.*, Cal., U.S.A.; on Pacific cst., 10 m. N. of Mexican border; naval installation; fine harbour, winter health resort; fish-canning, aircraft, marble, onyx, missiles, electronics; p. (1960) *573,224.*
San Felipe, *cap.*, Yaracuy St., Venezuela; sugar, cacao, cotton, maize, fruits, rice, hides; p. (1961) *29,274.*
San Felipe de Aconcagua, *t.*, Chile; nr. Valparaiso; agr. ctr., copper and gold mng.; p. (1961) *27,149.*
San Fernando, *t.*, Chile; agr. ctr.; p. (1961) *37,834.*
San Fernando, *t.*, B. of Cadiz, S. Spain; pt. has naval arsenal; salt mftg.; much of surrounding marshland now reclaimed; p. (1957) *41,196.*
San Fernando, *t.*, Venezuela; at confluence of Apuré and Portuguesa Rs.; ctr. cattle ranching region of upper Llanos; oil concessions not yet developed; p. (1961) *21,544.*
San Fernando, *spt.*, Trinidad I., W.I.; on W. cst. of Trinidad, 25 m. S. of Port of Spain; exp. sugar, asphalt, petrol; p. (estd. 1957) *38,850.*
San Francisco, *t.*, Argentina; on rly. between Córdoba and Santa Fé.
San Francisco, *c.*, *spt.*, Cal., U.S.A.; on the San

F. bay; entrance spanned by Golden Gate Bridge, second longest single-span bridge in the world; univ.; engin., canning, lumber mills, printing, publishing, chemicals, machin., petrol; p. (1960) *742,855.*

San Francisco Pass, Argentina–Chile; across Andes at alt. 15,505 ft.

San Francisco de Macoris, *t.,* Dominican rep., W. Indies; p. *18,108.*

San Geronimo, *t.,* Oaxaca st., Mexico; rly. junction.

San Giovanni a Teduccio, *t.,* S. Italy; at foot of Vesuvius; iron mines, rly. wkshps.; p. *27,475.*

San Giovanni in Persiceto, *t.,* N. Italy; nr. Bologna; p. *20,450.*

San Isidro, *t.,* E. Argentina; N. sub. Buenos Aires; resort; p. (1960) *80,000.*

San Jerônimo, *t.,* Rio Grande do Sul, Brazil; low-grade coal.

San Joaquin, *R.,* Cal., U.S.A.; trib. of Sacramento R.; length 400 m.

San José, *prov.,* Costa Rica, Central America; cap. San J.; p. (1963) *483,824.*

San José, *t., cap.,* Costa Rica; cath., univ., observ.; coffee tr.; p. (1963) *267,454.*

San José, *c.,* Cal., U.S.A.; in Santa Clara valley; nr. is Lick Observatory; resort; fruit and vegetable canning; lumber prod., woollens, leather; p. (1960) *204,196.*

San José, *dep.,* Uruguay; a. 2,688 sq. m.; cap. San J.; p. (1953) *96,848.*

San José, *t., cap.,* San José, Uruguay; grain, flour milling; p. (1963) *20,000.*

San Juan, *prov.,* Argentina; at foot of the Andes; a. 34,432 sq. m.; cap. San Juan; gold, copper; p. (1960) *352,000.*

San Juan, *t.,* cap. San Juan, Argentina; wine, fruit, cattle; p. *112,286.*

San Juan, *c., cap.,* Puerto Rico, Central America; cath.; univ.; naval sta., airport; distilleries, sugar; p. (1960) *431,705.*

San Juan R., Central America; divides Nicaragua and Costa Rica; plans made for its canalisation, which would give both countries a clear waterway from Caribbean to Pacific; length 90 m.

San Juan, *R.,* Mexico; trib. of Rio Grande; length 160 m.

San Juan del Norte (Greytown), *spt.,* S.E. pt. of Nicaragua on Caribbean Sea.

San Juan del Rio, *t.,* Durango, Mexico; p. *6,694.*

San Juan del Sur, *spt.,* Nicaragua, Central America; coffee, timber, sugar; p. (1960) *4,223.*

San Juanito, *spt.,* Lower Cal., Mexico; on W. cst.

San Lorenzo, *mtn.,* S. Argentina; alt. 12,000 ft.

San Lorenzo, *t.,* Argentina, 14 m. N. Rosario; lge. chemical wks.

San Lucas, *C.,* point of Lower Cal., Mexico.

San Luis, *prov.,* Argentina; oranges, grapes; a. 29,700 sq. m.; cap. S.L.; p. (1960) *174,000.*

San Luis, *t., cap.,* St. Luis, Argentina; cattle, grain, wines; onyx quarrying; p. (1960) *38,000.*

San Luis Obispo, *t.,* Cal., U.S.A.; p. (1960) *20,437.*

San Luis Potosi, *st.,* Mexico; agr. and mining; cap. San Luis Potosi; a. 24,415 sq. m.; p. (1960) *1,048,297.*

San Luis Potosi, *t., cap.,* San Luis Potosi st., Mexico; arsenic plant, clothing, cottons, rly. wks., lead-, silver- and gold-refining; sulphur fields; wool hides, cattle; p. (1960) *159,980.*

San Marco in Lanis, *t.,* Foggia, Italy; p. *19,275.*

San Marino, *small republic;* on spurs of Apennines, Italy; ch. exp.: wine, woollen goods, hides, building stone; farming, cattle-raising; wine; a. 23·8 sq. m.; cap. San Marino; p. (estd. 1962) *17,000.*

San Marino, *t., cap.,* San Marino; on hill-top, alt. over 1,200 ft., 12 m. S.W. of Rimini; tourists; wine, curios for sale to tourists; p. *2,200.*

San Martin, *dep.,* Peru; ch. t. Moyobamba; a. 17,448 sq. m.; p. (1961) *162,592.*

San Mateo, *t.,* Cal., U.S.A.; residtl. sub. San Francisco; p. (1960) *69,870.*

San Miguel, *c.,* El Salvador, Central America; on Rio Grande; nr. malarial swamps; cotton, sisal, coffee, cattle; p. (1960) *80,769.*

San Miguel, *principal I.,* Azores, Portugal; hot sulphur springs, oranges, etc.; 41 m. by 9 m.; cap. Ponta Delgada.

San Nicolas, *R. pt.,* Argentina; on Paraná R.; cattle, flour, agr. produce, distillery; steel plant; p. (1960) *55,000.*

San Pedro, *spt.,* Cal., U.S.A.; sub. Los Angeles; naval base; p. (1950) *36,527.*

San Pedro de Macoris, *t.,* Dominican Rep., W. Indies; p. (1948) *24,200.*

San Pedro Sula, *t.,* Honduras, Central America; ctr. for banana and sugar inds.; p. (1961) *58,931.*

San Quintin Bay, *spt.,* Lower Cal., Mexico.

San Rafael, *t.,* W. Argentina; agr., cattle, fruit; p. *32,663.*

San Remo, *sm. pt.,* Italy; famous winter seaside resort on Italian riviera; flower mkt., olive oil, lemons, wine; 12th cent. church; p. *31,625.*

San Roque, *C.,* E. Brazil.

San Roque, *t.,* Andalusia, Spain; nr. Gibraltar; p. (1957) *15,333.*

San Salvador or Watling's I., Bahama Is., W. Indies; discovered by Christopher Columbus, 1492; p. (1953) *694.*

San Salvador, *cap.,* El Salvador; univ., observatory; silks, cottons, cigars; p. (1960) *248,100.*

San Salvador de Jujuy, *t.,* Argentina; wheat, maize, sugar; minerals, timber; p. (1960) *52,000.*

San Sebastian, *c., spt., cap.,* Guipuzcoa, Spain; captured by Wellington 1813; gd. tr. and fisheries; sailcloth, cottons, paper, glass; p. (1959) *129,395.*

San Severo, *mkt. t.,* S. Italy; hill-top site, 15 m. N.W. of Foggia, Apulia; cath.; wine ctr., cream of tartar, bricks; p. (1961) *48,443.*

San'a, *cap.,* Yemen, Arabia; walled c. 7,270 ft. above sea-level; tr. in silk, cottons and china; jewellery, arms, fruit; p. (estd. 1965) *100,000.*

Sanchez, *spt.,* Dominican Rep., W. Indies; situated on the Bahia de Sumana, at E. end of Cibao lowland dist.; linked to Santiago by rail; exp. cacao, tobacco.

Sancti Spiritus, *c.,* Santa Clara, Cuba; in grazing dist.; sugar, tobacco; p. (1953) *37,740.*

Sandakan, *impt. tr. c.,* Sabah, E. Indies; N.E. cst.; fine natural harbour; exp. timber, rubber, copra, hemp, salt fish; p. (1960) *28,806.*

Sandalwood (Sumba), *I.,* in Malay Archipelago, S. of Flores, Indonesia; very fertile; horse-breeding; rice, maize, tobacco, timber, cinnamon; *cap.* Waingapu; a. 4,305 sq. m.; p. *251,126.*

Sanday, *I.,* Barra Is., Orkney, Scot.

Sandbach, *t., urb. dist.,* Cheshire, Eng.; 5 m. S.E. of Middlewich; salt, chemicals, motor vehicles; p. (1961) *9,856.*

Sandiacre, *vil.,* Derby, Eng.; 4 m. S. of Ilkeston; lace-mkg.; p. *6,071.*

Sandoa, *t.,* Congo; on upper Lulua R.; admin. ctr.; p. *5,000.*

Sandown-Shanklin, *t., urb. dist.,* I. of Wight, Eng.; on Sandown Bay; holiday resort; p. (1961) *14,257.*

Sandringham, *par.,* Norfolk, Eng.; Royal residence; farming. [p. *5,529.*

Sandur, *t.,* Mysore st., India; manganese, iron;

Sandusky, *c.,* Ohio, U.S.A.; on S. cst., L. Erie; tr. in coal, fruit, and foodstuffs; paper, farm implements, chemicals; p. (1960) *31,989.*

Sandwich, *t., mun. bor., Cinque pt.,* Kent, Eng.; at mouth of Stour R.; mkt., light inds., chemicals nearby; p. (1961) *4,234.*

Sandwich Is., *dependency* of Falkland Is., Brit. Crown Col. S. Atlantic.

Sandy, *t., urb. dist.,* Beds, Eng.; 3 m. N.W. of Biggleswade; mkt. gardening; p. (1961) *3,892.*

Sandy Hook, *peninsula,* N.J., U.S.A.; projecting into lower bay of N.Y.; yachting ctr.

Sanford, *t.,* Fla., U.S.A.; p. (1960) *19,175.*

Sanga, *R.,* trib. of Congo R., Equatorial Africa.

Sangir (Sangihe), *Is.,* Indonesia; between Philippines and Celebes; eruption of volcano on ch. I. killed 12,000 inhabitants, 1856.

Sankt Ingbert, *t.,* Saarland, N.E. of Saarbrücken; coal-mining, iron, glass, machin., textiles, leather; p. (1963) *28,700.*

Sankuru, *R.,* trib. of Kasai R., Congo, Central Africa.

Sanlucar, *t.,* Cadiz, Spain; nr. mouth R. Guadalquivir; wines and agr. produce; ruined cas.; p. (1957) *35,363.*

Sanniya Hor, *L.,* Iraq; linked to R. Tigris; shallow, acts as flood control reservoir.

Sannois, *t.,* Seine-et-Oise, France; p. (1954) *13,644.*

Sanok, *t.,* Poland; nr. Rzeszów; metallurgy; p. *11,176.*

Sanquhar, *burgh,* Dumfries, Scot.; in upper Nithsdale; carpets, coal, bricks; p. (1961) *2,182.*

Sansanding, *t.*, Mali, W. Africa; lge. barrage across R. Niger.
Santa Ana, *c.*, El Salvador, Central America; municipal palace, barracks; coffee, sugar; p. (1959) *130,976*.
Santa Ana, *t.*, Cal., U.S.A.; fruit farming, oilfields, mnfs. farm implements, preserved fruits; p.
Santa Bárbara, *dist.*, Honduras; Panama hats; p. (1962) *145,100*.
Santa Barbara, *t.*, *winter resort*, Cal., U.S.A.; at foot of Santa Inez mtns.; fruit, oil; p. (1960) *58,259*.
Santa Catarina, *st.*, Brazil; inc. Santa Catarina I.; a. 36,435 sq. m.; mineral wealth; cap. Florianopolis; p. (1960) *2,146,909*.
Santa Clara, *t.*, Cuba; at alt. over 1,200 ft.; sugar, tobacco, cattle; p. (1953) *77,398*.
Santa Clara Valley, Cal., U.S.A.; extends S. from San Francisco Bay; intensive fruit-growing under irrigation, prunes; ch. t. San José.
Santa Cruz, *spt.*, Patagonia, Argentina; sheep; p. *3,000*.
Santa Cruz, *prov.*, S. Argentina; sheep, horses; cap. Gallegos; a. 93,952 sq. m.; p. (1960) *53,000*.
Santa Cruz, *t.*, Bolivia; alt. 1,500 ft.; univ.; sugar, coffee, rice, cattle; oil refining; Japanese settlement nearby; p. (1962) *72,708*.
Santa Cruz, *dep.*, Bolivia; cap. S. C.; p. (1962) *326,900*.
Santa Cruz, *c.*, Cal., U.S.A.; on Monterey Bay; popular seaside resort, fruit, and vegetable canning; fishing; p. (1960) *25,596*.
Santa Cruz, *t.*, cap. Tenerife I., Canary Is.; p. (1962) *133,100*.
Santa Cruz Is., Pac. Oc.; Brit. Solomon Is.
Santa Cruz de la Sierra, *t.*, Bolivia; on R. Piray; sugar, flour; distilling; p. *33,000*.
Santa Cruz de Tenerife, *prov.* (Spanish), Canary Is., Atl. Oc.; inc. Is. of Tenerife, Palma, Gomera, Hierro; a. 1,329 sq. m.; p. (1962) *507,744*.
Santa Fé, *prov.*, Argentina; agr. and stock farming; cap. Santa Fé; a. 52,056 sq. m.; p. (1960) *1,866,000*.
Santa Fé, *t.*, Argentina; on I. in R. Salado; cath., univ.; dairy prod.; zinc and copper smelting; road tunnel to Panama under construction; p. (1960) *203,900*.
Santa Fé, *t.*, N.M., U.S.A.; at base of Sangre de Cristo range; oldest capital in U.S. founded by Spaniards 1610; p. (1960) *34,676*.
Santa Isabel, *cap.*, Fernando Po, Spanish Guinea, W. Africa; residence of Governor; p. (estd. 1957) *20,230*.
Santa Maria, *t.*, Rio Grande do Sul, Brazil; rly. ctr.; tanning, hats, brewing, maté, wine timber, rice; p. (1960) *78,682*.
Santa Maria, *t.*, Campania, Italy; on site of ancient Capua; cath.; glass, leather; p. *36,637*.
Santa Marta, *spt.*, *cap.*, Magdalena dep., Colombia, S. America; cath.; bananas; p. (1960) *64,400*.
Santa Maura, *see* **Levkàs.**
Santa Monica, *c.*, Cal., U.S.A.; sub. Los Angeles; residtl.; p. (1960) *83,249*.
Santa Rosa, *t.*, *cap.*, La Pampa terr., Argentina; p. (1960) *17,000*.
Santa Rosa, *t.*, Cal., U.S.A.; fruit, grain, dairying; p. (1960) *31,027*.
Santa Rosalia, *t.*, peninsula of Lower Cal., Mexico; located E. cst. on G. of Cal.; impt. copper-mines.
Santander, *dep.*, Columbia, S. America; E. of the Magdalena R.; cap. Bucaramanga; a. 12,379 sq. m.; p. (estd. 1959) *838,430*.
Santander, *prov.*, Spain; agr., grape growing, fisheries; cap. Santander; a. 2,108 sq. m.; p. (1959) *427,235*.
Santander, *spt.*, *cap.*, Santander prov., Spain; former summer resort of the Court; cath.; exp. iron and zinc ore; p. (1959) *113,116*.
Santarém, *t.*, Para, Brazil; rubber, cacao, Brazil nuts, sugar; p. (1960) *24,924*.
Santarém, *dist.*, Portugal; in fertile valley of R. Tagus; cap. S.; p. (1960) *480,038*.
Santiago, *prov.*, Chile; cap. Santiago; a. 5,557 sq. m.; p. (1961) *2,283,977*.
Santiago de Chile, *c.*, *cap.*, Chile; on R. Mapocho; most populous t. on Pacific side of S. America; cath., univ.; national library; leather, textiles, chemicals; p. (1961) *2,114,000*.
Santiago de Compostella, *c.*, Corunna, Spain; on R. Sar; cath. (with tomb of St. James); univ.; beer, spirits, paper, linen; p. (1950) *55,553*.
Santiago de Cuba, *c.*, *spt.*, Cuba, W. Indies; on S. cst.; former cap. of I.; cath.; iron foundries, tanneries, ctr. of mineral dist.; exp. sugar, coffee, tobacco; Spanish fleet destroyed by U.S.A. warships here 1898; p. (1953) *163,237*.
Santiago de las Vegas, *t.*, Cuba; nr. Havana; p. (1943) *21,265*.
Santiago de los Caballeros, *t.*, Dominican Rep., W. Indies; p. (1964) *329,808*.
Santiago del Estero, *t.*, Argentina; on R. Dulce; p. (1960) *92,000*.
Santiago del Estero, *prov.*, Argentina; cap. S. del E.; a. 52,511 sq. m.; p. (1960) *477,000*.
Santiago-Zamora, *prov.*, Ecuador; p. (1950) *21,046*.
Säntis, *mtn.*, on bdr. Swiss cans. St. Gallen and Appenzell, alt. 8,216 ft., Europe's highest television transmitter on summit.
Santo Domingo, *spt.*, *cap.*, Dominican Rep.; cath., univ.; p. (1961) *367,053*.
Santoña, *spt.*, Spain; on N. cst., E. of Santander; p. *8,938*.
Santorene, *see* **Thera.**
Santos, *c.*, *spt.*, São Paulo, Brazil; world's ch. coffee pt.; also exp. sugar, rum, tobacco; p. (1960) *265,753*.
Santo Tomé de la Guayana, *c.*, S.E. Venezuela; new industl. c. nr. confluence of Orinoco and Caroni Rs.; iron mines, steel, hydroelec. power and aluminium plants in a.; vast industl. complex projected.
São Carlos, *t.*, São Paulo st., Brazil; 120 m. N.W. of São Paulo; ctr. of coffee-growing a.; textiles, refrigerators, furniture; p. (1960) *50,010*.
São Francisco, *R.*, Brazil; flows from Minas Gerais prov., to Atlantic; navigable for 150 m. below cataract of Paulo Afonso; length 1,600 m.
São Jeronymo, *t.*, Rio Grande do Sul st., S. Brazil; 40 m. W. of Porto Alegre; coal-mines.
São João, *t.*, Minas Gerais, Brazil; coffee, rice, cattle, cotton, sugar; p. (1947) *38,500*.
São Leopoldo, *t.*, Rio Grande do Sul st., S. Brazil; 20 m. N. of Porto Alegre, mkt. t; (1960) *41,023*.
São Luiz, *cap.*, Maranhao st., Brazil; cultural ctr.; p. (1960) *159,628*.
São Paulo, *st.*, Brazil, on Atlantic cst.; babacu nuts, rice, cotton, tucum fibre, hides, maize; salt pans along cst.; cap. S. Paulo; a. 95,454 sq. m.; p. (1960) *12,974,699*.
São Paulo, *c.*, *cap.* São Paulo st., Brazil; cath., monasteries; machin., rubber, elec. gds., textiles, chemicals, pharmaceutics, timber, cement; aluminium refinery projected; p. (1960) *3,776,581*.
São Roque, *c.*, Rio Grande do Norte st., N.E. Brazil; most N.E. point of S. America.
São Tomé with Principe Is. in the G. of Guinea; p. (1950) *60,159*.
Saône, *R.*, France; rises in Vosges, and flows to R. Rhône at Lyons; length 282 m.
Saône-et-Loire, *dep.*, France; mountainous; wines, coal, cereals, iron, steel, porcelain, oil, chemicals; cap. Mâcon; a. 3,331 sq. m. p. (1962) *535,772*.
Saône-Haute, *dep.*, France; cereals; fruit, iron, steel, cottons, coal; cap. Vesoul; a. 2,074 sq. m.; p. (1962) *208,440*.
Sapporo, *t.*, *administrative cap.*, Hokkaido, Japan; garrison; flour mills, flax, hemp, brewing; p. (1960) *524,000*.
Saqqara, *t.*, U.A.R.; tombs and pyramids; nr. site of Memphis.
Saragossa, *see* **Zaragoza.**
Sarajevo, *t.*, *cap.*, Bosnia and Herzegovina, Jugoslavia; the assassination here, on 28 June 1914, of the Archduke Francis Ferdinand precipitated the First World War; weaving carpets, pottery, flour, silks, sugar; p. (1959) *176,000*.
Saransk, *t.*, R.S.F.S.R.; Mordov A.S.S.R. 145 m. S.E. of Gorkiy; univ.; elec. equipment; engin;. p. (1959) *90,000*.
Sarapul, *R. pt.*, R.S.F.S.R., on R. Kama; boots, shoes, gloves, engin.; p. (1959) *68,000*.
Saratoga Springs, N.Y., U.S.A.; summer resort at foot of Adirondack mtns., mineral springs; p. (1960) *16,630*.
Saratov, *t.*, *pt.*, R.S.F.S.R.; on R. Volga; univ.; engin., ball-bearings, textiles, oil-refining, saw-milling; p. (1962) *631,000*.
Sarawak, *st.*, Malaysia; N.W. Borneo; exp. sago, rubber, oil, pepper; cap. Kuching; a. 47,071 sq. m.; p. (1960) *744,391*.
Sardinia, *I.*, *aut. region*, Italy; Mediterranean; mtnous.; sheep, cattle, fishing, wheat, barley,

fruit, wine; cap. Cagliari; part of former kingdom of Sardinia belonging to house of Savoy; a. 9,302 sq. m.; p. (1961) *1,413,289*.
Sargasso Sea, *zone,* situated in S.W. of North Atlantic; relatively still sea within swirl of warm ocean currents. Noted for abundance of gulf-weed on its surface, rich in marine life. Named by Columbus.
Sariwon, *t.*, Korea; p. *30,389*.
Sark, *I.*, Channel Is.; 6 m. E. of Guernsey; picturesque scenery; farming; tourist ctr.; a. 1,274 acres; p. inc. Brechou *560*.
Sark, *R.*, forms extreme W. bdy. between Scot. and Eng.
Sarnen, *cap.* half-can. Obwalden, Switzerland.
Sarnia, *t.*, Ontario, Canada; on St. Clair R.; car parts, machin., oil refineries, petro-chemical inds.; p. (1961) *50,976*.
Sarpsborg, *t.*, Norway; on R. Glommen; mftg. inds.; lgst. pulp and paper concern in kingdom; p. (estd. 1960) *13,500*.
Sarreguemines, *t.*, Moselle, France; 7 m. S.E. of Saarbrücken; porcelain, plush leather, matches; p. (1954) *14,947*.
Sarria, *t.*, Lugo, Spain; p. (1957) *16,142*.
Sarthe, *dep.*, N.W. France; undulating surface; farming, apples, livestock; coal, linen, potteries; cap. Le Mans; a. 2,412 sq. m.; p. (1962) *443,019*.
Sarthe, *R.*, France; trib. of R. Loire; l. 165 m.
Sârzana, *t.*, Liguria, Italy; nr. Spezia; cath.; silks; p. *13,650*.
Sasebo, *spt.*, Kyushu, Japan; p. (1962) *288,000*.
Saseno I., Adriatic Sea; off cst. of Albania; restored to Albania by Italy.
Saskatchewan, *prov.*, Canada; coniferous forests and plains; Rs. Saskatchewan and Churchill; many lge. Ls.; extreme climate; good rail communications; hydro-elec. power; gr. wheat prov.; livestock, dairying; oil, coal, copper, potash, helium, furs, fisheries; cap. Regina; a. 251,700 sq. m.; p. (1961) *925,181*.
Saskatchewan, *R.*, Canada; flows from Rocky mtns. through L. Winnipeg and thence by R. Nelson to Hudson Bay; length 1,450 m.
Saskatoon, *c.*, Saskatchewan Canada; univ.; flour, cement, oil refining; p. (1961) *95,526*.
Sasolburg, *t.*, O.F.S., S. Africa; oil from coal production; p. (1960) *12,557* (inc. *6,723* whites).
Sasovo, *t.*, R.S.F.S.R.; wood inds.; p. *10,000*.
Sassari, *t.*, Sardinia, Italy; nr. G. of Asinara; cath., univ., palaces; tobacco and macaroni wks.; oil, grain; p. (1961) *89,482*.
Satara, *t.*, Maharashtra, India; p. (1961) *48,709*.
Satu-Mare, *t.*, N.W. Romania; pottery, textiles; p. (1956) *52,096*.
Saudi Arabia, *lgst. kingdom,* peninsula of Arabia; cap. Riyadh; formerly kingdom of Hejaz (cap. Mecca) and Nejd (cap. Riyadh); mainly desert; nomadic pop; Moslem; dates, wheat, barley; impt. oil concessions; a. 1,500,000 sq. m.; p. (estd.) *6,000,000*.
Sauerland, *dist., Land,* N. Rhine-Westphalia, W. Germany; plateau, alt. from 500 to 1,500 ft., E. of Rhine and between valleys of Sieg and Ruhr; agriculturally poor, largely forested; crossed by R. Wupper, with which are associated industl. ts. Wuppertal (textiles), Solingen and Remscheid (cutlery and special steel).
Sault Ste. Marie, *c.*, Mich., U.S.A.; on L. Superior at rapids; flour, woollens, locomotives; p. (1960) *18,722*.
Sault Ste. Marie, *c.*, Ontario, Canada; on L. Superior at rapids; pulp, paper, iron, steel; p. (1961) *43,088*.
Saulte Ste. Marie Canals ("Soo"), Canada and U.S.A.; twin canals on Canadian and American side of shallow channel linking L. Superior and L. Huron; traversed by all wheat and iron-ore traffic from L. Superior pts.; length (Canadian) 1 m.; depth 18 ft.
Saumur, *t.*, Maine-et-Loire, France; on R. Loire, 30 m. S.W. of Tours; wines, enamels, tinware; p. (1954) *18,169*.
Saurashtra, *former st.*, India; now absorbed into [Gujarat st.
Sava or Save, *R.*, N. Jugoslavia; trib. of Danube; length 550 m.
Savage or Niue, Cook Is., Pac. Oc.; under N.Z.; ch. exp. native plaited ware, bananas, copra, and sweet potatoes; ch. pt. Alofi; a. 100 sq. m.; p. (1948) *4,318*.
Savaii I., *lgst. of Samoan gr.*, Pac. Oc.; a. 703 sq. m.
Savannah, *c.*, *spt.*, Ga., U.S.A.; Kraft paper, sugar refining, ship bldg. and repair, fertilisers, paint; p. (1960) *149,245*.
Savannah, *R.*, U.S.A.; flows between Ga. and S.C., to Atl. Oc.; length 450 m.
Save, *R.*, France; trib. of R. Garonne; 65 m. l.
Saverne, Col de, *low pass,* N.E. France; carries trunk rly. from Paris to Strasbourg and the Orient between Vosges and Hardt Mtns.; gradual approach from W., steep descent to E. into Rhine valley.
Savigliano, *t.*, Piedmont, Italy; silk; p. *18,725*.
Savoie or Savoy, *dep.*, S.E. France; on Italian border; mountainous; mineral springs, pastoral, dairying; cap. Chambéry; Vanoise Park (1st French nat. park); a. 2,389 sq. m.; p. (1962) *266,678*.
Savoie (Haute), *dep.*, France; mountainous; farming, wine, cheese; cap. Annecy; a. 1,774 sq. m.; p. (1962) *329,230*.
Savona, *spt.*, Genoa, Italy; cath.; iron, shipbldg., glass and tinplate wks.; exp. preserved fruits and tomatoes; p. (1961) *71,007*.
Sawbridgeworth, *t.*, *urb. dist.*, Herts, Eng.; on R. Stort, 4 m. S. of Bishops Stortford; malting, fruit preserving; p. (1961) *4,633*.
Saxmundham, *mkt. t.*, *urb. dist.*, Suffolk, Eng.; 18 m. N.E. of Ipswich; p. (1961) *1,538*.
Saxony, *former Land,* E. Germany; farming, printing, type-founding, toys, textiles, lace, spirits, beer, coal, iron, mineral springs; ch. ts. Dresden, Leipzig, Karl-Marx-Stadt.
Saxony-Anhalt, *former Land,* E. Germany
Sayan Mtns., *range of mtns.*, between Rs. Yenisei and Angra, R.S.F.S.R.
Scafell Pike, *mtn.*, Cumberland, Eng.; in N. Pennines; highest in Eng.; alt. 3,210 ft.
Scalby, *t.*, *urb. dist.*, N.R. Yorks, Eng.; 3 m. N.W. of Scarborough; p. (1961) *7,251*.
Scalpay, *I.*, off E. cst. of Skye, Scot.
Scalpay, Harris, Outer Hebrides, Scot.
Scalloway, Shetlands, on W. cst. of Mainland; the anc. cap.; ruined castle.
Scandinavia, Sweden, Norway and Denmark.
Scania, *see* Skåne.
Scapa Flow, *strait,* N. Scot.; between Pomona and Hoy, Orkney Is., surrendered German fleet scuttled, 1919.
Scarba, *I.*, Argyll, Scot.; off N. end of Jura.
Scarborough, *t.*, *mun. bor.*, N.R. Yorks, Eng.; on E. cst. 18 m. N.W. of Flamborough Head; seaside resort; p. (1961) *42,587*.
Scarpanto, *I.*, Dodecanese, Greece; E. Mediterranean; between Rhodes and Crete,; p. *8,747*.
Schaan-Vaduz, *t.*, Liechtenstein; point where Arlberg Express (Paris–Vienna) passes through the principality.
Schaffhausen, *most N. can.*, Switzerland; on R. Rhine; pastoral and afforested; cap. Schaffhausen; p. (1961) *65,981*.
Schaffhausen, *t.*, cap. Schaffhausen can., Switzerland; on the Rhine; cath., cas.; famous falls, iron, steel, aluminium, cottons, brewing, distilling; p. (1957) *25,971*.
Schaumburg-Lippe, *former st.*, between provs. of Hanover and Westphalia, Germany, now part of Lower Saxony; farming; coal-mining.
Schefferville, *t.*, Canada; 360 m. N. of St. Lawrence estuary and connected to it (at Seven Islands) by rly.; ctr. of iron-ore mines of Quebec-Labrador trough; p. (estd.) *3,500*.
Schelde (Scheldt), *R.*, France, Neth. and Belgium; rises in Aisne, France, flows to N. Sea; 248 m.
Schenectady, *c.*, N.Y. U.S.A.; foundries, wireless-transmitting apparatus, locomotive; synthetic diamonds; p. (1960) *81,682*.
Scheveningen, *seaside resort,* Neth.; 2 m. N.W. of the Hague; fishing.
Schiedam, *t.*, Neth.; N.W. of Rotterdam; distilleries, gin; shipyds, mnfs.; p. (1960) *80,088*
Schichallion, *mtn.*, Perth, Scot.; alt. 3,547 ft.
Schiltigheim, *t.*, Bas-Rhin, France; machin., factory equipment; p. (1954) *22,798*.
Schlei, *narrow inlet* of Baltic, Schleswig-Holstein Germany; 25 m. long.
Schleswig, *c.*, *pt.*, Schleswig-Holstein, Germany cath., cas.; rope wks., tanning, freighting p. (1963) *33,600*.
Schleswig-Holstein, *Land,* N. Germany; retroceded from Denmark 1920; cap. Kiel; moors and plain farming, livestock; textiles, tobacco oil; a. 6,048 sq. m.; p. (1961) *2,316,000*.
Schlettstadt, *see* Sélestat.
Schneidemühl, *see* Pila.

Schönebeck, *t.*, Magdeburg, E. Germany; on R. Elbe; metals, chemicals, brewing; p. (1963) *45,035*.
Schouten I., West Irian, Indonesia; in Geelvink [Bay; p. *25,487*.
Schouwen I., Zeeland, Neth.; in N. Sea.
Schuylkill R., Penns., U.S.A.; flows into Delaware R.; length 130 m.
Schwabach, *t.*, Bavaria, Germany; S. of Nürnberg; metal inds.; p. (1963) *23,900*.
Schwäbisch-Gmünd, *c.*, Baden-Württemberg, Germany; E. of Stuttgart; cath.; clocks, glass, optical, precious metal and jewellery inds.; p. (1963) *40,500*.
Schwarzwald (Black Forest), *forest belt, Land* Baden-Württemberg, W. Germany; a. 1,844 sq. m.; highest peak Feldberg, alt. 4,900 ft.
Schwechat, *t.*, Austria; nr. Vienna; oil refining; oil pipeline to Trieste; p. (1961) *13,403*.
Schwedt, *t.*, Frankfurt, E. Germany; on R. Oder; lge. oil refinery; oil pipeline from Mozyr; p. (1963) *14,775*.
Schweinfurt, *t.*, Bavaria, Germany; on R. Main, N.E. of Würzburg; metals, machin., ball bearings, dyes, brewing; p. (1963) *57,800*.
Schwelm, *t.*, N. Rhine-Westphalia, Germany; E. of Wuppertal; metals, machin., textiles, paper; p. (1963) *34,200*.
Schwenningen, *t.*, Baden-Württemberg, Germany; clocks, metals, footwear; p. (1963) *32,600*.
Schwerin, *cap.*, Schwerin, E. Germany; indust. and educational; cath., palace; p. (1963) *94,786*.
Schwyz, *forest can.*, Switzerland; cap. Schwyz; a. 350 sq. m.; p. (1961) *78,048*.
Schwyz, *t.*, Switzerland; nr. L. of Lucerne; p. (1957) *12,464*.
Sciacca, *spt.*, Sicily, Italy; nr. Agrigento; cath.; H.Q. of Mediterranean coral fishery; sardines, olives; mineral springs; p. approx. *25,000*.
Scilla, *promontory*, Strait of Messina, Calabria, Italy.
Scilly Is., *gr.*, 30 m. S.W. of Land's End, Cornwall, Eng.; total a. 10 sq. m.; lgst. I., St. Marys; cap. Hugh Town; flowers, vegetables; p. (1961) *2,273*.
Scioto, *R.*, Ohio, U.S.A.; joins Ohio at Portsmouth; length 250 m.
Scone, *par.*, Perth, Scot.; place of residence and coronation of early Scottish kings; from here Edward I. removed the Stone of Destiny to Westminster Abbey in 1297; tourist ctr.; civil aerodrome.
Scotland, Brit. Is.; N. part of Gr. Britain; contains 33 cos.; home affairs administered by Dep. of Secretary of State for Scot.; physically divided into Highlands (many islands on W.), Middle Lowlands and S. Uplands; highest peaks, Ben Nevis 4,406 ft. and Ben Macdhui 4,296 ft.; ch. Ls., L. Lomond, L. Ness; ch. Rs., Clyde, Tweed, Tay, Spey, Dee, Forth; climate, maritime; agr. in E., grazing in W.; oats, barley, wheat, potatoes, fruit; coal, iron, oil-shale, granite; fisheries; mnfs., textiles, shipbldg.; machin., distilling, sugar-refining, printing; hydroelectric development in Highlands; cap. Edinburgh; Glasgow, ch. comm. and industl. t.; a. 29,796 sq. m.; p. (1961) *5,178,490*.
Scranton, *c.*, Penns., U.S.A.; on R. Susquehanna; anthracite, iron foundries, steel wks., locomotives, and silk mnfs.; p. (1960) *111,443*.
Scunthorpe, *t.*, *mun. bor.*, Lindsey, Lincs, Eng., on Lincoln Edge, 6 m. S. of the Humber; iron-mng. and smelting, steel girders, engin., chemicals, tar distillation, hosiery, lt. inds.; p. (1961) *67,257*.
Scutari (Albania), *see* **Shkodra.**
Scutari (Turkey), *see* **Usküdar.**
Seaford, *t.*, *urb. dist.*, E. Sussex, Eng.; 3 m. E. of Newhaven; seaside resort; p. (1961) *10,994*.
Seaforth Loch, Lewis, Outer Hebrides, Scot.; 14 m. long.
Seaham, *spt.*, *urb. dist.*, Durham, Eng.; Seaham Harbour, on E. cst. 4 m. S. of Sunderland; modern colly. workings, extending under sea; p. (1961) *26,048*.
Seathwaite, *vil.*, Cumberland, Eng.; 7 m. from Keswick, close to Styhead (1,430 ft.); exceptionally heavy annual rainfall (above 150 in.).
Seaton, *t.*, *urb. dist.*, S. Devon, Eng.; on Lyme Bay at mouth of R. Axe; seaside resort; freestone quarries; p. (1961) *3,410*.
Seaton Valley, *t.*, *urb. dist.*, Northumberland, Eng.; nr. Blyth; coal-mining; p. (1961) *26,086*.
Seattle, *spt.*, Wash., U.S.A.; univ., cath.; shipbldg., aeroplanes, glass, fish-canning, fishing, packing, lumbering, chemicals, trucks, buses; p. (1960) *557,087*.
Sebnitz, *t.*, Dresden, E. Germany; p. (1963) *14,520*.
Secunderabad, Andhra Pradesh, India; military [sta.; p. (1961) *78,412*.
Sedalia, *c.*, Mo., U.S.A.; farming, meat-packing; machin., textiles, coal; rly. ctr. and wks.; p. (1960) *23,874*.
Sedan, *t.*, Ardennes, France; on R. Meuse; weaving; machin., metal ware, woollens, flour; battle 1870; p. (1954) *17,637*.
Sedgley, *industl. t.*, *urb. dist.*, Staffs, Eng.; nr. Wolverhampton; coal-mng., metal wks., bricks, engin., fireclay goods; p. (1961) *27,927*.
Segezha, *t.*, R.S.F.S.R.; on L. Vyg; cellulose, paper, sawmilling.
Sego, *L.*, R.S.F.S.R.; 20 by 20 m.; N.W. of L. Onega; outlet into White Sea.
Ségou, *t.*, *R. pt.*, Mali, W. Africa; on R. Niger; ctr. of irrigation scheme; cotton, hides, cattle, wax, salt; p. (1957) *21,000*.
Ségou Canal, W. Africa; leaves R. Niger 4 m. below Bamako, extends 130 m. N.E. to Ségou; irrigates 3,000 sq. m. on right bank of Niger and assists navigation.
Segovia, *prov.*, Old Castile, Spain; agr., stock-keeping, and mftg.; cap. Segovia; a. 2,682 sq. m.; p. (1959) *204,484*.
Segovia, *c.*, Spain; nr. R. Eresma; cath.; iron-ware, cloth, earthenware, paper, flour; p. (1957) *34,700*.
Segre, *R.*, Lérida, N.E. Spain; rises in E. Pyrenees, flows S.W. into R. Ebro; water irrigates the a. around Lerida, the lgst. block of irrigated land in Spain; length approx. 170 m.
Segura, *R.*, Spain, flows to Mediterranean at Guardamar; 180 m.
Seikan Tunnel, project to link main Japanese I. of Honshu with northern I. of Hokkaido under Tsugaru Straits; length 23 m. (14 m. under sea-bed); expected completion 1970.
Seim, *R.*, Ukrainian S.S.R.; trib. of R. Desna; length 300 m.
Seine, *dep.*, France; mkt. gardens; gypsum, freestone; a. 185 sq. m.; cap. Paris; p. (1962) *5,646,446*.
Seine, *R.*, France; rising in Côte d'Or dep., and flowing past Paris and Rouen to English Channel at Havre; length 473 m.
Seine-et-Marne, *dep.*, N. France; agr., stock-raising, dairying; "Brie" cheese; porcelain, gypsum, flagstone; cap. Melun; a. 2,275 sq. m.; p. (1962) *537,543*.
Seine-et-Oise, *dep.*, N. France; mkt. gardening, vineyards, wheat; machin., chemicals, porcelain, gunpowder, stone; cap. Versailles; a. 2,185 sq. m.; p. (1962) *2,344,108*.
Seine-Maritime, *dep.*, N. France; undulating and fertile; grain, dairying, textiles, iron, shipbldg., flax, chemicals; fisheries; cap. Rouen; a. 2,448 sq. m.; p. (1962) *1,035,844*.
Seistan and Baluchistan, *twin prov.*, Iran; co. ts. Zabol, Zahedan (rly. term. Pakistan rly. from Quetta through Mirjaveh, the customs post on Iranian frontier).
Sekondi, *spt.*, Ghana, W. Africa; connected with and largely superseded as a pt. by Takoradi harbour; p. (1948) *44,130* (inc. Takoradi).
Selangor, *st.*, Malaysia; central Malaya; cap. Kuala Lumpur (to relieve congestion, Klang designated future cap.); a. 3,150 sq. m.; p. (1961) *1,180,413*.
Selby, *mkt. and industl. t.*, *urb. dist.*, W.R. Yorks, Eng.; on R. Ouse, 13 m. S. of York; ancient abbey church; flour-milling, flax, oil-cake; p. (1961) *9,869*.
Sele, *R.*, S. Italy; rises in S. Apennines, flows W. into G. of Salerno; headwaters now carried E. through gr. Apennine tunnel (7 m.) to irrigate plateau of Apulia in S.E. Italy.
Selenga, *R.*, Mongolia and Siberia; flows into L. Baikal; length 750 m.
Sélestat, *t.*, Bas-Rhin, France; on R. Ill; two caths.; p. (1954) *11,705*.
Selkirk, *co.*, Scot.; mountainous (Broad Law 2,723 ft.); sheep, oats, woollens; cap. Selkirk; a. 267 sq. m.; p. (1961) *21,055*.
Selkirk, *bor.*, *co. t.*, Selkirk, Scot.; on Ettrick Water; 4 m. S. of Galashiels; tartans, tweeds; p. (1961) *5,634*.
Selkirk, *t.*, Yukon, Canada; on junction of Macmillan and Lewes Rs.
Selkirk Mtns., B.C., Canada; run N.W. to S.E.

parallel with Rocky Mtns. and occupy inside of the great bend of R. Columbia; ancient rocks, highly mineralised; pierced by Connaught Tunnel on Canadian Pacific Rly. route through Kicking Horse Pass to Vancouver; rise to over 9,000 ft.

Selma, *c.*, Ala., U.S.A.; on Alabama R.; in cotton-growing dist.; also dairying, lumbering, ironwks., fertilisers; p. (1960) *28,385*.

Selsey, *t.*, Sussex, Eng.; on Selsey Bill, 7 m. S. of Chichester; coastal resort; fishing.

Selsey Bill, *peninsula*, between Bognor Regis and Portsmouth, Sussex, Eng.

Selukwe, *t.*, Rhodesia; alt. 4,734 ft.; gold-mining, chrome ore, molybdenum; ranching and agr.

Selwyn Range, *mtns.*, Queensland, Australia; extends 350 m. W. from Gr. Dividing Range; forms divide between Rs. flowing N. to G. of Carpentaria and Rs. flowing S. to Darling; gold, copper; alt. mainly below 1,500 ft.

Semarang, *spt.*, Java, Indonesia; exp. sugar, tobacco, tapioca, kapok; shipbldg., rly. repairs, cement, sawmills; p. (1961) *503,000*.

Seminole, *t.*, Okla., U.S.A.; p. (1960) *11,464*.

Semipalatinsk, *t.*, Kazakh. S.S.R.; on R. Irtysh; lge meat-packing plant; textiles, sawmilling, engin.; p. (1959) *155,000*.

Semlin, *see* **Zemun**.

Semmering Pass, *low pass*, Austria; provides route across E. Alps for rly. from Vienna to Venice; alt. below 3,000 ft.

Sena, *t.*, Mozambique, Port. E. Africa; on R. Zambesi. [425,000.

Sendai, *t.*, Honshu, Japan; salt, fish; p. (1960)

Senegal, *R.*, W. Africa; flowing from Kong mtns. W. and N.W. to Atlantic at St. Louis, above Cape Verde; length 1,000 m.

Senegal, *indep. sovereign st.*, within Fr. Community; N. of R. Gambia; groundnuts; chromium 375 m. E. of D.; cap. Dakar; a. 78,000 sq. m.; p. (1961) *2,973,000*.

Senekal, *t.*, O.F.S., S. Africa; tr. ctr.; wool, wheat; p. (1960) *7,409* (inc. *1,984* whites).

Senigallia, *t.*, Italy, N.W. of Ancona; p. *26,345*.

Sennar, *t.*, Sudan; on Blue Nile, on rly. route to Khartoum, Suakin, Pt. Sudan; dam for irrigation and control of Nile floods; hydro elec. power sta.; p. *1,000*.

Sennin, *see* **Kamaishi**.

Sens, *t.*, Yonne, France; on R. Yonne; cath., the ancient Agedincum; farm implements, boots, chemicals, cutlery; p. (1954) *18,612*.

Sensuntepeque, *t.*, E. Salvador, Central America; pottery, distilling; p. (1960) *27,070*.

Senta, *t.*, Jugoslavia; on R. Tisa; flour, leather, sugar, wine, agr., machin., chemicals, paper; p. (1959) *20,000*.

Seoul, *cap.*, S. Korea; brassware, pottery, silk; p. (1962) *2,983,000*. [alt. 7,611 ft.

Septimer, *mtn. pass*, Swiss Alps, can. Grisons;

Seraing, *t.*, Liége, Belgium; extensive ironwks.; engin.; p. (1962) *40,706*.

Serampore, *t.*, W. Bengal, India; former Danish settlement; cotton and silk weaving, pottery, jute- and paper-mills; p. (1961) *91,521*.

Serang, *I.*, Malaya Archipelago, Indonesia, N. of Amboyna; a. 6,612 sq. m.; tobacco; p. (estd.) *105,000*.

Serbia, *fed. unit*, Jugoslavia; former independent kingdom; a. 33,930 sq. m.; cap. Belgrade; p. (1960) *7,593,000*. [*25,000*.

Seremban, *t.*, cap., Negri Sembilan, Malaya; p.

Seres, *see* **Sérrai**. [290 m.

Sereth, *R.*, Romania; trib. of R. Danube; length

Sergipe, *cst. st.*, Brazil; forested; tobacco, maize, sugar, cotton; oil deposits; cap. Aracaju; a. 8,129 sq. m.; p. (1960) *760,273*.

Sergo, *see* **Kadiyevka**.

Seria, *t.*, Brunei; oil ctr.; linked by pipe-line with Lutong. [Ægean Sea.

Sériphos, *I.*, Cyclades gr., Grecian Archipelago,

Serov, *t.*, R.S.F.S.R., in Urals; iron and steel; natural gas pipeline from Ingrim; p. (1959) *98,000*. [Africa; p. *15,935*.

Serowe, *c.*, Bamangwato tribe, Botswana, S.W.

Serpukhov, *t.*, *R. pt.*, R.S.F.S.R.; on R. Oka, S. of Moscow; engin., textiles; p. (1959) *105,000*.

Serra da Mantiqueira, *mtn. range*, highest in Brazil;

Serra do Espinhaco, *mtns.*, Brazil; highest peak, Itambe, 6,705 ft.; iron-ore deposits.

Serra do Mar, *mtns.*, Brazil; form steep E. edge of Brazilian Plateau S. from Rio de Janeiro.

Sérrai (Seres), *prefecture* Macedonia, Greece; cap. Sérrai; p. (1961) *248,045*.

Sérrai (Seres), *t.*, Macedonia, Greece; on Struma R.; woollens, cottons, carpets; p. (1961) *40,063*.

Sesto San Giovanni, *sub.*, N.E. Milan, Italy; machin., glass, chemicals, plastics; p. (1961) *71,384*.

Sète (formerly **Cette**), *spt.*, Hérault, France; on Mediterranean cst.; chemicals, fisheries; exp. oysters, brandy, wine; oil pipeline under the sea to Frontignan; p. (1954) *33,454*.

Setif, *mkt. t.*, E. Algeria; alt. 3,596 ft.; cereals, horses; p. (1948) *51,674*.

Setouchi, *coastal region*, S.W. Honshu, N. Shikoku, Japan; flanks shores of Inland Sea; sm. plains backed by terraced hillsides; intensive agr., rice, mulberry, tea, citrus fruits; many sm. ts. engaged in fishing, local tr. and varied inds. inc. textiles, salt-extraction from brine.

Setté Cama, *spt.*, Gaboon, Equat. Africa; open roadstead, landing difficult owing to swell; exp. timber.

Settle, *mkt. t.*, *rural dist.*, W.R. Yorks, Eng.; on R. Ribble in heart of Craven dist.; caves with remains of extinct fauna; thread, cotton; p. (rural dist 1961) *13,782*.

Settsu Plain, S. Honshu, Japan; located at head of Osaka Bay at E. end of Inland Sea; intensively cultivated alluvial lowlands, ch. crops, rice, vegetables, oranges; gr. industl. belt extends along cst. through Kobe, Osaka, Kishiwada; engin., chemicals, textiles; a. 500 sq. m.

Setubal, *c.*, *spt.*, Lisbon, Portugal; on R. Sado; boatbldg., fishing, sardine-curing, lace, salt, fertilizers, etc.; p. (1950) *44,030*.

Seul Lac, *L.*, S. of St. Joseph L., Ontario, Canada.

Sevan (Gokcha), *lge. L.*, Armenian S.S.R.; alt. 6,340 ft.; never freezes; surrounded by high, barren mtns. [elec. power sta.

Sovan, *t.*, Armenian S.S.R.; underground hydro-

Sevastopol, *spt.*, Ukrainian S.S.R.; built on ruins left after famous siege 1855; Black Sea resort; naval arsenals; leather, tiles, machin.; exp. grain; p. (1959) *148,000*.

Seven Islands, *pt.*, on St. Lawrence, Quebec, Canada; iron brought by rail from Schefferville; airline service but no highway.

Sevenoaks, *mkt. t.*, *urb. dist.*, Kent, Eng.; in Vale of Holmesdale, 5 m. N.W. of Tonbridge; residtl.; agr., light inds.; Knole Park; p. (1961) *17,604*.

Severn, *R.*, W. of Eng. and N. Wales; rises in Montgomery and flows to Bristol Channel; length 200 m.

Severn, *R.*, Ontario, Canada; flows to Hudson Bay; length 350 m.

Severn Tunnel, Eng.; under estuary of R. Severn between Pilning (Glos.) and Severn Tunnel Junction (Mon.); carries main rly. from London to S. Wales; longest main-line rly tunnel in Brit. Is.; length nearly 4½ m.

Severodvinsk, *t.*, R.S.F.S.R.; on Dvina Bay, White Sea; metals, bldg. materials; p. (1959) *79,000*.

Seville, *prov.*, Spain; agr., mining; cap. Seville; a. 5,430 sq. m.; p. (1959) *1,226,730*.

Seville, *pt.*, *cap.*, Seville, Spain; on R. Guadalquivir; Gothic cath.; palace, univ.; ironware, machin., cigars, silks, porcelain, brewery, cotton and wool mills, aircraft; exp. lead, iron, mercury, cork, oranges, lemons, wine; birthplace of Velasquez and Murillo; p. (1959) *424,757*.

Sevran, *t.*, Seine-et-Oise, France; p. (1954) *12,956*.

Sèvres, *t.*, Seine-et-Oise, France; on R. Seine; celebrated porcelain mnfs.; p. (1954) *17,109*.

Sevres (Deux), *dep.*, N. France; p. (1962) *321,118*

Seychelles Is., *Brit. col.*, Indian Ocean; consisting of 92 Is., lgst. I. Mahé; cap. Victoria; export prods. of coconut palm, phosphate, essentia[l] oils and spices; famous for species of nut; tota[l] a. 156 sq. m.; p. (estd. 1965) *46,000*.

Seyne or **La Seyne-sur-Mer**, *t.*, Var, France nr. Toulon; shipbldg.; p. (1954) *26,672*.

Sfax, *spt.*, Tunisia; admin. ctr.; exp. phosphate olive oil, salt, esparto grass, cereals, dates hides; imports food, coal, textiles, soap sponges; fishing; natural gas found in a p. (1956) *65,635*. [3,483 ft

Sgurr Mor, *mtn.*, Ross and Cromarty, Scot.; alt

Shabani, *t.*, Rhodesia; asbestos; p. (1958) *7,93* (incl. *1,700* Europeans).

Shadrinsk, *t.*, R.S.F.S.R.; W. Siberia, 160 m. S.E of Sverdlovsk; car parts, printing presses; p. (1959) *52,000*.

Shaftesbury, *mkt. t., mun. bor.*, Dorset, Eng.; 10 m. N. of Blandford; agr. implements, chemicals, glove mftg.; p. (1961) *3,366.*

Shahjahanpur, *c.*, Uttar Pradesh, India; on Deoha R.; sugar; p. (1961) *117,702.*

Shahpur, *t.*, W. Punjab, Pakistan; cotton; p. *8,545.*

Shaker Heights, *t.*, Ohio, U.S.A.; p. (1960) *36,460.*

Shakhty (Alexandrovsk Grushevski), *t.*, R.S.F.S.R.; coal, engin., elec. power; p. (1959) *196,000.*

Shamaldy-Say, *t.*, Kirghiz S.S.R.; new town on site of Uch-Kurgan hydroelec. sta.

Shamokin, *bor.*, Penns., U.S.A.; iron mftg., anthracite; p. (1960) *13,674.*

Shan State, *div.*, Burma; a. 57,500 sq. m.; p. *2,500,000*; elevated plateau through which flows R. Salween; iron, lead, silver, zinc; former Federated Shan States and Wa States, E. Burma.

Shandakan Tunnel, N.Y. st., U.S.A.; carries water under Catskill Mtns. to augment water supply of c. of N.Y.; length 18 m.

Shanghai, *c., pt.*, Kiangsu, China; on Whangpoo trib. of Yangtze-Kiang; most impt. of the former Chinese treaty pts., considerable exp. silk and **tea**; mnfs. paper, cigarettes, cotton; shipbldg., engin.; p. (estd. 1957) *7,100,000.*

Shangkiu (Shangqiu), *c.*, Honan prov., China; agr. ctr.; silk weaving; p. (1953) *134,000.*

Shanklin, *see* Sandown-Shanklin.

Shannon Airport, Clare, Ireland, *see* **Foynes.**

Shannon, *R.*, Ireland; separating Connaught from provs. of Leinster and Munster, and flowing to Atlantic at Loop Head; length 224 m.

Shansi (Shanxi), *inland and hilly prov.*, N. China, bounded W. and S. by the Hwang-Ho; coal, iron ore, petroleum, salt; cap. Taiyuan; a. 60,394 sq. m.; p. (1953) *14,314,485.*

Shantung (Shandong), *maritime prov.*, China, on the G. of Chihli and the Yellow Sea; fertile plain; grain, silk, fruit; coal, iron, lead, copper; cap. Tsinan; a. 56,447 sq. m.; p. (1953) *48,876,548.*

Shaohing (Shaoxing), *c.*, Ckekiang prov., China; rice, wheat, cotton; p. (1953) *131,000*

Shaoyang, *c.*, Hunan prov., China; coal and iron mng.; timber; p. (1953) *127,000.*

Shap, *par.*, Westmorland, Eng.; near by is Shap Summit 914 ft., an impt. pass traversed by rly. and by a main road; granite.

Shapinsay, Orkney Is., Scot.

Shari, *R.*, Mali, W. Africa; flows from the S. to L. Chad; navigable for greater part of course; length 700 m.

Sharon, *plain*, Israel; citrus fruits, vines, poultry.

Sharon, *c.*, Penns., U.S.A.; ironwks., bricks, elec. goods; p. (1960) *25,267.*

Sharpness, *vil.*, Glos., Eng.; on S. shore, Severn estuary 18 m. N.E. of Avonmouth; entrance to Berkeley Canal.

Shasta, *mtn.*, Cal., U.S.A.; 14,380 ft.

Shatt-al-Arab, *R.*, Iraq; formed by union of Tigris and Euphrates, flows thence to head of Persian G.; length 120 m.

Shatura, *t.*, R.S.F.S.R.; E. of Moscow; elec. power-plant; p. (1954) *50,000.*

Shawinigan Falls, *c.*, Quebec, Canada; pulp and paper; p. (1961) *32,169.*

Shawnee, *c.*, Okla., U.S.A.; cottons, meat-preserving; p. (1960) *24,326.*

Sheaf, *R.*, W.R., Yorks, Eng.; rises in S.E. Pennines, flows N.E. to join R. Don at Sheffield; for last 2 m. narrow valley crowded with smaller factories of Sheffield; valley provides main route to S. (Chesterfield) and S.W. (Manchester via Totley); length 11 m.

Shebelinka, natural gas fields nr. Kharkov, Ukraine; pipelines to Kharkov-Bryansk and Dnepropetrovsk–Odessa.

Sheboygan, *c.*, Wis., U.S.A.; on L. Michigan; furniture mftg., pianos, gloves, enamelled ware; p. (1960) *45,747.*

Shechem, *see* **Nablus.**

Sheerness, *spt., urb. dist.*, Kent, Eng.; on I. of Sheppey at entrance to estuary of R. Medway; former royal dockyard and garrison; electronics, furniture, coach bldg.; p. (1961) *14,123.*

Sheffield, *c., co. bor.*, W.R. Yorks, Eng.; on cramped site at confluence of Rs. Sheaf and Don; univ.; gr. cutlery, steel, iron, brass mftg. ctr., machin., instruments, electro-plate; p. (1961) *493,954.*

Shelbyville, *t.*, Ind., U.S.A.; on Big. Blue R.; mftg. ctr. in colly. and agr. region; p. (1960) *14,317.*

Shellal (Esh Shellal), *t., R. pt.*, Upper U.A.R., N.E. Africa; on right bank of R. Nile, 2 m. above Aswan Dam; S. terminus of Egyptian rly. system; river-steamer service connects with Wadi Halfa, 160 m. upstream, N. terminus of Sudan rly. system.

Shellhaven, *oil refineries*, Essex, Eng.; on N. side of Thames estuary, nr. Stanford-le-Hope.

Shelton, *t.*, Conn., U.S.A.; old vil. of Huntingdon, has 18th-century houses; p. (1960) *18,190.*

Shenandoah, *t.*, Penns., U.S.A.; anthracite; p. (1960) *11,075.*

Shenandoah, *R.*, Va., U.S.A.; trib. of Potomac R.

Shendi, *t.*, Sudan; on R. Nile; p. *14,300.*

Shensi (Shenxi), *prov.*, China; W. of Hwang-Ho; wheat, cotton; coal, petroleum; cap. Sian; a. 72,919 sq. m.; p. (1953) *15,881,281.*

Shenyang, *see* **Mukden.**

Shepherd's Bush, *residtl. sub.*, W. London, Eng.

Shepparton, *t.*, Victoria, Australia; 118 m. N.N.E. of Melbourne; p. (1961) *13,574.*

Sheppey, I. of, Kent, Eng.; in Thames estuary E. of mouth of R. Medway; 9 m. long, 5 m. wide; cereals, sheep-raising.

Shepshed, *t., urb. dist.*, Leicester, Eng.; 3 m. W. of Loughborough; gloves, boots, shoes, needles; p. (1961) *7,179.*

Shepton Mallet, *mkt. t., urb. dist.*, Somerset, Eng.; at foot of Mendip Hills, 5 m. S.E. of Wells; shoes, cider; p. (1961) *5,518.*

Sherborne, *mkt. t., urb. dist.*, Dorset, Eng.; 4 m. E. of Yeovil; famous abbey and school; p. (1961) *6,062.*

Sherbrooke, *c.*, Quebec, Canada; at confluence of Rs. St. Francis and Magog; woollens, cottons, carpets, machin., sawmills; p. (1961) *66,554.*

Sherchell, *sm. spt.*, Algeria; mkt.; p. *12,650.*

Sheridan, *t.*, Wyo., U.S.A.; p. (1960) *11,651.*

Sheringham, *t., urb. dist.*, Norfolk, Eng.; on E. cst. 4 m. W. of Cromer; seaside resort; fishing; p. (1961) *4,836.*

Sherman, *t.*, Texas, U.S.A.; tr. in locally produced cotton and corn; p. (1960) *24,988.*

Sherwood Forest, *ancient royal woodland*, Notts, Eng.

Shetland Is., Scot.; in Zetland co., 50 m. N.E. of the Orkneys; about 100 in gr., ch. I., Mainland; textile, fishing; cattle, sheep, ponies; potatoes; ch. t. Lerwick; a. 551 sq. m.; p. (1961) *17,809.*

Sheyenne, *R.*, Dakota, U.S.A.; trib. of Red R.; length 325 m.

Shifnal, *mkt. t., rural dist.*, Shropshire, Eng.; 5 m. S.E. of Wellington; malting, coal, iron; p. (rural dist., 1961) *14,234.*

Shigatze, *t.*, Tibet; on R. Tsangpo; tr. ctr. on main caravan routes; p. *9,000.*

Shihkiachwang (Shijiazhuang), *c.*, Hopeh prov., China; cotton milling, glass mftg.; p. (1953) *373,000.*

Shikarpur, *t.*, N. Sind, Pakistan; tr. ctr., gems and silk; p. over *62,000.*

Shikoku, *one of the lge. Is.* Japan; S. of Honshu; rice, fruit, sugar-cane; copper; a. 7,248 sq. m.

Shildon, *t., urb. dist.*, Durham, Eng.; 3 m. S. of Bishop Auckland; rly. wks.; p. (1961) *14,372.*

Shilka, *R.*, E. Siberia; R.S.F.S.R.; trib. of R. Amur; length 760 m.

Shillong, *cap.*, Assam, India; at alt. 4,500 ft. in Khasi Hills; ctr. of impt. tea-growing dist.; p. (1961) *102,398.*

Shimbara, *t.*, Japan; holiday resort; p. (1947) *38,510.*

Shimisu, *spt.*, Japan; tea ctr.; oranges, paper, tinned fruit and fish; p. (1947) *68,892.*

Shimoda, *spt.*, Honshu, Japan; between Nagoya and Yokohama; p. *10,000.*

Shimonoseki, *spt.*, Honshu I., Japan; at extreme S.W. of I.; tunnel links island of Kyushu; p. (1962) *259,000.*

Shin, *Loch*, Sutherland, Scot.; 16½ m. long; drained by R. Shin to the R. Oykell.

Shipka Pass, Bulgaria; over the Balkan Mtns., 47 m. N.E. of Plovdiv.

Shipley, *t., urb. dist.*, W.R. Yorks, Eng.; on R. Aire, 8 m. N.W. of Leeds; worsted mnfs.; p. (1961) *29,762.*

Shipston-on-Stour, *mkt. t.*, Warwick, Eng.; in Cotswold Hills, 4 m. E. of Chipping Camden; rope, farming; p. *1,365.*

Shiraz, *c., cap.*, Fars, Iran; beautifully sited in

vine-growing dist.; mosaics, carpets, silk; p. (1956) *169,088.*

Shire, *R.*, flows from L. Malawi to R. Zambesi; on it are the famous Murchison Falls, up to which the R. is navigable; length 380 m.

Shirwa or Chilwah, *shallow L.*, nr. Malawi, Africa; 40 m. long, 14 m. wide; has 4 Is.

Shizuoka, *spt.*, Honshu, Japan; tea refining, blending, packing; oranges, fruit tinning; woodwork; textiles; p. (1960) *329,000.*

Shkodra (Scutari), *L.*, 29 m. long; on borders of Montenegro and Albania; outlet via R. Bojana into Adriatic.

Shkodra (Scutari), *t.*, Albania; stands at foot of S. L. (ancient cap. Illyria); cas. cath.; tobacco ind., cement; p. (1960) *41,000.*

Shoa, *st.*, Ethiopia; S.E. Amhara.

Shoalhaven, *t.* and *R.*, N.S.W., Australia; tourist resort.

Shoeburyness, *t.*, Essex, Eng.; on N. side of Thames estuary, 3 m. E. of Southend; barracks, gunnery school, bricks; p. (1961) *10,855.*

Sholapur, *c.*, Maharashtra, India; between Hyderabad and Poona; lge. bazaar, temples, etc., silk, cotton cloth; p. (1961) *337,583.*

Shoreditch, *see* **Hackney.**

Shoreham-by-Sea, *t.*, *urb. dist.*, W. Sussex, Eng.; at mouth of R. Adur, 4 m. E. of Worthing; old spt. and mkt. t.; boat bldg., chemicals, soap, preserves; p. (1961) *17,391.*

Shoshone Falls, on Snake R., Idaho, U.S.A.; height 200 ft.

Shott esh Shergui, lgst. saline L., Algeria.

Shotts, *plateau*, N. Africa; upland region with salt Ls., within Atlas mtns.

Shreveport, *c.*, La., U.S.A.; industl. ctr. in cotton-growing dist.; petroleum; p. (1960) *164,372.*

Shrewsbury, *co. t.*, *mun. bor.*, Salop, Eng.; on R. Severn 12 m. above Ironbridge gorge between The Wrekin and Wenlock Edge; agr. and dairy equipment, machin., elec. goods; impt. cattle and sheep mkt.; famous public school; fine churches, Shire Hall, Guildhall, p. (1961) *49,726.*

Shropshire (Salop), *N.W. midland co.*, Eng.; bordering on Wales; fine pastoral country with hills and woodland, agr. and dairying; iron; mnfs.; cap. Shrewsbury; a. 1,347 sq. m.; p. (1961) *297,313.*

Shumen (Kolarovgrad) *t.* Bulgaria; S.E. of Ruse; cloth; occupied by Russians, 1878; p. (1956) *41,670.*

Shurma, *t.*, Hejaz, Saudi Arabia; S. of Medina.

Shusha, *t.*, Azerbaydzhan S.S.R.; spa; p. massacred by Moslems 1926; p. (1956) *5,700.*

Shustar, *t.*, Iran; carpets, woollens, pottery, etc.; shallow-draught boats can reach Shallili, nr. S. by R. Karun; p. *20,000.*

Shuya, *t.*, R.S.F.S.R.; engin., textiles; p. (1959) *64,000.* [p. *11,286.*

Shwebo, *t.*, Central Burma; on R. Irrawaddy;

Si Kiang, *ch. R.*, S. China; headstreams rise in Yunnan plateau, form main R. nr. Sunchow; R. then flows E., enters S. China Sea through lge. delta nr. Hong Kong; lower valley intensively cultivated, rice, sugar-cane, tea; tropical climate permits continuous cultivation of most crops throughout year; valley very densely populated.

Sialkot, *t.*, W. Pakistan; N.E. of Lahore; sports goods, musical and surgical instruments, paper; p. (1961) *164,346.*

Siam. *See* **Thailand.** [N.W. to S.E.

Siam, G. of, *lge. inlet*, S. China Sea; 385 m. from

Sian (Xian), *c.*, *cap.*, Shensi, China; mkt.; oil- and saw-mills; p. (estd. 1957) *1,500,000.*

Siangtan (Xiangtan), *c.*, Hunan prov., China; tea ctr.; rice, cotton, hemp; coal-mng. in a.; p. (1953) *184,000.*

Siauliai, *t.*, Lithuanian S.S.R.; 115 m. N.W. of Vilnius; impt. rly junction; food inds.; p. (1959) *60,000.*

Šibenik, *t.*, Jugoslavia; naval base; fishing, weaving, woollens, chemicals; bauxite; p. (1959) *23,000.*

Siberia, *terr.*, U.S.S.R.; from the Ural Mtns. to Sea of Okhotsk and Bering Strait, bounded by the Arctic on the N., and on the S. by Mongolia and Turkestan; climate mostly severe; ch. ts. Novosibirsk (cap. W.S.) and Irkutsk (cap. E.S.); rich in coal, iron, minerals; oil and gas in W. Siberian lowland; resources not yet fully known; a. 4,210,420 sq. m.; p. (1959) *18,228,000.*

Siberut, *I.*, S. of Sumatra, Indonesia.

Sibi, *t.*, W. Pakistan; gypsum mng.

Sibiu, *t.*, Central Romania; linen, leather, brewing; p. (1959) *95,878.*

Sibu, *t.*, Sarawak, Malaysia; 80 m. up R. Rejang; p. (1960) *29,630.*

Sicily, *the lgst. I.*, Mediterranean Sea; former kingdom and now an aut. region of Italy; produces corn, oranges, olives, silk, almonds, sardines, sulphur and salt; oil in dist. of Ragusa, Gela Fontasarossa; pleasant climate; mountainous, highest point the volcano Mt. Etna; ch. ts. Palermo, Catania, Messina; a. 9,926 sq. m.; p. (1961) *4,711,783.*

Sicuani, *t.*, S. Peru, S. America; alt. 11,650 ft.; agr. and pastoral dist. ctr.; p. *15,000.*

Sidamo, *see* **Galla and Sidamo.**

Sidi-bel-Abbès, *t.*, W. Algeria; wheat, barley, tobacco, olives, vines; cattle, wool; footwear, bricks, furniture, cheese, macaroni; p. (1954) *81,000.*

Sidi-Kacem (Petit Jean) *t.*, Morocco, N.W Africa; oilfield and refinery; p. (1960) *19,478.*

Sidlaw Hills, *low mtn. range*, Angus, Perth, Scot.

Sidmouth, *mkt. t.*, *urb. dist.*, Devon, Eng.; on S. cst., 15 m. S.E. of Exeter; seaside resort; Honiton lace, gloves; p. (1961) *11,139.*

Sidon, *cst. t.*, Lebanon; on Mediterranean, S. of Beirut; terminal of oil pipe-line from Saudi Arabia; refinery; p. *17,695.*

Siedlce, *t.*, Poland; E. of Warsaw; p. (1960) *32,000.*

Siegburg, *t.*, N. Rhine–Westphalia, Germany; on R. Sieg; Benedictine abbey; dyes, iron, ceramics.; p. (1963) *34,100.*

Siegen, *t.*, N. Rhine–Westphalia, Germany; on R. Sieg; 2 cas.; iron-mining and smelting, machin., leather; p. (1963) *49,600.*

Siemianowice Slaskie, *t.*, Poland; nr. Katowice; (1960) *62,000.*

Siena, *hill-town*, Tuscany, Italy; 32 m. S. of Florence; spreads over three hilltops with Piazza del Campo in between where celebrated Palio festival (horse-races) are held; 13th- and 14th-cent. arch., cath.; agr. mkt., tanning, glass, textiles, bricks; *panforte* confectionery; tourist ctr.; p. (1961) *62,215.*

Siero, *t.*, Oviedo, Spain; on R. Nora; agr., livestock-raising, coal-mining; p. *30,931.*

Sierra da Estrella, *see* **Estrella, Sierra da.**

Sierra de Baudo, *mtn. range*, Columbia, S. America.

Sierra de Gata, *mtn. range*, Portugal–Spain.

Sierra de Gredos, *mtn. range*, Central Spain.

Sierra de Guadarrama, *mtn. range*, Central Spain.

Sierra Leone, *ind. sov. st.* within British Commonwealth (1961), W. Africa, situated between Guinea and Liberia; covered with ranges of hills; ch. prod., palm kernels, ginger, piassava, kolas; iron ore, diamonds, chromite, gold; cap. Freetown; a. 27,925 sq. m.; p. (1963) *2,183,000*

Sierra Madre, *mtn. range*, W. cst., Mexico and Guatemala.

Sierra Mojada, *mtn. range*, Central Mexico.

Sierra Morena, *mtn. range*, Spain; between Guadalquivir and Guadiana basins, highest point 5,500 ft.

Sierra Nevada, *mtn. range*, Granada, Spain, highest summit, Mulhacen.

Sierra Nevada, *mtn. chain*, Cal., U.S.A.; highest peak Mt. Whitney, alt. 14,898 ft.

Sierra Nevada de Mérida, *mtn. range*, W. Venezuela S. America; extends N.E. from San Cristóba to Barquisimeto; extension of E. range o Andes, alt. over 16,000 ft.; impt. coffe plantations from 3,000 to 6,000 ft. on slopes.

Sierra Nevada de Santa Marta, *mtns.*, Colombia S. America; summits over 19,000 ft.

Sighet, *t.*, N. Romania on U.S.S.R. frontier; p (1956) *22,361.*

Siglufjörd, *spt.* N. Iceland; herrings; p. (1962 *2,625*

Siguiri, *t.*, Guinea, W. Africa; on R. Niger; gold p. *11,000.*

Siirt, *t.*, Turkey; S. of Bitlis; p. (1960) *22,898.*

Sikang, *former prov.*, China; included in Szech wan prov. 1955. [*13,000*

Sikasso, *t.*, Mali, W. Africa; mkt., route ctr.; p

Sikkim, *st.* E. Himalayas, adjoining Tibet, Nepa and Bhutan; dense forests, with rich flora an orchidaceæ, but rice and corn grown in clearings India–Tibet tr. routes run through st.; cap Gangtok; lge. copper deposits nr. Ranikhola Gangtok; a. 2,745 sq. m.; p. (1961) *161,080.*

Sila La, *mtn. massif*, Calabria, S. Italy; granit

mass occupying full width of peninsula; alt. over 3,500 ft., max. 6,327 ft.

Silchester, *par.*, Hants, Eng.; between Basingstoke and Reading; impt. ctr. of the Roman road system; many Roman remains.

Silesia (Polish **Ślask**, Czech **Slezsko**), *geographical region*, Europe; extends on both sides of Oder R.; rich in coal, zinc, iron, arsenic; farming, sugar-beet, cereals, fruit, general ind.; has frequently changed hands, in 1919 was divided between Germany (70%), Poland (25%), and Czechoslovakia (5%); in 1945 the former German part became Polish, now forms 2 provs., caps. Katowice and Wroclaw; p. *4,764,500*; the Czechoslovakian part is united with Moravia; p. *200,000*.

Silistra, *t.*, Bulgaria; on N.E. Romanian border, on Danube R.; cloth, distilleries, sawmills, grapes; p. (1956) *20,350*.

Silkeborg, *t.*, Jutland, Denmark; W. of Aarhus; paper, textiles; (1960) *24,465*. [coal, grain.

Silloth, *resort*, on Solway Firth, Cumberland, Eng.;

Silsden, *t.*, *urb. dist.*, W.R. Yorks, Eng.; on R. Aire, 4 m. N.W. of Bingley; p. (1961) *5,142*.

Silva Porta, *t.*, Angola, Africa; admin. t.; cattle, agr. ctr.; p. *4,671*.

Silver City, *t.*, N.M., U.S.A.; gold, iron, silver; cattle; health resort; p. (1960) *6,972*.

Silver Spring, *t.*, Md., U.S.A.; sub. to Wash.; p. *43,294*.

Simalur, *I.*, S. of Sumatra, Indonesia.

Simcoe, *L.*, N. of L. Ontario, Canada; 30 m. by 18 m.

Simeto, *R.*, Sicily, Italy; rises in central Sicily, flows E. across plain of Catania into Mediterranean; lower course bordered by malarial marshes; length 54 m.

Simferopol, *t.*, Ukrainian S.S.R.; on R. Salghir nr. Sevastopol; soap, candles, fruits, engin.; p. (1959) *189,000*.

Simla, *t.*, Punjab, India; alt. 7,075 ft. above sea, with sanatorium; p. (1961) *42,597*.

Simonstown, W. Cape Prov., S. Africa; naval sta., docks; p. (estd. 1963) *10,220* inc. *5,120* Europeans.

Simplon, *mtn.*, Switzerland; alt. 11,695 ft.; the pass over the Simplon (alt. 6,594 ft.) from Domodossola, Italy, to Brig in the Rhône valley, Switzerland, was originally made by Napoleon I. The Simplon rly. tunnel leads from Brig on the Swiss side to Iselle in the Val di Vedro on the Italian and is the longest in the world, 12¼ m.

Simpson Desert, S.E. of Alice Springs, Northern Terr., extending into S. Australia.

Sinai, *peninsula*, between Gs. of Aqaba and Suez, at head of Red Sea; a. 11,055 sq. m., mainly desert in N., granitic ridges in S. rising to 8,500 ft. at Jebel Katrun; Jebel Musa or Mt. Sinai (7,359 ft.) is one of numerous peaks; mineral resources; coalmine at Maghâra.

Sinaloa, *st.*, Mexico; on G. of Cal.; agr. and mining, rich in gold, silver, copper, iron and lead; cap. Culiacán; a. 22,580 sq. m.; p. (1960) *838,404*.

Sind, *prov.*, W. Pakistan; lower Indus valley; agr. depends on irrigation; Gudda barrage (1963) to irrigate large a.; adm. ctr. Karachi; cereals, hemp, cotton, indigo; a. 50,443 sq. m.; p. (1951) *4,619,000*.

Sindara, *t.*, Gabon, Africa; admin. ctr.

Sines, *spt.*, S. Portugal; birthplace of Vasco da Gama; p. *6,094*.

Singapore, *I.* and *c.*, S. E. Asia; at tip of Malay pen.; indep. sovereign st. within Brit. Commonwealth on secession from Malaysian Fed. 1965; Brit. Govt. retained right to maintain military base; univ.; vast *entrêpot* tr.; a. 291 sq. m.; p. (1959) *1,550,000*.

Singen, *t.*, Baden-Württemberg, Germany; N.W. of L. Constance; foodstuffs, metals; p. (1963) *35,500*.

Singhbhum, *dist.*, Bihar, India; iron- and steel-wks; a. 5,191 sq. m.; p. (1961) *2,049,911*.

Sinhailien (**Xinhailion**), *c.*, Kiangsu, China; formed by merger of Sinpu, Tunghai and Lienyienkang; p. (1953) *208,000*.

Sining (**Xining**), *c.*, Tsinghai prov., China; wool, salt, timber; p. (1953) *94,000*.

Sinkiang-Uighur (**Xinjiang**), *aut. region*, China, bordering on Soviet Union and Kashmir; cereals, cotton, wool, silk; cap. Urumchi; a. 705,962 sq. m.; p. (1953) *4,873,608*.

Sinneh, *t.*, Iran; carpets; p. *32,000*.

Sinop, *Turkish t.*, on Black Sea in *I.* of same name; timber, silk; p. (1960) *8,999*.

Sinsiang (**Xinxiang**), *c.*, Honan prov., China; cotton weaving, flour milling; p. (1953) *171,000*.

Sintra (**Cintra**), *t.*, Portugal; summer resort, 18 m. from Lisbon; convention of S., 1808.

Sion, *cap.*, Valais, Switzerland; on R. Rhône; built on two castled hills; cath.; hydroelec. plant nearby; p. (1957) *10,904*.

Sioux City, Iowa, U.S.A.; on R. Missouri; meat-packing, foundries, elec. goods, cement; p. (1960) *89,159*.

Sioux Falls, *t.*, S.D., U.S.A.; on Big. Sioux R.; in rich wheat region; machin., cars, farming implements; nuclear reactor; p. (1960) *65,466*.

Sir Edward Pellew, *gr. of Is.*, N. Australia; in G. of Carpentaria.

Sirmur, *former Punjab st.*, India; now in Himachal Pradesh; p. (1961) *197,551*. [*53,884*.

Sitapur, *t.*, Uttar Pradesh, India; p. (1961)

Sitka (formerly **Novo Archangelsk**), *t.*, S.E. Alaska, U.S.A.; on Baranof I., in Sitka Sound; was ch. pt. of former Russian America; gold-mines; lumbering, canning; naval and coaling sta.; p. (1960) *3,237*.

Sitra, *I.*, Persia G.; forming part of st. of Bahrain, Arabia, 3 m. long and 1 m. wide; oil pipeline and causeway carrying road extends out to sea for 3 m. to deep-water anchorage.

Sittang, *R.*, Burma; rises in Pegu Yoma, flows S., enters G. of Martaban, Andaman Sea through delta; valley intensively cultivated, rice; delta forested; length 610 m.

Sittingbourne and Milton, *mkt. t.*, *urb. dist.*, Kent, Eng.; on Milton Creek, 9 m. E. of Chatham; paper-mills, brick-wks.; cement; insecticides; ctr. of fruit-growing dist.; p. (1961) *23,616*.

Sivas, *Turkish I.*, rich in minerals, has mineral springs with fertile grain-growing soil, fine orchards and vineyards, besides timber forests; cap. Sivas; p. (1960) *674,063*.

Sivas, *t.*, Turkey; in the Kizil Irmak valley; mnfs. woollens; p. (1960) *93,849*. [U.S.S.R.

Sivash or **Putrid Sea**, lagoon on E. side of Crimea,

Siwa, *oasis*, Egypt; in Libyan Desert, 300 m. S.W. of Alexandria; dates, olives, remains of temple of Ammon and the fountain of the Sun; 20 m. long, 1 m. wide; p. *1,000*.

Sizewell, Suffolk, Eng.; nuclear power sta.

Sjælland, I., Denmark; lgst. I.; agr., fishing, mnfs.; ch. t. Copenhagen; a. 2,840 sq. m.; p. (1960) *1,771,557*.

Skagen, *t.*, N. Denmark; on cst. of the Skagerrak; fishing, tourism; p. (1960) *10,390*.

Skagerrak, arm of N. Sea, giving access to the Kattegat, between Norway and Denmark, 70–90 m. wide.

Skagway, *sm. spt.*, Alaska, U.S.A.; at head of Lynn Canal inlet, 400 m. N.W. of Prince Rupert; linked by rly. to Whitehorse on Upper R. Yukon; boomed in gold rush (in 1898, p. *15,000*), subsequently declined; p. (1960) *659*.

Skåne (**Scania**), *peninsula*, extreme S. of Sweden; corresponds approx. to cos. Malmöhus, Kristianstad; most favoured part of Sweden in relief, soil, climate; intensive farming, wheat, barley, sugar-beet, fodder crops, dairy cattle; ch. ts. Malmo, Lund, Hälsingborg; a. approx. 4,000 sq. m. [*250,180*.

Skaraborg, *co.*, Sweden; a. 3,269 sq. m.; p. (1961)

Skarzysko-Kamienna, *t.*, Kielce, Poland; p. (1960) *35,000*.

Skaw, The (**Grenen**), *C.*, at extreme N. of Denmark.

Skeena, *R.*, B.C., Canada; rises in N. Rocky Mtns., flows S.W. to Pac. Oc. at Prince Rupert; lower valley used by Canadian National Rly. from Edmonton (Alberta) to Prince Rupert via Yellowhead Pass; length approx. 400 m.

Skegness, *t.*, *urb. dist.*, Lindsey, Lincoln, Eng.; on E. cst. at entrance to The Wash; farming, vegetables; resort; light engin.; p. (1961) *12,843*.

Skelleftea, *t.*, N. Sweden; on Bothnia G., mng., chiefly copper, gold,; p. (1961) *22,730*.

Skelmersdale, *t.*, *urb. dist.* Lancs. Eng.; coal, bricks, drainpipes; designated "New Town" 1961; p. (estd. 1965) *8,695*.

Skelton and Brotton, *t.*, *urb. dist.*, N.R. Yorks, Eng.; at N. foot of Cleveland Hills, 10 m. E. of Middlesbrough; steel flooring; p. (1961) *13,186*.

Skerries, *spt.*, Dublin, Ireland; fishing; muslin, stones; p. (1951) *2,457*.

Skibbereen, *mkt.*, *spt.*, *urb. dist.*, Cork, Ireland; farming; p. (1961) *2,015*.

Skiddaw, *mtn.*, Cumberland, Eng.; E. of Bassenthwaite L.; alt. 3,054 ft.
Skien, *spt.*, Bratsberg, Norway; on R. Skien; saw-mills, ice, and timber tr.; p. (1960) *15,502.*
Skierniewice, *t.*, Lodz, Poland; S.W. of Warsaw; p. (1960) *22,000.*
Skipton, *t.*, *urb. dist.*, W.R. Yorks, Eng.; on R. Aire, 6 m. N.W. of Keighley; cotton and rayon; cas.; p. (1961) *12,988.*
Skive, *t.*, N. Jutland, Denmark; fishing; rly. ctr.; p. (1960) *15,558.* [engin.; p. *16,740.*
Skopin, *t.*, R.S.F.S.R.; S.E. of Moscow; lignite,
Skopje, *t.*, *cap.*, Macedonia, Jugoslavia; the ancient Scupi, one of oldest ts. in Balkans; almost completely destroyed by earthquake 26 July 1963 (over 1,000 deaths); chrome mines in neighbourhood; p. (1959) *167,000.*
Skövde, *t.*, Sweden; between Ls. Vänern and Vättern; garrison t., cars, cement; p. (1961) *23,946.*
Skowhegan, *t.*, Me., U.S.A.; p. (1950) *6,183.*
Skye, *I.*, lgst. of the Inner Hebrides, Inverness, Scot.; mountainous; sheep-farming and fisheries; only town, Portree; a. 547 sq. m.
Skyros, *I.*, Grecian Archipelago, E. of Evvoia (Euboea).
Slagelse, *old t.*, Sjaelland, Denmark; food inds.; iron and silver wks.; p. (1960) *20,562.*
Slaithwaite, *mkt. t.*, W.R. Yorks, Eng.; S.W. of Huddersfield.
Slanic, *t.*, Wallachia, Romania; on S. flank of Carpathian Mtns., 22 m. N. of Ploesti; impt. salt deposits; p. (1956) *6,842.*
Śląsk, *see* **Silesia.**
Slatina, *t.*, Romania; on R. Olt, 87 m. W. of Bucharest; ancient churches; p. (1956) *13,381.*
Slave, *R.*, N.W. Terr., Canada; flows into Gr. Slave L.
Slave Coast, portions of Guinea cst., W. Africa, embracing Dahomey and Nigeria.
Slavonia, former Crown land (with Croatia) of Hungary; now Jugoslavia.
Slavyansk, *t.*, Ukrainian S.S.R.; coal, chemicals, salt, engin.; p. (1959) *83,000.*
Sleaford, *mkt. t.*, *urb. dist.*, Kesteven, Lincoln, Eng.; 12 m. N.E. of Grantham; agr. and agr. implements, malting, seeds; p. (1961) *7,834.*
Sleepers, The, *gr. of Is.*, Hudson Bay, Canada.
Slezsko, *see* **Silesia.**
Slieve Bloom, *hill range*, Offaly and Laoghis cos., Ireland; highest point 1,733 ft.
Slieve Donard, *mtn.*, N. Ireland; highest of the Mourne Mtns., co. Down; alt. 2,796 ft.
Sligo, *cst. co.*, Connacht, Ireland; pasture, tillage, barren mtn., and turf; livestock, fishing; a. 737 sq. m.; p. (1961) *53,558.*
Sligo, *t.* Sligo, Ireland; on Sligo Bay; distilling, flour, fisheries; p. (1961) *13,138.*
Slioch, *mtn.*, Ross and Cromarty, Scot.; 3,217 ft.
Sliven, *t.*, E. Roumelia, Bulgaria; famous for black wine; p. (1956) *46,383.*
Slough, *t.*, *mun. bor.*, Bucks, Eng.; on river terrace N. of R. Thames, 23 m. W. of London; many light inds.; p. (1961) *80,503.*
Slovakia, *old prov.*, ČSSR.; consists largely of Carpathian Mtns.; ch. t. Kosice; a. 18,902 sq. m.; p. (1961) *4,175,017.*
Slovenia, *fed. unit*, Jugoslavia; cap. Ljubljana (Laibach); a. 6,266 sq. m.; p. (1959) *1,589,000.*
Slupsk (Stolp), *t.*, Pomerania, Poland; German before 1945; cas.; machin., agr. implements; p. (1960) *53,000.*
Småland, *dist.*, S. Sweden; barren upland area S. of L. Vättern; moorland, deciduous forest; contrasts greatly with remainder of S. Sweden.
Smederevo, *t.*, Serbia, Jugoslavia; nr. Belgrade; p. (1959) *22,000.*
Smethwick, *co. bor.*, Staffs, Eng.; N.W. sub. of Birmingham; machin., engin., iron, glass; p. (1961) *68,372.*
Smichov, *t.*, ČSSR.; on R. Vltava; connected by bridge with Prague; mnfs.; p. *54,370.*
Smith Sound, Arctic Canada; connects Kane Bay with Baffin Bay.
Smith's Falls, *t.*, Ont., Canada; rly. ctr.; p. (1961) *9,603.*
Smoky Hill, *R.*, Col., Kan., U.S.A.; trib. of Kansas R.; length 400 m.
Smolensk, *c.*, R.S.F.S.R.; on both banks of the R. Dnieper; tallow, linen, iron and copper smelting, engin.; p. (1959) *146,000.*
Smyrna, *see* **Izmir.**
Snaefell, *highest mtn.*, I. of Man; alt. 2,034 ft.
Snake R. or **Lewis Fork**, trib. of Columbia R., flows from Wyo. to Wash., U.S.A.; length 1,050 m. [mnfs.; p. *16,820.*
Sneek, *t.*, Friesland, Neth.; nr. Leeuwarden;
Sneeuwbergen, *mtn. range*, Cape Prov., S. Africa.
Snizort, Loch, *arm of sea* (14 m. long), N. of I. of Skye, Scot. [Norway; alt. 7,565 ft.
Snohetten, *mtn.*, highest in Dovrefjeld range,
Snowdon, *mtn.*, nr. Caernarvon, Wales; (highest in Eng. and Wales); alt. 3,571 ft.
Snowy, *R.*, N.S.W. and Victoria, Australia; rises in Mt. Kosciusko, flows S. into Bass Strait 80 m. W. of C. Howe; length 220 m. Snowy Mtns. project (1950–75) to provide hydroelec. power and irrigation.
Soar, *R.*, Leicester, Nottingham, Eng.; rises in uplands of S. Leics, flows N.W. through Leicester, Loughborough, into R. Trent nr. Long Eaton; hosiery and knitwear inds. in lower valley; 43 m. long.
Sobat, *R.*, Sudan, N.E. Africa; rises in S.W. of Abyssinian Highlands, flows N.W. into R. Nile 80 m. below L. No; one of ch. sources of Nile flood-water; Abyssinia receives monsoon rains April to Oct., max. discharge into White Nile, Nov. and Dec.; length over 500 m.
Soche, *see* **Yarkand.**
Sochi, *t.*, R.S.F.S.R.; on Black Sea at foot of main Caucasian range; health resort with subtropical climate and sulphur springs; developed since 1933; p. (1959) *95,000.*
Society Is., *archipelago*, S. Pac. Oc.; between the Tuamotu Archipelago and Friendly Is., under Fr. protection; ch. I. Tahiti; ch. prod. phosphate and copper; cap. Papeete; p. *37,303.*
Socotra, *Brit. I.*, G. of Aden, Indian Ocean; S. of Arabia and E. of C. Guardafui; livestock; exports "Dragon's Blood", myrrh, frankincense, aloes; a. 1,382 sq. m.; p. *c. 9,000.*
Sodbury, *rural dist.*, Glos, Eng.; aircraft, bricks, quarrying, coal-mining; p. (1961) *44,826.*
Söderhamn, *spt.*, Sweden; on G. of Bothnia, N. of Gavle; timber, wood-pulp, iron, engin.; p. (1961) *13,010.*
Södermanland, *co.*, Sweden; S.W. of Stockholm; a. 2,634 sq. m.; p. (1961) *227,615.*
Södertälje, *t.*, Sweden; on L. Malar; engin., tools, machin., cars, aluminium; p. (1961) *33,152.*
Soerabaya or **Surabaya**, *spt.*, Java, Indonesia; dockyards and arsenal; oil; exp. coffee, rice, cotton, sugar, tapioca; p. (1961) *1,007,000.*
Soerakarta, or **Solo**, *t.*, Java, Indonesia; p. (1961) *368,000.*
Soest, *c.*, N. Rhine–Westphalia, Germany; cath.; iron ind.; p. (1963) *34,200.*
Sofala and Manica, *prov.*, Mozambique; N. of Inhambane; by some identified with the "Land of Ophir" of the Bible; cap. Beira.
Sofia, *t.*, *cap.*, Bulgaria; the ancient Sardica, and the Triaditza of the Byzantine Greeks; on Golem Isker R.; univ.; sugar, beer, flour, leather, silk, tobacco, maize, linen, engin., chemicals; p. (1959) *671,000.*
Sogn og Fjordane, *co.*, Norway; a. 7,135 sq. m. p. (1963) *100,467.*
Sogne Fjord, longest in Norway.
Sohâg, *t.*, U.A.R.; on R. Nile; p. (1960) *62,000.*
Soignies, *t.*, Belgium; on R. Senne; granite, flax p. (1962) *10,946.*
Soissons, *t.*, Aisne, France; iron, copper, farm implements, glass, sugar; p. (1954) *20,484.*
Söke, *t.*, Turkey; liquorice, fruits, cereals, livestock; emery, lead; p. (1960) *23,442.*
Sokoto, *t.*, Nigeria, W. Africa; groundnuts, rice cotton, cattle, hides and skins. Founded 180 as cap. of native st. of S., pop. mainly Haus and Fulani. p. *48,000.*
Sol Iletsk, *t.*, R.S.F.S.R.; near Kazakhsta border; potash; p. *10,000.*
Soleftea, *t.*, Västernorrland, Sweden; on G. o Bothnia; p. (1961) *9,888.*
Solent, The, *strait* separating the I. of Wight fror the mainland; extends from Hurst Castle t Calshot.
Soleure (Solothurn), *can.*, N. Switzerland; arabl pastoral, and afforested; a. 306 sq. m.; (1961) *200,816.*
Solihull, *co. bor.*, Warwick, Eng.; 5 m. S.W. Birmingham; motor wks., drawing office equi ment, stellite alloys mftg.; p. (1961) *96,010.*
Solikamsk, *t.*, R.S.F.S.R.; on R. Kama; potas and magnesium salts; chemicals, fertiliser paper; p. (1956) *41,200.*

Solingen, *t.*, N. Rhine-Westphalia, Germany; 15 m. E. of Düsseldorf; cutlery ctr.; p. (1963) *172,200.*
Sóller, *t.*, Majorca, Spain; p. (1957) *9,377.*
Solna, *t.*, nr. Stockholm, Sweden; p. (1961) *51,094.*
Solnechnyy, *t.*, R.S.F.S.R.; New Town 35 m. W.N.W. Komsomolsk; tin-mng.
Solomon Is., *Brit. prot.*, S. Pac.; inc. all Is. in 900-m. archipelago, S. and S.E. of large I. of Bougainville; copra, trochus shell, timber; a. 11,500 sq. m.; p. (1959) *124,076.*
Solor I., Lesser Sunda Is., Indonesia; a. 114 sq. m.
Solothurn, *can.*, N.W. Switzerland; crossed by Jura mtns. and R. Aar; agr., pastoral, industl.; a. 306 sq. m.; p. (1961) *200,816.*
Solothurn (Soleure), *t.*, *cap.*, can. Solothurn, Switzerland; on R. Aar; watches, jewellery, cottons, motor production; p. (1957) *16,744.*
Sölvesborg, *spt.*, Sweden; tanneries; p. *4,246.*
Solway Firth, *arm* of Irish Sea, between Dumfries, Kirkcudbright, Scot., and Cumberland; length 40 m.
Somaliland, *region*, N.E. Africa; "the Eastern Horn of Africa," from the Strait of Bab-el-Mandeb S. to the Equator.
Somaliland, French, *col.*, N.E. Africa; extends inland. 90 m. from straits of Bab-el-Mandeb; comprised of plain, mainly below 600 ft. alt.; hot, dry climate; shark and mother of pearl fisheries; salt, coffee, hides, oil-seed; cap. Djibouti (linked by rly. to Addis Ababa); a. 8,900 sq. m.; p. (estd. 1960) *67,000.*
Somali Republic, *ind. sovereign st.* since 1 July 1960, comprising former U.N. trust terr. under Italian adm. (cap. Mogadishu) and former British Somaliland Prot. (cap. Hargeisa) which achieved ind. June 26, 1960; consists of torrid coastal strip from bdy. of Kenya N. along Indian Oc. up to 300 m. inland and strip along G. of Aden, up to 150 m. inland; hot, dry climate (tempered inland by alt.); cattle, maize, food-crops, hides; total a. 246,200 sq. m.; p. (1961) *1,990,000.*
Sombor, *t.*, Serbia, Jugoslavia; cattle, grain; p. [(1962) *37,800.*
Sombrero I., Brit. Leeward Is., W.I.; phosphate of lime; Board of Trade lighthouse.
Somerset, *S.W. co.*, Eng.; bounded inland by Glos, Devon, Wilts and Dorset; pasture, arable, orchard and woodland, with mines, quarries and mnfs.; impt. fisheries; co. t. Taunton; a. 1,620 sq. m.; p (1961) *598,556.*
Somerset West, *t.*, Cape Province, S. Africa; wine, fruit, veg.; explosives, fertilisers, chemicals; p. (1960) *8,234* inc. *4,225* whites.
Somersworth, *t.*, N.H., U.S.A.; on Salmon Falls R.; mnfs.; p. (1960) *8,529.*
Somerville, *c.*, Mass., U.S.A.; sub. of Boston; varied mnfs.; p. (1960) *94,697.*
Somme, *dep.*, N. France; mainly agr. with thriving textile inds.; cap. Amiens; a. 2,443 sq. m.; p. (1962) *488,225.*
Somme, *R.*, France; flows in deps. Aisne and Somme to English Channel; length 116 m.
Sommen, *L.*, Sweden (25 m. by 8 m.) 15 m. E. of L. Vättern.
Somport Tunnel, on bdy. France–Spain; carries main rly. from Pau to Zaragoza under Central Pyrenees; length 5 m.
Sönderborg, *spt.*, S. Jutland, Denmark; resort; cas. (military barracks); p. (1960) *20,653.*
Sondrio, *prov.*, Lombardy, Italy; silk; a. 1,233 sq. m.; cap. Sondrio; p. (1961) *18,717.*
Songea, *t.*, Tanzania, E. Africa; admin. ctr.; wheat, coffee, tobacco.
Song-koi (Red R.), *R.*, rises in Yunnan plateau, S.W. China, flows S.E. through N. Vietnam, enters G. of Tongking; Hanoi is nr. head of delta; Haiphong nr. one of R. mouths; lower valley densely populated and intensively cultivated; length approx. 800 m.
Sonneberg, *t.*, Suhl, E. Germany; toys; p. [(1963) *29,231.*
Sonora, *st.*, Mexico; on G. of Cal.; silver-mines, stock-raising, grain, cotton, sugar, fruit, tobacco growing; cap. Hermosillo; a. 70,477 sq. m.; p. (1960) *783,378.*
"Soo" Canals, *see* **Saulte Ste. Marie Canals.**
Soochow (Suzhou), *c.*, Kiangsu, China; nr. Shanghai; former treaty pt.; silk, weaving and exp.; cotton, rice; p. (1953) *474,000.*
Sopot, *spa, seaside resort*, Poland; on W. shore of Gdańsk B.; p. (1960) *44,000.*
Sopron, *t.*, N.W. Hungary; on R. Hunte; holiday resort; p. (1962) *42,333.*
Sorata, *t.*, Bolivia; 57 m. W. La Paz; nr. Andes peak of Ancohuma (Illampú); p. *2,000.*
Sorau, *see* **Zary.**
Sorel, *t.*, Quebec, Canada; sawmills, foundries, engin.; p. (1961) *17,147.*
Soria, *prov.*, Old Castile, Spain; agr. and cattle-rearing, with cheese, timber, wool and salt exp.; cap. Soria; a. 2,977 sq. m.; p. (1959) *154,987.*
Soria, *t.*, *cap.*, Soria, Spain; on R. Douro; p. [(1957) *21,500.*
Soriano, *dep.*, Uruguay; a. 3,561 sq. m.; cap. Mercedes; p. (1953) *99,927.*
Sormova, *industl. sub.*; 6 m. W. of Gorkiy on R. Volga; Byelorussian S.S.R.; machin., diesel motors, boilers, ships, tanks.
Soro, *t.*, Själland, Denmark; p. *3,191.*
Sorocaba, *t.*, Brazil; rly. wks.; textiles, cement, footwear, wines, fertilisers; p. (1960) *109,258.*
Soroti, *t.*, Uganda; E. Africa; on Kioga L.; admin. ctr.; cotton ginning.
Sorrento, *cst. t.*, S. Italy; nr. S. extremity G. of Naples; popular resort, anciently celebrated for its fine wines; p. *26,325.*
Sör-Tröndelag, *see* **Tröndelag.**
Sosnowiec, *t.*, S.W. Poland; rly. junction; coal, iron, textiles; p. (1960) *132,000.*
Sotteville-lès-Rouen, *t.*, Seine-Maritime, France; rly. wks.; p. (1954) *25,625.*
Soudan, French. *See* **Mali.**
Soufrière, *mtn.*, Basse-Terre I., Lesser Antilles Gr. W. Indies; volcanic; highest peak in Lesser Antilles; alt. 4,869 ft.
Sound, The, *channel* between the Kattegat and the Baltic, 3 m. across at narrowest part from Sweden to the Zealand cst.
Sousse (Susa), *spt.*, Tunisia; p. (1956) *48,172.*
South Africa, Republic of, *ind. rep.* (withdrew from Br. Commonwealth May 31, 1961), compr. provs. Cape Province, Natal, Transvaal and O.F.S.; climate, Mediterranean to tropical; vegetation, evergreens in C. region, grassland (veld) in E.; cereals, cotton, sugar, vines, citrus fruit, sheep and cattle, ostriches, gold, diamonds, coal, copper, tin, various mnfs.; admin. cap. Pretoria, legislative cap. Cape Town; a. (inc. Walvis Bay) 472,685 sq. m.; p. (1960) *15,982,664.*
South America, *continent*; physical features, cst. regular except in S.W.; Andes Mtns. along whole of W. cst., Brazilian Highlands on E. cst., rolling plains in ctr.; climate, diverse, varying with latitude and alt.; equatorial, hot and wet; Atacama, a rainless desert on middle W. cst. In S. temperate; vegetation, varying with latitude, alt., climate, from coniferous, deciduous and tropical forest to tropical and temperate grasslands and deserts; ch. inds.; temperate and tropical agr.; cocoa, coffee, sugar-cane, rubber, cereals; cattle, sheep; minerals; gold, silver, copper, tin, diamonds, nitrates; factory inds. developing gradually; races: Europeans, mainly of Spanish and Portuguese descent, Indians, Negroes, mulattoes and mestizos (mixed races); a. 7,300,000 sq. m.; p. (estd.) *80,000,000.*
South Arabia, Federation of, comprises 17 member sts. mainly in the former W. Aden Prot.; amirates of Dhala and Beihan, sultanates of Lahej, Audhali, Lower Aulaqi, Upper Aulaqi, Fadhli, Lower Yafa, Haushabi and Wahidi, sheikdoms of Aqrabi, Upper Aulaqi, Alawi and Mallahi, sts. of Dathina and Shaibi, and Aden.
South Bend, *c.*, Ind., U.S.A.; carriage and wagon wks., iron foundries, paper- and flour-mills, farming implements, aeroplanes; seat of Notre Dame University; p. (1960) *132,445.*
South Carolina, *st.*, U.S.A.; level in E., and mtns. in W.; cereals, cotton, tobacco; textiles, chemicals, lumber; cap. Columbia; ch. pt., Charleston; a. 31,055 sq. m.; p. (1960) *2,382,594.*
South Coast, *t.*, Queensland, Australia; p. (1957) *22,800.*
South Dakota, *st.*, U.S.A.; mixed farming, wheat; gold, silver, gypsum, lumbering, flourmilling, butter, cheese, meat-packing; cap. Pierre; a. 77,047 sq. m.; p. (1960) *680,514.*
South Downs, *range chalk hills*, Sussex and Hants, Eng.
Southern Arabia, Protectorate of, the name adopted by Aden on accession to Federation (Jan. 1963).
South Gate, *industl. t.*, Cal., U.S.A.; paint, chemicals, tiles, furniture, tires, machin.; p. (1960) *53,831.*

South Georgia, *Brit. I.*, S. Atl. Oc.; a. 1,450 sq. m.; mtns., whaling ctr.
South Holland, *prov.*, Neth.; flat, intersected by Rs. and dykes; cap. The Hague; a. 1,130 sq. m.; p. (1960) *2,706,810*.
South I., *lge. I.*, N.Z.; contains S. Alps (highest Mt. Cook, 12,349 ft.), Canterbury Plains; wool, mutton, dairy prod., fruit; Benmore hydroelec. sta., on Waitiki R.; a. 58,093 sq. m.; p. (1961) *729,925* inc. *6,920* Maoris.
South Kensington, *dist.*, in W. London; contains Victoria and Albert Museum, Geological and Science Museums, British Museum of Natural History, Commonwealth Institute, Albert Hall.
South Molton, *mkt. t.*, *mun. bor.*, Devon, Eng.; at S. foot of Exmoor, 10 m. S.E. of Barnstaple; textiles, cosmetics; p. (1961) *2,994*.
South Orange, *t.*, N.J., U.S.A.; p. (1960) *16,175*.
South Orkney Is., Antarctica; whaling; met. sta.
South Portland, *c.*, Me., U.S.A.; on Portland harbour; p. (1960) *22,788*.
South Sandwich Is., Antarctica; whaling.
South Shetland, *Brit. archipelago*, S. Atlantic; 400 m. S. C. Horn.
South Shields, *t.*, *co. bor.*, Durham, Eng.; on S. bank at mouth of R. Tyne; coming holiday resort; coal, engin., lingerie; p. (1961) *109,533*.
Southall, *t.*, *former mun. bor.*, Middlesex, Eng., now inc. in Ealing outer bor. Greater London (*q.v.*); residtl.; many varied light inds.; p. (1961) *52,983*.
Southam, *mkt. t.*, *rural dist.*, Warwick, Eng.; 5 m. S.E. of Leamington; lime, cement, mineral spring; p. (1961) *15,457*.
Southampton, *c.*, *spt.*, Hants, Eng.; at head of Southampton Water on peninsula between estuaries of Rs. Test and Itchen; univ.; extensive docks for passenger-liners and other shipping, engin.; p. (1961) *204,707*.
Southampton, *C.*, S. pt. of Coates I., Hudson Bay, Canada.
Southampton Water, *inlet*, Hants, Eng.; comprises drowned estuaries of Rs. Itchen and Test; gives access from Solent and Spithead to spt. of Southampton; length 9 m., width 1–1½ m.
Southborough, *t.*, *urb. dist.*, Kent, Eng.; in ctr. of The Weald, 2 m. N. of Tunbridge Wells; residtl.; chalybeate spring; p. (1961) *9,770*.
Southbridge, *t.*, Mass., U.S.A.; optical instruments and cutlery; p. (1960) *15,889*.
Southend-on-Sea *t.*, *co. bor.*, Essex, Eng.; on N. side of Thames estuary; wireless factory, varied light inds.; air ferry terminal; p. (1961) *165,093*.
Southern Alps, *range of mtns.*, S.I., N.Z.
Southern Cross, *t.*, *rly. junction*, W. Australia; on main Transcontinental Rly. 220 m. E. of Perth; gold-mines, now declining.
Southern Ocean, surrounds Antarctica; pack ice.
Southern Rhodesia, *see* **Rhodesia**.
Southgate, *former mun. bor.*, Middlesex, Eng.; now inc. in Enfield outer bor. Greater London (*q.v.*); residtl.; p. (1961) *72,359*.
Southland, *prov.*; S.I., N.Z.; cap. Invercargill; big agr. a.; wheat, meat, wool; a. 11,170 sq. m.; p. (1961) *93,697*.
Southport, *t.*, *co. bor.*, Lancs, Eng.; on S. side of Ribble estuary; 18 m. N. of Liverpool; seaside resort; residtl.; p. (1961) *81,976*.
Southport, *wat. pl.*, Queensland, Australia; 50 m. S. of Brisbane; pastoral, dairying, fruit-growing and timber dist.; p. (1947) *8,432*.
Southsea, *dist.*, Portsmouth, Hants, Eng.; seaside resort.
Southwark, *inner bor.*, London, Eng.; incorporating former bors. of Bermondsey and Camberwell; p. (1964) *312,687*.
Southwell, *mkt. t.*, *rural dist.*, Notts, Eng.; cath.; coal-mining, agr.; p. (rural dist. 1961) *45,818*.
South-West Africa, mandate of Rep. of S. Africa; mostly desert, scanty rainfall; cattle, ostriches; diamonds, tin, copper; cap. Windhoek; a. 318,261 sq. m.; p. (1961) *525,064*.
Southwick, *urb. dist.*, W. Sussex, Eng.; on S. cst. 4 m. W. of Brighton; p. (1961) *11,874*.
Southwold, *spt.*, *mun. bor.*, E. Suffolk, Eng.; on E. cst. 8 m. S. of Lowestoft; fishing; resort; p. (1961) *2,228*.
Soviet Harbour, *spt.*, G. of Tartary, R.S.F.S.R.; sawmilling; p. (1954) *75,000*.
Sowerby Bridge, *t.*, *urb. dist.*, W.R. Yorks, Eng.; on R. Calder, 3 m. W. of Halifax; woollens; p. (1961) *16,224*.
Sowjetsk (Tilsit), *t.*, R.S.F.S.R.; German before 1945; on R. Memel; cas.; foodstuffs, machin., wood; p. (1956) *34,100*.
Sozh, *R.*, Ukrainian S.S.R.; trib. of R. Dnieper; length 240 m. [p. (1962 *9,040*.
Spa, *t.*, Liége, Belgium; mineral springs, resort;
Spain, *kingdom* (without a sovereign), S.W. Europe; interior plateau; climate varied, very hot summers, warm rainy winters, N.W. mild, and wet, central plateau extremes of heat and cold; evergreen trees and shrubs; cereals, vines, citrus fruits, olives, nuts; sheep, goats, pigs; coal, copper, iron, lead, zinc, mercury, colophony, turpentine, cork; mnfs. wine, sugar, silk, brewing; leading ind. tourism; cap. Madrid; a. 189,890 sq. m.; p. (1950) *27,976,755*.
Spalding, *mkt. t.*, *urb. dist.*, Holland, Lincoln, Eng.; in The Fens, 10 m. up the R. Welland from The Wash; agr., bulb mkt., agr. machin., sugar-beet, fruit canning; p. (1961) *14,821*.
Spandau, *t.*, Potsdam, E. Germany; firearms, gunpowder; previously gr. military ctr.
Spanish Guinea, *Spanish col.*, Central West African cst.; divided into two provs. with aut. status; Rio Muni (cap. Bata) and Fernando Po (cap. Santa Isabel); a. 10,800 sq. m.; p. (estd. 1960) *214,000*.
Spanish Sahara, *Spanish col.*, N.W. African cst.; comprising Rio de Oro and Saguia el Hamra; a. 105,000 sq. m.; p. (estd. 1963) *26,000* (nomadic). [*665*.
Spanish Wells, *I.*, Bahamas, W. Indies; p. (1953)
Sparrows Point, *t.*, Md., U.S.A.; situated on Chesapeake Bay at entrance to Bear Creek; impt. iron and steel ind.
Sparta, *famous ancient c.*, the Morea, Greece; on the R. Eurotas; passed under Roman rule, 146 B.C.; p. (1961) *10,412*. [*44,352*.
Spartanburg, *t.*, S.C., U.S.A.; cotton; p. (1960)
Spartel, *C.*, International Zone, N.E. Africa.
Spartivento, *C.*, Italy; most S. point of Italian mainland.
Spenborough, *mun. bor.*, W.R. Yorks, Eng.; textiles, plastics, wire; p. (1961) *36,412*.
Spencer Gulf, *lge. inlet*, S. Australia; penetrates 240 m. inland, max. width 75 m.
Spennymoor, *t.*, *urb. dist.*, Durham, Eng.; 5 m. S. of Durham; mnfs.; p. (1961) *19,104*.
Sperrin Mtns., Tyrone and Londonderry, N. Ireland.
Spey, *R.*, Inverness, Moray, and Banff, the most rapid in Scot., flows N.E. to Moray Firth; length 107 m.
Speyer, *c.*, Rhineland-Palatinate, Germany; cas., its famous Diet of 1529 condemning the Reformation gave rise to the term "Protestant"; textiles, tobacco, machin., footwear, beer, sugar, paper; p. (1963) *39,800*.
Spezia, La, *spt.*, Liguria, Italy; on Bay of Spezia; arsenal, docks, maritime inds., elec. machin., and olive oil; p. (1961) *121,191*.
Spice Is., *see* **Moluccas**.
Spitalfields, *par.*, E. London, Eng.; former silk-weaving dist., introduced by Huguenots, 17th. cent.
Spithead, *roadstead*, between Portsmouth and the I. of Wight, Eng.; used by ships of Royal Navy.
Spitsbergen (Svalbard), *I. gr.*, belonging to Norway; well within Arctic Circle; mountainous; sealing and whaling; coal-mining; asbestos, copper, gypsum, iron, marble, mica, zinc and phosphate deposits; a. 24,294 sq. m.; p. (1956) Norwegian *1,530*, Russian *2,746*.
Split (Spalato), *c.*, Jugoslavia; wine, olive oil, bauxite, shipping; p. (1959) *84,000*.
Splügen Pass, Rhaetian Alps; between Lombardy and Grisons, Switzerland; alt. 6,939 ft.
Spokane, *R.*, Idaho, U.S.A.; flows to the R. Columbia at Washington; length 120 m.
Spokane, *t.*, Wash., U.S.A.; on R. Spokane, at the fall which is used for hydro-elec. power; gr. timber tr., flour and sawmills, mng.; cement, elec. goods; p. (1960) *181,608*.
Spoleto, *t.*, Perugia, Italy; truffles; p. *32,600*.
Spondon, *t.*, Derby, Eng.; on R. Derwent, 3 m. E. of Derby; textiles; nylon plant projected 1964.
Sporades, *I.*, Grecian Archipelago in the Ægean and neighbouring seas; belonging to Greece, includes Samos, Kos, etc.
Spree, *R.*, E. Germany; flowing W. past Berlin to the Havel at Spandau; length 227 m.
Spremberg, *t.*, Cottbus, Germany; on R. Spree; lignite, mining, glass, elec., metals, cloth, bicycles, machin.; p. (1963) *22,931*.

Springbok, *t., cap.,* Namaqualand, Cape Prov., S. Africa; copper-mining; p. (1960) *3,111.*
Springfield, *c., cap.,* Ill., U.S.A.; gr. rly. ctr.; iron, watches, etc.; p. (1960) *83,271.*
Springfield, *c.,* Mass., U.S.A.; mnfs. cars, elec. apparatus and paper; p. (1960) *174,463.*
Springfield, *c.,* Mo., U.S.A.; flour milling; Congregational college; p. (1960) *95,865.*
Springfield, *c.,* Ohio, U.S.A.; agr. implements, motor lorries; p. (1960) *82,723.*
Springfontein, *t.,* O.F.S., S. Africa; rly. ctr.; p. (1960) *2,850* inc. *758* whites.
Springs, *t.,* Transvaal, Rep. of S. Africa; E. of Johannesburg; gold mng., engin., machin., cars, elec. goods; uranium plant; p. (1960) *135,231* inc. *36,445* whites.
Springsure, *t.,* Queensland, Australia; rly. term.; wheat; p. *1,113.*
Spurn Head, *C.,* E. Yorks, Eng.; at mouth of Humber estuary.
Sretensk, *t.,* R.S.F.S.R.; coal, machin., leather, woodworking.
Srinagar, *t., cap.,* Kashmir, India; on R. Jhelum in W. Himalayas; 5,263 ft. above sea-level; silver and copper wares, carpet weaving, paper; univ.; p. (1961) *285,257.*
Sriracha, *t.,* Thailand; sawmills; oil refinery being built; p. *81,471.*
Stade, *t.,* Lower-Saxony, Germany; nr. Hamburg; leather, wood, textiles; p. (1963) *31,400.*
Staffa, *I.,* the Inner Hebrides, W. Scot.; 6 m. N. Iona, off W. cst. Mull; Fingal's Cave, 227 ft. long, with other basaltic caves.
Stafford, *co. t., mun. bor.,* Staffs, Eng.; on R. Sow, 15 m. N. of Wolverhampton; elec. engin., concrete; engin., footwear, salt; p. (1961) *47,814.*
Staffordshire, *W. midland co.,* Eng.; rich in iron and coal, the "Black Country" being famous; also lge. Potteries dist., famous breweries, and many thriving mnfs.; co. t. Stafford; a. 1,153 sq. m.; p. (1961) *1,733,887.*
Staines, *mkt. t., urb. dist.,* Middx., Eng.; on R. Thames, 4 m. S.E. of Windsor; linoleum, machin., petrol engines; p. (1961) *49,838.*
Stainmore, *pass,* N.R. Yorks, Eng.; crosses N. Pennines from Greta valley into upper Eden valley; used by main road but only minor rly.; alt. 1,370 ft.
Stalin, *see* **Brasov.**
Stalin Canal, *see* **Volga Baltic Waterway.**
Stalinabad *see* **Dushanbe.**
Stalingrad, *see* **Volgograd.**
Stalino *see* **Varna.**
Stalino, *see* **Donetsk.**
Stalinogorsk, *see* **Novomoskovsk.**
Stalinsk, *see* **Novokuznetsk.**
Stalybridge, *t., mun. bor.,* Cheshire, Eng.; on R. Tame, 5 m. E. of Manchester; cotton and wool, engin., plastics, rubber goods, elec. cables; p. (1961) *21,940.*
Stamboul, *see* **Istanbul.**
Stamford, *c.,* Conn., U.S.A.; on shore of Long I. Sound; p. (1960) *92,713.*
Stamford, *mkt. t., mun. bor.,* Kesteven, Lincoln, Eng.; 10 m. N.W. of Peterborough; agr. inds., elec. goods, plastics; p. (1961) *11,743.*
Standerton, *t.,* Transvaal, S. Africa; on R. Vaal; livestock, oats; p. (1960) *16,868* inc. *6,698* Europeans.
Standish-with-Langtree, *urb. dist.,* Lancs, Eng.; 4 m. N.W. of Wigan; coal-mining, silk mftg.; p. (1961) *9,689.*
Stanger, *t.,* Natal, S. Africa; tea, sugar, maize, wattle; p. (1960) *9,557* inc. *1,740* whites.
Stanimaka *see* **Asenovgrad.**
Stanislaus, *R.,* Cal., U.S.A.; trib. of the San Joaquin R.; length 200 m.
Stanislav, *see* **Ivano-Frankovsk.**
Stanley, *t., urb. dist.,* Durham, Eng.; 10 m. N.W. of Durham; mnfs.; p. (1961) *46,280.*
Stanley, *spt., cap.,* Falkland Is.; whaling; p. (estd. 1958) *1,135.*
Stanley, *urb. dist.,* W.R. Yorks, Eng.; p. (1961) *16,749.*
Stanley Falls, on the Upper Congo R., Congo, Africa; nr. the Equator, named after the explorer, Sir H. M. Stanley.
Stanley Pool, an expansion of the Lower Congo, Africa; 25 m. long, 16 m. wide.
Stanleyville, *t.,* Congo, Africa; on R. Congo nr. Stanley Falls; named after the explorer; p. *27,312.*
Stanlow, inc. in Ellesmere Port, urb. dist., Cheshire; petrol ref., oil-storage dks. and terminal; chemicals.
Stanovoi Mtns., *range of mtns.,* U.S.S.R.; extends from N. of R. Amur to nr. Sea of Okhotsk.
Stans, *cap.,* half-can. Nidwalden, Switzerland.
Star of the Congo, *t.,* Katanga, Congo, Africa; copper-mining.
Stara Planina (Balkan Mtns.), Bulgaria; highest peak, 7,780 ft.
Stara Zagora, *t.,* Central Bulgaria; copper smelting, mineral springs; nitrogen fertiliser plant; p. (1956) *55,322.*
Stargard Szczecinski, *t.,* Poland; prev. in Prussia; woollens, machin., cottons, spirits; p. (1960) *31,000.*
Start Point, *C.,* nr. Dartmouth, Devon, Eng.
Stassfurt, *t.,* Magdeburg, E. Germany; potash salts, chemicals, machin., metals; p. (1963) *26,166.*
Staten I., the most S. point N.Y. st., U.S.A.; shipyards; linked with Brooklyn by Verrazano–Narrows bridge (opened 1964); also island off Tierra del Fuego, S. America, 45 m. long.
States of the Church or **Papal States,** former indep. terr. under the temporal rule of the popes, prior to 1870; comprised Latium, Umbria, the Marches, E. Emiglia-Romagna.
Stavanger, *spt.,* Rogaland, Norway; margarine and preserved-food, woollen mills, fish curing and canning, shipbldg.; oil refinery at Sola under construction; p. (1960) *52,799.*
Staveley, *t., urb. dist.,* Derby, Eng.; 3 m. N.E. of Chesterfield; coal, iron, chemicals; p. (1961) *18,071.*
Stávnice, *t.,* ČSSR.; impt. mining ctr., producing silver, copper, lead.
Stavropol, *t.,* S. terr., R.S.F.S.R., U.S.S.R.; engin., natural gas; p. (1959) *140,000.*
Stawell, *t.,* Victoria, Australia; 150 m. N.W. of Melbourne; gold-mining, agr., pastoral and tobacco growing dist.; p. (1957) *5,720.*
Steelton, *bor.,* Penns., U.S.A.; steel foundries; p. (1960) *11,266.*
Steep Holm I., Bristol Channel, Eng.
Steep Rock, *see* **Atikokan.**
Stellenbosch, *t.,* C. Prov., Rep. of S. Africa; 25 m. E. of Cape Town; univ.; wines, sawmilling, brick and tile mkg.; p. (1960) *22,233* inc. *10,673* Europeans.
Stendal, *c.,* Magdeburg, E. Germany; cath.; iron, sugar wks.; p. (1963) *37,204.*
Stepney, *see* **Tower Hamlets.**
Sterlitamak, *t.,* Bashkir, R.S.F.S.R.; on S.W. flank of Ural Mtns., 120 m. N.E. of Chkalov (Orenburg); impt. oil-refineries on "Second Baku" oilfield; linked by pipeline to Stavropol; p. (1959) *111,000.*
Šternberk, *t.,* Moravia, ČSSR.; N. of Olomouc; textile mftg.; p. (1961) *11,215.*
Stettin, *see* **Szczecin.**
Steubenville, *c.,* Ohio, U.S.A.; iron, steel, paper, glass, coal, natural gas; p. (1960) *32,495.*
Stevenage, *t.,* Herts, Eng.; 4 m. S.E. of Hitchin; one of "New Towns" designated 1946; agr., light engin., school furniture, elec. goods, chemicals, aircraft parts; p. (estd. 1965) *54,149.*
Stevenston, *sm. burgh,* Ayr, Scot.; p. (1961) *10,174.*
Stewart, *R.,* trib. of R. Yukon, N.W. Terr., Canada.
Stewart I., S. or S.I., N.Z.; a. 670 sq. m.; oysters.
Stewarton, *burgh,* Ayr, Scot.; 5 m. N. of Kilmarnock; woollens, carpets; p. (1961) *3,387.*
Steyning, *vil.,* E. Sussex, Eng.; on R. Adur, 4 m. N. of Shoreham at entrance to gap through S. Downs; residtl.; p. *1,875.*
Steyr, *t.,* Austria; on R. Enns, nr. Linz; bicycles, lorries, small-arms factories; p. (1961) *38,306.*
Stilton, *vil.,* Huntingdon, Eng.; 6 m. S.W. Peterborough; famous for cheese.
Stinchar, *R.,* Ayr, Scot.; flows W. to sea at Ballantrae; length 30 m.
Stirling, *ancient burgh,* Stirling, Scot.; on R. Forth in gap between Campsie Fells and Ochil Hills; cas.; univ.; coal-mng., engin., concrete, rock, wool, rubber gds; p. (1961) *27,553.*
Stirling, *midland co.,* Scot., borders Firth of Forth; coal-mining, agr., textiles; a. 466 sq. m.; p. (1961) *194,858.*
Stockerau, *t.,* Austria; machin., chemicals; p. (1961) *11,853.*
Stockholm, *c., cap.,* Sweden; on Is. at outlet of L. Malar; called the "Queen of the Baltic" for

the beauty of its surroundings; comm. ctr.; machin., textiles, leather, sugar, chemicals; many academic institutions; p. (1961) *808,484.*
Stockport, *t., co. bor.,* Cheshire, Eng.; on R. Mersey, 5 m. S.E. of Manchester; cotton, hats, engin.; p. (1961) *142,469.*
Stocksbridge, *urb.dist.,* W.R. Yorks; p. (1961) *11,137.*
Stockton, *t.,* Cal., U.S.A.; farm implements, flour, lumber; p. (1960) *86,321.*
Stockton-on-Tees, *mkt. t., mun. bor.,* Durham, Eng.; 4 m. W. of Middlesbrough; impt. iron and steel inds., plywood; first rly. for passenger traffic opened in 1825 between Stockton and Darlington; 18th cent. town hall; racecourse; p. (1961) *81,198.*
Stoke-on-Trent, *c., co. bor.,* Staffs, Eng.; at S.W. foot of the Pennines; formed in 1910 by union of the "five towns" of Arnold Bennett's novels, Hanley, Burslem, Tunstall, Longton, and Fenton (with Stoke-upon-Trent); ceramics, coal, iron and steel, engin., brick and tile wks., precast concrete; p. (1961) *265,506.*
Stoke Newington, *see* **Hackney.**
Stokesley, *mkt. t., rural dist.,* N.R. Yorks, Eng.; 7 m. S. of Middlesbrough; agr.; p. (rural dist. 1961) *25,571.*
Stolberg, *t.,* N. Rhine–Westphalia, Germany; E. of Aachen; metals, glass, wood, chemicals; p. (1963) *38,200.*
Stolp, *see* **Slupsk.**
Stone, *mkt. t., urb. dist.,* Staffs, Eng.; on R. Trent, 7 m. S. of Stoke-on-Trent; footwear, tiles, porcelain, scientific glassware; p. (1961) *8,791.*
Stoneham, *t.,* Mass., U.S.A.; boots and shoes; p. (1960) *17,821.*
Stonehaven, *fishing t., burgh,* Kincardine, Scot.; on E. cst., 14 m. S. of Aberdeen; distilling, net mftg.; p. (1961) *4,500.*
Stonehenge, *prehistoric gr. of monumental stones,* on Salisbury Plain, Wilts, Eng.; date of erection estd. between 1860–1560 B.C.
Stonehouse, *par.,* Lanark, Scot.; coal, linen; p. *4,204.*
Stony Stratford, *mkt. t.,* Bucks, Eng.; on R. Ouse, nr. Buckingham; engin., lace.
Stornoway, *spt., burgh,* Ross and Cromarty, Scot.; on E. cst. of I. of Lewis, Outer Hebrides; ctr. Harris Tweed ind.; fishing ctr.; p. (1961) *5,221.*
Stour, *R.,* Kent, Eng.; flows past Canterbury to Pegwell Bay; length 40 m.
Stour, *R.,* Somerset, Dorset, and Hants, Eng.; trib. of R. Avon; length 55 m.
Stour, *R.,* Suffolk and Essex, Eng.; flows E. to sea at Harwich; length 42 m.
Stour, *R.,* Worcs, and Staffs, Eng.; trib. of R. Severn; length 20 m.
Stourbridge, *t., mun. bor.,* Worcs, Eng.; on R. Stour, 9 m. W. of Birmingham; coal, iron and steel, brick and glass wks.; p. (1961) *43,917.*
Stourport-on-Severn, *urb. dist., mkt. t.,* Worcs, Eng.; at confluence of Rs. Stour and Severn; carpets, iron and steel goods, porcelain, ceramics; p. (1961) *11,751.*
Stowmarket, *t., urb. dist.,* Suffolk, Eng.; on R. Gipping, 11 m. N.W. of Ipswich; I.C.I. paint factory ctr.; p. (1961) *7,790.*
Strabane, *t., urb. dist.,* Tyrone, N. Ireland; salmon fishing, agr. ctr.; p. (1961) *7,786.*
Straits Settlements, *former Brit. crown col.,* Malay Peninsula; comprised Penang, Malacca, and Singapore, estbl. 1867, dissolved 1946; Christmas I., the Cocos Is. and Labuan were at various times part of the col. *See* **Malaya, Malaysia.**
Stralsund, *spt.,* Rostock, E. Germany; opposite Rügen I.; grain tr., machin., metals, fish smoking, shipbldg.; p. (1963) *68,791.*
Strand, *t.,* Cape Province, S. Africa; resort; p. (1960) *13,313* inc. *7,067* whites.
Strangford Lough, *arm of sea,* Down, N. Ireland; 18 m. long, 6 m. wide at entrance.
Stranraer, *burgh,* Wigtown, Scot.; at head of Loch Ryan; steamer service to Larne, Antrim, N. Ireland; creameries, brewing, knitwear; p. (1961) *9,249.*
Strasbourg, *fortfd. c., cap.,* Bas-Rhin, France; on R. Ill just above confluence with R. Rhine; captured 1870, regained 1918; fine cath., univ., imperial palace, many handsome new public bdlgs.; extensive tr.; oil refining; machin., tanning, jewellery, printing, hardware; exp. hops, sausages, famous pies, beer; p. (1962) *233,549.*
Stratford, *dist.,* E. London, Eng.; in bor. Newham; mftg.
Stratford, *c.,* Ontario, Canada; woollens, farm machin., flour, sawmills, engine wks.; p. (1961) *20,467.*
Stratford, *t.,* on R. Housatonic, Conn., U.S.A.; aircraft; p. (1960) *44,712.*
Stratford-on-Avon, *t., mun. bor.,* Warwick, Eng.; on R. Avon, 11 m. S.W. of Leamington; birthplace of Shakespeare; memorial theatre, library, tourist ctr.; light inds.; p. (1961) *16,847.*
Strathaven, *t.,* Lanark, Scot.; cas.; knitwear, agr. engin., fibre glass; p. *4,207.*
Strathmore, *lowland belt.,* central Scot.; extends from Crieff N.E. to Montrose; flanked to N. by Scot. Highlands, to S. by Sidlaw, and Ochil Hills; drained by Rs. Earn, Tay, Isla, S. Esk; famous for cereals and small fruits; length 60 m., width 7–10 m.
Strathpeffer, *wat. pl.,* Ross and Cromarty, Scot.; 5 m. W. of Dingwall; spa.
Strathspey, *valley of the Spey,* Scot.; 70 m. long.
Stratton and Bude, *resort,* N. Cornwall, Eng.; 12 m. S. of Hartland Point; p. (1961) *5,095.*
Straubing, *t.,* Bavaria, Germany; on R. Danube; cas.; brewing, tiles, chemicals, machin.; p. (1963) *36,700.*
Strawberry, *R.,* Utah, U.S.A.; on E. slopes of Wasatch Mtns. 80 m. S.E. of Salt Lake City; dammed to supply irrigation water, led through 3½ m. tunnel under Wasatch Mtns. to 100 sq. m. cultivable land round L. Utah.
Streator, *c.,* Ill., U.S.A.; bricks, glass, hardware, farm implements; p. (1960) *16,864.*
Street, *t., urb. dist.,* Somerset, Eng.; at foot of Polden Hills, 7 m. S.W. of Wells; footwear, leather, vehicle wks.; p. (1961) *6,660.*
Stresa, *vil.,* Piedmont, Italy; favourite health resort on L. Maggiore; p. (estd.) *4,500.*
Stretford, *mun. bor.,* S.E. Lancs, Eng.; sub. of Manchester; engin., chemicals; p. (1961) *60,331.*
Stromboli, *I.,* Lipari Is., N. of Sicily, Tyrrhenian Sea; active volcano, alt. 3,038 ft.; p. *853.*
Stromness, *mkt. burgh, pt.,* Mainland, Orkney Is., Scot.; 13 mm. W. Kirkwall; p. (1961) *1,477.*
Stromstad, *spt.,* Sweden; on Skagerrak; seaside resort; shipbldg.; fishing; p. (1961) *4,039.*
Stronsay, Orkney Is., Scot.
Stroud, *mkt. t., urb. dist.,* Eng.; in Cotswold Hills, on R. Frome; cloth, carpets, plastics, engin.; p. (1961) *17,461.*
Strumble Head, *promontory,* N. Pembroke, Wales.
Stryj, *R.,* Poland; trib. of R. Dniester.
Stryj, *t.,* Poland; sawmills, matches; p. *25,000.*
Sturminster Newton, *mkt. t., rural dist.,* Dorset, Eng.; on R. Stour, 6 m. N.W. of Blandford; creameries; p. (rural dist. 1961) *9,566.*
Sturt Desert, area N.E. of S. Australia.
Stuttgart, *c. cap.,* Baden-Württemberg, Germany; on R. Neckar; cas., cath.; cars, machin., elec. engin., hosiery, knitwear; route ctr.; oil refinery nearby; p. (1963) *640,500.*
Styr, *R.,* Poland; trib. of R. Prypei (Pripet); length 250 m.
Styria, *prov.,* Austria; grain, wine and fruit; stock-rearing, tourist tr.; a. 6,326 sq. m.; p. (1961) *1,137,865.*
Styrian Alps, that portion of the Alpine mtn. system E. of the Hohe Tauern.
Suakin, *former pt.,* Sudan, N.E. Africa; on Red Sea; now used only for pilgrim traffic to Jeddah.
Suanhwa (Xuanhua), *c.,* Hopeh prov., China; iron mng.; p. (1953) *114,000.*
Subotica, *t.,* Serbia, Jugoslavia; boots, rly. material, farming, stock-raising; p. (1959) *80,000.*
Suceava, *t.,* S. Bukovina, Romania; former residence of Moldavian princes; fancy leather; p. (1959) *23,000.*
Suchan, *t.,* R.S.F.S.R.; coal; p. (1956) *48,900.*
Süchow (Suzhou), *c.,* Kiangsu, China; on Tai-Hu, 40 m. W. of Shanghai; gr. comm. and industl. ctr., silks, cottons, rice; p. (1953) *c. 373,000.*
Sucre, *cap.,* Chuquisaca dep. and legal cap. of Bolivia; univ. and cath.; cement plant.; p. (1962) *54,270.*
Sucre, *st.,* Venezuela; cap. Cumana; p. (1961) *401,992.*
Sudan, The, *ind. sovereign st.* since Jan. 1956, N.E. Africa; formerly Anglo–Egyptian condominium; bounded by Egypt, Libya, Chad, Central African Rep., Congo, Uganda, Ethiopia, and Red Sea; cotton, gum arabic, hides, ground

nuts, sugar; cap. Khartoum; a. 967,500 sq. m.; p. (1961) *12,109,000*.

Sudanese Republic. *See* **Mali.**

Sudbury, *t., mun. bor.,* W. Suffolk, Eng.; on R. Stour, 12 m. N.W. of Colchester; p. (1961) *6,643*.

Sudbury, *t.,* Ontario, Canada; nickel, copper; p. [(1956) *46,025*.

Sudeten Mtns., *range,* Poland, Czechoslovakia; separating Bohemia and Moravia from Silesia.

Suez, *spt.,* U.A.R., N.E. Africa; at head of G. of Suez (arm of Red Sea) and S. entrance of Suez Canal, which crosses the Isthmus of Suez to the Mediterranean at Port Said and is of very gr. value to shipping; the ancient Arsinoë; Port Tewfiq adjoining has quay and docks; p. (1960) *203,000*.

Suez, *G.,* Red Sea; N.W. arm of Red Sea between Arabian Desert and Sinai Peninsula, Egypt; southern approach to Suez Canal; length 190 m. width varies from 12 to 25 m.

Suez Canal, *ship canal,* U.A.R., N.E. Africa; connects Mediterranean Sea (Pt. Said) with Red Sea (Suez) through Ls. Manzala, Timsah and Bitter; saves over 4,000 m. on journey N.W. Europe to India, 1,000 m. to Australia; opened 1869; length, 101 statute m.

Suffolk, *most E. maritime co.,* Eng.; bounded by Essex, Norfolk, Cambridge and the N. Sea; mixed agr., dairying; fisheries; mnf. of agr. implements; civil nuclear power-sta. at Sizewell, due 1966; co. t. Ipswich; a. 1,482 sq. m. divided for admin. purposes into Suffolk E. p. (1961) *342,696* and Suffolk W. p. (1961) *129,969*.

Suhl, *t.,* Suhl, E. Germany; toys, armaments; p. (1963) *26,907*

Suir, *R.,* Ireland; flows E. to Waterford Harbour.

Suiyuan, *former prov.,* China; now incorporated in Inner Mongolia Aut. Reg.

Sukhumi, *spt.,* Georgian S.S.R.; resort; sawmilling; p. (1959) *64,000*.

Sukkur, *t.,* Pakistan; on. R. Indus, 230 m. N.E. of Karachi; gr. dam for irrigation; thermal sta. under construction; p. (1961) *103,000*.

Sulaiman, *mtns.,* Asia; range bounding the Punjab and Baluchistan. [*272,442*.

Sulaimaniya, *liwa,* Iraq; a. 4,554 sq. m.; p. (1956).

Sulawesi (Celebes), *I.,* Indonesia; mtnous., forested; copra, coffee, bauxite; ch. pt. Menado, Makasar; a. 73,160 sq. m.; p. (1961) *7,079,349*.

Sulina, *t.,* Romania; at mouth of Sulina branch of Danube R.; considerable grain tr.; p. *3,622*.

Sullana, *t.,* N. Peru; rly. ctr.; maize, cotton, cinchona bark, fishing, whaling; p. (1961) *23,000*.

Sultanabad, *t.,* Persia; carpet mftg.; p. *55,000*.

Sulu Is., Philippines; archipelago between Borneo and the Philippines; a. 950 sq. m.; acquired by the U.S.A. 1898.

Sumatra, *I.,* Malay Archipelago, Indonesia; coffee, sugar, rice, pepper; gold, tin, petroleum, coal; a. 161,612 sq. m.; p. (1961) *15,739,363*.

Sumba, *I.,* Indonesia; part of Timor Archipelago.

Sumbawa, one of the Nusa Tenggara Is., Indonesia; in E. Indian Archipelago, E. of Lombok; a. (inc. nearby Is.) 5,240 sq. m.; p. *314,843*.

Sumgait, *t.,* Azerbaydzhan S.S.R.; on Caspian Sea; 25 m. N.W. of Baku; metallurgical ind.; chemicals; p. (1959) *52,000*.

Sumy, *t.,* Ukrainian S.S.R.; engin., chemicals, textiles; p. (1959) *97,000*. [m. long.

Sunart, Loch, *sea arm,* Argyll cst., W. Scot.; 19½

Sunbury-on-Thames, *urb. dist.,* Middx., Eng.; W. of London; residtl., water wks., gravel pits; petrol research establishment; p. (1961) *33,437*.

Sunda Strait, between Java and Sumatra, In donesia; 13 m. wide, contains the volcanic I. of Krakatao.

Sundarbans, The, *tract of forest and swamps,* fringing the delta of the Ganges, E. Pakistan; 165 m. long, 81 m. wide; rice grown in N.; tigers and crocodiles found in S.

Sunday I., lgst. of Kermadec Is., N.Z.; 20 m. in circuit and with a p. of *10* is the only one of the Kermadec Is. that is inhabited; met. and radio sta. established on I.

Sunday, *R.,* Cape Prov., S. Africa; flows into Algoa Bay; length 200 m.

Sunderland, *spt., co. bor.,* Durham, Eng.; at mouth of R. Wear; gr. shipbldg. and coal-exp. ctr. (inc. Monkwearmouth and parts of Bishopwearmouth), best gas coal, also engin., glass, paper and rope; fine harbour, piers and docks; p. (1961) *189,629*.

Sundsvall, *spt.,* Västernorrland, Sweden; on a wide bay of the Baltic nr. Hernösand; timber and wood-pulp inds.; p. (1961) *29,493*.

Sungari, *R.,* N. China; trib. of R. Amur; inc. the Nonni; length over 1,000 m.

Sungpan, *t.,* Szechwan, China; silver, gold, lead; linseed oil, paper; smelting, engin.

Superior, *c.,* Wis., U.S.A.; at head of L. Superior; gr. tr. in grain, timber, coal, shipbldg. and flour mills; oil refining; p. (1960) *33,563*.

Superior, *L.,* N. America; lgst. sheet of fresh water in the world; lies between Canada and the U.S.A.; one of the chain of gr. Ls. in the St. Lawrence system; outlet to L. Huron by the St. Mary's R., receives the waters of the St. Louis, Pigeon and Nipigon; a. 32,000 sq. m.

Surat, *c.,* Gujarat, India; on R. Tapti; cotton, silk, embroidery; p. (1961) *288,026*.

Surbiton, *former mun. bor.,* Surrey, Eng., on R. Thames, nr. Kingston; now inc. in Royal Borough of Kingston-upon-Thames (*q.v.*); residtl.; light engin., bricks, tiles, elec. components; p. (1961) *62,940*.

Suresnes, *t.,* Seine, France; p. (1962) *40,151*.

Surinam, *R.,* Neth. Guiana, S. America; flows N. to Atl. Oc. nr. Paramaribo; length 300 m.

Surinam (Neth. Guiana), *Dutch col.,* S. America; ch. exp. bauxite, timber, rubber, rice, fruit; cap. Paramaribo; a. 55,000 sq. m.; p. (1959) *264,372*.

Surinumu Dam, 30 m. from Port Moreby, Papua; part of hydro-elec. scheme; opened 1963.

Surrey, *S. co.,* Eng.; S. of R. Thames; cereals, livestock, vegetables; residtl.; a. 722 sq. m.; p. (1961) *1,733,036*.

Sus, *R.,* S. prov. Morocco, N. Africa; flowing to the Atlantic nr. Agadir; length 130 m.

Susa, *see* **Sousse.**

Susquehanna, *R.,* N.Y., Penns., and Md., U.S.A.; flows to Chesapeake Bay through highly industl. a.; routeway, W. from Philadelphia and Baltimore across Appalachian Mtns.; length 422 m.

Sussex, *maritime co.,* S.E. Eng.; adjoining Surrey, Kent and Hants, and washed by Eng. Channel; traversed E. to W. by the S. Downs; co. t. Lewes; a. 1,457 sq. m.; divided administratively into Sussex E. p. (1961) *664,669* and Sussex W. p. (1961) *411,224*.

Susten Pass, *modern alpine road,* alt. 7,296 ft., between Haslital and Reuss valley, links Bernese Oberland with Gotthard road.

Sutherland, *N. co.,* Scot.; N.W. Moray Firth, washed by Atlantic and N. Sea; grazing and forest land, most sparsely pop. in Scot.; mountainous, with many lochs; co. t. Dornoch; a. 2,102 sq. m.; p. (1961) *13,442*.

Sutherland Falls, Milford Sound, S.I., N.Z.; height 1,904 ft.

Sutlej, *R.,* West Pakistan; rises in the Himalayas and flows to the R. Indus; used for lge.-scale irrigation; length 1,000 m.

Sutton, *outer bor.,* Greater London, Eng.; inc. former bors. of Beddington and Wallington, Sutton and Cheam, and Carshalton; p. (1964) *169,019*.

Sutton Coldfield, *t., mun. bor.,* Warwick, Eng.; 6 m. N.E. of Birmingham; hardware, plastics; television transmitter; p. (1961) *72,143*.

Sutton-in-Ashfield, *t., urb. dist.,* Notts, Eng.; 3 m. S.W. of Mansfield; coal, light engin.; hosiery; p. (1961) *40,438*.

Suva, *c., cap.,* Fiji Is.; on Viti Levu I., fine harbour; p. (1956) *37,371*.

Suwalki, *t.,* N.E. Poland; nr. Lithuanian S.S.R. bdy.; timber, grain, woollens; p. (1960) *20,000*.

Suwannee, *R.,* Fla., and Ga., U.S.A.; flows to G. of Mexico; known as "Swanee River," length 250 m.

Svalbard, *see* **Spitsbergen.**

Svendborg, *spt.,* Fyn, Denmark; mnfs., earthenware, tobacco, exp. butter; p. (1960) *23,892*.

Sverdlovsk, *t.,* R.S.F.S.R.; on R. Iset, at E. base of the Ural Mtns.; steel, engin., chemicals, textiles; p. (1962) *853,000*. [of White Sea.

Sviatoi Nos, *C.,* Arctic cst., U.S.S.R.; nr. entrance

Svir, *R.,* U.S.S.R.; flowing between L. Onega and L. Ladoga; length 125 m.

Svistov, *t.,* Bulgaria; on R. Danube, Romanian border; p. (1956) *18,448*.

Svobodnyy, *t.,* R.S.F.S.R.; on R. Zeya, 105 m. N. of Blagoveshchensk; agr. equipment, sawmilling; p. (1959) *57,000*.

Svolær, *spt.,* Norway; ch. t. Lofoten Is.; fishing; p. (1961) *3,821*. [cap. Augsburg.

Swabia, *dist.,* Bavaria, Germany; a. 3,807 sq. m.;

Swabian Alps, *mtns.*, Württemberg, Germany; inc. the Swabian Jura range between valleys of Neckar and Danube.

Swadlincote, *t., urb. dist.*, Derby, Eng.; 3 m. E. of Burton-on-Trent; collys., potteries, engin., clothing; p. (1961) *19,222.*

Swaffham, *mkt. t., urb. dist.*, Norfolk, Eng.; forestry; p. (1961) *3,210.*

Swale, *R.*, N.R. Yorks, Eng.; joins R. Ure to form R. Ouse; length 60 m.

Swale, *channel*, between I. of Sheppey and Kentish mainland, Eng.; 16 m. long. [nr. Perth.

Swan, *R.*, W. Australia; flows to Indian Ocean,

Swan Hill, *t.*, Victoria, Australia; fruit growing and dairying under irrigation; p. (1957) *5,740.*

Swanage, *mkt. t., urb. dist.*, Dorset, Eng.; on bay, E. cst. I. of Purbeck; seaside resort; stone quarries; p. (1961) *8,112.*

Swanland, *region*, W. Australia; consists of extreme S.W. corner of W. Australia; hot, dry summers and mild winter with adequate rain; forests of Karri and Jarrah; agr. vines, citrus and deciduous fruits, wheat; highest pop. density in W. Australia; ch. ts. Perth, Fremantle, Bunbury.

Swansea, *spt., co. bor.*, Glamorgan, Wales; on Swansea Bay, Bristol Channel; univ. coll.; coal and iron, copper, steel, zinc, chemicals; lge. exp. anthracite, aluminium wire and cable, refrigerators; p. (1961) *166,740.*

Swat, *dist.*, Malakand, N.W. Frontier Agencies and Tribal Areas, Pakistan.

Swatow (Shantou), *c., spt.*, Kwangtung, S. China; on S.E. cst. nr. mouth of Han Kiang, 200 m. N.E. of Hong Kong; gd. harbour; fishing; sm. coastal tr., mainly with Hong Kong; exp. tangerines; p. (1953) *280,000.*

Swaziland, *Brit. prot.*, S. Africa; S.E. of the Transvaal; agr., maize, tobacco, fruit, cattle, asbestos, gold, tin, barytes, paper mills; seat of administration, Mbabane; a. 6,704 sq. m.; p. (estd. 1965) *285,000.*

Sweden, *kingdom*, N. Europe; forming E. (and larger) part Scandinavian Peninsula; mountainous W., but otherwise flat and dissected by Rs. and many Ls., while one-fourth of the land is forest; gr. timber exp. and mining of iron ore, lead, silver, arsenic; cereals, root crops, hay, livestock; mnfs., textiles, matches, machin., glass, chemicals, etc.; cap. Stockholm; a. 173,426 sq. m.; p. (1961) *7,495,129.*

Swidnica (Schweidnitz), *t.*, Lower Silesia, Poland; German before 1945; textiles, machin.; p. (1960) *39,000.*

Swift Current, *t.*, Saskatchewan, Canada; p. (1961) *12,186.*

Swilly, Lough, *arm of the Atlantic*, cst. of Donegal, Ireland; 25 m. long.

Swindon, *t., mun. bor.*, Wilts, Eng.; in upper Thames Valley (Vale of White Horse), 27 m. S.W. of Oxford; gr. rly. wks.; impt. rly. junction; mkt. for local dist.; heavy engin., textiles, tobacco, cars; p. (1961) *91,736.*

Świnemünde, *see* Świnoujście.

Świnoujście (Swinemünde), *spt.*, Pomerania, Poland, German before 1945; on I. of Usedom (Uznam), Baltic Sea; spt. for Szczecin; spa and summer resort; p. (1946) *5,771.*

Swinton, *t., urb. dist.*, W.R. Yorks, Eng.; in Don valley, 3 m. N.E. of Rotherham; coal, iron, potteries, bricks and tiles; p. (1961) *13,420.*

Swinton and Pendlebury, *mun. bor.*, Lancs, Eng.; 5 m. W. of Manchester; cotton spinning, coal, engin., accumulator mftg.; p. (1961) *40,450.*

Switzerland, *fed. rep.*, Cen. Europe; upland region, with Jura Mtns. on N. and Alps to S.; dairying, butter, cheese, chocolate, etc., wine; watches and clocks, elec. machin.; very dependent on lge. tourist tr.; 4 national languages; cap. Bern; a. 15,944 sq. m.; p. (1961) *5,429,061.*

Sydenham, *S.E., sub.*, London, Eng.; residtl.; site of the Crystal Palace, burnt down 1936.

Sydney, *c., cap.*, N.S.W., Australia; principal spt. on shore of Pt. Jackson Bay; many beautiful bdlgs. and parks, stretching S. to Botany Bay; univ.; lge. comm. and active inds.; magnificent bridge, harbour and docks; six-lane highway bridge under constr. p. (1961) *2,181,211.*

Sidney or S. Sydney, *spt.*, C. Breton I., Nova Scotia; iron and steelwks., coal, chemicals; p. (1956) *32,162.*

Sydney Mines, *t.*, Nova Scotia, Canada; coal; p. (1961) *9,122.*

Syktyvkar, *t.*, R.S.F.S.R.; on Vychegda R.; sawmilling, engin.; p. (1959) *64,000.*

Sylhet, *t.*, E. Pakistan; weaving and bamboo goods; p. *28,128.*

Syra, *I.* of the Cyclades, Ægean Sea; part of Greece; p. (1951) *33,775.*

Syracusa, *t.*, Sicily, Italy; on I. of Ortygia, off E. cst.; cath.; exp. olive oil, oranges, lemons, locust beans, almonds, wine, chemicals, pottery, etc; chemicals at Priolo; p. (1961) *90,333.*

Syracuse, *c.*, N.Y., U.S.A.; air conditioners, electronic equipment, jet engines; chemicals, salt, machin., cars, seat of Syracuse Univ.; p. (1960) *216,038.*

Syr Darya, *R.* Kazakhstan, U.S.S.R.; flowing into Aral sea.

Syrian Arab Republic, *rep.*, S.W. Asia; seceded from United Arab Rep. 28 Sept. 1961; stretches along E. shore of Mediterranean and E. to the R. Euphrates; chiefly agr.; cereals, olives, fruit, goats, sheep; silk, wool, cement, soap; cap. Damascus; a. 66,046 sq. m.; p. (estd. 1962) *4,839,000.*

Syzran, *t.*, R.S.F.S.R.; on R. Volga; petroleum refining, engin.; p. (1959) *148,000.*

Szarvas, *t.*, Hungary, S. of Mezötúr; industl; p. (1962) *18,950.*

Szczecin, *prov.*, Poland; cap. Szczecin; a. 12,100 sq. m.; p. (1961) *779,000.*

Szczecin (Stettin), *spt.*, Pomerania, Poland, German before 1945; at mouth of R. Odra (Oder); cas.; engin., iron, textiles, paper; p. (1960) *269,000.*

Szczecinek (formerly German Neustettin), *t.*, W. Polish Pomerania; p. (1960) *23,000.*

Szechwan (Sichuan), *prov.*, China; cereals, sugar, tea, cotton, silk, coal, iron, salt, petrol; cap. Chengtu; a. 144,996 sq. m.; p. (1953) *62,303,999.*

Szeged, *t.*, Hungary; on Theiss R., 100 m. S.E. of Budapest; univ.; cath.; gr. comm. and indstl. ctr.; leather, breweries, textiles; p. (1962) *102,000.*

Székesféhervár, *t.*, Hungary; nr. Budapest; wine, shoes; p. (1962) *57,757.*

Szentes, *t.*, Hungary; p. (1962) *30,979.*

Szeping (Siping), *c.*, Kirin prov., China; agr. distributing ctr.; cement; p. (1953) *126,000.*

Szolonok, *t.*, Hungary; on R. Tisza, E. of Budapest; machin., paper ind.; p. (1962) *47,919.*

Szombathely, *t.*, Hungary; rly. ctr.; textiles, wine, agr. implements; p. (1962) *55,849.*

Szóny, *t.*, Hungary; oil refining, linked to U.S.S.R. by "Friendship Oil Pipeline;" p. (1962) *4,600.*

T

Taasinge, *I.*, Denmark; S. of Fyn; 9 m. long; p. (1960) *4,866.*

Tabarka, *spt.*, Tunisia; mkt. exp. cork, tanning, charcoal; fishing; p. *1,500.*

Tabasco, *maritime st.*, Mexico; on Bay of Campeche, adjoining Guatemala; cacao, sugar-cane, tobacco, rubber, pepper, maize, rice and hard-woods; cap. Villa Hermosa; a. 9,782 sq. m.; p. (1960) *496,340.*

Tabatinga, *t.*, Brazil; on junction of Rs. Javari and Amazon.

Table Bay, *inlet of Atlantic*, cst. of C. of Gd. Hope, S. Africa; site of Cape Town.

Table Mountain, Cape Prov., S. Africa, nr. Cape Town; alt. 3,549 ft.

Tabor, *t.*, ČSSR.; S. of Prague, on R. Luznice; cigars, beer; p. (1961) *19,561.*

Tábor, Mt., N. Palestine; S.E. of Nazareth.

Tabora, *t.*, Central Tanzania; E. Africa; at junction of rlys. from Dar es Salaam and L. Victoria; agr.; p. (1960) *15,350.*

Tabriz, *prov. cap.*, Azerbaijan, Iran; gr. comm. ctr., formerly ch. emporium for the tr. of Persia in the W., much of which is now diverted by the rly. through the Caucasus; dried fruits, carpets; match factories; famous Blue Mosque; p. (1960) *319,000.*

Tabu, *spt.*, Ivory Cst., W. Africa; exp. palm oil, rice, cocoa, coffee.

Tachira, *st.*, Venezuela, S. America; cap. San Cristobal; p. (1961) *399,163.*

Tacna, *dep.*, Peru; terr. transferred by treaty from Chile, 1929; mainly desert; nitrate of soda, silver, copper; subject to earthquakes; a. 4,930 sq. m.; ch. t. T.; p. (1961) *69,176.*

Tacna, *t.*, Peru, airport, p. (1961) *18,000.*

Tacoma, *spt.*, Wash., U.S.A.; on Puget Sound; shipping, fishing, iron, steel, copper, electro-chemicals, aluminium; p. (1960) *147,979.*

Tacuarembo, *dep.* Uruguay, S. America; a. 8,112 sq. m.; cap. Tacuarembo; p. (1953) *119,658.*

Tadcaster, *rural dist.*, *mkt. t.*, on R. Wharfe, W.R. Yorks, Eng.; brewing, stone, paper board; p. (rural dist. 1961) *26,725.*

Tadmor, *see* Palmyra.

Tadoussac, *t.*, Quebec, Canada; on left bank of R. Saguenay, where it enters St. Lawrence R.; tourist ctr.; oldest settlement in Canada (1599).

Tadzhik, *constituent rep.*, U.S.S.R., cereals, cotton, fruit, horticulture, cattle breeding; minerals, gold, petroleum, coal; cap. Dushanbe; a. 55,700 sq. m.; p. (1959) *1,982,000.*

Taegu, *c.*, S.Korea; silk-spinning and cotton-ginning mills; p. (1962) *717,000.*

Taejon, *t.*, S. Korea; S. of Seoul; fish, petroleum, cereals; p. (1962) *269,000.*

Taff, *R.*, Glamorgan, Brecknock, Wales; rises in Brecon Beacons, flows S.E. across coalfield to Bristol Channel at Cardiff; length 40 m.

Tafilalet, Morocco, N. Africa; oasis of the Sahara, E. of Atlas; ch. t. Abuam; dates.

Taganrog, *spt.*, R.S.F.S.R.; on Sea of Azov; steel, engin.; p. (1959) *201,000.*

Tagliamento, *R.*, N.E. Italy; rises in Carnic Alps, flows S. into Adriatic Sea (G. of Venice); valley used by rly. from Venice to Vienna via Semmering Pass; length 100 m.

Tagus, *R.*, Spain and Portugal; flows W. across Meseta to Atlantic at Lisbon; length 540 m.

Tahiti, *principal I.*, of Society gr, French Polynesia; Pac. Oc.; fertile cst. land, picturesque; a. 402 sq. m.; cap. Papeete; p. (1962) *45,430.*

Tahoe, *L.*, Cal., Nevada, U.S.A.; in Yosemite National Park, Sierra Nevada, at alt. 6,225 ft., surrounded by summer resorts; a. 200 sq. m.

Taichow (Taizhou), *c.*, Kiangsu prov., China; rice ctr.; p. (1953) *160,000.*

Taif, *t.*, Hejaz, Saudi Arabia; 50 m. W. of Mecca; 5,900 ft. above sea-level; summer resort; honey, fruit, mat mkg., boat bldg.; p. *25,000.*

Taihape, *t.*, N.I., N.Z.; 161 m. N.E. of Wellington; in the King Country, on Hautapu R.; sheep and dairy farming, saw-milling; p. (1961) *2,684.*

Tai Hu, *L.*, Kiangsu, China; focus of intensive system of sm. canals and waterways 60 m. N. of Shanghai; a. approx. 100 sq. m.

Taima, *t.*, Saudi Arabia; cereals, dates, fruit, tobacco, rock salt.

Taimyr Peninsula, N. cst., Siberia, U.S.S.R.; terminates with C. Chelyuskin.

Tain, *burgh*, Ross and Cromarty, Scot.; on S. side of Dornoch Firth, 20 m. N.E. of Dingwall; p. (1961) *1,699.*

Tainan, *t.*, Taiwan, China; sugar, rice; p. (1957) *[229,500.*

Taipei, *cap.*, Taiwan; p. (1962) *927,000.*

Taiping, *t.*, Malaya; p. *41,361.*

Taiwan (Formosa), *I.*, China, 100 m. E. of mainland; U.S.A. protection; fishing, rice, tea, sugar, coal, gold, oil, natural gas; cap. Taipei; a. 13,890 sq. m.; p. (1959), *10,431,341* (excluding armed forces *600,000*).

Taiyuan, *c.*, Shansi, China; on Fuen-Ho; p. (1953) *721,000.*

Takamatsu, *t.*, Japan; N. cst. Shikoku; gr. tr.; [p. (1955) *212,537.*

Takaoka, *t.*, Honshu, Japan; ctr. of rice tr.; lacquer wk.; p. (1950) *142,046.*

Takasaki, *t.*, Honshu, Japan; coal mines, raw silk; radiation chemistry research ctr.; p. (1947) *82,582.*

Takoradi, *spt.* Ghana, West Africa; as spt. has superseded Sekondi; rly. to Kumasi thence to Accra; exp. cocoa, palm-oil, rubber, bauxite, gold, manganese, industl. gases; p. (1960) *41,000.*

Talara, *t.*, N. Peru, S. America; on C. Pariñas; oil refining; p. (1961) *40,000.*

Talavera, *c.*, Spain; on Tagus R.; cloth, leather, wine; p. (1957) *22,152.*

Talca, *prov.*, Chile; cap. Talca; a. 3,721 sq. m.; p. (1961) *226,052.*

Talca, *t.*, cap. Talca prov., Chile; S. of Santiago; lge. mftg. ctr.; matches, footwear, paper and flour mills, foundries; p. (1961) *80,277.*

Talcahuano, *spt.*, Chile, nr. Concepción; naval sta.; grain and exp. ctr.; steel plant at Huachipato; p. (1961) *99,231.*

Talence, *t.*, Gironde, France; p. (1954) *22,695.*

Talien (Dairen), *c.*, *spt.*, S. Liaoning prov., China; on Liaotung pen., Bay of Korea; together with Port Arthur adm. as part of special mun. of Luta (*q.v.*); p. (estd.) *1,432,000.*

Tallahassee, *c.*, Fla., U.S.A.; cigars; p. (1960) *48,174.*

Tallahatchee, *R.*, trib. of Miss., U.S.A.; flows S.W. and becomes R. Yazoo; length 240 m.

Tallin, *spt.*, *cap.*, Estonian S.S.R., U.S.S.R.; timber, shipbldg., textiles; p. (1962) *305,000.*

Taltal, *spt.*, Chile; S. of Antofagasta; exp. nitrates and silver; p. (1961) *5,897.*

Tamale, *ch. t.*, Northern Terr., Ghana, W. Africa; aerodrome; p. (1960) *49,223.*

Tamar, *R.*, Devon and Cornwall, Eng.; flows S. to Plymouth Sound; length 45 m.

Tamar, *R.*, Tasmania, Australia; formed at confluence of North Esk and South Esk at Launceston, flows into Bass Strait nr. Georgetown.

Tamatave, *one of the ch. pts.*, Malagasy; lge. meat-preserving factories; exp. graphite, hides, raffia; oil refinery; p. (1959) *48,627.*

Tamaulipas, *st.*, Mexico; on G. of Mexico, S. of Texas; nitrates, cereals, sugar, coffee, cattle, petroleum; cap. Ciudad Victoria; a. 30,731 sq. m.; p. (1960) *1,024,182.*

Tambov, *t.*, R.S.F.S.R; on R. Oka; synthetic rubber, engin., chemicals; p. (1959) *170,000.*

Tampa, bay on W. cst. Fla., U.S.A.; 40 m. long.

Tampa, *c.*, Fla., U.S.A.; popular winter resort, cigar factories, phosphates, electronics; fruit growing and canning; p. (1960) *274,970.*

Tampere (Tammerfors), *t.*, S. Finland; on rly. between Helsinki and Vaasa; textiles, leather, paper; p. (1961) *128,200.*

Tampico, *spt.*, Mexico; on the R. Panuco, 9 m. from the G. of Mexico; fruits, sugar, maize; p. (1960) *122,197.*

Tampico, *R.*, Mexico, flows to G. of Mexico; length 200 m.

Tamworth, *t.*, N.S.W., Australia; on R. Peel; milling; ch. comm. ctr. of Northern Tableland; p. (1961) *19,064.*

Tamworth, *t.*, *mun. bor.*, Staffs, Eng.; on R. Tame, 5 m. S.E. of Lichfield; ancient cas.; coal, light engin.; p. (1961) *13,555.*

Tana, *lge. L.*, N. Ethiopia, nr. Gondar, source of Blue Nile, 45 m. long, 40 m. wide; surrounded by marsh, papyrus swamp.

Tana, *R.*, forming part of bdy. between Finland and Norway, flows into Arctic Ocean.

Tana R., *ch. R.*, Kenya, E. Africa.

Tananarive, *c.*, *cap.*, Malagasy; air-line to Paris; ctr. of commerce and communications; lge. meat-preserving factories; p. (1959) *206,324.*

Tanaro, *R.*, N. Italy; trib. of R. Po; 125 m. long.

Tandil, *t.*, Argentina; resort; granite quarried nearby; p. (1960) *70,000.*

Tandjoengbalei, *spt.*, Sumatra, Indonesia; exp. tobacco, copra, shipyards.

Tanga, *spt.*, Tanzania, E. Africa; rly. terminus; on plateau overlooking Tanga Bay; hydro-elec. sta; p. *38,000.*

Tanganyika, *gr. L.*, E. Central Africa; 400 m. long, greatest width 45 m.; a. about 12,700 sq. m.; 2,800 ft. above sea; discovered by Burton and Speke in 1868, and since explored by Livingstone, Stanley and others.

Tanganyika, Rep. of, *see* **Tanzania.**

Tanimbal Is., S. Moluccas, Indonesia; gr. of 66 islands; forests, swamps; maize, rice, coconuts, sago; p. *31,847.*

Tangier, *free pt.*, Morocco, N. Africa; on Strait of Gibraltar; no longer internationalised zone but integral part of kingdom of Morocco; summer cap.; shipyd.; cigarettes, fishing; p. of t. (1960) *141,714.*

Tangshan, *c.*, Hopeh prov., China; mun. limits incl. whole Kailan coal mng. a.; p. (1953) *693,000.*

Tanjong Pandan, *spt.*, Billiton, Sumatra, Indonesia; exp. tin; p. *11,589.*

Tanta, *t.*, Lower U.A.R.; 55 m. N. of Cairo; impt. rly. junction; religious fairs; p. (1960) *184,000.*

Tanzania, United Rep. of, *indep. sov. st.*, E. Africa; within Brit. Commonwealth; comprising former sts. of Tanganyika and Zanzibar; climate tropical, varies with elevation; ch. prod., sisal, coffee, cotton, groundnuts, pyrethrum, copra, cloves, ebony, hardwoods; sugar mill and refinery projected in Kilombero Valley; cap. Dar es Salaam; a. 363,708 sq. m.; p. (estd. 1964) *9,710,000.*

Tapachula, *ch. t.*, S. Mexico; coffee, cattle, tobacco, sugar refineries, sawmills; p. (1940) *43,032.*
Tapajóz, *R.*, trib. of R. Amazon.
Tapti, *R.*, W. India; flows W. to G. of Cambay at Surat from Betul dist., Madhya Pradesh; length 450 m.
Tapungato, *mtn.*, W. Argentina; alt. 22,300 ft.
Taquari, *R.*, Brazil; trib. of R. Paraguay; length 400 m.
Tara, *R.*, Siberia, R.S.F.S.R.; trib. of R. Irtysh, length 200 m.
Tarakan, *spt.*, Borneo, Indonesia; on Tarakan I.; oil; p. (of I.) *12,000.*
Taranaki, *prov.*, N.I., N.Z.; a. 3,750 sq. m.; p. (1961) *99,721.*
Taranto, *t.*, Lecce, Italy; on G. of Taranto, inlet of Ionian Sea; maritime arsenal with gr. comm. and industl. interests; strong cas.; cottons, velvets, soap, oil; steel wks.; famous for its oyster and mussel fisheries; p. (1961) *191,515.*
Tarapaca, *prov.*, N. Chile; nitrates, silver; cap. Iquique; a. 21,340 sq. m.; p. (1960) *133,775.*
Tarapore, *t.*, Maharashtra, India, nr. border of Gujarat; 62 m. N. of Bombay, atomic power sta. projected.
Tarascon, *t.*, Bouches-du-Rhône, France; connected by bridges with Beaucaire on opposite bank of R. Rhône; old cas., famous festival; silk and fruit; p. (1954) *7,744.*
Tarbat Ness, *promontory*, N. Side of Moray Firth, Ross and Cromarty, Scot.
Tarbes, *t.*, *cap.*, Hautes-Pyrénées, France; on R. Adour; cath., paper, flax, woollens, machin., aircraft, leather; p. (1962) *50,715.*
Taree, *t.*, N.S.W., Australia; dairying, agr., fishing, oysters, timber, limestone; p. (1961) *10,053.*
Târgu-Jiu, *t.*, Romania; coal, petroleum, timber; p. *17,698.*
Târgul-Mures, *t.*, Romania; on R. Maros; famous old fort, with Gothic Calvinist cath., where in 1571 religious liberty was promulgated for the first time in Europe; gd. tr.; p. (1945) *41,118.*
Tarifa, *c.*, Spain; on Gibraltar Strait; most S. point of mainland of Europe; fish tr., cereals, oranges, wines; p. (1957) *18,098.*
Tarija, *prov.*, Bolivia; cap. Tarija; a. 24,786 sq. m.; p. (1962) *142,600.*
Tarija, *t.*, *cap.*, Tarija prov., Bolivia; S.E. of Potosi; maize, wheat, vines; p. (1962) *20,851.*
Tarim, *t.*, Protectorate of Southern Arabia (Aden); mkt.; religious teaching ctr.
Tarma, *t.*, Peru, S. America; alt. 9,980 ft.; maize, cotton, oranges, bananas; p. (1961) *7,860.*
Tarn, *R.*, France; trib. of R. Garonne; has famous rocky gorge 31 m. long in its upper course; length 235 m.
Tarn, *dep.*, S. France, watered by Tarn and its tribs.; wheat and wine; cap. Albi; a. 2,232 sq. m.; p. (1962) *319,560.*
Tarn-et-Garonne, *dep.*, W. France; corn, wine, woollens, paper, silk; cap. Montauban; a. 1,440 sq. m.; p. (1962) *175,847.*
Tarnow, *t.*, Poland; E. of Kraków; agr.; farm implements, glass; industl. development since 1950; p. (1960) *71,000.*
Tarragona, *prov.*, Spain; on the Mediterranean; vineyards and agr.; cap. Tarragona; a. 2,426 sq. m.; p. (1959) *364,075.*
Tarragona, *fortfd. spt.*, cap. Tarragona, Spain; at mouth of R. Franconi; mnfs. alcohol, liqueurs, chocolate, paper, silk, fish-salting; p. (1957) *42,000.*
Tarrasa, *t.*, Barcelona, Spain; in fruit and vine-growing dist.; royal college; thriving inds.; p. (1959) *86,469.*
Tarsus, *ancient c.*, Turkey; nr. Adana, opposite Cilician Gates; orange and citron groves; ruined Roman temple; birthplace of Apostle Paul; exp. cotton, wool, hides; p. (1960) *51,310.*
Tartary or **Tatary**, *region*, Central Asia; now divided into Chinese or E. Turkestan, and W. Turkestan, U.S.S.R.
Tartary, Gulf of, *arm of the Sea of Japan*, separating Sakhalin from the Siberian mainland.
Tartu (formerly **Dorpat**), *t.*, Estonian S.S.R.; univ.; saw milling, engin.; p. (1959) *74,000.*
Tarudant, *t.*, Morocco, N. Africa; mkt., orange water, leather, pottery, copper, brass; p. *12,877.*
Tashkent, *cap.*, Uzbek. S.S.R. on Syr Darya R.; univ.; extensive silk mnfs.; engin; pipeline from Gazil natural gas field; p. (1962) *1,002,000.*
Tasman Bay, *lge. inlet*, S.I., N.Z.; penetrates N. cst., between Separation Point and D'Urville I.; enclosed by mtns., sheltered, fertile, coastal fringe; ch. ts. Nelson, Motueka.
Tasman Glacier, S.I., N.Z.; one of the lgst. in the world.
Tasmania (formerly **Van Dieman's Land**), *I.*, *st.*, Australia; plateau with fertile valleys; temperate climate; forest and grasslands, grain, fruit, cattle-raising; aluminium, copper, coal, zinc, lead, tin, silver; whaling; electro-metallurgical inds.; cap. Hobart; a. 26,215 sq. m.; p. (1964) *375,946.*
Tatar, A.S.S.R., U.S.S.R.; oil, natural gas; ch. t. Kazan on R. Volga; p. (1956) *2,847,000.*
Tatra Mtns. (**High Tatra**), highest Carpathian gr., Czechoslovakia, alt. 8,743 ft.
Tatung (**Datong**), *c.*, Shansi prov., China; impt. coalfield; p. (1953) *229,000.*
Taubaté, *t.*, Brazil; p. (1960) *64,863.*
Tauber, *R.*, Germany; trib. of R. Main; l. 74 m.
Taunton, *co. t.*, *mun. bor.*, Somerset, Eng.; on R. Tone at W. end of Vale of Taunton; old cas.; apples, cider, clothing tr., engin., plastics; p. (1961) *35,178.*
Taunton, *c.*, Mass., U.S.A.; cotton, iron foundries; p. (1960) *41,132.*
Taunus, *mtn. range*, Hessen, Germany; between the R. Lahn and the Rs. Rhine and Main.
Taupo, *L.*, N.I., N.Z.; lgst. L. in N.Z.; geysers, hot springs in vicinity; 25 m. by 17 m.
Taurida or **Krim**, *dist.*, Crimean Peninsula, U.S.S.R., separated from Ukraine by Perekop Peninsula, divided by R. Salgir; a. 24,540 sq. m.; wheat, tobacco, fruit.
Taurus Mtns., *range*, S. Turkey.
Tavastehus (**Häme**), *dep.*, Finland; cap. Tavastehus; a. 7,118 sq. m.; p. (1958) *573,444.*
Tavira, *t.*, S. Portugal; fishing; p. *12,364.*
Tavistock, *mkt. t.*, *urb. dist.*, Devon, Eng.; on R. Tavy, 12 m. N. of Plymouth; impt. mkt.; p. (1961) *6,086.*
Tavoy, *t.*, Burma; between Thailand and the Bay of Bengal, W. of Bangkok; rice, tin-mining; p. *29,018.*
Tavy, *R.*, Devon, Eng.; trib. of R. Tamar; length 20 m.
Taw, *R.*, Devon, Eng.; flows from Dartmoor to Barnstaple Bay; length 50 m.
Taxco, *t.*, Mexico; alt. 5,600 ft.; gold- and silver-mining; tourist ctr.; p. (1960) *10,076.*
Tay, *R.*, Scot.; flows S.E. from Loch Tay in Perth to the Firth of Tay; longest R. in Scotland.
Tay Bridge, *rly. bridge*, E. Scot.; spans Firth of Tay from Wormit (Fife) to Dundee (Angus); carries main E. cst. rly. from Edinburgh to Aberdeen; length 2 m.; road bridge between Dundee and Newport under constr.
Tay, Firth of, *lge. inlet*, E. cst. Scot.; extends inland almost to Perth; length 27 m., max. width 3 m.
Tayabas, *t.*, Luzon, Philippines; on slope of extinct volcano Banajao; in rice- and coconut-growing dist.
Tayeh, *industl. t.*, Hupeh, China; lies to S. of Yangtze-Kiang, 42 m. S.E. of Wuhan; ctr. of very impt. iron-ore deposits; iron and steel inds., heavy engin.
Tayport, *burgh*, Fife, Scot.; at entrance to Firth of Tay; opposite Broughty Ferry; linen, jute; p. (1961) *3,151.*
Taz, *R.*, Siberia, R.S.F.S.R.; flows to Bay of Tazovsk in Gulf of Obi; length 300 m.
Tbilisi (**Tiflis**), *cap.*, Georgian S.S.R., petroleum refining, engin., textiles; natural gas pipeline to Ordzhonikidze; p. (1962) *743,000.*
Tczew (**Dirschau**), *t.*, Pomerania, Poland; on R. Vistula; rly. wks., sugar, agr. implements; p. (1960) *34,000.*
Team Valley, Durham, Eng.; impt. trading estate has been developed here.
Te Aroha, *t.*, N.I., N.Z.; between Hamilton and Thames; one of the ch. resorts in the thermal springs dist.; p. (1961) *3,058.*
Te Awamutu, *t.*, N.I., N.Z.; S. of Hamilton agr. and dairying dist.; p. (1961) *5,423.*
Tebessa, *t.*, Algeria; alt. 2,789 ft.; mkt.; embroidery, carpets; phosphate deposits near by; p. (1946) *18,293.*
Tecuci, *t.*, Romania; N.W. of Galati; battle, 1476 (between Stephen the Great and the Turks); p. (1956) *23,400.*
Teddington, *S.W. sub.* of London, inc. in Greater London outer bor. of Richmond-upon-Thames; National Physical Laboratory; p. (1961) *13,455.*

Tedzhen, *R.*, Turkmen and N. Persia; flowing into Hari-Rud.
Tees, *R.*, N. Eng.; flows E. from Pennines to N. Sea between Yorks and Durham; length 70 m.
Teffe, *R.*, Brazil; trib. of R. Amazon; length 500 m.
Tegal, *spt.*, Java, Indonesia; sugar; p. (1961) *89,016.*
Tegucigalpa, *c.*, *cap.*, Honduras, central America; lies on R. Choluteca; alt. 3,200 ft. above sea-level; univ.; inter-ocean highway, connecting the t. with both Caribbean Sea and Pacific constructed; bananas, p. (1961) *137,877.*
Tehran, *c.*, *cap.*, Iran; stands 70 m. due S. of the Caspian; alt. 3,447 ft.; a. (within the bastions) 7½ sq. m.; glass, small arms, ammunition, chemical and match factories; has twelve gates, closed at night; nuclear ctr. for Central Treaty Organisation; oil refinery and pipeline from Alborz field projected; p. of t. and dist. (1960) *1,664,000.*
Tehri-Garhwal formerly Himalayan princely st., India, now merged tog. with Kampur and Benares, into st. of Uttar Pradesh.
Tehuantepec, *t.*, Mexico; on the Tehuantepec R., nr. the Pacific cst. of the Isthmus; once an Indian cap.; cath.; p. *10,087.*
Tehuantepec, Isthmus of, separates G. of Mexico from the Pacific at narrowest point of Mexico; width 130 m.
Teifi, *R.*, S.W. Wales; rises in Cambrian Mtns. nr. Strata Florida, flows S.W. and W. into Cardigan Bay 14 m. N.E. of Fishguard; forms bdy. between Cardigan and Carmarthen, Cardigan and Pembroke; sm. flannel ind. in ts. and vils. in lower valley; length 94 m.
Teign, *R.*, Devon, Eng.; flows to sea at Teignmouth from Dartmoor; length 30 m.
Teignmouth, *t.*, *urb. dist.*, Devon, Eng.; at mouth of R. Teign, 13 m. S. of Exeter; resort; yacht-bldg.; p. (1961) *11,576.*
Tei-pei, *c.*, *cap.*, Taiwan, China; on cst. plain at N. end of I. of Taiwan; p. (1957) *759,200.*
Tekirdag, *t.*, Turkey; on Sea of Marmara, W. of Istanbul; grain; p. (1960) *23,905.*
Tela, *spt.*, Honduras Central America; on Atlantic cst.; p. (1961) *13,408.*
Tel Aviv, *c.*, Israel, founded by Zionists, 1909; first all-Jewish c.; many mnfs.; p. with Jaffa (1960) *387,000.* [*152,073.*
Telemark, *co.*, Norway; a. 5,837 sq. m.; p. (1963)
Tellicherry, *t.*, *spt.*, Kerala, India; exp. coffee, cardamoms, sandalwood, andc oconuts; p. (1961) *44,763.*
Telok Anson, *t.*, Perak, Malaya; p. *23,055.*
Telok Betong, *spt.*, Sumatra, Indonesia; exp. pepper, agr. products; p. *25,170.*
Tema, *new pt.*, *t.* nr. Accra, Ghana, opened 1962; big industr. devel., incl. aluminium smelter, deep-water harbour, oil refinery.
Teme, *R.*, on border of Wales and Worcester, Eng.; trib. of R. Severn; length 70 m.
Temes, *R.*, S.W. Romania; flows to R. Danube, nr. Belgrade; length 180 m.
Temir-Tau, *t.*, Kazakh S.S.R.; iron, steel, synthetic rubber, soda; lge thermal power sta.; p. (1959) *54,000.*
Temperley, *t.*, nr Buenos Aires, Argentina; impt. rly. junction; p. (1960) *105,000.*
Temple, *rly. t.*, Texas, U.S.A.; in cotton-growing dist.; p. (1960) *30,419.*
Templemore, *mkt. t.*, *urb. dist.*, Tipperary, Ireland; on R. Suir; p. (1961) *1,775.*
Temuco, *c.*, cap. Cautin prov., Chile; cath.; cereals, apples, timber; p. (1961) *117,115.*
Tenasserim, *div.*, lower Burma; on Siamese border; tin, rice; p. *2,110,420.*
Tenasserim, *t.*, lower Burma; on cst. at mouth of R. Tenasserim; length 250 m.; p. *10,000.*
Tenby, *mkt. t.*, *mun. bor.*, Pembroke, Wales; on W. side of Carmarthen Bay, Bristol Channel; seaside resort; p. (1961) *4,752.*
Tenedos, *I.*, Ægean Sea; off W. cst. Turkey; 7 m. long; Turkish possession.
Tenerife, *I.*, Canary Is.; tourist resort; wheat, fruits, wines, oil refining; contains extinct volcanic peak of Tenerife; alt. 12,182 ft.; cap. Santa Cruz; a. 782 sq. m.; p. (1962) *394,466.*
Tengri-Nor, *L.*, Tibet; N.W. Lhasa; 80 m. long, 40 m. wide.
Tennant Creek, *t.*, situated centre of Northern Terr., Australia; gold, copper.
Tennessee, *R.*, Tenn., Ky., U.S.A.; lgst. and most impt. branch of the Ohio; its valley once liable to flooding, now controlled by dams, and land improved by the Tennessee Valley Authority; length 782 m.
Tennessee, *S. central st.*, U.S.A.; between Mississippi R. and the Appalachian Mtns.; agr.: cotton, pecans, sorghum, maize; oil, natural gas, lignite, cement, salt; inds.: chemicals, synthetic rubber, primary magnesium (from sea-water), steel wks.; cap. Nashville; ch. pt. Memphis; a. 42,244 sq. m.; p. (1960) *3,567,089.*
Tenos, *I.*, Greek Archipelago, Ægean Sea; one of the Cyclades.
Tenterden, *mkt. t.*, *mun. bor.*, Kent, Eng.; 8 m. N. of Rye; church with famous steeple; p. (1961) *4,935.*
Tepic, *cap.*, Nayarit st., Mexico, p. *29,500.*
Teplice, *wat. pl.*, ČSSR., N.W. of Prague; textile and hardware inds.; p. (1961) *42,893.*
Teramo, *prov.*, Abruzzi, Italy; a. 1,067 sq. m.; cap. Teramo; p. (1961) *238,303.*
Teramo, *t.*, Italy; pottery and silks; ancient Interamnium; p. (1961) *41,629.*
Terek, *R.*, N. Caucasia, R.S.F.S.R.; flows to Caspian Sea; length 350 m.
Teresina, *t.*, *cap.*, Piaul st., Brazil; cotton, sugar, rice, cereals; p. (1961) *144,799.*
Termini, *spt.*, Sicily, Italy; S.E. of Palermo; tunny fishing, macaroni, olive oil; wine, sulphur; p. *19,050.*
Ternate, Moluccas Is., Indonesia; sago, spices; p. (estd.) *9,000.* [*11,494.*
Terneuzen, *t.*, Neth.; on W. Schelde R.; p.
Terni, *t.*, Perugia, Italy; amongst the Apennines; iron and steelwks., arms factory, jute; p. (1961) *94,015.*
Ternopil (Tarnopol), *t.*, Ukrainian S.S.R.; E. of Lvov; engin.; p. (1959) *52,000.*
Terranova, *t.*, Sardinia, Italy; on N.E. cst.; textiles, fishing; p. *10,157.*
Terre Adélie, name given to Fr. terr. and I. in Antarctic; estd. a. 160,000 sq. m.
Terre Haute, *c.*, Ind., U.S.A.; coal, natural gas, flour, paper, glass, foundries; p. (1960) *72,500.*
Terschelling, *I.*, Frisian Is., Neth.; at entrance to Zuyder Zee.
Teruel, *prov.*, S. Aragon, Spain; timber forests, coal, weaving, etc.; cap. Teruel; a. 5,721 sq. m.; p. (1959) *225,434.*
Teruel, *t.*, *cap.*, Teruel prov., on R. Turia; cath.; p. (1949) *19 047.*
Teslin Lake, S. of Yukon, N.W. Terr., Canada; source of R. Lewes.
Test or Anton, *R.*, Hants, Eng.; flows to head of Southampton Water.
Tettenhall, *urb. dist.*, Staffs, Eng.; industl.; p. (1961) *14,800.* [*101,352.*
Tetuan, *ch. spt.*, Morocco, N. Africa; p. (1960)
Tetyukhe, *t.*, R.S.F.S.R.; on cst N.E. of Vladivostock; cadmium refinery; p. *5,000.*
Teutoburger Wald, *mtn. range*, Germany.
Teviot, *R.*, Roxburgh, Scot.; trib. of R. Tweed; length 37 m.
Tewkesbury, *mkt. t.*, *mun. bor.*, Glos, Eng.; on R. Avon, 1 m. above confluence with R. Severn; old houses, Norman Abbey, milling, light engin.; p. (1961) *5,814.*
Texarkana, *c.*, Texas and Ark., U.S.A.; bdy. passes down middle of main street, timber and cotton region; rly. wkshps.; total p. (1960) *50,006.*
Texas, *st.*, S.W. U.S.A.; a. 263,644 sq. m.; prairie, mtns. in W.; chemicals, oil, gas, wood and leather products; meat pkg., fishing, mng.; agr. cotton; cap. Austin; ch. pt. Galveston; a. 267,339 sq. m.; p. (1960) *9,579,677.*
Texel, *I.*, W. Frisian Is., Neth.; a. 83 sq. m.; scene of several naval battles.
Tezcuco or Texocco, *L.*, Mexico; a. 77 sq. m.; less than 2 ft. deep; contains no fish.
Thailand (Siam), *kingdom*, S.E. Asia; much jungle; hot, abundant summer rainfall; rice, rubber, teak-wood, tin, cotton, tobacco, iron ore, chemicals; cap. Bangkok; a. 200,148 sq. m.; p. (1960) *25,519,965.*
Thame, *mkt. t.*, *urb. dist.*, Oxford, Eng.; on R. Thame, 7 m. S.W. of Aylesbury, p. (1961) *4,197.*
Thame, *R.*, trib. of R. Thames, Eng.; length 35 m.
Thames, *R.*, Eng.; rises in the Cotswold Hills, Glos, and flows past Oxford, Reading, Windsor and London to the Nore; length 209 m.
Thames, *R.*, Ontario, Canada; flows into L. St. Clair; length 160 m. [length 86 m.
Thames, *R.*, N.Z., flows N. to G. of Hauraki;

Thameshaven, *lge. oil refinery*, Essex, Eng.; on N. cst. of Thames estuary 8 m. below Tilbury.
Thanet, I. of, *lge. promontory*, N.E. extremity, Kent, Eng.; formed by bifurcation of R. Stour; contains Margate, Ramsgate and Broadstairs, with other seaside resorts.
Thanjavur, *t.*, Madras, India; silks, carpets, jewellery, inlaid metals; impt. Brahman ctr.; p. (1961) *111,099*.
Thar Desert, on bdy. between India and W. Pakistan; covers slopes between N.W. Deccan and irrigated valley of R. Indus; completely barren, lack of Rs. or level land prevents irrigation; crossed only by caravan routes.
Tharawaddy, *dist.*, Pegu, Lower Burma; mainly forest, with rice fields in the clearings; a. 2,815 sq. m.; p. of *dist. 508,319*; of *t. 7,131*.
Thaton, *dist.*, Tennasserim div., Burma; rice and tobacco. [length 130 m.
Thaya, *R.*, Austria; trib. of the R. March;
Thebes, *ruined ancient cap.*, Upper U.A.R.; on both banks of R. Nile; site now partly occupied by vils. Karnak and Luxor; impt. arch. discoveries in Valley of the Kings in 1923.
Theiss, *see* **Tisa.**
Theodore *t.*, Queensland, Australia; on R. Dawson; irrigation; cotton, fodder crops.
The Pas, *t.*, Manitoba, Canada; on R. Saskatchewan 80 m. upstream from L. Winnipegosis; rly. junction on line from Prairie Provs. to Churchill on Hudson Bay; branch line to Flin Flon.
The Sound, *see* **Sound, The.**
The West Indies Federation comprised British colonies of Antigua, Barbados, Dominica, Grenada, Jamaica, Montserrat, St. Kitts-Nevis and Anguilla, St. Lucia, St. Vincent, and Trinidad and Tobago. With independence and secession of Jamaica, Trinidad and Tobago, Fed. dissolved May 1962. Proposed East Caribbean Federation would comprise the other colonies except Grenada. *See* **K190.**
Thera, *volcanic I.*, Greek archipelago, Ægean Sea; 10 m. long; cap. Thera.
Thermopylæ or **Pylæ,** celebrated pass between Mt. Æta and the sea, N.E. Greece; battle between Persians and Spartans, 480 B.C.
Thesprotia, *prefecture*, Epirus, Greece; cap. Hegoumenitsa; p. (1961) *52,075*.
Thessaloniki (Salonika), *prefecture*, Greece; p. (1961) *542,880*.
Thessaloniki, *t.*, Greece; at head of G. of Thessaloniki; woollens, soap, cottons, brewing, import and exp. tr.; contains fiscal free zone; p. (1961) *250,920*.
Thessaly, *dist.*, Central Greece; containing two main prefectures, Larisa and Trikkala; horse-breeding; a. 5,208 sq. m.; p. (1961) *695,385*.
Thetford, *t.*, *mun. bor.*, Norfolk, Eng.; on Little R. Ouse; industl. estate for London overspill projected; fruit and vegetable canning, pulp mftg., engin.; p. (1961) *5,398*.
Thetford Mines, *t.*, Quebec, Canada; asbestos mining ctr.; p. (1956) *19,316*.
Thibodaux, *t.*, S.E. La., U.S.A.; comm. and mkt. ctr. for agr. dist.; petroleum nearby; p. (1960) *13,043*.
Thielt, *t.*, Belgium; 17 m. W. of Ghent; lace, wool, cotton, linen; p. (1962) *3,732*.
Thiers, *t.*, Puy-de-Dôme, France; cutlery; p. (1954) *16,243*.
Thiès, *t.*, Senegal, W. Africa; rly. ctr. and wkshps.; groundnuts; p. (1957) *39,100*.
Thionville, *t.*, Moselle, N. France; nr. Luxembourg border; fruit, vegetables, tanning, brewing; p. (1954) *23,054*.
Thirlmere, *L.*, Cumberland, Eng.; 3 m. long; furnishes part of the water supply of Manchester by a conduit of 96 m.
Thirsk, *mkt. t.*, *rural dist.*, N.R. Yorks, Eng.; in wide gap between Pennines and Cleveland Hills, 7 m. S.E. of Northallerton; flour; p. (rural dist. 1961) *13,060*.
Thisted, *t.*, Thyland, Denmark; on Lim Fjord; p. dairy prod., brewing; p. (1960) *8,768*.
Tholen, *I.*, S.W. Netherlands; a. 46 sq. m.; p. *15,000*.
Thok-Jalung, *t.*, Tibet; in Aling Kangri Mtns.; gold-mining ctr. [*11,333*.
Thomar, *t.*, Portugal; paper, cheese; route ctr.;
Thomasville, *c.*, Ga., U.S.A.; cotton region; p. (1960) *18,246*.
Thompson, *R.*, B.C., Canada; rises in Monashee Mtns. flows S.W. into R. Frazer 140 m. upstream from Vancouver; valley forms impt. routeway used by trunk rlys. from Vancouver E. towards Yellowhead Pass (Canadian National Rly.) and Kicking Horse Pass (Canadian Pacific Rly.); length approx. 280 m. [ducing a.
Thompson, *t.*, Manitoba, Canada; nickel pro-
Thonon-les-Bains, *t.*, Haute Savoie, France; resort on L. Geneva; p. (1954) *14,016*.
Thorez, *t.*, Ukrainian S.S.R.; formerly Chistyakovo; coalmng.; p. (1959) *92,000*.
Thornaby-on-Tees, *t.*, *mun. bor.*, N.R. Yorks; opposite Stockton-on-Tees; iron and steel mnf., heavy engin., wire ropery, flour and sugar milling; p. (1961) *22,786*.
Thornbury, *mkt. t.*, *rural dist.*, Glos, Eng.; 10 m. N. of Bristol; aircraft mftg.; p. (rural dist. 1961) *30,685*.
Thornton Cleveleys, *t.*, *urb. dist.*, Lancs, Eng.; 4 m. N.E. of Blackpool; p. (1961) *20,642*.
Thörshavn, *cap.*, *pt.*, Faroe Is.; p. (1960) *7,447*.
Thousand Isles, *L.*, at outfall of L. Ontario; the islets really number 1,500–1,800, and are partly situated in N.Y. State and partly in Canada.
Thrace, ancient name of terr. in S.E. Europe, part of which has been added to Greece; successively under Macedonian, Roman, Byzantine and Turkish rule, before passing to Greece; tobacco; a. 3,315 sq. m.; p. (1961) *356,555*.
Three Points, *c.*, Ghana; W. extremity of Bight of Benin.
Three Rivers (Trois Rivières), *c.*, *pt.*, Quebec, Canada; at confluence of St. Maurice and St. Lawrence Rs.; wood-pulp mnf.; exp. grain, cattle; p. (1956) *50,483*.
Thule, N.W. Greenland; 1,000 m. from N. Pole; American air base and site of ballistic missile early warning sta.; spt. open 2–3 mths. p.a.
Thun, *L.*, Berne can., Switzerland; occupies valleys of R. Aar where it leaves Alpine region; separated from L. Brienz by deltaic neck of land on which is Interlaken; a. 38 sq. m.
Thun, *t.*, Berne, Switzerland; on N.W. end of L. Thun, 16 m. S.E. of Berne; mil. training ctr.; cas. on hill above t.; p. (1957) *24,157*.
Thur, *R.*, Switzerland; flows to R. Rhine, nr. Schaffhausen; length 70 m.
Thurgau, *can.*, N.E. Switzerland, on L. Constance, watered by Thur R.; dairying, fruit, textiles; cap. Frauenfeld; a. 388 sq. m.; p. (1961) *166,420*.
Thuringia, *former Land*, E. Germany, bordered on Bavaria to S., Saxony-Anhalt, Lower Saxony and Hesse to N. and E.; drained by Rs. Saale and Werra; crossed by Thuringer Wald and extending to Harz mtns.; cap. Weimar; now dists. of Erfurt, Suhl and Gera.
Thuringian Forest or **Thüringer Wald,** *wild, wooded hill range*, Central Germany; 95 m. long; famous for romantic scenery and legends.
Thurles, *mkt. t.*, Tipperary (N. Riding), Ireland; on R. Suir; horse fair; p. (1961) *6,421*.
Thursday, *I.*, Torres Strait, Queensland; pearl and trochus fishery ctr.; p. (1957) *1,550*.
Thurso, *burgh*, Caithness, Scot.; on Thurso Bay; most N. t. on Scottish mainland; ancient stronghold of the Northmen; p. (1961) *8,038*.
Tiaret, *t.*, W. Algeria, N. Africa; in strategic pass; walled; agr. mkt.; cereals, wool, cattle; p. *22,344*.
Tiber, *R.*, Italy; flows from Apennines to Mediterranean, passing through Rome; l. 220 m.
Tiberias, *t.*, Israel; on Sea of Galilee (Lake Tiberias); gypsum quarried near by; inland pt.; p. (1946) *11,810*.
Tibesti, *mtns.*, on bdy. between Libya and Chad, Equatorial Africa; barren in spite of slight rainfall; mainly above 6,000 ft., maximum alt. 11,155 ft.
Tibet, *aut. reg.*, China; lofty plateau, called "the roof of the world", its lowest plains being 12,000 ft. above sea-level; semi-desert; Chinese suzerainty restored, 1951; network of roads being built, inc. one across Himalayas to Katmandu.; exp. wool, musk, gold, skins, and drugs; cap. Lhasa; a. 70,003 sq. m.; p. *c. 6,000,000*.
Ticino or **Tessin,** *can.*, Switzerland; forests, vineyards, olives, agr.; contains parts of Ls. Maggiore and Lugano; cap. Bellinzona; lgst. t. Lugano; a. 1,086 sq. m.; p. (1961) *195,566*.
Ticino, *R.*, Switzerland and Italy; trib. of Po; forms S. approach to St. Gotthard Pass; length 150 m.

Tickhill, *urb. dist.*, W.R. Yorks, Eng.; cas.; p. (1961) *2,584*.
Tidore I., Moluccas, Indonesia; coffee, tobacco, fruit; a. 30 sq. m.; p. *19,126*.
Tien Shan or Celestial Mtns., *lofty chain*, N. frontier China, Sinkiang-Kirghizia; hgst. peak 24,000 ft.
Tientsin (Tianjing), *c.*, *former treaty pt.*, *mun. prov.*, Hopei, China; 70 m. S.E. Peking; cottons silks; exp. wool, skins, soya-beans; p. (1953) *2,693,831*.
Tierra del Fuego, *archipelago*, extreme S. America, separated from Patagonia by Strait of Magellan, divided politically between Chile and Argentina; a. (Argentine part) 8,344 sq. m.; p. *7,500*; oil field at Rio Grande.
Tiffin, *c.*, Ohio, U.S.A.; milling, brewing, foundries; p. (1960) *21,478*.
Tigre, *st.*, Ethiopia, formerly an independent kingdom; cap. Adua.
Tigre, *R.*, S. America; rises in Ecuador and flows mainly through Peru to the R. Marañon (Amazon); length 400 m.
Tigris, *R.*, Turkey; rising in mtns. of Armenia and Turkestan, flowing S.E. to join the Euphrates 40 m. N.W. of Basra; length 1,100 m.; dam projected 35 m. N. of Mosul.
Tikhvin, *t.*, R.S.F.S.R.; on R. Syas; aluminium ores; p. (1954) *50,000*.
Tilburg, *t.*, N. Brabant, Neth.; nr. Breda; flourishing woollens, mnfs., tobacco, leather; p. (1960) *136,991*.
Tilbury, *t.*, Essex, Eng.; on N. bank of R. Thames, 20 m. E. of London; docks; shoe mftg; p. (1961) *18,387*.
Till, *R.*, N. Northumberland, Eng.; trib. of R. Tweed; length 32 m.
Tillicoultry, *burgh*, Clackmannan, Scot.; on Devon R.; woollen, worsted, paper mkg.; p. (1961) *3,963*.
Tilmanstone, *mining vil.*, Kent, Eng.; on N. flank of N. Downs, 4 m. S.W. of Deal; on Kent coal-field, coal despatched by overhead cable to Dover.
Timaru, *t.*, S.I., N.Z.; wool, milling, skins; p. (1961) *26,419*.
Timbuktu, Mali, Africa; 8 m. N. of the N. bend of R. Niger, on border of the Sahara desert; agr. tr. ctr.; p. (1957) *7,000*; flourished as comm. mart. and Moslem ctr., 14–16th cent.
Timisoara, *t.*, W. Romania; impt. comm. and industl. ctr., tobacco, petroleum, paper; fortress, cas., cath.; p. (1959) *112,000*.
Timmins, *t.*, Ontario, Canada; gold running out; vast deposits of copper, zinc, silver, discovered 1964; p. (1961) *29,270*.
Timor, *Portuguese possession*, E. Indies; consists of E. part of T.I. in Malay Archipelago, together with Ambeno, Pulo Cambing and Pulo Jako; ch. products coffee, sandalwood, copra, wax; cap. and ch. spt. Dili; total a. 7,330 sq. m.; p. (1950) *442,378*.
Timor Archipelago, *gr. of Is.*, Indonesia; of which the lgst. is Timor (E. part Portuguese; remainder Indonesian); total a. 24,450 sq. m.; fishing, exp. copra; p. *1,657,376*.
Timor Sea, that part of the Indian Ocean N.W. of W. Australia, and S. of Timor I.
Timsah, *L.*, U.A.R., N.E. Africa; sm. L. midway along Suez Canal; formerly used for recreational purposes by Brit. garrison in Canal zone.
Tinogasta, *t.*, Catamarca prov., Argentina; in E. foot-hills of Andes 120 m. N.W. of Catamarca; impt. copper-mines.
Tintagel, *vil.*, Cornwall, Eng.; ruined cas.; reputed birthplace of King Arthur; tourists.
Tinto, *R.*, Huelva, Spain; flows W. to the Atlantic; length 65 m.
Tinto Hills, Lanark, Scot.; highest peak 2,300 ft.
Tipperary, *inland co.*, Munster, Ireland; a. 1,659 sq. m.; divided into Tipperary co. (N.R.), p. (1961) *53,689*; and Tipperary co. (S.R.), p. (1961) *70,090*.
Tipperary, *t.*, Tipperary, Ireland; 29 m. S.E. Limerick; mftg., butter, lace; p. (1961) *4,703*.
Tipton, *t.*, *mun. bor.*, Staffs. Eng'; 2 m. W. of W. Bromwich; metals, engin.; p. (1961) *38,091*.
Tiranë, *t.*, *cap.*, Albania; univ.; textiles, metallurgy; p. (1960) *130,000*.
Tiraspol, *t.*, Moldavian S.S.R.; on R. Dniester; heat and power-sta. recently constructed; milling, tobacco; p. (1959) *62,000*.
Tire, *t.*, Aydin, Turkey; raisins, tobacco, cotton; p. (1960) *26,530*.
Tiree, *I.*, Inner Hebrides, Scot.; off cst. of Mull; sm. fresh-water lochs and Scandinavian forts.
Tirlemont (Flemish Thienen), *t.*, ctr. of Belgian sugar-refining; Brabant, Belgium; machin., woollens, leather; captured by Marlborough, 1705; p. (1962) *22,766*.
Tiruchirapalli, *formerly* Trichinopoly, *t.*, Madras, India; on R. Cauvery; cigars, goldsmith's wk.; boiler plant; p. (1961) *249,862*.
Tisa (Tisza), *R.*, U.S.S.R., Hungary, Jugoslavia; rises in E. Carpathians, flows N.W. to Cop, thence S. across flat, agr. plain of Gr. Arföld into R. Danube 45 m. below Novi Sad; approx. length 600 m.; navigable in part.
Tiszapalkonya, *t.*, Hungary; new town; chemical ctr.
Titicaca, *L.*, Bolivia, Peru, S. America; between 2 ranges of the Andes, on borders of Bolivia and Peru; 12,645 ft. above the sea; a. 3,200 sq. m.; average width 27 m. length 101 m.; almost cut in two by peninsula of Copacabana; nearly 700 ft. deep on E. side, shallow W. and S.; contains numerous Is., lgst. Titicaca; it is drained on the S. side by the R. Desaguadero.
Titograd (Podgorica), *t.*, Montenegro, Jugoslavia; nr. Albanian frontier; p. (1959) *22,000*.
Titov Veles, *t.*, Jugoslavia; on R. Vardar, and main rly. to Belgrade; maize, silk; p. (1960) *25,100*.
Tiverton, *mkt. t.*, *mun. bor.*, Devon, Eng.; 14 m. N. Exeter; lace and silk mftg.; p. (1961) *12,296*.
Tivoli, *t.*, Rome, Italy; sulphur baths.
Tiztuzu, *t.*, Algeria, N. Africa; admin. ctr.; livestock, honey, oil, corn; p. *40,526*.
Tjirebon, *t.*, Java, Indonesia; oil refining; p. (1961) *158,299*.
Tlaxcala, *st.*, Mexico; adjoining Puebla; a. 1,555 sq. m.; cap. Tlaxcala; p. (1960) *346,699*.
Tlemcen, *t.*, Algeria, N. Africa; exp. textiles, carpets, ostrich feathers, olive oil, grain and onyx; p. (1954) *73,000*.
Tobago, *I.*, with Trinidad *indep. st.* within Brit. Commonwealth (1962); exp. sugar, rum, rubber, cotton, tobacco, coffee, etc.; cap. Scarborough on S. side; a. 116 sq. m.; p. (1960) *33,200*, nearly all Negroes.
Tobata, *c.*, *spt.*, N. Kyushu, Japan; now part of Kitakyushu City newly formed 1963 (*q.v.*) on S. shore of Shimonoseki Strait at ent. to Tokai Bay; iron and steel ind., engin., sugar-refining, glass, bricks; lge. mod. coal docks; p. (1947) *84,260*.
Tobermory, *burgh*, Argyll, Scot.; on I. of Mull at N. entrance to Sound of Mull; p. (1961) *668*.
Tobol, *R.*, W. Siberia, R.S.F.S.R.; trib. of R. Irtysh; length 500 m.
Tobolsk, *t.*, W. Siberia, R.S.F.S.R.; on R. Irtysh; shipbldg., sawmilling, fishing; p. (1956) *35,300*
Tobruk, *spt.*, Libya, N. Africa; on cst. 220 m. E. of Benghazi; p. (estd. 1951) *2,500*.
Tocantins, *R.*, provs. Pará and Goiaz, Brazil; flows N. through the Pará estuary to the Atlantic; navigation interrupted by rapids 200 m. above Pará; length, 1,700 m.
Toce, *R.*, N. Italy; rises in Lepontine Alps, flows S. and S.E. into L. Maggiore; valley used by trunk rly. from Milan to Berne as S. approach to Simplon Tunnel; length, 54 m.
Tocopilla, *spt.*, Chile; exp. nitrate, copper ore, sulphates, iodine; p. (1960) *22,244*.
Todmorden, *mkt. t.*, *mun. bor.*, W.R. Yorks, Eng.; nr. source of R. Calder, 6 m. N.E. of Rochdale; cottons, machin.; p. (1961) *17,416*.
Togo Republic of, *indep. sov. st.* (April 1960), W. Africa, formerly U.N. trust terr. under French adm.; cap. Lomé; mainly agr.; yams, sweet potatoes, green peppers, beans, millet, sorghum, coffee, cocoa; phosphate plant; a. 21,220 sq. m.; p. (1961) *1,440,000*. (Br. Togoland integrated in Ghana on achieving independence 1957.)
Tokaimura, *vil.*, Ibaraki, Japan; nuclear reactor and lge. nuclear power sta.
Tokat, *t.*, Turkey; on Tokat I., N. of Sivas; copper and yellow leather mftg.; Armenian massacre 1895; p. (1960) *32,725*.
Tokelau or Union Isles, *gr.* of 3 Is., Brit. col., Pac. Oc.; 300 m. N. of W. Samoa administered by N.Z.; a. 4 sq. m.; p. (1959) *7,861*.
Tokio, *c.*, *spt.*, *cap.*, Japan; on Tokio Bay, S.E. cst. of Honshu; univ., imperial palace; gr. comm. ctr; silks, machin., lacquer, pottery, "chlorela" artificial food production, metal tableware; p. (1964) *10,609,000*.
Tokoroa, *t.*, N.I., N.Z., township to serve Kinleith; kraft paper, pulp, and sawn timber; p. (1961) *7,054*.

Tokushima, *t.*, E. cst. Shikoku, Japan: cottons, reed organs; p. (1955) *176,419*. [*42,815*.
Tolbukhin, *t.*, Bulgaria, former Dobrich; p. (1956)
Toledo, *prov.*, Spain; mtnous.; agr., vineyards, stock-raising; a. 5,925 sq. m.; p. (1959) *531,824*.
Toledo, *ancient c.*, *cap.*, Toledo, Spain; on R. Tagus; with cath., and many specimens of Gothic, Moorish and Castillian architecture in its picturesque narrow streets; famous Alcázar palace citadel; sword-mkg. still flourishes; p. (1957) *46,465*.
Toledo, *c.*, Ohio, U.S.A.; on Maumee R.; gr. rly. ctr. covering 28½ sq. m.; glass, car parts, oil refining; p. (1950) *318,003*.
Tolima, *volcano*, Andes, Colombia, S. America; alt. 18,143 ft.
Tolima, *dep.*, Colombia, S. America; a. 8,874 sq. m.; cap. Ibague; p. (estd. 1961) *875,650*.
Toluca, *t.*, Mexico; brewing, flour, cottons; p. (1960) *60,000*. [length 400 m.
Tom, *R.*, Siberia, R.S.F.S.R.; trib. of R. Obi;
Tomaszow Mazowiecki, *c.*, Lodz prov., Poland; woollens, synthetic fibres, agr. tools; p. (estd.) *50,000*.
Tombigbee, *R.*, Miss., U.S.A.; flows S. to form the Mobile; length 500 m.
Tommot, *t.*, Yakutsk, R.S.F.S.R.; on R. Aldan; gold; p. *10,000*.
Tomsk, *region*, Siberia, R.S.F.S.R.; adjoining Chinese frontier; agr., dairying, stock-raising, fisheries, mining, mftg.
Tomsk, *c.*, Siberia, U.S.S.R.; on R. Tom, and branch of Trans-Siberian rly.; univ., cath.; engin., chemicals; p. (1962) *275,000*.
Tonawanda, *t.*, N.Y., U.S.A.; on Niagara R.; mnfs.; p. (1960) *21,561*.
Tonbridge, *t.*, *urb. dist.*, Kent, Eng.; on R. Medway, 13 m. S.W. of Maidstone; malting, brewing, rly. wks., elec. apparatus, light inds.; p. (1961) *22,141*.
Tönder, *t.*, Denmark; old houses; cattle-breeding; lace; p. (1960) *7,192*.
Tonga Is., *see* Friendly Is.
Tongariro, *volcanic peak*, N.I., N.Z.; in ctr. of volcanic dist.; alt. 6,458 ft.; hydroelec. plant projected.
Tongeren (Tongres), *episcopal c.*, Belgium; mineral springs; p. (1962) *16,240*.
Tongking, *region*, N. Viet-Nam; formerly within French Union; rice, sugar-cane, tobacco, coffee, cotton, silk, coal, tin, limestone; a. 40,530 sq. m.; ch. t. Hanoi; ch. pt. Haiphong
Tonk, *t.*, Rajasthan, India; mica; p. (1961) *43,413*.
Tonlé Sap, *L.*, Cambodia, Indo-China.
Tönsberg, *t.*, Norway; on Bay nr. entrance to Oslo fjord; tr. ctr.; shipping; H.Q. of sealing- and whaling-fleet, oil mills; p. (estd. 1960) *12,500*.
Toowoomba, *c.*, Queensland, Australia; wheat, pastoral and dairying dist., flour-milling, tanning, brewing, wine; p. (1961) *50,107*.
Topeka, *t.*, *cap.*, Kan., U.S.A.; on Kansas R.; flour-milling, engin., machin., lge. tr.; p. (1960) *119,484*.
Torcello, *I.*, with ancient Byzantine cath., on lagoon nr. Venice, Italy.
Torhout, *t.*, W. Flanders, Belgium; textiles; p. (1962) *13,599*.
Tormes, *R.*, Spain; trib. of Douro; length 150 m.
Toronto, *c.*, *pt.*, *metrop. a.*, *cap.* Ontario, Canada; on Bay of Toronto, L. Ontario; spacious harbour; univ.; extensive tr. and mnfs.; oil refining; fine parliament bldgs., parks; a. 240 sq. m.; p. (1961) of met. a. *1,824,481*; of c. *672,000*.
Torontoy, *gorge*, Cuzco dep., Peru; located on R. Urubamba 50 m. N.W. of Cuzco.
Torpoint, *urb. dist.*, Cornwall, Eng.; on Plymouth Sound; p. (1961) *4,260*.
Torquay, *t.*, *mun. bor.*, S. Devon, Eng.; on N. side of Tor Bay; seaside resort with all-year season; p. (1961) *53,915*.
Torre Annunziata, *t.*, *spt.*, Italy; on Bay of Naples; arms factory, macaroni mftg., sericulture; p. (1961) *58,400*.
Torre del Greco, *spt.*, Italy; on Bay of Naples; at foot of Mt. Vesuvius; seaside resort; lava quarries, shipbldg; p. (1961) *77,576*.
Torredonjimeno, *t.*, Jaen, Spain; wine, wheat, fruit; p. *16,069*.
Torremolinos, cst. resort, Spain; S. of Malaga.
Torrens, *L.*, S. Australia; 130 m. long, 20 m. wide; varies from brackish lake to salt marsh.
Terreón, *t.*, Coahuila, Mexico; ctr. of comm. agr.; oil pipe-line connects to Chihuahua; thermo-elec. plant; p. (1960) *179,955*.
Torres Strait, between C. York, Queensland, Australia, and New Guinea; 90 m. wide, dangerous navigation.
Torridge, *R.*, Devon, Eng.; flows from Hartland Dist. to Bideford Bay; length 53 m.
Torrington, *t.*, Conn., U.S.A.; metal-plate wk., woollens; p. (1960) *30,045*.
Torrington, *t.*, *rural dist.*, Devon, Eng.; on R. Torridge, 4 m. S.E. of Bideford; ball clay; p. (rural dist. 1961) *6,945* [cath.; p. *21,813*.
Tortona, *t.*, N. Italy; the Roman Dertona;
Tortosa, *fortfd. t.*, Spain; on R. Ebro; wine, oil, fruit, paper, leather; p. (1957) *45,672*.
Tortuga, *I.*, Caribbean Sea; off N.W. cst. of Hispaniola; provides shelter from N.E. trade winds for Port de Paix; 25 m. by 10 m.
Torun (Thorn), *t.*, S. Pomerania, Poland; on R. Vistula; univ.; grain, timber; p. (1960) *105,000*.
Tosya, *t.*, Turkey; grapes, rice, cotton, wool, mohair, weaving; p. (1960) *13,690*.
Totana, *t*, Murcia, Spain; wheat, olives, oranges; p. (1957) *14,763*.
Totnes, *t.*, *mun. bor.*, Devon, Eng.; on R. Dart, 6 m. N.W. of Dartmouth; cider; p. (1961) *6,064*.
Totonicapan, *t.*, Guatemala, Central America; hot springs, gardens; pottery, furniture, textiles; p. (estd. 1960) *40,100*.
Tottenham, *former mun. bor.*, Middx., Eng.; now, inc. in Haringey outer bor., Greater London (*q.v.*); industl. and resdtl.; p. (1961) *113,249*.
Tottington, *urb. dist.*, Lancs, Eng.; cotton and artificial silk goods; p. (1961) *6,133*.
Touggourt or **Tuggurt**, *t.*, S. Algeria; on edge of Sahara Desert; rly. terminus; dates; p. *243,363*.
Toul, *t.*, Meurthe-et-Moselle, France; on R. Moselle; wines, brandy, earthenware, lace; p. (1954) *12,134*.
Toulon, *c.*, *spt.*, *naval sta.*, Var, France; on Mediterranean cst.; arsenal, fine bldgs., shipbldg, lace-mkg., vines, olive oil, fisheries; Port-Cros nat. park nearby; p. (1962) *172,586*.
Toulouse, *t.*, Haute-Garonne, S. France; on R. Garonne; cath.; paper, leather, stained glass, aircraft engin.; projected aeronautical and space research ctr.; p. (1962) *330,570*.
Touraine, *former prov.*, France; now divided into into Indre-et-Loire and part of Vienne deps.
Tourcoing, *t.*, Nord France; 10 m. N.E. of Lille; textiles, carpets, cement; p. (1962) *90,105*.
Tournai, *t.*, Hainaut, Belgium; on R. Scheldt; nr. Mons; famous cath.; textiles, carpet mftg.; p. (1962) *33,346*.
Tours, *t.*, Indre-et-Loire, France; cath.; iron, steel, wines, leather, textiles; p. (1962) *96,472*.
Towcester, *mkt. t.*, *rural dist.*, Northants, Eng.; 9 m. S.W. of Northampton; boot-mkg.; p. (rural dist. 1961) *15,198*.
Tower Hamlets, *inner bor.*, E. London, Eng., incorporating former bors of Bethnal Green, Stepney and Poplar; industl.; p. (1964) *205,375*.
Tow Law, *urb. dist.*, Durham, Eng.; in Wear Dale, 10 m. N.W. of Bishop Auckland; p. (1961) *2,920*.
Townsville, *spt.*, Queensland, Australia; on E. cst., 400 m. N. of Rockhampton; 2nd pt. of st.; exp. prods. of rich dairying, pastoral, and mining terr.; gen. inds.; p. (1961) *51,224*.
Towy, *R.*, S. Wales; flows S.W. to Carmarthen Bay; length 65 m.
Towyn, *mkt. t.*, *urb. dist.*, Merioneth, Wales; on cst. of Cardigan Bay, 3 m. N.W. of Aberdovey; p. (1961) *4,466*.
Toyama, *c.*, Honshu, Japan; located centrally on Etchu plain to E. of Noto Peninsula; administrative and comm. ctr. of region; aluminium smelting; p. (1960) *135,190*.
Trabzon, *spt.*, Turkey; on Black Sea cst.; caravan ctr.; exp. tobacco, carpets, hides; reputed to be the ancient Trapezus; p. (1960) *52,680*.
Trafalgar, *C.*, S.W. cst., Cadiz, Spain; Nelson's famous victory, 1805.
Trail, *t.*, B.C., Canada; lgst. metallurgical smelter in Brit. Commonwealth; p. (1961) *11,580*.
Tralee, *cst.*, *t.*, Kerry, Ireland; on R. Lee; exp. grain, butter; p. (1961) *10,714*.
Tranent, *burgh*, E. Lothian, Scot.; 10 m. E. of Edinburgh; coal; p. (1961) *6,317*.
Trani, *spt.*, Apulia, Italy; on the Adriatic; 12th-century cath.; p. *30,551*.

Transbaikal, *dist.*, Siberia, R.S.F.S.R.; E. of L. Baikal; mineral wealth; ch. t., Chita.

Transcaucasia, name given to region of U.S.S.R. which comprises the constituent reps. of Georgia, Armenia, and Azerbaydzhan; ch. t., Tbilisi.

Transkei, *Bantu reserve*, E. Cape, S. Africa; cereals, fruits, cattle, sheep; limited Bantu self-gov., pop. mainly employed in mines in Transvaal and Orange Free State; cap. Umtata; a. *16,544* sq. m.; p. (1963) *1,300,000*.

Transvaal, *prov.*, Rep. of S. Africa; hot summers, temperate winters; grassland, agr., maize, tobacco, sheep, wool, cattle, gold, diamonds; coal, copper, tea, engin., brewing, pottery; a. 110,450 sq. m.; cap. Pretoria; nuclear reactor in the N.; p. (1960) *6,273,477* (inc. *1,468,305* whites).

Transylvania, *former prov.*, Hungary, now in Romania; cereals, tobacco, sheep, cattle, horses; surrounded and traversed by the Carpathians; p. (1948) *3,420,859*.

Transylvanian Alps, *range of high mtns.*, Romania.

Trapani, *fortfd. spt.*, W. Sicily, Italy; salt, wine, olive oil, fish, alabaster, coral, mother-of-pearl; exp.; p. (1961) *75,537*.

Trasimeno, *L.*, Umbria, central Italy; occupies lge. extinct volcanic crater; drained S. to R. Tiber; a. approx. 60 sq. m.

Trás-os-Montes e Alto-Douro, *prov.*, N. Portugal; ch. t. Tua; a. 47,340 sq. m.; p. (1950) *636,322*.

Traun, *R.*, Austria; trib. of R. Danube; enters L. known as Traun See; length 100 m.

Travancore-Cochin, *former st.*, S. India; included in Kerala st. 1 Nov., 1956; rice, coconuts, pepper, tapioca, hardwoods; univ.

Traverse City, *t.*, Mich., U.S.A.; timber inds., tr.; p. (1960) *18,432*. [p. (1961) *1,951*

Trawden, *urb. dist.*, Lancs. Eng.; cotton, engin.;

Trawsfynydd, Merioneth, Wales; within N. Wales Nat. Pk.; atomic power sta.

Trebizond, *see* Trabzon.

Tredegar, *mining t.*, *urb. dist.*, Monmouth, Eng.; in narrow valley 3 m. W. of Ebbw Vale; p. (1961) *19,792*.

Treforest, *t.*, Glam., Wales; on R. Taff; lge. trading estate established in 1930s to alleviate unemployment in primary inds. of S. Wales; aircraft accessories, electronics, chemical, pharmaceutical, rayon, metal wks.

Treinta y Tres, *dep.*, Uruguay; a. 3,682 sq. m.; cap. Treinta y Tres; p. (1953) *72,063*.

Trelew, *t.*, Patagonia, Argentina; ch. comm. t.; sheep; p. (1960) *11,500*.

Trelleborg, *spt.*, S. Sweden; most impt. rubber fact. in cty.; p. (1961) *19,209*.

Tremadoc Bay, N. Wales; N. part of Cardigan Bay between Lleyn pen. and Merioneth cst.

Trengganu, *st.*, Malaysia; N. E. Malaya; rice, rubber, coconuts; tin, iron; cap. Kuala Trengganu; a. 5,050 sq. m.; p. (1961) *320,431*.

Trent, *R.*, Eng.; rises in N. Staffs, and flows to join the Ouse in forming the estuary of the Humber; length 170 m.

Trentino-Alto Adige, *aut. region*, N. Italy; a. 5,252 sq. m.; p. (1961) *785,491*.

Trento, *t.*, *cap.*, Venezia Tridentina, N. Italy; on R. Adige; p. (1961) *74,766*.

Trenton, *c.*, *cap.*, N.J., U.S.A.; on Delaware R.; ironwks., pottery, rubber, and other mnfs.; p. (1960) *114,167*. [ctr.; p. (1960) *40,000*.

Tres Arroyos, *t.*, E. Argentina; agr. and livestock

Treviglio, *t.*, Lombardy, Italy; E. of Milan; silk mftg.; p. *19,615*.

Treviso, *t.*, Lombardy, Italy; cath.; majolica ware, silks, woollens; p. (1961) *75,217*.

Trichinopoly, (*see* Tiruchirapalli).

Trier, *c.*, Rhineland-Palatinate, Germany; on R. Moselle; cath.; Roman antiquities (Porta Nigra); wine cellars, tobacco, leather, textiles, machin., brewing; p. (1963) *87,400*.

Trieste Free Territory, *former free st.*, on the Adriatic; constituted by Peace Treaty with Italy, 1947, as compromise between conflicting Jugoslav and Italian claims; a. 287 sq. m.; military government terminated Oct. 1954; Zone A handed over to Italy, Zone B to Yugoslavia.

Trieste, *spt.*, *cap.* Friuli-Venezia Giulia, N. E. Italy; shipbldg., fishing; cath., cas., Roman antiquities; oil pipeline to Schwechat, nr. Vienna; p. (1961) *273,390*.

Trikkala, *prefecture*, Thessaly, Greece; cap. Trikkala; p. (1961) *142,450*.

Trikkala (the ancient Trikal), *t.*, Thessaly, Greece; nr. Larissa; mosques; grain p. (1961) *27,876*.

Trincomalee, *t.*, *naval sta.*, N.E. cst., Ceylon; gd. harbour; tobacco, rice, palms; p. *32,507*.

Tring, *mkt. t.*, *urb. dist.*, Herts, Eng.; in gap through Chiltern Hills, 9 m. N.W. of Hemel Hempstead; dairy farming; p. (1961) *6,051*.

Trinidad, *c.* Col., U.S.A.; on Purgatory R.; rly. wks., coal; p. (1960) *10,691*.

Trinidad, *I.*, with **Tobago,** *indep. st.*, within Brit. Commonwealth (1962); W.I.; oil, natural gas, asphalt, sugar, rum, coconut oil, molasses, cocoa, citrus fruits; cap. Pt. of Spain; a. 1,864 sq. m.; p. (estd. 1964) *850,000* inc. Tobago.

Trinidad, *cap.* Beni, Bolivia; p. (1962) *14,505*.

Trinidad, *t.*, Cuba, W.I.; exp. honey; p. *16,756*.

Trinity, *R.* Texas, U.S.A.; flows S.E. to Galveston Bay; length 500 m.

Trino, Piedmont, N. Italy; 11 m. S.S.W. of Vercelli; nuclear power sta.

Tripoli, *spt.*, Lebanon; S.W. Asia; terminus of oil pipe-line from Iraq; p. (estd. 1956) *80,000*.

Tripoli, *prov.*, Libya, N. Africa; extends W. to Tunisia, E. to Cyrenaica, S. into Sahara Desert; largely composed of desert, scattered oases; cap. Tripoli; p. (1954) *746,064*.

Tripoli, *t.*, *cap.* Tripoli prov. Libya, N. Africa; expanded under Italian colonial administration; exp. wool, hides; p. (1958) *172,202*.

Tripolis, *cap.*, Arcadia, Peloponnese, Greece; tapestries, leather; p. (1961) *18,500*.

Tripura, Union Terr., India; hilly; rice, jute, cotton, sugar cane; cap. Agartala; a. 4,036 sq. m.; p. (1961) *1,142,005*.

Tristan da Cunha, *sm. gr. of Brit. Is.*, S. Atl. Oc.; ch. I. Tristan; evacuated Oct. 1961 (volcanic eruption) but resettled Nov. 1963 by nearly all previous islanders; p. (1964) *270*.

Trivandrum, *t.*, Kerala, S. India; univ.; wood-carving; p. (1961) *239,815*.

Trnava, *t.*, ČSSR.; on R. Vah; cloth, sugar; p. (1961) *31,732*.]*16,182*.

Trnovo (Tirnovo), *t.*, Bulgaria; copper wk.; p.

Troitsk, *t.*, S. Urals. R.S.F.S.R.; leather, knitwear; lge. thermal power sta.; p. (1959) *76,000*.

Trollhättan, *t.*, Sweden; famous waterfalls, with generating-sta.; cars; p. (1961) *32,051*.

Trombay, *I.*, off Bombay, India; oil refining; atomic reactor; zirconium metal produced.

Troms, *dist.*, Norway; a. 10,006 sq. m.; p. (1963) *129,219*.

Tromsö, *spt.* Troms, Norway; on sm. I. of Tromsö, in Tromsö Sound; seal and walrus fishing; canning; p. (1960) *12,316*.

Tronador, *volcano*, Andes, S. America; on Argentine–Chilean bdy.; alt. 11,352 ft.

Tröndelag, N., *co.*, Norway; a. 8,659 sq. m.; p. (1963) *116,469* [p. (1963) *215,274*.

Tröndelag, S., *co.*, Norway; a. 7,241 sq. m.;

Trondheim, *spt.*, Norway; on W. cst. on S. side of Trondheim Fjord; shipbldg., engin.; exp. timber and wood-pulp, butter, fish, copper; contains ancient cath., burial place of early Norwegian kings and place of coronation of recent sovereigns; p. (1960) *59,271*.

Troon, *burgh*, Ayr, Scot.; on Firth of Clyde, 6 m. N. of Ayr; gd. harbour and graving docks; shipbldg., hosiery; p. (1961) *9,932*.

Troppau, *see* **Opava.**

Troste, nr. Llanelly, Wales; steel strip mill, tin plate; newly developed 1952.

Trossachs, *mtn. defile*, Perth, Scot.; tourist resort.

Trouville, *spt.*, Calvados, France; resort, boatbldg., fishing; p (1954) *7,040*.

Trowbridge, *mkt. t.*, *urb. dist.*, Wilts, Eng.; 3 m. S.E. of Bradford-on-Avon; cloth wks., bacon curing, dairying, engin.; p. (1961) *15,833*.

Troy, *c.*, N.Y., U.S.A.; at confluence of Rs. Hudson and Mohawk; great shirt-mftg. ctr.; p. (1960) *67,492*.

Troyes, *c.*, Aube, France; on R. Seine; former cap. Champagne; magnificent cath., hosiery, iron, looms, mnfs.; p. (1962) *68,898*.

Trujillo, *spt.*, Honduras, Central America; on Atlantic cst.; p. (1958) *3,016*.

Trujillo, *ch. t.*, La Libertad, Peru; univ.; cath.; cocaine mftg., sugar, brewing, tanneries, rice mills; p. (1961) *122,000*.

Trujillo, *old t.*, Spain; N.E. Bardajoz; wheat, wine, fruit; birthplace of Pizarro; p. (1957) *14,587*.

Trujillo, *st.*, Venezuela, S. America; cocoa, coffee; cap. T.; p. (1961) *326,634*.

Truk Is., Caroline Is., Pac. Oc., U.S.A. Trusteeship; coral, copra, dried fish; a. 50 sq. m.; p. (1958) *19,807*.

Truro, *c.*, *mun. bor.*, Cornwall, Eng.; at confluence of Rs. Kenwyn and Allen; cath.; tin smelting, jam wks., light engin., textiles; p. (1961) *13,328*.

Truro, *t.*, Nova Scotia, Canada; on Salmon R.; hosiery; p. (1961) *12,421*.

Trutnov, *t.*, ČSSR.; at foot of Riesengebirge; coal, linen; p. (1961) *22,961*.

Tsamkong (Zhanjiang), *c.*, Kwangtung prov., China; cotton milling, leather mnfs.; p. (1953) *166,000*.

Tsangpo, *R.*, Tibet; one of the headstreams of the R. Brahmaputra; length 850 m.

Tschenstokov, *see* Czestochowa.

Tselinograd, *t.*, Kazakhstan, S.S.R.; nr. Karaganda coalfield; engin.; p. (1959) *101,000*.

Tsinan (Jinan), *c.*, Shantung, China; on the right bank of the Hwang Ho, 100 m. from the G. of Chihli; mnfs. glass, textiles, precious stones; p. (1953) *680,000*.

Tsinghai (Qinghai), *prov.*, China; between Nan Shan and Kunlun mtns.; cap. Sining; a. 269,187 sq. m.; p. (1953) *11,676,534*.

Tsingtao (Qingdao), *c.*, Shantung, China; salt, silk; former treaty pt.; p. (1953) *917,000*.

Tsitsihar (Qiqihar), *c.*, Heilungkiang, N. China; on the Vladivostock portion of the Trans-Siberian rly.; p. (1953) *345,000*.

Tsugaru Strait, Japan; separates Is. Hokkaido and Honshu; links Sea of Japan with Pac. Oc.; length 45 m., width 15–20 m.

Tsumeb, *t.*, S.W. Africa; rly. terminus; copper, lead, zinc; p. (1960) *7,769* inc. *2,987* whites.

Tsuruga, *spt.*, Japan; on W. cst. Honshu; rayon textiles, cotton, atomic power plant projected; p. (1947) *24,223*.

Tuam, *mkt. t.*, *rural dist.*, Galway, Ireland; Roman Catholic and Protestant caths.; p. (1961) (of dist.) *25,676* (of t.) *3,500*.

Tuamotu, *coral archipelago*, S. Pac. Oc.; belonging to France; a. of gr. 330 sq. m.; pearl fisheries; p. of gr. (1962) *7,097*.

Tuapse, *spt.*, R.S.F.S.R., U.S.S.R.; at foot of Caucasus Mtns. on N. cst. of Black Sea; at W. end of oil pipe-line from Baku and Makhach Kala; impt. oil refineries; p. (1954) *50,000*.

Tubarao, *t.*, Santa Catarina st., S. Brazil; on E. cst., 175 m. N. W. of Porto Alegre; coal-mines; p. (1960) *29,615*.

Tübingen, *t.*, Baden-Württemberg, Germany; on R. Neckar; univ., cas.; machin., paper, textiles; p. (1963) *53,300*.

Tucson, *c.*, Arizona, U.S.A.; on Santa Cruz R.; founded in 1560 by a Jesuit mission, and from 1867 to 1877 was the cap. of Arizona; seat of Univ. of Arizona; winter resort; aircraft, electronics, clothing; p. (1960) *212,892*.

Tucumán, *prov.*, Argentina; agr. and stock-raising; cap. Tucumán; a. 8,817 sq. m.; p. (1960) *780,000*.

Tucumán, San Miguel de, *c.*, cap. Tucumán prov., Argentina; on R. Sali; univ.; breweries, sawmills, flourmills, sugar; p. (1960) *290,000*.

Tugela, *R.*, Natal, S. Africa; rises in Drakensberg Mtns. and flows to Indian O.; length 300 m.

Tuggurt, *see* Touggourt.

Tula, *region*, R.S.F.S.R., U.S.S.R.; S. of Moscow; pasturage, stock-keeping, iron and coal.

Tula, *t.*, R.S.F.S.R., U.S.S.R.; on both banks R. Upa; engin., iron ore nearby; p. (1962) *342,000*.

Tulare, *L.*, S. Cal., U.S.A.; ctr. of inland drainage 40 m. S. of Fresno; streams feeding it used for irrigation; in drought years L. dries up completely; a. 90 sq. m.

Tulbagh, *t.*, Cape Prov., Rep. of S. Africa; on Gr. Berg R., 65 m. N.E. of Cape Town.

Tulcea, *t.*, Dobroja, Romania; on Danube; chemicals, copper; p. (1956) *24,639*.

Tulenovo, Balchik dist., on Black Sea, Bulgaria; oil production. [p. (1961) *19,343*.

Tulkarm, *t.*, Jordan; agr. ctr.; rly. junction;

Tullamore, *mkt. t.*, *urb. dist.*, Offaly, Ireland; on Grand Canal; farming, distilling, brewing; p. (1961) *6,243*. [*19,372*.

Tulle, *t.*, *cap.*, Corrèze, France; cath.; p. (1954)

Tulsa, *c.*, Okla., U.S.A.; 2nd lgst. c. in st.; oil-well machin., aeroplanes; p. (1960) *261,685*.

Tumbes, *dep.*, Peru, S. America; cap. Tumbes; a. 1,590 sq. m.; p. (1961) *52,403*.

Tummel, *R.*, Perth, Scot.; trib. of R. Tay; used by Perth to Inverness rly. as S. approach to Drumocheter Pass.

Tunbridge Wells, *mkt. t.*, *Royal mun. bor.*, Kent, Eng.; on border of Sussex, 5 m. S. of Tonbridge; chalybeate waters; p. (1961) *39,855*.

Tung Hai or Eastern China Sea, name of part of the Pac. Oc. bordering S. China.

Tunghwa (Tonghua), *c.*, Kirin prov., China; p. (1953) *129,000*.

Tungting Hu, *lge. L.*, Hunan, China; on S. margin of Yangtze-Kiang plain; receives waters of Yuan Kiang and Siang Kiang, drains N. to Yangtze-Kiang; surrounded by flat, intensively cultivated land, rice, sugar, mulberry; size varies greatly with season; maximum a. (in late summer) 2,500 sq. m.

Tunguska, Upper, Stony and Lower, *Rs.*, Siberia, U.S.S.R.; all rise in Sayan Mtns. nr. L. Baikal and flow N.W. through forested country into R. Yenesei.

Tunis, *ch. t.*, Tunisia, N. Africa; spt. on bay off G. of Tunis; univ., notable mosques; tourist ctr.; many inds., much tr.; the ruins of ancient Carthage are to the N.E.; p. (1956) *680,000*.

Tunisia, *ind. sovereign st.* since March 1956, formerly French prot., N. Africa; agr., stock-rearing, mineral and phosphate wkg., silk and carpet weaving, pottery mftg., fishing (inc. sponges), also fruit- and flower-growing and perfume distillation; lge. steelwks. at Menzel-Bourguiba projected; oil deposits in El Borma a.; cap. Tunis; a. 48,330 sq. m.; p. (1961) *4,168,000*. [*63,500*

Tunja, *t.*, cap. Boyaca, Colombia; p. (estd. 1959)

Turda, *t.*, Transylvania, Romania; salt-mines; p. (1956) *33,614*.

Turfan (Tulufan), *c.*, Sinkiang, China; below sea-level on the S. side of the Tian-Shan Mtns.

Turgai, *dist.*, U.S.S.R.; N. of Sea of Aral, forms part of Kazakh. rep.; a. 175,219 sq. m.; agr. and cattle-breeding; antimony p. *500,000* (largely nomadic Kirghiz).

Turgutlu (Kassaba), *t.*, Manisa prov., Turkey; 30 m. E.N.E. of Izmir; lignite, cotton, melons; p. (1960) *31,697*.

Turin, *c.*, N. Italy; on Rs. Po and Dora; former cap. Piedmont and Sardinian sts.; cath., univ., royal palace and cas., and Palazzo Carignano; leather, textiles, engin.; extensive tr.; p. (1961) *1,019,230*.

Turkestan E., terr. included in Sinkiang, China; separated from W. or former Russian Turkestan by Pamir plateau; mainly desert.

Turkey, *rep.*, Europe and Asia; has lost much of 19th-century terrs.; evergreen trees, shrubs, livestock, cereals, tobacco, figs, fruits, copper, silver, coal, carpets, silk, wine, olive oil; oil nr. Iskenderun and along shores of Marmara Sea; cap Ankara; lgst. t. Istanbul; a. 296,107 sq. m.; p. (1955) *24,111,778*.

Turkmenistan, *const. rep.*, U.S.S.R.; agr. based on irrigation, fruit, cotton, wool; sulphates, petroleum, mnfs., carpets; cap. Ashkhabad; a. 189,603 sq. m.; p. (1959) *1,520,000*.

Turks and Caicos, *Is.*, Caribbean Sea; West Indies; about 30 sm. Is., geographically the S.E. continuation of the Bahamas; Caicos Is. separated by narrow channel from Turks Is.; ch. prod., salt, conches, sisal, sponges. Total a. 166 sq. m.; p. (estd. 1965) *6,272*.

Turku (Abo), *spt.*, S. Finland; Swedish and Finnish univs., archiepiscopal see; p. (1961) *125,450*.

Turku (Åbo), *spt.*, S. Finland; Swedish and Finnish univs. archiepiscopal see; p. (1961) *125,450*

Turku-Pori (Åbo-Björneborg), *dep.*, Finland; a. 8,500 sq. m.; p. (1961) *660,269*.

Turner Valley, *dist.*, Alberta, Canada; oilfield; natural gas.

Turnhout, *t.*, Belgium; nr. Antwerp; textiles, lace, playing-card mnf.; p. (1962) *36,701*.

Turnu Severin, *t.*, Romania; below the Iron Gate cataracts of R. Danube; grain, salt, petroleum; p. (1956) *32,486*. [p. (1961) *2,686*.

Turriff, *burgh*, Aberdeen, Scot.; nr. R. Deveron;

Turton, *t.*, *urb. dist.*, Lancs, Eng.; 4 m. N. of Bolton; mnfs.; p. (1961) *13,673*. [*63,370*.

Tuscaloosa, *t.* Ala., U.S.A.; st. univ.; p. (1960)

Tuscany, *region*, *former grand duchy*, Italy; includes provs. Arezzo, Florence, Leghorn, Siena, Grosseto, Lucca, Pisa, and Massa and Carrara;

cereals, olive oil, wine, copper, lead, mercury, marble, textiles, porcelain; a. 8,876 sq. m.; p. (1961) *3,267,374*.

Tushino, *t.*, R.S.F.S.R., 10 m. N.W. of Moscow; textiles; absorbed by Moscow 1960; p. (1959) *90,800*

Tuticorin, *spt.*, Madras, India; cotton-spinning, salt, pearls; p. (1961) *124,273*.

Tuttlingen, *t.*, Baden-Würtemberg, Germany; on R. Danube; musical instruments, tanning, footwear, steel, textiles; p. (1963) *25,200*.

Tuva, *aut. rep.*, U.S.S.R.; formerly Tannu Tuva rep., bounded on E., W., and N. by Siberia, and on S. by Mongolia; cap. Kyzyl; pastoral; a. about 64,000 sq. m.; p. (1959) *172,000*.

Tuxtla Gutierrez, *t.*, Chiapas, Mexico; alt. 1,500 ft.; ctr. for sisal, tobacco, coffee, cattle; p. (1960) *28,262*.

Tuy, *t.*, Spain; cath.; mineral springs; p (1957) *13,865*.

Tuzla, *t.*, Jugoslavia; salt-springs, coal, timber, livestock, grain, fruit; p. (1959) *49,000*.

Tweed, *R.*, S.E. Scot.; rises in Peebles, and reaches sea at Berwick; dividing Berwick from the Eng. co. Northumberland; famous for its salmon fisheries; length 97 m.

Twelve Pins, star-shaped *mtn. range*, Galway, Ireland; Benbaum, alt. 2,395 ft.

Twickenham, *former mun. bor.*, Middx., Eng., now inc. in Richmond upon Thames (*q.v.*); Rugby Football Union ground; p. (1961) *100,822*.

Tychy, *t.*, Katowice, Poland; p. (1960) *50,000*.

Tyldesley, *t.*, *urb. dist.*, Lancs, Eng.; 4 m. S. of Bolton; mnfs.; p. (1961) *16,813*.

Tyler, *c.*, Texas, U.S.A.; fruit, livestock, cotton; p. (1960) *51,230*.

Tynagh, *mine* on Longhrea, Galway, R.O.I.; lead, zinc, copper.

Tyne, *R.*, Durham and Northumberland, Eng.; formed by junction of N. and S. Tyne at Hexham; flows E. to sea at Tynemouth and S. Shields; valley gives easy route across mtns. from Newcastle to Carlisle; forms a continuous harbour (with shipbldg. and other wks.) from Newcastle to Tynemouth; length 80 m.; road tunnel between Wallsend and Jarrow under constr.

Tynemouth, *t.*, *spt. co. bor.*, Northumberland, Eng.; at mouth of R. Tyne, on its N. bank; inc. in its a. the townships of Tynemouth, N. Shields, Cullercoats, Chirton, Preston, Percy Main, E. Howden and New York; favourite wat. pl. with old priory and cas.; gd. harbour; fishing, ship repairing, coal bunkering, laminated plastics; oil storage; p. (1961) *70,112*.

Tyneside, *lge. conurbation*, S.E. Northumberland, N.E. Durham, Eng.; comprises highly industl. built-up a. astride R. Tyne for 14 m. from its mouth to Scotswood Bridge; huge exp. of coal, abroad and round Brit. csts.; shipbldg., heavy engin.; a. 90 sq. m.; p. (1961) *852,341*. *See also under* **Gateshead, Newcastle upon Tyne, S. Shields, Tynemouth, Jarrow, Wallsend, Felling, Hebburn, Gosforth, Longbenton, Newburn, Whickham, Whitley Bay.** [p. *9,455*.

Tyre, or **Sur**, *t.*, Lebanon, S.W. Asia; on W. cst.;

Tyrol, *mountainous region*, Alps, Europe; falls within Austria and Italy; between Munich and Verona, which are linked by the Brenner Pass; the Tyrol embraces all the highest peaks of the Austrian Alps, culminating in the Ortler Spitz; two-fifths forest; cap. Innsbruck; mtn. pasture, vineyards, silk inds.; a. 4,884 sq. m.; p. of Austrian T. (1961) *462,899*.

Tyrone, *inland co.*, N. Ireland; agr. and dairying; cap. Omagh; a. 1,260 sq. m.; p. (1961) *133,930*.

Tyrrhenian Sea, part of Mediterranean between Italy and Corsica, Sardinia and Sicily.

Tyumen, *t.*, R.S.F.S.R.; on R. Tura, engin., textiles; natural gas nearby in Berezovo vil.; p. (1959) *150,000*.

Tzekung (Zigong), *c.*, Szechwan, China; petroleum, natural gas, salt wks.; p. (1953) *291,000*.

Tzepo (Zibo), *c.*, Shantung, China; formed by merging 1950 coal mng. ts. of Tzechwan and Poshan and 1954 addition of Changchow; p. (estd.) *284,000*.

U

Uanapú or **Anapú**, *R.*, Brazil; trib. of R. Pará; length 400 m.

Ubangi, *R.*, central Africa; trib. of R. Congo; with R. Congo forms W. bdy. between Central African Rep. and Congo; length 1,400 m.

Ubangi-Shari, *see* **Central African Republic.**

Ube, *spt.*, S. Honshu, Japan; chemical cement machin., coal; p. (1950) *128,569*.

Ubeda, *t.*, Jaen, Spain; on R. Guadalquivir; in vineyard and fruit-growing dist.; old walls; p. (1957) *30,249*.

Uberaba, *t.*, Minas Gerais, Brazil; cattle, maize, manioc, rice, sugar; p. (1960) *72,053*.

Ucayali, *R.*, Peru, S. America; head-stream of R. Amazon; over 1,400 m. long navigable for 1,000 m. [(1962) *73,169*.

Uccle, *t.*, Belgium; nr. Brussels; industl.; p.

Ucha Reservoir, *see* **Moscow Sea.**

Uckfield, *mkt. t.*, *rural dist.*, E. Sussex, Eng.; 8 m. N.E. of Lewes; p. (rural dist. 1951) *43,132*.

Udaipur, *t.*, Rajasthan, India; 2,469 ft. above sea-level; marble palace of the Maharajah; temple of Siva; embroidery, cotton cloth; p. (1961) *111,139*.

Uddevalla, *spt.*, S. Sweden; N. Göteborg; prefab. houses, timber, granite quarrying, textiles; p. (1961) *34,290*.

Udi, *t.*, S. Nigeria, W. Africa; 100 m. N. of Pt. Harcourt; impt. mining ctr. on Enugu coal-field; linked by rail to Kaduna and Pt. Harcourt.

Udine, *t.*, N.E. Italy; between Alps and G. of Venice; old cas. (now barracks); silk, velvet, and cotton inds.; p. (1961) *85,205*.

Udmurt, *autonomous Soviet Socialist Rep.*, part of R.S.F.S.R., U.S.S.R., cap. Izhevsk.

Uelzen, *t.*, Lower Saxony, Germany; on Lüneberger Heath; machin., chemicals, sugar; p. (1963) *24,500*.

Ufa, *t.*, R.S.F.S.R.; in W. Urals at confluence of Rs. Ural and Belaia; iron and copper foundries and machin. wks., saw-mills, textiles, oil; p. (1962) *610,000*.

Uganda, *indep. sov. st.* within Br. Commonwealth (1962); E. Central Africa; ch. R. Nile; Ruwenzori Range, Mt. Elgon on Kenya border; Ls. inc. parts of Victoria, Edward, Albert, Rudolf and whole of Kioga; moderate rainfall; cotton, coffee, tea, oilseeds, tobacco, groundnuts, maize; copper, beryl, tin; timber; Owen Falls hydro-elec. power plant; cap. Kampala; a. 93,981 sq. m. inc. 13,680 sq. m. swamp and water; p. (estd. 1964) *6,845,000*.

Uinta, *mtn. range*, Utah, U.S.A.; its highest points are Emmons (13,694 ft.), Gilbert Peak (13,687 ft.), and Wilson (13,300 ft.).

Uist, N., *I.*, Outer Hebrides, Inverness, Scot.; separated from I. of Skye by Little Minch; length, 17 m., width 3–13 m.

Uist, S., *I.*, Outer Hebrides, Inverness, Scot.; most S. lge. I. of Outer Hebrides gr.; length 22 m., width 8 m.

Uitenhage, *t.*, Cape Prov., S. Africa; summer resort, fruit, wool, rly. wks., tyres, car assembly, textiles; p. (1960) *48,755* inc. *17,531* whites.

Ujiji, *t.*, in sm. terr. same name (a. 920 sq. m.) on E. shore L. Tanganyika, E. Africa; where Stanley found Livingstone, 1871; p. (1957) *12,149*. [p. (1947) *63,093*.

Ujiyamada, *t.*, Japan; sacred c. of Shintoism;

Ujjain, *t.*, Madhya Pradesh, India; sacred c. and formerly cap. of Malwa; univ.; p. (1961) *144,161*. [p. *76,000*.

Ujpest, *t.*, Hungary; nr. Budapest; elec. engin.;

Ukerewe, *I.*, on L. Victoria, Central Africa.

Ukraine, *constituent rep.*, U.S.S.R.; fertile "black earth" region; agr., wheat, maize, barley; tobacco, sheep, pigs; coal, iron-ore, manganese; mnfs., flour, sugar, brewing, chemicals, smelting, hydro-elec., oil; cap. Kiev; a. 225,000 sq. m.; p. (1959) *41,893,000*.

Ulan Bator, *t.*, *cap.*, Mongolian People's Republic; in stock-raising region; comm. ctr.; formerly called Urga; p. (1951) *70,000*.

Ulan-Ude, **(Verkhneudinsk)**, *t.*, Siberia, R.S.F.S.R.; on L. Baikal; engin., textiles, glass, leather; p. (1959) *174,000*.

Ulcinj, *ancient c.*, Montenegro, Jugoslavia; tobacco, olive oil; p. *5,000*.

Uleåborg (Oulu), *spt.*, Finland; on G. of Bothnia; shipbldg., exp. pitch, timber, hides, butter; p. (1961) *59,163*.

Ulhasnagar, *c.*, Maharashtra, India; new c. built for refugees from Pakistan; p. (1961) *107,760*.

Ullswater, *L.*, on border Cumberland and Westmorland, Eng.; 8 m. long; outlet by R. Eamont to the Eden.

Ulm, *c.*, Baden-Württemberg, W. Germany; on R. Danube; cath.; machin., textiles, cars, radios; rly junction; p. (1963) *94,400.*

Ulster, *anc. Irish prov.*; comprised nine counties: six of these (Down, Antrim, Armagh, Fermanagh, Londonderry and Tyrone) now form Northern Ireland, a. 5,238 sq. m.; p. (1961) *1,423,127*; three counties (Cavan, Monaghan, Donegal) are in the Rep. of Ireland; largely agr. a. 3,123 sq. m.; p. (1961) *217,489.*

Ulva, *I.*, Argyll, Scot.; off W. cst. of Mull; 5 m. long.

Ulverston, *t., urb. dist.*, N.W. Lancs, Eng.; nr. Morecambe Bay; paper-mills, hardware mftg.; iron, corn, brewing; p. (1961) *10,515.*

Ulyanovsk, *t.*, R.S.F.S.R.; on R. Volga; engin., textiles; p. (1959) *205,000.*

Uman, *t.*, Ukrainian S.S.R.; iron; p. (1954) *50,000.*

Umbria, *region*, Italy; between Tuscany and the Marches, and Rome and the Abruzzi; comprising the prov. of Perugia; mtnous., fertile valleys; a. 3,271 sq. m.; p. (1961) *788,546.*

Ume älv, *R.*, Sweden; flows S.E. to the G. of Bothnia; length 250 m.

Umeå, *t.*, Sweden; at mouth of Ume älv; wood-pulp; cultural ctr.; p. (1961) *22,623.*

Umtali, *t.*, Rhodesia; impt. distr. ctr., timber, fruit, veg., car assembly, engin., textiles; oil refinery at Feruka; pipeline to Beira p. (1961) *41,900* inc. *8,410* whites.

Umtata, *c.*, S. Africa; cath.; veg., dehydration, refinery at Feruka; pipeline to Beira; p. (1961) *41,900* inc. *8,410* whites.

Una, *R.*, N. Jugoslavia; trib. of R. Sava.

Unalaska, *lge. I.*, Alaska, U.S.A.; in Aleutian gr.; mtnous., treeless; ch. pt. of Bering Strait.

Uncia, *t.* Oruro dep., Bolivia; alt. 13,000 ft. in E. Cordillera of Andes, 60 m. S.E. of Oruro; site of impt. Patino tin-mines.

Ungava Bay, *arm of Hudson Strait*, projecting into Labrador, N.E. Canada; lge. forests in the S., minerals abundant, recent exploitation of impt. medium and low-grade iron deposits.

Union of African States, union formed by Ghana, Guinea, Mali (1 July, 1961).

Union of South Africa—*see* **South Africa, Rep. of.**

Union of Soviet Socialist Republics, *cty.*, Europe, Asia; stretches across two continents from the Baltic Sea to the N. Pac. Oc. and from the Arctic to the Black Sea, bounded on the W. by Finland, Poland, Hungary and Romania, on the S. by Turkey, Persia, Afghanistan, and China; The Union consists of 15 Union Republics; R.S.F.S.R., Ukranian, Byelorussian, Azerbaydzhan, Georgian, Armenian, Turkmen, Uzbek, Tadzik, Kazakh, Kirghiz, Moldavian, Estonian, Lithuanian and Latvian S.S.R.'s. These reps. are divided into 126 terrs. and regions which include 18 autonomous reps., 10 autononomous regions and 10 national areas. European portion, separated in the E. from Asia by Ural Mtns., is a vast low plain with Caucasus Mtns. in the S. In Asia the ctr. and N. is occupied by the vast plain of Siberia, rising in the S. to lofty mtn. ranges, Pamirs, Tien Shan, Sayan, Yablonovy, Stanovoi, etc. Rs. are impt.: Dnieper, Volga, Ural and Don in Europe flowing southwards; Ob, Yenisei and Lena in Asia flowing northwards into Arctic Ocean; and Amur into Pac. Oc. N. and central regions—long, cold winters; short, cool summers, S. regions—temperate and sub-tropical; desert and semi-desert E. of Caspian Sea. In N. tundra and immense forests with lumbering and associated inds.; agr., wheat, oats, barley, rye, flax, potatoes, sugar-beet, tobacco, cotton, silk, rubber, vines, tea, rice; rich fisheries; impt. minerals; coal, oil, lignite, iron ore, manganese, chrome ore, platinum, copper, lead, zinc, nickel, uranium, asbestos, mica, apatite, nepheline bauxite; many hydro-elect. plants inc. lgst. in Europe; nuclear power stas.; good rly. and canal systems; highly developed inds. inc. metallurgical prods., textiles, chemicals, cellulose-paper and lumbering, leather goods, food-stuffs preparation. Ch. spts. Leningrad, Murmansk, Arkhangelsk, Vladivostok (kept open by icebreakers), Odessa, Sevastopol, Novorossik, Batumi; cap. Moscow; a 8,708,070 sq. m.; p. (1963) *225,000,000.*

Union City, *t.*, N.J., U.S.A.; p. (1960) *52,180.*

Uniontown, *bor.*, Penns., U.S.A.; glasswks., iron foundries; p. (1960) *17,947.*

United Arab Republic (Egypt), *ind. sovereign st.*, since Feb. 1958; desert, except fertile Nile valley; agr. depends on annual rise of the Nile waters and irrigation (Aswan High Dam); climate: hot, dry summers, warm winters with little rain; agr.; wheat, barley, rice, onions, cotton; phosphates; communications: Nile rly. Cairo–Aswan. caravan routes across desert; Moslem; cap. Cairo; chief spt. Alexandria; a. 386,100 sq. m.; p. (1961) *26,059,000.*

United Arab States, Federation of United Arab Republic and Yemen.

United Kingdom, *cty.*, N.W. Europe; separated from continent of Europe by Eng. Channel; consists of Gr. Britain (Eng., Wales, Scot.) and N. Ireland. *See under separate headings.*

United Provinces, India. *See* **Uttar Pradesh.**

United States, *federal rep.*, N. America; ch. physical features: Great Ls., lgst. freshwater a. in the world; ch. Rs.: Mississippi–Missouri, Rio Grande del Norte, Colorado, Hudson, Susquehanna, Savannah, Columbia; ch. mtns.; Rocky Mtns., Coast Range, Sierra Nevada, Appalachian Mtns.; Great Basin, great plains, Piedmont plateau, coastal plains; climate in N.E.—cool, temperate, rainfall all year round, warm summers, cold winters; in central plains and Gr. Basin—continental climate of extremes; in N.W.—cool temperate with abundant rainfall warm summers, cold winters; in S.W. on Pacific cst.—Mediterranean climate of very warm summers and drought, mild winters with rainfall, dense fogs off Pacific cst.; in S. and S.E. sub-tropical, hot summers, mild winters with abundant rainfall in the S.E. decreasing towards the W.; ch. inds.: agr., maize, wheat, oats, etc., fruit, potatoes, hay, alfalfa, cane- and beet-sugar, cotton, tobacco; pastoral farming, ranching, dairying, sheep, wool, cattle, pigs, horses; lumbering, timber, wood-pulp; fishing off Grand Bank, Newfoundland, for cod, etc., and in W for salmon; minerals: coal, petroleum, natural gas, phosphate, iron ore, copper, lead, gold, silver, zinc, aluminium, mercury; mftg. of all kinds; commerce; comprises 50 sts. and Dist. of Columbia; cap. Washington; lgst. ts. New York, Chicago, Philadelphia; total land a. (inc. extra-territorial possessions); a. *3,608,787* sq. m.; p. (1964) *191,334,000.*

University City, *t.*, Mo., U.S.A.; p. (1960) *51,249.*

Unna, *t.*, N. Rhine–Westphalia, Germany; coal-mng., machin., iron; p. (1963) *31,000.*

Unst, *I.*, Shetlands; most N. of gr.; length 12½ m.

Unstrut, *R.*, Saxony, Germany; trib. of R. Saale, length 110 m.

Untersee, W. portion of L. of Constance.

Unterwalden, *old can.*, Switzerland; now subdivided into Obwalden and Nidwalden; dairying, fruit and livestock; ch. ts. are Sarnen and Stans.

Unter-Yberg, *vil.*, Switzerland; medicinal springs.

Upholland, *t., urb. dist.*, Lancs, Eng.; 4 m. W. of Wigan; bricks; p. (1961) *7,451.*

Upper Austria, *prov.*, Austria; cap. Linz; a. 4,625 sq. m.; p. (1961) *1,131,623.*

Upper Nile, *prov.*, Sudan, N.E. Africa; cap. Malakal; a. 92,270 sq. m.; p. (estd. 1951) *852,200.*

Upper Seal Lake, Labrador, Newfoundland, Canada.

Upper Volta, see **Voltaic Republic.**

Uppingham, *mkt. t., rural dist.*, Rutland, Eng.; 4 m. S. of Oakham; p. (rural dist. 1961) *5,340.*

Uppsala, *co.*, E. Sweden: N. of L. Mälar; cap. Uppsala; a. 2,056 sq. m.; p. (1961) *167,735.*

Uppsala, *t.*, cap. Uppsala, Sweden; on R. Sala; 45 m. from Stockholm; univ., cath.; lt. inds.; p. (1961) *77,518.*

Ur, *ancient* Chaldean *c.* Iraq; 130 m. W.N.W. of Basra; ruins; flourished about 3,000 B.C.

Ural Mtns., R.S.F.S.R.; mtns. separating Asia from Europe; 2,050 m. long; highest summit, Tolposis Mtn., 5,430 ft.

Ural, *R.*, R.S.F.S.R.; flows S.W. and S. to the Caspian Sea; length 1,500 m.

Uralsk, *t.*, Kazakh S.S.R.; on R. Ural; grain-trading and cattle-mart. ctr.; flour, leather, woollens, iron-ware; p. (1959) *105,000*

Uranium City, N. Saskatchewan, Canada; nr. N. shore of L. Athabasca, ctr. of Beaverlodge uranium-mining a.; founded 1951; p. (1953) approx. *500.*

Urbana, *c.*, Ill., U.S.A.; on Embarrass R.; seat of st. univ.; p. (1960) *27,294.*

Urbino, *t.*, N. Marche, Italy; cath., univ.; silk, cheese, olive oil; p. *20,375.*

Ure, *R.*, N.R.; Yorks, Eng. flows E. and S.E. to the Swale to form the Ouse; length 50 m.
Urfa, *t.*, Turkey; nr. Syrian border; gd. local tr.; p (1960) *59,910.*
Urga, *see* **Ulan Bator.**
Uri, *can.*, Switzerland; S. of L. of Lucerne; forest and mtn.; traversed by St. Gotthard Rly. and R. Reuss; cap. Altdorf; a. 415 sq. m.; p. (1961) *32,021.*
Urmia (Rizaieh), *t.*, Azerbaijan, Iran; birth-place of Zoroaster; p. *64,000.*
Urmia, L. of, nr. Tabriz, N.W. Iran; 85 m. by 30 m.; salt and shallow.
Urmston, *urb. dist.*, Lancs, Eng.; p. (1961) *42,983.*
Urubamba, *R.*, Peru, S. America; rises in E. Cordillera of Andes; forms one of head streams of R. Amazon; length 350 m.
Uruguaiana, *t.* Brazil; on R. Uruguay; cattle ctr.; jerked beef, soap, candles; p. (1960) *48,358.*
Uruguay, *rep.*, S. America; climate, temperate; moderate rainfall; vegetation temperate and sub-tropical grasslands; language, Spanish; religion, R. C.; cattle- and sheep-rearing, wheat, olives, grapes, gold, textiles; cap. Montevideo; a. 72,153 sq. m.; p. (estd. 1956) *2,668,130.*
Uruguay, *R*, S. America; rises n S. Brazil, and flows between Argentina and Brazil and Uruguay to Rio de la Plata; length 850 m.
Urumchi (Wulumuchi), *c.*, Sinkiang, China; p. (1953) *141,000*
Urup, *I.*, Kurile gr., Pac. Oc.; 50 m. long; 12 m. wide.
Usa, *R.*, U.S.S R.; flows E. from the Urals to the Pechora; length 220 m.
Usak, *t.*, Turkey; connected by rail with Izmir; noted for pile carpet-weaving; p. (1960) *28,927.*
Usedom (Uznam), *I.*, Baltic Sea; off mouth of R. Oder; since 1945 the E. part belongs to Poland, the W. (the larger part) to Germany; I. is 30 m. long and 14 m. wide.
Ushant, *I.*, off cst. of Finisterre, France; at entrance to Eng. Channel; it was off Ushant that Lord Howe gained his great naval victory on the "glorious first of June," 1794.
Ushuaia, *t.*, Argentina; most southerly t. in world; sheep farming, timber, furs; freezing plant; p. *2,500.*
Usk, *R.*, S. Wales and Monmouth, Eng.; flows S. to Bristol Channel; length 57 m.
Usküdar (Scutari), *t.*, Turkey; on the Bosporus, opposite Istanbul; silks, cottons, muslin; p. (estd. 1960) *85,000.*
Uspallata Pass, Andes, Argentina; used by the Mendoza–Valparaiso Transandine rly.
Ussuriysk (Voroshilov), *t.*, R.S.F.S.R.; 70 m. N. of Vladivostok; rly. junction; soya oil, sugar; p. (1959) *104,000.*
Ust Kamenogorsk, *t.*, Kazakhstan, U.S.S.R.; lead refining; hydro-elec. power sta. nearby on R. Irtish; p. (1959) *117,000.*
Ustica, *I.*, Italy; hilly; fruit, olives, grain, osiers; fishing; a. 3 sq. m.
Usti Nad Labem, *t.*, ČSSR.; on the Elbe; chemicals, coal; p. (1962) *63,819.*
Usumacinta, *R.*, Mexico and Guatemala, Central America; trib. of R. Tabasco; length 400 m.
Usumbura, *t.*, Burundi, Africa; cotton ginnery, soapwks.; exp. cotton, coffee, hides; p. (estd. 1949) *17,188.*
Ussuri, *R.*, N. China; flows to R. Amur; length 340 m.
Utah, *W. st.*, U.S.A.; Mormons form about 91% of the church membership of the st.; farming, wheat, maize, barley, rye, livestock, sugar-beet, fruits; copper, silver, lead, gold, coal, uranium, vanadium; petroleum; fruit-canning; cap. Salt Lake City; a. 84,916 sq. m.; p. (1960) *890,627.*
Utah, *L.*, U.S A.; 23 m. long and 4,400 ft. above sea-level, discharges by R. Jordan to the Gr. Salt L
Utica, *c.*, N.Y., U.S.A.; on Mohawk R.; clothing and other mnfs.; p. (1960) *100,410.*
Utiel, *t.*, Spain; W. of Valencia: brandies, wines; p. (1957) *13,365.*
Utrecht, *prov.*, Neth.; between Guelderland and N. and S. Holland; fertile agr., stock-raising and horticultural dist. S. of the Zuider Zee; a. 526 sq. m.; p. (estd. 1959) *673,601.*
Utrecht, *c.*, Neth.; on Old R. Rhine; univ., cath.; chemical and cigar factories; printing, machin., woollens, silks, velvets; p. (1960) *254,186.*
Utera, *t.*, Spain; S.E. of Seville; industl.; p. (1957) *34,893.*
Uttar Pradesh, *st.*, India; Himalayas on N. bdy., drained by Ganges and Jumna; splendid irrigation; wheat, rice, millet, barley, maize, cotton, sugar, oil-seeds; ch. ts. Allahabad, Lucknow (cap.), Varanasi, Cawnpore, Agra, Meerut; a. 113,410 sq. m.; p. (1961) *73,746,401.*
Uttoxeter, *t.*, *urb. dist.*, Staffs, Eng.; on R. Dove, 10 m. N.W of Burton-on-Trent; machin., biscuit mftg.; p. (1961) *8,168.*
Uusimaa, *dep.*, Finland; a. 4,435 sq. m.; cap. Helsinki; p. (1961) *832,936.*
Uvira, *pt.*, Congo, Central Africa; on N.W. cst. of L. Tanganyika; exp. coffee, cotton, hides; bricks, cotton ginning.
Uxbridge, *mkt. t.*, *former mun. bor.*; Middx. Eng.; on R. Colne; now inc. in Hillingdon outer bor., Greater London; residtl.; light inds., film studio; p. (1961) *63,941.*
Uzbekistan, *constituent rep.*, U.S.S.R.; intensive farming based on irrigation; rice, cotton, fruits, silk, cattle, sheep; cap. Tashkent; a. 159,170 sq. m.; p. (1959) *8,113,000.*
Uzen, (Gr. and Little), *Rs.*, U.S.S.R., flowing 250 m. to the Caspian Sea.
Uzgen, *region*, Kirghiz, S.S.R., U.S.S.R.; coal cotton. engin.
Uzhgorod, *t.*, Ukrainian S.S.R.; univ.; wood-workings, food inds.; engin.; p. (1959) *47,000.*
Uzhoi Cape, *promontory*, on Ob. Bay, N. Siberia, U.S.S.R.
Uzlovaya, *t.*, R.S.F.S.R.; 30 m. S.E. of Tula; coal mng.; impt. rly. junction; p. (1959) *54,000.*

V

Vaal, *R.*, S. Africa; rises in Drakensberg Mtns., and flows between the Transvaal and Orange Free State to join the Orange R. nr. Kimberley; length 560 m.
Vaasa (Vasa), *dep.*, Finland; cap. Vaasa; p. (1961) *443,505.*
Vaasa, *t.*, *pt.*, *cap.*, Vaasa Finland; on G. of Bothnia; oats, butter, cattle exp.; p. (1961) *43,721.*
Vác, *t.*, Hungary; on R. Danube; chemicals, surveying instruments; p. (1962) *26,679.*
Vaduz, *t.*, *cap.*, Liechtenstein; p. (1950) *2,735.*
Váh, *R.*, Czechoslovakia; trib. of R. Danube; length 200 m.
Val de Chiana, *see* **Chiana, Val de.**
Valais, *can.*, Switzerland; comprising upper valley of R Rhône; surrounded by high mtns.; cap. Sion; a. 2,021 sq. m.; p. (1961) *177,783.*
Valdai Hills, U.S.S.R.; N.W. of Moscow; highest summit 1,100 ft.
Valdecañas, Spain, 120 m. S.W. Madrid; dam and power sta.
Valdepeñas, *t.*, Central Spain; mineral springs, wine; p *26,000*
Valdivia, *prov.*, S. Chile: cap. Valdivia: a. 7,721 sq. m.; p. (1960) *302,779.*
Valdivia, *t.*, cap. Valdivia, S. Chile; on R. Calle-calle nr. the sea (pt. Corral); damaged by earth-quake and tidal wave, May 1960; univ.; metal, wood and leather goods; paper, flour, brewing; p. (1961) *85,000.*
Valdosta, *t.*, Ga., U.S.A.; rly. ctr., cotton mills, light engin.; p. (1960) *30,652.*
Valence, *t.*, cap. Drôme, France; on left bank of R. Rhône; metal-founding, silks, hosiery, vineyards; p. (1962) *55,023.*
Valencia, *prov.*, Spain; on Mediterranean; agr., vineyards, olive-, fig-, and orange-growing, stock-rearing, silk, tapestry carpet mftg.; cap. Valencia; a. 4,239 sq. m.; p. (1959) *1,451,037.*
Valencia, *t.*, cap. Valencia, Spain; on R. Turia, 3 m. from the Mediterranean; univ., museum, cath.; active industl. and comm. ctr.; mnfs., linen, leather, cigars, silks, exp. wine, fruits, corn, etc.; p. (1959) *543,736.*
Valencia, *I.*, S.W Kerry, Ireland; 6 m. by 2 m.
Valencia, *t.*, Venezuela, S. America; univ.; ctr. of agr. a.; most industrialised town in rep.; p. (1961) *161,410.*
Valencia, *L.*, Venezuela; a. 216 sq. m.; surrounded by swampy flats used for cattle-grazing.
Valenciennes, *fortfd. t.*, Nord. France; on R. Escaut; lace; metallurgical inds., starch, chemicals, coal, iron; p. (1962) *46,643.*
Valera, *t.*, Trujillo, Venezuela; airport; p. (1961) *44,820.*
Valladolid, *prov.*, Central Spain; agr., vineyards, livestock, mnfs.; cap. Valladolid; a. 3,155 sq. m.; p. (1959) *368,049.*
Valladolid, *t.*, cap. Valladolid, Spain; on R.

Pisuerga; seat of army corps, univ., cath.; thriving inds. and tr.; p. (1959) *145,213.*
Vallecas, *sub.* Madrid, Spain.
Valle d'Aosta, *aut. region,* N.W. Italy; a. 1,260 sq. m.; p. (1961) *99,754.*
Valle del Cauca, *dep.,* Colombia, S. America; cap. Cali.; a. 8,083 sq. m.; p. (estd. 1959) *1,596,650.*
Vallejo, *c.,* Cal., U.S.A.; exp. fruit and corn, milling; p. (1960) *60,977.*
Vallenar, *t.,* Atacama prov., Chile; agr. ctr.; dried fruit, wines; iron ore nearby; p. (1960) *30,793.*
Valletta, *ch. t., spt.,* Malta; on N.E. cst. of I.; strongly fortfd., fine harbour; univ.; cath.; p. (1960) *18,000.*
Valleyfield, *t.,* Quebec, Canada; textiles, glazed paper; p. (1961) *27,297.*
Valona, *see* Vlonë.
Valparaiso, *prov.,* Chile; cap. Valparaiso; a. 1,860 sq. m.; p. (1961) *648,449.*
Valparaiso, *c., spt.,* cap. Valparaiso, Chile; the most impt. pt. on the Pacific cst. of S. America, and the ch. mftg., comm. and industl. ctr. of the Rep. of Chile; locomotives rolling-stock, sugar-refining, textiles, chemicals, tanneries; p. (1961) *259,241.*
Van, *fortfd. c.,* Turkey; on E. side of L. Van, S. of Erzurum; p. (1960) *22,018.*
Van, *I.,* Turkey; mtnous., pastoral; sulphur springs, petroleum wells; p. (1945) *126,919.*
Vancouver, *spt.,* B.C., Canada; international airport and terminus of trans-continental rly.; univ.; lumbering, shipbldg., fishing; oil- and sugar-refining; p. (1961) *790,165.*
Vancouver, *t.,* Wash., U.S.A.; dairying, milling, fruit, lumbering, canning; p. (1960) *32,464.*
Vancouver, *I.,* B.C., Canada; off W. cst.; forestry, fishing, dairying, coal, tourism; cap. Victoria; a. 12,408 sq. m.; p. (1956) *361,952.*
Vanderbijlpark, *t.,* Transvaal, S. Africa; on Vaal R.; ctr. for steel wks.; p. (1960) *41,318* (inc. *21,857* whites.)
Van Diemen Gulf, between Darwin and Coburg Peninsula, N. Terr., Australia.
Vänern, *lge. L.,* Sweden; W.N.W. of L. Vättern, with which it is connected by canal (and thence with the Baltic); a. 2,149 sq. m.
Vänersborg, *L. pt.,* Sweden; on a tongue of land between the R. Göta and the Vasobotten (the southernmost bay of L. Vänern); footwear, wood and sulphite pulp; p. (1961) *18,491.*
Vannes, *ch. t.,* Morbihan, France; on S. cst. Brittany; shipbldg., ironwks., breweries, ropes, leather, oysters; p. (1954) *28,403.*
Var, *R.,* Alpes-Maritimes, France; flows S. to the Mediterranean Sea; length 60 m.
Var, *dep.,* S. France; on the Mediterranean; pasture, vineyards, sericulture, wines, olives, paper; cap. Draguignan, Toulon lgst. c.; a. 2,333 sq. m.; p. (1962) *469,557.*
Varanasi (formerly **Benares**) *t.,* India; on Ganges, Hindu holy city; annual pilgrimage; temples, mosques, palaces, univ.; brocade, gold, silver, lacquer; p. (1961) *489,864.*
Varanger Fjord, an inlet of the Arctic Ocean into Finnmark, Norway's most N. prov
Varazdin, *t.,* Croatia, Jugoslavia; on R. Drava; woollens, coal; p. (1959) *23,000.*
Varberg, *spt.,* Halland, Sweden; resort; granite quarries; p. *11,874.*
Vardar, *R.,* Jugoslavia, Greece; flows S. into G. of Thessalonika; length 280 m.
Varde, *t.,* W. Jutland, Denmark; recently developed as agr. and route ctr.; food processing; steelwks.; p. (1960) *9,577.*
Varese, *t.,* N. Italy; silk-spinning, wine, paper, leather, aircraft; p. (1961) *64,977.*
Värmland, *co.,* Sweden; a. 7,427 sq. m.; p. (1961) *291,085.*
Varna, *fortfd. spt.,* Bulgaria; on Black Sea; univ.; shipbldg., textiles, grain; trading ctr.; p. (1956) *119,769.*
Varpalota, *t.,* Hungary; lignite mines; aluminium; [p. (1962) *22,853.*
Vasa, *see* Vaasa.
Vásárhely or **Hódmezö Vásárhely,** *t.,* Hungary; wine, tobacco.
Västerås, *t., cap.,* Västmanland, Sweden; on N. bay of L. Malar; Gothic cath. (with episcopal library), 16th-century cas.; impt. elec. inds.; power sta.; p. (1961) *77,946.*
Västerbotten, *co.,* Sweden; a. 22,839 sq. m.; p. (1961) *239,625.*
Västernorrland, *co.,* Sweden; a. 9,925 sq. m.; p. (1959) *288,231.*
Västervik, *t.,* Sweden; on Baltic cst.; engin., iron, wire, nails, chemicals, paper; p. (1961) *18,193.*
Västmanland, *co.,* Sweden; N. of L. Malar; cap. Västeras; a. 2,611 sq. m.; p. (1961) *232,589.*
Vathéos, *spt.,* Samos I., Greece; exp. wine, olive oil, leather, tobacco, raisins.
Vatican City, the Papal st. of Italy; a. 108.7 acres; p. (estd.) *1,000.*
Vatna Jökull, *mtn.,* Iceland; elevated snowfield.
Vättern, *L.,* Sweden: 25 m. S.E. L. Vänern; a. 733 sq. m.
Vaucluse, *dep.,* S.E. France; agr., wines, sericulture, linen, silks, pottery; cap. Avignon; a. 1,381 sq. m.; p. (1962) *303,536.*
Vaud, or **Pays de Vaud,** *can.,* W. Switzerland; N. of L. of Geneva; timber, forests and vineyards; cap. Lausanne; a. 1,239 sq. m.; p. (1961) *429,512.*
Växjö, *t.,* S. Sweden; engin., timber wks., hosiery; p. (1961) *24,041.*
Vecht, R., Neth.: branch of Rhine, flows into Ijsselmeer.
Vecses, *t.,* Hungary; p. (1962) *15,540.*
Véjer de la Frontera, *t.,* Spain; nr. C. Trafalgar; agr. and stock-rearing; p. (1957) *12,569.*
Vejle, *spt.,* Jutland, Denmark; gd. harbour and tr.; textiles, iron ind., leather, soap; p. (1960) *31,362.*
Velbert, *t.,* N. Rhine-Westphalia, Germany; N.W. of Wuppertal; metal ind. locks and keys; p. (1963) *53,000.*
Veliki Bečkerek, *see* **Zrenjanin.**
Veles, *see* Titov Veles.
Velez Málaga, *c.,* Malaga, Spain; famous for wine, raisins, sugar, olive oil; p. (1957) *31,610.*
Veliki Ustyug, *t.,* R.S.F.S.R.; on R. Sukhona; shipbldg., silver craft; p. (1956) *35,800.*
Velletri, *t.,* Italy; foot of the Alban Hills overlooking Pontine Marshes; gd. wine; at this spot Garibaldi gained a victory over the King of Naples, 1849; p. (1961) *40,053.*
Vellore, *t.,* Madras, India; perfumes, etc.; p. (1961) *113,742.*
Veluwe, *dist.,* Gelderland, Neth.; between Arnhem and Ijsselmeer (Zuiderzee); low hills of glacial sands and sand-dunes; heathland and pinewoods; relatively low p. density.
Vendée or **La Vendée,** *dep.,* W. France; on Bay of Biscay; agr. pasturage, vineyards, fishery, sea-salt, coal and some mnfs.; cap. La Roche-sur-Yon; a. 2,692 sq. m.; p. (1962) *408,928.*
Vendôme, *t.,* Loir-et-Cher, France; on R. Loire; leather goods, cottons; p. (1954) *10,811.*
Venetia (Veneto or Venetia Euganea), *div.* N.E. Italy; between the Alps and the Adriatic; embraces provs. Vicenza, Verona, Venice, Udine, Treviso, Padua, Belluno and Rovigo; cap. Venice; a. 7,098 sq. m.; p. (1961) *3,833,837.*
Venetia Tridentina, *div.,* N Italy; mountainous lying between Austrian and Swiss frontier and L. Garda; embraces provs. Trento and Bolzano; cap. Trento; a. 5,250 sq. m.; p (1961) *747,221.*
Venezia Giulia, *see* **Friuli-Venezia Giulia.**
Venezuela, *rep.,* S. America; on Caribbean cst. climate tropical, with temperate uplands, we summers, dry winters, tropical forests, an grasslands (llanos); petroleum (one of the lgst oil producing ctys. of the world), gold, copper iron ore, coal, asphalt; new inds. in petrol a inc. aluminium, cars, textiles, glass, agr. imple ments; pearl fishing, coffee, cocoa, sugar, maize cotton, indigo, balata, tobacco; cap. Carácas a. 352,143 sq. m.; p. (1963) *8,255,456.*
Venice, *maritime c.,* Italy; built on group of islet within a lagoon in G. of Venice, at head of th Adriatic; splendid architecture; rich in a treasures and historic associations; glasswar gold, silver, embroidery, lace, damask, shi bldg.; p. (1961) *336,184.*
Venlo, *t.,* Neth.; on the Maas; brewing, leathe needles, tobacco; p. (1960) *54,516.*
Vennachar, *Loch,* Perth, Scot.; expansion R. Teith.
Ventimiglia, *t., cst. resort,* Italy; on Mediterranea cst. nr. Fr. border; cath.; p. *17,081.*
Ventnor, *t., urb. dist.,* I. of Wight, Eng.; on S. cs 11 m. S. of Ryde; mild climate, tourist ar health resort; p. (1961) *6,410.*
Ventolene I., Pontine Is., Italy; vineyard fruit.
Veracruz, *c., pt.,* Veracruz, Mexico; on G.

Mexico; exp. ores, precious metals, textiles, raw cotton and petrol; p. (1960) 144,232.

Veracruz, prov., Mexico; contains volcano Orizaba; cap. Jalapa; a. 27,736 sq. m.; p. (1960) 2,727,899.

Veraguas, prov., Panama, central America; cap. Santiago; p. (1950) 106,998.

Vercelli, c., Piedmont, Italy; cath.; cottons, woollens, machin., aircraft parts; exp. rice; p. (1961) 50,197.

Verde, C., most W. point, Africa, Senegal.

Verden, c., Lower Saxony, Germany; S.E. of Bremen; cath.; machin., glass, tobacco; p. (estd. 1954) 19,900.

Verdun, t., Quebec, Canada; p. (1961) 78,317.

Verdun, fortfd. t., Meuse, France; on R. Meuse; 12th-century cath.; confectionery, liqueur, hardware factories; scene of famous battle in First World War; p. (1954) 18,831.

Vereeniging, t., Transvaal, S. Africa; coal, iron and steel, bricks; Treaty of Vereeniging (31 May 1902) ended Boer War; p. (1962) 88,008 inc. 26,234 whites.

Verkhneudinsk, see Ulan-Ude.

Verkhneuralsk, t., R.S.F.S.R.; on Upper Ural R.; tanneries, distilleries; p. (1956) 11,000.

Verkhoyansk, t., Yakutsk A.S.S.R., R.S.F.S.R.; in N.E. Siberia; coldest place in world; mean January temp. of –59° F.; ctr. of fur trapping a.; p. (1956) 1,800.

Vermont, st., New England, U.S.A.; adjoining Quebec prov., Canada; traversed by the Green Mtns.; farming, dairying, stock-raising, lumbering, quarrying, machin. tool and textile mnftg.; cap. Montpelier; a. 9,609 sq. m.; p. (1960) 389,881.

Vernon, t., B.C., Canada; fruit, farming, canning; p. (1961) 10,250.

Verona, fortfd. c., Venetia, Italy; on R. Adige; beautiful cath.; Roman antiquities; active tr. and inds.; iron goods, machin., paper, silk; p. (1961) 221,138.

Verona, prov. of Venetia region, Italy; a. 1,188 sq. m.; p. (1961) 665,053.

Verroia, t., N. Greece; S.E. of Thessaloniki; ancient Berea; p. (1961) 25,765.

Versailles, c., Seine-et-Oise, France; 12 m. W.S.W. of Paris; famous royal palace; mkt. gardening, distilleries, etc.; Treaty of Versailles 1919; p. (1962) 95,149.

Verulam, t., Natal, S. Africa; sugar, tobacco, fruit plantations; p. 1,878

Verulamium, site of ancient Roman t., Herts, Eng.; on R. Ver, opposite St. Albans; impt. during Roman occupation.

Verviers, t., Belgium; nr. Liége; cloth mnfs., glass, polystyrene mftg.; p. (1962) 35,125.

Vest Fjord, strait, separates Lofoten Is., from mainland, Norway.

Vestfold, co., Norway; a. 96,359 sq. m.; p. (1963) 177,438.

Vesuvius, famous active volcano, S. Italy; on side of Bay of Naples; alt. 3,984 ft.; its eruption in A.D. 79 destroyed Pompeii and Herculaneum, and frequent eruptions have since occasioned havoc; funicular rly. from the base of the mtn. to the edge of the crater since 1880.

Veurne (Furnes), t., W. Flanders, Belgium; sugar-refining; warehouses; p. (1962) 7,315.

Vevey, t., Vaud, Switzerland; on N.E. shore of L. of Geneva; chocolate, watches, machin.; p. (1957) 14,264.

Viacha, t., Bolivia, S. America; rly. junction nr. La Paz; cement; p. 2,000.

Viana do Castello, dist., Portugal; cap. Viana do Castello; a. 814 sq. m.; p. (1950) 275,969.

Viana do Castello, t., Portugal; at mouth of R. Lima, nr. Oporto; p. (1960) 282,611.

Viareggio, spt., resort, Italy; on Mediterranean, nr. Pisa; monument to the poet Shelley; p. (1961) 47,323.

Viazma, t., R.S.F.S.R.; N.E. of Smolensk, industl.

Viborg, t., Jutland, Denmark; comm. and admin. ctr., knitted goods; cath.; p. (1960) 23,265.

Viborg (Viipuri), spt., R.S.F.S.R., U.S.S.R.; on G. of Finland; impt. industl. and transport ctr.; agr. machin., timber; p. (1959) 51,000.

Vicente Lopez, t., Buenos Aires, Argentina; p. 25,600.

Vicenza, c., Italy; woollens, cottons, silks, pottery, furniture mkg.; p. (1961) 97,617.

Vich (Vique), c., Spain; nr. Barcelona; cath.; mnfs.; p. (1957) 16,975.

Vichuga, t., R.S.F.S.R., N.E. of Ivanovo; ctr. of cotton ind.; p. (1959) 51,000.

Vichy, t., wat. pl., Allier, France; 35 m., S. of Moulins; mineral springs, lge. exp. of waters; seat of Gov. during German occupation. p. (1954) 30,403.

Vicksburg, c., Miss., U.S.A.; on cliffs above a "cut-off" L. on R. Mississippi; furniture, machin.; mftg. ctr. in cotton and timber region; prominent in American Civil War, Confederate surrender 1863; p. (1960) 29,130.

Victoria, st, Australian Commonwealth; mixed farming, grapes, mnfs., machin., hardware, textiles, wine, gold, coal, tin; oil refining at Crib Point, 45 m. from Melbourne; cap. Melbourne; a. 87,884 sq. m.; p. (1964) 3,161,537.

Victoria, c., cap., B.C., Canada; on Vancouver I., sawmills, cement, chemicals, fish-canning; p. (1961) 154,152. (p. 42,873.

Victoria, spt., cap., Espirito Santo st., Brazil;

Victoria, t., cap., Seychelles, Ind., Oc.; gd. harb.

Victoria, t., cap., Labuan I., Sabah; fine harbour; p. (estd. 1957) 2,526.

Victoria, t., cap., Hong Kong; built on reclaimed land; p. (estd. 1948) 766,800.

Victoria Falls, on the R. Zambesi, Zambia, discovered by Livingstone in 1855; falls are 1,860 yd. wide and broken by islands and rocks.

Victoria, L., Kenya, Uganda, Tanzania, E. Africa; lgst. L. of Africa; lies on the Equator; a. 25,000–26,000 sq. m.; discharges to the N. by R. Nile; 3,705 ft. above sea; discovered by Captain Speke in 1858.

Victoria, L., on Gr. Pamir, Central Asia; 13,870 ft. above sea-level; supposed to be ch. source of the R. Oxus.

Victoria, R., flows into Queens Channel, N.W. cst. of Northern Terr. Australia.

Victoria Land, terr., N. Canada; S.E. of Prince Albert Land.

Victoria Land, region, Antarctica; discovered by Ross in 1841.

Victoria Nile, R., Uganda, E. Africa; name of R. Nile from its source at L. Victoria until it enters L. Albert.

Victoria Strait, separates Victoria I. from King William I., Arctic Canada. [2,535.

Victoria West, t., Cape Province, S. Africa; p.

Victoriaville, t., Quebec, Canada; woodworking; p. (1961), 18,720.

Vidin, fortfd. t., Bulgaria; on R. Danube; ruined mosque and palace; p. (1956) 23,932.

Viedma, t., cap., Rio Negro, Argentina; p. (1960) 7,000

Vienna (Wien), cap., Austria; on branch of R. Danube; ranks also as prov.; univ., gothic cath. (St. Stephen's Church), Rathaus, Parliament bldgs., magnificent Prater park; thriving comm. and mnfs., silks, iron, steel, breweries, etc.; p. (1961) 1,627,566.

Vienne, R., France; trib. of the Loire; l. 220 m.

Vienne, dep., W. France; grain, wine, cutlery, arms; cap. Poitiers; a. 2,711 sq. m.; p. (1962) 331,619.

Vienne, t., Isère, France; nr. Grenoble, on R. Rhône; textiles, gloves; p. (1954) 25,669.

Vienne, Haute (Haute-Vienne), dep., France; fruits, cereals, livestock, porcelain; cap. Limoges; a. 2,119 sq. m.; p. (1962) 332,514.

Vientiane, cap., Laos; p. (estd. 1962) 100,000.

Viersen, t., N. Rhine–Westphalia, Germany; S.W. of Krefeld; textiles, machin., furniture, paper ind.; p. (1963) 42,200.

Vierzon, t., Cher, France; nr. Bourges; mnfs.; p. (1954) 28,627.

Viet-Nam, S.E. Asia; formerly within the French Union, covering 3 countries of Tongking, Annam and Cochin-China. Since 1954 div. into 2 zones. S. zone (Rep. of Vietnam) a. 66,300 sq. m., p. (estd. 1960) 14,100,000; cap. Saigon; rice, rubber. N. zone (Dem. Rep. of Vietnam) a. 63,000 sq. m., p. (1960) 15,903,000; cap. Hanoi; rice, coal, cement, apatite (phosphate).

Vigevano, t., Lombardy, Italy; on R. Ticino; cath.; silks; p. (1961) 57,069.

Vigo, fortfd. t., Galicia, Spain; on Rio de Vigo; impt. fishery and shipping inds.; flour, sugar, petroleum, leather; p. (1959) 165,682.

Vijyavada, t., Andhra Prad., India; irrigation dam, Kistna R., rice; p. (1961) 230,397.

Vila de João Belo (Chai Chai), t., Mozambique, Port. E. Africa; on R. Limpopo; exp. sugar, rice, timber, maize; p. 4,000.

Vila Nova de Gala, t., Portugal; sub. of Oporto;

on R. Douro; pottery, wine-casks, tobacco and glass factories; p. (1940) *34,398*.
Vila Real, *dist.*, Portugal; a. 1,636 sq. m.; p. (1960) *333,156*.
Villa Franca de los Barros, *t.*, Badajoz, Spain; wine and corn; p. *15,360*.
Villa Hermosa, *cap.*, Tabasco, Mexico; p. (1960) *33,587*.
Villa Maria, *t.*, Argentina; rly. junction; grain, timber, dairying; p. (1960) *50,000*.
Villach, *t.*, Austria; iron, timber, leather, beer; tourist ctr.; p. (1961) *32,971*.
Villanueva de la Serena, *t.*, prov., Badajoz, Spain; wine, wheat, hemp and fruit; p. (1957) *18,391*.
Villanueva y Geltrú, *spt.*, Spain; nr. Barcelona; cotton spinning and weaving, tyres; p. (1957) *19,483*.
Villarrica, *t.*, Paraguay; cath.; tobacco, cotton, sugar, yerba-maté, hides, wines; p. (estd. 1960) *30,700*.
Villavicencio, *t.*, cap. Meta, Colombia, S. America, cattle raising; p. (estd. 1962) *48,355*.
Villaviciosa, *spt.*, Spain; on N. cst. 10 m. E. of Gijon; p. (1957) *20,348*.
Villefranche, *t.*, Rhône, France; on R. Rhône, nr. Lyons; cottons, wines; p. (1954) *21,703*.
Villejuif, *t.*, Seine, France; p. (1962) *46,130*.
Villena, *t.*, Alicante, Spain; silk, salt, brandy; p. (1957) *19,994*.
Villeneuve St. Georges, *t.*, Seine-et-Oise, France; marshalling yards; p. (1954) *21,596*.
Villeurbanne, *t.*, Rhône, France; sub. Lyons; silk, rayon, metallurgy, chemicals, leather, glass; p. (1962) *107,630*.
Villingen, *t.*, Baden-Württemberg, Germany; in the Black Forest; clocks, elec., metals; p. (1963) *34,000*.
Vilnius (Wilno, Vilna), *cap.*, Lithuanian S.S.R.; Polish from 1919 to 1939; univ., cath.; timber, chemicals, engin.; p. (1962) *264,000*.
Vilvorde, *t.*, Brabant, Belgium; on R. Senne; oil and chemical factories; p. (1962) *32,133*.
Viña del Mar, *t.*, Chile; social resort; textiles, sugar; p. (1960) *126,441*.
Vincennes, *t.*, Ind., U.S.A.; milling, glass, steelwks.; p. (1960) *18,046*.
Vincennes, *sub.*, Paris, France; p. (1962) *50,499*.
Vindhya, *mtn. range*, Madhya Prad., India; separating the Deccan from the Ganges basin
Vindhya Pradesh, *former st.* Indian Union; now absorbed into Madhya Pradesh 1 Nov. 1956; cereals, oil seeds; coal, iron, copper, bauxite.
Vinnitsa, *t.*, Ukrainian S.S.R.; on R. Bug, 120 m. S.W. of Kiev; agr. mkt. t.; engin., chemicals, textiles; p. (1959) *121,000*.
Virginia, *st.*, U.S.A.; S. of Md.; tobacco culture; famous for natural bridge in Rockbridge County and mineral springs; "Virginia Leaf" tobacco is the finest the U.S. produces; rayon, shipbldg., iron, coal, chemicals; cap. Richmond; a. 40,815 sq. m.; p. (1960) *3,966,949*. *See also* **W. Virginia.**
Virginia Water, *artificial L.*, nr. Windsor, Berks, Eng.
Virgin Is. (Brit.), part of Leeward Is. gr., W. Indies, a. 67 sq. m.; lgst. I. Tortola; fruit, vegetables, charcoal, rum, sugar, tobacco; p. (estd. 1965) *8,500*.
Virgin Isles (U.S.A.), gr. in the W. Indies; E. of Puerto Rico; purchased by U.S.A. from Denmark 1917, comprising the Is. of St. Croix, St. Thomas and St. John, and about 50 sm. Is.; total a. 133 sq. m.; p. (1950) *26,665*.
Visby, *old spt.*, Sweden; on Gotland I. in Baltic Sea; rich in historic interest; Gothic churches; resort; p. (1961) *15,604*.
Viscaya, *Basque prov.*, Spain; on Bay of Biscay; mineral inds., shipping, etc.; cap. Bilbao; a. 836 sq. m.; p. (1959) *722,030*.
Vistula, *R.*, Poland; rising in Silesia, and flowing past Krakow and through Poland to the Baltic nr. Gdańsk; navigable from Krakow to the sea; length 693 m.
Vitebsk, *t.*, Byelorussian S.S.R.; on R. Dvina, 354 m. W. of Moscow; textile, machin. tools, food inds.; rly. junction; p. (1959) *148,000*.
Viterbo, *c.*, Italy; N. of Rome; alum mines, matches; p. (1961) *49,543*.
Vitim, *R.*, E., Siberia, R.S.F.S.R.; flows to R. Lena; length 900 m.
Vitória, *spt.*, Brazil; exp. coffee, cocoa, fruit, iron ore; sugar refining, boots, shoes, textiles, cement; p. (1960) *85,242*.
Vitoria, *cap.*, Alava, Spain; wine, hardware, mules, horses; p. (1959) *60,148*.
Vittoria, *t.*, Sicily, Italy; silk mftg.; p. *38,628*.
Vittorio Veneto, *t.*, Italy; N. of Venice; resort; mineral springs; silk; p. *24,234*.
Vizagapatam, *impt. spt.*, E. cst. India; Andhra Prad.; exp. manganese and other mineral ores, tobacco, oil-seed, myrabalams and coir; sm. shipyard; oil-refining; p. (1961) *182,004*.
Vizcaino Bay, Lower Cal., Mexico.
Vizcaya, *prov.*, N. Spain; cap. Bilbao; a. 836 sq. m.; p. (1950) *569,188*.
Vizeu, *dist.*, Portugal; cap. Vizeu; a. 1,955 sq. m.; p. (1960) *498,292*. [*76,808*.
Vizianagram, *t.*, Andhra Prad., India; p. (1961)
Vlaardingen, *fishing t.*, S. Holland, Neth.; on R. Maas; p. (1960) *68,129*.
Vladimir, *c.*, R.S.F.S.R.; between Gorki and Moscow; cath.; farm produce, fruit, tobacco, engin., chemicals; p. (1959) *154,000*.
Vladivostok, *t.*, *ch. spt.*, Siberia, U.S.S.R.; univ., H.Q. Army of the Far East; terminus of the Trans-Siberian rly. and airline from Moscow; oil-refining; p. (1962) *325,000*. [Neth.
Vlieland, *Friesian I.*, at entrance to Ijsselmeer.
Vlonë, *spt.*, Albania; on Strait of Otranto, Adriatic Sea; salt; oil pipe-line connects from Kuçovë; p. (1960) *33,000*.
Vltava, *R.*, Bohemia, Czechoslovakia; flows to R. Elbe, below Prague; length 262 m.
Voghera, *t.*, Italy; silks; p. *30,422*.
Voi, *t.*, *impt. rly. junction*, Kenya, E. Africa; 90 m. N.W. of Mombasa on rly. to Nairobi; branch connection with Tanzania rly. system allows agr. produce from Arusha and Moshi dists. to pass through Mombasa as alternative to Tanga.
Voiron, *t.*, Isère, France; on R. Isère nr. Grenoble; p. (1954) *13,551*.
Volga, *R.*, U.S.S.R.; rises on Vladai plateau, flows in a serpentine course to the Caspian at Astrakhan; frozen in winter; 2,325 m. long.
Volga Baltic Waterway (Mariinsk Waterway), R.S.F.S.R.; inland deep water navigation network linking Black Sea and Caspian Sea in S. with Baltic Sea and White Sea in N.
Volgograd (former **Stalingrad**), *c.*, R.S.F.S.R.; on R. Volga, S. of Saratov; steel, engin., chemicals, oil-refining, hydro-elec. sta.; fierce siege and successful defence Sept. to Nov. 1942 turning point of the last war; p. (1962) *649,000*.
Volhynia, *dist.*, part of Ukraine S.S.R., U.S.S.R.; on Polish frontier (Polish 1919–39); a. 13,750 sq. m.; now prov. of Lutsk and Rovno.
Volkhov, *R.*, R.S.F.S.R.; flows from L. Ilmen to L. Ladoga; length 130 m.
Völklingen, *t.*, Saarland; on R. Saar; coal-mining metallurgy; p. (1963) *42,900*.
Volksrust, *t.*, Transvaal, S. Africa; dairying; rly wkshps.; p. (1960) *8,096* inc. *3,776* Europeans
Vologda, *t.*, R.S.F.S.R., U.S.S.R.; engin., textiles sawmilling; p. (1959) *138,000*.
Vólos, *spt.*, Greece; at head of G. of Vólos; p (1951) *51,134*.
Volpiano, nr. Turin, Italy; oil refinery unde construction; pipeline to Geneva projected.
Volsk, *t.*, R.S.F.S.R.; on R. Volga; gd. tr.; iron wks., tanneries, milling; p. (1959) *62,000*.
Volta Redonda, Rio de Janeiro, Brazil; stee plants; p. (1960) *83,973*.
Volta (White Volta), *R.*, drains extensive terr. i Niger Bend, flows S. through Ghana to delt on Guinea cst. 70 m. E. of Accra; forms mai means of communication; rapids make throug navigation impossible; length 950 m. Volta R project for industrialisation of Ghana: dam an power plant at Akosombo, aluminium smelter a Tema. *See also* **Black Volta.**
Voltaic Republic (former **Upper Volta**), *ind. so st.*, W. Africa; cap. Ouagadougou; a. 122,00 sq. m.; p. (1961) *3,635,000*.
Volterra, *hill t.*, Tuscany, Italy; Etruscan an mediaeval walls; alabaster; p. *19,054*. [*10,00*
Voltri, *t.*, Italy; shrine, shipbldg., ironwks.; p
Volzhskiy, *t.*, R.S.F.S.R.; new town 10 m. E. o Volgagrad; p. (1959) *67,000*.
Vorarlberg, *prov.*, Austria; cap. Bregenz (*q.v.*) a. 1,004 sq. m.; p. (1961) *226,323*. [*11,78*
Vordingborg, S., *t.*, Zealand, Denmark; p. (196
Vorkuta, *dist.*, Siberia, R.S.F.S.R.; about 120 m W. of mouth of R Ob; new coal-minin ctr. which supplies entire European nort U.S.S.R.; p. of Vorkuta t. (1959) *55,000*.
Voronezh, *region*, R.S.F.S.R., U.S.S.R.; agr

stock-rearing, woodwork and domestic mnfs.; cap. Voronezh.

Voronezh, *t.*, R.S.F.S.R., U.S.S.R.; on R. Voronezh nr. its junction with R. Don; univ.; impt. comm. ctr.; synthetic rubber, engin.; p. (1962) *516,000*.

Voroshilovgrad *see* **Lugansk.**

Voroshilovsk, *t.*, Ukrainian S.S.R.; 25 m. S.W. of Lugansk; ctr. of iron, steel and coking inds.; p. (1956) *98,000*.

Vosges, *mtn. chain*, E. France; 190 m. long; highest summit, the Ballon de Guebwiller (4,672 ft.).

Vosges, *E. frontier dep.*, France; agr., dairying, vineyards, textiles, coal, stone; cap. Epinal; a. 2,305 sq. m.; p. (1962) *380,676*.

Voskresensk, *t.*, R.S.F.S.R.; S.E. Moscow; lignite, chemicals, fertilisers; p. (1954) *50,000*.

Votkinsk, *t.*, R.S.F.S.R.; 38 m. N.E. of Izhevsk; lge. engin. plant; p. (1959) *59,000*.

Voyusa, *R.*, rises in Greece, flows N.W. through Albania into Strait of Otranto.

Vranja, *t.*, Jugoslavia; flax and hemp culture and mnf.; nr. is health resort of Vranyskas Banya; p. (1959) *15,000*.

Vratca, *t.*, Bulgaria; on R. Vratcanska; jewellery, wine, silk, tanning; p. (1956) *26,582*.

Vrede, *t.*, O.F.S., S. Africa; agr. ctr.; horse-breeding; p. (1960) *6,770* (inc. *2,106* whites).

Vrsac, *t.*, Jugoslavia; milling, wine, brandy; p. (1959) *30,000*.

Vryburg, *t.*, Cape Province, S. Africa; gold field in a.; stock-raising; p. (1960) *14,597* (inc. *4 809* whites).

Vryheid, *t.*, Natal, S. Africa; coal, iron, copper, gold, silver, lead mines; p. (1960) *10,783* (inc. *4,920* whites).

Vulcan Pass, in the Carpathian Mtns., between Romania and Transylvania.

Vulcano, *I.*, Lipari gr., Tyrrhenian Sea; located 12 m. off N.E. cst., Sicily; active volcano; gave its name as generic title for this type of mtn.

Vychegda, *R.*, Komi A.S.S.R., R.S.F.S.R.; flows W. to N. Dvina R.; length 700 m.

Vyrnwy, *L.*, *artificial reservoir*, Montgomery, Wales; with a dam 1,180 ft. long furnishing water for Liverpool; 5 m. long; a. 1,121 acres

Vyshni-Volochek, *t.*, R.S.F.S.R., U.S.S.R.; 74 m. N.W. of Kalinin; flour-milling, textiles, glass inds.; p. (1959) *66,000*.

W

Waag, *see* **Vah.**

Waal, *R.*, Neth.; S. arm of R. Rhine.

Wabana, *see* **Bell I.**

Wabash, *c.*, Ind., U.S.A.; rly. ctr.; p. (1960) *12,621*.

Wabash, *R.*, Ohio and Ind., U.S.A.; trib. of R. Ohio; length 550 m.

Wabash and Erie, *canal*, Ind., U.S.A., longest canal in U.S.A.; 476 m. long.

Wabush, *t.*, Labrador, Canada; iron ore mines; p. (1965) *2,700*.

Waco, *c.*, Texas, U.S.A.; on Brazos R.; univ.; cotton ctr., woollens, grain, iron, leather; p. (1960) *97,807*.

Wadai, *dist.*, Equatorial Africa; nr. L. Chad; desert and oases; pastoral; ivory, ostrich feathers; a. 17,000 sq. m.; p. (1947) *1,000,000*.

Wadden Zee, *G.*, between W. Frisian Is. and N. Neth.

Waddington, *mtn.*, B.C., Canada; alt. 13,260 ft.

Wadebridge, *spt.*, *rural dist.*, Cornwall; at head of Camel estuary 6 m. N.W. of Bodmin; china clay; p. (rural dist. 1961) *14,907*.

Wädenswil, *t.*, Zürich, Switzerland; on L. Zürich; silk, wool, textiles; wine, fruit; p. *10,000*.

Wadi Halfa, *t.*, Sudan, N.E. Africa; on R. Nile; at 2nd cataract; rly. terminus of Sudan rlys.; to be inundated by Aswan L.; new t. Khashm el Girba for inhabitants.

Wad Medani, *t.*, *cap.*, Blue Nile Prov., Sudan, Africa; grain, oil, soap; p. (1956) *57,000*.

Wadsworth, *t.*, Ohio, U.S.A.; matches, valves, engin.; p. (1960) *10,635*.

Wagadugu, *see* **Ouagadougou.**

Wager Bay, *inlet*, of Hudson Bay, N.W. Terr., Canada.

Wagga Wagga, *t.*, N.S.W., Australia; on R. Murrumbidgee; wheat, agr., pastoral ctr., dairying; large stock mkt.; p. (estd.) *23,000*.

Wahiawa, *t.*, Oahu I., Hawaii; pineapples; p. (1960) *15,512*.

Waigeo, *I.*, off N. cst., Dutch New Guinea, Indonesia.

Waihi, *t.*, N.I., N.Z.; gold-mining; p. (1961) *3,164*.

Waikaremoana, *L.*, N.I., N.Z.; hydro-elec. power plant.

Waikato, *R.*, N.I., N.Z.; the longest in N.Z.; length 220 m.

Waimate, *t.*, S.I., N.Z.; agr. ctr., soft fruits; p. (1961) *3,308*.

Wairakei, *t.*, N.I., N.Z.; on L. Taupo; health resort; geothermal power sta. opened Nov. 1958.

Wairoa, *t.*, N.I., N.Z.; on R. Wairoa; p. (1961) *4,301*.

Waitaki, *t.*, Otago, S.I., N.Z.; Benmore hydro-elec. power plant projected; p. (1961) *11,018*.

Waitzen, *t.* Hungary; on R. Danube.

Wakamatsu, *t.*, Honshu, Japan; silk reeling; p. (1947) *56,275*.

Wakamatsu, *t.*, Kyushu, Japan; now part of Kitakyushu City newly formed (1963) (*q.v.*); lacquer ware, mnfs.; p. (1960) *106,975*.

Wakatipu, *L.*, Otago, S.I., N.Z.; 52 m. long, 3 m. wide; 1,200 ft. deep; 1,070 ft. above sea-level.

Wakayama, *spt.*, Honshu, Japan; cotton; p. (1960) *285,000*.

Wake I., Pac. Oc.; between Marianas and Hawaii; calling-place on trans-Pacific air-routes; belongs to U.S.A.

Wakefield, *c.*, *co. bor.*, W.R. Yorks, Eng.; on R. Calder; 8 m. S. of Leeds; cath.; woollens, brewing, coal, iron, boiler mkg., chemicals, glass, engin.; p. (1961) *61,591*.

Wakefield, *t.*, Va., U.S.A.; George Washington's birthplace; p. *687*.

Walachia, *dist.*, S. Romania; cereals, fruits; ch. t. Bucharest; a. 29,561 sq. m.; p. *5,029,212*.

Walbrzych (Waldenburg), *t.*, Silesia, Poland; German before 1945; textiles, coal, porcelain, iron ware; p. (1960) *117,000*.

Walcheren, *I.*, Neth.; 12 m. long, low-lying, agr.; was flooded to stop German advance in Second World War.

Waldeck, *see* **Hessen-Nassau.**

Waldenburg, *see* **Walbrzych.**

Wales, *principality*, S.W. of Gr. Britain; flanked by Irish Sea, St. George's Channel and Bristol Channel; mtns.; coal, slate, oats, barley, good pasturage, smelting tin, copper, iron; cap. Cardiff; a. 7,388 sq. m.; p. (1961) *2,196,943* (excluding Monmouthshire).

Walhalla, *t.*, Victoria, Australia; gold-mining; p. *2,000*.

Walker, *t.*, Northumberland, Eng.; on R. Tyne; industl. sub. of Newcastle.

Wallaceburg, *t.*, Ontario, Canada; glass, brass, iron; sugar, flour; p. (1961) *7,881*.

Wallaroo, *spt.*, S. Australia; copper-mining; p. *2,140*.

Wallasey, *co. bor.*, on Mersey estuary, adjoining Birkenhead, Cheshire, Eng.; residtl., seaside resort (New Brighton); p. (1961) *103,213*.

Walla Walla, *t.*, Wash., U.S.A.; on Mill Creek; cereal and fruit ctr., agr. tools, flour, leather; p. (1960) *24,536*.

Wallensee, *L.*, Switzerland; 11 m. long.

Wallingford, *t.*, *mun. bor.*, Berks, Eng.; on R. Thames, to N. of its gap between Chiltern Hills and Lambourn Downs; p. (1961) *4,829*.

Wallingford, *t.*, Conn., U.S.A.; steel, brass, silver and nickel ware; tools, wire; p. (1960) *29,920*.

Wallington, *t.*, N.J., U.S.A.; curtains, paints; p. (1960) *9,261*.

Wallis Archipelago, *I. gr.*, S. Pacific; a. 40 sq. m.; status as overseas terr. Fr. Community (1962); p. (1959) *6,000*.

Wallsend, *t.*, *mun. bor.*, Northumberland, Eng.; on N. bank of R. Tyne; 4 m. below Newcastle; coal-mining, shipbldg., engin., iron, plywood, plastics and quartz glass; p. (1961) *49,785*.

Walmer, *t.*, Kent, Eng.; 2 m. S. of Deal; holiday resort; cas., residence of Warden of Cinque Ports; p. *5,335*.

Walney, *I.*, off cst. of Lancs, Eng.; opposite Barrow.

Walpole, *t.*, Mass., U.S.A.; nr. Boston; p. (1960) *14,053*.

Walpole, *I.*, dep. of New Caledonia; Pac. Oc.; Fr. possession, lies S.E. of Maré (Loyalty Is.).

Walsall, *t.*, *co. bor.*, Staffs, Eng.; 5 m. E. of Wolverhampton; leather and iron goods, engin. steel tubes; p. (1961) *117,836*.

Walsham, N., *see* **North Walsham.**

Walsingham, *C.*, on Cumberland Peninsula, Baffin I., Canada.

Walsum, *t.*, N. Rhine-Westphalia, Germany; at

confluence of Emscher and Rhine; coal-mining, paper, cellulose; p. (1963) *46,400*.
Waltham, *c.*, Mass., U.S.A.; nr. Boston; watch-mkg., textiles, motors, furniture, shoes, paper; p. (1960) *55,413*.
Waltham Forest, *outer bor.*, E. London, Eng.; incorporating former bors. of Chingford, Leyton, Walthamstow; industl. and residtl.; p. (1964) *248,422*.
Waltham, Holy Cross, *t.*, *urb. dist.*, Essex, Eng.; on R. Lea, 11 m. N. of London; abbey; mkt. gardening, cordite, light inds.; p. (1961) *11,655*.
Walthamstow, *see* **Waltham Forest**.
Walton and Weybridge, *urb. dist.*, Surrey, Eng.; on R. Thames, 17 m. S.W. of London; engin., aircraft; anglers' resort; p. (1961) *45,497*.
Walton-le-Dale, *t.*, *urb. dist.*, N.E Lancs, Eng.; on R. Ribble, 2 m. E. of Preston; mkt. gardening, cottons, timber; p. (1961) *19,061*.
Walvis Bay, *dist.* and *spt.*, administered by S.W. Africa; a. 374 sq. m.; fishing, whaling; p. (1961) *16,490* (inc. *5,067* Europeans).
Wandsbeck, *t.*, Germany; sub. of Hamburg; beer, brandy, tobacco; p. *40,000*.
Wandsworth, *inner bor.*, S.W. London, Eng.; inc. Battersea; on R. Wandle at influx into Thames; oil-mills, metal-wks., paper, brewing; p. (1964) *335,367*.
Wanganui, *c.*, N.I., N.Z.; on R. Wanganui; wool, grain, meat, dairy prod.; p. (1961) *35,718*.
Wanganui, *R.*, N.I., N.Z.; l. 160 m., famous for its beauty.
Wangaratta, *t.*, Victoria, Australia; 145 m. from Melbourne; agr. dist.; p. (1961) *13,812*.
Wankie, *t.*, Rhodesia: site of coalmng. ind.; 215 m. N.W. Bulawayo; p. (1958) *19,610* (incl. 2,460 Europeans).
Wanlockhead, *vil.*, Dumfries, Scot.; in Lowther Hills; lead-mines.
Wanne-Eickel, *t.*, N. Rhine–Westphalia, Germany; N.W. of Bochum; coal-mining, chemicals; p. (1963) *107,800*.
Wansbeck, *R.*, Northumberland, Eng.; flows E. from Pennines into N. Sea 3 m. N. of Blyth; length 23 m.
Wanstead and Woodford, *see* **Redbridge**.
Wantage, *mkt. t.*, *urb. dist.*, Berks, Eng.; in Vale of the White Horse; hempen cloth, brass; p. (1961), *5,940*.
Wapping, *Thames-side dist.*, London, Eng.; contains the London Docks; industl.; p. *3,200*.
Warangal, *t.*, Andhra Prad., India; p. (1961) *156,106*.
Waratah, *t.*, N.S.W., Australia; sub. of Newcastle; coal, copper-mines; p. (1947) *20,313*.
Waratah, *t.*, N. Tasmania, Australia; tin-mining ctr.; p. *1,009*.
Warburg, *t.*, Germany; on R. Diemel; industl.
Wardha, *R.*, Madhya Pradesh, India; trib. of R. Wainganga; length 254 m.
Ware, *mkt. t.*, *urb. dist.*, Herts, Eng.; on R. Lea; 2 m. N.E. of Hertford; malting, bricks; p. (1961) *9,987*.
Wareham, *mkt. t.*, *mun. bor.*, Dorset, Eng.; on R. Frome, on N. of I. of Purbeck, 8 m S.W. of Poole; agr. engin., pipes; p. (1961) *3,094*.
Waremme (Borgworm), *t.*, Belgium; p. (1962) *6,818*.
Waren, *t.*, Neubrandenburg, E. Germany; on Müritzsee; timber, dairying, iron; p. (1963) *19,693*.
Warminster, *t.*, *urb. dist.*, Wilts, Eng.; on Wylye watershed at edge of Salisbury Plain; agr. mkt., gloves, silk; p. (1961) *9,855*.
Warnemünde, *spt.*, Germany; ferry pt. for rail traffic between Berlin and Copenhagen; shipbldg., resort; p. *6,374*.
Warragamba Dam, 40 m. W. Sydney, New S. Wales, Australia; 450 ft. high, opened Oct. 14, 1960; when in full operation a 36-mile lake will be formed behind dam, impounding 460,000 millions gallons of water.
Warrego, *R.*, Queensland, N.S.W., Australia; trib. of R. Darling; length 400 m.
Warren, *c.*, Ohio, U.S.A.; on Mahoning R.; coal- and iron-mining, iron and steel mftg.; p. (1960) *59,648*.
Warren, *bor.*, Penns., U.S.A.; on Allegheny R.; natural gas, petroleum, oil-refining; furniture, tools; p. (1960) *14,505*.
Warrenpoint, *spt.*, *urb. dist.*, Down, N. Ireland; at head of Carlingford Lough; holiday resort; p. (1961) *3,238*.
Warrenton, *t.*, Cape Province, S. Africa; cheese-mkg.; p. (1960) *5,980* (inc. *1,559* whites).
Warrington, *t.*, *co. bor.*, Lancs, Eng.; on R. Mersey, 18 m. E. of Liverpool; aluminium rolling and drawing, soap, chemicals, iron and steel; p. (1961) *75,533*.
Warrnambool, *spt.*, Victoria, Australia; mkt., agr., dairying; p. (1961) *15,697*.
Warsak Dam, W. Pakistan; on Kabul R., 15 m. N. of Peshawar, nr. Khyber Pass; hydroelec. power and irrigation project.
Warsaw or Warszawa, *prov.*, Poland; on Vistula and Bug Rs.; a 10,900 sq. m.; p. (1961) *2,372,000*.
Warsaw or Warszawa, *cap.*, Poland; on R. Vistula; cath., univ.; rly. ctr.; iron and steel, engin., textiles, chemicals; p. (1961) *1,171,000*.
Warsop, *t.*, *urb. dist.*, Notts, Eng.; 4 m. N.E. of Mansfield; limestone, gravel; p. (1961) *11,596*.
Warta, *R.*, Poland; trib. of R. Oder; length 450 m.
Warwick, *t.*, Queensland, Australia; coal, agr., sawmilling; p. (1962) *9,813*.
Warwick, *co.*, Eng.; coal, iron, limestone, fruit, livestock, motors, metal goods; co. t. Warwick; a. 976 sq. m.; p. (1961) *2,023,289*.
Warwick, *co. t.*, *mun. bor.*, Warwick, Eng.; on R. Avon, 8 m. S.W. of Coventry; cas.; agr. implements, brewing, malting, rope, iron; p. (1961) *16,032*.
Warwick, *c.*, R.I., U.S.A.; on Narragansett Bay; cotton mnfs.; p. (1960) *68,504*.
Wasatch Mtns., *range*, Utah and Idaho, U.S.A.
Wash, The, *bay*, N. Sea between Lincs and Norfolk, Eng.; 22 m. long, 15 m. wide; partly reclaimed.
Washa, *L.*, La., U.S.A.; 14 m. long.
Washburne, *mtn range*. Yellowstone National Park, U.S.A.; highest summit 10,345 ft.
Washington, *t.*, *urb. dist.*, Durham, Eng.; 5 m. S.E. of Gateshead; coal, iron and steel, stone quarrying, chemicals; designated "New Town" 1964; p. (estd. 1965) *20,000*.
Washington, *st.*, U S.A.; coal, iron, minerals, forests, agr.; cap. Olympia; ch. ts. Seattle and Tacoma; a. 68,192 sq. m.; p. (1960) *2,853,214*.
Washington, *c.*, *cap.*, U.S.A.; in Dist. of Columbia, on Potomac R.; White House, Capitol, 4 univs., etc.; printing and engraving; world's first weather ctr. 1965; p. (1960) *746,958*.
Washington, *t.*, Penns., U.S.A.; coal, petroleum, steel, glass, chemicals; p. (1960) *23,540*.
Washington I., Pac. Oc. (Gilbert and Ellice Is. col.); a. 6 sq. m., coral atolls; copra; p. *86*.
Washita, *R.*, Ark. and La., U.S.A.; trib. of Red R.; length 400 m.
Wasmes, *t.*, Belgium; nr. Mons; coal-mining; p. (1962) *13,923*.
Wasquehal, *t.*, Nord, France; textiles, chemicals, oil-refineries; p. (1954) *12,363*.
Wast Water, *L.*, Cumberland, Eng.; 3 m. long.
Watchet, *t.*, *urb. dist.*, Somerset, Eng.; on cst. of Bristol Channel; 5 m. E. of Minehead; paper mkg., fishing; p. (1961) *2,596*.
Waterbury, *c.*, Conn., U.S.A.; on Naugatuck R.; watches, pins, brass goods, elec. and photographic goods, chemicals; p. (1960) *107,130*.
Waterford, *co.*, Munster, Ireland; agr., livestock, fisheries; co. t., Waterford; a. 721 sq. m.; p. (1961) *71,343*.
Waterford, *co. t.*, *spt.*, Waterford, Ireland; on R. Suir; cath.; brewing, fishing; p. (1961) *28,138*.
Waterloo, *vil.*, Belgium; battle, 1815; p. (1962) *12,261*.
Waterloo, *c.*, Iowa, U.S.A.; on Cedar R.; agr. produce and tools; p. (1960) *71,755*.
Waterloo, *t.*, N.Y., U.S.A.; on L Seneca; p. (1960) *5,098*.
Waterloo, *t.*, Ontario, Canada; p. (1961) *21,366*.
Waterloo-(with-Seaforth), *urb. dist.*, Lancs, Eng.; at mouth of R. Mersey; N. sub. of Liverpool; residtl.; p. *15,447*.
Waterpoort, *t.*, Transvaal, S. Africa; on R. Sand; cattle; agr. ctr.
Watertown, *t.*, Conn., U.S.A.; plastics, textiles, hardware, wire prods.; p. (1960) *14,812*.
Watertown, *t.*, Mass., U.S.A.; on Charles R.; arsenal; p. (1960) *39,092*.
Watertown, *c.*, N.Y., U.S.A.; on Black R.; carriage wks., steam-engines, silk, agr. tools; p. (1960) *33,306*.
Watertown, *t.*, S.D., U.S.A.; machin., meat-packing; p. (1960) *14,077*.
Watertown, *c.*, Wis., U.S.A.; on Rock R.; univ.; mnfs.; p. (1960) *13,943*.
Waterville, *c.*, Me., U.S.A.; on Kennebec R.; univ.; cotton mnfs., rly. wks.; p. (1960) *18,695*.
Watervliet, *c.*, N.Y., U.S.A.; on Hudson R.;

arsenal; iron goods, woollens, asbestos goods; p. (1960) *13,917*.

Watford, *t., mun. bor.*, Herts, Eng.; on R. Colne, 16 m. N.W. of London; mkt.; many varied inds., inc. light and elec. engin., paper, printing; p. (1961) *75,622*.

Wath, *t., urb. dist.*, W.R. Yorks, Eng.; 4 m. N. of Rotherham; coal, quarrying; p. (1961) *15,191*.

Watling, *Brit. I.*, Bahamas, W. Indies; reputed landing place of Columbus.

Watlington, *t.*, Oxford, Eng.; at N. foot of Chiltern Hills, 5 m. S.W. of Princes Risborough; lace; p. *1,386*.

Watson's Bay, N.S.W., Australia; nr. Sydney; holiday resort.

Wattenscheid, *t.*, N. Rhine-Westphalia, Germany; E. of Essen; coal, metals, footwear; p. (1963) *79,700*.

Wattrelos, *t.*, Nord, France; nr. Lille; textiles, mnfs.; p. (1962) *41,319*.

Watu Bella Is., Moluccas, Indonesia; coconuts, sago.

Wau, *cap.*, Bahr-el-Ghazal, Sudan, N.E. Africa; p. *6,000*.

Waukegan, *c.*, Ill., U.S.A.; on L. Michigan; summer resort; steel, brass, motors, sugar refining; livestock, agr. ctr.; p. (1960) *55,719*.

Waukesha, *t.*, Wis., U.S.A.; health resort; p. (1960) *30,004*.

Wausau, *c.*, Wis., U.S.A.; on Wisconsin R.; timber, paper, machin., leather, silver-fox farms; p. (1960) *31,943*.

Wauwatosa, *c.*, Wis., U.S.A.; sub. of Milwaukee; p. (1960) *56,923*.

Waveney, *R.*, Norfolk and Suffolk, Eng.; length 50 m.

Waverly, *t.*, N.Y., U.S.A.; dairying, tr. ctr.; p. (1960) *5,950*.

Waxahachie, *t.*, Texas, U.S.A.; rly. ctr.; p. (1960) *12,749*.

Waycross, *t.*, Ga., U.S.A.; rly. wks., timber, naval stores, machin., agr. prods.; p. (1960) *20,944*.

Waynesboro, *t.*, Penns., U.S.A.; industl.; p. (1960) *10,427*.

Wazan or **Ouezzan,** *sacred c.*, Morocco; p. (1960) *26,203*.

Waziristan, *dist.*, N.W. frontier, Pakistan; mtns.; a. 5,000 sq. m.; p. (1951) *264,000*.

Weald, The, wooded and pastoral tracts S.E. Eng., extending from Folkestone, Kent, through Surrey, Hants and Sussex to the sea about Beachy Head.

Wear, *R.*, Durham, Eng.; rises in the Pennines, flows through Durham to N. Sea at Sunderland; length 60 m.

Weaver, *R.*, Cheshire, Eng.; trib. of R. Mersey; length 45 m.

Weaver Hills, Staffs, Eng.; alt. 1,300 ft.

Webb City, *c.*, Mo., U.S.A.; lead, zinc mining; p. (1960) *6,740*.

Webster, *t.*, Mass., U.S.A.; on French R.; textiles, footwear; p. (1960) *12,072*.

Webster Grove, *t.*, Mo., U.S.A.; p. (1960) *28,990*.

Weddell Sea, arm of S. Atl. Oc., Antarctica; whaling and sealing.

Wednesbury, *t., mun. bor.*, Staffs, Eng.; 8 m. N.W. of Birmingham; iron, aluminium, metal inds.; rly. carriages, elec. goods; p. (1961) *34,511*.

Wednesfield, *urb. dist.*, Staffs, Eng.; nr. Wolverhampton; locks and keys, metal refining, engin.; p. (1961) *32,986*.

Wed Zem, *t.*, Morocco; impt. production of phosphate; p. *12,223*.

Weehawken, *t.*, N.J., U.S.A.; coal depot, rly. ctr.; mnfs.; p. (1960) *13,504*.

Weerdt, *t.*, Neth.; industl.; p. (1960) *28,184*.

Wei *R.*, Shensi, China; rises in highlands of Kansu, flows E. between highlands of Shansi and Tsinling Shan to join Yellow River nr. Tungkwan; valley contains very fertile loess soils; formed cradle of Chinese civilisation; length approx. 500 m.

Weiden, *t.*, Bavaria, Germany; porcelain, glass, textiles; p. (1963) *42,200*.

Weifang, *c.*, Shantung, China; coal-mng. ctr.; tobacco processing; p. (1953) *149,000*.

Weihai, *spt.*, Shantung, China; cotton, silk, oilseed; summer resort; p. *222,000*.

Weimar, *t.*, Erfurt, E. Germany; on R. Ilm; 2 cas., Goethe and Schiller houses; cultural institutes; elec., metal, footwear, textiles, machin.; p. (1963) *64,406*.

Weinheim, *t.*, Baden-Württemberg, Germany; cas.; leather, machin., rubber; p. (1963) *28,800*.

Weipa, Queensland, Australia; new t., pt., and alumina plant; bauxite.

Weissenfels, *t.*, Halle, E. Germany; on R. Saale; cas.; footwear, paper, metals; p. (1963) *46,600*.

Weisshorn, *mtn. peak*, Switzerland; alt. 14,770 ft.

Weisskirchen, *see* Bela Crkva.

Wejh, *spt.*, Hejaz, Saudi Arabia.

Welkom, *t.*, O.F.S., S. Africa; ctr. of O.F.S. goldfields; p. (1964) *128,000*.

Welland, *t.*, Ont., Canada; on Welland Canal; farm machin., steel tubing, castings, rope; p. (1956) *15,935*.

Welland, *R.*, Northants and Lincs, Eng.; rises in Northampton Heights, flows N.E., enters The Wash 10 m. below Spalding; length 70 m.

Welland Ship Canal, Ontario, Canada; connects Ls. Erie and Ontario; length 27 m.; 2-lane waterway projected. 1963

Wellesley, *t.*, Mass., U.S.A.; residtl.; p. (1960) *26,071*.

Wellesley Is., *gr.*, in the Gulf of Carpentaria, belonging to Queensland, Australia.

Wellingborough, *t., urb. dist.*, Northants, Eng.; on R. Nene, 9 m. N.E. of Northampton; mkt., footwear, iron smelting, brewing; p. (1961) *30,579*.

Wellington, *mkt. t., urb. dist.*, Shropshire, Eng.; 12 m. E. of Shrewsbury; steel wks., brewing, toys, storage tanks, timber yds., agr.; its ancient name was Watling Town, because it stood on the line of Watling Street; p. (1961) *13,630*.

Wellington, *mkt. t.*, Somerset, Eng.; 6 m. S.W. Taunton, anc. woollen ind. still survives; dairy prod.; p. (1961) *7,523*.

Wellington, *c., spt.*, N.I., cap. N.Z.; univ.; foundries, cold storage, soap, candles, footwear; p. (1961) *150,537*, of c. *123,948*.

Wellington, *prov.*, N.I., N.Z.; a. 10,870 sq. m.; p. (1961) *473,621*.

Wellington, *t.*, Cape Prov., S. Africa; tanning, dried fruits, wine, jam, textiles; p. (1960) *10,330* (inc. *3,736* whites).

Wellington, *L.*, Gippsland, Victoria, Australia; shallow; fishing.

Wells, *c., mun. bor.*, Somerset, Eng.; at W. foot of Mendip Hills; cath., bishop's palace; paper, brushes, textiles, scientific inst.; p. (1961) *6,691*.

Wells-next-the-Sea, *t., urb. dist.*, Norfolk, Eng.; ancient pt. on N. cst. of E. Anglia, 14 m. W. of Sheringham; whelks, cockles and mussels; p. (1961) *2,490*.

Wellston, *c.*, Ohio, U.S.A.; rly. ctr.; furniture; p. (1960) *5,728*.

Wellsville, *c.*, Ohio, U.S.A.; on Ohio R.; coal-mining, agr.; p. (1960) *7,117*.

Wels, *t.*, Austria; machin., leather, paper; natural gas; p. (1961) *41,060*.

Welshpool, *mkt. t., mun. bor.*, Montgomery, Wales; on R. Severn, 7 m. N. of Montgomery; nr. is Powis Castle; lt. inds. based on agr., hoisery; p. (1961) *6,332*.

Welwyn Garden City, *urb. dist.*, Herts, Eng.; 21 m. N. of London. Founded by Sir Ebenezer Howard in 1920 as the first of the satellite ts. of London; one of the "New Towns" designated 1948, inc. Hatfield, Hertford, and Welwyn rural dist.; pharmaceutics, plastics, radio, and electronics, light inds.; p. (estd. 1965 *42,069*.

Wem, *t., urb. dist.*, Salop, Eng.; nr. Shrewsbury; mkt., flour, tanning, malting; p. (1961) *2,603*.

Wembley, *former mun. bor.*, Middx., Eng.; now inc. in Brent outer bor. Greater London, (*q.v.*); light ind., sports ctr.; p. (1961) *124,892*.

Wemyss, *par.*, Fife, Scot.; fishing pt., coal-mining; p. *26,619*.

Wemyss Bay, *t.*, Renfrew, Scot.; holiday resort, residtl.; impt. ctr. for Clyde steamers.

Wenatchee, *t.*, Wash., U.S.A.; fruit (apple) ctr. and inds.; p. (1960) *16,726*.

Wenchow (Wenzhou), *c., spt.*, Chekiang, China; nr. mouth of Wu Kiang 230 m. S.W. of Shanghai; textile, silk inds.; exp. wood, tea, agr. prod.; fishing; coastal tr.; p. (1953) *202,000*.

Wendover, *t.*, Bucks, Eng.; at N. foot of Chiltern Hills, 4 m. S.E. of Aylesbury, at entrance to wind gap; agr. mkt.; p. *2,500*.

Wengen, *vil.*, Bernese Oberland, Switzerland; alt. 4,200 ft.; resort; p. *1,230*.

Wenlock or **Much Wenlock,** *t., mun. bor.*, Salop, Eng.; on N.E. end of Wenlock Edge, 11 m.

S.E. of Shrewsbury; iron and coal; p. (1961) *14,929*.

Wenlock Edge, *narrow ridge*, Shropshire, Eng.; extends 18 m. S.W from Much Wenlock to Craven Arms; limestone; moorland, woodland on margins, particularly steep N.W. flank; width 1-1½ m., mainly above 950 ft. alt.

Wensleydale, N.R. Yorks, Eng.; valley in N. Pennines drained E. by R. Ure; cattle reared for fattening on lowland farms; some dairying (cheese); length 35 m.

Wensum, *R.*, Norfolk, Eng.; flows to R. Yare at Norwich; length 30 m.

Wentworth, *t.*, *R. pt.*, N.S.W., Australia; at confluence of Rs. Murray and Darling; ships wool downstream to Morgan and round to Adelaide.

Werdau, *t.*, Karl-Marx-Stadt, E. Germany; on R. Pleisse; textiles, machin., tools; p. (1963) *24,634*.

Werdohl, *t.*, N. Rhine–Westphalia, Germany; metal goods, glass; p. (1963) *22,800*.

Wermelskirchen, *t.*, N. Rhine–Westphalia, Germany; S.E. of Remscheid; footwear, iron, textiles; p. (1963) *25,200*.

Wernigerode, *t.*, Magdeburg, E. Germany; cas.; elec., glass, wood, metals, sugar; p. (1963) *33,161*.

Wervicq, *t.*, Belgium; nr. Ypres; tobacco factories; p. (1962) *12,384*.

Wesel, *c.*, N. Rhine–Westphalia, Germany; at confluence of Rs. Lippe and Rhine; cath.; machin., potteries; p. (1963) *32,100*.

Weser, *R.*, Germany; flows N. to N. Sea at Bremerhaven; navigable for 270 m.; total length 440 m.

Wesermünde, *t.*, Bremen, Germany; nr. mouth of R. Weser; adjoins Bremerhaven; brewing, bricks; p. (1946) *77,491*.

Wesseling, *t.*, N. Rhine–Westphalia, Germany; on R. Rhine, S. of Cologne; oil refining, petrochemicals; p. (1963) *21,200*.

Wessex, *ancient kingdom*, S. Eng.; inc. Berks, Hants, Wilts, Dorset, Somerset and Devon.

West Allis, *t.*, Wis., U.S.A.; iron and steel goods; p. (1960) *68,157*.

West Bengal, *st.*, India; delta of Ganges; rice, jute, oilseeds; cap. Calcutta; a. 33,945 sq. m.; p. (1961) *34,967,634*.

West Bridgford, *t.*, *urb. dist.*, Notts, Eng.; at junction of Grantham canal with R. Trent; p. (1961) *26,957*.

West Bromwich, *t.*, *co. bor.*, Staffs, Eng.; on R. Thame, 5 m. N.W. of Birmingham; heavy engin. and allied inds., chemicals, springs, oil ref.; p. (1961) *95,909*.

West Calder, *see* **Calder, W.**

West Chester, *bor.*, Penns., U.S.A.; residtl. sub. Philadelphia; mkt gardening, dairying, agr. tools; p. (1960) *15,705*.

West Dean, *rural dist.*, Gloucester, Eng.; coal-mining, forestry; p. (1961) *17,472*.

West Ham *former co. bor.*, Essex, Eng.; sub. to E. of London; bordered by Rs. Thames and Lea; now inc. in Newham bor., Greater London; residtl.; extensive docks, rubber, soap, jute-wks., engin., smelting, chemicals; p. (1961) *157,367*.

West Hartford, *t.*, Conn., U.S.A.; residtl. sub. of Hartford; metal goods, ctr. for dairying, tobacco-growing dist.; p. (1960) *62,210*.

West Hartlepool, *see* **Hartlepool, W.**

West Haven, *bor.*, Conn., U.S.A.; sub. of New Haven; p. (1960) *42,567*.

West Indies or Antilles, *I. grs.*, Atl. Oc.; extend between the csts of Florida and Venezuela, separating the Caribbean Sea and the G. of Mexico from the Atlantic; sugar, tobacco, fruits, cotton, coffee, cocoa; p. *16,494,000*. *See* **The West Indies.**

West Irian, Indonesia; formerly West New Guinea and Dutch col.; came under Indonesian adm. 1 May 1963; cap. Kota Baru (formerly Hollandia); a. (inc. Ternate) 115,861 sq. m.; p. (1961) *758,396*.

West Lothian, *co.* Scot.; agr., coal, iron, bricks, engin., hosiery; co. t. Linlithgow; a. 120 sq. m.; p. (1961) *92,764*.

West New York, *t.*, N.J., U.S.A.; on Hudson R.; grain elevators, silks rubber goods, cotton-seed oil; p. (1960) *35,547*.

West Orange, *t.*, N.J., U.S.A.; industl.; p. (1960) *39,895*.

West Pakistan, *prov.*, Pakistan; divided into 10 divs.: Karachi, Hyderabad, Khairpur, Bahawalpur, Quetta, Dera Ismail Khan, Peshawar, Lahore, Rawalpindi, and Kalat; ch. c. Lahore; 5 gt. Rs.: Indus with tribs. Jhelum, Chenab, Ravi, and Sutlej; wheat, cotton, rice, oilseeds, rocksalt; a. 300,839 sq. m.; p. (1961) *40,815,000* (excl. Fed. terr. of Karachi).

West Point, *military sta.*, N.Y., U.S.A.; on Hudson R.; Military Academy; p. *1,350*

West Springfield, *t.*, Mass., U.S.A.; industl.; p. (1960) *25,385*.

West Virginia, *st.*, U.S.A.; coal, salt, petroleum, agr. (cereals, tobacco), pastoral; cap. Charleston; a. 24,181 sq. m.; p. (1960) *1,860,421*.

West Warwick, *t.*, R.I., U.S.A.; p. (1960) *21,414*.

Westbrook, *c.*, Me., U.S.A.; paper, cottons, silks; p. (1960) *13,820*.

Westbury, *t.*, *urb. dist.*, Wilts, Eng.; at N. foot of Salisbury Plain; rly. junction; woollens, bricks, glove mnfs.; p. (1961) *5,409*.

Westerwald, *plateau of old volcanic rocks*, W. Germany, ending in steep slope E. of R. Rhine between Koblenz and Bonn; drained to Rhine by R. Lahn and R. Sieg; fertile soil; pasture-land or deciduous woodland; sm. quantities of iron ore in Siegerland.

Westfield, *t.*, Fife, Scot.; Lurgi gas plant.

Westfield, *c.*, Mass., U.S.A.; cigars, paper, machin., bicycles, radiators; p. (1960) *26,302*.

Westfield, *t.*, N.J., U.S.A.; p. (1960) *31,447*.

Westgate-on-Sea, *t.*, Kent, Eng.; nr. Margate; agr., seaside resort; p. *4,554*.

Westhoughton, *urb. dist.*, S.E. Lancs, Eng.; coal-mining cottons; p. (1961) *16,254*.

Westland, *prov.*, S.I., N.Z.; coal, timber, gold; cap. Hokitika; a. 4,880 sq. m.; p. (1961) *17,954*.

Westmeath, *co.*, Leinster, Ireland; pasture, agr., dairying; with much bog; co. t. Mullingar; a. 708 sq. m.; p. (1961) *52,774*.

Westminster, City of, *inner bor.*, London, Eng.; on N. bank of R. Thames; W. of City of London; incorporates former bors. of Paddington and St. Marylebone; contains Houses of Parliament, Westminster Abbey, Government offices, Royal Palaces (Buckingham Palace and St. James's); p. (1964) *269,379*.

Westmorland, *co.*, N.W. Eng.; covering part of the Lake Dist. (Windermere, Ullswater, Grasmere, etc.); sheep, oats, bldg.-stone, tourist ind.; cap. Appleby; most populous t., Kendal; a. 789 sq. m.; p. (1961) *67,222*.

Westmount, *t.*, Que. Canada; p. (1961) *25,012*.

Weston-super-Mare, *t.*, *mun. bor.*, Somerset, Eng.; on Bristol Channel, 20 m. S.W of Bristol; holiday resort; p. (1961) *43,923*.

Westphalia, *see* **N. Rhine–Westphalia.**

Westport, *spt.*, *urb. dist.*, Mayo, Ireland; on Westport Bay; mkt., cereals; p. (1961) *2,883*.

Westport. *spt.*, S.I., N.Z.; on R. Buller; cst. shipping; coal; p. (1961) *5,464*.

Westport, *t.*, Conn., U.S.A.; residtl.; woollens, twine, soap, disinfectants; p. (1950) *11,667*.

Westray, *I.*, Orkney Is., Scot.; 10 m long; p. *1,270*.

Westward Ho!, *vil.*, N. Devon, Eng.; on Bideford Bay; seaside resort.

Westwood, *t.*, Queensland, Australia; coal-mining.

Wetherby, *t.*, W.R. Yorks, Eng.; on R. Wharfe; mkt., malting, brewing; p. *2,126*.

Wethersfield, *t.*, Conn., U.S.A.; oldest regular settlement in C.; lge. st. prison; agr. implements, seeds; p. (1960) *20,526*.

Wetteren, *t.*, Belgium; on R. Schelde; textiles; p. (1962) *20,250*.

Wetterhorn, *mtn.*, Switzerland; alt. 12,165 ft.

Wetzlar, *c.*, Hessen, Germany; on R. Lahn; cath.; optical instruments, metals, radios, textiles, footwear; p. (1963) *37,800*.

Wewoka, *t.*, Okla., U.S.A.; oil wells; agr., bricks, petrol; p. (1960) *5,954*.

Wexford, *maritime co.*, Leinster, S.E. Ireland; pasture, agr., dairying, fishing; cap. Wexford; a. 901 sq. m.; p. (1961) *83,259*.

Wexford, *t.*, *cap.*, Wexford; Leinster, S.E. Ireland; on R. Slaney; p. (1961) *10,002*.

Wey, *R.*, Hants, Surrey, Eng.; rises in W. Weald, flows N. into R. Thames nr. Weybridge; cuts impt. gap through N. Downs at Guildford; length 35 m.

Weybridge, *see* **Walton and Weybridge.**

Weymouth and Melcombe Regis, *t*, *mun. bor.*, Dorset, Eng.; on Weymouth Bay, 8 m. S. of Dorchester; torpedo and boatbldg., bricks, tiles, engin.; holiday resort; p. (1961) *40,962*.

Weymouth, *t.*, Mass., U.S.A.; footwear mnf.; p. (1960) *48,177*.

Whakatane, *t.*, N.I., N.Z.; on Bay of Plenty; board mills; p. (1961) *7,169*.

Whales, Bay of, *inlet* in Ross Dep., Antarctica; exploration base.

Whangarei, *t.*, N.Z.; agr., fruit; oil refining; natural gas pipeline from Kapuni; p. (1961) *17,865*.

Whangpoo, *R.*, Kiangsu, China; tidal creek upon which Shanghai is situated; runs 14 m. inland from Yangtze-Kiang estuary nr. Woosung.

Wharfe, *R.*, W.R. Yorks, Eng.; trib. of R. Ouse; length 60 m.

Wheeling, *c.*, W. Va., U.S.A.; on Ohio R.; rly. and comm. ctr., iron and steel, pottery; p. (1960) *53,400*.

Whernside, *mtn.*, W.R. Yorks, Eng.; alt. 2,414 ft.

Whickham, *t.*, *urb. dist.*, Durham, Eng.; nr. Gateshead; coal-mining, iron and steel, chemicals, rope mnf.; p. (1961) *24,791*.

Whitburn, *burgh*, W Lothian. Scot.; 20 m. S.W. of Edinburgh; coal, limestone; p. (1961) *5,902*.

Whitby, *spt.*, *urb. dist.*, N.R. Yorks, Eng.; at mouth of R. Esk. 17 m. N.W. of Scarborough; abbey; holiday resort; fisheries; potash to be mined nearby; p. (1961) *11,662*.

Whitby (formerly **Windsor**), *t.*, Canada; on L. Ontario; p. (1961) *14,685*.

Whitchurch, *t.*, *urb. dist.*, Salop, Eng.; 13 m. S.W. of Crewe; mkt., malting, cheese; p. (1961) *7,159*. [length 350 m.

White, *R.*, Ark., U.S.A.; trib. of Mississippi R.;

White, *R.*, Ind., U.S.A.; trib. of Wabash R.; length 330 m.

White, *R.*, Ark., Mo., U.S.A.; trib. of Mississippi R.; 300 m. navigable; length 800 m.

White Mtns., part of Appalachian system, N.H., U.S.A.; highest summit, Mt. Washington, 5,805 ft.

White Nile (**Bahr-el-Abiad**), *R.*, Sudan, N.E. Africa; strictly, name applied to stretch of R. Nile between L. No and Khartoum; distance over 500 m.

White Plains, *t.*, N.Y., U.S.A.; on Bronx R.; residtl.; battle 1776; p. (1960) *50,485*.

White Russia, *see* **Byelorussia.**

White Sea or G. of Arkangelsk, *inlet* of the Arctic Ocean, R.S.F.S.R.; a. 47,346 sq. m.

Whiteadder, *R.*, Berwick, Scot.; trib. of R. Tweed; length 34 m. [p. (1961) *14,370*.

Whitefield, *urb. dist.*, Lancs, Eng.; cotton mnf.;

Whitehall, *t.*, N.Y., U.S.A.; at head of L. Champlain; timber tr.; p. (1960) *4,016*.

Whitehaven, *spt.*, *mun. bor.*, Cumberland, Eng.; on Solway Firth, 3 m. N. of St. Bees Head; coal, methane gas, tanning, chemicals, flour and silk mills; p. (1961) *27,541*.

Whitehead, *t.*, *urb. dist.*, Antrim, N. Ireland; at entrance to Belfast Lough; seaside resort; p. (1961) *2,174*.

Whithorn, *royal burgh*, Wigtown, Scot.; 9 m. S. of Wigtown; cath.; p. (1961) *986*.

Whitehorse, *c.*, cap. Yukon Terr., Canada; ctr. coal and copper mng., hunting and fur trapping; once a gold " boom town "; H.Q. Royal Canadian Mounted Police; end of Alaska highway linking Edmonton, Alberta; p. (1961) *5,031*.

Whitley Bay, *bor.*, Northumberland, Eng.; 3 m. N. of Tynemouth; seaside resort; plastics; p. (1961) *36,519*. [alt. 14,898 ft.

Whitney, *mtn.*, Sierra Nevada, Cal. U.S.A.;

Whitstable, *spt.*, *urb. dist.*, Kent, Eng.; on Thames estuary, 6 m. N. of Canterbury; holiday resort, oysters; p. (1961) *19,534*.

Whittington or Whittington Moor, *par.*, Derby, Eng.; nr. Chesterfield; coal-mining, iron, steel; p. *8,317*.

Whittlesey, *t.*, *urb. dist.*, I. of Ely, Eng.; in The Fens, 8 m. W. of March; bricks, mkt. gardening; p. (1961) *9,324*.

Whitworth, *urb. dist.*, S E. Lancs, Eng ; cottons, coal, slate; p. (1961) *7,031*.

Whyalla, *spt.*, S. Australia; impt. steel and shipbldg. inds.; exp ironstone and pig-iron; p. (1961) *14,076*.

Wichita, *c.*, Kan., U.S.A.; in Arkansas valley; rly. wks.; oil refineries and equipment; meat-packing ctr. in agr. and stock-raising region; p. (1960) *254,698*. [length 225 m.

Wichita, *R.*, Texas, U.S.A.; trib. of Red R.;

Wichita Falls, *c.*, Texas, U.S.A.; oil-refining; p. (1960) *101,724*.

Wick, *spt.*, *burgh*, Caithness, Scot.; on E. cst. 14 m. S. of John O'Groats; herring-fisheries ctr.; p. (1961) *7,397*.

Wicklow, *maritime co.*, Leinster, Ireland; pastoral and agr.; cap. Wicklow; a. 781 sq. m ; p. (1961) *58,449*.

Wicklow, *t*, *cap.*, Wicklow, Leinster, Ireland; on S.E. cst., 35 m. S. of Dublin; mkt.; sm. seaside resort; p. (1961) *3,117*.

Wicklow, *mtns.*, Wicklow, Ireland; highest summit, Lugnaquillia, 3,039 ft.

Widnes, *t.*, *mun. bor.*, Lancs, Eng.; on R. Mersey, 12 m. E of Liverpool; anhydrite acid, asbestos, cement, wire cables, chemicals, explosives, fertilisers, copper and zinc; p. (1961) *52,168*.

Wiener Neustadt, *t.*, Lower Austria; 20 m. S. of Vienna; machin., pottery; p. (1961) *33,845*.

Wieringermeer Polder, *reclaimed a.*, N. Holland, Neth.; located in N.W. of Zuider Zee; reclaimed in 1930, flooded by Germans and drained again 1945; largely meadowland; a. 78 sq. m.

Wiesbaden, *cap.*, Hessen Germany; at S. edge of the Taunus; spa; cas.; chemicals, cement, engin.; p. (1963) *258,000*.

Wigan, *t.*, *co. bor.*, S.W. Lancs, Eng.; 16 m. N.E. of Liverpool; coal, cotton, engin., chemicals, cement; p. (1961) *78,702*.

Wight, I. of, *co.*, Eng.; Eng. Channel, separated from Hants by Spithead and The Solent; wheat, sheep, cement; holiday resort; ch. ts.: Newport, Cowes, Ryde; a. 147 sq. m.; p. (1961) *95,479*.

Wigston, *t.*, *urb. dist.*, Leic., Eng.; 4 m. S. of Leicester; rly. wks., engin., hosiery; p. (1961) *21,405*.

Wigton, *t.*, Cumberland, Eng.; mkt., textiles, malting; p. *3,521*.

Wigtown, *maritime co.*, S.W. Scot.; agr. mainly dairying, creameries; agr. implements; cap. W.; a. 485 sq. m.; p. (1961) *29,107*.

Wigtown, *burgh*, Wigtown. Scot.; on Wigtown Bay, Solway Firth; fishery; creamery, distillery; p. (1961) *1,201*.

Wilcannia, *t.*, *R. pt.*, N.S.W., Australia; on R. Darling, 350 m. upstream from Wentworth; sends wool and minerals downstream to Morgan, Murray Bridge, Echuca for transhipment by rail to Adelaide or Melbourne.

Wilhelmshaven, *spt.*, Lower Saxony, Germany; 40 m. N.W. of Bremen; shipbldg., machin., textiles, furniture, elect., wood, leather; harbour; oil pipeline; p. (1963) *100,400*.

Wilkes-Barre, *c.*, Penns., U.S.A.; on Susquehanna R.; anthracite-mining, machin., locomotives, iron and steel, textiles; p. (1960) *63,551*.

Wilkes Land, Antarctica; featureless plateau, alt. 9,500 ft.; immense glaciers; U.S. base taken over by Australia in 1959.

Wilkinsburg, *bor.*, Penns., U.S.A.; Pittsburgh sub.; residtl.; timber wks.; p. (1960) *30,066*.

Willamette, *R.*, Ore., U.S.A.; rises in Cascade Mtns., flows N. into Columbia R. below Portland; valley gives rich agr. land, wheat, root-crops, dairy produce, hard and soft fruits; ch. ts. Portland, Salem; length approx. 300 m.

Willemstad, *pt.*, *cap.*, Neth. Antilles; on Curaçao I.; oil refining; p. (estd. 1963) *60,000*.

Willenhall, *urb. dist.*, Staffs, Eng.; 4 m. E. of Wolverhampton; lock and key drop forgings, castings, car accessories; p. (1961) *32,317*.

Willesden, *former mun. bor.*, Middx,. Eng.; now inc. in Brent outer bor., Greater London, (*q.v.*); impt. rly. junction; residtl. and industl.; p. (1961) *171,001*.

Williamsburg, *c.*, Va., U.S.A.; oldest incorporated c. in America; p. (1960) *6,832*.

Williamsport, *c.*, Penns., U.S.A.; on Susquehanna R.; rly. ctr., timber, machin., silks; summer resort; p. (1960) *41,967*.

Williamstown, *spt.*, *sub.*, Melbourne, Victoria, Australia; at mouth of Yarra R.; naval dockyds., shipbldg., railway wks., rifle range; p. (1958) *30,388*.

Willimantic, *c.*, Conn., U.S.A.; on Willimantic R.; textiles, thread; p. (1960) *13,881*.

Wilmette, *t.*, Ill., U.S.A.; residtl. sub. Chicago; p. (1960) *28,268*.

Wilmington, *c.*, *spt.*, Del., U.S.A.; on Delaware R.; shipbldg., gunpowder, machin., iron- and steel-wks.; chemicals; leather, cork, rubber goods; p. (1960) *95,827*.

Wilmington, *spt.*, N.C., U.S.A.; exp. cotton, tobacco, timber, fertilizers; shipbldg., textiles, chemicals; p. (1950) *45,043*.

Wilmslow, *t., urb. dist.*, Cheshire, Eng.; on R. Bollen, 6 m. S.W. of Stockport; residtl., cotton mnfs.; p. (1961) *21,393*.
Wilsden, W.R. Yorks, Eng.; nr. Bradford; worsted mnfs.; p. *2,500*.
Wilson, *t.* N.C., U.S.A.; tobacco, cotton, timber; p. (1950) *23,010*. [Victoria, Australia.
Wilson's Promontory, juts into Bass Strait,
Wilton, *t., mun. bor.*, Wilts, Eng.; on R. Wylye, 3 m. W. of Salisbury; agr. mkt., carpets, felt; p. (1961) *3,404*.
Wilton, *industl. estate*, Cleveland, Yorks.; S. side of Tees estuary; heavy organic- and petro-chemicals; nylon polymer plant projected 1964.
Wiltshire, *S.W. inland co.*, Eng.; agr. and pastoral; cap. Salisbury; a. 1,345 sq. m.; p. (1961) *422,753*.
Wimbledon, *former mun. bor.*, Surrey, Eng.; now inc. in Merton outer London bor.; residtl.; famous common and internationally famous tennis tournament; p. (1961) *56,994*.
Wimborne Minster, *t.*, Dorset, Eng.; on R. Stour; agr. machin., car body bldg.; p. (1961) *4,156*.
Wimmera, *N.W. dist.*, Victoria, Australia; a. 24,000 sq. m.; pastoral areas of fruit-growing under irrigation.
Winburg, *t.*, O.F.S., S. Africa; was the first cap. of O.F.S.; tr. ctr.; p. (1960) *1,454* whites.
Wincanton, *t.*, Somerset, Eng.; at N.W. foot of Salisbury Plain; mkt., agr., cheese; p. *2,047*.
Winchcomb, *t.*, Gloucester, Eng.; nr. Cheltenham; silk, flour, tanning; cas.; p. *2,546*.
Winchelsea, *ancient t.*, Sussex, Eng.; 2 m. S.W. of Rye; formerly an impt. walled spt., now 2 m. inland; p. *693*.
Winchester, *c., mun. bor.*, Hants, Eng.; on R. Itchen, 12 m. N. of Southampton; ancient cap. of the Saxons; cath., famous Public School, barracks; brewing, malting, agr. produce; p. (1961) *28,643*.
Winchester, *t.*, Ky., U.S.A.; agr., livestock; p. (1960) *10,187*. [1960) *19,376*.
Winchester, *t.*, Mass., U.S.A.; sub. of Boston; p.
Winchester, *c.*, Va., U.S.A.; in Shenandoah valley; p. (1960) *15,110*.
Windermere, *lgst. Eng. L.*, in Westmorland and Lancs; outlet to Morecambe Bay; 10 m. long, 1 m. wide.
Windermere, *urb. dist.*, Westmorland, Eng.; on E. shore of L.; tourist ctr.; p. (1961) *6,556*.
Windhoek, *cap.*, S.W. Africa; fruit, silver, copper, lead; p. (1962) *43,000* inc. *25,200* Europeans.
Windorah, *t.*, Queensland, Australia; pastoral, sheep and cattle.
Wind River Mtns., Wyo., U.S.A.; range of Rockies; Fremont's Peak, 13,576 ft.
Windrush, *R.*, Oxford, Gloucester, Eng.; trib. of R. Thames.
Windscale, Cumberland, Eng.; nuclear reactors for defence purposes. [(1961) *12,015*.
Windsor, *t.*, N.S.W., Australia; farming ctr.; p.
Windsor, *c., pt.*, Ontario, Canada; linked to Detroit, U.S.A., by tunnel bridge and ferry; cars, tyres, paint, drugs, salt; p. (1961) *193,365*.
Windsor, *t.*, Conn., U.S.A., on Connecticut R.; p. (1960) *19,346*.
Windsor, New, *t., mun. bor.*, Berks, Eng.; on R. Thames, 20 m. W. of London; famous royal cas. (founded by William the Conqueror) and park, St. George's Chapel and the Royal Mausoleum; p. (1961) *27,126*.
Windward, Is., W.I., consisting of Grenada, St. Vincent, St. Lucia and Dominica; a. 826 sq. m.; p. *290,000*.
Windward Is., (Neth.), part of Neth. Antilles, W. Indies; consisting of 3 Is.; Curaçao (a. 447 sq. m.; p. (1948) *91,450*), Aruba (a. 181 sq. m.; p. (1948) *47,932*), Bonaire (a. 290 sq. m.; p. (1948) *5,356*).
Windward Passage, *channel*, 60 m. wide, between Cuba and Haiti.
Winfield, *c.*, Kan., U.S.A.; on Walnut R.; educational and comm. ctr., agr.; p. (1960) *11,117*.
Winfrith Heath, Dorset, Eng.; UKAEA Atomic Energy Establishment (ENEA *Dragon* project inaugurated 1964).
Winneba, *t.*, Ghana, W. Africa; p. (1960) *25,000*.
Winnebago, *L.*, Wis. U.S.A.; 27 m. long.
Winnipeg, *c., cap.*, Manitoba, Canada; at junction of Red and Assiniboine Rs.; caths., univ.; rly. ctr.; ch. world wheat mkt.; meat packing and food processing plants; lgst. garment mnf. ctr. in Canada; p. (1961) *475,989*.
Winnipeg, *L.*, Manitoba, Canada; 40 m. N. of Winnipeg; 260 m. long, 25–60 m. wide; contains several lge. Is. (Reindeer, 70 sq. m.; Big I., 60 sq. m.).
Winnipegosis, *L.*, Manitoba and Saskatchewan, Canada; a. (exclusive of Is.) 2,000 sq. m.; 50 m. W. of L. Winnipeg, into which it drains.
Winnispesaukee, *L.*, N.H., U.S.A.; 24 m. long.
Winona, *c.*, Minn., U.S.A.; on R. Mississippi; rly. ctr., timber, grain tr., medicines, shoes, furs.; p. (1960) *24,895*.
Winooski or Onion, *R.*, Vt., U.S.A.; length 90 m.
Winsford, *urb. dist.*, Cheshire, Eng.; on R. Weaver; 4 m. S. of Northwich; only rock salt mine still working in Brit. Is.; p. (1961) *12,738*.
Winslow, *t.*, Bucks, Eng.; mkt., agr. ctr.; p. *1,539*.
Winston-Salem, *c.*, N.C., U.S.A.; tobacco and cotton mnfs.; p. (1960) *111,135*.
Winterswijk, *t.*, Neth.; industl.; p. (1960) *24,532*.
Winterthur, *t.*, Zurich, Switzerland; on Eulach R.; rly. ctr., locomotives, machines, cottons, wine; p. (1961) *84,300*.
Winthrop, *cst. t.*, Mass., U.S.A.; residtl. sub. of Boston, summer resort; p. (1960) *20,303*.
Wipper, *R.*, Germany, trib. of R. Rhine; length 50 m.
Wiri, *t.*, New Zealand, 15 m. S. of Auckland; aluminium fabricating mill.
Wirksworth, *t., urb. dist.*, Derby, Eng.; in Pennines, 5 m. S. of Matlock; lead-mng., limestone, fluorspar wks.; p. (1961) *4,930*.
Wirral, *urb. dist.*, W. Cheshire, Eng.; between estuaries of Dee and Mersey; residtl.; p. (1961) *21,847*.
Wisbech, *t., mun. bor.*, of Ely, Cambs, Eng.; on R. Nene, 11 m. from its mouth in the Wash; mkt. gardening, fruit growing and canning, agr. implements; p. (1961) *17,512*.
Wisconsin, *st.*, U.S.A.; leading dairy st. of Union; timber, iron ore, lead, zinc, stone, sand, and gravel; agr. machin., cars, engin.; cap. Madison; ch. t. Milwaukee; a. 56,154 sq. m.; p. (1960) *3,951,777*.
Wisconsin, *R.*, Wis., U.S.A.; trib. of R. Mississippi; length 600 m.
Wishaw, *burgh*, Lanark, Scot., joined with Motherwell; rly. wks., engin., coal, iron, steel.
Wiske, *R.*, N.R. Yorks, Eng.; trib. of R. Swale; length 24 m.
Wismar, *spt.*, Rostock, E. Germany; on Baltic Sea, N. of Schwerin; metals, sugar, canning, shipbldg.; p. (1963) *57,277*.
Witbank, *t.*, Transvaal, S. Africa; power sta.; coal-mng.; carbide, cyanide, steel; p. (1960) *24,510* (inc. *8,482* whites).
Witham, *R.*, Rutland and Lincs, Eng.; flows into The Wash; length 80 m.
Witham, *t., urb. dist.*, Essex, Eng.; 9 m. N.E. of Chelmsford; agr., mkt. gardening; malting, metal windows; p. (1961) *9,459*.
Withernsea, *t., urb. dist.*, E.R. Yorks, Eng.; on E. cst. 15 m. E. of Hull; holiday resort; agr., fishing; p. (1961) *4,963*.
Withnell, *t., urb. dist.*, Lancs, Eng.; at N. foot of Rossendale Fells, 3 m. S.W. of Blackburn; textiles, stone, paper; p. (1961) *2,840*.
Witney, *t.*, Oxford, Eng.; on R. Windrush, 10 m. W. of Oxford; woollens, blankets, gloves; p. (1961) *9,217*.
Witten, *t.*, N. Rhine–Westphalia, Germany; on R. Ruhr; glass, machin., metals, chemicals, optical inds.; p. (1963) *97,400*.
Wittenberg, *t.*, Halle, E. Germany; on R. Elbe; cas.; ctr. of Reformation and burial place of Luther; he burnt Papal bull against him here in 1520; iron, machin., textiles; p. (1963) *46,544*.
Wittenberge, *t.*, Schwerin, E. Germany; on R. Elbe; woollens, machin., rly. junction; p. (1963) *32,828*.
Witwatersrand, *dist.* Transvaal, S. Africa; gold-mining.
Wivenhoe, *t., urb. dist.*, Essex, Eng.; on R. Colne; boatbldg., oysters, lt. inds.; p. (1961) *2,729*.
Wloclawek, *t., pt.*, N. Poland; on R. Vistula; brewing, iron-wks., pottery; p. (1960) *63,000*.
Woburn, *t.*, Bedford, Eng.; 5 m. N.E. of Leighton Buzzard; Woburn Abbey (seat of Dukes of Bedford).
Woburn, *c.*, Mass., U.S.A.; chemicals, footwear; p. (1960) *31,214*.
Woking, *t., urb. dist.*, Surrey, Eng.; 4 m. N. of

Guildford; wireless parts, aeroplane equipment; mkt., residtl.; p. (1961) *67,485*.
Wokingham, *t.*, *mun. bor.*, Berks, Eng.; 5 m. S.E. of Reading; mkt., agr. and agr. machin., bricks; p. (1961) *11,400*.
Wolds, The, *chalk hill range*, Lincoln, E.R. Yorks, Eng.; pastoral; 45 m. long.
Wolf Rock, *isolated rock, lighthouse*; at approach to Eng. Channel from Bay of Biscay; 9 m. S.W. of Lands End, Cornwall.
Wolfe, *I.*, in L. of 1,000 Is., St. Lawrence R., Canada.
Wolfenbüttel, *t.*, Lower-Saxony Germany; S. of Brunswick; cas., Lessing museum; textiles, machin., canning; p. (1963) *39,700*.
Wolfsburg, *t.*, Lower Saxony, Germany; on R. Aller N.E. of Brunswick; Volkswagen wks.; p. (1963) *74,100*.
Wollaston, *L.* N.W. Terr., Canada; 50 m. long.
Wollongong, Greater, *t.*, N.S.W., Australia; coal-mining, iron- and steel-wks., dairying; p. (1961) *131,758*.
Wolmaransstad, *t.*, Transvaal, S. Africa; diamonds; p. (1960) *6,041* inc. *2,474* whites.
Wolsingham, *t.*, Durham, Eng.; on R. Wear; woollens, coal, agr. tools, marble; p. *3,535*.
Wolverhampton, *t.*, *co. bor.*, Staffs, Eng.; 15 m. N.W. of Birmingham; ironwks., coal, metal goods, elec. engin., elec. apparatus, car and cycle components, rayon, nylon, rubber goods; p. (1961) *150,385*.
Wolverton, *t.*, *urb. dist.*, Bucks, Eng.; on R. Ouse, 15 m. S.W. of Bedford; rly.-carriage wks.; p. (1961) *13,116*.
Wolyn (*former* Wollin), *I.*, Baltic Sea; off mouth of R. Oder; Polish; a. 133 sq. m.; p. *21,000*.
Wombwell, *urb. dist.*, W.R. Yorks, Eng.; at E. foot of Pennines, 7 m. N. of Sheffield; coal-mining, bricks; p. (1961) *18,701*.
Wonokromo, *sub.* of Soerabaya, Indonesia; oil refining.
Wonsan, *spt.*, N. Korea; exp. rice, cattle, hides, fish; p. (estd. 1942) *122,185*.
Wonthaggi, *t.*, Victoria, Australia; coal; p. (1957) *4,530*.
Woodbridge, *t.*, *urb. dist.*, E. Suffolk, Eng.; on R. Deben; engin., brush mkg.; p. (1961) *5,927*.
Woodbridge, *t.*, N.J., U.S.A.; tiles, bricks, terracotta; p. (1960) *78,846*.
Woodbury, *t.*, N.J., U.S.A.; nr. Philadelphia; (1960) *12,453*.
Wood Green, *former mun. bor.*, Middx., Eng.; now inc. in Haringey outer bor., Greater London, (*q.v.*); p. (1961) *47,945*.
Woodhall Spa, *t.*, *urb. dist.*, Lindsey, Lincs, Eng.; 4 m. S.W. of Horncastle; health resort; p. (1961) *1,990*.
Woodside, *burgh* Aberdeen, Scot.; on R. Don; paper; p. *7,698*.
Woodstock, *t.* Ontario, Canada; on R. Thames; dairying, woollens, agr. tools; p. (1961) *20,486*.
Woodstock, *t.*, *mun. bor.*, Oxford, Eng.; on Glynne R. 7 m. N.W. of Oxford; glove mnfs.; Blenheim Palace; p. (1961) *1,808*.
Wookey Hole, *cave*, Mendip Hills, Somerset, Eng.; at foot of limestone hills, 2 m. N.W. of Wells; R. Axe emerges from the cave.
Woolgar, *t.*, Queensland, Australia; gold.
Woolwich, *former met. bor.*, London, Eng.; a. S. of R. Thames incorporated in Greenwich; a. N. of Thames incorporated in Newham; Royal Ordnance Factory (Woolwich Arsenal) to be closed by 1966; of total Defence Department estate of 1,193 acres, 500 acres to be developed by GLC for housing purposes; free ferry across Thames; p. (1961) *146,603*.
Woomera, S. Australia; about 270 m. N.W. of Adelaide; base for joint U.K.–Australian guided-weapon testing range extending N.W. across the continent; established 1947.
Woonsocket, *c.*, R.I., U.S.A.; on Blackstone R.; textiles, rubber goods; p. (1960) *47,080*.
Wooster, *c.*, Ohio, U.S.A.; univ.; agr. ctr.; p. (1960) *17,046*.
Wootton Basset, *see* **Cricklade and Wootton Bassett.**
Worcestershire, *midland co.*, Eng.; W. of Warwick; agr., pasturage, hops, orchards, minerals, mnfs.; co. t. Worcester; a. 699 sq. m; p. (1961) *568,642*.
Worcester, *c.*, *co. bor.*, Worcester, Eng.; on R. Severn, 24 m. N. of Gloucester; cath.; porcelain wks., glove mkg.; p. (1961) *65,865*.
Worcester, *t.*, C. Prov., S. Africa; wines, dried fruits, engin., bricks., textiles; p. (1960) *32,301* inc. *10,858* Europeans.
Worcester, *c.*, Mass. U.S.A.; univ.; iron, footwear, tools; p. (1960) *186,587*.
Workington, *spt.*, *mun. bor.*, Cumberland, Eng.; on Solway Firth, at mouth of Derwent R.; coal, iron, steel, shipbldg., cycles, motors; p. (1961) *29,507*.
Worksop, *t.*, *mun. bor.*, Notts, Eng.; 15 m. S.E. of Sheffield; coal-mining, timber, glasswks., knitwear, refractory bricks; quarrying; p. (1961) *34,237*.
Worms, *c.*, Rhineland-Palatinate, Germany; on R. Rhine, cath.; "Nibelungen city"; wine ctr.; chemicals, leather, textiles, machin., metals; p. (1963) *63,100*.
Worms Head, *promontory*, on Glamorgan cst., Gower Peninsula, Wales.
Worsborough, *urb. dist.*, W.R. Yorks, Eng.; coal-mng., timber, gunpowder; p. (1961) *14,577*.
Worsley, *urb. dist*, S.E. Lancs, Eng.; cottons, iron, coal; p. (1961) *40,948*.
Worthing, *t.*, *mun. bor.*, W. Sussex, Eng.; on S. cst., 10 m. W. of Brighton; holiday resort, mkt. gardening, horticulture; p. (1961) *80,143*.
Wotton-under-Edge, *t.*, Gloucester, Eng., nr. Stroud; mkt., agr. ctr., woollens; p. *3,121*.
Wowoni I., Celebes, Indonesia.
Wrangel *I.*, Arctic Ocean; off N. cst., R.S.F.S.R.
Wrangel, *t.*, Alaska, U.S.A.; p. (1960) *1,315*.
Wrangell, *mtn.*, Alaska, U.S.A.; alt. 17,500 ft.
Wrath, *C.*, N.W. Sutherland, Scot.
Wrekin, *hill*, Salop, Eng.; alt. 1,320 ft.
Wrexham, *t.*, *mun. bor.*, Denbigh, Wales; 11 m. S.W. of Chester; steel, engin., textiles, brick wks., chemicals, tanning; p. (1961) *35,427*.
Wroclaw (**Breslau**), *prov.*, Poland–Lower Silesia; industl., coal, ironwks., agr.; cap. Wroclaw; a. 9,552 sq. m.; p. (1961) *1,853,000*.
Wroclaw (**Breslau**), *c.*, Silesia, Poland; German before 1945; on R. Oder; univ., cath.; metals, textiles, machin., foodstuffs; p. (1961) *443,000*.
Wrotham, *t.*, Kent, Eng.; nr. Sevenoaks; hops, fruit; p. *4,510*
Wuchang, *c.*, Hupeh, China; on Yangtze-Kiang, opp. Hankow; cottons, tea; comm. ctr. *See* **Wuhan.**
Wuchow (**Wuzhou**), *R.pt.*, Kwangsi, China; on Si-Kiang; tr. ctr.; exp. tung oil, hides, aniseed; p. (1953) *111,000*.
Wuhan, *industl. c.*, Hupeh, China; at head of navigation by ocean-going steamers of Yangtze-Kiang; formed by amalgamation of Hankow, Hanyang, Wuchang; combined p. (1953) *1,427,000*. *See also under separate headings.*
Wuhu, *c.*, Anhwei, China; on Yangtze-Kiang; tea, silk, coal; p. (1953) *242,000*.
Wupper, *R.*, Germany; trib. of R. Rhine; length 40 m.
Wuppertal, *t.*, N. Rhine–Westphalia, Germany; formed by amalgamation of Barmen and Elberfeld; textiles, rubber goods, paper, metals, pharmaceuticals; p. (1963) *422,900*.
Württemberg-Hohenzollern, *Land*, Germany; formed in 1947 from portion of Württemberg and former Prussian dist. of Hohenzollern; cap. Tübingen; a. 4,017 sq. m.; p. (1950) *1,242,204*.
Würzburg, *c.*, Bavaria, Germany; on R. Main; univ.; machin., metals, chemicals, printing, engin.; route ctr.; p. (1963) *119,700*.
Wurzen, *c.*, Leipzig, E. Germany; on R. Mulde; cath., cas.; machin., furniture, leather, foodstuffs; p. (1963) *23,824*.
Wusih (**Wuxi**), *c.*, Kiangsu, China; on N. shore of Tai Hu, 75 m. W. of Shanghai; silk, cotton-weaving; p. (1953) *582,000*.
Wutungkiao (**Wutongqiao**), *c.*, Szechwan prov., China; 15 m. S.E. of Loshan; p. (1953) *199,000*.
Wyalong, N.S.W., *see* **West Wyalong.**
Wyandotte, *c.*, Mich., U.S.A.; on Detroit R.; chemicals; p. (1960) *43,519*.
Wye, *R.*, Bucks, Eng.; rises in Chiltern Hills above High Wycombe, flows S.E. to R. Thames at Cookham. length 20 m.
Wye, *R.*, Derby, Eng.; trib. of R. Derwent;
Wye, *R.*, Eng. and Wales; rises in Plynlimmon, flows S.E. into R. Severn at Chepstow; length 130 m.
Wylfa Head, Anglesey, N. Wales; nuclear power sta. projected.
Wymondham, *t.*, Norfolk, Eng.; 9 m. S.W. of Norwich; mkt.; brush-making; Benedictine abbey, founded 1107; p. (1961) *5,896*.

Wyoming, *st.,* U.S.A.; livestock, agr., coal-mining, minerals, petroleum; cap. Cheyenne; a. 97,914 sq. m.; p. (1960) *330,066.*
Wyoming, *valley,* N.E. Penns., U.S.A., on Susquehanna R.; coal; length 30 m.
Wyre, *R.,* Lancs, Eng.; rises in Pennines, flows W. into Lancaster Bay at Fleetwood; length 28 m.
Wyvis, Ben, *mtn.,* Scot., *see* **Ben Wyvis.**

X

Xaltocán, *L.,* Central Mexico.
Xanten, *t.,* Rhine prov., Germany; cath.; p. *5,057.*
Xanthi, *t.,* Thrace, Greece; on R. Mesta; tobacco; p. (1961) *26,377.*
Xanthus, *ruined c.,* Turkey; on R. Xanthus.
Xanxere, *t.,* Brazil; nr. R. Peixe.
Xauen, *t.,* Morocco, N. Africa; p. *14,473.*
Xenia, *c.,* Ohio, U.S.A.; in Miami valley; twine, footwear, agr. ctr.; p. (1960) *20,445.*
Xeres, *see* **Jerez de la Frontera.**
Xilitla, *t.,* Mexico; p. *2,092.*
Xingu, *R.,* Brazil; trib. of the Amazon; navigable for steamers 110 m.; length 1,300 m.
Xochicalco, *ruins,* Mexico.
Xochimilco, *L.,* Mexico; formerly contiguous with L. Tezcuco.
Xochimilco, *t.,* Mexico; on L. Xochimilco; p. *14,370.*
Xois, *ancient c.,* Lower U.A.R.; cap. in 17th century B.C.
Xucar or Juvar, *R.,* Spain; length 200 m.

Y

Y or Ij, *inlet* Zuider Zee, now separated by locks, forming part of canal system of Amsterdam.
Yablonovy, *mtn. range,* Siberia, Asiatic R.S.F.S.R.; E. of L. Baikal; highest peak, Sokhondo, *c.* 8,230 ft.; crossed by Trans-Siberian rly.
Yaila Mtns., Ukrainian S.S.R., U.S.S.R.; form S.E. margin of Crimea Peninsula, extend from Sevastopol to Kerch; forested on middle slopes, pasture on upper slopes; forms marked climate barrier between mild winters of Mediterranean cst. to the S. and cold winters to the N.
Yakima, *t.,* Wash., U.S.A.; agr., livestock; p. (1960) *43,284.*
Yakima, *R.,* Wash., U.S.A.; trib. of Columbia R.; length 208 m.
Yakova, *t.,* Albania; nr. Shkodra.
Yakushima, *I.,* Osumi Gr., Japan; S. of Kyushu; mtns., forest.
Yakut, A.S.S.R., U.S.S.R.; gold-mining; a. 1,530,253 sq. m.; p. (1959) *247,000.*
Yakutsk, *t.,* R.S.F.S.R.; on R. Lena; p. (1959) *74,000.*
Yala, *t.,* S. Thailand; tin-mining.
Yalta, *spt.,* Ukrainian S.S.R.; on Black Sea; p. (1956) *34,100.*
Yalu, *R.,* forms bdy. between Manchuria and N. Korea; flows into Yellow Sea.
Yamagata, *t.,* Honshu, Japan; mnfs.; p. (1955) *160,245.*
Yamaguchi, *t.,* Honshu, Japan; p. (1955) *81,177.*
Yamal, *peninsula,* R.S.F.S.R.; jutting into Arctic Ocean.
Yambol, *t.,* Bulgaria; on R. Tunja; ruined mosque; corn tr.; p. (1956) *42,038.*
Yamethin, *dist.,* Upper Burma; teak forests, rice; ch. t. Yamethin; p. *9,291.*
Yamina, *t.,* Gambia, W. Africa; p. *6,700.*
Yamina or Nyamina, *t.,* Nigeria, W. Africa; on R. Niger; tr. ctr.
Yana, *R.,* Siberia, U.S.S.R.; length 1,000 m.
Yanago, *t.,* Japan; business ctr.; cotton textiles; p. (1947) *50,027.*
Yanaon or Yanam, *prov., t.* formerly Fr. Orissa, united with India 1954; p. (1961) *7,032.*
Yanbu, *spt.,* Arabia; on E. cst. of Red Sea; pt. for Medina.
Yanco, *t.,* N.S.W., Australia; fruit, rice, dairying.
Yangchow (Yangzhou), *c.,* Kiangsu, China; on Grand Canal; comm. ctr.; p. (1953) *180,000.*
Yangchuan (Yangqan), *c.,* Shansi prov., China; ironworking ctr.; p. (1953) *177,000.*
Yangi-yer, *t.,* Uzbek S.S.R., founded 1957 as ctr. for new irrigated cotton lands of the Hunger steppe.
Yangtze River, China; rises in plateau of Tibet, flows E. to E. China Sea, Pac. Oc. nr. Shanghai; traverses "Red Basin" of Szechwan, a deep gorge above Ichang, and finally a broad, level plain; many lge. cs. on its banks, Chungking, Ichang, Wuhan (Hankow, Hayang, Wuchang), Nanking, Chinkiang; navigable by ocean-going vessels 1,800 m. to Ichang; total length 3,500 m.
Yannina, *see* **Ioánnina.**
Yaoundé, *cap.,* Cameroun Rep., W. Africa; p. (1955) *38,000.*
Yap, *I.,* Carolines, Pac. Oc., U.S.A. trusteeship; a. 79 sq. m.; cable sta.; p. (1958) *5,459.*
Yapura, *R.,* Brazil and Colombia, S. America; trib. of R. Amazon; navigable for 600 m.; length 1,500 m.
Yaracuy, *st.,* Venezuela; cap. San Felipe; p. (1961) *175,291.*
Yare, *R.,* Norfolk, Eng.; flows E. to N. Sea at Gorleston; length 50 m.
Yaritagua, *t.,* Venezuela; tobacco, coffee, cocoa, sugar; p. *5,399.*
Yarkand (Soche), *c.,* Sinkiang, China; tr. ctr.; wheat, rice, beans, fruit, carpets, textiles; p. (estd.) *60,000.*
Yarkand, *R.,* Sinkiang, China; trib. of Tarim R.; length 500 m.
Yarmouth, *spt.,* Nova Scotia, Canada; shipbldg., fisheries; p. (1961) *8,636.*
Yarmouth, *par.,* I. of Wight, Eng.; on N.W. cst., 8 m. W of Newport; holiday resort; p. *893.*
Yarmouth, Great, *spt., co. bor.,* Norfolk, Eng.; at mouth of R. Yare; holiday resort; fisheries, herrings, timber, shipyds.; p. (1961) *52,860.*
Yaroslavl, *t.,* R.S.F.S.R.; on R. Volga; cath.; synthetic rubber, engin., textiles, chemicals, sawmilling; p. (1962) *443,000.*
Yarra, *R.,* Victoria, Australia; length 100 m.
Yatschushiro, *t.,* Kyushu, Japan; p. (1947) *41,281.*
Yavary, *R.,* S. America; on Brazilian–Peruvian frontier; trib. of R. Marañon; length 450 m.
Yawata, *t.,* Kyushu, Japan; now part of Kitakyushu City newly formed 1963 (*q.v.*); chemicals, iron and steel; p. (1960) *332,000.*
Yazoo, *c.,* Miss., U.S.A.; on Yazoo R.; agr. tr.; p. (1960) *11,236.*
Yazoo, *R.,* Miss., U.S.A.; trib. of R. Mississippi; length 280 m.
Yazoo, *dist.,* Miss., U.S.A.; very flat, low-lying flood plain of R. Mississippi and R. Yazoo, extends 220 m. along R. from Memphis to Vicksburg; very fertile alluvial soil, but subject to disastrous floods; one of ch. cotton-growing dists. in U.S.A.
Yecla, *t.,* Spain; mkt.; p. (1957) *24,046.*
Yeddo, old name of Tokyo, Japan.
Yegoryevsk, *t.,* R.S.F.S.R.; 72 m. S.E. of Moscow; lge. textile ind.; p. (1959) *59,000.*
Yekabpils, *t.,* Kurland, Latvian S.S.R.; on R. Dvina.
Yeletz, *t.,* R.S.F.S.R.; on R. Sosna; grain and cattle tr.; p. (1959) *78,000.*
Yell, *I.,* Shetlands, Scot.; 17 m. long; p. *1,883.*
Yellow R., *see* **Hwang Ho.**
Yellow Sea (Hwang-hai), *arm* of Pacific Ocean, between China and Korea; length 600 m., greatest width 400 m.; max. depth 500 ft.
Yellowhead Pass, B.C., Alberta, Canada; most N. and lowest of main passes across Rocky Mtns.; carries Canadian National Rly. on route from Edmonton to Vancouver and Prince Rupert; summit alt. 3,700 ft.
Yellowknife, *t.,* N.W. Terr., Canada; on N. shore of Gr. Slave L.; ctr. of impt. gold-mining dist.; linked by air to Edmonton, Alberta.
Yellowstone, *L.,* Wyo., U.S.A.; 20 m. long, 15 m. wide; alt. 7,740 ft.; in Y. National Park.
Yemen, *republic,* Arabia; federated with United Arab Republic to form United Arab States, March 1958; barley, wheat, millet, coffee, hides; cap. Sana; a. 75,000 sq. m.; p. (estd. 1958) *8,000,000.*
Yenakievo, *t.,* Ukrainian S.S.R.; coal, iron and steel; p. (1959) *92,000.*
Yenangyaung, *t., R. pt.,* Burma; on left bank of R. Irrawaddy, 280 m. N. of Rangoon; ctr. of Burma oilfields.
Yenchow (Tzuyang), *t.,* Chekiang, China; S. of Hangchow.
Yenesei, *R.,* Siberia, R.S.F.S.R.; rises in Sayan Mtns., flows N. into Arctic Ocean; ch. tribs. Upper, Stony and Lower Tunguska Rs.; length 3,300 m.
Yentai, *see* **Chefoo.**
Yeo or Ivel, *R.,* Dorset, Somerset, Eng.; trib. of R. Parrett; length 24 m.

Yeovil, *t., mun. bor.*, Somerset, Eng.; on R. Yeo; 22 m. S.E. of Taunton; glove mnf., aeroplane wks. engin.; dairying; p. (1961) *24,552.*
Yerevan, *cap.*, Armenian S.S.R.; engin., chemicals, synthetic rubber, textiles, aluminium; p. (1962) *583,000.*
Yeshil-Irmak, *R.*, Turkey; flows N. to Black Sea; length 200 m.
Yeshil Kul, *L.*, Chinese Turkestan (Sinkiang).
Yes Tor, *2nd highest summit*, Dartmoor, Devon, Eng.; alt. 2,028 ft.
Yevpatoriya (Eupatoria), *spt.* Ukrainian S.S.R.; chemicals, leather, locks, dried fish; new port being built 1963; p. (1959), *57,000.*
Yeysk, *t.*, R.S.F.S.R.; N. Caucasus, pt. on Taganrog Bay; resort; engin.; p. (1959) *55,000.*
Yezd, *t., prov. cap.*, Iran; caravan ctr.; p. (estd. 1949) *56,000.*
Yezo, *see* **Hokkaido.**
Yiewsley and West Drayton, *former urb. dist.*, Middx., Eng.; now inc. in Hillingdon outer bor. Greater London; varied light inds.; p. (1961) *23,723.*
Yingkow (Yingkou), *c.*, Liaoning prov., China: 20 m. up R. from mouth of Liao-ho; soyabean prods.; p. (1953) *131,000.*
Ykspihlaja, *sub.* of Kokkola, W. Finland; foundries, chemicals.
Yokkaichi, *industl. c., spt.*, S. Honshu, Japan; on W. cst. of Ise Bay, 23 m. S W. of Nagoya; silk, cotton and woollen goods, petro chemicals, synthetic rubber; p. (1950) *123,870.*
Yokohama, *ch., spt.*, Honshu Japan; W. side of Tokyo Bay; silks, tea, cars; p. (1962) *1,499,000.*
Yokosuka, *spt.*, Honshu, Japan; S. of Tokyo; holiday resort; thermal power sta.; p. (1962) *295,000.*
Yola, *t.*, N. Nigeria, Africa; nr. R. Benue; agr. tr.; p. *5,310.*
Yonkers, *c.*, N.Y., U.S.A.; on Hudson R.; light inds.; p. (1960) *190,634.*
Yonne, *dep.*, France; agr., wines, minerals; cap. Auxerre; a. 2,894 sq. m.; p. (1962) *269,826.*
York, *c., co. bor., co. t.*, Yorks, Eng.; on R. Ouse; in central position in Vale of York; cath., cas. univ.; mkt., confectionery; p. (1961) *104,468.*
York, *I. gr.*, Torres Strait (between New Guinea and Australia).
York, *R.*, tidal estuary of Chesapeake Bay, U.S.A.
York, *c.*, Nebraska, U.S.A.; rly. ctr.; p. (1960) *6,173.*
York, *c.*, Penns., U.S.A.; agr. tools, confectionery, tobacco; p. (1960) *54,504.*
York, *C.*, Hayes Peninsula, Greenland
York, *C.*, Queensland, Australia; most N. point on mainland of Australia.
York Factory, *t.*, on Nelson R., Hudson Bay, Manitoba, Canada.
York, Vale of, *broad lowland*, Yorks, Eng.; extends N. to S. between Pennines to W. and N. Yorks Moors and Yorks Wolds to E.; drained to Humber by R. Ouse and tribs. from N. by Rs. Don and Trent from S.; flar apart from low transverse ridge Stamford Bridge to Harrogate; glacial and alluvial soils have required draining; crop farming, wheat, barley, root-crops, associated with fattening of beef cattle; settlement mainly marginal; ch. t. York; length 60 m.; width varies from 10 m. in N. to 30 m. in S.
Yorke, *peninsula*, S Australia; separates Spencer G. and G. of St. Vincent; 100 m. long, 30 m. wide.
Yorkshire, *lgst. co.*, Eng.; divided into 3 Ridings, N., E. and W.; cap. York; a. 6,081 sq. m; p. (1961) *4,722,661.*
Yorkshire, East Riding, *admin. co.*, Yorks, Eng.; farming, pastoral on Wolds, arable elsewhere; ch. t. Hull; a. 1,172 sq. m.; p. (1961) *527,051.*
Yorkshire, North Riding, *admin. co.*, Yorks, Eng; farming, pastoral on Moors, mixed elsewhere; iron-ore mng. in Cleveland Hills; heavy inds. around Middlesbrough; ch. t. Middlesbrough; a. 2,128 sq. m.; p. (1961) *554,382.*
Yorkshire, West Riding, *admin. co.*, Yorks, Eng.; pastoral farming on Pennines, but highly industl. on coalfield at foot of Pennines; woollens, steel, engin.; ch. ts. Leeds (in N.), Sheffield (in S.); a. 2,780 sq. m.; p. (1961) *3,641,228.*
Yorkshire Moors, *hills*, N.R. Yorks, Eng.; inc. North Yorks Moors, Cleveland Hills and Hambleton Hills; bounded to N. by Tees Valley, S. by Vale of Pickering, W. by Swale Valley, E. by sea; composed of oolitic limestone; good sheep pastures; impt. iron-ore deposits worked in Cleveland Hills; maximum alt. 1,489 ft.
Yorkshire Wolds, *hills*, E.R., Yorks, Eng.; extend N.E. from Humber and terminate in Flamborough Head; composed of chalk; smooth slopes and short grass give gd. sheep pasture; average alt. 600 ft.
Yorkton, *t.*, Saskatchewan, Canada; agr. ctr.; p. (1961) *9,995.*
Yoruba, *dist.*, Nigeria; ch. ts., Oyo, Ibadan, Abeokuta and Illorin.
Yosemite Falls, 3 cataracts, of Yosemite Creek, Cal., U.S.A.
Yoshkar-Ola, *t.*, Mariy A.S.S.R.; R.S.F.S.R.; 80 m. N.W. of Kazan; wood processing, food inds.; p. (1959) *88,000.*
Youghal, *spt., urb. dist.*, Cork, Ireland; on estuary of the Blackwater, Cork, Ireland; fisheries; p. (1961) *5,043.*
Youngstown, *industl. c.*, Ohio, U.S.A.; on Beaver R., 60 m. N.W. of Pittsburgh; iron- and steel-mkg., heavy engin.; p. (1960) *166,689.*
Yoyang, *c.*, Hunan, China; at outlet of Tung Ting L. on the bank of the R. Yangtze; p. *4,800.*
Yozgat, *t.*, Turkey; p. (1960) *18,263.*
Ypres (Ieper), *t.*, Belgium; automatic textile loom mkg.; 2 battles, First World War; p. (1962) *18,213.*
Ypsilanti, *c.*, Mich., U.S.A.; on Huron R.; agr. mkt., mnfs.; p. (1960) *20,957.*
Yssel (Zuider Zee), *L.*, Neth.; *see* **Ijsselmeer.**
Yssingeaux, *t.*, Haute-Loire, France; nr. Le Puy; mnfs.; p. (1954) *5,653.*
Ystad, *spt.*, S. Sweden; on Baltic Sea; agr. machin., soap; p. (1961) *13,711.*
Yuba, *R.*, Cal., U.S.A.; trib. of Feather-Sacramento R.
Yucatan *st.*, Mexico; cereals, cotton; cap. Merida; a. 23,926 sq. m.; p. (1960) *614,049.*
Yucatan, *strait*, connects G. of Mexico with Caribbean Sea.
Yudanamutana, *dist.*, S. Australia; copper-mining.
Yuan Kiang, *R.*, Hunan, China; length 400 m.
Yugoslavia, *see* **Jugoslavia.**
Yukon, *R.*, Canada–Alaska; flows N.W. and W. into Bering Strait; navigable for 1,200 m.; length 2,000 m.
Yukon, *terr.*, Canada; mountainous; coal, minerals; chief ts. Dawson, and Whitehorse (cap.); a. 207,076 sq. m.; p. (1961) *14,628.*
Yuma, *t.*, Arizona, U.S.A.; at confluence of Rs. Gila and Colorado nr. Mexican–U.S.A. bdy.; ctr. of irrigated agr., obtaining water from Laguna and Imperial Dams; cotton, citrus fruits, alfalfa; p. (1960) *23,974.*
Yunnan, *S.W. prov.*, China; adjoining Burma; mountainous; agr., minerals; cap. Kunming; a. 162,342 sq. m.; p. (1953) *17,472,737.*
Yuzhno-Sakhalinsk, *t.*, R.S.F.S.R.; at S. end of Sakhalin I; paper, light inds.; p. (1959) *86,000.*
Yverdon, *t.*, Switzerland; cas.; tourist ctr.; p. *10,865.*

Z

Zaandam, *t.*, N. Holland, Neth.: paper, oil, timber, cement; p. (1960) *48,910.*
Zabrze (Hindenburg), *t.*, Upper Silesia, Poland; German before 1945; steel, coal, engin., chemicals; p. (1960) *189,000.*
Zacapa, *t.*, Guatemala, Central America; sulphur springs; tobacco; p. (estd. 1960) *35,300.*
Zacatecas, *st.*, Mexico; silver-mines; cereals, fruit, sugar; a. 28,122 sq. m.; p. (1960) *817,831.*
Zacatecas, *t., cap.*, Zacatecas, Mexico; silver, pottery, comm. ctr.; p. (1960) *24,454.*
Zacatecoluca, *t.*, El Salvador, Central America; cigar mkg., hand looms; coffee, cotton, sugar, vanilla in a.; p. (1960) *30,810.*
Zadar (Zara), *spt.*, Jugoslavia; formerly Italian; cath.; maraschino, flour, glass; p. (1959) *22,000.*
Zagan (Sagan), *t.*, Silesia, Poland; German before 1945; on R. Bober; cas.; textiles, paper, lignite; p. (estd. 1939) *23,000.*
Zagazig, *t.*, Egypt; on Nile Delta; cotton, grain tr.; p. (1960) *124,000.*

Zagorsk, *t.*, R.S.F.S.R.; 44 m. N.E. of Moscow; woodcarving, toy mkg.; p. (1959) *73,000*.

Zagreb, *t.*, Jugoslavia; on R. Sava; cath., univ.; engin., textiles, chemicals, paper, asbestos; p. (1961) *457,000*.

Zagros, *mtns.*, Persia; highest, Zardeh Kuh, 14,921 ft.

Zahle, *t.*, Lebanon, S.W. Asia; on slopes of L. mtn.; p. (estd 1950) *78,031*.

Zakopane, *t.*, Poland; in High Tatra mtns.; tourist resort; p. (1960) *25,000*.

Zakynthos, *Ionian I.* Greece; cap. Zante; currants; devastated by severe earthquake, 1953; a. 277 sq. m.; p. (1961) *35,451*.

Zambesi, *R.*, S.E. Africa; flows E. to Mozambique Channel, Indian Ocean; navigable for 1,700 m.; length 2,200 m.

Zambesia, *prov.*, Mozambique; ch. t., Quelimane; p. (1962) *1,369,961*.

Zambia, *indep. sov. st.* within Brit. Commonwealth (1964), Central Africa; landlocked, bordering Congo, Angola, South-West Africa, Rhodesia, and Bechuanaland (50-yd. frontier across Zambesi); tropical climate, moderate rains; savannah vegetation; maize, tobacco, wheat, coffee; zinc, copper, vanadium, gold, ivory; fishing ind.; irrigation system under development on Kafue Flats; mica in the Lundazi a.; cap. Lusaka; a. 288,130 sq. m.; p. (estd. 1964) *3,500,000*.

Zamboanga, *t.*, Mindanao, Philippines; rice, sugar, tobacco, timber; p. (1960) *131,489*.

Zamora, *prov.*, Spain; cap. Zamora; a. 40,825 sq. m.; p. (1959) *320,335*.

Zamora, *t.*, *cap.*, Zamora, Spain; on R. Duero; olive oil, wines; p. (1957) *45,000*.

Zamosc, *old t.*, Poland; bentwood furniture mnf.; p. (1960) *28,000*.

Zanesville, *t.*, Ohio, U.S.A.; textiles, pottery, machin.; p. (1960) *39,077*.

Zante, *t.*, Zakynthos, Greece; p. (1961) *9,506*.

Zanzibar, *see* **Tanzania**.

Zapala, *t.*, W. Argentina; in Andes; rly. term.; [oilfield.

Zaporozhe (Dneprostroy), *industl. t.*, Ukrainian S.S.R.; on R. Dnieper, 45 m. S.E. of Dnieperpetrovsk; nr. Lenin (Dnieper) Dam and hydro-elec. power-sta. (558,000 kW.); iron- and steel-wks., ferro-alloys, engin., aluminium, chemicals, cars, elec. equipment; p. (1962) *490,000*.

Zapotitlán, *t.*, Mexico; local tr. ctr.; p. *2,218*.

Zara, *see* **Zadar**.

Zaragoza, *prov.*, Spain; cap. Zaragoza; a. 6,611 sq. m.; p. (1959) *643,825*.

Zaragoza, *t.*, Spain; on R. Ebro; 2 caths., univ., citadel; captured by Moors 8th century, once cap. of Aragon; beer, spirits, woollens, iron ware; p. (1959) *301,569*.

Zarate, *t.*, Entre Rios, Argentina; paper wks,; p. (1960) *52,000*.

Zaria, *t.*, N. Nigeria, Africa; univ.; cotton ctr.; p. (1953) *54,000*.

Zaruma, *t.*, Ecuador; mnfs.; p. *12,975*.

Zary (Sorau), *t.*, Brandenburg, Poland; German before 1945; textiles, pottery; p. (1960) *25,000*.

Zastron, *t.*, O.F.S., S. Africa; alt. 5,507 ft.; agr. ctr.; p. (1960) *4,440* inc. *1,625* whites.

Zawiercie, *t.*, Poland; coal, iron, textiles, glass; p. (1960) *33,000*.

Zdunska Wola, *t.*, Poland; nr. Lodz; p. (1960) *25,000*.

Zealand (Sjaellan), *I.*, Denmark; between Kattegat and Baltic; a. (with Is. attached) 2,840 sq. m.; ch. t. Copenhagen; p. *1,251,661*.

Zeebrugge, *spt.*, Belgium; connected with Bruges by ship canal; glass ind.; petrol storage and conditioning depot; oil refinery; rolling mill equip.; p. (1947) *8,450*.

Zeeland, *prov.*, Neth.; fishing; cap. Middelburg; a. 690 sq. m.; p. (estd. 1959) *283,721*.

Zeilah, *t.*, Somali Rep., E. Africa; on G. of Aden; p. *1,000*.

Zeist, *t.*, Neth.; metalware; p. (1960) *51,543*.

Zeitz, *t.*, Halle, E. Germany; S.W. of Leipzig; cas., cath.; machin., sugar, wood, leather, chemicals; p. (1963) *46,301*.

Zelenodolsk, *t.*, R.S.F.S.R., on R. Volga 25 m. W. of Kazan; rly. junction; sawmills; p. (1959) *60,000*.

Zelten, Libya, N. Africa; 200 m. S. of Benghazi; oil field.

Zemun, *t.*, Jugoslavia; p. (1947) *28,083*.

Zenica, *t.*, Jugoslavia; lge. iron and steel wks; p. (1959) *47,000*.

Zenjan or **Zanian**, *t.*, cap. Khamseh, Persia; comm. ctr., carpets; p. *30,109*.

Zerbst, *t.*, Magdeburg, E. Germany; on R. Nuthe, S.E. of Magdeburg; cas.; machin.; p. (1963) *18,862*.

Zermatt, *vil.*, Valais, Switzerland; at foot of Matterhorn; tourist ctr., p. *1,000*.

Zgierz, *t.*, Poland; nr. Lodz; linens; p. (1960) *37,000*.

Zhdanov (Mariupol), *spt.*, Ukrainian S.S.R.; on Azov Sea; iron and steel, zirconium, chemicals; p. (1962) *321,000*.

Zhitomir, *t.*, Ukrainian S.S.R.; engin.; p. (1959) *105,000*.

Zielona Gora (Grünberg), *t.*, Silesia, Poland; German before 1945; lignite mining, viticulture; p. (1960) *51,000*.

Zile, *t.*, Turkey; cereals, fruit, wool, rugs; p. (1960) *21,436*.

Zillertal, *valley*, Tyrol, Austria; drained by R. Ziller, trib. of R. Inn; length 50 m.

Zillertal Alps, *mtns.*, Austria; in Tyrol.

Zinder, *t.*, Niger, W. Africa; terminus of trans-Saharan motor route; tr. ctr.; p. *12,000*.

Zipaquira, *t.*, Colombia; 30 m. N. of Bogota; cattle farming; salt mines; p. (estd. 1959) *29,880*.

Zittau, *t.*, Dresden, E. Germany; on R. Mandau; woollens, linens, machin., cars, chemicals; p. (1963) *42,863*.

Žižkov, *t.*, ČSSR.; sub. of Prague; p. *91,082*.

Zlatoust, *t.*, R.S.F.S.R.; in the Ural Mtns.; steel, chemicals, sawmilling; p. (1959) *161,000*.

Zlin, *see* **Gottwaldov**.

Znojmo or **Znaim**, *t.*, ČSSR.; pottery, textiles, mkt. gardening; p. (1961) *23,956*.

Zomba, *t.*, Malawi, 2,900 ft. above sea level on slopes of Zomba mtn., 42 m. N.E. Blantyre; univ.; p. *7,800* (incl. *800* Europeans).

Zona Militar de Comodoro Rivadavia, *terr.*, Argentina, separated from Chubut terr. in 1946.

Zonguldak, *t.*, Turkey; p. (1960) *54,026*.

Zorritos, *t.*, Tumbes dep., Peru, S. America; on cst., 10 m. from Ecuador bdy.; oilfield.

Zoutpansberg, *dist.*, N.E. Transvaal, S. Africa; goldfields, mtns.

Zrenjanin (Veliki Bečkerek), *t.*, Vojvodina, Jugoslavia; on R. Begej; flour, leather, timber, sugar, wine, paper, agr., machin.; p. (1960) *52,100*.

Zug, *can.*, Switzerland; cap. Zug; a. 93 sq. m.; p. (1961) *52,489*.

Zugspitze, *mtn.*, Bavarian Alps, highest peak in Germany, 9.722 ft.

Zuider Zee, *see* **Ijselmeer**.

Zulia, *st.*, Venezuela, S. America; cap. Maracaibo; p. (1963) *1,044,000*.

Zululand, *prov.*, Natal; livestock, cereals, fruit, sugar, coffee, tea, gold, coal; a. 10,427 sq. m.

Zungeru, *t.*, Nigeria, Africa; on Lagos–Kano rly.; p. *1,000*.

Zurich, *can.*, Switzerland; cottons, silks; a. 668 sq. m.; p. (1961) *952,304*.

Zurich (Zürich), *c.*, Switzerland; on L. Zurich and R. Limmat, lgst. t.; cap. of Z. prov.; cath., univ.; paper, silks, cottons, machin.; p. (1961) *439,600*.

Zutphen, *t.*, Neth.; on R. Yssel; paper, tanning, engin.; p. (1960) *25,036*.

Zwartebergen, *mtns.*, Cape Province, Rep. of S. Africa; extending 200 m. E. to W. flanked by Gr. Karroo to N. Little Karroo to S.; form impenetrable barrier except where broken across by headstreams of R. Gouritz; rise to over 7,000 ft.

Zwartsluis, *t.*, Neth.; nr. Zwolle; p. *3,348*.

Zweibrücken, *t.*, Rhineland-Palatinate, Germany nr. Saarbrücken; cas.; machin., footwear textiles; p. (1963) *33,300*.

Zwickau, *t.*, Karl-Marx-Stadt, E. Germany; on R. Zwickhauser Mulde; cas.; coal, motors machin., textiles; p. (1963) *129,389*.

Zwolle, *c.*, Neth.; canal ctr.; cattle mkt., cottons ironwks.; p. (1960) *55,523*.

Zyrardow, *t.*, Poland; nr. Warsaw; mnfs.; p (1960) *30,000*.

Zyryanovsk, *t.*, Kazakhstan S.S.R.; lead, zinc p. (1959) *54,000*.

THE BRITISH COMMONWEALTH

The British Commonwealth is a free association of independent member nations together with their dependencies at various stages of political advance. Member nations include Britain, Canada, Australia, New Zealand whose membership of the Commonwealth dates from the Statute of Westminster, 1931, India (1947), Pakistan (1947), Ceylon (1948), Ghana (1957), the Federation of Malaya (1957), which in 1963 became Malaysia, the Federation (now the Federal Republic) of Nigeria (1960), Cyprus (1961), Sierra Leone (1961), Tanganyika (1961), which in 1964 united with Zanzibar (1963) to become Tanzania, Jamaica (1962), Trinidad and Tobago (1962), Uganda (1962), Kenya (1963), Malawi (1964), Malta (1964), Zambia (1964), the Gambia (1965), Singapore, which seded from the Malaysian Federation (1965), Botswana (1966), and Guyana (1966).

See also the chapter on the British Commonwealth in Section C which contains definitions of the status of the various countries of the Commonwealth.

I.—MEMBERS OF THE COMMONWEALTH

(including territories for which members other than the U.K. are responsible).

Country	Land Area (sq. miles)	Recent Population Estimates
United Kingdom	94,209	51,985,000
Canada (incl. Newfoundland and Labrador)	3,851,809	18,928,000
Australia (Commonwealth of)	2,974,581	11,250,708
Cocos Islands	5	607
Christmas Island	55	3,099
Norfolk Island—*Colony*	13⅓	1,048
Papua—*Colony*	90,540	523,000
New Guinea—*Trusteeship*	93,000	1,449,000
Nauru—*Trusteeship with Australia, New Zealand and the U.K.*	8¼	4,613
Antarctic territory	2,333,624	—
New Zealand	103,736	2,414,064
Island Territories	194	24,121
Ross Dependency	160,000 (estimated)	198
India (Republic of)	1,178,995	439.235,082
Pakistan (Republic of)	365,529	93,831,982
Ceylon	25,332	9,404,000
Ghana (Republic of)	91,843	6,691,000
Nigeria (Federal Republic of)	356,669	35,752,000
*Cyprus (Republic of)	3,572	577,639
Sierra Leone	27,925	2,183,000
Tanzania (United Republic of)	363,708	9,710,000
Uganda	93,981	6,845,000
Jamaica	4,411	1,638,000
Trinidad and Tobago	1,980	850,000
Kenya (Republic of)	224,960	8,676,000
Malaysia (Federation of)	127,298	8,416,345
Malawi (Republic of)	45,747	3,000,000
Malta and Gozo	122	329,000
Zambia (Republic of)	288,130	3,500,000
Gambia	4,003	315,999
Singapore (Republic of)	291	1,550,000
Botswana (Republic of)	222,000	548,000
Guyana	83,000	650,000

* The United Kingdom retains sovereignty over areas totalling about 99 sq. m.

Brunei (area: 2,226 sq. m.; p. 84,000), for whose defence and external relations Britain is responsible, and Rhodesia (area: 150,333 sq. m.; p. 4,210,000) come within the jurisdiction of the Secretary of State for Commonwealth Relations.

II.—TERRITORIES FOR WHICH THE U.K. IS RESPONSIBLE AND WHICH ARE ADMINISTERED THROUGH THE COLONIAL OFFICE.

(Some of the very small, or practically uninhabited, islands have been omitted.)

Region and Territory	Status	Land Area (sq. miles)	Recent Population Estimates
South Africa:			
Basutoland	Colony	11,716	733,000
Swaziland	Protectorate	6,704	285,000
Far East:			
Hong Kong	Colony	398	3,692,000
Mediterranean:			
Gibraltar	Colony	2¼	24,386
Caribbean:			
Antigua (including dependencies)	Colony	171	60,000
Barbados	Colony	166	242,000
Dominica	Colony	290	64,000
Montserrat	Colony	32	13,000
St. Kitts—Nevis—Anguilla	Colony	138	59,000
St. Lucia	Colony	238	94,000
St. Vincent	Colony	150	85,000
Grenada	Colony	133	93,000
Cayman Is.	Colony	100	8,853
British Honduras	Colony (Intern. self-gov.)	8,866	103,000
Virgin Islands	Colony	59	8,500
Western Pacific:			
Fiji	Colony	7,095	449,000
Pitcairn	Colony	2	186
Tonga	Protected State	270	71,000
Western Pacific High Commission Territories:			
British Solomon Islands Protectorate	Protectorate	11,500	137,000
Gilbert and Ellice Islands Colony	Colony	369	50,000
New Hebrides	Anglo-French Condominium	5,700	66,000
Atlantic Ocean:			
Falkland Islands	Colony	4,700	2,117
Dependencies:			
S. Georgia	Dependency of Falkland Islands	1,450	521
S. Sandwich Is.	Dependency of Falkland Islands		Uninhabited
British Antarctic Territory:			
S. Shetlands, S. Orkneys, Graham's Land	Colony	500,000	No permanent inhabitants
Bahamas	Colony (Intern. self-gov.)	4,404	134,000
Turks and Caicos Is.	Colony	166	6,272
Bermuda	Colony	21	48,000
St. Helena	Colony	47	4,526
Ascension	Dependency of St. Helena	34	374
Tristan da Cunha	Dependency of St. Helena	38	270
Indian Ocean:			
*Aden	Colony	75	220,000
*Protectorate of South Arabia	Protectorate	111,000	1,000,000
‡Mauritius (including dependencies)	Colony (Intern. self-gov.)	805	741,000
Seychelles	Colony	156	46,000
†British Indian Ocean Territory			1,400

* Aden and 16 of the 19 States of the Protectorate have joined together in the Federation of South Arabia which has a common legislature and executive. The State of Aden and the Protectorate of South Arabia, however, remain the territorial units.

† This territory consists of the Chagos Archipelago (formerly part of Mauritius) and Aldabra Farquhar and Desroches Islands (formerly part of Seychelles).

‡ Mauritius was to become an independent State within the Commonwealth by the end of 1966.

GENERAL INFORMATION

GENERAL INFORMATION

A

Aard-vark (Dutch *aarde* = earth + *vark* = pig), name given by the Boers to a genus of ant-eating mammals peculiar to Africa. They are nocturnal and burrowing, with an arched back, and usually grow to a length of 5 ft.

Abacus, a device for making arithmetical calculations, consisting of parallel bars on which are strung movable coloured beads. The earliest form of this instrument was used in Mesopotamia about 3000 B.C., and its use spread westwards throughout the Græco–Roman world and eastwards to China. An efficient form of the abacus is still used today in parts of Asia.

Abdication. The term usually refers to the renunciation of the royal office by a reigning monarch. Both Edward II (1327) and Richard II (1399) were forced to abdicate, James II left the throne vacant without waiting for a formal deposition, and the abdication of Edward VIII was effected by the Declaration of Abdication Act, 1936. Since 1688 when Parliament declared James II to have abdicated by reason of desertion and subversion of the constitution, no British monarch can abdicate without the consent of Parliament.

Aberration, in astronomy, is the apparent displacement of a star due to the speed of the observer with the earth (see Parallax). In optics (i) spherical aberration, causing blurring of an image, is due to failure of lens to bring light to a single focus, (ii) chromatic aberration, causing coloured fringes to an image, is due to the refractive index of glass being different for light of different colours. For instance, violet light is bent more than red.

Abiogenesis, or spontaneous generation; the origination of living from non-living matter. The term is applied to such discredited ideas as that frogs could be generated spontaneously by the action of sunlight on mud, or maggots arise spontaneously in dead meat without any eggs from which the maggots hatch being present. Spallanzani (1729–99) upset the hypothesis of spontaneous generation; Pasteur dealt it a death-blow.

Abominable Snowman. *See* **Yeti.**

Aborigines, a term first applied to an ancient mythical people of central Italy, derives from the Latin *ab origine* = from the beginning. It now signifies the original inhabitants of any country, in particular the aboriginal tribes of Australia. In contrast to their highly complex social and religious customs, the material culture of Australian aborigines is very low and ill adapted to stand up to contact with European civilisation. Originally estimated at 300,000, their number has dropped in the last 200 years to some 30,000; the 18,000 who live in the Northern Territory received full citizen rights in 1964.

Absolution, an ecclesiastical term denoting the liberation of a person guilty of sin from its consequences by the act or intercession of religious authority.

Abstract Art, a term applied to 20th cent. plastic arts in which form and colour possess aesthetic value apart from the subject. Usually represented as a modern movement beginning with Cézanne. The idea is ancient, abstract design being found in the Neolithic period, in folk-art, and particularly in Moslem art (which forbids naturalistic representations especially of the human figure). Among those in the tradition are Kandinsky, Braque, Mondrian, Calder.

Acetic Acid, an organic acid produced when ordinary (ethyl) alcohol is fermented by the organism called *Acetobacter aceti*. The same oxidation process yields vinegar; this is a weak and crude solution of acetic acid obtained by trickling dilute alcoholic liquor over beechwood shavings at 35° C. The souring of wine is due to the same process. Acetic acid is used as a food preservative and flavouring material, and in the manufacture of cellulose acetate and white lead.

Acetylene, a compound of carbon and hydrogen prepared from calcium carbide and water. A very reactive gas, it is used industrially on a large scale to prepare acetaldehyde, chlorohydrocarbon solvents, and many intermediates for plastics manufacture. Burns in air with a highly luminous flame formerly used for lighting purposes, but is now widely used, with oxygen, in welding. For safe storage and transportation it is dissolved in acetone.

Acids, substances having a tendency to lose a positive ion (a proton). This general definition overcomes difficulties of earlier views which merely described their properties and asserted that they are chemically opposite to bases. As a whole acids contain ionisable hydrogen, replaceable by a metal, to form a salt. Inorganic acids are compounds of non-metals or metalloids, *e.g.*, sulphuric, phosphoric acid. Carboxylic acids contain the group –COOH.

Acolyte, one who assists the priest at Mass by saying the responses and by waiting on him.

Act of God, a natural catastrophe that could not be foreseen or averted.

Advent, a period devoted to religious preparation for the coming celebration of the Nativity (Christmas). It comprises four Sundays, and commences on the one nearest to St. Andrew's Day (Nov. 30). Advent was not observed before the 4th cent.

Advocatus Diaboli (" the devil's advocate "), a Roman Catholic functionary who presents opposing evidence in regard to the life of any deceased person it may be proposed to canonise.

Aeolian Harp, a musical instrument once very popular. It consists of catgut stretched over a wooden sound-box which, when placed out of doors in the wind, can be made to emit many pleasing harmonies.

Aerenchyma. Plant tissue which is spongy because there are large air spaces between the cells in which gases can circulate. This aerating tissue is characteristic of marsh and water-plants.

Aerodynamics, the science of gases (especially air) in motion, particularly in relation to aircraft (aeronautics). The idea of imitating the birds by the use of wings is of ancient origin. Leonardo da Vinci first carried out experiments in a scientific manner. The invention of the balloon in 1783 and the researches of scientists and engineers in the 19th cent. ultimately led to the development of the aeroplane.

Aerolites, the name given to the class of meteorites composed chiefly of heavy silicates. The other two main classes are *siderolites* (nickel–iron and silicates) and *siderites* (nickel–iron).

Aerosol, a suspension of a liquid in a gas; for example, a fog is very small drops of water suspended in air. Formed by spraying the liquid in air, aerosols are used to disperse liquid over a wide area in crop spraying, air freshening and pest control.

Aesthetics, the branch of philosophy dealing with the nature of the individual's appreciation of beauty. Basically there are three theories. (1) The theory of Plato that beauty is an objective reality belonging to the ideal world which lies behind our own shadowy existence; essentially this is the view taken by Clive Bell, whose theory of " significant form " (1914) suggests that the aesthetic emotion is a real and specific one, aroused by all true works of art. Beauty inheres in the external object, beheld with detachment, not as a means but implicit in itself. (2) The subjectivist view of Tolstoy that: (a) great art is that which transmits the original emotion felt by the artist to as many people as possible; (*b*) art has a moral function (*e.g.*, *King Lear* is bad art because its theme is immoral and Russian folk-music is good because it has given aesthetic pleasure to more people than the plays of Shakespeare). (3) The psychological theory of I. A. Richards and C. K. Ogden (*c.* 1920) which equates beauty with emotional satisfa tion. A beautiful object has the effect of temporarily integrating our ordinarily conflicting impulses, bringing a sense of meaningfulness and cessation of strife.

Afrikander, type of cattle bred in South Africa.

Afrikaner, an Afrikaans-speaking South African, usually of Dutch descent.

After-damp is a mixture of carbon dioxide and nitrogen that occurs in a mine after an explosion and causes suffocation to human beings. It is also called "choke damp" and "black damp."

Agape, a "love-feast" held by the early Christians in commemoration of the Lord's Supper. *See* **J28 (1).**

Agar-agar, a vegetable jelly obtained from seaweeds, widely used in jellies, canned meat and poultry, and as a constituent in medicinal and cosmetic preparations. Used by bacteriologists to solidify broth and blood upon which bacteria are cultivated. Before the war Japan had a virtual monopoly in agar-agar; U.S.A. and the British Commonwealth now make it in quantity.

Agaric, large fungi of the family *Agaricaceae*, which includes the mushroom and what are popularly called "toadstools," though the idea that these two lay terms sharply differentiate between edible and poisonous fungi is an incorrect one. Characteristic of the agarics is the presence of a cap or *pileus* (bearing underneath the spore-shedding gills) and a stalk or *stipe*.

Agate, a variety of chalcedony. Parallel bands of colour are often characteristic. Germany, Brazil. and India furnish the main supplies, and Scotland has a species of agate called Scotch pebble.

Agave, the American aloe or Century Plant which sometimes does not attain to flowering maturity under sixty or seventy years, and then dies. The flower spray may reach a height of 20 feet and in its development the rush of sap is so great that the Mexicans collect for brewing the strong spirit called mescal. 1,000 litres of sap can be obtained from a single plant. Some species of agave yield sisal used for making cord and rope.

Agnus Dei (Lamb of God), a short anthem said or sung at a certain point of the Roman Catholic Mass or Anglican communion service. (John i. 29.)

Air is a mixture of gases forming the atmosphere we breathe. Nitrogen, oxygen, and argon are always present in air; a typical sample of dry air might contain these gases in the following proportions (by volume): nitrogen, 78·06%; oxygen, 21%; argon, 0·94%. A small quantity of carbon dioxide is present, about 3 parts in 10,000 parts of air. This carbon dioxide is the source of carbon compounds built up by green plants in photosynthesis (**F29**); in the process carbon dioxide is absorbed from the air and oxygen returned, the reverse of the respiratory process of animals. Air also contains a quantity of water vapour, and traces of ammonia, nitrogen oxides, hydrogen, sulphur dioxide, hydrogen sulphide, ozone and of the rare gases helium, krypton, neon, and xenon. In a city smoke and dust particles may be as abundant as 100,000 particles per cc. A litre of air at 0° C. and 700 mm. pressure weighs 1·2932 grams. *See also* **Atmosphere, Pollution.**

Alabaster, a soft crystalline form of sulphate of lime, or granulated gypsum, easily worked for statuary and other ornamental articles, and capable of being highly polished. Volterra, in Tuscany, yields the finest; that in highest ancient repute came from Alabastron in Egypt, near to the modern Antinoë.

Alb, white vestment reaching to the feet, worn by priests in religious ceremonies.

Albatross, a large sea-bird of almost pure white, black and white, or brown plumage. It nests in colonies on remote islands, but at other times rarely approaches land. Of the thirteen species, nine are found in the southern oceans, one in the tropics, and the three others in the North Pacific.

Albert Memorial, a large Gothic monument designed by Sir George Gilbert Scott, and embellished with sculptures by eminent artists. Erected in memory of Prince Albert in Kensington Gardens at a cost of £120,000.

Alcázar, the palace at Seville, famed for the beauty of its halls and gardens, in ancient days the residence of the Moorish kings.

Alcohols. A class of organic compounds of general formula R–OH, where R is an aliphatic radical. "Alcohol" is the name used for ethyl alcohol (ethanol); this is produced by distilling fermented liquors, and synthetically from ethylene, a product of petroleum cracking. Industrially ethyl alcohol is used in the manufacture of chloroform, ether, perfumes, etc. Diluted with wood alcohol or other denaturants ethyl alcohol is called "methylated spirits"; the denaturants are varied according to the industrial purposes for which it is required, the methylated spirits then being largely exempt from duty. Wood alcohol (methyl alcohol or methanol) can be obtained by distilling wood, or synthetically from water gas.

Alcoholic Strength. In Great Britain the standard is the proof gallon which is an imperial gallon of spirits containing 49·28 per cent. of alcohol by weight or 57·1 per cent. by volume at 60° F. In Europe the strength of spirits is usually measured by the Guy-Lussac hydrometer. In the U.S.A., because of the smaller gallon, 1·37 U.S. proof gallons = 1 British proof gallon. In Britain the alcoholic content of spirits and liqueurs appears on the bottle in degrees proof. Whisky, for example, at 70° proof (or 30° under proof) contains 70/100 × 57·1 alcohol, or about 40 per cent. The alcoholic content of wines is not shown on the label.

Aldehyde, the generic term for a class of chemical compounds of general formula R–CHO, where R is an organic radical. Except for formaldehyde, which is a gas, aldehydes are volatile liquids. They are produced by oxidation of primary alcohols. Most important aldehyde is formaldehyde used in making the plastics described as formaldehyde resins. Formalin (formaldehyde solution in water) is much used for preserving zoological specimens.

Alder, a river-side tree of the genus *Alnus*, including some 30 species and found in north temperate regions and the Andes. The only species native to Britain is *A. glutinosa*, which has been described as "guardian of river-banks" because of the way its roots bind together the sand and stones, and so slow down erosion. The wood is used for furniture and charcoal.

Aldine Editions are the beautiful books printed in Venice by the Renaissance printer Aldo Pio Manuzio and his family between 1490 and 1597. Italics were first introduced in these books.

Algae, flowerless plants living mostly in water. Seaweeds and the green pond scums are the best known algae. The green powder found on trees is composed of a microscopic alga (*Protococcus*). *See* **F27 (2).**

Algebra, a branch of mathematics in which symbols are used in place of numbers. Sir Isaac Newton styled it the "universal arithmetic." The Chinese were able to solve the quadratic equation before the Christian era but it was Al-Khowarizmi, an Arab mathematician of the early 9th cent., who introduced algebra to Europe.

Alhambra, the ancient palace of the Moorish kings at Granada in Spain, built in the 13th and 14th cent. Though part of the castle was turned into a modern palace under Charles V., the most beautiful parts of the interior are still preserved—the graceful halls and dwelling-rooms grouped round the Court of Alberca and the Court of Lions, with their fountains, arcades, and lovely gardens.

Aliphatic describes derivatives of hydrocarbons having chains of carbon atoms, as distinct from rings of carbon atoms as in benzene (*see* **Aromatic**). The gas butane is aliphatic.

Alkali, the general name given to a number of chemicals which are bases (*q.v.*). The term should be limited to the hydroxides of metals in the first and second group of the periodic table and of ammonia, *e.g.*, NaOH, KOH. They are used commercially in the manufacture of paper, glass, soap, and artificial silk. The word comes from the Arabic *al-kali* meaning calcined wood ashes. Alkalis are extremely soluble in water and neutralise acids to form salts and water.

Alkaloids, a large group of natural products which contain nitrogen; they are usually basic. Isolated from plants and animals, they include some hormones, vitamins, and drugs. Examples are nicotine, adrenalin, and cocaine. Many alkaloids are made synthetically for medicinal use, *e.g.*, morphine, quinine. Their function in plants is not well understood. *See* **Belladonna.**

Alligator, the crocodile of America, common in the lower Mississippi and adjacent lakes and marshes, varying in length from 2 to 20 feet.

Allopathy, medicine as ordinarily practised in which remedies are given to produce results opposed to the symptoms. The name is rarely used save to contrast it with homoeopathy (founded by Hahnemann of Leipzig about 1796) in which remedies are given which produce the *same* effects as the symptoms. In fact modern medicine is increasingly based on the results of scientific research and, unlike homoeopathy, is based on no one theory and no single technique.

Alloys are combinations of metals. They are made because of their valuable special properties, *e.g.*, durability, strength, lightness, magnetism, rust-resistance, etc. Some well-known ones are brass (zinc + copper), coinage bronze (copper + zinc + tin), steels (iron + carbon + various other materials), soft solder (tin + lead), dental fillings (mercury + various ingredients).

All Saints' Day (Nov. 1) is common to both the English and Roman Catholic Churches, and is in commemoration of the saints generally, or such as have no special day set apart for them. Instituted by Pope Boniface IV., early in the 7th cent., this ecclesiastical festival was formerly called " All Hallows."

All Souls' Day (Nov. 2) is a festival of the Roman Church, intended for the mitigation by prayer of the sufferings of souls in purgatory. The commemoration was enjoined by Abbot Odilo of Cluny during the 11th cent. upon the monastic order over which he presided, and was afterwards adopted generally throughout the Roman Communion.

Allspice, a flavouring obtained from a West Indian tree of the myrtle family, *Pimenta officinalis.* The essential oil of its unripe fruit is a powerful irritant, and the bruised berries are carminative.

Alluvium, accumulations of sand, mud, gravel, etc., washed down by rivers and forming distinct deposits.

Almond, the fruit of the *Amygdalus communis,* originally indigenous to Persia, Asia Minor, and N. Africa; now cultivated in Italy, Spain, France, the U.S.A., and Australia. It yields both bitter and sweet oil. Bitter almond oil is obtained by macerating and distilling the ripe seeds; it is used for flavouring and scenting purposes, its fragrant odour being due to the presence of benzaldehyde and hydrogen cyanide. When the seeds are pressed sweet almond oil results: this is used in perfumery, and also as a lubricant for very delicate machinery.

Almuce, a fur stole worn by certain canons.

Aloe, large plants of the lily family, with about 180 species found mainly in the S. African veldt and Karroo. The bitter purgative drug (aloes) is prepared by evaporating the plant's sap. *See* **Agave.**

Alpaca, a South American ruminant related to the llama whose long, fine wool is woven into a soft dress fabric known by the same name. Sir Titus Salt first manufactured alpaca cloth (1836). Saltaire, near Bradford, remains to evidence the success which for many years attended the enterprise.

Alpha Particle, or **alpha-ray,** fast-moving helium nucleus ejected by some radioactive atoms, *e.g.*, polonium. It is a combination of 2 neutrons and 2 protons. *See* **F11(1).**

Alphabet (so called from the first two letters of the Greek alphabet—alpha, beta) is the term applied to the collection of letters from which the words of a language are made up. It grew out of the knowledge that all words can be expressed by a limited number of sounds arranged in various combinations. The Phoenicians were the first to make use of an alphabetic script derived from an earlier Semitic alphabet (earliest known inscriptions *c.* 1500–950 B.C.) from which all other alphabets have sprung. The stages in the development of the alphabet were mnemonic (memory aids), pictorial (actual pictures), ideographic (symbols), and lastly phonetic. All the ideographic systems died out, with the exception of that of the Chinese.

Altimeter, an instrument used in aircraft to estimate altitude; its usual essential feature is an aneroid barometer which registers the decrease of pressure with height. Roughly 1 millibar corresponds to 30 ft. To read an aircraft altimeter correct for its destination, the zero setting must be adjusted for difference of ground height and difference of surface pressure, especially when pressure is falling or when flying towards low pressure.

Altitude, an astronomical term used to signify the angular elevation of a heavenly body; this is measured with a quadrant or sextant. In aeronautics it is the height (in feet or metres) above sea-level.

Alto, the second voice of a male-voice church choir, *i.e.*, below treble and above tenor. The term may also be applied to an instrument to distinguish it from others of similar design but different register: *e.g.*, alto saxophone.

Alto-Relievo, a term applied to sculptured designs which are depicted in prominent relief on a flat surface, technically signifying that the projection exceeds one-half the true proportions of the objects represented. Basso-relievo is carving kept lower than one-half such projection.

Alum is a compound salt used in various industrial processes, especially dyeing, its constituents being the sulphate of one univalent metal or radical (*e.g.*, potassium, sodium, ammonium, rubidium, caesium, silver, thallium) and the sulphate of a tervalent metal (*e.g.*, aluminium, iron, chromium, manganese), and water of crystallisation.

Alumina is the oxide of aluminium. Very valuable as a refractory material. The ruby is almost 100 per cent. alumina; so also are the emerald, oriental amethyst, etc. An hydrated aluminium oxide is bauxite, chief ore of aluminium from which the metal is extracted electrolytically.

Aluminium is a light metal which conducts electricity well. Its specific gravity at 20° C. is 2·705. Melting point of aluminium is 660·2° C. It is made commercially by electrolysing bauxite dissolved in cryolite (double fluoride of aluminium and sodium). Aluminium alloys because of their strength and lightness are being increasingly used for the construction of railway coaches, automobiles, aeroplanes, etc.

Amadavat, a popular cage bird of the weaver family, mainly crimson with white spots, so named because the first specimens came from Ahmadabad in India about 1700.

Amalgam is the term applied to any alloy of which mercury forms a part.

Amber, a brittle resinous substance; in origin, fossilised resin. Obtained mostly from the Baltic coasts, and used for ornaments, pipe mouth-pieces, etc.

Ambergris is a waxy substance produced in the intestines of the sperm whale, and generally found floating on the sea. It is a valuable perfumery material.

Amblycephalus, a genus of homoptera including the froth-fly, which is destructive in many hop gardens in July and August, sucking the sap from the vine.

Amblyopsis, a species of fish, practically sightless and with inoperative organs of hearing and feeling, that inhabit the Mammoth Cave of Kentucky. A remarkable illustration of the failure of senses not brought into use.

America's Cup, a prize trophy first offered in 185 by the Royal Yacht Squadron and open t yachts of all nations. It was won in the firs year by the " America," a New York yacht and has remained on that side of the ocean eve since, despite attempts to recapture it by Lor Dunraven, Sir Thomas Lipton, Mr. T. O. M Sopwith, and others. The last attempt by Grea Britain was in 1964, when *Sovereign* was beate by the American *Constellation.* Australi challenged for the first time in 1962 with *Grete* but unsuccessfully.

Amethyst, the violet variety of quartz, used as precious stone, containing traces of manganes titanium, and iron. The finest coloure specimens come from Brazil and the Urals.

Amice, a linen vestment worn about the neck b Roman and many Anglican priests over th alb when officiating at Mass or Holy Eucharis Formerly worn on the head by priests an pilgrims.

Amines, organic chemicals composed of carbo hydrogen, and nitrogen. They are deriv from ammonia, which they resemble in smell and chemical characteristics. The smell of bad fish is due to the presence of amines. Important industrially as intermediates in a wide variety of products, for example, the synthesis of dyestuffs and man-made fibres such as nylon.

Amino-acids, organic compounds containing an amine group and an acid group. They are the "building bricks" of proteins (*q.v.*)

Ammeter, an nstrument for measuring the current flowing in an electric circuit. A contraction of ampere-meter. (*See* **Ampere.**)

Ammonia, a colourless gaseous compound comprising three atoms of hydrogen to one of nitrogen. Formerly it was made by heating the horns and hoofs of deer, acquiring the name of spirits of hartshorn. The ammonia of commerce is now procured by coal decomposition in the course of gas-making and by direct synthesis. In the very important Haber process of ammonia production by fixation of atmospheric nitrogen, the nitrogen is made to combine with hydrogen and the ammonia so prepared is converted into nitric acid, ammonium nitrate or ammonium sulphate. The Haber process made Germany self-sufficient in nitrates in the first world war, and was afterwards exploited all over the world.

Ammonites, extinct animals related to the Nautilus. The chambered shell is coiled, usually in a plane spiral, and they are confined to Mesozoic rocks.

Ammonium, the basic radical of ammonium salts. Composed of one atom of nitrogen and four of hydrogen, it behaves chemically like an ion of a monovalent alkali metal. Ammonium chloride is known as "sal ammoniac." "Sal volatile" is ammonium carbonate.

Amnesty, an act of grace by which a ruler or governing power pardons political offenders.

Amorphous, a term used to indicate the absence of crystalline form in any body or substance.

Ampere, the most commonly used unit of electric current; often abbreviated to "amp," named after André Marie Ampère, who in the 1820s helped to lay the foundations of modern electro-magnetism. *See* **N13(1).**

Amphibia. *See* **F23(1).**

Amphioxus *or* **Lancelet**, a primitive chordate occurring in sand-banks around British shores and elsewhere.

Ana, a collection of criticisms, observations, or opinions about a particular person, place or subject. Used as a suffix especially applies to a person's memorable sayings, anecdotes about or publications bearing on, as in *Johnsoniana, Alexandriana, Victoriana.*

Anarchism. *See* **J3.**

Anchor, an instrument used for keeping ships stationary. Great improvements have been introduced in recent years, stockless anchors being now chiefly used, consisting of a shank and a loose fluke. Lloyds' rules prescribe the number and weight of anchors which must be carried by merchant ships.

Anchorite is a religious person who retires into solitude to employ himself with holy thoughts. Among the early Christians, anchorites were numerous, but in the Western Church they have been few. Their reputation for wisdom and prescience was high, and kings and rulers in olden days would visit their cells for counsel. An anchorite or "ankret" was in mediæval times a source of fame and profit to the monastic house within which he was voluntarily immured.

Anchovy, a fish of the herring family, distinguished by its large mouth and projecting snout, plentiful in the Mediterranean and much esteemed when cured.

Ancient Lights are rights of light enjoyed by a property owner over adjoining land. Such a right is obtained either by uninterrupted enjoyment for twenty years, or by written authority, and once legally established cannot be upset, no building being permissible that would seriously interfere with the privilege.

Anemometer, an instrument for measuring the strength of the wind. In the most widely used pattern the rotation, about a vertical axis, of a group of hemispherical or conical cups gives a measure of the total flow of air past the cups, various registering devices being employed. The Dines anemograph provides a continuous record of the variation in both velocity and direction; changes of pressure produced in a horizontal tube, kept pointing into the wind by a vane, cause a float, to which a pen is attached, to rise and fall in sympathy with the gusts and lulls. The recently devised hot-wire anemometer, depending upon the change of electrical resistance experienced by a heated wire when cooled, enables very gentle air currents to be investigated.

Aneroid is the kind of barometer which does not depend upon atmospheric support of a mercury (or other liquid) column. It consists of a metallic box, partially exhausted of air, with a corrugated lid which moves with atmospheric changes. A lever system magnifies the lid movements about 200 times and atmospheric pressure is read from a dial. The construction of the vacuum chamber provides automatic compensation for temperature changes. An aneroid barometer is the basic component of an altimeter.

Angelica, an aromatic plant of the Umbelliferae order, *Angelica officinalis*, valuable as a flavouring and possessing medicinal properties. In olden times supposed to protect against poison.

Angelus, a church bell rung in Roman Catholic countries, at morn, noon, and sunset, to remind the faithful to say their Angelic Salutation.

Angevin Dynasty includes the Plantagenet kings from Henry II. to Richard II. The name was derived from Henry II.'s father, Geoffrey, Count of Anjou.

Angles, a northern tribe originally settled in Schleswig, who with the Saxons and Jutes invaded Britain in the 5th cent.

Angstrom, a unit of wavelength, named after the Swedish physicist A. J. Angstrom (1814–74), equal to one hundred-millionth of a centimetre (10^{-8} cm.). It is used to measure wavelengths of light, X-rays, etc.

Aniline, a simple aromatic compound related to benzene and ammonia. It is obtained from coal-tar. The name recalls the fact that it was first prepared by distilling indigo (*anil* is Portuguese for indigo). In 1856 W. H. Perkin (1838–1907) discovered the first aniline or coal-tar dye, mauve, and thus founded the modern dyestuff industry.

Animal Kingdom. *See* **F22–27.**

Anise, an umbelliferous plant (*Pimpinella anisum*) found in Egypt and the Levant, and valued for its fruit, aniseed, possessing certain medicinal properties and yielding an aromatic, volatile oil. Also used in cooking. The anise of the Bible is *Anethum graveolens, i.e.,* dill.

Annates were acknowledgments formerly paid to the pope by way of fee or tax in respect of ecclesiastical preferment, and consisted usually of a proportion of the income (" first-fruits ") of the office. Introduced into England in the 13th cent.; annexed to the Crown under Henry VIII; transferred to a perpetual fund for the benefit of the poorer clergy in 1704. *See* **Queen Anne's Bounty.**

"Annual Register," a yearly record of political and literary events, founded by Edmund Burke (as editor) in 1759 and Robert Dorsley, the bookseller.

Annunciation, Feast of the (March 25), is a church festival commemorating the message of the incarnation of Christ brought by the angel Gabriel to the Virgin Mary, hence the title Lady Day.

Anointing is the pouring of consecrated oil upon the body as a mark of supreme honour. In England it is restricted chiefly to the ceremony of the monarch's coronation, and the spoon with which the oil is applied forms part of the English regalia. In the Roman Catholic Church anointing represents the sacrament of extreme unction.

Ant. There are about 6,000 species of ants, which belong to the same order (Hymenoptera) as the bees, wasps, and ichneumon flies. They are social in habit, living in communities of varying size and development. There are three basic castes in ants—the females or *queens*, the *males*, and the *workers* (the last-named being neuter), although specialised forms of workers are sometimes found, *e.g.*, the *soldiers* of the harvesting ants. In the communities of those species of ants which evolved most recently there is a highly complex social life and well-developed division of labour. Some species of these ants make slaves of other species, stealing the cocoons before the adult forms emerge. Many ants "milk" greenflies, which they protect for their honey-like secretion, and most ants' nests contain many "guests," such as beetles and silver fish. Some ants harvest grains of corn, and others, from S. America, live on fungi which they cultivate in underground "mushroom beds."

Antarctic Exploration. In earlier centuries it was thought that a great continent must exist in the southern hemisphere, around the South Pole, to balance the known land masses in the north. Its supposed extent was greatly reduced in the 18th cent., particularly when Capt. Cook sailed for the first time south of the Antarctic Circle and reached the edge of the ice pack. A portion of the ice-covered continent—the coast of Graham Land—was first sighted by Lieut. Edward Bransfield in 1820. Explorers of several other nations sighted portions of the coast-line in other quarters, but the first extensive exploration was made by Capt. James Clarke Ross, who with the *Erebus* and *Terror* penetrated into the Ross Sea in 1841, and discovered the great Ross Ice Barrier in 78° South lat. Interest in the Antarctic did not revive until after 1890, when an international scheme of research was drawn up. A Norwegian, C. E. Borchgrevink, in 1898–1900, was the first to winter in the Antarctic and to travel on the ice barrier. The British share in this work was carried out by Capt. R. F. Scott's expedition in the *Discovery*, 1901–4. Scott's party sledged across the barrier to 82° 17′ South, then a record "farthest south." A little later, Ernest Shackleton beat this by travelling to within 100 miles of the South Pole. In 1910 Scott organised his second expedition of the *Terra Nova*, and became engaged against his will in a "race for the Pole," when, after his departure, the Norwegian Arctic explorer, Roald Amundsen, suddenly announced that he was sailing for the Antarctic. Amundsen set up his base at the eastern end of the Barrier, and, relying on dog teams for hauling his sledges, reached the Pole on December 14, 1911. Meanwhile Scott and his party, their start delayed by adverse weather, were marching southwards, man-hauling their sledges, for Scott was against the use of dogs. After an arduous journey they reached the Pole one month after Amundsen. The return was a struggle against the weather and increasing weakness, probably due to scurvy, until at last they perished within a few miles of their base. After the First World War the development of the whaling industry greatly stimulated further exploration. Outstanding expeditions included that of Admiral R. E. Byrd, 1929, when he flew over the South Pole; The British Graham Land expedition, 1934, which carried out the first extensive mapping of any part of the Antarctic continent; and the U.S. Navy's Antarctic Expedition of 1940, when the whole continent was circumnavigated and great areas photographed from the air. In recent years valuable work has been done by the first International expedition, the Norwegian–British–Swedish Expedition to Queen Maud Land, and by the French in Adélie Land. The Falkland Island Dependencies Survey, set up during the war, has continued the scientific exploration of Graham Land. The Antarctic was the scene of high adventure during the International Geophysical Year (1957–58), when scientists from many countries participated in the explorations. The Commonwealth Trans-Antarctic Expedition set out from opposite sides of the continent and met at the South Pole, the U.K. party, led by Sir Vivian Fuchs, from the Falklands, and Sir Edmund Hillary and his party from New Zealand. The U.K. party accomplished the first crossing of the White Continent in 99 days. Their scientific work included the making of seismic and complementary gravimetric studies at frequent intervals along the 2,200-mile traverse. Since the Antarctic is becoming important for many reasons, in weather forecasting, in the whaling industry, and as a possible centre for world air routes, the tempo of exploration and research will become even faster in the future.

Anteater. There are two unrelated families of anteaters, the Myrmecophagidae and the Manidae. Among the former the Great Anteater (*Myrmecophaga jubita*) is the largest species, over 6 ft. in length, occurring in Central and S. America. Only half its size is the lesser Anteater (*Tamandua tetradactyla*); this is found in forests of tropical America and Trinidad. The Two-toed Anteater (*Cyclopes didactylus*) belongs to South America and Trinidad. These three animals live mostly on termites; they are adapted to this diet, having large claws for digging out ants, and a tubular mouth with a long sticky tongue. The Manidae are the Scaly Anteaters or Pangolins, widely distributed over Africa and the Orient. The difference between the two families is that the first has hair covering the body, the latter has horny scales instead.

Antennae, paired feelers of insects and crustacea.

Anthem, a choral composition, with or without instrumental accompaniment, usually sung after the third collect in the Church of England service. The words are from the Scriptures, and the composition may be for solo voices only, for full choir, or for both. Among the chief British composers of anthems are Tallis, Purcell, Croft, Boyce, Goss, and Stainer.

Anthracite is a black coal with a brilliant lustre. It contains 92% and over of carbon and burns slowly, without smoke or flame.

Anthropoid, meaning "resembling man," a sub-order of the primate mammals including man and also the gibbon, chimpanzee, orang-utan, and gorilla.

Anticyclone, a region where barometric pressure is greater than that of its surroundings. Such a system is distinguished on weather charts by a pattern of isobars, usually circular or oval-shaped, enclosing the centre of high pressure where the air is calm. In the remaining areas light or moderately strong winds blow spirally outwards, in a clockwise direction in the Northern Hemisphere (and in the reverse direction in the Southern Hemisphere), in accordance with Buy's Ballot's law (an observer with back to wind in Northern Hemisphere has lower pressure to left; in Southern to right). Over the British Isles anticyclonic weather is generally quiet and settled, being fair, warm, and sunny in summer and either very cold and often foggy or overcast and gloomy in winter. These systems move slowly and sometimes remain practically stationary for days at a time, that over Siberia being particularly well defined. Extensive belts of almost permanent anticyclones occur in latitudes 30° N. and 30° S. Persistent anticyclonic weather with easterly winds during the months December to March 1962–3, brought the coldest and hardest winter to Britain since 1740 (taking the Midlands a representative).

Antimony. Metal element, symbol Sb. In grou V of the periodic table. Exists in various forms the stable form being a grey brittle metal with layer structure. The other forms are non conductors. On being burned, it gives o dense fumes of oxide of antimony. By itsel it is not of special utility; but as an alloy fo hardening other metals, it is much used. As a alloy with lead for type-metal, and with tin an copper or zinc for Britannia-metal, it is of grea value. Most important antimony ore is stibnit (antimony sulphide).

Anti-Pope, one elected in opposition to one he to be canonically chosen; commonly applied t the popes Urban VI. and Clement VII., wh resided at Avignon during the Great Schis (1378–1417).

Anti-proton, the "negative proton," an atom particle created in high energy collisions nuclear particles. Its existence was confirme in Oct. 1955. *See* **F13 (1), 14.**

Antisemitism. *See* **J3.**

Antlers are the branched horns of deer, th branches being called tines. Antlers origina as outgrowths of the frontal bone, and a usually shed once a year. Except in the rei deer and caribou they are restricted to the ma

Apartheid. *See* **J4.**

Ape, a term applied to the gorilla, chimpanze orang-utan, and gibbon—the anthropoid apes

Aphelion, the point in the orbit of a planet farthe from the sun: the opposite of perihelion.

Aphids. *See* **T28 (2).**

Apis, the sacred bull worshipped by the ancient Egyptians; also the scientific name for the bee.

Apocalyptic writings are those which deal with revelation and prophecy, more especially the Revelation of St. John.

Apocrypha (hidden writings), the books which were included in the Septuagint (Greek) and Vulgate (Latin) versions of the Old Testament but excluded from the sacred canon at the Reformation by the Protestants on the grounds that they were not originally written in Hebrew nor regarded as genuine by the Jews. The books include: 1 and 2 Esdras, Tobit, Judith, additions to Esther, Wisdom of Solomon, Ecclesiasticus, Baruch, Song of the Three Holy Children, History of Susannah, Bel and the Dragon, Prayer of Manasses, 1 and 2 Maccabees. The term is usually applied to the additions to the old Testament, but there are also numerous Christian writings of the same character.

Apogee, that point in the orbit of a heavenly body which is farthest from the earth; used in relation to the sun, moon, and artificial satellites. The sun's apogee corresponds to the earth's aphelion; the moon's apogee is the point in its orbit most remote from the earth. *See* **Perigee.**

Apostasy is a revolt, by an individual or party, from one form of opinions or doctrine to another. Julian, the Roman Emperor (331–63), brought up as a Christian, became converted to paganism and on coming to the throne (361), proclaimed religious toleration. Hence his name, Julian the Apostate.

Apostles. The twelve apostles who were disciples of Jesus were: Simon Peter and Andrew (his brother), James and John (sons of Zebedee), Philip, Bartholomew, Thomas, Matthew, James, Thaddaeus, Simon, and Judas Iscariot. After the Ascension Matthias was chosen to take the place of Judas. St. Paul is always referred to as the chief apostle, though he is not one of the twelve. St. Barnabas has also been called an apostle.

Apostles' Creed, applied to the most ancient of the Church's statements of its belief: "I believe in God the Father Almighty; and in Jesus Christ his only Son our Lord, who was born of the Holy Ghost and the Virgin Mary. . . ." A later version is used in the Church of England at morning and evening prayer.

Apostolic Fathers were the immediate disciples or followers of the Apostles, especially such as left writings behind. They included Barnabas, Clement of Rome, Ignatius of Antioch, Hermas, Papias of Hieropolis, and Polycarp.

Appeasement Policy. The name of the policy during 1937 and 1938 of yielding to the demands of Hitler and Mussolini in the hope that a point would be reached when the dictators would co-operate in the maintenance of peace. The policy culminated in the Munich Agreement (which was the subject of much criticism) after a series of concessions including the recognition of the Italian conquest of Abyssinia and the German annexation of Austria. The policy was finally demonstrated as futile when Hitler seized Czechoslovakia in March 1939.

Appian Way, the oldest and finest of the Roman roads originally laid by Appius Claudius (312 B.C.) from Rome to Capua and thence to Brundisium (Brindisi).

Approved Schools are residential schools for the training of young persons under 17 who, because of disturbed behaviour as a result of unfavourable influences such as bad environment or parental neglect, are guilty of offences or in need of care and protection and have been sent to them by magistrates from juvenile or other courts. *See also* **Detention Centre, Borstal.**

April, the fourth month of the year, from the Roman *Aprilis* derived from *aperire* "to open"—the period when the buds begin to open.

Apse is a semicircular recess, arched or dome-roofed, at the end of the choir, aisles, or nave of a church.

Aquatint is a method of etching on copper, by which imitations of drawings in water-colours, Indian ink, bistre, and sepia are produced.

Aqueducts are conduits in which water flows or is conveyed from its source to the place where it is to be used. Most famous builders were the Romans and the oldest Roman aqueduct was the Aqua Appia, which dates from about 310 B.C. Among modern aqueducts may be mentioned that of Glasgow, which brings water to that city from Loch Katrine; that of Manchester, which taps Thirlmere; that of Liverpool, with Lake Vyrnwy in North Wales as its source, and the Fron Aqueduct, Radnorshire, which carries water from the Elan Valley to Birmingham.

Arabesque, the term applied to the elaborate decoration based on flowing lines used in Moorish art.

Arabian Nights, a collection of fascinating tales of the Orient, of mixed Indian, Persian, Arabic, and Egyptian origination, and first made known in Europe by Antoine Galland, a French Oriental scholar whose original translation was called *The Thousand and One Nights.*

Arabic Numerals, consisting of the characters, 0, 1, 2, 3, 4, 5, 6, 7, 8, 9, had their roots in India, whence they passed to Baghdad in the second half of the 8th cent. and were introduced by way of Spain to Europe in the 12th cent., taking the place of the Roman numerals.

Aragonite, the unstable form of calcium carbonate found as a mineral in some young deposits. It crystallises in the orthorhombic system but tends to revert to calcite (*q.v.*).

Aramaic Languages, the Semitic dialects current in Mesopotamia and the regions extending south-west from the Euphrates to Palestine from about the 12th cent. B.C. until after the rise of Islam, when Aramaic was superseded by Arabic. Both Aramaic and Greek were spoken in Palestine during the time of Christ.

Archaeopteryx, a fossil bird providing a connecting link between reptiles and birds. It had feathers, jaws with teeth, no bill, reptilian bones and skull, a long tail, and it probably used its fore-limbs for gliding flight. The first specimen, found in 1861, in the Solenhofen limestone of Bavaria, is in London's Natural History Museum. *See* **F32(1).**

Archbishop, the chief of the bishops of an ecclesiastical province in the Greek, Roman, and Anglican churches. In the Church of England there are two archbishops, the Archbishop of Canterbury, called the Primate of *all* England, and the Archbishop of York, styled the Primate of England.

Archimedes' Principle. When a body is weighed in air and then in any fluid, the apparent loss in weight is equal to the weight of fluid displaced. This scientific fact was noted by the Syracusan philosopher Archimedes (287–212 B.C.) and is frequently used as a basis for density measurements.

Architecture, the art and science of building. The provision of shelter for mankind by the orderly arrangement of materials in a manner which expresses man's attitude to living. The forms which buildings take are the outcome of the function for which they are to be used, of the architect's aesthetic sensibility and of the structural method adopted. Until the last hundred years structural methods were limited to timber frames, and columns, lintels, load-bearing walls, arches, vaults, and domes in brick or stone. From these few basic elements have evolved the great variety of historic styles of building to be found throughout the world. To give but one example, the Greeks created those systems of decorated columns and beams, known as the Orders, which were adapted by the Romans, revived decoratively rather than structurally during the Renaissance and are still used in debased form on the more presumptuous type of modern building. In recent years, however, architecture has taken on a new meaning. Once confined to the rich, in the form of Church, State, or Commerce, it is now, with the coming of democracy, recognised as an essential social service for all. This, and the development of new structural techniques and materials (steel, aluminium, sheet glass, reinforced concrete, plastics, and plywoods, to name a few), have made the interest in historic styles, the mainstay of the older architect, of secondary importance. Modern architecture is the creation of buildings with the highest possible standards of functional performance in terms of efficient planning and structure, good artificial and natural lighting, adequate heating or cooling, and proper acoustic conditions consistent with the price the client can afford to pay. At the same time the architect's task is to design a structure, and the spaces the structure delimits, internally and externally, which are æsthetically stimulating and satisfying, and well related to the land and buildings around.

Arctic Exploration. Modern exploration of the Arctic begins in the 16th cent., when men sought to reach the East Indies by sailing through the Arctic to the Pacific Ocean. The North-east Passage, via the shores of northern Asia, was the first attempted. In 1553 and 1554 the English navigators Sir Richard Chancellor and Stephen Burrough sailed into the White Sea, but were prevented by storms and ice from advancing farther eastwards. The project was later revived by the Dutch; Barendts in 1594 discovered Spitsbergen, but also failed to get beyond Novaya Zemlya. It was not, in fact, until 1879 that the Swede, A. E. Nordenskiöld, in the *Vega*, succeeded in reaching the Pacific. The attempts to find a North-west Passage were more numerous and determined. In 1585 John Davis penetrated Davis Strait and coasted along Baffin Island. Hopes ran high when Henry Hudson discovered Hudson Bay in 1610, but a practicable passage continued to elude explorers. The problem was to find a navigable route through the maze of channels in the short summer season, and to avoid being frozen in with supplies exhausted. After the Napoleonic Wars the Admiralty sent out many naval expeditions which culminated in Sir John Franklin's expedition with the *Erebus* and *Terror* in 1845. The ships were beset by ice in Victoria Channel and, after Franklin's death, were abandoned by their crews, who perished from scurvy and starvation on their march southwards. To ascertain their fate, several further expeditions were despatched, and the crew of the *Investigator*, commanded by R. J. M'Clure, sailing eastwards from Bering Strait, were the first to make the Passage, though in doing so they were obliged to abandon their ship. It was thirty years before the Norwegian, Roald Amundsen, succeeded in sailing the *Gjoa* from east to west. In the meantime, the North Pole had become the goal of explorers. Nansen, in 1893, put the *Fram* into the ice-pack to drift across the Polar basin, and himself made an unsuccessful attempt on the Pole across the pack. This was eventually achieved by the American explorer Robert E. Peary, who after several expeditions in the North Greenland region, sledged to the Pole with Eskimo companions in 1909. The next phase was the employment of airships and aeroplanes in Arctic exploration. In 1926 Admiral Byrd made the first flight over the Pole, and in the same year Amundsen and Lincoln Ellsworth flew the airship *Norge* from Spitsbergen to Point Barrow, Alaska. Two years later, the *Italia*, commanded by the Italian, Nobile, was wrecked on a return flight from the Pole, and Amundsen lost his life in an attempt to rescue the survivors. With modern developments in aircraft and navigation, flights over the Polar basin are almost a routine matter, and passenger flights between Europe and America via northern Greenland are being pioneered. The first voyage under the North Pole was made in August 1958 by the American nuclear-powered submarine *Nautilus*.

Arenaceous Rocks, the rocks composed of grains of sand, chiefly sandstones; quartz is the most abundant mineral in these rocks.

Argillaceous Rocks are a sedimentary group, including the shales and clays.

Argon, chemical element, symbol A. This was the first of the inert gases (*q.v.*) to be isolated from air by Rayleigh and Ramsay in 1894. Argon is used for filling gas-filled metal filament electric lamps. In gas discharge tube it gives a blue glow.

Aria, a song consisting of a first part, a second part, and a repetition of the first part. Songs of this type commonly occur in 18th-cent. operas and oratorios. The term has been loosely extended to cover airs rendered solo by principal characters in opera.

Aries, the Ram, the first of the signs of the Zodiac.

Arithmetic, the branch of mathematics that deals with numerical calculations as in counting, measuring, weighing. The early civilisations used simple arithmetic for commercial purposes, employing symbols and later letters of the alphabet as numerals. When Hindu-Arabic numerals replaced Roman numerals in the Middle Ages it meant a great step forward and led to rapid developments—the invention of logarithms, slide-rule, calculating machines.

Ark of the Covenant was the sacred chest, overlaid with gold, which occupied the inner sanctum of the Temple, and symbolised God's covenant with his people.

Armada, Spanish, the naval expedition fitted out by Phillip II. of Spain in 1588 against England, commanded by the Duke of Medina Sidonia. It comprised 129 ships, was manned by 8,000 sailors and carried 19,000 soldiers and more than 2,000 cannon. Against this formidable force Elizabeth had only 80 ships, manned by 9,000 sailors, under Lord Howard of Effingham, under whom served Drake, Hawkins, and Frobisher. The British Fleet awaited the Armada off Plymouth, and at Tilbury there was a considerable defensive land force under the command of the Earl of Leicester. On July 19 the ships of the Armada were sighted off the Lizard, disposed in a crescent seven miles long from horn to horn. The excellent manoeuvring of the English, their fire-ships, and a gale from the N.W. combined so effectively to cripple the Spanish ships that the Armada was scattered in confusion, a very small remnant contriving to reach home via the North of Scotland. It was impossible to embark the army of Parma waiting in the Netherlands. Elizabeth had a medal struck bearing in Latin the inscription, "God blew, and they were scattered."

Armadillo, a genus of animals related to the sloths and anteaters, belonging to South America, and carrying a hard bony covering over the back, under which one species (*Tolypeutes*) can completely conceal itself when attacked, rolling itself up like a hedgehog.

Armageddon, according to the Revelation of St. John, the great battle in which the last conflict between good and evil is to be fought.

Armillary Sphere, an early form of astronomical apparatus with a number of circles representing equator, meridian, ecliptic, etc. Used by Hipparchus and Ptolemy and up to the time of Tycho Brahe for determining the position of the stars.

Aromatic. A term used by chemists, originally to describe compounds like benzene, having a characteristic smell. It is a term which implies a collection of chemical characteristics, the salient features being a flat ring structure and a general similarity to benzene.

Arpeggio, a chord whose notes are played in ascending or descending sequence, as on a harp.

Arsenic, a metalloid element, symbol As, in group V of the periodic table, usually met with as a constituent of other minerals, sometimes by itself. Its compounds are very poisonous. Lead arsenante is a powerful insecticide used for spraying fruit trees. The more stable allotropic form (grey) has a layer structure, and conducts electricity.

Artesian Wells take their name from Artois in France, where the first wells of this kind were constructed in 1126. They are to be found only when a water-bearing bed is sandwiched between two impervious beds. When a boring is made to the lower part of the bed, the pressure of water is sufficient to cause the water to overflow at the surface. Artesian wells were known to ancient Egypt and China, and have existed in the Sahara since the earliest times. The fountains in Trafalgar Square are fed by artesian wells sunk through the London clay into the chalk about 400 ft.

Arthropoda. *See* F22(2).

Arthur's Seat, a hill of volcanic origin, 823 ft. high, dominating Holyrood Park, to the south-east of Edinburgh.

Articles. The *Six Articles* are those contained in an Act of Henry VIII. and were of Roman Catholic origin. The *Thirty-Nine Articles* drawn up in 1563 comprise the doctrines of the Anglican Established Church, and must be subscribed to by all taking holy orders therein.

Art Nouveau, a term applied to the "new art" which spread across Europe and the U.S.A during the 1890s. It was mainly a style of architecture and interior decoration which attempted to break with the old traditions of darkness and "heaviness" by the use of the new materials of cement, steel, and glass from which it created patterns characterised by: (*a*) over-elaboration; (*b*) relatively naturalistic but tortuous representations of plants, etc.; (*c*) a ubiquity which left no surface undecorated. Typical of the extravagances of Art Nouveau are the cast-iron lilies with copper tendrils, the cupboard doors and chair-backs with heart-shaped holes, and the furniture shaped like animals, examples of which are still with us. In Britain the movement was basically a continuation of the Arts and Crafts movement of William Morris; Aubrey Beardsley represented this essentially fin-de-siècle school in his drawings.

Arts and Crafts Movement, the English revival of decorative art which began about 1875 as a revolt against the existing vulgarity of internal decoration and furnishings and the pettiness of academic art. Inspired by William Morris and Burne-Jones together with Rossetti, it was strongly influenced by the former's mediaevalism, his hatred of industrialism, and his own version of socialism which included the regeneration of man by handicrafts. His firm of Morris & Co. produced wallpapers, tapestries, furniture, stained-glass windows, carpets, and fabrics in a style totally different from that of contemporary Victorian decoration. The V. & A. Museum in London has a room entirely decorated with Morris products, and his Kelmscott Press did much to raise the standards of book design and printing in its day. *See* **Art Nouveau.**

Arum, a genus of plants of the Araceae family, of which there is but one British species, the wake-robin or cuckoo-pint, sometimes also styled "Lords and Ladies." Its pointed leaves and spikes of scarlet poisonous berries are familiar in the hedgerows.

Arundel Marbles, a collection of ancient Greek sculptures formed by Thomas Howard, Earl of Arundel, in the 17th cent. and presented to Oxford University by his grandson, Henry Howard, who became Duke of Norfolk.

Aryan is a term used to denote the lingual and ethnological groups otherwise known as Indo-European or Indo-Germanic. Comprises two branches, Western or European, and Eastern or Armenian. The Aryan languages show common origin by their vocabulary, syntax, and inflexions. The word *Aryan*, derived from the Sanskrit, means an "honourable lord of the soil"; the nearest to the parent tongue is Sanskrit, and the chief divisions in Europe are the Teutonic, Romance, Slav, and Celtic. The Turks, Magyars, Basques, and Finns are non-Aryan. India was invaded by Aryan people from Mesopotamia and Asia Minor, *c.* 1500 B.C.

Asafoetida, an acrid, strong-smelling gum resin exuded from the stem of an umbelliferous plant, *Ferula foetida*, found in Persia and Afghanistan. Formerly used medicinally to treat hysteria; still used in cooking in India, Iran, and France.

Ascension Day, or Holy Thursday, is the 40th day after Easter.

Ascot Races are an annual fashionable function dating from 1711 and taking place on Ascot Heath, only six miles from Windsor, in June. These races have always had royal patronage. The course is nearly two miles long.

Ash, a familiar deciduous tree of the genus *Fraxinus*, of over 60 species, native to North-temperate regions. The ash held an important place in Norse mythology, as it was supposed to support the heavens with its roots in Hell. The species native to Britain, and to Europe, is *F. excelsior*, a tall tree with compound leaves, greenish flowers, winged seeds, and black buds in winter. It is a valuable timber tree, tough and elastic, and largely used for wheels and handles. The rowan, or mountain ash, *Sorbus aucuparia*, with similar leaves and orange berries, belongs to a different family. *F. pendula* or weeping ash is a weeping strain which makes an ideal natural summer house.

Ashes, The, the symbol which distinguishes the winning cricket team in the Australian Test Matches. In 1882 the Australians won at the Oval by 7 runs. After the match the following epitaph appeared in the *Sporting Times*: "In affectionate remembrance of English Cricket which died at the Oval on Aug. 29, 1882, deeply lamented by a large circle of sorrowing friends and acquaintances. R.I.P. NB. The body will be cremated and the ashes taken to Australia." When the English Eleven went to Australia the same winter it was said that they had come to recover the "ashes." England won two out of three matches, and after the third match the ashes of what is now generally believed to have been a stump were presented in an urn to Ivo Bligh, later Lord Darnley. He bequeathed the urn to the M.C.C., and it now stands in the Memorial Gallery at Lord's.

Ash Wednesday, first day of Lent, being the seventh Wednesday before Easter, on which ashes are sprinkled on the head as sign of penitence, a practice dating from the Middle Ages.

Asp, a small poisonous snake, often mentioned in ancient literature and traditionally supposed to have been used by Cleopatra in killing herself. Probably the Egyptian Horned Viper (*Cerastes*).

Assassination, treacherous murder for political ends, usually of a ruler or distinguished person. Among the most famous assassinations of history were: Julius Caesar, 44 B.C.; Thomas à Becket, 1170; David Rizzio, 1566; William the Silent, 1584; Henry IV. of France, 1610; Jean Paul Marat, 1793; Abraham Lincoln, 1865; Alexander II. of Russia, 1881; Archduke Francis Ferdinand of Austria, 1914; Dr. Dollfuss, 1934; King Alexander of Yugoslavia, 1934; Mahatma Gandhi, 1948; King Abdullah of Jordan, 1951; Liaquat Ali Khan, 1951; King Feisal of Iraq, 1958; Mr. Bandaranaike, 1959; President Kennedy, 1963.

Assassins. *See* **J5.**

Asteroids are minor planets most of whose orbits lie between those of Mars and Jupiter; they were unknown until the discovery of Ceres by Piazzi in 1801. More than a thousand have been named and many thousands are believed to exist. After 1891 they were identified by their paths on exposed photographic plates. Most of them have a diameter of well under 50 miles. Ceres, with a diameter of *c.* 480 m., is the largest, then there are Pallas (*c.* 304 m.), Juno (120 m.), Vesta (240 m.), Astraea, Adonis, Hermes, Hidalgo, Eros, Amor, Apollo, and the Trojan group which all take their names from Homer's *Iliad*—Achilles, Patroclus, Hector, Nestor, Priam, Agamemnon, Ulysses, Aeneas, Anchises, Troilus, Ajax, and Diomede. A full list with explanation of all the names has recently been issued by the Spanish astronomical historian, Prof. A. Paluzie-Borrell.

Astrolabe, a mediæval scientific instrument for taking altitudes, observing the sun by day and the stars by night, and used for telling the time and finding the latitude. Used by the ancient Greeks, later by the Arabs and Persians, and introduced into Europe by way of Spain in the 14th cent. Chaucer is said to have sent his son Lois, a ten-year-old student at Oxford, an astrolabe with a treatise on its use in 1391.

Astronomical unit, the mean distance from the centre of the earth to the centre of the sun, or half the major axis of the earth's elliptical orbit. It has been known for some 300 years that the earth–sun distance is roughly 93 million miles, but over the past 60-odd years astronomers have attempted to determine it with ever-greater accuracy, using various methods of computation. Spencer Jones (1931) deduced a value of 93,004,000 miles; the American astronomer E. K. Rabe (1950) obtained a value of 92,914,800 miles; and data from the *Pioneer V* space probe gave a value of 92,925,100 miles. The earth–sun distance is a fundamental value in astronomy.

Astrology. *See* **J4.**

Astronomy, the oldest and one of the most fascinating of sciences, was in early times associated with astrology, but by a long series of observations and mathematical calculations a gradual knowledge of the movements of the heavenly bodies grew up. Pythagoras (520 B.C.) understood the revolution of the earth upon its axis, but it was not until two thousand years later that his theory gained general acceptance, when the keen and spacious minds, first of Copernicus, and then of Tycho Brahe and Galileo, demonstrated the truth of the

Pythagorean theory. With the setting forth of the Copernican system, astronomy was placed on a sure foundation, and the movements of the planets began to be more clearly comprehended. The studies of Kepler and Galileo, making their observations with the telescope, resulted in an immense increase of astronomical knowledge. Newton, to whom we owe the discovery of the law of gravitation, the improvement of the telescope and many other discoveries, placed physical astronomy on well-defined lines. Two great landmarks in more recent times were the discovery of Uranus by Herschel in 1781 which extended the solar system as then recognised, and the estimation by Hubble in 1924 of the distance of Andromeda of nearly a million light years (more recent determinations give 1,500,000 light years), which showed that our Galaxy was just one of many. Today radio-astronomy is advancing astronomical knowledge and making it possible to explore regions beyond the scope of optical telescopes. *See* F5–7.

Astrophysics, a branch of astronomy concerned with the physical nature and constitution of celestial bodies. Since the second half of the 19th cent. the application of spectroscopy and photometry has been responsible for the great advance in this branch of science.

Athanasian Creed, one of the three ancient creeds of the Christian Church, often referred to as the *Quicunque Vult*, is a statement of the doctrine of the Trinity and the Incarnation, and though named after St. Athanasius, the view is now widely held that it is the work of St. Ambrose (339–97). *See also* **Apostles' Creed** and **Nicene Creed**.

Athodyd, also called "Ramjet" or "Propulsive Duct." This can be considered as an extremely simple gas-turbine engine, without any rotating parts. A power plant with great possibilities for high-speed aerial flight, it consists of a diffuser, combustion chamber, and exhaust chamber; its thrust results from the fact that the gases leaving the athodyd have a higher velocity than the gases entering it.

Atmosphere is the gaseous envelope of the earth, and consists of a mixture of gases (*see* **Air**) and water vapour, the variability of the latter being of great importance meterologically. The ozone layer, which absorbs ultra-violet radiation which would be lethal to plant life if it reached the ground, is concentrated at about 20 miles above the earth but extends to about twice that height. The lower level of the atmosphere up to a height of about 7 miles (6 miles at the Poles and 10 miles at the Equator) is known as the *troposphere*, and it is in this region that nearly all weather phenomena occur. This is the region of most interest to the forecaster studying temperature, humidity, wind-speeds, and the movement of air masses. Temperature falls with height by about 1° C. per 500 ft. in this layer. The *tropopause* is the boundary between the troposphere and the *stratosphere*. Temperature varies little in the lower levels of this region: it is mainly cloudless, and has no vertical currents. Strangely enough, the lowest temperatures of the atmosphere are to be found not at the Poles, but at about 11 miles above the Equator, where a temperature as low as −80° C. has been recorded! Temperatures begin to rise about 20 miles from the earth's surface at about the same rate as they fall in the troposphere, owing to the absorption of solar radiation by the concentration of ozone. The stratospheric air is extremely dry. Near the 60-mile level a number of important atmospheric phenomena occur. Above this level the oxygen becomes predominantly monatomic in contrast to the normal diatomic form at lower altitudes. This is the *ionosphere*, extending to heights over 500 miles from the earth's surface. This layer acts as an electrical radio mirror which makes long-distance radio transmission possible. The auroras are most frequently observed at altitudes near 60 miles but do extend at times far higher. *See also* **Ionosphere**.

Atmospherics are electrical impulses which are believed to originate in atmospheric electrical discharges such as lightning. They give rise to crashing background noises in the loudspeakers of radio sets, interfering with reception at distances of up to 4,000 miles from the centre of the disturbance. The location of atmospherics with the aid of radio direction-finding methods gives warning of the approach of thunderstorms.

Atom. *See* **F9–14.**

Atomic Pile, an apparatus containing a fissionable element and a moderator, such as heavy water or graphite, in which a self-sustaining fission process proceeds at a controllable rate. The first atomic pile, constructed on a squash court at Chicago, was operated for the first time on December 2, 1942, under the direction of Dr. Enrico Fermi. The pile contained 12,400 lb. of uranium. *See* **Nuclear Reactors.**

August, named after the Emperor Augustus, because it was his "lucky" month.

Auks, duck-like sea-birds, black and white, with short, narrow wings, compact bodies, and legs set well back. Breed in colonies on rocky coasts of N. Europe (incl. British Isles) and spend most time in coastal waters. Migrate south in winter. The Auk family includes the Razorbill, Little Auk, Guillemot, and Puffin. The Great Auk became extinct in the 19th cent. after ruthless hunting for the sake of its feathers. Except for the Black Guillemot, they lay only one egg a year.

Aulic Council, a supreme court of the Holy Roman Empire, established by Maximilian I., in 1501.

Aurora polaris. This wonderful phenomenon of the night sky is a common sight in some high latitudes, north and south. It is visible less often in temperate latitudes, and only very seldom in the tropics. As seen in the northern hemisphere it is called the aurora borealis or northern lights, and in the south, the aurora australis or southern lights. The zone of maximum frequency surrounds the north magnetic pole and includes Greenland, northern Canada, and the north coast of Alaska. Auroral displays may take several forms, *e.g.*, a faint glow, a diffuse ribbon of light crossing the heavens, great folded waving curtains like draperies; the whole sky may be a grand panoply of light. Both the aurora and the magnetic storm associated with it are ascribed to the envelopment of the earth in a great cloud or stream of solar gas shot out from stormy areas on the sun (sunspots) that has travelled to the earth at a speed of over a thousand miles a second. The gas is mainly atomic hydrogen, but the atoms are broken up into their two parts, protons and electrons. These are both electrically charged. This renders them subject to the influence of the earth's magnetic field, which deflects many of them to the high latitudes where the aurora is most commonly seen. The aurora is a kind of light essentially different from that of the rainbow which is a partly subjective phenomenon. Each beholder sees his own rainbow, whose light is sunlight refracted and reflected by many raindrops. The raindrops that produce his rainbow depend on his position as well as on the direction of the sun. The aurora, on the contrary, is a light as objective as that of a candle, though produced differently. It is a self-luminescence of the air in particular regions of the atmosphere that lie far above the clouds. By simultaneous observation from stations twenty or more miles apart it is possible to locate the position of the luminous air, *i.e.*, to determine the height of the aurora, its location in plan, and its form and volume.

Austerlitz, Battle of, was fought near Brünn, in Moravia, on December 2, 1805, when Napoleon defeated the Russians and Austrians under Kutuzon.

Auto-da-Fé, or Act of Faith, was the ceremony connected with the sentencing of heretics under the Inquisition of Spain and Portugal, the persons found guilty being imprisoned or burned alive. The ceremony took place in some public square, sometimes in the presence of the king and court.

Automation is a recently coined word, used to designate the adoption of methods of automatic control either of manufacturing processes or of any business process involving a large mass of routine work. The word is used in broader and narrower senses. In its broadest sense it covers any form of mechanisation which largely re places human labour by the work of automatic or semi-automatic machines, such as has been in progress continuously since the Industrial Revolution; but it is better kept to a narrower meaning, in which it is confined to the recent development of electronic or similar devices which eliminate human labour, except that needed for watching and maintaining the elaborate machines used. In this sense, automation began mainly in the United States, but has been spreading rapidly to other advanced countries. *See* G16(2).

Autumn, the third season of the year, begins with the autumnal equinox, and ends with the winter solstice, but the term is generally understood as covering the period from mid-August to mid-November.

Auxins, "plant hormones," organic substances produced by plants to regulate growth. Synthetic auxins are now widely used, *e.g.*, for promotion of root formation in cuttings, differential weed control, prevention of premature dropping of fruit, in storage of potatoes and hard fruit, and to overcome frost damage to fruit buds.

Avocet, a graceful wading bird related to the stilts, of black-and-white plumage, bluish legs, and slender upturned bill. There are four species. Avocets nest in colonies and there is one in the sanctuary on Havergate Island, Suffolk.

Avogadro's Hypothesis. This is a fundamental concept of chemistry. Equal volumes of all gases under the same conditions of temperature and pressure contain the same number of molecules. This law was instrumental in assigning the formulæ of molecules. The hypothesis was put forward in 1811, but was not generally accepted until 1860.

Aztecs, the name of a native and powerful race found in Mexico when the Spaniards first discovered that country, and with difficulty subdued.

B

Babiroussa, a ferocious, long-legged wild pig, native of the Celebes, sometimes called the horned-hog, because of the long upper tusks in the male, which are developments of the canine teeth which grow upwards, piercing the upper lip, and curving backwards, often broken in fighting.

Baboon, monkeys belonging to the African genus *Papio*. They are considered the lowest of the Old World (Catarrhine) monkeys, and walk on all fours. In the main terrestrial, but take to trees after food. The mandrill is closely related.

Babylonian Captivity, the period spent by the Jews in Babylon after Jerusalem was captured by Nebuchadnezzar, the Babylonian emperor, in 586 B.C. Traditionally the captivity lasted 70 years, but when Babylon was in turn taken by Cyrus in 538 B.C., the exiles were permitted to return to Jerusalem. The term is also applied in church history to the period 1309–78 when the papacy moved to Avignon, into the control of the French monarchy.

Badger, a carnivorous mammal related to the weasel, of nocturnal and burrowing habits, inoffensive, subsisting chiefly on roots and insects, though sometimes mice, young rabbits, and eggs form part of its diet. Badger-baiting was a favourite sport in Britain until it was prohibited in the middle of the 19th cent.

Bagpipe. Once popular all over Europe, this instrument is still played in Scotland, Ireland, Brittany, and elsewhere. The bag acts as a reservoir of air and, when squeezed by the player's arm, forces air through the pipes. One of these, the Chanter pipe, provides the tune and is played by the fingers as in a flageolet. The remainder, the Drone pipes, give a continuous, unvarying note.

Bailey Bridge, invented by Sir Donald Bailey and first used in N. African campaign 1942–3. Built up of pre-fabricated girders, it can be easily transported and erected.

Bailie, is a Scottish term for the magistrate of a municipal corporation or royal burgh.

Bailiwick, a feudal term denoting the limits of a bailiff's jurisdiction. The term has survived in the Channel Islands, where Jersey and Guernsey are Bailiwicks.

Bakelite. A plastic material made from phenol, formaldehyde, and urea. It is used in the manufacture of electrical fittings because of its insulating properties.

Balance of Power was the doctrine in British policy whereby European groups should be so balanced as to prevent the emergence of a dominating Power. Thus the balance was maintained between the Triple Alliance (Germany, Austria and Italy) and the Triple Entente (Great Britain, France and Russia) and preserved peace from 1871 to 1914. After the first world war there was tentative support of Germany's recovery to counterweight a possible French hegemony; but when Germany's power grew under Hitler culminating in the second world war, Britain, France and Russia again became allies. With the growing power of Russia, a new system of alliances is being attempted, based on the so-called nuclear deterrent.

Baldachin (It. *Baldachino*), a canopy usually supported by four pillars over throne, altar, or other sacred object. The name is also applied to the silken canopy used in processions and borne by the priest who carries the Host.

Balearic Crane, the crowned crane of the Balearic Islands in the Mediterranean and the North African mainland, distinguished by its yellowish, black-tipped occipital tuft and by its trumpet note.

Baleen *or* **"whalebone"** the name given to a series of horny plates growing from the roof of the mouth in those whales classified as Whalebone or Baleen Whales (Mystacoceti) There are 300–400 or so plates on each side, and their inner edges are frayed, the whole system constituting a filter for collecting minute organisms used for food. The Baleen Whales include the Right-Whales, the Pacific Grey-Whale, and the Rorquals. *See* **Whales.**

Ballade, a piece of piano music which may fancifully be regarded as the musical equivalent of the poetic ballad: *e.g.*, the Ballades of Chopin.

Ballet is a combination of four arts; dancing, music, painting and drama, each of which is ideally of equal importance. The movement of the individual dancers and the "orchestration" of the whole group is in the hands of the choreographer. The dancer's training follows certain basic rules but save in classical ballet there is considerable freedom of movement. Ballet as we know it today developed professionally at the Court of King Louis XIV. of France, though it owes its origins to Italy and in the earliest times to Greece and Rome. Its movements were made up from the dances of courtiers, country folk and tumblers. Technique grew more complex as costume became modified, the body gaining complete freedom with the invention of tights. A succession of great dancers—French, Italian and latterly Russian left their imprint on the art. Contemporary ballet reflects the aesthetic of the Russian, Sergei Diaghilev. In England Dame Ninette de Valois has laid the foundation of a national ballet, at Sadler's Wells and Covent Garden, with a personality that reflects the national character. A Royal Charter was granted in Jan. 1957 setting up the Royal Ballet to co-ordinate the activities of the Sadler's Wells group.

Ballistics, the science dealing with the motion of projectiles, especially shells, bombs, and rockets. Great advances have been made in this science in recent years.

Balloon, the modern balloon consists of a bag of varnished cloth or gold-beater's skin inflated with a gas lighter than air. The first ascent by man in a hot-air balloon was made on Nov. 21, 1783, and in a hydrogen balloon on Dec. 1, 1783. The most famous of the early scientific flights by manned balloons were those of the Englishmen Coxwell and Glaisher, in 1862, when a height of 7 miles was reached. The first aerial crossing of the English Channel by Blanchard and Jeffries was made on 7 Jan. 1785. Piccard's ascent to 10 miles, in 1931, marked the conquest of the stratosphere. Four years later the huge American balloon Explorer II. inflated with nearly 4 million cubic feet of helium, carried a team of scientists with their floating laboratory to an altitude of 14 miles. In 1957 a pressurised balloon carrying an American doctor rose 19 miles above the Earth. Captive kite-balloons were widely used in the war as defensive measures against air attack. Meteorologists send their instruments up in balloons to collect data about the upper atmosphere, and of recent years physicists have learned much about cosmic radiation from the study of photographic plates sent to the upper regions in balloons. An American balloon earth satellite, *Echo I*, was carried into orbit 1,000 m. high by a three-stage rocket in Aug. 1960, and, as the brightest of the earth satellites, can still be seen with the naked eye.

Balsam, a big genus (140 species) of flowering plants. Many species are cultivated for their showy flowers, *e.g. Impatiens noli-me-tangere*, the yellow balsam or "touch-me-not," so called because the fruit explodes when touched, slinging out the seeds. Balsam fir is a conifer (*Abies balsamea*) from which Canada balsam gum is obtained.

Baltimore Bird, a lively black-and-orange bird of the oriole sub-family extending from Brazil to Canada; builds a well-constructed hanging nest, and has a fine voice.

Bamboo, a genus of strong grasses, some species growing to over 120 ft. in height; much used by oriental peoples for all kinds of purposes. The young shoots of some species are tender and esculent. *See* **T4**(2).

Banana (family *Musaceae*), a large herbaceous plant cultivated in moist regions of the tropics, and one of the most productive plants known. The main areas of commercial cultivation are in tropical America, the Canary Islands, and West Africa. World production is estimated at 20 million tons, of which only 3 million are for trade.

Bandicoots, Australasian marsupial mammals, of the size of a large rat or rabbit. They are burrowing animals living largely on insects. The rabbit-eared bandicoot, restricted to Australia, has shrew-like snout, long ears like a rabbit, long crested tail, and a silky coat. The long-nosed bandicoot has a spiny coat and comes from E. Australia. The pig-footed bandicoot has two functional toes on the foot, like a pig.

Bantu, ethnic and linguistic group of African Negro peoples, widely spread over Africa south of the Congo. There are an enormous number of Bantu languages and dialects, including Swahili, Zulu, Luba, Kongo, and Ganda. The Bantu tribal groups, of which there are many, include the Zulu, the Matabele, the Basuto, and the Mashona.

Baobab, a tropical African tree. The species *Adansonia digitata* is one of the largest trees known, though not the tallest; the trunk can reach 30 ft. in thickness. The fruit is woody, but its juice provides a cooling beverage. The bark yields a fibre used for making rope and cloth.

Barbary Ape, a large monkey belonging to the genus *Macaca*. It is the only monkey living in relative freedom in Europe, a small colony being found on the Rock of Gibraltar. It has no tail.

Barberry, a genus of berry-producing shrubs containing a hundred species. Several species are cultivated for their flowers and bright berries. Has an interesting pollination mechanism; the base of each stamen is sensitive to touch, and insects probing for nectar cause top of stamen to spring inwards, so dusting visitor's head with pollen which can then be carried to the next flower visited. The common barberry (*Berberis communis*) harbours one stage of the fungus that causes rust of wheat.

Barbican, a fortified entrance to a castle or city, with projecting towers. In the London street called Barbican there was formerly a barbican in front of the city gates.

Barbiturates. A group of drugs derived from a parent compound called barbituric acid: phenobarbitone is the best-known example. They induce sleep and are used in the manufacture of sleeping pills and sometimes as anaesthetics, but they have the disadvantage of being habit forming. *See also* **P23**(2).

Barbizon School, a school of mid-19th-cent. landscape painters whose main tenet was a return to nature with an exact rendering of peasant life and country scenery painted on the spot. It was named after the village of that name in the Forest of Fontainebleau, where its chief members—Millet, Theodore Rousseau, Daubigny, and Diaz—made their home. Their practice of painting direct from nature, which was far from universal at that time, made them the precursors of Impressionism (*q.v.*).

Barcarolle, a Venetian gondolier's song applied to instrumental as well as vocal compositions.

Bard, among the ancient Celts a poet or minstrel whose mission was to sing of heroic deeds. He was supposed to have the gift of prophecy, and was exempt from taxes and military service.

Barilla, soda carbonate or soda ash obtained by burning certain salt-marsh plants (*e.g.* the saltwort, *Salsola kali*). It used to be in great demand, until the product of the Leblanc and then the Solvay ammonia-soda process was made available by the chemical industry.

Baritone, a male voice whose pitch lies between those of a tenor and a bass.

Barium, metal element, symbol Ba. In group II of the periodic table. The metal is soft and easily cut. It occurs as the sulphate and carbonate in nature. It was first prepared by Sir Humphry Davy in 1808, as an amalgam, by electrolysis of barium chloride. The pure metal was not isolated until 1901.

Barium meal. Barium sulphate is opaque to X-rays and before taking X-ray pictures of the alimentary canal radiologists give a "barium meal" to the patients so that the alimentary canal shows up more clearly.

Barnacles constitute a sub-class (*Cirripedia*) of the Crustacea. The barnacle fouling the bottom of ships is the Goose Barnacle, which has a long muscular stalk and a shell composed of five plates. The Acorn Barnacles, which cover rocks, breakwaters, etc., just below high-water mark are similarly constructed, but have no stalk. The manner of feeding of barnacles was vividly described by T. H. Huxley, who said the barnacle is "a crustacean fixed by its head kicking the food into its mouth with its legs." It was a naval surgeon, J. Vaughan Thompson, who discovered in 1830 that barnacles have a free-swimming larva (or nauplius). In the Middle Ages a curious myth grew up to the effect that the Barnacle changed into a sea-bird called, for that reason, the Barnacle Goose.

Barometer is an instrument for measuring atmospheric pressure, invented at Florence by Torricelli, pupil of Galileo, in 1644. The standard method consists of balancing the air column against a column of mercury, used on account of its high density. The mercury is contained in a long glass tube, closed at one end, and inverted in a cistern also containing mercury. The height of the mercury column, supporting the air column, is taken as the pressure at the time, and can be read off very accurately by means of a vernier scale. Present-day tendency is to express the readings in units of pressure instead of length, the millibar being adopted (1 mb = 1000 dynes per sq. cm.; 1000 mb $\equiv$ 29·53 inches of mercury approx.). The standard instrument is correct for pressures at 0° C. in Lat. 45°, so that corrections have to be applied for temperatures and latitudes other than these. Also a correction has to be made for reducing the pressure to mean sea level. *See* **Aneroid.**

Baron, title given in feudal England to a man who held his land directly from the king by military or other honourable service. The first baron created by letters patent was John Beauchamp de Holt, Baron of Kidderminster, on Oct. 10, 1387. The title derives from the Latin "baro" meaning "a man." In old legal diction "baron et feme" meant "man and wife." To-day a baron is a member of the fifth and last grade of the peerage and is addressed as "Lord."

Baronet, a title instituted by James I. The first baronet was Sir Nicholas Bacon, but numerous others were made about the same time, the fee charged for the honour in each case being about £1,000. It is the lowest hereditary title, and is freely dispersed among those who distinguish themselves in trade, industry, politics, or special civic service. James I. limited the number of baronets to 200, but to-day no number is specified. A royal warrant in 1910 commanded an official list of baronets to be prepared.

Baroque, a term used for the art style of the period *c.* 1600–1720 which was the artistic accompaniment of the Jesuit counter-Reformation. Its most obvious characteristics are: (*a*) its emotional appeal and dramatic intensity both related to its deliberate intention as propaganda ("a good picture makes better religious propaganda than a sermon" said one of its exponents); (*b*) in architecture, a style which is heavily and sometimes almost grotesquely ornate, plentifully covered with voluptuous sculpture on which draperies float rather than hang, with twisted and spiral instead of plain or fluted columns, and unnecessary windows or recesses added for ornament rather than use; (*c*) its emphasis on the whole at the expense of the parts such that a building's sculpture merges into its architecture and both into its painting (Baroque paintings are as closely knit as a jig-saw puzzle so that one cannot isolate individual figures as would be possible in a Renaissance one). Baroque architecture owing to its origin is found mainly in the Catholic countries; Italy, France, Austria, Bavaria, *e.g.*, the Barberini Palace, Rome, designed by its greatest exponent Bernini and others; the Church of the Invalides, Paris. Baroque artists include Caravaggio, Guido Reni, Murillo, and Rubens, the greatest Northern Baroque painter. The Baroque style merges gradually into **Rococo** (*q.v.*).

Barque, a small sailing vessel with three or four masts. A three-masted barque has fore- and mainmasts square-rigged, the mizzenmast fore-and aft-rigged.

Barrel Organ, a musical instrument in which the music is made by a barrel or cylinder, set with pins and staples, which rotate so as to open the valves for admitting the wind to the pipes.

Barrow is an ancient artificial mound of earth or stone raised over the site of a burial. In Britain barrows were built from 2500 B.C. until the late Saxon period, but the Egyptian are the earliest barrows known, the great pyramids being a spectacular development of the custom of ceremonial burial.

Bartholomew, Massacre of St., occurred in Paris on the night of Aug. 24, 1572, when over two thousand Huguenots were massacred by order of the Catholic French Court.

Basalt Rocks are fine-grained, dark coloured, of igneous origin and occur either as lava flows as in Mull and Staffa, or as intrusive sheets, like the Edinburgh Castle Rock and Salisbury Craig. One of the most noted examples of columnar basalt is that of the Giant's Causeway in Ireland.

Basanite, A smooth black siliceous mineral, or flinty jasper; a crypto-crystalline quartz, sometimes styled the Lydian Stone. An alloyed metal being rubbed across basanite, the mark of colour left will indicate the nature and depth of the alloy, hence it obtains its name, which signifies, in Greek, "a touchstone."

Base, a substance having a tendency to accept a proton (H^+). This is a wide definition and covers unconventional types of compounds. In aqueous solution bases dissolve with formation of hydroxyl ions, and will neutralise an acid to form a salt. In non-aqueous solvents, like liquid ammonia or hydrogen fluoride, compounds classically regarded as salts can be bases, *e.g.*, sodium fluoride is a base in hydrogen fluoride solution.

Bashi-Bazouks, name formerly given to irregular troops in the pay of the Turkish sultans. They were a rough but brave class of men.

Basilisk, is a lizard of aquatic habits, with an elevated crest (which it can erect or depress at will) down the centre of its back.

Basques, people of N. Spain and S.W. France, oldest surviving racial group in Europe, who have preserved their ancient language which is unrelated to any other tongue.

Bas-Relief ("low relief"), a term used in sculpture to denote a class of sculptures the figures of which are only slightly raised from the surface of the stone or clay upon which the design is wrought.

Bass, the fourth or lowest voice in a male voice church choir and therefore the lowest voice in a mixed choir. The term may also be applied to instruments having a lower register than others of their class: *e.g.*, bass clarinet.

Basset horn (= corno di bassetto). An alto form of the clarinet. This instrument is rarely used in modern orchestras.

Bassoon, a bass version of the oboe in which the tube, being 9 ft. long, is bent back on itself for convenience. There is also a double-bass oboe which is called the contra-bassoon.

Bastille, a castle or fortress in Paris, built in the 14th cent., and used as a state prison, especially for political offenders. Its bad repute as an instrument of despotism excited the hatred of the populace, who stormed and demolished it on July 14, 1789, at the beginning of the Revolution.

Bastinado, an oriental punishment, by beating with a pliable rod or cane on the soles of the feet.

Bats. These mammals fly by means of a membrane stretched between each of the long fingers of the hand and between the fifth finger and the body. Another membrane stretches between the legs and the tail. There are twelve British species; namely, the Noctule, Leisler's B., Serotine, Pipistrelle, Long-eared B., Daubenton's B., Natterer's B., Whiskered B., Bechstein's B., Barbastelle, Greater Horseshoe, and Lesser Horseshoe Bats. Bats echo-locate obstacles by means of supersonic sound waves; this explains their ability to fly perfectly at night and in dark woods and caves. Blindness does not affect this ability but deafness leaves them comparatively helpless. Bats are mostly insectivorous, catching the insects in their open mouths while flying; some eat fruit. The Vampire Bats, feeding exclusively on blood, are confined to tropical America.

Bath, Order of the, believed to have been established by Henry IV. at his coronation in 1399; remodelled in 1725 as a military order; formally instituted in three classes in 1815; civil division added in 1847. In the Order are three classes: G.C.B., or Knight Grand Cross of the Bath; K.C.B., or Knight Commander of the Bath; C.B., or Companion of the Bath. Companionship of the Bath does not carry knighthood nor entitle the holder to the prefix "Sir." The motto of the order is *Tria juncta in uno* (Three joined in one). The insignia for civil and military and the three classes vary. *See* **Knighthood.**

Batteries. A battery is a device for converting stored chemical energy into electricity, which can then be used for heat, light, traction, or any desired purpose. Primary electrical power, from an oil or nuclear station, must first be available, since batteries have to be fabricated in a power-using factory and the necessary chemicals have to be produced. After that, the battery may need charging periodically like the well-known lead–acid accumulator. The most well-known battery is the Leclanché dry cell used in torches. It is interesting that to-day, about a century after it came into common use, it is still the chief source of power in the tactical electronic equipment of the highly mechanised U.S. army. There are, however, many other types of cell, some under active development as space travel and missile warfare call for batteries of lighter weight and utmost reliability.

Bauhaus, a German institution for the training of architects, artists, and industrial designers, founded in 1910 at Weimar by Walter Gropius. It was closed by Hitler in 1932 and re-opened at Chicago in 1937 under the name of The Institute of Design. The Bauhaus doctrine held that there should be no separation between architecture and the fine and applied arts; that art, science, and technology should co-operate to create "the compositely inseparable work of art, the great building." The original institution, at the instigation of Gropius, included on its teaching staff not only architects and technicians but also such noted artists as Paul Klee and Wassily Kandinsky.

Bauxite, the chief ore of aluminium. Chemically it is aluminium oxide. Aluminium metal is made industrially by electrolysing purified bauxite dissolved in fused cryolite. Chief producing areas: Surinam, Br. Guiana, U.S.A., France, Hungary, Indonesia, U.S.S.R., Yugoslavia, Italy.

Bayeux Tapestry, a famous tapestry representing the conquest of England by William the Conqueror. It is embroidered on a band of linen 231 ft. long and 20 in. wide in blue, green, red, and yellow, divided into 72 scenes ranging over the whole story of the conquest. The accepted view is that the tapestry was commissioned for Bayeux Cathedral, but a new interpretation is that it is an Anglo-Norman secular work of art, much influenced by the contemporary *chansons de geste*, executed by English embroiderers for a Norman patron. A representation can be seen in the Victoria and Albert Museum in London.

Beagle, a small hound that tracks by scent, and formerly used for hare hunting.

Bears belong to the Ursidae family of the Carnivora. They are plantigrade mammals, walking (like man) on the soles of their feet. Found in most parts of the world except Australia. The common Brown Bear was once spread over the whole of Europe; it became extinct in England about the 11th cent.: 7–8 ft. in length, and stands 3 ft. or more at the shoulder. The Grizzly Bear of N. America is larger, and the coat is shorter and greyer. The Polar Bear is remarkable in having a white coat all the year round; it spends much time in water, and unlike the other bears it is entirely carnivorous. Bear-baiting was made illegal in England in 1835.

Beat Generation. *See* **J5.**

Beaufort Scale of wind force is used to specify numerically the strength of the wind. Since the introduction of anemometers to measure the actual velocity, equivalent values of the ranges in miles per hour at a standard height in the open have been assigned to the Beaufort numbers. *See* **N13.**

Beaver, a genus of mammals of the Rodentia order, with short, scaly ears, webbed hind feet, and a long broad scaly tail. They grow up to 4 ft. long, and live in communities, constructing dams and lodges where they breed. Found in N. America, Russia, and Poland. Valuable commercially for their fur.

Bedford Level comprises parts of Norfolk, Suffolk, Huntingdon, Northampton, Lincoln, and Cambridge, generally called the Fens, 70 miles long and 20 to 40 miles broad. It was reclaimed and drained in the 17th cent. by the Earl of Bedford and the Dutch engineer Cornelius Vermuyden.

Bedlam (a corruption of Bethlehem) was a priory in Bishopsgate, afterwards converted into a hospital for lunatics. The asylum was transferred to St. George's Fields, Lambeth, in 1815. The term "bedlamite" came to be applied to any person behaving like a madman.

Beech, a deciduous tree belonging to the genus *Fagus* of some eight or nine species found in north temperate regions. The common beech, *F. sylvatica*, is believed to be native to Britain and is one of our finest trees, with massive trunk, long, pointed winter buds, and smooth, grey bark. There is little undergrowth under its dense shade. It is shorter lived than the oak, taking about 200 years to reach full size and then declining. The timber of beech has a variety of uses, *e.g.*, spoons, handles, tools, and chairs.

Bee-eater, name of a family of brilliantly coloured birds closely related to the rollers and kingfishers inhabiting the tropical and sub-tropical parts of Africa, Asia and Europe. The European species successfully nested in Britain for the first time in 1955 and a pair nested in Alderney in 1956. With their long curved beaks they catch insects on the wing, especially bees and butterflies, and lay their eggs in dark nest tunnels.

Beefeater. *See* **Yeomen of the Guard.**

Beeswax, the secretion of the bee, used for the formation of the cells or honey-comb of the hive; when melted it is what is commercially known as yellow wax, white wax being made by bleaching. Being impervious to water, it acts as a good resistant and is an article of much utility.

Beetles (Coleoptera) constitute one of the biggest orders of insects, numbering over 200,000 species. There are two pairs of wings; the hind pair are used for flight, while the front pair are hardened to form a pair of protective covers (elytra). Some beetles have lost the power of flight and then the elytra are joined together.

Bel and the Dragon is the title of certain supplementary chapters to the "Book of Daniel" of an apocryphal character. First appeared in the Septuagint, but the Jewish Church did not accept it as inspired. In 1546 the Council of Trent declared it to be canonical.

Bell, a hollow body of metal used for making sounds. Bells are usually made from bell-metal, an alloy of copper and tin. Small bells used for interior functions are often made of silver, gold, or brass. Ordinary hand-bells are of brass. From the 7th cent. large bells have been used in England in cathedrals, churches, and monasteries. The greatest bell in the world is the "King of Bells" in the Kremlin at Moscow, which weighs about 198 tons, is 20 ft. 7 in. high and 22 ft. 8 in. in diameter. It was cast in 1733, but cracked in the furnace (the broken part weighed 11 tons) and is now preserved as a national treasure. Other large bells in Russia, include the 171-ton one at Krasnogvardersk, near Leningrad, and the one of 110 tons at Moscow. The Great Bell (Great Paul) at St. Paul's, cast in 1881, weighs 16¾ tons, and is the largest in the United Kingdom. Other gigantic bells are the Great Bell at Peking (53 tons); Nanking (22 tons); Cologne Cathedral (25 tons); Big Ben, Westminster (13½ tons); Great Peter, York Minster (10 tons). The Curfew bell is rung in some parts of England to this day, notably at Ripon. The number of changes that can be rung on a peal of bells is the *factorial* of the number of bells. Thus four bells allow 24 and eight bells 40,320.

Belladonna *or* **Deadly Nightshade** (*Atropa belladonna*), a well-known poisonous wild plant found in Southern Europe and Western Asia. The alkaloid atropine it contains is valuable in medicine, although a large dose is poisonous.

Bell, Book, and Candle. To curse by "bell, book, and candle" was a form of excommunication in the Roman Church ending with the words: "Do to the book, quench the candle, ring the bell."

Benedicite, the canticle in the Book of Common Prayer, known also as "The Song of the Three Holy Children."

Benedictines are monks and nuns of the Benedictine Order who live under the rule of St. Benedict—the monastic code whose influence on the religious and cultural life of the West has been so powerful. The rule is marked by an absence of extravagant asceticism. The greatest of the early Benedictines was Pope Gregory I (590–604) who sent St. Augustine of Canterbury to Anglo-Saxon England. Gregorian plainsong is named after him. *See also* **J30(1).**

Benedictus, a canticle used in the morning service of the English Church, and deriving its name from the first word of the Latin verse, *Benedictus*, blessed.

Benzene. An aromatic hydrocarbon obtained from coal tar and some petroleum fractions. It is a volatile inflammable liquid with a characteristic smell. The molecule consists of a flat ring of six carbon atoms, each bound to one hydrogen atom. Benzene is the parent member of many aromatic organic compounds and is widely used in industry to synthesise intermediates for fibres, dyestuffs, explosives, and pharmaceutical chemicals.

Bergamot, an essential oil obtained from the rind of a species of citrus grown chiefly in Calabria, and largely used in perfumery. Also a hardy herbacious perennial.

Beryl, a mineral, of which the emerald is a grass-green variety. Composed of beryllium and aluminium silicates. The pure mineral is colourless; the colour of most beryl comes from traces of impurities, notably iron and chromium. Otherwise it is yellowish, greenish-yellow, or blue, and is found in veins which traverse granite or gneiss, or embedded in granite, and sometimes in alluvial soil formed from such rocks.

Beryllium. Metallic element, symbol Be. Very similar to aluminium, it is stronger than steel and only one-quarter its weight. It is not very abundant, its main source is the mineral, beryl. Copper containing 2% beryllium is used for making springs. Because of its special properties the metal is used as a component in spacecraft, missiles and nuclear reactors. This accounts for its recent development on a technical scale. The metal powder is toxic.

Bessemer Process, for making steel depends on the forcing of atmospheric air into molten pig iron to burn out the impurities. *See* **Steel.**

Betel, the leaf of an Indian climbing plant, of pungent, narcotic properties. It is destructive to the teeth, and reddens the gums and lips.

Bhang, the Indian name for the hemp plant *Cannabis sativa*, the leaves and seed-capsules of which are chewed or smoked. The potent drug which comes from flowers of the female plant is called hashish in Arabia and marihuana in the United States and Mexico. *See* **P23(2)**.

Bible—The Old Testament and the New Testament. The Old Testament—the prehistoric portion—consists of 39 books, and is divided into three parts: (1) the Law, (2) the Prophets, (3) Miscellaneous Writings. The Old Testament was written in Hebrew except for parts of Ezra and Daniel, which were in Aramaic. It was not until the 9th cent. A.D. that a complete Hebrew text was made, the so-called Massoretic text. Before that the main versions were the Alexandrian Greek translation (Septuagint) made in the 2nd cent. B.C. and St. Jerome's Latin Vulgate of the 4th cent. A D. Portions were translated into the Anglo-Saxon in the 8th cent. and the Venerable Bede put the preater part of St. John's gospel into English, but it was not until 1535 that a complete printed English version appeared—the Coverdale Translation. The Authorised Version dates from 1611 in the reign of James I., and because of its beautiful phraseology it has had a lasting appeal. The Revised Version dates from 1885. A new translation of the Bible in the English language of today is in progress (*The New English Bible*); the New Testament was published in 1961 and the Old Testament and the Apocrypha will be ready later. The finding of the Dead Sea Scrolls (since 1947) has added to our knowledge of Scripture.

Bill of Rights, or Declaration of Rights, was the document setting forth the conditions upon which the British throne was offered to William and Mary in 1688. This was accepted and ultimately became an Act of Parliament.

Birch, a genus of deciduous trees including about 40 species and found only in northern regions. Birches native to Britain, and to Europe generally, are of two species—the silver birch, *Betula pendula*, with its graceful, drooping branches and triangular leaves, and the white birch, *Betula pubescens*, which has erect branches and soft oval leaves. Birch timber is an important plywood timber, the bark is used for tanning leather, and wintergreen oil comes from the bark of black birch, *Betula lenta*, a North American species. The birch is not a long-lived tree, few standing for more than a hundred years. The tallest recorded is at Woburn in Bedfordshire, 102 ft. high.

Birds, or Aves, are, next to mammals, the highest class of animal life (**F23(2)**. There are two kinds of modern birds—*Carinatae*, possessing keeled breast-bones and having power of flight; *Ratitae*, having raft-like breast-bones, and incapable of flight; and a sub-class of fossil birds, *Archaeornithes* (**F30(2)**) *and* **Archaeopteryx**. It is estimated that there are about 120 million land birds breeding in Great Britain, including 10 million each of the chaffinch and blackbird, 7 million each of the starling and robin and about 2 million sparrows.

Bird Arrivals. The wheatear is usually the first of the migratory birds to return, often reaching Britain at the end of February and always before the middle of March; the sand martin is the first of the "early swallows" to return, followed by the house martin. The first cuckoo arrives about the middle of April, and the whinchat, garden warbler, and sedge warbler during the last week in April. The nightjar, spotted flycatcher, and red-backed shrike are not seen until the first week in May. The swift is among the last to return from Africa and the earliest to depart. *See also* **Z21**.

Birds of Paradise, over 40 species of tropical birds inhabiting the dense forests of New Guinea and neighbouring islands. The male birds are remarkable for their brilliant plumage, long tail feathers, and ruffs on wings and neck, which are displayed to advantage during courtship. Related to the Bower Birds of Australia, and crows.

Biretta, a four-cornered head-covering worn by ecclesiastics of the Roman Church and varying in colour according to the rank of the wearer. A cardinal's biretta is red, a bishop's purple, a priest's black.

Bise, a keen dry north wind prevalent in Switzerland and South France.

Bishop is a Christian ecclesiastic, a person consecrated for the spiritual government of an area, a diocese or province, to the spiritual oversight of which he has been appointed (diocesan bishops), or to aid a bishop so appointed (suffragan bishops). In the Church of England there are forty-three diocesan bishops, all nominated by the Crown. Two, Canterbury and York, are archbishops having primacy in the respective provinces. The archbishops of Canterbury and York and the bishops of London, Durham, and Winchester and twenty-one other diocesan bishops in the order of seniority are spiritual peers, and sit in the House of Lords. The (Disestablished) Church of Ireland has two archbishops and twelve bishops; the (Disestablished) Church of Wales an archbishop and five bishops and the Episcopal Church in Scotland seven bishops. *See also* **Cardinal.**

Bismuth, metallic element, symbol Bi, in group V of the periodic table. Like antimony, the stable form is a grey, brittle, layer structure; electrical conductor. It is readily fusible, melting at 264° C. and boiling at about 1420° C. Wood's metal, an alloy with one of the lowest melting points (under 150° F., so that a spoon made of it will melt when placed in a cup of hot tea), contains four parts bismuth, two parts lead, one part tin, one part cadmium.

Bison, a genus of wild cattle, distinguished from the ox by its shorter, wider skull, beard under the chin, high forequarters, and, in winter, a great mane of woolly hair covering head and forequarters. There are two species, the European and the American bison, both now protected in game preserves.

Bittern, a bird of the heron genus, with long, loose plumage on the front and sides of the neck. It is a solitary bird inhabiting marshes, but rare in Britain.

Bivalves, shell-fish whose shell consists of two hinged valves, lying one on each side of the body, such as mussels, oysters, and cockles.

Blackbird, or Merle, a member of the Thrush family, a familiar song bird in Britain. Male is all-black with orange bill; female is mottled brown with brown bill; the young are spotted brown.

Blackcock and Greyhen (as the female is called) are closely related to the Capercaillies but smaller. They nest on the ground and prefer wooded country to open moors. Found in northern half of northern hemisphere. Polygamous, they perform excited courtship dances; the male is a handsome blue-black bird with white undertail, the female dark brown mottled.

Black Death, the plague which swept across Europe in the years 1348–50, beginning in the ports of Italy, brought in by merchant ships from Black Sea ports. It was the worst scourge man has ever known; at least a quarter of the European population was wiped out in the first epidemic of 1348. It reached England in the winter of that year. The disease was transmitted to man by fleas from black rats, though this was not known at the time, the specific organism being *Bacillus pestis*. The disease continued to ravage Europe in recurrent outbreaks up to the late 17th cent. The epidemic which raged in England in 1665 wiped out whole villages and one-tenth of London's population of 460,000. Samuel Pepys wrote a grim account of it in his *Diary*. *See also* **Labourers, English Statute of.**

Black Hole of Calcutta, the name given to the place where a captured British garrison was confined in 1756, during the struggle for India between the French and British, by order of Suraj-ud-daula, the nawab of Bengal. Into a noisome space, about 20 ft. square, 146 persons were driven, and only 23 were found alive the next morning.

Black-letter, the Old English or Gothic type first used in printing blocks.

Black Woodpecker (*Dryocopus martius*), a large, black bird about the size of a rook, with slightly crested scarlet crown, found in many parts of Europe.

Blenny, a group of marine fishes with spiny rays

part of the fin running along the back. Several species are found around the British coast.

Bloody Assizes, the assizes, conducted in 1685 by George Jeffreys, Lord Chief Justice, at which participants in the Duke of Monmouth's rebellion against King James II. were tried. They were marked by relentless cruelty.

Bluebird, a migratory bird of North America, deriving its name from its deep blue plumage. It is one of the few song birds of America, and familiar in the woods from early spring to November. In India and Malaya there is the Fairy Blue-bird; the male is black with shiny blue upper parts. The bluebird was used as the symbol of happiness by Maeterlinck in his play *The Blue Bird*.

Blue Peter, a blue flag with a white square in the centre, is hoisted 24 hours before a ship leaves harbour (the letter P in the alphabet of the International Code of Signals).

Blue Ribbon, a term in general use to denote the highest honour or prize attainable in any field or competition. Thus the Derby is the blue ribbon of the turf. The expression is derived from the highest Order of Knighthood in the gift of the British Crown, the insignia of which is a garter of blue velvet.

Blue Stocking, a term used to describe a learned or literary woman, particularly if pedantic and undomesticated. It is said that the term derives from the Bas-Bleu club of Paris, which was attended by the literary savantes of the 17th cent. In England a similar literary club was formed about 1780, whose members were distinguished by their blue stockings.

"Blue" Sun, Moon, etc., a phenomenon caused by the scattering of sunlight by transparent particles suspended in the atmosphere, the effect being that blue light is transmitted and red light extinguished to direct vision. The dust from the Krakatoa eruption in 1883 and the drifting layer of smoke from the forest fires in Alberta, Canada, in September 1950 gave rise to "blue" moons and suns, phenomena sufficiently rare to be described as occurring "once in a blue moon." In the cold climatic conditions of the Pamirs and the far north, vegetation is said to look "blue" on account of the rays of high calorific value (red, yellow, green) being absorbed, while only the blue and violet are transmitted. It was Tyndall who first explained the blue colour of the sky.

Boa, a term applied to a family of snakes of large size, some attaining a length of 30 ft. They are not poisonous, but kill their prey by crushing—constriction—hence the name "boa constrictor." They occur both in the Old World and the New, but are more abundant in the latter. Most Boas retain the eggs within the body until young are fully developed, whereas the Pythons almost all lay leather-shelled eggs.

Boar, or Wild Hog, an animal largely distributed over the forest regions of Europe, Asia, Africa, and South America. It has a longer snout and shorter ears than its descendant the domestic hog, and is provided with tusks. Having to forage for itself, it is a more active and intelligent animal than the pig of the sty, and offers good sport to the hunter.

Boat, an open vessel, propelled by oars or sails, or both. The boats of a ship of war are the launch, barge, pinnace, yawl, cutters, jolly boat, and gig; of a merchant vessel, the launch, skiff, jolly boat or yawl, stern boat, quarter-boat, and captain's gig. Every ship is compelled to carry adequate, fully provisioned and equipped life-boats.

Bode's Law, a numerical relationship formulated by Bode in 1772, which states that the relative mean distances of the planets from the sun are found by adding 4 to each of the terms 0, 3, 6, 12, 24, 48, 96. The actual mean distances (in millions of miles) are: Mercury, 36; Venus, 67·2; Earth, 92·9; Mars, 141·6; Jupiter, 483·3; Saturn, 886·0; Uranus, 1782·8. The gap between Mars and Jupiter caused Bode to predict the existence of a planet there, which was later confirmed by the discovery of Ceres and other minor planets. The law breaks down, however, for Neptune and Pluto.

Boer War, lasted from Oct. 11, 1899, when the Boers invaded Natal, to May 31, 1902, when the Treaty of Vereeniging ended hostilities. At first the operations of the British troops in Cape Colony were unsuccessful and disastrous reverses were sustained. Lord Roberts was then sent out as Commander-in-Chief, with Lord Kitchener as Chief-of-Staff, and from February, 1900, when Kimberley was relieved and Cronje was compelled to surrender and Ladysmith and Mafeking were relieved, the struggle was practically over.

Boiling-point is the temperature at which a liquid boils. At that point the pressure of the vapour is equal to the pressure of the atmosphere. Under increased pressure the b. p. rises and under less pressure, as on the top of a mountain, it is lower. As represented on the Centigrade scale the b. p. of water is 100°; alcohol 78·4°; and ether, 35·6°. On the Fahrenheit scale, the b. p. of distilled water is 212°. Boiling points are given for a standard pressure (760 millimetres of mercury).

Books are technically described, according to their sizes, as 4to, 8vo, 16mo (*quarto, octavo, duodecimo*), the names indicating the number of folds in a sheet. For Standard Sizes of British Books *see* **N13**.

Books, Classification of. All libraries are classified to facilitate reference, but the favourite system is the Dewey Decimal System, which divides the whole field of knowledge into ten Main Classes: General Works; Philosophy; Religion; Sociology; Philology; Natural Science; Useful Arts and Applied Science; Fine Arts; Literature; History (including geography and travel and biography). Each of these Main Classes is again subdivided into ten main divisions. As an example: the main class of Sociology receives the number 300. This range 300 to 400 (the next main class) is graduated into tens, and Economics is 330. The range 330 to 340 is again graduated, and the subject of Labour and Capital is 331. This process is carried on by decimals so that 331·2 deals with Remuneration for Work, 331·22 with Wage Scales, and 331·225 with Extra Pay.

Borax (Sodium Pyroborate) is a white, soluble, crystalline salt. It is widely and diversely used, *e.g.*, as a mild antiseptic, in glazing pottery, in soldering, in the making of pyrex glass, as a cleansing agent and sometimes as a food preservative. Borax occurs naturally in the salt lakes of Tibet, where it is called tincal, in California (Borax Lake, Death Valley), and elsewhere.

Boron. A metalloid element, symbol B There are two forms, one crystalline, the other amorphous. It is not very abundant in nature but occurs in concentrated deposits. It is best known in boric acid, which is used as a mild antiseptic (called boracic acid) and borax (*q.v.*). Boron compounds are essential to some plants, *e.g.*, beans. Used in the preparation of various special-purpose alloys, such as impact resistant steel. Compounds of boron and hydrogen are used as rocket fuels.

Borstal, an institution where young delinquents between 15 and 21 on conviction may be sent for detention and reform by a court of quarter sessions or assize. The first was opened in 1902 at the village of Borstal, near Rochester in Kent. Administered by the Home Office. *See* **D35**.

Boston Tea Party, an incident which occurred on Dec. 16, 1773, on board some tea-ships in Boston Harbour. High taxation imposed by the British Parliament under George III. had caused bitter feelings, and instigated by popular meetings, a party of citizens, disguised as Indians, boarded the tea-ships and threw the tea overboard. This incident was a prelude to the American War of Independence (1775–83).

Bounds Beating, an old Anglo-Saxon custom. The parish clergyman and officials go round the parish boundaries accompanied by boys who beat the boundary stones with long sticks of willow. The ceremony takes place on the Rogation days preceding Ascension Day.

Bourgeoisie, a term used by Marxists to indicate those who do not, like the proletariat, live by the sale of their labour. They include, on the one hand, industrialists and financiers or members of the liberal professions and, on the other, small artisans and shop-keepers who, although their standard of living may not be appreciably higher (and today is often lower) than that of the proletariat, are described as the "petty bourgeoisie." According to the Marxist view of history, the bourgeoisie arose with modern industrialism after it had overthrown the old feudal aristocracy and replaced it as ruling class. It is associated in politics with liberalism—which was necessary to break up the old feudal ideas—and in religion with Protestantism, especially of the nonconformist type. Marxists believe that the bourgeoisie are to be followed by the proletariat as ruling class, that fascism is an attempt by the bourgeoisie to prevent this happening, and that, according to their "law of concentration," at this stage the petty bourgeoisie gradually become proletarianised as capital becomes concentrated in fewer and fewer hands (*e.g.*, combines and trusts).

Bow, an instrument for propelling arrows, and, in the days when it was a weapon of war, was usually made of yew or ash, and was about 6 ft. long, with an arrow 3 ft. long. It was the weapon with which Crécy, Poitiers, and Agincourt were won. The cross-bow was Italian and was adopted in France, but did not become popular in Britain.

Bow Bells is the peal of the London church of St. Mary-le-Bow, Cheapside, within sound of which one must be born to be entitled to be called a "cockney." Bow Bells had not been heard since 1939, but they once again rang out over the City of London on Dec. 20, 1961.

Bowdlerize, to expurgate a book. Derived from Thomas Bowdler (1754–1825), the editor of the Family Shakespeare, in which "those words and expressions are omitted which cannot with propriety be read aloud in a family." He treated Gibbon's *History of the Decline and Fall of the Roman Empire* in the same way, omitting "all passages of an irreligious and immoral tendency." Such prudery met with ridicule and hence the words "bowdlerism," "bowdlerist," etc.

Bower Bird, native to Australia and New Guinea and related to the Bird of Paradise, though often less striking in appearance. In the mating season the male builds a "bower" of sticks and grasses for courtship displays and as a playground. The Gardener Bower Bird of Papua makes a lawn in front of his bower and adorns it with bright coloured pebbles and flowers which are replaced as they wither. The female builds her nest away from the bower.

Boycott, a term used in connection with a person that the general body of people, or a party or society, refuse to have dealings with. Originally used when Captain Boycott (1832–97) was made the victim of a conspiracy by the Irish Land League which prevented him making any purchases or holding any social intercourse in his district. He had incurred the League's hostility by a number of evictions.

Brass, an exceedingly useful alloy of copper and zinc. Much brass is about two-thirds copper, but different proportions give different properties. It is harder than copper and easily worked. Brass in the Bible (Matt. x, 9) probably refers to bronze.

Brass-wind, a collective term for those instruments in an orchestra which are made of brass (or other metal) and which are sounded by blowing so as to cause the lips to vibrate within a cup- or funnel-shaped mouthpiece. The shape of the mouthpiece affects the tone, *e.g.*, cornet, trumpet, horn, trombone, tuba.

Breadfruit Tree (*Artocarpus altilis*), a native of the South Sea Islands; the fruits are a brownish green, about the size of a melon, and contain a white pulpy substance which is roasted before being eaten. The tree grows 40 ft. or more. Captain Bligh's ship *Bounty* was on a voyage to Jamaica carrying a cargo of 1,000 breadfruit trees when the mutiny occurred.

Breviary (Lat. *breviarium*=abridgment), the short prayer-book of the Roman Catholic Church which gives the Divine Office, *i.e.*, the canonical hours or services. The directions for Mass are in the Missal. The modern Roman breviary is a reformed version of the 11th-cent. breviary and was produced by Pope Pius V. in 1568 in response to a decree of the Council of Trent. All Roman Catholic priests are required to recite the whole of the breviary services allotted for each day. *See also* **Matins**.

Brick, a moulded block of clay, either burnt in a kiln or sun-dried, used for building. All the ancient nations made bricks, at first only baking them in the sun, and afterwards by means of fire. The Israelites were employed in brick-making during their captivity in Egypt. The Romans used bricks for all ordinary purposes, and introduced them into England. In these days brick-making is mainly done by machinery—digging the clay, grinding, screening tempering (pugging), moulding, drying, burning (firing). The standard size, proved by centuries of experience to be the easiest to handle and the most economical, is approx. 9 in. × 4½ in. × 3 in. The processes of tile-making are similar. A plain tile is 10½ in. × 6½ in. × ⅜–⅞ in. Many varieties of bricks and tiles are produced for different purposes.

Bridges are structures for continuing a road, railway, or canal across a river, valley, ravine, or a road or railway at a lower level. From early times bridges were made of timber, stone, or brick, and it was not until the 19th cent. that wrought- and cast-iron were used. Today the materials mostly used are steel and reinforced concrete. Among the most famous of ancient bridges is that of S. Angelo at Rome, built by Hadrian as the Pons Aelius, A.D. 134. The Rialto bridge at Venice dates from 1588. The Ponte Santa Trinita at Florence, one of the finest Renaissance bridges and deemed the most beautiful in the world, was destroyed by German mines in 1944 but has now been reconstructed just as it was before. The first stone bridge across the Thames was begun in 1176. It had 19 arches and was lined with houses and stood until 1831 when it was replaced by the present granite bridge designed by Sir John Rennie. It is planned to replace it by 1970 by a new three-span concrete bridge with a six-lane carriageway and two footways. The first cast-iron bridge was Telford's famous Menai suspension bridge with a span of 580 ft., built 1819–26, which lasted until 1940, when it was completely reconstructed. Another example of Britain's supremacy in constructional ironwork was Robert Stephenson's tubular bridge across the Menai Straits, the prototype of all modern plate girder railway bridges. Other famous bridges are the Niagara (suspension), Forth railway bridge (cantilever), London Tower bridge (suspension), Tay bridge in Scotland, Victoria Jubilee bridge across the St. Lawrence at Montreal (an open steel structure), Sydney Harbour bridge, Lower Zambesi bridge, Storstrom bridge in Denmark, Howrah bridge at Calcutta, with the third largest cantilever span in the world, the Volta bridge of Ghana and the Auckland Harbour bridge, both built in recent years, the Verrazano-Narrows bridge spanning New York's harbour from Brooklyn to Staten I., the world's longest bridge, exceeding by 60 ft. the centre span of San Francisco's Golden Gate bridge, until 1964 the world's longest. Britain is engaged in the largest bridge building programme for over a century. The new road suspension bridge across the Firth of Forth, completed in 1964, has the largest single span in Europe (3,300 ft.). The Medway bridge, completed in 1963, is the largest pre-stressed concrete structure of its kind in the world. The Severn bridge was completed in 1966.

Britannia Metal, an alloy of tin, antimony, and copper, harder than pure tin, corrosion-resistant, and used for teapots, and jugs (often electroplated).

British Association for the Advancement of Science, The, was founded in 1831 by a group of British scientists under the leadership of Charles Babbage (1792–1871) to stimulate scientific inquiry and promote research in the interest of the nation. Its meetings are held annually in different cities of the United Kingdom. It is divided into sections which include the chief physical and biological sciences, economics, anthropology and archaeology, psychology and education, engineering, forestry, agriculture, and there is also a division for studying the social and international relations of science. Sir Joseph Hutchinson, Draper's professor in the University of Cambridge, was elected President for 1966, when the meeting was to be held in Nottingham. Membership is open to laymen as well as scientists.

British Museum, was created by an Act of Parliament in 1753, when the Sir Hans Sloane collection, which the British Government had acquired for £20,000, was added to the Cottonian Library and the Harleian Manuscripts. It was opened to the public in 1759 at Montagu House, Bloomsbury. The acquisition of the library of George III. (now known as the King's Library) in 1823 made larger premises necessary, and the present building in Great Russell Street was completed in 1847 from designs by Sir Robert Smirke. The great domed Reading Room was opened in 1857, and the Natural History Department was transferred to South Kensington in the eighties. As a museum it is perhaps the most famous in the world, since, apart from its colossal library of books and manuscripts, it has many priceless collections of sculptures, antiquities, prints and drawings, coins and medals. Under the Copyright Acts the British Museum has the right to receive *gratis* a copy of every book published in the United Kingdom. The Reading Room contains original sources, books, and periodicals which cannot be found elsewhere; its use is restricted to those who require a wider range of books on the subject of their study than can be found in other libraries. The modernisation programme announced in 1963 includes the building of a new library on a site adjacent. The Natural History Museum at South Kensington became a separate institution in 1963 and is now known as the British Museum of Natural History.

British Railways. The name under which the railways of Britain were unified on January 1, 1948. Instead of the former four main railway systems six regions were formed: London Midland region (former L.M.S.R.) Western (former G.W.R.), Southern (formerly S.R.), Eastern (southern area of former L.N.E.R.), N.E. region (N.E. of former L.N.E.R.), Scottish region (Scottish system of the former L.M.S.R. and L.N.E.R.). The most far-reaching change in the modernisation and re-equipment programme announced in 1955 has been the replacement of steam traction by electric and diesel locomotives. Under the chairmanship of Dr. Richard Beeching the British Railways Board published its first report, *The Reshaping of British Railways*, in 1963 and its plans for establishing a viable railway system by closing uneconomic branch lines and by developing new services on the liner train principle are in progress. The second Beeching report, *The Development of the Major Railway Trunk Routes*, issued in 1965 studies the selective development and intensive utilisation of a more limited trunk route system. The name was changed to British Rail in 1964.

Brocken-spectre or Glory. The series of coloured rings which an observer sees around the shadow of his own head (or an aeroplane in which he is travelling) as cast upon a bank of mist or thin cloud. This effect is produced by reflection and refraction of sunlight in minute water-droplets in the air just as in a rainbow.

Bromine. A non-metal element, symbol Br, member of the halogen family (*q.v.*). It is a red, evil-smelling liquid (Greek *bromos*, a stink). It is an abundant element. In the U.S.A. bromide is extracted from sea-water on a large scale. It unites readily with many other elements, the products being termed bromides. Its derivatives with organic compounds are used in synthetic chemistry. Bromoform is a liquid resembling chloroform. Bromides are used in medicine to calm excitement.

Bronze is primarily an alloy of copper and tin, and was one of the earliest alloys known, the Bronze Age in the evolution of tool-using man coming between the Stone Age and the Iron Age. Some modern bronzes contain zinc or lead also, and a trace of phosphorus is present in "phosphor-bronze."

Bubble Chamber. An instrument used by physicists to reveal the tracks of fast fundamental particles (*e.g.*, those produced in large accelerating machines) in a form suitable for photography; closely related to the Wilson cloud chamber (*q.v.*), but the particles leave trails of small bubbles in a liquid (often liquid hydrogen) instead of droplets of liquid in a gas; invented in 1952 by the American physicist, Dr. D. Glaser, Nobel Prizeman, 1960.

Buckingham Palace, London residence of British sovereigns since 1837. Originally built for the Duke of Buckingham (1703); bought by George III. in 1762 and remodelled by Nash 1825–36.

Buddhism. *See* **J6.**

Bulk Purchase. Arrangements for bulk purchase involve undertakings by a country, or by some agency within it, to buy from another country specified quantities of its products, either at prices fixed in advance or with provision for adjusting the prices at specified intervals to take account of general price movements. Such long-term arrangements may be, but need not be, combined with undertakings by the seller to buy specified quantities, or specified values, of the products of the purchasing country in exchange. The purpose of bulk-purchase arrangements is, on the one hand, to provide the seller of the goods in question with assured markets and, on the other, to assure the buyers of needed supplies of their goods.

Buntings, name of a group of finches, seed-eating birds, usually found in open country. The Yellowhammer, Reed Bunting, Corn Bunting, and Cirl Bunting are resident in Britain; the Snow Bunting (which breeds in small numbers in Scotland) and Lapland Bunting are regular winter visitors, and the Ortolan is among the rare visitors.

Busby, a military head-dress of fur: the fur *busby* worn by the Hussars and the *bearskin* busby, introduced in 1832 and properly called "bearskin," worn by the Guards.

Byzantine Art developed in the eastern part of the Roman empire after Constantine founded the city of Constantinople (A.D. 330). It has many sources—Greek, Syrian, Egyptian, and Islamic—and reached its zenith in the reign of Justinian (527–65). The major art form was ecclesiastical architecture, the basic plan of which was Roman—either basilican (symmetrical about an axis) or centralised (symmetrical about a point). Arched construction was developed, and the dome became the most typical feature, although, unlike the Roman dome which was placed on a round apartment, the Byzantine dome was placed on a square one on independent pendentives. Frequently small domes were clustered round a large one as in the case of the great church of Santa Sophia (537), the climax of Byzantine architecture. Usually the churches were small and include those of SS. Sergius and Bacchus, Sta. Irene (in Constantinople), S. Vitale in Ravenna, and the much later and larger St. Mark's in Venice. Byzantine art also took the form of miniatures, enamels, jewels, and textiles, but mosaics, frescos, and icons (*q.v.*) are its greatest treasures.

C

Cacao, *Theobroma cacao*, is an evergreen tree, from 15 to 20 ft. high, growing abundantly in tropical America, West Africa, the West Indies, Ceylon, etc., yielding seeds, called cocoa beans, from which cocoa and chocolate are manufactured. The fruit is 7–10 in. long, hard and ridged; inside are the beans, covered with a reddish-brown skin, which are first fermented, then dried. The trees mature at five to eight years and produce two crops a year.

Cactus, a family of flowering plants numbering about a thousand species adapted to living in very dry situations. The stem is usually fleshy, being composed of succulent tissue, remarkably retentive of water; commonly equipped with sharp thorns which deter animals from eating them. The roots are generally very long, tapping soil water over large area; a "prickly pear" cactus may have roots covering a circular area 25 ft. or more in diameter. The leaves are commonly insignificant or absent, and the stem takes over the photosynthetic leaf function and becomes accordingly flattened to expose greater area to sunlight and air. In some kinds of cactus (*e.g. Echinocactus*) the stem is shaped almost like a sea-urchin.

Cadmium. A metallic element, symbol Cd, chemically similar to zinc and mercury. Used in alloys to lower the melting point, as in Wood's metal with bismuth and tin. Alloyed with copper to make electric cables. Like zinc, it is a protective metal and is used in electro-plating. The cadmium-vapour lamp gives a characteristic frequency used in measuring wavelength.

Caesium, also spelt **Cesium**, is an alkali metal element, symbol Cs, in first group of the periodic table. It resembles rubidium and potassium and was discovered by Bunsen and Kirchhoff in 1860. It was the first element whose existence was discovered spectroscopically. The caesium atom consists of a heavy nucleus surrounded by 55 electrons, 54 of which are arranged in stable orbits, and one of which, known as the valency electron, is in a less stable orbit surrounding them. Used in the construction of photo-electric cells and as an accurate time standard (atomic clock).

Calcite, the stable, naturally-occurring form of calcium carbonate; very abundant; crystallises in the hexagonal system.

Calcium, a silvery-white metallic element, symbol Ca. It melts at 810° C. and is very reactive. It was discovered by Sir Humphry Davy in 1808, but not until 1898 was it obtained pure, by Moissan. Does not occur as metal in nature, but calcium compounds make up a large part of the earth's crust. Most important calcium sources are marble, limestone, chalk (all three are, chemically, calcium carbonate); dolomite, which is the double carbonate of calcium and magnesium; gypsum, a hydrated calcium sulphate; calcium phosphate and calcium fluoride. Igneous rocks contain much calcium silicate. Calcium compounds are essential to plants and are used in fertilisers. Animals require calcium and phosphorus for bone and teeth formation; deficiency is treated by administration of calcium phosphate. Strontium is chemically similar to calcium, and the radioactive strontium 90 from atomic "fall-out" is therefore easily assimilated by the body.

Calculating machines are inventions to relieve men and women of the tedium of long routine or involved computations. The calculating machine seems to date from 1642, when Pascal constructed one which could be used for addition and subtraction. General interest was lacking, however, and almost two hundred and fifty years elapsed before Ohdner in Sweden produced the first numerical arithmetical machines of the type now in general use. Before very long the electric motor replaced the hand in providing the motive power, and so the electric calculating machine was invented. But at all stages of any calculation on hand-operated or electric machines human operators have to supply them with numbers. The principal feature of the more modern machines is that they are automatic; that is, once a sequence of an arithmetical operation has been decided, and instructions given to the machine in suitable form, such as holes punched into cards or tape, or in some other way, the machine carries out its work without further human intervention. In some calculations these machines frequently give the impression that they are "thinking," or "choosing" a way to carry out the calculations as quickly as possible. But even in such cases the criteria for judgment are actually contained in the initial instructions. The idea of automatic computation by machinery is due to the English mathematician Charles Babbage (1792–1871). He made a small machine of this type, based on the idea of the Jacquard loom for lace-making. He next planned, but never completed, two separate automatic machines, a "difference engine" to help in making mathematical tables, and an "analytical engine," which was to be a general-purpose, programme-controlled, machine possessing all the features of modern calculating machines. But Babbage's inventions were designed to be operated mechanically; it was left to the electronic engineers of the 20th cent. to bring Babbage's ideas to full fruition. The next important step was taken in 1937, when Aiken of Harvard started to construct, and subsequently completed, the first of the electronic machines. In these electricity is conducted either through an evacuated space, or a gas, or a semi-conductor. All calculating machines are of the "Analogue" or "Digital" types. In the analogue type, numbers are represented by physical quantities, for example, electric currents, of which the numbers themselves are the measures. The most important of this class is the Differential Analyser invented by Vannever Bush of America. In the digital machines the numbers are stored in it, and are represented by discrete objects, such as the teeth of a gear-wheel. Most of the important modern machines are of the digital variety. Almost all the ideas underlying the more advanced of these machines can be found in a remarkable mathematical paper published in 1936 by Turing of Manchester. In their earliest form digital computers were suitable only for scientific calculations, and some of the more spectacular applications at this period included the evaluation of π to 3,000 decimal places. After a period of increasing technological application the main emphasis passed to business operations of the types exemplified by the calculation of P.A.Y.E., and to integrated data processing, in which all of the operations of management and accountancy are carried out within the machine, and human intervention is required only for the higher administrative and policy decisions. The invention of the modern calculating machine may be as important to the world as was that of the Hindu–Arabic numerals to the Middle Ages.

Calendar, a collection of tables showing the days and months of the year, its astronomical recurrences, chronological references, etc. The Julian Calendar, with its leap year, introduced by Julius Cæsar, fixed the average length of the year at 365¼ days, which was about 11 minutes too long (the earth completes its orbit in 365 days 5 hours 48 minutes 46 seconds of mean solar time). The cumulative error was rectified by the Gregorian Calendar, introduced in Italy in 1582, whereby century years do not count as leap years unless divisible by 400. This is the rule we now follow. England did not adopt the reformed calendar until 1752, when she found herself 11 days behind the Continent.

Calends, the first day of the month in the Roman calendar, when interest fell due, and proclamations as to the order of days were made.

Calorie. Unit of quantity of heat. The "small" or fundamental calorie is the amount of heat required to raise the temperature of 1 gram of water from 14·5° to 15·5° C. This is the gram-calorie used in physics and chemistry. The large Calorie (written with a capital C), commonly used in nutritional connotations, is equal to 1000 small calories and is called the kilogram-calorie. *See also* **P39(2)**.

Calvinism. *See* **J7**.

Calypso, West Indian song in the form of a doggerel lampoon composed spontaneously and sung to a guitar.

Cambridge University had a sufficiently good teaching reputation to attract Oxford students in 1209, when lectures at their own university were suspended. In 1226 it had a Chancellor who was recognised by King and Pope. The first college to be founded was Peterhouse in 1284. The university was reorganised and granted a Charter of Incorporation by an act of Elizabeth in 1571. The colleges with their dates of foundation are Christ's (1505), Churchill (1960), Clare (1326), Corpus Christi (1352), Darwin (1964), Downing (1800), Emmanuel (1584), Gonville and Caius (1348), Jesus (1496), King's (1441), Magdalene (1542), Pembroke (1347), Peterhouse (1284), Queens' (1448), St. Catherine's (1473), St. Edmund's House (1896), St. John's (1511), Selwyn (1882), Sidney Sussex (1596), Trinity (1546), Trinity Hall (1350), Fitwilliam House (1869). The four women's colleges are: Girton (1869), Newnham (1875), New Hall (1954), and Hughes Hall (formerly Cambridge T.C.) (1885). Women were admitted to degrees (though not allowed to sit for examination) in 1920, and to full membership of the University in 1948.

Camel, a large ruminant quadruped, inhabiting Asia and Africa, where it is largely used as a beast of burden. There are two species—the Arabian camel or dromedary, with only one hump; and the Bactrian, or double-humped camel. There are no wild dromedaries, and the only wild bactrians occur in the Gobi Desert. The camel is able to go for long periods without water, not, as was formerly believed, because it stored water in its hump, but because of the unique mechanism of its physiology which enables it to conserve water at the expense of not sweating until 104° F. is reached.

Campanile, or bell-tower, is separate from but usually adjoining its parent church. The most famous are in Italy. Giotto's tower at Florence, adjoining the cathedral of Santa Maria del Fiore, is architecturally the finest in the world. Others are at Cremona, the loftiest in Italy (364 ft.) and Pisa (the leaning tower). The magnificent pointed campanile of St. Mark's, Venice, which collapsed in 1902 and has since been rebuilt in its original form, was begun in 902.

Canal, an artificial watercourse used for navigation which changes its level by means of locks. The completion of the Bridgewater Canal in 1761 to take coal from Worsley to Manchester marked the beginning of canal building in industrial Britain. There are some 2,500 miles of navigable inland waterways in Great Britain today, 1,850 miles of which are under the control of the British Waterways Board set up by the Transport Act, 1962. The English network is based on the four great estuaries Mersey, Humber, Severn, and Thames.

Canary, a light, sweet wine from the Canaries and chief export until the grape blight of 1853. Much consumed in Britain from Tudor to Georgian times. Also, a popular cage bird bred from a small finch, *Serinus canarius*. *See* **Z22**.

Candela, unit of luminous intensity, replacing the former *international candle* as standard. So defined that the brightness of a total radiator, or black body, at the temperature of solidification of molten platinum is 60 candelas per sq. cm.

Candlemas, an English and Roman Church festival in celebration of the Purification of the Virgin when she presented the infant Jesus in the Temple, and deriving its name from the great show of candles made on the day (February 2) in the Roman celebrations.

Canon, a term applied to signify a recognised rule for the guide of conduct in matters legal, ecclesiastical, and artistic, or an authoritative ordinance: thus we have Canonical Scriptures, Canon Law, etc. A Canon is also a dignitary of the Church, usually a member of a cathedral chapter in the Anglican communion, or in the Roman Church a member of an order standing between regular monks and secular clergy.

Canonical Hours were seven in number in the Western Church; Matins and Lauds, before dawn; Prime, early morning service; Terce, 9 a.m.; Sext, noon; Nones, 3 p.m.; Vespers, 4 p.m.; Compline, bed-time.

Canonisation, the entering of one of the faithful departed on the list of saints of the Roman Catholic Church, after proof of purity and distinction of life has been accepted. A day is then named for the future keeping of the anniversary of the saint's death. Beatification, by which a person is called blessed, is usually followed by canonisation, but not necessarily.

Cantata, originally a long piece for solo voice, *i.e.*, the vocal counterpart of a sonata. The term is now used to cover a small oratorio.

Canticles, the name given to the scriptural passages from the Bible sung by the congregation in the various Christian liturgies. They are the *Benedicite, Benedictus, Magnificat, Nunc Dimittis*.

Capercaillie, the largest of the grouse family, found in the Scottish highlands and the pine forests and mountainous regions of Northern and Central Europe and Asia.

Capet, the family name of a race of French kings, founded by Hugh Capet in 987 with its collateral branches. Reigned until 1848, except for the period of the French Revolution and Napoleon.

Capitalism. *See* **J7**.

Capricorn, a zodiacal constellation between Sagittarius and Aquarius, figured out in ancient times as having the head of the goat and the hind part shaped like a fish.

Capuchins are members of a mendicant order of Franciscans, founded in the 16th cent. with the aim of restoring the primitive and stricter observance of the rule of St. Francis, so called from the capuce or pointed cowl worn by them.

Carat, a term used in assessing the value of gold and precious stones. In connection with gold, it represents the proportion of pure gold contained in any gold alloy, and for this purpose the metal is divided into 24 parts. Thus 24-carat indicates pure gold, and any lesser number of carats shows the proportion of gold contained in the alloy. The carat as a measure of weight is now obsolete, having been replaced by the *metric carat* of 0·2 grams.

Caravan, a band of travellers or traders journeying together for safety across the Eastern deserts, sometimes numbering many hundreds. There are several allusions to caravans in the Old Testament. The great caravan routes of this period from Egypt to Babylon and from Palestine to Yemen linked up with the Syrian ports and so with western sea commerce. Many wars have been fought in the past over their control.

Carbohydrates, group of organic compounds composed of carbon, hydrogen and oxygen, *e.g.*, sugars, starches, cellulose. Play an essential rôle in all living processes. *See* **P39**(2).

Carbon, a non-metallic chemical element which occurs in crystalline form as diamonds and graphite; amorphous forms of carbon include charcoal and soot, while coke consists mainly of elementary carbon. The biochemistry of plants and animals largely hinges upon carbon compounds. The study of carbon compounds is called Organic Chemistry. **Carbon 14.** A radioactive isotope of carbon, with a half-life *c.* 6,000 years, used in following the path of compounds and their assimilation in the body (**F21**(1)). Also used in determination of the age of carbon-containing materials such as trees, fossils, and very old documents.

Carbonari, members of a secret political society originated in Naples, and at one time very numerous. Their chief aim was to free Italy from foreign rule, and they exerted considerable influence in the various revolutionary movements in the first half of the 19th cent. Their name was adopted from the charcoal-burners (*carbonari*), and their passwords, signs, etc., were all in the phraseology of the fraternity.

Carbon dioxide. Commonest of the oxides of carbon. It is formed when carbon and its compounds are burnt with abundant supply of air, and when carbon compounds are oxidised in the respiration process of animals. The atmosphere contains carbon dioxide to the extent of about three parts in 10,000; this figure remains more or less constant because, while carbon dioxide is always being added by animal respiration and the burning of fuels, such as coal and oil by man, plants are constantly removing it in the process known as photosynthesis or carbon assimilation. A heavy gas and obviously not one capable of supporting respiration, it can accumulate in caves, etc., and cause asphyxiation; for instance, in the Grotto del Cane, near Naples, a dog entering the cave is suffocated, whereas a man whose head is above the carbon dioxide level can walk through it unharmed. Solid carbon dioxide is called "dry ice." The gas in aerated drinks and soda water is carbon dioxide.

Carbon monoxide is a colourless gas with no taste or smell. It is formed when coal and coke are burnt with a restricted supply of air; the blue flame to be seen in a coke brazier, for instance, is the flame of carbon monoxide. This gas is very poisonous, forming with the haemoglobin of the blood a compound which is useless for respiration and cherry red in colour, which gives a visible symptom of poisoning by carbon monoxide. With nickel it forms a volatile compound, called nickel carbonyl, and this reaction is the basis of the Mond process for extracting nickel.

Cardinal, one of the chief dignitaries of the Roman Catholic Church who constitute the Pope's council, or Sacred College, and when the papal chair is vacant elect a Pope from among themselves. There are three orders: cardinal bishops, members of the Roman Curia (the central administration of the Church) and bishops of sees near Rome; cardinal deacons, also members of the Curia, holding titular bishoprics; and cardinal priests who exercise pastoral duties over sees removed from Rome, though some are members of the Curia. Their numbers were fixed by Pope Sixtus V in 1586 at 6, 14, and 50 respectively. Both Pope John XXIII and Pope Paul increased the number and since 22 February 1965 there have been 103, the highest number in the history of the Church.

Cardinal Virtues, according to Plato these were justice, prudence, temperance, fortitude—*natural* virtues as distinct from the *theological* virtues of the Roman Catholic Church, faith, hope, charity. The phrase "seven cardinal virtues," combining the two, figures in mediæval literature. *See* **Sins, Seven Deadly.**

Carlovingians, the second dynasty of the French kings (established 751), included such notable rulers as Charles Martel and Charlemagne. In 987 the Capet dynasty succeeded.

Carmelites, a body of mendicant friars taking their name from Mount Carmel, where the order was first established in the 12th cent. The original rule of the order required absolute poverty, abstinence from meat and a hermit life. The rigidity of the rule of the order was mitigated by Innocent IV. They wear a brown habit with white mantle, hence their name of White Friars. The order of Carmelite nuns was instituted in the 15th cent.

Carnivora. *See* **F23**(2).

Carp, a well-known fresh-water fish, found in plenty in most European and Asiatic still waters; reaches a length of about 2 ft. and under favourable conditions lives for about 40 years. Familiar British members of the family are the roach, rudd, dace, chub, gudgeon, tench, minnow, barbel, bream, and bleak. The goldfish, popular in ornamental ponds, is the domesticated variety of a Far Eastern member of the carp family.

Carthusians, an order of monks founded in 1084 by St. Bruno at the Grande Chartreuse near Grenoble, and introduced into England about a century later. They built the Charterhouse (corruption of Chartreuse) in London in 1371. The chief characteristics of the order are a separate dwelling-house in the precincts of the charterhouse for each monk, and the general assembly in the Church twice in the day and once at night. They wear a white habit, with white scapular and hood. The liqueur *Chartreuse* was invented by the order and is still their secret. For many years they have derived large revenues from its sale. The order of Carthusian nuns was founded in the 12th cent.

Casein, the chief protein in milk and cheese. It is coagulated by the action of rennet or acid. An important class of plastics ("casein plastics") are produced from it, and these plastics are converted into buttons, knitting-needles, etc. 8000 gallons of milk yield about a ton of casein.

Cassowary, a genus of ostrich-like birds which, together with the emu, form a separate order found only in Australasia. All species are black, with brightly coloured necks, and with a horny crest on the head. Noted for fleetness.

Castor-oil Plant (*Ricinus communis*), an African shrub now cultivated in most tropical countries. It has broad palmate leaves and bears a spiny fruit containing seeds which when pressed yield the well-known oil.

Cat, the general name for all members of the class *Felidae* of the carnivorous order, from the lion down to the domestic cat. The latter is believed to be descended from the European and African wild cats. Egypt is credited with having been the first country in which the cat was domesticated. *See* **Z9–12.**

Catalyst. A substance which speeds up a chemical reaction without being changed itself. Various aluminium and titanium compounds are catalysts in the formation of polythene from ethylene. Palladium catalyses the reaction of hydrogen with oxygen (hence its use in gas lighters). Enzymes in the body hasten the breakdown of carbohydrates and proteins by catalytic action.

Cataracts are gigantic waterfalls. The most famous are those of Niagara in North America, the Orinoco in South America, the Victoria Falls on the Zambesi in Africa, the Falls of the Rhine at Schaffhausen, and the Cascade of Gavarni in the Pyrenees.

Catechism, an elementary book of principles in any science or art, but more particularly in religion, in the form of questions and answers. There is a great variety of these, including the Lutheran, prepared by Luther in 1529. Calvin's Geneva (in 1536), and the Anglican, in the Book of Common Prayer.

Catechumens, a term applied in the primitive Church to children of Christian parents, who were admitted as neophytes, and occupied a place apart in the church.

Caterpillar, the larva of a butterfly or moth, worm-like in its segmented body, with 3 pairs of jointed true legs often curiously marked and coloured, and frequently more or less hairy.

Cathedral, the chief church of a diocese, so called from its containing a Bishop's seat, or episcopal chair. The town in which it is situated is a cathedral city. Some celebrated cathedrals are St. John Lateran of Rome, Notre Dame of Paris, the cathedrals of Cologne and Milan, St. Paul's in London, Canterbury Cathedral, York Minster, and the cathedrals of Durham, Bristol, Gloucester, Peterborough, Exeter, Liverpool, and Coventry (destroyed by bombs, now rebuilt).

Catholicism. *See* **J7.**

Cat's-eye, a kind of quartz, much valued as a gem, opalescent, and of various shades.

Cavalier, a name adopted during the troubles of the Civil War to designate the Royalist party; it is also used generally in reference to a knightly, gallant, or imperious personage.

Caves, natural hollow places in the earth, frequently found in limestone, less frequently in volcanic rocks. Popular caves in Britain are Kent's cavern near Torquay, Cheddar and Wookey hole in the Mendips; Fingal's Cave in Staffa (Inner Hebrides) is noted for its splendid range of basalt columns. The scientific study of caves is known as spelaeology. The first discovery of Palæolithic paintings (the celebrated bulls) was made in the Altamira caves in Spain in 1879.

Cedar, a dark-leaved, cone-bearing, horizontal-branched evergreen tree that grows to a considerable height and girth, the best known species in Britain being the Lebanon Cedar, which was introduced in the 17th cent.

'Cello. *See* **Violoncello.**

Celluloid, one of the first synthetic thermoplastic materials, discovered by Alexander Parkes in 1865 when he was attempting to produce synthetic horn. It is made by treating cellulose nitrate with camphor and alcohol. Photographic film is made of a similar, but less-inflammable material, formed by the use of cellulose acetate instead of the nitrate.

Cellulose, a carbohydrate, and a constituent of nearly all plants. Cellulose occurs in an almost pure state in the fibres of linen (flax), absorbent cotton, jute, and filter-paper (used in laboratories).

Celts, an ancient race of W. Europe, originally from southern Germany (2nd millennium B.C.), united by a common language and culture, who spread westward into Spain, northward into Britain, eastward to the Black Sea, reaching Galicia in Asia Minor. The "La Tène" iron age Celts invaded Britain 250 B.C. After Britain was conquered by the Romans and invaded by the Angles and Saxons there remained as areas of Celtic speech only Wales (Brythonic speakers), Ireland, Scotland, Isle of Man (Gaelic speakers). The late Celtic period in Britain produced a distinctive Christian art (*e.g.*, the Lindisfarne Gospel *c.* 700, and the Irish Book of Kells, dating from about the same time).

Cerium, a scarce metallic element discovered by Berzelius in 1803. A mixture of cerium and thorium nitrates is used in the manufacture of gas mantles, which owe their incandescent property to the deposit of cerium and thorium oxide with which they are coated.

Cetacea, the order of mammals including the whales, dolphins, and porpoises, which, though strictly aquatic, breathe air, suckle their young, and are warm-blooded.

Chain reaction. *See* **F12**(1).

Chalcedony, a mixture of crystalline silica and amorphous hydrated silica, *i.e.*, of quartz and opal. It has a waxy lustre, and is much used by jewellers for necklaces, bracelets, etc. Commonly it is white or creamy. Its bright orange-red variety is called carnelian; its brown variety, sard. Chrysoprase, plasma, bloodstone are varieties which are respectively pale apple-green, dark leek-green, green with red spots.

Chalk, a white limestone, calcium carbonate, found in the Upper Cretaceous deposits (formed from the shells of minute marine organisms). In southern England the chalk is a soft rock, but in Yorkshire, Scotland, and Ireland it is solid limestone. French chalk is hydrated magnesium silicate, a variety of talc.

Chama, a genus of large bivalves, "hoof shells" of the clam family, found in tropical waters, especially amongst coral reefs. *Chama gigas* weigh sometimes as much as 300 lb., and one valve has been employed as the basin of baptismal fonts in various churches.

Chamberlain, Lord, the senior officer of The Royal Household who is responsible for all ceremonial within the palace (levées, courts, garden parties, entertainment of foreign royalties and heads of state) but not the coronation or state opening of parliament. He is also in charge of appointments to The Royal Household and is examiner and licenser of plays.

Chamberlain, Lord Great, one of the great officers of state whose duties are now mainly ceremonial. He attends the monarch at the state opening of parliament and at the coronation and is custodian of the Palace of Westminster (Houses of Parliament). The office is hereditary, dating from Norman times, and is held for one reign in turn by the descendants of the De Veres, Earls of Oxford.

Chamber Music, strictly, signifies music suitable for playing in a small room, but is used to cover music specially composed for small combinations of instruments; *e.g.*, string quartets, etc.

Chameleon, a family of lizards with numerous species. Their ability to change colour is well known, but exaggerated, and is due to the movement of pigment cells beneath the skin. They are slow in movement, arboreal, and mainly insectivorous. Found in Africa, India, Ceylon, Madagascar, and Arabia.

Chamois, a species of antelope, native of Western Europe and Asia. About the size of a goat, it lives in mountainous regions, and possesses wonderful leaping power, so that it is very difficult to capture. Its flesh is much esteemed, and from its skin chamois leather is made, although to-day sheep and goat skins are usually substituted. The mating season is Oct.–Nov. and the fawns are born in May or June. Live to be 20–25 years old.

Channel Tunnel, a scheme to bore a tunnel through 20–30 miles of chalk under the sea between Dover and Calais has been a subject for discussion ever since Albert Mathieu first conceived the idea as a practical possibility in 1802. In the 1830s proposals for a bridge were made. Investigations have been undertaken from time to time, the most recent being that of the Channel Tunnel Group, composed of British, French, and American interests, which was set up in 1957. In Feb. 1964 it was announced that the British and French Governments had decided in principle to go ahead with a rail tunnel, thus accepting the recommendations of the Anglo-French study group published in Sept. 1963. New techniques in the field of geophysics and palæontology are being used to study the soil and rock conditions.

Chapel Royal, the church dedicated to the use of the Sovereign and Court. There are, among others, chapels royal at St. James's Palace, Buckingham Palace, Windsor, Hampton Court, the Tower, and Holyrood.

Characterology. *See* **J7.**

Charcoal, a term applied to wood that has been subjected to a process of slow smothered combustion. More generally it refers to the carbonaceous remains of vegetable, animal, or combustible mineral substances submitted to a similar process. Charcoal from special woods (in particular buckthorn) is used in making gunpowder. Bone charcoal finds use in sugar refining, as it removes dark colouring matter present in the crude syrup.

Charterhouse, a famous school that was in Aldersgate Street, London, but removed to Godalming. In connection with the school is an almshouse on the old London site, endowed by Thomas Sutton in 1611. Thackeray, as well as Addison, Grote, and other eminent men, were Charterhouse scholars.

Chasuble, a sleeveless vestment worn by ecclesiastics over the alb during the celebration of Mass. It is supposed to symbolise the seamless coat of Christ. Its use in English churches was prohibited in 1552, but again permitted after 1559. It gradually fell into disregard, however, but about 100 years ago its use was revived in the Church of England.

Cheese, an article of food made from the curd of milk, which is separated from the whey and pressed in moulds and gradually dried. There are about 500 varieties differing with method of preparation and quality of milk. They used to be made in the regions after which they are named but nowadays many of them are mass-produced, *e.g.*, Cheddar is made not only in all parts of Britain but in Canada, New Zealand, Australia, Holland, and the U.S.A. Cheeses may be divided into 3 main classes: (1) soft, *e.g.*, Camembert, Cambridge, Port l'Evêque; (2) blue-veined, *e.g.*, Stilton, Gorgonzola, Roquefort (made from ewe's milk), (3) hard-pressed, *e.g.*, Cheddar, Cheshire, Gruyère, Parmesan, Gouda.

Cheetah or "hunting leopard," the large spotted cat of Africa and Southern Asia whose ability to reach a speed of 45 m.p.h. makes it the swiftest four-footed animal alive.

Chemistry is the science of the elements and their compounds. It is concerned with the laws of their combination and behaviour under various conditions. It had its rise in alchemy (**J2**) and has gradually developed into a science of vast magnitude and importance. Organic chemistry deals with the chemistry of the compounds of carbon; inorganic chemistry is concerned with the chemistry of the elements; physical chemistry is concerned with the study of chemical reactions and with the theories and laws of chemistry.

Chestnut, the fruit of the chestnut tree; those of the Spanish chestnut, *Castanea vesca*, furnish a favourite esculent. The wood is used in carpentry; while the horse-chestnut (*Æsculus hippocastanum*) is much employed in brush-mounting and in cabinet work.

Chiaroscuro, a term used in painting to denote the arrangement of light and shade in a picture.

Chiltern Hundreds, three hundreds—Stoke, Burnham, and Desborough—the stewardship of which is now a nominal office under the Chancellor of the Exchequer. Since about 1751 the nomination to it has been used as a method of enabling a member of Parliament to resign his seat on the plea that he holds an office of honour and profit under the crown. (This has been a disqualification for Parliament since 1707.)

Chimpanzee, a large anthropoid ape, a native of tropical West Africa, of a dark brown colour, with arms reaching to the knee, and capable of walking upright. Its brain is about a third of the weight of the human brain, but is anatomically similar. The animal has considerable intelligence and powers of learning. A suitable subject for space flight experiments.

China Lobby, the name applied to the body of opinion and pressure in American politics which strenuously opposes recognition of Communist China, and advocates support of Chiang Kai-shek.

Chinchilla, a South American burrowing rodent. Grey in colour, and white underneath. It is greatly esteemed for its beautiful fur.

Chippendale Furniture was introduced in the reign of George I. by Thomas Chippendale, a Worcestershire cabinet-maker who migrated to London and set up for himself in St. Martin's Lane, Charing Cross. He was fonder of inventing designs for furniture than of making it, and in 1752 published a book of patterns; the London furniture-makers of the day soon began to model their work upon it.

Chirognomy. *See* **J8.**

Chivalry, an international brotherhood of knights formed primarily during the 13th cent. to fight against the infidels in the Crusades. For the French the major battle was against the Moslems in the Holy Land and North Africa, the Spaniards fought the same enemy in their own country, and the Germans were concerned with the heathen of Baltic lands, but Chaucer's "very perfect gentle knight" had fought in all these areas. One did not easily become a knight who had to be of noble birth and then pass through a period of probation, beginning as a boy page in the castle of some great lord, serving his elders and betters humbly while he was taught good manners, singing, playing musical instruments, and the composition of verse. Probably he learned Latin, but he certainly learned French, which was the international language of knights as Latin was of scholars. At fourteen he became a squire and learned to fight with sword, battle-axe, and lance, and to endure conditions of hard living while carrying out his duties of waiting on his lord, looking after his horses, and in time accompanying him in battle. Only if he showed himself suitable was he finally knighted by a stroke of the hand or sword on the shoulder from the king or lord. Knighthood was an international order and had its special code of behaviour: to honour one's sworn word, to protect the weak, to respect women, and defend the Faith. To some extent it had a civilising effect on the conduct of war (*e.g.*, knights of opposing sides might slaughter each other in battle but feast together after), but, since war was regarded as the supreme form of sport, it cannot be said to have contributed to peace.

Chlorine, a gaseous element of the halogen family, first isolated in 1774 by Scheele by the action of manganese dioxide on hydrochloric acid. It unites easily with many other elements, the compounds resulting being termed chlorides. The gaseous element is greenish-yellow, with a pungent odour. It is a suffocating gas, injuring the lungs at a concentration as low as 1 part in 50,000, and was used during the first world war as a poison gas. Has a powerful bleaching action, usually being used in form of bleaching powder, made by combining lime and chlorine. Also a valuable disinfectant; used, for instance, in rendering water of swimming baths sterile.

Chloroform, a volatile colourless liquid, compounded of carbon, hydrogen, and chlorine. It is a powerful solvent, not naturally occurring but synthesised on a large scale. When the vapour is inhaled it produces unconsciousness and insensibility to pain. It owes its discovery to Liebig, and its first application for medical purposes to Sir James Young Simpson (**P5**(2).

Chlorophyll, the green pigment contained in the leaves of plants, first discovered by P. J. Pelletier (1788–1829) and J. B Caventou (1795–1877) in 1818. Enables the plant to absorb sunlight and so to build up sugar. The total synthesis of chlorophyll was reported in 1960 by Prof. R. B. Woodward. This is an outstanding achievement in the field of organic chemistry. *See* **F29(1).**

Chorale. Originally a Lutheran hymn-tune, but used, especially by J. S. Bach, as a basis for instrumental or choral pieces, *e.g.*, Chorales and Choral Preludes.

Chordate. *See* **F22**(1).

Chouans, the name given to the band of peasants, mainly smugglers and dealers in contraband salt, who rose in revolt in the west of France in 1793 and joined the royalists of La Vendée. Balzac gives a picture of the people and the country in which they operated in his novel *Les Chouans*. They used the hoot of an owl as a signal—hence the name.

Chough, a member of the crow family, of glossy blue-green-black plumage, whose long curved bill and legs are coral red. It used to be abundant on the cliffs of Cornwall, but its haunts are now restricted to the rocky outcrops of the western coasts and in the mountains near by. It nests in cleft rocks and caves. The Alpine chough with yellow bill inhabits the mountainous districts of Europe and Asia and is not found in Britain. It was found at 27,000 ft. on Everest.

Christmas means "mass of Christ" from the old English *Cristes maesse*, which is celebrated by the Western church on December 25. The actual day on which Christ was born is not known and there is some uncertainty about the year. December 25 as the day of Nativity was not generally observed until the 5th cent. A.D., though, as the winter solstice, it had long been observed as a pagan festival of *sol invictus* (unconquered sun). The first Christmas card dates from about 1843 and the Christmas tree, of pagan origin, was introduced into England from Germany by Queen Adelaide, wife of William IV. Santa Clause is a corruption of Saint Nicolas, patron saint of children, whose feast day properly falls on December 6.

Chromatic Scale, a scale proceeding in intervals of one semitone. *E.g.*, chromatic scale in C C–D♭–D–E♭–E–F–G♭–G–A♭–A–B♭–B–C.

Chromium, a very hard, bluish-white metal element, symbol Cr, melting at a very high temperature (above 1900° C.). Its chief ore is chromite or chrome iron-ore (ferrous chromite). "Ferro-chrome" is produced by heating chromite and anthracite in an electric furnace, and chrome steels are prepared by adding the pre-calculated amount of ferro-chrome to melted steel. Best known chrome steel is stainless steel first made by Brearley in 1912 and since then developed greatly at Sheffield. A typical formula is 18 per cent. chromium, 8 per cent. nickel, 74 per cent. iron. Equally important are Stellite alloys, containing chromium, cobalt, tungsten (or molybdenum), which have made possible modern high-speed cutting tools. Dies used in manufacture of plastics are commonly of chrome steel. The elementary metal finds little use alone except in chromium-plating for motor cars, etc.

Chromosomes, the structures contained within the nucleus of every animal and plant cell by which genetic information is transmitted. The chromosome number in somatic (body) cells is constant for each species of plant and animal, *e.g.*, man (46), cat (38), mouse (40), honey bee (16), fruit fly *Drosophila* (8), potato (48). Chromosomes are long molecules composed of deoxyribonucleoproteins (*i.e.*, proteins and DNA). Human chromosomes have been the subject of much recent research since it has been found that certain disorders are associated with chromosomal aberration, *e.g.*, in Mongolism an extra chromosome is present. *See also* **Genes, Meiosis,** and **Cell Division, F19–21.**

Church Commissioners. The Church Commissioners were established in 1948 by the amalgamation of Queen Anne's Bounty (established 1704) and the Ecclesiastical Commissioners (established 1836) to administer Church revenues and to manage Church property generally. The Commissioners own in investments and real estate a total of over £300 million.

Church of England. *See* **J9.**

Cid, The, a famous Spanish hero of the 11th cent Don Rodrigo Diaz de Vivar, who, before he was twenty, led a Spanish force against the Moors, and drove them out of Spain. He is celebrated in poem, play, and romance.

Cinchona, the tree native to the Andes which is famous for its bark, source of the drug quinine. It was introduced into Ceylon, India, and Java, the latter becoming the main supplier of quinine.

Cinque Ports, a number of seaport towns on the coast of Kent and Sussex, originally five: Hastings, Romney, Hythe, Dover, and Sandwich. Winchelsea and Rye were added later. These ports were required to furnish a certain number of ships, ready for service, and in return they were granted many privileges. The official residence of the Lord Warden is Walmer Castle, near Dover.

Cistercians, an order of monks and nuns taking their names from Cîteaux, near Dijon, where their first monastery was established in 1098. The order was noted for the severity of its rule. They were famous agriculturists. The habit is white, with a black cowl or hood. The order declined, and in the 17th cent. there was a reform movement instituted by the Trappists, who were later organised into a separate order.

Citron, a species of citrus (*Citrus medica*) related to the lemon, whose fruit has thick rind used for candied peel.

Civil List is the annual sum payable to the Sovereign to maintain the Royal Household and to uphold the dignity of the Crown. The amount is granted by Parliament upon the recommendation of a Select Committee and has to be settled afresh in the first six months of a new reign. The Civil List of Queen Victoria was £385,000; Edward VII. and George V., £470,000; Edward VIII. and George VI., £410,000; Elizabeth II., £475,000. The annuities payable to members of the Royal Family do not form part of the Civil List but are a charge on the Consolidated Fund; Queen Mother, £70,000; Duke of Edinburgh, £40,000; Duke of Gloucester, £35,000; Princess Royal, £6,000; Princess Margaret and Princess Anne, £6,000 (£15,000 on marriage),

Prince Charles has his own income from the Duchy of Cornwall.

Clarinet, a wood-wind instrument with a single reed which gives forth a rich, smooth tone. The reed is "tongued" and the note selected by operating keys which open or close holes in the wooden tube. A larger instrument of lower pitch is known as the bass clarinet.

Classicism (classic, or classical), a rather vague term often used, especially in the forms in parentheses, to signify that which is of accepted excellence, cited as a model or standard, or of ancient origin. Hence the "classic" horse races—Two and One Thousand Guineas, Derby, Oaks, St. Leger—and classic writers, the former in the sense of standard and accepted, the latter signifying Latin and Greek writers with or without merit. In art the term implies that form of painting or sculpture where the artist is mainly concerned with producing a work based on formal principles rather than with expressing a subjective mood as in Romantic art (*q.v.*). Classic art is derived (or the artist believes his own version of it to be derived) from the art of classical Greece which is disciplined and primarily intellectual in appeal. Its passion for rules and Academies led to the Romantic reaction with its love of drama and the exotic often carried to an absurd degree. Throughout history art has tended to fluctuate between one attitude or the other: thus in France, Ingres and Delacroix, although contemporaries, were the living embodiments of the two approaches, the former classical, the latter romantic. Similarly, Cubism in its attachment to form is classical, Surrealism in its concern with content, romantic.

Cleopatra's Needle on the Thames Embankment is of the time of Tuthmosis III. (1500–1450 B.C.). Presented to the British Government by Mehemet Ali in 1819, but not brought to this country until 1878. Its weight is 180 tons and it is 68½ ft. in height.

Climate is a generalised representation of the day-to-day weather conditions throughout the year, the combination of all weathers thus determining the climate of a place. Averages and extremes of temperature, variation of humidity, duration of sunshine and cloud cover, amount of rainfall and frequency of snow, frost, gales, etc., are amongst the data normally investigated. The interiors of great land masses are characterised by large ranges of temperature and low rainfall (continental climate), while proximity to oceans has an ameliorating effect with increase in rainfall (oceanic climate). Presence of mountain ranges and lakes and configuration generally produce local modifications of climate, also apparent between the centre and the outlying suburbs of a city. There is evidence that vast changes of climate have occurred during geological time. Since the mid-19th cent. most of the world has shown a tendency to be warmer; the rise in annual mean temperature is now over 1° C. But this trend now seems to be easing off. Latitude introduces zones of climate, *e.g.*, tropical rain, subtropical steppe and desert, temperate rain and polar.

Clock, a device for measuring the passage of time. The earliest timekeeper was the shadow-clock, a primitive form of sundial, used in Ancient Egypt about 1500 B.C. To find the time at night the water-clock or clepsydra was used. The sand-glass dates from the 15th cent. No one knows when the first mechanical clocks were invented, but it is known that a complicated mechanical clock driven by water and controlled by a weighbridge escapement was built in Peking in 1090. The Dover Clock in the Science Museum is not the earliest surviving clock in England, as was once believed, but early 17th cent. The Salisbury Cathedral clock dates from 1386 and that of Wells Cathedral from 1392. The pendulum clock was invented by the Dutch scientist Christiaan Huygens (1625–95). The first watches were made in Nuremberg shortly after 1500. The marine chronometer is a high-precision timepiece used at sea for giving Greenwich mean time. The quartz-crystal clocks are accurate to one thousandth of a second a day, and the improved atomic clock, recently developed at the British National Physical Laboratory, which makes use of the natural vibrations of the caesium atom, is said to be an almost absolute measure of time (accurate to 1 sec. in 3,000 years).

Cloisonné, a kind of fine pottery with enamelled surface, decorated with elaborate designs, the outlines of which are formed by small bands or fillets of metal. The Byzantines excelled in this work, but in the 20th cent. Japan and China led in Cloisonné-ware.

Cloud chamber, an apparatus invented by C. T. R. Wilson in which the tracks of atomic particles can be made visible. Just as the vapour trails tell of the track of an invisible aircraft high up in the air, so the vapour trails of an unseeable particle can tell of its behaviour. The rays under investigation pass through a chamber containing a gas, *e.g.*, air thoroughly cleansed of dust, supersaturated with water- or alcohol-vapour. As the particle passes through it forms a track of tiny water droplets which can be photographed. Another ingenious device for tracking fast fundamental particles is the Bubble chamber (*q.v.*).

Clouds are formed by the ascent of moist air, the type depending on the way the air ascends and the height at which condensation occurs. There are three main classes: (1) high cloud (above 20,000 ft.)—cirrus (delicate and fibrous), cirrostratus (thin white veil), and cirrocumulus (delicately rippled) consisting of ice crystals; (2) medium cloud (above 7,000 ft.)—altostratus (dense, greyish veil) and altocumulus (broken flattened cloudlets)—chiefly water particles, often supercooled; (3) low cloud (from near ground to 7,000 ft.)—cumulus (fair weather, broken, dome-topped), cumulonimbus (heavy, towering to great heights), stratocumulus (layer of globular masses or rolls), stratus (like fog but off the ground), nimbostratus (low, rainy cloud). The highest clouds of all, and the rarest, are the noctilucent, seen only on summer nights in high latitudes. They form at about 50 miles above the earth and consist of ice-coated dust from meteors.

Clover, plants of the *Trifolium* genus, family *Leguminosae*, with about 250 species. These are "nitrogen fixing" plants and are cultivated extensively for fodder and green manure. The most widely used are Red Clover, White Clover (also an important source of honey), Alsike Clover, and Crimson Clover. Other interesting species are Subterranean Clover whose ripe flower heads reflex and bury themselves in the ground; strawberry clover, tolerant to soil salinity, found on shingle with fruits resembling strawberries, and shamrock.

Cloves are the dried flower-buds of a species of myrtle (*Eugenia caryophyllata*) grown principally in Zanzibar and Madagascar.

Clubmosses *or* **Lycopods.** *See* **F28(1).**

Coal is a carbonaceous mineral substance, commonly black and easily breakable, and may be either dull or shiny. It is very inflammable, and has formed for a long period the most important substance for fuel in employment in most civilised lands. It is composed of chemically altered vegetable matter, chiefly the timber of long extinct lycopodiaceous trees (*see* **Clubmosses**) and is found as a sort of stratified rock in the coal measures. Anthracite coal has lost nearly all its hydrocarbon by change or by pressure, and this and the more highly bituminous coals are greatly employed in manufacturing industries the world over, while those less so are used for household purposes. A ton of coal will yield by high temperature carbonisation from 10,000 to 15,000 cu. ft. of gas, 8 to 12 galls. of tar, 13¼ cwts. of coke and about 20 galls. of ammoniacal liquor, varying according to the class of coal used. It is calculated that in seams of one foot thickness or more to a depth of 4,000 ft., the proved resources of coal in Great Britain amount to 120,000,000,000 tons. Output in Great Britain is expected to be 170–180 million tons a year by 1970. In 1947 the British coal industry was brought under public ownership and all its assets were vested in the National Coal Board.

Coal Tar. A by-product in coal-gas and coke manufacture, it is a valuable source of organic intermediates, indeed over 20 different compounds have been isolated, many of which find use in such fields as the manufacture of soaps, fuel, cosmetics, detergents, and drugs as well as dyes. *See* **Benzene, Aniline.**

Coat of Arms, in heraldry, is a device containing a family's armorial bearings. In mediæval times it was an actual coat upon which such device was embroidered, and knights wore it over their armour.

Cobalt, a white metal melting at 1490° C. Two main ores are *cobalt glance* (in which the element is combined with arsenic and sulphur) and *smaltite* (cobalt arsenide). The principal sources are Ontario and the Congo. Various cobalt alloys are important, *e.g.*, stellite, ferrocobalt and carboloy. Its monoxide is an important colouring medium, and is used for colouring glass and porcelain-blue.

Cobra, hooded and very venomous snakes. The best known species are the Indian Cobra, the Egyptian Cobra, and the Black-necked Cobra. Their food consists chiefly of small rodents. The King Cobra is almost exclusively a snake-eater. "Spitting" Cobras (or Ringhals) of S. Africa are a related genus, capable of spitting their venom several yards.

Coca, a S. American shrub, *Erythroxylon coca*, also cultivated in Java. The leaves yield cocaine, classified as a dangerous drug; used medicinally as a local anaesthetic, especially on the eyes and in dentistry. When the natives chew the leaves they are enabled to withstand astonishing amounts of hunger and fatigue, as cocaine acts both as a mental stimulant and as an anaesthetic on the mucous lining of the stomach.

Cochineal *or* **Carmine,** a dyestuff consisting of the dried bodies of the female scale insect (*Dactylopius coccus*) which feeds on cacti. Of ancient origin, the dye was well known to the Aztecs, and was used widely in the Middle Ages. The famous scarlet tunics worn by the English during the Napoleonic wars owed their colour to carmine. To-day it is almost entirely replaced by aniline dyes.

Cockatoo, a member of the parrot family, bearing a crest of feathers on the head, native to Australia and adjacent regions. Predominant colour is white tinged with yellow or scarlet while some species have dark plumage. The great black cockatoo of New Guinea is slaty black with pale red cheeks and can crack Kanary nuts which usually require a hammer to break them open.

Cockchafer (*Melolontha*), one of the most destructive of beetles, the larvae feeding on roots. It is about 1 inch in length, of a brownish colour, and emits a loud whirring sound when flying.

Cockle, the popular name of the bi-valve shell-fish of the genus *Cardium*, found plentifully in sandy bays near low-water line; there are numerous British species.

Cockroach, inaccurately called the "black beetle"; a pest of bakeries and kitchens. In Britain two species are commonly found: the Common Cockroach (*Blatta orientalis*), resident since the time of Elizabeth I, dark brown, about an inch long, with the wing covers long in the male and short in the female; and the German Cockroach (*Blatta germanica*), now the most common, half the size, dark yellow, with both sexes fully winged. All species have long antennae and flattened, leathery, shiny bodies. They are nocturnal and omnivorous.

Cocoa. *See* **Cacao.**

Coconut Palm (*Cocos nucifera*), a tropical tree, growing to a height of 100 ft., with a slender, leaning trunk surmounted by giant feather-like leaves. One of the most important sources of food and raw material for people living in the tropics. The juice of the fruit, or coconut, is drunk; the kernel is eaten fresh or dried to form copra, which yields animal feeding stuffs and oil, used in the manufacture of soap, margarine, cosmetics, synthetic rubber, etc.; leaves are used for thatching; leaf stalks for canes, fence posts, needles, etc., and the trunk for houses and bridges. Main producing areas: Indonesia, Philippines, Malaya, Ceylon, and S. India.

Codes, a term used to designate a system of laws properly classified. The Code of Hammurabi, king of Babylon, *c.* 1700 B.C., had extensive influence over a long period. The Romans formulated several codes of historic importance including the Theodosian Code which summarised the Roman laws from the time of Constantine to 438 A.D. The final codification was made under order of the Emperor Justinian by his chief minister Tribonian and published in 529 with a new edition in 534. The most important of modern codes is the *Code Napoléon*, compiled between 1803 and 1810, and still in force. It has been used as an example for the codification of the laws of a number of countries from America to Japan. Under Frederick the Great the law of Prussia was codified. English law has never been codified, although the law on certain subjects has been gathered up into a single statute. A plan to codify and simplify the law was announced by the Government in 1965. *See* **C29(1).**

Codex, a manuscript volume of the Scriptures comprising the Sinaitic codex of the 4th cent., the Vatican codex of the same period, the Alexandrine codex of the 5th cent., and others. The British Museum, in 1933, purchased the *Codex Sinaiticus* from the Soviet Government for £100,000.

Coffee, a shrub found originally in Arabia and Abyssinia, but now extensively grown in the West Indies, Brazil, India, and Central America. It yields a seed or berry which, after undergoing the necessary preparation, is ground and largely used in most countries as a popular breakfast beverage. The best coffee is the Mocha, an Arabian variety. The stimulating effect of coffee is due to the caffeine, which is also present in tea. The beverage was introduced into Europe in the 16th cent., and the first London coffee shop was opened in 1632.

Coke is the solid residue remaining when coal is carbonised and nearly all the volatile constituents have been driven off. Used as fuel, and as an agent for reducing metallic oxides to metals, *e.g.*, iron ore to iron, in the manufacture of steel.

Colorado Beetle, a serious pest of potato crops. Both adults and larvae feed on the foliage where the orange eggs are laid. The grub is reddish, with two rows of small black spots on each side. The adults are about ½ in. long with yellow and black striped wing cases. The beetle is avoided by birds because of its nasty taste, and is controlled by arsenical sprays.

Colosseum, the name of the Flavian amphitheatre at Rome, begun by Vespasian and finished by Titus A.D. 80. In general outline it still remains one of the most magnificent ruins in the world. In the arena of this great building the famous gladiatorial displays and mimic naval battles used to be given, and about 50,000 spectators could be accommodated.

Colossus is the name which the ancients gave to any statue of gigantic size. The Colossus at Rhodes, which was a bronze statue of the sun god, Helios, was the most famous, and reckoned among the seven wonders of the world. It stood over 100 ft. high at the mouth of the harbour. There is no truth in the legend that ships could pass between its legs. It fell in an earthquake in 224 B.C.

Coluga, also known as "**flying lemur**", **caguan** or **kubuk**, a remarkable mammal which may be regarded as an aberrant insectivore or an aberrant form of the earliest ancestor of the bats. It has nothing to do with lemurs. There are two genera, one inhabiting the Philippines and one inhabiting Malaya. They have a parachute-like membrane which covers them from the neck to the tip of the tail, by means of which they can glide from treetop to ground a distance of up to 70 yards.

Column, in architecture, is an upright solid body serving as a support or decoration to a building. Columns consist of a pedestal, a shaft, and a capital, over which the supported entablature rises. They are named according to the styles of architecture of which they form part, being Doric, Tuscan, Ionic, Corinthian, or Composite as the case may be.

Comets are celestial bodies which move about the solar system in elliptical or hyperbolic orbits. Usually these star-like bodies are accompanied by a long shining tail. The hyperbolic comets are seen once only, and do not reappear; the elliptical comets are periodic, and their recurrence can be calculated with accuracy. The head of a comet is believed to consist of small lumps of solid matter accompanied by dust particles and gases such as carbon dioxide and methane. It used to be thought that the tail was produced by the pressure of sunlight on the cometary material but a modern explanation is that it is produced by the combined action of the solar wind (a continuous stream of ionised hydrogen originating in the sun) and the interplanetary magnetic field. When they run parallel the effect is to produce a long streaming tail pointing away from the sun. Chief among the periodic comets is Edmund Halley's, the first to return as predicted in 1757. It reappears about every 76 years and is next due in 1985. The most spectacular comet of the 19th cent. was that found by Donati in 1858.

Common Law, *See* **D4.**

Commons are unenclosed tracts of land sometimes dedicated to the use in common of the inhabitants of the township in which they lie. Many of these common lands were enclosed during the agrarian revolution in the Tudor period. The four chief rights of common are: (1) estovers—the right of taking wood for house building or firewood; (2) pasture, or right of grazing beasts; (3) turbary, or right of digging turf; (4) piscary, or the right to fish. *See* **Registration of Commons, C11.**

Commons, House of, the Lower House of the British Parliament. *See* **Section C, Part II.**

Commune of Paris has twice played a dramatic part in the history of France. In 1792 it was able, through its control of the administrative organisation of Paris, to override the National Assembly. In 1871, after the withdrawal of the Prussian troops, it tried to assert its authority. Public buildings were destroyed by members of the Commune and civil war raged during April and half May, but Government troops suppressed the rising.

Communism. *See* **J9.**

Compass *or* **Mariner's Compass** is an instrument by which the magnetic meridian is indicated, and comprises a horizontal bowl containing alcohol and water, a card upon which the thirty-two points of the compass are marked, and the steel needle which always points to the meridian. Although the discovery of the directive property of a magnet is credited to the Chinese, the first practical use of this property in a compass was made in western Europe in the 12th cent. Aircraft and ships now largely employ gyrostatic compasses which are not affected by electrical and magnetic disturbances. Sperry, Brown, and Anschutz are three important types of gyroscopic compass.

Concerto, a kind of hybrid between the Symphony and the Sonata. It may be regarded as a Symphony in which one instrument has a preponderance of solo passages or as a Sonata in which the solo instrument is accompanied by full orchestra.

Conclave, an assembly of Roman Catholic cardinals met together to elect a pope. The last Conclave was held in the Vatican in June 1963 when Cardinal Montini, archbishop of Milan, was elected Pope Paul VI.

Concordat, an agreement or convention between the pope and a secular government regarding ecclesiastical matters. The Concordat of Worms in 1122 between Calixtus II. and the Emperor Henry V. was famous as deciding a long struggle in regard to investiture. In 1801, Napoleon concluded a concordat with Pius VII. defining the restored relations between the head of the Church and the French Roman Catholics.

Condor, a large eagle of brilliant black plumage with a circlet of white feathers round its neck. It is a native of the Andes.

Confederation is a free association of sovereign states united for some common purpose. It is to be distinguished from a **Federation,** which is a union of states with one central government, each state relinquishing its sovereignty, though retaining some independence in internal affairs.

Confucianism. *See* **J10.**

Coniferae are cone-bearing trees, including firs, pines, cedars, cypresses, junipers, yews, etc., and are widely distributed in temperate regions.

Conservatism. *See* **J10.**

Consistory, a council or meeting of councillors; also the higher ecclesiastical courts and senates of the Anglican and Roman Churches.

Constable, an office of high rank in mediaeval times, and still, in some few offices, representing considerable dignity. The office of Lord High Constable of England existed until 1521, since when it has been revived temporarily for special occasions such as Coronations. Before the introduction of the police system in England, every hundred and parish had its constables upon whom devolved the duty of keeping the peace. The official designation of a policeman is police constable.

Constitution, the fundamental organic law or principles of government of a nation, state, society, or other organised body, embodied in written documents, or implied in the institutions and customs of the country or society. The government of the U.S.A., unlike Great Britain, works upon a written Constitution. It was framed when the U.S.A. came into existence as a sovereign body, when the Constitution built a republic out of a federation of thirteen states, based on representative government. The constitution was adopted in 1789, and its strength has been tested by the fact that, substantially unchanged, it is now the groundwork for a federation which now comprises fifty states.

Continent, a word used in physical geography to denote the larger continuous land masses in contrast to the great oceans of the earth. They are: Eurasia (conventionally regarded as 2 continents, Europe and Asia), Africa, North America, South America, Australia, and Antarctica.

Contralto, the feminine equivalent of the male alto. Where altos and contraltos are present in the same choir they sing the same part. But, whereas the alto is the highest adult male voice, the contralto is the lowest female voice.

Conurbation, a term which has been defined as "an area occupied by a continuous series of dwellings, factories, and other buildings, harbours, and docks, urban parks and playing fields, etc., which are not separated from each other by rural land; though in many cases in this country such an urban area includes enclaves of rural land which is still in agricultural occupation." The term has been widely adopted for the contiguous densely populated areas which form continuous urban areas. The seven officially recognised in Britain are: Greater London, West Midlands, S.E. Lancashire, West Yorkshire, Merseyside, Tyneside, Clydeside.

Convention is an assembly of delegates, representatives, members of a party met to accomplish some specific civil, social, political, ecclesiastical or other important object.

Convocation, an assembly called together to deliberate ecclesiastical affairs. In the Church of England the provinces of Canterbury and York each have their convocation. The term is also applied to assemblies of the graduates of certain universities.

Coot. A very widely distributed bird of the rail family and a common resident of the British Isles. The adult is black with a conspicuous white bald shield on the forehead and a white bill. The juvenile is brownish grey with whitish breast and throat. The coot flies heavily, but swims well. It dives frequently and can remain submerged for a considerable time. It is pugnacious and in winter gregarious. The food is chiefly vegetable. The large nest is usually built among aquatic vegetation and the young are fed by both parents. Another species, the Crested Coot, occurs in S. Europe.

Copper, one of the most familiar of metals, symbo Cu, used in ancient times as an alloy with tin in producing bronze, and preceding iron as an industrial material. Copper ores are mos abundant in the U.S.A., Chile, Canada, Zambia and the Congo. All copper compounds ar poisonous. Copper sulphate is largely used i calico-printing and in the production of blu and green pigments.

Copyright. Under the Copyright Act, 1956, copy right subsists in every original literary, dramatic musical, and artistic work if the author is British subject or a citizen of the Republic c Ireland or resident in the United Kingdom, c if the work is first published in the Unite Kingdom. The Act provides that, except i certain special cases, the author of the wor shall be the first owner of the copyright, and there are no formalities, such as registration or payment of fees, to be accomplished. Copyright includes the right to reproduce the work in any material form, to perform the work in public, or, if the work is unpublished, to publish the work. The Act also protects sound recordings, films, and television and sound broadcasts. Literary, dramatic, musical, and artistic works which enjoy the protection of the Act are automatically protected in those countries which are parties to the Berne Copyright Convention or the Universal Copyright Convention. In general, copyright in literary, dramatic, musical, and artistic works is vested in the author for the period of his lifetime and 50 years following, after which it passes into the public domain and becomes freely available to any who wish to make use of it. The Copyright Libraries, entitled to receive *gratis* copies of books published in the United Kingdom, are the British Museum, the Bodleian at Oxford, the University Library, Cambridge, the Scottish National Library, Edinburgh, Trinity College, Dublin, and with certain exemptions the National Library of Wales. The Government Department responsible for matters in connection with copyright is the Industrial Property Department, Board of Trade, 25, Southampton Buildings, London, W.C.2.

Coral, an order of small marine animals closely related to the sea-anemone, but differing from it in their ability to develop a limy skeleton. They multiply sexually and by budding. The structure of the coral secretions assumes a variety of forms, fan-like, tree-like, mushroom shape, and so forth. Red coral (the skeleton of *Corallium rubrum*) is mainly obtained from the Mediterranean. The coral reefs of the Pacific and Indian Oceans are often many miles in extent. Living corals occur only in warm seas at about 23° C. *See* **F22(2)**.

Cor Anglais (English horn = *corno inglese*). A tenor version of the oboe.

Cordite, a smokeless explosive adopted for small arms and heavy artillery by the British Government in the naval and military services in 1889, and composed of 58 parts of nitro-glycerine, 37 of gun-cotton, and 5 of vaseline. It is a jelly or plastic dough, and used in the form of sticks.

Cork, the bark of a species of oak, *Quercus suber*, grown largely in the South of Europe and North America. The cork tree is said to yield bark every six to ten years for 150 years, and grows to a height of from 20 to 40 ft. Its lightness, impermeability, and elasticity enable it to be used for a variety of commercial purposes, especially for stoppers of bottles.

Cormorant, a large, long-billed water-bird which captures fish by diving. It has bronze-black plumage with white cheeks and sides and is found around the sea coasts of most parts of the world, including the British Isles. It nests in colonies on sea cliffs and rocky ledges. The Shag or Green Cormorant is a smaller bird with green-black plumage and a crest.

Corncrake. *See* **Landrail.**

Cornet, an instrument which is fundamentally a small trumpet. Its tone is neither so bold nor so powerful as that of the trumpet, and it is therefore of use in small orchestras whose balance would be upset by the inclusion of trumpets.

Corn Laws were statutes intended for the benefit of British agriculture, and restricted import and export of grain. From the 14th to the mid-19th cent. such laws were in force, and were often of a stringent nature. They became so oppressive and caused corn to reach so high a price that the poorer classes were plunged into distress. A powerful anti-corn law agitation was organised, of which Cobden, Bright, and Villiers were the leaders, and Sir Robert Peel, in 1846, at the time of the Irish potato famine, carried through free trade. The repeal of the Corn Laws marked an important phase in the transformation of an agricultural to an industrial Britain.

Coronae, series of luminous rings surrounding sun or moon produced by the diffraction of light by water droplets in the atmosphere. Usually seen when sun shines through altostratus clouds. The outside of the ring is red and the inside bluish. *See* **Halo.**

Corpus Christi Festival is one of the great celebrations of the Roman Catholic Church, and takes place on the Thursday after Trinity. It was instituted by Pope Urban IV. in 1264.

Cortes, the name of the Parliamentary assemblies of Spain and Portugal.

Cosmic Rays, a form of radiation coming from outer space, of deep penetrating power and of great scientific interest. The rays are believed to consist chiefly of fast protons, with a few α-particles and other positive nuclei. By interacting with the gas of the atmosphere, these rays initiate a complex series of events, in the course of which other particles ("secondary radiations") are generated. The secondary rays contain virtually all the particles listed on **F14**; indeed, several particles were first discovered as secondary cosmic rays. Cosmic rays are investigated at and below sea-level, on mountains, in mines, in balloons, rockets, and satellites. Origin still unknown. *See* **F3(2)**.

Cotton, the name of a plant of several species, bearing large yellow flowers with purple centres. These centres expand into pods, which at maturity burst and yield the white fibrous substance known as cotton. The raw cotton contains a large proportion of seeds which are removed by "ginning." Long before the Christian era, cotton had been grown and used with great skill in India to make fabrics. The industry was not introduced into England until the middle of the 17th cent. when Protestant refugees from Flanders came to settle in the wool textile districts of East Anglia and Lancashire. With improvements in machinery and expansion of overseas trade in the 18th and 19th cent., Lancashire became the centre of the world's cotton industry. Since the first world war there has been a marked decline in Britain's cotton industry. Cotton reacts with nitric acid to form gun cotton, which is combined with more sensitive explosives to give a more safely handled substance.

Coulomb, a unit of electric charge, named after the French naval engineer, Charles Augustin de Coulomb (1736–1806), equal to the quantity of electricity transferred in one second by a current of one ampere. *See* **N13**.

Counterpoint (adj. **contrapuntal**). The weaving together of two or more distinct melodies to create harmony.

County. The word county was introduced after the Norman conquest as an equivalent of the old English "shire." England has 41 geographical counties, Wales 13, Scotland 33, and Ireland 32. The number of administrative counties differs from the number of geographical counties because the division for Local Government purposes is made on grounds of convenience. Under the London Government Act, 1963, the county of Middlesex was completely absorbed in Greater London.

Coup d'Etat, a violent change in the government of a state carried out by force or illegally. Examples are the overthrow of the French Republic in 1851 by Louis Napoleon, who then became Emperor, and more recently the military *coups* in the Middle East which brought about the abdication of Farouk of Egypt in 1952 and the assassination of Feisal of Iraq in 1958.

Court Leet, a court of record held annually before the steward of any particular manor or lordship; originally there was only one court for a manor, but in the time of Edward I. it branched into two, the court baron and the court leet.

Coypu or **Nutria rat**, a large beaver-like rodent found in S. America; now wild in E. Anglia, where it is causing damage to dykes, reeds, and crops, having escaped from farms where it is bred for its fur.

Crane, a large, graceful wading-bird with elegant long legs and neck, greyish plumage, superficially resembling the heron and related to the bustard. They migrate in V or W formation and have trumpet-like voices. There are several species, found in all continents except S. America, including the Crowned Crane with golden coronet and the Demoiselle with tuft-like crest of white feathers. The Common Crane nested in East Anglia in mediaeval times but now comes only as a rare visitor from the Continent.

Credit is an advance of money or of goods or services in consideration of a promise of payment later. Trade credit is such an advance from trader to customer; bank credit is an advance of money by a bank to a client, whether a business firm or a private person, in consideration of an interest payment by the borrower.

Creed, a brief enumeration of a particular belief or religion. The three important Christian creeds are the Apostles' Creed, the Nicene Creed, and the Athanasian Creed.

Cremation, the ancient custom, revived in modern times, of burning the dead. Many scientific men commend the practice on hygienic grounds, particularly in densely populated countries. Cremation was first legalised in Great Britain in 1885 and the first crematorium opened at Woking in that year. Application for cremation must be accompanied by two medical certificates.

Cricket, a genus of insects of the grasshopper order which move by leaps. The male produces a chirping noise by rubbing its wing-covers together.

Crimean War (1853–56). This war between Russia and the allied powers of Turkey, England, France, and Sardinia, was connected with the Eastern Question (*q.v.*) and the desire of Russia for a port on the Mediterranean. Chief engagements were the Alma, Balaclava, and Inkerman. Fighting virtually ceased with fall of Sevastopol in Sept. 1855. Treaty of Paris signed March 30, 1856.

Crocodile, the name of the largest existing reptile, and classed with the alligator and the gavial. The crocodile inhabits the Nile region, the alligator the lower Mississippi, and the gavial is found in many Indian rivers.

Crow, a family of birds including many well-known species such as the rook, raven, jackdaw, carrion crow, hooded crow, magpie, nutcracker, jay, and chough.

Crusades were military expeditions undertaken by some of the Christian nations of Europe with the object of ensuring the safety of pilgrims visiting the Holy Sepulchre and to retain in Christian hands the Holy Places. For two centuries nine crusades were undertaken: First, 1095–99, under Godfrey of Bouillon, which succeeded in capturing Jerusalem; Second, 1147–49, led by Louis VII. of France, a dismal failure, which ended with the fall of Jerusalem; Third, 1189–92, in which Richard I. of England took part, making a truce with Saladin; Fourth, 1202–4, led by French and Flemish nobles, a shameful expedition, resulting in the founding of a Latin empire in Constantinople; Fifth, 1217–21, led by John of Brienne; Sixth, 1228–29, under the Emperor Frederick II.; Seventh, 1248–54, under St. Louis of France; Eighth, 1270, under the same leadership, but cut short by his death on an ill-judged expedition to Tunis; Ninth, 1271–72, led by Prince Edward of England, which accomplished nothing. Millions of lives and an enormous amount of treasure were sacrificed in these enterprises and Jerusalem remained in the possession of the "infidels." The chief material beneficiaries were the Italian maritime cities; the chief spiritual beneficiary was the pope; but in literature and the arts both Europe and the Levant benefited enormously from the bringing together of the different cultures.

Crystal, in everyday usage, a solid chemical substance bounded by plane surfaces which show a regular geometrical arrangement as, *e.g.*, quartz crystals, rock salt, snow flakes. In physics the term means any solid whose atoms are arranged in a regular three-dimensional array. This includes most solids, even those not particularly crystalline in appearance, *e.g.*, a lump of lead. Common *non*-crystalline substances are liquids, jellies, glass.

Cubism, the name of a revolutionary movement in art created in the years 1907–9 by the two painters Picasso and Braque. Rejecting purely visual effects, they approached nature from an intellectual point of view, reducing it to mathematical orderliness. Its respectable grandparent was Cézanne who had once written: "you must see in nature the cylinder, the sphere, and the cone"—a concept which, together with the contemporary interest in Negro sculpture, moved the two founders of the movement to experiment with the reduction of natural forms to their basic geometrical shapes. In practice, this meant combining several views of the object all more or less superimposed in order to express the idea of the object rather than any one view of it. The name Cubism was derisive and the movement aroused the same opposition as Impressionism, Fauvism, and the later Futurism. Picasso's *Young Ladies of Avignon* was the first Cubist painting and his "Head" (1909) the first Cubist sculpture. Three phases are recognised: (1) Cubism under the influence of Cézanne; (2) high or analytical Cubism (*c.* 1909–12) concentrating on the breaking-down of form to the exclusion of interest in colour; (3) synthetic Cubism (*c.* 1913) making use of *collage* in which pieces of pasted-on paper (illustrations, wallpaper, newspaper) and other materials were used in addition to paint. Amongst other early cubist painters were Metzinger, Gris, Duchamp, and Léger.

Cuckoo, a well-known migratory bird which is found in Great Britain from April to July, hawk-like in shape, with a very characteristic note, uttered during the mating season only by the male. The hen has a soft bubbling call. It lays its eggs in the nests of other birds, *e.g.*, the meadow pipit and hedge sparrow, but only one egg in each nest. Feeds mainly on insects, particularly hairy caterpillars.

Cuneiform, the term applied to the written arrow-headed characters found in Assyria, Persia, and Mesopotamia. Good examples may be seen in the British Museum, some of them several thousand years old.

Curfew, the bell which William the Conqueror ordered to be rung at eight o'clock each night in the towns and villages of Britain, as a signal to the inhabitants to extinguish lights and go to bed. It originated in the fear of fire when most cities were built of timber. It was abolished in 1100, but at Ripon, Sandbach, Chesham, Penrith, Ibberton, Wokingham, it is still rung as a matter of custom.

Curie, a measure of the rate at which radioactive material emits radiation. One curie is a disintegration rate of $3{\cdot}7 \times 10^{10}$ disintegrations per second.

Curlew, a wading-bird of which there are several species. It frequents marshy places, feeds on worms, insects, molluscs, and berries and possesses a very long, down-curved bill.

Currency is the name given to the types of cash money—metal or paper—in use in an area (*e.g.* pound, sterling, dollar, franc). It also designates the actual coins or notes issued. Its amount is usually subject to regulation by the Government, or by a Central Bank acting on the Government's behalf. *See also* **N9, 26.**

Cybernetics, the science concerned with the automatic control and communication processes in both animals and machines. Thus it is concerned with brain function, information theory, electronic computers, and automation.

Cyclone, a term usually applied to a tropical revolving storm. Cyclones often occur towards the end of the hot seasons and are mainly confined to tracks in the western areas of the oceans, being known as hurricanes (Caribbean and Pacific), cyclones (Indian Ocean), and typhoons (China Seas). The circulation of air in a cyclone is similar to that in the *depression* of temperate latitudes, but the region of low pressure is much more localised and the pressure gradients steeper. Winds of hurricane strength and torrential rain occur generally, although at the centre of the storm there is a small area, known as the "eye," where fair, calm weather prevails.

Cyclotron, a machine for accelerating charged particles such as protons to very high energies. Devised by E. O. Lawrence in California in 1930, it uses a magnetic field to make the particles traverse nearly circular paths and an electric field to give them an additional pulse of energy each time round. The accelerated particles impinge on targets, and the resulting events are a basic source of information for nuclear physicists. The cyclotron is obsolescent and has led to the development of other machines, *e.g.*, betatrons, synchrotrons.

Cyrogenics, the technology concerned with the production, maintenance and employment of temperatures close to absolute zero (−273° C) and with the study of the physical phenomena which manifest themselves in these conditions; a subject of intensive research in Britain.

D

Dactylopterus, a fish of the gurnard family, with wing-like pectoral fins; sometimes known as the flying fish, though that appellation is more generally given to *Exocaetus exiliens*.

Dadaism (French *Dada* = hobby-horse) was a hysterical and nihilistic precursor of **Surrealism** (*q.v.*) resulting from the shock produced by the first world war. Beginning in Zurich about 1915, it spread to other continental cities, such as Berlin and Paris, dying out in 1922. The movement was deliberately anti-art, destructive, and without meaning; it intended to scandalise by such tricks as "compositions" made out of anything that came to hand—buttons, bus tickets, pieces of wire, bits of tin, etc. Other excesses included incoherent poetry, Dada night-clubs, plays, and short-lived newspapers. Many Dadaist painters became Surrealists at a later stage, but where Surrealism is a deliberate attempt to present subconscious and dream-like images, Dadaism was sheer anarchism. Among its chief exponents were Hans Arp, Marcel Duchamp, André Breton, Guillaume Apollinaire, and Max Ernst, all of whom subsequently became noted in more reputable ways.

Daddy Longlegs, or **Crane-fly,** a slender long-legged fly of the family Tipulidae. The larvae which do damage to lawns and plants are called leather-jackets. The Americans call Harvest-men (*q.v.*) daddy longlegs.

Dafila, a genus of river duck, with long, supple tail, found in Europe, Asia, and America, related to the pintail duck.

Daguerreotype, a first practical photographic process, invented in Paris by M. Daguerre during the years 1824–39. The light-sensitive plate was prepared by bringing iodine in contact with a plate of silver. After exposure a positive image came by development of the plate in mercury vapour. Even for open-air scenes the first daguerreotypes involved exposure of 5–10 minutes. The wet collodion process (1851) rendered the technique obsolete.

Dail Eireann, the name of the national parliament of the Irish Republic.

Dalmatic, a wide-sleeved ecclesiastical vestment, reaching below the knee. Worn by bishops and deacons over the alb or stole.

Dama, the generic name of the fallow deer, which is fawn coloured or brown, with white spots.

Damaskeening, the art of inlaying one metal upon another, largely practised in the East in mediaeval times, especially in the decoration of sword blades.

Dandies, the name given to a class of exquisites prominent in early Victorian days, and who attracted attention by excessive regard for dress. Their feminine counterparts were the dandizettes.

Danegeld, a tax imposed in England in Anglo-Saxon times to raise funds for resisting the Danes or to buy them off. Edward the Confessor abolished the tax, but it was revived by the Conqueror and subsequently retained, under another name, after the danger from the Danes was past. It is the basis of all taxation in this country. Domesday Book (*q.v.*) was originally drawn up for the purpose of teaching the State how to levy the tax.

Danelaw, the law enforced by the Danes in the kingdoms of Northumbria, East Anglia, and in the districts of the five (Danish) boroughs—lands grouped round Leicester, Nottingham, Derby, Stamford, and Lincoln—which they occupied during the Viking invasions of the 9th and 10th cent. The country occupied was also called the Danelaw or Danelagh.

Darter, 1. Snakebirds, a genus of the pelican family, with long, pointed bill and serpent-like neck and resembling cormorants in appearance. There are 5 species. 2. Numerous species of small freshwater fish belonging to the Perch family, found in N. America.

Date Palm, *Phoenix dactylifera*, one of the oldest known food plants widely cultivated in N. Africa and W. Asia. It grows to 100 ft. and continues to bear for 2 or 3 centuries, its fruit being of great value as a food. From the leaves the Africans make roofs for their huts; ropes are made from the fibrous parts of the stalks; and the sap furnishes a stimulating beverage.

Dauphin, the title borne by the eldest sons of the Kings of France from 1349 to the Revolution of 1830.

Day is the most natural unit of time and may be defined as the period of rotation of the earth relative to any selected heavenly body. Relative to the sun it is called the *solar day*. Relative to a fixed star it is called the *sidereal day*. Owing to irregularities in the earth's movements, the time taken for the earth to rotate through 360° relative to the sun is variable, and so the *mean solar day* of 24 hours has been introduced, which is the average throughout the year. The *mean solar day* is our standard, used for purposes of the calendar, and astronomers use *sidereal* clocks to check mean solar time. In practice, for convenience, the sidereal day is determined by the earth's rotation relative to the vernal equinox or first point of Aries, and is equal to 23 hours 56 minutes and 4·091 seconds of mean solar time (*i.e.*, about 4 minutes shorter than a solar day).

D.D.T. (dichloro-diphenyl-trichloroethane). A very powerful insecticide which has had wide success in the control of diseases, such as malaria and typhus, which is carried by insects. Mosquito swamps are sprayed with D.D.T. to kill the carriers.

Deacon, an ecclesiastical official, who assists in some of the smaller ministerial duties in church or chapel; in the Anglican Church he ranks below a priest.

Dead Languages are such as the ancient Greek and Roman tongues, which are no longer spoken but are preserved in literature.

Dead Sea Scrolls, a group of ancient Jewish documents, consisting of scrolls and fragments which have been recovered since 1947 in the vicinity of Qumran near the Dead Sea and which represent one of the most important finds ever made in the field of biblical archæology and Christian origins. The scrolls, written in Hebrew or Aramaic, were found in caves, the first by chance by an Arab shepherd in 1947. These consisted of biblical texts older by a thousand years than the earliest Hebrew manuscript of the Old Testament (A.D. 895). Many fragments have since been discovered, comprising the whole of the Old Testament with the exception of Esther. In addition there are commentaries and other non-biblical writings, including one called "The War of the Sons of Light with the Sons of Darkness." The writing on the scrolls indicates that they were written over a period of two centuries, the greater proportion before the birth of Christ. A nearby ruin is believed to have been the home of a religious sect to whom the scrolls belonged. By the aid of the latest scientific techniques, including radiocarbon tests, the age of the scrolls is being accurately determined.

Dean, a Church of England dignitary, ranking below a bishop, and the head of the chapter of a cathedral. A rural Dean supervises a *deanery* or group of parishes. There are also Deans of Faculties in some universities, and at Oxford and Cambridge the *Dean* is in charge of chapel services and disciplinary arrangements.

Death Watch Beetle (*Xestobium rufovillosum*), a wood-boring beetle, larger than the common furniture beetle, found chiefly in the old oak beams of churches and other historic buildings. The grub bores from 4–12 years. The name "death watch" comes from the superstition that the ticking sound, made by the beetle striking its head against the wood, is a sign of approaching death. *See also* **Furniture Beetle, Woodworm.**

Decalogue, name given to the Ten Commandments of the Old Testament. There are two versions of them, differing in detail: Exodus xx. 2–17 and Deuteronomy v. 6–21. They are of Hebrew origin and are recognised by Jews and Christians as the divine law given by God to Moses on Mt. Sinai. Most of them are prohibitions in contrast to the beatitudes (pronounced by Christ in the Sermon on the Mount) which are positive, *e.g.*, Blessed are the merciful.

December, the last month of the year in our calendar, and the tenth in the old Roman.

Deciduous Trees are such as shed their leaves at certain seasons as distinguished from evergreens or permanent foliaged trees or shrubs.

Decimal System is based on the unit of **10. Duodecimal System** is based on the unit of 12. Fractional numbers are expressed as divisions of 10 and 12 respectively. Thus:

Fraction	*Decimal*	*Duodecimal*
$\frac{1}{2}$	0·5	0:6
$\frac{1}{3}$	0·3333	0:4
$\frac{1}{4}$	0·25	0:3
$\frac{1}{5}$	0·2	0:2497
$\frac{1}{6}$	0·1666	0:2
$\frac{1}{8}$	0·125	0:16
$\frac{1}{12}$	0·0833	0:1
$\frac{1}{24}$	0·04166	0:06

Decimal currency was imposed on France in 1795. A changeover to decimal coinage in 1971 has been accepted by the British government. *See* **Metric System.**

Declaration of Independence was an Act by which the American Congress, on July 4, 1776, declared the American colonies to be independent of Great Britain. "Independence Day" is a holiday in the United States.

Deemster is the title of the two judges in the Isle of Man.

Defender of the Faith (*Defensor Fidei*), a title conferred upon Henry VIII. by Pope Leo X. in 1521 for entering the lists against Luther with his book on *The Assertion of the Seven Sacraments.* In 1554 the title was confirmed by Parliament and has been used even since by English sovereigns.

Deflation is a policy designed to bring down costs by reducing the supply of means of payment. It is usually advocated as a remedy for inflation, and in this connection is often referred to as Disinflation. It usually results in a fall in employment. The "credit squeezes" in Great Britain were designed to have a disinflationary effect.

Dehydrate, to eliminate the water from a substance. The process of dehydration is now used in the food industry, as a result of wartime research, in making such things as dried egg and packet soups. Most vegetables contain over 90% of water, and much of this can be removed under vacuum at low temperatures without appreciably impairing the flavour. The lightness of the dehydrated products is an advantage to expeditions and the army in transporting supplies.

Deliquescence, the process of dissolving by the absorption of moisture from the atmosphere. For instance, chromic acid crystals on exposure to the air quickly deliquesce.

Delta, a triangular tract of land between diverging branches of a river at its mouth, and so called from its general resemblance to the Greek letter Δ *delta.* The best-known examples are the deltas of the Nile, the Ganges, the Niger, and the Mississippi.

Deluge, a flood, commonly applied to the story of the Deluge in the Bible, in which Noah and the Ark figure. A similar tradition lingers in the mythologies of all ancient peoples.

Democratic Party, one of the two great American political parties, originated about 1787, advocating restrictions on the federal governments and in opposition to the federalists. It was in 1825 that a group who were in favour of high tariffs seceded later to become the Republican Party. In 1960 Kennedy narrowly won the Presidency and in 1964 Lyndon Johnson swept in with a landslide victory over the Republican candidate.

Demoiselle, the Numidian crane, a wading-bird. Also, a sub-order of dragon flies which close their wings over their backs when at rest.

Dendrite, any stone or mineral on or in which appears natural tracery resembling trees, leaves, or flowers, the result of the action of the hydrous oxide of manganese.

Density, a measure of the mass per unit volume of a material, usually expressed in grams per cubic centimetre. *Specific gravity* is the ratio of the density of a material at the temperature under consideration to that of water at the temperature of its maximum density (4° C.). In grams per cubic centimetre the density of gold is 19·3, silver 10·5, lead 11·3, water 0·99997, air 0·00129.

Depreciation of a currency is a fall in its relative value in terms of gold or of other currencies. The term is most often used to indicate a fall in the value of one country's money in relation to others.

Depression, a region where barometric pressure is lower than that of its surroundings. These areas of low pressure enclosed by the isobars are usually less extensive than anticyclones and may vary from 100 to 1,000 miles in diameter. The winds, often of gale force when the depression is deep, blow round the system in an anticlockwise direction in the Northern Hemisphere (in the reverse direction in the Southern Hemisphere) and inwards across the isobars. The majority of depressions which cross the British Isles travel from the Atlantic, sometimes in series or families, at rates of between a few miles and 700 miles in a day, bringing their generally unsettled weather with them.

De Profundis (out of the depths), the first two words of the Latin version of the 130th Psalm, and commonly used to designate this psalm.

Descant. An additional contrapuntal part, often much ornamented, woven in with an existing part. The vocal descant is one of the earliest uses of counterpoint.

Deserts, vast, barren, stone or sandy wastes where there is almost no rainfall and little or no vegetation. These regions are found in the interior of the continents Africa, Asia, and America between 20° and 30° north and south of the equator. Europe is the only continent without deserts. The most famous are the Sahara, the largest in the world, the Gobi desert of central Asia, the Kalahari desert of south-west Africa, and the great Australian desert.

Detention Centres in Britain are for young people (boys and girls) aged at least 14 but under 21 who have been found guilty of an offence for which an adult could be sent to prison. *See* **D36.**

Detergent, a cleansing agent. Grease and fats are not soluble in water, but detergents cause water to spread out (*see* **Surface Tension**) and wet the surface of greasy articles, so dissolving the grease and removing dirt. Detergent molecules have two distinct parts: one is water soluble, the other is fat soluble, and they act by dissolving in both fat and water and taking the fat, as a fine suspension, into the water.

Deuterium or "heavy hydrogen." The second isotope of hydrogen; the third is called tritium. Deuterium atoms have in their nuclei a neutron as well as a proton; tritium nuclei have two neutrons and one proton. In ordinary hydrogen gas about one out of every 5,000 atoms is a deuterium atom. Deuterium was discovered in 1932 by Professor Harold Urey. The oxide of deuterium corresponding to water is called "heavy water." The nucleus of the deuterium atom is called a deuteron. An anti-deuteron consisting of an anti-proton and an anti-neutron was produced at Brookhaven in 1965, the first compound anti-nucleus ever to be produced.

Devaluation is a definite, official downward valuation of a country's currency in terms of its exchange value with other currencies.

Devil-fish, a strange marine fish of large size and o[f] several species. As it is met with in Europea[n] waters it is called the fishing frog, and the chie[f] American species is the giant ray.

Devonian System in geology refers to the strat[a] between the Silurian and the Carboniferou[s] Formations. It includes the Old Red Sand[-]stone Formation. The fauna of the Devonia[n] include the group of fishes known as the Rhipid[-]istra (on the evolutionary route towards th[e] amphibians), Actinistia (cœlacanth), and th[e] Dipnoi or lung fishes. *See* **F30.**

Dew, moisture deposited by condensation of wate[r] vapour on exposed objects especially durin[g] calm, cloudless nights. The loss of heat fro[m] the ground after sunset, by radiation, cause[s] the layer of atmosphere close to the surface to b[e] chilled below the temperature, known as th[e] dew-point, at which the air is saturated wit[h] vapour. Part of the vapour condensed may b[e] transpired from blades of grass and foliage o[f] plants.

Dew Pond is a shallow artificial pond which is o[n] high ground and rarely dries up, even durin[g] prolonged droughts, despite being used b[y] cattle and sheep as a drinking source. Th[e] name arose from the belief that dew deposits a[t] night provided the moisture for replenishmen[t]. Drainage of rain-water and mist condensed o[n] neighbouring trees and shrubs are probab[ly] more important factors.

Dextrin, a white, odourless, viscid substance of the same composition as starch, from which it is obtained. It is used as gum, being the material put on the backs of postage stamps and other articles which are required to be made adhesive. It also is utilised in calico printing.

Dialectical Materialism. *See* **J12.**

Diamond, a mineral, one of the two crystalline forms of the element carbon (the other is graphite), the hardest known substance, used as a gem and in industry. India was the first country to mine diamonds (the Koh-i-noor, known since 1304, came from Golconda near Hyderabad). The celebrated diamond mines of South Africa were discovered in the 1870s. Other important diamond producing countries are Angola, Sierra Leone, Congo, Tanzania, Guyana, and the Soviet Union. Antwerp is the most important diamond centre in the World.

Diapason. The concord of the first and last tones of an octave and the fixed rule by which organ pipes are arranged to proper pitch. The open metal flue pipes which form the basis of an organ are called the diapason "stops." Their pitch is expressed in terms of length, *e.g.*, 4-ft. diapason, 8-ft. diapason, 16-ft. diapason. The pitch of other pipes is related to that of the diapason: *e.g.*, a trumpet, which is a reed stop, may be said to have an 8-ft. tone, *i.e.*, its pitch is the equivalent of an 8-ft. diapason.

Diatoms. One-celled algae, common in fresh and salt water. Distinctive feature is the siliceous wall which is in two halves, one fitting over the other like the lid of a box. These walls are often very finely and beautifully sculptured. The diatoms constitute a class of the plant kingdom known as the Bacillariophyta. *Diatom ooze* is a deep-sea deposit made up of diatom shells. *Diatomite* or *diatomaceous earth* is the mineral form that such diatom oozes assume (sometimes known as kieselguhr which mixed with nitroglycerine yields dynamite).

Diatonic Scale. The ordinary major and minor scales on which most European music is built, *e.g.*,

C major C – D – E – F – G – A – B – C
Tone intervals 1 – 1 – ½ – 1 – 1 – 1 – ½
C minor C – D – E♭ – F – G – A♭ – B – C
Tone intervals 1 – ½ – 1 – 1 – ½ – 1½ – ½

Dies Irae (the Day of Wrath), a famous 13th-cent. Latin hymn, sung at burial services, and taking its place in translated form in the English hymnology.

Diesel Engine. A compression-ignition engine. The air in the cylinder is compressed to over 500 lb. per sq. in. and its temperature is about 800° F.; oil injected into the hot compressed air ignites immediately. The modern oil engine has been evolved mainly from the principles enunciated by Herbert Akroyd-Stuart in his patent of 1890 and, like the steam and other inventions, represents the improvements achieved by many men including those by Rudolf Diesel of Germany, in respect of high compression pressures and greater fuel economy.

Diet, in German history, an assembly of dignitaries or delegates called together to debate upon and decide important political or ecclesiastical questions. The most famous imperial Diets were those held at Worms (1521), Speyer (1529), and Augsburg (1530), all of which dealt with matters of religious conflict arising from the Reformation.

Diffusion is the process of mixing which occurs when two liquids or gases are in contact. It is most rapid between gases, and, as laid down by Graham's law, "the rates of diffusion of different gases are in the inverse proportion to the square roots of their relative densities." Diffusion arises through the continual movement of molecules. Even in solids diffusion can occur. If a block of gold and a block of silver are welded together, after some time particles of gold are found in the silver, and *vice versa*.

Dimensions in common speech are the magnitudes of length, breadth, and thickness giving the size of an object, thus a line has only one dimension: length; a plane surface two: length and breadth; and a solid three: length, breadth, and thickness. In mathematics, hypothetical objects with any number of dimensions are considered. In physics and mechanics, dimensions are numbers which relate the units in which any quantity is measured to the so-called fundamental units. The latter are usually but not necessarily those of length, mass, and time. "Dimensional analysis" is an important technique of scientific reasoning.

Dimorphism, the quality of assuming two distinct forms. For instance, carbon, which is graphite in one form, is the diamond in another.

Dinosaur, the name given to a group of extinct reptiles of the Mesozoic period, some of which were of immense size—much larger than crocodiles. *See* **Diplodocus.**

Diocese, a territory under the pastoral authority of a bishop. The term originated in the time of the Roman Empire, and represented then an administrative rather than an ecclesiastical territory.

Diopside, a variety of pyroxene occurring in prismatic crystals, chemically calcium magnesium silicate. Two light-green varieties, malacolite and alalite, are gemstones.

Dioptase, or emerald copper, a scarce copper ore occurring in prismatic emerald green crystals, and composed of silicate of copper.

Diorite, an igneous rock of crystalline structure composed of felspar and hornblende. It used to be classed as greenstone.

Dip Needle. Instrument for measuring the *dip* or inclination of the earth's magnetic field.

Diplodocus, one of the best known of the extinct mammoth dinosaurs. Fossil remains have been discovered in the Jurassic rocks of the United States. Some reached a length of over 80 ft.

Dipnoi *or* **Lung Fishes.** These have the air bladder adapted to function as a lung, and they can remain alive when the stream or marsh in which they live dries up. Species of lung fish occur in Australia, Africa, and S. America.

Diptera, an order of insects. Their main characteristic is that they are two-winged, and the common house-fly is the best-known example. There are at least 50,000 species of these insects, including gnats, blow-flies, mosquitoes, tsetses.

Diptych was a folding two-leaved tablet of wood, ivory, or metal, with polished inner surfaces, utilised for writing with the style by the ancient Greeks and Romans. The same term was applied to the tablets on which the names of the persons to be commemorated were inscribed in the early Church. In art any pair of pictures hinged together is styled a diptych.

Dirge, a hymn or song of mourning and lamentation, usually a combination of music and words.

Discus, a circular piece of metal or stone about 12 in. in diameter, used in athletic contests by the ancient Greeks and Romans. Throwing the discus was a very favourite game, which was deemed worthy of celebration in Myron's famous *Discobolus* (*c.* 460 B.C.–450 B.C.), the best copy of which is in Rome.

Disk, an astronomical term denoting the seemingly flat surface of celestial bodies as seen by the eye.

Distillation, a process used to separate liquids of different boiling points. This is effected by placing the mixture in a distillation apparatus and heating. The liquid with the lower boiling point distils over first, the vapour being condensed and collected, forming the first *fraction*. With continued heating the second liquid reaches its boiling point, distils over and the mixture is said to be *fractionated*. Mixtures of liquids with close very high boiling points require more elaborate apparatus. Fractional distillation is a common process in the chemical industry, particularly in the refining of petroleum.

Divertissement, a short musical entertainment which is usually accompanied by dancing.

DNA (**Deoxyribonucleic acid**), a polymer molecule in the form of a double-strand helix containing many thousands of sub-units. Contains the genetic information coded in sequences of sub-units called bases. *See* **Nucleic Acids.**

Docks are enclosed water spaces where ships rest while being loaded or unloaded, or waiting for cargo. There are three main types: the wet dock (*e.g.*, King George V dock, London) is for loading and unloading; the dry dock, or graving dock (*e.g.*, King George V. dock, Southampton) is for overhauling and repairing vessels, and is so constructed that, after a ship has been docked, the water can be drawn off; the floating dock is a type of dry dock.

Dodo, an extinct bird, giant and flightless, which lived on the island of Mauritius up until 250 years ago. Another species, the white dodo, lived on Réunion. Some reached exceptional sizes. By the end of the 17th cent. Mauritius, Rodriguez, and Réunion had all been colonised, and the dodo along with many other birds vanished forever because of their inability to stand up to man and the animals imported into the islands.

Dog-days, a period of 40 days (3 July–11 Aug.) when Sirius rises and sets with the sun. The ancient superstition, which can be traced back in Greek literature to Hesiod (8th cent. B.C.), was that this star exercised direct influence over the canine race.

Doge, the chief magistrate in the former republics of Venice (697–1797) and Genoa (1339–1797, 1802–5).

Dogfish, a large family of small sharks, seldom more than 3 ft. in length. The flesh is sold as "rock salmon." The eggs are contained in horny cases called "mermaid's purses." The commonest of the British dogfishes are the spur-dogs.

Dog Licences are necessary for household dogs of six months of age or over. The cost per dog is 7*s.* 6*d.*, and the licence can be obtained at any Post Office. Dogs for tending sheep or cattle, or for leading blind persons, are exempt.

Dolce, a musical term indicating that the music has to be rendered softly and sweetly.

Doldrums, a nautical term applied to those areas of the Atlantic and Pacific towards which the trade winds blow and where the weather is calm, hot, and sultry but liable to change suddenly to squall, rendering navigation difficult.

Dolomite, a name applied to a limestone containing appreciable magnesium; also the mineral dolomite, a double carbonate of magnesium and calcium.

Doloroso, a musical term denoting a sorrowful or plaintive style of playing.

Dolphin, an ocean mammal of the whale order, from 6 to 8 ft. long, with a long, sharp snout, and of an active disposition. They abound in most temperate seas and swim in shoals. A few species live in large rivers (Ganges and Amazon). They can cruise for long periods at around 15 knots and produce bursts of speed in the region of 20 knots, the water apparently flowing smoothly past their bodies.

Dome, a large cupola, hemispherical in form, rising over the main building of a cathedral or other prominent structure. The finest existing dome, that of the Pantheon at Rome, is also the oldest, dating from the time of the Emperor Hadrian. It is 142 ft. in diameter and about the same in height. The dome of St. Peter's, in the same city, has a double shell, is 330 ft. high and 140 ft. in diameter. The dome of the cathedral at Florence is 139 ft. in diameter and 310 ft. high, and that of St. Paul's, London, has 3 shells and is 112 ft. in diameter and 215 ft. high. The circular reading-room of the British Museum has a dome 140 ft. in diameter and is 106 ft. high. Malta's Mosta dome is also famous.

Domesday Book is the famous register of the lands of England framed by order of William the Conqueror. According to Stowe, the name was derived from *Domus dei*, the name of the place where the book was deposited in Winchester Cathedral; though by others it is connected with doom in the sense of judgment. Its compilation was determined upon in 1084, in order that William might compute what he considered to be due to him in the way of tax from his subjects. William sent into each county commissioners to make survey. They were to inquire the name of each place, the possessor, how many hides of land were in the manor, how many ploughs were in demesne, how many homagers, villeins, cottars, serving men, free tenants, and tenants in soccage; how much wood, meadow, and pasture; the number of mills and fish ponds; what had been added to or taken away from the place; what was the gross value at the time of Edward the Confessor. So minute was the survey that the Saxon chronicler of the time reports "there was not a single hide, nor one vintage of land, nor even, it is shame to tell, though it seemed no shame to do, an ox, nor a cow, nor a swine was left that was not set down." The record, which did not take in Northumberland, Cumberland, Durham, and parts of Lancashire and Westmorland, was completed on Nov. 15, 1085, and was comprised in two volumes—one a large folio, sometimes called the Little Domesday, which deals with Essex, Norfolk, and Suffolk, the other a quarto, sometimes called the Great Domesday. The first is written on 384 double pages of vellum in one and the same hand, and in a small but plain character, each page having a double column. The quarto is written on 450 pages of vellum, but in a single column and in a large, fair character. The original is preserved in the Public Record Office. *See also* **Danegeld.**

Domesday Machine, a hypothetical weapon which would give its owners the power to wipe out the whole of humanity. This evil idea follows logically from present-day arms-race military thinking. The argument is that with the development of nuclear weapons of ever greater explosive power one or both sides in the "cold-war" may become so powerful that only a weapon so terrible could act as the ultimate "deterrent." The A-bomb (now a mere "tactical" weapon) and the H-bomb have also played this rôle.

Dominant, in music, the fifth tone of the modern scale, and the reciting tone in the Gregorian scale.

Dominicans, an order of mendicant preaching friars founded by St. Dominic in Languedoc in 1215 and confirmed by the Pope in 1216. The rule of the order was rigorous. The dress was a white habit and scapular with a long black mantle. This gave them the name of Black Friars. Their official name is Friars Preachers.

Don, originally a Spanish title of nobility, but now accorded as a courtesy title. Also applied to a person with an academic appointment at the Universities of Oxford and Cambridge.

Donjon, the keep, or inner tower of a castle, and the strongest and most secure portion of the structure. This was the last refuge of the garrison, and there was usually a prison on the lower floor, hence the name *dungeon*.

Don Juan, the legendary hero of many famous works, supposedly based on the life and charac-ter of the unscrupulous gallant Don Juan Tenorio of 14th-cent. Seville. The first drama-tisation of the legend and the most famous is Tirso de Molina's *El Burlador de Sevilla*. Don Juan was also the subject of Molière's *Le Festin de Pierre*, Mozart's *Don Giovanni*, Byron's *Don Juan*, and José Zorilla's *Don Juan Tenorio*. The latter is played on All Saints' Day through-out Spanish-speaking countries.

Don Quixote, the "knight of the doleful counten-ance," the hero and title of Cervantes' classic novel of 16th-cent. Spain. Don Quijote de la Mancha, a gentle country gentleman of lofty but unpractical ideals, having read many chival-ric romances, believes he is called upon to redress the wrongs of the world. Mounted on his nag Rosinante and accompanied by his companion Sancho Panza, a hard-headed and practical peasant, he sets out on his journeys of knight-errantry

Dormouse, a family of small, squirrel-like rodents widely distributed throughout Europe and Asia, and living mainly on fruit and nuts. It is of nocturnal habits and sleeps through the winter.

Dot, a French term indicating the property which a wife brings to her husband on marriage and is usually settled on the woman, being her separate property, though the income from it may go towards the general household expenses.

Dotterel, a handsome bird of the plover family found in northern Europe and Siberia. Nests in the Cairngorms, the Grampians, and E. Ross. Very tame.

Double-Bass. The largest and deepest-toned instrument of the Violin family. The Violon-cello corresponds with the vocal bass so the the pitch of the Double Bass has no vocal counterpart—hence its name.

Double-entendre, a corruption of the French phrase "double entente," and used in English to indicate a word or sentence of indelicate double meaning.

Doukhobors. *See* J12.

Drachm (or **Drachma**), an ancient Greek silver coin and weight. One drachma was equivalent to six obols. The word has survived as the name of a weight: Avoirdupois, one-sixteenth part of an ounce; Apothecaries' Weight, one-eighth part of an ounce.

Drag. Term used in mechanics for resistance offered by a fluid to the passage of a body moving through it. When speed of sound is reached drag increases abruptly. The lift/drag ratio gives the aeroplane designer his measure of aerodynamic efficiency.

Dragon, a fabulous monster common to folk-lore in most countries; generally represented as a winged reptile with fiery eyes and breath of flame. A dragon guarded the garden of the Hesperides; in the New Testament there is mention of the "dragon, that old serpent, which is the devil"; St. George, England's patron saint, is supposed to have overcome the dragon; mediaeval legend abounds in dragons. In heraldry it has also a conspicuous place; and in China was the imperial emblem.

Dragonade, the term given to the series of persecutions of Huguenots in France in the reign of Louis XIV., just before and after the revocation of the edict of Nantes, dragoons being chiefly employed in the work. Since then the term has been used in reference to any onslaught on the people by soldiers.

Dragonet, the name of the fish of the *Callionymus* genus, beautifully coloured, and about a foot in length. They are common on the British coast and in the Mediterranean.

Dragon Fly, the common name of a well-known order of insects having two pairs of membraneous wings, and often of very brilliant colours. They are swift of flight and may be seen hovering over sheets of water in the sunshine all through the summer. Their chief food is mosquitoes.

Dragon's Blood, a dark-red resinous substance obtained from the fruit of a Malay palm, and possessing medicinal virtues. In a special technique used for making line blocks in printing, dragon's blood is used.

Drama. The word *drama* comes from a Greek word meaning to do or to act, and it is from Greece that the play originates (at least, so far as the West is concerned). Plays have their origin in the long-ago past when players dressed up as various supernatural beings to perform rituals designed to make the gods carry out desired actions. Three or four hundred years B.C. such playwrights as Aeschylus, Sophocles, and Euripides began to write plays partly religious and partly secular for the pleasure of their audiences: this was one of the greatest periods the theatre has seen, and such plays as *Oedipus Rex* and *Antigone* still give pleasure in our own theatres. Roman drama was of little significance in general, and the next important stage in the history of the theatre is the Catholic mystery play of the Middle Ages, which, at the time of the Renaissance, developed into the play as we know it now. In England the great Elizabethan playwrights Webster, Ford, Shakespeare were in the forefront of this movement. Cromwell disapproved of the theatre, and the next important stage is the Restoration Drama following the Restoration of the monarchy in 1660. The only European achievement comparable to that of Britain in the history of the stage is that of France with such great playwrights as Molière and Racine. In the 19th and 20th cent. the great playwrights have been Oscar Wilde, Shaw, and others in Britain; Pirandello in Italy; Ibsen in Norway; Strindberg in Sweden; Hauptmann in Germany; Chekov and Turgenev in Russia. There are signs that the drama in verse is once more becoming popular in this country with such writers as T. S. Eliot and Christopher Fry. A summary such as the foregoing cannot include the great dramas stemming from another tradition in Asia—the plays of Japan, China, and India. The characteristics of modern English drama are dealt with in **Section I.**

Drawbridge, a bridge that can be lifted up so that no passage can be made across it. It was a usual feature of a fortified castle in the Middle Ages, and was raised or lowered by chains and levers. It spanned the fosse, and on the approach of an attacking party was raised and formed a special barricade to the gate. Modern drawbridges are such as are raised to allow of the passage of boats up and down a river or estuary. The Tower Bridge is a famous London bridge of this type.

Drongo. The King Crow or Indian Black Drongo is frequently seen in India perched on branches or telegraph wires, darting suddenly to catch insects and to attack crows and hawks. Other members of the family are found in Asia, Africa, and Australia. Its plumage is black with steel-blue gloss.

Drosophila *or* **Fruit Fly.** More has been learnt by geneticists from breeding experiments with this insect than with any other.

Dross, the name generally applied to the refuse of molten metal, composed of slag, scales, and cinders.

Drought, a period of dry weather, is a normal and recurring condition in many warm climates, and is frequently provided against by irrigation. In the British Isles really long rainless spells are somewhat rare, and an "absolute drought" is defined officially as a period of at least fifteen days on each of which the rainfall is less than $\frac{1}{100}$ inch. The summer of 1959 was wholly without precedent in all parts of Britain for lack of rainfall, abundant sunshine, and warm weather. In South Yorkshire an absolute drought lasted 59 days, the longest period in British records.

Drum. There are three main kinds of drum: the bass drum, the side drum, and the kettle drum.

BASS DRUM: a large shallow wooden cylinder whose ends are covered with skin or parchment rendered taut. It is used in a vertical position and beaten on both sides with padded leather hammers. Much used by military bands to beat out the rhythm of a march.

SIDE DRUM. A smaller version of the bass drum, sometimes with a metal body. It is used horizontally and played on the upper side with a pair of wooden drumsticks or, in dance bands, with a wire brush. Jazz-drummers use a combination of bass drum and several side drums on which complicated solo passages may be performed. To increase the rattle, strings of catgut may be strung across the lower parchment. The drum is then called a snare drum.

KETTLE DRUM: a large copper bowl whose mouth is covered with parchment. The tension of the parchment may be altered by means of hand-screws so that the drum may be tuned to a particular note. In a normal orchestra there are two kettle drums known collectively as the tympani.

Drupe is the scientific term for stone fruit. The stone forms the inner part (endocarp) of the fruit, and encloses a seed or kernel which is liberated after the fleshy part (pericarp) has rotted.

Dry-rot, the term was first used about 1775 to describe the fungal decay of timber in buildings. Creosote distilled from coal tar is the standard material for preservation of timber, and pentachlorophenol and copper naphthenate are two compounds now extensively used. Dry wood always escapes dry-rot. Chief fungi causing dry-rot are *Merulius* and *Poria*.

Duck, water bird smaller than the related goose and swan, which together form the family Antidae. Duck refers to the female, drake to the male. The duck family falls into two separate groups: the river or freshwater (surface feeding) ducks, such as the mallard, pintail, wigeon, shoveler, mandarin, teal, garganey; and the sea (diving) ducks, such as the goldeneye, pochard, scoter, eider, and the fish-eating mergansers or "sawbills." The ancestor of all domestic breeds, with the exception of the muscovy, is the mallard.

Duck-bill, *Ornithorhynchus anatinus*, also duck-billed platypus, a fur-covered, egg-laying, nest-building mammal inhabiting Australia and Tasmania. It has webbed feet and a muzzle like a duck's bill and is about 20 in. long.

Ductility is a property possessed by most metals which renders them capable of being stretched without breaking. Gold is the most, and lead the least ductile of metals, the order being gold, silver, platinum, iron, copper, palladium, aluminium, zinc, tin, lead. In animated nature the spider and the silkworm produce secretions of notable ductility.

Dugong. A marine mammal, belonging to the order Sirenia (sea-cows). Inhabits Red Sea and Indian Ocean; also found as far East as the Philippines and Australia. Lives on seaweed. Related to the Manatee.

Duke, the highest rank in the British peerage next to that of a royal prince. Edward, the Black Prince, eldest son of Edward III., who died before his father, was the first English duke, being created Duke of Cornwall in 1337. Since then all Princes of Wales have held that title.

Dukeries, a range of English woodland and park country, mainly in Nottinghamshire, comprising the adjacent demesnes of several English dukes and nobles. The Dukeries include Sherwood Forest and the estates of Welbeck Abbey, Clumber Park, Worksop Manor, and Thoresby Hall.

Dulcimer. An instrument of stretched wires which are struck by hammers held in the hands. It is the logical precursor of the pianoforte.

Dunes. Sand dunes are elliptical or crescent-shaped mounds of loose sand produced by wind action. The dune has a gentle slope on windward side; a steep slope on the leeward side.

Dunlin, very common small wading-bird of the Sandpiper family nesting in Britain. Its range extends to other areas where it also breeds.

Dunmow Flitch, a custom which originated in the parish of Little Dunmow, Essex, in the reign of Henry III., which was that the husband who was prepared to swear before the prior, convent, and townsfolk of Dunmow that he had not repented of marriage or quarrelled with his wife for a year and a day, should be rewarded with the gift of a flitch of bacon. The custom has frequently been revived.

Dunnock (*Prunella modularis*), a small bird of rich brown and dark grey plumage common in gardens and hedgerows. Sings a cheerful song all the year round. Called hedge-sparrow in southern England. Another member of the same family, the larger Alpine Accentor (*Prunella collaris*), is found on rocky mountain slopes of Europe and Asia.

Duodecimo, a sheet of paper folded into twelve leaves, written "12mo."

Durbar, a term used in India from the Persian word *darbár* meaning "court" or "audience." It may be either a council for administering affairs of state, or a purely ceremonial gathering. The word was applied to great ceremonial gatherings like Lord Lytton's durbar for the proclamation of the Queen-Empress in 1877 and the Delhi durbar of 1911.

Dust, solid particles of matter floating in the atmosphere, produced chiefly by volcanic eruptions, sand-storms in desert regions, and industrial and domestic smoke. When the island of Krakatoa erupted in 1883, more than 1 cubic mile of dust was thrown into the air and carried three times round the earth by the explosion wave. The particles in dust-storms are much finer than those in sand-storms and are swept up to far greater heights. The local whirlwinds which form over loose dry soils are termed dust-devils.

Dyke. A wall-like intrusion of igneous rock which cuts across the bedding or other layered structure of the country rock; the word also signifies in alternative usage, a sea-wall and an open drain.

Dynamite, a powerful explosive whose chief element is nitro-glycerine. It was discovered by Nobel in 1867, who absorbed nitro-glycerine in kieselguhr; has a disruptive force of about eight times that of gunpowder.

Dynamo. Machine for transforming mechanical energy into electrical energy. Depends on principle of electromagnetic induction whereby a current is produced in a conductor (*e.g.*, copper wire) traversing a magnetic field. The two essential parts of a dynamo are the conductors or *armature* and the *field magnets*.

Dynasty, a succession of monarchs of the same family, as the Carlovingian dynasty, the Bourbon dynasty, the Plantagenet dynasty, etc.

E

Eagle, large bird of prey with huge hooked bill, related to the buzzard, kite, hawk, harrier, falcon, and vulture, together forming the family Falconidae. There are many species to be found throughout the world, the Golden, Imperial, Tawny, Spotted, and Lesser Spotted being found in Europe. The Golden Eagle, a magnificent-looking bird, nests in the Scottish Highlands, and the White-tailed Sea Eagle, which used to breed in Britain, is now only an occasional visitor. The eagle has been the symbol of royal power since the earliest times, and the American or Bald Eagle is the emblem of the United States.

Earl, a British title of nobility of the third rank, duke and marquis coming first and second. The title dates from Saxon times, and until 1337 ranked highest in our peerage.

Earl-Marshal, in England ranks as the eighth of the great officers of state, is head of the College of Arms, attends the sovereign in opening and closing the session of Parliament, arranges state processions (especially coronations) and assists in introducing newly created peers in the House of Lords. The office is hereditary in the family of the Dukes of Norfolk.

Earth, our habitable globe, is the third of the planets of the solar system in order from the sun, and on an average throughout the year takes 24 hours to turn completely round relative to the sun, the whole earth revolving round the sun in a slightly elliptical orbit once in a year of 365·2564 days. The mean distance of the earth from the sun is 93,004,000 miles. The shape of the earth is that of an oblate spheroid, its equatorial and polar axes measuring 7,926 miles and 7,900 miles respectively. Earth satellite studies have shown that it is also slightly pear-shaped, with the stalk towards the north pole. The scale of this effect is such that the south pole is 50 ft. nearer the centre of the earth than the north pole. The crust consists of an outer layer of surface soil of varying thickness, beneath which there is a mass of hard rock several miles deep, the percentage (by weight) of the principal elements present being oxygen 47, silicon 28, aluminium 8, sodium and potassium 5, iron 4·5, calcium 3·5, magnesium 2·2, titanium 0·5, hydrogen 0·2, carbon 0·2, phosphorus and sulphur 0·2. Mass of the earth is estimated to be 6,000 million million million tons. Two-thirds of the earth's surface is covered with water. It has only one satellite, the moon. The earth receives more light from the sun in 13 seconds than it does from the moon in one year. Weather changes are independent of the moon. A recent estimate of the age of the earth's crust is 5,300 million years. Recent discoveries suggest that the earth is embedded in the atmosphere of the sun and that some of the heat that reaches us from the sun gets here by direct conduction through interplanetary space. *See* **F8–9.**

Earthquake, a sudden violent disturbance of the earth's crust; the region of the surface immediately above the "focus," or source where the earthquake originates, is termed the "epicentre." On account of their destructive power earthquakes have attracted attention from the earliest times, but accurate study dates only from the last century and the development of a world-wide network of recording stations from the present one. The majority of severe earthquakes result from fractures, usually along existing faults, in underlying rock strata subjected to great strains, the shearing movement sometimes extending to the surface. These dislocations set up vibrations which are propagated as waves throughout the bulk of the earth or round the crust. Frequently the main shock is followed by a series of smaller aftershocks. Minor local earthquakes may be attributed to the effects of volcanic activity, but most of the larger ones originate in non-volcanic regions along well-marked lines of weakness in the earth's crust. Generally the ground is felt to tremble, undergoing oscillations which may gradually or suddenly increase to a maximum and accompanied by sounds. Where there is movement of the sea-bed a tidal wave may result. One of the greatest of historic times was that which destroyed and flooded Lisbon in 1755. Among the notable shocks of the present century rank those of San Francisco (1906), Messina, Italy (1908),

Tokyo, Japan (1923), Napier, New Zealand (1931), N.E. Assam (1950), Ionian Is. (1953), Agadir (1960), Chile (1960), Skopje, Yugoslavia (1963).

Earthworm, of which there are several species, has a cylindrical body, tapering at both ends, and segmented into rings. It moves by contraction of its rings, aided by retractive bristles; is eyeless, but has a mouth, gullet, and stomach. Earthworms exist in immense numbers, and perform an important part in the scheme of nature by loosening the soil and rendering it more amenable to tillage. They also form a valuable food for birds and many mammals, and are unequalled as bait for certain kinds of fish. *See* **F22(2).**

Earwig, a genus of insects possessing two pairs of wings and anal forceps. It is nocturnal lives on vegetable matter, and hides by day under stones or in flowers, *e.g.*, dahlias. The old belief that it deliberately creeps into people's ears is altogether unfounded. *See* **T29(2).**

Easter, the annual Christian festival in commemoration of the resurrection of Christ, the English name being derived from Eostre, goddess of Spring. The date cannot fall earlier than March 22 nor later than April 25. Many disputes arose among the early Christians as to the proper time to celebrate this day which governs all other movable feasts. It was eventually ruled at the Council of Nicaea in 325 that Easter Day should be the first Sunday after the full moon following the vernal equinox. If this happens to be a Sunday, then Easter Day is the Sunday after. It should be remembered, however, that this moon is a hypothetical moon of the ecclesiastical calendar, quite imaginary, and generally one or two days later than the real moon we see in the heavens. In fact the reverend fathers at Nicaea did us a bad turn in having anything to do with the moon but then they had no Astronomer Royal to advise them of the complications. *See also* **N24.**

Eastern Question, a term formerly applied to the problems arising from the instability of the Mohammedan power of Turkey and its relations with the other nations of Europe. Later connected with other problems of the Near East, such as the possession of Constantinople and the position of the Balkan states.

East India Company was incorporated by Elizabeth in 1600. In 1613 the Company set up a factory at Surat, India, and in 1662 Bombay came under the Company's influence and developed into an important trading port. Dupleix wanted to establish French power in India and a struggle for supremacy took place. Clive gained the victory for England and thenceforward British dominion in India remained undisputed except by native princes. In 1772 Warren Hastings was appointed the first Governor-General and in 1784 Pitt's India Act established a Board of Control for the India Company. A great increase of trade resulted, and this rule continued down to 1858, when, as a result of the mutiny, the Crown assumed the sovereignty. With the passing of the Indian Independence Act of 1947, British dominion ended and India was handed back to the Indians.

Eau-de-Cologne, a popular distilled perfume first manufactured at Cologne in the 18th cent. by Johann Maria Farina, an Italian, and since made in large quantities in Cologne and elsewhere.

Ebony, a name applied to various hard black woods, the best of which are grown in Mauritius and Ceylon. There are also Indian and American varieties. Only the inner portions, the heartwood, of the trees are of the necessary hardness and blackness. Ebony is largely used in ornamental cabinet work, for piano keys, canes, etc.

Ecce Homo ("Behold the Man!"), used in reference to the pictures and sculptures representing Christ crowned with thorns.

Ecclesiastical Courts, courts for administering ecclesiastical law and maintaining the discipline of the Church of England. Introduced by the Normans. Originally they had jurisdiction over both clergy and laity. *See also* **D24(1).**

Echidna. *See* **F23(2).**

Echinodermata. *See* **F23(1).**

Eclipse, an obscuration of the light of the sun, moon, or other heavenly body by the passing of another body either between it and the eye or between it and the source of its light. The sun is eclipsed by the moon intervening between it and the earth; the moon by the earth passing between it and the sun. Total eclipses of the sun have occurred over parts of the British Isles in the years 1424, 1433, 1598, 1652, 1715, 1724, 1927, 1954 (visible from the Shetland Is.), and the next will be seen only from near Land's End on Aug. 11, 1999.

Ecliptic is the sun's apparent path in the sky: the great circle described by the sun from west to east in the course of a year. The sun is exactly on the equator on approx. March 21, and Sept. 23, and the points where the celestial equator and ecliptic intersect on these days are called the *equinoctial points.* On approx. June 21 and Dec. 22 the sun reaches its greatest and least midday elevation and its greatest distance north and south of the equator, and the points on the ecliptic on these days are called the *solstices* (*see* **Seasons, N24**). These four points are equidistant from each other by 90°. The equinoctial points are not fixed. The angle of inclination of the ecliptic to the equator is called the obliquity of the ecliptic, which is also variable, being influenced by the gravitational action of the other planets on the earth. At present the angle is 23½°.

Ecumenical Council. *See* **Oecumenical Council.**

Edda, the name given to two important collections of early Icelandic literature—*the Elder or Poetic Edda,* poems handed down from the 9th and 10th cent., probably Norwegian in origin, and the *Younger* or *Prose Edda* of Snorri Sturluson compiled about 1230. They treat of mythical and religious legends of an early Scandinavian civilisation.

Eddystone Lighthouse stands on a group of rocks about 9 miles from the Cornish coast and 14 from Plymouth. The present structure is the fourth that has occupied this dangerous position. The first was of wood, completed by Winstanley in 1700, but three years later washed away, its architect with it. In 1709 a second and stronger wood lighthouse was built by Rudyard. This lasted until 1755, when it was destroyed by fire. Smeaton built the third lighthouse, of granite and Portland stone, on the model of an oak trunk, and this, which was finished in 1759, withstood the storm and tempest for over a hundred years, being superseded by the present building, erected in 1879–82 by Sir James Douglas. It is wholly of granite. Its light can be seen over 17 miles, and in foggy weather it gives an explosive signal every 5 minutes.

Edelweiss, a white perennial flower of the daisy order, common in Alpine regions.

Edentata. *See* **F23(2).**

Education, History of. *See* **J13.**

Eels, edible fishes of the order Apodes, with snakelike body covered with minute scales embedded in the skin. The common or freshwater eel *Anguilla anguilla* is found in the Atlantic coastal areas of N. America and Europe and in the Mediterranean, and breeds S.E. of Bermuda. The electric eel of S. America is a variety of great interest, being able to cause electric shocks.

Egg-plant *or* **Aubergine,** a plant cultivated for its ovate fruit, varying in colour from dark purple to white.

Egret, a slender, graceful bird of the heron family, of pure white plumage, famed for its beautiful silky plumes (aigrettes), which appear in the breeding season, and for which it was ruthlessly hunted and would have been exterminated had not international action been taken to protect it. The Little Egret with black bill, black legs, and yellow feet breeds in Mediterranean lands.

Ego. *See* **Freudian Theory, Section F, Part III.**

Egyptian Vulture is smaller than other vultures. Found in S. Europe, frequents native villages and scavanges for offal.

Eider, a large diving duck, found along the rocky coasts of northern latitudes, well known for the beautifully warm soft down, called "eider down," which the female bird plucks from her breast to line her nest. In Norway and Iceland the haunts of the eider are preserved and the birds protected by law on account of the much prized "eider down," which is collected from the nests just before the breeding season. "Eider down" is so elastic that a pound or two of it will fill an ordinary bed covering.

Eiffel Tower, built by the French engineer Alexandre Gustave Eiffel (1832–1923) for the Paris Exhibition of 1889. The tower which is made of iron is 985 ft. high and weighs about 7,000 tons.

Eisteddfod (a sitting) was originally a congress of Welsh bards and minstrels, and dates from before the 12th cent. These assemblies, discontinued for a long period, were resumed in 1819, and have been held yearly since, each lasting three or four days. Their object is to foster the Welsh patriotic spirit; they are devoted to orations and competitions in poetry, singing, and harp-playing, prizes being awarded to the successful contestants.

Eland, the largest species of antelope, a native of Africa; has large pointed horns, stands 5 feet highat the withers, and weighs several hundred pounds.

Elateridae, a family of beetles of numerous species with short legs and indented antennae. Commonly known as Click-beetles or Shipjacks. Their larvae are the wireworms which cause so much damage to farm crops.

Elder, small trees of the *Sambucus* genus, with pinnate leaves, and clusters of white flowers and, later, small purplish-black berries. The black elder, the best known, is common in most parts of Europe, and thrives in Britain. A wine is made from its berries.

El Dorado, a "golden land," was an idea much favoured in the days of the early Spanish explorers. It was believed that somewhere on the South American continent there was a country abounding in gold and precious stones. Many expeditions were fitted out to discover it. Sir Walter Raleigh also went forth on this illusive quest. The term is still used in regard to any place of rich promise.

Electret, a piece of solid matter which retains a permanent electric polarisation analogous to the magnetic polarisation of a permanent magnet. There are various recipes for making them; carnauba wax is a common constituent.

Electric Light is produced in several ways, commonly by causing a tungsten wire to heat up to incandescence by passing a current through it. Current may also be forced through ionised gases, causing them to glow. Such discharges include neon lights, sodium and mercury-vapour street-lamps, and various intense electric arcs used for technical purposes. In fluorescent lights an electric discharge causes ultra-violet (invisible) light, which then excites luminosity in certain chemical substances called luminescent materials. Other forms of electric lighting are being investigated.

Electric Telegraph may be said to date from 1836, when Sir Charles Wheatstone and his co-inventor Cooke introduced their Single-Needle instrument, which was soon followed by the Double-Needle apparatus. Morse, in 1837, invented his famous recording instrument. The first electric cable was between Dover and France, and was laid in 1850. The first Atlantic cable was laid in 1858, and the second in 1866. It was in 1899 that the first Marconi wireless telegraph messages were sent between England and France.

Electrolysis is the condition established when an electric current passes through a conducting substance, between electrodes, resulting in decomposition and separation into constituents. Water thus becomes decomposed into hydrogen and oxygen.

Electrometer, an instrument for measuring differences of electrical potential. The moving part, perhaps a needle, is affected by electrostatic forces and no current flows through the instrument. High sensitivity can be obtained.

Electron. *See* **F10, 14.**

Electron Microscope. A microscope in which beams of electrons are focused by magnetic lenses in a manner analogous to the focusing of light beams in the ordinary optical microscope. Modern electron microscopes have very high resolving power and can magnify up to 1,500,000 times, making it possible to explore the cell and the virus. A development of the electron microscope is the scanning electron microscope (stereoscan), recently developed at Cambridge, which can examine an essentially thick object, giving a very large depth of focus. *See also* **F20(1).**

Electron-volt, unit of energy used in nuclear physics. 1 Mev = 1 million electron-volts, 1 GeV = 1000 million electron-volts.

Electronics. The science which deals with the behaviour and control of free electrons. It started with the discovery of the electron by Sir J. J. Thomson in 1897. The practical applications, constituting electronic engineering, have given us radio, radar, photo-electric cells, cathode-ray oscillographs, electron microscopes, television. Nowadays electronics uses devices like transistors such that the electrons move inside solid matter instead of *in vacuo*. This is sometimes referred to as "solid state electronics." *See* **Microelectronics, Section F.**

Electrophorus, a simple device for producing static electricity, consisting of a smooth disc of resin or ebonite mounted on a metal base and with a metal cover carrying an insulated handle. The disc is first electrified (negatively) by rubbing it with a dry catskin or flannel and the cover replaced, the upper surface receiving a positive charge and the lower a negative. On lifting off the cover, after having touched it with the finger, the negative charge leaks away to earth and the positive charge is isolated on the cover. The action may be repeated a number of times before it is necessary to replenish the original charge on the disc. Of historical interest only.

Elements. In chemistry, an element is a substance in the simplest form to which it has been reduced. Ninety elements are found naturally on the earth, one is observed spectroscopically in the stars, and a further twelve have been made artificially. Between them these elements can appear in some 1,200 different isotopes, of which 317 occur in Nature. (There are 274 stable isotopes among 81 stable elements.) *See* **F9(2), N32.**

Elephant, a proboscidian mammal of which only two species survive—the Asiatic, in India, and the African elephant. No other animals possess a trunk. Both males and females have large ivory tusks, of considerable commercial value. The Indian elephant is usually about 9 ft. high and weighs about 3 tons; African elephants are larger, weigh about 6 tons, and are usually much fiercer. Several fossil elephants of still larger bulk have been discovered, including the mammoth and the mastodon. The Indian elephant is domesticated and used as a beast of burden, and may live 70 years.

Eleusinian Mysteries, festivals common throughout ancient Greece, agricultural in their symbolism.

Elgin Marbles, a collection of ancient Greek sculptures and architectural fragments got together by the 7th Earl of Elgin and brought to England between 1802 and 1812. These celebrated treasures had originally formed part of the Parthenon at Athens, and were probably carved by pupils of the sculptor Phidias. Lord Elgin expended over £70,000 upon them, and they were purchased for £35,000 for the British Museum, where they can now be seen displayed.

Elk, the largest animal of the deer family, possessing enormous antlers, and standing, when mature, about seven feet high. The American moose is of the same family.

Elm, a stately, wide-spreading tree having some 20 species spread over north-temperate regions, several of which are native and peculiar to Britain. The grandest of the field elms is the English elm, *Ulmus procera*, which may reach a height of 140 ft. and a girth of 25 ft. The wych elm, *U. glabra*, or Scots elm, is a valuable hardwood and used in boat-building.

Elzevir, the name of a celebrated family of Dutch printers, who produced editions of Latin, French, and German classics, which were highly valued for their beauty of type and accuracy of printing. They flourished in the 17th cent.

Embalming, the process by which dead bodies are preserved from decay by means of spices and drugs. The art reached perfection in ancient Egypt, as the mummies which still exist so powerfully testify. In modern times many experiments in embalming have been tried, with various degrees of success.

Ember-days are set apart for fasting and prayer in the Western Church, at the periods appointed for ordination, viz., the Wednesday, Friday, and Saturday after the first Sunday in Lent, Whit-

Sunday, Sept. 14 (Holy Cross Day), and Dec. 13 (St. Lucia's Day). They are of very ancient origin.

Embossing, the art of stamping in relief letters or designs upon pliant substances.

Embryology, that branch of biology which deals with embryos, tracing their development from fertilisation of the germ or seed to birth.

Emerald. The rich green variety of beryl (beryllium aluminium silicate). The colour is due to the presence of chromium oxide.

Emery, a granular substance of the corundum order, generally mixed with other metallic substances, and used in a powdered state for polishing and grinding purposes. Emery is mined in Asia Minor and the Grecian archipelago.

Enamel, a vitrified substance applied as a coating to pottery and porcelain. The art was practised by the Assyrians and Egyptians, and was introduced into Europe by way of Greece. Enamels are all either of the transparent or opaque kind, and are susceptible to an immense variety of colouring, according to the metallic oxides introduced.

Encaenia, a festival commemorating a dedication; at Oxford University the annual commemoration of benefactors, accompanied by the conferring of honorary degrees, is held in June.

Encyclical Letters, a term used in reference to letters addressed by the Pope to his bishops upon matters of doctrine or discipline.

Encyclopaedists, a term first applied to the eminent writers who collaborated in the French *Encyclopédie* (1751–65). They included Diderot, D'Alembert, Voltaire, Helvetius; their writings generally were sceptical as to religion, destructive as to politics, and had great influence in popularising the social ideas which afterwards resulted in the French Revolution.

Energy. One of the most fundamental concepts of science A body in motion possesses *kinetic energy* as a result of the *work* done by the forces creating the motion. But a force which does work to stretch a spring does not create motion. Instead, the work is stored up in the spring and is one example of *potential energy*. A raised body also possesses potential energy which turns into kinetic when the body falls. The *heat energy* contained in a body is the sum of the kinetic and potential energy of the constituent atoms which are vibrating all the time. Heat and motion are obtainable from electrical, magnetic, chemical, atomic, and other sources, and physicists therefore define corresponding forms of energy. The vital point is that all forms of energy are transferable into one another *without loss or gain*. This is the Law of Conservation of Energy. It is one of the most fundamental laws of science, and its general validity is the reason why energy is an important idea. Since Einstein, it has been recognised that mass also is interchangeable with energy. *See* **F13**, *also* **Nuclear Energy.**

English Language is composed of many elements. Anglian, Saxon, Norman French, Scandinavian, Dutch, and the various underlying contributions from Latin and Celtic sources. The result is a strong, expressive, composite language now spoken by all races of English descent, and is the mother tongue of over 200 million people living in Britain and the Commonwealth and the United States of America. *See* **A7**, 1362.

Engraving is the art of cutting or otherwise forming designs of pictures on wood, stone, or metal surfaces for reproduction by some method of printing. Wood-engraving was the earliest in the field, dating from the 15th cent. Later, engraving on steel and copper plates was introduced, and mezzotint, lithography, stipple, aquatint, etc. With the development of photography, and an increased knowledge of the use of acids, many readier methods of engraving were adopted, and now wood-engraving, which was formerly resorted to for all general engraving purposes, is comparatively little used. What is styled "process" engraving is the most utilised.

Ensilage, a method of storing and preserving fodder, vegetables, etc., in pits dug in the ground and excluded from air or light. The system was practised in ancient Rome and revived in England in the 19th cent.

Entablature, that portion of a building which surmounts the columns and extends to the roof of the tympana of the pediments; it comprises the architrave, the frieze, and the cornice.

Entomology is the study of insects. *See* **Insects.**

Entrepreneur. An entrepreneur or undertaker, is a firm which brings together the factors of production needed for producing goods or services, undertaking the risks and uncertainties involved—though it may transfer some of them by insurance or by other methods. The entrepreneur may be either an individual or a company or corporation, private or public.

Enzyme. Organic catalysts which accelerate chemical processes occurring in living organisms. Examples are: *lipase*, which speeds the hydrolysis of fats; *diastase*, which is involved in the conversion of starch to glucose. Fermentation of sugars to alcohol requires the presence of the enzyme *zymase*. *See* **Catalyst,** *also* **F21(1), F33(2).**

Epaulette, a shoulder badge fringed with cord, worn by English army officers until 1855; now confined to naval officers, and varying in form and richness according to the rank of the wearers.

Ephemoptera *or* **May-flies**, an order of insects. In the larval condition they exist from two to three years aquatically, but no sooner do they arrive at maturity than their lives are hurried to a close. They rise up in pyramids on warm summer nights, take no food, propagate, and perish. The Latin name expresses the fact that the adults have an ephemeral existence.

Ephod, a vestment worn by a Jewish high priest, and sometimes by priests of lower rank. In olden times it was of rich texture and set with gems.

Epiglottis, a lamella or cartilage in mammals, designed to cover and protect the entrance to the larynx during the process of food swallowing.

Epiphany, a church festival celebrated on January 6, Twelfth Day.

Equator, the imaginary great circle of the earth, every point of which is 90 degrees from the earth's poles, and dividing the northern from the southern hemisphere. It is from this circle that the latitude of places north and south is reckoned. The celestial equator is the circle in which the plane of the earth's equator meets the celestial sphere (the imaginary sphere, in which the observer is at the centre, used for representing the apparent positions of the heavenly bodies).

Equinox, the time when the sun crosses the plane of the earth's equator, making day and night of equal length. *See* **N24.**

Eras are distinctive periods of time associated with some remarkable historical event or personage. *The Christian era* is computed according to a 6th-cent. reckoning to begin with Jesus's birth, A.D. 1. The date is placed some years too late. Scholars now believe that Jesus was born *c.* 6 B.C. The *Jewish era* dates from 3761 B.C.; the *Julian era* from the alteration of the calendar by Julius Caesar, 45 B.C.; the *Mohammedan era* from the date of the *Hejira*, or the flight of Mohammed from Mecca to Medina, which is A.D. 622, July 16, in the Gregorian Calendar.

Erbium, belongs to the group of rare-earth metals discovered by Mosander in 1842.

Erg, the unit of work and energy in the centimetre-gram-second system; the energy involved when a force of 1 dyne moves its point of application through a distance of 1 cm.

Erl-King, a forest fiend of German mythology, who lured children from their homes and carried them off. In Goethe's ballad the "Erlkönig" it is a traveller's child who is lured to destruction.

Ermine. *See* **Stoat.**

Ernie, the name given to the "electronic random number indicator equipment", the electronic machine which selected the prizewinning numbers in the first Premium Bond draw held June 1–2, 1957.

Eros. This asteroid is 15–20 miles in diameter. It comes closer to the earth than any other member of the solar system with the exception of the moon and several very small asteroids. Determination of solar parallax based on observations of Eros in 1930–31 yielded the most accurate estimate of the distance of the sun from the earth (93,004,000 miles).

Erse, a term used by Lowland Scottish, and English writers for the Gaelic language spoken in the Highlands of Scotland. Sometimes erroneously applied to Irish, the Gaelic language as spoken in Ireland and revived as an official language in recent times. Dr. Johnson, Sir Walter Scott, and other writers used "Erse" to signify Scottish Gaelic. The language of the Scottish Lowlands (that used by Robert Burns) is related to the English language and not to Gaelic and is variously termed Scots, Braid Scots, the Doric, the Scottish vernacular, and, fashionably of late, Lallans.

Escutcheon, a shield-shaped surface called a field, upon which a man's armorial bearings are represented. A woman's escutcheon is lozenge-shaped.

Espalier, lattice work upon which to train fruiting or ornamental trees.

Esparto Grass grows in great abundance in Spain and North Africa, and the pulp is largely used for paper-making as well as for other purposes.

Esperanto, an artificial international language created by L. Zamenhof of Warsaw and first published in 1887. It does not seek to replace national languages but to serve as a second language for international communication. It is based on the internationality of many words in The principal modern languages, and is entirely phonetic in spelling and pronunciation.

Esquire, formerly a title applied to a young man of noble birth who attended on a knight and carried his shield. The title ranked next below that of knight and was applied to the eldest sons of knights and the younger sons of peers. Later it became a courtesy title and given to any man as a mark of respect.

Essential Oils are oils derived from plants by distillation or expression, and much used in perfumery as well as to some extent in medicine.

Estate Duty is the duty payable upon the value of all property passing on the death of any person. As from 4 April 1963 the rates are: not exceeding £5,000, nil; £5,000–£6,000, 1%; £6,000–£7,000, 2%; £7,000–£8,000, 3%; rising gradually to 80% on estates exceeding £1,000,000. Gifts made by deceased during his life for public or charitable purposes are liable for duty, unless made more than 1 year before death; other gifts are liable for duty, unless made more than 5 years before death, although there are graduated rates for gifts made more than two, three, or four years before death of 15 per cent, 30 per cent, and 60 per cent respectively. Gifts made in consideration of marriage (parties to the marriage and their issue) are exempt from estate duty as are buildings and land of special interest bequeathed to non-profit-making bodies for preservation. Gifts not exceeding £100 in value (or in certain circumstances £500) also exempt.

Estates of the Realm in Great Britain are the Lords Spiritual, the Lords Temporal, and the Commons. They are the great classes invested with distinct political powers, and whose concurrence is necessary to legislation.

Esters. Organic chemicals formed by combining an alcohol with an acid. They have a pleasant smell, and occur naturally in plants as the scent of flowers. Manufactured for use in the perfumery industry, and as flavourings in food. Some esters are used as solvents, notably amyl-acetate ("pear drops") in quick-drying paints. The polymeric fibre "Terylene" consists of chains of molecules containing many ester groups, formed by reacting an alcohol having two alcoholic (OH) groups with an acid having two acid (COOH) groups.

Etching, a process of engraving, on copper usually, the design being drawn with a steel needle, and the lines produced by the action of an acid or mordant.

Ether, a volatile liquid, composed of carbon, oxygen, and hydrogen. It is a valuable anaesthetic obtained by heating alcohol with sulphuric acid.

Ethylene. A gas compounded of carbon and hydrogen, it is related to acetylene and ethane. Industrially it is obtained as a by-product in petroleum refining. It has wide uses as a starting material in the industrial manufacture of intermediates, especially alcohol. Its most important application is in the production of polythene (poly-ethylene). *See* **Catalyst.**

Etruscans, people believed to have come from Asia Minor who colonised Italy about 900 B.C., settled in what is now Tuscany and part of Umbria, reached the height of their civilisation about 500 B.C., and were ultimately absorbed by the Romans. They were skilled technicians in bronze, silver, and goldwork, and excelled in the art of granular decoration.

Etude. *See* **Study.**

Etymology treats of the science and structure of words, including classification and derivation.

Eucalyptus. This genus includes 300 species of evergreen, leathery-leaved trees native to Australia. The oils yielded by different species vary a great deal in their scent and other properties and are chiefly used in pharmacy and perfumery; about 30 species produce oils suitable for medicinal purposes. Various species produce timber.

Euphonium, alternative name for the Bass Saxhorn in B♭. A large brass instrument of the trumpet type played by operating three valves.

Eurasian, a half-caste or person of mixed European and Asiatic parentage.

Europium, element discovered by Demarcay in 1906. A member of the rare-earth metal group.

Evaporation is the process by which a solid or liquid is resolved into vapour by heat. As it is rarely that the atmosphere is completely saturated, evaporation is nearly always going on at the surface of the earth, especially over the sea and other water surfaces, the vapour rising and, being lighter than the air, forming clouds which afterwards break, the vapour thereupon falling to earth again as rain. The same process occurs over smaller surfaces, the rate of evaporation being dependent on the general atmospheric conditions.

Everest Expeditions. For many years after Mt. Everest had been shown to be the highest mountain in the world, political conditions in Nepal, lying south of the summit, and in Tibet, to the north, prevented mountaineers from attempting an ascent. At last in 1921 the Tibetan authorities gave permission, and the first expedition, organised, as were all subsequent British expeditions, by a joint committee of the Royal Geographical Society and the Alpine Club, and led by Col. C. K. Howard-Bury, was sent out. This was primarily a reconnaissance; besides mapping the northern flanks, it found a practicable route up the mountain. By 1939, six further expeditions had climbed on the northern face. Some were baulked by bad weather, others by problems previously little known, such as the effect of high altitudes on the human body and spirit. Nevertheless, notable climbs were accomplished. In 1924, for example, Col. E. F. Norton reached 28,163 ft., and it was on this expedition that G. L. Mallory and Andrew Irvine were seen going well at about the same height. They never returned, however, and what disaster befell them is not known. After the war, political conditions again closed the Tibet route: permission was eventually obtained from the Nepalese Government to make the attempt from the south. In 1951 a reconnaissance expedition under Eric Shipton reached the ice-fall at the exit of the Western Cwm (a high valley lying south-west of the massif), and reported favourably on the prospects for an ascent. The first attempt from this side was made the following year by a Swiss expedition led by Dr. E. Wyss-Dunant, two members of which made an attempt on the summit, but were stopped at approx. 28,200 ft. by the intense cold and the very strong winds. When the British 1953 Expedition, led by Col. (now Brig. Sir) John Hunt, was being organised, stress was laid on three main points: proper acclimatisation of the climbers; use of oxygen for the final stages; and the establishment of very high altitude camps, so that the final assault parties would set out fresh and unencumbered. Great attention was also paid to recent developments in diet, clothing, and equipment. In all these matters the 1953 expedition was able to draw on the accumulated experience of their predecessors. By the end of April, a base camp had been established below the ice-fall, and with the aid of thirty-four Sherpa porters supplies had been carried up into the Western Cwm. The next critical stage was the ascent of the steep head of the cwm, the Lhotse face, with the threat of avalanches always present. By most strenuous efforts, a camp was established on the South Col (25,800 ft.) on May 21. From this camp on May 26, T. D. Bourdillon and R. C. Evans climbed the South Peak of Everest (28,720 ft.), then the highest altitude ever attained. On May 28, Edmund Hillary and the Sherpa leader, Tenzing Norkey, spent the night at the highest camp (27,900 ft.) and on the following day, May 29, climbed to the South Summit, negotiated the difficult final ridge, and reached the summit of Everest—the climax of a long, arduous, and stirring endeavour.

Evolution, in the words of Sir Julian Huxley, "a natural process of irreversible change which generates novelty, variety, and increase of organisation." The theory, as laid down by Darwin, is that all existing species, genera, and classes of animals and plants have developed from a few simple forms by processes of change and selection. Up to the time of Darwin a large part of the civilised world believed that life had been created suddenly at the beginning of the world which God had created, according to Archbishop Usher, on 22 Oct. 4004 B.C. The evidence of the rocks, however, has given a more convincing theory of creation, and by studying the fossils preserved in the various layers of the earth's crust the past history of the earth's life has been pieced together. Darwin has been called the Newton of biology. *See* **F31–33**.

Excommunication, exclusion from the rights and privileges of the Church. It is of two kinds—the major, which means a total cutting off, and the minor, which shuts out only from participation in the Eucharist. In mediæval times, major excommunications were often launched against rulers and leaders.

Exchequer, which derives its name from the checkered tablecloth on which accounts were calculated in early Norman times, is a term connected with the revenues of the Crown. In former times it had jurisdiction in all revenue matters. The term Exchequer is now applied to the Governmental department which deals with the public revenues, the working head of which is the Chancellor of the Exchequer.

Existentialism. *See* **J15**.

Exploration. Modern exploration began in the second half of the 15th cent. with the voyages of the great Portuguese and Spanish discoverers. They were followed by sailors of other European nations, who profited from their developments in navigation and from their charts, and in less than one hundred years the coast-lines of much of the Americas, Africa, and south-west Asia had been revealed and the globe circumnavigated. The motives of these early explorers were mixed: they were seeking adventure, trade, plunder, national power, and the conversion of the heathen. Few if any were directly interested in advancing scientific knowledge. But from the reports of their voyages and travels, scholars at home compiled descriptions of the strange new world which stimulated their successors to undertake more systematic enquiries. One of the earliest English expeditions to be despatched for scientific research was that of William Dampier on the *Roebuck*, which was sent out by the Admiralty in 1699 to examine the coasts of North-west Australia. In the 18th cent. British explorers were at work mainly in the Pacific Ocean, with the object of breaking the Spanish monopoly of trade. Capt. James Cook sailed thither in 1769 to observe first the transit of Venus at Tahiti, and then to search for the alleged great southern continent. On this voyage he discovered and charted much of the coasts of New Zealand and the east coast of Australia. On his second voyage he was the first to sail across the Antarctic Circle, and he showed that the southern continent was much smaller than had been supposed. By 1800 the general outlines of the continents, except for Antarctica were known, and explorers in the 19th cent. were largely engaged in opening up the interiors. In Africa British explorers solved two problems which had puzzled men for centuries: Mungo Park and Richard Lander established the true course of the River Niger, and Sir Richard Burton, J. H. Speke, Sir Samuel Baker, and others revealed the true sources of the Nile. The greatest African explorer of that age was undoubtedly David Livingstone, the missionary, who in three great journeys explored the Zambesi and the region of the Great Lakes, spreading the Gospel, fighting the slave trade, and opening up the interior to settlement and trade. In North America Alexander Mackenzie was the first to cross the main breadth of the continent from sea to sea. In Asia motives were also mixed; men like Charles Doughty, who explored in Arabia, and Sir Francis Younghusband, who journeyed from China to India across the Gobi and the Himalaya, were impelled by a love of adventure and the quest for knowledge, but political considerations were often involved. In recent years, with the main features of the world's surface known, exploration has become more intensive. Teams of scientists go out to study restricted areas in detail. An Antarctic expedition can contribute to our knowledge of world weather, or by biological research into the life history of whales, can help to improve our food supplies. Similarly, expeditions in Africa can help to check the loss of valuable agricultural land through soil erosion, or to develop areas of settlement by schemes for irrigation and power. And there are still great areas to be adequately mapped. All these problems are inter-related, and in solving them the modern explorer can call on many improved techniques and instruments—the aeroplane, the aerial camera, tracked motor vehicles, radio, in fact all the resources of modern science. But the human element is still vital, and for those with the old explorers' spirit there will always be problems left to solve.

Explosives, substances which burn violently to produce gases in such volume that an explosion is induced. Gunpowder was the first explosive to be used; Roger Bacon's powder, consisting of charcoal, sulphur, and nitre, was the only practical explosive for centuries. 1845 brought gun-cotton, made by treating cotton with a mixture of sulphuric and nitric acids; but it was not until 1865 that Sir Frederick Abel perfected the process of manufacture that made it safe enough to store and use. In 1867 Alfred Nobel discovered how to make dynamite by absorbing nitro-glycerine in kiesulguhr; in 1886 he produced cordite, evaporating a solution of gun-cotton and nitro-glycerine in acetone, the resultant jelly being squeezed through jets to form cords. Cordite came into general use as a propellant. High explosives, providing bursting charge for shells and bombs, include: T.N.T. (trinitrotoluol), picric acid (known as lyddite, melinite, etc.), cyclonite (R.D.X.). Chemical explosives have been eclipsed by nuclear explosives which have developed from the first atom bomb (dropped on Hiroshima 6 August 1945) to the 100-megaton hydrogen bomb.

Expressionism, a modern art movement confined primarily to the non-Latin countries of Europe which sought to give expression to intimate and personal emotions by means of distortions of line and colour and simplified style which carried a greater impact in terms of feeling. Broadly speaking, this has been characteristic of northern art in general. (*See* **Gothic**) The term is usually used of the modern movement which influenced the Post-impressionists and subsequent movements in France. Tired of the naturalism of the Impressionists, such artists as van Gogh, Gauguin, Matisse, and Rouault together with the Fauvists (*q.v.*) made use of simple outlines and strong colours. Apart from Toulouse-Lautrec, the principal Expressionists were Norwegian, like Munch, or German, like the painters of *Die Brücke* and *Der Blaue Reiter* groups. Individual artists were Ensor, Kokoschka, Nolde, Rouault, and Soutine.

Extreme Unction, the final sacrament of the Roman Catholic and Greek Churches, administered to a dying person, and consisting of the anointing with holy oil, after confession and absolution.

F

Fabian Society. *See* **J16**.

Fables are fictitious narratives intended to enforce some moral precept, and may be either in prose or verse, and deal with personified animals and objects or with human beings. Aesop in ancient times and Hans Christian Andersen and the Brothers Grimm (in many of their stories) in later days, have given fables. Mention must also be made of La Fontaine's and Krylov's fables.

Faience, a kind of decorated glazed earthenware invented in Faenza, Italy, about the end of the 13th cent. Wedgwood-ware is a notable example of modern faience.

Fairs were established in mediæval times as a means of bringing traders and customers together at stated periods, and formed the chief means of distribution. The great English fairs of early times were those of Winchester and Stourbridge near Cambridge. Traders from the Netherlands and the Baltic gathered there with the great merchants of London, and goods of every kind, wholesale and retail, were sold. The British Industries Fair is the modern counterpart of the mediaeval trade fair. One of the biggest trade fairs was at Nijni-Novgorod, founded in the 17th cent.; other big continental fairs are those of Leipzig (founded in the 12th cent.), Lyons, and Prague.

Fairy Rings are the circles caused in grassland by certain fungi. The circles expand outwards as the fungus spreads, the fruiting bodies being at the periphery. Farther inward where the fungi are decaying the grass grows more strongly, fertilised by the nitrogen released from the rotting fungi. In olden times these rings were held to be the scene of fairy dances.

Falcon, name given to diurnal birds of prey which belong to the same family, *Falconidae*, as the hawk, eagle, buzzard, kite, and harrier. They are swift of wing and feed on birds and small mammals. These birds have long, pointed wings, strong, hooked and notched bill, long, curved claws, and an eye of great power. They are found all over the world. Those that breed in Britain are the Kestrel (the most common), Hobby (one of the swiftest of European birds), Merlin, and Peregrine, a swift and magnificent bird with slate-grey back, blackish crown, black "moustache" and whitish breast. Other members of the family are the Gyr Falcon from northern latitudes, Iceland and Greenland, which is a winter visitor to Britain, the Lanner, Saker, Eleonora's falcon, Red-footed falcon, and the Lesser Kestrel. The Gyr Falcon and the Peregrine were used in the sport of falconry in olden times. Because of its fearlessness and larger size, the female bird was used. When the quarry was sighted, the bird was unhooded, set free, and after mounting high into the air would dart swiftly down to strike the prey. The heron was the usual victim.

Falculia, a black-and-white bird only found in Madagascar, possessing a bill shaped like a sickle.

Fall-out. Radioactive material produced by nuclear explosions which may cause bodily and genetic damage. (1) *Local fall-out*, due to the return to earth of larger particles, occurs locally, and within a few hours after the explosion; (2) *Tropospheric fall-out*, due to particles which remain in the troposphere and come down within a month or so, possibly all over the world, but within the altitude in which the explosion occurred; (3) *Stratospheric fall-out*, which comes from fragments taken up into the stratosphere and then deposited, in the course of many years uniformly all over the globe. The two radioactive materials which have given rise to the greatest concern for the health of the individual are strontium-90 and iodine-131. Both these materials are liable to become concentrated in certain parts of the human body, strontium-90 in bone and iodine-131 in the thyroid gland. Iodine-131 gives off radiation, but after a few weeks this becomes negligible; the risk is likely to be limited to children under one year old. Strontium-90 continues to give off radiation for many years, and particular attention is therefore paid to levels of strontium-90 in milk and in the bones of young children who are growing rapidly. Radiation exposure may produce genetic effects, that is effects which may show up in succeeding generations. So far as these genetic effects are concerned, the most important components of fall-out are caesium-137 and carbon-14.

Fallow Deer received its name from its fallow or yellow colour. It is smaller than the red deer, and has cylindrical antlers with palmated ends. It is native to many parts of Europe.

Falsetto, tones of a voice, particularly the male voice, which are pitched higher than the natural tones of the voice. Used in choral singing by male altos.

Fandango, a lively Spanish dance executed by two persons, who usually mark time with castanets.

Fantail, a variety of the domestic pigeon; also a genus of Australian birds of the *Muscicapidae* family. A small New Zealand bird is called a fantail.

Fantasia, a composition for orchestra or solo pianoforte which is not bound by the rules governing formal compositions, *i.e.*, symphonies, sonatas, etc.

Fan Tracery, a complicated style of roof-vaulting, elaborately moulded, in which the lines of the curves in the masonry or other material employed diverge equally in every direction. It is characteristic of the late Perpendicular period of Gothic architecture, and may be seen in St. George's Chapel at Windsor and the Chapel of Henry VIII. at Westminster Abbey.

F.A.O. (Food and Agricultural Organisation of the United Nations). *See* **Section C, Part I.**

Farmer-General, the name given to the financiers who in the days of the old French monarchy farmed certain taxes, contracting to pay the Government a fixed sum yearly, on condition that the specified taxes were collected and appropriated by themselves. The revolution of 1789 swept Farmers-General away.

Fascism. *See* **J16.**

Fata Morgana, the name given to a curious mirage often observed over the Straits of Messina, attributed to the magic of the fairy Morgana, half-sister of King Arthur, who was fabled to live in Calabria.

Fathers of the Church were early writers who laid the foundations of Christian ritual and doctrine. The earliest were the Apostolic Fathers, (*q.v.*). The Four Fathers of the Latin Church were St. Ambrose, St. Jerome, St. Augustine, and St. Gregory the Great. The Four Fathers of the Greek Church were St. Basil, St. Gregory Nazianzen, St. John Chrysostom, and St. Athanasius.

Fats are important foodstuffs. In physiology they constitute a valuable form of reserve food. They contain carbon, hydrogen and oxygen; chemically they are described as esters of glycerol (glycerine). Commonest fats are stearin, palmitin, and olein, esters formed by the combination of glycerol with stearic, palmitic, and oleic acid respectively. Fats are converted into soap by alkali; this process (saponification) also releases glycerol.

Fault, a term designating a breakage coupled with displacement of geological strata.

Fauvism (Fr. *fauve* = wild beast), a term contemptuously applied to the work of a group of French painters led by Matisse who exhibited at the Salon d'Automne in Paris in 1905. Their belief was that a painting must be not only a consistent and harmonious decoration but the expression of an idea or feeling. Forms and colours are emotive in their own right. The objects painted by the Fauves, though simplified, distorted, and often violently coloured, are easily recognisable. Inspiration for their highly decorative canvasses came from many sources: Byzantine and Persian art in the case of Matisse; German Expressionism in the case of Derain and Vlaminck. The Fauves paved the way for the Cubists (Braque joined Picasso in 1909) who approached nature in more arrogant mood, from a more intellectual point of view.

February, the second month of the year, contains in ordinary years 28 days, but in leap years 29 days. When first introduced into the Roman calendar by Numa *c.* 700 B.C. it was made the last month of the year, preceding January, but in 452 B.C. the position of the two months was changed, February following January.

Federation. *See under* **Confederation.**

Félibrige, a movement founded in 1854 to revive the ancient glories of Provence, initiated by the French poet Frédéric Mistral.

Felspar, the name given to a group of minerals, silicates of aluminium with some calcium and sodium, or potassium, which make up probably more than half of the earth's crust. It is formed in granite and other rocks, both igneous and metamorphic.

Fenestella, the niche set apart on the south side of the altar for the piscina in Roman Catholic churches.

Fermentation, the action of chemical ferments or *enzymes* in bringing about chemical changes in the materials of living animals and plants, *e.g.*, the breaking-down of sugar by yeast into alcohol.

Ferret, a carnivorous animal of the Pole-cat family, with a pointed head and long sinuous body, well adapted for following rabbits and game into their burrows and hiding-places, it being kept in this country for that purpose. It is a native of Spain and Africa, and does not exist in England in a condition of natural freedom. *See* **Z12.**

Ferrites are compounds containing iron, oxygen, and one or two of a certain range of other possible metallic elements. Ferrites have recently become very important technically, because, unlike ordinary magnetic materials, they combine strong magnetism with electrical insulating properties. Ferrite-rod aerials are now common in portable radios, and ferrite devices are used in radar.

Feudalism. *See* **J17.**

Fieldfare, the largest member of the thrush family, a regular winter visitor to Britain from Scandinavia. It is brown in colour with a lighter spotted breast and a grey head.

Field-Marshal, the highest ranking title in the British army, and only bestowed on royal personages and generals who have attained great distinction. The first British Field-Marshal was created in 1736, when John, Duke of Argyll, had the title conferred upon him by George II.

Fife. A small flute with a compass of about two octaves used only in military drum-and-fife bands.

Fifth Column. When Franco, the Spanish dictator, revolted against the Spanish Republic in 1936 and attacked Madrid with four armies, he declared that a group of fascists within the city was assisting the besiegers. The term is used to describe a body of spies behind a fighting front.

Figaro, a well-known comic character in drama and opera, invented by Beaumarchais, adopted by Mozart, and the name of a popular paper of Paris.

Fighting-Fish, small pugnacious Siamese fish with long caudal and ventral fins. They are kept in glass globes in Siam, and when brought into contact will fight to the death, these encounters being the occasion of much gambling.

Filibuster, a name first given to pirates and buccaneers in the 17th cent. who took possession of small islands or lonely coast lands, and there maintained themselves apart from any governing authority. In later times the term was used to specify men taking part in expeditions whose object was to appropriate tracts of country, and settle upon them in disregard of international law. The most notable expeditions of this kind in modern times were those of Narcisco Lopez against Cuba in 1850–51, and of William Walker against Nicaragua, between 1855 and 1860. Both leaders were captured and executed. The term is also used to express the right of a minority in the United States Senate for unlimited debate, which is used on occasions to delay legislation for an unlimited period.

Finches, a large family of small birds belonging to the Passerine or perching order of birds. There are about 200 species, including greenfinch, hawfinch, chaffinch, goldfinch, siskin, bullfinch, crossbill, linnet, twite, and buntings.

Fir, a cone-bearing tree with small evergreen leaves and of considerable use as timber. There are two types: the Silver Firs and the Douglas Firs numbering about 25 species. All these firs attain to a considerable height, and all yield turpentine or other resinous material.

Fire-Fly, a small winged insect of the *Eleteridae* family, is able to throw out a strong phosphorescent light in the dark. There are some remarkable specimens in tropical countries.

Fire of London, of 1666, extended from East to West, from the Tower to the Temple church, and northward to Holborn Bridge. It broke out in a baker's shop in Pudding Lane, and lasted four days, and destroyed 87 churches, including St. Paul's Cathedral, and many public buildings, among them the Royal Exchange, the Custom House, and the Guildhall. In the ruins were involved 13,200 houses and 400 streets. The plague had not disappeared from London when the fire occurred.

Firkin, a former measure of capacity, the fourth part of a barrel, now only used in reference to a small cask or tub for butter, lard, tallow, etc.

Fischer-Tropsch Process. A process for making synthetic petrol from carbon monoxide and hydrogen. The synthesis is accelerated by cobalt-thoria and nickel-thoria catalysts.

Fish Louse. Parasitic crustacea found on marine and fresh-water fishes and whales.

Fission, Nuclear. A nuclear reaction in which the nucleus of an atom (*e.g.*, uranium 235, plutonium) captures a neutron, and the unstable nucleus so produced breaks into two nearly equal fragments and throws out several neutrons as well. In biology the term fission is applied to reproduction by fragmentation of a single-cell organism, as in amœba. *See* **F12(1).**

Flageolet. A sweet-toned instrument which is in effect a portable organ pipe whose length, and therefore pitch, may be varied by opening or closing holes in the pipe with the fingers. Sometimes called the English Flute or "Penny Whistle."

Flag Officer, a British naval officer who enjoys the right of carrying a flag at the mast-head of his ship, and is of the rank of Admiral, Vice-Admiral, or Rear-Admiral.

Flagship, the ship that flies the Admiral's flag, and from which all orders proceed.

Flamingo, a strangely beautiful, extremely slender wading bird of white and rose-pink plumage with long, slender legs and neck and a long, down-curved bill with which it rakes the mud and obtains its food of worms and molluscs. The wings are bright crimson, bordered with black, and a flock in flight is a picture of singular beauty. There is a large and famous colony in the Camargue.

Flash-Point. This is found by heating an oil in a special cup and taking the temperature at which sufficient vapour is produced to ignite when a small flame is applied. It is an index of the inflammability of oils.

Flat. A keyboard instrument has white keys and black keys. The notes played by the white keys are called "naturals." There are eight of these to each octave and they are called A, B, C, D, E, F, G, A. The black key immediately below a natural (one semitone interval) is called its "flat," *e.g.*, the black note below B is B flat and is written B♭. Conversely the black key above a natural (one semitone interval) is known as its "sharp," *e.g.*, the black note above A is A sharp and is written A♯. Since B natural is a full tone above A natural, it follows that B flat and A sharp are the same note.

Flea. Fleas are small parasitic insects belonging to the order *Aphaniptera* (so called because these creatures have no wings). They obtain their food by sucking blood from their host. They are laterally compressed, which immediately distinguishes them from lice. The human flea (*Pulex irritans*) is able to jump vertically a distance of over 7 in.

Fleet Prison, a noted debtors' prison that stood in Farringdon Street, London, where the Congregational Memorial Hall now stands, taking its name from the Fleet Ditch. Notorious for the cruelties inflicted on prisoners. It was pulled down in 1846.

Fleet Street, a famous thoroughfare in London, now the centre of journalism and newspaperdom, though it was long celebrated for its taverns where the literary coteries of the day were wont to meet. It takes its name from the Fleet stream which used to run from Hampstead through Holborn to the Thames at Blackfriars.

Flemings, the people of Flanders, whose ancestors of mediaeval times excelled in the textile arts; England owes its early eminence as a manufacturing nation to the migration of numbers of

Flemings to this country in the 16th and 17th cent.

Fleur de Lis, the former national emblem of France, the flower of the lily. It was superseded by the Tricolour in 1789, but is still adhered to by the supporters of the old French royalties.

Flint, consists of granular chalcedony with some opaline silica, and occurs as nodules and bands in the Chalk. It is hard and has a conchoidal fracture, so enabling it to be used in making cutting implements in prehistoric times. Before the invention of lucifer matches, it was used along with steel for striking lights.

Flint implements are objects found in the younger geological strata, and constituting evidence of the condition and life of the period. They include knives, clubs, arrow-heads, scrapers, etc., used as weapons, tools and possibly as surgical instruments and in religious ceremonies. At the end of the Neolithic Period and the beginning of the Bronze Age a people using a new type of stone axe became evident in Europe, advancing towards the south and central regions, and supposed by many to be the ancestors of the present European stock, or Aryans. Similar to prehistoric specimens are the flint and obsidian implements of some of the primitive peoples of today. Ritual weapons and sacrificial knives continued to be made of stone long after the introduction of metals for practical purposes.

Flounder, one of the most familiar of the smaller flat fishes common round the British coasts, and seldom attaining a weight of over three pounds.

Fluorine, a chemical element, member of the halogen family, symbol F, it is found in combination with calcium in fluorspar, and occurs in minute quantities in certain other minerals. Discovered by Scheele in 1771, it was first obtained by Moissan in 1886. A pale yellow gas, it is very reactive and combines with most elements except oxygen. Its acid, hydrogen fluoride, etches glass, the fluorine combining with the silicon to form volatile silicon fluoride. Organic fluorine compounds have found use as very stable polymers which resist a wide variety of chemical actions.

Fluorescent Lamp. *See* **Electric Light** and **Ultra-Violet Rays.**

Fluorspar, a mineral; chemically, calcium fluoride. Can be colourless, green, or yellow, but is most commonly purple. Blue fluorspar under the name of Derbyshire "blue John" has been used for ornamental purposes.

Flute. A wooden musical instrument, part of the wood-wind of an orchestra, played by blowing across a mouth-hole, the notes being produced by pressing the fingers on finger-holes or keys. It has a compass of three octaves and a singular purity of tone. In simple form the flute has been known since Greek times, but the modern flute dates from the 18th cent.

Fly, the popular name for a large number of insects with one pair of wings and a proboscis terminating in a sucker through which fluid substances can be drawn up. The best-known species are the common house-fly, the bluebottle, and the blow-fly. In the larval form flies are maggots, and feed upon decaying substances, animal flesh, etc. Flies are able to walk upon ceilings or upright surfaces by having suckers at the soles of their feet. *See* **Diptera.**

Flycatcher, name of a large family of small birds, the Muscicapidae. They are insect feeders, catch their food in the air, and are distributed over most countries of the world. The spotted and the pied nest in Britain, which they visit from April to September.

Flying Fish are frequently to be seen in southern waters, and are capable of gliding considerable distances without touching the water. To build up speed for its "take-off" the fish swims rapidly, to break the surface at 15–20 miles an hour. Maximum air speed is about 40 m.p.h.

Flying Fox, a member of the bat family, but of much larger size, and confined to the tropical and sub-tropical Old World. Like the bats, it is nocturnal, but it feeds entirely on fruits.

Flying Lemur. *See* **Colugo**

Flying Lizard, or *Draco*, an Asiatic lizard, possessing wing-like projections from each side, which enable it to make flying leaps through the air, though not sufficient for continuous flight.

Flying Saucers, the name given to certain saucer-like shapes which have on occasion been seen travelling through the atmosphere. For some time speculation was rife, especially in America, but it is now believed that when not hallucinations, meteorological or cosmic-ray balloons, they are nothing more than atmospheric phenomena like mirages or mock suns caused by unusual atmospheric conditions. Described by Dr. Menzel, astrophysics professor at Harvard, "as real as rainbows are real, and no more dangerous".

Flying Squirrel, rodents of which there are several species in Europe, Asia and America. It possesses a parachute-like fold of skin by means of which it projects itself through the air. In appearance they are much like ordinary squirrels, to which they are related. The African flying squirrels belong to a different family.

Fog is caused by the presence of particles of condensed water vapour or smoke in the surface layers of the atmosphere, the term being applied meteorologically when the resulting obscurity is such as to render objects invisible at distances of up to 1 km. Fogs are frequently formed when the air near the ground is cooled below its dew-point temperature by radiation on a still, cloudless night; by flowing over a relatively cold land or water mass; or by mixing with a colder air stream. An accumulation of smoke over a large city may cause a high fog cutting off the daylight and producing gloom. *See* **Pollution** *and also* **Aerosol.**

Foliation, a geological term applied to rocks whose component minerals are arranged in parallel layers as the result of strong metamorphic action.

Folio, a printing term for a sheet of paper folded once, a half sheet constituting a leaf.

Folklore concerns itself with the mental and spiritual life of the people—both civilised and primitive—as expressed in the traditional beliefs, customs, institutions, and sayings that have been handed down from generation to generation by word of mouth, and with the observation, recording, and interpretation of such traditions. (The word *folklore* itself was first suggested and used—as two words *Folk Lore*—by W. J. Thoms in the *Athenæum* of August 22nd, 1846, and was at once absorbed into the English language.) Traditional lore of the kind included in the term folklore takes many forms and ranges from omens of good and bad luck (spilling the salt, breaking a mirror, dropping an umbrella, etc.) and the wearing of amulets or the possession of talismans (such as the horse-shoe) as protection against misfortune, to elaborate ceremonial dances such as the Abbots Bromley Horn Dance, the Hobby horses of Padstow and Minehead, the Northern sword-dances, and the Christmas mummers' plays. Especially important are the beliefs and customs associated with birth, babyhood, marriage, and death, such being occasions when the individuals concerned require special protection or when unusual happenings can be used for foretelling their future. The child born on a Sunday will be the luckiest; rocking an empty cradle will ensure the speedy arrival of a new baby; throwing an old shoe after a newly-married couple brings them luck; the bride should be carried over the threshold of the new home; on the sea-coast, death is believed to take place at the ebb-tide; the bees must be told of the death of the master of the house, or they will leave the hive. Another very large section of the subject deals with the traditional sayings and practices associated with particular days and seasons of the year—calendar customs, as they are called. The eating of pancakes on Shrove Tuesday; Mother Sunday customs and the simnel cake; Good Friday as the right day for planting potatoes, but emphatically the wrong day for washing clothes or cutting one's finger-nails; the necessity of wearing something new on Easter Sunday; the children's maypole dances and May garlands; midsummer fires; All Hallowe'en as the most favourable occasion for divining the future—especially in respect of marriage—and for games and sports such as apple-bobbing; the numerous practices accompanying the harvest. All these are examples of calendar customs; their full story would occupy several volumes. Folklorists are interested in all such oral tradition because they think that to a large extent it represents what folk have mentally stored up from the past and transmitted to their descendants throughout the centuries, and because therefore it is able to assist other historic methods—ethnographical linguistic, archaeological, etc.—in the elucidation of the early story of man. In those countries with a great diversity of peoples in all stages of culture, a knowledge of folklore and what it can teach of the mind of man is of great importance to administrators. The Folk-Lore Society was founded in 1878, and that part of the subject represented by song and dance has now its own organisation in the English Folk Dance and Song Society.

Force, as a term in physics, signifies an influence or exertion which, when made to act upon a body, tends to move it if at rest, or to affect or stop its progress if it be already in motion. In the c.g.s. system of units the unit of force is the dyne; in the foot-pound-second system it is the poundal.

Formaldehyde. Chemically it lies between methyl alcohol and formic acid; oxidation of methyl alcohol yields formaldehyde, and oxidation of formaldehyde produces formic acid. It is used as a disinfectant, in silvering mirrors, and in the manufacture of phenol-formaldehyde plastics (of which bakelite is the best-known example). Solutions of formaldehyde in water, formalin, are used to preserve biological specimens.

Forme, a body of letterpress type, composed and secured for printing from; or a stereotype or electrotype. The former is used more for newspaper formes and the latter in good book work.

Formic Acid can be obtained from a colourless fluid secreted by ants and other insects and plants. It is a strong irritant. Commercially it is obtained from sodium formate, which is synthesised by the absorption of carbon monoxide in caustic soda. It is used in the electroplating, tanning, and textile industries.

Formula, in mathematics and physics a statement of certain facts in symbolical form. In chemistry a representation of the composition of a compound.

Forte, a musical term signifying "loud," and represented by the letter "f"; "ff" (fortissimo) indicating "very loud."

Fossils. Remains of animals and plants, or direct evidence of their presence, preserved in rocks. They include petrified skeletons and shells, leaf imprints, footprints, etc. *See* **F29(1)**.

Four Freedoms, a phrase coined by President Roosevelt in January, 1941, embodying what should be the goal of the Allies. They were (1) Freedom of speech and expression; (2) Freedom of every person to worship God in his own way; (3) Freedom from want; (4) Freedom from fear.

Fox, carnivorous animal of the canine family, found in considerable numbers in most parts of the world. The common fox *Vulpes vulpes* of Europe is a burrowing animal of nocturnal habits, living upon birds, rabbits, and domestic poultry, in the capture of which it displays much cunning. The fox in Britain is preserved from extinction chiefly for hunting purposes. Among other notable species are the Arctic fox and the red fox of North America, of which the valuable silver fox, coveted for its fur, is a variety.

Fox-Shark, *or* **Thresher Shark**, a large species of shark common in the Atlantic and in the Mediterranean. It is very destructive to small fish, but although it attains a length of 15 ft. it is not dangerous to man.

Franciscans. *See* **Friars.**

Franco-German War (1870–71) was opened by a declaration of war by Napoleon III., but the Germans who were better prepared than the French, won victory after victory. In September Napoleon and the whole French army were made prisoners at Sedan, a republic was then proclaimed, and Paris sustained a four months' siege. In the end France ceded Alsace and part of Lorraine to Germany, who claimed a war indemnity of over £20 million.

Francolin, a genus of birds closely related to the common partridge, belonging to Africa. It includes the spur-legged partridge, and the black partridge which ranges from Cyprus to Assam.

Frankincense is of two kinds, one being used as incense in certain religious services and obtained from olibanum, an Eastern shrub, the other is a resinous exudation derived from firs and pines, and largely used in pharmacy.

Franklin, the name given in feudal times to a country landowner who was independent of the territorial lord, and performed many of the minor functions of local government, such as serving as magistrate.

Fresco, a painting executed upon plaster walls or ceilings, a technique which has remained unchanged since it was practised by the great Renaissance artists.

Freshwater Shrimp, a small crustacean abounding in British streams, and feeding on dead fish or other decomposing matter. Although of shrimp-like form it is not closely related to salt-water shrimps. Its generic name is *Gammarus*.

Friars, members of certain mendicant orders of the Roman Catholic Church. The four chief orders are the Franciscans or Grey Friars, the Dominicans or Black Friars, the Carmelites or White Friars, and the Augustinians (Austin Friars).

Friday, the 6th day of the week, named after Frigga, the wife of Odin. It is the Mohammedan Sabbath, a general abstinence day of the Roman Catholic Church, and according to popular superstition, an unlucky day.

Friends, The Society of. *See* **J17.**

Frigate-Bird, a web-footed bird widely distributed over tropical latitudes, and deriving its name from its great expanse of wing and forked tail, resembling the shape of a swift vessel. It feeds on flying fish mostly, being unable to dive and also steals from other birds. A frigate-bird was found dying on the Hebridean island of Tiree in July 1953: only twice previously had one been recorded in Europe—the first on the German coast in 1792, and the second on the coast of France in 1902.

Frog, a familiar amphibian, breathing through gills in the earlier (tadpole) part of its existence, and through lungs later. It remains three months in the tadpole stage. The frog hibernates underwater in the mud during the winter.

Frost occurs when the temperature falls to, or below, 0° C., which is freezing point. Hoar frost is applied to the needles or feather-like crystals of ice deposited on the ground, in the same manner as dew. Glazed frost is the clear icy coating which may be formed as a result of rain falling on objects whose temperatures are below the freezing point. These layers of ice, often rendering roads impassable for traffic, damaging overhead power and communication systems and endangering aircraft, can also be caused by condensation from warm, damp winds coming into contact with very cold air and freezing surfaces.

Froth-Hopper *or* **Frog-Hopper.** A family of bugs (belonging to the insect order *Hemiptera*) which in the larval stage surround themselves with a protective mass of froth ("cuckoo spit"). These insects, which suck the sap of plants, bear a faint resemblance to frogs, and the adults possess great leaping powers.

Fuel Cells. A recent development is a type of battery into which the active chemicals are fed from external fuel tanks. This is the *fuel cell*, which is being developed in several countries. In August 1959 F. T. Bacon of Cambridge University demonstrated his fuel cell driving a fork-lift truck and a welding machine. The Bacon fuel cell consists of two electrodes of porous nickel dipping into a solution of caustic potash in water. One electrode is supplied with hydrogen gas from an outside cylinder and the other with oxygen. These gases, forming layers on the nickel, are the active chemicals. The oxygen combines with water to make two negatively charged ions, each consisting of an oxygen and a hydrogen atom joined together (a hydroxyl ion). The hydroxyl ions travel through the solution to the hydrogen electrode, where they combine with hydrogen to form neutral water. Their negative charge (one electron per ion involved) has now arrived at the hydrogen electrode and is ready to flow back to the other electrode through any outside circuit that is provided. This flow constitutes the useful electric current, and it has been provided at the expense of creating water out of the original hydrogen and oxygen. The water can be removed in the form of steam. What is the advantage of all this? In the first place the fuel gases are easy to make and to store in cylinders. Supplying a new gas cylinder is easier and quicker than recharging an ordinary accumulator. Furthermore, a fuel cell is lighter for a given power than an accumulator; satellite designers have found them useful. The fuel cell is not damaged by heavy overloading, and this is valuable for application to vehicle driving. Fuel-cell-driven buses could combine the advantages of diesel buses and trolleybuses. Fuel cells are still in the development stage. It is not certain how they will compete with combustion engines or, in the oil-less future, with improved ordinary batteries.

Fugue. A contrapuntal piece of music in which the several " voices " take up the theme in turn.

Fulani, a non-Negro people of Hamitic stock widely distributed in N.W. Africa, chiefly in Nigeria. There are two main branches: the dark-skinned Fulani, settled farmers and city dwellers, Moslem in religion, and the light-coloured Bororo'en who are semi-nomadic herdsmen. The Fulani are different from any tribe in W. Africa though they resemble in some ways the Masai of E. Africa. The Fulani conquered the Hausa states at the beginning of the 19th cent. which passed under British suzerainty after 1903. Sokoto, built in 1810, was capital of the Fulani empire.

Fuller's Earth, a special kind of clay or marl possessing highly absorbent qualities, originally used in the " fulling "—that is, cleansing and felting—of cloth. Now used in clarifying oils. Deposits in America and in south of England.

Function. In mathematics, one quantity y is said to be a function of another quantity x, written $y = f(x)$, if a change in one produces a change in the other. Thus the pressure of a gas is a function of its density and its temperature ($PV = RT$).

Functionalism, in architecture, a movement originated by Le Corbusier, Swiss-born French architect and town-planner, who applied the austere principles of the Purist movement in painting to his own art. From about 1924 he designed in concrete, steel, and glass, buildings in which every part had a significance in terms of function on the theory that objects created to carry out their particular function to perfection cannot help being beautiful. " A house is a machine for living in." The style was in vogue between the two wars, and although its severity became somewhat modified, it is still the basis of most modern architecture.

Fungi, a class of simple plants, which reproduce from spores and lack the green colouring matter *chlorophyll*. It includes moulds, rusts, mildews, smuts, mushrooms, etc. Potato blight is a fungus disease which caused the failure of the potato crop in Ireland in 1846. 50,000 different fungi are known. *See also* **F27**(2), **P8**(1).

Furniture Beetle (*Anobium punctatum*). The common furniture beetle is responsible for 80 per cent of all woodworm damage and is the great pest of the comparatively modern house, causing damage in the main to softwood roofing and flooring timbers. Adults one-eighth of an inch long. The grub tunnels for about 33 months. *See also* **Woodworm, Death Watch Beetle.**

Futurism, the only important modern art movement to arise outside France, initiated by Marinetti, an Italian writer and mountebank friend of Mussolini at a later period. Its origin took the form of a manifesto published in Paris in 1909 in which Marinetti glorified violence, war, and the machine age. In its aggression it favoured the growth of fascism. One of the distinctive features of Futurist art was the use of the principle of " simultaneity " in which the same figure (*e.g.*, a woman descending a flight of stairs) is represented in successive positions like film " stills " superimposed on each other. In spite of two further manifestos it was not until 1911 that the first examples of Futurist painting and sculpture appeared by the artists Severini, Balla, and Boccioni. Apart from the principle of simultaneity, Futurism derived from Cubist and Post-impressionist techniques. The movement faded out early in first world war.

G

Gabardine, a long, loose, coarse, over-garment, worn by men of the common class in the Middle Ages, and prescribed by law as the distinctive garment of the Jews. The name is now given to a closely woven cloth of wool and cotton used to make raincoats.

Gabbro, a kind of igneous rock, often very coarse-grained, containing a good deal of plagioclase felspar, and monoclinic pyroxene; it may occasionally also include biotite, magnetite, ilmenite, and hornblende. A gabbro containing nickel at Sudbury in Canada is one of the richest sources known of that metal.

Gadfly, a widely distributed family of flies with only one pair of wings, including the horse fly. The females are very voracious, being able to bite through the skin and suck the blood of animals. The males are harmless.

Gadolinium. An element belonging to the rare-earths metals discovered in 1886 by Marignac.

Gaelic, relating to the Gaels and their language, a term now applied only to the Celtic people inhabiting the Highlands of Scotland, but formerly also to the Celts of Ireland and the Isle of Man.

Galago, " Bush Babies," related to the lemur, native to Africa, large-eyed, in keeping with its nocturnal characteristics.

Galaxy *or* **Milky Way Galaxy** is the huge disk-shaped cloud of gas and stars (some 100,000 million, one of which is the sun) that is turning in space like a great wheel, with a diameter of about 100,000 light years. The Milky Way (that part of the heavens in Milton's words " powdered with stars ") is really only a small part of this disk, and every star in the galaxy is moving round the centre under the gravitational control of the whole. The sun and planets lie near the edge of the disk, and it takes them about 250 million years to travel once round. The number of stars that can be seen with the unaided eye is about 3,000, and they all belong to the Milky Way Galaxy, as do most of the stars that can be seen with anything but the greatest telescopes. With the large modern optical and radar telescopes many other systems, similar in size and weight to our galaxy, have been discovered, scattered more or less uniformly through space, and the universe is said to include at least 10,000 million such galaxies. *See also* **F3–6.**

Gale, a high wind now technically defined as one of at least Beaufort force 8. Between thirty and forty gales a year occur on the north and west coasts of the British Isles and only about half of this number in the south-east. At St. Ann's Head, Pembroke, the anemometer registered a gust of 113 m.p.h. on Jan. 18, 1945, which is a record for these islands. Gusts exceeding 70 m.p.h. are rarely experienced in London. Gale warnings are issued for specified areas by the Meteorological Office, the warnings taking the form of radio broadcasts and the hoisting of storm signals at certain points on the coast. *See* Beaufort Wind Scale, **N13.**

Gall, abnormal vegetable growths caused by insects, mites, bacteria, or fungi, found on all parts of the plant. Oak-apples, Robin's pin-cushion (on wild rose), " witches brooms " (on trees) are examples. Some are useful commercially, *e.g.*, oak apples yield tannic acid and the black oak gall is used in America as animal food.

Galleon, the name given to the old three-decked Spanish treasure vessels employed in conveying the precious minerals from the American colonies to Spain. The term is often applied to any large, especially stately, sailing vessel.

Galley, an oar-propelled sea-boat used by the ancient Greeks and Romans for transport purposes, manned by slaves. Boats of a similar class were used by the French down to the middle of the 18th cent., and manned by convicts.

Gallic Acid, obtained from gall nuts, sumach, tea, coffee, and the seeds of the mango, is used in the manufacture of inks and as an astringent in medicine. It was discovered by C. W. Scheele (1742–86), a Swedish chemist.

Gallium, a white metal, symbol Ga, related to aluminium, but which can be cut with a knife. It was discovered spectroscopically by L. de Boisbaudran in 1875. Long before Mendeleyev had predicted that an element with its properties would be found to fill the then existing gap in the Periodic Table; this gap came immediately below aluminium, so he suggested the name "eka aluminium" for it.

Gallup Poll, a system, introduced by Dr. Gallup of the United States, for testing public opinion on topical subjects by taking a test poll on questions framed to elicit opinions.

Galvanised Iron is iron coated with zinc. The name comes from the fact that such a coat protective against rust could be deposited electrolytically. Electrodeposition is sometimes used, but the cheaper and more common process depends on dipping the iron in a bath of molten zinc.

Gamboge, a resinous gum obtained from the sap of *Garcinia morella*, a tree native to Thailand, Cambodia, and Ceylon, and used as a yellow pigment in paints and also as a purgative.

Game is the term applied to wild animals which are protected from indiscriminate slaughter by Game Laws. In the United Kingdom game comprehends deer, hares, pheasants, partridges, grouse, black game, moor game, woodcocks, bustards, and certain other birds and animals of the chase. Game can only be killed (with few exceptions) by persons holding game licences. Occupiers of land and one other person authorised by them in each case are allowed to kill hares and rabbits on their land without licence. Game cannot be sold except by a person holding a proper licence. There is a "close time" prescribed for the different classes of game; for instance, the selling or exposing for sale of any hare or leveret during March, April, May, June, or July is prohibited by law. Grouse cannot be shot between Dec. 11 and Aug. 11; patridges between Feb. 2 and Aug. 31; pheasants between Feb. 2 and Sept. 30; and black game between Dec. 11 and Aug. 10. In regard to foxes, stags, and otters, custom and not Parliament prescribes a certain law which sportsmen rigidly adhere to. Game reserves are legally protected areas where natural vegetation and wild life are allowed to remain unmolested by sportsmen or those who might destroy for economic ends. *See* British Game Seasons, **N24**.

Gaming, *or* **Gambling**—*i.e.*, staking money on the chances of a game—differs from betting in that it depends upon the result of a trial of skill or a turn of chance. The Betting and Gaming Act of 1959 replaced all the old laws on gaming, which went back to an Act of 1541 entitled "An Acte for Mayntenance of Artyllarie and debarringe of unlauful games," under which some games were unlawful if played for money in any circumstances. Roulette and any game of dice were among such games. Under the new Act any game is lawful, subject to certain conditions.

Gammexane, a powerful insecticide, used particularly to kill the tsetse fly and mosquito.

Gamut. The set of lines and spaces on which music is written.

Gangue. Useless minerals associated with metallic ores.

Gannet, a fish-eating bird which dives on its prey from a great height, swallowing it under water; is found in large numbers off the coast of Scotland, and has breeding stations in the Hebrides, St. Kilda, Ailsa Craig, the Bass Rock, Grassholme Island, and on Ortac and Les Etacs (rocks off Alderney). It is a bird of white plumage, black tips to long narrow wings and wedge-shaped tail, and weighs about 7 lb. The gannet breeds in colonies on ledges of steep, rocky, island cliffs. Related to the cormorants, pelicans, and frigate-birds.

Garden Cities in England were founded by Ebenezer Howard (1850–1928), and his ideas were put forward in his book *Tomorrow—A Peaceful Path to Real Reform* (later re-issued as *Garden Cities of Tomorrow*). New towns should be so placed and planned as to get the best of town and country life, an adaptation of the model villages of certain industrial philanthropists such as Salt, Richardson, Cadbury, Leverhulme, and others. The Garden City Association (later the Town and Country Planning Association) was formed in 1899, and the first garden city was begun at Letchworth in 1904 and successfully established. Welwyn Garden City was also Howard's foundation, established in 1919.

Gardener-Bird, a bird possessing many of the characteristics of the bower-bird, and found only in Papua–New Guinea. *See also* **Bower Bird.**

Gargantua, the giant hero of Rabelais' satire, of immense eating and drinking capacity, symbolical of an antagonistic ideal of the greed of the Church.

Gargoyle, a projecting spout for carrying off water from the roof gutter of a building. Gargoyles are only found in old structures, modern water-pipe systems having rendered them unnecessary. In Gothic architecture they were turned to architectural account and made to take all kinds of grotesque forms—grinning goblins, hideous monsters, dragons, and so forth.

Garlic, a bulbous plant of the same genus as the onion and the leek, and a favourite condiment among the people of Southern Europe. It possesses a very strong odour and pungent taste and its culinary use is agelong.

Garnet, a group of minerals; chemically they are orthosilicates of the metals calcium, magnesium, titanium, iron, aluminium. Garnets can be coloured yellow, brown, black, green, or red; the blood-red garnet is an important gemstone.

Garrotte, a method of strangulation used as capital punishment in Spain, and consisting of a collar which is compressed by a screw that causes death by piercing the spinal marrow. Garroting was also applied to a system of highway robbery common in England in 1862–63, the assailants seizing their victims from behind, and by a sudden compression of the windpipe disabling them until the robbery was completed.

Garter. The Most Noble Order of the Garter was founded (*c.* 1348) by King Edward III., and is the premier order of knighthood in Great Britain. The traditional story associating the garter and the motto with the Countess of Salisbury, who it was said dropped her garter while dancing with the King, who remarked "honi soit qui mal y pense" cannot be accepted. The order was originally limited to the Sovereign and 25 knights, but the number has been extended, and it may now be bestowed on royal personages and leading representatives of the British peerage. The insignia of the order are the garter of dark-blue velvet with the motto in letters of gold, the mantle of dark-blue velvet lined with white silk, the surcoat and hood, and the gold-and-enamel collar. The garter is worn on the left leg below the knee and by women as a sash over the left shoulder. *See* **Knighthood.**

Gas is an elastic fluid substance, the molecules of which are in constant rapid motion, and exerting pressure. The technique whereby gases are liquefied depends on increasing pressure and diminishing temperature. Each gas has a critical point; unless the temperature is brought down to this point no amount of pressure will bring about liquefaction. Last gas to be liquefied was helium (1908) which boils at —209° C. *See* **Gas Laws, N32,** *and* **F16(2).**

Gas from Coal for lighting and heating purposes is obtained from bituminous coal. Such a gas was produced and used for illuminating purposes by William Murdoch towards the end of the 18th cent. in Birmingham, and about 1807 the illuminant was introduced in London, one side of Pall Mall being lighted with it. It soon supplanted oil and candles for outdoor and indoor lighting, and is still, in spite of the advances of electric light, a common illuminant, its power having been greatly increased by the incandescent burner. It is widely used for space heating and cooking. *See* **Underground Gasification.**

Gas, Natural, natural mixture of gases often present with deposits of petroleum, found issuing from the ground in many parts of the world—in the oilfields of Venezuela and the Caucasus, in China, Saudi-Arabia, but chiefly in North America. Its chief component is methane. Large industrial centres have made use of this gas since the latter part of the 19th cent., but much of this valuable fuel still goes to waste. Pipelines have been constructed to deliver the gas to where it is wanted. Britain began to ship liquid methane from the Saharan oilfield in 1964. *See also* **Methane.**

Gas Turbine. This kind of engine has recently become a competitor of the internal combustion engine. Mechanical movement is produced by a jet of gas impinging on a turbine wheel. Gas turbines are being used in aeroplanes, locomotives, and ships. These engines are mechanically simple compared with internal combustion engines, and require less maintenance. It has been stated that the jet-propelled Comet cruises at 450 m.p.h. burning less than ½ lb. of kerosene per passenger mile.

Gauge, a standard dimension or measurement, applied in various branches of construction. Thus, the standard railway gauge is 4 ft. 8½ in. in the United Kingdom, United States, Canada, France, Germany, Austria, Holland, Egypt, Belgium, Denmark, Italy, Hungary, Sweden, Switzerland, and Turkey. In India, Ceylon, and Spain the gauge is 5 ft. 6 in. In Soviet Russia and Finland, 5 ft., Ireland, 5 ft. 3 in. Narrow railway gauges of different standards are in use on very steep inclines in various countries. Other standard gauges are fixed in building and gun-boring.

Gauls were inhabitants of ancient Gaul, the country which comprised what is now France, Belgium, and parts of the Netherlands, Switzerland, and Germany.

Gault, a stratum of blue clay between the Lower Greensand and the Chalk. A typical section of the Gault can be seen at Folkestone.

Gauss, a unit of magnetic induction in the c.g.s. system, named after the great German mathematician and astronomer, K. F. Gauss.

Gavelkind, an old English custom of land tenure in Kent and other places in England, whereby on the death, intestate, of a property owner, his property is divided equally among his children and not according to the law of primogeniture. Abolished by the Law of Property Act, 1922, and the Administration of Estates Act, 1925.

Gazelle, an animal of the antelope family, of small and delicate shape, with large eyes and short cylindrical horns. It is of a fawn colour, a native of North Africa, and easily domesticated.

Gecko, the name of a family of drab lizards common in or near the tropics. They are nocturnal, insectivorous, and harmless.

Geiger Counter, an electrical device, invented by Geiger, which can detect individual atomic particles, *e.g.*, electrons, protons, etc. It often consists of a tube of gas at a few cm. Hg pressure, fitted with two electrodes—a cylinder and an axial wire. A high voltage is kept across the electrodes, and the passage of a charged particle through the gas releases ions which permit a momentary discharge between the electrodes. Electronic circuits register this discharge as a "count." Geiger counters are widely used to detect and measure radioactivity and cosmic rays, both for technical and research purposes.

Gelatine, a transparent, tasteless, organic substance obtained from animal membranes, bones, tendons, etc., by boiling in water. It is of various kinds, according to the substance used in making it. Isinglass, the purest form of it, is made from air-bladders and other membranes of fish, while the coarser kind—glue—is made from hoofs, skin, hides, etc. Its constituents are carbon, hydrogen, oxygen, and nitrogen. Gelatine is applied to an immense variety of purposes, from the making of food jellies to photographic materials.

Gemini, one of the signs of the Zodiac lying east of Taurus and containing numerous stars, only two of which—Castor, the upper and brighter one, and Pollux, the lower one—are visible to the naked eye. The stars are named after twin divinities of classical mythology.

Gemsbok, a large South African antelope, with long straight horns and tufted tail. Light fawn in colour, it has a black streak across its face, and is very fleet of foot.

General, a military title next in rank to that of Field-Marshal, the highest officer in the army. Ranking below full General are Lieutenant-General, Major-General, and Brigadier.

Generation, a time-measure reckoned at about 30 years when children are ready to replace parents; also the body of persons existing at the same time or period.

Generation, Spontaneous. *See* **Abiogenesis.**

Genes, the elementary units of heredity. They exist as highly differentiated regions arranged along the length of the chromosomes which the nuclei of cells carry. A chromosome may carry hundreds or even thousands of genes, each with its own particular structure and specific properties. The position of a particular gene on a chromosome is called its locus. *See* **Cell Division F19–21.**

Genesis, the first book of the Pentateuch, compiled in the 5th cent. B.C. from earlier documents, which carries the scriptural narrative from the creation to the death of Joseph. Sometimes there is disagreement, as in the story of the creation, Gen. i and ii. Gen. i reflects the views of the ancient Greek scientist Thales (*c.* 640–546 B.C.) and may be said to be the first scientific account of the creation of the world. The conditions described around the figures of Abraham, Isaac, Jacob, and Joseph have a genuine historical basis.

Genet, one of the smaller carnivorous animals, about the size of a cat, but with longer tail and spotted body. It is a native of Southern Europe, North Africa, and Western Asia, and is valued for its fine soft fur, and also for a perfume it produces.

Geneva Convention, an agreement made by the European Powers at Geneva in 1864, establishing humane regulations regarding the treatment of the sick and wounded in war and the status of those who minister to them. All persons, hospitals, hospital ships are required to display the Geneva cross—a red cross on a white ground. A second conference held at Geneva in 1868 drew up a supplementary agreement. An important result of this Convention was the establishment of the Red Cross Society in 1870.

Genouillieres, ancient metal caps for covering the knees of an armed man; an example may be seen on the Black Prince's monument in Canterbury Cathedral.

Genre, an art term used to describe a style of painting which deals with subjects of homely life, but also applied to other kinds of paintings, *e.g.*, genre du paysage (landscape painting), genre historique (historical painting).

Gentian, the name for plants of the *Gentiana* genus, many of which have intensely blue flowers. The gentian-root of *G. lutea* is used in pharmacy.

Genus, a term applied in biology to designate a group of similar species. A group of similar genera is called a family.

Geodesy, the science of calculating the configuration and extent of the earth's surface, and determining exact geographical positions and directions, with variations of gravity, etc. Land-surveying is a branch of geodesy.

Geography, the science which describes the earth's surface, its physical peculiarities, and the distribution of the various animals and plants upon it. It is usual to divide the subject into two main branches—physical geography, which deals with the composition of the earth's surface and the distribution of its living occupants, animate and inanimate; and human geography, which includes economic, political, and social geography.

Geology, the science which deals with the condition and structure of the earth, and the evidence afforded of ancient forms of life. The geological strata are classified in the following categories: *Primary* or *Palaeozoic* (the oldest fossil-bearing rocks including the Cambrian, Ordovician, Silurian, Devonian, Carboniferous, Permian); *Secondary* or *Mesozoic* (Triassic, Jurassic, Cretaceous); *Tertiary* or *Cainozoic* (Eocene, Oligocene, Miocene, Pliocene, Pleistocene); *Post tertiary* (most recent rocks). *See* **F30.**

Geometrical Progression is a term used to indicate a succession of numbers which increase or decrease at an equal ratio—as 3, 9, 27; or 64, 16, 4.

Geometry is the branch of mathematics which demonstrates the properties of figures, and the distances of points of space from each other by means of deductions. It is a science of reason from fundamental axioms, and was perfected by Euclid about 300 B.C. The books of Euclid contain a full elucidation of the science, though supplemented in modern times by Descartes,

Newton and Carnot. Of recent years non-Euclidean geometry has been developed.

Geophysics, the branches of physics which are concerned with the earth and its atmosphere. Meteorology, geomagnetism, aurora and air-glow, ionosphere, solar activity, cosmic rays, glaciology, oceanography, seismology, nuclear radiation in the atmosphere, rockets, and satellites—all these are geophysical subjects. The object of the International Geophysical Year, 1957–58, was to investigate the physical phenomena occurring on and around the earth by means of carefully co-ordinated observations made simultaneously all over the globe. *See also* F9(1).

George-Noble, a gold coin, so called from St. George and the dragon depicted on its obverse. First issued in the reign of Henry VIII.

German Silver, an alloy of copper, zinc, and nickel, and used in the manufacture of table-ware, such as spoons, forks, etc.

Germanium. A grey, hard, brittle chemical element, symbol Ge, chemically related to silicon and tin. Discovered by Winkler in 1886. Its richest ore is germanite containing 6% of the metal. Coal is also a relatively rich source. Since 1948 it has assumed great importance as a semi-conducting material for making transistors (*q.v.*). Because of this it has been so intensively studied that more is known about it than about any other element.

Gesta Romanorum (Latin = deeds of the Romans), a mediaeval collection of Latin stories of unknown authorship which circulated widely in Europe during the Middle Ages. First printed in the 15th cent. The stories were used by Chaucer, Shakespeare and other writers who found many romantic incidents and legends which they were able to turn to good account.

Gestation, the carrying of young in animals during pregnancy, varies considerably in its length. In the case of an elephant, the period is 21 months; a camel, 12 months; a cow, 9 months; a cat, 8 weeks; a horse, 48 weeks; a dog, 9 weeks; and a pig, 16 weeks. Hens "sit" for 21 days; geese, 30; swans, 42; turkeys, 28; pigeons, 18.

Geysers, hot springs of volcanic origination and action, are remarkable for the fact that they throw out huge streams of boiling water instead of lava as in the case of a volcano. The most famous geysers are those of Iceland, which number over a hundred, the principal one having an opening 70 ft. in diameter and discharging a column of water to a height of 200 ft. There are also geysers in the Yellowstone region of America, and some in New Zealand. Also a device now in common domestic use for heating running water quickly by gas or electricity.

Ghost-Moth or Ghost Swift, an interesting nocturnal insect (*Hepialus humuli*), common in England, possessing in the male a white collar and known for its habit of hovering with a pendulum-like action in the twilight over a particular spot where the female is concealed.

Giambeaux, metal armour for the legs and shins, worn by the warriors of Richard II.'s reign.

Gibbon, the name of a long-armed ape mainly inhabiting S.E. Asia. It is without tail, and possesses the power of very rapid movement among the trees of the forests.

Gin, a well-known spirit distilled from malt or barley and flavoured with the juniper berry. The principal varieties are the English and American, known as "Gin" or "Dry Gin", and the Dutch, referred to as "jenever" or "Hollandse jenever". In Germany and Austria it is called "Schnapps". The word "Gin" is an abbreviation of "Geneva", both being primarily derived from the French genièvre (juniper).

Ginger is obtained from a reed-like perennial plant grown in tropical countries. There are two varieties, black ginger and grey ginger. The former is obtained by peeling and drying the root, the latter by scalding and drying. Ginger is largely used as a condiment

Giraffe, the tallest of existing animals, reaching a height of from 18 to 20 ft. when full grown. Its sloping back and elongated neck seem to be the natural evolution of an animal that has to feed on the branches of trees. It is a native of Africa, is of a light fawn colour marked with darker spots, and has a prehensile tongue.

Giralda, a beautiful and remarkable example of Arabian art, erected in 1195 at Seville, still in existence. Minarets similar to the Giralda are to be found at Morocco, Tunis, and Tetuan.

Glaciers form in the higher Alpine ranges, and are immense consolidated masses of snow, which are gradually impelled by their force down the mountain-sides until they reach a point where the temperature causes them to melt, and they run off in streams. From such glaciers the five great rivers, the Rhine, the Po, the Rhône, the Inn, and the Adige, have their source. The longest of the Swiss glaciers is the Gross Aletsch, which sometimes extends over 10 miles. Some of the glaciers of the Himalayas are four times as long. The Muir in Alaska is of enormous magnitude, and that of Justeldals Brae in Norway is the largest in Europe.

Gladiators were professional athletes and combatants in ancient Rome, contesting with each other or with wild beasts. At first they were drawn from the slave and prisoner classes exclusively, but so much were the successful gladiators held in esteem that men came to make a profession of athletics, and gladiatorial training schools were established. When a gladiator was vanquished without being killed in combat, it was left with the spectators to decide his fate, death being voted by holding the hands out with the thumb turned inward, and life by putting forth the hands with the thumb extended. Gladiatorial shows were the chief public displays in Rome from the 3rd to the 4th cent. A.D.

Glass, a substance obtained from the fusion of silica (sand) with various bases, and is more or less transparent. There are numerous kinds of glass, but they group themselves under one or other of the following classifications:—Flint glass, or crystal, whose components are potash, silica, and oxide of lead; window glass, made from soda, lime, and silica; Bohemian glass, containing potash, lime, and silica; and bottle glass, composed of soda, lime, alumina, silica, and oxide of iron. Heat-proof glasses used for making cooking utensils contain boron. Glass was made by the Phoenicians, and was familiar in ancient Egypt. The Egyptians introduced it into Rome. In the Middle Ages Venice was famed for its glass manufactures, but after the 17th cent. Bohemia acquired pre-eminence. English glass reached its highest level of artistic design in the 17th and 18th cent. Window glass was not used in this country for dwellings until the end of the Middle Ages.

Glass-Snake, genus, *Ophisaurus*, of legless lizards with long fragile tails capable of re-generation when broken. Six species are known; in S.E. Europe, S.W. Asia, Indo-China, and N. America. Attains a length of about 2 ft.; main colouring, green, with black and yellow markings.

Glauconite. A green mineral, chemically a hydrated silicate of potassium and iron. Commonly found in marine sands (hence these rocks are known as "greensands") and sandstones.

Glaucus is a curious genus of sea slugs often called the Sea Lizard belonging to the molluscs. It is without shell and has a soft body, with horny mouth and four tentacles. It is a native of the Atlantic, and is not more than 12 in. in length.

Glee, an unaccompanied piece for three or more voices. Glee-singing was popular in England during the 18th and early 19th cent. and glee-clubs are still in existence.

Globigerina, an oceanic unicellular animalcule with a perforated shell, and occurring in certain parts of the Atlantic in such vast numbers as to form a bed of chalk ooze with their empty shells.

Glockenspiel, an instrument composed of metal bars each of which is tuned to a note. The bars are struck by hand-hammers and give forth chiming sounds.

Gloria in Excelsis ("Glory to God in the highest") is the opening of the Latin hymn adapted from Luke ii. 4, and the most prominent hymn of the ecclesiastical rites in the Christian liturgies.

Gloria Patri, the lesser Doxology, with which chants are generally concluded in the English Church service—"Glory be to the Father, and to the Son."

Glow-worm, a beetle, possessing the power (much stronger in the female than the male) of emitting phosphorescent light from the hind end of the body. The female is wingless.

Glucinium. *See* **Beryllium.**

Glucose, Dextrose *or* **Grape Sugar** is a carbohydrate (*q.v.*). It is produced by hydrolysis from cane sugar, dextrine, starch, cellulose, etc., by the action of reagents. It also occurs in many plants, fruits, and honey. For brewing purposes glucose is prepared by the conversion of starch by sulphuric acid. Malt also converts starch into glucose.

Glutton *or* **Wolverine,** the biggest animal of the weasel family, inhabits the northernmost parts of Europe and America. In build it resembles the bear, and is rather larger than a badger. Its fur is of a brown-black hue, but coarse.

Glycerine *or* **Glycerol,** occurs in natural fats combined with fatty acids, and is obtained by decomposing those substances with alkalies or by superheated steam. It is colourless and oily and sweet, and is put to a variety of commercial uses, being widely utilised for medicaments, for lubricating purposes, and in the manufacture of nitro-glycerine.

Glycols. Organic compounds containing two alcohol groups. Ethylene glycol is the most widely known example: it is used as an anti-freeze in motor-car radiators on account of its property of greatly reducing the freezing point of water. Also used in the manufacture of "Terylene". *See* **Esters.**

Glyptoden, an extinct species of gigantic armadillo, fossil remains of which have been discovered in S. America. It was some 9 ft. long, carried a huge tortoise-like shell, and had fluted teeth.

Gneiss, a metamorphic rock usually containing quartz, felspar, and mica. It is banded, the light-coloured minerals being concentrated apart from the dark minerals.

Gnosticism. *See* **J18.**

Gnu, an animal of the antelope family, combining the characteristics of the buffalo in its head and horns, the ass in its neck and mane, and the horse in its long and bushy tail. There are two species, the common and the brindled, and they are about the size of an ass. They abound in Africa and congregate in herds.

Goat-Moth (*Cossus cossus*), a large moth of the *Cossidae* family, common in Britain, evil-smelling, and very destructive in the larval stage to trees of the poplar and willow genus, into the wood of which the caterpillar bores during its three years' period of development.

Goats are horned ruminant quadrupeds, indigenous to the Eastern Hemisphere, but now domesticated in all parts of the world. Though related to the sheep, they are a much hardier and more active animal. The male has a tuft of hair under the chin. Many species, including those of Cashmere and Angora, are valuable for their hair, which is used for fine textile fabrics. The milk of the goat is nutritive, and goat-skins are in good demand for leather for gloves, shoes, etc.

Gobelin Tapestry was originated by a family of dyers named Gobelin in the 15th cent. in Paris. The Gobelin establishment, which produced this beautiful tapestry, made of silk and wool, or silk and cotton, was taken over by the Government of Louis XIV., in 1662, and since then has been the French national factory for that class of fabric.

God and Man. *See* **J18.**

Gog and Magog, two legendary City of London giants, supposed to be the offspring of certain wicked daughters of the Emperor Diocletian and a band of demons. They were brought captive to London and made to serve as prisoners at the Palace of Brute, which stood on the site of Guildhall. Effigies of the giants have stood in Guildhall since the time of Henry V. They were destroyed in the Great Fire of 1666, replaced in 1672, and used to be carried through the streets of London in the Lord Mayor's Show. The present figures, newly carved in lime wood by Mr. David Evans, replaced those carved in 1708 by Richard Saunders, which were destroyed in an air raid during the last war.

Gold. Metallic element, symbol Au (Latin *Aurum*) related to silver and copper, the coinage metals. The greatest amount of gold is obtained by treating gold-bearing quartz by the cyanide process. The gold is dissolved out by cyanide solution, which is then run into long boxes filled with zinc shavings when the gold is precipitated as a black slime. This is melted with an oxidising agent which removes the zinc.

Gold-Beaters' Skin is the outside membrane of the large intestine of the ox, specially prepared and used by gold-beaters for placing between the leaves of gold while they beat them. This membrane is of great tenacity, and gets beaten to such extreme thinness that it is used to put on cuts and bruises.

Gold Standard. This consists in the fixing of the value of a currency in terms of a weight of gold of a certain fineness. Countries working under the gold standard lay down a fixed (or only slightly varying) weight of gold as equivalent to a unit of their currency, and their Central Banks undertake to supply gold, either freely or subject to certain limitations, in exchange for the national currency at this rate. Accordingly, their Central Banks need to keep a Gold Reserve sufficient to meet demands for such exchanges of the currency for gold. In practice under present conditions, the possession of dollars or of other gold-standard money is treated as equivalent to that of gold.

Golden Age, according to the Greek and Roman poets, was the age of peace and innocence when mankind lived in a state of ideal prosperity and happiness.

Goldeneye, a species of wild duck, widely distributed over Arctic regions. It is a passage-migrant and winter-visitor to the British Isles. Has nested in Cheshire. Distinguished by a large white spot in front of each eye on a dark ground.

Golden Number, the number of any year in the metonic cycle of 19 years, deriving its name from the fact that in the old calendars it was always printed in gold. It is found by adding 1 to the number of the year A.D. and dividing by 19, the remainder being the Golden Number; or, if no remainder, the Golden Number is 19. The only use to which the Golden Number is put now is in making ecclesiastical calculations for determining movable feasts.

Goldsmiths Company, one of the richest London City Companies; the official assayers of gold and silver, invested with the power of "hall-marking" the quality of objects made from these metals. First charter granted in 1327.

Gondola, the old regulation black boats so common on the canals of Venice, propelled by a gondolier with one oar who stands at the stern, his passengers being accommodated in a covered space in the centre.

Gonfalon, the pennon affixed to a lance, spear, or standard, consisting usually of two or three streamers, and made to turn like a weather-cock.

Gophers. Rodent mammals. The pocket gophers are stout-bodied burrowers common in the U.S.A. The slender burrowing gophers, also called "ground squirrels," occur in central and western U.S.A. The sisel or suslik is a related European species. They are a great pest among grain crops.

Gordon Riots of 1780 were an anti-popery agitation fomented by Lord George Gordon. Called also "No-Popery Riots."

Gorilla, the largest of the anthropoid apes, found in the forests of Equatorial Africa, and at maturity standing from 4 to 5 ft. high.

Goshawk (*Accipiter gentilis*), a diurnal bird of prey fearless and extremely agile; loves wooded country and is very destructive of poultry and game-birds. It resembles the peregrine falcon in appearance, but has shorter, rounded wings. This bird was a great favourite of falconers in mediaeval times. It is still a familiar sight in parts of Europe, was once common in England where it is said to have bred again in recent years.

Gospels are those portions of the New Testament which deal with the life, death, resurrection and teachings of Christ. They are the gospels of Matthew, Mark, Luke, and John, and the first three are called the *synoptic gospels* because of their general unity of narrative. That of John is of somewhat wider scope, and gives in addition to the story of the Passion an account of the ministry in Judaea.

Gothic. A term applied to a style of architecture which followed the Romanesque, appeared i

France during the 12th cent., and is typical of northern Europe. It was not generally appreciated south of the Alps. The high and sharply pointed arches, the walls supported outside by flying buttresses, the traceried windows, often filled with stained glass, and the lofty spires are in sharp distinction to the semicircular arches and the massive walls characteristic of the more sturdy Romanesque style. Yet the transition was gradual. The cathedrals of Chartres, Laon, and the Benedictine church of St. Denis just outside Paris are typical of early Gothic. The style found its full expression in the French cathedrals of the 13th and 14th cent.: Reims, Notre Dame, Beauvais, Bourges, and Amiens. From France the style spread to other lands in each of which it developed its own characteristics; thus the English churches tended to have massive towers and delicate spires and, as at Salisbury, were often set in open grounds surrounded by lawns; Flemish and Dutch churches were sometimes built of brick as were those in north Germany and Scandinavia; in Spain the Flamboyant style was followed. The main Gothic cathedral in Italy, that of Milan, although begun in 1386 was not completed until the early 19th cent. The lofty character of Gothic has been attributed by the romantic to pious aspiration, as if the spires were striving towards heaven and this concept may well have played a part. The more concrete reasons however were somewhat different: Romanesque churches were thick-walled, sturdy, small-windowed, and set often in open country or on heights (*a*) because architects had not yet discovered how to support a heavy roof without massive walls; and (*b*) because, being built in dangerous times, they had a defensive function. Gothic churches began to be raised in less troublesome times and were tall for the same reason that New York skyscrapers are tall (*i.e.*, the increasing price of land). Also they were built in growing cities where not much space was available and they were lavish in style because wealth was increasing and rich merchants were willing to contribute. Late English Gothic is seen, for example, at King's College Chapel, Cambridge, Henry's Chapel at Westminister, and St. George's Chapel at Windsor (all *c.* 1500). Gothic is also found in secular buildings, *e.g.*, Little Wenham Hall in Suffolk, the castle at Ghent, the town halls of Louvain and Middelburg, and the streets of Gothic houses in Bruges still in use today. Virtually Gothic as a style (excluding the "Gothic revival" of 19th cent. England) ended at the close of the 15th cent. Gothic art is best seen in the illuminated manuscripts of the 13th and 14th cent. and in the church sculpture. Its characteristic is a complete departure from the cool, perfectionist realism of classical times with distortion to produce emotional effects. The human figures are not ideal forms but recognisable as people we might meet in the street; yet there was also the element of wild imagination, intricate design, and a wealth of feeling which might be grotesque, humorous, macabre, or even obscene. This element of distortion and sometimes wildly "unrealistic" colouring which produced an effect more dramatic than the literal representation of the classic schools remained an important element in German art (*see* Expressionism) right up to modern times and is used by other modern schools.

Goths. A Teutonic people who originally came from southern Sweden (Gotland) and by the 3rd cent. were settled in the region north of the Black Sea. They began to encroach on the Roman Empire and early in the 4th cent. split into two divisions: the Visigoths or West Goths, and the Ostrogoths or East Goths. The Ostrogoths were conquered by the Huns *c.* 370, while the Visigoths under Alaric devastated Greece and sacked Rome in 410. Eventually the Visigoths spread to France and Spain and their last king Roderick fell in battle against the Moors in 711. The Ostrogoths regained their independence on the death of Attila in 453 and under their king Theodoric the Great conquered Italy in 493. They lost their identity after Justinian regained Italy, 525–552.

Gourd Family *or* **Cucurbitaceæ.** This family of about 650 species of flowering plants includes the gourds, pumpkins, cantaloupes, cucumber, gherkin, water-melon and squashes. Most abundant in the tropics, the cucurbits are mainly climbing annuals with very rapid growth. The bath-room loofah is the skeleton of one curcurbit fruit, *Luffa cylindrica*. The squirting cucumber is another member of the family.

Governor. A device attached to an engine, turbine, compressor, etc., which automatically controls the engine's speed in accordance with power demand. Most governors depend upon the centrifugal action of two or more balls which are thrown outwards as their speed of rotation increases and actuate a throttle valve or cut-off. The centrifugal governor was invented by Thomas Mead, patented by him in 1787, and used on windmills. Watt adapted it to the steam engine.

Grail, Legend of the Holy, a tale of Celtic origin which became part of Arthurian legend and the subject of many mediaeval quest-romances. According to the Christian version the grail was the cup which Christ used at the Last Supper, brought to England by St. Joseph of Arimathea.

Grand Prix, the "French Derby," was established by Napoleon III., in 1863. It is the chief French race and is an international competition of three-year-olds.

Granite is a coarsely crystalline igneous rock consisting of quartz and alkali felspars plus mica or hornblende. It is a much used ornamental and building stone; it forms the high ground of Dartmoor and Bodmin Moor.

Graphite *or* **Plumbago,** commonly called black-lead, is a form of carbon occurring in foliated masses in marble, schist, etc. It is soft, will make black marks on paper or other plain surfaces, and is mainly used for lead pencils. It is also a valuable lubricant. Pure graphite has found a new use with the construction of atomic piles. Important deposits occur in Siberia, Ceylon, Madagascar, Canada, and the U.S.A.

Graptolites, fossil animals confined to Cambrian, Ordovician and Silurian strata. Once classified as hydrazoa but now considered more likely to be hemichordates.

Grasshopper. There are many species of these leaping insects which are related to the locusts and crickets. Most are vegetarians; some eat flies and caterpillars also. The chirping sound they make is made by scraping the hind legs against the wings; in some species a noise is produced by rubbing the wings together.

Gravitation. The nature of the force of gravity is not properly understood. This is partly due to the fact that gravitational forces are very weak unless at least one of the interacting bodies is very large. Einstein's General Theory of Relativity is the only theory at present extant which attempts to interpret gravitational forces in terms of more fundamental concepts. *See* **F15(1).**

Graylag, the ordinary wild grey goose of Europe, the species from which domestic geese are derived; frequents fens and marshes; breeds in Iceland, Scandinavia, and Scotland; distinguished by pinkish legs and feet and lack of black markings on bill.

Grayling, a fresh-water fish of the salmon family having a large dorsal fin, and averaging about 1 lb. in weight.

Grebe, a diving bird of beautiful plumage found over a great part of the world on lakes and oceans. The two species familiar in Great Britain are the Dabchick or Little Grebe and the large and handsome Great Crested Grebe, which has a feathery tuft, lost in the autumn, on each side of the head. Grebes have remarkable courtship displays. The breast feathers are of a downy softness and silver lustre, for which they were formerly much hunted.

Greek Art. *See* **Hellenic Art.**

Greek Fire, a combustible, supposed to have been composed of sulphur, nitre, naphtha, and asphalt, used with destructive effect by the Greeks of the Eastern Empire in their wars.

Greek Kalends, equivalent to never, as only the Romans, not the Greeks, had kalends.

Gregorian Calendar. *See* **Calendar.**

Gregorian Chant, ritual music with a system of harmony suitable for church use. First established by Pope Gregory I.

Gresham's Law states that if good money, *i.e.*, money with the higher intrinsic value, and bad money are in circulation together, the bad money will tend to drive out the good money from circulation. For instance, the good money is more likely to be melted down or demanded in payment by foreign creditors.

Gretna Green, a celebrated village in Dumfries, just over the border from England, where runaway marriages were performed from 1754 to 1856, though only completely stopped during present century.

Griffin, in ancient mythology, a winged creature with an eagle's head and body of a lion, found in ancient sculptures of Persia and Assyria. Its origin is traced to the Hittites. It had the same religious significance as the winged sphinx of Egypt. The griffin vulture is a bird named after the mythological creature, found in Europe, Africa and India.

Grilse, a young salmon that has only been once to the sea.

Grimm's Law, formulated by Jacob Grimm, an eminent German philologist, lays down a principle of consonantal change in the Germanic languages. For instance, Lat. *pater*, Eng. *father*, Ger. *Vater*; Lat. *frater*, Eng. *brother*, Ger. *Bruder*; Lat. *decem*, Eng. *ten*, Ger. *zehn*.

Grog, the beverage served out to sailors, and compounded of spirit and water in prescribed proportions. The name, it is said, was derived from the fact that Admiral Vernon, who introduced it into the English navy in 1745, wore Grogram breeches.

Grogram (French = *gros grain*), a kind of rough fabric made of wool and some other fibre, such as silk, mohair, or cotton, formerly much used for commoner kinds of wearing apparel.

Grotto, a natural or artificial cave. Among the most famous are the blue grotto of Capri and the stalactite grotto of Antiparos (Cyclades, Aegean). The latter has been known since 1673 and is of singular picturesqueness.

Ground Wave, that part of the energy emitted by a radio transmitter which travels along the ground; as opposed to the sky wave which is reflected back to earth by the ionosphere. With the lower radio-frequencies, the ground wave can be picked up over several thousand miles; in the broadcasting band, over a hundred or so miles; it is virtually useless at high frequencies.

Grouse, game bird of the northern latitudes where some 20 species occur. They are stout, compact, ground-dwelling birds, protectively plumaged (the willow grouse turns white in winter), the male usually being larger and more brightly coloured than the female. The red grouse of the British moorlands has been introduced into Belgium and W. Germany. Of the same family are the blackcock, ptarmigan, capercaillie, American prairie-hen, and the common partridge. Grouse shooting begins in Britain on Aug. 12.

Guanaco, a large species of llama, common to South America, and utilised as a beast of burden.

Guano, the excrement of sea-birds, found in large quantities on the rocky islands of the western coasts of South America and Nauru Is. It forms a useful fertilising agent, being rich in phosphate and ammonia, and first came into use in 1841, since which time Peruvian guano has been a recognised article of commerce. Beds of guano from 50 to 60 ft. in thickness are not uncommon. Fish guano and bat guano from caves in South America and the Bahamas are also used as fertilisers.

Gudgeon, a small fresh-water fish of the carp family with 2 small barbels on the upper lip.

Guelph and Ghibelline, italianised forms of the German words "Welf" and "Waiblingen," the names of two rival princely families whose conflicts made much of the history of Germany and Italy during the Middle Ages. The feuds between these two factions continued in Italy during the campaigns of Emperor Frederick I., and later developed into the fierce struggles of the 13th cent. between emperor and pope. In Italy the Ghibellines supported the side of the German emperors and the Guelphs the cause of the pope. The present Royal Family of England is descended from the Guelphs, through the ducal House of Brunswick (the name of Windsor was assumed during the first world war).

Guildhall, the place of assembly of the members of a guild, and at one time, when guilds were in full strength, was practically the Town Hall. The London Guildhall is to-day the hall of meeting for the City of London Corporation.

Guilds for the fostering and protection of various trades have existed in England since Anglo-Saxon times, and from the 12th to the 16th cent. exercised great influence and enjoyed many privileges. There were trades' guilds and craftsmen's guilds, and in all large cities and towns there was a guild hall. Their successes in the Middle Ages led to many monopolistic abuses, and in the end it became necessary to free the country from their restrictive power. The City Guilds (Livery Companies of the City of London) derive their name from the distinctive dress assumed by their members in the 14th cent. There are 83 Guilds in existence.

Guild Socialism. *See* **J21**.

Guillemot, a genus of sea-birds of the auk family, common in Northern Europe, two species—the Common Guillemot and the Black Guillemot—being natives of our own sea coasts, nesting on the cliffs. Brünnich's Guillemot, an Arctic species, is a rare straggler in the British Isles.

Guinea, an English gold coin of the value of twenty-one shillings, current from 1663 to 1817, and deriving its name from the first guinea coinage having been struck from gold obtained on the coast of Guinea.

Guinea-Pig, a rodent of the cavy family about 10 in. in length and with a tail so short that it does not project outside the body. It makes an excellent pet, though easily frightened. Its ancestors were species of the wild cavy of S. America said to have been domesticated by the Incas of Peru. *See* **Z15**(2).

Guitar, a six-stringed instrument with a hollow resonant body, the strings being plucked by the fingers. The instrument seems to have originated in Spain, but there is a variant known at the Hawaiian Guitar. A recent development is the Electric Guitar, in which the mechanical vibrations of the strings are converted into electromagnetic vibrations, amplified, and reproduced by a loud-speaker.

Gules, a heraldic term, denoting a rose of red tincture, indicated by vertical lines drawn or engraved without colour.

Gulf Stream is confined entirely to the western side of the N. Atlantic and is the warm-water current flowing through the Straits of Florida from the Gulf of Mexico parallel to the American coast up as far as Cape Hatteras. From there it continues north-eastwards as a slower, broader, cooler (yet even so, relatively warm) drift of water, merging with the North Atlantic Drift and losing its identity about 40° N. Lat., 60° W. Long. It is a common error to attribute the warmth of the British Isles and Western Europe generally to the Gulf Stream but this has no influence whatever except in so far as it feeds the North Atlantic Drift. Both the Gulf Stream and the North Atlantic Drift owe their movement to the direction of the prevailing winds, and it is the south-westerly airstream coming from warmer regions and passing over the surface waters of the Atlantic Drift that brings the warmth inland to influence the climate of Western Europe.

Gull. An extremely well-known, long-winged seabird with rather short legs and webbed feet. In almost all adults the body and tail are white whilst the back and most of the wings are grey or black. In the majority of cases the plumage of juveniles is partly or entirely dusky. Gulls are omnivorous, and are very useful as scavengers. They follow ships and quickly seize upon any refuse which may be thrown overboard. There are 44 species, which vary in size from moderately small to large. With certain exceptions, such as the Kittiwake in the North Atlantic, they are not found very far from land. They are sociable and mostly breed in colonies on cliff-ledges, on islands, beaches and sandhills, and among vegetation in swamps, sometimes a long way from the sea. The nest is usually substantial, and the eggs generally number from two to three. Of the 29 species breeding in the northern hemisphere, 14 occur in the British

Isles. The pure white Ivory Gull is the most northerly of birds. Sabine's and the Swallow-tailed Gull have forked tails. Ross's Gull has a black ring round the neck and one species, Franklin's Gull, migrates from the North, where it breeds, to pass the winter in the Southern hemisphere.

Gulliver, the hero of Swift's satire, *Gulliver's Travels,* who, in Lilliput and Brobdingnag, passed through a series of adventures which were so contrived as to reflect the humour, follies, and shortcomings of Swift's day.

Gums are glutinous compounds obtained from vegetable sources, soluble in cold or hot water, but not in alcohol. There are innumerable varieties. Gum Arabic is exuded from a species of acacia grown in Senegal, the Sudan, Arabia, India and other countries, and is a valuable commercial product, used in dyeing, ink-making, as a mucilage, and in medicine. India-rubber is an elastic gum. Gums are also made from starch, potatoes, wheat, etc., from seeds, bark, roots, and weeds. Many so-called gums are resins.

Gun-Cotton, a powerful explosive manufactured by subjecting a prepared cotton to the prolonged action of a mixture of three parts sulphuric acid and one part of nitric acid. It burns without explosion on ignition, but by percussion explodes with a force five times greater than that of gunpowder.

Gunpowder, also called "black powder," the oldest of explosive mixtures, consists of saltpetre, sulphur, and charcoal, intimately mixed, the proportions being varied for different intended uses.

Gunpowder Plot was a conspiracy by a desperate band of Roman Catholics in the reign of James I. to avenge the harsh treatment to which Catholics were subjected. Barrels of gunpowder were secreted in the vaults underneath the Houses of Parliament, and it was proposed to fire these when the King and his Ministers assembled on Nov. 5, 1605. The plot was betrayed and Guy Fawkes and his co-conspirators were arrested and executed. The date serves to perpetuate the ancient custom of burning the effigy of Fawkes, a custom in which young people are the most enthusiastic participants, with bonfires, fireworks, etc.

Gunter's Chain, a surveyor's chain, 22 yd. long divided into 100 links, invented by Edmund Gunter (1581–1626), Professor of Astronomy at Gresham College, for the measurement of areas. 1 acre contains 100,000 square links.

Gurnard, a sea-fish, with large, bony head and diminutive body, of which there are some forty species. They are plentiful in British waters.

Gymnasium, originally the name given in ancient Greece to the public places where Greek youth used to exercise and receive instruction. Plato, Aristotle, and other great teachers lectured there. The Greek institution was never very popular with the Romans, and it was not until the 18th and 19th cent. that the cult of combining physical with intellectual activity again found a place in educational systems. In Germany the name was applied to the classical grammar school; in this country and America to the halls where gymnastics were practised.

Gymnosperms. *See* **F28(1).**

Gypsies, a nomadic race, believed to be of Indian origin; their language, Romany, certainly seems related to Hindustani. They are spread over many parts of the world, but are most common in Europe, having appeared in Western Europe in 1417, finding their way to England at the beginning of the 16th cent. They give evidence of their Eastern origin in their dark skins, large black eyes, black hair, and pearly white teeth. They are born wanderers, and pass from place to place following certain small occupations such as tinkering, basket-making, and the like.

Gypsum, a whitish mineral consisting of hydrated sulphate of calcium. The finest gypsum is alabaster. When heated gypsum is converted into the powder called Plaster of Paris; the water it loses can be taken up when the plaster is wetted, and the reconversion of Plaster of Paris into gypsum accounts for the way in which the former sets hard. The name "Plaster of Paris" came from the location of important gypsum quarries in the Montmartre district of Paris. It was found after the flood disasters of Jan. 1953 that gypsum could undo the effect of sea-water. By spreading it for the rain to wash into the soil, thousands of acres of farmland in Holland and Britain were made productive again.

Gyroscope, an application of the principle of the spinning top to a single-rail railway, the steering of ships, and the steadying of torpedoes. A high-accuracy gyroscope combined with a highly sensitive accelerometer in what is known as an inertial navigation system was used by the *Nautilus* when it made its journey under the North Pole in 1958.

H

Habeas Corpus, the name given to a writ ordering the body of a person under restraint or imprisonment to be brought into court for full inquiry into the legality of the restraint to be made. The first Habeas Corpus Act was passed in 1679, though nominally such a right had existed from Magna Carta, but some of the more despotic kings had disregarded it. In times of public peril the privilege of *habeas corpus* is sometimes temporarily suspended, many instances occurring in the history of Ireland and during the First and Second World Wars.

Haber Process, the important industrial process for synthesising ammonia from atmospheric nitrogen. Nitrogen and hydrogen are made to combine at high pressure (200 atmospheres or upwards) in an electric arc.

Haddock, one of the best-known fishes abounding in northern seas and averaging about 4 lb. in weight. Related to the cod. Largely used for curing, and sold as "finnan haddies."

Hade of veins, a mining term indicating the particular inclination that any vein, seam, or strata may have from the perpendicular; thus, in Weardale the veins mainly "hade" to the north.

Hadrian's Wall. *See* **Roman Walls.**

Haematite, ferric oxide, one of the principal iron ores, containing about 70% of the metal. It is usually found in kidney-shaped masses, and is specular, red or brown, in thin fragments, but greyish in bulk.

Haemocyanin, the respiratory pigment of crustaceans and molluscs. It functions like haemoglobin, from which it differs in containing copper instead of iron and being blue when oxidised instead of red.

Haemoglobin, the pigment containing iron which gives red blood corpuscles their colour. It is a respiratory pigment, having the property of picking up oxygen when the blood passes through the lungs to produce the compound known as oxyhaemoglobin. In other parts of the body the oxyhaemoglobin breaks down, liberating oxygen, which is used in the oxidation process (respiration) that the body tissues carry on. *See also* **F25.**

Hafiz, besides being the pseudonym of a famous Persian poet, is a title conferred upon any Mohammedan who has committed the whole of the Koran to memory.

Hafnium, a metallic element discovered by Coster and Hevesy in 1922 and important in the atomic-energy field. It occurs in most zirconium minerals to the extent of about 5 per cent.

Hag-fish, a blind, eel-like parasitic sea-fish with soft backbone; found within the bodies of other fish, and called sometimes the "borer," or "the glutinous hag-fish." Related to the Lamprey.

Hagiarchy, the rule or order of Saints.

Hagiology, a branch of literature that is wholly given up to the history of the saints, and the setting forth of the stories and legends associated with their names.

Hail, hard, roughly spherical balls of ice, consisting of white cores covered by layers of both transparent and opaque ice, frequently falling during thunderstorms. They usually do not exceed 1 in. in size, but hailstones larger than apples and weighing more than 2 lb. have been observed. The general theory of a hailstone is that near the top of a cumulonimbus cloud a raindrop becomes frozen, grows in size by condensation and through collisions with snow particles, and eventually becomes so weighty as to overcome the ascending air currents in the cloud. Falling, it first encounters supercooled water drops, immediately freezing on it, increasing the white core, and then at lower levels ordinary water drops, freezing more slowly, producing a layer of clear ice. Before the hailstone arrives at the ground gusts and lulls may transport it several times up and down both regions, adding alternate coatings of soft white and hard clear ice.

Hake, a fish of the cod family, found in large numbers in the seas of Europe, but not in high favour for the table with fastidious feeders.

Halcyon, a term associated in olden times with the kingfisher and days of soothing calm, " halcyon days " being a frequently used expression. The legend was that the kingfisher laid its eggs on the surface of the sea at the time of the winter solstice when the sea was specially calm.

Halibut, one of the largest of the flat fishes, averaging when full grown from 4 to 6 ft. in length, and highly esteemed for the table. Specimens of still larger size occasionally occur. It is plentifully distributed. Its two eyes are on the right side of the head.

Hall-mark. A mark or group of marks, impressed by an assay office on gold or silver articles guaranteeing the standard of fineness of the precious metal used in them. These marks, which have been applied to silver made in London since the beginning of the 14th cent. and perhaps earlier, make it possible to establish the year and place of assay as also the name of the maker. English pieces of silver usually have not less than four marks, viz., (1) town mark; (2) maker's mark; (3) date letter; (4) sterling mark.

The town mark is rarely changed; in London a crowned leopard's head was used from the earliest days until 1820 with only minor modifications, except for the period 1697–1720 when a lion's head erased was substituted; since 1820 the crown has been omitted.

Until the late 17th cent. a symbol was often used as a maker's mark, from 1696 to 1720 the first two letters of the maker's surname, and subsequently the maker's initials. Owing to the destruction of the earlier mark plates at Goldsmiths' Hall no maker's name prior to the late 17th cent. can be identified with certainty.

The London date letter is changed at the end of May each year, so each letter covers seven months of one year and five months of the following. The London date cycle has usually consisted of twenty letters: the alphabet of each cycle is of different style, and the letters are enclosed in shields of different shape.

The sterling mark, the lion passant, was introduced in 1544 and continued in use until 1697, when the higher Britannia standard was introduced in order to discourage the practice current amongst goldsmiths of melting down coin of the realm to make plate. The leopard's head crowned and the lion passant were then replaced by a figure of Britannia and a lion's head erased. Though the regulation imposing the higher standard was withdrawn in 1720, a small amount of Britannia standard silver continued to be made and still is made

From 1784 until 1890 a plate tax was levied on all silver assayed in Great Britain and an additional duty mark, the sovereign's head, was used during this period. A Jubilee mark bearing the head of George V and of Queen Mary was used in between the years 1933 and 1935, and in 1953 a coronation mark with the head of Queen Elizabeth was introduced.

The tables of hall-marks in Gen. Comp. (**N15–17**) give the London date letter cycles from 1598 to 1955. The form of town mark and sterling mark used during each cycle is given at the head of each column. Where a major alteration took place in either of these marks during a date-letter cycle, the alternative forms are also shown. The date of the change can be established by reference to the notes above. At the bottom of each page the marks used by the major provincial, Scottish and Irish assay offices are shown. Owing to lack of space, the complete date-letter cycles are not shown, but two examples only from the 17th, 18th or 19th cent. Where a provincial assay office was established in the 17th cent. or earlier, the marks of one year in the 17th and 18th cent. respectively are shown, where the office was not established until the 18th cent., the marks of one year in the 18th and 19th cent. are given.

Halloween (Oct. 31), the eve of All Saints' Day, a time associated, especially in Scotland, with certain pleasing superstitions attractively set forth in Burns's famous poem " Hallowe'en." It is the night when young men and maidens are supposed, by observing certain rites, to have their future wives and husbands disclosed to them.

Halo, a luminous circle usually of 22° radius, surrounding sun or moon, produced by the refraction and reflection of light by ice crystals of high cirrus cloud. It is a very common occurrence, in the British Isles almost one day in three. The inner side is red and the outer a whitish-yellow colour. " Mock suns," *i.e.*, patches of light at the same elevation as the sun are much rarer occurrences, sometimes being of great beauty and brilliance. *See* **Coronae.**

Halogens, the group name for the four non-metallic elements fluorine, chlorine, bromine, and iodine. The term " halogen " means " salt-producer."

Halteres, the modified hind-wings of the two-winged flies or *Diptera* (*e.g.*, the house-fly). The equilibrium in flight of these insects depends on the halteres, which are commonly called " balancers."

Hampton Court Conference, presided over at Hampton Court Palace by James I. in 1604 and which brought about his authorised translation of the Bible, had an important bearing on the religious differences of the time. James refused to grant tolerations to the Puritans. This sowed the seeds of civil war. Following the conference three hundred English Puritan clergy were ejected from their livings.

Hanaper Office, a former Chancery office, deriving its name from the fact that its writs and papers were kept in a hanaper (hamper). The Chancellor's officer thus came to be known as the Hanaper. The Comptrollers of the Hanaper were abolished in England in 1842.

Hand, a measure of four inches, the average size of the palm; used in reckoning height of horses.

Handfasting, an informal marriage custom once prevalent in Scotland, whereby a man and woman bound themselves to cohabit for a year and a day, and at the end of that period either confirmed their contract by a regular marriage or separated.

Hansard, the title given to the official reports of Parliamentary debates, so named after Luke Hansard who in 1774 became partner in a firm of printers to the House of Commons. His son T. C. Hansard was first the printer and then the publisher of an unofficial series of parliamentary debates inaugurated by William Cobbett in 1803. In 1909 production was taken over by H.M. Stationery Office and today's volumes contain full substantially verbatim reports of what is said in both Houses of Parliament.

Hanseatic League was a confederation of North German towns established about 1241 for purposes of mutual protection in carrying on international commerce. The League became so powerful that it was able to dominate the foreign trade of Norway, Sweden, Denmark, and even to some extent of London. A branch was established in London and had its guild hall in Cannon Street for hundreds of years. The League existed down to the middle of the 17th cent. Hamburg, Lübeck, and Bremen are the only cities which, as free ports, still by commercial courtesy retain the name of Hanse towns.

Hansom, a two-wheeled one-horse cab, invented by Joseph A. Hansom in 1843. It was, until the introduction of the taxi, the cab in most ordinary use in London and other large cities Lord Beaconsfield styled it the " gondola of London." The driver sat on a " dickey " behind, level with the roof of the cab.

Hara-kiri, the custom of suicide by compulsion, or " happy despatch," once common in Japan, but no longer permitted. The condemned person gave himself the first cut, and if his courage then failed him, the fatal blow was dealt by a friend.

Hard Water. Water containing appreciable quantities of dissolved salts of calcium and magnesium. It is difficult to form a lather with soap in hard water, and the impurities block up water pipes. *See* **Water.**

Hare, species of the *Lepus genus,* distributed widely through the N. hemisphere. Noted for having four upper front teeth, one pair behind the other, short tufted tail, a cleft upper lip and longer ears and limbs than the rabbit. It does not burrow. The young are born with hair and able to see. A swift animal hunted with greyhounds in the sport called "coursing." *See* **Game.**

Harleian MSS. comprise some thousands of volumes of MSS. and documents, collected by the first Earl of Oxford (1661–1724) and his son Edward. After the death of the latter, his widow handed the MSS. over to the nation for £10,000, a sum that did not represent a quarter of their value, and they are deposited in the British Museum.

Harlequin, the buffoon of ancient Italian comedy. As adapted to the British stage, however, harlequin is a pantomime character only, in love with Columbine, appearing in parti-coloured garments and carrying a wand, by which he exercises a magic influence in thwarting the fantastic tricks of the clown and pantaloon.

Harmattan, a dry wind which may blow between January and May across the Sahara to the Gulf of Guinea. Although affording relief from the tropical heat, vegetation withers because of its extreme dryness and much irritation is caused by the clouds of fine dust which it carries.

Harmonic Motion, regular periodic motion of the kind exemplified by a ball bobbing up and down at the end of a spring, and by the piston in a steam engine. It may be simple (simple harmonic motion) or composed of two or more simple harmonic motions. In simple harmonic motion the acceleration is proportional to the distance of the moving body from its original rest position.

Harmonics. Flute-like tones which can be produced by touching the strings of a violin in a certain way. The effect is due to the suppression of the fundamental frequency at which the string would normally vibrate. In consequence only the harmonics or overtones (notes one octave or more above the fundamental which combine to give the characteristic timbre of the instrument) are heard.

Harmonica *or* **Mouth Organ,** a small instrument consisting of reeds enclosed in separate chambers through which air is blown or sucked by the mouth. Recent improvements and elaborations have made of it a versatile solo instrument in the hands of an expert.

Harmonium *or* **American Organ,** a small organ of one or two manuals consisting entirely of reed stops. There is no pedal organ, the feet being used to operate the bellows.

Harp, a musical instrument of ancient origin consisting of many strings stretched on a frame. The player stands beside it and plucks the strings with his fingers. Used orchestrally in early Italian operas (17th cent.).

Harp-seal, the ordinary Greenland seal, with a dark harp-shaped marking on its back, hence its name. It abounds in Newfoundland waters and further northward towards the Arctic.

Harpsichord, a keyboard instrument with a compass of up to six octaves in which stretched strings are plucked by quills. The harpsichord was an instrument of great importance from the 16th to the 18th cent., but it was eclipsed by the pianoforte, in which the plucking action (*cf.* **Harp**) was replaced by a striking action (*cf.* **Dulcimer**). Recently it has regained much of its former popularity.

Harpy Eagle, a large bird of prey named from the winged monsters of Greek mythology, inhabiting the forest regions of Central and South America. There are eight species, one with handsome grey plumage and large crest which attacks and kills animals much larger than itself, and was called by the Aztecs "winged wolf."

Harrier, a bird of prey of the falcon family; of the various species distributed over the world, three breed in Britain: the moorland Hen harrier, the Marsh harrier, and Montagu's harrier. They are large birds with long tails, long legs, long wings, and gliding flight. They nest on the ground and eat small mammals, frogs, lizards, and small birds.

Hartebeest, common African antelope of a grey-brown colour, with ringed and knotted horns bending backward and tapering to sharp points; gregarious, of large size, and capable of domestication. There are several species.

Harvest Bug, a very small insect, of a dark red colour, which appears in large numbers in the fields in autumn, and is peculiarly irritating to animals and man by the tenacity with which it attaches itself to the skin and burrows underneath. Probably the larvae of spinning mites (Trombidoids). In the U.S.A. they are called "chiggers."

Harvest Moon, the full moon that occurs nearest to the autumn equinox, in September. It rises for several nights running about the same time, and yields an unusually brilliant series of moonlight nights.

Harvestmen are, like spiders, members of the arachnid class but belong to the distinctly different order of Phalangida. They are common in the countryside in autumn and have small oval bodies and eight long slender legs which besides being mere organs of locomotion also act as sense organs. Known as "daddy longlegs" in America.

Hashish, an Arabic word for the narcotic substance prepared from the hemp plant (*Cannabis sativa*). It is known by a variety of names, *e.g.*, bhang in India and marijuana in America.

Hatchment, in heraldry, is a square board, in vertical diagonal position, placed outside a house or on the tomb at the death of a member of a family and so arranged that it indicates the sex and condition of the deceased.

Hawfinch, a well-known European bird of the finch family, having a variegated plumage, a sturdy bill, and black-and-white tail. In England it is found in the Midland and Eastern Counties, and locally in Scotland.

Hawk. This name is applied to almost any diurnal bird of prey other than eagle, falcon, or vulture, but in its strict sense applies only to the *Accipiter* genus—the small Sparrow Hawk and the larger Goshawk, round-winged, long-tailed birds with barred under-parts. They prey upon small birds captured in flight and small mammals.

Hawk-moths, large species of moths, thick of body and strong of wing, which fly with rapid swooping motion, hence its name. There are numerous handsome species in Britain.

Hearth-Money was a tax laid on hearths (in all houses paying the church and poor rates). Charles II. introduced it in 1662, and it was repealed in the reign of William and Mary.

Heat, after prolonged controversy over whether or not heat is a "substance" (formerly called "caloric"), it was established in the 19th cent. that heat is a form of energy; it is in fact the combined kinetic and potential energy of the atoms of which a body is composed. Heat can be turned into other forms of energy, *e.g.*, a red hot body loses heat by radiating it in the form of electromagnetic waves ("radiant heat"—chiefly infra-red rays). Heat may also be transferred from one place to another by conduction and, in fluids, by convection. All three processes occur when a glowing fire heats a room. A unit quantity of heat is the calorie, which is the amount of heat sufficient to raise the temperature of 1 gm. of water by 1° C. In general, adding heat to a body raises its temperature. The number of calories required per gm. of material to raise the temperature 1° C. is called the *specific heat* of the material. However, adding heat may not raise the temperature but may instead cause a change of state, *e.g.* from solid to liquid (melting) or liquid to gas (evaporation). The amount of heat required to melt 1 gm. of a solid is called the latent heat of melting. Similarly, there is a latent heat of evaporation. Strictly speaking, the specific and latent heats of a substance depend on how much its pressure and volume are allowed to vary during the measurements. Water has a high specific heat, and this makes the oceans a vast heat reservoir, a factor of great meteorological significance. The science of heat is called thermodynamics, and is of great importance in physics and chemistry. *See* **F16.**

Heath, flowering plants of the *Ericaceae* family. Heaths are widely distributed over uncultivated spaces of Europe and Africa. In Britain they are represented by heather (of which there are several species) and ling (*Calluna vulgaris*), which cover thousands of acres of moorland. Some of the African or Cape heaths are very beautiful and much prized by florists. One species of heath (*Erica arborea*) which grows in S. Europe and N. Africa has close-grained woody root-stock used for making briar pipes. *See* **T6**(2).

Heat Wave is a spell of very hot weather, due chiefly in the British Isles to a warm southerly current of air caused by the presence of an anticyclone over western or central Europe at the same time as a depression is stationary over the Atlantic. High humidity increases the discomfort.

Hegira, an Arab term signifying departure or flight, and used in reference to Mohammed's departure from Mecca for Medina, A.D. 622, from which date the Mohammedan era is reckoned.

Helicopter, heavier-than-air aircraft which obtains its lift from blades rotating above the fuselage in windmill-fashion. The first successful helicopters were the Focke-Wulf 61, a German machine (1936), and the VS-300, designed by Igor Sikorsky, flown in 1937. Helicopters can hover, and rise and descend vertically, in addition to being capable of horizontal flight.

Heliotrope, a favourite sweet-scented flowering plant, common in tropical and sub-tropical countries; the Peruvian heliotrope is the "cherry pie" of our summer garden borders. *See* **T8**(1).

Helium, a gaseous element first discovered by means of the spectroscope in the sun's atmosphere. This discovery, made in 1868 by the astronomer Sir Norman Lockyer, was followed in 1895 by Sir William Ramsay's proof that the element existed on earth. He found it in the uranium ore, clevite. Later it was established that helium is formed by the radioactive decay of many elements which emit α-particles (nuclei of helium atoms) and is contained in all radioactive minerals. The largest source of helium is natural gas, the richest in helium being the gas from certain wells in Utah, U.S.A. Next to hydrogen, helium is the lightest gas known, has a lifting power equal to 92% of hydrogen and the advantage that it is inert and non-inflammable. It is used for inflating airships. Ordinary air contains 1 part in 200,000 of helium. It was the last gaseous element to be liquefied, this being achieved by Onnes in 1908 in Leyden. Hydrogen fusion in the "H bomb" produces helium.

Hellebore, a plant of the *Ranunculaceae* (buttercup) family. The best-known British examples are the green and stinking varieties. There is also a garden kind which flowers in December called the Christmas Rose. Hellebore yields a bitter substance which forms a drastic purgative, but is now little used. *See* **T8**(1).

Hellenic Art. The art of ancient Greece may be roughly divided into three periods: the prehistoric period (*c.* 1500–1000 B.C.) of the bronze age Mycenaeans; the archaic period (*c.* 600–500 B.C.); and the classical period (*c.* 500–300 B.C.). Of the first period centred on Mycenae in Peloponnesus but extending to the coasts of Asia and the city of Troy we can mention only the massive stone gateways and the shaft graves of Mycenae, where the archaeologist Schliemann discovered painted vases, gold cups, bronze swords, and ornaments of what had once been a great, if primitive, civilisation. During the archaic period sculpture was the principal form of art expression. The magnificent male and female figures are reminiscent of Egyptian art, but are distinctive in liveliness of facial expression. The vase-paintings of this period became more elaborate, depicting scenes from mythology or ceremonial events. Typical of classical Greek art is the representation of the beautiful and healthy human body deliberately posed and often carrying out heroic or athletic acts. The vast majority of these statues are known to us only through Roman copies. The *Hermes* of Praxiteles (born *c.* 385 B.C.) is possibly the only existing statue which can be assigned with any degree of certainty to an individual artist. Almost the whole of the Greek genius in architecture was expended on temples which are all basically similar in design—a rectangle with a low-pitched gabled roof resting on side walls. The three orders Doric, Corinthian, and Ionic mainly referred to the type of column used, but naturally the whole building was influenced thereby. Some of the main buildings are on the Acropolis, a hill outside Athens, on which stand the Parthenon (from the outer frieze of which the Elgin marbles, now mostly in the British Museum, were taken), the Erechtheum, famous for its Porch of Maidens, and the gateway known as the Propylaea with its broad flight of marble steps. Apart from that on vases, no Greek painting has come down to us, although Greek painters existed and were noted in their time. All we have are copies in mosaic and fresco made by the Romans, at Naples and Pompeii. Of Greek literature in prose, verse, and the drama little can be said here. To the early period (*i.e.*, the archaic age) belong Homer's *Iliad* and *Odyssey*, Hesiod's long poem *Work and Days*, and Sappho's love poems, and Pindar's Odes. The period of Pericles in the 5th cent. B.C. produced more great literature than any comparable period in history: the philosophical writings of Plato and Aristotle, the tragedies of Aeschylus, Euripides, and Sophocles, the comedies of Aristophanes—all these are still part of the European tradition, and together with Greek architecture played a major part in the Renaissance (*see* **J38**).

Hellenistic Art, the art of the period of Greek civilisation which began with the conquests of Alexander the Great (356–323 B.C.) and lasted until his former empire (which encompassed most of the Middle East and part of North Africa) was conquered by the Romans in 146 B.C. Culturally it was an important period because it spread Greek culture far beyond its original boundaries—even as far as the north of India, and its centres spread from Athens to the cities of Alexandria in Egypt, Antioch in Syria, and Pergamum in Asia Minor. But equally Eastern culture spread to the West: democracy was replaced by absolute monarchy, cosmopolitanism took the place of the Greek tendency to believe that all who were not Greeks were barbarians, and mystical philosophies took the place of Greek rationalism. This was a sensuous, secular, pleasure-loving, rootless society, and these tendencies were reflected in its art. Hellenistic sculpture was sensual, effeminate, and violently emotional, yet it depicted individuals and not always noble or beautiful ones. (Classical Greek sculpture was idealistic, showed types rather than individuals, and appealed to the intellect rather than the emotions.) Some of the best examples came from the school at Pergamum and later from the island of Rhodes, and the titles themselves speak of their nature: *The Dying Gaul*, *Gaul Slaying his Wife and Himself*, and the famous *Laocoön* (representing Laocoön and his two sons being crushed by two enormous serpents). All these date from about 240 to 50 B.C.—for the culture did not immediately end with the Roman conquest. The enormous frieze of the altar of the temple in Pergamum depicts a battle between gods and giants with tremendous realism and brutal violence far removed from the serene art of classical times. Portrait sculpture is typical of Hellenistic art, where it may almost be said to have been invented, since such ventures in the past had been idealistic rather than realistic. The great Hellenistic cities were geometrically planned and fine public buildings made their appearance in which the slender and graceful Ionic or the ornate Corinthian columns took the place of the more austere and heavy classical ones. Alexandria was famed for its library of 700,000 books and was the centre of philosophical schools such as the Stoics and Epicureans. Here too worked the mathematicians Euclid and Archimedes, the physicians Erasistratus and Herophilus, and the geographer Pytheas. But Hellenistic literature was a pale reflection of the glories of the past and we mention only the comedies of Menander and the pastoral verse of Theocritus of Syracuse.

Hemiptera, the order of insects to which belong the true bugs. Their wing structure is in most species incomplete, hence the term hemiptera. This order includes the familiar water insects, the water boatman and water skater, also the aphids, cicadas, leaf hoppers, scale insects. *See* **T28(2).**

Hemlock, a plant of the *Umbelliferae* family, growing in all parts of Britain, and containing a strong alkaloid poison. Used medicinally, this alkaline substance is of considerable service, being a powerful sedative. According to Pliny, hemlock was the poison used by the Athenians in putting criminals to death.

Hemp (*Cannabis sativa*), name of a plant native to Asia, now cultivated widely for the valuable fibre contained in the stalk or in some species in the leaves. Hemp fibre has been replaced by cotton for textiles and by jute for sacks and is now chiefly used for cordage and twine. It contains a resinous substance from which the narcotic hashish is made. The seed yields a valuable oil. The term hemp is also used for other fibre plants, including manila hemp from the Philippines, sunn hemp from India, sisal from W. and E. Africa and phorium from New Zealand.

Henbane, a plant found in Britain and other parts of Europe and Northern Asia. It belongs to the potato family *Solanaceae*, grows mostly on waste ground, and bears yellow-brown flowers veined with purple. The leaves yield a poisonous alkaloid substance which, medicinally prepared and administered, is of great use. Tincture of henbane is often preferred to laudanum.

Heptarchy, a word derived from the Greek *hepta*, seven, and denoting the seven kingdoms (*archai*) into which Anglo-Saxon England was divided before 900. The seven were Kent, Essex, Sussex, Wessex, Mercia, East Anglia, and Northumbria.

Heracleum, a plant of the *Umbelliferae* family, common in southern and central Europe, though only one species, the cow parsnip, grows in England. It has a bitter root, and from the juice of the stem an intoxicating liquor is occasionally prepared.

Herald, an officer of state empowered to make formal proclamations and deliver messages from the sovereign or other high personage whom he serves. In the developments which took place in armorial bearings, the herald was the functionary charged with the duty of their proper depiction.

Heraldry, the knowledge of armorial bearings, was mainly the outcome of the love of outward distinction which prevailed in mediaeval times. "Heraldry," says Stubbs, "became a handmaid of chivalry, and the marshalling of badges, crests, coat-armour, pennons, helmets, and other devices of distinction grew into an important branch of knowledge." The *shield*, or *escutcheon*, is the ground upon which armorial signs are traced, the colour of the shield being called the *tincture*, the signs recorded the *charges*. There are seven *tinctures—or* (gold), *argent* (silver), *gules* (red), *azure* (blue), *vert* (green), *purpure* (purple), and *sable* (black). The *charges* are classed as "Honourable" and "Subordinate" ordinaries, comprising lines and geometrical forms; and "Common" ordinaries, which latter includes all representations of natural objects. There is also a system of external signs, such as crowns, coronets, mitres, helmets, mantlings, wreaths, and crests, each having its distinctive significance. For other distinguishing marks see **Hatchments, Quartering, Rampant, Pean.**

Heralds' College or College of Arms, was incorporated by Richard III. in 1483. Its head is the Earl Marshal (an office hereditary in the family of the Dukes of Norfolk), and there are three Kings of Arms, six Heralds, and four Pursuivants. The business transacted is wholly connected with the tracing of genealogies and the granting of armorial bearings. In Scotland the Heraldic functions are performed by the Lord Lyon King of Arms.

Herbarium, a systematically classified collection of preserved plants. One of the largest in the world is at the Royal Botanic Gardens at Kew.

Heredity is the study of the transmission of physical and mental characteristics from one generation to another. Gregor Mendel (1822–84), a great experimenter in the field of inheritance, established the principle embodied in Mendel's law in his work published in 1866. The ideas which he then put forward were forgotten until the early years of this century, but today they form the basis of the modern study of genetics. Genes are the units of heredity. They are contained in the chromosomes of the cell nucleus. It is in the development of personality that the interplay between heredity and environment becomes most apparent. *See* **The Evolution of Organisms, F31–2,** *and* **Section Q, Part I.**

Hermaphrodite, animals or plants possessing both male and female reproductive organs, *e.g.*, snail, earthworms, most flowering plants.

Hermit Crab, a decapod, with a soft asymmetrical body which it protects by thrusting it into an empty gastropod shell, *e.g.*, whelk, which it carries about, only abandoning it when necessary for a larger one. Found in all seas, many live in commensal relationship with sea anemones, etc.

Heron, a large wading bird with long curved neck and pointed bill, is a member of the *Ardeidae* family, of which there are many species. Egrets and bitterns are included as herons. Herons are to be met with in marsh lands and near rivers and lakes, where they feed on fish and frogs. They nest in trees in large numbers, these colonies being called heronries. The common heron is native to England, and other species from the Continent are frequent visitors.

Herring, a common sea-fish, related to the sardine and pilchard, abounding in northern seas and found in large numbers round the British coasts. The herring fishing is the most important fish industry in this country, a large fleet being engaged in it. The fishing season proper lasts from May to October, the enormous shoals being followed as they move from place to place. The spawning season is about the end of August. One female herring may produce 20 to 50 thousand eggs, which sink to the sea-bed, where they develop.

Hibernation, the dormant condition in which numerous mammals, reptiles, amphibians, insects, plants, etc., pass the winter. The rate of metabolism slows down, and the body temperature drops to that of the surroundings. Work on these low temperatures and their physiological effect has led to improved surgical techniques (*see* **P30**). Animals of the torrid regions pass through an analogous period (aestivation) during the hot season, when the sources of food are dried up.

Hickory, several species of American tree of the walnut family, remarkable for its very hard, solid, heavy white wood, and bearing an edible, four-lobed nut.

Hieratic Art, a type of art (typified by the major part of the art of ancient Egypt) which is (*a*) exclusively religious, and (*b*) conventionally based on earlier forms and traditions.

Hieroglyphics are the earliest form of pictured symbolic expressions, and are supposed to have been introduced by the ancient Egyptians. They consist of rude depictions of animals, plants, signs, and objects, and in their later examples express, in abridged form, ideas and records from which significant historical information has been gleaned. The deciphering of Egyptian hieroglyphics long formed an ardent study, but gradually the key to the riddle was discovered, and most of the ancient records can now be understood. Besides the Egyptian there are also Hittite, Minoan and Mayan hieroglyphic scripts. *See* **Rosetta Stone.**

Hindi, the great Aryan vernacular language of Northern India. In the Indian Constitution, adopted in 1950, it was laid down that Hindi in the Devanagari script should within 15 years replace English as the official language of the Indian Union. However, under the Official Language Act, 1963, English can still be used after that time in addition to Hindi.

Hinduism. *See* **J21.**

Hindustani, the *lingua franca* of India, a Sanskritised Hindi vernacular introduced by the British in 1837 to replace the official Persian. It is written in Devanagari (Sanskrit) characters. The Persianised Hindi vernacular is known as Urdu.

Hippogriff, a fabulous animal, like a horse in body, but with the head, wings, and front legs and claws of an eagle. The monster frequently appears in the romances of the Middle Ages.

Hippopotamus or "river-horse," the largest living

representative of the hog family, widely distributed over Africa, where it lives in herds. It is of immense bulk, attaining a length of 12 ft. and a weight of 4 tons and stands about 5 ft. high. Its skin is hairless and about 2 in. thick, and it has a pair of tusks often weighing as much as 6 lb. It spends most of its time in the water, and lives entirely on vegetation, both aquatic and terrestrial. The pigmy hippopotamus, which occurs in forests and swamps in W. Africa, is only half the size.

Histology is the study of the structure of plant and animal tissues. These mainly consist of groups of cells with similar functions, *e.g.*, muscle, brain tissue.

Hittites, an ancient race (often mentioned in the Old Testament) who inhabited Asia Minor and N. Syria from the third to the first millennium B.C. Excavations have revealed that they attained a high level of civilisation round about 1350 B.C. They were rivals of Egypt, disputing with Pharaoh the mastery of the Middle East.

Hobby, a bird of the falcon family, 12–14 in. long. Local breeding visitor to England and Wales, April–Sept.; irregular visitor to Scotland and Ireland. They winter in Africa.

Hog, the common name of animals of the Suina family, including the wild boar, pig, and sow. The wild boar, *Sus scrofa*, is the common ancestor. The skin of the hog is covered with bristles, the snout truncated, and each foot has four hoofed toes. Hogs are omnivorous feeders and eat almost anything that is given them.

Hogmanay, the Scottish New Year's Eve festival and a national holiday of the country. The custom of demanding Hogmanay bread is still upheld in many parts of Scotland.

Hogshead, a cask of varying capacity, also a specific measure. In the old English measure a hogshead was 52½ imperial gallons, or 63 old gallons of wine. Of beer 54 old gallons make a hogshead.

Hollands, Schiedam, or **Schnapps,** a kind of gin made mostly in Holland from rye and malt, with a flavouring of juniper berries.

Holly, a hardy evergreen shrub, largely grown in England. Its bright dark green prickly curved leaves and clusters of red berries are familiar in all parts of the country, and used as house decoration between Christmas Eve and Twelfth Night, probably a relic from Roman and Teutonic customs. Its wood is white and hard, valued for carved work, while its bark yields a gummy substance which is coverted into birdlime.

Holy Alliance, an alliance ostensibly for conserving religion, justice and peace in Europe, but used for repressing popular tendencies towards constitutional government. Formed by Alexander I. of Russia, Francis I. of Austria and Frederick William III. of Prussia, at Paris on Sept. 26, 1815. Subsequently joined by all the sovereigns of Europe, except the Pope and the King of England. It ended after the 1830 revolution in France.

Holy Coat of Trèves, a garment preserved in the Cathedral of Trèves and said to have been worn by Christ. It was brought from Jerusalem by the Empress Helena in the fourth century.

Holy Rood, an annual Roman Catholic festival held on Sept. 14 to celebrate the Elevation of the Cross in commemoration of its re-erection in Jerusalem by the Emperor Heraclius in 628 after it had been lost for nearly 300 years and had fallen into the hands of the Persians. Also included in the Church of England calendar.

Holyrood, the ancient royal palace at Edinburgh, dating from the 15th cent., and inhabited by many Scottish sovereigns, notably Mary Stuart, the rooms occupied by her (including the one in which Rizzio was murdered) being still shown. It is now known as Holyrood House and is still used as a royal residence.

Holy Roman Empire, the title which the German Empire received in 962 when Pope John XII. crowned Otto I. at Rome. It endured until 1806 when Francis II. became Emperor of Austria.

Holy Water, water blessed by a priest and kept in small fonts at the entrance to Roman Catholic churches, and used by worshippers going in, and out, or by priests in sprinkling.

Holy Week is the week preceding Easter Sunday, and includes the days of the Sufferings of Christ, ending on Good Friday.

Honey, the sweet syrup formed by bees from the nectar of flowers, the sucrose in the nectar being converted into a mixture of the simple sugars, glucose and fructose.

Honey-eater, an Australian bird (of which there are many species) provided with a long curved bill and tufted tongue. It lives by sucking the "nectar" from the flowers which abound in rural parts of Australia and New Zealand.

Hookah, an Oriental pipe for tobacco smoking, the smoke being drawn through the water of a goblet (commonly a coconut shell) by means of a long flexible tube.

Hoopoe, a remarkably handsome bird with vivid black and white-barred wings and tail and black-tipped crest which opens like a fan. Ranges over Europe, Asia, and Africa. It has bred in England and Wales and occurs in the British Isles in small numbers at all seasons. Other species are confined to Africa, Madagascar, and India.

Hops, the female "cones" of the hop plant used in brewing; their essential oils give beer an aromatic flavour, and their tannin and resin act as a preservative as well as accounting for the bitter taste desired. The hop is a perennial climber belonging to the mulberry family. The male and female organs are on separate plants; as only the female flower-heads are commercially useful, female plants predominate in a hop garden, only a very few male plants being grown so that the female flowers can be fertilised.

Horizon, the limit of vision, the apparent line where sea and sky, or land and sky meet. This is termed the *sensible* or visible horizon. An ordinary person at the height of 5 feet can see for 3 miles, at 20 feet 6 miles, at 50 feet 9¼ miles, and at 1,000 feet 42 miles. The figures are approximate.

Horn *or* **French Horn,** a brass instrument of the trumpet family (*i.e.*, played by three valves) whose tube is very thin and long (Horn in F = 12 ft.). In consequence the tube is curled in a complicated manner. Owing to the sweet tone it is capable of producing, the Horn sometimes plays as part of the wood-wind.

Hornbill, large bird found in Africa and oriental regions, remarkable for its having an immense horned upward-curved helmet, growing over its downward curved beak. It inhabits tropical regions, and feeds on fruits. When the female has laid her eggs in the hollow of a tree, the male bird stops up the entrance, and keeps her imprisoned until the hatching is completed and the young ones are able to fly. There are about 45 species.

Horneblende, the commonest member of the amphibole group of minerals, a silicate of calcium, magnesium, iron and aluminium, of a dark green colour. It is a constituent of numerous rocks, including diorite, syenite, and hornblende schist.

Horned Viper, a curious African genus of *Viperidae*, with a small pointed bone over each eyebrow; a venomous species, found in Egypt, is thought by some to be identical with the "adder" mentioned in Genesis xlix. 17.

Hornet, a general name for many of the bigger wasps. It usually nests in hollow trees, and despite its rather fiercesome appearance does not sting unless unduly provoked.

Horology, the science of time-measurement, including the construction and management of clocks, watches, etc. Instruments of this kind are not known to have existed before the 12th cent. and until the introduction of the pendulum in the 17th cent., clocks were ill-regulated and inaccurate. The time-recording mechanisms of the present day include (*a*) the *clock*, which shows the hours and minutes by hands, and strikes the hours, and sometimes quarters; (*b*) the *timepiece*, which is not generally a fixture and shows the time, but does not strike; (*c*) the *watch*, which is a pocket time-keeper; (*d*) the *chronometer*, which indicates the minutest portions of time; (*e*) electric timepieces, mains electric clocks; (*f*) the highly accurate quartz crystal and atomic clocks used for astronomical purposes. *See* **Clocks.**

Horse Chestnut, one of the large forest trees, with ample branches, and full foliage, and much esteemed for parks and ornamental grounds. The bark and fruit seeds yield substances of commercial value, but the timber is not worth much. The tree came originally from Asia about the 16th cent.

Horse Guards, the building in Whitehall which until 1872 was the headquarters of the Commander-in-Chief of the British Army. The archway is still sentinelled by mounted guards.

Horse Latitudes, the latitudes of the sub-tropical high pressure systems, between the trade winds and the prevailing westerlies, characterised by light variable winds and low humidity.

Hospitallers, Knights, were of the order of St. John of Jerusalem, at first devoted to the aid of the sick, but afterwards military monks, who became prominent figures in the Crusades of the 12th cent. They adopted the Benedictine black habit with the eight-pointed cross worn by the modern St. John's Ambulance Brigade. In 1309 they took Rhodes, but were expelled by the Ottomans in 1522. In 1530 the emperor Charles V gave them the island of Malta, which, as Knights of Malta, they held until 1798, when they were dislodged by Napoleon. The Knights still survive as a sovereign order, with headquarters in Rome. *See* **Templars** and **Teutonic Order**.

Hottentots, name given to certain African natives by Dutch settlers in the 17th cent. They used to occupy the greater part of Cape Colony, and though driven out a number still survive in S.W. Africa. Appear to be related to the Bushmen, though their culture is more advanced. In addition to herding, they practise some farming and know how to smelt iron.

Hounds are dogs that were originally bred and trained for hunting, such as the greyhound, foxhound, bloodhound, wolfhound, deerhound, beagle, harrier, etc., but now often kept also as domestic dogs. The greyhound, deerhound, and wolfhound hunt by sight, the others, with the bloodhound first in order, track by scent.

Hour-glass, a glass instrument tapering to the middle to a narrow orifice, through which a sufficient quantity of fine sand gravitates to mark an hour of time. When the sand has run through from one end, it can be reversed and made to count the hour in the opposite direction. The same kind of glass with smaller supplies of sand will indicate shorter periods, as an egg-glass, which runs its course in three minutes—time to boil an egg by, or to gauge the length of a telephone trunk call.

House Flies are world-wide and prolific. Their eggs are hatched within 24 hours of being laid, and full maturity is attained in a month. They feed mainly on decayed animal and vegetable matter.

Howler Monkey, a genus of South American monkey noted for a laryngeal conformation which enables it to emit a loud reverberant noise something between a yell and a howl, as the name suggests.

Huanuco-bark, a medicinal bark, brought from the Peruvian town of that name, and derived from the *Cinchona micrantha* tree. *See* **Cinchona**.

Huguenots, a name applied to the French Protestant communities of the 16th and 17th cent. Henry of Navarre, by the Edict of Nantes in 1598, granted them religious freedom, but more than a quarter of a century before—Aug. 24, 1572—thousands had been put to death in the massacre of St. Bartholomew. The revocation of the Edict of Nantes by Louis XIV. in 1685 drove thousands into exile in England, Holland, Germany, and America.

Humanism. *See* **J21**.

Humble-bee or **Bumble-bee**, the common name of the insects of the genus *Bombus*, of the Hymenoptera order. They live in small communities comprising males, females, and drones, their habitations being underground. They do not have one queen bee only like the hive bee, but several females occupy the same nest, and these alone live through the winter, breeding and forming new colonies in the spring. Although this large bee buzzes loudly, it does not sting.

Humidity, the state of the atmosphere with respect to the water-vapour it contains. "Absolute humidity" is defined as the density of the vapour present, while "relative humidity," more frequently employed, indicates the degree of saturation, *i.e.*, the ratio of the actual vapour pressure to the saturation vapour pressure at the particular temperature, expressed as a percentage.

Humming Birds are so called because of the humming noise made by the vibration of their wings in flying. They are of radiant plumage, and are among the smallest birds. The smallest bird in the world is the Fairy or Princess Helen's humming bird of Cuba. The body is 2 in. long and the eggs are $\frac{3}{10}$ in. long. There are from four to five hundred species, and they are confined wholly to North and South America, being most numerous in the tropical latitudes. They have long, slender bills and tubular tongues which reach down into flowers to suck up the nectar on which they feed.

Hummum, the original name for what is now called the Turkish Bath in this country. One of the first of these baths to be established in London was the Hummums in Covent Garden.

Hundred, the ancient divisional name given to a portion of a county for administration or military purposes. It is supposed to imply the territory occupied by a hundred families; or the space of a hundred hides of land, or the capacity of providing 100 soldiers. Each hundred had its hundred court, with powers similar to those of a manor court, but this was abolished in 1867 by County Court Act.

Hundred Days, the interval of time between Napoleon Bonaparte's entry into Paris after his escape from Elba and his departure after his abdication, extending from March 20, 1815 to June 28. During this period occurred the battle of Waterloo, June 18.

Hundred Years' War, a term applied to the almost incessant contest between England and France, lasting from 1338 to 1453, including such famous battles as Crécy, Poitiers, and Agincourt, and engaging successively Edward III., Henry V., and Henry VI., among English kings.

Huns, a fierce Asiatic race which swept over eastern Europe in the 4th cent. Under Attila about the middle of the 5th cent. they obtained control of a large portion of central and eastern Europe, forcing even Rome to pay tribute. Their defeat at Châlons-sur-Marne in 451 and the death of Attila in 453 terminated their empire.

Hurdy-Gurdy, an Italian rustic so-called musical stringed instrument of the lute order, the sounds of which are produced by the action of a rosined wheel turned by the left hand, the notes being made by the fingering of the right hand.

Hurricane. *See* **Cyclone** *and* **Wind**.

Hydra, an aquatic animal of simple structure, whose body is in the form of a cylindrical tube, with a disc-shaped base by which it attaches itself to any shifting substance. Its mouth is surrounded by tentacles by which it catches its food. The Hydra has the power of reproducing lost parts. *See also* **F22(2)**.

Hydrates are compounds containing water of crystallisation.

Hydraulic Ram, a form of automatic pump, used to raise water to a height by the action of its own falling velocity.

Hydraulics, the science of applied hydrodynamics, or water-machine engineering, ranging from pumps to marine engines.

Hydrocarbons are compounds of carbon and hydrogen. They include the *paraffins*, which are saturated compounds (*e.g.*, methane); the ethylene, acetylene and other series which are unsaturated; compounds with ring structures, *e.g.*, benzene, naphthalene, and anthracene. Petroleum is composed almost entirely of hydrocarbons.

Hydrochloric Acid, a solution of hydrogen chloride gas in water, and resulting in considerable quantities as a by-product of the soda-ash or salt-cake manufacture. Its solution forms the common hydrochloric or muriatic acid of commerce. It is present to the extent of nearly half a per cent. in the digestive juice secreted by the stomach.

Hydrocyanic Acid, cyanide of hydrogen or prussic acid; very poisonous, and of the odour of bitter almonds. It is formed by the action of acids on sodium or potassium cyanide. Used to kill wasps (and in the gas chamber in the U.S.A.). It is a very important chemical on account of the reactions of its derivatives in many synthetic fields. Discovered by Scheele in 1782.

Hydrodynamics, the science of fluids in motion.

Hydrofluoric Acid is obtained by distillation of fluorspar with sulphuric acid, and is a compound of fluorine and hydrogen. Its action is highly corrosive; a valuable agent in etching on glass, and a rapid decomposer of animal matter.

Hydrogen, Symbol H, the simplest element, atomic number (*q.v.*) of 1, colourless, and the lightest of all substances. Cavendish in 1766 was the first to recognise that it was an element. It is 14·4 times as light as air, and is found in a free state in volcanic regions. It can be obtained by the action of metals on acids, and forms an explosive mixture with air, burning with oxygen to form water. Commercially it is used to produce the very hot flame of the oxy-hydrogen blowpipe for cutting metals; to fill balloons and airships; to harden certain oils and render them suitable for margerine- and soap-production. The gas can be liquefied, and the presence of the isotope deuterium was detected by Urey in 1931 in the residue of the evaporated liquid. The third isotope, tritium, is very rare. *See also* **Deuterium, Tritium.**

Hydrography, the science of water measurement, as applied to seas, rivers, lakes, currents, rocks, reefs, etc., and embracing the whole art of navigation.

Hydrometer, an instrument for measuring the specific gravity of liquids, especially for ascertaining the strength of spiritous liquors and solutions. It is usually in the form of a glass bulb, to the lower end of which a smaller bulb, containing mercury, is attached, which forces the instrument to sink into the liquid which it is to test. The larger bulb has a scale fixed to it, and the indication on this scale of the sinking point shows the specific gravity. There are many varieties: Twaddell's—a pear-shaped bulb containing mercury: Beaumé's, of similar construction, but applicable to liquids both heavier and lighter than water: Sykes's, largely employed for determining the strength of alcohol: and Nicholson's, used for taking the specific gravities of solids.

Hydropathy, the method of treating disease with water, either by bathing or drinking. Natural springs of special chemical and therapeutic properties, such as sulphur springs, and other mineral sources, have been used since prehistoric times for this purpose. It is probably one of the most ancient methods of cure. Recently the beneficial effects of pure water treatment have been advocated. Hydropathic establishments have been set up in many health resorts.

Hydroponics, the culture of plants without soil. The plants are grown with their roots dipping into a solution of nutritive mineral salts; or they may be rooted in sand which is watered with such a solution.

Hydrostatics, the science of the pressure and equilibrium of liquids that are non-elastic.

Hydrozoa are a class of water animals of the *Coelenterata phylum* to which Hydra (*q.v.*) belongs. In one order of the Hydrozoa, free-swimming colonies showing marked division of labour between the individual units occur; this order includes the Portuguese man-of-war. *See* **F22**(2).

Hyena, a nocturnal carnivore with powerful jaws. The striped hyenas inhabit N. Africa, India, and S.W. India. The brown hyenas with long shaggy hair are natives of S. Africa. The spotted, or laughing hyena, noted for the peculiar cry from which its name is derived, is also confined to Africa.

Hygrometer, an instrument for measuring the amount of water vapour in the atmosphere. A simple form of hydrometer, known as the wet-and-dry bulb, consists of two vertical thermometers affixed to a frame. One bulb is exposed to the air, and the other is covered with muslin which dips into a water-bath to keep it moist. If the air is saturated, it takes up no moisture from the wet bulb and the two thermometers read the same. If the air is not saturated, evaporation takes place from the wet bulb, latent heat is absorbed from the air, and the temperature of the wet bulb is lower than that of the dry bulb. Relative humidity and dew-point of the air can then be derived from suitable tables. Hygrometers depending upon the expansion of human hair and gold-beater's skin and the deposition of dew on a polished surface, when cooled sufficiently, are also in general use. *See* **Humidity.**

Hymenoptera, the order of insects to which bees, wasps, hornets, ants and sawflies belong. They have a well-defined waist, two pairs of membranous wings coupled together, mouth parts modified for biting or sucking; the females possess an ovipositor used for depositing eggs and is sometimes modified for stinging. There are about 70,000 species in this order and many live in highly organised communities. *See also* **Ichneumon Fly.**

Hypocaust, an arched fire vault or chamber through which heat is distributed to rooms above. Used in the baths of ancient Rome.

Hypostyle, an architectural term, designating a colonnade or pillared hall, such as in the ancient Egyptian temple of Karnak.

Hypsometer, an instrument formerly used by mountaineers to find the height above sea-level by indirectly measuring the atmospheric pressure by determining the boiling point of water at the particular height. Based on the fact that as pressure decreases with height so the boiling point is lowered. Superseded by the aneroid barometer.

I

Ibex, wild goats of several species found in the mountain regions of Europe, Asia, and Africa. The male has exceedingly large curved ridged horns. The species that lives in the Alps is called the steinbock or bouquetin.

Ibis, belongs to a family of birds related to the stork. The sacred ibis of ancient Egypt is now extinct in Egypt but is found in the lakes and swamps of the Sudan near the Upper Nile. It has white and black plumage and a long curved beak. Other species are found elsewhere, the Glossy Ibis (black plumage glossed with purple and green) occasionally visiting England.

Ice is frozen water. It is a colourless, crystalline and brittle solid. Being only 92% as dense as water, it floats on the latter; the expansion which occurs as water changes into ice causes the fracture of water-pipes, though the fracture only becomes obvious when the ice melts and leaks out through the crack. The temperature at which ice forms is 0° C., 32° F. Ice can be melted by pressure, and the ease and smoothness with which one is able to skate on ice depend on this phenomenon.

Ice Ages. Periods during which the continents were partly or largely covered by ice-sheets and glaciers. The present-day ice-sheets of Greenland and Antarctica are relics of the latest Ice Age, which began in the Pleistocene. Much of the southern hemisphere experienced an ice age at the end of the Carboniferous Period; ice ages are recorded from isolated localities during the Pre-Cambrian, but there is no evidence that these were simultaneous. *See* **F9**(1), **31**(1), **A2.**

Icebergs are detached masses of glacier which subside into the sea and float as wind or current may take them. About one ninth of an iceberg is above sea-level. The North Atlantic is the chief home of icebergs, which reach the ocean from the ice-clad plateaux of Greenland. Some of these floating masses of ice are of enormous proportions, and constitute in the spring and early summer seasons a great menace to the safety of ships, as was disastrously shown in the *Titanic* catastrophe of 1912. For some years past these menaces to N. Atlantic shipping have been kept under close observation by vessels specially detailed for this work.

Ice-breaker, a special heavy bow-plated ship for forcing a way through ice and used especially at ports of the Baltic Sea and the Great Lakes region of Canada which freeze during the winter months. The Soviet atomic ice-breaker *Lenin*, the first of its kind in the world, launched in Dec. 1957, is designed to cut a channel through ice of any thickness. Her icebreaking performance will allow the sea-route to the north of Siberia to be kept open throughout the year.

Icelandic Literature, the Old Norse literature, centred about Iceland, which includes numerous works of poetry, mythology, and history of interest and importance. Much of this literature is in the saga form. *See also* **Edda.**

Iceland Moss, a kind of lichen (*Cetrario islandica*) which grows in great quantities in the mountain regions of Iceland and other Northern countries. It possesses certain nutritive qualities and is of some value in medicine.

Iceland Spar, a colourless form of calcite (calcium carbonate), frequently found in association with metallic ores; it has the power to produce strong double refraction of light so that two images are seen of an object viewed through a piece of Iceland spar. It was formerly used in optical apparatus for producing polarised light.

Iceni, an ancient British race who in early times lived in Norfolk and other parts of Eastern England. Their most famous ruler was Queen Boadicea, who led her people against the Romans in A.D. 61.

Ice Plant, also called "dew plant" and "diamond plant." A South African mesembryanthemum commonly grown in British gardens. Introduced in 1690.

Ice Saints, St. Mamertus, St. Pancras and St. Servatius, so called because of the legendary cold on these Saints' Days, namely, May 11–13.

Ichneumon, the Egyptian mongoose, popularly known as "Pharaoh's Rat." It is of great use in checking the multiplication of reptiles. It is frequently domesticated.

Ichneumon Fly, a numerous group of parasitic hymenopterous insects abounding in many lands, and all having the peculiarity of depositing their eggs in the bodies of other insects. It destroys swarms of caterpillars, which become the unwilling hosts of its progeny.

Ichthyology, the natural history of fishes.

Ichthyosaurus was a gigantic marine reptile of the Mesozoic age. The fossils are mostly found in the lias formation. Some were over 30 ft. in length.

Icons. Icons are religious paintings designed for devotional use either by the individual or in church rituals. In size they range from the very small to large ones in two or three panels on church screens dividing the nave from the chancel (these are known as diptych and triptych respectively). The icon style of painting derives from the tomb paintings of Hellenistic and Roman Egypt, where it had become the custom to leave a portrait of the dead over the mummy's face. Icons of the earlier periods are rare, those of the 6th cent. probably having been destroyed and those of the 9th–12th cent. mostly removed to Russia. They were essentially simple with the Virgin and Child, or the Virgin, Christ, and John the Baptist as subject. From the 13th cent. icons were more complex, dealing with New Testament scenes or scenes from the lives of the saints, and by this time schools of painting, each with their own style, were arising in other countries, including Russia, which accepted the Eastern Church. The 16th-cent. icons begin to show Italian influence just as Italian painting was influenced by Byzantine. Most icons were painted on wood, but mosaic was sometimes used, and some icons were of metal.

Ides, in the ancient Roman Calendar, the 15th of March, May, July, October, and the 13th of all other months; always the eighth day after the Nones.

Idiom, an expression characteristic of a country, district, dialect or language, which usually gives strength and force to a phrase or sentence. The idioms of a language are its distinctive marks, and the best writers are the most idiomatic.

Idris, a famous giant belonging to the myths of Wales, commemorated by a chair of rock on the top of the Cader Idris mountain in Merionethshire.

Igneous Rocks are such as have been molten under conditions of great heat at some stage in their history: *e.g.*, granite, basalt. *See* **F8**(2).

Ignis Fatuus *or* **"Will-o'-the-wisp,"** a phosphorescent light which may often be seen on summer and autumn evenings hovering over marshy ground or graveyards. Its nature is hardly understood, though it is generally believed to be the result of the spontaneous combustion of the gases from decaying organic matter. In olden times when marshy grounds were more common than now, this "dancing light" was very frequently visible and was regarded with superstition.

Iguana, large South American lizards, with a long tail, a scaly back and head, a thick fleshy tongue and a prominent dew-lap in the throat. Specimens of the different species average 4–5 ft. in length, and they live mostly in trees, though they are equally at home on land or in the water. The flesh of some species is good eating, as are also the eggs.

Iguanodon, a genus of extinct dinosaurs, whose fossils are found in the Jurassic and Cretaceous rocks. Iguanodons were 15–25 ft. long, and walked on their hind legs, the front legs being small and adapted for grasping the branches of trees on the leaves of which they fed.

Ilex, mentioned by classical authors, is the holm- or holly-oak, which flourishes round the Mediterranean. To botanists Ilex is the genus to which the holly and maté plant belong. *See* **T8**(2).

Iliad, the great epic poem of ancient Greece attributed to Homer (*c.* 700 B.C.). It consists of ancient folk tale and saga, welded into an artistic unity, having as plot the carrying off of Helen by Paris to Troy and the subsequent siege of Troy. *See* **H19.**

Illuminated MSS. of great value and beauty of decoration exist in most public museums and in many private collections, some of them being of great antiquity, especially those of ancient Egypt executed on papyri. Greek and Latin specimens are also numerous, and the British Museum contains fine examples of all these kinds and also an extensive collection of mediæval English MSS.

Ilmenite, a mineral widespread in igneous rocks: chemically it is an oxide of iron and titanium. Rich deposits have recently been found in the Allard Lake area of Quebec; the Travancore sands are also a source of ilmenite.

Immortality. *See* **J22.**

Immortelles are wreaths, crosses, or other designs made from what are called everlasting flowers, which are obtained from certain plants of the Composite order, and retain their colours and compactness for a long time. Immortelles are largely used as mementoes for decorating graves, especially in France.

Impeachment, a special arraignment, usually before Parliament or other high tribunal, of a person charged with some offence against the State. The custom in England was for the impeachment to be made in the House of Commons, and the trial to be before the House of Lords. The first instance occurred in 1376 when Lord Latimer was impeached. With present parliamentary procedure, impeachment is no longer necessary, since the Cabinet is responsible for the individual actions of its ministers, who, acting as a team, must carry the Commons with them, or resign, when it falls to the Leader of the Opposition to form a new Cabinet. Other famous impeachments were those of the Lord High Chancellor Francis Bacon (1621), Earl of Strafford and Archbishop Laud (1640), Warren Hastings (1788), the last being that of Lord Melville (1805). Under the constitution of the United States public officials may be impeached by the House of Representatives and tried by the Senate. The most famous case was that of President Andrew Johnson.

Imperialism. *See* **J22.**

Impluvium, a basin or tank in the hall or atrium of an ancient Roman house, serving the purpose of receiving the rain that dropped through the open space in the roof.

Impressionism, the name given contemptuously to the first modern movement in painting, being derived from the title of Claude Monet's picture *Impression: soleil levant*, which showed the play of light on water with the observer looking straight into the rising sun. Although intended to be the ultimate form of naturalism the inspiration of the school had been the scientific study of light with an attempt to render the play of light on the surface of objects. Feeling that putting a line around a form was bound to cause it to look unnatural, they used bright colours corresponding to the spectrum and unmixed on the palette, and noted that an object of any given colour casts a shadow tinged with the complementary one (*e.g.*, red-green, yellow-blue). Hence bright sunlight was represented in clear yellows and orange with violet shadows. The first Impressionist exhibition held in Paris in 1874 aroused derision with its paintings by Monet, Renoir, Sisley, Pissaro, Cézanne, and Degas among others. Impressionism subsequently led to the entirely artistic and anti-naturalist movement of Post-impressionism. Cézanne, who felt that he wanted to produce "something solid and durable, like the art of the museums," was only dubiously impressionist, as were also Degas and Renoir. Of course, in the wider sense of the word (*i.e.*, the recording of an ephemeral impression of a scene), Whistler, Turner, and even Rembrandt used the technique.

Impressment, the forced seizure of persons for military service resorted to by many countries before the establishment of conscription. Press gangs forcibly recruited men for British warships especially during the Napoleonic wars, but such measures were abandoned after about 1850.

Imprimatur, originally an official licence to print, and an important formula in the early days of printing. The term is now used in the wider significance of authority, or endorsement.

Impromptu, a piece of music for orchestra or solo instrument of informal construction and composed without preparation.

Inbreeding, mating of closely related animals and plants. Close inbreeding has long been held to be harmful, but this is not necessarily so, for if practised with selection, stock can be purged of the undesirable qualities and the race improved.

Incas, an Indian people who inhabited ancient Peru, founded a great empire, and reached a high level of civilisation: overthrown by the Spaniards in 1533.

Incense, an aromatic resinous substance which, under combustion, exhales a pungent odour, and is used, mixed with certain fragrant perfumes, in the celebration of Mass in Roman Catholic churches. Olibanum or frankincense is ordinarily the leading ingredient.

Incisors, the sharp-edged cutting teeth at the front of mammalian jaws. Elephant tusks are modified incisors.

Income Tax, a tax on annual income charged under the following schedules:

Schedule A.—On the beneficial occupation of land (including buildings). Abolished as from 1963–64 for owner-occupiers. Abolished altogether as from 1964–65.

Schedule B.—Abolished as from 1963–64 on amenity lands (parks, gardens). Restricted to woodlands managed on a commercial basis.

Schedule C.—On dividends, interest, annuities from public revenue. Income Tax deducted at source.

Schedule D.—On profits from trade, profession, or vocation; remittances from abroad; interest on government stocks not taxed at source, Post Office Savings, etc.; sundry profits, short-term gains, etc.

Schedule E.—On salaries, wages, pensions, emoluments, directors' fees, etc. Taxed under P.A.Y.E.

The income-tax year is from April 6 to the following April 5. Rates of tax on taxable income for the year 1965–66 are as follows:—on the first £100, 4*s.* in the £; on the next £200, 6*s.*; and on the balance 8*s.* 3*d.* in the £. *Taxable* income is found by deducting from *Total* income certain allowances.

(1) *Earned Income* allowance of two-ninths to £4,005 and one-ninth to £9,945.

(2) *Personal* allowance of £220 to single persons and married women in employment; to married man living with his wife, or if wife though not living with, is wholly maintained by means of a voluntary allowance, £340. If the wife is maintained under a Court Order or under a binding legal agreement the allowance is reduced to £220.

(3) *Child* allowance of £115 for each child under 11; £140 over 11; and £165 over 16 if still being educated; provided child does not have income in own right of more than £115.

(4) *Dependent Relative* allowance of £75 for each relative or wife's relative maintained whose own income does not exceed £210. Relief reduced by £1 for every £1 by which relative's own income exceeds £210. The dependent person must not be in receipt of an income exceeding £285.

(5) *Widow and Widower* allowance of £40 (certain restrictions).

(6) *Daughter's Services,* necessary owing to old age or infirmity, allowance of £40.

(7) *Housekeeper* allowance of £75 (certain restrictions).

(8) *Age* allowance of two-ninths of unearned income where taxpayer (or his wife) is over 65 and total income does not exceed £900. Marginal allowances.

(9) *Life Insurance.* Subject to certain restrictions, an allowance for the premiums paid for life-insurance of tax-payer and his wife, but not on life of his child or any other person, to a maximum of two-fifths on premiums over £25.

Age Exemption: no tax payable by single persons aged 65 or over if income does not exceed £390; £625 for married couples where either is 65 or over. Appropriate marginal allowances.

Pensions qualify for the earned income relief of two-ninths.

Small Income Relief. All incomes up to £450 are treated as Earned Income.

Surtax is on a sliding scale, increasing from 2*s.* in the £ with the size of the income. For 1965–66 (payable Jan. 1, 1967) surtax on earned income begins, in effect, at £5,000, or more if personal reliefs are due. (*See* **L110.**)

Independence Day, commemorates the adoption of the Declaration of Independence on July 4, 1776. July 4 is celebrated as a holiday in the United States.

Index. The name given to a list of books, prepared by papal authority, which are declared to be dangerous to faith and morals, and therefore forbidden to Roman Catholics. The *Index Expurgatorius* covers books which may be read with offending passages removed; the *Index Librorum Prohibitorum* those which may not be read at all. The first *Index* was issued by Pope Pius IV, in 1559.

India Office Library (since 1947 called the **Library of the Commonwealth Relations Office** (**Division B**)). This is an orientalist library, which specialises in Indian studies. It was founded in 1801 by the East India Company, and contains 20,000 manuscripts in European languages and in Sanskrit, Persian, modern Indian, and other oriental languages, and a quarter-of-a-million printed books, of which three-quarters are in oriental languages. There are also collections of drawings, photographs, and other objects of oriental interest. It was announced in 1965 that a judicial tribunal was to decide on legal ownership of the library.

Indian Ink, a pigment made from lampblack and gum or glue, originally prepared in China and Japan. It is dried and marketed in small sticks and used mainly by artists for shading and lettering.

Indian Mutiny. This turning-point in the history of modern India occurred in 1857–58. The ostensible cause was the serving out to the native troops of cartridges greased with animal fat, for contact with this was forbidden both by the Hindu and Mohammedan faiths. A rebellious feeling, however, had long been developing, and when the Sepoys at Meerut in May 1857 refused to obey the English officers, overpowered and put them to death, the mutiny spread like wildfire. The rebels took Delhi and Lucknow, and for many months terrible massacres and atrocities were committed; men, women and children were slain in thousands. Order was re-established in the autumn of 1858 when the governing power was transferred from the East India Company to the Crown.

Indian Summer is applied to a warm spell of weather occurring in the late autumn.

Indicators, substances which by a marked change in colour are used to indicate the course of a chemical reaction. Litmus paper, for instance, is red with acids and blue with alkalis. In biological work some radioactive substances are used as tracer elements.

Indigo, the substance obtained from the plant *Indigofera tinctoria,* a native of S. Asia, India being the chief producing country. The colouring matter is the result of the decomposition and fermentation of a glucoside contained in the plant. This is afterwards dried and becomes the caked indigo of commerce. Natural indigo has been eclipsed by artificial indigo, a coal-tar dye which came into commercial production at the end of the last century, which is cheaper and more uniform in quality.

Indium, a scarce lead-coloured metal, symbol In, found in zinc blende in Saxony and certain other ores. This element was discovered in 1863 by Reich and Richter. It is an important material in the manufacture of transistors.

Indo-European, a term used to designate the great Aryan family of languages, which embraces Indo-Iranian, Celtic, Greek, Italic, Slavonic, and Germanic. Basque, Magyar, Turkish, and Finnish do not belong to this family.

Indulgence. In the Roman Catholic Church the remission granted by ecclesiastical authority to a repentant sinner of the temporal punishment still due after the guilt of sin has been forgiven by God. The indiscriminate sale of Indulgences by Tetzel and other Papal agents in the 16th cent. was one of the grievances which led to the Reformation (*see* **J38**).

Indulgence, Declaration of, was the proclamation by which James II. suspended the penal laws against Roman Catholics and Dissenters. It was issued in 1688, but the clergy as a body refused to obey, and the trial of the Seven Bishops and their acquittal by a jury followed. An invitation was thereupon sent to William of Orange to become King.

Industrialisation is simply a name for industrial development. It is customarily used in particular to designate the course of events in a hitherto underdeveloped country which is seeking to increase its wealth and productivity by the introduction of more advanced techniques and by the establishment of industries previously not carried on within it. The word usually covers not only the development of modern industrial production but also the provision of electric power-stations, irrigation works, and transport and other developments designed to improve production in any field by methods involving large capital investments. The outstanding example in our time of rapid industrialisation has been the Soviet Union, which, unable to get the capital from abroad, has had to carry it through by ruthless restriction of the people's consuming power so as to achieve an unprecedentedly high ratio of investment to total production. Industrialisation has in practice meant a high concentration on the expansion of the basic heavy industries and of power supply, coupled with much slower development of the industries supplying consumers' goods and of agricultural production; but there is no reason why this should always be the case. It may well be that in most underdeveloped countries development can but be devoted largely to the industries making consumers' goods and to measures designed to increase agricultural production and productivity.

Inertia, a term used in mechanics for the property of matter by which it offers resistance to a change in its state of rest or in its state or direction of motion.

Inertial Navigation, an automatic method of dead-reckoning which at present finds its chief application in guided missiles, submarines, and aircraft. Navigation by this means is carried out with reference to inertial space (*i.e.*, space which is stationary with respect to the fixed stars) and not to the surface of the earth as in normal navigation (latitude and longitude). This is done by means of high-accuracy gyroscopes combined with highly sensitive accelerators in an apparatus known as the Ship's Inertial Navigation System. The American nuclear-powered submarine *Nautilus* pioneered the new north-west passage under the polar ice pack by this method of dead-reckoning in Aug. 1958.

Inflorescence, a flowering shoot. Many arrangements of the flowers are possible and there are many kinds of inflorescence; *e.g.*, the spike, catkin, umbel, capitulum (in composites).

Inflation. *See* **G4**(2).

Infra-red Rays *or* **Radiation.** This is the range of rays which come between the visible red rays and the ultra-short Hertzian radiation. The wave-lengths involved range from about 0·00076 millimetre (7,600 Angstrom units) to 0·4 millimetre. Infra-red rays penetrate haze; hence landscapes obscured by haze or cloud can be photographed using plates sensitive to infra-red. Many substances strongly absorb these rays and thereby become hot; this happens in toasting bread. Many industries use infra-red lamps for drying paints and lacquers. Very important to chemists, as a tool in the investigation of the structure of compounds, since various groups of elements absorb infra-red radiation at a characteristic frequency.

Infula, a sacred fillet, of woollen material, worn on the forehead by priests, magistrates and rulers in Roman times, also by persons fleeing for protection to sanctuary. Later, each of the two lappets of a bishop's mitre.

Ingoldsby Legends, a series of whimsical metrical tales full of droll humour written by the Rev. R. H. Barham, and first published in *Bentley's Miscellany* in 1837. The best known is the *Jackdaw of Rheims*.

Ink, a liquid pigment ordinarily made from an infusion of nut-galls, copperas, and gum arabic. Shumac is substituted for nut-galls for inferior inks. An acid is sometimes added to prevent oxidation, and for the blue-black inks a small quantity of solution of indigo serves for colouring. Copying ink contains glycerine or sugar, which keeps the ink moist. Lampblack used to be the leading ingredient in printer's ink but now new methods of manufacturing have been developed. Marking ink is composed of a solution of nitrate of silver, gum, ammonia, and carbonate of soda. For red, blue, and other coloured inks, colouring solutions are used, for example, Prussian blue. The earliest examples of ink writing (on wooden tablets) ever found in Britain were recovered from the well of a Roman villa (3rd cent A.D.) during excavations in 1954 at Chew Stoke, Somerset.

Ink Sac, a glandular organ found in squids and other cephalopods which contains an inky solution. When roused the animal discharges the contents of the ink sac into the water, to make a cloud through which its enemies cannot see. The pigment, sepia, comes from the ink sac of the cuttlefish.

Inlaying is the introduction of one class of substance into another in some artistic or other design, such as silver let into zinc, copper, or lead, and called *bidri*; the insertion of gold and silver into iron or steel, which is *damascening*; the mingling of brass with tortoiseshell, *buhl work*; the inlaying of woods, *marquetry*; of stone, *pietra dura*; and of the arrangement of small pieces of stone, for floors, walls, etc., *mosaic*.

Innocents' Day, a festival day in Roman, Greek, and Anglican Churches in commemoration of the killing of the children of Bethlehem by Herod, Dec. 28.

Inns of Court, the four bodies in London which enjoy the privilege of calling candidates to the bar after they have studied for a certain number of terms and passed certain examinations. The Inns are: the Inner Temple, the Middle Temple, Lincoln's Inn, and Gray's Inn.

Inquisition, a Roman Catholic ecclesiastical court which became a formidable weapon of the Church in the 13th cent. under Pope Innocent III. in dealing with charges of heresy. It was effectively set up in the various Catholic countries of the Continent, obtaining its fullest and most sweeping organisation in Spain in the days of Ferdinand and Isabella, when Torquemada was made Grand Inquisitor, and used its powers with terrible severity. *See* **Auto-da-fé.** In the 18th cent. its influence began to wane, and although the Congregation of the Holy Office still exists at Rome, its jurisdiction is limited to the suppression of heretical literature.

Insectivorous Plants, plants which trap insects with special mechanisms. Plant enzymes or bacteria digest the prey, providing the plants with nitrogen usually scarce in the soil in which they grow. The most common British species are the Sun-dew and the Bladderwort.

Insects. This huge class of invertebrate animals (*see* **Arthropoda, (F22)**) includes about 100,000 species. Insects are ubiquitous except in the sea, only a very few species being adapted to marine existence. Characteristic features are: the body is divided into three parts, head, thorax, and abdomen: the head carries a pair of antennae, the thorax three pairs of legs, and usually two pairs of wings. The most primitive insects constituting the sub-class *Apterygota* are wingless. The other sub-class, *Pterygota*, is divided into the *Exopterygota* (*Hemimetabola*), which have a simple metamorphosis, *e.g.*, cockroach, and the *Endopterygota* (*Holometabola*), with a complex metamorphosis, *e.g.*, butterfly, bee. Although many are parasitic on man, animals and plants, innumerable animals and some plants use them as food, and many flowering plants are dependent on a variety of insects for pollination leading to the development of seeds and fruits. *See* **F23**(1), **F28**(2), **T27**(1).

Insignia, marks or badges of office or honour, such as stars, ribbons, crosses, medallions or other designating objects, worn by members of special Orders or holders of prominent offices.

Institut de France was formed in 1795, and after various modifications was in 1832 organised on its present basis. Its five academies are—the Académie Française, Académie des Inscriptions et Belles-Lettres, Académie des Sciences, Académie des Beaux-Arts, Académie des Sciences morales et politiques. It is restricted to 40 members.

Instruments, Musical. Musical instruments may be classified in a number of ways, but in general they fall into one of the three main classes, String, Wind, and Percussion, according to how the sound is produced. **Stringed Instruments** are those which produce the sound by the vibration of a string: (*a*) by plucking, as in Harp, Lyre, Psaltery, Zither, Lute, Guitar, Balalaika, Ukelele, Harpsichord; (*b*) by friction (bowed), as in Crwth, Rebec, Viol, Violin, Marine Trumpet, Hurdy-Gurdy; (*c*) by striking (hammered), as in Dulcimer, Pianoforte, Clavichord; (*d*) by wind (blown), as in the Aeolian Harp. **Wind Instruments** are those in which the air in the instruments is set in vibration: (*a*) by blowing into a tube (flue-voiced), as in Recorder, Pandean Pipe, Flute, Organ; (*b*) by means of reeds (reed-voiced), as in Oboe, Clarinet, Saxophone, Bagpipe, Cor Anglais, Bassoon, Organ reed-stops; (*c*) those in which the sound is produced by the vibration of the player's lips against the mouthpiece (lip-voiced), as in Bugle, Horn, Trumpet, Tuba, Trombone, Saxhorn, Flügelhorn, Cornet. In a modern orchestra these are known as the *Brass*: instruments of the flute, oboe, and clarinet families as the *Woodwinds*. Then there are the **Percussion Instruments**, which include the Drums, Cymbals, Tambourines, Castenets.

Insulation, the condition in which an electrified body is prevented from communicating electricity to contiguous bodies by the interposition of a non-conducting material. Important insulators are rubber, plastics, some fibres, *e.g.*, silk, ceramics, oil.

Insulin is a hormone which controls the supply of sugar from the blood to muscles. The breakdown of sugar provides energy. In diabetes there is a lack of insulin, causing a build-up of blood sugar which can be released by the injection of insulin. It is secreted by the islet tissue of the pancreas, from which it was isolated in 1922 by Banting and Best. Dr. F. Sanger of Cambridge University was awarded the 1958 Nobel Prize for his work in determining the chemical structure of insulin. *See* **P39**(1). **50**(1).

Intaglio, engraving or carving on a sunken ground, a method frequently adopted in the ornamentation of stones and rings.

Intelligence. Intelligence has been variously defined as "the ability to see the relationships between things" and "the ability to profit from experience." The idea of intelligence testing was first devised by the French psychologist Binet at the beginning of this century. He was asked by the French government to invent a test which would weed out backward children in state schools, and thus save public money and avoid holding back the work of the class by teaching children who were incapable of learning at a given standard. Briefly, a series of problems are given to a large number of children and it is thus found out which series can be solved by the average child of a given age-group; if a child of 7 can only pass the tests suitable to the average child of 6, then his mental age is 6. The intelligence quotient or I.Q. is discovered by dividing his mental age by his chronological age. For example, if a child is 7 years and 1 month old, we may begin by giving him tests at the 6-year level. If he passes all these plus four for age 7, three for age 8, and one for age 9, his mental age is calculated by crediting him with 72 months for passing all tests at age six and two months mental credit for each additional test passed, *i.e.*, 8 months at age 7 (4 out of 8 tests), 6 months at age 8, and 2 months at age 9. His total mental age (M.A.) is therefore 88 months, and since his chronological age is 85 months, the I.Q. is 88/85. To remove the decimal point, the result is multiplied by 100, giving an I.Q. of 104. *See also* **Section Q, Part I.**

Interest is the payment made for the use of borrowed money over time. The rate of interest is the rate per cent per annum charged for such loans. There are many such rates, varying with the plenty or scarcity on borrowable money, with the length of time for which the loans are made, and with the degree of risk, if any, that the loans will not be duly repaid. Short-term loans are usually cheaper than long-term: the lowest rates are usually for "call money" repayable immediately on demand. These are used principally in short-term financial transactions, such as bill discounting. Bank loans, though usually made for fairly short terms, command higher rates. Long-term loans are made chiefly to public authorities, or as bonds or debentures to business concerns. The rates obtained vary with the demand and the supply of such accommodation.

Interferon, the name given to a substance discovered in 1957 by Drs. Isaacs and Lindenmann at the National Institute for Medical Research. It is produced by the interaction of viruses with living cells and has the important property of inhibiting virus reproduction. Its development may lead to a new approach to the therapy of viral diseases.

Interlude, any short stage piece, or brief musical composition, for performances between more important pieces. In the strict musical sense an interlude is an *instrumental* composition played between the acts.

International Date Line, a line along the 180° meridian, marking the difference in time between E. and W. For the westward-bound traveller crossing the line the date would be put forward one day, for the eastward-bound, back one day. To avoid difference of date in adjacent land areas, the line deviates from the 180° meridian where this crosses land.

Interval, in music indicates the differences in pitch between two notes. This is often expressed numerically. Thus the interval between C and the E above it is a major third, that between C and E flat is a minor third, that between C and G is a fifth, that between C and A is a sixth.

Introit, the psalm or hymn in common use in the Anglican Church, which is sung as the clergy enter the church to commence the divine service of Holy Eucharist.

Invention of the Cross, a Roman Catholic festival held on May 3, to celebrate the finding of the alleged True Cross at Calvary by the Empress St. Helena in 326. Also included in the Church of England calendar. *See* **Holy Rood.**

Investiture, the ceremony of conferring honour, office, or possession—the investment of the recipient with badge, token, or public recognition.

Iodine, a non-metal element, symbol I, member of the halogen family (*q.v.*), a substance formerly exclusively obtained from the ribbon-wrack seaweeds. These were burnt and the ashes (kelp) extracted with water. After concentrating the iodides, these were distilled with manganese dioxide and sulphuric acid to yield iodine vapour which was condensed in stoneware bottles. Nearly all iodine now in use is derived from the iodine salt present in Chile saltpetre (sodium nitrate). Iodine is used in photography, as an antiseptic solution in alcohol or potassium iodide (tincture of iodine), and in medicine. Discovered by Courtois in 181

Ions, electrically charged atoms, or groups of atoms. Atoms of the metals lose electrons to become positively charged ions, *e.g.*, the sodium ion (Na^+) has one electron less than the atom. The non-metal ions are negatively charged, *e.g.*, the chloride ion (Cl^-) has one electron more than the atom. Similarly, a group like the sulphate ion (SO_4^{2-}) has more electrons than the constituent atoms. Thus, the hydrogen atom without its electron is a hydrogen ion or *proton* and the helium atom without its two electrons is a helium ion or *alpha-particle*. When an electric force is applied to certain solutions, the ions into which molecules of the dissolved substance are broken up are attracted to the oppositely charged electrodes, their movements constituting an electric current through the solution. In the same way gases, including air, conduct electricity by virtue of free ions (*see* **F12(2)**). Combustion, radioactivity, and ultra-violet and cosmic radiations produce ionisation.

Ionic Order of architecture is one of the five classic orders, its leading characteristics being the volute of its capital, which has on each side distinctive curved or scrolled ends.

Ionosphere, a succession of ionized layers of the earth's atmosphere lying above the stratosphere. In this region free electrically charged particles —electrons and positive ions—occur in sufficient concentration to affect substantially the propagation of radio waves through the region. It extends upwards from a height of 60 miles to several hundred miles, being most concentrated at an altitude of 200 miles. The behaviour of the upper atmosphere is strongly influenced by the sun. A great deal of new information about the ionosphere above an altitude of 150 miles (the topside ionosphere) has been obtained by the use of instruments carried in satellites. *See also* **Atmosphere.**

Ipecacuanha, a flowering plant of the Brazilian forests. Various alkaloids are isolated from ipecacuanha, one is emetine, which is used in medicine to cause vomiting and so remove poisons from the stomach. Another is used as an expectorant in cough mixtures.

Iridium, a white and very hard metal, symbol Ir, discovered by Tennant in 1804. It occurs naturally as an alloy with platinum or osmium; tips for fountain-pen nibs have been made from the former native alloy. The former standard metre was composed of platinum–iridium alloy (*see* **Metre**) as are parts of scientific apparatus and surgical tools that must be non-corrodible.

Iris, the typical genus of the botanical order *Iridacae*, with tuberous rhizomes and sword-shaped leaves, many of the family having beautiful flowers. About 100 species of Iris are recorded from the northern temperate zone, the most common species wild in Britain being the yellow flag. Orris root, used in perfumery, comes from another iris species.

Iron is a metallic element, symbol Fe (Latin *ferrum*), ocurring widely in nature in such ores as haematite, loadstone (magnetic iron oxide), spathic ore, and iron pyrites. It is extracted by a process known as smelting, with coke and limestone in a furnace. Its many uses are familiar, the most important being in the manufacture of cast- and wrought-iron products and of steels, which are alloys mainly of iron with added carbon and various metals. Iron rust is formed by the action of oxygen and water, and is a coating of iron oxide. *See* **Smelting.**

Ironclads, ships of war cased in iron or steel plates of sufficient thickness to resist projectiles. They were first introduced (1858) in the French Navy, and in 1860 the first British ironclad, the *Warrior*, was launched.

Iron Curtain. In a speech at Fulton, U.S.A., on March 5, 1946, Sir Winston Churchill used this phrase to describe the dividing line behind which, he said, lie all the capitals of the ancient States of Central and Eastern Europe—Warsaw, Berlin, Prague, Vienna, Budapest, Belgrade, Bucarest, and Sofia. These famous cities and the populations around them, said Sir Winston, lie in the Soviet sphere and are subject "to a very high and increasing measure of control from Moscow."

Ironsides were Cromwell's special troopers, so called because of their solidity and firmness in battle.

Irredentists, a political party organised in Italy about 1878 with the object of incorporating within Italy neighbouring regions. Also a person, group, or party advocating policies for the restoration to their country of territory formerly belonging to it but later lost.

Irrigation, an artificial method of providing water for the growth of plants on lands where the natural supply of water is deficient. The science has made immense progress during the last fifty years, and has been the means of bringing into profitable cultivation vast tracts of territory in India and Western America which had previously been arid wastes. The systems are various and are utilised according to the special conditions of the land to be irrigated, but the success which has attended these experiments has been very gratifying. In fact, irrigated lands are often more productive than lands which receive a fair amount of moisture from the elements; the irrigation supply can be distributed and regulated exactly according to requirements. Irrigation also serves the purpose of supplying *warmth* in winter; *e.g.*, in the English water-meadows, and in the more highly developed Italian *marcite* and winter-meadows, where the water is mostly applied in winter when there is plenty of rain. There are several other functions of irrigation; *e.g.*, washing out of excess salts.

Isinglass, a gelatinous substance manufactured from the swim bladders of certain fish; used to preserve eggs, to keep beer free from sediment, and to make a glue.

Islam. *See* **J23.**

Isobars are the lines drawn on charts linking together points of equal barometric pressure.

Isochasms, lines connecting places at which there is an equal probability of seeing an aurora, taking the average over a number of years, based on the auroral catalogue of Fritz.

Isomers are chemical compounds having the same composition but different structural arrangements, and consequently different physical and chemical properties. For example, ethyl alcohol and methyl ether are isomers, since the molecules of both are built up of two atoms of carbon, six of hydrogen, and one of oxygen, *viz.*, C_2H_6O; ethyl alcohol, C_2H_5OH; and methyl ether, CH_3OCH_3.

Isotherms are lines drawn on charts through points of equal temperature.

Isotopes. When one talks of an element, say, uranium or lead, the name of the element is a generic name for a collection of uranium species and lead species. The different species are called isotopes. For any particular element, the number and arrangement of electrons around the nucleus are the same in all the isotopes, so all the isotopes have the same chemical properties. Soddy has described isotopes as "elements, the atoms of which have similar outsides but different insides." For example, in the nucleus of the uranium isotopes, U 235, U 238, and U 239, there are respectively 143, 146, and 147 neutrons, but all have 92 protons. The isotopes have different atomic weights, in this instance respectively 235, 238, and 239. But all have the same chemical properties.

Ivory, the dentine substance of which the tusks of the elephant, hippopotamus, walrus, etc., are composed. The tusks of the African elephant sometimes weigh as much as 100 lb., and reach a length of 8 or 9 ft.

Ivory Gull, a small, beautifully shaped sea-bird with striking all-white plumage and black legs which breeds on the rocky shores of the Arctic, being found farther north than any other bird; it occasionally wanders south in the winter.

Ivy, the well-known climbing shrub, chiefly evergreen; furnishing a sudorific, the berries having also emetic properties.

J

Jabiru, the Brazilian name for the giant stork of South America.

Jacamar, from *Jacameri*, the Brazilian name for a smallish bird with long, sharply pointed bill and brilliant plumage which inhabits the tropical regions of South America east of the Andes. These birds are seen sitting motionless on trees, darting off at intervals, like flycatchers, to catch insects on the wing.

Jacana, a tropical bird (the water-hen of Brazil and the warmer parts of America) of wide range, beautiful of plumage, with slim body and narrow wings, and long, pointed beak. It feeds on seeds and insects, inhabits marshy lands, and is related to the plovers.

Jack, a small schooner-rigged vessel, used in the Newfoundland fisheries; a pike; an oscillating lever; a device used in roasting meat.

Jackal, *Canis aureus*, a small wild dog related to the wolf and resembling a fox. The Common Jackal is found in S.E. Europe, India, and Ceylon; other species inhabit Africa and Egypt. The jackal is a well-known scavenger.

Jackdaw, one of the smaller members of the Crow family. This European bird is typically black with grey collar. It is easily tamed, makes an amusing pet, and delights in making off with and taking to its nest bright objects, such as silverware.

Jacobins, a French revolutionary club or party, formed in 1789, and accustomed to meet at a Jacobin convent, hence the name. It became a controlling force in the Revolution, especially in the movement which led to the Terror. Robespierre was its chief spokesman.

Jacobites, adherents of the Stuart cause after the abdication of James II. First James himself, then his son (the Old Pretender), and later his grandson (the Young Pretender) tried to fan the flame of rebellion in Scotland and Ireland, but after the defeat at Culloden in 1746 the cause was lost. Also the name of the monophysite heretics of Syria (*see* **Section J**), so named after their leader Jacobus Baradaeus in the 6th cent. A.D.

Jade, a green mineral found in China, America, and New Zealand, and used for making vases, bracelets, and other ornamental articles. There are many varieties, and there is evidence that the stone was in common use in prehistoric times for weapons and utensils.

Jaguar, a South American carnivorous animal resembling the leopard, but much larger and more powerful, the largest of the Felidae.

Janeite, a devotee of Jane Austen and her writings.

Janissaries, an élite band of Turkish foot soldiers who acted as the Sultan's bodyguard, noted for their turbulence and cruelty. They gained great power under the Ottoman Empire. In 1826 the Sultan Mahmud II had them massacred.

January, the first month of the year, named after Janus, the two-faced god of the Romans. It was the *Wolf monath* and *Aefter Yule* of the Saxons.

Jasmine, a graceful climber belonging to the olive family with odoriferous blossom, originally a Persian plant, but now acclimatised in many varieties in almost all parts of the world. Two species of jasmine (the common jasmine and the Spanish jasmine) yield oils used in perfumery.

Jasper, a precious stone of the chalcedony variety, opaque, and coloured red, brown, yellow and sometimes green. It was greatly esteemed by the ancients, the Bible having numerous allusions to it.

Jay, a gaily-coloured bird of the Crow family, of many species—the Blue jay of N. America, the Canada jay, sometimes called "whisky jack," the Siberian jay, and the British jay, fawn-coloured with black and whitish crest and bright blue feathers in the wings. It lives in woods and like the magpie, takes the eggs and young of small nesting birds.

Jazz, a rhythmical syncopated music characterised by a strong element of improvisation in the performance, probably originating among the Negro population of the Southern States of the U.S.A. It became popular during the first world war and, in a commercialised form, has held the popular field ever since. Modern dance music and popular songs are based on the jazz idiom, which has also had a profound effect upon contemporary music of a more serious kind.

Jean, a stout kind of twilled cotton cloth much worn in olden times, and resembling fustian. Blue *jeans*, adopted by American city youngsters from farmworkers, are now the fashion elsewhere and worn not only as overalls by workmen but by both sexes in leisure time.

Jelly-fish. The jelly-fishes, which have gelatinous, translucent bodies fringed at the margin with delicate tentacles, constitute the coelenterate order *Scyphozoa*. The mouth, with a squarish opening, is seen on the underside, and there are four horseshoe-shaped sex organs.

Jerboa, small jumping mammals of the Rodent order. These mice-like animals have long tufted tails and very long hind legs, the front legs not being used for locomotion.

Jeremiad, any utterance or writing in which sorrow or complaint is the chief characteristic, so named as recalling the style of the "Lamentations of Jeremiah," in the Old Testament.

Jerusalem Chamber, a room in Westminster Abbey, deriving its name from the circumstance of its having originally been decorated with a view of Jerusalem. Henry IV. died in this chamber, and the Committee for the Revision of the Bible met there in 1870 and later.

Jesuits, members of the Roman Catholic teaching order founded by Ignatius Loyola in 1534. A long and vigorous course of study is prescribed before they are admitted into the privileges of full membership. They are required to take the vows of voluntary poverty, perfect chastity, perfect obedience, and complete submission to the Pope. The Society played an important part in politics.

Jet, a deep black fossil substance admitting of a high polish and much used for jewellery, ornaments, and trimming. It is a form of lignite, the most important British deposit being found near Whitby, where jet manufacture has been an established industry for a long period.

Jet Engine, an aeroplane engine which derives its thrust from the high velocity of the gases it ejects. The essential units in a jet engine are a rotary compressor and a gas turbine, the latter driving the compressor. The first reliable, high-performance jet propulsion engine for aircraft was invented by Air Commodore Sir Frank Whittle.

Jet Stream, a meteorological term coined in 1946 to describe the relatively narrow belt of strong winds (100–200 m.p.h.) at levels in the atmosphere from 3 to 7 miles. These winds are important in forecasting weather, and can be a valuable aid to aircraft. From the ground, where there may be little wind, the jet stream can sometimes be seen as high cirrus cloud moving across the sky at high speed.

Jewish Calendar is supposed to date from the Creation, which according to their reckoning occurred on Oct. 7, 3761 B.C.

Jew's Harp. The name is believed to be a corruption of "jaws harp." This instrument consists of a metal frame with a central tongue of spring steel. The frame is pressed against the teeth, and the tongue of the harp is twanged with the finger, the mouth acting as a resonating chamber. By altering the shape of the mouth the resonant frequency and therefore the note can be varied.

Jimson Weed, corruption of Jamestown Weed, a synonym for the Thorn Apple of the Nightshade family.

Jockey Club, the governing body that, although possessing no legal status, frames rules and laws by which horse-racing and turf matters generally are regulated. The club-house is at Newmarket.

John Bull, the typical figure of an Englishman, bluff, big, and burly. Arbuthnot's *History of John Bull* is supposed to have originated the character.

John Dory, a well-known sea-fish of which there are six species. It is of a golden-yellow colour (*jaune doré*), has a high dorsal fin with long filaments projecting from the spines, and is much valued as a table fish. It is sometimes found in British waters, but the Mediterranean is its chief habitat.

John o' Groat's House, W. of Duncansby Head, Caithness, popularly named as the northernmost point of Scotland. According to legend the house, which has now disappeared, was built in octagonal form by a Dutchman Jan de Groot who came to live there in the 16th cent. The site is marked and an inn was erected near it in 1876.

Jongleurs were minstrels and jesters who wandered from town to town singing songs, playin musical instruments, dancing, and giving entertainments in mediæval France and Norman England. Jongleurs were low-born in contrast to the Troubadours, who were often of the nobility.

Joule, a unit of energy equal to 10^7 ergs; this is about $\frac{3}{4}$ of a foot-pound. Named after J. P. Joule (1818–89). The relationship between mechanical energy and heat energy is called the mechanical equivalent of heat and was found by Joule to be 778 ft. lb. in lb. °F. units or $4{\cdot}18 \times 10^7$ ergs in gram °C. units. *See* **F16** (2).

Jousts were military tiltings in the nature of tournaments, where the contestants strove against each other on horseback with blunted lances. It was the sport of nobles in feudal times.

Judaism. *See* **J24.**

Julian Calendar, named after Julius Cæsar, who in 46 B.C., finding the Roman year 90 days in advance of the real time, was the first to adopt the calculation of time by the solar year, the average length being fixed at 365¼ days. There was still an overplus of a few minutes every year, and this was rectified by the Gregorian Calendar, introduced in Italy in 1582 and adopted in England in 1752, from which date what is called the "New Style" begins.

Julus, a genus of millipedes with cylindrical bodies and two pairs of legs to each segment, the latter being 40 to 50 in number. In South America specimens 5 or 6 in. long are frequent, but those found in England are small.

July, the seventh month of the year, named after Julius Caesar. It was the *Maed monath* (Mead-month) of the Saxons.

June, the sixth month of the year, containing 30 days and deriving its name from Juno. It was the *Sear* (Dry) *monath* of the Saxons.

Jungle-Fowl, birds related to the peacocks and peacock-pheasants. At least four species are known from the jungles of India, Ceylon, and Java. The domestic chicken has been derived from the Red Jungle-Fowl (*Gallus gallus*).

Junkers, name of the ruling class of Prussia, military in spirit, who were the party of reaction and defenders of the landed interests. Supported Bismarck prior to the Franco-Prussian war and helped bring Hitler to power.

Jupiter, the largest planet. It is believed to have a rocky core surrounded by ice layers thousands of miles thick. There is an outer atmosphere containing ammonia and methane, both presumably in the liquid or solid state owing to the very low temperatures of the outer layers (−120° C.). In 1610 Galileo made history by discovering the four major satellites of Jupiter, which he named Medicean planets after his patron Cosimo Medici; these are visible with good field-glasses. There are eight others. For distance of Jupiter, etc., *see* **F7.** Also the supreme mythical deity of the Romans, identified with the Greek Zeus (**H38**).

Jurassic Formation, a series of rocks (the evidences of which are most marked in the Jura Mountains) coming between the Cretaceous and Triassic groups and including the Oolite and the Lias. It is a formation rich in fauna, abounding in echinoids, lamellibranchs, ammonites, and belemnites; large reptiles, marine and land, are common, as are the plants called cyads. In Britain the Jurassic outcrop extends from the Dorset coast to the Yorkshire moors. *See* **F30.**

Jury, a body of private citizens chosen and sworn to hear and pass verdict upon evidence brought forward at a trial, inquest, or inquiry. The origin of the English jury is obscure, but it is thought to have been introduced by the Normans. The jurors are the judges of fact upon the evidence laid before them. Verdicts (in criminal cases) not guilty or guilty, and unless all 12 agree, cases must be retried with fresh jurors. In Scotland 45 jurors are summoned in criminal cases, of whom 15 are chosen by ballot, and majority verdicts are accepted: not guilty, not proven, and guilty.

Jute, the name given to the fibre of a plant grown largely in Pakistan in the Ganges delta and used for the manufacture of coarse cloths, cordage, and packs. Calcutta is the biggest jute-manufacturing centre of the world, as Dundee was in the 19th cent.

Jutes, a Low German race who in the 5th cent. invaded the south-eastern part of England, establishing themselves in Kent and making Canterbury their capital.

K

Kaffirs, Bantu-speaking negro tribes of South Africa, whose occupations are cattle-raising, farming, and hunting.

Kagu, native name for a curious bird related to the sun-bittern and the only member of the Rhinochetinae family, found inhabiting New Caledonia when that island was colonised by the French.

Kakapo, the Maori name for the New Zealand owl-parrot, a peculiar and interesting species, possessing wings but not able to use them for flight (though it can glide); of sap-green plumage, nocturnal in its habits, and nesting in burrows. Still to be found in the larger forest areas of the South I.

Kangaroo, pouched (marsupial) mammals of Australia and adjacent islands. There are over 20 species, the smaller ones being known as "wallabies." Kangaroos leap in a succession of springy bounds 10–20 ft. long, the forefeet not touching the ground. They can reach a height of over 6 ft. and a weight of 200 lb. First seen by white men when Capt. Cook's expedition visited Australia in 1770. Related genera include the tree kangaroos, rat kangaroos, and the Tasmanian Jerboa kangaroo.

Kaolin *or* **Kaolinite**, a fine clay much used in the manufacture of high-class pottery. It results from the decomposition of felspar, and is found in China, Japan, Devon, Cornwall, at Limoges in France, and in parts of the United States.

Karst, geological formations typical of limestone regions in which the drainage is by underground channels. Rain water carries part of the limestone away in solution, leaving the surface dry and barren and pitted with innumerable hollows. The name comes from the Karst (Slav *Kras*) region of N.W. Yugoslavia where the rocks are massive pure limestone; the barren plateau is characterised by fissures, caves and subterranean rivers.

Katydid, large long-horned insects of the grasshopper family, common throughout the United States east of the Rockies. Their name comes from the sound these insects make.

Kauri Pine, a large coniferous tree yielding a fine copal resin which ranges from Malay to New Zealand. The New Zealand Kauri, *Agathis australis*, is found only in N. Island. Some of the best Kauri gum comes from fossilised pines and is dug out of the soil far from any living trees.

Kava, a refreshing drink made from the pounded root of the pepper plant (*Piper methysticum*) and the national drink of Tonga.

Keep, the central tower or chief stronghold of an ancient castle, sometimes called the donjon.

Kelvin, a degree on the thermometer scale that takes absolute zero as 0° K, so that there are no negative readings. The freezing point of water at a pressure of one atmosphere is 273·16° K and the boiling point at the same pressure is 373·16° K. The intervals on the Kelvin scale are the same as those on the Celsius or Centigrade scale.

Kentish Rag, a fossiliferous clayey limestone of Cretaceous age found in Kent. Used in building.

Keratin, a hard protein material of which horns, nails, claws, hoofs, and reptiles' scales are made.

Kestrel, the most common British falcon, well known for its habit of hovering for minutes at a time with vibrating wings and then swooping down to attack mice and insects. The male has spotted chestnut-brown back, greyish head and tail, which has a broad black band near tip.

Ketones. A class of organic compounds, related to aldehydes, of general formula R_2CO (where R is an organic radical). The simpler ketones, especially acetone, are widely used as solvents for lacquers, synthetic rubber, and polymers, such as cellulose acetate and perspex. More complex ketones occur in nature, and some are used in the perfumery industry, muscone (from the musk deer (*q.v.*)) is an example.

Kew Gardens, officially known as the Royal Botanic Gardens, are among the most celebrated gardens in the world. They were started in 1759 by Princess Augusta of Saxe-Gotha, widow of Frederick, Prince of Wales, and mother of George III. They remained private property until 1841, when control passed to the Commissioners of Woods and Forests. They now cover 300 acres and are administered by the Min. of Agriculture, Fisheries, and Food. Since 1841 the gardens have been open to the public, and form one of the most attractive resorts near London.

Key, a musical term indicating the central dominating note that gives the melodic order in which the tones of a tune or composition are arranged. It is the starting-point, and different starting-points demand different scales. The natural key of C, for instance, requires no flats or sharps; all other keys require the use of sharps or flats to bring the notes of their scales into proper relation.

Keys, House of, is the Manx representative assembly. *See* **Tynwald.**

Keystone, the stone which occupies the centre and highest point of an arch and is usually the last to be inserted.

Khaki, a clay-coloured cloth adopted for uniforms in the British Army in the time of the war with the Boers, and used in the first and second world wars. First used by Indian regiments.

Kilderkin, once a common liquid measure in England, representing 18 gallons.

Kilogram, unit of mass, defined as the mass of the international prototype kilogram of platinum-iridium kept at the International Bureau of Weights and Measures at Sèvres. A new determination of the imperial standard pound in terms of the international kilogram was made recently by the National Physical Laboratory (1 international pound = 0·45359237 kilogram). *See also* **N11, 12.**

Kilowatt. *See* **N13(2).**

Kinetic Energy, the energy (*q.v.*) possessed by a particle or body in virtue of its motion. If the motion is destroyed, *e.g.*, by the impact of the body with an obstacle, the kinetic energy vanishes, being turned into some other form of energy such as heat and sound. If the body has mass m and speed v its kinetic energy (leaving out corrections due to relativity) is $\frac{1}{2}mv^2$.

Kinetic Sculpture, a development of equipoised sculpture (*i.e.*, sculpture independent of gravity in the sense of resting on a base either horizontally, vertically, or obliquely) intended to appear as " a weightless poising of volumes, relationships, and interpenetrations." Since in the literal sense this is impossible, the Constructivists (Pevsner, Gabo, and Moholy-Nagy) used glass and invisible wire as supports, giving the impression that their creations were in fact independent of gravity. However, the American, Alexander Calder, has made constructions of balls and wire which he calls " mobiles," and in this form they are now known to everyone as they delicately dangle and rotate suspended from the ceiling.

King Crab, remarkable arthropods now classified separately from both Arachnids and Crustacea which they resemble, inhabiting the sea coasts of America, Japan, India, and Malay Peninsula, carrying a shield-shaped shell, and having a long pointed spine projecting from the posterior. The body comprises three separate sections articulated together. These crabs—in America known commonly as the horseshoe crab because of their shape—are from 18 in. to 2 ft. in length. Fossil king-crabs are found as far back as the Silurian. There are about six living species.

Kingfisher, a well-known family of brilliant-plumaged birds, found in all continents, comprising some 250 species and sub-species. The British kingfisher, *Aceldo atthis*, haunts the rivers and streams, and is one of the most beautiful of native birds, having iridescent blue-green, white, and rich chestnut in its plumage and bright-red feet. All kingfishers have long, dagger-shaped bills. In the Malayan region, New Guinea, the Moluccas, and Australia the varieties are very numerous. The quaint *Laughing Jackass* of Australia is among the largest of the kingfisher family. The European kingfisher is the bird of the Greek legend of the Halcyon.

King-of-Arms, the name of the chief officials of the Heralds' College. There are several in England —the principal being those of the Garter, Norroy and Ulster, Clarenceux. *See* **Heralds' College.**

Kiosk, a word of Russian or Turkish origin meaning a small open pavilion of light construction much used in Eastern countries as a place of shade and rest. Similar structures are common in the streets of Paris as news and advertisement stands, and in London as telephone offices.

Kirimon (*Kiri no go Mon*) and **Kikumon** (*Kiki no go Mon*), the two Japanese imperial crests, the first a design of leaves, stems, and flowers of the Paulownia plant, and the other representing the sixteen-petalled chrysanthemum.

Kite, name of several birds of prey, widely distributed, related to the hawks and eagles, graceful in flight, and distinguished by their long wings and deeply forked tails. The red kite, light chestnut brown, once the most familiar bird of prey in Britain, seen scavenging the streets of London, is now the rarest, and found only in Wales. The Egyptian kite and the pariah kite of India, notorious for their daring thefts, are closely related to the black kite, a smaller European species, with less forked tail and blackish-brown plumage.

Kittiwake, a beautiful white and pearl-grey gull with black legs, dark eyes, and greenish-yellow bill. Its range is wide, and includes the British Isles, where it is a local resident. The flight of this only truly oceanic gull, which excepting in the breeding-season, is generally found off-shore is graceful, swift, and buoyant. A triangular black patch, noticeable on the ends of the wings when open, is characteristic of the species, as is the call kitti-wake, from which the bird derives its name. It nests in colonies on the ledges of caves and steep cliffs.

Kiwi, flightless, stoutly-built birds of New Zealand, now very rare and carefully protected by the Government. They are little larger than a domestic hen, and lay astonishingly large eggs for their size. Incubation and care of chicks fall to the male bird. They have rudimentary wings concealed by the plumage, and the feathers are hair-like. They are nocturnal in habit.

Knighthood is a degree of honour or title common in Europe since the Middle Ages, and was at first exclusively a military order. In Great Britain the four main orders of knighthood are those of the Garter, the Bath, the Thistle, and St. Patrick; in addition to which there are several other orders, such as the Order of St. Michael and St. George, the Star of India, etc. There are also Knights Bachelors, such as are not associated with any special order. The title is not hereditary, and therefore ranks below that of a baronet, though both are entitled to the prefix " Sir."

Knot, a nautical measure of speed (1 sea mile per hour), and formerly measured by a log-line, divided by knots at equal distances $\frac{1}{120}$ of a geographical mile. The number of knots travelled by the ship in half a minute corresponded to the number of sea miles it travelled per hour. A sea mile is equal to about $1\frac{1}{8}$ of a statute mile. Also, a grey and white wading bird, usually a winter visitor to Britain found in flocks on the coast.

Knout, formerly a Russian instrument of punishment, consisting of a whip of many thongs, used upon Russian criminals since the 15th cent. A hundred and twenty strokes were considered equivalent to a sentence of death, half that number sufficing to kill in many instances. Tsar Nicholas I., however, changed the form of the knout, and made it a much milder instrument.

Koala, the Australian arboreal marsupial mamma that looks like a toy teddy-bear, with ashy-gre fur, bushy ears, and rudimentary tail. It feed on the leaves and shoots of certain eucalyptu trees, and is not more than 2 ft. in length.

Kohl, a powder prepared from antimony or burn almond shells, and in common use by th women of the East for darkening the eyelids.

Koto, a musical instrument in general use in Japa consisting of a series of 13 silken strings stretche across a curved wooden surface, and playe with the fingers. Each string is 5 ft. long, an has a separate bridge so fixed as to give th vibration necessary for the note it has to pro duce. It is a sort of horizontal harp, and in th hands of an expert player is capable of givin forth excellent music.

Kremlin, the citadel or walled city within Russian city which during the Middle Ag served as an administrative and religious cent and offered protection. That of Moscow, no the headquarters of the Russian government, contains the cathedral where the Tsars were crowned, an imperial palace, and the bell-tower of Ivan the Great. Its walls which are topped with towers were built in the 15th cent.

Krypton, one of the rare gases, symbol Kr, occurring in the air to the extent of 1 part in 20 million. It was discovered in 1898 by Ramsay and Travers. It is used in gas-filled electric lamps.

Kussier, a Turkish musical instrument consisting of five strings stretched over a sort of kettle-drum.

Kusti, the sacred cord or girdle of the Parsees, consisting of 72 threads—the number of the chapters of the Izashue—and two branches, each branch containing six knots, together standing for the 12 months of the year.

Kutch, the packet of vellum leaves in which gold is placed for the first beating; the gold-beaters' skin packet into which the leaf is placed for the second beating is known as the "shoder."

Kyrie Eleison ("Lord, have mercy"), the name of a common form of prayer in the Anglican, Roman Catholic, and Greek Churches; also applied to the English Church responses after the recital of the commandments.

Kyrle Society, named after Pope's "Man of Ross," John Kyrle, founded by Miss Miranda and Miss Octavia Hill in 1875, and having for its object, the decoration of workmen's clubs, hospitals, etc. and the promotion among the poor of a taste for literature, music, and outdoor recreation.

L

L.S.D., from the Latin libra (a pound), solidus (a shilling), and denarius (a penny), introduced by the Lombard merchants.

Labarum, the standard of Constantine the Great, adopted after his conversion to Christianity, marked with his seal, and represented upon the coinage.

La Belle Sauvage, a site on the north side of Ludgate Hill, famous for the inn that stood there from the 15th cent. to the early 19th. The site was blitzed during the second world war.

Labourers, English Statute of, was passed 1350–51, with the object of compelling labourers to accept a certain rate of wages and not leave their employers' service, the Plague having rendered labourers so scarce that they were in great demand and had been insisting on higher pay. These enactments were bitterly opposed and led to the "Peasants' Revolt," headed by Wat Tyler.

Labradorite, a felspar rich in calcium and of a pearly lustre on cleavage, found in masses in igneous rocks, the best samples of which come from Labrador.

Labyrinth, or Maze, a combination of roads and passages so constructed as to render it difficult for anyone ignorant of the clue to trace the way to the central part. The Egyptian labyrinth near Lake Moeris had 3,000 rooms, half of them subterranean and the remainder above ground. The labyrinth in Crete, according to Greek myth, was built by Dædalus to house the Minotaur. There was one at Lemnos, renowned for its stalactite columns; and another at Clusium constructed by Porsenna, King of Etruria, about 520 B.C. The labyrinth in which Fair Rosamond was concealed was at Woodstock. Hampton Court maze dates from the 16th cent.

Labyrinthodonts, gigantic fossil amphibians which get their name from the curious labyrinthine structure of their teeth, probably an evolutionary link between fishes and reptiles. They occur in the Carboniferous, Permian, and Triassic formations, and remains have been found in Britain and other parts of Europe. Their heads were several feet long, and their footprints, by which they were discovered, closely resemble the prints of the human hand.

Lac, a resinous matter deposited on the branches of a number of tropical trees by the females of the lac insect, the exudation including eggs and a viscous covering. At the gathering time the twigs are broken off and dried in the sun, when the insects die, and the lac that remains is termed *stick-lac*. From this, by the removal of extraneous accretions and dissolving, *seed-lac* is produced. *Shell-lac* is seed-lac after it has been melted and otherwise prepared, and this is the best known of the lacs, being used in printing and the manufacture of varnishes and sealing-wax, and for other commercial purposes.

Lace, a delicate fabric of linen, silk, or cotton threads, made by hand or machinery, and worked in various ornamental designs. The kinds of lace are many, deriving their distinctive names either from the method employed in production or from the place where any special variety was originally made. The best-known makes are pillow or bobbin-lace, woven and plaited by hand; needle-point lace, worked by the needle over a traced design; and machine lace, which practically dates from Heathcote's invention of the early part of the 19th cent. Some of the most famed laces are the following: *Alencon*, a needle-point lace; *Brussels*, a very fine kind, with needle-point sprigs and flowers; *Chantilly*, a silk variety with flowers and open-work; *Cluny*, a netlace with darned stitch; *Honiton*, a delicate kind with dainty sprigs and figures; *Mechlin*, generally made in one piece and very varied in design; and *Valenciennes*, or bobbin lace, of great durability, the pattern and ground of which are made at the same time, being one of the best and most costly of laces, now manufactured mainly in Belgium. Nottingham is famous for its lace.

Lace-Wings, insects with frail, transparent, and much-veined wings whose grubs eat large numbers of insect pests such as aphids. The eggs are borne at the ends of threads attached to plants.

Lachesis, a genus of venomous snakes of the rattle-snake family confined to tropical countries, and including the "deadly bushmaster," of Surinam, and several Crotalidae pit-vipers of Guiana and Brazil.

Lacquer, a varnish made from shellac and certain colouring matters, and utilised for imparting lustre to various surfaces of metal or wood. In China and Japan the production of lacquer ware of a decorative character has long been an important industry, bringing into use gold, coral, vermilion, sprinkled, and other lacquers, with pleasing effect.

Lacrimoso, a musical term denoting a mournful method of playing; sadly, with feeling.

Ladybird, the common name of a large family of beetles—the *Coccinellidae*. The insect is usually of a red or yellow colour with small black or coloured spots. Ladybirds are of good service to the gardener because their larvae feed on aphids. There are about 2,000 species.

Lady-Day, the day of the festival of the Annunciation of the Virgin Mary, Mar. 25. One of the four English quarter days.

Lagoon, a stretch of shallow water opening out upon the sea. Venice is built on lagoons.

Lake Dwelling, the name given to certain pre-historic habitations which were thought to have stood on platforms over lakes, like villages in certain Pacific islands. Recent excavations at the Lake of Burgäschi in Switzerland show that the prehistoric Swiss pile dwellings probably stood on the shores of lakes, not on platforms over the water.

Lakes are bodies of water collected in depressions of the earth's surface. The most notable lakes are the Great Lake series of North America, including Superior, Michigan, Huron, Erie, and Ontario, all discharging into the St. Lawrence River. Africa has an enormous area of lakes, including the Albert Nyanza and the Victoria Nyanza, forming the sources of the White Nile, Lakes Tanganyika, Nyassa, Tchad, etc. Smaller lakes are numerous in other countries—Switzerland, Germany, Italy, England, Ireland, Scotland, all having their lake regions, where the scenery is invariably beautiful and romantic.

Lake School, the name given, at first in ridicule, to a distinguished trio of poets—Wordsworth, Coleridge, and Southey—who made their homes in the English Lake District.

Lamellibranchs (Pelecypods), the class of aquatic, bi-valve molluscs to which the oysters, cockles, mussels, clams, and scallops belong. In these animals the body, which is compressed laterally, is enclosed in two hinged shells held together by muscular action. The gills are thin plates, hence the name "lamellibranch."

Lamellicornia, a sub-order of beetles, distinguishable because the antennae, made up of a number of plates, appear club-shaped. The Lamellicorn beetles are herbivores and number several thousand species, the best-known being the stag-beetles, cockchafers, and scarabs.

Lamination, stratification on a very fine scale, as in shales.

Lammas Day is one of the oldest of the Church festivals, probably derived from the loaf-mass (hlafmæsse) of the Anglo-Saxons. It occurs on August 1. In the olden times it was the day when loaves were given in place of first-fruit offerings.

Lammergeyer, the bearded vulture of alpine regions, resembling an eagle in appearance. It has a white head with black tufts at base of the bill, and its general plumage is dark brown, nearly black. It is found in the remote mountain ranges from Southern Spain to China, and is becoming scarce.

Lampblack, a carboniferous pigment obtained from flame-smoke, and now produced in specially constructed furnaces in which bodies rich in carbon, such as tar, resin, petroleum, etc., are burned. The smoke or soot resulting is collected from the sides of the furnace, and forms lampblack. It finds use in making printer's ink, black paint, etc. Being a very pure form of carbon, it is also utilised in the manufacture of dynamo brushes and arc-lamp carbons.

Lamprey. Eel-like fish having no scales, bones, paired fins, or jaws. They attach themselves by their mouths to fish whose blood they suck. Together with the hagfishes, the lampreys are placed in a special class—the Cyclostomes. There are three British lampreys.

Lancelet. *See* **Amphioxus.**

"Lancet," the name of a noted English medical journal, established in 1823 by Dr. Wakley.

Land Crab, a family of crabs (*Gecarcinidae*) which live mainly on land, though migrating to the sea to deposit their eggs.

Land League, an association formed in 1879, with Parnell as president, for compelling a reduction in the rents of land, and a reconstruction of the land laws in Ireland, and in case of non-compliance refusing to pay rent. For a time this League exercised great political influence and was an important aid to the Home Rule agitation.

Landrail, popularly known as the Corncrake, is a regular summer visitor to Britain, and is well known by its harsh and piercing note, so familiar in cornlands in the night time.

Landslip, a sudden downward sliding under gravity of large masses of rock, soil, etc.; often set off by earthquake shock or saturation of a particular stratum with water. Many serious landslides have occurred from time to time. In 1618, an earthfall happened at Plurs, on Lake Como, involving the destruction of many buildings and the loss of numerous lives. In 1806 a portion of Rossberg mountain in Switzerland slipped from its position, and falling into the valley below buried many villages and hamlets and over 800 people. A chalk cliff from 100 to 150 ft. high and three-quarters of a mile long fell at Lyme Regis, in Dorsetshire, in 1839, doing great damage. Over 200 people were killed by a landslip in Naini Tal, in India, in 1880; and at Quebec, in 1889, a rocky eminence called Cape Diamond gave way, many buildings being destroyed and lives lost. Notable landslips in recent times have occurred at Amalfi (Italy) in 1924, and at Murchiston (New Zealand) in 1929.

Langue d'oc and Langue d'oïl, the two principal mediæval French dialects, *oc* and *oïl* being their respective words for the affirmative particle (modern French *oui*). *Langue d'oc*, spoken south of the Loire, was the language of the troubadours. Provençal, one of its dialects had a literary revival in the 19th cent. under the influence of the poet Frédéric Mistral. *Langue d'oïl* was spoken in northern France, and it was the dialect of the Paris region which developed into modern French.

Lantern Fly, bugs belonging to the family *Fulgoridae* in which the head is drawn out to form a lantern-like structure. In no instance is the "lantern" luminous, though naturalists used to think it was.

"Lantern of England." Bath Abbey possesses so many windows that it is called sometimes the "Lantern of England." Among numerous interesting monuments Bath Abbey contains that of Malthus, author of *Essay on Population.*

Lanthanum, a metal belonging to the rare earth group of metals, discovered by Mosander in 1839.

Lapidary, a cutter of, or dealer in, precious stones; also used in adjective form in regard to the working, engraving, or setting of stones.

Lapis Lazuli, an azure-blue mineral, being a silicate of aluminium and sodium. The pigment ultramarine is made by grinding it, though artificial ultramarine has largely superseded it. The mineral (also called *lazurite*) has been used as a gemstone since ancient times.

Lapwing *or* **Green Plover**, familiar British bird on moors and marshlands with iridescent greenish-black plumage, white underparts, and black crest. Often called "peewit" from its cry.

Larboard is the old nautical term indicating the left-hand side of a ship, and changed by Admiralty order to "port" in 1844. Starboard is the right-hand side.

Larch, a familiar coniferous tree in the mountain regions of northern Europe, and though not native to Britain, the Common Larch is successfully cultivated in various parts of the kingdom. It is one of the best of all turpentine-yielding trees, and the bark is valued for tanning. The larch is an unusual conifer in being deciduous.

Larid, a bird of the *Laridae* or gull family.

Lark, a family of song birds (*Alaudidae*) of many species, some of which—notably the skylark—are famed for their habit of soaring into the air, singing all the while. They build their nests on the ground in the open country and, except for the black lark of Russia, have streaked brown plumage. The skylark and woodlark are the best known British species, while the crested lark and shore lark are among the occasional visitors. Africa has the greatest number of larks; America has only one species, the horned lark.

Larkspur, the common name of the genus *Delphinium*, a favourite flower introduced into British gardens from Switzerland in 1573. The common larkspur is *D. consolida.*

Larva, the undeveloped form of any animal which, before maturity, undergoes metamorphosis, usually different from the adult in structure and habits.

Laser. *See* **Section F, Part IV.**

Latent Heat is the quantity of heat required to convert 1 gram of a substance from one form into another. For example, when a solid changes into a liquid or a liquid into a gas, the addition of heat to bring about the change produces no rise in temperature, the energy being absorbed in the form of latent heat. An equal amount is released when the process is reversed. The latent heat of fusion of ice is about 79·6 calories per gram, that of the vaporisation of water about 539 calories per gram.

Lateran Councils were the religious conventions held in the Lateran basilica at Rome for deciding important questions of Church doctrine. The most brilliant was that of 1215, which pronounced in favour of a Crusade, *See* **Oecumenical Councils.**

Laterite, a residual deposit formed in the tropics by weathering and decomposition of igneous rocks. It consists mainly of hydrated ferric and aluminium oxides and is difficult to cultivate.

Latin America. The Spanish-speaking, Portuguese-speaking, and French-speaking countries of N. America, S. America, Central America, and the W. Indies. *See* **K93.**

Latitude of a point on the earth's surface is its angular distance from the equator, measured on the surface of the earth in degrees, minutes, and seconds. Thus the equator is 0° Lat. and the poles 90° Lat. (N. or S.). First determined by Hipparchus of Nicaea about 160 B.C.

Laughing Gas. *See* **Nitrous oxide.**

Launce *or* **Sand Eel**, a family of eel-like sea fishes found in large numbers on the coasts of North America and Europe. There are two species common to British waters. These fishes are of a bright silvery hue, and live much in the sand underneath the water. They are prized as bait.

Laurentian Shield refers to the Pre-Cambrian rocks in the region of the Upper Lakes of Canada, nearly 2 million sq. m. in extent. Of enormous importance to Canada on account of the mineral wealth, forests yielding valuable timber and wood-pulp, and water-power.

Lava, the molten rock which is erupted from a volcanic vent or fissure. Also the same material which has cooled and solidified.

Lawn, very fine sun-bleached linen, in olden time called "cloth of Rheims."

Lead, a soft malleable metal, symbol Pb (Latin *plumbum*), occurring in numerous ores, which are easily smelted. Its most important source is the mineral galena which consists chiefly of lead sulphide; rarely is it found free. Lead is largely used in plumbing on account of its pliability, and in nuclear reactors as a shield against radiation because of its very high density. As an alloy element it combines in the formation of type metal, stereo metal, shot metal, pewter, and many other compounds. Oxides of lead are used in some types of glass and in the manufacture of paints (red lead). All lead compounds are poisonous. Leading producers of lead are the United States (Missouri), Australia (Broken Hill) and the Soviet Union.

Leaf Insect, a group of insects related to the locusts, grasshoppers and stick insects which in colour and form closely resemble leaves.

Leaf Miners, insect larvae which tunnel between the upper and lower skins of leaves. Most leaf miners are caterpillars of tiny moths; some sawfly larvæ have the same habit.

Leagues, or combinations of kings, countries, communities, have been frequent since the kings of Canaan united against the Israelites. Among the most famous leagues may be mentioned the Holy or Catholic League, which prevented the accession of Henry IV. of France until he became a Roman Catholic; and the League of Augsburg against Louis XIV. of France in 1686.

League of Nations, was founded on Jan. 10, 1920, with the object of promoting international peace and security. The original members were the signatories to the Peace Treaties at Versailles, and membership grew to fifty-three as new nations and ex-enemy States were admitted. Two notable absentees were the United States and Soviet Russia, the latter not being represented until 1934. Germany was a member from 1926 to 1933. The League had an Assembly which met at Geneva every year and a Council which met five or six times a year. The Permanent Court of International Justice sits at The Hague. The final Assembly of the League was held at Geneva between April 8 and 18, 1946. Its place has been taken by the United Nations. The International Labour Organisation, set up by the League of Nations met on April 20, 1944, at Philadelphia and resumed its old quarters at Geneva under the new organisation in 1946.

Leap Year *or* **Bissextile**, was fixed by Julius Cæsar, 45 B.C., the addition of one day in every four years bringing the measure of the calendar year even with the astronomical year, with three minutes per year over. The Gregorian Calendar corrected this by dropping leap year at the centuries not divisible by 400. For instance, 1700, 1800, and 1900 were not leap years.

Leather was made in ancient Egypt, Greece, and Rome, and has through succeeding centuries played an important part in the service of man. It consists of the dressed hides or skins of animals after the process of tanning has been gone through. Untanned skins are known as pelts. Leather is classed either according to the skins from which it is made or the system of preparation employed. The best-known kinds are morocco, kin, Russian, chamois, Cordovan, grained, patent, russet, tan, calf, Hungarian.

Lebensraum, a German slogan for "living space."

Leech, an aquatic blood-sucking worm, mostly found in fresh-water ponds. Each end of the body is provided with a sucker, but that at the head end has jaws and teeth. The medicinal leech has three jaws. The leech attaches itself with avidity to animal bodies and sucks until glutted. Its saliva contains an anti-coagulant.

Leeward, a nautical term, meaning the sheltered side of a vessel—that is, the opposite side to that from which the wind is blowing.

Legion, a body of Roman troops, varying in numbers at different periods. A legion was divided into 10 cohorts, and every cohort into three maniples. Three legions composed the Roman army of occupation in Britain.

Legion of Honour, the French order for distinguished services, military or civil, was instituted by Napoleon I. in 1802, and confirmed and modified under later rules. There are five grades—Grands Croix, Grands Officiers, Commandeurs, Officiers, and Chevaliers.

Legume, the fruit typical of the pea, bean family, or *Leguminosae*.

Leitmotif, a musical theme intended to represent a particular idea and introduced whenever the composer wishes that idea to be held in mind. Wagner made use of the leitmotif to such an extent that his enemies said that each of his characters presented a visiting-card.

Lemming, small light-brown rodents with dark spots, abounding in Scandinavian countries and in Siberia, about 5 in. long, with a short stump of a tail. The migrations of the lemming are famous, probably caused by overbreeding when food is plentiful. So insistent is the urge to keep moving that these animals will march on into the sea in their thousands and be drowned.

Lemur, the most primitive member of the Primate order of mammals (to which man, apes, and monkeys also belong). They are noted for having strong pliant toes enabling them to use their feet as hands, and also well-developed thumbs on the hands. They have long squirrel-like tails, fox-shaped heads, and large staring eyes, and are distributed over the tropical parts of the Old World, being most abundant in Madagascar.

Lend-Lease, an arrangement made by the U.S.A. in March 1941 to provide goods, services, and capital facilities to nations whose fighting contributed to her own defence. The principal beneficiaries were Great Britain and Soviet Russia. There was to be payment or repayment in kind, property, or other benefits to the U.S.A., but when the time of settlement came goods already consumed were written off the account and the recipient countries were asked to make some payment for what remained in existence. By the end of the war practically all the Allies were giving each other Mutual Aid, as it was called, making available their own resources for the use of others in the task of defeating the common enemy. It is estimated that Lend-Lease aid given by the U.S.A. amounted to over £12,000 million and Mutual Aid given by Great Britain to over £2,000 million.

Lenses, pieces of transparent material designed to focus an image of an illuminated object. Usually of glass, but plastic lenses are common, and quartz, etc. are used for special purposes. The surfaces of the simplest lenses are parts of spheres. Lenses which are thickest, or thinnest, at the centre are called convex and concave respectively. Lenses of complex shape are often used in microscopes, etc. Electron lenses are arrangements of electric or magnetic fields which focus beams of electrons, *e.g.*, on to television screens.

Lent, the forty days' period of fasting that precedes Easter.

Leo, one of the twelve signs of the Zodiac, bounded on the west by Cancer, and on the east by the Virgin. The constellation consists of seventy-five stars, of which Regulus (a double star) is the brightest. The Leonids, the best-known of meteor showers, radiate from a point in this constellation.

Lepidodendron, a fossil plant of gigantic height (nearly 100 ft.) bearing a cone-like fruit, frequently met with in the coal strata. *See* **F28**(1).

Lepidoptera, the order of insects with scaly wings and bodies, to which the 90,000 butterflies and moths gelong.

Lepidosiren, a genus of S. American lung-fishes. In times of drought these fish burrow in the mud, and breathe by means of the air bladder which functions as a lung.

Lepus, the constellation of the Hare, situated

under the Orion group, and one of the constellations with which the ancients were familiar.

Lernaea, or *Lernaeocera*, a parasitic crustacean, a "fish louse," with two hosts: first, a flat fish, and later a cod, haddock or whiting.

Lettres de Cachet, sealed letters which the kings of France issued to their agents to secure the imprisonment of distrusted or disliked persons without trial. Abolished in 1789.

Levée, a State reception held by the Sovereign or his representative and attended by men only.

Lever, a rigid bar of metal or wood used for raising heavy bodies, and worked by means of a support called the fulcrum placed underneath the lever.

Lewis, a contrivance for stone-lifting, the principle of which was known to the ancient Romans; it consists of two dovetail tenons of iron or other metal, expanded by an intervening key in a dovetail-shaped mortice in the stone, and shackled by a ringed bolt to the hoisting chain.

Leyden Jar, the earliest form of electrical condenser. Its invention is usually credited to Muschenbroeck of Leyden (1745). It consisted of a jar coated inside and out with tinfoil for about two-thirds of its height and having its inner coating connected with the top by a brass knob and chain. The jar was charged by connecting it to an electrostatic machine.

Lias, a geological term referring to the lower section of the Jurassic group, and mainly comprising shales and limestones.

Liberalism. *See* **J25.**

Libra, the Scales, one of the twelve Signs of the Zodiac, lying east of the Scorpion.

Libraries, before the invention of printing, were few, and collected together at enormous cost. At Nineveh remains of libraries, consisting of tablets of baked clay, have been discovered. There were two libraries at Alexandria containing a vast collection of rolls or volumes, founded by Ptolemy I Soter (367–283 B.C.) and established by Ptolemy II Philadelphus (309–246 B.C.). Among the great libraries of later times may be mentioned the Vatican Library at Rome, moved to its present premises in 1588; the Royal Library in Paris which later became the Bibliothèque Nationale; The Astor Library, New York; and in England, the Bodleian Library, Oxford, and the British Museum Library at Bloomsbury. Since 1850 public libraries have been established in all the chief cities and towns of the kingdom. The first lending library was opened in Edinburgh in 1726. In most villages there is a "county library centre" to which collections of books are sent by the County Library. In Great Britain there are 24,000 centres of this kind in village clubs, halls, shops, schools, and even homes. In some counties there is a library van or the bibliobus, as it has been called by a French writer. This travelling library tours on a pre-arranged time-table so that everyone knows exactly when it will arrive. Four of the best special libraries in the world are open to the public in London. They are:

1. The Library of the Natural History Museum (for zoology, geology, and related subjects).
2. The Library of the Science Museum (all branches of science and technology, except medicine).
3. The Patent Office Library.
4. The Library of the Victoria and Albert Museum, which is the national art library containing volumes and photographs on all aspects of fine, applied, and decorative art.

Full details of the large number of specialist libraries in London (including that of the British Library of Political and Economic Science, one of the best collections in the world on this subject, at the London School of Economics) will be found in *The Student's Guide to the Libraries of London*, by R. A. Rye, published by the University of London Press and *The Libraries of Greater London*, by L. M. Harrod, published by G. Bell. *See also* **British Museum, India Office Library.**

Libration, an astronomical term referring to an apparent irregularity in the moon's course, which may be libration in longitude or latitude, or diurnal, and due to a variety of causes.

Libretto, the word-book of an opera or oratorio. Usually the composer and the librettist collaborate in the writing of an opera, but several composers (*e.g.*, Wagner) wrote their own libretti. Boito, librettist to Verdi for *Otello* and *Falstaff*, himself composed two operas, *Mefistofele* and *Nerone*.

Licence is a permission given to do some act, which, without such permission, it would be unlawful to do. It usually refers to permits issued on payment of excise duty. Licences are required for keeping carriages, dogs, for operating a television or wireless set, for driving a motor vehicle, for shooting game, for setting up as a bookmaker, for hawking and peddling, for selling beer, ale, wines and spirits, tobacco, etc.

Lichens. In every lichen, two plants are associated, one being an alga and the other a fungus. The fungus derives its food from the alga; probably the alga gains too from the association, being protected against desiccation by the fungus (an example of symbiosis). Lichens are the first plants to colonise bare rocks.

Lieder, the plural form of the German word *Lied* meaning song. It is applied particularly to poems set to music by the German romantic composers, Schubert, Schumann, Brahms, and Hugo Wolf.

Life-Boat was invented by three men, Lionel Lukin who converted a coble into a boat for saving life in 1785; William Wouldhave, who discovered how to make a boat right herself if she capsized, and Henry Greathead, who built a life-boat, partly from Wouldhave's model, in 1789. This boat was stationed at South Shields, which was the first permanent life-boat station to be established. It was not until 1851 that the first life-boat able to self-right was built, and a motor was first installed in a life-boat in 1904. Modern motor life-boats have engines of from twin-18 h.p. to twin-80 h.p., with a speed of nearly 10 knots. All coastal life-boats in this country are maintained by the Royal National Lifeboat Institution founded by Sir William Hillary in 1824.

Light, a particular kind of electromagnetic disturbance capable of travelling through space and some kinds of matter, and of affecting ou eyes to cause vision. Its finite speed was firs demonstrated by O. Römer, using observation of the eclipses of Jupiter's satellites in 1675 In 1860 Maxwell showed that light waves ar electromagnetic. Since Einstein's theory c relativity (1905) it has been generally realise that the speed of light is a fundamental natura constant. Visible light with wavelength between about 4 and 6×10^{-5} cm. is only a sma part of the electromagnetic spectrum. Subtl modern methods give the speed as $2{\cdot}997930 \times 10^{10}$ cm. per sec. (about 186,000 miles pe sec.).

Light Year. A measure of astronomical distanc equal to the distance light travels in the cours of a year. A light year is thus 5·88 millio million miles. *See also* **F3(2).**

Lighthouses, to warn ships of dangerous places an indicate coasts, points, harbours, etc., hav existed since the building of the Pharos, tower of white marble 600 ft. high, built b Ptolemy II Philadelphus at Alexandria abou 280 B.C. In early lighthouses the lights we simple fires. The most famous and one of th earliest British lighthouses is the Eddysto (which see). The introduction of parabol mirrors was a great improvement, providing reflecting medium which intensified the lig beam in the required direction. Further in provements were made by Fresnel, Stevenso and others. A new Dungeness lighthouse planned which will be revolutionary in desig and the first in Britain to be fully automat in operation. It will be powered by a small b extremely powerful lamp, and electronic equi ment will control all the operations fro switching on the main beam at nightfall to d tecting presence of fog and sounding fog signa The lighthouses of England and Wales, th Channel Islands, and Gibraltar are under t control of Trinity House; Commissioners Northern Lighthouses control those of Scotlan and the Commissioners of Irish Lights cont the coasts of Ireland. Particulars of lights in parts of the world are published for the guidan of navigation in the *Admiralty Lists of Lights*, compiled annually by the British Admiralty.

Lightning, the flash of a discharge of electricity between two clouds, or between a cloud and the earth, when the strength of the electric fields becomes so great as to break down the resistance of the intervening air. With "forked" lightning the actual path, often branched, is visible, while with "sheet" lightning the flash is hidden by the clouds which themselves are illuminated. "Ball" lightning or fireballs is the name given to the luminous balls which have been seen floating in the air during a thunderstorm. The Boys camera has provided much information regarding the sequence of events in a lightning discharge. It is found that a flash consists of a number of separate strokes, usually four or five, and that the discharge of electricity to earth begins with a faintly luminous "leader" moving downwards and branching at intervals. As the ground is approached a much brighter luminosity travels back along the conducting channels, lighting up the several branches. The multiple strokes which follow in fractions of a second have the same "return" nature and are rarely branched. Lightning flashes to earth damage structures, cause loss of life and endanger overhead power systems, often interrupting electricity supply. Such storms generally affect radio transmissions and present hazards to aircraft. Thunder-clouds may develop energy far exceeding the capacity of our largest power generating stations.

Lightning Conductor, a metal rod, the upper part of which is of copper with a conical point, the lower portion being iron, which extends into the earth. Its effect is to gather to itself the surrounding electricity and discharge it into the earth, thus preventing its falling upon the protected building. In ships, lightning conductors are fixed to the masts and carried down through the ship's keel-sheathing. Benjamin Franklin was the first to realise the possibilities of lightning protection and, in 1752, carried out his famous experiment of drawing electricity from thunder-clouds, with the aid of a sharp-pointed conductor fixed to a kite.

Lignin, a substance found in the cell walls of plants, making them strong and rigid. It forms 25–30 per cent of the wood in trees.

Lignite *or* **Brown Coal**, an intermediate substance between peat and coal; it is known as brown coal. The best-known deposits in Britain are the Bovey Tracey Beds in Devon.

Lillibulero, an old marching song composed by Purcell. With words by Wharton, it is said to have "sung James II. out of three kingdoms." During the second world war it was used by the B.B.C. as a station identification signal preceding news bulletins.

Lily Family (Liliaceae), one of the largest families of flowering plants, with 200 genera and 2,500 species. It includes the true lilies (*Lilium*), tulips and hyacinths. Useful vegetables belonging to the family are the onion and asparagus. Most members are herbaceous plants; shrubs or small trees occur in the genera *Aloe* (Yucca) and *Dracaena* (Dragon-tree).

Lime, an alkaline earth obtained from kiln-heated limestone, and used in making mortars and cements; valuable in agriculture in treatment of acid and clay soils.

Limes, trees of the genus *Tilia*, including some 30 species spread over north temperate regions. The word is a corruption of "linden." Limes native to Britain are the small-leaved *T. cordata* and the broad-leaved *T. platyphyllos*. The hybrid *T. vulgaris* was introduced into Britain from the Continent during the 17th cent. and is frequently seen in streets and parks. Lime-wood was used by Grinling Gibbons for his fruit, flower, and bird decorations.

Limestone is carbonate of calcium. It is found in every geological formation, and is often highly fossiliferous. Marble is limestone that will polish after cutting.

Limpet, a marine mollusc with a single-valved shell, generally found sticking close to sea-washed rocks.

Linen, a textile fabric manufactured from flax fibre, known to the ancient Egyptians, and first manufactured in England under Henry III. by Flemish weavers. The chief seat of the manufacture is Ulster, with Belfast as the centre. Dunfermline (famous for its damasks) and Manchester are also large linen-producing towns.

Ling, a sea-fish common on the coasts of Britain, and abounding in more northern waters. It averages from 3 to 4 ft. in length, and is a voracious feeder, living chiefly on small fish. Ling is also the name applied to *Calluna vulgaris*, the plant which most people called "heather."

Linseed, the seed of the flax plant, containing, apart from its fibrous substance, certain oily and nitrogenous matter of considerable commercial value. This yields linseed oil, and some of the residue is used to make cattle food.

Lion, the most impressive of the Cat tribe (Felidae) of the order Carnivora. It is chiefly found in Africa, being comparatively rare in Asia. Its large square head, its flowing mane (in the males only), and its tufted tail distinguish it. From tip to tip it can reach a length of 10 ft.; a weight of 500 lb.

Lion and Unicorn, the supporting figures of the royal arms of Great Britain, date from the union of Scotland with England at the accession of James I. (James VI. of Scotland), the lion representing England and the unicorn Scotland.

Liqueurs are essences combined with alcoholic liquid, and are of many kinds, named according to their flavourings or place of production, and include Maraschino, Chartreuse, Curacoa, Benedictine, Noyau, Kümmel, etc.

Liquid, the name given to matter in such state that it takes its shape from the containing vessel. The volume it occupies is independent of the container, however. *See* **F17(1)**.

Litanies were first used in church processions in the 5th cent. The first English litany was commanded to be recited in the Reformed churches by Henry VIII. in 1544.

Lithium, a soft metallic element, symbol Li, similar to sodium. It is very reactive and is stored under paraffin oil. It is the lightest metal element.

Lithography, the art of drawing on stone and printing therefrom, was discovered by Alois Senefelder about 1796, and was introduced into England a few years later. Many improvements in the art have been made in recent years, especially in chromo-lithography and photo-lithography.

Litmus, a special kind of colouring matter produced from certain lichens. The resulting colour is violet; is turned red by acids and blue by alkalis.

Litre, a metric measure, abolished 1964 as a scientific unit of volume.

Liturgy, the name given to the Church ritual, though strictly applying only to the portion used in the celebration of the Eucharist or Lord's Supper. The Anglican liturgy is laid down in the Book of Common Prayer (1662). Parliament gave its consent in 1965 for changes in the form of worship.

Liverworts (Hepatics), a class of simple green plants related to the mosses. There is no differentiation into stem and leaves. Liverworts are most common in damp situations, such as the banks of ditches. *See* **F27(2)**.

Lizard, the name given to a diversified order of reptiles, of which there are about 1,600 species. Included among the lizards are the geckos, chameleons, glass snakes, skinks, and blind worms.

Llama, mammals related to the camels, from which they differ in small size, absence of humps, and more woolly coat. The domestic llama of S. America is used as a beast of burden, also providing wool, meat, and milk. *See also* **Alpaca, Guanaco.**

Loadstone *or* **Lodestone**, an oxide of iron, found chiefly in Sweden and Norway. Its scientific name is magnetite. It has the power of attracting pieces of iron and served as the first magnets used in compasses. One of the class of non-metallic magnetic materials nowadays known as "ferrites."

Lobby Correspondents are political correspondents of newspapers who do not report the actual proceedings of Parliament—this is done by Parliamentary Correspondents—but interpret political news and events.

Lobsters are marine crustacean animals existing in large numbers in the northern seas of Europe and America, and in fair proportion on some parts of the British coasts, especially in the neighbourhood of the Channel Islands.

Locarno, Treaty of, 1925, whereby Germany, France, and Belgium undertook to maintain their present frontiers and to abstain from the use of force against each other. Hitler broke the pact by re-occupying the Rhineland, the demilitarisation of which had been recognised by Germany.

Locust, insects of the grasshopper family, but much more powerful. They are inhabitants of hot countries, and often make their appearance in untold millions, like clouds, devastating all the vegetation that comes within their course. The locust-tree (*Ceratonia siliqua*) is supposed to have furnished food to St. John the Baptist in the wilderness, and its "beans" have accordingly been styled "St. John's Bread."

Loess, a deposit of silt or marl laid down by wind action. The biggest loess deposits are in Asia, the source of the dust of which they are composed probably being the deserts of Central Asia.

Log, a line used for reckoning the speed at which a ship is travelling. It was first used in the 16th cent. The line is divided into spaces of 50 ft. marked off by knots and measured by a half-minute sand glass, bearing the same proportion to an hour as 50 ft. bear to a mile.

Logarithms, a system of calculation invented by John Napier in 1614, and developed by Henry Briggs a few years later. Thus if a number is expressed as the power of another number, *i.e.*, if $a = b^n$, then n is said to be the logarithm of a to base b, written $\log_b a$. Common logs are to base 10 and Napierian to base 2·7182818 . . ., expressed as e. Their use represents a great saving of time.

Logical Positivism. *See* **J25.**

Lollards. *See* **J25.**

Lombards, a German people, originating on the Elbe, who settled in Italy in the 6th cent., occupying northern and central regions, and establishing a kingdom with Pavia as capital. They were conquered by Charlemagne in 774, but left their name to the region of Lombardy. Lombard Street, London, takes its name from the Lombard merchants and bankers who came to settle there in the 12th cent.

London Clay, geological stratum which occupies much of the London Basin and part of the Hampshire Basin. It represents the lower stratum of the Eocene. Outside the metropolis, brickfields utilise the clay for brickmaking. Water held above this impervious stratum is tapped by a number of artesian wells in London. The tunnels of the Capital's underground railways run through the London Clay.

London University comprises nearly one-third of the academic activity of the United Kingdom, and is recognised as one of the great universities of the world. Originated in the foundation of a non-sectarian college in Gower Street in 1828. Among the chief colleges are: University, Kings, Imperial College of Science and Technology, London School of Economics, School of Oriental and African Studies, Queen Mary, Birkbeck, Royal Holloway, Bedford, Westfield, and Queen Elizabeth College. London University was the first to throw open all degrees to women (1878).

Long Distance Routes. The National Parks and Access to the Countryside Act 1949 provided for the establishment in England and Wales of Long Distance Footpaths and Bridleways. The following have been approved but only the Pennine Way has been completed: Pennine Way (a magnificent hill walk of 250 miles from Edale in Derbyshire along the Pennines over the Cheviots to the Scottish border); Pembrokeshire Coast Path; Offa's Dyke Path (168 miles along the marches of Wales); South Downs Way (Beachy Head to Salisbury); South-West Peninsula Coast Path (North Cornwall, South Cornwall, South Devon, Somerset and North Devon, Dorset); Yorkshire Coast and North York Moors. *See also* **National Parks.**

Longitude of a point on the earth's surface is the angle which the meridian through the poles and that point makes with some standard meridian. The meridian through Greenwich is usually accepted as the standard meridian and the longitude is measured east or west of that line. As the earth revolves through 360° in 24 hrs., 15° longitude represent 1 hour's difference in apparent time.

Long Parliament (1640–60), marked the end of Charles I's 11-year attempt to govern without parliament. It carried through what has come to be called "the English Revolution" and was the parliament of the civil war (1642–49).

Lord, a title of honour held by such as are peers of the realm, and bestowed on persons who have achieved distinction or inherited by descent. It is also borne by Bishops, on spiritual and ecclesiastical grounds, and is accorded as a courtesy to the eldest sons of dukes, marquises, and earls, to the younger sons of dukes and marquises, and to Judges of the High Court in England and Scotland.

Lord Lieutenant is the Queen's representative in the county, and his office is now largely ceremonial. On his recommendation the magistrates or Justices of the Peace are appointed by the Lord Chancellor. The office was created by Henry VIII. in 1549 to take over the military duties of the sheriff.

Lords, House of, the Upper House of the British Parliament composed of Lords Spiritual and Lords Temporal. The former consist of the two Archbishops and twenty-four English Bishops and the latter of Peers and Peeresses. The full membership is about 900. The right of the Lords to veto Bills passed by the Commons is restricted by the Parliament Acts of 1911 and 1949. The Lord High Chancellor presides over the House of Lords. *See* **Section C, Part II.**

Louse, parasitic insect found on the skin of birds and mammals. The bird or biting lice make up one order (*Mallophaga*); the true or sucking lice belong to another order, called *Anoplura*. Two species of lice parasitise man, and one of these, the body louse, is a carrier of typhus.

Louvre, one of the old royal palaces of Paris, was built in its present form partly by Francis I., and added to by later monarchs, Louis XIV. completing the edifice. Napoleon I. turned it into a museum and enriched it with the plunder of many foreign art galleries. The great extension to the Louvre building begun by Napoleon I. was completed under Napoleon III. in 1857. Much injury was done to the building during the Commune of 1871. Amongst other famous treasures it houses the Venus de Milo and Leonardo da Vinci's masterpiece, *La Gioconda*.

Lovebird, a vivid little bird native to Africa, resembling a parrakeet but with a short, wide tail and short body.

Luddites, a combination of workmen formed in 1811, in a period of great distress, with the object of destroying the new textile machinery then being largely adopted, which they regarded as the cause of their troubles. Their first outbreak was at Nottingham, and was stated to have been started by a young apprentice named Ned Ludd. Afterwards, serious Luddite riots occurred in various parts of the country, especially in the West Riding of Yorkshire, where many people were killed, mills were destroyed, and numbers of rioters were tried and executed. Charlotte Brontë used the period in her novel, *Shirley*.

Lunar Month. *See* **Month.**

Lung Fishes *or* **Dipnoi.** *See* **Dipnoi.**

Luniks, the name of the Soviet moon rockets. *Lunik I*, launched 2 Jan. 1959, with payload of 800 lb. and max. velocity of 25,500 m.p.h., entered a solar orbit between Earth and Mars to become the first man-made planet. *Lunik II*, launched 2 Sept., 1959, landed on the moon. *Lunik III*, launched 6 Oct. 1959, circumnavigated the moon and took a photograph of its hidden side which it televised back to Earth. Since then the Russians have used the name *Luna* for their moon probes. *Luna 9* made a soft landing on 3 Feb. 1965; *Luna 10* on 3 April 1966 became the first lunar orbiter.

Lute, a stringed instrument of the guitar type of unknown antiquity. Its name is Arabian. Lute music was very popular in England in the 17th cent. There has been a revival in this cent.

Lutecium, element of the rare-earth metal group discovered in 1907 by Urbain.

Lutheranism. *See* **J25.**

Lynx, cats of sturdy build, with tufted ears and spotted fur, inhabiting many parts of the world, including Northern and Central Europe. They commit serious ravages among sheep and goats and are very fierce.

Lyon King of Arms, the President of the Scottish Lyon Court, and head of the heraldic organisation for Scotland.

Lyre, an upright stringed instrument rather like a miniature harp. It was the universal musical instrument of classical Greece and Rome.

Lyre-Bird, a remarkable family of Australian birds, the males of which possess a beautiful lyre-shaped tail. The bird is not more than 15 in. long, but its tail, displayed during its remarkable courtship dance, is 23 in. in length. There are two species: the Superb and Albert's Lyrebird.

M

Macaque. A family of monkeys which include the Barbary ape (specimens of which live on Gibraltar), the Rhesus macaque (the organ grinder's monkey and the one used for experimental work in the investigation of disease), the Bonnet monkey of southern India and Ceylon, the Crab-eating, and the Pig-tailed monkeys of south-eastern Asia.

Macaw, a genus of large parrots with brilliant scarlet and sky-blue plumage, with interminglings of green. Native to South and Central America.

Mace, originally a weapon of offence, now an ensign of authority borne before officers of state and other dignitaries. In the House of Commons the mace is handed to an official of the Crown by the Sergeant-at-Arms at the close of a parliamentary session.

Mach Number. Unit of flight speed. The ratio of speed of flight to speed of sound under same conditions of pressure and density. Speed of sound at sea-level is 762 m.p.h., so flight speed of 381 m.p.h. is equivalent to a Mach Number of ½. At supersonic speeds the Mach Number is greater than 1; subsonic speeds, less than 1.

Mackerel, a familiar sea-fish existing in large numbers in the northern waters of both hemispheres. In May and June immense shoals are to be found round the British coasts.

Madder, one of the most important of dye-stuffs, largely used in producing Turkey-red dye, but now superseded by synthetic alizarin. Natural madder is the root of the *Rubia tinctorum*.

Madrier, a term in military engineering denoting a beam used to support the earth in a mine or fortification, or to receive the mouth of a petard.

Madrigal, a style of unaccompanied composition for three or more voices. Developed in the Netherlands, it reached perfection in 13th-cent. Italy. Brought to England during the Renaissance it achieved great popularity and many English composers became famous for their madrigals.

Maelstrom, a great whirlpool. The most famous is that off the coast of Norway, between the islands of Moskenēs and Mosken, of the Lofoten group, the power of which has been much exaggerated.

Mafia, a secret Sicilian society formed for purposes of vengeance, private and public, prominent about 1860, and again after the second world war. Signor Dolci (*see* **B26**) is working to end Mafia exploitation, intimidation, and violence in Sicily. It was not until 1962 that the Italian Parliament finally admitted that the Mafia existed and decided to set up a commission to study it and the means of eradicating it.

Magellan, Clouds of, the name given to a pair of small galaxies, satellite systems of our own galaxy, visible only from the southern hemisphere. On account of their relative nearness to the earth (186,000 light-years), they are receiving much attention from astronomers.

Magenta, a blue-red aniline dye discovered in 1859 by Sir W. H. Perkin, and named after the great battle of that year between the French and Austrians.

Magic. *See* **J26.**

Magistrates *or* **Justices of the Peace** preside over courts of petty sessions, and are appointed by the Lord Chancellor on the recommendation of the Lord Lieutenant of the County. Most J.P.s are laymen and are unpaid. Mayors during their time of office are J.P.s *ex officio*. In certain big towns a legally-qualified, paid, full-time magistrate is appointed, known as a stipendiary magistrate. In London stipendiaries are known as Metropolitan Stipendiary Magistrates. **D37.**

Magma, molten rock material rich in volatile constituents prior to its eruption at the surface. On eruption and loss of volatiles it becomes lava.

Magna Carta was sealed by King John at Runnymede on June 15, 1215, in obedience to the insistent demands of the barons, and has been confirmed many times by later monarchs. It was not a revolutionary document. It laid down what the barons took to be the recognised and fundamental principles for the government of the realm and bound king and barons alike to maintain them. Its main provisions were that no man should be punished without fair trial, that ancient liberties generally should be preserved, and that no demands should be made by an overlord to his vassal (other than those recognised) without the sanction of the great council of the realm.

Magnesium, a metallic element, symbol Mg, first isolated in 1808 by Sir Humphry Davy, who prepared it by electrolysing the chloride. Its chief ores are magnesite and dolomite. Industrially it is obtained by electrolysis. Many important light alloys contain magnesium. The metal burns with a very bright light, and for this reason it is used in photographers' flash bulbs and also in firework manufacture.

Magnetic Poles are at a considerable distance, of the order of 1,000 miles, from the geographical poles, and are not antipodal to one another. The poles do not remain fixed, and the North pole wanders more than the South. The position of the North magnetic pole is in the region of lat. 74° N.; long. 100° W., considerably north of Amundsen's observations of 1904. The South magnetic pole is not far from lat. 70° S.; long. 150° E.

Magnetic Storms, large irregular disturbances superimposed upon the normal magnetic field of the earth. They may occur at any time, but are most frequent during equinoctial months and in years of sunspot maxima. World-wide in extent, magnetic storms are most pronounced in the polar regions, being due apparently to intense electric currents located in the upper atmosphere near to the zones of greatest auroral frequency. One theory attributes the high ionisation of these belts to solar radiation. Magnetic storms cause radio fade-outs and interfere with telegraphic communication.

Magnetism, originally the name given to the quality of attraction for iron possessed by lodestone (*q.v.*). Now known to be a phenomenon inseparably connected with electricity (**F18**). Strong magnetic attraction is possessed by a comparatively small class of substances; iron, nickel, and cobalt are the most common elements, but there are several less well known, *e.g.*, gadolinium. Many alloys have valuable magnetic properties which make possible numberless technical devices. New magnetic substances are always being developed (*see* **Ferrite**). The earth acts like a huge magnet with its axis inclined at about 10° to the axis of rotation, the magnetic poles being on the Boothia Peninsula (North Canada) and South Victoria Land (Antarctica). The magnetic field at the surface consists of the regular field of a magnetised sphere with an irregular field superimposed upon it. Variation in the magnetic forces occurs from place to place and from time to time, and maps showing the distribution over the globe of points of the same declination (*i.e.*, the angle which the magnetic meridian makes with the geographical one) are of the utmost importance in navigation. In the south-east of the British Isles, at present, a magnetic needle points 9° and in the north-west 14° west of true north. Little is known regarding the origin of the main (regular) field of the earth, but it is believed that the irregularities are due to the presence of intense electric currents in the upper atmospheres and local magnetisation of rock strata.

Magnetohydro-dynamics. A current-carrying wire always experiences a force if it is in a magnetic field. This is the well-known electrodynamic force, and electric motors work because of it. If the current is carried in a fluid, *e.g.*, a liquid metal or a plasma, these forces cause bodily movements of the fluid, which are in general very difficult to calculate. The forces are then called *magnetohydro-dynamic forces*. Now magnetic fields are themselves produced by electric currents; so a current flowing in a fluid produces a magnetic field, which then reacts on the fluid itself by means of the magnetohydrodynamic forces. In the Harwell machine Zeta, used in studying the technical problems of thermonuclear reactions, this effect acts so as to constrict the electric discharge on to the axis of the tube and thus keeps it away from the walls. This action is assisted by an extra magnetic field produced by a separate current flowing in metallic conductors outside the tube. Thus the hot plasma is contained by magneto-hydro-dynamic forces and not at all by the material tube wall. In practical devices of the future magnetic forces may have to sustain plasma pressures of 60 atmospheres—a pressure for which a thick steel wall would normally be used! *See also* **Plasma Physics.**

Magnificat, the hymn of the Virgin Mary, given in Luke 1, 46 beginning in the Vulgate with the words "Magnificat anima mea Dominum" ("My soul doth magnify the Lord"), and used in the services of all Christian Churches.

Magnitude in astronomy is a measure of the apparent brightness of a star, which is inversely proportional to the square of its distance. A low number indicates a bright star, and a high one a faint star. The *absolute magnitude* is a measure of *real* brightness, *i.e.*, the brightness a star would have at a standard distance away of 32·6 light years. The distance can be calculated if the apparent and absolute magnitudes are known.

Magnolia, species of the family *Magnoliaceae* comprising many beautiful trees, and shrubs with large and fragrant flowers, and chiefly native to North America and Asia. Introduced in 1688.

Magpie, a well-known bird of the crow family, of glossy black and white plumage, famed for its mischievous propensities.

Magyars, the Hungarian race who came to eastern Europe from S.W. Asia and settled in Hungary in the 10th cent. Their language belongs to the Finno-Ugrian group.

Mahdi, an Arab leader of great influence, invested with powers akin to those of a Messiah in the Mohammedan mind. The title was taken by Mohammed Ahmed, who overran the Egyptian Sudan, and in 1885 captured Khartoum.

Mahogany, a fine hard wood susceptible of a very high polish, and distinguished for the beauty of its colour and markings. Obtained chiefly from the trees of the genera *Swietenia* (Spanish or Cuban mahogany) and *Khaya* (African mahogany) of the family Meliacaea. According to tradition Raleigh had a mahogany table made for Queen Elizabeth.

Maidenhair Tree *or* **Ginkgo.** This tree takes its name from the shape of its leaves, which resemble those of the maidenhair fern. Widely cultivated in China and Japan. It is the only survivor of an order of gymnosperms which flourished in Mesozoic times. Botanically interesting because the male gametes are motile. *See also* **F28**(1).

Major Scale. *See* **Diatonic Scale.**

Malacostraca, the sub-class of the Crustacea to which the lobsters, crayfish, shrimps, belong.

Malmaison, château at Rueil-Malmaison, a western suburb of Paris. It derives it name from having been inhabited in the 11th cent. by the Norman brigand Odon, and afterwards, according to the tradition, by evil spirits, exorcised by the monks of St. Denis. It was the residence of Napoleon and of the Empress Josephine after her divorce. She died there in 1814 as the result of a chill caught while showing the Russian Emperor round the grounds. In 1900 it was given to the nation.

Malmsey, a strong, sweet wine originally made in Greece, but now also in Spain, Madeira, and the Azores; known also as Malvoisie.

Maltose, a sugar formed in cereal grains during germination. It is produced by hydrolysis of starch, and further hydrolysis converts the maltose into glucose.

Mamluks, commonly known as Mameluks, were originally—in the 13th cent.—a bodyguard of Turkish and Circassian slaves in the service of the Sultan of Egypt, and attained such influence that in 1250 they were strong enough to appoint one of their own body to the throne of Egypt. After that a succession of Mamluk Sultans reigned down to 1517. Then the Turks annexed Egypt, and the Mamluks were taken into the service of the Beys. They again came to the front after Napoleon's conquest of Egypt, and for a time resumed governmental sway; but in 1811 they were decoyed into the citadel of Cairo and massacred by order of Mehemet Ali.

Mammalia. *See* **F23**(2).

Mammoth, extinct elephants of gigantic size. In 1799 the first perfectly preserved specimen was found in Siberia in a block of ice. It was in prehistoric times an inhabitant of Britain and other parts of Europe, as well as of Asia and America.

Mammoth Cave of Kentucky, about 10 miles long, is one of a series of spacious caverns formed in the limestone rock formation, and is from 40 to 300 ft. wide and at one point 300 ft. high. Stalactites and stalagmites abound.

Manatee, an aquatic mammal of the sea cow (Sirenia) order of mammals, averaging when full grown from 10 to 12 ft. in length, with shovel-shaped tail, and four limbs and nails which almost give the appearance of arms and hands. In spite of their ungainly aspect, these creatures are believed to have given rise to the legend of mermaids.

Manchus, the original nomadic race inhabiting northern Manchuria who invaded China early in the 17th cent. A Manchu dynasty occupied the imperial throne of China from 1644 to 1911.

Mandarin, the name given to a powerful Chinese official, civil or military under the old régime, whose rank was shown by the wearing of a button on the cap. In Chinese the name is Kwan.

Mandible, the lower jaw in human anatomy. The two parts of a bird's beak are known as the upper and lower mandible. The term is also used for biting jaws in arthropods.

Mandoline, an Italian fretted guitar, so called from its almond conformation.

Manganese, a metallic element, symbol Mn, discovered by Scheele in 1774. It is silver-white, not very hard (it forms a hard alloy with carbon), brittle, and tarnishes when exposed to air. Its chief ore is pyrolusite (manganese dioxide). Steels containing manganese are very tough, and used for making machine parts.

Manikin, a dwarf or pigmy; an artificial figure employed in anatomical demonstrations, made sometimes of papier-mâché.

Maniple, eucharistic vestment worn over left arm.

Manna, a tree of the ash genus, *Fraxinus ornus*, growing in the South of Europe and in the East and exuding a sweet substance which is gathered, boiled, and eaten.

Manometer, instrument used to measure gas pressure. Usually a U-tube containing water or mercury, one end open to the atmosphere, the other to the gas whose pressure is to be measured. More sensitive for small pressures than the Bourdon gauge.

Manors were estates originally granted in Anglo-Saxon times as rewards for knightly service, and included the privilege of a special court with jurisdiction, criminal and civil, within the manorial territory. *See* **Court-Leet.**

Mansion House, the official residence of the Lord Mayor of London, stands opposite to the Bank of England, and was erected in 1739–53 from the designs of George Dance.

Mantis. Large insects belonging to the same order as the locusts and grasshoppers. The manner in which the forelegs are held, as though in suppliance, has gained for these insects the common name of "praying mantis." They are distributed throughout the warmer countries of the world.

Manuals, the keyboards of an organ which are operated by the hands as apart from the pedals which are worked by the feet. In a large organ there may be four manuals, each controlling a group of stops. These groups are called great organ, swell organ, choir organ, solo organ.

Manx, the original Celtic inhabitants of the Isle of Man, where a Celtic dialect still lingers.

Maoris, the race found in New Zealand at the time of its discovery by Europeans. The Maoris are believed to have migrated from Polynesia about 1350. They number 165,000 (1961), and being very intelligent people have adapted themselves with considerable success to the conditions of civilised life. Until 1870 they were frequently in arms against the Government, but since then have settled down with the Whites as equal citizens.

Maple, trees native to the northern hemisphere. There are over 100 species. The sycamore is the best-known species growing in Britain. The sugar maple abounds in Canada and the eastern parts of the United States. The sugar is tapped by boring holes in the tree in Feb. and Mar., and the juice that escapes is collected and evaporated. The maple-leaf is the Canadian national emblem.

Maquis, name of the dense scrub in Mediterranean France and Corsica, providing good cover for bandits and outlaws. The French resistance movement adopted the name Maquis during the German Occupation, 1940–45.

Marabouts, Mohammedan hermits or monks, especially amongst the Moors and Berbers of N.W. Africa. They live in monasteries or attached to mosques and are held in great veneration by the Berbers.

Marble is limestone in its hardest and most crystalline form. There are many varieties—33 were used in the building of the Paris Opera House—but white is the purest and rarest. White marble was used by the ancient Greeks for their temples and statues. Among the famous marbles of Italy are the Carrara and Siena marbles, which were used by Renaissance sculptors. Devonshire and Derbyshire yield some beautiful marbles and Connemara furnishes a serpentine-marble.

March, the third month of the year, and the first of the old Roman Calendar. It was named after the god Mars, and was the *Hlyd* (storm) *monath* of the Anglo-Saxons.

Mardi Gras, the last day of the Carnival in France, Shrove Tuesday.

Marionettes are puppets moved by strings. They originated in the *Fantoccini* of the 15th cent. which had such a vogue in Italy and elsewhere on the Continent. The English *Punch and Judy* is a version of Punchinello. Puppet shows were known in the earliest civilisations.

Marl, a rock composed partly of clay and partly of carbonate of lime.

Marlinspike, a pointed iron tool used by sailors to splice wire. The instrument used when rope splicing is called a fid.

Marmoset, small monkeys confined to the New World. Very squirrel-like in appearance, with long bushy tails, and thick woolly fur, they are pretty little animals and the smallest of all monkeys. There are claws, not nails, on their digits, the big toe excepted.

Marprelate Tracts, seditious pamphlets written with great maliciousness by a group of Elizabethan puritans about 1586, and intended to discredit the episcopacy, caused a great sensation in their time, and led to the execution of their supposed author, John Penry.

Marquess *or* **Marquis**, the title next in precedence to that of duke. The first English marquess was Rovery de Vere, Earl of Oxford, who had the honour conferred upon him by Richard II. in 1385.

Marquetry, a kind of inlaying in which thin layers of coloured woods are wrought into a design, and mainly used in ornamental floors.

Mars, the fourth nearest planet to the sun, being 141,500,000 miles distant. Its diameter is 4,215 miles as against the earth's 7,920. There has been much speculation about certain dark lines which some observers have seen on the surface of Mars: photographs give no support to the theory of an artificially constructed network of canals, but it is possible they represent areas covered by some simple form of vegetation of the lichenous type. The temperature of the planet's surface would allow living organisms as we know them to exist, but the quantity of oxygen in the atmosphere would be almost certainly too little to support animal life. American (*Mariner IV*) and Russian (*Zond II*) spacecraft launched in 1964 reached the planet in the summer of 1965. *Mariner IV* took close-up pictures of 1 per cent of the Martian surface. Like the moon it is pitted with craters. Mars has two small moons—Phobos and Deimos.

Marseillaise, the French national hymn, written and composed by Rouget de L'Isle, a French engineer officer, who was inspired to write it in 1792 to encourage the Strasburg conscripts. It immediately became popular, and received its name from the fact that it was sung by the Marseillaise troops while marching into Paris.

Marshalsea Prison, a once well-known house of detention in Southwark. It stood near St. George's Church, and was originally a prison for royal servants convicted of offences, but from 1842 to 1849 was a debtors' prison. It was abolished in 1849. Dickens described it in *Little Dorrit*.

Marsh Gas. *See* **Methane.**

Marsh Tortoise, an amphibious animal of the order *Chelonia*, spread over many countries and inhabiting ponds and small rivers. There are 42 species, and they are all carnivorous.

Marston Moor, near York, was the scene of the famous battle between Prince Rupert and Cromwell on July 2, 1644. Cromwell's victory was the turning-point in the Civil War.

Marsupials, members of the order of pouched animals. Except for the oppossums of America, all marsupials occur in Australasia. Well-known marsupials are the kangaroos, wallabies, and wombats. *See* **F23**(2).

Martello Towers, circular forts erected on the coasts of England early in the 19th cent. as defences against the threatened Napoleonic invasion. So called from the circular fort at Mortella (Corsica), which resisted an English fleet in 1794.

Marten, carnivorous animals of the weasel family, one species of which was once common in Britain, but now seldom met with. Many valuable furs come from martens, *e.g.*, the sable of N. Asia and the marten of N. America.

Martial Law is a term loosely employed to indicate the suspension of the administration of normal civil law and its replacement by military authority when this is rendered desirable by such circumstances as war or rebellion.

Martin, a well-known bird-visitor to Britain. It belongs to the swallow family, and the two species that spend their summers here are the house-martin, which makes its nest of mud under the eaves of houses, and the sand martin, which builds in sandy banks.

Martingale, a long strap or thong of leather, one end of which is fastened to the girth of a horse, between the fore legs, and the other to the bit, or to a thin mouthpiece of its own.

Martinmas *or* **St. Martin's Day**, falls on Nov. 11, and is one of the Scottish quarter days. St. Martin was a popular Saint with our ancestors, and Martinmas was a busy time for the mediæval housewife. It was the date when "Martlemas Beef" was dried in the chimney, and enough bacon and mutton cured to last until the spring, because, owing the the scarcity of winter fodder, fresh meat could seldom be obtained. This diet of dried meat without vegetables caused scurvy, King's evil, leprosy, and other maladies. Originally the goose belonged to Martinmas, not to Michaelmas, the legend being that when Martin was elected Bishop of Tours he hid himself, but was betrayed by the cackling of geese. He died in the 4th cent. The spell of fine weather sometimes occurring at Martinmas is called St. Martin's Summer.

Martyrs. People who suffer death in testimony to their faith. Stephen was the first Christian martyr in 39. The first English martyr was St. Alban, 286, and in Tudor times many eminent churchmen went to the stake at West Smithfield, in London, and at Oxford, where now exists the "Martyrs' Memorial." There is a Martyrs' Memorial Church in St. John St., Clerkenwell, near the scene of the Smithfield fires.

Marxism. *See* **J27.**

Mason and Dixon's Line is the boundary line separating the old slave states of America from the free state of Pennsylvania. It was drawn by two English surveyors, Charles Mason and Jeremiah Dixon, between 1763 and 1767.

Masques were light dramatic compositions set to music and performed on special occasions. One of the best-known examples is Milton's "Comus," which was given at Ludlow Castle in 1634.

Mass, the service in the Roman Catholic Church in which are enacted and enshrined Christ's words and actions at the Last Supper. It is high or low, *i.e.*, performed with full choral service, or merely by the rehearsal of prayers without singing. Mass was first celebrated in Latin in the 4th cent., and was introduced into England in the 7th cent. The use of a vernacular language was sanctioned by the Second Vatican Council (1965).

Mass Spectrograph, an instrument for separating isotopes. It works by sorting electrified particles according to their masses; the particles stream through a magnetic and possibly an electric field, and the lightest particles undergo the greatest deflection.

Massorah, a collection of criticisms on the Hebrew text of the Scriptures, and rules for its correct interpretation.

Mast, a long round piece of timber or tubular steel or iron, standing upright in a vessel, and supporting the yards, sails, and rigging in general. The earliest ships had only one mast, carrying a simple sail. The number increased until there were 4 or 5, or even more. Above the lower mast of a sailing-ship comes the topmast, and above that, the topgallantmast and royalmast. The position of each mast is indicated by a prefix, as foremast, foretopmast, foretopgallantmast, foreroyalmast, mainmast, maintopmast, etc. The foremast is in the fore of the ship, the mainmast in the centre, and the mizzen nearest the stern. In large vessels nowadays the mast does not extend to the keel, as it formerly did, but is usually stopped at the second deck.

Master of the Revels was an important Court official upon whom devolved the arrangement of Court festivities. The office is at least as old as the time of Edward III. By 1737 it seems to have died.

Master of the Rolls, one of the English judges, formerly a judge of Chancery, but since 1881 a judge of the Court of Appeal only. In addition he has charge of the rolls or records of Chancery and ranks next to the Lord Chancellor and Lord Chief Justice.

Mastodon, an extinct order of quadruped closely resembling the elephant in structure, but much larger.

Mathematics is the language of physics, and uses symbols for expressing measurements, theories, and laws. Mathematical formulae summarise and condense in exquisite simplicity the results of vast numbers of observations and experiments.

Matins, the first of the canonical hours or services of the day in the Roman Catholic Church and Morning Prayer in the Anglican Church. The daily service in the Roman breviary (*q.v.*) consists of eight offices or "hours," fixed by canon, for prayer and devotion. Formerly, Matins was recited or sung at midnight, Lauds at sunrise, Prime at 6 a.m., Terce at 9 a.m., Sext at midday, Nones at 3 p.m., Vespers at sunset, and Compline before retiring for the night. Lauds are now commonly joined to Matins.

Mau-Mau, a secret, anti-European, terrorist movement which agitated the Kikuyu tribe of Kenya during the years 1953–57. Mau-mau was a symptom of native insecurity and discontent; emergency powers were lifted in Nov. 1959, and large-scale reforms were instituted. Kenya attained independence in Dec. 1963 with Mr. Jomo Kenyatta as Prime Minister.

Maundy Thursday, the day before Good Friday, commemorates the Last Supper. "Maundy" derives from Christ's command (mandatum) to his disciples on that day to love one another. It was the custom in the monasteries for the monks to wash the feet of the poor on this day, and for many centuries the sovereigns of England, through their almoners, have distributed money, food, and clothing to "as many old men and as many old women as the Sovereign is years of age." The Royal Maundy ceremony is still observed, special silver money granted by the Royal Almonry is coined for the occasion and the distribution takes place in Westminster Abbey. *See* **U.K. Coinage, N9.**

Mausoleum, a special place of sepulture, generally for the reception of the remains of members of a royal or other family of distinction. The name is derived from the tomb of King Mausolus at Halicarnassus, erected about 350 B.C., and forming one of the seven wonders of the world.

Mauve, a colouring matter produced from lichens by Dr. Stenhouse in 1848, but in 1856 obtained from aniline by William Perkin (1838–1907), who gave it the name Mauveen. This was the first synthetic organic dyestuff ever to be produced, which led to the building up of the great synthetic dyestuffs industry.

May, the fifth month of the year, but the third of the ancient Roman calendar. Supposed to be named after Maia, the mother of Mercury, to whom sacrifices were offered on the first day of this month. In England in former days May Day was made the occasion of many festivities, including the crowning of the May Queen, dancing round the Maypole, etc.

"Mayflower," the name of the ship which in 1620 conveyed the Pilgrim Fathers, 101 in number, from England to America. *See* **Pilgrim Fathers.**

May Fly. *See* **Ephemoptera.**

Mazarin Bible, an edition of the Latin Vulgate, acknowledged as the masterpiece of the Gutenberg press (1456). It was the first book completely printed from movable types. It is called the Mazarin Bible because the first copy to capture the attention of scholars was found in the library of Cardinal Mazarin, in Paris. Sometimes called the Gutenberg or the 42-line Bible.

Mazurka, a Polish dance in 3-beat time. Chopin wrote many Mazurkas as concert-pieces for the pianoforte.

Meal-Worm is the larva of a beetle—*Tenebrio molitor*—and is found in corn mills, granaries, and bakeries, where it does considerable damage. It is largely used for feeding birds.

Mean. In mathematics generally understood to be the arithmetic mean, *i.e.*, the average. The geometric mean between two quantities is the square root of their product.

Mechanical Equivalent of Heat. *See* **Joule.**

Medals, as decorations for military service, were first issued in this country by Charles I., who ordered medals for gallantry to be distributed to certain soldiers in 1643. Medals were also issued to officers and men who were victorious against the Dutch fleet in 1653. After Lord Howe's victory in 1794 a naval medal was instituted. Medals were also struck for the victory of Waterloo, and since that time special medals have been issued in connection with all our wars. The Victoria Cross, a special reward for personal gallantry in the Navy, Army, and Air Force, was instituted in 1856. The George Cross for gallantry instituted in 1940 ranks next to the Victoria Cross. The Military Cross was instituted in 1914.

Medlar, a tree of which the fruit is about 1 in. in diameter and hard fleshed when gathered, but after being stored for a few weeks it softens. It has a peculiar flavour. Its large white flowers give it a decorative appearance.

Meerschaum, a white or yellow-white earthy mineral, found in beds in Asia Minor, Greece, and other places, is a silicate of magnesium allied with water. Its chief use is in making pipe-bowls.

Megalith, a prehistoric monument, consisting of a large single stone or a group of such stones, in a circle as at Stonehenge or in burial chambers as at New Grange, Ireland. Megalithic monuments have been constructed by different peoples in different parts of the world since the third millennium B.C.

Meiosis, a process of plant or animal cell division, in which the number of chromosomes is halved, only one member of each pair of chromosomes appearing in each gamete or sex-cell. The gametes in man each contain 23 chromosomes.

Melody, a succession of single notes forming a pattern around which the rest of the composition (harmony, counterpoint) is woven. The theme (of a fugue, for instance) is a short melody.

Mendelian Law. The first statistical rules of inheritance, determining the ratio of variation of characteristics in the offspring of differing individuals, and the classification of characters discontinuously inherited, were first formulated by the Austrian monk Gregor Mendel. The results of his most important experiments in the crossing of peas were published in 1866, and showed that when two races are crossed, the resultant hybrids will exhibit the dominant features of one parent, but the offspring of the second generation will show those of both grandparents. *See* **F32.**

Mendicant Friars, certain religious orders which spread over Europe in the 13th cent., and comprised the Franciscans, Dominicans, Augustines, and Carmelites. Originally they depended entirely on alms.

Mercator's Projection, a method of indicating meridians and parallels of latitudes on maps, introduced by Mercator in the 16th cent., and still universally used in navigator's charts.

Mercury, one of the smaller planets and the nearest to the sun, being 36 million miles distant. It has no satellite. *See* **F7.**

Mercury *or* **Quicksilver**, symbol Hg (Latin *hydrargyrum*) is one of the oldest-known metals, whose chief ore is the sulphide, cinnabar, found in certain parts of Spain, China, Japan, Mexico, and South America. It is liquid at ordinary temperature and is used in the construction of barometers and thermometers. Alloys of mercury are called amalgams. It is also of great value in medicine. The metal is used in the mercury-vapour (or "sunlight") lamp, since the vapour gives a bright yellow-white glow in an electric discharge.

Mercy Killing. *See* **D6**(2).

Meridian, an imaginary circle extending through the North and South Poles and any given place. When the sun is at its midday height at any place it is "on the meridian"; hence the terms ante-meridian (a.m.) and post-meridian (p.m.).

Merino Sheep were imported into England from Spain in 1788, and had great influence in improving native breeds, especially in regard to the quality of the wool.

Merit, Order of, founded by King Edward VII. in 1902 as a special distinction for eminent men and women without conferring a knighthood upon them. The Order has twenty-four British companions in addition to foreign honorary members limited in number, as the choice of members is, by the Sovereign's pleasure. Lord Kelvin was the founder companion. General Eisenhower (1945), and Dr. Sarvepalli Radhakrishnan (1963) are honorary members. Florence Nightingale (1907) and Professor Dorothy Hodgkin (1965) are the only women to have received this coveted decoration.

Merovingians, the name given to the family that ruled over France from about 500 to 750. Clovis was first of the line and Chilperic the last.

Mesons (from Greek *meso* = middle), a family of unstable particles of mass between that of an electron and that of a proton. Some are positive, some negative, some neutral. No stable meson is known, the longest-lived particle having a lifetime of only two-millionths of a second. The first of these particles was discovered in cosmic radiation in 1937 and called the mu-meson or *muon*. In 1947 a heavier type was discovered called the pi-meson or *pion*, which behaved like the meson predicted on theoretical grounds by Yukawa in 1935. The pion is connected with the theory of nuclear forces. *See also* **F13, 14.**

Mesozoic. The geological era which includes the Triassic, Jurassic, and Cretaceous rocks. *See* **F30.**

Metalloid, an element which has properties intermediate between those of a metal and a nonmetal. Arsenic is a metalloid.

Metamorphic Rocks are such geological deposits as have undergone alterations of structure and mineral reorganisation. The most active agents in producing these metamorphic changes are heat, water, and pressure. *See* **F8**(2).

Metamorphosis, period of development from egg to adult, during which the animals have different forms, as found, *e.g.*, in the life histories of frog and butterfly.

Meteorites. The word meteor originally signified any natural phenomenon, but in modern usage meteors are small bodies coming from interplanetary space which become luminous by friction on entering the earth's atmosphere. Popularly called "shooting stars." Larger meteors are known as fireballs. Some of these reach the ground. The object which has been a meteor in flight then becomes a meteorite. In some meteorites iron is the predominating element, others are like rock. The iron meteorites are more common amongst those which have been preserved, but falls of rock-like meteorites occur more frequently. At l'Aigle in France in 1803 from 2000 to 3000 meteorite stones fell; this fall is famous because it convinced scientists that meteorites really came from outside our atmosphere. (The largest meteorite stone actually known to have fallen to earth is one which descended in Emmott County, Iowa, in 1870, weighing 437 pounds.) A meteorite weighing no less than 36½ tons found in Greenland is now in New York. On June 30, 1908, an enormous meteor fell in Siberia in a sparsely-inhabited region. A hot blast destroyed all trees within a radius of about 5–10 miles, the explosion waves being recorded by barographs as far distant as London, Washington, and Batavia. For the next few nights there was in Europe in the northern sky brilliant illumination due to sunlight falling on clouds of dust at a great height in the atmosphere. Whether this dust had accompanied the meteor in its journey through space like the tail of a comet or whether the dust had come from Siberia is unknown. When the place where the meteor fell was visited in 1927 some 200 craters were found, but no considerable meteorite has been recovered. Meteorites are possibly débris from the disintegration of a body in the solar system.

Meteorology, the science of the atmosphere considered as a heat engine. Deals with weather, climate, optical phenomena, atmospheric electricity, physical processes such as radiation and precipitation, the dynamics and structure of cyclones, anticyclones, etc. Wide application to problems of aviation, agriculture, commerce and shipping. Meteorological observing stations are in operation all over the world, and on the simultaneous or synoptic reports of their instrument readings and estimates of pressure, temperature, humidity, speed and direction of wind, rain, character and amount of cloud, visibility, etc., forecasts, gale, snow and frost warnings are based. Instruments carried by earth satellites outside the atmosphere can make systematic observations on a world-wide basis of the atmospheric circulation, through observation of cloud cover and of the thermal radiation into space from the atmosphere. Such observations are of great importance for meteorology. For example, in 1961, the development of a hurricane in mid-Atlantic was first detected by an American weather satellite, one of the *Tiros* series which have since been used for Weather Bureau routine forecasts.

Methane. The simplest hydrocarbon, compounded of one carbon atom and four hydrogen atoms. This gas occurs over marshes and swamps, where it is liberated in the decay of vegetable matter. It is the main constituent of natural gas, and also occurs in coal-mines, where it is called "fire-damp" because of the explosive character of its mixture with air. Formerly this natural gas was removed from the coal seams and ran to waste; now in many countries (including Britain) it is being used for commercial purposes.

Methodism. *See* **J27.**

Methylated Spirit, a mixture of 90 parts by volume ethyl alcohol, 9½ parts wood naphtha (methyl alcohol), ½ part crude pyridine, together with small amounts of petroleum oil and methyl violet dye. Industrial methylated spirit consists of a mixture of 95 parts by volume ethyl alcohol and 5 parts wood naphtha. It is used as a solvent and a fuel.

Metre. *See* **English Verse, M2.**

Metre, unit of length in the metric system; since 1958 the wavelength of the orange-red light of krypton 86 has been adopted as the basis of the international unit of length. Before that (since 1889) the platinum–iridium bar kept at Sèvres was the international prototype metre.

Metric System, the system of weights and measures based on the gram and the metre, smaller and larger units being decimals and multiples of the primary units respectively. A decimal currency was adopted in France in 1795 and the metric system of weights and measures in 1799. (In that year the quadrant of the earth was surveyed and the standard metre adopted.) Nevertheless the change was accepted slowly, and as late as 1837 the French Government had to pass a law forbidding the use of the old measures. Since then the metric system has been adopted in most of the continental countries and is used universally in scientific work. Although there have been many attempts to get the system adopted in Britain, it was not until 1965 that the Government announced that it was encouraging the adoption of the metric system of weights and measures. *See* **N11**.

Mezzotint, an engraving from copper or steel produced by instruments which burnish and scrape away portions of the surface, and yield an impression effectually graded in light and shade.

Mica. The mica of commerce is a nearly transparent mineral, which has great heat-resisting power, and can be split into thin plates. The most important micas are muscovite (potassium mica), the commoner variety, phlogopite (magnesium mica), and biotite, the magnesium and iron mica.

Michael, St., and George, St., an order of knighthood originally founded for the Ionian Isles and Malta in 1818, and reorganised in 1869, so as to admit Crown servants connected with the Colonies. The Earl of Derby, Earl Russell, and Earl Grey were the first of the new knights.

Michaelmas Day, the festival day of St. Michael and All Angels, Sept. 29th, one of the English quarter days.

Microbe, a term proposed by Sédillot in 1878 to denote any microscopic organism, vegetable or animal, or found on the borderland between the two great natural kingdoms. The term is commonly used, but not by scientists.

Micrometer, an instrument for measuring minute distances; usually attached to the eye-pieces of a microscope or telescope, and consisting of two very fine hairs or wires stretched across the field of view, one fixed, the other movable. It was invented by William Gascoigne in the 17th cent. and improved by later inventors. Sir Joseph Whitworth made one in 1858 to measure the millionth part of an inch.

Microphone, device for converting the acoustic energy of sound waves into waves of electrical energy, used in sound amplifying systems. Developed independently by Edison (1877) and Hughes (1878).

Microscope, invented about 1590 by Janssen, and improved by Galileo, Fontana, and others, is an instrument which by a lens system magnifies minute objects. Microscopes are simple, compound, and binocular. The more powerful instruments have a magnifying capacity of as much as 10,000 diameters. *See also* **Electron Microscope**.

Middle Ages (*c.* A.D. 400–1500), usually considered to be the period between the decline and fall of the Western Roman Empire and the fall of Constantinople to the Turks (*see* **A4-7**). The period covers (*a*) an earlier part ending with the 12th cent. (sometimes called the Dark Ages) when science was dead, when theology was the main preoccupation, and when the language of the learned West was Latin; and (*b*) a later age of Arabian influence when alchemy and astrology (at that time indistinguishable from astronomy) were central interests, technology was advancing, and Greek learning was transmitted by Arab scholars. Characteristic features of the mediaeval scene were monasticism (**J29**), the Crusades (*q.v.*), Gothic art (*q.v.*), feudalism (**J17**), and the supremacy of Islam in the field of learning. The period came to an end with the ushering in of the Renaissance (**J38**).

Midrash, name given to the homiletical interpretation of some of the Hebrew Scriptures in which allegory and legendary illustration were freely used. Compiled by Jewish rabbis from *c.* A.D. 200.

Millenary Petition was presented to James I. in 1603, on behalf of nearly 1,000 Puritan Ministers against certain of the rites and ceremonies of the Church of England. The Hampton Court Conference was the outcome of this petition.

Millennium, a period of a thousand years. The term is specifically used of the period of a thousand years during which, according to Rev. xx. 1–5, Christ will reign in person on earth. The Millenarians are a sect that interprets the "Millennium" as beginning with the commencement of the 6001st year from the Creation, which, according to Archbishop Ussher (1581–1650), was in 4004 B.C.

Millipede. Arthropods allied to the centipedes, from which they differ in having two pairs of legs to each body segment (except the first three) instead of one pair. Worm-like in shape but with a pair of antennæ on the head, they are vegetarians and can do much harm to garden plants. *See* **T28(1)**.

Millstone-Grit, a series of grits and sandstones of deltaic origin underlying the coal measures of the Carboniferous system and attaining in England a thickness in parts of 5,000 ft. It is from this rock that millstones have been made from time immemorial.

Mimicry, protective similarity of an animal to another animal or to inanimate objects. Examples of the former are the hover flies, which mimic wasps and bees; of the latter, leaf insects, stick insects, and caterpillars that look like dead twigs.

Mind and Matter. *See* **J28**.

Minim, a musical term denoting a note equal to two crochets, or half the value of the semibreve; also pharmaceutical term for $\frac{1}{480}$th part of a fluid ounce.

Mink. Semi-aquatic mammals closely related to polecats. There is one American species and one European. The fur, which varies light to dark brown, is soft and thick, and is among the most valuable of commercial furs.

Minnesingers were minstrel poets of Germany who, during the 12th and 13th cent., composed and sang verses of heroism and love. They were of knightly rank, the counterpart of the French troubadours.

Minnow, a small fresh-water fish of the carp family, abounding in all the waters of Europe; it has a mottled back and silvery belly, and forms a popular bait for trout.

Minor Scale. *See* **Diatonic Scale**.

Minstrels were originally specially appointed instrumentalists and singers—pipers, harpers, and gleemen—engaged by barons and manorial lords to amuse their tenants. Later, minstrels assumed nomadic habits, made their way into the houses of the great, and were generally welcome. By Elizabeth's time, however, they were too numerous, and were classed as "rogues and vagabonds," along with actors.

Minuet, a composition in 3-beat time and in the rhythm of the minuet dance. A movement of a sonata or symphony may be in minuet form.

Miracle Plays, which were very popular in England in the 15th cent., were usually religious in character, representing some of the dramatic incidents of the Bible. Staging of plays was one of the many activities of the Guilds of those days.

Mirage, an optical illusion often observed in desert regions when the objects on the surface of the earth often some distance away appear as if reflected in a surface of water. Mirage is due to the unequal heating of the different parts of the atmosphere, which bends the light rays and so produces distorted images.

Mishna, the first part of the Talmud, setting forth the "Oral Law" of the Jews.

Missal, the name of the mass-book of the Roman Church compiled 492–96 by Pope Gelasius I. and revised by Gregory I., 590–604. The present Roman Missal was sanctioned by the Council of Trent 1545–63. In the Anglican Communion the Book of Common Prayer superseded the Missal in 1549.

Mistle-thrush receives its name from its partiality to the mistletoe-berry. Larger than the song thrush, with spotted breast rather than speckled.

Mistletoe, a parasitic evergreen with white berries used as a decoration at Christmas-time. The familiar mistletoe of Europe is the *Viscum album*, which grows on the boughs of lime, willow, apple, poplar, maple, ash, hawthorn but seldom on oak-trees. It was sacred to the Druids, and in Norse mythology it was a mistletoe dart that killed the god Baldur.

Mistral, a cold, dry, northerly wind peculiar to the French coast of the Mediterranean.

Mites, minute animals related to spiders, but without the well-marked division of the body exhibited by the latter. Some are parasites, *e.g.*, the scab mite and mange mite. The garden pest called the "red spider" is really a mite.

Mitre, the twofold pointed head-dress of bishops and certain abbots of the Western Church, and occasionally of other ecclesiastics.

Moa, the name for several species of ostrich-like extinct birds related to the New Zealand kiwi. The largest species, *Diornis maximus*, stood 8 ft. 7 in. high. Became extinct about 500 years ago.

Moabite Stone, a stone of the 9th cent. B.C. containing the earliest known inscription in Phoenician characters, and discovered in the highlands of Moab in 1868. It is now in the Louvre, Paris. It records the campaign between Moab and Israel, a differing account of which is given in the Old Testament.

Moderator, a material used to slow down neutrons in an atomic pile. Examples of moderators are pure graphite and heavy water. *See* **Nuclear Reactors.**

Mohole Project, a scheme to bore through the earth's crust to take samples of the mantle rocks beneath. Drilling trials, led by an American team of geophysicists, began in 1961 near the island of Guadalupe off the Mexican coast in the Pacific. When a suitable site has been selected the drill is expected to reach a depth of some 6–7 miles below the ocean surface. Sea-bed sediment samples will also be taken. The drilling craft will act as a floating island capable of moving under its own power at 10 knots. Russian geophysicists are also engaged in a similar experiment, but are boring through land rocks where the digging will have to be much deeper and higher temperatures are likely to be met with. The boundary between the earth's crustal and mantle rocks is known as the Mohorovičić Discontinuity, or, more simply, as the Moho. *See* **F8(1).**

Molasses, sugar-cane juice in its uncrystallised form after boiling. The crystallised part is the raw sugar. Used to make rum.

Mole, a small burrowing animal with long, sensitive nose, about the size of a small rat, with short legs and forefeet armed with strong claws for digging in the earth. Their subterranean dwellings are of curiously ingenious construction, and they do not often leave them except to make raids on mice, frogs, snails, etc. The earth worm, however, is the mole's chief item of food. Not to be confused with the vole which has a blunt nose.

Molecular Biology, a rapidly expanding branch of science concerned with cell structure and function at a molecular level. The European Molecular Biology Organization (EMBO) hopes to establish a laboratory on an international basis similar to the high-energy physics laboratory at Geneva (CERN). *See* **F19–21.**

Molecule. *See* **F12(2).**

Mollusca. *See* **F23(1).**

Molybdenum, symbol Mo, a fairly hard white metal with properties resembling those of chromium. Its commonest ore is the sulphide, molybdenite. The chief use of the metal is in the manufacture of alloy steels.

Monasticism. *See* **J29.**

Monazite, a cerium mineral containing some thorium. Occurs as grains, often as sand ("monazite sands"), derived from granites. Deposits occur in India (Travancore), Russia, Norway, Madagascar, S. Africa, Brazil, U.S.A.

Monday, the second day of the week, called by the Anglo-Saxons *Monandaeg* (moon-day).

Mongoose, species of mammals related to the civets, feeding on vermin and reptiles. These animals, which have long tails and short legs, occur in Africa and Asia (especially India). The biggest mongoose is the Egyptian ichneumon, and this has been introduced into the W. Indies because of its ability to kill large poisonous snakes.

Monitor, a family of lizards most resembling dragons. There are about 30 species widely distributed over the tropical parts of Asia, Australia, and Africa.

Monocotyledons. *See* **F29(1).** Most monocotyledons are herbs; many are cultivated for their beautiful flowers, *e.g.*, lilies, tulip, daffodil, iris, orchids, and cannas. A few are tree-like, *e.g.* bananas, pineapples, bamboo, and palms.

Monroe Doctrine, a principle of American policy declining any European intervention in political affairs of the American continent, outlined by President Monroe in 1823. At the same time interference was disclaimed with existing European colonies in the Western Hemisphere. The American Civil War hampered the application of the doctrine for some time, but afterwards the United States firmly insisted on it. The Doctrine is not international law, but a national policy of the U.S.A.

Monsoons, regular persistent winds which blow at certain seasons in middle latitudes, mainly in South and East Asia. Their occurrence is related to the great changes of pressure which take place between summer and winter over the land mass. In India the south-west monsoon (June–Oct.) is moisture-laden from its long passage over the sea and in the higher regions, especially, there is heavy rainfall. Sudden reversal of the wind results in the cold north-east monsoon (Oct.–March) which is dry on account of the shelter afforded by the mountain ranges to the north. Frequently the term "monsoon" is applied to denote the associated rainfall without reference to the actual winds.

Monstrance, an ornamental transparent receptacle in which the Sacred Host is carried in procession or exposed for adoration.

Month, the 12th part of the calendar year. A lunar month is the interval of new moon to new moon or full moon to full moon; mean length, 29 days, 12 hours, 44 minutes, 2·87 seconds. A sidereal month represents the time of the moon's revolution from a given star back to the same again, 27 days, 7 hours, 43 minutes, 11·5 seconds. In English law, since 1926, a month, unless otherwise expressed, means a calendar month.

Monument of London, a 202 ft. column, overlooking Billingsgate, designed by Wren and erected (1671–77) to mark the starting-point of the Great Fire of London (1666). The original inscription upon it ascribed the fire to "the treachery and malice of the popish faction," which stood down to 1831, when the words were erased as objectionable. The black marble staircase has 345 steps (311 to the balcony).

Moon, the earth's satellite, 2,160 miles in diameter and 238,857 miles distant from the earth. In 1959 Russia launched her first three moon probes. The second succeeded in hitting the moon and recorded no magnetic field. The third photographed that part of the moon's surface which is never visible from the earth. The U.S. *Ranger VII* in 1964 and *VIII* and *IX* in 1965 each took a series of photographs of the surface. From these pictures and from those taken by the Russian *Luna 9*, which made a soft landing in 1966, it is clear that there are craters on the moon's surface. From their shape and distribution it is a reasonable conclusion that the surface is not covered by any great thickness of soft dust. This removes one of the possible objections to the feasibility of a manned spacecraft making a landing on the moon.

Moorhen, a widely distributed bird of the rail family, a common resident in the British Isles. The adult is blackish with white under tail-coverts, a white line on the flanks, and a yellow-tipped bill. The frontal shield and the base of the bill are vermilion. It bobs its head, flirts its tail, and dives well. The nest is usually placed close to the water's edge or on an overhanging branch. In feeding the young the parents are sometimes helped by their offspring of a previous brood of the season. In N. America the bird is known as the Florida Gallinule.

Moors, the name given to the Moslems who live in N.W. Africa and to those who once lived in Spain. In 711 Moorish Arabs invaded Spain and spread beyond the Pyrenees into France, where they were driven back by the end of the century. Spain, however, remained virtually under Moorish domination until the 11th cent., and during that period was the most civilised and prosperous part of Western Europe. In the arts and sciences the impact of Moorish culture was profound and lasting. Examples of the brilliant splendour of Moorish architecture are still to be seen in Toledo, Córdoba, Seville, and Granada. During the long struggle for the Christian reconquest thousands were killed and expelled, and in 1492 Granada, their last remaining kingdom, was forced to surrender They were virtually exterminated by the Inquisition, and the last were expelled in 1609.

Moose, the largest members of the deer family. The N. American Moose stands 5½–6¾ ft. high, and has huge palmate antlers. There is another New World species, occurring in Alaska. The European species is known as the elk.

Morris Dance, an old English country dance of the reel order.

Morse Alphabet, a system of dots and dashes, intended to be used in combination with the indicator in telegraphy; but usually read by sound, the receiving operator writing down the words in the system as transmitted. This system of signals was invented by the American inventor and artist Samuel Finley Breese Morse (1791–1872) of Charlestown, Massachusetts.

Mosaic, art of arranging small pieces of coloured glass, marble, or other materials in such a fashion as to produce a decorative pattern. Some of the best examples of Byzantine mosaics are to be seen at Ravenna, Rome, Venice, and Sicily.

Mosque, a Mohammedan church, the greatest being that of Santa Sophia at Istanbul, now converted into a museum of Byzantine art.

Mosquito, small two-winged flies with long legs and and slender body. Their larvae are aquatic. The females of some species are blood-suckers, and thus come to transmit the blood parasites which cause malaria and yellow fever, for example. *See* **D.D.T.** *and* **Gammexane.**

Mosses. Most mosses live in moist habitats, but there are some species that can withstand desiccation and are adapted to live on rocks and tree-trunks. *See* **F27(2).**

Motet, an unaccompanied anthem of the Catholic and Lutheran Churches. Many fine motets which were settings of sacred writings or paraphrases and which were written mostly in the 15th cent. still survive.

Moths, of the insect order, *Lepidoptera*, differing from butterflies which have clubbed antennae, in having feathery, sometimes thin, pointed antennae, rarely clubbed. Most are nocturnal, and the pupae are usually brown and enclosed in a cocoon unlike those of the butterfly, which are usually naked. *See also* **Lepidoptera.**

Motion, Laws of. According to Newton: (1) A body continues in its state of rest or uniform motion in a straight line except in so far as it is compelled by external forces to change that state. (2) Rate of change of momentum is proportional to the applied force, and takes place in the direction in which the force acts. (3) To every action there is an equal and opposite reaction. These laws are the basis of almost all engineering and everyday mechanics. Corrections to them have been made by relativity and the quantum theory. *See* **F13, 14.**

Movement, one of the contrasting pieces which together make up a Sonata, Symphony, or Concerto. A typical sonata has three movements, while a typical symphony has four.

Mule, a hybrid between horse and ass. Also the name of the spinning machine invented by Crompton in 1779 which combined the principle of Hargreaves' spinning jenny with the machine invented by Arkwright.

Mullions, the vertical bars dividing the lights in a window, forming a highly decorative feature in the Tudor period of English Gothic architecture. The cross-beam or horizontal bar of wood or stone in a mullioned window is styled a transom. *See* **Windows.**

Munich Agreement. In Sept. 1938 Mr. Neville Chamberlain and M. Daladier, British and French Premiers, reached agreement with Hitler at Munich for the dismemberment of Czechoslovakia, primarily for the benefit of Germany. Czechoslovakia itself was not consulted, nor Russia who with Britain and France had jointly pledged themselves to uphold the independence of Czechoslovakia. Hitler had been threatening that country for some time, but every concession had been met by further demands. After three visits to Germany, during which Hitler raised his demands, the British and French statesmen gave way. Mr. Chamberlain declared on return that he had secured "Peace in our Time." The Agreement was the subject of much controversy. Hitler seized Czechoslovakia in March 1939.

Musk Deer, a small deer of the Himalayas, standing about 20 in. high. It is grey in colour, slightly brindled, and carries a small pouch in the abdominal region, containing what is commercially known as musk, an article which is of great value in the manufacture of various perfumes. The active constituent of musk, muscone, is now made synthetically. The species was becoming rare on account of its slaughter for its musk.

Mutton Bird, an Australasian name of controversial origin for a shearwater or petrel, *e.g.*, the Short-tailed and Sooty Shearwaters and the Great-winged, Kermadec, and White-headed Petrels. The young are taken by hand from their burrows for human food.

Myrrh, a resinous substance obtained from a tree of the natural order *Amyridaceae*, growing plentifully in Abyssinia and Arabia. Its use for embalming, medical, and aromatic purposes may be traced back to the most remote times.

Mysteries, Greek, secret mystic ceremonies of the ancient Greeks, religious drama accompanied by dancing, the most well known being the Eleusinian and Orphic ceremonies.

Mystery Plays were the mediaeval religious dramas performed by the priests at great ecclesiastic festivals, particularly in France and Bavaria, staging the Nativity, Passion, and Resurrection.

N

Nadir, one of the two poles of the horizon, the other being the zenith. The nadir is the pole vertically below the observer's feet.

Nahum, one of the books of the Minor Prophets of the Old Testament. It is a prophecy of doom on the approaching sack of Nineveh which fell in 612 B.C. to the Medes and Babylonians.

Naiad, a water-nymph of classic mythology, beautiful and mystic; celebrated by Virgil, Ovid, Homer, and other ancient writers.

Nantes, Edict of, was a decree promulgated by Henry IV. of France in 1598, giving full freedom of worship to the Protestants of the country. It was the revocation of this edict in 1685 by Louis XIV. that drove hundreds of thousands of French Huguenots to this country.

Naphtha, a liquid combustible believed to have been one of the ingredients of "Greek fire." Naphtha is a light, highly inflammable oil obtained by distilling petroleum, shale oil, or coal tar. The petroleum naphtha consists of a mixture of paraffins; that from shale contains olefines as well as paraffins. Coal-tar naphtha contains xylol.

Naphthalene is an aromatic hydrocarbon; it is obtained from coal tar, and its derivatives are much used in the manufacture of colours for dyers and printers. "Moth balls" are made of naphthalene.

Narcotic, a medical dictionary definition is that a narcotic is a drug that produces stupor, complete insensibility, or sleep. In terms of drug addiction, a narcotic has been defined as altering and distorting the user's perception of himself and of the external world, being taken primarily for that purpose. *See* **P22–24.**

Nardus, a genus of coarse grasses, growing on bleak upland heaths and hill slopes. *Nardus stricta*, known as "mat-weed," is a British species.

Narghile, an oriental tobacco pipe so constructed that the smoke passes through water and up a long flexible tube before reaching the lips of the smoker.

Narrative Art, a type of art popular during the late 19th cent. based on the principle: "every picture tells a story"—*e.g.*, such paintings as the little Royalist boy surrounded by his anxious family and confronted across a table by the Roundheads bearing the title: "When did you last see your father?" The term, although often applied derisively, suitably describes many works of considerable artistic merit: *e.g.*, Hogarth's *Marriage à la Mode*, his series of eight engravings entitled *A Rake's*

Progress, the Bayeux Tapestry, and many Babylonian and Egyptian friezes.

Naseby, Battle of, was fought on June 14, 1645, between the Royalists under the command of Prince Rupert and the King, and the Parliamentarians under Fairfax and Cromwell. It resulted in a complete defeat for Charles.

National Anthem, a musical composition with words, officially adopted for ceremonial use as an expression of patriotism and loyalty to a national cause. The national anthem of the United Kingdom is "God Save the Queen" which has been in use since about the middle of the 18th cent. There is some doubt about its origin. It has been variously attributed to Dr. John Bull, Henry Carey, and James Oswald.

National Assembly, the name taken by the body responsible for the opening stages of the French Revolution and subsequently by other sovereign bodies in France and elsewhere.

National Covenant, an oath and declaration subscribed to by the Scottish Presbyterians in 1638 to maintain their religion against Charles I.'s episcopalianising designs.

National Gallery, established in 1824 at Pall Mall, London, with the Angerstein Collection of 38 pictures, purchased for £60,000 as a nucleus. The existing building which was opened in 1838 has been enlarged several times. The National Gallery at Millbank, known as the Tate Gallery, was given to the nation by Sir Henry Tate in 1897.

Nationalisation is the taking over by the State of the ownership and operation of an industry or service—*e.g.*, coal-mining, railway transport, gas, and electricity. Where this is done without revolution, compensation is usually paid to the previous owners at what is regarded as a fair market price; the compensation is sometimes paid in cash, but more often in fixed-interest-bearing bonds issued either by the State or by the administration of the nationalised service, which is usually a publicly appointed Board or Corporation acting, with greater or lesser autonomy, under the direction of a Minister responsible to Parliament. In some cases the State becomes a partner with private investors in the ownership of a particular enterprise, *e.g.*, oil companies, such as the former Anglo-Iranian and some recent French examples. Nationalisation is usually brought about by a separate Act of Parliament relating to each industry or service taken over. These Acts, in Great Britain, include provision for joint consultation at all levels between the administering boards or commissions and the workers employed and their Trade Unions. When, as in the Soviet Union, nationalisation occurs as an outcome of social revolution no compensation is paid to the dispossessed owners.

National Parks. Under the National Parks Act 1949 a National Parks Commission was set up to create National Parks in England and Wales. Ten have been established: Peak District, Lake District, Snowdonia, Yorkshire Dales, Exmoor, Brecon Beacons, Dartmoor, Pembrokeshire Coast, North Yorks Moors, and Northumberland. It is not intended to change the character of these territories but to control their development so as to harmonise with the two dominant principles: (*a*) that the characteristic beauty of the landscape within the Park area shall be preserved and (*b*) that the visiting public shall have ample access and facilities for recreation and enjoyment. The National Parks Commission also has power to designate areas in England and Wales outside the national parks as "areas of outstanding natural beauty." Eighteen areas had been designated by 1965: Gower, Quantock Hills, Lleyn, Surrey Hills, Dorset, Northumberland Coast, Cannock Chase, Shropshire Hills, Malvern Hills, Cornwall, N. Devon, S. Devon, E. Devon, E. Hampshire, Isle of Wight, Forest of Bowland, Chichester Harbour, and Solway Coast. *See also* **Long Distance Routes.**

National Physical Laboratory, situated at Teddington, is one of the world's largest and best-equipped laboratories. It was first established in 1900 under the control of the Royal Society. In 1918 DSIR took over financial liability and in 1964 it became part of the Ministry of Technology. It conducts research in various branches of non-nuclear physics and maintains British primary standards and physical units.

National Portrait Gallery, established in 1856, and now located in a building in St. Martin's Lane adjoining the National Gallery. Contains portraits of eminent people in history, literature, art, etc., and a valuable collection of medals and autographs.

National Trust, founded in 1895. "A non-profit-making organisation incorporated by Act of Parliament for the purposes of promoting the permanent preservation of lands and buildings of historic interest or natural beauty for the benefit and access of the people." As a consequence of gifts of public-spirited individuals the Trust now owns many acres of magnificent scenery and property, including mediaeval castles, bird sanctuaries, ancient monuments, birthplaces and homes of famous men, and classic examples of domestic architecture, preserved for the enjoyment of present and future generations. Since 1946 lands and houses of interest to the nation may be given to the National Trust in lieu of death duties.

Nativity. There are three nativity festivals of the Christian Church: Christmas, 25 December, the festival of the birth of Christ; the birthday of the Virgin Mary (8 Sept.); and of St. John the Baptist (24 June).

Natterjack, a curious warty, prominent-eyed, brown toad (*Bufo calamita*), having a bright yellow line down the middle of its back. It utters a muttering sort of croak, hence its name.

Natural Law. *See* **J32.**

Naturalisation, the grant of British nationality to an alien. Before an application can be made to the Secretary of State for the grant of a certificate an alien must have qualified by 5 years' residence in the U.K. or service under the Crown, during the 8 years immediately passed.

"Nautical Almanac," published under the authority of the Admiralty, is always issued four years in advance, and contains information specially prepared for the use of navigators and astronomers. It first appeared in 1767.

Nautilus, a term now applied only to the pearly-shelled nautilus, the sole surviving example of the four-gilled section of the *Cephalopoda*. Its fossil relatives are called Ammonites. The spiral shell is divided into a number of compartments, the animal living in the last and largest chamber. There are three or four species, all living in tropical seas. The Paper Nautilus is not related to the Pearly Nautilus, belonging to the same order as the octopus.

"Nautilus," the name of the American nuclear-powered submarine which made the first voyage under the North Pole in Aug. 1958, having navigated a new north-west passage without stars, compass, radio, or radar but using a piece of equipment known as an "inertial navigator." *See* **Inertial Navigation.**

Nave is the body or main open portion of a cathedral or church, and extends from the chief entrance to the choir, or chancel, and is usually flanked by aisles. A nave, in mechanics, indicates the "hub" or central part of a wheel.

Neandertal, the name of the valley lying between Düsseldorf and Wuppertal, where in a limestone cave a now famous skull of a very early species of prehistoric man was discovered in 1856. Fossils of Neandertal man have been found over a wide area, and from archaeological evidence he began to disappear from Europe during the last Ice Age, about 40,000 B.C. *See also* **F34**(2).

Necromancy, "the black art," was in olden times much believed in, and supposed to be an occult power by which its practitioners could converse with the spirits of the dead and learn the future.

Negroes are the dark-skinned, woolly-headed races, natives of tropical Africa, or descendants of such natives. There are many different racial types, but the most typical Negroes are found in W. Africa—the Ashanti of Ghana, and the Yoruba of Nigeria. There are the Pygmies living in the forests north and south of the equator, the Bushmen of the Kalahari Desert, the Hottentots of South Africa, who however have largely lost their identity, the Bantu peoples, and many others. Their culture is rich in folk-lore, and they have a great gift for music and dancing. About 25 million people of Negro descent are in N. and S.

America, the European slave trade having taken them there from their homes in W. Africa.

Negus, the name given to any mixture of wine and water, and said to have been named after Colonel Francis Negus about 1714. The sovereign of Abyssinia is styled the Negus.

Nekton, term used to differentiate actively swimming aquatic organisms (*e.g.*, fishes) from the "drifters" or plankton.

Nelson Column, in Trafalgar Square, London, designed by Mr. William Railton, was chosen from among a number of designs—temples, obelisks and various sculptural groups—sent in as a result of a competition held in 1839. The erection of the column was begun in 1840. Twenty-six years later the lions designed by Landseer were set up at the foot of the completed column. The statue of Nelson himself was made by E. H. Bailey and the bronze reliefs at the base executed by Carew, Woodington, Ternouth, and Watson, representing the Battles of the Nile, St. Vincent, Copenhagen, and Trafalgar. Height 170 ft., executed in Portland stone instead of granite, as originally planned, at a cost of £46,000.

Nematodes, the roundworms or threadworms. Some parasitise man and domestic animals.

Néné or Hawaiian Goose. At the Severn Wildfowl Trust at Slimbridge Mr. Peter Scott has saved this bird from extinction.

Neo-Classical School of Art, a French school of painting and sculpture belonging to the late 18th and early 19th cent. and founded by Jacques David, the Academician, republican, and later admirer of Bonaparte. His classicism probably arose from his republican sympathies, which caused him to paint such works as the *Oath of the Horatii* (Louvre) drawing analogies between revolutionary France and Rome. Because of these views he revolted against the romantic and sensual art of Watteau and Greuze and equally against the realism of Chardin. Among his many famous pupils was Ingres, who later assumed leadership of the school.

Neodymium, an element belonging to the rare earth metal group. Discovered by Welsbach in 1885.

Neo-Impressionism, a development of Impressionism (*q.v.*) by Seurat and Signac during the 1880s who devised the method of painting known as *pointillism* (the application of pure colours in minute touches to form a composite whole, based on a knowledge of the laws of colour and optics). One of the best-known examples of this technique is Seurat's *Sunday Afternoon on the Grand Jatte*.

Neon, inert gas present in air to the extent of about 1 part in 65,000. The crimson glow produced when an electric discharge passes through the gas is familiar in advertising signs.

Neoprene, generic name for a class of synthetic rubbers made from acetylene.

Nepotism, the bestowal of patronage by reason of relationship rather than of merit. It had its origin in the custom of certain Popes to enrich their families out of the offices of the Church.

Neptune. Apart from Pluto this is the most distant of the planets, estimated to be about 2,793 million miles from the sun, and taking about 165 years to revolve around it. Discovered by the German astronomer Galle on Sept. 23, 1846, after its existence had been predicted by Leverrier and Adams.

Neptunium, element 93, one of the four new elements discovered during the progress of the atomic bomb project in the second world war. Neptunium is formed when a neutron enters a nucleus of Uranium 238, and it decays radioactively to yield plutonium.

Neuroptera, an order of insects which includes lacewings, alder-flies, ant-lion flies, etc.

Neutrino, a neutral particle which carries energy and spin and although possessing little or no mass plays an important part in the interaction of other fundamental particles. The discovery that there are in fact two distinct neutrinos, each with its counterpart, was discovered in 1962 as a result of an experiment made with the 30,000 million-electron-volt proton accelerator at Brookhaven. *See* **F13, 14.**

Neutron, a neutral particle present in all atomic nuclei except the hydrogen nucleus which is a single proton. In the development of nuclear science and technology the neutron has played a most important role and neutrons produce the radioisotopes now widely used in medicine, agriculture, and industry. Neutrons and protons are termed nucleons. *See* **F10, 14.**

New Deal. The measures taken by President Roosevelt in U.S.A. in 1933 to overcome the great economic crisis which broke out at the end of 1929 and to restore the social security threatened by it. The measures were drawn up by a group of experts called a Brains Trust and they provided for recovery by a programme of public works, including large-scale construction of houses and large-scale assistance to farmers. Loans were granted and authorities formed to stimulate activities which reduced the workless from 17 millions to between 7 and 10 millions. Unemployment relief was regulated and enlarged; and social insurance (which for decades had been a subject of dispute, being held to be contrary to American principles of self-help) was introduced. Many of the changes have become a permanent part of American legislation though some laws were repealed by the U.S. Supreme Court as being unconstitutional.

Newgate Prison, now pulled down and replaced by the Central Criminal Court, opened in 1907, was situated near the point where once stood one of the old London city gates. There is a record of a prison upon this spot in the 13th cent. Later a new one was built by the executors of Richard Whittington, but this was destroyed by the Great Fire in 1666. Still another new prison on this site was erected between 1778 and 1780. In the Gordon Riots of the latter year it was destroyed by fire and re-erected. It was not used as a prison after 1880.

News Letters were an early form of newspaper, popular in the time of Charles II. They consisted of items of news and gossip collected at the various coffee-houses and other places of public resort. They often included blank pages on which readers wrote their private letters.

Newspapers. The first news-books to be published at regular intervals in Britain appeared in 1662 with news of what was going on abroad translated from German and Italian news-sheets. Licence to print was obtained from the Star Chamber, which until its abolition in 1641 allowed only the printing of foreign news. With the lifting of the ban on domestic news the Press became free. In the reign of Queen Anne English newspapers employed writers of great intellectual power and versatility. Despite the newspaper tax introduced in 1712, the number of newspapers published in London in 1776 had increased to 53, though the standard of writing was below that of earlier times. The development of the Press was greatly assisted in the 19th cent. by the abolition of the "taxes on knowledge," by the introduction of the cheap postal system, and by improvements in printing, distribution, collection of news, and advertising. The *London Gazette*, founded in 1665 (and still appearing twice weekly as the official organ of the Government), is the oldest newspaper living. *The Times*, known throughout the world, began as the *London Universal Register* in 1785, and adopted its present title in 1788. The *Manchester Guardian* (renamed *Guardian* in 1959), once a provincial but now a national newspaper with a world-wide reputation, began as a weekly in 1821, and became a daily in 1855. The *Scotsman*, founded as a weekly in 1817 and established as a daily in 1855, and the *Glasgow Herald*, which began as the *Glasgow Advertiser* in 1783, are the leading Scottish newspapers. The London Press, which is national, publishes 11 daily, 2 evening, and 8 Sunday newspapers.

Newt, amphibians of lizard shape and mottled markings. There are three British species, the largest being the Great-Crested Newt (*Triturus cristatus*), which attains a length of 6 in.

Newton's Rings. Concentric circular rings, due to the phenomenon of interference, which are seen around the point of contact of a slightly convex lens with a flat plate of glass.

New Towns. The new towns in Britain established under the provisions of the New Towns Act 1946, are at Basildon, Bracknell, Crawley, Dawley, Harlow, Hatfield, Hemel Hempstead, Stevenage, Welwyn Garden City, Corby, Newton

Aycliffe, Peterlee, Skelmersdale, Runcorn, Redditch, and Washington in England; at Cwmbran in Wales; and at East Kilbride, Glenrothes, Cumbernauld, and Livingston in Scotland. In addition, a new town is to be built in the Leyland-Chorley area in Lancashire to take population from Manchester, in North Buckinghamshire, to provide housing for people from London, in mid-Wales, and at Irvine in Scotland. It is also proposed to expand Ipswich, Peterborough, and Northampton, and to provide large sites for housing in London. New cities for the Southampton–Portsmouth, Bletchley, and Newbury–Hungerford areas, as proposed in *The South East Study* (1964), to deal with the expected population increase over the next two decades are under review. It is also planned to create a new city in Northern Ireland and to expand a number of towns.

New Year's Day, Jan 1. The first New Year's festival of which we have record is that constituted by Numa 713 B.C., and dedicated to Janus.

Nibelungenlied, the German epic of the early 13th cent. comprising numerous mythical poems or sagas of which several English translations exist. Wagner's *Der Ring des Niebelungen* was based largely on Norse legends and on the Niebelungenlied.

Nicene Creed, a summary of the principles of Christian faith, first issued in 325 by the Council of Nicaea (summoned by the emperor Constantine the Great) for the purpose of thwarting the Arian heresy and asserting the godhead of Christ. Date of Easter fixed at Council of Nicaea.

Nickel, silver-coloured metal, symbol Ni, fairly soft though harder than iron. Chief source of the metal is the nickel sulphide in iron–copper pyrites deposits in Ontario. Chief uses are: in electroplating, in coins, as an element in alloy steels. A novel method of making pure nickel (by treating the metal with carbon monoxide and heating the resulting liquid, nickel carbonyl) was developed in 1890 by Mond. This discovery led to many technical advances in industrial chemistry, one of which is the production of catalysts for a variety of processes.

Nicolo, a large brass reed instrument, common in the 17th cent. but now superseded by the bassoon.

Niello Work was in considerable vogue in the Middle Ages, and is said to have suggested the idea of engraving upon copper. It was produced by rubbing a mixture of silver, lead, copper, sulphur, and borax into engravings on silver, and some highly decorative results were obtained.

Night-heron, a stocky, short-legged heron of black and white plumage, red eyes, and yellowish legs, crepuscular except in breeding season, and an occasional visitor to Britain.

Nightingale, a familiar singing bird which visits the southern counties of England every summer, and is sometimes found as far north as Yorkshire. It is a shy, brown bird, not often seen, but the song of the male, usually heard in the late evening or at early morn, is of remarkable sweetness and variety. After its wooing period is over its song ceases.

Night-jar, nocturnal, insectivorous bird, owl-like in appearance, with mottled brown plumage of "dead leaf" pattern, and a churring song. It is a common breeding visitor to the British Isles, Apr. to Sept., and lays its eggs on bare ground.

Niobium is a metal element, symbol Nb, related to vanadium. Technical development has been slow because of its rare occurrence, although niobium is now used in ferrous alloys to increase resistance to corrosion and produce steel which can be used at high temperatures.

Nitre *or* **Saltpetre**, is now mostly manufactured by the double decomposition of sodium nitrate and potassium chloride. Its chief use is the manufacture of gunpowder and fireworks. It has been manufactured in England since 1625.

Nitrogen, a non-combustible gaseous element, symbol N, devoid of taste or smell, and constituting nearly four-fifths of the atmospheric air. Nitrogen compounds are essential to plants and animals, and are used in fertilisers.

Nitro-Glycerine, an explosive yellow fluid produced by mixing small quantities of glycerine with a combination of one part of nitric acid and two parts of sulphuric acid. By itself it is a dangerously explosive substance to handle. In 1867, Nobel produced dynamite, a safe explosive made by absorbing nitro-glycerine in kieselguhr.

Nitrous Oxide, a compound of nitrogen and oxygen possessing mild anaesthetic power. Termed "laughing gas" on account of its exhilarating effect. It is still used in dentistry, and for minor operations and has proved useful in a new technique for finding leaks in water mains.

Nocturne, a short piece of music, romantic in character, generally for the pianoforte. The nocturne was invented by John Field, from whom Chopin borrowed the idea. After this the nocturne became popular all over Europe, being known in Italy as "notturno" and in Germany as "nacht-musik."

Nones were dates of the Roman calendar which fell on the 5th of each month, excepting Mar., May, July, and Oct., when they fell on the 7th.

Nonet, a musical composition for nine voices or instruments.

Non Nobis Domine! ("Not unto us, O Lord!"), a musical canon, sung as a grace at public feasts (traditionally attributed to Byrd).

Norman Architecture is English Romanesque (*q.v.*), which flourished from the time of the Norman Conquest and was gradually superseded through a transition period (*c.* 1175–1200) by the introduction of the pointed arch characteristic of the Early English (first Gothic style). Typical of Norman churches are the round arches, thick walls, massive cylindrical columns, with throughout the basic pattern of the square and the circle. Some churches (*e.g.*, the Temple church in London or the chapel at Ludlow Castle) are wholly circular. Roofs in the early days were flat and towers, usually placed at the "crossing," were square but occasionally round; the spires of all these towers have perished, but it seems likely that they were squat and pyramidal.

North-East Passage, from the North Atlantic to Bering Strait has been rapidly developed by the U.S.S.R. in recent years as a northern sea route to render accessible vast areas of northern Siberia. Attempts to find a north-east passage were made by Englishmen and Dutchmen in the 16th cent. but they were always defeated by the ice, for the sea is completely frozen for some 3,000 miles for 9 months of the year. A Swede succeeded in sailing from Europe to Japan via the Arctic in the late 19th cent. *See also* **Arctic Exploration.**

North-West Passage, from the Atlantic to the Pacific through the Arctic Seas, has been the dream of navigators for centuries. Attempts to find it were made in the 16th and early 17th cent. by John and Sebastian Cabot, Frobisher, Gilbert, Davis, Hudson, and Baffin. Two centuries later Ross, Parry, Franklin, and others made the attempt; but it was not until 1903–5 that Amundsen, discoverer of the South Pole, made the complete voyage. The American nuclear-powered submarine, *Nautilus*, opened up a new short sea route between the Atlantic and the Pacific when she made her epic voyage under the North Pole in Aug. 1958.

Notre Dame, the famous Paris cathedral, was founded in 1163, and is one of the finest specimens of Gothic architecture in Europe. The best descriptions of the buildings are to be found in Victor Hugo's "Hunchback of Notre Dame."

November, the 9th month of the year originally, but from *c.* 700 B.C., when Numa added Jan., and Feb., it became the 11th month.

Nuclear Energy. Atomic nuclei consist of protons and neutrons joined in various proportions (**F10**). The heaviest naturally occurring nucleus contains 238 particles (92 protons, 146 neutrons) and is uranium 238 (U^{238}); the lightest is hydrogen, which consists of 1 proton. Neutrons and protons attract one another by very strong forces which are not at all well understood; they are called *nuclear forces*. Consequently it requires energy to be supplied if a nucleus is to be pulled apart into its constituent particles. The energy is required to overcome the attractions of the nuclear forces. Conversely, when the particles rush together to form a nucleus, energy is released in the form of heat or radiation. The energy released when protons and neutrons coalesce to form a nucleus is called

Binding Energy. The binding energy of a nucleus divided by the number of particles involved is called the binding energy per particle, which we will call B. It is very difficult to overestimate the importance of B to the human race. B varies from nucleus to nucleus, and the exact form of its variation is only roughly understood at the present time. But the most significant thing is that B is greatest for elements of medium atomic weight and lowest at the heavy (uranium) and light (hydrogen) ends of the periodic table. This means that if middleweight nuclei can be formed either from heavy ones or from light ones, B increases and *energy is released in either case.*

Nuclear Fission. *See* **F12(1).**

Nuclear Fusion. If light nuclei are hurled at high speeds into intimate contact they sometimes coalesce and release binding energy (*see* **Nuclear Energy**). This has been studied in laboratories where powerful and energy-consuming machines accelerate small numbers of particles for purely experimental purposes. If useful amounts of energy are to be gained these fusion reactions will have to occur on a bigger scale in an apparatus from which the resulting heat can be extracted in a controlled way. The one "useful" fusion device so far made is the thermonuclear bomb ("H-bomb"). Thermonuclear is the important word. If a suitable gas can be raised to a very high temperature the nuclei are stripped of their electrons and all particles move with very high speeds. The gas is then called a plasma. High enough temperatures will make speeds great enough for fusion reactions to occur and nuclear energy to be released. This is a thermonuclear reaction. For example, in deuterium gas, at temperatures over a million degrees Centrigrade, the deuterium nuclei (*i.e.*, heavy hydrogen nuclei consisting of 1 proton joined to 1 neutron) interact to produce helium nuclei. To obtain a net gain in energy from this process, the temperature must be raised to about 300 million degrees C. and maintained long enough; otherwise the energy released is less than that required to heat the fuel and to make up for heat losses. Many attempts to study the staggering technical problems are being made. In the Harwell machine Zeta (1957) the deuterium gas was contained in a metal tube shaped like a tyre 3 metres across. The temperature was raised by passing a huge electric current (about 200,000 amps.) through the gas for a few thousandths of a second. Temperatures up to 5 million degrees were produced, and new apparatus has since stepped this up. Neutrons have been detected, but the original view that these were evidence of true thermonuclear reactions has not survived later studies. Fusion research is very active in Britain, the U.S.A. and Russia.

Nuclear Power Stations. The nine British nuclear power stations at Berkeley (1962), Bradwell (1962), Hinckley Point (1964), Hunterston (1964), Trawsfyndd (1964), Dungeness "A" (1965), Sizewell (1965), Oldbury (1965–6), and Wylfa, in Anglesey (1968–69) have all been developed from the classic Calder Hall type, burning natural uranium inserted in a graphite moderator and cooled by carbon dioxide gas. They are called Magnox stations because the fuel elements of natural uranium rods are encased in magnesium alloy cans. The second nuclear power programme announced for 1970–75, is to be based on the advanced gas-cooled reactor system; the first of the new stations will be Dungeness "B" (1969–70). The third programme which will begin by the end of the 1970s is expected to be based on the fast breeder reactor.

Nuclear Reactors are pieces of apparatus designed to permit nuclear chain reactions to occur under controlled conditions. (Uncontrolled chain reactions are dangerous, *e.g.*, atomic bombs.) The success of a reactor depends on the neutrons reaching the U^{235} nuclei to produce more fissions and not being wasted in irrelevant processes or simply escaping through the wall of the apparatus (neutrons are quite difficult to contain). The neutrons leaving the scene of fission are rapidly moving, and they stand more chance of causing another fission if they are slowed down. Consequently a material other than the uranium has to be present to facilitate this, and it is called a moderator. A useful moderator is pure graphite. Thus a reactor may consist of alternate blocks of uranium and graphite. If the reactor is too small so many neutrons escape that there are not enough to keep the chain reaction going. The reactor must therefore be greater than a certain *critical size.* In order to intensify or damp down the chain reaction, it is arranged for pieces of neutron-absorbing material, such as cadmium, to be inserted or withdrawn as required. While the chain reaction is proceeding countless numbers of fissions are occurring, each one liberating energy which turns into heat. The temperature therefore increases, and to prevent a catastrophic rise, cooling has to be provided. The reactor therefore has cooling pipes through which a fluid coolant is pumped. The coolant carries the heat away and, in a reactor designed to produce electrical power, the heat is taken to steam-raising boilers and the high-pressure steam is led to turbines which drive the electric generators. What has been briefly described is the type of reactor first used for serious power production at Calder Hall. This is a graphite-moderated, gas-cooled reactor using as fuel natural uranium (*i.e.*, fissile U^{235} greatly diluted with U^{238}). It is also possible to make reactors work without slowing the neutrons with a moderator; these are called *fast reactors.* The design of the prototype fast reactor (PFR) to be built at Dounreay in N. Scotland is based on experience gained with the Dounreay experimental fast breeder reactor which was the first in the world to produce electricity on a commercial scale (1962) and has achieved the highest power output of any of its type in the world. These fast reactors can produce new nuclear fuel in the course of their operation and therefore offer great economies. The British-designed advanced gas-cooled reactor (AGR) successfully developed at Windscale and chosen for the new Dungeness "B" nuclear power station, promises to produce electricity more cheaply than conventional sources. The Americans have had spectacular successes with their nuclear-powered submarines, proving that it is quite practicable to use reactors in propulsion plant. Their n.s. *Savannah*, a merchant ship of 21,000 tons, is the first nuclear cargo ship, and it raised and solved many new problems of marine engineering. But the question still remains, can a nuclear-powered merchant ship compete economically with one driven by conventional machinery?

Nucleic Acids. Living matter is built up of cells, each of which has a nucleus surrounded by cytoplasm. Cell nuclei are composed chiefly of substances called nucleoproteins, which consist of a protein attached to a nucleic acid (this original name is still used, although nucleic acids are found in the cytoplasm as well as the nucleus). Nucleic acids are complex organic structures made up of chains of compounds called nucleotides (**F20** (2). Nucleotide molecules have a sugar group attached to a nitrogenous base and a phosphate group. Only two sugar groups are found in the nucleotides, ribose, giving rise to ribonucleic acids (R.N.A.s, found mainly in the cytoplasm) and deoxyribose, which forms deoxyribonucleic acids (D.N.A.s, found mainly in cell nuclei). Seven different nitrogenous bases have been isolated, so that a number of different nucleotides are possible. A repeating, regular pattern of nucleotides is linked by the phosphate groups, forming nucleic acids. The functions of nucleic acids are of fundamental importance. They are concerned in the process of transmission of inherited qualities in reproduction and in building up body proteins. Lord Todd of Cambridge University was awarded the 1957 Nobel Prize in Chemistry for his work on the structures of nucleic acids; the 1962 Nobel Prize in Medicine (*see* **L126**) was awarded for the discovery of the molecular structure of D.N.A. *See* **F20** (2).

Nuncio, a permanent official representative of the Holy See at a foreign court. Nuncios were permanently established during the 16th cent.

Nuremberg Trial. On Nov. 21, 1945, an International Military Tribunal, consisting of one American, one British, one Russian, and one French member, began the trial of twenty-four

Nazi leaders. There were four counts: the conspiracy of Nazism; wars of aggression; war crimes; and crimes against humanity. Twelve were condemned to hanging of whom ten were hanged on Oct. 16, 1946. Goering committed suicide; Bormann has never been found; Papen, Schacht, and Fritsche were acquitted. The rest received varying terms of imprisonment.

Nuthatch, name of a number of tree-creeping birds, plump, with short tail, bluish-grey plumage, and black stripe under eye. Nest in holes and wedge nuts in bark of trees, hammering them to get a kernel. There are three European species, one, *Sitta europaea*, resident in England.

Nylon, a generic term for any long-chain synthetic polymeric amide which has recurring amide groups as an integral part of the main polymer chain, and which is capable of being formed into a filament in which the structural elements are orientated in the direction of the axis. The first nylon of commerical interest was made in 1935, and the world's first nylon factory—in the United States—began production in 1940.

O

Oak, a tree of the genus *Quercus*, including some 300 species distributed over the northern hemisphere and into the tropics. Two species are native to Britain, where the oak is the commonest tree (1 in 3)—*Q. petraea*, more common in the west and north on shallower, lighter soils, and *Q. robur*, more common in the south on deeper, heavier soils. Oak timber is much prized for its strength and durability, and from the time of the Spanish Armada to Nelson's day was in great demand for naval construction. It has always been used for building, flooring, furniture, and cabinet work. The oak is attacked by many insects, the round nut-like oak galls, or oak-apples, being produced by the sting of certain minute gall wasps.

"Oaks," a famous race for three-year-old fillies run at Epsom two days after the "Derby."

Obbligato, originally, as the name suggests, a part which must be played (= obligatory). Now, by a curious misuse of the word, a part which need not be played, *e.g.*, a "violin obbligato"—additional to the pianoforte accompaniment and may be omitted if desired.

Obelisk, a tapering monolithic column, square at the base and pyramidal at the top, regarded by the ancient Egyptians as a sacred stone and usually found at the entrance to the sun temples. Many were transported from Egypt and set up at various times: there is one in the Place de la Concorde in Paris, and one on the Thames Embankment in London—Cleopatra's Needle—originally erected at Heliopolis, centre of the sun-cult, by Tuthmosis III *c.* 1500 B.C.

Oboe, (old spelling: hautbois). A reed wood-wind instrument rather similar to the clarinet in appearance, but having a double reed. The tone of the oboe is more thin and penetrating than that of the clarinet. The tenor oboe is called the Cor Anglais, while the bass oboe is the Bassoon. There is also a "double-bass" oboe called the contra-bassoon.

Observatories existed in ancient Babylon and Egypt. They were erected on tombs and temples. The most famous observatory of Egypt was that of Alexandria, erected by Ptolemy Soter, 300 B.C. It was not until the 16th cent., however, that an observatory adequately equipped for astronomical investigations was built. This was at Cassel. Tycho Brahe's observatory at Uranienburg was erected in 1576. The Royal Observatory at Greenwich was completed in 1675. Mount Wilson Observatory in California has had a 100-in. reflector telescope working since 1917 but Mount Palomar Observatory, also in California, has a 200-in. reflector—the largest in the world, completed in 1949—which can reveal remote galaxies out to a limiting distance of 2,000 million light years. It is known as the *Hale* telescope in memory of Dr. George Ellery Hale, the founder of the Mount Wilson Observatory. A 98-in. telescope, the *Isaac Newton*, is being installed at the new Royal Greenwich Observatory at Herstmonceux Castle. A number of observatories are devoted to meteorological and geophysical work, the most important in the British Isles being those at Eskdalemuir (Dumfries), Kew, Lerwick, and Valencia (Eire). *See also* **Astronomy** *and* **Telescopes.**

Obsidian, a form of volcanic rock of vitreous structure, and usually a silicate of aluminium, lime, magnesium, etc. Produced when acid lavas are rapidly congealed, it is usually black and fractures like pitch.

Ocarina, a simple kind of musical instrument usually made of terra-cotta. The whistle mouthpiece is at right angles to the bulbous body, in which are a number of finger-holes. The tone resembles that of a mellow flageolet.

Occam's Razor. *See* **J32.**

Occultation, in astronomy, refers to the concealment of a celestial body by the passing before it of some other heavenly body. The most frequent occultation is the eclipse of a star or planet by the moon.

Ocean comprises the great body of water which covers five-eighths of the surface of the earth, and has an average depth of 2 miles. The principal oceans are the Pacific, Atlantic, Indian, and Arctic. *See* **F9.**

Ocean Currents are well-defined streams running over certain portions of the ocean and caused mainly by wind-friction, slope of the sea surface and differences in density of the water, all movements being influenced by the deflective forces due to the earth's rotation. The climatic importance of the great ocean currents is that they constitute one of the means whereby heat is transferred from lower to higher latitudes.

Ocelot, the most common wild cat of S. America. It is about 4 ft. in length, including tail, and of a grey or tawny colour and spotted. Closely related to the Leopard cats.

Octane Number, the index of the knock-rating of petrol. It is based on the arbitrary scale in which iso-octane (which does not cause "knocking") has a value of 100, and normal heptane (which is prone to "knocking") has a value of 0. A good fuel for modern cars must have an octane number greater than 80.

Octarch, the kings of the English heptarchy, Hengist (455) being the first, and Egbert (800) the last.

Octave, an interval of an eighth (*see* **Interval**). The interval between one note and the same note pitched higher. A pure note is an air vibration of fixed frequency. Middle C is thus 256 vibrations per second. The note an octave above middle C is exactly twice this frequency, *i.e.*, 512 vibrations per second.

Octet, a musical composition for eight voices or instruments.

October, the 10th month, but the 8th in the old Roman calendar. It was held sacred to Mars.

Octopus, a genus of marine molluscs with eight tentacles that bear suckers.

Odyssey, Homer's epic setting forth the incidents of the wanderings of Odysseus on his way back to Ithaca after the Siege of Troy. *See* **H23.**

Oecumenical Council, a general council of the Christian Church summoned when important questions of Church doctrine and policy are to be decided. The early councils were predominantly Greek and convoked by the emperor. Those summoned by the pope when they meet at the Lateran Palace in Rome are called Lateran Councils; others have met at Constance, Florence, Trent, and the Vatican. Their decisions are not binding on the rest of Christendom. Only 21 Oecumenical Councils have been held in the history of Christendom. The first was held at Nicaea in 325 when the mystery of the Trinity was defined. The 21st (known as the 2nd Vatican Council), convened by Pope John, opened in Oct. 1962 in St. Peter's Rome, and ended in Dec. 1965. Two of the principal themes were the reunion of all Christians with the Church of Rome and the Church's place in the modern world. At the last session of the Council the Pope announced his decision to establish for the first time an international synod of bishops in Rome for consultation and collaboration in the government of the Roman Church. This Senate of Bishops will provide the balancing factor alongside the Curia, which represents the Papacy and not the episcopasy.

Oeil-de-boeuf, meaning bull's eye, is the name of a small octagonal vestibule lighted by a small round window in the palace of Versailles. The term is used in architecture for a small round or oval window in friezes, roofs, or domes of buildings.

Oersted, a unit of magnetic-field intensity in the c.g.s. system.

Ohm's Law, propounded by G. S. Ohm in 1827, is expressed in the equation: electromotive force (in volts) = current (in amperes) × resistance (in ohms). The ohm is the unit of electrical resistance in the metre-kilogram-second system.

Olbers' Comet was discovered in 1815 by Olbers the German astronomer. Olbers also discovered the asteroids Pallas and Vesta (1802–07).

Old Red Sandstone, the continental rocks formed during the Devonian. *See* **F30**.

Olefines, a series of hydrocarbons, in which the hydrogen atoms are double the number of carbon. The first member of the series is ethylene.

Oleic Acid, an important fatty acid present in lard and olive- and cotton-seed oils. Used in soap-making. Olein is the ester formed by the reaction of oleic acid and glycerine.

Oléron Laws or Judgments, were a code of maritime laws, introduced into England in the reign of Richard I. in the 12th cent. Oléron is an island off the west coast of France, opposite the mouth of the Charente.

Olive. This small tree, whose fruit yields olive oil, is a native of the eastern Mediterranean countries, but has been introduced into cultivation elsewhere. Its oil is used for cooking, in packing sardines, and in soap making; the green unripe fruit is pickled for table olives.

Olympiads were periods of four years which elapsed between each celebration of the Olympic games, instituted in honour of Zeus by the Greeks, and held at Olympus in the Peloponnesus. These festivals included competitions in literature, art, drama, rhetoric, music, and gymnastics, and they were continued, with intervals, from 776 B.C. to A.D. 394. Athletic revivals have taken place at Athens 1896, Paris 1900, St. Louis 1904, London 1908, Stockholm 1912, Antwerp 1920, Paris 1924, Amsterdam 1928, Los Angeles 1932, Berlin 1936, London 1948, Helsinki 1952, Melbourne 1956, Rome 1960, Tokyo 1964, and it is planned to hold the 1968 Olympic Games in Mexico City. *See* **U36**.

Onyx or **Sardonyx**, a variety of chalcedony built up of different-coloured layers, which are parallel and straight (not curved as in agate).

Oolite, a geological term for the Jurassic oolitic limestones existing through a long stretch of country extending from Yorkshire to Dorsetshire. It abounds in fossils of molluscs and reptiles. The term "oolite" derives from the fact that these rocks are made of egg-shaped particles of calcium carbonate.

Opal, a mineral consisting of hydrous silica, occurring in numerous varieties and colours. Precious opal displays a beautiful internal opalescence, the result of the interference of light waves on the surfaces of layers differing in their water-content. Opal miners are called gougers. Chief source, the Andamooka and Coober Pedy fields of South Australia.

Opera derives, like drama, from the religious plays of mediaeval times. These plays were always accompanied by music, but, whereas drama has relegated music to the entr'acte, opera has developed it to the point of being the most important feature of the performance. The first true opera was produced at Florence in 1597. It was written by Rinuccini and composed mainly by Peri and called *La Dafne*. Rinuccini and Peri followed this in 1600 with *Euridice*—the earliest opera of which we have a complete record. The first opera house was opened in Venice by Caralli in 1637. Cardinal Mazarin tried to introduce Italian opera into France, bringing in Caralli in 1660, but the experiment was a failure. Native French opera began in 1672 under the patronage of Louis XIV. with Lulli's *Les Fêtes de l'Amour et de Bacchus*. In England musical plays were being performed at this time, but the first real opera was Purcell's *Dido and Aeneas* written in 1689. At this time Scarlatti was writing operas in Naples and shaping the Italian opera into the form in which we know it to-day. Handel produced nearly forty operas in thirty years, his first being *Rinaldo* at the Haymarket, London, in 1711. The comic opera seems to have originated in Naples. The first English comic opera, the *Beggar's Opera* by Gay, was given in London in 1727. Mozart, after producing his magnificent *Idomeneo* at the age of 25, wrote a succession of comic operas: *Seraglio* (1782), *Figaro* (1786), *Don Giovanni* (1788), *Cosi fan tutte* (1790). These laid the foundations for all future comic opera. *The Magic Flute* (1791) was the first of what might be called "opera for the people." Beethoven made a single excursion into opera: *Fidelio* (1805). Rossini is best known for *The Barber of Seville* (1816), a comic opera, although his reputation was made with a serious opera *Tancredi* (1813). The operas of Bellini are rarely performed outside Italy, but these had considerable influence on the work of Chopin and Liszt. Bellini's successor Donizetti is best known for his comic operas *Don Pasquale* and *L'Elisir d'Amore*. This period in French opera is best represented by Auber's *Fra Diavolo*. German opera, slow to take root, developed at this time through Weber and Meyerbeer to Wagner, whose first important opera, *Rienzi*, was performed in 1842. The complete *Ring* was first given at Bayreuth in 1876 and Wagner's last opera, *Parsifal*, in 1882. The most successful exponent of comic opera at this time was Offenbach, although Strauss in Vienna and Sullivan in England enjoyed considerable local success. Italian opera underwent a revival with the advent of Verdi. Of his earlier operas, *Rigoletto* (1851), *Il Trovatore* (1853) and *La Traviata* (1853) alone have retained their popularity. *Aïda* (1871) is a more mature work, while *Otello* (1887), and *Falstaff* (1839), for which Boito wrote the libretti, are works of high merit. Several French operas of this period retain their popularity: Gounod's *Faust* (1859), Bizet's *Carmen* (1875), Massenet's *Manon* (1884), Saint-Saëns *Samson et Dalila* (1877). In 1890 Mascagni achieved startling success with *Cavalleria Rusticana*. This was followed almost immediately by Leoncavallo's *I Pagliacci* and the two are now inseparable. Of the operas produced in the 20th cent., the most popular have been Puccini's *La Bohème* (1896), *Tosca* (1900), *Madame Butterfly* (1904), Richard Strauss's *Der Rosenkavalier* (1911) and Debussy's *Pelléas et Mélisande* (1902).

Ophicleide, a brass instrument invented in the 19th cent. Mendelssohn and Berlioz wrote scores for the ophicleide, but the instrument has fallen out of general use.

Opium was known to the ancients, and used by them as a medicine. It is obtained from the poppy (*papaver somniferum*), the unripe "head" or seed capsule of that flower yielding a juice which when dried becomes the opium of commerce. The poppy is cultivated in India, Persia, Turkey, Macedonia, and China for the sake of this juice, which yields various alkaloids, such as morphine, narcotine, codeine, etc. These days the drug is rarely used medicinally. *See also* **P22**(2).

Opossum, marsupial mammals found in the more southerly of the United States, South America, and Australasia. They are arboreal except for the water-oppossum, which eats fish.

Optics, the branch of physics which investigates the nature and properties of light and the phenomena of colour. Burning lenses were known to the ancient Greeks and Ptolomy wrote a treatise on optics A.D. 150. Lenses as visual aids were known in ancient China but eyeglasses were not in use until the 13th cent. Spectacles were in more general use after the invention of printing in the 15th cent. The camera obscura was invented in the 16th cent. and the telescope and microscope at the beginning of the 17th cent.

Opus, a term used in cataloguing a composer's works, *e.g.*, Opus 1, Opus 2, etc. If several pieces are included in a single opus they are listed as Opus 1, No. 1., etc.

Oracles were in ancient times supposed to be words spoken by the gods, and it was the custom on important occasions to consult them about the future. The Greeks had the Oracles of Zeus at Dodona, and Apollo at Delphi, while the Romans consulted the Oracles of Mars, Fortune, and others.

Orange, a fruit growing in most sub-tropical

climates and in universal demand. It is grown on an evergreen tree that attains a height of about 20 ft. at maturity.

Orang-utan, one of the largest of the anthropoid apes, found only in the swampy forests of Borneo and Sumatra. When full-grown it stands over 4 ft. in height and weighs about 150 lb.

Oratorio, a sacred work for solo voices, chorus, and orchestra. The word applies to a special composition and not to a musical setting for a normal part of the church service.

Orchestra, a group of instruments and instrumentalists whose playing is under the direction of a conductor. The composition of a typical symphony orchestra is as follows: STRINGS: 1st Violin (16), 2nd Violin (16), Viola (12), Violoncello (12), Double Bass (8). WOOD-WIND: Flute (3–4), Piccolo (1), Oboe (3), Cor Anglais (1), Bass Oboe (1), Clarinet (3), Bass Clarinet (1), Bassoon (3), Contra-bassoon (1). BRASS: Horn (6), Trumpet (5), Trombone (3–4), Tuba (2). PERCUSSION: Timpani (3–6), Side Drum (1), Bass Drum (1), Cymbals (1), Harp (2).

Orders in Council are issued by the sovereign on the advice of a few selected members of the Privy Council. They must not seriously alter the law of the land. Another class of Orders in Council are issued by authority of an Act of Parliament for the carrying out of its provisions.

Ordination, the ceremony of installing ministers or clergymen in clerical offices, has existed from the earliest times. In the Anglican and Roman Catholic Churches the rites of Ordination are performed by bishops; among Nonconformists the power of ordination rests with the governing bodies of the different Churches.

Organ is a musical wind instrument of ancient origin whose tones are produced by the vibrations of air in pipes of varying length. Basically, an organ consists of a number of pipes grouped in rows or ranks according to their special tone-character. The air is fed by bellows or, in modern organs, by a rotary fan, electrically driven. Each rank is controlled by a slider, and the knob that controls the slider is called a stop. The organist pulls out the stops to give the tones he wants, the other pipes being kept out of action by the slider. When a particular note on the keyboard is depressed the player may hear, by pulling out the appropriate stop, not only the normal pitch but the note in several octaves. A stop of which the notes are of normal pitch is called an 8-foot stop, a 16-foot stop would give an octave lower, a 4-foot stop an octave higher, and a 2-foot stop two octaves higher. The hand keyboard is called a manual, and the foot keyboard the pedal board. The basic tone of an organ is its diapason tone, and is normally of 8-foot length and pitch. Most large organs have four manual keyboards and one pedal board. The most important manual is the great organ which comprises the majority of basic stops. The next in importance is the swell organ, so called because the pipes are enclosed in a box fitted with movable shutters operated by a swell-pedal. The effect provides a controlled crescendo or diminuendo. The tone of a typical English swell has a reedy character. The third manual controls the choir organ—a collection of stops suitable for vocal accompaniment. The fourth manual controls the solo organ—a group of stops which, singly or in combination, may provide a solo melody which the remainder of the organ accompanies. The pedal keyboard controls most of the bass stops. In some very large organs there is a fifth manual controlling the echo organ. This is a small group of stops usually set high in the roof of the building to give the effect of distant music. Most church organs have two or three manuals. Modern cinema organs may have some normal stops but rely chiefly on a number of effects unknown to the straight organ.

Orguinette, a musical instrument composed of reeds which are played upon by a bellows. A strip of paper passes over the holes of the reeds, moved by a crank, and the paper is cut into holes to represent the required sounds. As the rollers turn the bellows the melody is "ground out."

Oriel Window is a window projected from the front of a building, rectangular, triangular, or pentagonal. The ordinary bay window and bow window are varieties of Oriel. When an Oriel window does not reach to the ground it usually rests upon moulded sills supported by corbels.

Oriflamme, the name of the original banner of the abbey of St. Denis, and adopted by Louis VI. as his standard. It remained the national emblem of France for three centuries. The flag was of red silk, the outer edge being cut in the form of flames.

Original Sin, according to Christian doctrine the corruption that is born with us, as a result of Adam's fall.

Orioles, brilliantly coloured birds, members of the passerine family *Oriolidae*, found in the tropical regions of Asia, Africa, and Australia. The golden oriole, perhaps the most beautiful of them all, with brilliant yellow plumage, black wings and tail, winters in Africa, visits England, and is known to have nested here.

Orion, a famous constellation of the heavens, comprising nearly a hundred stars, all visible to the naked eye. It contains three stars of the second magnitude in a line, and these are called "Orion's Belt."

Ormer, a shellfish (*Haliotis tuberculata*) which occurs in the Channel Islands and on parts of the French coast. It is considered a great delicacy.

Ornithology, the scientific study of birds.

Ornithorhynchus. *See* **Duck-bill.**

Orogeny, large-scale earth movements, including faulting and folding and sometimes igneous activity, which produce a linear belt of mountains, *e.g.*, the Alpine orogeny in Europe which produced the Alps.

Orphism. *See* **J33, H117–128.**

Orphrey, the name of an ornamental border of gold and silver embroidered on ecclesiastical vestments.

Orrery, an instrument used in the 18th and early 19th cent. which showed the motions of the planets round the sun and the satellites round their primaries. The first orrery made was named after Charles Boyle, Earl of Orrery.

Orthodox Eastern Church. *See* **J33.**

Orthoptera. The large order of insects including grasshoppers, crickets, locusts, mantises, stick insects, cockroaches, etc. These insects have biting mouth parts, and wings, if present, are in two pairs, the front pair being hardened to protect the membranous hind wings which are folded under the front ones when at rest.

Osborne House, near Cowes, in the Isle of Wight, Queen Victoria's favourite winter-residence, and where she died. It was given to the nation by Edward VII., and is now a convalescent home.

Osier, a species of willow growing in damp soils and yielding branches utilised in basket-making.

Osmium, a very hard, bluish-white metal, symbol Os, of the platinum group and one of the heaviest of known metals. It is obtained from certain sands of South America, California, Australia, and Russia. The alloy of osmium and iridium (osmiridium) provides long-wearing tips for gold fountain-pen nibs.

Osmosis, The process by which absorption of liquids through semi-permeable membranes takes place. A solution exerts osmotic pressure (O.P.) or suction in proportion to concentration but also depending on kind of dissolved substance. The roots of the higher plants are covered with fine root-hairs, within the cell-walls of which the sap is normally of a higher concentration than the dissolved matter in the surrounding soil. The root-hairs, therefore, draw into themselves these weaker salt-solutions. (The explanation of water and salt exchanges is complicated by the selective ability of some cells (*e.g.*, roots) to accept or reject particular dissolved substances along with the water. The absorption of salts by a plant is selective, each plant selecting through the semi-permeable membranes of its root-hairs those substances which are most suited to itself.)

Osprey (*Pandion haliaëtus*), a large and magnificent bird of prey, dark brown above and nearly white below. The head is whitish with a dark band from eye to nape. To the British Isles it is a rare passage migrant. In 1959, thanks to the energy and vigilance of the Royal Society for the Protection of Birds, a pair nested in a

Scots pine in Inverness-shire and reared three young. Since then more young ospreys have been safely fledged in this sanctuary. The food consists almost entirely of fish, which the bird seizes with its talons. The so-called osprey plumes do not come from this bird but from the egret.

Ostrich, the largest living bird, related to the rhea, emu, and extinct moa, now found only on the sandy plains of Africa and parts of S.W. Asia. The male has beautiful white plumes on wings and tail. The wings are useless in flight, but the birds have a fleetness of foot exceeding that of the swiftest horse. An ostrich's egg weighs 3 lb.

Otary, any seal which has external ears (as opposed to the *true seals* which lack them). The eared seals make up the family *Otariidae*, which includes the Sea-Lion and the Fur-seal of the N. Pacific.

Otter, an aquatic carnivorous mammal widely distributed over Europe, and at one time very common in England and Wales. Otter hunting, indeed, is still a country sport in some districts, and a breed of dogs called otter-hounds is kept for the purpose. The otter averages about 2 ft. in length, exclusive of tail, has web-feet, and is a very expert swimmer.

Ounce, a carnivorous member of the cat family, spotted like a leopard and having a long bushy tail. It is only found at high altitudes on the Himalayas, and is often called the "snow leopard."

Outcrop. Where a bed of rock appears at the surface of the ground, there is an outcrop of the particular rock. Outcrop coal is surface coal; the mining of such coal is called open-cast mining.

Overture, introductory piece to an opera or oratorio, often including the main themes to be elaborated later. Many so-called overtures have been composed as separate concert pieces.

Oviparous, a zoological term referring to animals which lay eggs to be hatched outside the body of the parent.

Ovipositor, the organ by means of which female insects lay their eggs.

Owls, nocturnal birds of prey, distributed over the greater part of the world. Their forward-looking eyes, embedded in rings of feathers, give them a characteristic "owl-like" appearance, and their plumage, usually a mottled blend of browns and greys, is so soft that their flight is almost noiseless. Owls live on small mammals, reptiles, birds, insects, and fish, and are very valuable birds to the farmer. British owls include the barn owl (screech owl), short-eared owl, long-eared owl, tawny owl, little owl.

Ox, the popular name of the mammals included in the genus *Bos*. They are hollow-horned ruminants and hoofed quadrupeds, and include the various classes of domestic cattle as well as the different wild species. The adult male is called a bull, the female a cow, and the young a calf. The best-known breeds of domesticated cattle are the Durham or Shorthorn, the Angus, the Jersey, Ayrshire, Suffolk, and Hereford.

Oxalic Acid, an organic acid obtained from numerous plants, such as sorrel and rhubarb, and produced artificially for commercial purposes from sawdust, treated with caustic potash or caustic soda. It combines with metals to form oxalates; used in the manufacture of ink.

Oxford Clay, a geological formation consisting of a bed of blue clay hundreds of feet thick, and forming the lower portion of the Upper Jurassic. It makes good bricks.

Oxford University. The early history of the university is obscure. There was a school at Oxford as early as 1115 and it is known that Robert Pullen, a theologian from Paris, lectured there in 1133. Allusions to Oxford as the most celebrated centre of learning in England occurred in a work of Gerald of Wales in 1184–5. The earliest colleges to be founded were University College (1249), Balliol (about 1263), Merton (1264). In 1571 the university was reorganised and granted a Charter of Incorporation by an Act of Elizabeth. Other colleges, halls, and societies with their dates of foundation are: All Souls (1438), Brasenose (1509), Christ Church (1546), Corpus Christi (1517), Exeter (1314), Hertford (1874), Jesus (1571), Keble (1868), Lincoln (1427), Magdalen (1458), New College (1379), Oriel (1326), Pembroke (1624), Queen's (1340), St. Edmund Hall (1270), St. John's (1555), Trinity (1554), Wadham (1612), Worcester (1714), St. Peter's (1929), St. Antony's (1950), St. Catherine's (1962), Campion Hall (1962), St. Benet's Hall (1964), Mansfield (1886), Regent's Park (1958), Greyfriars Hall (1953), Nuffield (1937), and Linacre House (1962). The women's colleges are:—Lady Margaret Hall (1878), Somerville (1879), St. Hugh's (1886), St. Hilda's (1893), St. Anne's (1952). Women were not admitted to degrees (though allowed to sit for examination) till 1920.

Oxygen is the most abundant of all terrestrial elements, symbol O. In combination, this gaseous element forms about 46% of the earth's crust; one-fifth of the atmosphere, eight-ninths by weight of all water. Joseph Priestley in 1774 was the first to separate it from red oxide of mercury. It is colourless, tasteless, and odourless, and forms the chief life-supporting element of animal and vegetable life.

Oyster, a bivalve mollusc, of the genus Ostrea, having very numerous species and abounding in nearly all seas. The shell is rough and irregular. Oysters are exceedingly prolific, spawning in May and June. In England and Scotland deep-sea oysters are not allowed to be sold between June 15 and Aug. 4, and other kinds between May 14 and Aug. 4. In Ireland, no oysters may be taken between May 1 and Sept. 1, except in certain waters. The Whitstable oyster beds have existed since pre-Roman times; "clocks" are dead oysters.

Oystercatcher, a wading bird with black-and-white plumage and long, orange bill, inhabiting estuaries and sea-shores. Feeds on mussels, shell fish, etc., but not oysters.

Ozone, a modified form of oxygen, containing three atoms of oxygen per molecule instead of two. It is prepared by passing oxygen through a silent electric discharge. When present in air to the extent of 1 part in 4 million parts of air it kills bacteria, and has been used for this purpose in ventilating systems, *e.g.*, that of underground railways. It is present in extremely small quantities in the lower atmosphere but is comparatively plentiful at heights of about 20 miles. The belief widely held that seaside air is particularly rich in ozone is untrue. As ozone absorbs ultra-violet light of certain wavelengths spectroscopic methods, involving the analysis of sunlight, are chiefly used in ozone determinations. *See also* **Atmosphere.**

P

Paca, a genus of large rodents found in Central and South America, and resembling the guinea-pig. It is of nocturnal habits, has a streaked and spotted fur, and lives on fruits and plants.

Pacific Ocean. The first European to recognise the Pacific as distinct from the Atlantic was the Spanish explorer, Vasco Nuñez de Balboa, who discovered its eastern shore from a peak in Panama in 1513. The first European to sail upon it was Magellan, who entered it by the strait that bears his name in 1520. Sir Francis Drake was the first Englishman to sail upon it in 1577. The world's greatest ocean depth (6,297 fathoms or just over 7 miles) was established by a British survey ship in 1962 in the Mindanao trench in the Philippine Sea.

Pagan, a person who does not worship God; a heathen. The word is derived from the Latin *paganus* (a countryman or uncultivated person). In the Middle Ages the term was used largely to describe Mohammedans (Moors, Saracens, etc.).

Pagoda, the name given in China, India, and other Asiatic countries to a high pyramidal tower, usually, but not necessarily, connected with a temple.

Palaeontology, the science which is devoted to the investigation of fossils: animal (palaeozoology) and plants (palaeobotany). By studying the markings and fossils of living things in the stratified rocks, palaeontologists have been able to establish with astonishing accuracy a record of the evolution of life through geological time. The geologist at the same time with the evidence of the fossils has been able to work out the order and the age of the rocks. *See also* **F29–31.**

Palaeotherium, a genus of extinct tapir-like animals of large size, discovered in the Paris basin and elsewhere, of the Upper Eocene Age.

Palatinate, a term formerly applied to two German electorates or provinces, the Upper and Lower Palatinates. They are now provinces of Bavaria.

Pale, the name given to the part of Ireland colonised by the English and comprising portions of the counties of Louth, Dublin, Meath, and Kildare. The Anglo-Saxon rulers were styled "Lords of the Pale."

Palimpsests are ancient MSS. or parchments which have been partly effaced and used for fresh writings. Many valuable MSS. were thus lost, but sometimes the second writing has been washed out, enabling the original writings to be deciphered. Among such restorations are a dialogue of Cicero's, a portion of a book of Livy, etc.

Palladium, a scarce metallic element, symbol Pd, similar to platinum, with which it is usually found. It is an expensive metal, with desirable properties as a catalyst in reactions involving hydrogen, since it has a remarkable capacity for absorbing this gas; for example, coal gas and air will inflame in the presence of palladium at room temperature. It forms a silver-white alloy with gold, and this is used in some kinds of jewellery. It is used in expensive watches to make non-magnetic springs.

Pallium, a vestmental ornamentation of white wool presented by the Pope to archbishops on their appointment, and the sign of Papal confirmation.

Palm, a large straight-trunked plant or tree common to tropical countries, and usually fruit-yielding, such as dates, coconuts, etc. Many commodities useful to man are obtained from plants of the Palm family (*Palmaceae*).

Palm Sunday, the Sunday before Easter, upon which occasion it is customary to carry palms to the churches in some countries, in commemoration of Christ's entry into Jerusalem for the Feast of the Passover, when the people went forth to greet Him with palm branches.

Panama Canal. In 1903 the United States signed a treaty with Panama (which had previously seceded from Colombia) which gave the United States rights in perpetuity over a ten-mile-wide strip of land extending across the isthmus for the purposes of building and running the canal. The canal connects the Atlantic and Pacific Oceans, is just over fifty miles long (with sea approaches), and the depth varies from 41 to 85 ft. It is constructed above sea-level, with locks, and has been available for commercial shipping since Aug. 3, 1914. Studies are in progress for the building of a new sea-level canal to replace the present one.

Panda, *or* **Cat-Bear,** is related to the Raccoon, Dogs and the Bear. There are two kinds, the Red or True Panda, resembling a large domestic cat, which lives in the eastern Himalayas and S.W. China, and the Giant Panda, which is more like a bear in appearance and inhabits the mountains of western China. Both frequent the dense bamboo forests of these regions.

Pangolin, the scientific name of the "scaly ant-eater," a member of the armadillo family, found in Africa and Southern Asia. It has an extensive tongue, covered with glutinous matter, which it uses in catching ants, its chief food. When once caught on the tongue, the insects cannot escape. When attacked the pangolin rolls itself into a ball, and its scales assume the form of sharp spikes. *See* **Anteater.**

Pantagruel, the leading character in one of the satires of Rabelais.

Pantheon, the famous temple in Rome, originally consecrated to the gods, built by Agrippa in 27 B.C. and rebuilt in the 2nd cent. by Hadrian. Its splendid dome and portico make it one of the most interesting architectural monuments of ancient days. Since the 7th cent. it has been used as a Christian church.

Panther, another name for the leopard, *Panthera pardus,* related to the lion, carnivorous, active climber, found in India, and other parts of Asia, also in Africa.

Papal Infallibility. *See* **J33.**

Paper has been known in one form or another from very early times. The papyrus reeds of the Nile swamps served the ancient Egyptians for sheets upon which to inscribe their records. The Chinese and Japanese, centuries later, were using something more akin to modern paper in substance, an Asiatic paper-mulberry, yielding a smooth fibrous material, being utilised. With the spread of learning in Western Europe the necessity of a readier medium made itself felt and paper began to be manufactured from pulped rags and other substances. The first known English paper-mill was Sele mill near Stevenage, built about 1490, which produced the paper for an edition of Chaucer in 1498. Other mills were set up under Elizabeth, using linen and cotton as raw material. Other papermaking staples were later introduced, such as surat, esparto grass, and wood-pulp. The chief raw material in the world paper industry is wood-pulp, the main exporters being the timber-growing countries of Canada, Sweden, and Finland. Canada is the world's chief producer of newsprint and supplies a large proportion of U.S. requirements.

Papier mâché means pulped-paper and is a composition of paper pulp and other substances, to which, when moulded into form, coatings of japan, with gilt and coloured inlayings, are added. Elegant and decorative objects are made of papier-mâché. A ceramic papier-mâché is very durable.

Papyrus, the earliest known paper made in Egypt at a very remote period from a large species of reed, *Cyperus papyrus.* This plant is to be found all over tropical Africa, especially in the "sudd" region of the White Nile.

Parachute, the umbrella-shaped safety device used in emergency by the crew and passengers of aircraft. The first parachute descent from a great height was made in 1797 by André Garnerin who dropped 3,000 ft. from a balloon. *See also* **Parachute Jumping, U24.**

Paraclete (the Holy Ghost, or Comforter), the name used in the English translations of St. John's Gospel, and adopted by Abelard to designate the convent in Champagne founded by him, and of which Héloïse became the abbess.

Paradise, a Persian word used by the translators of the Old Testament to designate the Garden of Eden, and since meaning any place of happiness.

Paraffin, a mixture of hydrocarbons of higher boiling point than petrol. Paraffin was first obtained by distillation of coal, the process being discovered about 1830. About 1848, Mr. James Young procured it from mineral oil, and Irish peat also yielded it. The main source of paraffin supply to-day is crude petroleum. It is largely used in the manufacture of candles, for waterproofing, and numerous other purposes.

Parakeets, various small parrots of vivid plumage native to Australia, Polynesia, Asia, and Africa. One of the loveliest of the parakeets is the budgerigar of Australia. *See* **Z21, 23.**

Parallax, the change in direction of a body caused by a change in position of the observer. If the parallax is measured (in degrees of angle) and the distance between the two observation points is known the distance of the observed body can be calculated. The distance of heavenly bodies has been found this way. The first stellar distances were so obtained in 1838 by Henderson, Struve, and Bessel. Stellar distances are so great that even when the two observations are made at opposite points of the earth's orbit round the sun the parallax is always less than 1·0″ of arc. *See* **Aberration.**

Parchment, made chiefly from the skins of animals, usually of goats and sheep, was employed in olden times before printing was invented and superseded papyrus as writing material. Vegetable parchment, invented by W. E. Gaine in 1853, though not equal in strength and durability to skin parchment, is about five times stronger than ordinary paper. Vellum is parchment made from the skins of young calves or lambs.

Paris University, of which the Sorbonne forms a part was founded in the 12th cent. and is one of the greatest educational institutions of Europe.

Parliament, is the name given to the supreme legislature of the United Kingdom. It consists of the Queen, the Lords spiritual and temporal, and the Commons. It meets in two houses: the House of Lords (the Upper or Second

Chamber) and the House of Commons. It derives from the Anglo-Saxon *Witans* (*see* **Witan**). The Statute of Westminster (1275) first uses " parlement " of the Great Council in England, which comes from the French word meaning discourse. *See* **Outline of Central Government, Section C,** *also* **D5.**

Parliamentary Correspondents sit in the Press Gallery of the House of Commons and describe its proceedings for newspapers either by impressions or a summary of the debate.

Parquetry, the name of a style of flooring consisting of small rectangular wooden blocks laid down according to geometrical pattern.

Parrot, the popular name of a widely distributed family of tropical birds, including the African grey parrot, the green parrot of South America —both familiar cage pets in this country—and the various parakeets, cockatoos, macaws, lories, etc. Many of these birds possess a remarkable gift of imitating sound, especially that of the human voice.

Parsec, unit of distance used by astronomers for expressing distances between stars; equivalent to about three and a quarter light-years.

Parthenogenesis. The development of animals from unfertilised eggs. The drones of the honey bee are parthenogenetic, and the phenomenon is also common among aphids.

Parthenon, the famous Temple of Athena on the Acropolis at Athens, was built under the rule of Pericles between 447 B.C. and 432 B.C. It was made wholly of marble without mortar. The famous sculptured friezes, known as the Elgin Marbles, are now in the British Museum.

Partridge, a well-known British game bird the shooting of which forms a considerable attraction to sportsmen in the season, which opens on Sept. 1. Two species are common in Britain.

Passeriformes, the order of perching birds which includes about half the known species.

Passport is an official document issued to a person by his own government, certifying to his citizenship and permitting him to travel abroad. Passports to British subjects are granted by the Foreign Office, authorise bearer to leave the country and guarantee him the state's protection. Fee £1 10*s*. Valid for 5 years. Renewable for a further period of 5 years for a fee of £1. A simplified form of travel document (British Visitors' Passport) was introduced in 1961 for British subjects wishing to pay short visits to certain foreign countries for a fee of 7*s*. 6*d*., valid for 12 months.

Paten, the dish used for holding the consecrated bread in the Eucharistic service.

Patricians, the aristocracy of ancient Rome.

Paul's Cathedral, St., is the third cathedral church to be built on the site. It was preceded by a Norman building which was practically destroyed by the Great Fire in 1666. This followed a Saxon church which was burnt in 1086. The present building was designed by Sir Christopher Wren. The foundation stone was laid in 1675 and the structure was completed in 1710. It cost a little under £748,000. Its central feature is the dome, crowned by its cupola and lantern with the golden ball and cross. It escaped serious damage during the air raids of the second world war, but many of the surrounding buildings were laid waste.

***pC* Value,** introduced by Dr. C. L. Whittles in 1935 as a measure of salinity of aqueous solutions (soil extract, irrigation water, etc.); defined as the negative logarithm of specific electrical conductivity in reciprocal ohms. Alone or joined with *pH* (below) is useful as an index of osmotic pressure (*see* **Osmosis**) and related hindrance to plant growth resulting from excess of fertiliser or soil salts. If manuring is balanced, growth is best about *pC* 3.3.

Peacock, a bird of large size and beautiful plumage, its characteristic feature being a tail of brilliant " eyed " feathers, which it can erect and spread out, the males possessing resplendent feathering to a much greater extent than the females. It is related to the pheasant; one species is found wild in the forests of India, and another inhabits Burma and the Malayan regions, in Africa there is the Congo Peacock.

Pean, a term in heraldry indicating one of the furs borne in coat armour, the ground of which is black, with ermine spots of gold.

Peanut, Ground Nut *or* **Monkey Nut.** A member of the pea family native to S. America, but now cultivated in many parts of the world. After pollination, the flower stalk bends down and buries the pod containing the peas (" nuts ") in the ground. The oil from these " nuts " can be used for margarine manufacture.

Pearl is produced by certain shelled molluscs, chiefly the oyster. The inner surface of the shells of the pearl oyster yield " mother-of-pearl," and distinct pearls are believed to be morbid secretions, caused by some external irritation. Many fine pearls are found in the actual body of the oyster. The Persian Gulf, Ceylon, the north-west coast of Western Australia, many Pacific islands, and the Gulf of Mexico are among the most productive pearl-fishing grounds. In ancient times Britain was renowned for its pearl fisheries, the pearls being obtained from a species of fresh-water mussel. Western Australia has produced a 40-grain pearl, the finest the world has seen. The largest pearl ever found was the " Beresford-Hope Pearl," which weighed 1,800 grains, over six times as much as the oyster that produced it.

Peat, decayed vegetable matter found mostly in marshy positions, and common in Ireland and Scotland. Peat is coal in its first stage of development; burnt for fuel in many cottage homes.

Peccary, a pig-like animal native to the Americas. There are two species: the collared peccary and the white-lipped peccary, the latter being a vicious and dangerous animal.

Pelican, a genus of bird with long depressed bill pouched underneath so that it can hold a number of fish in reserve for future consumption. It has immense wings and webbed feet.

Pemmican, venison or other meat, sliced, dried, pounded and made into cakes, used by explorers and others when out of reach of fresh meat.

Penguin, a genus of flightless, fish-eating sea-birds of the southern hemisphere. They are stout-bodied, short-necked, and of small, moderate, or large size. The Emperor and King Penguins make no nest but protect and incubate the single egg by carrying it in the down feathers between the feet and the body. Other species brood in the usual way and may lay as many as three eggs. Penguins use their flippers for swimming under water. All 16 species are bluish-grey or blackish above and white below. They are very sociable and breed in colonies.

Penicillin. An antibiotic drug produced by the mould *Penicillium notatum*, and discovered by Sir Alexander Fleming in 1928. It is one of the most effective chemotherapeutic agents known. The mould produces a number of penicillins, all of which are effective antibiotics. *See* **P4(2), 9(1).**

Peninsular War lasted from 1808 to 1814. Fought in Spain and Portugal (the Iberian peninsula) by the British, Spanish, and Portuguese forces, chiefly under Wellington, against the French. The latter were defeated.

Pentagon, government office in Washington (the largest in the world), housing many thousand of military and civilian workers in the War Department of the United States (Army, Navy and Air Force).

Pentateuch, the first five books of the Old Testament—Genesis, Exodus, Leviticus, Numbers and Deuteronomy.

Pentatonic Scale, the scale of five notes prevalent in Chinese, Japanese, Javanese, and some Negro music. Music based on the pentatonic scale is almost incomprehensible to an ear accustomed to the diatonic scale.

" Pepys Diary," by Samuel Pepys, was first published in 1825. The original MS. is deposited at Magdalene College, Cambridge. The " Diary " gives a picture of the social life of the period between Jan. 1, 1660, and May 31, 1669

Perch, a well-known family of fresh-water fish with dark striped sides. The common perch of British rivers and lakes falls an easy prey to the angler because of its voracity.

Percussion Instruments, a collective term covering the instruments of an orchestra that give forth sound when struck, *e.g.*, timpani, drums, cymbals, tambourine, triangle, glockenspiel. In some modern orchestral works the pianoforte is used as a percussion instrument instead of in its usual role as a solo instrument.

Perfumes are essences or odours obtained from

floral and other substances. The chief flower perfumes are those obtained from rose, jasmine, orange flower, violet, and acacia. Heliotrope perfume is largely obtained from vanilla and almonds. Among the aromatic herbs which yield attractive perfumes are the rosemary, thyme, geranium, lavender, etc., while orange peel, citron peel, musk, sandalwood, patchouli, and other vegetable products are largely drawn upon. In recent times chemistry has been called into play in aid of the perfumer, and many of the popular perfumes of to-day are chemically prepared in simulation of the scents of the flowers or other natural substances the names of which they bear. *See* **Musk Deer.**

Periclase, a mineral form of magnesium oxide.

Perigee. The moon or the sun is said to be in perigee when it is at its least distance from the earth. The opposite of apogee (which see).

Perihelion. That point in a planet's orbit when it is nearest to the sun. The opposite of aphelion.

Peripatus, an animal which stands as a link between the annelid worms and the arthropods. Wormlike with short unjointed legs it breathes by a system of air tubes like those in insects. Certain other points of internal structure point to a relationship with annelid worms. There are some fifty species, the best known being the S. African *Peripatus capensis.*

Perjury, the offence of giving false evidence. The ancient Romans threw the perjurer from the Tarpeian Rock, and after the Empire was Christianised, those who swore falsely upon the Gospel had their tongues cut out. The usual punishment in England from the 16th to the 19th cent. was the pillory, fine, and imprisonment.

Permian Formation, a group of rocks lying between the Trias and the Carboniferous strata. It has three subdivisions, Upper, Middle and Lower Permian. *See* **F30.**

Per Procurationem signature means that the subject of the correspondence has been put into the writer's care by his principal for him to use his personal judgment in the matter, and that he is authorised to sign on behalf of his principal. Normally contracted to *per pro* or *p.p.*

Peruke, the name given to the wigs worn by men in the latter half of the 18th cent. The custom of wearing wigs was gradually superseded by powdering the natural hair. Wigs are still worn by the Speaker of the House of Commons, judges, and barristers.

Petrel, the name given to a member of a large, widely-distributed family of sea-birds of great diversity of size and colouring and distinguished by tube-like external nostrils. They usually skim low over the waves, and some, for this reason, are known as shearwaters. The storm petrel or Mother Carey's chicken occasionally patters along the surface, and is often called Little Peter—a reference to St. Peter walking on the water. Except when breeding, petrels are always at sea. They mostly nest in holes and crevices on islands and lay one egg, which is invariably white. The storm petrel, Leach's petrel, Manx shearwater, and the fulmar petrel are resident in the British Isles. *See also* **Mutton Bird.**

Petroleum, a mineral oil composed of a very complex mixture of hydrocarbons, occurring naturally in the earth and recovered from wells drilled often to several thousands of feet. Rarely the oil is under high pressure due to natural gas (*q.v.*) and may reach the surface as a gusher. More commonly the oil has to be pumped to the surface. The composition of the crude oil varies according to source and may be divided roughly into two types: paraffinous and naphthenic. The crude oil is subjected to fractional distillation which separates out the various grades of petroleum with their different boiling points. "Cracking" converts, by heating under pressure, oils of high boiling point into more volatile oils suitable for petrol engines. A great industry has grown up around petroleum, and the by-products, which used to be regarded as waste, form the basis of the modern synthetic-chemical industry (rubber, plastics, etc.). Chief sources are: U.S.A., Middle East, Caribbean, U.S.S.R., and Eastern Europe. The oil is carried in pipelines sometimes for hundreds of miles from oilfield to port.

Pewter, alloy of tin and lead formerly much used for making household utensils and ornaments.

***pH* Value.** Introduced in 1909 by the Danish chemist Sørensen to indicate hydrogen-ion concentration on the basis of electrical conductivity and a view of ionisation since discarded; is now taken as a logarithmic scale of acidity or alkalinity of aqueous solutions: acidity 0–7, neutrality at 7·0, alkalinity 7–14. The *pH* of blood is about 7·6 (faintly alkaline).

Phalanger, pouched marsupial mammals. They are arboreal and superficially resemble squirrels. There are two genera of flying phalangers or flying squirrels, which have a remarkable membrane along each side of the body enabling the animals to glide through the air. The members of the phalanger family are confined to the Australasian and oriental regions.

Phalangid, a member, of the arachnid family Phalangida: popularly known as "harvesters."

Phalanx, a name applied by the ancient Greeks to a body of troops drawn up in close array, with overlapping shields, and eight, ten, or more rows deep. The Macedonians stood sixteen deep. A Greek phalanx consisted of 8,000 men.

Pharmacopoeia, an official publication containing information on the recognised drugs used in medicine. Each country has its own pharmacopoeia. The British Pharmacopoeia (B.P.) is published under the direction of the General Medical Council. The Pharmaceutical Society issues the British Pharmaceutical Codex (B.P.C.); there is also an International Pharmacopœia (2 vols.) which is issued by the World Health Organisation.

Pharos, the name of the first lighthouse, built by Ptolemy II. about 280 B.C., on the Isle of Pharos, at the entrance to the harbour of Alexandria. It was 600 ft. high, and one of the "seven wonders."

Pheasant, game birds related to the partridges, quails, peacocks, chickens, and turkeys, distinguished by their brilliant plumage and long tapering tail. First found by the Greeks in Georgia where the River Phasis flows through to the Black Sea.

Phillippics, the orations delivered by Demosthenes, 352–341 B.C., against Philip of Macedon—remarkable for their acrimonious invective. The word was also used for Cicero's speeches against Antony. In modern use, any impassioned invective.

Philosopher's Stone. *See* **Alchemy, J2.**

Phoenix, a fabled bird of Egyptian mythology.

Phosphorus is a non-metal element, symbol P. Most familiar as a waxy, yellow solid which is spontaneously inflammable in air. It has chemical similarities to arsenic, like which it is very poisonous. It was discovered by Brandt in urine in 1669. It is found in most animal and vegetable tissues. It is an essential element of all plants and of the bones of animals. In combination with various metals it forms different phosphates, which are largely utilised as manures. The chief commercial use of phosphorus is in the preparation of matches.

Photoelectric Cell, a device which gives a useful electrical response to light falling on it. There are several kinds depending on the different effects which light may have on a suitably chosen solid (usually a semiconductor), viz., the emission of electrons from the surface ("photo-emissive cell"); change in electrical resistance ("photoconducting cell"); generation of electric current from a specially designed sensitive structure ("barrier layer" or "photovoltaic cell", "solar battery"). Different cells respond differently to lights of various wavelength and must be chosen for each application. *See also* **Solar Battery.**

Photogrammetry, the science of measurement from photographs taken from an aircraft. Aerial photography has many uses and is of great value to military intelligence and for map-making.

Photosynthesis. *See* **F29(1).**

Phrenology. *See* **J34.**

Phylloxera, a genus of plant-lice related to the aphids, which attacks the grape vine. Many vineyards of France, in common with the rest of Europe, were replanted with native vines grafted on immune stocks from California in

1879 after being ravaged by the insect (which came from America). Curiously enough, the remedy also came from America, the vine stocks there being immune to *phylloxera*.

Piano-Accordion, a small, portable reed-organ whose melody is played by the right hand on a short piano-type keyboard. The left hand operates up to 120 stud-like bass keys, each of which produces a standard chord. The instrument is slung from a strap across the shoulders and wind for the reeds is provided by a central bellows operated by the movement of the left arm. The piano-accordion is an Italian development of the older accordion or concertina.

Pianoforte. Fundamentally a mechanical dulcimer whose hammers are operated from a keyboard, just as the harpsichord is a mechanical harp whose strings are plucked by quills operated from a keyboard. Historically, however, the pianoforte followed the harpsichord, on which it was regarded as an improvement. The name itself (piano-forte = soft-loud) was chosen to point out that the new instrument gave a much wider control of volume than did the harpsichord. The pianoforte first appeared in the 18th cent. and its invention is generally attributed to an Italian, Cristofori, who produced an instrument called the "piano e forte" in 1711. England first saw the pianoforte in the 1760s. Probably the most famous makers of pianofortes are Pleyel (France) and Blüthner and Bechstein (Germany). Good English pianos have been made by Broadwood, Collard, etc.

Piccolo, a small flute with a high, piercing note. When required, the piccolo is usually played by one of the flautists in an orchestra.

Picts, inhabitants of Scotland in pre-Roman times, are held by some historians to be a branch of the old Celtic race, by others to have been of Scythian origin. They occupied the Lowland portion of Scotland, and were subdued by the Scots in the 9th cent. Kenneth II, becoming king of the whole of Scotland.

Pike, a familiar fresh-water fish abundant in the temperate regions of both hemispheres. It forms good sport for the angler in rivers and lakes, and sometimes attains a weight of from 20 to 30 lb. It is extremely voracious, is covered with small scales, and has a ferocious-looking head

Pilchard, a fish of the herring family, but with smaller scales and more rounded body. It appears off the Cornish coasts in vast shoals every summer.

Pilgrimage, the undertaking of a journey to a distant place or shrine to satisfy a religious vow or secure spiritual benefit, was resorted to in early Christian times The first recorded pilgrimage is that of the Empress Helena to Jerusalem in 326. In the Middle Ages pilgrimages became common, and were undertaken by monarchs and people of rank in all Christian countries. Moslems have been making pilgrimages to Mecca since the death of the Prophet, such duty being enjoined by the Koran. Among the great centres of Christian pilgrimages are Jerusalem, Rome, the tomb of Becket at Canterbury, and the holy places of Lourdes and La Salette in France.

Pilgrim Fathers, the 101 English Puritans, who, after living some years in exile in Holland, to escape persecution in their own country, set sail for America in the *Mayflower*, Sept. 6, 1620, landing at Plymouth, Mass., Dec. 4. They founded the settlement of Plymouth, and are regarded as the pioneers of American colonisation although 13 years earlier a small Virginian colony had been established.

"Pilgrim's Progress," Bunyan's famous allegory, written in Bedford gaol. The first part was issued in 1678. It is the greatest work of its kind. *See* **M12 (1).**

Pillory, a wooden instrument of punishment in use in England until 1837. It consisted of a pair of movable boards with holes through which the culprit's head and hands were put, and was usually erected on a scaffold. While a person was undergoing this punishment the mob generally pelted him with stones and rubbish, sometimes to his serious injury. People convicted of forgery, perjury, or libel were often condemned to the pillory, but from 1816 to 1837 the only offence for which it could be inflicted was perjury.

Pine, a conifer of the genus *Pinus*, which flourishes all over the northern hemisphere and includes 80–90 species, which afford valuable timber and yield turpentine and tar. The Scots Pine, *Pinus silvestris*, with its blue-green, short needles, set in pairs, and its rosy-orange branches, is native to Britain, as it is to the whole of Europe. It provides the red and yellow deal in everyday use.

Pipa, a species of toad inhabiting Guiana, and not found elsewhere. It is of considerable size, and is remarkable for the fact that the female carries its eggs on its back until they are hatched, herself depositing them in that position. Generally known as the "Surinam toad."

Pitcairn Islanders were originally the mutineers of the *Bounty*. They took possession of the island in 1790, and it was not until 1814 that their whereabouts was ascertained, accidentally, by a passing ship. The mutineers, under their leader, Adams, had settled down to a communal existence, married Tahitian women, and increased so in numbers that in the course of years they were too many for the island to support, and in 1856 they were removed by the British Government to Norfolk Island. A small number returned to Pitcairn.

Pitchblende *or* **Uraninite**, a relatively scarce mineral. It is nearly all uranium oxide, but lead, thorium, etc., are also present. Pitchblende from Joachimstal in Czechoslovakia was the material in which radium was discovered by the Curies. Pitchblende also occurs in Saxony, Rumania, Norway, Cornwall, the Congo, and at Great Bear Lake in Canada.

Plague. *See* **Black Death.**

Plainsong, a style of musical composition sung in unison (all voices singing the same tune without harmony), familiar in the Western Church from very early times and still performed, principally in the Roman Catholic Church. Though restrained and contemplative in spirit, it is capable of expressing deep emotion.

Planetarium, a complex optical system which projects into the interior of a dome a replica of all the phenomena of the sky that can be seen by the naked eye, *e.g.*, sun, moon, planets, stars, comets, meteors, aurora, eclipses, and clouds. There is a planetarium in the Marylebone Road, London, and another (opened in 1966) at Armagh Observatory, N. Ireland.

Planets, the name give to such celestial bodies as revolve round the sun in elliptical orbits. The name was first used by the Greeks to indicate their difference from the fixed stars. There are nine planets, Mercury, Venus, Earth, Mars, Jupiter, Saturn, Uranus, Neptune, Pluto. Many important questions can be answered by means of probes sent to the neighbourhood of the planets. These include the measurement of the magnetic field, if any, of the planets, the study of their atmospheres, much of which can be done without actually penetrating to the surface. With instruments landed gently on the surface it will be possible to investigate surface conditions and composition by many methods. Even without a soft landing information on these questions can be obtained by photography and subsequent transmission of the picture back to earth by some form of television scanning. For example, the American Mars probe, *Mariner IV*, transmitted pictures of the Martian surface in 1965 when it was at its closest approach to the planet. *See* **F7.**

Plankton, a word which first came into biological use in 1886 to describe the usually microscopic plants and animals floating, swimming, and drifting in the surface waters of the sea. To be distinguished from *nekton* (swimming animals like fishes and squids) and *benthos* (plants and animals living on the sea bottom, like fixed algae, sponges, oysters, crabs, etc.). Of great economic importance, providing food for fish and whales.

Plantagenets, the kings who reigned in England between 1154 and 1485 and included the Houses of Lancaster and York. More correctly they are styled Angevins, from Anjou, of which Geoffrey, father of Henry II., was Count, and whose badge was a sprig of broom (*planta genista*).

Plasma Physics is the physics of wholly ionised gases, *i.e.*, gases in which the atoms initially present have lost practically the whole of the electrons that usually surround their nuclei, so that the gas consists of a mixture of two components, positively charged ions and negatively charged electrons. The problems to be solved in the controlled release of the energy of fusion reactions are problems in plasma physics. A new professorship of Theoretical Plasma Physics was established at Oxford in 1962 and research is carried out at the Culham Laboratory of the UKAEA. The physical properties of a *plasma* are very different from those of an un-ionised gas. In particular, a plasma has a high electrical conductivity and can carry large currents. *See also* **Nuclear Fusion.**

Plastics, a broad term covering those substances which become plastic when subjected to increased temperatures or pressures. The Plastics Industry is based on synthetic organic examples of this group. There are two classes of plastics: the *thermoplastic*, which become plastic every time they are heated (*e.g.* cellulosic plastics) and *thermosetting*, which undergo chemical change when heated, so that once set they cannot be rendered plastic again (*e.g.* Bakelite). Plastics are composed of long-chained molecules, *e.g.*, polyethylene.

Platinum, a metal element, symbol Pt. It is a scarce white metal generally allied with iridium, osmium, ruthenium, and palladium. It can only be melted in an oxyhydrogen or electric furnace, but can be rolled out into a film-like sheet, or drawn out to the finest wire; being resistant to acids it is termed a noble metal.

Platyhelminthes *or* **Flat-worms.** *See* **F22(2).**

Plebeians were the ordinary citizens of Rome as distinct from the patricians. There was a long struggle between the two orders for political equality.

Pleiades, famous cluster of stars in the constellation of Taurus. Of the seven principal stars in the group, one is rather faint, and many myths have sprung up about this "lost pleiad".

Pleistocene the geological period that succeeded the Pliocene. It is supposed to have begun more than half a million years ago. During the Pleistocene, also known as the *Great Ice Age*, there were four cold periods, when the ice sheets covered northern Europe and N. America, separated by warm periods when the glaciers drew back into the mountains. *See* **F30, 31.**

Pliocene, the geological period preceding the Pleistocene, and the last major division of the Tertiary strata. It began about fifteen million years ago. *See* **F30.**

Plough Monday, the first Monday after the Epiphany, when in olden times the rustic population returned to work after the Christmas festivities.

Plover, wading birds, widely distributed over marshy places of Europe. Several species occur in Britain, including the Golden-plover, which breeds on the moors of Devon, Somerset, Wales, N.E. Yorkshire, and Scotland, and the Ringed plover, Kentish plover, and Dotterel.

Pluto, the last planet to be discovered; existence established by C. W. Tombaugh at the Flagstaff Observatory in Arizona in Jan. 1930 from reckonings made by P. Lowell in 1914. It is the most distant of all the known planets; diameter about 3,650 miles. Mean distance from the sun estimated at 3,671 million miles.

Plutonium, a chemical element, symbol Pu, capable of nuclear fission in the same way as Uranium 235. Not until after it had been synthesised in atomic piles during the second world war was it shown to occur in infinitesimally small traces in nature. Its synthesis in the atomic pile depends on the capture by Uranium 238 nuclei of neutrons; immediate product of this reaction is the element neptunium, but this undergoes rapid radioactive disintegration to plutonium.

Poet Laureate is the poet attached to the royal household, an office officially established in 1668, though its origins go back to the early Middle Ages, when minstrels were employed at the courts of English kings. Chaucer, Skelton, and Spenser, though not court poets, were all unofficial poets laureate. Ben Jonson has been called the first "official laureate" (1616), but the office was not officially recognised until 1668, when Dryden was formally granted the office. It is customary for the poet laureate to write verse in celebration of events of national importance. John Masefield succeeded Robert Bridges as poet laureate in 1930.

Pogrom. Russian word meaning "destruction." First used to describe the Tsarist attacks on the Jews in 1881 in Russia. In 1938 Hitler ordered a general pogrom in Germany: all synagogues were destroyed and nearly all Jewish shops and homes, Jewish hospitals and children's homes suffered. During the subsequent war Jews of central Europe were systematically exterminated in cold blood by the Nazis.

Poitiers, Battle of, was fought on Sept. 19, 1356, during the Hundred Years' War, when Edward the Black Prince gained a complete victory over John, King of France, who was taken prisoner and brought to London.

Pole-Cat, an animal of a dark-brown colour, about 18 in. in length, exclusive of tail; the ears and face-markings are white or light brown. It is carnivorous and belongs to the weasel family. Like the skunk, it emits an offensive odour.

Pole-Star is of the second magnitude, and the last in the tail of the Little Bear constellation. Being near the North pole of the heavens—never more than about one degree from due north—it always remains visible in the Northern hemisphere; hence its use as a guide to seamen.

Police, a regular force established for the preservation of law and order and the prevention and detection of crime. The powers they have vary from country to country and with the type of government; the more civilised and democratic the state, the less police intervention. England, compared with countries abroad, was slow to develop a police force, and it was not until 1829 that Sir Robert Peel's Metropolitan Police Act established a regular force for the metropolis, later legislation establishing county and borough forces maintained by local police authorities throughout England and Wales. Up to that time police duties were discharged by individual constables and watchmen appointed by local areas in England and Wales. The existing organisation of police forces is complicated. There are at present 152 regular police forces in Great Britain: 121 in England and Wales, and 31 in Scotland. Those in England and Wales are:—

1. County forces, under a Joint Standing Committee (half the members from the county council and half Justices of the Peace).
2. Borough forces, under Watch Committees, elected by the borough councils.
3. Combined forces covering more than one county or borough, under a body representing the constituent areas.
4. The Metropolitan Police Force, covering a 15-miles radius from Charing Cross, under the control of the Home Secretary.
5. The City of London force, under a committee of the Common Council.

Before the 1966 General Election it was announced by the Labour Government that if re-elected it would deal with the problem of undermanned police forces and provide the police with the form of organisation and the most modern scientific equipment best suited to the battle against crime.

Pollution of the atmosphere is due chiefly to the incomplete combustion of fuels, especially coal, large particles of soot being deposited fairly quickly close to their place of origin and smaller particles (including smoke) remaining suspended in the air for a long time. Corrosion of exposed objects and damage to buildings result from the production of sulphuric acid. The introduction of more efficient furnaces, the washing of flue gases and the introduction of smokeless zones have assisted in the abatement of smoke and other forms of pollution. Estimation of polluting substances is carried out systematically in Great Britain by the Department of Scientific and Industrial Research, the dust and matter brought down with the rain being collected in large deposit gauges; automatic filters provide continuous records of the variation of the floating solid impurities; and apparatus is employed to measure the concentration of sulphur dioxide.

Nuclear tests add to the load of pollution in the atmosphere (*see* **Fall-out**). "Smog" (smoke-laden fog) which reduces visibility to zero and affects the respiratory organs, is liable to occur when the air near the earth is cooled below the dew-point temperature by radiation on a still, cloudless night when an accumulation of smoke over a large city cuts off daylight and produces gloom, and absence of wind or vertical currents prevents the lower layers of the air from getting away. Such conditions are associated with the smoke-laden atmosphere of large industrial towns during a winter anticyclone. During the great London smog of 1952 there were 2,000 deaths over and above those expected for the time of year. Since the Clean Air Act of 1956 the pall over London has been thinned by 37 per cent though the amount of sulphur dioxide has gone up slightly.

Polonium, a radioactive element, symbol Po, discovered by Madame Curie in 1898, and named after her native land of Poland.

Poltergeist. *See* **J35.**

Polymerisation is the linking together of small molecules to make a large long-chain molecule. The general name for polymers of ethylene is Polythene, a wax-like plastic solid which because of its special qualities is used in a variety of ways today.

Polytheism. *See* **God and Man, J18.**

Pomander, name of a small ball or box containing perfumes and spices, formerly carried suspended from the neck or girdle as a protection against infection so it was believed.

Pomology, the science of fruit-growing.

Pontifex, the title assigned in ancient Rome to members of the college of pontifices. "Pontifex maximus" was the official head of Roman religion. It was as "pontifex maximus" that Julius Caesar revised the calendar in 46 B.C., and when after the rise of Christianity the popes took over the title the revision of the calendar fell to them.

Pope, The, the head of the Roman Catholic Church, recognised by that Church as the lawful successor of St. Peter. He is elected by the body of Cardinals. Since 1870, when the King of Italy deposed the holder from temporal power, no pope had left the Vatican between appointment and death until 1929, when peace was made between the Church and State in Italy and compensation was paid to the Holy See for the loss of temporal power. Cardinal Montini, Archbishop of Milan, was elected Pope Paul VI in 1963 on the death of Pope John XXIII.

Porcelain. The word is thought to be derived from the Italian *porcellana*, indicating the texture of a piglet. The majority of porcelain made on the continent was of "hard-paste", or true porcelain, similar to that discovered by the Chinese as early as the T'ang Dynasty (A.D. 618–907). It was composed of *kaolin* (china-clay) and *petuntse* (china-stone) which when fired in a kiln at a temperature of *c.* 1300° C. became an extremely hard and translucent material. The recipe of "hard-paste" porcelain remained a secret of the Chinese until 1709, when it was re-discovered in Europe by Johann Böttger of the Meissen factory (popularly known as Dresden). Aided by disloyal Meissen workmen, factories were later established at Vienna, Venice and in many parts of Germany. Plymouth and Bristol were the only English factories to produce this type of porcelain, from 1768 to 1781. Elsewhere, both in England and France, the material manufactured was known as "soft-paste" or artificial porcelain which was made by blending varying white-firing clays with the ingredients of glass. The French factory of Sèvres began to make some hard-paste porcelain by 1768 and by the 19th cent. such porcelain was the only type being made throughout the whole of the continent. In England Josiah Spode is credited with the introduction of "bone-china" about 1794. This hybrid-paste was quickly adopted by many other factories and today remains the most popular type of English porcelain. *See* **Pottery and Porcelain Marks, N18–23.**

Porcupine, a rodent whose back is covered with long, sharp, black and white spikes, which form a powerful means of defence. There are two families of porcupines; one is confined to the Old World and the other contains the American porcupines.

Porphyry, a form of crystalline rock of many varieties that in ancient Egypt was quarried and used for the decorative portions of buildings and vessels. The term is applied generally to the eruptive rocks in which large well-formed crystals of one mineral are set in a matrix of other minerals.

Porpoise, a highly intelligent marine mammal of the dolphin and whale family, and a common inhabitant of northern seas. Porpoises travel in shoals, their progression being marked by constant leapings and plungings. Their average length is from 4 to 5 ft. There are several species, nearly all being confined to northern oceans.

Port, a special kind of red Portuguese wine, taking its name from Oporto. It was little known in England until the Methuen Treaty of 1703, when it was permitted to be imported at a low duty.

Portcullis, a strong, movable timber or iron grating let into the wall of the gateway to a feudal castle, and capable of being lowered or raised at will. It formed an effective protection against attack in the days before firearms.

Portland Cement is a mixture of about 20 parts of clay with 80 parts of chalk, specially prepared in kilns, and forming a substance which, after admixture with water, will set hard and solid.

Portland Vase, one of the most renowned specimens of Greek Art, long in the possession of the Portland family. In 1810 it was loaned to the British Museum. Here it was shattered in 1845 by a stone from a maniac's hand, but has been skilfully restored. It is said to have been found in the 17th cent. in an ancient tomb near Rome. It was purchased from the Barberini family in 1770 by Sir Wm. Hamilton, subsequently sold to the Duchess of Portland. The vase, which is actually a two-handled urn, stands about 10 ins. high, is of transparent dark blue glass, ornamented with figures in relief in white enamel. It was purchased by the British Museum in 1945.

Portreeve in olden times was an official appointed to superintend a port or harbour, and before the name of mayor was used the chief magistrate of London was styled the Portreeve.

Positivism. *See* **J35.**

Positron, the "positive electron," an atomic particle having the same mass but an electric charge equal but opposite to that of an electron. It was discovered in 1932. *See also* **F14.**

Post-Impressionism, a term introduced by Roger Fry to describe the exhibition of paintings sponsored by himself in London (1910–11) officially entitled "Manet and the Post-Impressionists." The exhibition included paintings by Manet, Cézanne, Gauguin, Van Gogh, Seurat, Signac, works by Matisse, Rouault, and the *Fauves* (*q.v.*), and sculpture by Maillol. In a second exhibition, held in 1912, Picasso and the Cubists were also represented. The term therefore refers to the movement in modern art which reacted against the transient naturalism of the Impressionists by concerning itself primarily with colour, form, and solidity. Most artists today would include Cézanne, Van Gogh, and Gauguin as the main Post-Impressionists and maintain that it prepared the way for Fauvism, Cubism, and Expressionism.

Potassium, a metal, symbol K (German *Kalium*). It is similar to sodium, like which it reacts violently with water. It was discovered by Sir Humphry Davy in 1807, and now generally obtained by the electrolysis of fused potassium hydroxide or chloride/fluoride mixture. Its principal minerals are carnallite and kainite, and it is relatively common in rocks, accounting for about 2½% of the earth's crust. An essential element for healthy plant growth; the ashes of plants are relatively rich in potassium.

Potsdam Agreement was signed by Truman, Stalin, and Attlee in Aug., 1945. By this Agreement a Council of Foreign Ministers was established, representing the five principal Powers: China, France, Soviet Russia, the United Kingdom, and United States of America, with the task of drawing up the peace treaties for submission to the United Nations. It laid down, *inter alia* that German militarism and Hitlerism should be destroyed; that industrial power should be so reduced that Germany would never again be in a position to wage aggressive war; that surplus equipment should be destroyed or transferred to replace wrecked plant in allied territories; that Germany should be treated as an economic whole; and that local self-government should be restored on democratic lines as rapidly as was consistent with military security. The Potsdam Agreement has become a dead letter by the creation of a Communist régime in the Russian zone of Germany.

Prado Gallery, the great public picture collection of Madrid, containing a superb collection of paintings by Velasquez, Murillo, Raphael, Titian, Dürer, Van Dyck, Rubens, Holbein, etc.

Pragmatism. *See* **J35.**

Prairie Dogs are common rodents in Western America and very like the marmot in general structure. They live in communities in burrows.

Prawns, crustaceans related to lobsters, shrimps, and cray fishes.

Prebendary, a clergyman who receives a prebend or stipend because of his special connection with a cathedral or cathedral church.

Prefect, chief magistrates in ancient Rome. The title is now applied to the chiefs of administration of the departments of France.

Prelude, a piece of music intended to precede another piece, *e.g.*, Prelude and Fugue. The name has been used by many composers (*e.g.*, J. S. Bach, Chopin) to describe short compositions for which no following piece was written.

Pre-Raphaelite Brotherhood was the name given to their school of thought by three British artists, Dante Gabriel Rossetti, J. E. Millais, and W. Holman Hunt, who in 1848 revolted against the academic art of their time and advocated a return to the style of the Italian painters prior to Raphael—the simple naturalism of the Primitives, such as Botticelli, Fra Angelico and Fillipo Lippi. Thus they avoided the use of heavy shadows and painted on a white ground in bright colours—a technique which aroused the ire of those used to the dark and murky canvases of the contempoary romantic artists. Although they held these principles in common the three members of the "P.R.B.", as it was popularly called, were really quite different in other respects. Thus Rossetti (who for some reason is always thought of as the typical Pre-Raphaelite) produced works of a highly romanticised mediaevalism which, apart from certain aspects of technique, bear not the slightest resemblance to the sentimental naturalism of Millais or the much more dramatic realism of Holman Hunt (*e.g.*, in *The Scapegoat*). The Brotherhood was later joined by a number of lesser artists, but its works are not commonly accepted with enthusiasm to-day when the general feeling is that they are sentimental and religiose rather than the product of deeply-felt emotions. Ruskin in his writings defended their work but the movement came to an end in 1853.

Presbyterianism. *See* **J35.**

Press-Gang, a body of sailors employed to impress men into naval service, frequently resorted to in England, especially during the war with France in the early 19th cent. Press gangs were not used after about 1850.

Primate. *See* **F24(1).**

Primitive Art. The word "primitive" has a number of different meanings: (1) the art of prehistoric communities (*e.g.*, the famous animal cave-drawings of the Aurignacians, *c.* 25,000 B.C., at Altamira in Spain); (2) the art of modern primitive communities (*e.g.*, Bushman rock-paintings); (3) child art; (4) peasant art which springs from a spontaneous desire to impart beauty to objects of daily use and shows a tendency towards abstraction. Peasant art has many features in common the world over, the woodcarving of the Norsemen being almost indistinguishable from that of the Maoris; (5) the modern school of primitive painting in which naïveté of presentation is either the aim of a highly sophisticated mind (*e.g.*, the self-taught French painter Le Douanier Rousseau (d. 1910)), or arises naturally from a simple one (the American "grandma" Moses (d. 1961) who began to paint in her seventies).

Printing by movable types was first used in Europe in 1454 by Johann Gutenberg, a citizen of Mainz. The invention is also claimed for Laurens Koster of Haarlem. It was introduced into England by Caxton, who set up a printing press in Westminster in 1476. Gothic characters were first used, being superseded by Roman letters in 1518. In 1798 Earl Stanhope replaced the wood printing press by one of iron. In 1814 Friedrich Koenig applied the principle of steam power to the press. Mr. John Walter, of *The Times* newspaper, was the first to use the steam press which printed 1,100 sheets per hour. Improvements were introduced by Applegath and Cowper in 1828 and great strides were made in 1858 when the Hoe machine, which turned out 20,000 impressions an hour, was put on the market. Then came the Walter press in 1866 which printed on continuous rolls of paper from curved stereotyped plates. Modern Hoe machines can print a 48-page paper at 28,000 copies an hour (max. speed 50,000). The Monotype machine casts single letters and the Linotype whole lines.

The Privy Council is the Queen's own Council, consisting of over 300 distinguished men drawn from all walks of life. Its function is to give private advice to the Queen. From it have sprung many organs of the constitution. For example, the Judiciary or courts of justice have grown from the Queen's Council sitting as a Court of Justice, and today the Judicial Committee of the Privy Council is a body of distinguished lawyers acting as a Court of Appeal from courts of the Commonwealth. Many of our Government Departments have grown from Committees of the Privy Council.

Productivity. Physical productivity is the output of products during a time unit, *e.g.*, so many products per man hour, or day, or year. Total productivity is the sum of all the units of product created during the given time. Labour productivity is the part of the total that is attributed to labour as a factor of production. Productivity of capital is the element attributed to capital as a factor. Productivity of land is the element attributed to the natural powers of the soil, as distinct from what is contributed by the application to it of capital or labour. The term productivity is also used to refer not to the quantity of output, but to its money value. There have been many attempts to compare the productivities of different economies—*e.g.*, Great Britain and the United States or advanced and underdeveloped countries.

Proteins are the main chemical substances of living matter: they are a part of every living cell and are found in all animals and plants. Proteins have many functions, and occur in structural matter such as bones, tendons, skin, hair, and hoof, and in some vitamins and hormones. Lean meat, fish, and eggs are almost entirely proteins. Their composition varies with the source, but all proteins are basically constructed of carbon, hydrogen, oxygen, and nitrogen, and some contain sulphur, phosphorus (nucleoproteins), and iron (haemoglobin). Proteins are built up of very long chains of amino-acids connected by amide linkages (the synthetic polymers such as "nylon" and casein plastics (from milk) are built up of the same linkages). Enzymes, which bring about chemical reactions in living cells, are proteins having specific properties. *See* **F21.**

Proton, a basic constituent of the atomic nucleus, positively charged, having a mass about 1836 times that of the electron. It is a positive hydrogen ion. *See* **F10(2), 14.**

Protoplasm. *See* **F20(1).**

Provost, a Scottish official similar in rank to an English mayor. The Provosts of Edinburgh, Glasgow, Aberdeen, Perth, and Dundee are styled Lords Provost. The title of provost is also given to the heads of various English colleges.

Prud'hommes (Prudent Men), **Councils of**, were French trade tribunals, of masters and workmen, formed to decide on disputes. Originally a mediaeval institution, they were revived by Napoleon in 1806, and were carried on by the Third Republic.

Psalms, Book of, for many years attributed to David, but present-day scholars are of opinion that the psalms were written by a series of authors at different times and for different purposes, and that few, if any, were written by David. The Holy Scriptures contain 150.

Psychic Research. *See* **J36.**

Psychology. *See* **Sections J and Q under appropriate headings.**

Ptarmigan, birds of the grouse family, one species of which occurs in Britain, inhabiting the Scottish Highlands. In the winter assumes a white plumage.

Ptomaines, amino acids produced during the putrefaction of proteins of animal origin. Not a cause of food poisoning, as was once generally supposed, which is almost invariably due to certain specific bacteria.

Publicans, under the Roman Empire, were people who farmed the public taxes. It is this class of officials that is alluded to in the "publicans and sinners" phrase in the New Testament.

Public Corporations. A method of operating large-scale industries transferred from private to public operation. Thus the Port of London Authority is an independent corporation governed by users of the port and representatives of municipal interests and labour. The Forestry Commission, the Electricity Authorities, the British Railways Board, the National Coal Board, the Gas Council, and the B.B.C. follow a varied pattern.

Public Schools. The Public Schools Act of 1864 named nine "public" schools: Eton, Harrow, Rugby, Winchester, Westminster, Shrewsbury, Charterhouse, St. Paul's, and Merchant Taylors. Today the term embraces many more, and can be applied to all those schools which are financed by bodies other than the State and whose headmasters belong to the Headmasters' Conference as distinct from the Headmasters' Association. There are about 200 such schools in Britain, including among others: Bedford Grammar School (founded 1552); King Edward's School, Birmingham (1552); Brighton College (1845); Charterhouse School, Godalming (1611); Cheltenham College (1841); Christ's Hospital, West Horsham (1552); City of London School (1442); Clifton College, Bristol (1862); Dulwich College (1619); Eton College (1440); Felsted School (1564); Haileybury College (1862); Harrow School (1571); Malvern College (1865); Manchester Grammar School (1515); Marlborough College (1843); Merchant Taylors' School (1561); Mill Hill School (1807); Oundle (1556); Radley (1847); Repton School, Derbyshire (1557); Rugby School (1567); St. Paul's School (1509); Sherborne School (1550); Shrewsbury School (1552); Stonyhurst College (1594); Tonbridge School (1553); Uppingham School (1584); Wellington College (1859); Westminster School (1339); Winchester College (1387); and Warwick (1545). Public schools for girls include: Christ's Hospital, Hertford (1552), Cheltenham Ladies College (founded by Miss Beale in 1853), North London Collegiate School (founded by Miss Buss in 1850), Roedean (1885), Wycombe Abbey (1896).

Puma, a carnivorous mammal of the cat family found in the New World from Canada to Patagonia.

Pyramids of Egypt, on the west bank of the Nile, are vast stone or brick-built structures with inner chambers and subterranean entrances, built by the Pharaohs as royal tombs and dating from about 3000 B.C. The most celebrated are at Giza built during the 4th dynasty. The largest, originally 481 ft. high, is called the Great Pyramid, one of the seven wonders of the world, built by the Pharaoh Khufu, better known as Cheops, and there he was buried. 100,000 men, according to Herodotus, being employed for 20 years upon it. Chephren, successor of Cheops, erected the second pyramid, and the third was built by Mycerinus, a son of Cheops. The pyramid at Meidum built by King Snefru, founder of the 4th dynasty, is the most imposing of all.

Pyrite, the brassy-yellow crystalline form of iron disulphide. It can often be seen in coal; known as "fool's gold".

Pythons, large snakes, non-poisonous, and destroying their prey by crushing it. Some species average 30 ft. in length, and prey upon deer and other small mammals. Found in Asia, Africa, and Australia. They lay eggs.

Q

Quadrant, an astronomical instrument for measuring altitudes, superseded for navigational purposes in modern times by the sextant. It consists of a graduated arc of 90° with a movable radius for measuring angles on it.

Quadrille, adapted from an old French country dance, became fashionable throughout Europe in the early part of the 19th cent., but seldom danced now.

Quai d'Orsay. An embankment in Paris where the French Foreign Office is situated.

Quail, an edible bird of the partridge family, of which only one species, the Common Quail, is found in England. It is not more than 8 in. long. It is found in most of the warmer regions of the world. In England and Wales the Quail is covered by the Wild Bird Protection Acts.

Quair, an old name for a pamphlet or little book.

Quantum Theory. *See* **F13(1).**

Quartering, in heraldry, is the disposition of various escutcheons or coats of arms in their proper "quarters" of the family shield, in such order as indicates the alliances with other families.

"Quarterly Review," the great Tory quarterly was started in 1809, in opposition to the *Edinburgh Review*, the Whig organ, est. in 1802.

Quartermaster, a military officer charged with the provisioning and superintendence of soldiers in camp or barracks, and holding the equivalent rank to a lieutenant. The Quartermaster-General is an officer who presides over the provisioning department of the whole army. A Quartermaster in the Navy is a petty officer responsible to the Officer of the Watch; at sea for the correct steering of the ship and in harbour for the running of the ship's routine.

Quartet, a musical composition for four voices or instruments. If for stringed instruments (*e.g.*, first and second violin, viola, violoncello) it is called a string quartet. If for three strings and another instrument it is called by the name of the fourth instrument, *e.g.*, piano quartet. The name is often misapplied to the musicians instead of to the music. Thus a four-piece string orchestra will be called a string quartet. This misuse is also found with quintet, sextet, etc.

Quarto, a sheet of paper folded twice to make four leaves, or eight pages; usually abbreviated to "4to."

Quartz is a common and usually colourless mineral, occurring both crystallised and massive. In the first form it is in hexagonal prisms, terminating in pyramids. When pure its specific gravity is 2·66. It is one of the constituents of granite, gneiss, etc. Among the quartz varieties are *rock crystal* (colourless), *smoky quartz* (yellow or brown), *amethyst* (purple), *rose quartz* (pink), and *milky quartz* (white). Quartz veins in metamorphic rocks may yield rich deposits of gold. Mining for gold in the rock is termed quartz-mining.

Quaternary Deposits *or* **Post-Tertiary,** are the latest stratified rocks of the earth's crust, and include the Pleistocene ("Great Ice Age") and recent systems.

Quaver, a note of music, equal to one-eighth of a semibreve and one-fourth of a minim.

Queen Anne's Bounty, established by Queen Anne in 1704 for the augmentation of the maintenance of the poor clergy. Since April 1, 1948, Queen Anne's Bounty and the Ecclesiastical Commissioners ceased to exist and became embodied in the Church Commissioners for England.

Queen's (or King's) Speech is the speech prepared by the Government in consultation with the Queen and delivered by Her Majesty in person or by her deputy, at the opening or closing of a Parliamentary session.

Quicksilver. *See* **Mercury.**

Quince, a well-known hardy orchard tree of the pear family, bearing fragrant, yellow, pear-shaped fruit, largely used for preserves. A mucilage is made from the seeds, which also possess medicinal virtues.

Quinine, a vegetable alkaloid obtained from the bark of several trees of the *Cinchona* genus. It is colourless and extremely bitter. The drug, sulphate of quinine, is one of the most valuable medicines, forming a powerful tonic. It is antiperiodic, antipyretic, and antineuralgic. In cases of malaria it is the most efficacious remedy of natural origin known.

Quintal metrique, a French weight of 100 kilogrammes, or 220 lb. avoirdupois.

Quintet, a musical composition for five voices or instruments. If all five instruments are strings the piece is a string quintet. A clarinet quintet, for example, is a piece scored for "four strings" and a clarinet.

Quirinal, one of the seven hills of Rome.

Quisling, term which came into use during the second world war to denote traitor, collaborator, or fifth-columnist. After Vidkun Quisling, who became head of the puppet government after the German invasion of Norway in 1940.

Quorum, the number of members of any body or company necessary to be present at any meeting or commission before business can be transacted. Forty form a quorum in the House of Commons.

Quo Warranto ("By what authority") a form of writ which has existed in England since 1278, and is a direction to the proper authorities to inquire into the circumstances under which any office or franchise is held.

R

Rabbi, a Jewish term applied to specially ordained officials who pronounce upon questions of legal form and ritual, and also generally accorded to any Jewish scholar of eminence.

Rabbit. *See* **Z17**.

Raccoon, plantigrade carnivorous mammals common to the American continent. There are several species. The common Raccoon (*Procyon lotor*) is about 2 ft. long, with a bushy ringed tail and sharp snout. Its skin is valuable.

Race. In the old text-books anthropologists were much concerned with the differences between the various races of Man: they described the Black Man (Negro), the Yellow Man (Mongol), the Red Man (American Indian), the Brown Man (Indian), and the White Man (European). Those who study Man from this point of view further subdivide each group into others. Thus White Man may be divided into Nordic, Alpine, and Mediterranean; Black Man into Hamitic, Bushman, and so on. Each of these groups tends to have physical traits which its members hold in common, although, of course, there are no *pure* racial types. All existing races have been fairly thoroughly mixed. What, in view of recent experience, is really important, is that races or even nations do not have psychological traits—at least not *innate* traits. Anthropology dismisses all theories of a superior race as unscientific: there is not the slightest evidence that one race differs in any way from another in its psychological potentialities. Jews, Irish, Scots, Italians do differ (so do the inhabitants of Edinburgh and London): but their differences are due to their situation and not to anything inborn. *See* **F35**(2).

Raceme, an inflorescence in which the main stem bears stalked flowers, *e.g.*, lupin, foxglove. The youngest flowers are at the tip of this axis.

Radar. The basic principle of radar is very similar to that of sight. We switch on a light in the dark, and we *see* an object because the light waves are reflected from it and return to our eye, which is able to detect them. Similarly, the radar station *sees* an object because the invisible radio waves sent out from the transmitter are reflected from it and return to the receiver, which is able to detect them.

The utilisation of radio waves for the detection of reflecting surfaces began with the classical experiment of Dr. (now Sir) Edward Appleton in 1925, which he conducted in order to demonstrate the existence of the Heaviside layer in the upper atmosphere. During the course of the last war developments took place which tremendously improved the methods and instruments used. As in the case of so many of the inventions primarily developed for the purpose of waging war, many useful applications have been found for radar in times of peace, and, in particular, it has proved of great service as an aid to aerial and marine navigation, and in meteorology and astronomy.

Radiation, energy emitted in the form of a beam of rays or waves, *e.g.*, acoustic (sound) radiation from a loudspeaker, radiant heat from a fire, β-radiation from a radioactive substance. The radiation of electromagnetic waves from a body depends on its temperature, the amount of energy radiated per second being proportional to the fourth power of the absolute temperature. The hotter the body, the shorter the wavelengths of the radiation; thus the colour of a glowing body depends on its temperature. Of paramount importance to us is radiation from the sun. Amongst other radiations, the sun sends ultra-violet, visible, and infra-red (heat) waves. The principal gases of the atmosphere are transparent to practically all of the solar and sky radiation and also that which the earth re-transmits to space. Carbon dioxide and water vapour, however, strongly absorb certain types, the latter, as clouds, playing an important rôle in regulating the temperature of the globe. The cooling of the ground on a clear night is a result of the outgoing long-wave radiation exceeding that coming down from the sky: at sunrise cooling ceases as the incoming radiation becomes sufficient to compensate for the loss of heat.

Radiation, Cosmic. *See* **F3**(2).

Radioactivity. *See* **F11**.

Radiosonde, a weather station in miniature carried aloft by a free balloon to heights normally in the neighbourhood of 10 miles. Signals representative of values of atmospheric pressure, temperature and humidity are transmitted simultaneously by radio to receiving apparatus on the ground. The position of the balloon at any instant can be determined by radar, enabling the speed and direction of the upper winds to be deduced.

Radium, a radioactive metal, symbol Ra, discovered by Marie and Pierre Curie in 1898. Atomic weight 226. The Radium Institute, founded and equipped by Lord Iveagh and Sir Ernest Cassel, was opened in 1911 for the treatment of patients and research into the effect of radium on the human system. Radiotherapy (use of X-rays from radium) is used in the treatment of cancer.

Radon, a radioactive gaseous element, symbol Rn, formed by radioactive decay of radium. Its discovery completed the series of elements known as the inert (or rare) gases.

Rail, a well-known genus of the *Rallidae* family, including the Water Rail, the Moorhen, Corncrake, and Coot, resident in the British Isles.

Rain. When moist air rises into lower temperatures and becomes saturated, condensation takes place on the numerous hygroscopic particles present in the atmosphere. If the temperature is above freezing a cloud of small droplets is formed, and as the air continues to rise they grow in size until the weight is great enough to make them fall to the earth as rain. The formation of large raindrops has been attributed to coagulation of smaller drops of different sizes, while another mechanism depends upon the presence in the cloud of ice crystals as well as water drops. In temperate latitudes snowflakes falling from the freezing level melt in the warmer air below, producing large raindrops which grow in their flight through the lower part of the cloud.

Rainbow, a beautiful colour effect visible to an observer with back to the sun and facing a rain shower, caused by the refraction and reflection of sunlight in minute water-droplets in the air. From high in the air it would be possible to see a rainbow as a complete circle, but from the ground the most that can be seen is a semicircle when the sun is just on the horizon; the higher the sun is, the smaller the arc of the rainbow. When conditions are suitable two bows are seen, the secondary with the colours of the spectrum reversed. The colours of the rainbow are seven: red, orange, yellow, green, blue, indigo, and violet—the colours of the spectrum. *See also* **Aurora**.

Raingauge, an instrument consisting of a deep metal funnel whose stem dips into a graduated glass jar from which the depth of the rain water collected can be read. Continuous records of rainfall are provided by self-registering instruments.

Rambouillet, a royal French château (14th cent., rebuilt 18th cent.), near Paris, and the official summer residence of the President of the French Republic. Also the name of the famous literary salon of the Marquise de Rambouillet (1588–1665).

Rampant, in heraldry, is a term applied to the figure of an animal with forelegs elevated, the dexter uppermost. When the animal is shown side-faced it is *rampant displayed*, when full-face, *rampant guardant*; when looking back, *rampant reguardant*; and when in sitting position *rampant sejant*.

Rape, a cruciferous plant yielding coleseed or rape-seed, extensively grown in all parts of Europe and India. Rape oil or colza is made from the seeds, and the leaves and refuse are used for sheep-food. Rape oil is a yellow, thick oil, of considerable commercial importance as a lubricant and for other purposes. It was at one time much used as an illuminant.

Rare Gases (also called **Inert Gases**). These are a group of elements which are chemically inert, comprising helium, neon, argon, krypton, xenon, and radon. Cavendish in 1785 noticed that there was in air some gas which was not oxygen, nitrogen, or carbon dioxide, but it was not until 1894 that the first of the rare gases was found by Rayleigh and Ramsay. This they called argon (inert). After the discovery of helium in 1895 Kayser, Rayleigh and Travers soon isolated the other gases except radon, which was later detected as a radioactive decay product of radium. Some of these inert gases are used to fill electric-light bulbs, and helium is used in balloons, since it is very light. That they are not completely inert has only recently been discovered, *e.g.*, one uranium-235 atom in 3,000 undergoing fission produces a krypton-85 atom, which has a half-life (*see* **F11**) of nine years. This gas is a radioactive waste product of nuclear fission and could, if not removed, consitute yet another radiation hazard.

Rat, a well-known order of rodent embracing many species. The *brown rat* appeared in Europe early in the 18th cent., coming from the East and entering by way of Russia; now it is widespread and met with in Britain and all parts of the Continent. The *black rat*, which was the common rat before the arrival of the brown species, is a smaller animal and now comparatively scarce. There are numerous other kinds, all of them gross feeders, and existing in such numbers in many places as to constitute a pest. *See* **Z13**.

Rationalism. *See* **J37**.

Rattlesnake, venomous snakes which obtain their name from the possession of a rattle in the end of their tail, consisting of horny pieces so arranged that when vibrated they make a rattling sound. They are only found in N. and S. America.

Raven, a black-plumaged bird of the crow family, with raucous voice and massive bill. Occurs in many parts of Europe, Asia, and America. Ravens are easily domesticated and form interesting pets. Dickens had one which he described in *Barnaby Rudge*.

Ray, fish with a very flat body and broad and fleshy pectoral fins, related to the sharks. There are about 140 species. In Britain they are generally called *skate*.

Razorbill, a sea-bird of the auk family, having a high, furrowed bill and black-and-white plumage. It inhabits rocky cliffs during the breeding season, and at other times is mostly out on the open sea.

Realism is a vague term. For its use in philosophy *see* **J38(1)**. As a movement in art it can be said to have started with Gustave Courbet in the mid-19th cent. in his revolt against the classicism of Ingres and the romanticism of Delacroix. He was a man of strong radical views, and like Zola, Balzac, and Flaubert in literature, turned to the actuality of everyday life, recording it with frankness and vigour. Some young English painters, notably Bratby, of the "kitchen sink" school, practise what some describe as social realism. In another sense, realism is an attitude concerned with interpreting the essential nature of the subject, revealing truths hidden by the accidentials of ordinary visual appearance. Thus form becomes more significant than content. Beginning with Cézanne and Van Gogh this trend passes on to Cubist and Abstract painting.

Recitative, a style of singing only slightly removed from ordinary speaking, used in the narrative portions of operas and oratorios. In older operas "recitativo secco" (dry recitative) was used, the voice being accompanied by the harpsichord alone. After Scarlatti the orchestra was used to give a more dramatic touch to the recitative, while Verdi introduced a type of recitative that was half-way to an aria.

Record Office, in Chancery Lane, London, the place where the Public Records of England are now preserved, including Domesday Book, the various Rolls of Charters, and important historical documents from a remote period.

Recusants, people who refused to attend the Anglican Church or to acknowledge the ecclesiastical supremacy of the Crown in the 16th and 17th cent.

Red Crag, the name given to a strata of gravel or sand, containing certain fossil mollusc deposits, found on the Suffolk and Norfolk coasts.

Red Cross. *See* **Geneva Convention**.

Rede Lecture, at Cambridge University, was instituted and endowed in 1524 by Sir Robert Rede, Chief Justice of Common Pleas. These lectures were superseded by an annual oration, which is usually given by an eminent scientist.

Red-Letter Day, a Church festival day indicated in the Prayer Book by red letters, now a popular term for any day of special significance.

Redstart, a small bird of the Thrush family of handsome plumage and striking song. Two species visit Great Britain; the Common Redstart, with bright chestnut rump and tail white forehead, and black cheeks, favours wooded country, and the Black Redstart, with black breast and throat, chestnut tail and white wing bars, prefers rocky ground or bombed buildings, and has recently begun to breed in S England.

Redwing, a bird of the Thrush family which finds its way to this country for the winter. Resembles the song thrush, but distinguished by smaller size, buffish-white eye-stripe, chestnut flanks and underwings. It has bred in Scotland and on Fair Isle.

Redwood *or* **Sequoia.** This genus of coniferous tree comprises two species of Redwoods occurring in N.W. America. Specimens of one species, the Giant Redwood, reach a height of over 300 ft and a thickness of 36 ft. The age of the largest, the General Sherman tree, is put at 3,500 years.

Reed, the sound-producing agent (of thin cane or metal) of many musical instruments. Reeds are described as *free* or *beating*, and the latter a single or *double*, *i.e.*, two reeds placed togethe which vibrate when wind is forced between Reed instruments include clarinet, harmonium bassoon, oboe, bagpipe, mouth organ.

Referendum and Initiative, two methods by whic the wishes of electors may be expressed with re gard to proposed legislation. It is developed t the highest extent in Switzerland. In a re ferendum some specific matter is referred to th electors. The Initiative is the means by whic electors can compel their representatives to con sider a specific issue. After consideration by th legislature it must then be submitted to th electorate for approval (*i.e.*, a referendum Gen. de Gaulle has made use of the referendu in seeking the consent of the French nation fo his policies. In a democracy a referendu should be preceded by a programme of educatio and public debate.

Reformation. *See* **J38, 25**.

Reform Bills. The principal Bills have bee passed for the reform of the Parliamenta franchise. The first was the great Reform B of 1832, introduced by Lord John Russell a enacted under the Whig administration of Lo Grey. In addition to a sweeping redistributi of seats, this Act greatly extended the franchi but still left many people without the right vote. The second Bill, passed in 1867, furth redistributed the seats and gave the vote workers in towns. A third Bill, passed in 18 under a Gladstone ministry, removed t distinction between borough and coun franchises, enfranchised agricultural worke and thus gave the vote to all men over Women had to wait until 1918 to get the vote the age of 30. The Representation of the People (Equal Franchise) Act, 1928, gave them the right to be registered as Parliamentary electors at the age of 21, thus making England into a true democracy. The Representation of the People Act, 1948, abolished the representation of the universities and the separate representation of the City of London and the business-premises vote.

Refraction. The change of direction which light rays and other rays undergo when passing from one medium to another. The phenomenon is due to the fact that in different media light (and other forms of radiation) has different speeds.

Refractory, a substance capable of standing high temperatures and therefore useful for making furnaces and allied apparatus. Some insulating refractories are fire-clay, alumina, porcelain, carborundum, graphite, and silica. Some refractory metals are platinum, molybdenum, tungsten, tantalum, and the alloys nichrome, chromel, alumel.

Reindeer, a genus of deer horned in both sexes, occurring only in northerly regions. It has an average height of 4 ft. 6 in., is very fleet of foot, and the Laplanders utilise it for draught purposes and for food.

Relativity. The laws of relativity have been substantially proved and have revolutionised our ideas as to the nature of space, time, matter, and energy and forced us to think along new lines. In 1949 a new theory by Einstein was announced which sets forth in a series of equations the laws governing both gravitation and electromagnetism, which is said to bridge the gap that separates the universe of the stars and galaxies and the universe of the atom. At present the one is explained by relativity, and the other rests on the quantum theory. *See* **F14.**

Relief in sculpture is of three kinds—high relief (*alto-relievo*), in which the figures stand out to the extent of one-half of their natural proportions, low-relief (*basso-relievo*) when the figures project but slightly; and middle-relief (*mezzo-relievo*), when the projection is intermediate.

Renaissance. *See* **J38.**

Reptilia, the class of vertebrate animals including tortoises, lizards, snakes, crocodiles. *See* **F23**(2).

Republican Party of the United States was born by the fusion in 1854 of the group who called themselves National Republicans, having split from the Democrats over tariffs in 1825, and the northern Democrats, both of them being opposed to slavery. It came to power on Abraham Lincoln becoming President in 1861 and remained in power (with the exception of four Administrations) until 1912. On coming to power in 1920 the Republicans withheld the U.S. ratification of the Treaty of Versailles, which had been negotiated by Woodrow Wilson. It was defeated in 1932 largely as a result of the economic depression. Once isolationist in foreign policy, the Party now advocates an active policy, especially in Asia. Except for the Eisenhower administration (1953–61), the Republican Party has not held power since 1933, Nixon narrowly failing to defeat Kennedy in 1960, and Goldwater being decisively beaten by Lyndon Johnson in 1964. The symbol of the party is an elephant.

Requiem. Properly a mass for the dead, the term is extended to cover musical settings by Palestrina, Mozart, Verdi, and others.

Reredos, the ornamental screen at the back of the altar or communion table. It is often of a highly decorative character and is an architectural feature in many churches in Spain. Other examples are to be found in the following cathedrals in England: Southwark, St. Albans, Winchester, Durham, and Liverpool.

Resins, natural resins are vegetable compounds largely employed in the industrial arts. They comprise india-rubber, amber, mastic, copal, etc. "Synthetic resins" is a term sometimes used as a synonym for "plastics."

Rest, a musical term denoting silence or cessation from playing for the period represented by the character of the rest, *e.g.*, minim, semibreve, quaver.

Reuter, an international news agency, organised since 1941 as a trust and owned by the newspapers of Britain, Australia, and New Zealand, founded by Baron J. de Reuter in 1849.

Rhapsody, an instrumental composition, not in symphonic form, which suggests that it was composed to express some powerful emotion or ecstasy. Liszt's "Hungarian Rhapsodies" are based on old folk tunes, while it is believed that Gershwin's "Rhapsody in Blue" is intended to express the mood of America at the time it was written.

Rhea, a large flightless bird, the "ostrich" of S. America, distinguished from the ostrich proper by smaller size, longer beak, larger wings, no tail and 3 toes instead of 2. There are 2 species.

Rhinoceros, a large hoofed quadruped, of which there are nine existing species native to the river and marsh regions of Africa, India, Borneo, and Java. It is remarkable for its thick hide and upturned snout, from which springs a long horn. The white rhinoceros, which is scarce, is the biggest species, attaining a length of 10–12 ft. and a height of from 5 to 6 ft.

Rhodium, a metallic element, symbol Rh, discovered by Wollaston in 1804. It is found in platinum ores in small amounts, generally less than 2 per cent. With platinum it gives a very hard and durable alloy. It is also used, instead of silver, in putting the reflecting layer on a mirror.

Rialto, a famous bridge that crosses the Grand Canal at Venice, and dates from 1591.

Ribbon Fish *or* **Oarfish,** a deep-sea fish, deriving its name from its ribbon-like shape. Though many feet in length, it is only an inch or two thick. The ribbon fish is rarely met with because of its habitat, and most of what is known about it has been learnt from specimens occasionally cast ashore during storms.

Riboflavin. Vitamin B_2, it is essential in the diet of man and many animals; its absence causes stunted growth and loss of energy. It is a nitrogenous base attached to a sugar group, found in milk, yeast, liver, and eggs, and it occurs in some enzymes and nucleic acids.

Rice, a grain-yielding grass, of which thousands of strains are known today, extensively cultivated in China, India, and certain parts of America, and forming the main food of the peoples of China, Japan, India, and the Malayan regions. Some 95 per cent. of the world's rice is produced and consumed in the Orient. The grain with the husk is known as "paddy." Arrack, an alcoholic liquor, is made from fermented rice seeds.

"Rights of Man," the title of the declaration of the French National Assembly in 1789, proclaiming that all men have equal rights. Also the title of a famous book by Tom Paine, justifying the Revolution.

Rime, a crystalline deposit of ice formed on objects exposed to wet fog at the same time as frost.

Rinderpest *or* **Cattle Plague,** is a highly contagious disease affecting cattle, sheep, and other ruminants. In Europe the disease has been eradicated, but it was formerly very widespread and caused great loss of life amongst cattle. The disease is caused by a filtrable virus, and is attended by fever and congestion of the mucous membranes.

Ring Dove *or* **Wood Pigeon,** a blue-grey bird, distinguished from other pigeons by larger size (16 in.), white wing-bar, glossy green-and-purple neck, and white half-collar. It is very common in Britain.

Rituale, the book of rites used in the Roman Catholic Church for the administration of certain sacraments and other church ceremonies. Like the Roman breviary, it dates in its present form from the Council of Trent.

RNA. (Ribonucleic Acid). *See* **Nucleic Acids.**

Roaring Forties, name applied to the prevailing westerly winds over the oceans in the temperate latitudes of the Southern Hemisphere.

Robin (or Redbreast). A small bird with olive-brown upper parts and orange-red forehead, throat, and breast, both sexes alike. The young are speckled, lacking the red breast. Its wide European distribution includes the British Isles, where it is the national bird. It also occurs in N. Africa and W. Asia. The nest is placed in a great variety of situations including holes in banks, trees, and walls; in sheds, amongst ivy, and sometimes in old tins. Nesting-boxes are readily adopted, but care should be taken to ensure that the entrance-hole is small enough to exclude starlings. Robins are pugnacious and defend their territories with vigour. Their attractive appearance, trustful disposition, engaging ways, and sweet song make them extremely popular. The name robin is also applied to a number of very different birds, one of which, the American Robin, occasionally wanders to Europe.

Rock Dove, the grey pigeon *Columba livia* of Europe and Asia, ancestor of the domestic pigeons as Darwin was the first to show.

Rockets for use in war were first studied by Sir William Congreve early in the 19th cent., and proved very destructive in siege operations. They were invented by the Chinese as long ago as the 11th cent. The Germans devised the huge V2 rocket, carrying a ton of explosive, which was used near the end of the war to bombard London. Rockets are propelled by the burning of fuel (*e.g.*, oxygen or nitric acid), the exhaust, being ejected at high velocity, thrusts the rocket forward. For the study of the properties of the atmosphere vertical sounding rockets are used. Rocket flight in outer space was first presented as practicable by the Russian rocket expert, K. E. Tsiolkovsky, in 1903. The provision of sufficient launching velocity involves the use of rocket motors with adequate thrust. To launch a satellite into an orbit circulating within a few hundred miles of the surface a velocity of 18,000 m.p.h. must be imparted. This may be done by using a multi-stage launching system. When the first-stage motor has burned out it drops off, so that, when the second-stage motor ignites, it does not have to support the weight of the first-stage, and so on. If the launching velocity is increased to 25,000 m.p.h. the vehicle will not return to the neighbourhood of the earth but pass out of the range of the earth's gravitational pull completely. Unless the launching velocity reaches 100,000 m.p.h. it will not escape from the sun and will become an artificial planet. *See also* **Space Research.**

Rococo, an architectural style which was, in effect, the final stage of **Baroque** (*q.v.*). The name first came into use about 1830 to describe the period 1720–70 and means "shell-shaped" (French *Rocaille*), since the shell was a favourite motif in Rococo ornamentation. About the beginning of the early 18th cent. the heavy older type of Baroque began to show even less restraint than had characterised it in the past; it became still less utilitarian, and showed a kind of playful lighthearted vitality which manifested itself in a wealth of ornamental invention. Baroque was flamboyant and robust, Rococo frivolous. In architecture Rococo is naturally found in those areas where the Baroque had flourished, *i.e.*, Munich, Prague, Vienna, and Dresden. In painting, the best expressions of Rococo are to be seen in the works of the French painters Watteau (d. 1721), Boucher (d. 1770), a favourite of Mme de Pompadour, and famous as a decorator of boudoirs, and Fragonard (d. 1806). (As in the case of Baroque, it was typical of Rococo that the sculpture, painting, and the decorative arts of a building all expressed the same spirit.)

Roe, popular name given to organs in fish which produce eggs and sperms. "Hard roe" is that of the female and consists of eggs; that of the male is the soft roe or milt.

Roebuck, a deer that was formerly common in the forests and parks of Britain, but is now only found at large in the northern parts of Scotland.

Roller, a tropical Old World bird of the *Coraciidae* family, related to the hoopoe, kingfisher and bee-eater, of strikingly brilliant blue, chestnut, greenish-blue plumage. There are fifteen species, one of which breeds in the far north and visits the British Isles on its migrations to and from its winter quarters in Africa.

Romanesque Architecture, prevailed throughout Europe from the mid-10th to the 13th cent., and implies an art which developed from that of the Romans. Notable in Romanesque style were the rounded arch and masonry vaulting. Romanesque led to the graceful and more complex Gothic (*q.v.*). The Italians never regarded Gothic highly and Romanesque churches, generally based on the basilican plan (oblong with double colonnades and a semi-circular apse at the end), continued to be built there until the beginning of the 15th cent. Some of the best examples can be seen at Pisa (11th cent.), Florence (San Miniato, 1013), Lucca (12th cent.), and Milan (the 12th cent. San Ambrogio, most famous of all). In Germany Romanesque architecture flourished longer than in France or England; the most famous churches are in the valley of the Rhine, at Cologne (completely destroyed during the second world war), Mainz and Speyer. In France Romanesque churches are found in Burgundy, Provence and Normandy. For English Romanesque *see* **Norman Architecture.**

Roman Roads, highways constructed by the Romans. They were of great durability. The best known British roads were Ermine Street (London, Lincoln, York), Fosse Way (Lincoln through Leicester, Cirencester, Bath, Exeter), Watling Street (London to Shropshire).

Romanticism, a term for a movement in the arts—whether in music, painting, sculpture or literature—which seeks to give expression to the artist's feelings about his subject rather than to be concerned with form or reality. The romantic view is that art is nature seen through a temperament; the realist view is that art is a slice of life. Just as Descartes (1596–1650) was the herald of the Age of Reason, so Jean Jacques Rousseau (1712–78) was the herald of the Age of Romance, the first to give it full expression. His influence cannot be overemphasised (*See* **J14**). In painting Delacroix (1798–1863) is the romantic artist par excellence with his uncontrolled expression of the passions and love of the exotic. In literature the Romantic movement reached its finest form in the works of Goethe, Schiller, and Heine; in the poetry of Byron, Keats, Wordsworth, Shelley and Blake; and in the writings of Victor Hugo. Since Romanticism is partly a matter of temperament in the artist just as Classicism is, it may be found at all times and places, although whether or not it becomes predominent depends on contemporary taste. Cubism, for example, with its attention to form is classical, whereas Surrealism with its attention to content is romantic.

Roman Walls were built as frontier barriers under the Emperors Hadrian (76–138) and Antoninus Pius (86–161). Hadrian's works, linking Wallsend-on-Tyne with Bowness-on-Solway, comprised a twenty-foot stone wall, ditches, turrets "milecastles," fortresses, and a double earther mound, or "Vallum." Impressive ruins are stil visible at Chesters and Housesteads. Antoninus Pius, Hadrian's successor, made a further advance, but the turf wall which he built betweer Forth and Clyde was soon abandoned. Septimius Severus (146–211) restored Hadrian's wall after the assassination of Commodus and the subsequent civil wars. It was finally abandoned between 380 and 390.

Rome, Treaty of, 1958. *See* **G35, C45.**

Rondo, a piece of music in which a principa theme is repeated several times with othe themes in between. In the typical Rondo c Beethoven (*e.g.*, third movement of Sonat Pathétique) the order is 1, 2, 1 — 3 — 1, 2, 1.

Rood Screen, an ornamental partition, separatin the choir from the nave in a church, and sup porting a crucifix or rood.

Rook, a member of the crow family, abounding i most parts of the British Isles and found i Europe, Asia, and N. Africa. It has been intrc duced into New Zealand. Rooks usually nes in colonies in tall trees. They are highly ir telligent birds, and their ways have long bee the subject of much careful study.

Rosary, a circular chain of beads, used by Catholic when reciting a particular form of sustaine prayer. Each bead represents an entire praye and the combined prayers constitute the Rosar

Roses, Wars of the (1455–85), between the riv houses of York and Lancaster, for the possessic of the English crown, began in the reign Henry VI. and ended with the death of Richar III. on Bosworth Field. The emblem or bad of the Lancastrians was the red rose and of th Yorkists the white rose. All rivalry betwee the Roses ended by the marriage of Henry VI the Lancastrian, with the Princess Elizabet daughter of Edward IV., the Yorkist.

Rosetta Stone, discovered in 1799 by the French Rosetta in Egypt, and deposited in the Britis Museum. It is a piece of black basalt about 3

long, and contains a decree of the Egyptian priests of Ptolemy V. Epiphanes (205–181 B.C.) in (1) hieroglyphics, (2) demotic, and (3) Greek characters. It was by means of the three different inscriptions on the same stone that hieroglyphic writing was first able to be deciphered.

Rotten Row, a corruption of *route de roi* (king's drive), the famous riding resort in Hyde Park.

Rouge et Noir, a well-known gambling card game played on a table divided into two sections and marked with two black and two red lozenges. Any number of players can take part, and the money is staked on the red or black spaces. The cards are dealt out, first to Noir, until the pips aggregate more than 30; then in like manner to the Rouge, and the packet coming nearest to 31 wins the stakes.

Roulette, a gambling game played on a table carrying a revolving wheel divided into 37 compartments. Each compartment bears a number, 0 (zero) and 1 to 36. The numbers are mixed and do not follow any particular order. Of these 37 numbers 18 are black and 18 are red, whereas zero is green. The players stake their money on any compartment, colour, or combination of numbers they please. The wheel is whirled round and a ball is set rolling in the opposite direction, dropping finally into one of the compartments, thus deciding the winning number and colour.

Round, a musical composition in several parts, taken up by each participator at a different point from the other, and effecting a harmonious combination throughout. A Catch is similar in form, but usually allied to humorous words.

Roundhead. In the reign of Charles I. and later, a Puritan or member of the Parliamentary party who wore his hair cut short. It was originally a term of derision applied by the Royalists, who usually wore ringlets.

Round Towers, high circular towers with conical roof and massive masonry walls, built during the early Middle Ages (*c.* 10th cent.) It is believed that they served as refugees and lookouts. These buildings are numerous in Ireland, and three remain in Scotland, including that at Brechin which is attached to the church.

Royal Academy of Arts was founded in London in 1768, under the patronage of George III. The early exhibitions of the Academy were held first in Pall Mall, and after in Somerset House, where the exhibitions continued to be held until 1836, when the National Gallery being built, the Academy moved its quarters to that building. In 1869 the present Royal Academy at Burlington House was opened. The Academy numbers 58 R.A.s and about 30 A.R.A.s. List of presidents: Sir Joshua Reynolds (1768), Benjamin West (1792), James Wyatt (1805), B. West (1806), Sir Thomas Lawrence (1820), Sir M. A. Shee (1830), Sir C. Eastlake (1850), Sir F. Grant (1866), Lord Leighton (1878), Sir J. E. Millais (1896), Sir E. J. Poynter (1896), Sir Aston Webb (1919), Sir F. Dicksee (1924), Sir William Llewellyn (1928), Sir E. Lutyens (1938), Sir A. J. Munnings (1944), Sir Gerald F. Kelly (1949), Sir A. E. Richardson (1954) and Sir Charles Wheeler (1956). The Academy holds an exhibition of pictures, statuary, and architectural designs every summer, to which non-members can, subject to selection, send their work.

Royal Hospital, Chelsea, built by Wren, was opened in 1694 as an institution for invalid soldiers.

Royal Institution, established 1799, and incorporated by Royal Charter in 1800 for "the promotion, extension, and diffusion of Science and of Useful Knowledge." It was in the building of the Institution that Faraday conducted his experiments. It supports four professors: natural philosophy, astronomy, chemistry, and physiology. Famous also for its Christmas lectures designed for a juvenile audience.

Royal Society was founded in 1660 and incorporated by Royal Charter in 1662, Viscount Brouncker being named the first president. Its *Philosophical Transactions* date from 1665. Among those who served as president of the Royal Society are Sir Christopher Wren, Pepys, Sir Isaac Newton, Sir Joseph Banks, Sir Humphry Davy, Prof. T. H. Huxley, Lord Rayleigh, Sir Archibald Geikie, Sir J. J. Thomson, O.M., Prof. Sir C. S. Sherrington, O.M., G.B.E., Lord Rutherford, O.M., Sir William Henry Bragg, O.M., Sir Henry Dale, O.M., Sir Robert Robinson, O.M., Lord Adrian, O.M., Sir Cyril Hinshelwood, O.M., Lord Florey, O.M., and Prof. P.M.S. Blackett (1966).

Rubber, produced from the juice of certain trees and shrubs of tropical countries, is in such extensive demand now for tyres and other purposes that rubber plantations have been established in almost every part of the world where rubber can be grown, particularly in Malaya and Indonesia. The best kinds come from the Amazon valley. In recent years great advances have been made in the production of synthetic rubber.

Rubicon, a small river falling into the Adriatic, and forming one of the Italian boundaries, the crossing of which anciently involved decisive action and constituted a declaration of war. Thus the phrase "crossing the Rubicon", denoting an act from which there is no withdrawal.

Rubidium, a metallic element, symbol Rb, most closely resembling potassium. It is silver-white and very soft, and was discovered in 1861 by Bunsen and Kirchoff, using the spectroscope. It is rare, occurring in small amounts in the mica called lepidolite and in potash salts of the Strassfurt deposits in Germany.

Rubrics are instructions in regard to the ceremonies of the Church, appearing in red in the Prayer Book.

Ruby is a deep red variety of Corundum (aluminium oxide); one of the most valued of precious stones. Burma yields some of the finest, and rubies of inferior colour are found in Siam, Ceylon, South Africa, and Brazil.

Rudd, a fresh-water fish of wide distribution, plentiful in the rivers of Britain, and found in most other parts of Europe, also in Asia Minor. It is of a reddish-gold colour, with a greenish-blue beard.

Ruff, a bird related to the common sandpiper, at one time common in the Fen districts. The males have a ruff of feathers round the neck in the breeding season. The female is the Reeve.

Ruffe *or* **Pope,** a small fresh-water fish common in most parts of central Europe, and similar in appearance to the ordinary perch. It is found in British rivers.

"Rule, Britannia!" the national sea-song of England, was written by James Thomson (1700–48), the author of the "Seasons," and set to music by Dr. Arne about 1740. The poet's words were "Britannia, rule the waves!" but it is usually rendered "Britannia rules the waves."

Rum, an ardent spirit distilled from molasses, and containing from 40 to 50 per cent. of alcohol. It is chiefly manufactured in the West Indies, and derives its special flavour from a volatile oil.

Ruminants, animals that chew the cud, being provided with a compartmented stomach, enabling them to swallow food, and later to bring it back to the mouth for mastication; *e.g.,* sheep, goats, oxen, etc. While in the rumen, or storage compartment, some digestion of food, especially cellulose, takes place by bacterial action.

Runcible spoon, a kind of fork used for pickles having three broad prongs. The word was used by Edward Lear about 1870 as a nonsense word and may be derived from *Rouncival* meaning large or huge from the bones said to have been dug up at *Roncesvalles* where Roland fell. Rouncival peas are the large peas called "marrowfats."

Runes, certain characters of an alphabet found in inscriptions in the Germanic languages, discovered cut upon stone monuments and implements found in many parts of Europe, including England. The runic alphabet originally had 24 letters. Scholars agree that some of the runes derive from Greek and others from Latin.

Rural Dean, an ecclesiastical officer whose chief duty is to assist the Bishop in the duties of his diocese.

Ruskin College, the first residential college for working people, founded at Oxford in 1899 by Mr. Walter Vrooman, an American.

Rusts, parasitic fungi, some common species of which have reddish spores which in a mass have a rusty appearance. A well-known species is the Wheat Rust (*Puccinia graminis*), which has an alternative host in the barberry.

Ruthenium, a greyish-white metallic element, symbol Ru, discovered by Claus in 1845. It is harder and more brittle than platinum, in whose ores it occurs.

Rutile, mineral titanium dioxide. It is found in many igneous rocks, and in gneisses and schists. Its commonest colour is reddish-brown.

S

Sabaoth, a Hebrew word, meaning an army or host, and applied sometimes to the Supreme Being, *e.g.*, " the Lord of Hosts " (Rom. ix. 29).

Sabbath, the Bible name for the seventh day of the week, designated as the day of rest in the fourth commandment. It corresponds with Saturday in the modern calendar. The Christian " Sunday " is the first day of the week. It is nowhere in Scripture called the Sabbath, though this name is sometimes erroneously applied to it.

Sabbatical Year was instituted by the Jews in ancient times for the purpose of giving the soil a rest from cultivation. This was every seventh year.

Sable, a furred mammal of the weasel family mainly inhabiting Siberia. It is bright brown in colour, and has a long, bushy tail. American sable is a marten.

Saccharin, a white crystalline solid manufactured from toluene, 550 times as sweet as cane sugar. It is used as a sweetening agent; as a substitute for sugar when sugar is forbidden, as in certain diseases, or when there is a shortage. It has no value as a food.

Sack, the white dry wines of Spain and Madeira, canary being the most popular.

Safety Lamp, as used in coal mines, was invented by Sir Humphry Davy in 1816. The flame is enclosed in a cage of fine-meshed wire which allows air to enter and promote burning, but conducts away the heat generated in combustion so that no product of combustion escapes at a temperature high enough to ignite explosive gases in the mine.

Sagittarius *or* **" the Archer,"** one of the celestial constellations situated between Cygnus and Aquila. Sagittarius is another of the zodiacal constellations of 69 stars, which ancient astronomers worked into the representation of an archer. It lies between Scorpio and Capricornus.

Sainfoin, a widely cultivated forage plant, especially adapted for sheep. It is of strong, leafy growth and bears bright red flowers. It belongs to the same family of flowering plants as peas and beans.

St. Elmo's Fire, a glowing brush-like discharge of electricity which takes place from sharp-pointed objects on mountains or the masts of ships exposed to the intense electric fields of thunder-clouds.

Salamanders are amphibia superficially resembling lizards, from which they differ in having a moist skin and no scales.

Salic Law was probably instituted in France in the 5th cent. for the purpose of excluding females from inheriting the Crown. The Bourbons introduced the same law into Spain, but this was abolished by decree in 1830 to enable Isabella II. to succeed.

Salicylic Acid can be obtained from the flowers of the meadow-sweet, and from oil of wintergreen, but is now usually prepared by the action of carbon dioxide on sodium phenate under pressure. The acid is then prepared from the sodium salicylate. It is used as an antiseptic and has been used as a food preservative. Aspirin is a derivative of salicylic acid.

Salmon, a familiar fish notable for its habit of ascending rivers from the sea in the autumn and there depositing its spawn, not returning to the sea until the early spring. The salmon fishing season varies from place to place.

Saltpetre. *See* **Nitre.**

Salvarsan, the organic arsenical compound arsphenamine, which Ehrlich discovered was able to kill inside the human body the spirochæte germ that causes syphilis. Also known as "606." It has been superseded by neosalvarsan.

Salvation Army. *See* **J39.**

Sanctuaries were places where offenders against the law were free from arrest, and previous to 1697, when sanctuaries were suppressed, several parts of London were treated as sanctuaries. The chief of these refuge localities was in Whitefriars. There were others in the Minories, Mitre Court, the Savoy, Westminster, and the Mint. Other sanctuaries were at Beverley and at St. Burian's in Cornwall.

Sanderling, small wading bird of sandpiper family; breeds in tundra regions of far north, and is seen on sandy beaches of Britain as a winter visitor. Conspicuous white wing stripe and, like Curlew, Sandpiper, Knot, Dunlin, and other members of sandpiper family, has marked change of plumage between winter and summer.

Sandpiper, small- to medium-sized wading birds of several species whose migratory powers are so great that they are found in most parts of the world. They include the Common Sandpiper, a bird about 7 in. long, greenish-brown head and back, white under-parts; beak long and slender. Other species met with in Britain are the Green, Purple, Wood, and Curlew-Sandpipers.

Sans-culottes (French = without knee breeches), a term applied by the French aristocrats to the revolutionary leaders during the French Revolution who wore long trousers instead of knee breeches.

Sanskrit is the language of ancient India, spoken by the Brahmins, and existing in early Oriental literature. It was the language of literature and government and is now confined to temples and places of learning. Its relationship to the modern Indian languages is rather like that of Latin and Greek to modern European languages.

Saponin. The term is a generic one applied to a range of organic compounds which produce frothy, soapy solutions. Saponins are extracted from the soapwort root, horse chestnut seeds, etc. Saponin is the basis of the " foam " used for fire fighting; it can be used like soap to make insecticides and fungicides adhere to the leaves of plants. Also used as detergents.

Sapphic Verse, a form of verse said to have been invented by Sappho, the lyric poetess of Lesbos, who flourished about 600 B.C.

Sapphire, a valuable deep blue variety of Corundum (aluminium oxide) found mostly in India, Ceylon, and Northern Italy. Synthetic sapphire is often used for gramophone styli.

Saprophytes. A term applied to plants which feed on dead organic matter. Many fungi are saprophytes.

Saracen, the name given in classic times to the Arab tribes of Syria and adjacent territories. In the Middle Ages the current designation among the Christians for their Muslim enemies.

Sarcophagus, the name given to a stone coffin, such as was used by the ancient Egyptians, Greeks, and Romans, for receiving the remains of their famous dead. These sarcophagi were often decorated with rich carvings and sculptures.

Sardonyx. *See* **Onyx.**

Sarrusophone, bears the same relation to the Oboe as the Saxophone does to the Clarinet (*i.e.*, it has a metal tube and a double-reed mouthpiece). The Contrabass Sarrusophone is sometimes used instead of the Double Bassoon.

Sassanides were a dynasty of Persian rulers descended from Artaxerxes from 226 to 652.

Satellites are small planets revolving round the larger ones. The moon is the earth's only satellite. Jupiter has twelve; Saturn, nine; Uranus, five; Mars, two; and Neptune, two. A number of artificial earth satellites have been launched by America and Russia since Oct. 1957.

Satin-Bird, one of the bower birds of Australia; the male is silky blue-back and the female greyish green. *See* **Bower bird.**

Satinwood, the timber of a tree plentiful in India and Ceylon, and valued for cabinet work. It is of fine grain and very hard. Varieties also exist in the West Indies, Florida, and Tasmania.

Satrap, the name given in ancient times to a Persian Governor of a Province.

Saturday, the seventh day of the week (the Jewish Sabbath), derived its name from Saturn, or as some hold, is called after the Saxon idol Saterne, which was worshipped on this day.

Saturn, a planet, the sixth from the sun, from which it is distant about 886 millions of miles and around which it makes a revolution in about twenty-nine and a half years. It is about 71,500 miles in mean diameter, or nine times a large as the earth, and rotates on its axis in ten and a quarter hours. It is surrounded by a series of rings composed of myriads of tiny satellites. It has nine small satellites. *See* **F7.**

Saturnalia, festivals held in ancient Rome in honour of the god Saturnus. They were made the scene of the most boisterous festivities, and were continued for several days at the end of December.

Sawfish, a large marine ray found in tropical America and Guinea, whose snout often attains the length of several feet, and is provided with saw-like teeth. This " saw " is swung from side to side among a shoal of fish which form the food of this ray.

Sawfly. These insects are considered to be the most primitive members of the order (*Hymenoptera*) to which the bees and wasps belong. In appearance they resemble somewhat the latter, but there is no waist separating thorax and abdomen. The ovipositor is never used as a sting; usually it is saw-like so that the female can use it to make incisions into tissues of plants where the eggs are laid. The larvae look like caterpillars of butterflies and moths. One of the commonest species occurs on gooseberry bushes.

Saxhorns, large brass instruments on the cornet model invented by Sax. They are much used in military and other brass bands. The Tuba is the Bass Saxhorn in E flat or F. The Euphonium is the Bass Saxhorn in B Flat. The Contrabass Saxhorn in B flat (*i.e.*, one octave lower than the Euphonium) is called the Bombardon, but this term may be applied to the E flat Tuba.

Saxons, a Teutonic race originally inhabiting what is now Holstein. By the 7th cent. they had, with the Angles and Jutes, conquered and colonised most of England.

Saxophone, a musical instrument best described as a metal clarinet with a wide, curved tube. It is rarely used in serious music but is an important component of dance bands and the like. It is also used in military bands.

Scale (Musical), the series of notes on which a musical composition is built. Most European music is constructed upon the Major and Minor Diatonic Scales (*q.v.*).

Scald, the name of the Norse poets, who were similar to the bards of Wales. They had to celebrate the achievements of their warriors and leaders.

Scallop, marine bivalve molluscs of the genus *Pecten*, which is widely distributed. The scalloped edge to the shell results from a pattern of radiating grooves. Related to the oyster.

Scandium, a metal element, symbol Sc. It was discovered in 1879 by Nilson, and occurs in small quantities in certain rarer minerals such as wolframite.

Scapular, a vestment hanging from the shoulder to the knees, worn by members of certain Roman Catholic orders. The name is also given to two small pieces of cloth worn over the shoulders by lay members of the Church in honour of the Virgin.

Scarabaeidae, a family of beetles (Scarabs) widely distributed through Africa and Asia and the inner parts of Europe. It is to this genus that the " Sacred Beetle " of the Egyptians belongs, and numerous representations of it are found on ancient monuments.

Sceptre, the staff or rod constituting the symbol of supreme authority. Tarquin, the elder, was the first Roman to assume the sceptre in 468 B.C. The French kings of the 5th cent. made a golden rod their sceptre.

Scherzo. The word signifies a *joke*. It is used to describe a piece of music in light or jocular vein. Beethoven used the Scherzo as a middle movement in a number of Symphonies and Sonatas, since when it has tended to displace the more formal minuet.

Schism, an ecclesiastical term for division in a church. The Great Schism was the separation of the Greek Church from the Latin, finally established in 1054. The Western Schism was the division in the Roman Catholic Church from 1378 to 1417, when there were two lines of popes, one at Rome and one at Avignon, which arose over the election of Urban VI. and Clement VII. to the papacy and was more a matter of persons and politics than a question of faith.

Schist, the geological name of certain metamorphic rocks composed for the most part of minerals with thin plate-like crystals (*e.g.*, mica) so that the layers of a schist are closely parallel. Quartz occurs in schists, and where it preponderates the term " quartz schist " is applied.

Schoolmen, the great scholastic philosophers of the Middle Ages who devoted themselves to the study and exposition of questions of religious inquiry, and attempted to reconcile the teaching of the Church with that of Aristotle. The chief Schoolmen were Archbishop Anselm, Albertus Magnus, Thomas Aquinas, Peter Lombard, Duns Scotus. *See also* **J39**(2).

Scorpion. The scorpions constitute an order of the arthropods. Distinctive features are the pair of powerful claws at the head and a " sting " at the tail, which curves over the back in attack or defence so that it points forwards. The poison injected by the sting is potent, causing instant death in spiders, centipedes, etc., and acute discomfort to humans. The idea that a cornered scorpion can sting itself to death is a myth; scorpions are immune to their own poison.

Scorpion Fly. The scorpion fly, of which there are less than 500 species, constitute a separate order of insects, the *Mecoptera*. They have 2 pairs of membranous wings, and gain their popular name because in some species the end of the abdomen is turned up, though it does not function as a sting.

Scree *or* **Talus,** the mass of loose, angular rock fragments which accumulate towards the bottom of hill-sides and mountain-sides. These fragments have been detached by weathering processes, in particular frost action.

Scyphozoa. *See* **Jelly Fish.**

Scythians, nomadic conquerors and skilled horsemen of ancient times (9th–3rd cent. B.C.) who inhabited much of Southern Europe and Asiatic Russia.

Sea Anemones *or* **Actinaria,** an order of marine animals of the cœlenterate class *Anthozia*. They form a large and varied group of about 1,100 species and occur in many beautiful colours, flower-like in form.

Sea Butterfly, marine molluscs which propel themselves by two " wings," or side expansions of the foot. They constitute the order called *Pteropoda*.

Sea Cow. *See* **Manatee.**

Sea Cucumbers *or* **Holothurians.** These animals constitute the class of echinoderms called *Holothuroidea*. They are elongated and worm-like, with a ring of about twenty tentacles round the mouth. There are about 500 species.

Sea Eagle, a genus of flesh-eating birds related to the true eagles, kites, and other birds of prey. Examples are the Bald Eagle, emblem of the U.S.A., White-tailed Eagle (Grey Sea Eagle), and Steller's Sea Eagle of the Pacific coast of Asia. Last known in Britain in 1911.

Sea Elephant *or* **Elephant Seal,** a curious genus of seal, the males of which possess a proboscis a foot or more in length that suggests an elephant's trunk. They are found on the coast of California and in certain parts of the Southern Ocean; their blubber has a commercial value.

Sea Gravimeter, a new instrument to determine the density of the earth's crust beneath the oceans of the world. Designed by Dr. A. Graf of Munich and Dr. J. Lamar Worzel of Columbia University, it can detect changes of one-millionth of the value of gravity at the earth's surface and is being used in the oceanographical research programme of the I.G.Y.

Sea Hare, a genus of molluscs (*Aplysia*), so-called because of resemblance to a crouching hare. The shell is thin curved plate largely sunk in the animal's body. They have four tentacles, occur in Britain in the laminaria or ribbon-wrack zone, and discharge a purple fluid when molested.

Sea Horse, a sea-fish (*Hippocampus*), very numerous in the tropics and comprising some twenty species. Their bodies are ringed and they have prehensile tails. Their heads are horse-shaped, and they swim in a vertical position.

Sea Lily. A class of echinoderms, the sea lilies may be roughly described as " stalked starfishes." There are about 400 living species, and several thousand extinct species are known. Otherwise called Crinoids.

Sea Mouse, a genus of marine worms called *Aphrodite*, oval in shape, 8 or 9 in. long, iridescent, covered with fine bristles.

Sea Squirts *or* **Tunicates**. These animals are placed in the sub-phylum called *Urochorda*; found growing in rounded, jelly-like masses on rocks near low-water level. They get their name through the water jets they discharge.

Sea Urchin, species forming the class *Echinoidae*. The body is globular and covered with spines which may be used for both defence and locomotion. The main organs of locomotion are, however, the tube feet, as in starfishes. Much has been learnt of recent years by marine biologists from experiments with the purple sea-urchin *Arbacia*.

Seasons comprise the four natural divisions of the year, and are due to the inclinations of the earth's axis to the plane of the elliptic. *See* Equinox, *also* **N24**.

Secondary Sexual Characters. Characters of animals which are distinctive of sex, but have no direct connection with the reproductive process. Examples are: the mane of the lion and the antlers of some deer.

Secretary Bird, so called because of the quill-like plumes about its ears, is a bird of prey related to the eagles and vultures; common in Africa, and of considerable service as an exterminator of snakes. It is a large bird about 4 ft. in height.

Sedimentary Rocks. *See* **F8**(2).

Seismology, the branch of geophysics devoted to the study of earthquakes and other earth movements. The instruments used for the registration of earth tremors are termed seismographs and consist in principle of a pendulum system, the supporting framework following the ground movement and the bob remaining at rest, thus setting up a relative movement between two parts. In order to record the displacements completely, at one station, three seismographs are necessary to show the two horizontal and the vertical components of the motion. Apart from detection and study of waves from earthquakes, sensitive seismographs are now widely used in geophysical prospecting, particularly in the search for possible oilfields.

Selenium, a non-metallic element, symbol Se, related to sulphur, it is a dark red colour, and solid, found associated with sulphur, iron, pyrites, etc., though only in small quantities. It is a semiconductor (**F18**) and its special electrical properties have led to its use in photo-electric cells and rectifiers. Selenium is widely used in the chemical industry as a catalyst (*q.v.*) in producing aromatic hydrocarbons from less useful hydrocarbons. Also used in making some types of glass.

Semi-Conductors. Many of the functions of thermionic valves are nowadays being performed by various types of semi-conductors, the increasing use of which promises to effect big changes in the design of radio receivers and other radio equipment. It is interesting to note that the crystal detector, which was in use for many years before the advent of the valve detector, was itself a particular example of the use of a semi-conducting device. During recent years the properties of certain crystalline materials have been more closely investigated, and as a result crystal diodes have been produced which possess several advantages over valves. But, more important, it was soon found that crystals, if built up or arranged in a suitable manner, could provide amplification, and thus could be used as amplifiers or as oscillators, in many instances in the place of valves. The crystal material used is principally germanium into which an impurity has been introduced, or sometimes silicon similarly treated. *See* **Microelectronics, Section F, Part IV**.

Semitic Languages are divided into two main sections; one including the Assyrian, Aramaic, Hebrew, and Phœnician groups; the other embracing the Arabic and the Ethiopian.

Semitone, the smallest interval in music—half a tone in the diatonic scale.

Senate, the higher governing Assembly of a Legislature. The word, applied primarily to the Roman council, is also used to denote the upper chamber in the legislatures of France, the United States, and other countries. In certain universities the governing body is also called the Senate.

Sensitive Plant. A species of Mimosa (*Mimosa pudica*), whose leaves are extremely sensitive to touch, shaking, and burning.

Sepia, the "ink" of the cuttlefish. *See* **Ink Sac**.

September, the ninth month of the year, and the seventh of the old Roman calendar; hence the name, from Septimus. The designation was several times changed by the Emperors, but none of the new names survived for long.

Septet, a musical composition for seven voices or instruments.

Septuagesima Sunday, the third Sunday before Lent.

Septuagint, the Greek translation of the Old Testament made by Alexandrian Jews between 250 B.C. and 100 B.C. from Hebrew texts now lost. There are many differences between the Septuagint and the Massoretic version (A.D. 900), and therefore it is of great value for textual criticism. The symbol for the Septuagint is LXX.

Serfs, the name given to the slaves formerly existing in Russia, who answered to the condition of the feudal "villeins" of England. They were attached to the soil and were transferred with it in all sales or leases. Serfdom existed in Prussia until 1807 and in Russia until 1861.

Serpentine, a mineral: chemically a hydrous silicate of magnesium. Green serpentine is used as an ornament stone. Fibrous serpentine is called asbestos.

Serval, a small carnivorous animal of the lynx order, with black spots on a tawny ground. It is numerous in Africa, preys upon the smaller animals of the deer family, and is sometimes styled the "Tiger Cat."

Settlement, Act of, passed in 1701, assigned the Crown to the House of Hanover in case of Anne's death without children. The decision represented the determination of the squires and the Anglican Church never again to trust themselves to a Roman Catholic king.

Seven Champions of Christendom, as set forth in mediæval literature, were St. George of England, St. Andrew of Scotland, St. Patrick of Ireland, St. David of Wales, St. James of Spain, St. Denis of France, and St. Anthony of Italy.

Seven Churches of Asia, referred to in the Revelation of St. John, were those of Ephesus, founded by St. Paul in 57, Smyrna, Pergamos, Thyatira, Sardis, Philadelphia (Lydia), and Laodicea (Phrygia), all in W. Asia Minor.

Seven Wonders of the World were: 1, the Pyramids of Egypt; 2, the tomb of Mausolus, King of Caria (hence the word mausoleum); 3, the Temple of Diana at Ephesus; 4, the Walls and Hanging Gardens of Babylon; 5, the Colossus at Rhodes; 6, the Ivory and Gold Statue of Jupiter Olympus; and 7, the Pharos, or Watch Tower, built at Alexandria by Ptolemy Philadelphus, King of Egypt.

Seven Years' War was waged by Frederick the Great and England against Austria, France, and Russia, from 1756 to 1763. It resulted in the secession of Silesia to Prussia, of Canada to England, and in the strengthening of our Indian Empire.

Sexagesima Sunday is the 2nd Sunday before Lent.

Sextant, an instrument which has superseded the quadrant as a measurer of angles between distant objects. It is of special importance in navigation and surveying, and contains 60 degrees described on a graduated arc. A small telescope is attached and there are also a couple of mirrors which reflect the distant objects so as to enable them to be accurately observed. The invention is attributed to John Hadley, and to Thomas Godfrey independently, about 1730.

Sextet, a musical composition for six voices or instruments.

Shad, a marine fish belonging to the same genus as the herring. It is found along the Atlantic Coast of the U.S.A., and ascends rivers to spawn.

Shagreen, shark's skin: also untanned leather of peculiar grain made from skins of wild asses, camels, and horses.

Shalloon, a kind of cloth manufactured from wool and worsted, and used chiefly for women's dresses and coat linings. It gets its name from the fact that it was originally made at Chalons.

Shamrock, the three-leaved clover-like plant native to Ireland and its national emblem.

Shark, a large and powerful ocean fish, comprising many species, very widely distributed, but most numerous in tropical seas. They have formidable teeth and are the most carnivorous of all fishes. They usually attain a large size, the whale-shark being often of a length of 50 ft. Commercially the shark yields shagreen from its skin, the fins are made into gelatine, and an oil is obtained from the liver.

Sharp. *See* **Flat.**

Sheep, a well-known family of ruminants of great utility as wool-producers, and for food. From the earliest times sheep have been a source of wealth to England. So much were they valued in the 15th and 16th cent., that their exportation was frequently prohibited. Sheep are classified under (1) longwools; (2) shortwools; and (3) mountain breeds. Most of the longwools carry Leicester blood in their ancestry and the shortwooled Down breeds carry the blood of the Southdown. The Southdown produced the present Suffolk, one of the most popular breeds. Cheviot is an important mountain breed. Of the foreign breeds the most valued are the Merino sheep of Spain, which yield a fine long wool. Australia, U.S.S.R., Argentina, India, U.S.A., New Zealand, and S. Africa are the chief wool-producing countries in the world.

Shelduck, a handsome genus of surface-feeding ducks, one of which, the common shelduck, is an inhabitant of this country. It is a beautiful white-and-chestnut plumaged bird with dark-green head and neck and red bill. Another species, the ruddy sheldrake, appears in Britain only occasionally.

Shellac. This resin is the secretion of the lac insect (*Coccus lacca*), which occurs in forests of Assam and Siam. It is used for making varnish and in the manufacture of gramophone records. *See also* **Lac.**

Sherardizing. Process for coating steel or iron parts with zinc to prevent corrosion; this is done by heating the parts in a closed rotating drum containing zinc dust.

Shilling has been an English coin from Saxon times, but is was not of the value of 12 pence until after the Conquest. The present style of shilling dates from the time of Henry VII.

Ships have existed from prehistoric times. There is mention of one that sailed from Egypt to Greece in 1485 B.C., and in 786 B.C. the Tyrians built a double-decked vessel. No double-decked ship was known in England, however, before the *Royal Harry* was built by Henry VII., and it was not until the 17th cent. that shipbuilding was carried on in this country as a prominent industry.

Ship-worm. *See* **Teredo.**

Shoddy, the name given to a kind of cloth mainly composed of woollen or worsted rags, torn up and re-fabricated by powerful machinery. It was first made at Batley in Yorkshire about 1813, and became a very important industry employing many thousands of people at Batley and the neighbouring town of Dewsbury.

Shot, the name given to solid projectiles fired from guns. In the time of Henry V. stone shot was used, later leaden shot, then iron shot, and finally steel shot, introduced by Sir Joseph Whitworth.

Shrike, a large and varied family of birds of hawk-like behaviour found in all continents except S. America. The Red-backed Shrike, which winters in Africa, is a breeding visitor to England and Wales. It is commonly called the " Butcher Bird " from the way it impales its prey (small birds and insects) on thorn-twigs. The other species on the British list are the Great Grey Shrike, the Lesser Grey Shrike, the Woodchat Shrike, and the Masked Shrike.

Shrove Tuesday, the day before the first day of Lent, receiving its name from the old custom of shriving, or making confession, on that day. In England the day has always been associated with the making of pancakes.

Sicilian Vespers, the term applied to the terrible massacre of French people in Sicily in 1282. The French under Charles of Anjou were then in occupation of the island, and had been guilty of many cruelties. It began at Palermo on Easter Monday at the hour of vespers and resulted in the expulsion of the French king and the introduction of Spanish rule.

Silence, Tower of, or *dakhma*, a tower about 25 ft. high, built by the Parsees for their dead. The corpse is taken inside by professional corpse-bearers and left to be consumed by vultures. Parsees do not burn or bury their dead, and the *dakhma* is to protect the living and the elements from defilement.

Silhouette, a form of black profile portrait, invented by Etienne de Silhouette in 1759, and formed by an outline cutting made with scissors or other sharp instrument from cloth, paper, or other flat substance.

Silicon, an important non-metallic element, symbol Si, it is related to carbon. Next to oxygen, it is the most abundant constituent of the earth's crust (27% by weight). It occurs in many rocks, and its oxide occurs in many forms (*e.g.*, quartz, sand, flint, agate, chalcedony, opal, etc.). Coming into use as a semi-conducting material for making transistors and similar devices.

Silicones are synthetic organic derivatives of silicon which because of their high resistance to heat and moisture have special uses, *e.g.*, lubricants, heat-resistant resins and lacquers, and water-repellent finishes. Silicones are compounds in which the molecules consist of chains of atoms of silicon and oxygen alternately. Silicones were developed in the United States from discoveries first made by Prof. F. S. Kipping at Nottingham University. Manufacture began in Britain in 1950, and in the form of fluids, resins, rubbers, and greases they find wide use in industry. The largest plant in Europe is in Glamorgan.

Silk, the name given to a soft glossy fabric manufactured from the fine thread produced by the silkworm. It was known to, and highly prized by, the ancients, being at one time paid for, weight for weight, with gold. The manufacture of silk was carried on in Sicily in the 12th cent., later spreading to Italy, Spain, and the south of France. It was not manufactured in England before 1604; but when certain French refugees established themselves at Spitalfields in 1688, the industry was developed and became of importance. In the 18th cent. the Lombes of Derby achieved great success in this industry. Japan, China, Italy, Korea, and the Soviet Union are the chief silk-producing countries.

Silkworm, the larva of a species of moth, *Bombyx mori*. It is native to China, and has been cultivated with success in India, Persia, Turkey, and Italy. The silkworm of commerce feeds on mulberry leaves and produces a cocoon of silk varying in colour from white to orange. The cocoon is the silken habitation constructed by the worm for its entrance upon the pupal condition, and to obtain the silk the pupa is killed by immersion in hot-water.

Sill, a sheet-like mass of igneous rock which has been intruded parallel with the stratification of the country rock, cf. a dyke.

Silurian. This geological period is one of the major subdivisions of the Palaeozoic era. Its beginning is estimated at 440 million years ago, and the period lasted about 40 million years. Maximum thickness of the Silurian strata in Britain measures 15,000 ft. *See* **F30.**

Silver, a white precious metal, symbol Ag (Latin *argentum*), found in a free state, also in certain combinations, and in a variety of ores. The chief silver-producing regions are the Andes and Cordilleras. Peru, Bolivia, and Mexico have yielded vast supplies of the metal since the 16th century, and Colorado and Nevada in the United States have also been very prolific in silver yield. In England standard silver (that used for coinage) formerly contained 92½ per cent. fine silver and 7½ per cent. alloy, but when the price rose to 89½*d.* per oz. and the coins became worth more than face value, the Coinage Act of 1920 was passed, reducing the fineness to half. To provide silver bullion for industry and for a fund towards the redemption of our silver debt to America, it was decided in 1946 to replace the United Kingdom silver coinage by one made of cupro-nickel (75 per cent. copper, 25 per cent. nickel). Maundy money, however, is of the original silver standard. Silver chloride and bromide are light-sensitive compounds and are used in photography.

Silverfish, a primitive wingless insect (*Lepisma*) found commonly in old papers and under floor coverings.

Simony, the offence of trading in church offices, has been contrary to English law since the time of Edward VI. Elizabeth also promulgated laws against simony. In 1879 a Royal Commission reported on the law and existing practice as to the sale, exchange, and resignation of benefices. The position is now controlled by the Benefices Act 1898, the Amendment Measure 1923, and the Benefices Rules 1926.

Sinn Fein (*Irish* = ourselves alone), an Irish nationalistic movement founded in 1905 which developed into a mass republican party and triumphed in the establishment of the Irish Free State. A small extremist group has survived which represents politically the outlawed I.R.A.

Sins, The Seven Deadly or Capital Sins are pride, avarice, lust, anger, gluttony, envy, sloth.

Sirius, the dog-star, so called because of its situation in the mouth of the Dog (Canis Major): it is the brightest of all the fixed stars, and is also one of the nearest to us.

Sirocco, a warm, southerly, often dust-laden, wind blowing across Mediterranean lands from the Sahara, in advance of an eastward-moving depression over the Mediterranean.

Siskin, a small bird of the finch family, common in Northern regions, nesting in Britain. The common Siskin has a yellow-green colour and is a lively, swift-flying bird with a stout bill.

Sistine Chapel, the chapel of the Pope in the Vatican, renowned for its frescos by Michelangelo.

Six Articles, The Statute of the, was passed in 1539 for compelling adhesion to the chief doctrines of Roman Catholic faith; transubstantiation, communion in one kind only for the laity, vows of chastity, celibacy of the clergy, private masses, and auricular confession: those who refused to subscribe to the Articles were treated as heretics. The Act was repealed in 1547.

Skate, a genus of sea-fishes related to the Rays.

Skink. The skinks constitute a large family of lizards with large smooth scales, under each of which is a bony plate. The largest species, found in Australia, is about 2 ft. long. Some skinks have adopted a burrowing habit and degeneration of the limbs is associated with this. The Common Skink is a small species about 5 in. long, living in the deserts of N. Africa.

Skua, falcon-like marine birds related to the gulls, found throughout the world. Known as "Robber Birds" because they steal not only the young and eggs of other birds (including penguins) but also their food, which they force them to disgorge in mid-air. The Arctic Skua breeds as far south as Scotland. The Great Skua breeds in both Antarctica and Arctica. Other species are the Pomarine, the Long-tailed, and McCormick's Skua.

Skunk, a North American mammal of the weasel family, with short legs and long bushy tail. All fifteen species are black and white, some being striped and the rest spotted. It secretes and ejects at will a foul-smelling fluid. Anything tainted with this retains the odour for days.

Sky. The blue colour of the sky on a summer's day is the result of the scattering of light waves by particles of dust and vapour in the earth's atmosphere. Blue light having almost the smallest wavelength in the visible spectrum (0·00004 cm.) is scattered laterally about 10 times as much as the red (0·00007 cm.).

Skyscraper. Owing to lack of ground space, increasing cost of land, and growth of modern cities, buildings are being made higher than broader; hence the name. The structures are constructed of a steel framework usually clothed in concrete or reinforced concrete. Among the highest New York skyscrapers are the Empire State Building (102 stories, 1,250 ft.), Chrysler (77 stories, 1,046 ft.), and the Rockefeller Center (67 stories, 950 ft.). The tallest building in Britain is the 620 ft. Post Office radio tower (basic diameter 52 ft.) near Tottenham Court Road, London.

Slate, fine-grained clayey rocks which have undergone metamorphism. They cleave easily, and it is this property of cleavage which makes them a valuable source of roofing material. Welsh slates are among the best, there being important quarries at Penrhyn, Llanberis, and Ffestiniog.

Slavery. In its earlier forms, as in the times of ancient Greece and Rome, in the feudal ages, when vassalage and villeinage existed, and in the serfdom of Russia and other northern nations, slavery was attended by many inhumanities and evils; but perhaps in the negro slavery system which prevailed in the British colonies for upwards of 200 years and in certain parts of the United States up to 1865, it attained its highest point of cruelty. Since 1833 no slavery has existed in the British possessions, though to the world's shame it is still prevalent in parts of Arabia, and, in the form of forced labour, in parts of Africa and elsewhere.

Slide Rule, an instrument which in its simplest form consists of two logarithmic scales sliding alongside each other. By its use multiplication, division, extraction of roots, etc., are speedily carried out.

Sloth, a curious family of mammals, only found in Central and South America. They dwell almost entirely in the trees, proceeding from branch to branch with their bodies hanging downwards, their weight being supported by their large hook-like claws. They eat foliage.

Slow-Worm, a species of lizard found in Britain which lacks legs. Silver with longitudinal brown stripes, it lives almost entirely on slugs.

Smelting. The process of heating an ore with a reducing agent to convert ore into metal, and with a flux to convert rocky impurities into a slag that will float on top of the molten metal. Slag and metal can then be tapped separately. An example is iron smelting; the reducing agent is coke, and limestone is added as the flux; the smelting is carried out in a blast furnace.

Snake. The snakes constitute the important reptilian order *Ophidia*. Snakes have a scaly, cylindrical, limbless body, lidless eyes, forked tongue, and the upper and lower jaws joined by an elastic ligament. Their locomotion is accomplished by means of the excessive mobility of their numerous ribs. All snakes have teeth used for seizing prey, and the poisonous varieties are furnished with poison fangs in the upper jaw. These fangs are hollow modified teeth and the venom passes into them from a special gland situated behind the angle of the mouth. Some 2,500 species of snakes are known, divided into 13 families.

Snipe, a wading bird, long-legged, with long, slender, straight bill, brown plumage, and zigzag flight. The Common Snipe breeds locally throughout Britain; the Great Snipe and small Jack Snipe are occasional visitors. The close season is Feb. 1 to Aug. 11.

Snort (*Ger.* Schnorchel), a tubular device of modern invention used in submarines. It contains two pipes for the intake of air and outlet of gases, and can be maintained above the level of the surface of the water. When a submarine is submerging with snort at the surface it is said to be *snorting*.

Snow. When water vapour condenses at high levels at a temperature below freezing, a cloud of ice particles is formed. If these frozen droplets are small, they fall slowly and gradually assume a feathery crystalline structure, reaching the earth as snowflakes if the temperature remains below freezing.

Socialism. *See* **J40**.

Sociology is the study of society, but the science is so vast that sociologists differ in what they consider to be its subject-matter. One of the leading sociologists, however, Professor Ginsberg of London, lists the problems of the worker in this field as follows: (1) the investigation of the quantity of the population and its quality; the study of the various types of social structure and classification of social groups and institutions; (2) social control—the study of law, morals, religion, convention, and fashion—the regulating agencies of society; (3) social processes—study of the various types of interaction between individuals and groups—co-operation, conflict, etc.; (4) social pathology—the study of social maladjustment and disturbances. Sociology, like psychology, has been for long considered a field for arm-chair philosophy;

most of the great philosophers from Plato and Aristotle onwards to Marx and Engels have produced theories on the nature of society, but such theories often tell more about the individual who composed them and his political prejudices than about facts. Recently, however, there are signs that sociology is becoming a science in its own right. *See* **Section Q, Parts II and III.**

Soda, carbonate of sodium, is now mainly obtained by certain processes of manufacture from common salt. It was formerly obtained from the ashes of plants. Bicarbonate of sodium is the primary product in the Solvay or Ammonia-soda method for commercial manufacture of soda; it is also formed when carbon dioxide is passed into strong soda solution. The bicarbonate is used in medicine and in the preparation of baking powder.

Sodium, a metallic element, symbol Na (Latin *Natrium*), first obtained by Sir Humphry Davy in 1807 from caustic soda by means of the electric battery. Its chloride is *common salt*; the deposits of salt (*e.g.*, in Cheshire and at Stassfurt) have come into existence through the drying up of inland seas. Salt occurs in sea-water to the extent of about 3 per cent.; the Dead Sea contains about 22 per cent. The blood of animals is maintained at a level of about 0·6% sodium chloride. That there is sodium in the sun's atmosphere was confirmed in 1859 by Kirchhoff from his spectroscopic observations.

Soil, the superficial covering of land areas composed mainly of disintegrated rock material and the remains of dead plants and animals (humus) and containing in varying amounts trace elements and other nutriments essential for plant growth.

Solar Battery, one of the innumerable devices made possible by the development of semi-conducting materials, notably germanium and silicon. This device creates an electric current from light falling on it. The current can be put to use or stored in storage batteries. The energy of the current is derived from the sunlight, and the solar battery is thus an *energy converting* apparatus. Solar batteries have provided power for the instruments in satellites. In London in 1960 a car (developed in the U.S.A.) was demonstrated running on the power from sunlight and solar batteries.

Solar Wind, a continuous stream of electrically charged particles blowing outwards from the sun, supplemented from time to time by intense outbursts from particular regions of the sun's surface. These streams of protons and electrons on encountering the earth's magnetic field cause magnetic storms and aurorae.

Solstice, an astronomical term indicating the point at which the sun is most distant from the equator. *See* **N24.**

Sonata. Properly the instrumental equivalent of a Cantata, *i.e.*, an extended piece for a solo instrument, *e.g.*, pianoforte or violin with pianoforte accompaniment. A typical sonata (*e.g.*, Beethoven's Pathétique, Op. 13) consists of three movements. Each movement (*see* **Movement**) consists of two or more subjects interwoven in a characteristic way. The first movement is longer than the others. A solemn introduction leads to an agitated first subject which is connected by a bridge to the second subject. This is followed by a small coda. This first part comprises the Exposition. There follows a short Development of themes found in the Exposition, this leading to a recapitulation of the first and second subjects, the latter with a change of key. The movement ends with a Coda consisting of themes from the Introduction and first subject. This treatment is typical of sonata form. The second movement is in complete contrast and is one of the loveliest slow movements ever written. Its form is that of a simplified Rondo. 1, 2, 1–3–1, Coda. The third movement is again in contrast. It is rapid but has not the tragic character of the first movement. The form is that of a full Rondo.

Soundings at sea, to determine depth at any point, have been taken in all seas, and with considerable accuracy. A deep reading was that of the *Challenger* expedition in 1873, near St. Thomas's in the North Atlantic, when 3,875 fathoms were sounded. In 1851 H.M.S. *Challenger* recorded the then maximum ocean depth in the Marianas Trench (W. Pacific) by echo-sounding as between 5,882 and 5,940 fathoms. Another deep was located in the S. Pacific in 1952–53 of 5,814 fathoms in the Tonga Trench, 180 miles S. of Tonga Tabu. Since then even greater depths have been recorded, in the Marianas Trench and the Mindanao Deep. *See* **Pacific Ocean.**

Southern Cross, popular name of *Crux*, a constellation of the Southern hemisphere, consisting of four bright stars in the form of a Latin cross. It has been called the pole-star of the south and is indispensable to seafarers.

South Sea Bubble, the name given to a series of financial projects which began with the formation of the South Sea Company in 1711 and ended nine years later in disaster after a mania of speculation. The idea behind the parent scheme was that the state should sell certain trading monopolies in the South seas in return for a sum of money to pay off the National Debt (which stood at £51,300,000 in 1719 when the scheme started). The idea fascinated the public, fabulous profits being dreamt of, and the price of the stock rose out of all proportion to the earnings of the Company. Many dishonest speculative ventures sprang up in imitation with the inevitable result that thousands were ruined. All classes had joined in the gamble and a Committee of Secrecy set up by the House of Commons in Dec. 1720 to investigate the affairs of the Company proved that there had been fraud and corruption on a large scale in the affairs of the Company. Sir Robert Walpole who had been an opponent of the scheme from the outset dealt with the crisis.

Soya Bean. This is the bean of a leguminous plant (*Glycine soja*) found in Asia. The bean meal, which is rich in protein and oil, is familiar in Britain as "soya flour."

Space Flight. The Soviet Union was the first country to launch a man into space and bring him safely back to earth. This epoch-making event took place on April 12, 1961, when Yuri Alexeyevich Gagarin, an officer in the Soviet Air Force, girdled the earth in a spaceship weighing about $4\frac{3}{4}$ tons. It was launched by rocket in an elliptical orbit with greatest height 187 miles and least 109 miles. The inclination of the orbit to the equator was 65 deg. 4 min. and the period of revolution was 89 min. 6 sec. Since then, the Russians Titov (17 orbits), Nikolayev (64 orbits), Popovich (48 orbits), Bykovsky (81 orbits), Tereshkova, the first woman astronaut (48 orbits), Komarov, Feoktiskov, and Yegorov (16 orbits), Leonov and Belyaev (26 hrs.), and the Americans Glenn (3 orbits), Carpenter (3 orbits), Schirra (5 orbits), Cooper (22 orbits), Grissom and Young (3 orbits), McDivitt and White in *Gemini 4* (62 orbits), Cooper and Conrad in *Gemini 5* (120 orbits), Schirra and Stafford in *Gemini 6*, who made a successful rendezvous with Borman and Lovell in *Gemini 7* in December 1965, have completed successful missions in space. Leonov was the first man to leave an orbiting space ship and float freely in space. He was tethered to his ship by a 15 ft. lifeline and was travelling at a speed of 5 miles a second.

Space Research. By space research we mean scientific research work which can only be carried to otherwise inaccessible observing locations by rocket propulsion. Such propulsion does not rely on the presence of an atmosphere to provide oxygen so that it is capable in principle of conveying objects to unlimited distances. The subject of space research is, therefore, one which is concerned with scientific applications in various fields of a single highly specialised and powerful technique. It is not a single discipline, but can provide data of great importance for many, such as the physics of the earth, the sun, moon, and other bodies of the solar system, astronomy, geodesy, and the study of gravitation. The prospect of investigating the biological conditions on different planets such as Mars and Venus is also opened, as well as that of experimental biological studies under conditions of zero gravity. Although the results of many aspects of space research are vital for those concerned with the practical realisation of manned travel in space, space research is largely a branch of pure science, independent of any applications which may stem from it. The major technical problems involved in space research are:

(*a*) Launching of the instrument-containing vehicle with the necessary velocity.

(*b*) Guidance and control of the vehicle so it pursues the desired path.

(*c*) Tracking the vehicle to determine its actual path and the position on the path at any time.

(*d*) Transmission of the data, recorded by the instruments, back to the earth.

(*e*) Satisfactory operation of scientific instruments in the environment within the vehicle.

(*f*) Provision of adequate power supplies to operate the equipment within the vehicle for sufficiently long periods.

Spanish Civil War, 1936 to 1939. The war commenced by a revolt by the Fascist General Franco against the Republic which had succeeded the Monarchy in 1931. Germany and Italy aided the rebels who besieged Madrid for over 2 years. An International Brigade was formed to help the Republic, but the Spanish Government was faced by the greater part of the Army, and very effective assistance from Italy and Germany. Those powers seized the opportunity to have a curtain-raiser to the world conflict which they intended to precipitate. After a total loss of a million men the Fascists overpowered the Republic.

Sparrow, name given to finch-like birds found in most parts of the world, of which the House Sparrow *Passer domesticus*, is the most familiar of British birds. Also native to Britain is the rural Tree Sparrow, distinguished from the male House Sparrow by its chestnut crown. Other European species are the Italian, Spanish and Rock Sparrows.

Specific Gravity, defined as the ratio of the mass of a particular volume of a substance to the mass of an equal volume of water at 4° C. *See* **Hydrometer.**

Spectroscope, an instrument for spectrum analysis or observation. It consists in its simplest form of a tube through which the light, in whose spectrum the observer is interested, is conveyed to a collimating lens, which focuses it on to a prism, and a telescope through which to view the spectrum. The first flame spectrometer was constructed by Kirchhoff in 1859. High-precision spectroscopy is a very important technique in physics, chemistry, and astronomy, and is facilitated by numerous elaborate instruments. *See* **F12**(2).

Spectrum. When light is refracted by a prism the rays of different wave-length are refracted slightly differently. Thus white light is broken down to give its spectrum colours, ranging from red (longest wave-length) to violet (shortest wave-length). This phenomenon was discovered by Newton in 1672. Outside the wave-length range of visible light are other electromagnetic waves ranging from very long radio waves to very short γ-rays (*see* **F13**). This extended series of radiations is called *the electromagnetic spectrum. See* **Section F, Part IV.**

Sphinx, in Greek mythology, a winged creature with a woman's head and a lion's body. The sphinx of ancient Egypt represented the pharaoh in a divine form. The most famous is the Great Sphinx at Giza, sculptured out of natural rock.

Spinet, a sort of boudoir harpsichord popular in the 17th cent. The name derives from that of its inventor, Spinetti.

Spiritualism. *See* **J41.**

Spirituals, negro melodies with religious inspiration and which are still spontaneously created, but have also passed into art-music.

Sponge, a marine organism consisting of a colony of cells organised in a more primitive way than most multi-cellular organisms without a nervous system. While the sponge lives a current of water circulates through the main apertures. It is the dead skeleton of this mass that forms the sponge of commerce. *See* **F22**(2).

Spoonbill, a long-legged, marsh bird, closely related to the ibis and stork, remarkable for its snow-white plumage and broad, flat, spoon-shaped bill. The European species has not bred in England since the beginning of the 17th cent., but is still a regular summer visitor from Holland, where it nests in colonies in reed-beds and islets.

Sputniks, the name of the Russian earth satellites first launched during the period of the International Geophysical Year. *Sputnik I*, launched 4 Oct. 1957, became the first man-made earth satellite. *Sputnik II*, launched a month later, carried a dog as passenger. *Sputnik III*, launched in May 1958, and weighing well over 2 tons, became the first fully-equipped laboratory to operate in space. The father of space travel with rockets was a Russian—Konstantin Eduardovich Tsiolkovsky—the centenary of whose birth practically coincided with the launching of the first earth satellite.

Squirting Cucumber, *Ecballium eletarium*, so named from the fact that when ripe it breaks from the stalk and ejects its seeds and juice from the hole made by the breakage.

Stainless Steel. The development of stainless steel for cutlery manufacture, etc., began with the discovery of Harry Brearsley in 1912 that steel containing 12 per cent. of chromium is rust-proof.

Stalactites are deposits of calcium carbonate formed on the roofs and sides of limestone caves, and in tunnels, under bridges, and other places where the carbonic acid of rain-water percolates through and partly dissolves the limestone, resulting in the growth of icicle-like forms that often assume groupings. The water that drops from these may deposit further calcium carbonate, which accumulates and hardens into a series of sharp mounds or hillocks called stalagmites.

Starch is an organic compound occurring in granules in nearly all green plants, and especially in the seeds of dicotyledonous and cereal plants, potatoes, etc. In its pure form starch is a tasteless, odourless white powder, and is a carbohydrate consisting of carbon, hydrogen, and oxygen.

Star Chamber, an ancient tribunal of State in existence in 1487 and possibly earlier, charged with the duty of trying offences against the Government, unfettered by the ordinary rules of law. It was in effect a Privy Council entrusted with judicial functions. Under Charles I. the Star Chamber was used by the King and his party to persecute opponents; and in 1641 a Bill carried in both Houses abolished it.

Starling (*Sturnus vulgaris*), a well-known European bird now common in many parts of the world. It has handsome iridescent blackish plumage and nests in holes and crevices. Flocks of starlings are often seen wheeling in the air; thousands roost on buildings in the heart of London. Other European species are the Spotless and Rose-coloured starlings. The latter sometimes wanders to the British Isles.

States-General, national assembly in which the chief estates of the realm were represented as separate bodies. The name, though not the institution, has survived in the Netherlands, where the two houses of parliament are known as states-general. In France the states-general consisted of three orders, clergy, nobility, and commons. Philip IV. first summoned it in 1302 to support him in his quarrel with Pope Boniface VIII. While absolute monarchy was establishing itself it met rarely, and not at all from 1614 until 1789, when it was convoked as a last resort by Louis XVI. But when it met it declared itself the National Assembly which marked the beginning of the revolution.

Statute of Westminster, 1931. An Act of parliament which gave a basis of equality to the British Dominions. The Dominions as well as the United Kingdom were defined by the Balfour Memorandum of 1926 as "autonomous communities within the British Empire, equal in status, in no way subordinate one to another in any aspect of their domestic or external affairs, though united by a common allegiance to the Crown, and freely associated as members of the British Commonwealth of Nations." The Statute was the sequel. The Dominions are sovereign States governed solely by their own Parliaments and Governments.

Steam Engine, a machine whereby steam becomes the active agent of the working of machinery, and of very wide application. The leading types of steam engine are: (*a*) condensing, or low-pressure engines, where the steam is generated by a boiler; (*b*) non-condensing, in which the cylinder exhausts its steam into the open air. Engines of the latter type are used where portable engines are required.

Steam Hammer, invented by the Scottish engineer James Nasmyth (1808–90) in 1839, which proved of great utility in the development of the iron trade. The hammer itself, which is fixed to the end of a piston-rod passing through the bottom of an inverted cylinder, often weighs as much as 80 or 100 tons, and is so perfectly controlled by the steam power that its action can be so accurately gauged that it could be made to crack the glass of a watch without actually breaking it, or brought down upon a mass of molten iron with a force representing many hundreds of tons.

Stearin is the portion of fatty matters and oils which remains solid at an ordinary temperature, and is a compound of stearic acid with glycerine. It is largely used in the manufacture of candles and for other commercial purposes. With caustic soda stearin forms a soap (sodium stearate), which is present in most commercial soaps which contain sodium palmitate and oleate in addition.

Steel, an alloy of iron and carbon, with varying proportions of other minerals. The famous blades of Damascus and steels of Toledo were made by the cementation and crucible method. The metal produced by the "Bessemer process" (*q.v.*) is of the highest value for structural purposes, rails, etc. In recent years the technique known as continuous casting has been developed which bypasses some major steps in the conventional process of steel-making. *See also* **Stainless Steel.**

Stellite, an important alloy for the manufacture of cutting tools. It contains chromium, cobalt, usually some tungsten, and a small quantity of carbon.

Stereotype, a metal cast taken from movable type which has been set up in the ordinary way. The first to introduce the process in practical form in this country was William Ged, of Edinburgh, who made stereotype plates in 1730. An impression of the type matter is first taken by means of a mould of prepared plaster of Paris or moistened sheets of specially prepared paper, and when molten stereo metal is poured upon the mould and allowed to cool and harden, the stereo plate is formed, and can be printed from as a solid block for some time.

Steroids. A class of structurally related compounds, based on a system of condensed rings of carbon and hydrogen, which are widely distributed in animals and plants. Included in the steroid family are sterols, found in all animal cells, vitamin D, sex hormones, bile acids, and cortisone, a drug used in the treatment of rheumatic fever.

Stethoscope, an instrument by which the action of the heart and other organs of the chest can be heard and gauged. It was invented by Laënnec, of Paris, in 1816, and consists of a cylinder, one end having a funnel-shaped opening which is placed against the chest, while the other end is held to the listener's ear. There is also a binaural stethoscope, which has two india-rubber tubes for the ears.

Stibnite, the chief ore of antimony; chemically it is antimony sulphide. Steely-grey in colour.

Stickleback, a family of small spiny-finned fish widely distributed in both fresh and salt water. Male constructs roofed nest held together by sticky secretion from glands near kidneys. Several females deposit eggs therein which he jealously guards until after young are hatched.

Stirrup, a loop of metal U-shaped strap suspended from the sides of the saddle, used for mounting and to support the horseman's foot. Some authorities allege their use as far back as the early Iron Age, and it is generally believed that they were used in battle in A.D. 378, when the Gothic cavalry defeated the legionaries of the Emperor Valens at Adrianople. Stirrups relieved the tension on the rider's knees and so enabled him to be armed from top to toe.

Stoat, a slender, carnivorous mammal with short legs, related to the weasels. The stoat is distinguished from the latter by its longer tail, which has a black tip. The black tip is retained even in the winter when the animal turns white, the fur then being known as "ermine." It is found in northern latitudes, and is abundant in Arctic America.

Stoma (pl. **stomata**), microscopic pores on the surfaces of leaves through which gaseous exchanges take place and water is lost. It has been estimated that a single maize plant bears 200 million stomata, usually closed at night.

Stone-Flies, comprise the order of insects called *Plecoptera*, which includes some 700 species, of which about thirty occur in Britain. The wings are membranous, and two long, thread-like feelers protrude at the tail end. The larvae are aquatic.

Stonehenge, a remarkable collection of Bronze Age monuments arranged in two circles, 340 ft. in diameter, standing on Salisbury Plain, Wiltshire. Modern archaeological research dates origin back to between 1860 and 1500 B.C. There is some evidence to suggest that the monument may have been built for astronomical purposes, providing a method of keeping a calendar for predicting the seasons and foretelling eclipses of sun and moon. *See also* **J13(1).**

Stork, a family of heron-like birds with long bills, freely distributed over Europe, Asia, Africa, and S. America. The White Stork is an occasional visitor to England, and, more rarely, the Black Stork; these are the only two European storks.

Stratosphere, a layer of the earth's atmosphere, which begins 6–7 miles above the earth. The attraction of the stratosphere as a medium for air travel rests upon the absence of storms; indeed weather phenomena as commonly understood do not occur, there being no vertical temperature gradient in the stratosphere and no convection currents.

Stratum (pl. **strata**), a bed or layer of rock.

Strontium. This silver-white metallic element was discovered by Hope and Klaproth in 1793, and isolated by Sir Humphry Davy in 1808. The chief strontium minerals are celestite (sulphate) and strontianite (carbonate). Compounds of strontium give a brilliant colour to fireworks and signal flares. Radioactive isotopes of strontium (strontium-90) are formed as fission products in nuclear explosions and tend to collect in bone on account of the chemical similarity of strontium and calcium (*q.v.*). This genetic hazard is a cause of great alarm. *See* **Fall-out.**

Sturgeon, a large fish found in northern seas and rivers with five rows of bony plates along the back and sides and pointed mouth with four barbels. Caviare is prepared from sturgeon ova. Since the reign of Edward II. all sturgeon caught off the coasts of Britain, except in certain privileged places, have belonged to the Sovereign.

Sublimation, when a solid substance is heated and turns into vapour without passing through the liquid stage and then condenses as a solid on a cold surface, it is said to "sublime" and the process is called "sublimation". Iodine behaves in this way, and sublimation is used as a method of purifying it. For the psychological meaning, *see* **Freudian Theory, Section F, Part III.**

Submarine, the first submarine, the *Nautilus*, was designed by Robert Fulton and tried out in the river Seine and in the sea off Brest in 1801. The idea was too revolutionary to find acceptance and it was not until electricity for under-water propulsion became available that the submarine underwent extensive development. Britain became interested about 1900 and the Germans developed it and made it into an instrument of warfare. The Royal Navy's Dreadnought-class submarines have all been launched: *Dreadnought* (Oct. 1960), *Valiant* (Dec. 1963) and *Warspite* (Sept. 1965). The first voyage under the North Pole was made in 1958 by the American nuclear-powered submarine *Nautilus* (*q.v.*). In Sept. 1964 the world's deepest-diving submarine, the American *Aluminaut*, was launched to carry out oceanographic research.

Suez Canal, connecting the Mediterranean and the Red Sea, was built by the French engineer Ferdinand de Lesseps and opened in 1869. An Egyptian company, *Canal Maritime de Suez*, was formed in 1866 with a capital of 200 million francs. The British Government acquired 176,602 shares out of a total of 400,000 for £4 million (value Mar. 31, 1956, £28,982,544). Its length is 101 statute miles, minimum width 196 ft. 10 in. (navigation channel). Under the Convention of 1888 all nations were granted freedom of navigation without discrimination in peace or war. The right was recognised by Egypt in the Anglo-Egyptian Agreement of 1954, under which Britain agreed to give up the Suez base. The Suez Canal Company was nationalised by the Egyptian Government without warning on July 28, 1956, since when it has been widened and deepened and the average time of transit reduced.

Suffragette, member of the Women's Suffrage Movement who in the early part of this century agitated to obtain the parliamentary vote. The movement ended in 1918, when women of 30 were given the vote. In 1928 a Bill was passed which granted equal suffrage to men and women. The leaders of the Women's Suffrage Movement were Mrs. Pankhurst and her two daughters, Sylvia and Dame Christabel, Mrs. Fawcett, Nellie Kenny, and others.

Sugar, to the chemist the term is a generic one covering a group of carbohydrates, including cane sugar (sucrose), glucose, fructose, and maltose. In ordinary parlance sugar means sucrose, which is obtained from the sugar cane, sugar beet, or sugar maple.

Sulphur, an elementary, brittle, crystalline solid, symbol S, abounding in the vicinity of volcanoes. It is yellow in colour. It occurs in combination with other elements, as sulphates and sulphides, and allied with oxygen, hydrogen, chlorine, etc., is of great commercial utility. Used in its pure state it constitutes the inflammable element in gunpowder; it is also used for matches and for making sulphuric acid.

Sulphuric Acid, a compound of great commercial importance, used in a variety of manufactures, and composed of sulphur, oxygen, and hydrogen.

Summer Time. In 1916 an Act was passed advancing Greenwich Mean Time by one hour during the summer months, calculated to save light and fuel by making use of an extra hour of daylight. This Act was made permanent in 1925, and summer time was to begin on the day following the third Saturday in April, or if that day was Easter Sunday, the day following the second Saturday, and end on the day following the first Saturday in Oct. By the Summer Time Act, 1947, the periods of summer time are now fixed each year by Order in Council.

Sumptuary Laws. Both the Greeks and Romans passed laws against luxury. In England regulations against luxury in food were promulgated under Edward II. and subsequently. A series of Acts of Parliament, beginning in 1363, placed restrictions on apparel, graduated according to rank. In 1603, most of these laws, which had already fallen into abeyance, were repealed.

Sun, one of the millions of stars in the universe, the centre of the solar system, estimated to be distant from the earth 93,004,000 miles, to have a diameter of 865,000 miles, and a volume a million times that of the earth. It rotates on its axis from east to west, though not as a solid, the solar equator turning once in about 25½ days and the poles in about 34 days. Large spots are observed on the sun—varying in size from 30,000 miles in diameter—which form and disappear at irregular intervals. The area of the disc covered by the spots, however, reaches a maximum roughly every 11 years, when the sun's heat seems rather greater than usual and magnetic storms more frequent (sunspot cycle). Spectrum analysis show that the sun is composed of many elements found in the earth. Its surface temperature is about 6,000° C. Observations made in 1964–65 (Year of the Quiet Sun) complemented those obtained during the International Geophysical Year 1957–58, when the sun was remarkably active. The earth is in the outer atmosphere of the sun and subject to its winds and storms. The apparently inexhaustible heat of the sun, which has maintained life on the earth for millions of years, is derived from the destruction of matter, involved in the transmutation of hydrogen nuclei into helium nuclei, in which process about four million tons of matter is destroyed every second. At this rate of conversion the sun will go on radiating for 30,000 million years. The Soviet space rocket *Lunik I*, fired on 2 Jan. 1959, became the first artificial planet of the sun. *See also* **F7** and for an account of the aurora, **L10.**

Supersonic, pertaining to speeds greater than the speed of sound waves. In air at sea-level sound waves travel at about 760 m.p.h., and a plane or projectile moving faster than this (at sea-level) would be *supersonic*. Not to be confused with **ultrasonic** (*q.v.*). Aircraft travelling at supersonic speeds produce shock waves in the air somewhat analogous to the bow waves of fast-moving ships. These shock waves are regions of intensely disturbed air which produce the sonic boom effect so distressing to people living near supersonic routes. *See also* **Mach Number.**

Surface Tension. The surfaces of fluids behave in some respects as though they were covered by a stretched elastic membrane. This property is called "surface tension." The action of detergents may be attributed in part to a reduction in the surface tension of water, allowing it to wet the surface of dirty articles.

Surrealism. The aim of the Surrealist school of painting and sculpture is to overcome the barriers between conscious and unconscious mind, the real and unreal worlds of waking and dreaming. As such it has a long and respectable ancestry, although the term was not in use until 1922 when it was picked by André Breton from Guillaume Apollinaire who had used it in connection with certain works by Chagall. However, Bosch in the 15th cent., Fuseli and Goya in the 18th, and many other purveyors of the weird and fantastic were the forerunners of modern Surrealism. The modern movement has broadly speaking taken two different directions: the first was towards complete fantasy and absurdity which took the form of "found objects"—*e.g.*, a bird-cage filled with sugar-cubes and a thermometer, a bottle-dryer, a bicycle wheel, or abstract works with strange and apparently irrelevant titles such as Paul Klee's *Twittering Machine*; the second towards highly detailed and realistic paintings of objects placed in strange juxtapositions—*e.g.*, Salvator Dali's trees with limp watches drooping over their branches or Georgio de Chirico's deserted and classical-looking streets with long arcaded perspectives and a lone statue or a bunch of bananas in the foreground. On the whole Surrealism has spent its initial force and become almost respectable; its idea of strange juxtapositions, now widely commercialised, finds a place in advertisement illustrations and in the more sophisticated forms of window-dressing.

Surtax an additional duty of income tax, chargeable on total income in excess of £2,000. The starting level on *earned* income is £5,000 or more depending on personal allowances. Payable on Jan. 1 following year of assessment, so that surtax for 1965–66 is payable on Jan. 1, 1967. Charged on a sliding scale. *See* **L60.**

Swans, large, graceful birds which together with the ducks and geese form the family Anatidae. There are three European species with white plumage; the Mute Swan, distinguished by its orange bill with black knob, being the best known and a familiar sight on the rivers and ornamental lakes of this country. Two wild swans are winter visitors here, the Whooper and Bewick's Swan. The "pen" (female) and "cob" (male) mate for life and the young swans are called "cygnets."

Swan-upping. The annual marking of the Thames swans which takes place during the third week of July. This ancient ceremony dates back to the 15th cent. when all the Thames swans were declared to be Royal birds owned by the Crown. Two city guilds—the Vintners' and Dyers' Companies—own one third of the 600 swans now on the Thames. This privilege was granted to them by King Edward IV. in return for money grants. Vintners' birds are marked with a nick on each side of the bill, the Dyers' with a nick on the right side only. The Queen's birds are unmarked.

Sweet Potato. This plant (*Ipomoea batatas*), which is a climbing perennial belonging to the convolvulus family, has thick roots that are rich in starch, and are eaten like potatoes. A native of the W. Indies and Central America, new varieties of sweet potato have been bred which stand cooler climates and can be grown as far north as Cape Cod. The sweet potato of New Zealand is called the Kumara.

Swift, a bird so-called from the extreme speed of its flight, resembling a swallow but related to the humming-bird. It has long, scythe-like wings, sooty-black plumage and greyish-white chin. There are several species inhabiting most parts of the world, particularly the tropics. The British breeding bird is among the latest to return from Africa and the earliest to go. Swifts are the only birds to use saliva for their nests. One oriental species builds its nest entirely from saliva.

Sword, weapon used in personal combat, originally made of bronze. The Romans introduced the iron sword, 20 in. long. During the Middle Ages the most famous blades were those made by the Arabs at Damascus and those made at Toledo.

Symbiosis. When two organisms live together and both derive mutual benefit from the association, the partnership is known as symbiosis. An example is the symbiosis of an alga and a fungus in lichens; another is the ordinary pea plant and the bacteria which live in the nodules on the pea's roots.

Symphony, a "sonata for full orchestra," usually consisting of four movements. In Beethoven's Third Symphony the first movement is in typical sonata form, consisting of an exposition of two subjects followed by a development. The second movement is a funeral march on a ternary plan (*i.e.*, 1–2–1). The third movement is a Scherzo on two subjects, while the fourth movement is an air with variations.

Syncopation, a displacement of the accent in music. For instance, in four-beat time the accent is normally on the first beat. If it were on any of the other beats the music would be syncopated. This device has frequently been used in classical music, but it is the very essence of jazz.

Synod, an assembly of the clergy of a particular church, state, province, or diocese. The Synod of Whitby (663) settled the dispute between the Celtic and the Roman churches in the matter of Easter in favour of the Roman system of reckoning.

Synoptic Charts. These are meteorological charts used in forecasting on which weather conditions at a network of stations, at a standard hour of observation, are recorded, using symbols of the international weather code.

T

Tabard, a cloak or outer garment worn in mediæval days by the peasantry. The name was also applied to a garment worn by knights over their armour.

Tailor-Bird, name of a small group of warblers, familiar in India and China, and remarkable for their habit of sewing leaves together to enclose their nests. The bill is used as needle, vegetable fibre as thread, and a knot is tied to prevent it slipping.

Taj Mahal, the white marble mausoleum built at Agra by Shah Jehan in memory of his favourite wife who died in 1629. Over 20,000 men were occupied for over twenty years in its erection.

Takahe or Notornis, large New Zealand bird of the rail family which for many years was believed to be extinct. Small colony found in 1948 in remote valley of mountainous part of the S. Island. The bird is strictly protected.

Take-over Bid describes an offer made to all the shareholders of a company to purchase their shares at a named price and conditional upon acceptance by the holders of a named proportion of the total share issue. If accepted the purchaser thus gains control of the company.

Tallage, in Norman times, were taxes levied by the Crown upon lands of the royal demesnes. The levying of tallage was taken away by a statute of 1340 which required the consent of Parliament for all direct taxes.

Tallow, the more solid portions of animal fat, and prepared from beef, mutton, etc., by melting at a low temperature. Stearin is its chief constituent. Used for making candles, soap, etc.

Tally Office, in the Exchequer, was the department of the Government in which tallies were kept, representing the acknowledgment of moneys paid or lent; in 1834 the Houses of Parliament were burnt down through the overheating of a stove with discarded Exchequer tallies.

Tambourine, a light, small, single-headed drum with loose metal discs let into the side of the hoop so that they jingle when the tambourine is shaken. An older name for it is the timbrel.

Tammany, a New York democratic organisation, sprang out of an old benevolent society named after an Indian chief, and has exerted a powerful influence over political movements in New York. The leaders of the organisation have used their power when their party has been successful at the polls to appoint their nominees to every prominent office, and have exacted bribes for concessions and privileges, and generally Tammany rule has meant wholesale corruption. Of this there is ample evidence in the disclosures of the Tweed and other Tammany frauds, and in the fact that the "Boss" usually contrived to make himself wealthy.

Tannins are chemical substances obtained from a variety of plants and trees, from oak-bark, and from galls. They are used in the leather trade, the tanning process making the skins resistant to decay.

Tantalum, a scarce bluish metallic element, symbol Ta, discovered by Ekeberg in 1802. Chemically related to vanadium and niobium, it is usually associated with the latter in nature. For several purposes it can be used in place of platinum, and it finds application in the making of surgical instruments. Tantalum is very hard, and resistant to acids (other than hydrofluoric acid); it is used in alloys.

Taoism. *See* **J42.**

Tapestry, a fabric largely used in former times for wall decoration and hangings. It was known to the ancient Greeks, but in its modern form came into prominence in the 15th and 16th cent., when it was manufactured in a marked degree of excellence by the weavers of Flanders, especially those of Arras. The manufacture was introduced into England early in the 17th cent., and was attended by considerable success. At the present day the term is applied to worsted cloths for furniture coverings, and there are also various kinds of tapestry carpets now made. The most famous tapestries of olden times were the Aubusson Tapestry and the Savonnerie. The Gobelin Tapestry factory, originated in Paris in the reign of Francis I., is still a national establishment. *See also* **Bayeux Tapestry.**

Tapioca, a food-substance yielded by the tuber of a tropical plant, called the manioc or cassava plant, poisonous in its raw state, but purified by roasting.

Tapirs. The tapirs constitute a family close to the horse family and the rhinoceros in the Ungulate order. They have four toes on the front feet and three on the hind. The snout is drawn out into a short trunk. The largest tapir is the Malayan tapir, which stands 3½ ft. at the shoulder. Four species occur in Central and S. America.

Tar is a dark viscid product obtained from the destructive distillation of wood, coal, peat, etc. Wood tar is acid owing to the presence of acetic acid ("pyroligneous acid"). The highest proportion of coal tar goes into road making. Distillation of coal tar yields many valuable compounds, including benzene, phenol (carbolic acid), naphthalene, and creosote; the final residue after distillation is pitch. Based on the chemical manipulation of compounds from coal tar is the preparation of many perfumes, food essences, drugs, antiseptics, and plastics.

Tarantula, the name given to a large range of big hairy spiders. Music was supposed to cure their sting, hence the Tarantella dance.

Tarpeian Rock at Rome received its named from the tradition that Tarpeia, the daughter of the Governor of the Citadel who betrayed the fortress to the Sabines, was crushed to death by their shields and buried beneath the rock. From this height persons guilty of treason were hurled to death.

Tartaric Acid is prepared from tartar (potassium hydrogen tartrate) deposited in wine vats during fermentation. "Cream of tartar" is purified potassium hydrogen tartrate, which is incorporated in baking powder. Tartaric acid is also used in the manufacture of effervescent salts, and in medicine (*e.g.*, "tartar emetic").

Tate Gallery, named after its founder, Sir Henry Tate, at Millbank, S.W., was opened in 1897; Sir Henry Tate bore the cost of the building (£80,000) and also contributed the nucleus of the present collection. "The Turner Wing," the gift of Sir Joseph Duveen, was added in 1910. The collection is thoroughly representative of British art and has been extended several times to include modern foreign art.

Tay Bridge spans the Tay at Dundee, is over two miles in length, and was opened for traffic on June 20, 1887. A previous bridge, completed in 1877, was blown down on Dec. 28, 1879, as a railway train was passing over it. Work has started on a new bridge across the Firth of Tay.

Tea was introduced into England about the middle of the 17th cent., when it was a great luxury, and fetched from £6 to £10 a pound. It is an Asiatic plant, native properly to China, Japan, and India. Up to about 1885 most of the tea imported into this country came from China; the bulk now comes from India and Ceylon.

Teal, the smallest of the European ducks and next to the Mallard the commonest British species. It is a handsome bird and a very swift flier, but not as swift as the Garganey or Summer Teal.

Te Deum, the song of praise ("Te Deum laudamus"—"We praise Thee, O God"), is supposed to have been the composition of St. Ambrose in the 4th cent. and is used in Roman Catholic and English Church services.

Telecommunications. The sending of messages over a distance. The term is generally applied to the sending of messages by telegraph, telephone, radio, television or radar. The first submarine telegraph cable between England and France was laid in 1850 and, following Hertz's investigations into electric waves, Marconi's invention led to Britain being linked with Europe by wireless telegraphy in 1899. The first permanently successful telegraph cable across the Atlantic was laid in 1866. The first telephone service between London and Paris was opened in 1891. The electro-magnetic telephone was invented by Alexander Graham Bell, a Scottish-born American, in 1876. The first submarine telephone cable to span the Atlantic was laid in 1955, which enables speech to be transmitted over a distance of 2,000 miles. Before that, transatlantic communication was by radio-telephone. The rapid advance of scientific discoveries and technical capacity makes it certain that new telecommunication facilities will be available in the near future for data transmission, *e.g.*, traffic control systems, automatic processes, reading of supply meters. The performance of *Telstar* in July 1962 and of *Early Bird* in April 1965 showed that intercontinental communication by satellites in space is practical.

Telemetry, measurement at remote distances by means of a radio-link from the object (missile or satellite) to the ground. The third Russian sputnik, for instance, carried apparatus for measuring, among other things, the pressure and composition of the atmosphere, and the intensity of different kinds of radiation from the sun. Its radio transmitter, powered by solar-energy batteries, sent out the information in coded form by means of uninterrupted signals at 20·005 megacycles with a duration of 150–300 milli-seconds. Radio telemetry from inside the body is being increasingly used in medical and biological research; miniature radio transmitters can be swallowed or implanted in man or animal to detect various physiological conditions.

Telepathy and Clairvoyance. *See* **J43.**

Teleprinter, a telegraph transmitter with a type-writer keyboard, by which characters of a message are transmitted electrically in combinations of 5 units, being recorded similarly by the receiving instrument, which then translates the matter mechanically into printed characters. The telex or public teleprinter service provides direct person-to-person transmission of written messages.

Telescope, an optical instrument for viewing objects at a distance, "the astronomer's intelligencer." Lippershey is credited with construction of the first in 1608; Galileo constructed several from 1609 and Newton was the first to construct a reflecting telescope. The ordinary telescope consists of an object-glass and an eye-lens, with two intermediates to bring the object into an erect position. A lens brings it near to us, and the magnifier enlarges it for inspection. A refracting telescope gathers the rays together near the eye-piece and is necessarily limited as to size, but the reflecting telescope collects the rays on a larger mirror, and these are thrown back to the eye-piece. The world's largest reflectors are at Mount Palomar Observatory, California (200 in.), Mount Wilson Observatory, California (100 in.), the McDonald Observatory at Mount Locke, Texas (82 in.), and the Victoria B.C. Observatory (72 in.). At the Royal Observatory, formerly at Greenwich, now at Herstmonceux, Sussex, a 98 in. *Isaac Newton* telescope is being installed. The *Hale* 200 in. telescope at Mount Palomar is the largest ever made and has revealed objects never before photographed; it is able to probe space and photograph remote galaxies out to a limiting distance of 2,000 million light years. The *Schmidt* telescope at Mount Palomar has been used to make a huge photographic map of the universe. The giant steerable radio telescope built by Manchester University at Jodrell Park, Cheshire, has a 250 ft. reflector with a beam width of 12 minutes of arc. Early in its career it tracked the Russian earth satellites and the American lunar probes. Another instrument of radio astronomy is the interferometer which consists of two spaced aerials. *See also* **Observatories.**

Television, or the transmission of images of moving objects by radio. True television was first demonstrated by J. L. Baird at the Royal Institution in London in 1926. The B.B.C. began television broadcasts in 1930. The first television exchange across the Atlantic was made in July 1962 by way of the *Telstar* satellite.

Tellurium, a relatively scarce element, symbol Te, discovered in 1782 by Reichenstein. Chemically it behaves rather like sulphur; its salts are known as tellurides. It occurs chiefly combined with metals in ores of gold, silver, copper, and lead. It is a semiconductor, and some of its compounds (also semiconductors) are coming into use in technical devices.

Templars were soldier knights organised in the 12th cent. for the purpose of protecting pilgrims in their journeyings to and from Jerusalem, and obtained their name from having had granted to them by Baldwin II. a temple for their accommodation. At first they were non-military, and wore neither crests nor helmets, but a long wide mantle and a red cross on the left shoulder. They were established in England about 1180. During the crusades they rendered valuable service, showing great bravery and devotion. In the 12th cent. they founded numerous religious houses in various parts of Europe and became possessed of considerable wealth. It was this that caused their downfall. Kings and Popes alike grew jealous of their influence, and they were subjected to much persecution, and Pope Clement V. abolished the Order in 1312. Edward II. in 1308 seized all the property of the English Templars. The English possessions of the Order were transferred to the Hospitallers of St. John, afterwards called the Knights of Malta. *See also* **Hospitallers, Knights, Teutonic Order.**

Temple, a building dedicated to the worship of a deity or deities. Those built by the ancient Greeks at Olympia, Athens, and Delphi were the most famous. The Temple of Diana at Ephesus was another. The Temple of Solomon at Jerusalem was destroyed and rebuilt several times; Herod's Temple was destroyed by the Romans in A.D. 70.

Temple Bar, an historic gateway that until 1879 stood at the western entrance to Fleet Street near the bottom of Chancery Lane. In olden times it was the custom to impale the heads of traitors over this gateway. It has been at Theobald's Park, Cheshunt, since 1888.

Tempo, a musical expression referring to the pace at which a composition is to be played, and generally used in combination with a qualifying word, as "Tempo Ordinario," ordinary time.

Tenor, the third voice in a male voice choir, *i.e.*, between alto and bass. The name is also applied to instruments of equivalent pitch, *e.g.*, tenor saxophone.

Terbium, an element, symbol Tb, discovered in 1842 by Mosander, belonging to the group of rare-earth metals.

Teredo, the scientific name of the ship-worm, a peculiar bivalve mollusc, which lodges itself when young on the bottoms of wooden ships and bores its way inwards, causing much injury.

Termites, also known as *White Ants*, though they are not related to the true ants and are placed in an entirely different insect order (*Isoptera*). They abound in the tropics and also occur in temperate countries, though only two species are common in Europe. There is no British species. They live in colonies and their nests take the form of mounds of earth and wood, cemented together with saliva, and up to 20 ft. in height. Five separate castes are recognised, three of them being capable of reproduction, and the other two are sterile.

Tern. This slender, gull-like bird has long pointed wings, a deeply-forked tail, pale grey and white plumage, black cap, and is a very graceful flier. There are several species, some of which are summer migrants to Britain. The Arctic tern winters in the Antarctic, returning to find a nesting place in the spring.

Terrapin, a kind of fresh-water tortoise. There are several species widely distributed in the Northern Hemisphere.

Tertiary Rocks, in geology the rocks formed during the Caenozoic era comprising the Eocene, Oligocene, Miocene, Pliocene and Pleistocene periods. *See* **Geological Time Scale, F30.**

Teutonic Order, of German military knights, was founded in the Holy Land at the end of the 12th cent. for succouring the wounded of the Christian army before Acre. They were dispersed in the 15th cent. but the Order continued to exist until 1809, when Napoleon I. confiscated its properties. In 1840 the order was resuscitated in Austria as a semi-religious knighthood. *See also* **Hospitallers, Knights, Templars.**

Thallium, a blue-grey metallic element, symbol Tl, discovered by Crookes in 1861. It is obtained from the flue dust resulting from the burning of pyrites for sulphuric acid manufacture.

Thallophytes *or* **Thallophyta**, the division of the plant kingdon which includes fungi, algae, and bacteria. *See* **F27**(1).

Theodolite. The instrument used by surveyors for measuring angles in the horizontal and vertical planes; also used in meteorology for following balloons to measure the speed and direction of wind.

Therm. The charges for gas for lighting and heating (formerly reckoned at per cubic foot) are now based on the calorific, or heat, value of the gas, and the unit used is termed a therm. The therm is 100,000 British thermal units.

Thermodynamics, a term first applied by Joule to designate that branch of physical science which treats of the relations of heat to work. What is called the first law of thermodynamics is thus stated by Clerk Maxwell: "When work is transformed into heat, or heat into work, the quantity of work is mechanically equivalent to the quantity of heat." In one of its many formulations, the second law asserts that "the heat tends to flow from a body of hotter temperature to one that is colder, and will not naturally flow in any other way." *See* **F16**(2).

Thermo-electric Devices. If two wires of different materials are formed into a loop and if the two joins are kept at different temperatures a current flows in the loop. This was discovered by Seebeck in 1822, and the device is called a thermocouple. The electric current could in principle be made to drive some useful machine, and the energy comes from the heat that is absorbed by the thermocouple—if one part of the thermocouple is not hotter than the others it will not work. It has long been realised that this is a device that converts heat directly into electricity without raising steam and driving dynamos as in a power-station. However, until recently nobody has used thermocouples for much besides temperature measurement, for which they are exceedingly useful. The new development is the manufacture of semiconductors (*q.v.*); for the thermoelectric effects of these new materials are much greater than those of metals. A material much studied in this connection is a compound of bismuth and tellurium, bismuth telluride. It now seems practicable to generate useful electricity from suitably designed thermocouples. For example, the U.S.S.R. produces a thermoelectric device which uses the heat from the chimney of a domestic oil-lamp to produce enough electricity to work a radio. Presumably this is very useful in remote parts with no electricity supply. But the possibilities do not stop there. Indeed, an eminent Russian authority has stated that thermocouples could produce electricity direct from the warmth of sunlight on a scale and at a cost comparable with conventional fuel-burning power-stations. Even if solar energy cannot be so used, it might be possible to use the heat of nuclear reactors, but this means that the thermoelectric devices would have to stand up to very heavy radioactivity and still work. It is not surprising, however, that many firms are showing great interest in thermoelectricity these days.

Thermometer, an instrument by which the temperature of bodies is ascertained. The most familiar kind of thermometer consists of a glass tube with a very small bore, containing, in general, mercury or alcohol. This expands or contracts with variation in the temperature, and the length of the thread of mercury or alcohol gives the temperature reading on a scale graduated in degrees. Various forms of thermometer are used for particular purposes.

Thermonuclear Reactions. *See* **Nuclear Fusion.**

Thirty-nine Articles. *See* **Articles.**

Thistle, Order of. *See* **Knighthood.**

Thorium, a scarce, dark grey, metal element, symbol Th, discovered by Berzelius in 1828. All substances containing thorium are radioactive. Chief source of thorium is monazite sand, big deposits of which occur in Travancore (India), Brazil, and the U.S.A. Considered important as a potential source of atomic energy since the discovery that it can be transmuted into U233, which is capable of fission like U235.

Thorough Bass, a musical term applied to a voice part accompanied by numerals, showing the chord applicable to each note. The term also refers to the entire science of harmonic composition.

Thrush, a large family of song-birds of the *Passeriform* order, distributed all over the world. The British species include the robin, redstart, nightingale, song-thrush (or mavis), blackbird, mistle-thrush, ring-ouzel of the mountains, and large numbers of migrant fieldfares and redwings from northern Europe are winter visitors.

Thunder, the sound heard after the occurrence of a lightning flash. It is due to vibrations of the air along the path of the flash, which are set up by the sudden heating (and expansion) followed by the rapid cooling (and contraction) to which the air is subjected. It is unusual for thunder to be heard more than 10 miles away, the distance being estimated roughly by allowing 1 mile for every 5 seconds which elapse between seeing the flash and hearing the thunder. Continued rolling of thunder results from the zig-zag nature of the flash and the multiple strokes of which it is composed, variations in the energy developed along the path, and echo effects. Thunderstorms are caused by powerful rising currents of air within towering cumulonimbus clouds and are most frequent during the afternoons and evenings of sunny summer days.

Thursday, the 5th day of the week, named after Thor, the Scandinavian deity. To the ancient Romans Thursday was *dies Jovis*, or Jupiter's day.

Tides, the periodical rise and fall of the waters of the ocean and its arms, are due to the gravitational effect of the moon and sun. Newton was the first to give a general explanation of the phenomenon of the tides. He supposed the ocean to cover the whole earth, and to assume at each instant a figure of equilibrium, under the combined gravitational influence of earth, sun, and moon, thus making and controlling the tides. At most places there are two tides a day, and the times of high- and low-water vary according to the positions of the sun and moon relative to the earth. When earth, moon, and sun are in line (at full moon and new moon) the gravitational pull is greatest and we get "spring" tides. When sun and moon are at right angles (first and third quarters of the moon's phases) we get the smaller "neap" tides.

Tiers Etat, the lowest of the three estates of the realm as reckoned in France—nobility, clergy, and commons (*tiers état*)—prior to the Revolution.

Tiger, a powerful carnivorous animal of the cat family, which occurs in India and certain other parts of Asia. Its skin is of a tawny yellow, relieved by black stripings of great beauty of formation. Some tigers attain a length of from 9 to 12 ft.

Timpani, the kettledrums in an orchestra. *See* **Drums.**

Tin is a white, metal element, symbol Sn (Latin *Stannum*), whose commonest ore is cassiterite (tin oxide), which occurs in Malaya, Indonesia, Bolivia, Congo, Nigeria, and Cornwall. It protects iron from rusting, and the tin coating on tinplate is applied by dipping the thin steel sheet in molten tin or by electrolysis. Tin alloys of importance include solder, bronze, pewter, and Britannia metal.

Tit *or* **Titmouse**, a small insectivorous bird of the woodlands and forests, bright of plumage and very active and agile, often seen hanging upside down searching for food. There are over fifty species, eight of which occur in Britain: the Great and Blue Tits, familiar in gardens and countryside, the Cole Tit, Marsh Tit, Willow Tit, Bearded Tit, Long-tailed or "Bottle" Tit, and the Scottish Crested Tit.

Titanium, a scarce metal, symbol Ti, difficult to extract from ores, found in association with oxygen in rutile, anatase, and brookite, as well as with certain magnetic iron ores. It combines with nitrogen at a high temperature. Discovered by the Rev. William Gregor in 1791. Titanium alloys, being very resistant to stress and corrosion, and combining strength with lightness, are finding wide application not only in marine and chemical engineering but in the building of aircraft, rockets, and the nuclear-energy field. Titanium dioxide is now widely used in making paints.

Tithes, an ecclesiastical tax consisting of a tenth part of the annual produce known to the ancient Jews, and first imposed by Christian authorities in the 4th cent., although not made compulsory in England before the 9th cent. Tithes derived from land are termed "praedial," those derived from cattle being styled "mixed," while others are personal. After the passing of the Tithes' Commutation Act of 1836, tithes were gradually converted into rent charges, and to-day the old form of tithes exists only to a small degree. Consult Tithe Act of 1936.

T.N.T. (Trinitrotoluene). A high explosive formed by the action of a mixture of nitric and sulphuric acids on toluene. Not highly sensitive to shock, it can be used in shells without danger, and is exploded by a time, or detonator, fuse. Apart from wartime applications, it is used in blasting in quarries and mines.

Toad, an amphibian, differing from the frog in having a dry, warty skin, a heavier, squat build and shorter limbs. It has a similar metamorphosis, is largely nocturnal, and will wander far from water after the breeding season. Two toads occur in Britain, the Common Toad and the Natterjack. The latter can be identified by the narrow light stripe running down the middle of the back.

Tobacco is made from the leaves of various narcotic plants of the *Nicotiana* family, which contain a volatile oil and an alkaloid called nicotine. Tobacco is largely grown in America, India, Japan, Turkey, Greece, Canada, Italy, Indonesia, Bulgaria, Philippines, France, Congo, China, Rhodesia, Zambia, S. Africa, S. America, and other countries of a warm climate. It undergoes various processes of preparation. The leaves are first dried, then cut into small pieces, moistened and compressed, and in this form it is known as cut or "shag" tobacco; when moistened with syrup or treacle and pressed into cakes, it is Cavendish; when twisted into string form, it is "twist" or "pig-tail." For cigars the midribs of the dry leaves are removed, and what is left is moistened and rolled into cylindrical shape. For snuff, the tobacco leaves are moistened and allowed to ferment, then dried, powdered and scented. *See* **P32**(2) for the connection between tobacco-smoking and lung cancer.

Toga, an outer robe worn by the ancient Romans and corresponding to the pallium of the Greeks. It was white and made of wool.

Tolls. Payments for privileges of passage were first exacted in respect of ships passing up rivers, tolls being demanded on the Elbe in 1109. Tolls for land passage are said to have originated in England in 1269, toll-bars being erected at certain distances on the high-roads in the 17th cent., where toll had to be paid for all vehicles passing to and fro. After about 1825 they began to disappear, but still linger on some country roads and bridges. Tolls on London river bridges ceased in 1878–79.

Tone Poem *or* **Symphonic Poem**, a musical work of a serious nature and of symphonic dimensions in which the composer has not adopted the forms and conventions of the true symphony.

Tonic Sol-Fa, a system of musical notation in which monosyllables are substituted for notes. Thus the major diatonic scale is represented by Doh, Ray, Me, Fah, Soh, La, Te, Doh. The system was invented by a Miss Glover of Norwich in about 1840 and has proved of great assistance in the teaching of music in schools.

Tonsure, the shaven part of the head of a Roman Catholic ecclesiastic, dates from the 5th or 6th cent. In the Roman Catholic Churches only a circle, or a crown, is shaved, while in the Greek Church shaving is forbidden.

Topaz, a transparent mineral gem, being a silicate and fluoride of aluminium and generally found in granitic rocks. Its colour is yellow, but it also occurs in pink and blue shades. The best kinds come from Brazil.

Topiary, the art of clipping and trimming trees, shrubs, etc., into ornamental shapes. This art goes back to Elizabethan times when gardens were formal and the shapes simple and symmetrical. By the end of Queen Anne's reign topiary had become much more elaborate, and all kinds of fanciful shapes were produced.

Tornado, a violent whirlwind, characterised by a black, funnel-shaped cloud hanging from heavy cumulonimbus. Usually tornadoes are only a few hundred feet in diameter and occur frequently in the Mississippi region of the U.S.A., where it has been estimated that the wind speeds within them may exceed 200 m.p.h. In West Africa the term is applied to thundery squalls.

Tortoises and **Turtles**, are cold-blooded reptiles, four-footed, and encased in a strong shell protection, the shells of some species being of beautifully horny substance and design, in much demand for combs, spectacle frames, and ornamental work. It is the custom to designate the land species as tortoises and the aquatic kinds as turtles. The green turtle, so called because its fat has a green tinge, is in great demand for soup. Together the tortoises and turtles make up the reptilian order called *Chelonia*, the biggest representatives of which are the giant land tortoises of the Galapagos Islands, reaching a weight of 500 lb. and living a century. Some of these giant tortoises are even said to have reached 200 or 300 years of age.

Toucan, a South and Central American family of brilliantly coloured birds, remarkable for their huge bills. Toucans live on fruit, are of arboreal habits, and nest in holes. There are about 37 species.

Touchstone, a kind of jasper called by the ancients "Lydian stone," of economic value in testing the quality of metal alloys, especially gold alloys. The testing process is very simple. The alloy is drawn across the broken surface of the Touchstone, and from the nature of the mark or streak it makes the quality of the alloy can be ascertained.

Tourmaline, a mineral occurring in different colours in prismatic crystals. It is a well-known example of a pyro-electric crystal, *i.e.*, one that has a permanent electric polarisation. It is a double silicate of aluminium and boron, and occurs in Cornwall, Devon, South America, and Asia.

Tournaments were equestrian contests between military knights and others armed with lances, and frequent in the Middle Ages. The Normans introduced them to England.

Tower of London was a royal palace from the time of the Conqueror, who began the building of the White Tower in 1078. Later kings made considerable additions. Between the 15th and 18th cent. many princes and nobles were executed or imprisoned here, and here Henry VI., Edward V., and his brother were put to death. The Crown Jewels are kept at the Tower, and in the Armoury a fine collection of armour of various dates is preserved. The attendant staff are called Yeomen Warders of the Tower. Their style of dress is of the Tudor period.

Trade-Mark, a mark used in relation to goods for the purpose of indicating a connection in the course of trade between the goods and some person having the right, either as a proprietor or registered user, to use the mark. Trade-marks can be registered, the registration holding good for 7 years and being renewable thereafter indefinitely for periods of 14 years. Infringement of a registered trade-mark renders the infringer liable to damages.

Trade Winds form part of the circulation of air round the great permanent anticyclones of the tropics and blow inwards from north-east and south-east towards the equatorial region of low pressure. Atlantic trades are more regular than those of the Pacific. The belts may extend over 1,500 miles of latitude and, together with the Doldrums, move north and south in sympathy with the seasonal changes in the sun's declination, the average annual range being about 5 degrees of latitude. The discovery of the regularity of the trade winds is usually credited to Columbus.

Trafalgar, Battle of, was fought off Cape Trafalgar on Oct. 21, 1805, between the British under Nelson and the French and Spanish under Villeneuve and Gravina. It was a complete victory for the British, but Nelson was killed.

Trafalgar Square. The site has often been referred to as the finest in Europe. It was conceived originally as a square by John Nash (1752–1835) when the project was considered of linking Whitehall with Bloomsbury and the British Museum. It was to be named after the new monarch as King William the Fourth's Square but on the suggestion of George Ledwell Taylor (a property owner near the site) alteration to the more popular name Trafalgar Square was agreed to by the King. On the north side the National Gallery was planned by Nash and erected by William Wilkins on the place of the Royal Mews—a work of William Kent a century before. The lay-out was the idea of Charles Barry but he did not approve the erection of the Nelson column (which see). His idea was for the square to have a grand flight of steps from the north side with sculptural figures of Wellington and Nelson but the Commons decided otherwise and the column as designed by William Railton was begun in 1840. The two fountains by Barry were supplanted in 1948 by ones designed (1938) by Sir Edwin Lutyens. Executed in Portland stone they are flanked by some bronze sculptures. In the same year memorial busts of Lords Jellicoe and Beatty were placed by the north wall.

Transept, the portion of a church which extends across the interior between the nave and the choir.

Transistor. An electronic device consisting of a small piece of semiconducting solid (usually germanium or silicon) to which contact is made at appropriate places by three wires. The three parts resemble in function (not construction or behaviour) the cathode, anode, and grid of a thermionic valve, and transistors can perform many of the operations that valves have hitherto been used for in radio, television, etc. They possess several advantages over valves since there is no need for evacuated glass bulbs nor for a heated emitter to give off electrons. This leads to much greater compactness and economy as well as to a much longer life. Nevertheless, there are certain limitations to their use, and they are not yet suitable as substitutes for valves in all cases. The device was invented by the Americans Bardeen, Brattain, and Shockley in 1948. *See* **Microelectronics, Section F, Part IV.**

Transubstantiation. *See* **J43.**

Treasure-Trove, a legal term applying to treasure (coin, bullion, gold or silver articles) found hidden in the earth or other place, for which no owner can be discovered. The treasure legally belongs to the Crown, but it is the practice to return to the finder all articles not required for national museums and to reward him with the full market value of such as may be retained. It is the duty of the finder to report to the Coroner for the district in which the find is made who holds an inquest to find whether the discovery be treasure-trove or no. In England concealment is a criminal offence.

Treble, the highest voice in a male voice choir This is, of course, a boy's voice, the highest adult male voice being the alto. In a mixed choir the treble part is sung by sopranos.

Tree Frog, occurs most commonly in America and Australasia. The common European tree frog is a brilliant green animal, the adhesive discs at the tips of its fingers and toes enabling it to cling to trees, etc., wth ease.

Tree Shrew, an arboreal insectivorous mammal of Asia belonging to the family *Tupaiidae*. Tree shrews are related to the shrews, though in appearance they resemble squirrels except for their sharply pointed snout. They occur in Borneo, Siam, China, and Malaya. Some zoologists classify them as primitive primates.

Trent, Council of, the longest and one of the most important in the history of the Roman Catholic Church, was convened to combat the doctrines of Martin Luther. It first sat in 1545, the last sitting being in 1563. At this Council the general policy, principles, and dogmas of the Roman Catholic Church were authoritatively settled.

Triassic *or* **Trias**, the earliest geological period in the Mesozoic era, which began some 225 million years ago. Triassic formations 25,000 ft. thick occur in the Alps. *See* **F30.** Modern insects were appearing, and also small reptile-like mammals. Other important Triassic animals were: dinosaurs, ichthyosaurs (marine reptiles), and pterosaurs (flying reptiles).

Tribunes, name assigned to officers of different descriptions in ancient Rome. The original tribunes were the commanders of contingents of cavalry and infantry. The most important tribunes were the tribunes of the plebs, first elected in 494 B.C. as the outcome of the struggle between the patrician and the plebeian orders. They held the power of veto and their persons were sacred.

Trichoptera. This is the insect order comprising the Caddis-flies. These are moth-like insects, having hairs on the wings. They are usually found fluttering weakly near water. The larvae are aquatic and are remarkable for the cases (caddis cases) which they build out of sticks, small stones, sand grains, and shells.

Tricolour, the flag of the French Republic since 1789, consisting of three nearly equal vertical bands of blue, white, and red (ratio 90 : 99 : 111).

Trilobites, extinct marine arthropods, most abundant in the Cambrian and Ordovician systems. Their appearance may be roughly described as resembling that of a woodlouse, and like that animal the trilobites were capable of rolling their bodies up into a ball.

Trinity. The Christian doctrine that God exists in three persons, all co-equal, and indivisible, of the same substance—God the Father, God the Son (who became incarnate as Jesus), begotten of the Father, and God the Holy Ghost, proceeding from Father and Son. The system denying the Trinity is Unitarianism (*see* **J43**).

Trinity House, on Tower Hill, London, was incorporated in 1514 as an association for piloting ships, and has ever since been entrusted with various matters connected with the regulation of British navigation. Since 1854 the lighthouses of the country have been under its supervision. The acting Elder Brethren act as Nautical Assessors in Marine causes which are tried by the High Court of Justice.

Trio, strictly a musical composition for three voices or instruments. The third movement, of a classical symphony is usually in three-beat time and the second subject of the movement, which is of ternary form, is often called the Trio. Thus, Minuet and Trio, Scherzo and Trio.

Triptych, a picture, carving, or other representation, with two swing doors, by which it could be closed in; frequently used as an altar-piece. Also a writing tablet in three parts, two of which folded over the one in the centre.

Trireme, an ancient vessel with three rows of oars of great effectuality in early naval warfare. Mentioned by Thucydides. It was a long, narrow vessel propelled by 170 rowers. The Romans copied it from the Greeks.

Trisagion ("thrice holy"), an ancient Jewish hymn, still regularly sung in the service of the Greek Church. A version of it—"Tersanctus"—also forms part of the Anglican Eucharistic service.

Tritium, a radioactive isotope of hydrogen which has three times the weight of the ordinary hydrogen atom. It is produced by bombarding an isotope of lithium with neutrons and has a half-life of 12¼ years, decaying with the emission of β-particles (electrons).

Triumvirate, a term used to denote a coalition of three persons in the exercise of supreme authority. The first Roman triumvirate was that of Pompey, Julius Caesar, and Crassus, 60 B.C.; the second was that of Mark Antony, Octavus, and Lepidus, 43 B.C.

Trombone, a bass wind instrument which has a tube of variable length. By moving the slide, which shortens or lengthens the tube, the player causes the trombone to emit different notes.

Tropic-Bird, a long-tailed sea bird, of which there are 3 species (the Red-billed, the White-tailed, and the Red-tailed), frequenting the tropical regions of the Atlantic, Pacific, and Indian oceans. They are commonly called Bo'sun Birds.

Troposphere. The atmospheric layer which extends from the earth's surface to the stratosphere. As a general rule the temperature in the troposphere falls as altitude increases. *See* **Atmosphere.**

Troubadours, lyric poets who flourished from the 11th to the end of the 13th cent., chiefly in Provence and the north of Italy. They were often knightly amateurs, and cultivated a lyrical poetry intricate in metre and rhyme and usually of a romantic amatory strain. They did much to cultivate the romantic sentiment in days when society was somewhat barbaric and helped considerably in the formation of those unwritten codes of honour which served to mitigate the rudeness of mediaeval days. *See also* **Jongleurs.**

Trouvère *or* **Trouveur**, mediaeval poet of northern France, whose compositions were of a more elaborate character—epics, romances, fables, and chansons de geste—than those of the troubadour of the south. Flourished between the 11th and 14th cent.

Truffles are subterranean edible fungi much esteemed for seasoning purposes. There are many species, and they are found in considerable quantities in France and Italy, less commonly in Britain. They are often met with under beech or oak trees, and prefer calcareous soils, but there are no positive indications on the surface to show where they are, and they are not to be cultivated. Hogs, and sometimes dogs, are used to scent them out, the former, by reason of their rooting propensities, being the most successful in the work.

Trumpet, a brass wind musical instrument in which different notes are produced by the operation of three "valves."

Tsetse, an African dipterous fly belonging to the same family as the house-fly. It is a serious economic pest as it transmits the protozoon causing African sleeping sickness when it pierces human skin in order to suck blood, which forms its food. *See* **Gammexane.**

Tuatara or *Sphenodon punctatum*, a primitive lizard found in New Zealand. It has a rudimentary third eye on the top of the head; this is called the pineal eye and corresponds to tissue which in mammals forms the pineal gland.

Tuba, an alternative name for the Bass Saxhorn in E flat or F. *See* **Saxhorn.**

Tube Foot, the characteristic organ of locomotion of starfishes and kindred animals. They are arranged in pairs along the underside of the arms, and their sucker-like ends can grip a surface very tightly. The action of the suckers depends on hydraulic pressure.

Tudor Period extends from 1485 to 1603. The first Tudor sovereign was Henry VII., descended from Owen Tudor; then followed Henry VIII., Edward VI., Mary, and Elizabeth, the last of the line.

Tuesday, the third day of the week, named from the Saxon deity Tuisto, Tiw, or Teusco. To the Romans it was the day of Mars.

Tuileries, a French royal and imperial palace dating from 1564. It was attacked by insurgents during the outbreaks of 1792, 1830, and 1848, and was burned down during the Commune of Paris in 1871.

Tumulus, a mound of earth raised over the bodies of the dead. The mound of Marathon, enclosing the bodies of the Athenians who were killed in the famous battle with the Persians, is a celebrated tumulus. Such mounds were commonly raised over the tombs of the distinguished dead in ancient times, and sometimes enclosed heavy structures of masonry. The Roman "barrows" were tumuli. Evidences of such mounds are frequent in prehistoric remains.

Tuna *or* **Tunny**, a large marine fish belonging to the mackerel family, frequenting the warm waters of the Atlantic, Pacific, and Mediterranean. Tuna fisheries are an important industry.

Tundra, the vast barren treeless plains with small lakes and morasses lying in the arctic regions of northern N. America and northern Russia where the winters are long and severe and the subsoil permanently frozen. Sparsely inhabited by nomadic peoples—Lapps, Samoyeds, and Eskimos—who support themselves by hunting and fishing. The reindeer is domesticated and supplies most of their needs.

Tungsten, a hard, brittle metal, symbol W (it was formerly called wolfram), silver to grey in colour. Its chief ores are wolframite (iron and manganese tungstate) and scheelite (calcium tungstate). Tungsten is alloyed in steel for the manufacture of cutting tools; also in the non-ferrous alloy stellite (*q.v.*). Electric lamp filaments are made from tungsten. Tungsten carbide is one of the hardest substances known and is used for tipping tools.

Turbines propelled by steam provide power for the propulsion of many ships, and on land steam turbines are a principal source of power, being used in large central electricity stations, for instance, to convert heat energy into electrical energy. Gas turbines have recently come into use in aeroplanes, and gas-turbine railway locomotives are being developed. The first gas-turbine ship had its trials in 1947, just half a century after the first steam-turbine ship.

Turbot, a large flat fish, highly valued as food. It often attains from 30 to 40 lb. in weight. Its flesh is white and firm. It is confined to European waters, and is caught by line or trawl.

Turkey, a fowl of American origin, brought to Europe from America soon after the discovery of that country. It was a domesticated bird in England in the first half of the 16th cent.

Turpentine, an oily substance obtained from coniferous trees, mostly pines and firs. It is widely used especially in making paints and varnishes, and also has medicinal properties.

Turquoise, formerly called Turkey-Stone, is a blue or greenish-blue precious stone, the earliest and best specimens of which came from Persia. It is composed of a phosphate of aluminium, with small proportions of copper and iron. India, Tibet, and Silesia yield turquoises, and a variety is found in New Mexico and Nevada. It derives its name from the fact that the first specimens were imported through Turkey.

Turtle Dove, a summer visitor from Africa to southern England. It is a small, slender bird with reddish-brown upper parts, pinkish throat, black tail with white edges, and a repeated purring note.

Tweed. A rough-surfaced fabric of the twilled type usually all-wool, though cheaper kinds may include cotton. Of a soft, open, flexible texture it may have a check, twill, or herringbone pattern. Harris, Lewis, Bannockburn, and Donegal tweeds are well known. "Tweeds" is said to have been written in error by a clerk for "twills."

Twelfth Night is the eve of the feast of the

Epiphany, and in olden times was made the occasion of many festivities. It was the most popular festival next to Christmas, but is now little observed.

Twilight is the light which is reflected from the upper portion of the earth's atmosphere when the sun is below the horizon (before sunrise or after sunset). The term is most usually understood to refer, however, to the evening light; the morning light we call dawn. The twilight varies in duration in different countries, according to the position of the sun. In tropical countries it is short; in the extreme north it continues through the night.

Tyburn, a former small tributary of the Thames, which gave its name to the district where now stands the Marble Arch, Hyde Park. Here public executions formerly took place.

Tycoon, the title by which the commander-in chief of the Japanese army (virtually the ruler of Japan) was formerly described by foreigners. (In Japanese *taikun* means great lord or prince.) The term is now applied, usually in a derogatory sense, to an influential business magnate.

Tympanum is, in architectural phraseology, the triangular space at the back of a pediment, or, indeed, any space in a similar position, as over window or between the lintel and the arch of a doorway. In ecclesiastical edifices the tympanum is often utilised for sculptured ornamentation.

Tynwald, the title given to the Parliament of the Isle of Man, which includes the Governor and Council (the Upper House), and the House of Keys, the representative assembly. This practically constitutes Home Rule, the Acts passed by the Tynwald simply requiring the assent of the Sovereign.

Typhoon. The tropical cyclone of the China Seas which brings winds of hurricane strength and torrential rains, most frequently in late summer or early autumn.

U

Uhlan, a light cavalry soldier armed with lance, pistol, and sabre and employed chiefly as skirmisher or scout. Marshal Saxe had a corps of them in the French Army; and in the Franco-German war of 1870 the Prussian Uhlans won fame.

Ultramarine, a sky-blue pigment obtained from *lapis lazuli*, a stone found in Tibet, Persia, Siberia, and some other countries. A cheaper ultramarine is now produced by grinding and heating a mixture of clay, sulphur, carbonate of soda, and resin.

Ultrasonics, sound waves of frequency so high as to be inaudible to humans, *i.e.*, about 12,000 cycles per sec. and upwards. Ultrasonic waves are commonly produced by causing a solid object to vibrate with a suitably high frequency and to impart its vibrations to the air or other fluid. The object may be a quartz or other crystal in which vibrations are excited electrically, or a nickel component which is magnetically energised. There are numerous technical applications, *e.g.* submarine echo sounding, flaw detection in castings, drilling glass and ceramics, emulsification. Ultrasonic waves are an important tool of research in physics.

Ultra-Violet Rays. These are invisible electromagnetic rays whose wavelengths are less than 3,900 A. (Angstrom = one-hundredth of a millionth of a centimetre). The sun's radiation is rich in ultra-violet light, but much of it never reaches the earth, being absorbed by molecules of atmospheric gases (in particular, ozone) as well as by soot and smoke particles. One beneficial effect of ultra-violet light on human beings is that it brings about synthesis of vitamin-D from certain fatty substances (called sterols) in the skin. The wave-lengths which effect this vitamin synthesis also cause sun tan and sun burn. Ultra-violet lamps (which are mercury-vapour discharge lamps) are also used for sterilising the air inside buildings, their rays being lethal to bacteria. Many substances fluoresce under ultra-violet light; for instance, zinc silicate glows green, while cadmium borate throws out red light. This phenomenon is applied practically in fluorescent lamps, the light of requisite hue being secured by judicious mixture of the fluorescent materials which coat the lamp. *See* **Electric Light.**

Umbra, the full shadow of the earth or moon during an eclipse; the half shadow is called penumbra.

Uncials were a form of written characters used in times prior to the 10th cent.; while smaller than capitals they were larger than the later minuscule. The term uncial was a misapplication of St. Jerome's *literae unciales*, "inch-high" letters.

Unction, the act of anointing with oil, a symbol of consecration practised in the Roman Catholic, Greek, and other Churches, but not in the Protestant. *Extreme unction* is the rite of anointing a dying person with holy oil. This function consists in anointing the eyes, ears, nostrils, mouth, the palms of the hands, and the soles of the feet.

Underdeveloped Countries are countries in which primitive methods of production still largely prevail. Most of the population are peasants, carrying on agricultural pursuits on small-holdings without much use of capital, and the industrial production is largely in the hands of individual craftsmen working without expensive capital instruments. Many of these countries are now trying to carry through large plans of industrialisation, but are severely hampered by lack of capital resources, as they need to import capital goods for which they find it difficult to pay with exports, especially when the "terms of trade" (*see* **G7**) are unfavourable to primary producers. The need for capital imposes on such countries the necessity of a high rate of saving out of their national incomes; but this is difficult to enforce in view of the deep poverty of most of the people. They accordingly stand in need of help from the advanced countries, both with capital loans at low interest rates and gifts. *See* **G11.**

Underground Gasification, the process of converting coal into gas underground. Briefly an "underground gasworks" comprises two approximately vertical shafts connected by a gallery through the coal seam, which is ignited. Air is led down one of the shafts, and the gas produced is drawn off from the second shaft. The technique was worked out by the British chemist, Sir William Ramsay, but it was not until 1933 that it was tried seriously—in the Donetz coalfield in Russia. America, Italy, and Belgium are experimenting with underground gasification; British experiments ended in 1959.

Unicorn, a fabulous single-horned animal. In heraldry its form is horse-like, with the tail of a lion and pointed single horn growing out of the forehead. In the Middle Ages the unicorn was a symbol of virginity.

Union of Great Britain and Ireland was proposed in the Irish Parliament in Jan. 1799 after the 1798 Rebellion and came into force on Jan. 1, 1801. The troubled history of Ireland, associated with the question of self-government, nationalism, land, and religion, culminated in the Easter revolution of 1916. A treaty giving the 26 southern counties independence in 1921, as the Irish Free State, was followed by a period of internal dissention. In 1937 a new constitution was enacted in Eire in which no reference was made to the Crown. This, however, left in force the External Relations Act of 1936 and with its repeal in 1948, Eire separated itself from the British Crown and thus severed the last constitutional link with the Commonwealth, and became an independent Republic.

Union, Treaty of, was the treaty by which Scotland became formally united to England, the two countries being incorporated as the United Kingdom of Great Britain, the same Parliament to represent both, Scotland electing sixteen peers and forty-five members of the House of Commons. Uniformity of coins, weights, and measures was provided for, Scottish trade laws and customs were assimilated to those of England, and as regards religion and the practices of the law, Scotland was to continue as before. This Act was ratified on May 1, 1707.

United Nations. *See* **Section C.**

Universe in astronomy means not only the star system (of which the sun and planets are a small part) but all the countless star systems or nebulae which may be separated from each other by millions of light-years. *See* **F3–7.**

Universities are institutions of higher education whose principal objects are the increase of knowledge over a wide field through original thought and research and its extension by the teaching of students. Such societies existed in the ancient world, notably in Greece and India, but the origin of the University as we know it today lies in mediaeval Europe, the word *universitas* being a contraction of the Latin term for corporations of teachers and students organised for the promotion of higher learning. The earliest bodies to become recognised under this description were at Bologna and Paris in the first half of the 12th cent.; Oxford was founded by an early migration of scholars from Paris, and Cambridge began with a further migration from Oxford. Other Universities sprang up all over Europe, including three in Scotland—St. Andrews (1412), Glasgow (1451), and Aberdeen (1494)—which were followed by Edinburgh in 1582. These six bodies remained the only Universities in Great Britain until the foundation in 1826–29 of University and King's Colleges in London (resulting in the establishment of the University of London in 1836) and of the University of Durham in 1832. There are (1966) twenty-five Universities in England (Birmingham, Bristol, Cambridge, Durham, East Anglia, Essex, Exeter, Hull, Keele, Kent, Lancaster, Leeds, Leicester, Liverpool, London, Manchester, Newcastle, Nottingham, Oxford, Reading, Sheffield, Southampton, Sussex, Warwick, and York); one in Wales (the University of Wales with Colleges at Aberystwyth, Bangor, Cardiff and Swansea); five in Scotland (Aberdeen, Edinburgh, Glasgow, St. Andrews, and Strathclyde—Britain's first technological University); and one in Northern Ireland (Queen's University, Belfast). In addition, St. David's College, Lampeter, confers two degrees (in Arts and Theology). The distribution of university status among the county towns of England came to an end when the Government decided in 1965 that no more new Universities were to be created in Britain in the next decade, with the possible exception of a new technological University in north-east England, but that existing Universities should be expanded to meet the needs of the increased number of students which was expected to reach 218,000 by 1973–4. This decision does not affect the creation of a new University at Stirling, nor the granting of university status to Queen's College, Dundee, and to the Heriot-Watt College, Edinburgh. The Colleges of Advanced Technology (CATs) are all preparing for university status. Three are moving to new sites: Bristol (the proposed University of Bath), Battersea (the proposed University of Surrey) at Guildford, and Brunel (the proposed Brunel University) at Uxbridge. The Royal Colleges of Art, and the Cranfield College of Aeronautics are also to be granted university status. The new creations will bring the total number of Universities to forty-five instead of sixty as proposed by the Robbins Committee. The Republic of Ireland has Trinity College, Dublin (founded in 1592), and the National University of Ireland, with its three constituent University Colleges at Dublin, Cork, and Galway. The 19th cent. also saw a wide extension of the University movement throughout the British Empire, the early important foundations being McGill (1821), Toronto (1827), and Laval (1852) in Canada; Sydney (1850) and Melbourne (1853) in Australia; New Zealand (1870); South Africa (1873); Bombay, Calcutta, and Madras in 1857 in India; and the University of the Punjab (1882) in the present Pakistan. Since the war a number of Universities and University Colleges have been instituted in Commonwealth countries—in the West Indies, in East and West Africa and Rhodesia, in Malaya, India, and Pakistan. In the U.S.A. the development of higher education has left the Universities less sharply defined than in Europe and the Commonwealth, the best-known being Harvard, Yale, Princeton, Columbia, and Chicago. In England a certain emphasis has always been placed on the provision of residential facilities for students. The Universities receive aid from the State mainly in the form of direct grants from the Treasury made on the advice of the University Grants Committee, a committee appointed by the Chancellor of the Exchequer from people with wide educational or industrial experience. But they are self-governing institutions free from State control. *See also* **N27–31.**

University Boat-race. *See* **U37.**

Uranium, a metal, symbol U, discovered by Klaproth in 1789 in pitch-blende. It is a white metal which tarnishes readily in air. Great developments have followed the discovery that the nucleus of the uranium isotope U^{235} undergoes fission, and uranium minerals have become very important since it was found that atomic energy could be released controllably by taking advantage of fission. Previous to the second world war the uranium content of all the uranium ores that were mined was estimated at 1,000 tons. Before atomic energy work began to take the major part of the world's output of uranium minerals, the chief users of uranium compounds were the ceramics and textile industries. *See also* **Nuclear Reactors, Nuclear Fission, F12(1).**

Uranus. This planet was discovered by Herschel in 1781. Its diameter is 32,000 miles and its average distance from the sun is 1,783 million miles. It has five small satellites.

Ursa Major, the Greater Bear, or "Charles's Wain," a constellation familiar to all observers because of the brilliance of the seven stars forming its outline. It never sets in these latitudes.

Ursa Minor, the Lesser Bear Constellation, has, like Ursa Major, seven prominent stars, of which the pole star is the brightest.

Utopias. *See* **J43.**

V

Vaccination, a system of inoculation against smallpox disovered by Dr. Jenner in the 18th cent. In Great Britain it is usual for all infants at the age of three months to be vaccinated unless the parent conscientiously believes that it would be harmful to the infant's health. *See* **P11(2).**

Valency. A term used by chemists to describe the combining ability of an element with respect to hydrogen. Thus oxygen, which forms water, H_2O, with hydrogen is said to have a valency of two, nitrogen (forms ammonia, NH_3) three, and carbon (forms methane, CH_4) four. Chlorine forms hydrogen chloride, HCl, and is said to be monovalent. This empirical approach cannot account for valency in such compounds as carbon monoxide, CO, which appears to require both elements to have the same valency. With the discovery of the electron it was realised that the concept of valency and chemical bonds is intimately concerned with the electronic structure of atoms, and theories have been advanced to explain why the same element can have different valencies in different compounds. Iron, for example, can have a valency of two ($FeCl_2$, ferrous chloride) or three ($FeCl_3$, ferric chloride). *See* **N32.**

Valentine's Day, the 14th Feb., is a festival in celebration of St. Valentine, one of the Christian martyrs of the 3rd cent. A sweetheart or Valentine is chosen on that day and letters or tokens sent secretly to the object of affection.

Valhalla, in Scandinavian mythology, is the special Paradise to which the souls of warriors slain in battle were transported. The term is also generally used to designate a burial place of great men.

Valkyries, the chosen handmaidens of Odin, appointed to serve at the Valhalla banquets. Their most important office, however, according to the Norse mythology, was to ride through the air at a time of battle and point out the heroes who were to fall. It is one of these Valkyries who is made the heroine of Wagner's opera "Die Walküre."

Vampire *or* **Werewolf,** according to ancient superstition, was a spectre in human form which rose from its grave in the night-time and preyed upon the living as they slept, sucking their blood, and then returning to the grave.

Vampire-Bats. blood-eating bats of tropical America. They puncture the skin with their incisor teeth, leaving a wound that bleeds profusely. The blood is lapped up by the bat, not sucked.

Vanadium, a scarce metallic element, symbol V, whose chief ores are carnotite and patronite. Some iron ores contain it. Most of the vanadium commercially produced finds its way into vanadium steels, which are used for tools and parts of vehicles, being hard, tough, and very resistant to shocks. The oxide is used as a catalyst in industry, especially in making sulphuric acid.

Van Allen Belts, two zones of high intensity particle radiation surrounding the earth, one concentrated at a distance of about 1,000 miles, the other at about 15,000 miles. A close relation exists between the shapes of the regions and the earth's magnetic field. Named after the American scientist who explained the puzzling data collected by the satellites *Explorers I* and *III*. Recent evidence suggests that Jupiter also is surrounded by a dense belt of trapped energetic particles.

Varnish is of two leading kinds: spirit varnish, made from resinous substances dissolved in spirit; and oil varnish, in which the dissolving agent is linseed oil and turpentine.

Vatican, the Papal residence at Rome, a famous palace on the hill adjacent to St. Peter's. Its museum is a rich treasure-house of literary and artistic objects.

Vauxhall Gardens, a famous London pleasure resort from the early part of the 18th to the middle of the 19th cent. It was here that many great singers appeared, where the earliest balloon ascents were made, and where there were fine displays of fireworks.

Vein. *See* **Lode.**

Venus, the brightest of all the planets, whose orbit lies between that of Mercury and the earth, second in order from the sun (*see* **F6**). It can approach the earth to within 25 million miles. At wide intervals Venus passes across the sun's disc ("transit of Venus"). The first transit was recorded in 1639, since then four have occurred, in 1761, 1769, 1874, and 1882, and the next is due in 2004. Little was known about the planet because of its obscuring atmosphere (much carbon dioxide and water vapour) until the American research spacecraft, *Mariner II*, passed within 21,600 miles of the planet in 1962 and gave data about its atmosphere, rotation period, etc. The surface temperature was found to be far too hot for life as known on earth, and no magnetic field was detected. Other scientific evidence suggests however that the planet may be cold at the surface, with its clouds composed of ice-crystals. Russia launched two Venus probes in 1965; the first passed within 15,000 miles of the planet and the other landed on the surface.

Venus Fly-trap, a well-known insectivorous plant (*Dionaea muscipula*) occurring in Carolina in damp mossy places. It is related to the Sundew. The leaf is the organ that catches the insects. The leaf blade is in two halves, hinged along the centre line. Each half bears three sensitive hairs called "trigger hairs." When an insect touches a trigger, the two halves of the leaf clap together, trapping the insect between them, when it is digested by a secretion (digestive enzymes) from the leaf, which afterwards absorbs the soluble products.

Vernalization. Seeds which, after being exposed to a low temperature, produce plants that flower earlier than usual are said to have been "vernalized." This technique of seed treatment devised by Lysenko is called vernalization. It is claimed to have been widely used in Russia to obtain cereal crops in places where climatic conditions are favourable for only a short season.

Versailles, Treaty of. The Peace Treaty, 1919, ending the first world war. The first half was devoted to the organisation of the League of Nations. Among the territorial changes Germany ceded Alsace-Lorraine to France, Posen and the Corridor to Poland. Germany undertook to disarm, to abolish universal military service, to keep only a small army of 100,000 and a small navy. Her colonies were to be shared out among the Allies under League Mandates. Reparations were to be paid, but were gradually reduced and entirely ceased in 1932. Hitler took unilateral action against the Treaty especially in regard to rearmament and the annexation of Austria. Hitler's attempt to change the eastern frontiers was the immediate cause of the Second World War.

Victoria and Albert Museum, in Kensington, London, was begun in 1852 as the Museum of Ornamental Art at Marlborough House. The present building was completed in 1909, and has the following nine departments: Architecture and Sculpture; Ceramics; Engraving, Illustration and Design; Metalwork; Paintings; Woodwork; Textiles; Library (of books on art) and Book-production; and the Dept. of Circulation. The Bethnal Green Museum is a branch of the V. and A.

Victoria Cross, an order of merit for conspicuous valour, awarded to members of the Army, Navy, and Air Force, was established in 1856. In July 1959 it was announced that all holders of the V.C. for whom the British Government is responsible would receive a tax-free annuity of £100.

Vienna Congress, sat at Vienna from Sept. 1814 to June 1815, and settled the delimination of the territories of the various European nations after the defeat of Napoleon. The Treaty of Vienna which resulted gave Ceylon, Mauritius, Cape Colony, Heligoland, Malta, and part of Guiana to England; France was not permitted to hold more territory than she had possessed at the outbreak of the Revolution in 1789; Austria took Northern Italy; Russia part of Poland; and Prussia, part of Saxony and the Rhenish province. Except for one or two changes the clauses of the treaty were maintained for over forty years.

Viet-Minh, the Indo-Chinese (Annamite) national movement led by Ho Chi-Minh which resisted French rule from 1945 to 1954, when Vietnam was partitioned as a result of the Geneva Conference. The National Liberation Front of South Vietnam is called the **Viet Cong.**

Vikings. Scandinavian pirates who from the 8th to the 10th cent. were the terror of northern waters. Sometimes the Viking raids reached south to the Mediterranean and east to the White Sea, and they ventured as far as Greenland and North America. Their leader Rurik founded the first Russian kingdom of Novgorod. They excelled in shipbuilding, were fine sailors and splendid craftsmen.

Vinegar. This condiment and preservative is a weak solution of acetic acid (3–9%) formed by the oxidation of ethyl alcohol by the action of bacteria on alcoholic liquor (wine, beer, cider, fermented fruit juices, or malted cereals). Wine vinegar is usually red; malt vinegar is brown. The name vinegar is derived from the latin *vinum aigre*, bad wine. *See also* **Acetic Acid.**

Vinyl Plastics are polymers made from derivatives of ethylene, examples are polyvinyl chloride (P.V.C.), which is used in making plastic pipes and kitchen utensils, among other things; polyvinyl acetate used in the paint industry and in bonding laminated articles like plywood; and polystyrene (poly vinyl benzene) used in making electrical fittings and for lenses.

Viola, a stringed instrument of the violin type but rather larger than the violin. Music for the viola is written mainly in the alto clef, though the treble clef is used for the higher notes.

Violin, a stringed instrument rather smaller than the ancient viol from which it derives. It is held under the chin for playing, the right hand bowing while the left hand "stops" the strings. The violin has been used in its present form since the 16th cent., the most famous maker being Antonio Stradivari of Cremona.

Violoncello, a member of the violin family of stringed instruments whose pitch corresponds with that of the bass voice. It is played while between the knees as was the old *viola da gamba*.

Viper, a family of poisonous snakes of which there is one example in Britain, the common viper or adder, only found in very dry localities.

Virginal, an English keyboard instrument of the harpsichord type greatly in vogue during Elizabethan times.

Virgo, the 6th constellation of the Zodiac, lying between Leo and Libra. It has seven prominent stars ranged in the form of the letter "Y." One of these stars is of the first magnitude, the other six being of the third magnitude.

Visibility is defined by the distance at which

the farthest of a series of objects, specially selected to show against the skyline or in good contrast with their background, can be distinguished. Visibility depends chiefly upon the concentration of water or dust particles suspended in the air. Instruments are available to measure the obscurity of the atmosphere more directly, including that at night. A large lapse rate of temperature and a strong wind are favourable to good visibility; a small lapse rate, calm or light wind favourable to bad visibility. Fog is when the visibility is less than 1,100 yds.; mist or haze when it is between 1,100 and 2,200 yds. *See* **Pollution.**

Viscount, a title of rank coming between that of Earl and Baron. The title originally stood for deputy-earl. The first English Viscount was Viscount Beaumont, created in 1440.

Vitamins, name of a group of organic substances found in relatively minute amounts in certain foodstuffs, essential for growth and the maintenance of normal bodily structure and function. The Hungarian biochemist Szent-Györgyi, who first isolated vitamin C or ascorbic acid, defined the vitamin as " a substance that makes you ill if you don't eat it!" *See* **P42**(2).

Volcanoes are vents through which magma reaches the surface as lava flows, or as the solid products, *e.g.*, ashes and bombs, of explosive eruption. The vent may be cylindrical or it may be a long fissure. The former type usually builds up cones, *e.g.*, Vesuvius. Notable active volcanoes are Etna, Vesuvius and Stromboli, in Italy; Hekla in Iceland; and Mont Pelée in Martinique. The last-named was in violent eruption in 1902, when the chief town of St. Pierre was completely destroyed. Volcanic eruptions are sometimes linked with brilliant sunset phenomena, *e.g.*, Krakatoa (1883), and Agung on the island of Bali (1963) which had been dormant for 120 years. A new fissure volcano (Surtsey) developed off the coast o Iceland in 1963.

Vole. There are three species of British vole; the Field-vole, the Bank-vole, and the Water-vole.

Volt, the electromotive force unit, named after Alessandro Volta (1745–1827), and defined in terms of the coulomb, the second, and the joule. *See* **N13**(1).

Vraic, a name for seaweed in the Channel Islands, where it is extensively used as a manure.

Vulgate, a term used to designate the Latin version of the Scriptures sanctioned by the Council of Trent.

Vulture, a famous bird of prey of two distinctive groups; that of the Old World, whose nostrils are separated by a bony partition, and the New World vulture, which has no such division. Vultures feed on carrion and are the great scavengers of tropical regions. The European species are the Egyptian vulture, Griffon vulture, Black vulture, and Bearded vulture. Vultures have no feathers on the head and neck.

W

Wading Birds, *Charadriiformes*, an order of migratory, long-legged, long-billed birds, frequenting marshes and shallow waters. They include the plovers, avocets, stilts, oystercatchers, curlews, phalaropes, godwits, dunlins, sandpipers, redshanks, greenshanks, snipe, woodcocks, the pratincole of the Mediterranean, and the sun bittern of tropical America. Many species breed in Britain.

Wagtails, familiar long-tailed small birds, the most common British species being the Pied or Water (with sub-species White) Grey and the Yellow (sub-species Blue.) Wagtails nest in holes and are active of habit.

Walloons, name given to the French-speaking population of the southern provinces of Belgium, in contrast to the Flemings or Dutch-speaking population of the northern provinces. The Walloon areas contain the mining and heavy industries of the country; the Flemish regions are more agricultural. Walloons number *c.* 3 million, Flemings *c.* 5 million. The *Mouvement Populaire Wallon* desires an autonomous Wallonia within the Belgian state.

Walpurgis Night, the night before May 1st, when witches and creatures of evil are supposed to have liberty to roam. Named after St. Walpurgis, an English nun, who went on a mission to Germany in the 8th cent. There is a famous Walpurgis night scene in Goethe's *Faust.*

Walrus, a very large marine mammal, related to the seals having in the upper jaw two large curved tusks, which average in length from 15 in. to 2 ft. It lives on bi-valve molluscs, and inhabits the Arctic seas. An adult walrus can exceed 12 ft. in length and weigh over a ton.

Wapentake, the ancient name given in the northern counties to territorial divisions corresponding to the Hundreds of southern counties.

Warblers, a family of small, lively song-birds closely related to the flycatchers and thrushes. Represented in Britain by about 36 species, including the chiffchaff, one of the earliest spring visitors, willow-wren, wood-warbler, blackcap, garden-warbler, whitethroats, sedge- and grasshopper-warbler.

Water is the simplest compound of hydrogen and oxygen. It is formed when an electric spark is passed through a mixture of the gases, and is a product of combustion of all hydrogen-containing compounds, *e.g.*, petrol, coal, coal gas, and wood. Water is essential to living matter, and is the medium which carries food to animals and plants. Salts in hard water may be removed by distillation of the water or by a process known as ion-exchange (water softening). Pure water freezes at 0° C. and boils at 100° C. and is used as a standard of temperature on this scale. It has a maximum density at 4° C. Heating water above 100° C. converts it into steam, which is used under pressure to convert heat energy into useful work, as in electrical power stations and steam engines. Water gas is a mixture mainly of carbon monoxide and hydrogen formed by blowing steam and oxygen through red-hot coke: it is used as a fuel. Water is one of the very few compounds which freezes from the surface down rather than from the bulk of the liquid up. This property has important consequences on the preservation of life in rivers and lakes when they are frozen over.

Water Hyacinth (*Eichhornia crassipes*), a beautiful aquatic plant native to Brazil which has spread to other favourable equatorial regions of the world causing havoc on account of its abnormal rate of reproduction away from its natural environment. In recent years it has invaded the Nile and the Congo, forming vast floating carpets which block the channels, clog the paddles of river craft and de-oxygenate the water, killing the fish. It is being held in check by spraying with the herbicide 2,4D.

Waterloo, Battle of, was fought on June 18th, 1815. The Allies (British. German, and Dutch) under Wellington and Blücher defeated the French under Napoleon. This ended Napoleon's career.

Waterloo Bridge, crossing the Thames, was built by Rennie, and opened in 1817. It had nine arches, each of 120 ft. span, was built of granite, and had a length (including approaches) of 2,456 ft. The present bridge, completed in 1942, and formally opened Dec. 10, 1945, is a fine example of reinforced concrete construction. (Architect, Sir Giles Gilbert-Scott.)

Water-Spider, an interesting little animal which spins a sac of silk on a water-plant, which it uses as a sort of diving bell. Into this bell it introduces bubbles of air, one at a time; thus the spider is enabled to remain below the surface a considerable time.

Waterspout, whirling tornado-like cloud, occurring at sea. It begins as a cone of cloud tapering slowly downwards, the sea surface becoming disturbed; on reaching the centre of the cloud of spray the spout takes on the appearance of a column of water. A number of these vortices may form fairly close together at about the same time, their duration ranging up to 30 minutes.

Watling Street, the name of the old Roman road which ran from the Channel ports by way of London to Shropshire. *See also* **Roman Roads.**

Watt. A unit of electrical power equivalent to 1 joule of work per second, named after James Watt (1736–1819). 1 horsepower = 745·7 watts. *See* **N13**(1).

Wax, the name applied to certain substances or mixtures which are solids having little crystalline form and may be regarded as solidified oils. They are used for various purposes, such as the making of wax candles, bleaching, and making artificial flowers and anatomical models, also in pharmacy for blending in the composition of plasters, ointment, etc. The best-known natural wax is beeswax, and there are others, such as spermaceti, obtained from the sperm whale, and Chinese wax, which is a cerotyl cerotate.

Waxbill, a small Oriental and African bird of the *Estrildidae* family, with wax-like bill and beautifully variegated plumage. The Java sparrow, and the Blue-breasted waxbill are attractive, and often find their way into cages.

Wayz-Goose, the name given to a festive gathering of people employed in printing and other works, so called from the fact that in earlier times a goose was the principal dish of the feast.

Weasel. A carnivore mammal found in Britain, smallest member of the group including the Stoat, Polecat, and Pine-marten, about 8 in. long. Its fur is reddish on the upper side of the animal, white on the under side; it may all turn white in winter with the exception of the tail.

Weather, the factors determining to-morrow's weather are so manifold, variable, and complex that the task of the meteorologist is no easy one. There are still people who cling to the idea that weather is determined by the phase of the moon, but their predictions have no scientific backing, and can be dismissed. Changes in temperature, humidity, and speed of air masses can best be measured by instruments designed for the purpose. By taking into account the peculiar character of any part of the country, whether coastal, high- or low-lying, industrial, sheltered, precise forecasts for that particular region can be made up to twenty-four hours ahead and sometimes longer. We need to know more about the heat exchange between oceans and the atmosphere before long-range forecasting is possible. The British Isles lie in the path of depressions moving north-eastward across the Atlantic. It is the frequency, intensity, and speed of these centres of low pressure, which give these islands such changeable weather. On the other hand, when an anticyclone builds up and embraces the British Isles, settled weather is fairly certain, the type of weather, whether dull or cloudless, warm or cold, depending mainly on the direction of the wind in the particular area concerned and the time of year. An American earth satellite, *Vanguard II*, was launched in Feb. 1959 to serve as the first "weather-eye" in space.

Weather Lore. Before instruments were invented to measure atmospheric conditions, man relied on his own observation of wind and sky, behaviour of birds and animals, and came to associate certain phenomena with types of weather. Many popular weather rhymes have survived the centuries, and as long as forecasting is confined to the next 24 hours there is perhaps something to be said for them, particularly those dealing with the winds. What is very unlikely is that next year's summer can be predicted from this year's winter, or that one month's weather is related to that of another. The study of past records reveals too many exceptions for such predictions to be of much use in forecasting.

Weaver Bird, the popular name for a large group of finch-like birds belonging to the family *Ploceidae*, found principally in Africa but also in Southern Asia, Australia, and Europe and remarkable for their habit of building nests formed of blades of grass dexterously interwoven and suspended from the boughs of trees.

Weaving has been practised since before any times of which we have record. The Egyptians credit the invention to Isis, the Grecians to Minerva. The main principle of the weaving loom is the same to-day as it was thousands of years ago; a warp extends lengthwise through the loom, the threads being held in separate regular order by being passed through a reed or "slay," while the weft is crossed through alternating threads of the warp by means of a shuttle which holds the weft. Thus the fabric is built up. Weaving was done by hand up to the early part of the 19th cent., when Cartwright's steam-power loom was introduced, and is now in universal use. The Jacquard loom for weaving figured designs dates from 1801.

Wedding Anniversaries are: first, Cotton; second, Paper; third, Leather; fourth, Fruit and Flower; fifth, Wooden; sixth, Sugar; seventh, Woollen; eighth, Salt; ninth, Copper; tenth, Tin; twelfth, Silk and Fine Linen; fifteenth, Crystal; twentieth, China; twenty-fifth, Silver; thirtieth, Pearl; thirty-fifth, Coral; fortieth, Ruby; fiftieth, Golden; sixtieth, Diamond; sixty-fifth, Blue Sapphire; seventieth, Platinum.

Wednesday, the 4th day of the week, derived its name from Woden or Odin, the Norse god of war.

Weever, a genus of sea-fishes which possess the power of inflicting stings by means of the dorsal fin and a spine on the gill cover.

Weevil. The term is applied to members of a group (called Rhynchophora) of beetles with a snout at the end of which is the mouth. Certain weevils are serious pests in granaries, while the cotton-boll weevil does enormous damage.

Weights and Measures. Crude standards of weights and measures existed in the ancient world. Weight was based on the wheat or barley grain, length on the natural proportions of the human body, *e.g.*, cubit, digit, hand. The avoirdupois standard of weight was established in England by Edward III in 1340. The Standards Department of the Board of Trade is responsible for the national standards of weights and measures in Great Britain. The International Bureau of Weights and Measures, Paris, is the custodian of accurate scientific measures. Britain is to change over to a decimal currency in 1971 and to the metric system of weights and measures over the ten-year period to 1975. *See* **N11–13.**

Werewolf, a man or woman, who according to mediaeval belief, could be turned by witchcraft or magic into a wolf, eat human flesh or drink human blood, and turn into himself again. This belief was widely held in Europe, and similar superstitions prevail among most primitive peoples, *e.g.*, the "leopard man" of certain African tribes. Lycanthropy (from Gr. = wolf-man) is a form of madness in which the patient imagines himself a beast.

Westminster Abbey stands on the site of an old church and Benedictine foundation of the 7th cent. It was rebuilt under Edward the Confessor, and again under Henry III., and important additions were made by Edward II., Edward III., Richard II., Richard III. and Henry VII., the latter erecting the beautiful eastern chapel in the perpendicular style which bears his name. The western towers and front were rebuilt by Wren in the 18th cent. It contains tombs of many sovereigns, of the Unknown Warrior, and many other illustrious men are commemorated by monuments.

Westminster Cathedral, seat of the Roman Catholic Archbishop of Westminster. It was designed by J. F. Bentley and built between 1895 and 1910. It is of red brick, in early Christian Byzantine style with a domed campanile, 283 ft. high, and a decorative interior.

Westminster Hall, adjoining the Houses of Parliament, was built as a Banqueting Hall by William Rufus, and many courtly festivals were held there in succeeding centuries. King John established the Law Courts there. It now forms a gigantic hallway, leading to the Houses of Parliament. Charles I., Sir Thomas More, and Warren Hastings were tried there.

Whale, a completely aquatic mammal; the fore-limbs are modified to form fin-like paddles and there is virtually no external trace of the hind-limbs. There are two major groups of whales—the *Toothed Whales*, including the Sperm-whale (Cachalot), Dolphins, Killer-whales, and Porpoises; and the *Whalebone Whales*. In the latter a series of whalebone plates grow down from the roof of the mouth, and, being frayed at their edges into a hairy fringe, together constitute a filtering mechanism. The animal takes in sea water containing minute organisms on which it feeds; the mouth is then closed and the tongue raised when the water is forced out through the filter, on which is left the food. As the tongue is lowered, the whalebone plates straighten up, flicking the food on to the tongue, which transfers it to the gut. Most whale oil is obtained from the thick layer of fat under the skin (blubber), but in the Sperm-whale there is a large reserve of oil in the head. The oil is used for making candles, margarine, and soap. Ambergris used in perfumery comes from the intestine of whales. The number of whales that may be killed in a season is limited by International Convention.

Whimbrel, a bird of the Curlew family, more common in Scotland than in England.

Whinchat, a small migratory bird, a breeding visitor to Britain (Apr. to Oct.); bright brown plumage, with prominent eye stripe.

Whip, an M.P. responsible to his Party for the organisation of the voting M.P.s. He is responsible for ensuring the presence of (or whipping up) a sufficient number of members to carry the vote through.

Whip-poor-Will, the name of the American nightjar, which gets its name from its three-syllable call-note. It is a nocturnal bird, catching its insect food on the wing. It has been known to hibernate for as long as three months.

Whirlpool, a circling current of water often of great power, capable of drawing into its centre and submerging small vessels. The most famous whirlpool is the maelstrom on the Norwegian coast.

Whirlwind, a sudden circular rush of opposing winds, which often causes much damage.

Whisky, an ardent spirit distilled from malt or other grain, and containing a large percentage of alcohol. It has a greater consumption than any other spirit, and is of many kinds, Scotch and Irish whiskies being chiefly consumed in this country, and being of pot still or patent still production, or a blend of the two. Whisky is the most heavily taxed product; in 1661 a duty of 4*d.* a gallon was imposed, today the duty is £10 10*s.* 10*d.* on a proof gallon. American whiskies are mostly distilled from corn (maize), or rye. *See* **Alcohol.**

Whitebait, the name given in Great Britain to young fish, mainly herring and sprat, sold and eaten when about 2 in. long. In New Zealand the whitebait is the juvenile of a native fish called "inanga." It is about 2 in. long, wholly transparent, and belongs to the family of freshwater fish *Galaxia*.

White Elephant, a term in common use to designate a gift that causes the recipient more trouble or cost than it is worth; derived from an old-time custom of the Kings of Siam who presented a white elephant to a courtier whom it was desired to ruin.

Whitehall Palace, erected within sight of Westminster Abbey in the 13th cent., was the residence of the Archbishops of York until Henry VIII. took possession of it in 1530. Thenceforward to 1697, when it was burned down, it continued to be the favourite town residence of royalty, and to the Stuarts especially it was a great centre of court festivities. In those days, with its grounds, it extended from the Strand to the river. The only portion of Whitehall Palace now standing is the Banqueting Hall built by Inigo Jones, on a scaffold projected from the front of which Charles I was beheaded. A block of new government buildings has recently been built on part of the site of the old Palace.

White House, the official residence at Washington of the President of the United States.

Whitsuntide, the festival celebrating the descent of the Holy Ghost and occurring seven weeks after Easter.

Whole-tone Scale, a musical scale all of whose intervals are tones. This scale has been popularised by Debussy.

Whydah Bird, the widow-bird of Equatorial Africa. The Paradise Whydah is remarkable for the long tail and handsome black-and-scarlet plumage of the male during mating season.

Widow Bird, certain species of African weaver birds with predominantly black plumage. In the breeding season the male birds are strikingly beautiful, with scarlet and buff markings and long tail feathers. They are social parasites and trick other birds into rearing their young.

Wigeon, a surface-feeding duck of northern Europe, known in Britain more as a winter visitor than a nesting bird. It feeds in flocks in the muddy estuaries and has a characteristic "whee-oo" call.

Willow, a water-side-loving tree of the genus *Salix*, to which the osiers belong. The best cricket-bat blades are made from a white willow, *S. alba* var. *caerulea*, a fine tree with bluish-green leaves, mostly found in Essex. Willow is also used for polo balls. Weeping willow, *S. babylonica*, is native to China and is the willow seen on Old China willow-pattern plates. It was introduced into England at the end of the 17th cent.

Wind, air set in motion by special atmospheric conditions, is of various degrees, from a slight rustling breeze to a hurricane. Winds are *constant*, as in trade winds or anti-trade winds; *periodic*, as in monsoons and other wind-visitations occurring according to influences of season; *cyclonic* and *anti-cyclonic*, when their motion is spiral; *whirlwinds*, *hurricanes*, and *tornados*, when high temperature and great density induce extreme agitation. Ordinarily, a wind is named from the point of the compass from which it blows, or it may be expressed in degrees from true north. The *sirocco*, the *mistral*, and the *simoom* are local forms of winds of great velocity. A *blizzard* is a biting blast of icy temperature. *See also* **N10.**

Windmills were in use in the East in ancient times, but were not much seen in Europe before the 13th cent. Wind sawmills were invented by a Dutchman in the 17th cent., and one was erected near the Strand in London in 1633. Great improvements have been made in these mills, especially in the United States, where, by the application of the windshaft principle, much space is saved and the mills can be used for pumping, grinding, and other purposes.

Windows (Old Norse *vindauga* = wind-eye), an opening in a wall of a building to admit light and air, and to afford a view of what is outside. In northern Europe windows, as the derivation of the word implies, were first used for ventilation and glass was not used in private houses before the end of the 12th cent. In early Gothic (12th cent.) windows were still small and narrow, with rounded heads. In Early English (13th cent.) they became longer and the heads pointed. In the Decorated period (14th cent.) windows were mullioned (divided by slender bars into panes) and the pointed heads often traceried. In Tudor times when the Renaissance had found its way to England, windows were larger and the bay-window (projecting from the wall) and the oriel window (*q.v.*) were much in vogue; in the late 18th cent. curved bays (called bow-windows) became fashionable. Sash windows (invented by the English) with wooden frames and divided into equal rectangular panes were used in Queen Anne and Georgian houses. Their design was influenced by a passion for symmetry; they were very efficient ventilators. The French window reaches to the floor and has double casements opening as doors. A Dormer window is a vertical window set on the sloping side of a roof. One of the main features of modern architecture is the large area devoted to windows, a development made possible by improved heating systems. Windows are now mass-produced in stock sizes and patterns.

Windsor Castle, the famous British royal residence on the banks of the Thames, as it now stands, was mainly built by Henry III., though a royal residence had existed there from the time of the Conqueror. Additions were made by Henry VIII., Elizabeth, and Charles II. Windsor Park and Forest comprise over 13,000 acres.

Wine, the fermented juice of the freshly-gathered grape. There are innumerable varieties, each obtaining its distinctive character from the species of wine producing the grape, the locality of the vineyard, method of cultivation, etc. Wines are of three main kinds: *sparkling*, as in champagne, due to their having been bottled before fermentation is complete; *beverage*, when the must has been fermented out before bottling. Such wines include the famous red and white wines of Burgundy, Bordeaux and the Rhone valley and the white wines of the Rhine Moselle and Loire valleys. Wines are *fortified* by the addition of alcohol either before fermentation (*e.g.* sherry) or during fermentation (*e.g.* port). The principal wine-producing areas of the world are: France, Italy, Algeria, Spain, Portugal, Rumania, Argentine, Yugoslavia, U.S.S.R., Greece, Germany, Hungary The alcoholic content of wine varies widely, but is usually in the range 8–20% by volume.

Wirebird, a species of plover confined to St. Helena where it is protected.

Wireworm, the larva of the click beetles, a serious pest of grass, cereal crops, potatoes, etc.

Witan *or* **Witenagemot,** the name given to the Great Council of the Anglo-Saxons, "the Council of the Wise Men," and composed of the leading nobility.

Witchcraft. *See* **J45.**

Woad, a plant (*Isastis tinctoria*) that in olden days was largely used in England for the blue dye obtained from the leaves. It is a biennial plant belonging to the same family (*Cruciferae*) as the wallflower and is still cultivated in some parts.

Wolves, well-known carnivorous animals still found in many parts of Europe, but not existing in Britain since the middle of the 17th cent.

Woodcock, a wading bird, greatly valued for its flesh. It is a member of the snipe family, and breeds in Britain. The parent bird is able to carry its young between its thigh and body when flying to and from the feeding spots. It is one of the birds protected by the Game Laws.

Wood-Louse, any terrestrial isopod crustacean of the *Oniscidae* family. They have segmented bodies and 14 legs, and feed mostly on decaying matter, animal and vegetable. The best known is the Pill Wood-louse (*Armadillidium*), which rolls itself into a ball when touched.

Woodpecker, a familiar tree-climbing, insectivorous bird of conspicuous plumage, of which three species are found in Britain, the green woodpecker or yaffle (because of its harsh cry), the great and lesser spotted woodpeckers. They build in the hollows of trees. Yaffle has a long sticky tongue for licking up ground insects, especially ants. The other two obtain insects by digging into tree trunks with strong, chisel-like bills, spearing the insects with a sharp tongue. The metallic drumming sound made by the birds in spring is thought to be caused by their beaks hammering away at some hard resounding substance.

Wood's Metal, an alloy with a very low melting point (65° C., which is under 150° F.) so that a spoon made of it will melt when used to stir a cup of tea. Contains bismuth 4 parts, lead 2 parts, tin 1 part, cadmium 1 part. Its use as a heat exchanger has now been largely superseded by silicone oils, which have a wider temperature range.

Woodworm. Four beetles are mainly responsible for woodworm damage: common furniture beetle (*Anobium punctatum*), powder post beetle (*Lyctus brunneus*), death watch beetle (*Xestobium rufovillosum*), and house longhorn beetle (*Hylotrupes bajulus*). Particular attention should be paid to wood in damp, dark, and out-of-the-way places, and the backs and underneaths of furniture. The most frequent cause of woodworm damage is the common furniture beetle (*q.v.*).

Wool is a fibre, made up of very long protein molecules. It has been largely grown and used in the manufacture of cloth in England since before the Roman invasion. It is grown on the backs of sheep, and is of various kinds, according to the breed of sheep from which it is derived. Wool differs from hair in that it has a wavy, serrated fibre, its curl being a notable characteristic, whereas hair has a smooth surface comparatively free from serratures. Long wools are mostly used for the manufacture of worsted goods, and short wools for woollen cloths, though the improvements in machinery in recent years have enabled manufacturers to utilise short wools to a great extent for dress fabrics as well as for woollens. The finest wools are obtained from the fleece of the Spanish merino sheep. Australia, New Zealand, and the Argentine are the greatest wool-producing countries.

Woolsack, the name given to the seat occupied by the Lord Chancellor in the House of Lords. It is a large square bag of wool, without back or arms, covered with red cloth. At the time when it was first used, in the reign of Edward III., wool was the great staple commodity of the country and, it is said, chosen for the seat of judges as a constant reminder of the main source of the national wealth. The Lord Chancellor is said to be "appointed to the woolsack."

Work. When a force moves its point of application, *e.g.*, when one exerts force in pushing a car along, the product of the force times the distance moved is a quantity known as "the work done." Work requires a source of energy (*q.v.*); conversely, energy can be converted into work. Machines are largely for converting suitable forms of energy into useful forms of work. Both work and energy are measured in the same units, *e.g.*, foot lb., ergs, joules (*q.v.*)

World Council of Churches. *See* **J45.**

World Population. According to the United Nations Statistical Yearbook (1964), the world's estimated population in 1963 was 3,160,000,000, of whom more than half lived in Asia. Highest growth rate was in Latin America (2·6 per cent a year) compared with world rate of 1·8 per cent, Africa 2·3 per cent, and Europe 0·9 per cent. Different countries are at different stages in a demographic transition from the stability provided by a combination of high birth rate and high death rate to that provided by a combination of low birth rate and low death rate. Their recent population history and current trend of growth, the age-structure of their population, and consequently their population potential for the near future are all widely different. By the beginning of the Christian era world population is believed to have been 200–300 million, rising to about 500 million by 1650, and it is estimated that about one in 25 of all human beings who have ever lived are alive today. *See also* **Demography Today, Section F, Part IV.**

Wren, a family o small passerine birds possessing upturned tails and most abundant in South America. The British species is an interesting singing bird with a surprisingly loud note for its size.

X

Xenon a rare gaseous element, symbol Xe, occurring in minute quantities in the atmosphere, discovered by Sir William Ramsay and M. W. Travers in 1898. *See* **Rare Gases.**

X-Rays were discovered in 1895 by Professor Röntgen, of Wurzburg, while experimenting with a Crookes vacuum tube, when the fact was accidentally revealed that a photographic plate, contained in a dark box and exposed to its rays, was affected. To the X-rays the box was transparent. X-ray photographs are now commonly taken to obtain information about objects enclosed within solid bodies; they enable bullets and any solid bodies of metal, as well as bones, etc., in the body to be perfectly located and investigated. The discovery has proved of great advantage in surgical operations. X-rays are used to determine the structure of matter; the atoms in a substance may be located and their relative positions determined by photographing reflections of the X-rays by the specimen. *See* **F11(1), 13(2).**

Xylem, the woody tissue of higher plants whose function is to conduct water and mineral salts upwards, and to provide mechanical support.

Y

Yacht, a light vessel now much used for pleasure trips and racing. The first yachting club was the Cork Harbour Club, started about 1720; and in 1812 the Royal Yacht Squadron was founded at Cowes. The Royal Thames Yacht Club dates from 1823. The most famous international yachting trophy is *The America's Cup.*

Yak, a curious, long-haired ox, found in Tibet, used as a beast of burden, and also kept for milk and meat.

Yard, a standard measure of 36 in., the word being derived from the Saxon gyrd, or rod. The yard and pound are now defined by reference to the metre and the kilogram: yard = 0·9144 of a metre; pound = 0·45359237 of a kilogram. By international agreement the metre is defined by reference to the wavelength of Krypton-86 light. *See* **N11.**

Yeast, a unicellular fungus which contains enzymes promoting fermentation. In brewing and wine-making the yeasts are important. The baker uses yeast to make bread rise; yeast is incorporated in the dough and ferments some of the starch present, yielding carbon dioxide gas which expands and aerates the bread in the baking process.

Yellowhammer, a common British bird of the bunting family, of lemon-yellow and brown plumage. Nests on or near the ground.

Yeomen of the Guard are a body of Foot Guards established in the reign of Henry VII. for the protection of the Royal Person. Yeomen are now about 100 in number, and their duties consist in being present on ceremonial State occasions, the yearly distribution of Maundy Money, and the searching of the vaults of the Houses of Parliament on Guy Fawkes' day. "Beefeater" is the nickname of both Yeomen of the Guard and Yeomen Warders of the Tower, and they both wear the style of dress of the Tudor period, but with one distinction, the Yeomen of the Guard wear a cross belt, the Warders do not.

Yeti, opinions differ as to whether this is a mythical inhabitant of the Himalayas, a primitive primate or bear. Evidence to date is inconclusive.

Yew, an evergreen tree, the wood of which in olden days was in great demand for bow-making.

Yoga. *See* **J45.**

York Minster, one of the oldest and finest of English cathedrals, is 524 ft. long, its nave is 240 ft. broad, and the central tower is 216 ft. high. The present edifice, in parts, dates back to the 12th cent., but a church stood on the site in the 7th cent. In 1829 it was set on fire by a lunatic named Jonathan Martin, and the destruction that then took place cost £60,000 to restore.

Ytterbium, a chemical element discovered by Urbain in 1907; one of the group of rare earth metals.

Yttrium, a chemical element discovered by Mosander in 1842. It is found in a few rare minerals such as gadolinite, xenotine, fergusonite, and euxenite. One of the group of rare-earth metals.

Z

Zaibatsu, great and powerful family trusts, including the Mitsui, Mitsubishi, Sumitomo, and Yasuda, who held a position of unparalleled influence in Japan before the second world war, for in their hands was concentrated almost the entire economy of the Japanese nation. It was a major war aim of the Allies to break these trusts, but their economic power has been largely restored.

Zamboni Pile, a dry galvanic battery, which can provide small amounts of high-voltage current over a very long time. At Oxford a couple of Zamboni Piles have kept a bell ringing for over a hundred years. These Piles in the second world war were perfected and produced in quantity, being the most convenient source of current for infra-red signalling devices.

Zebra, an African quadruped of whitish-grey colour, with regular black stripings, perhaps the most beautiful member of the Equine family. Rather larger than an ass and smaller than the horse, it has a tufted tail, is of light build, wild, and fleet of foot; there are several species, and the Quagga and Burchell's Zebra (ground colouring yellow), as well as the True Zebra, belong to the group.

Zebu, a species of oxen having a large hump on the shoulder and short horns. In India and some parts of Africa these animals are domesticated and used as beasts of burden. They are of a light grey colour and very docile. Their flesh makes good food-meat; the Hindus, however, do not slay them but regard them with much veneration.

Zen Buddhism. *See* **J46.**

Zenith, the highest point in the heavens above an observer's head, the opposite pole to the Nadir.

Zero, the cypher signifying nothing. The West is indebted to the Arabs for it, who probably got it from the Hindus and passed it to European mathematicians towards the end of the Middle Ages. The zero has also been found in Babylonian cuneiform. The Greeks had no such symbol, which hindered the development of their mathematics. The use of zero led to the invention of decimal fractions and to the later developments in astronomy, physics and chemistry. Absolute zero on the temperature scale is the lowest temperature theoretically possible (when no heat whatever is present) and equal to −273·15° C.

Zeta, the name given in former times to the closet or room, above a church porch, where the sexton lived and guarded the documents of the church. Zeta is also the name of the machine at Harwell (zero energy thermometer assembly) designed to solve some of the problems of thermonuclear reactions

Zinc, a familiar metallic element, symbol Zn, known to the ancients, and used by them in the making of brass. It occurs as the sulphide, carbonate, etc. The ores of zinc are crushed, roasted, and reduced with coal. In combination with copper it constitutes the familiar alloy called brass, and zinc itself is much used for roofing and other protective purposes. Zinc ores are mined in Canada, the U.S.A., Mexico, Poland, Australia, Russia, Italy, Spain, and many other parts of the world. Zinc smelting is carried on in most industrial countries, including Great Britain.

Zirconium, metallic element, symbol Zr, was discovered by Klaproth in the sand of the rivers of Ceylon in 1789. The crystalline metal is white, soft, and ductile; in its amorphous condition it is a blue-black powder. Zirconium is used in atomic reactors as containers for fuel elements, since it does not absorb neutrons.

Zither, an ancient musical instrument consisting of strings stretched on a frame which is held in the left hand. The right hand plucks the strings with a plectrum.

Zodiac, an imaginary zone or belt of the sky enclosing the circuit over which the principal planets travel. It is divided into 12 equal spaces of 30 degrees each, comprising respectively the 12 signs of the zodiac—Aries, Taurus, Gemini, Cancer, Leo, Virgo, Libra, Scorpio, Sagittarius, Capricornus, Aquarius and Pisces. The idea of the zodiac originated with the Babylonians about 2000 B.C. and passed by way of the Greeks to the Western world.

Zodiacal Light, a faint cone of light occasionally seen stretching along the zodiac from the western horizon after evening twilight or the eastern horizon before morning twilight. It is believed to be due to the scattering of the sun's light by dust particles in orbit round the sun and extending beyond the earth. Recent observations at the high altitude station at Chacaltaya in the Andes suggest that the dust is travelling round the sun in regular planetary orbits.

Zollverein, any of the customs unions successively formed under the leadership of Prussia among certain German states for maintaining uniform duties and tariffs against foreign countries and free trade among themselves. The administration was finally merged in the German Empire of 1871.

Zonda, a warm moist wind in Argentina of great velocity blowing from the north or northwest, and, like the Sirocco in Southern Europe, causes much discomfort. It happens when a depression is moving across the pampas, bringing with it a mass of air from the humid tropics. It is followed by a refreshing wind from the south-east.

Zone, an imaginary geographical belt encircling the earth. There are five zones—the Torrid Zone, from tropic to tropic; two Temperate Zones, from the tropics to the Polar Circles; and two Frigid Zones, from the Polar Circles to the North and South Poles respectively.

Zoological Gardens of London were opened in 1828, and belong to the Zoological Society of London. They contain one of the largest and most varied collections of living animals in the world. The Society maintains an open-air zo at Whipsnade, on the edge of Dunstable Downs this was opened in 1931.

Zoology, the science of animal biology, treating o the structure, classification, and distribution o the various members of the animal kingdom.

Zoroastrianism. *See* **J46.**

Zouaves, a body of French light infantry, firs recruited from an Algerian tribe; afterward composed of selected French soldiers retainin the Oriental uniform.

Zulus, a native African people occupying Zululand which later became part of Natal, Union of S Africa. They are a brave race, and in a wa with Great Britain in 1879 inflicted severe de feats upon our troops. The Zulu king, Cete wayo, was finally defeated and taken prisone and his country annexed.

NOBEL PRIZE WINNERS (1901–1965)

YEAR.	PHYSICS.	CHEMISTRY.	PHYSIOLOGY AND MEDICINE.	LITERATURE.	PEACE.
1901	W. C. Roentgen (G).	J. H. van't Hoff (D).	E. v. Behring (G).	R. F. A. Sully Prudhomme (F).	H. Dunant (Sw), F. Passy (F).
1902	H. A. Lorentz (D), P. Zeeman (D).	E. Fischer (G).	R. Ross (B).	T. Mommsen (G).	E. Ducommun (Sw), A. Gobat (Sw).
1903	H. Becquerel (F), P. Curie (F), Marie Curie (F).	S. Arrhenius (S).	N. R. Finsen (Da).	B. Björnson (N).	Sir W. R. Cremer (B).
1904	Lord J. W. S. Rayleigh (B).	W. Ramsay (B).	I. P. Pavlov (R).	F. Mistral (F), J. Echegaray (Sp).	Institut de Droit International.
1905	P. Lenard (G).	A. v. Bayer (G).	R. Koch (G).	H. Sienkiewicz (P).	Bertha von Suttner (Au).
1906	J. J. Thomson (B).	H. Moissan (F).	C. Golgi (I), S. R. y Cajal (Sp).	G. Carducci (I).	T. Roosevelt (A).
1907	A. A. Michelson (A).	E. Buchner (G).	C. L. A. Laveran (F).	Rudyard Kipling (B).	E. T. Moneta (I), L. Renault (F).
1908	G. Lippmann (F).	E. Rutherford (B).	P. Ehrich (G), E. Metchnikoff (R).	R. Eucken (G).	K. P. Arnoldson (S), F. Bajer (Da).
1909	F. Braun (G), G. Marconi (I).	W. Ostwald (G).	T. Kocher (Sw).	S. Lagerlöf (S).	A. M. F. Beernaert (Be), Baron d'Estournelles de Constant de Rebecque (F).
1910	J. D. van der Waals (D).	O. Wallach (G).	A. Kossel (G).	P. Heyse (G).	The Bureau International Permanent de la Paix, Berne.
1911	W. Wien (G).	Marie Curie (F).	A. Gullstrand (S).	M. Maeterlinck (Be).	T. M. C. Asser (D), A. H. Fried (Au).
1912	G. Dalén (S).	V. Grignard (F), P. Sabatier (F).	A. Carrel (A).	G. Hauptmann (G).	E. Root (A).
1913	H. Kamerlingh Onnes (D).	A. Werner (Sw).	C. Richet (F).	R. Tagore (In).	H. la Fontaine (Be).
1914	M. v. Laue (G).	T. W. Richards (A).	R. Bárány (Au).	—	—
1915	W. H. Bragg (B), W. L. Bragg (B).	R. Willstaetter (G.).	—	R. Roland (F).	—
1916	—	—	—	V. von Heidenstam (S).	—
1917	C. G. Barkla (B).	—	—	K. Gjellerup (Da), H. Pontoppidan (Da).	Comité International de la Croix-Rouge, Geneva.
1918	M. Planck (G).	F. Haber (G).	—	—	—
1919	J. Stark (G).	—	J. Bordet (Be).	C. Spitteler (Sw).	W. Wilson (A).
1920	C. E. Guillaume (F).	W. Nernst (G).	A. Krogh (Da).	K. Hamsun (N).	L. Bourgeois (F).
1921	A. Einstein (G).	F. Soddy (B).	—	A. France (F).	K. H. Branting (S), C. L. Lange (N).
1922	N. Bohr (Da).	F. W. Aston (B).	A. Hill (B), O. Meyerhof (G).	J. Benavente (Sp).	F. Nansen (N).
1923	R. A. Millikan (A).	F. Pregl (Au).	F. G. Banting (C), J. R. Macleod (C).	W. B. Yeats (Ir).	—
1924	M. Siegbahn (S).	—	W. E. Einthoven (D).	W. Reymont (P).	—
1925	J. Franck (G), G. Hertz (G).	R. Zsigmondy (G).	—	G. B. Shaw (B).	Sir A. Chamberlain (B), C. G. Dawes (A).
1926	J. Perrin (F).	T. Svedberg (S).	J. Fibiger (Da).	G. Deledda (I).	A. Briand (F), G. Stresemann (G).
1927	A. H. Compton (A), C. T. R. Wilson (B).	H. Wieland (G).	J. Wagner-Jauregg (Au).	H. Bergson (F).	F. Buisson (F), L. Quidde (G).
1928	O. W. Richardson (B).	A. Windaus (G).	C. Nicolle (F).	S. Undset (N).	—
1929	L. de Broglie (F).	H. v. Euler-Chelpin (S), A. Harden (B).	C. Eijkman (D), F. G. Hopkins (B).	T. Mann (G).	F. B. Kellogg (A).
1930	C. V. Raman (In).	H. Fischer (G).	K. Landsteiner (Au).	S. Lewis (A).	L. O. J. Söderblom (S).
1931	—	F. Bergius (G), K. Bosch (G).	O. Warburg (G).	E. A. Karlfeldt (S).	Jane Addams (A), N. M. Butler (A).
1932	W. Heisenberg (G).	I. Langmuir (A).	C. S. Sherrington (B), E. D. Adrian (B).	J. Galsworthy (B).	—
1933	P. A. M. Dirac (B), E. Schroedinger (Au).	—	T. H. Morgan (A).	Bunin (R).	Sir Norman Angell (B).
1934	—	H. C. Urey (A).	G. Minot (A), W. Murphy (A), G. Whipple (A).	L. Pirandello (I).	Arthur Henderson (B).
1935	J. Chadwick (B).	F. Joliot (F), I. Joliot-Curie (F).	H. Spemann (G).	—	C. von Ossietzky (G).
1936	V. F. Hess (Au), C. D. Anderson (A).	P. Debye (D).	Sir H. H. Dale (B), O. Loewi (G).	E. O'Neill (A).	C. de S. Lamas (Ar).

NOBEL PRIZE WINNERS (1901–1965), *continued*

YEAR.	PHYSICS.	CHEMISTRY.	PHYSIOLOGY AND MEDICINE.	LITERATURE.	PEACE.
1937	C. J. Davisson (A), G. P. Thomson (B).	W. N. Haworth (B), P. Karrer (Sw).	A. v. Szent-Dyörgyi (H).	R. Martin du Gard (F).	Viscount Cecil of Chelwood (B).
1938	E. Fermi (I).	R. Kuhn (G).	C. Heymans (Be).	Pearl S. Buck (A).	Office International Nansen pour les Réfugiés.
1939	E. O. Lawrence (A).	A. F. Butenandt (G), L. Ruzicka (Sw).	G. Domagk (G).	F. E. Sillanpää (Fi).	—
1940–42	—	—	—	—	—
1943	O. Stern (A).	G. Hevsey (H).	H. Dam (Da), E. A. Doisy (A).	—	—
1944	I. I. Rabi (A).	O. Hahn (G).	E. J. Erlanger (A), H. S. Gasser (A).	J. V. Jensen (Da).	Comité International de la Croix-Rouge, Geneva.
1945	W. Pauli (Au).	A. Virtanen (Fi).	Sir A. Fleming (B), Sir H. Florey (B), E. B. Chain (B).	G. Mistral (Ch).	Cordell Hull (A).
1946	P. W. Bridgman (A).	J. B. Sumner (A), J. H. Northrop (A), W. M. Stanley (A).	H. J. Muller (A).	H. Hesse (Sw).	Emily G. Balch (A), J. R. Mott (A).
1947	Sir Edward Appleton (B).	Sir Robert Robinson (B).	B. A. Houssay (Ar), C. F. Cori (A), G. T. Cori (A).	André Gide (F).	American and British Quaker Organisations.
1948	P. M. S. Blackett (B).	A. Tiselius (S).	P. Müller (Sw).	T. S. Eliot (B).	—
1949	H. Yukawa (J).	W. F. Giauque (A).	W. R. Hess (Sw), A. E. Moniz (Po).	W. Faulkner (A).	Lord Boyd-Orr (B).
1950	Cecil F. Powell (B).	Otto Diels (G), K. Alder (G).	E. C. Kendall (A), P. S. Hench (A), R. Reichstein (Sw).	Lord Russell (B).	Ralph Bunche (A).
1951	Sir J. Cockcroft (B), E. T. S. Walton (Ir).	E. M. MacMillan (A), G. T. Seaborg (A).	M. Theiler (A).	P. Lagerkvist (S).	Léon Jouhaux (F).
1952	E. Purcell (A), F. Bloch (A).	A. J. P. Martin (B), R. L. M. Synge (B).	S. Waksman (A).	F. Mauriac (F).	A. Schweitzer (F).
1953	F. Zernike (D).	H. Staudinger (G).	H. A. Krebs (B), F. A. Lipmann (A).	Sir W. S. Churchill (B).	Gen. G. Marshall (A).
1954	M. Born (B), W. Bothe (G).	L. Pauling (A).	J. F. Enders (A), F. C. Robins (A), T. H. Weller (A).	E. Hemingway (A).	U.N. High Commission for Refugees.
1955	W. E. Lamb (A), P. Kusch (A).	Vicent du Vigneaud (A).	Hugo Theorell (S).	Halldor Laxness (Ic).	—
1956	W. Shockley (A), J. Bardeen (A), W. H. Brattain (A).	Sir Cyril Hinshelwood (B), N. Semenov (R).	A. F. Cournaud (A), D. W. Richards (A), W. Forssmann (G).	J. Ramón Jiménez (Sp).	—
1957	T. Dao-lee (Chi), C. Ning-yang (Chi).	Sir Alexander Todd (B).	D. Bovet (I).	A. Camus (F).	L. B. Pearson (C).
1958	P. A. Čerenkov (R), I. M. Frank (R), I. Tamm (R).	F. Sanger (B).	G. W. Beadle (A), E. Tatum (A), J. Lederberg (A).	B. Pasternak (R).	Father George Pire (Be).
1959	E. Segré (A), O. Chamberlain (A).	J. Heyrovsky (Cz).	S. Ochoa (A), A. Kornberg (A).	S. Quasimodo (I).	P. J. Noel-Baker (B).
1960	D. A. Glaser (A).	W. F. Libby (A).	P. B. Medawar (B), Sir M. Burnet (Aus).	A. St. Léger (F).	A. Luthuli (S.A.)
1961	R. Hofstadter (A), R. Mossbauer (G).	M. Calvin (A).	G. von Bekesy (H.)	I. Andric (Y).	D. Hammarskjöld (S.)
1962	L. Davidovich (R).	M. F. Perutz (B), J. C. Kendrew (B).	F. H. C. Crick (B), M. H. F. Wilkins (B), J. D. Watson (A).	J. Steinbeck (A).	L. Pauling (A).
1963	Maria Goeppert-Mayer (A), J. H. D. Jensen (G), E. P. Wigner (A).	K. Ziegler (G), G. Natta (I).	A. L. Hodgkin (B), A. F. Huxley (B), Sir J. Eccles (B).	G. Seferis (Gr).	International Red Cross Committee and the International League of Red Cross Societies.
1964	C. H. Townes (A), N. G. Basov (R), A. M. Prokhorov (R).	Dorothy Hodgkin (B).	K. E. Bloch (A), F. Lynen (G).	Jean-Paul Sartre (F).	Martin Luther King.
1965	S. Tomonaga (J), J. Schwinger (A), P. Feynman (A).	A. B. Woodward (A).	F. Jacob (F), A. Lwoff (F), J. Monod (F).	M. Sholokhov (R).	UNICEF

A = American
Ar = Argentine
Au = Austrian
Aus = Australian
B = British
Be = Belgian
C = Canadian
Ch = Chilean
Chi = Chinese
Cz = Czech
D = Dutch
Da = Danish
F = French
Fi = Finnish
G = German
Gr = Greek
H = Hungarian
I = Italian
Ic = Icelandic
In = Indian
Ir = Irish
J = Japanese
N = Norwegian
P = Polish
Po = Portuguese
R = Russian
S = Swedish
S.A. = South African
Sp = Spanish
Sw = Swiss
Y = Yugoslav

LITERARY COMPANION

ENGLISH VERSE

This section of the *Cyclopaedia* is concerned with English verse since the time of Chaucer, with its different metres and rhymes. The poet's subtle verse patterns of metre and rhyme are indeed one of his most potent means of expression, and by keeping an attentive ear to them we are helped to catch his meaning.

A glance at any good anthology of English poems written during the last five or six centuries will show what a rich variety of traditional verse patterns the contemporary poet now has at his disposal, whatever may be his mood or theme. Our poet laureate, Masefield, has made great use of these time-honoured forms. For his leisurely "Dauber," he employs the stately "rhyme-royal" stanza that was no longer new even to Chaucer. His sonnets are of Shakespearean design, and for his brisk "Reynard the Fox" he uses the octosyllabic couplet in which the Puritan poet, Marvell, once hymned the newly discovered "remote Bermudas."

Many poets, however, find the traditional forms are not sufficiently flexible for modern needs, and they may so drastically modify them as to make them, at first sight, unrecognisable.

One of the most indefatigable experimenters has been Dame Edith Sitwell. In the notes to the Penguin selection of her poetry she says:

> "At the time I began to write, a change in the direction, imagery, and rhythms in poetry had become necessary, owing to the rhythmical flaccidity, the verbal deadness, the dead and expected patterns, of some of the poetry immediately preceding us.
>
> "Rhythm is one of the principal translators between dream and reality. Rhythm might be described as, to the world of sound, what light is to the world of sight. It shapes and gives new meaning."

Placing so high a value on rhythm, Edith Sitwell set herself, in her early "Facade," to tireless experiment in the effect on rhythm or metre of all kinds of subtle devices in the use of sound, until, as she says, her experiences led to the poem "Gold Coast Customs." This poem, written in 1929, is "about the state that led up to the second World War," and is prophetic in its vision of

"That sick thick smoke from London burning."

When we first read "Gold Coast Customs" we are shocked and stunned by this portrayal of the ruthless and heartless savagery of our so-called civilization. The shock is driven home by the metre, a savage staccato of stabbing lines, that echoes the fevered heart-beat of those indifferent to poverty and suffering, of the "rich man Judas, brother Cain." It also echoes "the beating of the drums that heralded the Customs, as they were called, in Ashantee, a hundred years ago, when, at the death of any rich or important person, slaves and poor persons were killed so that the bones of the dead might be washed by human blood."

Only when we recover from our shock and look carefully at the verse, do we realise that this blood-curdling metre, apparently entirely new, is written according to age-long principles, and uses for the most part an irregular tattoo of the iambs and anapæsts that are the ground beat of most of our finest verse.

As Day Lewis has said in the Preface to the Penguin selection of his poems:

> "We must never think of 'modern poetry' as something in a vacuum, or something that started in 1900 or 1917 or 1930. Every good poem has grown out of the compost of all the poetry ever written."

Of his own poems Day Lewis goes on to say, "Contrary to received opinion about modern verse, nearly all my poems 'rhyme and scan,'" and the same may be said of most of our highly original contemporary poetry, such as that of W. H. Auden or Dylan Thomas.

The poet's intensely individual music is played on the age-old instrument of metre and rhyme, and the better we understand the instrument, the keener will be our enjoyment of the poet's skill and genius.

Even verse that cannot be called poetry—verse that is mechanical, uninspired, lacking that intensity of insight and expression that we recognise as poetic—even this mediocre verse can teach us something of the poet's instrument. A homely nursery rhyme like "Humpty Dumpty" can help us to appreciate the metre of Ariel's unearthly song, "Where the bee sucks."

It is for this reason that the following guide to versification throws its net wide, gathering together for our consideration patterns as diverse as those of the mediæval ballad and the modern Frenchified triolet, of the flippant clerihew, and the grave blank verse of Wordsworth's "Prelude."

Reference

The following account of our verse is illustrated by quotations and by constant reference to the numbered poems in the new edition of "The Oxford Book of English Verse," 1939.

Thus "OBEV 16" means "Oxford Book of English Verse," New Edition, Poem No. 16.

I. INTRODUCTION. STRESS, METRE, AND RHYME.

If we listen carefully to spoken English, we shall observe that there is a natural tendency to stress some syllables more than others. In the following sentence, for example, the greater stress normally falls on the syllables whose vowels are marked with an acute accent, which is the usual way of indicating stress.

"The expréss léft Mánchester at séven."

It is obvious that in this sentence the stress falls in a quite haphazard way, and it is for this reason that we recognise the sentence as prose, for the essential difference between English prose and verse is that in prose the stress falls at random, while in verse the stressed syllables occur according to some regular pattern.

If we mark the stressed syllables in the following line from Wordsworth,

"And lóud hallóos and scréams and échoes lóud,"

it is immediately clear that the stress occurs regularly. The line is in fact, composed of a simple stress pattern of an unstressed syllable followed by a stressed (*e.g.*, and lóud) which is repeated throughout.

It is a regular pattern of stress, such as this that in English verse constitutes what we call "metre." Metre in Greek means simply "measure," and it is always by stress that we measure our verse.

Another feature that distinguishes our verse from prose is the use of rhyme, although rhyme unlike metre, is not essential to verse.

II. METRE.

Different Kinds of Feet.

In English verse the unit of stress pattern constitutes a foot, the foot of verse being comparable to the bar of music.

English verse uses several kinds of feet, some of two syllables, or disyllablic, some of three syllables or trisyllabic, and occasionally a foot of four syllables.

Disyllabic feet are of four kinds:

The Iamb, consisting of an unstressed syllable followed by a stressed, *e.g.* " retúrn."

The Trochee, consisting of a stressed syllable followed by an unstressed, *e.g.*, " ríver."

The Spondee, consisting of two stressed syllables, *e.g.*, " dóor mát."

The Pyrrhic, consisting of two unstressed syllables, *e.g.*, in the phrase " into tówn," " into " is a pyrrhic.

Trisyllabic feet are of four kinds:

The Anapæst, consisting of two unstressed syllables followed by a stressed, *e.g.*, " as you wísh."

The Dactyl, consisting of a stressed syllable followed by two unstressed, *e.g.*, " árchery."

The Amphibrach, very rarely used, consisting of a stressed syllable between two unstressed, *e.g.*, " delíghted."

The Tribrach, still more rare, consisting of three unstressed syllables, *e.g.*, last three syllables of " incommúnicable."

A four-syllabled foot is very occasionally found:

The Choriambus, which may be thought of as a trochee followed by an iamb, *e.g.*, " Tóll for the bráve."

Different Kinds of Metrical Line.

Based on the different kinds of feet are the different kinds of English metre, which may be compared with the " time " in music.

Disyllabic metres may be either iambic or trochaic, for it is impossible to speak at any length using only pyrrhic or spondees, and the most common trisyllabic metres are anapæstic or dactyllic. Examples of different kinds of metrical line follow.

Iambic Line.

" I stróve with nóne for nóne was wórth my
strífe."
[OBEV 584]

Trochaic Line.

" Hóme art góne and tá'en thy wáges."
[OBEV 150]

Anapæstic Line.

" With a héy and a hó and a héy noninó."
[OBEV 147]

Dactylic Lines.

" Wit with his wántonness,
Tásteth death's bítterness."
[OBEV 177]

Amphibrach Lines.

" Most fríendship is féigning, most lóving mere
fólly
Then héigh ho, the hólly!
This lífe is most jólly."
[OBEV 146]

Choriambic Line.

" Kéntish Sir Býng stóod for his Kíng."

Variations in Metre.

Satisfying poetry is rarely entirely regular. Mechanical regularity is soon wearisome to the ear and is a characteristic of doggerel. The poet satisfies our love of rhythm in a more interesting and subtle way by introducing all kinds of variations and inversions, while at the same time maintaining the throb of the basic metre. An account of the chief variations follows.

Elision.

Elision is the suppression in pronunciation of a vowel or a syllable.

In the anapæstic line,

" The Assýrĭan came dówn like a wólf on the fóld "

the second foot appears to have four syllables, but in fact the " i " of " Assýrĭan " is elided or dropped before the " a " as shown by the little bracket. The elision of " i," which is pronounced " y " and known as " consonantal y," is especially common, and occurs in such words as " familiar," " opinion." Elision is often shown by the use of the apostrophe as in " heav'n." In " heav'n " we see one of the many conventional elisions of poetry, like " 'tis," " 'twas," " did'st," " o'er," " e'er," " 'gainst," and many more.

Substitution.

Substitution is the use of a foot different from that of the metre in which the poem is written. In the following examples we can see the effect on iambic verse of some common substitutions.

Of a Trochee.

" Stíffen the sínews, súmmon úp the blóod."
Shakespeare, " Henry V."

Here the initial trochee gives force and emphasis.

Of a Spondee.

" Rócks cáves, lákes féns, bógs déns and shádes
of déath."

In this extraordinary line of Milton's the spondees slow down and weight the verse.

Of a Pyrrhic.

" They flý forgótten as a dréam "

Here the pyrrhic in the third foot gives lightness to the line.

Of a Dactyl.

" Cháttering his téeth for cóld that díd him chíll."

When a dactyl replaces an iamb it is usually in the first foot as in this typical instance from Spenser, where the dactyl gives emphasis and variety to the line.

Of Anapæsts.

" And the cóming wínd did róar more lóud
And the sáils did sígh like sédge."
[OBEV 562]

The initial anapæsts in these two lines from " The Ancient Mariner " give an effect of hurry and speed.

Additional Syllable.

An additional syllable may be added to either the beginning or end of a line.

Feminine Ending.

A feminine ending is an extra unstressed syllable that is added after the final stressed syllable of a line, giving a gentle falling inflexion. It is often used in blank verse and is a marked characteristic of Shakespeare's later plays, *e.g.*,

"Be not afear'd; the isle is full of noises,
Sounds and sweet airs that give delight and hurt not."

Anacrusis.

Anacrusis is the use of an extra syllable before the first regular foot of the line.

Dropped Syllable.

It sometimes appears that a line is a syllable, or syllables, short, until we realise that a suspense or pause occupies the time that would have been taken by the missing syllable. The dropped syllable can be indicated by the "caret" mark, thus ^. The following technical terms are used for lines that are short of syllables.

Catalectic Line.

This leaves off in the middle of the last foot, as in the trochaic line

"Éver lét the fáncy róam,"

or the dactylic line,

"Ríngs on her fíngers and béllś on her tóes."

The catalectic line is common in trochaic and dactylic verse, for it is in keeping with the tendency of English verse to end on a stressed syllable.

Acephalous Line.

This omits the first syllable of the line, as in the anapæstic line,

"That hóst with their bánners at súnset were séen."

The Cæsura.

The cæsura is a special kind of pause, quite different from that which indicates a dropped syllable. It is a pause about the middle of a line and is usually indicated by a pause in the sense, *e.g.*,

"Both hungered after death; both chose to win or die."

Two Ways of Describing Metre.

The Classical.

The actual names that we have been using for the different kinds of feet and metres are derived from Greek. It is most important, however, to realise that in the classical languages they had a different meaning, for Greek and Latin verse was written on a quite different principle from ours, and was scanned according to the "quantity" or length of the syllable, and not according to stress. Thus an iamb in Greek and Latin consisted of a short syllable followed by a long, marked thus, ∪ –, and a trochee of a long syllable followed by a short, marked – ∪.

In English verse the length of the syllable is totally irrelevant. For instance, the line,

"Pólly pút the kéttle ón and léts have téa"

begins with five trochees, all consisting of two *short* syllables.

The application of Greek words to English metres is confusing only if we forget that in English verse the criterion is stress.

The Modern.

Some writers, however, prefer new ways of describing our verse, and the most popular method is set out below:

A foot is called a period.
A disyllabic metre is called duple or double time.
A trisyllabic metre is called triple time.
A period with the stress on the first syllable is said to be falling.
A period with the stress on a second or third syllable is said to be rising.

III. RHYME.

Another thing that gives a formal pattern to English verse, and distinguishes it from prose, is rhyme. It is not essential to our verse, much of our verse being rhymeless.

Rhyme is a similarity in sound in words occurring normally at the ends of lines. In true rhyme the last stressed syllable and consonants following it are the same, while the sounds preceding the stressed vowel are different, *e.g.*, "cage/page," "pleasure/treasure."

The Types of Rhyme.

The most familiar division of rhyme is into masculine, feminine, and triple rhyme, but we also distinguish broken and Leonine rhyme.

Masculine, Male, or Single Rhyme.

The final syllable is stressed, *e.g.*, "cage/page," "joy/boy."

Feminine, Female, or Two-syllabled Rhyme.

The syllable before the last is stressed, and the final syllable unstressed, *e.g.*, "pleasure/treasure," "bending/lending."

Triple or Tumbling or Three-syllabled Rhyme.

The antepenultimate syllable is stressed. Triple rhyme is normally found in light or comic verse, like that of W. S. Gilbert or in this punning "Epitaph on a Dentist.":

"Stranger! Approach this spot with gravity!
John Brown is filling his last cavity."

In "The Bridge of Sighs" [OBEV 662] Hood dares to use it in a serious poem with such rhymes as "scrútiny/mútiny."

Broken Rhyme.

Broken rhyme, where more than one word is needed to complete the rhyme, is occasionally used, *e.g.*, "estate/their gate."

Leonine Rhyme.

Although rhyme normally occurs at the end of the line, we also find verse where the first half of the line rhymes with the second. This device, known as Leonine rhyme, is frequently used in Coleridge's "Ancient Mariner" [OBEV 562], *e.g.*,

"The ice did split, with a thunder-fit."

Poetic Licence in Rhyme.

The difficulty of rhyming in English is considerable, for many words have not a single rhyming word, some have only one, others very few. Certain licences are therefore allowed to the poet in the following ways:

Eye Rhyme or Printers' Rhyme.

Here words rhyme only to the eye, as "love/move." Keats in "Meg Merrilies" uses "rushes/bushes."

Identical Rhyme.

Here the same syllable or word is used twice so that the line rhymes with itself, *e.g.*, "part/impart" [OBEV 562], "universe/this verse" [OBEV 617]. The use of rhyming words spelt differently but pronounced identically is also a poetic licence, *e.g.*, "wright, write, right."

Cockney Rhyme.

Keats' use of Cockney rhymes has been much criticised, *e.g.*, "mourn/torn," "faces/vases," "briar/attire." There is still considerable difference between Northern and Southern pronunciation of English, and many eminent poets have availed themselves of a Southern pronunciation in rhyming "dawn/morn," although in the North of England the "r" of "morn" would be sounded.

Assonance.

Assonance is sometimes used instead of rhyme, and occurs frequently in early folk poetry and less formal verse. It consists in a similarity in the accented vowels and those which follow, but not in the consonants, *e.g.*, "feet/creep," "skin/swim."

Perversion of Rhyme.

Modern poets, following Wilfrid Owen, have sometimes used a deliberate perversion of rhyme, which should not be confused with assonance. Wilfrid Owen opens his bitter poem "A Terre" with the following stanza:

"Sit on the bed. I'm blind and three parts shell.
Be careful; can't shake hands now; never shall.
Both arms have mutinied against me,—brutes.
My fingers fidget like ten idle brats."

The deliberate falsity of rhymes like "shall/shell," and "brutes/brats" conveys Owen's horror at the disintegration and collapse of the First World War.

Recording of Rhyme Schemes.

The conventional way of noting rhyme schemes is to call the first series *a*, the second *b*, and so on. Normally each new series is indented, *e.g.*,

"Joyful, joyful!	*a*
When virginity	*b*
Seeks all coyful	*a*
Man's affinity.	*b*
Fate all flowery,	*c*
Bright and bowery	*c*
Is her dowery!	*c*
Joyful, joyful."	*a*

W. S. Gilbert, "Yeomen of the Guard."

IV. THE STANZA.

Some poems are divided into groups of lines, which strictly speaking are called "stanzas," though in popular language they are often known as "verses." Generally the stanzas of a poem are uniform, but sometimes they are varied as in Milton's "Lycidas" [OBEV 325].

V. ENGLISH VERSE FORMS.

English poetry uses an immense wealth of verse forms, distinguishable from each other by the predominating metre and also by the pattern of rhyme and the kind of stanza—or by the absence of rhyme and stanza. An account of these follows.

Iambic Metres.

The metre most natural to the English language is undoubtedly the iambic.

With Iambic Pentameter as Basis.

The iambic pentameter of five stresses and ten syllables, also called the iambic decasyllabic line, is more used than any other, and is the basis of the following forms.

Blank Verse. Blank verse, consisting of unrhymed iambic pentameters, is the metre of Shakespeare's plays, Milton's "Paradise Lost," Wordsworth's "Prelude," and Tennyson's "Idylls of the King." In the hands of such masters it is a most flexible instrument, especially when diversified with the eleven-syllabled line with a feminine ending. Shakespeare used the metre with increasing freedom, though it must be remembered that some apparent variations are due to the different pronunciation of Elizabethan times.

The following lines of blank verse occur in Wordsworth's "Prelude," Book III. He is describing his rooms in St. John's College, Cambridge.

"And from my pillow, looking forth by light
Of moon or favouring stars, I could behold
The antechapel where the statue stood
Of Newton with his prism and silent face,
The marble index of a mind for ever
Voyaging through strange seas of Thought, alone."

Heroic Couplet. The heroic couplet, consisting of iambic pentameters rhyming in pairs, was in Elizabethan times called "riding rhyme," possibly because it is the metre of The Prologue of Chaucer's "Canterbury Tales," and of many of the tales themselves. It became the most fashionable metre of the eighteenth century when it was used by Pope, Goldsmith, and Johnson. Keats later employed it in "Lamia."

The *Closed Couplet* was, in the heyday of the couplet's vogue, considered the most polished and correct. Here the sentence form exactly coincides with the couplet and the rhyme has a clinching effect, *e.g.*,

"True ease in writing comes from art, not chance,
As they move easiest who have learned to dance."

Pope was the supreme master of the closed couplet, and eschewed variations such as enjambement, or the Alexandrine.

Enjambement is a variation used by poets before Pope's time and revived by the Romantic poets. In enjambement the sentence flows over from one line or couplet to the next, and the click of the rhyme is submerged, *e.g.*, Keats' description of Lamia in her serpent form with skin of "dazzling hue."

"And full of silver moons, that, as she breathed,
Dissolv'd or brighter shone, or interwreathed
Their lustres with the gloomier tapestries."
Keats, "Lamia."

The Alexandrine, another variation, is a line of six iambic feet. Dryden made frequent use of the Alexandrine but Pope parodied it in the brilliant line that serves as a mnemonic.

"A needless Alexandrine ends the song,
That, like a wounded snake, drags its slow length along."

The triplet, another variation, consists of three lines rhyming together. The third line is frequently an Alexandrine.

Rhyme Royal. Rhyme royal has seven iambic pentameters, rhyming ABABBCC. Used by Chaucer in "Troilus and Cressida" [OBEV 14 and 15] and Shakespeare in "Lucrece," it was revived by Masefield in such poems as "Dauber."

Spenserian Stanza. The Spenserian stanza has eight iambic pentameters followed by an Alexandrine, rhyming ABABBCBCC. Invented by Spenser in "The Faerie Queene," it was used by Byron in "Childe Harold," Keats in "The Eve of St. Agnes," and Shelley in "Adonais."

Elegaic Stanza. The Elegaic stanza has four iambic pentameters, rhyming ABAB. It is also called the "heroic quatrain," quatrain meaning a four-lined stanza. This form is best known through Gray's "Elegy" [OBEV 465].

"Omar Khayyám" Stanza.

The "Omar Khayyám" stanza receives its name from its use by Fitzgerald in his translation of the "Rubaiyat." It has four iambic pentameters, rhyming AABA.

Ottava Rima. Ottava rima, also called the octave stanza, has eight iambic pentameters, rhyming ABABABCC. It was used by Byron in "Don Juan," and by Keats in "Isabella."

Terza Rima. Terza rima has stanzas of three iambic pentameters with a linking rhyme scheme: ABA, BCB, CDC, etc. The concluding stanza is rounded of with an extra line rhyming with its central line, *e.g.*, DEDE, constituting, in effect, a heroic quatrain. Used by Dante, the verse has been adapted by English poets. Shelley's "Ode to the West Wind" [OBEV 617] uses modified terza rima, the final rhymes being DEDEE.

The Sonnet. A sonnet has fourteen iambic pentameters. Perfected in Italy by Petrarch, who died in 1374, it was introduced into England in the sixteenth century. There are two chief types of sonnet.

The Petrarchan, or Italian, sonnet has an "octave" of eight lines, rhyming ABBAABBA, followed by a "sestet" of six lines, where some variety of rhyme schemes is found. The strictest Petrarchan sonnets have either two "tercets" of three lines each, with rhymes CDECDE, or else three pairs of lines rhyming CDCDCD.

An example of sestet rhyming CDECDE is Milton's "On His Blindness" [OBEV 327].

Examples of sestets CDCDCD are Wordsworth's "Upon Westminster Bridge" [OBEV 534] and Keats' "On First Looking into Chapman's Homer" [OBEV 641].

Not all of these examples observe the natural pause between octave and sestet which is characteristic of the strict Italian form, and many of our finest sonnets depart from the original rhyme scheme in both octave and sestet.

A lesser-known Petrarchan sonnet by Keats:

'To one, who has been long in city pent,
'Tis very sweet to look into the fair
And open face of heaven,—to breathe a prayer
Full in the smile of the blue firmament.
Who is more happy, when, with heart's content,
Fatigued he sinks into some pleasant lair
Of wavy grass, and reads a debonair
And gentle tale of love and languishment?
Returning home at evening with an ear
Catching the notes of Philomel,—an eye
Watching the sailing cloudlet's bright career,
He mourns that day so soon has glided by:
E'en like the passage of an angel's tear
That falls through the clear ether silently."

The *Elizabethan, or Shakespearean,* sonnet consists of three quatrains with the rhymes ABAB/CDCD/EFEF/ concluded by a couplet rhyming GG. The couplet often clinches the thought.

Examples are Shakespeare's sonnets [OBEV 155–174], and Keats' last sonnet [OBEV 644].

Other Iambic Metres.

Many of our iambic verse forms use a shorter or longer line than the pentameter.

The Octosyllabic Couplet. The octosyllabic couplet consists of lines of four stresses and eight syllables, and the lines rhyme in pairs. English poets like Marvell have used this metre effectively, *e.g.*, "A Garden" [OBEV 365, *see also* OBEV 367, 370]. It is the metre of Masefield's "Everlasting Mercy" and "Reynard the Fox."

The Ballad. There are two chief kinds of ballad metre.

(a) *Strict Ballad Form* consists of stanzas of four iambic lines, the first and third with four stresses, and the second and fourth with three, with the rhyme scheme ABCB. The fine old ballads "Sir Patrick Spens" [OBEV 381] and "The Wife of Usher's Well" [OBEV 388] are in this metre. Coleridge, in "The Ancient Mariner" [OBEV 562] shows how many varieties of stanza can be based on the simple ballad stanza.

"*Fourteeners*" is the name given to a form which is simply a re-arrangement of the ballad quatrain as a rhyming couplet of two iambic lines with seven stresses, as in Macaulay's "The Armada."

(b) *Less Strict Ballad Form, or Long Metre,* consists of stanzas of four iambic lines each with four stresses, the rhyme scheme being ABCB or ABAB. Many ancient ballads, such as "Thomas the Rhymer" [OBEV 379], are of this type.

"In Memoriam" Metre. This, the metre of Tennyson's "In Memoriam," is like the less strict ballad metre in having four iambic lines, each with four stresses, but its rhyme scheme is ABBA.

Short Metre. Short metre, rarely used, consists of iambic quatrains, each line having three stresses and the rhyme scheme being ABCB.

English Hymn Metres. Most English hymns are written in short iambic lines, and English hymnology names them according to the number of syllables. The most common are:

Common Metre, or 8686, with rhymes ABAB, *e.g.*, "O for a thousand tongues to sing" ["Songs of Praise" 595].

Long Metre, or 8888, with rhymes ABAB, *e.g.*, "When I survey the wondrous cross" ["Songs of Praise" 133].

Short Metre, or 6686, with rhymes ABCB, *e.g.*, "Blest are the pure in heart" ["Songs of Praise" 455].

Double Iambic Metre. When we are accustomed to hearing verse we come to realise that stresses are not always of equal weight. It is possible to distinguish in these "fourteeners" of Masefield a major stress, marked ″ and a minor stress marked ′.

" Oh sőme are fónd of Spǎ̋nish wíne, and sőme are fónd of Frĕ̋nch,
And sőme'll swállow tǎ̋y and stúff fit ő̆nly fór a wĕ̋nch."

Masefield's "Captain Stratton's Fancy" [OBEV 939]

The lines have in fact four major stresses, and between the major stresses intervene three syllables, of which the middle has a minor stress. It is this alternation in the weight of the stress which gives its characteristic swing to such a poem as Chesterton's "The Rolling English Road" [OBEV 930].

Trochaic Metres.

Pure Trochaic Metre.

English poets seldom use a pure trochaic metre, partly because of the difficulty of rhyming, and partly because the continual feminine ending that it involves is not pleasing to the English ear. A few very short lyrics in this metre can be found, as Browne's Song "For her gait, if she be walking" [OBEV 251], but the only poem of any length is Longfellow's "Hiawatha," and the metre of this *tour de force* tends to sound monotonous. It consists of unrhymed lines, each of four stresses, *e.g.*,

" Líke a yéllow léaf in áutumn
Líke a yéllow wáter-lily."

Modified Trochaic Metre.

Ever since the Middle Ages our poets have contrived to combine the advantages of a trochaic metre and of a masculine ending by the simple expedient of shortening the last foot of the line to a stressed monosyllable. This catalectic, or shortened, trochaic line is found both in couplets and in stanza forms. *The seven-syllabled trochaic couplet, also called the trochaic tetrameter*, consists of these catalectic, or shortened, lines rhyming in pairs, and is a gay, tripping measure, as in some passages of Milton's " L'Allegro " [OBEV 318].

" Háste thee nýmph and bríng with thée
Jést and yóuthful Jóllity."

Keats uses the metre in " Bards of Passion," and " Fancy " [OBEV 637 and 638].

Lyrics in modified trochaic metre are often found. Herrick uses the seven-syllabled lines rhyming in pairs in " Cherry Ripe " and other lyrics [OBEV 264, 279, 280, 281]. Edmund Blunden, in " Forefathers " [OBEV 965], uses it in a stanza rhyming ABABCC. George Herbert in his lyric " Discipline " [OBEV 291] brilliantly combines five- and three-syllabled lines rhyming ABAB, *e.g.*,

" Thrów awáy Thy ród,
Thrów awáy Thy wráth;
Ó my Gód,
Táke the géntle páth."

Further Variations in Modified Trochaic Metre.

The modified trochaic line is especially subject to further variation.

(*a*) It is often combined with a pure trochaic line, *e.g.*, in Hunt's poem " Jenny Kiss'd Me " [OBEV 600] where the catalectic and the complete trochaic line alternate regularly.

(*b*) It often has an extra unstressed syllable preceding it (anacrusis), as in the second of these lines from Keats' poem " Fancy " [OBEV 638].

" Ín a dárk conspiracý
To | bánish Éven fróm her ský."

The line that results might well be taken for iambic, and there are some passages in English poetry, such as lines in Milton's " L'Allegro " [OBEV 318], which can be described either as irregular trochaic or irregular iambic lines! It depends on what the hearer judges to be the *basic* stress.

Double Trochaic Metre.

Corresponding to double iambic metre there is a double trochaic metre. W. S. Gilbert effectively uses it in many of his patter songs, as in " Ferdinando and Elvira," *e.g.*,

" Thén we lĕ̈t off páper crăckers, éach of which contáined a mŏtto,
Ánd she lĭstened whíle I rĕad them, till her mŏther tóld her nŏt to."

These lines, like those in double iambic metre, have four major stresses (marked ″), and between the major stresses three syllables, of which the middle carries a minor stress.

A modified double trochaic metre, where the last foot is shortened to a stressed monosyllable, can be recognised in Tennyson's " Locksley Hall," or in Lewis Carroll's verses in " Alice in Wonderland ":

" ' Will you wălk a líttle făster? ' sáid a whĭting tó a snáil."

Trisyllabic Metres Generally.

Because of the irregularities incident to verse in anapæsts, dactyls, and amphibrachs, it is not easy to distinguish one trisyllabic metre from another. Swinburne, the past master of trisyllabic metres, often passes with great freedom from anapæstic to dactylic lines within the same stanza.

Anapæstic Metres.

Pure Anapæstic.

Anapæstic metre is used only in short poems, and often conveys a sense of speed and urgency. The chief variation is the omission of one or two of the unstressed syllables at the beginning of a line. Some of the best-known examples of anapæstic verse are Byron's " Sennacherib," Flecker's " The War Song of the Saracens," and Lewis Carroll's parodies, " 'Tis the voice of the lobster " and " You are old, Father William," from " Alice in Wonderland."

The Limerick.

The limerick may be defined as a single anapæstic stanza, having the first two lines of three feet, the next two lines of two feet and a concluding line of three feet, with the rhyme scheme AABBA.

The origin of the limerick is uncertain, but it became popular after the appearance in 1846 of Edward Lear's " Book of Nonsense." Lear's limericks differ from the contemporary type in that his final line is normally a repetition, adding nothing to the sense and repeating one of the previous rhyme words.

Most of our modern limericks are passed on by word of mouth, but some that concisely express some intellectual attitudes have appeared in print, as the following, on " Determinism "—

" There wás a young mán who said ' Dámn!
It appéars to me nów that I ám
Just a béing that móves
In predéstinate gróoves,
Not a táxi or bús, but a trám.' "

Dactylic Metres.

Pure Dactylic.

Like pure trochaic metre, pure dactylic metre has a feminine ending to the line, which makes rhyming difficult and does not satisfy the English ear. Very few serious poems keep consistently to a pure dactylic verse, and Robert Graves' " In the Wilderness " is most unusual in this respect, *e.g.*,

" Chríst of His géntleness
Thírsting and húngering
Wálked in the wilderness."

Modified Dactylic Metre.

Normally dactylic metre is modified in that a catalectic line is frequently used, where the final foot is shortened to a trochee or a stressed monosyllable, as in Hood's " Bridge of Sighs " [OBEV 662], the most remarkable dactylic poem in the language, *e.g.*,

" Óne more unfórtunate
Wéary of bréath
Ráshly impórtunate
Góne to her déath."

Shakespeare also uses the catalectic line in the refrain to " Where the bee sucks " [OBEV 140]—

" Mérrily mérrily sháll I live nów
Únder the blóssom that hángs on the bóugh."

It is interesting to note how the catalectic dactylic line of the refrain is matched by the catalectic trochaic line of the verse.

Amphibrach Metres.

Pure Amphibrach Metre.

The amphibrach metre is extremely rare in English, although it occurs occasionally in a few lines, or a refrain, like that to " Blow, blow thou Winter Wind " [OBEV 146]. Laurence Binyon's

"Bablock Hythe" is one of the few poems to use amphibrachs continuously, *e.g.*,

"Till súnset was rímming
The Wést with pale flúshes;
Behínd the black rúshes
The lást light was dímming."

Modified Amphibrach Metre.

The pure amphibrach line can be used alternating with a catalectic line, shorn of its last syllable, as in Goldsmith's drinking song in "She Stoops to Conquer," Act I, Scene 2, *e.g.*,

"Let schóol-masters púzzle their bráin
With grámmar and nónsense and léarning."

Choriambic Metre.

There are few poems in pure choriambic metre. Ruskin's quatrain "Trust Thou thy Love" [OBEV 753] is one of the few examples, *e.g.*,

"Trúst thou thy Lóve; if she be próud, is she not swéet?"

Choriambic effects are often obtained incidentally, especially in blank verse, when the first foot of a line is a trochee.

Lionel Johnson frequently achieves the same kind of effect in lyric verses by substituting a choriamb for two iambs, as in the poem "By the Statue of King Charles" [OBEV 909], *e.g.*,

"Cómely and cálm, he rides
Hárd by his ówn Whitehall."

Sprung Rhythm.

Sprung rhythm was practised by Gerard Manley Hopkins and his followers.

Its distinction lies in the fact that in a foot of verse the first syllable is always stressed, and this stressed syllable may be followed by any number of unstressed syllables from none to three, or even more, as the occasion demands. Hopkins has described sprung rhythm in the Preface to his "Poems."

Quantitative Classical Metres.

Since the Renaissance poets such as Spenser, Coleridge, and Tennyson have from time to time endeavoured to reproduce in English verse the complicated quantitative metres of Greek and Latin verse. The difficulty, if not impossibility, of putting the stress on the long vowel in English has for the most past rendered such experiments interesting only to the scholar.

It should always be remembered that the technical names, such as iamb and trochee, although borrowed from the classics, have in English verse a quite different meaning, referring never to quantity but always to stress.

Metrical Forms of French Origin.

It became fashionable during the last years of the nineteenth century for poets to imitate certain verse forms which had long been practised in France, some of them from the time of the troubadours.

Chaucer and Gower had in the fourteenth century used some of these forms, later English poets had occasionally experimented with some of them, and Swinburne, Austin Dobson, Edmund Gosse, and others did much to adapt and naturalise them, although their intricate rhyming patterns are very difficult to construct in a language so short of rhymes as English. The most popular were the triolet, villanelle, rondeau, ballade, and sestina.

Characteristic of the Anglicised versions are:

1. Freedom as regards metre and length of line.

2. Complicated and exacting rhyme schemes, which permit of no such poetic licence as identical rhyme.

3. A refrain line which recurs in certain stereotyped positions without any alteration of sound, although there may be significant alteration of meaning. Only the sestina is without a refrain.

Triolet.

A triolet is a single stanza of eight short lines. The first line is repeated as the fourth, and the first and second appear again as seventh and eighth. Only two rhymes are used, the scheme being: ABAAABAB.

The triolet was re-introduced into England by Bridges in 1873. Austin Dobson's "A Kiss" is a good example of the form.

"Rose kissed me today.
Will she kiss me tomorrow?
Let it be as it may,
Rose kissed me today,
But the pleasure gives way
To a savour of sorrow;—
Rose kissed me today,—
Will she kiss me tomorrow?"

See also Dobson's triolet "I intended an Ode" [OBEV 828].

Villanelle.

The villanelle has five stanzas, each of three lines, followed by one stanza of four lines. It has a refrain which consists of the first and third lines of the first stanza. These lines alternately form the last lines of the four middle stanzas, and reappear as a concluding couplet to the poem. Only two rhymes are employed throughout. Stanzas one to five rhyme ABA and stanza six ABAA.

Austin Dobson wrote several villanelles including the well-known "On a Nankin Plate." The following of Henley's is both a good example and description of the form.

Villanelle by W. E. Henley:

A dainty thing's the Villanelle
Shy, musical, a jewel in rhyme,
It serves its purpose passing well.

A double-clappered silver bell
That must be made to clink in chime,
A dainty thing's the Villanelle;

And if you wish to flute a spell,
Or ask a meeting 'neath the lime,
It serves its purpose passing well.

You must not ask of it the swell
Of organs grandiose and sublime—
A dainty thing's the Villanelle;

And, filled with sweetness, as a shell
Is filled with sound, and launched in time,
It serves its purpose passing well.

Still fair to see and good to smell
As in the quaintness of its prime,
A dainty thing's the Villanelle.
It serves its purpose passing well.

Rondeau.

A rondeau is a short and compact verse form. It has thirteen lines, usually of eight syllables, which use only two rhymes, and in addition a refrain, usually of four syllables, which introduces a third rhyme. This refrain consists of the first half of the opening line and is twice repeated, thus giving the rondeau fifteen lines all told. The rondeau is divided into three stanzas with the following rhyme scheme: AABBA: AAB + refrain, C: AABBA + refrain C.

Austin Dobson wrote many rondeaus to this exacting plan, including the ingenious "You bid me try" and "In After Days" [OBEV 830].

A Rondeau by Austin Dobson:

You bid me try.

You bid me try, Blue-Eyes, to write
A Rondeau. What!—forthwith?—to-night?
Reflect. Some skill I have, 'tis true;—
But thirteen lines!—and rhymed on two!
"Refrain," as well. Ah, hapless plight!

Still, there are five lines,—ranged aright.
These Gallic bonds, I feared, would fright
My easy Muse. They did, till you—
You bid me try!

That makes them eight. The port's in sight:—
'Tis all because your eyes are bright!
Now just a pair to end in 'oo'—
When maids command, what can't we do.
Behold!—the RONDEAU, tasteful, light,
You bid me try!

1876

Roundel.

The roundel is a variation of the rondeau. Swinburne in his "Century of Roundels" wrote a hundred, and his pattern is usually followed. It consists of nine full lines, plus the refrain (consisting of the opening half of the first line), which is twice repeated, giving eleven lines all told. Only two rhymes are used throughout. The roundel is divided into three stanzas with the following rhyme scheme: ABA + refrain B; BAB; ABA + refrain B.

Swinburne's roundel called "The Roundel" is especially interesting.

Rondel.

The rondel is a form of verse similar to the rondeau. The modern English version consists of fourteen lines all told. Only two rhymes are used, and the initial two lines are repeated as lines 7 and 8 and again as lines 13 and 14. The rondel is frequently arranged in three stanzas with a rhyme scheme as follows: ABBA; ABAB; ABBAAB.

The rondel was revived in the nineteenth century by Bridges, Dobson, Gosse and Henley, and Dobson's "Love comes back to his vacant dwelling" is one of the best known.

Ballade.

There are several kinds of ballade, but the most popular modern form consists of three eight-lined stanzas followed by an envoy of four lines. Each of the stanzas and the envoy end with a refrain. The rhymes of the eight-lined stanzas are ABABBCBC, and of the envoy BCBC.

Austin Dobson wrote several ballades of this kind, the best known being, "This was the Pompadour's fan," and "And where are the galleons of Spain?"

Chaucer's "Balade," "Hyd, Absolon, thy gilte tresses clere," is of an earlier seven-lined type without an envoy.

A ballade by Austin Dobson:

TheBallad of the Thrush.

Across the noisy street
I hear him careless throw
One warning utterance sweet;
This faint at first, and low
The full notes closer grow;
Hark! What a torrent gush!
They pour, they overflow—
Sing on, sing on, O Thrush!

What trick, what dream's deceit
Has fooled his fancy so
To scorn of dust and heat?
I, prisoned here below,
Feel the fresh breezes blow;
And see, thro' flag and rush,
Cool water sliding slow—
Sing on, sing on, O Thrush!

Sing on. What though thou beat
On that dull bar, thy foe!
Somewhere the green boughs meet
Beyond the roofs a-row;
Somewhere the blue skies show,
Somewhere no black walls crush
Poor hearts with hopeless woe—
Sing on, sing on, O Thrush!

Envoy.

Bird, though they come, we know,
The empty cage, the hush;
Still, ere the brief day go,
Sing on, sing on, O Thrush!

1883

The Chant Royal.

The chant royal is a longer form of ballade. It has five stanzas of eleven lines and an envoy of five lines.

The rhyme scheme is ABABCCDDEDE, and the envoy has rhyme DDEDE.

The Sestina.

The sestina has six stanzas, each of six lines. The end words to the lines of the first stanza are repeated as end words in the other five stanzas, but in a different and stereotyped order. The poem concludes with an envoy.

The first sestina published in English was in Spenser's "Shepheardes Calender" (1579). Swinburne wrote many, including "I saw my soul at rest upon a day."

The Clerihew.

The clerihew is an amusing quatrain, so called after its inventor Edmund Clerihew Bentley. It disdains regular metre and depends on the simple rhyme scheme AABB. The distinctive characteristic of the clerihew is that it is concerned with some eminent person, who is named in the first line and then described in a wilfully fanciful way, the matter being dictated by the exigencies of the rhyme, as in Bentley's clerihew on J.S. Mill.

"John Stuart Mill,
By a mighty effort of will,
Overcame his natural bonhomie
And wrote 'Principles of Political Economy.'"

We might invent a clerihew for Pears Cyclopædia, and say

"You will find *Pears Cyclopædia*
A simpler and speedier
Aid in your search for verity
If you do not use it with levity."

Free Verse or Vers Libre.

It is hardly possible to define anything so vague as Free Verse. It is characterised by a greater intensity of feeling and a more elevated language than is usual in prose, and has a rhythm that is different from that of poetry in that it is irregular; it has rhythm but not metre.

Free Verse is arranged in lines, but these lines have an indefinite number of syllables. They have balance but no regularly recurring pattern of stress, and no rhyme.

The best-known writer of Free Verse is Walt Whitman, whose "Leaves of Grass" was published in 1855.

VI. CONCLUSION.

The foregoing account is no more than a description of our traditional verse forms. It in no way implies that verse is written according to rules.

We have only to look at Shakespeare's lyrics [OBEV 133–174] to realise how brilliantly free and inventive the poet can be in devising new and delightful patterns of verse—many of them so subtle as to be very difficult to define All that the students and critics can do is to follow in the poets' wake, endeavouring to understand and elucidate the forms that the maker has created.

FIGURES OF SPEECH

We constantly use figurative language without realising it. When we say that we are "browned off," "fed up," "at the end of our tether," we do not expect to be taken literally. We are in fact employing metaphors.

An understanding of metaphors and other figurative expressions enables us to use our language with greater confidence and effectiveness. It also helps us to understand more fully what others have written. Especially is it valuable when we read a good novel, play, or poem, for to the creative writer figurative language is as natural as the air he breathes.

The following guide to our figures of speech is arranged alphabetically for ease of reference.

Alliteration. A kind of repetition. Two or more words in close succession begin with the same letter, or sound, usually a consonant. Up to the fourteenth century much English verse was written according to an alliterative principle, as in this modernised quotation from "Piers Plowman."

"I had *w*andered me *w*eary so *w*eary I rested me
On a *b*road *b*ank by a merry-sounding *b*urn."

A strong tendency to alliteration still survives in our poetry. Shakespeare ridicules it in the mechanical's play in "A Midsummer Night's Dream" (Act V, Scene 1) in such lines as—

"Whereat, with blade, with bloody blameful blade,
He bravely broach'd his boiling bloody breast."

Anti-climax. See Bathos.

Antithesis. A figure of speech where ideas are so set out that they are in sharp contrast to each other, *e.g.*,

"Better to reign in Hell than serve in Heav'n."
Milton.

"To err is human, to forgive divine."
Pope.

Apostrophe. A figure of speech where the speaker or writer suddenly breaks off and directly addresses some other person who may be present either in the flesh or only in the imagination. Often it is not a person but a thing, abstraction, or personification that is addressed, as in Milton's famous apostrophe, "Hail, holy light" in "Paradise Lost," Book III, line 1. Apostrophe can be used with comic effect, *e.g.*,

"She turns, O guardian angels stop her
From doing anything improper."

(This couplet is also, incidentally, an example of bathos.)

Assonance. (1) Assonance is correspondence of vowel sounds. For instance, in the opening lines of the "fairy song" in "A Midsummer Night's Dream" (Act II, Scene 3) there is a play on only three vowels, and this repetition helps towards the effect of a magic charm, *e.g.*,

"Philomel, with melody, Sing."

In Tennyson's poem "Break, break, break" the repetition of the "o" sound in the second line is like an outcry of grief, *e.g.*,

"On thy c*o*ld grey st*o*nes, *O* sea."

(2) Assonance is sometimes used instead of rhyme, especially in early folk poetry. Here there is correspondence of one word with another in the accented vowel and any vowels which follow, but not in the consonants, *e.g.*, in "King Estmere," "Spain" is rhymed with "same," and "barone" with "home."

Bathos or Anti-climax. A figure of speech that consists of a sudden and ludicrous descent from lofty to trivial things. In "The Rape of the Lock" Pope wittily used bathos to satirise the frivolity of the woman of fashion, who lacking all sense of proper feeling, casts the same "screams of horror," and "shrieks to pitying heav'n,"

"When *husbands* or when *lapdogs* breathe their last."

The careless writer may fall to bathos which is unintentionally comic in its effect. The word "bathos" in Greek means "depth."

Climax. A figure of speech where ideas are set out in such a way that each rises above its predecessor in fable. In Greek the word "climax" means a ladder. One of the finest examples is in Shakespeare's "The Tempest" (Act IV, Scene 1) when Prospero says,

"And like the baseless fabric of this vision
The cloud-capp'd towers, the gorgeous palaces,
The solemn temples, the great globe itself,
Yea, all which it inherit, shall dissolve."

Epigram. A concise and pointed saying, effective by its wit and ingenuity. It often uses antithesis. S. T. Coleridge's definition of this form is in itself an epigram, *e.g.*,

"What is an epigram? a dwarfish whole:
Its body brevity, and wit its soul."

Euphemism. A figure of speech where a harsh or distressing expression is replaced by one that is gentler, if less accurate. Thus we may call a lie a "flight of fancy," or a "terminological inexactitude." There is a striking instance of euphemism in "Macbeth" (Act I, Scene 5), when Lady Macbeth, planning the murder of her guest, Duncan, says, "He that's coming must be provided for."

Hypallage or **"Transferred Epithet."** A figure of speech where an adjective, or adverb, is separated from the word to which it belongs grammatically, and is transferred to some other word in the sentence, its unusual position giving it a kind of emphasis. The word "obsequious" is thus transferred in the sentence "A lacquey presented an obsequious cup of coffee."

Hyperbole. A figure of speech where there is a deliberate use of exaggeration for the sake of effect as in the phrase "tons of money." Lady Macbeth uses hyperbole when she says, "Here's the smell of blood still; all the perfumes of Arabia will not sweeten this little hand" (Act V, Scene 1).

Writers of film trailers frequently indulge in hyperbole.

Innuendo. A figure of speech where something is hinted at, or suggested, but not openly stated. Dickens uses innuendo to suggest Scrooge's stinginess by saying, "Darkness was cheap, and Scrooge liked it."

Irony. (1) A figure of speech where the speaker says one thing but intends the opposite to be understood. Shylock uses the word "courtesies" ironically when he says,

"Fair sir, you spit on me on Wednesday last,
You spurn'd me such a day; another time
You call'd me dog; and for these courtesies
I'll lend you thus much moneys."
"Merchant of Venice" (Act I, Scene 3).

The use of irony can clearly be seen in Shakespeare's "Julius Cæsar" in Antony's well-known speech to the citizens. They gradually realise that when Antony repeats that Brutus and the rest are "honourable men," he is speaking ironically, and intends the opposite. When they fully perceive this they cry, "They were traitors . . . villains, murderers." ("Julius Cæsar," Act III, Scene 2.)

(2) *Dramatic irony* is the use of words which have a second inner significance that is not realised by some of the actors in a scene. For instance, in Sheridan's "School for Scandal," Act IV, Scene 3, Sir Peter admires Joseph Surface's useful screen, and Surface replies, "Oh yes, I find great use in that screen." He and the audience know, but Sir Peter does not, that at that very moment the screen is concealing Peter's own wife who had rashly visited Joseph.

It is helpful to remember that in Greek the word "irony" means "dissimulation."

Litotes. A figure of speech which is really a special kind of understatement (or Meiosis). Instead of making a positive statement (*e.g.*, "This is a difficult task") we might use Litotes, and say "This is no easy task," thus expressing a positive by the negative of its opposite.

Malapropism. An amusing inaccuracy in vocabulary. Words that have an accidental similarity in sound may become confused in the speaker's mind and the wrong word may come uppermost. Thus Mrs. Malaprop complains that the disobedience of her niece gives her, not "hysterics," but "hydrostatics." It is not surprising that Mrs. Malaprop, of Sheridan's "The Rivals," has given her name to this kind of verbal confusion, though many before her time, including humble folk in Shakespeare's plays, have uttered malapropism. Bottom, in "A Midsummer Night's Dream," says that in the wood they "may rehearse more obscenely" when he means "obscurely."

Meiosis. A figure of speech where a deliberate understatement is made for the sake of effect. English people are especially fond of Meiosis and often use it colloquially, in such an expression as "He made a very 'decent' contribution," meaning a very "generous" contribution. The full meaning of what we intend is often conveyed by the tone of voice, *e.g.*,

"This is *some* war."

Metaphor. It is helpful to think of the figure of speech, metaphor, as a condensed simile. In metaphor one thing is not merely *compared* to another, as in simile, but is boldly spoken of as if it actually *were* that other. Thus Bacon, in the following metaphor, does not say books are *like* food, but speaks of them as if they actually *were* food, *e.g.*, "Some books are to be tasted, others to be swallowed, and some few to be chewed and digested."

Metaphor is usually defined as the transfer of a name, or descriptive term, to some object to which it is not properly applicable, thus making an implicit comparison. Shakespeare uses nautical terms to describe our human situation when Brutus says,

"There is a tide in the affairs of men which, taken at the flood, leads on to fortune" ("Julius Cæsar," Act IV, Scene 3).

In *Mixed Metaphor* two or more inconsistent metaphors are used of the same object, as when, speaking of a suspicion, someone said, "I smell a rat; I see it in the air; but I will nip it in the bud."

Metonymy. A figure of speech where a person or thing is not named directly, but by some associated thing. Instead of saying, "The prisoner addressed the magistrate," we might use metonymy, and say, "The prisoner addressed the bench." Similarly, "a speech from the Lord Chancellor" is sometimes called "a speech from the Woolsack."

Onomatopœia. The use of words which imitate or echo the sounds they suggest, *e.g.*,

"Seas half-frozen slushed the deck with slime."
Masefield.

Oxymoron. A figure of speech where words that are usually contradictory are combined in one expression, *e.g.*, "bitter-sweet."

"I know this is a joyful trouble to you."
"Macbeth," Act II, Scene 3.

Paradox. A figure of speech where a statement is made that at first sight seems contradictory, or absurd, *e.g.*,

"The rule of the road is a paradox quite:
If you keep to the left, you are sure to be right."

and

"The child is father of the man."
Wordsworth.

Pathetic Fallacy. A figure of speech where it is assumed that things of nature have feelings like those of human beings, *e.g.*,

"And daffadillies fill their cups with tears."
Milton.

In Greek "pathos" means "feeling."

Personification. A figure of speech where some abstraction, or some inanimate thing is represented as a person, *e.g.*,

"Rule, Britannia."

"But look the dawn in russet mantle clad
Walks o'er the dew of yon high eastern hill."
Hamlet, Act I, Scene 1.

Personification is really a special kind of metaphor.

Pun. The use of words so as to convey a double meaning, as in Belloc's couplet

"When I am dead, I hope it may be said
"His sins were scarlet, but his books were read.'"

In the three puns that follow there is a suggestion of a banking transaction! "The Egyptians received a check on the bank of the Red Sea which was crossed by Moses." Puns, which were popular in the nineteenth century, especially with Lamb and Hood, are now out of favour.

Simile. A figure of speech which makes a comparison pointing out a similarity between things otherwise unlike. It is usually introduced by "like" or "as," *e.g.*,

"Men fear death as children fear to go in the dark."
Bacon.

"His own thought drove him like a goad."
Tennyson.

Spoonerism. An accidental transposition of the sound of two words, so called after Rev. W. A. Spooner, warden of New College, Oxford, *e.g.*,

"You have hissed all my mystery lectures" for "You have missed all my history lectures."

Synecdoche. A figure of speech where the name of a part is used for the whole, or the whole for the part, *e.g.*,

"A fleet of a hundred sail",

meaning of a hundred ships.

Synecdoche is really a special kind of Metonymy.

Transferred Epithet. See Hypallage.

LITERARY FORMS

Allegory. A description or story which has a second and deeper significance below the surface. The characters are really personifications, usually representing some vice or virtue. Allegory flourished in the Middle Ages, but the best-known allegory in the world is Bunyan's "Pilgrim's Progress" (1678), which has been translated into over a hundred different languages and dialects. On the surface "The Pilgrim's Progress" is the story of a journey in which the hero encounters many difficulties but at last reaches his destination. Its inner meaning is the progress of the Christian soul through life on earth. Spenser's "Faerie Queene" (1589 and 1596) is a more subtle and complex allegory, capable of several interpretations, religious, ethical, and political. Allegory has been described as extended metaphor. *See* **M10–11.**

Autobiography. The story of a man's (or woman's) own life, written by himself. The autobiography is becoming increasingly popular, recent excellent examples being Stephen Spender's *World within World*, Richard Church's *Over the Bridge* and Laurie Lee's *Cider with Rosie*.

Ballad. There are two chief types of ballad:

1. A light song, often sentimental, as was the Victorian ballad, or a popular song, often of a personal kind, praising or attacking some notability.

2. A traditional poem, passed on by word of mouth. Many of our traditional ballads date from the 15th century. They tell some stirring tale, as do the many ballads about Robin Hood. Sometimes they record an actual occurrence, like the ballad "The Battle of Otterbourne," which tells of a Border skirmish, fought in 1388. Such ballads are enlivened by lively dialogue, and they use a special kind of stanza, which is described on **M5.**

Ballade. A short highly stylised poem, with a strict verse form. *See* **M9.**

Biography. A narrative telling the life story of some actual person, usually a well known figure. The most famous biographer of classical times was Plutarch, who in the 1st century A.D. wrote his series of parallel "Lives" of twenty-three Greeks and twenty-three Romans. The English translation of this provided Shakespeare with some of the plots of his plays. Boswell's *Life of Samuel Johnson* (1791) is our best-known English biography.

Burlesque. The aim of burlesque is to make us laugh by ridiculing the work of some other writer. Sometimes it treats his serious subject in a mocking way. Sometimes it takes the form of an absurd imitation or caricature of his style. Some of our most successful burlesques are dramatic in form, like Sheridan's "The Critic," produced in 1779. This has a play within a play, called "A Tragedy Rehears'd," a brilliant burlesque of the sentimental, historical plays so popular in his time. Danny Kaye's film, "The King's Jester," is a burlesque of pseudo-historical films.

Chant Royal. A poem of a strictly formal kind, French in origin. *See* **M9.**

Clerihew. A single-stanza verse form, four lines long *See* **M9.**

Comedy. A play which is happy and amusing in tone, but not necessarily light or superficial. A comedy always has a fortunate conclusion. Shakespeare's "Twelfth Night" and Oscar Wilde's "The Importance of being Earnest" are typical examples.

Drama. A play in verse or prose, where the story is unfolded and the characters represented through the actions and speeches of actors on a stage. It is essential to good drama that there should be some kind of dynamic action and some conflict between the characters. In comedy the conflict is usually open and external. "As You Like It," for instance, begins with a quarrel between Orlando and Oliver. But most of the world's finest tragedies reveal also an inner conflict in the soul of man. In "Hamlet" the hero is at odds with many people, including his mother, the king, Ophelia, Polonius, and Laertes, but all these struggles are of secondary significance, compared with the conflict in his own mind. Even a play like "Waiting for Godot," which reduces incident and conflict to a minimum, must make some concession to the demand of the audience for the dynamic. Drama cannot be static. Occasionally poets have written dramas which they knew were not practicable for the stage. Shelley's lyrical dramas, "Prometheus Unbound" and "Hellas," are of this kind. *See* **Section I.**

Eclogue. In classical literature a brief poem, usually in the form of a dialogue between shepherds. It was a popular form in the time of the Renaissance; Spenser's "Shepheardes Calendar" (1579) consists of twelve eclogues, one for each month of the year.

Elegy. A lyric poem of lamentation for the dead. Gray's "Elegy in a Country Church-yard" (1750) is the best-known English elegy. It reflects in a general way on the "destiny obscure" of the humble folk who are buried in a quiet church-yard, probably that of Stoke Poges, but most elegies mourn the death of only one person. Such are Shelley's "Adonais" (1821), on the death of Keats, and Matthew Arnold's "Thyrsis" (1867), commemorating his friend Arthur Hugh Clough. Tennyson's "In Memoriam" (1850) is unusual, in that it is not a single elegy, but a series of elegiac poems, inspired by the poet's grief for the death in 1833 of his friend Arthur Hallam.

Epic. A very long narrative poem, usually consisting of several books. The epic tells of the splendid deeds of some hero of history or legend and is frequently concerned with war. Some of the world's greatest epics are the Greek "Iliad" and "Odyssey," ascribed to Homer, the Latin "Aeneid" of Virgil, the Hindu "Mahabharata," and Milton's "Paradise Lost," whose hero is God himself. The epic is distinguished by its sustained dignity of style.

Epilogue. *See* **Prologue.**

Essay. The word essay, derived from the French, means literally an "attempt" or "endeavour," and as a literary term it applies to a short prose composition which attempts to present the author's reflections on any subject he chooses. As a literary form the essay derives from the French "Essais" of Montaigne, first translated into English by Florio in 1603. Our first English essayist was Francis Bacon, who published between 1597 and 1625 three volumes of his essays, brief, pithy, and objective in character. In course of time the essay has become more subjective and personal, especially in the hands of Lamb, Hazlitt, and contemporary writers.

Extravaganza. A composition, musical or literary, which uses improbable and fantastic elements and incidents. A good example of narrative extravaganza is Thackeray's *Rose and the Ring* (1855), in which, for instance, Gruffanuff's husband, the footman, is, because of his rudeness, turned into a door-knocker. Extravaganzas are frequently dramatic in form, and most pantomimes may be regarded as such.

Fable. A very brief story designed to teach some lesson or moral. The characters of the story are often animals, birds, or insects, which converse like human beings. The most famous of all fables are those attributed to Aesop, and those of La Fontaine, the French writer of the 17th century.

Farce. A species of dramatic comedy whose whole aim is to excite laughter. It does not scruple to use improbable characters and incidents and absurd situations. "Charley's Aunt" is a typical farce.

Lampoon. A coarse satire (q.v.) attacking an individual. Lampoons are usually short. The word itself is derived from a French word meaning "drinking song."

Limerick. A single-stanza verse form, 5 lines long and with a formal metre and rhyme scheme. *See* **M7.**

Lyric. In ancient Greece a lyric was originally a poem meant to be sung to the accompaniment of the lyre, a stringed musical instrument rather like a small harp. Later the word was used for a poem with song-like qualities: short, usually divided into verses, and expressing the feelings of the poet. The lyric flourished in England in the Elizabethan age as witnessed by the lovely lyrics scattered through Shakespeare's plays. Neglected in the 18th century, it became popular again with the Romantic poets of the 19th century. Odes, elegies, and sonnets are all species of lyrics.

Mask or Masque. A dramatic entertainment performed by amateurs and originating in the court masquerade. The action or plot of the masque is of the slightest and there is little concern with portrayal of character, for the masque gives pleasure by means of its verse, music, and dancing, and its elegant costume and scenery. It was very popular in the 16th and 17th centuries, and from 1605 Ben Jonson wrote many court masques, for which Inigo Jones designed original costumes and settings. Our best-known examples are Shakespeare's masque in Act IV of "The Tempest" and Milton's "Comus."

Melodrama. There are two meanings of the word melodrama.

1. In the early 19th century a melodrama meant a play, usually of a romantic and sensational kind, in which songs were inserted, and where an orchestra accompanied the action. The musical comedy of today might be regarded as its modern counterpart.

2. Today the word melodrama is used of an inferior kind of play, which deliberately excites the emotions by its sensational and violent happenings, but which has a happy ending. We should be careful to distinguish melodrama, which uses violence for its own sake, from serious plays, like "Hamlet" or "King Lear," where violent acts are only incidents necessary to a profound interpretation of human conduct.

Memoirs. The word is normally used of a record of events of which the author has some personal experience or special source of information.

Miracle Plays. Mediæval verse plays produced from the late 14th to 16th centuries by the town guilds and performed in the market-place, or other suitable open space. They consisted of a series of dramatised stories from the Bible or Lives of Saints. Each scene would be allotted to one of the guilds, which was then responsible for its production on a wheeled stage. As soon as the actors of one guild had completed their scene, their stage would be trundled off, sometimes to another rendezvous, and would itself be succeeded by another stage with its scene, until a whole cycle of episodes had been performed. Four great cycles of miracle plays are still extant called after the towns where they were probably performed, York, Coventry, Chester, and Wakefield. The Wakefield cycle is often called the Towneley cycle. The plays have not only a strong religious sense but also a lively comic spirit. The Towneley cycle has some especially racy comic scenes. One popular incident shows the noisy quarrel that results when Noah's wife refuses to go into the ark.

Mock Heroic. A species of parody (*q.v.*), caricaturing some play or poem written in a lofty and high-flown style. "The Rehearsal" (1672), by Villiers, is typical. It is an absurd imitation ridiculing the artificial and high falutin' heroic plays which were then in vogue.

Monody. In Greek literature an ode sung by a single voice, like our solo in music. In English literature it signifies a poem of mourning for someone's death. The elegies "Lycidas," by Milton, and "Thyrsis," by Matthew Arnold, were both called monodies by their authors.

Monologue. Originally a scene where one person of the drama spoke alone. Today it usually means a dramatic composition for a single actor, such as the well-known Lancashire monologues presented by Stanley Holloway. The word is also sometimes used as meaning soliloquy.

Moralities or Morality Plays. Mediæval verse plays of an allegorical kind, which attempted to teach lessons of virtue, the persons of the drama usually being not real people, but personifications. Most Moralities date from the 15th century, the best known being "Everyman," which is Dutch in origin. The hero, Everyman, is summoned by Death, and vainly appeals for help to his friends, Fellowship, Kindred, Goods, Knowledge, Beauty, and Strength, but all fail him. Only his own Good Deeds will consent to accompany him on his last journey.

Mysteries or Mystery Plays. Some modern writers use the term "Mystery play" instead of "Miracle play" (*q.v.*). It is really an alternative title. One critic tried to distinguish between "Mystery plays," as concerned with stories from the Gospels, and "Miracle plays," as concerned with the lives and deeds of Saints, but this distinction is not usually followed.

Novel. A lengthy prose fiction in narrative form, telling a realistic story of people and their doings. Its chief interest is in character and incident. The first English novelist was Samuel Richardson, whose novels, especially *Pamela* (1740–41) and *Clarissa Harlowe* (1747–48), had a European reputation. In the present century writers like James Joyce, and Virginia Woolf have written what have been called novels of the "stream of consciousness," where the interest lies not so much in the incidents as in the mind's response to events, and reflections.

Ode. In classical literature an ode was a poem to be sung. In English literature it signifies a lyric poem, usually in rhyme, and is seldom longer than 150 lines. It is usually in the form of an address, and lofty in its feeling and style. The ode was popular with the romantic poets. Some of our best known are Shelley's "Ode to the West Wind," and Keats' "Ode to a Nightingale," "Ode on a Grecian Urn," and "To Autumn," all of them published in 1820.

Parable. A parable is an arresting simile or metaphor from nature or common life, which may be elaborated into a life-like story. It presents a situation which at a certain point implies some correspondence with ethical or religious principle. *See* C. H. Dodd's *The Parables of the Kingdom*.

Parody. A literary caricature, which mimics the themes and style of some other author in such a way as to make his faults seem absurd and laughable. J. C. Squire's *Tricks of the Trade* is an amusing collection of his skilful parodies of such writers as Byron, Wordsworth, and Masefield.

Pastoral. A pastoral poem, romance, or play is one in which the life of shepherds or of simple rustic folk is portrayed in an idealised way. Originating in Greek literature, the pastoral was revived at the time of the Renaissance. Spenser's "Shepheardes Calendar" consists of twelve pastoral eclogues. Shakespeare's "As You Like It" is a pastoral play, Milton's "Lycidas" is a pastoral elegy and his "Comus" a pastoral masque. There is usually in the pastoral a deeper meaning below the surface. A critic has said, "The shepherd's cloak was the acknowledged disguise of the lover, the poet, the courtier, the pastor of souls, the critic of contemporary life." In the pastoral form the charm of a simple setting and deeper significance are combined.

Prologue and Epilogue. Generally speaking, a prologue means a foreword, or preface, and an epilogue an appendix to a literary work, but the terms are often used more specifically when referring to a play. Here the prologue is a short speech in verse or prose spoken to the audience by one of the actors before the play begins, the epilogue a similar speech after its conclusion. The prologue endeavours to put the audience into a receptive state of mind, the epilogue to ask for a kind reception to the play. Shakespeare's "Romeo and Juliet" has a prologue, his "As You Like It" an epilogue, spoken by Rosalind, who says, "Good plays prove the better by the help of a good epilogue." In the 18th century it was customary for a leading actor to speak the prologue and for a leading actress to make a plea for the play in the epilogue.

Romance. The romance of the early Middle Ages was a fictitious tale in verse, telling the adventures of some hero of chivalry, the interest being in the incidents, sometimes of a supernatural kind, rather than in character. The most famous of these early romances is the French "Chanson de Roland" of the early 12th century. In the later Middle Ages a romance might be written in prose. In the 16th and 17th centuries a romance meant a tale in either prose or verse in which the scenes and incidents were remote from those of real life. Sir Philip Sidney's "Arcadia" (1590), written to entertain his sister, is of this type. Today the word romance is rather vaguely used of a tale of somewhat improbable events. Sir Henry Rider Haggard wrote several such romances, including *King Solomon's Mines* (1886) and *She* (1887).

Rondeau. A poem of a strictly formal kind, French in origin. *See* **M8**.

Rondel. A poem similar in form to the rondeau. *See* **M9**.

Roundel. A variation of the Rondeau. *See* **M9**.

Saga. The word saga, which is of Norse origin, and means story, is applied to the mediæval prose narratives of Iceland and Norway, especially those concerned with the traditions of Icelandic families and Norwegian kings. William Morris, in his "Earthly Paradise," gives in "The Lovers of Gudrun" a version of the Icelandic Laxdæla Saga.

Satire. A work in either verse or prose attacking folly and vice. Pope's "Dunciad," in verse, published between 1728 and 1743, ridicules contemporary authors and literary follies in a massive attack on dulness and literary hacks. Swift's *Gulliver's Travels* (1726), which on the surface is a series of prose tales of travel to imaginary countries, is actually a comprehensive satire. It begins, in the first book on "Lilliput," with incisive ridicule of the squabbles between English political parties and religious sects, and culminates, in the final book on the Houyhnhnms, in a devastating attack on all that is bestial in human nature. Samuel Butler's *Erehwon* (an anagram of Nowhere), published in 1872, also uses a prose travel tale in his satirical exposure of Victorian convention and hypocrisy. Although not precisely satires, many of Shaw's plays are satirical in spirit. "Arms and the Man" may be considered in one of its aspects as a satire on war.

Sestina. A poem of a strictly formal kind, French in origin. *See* **M9**.

Skit. A light satire, often in the form of parody.

Soliloquy. In a soliloquy a man talks to himself, or utters his thoughts aloud regardless of the presence of others who may hear him. The word is usually applied to such utterances by a character in a play. The most famous soliloquies in literature are those of Hamlet.

Sonnet. A lyric poem of fourteen lines, with an intricate rhyme scheme. *See* **M6**.

Squib. A brief, sharp satire (*q.v.*) attacking an individual.

Threnody. A term from the Greek, seldom used today. It means a song of mourning, especially a lament for the dead.

Tragedy. A play, or other literary work, which is preoccupied with the serious and unhappy aspects of life. It is sombre in tone and ends with misfortune. Shakespeare's "Macbeth" and Ibsen's "Ghosts" are typical tragedies.

Tragi-Comedy. The word is used in two different ways:

(*a*) It may denote a play (or very occasionally a story) which combines both tragic and comic elements. Chekhov's "The Cherry Orchard" is a tragi-comedy of this type.

(*b*) It may also mean a play which is for the most part sombre in theme and tone, but which has a happy conclusion, like Shakespeare's "The Winter's Tale."

Trilogy. In Greek literature a series of three tragedies, like Aeschylus' trilogy, the "Oresteia," written when he was nearly seventy, in the 5th century B.C. In modern times the word trilogy is applied to any sequence of three literary works which are related to each other in subject and theme.

Triolet. A single-stanza verse form, eight lines long, and with a very formal pattern, French in origin. *See* **M8**.

Villanelle. A poem of a strictly formal kind, French in origin. *See* **M8**.

FAMILIAR FOREIGN PHRASES AND CLASSICAL QUOTATIONS

Fr., French. Gr., Greek. Ger., German. It., Italian. L., Latin. Sp., Spanish.

à bas (Fr.), down, down with.
ab extra (L.), from without.
ab incunabilis (L.), from the cradle.
ab initio (L.), from the beginning.
ab intra (L.), from within.
à bon chat, bon rat (Fr.), to a good cat, a good rat; well attacked and defended; tit for tat; a Rowland for an Oliver.
à bon marché (Fr.), cheap, a good bargain.
à bras ouverts (Fr.), with open arms.
absente reo (L.), the accused being absent.
absit invidia (L.), let there be no ill-will; envy apart.
ab uno disce omnes (L.), from one specimen judge of all the rest; from a single instance infer the whole.
ab urbe conditâ (L.), from the building of the city; i.e., Rome.
a capite ad calcem (L.), from head to heel.
à chaque saint sa chandelle (Fr.), to each saint his candle; honour where honour is due.
à cheval (Fr.), on horseback.
à compte (Fr.), on account; in part payment.
à corps perdu (Fr.), with might and main.
à couvert (Fr.), under cover; protected; sheltered.
ad astra (L.), to the stars.
ad calendas Græcas (L.), at the Greek calends; *i.e.*, never, as the Greeks had no calends in their mode of reckoning.
à demi (Fr.), by halves; half-way.
a Deo et rege (L.), from God and the king.
ad hoc (L.), arranged for this purpose; special.
ad hominem (L.), to the man; to an individual's interests or passions; personal.
adhuc sub judice lis est (L.), the case has not yet been decided.
a die (L.), from that day.
ad infinitum (L.), to infinity
ad interim (L.), in the meantime.
ad libitum (L.), at pleasure.
ad modum (L.), after the manner of.
ad nauseam (L.), to disgust or satiety.
ad referendum (L.), for further consideration.
ad rem (L.), to the purpose; to the point.
ad valorem (L.), according to the value.
affaire d'amour (Fr.), a love affair.
affaire d'honneur (Fr.), an affair of honour; a duel.
affaire de cœur (Fr.), an affair of the heart.
a fortiori (L.), with stronger reason.
à gauche (Fr.), to the left.
à genoux (Fr.), on the knees.
à haute voix (Fr.), aloud.
à huis clos (Fr.), with closed doors; secretly.
à la belle étoile (Fr.), under the stars; in the open air.
à la bonne heure (Fr.), well timed; all right; very well; as you please.
à l'abri (Fr.), under shelter.
à la mode (Fr.), according to the custom or fashion.
à la Tartufe (Fr.), like Tartuffe, the hero of a celebrated comedy by Molière; hypocritically.
al fresco (It.), in the open air; out-of-doors.
al più (It.), at most.
alter ego (L.), another self.
à merveille (Fr.), to a wonder; marvellously.
amor patriæ (L.), love of country.
amour-propre (Fr.), self-love; vanity.
ancien régime (Fr.), the ancient or former order of things.
anguis in herba (L.), a snake in the grass.
anno Christi (L.), in the year of Christ.
anno Domini (L.), in the year of our Lord.
anno mundi (L.), in the year of the world.
annus mirabilis (L.), year of wonders; wonderful year.
ante bellum (L.), before the war.
ante lucem (L.), before light.
ante meridiem (L.), before noon.
à outrance (Fr.), to the utmost; to extremities; without sparing.
à pied (Fr.), on foot.
à point (Fr.), to a point, just in time, exactly right.
a posse ad esse (L.), from possibility to reality.
ariston metron (Gr.), the middle course is the best; the golden mean.
arrière-pensée (Fr.), hidden thought; mental reservation.
au courant (Fr.), fully acquainted with.
audi alteram partem (L.), hear the other side.
au fait (Fr.), well acquainted with; expert.
au fond (Fr.), at bottom.
auf Wiedersehen! (Ger.), till we meet again.
au pis aller (Fr.), at the worst.
au revoir (Fr.), adieu till we meet again.
aut vincere aut mori (L.), either to conquer or to die; death or victory.
a verbis ad verbera (L.), from words to blows.
a vinculo matrimonii (L.), from the bond of matrimony.
à volonté (Fr.), at pleasure.
a vostra salute (It.), *à votre santé* (Fr.), *a vuestra salud* (Sp.), to your health.
bas bleu (Fr.), a blue-stocking; a literary woman.
beau monde (Fr.), the world of fashion.
beaux esprits (Fr.), men of wit; gay spirits.
beaux yeux (Fr.), fine eyes; good looks.
ben trovato (It.), well or cleverly invented.
bête noire (Fr.), a black beast; a bugbear.
bon gré mal gré (Fr.), with good or ill grace; willing or unwilling.
bonhomie (Fr.), good-nature; artlessness.
bonne bouche (Fr.), a delicate or tasty morsel.
bon vivant (Fr.), a good liver; a gourmand.
brutum fulmen (L.), a harmless thunderbolt.
canaille (Fr.), rabble.
candida Pax (L.), white-robed Peace.
casus belli (L.), that which causes or justifies war.
causa sine qua non (L.), an indispensable cause or condition.
caveat emptor (L.), let the buyer beware (or look after his own interest).
cela va sans dire (Fr.), that goes without saying; needless to say.
ceteris paribus (L.), other things being equal.
chacun son goût (Fr.), every one to his taste.
cogito, ergo sum (L.), I think, therefore I exist.
comme il faut (Fr.), as it should be.
compos mentis (L.), sound of mind; quite sane.
compte rendu (Fr.), an account rendered; a report or statement drawn up.
conditio sine qua non (L.), a necessary condition.
conseil de famille (Fr.), a family consultation.
consensus facit legem (L.), consent makes the law.
consilio et animis (L.), by wisdom and courage.
consilio et prudentia (L.), by wisdom and prudence.
constantia et virtute (L.), by constancy and virtue.
contra bonos mores (L.), against good manners.
contretemps (Fr.), an unlucky accident; a hitch.
cordon bleu (Fr.), blue ribbon; a cook of the highest class.
cordon sanitaire (Fr.), a line of guards to prevent the spreading of contagion or pestilence.
corpus delicti (L.), the body or substance of a crime or offence.
corrigenda (L.), things to be corrected.
coup de grâce (Fr.), a finishing stroke.
coup d'état (Fr.), a sudden decisive blow in politics; a stroke of policy.
coup de soleil (Fr.), sunstroke.
credat Judæus Apella (L.), let Apella, the superstitious Jew, believe it (I won't); tell that to the marines.
cucullus non facit monachum (L.), the cowl does not make the friar.
cui bono? (L.), For whose advantage is it? to what end?
culpam pœna premit comes (L.), punishment follows hard upon crime.
cum grano salis (L.), with a grain of salt; with some allowance.
cum privilegio (L.), with privilege.
currente calamo (L.), with a fluent pen.
da locum melioribus (L.), give place to your betters.
damnant quod non intelligunt (L.), they condemn what they do not comprehend.
data et accepta (L.), expenditures and receipts.
de bon augure (Fr.), of good augury or omen.
de bonne grâce (Fr.), with good grace; willingly.

de die in diem (L.), from day to day.
de facto (L.), in point of fact; actual or actually.
dei gratia (L.), by God's grace.
de jure (L.), from the law; by right.
de mal en pis (Fr.), from bad to worse.
de novo (L.), anew.
deo volente (L.), God willing; by God's will.
de profundis (L.), out of the depths.
dernier ressort (Fr.), a last resource.
deus ex machina (L.), one who puts matters right at a critical moment; providential intervention.
dies non (L.), a day on which judges do not sit.
distingué (Fr.), distinguished; of genteel or elegant appearance.
dolce far niente (It.), sweet doing-nothing; sweet idleness.
double entente (Fr.), a double meaning; a play on words.
dramatis personæ (L.), characters of the drama or play.
dum spiro, spero (L.), while I breathe, I hope.
ecce homo! (L.), behold the man!
eheu! fugaces labuntur anni (L.), alas! the fleeting years glide by.
einmal ist keinmal (Ger.), just once doesn't count.
en avant (Fr.), forward.
en badinant (Fr.), in sport; in jest.
en déshabillé (Fr.), in undress.
en famille (Fr.), with one's family; in a domestic state.
enfant terrible (Fr.), a terrible child, or one that makes disconcerting remarks.
enfin (Fr.), in short; at last; finally.
en passant (Fr.), in passing; by the way.
en plein jour (Fr.), in broad day.
en rapport (Fr.), in harmony; in agreement; in relation.
en règle (Fr.), according to rules; in order.
entente cordiale (Fr.), cordial understanding, especially between two states.
entre nous (Fr.), between ourselves.
en vérité (Fr.), in truth; verily.
e pluribus unum (L.), one out of many; one composed of many.
esprit de corps (Fr.), the animating spirit of a collective body, as a regiment, learned profession or the like.
et sequentes, et sequentia (L.), and those that follow.
et tu, Brute! (L.), and thou also, Brutus!
ex animo (L.), heartily; sincerely.
ex capite (L.), from the head; from memory.
ex cathedra (L.), from the chair or seat of authority, with high authority.
exceptio probat regulam (L.), the exception proves the rule.
ex curia (L.), out of court.
ex dono (L.), by the gift.
exeunt omnes (L.), all go out or retire.
exit (L.), he goes out.
ex mero motu (L.), from his own impulse, from his own free will.
ex nihilo nihil fit (L.), out of nothing, nothing comes; nothing produces nothing.
ex officio (L.), in virtue of his office.
ex post facto (L.), after the deed is done; retrospective.
face à face (Fr.), face to face.
façon de parler (Fr.), manner of speaking.
faire bonne mine (Fr.), to put a good face upon the matter.
fait accompli (Fr.), a thing already done.
fama clamosa (L.), a current scandal; a prevailing report.
faute de mieux (Fr.), for want of better.
faux pas (Fr.), a false step; a slip in behaviour.
festina lente (L.), hasten slowly.
fiat justitia, ruat cœlum (L.), let justice be done though the heavens should fall.
fiat lux (L.), let there be light.
fide et amore (L.), by faith and love.
fide et fiduciâ (L.), by fidelity and confidence.
fide et fortitudine (L.), with faith and fortitude.
fidei defensor (L.), defender of the faith.
fide non armis (L.), by faith, not by arms.
fide, sed cui vide (L.), trust, but see whom.
fides et justitia (L.), fidelity and justice.
fides Punica (L.), Punic faith; treachery.
filius nullius (L.), a son of nobody; a bastard.
finis coronat opus (L.), the end crowns the work.
flagrante bello (L.), during hostilities.
flagrante delicto (L.), in the commission of the crime.
floreat (L.), let it flourish.
fons et origo (L.), the source and origin.
force majeure (Fr.), irresistible compulsion; war, strike, Act of God, etc.
forensis strepitus (L.), the clamour of the forum.
fortuna favet fortibus (L.), fortune favours the bold.
functus officio (L.), having performed one's office or duty; hence, out of office.
gaudeamus igitur (L.), so let us be joyful!
genius loci (L.), the genius or guardian spirit of a place.
gradu diverso, via una (L.), the same road by different steps.
grande parure / *grande toilette* (Fr.), full dress.
guerra al cuchillo (Sp.), war to the knife.
Hannibal ante portas (L.), Hannibal before the gates; the enemy close at hand.
hiatus valde deflendus (L.), a chasm or deficiency much to be regretted.
hic et nunc (L.), here and now.
hic et ubique (L.), here and everywhere.
hic jacet (L.), here lies.
hic labor, hoc opus est (L.), this is a labour, this is a toil.
hic sepultus (L.), here buried.
hoc genus omne (L.), all of this sort or class.
hoi polloi (Gr.), the many; the vulgar; the rabble.
hominis est errare (L.), to err is human.
homme de robe (Fr.), a man in civil office.
homme d'affaires (Fr.), a man of business.
homme d'esprit (Fr.), a man of wit or genius.
honi soit qui mal y pense (O. Fr.), evil to him who evil thinks.
honores mutant mores (L.), honours change men's manners or characters.
hors de combat (Fr.), out of condition to fight.
hors de propos (Fr.), not to the point or purpose.
hors-d'œuvre (Fr.), out of course; out of order.
ich dien (Ger.), I serve.
idée fixe (Fr.), a fixed idea.
id est (L.), that is.
il a le diable au corps (Fr.), the devil is in him.
Ilias malorum (L.), an Iliad of ills; a host of evils.
il penseroso (It.), the pensive man.
il sent le fagot (Fr.), he smells of the faggot; he is suspected of heresy.
imperium in imperio (L.), a state within a state; a government within another.
in actu (L.), in act or reality.
in articulo mortis (L.), at the point of death; in the last struggle.
in capite (L.), in chief.
in curia (L.), in court.
index expurgatorius / *index prohibitorius* (L.), a list of books prohibited to Roman Catholics.
in esse (L.), in being; in actuality.
in extenso (L.), at full length.
in extremis (L.), at the point of death.
in memoriam (L.), to the memory of; in memory.
in nubibus (L.), in the clouds.
in petto (It.), in (my) breast; to one's self.
in re (L.), in the matter of.
in sano sensu (L.), in a proper sense.
in situ (L.), in its original situation.
in vino veritas (L.), there is truth in wine; truth is told under the influence of intoxicants.
ipse dixit (L.), he himself said it; a dogmatic saying or assertion.
ipsissima verba (L.), the very words.
ipso facto (L.), in the fact itself.
ipso jure (L.), by the law itself.
jacta est alea (L.), the die is cast.
je ne sais quoi (Fr.), I know not what.
joci causa (L.), for the sake of a joke.
labor omnia vincit (L.), labour conquers everything.
l'allegro (It.), the merry man.
lapsus linguæ (L.), a slip of the tongue.
lares et penates (L.), household gods.
laus Deo (L.), praise to God.
le beau monde (Fr.), the fashionable world.
lector benevole (L.), kind or gentle reader.
le jeu n'en vaut pas la chandelle (Fr.), the game is not worth the candle; the object is not worth the trouble.
le mot de l'énigme (Fr.), the key to the mystery.
le point du jour (Fr.), daybreak.
lèse-majesté (Fr.), high-treason.
lettre de cachet (Fr.), a sealed letter containing private orders; a royal warrant.
lex loci (L.), the law or custom of the place.
lex non scripta (L.), unwritten law; common law.
lex scripta (L.), written law; statute law.
locum tenens (L.), a deputy.

lucri causa (L.), for the sake of gain.
magnum opus (L.), a great work.
mala fide (L.), with bad faith; treacherously.
mal à propos (Fr.), ill-timed; out of place.
malgré nous (Fr.), in spite of us.
malheur ne vient jamais seul (Fr.), misfortunes never come singly.
malum in se (L.), evil or an evil in itself.
mardi gras (Fr.), Shrove-Tuesday.
mariage de convenance (Fr.), marriage from motives of interest rather than of love.
mauvaise honte (Fr.), false modesty.
mauvais goût (Fr.), bad taste.
mea culpa (L.), my fault; by my fault.
me judice (L.), I being judge; in my opinion.
mens agitat molem (L.), mind moves matter.
mens legis (L.), the spirit of the law.
mens sana in corpore sano (L.), a sound mind in a sound body.
meo periculo (L.), at my own risk.
meo voto (L.), according to my wish.
mise en scène (Fr.), the getting up for the stage, or the putting on the stage.
modus operandi (L.), manner of working.
more suo (L.), in his own way.
motu proprio (L.), of his own accord.
multum in parvo (L.), much in little.
mutatis mutandis (L.), with suitable or necessary alteration.
nervus probandi (L.), the sinews of the argument.
nihil ad rem (L.), irrelevant.
nil desperandum (L.), there is no reason to despair.
noblesse oblige (Fr.), rank imposes obligations; much is expected from one in good position.
nolens volens (L.), willing or unwilling.
nom de guerre (Fr.), a false or assumed name.
non compos mentis (L.), not of sound mind.
non sequitur (L.), it does not follow.
nosce te ipsum (L.), know thyself.
nota bene (L.), mark well.
nudis verbis (L.), in plain words.
obiter dictum (L.), a thing said by the way.
omnia vincit amor (L.), love conquers all things.
ora pro nobis (L.), pray for us.
O tempora! O mores! (L.), O the times! O the manners (or morals)!
ouï-dire (Fr.), hearsay.
padrone (It.), a master; a landlord.
par excellence (Fr.), by way of eminence.
pari passu (L.), at an equal pace or rate of progress.
particeps criminis (L.), an accomplice in a crime.
pas de quoi (Fr. abbrev. Il n'y a pas de quoi), don't mention it.
passim (L.), everywhere; in all parts of the book, chapter, etc.
pâté de foie gras (Fr.), goose-liver pie.
pater patriæ (L.), father of his country.
patres conscripti (L.), the conscript fathers; Roman senatore.
pax vobiscum (L.), peace be with you.
per ardua ad astra (L.), through rough ways to the stars; through suffering to renown.
per capita (L.), by the head or poll.
per contra (It.), contrariwise.
per diem (L.), by the day; daily.
per se (L.), by itself; considered apart.
pied-à-terre (Fr.), a resting-place; a temporary lodging.
pis aller (Fr.), the worst or last shift.
plebs (L.), the common people.
poco a poco (It.), little by little.
poste restante (Fr.), to remain in the post-office till called for.
prima facie (L.), at first view or consideration.
primus inter pares (L.), first among equals.
pro forma (L.), for the sake of form.
pro patria (L.), for our country.
pro tanto (L.), for so much; for as far as it goes.
pro tempore (L.), for the time being.
quid pro quo (L.), one thing for another; tit for tat; an equivalent.
qui m'aime, aime mon chien (Fr.), love me, love my dog.
qui tacet consentit (L.), he who is silent gives consent.
quod erat demonstrandum (L.), which was to be proved or demonstrated.
quod erat faciendum (L.), which was to be done.
quod vide (L.), which see; refer to the word just mentioned.
quo jure? (L.), by what right?
raison d'être (Fr.), the reason for a thing's existence.
re (L.), in the matter or affair of.
reculer pour mieux sauter (Fr.), to draw back in order to make a better spring.
reductio ad adsurdum (L.), the reducing of a position to a logical absurdity.
requiescat in pace (L.), may he (or she) rest in peace.
respice finem (L.), look to the end.
respublica (L.), the commonwealth.
revenons à nos moutons (Fr.), let us return to our sheep; let us return to our subject.
re vera (L.), in truth.
sans peur et sans reproche (Fr.), without fear and without reproach.
sans rime ni raison (Fr.), without rhyme or reason.
sans souci (Fr.), without care.
sartor resartus (L.), the botcher repatched; the tailor patched or mended.
sauve qui peut (Fr.), let him save himself who can.
savoir-faire (Fr.), the knowing how to act; tact.
savoir-vivre (Fr.), good-breeding; refined manners.
semper idem (L.), always the same.
seriatim (L.), in a series; one by one.
sic passim (L.), so here and there throughout; so everywhere.
sicut ante (L.), as before.
sine die (L.), without a day being appointed.
sine mora (L.), without delay.
sine qua non (L.), without which, not; indispensable condition.
sotto voce (It.), in an undertone.
spirituel (Fr.), intellectual; witty.
stet (L.), let it stand; do not delete.
sub judice (L.), under consideration.
sub pœna (L.), under a penalty
sub rosa (L.), under the rose; privately.
sub voce (L.), under such or such a word.
sui generis (L.), of its own or of a peculiar kind.
summum bonum (L.), the chief good.
tableau vivant (Fr.), a living picture; the representation of some scene by a group of persons.
tant mieux (Fr.), so much the better.
tant pis (Fr.), so much the worse.
tempora mutantur, nos et mutamur in illis (L.), the times are changing and we with them.
tempus fugit (L.), time flies.
tête-à-tête (Fr.), together in private.
tiers état (Fr.), the third estate; the commons.
to kalon (Gr.), the beautiful; the chief good.
to prepon (Gr.), the becoming or proper.
tour de force (Fr.), a feat of strength or skill.
tout à fait (Fr.), wholly; entirely.
tout à l'heure (Fr.), instantly.
tout de suite (Fr.), immediately.
tu quoque (L.), thou also.
ubique (L.), everywhere.
ubi supra (L.), where above mentioned.
ultra licitum (L.), beyond what is allowable.
ultra vires (L.), beyond powers or rights conferred by law.
urbi et orbi (L.), to the city (Rome) and the world.
utile dulci (L.), the useful with the pleasant.
ut infra (L.), as below.
ut supra (L.), as above stated.
vade in pace (L.), go in peace.
variæ lectiones (L.), various readings.
variorum notæ (L.), the notes of various commentators.
vede et crede (L.), see and believe.
veni, vidi, vici (L.), I came, I saw, I conquered.
verbatim et literatim (L.), word for word and letter for letter.
verbum sat sapienti (L.), a word is enough for a wise man.
ver non semper viret (L.), spring is not always green.
vexata quæstio (L.), a disputed question.
via media (L.), a middle course.
via trita, via tuta (L.), the beaten path is the safe path.
vice versâ (L.), the terms of the case being reversed.
videlicet (L.), that is to say; namely.
vi et armis (L.), by force of arms; by main force; by violence.
vigilate et orate (L.), watch and pray.
vita brevis, ars longa (L.), life is short; art is long.
vivat regina! (L.), long live the queen!
vivat rex! (L.), long live the king!
viva voce (L.), by the living voice; orally.
voilà (Fr.), behold; there is; there are.
voilà tout (Fr.), that's all.
volo, non valeo (L.), I am willing, but unable.
vox populi, vox Dei (L.), the voice of the people is the voice of God.

ABBREVIATIONS IN COMMON USE

A

a. = area; acre(s); are (100 sq. metres).
A.A. = Automobile Association; Alcoholics Anonymous.
A.A.A. = Amateur Athletic Association.
A.A.C.C.A. = Associate of the Association of Certified and Corporate Accountants.
A.A.I. = Associate of the Chartered Auctioneers' and Estate Agents' Institute.
A.A.L.P.A. = Associate of the Incorporated Society of Auctioneers and Landed Property Agents.
A.B. = able-bodied seaman; *Artium Baccalaureus* (Bachelor of Arts).
A.B.A. = Amateur Boxing Association.
A.B.I.C.C. = Associate of the British Institute of Certified Carpenters.
Abp. = Archbishop.
abr. = abridged.
a.c. (*or* A.C.) = alternating current.
A.C.A. = Associate of the Institute of Chartered Accountants.
A.C.C.S. = Associate of the Corporation of Certified Secretaries.
A.C.I.S. = Associate of the Chartered Institute of Secretaries.
A.Comm.A. = Associate of the Society of Commercial Accountants.
A.C.P. = Associate of the College of Preceptors.
ACSP = Advisory Council on Scientific Policy (replaced by CSP).
ACT = Advisory Council on Technology.
ACTH = adreno-cortico-trophic hormone.
A.C.W.A. = Associate of the Institute of Cost and Works Accountants.
A.D. = *anno domini* (in the year of our Lord).
A.D.C. = Aide-de-Camp.
Adm. = Admiral.
advt. (*or* adv.) = advertisement.
A.F.A.S. = Associate of the Faculty of Architects and Surveyors.
AEA = Atomic Energy Authority (UK).
AEC = Atomic Energy Commission (US).
AERE = Atomic Energy Research Establishment.
aet. (*or* aetat.) = *aetatis* (of age).
A.F.C. = Air Force Cross.
A.F.L. = American Federation of Labour.
A.F.M. = Air Force Medal.
A.G. = Adjutant-General.
AGR = Advanced Gas-cooled Reactor.
A.H. = *anno Hegirae* (in the year of the Hegira).
A.I.A. = Associate of the Institute of Actuaries.
A.I.A.C. = Associate of the Institute of Company Accountants.
A.I.B. = Associate of the Institute of Bankers.
A.I.B.P. = Associate of the Institute of British Photographers.
A.I.C.E. = Associate of the Institution of Civil Engineers.
A.I.C.S. = Associate of the Institute of Chartered Shipbrokers.
AID = Agency for International Development (U.S.).
A.I.I.A. = Associate of the Institute of Industrial Administration.
A.I.M.E. = Associate of the Institution of Mining Engineers.
A.I.Mech.E. = Associate of the Institution of Mechanical Engineers.
A.I.N.A. = Associate of the Institution of Naval Architects.
A.Inst.P. = Associate of the Institute of Physics.
A.I.R.I. = Associate of the Institution of Rubber Industry.
A.L.A. = Associate of the Library Association.
A.L.S. = Associate of the Linnean Society.
alt. = altitude.
A.M. = *anno mundi* (in the year of the world); *Artium Magister* (Master of Arts); amplitude modulation.
a.m. = *ante meridiem* (before noon).
A.M.D.G. = *ad majorem Dei glorium* (to the greater glory of God).
AMM = anti-missile-missile.
amp. = ampere(s).
A.M.I.C.E. = Associate Member of the Institution of Civil Engineers.
A.M.I.Chem.E. = Associate Member of the Institution of Chemical Engineers.
A.M.I.E.E. = Associate Member of the Institution of Electrical Engineers.
A.M.I.Mech.E. = Associate Member of the Institution of Mechanical Engineers.
A.M.I.Mun.E. = Associate Member of the Institution of Municipal Engineers.
A.M.T.P.I. = Associate Member of the Town Planning Institute.
ANC = African National Congress.
anc. = ancient.
ANF = Atlantic Nuclear Force.
anon. = anonymous.
ANZAC = Australian and New Zealand Army Corps.
ANZUS = Australian, New Zealand and U.S. Defence Pact (Pacific Security Treaty).
A.O.C. = Air Officer Commanding.
A.P. = Associated Press.
A.R.A. = Associate of the Royal Academy.
A.R.A.D. = Associate of the Royal Academy of Dancing.
A.R.A.M. = Associate of the Royal Academy of Music.
A.R.B.S. = Associate of the Royal Society of British Sculptors.
ARC = Agricultural Research Council.
A.R.C.A. = Associate of the Royal College of Arts.
A.R.C.M. = Associate of the Royal College of Music.
arch. = archipelago.
A.R.C.O. = Associate of the Royal College of Organists.
A.R.C.Sc. = Associate of the Royal College of Science.
A.R.I.B.A. = Associate of the Royal Institute of British Architects.
A.R.I.C. = Associate of the Royal Institute of Chemistry.
A.R.I.C.S. = Associate of the Royal Institution of Chartered Surveyors.
A.R.P.S. = Associate of the Royal Photographic Society.
A.R.W.S. = Associate of the Royal Society of Painters in Water Colours.
A.S. (*or* AS) = Anglo-Saxon.
A.S.A. = Amateur Swimming Association.
ASDIC = Anti-submarine detector indicator
ASLIB = Association of Special Libraries and Information Bureaux.
A.T.C. = Air Training Corps.
atm. = atmospheric pressure.
ATP = adenosine triphosphate.
A.T.S. = Auxiliary Territorial Service.
ATV = Associated Television Authority.
at.wt. = atomic weight.
A.U.C. = *ab urbe condita* (from the founding of the City (Rome)), *or*, *anno urbis conditae* (in the year of the founding of the City).
AV = Authorized Version.

B

b. = born; bowled.
B.A. = Bachelor of Arts.
B.A.A. = British Astronomical Association.
B.A.O. = Bachelor in the Art of Obstetrics.
BAOR = British Army of the Rhine.
B.Arch. = Bachelor of Architecture.
Bart. (*or* Bt.) = Baronet.
B.B. = Boys' Brigade.
B.B.C. = British Broadcasting Corporation.
B.C. = before Christ; British Columbia.
B.Ch. (*or* Ch.B.) = Bachelor in Surgery.
B.C.L. = Bachelor in Civil Law.
B.Com. = Bachelor of Commerce.
B.D. = Bachelor in Divinity.
B.D.A. = British Dental Association.
Bde. = Brigade.
B.D.S. (*or* B.Ch.D.) = Bachelor in Dental Surgery
BEA = British European Airways Corporation.
B.E.C. = British Employers' Confederation.
B.Ed. = Bachelor of Education.
B.E.M. = British Empire Medal.
B.Eng. = Bachelor of Engineering.
BIM = British Institute of Management.

BIS = Bank for International Settlements.
BISRA = British Iron and Steel Research Association.
B.Litt. = Bachelor in Letters.
B.M. = Bachelor in Medicine; British Museum.
B.M.A. = British Medical Association.
B.M.C. = British Motor Corporation.
B.Mus. = Bachelor in Music.
B.N.C. = Brasenose College, Oxford.
BOAC = British Overseas Airways Corporation.
bor. = borough.
B.O.T. = Board of Trade.
Bp. = Bishop.
B.Phil. = Bachelor of Philosophy.
Br. (*or* Brit.) = British.
Brit.Ass. = British Association for the Advancement of Science.
B.R. = British Railways; British Rail.
B.R.B. = British Rail Board.
B.R.C.S. = British Red Cross Society.
B.R.S. = British Road Services.
B.Sc. = Bachelor of Science.
B.S.I. = British Standards Institution.
BST = British summer time.
Bt. = Baronet; Brevet.
B.T.H.A. = British Travel and Holidays Association.
B.Th. = Bachelor in Theology.
BTU = British thermal unit.
B.U.A. = British United Airways.
B.V.M. = Blessed Virgin Mary.
B.V.M.S. = Bachelor in Veterinary Medicine and Surgery.
B.W.B. = British Waterways Board.

C

C. = Centigrade; Conservative.
c. (*or* ca.) = *circa* (about).
Cal. = Calorie (nutritional kilogram-calorie).
cal. = calorie (gram-calorie used in physics and chemistry).
Cantab. = of Cambridge.
Cantuar. = of Canterbury.
cap. = capital letter; capitulum (chapter).
CATs = Colleges of Advanced Technology.
C.B. = Companion of the Order of the Bath.
C.B.E. = Commander of the Order of the British Empire.
CBI = Confederation of British Industry (replaces BEC, FBI and NABM).
C.C. = County Council; County Councillor; Chamber of Commerce.
c.c. (*or* cc.) = cubic centimetre(s).
CCPR = Central Council of Physical Recreation.
C.D. = Civil Defence.
C.D.C. = Commonwealth Development Corporation.
C.D.S. = Chief of Defence Staff; Campaign for Democratic Socialism.
C.E. = Civil Engineer; Christian Era.
CEGB = Central Electricity Generating Board.
CENTO = Central Treaty Organisation.
CERN = European Organisation for Nuclear Research.
C.F. = Chaplain to the Forces.
cf. = *confer* (compare).
C.G.M. = Conspicuous Gallantry Medal.
C.G.S. = Chief of General Staff.
cgs = centimetre-gram-second.
CGT = Confédération Générale du Travail (French TUC).
C.H. = Companion of Honour.
Ch.M. = Master in Surgery.
C.I. = Lady of Imperial Order of the Crown of India; Channel Islands.
CIA = Central Intelligence Agency (US).
CID = Criminal Investigation Department.
C.I.E. = Companion of the Order of the Indian Empire.
Cie = Compagnie (Company).
c.i.f. = cost, insurance and freight.
C.-in-C. = Commander-in-Chief.
CIO = Congress of Industrial Organisations (US).
C.L. = Companion of Literature.
C.L.B. = Church Lads' Brigade.
cm. = centimetre(s).
C.M.G. = Companion of the Order of St. Michael and St. George.
C.M.S. = Church Missionary Society.
CND = Campaign for Nuclear Disarmament.
C.O. = Commanding Officer; Colonial Office; Conscientious Objector.
Co. = County; Company.
c/o = care of.
C.O.D. = Cash on Delivery.
C. of E. = Church of England.
COI = Central Office of Information.
CoID = Council of Industrial Design.
COMECON = Council for Mutual Economic Assistance (East European).
Con. (*or* C.) = Conservative.
COSPAR = Committee on Space Research.
CP = Communist Party.
CPC = Communist Party of China.
C.P.R.E. = Council for the Preservation of Rural England.
CPSU = Communist Party of the Soviet Union.
C.R.O. = Commonwealth Relations Office.
C.S.C. = Conspicuous Service Cross.
C.S.E. = Certificate of Secondary Education.
C.S.I. = Companion of the Order of the Star of India.
CSP = Council on Scientific Policy.
C.T. = Civic Trust.
C.T.C. = Cyclists' Touring Club.
CTR = Controlled thermonuclear research.
cu. = cubic.
C.V.O. = Commander of the Royal Victorian Order.
cwt. = hundredweight.

D

d. = *denarius* (penny), *denarii* (pence); died; daughter.
D.A.R. = Daughters of the American Revolution.
db = decibel(s).
D.C. = District of Columbia.
d.c. (*or* D.C.) = direct current.
D.C.L. = Doctor in Civil Law.
D.C.M. = Distinguished Conduct Medal.
D.D. = Doctor in Divinity.
D.D.R. = German Democratic Republic (E. Germany).
D.D.S. = Doctor in Dental Surgery.
DDT = Dichloro-diphenyl-trichloro-ethane.
del. = *delineavit* (he drew it).
D.ès L. = Docteur ès Lettres.
D.ès Sc. = Docteur ès Sciences.
D.F.C. = Distinguished Flying Cross.
D.F.M. = Distinguished Flying Medal.
D.G. = *dei gratie* (by the grace of God).
DIA = Design and Industries Association.
Dip.Tech. = Diploma in Technology.
D.L. = Deputy-Lieutenant.
D.Lit. (*or* D. Litt) = Doctor of Literature.
D.M. = Doctor in Medicine (Oxford).
DM = Deutschemark.
D.Mus. = Doctor of Music.
DNA = deoxyribonucleic acid.
D.N.B. = Dictionary of National Biography.
do. = *ditto* (the same).
D.O.M. = *dominus optimo maximo* (To God, the best, the greatest).
D.P. = Displaced Person(s).
D.P.H. = Diploma in Public Health.
D.Phil. = Dictor of Philosophy.
Dr. = Doctor; debtor.
dr. = drachm.
D.Sc. = Doctor of Science.
D.S.C. = Distinguished Service Cross.
DSIR = Department of Scientific and Industrial Research (to be abolished and replaced by SRC, IRDA, and NERC).
D.S.M. = Distinguished Service Medal.
D.S.O. = Companion of the Distinguished Service Order.
D.Th. = Doctor in Theology.
D.T.M. = Diploma in Tropical Medicine.
D.V. = *Deo volente* (God willing).
dwt. = pennyweight.

E

EAAFRO = East African Agriculture and Foresty Research.
E. and O.E. = Errors and omissions excepted.
Ebor. = of York.

EC = Electricity Council.
ECA = Economic Commission for Africa (UN).
ECAFE = Economic Commission for Asia and the Far East (UN).
ECE = Economic Commission for Europe (UN).
ECGD = Export Credits Guarantee Department.
ECLA = Economic Commission for Latin America (UN).
ECSC = European Coal and Steel Community.
EDC = European Defence Community.
EEC = European Economic Community (Common Market).
EFTA = European Free Trade Association.
e.g. = *exempli gratio* (for example).
ELDO = European Launcher and Development Organisation.
EMA = European Monetary Agreement.
EMBO = European Molecular Biology Organisation.
emf = electromotive force.
ENEA = European Nuclear Energy Agency.
EPU = European Political Union.
E.R. = Elizabetha Regina, *or* Edwardus Rex.
E.R.A. = Electrical Research Association.
ERNIE = electronic random number indicating equipment.
ERP = European Recovery Programme.
ESC = Economic and Social Council (UN).
ESRO = European Space Research Organisation.
et al. = *et alibi* (and elsewhere); *et alii* (and others).
etc. = *et cetera* (others; and so forth).
et seq. = *et sequens* (and the following).
et sqq. = *et sequentes, et sequentia* (and those following).
E.T.U. = Electrical Trades Union.
Euratom = European Atomic Energy Community.
ex lib. = *ex libris* (from the books of).

F

F. = Fahrenheit; Fellow.
f. = and the following page; ff. = and the following pages.
F.A. = Football Association.
F.A.C.C.A. = Fellow of the Association of Certified and Corporate Accountants.
F.A.I. = Fellow of the Chartered Auctioneers' and Estate Agents' Institute.
F.A.L.P.A. = Fellow of the Incorporated Society of Auctioneers and Landed Property Agents.
F.A.N.Y. = First Aid Nursing Yeomanry.
FAO = Food and Agriculture Organisation of the United Nations.
f.a.s. = free alongside.
F.B.A. = Fellow of the British Academy.
FBI = Federal Bureau of Investigation (U.S.).
F.B.I.M. = Fellow of the British Institute of Management.
F.B.O.A. = Fellow of the British Optical Association.
F.B.S. = Fellow of the Botanical Society.
F.C.A. = Fellow of the Institute of Chartered Accountants.
F.C.C.S. = Fellow of the Corporation of Certified Secretaries.
F.C.I.S. = Fellow of the Chartered Institute of Secretaries.
F.C.P. = Fellow of the College of Preceptors.
F.C.W.A. = Fellow of the Chartered Institute of Cost and Works Accountants.
F.D. = *Fidei Defensor* (Defender of the Faith).
Fed. = Federation; Federal.
ff. = folios; and the following pages; fortissimo.
F.F.A.R.C.S. = Fellow of the Faculty of Anaesthetics, Royal College of Surgeons.
F.F.R. = Fellow of the Faculty of Radiologists.
F.G.S. = Fellow of the Geological Society.
F.H. = Fire Hydrant.
F.I.A. = Fellow of the Institute of Actuaries.
F.I.B. = Fellow of the Institute of Bankers.
F.I.B.P. = Fellow of the Institute of British Photographers.
F. Inst.F. = Fellow of the Institute of Fuel.
F.I.I.A. = Fellow of the Institute of Industrial Administration.
F.Inst.P. = Fellow of the Institute of Physics.
F.Inst.Pet. = Fellow of the Institute of Petroleum.
F.I.R.E. = Fellow of the Institute of Radio Engineers.
F.J.I. = Fellow of the Institute of Journalists.
F.K.C. = Fellow of King's College (London).
fl. = *floruit* (flourished).
F.L.A. = Fellow of the Library Association.
F.L.A.S. = Fellow of the Land Agents' Society.
F.L.N. = (Algerian) National Liberation Front.
F.L.S. = Fellow of the Linnean Society.
FM = Frequency modulation.
FMC = Federal Maritime Commission (US).
F.N.S. = Fellow of the Newtonian Society.
F.O. = Foreign Office.
fo. = folio.
f.o.b. = free on board.
F.O.P. = Friendship Oil Pipeline (E.Europe).
F.P.S. = Fellow of the Pharmaceutical Society.
F.Ph.S. = Fellow of the Philosophical Society.
F.R.A.D. = Fellow of the Royal Academy of Dancing.
F.R.A.I. = Fellow of the Royal Anthropological Institute.
F.R.A.M. = Fellow of the Royal Academy of Music.
F.R.A.S. = Fellow of the Royal Astronomical Society.
F.R.Ae.S. = Fellow of the Royal Aeronautical Society.
F.R.B.S. = Fellow of the Royal Society of British Sculptors.
F.R.C.M. = Fellow of the Royal College of Music.
F.R.C.O. = Fellow of the Royal College of Organists.
F.R.C.O.G. = Fellow of the Royal College of Obstetricians and Gynaecologists.
F.R.C.P. = Fellow of the Royal College of Physicians.
F.R.C.S. = Fellow of the Royal College of Surgeons.
F.R.C.V.S. = Fellow of the Royal College of Veterinary Surgeons.
F.R.E.S. = Fellow of the Royal Empire Society.
F.R.Econ.S. = Fellow of the Royal Economic Society.
F.R.F.P.S. = Fellow of the Royal Faculty of Physicians and Surgeons (Glas.).
F.R.G.S. = Fellow of the Royal Geographical Society.
F.R.H.S. = Fellow of the Royal Horticultural Society.
F.R.Hist.S. = Fellow of the Royal Historical Society.
F.R.I.B.A. = Fellow of the Royal Institute of British Architects.
F.R.I.C. = Fellow of the Royal Institute of Chemistry.
F.R.I.C.S. = Fellow of the Royal Institution of Chartered Surveyors.
F.R.M.S. = Fellow of the Royal Microscopical Society.
F.R.Met.S. = Fellow of the Royal Meteorological Society.
F.R.P.S. = Fellow of the Royal Photographic Society.
F.R.S. = Fellow of the Royal Society.
F.R.S.A. = Fellow of the Royal Society of Arts.
F.R.S.C. = Fellow of the Royal Society of Canada.
F.R.S.E. = Fellow of the Royal Society of Edinburgh.
F.R.S.L. = Fellow of the Royal Society of Literature.
F.S.A. = Fellow of the Society of Antiquaries.
F.S.A.A. = Fellow of the Society of Incorporated Accountants and Auditors.
F.S.M.C. = Fellow of the Spectacle Makers Company.
F.S.S. = Fellow of the Statistical Society.
F.T.I. = Fellow of the Textile Institute.
F.Z.S. = Fellow of the Zoological Society.

G

g. = gram(s).
GATT = General Agreement on Tariffs and Trade.
G.B.E. = Knight (*or* Dame) Grand Cross of the Order of the British Empire

G.C. = George Cross; Gas Council.
G.C.A. = Ground Control Approach.
G.C.E. = General Certificate of Education.
G.C.B. = Knight Grand Cross of the Order of the Bath.
G.C.I.E. = Knight Grand Commander of the Indian Empire.
G.C.M.G. = Knight Grand Cross of the Order of St. Michael and St. George.
G.C.S.I. = Knight Grand Commander of the Star of India.
G.C.V.O. = Knight (*or* Dame) Grand Cross of the Royal Victorian Order.
Gen. = General; Genesis.
GeV = thousand million electron-volts.
G.H.Q. = General Headquarters.
G.I. = American soldier (from army term "Government Issue" applied to kit and equipment).
GLC = Greater London Council.
G.M. = George Medal.
G.M.C. = General Medical Council.
G.M.T. = Greenwich mean time.
g.n.p. = gross national product.
G.O.C. = General Officer Commanding.
G.O.P. = Grand Old Party (US Republican Party).
G.P. = General Practitioner.
G.P.O. = General Post Office.
gr. = grain(s).
G.S.O. = General Staff Officer.

H

ha = hectare (100 ares).
H.E. = His Excellency; His Eminence: high explosive.
H.H. = His (*or* Her) Highness.
hhd. = hogshead.
H.I.M. = His Imperial Majesty.
H.J.S. = *Hic jacet sepultus* (Here lies buried).
H.M. = His (*or* Her) Majesty.
H.M.I. = Her Majesty's Inspector.
H.M.S = Her Majesty's Ship; Her Majesty's Service.
H.M.S.O. = Her Majesty's Stationery Office.
H. of C. = House of Commons.
H. of L. = House of Lords.
Hon. = Honourable; Honorary.
ıp = horsepower.
H.P. = Hire purchase.
H.R. = House of Representatives (US).
H.R.H. = His (*or* Her) Royal Highness.
H.S.E. = *Hic sepultus est* (Here lies buried).
H.T. = high tension.
H.V. = health visitor.
H.W.M. = high water mark.

I

ADB = Inter-American Development Bank.
AEA = International Atomic Energy Agency (UN).
ATA = International Air Transport Association.
b. (*or* ibid.) = *ibidem* (in the same place).
BRD = International Bank for Reconstruction and Development (World Bank).
CAO = International Civil Aviation Organisation (UN).
CBM = Intercontinental ballistic missile.
CFC = Industrial and Commercial Finance Corporation.
CFTU = International Confederation of Free Trade Unions.
CI = Imperial Chemical Industries.
CJ = International Court of Justice (UN).
CSU International Council of Scientific Unions.
CT = International Computers and Tabulators.
CY = International Co-operation Year (1965).
d. = *idem* (the same).
DA = International Development Association.
e. = *id est* (that is)
FC = International Finance Corporation (UN).
gn. = *ignotus* (unknown).
GY = International Geophysical Year (1957–8).
HS = *Iesus Hominum Salvator* (Jesus Saviour of men)—repr. a Greek abbrev. of the word Jesus.
LEA = Inner London Education Authority.
LO = International Labour Organisation (UN).

I.L.S. = Instrument Landing System.
IMCO = Inter-Governmental Maritime Consultative Organisation (UN).
IMF = International Monetary Fund (UN).
Inc. = Incorporated.
Incog. = *incognito* (unknown, unrecognised).
inf. = infinitive; *infra* (below).
I.N.R.I. = *Iesus Nazarenus, Rex Iudaeorum* (Jesus of Nazareth, King of the Jews).
Inst. = Institute; Institution.
inst. = instant (the present month).
IOU = I owe you.
IQ = intelligence quotient.
IQSY = International Years of the Quiet Sun.
I.R. = Inland Revenue.
I.R.A. = Irish Republican Army.
IRBM = Intermediate-range ballistic missile.
IRC = International Red Cross.
IRDA = Industrial Research and Development Authority.
I.S.M.A. = Incorporated Sales Managers' Association.
I.S.O. = Imperial Service Order; International Standardisation Organisation.
I.T.A. = Independent Television Authority; Institute of Travel Agents; Industrial Transport Association; Invalid Tricycle Association.
I.T.O. = International Trade Organisation.
I.T.U. = International Telecommunication Union.
ITV = Independent Television.

J

J. = Judge; Jet (aircraft).
J.P. = Justice of the Peace.

K

K. = Kelvin; Carat; Köchel numeration (of Mozart's works).
KANU = Kenya African National Union.
k = kilo = thousand.
K.B.E. = Knight Commander of the Order of the British Empire.
K.C. = King's Counsel.
kc. = kilocycle(s).
K.C.B. = Knight Commander of the Order of the Bath.
K.C.I.E. = Knight Commander of the Order of the Indian Empire.
K.C.M.G. = Knight Commander of the Order of St. Michael and St. George.
K.C.S.I. = Knight Commander of the Star of India.
K.C.V.O. = Knight Commander of the Royal Victorian Order.
K.G. = Knight of the Order of the Garter.
kg = kilogram(s).
KJV = King James Version.
K.K.K. = Ku Klux Klan.
km = kilometre(s).
K.P. = Knight of the Order of St. Patrick.
K.T. = Knight of the Order of the Thistle.
Kt. = knight.
kV = kilovolt(s).
kW = kilowatt(s).
kWh = kilowatt hour(s).

L

L. (*or* Lib.) = Liberal.
L.A. = Local Authority.
Lab. = Labour.
L.A.C. = London Athletic Club.
LAMDA = London Academy of Music and Dramatic Art.
lat. = latitude.
lb. = *libra* (pound), *librae* (pounds).
l.b.w. = leg before wicket.
l.c. = lower case (small letter(s)).
LCC = London County Council.
L.C.P. = Licentiate of the College of Preceptors.
L.D.S. = Licentiate in Dental Surgery.
L.ès L. = Licencié ès Lettres.
L.F.B. = London Fire Brigade.
L.H.D. = *Litterarum Humaniorum Doctor* (Doctor of Humane Letters).

Lic.Med. = Licentiate in Medicine.
Lic.S. = Licentiate in Surgery.
Lit.Hum. = *Literae Humaniores* (Study of the Classics).
Litt.D. = *Litterarum Doctor* (Doctor of Letters; Doctor in Letters (Camb.)).
LL.B. = *Legum Baccalaureus* (Bachelor of Laws).
LL.D. = *Legum Doctor* (Doctor of Laws; Doctor in Law (Camb.)).
L.M. = Licentiate in Midwifery.
loc.cit. = *loco citato* (in the place sited).
log. = logarithm.
long. = longitude.
L.R.A.D. = Licentiate of the Royal Academy of Dancing.
L.R.A.M. = Licentiate of the Royal Academy of Music.
L.R.C.M. = Licentiate of the Royal College of Music.
L.R.C.P. = Licentiate of the Royal College of Physicians.
L.R.C.S. = Licentiate of the Royal College of Surgeons.
L.R.C.V.S. = Licentiate of the Royal College of Veterinary Surgeons.
L.S. = *loco sigilli* (place of the seal).
L.S.A. = Licentiate of the Society of Apothecaries.
L.s.d. = *Librae, solidi, denarii* (Pounds, shillings, pence).
L.S.E. = London School of Economics.
L.S.O. = London Symphony Orchestra.
L.T.A. = Lawn Tennis Association.
L.Th. = Licentiate in Theology.
Lt.-Gen. = Lieutenant-General.
L.W.M. = lower-water mark.
LXX = Septuagint.

M

M. = Member; Monsieur; mark (German coin); *meridies* (noon); mega (million times).
m. = metre(s); married; masculine; million; milli- (one-thousandth part).
M.A. = Master of Arts.
M.A.O. = Master in the Art of Obstetrics.
M.B. = Bachelor in Medicine.
M.B.E. = Member of the Order of the British Empire.
M.C. = Military Cross; Master of Ceremonies.
Mc = million cycles, *or* megacycle.
M.C.C. = Marylebone Cricket Club.
M.Ch. = Master in Surgery.
M.Ch.D. = Master in Dental Surgery.
M.Ch.Orth. = Master in Orthopaedic Surgery.
M.Com. = Master of Commerce.
M.C.S.P. = Member of the Chartered Society of Physiotherapy.
M.C.T. = Member of the College of Technologists.
M.D. = *Medicineae Doctor* (Doctor in Medicine).
M.D.S. = Master in Dental Surgery.
M.E. = Middle English.
mega = one million times.
MeV = million electron-volts.
M.F.H. = Master of Foxhounds.
mg = milligram(s).
Mgr. = Monsignor.
MHD = magnetohydrodynamics.
M.I. = Military Intelligence.
M.I.C.E. = Member of the Institution of Civil Engineers.
M.I.Chem.E. = Member of the Institution of Chemical Engineers.
M.I.E.E. = Member of the Institution of Electrical Engineers.
M.I.Mar.E. = Member of the Institute of Marine Engineers.
M.I.Mech.E. = Member of the Institution of Mechanical Engineers.
M.I.Min.E. = Member of the Institution of Mining Engineers.
M.I.N.A. = Member of the Institution of Naval Architects.
M.Inst.Met. = Member of the Institute of Metals.
M.I.Mun.E. = Member of the Institution of Municipal Engineers.
M.Inst.T. = Member of the Institute of Transport.
M.I.T. = Massachusetts Institute of Technology.
M.I.T.M.A. = Member of the Institute of Trade Mark Agents.
M.I.W.M. = Member of the Institution of Works Managers.
M.J.I. = Member of the Institute of Journalists.
MLF = Multilateral Force.
Mlle = Mademoiselle.
MM. = Messieurs.
mm = millimetre(s).
Mme = Madame.
Mods. = Moderations (Oxford).
M.O.H. = Medical Officer of Health; Ministry of Health.
M.P. = Member of Parliament; Military Police.
m.p.h. = miles per hour.
M.P.S. = Member of the Pharmaceutical Society; Member of the Philological Society; Member of the Physical Society.
M.R. = Master of the Rolls.
M.R.A.S. = Member of the Royal Asiatic Society; Member of the Royal Academy of Science.
M.R.Ae.S. = Member of the Royal Aeronautical Society.
M.R.C. = Medical Research Council.
M.R.C.P. = Member of the Royal College of Physicians.
M.R.C.P.(E.) = Member of the Royal College of Physicians (Edinburgh).
M.R.C.S. = Member of the Royal College of Surgeons.
M.R.C.V.S. = Member of the Royal College of Veterinary Surgeons.
M.R.I. = Member of the Royal Institution.
M.S. = Master in Surgery.
Ms., Mss. = Manuscript, Manuscripts.
M.S.A. = Mutual Security Agency.
M.Sc. = Master of Science.
M.T.B. = Motor Torpedo Boat.
M.T.P.I. = Member of the Town Planning Institute.
Mus.B. = *Musicae Baccalaureus* (Bachelor in Music).
Mus.D. = *Musicae Doctor* (Doctor in Music).
MV = million volts *or* megavolt.
M.V.O. = Member of the Royal Victorian Order.
MW = million watts *or* megawatt.
M.W.B. = Metropolitan Water Board.

N

NAAFI = Navy, Army and Air Force Institutes.
N.A.B.M. = National Association of British Manufacturers.
NASA = National Aeronautics and Space Administration (US).
NATO = North Atlantic Treaty Organisation.
NATSOPA = National Society of Operative Printers and Assistants.
N.B. = *nota bene* (note well).
NBS = National Bureau of Standards (US).
N.C. = Nature Conservancy.
N.C.B. = National Coal Board.
N.C.L.C. = National Council of Labour Colleges.
N.C.O. = Non-commissioned Officer.
N.C.U. = National Cyclists' Union.
n.d. = no date (of books).
NEDC = National Economic Development Council.
Nem.con. = *Nemine contradicente* (no one contradicting = unanimously).
Nem.diss. = *Nemine dissentiente* (no one dissenting = unanimously).
NERC = Natural Environment Research Council.
Net. (*or* Nett.) = free from, or not subject to, any deductions.
NHS = National Health Service.
NIC = National Incomes Commission.
NIRNS = National Institute for Research in Nuclear Science.
NLL = National Lending Library for Science and Technology.
No. = *numero* (number).
N.P. = Notary Public.
N.P.C. = National Parks Commission.
N.P.F.A. = National Playing Fields Association.
NPL = National Physical Laboratory.
NRDC = National Research Development Corporation.
N.S. = New Style in the calendar (in Gt. Britain since 1752)

N.S.P.C.C. = National Society for the Prevention of Cruelty to Children.
N.T. = New Testament; National Trust.
N.U.R. = National Union of Railwaymen.
N.U.T. = National Union of Teachers.
N.Y. = New York.
N.Z. = New Zealand.

O

OAS = Organisation of American States; Organisation de l'Armée Secrète (the clandestine army of the French colonists in Algeria).
OAU = Organisation of African Unity.
ob. = *obit* (died).
O.B.E. = Officer of the Order of the British Empire.
OCAM = Organisation commune africaine et malgache.
OCTU = Officer Cadets' Training Unit.
ODECA = Organisation of Central American States.
OECD = Organisation for Economic Co-operation and Development.
O.E.D. = Oxford English Dictionary.
O.F.M. = *Ordo Fratrum Minorum* (Order of Friars Minor = Franciscan).
O.H.M.S. = On Her Majesty's Service.
O.M. = Member of the Order of Merit.
O.P. = *Ordinis Praedicatorum* (Order of Preachers = Dominicans); opposite to prompter (stage term); out of print.
op. = *opus* (work).
op cit. = *opere citato* (in the work cited).
ORC = Overseas Research Council.
ORGEL = Organique et Eau Lourde (organic liquid and heavy water nuclear reactor).
O.S. = Old Style in calendar.
O.S.B. = *Ordo Sancti Benedicti* (Order of St. Benedict = Benedictines).
O.T. = Old Testament.
O.T.C. = Officers' Training Corps.
Oxon. = of Oxford.
oz. = ounce(s).

P

P.A. = Press Association.
PAYE = Pay as you earn (income tax scheme).
P.C. = Privy Councillor; Police Constable.
P.C.C. = People's Caretakers' Council (Nat. movement in Rhodesia).
p.c. = per cent.; postcard.
P.D.S.A. = People's Dispensary for Sick Animals.
P.E.N. = Poets, Playwrights, Essayists, Editors and Novelists (Club).
P.E.P. = Political and Economic Planning (Society).
per pro (*or* p.p.) = *per procurationem* (by proxy).
Ph.D. = *Philosophiae Doctor* (Doctor of Philosophy).
pinx = *pinxit* (he painted).
P.L.A. = Port of London Authority.
PLUTO = Pipe-line under the ocean.
P.M. = Prime Minister; Post master; *post meridiem* (afternoon).
P.M.G. = Postmaster General.
P.M.O. = Principal Medical Officer.
P.N.E.U. = Parents' National Education Union.
P.O. = Post Office; postal order; Petty Officer.
P. & O. = Peninsular and Oriental Steamship Co.
P.O.W. = prisoner of war.
pp. = pages.
P.P.C. = pour prendre congé (to take leave).
P.Q. = Parliamentary Question.
P.P.S. = Parliamentary Private Secretary.
P.R. = Proportional Representation.
P.R.A. = President of the Royal Academy.
P.R.B. = Pre-Raphaelite Brotherhood.
pro tem. = *pro tempore* (for the time being).
prox = *proximo* (of the next month).
P.R.S. = President of the Royal Society.
P.S. = *post scriptum* (postscript).
Ps. = Psalm.
Pss. = Psalms.
P.T. = Physical Training.
Pte. = Private.
P.T.O. = please turn over.

Q

Q. = Queen.
Q.B. = Queen's Bench.
Q.C. = Queen's Counsel.
Q.E.D. = *quod erat demonstrandum* (which was to be demonstrated).
Q.E.F. = *quod erat faciendum* (which was to be done).
Q.E.I. = *quod erat inveniendum* (which was to be found).
q.l. (*or* q.pl) = *quantum libet* (*or quantum placet*) (as much as one pleases).
Q.M. = Quartermaster.
Q.M.C. = Queen Mary College.
q.s. = *quantum sufficit* (a sufficient quantity).
QSEs = Qualified skills and engineers.
QSSs = Quasars (quasi stellar radio sources).
Q.T. = quiet (slang).
Qto. = quarto (folded in four).
q.v. = *quod vide* (which see).

R

R. = Réaumur; *Rex* (King); *Regina* (Queen); Right (stage direction).
R.A. = Rear Admiral; Royal Academy; Royal Academician; Research Association; Right Ascension (astron.).
R.A.C. = Royal Automobile Club.
R.Ae.S. = Royal Aeronautical Society.
R.A.E. = Royal Aircraft Establishment.
R.A.F. = Royal Air Force.
R.A.M. = Royal Academy of Music.
R.C. = Red Cross; Roman Catholic.
R.D. = Rural Dean; Royal Naval Reserve Decoration; Refer to Drawer.
R.D.C. = Rural District Council
R.D.I. = Designer for Industry of the Royal Society of Arts.
R.E. = Royal Engineers.
Reg. Prof. = Regius Professor.
R.E.M.E. = Royal Electrical and Mechanical Engineers.
Rep. = Representative; Republican.
R.G.S. = Royal Geographical Society.
R.H.S. = Royal Humane Society; Royal Horticultural Society.
R.Hist.S. = Royal Historical Society.
R.I. = Royal Institution; Royal Institute of Painters in Water Colours; Rhode Island; Religious Instruction.
R.I.B.A. = Royal Institution of British Architects.
R.I.I.A. = Royal Institute of International Affairs (Chatham House, London).
R.I.P. = *requiescat in pace* (may he rest in peace).
R.L.O. = Returned Letter Office.
R.M. = Royal Marines; Resident Magistrate.
R.M.C. = Royal Military College, Sandhurst.
R.N. = Royal Navy.
RNA = ribonucleic acid.
R.N.L.I. = Royal National Lifeboat Institution.
Ro. = *recto* (on the right-hand page).
R.P. = Member of the Royal Society of Portrait Painters.
rpm = revolutions per minute.
R.S.A. = Royal Society of Arts; Royal Scottish Academician.
R.S.M. = Regimental Sergeant Major.
R.S.P.C.A. = Royal Society for the Prevention of Cruelty to Animals.
R.S.V.P. = *Répondez, s'il vous plaît* (An answer is requested).
R.S.W. = Royal Scottish Society of Painters in Water Colours.
Rt. Hon. = Right Honourable.
Rt. Rev. = Right Reverend (of a Bishop).
R.U. = Rugby Union.
RV = Revised Version.
R.W.S. = Royal Society of Painters in Water Colours.
R.Y.S. = Royal Yacht Squadron.

S

S. = *San, Santa, Santo*, or *São* (Saint); SS. = Saints.
s. = *solidus* (shilling), *solidi* (shillings).

S.A. = Salvation Army; Sex Appeal; South America; South Australia; South Africa; Société Anonyme (Limited).
SACEUR = Supreme Allied Commander Europe.
SACLANT = Supreme Allied Commander Atlantic.
Sarum = of Salisbury.
S.C. = qualified to admission to Staff College.
sc. = *scilicet* (namely).
Sc.D. = *Scientiae Doctor* (Doctor in Science).
S.C.F. = Senior Chaplain to the Forces.
S.C.M. = State Certified Midwife; Student Christian Movement.
SEATO = South-East Asia Treaty Organisation.
S.G. = Solicitor-General; Scots Guards.
SHAPE = Supreme Headquarters, Allied Powers, Europe.
sic. = so written.
SINS = Ships Inertial Navigation System.
SISTER = Special Institution for Scientific and Technical Education and Research.
SOS = distress signal (wireless code signal, used especially by ships at sea).
s.p. = *sine prole* (without issue).
S.P.C.K. = Society for the Promotion of Christian Knowledge.
S.P.G. = Society for the Propagation of the Gospel.
sp. gr. = specific gravity.
sq. = square; *sequens* (the following).
sqq. = *sequentes, sequentia* (those following).
SRC = Science Research Council.
S.R.N. = State Registered Nurse.
SS. = Saints.
S.S. = Steamship.
S.S.C. = Solicitor before Supreme Court (Scotland).
S.T.D. = *Sacrae Theologiae Doctor* (Doctor of Theology); Subscriber Trunk Dialling.
St. = Saint; Street.
Ste = *Sainte* (Saint, feminine).
Stet = Let it stand (printing term).
S.T.P. = *Sacrae Theologiae Professor* (Professor of Divinity, old form of D.D.)
s.v. = *sub verbo* (under the entry).

T

TAB = Technical Assistance Board (UN).
T.B. = Tubercule bacillus (tuberculosis).
t.b. = torpedo boat.
T.C.D. = Trinity College, Dublin.
T.D. = Territorial Decoration; Tealta Dáil (Member of the Dáil).
T.F. = Territorial Force.
T.H. = Trinity House.
TNT = trinitrotoluene (high explosive).
Toc.H. = Talbot House.
tr. = transpose.
T.R.C. = Thames Rowing Club; Tithes Rent Charge.
T.T. = tubercular tested; teetotal.
TUC = Trades Union Congress.
TV = Television.
TVA = Tennessee Valley Authority.
T.V.W.B. = Thames Valley Water Board.
TWI = Training Within Industry for Supervisors.
T.Y.C. = Thames Yacht Club; Two-year Old (*or* Thousand Yards) Course.

U

U.A.M. = Afro-Malagasy Union.
U-boat = German submarine.
UAR = United Arab Republic.
UCL = University College, London.
U.D.C. = Urban District Council.
UDEAC = Union douanière et economique de l'Afrique centrale.
UGC = University Grants Committee.
UHF = ultra-high frequency.
U.K. (*or* UK) = United Kingdom.
UKAEA = UK Atomic Energy Authority.
ult. = *ultimo* (of the last month).
U.N. (*or* UN) = United Nations.
UNCTAD = United Conference on Trade and Development (UN).
UNEF = United Nations Emergency Force(s).
UNESCO = United Nations Education, Scientific, and Cultural Organisation.
UNICEF = United Nations Children's Fund.
UNRWA = United Nations Relief and Works Agency for Palestine Refugees.
U.P. = United Press.
U.P.U. = Universal Postal Union (UN).
U.S. (*or* US) United States.
U.S.A. (*or* USA) = United States of America.
USAEC = US Atomic Energy Commission.
U.S.S.R. (*or* USSR) = Union of Soviet Socialist Republics (Russia).

V

v. = *vide* (see); *versus* (against); volt(s).
V.A. = Vicar-Apostolic.
V. & A. = Victoria and Albert Museum, S. Kensington.
V.C.H. = Victoria County Histories.
V.D. = venereal disease; Volunteer Officers' Decoration.
v.d. = various dates.
V.E. Day = Victory in Europe Day, 8 May 1945.
Ven. = Venerable (of an Archdeacon).
Very Rev. = Very Reverend (of a Dean or a Provost).
v.g. = very good.
v.h.c. = very highly commended.
V.H.F. = very high frequency.
V.I.P. = very important person.
viz. = *videlicet* (namely).
V.J. Day = Victory over Japan Day, 15 August 1945.
V.L. = Vice-Lieutenant (of a County).
V.M. = Virgin Mary.
V.M.H. = Victoria Medal of Honour (Royal Horticultural Society).
Vo. = *verso* (on the left-hand page).
V.P. = Vice-President.
V.R. = *Victoria Regina* (Queen Victoria).
v.r. = variant, *or* various reading.
V.S. = veterinary surgeon; vital statistics.
VTOL = vertical take-off and landing (aircraft).

W

W. (*or* w.) = watt(s).
W.A. = Western Australia.
Wasps = White Anglo-Saxon Protestants.
WCC = World Council of Churches.
W.E.A. = Workers' Educational Association.
WEU = Western European Union.
WFTU = World Federation of Trade Unions.
WHO = World Health Organisation (UN).
WMO = World Meteorological Organisation (UN).
W.R.A.C. = Women's Royal Army Corps.
W.R.A.F. = Women's Royal Air Force.
W.R.N.S. = Women's Royal Naval Service.
W.S. = Writer to the Signet.
W.V.S. = Women's Voluntary Services.

X

X = Christ (X repr. first letter of the Greek word).
X's = expenses (slang).
xd = ex dividend.
Xmas = Christmas.

Y

y. = year(s).
yd. = yard(s).
Y.M.C.A. = Young Men's Christian Association.
Y.W.C.A. = Young Women's Christian Association.

Z

ZANU = Zimbabwe African National Union (Nat movement in Rhodesia).
ZAPU = Zimbabwe African People's Union (Nat movement in Rhodesia)

GENERAL COMPENDIUM

GENERAL COMPENDIUM

ENGLISH MONARCHS
(A.D. 827–1603)

Monarch	Accession	Died	Age	Reigned
I.—BEFORE THE CONQUEST.				
SAXONS AND DANES				
Egbert	827	839	—	12
Ethelwulf	839	858	—	19
Ethelbald	858	860	—	2
Ethelbert	858	865	—	7
Ethelred	865	871	—	6
Alfred the Great	871	899	50	28
Edward the Elder	899	924	54	25
Athelstan	924	939	45	15
Edmund	939	946	25	7
Eadred	946	955	32	9
Eadwig	955	959	18	3
Edgar	959	975	32	17
Edward the Martyr	975	978	17	3
Ethelred II ("the Unready")	978	1016	48	37
Edmund Ironside	1016	1016	27	Apr.–Nov.
Canute the Dane	1017	1035	40	18
Harold I	1035	1040	—	5
Hardicanute	1040	1042	24	2
Edward the Confessor	1042	1066	62	24
Harold II	1066	1066	44	Jan.–Oct.
II.—FROM THE CONQUEST TO THE PRESENT DAY.				
NORMANS				
William I	1066	1087	60	21
William II	1087	1100	43	13
Henry I	1100	1135	67	35
Stephen, Count of Blois	1135	1154	50	19
PLANTAGENETS				
Henry II	1154	1189	56	35
Richard I	1189	1199	42	10
John	1199	1216	50	17
Henry III	1216	1272	65	56
Edward I	1272	1307	68	35
Edward II	1307	dep. 1327	43	20
Edward III	1327	1377	65	50
Richard II	1377	dep. 1399	34	22
Henry IV (Lancaster)	1399	1413	47	13
Henry V (Lancaster)	1413	1422	34	9
Henry VI (Lancaster)	1422	dep. 1461	49	39
Edward IV (York)	1461	1483	41	22
Edward V (York)	1483	1483	13	Apr.–June
Richard III (York)	1483	1485	35	2
TUDORS				
Henry VII	1485	1509	53	24
Henry VIII	1509	1547	56	38
Edward VI	1547	1553	16	6
Jane	1553	1554	17	9 days
Mary I	1553	1558	43	5
Elizabeth I	1558	1603	69	44

BRITISH MONARCHS
(1603 to the Present day)

Monarch	Accession	Died	Age	Reigned
STUARTS				
James I (VI of Scotland)	1603	1625	59	22
Charles I	1625	beh. 1649	48	24
COMMONWEALTH DECLARED, MAY 19, 1649				
Oliver Cromwell, Lord Protector	1653–8	—	—	—
Richard Cromwell, Lord Protector	1658–9	—	—	—
STUARTS (RESTORATION)				
Charles II	1660	1685	55	25
James II (VII of Scotland)	1685	dep. 1688	68	3
Interregnum Dec. 11, 1688 to Feb. 13, 1689				
William III and Mary II	1689	1702 1694	51 33	13 6
Anne	1702	1714	49	12
HOUSE OF HANOVER				
George I	1714	1727	67	13
George II	1727	1760	77	33
George III	1760	1820	81	59
George IV	1820	1830	67	10
William IV	1830	1837	71	7
Victoria	1837	1901	81	63
HOUSE OF SAXE-COBURG				
Edward VII	1901	1910	68	9
HOUSE OF WINDSOR				
George V	1910	1936	70	25
Edward VIII	1936	Abd. 1936	—	325 days
George VI	1936	1952	56	15
Elizabeth II	1952			

SCOTTISH MONARCHS
(1057–1603)

Monarch		Accession	Died
Malcolm III (Canmore)	Son of Duncan I (slain by Macbeth)	1058	1093
Donald Ban	Brother of Malcolm Canmore	1093	—
Duncan II	Son of Malcolm Canmore, by first marriage	1094	1094
Donald Ban	Restored	1094	1097
Edgar	Son of Malcolm Canmore, by second marriage	1097	1107
Alexander I	Son of Malcolm Canmore	1107	1124
David I	Son of Malcolm Canmore	1124	1153
Malcolm IV (the Maiden)	Son of Henry, eldest son of David I	1153	1165
William I (the Lion)	Brother of Malcolm the Maiden	1165	1214
Alexander II	Son of William the Lion	1214	1249
Alexander III	Son of Alexander II, by second marriage	1249	1286
Margaret, Maid of Norway	Daughter of Eric II of Norway, granddaughter of Alexander III	1286	1290
John Baliol	Grandson of eldest daughter of David, Earl of Huntingdon, brother of William the Lion	1292	1296
Robert I (Bruce)	Great-grandson of 2nd daughter of David, Earl of Huntingdon, brother of William the Lion	1306	1329
David II	Son of Robert I, by second marriage	1329	1371
Robert II (Stewart)	Son of Marjorie, daughter of Robert I by first marriage, and Walter the Steward	1371	1390
Robert III	(John, Earl of Carrick) son of Robert II	1390	1406
James I	Son of Robert III	1406	1437
James II	Son of James I	1437	1460
James III	Eldest son of James II	1460	1488
James IV	Eldest son of James III	1488	1513
James V	Son of James IV	1513	1542
Mary	Daughter of James V, by second marriage	1542	1587
James VI (ascended the Throne of England 1603)	Son of Mary, by second marriage	1567	1625

THE ROYAL FAMILY

Showing the common descent of Queen Elizabeth and The Duke of Edinburgh from Queen Victoria and from Christian IX of Denmark.

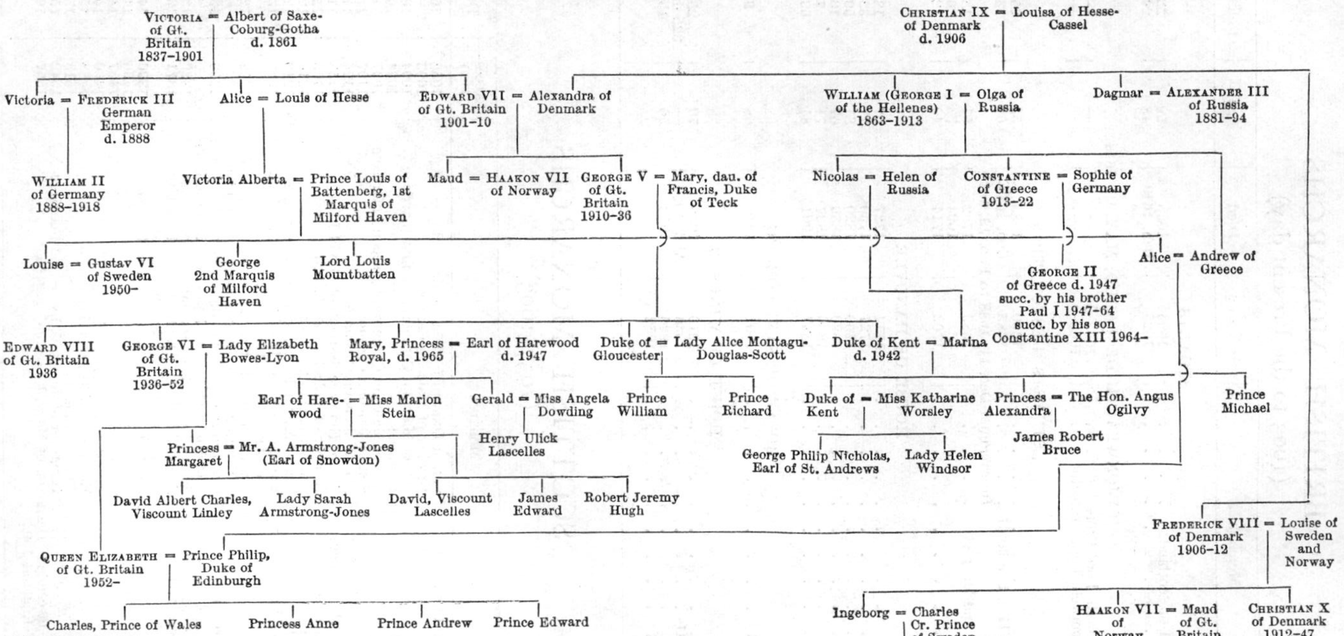

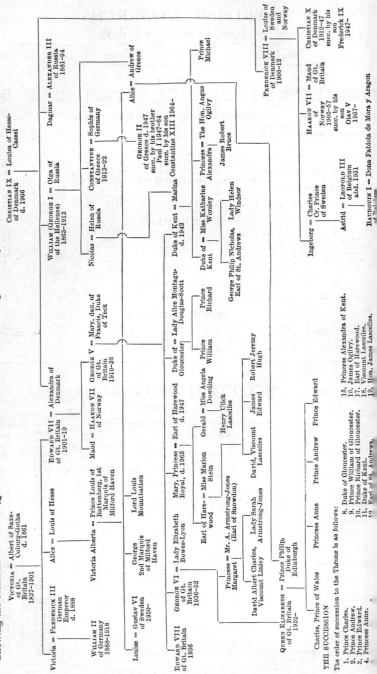

THE SUCCESSION

The order of succession to the Throne is as follows:

1. Prince Charles.
2. Prince Andrew.
3. Prince Edward.
4. Princess Anne.
8. Duke of Gloucester.
9. Prince William of Gloucester.
10. Prince Richard of Gloucester.
11. Duke of Kent.
12. Earl of St. Andrews.
15. Princess Alexandra of Kent.
16. James Ogilvy.
17. Earl of Harewood.
18. Viscount Lascelles.
19. Hon. James Lascelles.

PRECEDENCE IN ENGLAND

The Sovereign.

The Duke of Edinburgh.

The Prince of Wales.

Younger sons of the Sovereign.

The Duke of Gloucester.

The Duke of Windsor.

Archbishop of Canterbury

Lord High Chancellor.

Archbishop of York.

Prime Minister.

Lord President of the Council.

Speaker of the House of Commons.

Lord Privy Seal.

High Commissioners of Commonwealth Countries and Ambassadors of Foreign States.

Ambassadors and High Commissioners.

The five Great Officers of State:

1. Lord Great Chamberlain
2. Earl Marshal
3. Lord Steward
4. Lord Chamberlain
5. Master of the Horse

(Above all of their degree.)

Dukes, according to their creation:

1. Of England.
2. Of Scotland.
3. Of Great Britain.
4. Of Ireland.
5. Since the Union.

Ministers and Envoys.

Eldest sons of Dukes of Blood Royal.

Marquesses, in same order as Dukes.

Dukes' eldest sons.

Earls, in same order as Dukes.

Younger sons of Royal Dukes.

Marquesses' eldest sons.

Dukes' younger sons.

Viscounts, in same order as Dukes.

Earls' eldest sons.

Marquesses' younger sons.

Bishops of London, Durham, and Winchester.

All other English bishops, according to seniority of consecration.

Secretaries of State, if Barons.

Barons, in same order as Dukes.

Treasurer of H.M. Household.

Comptroller of H.M. Household.

Vice-Chamberlain of H.M. Household.

Secretaries of State under degree of Baron.

Viscounts' eldest sons.

Earls' younger sons.

Barons' eldest sons.

Knights of the Garter, if commoners.

Privy Councillors, if of no higher rank.

Chancellor of the Exchequer.

Chancellor of the Duchy of Lancaster.

Lord Chief Justice of England.

Master of the Rolls.

President of the Probate Court.

Lords Justices of Appeal.

Judges of the High Court of Justice.

Vice-Chancellor of County Palatine of Lancaster.

Viscounts' younger sons.

Barons' younger sons.

Sons of Life Peers.

Baronets according to date of patent.

Knights of the Thistle.

Knights of St. Patrick.

Knights Grand Cross of the Bath.

Members of the Order of Merit.

Knights Grand Commanders of the Star of India.

Knights Grand Cross of St. Michael and St. George.

Knights Grand Commanders of the Indian Empire.

Knights Grand Cross of the Royal Victorian Order.

Knights Grand Cross of Order of the British Empire.

Companions of Honour.

Knights Commanders of the above Orders.

Knights Bachelors.

Official Referees of Supreme Court of Judicature.

Judges of County Courts and of Mayor's and City of London Court.

Serjeants at Law.

Masters in Lunacy.

Companions and Commanders, *e.g.*, C.B.; C.S.I.; C.M.G.; C.I.E.; C.V.O.; C.B.E.; D.S.O.; M.V.O. (4th); O.B.E.; I.S.O.

Eldest sons of younger sons of Peers.

Baronets' eldest sons.

Eldest sons of Knights in order of their fathers.

M.V.O. (5th); M.B.E.

Younger sons of the younger sons of Peers.

Baronets' younger sons.

Younger sons of Knights in order of their fathers.

Naval, Military, Air, and other Esquires by Office.

Women take the same rank as their husbands or as their eldest brothers; but the daughter of a Peer marrying a Commoner retains her title as Lady or Honourable. Daughters of Peers rank next immediately after the wives of their elder brothers, and before their younger brothers' wives. Daughters of Peers marrying Peers of lower degree take the same order of precedency as that of their husbands; thus the daughter of a Duke marrying a Baron becomes of the rank of Baroness only, while her sisters married to commoners retain their rank and take precedence of the Baroness. Merely official rank on the husband's part does not give any similar precedence to the wife. Dames Grand Cross (G.C.V.O. or G.B.E.) rank after wives of Baronets and before wives of Knights Grand Cross. Dames Commanders (D.C.V.O. or D.B.E.) rank after wives of Knights Grand Cross and before wives of Knights Commanders.

Precedence is formed by statute, patent, or usage, but the chief regulations regarding the order of precedence were settled by Parliament in the reign of Henry VIII.

Precedence locally, in county or city, has not been promulgated by written code, but in Counties the Lord Lieutenant stands first, and secondly the Sheriff, and therefore in Cities and Boroughs the Lord Lieutenant has social precedence over the Mayor; but at City or Borough functions the Lord Mayor or Mayor will preside. At Oxford and Cambridge the High Sheriff takes precedence of the Vice-Chancellor.

PRECEDENCE IN SCOTLAND

The Sovereign.

The Duke of Edinburgh.

The Duke of Rothesay (eldest son of the Sovereign).

Younger sons of the Sovereign.

The Lord High Commissioner during sitting of General Assembly.

The Duke of Gloucester, the Duke of Windsor, uncles of the Sovereign.

Lord Lieutenants of counties, Lord Provosts of cities being ex-officio Lord Lieutenants of counties of cities, and Sheriffs Principal, when within their localities, in the order named.

Lord Chancellor of Great Britain.

Moderator of the Assembly of the Church of Scotland.

The Prime Minister.

Keeper of the Great Seal of Scotland (Secretary for Scotland), if a peer.

Keeper of the Privy Seal of Scotland, if a peer

Hereditary Lord High Constable of Scotland.

Hereditary Master of the Household in Scotland.

Dukes, as in English precedence.

Eldest sons of Dukes of Blood Royal.

Marquesses, as in England.

Eldest sons of Dukes.

Earls as in England.

Younger sons of Royal Dukes.

Eldest sons of Marquesses.

Younger sons of Dukes.

Keeper of the Great Seal of Scotland (Secretary for Scotland), if not a peer.

Keeper of the Privy Purse, if not a peer.

Lord Justice-General.

Lord Clerk-register.

Lord Advocate.

Lord Justice Clerk.

Viscounts, as in England.

Eldest sons of Earls.

Younger sons of Marquesses.

Barons, as in England.

Eldest sons of Viscounts.

Younger sons of Earls.

Eldest sons of Barons.

Knights of the Garter.

Privy Councillors not included in above ranks.

Lords of Session (by date of appointment).

Younger sons of Viscounts.

Younger sons of Barons.

Sons of Life Peers.

Baronets.

Knights of the Thistle.

Knights of St. Patrick.

Knights of other Orders as in England.

Solicitor-general for Scotland.

Lord Lyon King of Arms.

Sheriffs Principal (except as shown above).

Knights Bachelor.

Sheriffs Substitute.

Companions of Orders as in England.

Commanders of Royal Victorian Order.

Commanders of the British Empire Order.

Eldest sons of younger sons of Peers.

Companions of Distinguished Service Order.

Member of Fourth Class of Royal Victorian Order.

Officers of British Empire Order.

Eldest sons of Baronets.

Eldest sons of Knights of the Garter, of the Thistle, and of St. Patrick.

Eldest sons of Knights.

Members of Fifth Class of Royal Victorian Order.

Members of British Empire Order.

Younger sons of Baronets.

Younger sons of Knights.

Queen's Counsel.

Barons-feudal.

Esquires.

Gentlemen.

MODES OF ADDRESS TO PERSONS OF RANK

ROYALTY.

QUEEN.

Begin: Madam, *or* May it please Your Majesty, *or* Lord —— presents his duty to Your Majesty.
Address: The Queen's Most Excellent Majesty.
Speak to as: Your Majesty.

PRINCES AND PRINCESSES, DUKES AND DUCHESSES OF THE BLOOD ROYAL.

Begin: Sir (*or* Madam).
Address: His (*or* Her) Royal Highness the Prince (*or* Princess) ——.
His (*or* Her) Royal Highness the Duke (*or* Duchess) of ——.
Speak to as: Your Royal Highness.

NOBILITY.

DUKES AND DUCHESSES.

Begin: My Lord Duke.
Address: His Grace the Duke of ——, K.G., etc.
Speak to as: Your Grace.

Begin: Madam.
Address: Her Grace the Duchess of ——.
Speak to as: Your Grace.

MARQUESSES AND MARCHIONESSES.

Begin: My Lord Marquess, *or* My Lord.
Address: The Most Hon. the Marquess of ——.
Speak to as: Your Lordship.

Begin: Madam.
Address: The Most Hon. the Marchioness of ——.
Speak to as: Your Ladyship.

EARLS AND COUNTESSES.

Begin: My Lord.
Address: The Right Hon. the Earl of ——, *or* The Earl ——.
Speak to as: Your Lordship.

Begin: Madam.
Address: The Right Hon. the Countess of ——, or The Countess ——.
Speak to as: Your Ladyship.

VISCOUNTS AND VISCOUNTESSES.

Begin: My Lord.
Address: The Right Hon. Viscount, *or* Viscount ——.
Speak to as: Your Lordship.

Begin: Madam.
Address: The Right Hon. the Viscountess ——.
Speak to as: Your Ladyship.

BARONS AND BARONESSES.

Begin: My Lord.
Address: The Right Hon. Lord ——.
Speak to as: Your Lordship.

Begin: My Lady.
Address: The Right Hon. Lady ——.
Speak to as: Your Ladyship.

BARONETS.

Begin: Sir.
Address: Sir (Christian name and surname), Bt.

KNIGHTS BACHELOR.

As Baronet, except that the word Bt. is omitted.

THE CHURCH.

ARCHBISHOPS.

Begin: My Lord Archbishop, *or* Your Grace.
Address: His Grace the Lord Archbishop of ——.
Speak to as: Your Grace.

A retired archbishop is addressed as The Most Rev. Archbishop ——.

BISHOPS.

All Bishops, whether Diocesan or Suffragan, are addressed by the spiritual title "Lord."

Begin: My Lord Bishop.
Address: The Right Rev. the Lord Bishop of ——.
Speak to as: Your Lordship.

It is usual to accord to Colonial Bishops the courtesy title of "Lord Bishop," and they are addressed in the same manner as English Bishops. Assistant and retired Bishops are not addressed as "Lord Bishop" but as The Right Rev. Bishop ——, *or* The Right Rev. (surname), D.D.

Begin: Right Rev. Sir.

DEANS.

Begin: Very Reverend Sir.
Address: The Very Rev. the Dean of ——.

ARCHDEACONS.

Begin: Venerable Sir.
Address: The Venerable the Archdeacon of ——.

CANONS.

Begin: Reverend Sir.
Address: The Reverend Canon ——.
Speak to as: Canon ——.

THE POPE.

Begin: Your Holiness *or* Most Holy Father.
Address: To His Holiness the Pope.

CARDINALS.

Begin: My Lord Cardinal *or* My Lord.
Address: To His Eminence Cardinal ——.

THE CHIEF RABBI.

Begin: Very Rev. and Dear Sir.
Address: To the Very Rev. the Chief Rabb *or* To the Very Rev. (Dr.) ——

RABBIS.

Begin: Rev. and Dear Sir.
Address: To the Rev. Rabbi (Dr.) ——.

THE LAW.

LORD CHANCELLOR.

Begin: According to rank.
Address: The Right Hon. the Lord High Chancellor.
Speak to: According to rank.

LORD CHIEF JUSTICE.

Begin: According to rank, if a peer, otherwise as a Judge.
Address: The Right Hon. the Lord Chief Justice of England.

LORD JUSTICE OF APPEAL.

Begin: Sir.
Address: The Right Hon. the Lord Justice ——.
Speak to as: Your Lordship (addressed on the Bench as "My Lord").

LORD OF APPEAL IN ORDINARY AND HIS WIFE.

As Baron and Baroness.

JUDGES.

Begin: Sir (*or* Madam)
Address: The Hon. Mr. Justice —— *or* The Hon. Sir —— (if a Knight).
Speak to as: Your Lordship (*or* Ladyship) (addressed on the Bench as "My Lord" (*or* "My Lady").

JUDGES OF COUNTY COURT.

Begin: Dear Judge ——.
Address: His Honour Judge —— (addressed on the Bench as "Your Honour").

JUSTICES OF THE PEACE.

Address: The Right Worshipful ——, J.P. (addressed on the Bench as "Your Worship").

LORD MAYORS.
Begin: My Lord.
Address: The Right Hon. the Lord Mayor of —— (London, York, Dublin, Belfast, Adelaide, Sydney, Melbourne, Perth (Aust.), Brisbane and Hobart).
Speak to as: Your Lordship.

MAYORS.
Begin: Sir.
Address: The Right Worshipful the Mayor of —— (Mayor of a City). The Worshipful the Mayor of —— (Mayor of a Borough).
Speak to as: Your Worship.

LORD PROVOSTS.
Begin: My Lord Provost, *or* My Lord.
Address: The Right Hon. the Lord Provost of —— (Edinburgh and Glasgow). The Lord Provost of —— (Aberdeen, Dundee, Elgin, and Perth).
Speak to: Your Lordship.
(The Lord Provost's wife is called Lady Provost.)

DIPLOMATIC SERVICE.

AMBASSADORS (in charge of Embassies).
Begin: Sir, My Lord, etc., according to rank.
Address: His Excellency (in other respects according to rank) H.B.M. Embassy.
Speak to as: Your Excellency.

MINISTERS (in charge of Legations).
Rules as for ambassadors, except in the case of commoners when the envelope should be addressed: (Christian name and surname), Esq., H.M.B. Legation, ——.

CONSULS.
Begin: Sir.
Address: (Christian name and surname), Esq., H.B.M. Agent and Consul-General, *or* H.B.M. Consul-General, *or* H.B.M. Consul, *or* H.B.M. Vice-Consul.

GOVERNORS-GENERAL.
Begin: According to rank.
Address: His Excellency (ordinary designation), Governor of——.
Speak to as: Your Excellency.

PRIVY COUNCILLORS.
The courtesy title of "Right Honourable" is accorded all Privy Councillors (all members of the Cabinet are privy councillors, and the office is conferred for life). In the case of peers below the rank of Marquess, who already have a right to it in virtue of their peerage, the rank of Privy Councillor is indicated by the letters "P.C." after the name. Wives do not share the title.
Address: The Right Hon. ——.
Admiral the Right Hon. Sir ——.
The Right Rev. the Right Hon. the Lord Bishop of ——.
The Most Hon. the Marquess of ——, P.C.

BUSINESS LETTERS.
Business letters to persons of rank can either be written in the third person (grammatical pitfalls must be guarded against), in which case they are not signed, or in the first person plural.

ORDERS OF CHIVALRY

Garter
K.G.

The Most Noble Order of the Garter (1348). *Ribbon:* Garter blue, not worn in undress uniform. *Motto:* Honi soit qui mal y pense (*Evil to him who evil thinks*).

Thistle
K.T.

The Most Noble and Most Ancient Order of the Thistle (1687). *Ribbon:* Green, not worn in undress uniform. *Motto:* Nemo me impune lacessit (*No one provokes me with impunity*).

Saint Patrick
K.P.

The Most Illustrious Order of St. Patrick (1783). *Ribbon:* Sky blue, not worn in undress uniform. *Motto:* Quis separabit? (*Who shall separate?*).

Bath
G.C.B. (Knight Grand Cross), (Mil. & Civ).
K.C.B. (Knight Commander), (Mil. & Civ).
C.B. (Companion), (Mil.).

The Most Honourable Order of the Bath (1399). *Ribbon:* Crimson. *Motto:* Tria juncta in uno (*Three joined in one*). (Remodelled 1725 and 1815, and enlarged 13 times since.)

Order of Merit
O.M. (Mil. & Civ.)

The Order of Merit (1902). *Ribbon:* Blue and crimson. Ranks after G.C.B. before K.C.B.

Star of India
G.C.S.I. (Knight Grand Commander).
K.C.S.I. (Knight Commander).
C.S.I. (Companion).

The Most Exalted Order of the Star of India (1861). (Since enlarged 8 times.) *Ribbon:* Light blue, with white edges. *Motto:* Heaven's Light our Guide.

Saint Michael and Saint George
G.C.M.G. (Knight Grand Cross).
K.C.M.G. (Knight Commander).
C.M.G. (Companion).

The Most Distinguished Order of St. Michael and St. George (1818). *Ribbon:* Saxon blue, with scarlet centre. *Motto:* Auspicium melioris aevi (*Token of a better age*).

Indian Empire
G.C.I.E. (Knight Grand Commander).
K.C.I.E. (Knight Commander).
C.I.E. (Companion).

The Most Eminent Order of the Indian Empire (1877). (Since enlarged 8 times.) *Ribbon:* Imperial purple. *Motto:* Imperatricis auspiciis (*Under the auspices of the Empress*).

Victorian Order
G.C.V.O. (Knight or Dame Grand Cross).
K.C.V.O. (Knight Commander).
D.C.V.O. (Dame Commander).
C.V.O. (Commander).
M.V.O. (Member).

The Royal Victorian Order (1896). *Ribbon:* Blue, with red and white edges. *Motto:* Victoria.

British Empire
G.B.E. (Knight or Dame Grand Cross).
K.B.E. (Knight Commander).
D.B.E. (Dame Commander).
C.B.E. (Commander).
O.B.E. (Officer).
M.B.E. (Member).

The Most Excellent Order of the British Empire (1917). *Ribbon:* Rose pink edged with pearl grey with vertical pearl stripe in centre (Mil. Div.); without vertical stripe (Civ. Div.). *Motto:* For God and the Empire.

Companions of Honour
C.H.

Order of the Companions of Honour (1917). *Ribbon:* Carmine, with gold edges. Ranks after G.B.E. and before K.B.E.

Victoria and Albert
V.A.

The Royal Order of Victoria and Albert (for Ladies) (1862). (Since enlarged 3 times.)

Crown of India
C.I.

The Imperial Order of the Crown of India (for Ladies) (1878). *Ribbon:* Light blue watered edged white, worn as bow on left shoulder.

BRITISH PRIME MINISTERS

	Party	Served
George I, 1714–27		
George II, 1727–60		
Sir Robert Walpole	Whig	1721–42
Earl of Wilmington	Whig	1742–3
Henry Pelham	Whig	1743–54
Duke of Newcastle	Whig	1754–6
Duke of Devonshire	Whig	1756–7
Duke of Newcastle	Whig	1757–60
George III, 1760–1820		
Duke of Newcastle	Whig	1760–2
Earl of Bute	Tory	1762–3
George Grenville	Whig	1763–5
Marquis of Rockingham	Whig	1766
Duke of Grafton	Whig	1766–9
Lord North	Tory	1770–82
Marquis of Rockingham	Whig	1782
Earl of Shelburne	Whig	1782–3
Duke of Portland	Coalition	1783
William Pitt	Tory	1783–1801
Viscount Sidmouth	Tory	1801–4
William Pitt	Tory	1804–6
Lord Grenville	Whig	1806–7
Duke of Portland	Tory	1807–9
Spencer Perceval (assassinated)	Tory	1809–12
George IV, 1820–30		
Earl of Liverpool	Tory	1812–27
George Canning	Tory	1827
Viscount Goderich	Tory	1827
Duke of Wellington	Tory	1827–30
William IV, 1830–7		
Earl Grey	Whig	1830–4
Viscount Melbourne	Whig	1834
Sir Robert Peel	Tory	1834–5
Viscount Melbourne	Whig	1835–7
Victoria, 1837–1901		
Viscount Melbourne	Whig	1837–41
Sir Robert Peel	Tory	1841–6
Lord John Russell	Whig	1846–52
Earl of Derby	Tory	1852
Earl of Aberdeen	Peelite	1852–5
Viscount Palmerston	Liberal	1855–8
Earl of Derby	Tory	1858–9
Viscount Palmerston	Liberal	1859–65
Earl Russell	Liberal	1865–6
Earl of Derby	Conservative	1866–8
B. Disraeli	Conservative	1868
W. E. Gladstone	Liberal	1868–74
B. Disraeli	Conservative	1874–80
W. E. Gladstone	Liberal	1880–5
Marquis of Salisbury	Conservative	1885–6
W. E. Gladstone	Liberal	1886
Marquis of Salisbury	Conservative	1886–92
W. E. Gladstone	Liberal	1892–4
Earl of Rosebery	Liberal	1894–5
Marquis of Salisbury	Conservative	1895–1901
Edward VII, 1901–10		
Marquis of Salisbury	Conservative	1901–2
A. J. Balfour	Conservative	1902–5
Sir H. Campbell-Bannerman	Liberal	1905–8
H. H. Asquith	Liberal	1908–10
George V, 1910–36		
H. H. Asquith	Liberal	1910–15
H. H. Asquith	Coalition	1915–16
D. Lloyd George	Coalition	1916–22
A. Bonar Law	Conservative	1922–3
S. Baldwin	Conservative	1923–4
J. R. MacDonald	Labour	1924
S. Baldwin	Conservative	1924–9
J. R. MacDonald	Labour	1929–31
J. R. MacDonald	Coalition	1931–5
S. Baldwin	Coalition	1935–6
Edward VIII, 1936		
George VI, 1936–52		
S. Baldwin	Coalition	1936–7
N. Chamberlain	Coalition	1937–40
W. S. Churchill	Coalition	1940–5
W. S. Churchill	Conservative	1945
C. R. Attlee	Labour	1945–51
Sir W. S. Churchill	Conservative	1951–2
Elizabeth II, 1952–		
Sir W. S. Churchill	Conservative	1952–5
Sir A. Eden	Conservative	1955–7
H. Macmillan	Conservative	1957–63
Sir A. Douglas-Home	Conservative	1963–4
H. Wilson	Labour	1964–

PRESIDENTS OF THE UNITED STATES

The terms are for four years; only President F. D. Roosevelt has served more than two terms.

	Party	Served
1. George Washington	Fed.	1789–97
2. John Adams	Fed.	1797–1801
3. Thomas Jefferson	Rep.	1801–9
4. James Madison	Rep.	1809–17
5. James Monroe	Rep.	1817–25
6. John Quincy Adams	Rep.	1825–9
7. Andrew Jackson	Dem.	1829–37
8. Martin Van Buren	Dem.	1837–41
9. William H. Harrison (died in office)	Whig	1841
10. John Tyler	Whig	1841–5
11. James K. Polk	Dem.	1845–9
12. Zachary Taylor (died in office)	Whig	1849–50
13. Millard Fillmore	Whig	1850–3
14. Franklin Pierce	Dem.	1853–7
15. James Buchanan	Dem.	1857–61
16. Abraham Lincoln (assassinated)	Rep.	1861–5
17. Andrew Johnson	Rep.	1865–9
18. Ulysses S. Grant	Rep.	1869–77
19. Rutherford B. Hayes	Rep.	1877–81
20. James A. Garfield (assassinated)	Rep.	1881
21. Chester A. Arthur	Rep.	1881–5
22. Grover Cleveland	Dem.	1885–9
23. Benjamin Harrison	Rep.	1889–93
24. Grover Cleveland	Dem.	1893–7
25. William McKinley (assassinated)	Rep.	1897–1901
26. Theodore Roosevelt	Rep.	1901–9
27. William Howard Taft	Rep.	1909–13
28. Woodrow Wilson	Dem.	1913–21
29. Warren G. Harding (died in office)	Rep.	1921–3
30. Calvin Coolidge	Rep.	1923–9
31. Herbert C. Hoover	Rep.	1929–33
32. Franklin D. Roosevelt (died in office)	Dem.	1933–45
33. Harry S. Truman	Dem.	1945–53
34. Dwight D. Eisenhower	Rep.	1953–61
35. John F. Kennedy (assassinated)	Dem.	1961–3
36. Lyndon B. Johnson	Dem.	1963–

UNITED KINGDOM COINAGE

The Royal Mint is authorised to issue coins of the following denominations and specifications:—

Denomination.	Standard Weight.
Gold:	Grains.
Five Pound Piece	616·37239
Two Pound Piece	246·54895
Sovereign	123·27447
Half Sovereign	61·63723
Cupro-Nickel:	
Crown	436·36363
Half-Crown	218·18181
Florin	174·54545
Shilling	87·27272
Sixpence	43·63636
Silver:	
Maundy Fourpence	29·09090
Maundy Threepence	21·81818
Maundy Twopence	14·54545
Maundy Penny	7·27272
Nickel Brass:	
Threepence	105·00000
Bronze:	
Penny	145·83333
Halfpenny	87·50000

Gold Coinage in Britain consists of eleven-twelfths of fine metal and one-twelfth of alloy: millesimal fineness 916·6. Two hundred and forty troy ounces of standard gold are coined into 934 sovereigns and one half-sovereign; one troy ounce is, therefore, worth £3 17*s*. 10½*d*., and one ounce of pure gold is nominally worth £4 4*s*. 11½*d*. The minimum weight at which a sovereign is allowed to remain current unchallenged is 122½ grains; that of half-a-sovereign 61⅛ grains. Any person to whom it is tendered may break, cut, or deface any gold coin below the least current weight, but light gold coin which has not been illegally dealt with is received by the Bank of England on behalf of the Mint at its full face value.

Cupro-Nickel. The first change in the silver standard since the reign of Queen Elizabeth was made in 1920, when the degree of fineness was reduced to 500 parts in a thousand as against 925. 1946 marked the end of the silver coinage. Silver coins have been replaced by those made of cupro-nickel, composed of 75% copper and 25% nickel. Maundy money is, however, made of silver, at the standard of 925 parts per 1000.

Bronze is employed in minting United Kingdom coins and its composition has varied slightly from time to time. At present it consists of 97% copper, ½% tin, and 2½% zinc.

Nickel Brass. The twelve-sided threepenny piece is composed of copper 79%, zinc 20%, and nickel 1%.

No person is permitted to coin any token to pass for, or as representing, any British piece of money under a penalty of £20.

New Coinage. A proclamation approving new designs for coinage was signed by H.M. the Queen in Council on November 25th, 1952. These coins became legal tender on January 1st, 1953, and include coin in gold as well as in silver-cupro-nickel, nickel–brass, and bronze.

The principal design is that of the uncrowned head of Elizabeth II, which is the work of Mrs. Mary Gillick, C.B.E. The Queen is shown wearing a laurel wreath tied at the back with a flowing ribbon above two rows of curls at the nape of the neck. The inscription on the obverses of the cupro-nickel coins issued after the 1st January, 1954, reads "ELIZABETH · II · DEI · GRATIA · REGINA" and on the obverses of the gold, silver, nickel-brass and bronze coins "ELIZABETH · II · DEI · GRATIA · REGINA · F: D:".

The reverse sides of the coins are as follows:—

Half-crown, shield of the Royal Arms surmounted by the Crown; prepared by Mr. E. G. Fuller and modelled by Mr. Cecil Thomas, O.B.E., F.R.B.S.

Florin, circular pattern of thistles, shamrock, and leeks about a double rose. This is the first time a Welsh emblem has decorated the United Kingdom coinage as an integral part of the design; prepared by Mr. E. G. Fuller and modelled by Mr. Thomas.

Shilling, shield of the English quartering of the Royal Arms surmounted by the Crown; design prepared and modelled by Mr. W. M. Gardner, A.R.C.A., F.R.S.A. The Scottish shilling shows a shield of the Scottish quartering of the Royal Arms surmounted by the Crown; also designed and modelled by Mr. Gardner.

Sixpence, garland of interlaced rose, thistle, shamrock, and leek, designed by Mr. Fuller and modelled by Mr. Thomas.

Threepenny piece, chained portcullis surmounted by a coronet, designed and modelled by Mr. Gardner.

There is no change on the reverse of the bronze coinage (coppers), which will continue to bear, on the *penny*, the figure of Britannia, familiar since Charles II, and on the *half-penny*, a sailing-ship inspired by the *Golden Hind*, designed by Mr. T. H. Paget, O.B.E.

The coins of Colonial territories, in accordance with tradition, bear the crowned head of the Sovereign, designed for the present Reign by Mr. Thomas.

The *five-shilling pieces* issued to commemorate the Coronation bore on the obverses an equestrian effigy of Her Majesty by Mr. Gilbert Ledward, R.A., and on the reverses a design by Mr. Fuller modelled by Mr. Thomas, of the four quarterings of the Royal Arms each contained in a shield and arranged in saltire with, in the intervening spaces, a rose, a thistle, a sprig of shamrock and a leek. Upon the edges of the coins was the inscription, "FAITH AND TRUTH I WILL BEAR UNTO YOU".

The designs specified for *crown pieces* issued after the 1st January, 1954 are Mrs. Gillick's uncrowned effigy for the obverses and the same design as shown on the reverses of the Coronation crown pieces for the reverses.

Having regard to impending changes in the coinage of certain Commonwealth countries, a new royal effigy was approved by Her Majesty in 1964 for use on the coinages of the United Kingdom and Commonwealth countries, to come into use at such times as the Governments decide. The portrait is the work of the sculptor, Mr. Arnold Machin, R.A.

LEGAL TENDER

Bank of England Notes are issued for sums of 10*s*., £1, £5 and £10. 10*s*. and £1 bank notes are legal tender in Great Britain and Northern Ireland, £5 and £10 bank notes in England and Wales only. The old 10*s*. and £1 notes (without the portrait of Her Majesty the Queen), the old £5 and £10 notes (on white paper), and all notes of higher denominations have ceased to be legal tender; they are, however, still exchangeable at the Bank of England.

Gold Coins dated 1838 onwards, if not below the minimum current weight, are legal tender; but (unless exempted by reason of their numismatic value under the Collectors' Pieces Exemption Order, 1947, or other Treasury Authority) any held by persons resident in the United Kingdom must (under the Exchange Control Act, 1947) be offered for sale to an Authorised Dealer.

Silver and/or Cupro-Nickel Coins from 1816 onwards are legal tender for sums not exceeding £2, nickel-brass (3*d*.) from 1937 for sums not exceeding 2*s*., and bronze from 1860 (with the exception of the farthing which was demonetised from 1 January 1961) for sums not exceeding 1*s*. No one can demand "change".

WEIGHTS AND MEASURES

I. IMPERIAL WEIGHTS AND MEASURES.

AVOIRDUPOIS.

1 dram (dr.)	27·34375 grains (gr.)
16 drams	1 ounce (oz.) = 437·5 gr.
16 ounces	1 pound (lb.) = 7000 gr.
14 pounds	1 stone
28 pounds	1 quarter
4 quarters	1 hundredweight (cwt.) = 112 lb.
20 hundredweight	1 ton = (2240 lb.)

TROY WEIGHT.

1 pennyweight (dwt.)	24 grains
480 grains	1 ounce

The only unit of troy weight which is now legal for use in trade in this country is the ounce Troy, and weighings of precious metals are made in multiples and decimals of this unit.

The term *carat* is not a unit of weight for precious metals, but is used to denote the quality of gold plate, etc., and is a figure indicating the number of 24ths of pure gold in the alloy, *e.g.*, a 9 carat gold ring consists of nine parts of pure gold and fifteen parts of base metals.

CAPACITY MEASURE.

4 gills	1 pint
2 pints	1 quart
4 quarts	1 gallon
2 gallons	1 peck
4 pecks	1 bushel
8 bushels	1 quarter
36 bushels	1 chaldron

The gallon, as the capacity standard, is based upon the pound.

1 gallon = 277·274 cubic inches.

APOTHECARIES' WEIGHT.

20 grains	1 scruple
3 scruples	1 drachm
8 drachms	1 ounce

While the apothecaries' ounce is the same as the troy ounce, there is no such thing as an apothecaries' or troy pound of 12 ounces. The troy pound has been obsolete for many years.

The Avoirdupois system is normally used for retailing chemicals in quantities of a ¼ ounce and over, whilst the metric system is used for the newer drugs. The metric system (with apothecaries' equivalents) is also used for formulæ and prescriptions in the *British Pharmacopœia*.

APOTHECARIES' FLUID MEASURE.

60 minims (min.)	1 fluid drachm
8 fluid drachms	1 fluid ounce
20 fluid ounces	1 pint

There are 437½ grains weight of distilled water at 62° F. in 1 fluid ounce.

LINEAR MEASURE.

1 nail	$\frac{1}{16}$ yard
1 link	7·92 inches
12 inches	1 foot
3 feet	1 yard
22 yards	1 chain
10 chains	1 furlong
8 furlongs	1 mile = 1760 yards

SQUARE MEASURE.

144 sq. inches	1 sq. foot
9 sq. feet	1 sq. yard = 1296 sq. inches
484 sq. yards	1 sq. chain
1210 sq. yards	1 rood
10 sq. chains	1 acre
4 roods	1 acre
4840 sq. yards	1 acre
640 acres	1 sq. mile

CUBIC OR SOLID MEASURE.

1728 cu. inches	1 cu. foot
27 cu. feet	1 cu. yard

The primary standards are the yard, pound, metre and kilogram.

The international yard = 0·9144 metre
The international pound = 0·45359237 kilogram

Note.—The Government announced in 1965 that it was encouraging the adoption of the metric system of weights and measures and by 1975 the greater part of British industry should have effected the change.

2. METRIC WEIGHTS AND MEASURES.

LINEAR MEASURE.

10 millimetres (mm.)	1 centimetre (cm.)
10 centimetres	1 decimetre (dm.)
10 decimetres	1 METRE (m.)
10 metres	1 dekametre (dam.)
10 dekametres	1 hectometre (hm.)
10 hectometres	1 kilometre (km.)

SURFACE OR SQUARE MEASURE.

100 centiares	1 are = 100 sq. metres
100 ares	1 hectare = 10,000 sq. metres

CAPACITY.

10 millilitres (ml.)	1 centilitre (cl.) = 10 c.c.
10 centilitres	1 decilitre (dl.) = 100 c.c.

CAPACITY (*cont.*).

10 decilitres	1 LITRE (lit.) = 1000 c.c.
10 litres	1 dekalitre (dal.)
10 dekalitres	1 hectolitre (hl.)
10 hectolitres	1 kilolitre (kl.) = 1 cu. metre

WEIGHT.

1000 micrograms	1 milligram (mg.)
10 milligrams	1 centigram (cg.)
10 centigrams	1 decigram (dg.)
10 decigrams	1 GRAM (gm.)
10 grams	1 dekagram (dag.)
10 dekagrams	1 hectogram (hg.)
10 hectograms	1 kilogram (kg.)
The metric carat	0·2 gram

3. IMPERIAL AND METRIC EQUIVALENTS.

LINEAR MEASURE.

IMPERIAL TO METRIC

inch	2·54 centimetres
foot	30·48 centimetres
yard	0·914399 metre
chain (22 yards)	20·1168 metres
furlong (220 yards)	201·168 metres
mile (8 furlongs)	1·6093 kilometres

METRIC TO IMPERIAL.

1 millimetre	0·03937 inch
1 centimetre	0·3937 inch
1 decimetre	3·937 inches
1 metre	39·370113 inches.
1 metre	3·280843 feet
1 metre	1·0936143 yards
1 dekametre	10·936 yards
1 hectometre	109·36 yards
1 kilometre	0·62137 mile

SQUARE MEASURE.

Imperial to Metric		Metric to Imperial	
1 sq. inch	6·4516 sq. cm.	1 sq. cm.	0·15500 sq. inch
1 sq. foot	9·2903 sq. decimetres	1 sq. metre	10·7639 sq. feet
1 sq. yard	0·836126 sq. metre	1 sq. metre	1·1960 sq. yards
1 rood (1210 sq. yd.)	10·117 ares	1 are (100 sq. metres)	119·60 sq. yards
1 acre (4840 sq. yd.)	0·40468 hectare	1 hectare (100 ares or 10,000 sq. metres)	2·4711 acres
1 sq. mile (640 acres)	259·00 hectares		

CUBIC MEASURE.

Imperial to Metric.		Metric to Imperial.	
1 cu. inch	16·387 cu. cm.	1 cu. centimetre	0·0610 cu. inch
1 cu. foot (1728 cu. in.)	0·028317 cu. metre	1 cu. decimetre (1000 cu. cm.)	61·024 cu. inches
1 cu. yard (27 cu. ft.)	0·764553 cu. metre	1 cu. metre	35·3148 cu. feet
		1 cu. metre	1·307954 cu. yards

CAPACITY MEASURE.

Imperial to Metric.		Metric to Imperial.	
1 gill	1·42 decilitres	1 centilitre	0·070 gill
1 pint	0·568 litre	1 decilitre	0·176 pint
1 quart	1·136 litres	1 litre	1·75980 pints
1 gallon	4·546 litres	1 dekalitre	2·200 gallons
1 peck (2 gallons)	9·092 litres	1 hectolitre	2·75 bushels
1 bushel (8 gallons)	3·637 dekalitres		
1 quarter (8 bushels)	2·909 hectolitres		

Note: The *litre* was abolished in 1964 as a *scientific unit* of volume.

APOTHECARIES' MEASURE.

Imperial to Metric.		Imperial to Metric.	
1 minim	0·059 millilitre	1 pint	0·568 litre
1 fluid scruple	1·184 millilitres	1 gallon (8 pints or 160 fluid ounces)	4·546 litres
1 fluid drachm (60 minims)	3·552 millilitres		
1 fluid ounce (8 drachms)	2·84123 centilitres		

AVOIRDUPOIS WEIGHT.

Imperial to Metric.		Metric to Imperial.	
1 grain	0·0648 gram	1 milligram	0·015 grain
1 dram	1·772 grams	1 centigram	0·154 grain
1 ounce (16 drams)	28·350 grams	1 decigram	1·543 grains
1 pound (16 ounces or 7000 grains)	0·45359243 kilogram	1 gram	15·432 grains
1 stone (14 lb.)	6·350 kilograms	1 dekagram	5·644 drams
1 quarter (28 lb.)	12·70 kilograms	1 hectogram	3·527 ounces
1 cwt. (112 lb.)	50·80 kilograms = 0·5080 quintal	1 kilogram (1000 gm.)	2·2046223 lb. or 15,432·3564 grains
1 ton (20 cwt.)	1·0160 tonnes or 1016 kilograms	1 myriagram (10 kg.)	22·046 lb.
		1 quintal (100 kg.)	1·968 cwt.
		1 tonne (1000 kg.)	0·9842 ton

TROY WEIGHT.

Imperial to Metric.		Metric to Imperial.	
1 grain	0·0648 gram	1 gram	0·03215 ounce troy
1 pennyweight (24 grains)	1·5552 grams	1 gram	15·432 grains
1 troy ounce (20 pennyweights)	31·1035 grams		

APOTHECARIES' WEIGHT.

Imperial to Metric.		Metric to Imperial.	
1 grain	0·0648 gram	1 gram	0·2572 drachm
1 scruple (20 grains)	1·296 grams	1 gram	0·7716 scruple
1 drachm (3 scruples)	3·888 grams	1 gram	15·432 grains
1 ounce (8 drachms)	31·1035 grams		

ELECTRICAL UNITS.

Until 31st December, 1947, the electrical units in general use were the so-called International Units, having been defined by the International Conference on Electrical Units held in London in 1908. These units were based upon specifications for a column of mercury and a silver voltameter which defined the International Ohm and International Ampere respectively, as units which for practical purposes could be accepted as equivalent to the fundamental theoretical units derived by multiplying the corresponding centimetre, gram, second (C.G.S.) electromagnetic unit by an integral power of ten. The International Units were not exactly equal to the fundamental units, and as the accuracy of all measurements increased, the discrepancy became increasingly troublesome.

The International Committee of Weights and Measures, which had succeeded the 1908 Conference, met in Paris in 1946 and decided to abolish the International Units, and as from 1st January 1948, to use throughout the world the fundamental units themselves, which are known as Absolute Units. The decision meant that the units in common use at that time changed by various amounts up to 5 parts in 10,000.

The International Units and corresponding Absolute Unit values are as follows:—

OHM. The International Ohm is the resistance offered to an unvarying current by a column of mercury of height 106·3 cm., 1 sq. mm. cross section and weight 14·4521 grams at the temperature of melting ice (0° C.).

1 International Ohm = 1·00049 Absolute Ohm.

1 Absolute Ohm = 10^9 C.G.S. electromagnetic units.

1,000,000 Ohms = 1 Megohm.

AMPERE. The International Ampere is that steady current which in flowing through a specified solution of silver nitrate, deposits silver on the cathode at the rate of 0·001118 gram per second.

1 International Ampere = 0·99985 Absolute Ampere.

1 Absolute Ampere = 0·1 C.G.S. electromagnetic unit.

VOLT. The International Volt is that steady electromotive force which applied to the ends of a conductor, whose resistance is 1 International Ohm, causes a current of 1 International Ampere to flow.

1 International Volt = 1·00034 Absolute Volt.

1 Absolute Volt = 10^8 C.G.S. electromagnetic units.

1000 volts = 1 Kilovolt.

WATT. Energy is supplied to a circuit at the rate of 1 International Watt if the current in it is 1 International Ampere and the pressure across it is 1 International Volt.

1 International Watt = 1·00019 Absolute Watt.

1000 watts = 1 Kilowatt.

1 Kilowatt-hour = 1000 watts supplied for a period of 1 hour = Board of Trade Unit.

COULOMB. The unit of quantity, and is the quantity passing in 1 second when the mean current is 1 ampere.

1 Coulomb = 0·1 electromagnetic unit.

HENRY. The unit of inductance, defined as the inductance of a circuit in which the induced electromotive force is 1 volt when the inducing current changes at the rate of 1 ampere per second.

1 International Henry = 1·00049 Absolute Henry.

1 Absolute Henry = 10^9 C.G.S. electromagnetic units.

FARAD. The unit of capacity, and is that capacity which is charged to a difference of pressure of 1 volt by 1 coulomb.

1,000,000 microfarads = 1 farad.

1 International Farad = 0·99951 Absolute Farad.

1 Absolute Farad = 10^9 C.G.S. electromagnetic unit.

STANDARD SIZES OF BRITISH BOOKS

Size	Abbreviation	Inches	Size	Abbreviation	Inches
Foolscap octavo	F8	$6\frac{3}{4} \times 4\frac{1}{4}$	Demy quarto	D4	$11\frac{1}{4} \times 8\frac{3}{4}$
Crown octavo	C8	$7\frac{1}{2} \times 5$	Medium quarto	M4	$12 \times 9\frac{1}{2}$
Large crown octavo	lC8*	$8 \times 5\frac{1}{4}$	Royal quarto	R4	$12\frac{1}{2} \times 10$
Demy octavo	D8	$8\frac{3}{4} \times 5\frac{5}{8}$	Imperial quarto	Imp4	15×11
Medium octavo	M8	$9\frac{1}{2} \times 6$	Foolscap folio	F fol	$13\frac{1}{2} \times 8\frac{1}{2}$
Royal octavo	R8	$10 \times 6\frac{1}{4}$	Crown folio	Cfol	15×10
Imperial octavo	Imp8	$11 \times 7\frac{1}{2}$	Royal folio	Rfol	$20 \times 12\frac{1}{2}$
Foolscap quarto	F4	$8\frac{1}{2} \times 6\frac{3}{4}$	Imperial folio	Impfol	$22 \times 15\frac{1}{2}$
Crown quarto	C4	$10 \times 7\frac{1}{2}$			

* l = large, s = small may precede some abbreviations.

THE BEAUFORT SCALE OF WIND FORCE

Beaufort number	*Wind*	*Effect on land*	*Speed*	
			M.p.h.	*Knots*
0	Calm	Smoke rises vertically	Less than 1	Less than 1
1	Light air	Direction shown by smoke but not by wind vanes	1–3	1–3
2	Light breeze	Wind felt on face; leaves rustle; wind vanes move	4–7	4–6
3	Gentle breeze	Leaves and twigs in motion; wind extends light flag	8–12	7–10
4	Moderate breeze	Raises dust, loose paper and moves small branches	13–18	11–16
5	Fresh breeze	Small trees in leaf begin to sway	19–24	17–21
6	Strong breeze	Large branches in motion; whistling in telegraph wires; difficulty with umbrellas	25–31	22–27
7	Moderate gale	Whole trees in motion; difficult to walk against wind	32–38	28–33
8	Fresh gale	Twigs break off trees; progress impeded	39–46	34–40
9	Strong gale	Slight structural damage occurs; chimney pots and slates blown off	47–54	41–47
10	Whole gale	Trees uprooted and considerable structural damage	55–63	48–56
11	Storm	Widespread damage, seldom experienced in England	64–75	57–65
12	Hurricane	Winds of this force only encountered in tropical revolving storms	Above 75	Above 65

HOW TO CORRECT PRINTERS' PROOFS

Marginal mark	Meaning	Corresponding mark in text
δ/	Delete (take out)	Cross through
δ (with close-up)	Delete and close-up	Above and below letters to be taken out
stet	Leave as printed (when words have been crossed out by mistake)	.... Under letters or words to remain
caps	Change to capital letters	Under letters or words to be altered
s.c.	Change to small capitals	Under letters or words to be altered
caps & s.c.	Use capital letters for initial letters and small capitals for rest of words	Under initial letters and under the rest of the words
l.c.	Change from capitals to lower case	Encircle letters to be altered
bold	Change to bold type	Under letters or words to be altered
ital.	Change to italics	Under letters or words to be altered
rom.	Change to roman type	Encircle words to be altered
w.f.	(Wrong fount.) Replace by letter of correct fount	Encircle letter to be altered
↻	Invert type	Encircle letter to be altered
×	Replace by similar but undamaged character	Encircle letter to be altered
γ	Insert (or substitute) superior figure or sign	(Or encircle letters or signs to be altered)
γ	Insert (or substitute) inferior figure or sign	(Or encircle letters or signs to be altered)
⁀‿	Close-up—delete space between letters	Linking words or letters
#	Insert space	
eq.#	Make spacing equal	Between words
less#	Reduce space	Between words
trs.	Transpose	Between letters or words, numbered when necessary
centre	Place in centre of line	Indicate position with ⌐ ¬
⌐	Move to the left	
¬	Move to the right	
n.p.	Begin a new paragraph	Before first word of new paragraph
run on	No fresh paragraph here	Between paragraphs
spell out	The abbreviation or figure to be spelt out in full	Encircle words or figures to be altered
⋏	(Caret mark.) Insert matter indicated in margin	⋏
ʹ/ ʹ/	Insert single quotation marks	⋏ ⋏
"/ "/	Insert double quotation marks	⋏ ⋏

THE LONDON SILVER MARKS

1598	1618	1638	1658	1678	1697
9	19	39	59	79	97
1600	20	40	Chas. II. 60	80	98
1	21	41	61	81	99
2	22	42	62	82	1700
Jas. I. 3	23	43	63	83	1
4	24	44	64	84	Anne. 2
5	Chas. I. 25	45	65	Jas. II. 85	3
6	26	46	66	86	4
7	27	47	67	87	5
8	28	48	68	88	6
9	29	Cmwth. 49	69	W. & M. 89	7
10	30	50	70	90	8
11	31	51	71	91	9
12	32	52	72	92	10
13	33	53	73	93	11
14	34	54	74	94	12
15	35	55	75	Wm III. 95	13
16	36	56	76	96	Geo. I. 14
17	37	57	77		15

PROVINCIAL SILVER MARKS

BIRMINGHAM .	1800		1900	
CHESTER . .	1701		1800	
EXETER . .	1601		1800	

See also **Hall-mark,** Gen. Information.

THE LONDON

A	Geo. I. 1716	a	1736	A	1756	a	1776	A	1796	a	1816
B	17	b	37	B	57	b	77	B	97	b	17
C	18	c	38	C	58	c	78	C	98	c	18
D	19	dd	39	D	59	d	79	D	99	d	19
E	20	e	40	E	Geo. III. 60	e	80	E	1800	e	Geo. IV. 20
F	21	f	41	F	61	f	81	F	1	f	21
G	22	g	42	G	62	g	82	G	2	g	22
H	23	h	43	H	63	h	83	H	3	h	23
I	24	i	44	I	64	i	84	I	4	i	24
K	25	k	45	K	65	k	85	K	5	k	25
L	26	l	46	L	66	l	86	L	6	l	26
M	Geo. II. 27	m	47	M	67	m	87	M	7	m	27
N	28	n	48	N	68	n	88	N	8	n	28
O	29	o	49	O	69	o	89	O	9	o	29
P	30	p	50	P	70	p	90	P	10	p	Will. IV. 30
Q	31	q	51	Q	71	q	91	Q	11	q	31
R	32	r	52	R	72	r	92	R	12	r	32
S	33	s	53	S	73	s	93	S	13	s	33
T	34	t	54	T	74	t	94	T	14	t	34
V	35	u	55	U	75	u	95	U	15	u	35

PROVINCIAL SILVER MARKS

NEWCASTLE . . 1702  1800 

SHEFFIELD . . 1800  1900 

YORK . . 1700  1800 

SILVER MARKS

A	1836	a	1856	A	1876	a	1896	a	1916	A	Ed. VIII. 1936
B	Vic. 37	b	57	B	77	b	97	b	17	B	Geo. VI 37
C	38	c	58	C	78	c	98	c	18	C	38
D	39	d	59	D	79	d	99	d	19	D	39
E	40	e	60	E	80	e	1900	e	20	E	40
F	41	f	61	F	81	f	Ed. VII. 1	f	21	F	41
G	42	g	62	G	82	g	2	g	22	G	42
H	43	h	63	H	83	h	3	h	23	H	43
I	44	i	64	I	84	i	4	i	24	I	44
K	45	k	65	K	85	k	5	k	25	K	45
L	46	l	66	L	86	l	6	l	26	L	46
M	47	m	67	M	87	m	7	m	27	M	47
N	48	n	68	N	88	n	8	n	28	N	48
O	49	o	69	O	89	o	9	o	29	O	49
P	50	p	70	P	90	p	Geo. V. 10	p	30	P	50
Q	51	q	71	Q	91	q	11	q	31	Q	51
R	52	r	72	R	92	r	12	r	32	R	Eliz. II. 52
S	53	s	73	S	93	s	13	s	33	S	53
T	54	t	74	T	94	t	14	t	34	T	54
U	55	v	75	U	95	u	15	u	35	U	55

SCOTTISH AND IRISH SILVER MARKS

EDINBURGH . . 1700  1800 

GLASGOW . . 1700  1800 

DUBLIN . . 1700  1800 

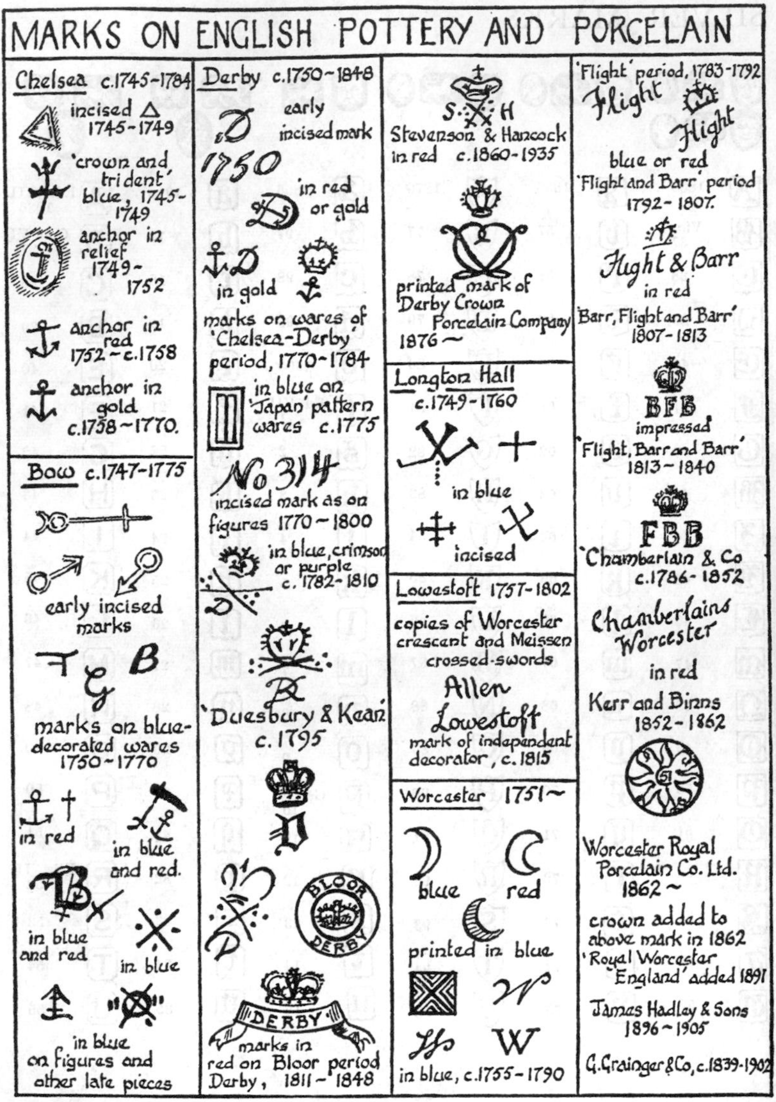

Many of the marks found on ceramics are merely the marks of painters and workman. Even when identified, they are not a sure guide to the place of manufacture, as these people would work in many different factories in the course of their careers. The throwers or "repairers" (the workers who assembled the various parts of figures, etc.) invariably used a mark scratched in the body of the ware prior to the biscuit-firing. These marks when *under* the glaze can safely be treated as genuine. A mark which has been ground in after firing, in order to deceive, will not have the characteristic burr or raised edge produced when soft clay is scratched.

Painters and gilders would generally use one of the colours in their palette or gilt to mark the wares upon which they worked. This was probably for the benefit of the management as payment was often on a piecework basis.

The marks used on English wares were applied in several different ways—by incising, impressing, painting, or by transfer-printing *under* the glaze

MARKS ON ENGLISH POTTERY AND PORCELAIN

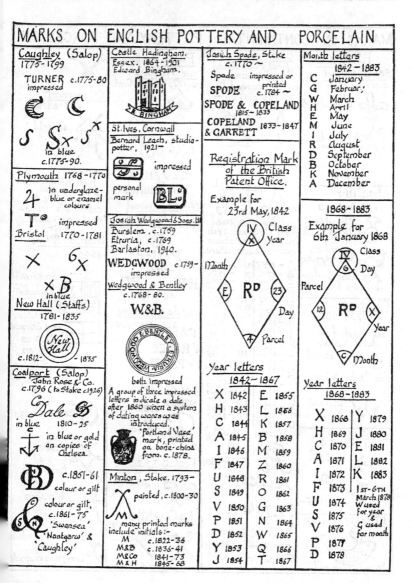

Caughley (Salop) 1775–1799

TURNER c.1775-80 impressed

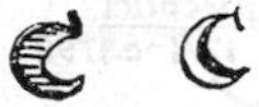

S Sx S in blue c.1775-90.

Plymouth 1768–1770

4 in underglaze-blue or enamel colours

T° impressed

Bristol 1770–1781

X 6X ×B in blue

New Hall (Staffs) 1781–1835

c.1812- -1835

Coalport (Salop) John Rose & Co. c.1796 (to Stoke c.1926)

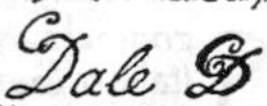

in blue 1810–25

in blue or gold on copies of Chelsea.

c.1851-61 colour or gilt

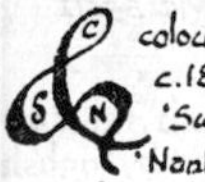

colour or gilt, c.1861-75 'Swansea' 'Nantgarw' & 'Caughley'

Castle Hedingham. Essex. 1864-1901 Edward Bingham.

St. Ives, Cornwall Bernard Leach, studio-potter, 1921–

impressed

personal mark

Josiah Wedgwood & Sons Ltd. Burslem, c.1759 Etruria, c.1769 Barlaston, 1940.

WEDGWOOD c.1759– impressed

Wedgwood & Bentley c.1768-80.

W.&B.

both impressed

A group of three impressed letters indicate a date after 1860 when a system of dating wares was introduced.

'Portland Vase' mark, printed on bone-china from c.1878.

Minton, Stoke. 1793–

painted, c.1800-30

many printed marks include initials:-

M	c.1822-36
M&B	c.1836-41
M&Co	1841-73
M&H	1845-68

Josiah Spode, Stoke c.1770–

Spode impressed or printed c.1784–

SPODE

SPODE & COPELAND 1815–1833

COPELAND & GARRETT 1833–1847

Registration Mark of the British Patent Office.

Example for 23rd May, 1842

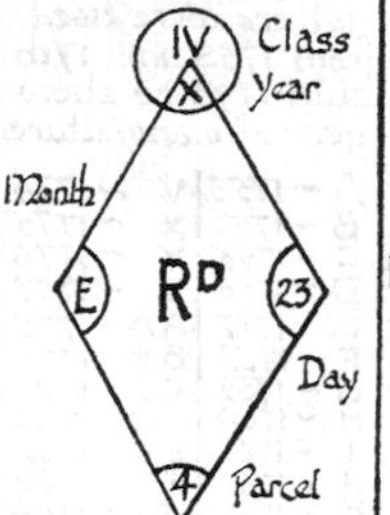

Year letters 1842–1867

X	1842	E	1855
H	1843	L	1856
C	1844	K	1857
A	1845	B	1858
I	1846	M	1859
F	1847	Z	1860
U	1848	R	1861
S	1849	O	1862
V	1850	G	1863
P	1851	N	1864
D	1852	W	1865
Y	1853	Q	1866
J	1854	T	1867

Month letters 1842–1883

C	January
G	February
W	March
H	April
E	May
M	June
I	July
R	August
D	September
B	October
K	November
A	December

1868–1883

Example for 6th January 1868

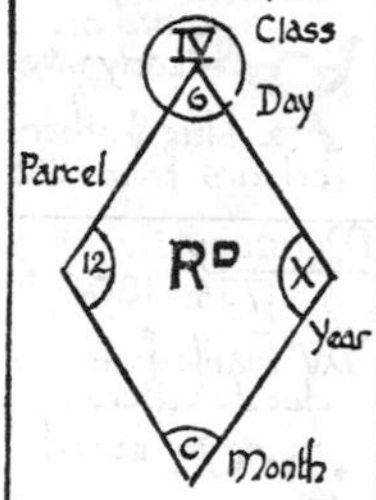

Year letters 1868–1883

X	1868	Y	1879
H	1869	J	1880
C	1870	E	1881
A	1871	L	1882
I	1872	K	1883
F	1873		
U	1874		
S	1875		
V	1876		
P	1877		
D	1878		

1st–6th March 1878 W used for year & G used for month

a blue (also in green after 1850). Marking by ainting, transfer-printing, or stencilling *over* the laze in enamel colours is always liable to be raudulent as these types of mark can be added at ny time after the piece has been made.

From 1842–83 many manufacturers' wares were arked with the "diamond-mark", illustrated bove. This was an indication that the design ad been registered with the British Patent Office. eramics was Class IV, indicated in the topmost section of the mark. This gave copyright protection for three years. After 1883 the mark was written as a number, *e.g.*, Rd. No. 12345.

A further indication of late wares is the inclusion of the word "England" in the mark. This was necessary to comply with the American McKinley Tariff Act of 1891. The full term "Made in England" is an indication of 20th century manufacture.

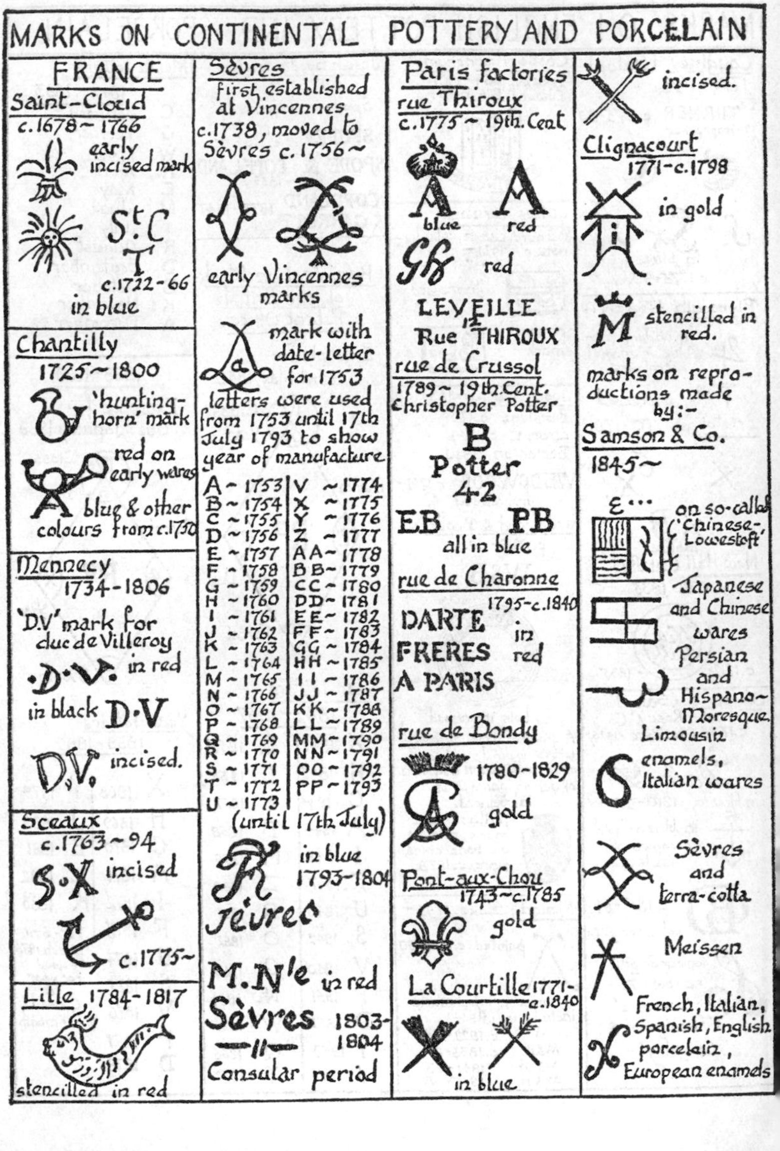

It was not until the adoption on Meissen porcelain in 1723 of the "K.P.M." and in 1724 of the cross-swords (from the arms of Saxony) that marks began to be used at all regularly in Europe. The placing of the mark underneath and the use of blue are clear indications that the Chinese model was being followed. The Meissen practice was then adopted by other German and, indeed, by most porcelain factories of repute.

Throughout the 18th century the practice was never regularised, and except for a brief period i France from 1766, and two years later in the Dutc town of Delft, there was no compulsory marking o wares. The factories of repute, proud of the productions, added a recognised mark and eve used it, as at Nymphenburg, as part of the decora tion. Their imitators left their wares unmarke or employed a mark likely to be mistaken for more famous one: Weesp and Tournay bot adopted a version of the Meissen crossed-sword

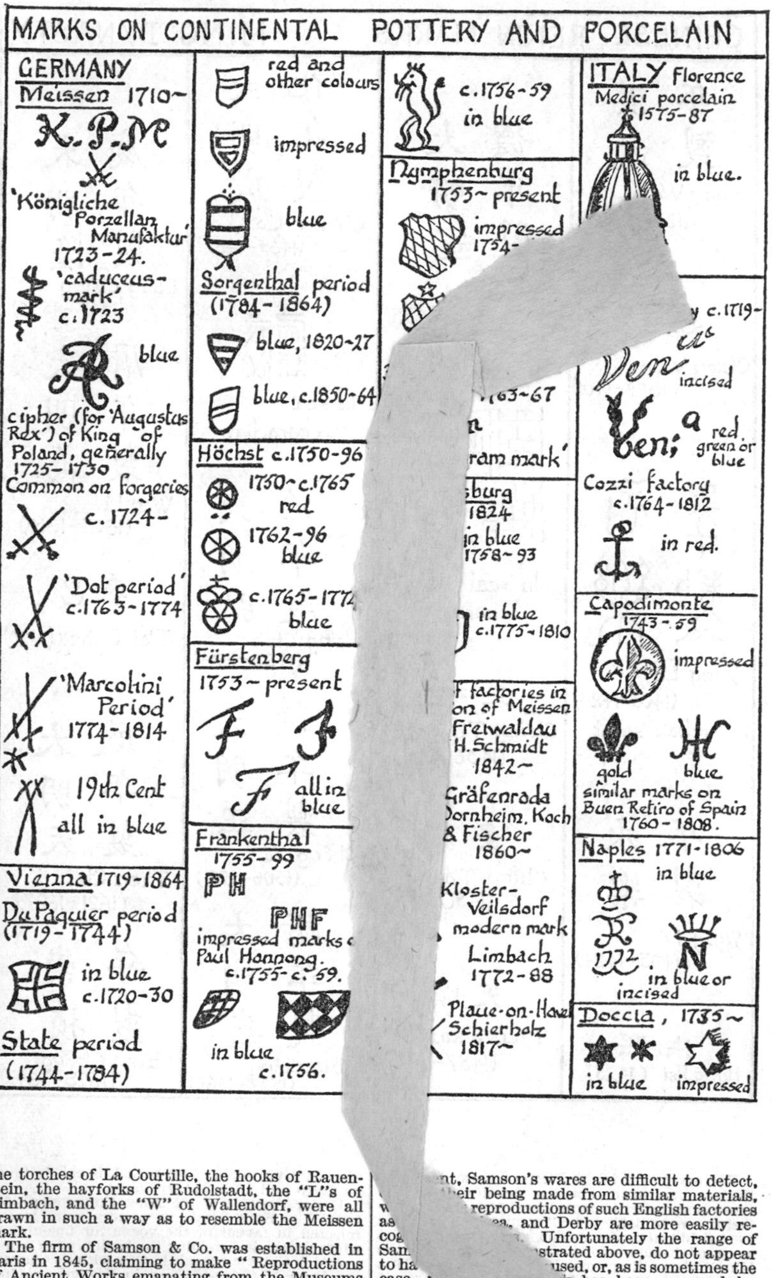

the torches of La Courtille, the hooks of Rauenstein, the hayforks of Rudolstadt, the "L"s of Limbach, and the "W" of Wallendorf, were all drawn in such a way as to resemble the Meissen mark.

The firm of Samson & Co. was established in Paris in 1845, claiming to make " Reproductions of Ancient Works emanating from the Museums and from Private Collections ". When imitating the true hard-paste porcelain of the Far East or the

...nt, Samson's wares are difficult to detect, ...eir being made from similar materials, w... reproductions of such English factories as ...ea, and Derby are more easily recog... Unfortunately the range of Sam... strated above, do not appear to ha... used, or, as is sometimes the case, t... has been removed by grinding ... ay with acid, and a replica of a ... mark added.

CHINESE REIGN MARKS MING DYNASTY

洪武年製
Hung Wu (1368–1398)

建文
Chien Wên (1399–1402)

Yung Lo (1403–1424)
In archaic script

永樂年製
Yung Lo (1403–1424)

洪熙
Hung Hsi (1425)

大明宣德年製
Hsüan Tê (1426–1435)

In seal characters

正統
Chêng T'ung (1436–1449)

景泰
Ching T'ai (1450–1457)

天順
T'ien Shun (1457–1464)

大明成化年製
Ch'êng Hua (1465–1487)

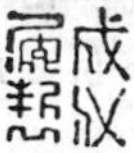

In seal characters

大明弘治年製
Hung Chih (1488–1505)

大明正德年製
Chêng Tê (1506–1521)

大明嘉靖年製
Chia Ching (1522–1566)

大明隆慶年製
Lung Ch'ing (1567–1572)

大明萬曆年製
Wan Li (1573–1619)

泰昌
T'ai Ch'ang (1620)

大明天啟年製
T'ien Ch'i (1621–1627)

崇禎年製
Ch'ung Chêng (1628–1643)

Factory marks in the Western sense are practically unknown on Chinese porcelain wares, while those purporting to record the period of manufacture are so liable to be "commemorative", or even deliberately fraudulent, as to be a frequent cause of dispute among students. Marks of the Ming Chinese Emperors, Hsüan Tê, Ch'êng Hua and Chia Ching are commonly found on wares of the reign of the Ch'ing Emperor K'ang Hsi, while the reign name of K'ang Hsi himself, rare on the abundant porcelain of his period, is chiefly found on 19th- and 20th-century wares.

Under the rule of the Ming Emperors (1368–1644) the Sung ideals in pottery were largely rejected in favour of the vogue for fine-grained white porcelain heralding the beginning of a new period in Chinese ceramic history with its centre in the town of Ching-tê Chên in Kiangsi province where a new Imperial factory was started in 1369 with a prolific output of early Ming blue-and-white

CHINESE REIGN MARKS CH'ING DYNASTY

Drawn by J. P. Cushion, Victoria and Albert Museum.

and fine enamel-painted porcelain both for the court and later for general use and export.

Following the fall of the Ming Dynasty in 1644 their declining culture was revived by the Ch'ing Emperor K'ang Hsi (1662—1722) who was a great patron of the arts. The European influence of the French and Netherlandish Jesuits at his courts is seen in the Baroque character of the early Ch'ing porcelain.

There was a backward-looking tendency during the reigns of Yung-Chêng (1723–35) and Ch'ien Lung (1736–95) when exact copies of the classical Sung wares and the early Ming painted porcelain were made.

The Imperial porcelain of the 19th century was as a rule carefully and weakly correct in following earlier styles and models. The factory was burnt in 1853 by the T'ai-ping rebels and hardly recovered before the 1911 revolution ended the Dynasty.

BANK AND PUBLIC HOLIDAYS

In *England, Wales, N. Ireland* and *The Channel Islands* there are Bank Holidays on Easter Monday, Whit Monday, first (or last) Monday in August, Boxing Day (first weekday after Christmas). The Channel Islands have in addition special Bank Holidays on New Year's Day and Liberation Day.

Note:—There are to be further experiments with Bank Holidays, including separation of Bank Holiday from Whit Monday in 1967 and a Bank Holiday in Sept. instead of August in 1968.

	1966.	1967.
Easter Monday .	Apr. 11	Mar. 27
Whit Monday . .	May 30	May 15

N. Ireland has a special holiday on St. Patrick's Day, March 17th, and on July 12th (commemorating the Battle of the Boyne, 1690).

The Queen's birthday (when decreed) is observed in the Customs and certain other Government establishments as a holiday.

In *Scotland* Bank Holidays are observed on New Year's Day, first Monday in May, first (or last) Monday in August. There are also special Spring and Autumn holidays in most towns in Scotland.

THE SEASONS

1966.

Vernal Equinox—Spring begins Mar. 21, 2 a.m.
Summer Solstice—Summer begins June 21, 9 p.m.
Autumnal Equinox—Autumn begins Sept. 23, 12 noon
Winter Solstice—Winter begins Dec. 22, 7 a.m.

1967.

Vernal Equinox—Spring begins Mar. 21, 7.37 a.m.
Summer Solstice—Summer begins June 22, 2.23 a.m.
Autumnal Equinox—Autumn begins Sept. 23, 5.38 p.m.
Winter Solstice—Winter begins Dec. 22, 1.17 p.m.

(These times are G.M.T.)

QUARTER DAYS

ENGLAND, WALES, AND N. IRELAND.

Lady Day	March 25	Michaelmas	September 29
Midsummer	June 24	Christmas	December 25

SCOTLAND.

Candlemas	February 2	Lammas	August 1
Whitsun	May 15	Martinmas	November 11

HALF QUARTER DAYS

ENGLAND

February 8.	May 9.	August 11.	November 11.

GAME

Game is defined under the game laws as including hares, pheasants, partridges, grouse, heath or moor game, black game, deer, rabbits and (in Scotland) ptarmigan. The close times for game are as follows (the dates given are inclusive).

Black (or Heath) Game	Dec. 11 to Aug. 19 (Aug. 31 in Somerset, Devon, and New Forest).
Grouse (or Moor Game) and (in Scotland) Ptarmigan . . .	Dec. 11 to Aug. 11.
Partridge	Feb. 2 to Aug. 31.
Pheasant	Feb. 2 to Sept. 30.

Deer, hares and rabbits are also protected to a limited extent.

CLOSE TIMES FOR SPORTING BIRDS

Birds for which the close season is Feb. 1 to Aug. 31 (inclusive):—

Godwit, bar-tailed; Plover, grey; Coot; Redshank, common; Curlew (other than Stone Curlew); Moorhen; Whimbrel; Plover, golden

Birds for which the close season is Feb. 1 to Aug. 31 (inclusive) (except below high water mark when it is Feb. 21 to Aug. 31 (inclusive):

Wild duck of the following species:—

Common pochard	Long-tailed duck	Teal
Common Scoter	Mallard	Tufted Duck
Gadwall	Pintail	Velvet Scoter
Garganey Teal	Scaup-duck	
Goldeneye	Shoveler	Wigeon

Wild geese of the following species:—

Bean-goose	Grey Lag Goose	White-fronted Goose
Canada Goose	Pink-footed Goose	

Birds for which the close season is Feb. 1 to Sept. 30 (inclusive):—

Capercaillie; Woodcock (in Scotland Feb. 1 to Aug. 31).

Birds for which the close season is Feb. 1 to Aug. 11 (inclusive):—

Snipe, common; Snipe, jack.

THE COUNTRY CODE

GUARD AGAINST THE RISK OF FIRE. Great damage is done every year to crops, plantations, woodlands, and heaths. A match or cigarette thrown away or a pipe carelessly knocked out, picnic fires not properly put out or lighted near dry crops, can quickly start a blaze.

FASTEN ALL GATES. If animals get out of a field they stray. As a result they may do serious damage to crops, suffer injury on the roads, or eat food that is harmful.

KEEP DOGS UNDER CONTROL. Animals are easily frightened, even by small, playful dogs. Stillbirths may be the result.

KEEP TO THE PATHS ACROSS FARM LAND. Crops are damaged by treading; flattened crops are difficult to harvest. Grass is a valuable crop.

AVOID DAMAGING FENCES, HEDGES, AND WALLS. If these are damaged, gaps will be caused. Where a man goes, an animal may follow.

LEAVE NO LITTER. Litter is not just unsightly, but often a danger as well. Broken glass and tins may injure animals and harm machinery

SAFEGUARD WATER SUPPLIES. Countrymen often depend on wells and streams for water for themselves and for their animals.

PROTECT WILD LIFE, PLANTS, AND TREES. Wild animals should not be disturbed, plants uprooted, or trees treated roughly.

GO CAREFULLY ON COUNTRY ROADS. If there is no footpath, walkers are generally safer on the right, facing on-coming traffic. Care and patience are needed by motorists when passing farm animals.

RESPECT THE LIFE OF THE COUNTRYSIDE. Many of the machines and much of the business stock on which the farmer depends for his livelihood have to be kept in the open. Take care not to damage them.

SUNRISE AND SUNSET, LONDON 1966–7

(These times are given in G.M.T. throughout.)

Sundays, 1966 Date		Sunrise a.m.	Sunset p.m.
July	3	3.48	8.19
	10	3.55	8.15
	17	4.02	8.09
	24	4.11	8.01
	31	4.21	7.50
August	7	4.32	7.38
	14	4.43	7.25
	21	4.54	7.11
	28	5.05	6.56
September	4	5.17	6.41
	11	5.28	6.25
	18	5.38	6.09
	29	5.50	5.53
October	2	6.02	5.37
	9	6.13	5.21
	16	6.25	5.06
	23	6.37	4.51
	30	6.49	4.37
November	6	7.01	4.26
	13	7.13	4.14
	20	7.26	4.05
	27	7.37	3.58
December	4	7.47	3.53
	11	7.55	3.51
	18	8.01	3.52
	25	8.04	3.55

Sundays, 1967 Date		Sunrise a.m.	Sunset p.m.
January	1	8.05	4.01
	8	8.04	4.09
	15	7.59	4.19
	22	7.52	4.31
	29	7.43	4.44
February	5	7.32	4.56
	12	7.21	5.09
	19	7.07	5.22
	26	6.52	5.34
March	5	6.37	5.47
	12	6.22	5.59
	19	6.06	6.11
	26	5.50	6.23
April	2	5.35	6.34
	9	5.19	6.46
	16	5.03	6.58
	23	4.48	7.10
	30	4.35	7.20
May	7	4.22	7.32
	14	4.10	7.43
	21	4.00	7.54
	28	3.53	8.02
June	4	3.47	8.10
	11	3.43	8.16
	18	3.42	8.20
	25	3.44	8.21

Sundays, 1967 Date		Sunrise a.m.	Sunset p.m.
July	2	3.48	8.20
	9	3.54	8.16
	16	4.01	8.10
	23	4.10	8.02
	30	4.20	7.42
August	6	4.31	7.40
	13	4.42	7.27
	20	4.52	7.14
	27	5.04	6.58
September	3	5.15	6.43
	10	5.26	6.27
	17	5.37	6.11
	24	5.48	5.55
October	1	6.00	5.39
	8	6.11	5.24
	15	6.23	5.08
	22	6.35	4.53
	29	6.48	4.39
November	5	6.59	4.27
	12	7.12	4.16
	19	7.24	4.06
	26	7.35	3.59
December	3	7.46	3.54
	10	7.54	3.51
	17	8.00	3.52
	24	8.04	3.55
	31	8.06	4.00

MOON'S PHASES, 1966–7

(These times are given in G.M.T. throughout.)

1966.

New Moon	May	20	9.42 a.m.
First Quarter		27	8.50 a.m.
Full Moon	June	3	7.40 a.m.
Last Quarter		11	4.58 a.m.
New Moon		18	8.09 p.m.
First Quarter		25	1.22 p.m.
Full Moon	July	2	7.36 p.m.
Last Quarter		10	9.43 p.m.
New Moon		18	4.30 a.m.
First Quarter		24	7.00 p.m.
Full Moon	August	1	9.05 a.m.
Last Quarter		9	12.56 p.m.
New Moon		16	11.48 a.m.
First Quarter		23	3.02 a.m.
Full Moon		31	12.14 a.m.
Last Quarter	September	8	2.07 a.m.
New Moon		14	7.13 p.m.
First Quarter		21	2.25 p.m.
Full Moon		29	4.47 p.m.
Last Quarter	October	7	1.08 p.m.
New Moon		14	3.52 a.m.
First Quarter		21	5.34 a.m.
Full Moon		29	10.00 a.m.
Last Quarter	November	5	10.18 p.m.
New Moon		12	2.26 p.m.
First Quarter		20	12.20 a.m.
Full Moon		28	2.40 a.m.
Last Quarter	December	5	6.22 a.m.
New Moon		12	3.13 a.m.
First Quarter		19	9.41 p.m.
Full Moon		27	5.43 p.m.

1967.

Last Quarter	January	3	2.19 p.m.
New Moon		10	6.06 p.m.
First Quarter		18	7.41 p.m.
Full Moon		26	6.40 a.m.
Last Quarter	February	1	11.03 p.m.
New Moon		9	10.44 a.m.
First Quarter		17	3.56 p.m.
Full Moon		24	5.43 p.m.
Last Quarter	March	3	9.10 a.m.
New Moon		11	4.30 a.m.
First Quarter		19	8.31 p.m.
Full Moon		26	3.21 a.m.
Last Quarter	April	1	8.58 p.m.
New Moon		9	10.20 p.m.
First Quarter		17	8.48 p.m.
Full Moon		24	12.03 p.m.
Last Quarter	May	1	10.32 a.m.
New Moon		9	2.55 p.m.
First Quarter		17	5.18 a.m.
Full Moon		23	8.22 p.m.
Last Quarter		31	1.52 a.m.
New Moon	June	8	5.13 a.m.
First Quarter		15	11.12 a.m.
Full Moon		22	4.57 a.m.
Last Quarter		29	6.39 p.m.
New Moon	July	7	5.00 p.m.
First Quarter		14	3.53 p.m.
Full Moon		21	2.39 p.m.
Last Quarter		29	12.14 p.m.
New Moon	August	6	2.48 a.m.
First Quarter		12	8.44 p.m.
Full Moon		20	2.27 a.m.
Last Quarter		28	5.35 a.m.
New Moon	September	4	11.37 a.m.
First Quarter		11	3.06 a.m.
Full Moon		18	4.59 p.m.
Last Quarter		26	9.44 p.m.
New Moon	October	3	8.24 p.m.
First Quarter		10	12.11 p.m.
Full Moon		18	10.11 a.m.
Last Quarter		26	12.04 p.m.
New Moon	November	2	5.48 a.m.
First Quarter		9	1.00 a.m.
Full Moon		17	4.52 a.m.
Last Quarter		25	12.23 a.m.
New Moon	December	1	4.10 p.m.
First Quarter		8	5.57 p.m.
Full Moon		16	11.21 p.m.
Last Quarter		24	10.48 a.m.
New Moon		31	3.38 a.m.

ONE HOUR must be ADDED to the above times when SUMMER TIME is in operation.

LIGHTING-UP TIME is from half an hour after local sunset to half an hour before local sunrise throughout the year.

FOREIGN CURRENCIES IN RELATION TO STERLING

Country	Currency	Parity[1] value to £ at 16.1.66	Approximate rate at 12.3.66 or latest date available
Argentine	Peso		525.00[4]
Australia	Pound	1·25[7]	(A£1·25) A$2·50
Austria	Schilling	72·80	72·235
Belgium/Lux.	Franc	140·00	139·175
Bolivia	Peso Boliviano		33·063[4]
Brazil	Cruzeiro		6,195·00[4]
British Honduras	Dollar	4·00	4.00
Burma	Kyat	13·333	13·333
Canada	Dollar	3·027	3·009
Ceylon	Rupee	13·333	13·31
Chile	Escudo		12·20[2]
China	Peoples Bank $		6·893
Colombia	Peso		49·50[4]
Congo (Leopoldville)	Franc		504·00(Imp.) 420·00(Exp.)
Costa Rica	Colon	18·55	18·55
Cuba	Peso		2·796
Czechoslovakia	Koruna		20·16[3]
Denmark	Krone	19·34	19·283
Dominican Republic	Peso	2·80	2·796
Ecuador	Sucre	50·40	52·70[4]
Egypt (U.A.R.)	Pound	0·975	1·22
El Salvador	Colon	7·00	7·04[4]
Ethiopia	Dollar	7·00	7·00
Finland	Markka	8·96	9·00
France	Franc	13·824	13·704
French monetary a. in C. and W. Africa and Malagasy	C.F.A. Franc		685·188
Germany (Fed. Rep.)	D. Mark	11·20	11·216
Greece	Drachma	84·00	83·75
Guatemala	Quetzal	2·80	2·796
Guyana	Dollar	4·80	4·80
Haiti	Gourde	14·00	13·978
Honduras Rep.	Lempira	5·60	5·591
Hong Kong	Dollar	16·00	16·067
Iceland	Krona	120·40	120·64
India	Rupee	13·333	13·333
Indonesia	New Rupiah=1,000 old		28·—[5]
Iran	Rial	212·10	212·10
Iraq	Dinar	1·00	1·00
Israel	Pound	8·40	8·40
Italy	Lire	1,750·00	1,747·125
Jamaica	Pound	1·00	1·00
Japan	Yen	1,008·00	1,012·25
Jordan	Dinar	1·00	1·00
Lebanon	Pound	6·136	8·65[4]
Malaysia	Dollar	8·571	8·571
Morocco	Dirham	14·169	14·064
Mexico	Peso	35·00	34·92
Netherlands	Guilder	10·136	10·11
Netherlands W.I.	Guilder	5·28	5·25
New Zealand	Pound	1·007	1·007
Nicaragua	Cordoba	19·60	19·569[4]
Norway	Kroner	20·00	19·99
Pakistan	Rupee	13·333	13·333
Panama	Balbao	2·80	2·796
Paraguay	Guarani		351·07[4]
Peru	Sol		74·92[4]
Philippines	Peso	10·92	10·90[4]
Poland	Zloty		11·20[6]
Portugal	Escudo	80·50	80·17
Rwanda	Franc		139·175[3,5]
South Africa	Rand	2·00	2·00
Spain	Peseta	168·000	167·50
Sweden	Kronor	14·485	14·406
Switzerland	Franc		12·138
Syria	Pound	6·136	11·50[4]
Thailand	Baht	58·24	57·97
Trinidad & Tobago	T.T. $	4·80	4·80
Tunisia	Dinar	1·47	1·45
Turkey	£ (Lira)	25·20	25·31
U.S.A.	Dollar	2·80	2·796
Uruguay	Peso	20·72	183·00[4]
Venezuela	Bolivar	9·38	12·54[4,5]
Yugoslavia	New Dinar=100 old		35·00

[1] Established under agreement with the I.M.F which requires that the par value of the currency of each member be expressed in terms of gold or U.S. Dollars.
[2] Rate which in general is applicable to financial transactions. [3] Official rate. [4] Free market rate.
[5] Not necessarily the effective rate for all transfers.
[6] Basic rate.
[7] With effect from 14.2.66 the Australian pound has been replaced by the Australia dollar ($A) as the new currency unit. The new unit which is divisible into 100 cents, is equivalent to 10 shillings of the old unit.

THERMOMETER COMPARISONS

Centigrade, 100°	Fahrenheit, 212°	Centigrade, 100°	Fahrenheit 212°
95	203	20	68
90	194	15·5	60
85	185	12·8	55
78·9	174	10	50
75	167	7·2	45
70	158	5	41
65	149	1·7	35
60	140	0	32
55	131	− 1·1	30
52·8	127	− 5	23
50	122	− 6·7	20
45	113	− 10	14
42·2	108	− 12·2	10
40	104	− 15	5
36·7	98	− 17·8	0
35	95	− 20	− 4
32·2	90	− 25	− 13
30	86	− 30	− 22
26·7	80	− 35	− 31
25	77	− 40	− 40

To reduce Fahrenheit to Centigrade, subtract 32 degrees and multiply by 5/9; to reduce Centigrade to Fahrenheit, multiply by 9/5 and add 32 degrees.

An alternative method, perhaps easier to remember, is to add 40 to the given figure, multiply by 5/9 (°F to °C) or 9/5 (°C to °F) and subtract 40.

ROMAN NUMERALS

I	1	LXX	70
II	2	LXXX	80
III	3	LXXXVIII	88
IV	4	XC	90
V	5	IC	99
VI	6	C	100
VII	7	CX	110
VIII	8	CXI	111
IX	9	CXC	190
X	10	CC	200
XI	11	CCXX	220
XII	12	CCC	300
XIII	13	CCCXX	320
XIV	14	CD	400
XV	15	D	500
XVI	16	DC	600
XVII	17	DCC	700
XVIII	18	DCCC	800
XIX	19	CM	900
XX	20	XM	990
XXX	30	M	1000
XL	40	MD	1500
L	50	MDCCC	1800
LV	55	MCMLXI	1961
LX	60	MM	2000

RUSSIAN ALPHABET

А а	a	Р р	r
Б б	b	С с	s
В в	v	Т т	t
Г г	g	У у	u
Д д	d	Ф ф	f ph
Е е	e	Х х	kh[1]
Ж ж	zh	Ц ц	ts
З з	z	Ч ч	ch[2]
И и й	i	Ш ш	sh
К к	k	Щ щ	shch[3]
Л л	l	Ы ы	y[4]
М м	m	Э э	e[5]
Н н	n	Ю ю	yu[6]
О о	o	Я я	ya
П п	p	Ѳ ѳ	f

[1] as in " loch ". [4] as in " bit ".
[2] as in " church ". [5] as in " epic ".
[3] as in " Ashchurch ". [6] as in " you ".

UNIVERSITY DEGREES—COLOURS OF HOODS

Aberdeen

M.A.	Black silk, lined with white silk.
D.Litt.	Scarlet cloth, lined with white silk.
Ph.D.	Scarlet cloth lined with black ribbed silk, the ribs running horizontally.
B.Sc.	Black silk, lined with green silk.
B.Sc.Agr.	Black silk, edged with green silk.
B.Sc.For.	Black silk edged with waved green silk.
B.Sc.Eng.	Black silk edged with green silk and bordered inside, within the green edging, with white cloth (½″)
D.Sc.	Scarlet cloth, lined with green silk.
B.D.	Black silk, lined with purple silk, and bordered inside with white silk (1″)
D.D.	Scarlet cloth, lined with purple silk.
B.L.	Black silk edged with pale blue silk.
LL.B.	Black silk, lined with pale blue silk.
LL.D.	Scarlet cloth, lined with pale blue silk.
M.B., Ch.B	Black silk, lined with crimson silk.
M.D.	Scarlet cloth, lined with crimson silk.
Ch.M.	White silk, lined with crimson silk.
Ed.B.	Black silk edged with white silk.
M.Sc.	White silk lined with green silk.

Note:—All the hoods of this University are of uniform pear shape of a cloth or silk foundation and lined or edged with the colour peculiar to the Faculty or Degree.

Belfast, The Queen's University

B.A.	Black ribbed silk edged with white fur and the neck edged with blue watered silk.
M.A.	Black ribbed silk lined with blue silk and edged with blue watered silk.
D.Lit.	Scarlet superfine cloth lined with white silk and edged with blue watered silk.
B.D.	Black ribbed silk lined with white silk and edged with blue watered silk.
D.D.	Scarlet superfine cloth lined with black silk and edged with blue watered silk.
LL.B.	Black ribbed silk lined with pink silk and edged with blue watered silk.
LL.M.	Royal blue ribbed silk, lined with pink silk and edged with blue watered silk.
LL.D.	Scarlet superfine cloth lined with pink silk and edged with blue watered silk.
M.B., B.Ch., B.A.O.	Black ribbed silk lined with scarlet silk and edged with blue watered silk.
M.Ch.	Red ribbed silk lined with white silk and edged with blue watered silk.
M.D.	Scarlet superfine cloth lined with scarlet silk and edged with blue watered silk.
M.A.O.	Black ribbed silk lined with purple silk and edged with blue watered silk
B.Ed.	Black ribbed silk lined with mauve silk and edged with blue watered silk.
B.Mus.	Blue silk lined with white silk and edged with blue watered silk.
D.Mus.	Scarlet superfine cloth lined with blue silk and edged with blue watered silk.
Ph.D.	Scarlet superfine cloth lined with violet silk and edged with blue watered silk.
B.Sc.	Black ribbed silk lined with green silk and edged with blue watered silk.
M.Sc.	Red ribbed silk lined with green silk and edged with blue watered silk
D.Sc.	Scarlet superfine cloth lined with green silk and edged with blue watered silk.
B.Sc.(Econ.)	Black ribbed silk lined with rose pink silk and edged with blue watered silk.
M.Sc.(Econ.)	Rose pink silk lined with white silk and edged with blue watered silk.
B.D.S.	Black ribbed silk lined with dove-grey silk and edged with blue watered silk.
M.D.S.	Scarlet ribbed silk lined with dove-grey silk and edged with blue watered silk.
B.Agr.	Black ribbed silk lined with primrose silk and edged with blue watered silk.
M.Agr.	Red ribbed silk lined with primrose silk and edged with blue watered silk.

Note:—Bachelors' and Masters' hoods are of the simple shape and Doctors' of the full shape. All the hoods have the neck portion at least edged with the pale blue watered silk peculiar to this University.

Birmingham

B.A.	Black ribbed silk lined for 3″ with electric blue watered silk.
M.A.	Black ribbed silk fully lined with electric blue watered silk
B.D.	Black ribbed silk lined with cobalt blue watered silk.
D.D.	Scarlet superfine cloth lined with cobalt blue watered silk.
LL.B.	Black ribbed silk lined for 3″ with bronze green watered silk.
LL.M.	Black ribbed silk fully lined with bronze green watered silk.
LL.D.	Scarlet superfine cloth lined with bronze green watered silk.
M.B., Ch.B.	Black ribbed silk lined for 3″ with cardinal watered silk.
Ch.M.	Black ribbed silk fully lined with cardinal watered silk.
M.D.	Scarlet superfine cloth lined with cardinal watered silk.
B.Mus.	Black ribbed silk lined for 3″ with orange watered silk.
M.Mus.	Black ribbed silk lined orange watered silk.
D.Mus.	Scarlet superfine cloth lined with orange watered silk.
Ph.D.	Crimson cloth, lined with the watered silk of the Faculty colour.
B.Sc.	Black ribbed silk lined for 3″ with grey watered silk.
M.Sc.	Black ribbed silk fully lined with grey watered silk.
D.Sc.	Scarlet superfine cloth lined with grey watered silk.
D.Litt.	Scarlet superfine cloth lined with electric blue watered silk.
B.D.S.	Black ribbed silk lined for 3″ with dark red watered silk.
M.D.S.	Black ribbed silk fully lined with dark red watered silk.
B.Com.	Black ribbed silk lined for 3″ with terra-cotta watered silk.
M.Com.	Black ribbed silk fully lined with terra-cotta watered silk.
B.Soc.Sc., M.Soc.Sc.	Follow the scheme for Bachelors and Masters above with 3″ of the watered silk of the Faculty colour.
D.Soc.Sc.	Scarlet superfine cloth lined with terra-cotta watered silk, bound with grey silk at top edge.

Note:—All hoods are of the full shape, similar to London, all the capes having well-rounded corners.

Bristol

B.A., M.A., LL.B., LL.M., LL.D., M.B., Ch.B., Ch.M., M.D., B.Mus., D.Mus., Ph.D., B.Sc., M.Sc., D.Sc., D.Litt., B.D.S., M.D.S., B.Sc.(Dom.Sc.), B.V.Sc.

All hoods are of the full shape, similar to Cambridge. Hoods are made of the University's special red stuff or silk Bachelor's hoods are partly lined with a silk of a somewhat lighter shade of University red. Masters' hoods are fully lined with white silk, and Doctors' are fully lined with salmon-coloured silk. The M.B., Ch.B. hood is fully lined with light red silk and edged inside the hood proper with ¾″ of white silk. The LL.B. hood is fully lined with the lighter shade of University red and edged with ¾″ violet silk. The B.Mus. hood is fully lined with lavender silk and edged with ¾″ lavender silk. The Ph.D. hood is of red silk fully lined with dark violet silk. [This is an unconventional system.]

Cambridge

D.D.	Scarlet cloth lined with dove-coloured silk, that is silk of a turquoise-blue shot with rose-pink.
LL.D.	Scarlet cloth lined with light-cherry silk.
M.D.	Scarlet cloth lined with mid-cherry silk.
Sc.D.	Scarlet cloth lined with pink silk shot with light blue.
Litt.D.	Scarlet cloth lined with scarlet silk to match the cloth.
Mus.D.	Cream damask lined with dark-cherry satin.
B.D.	Black corded silk lined with black silk.
Ph.D.	Black corded silk lined with scarlet cloth.
M.Chir.	Black corded silk lined mid-cherry silk.
M.A.	Black corded silk lined with white silk.
LL.M.	Black corded silk lined light-cherry silk.
Mus.M.	Black corded silk lined dark-cherry satin.
M.Sc.	Black cloth lined pink silk shot light blue.
M.Litt.	Black cloth lined with scarlet silk.
M.B.	Mid-cherry silk part-lined with white fur, the tippet edged with white fur.
B.Chir.	Mid-cherry silk part-lined with white fur but with no fur edging to the tippet.
B.A.	Black stuff, part-lined with white fur, the tippet edged with white fur (or black stuff, part-lined with white, the tippet edged with white).
LL.B.	Light-cherry silk part-lined with white fur, the tippet edged with white fur.
Mus.B.	Dark-cherry satin part-lined with white fur, the tippet edged with white fur.
Vet.M.B.	Mid-cherry silk part-lined white fur, with white fur edging (2″) to the tippet.

Note:—The neck band of the hood is of the outer colour, with no edging of the lining material. The corners of tippets are square. All hoods are of the full shape.

Durham

B.A.	Black and white fur lining.
M.A.	Black and Palatinate purple.
B.D.	Black and black.
D.D.	Scarlet and Palatinate purple.
B.C.L.	Palatinate purple and white fur.
D.C.L.	Scarlet and white.
LL.M.	Maroon and Palatinate purple
M.B., B.S.	Scarlet, Palatinate purple and white fur edging.
M.S.	Rose and Palatinate purple.
D.Ch.	Scarlet, rose and Palatinate purple.
M.D.	Scarlet, scarlet and Palatinate purple.
B.Mus.	Palatinate purple and brocaded satin.
D.Mus.	Brocaded satin and Palatinate purple.
Ph.D.	Scarlet, scarlet and Palatinate purple silk edging 1″.
B.Sc.	Palatinate purple, fur, edged scarlet silk ($\frac{1}{2}$″)
M.Sc.	Black, Palatinate purple, edged scarlet ($\frac{1}{2}$″)
D.Sc.	Palatinate purple and scarlet.
D.Litt.	Scarlet and gold.
B.Hy.	Black, Palatinate purple, scarlet, white fur.
D.Hy.	Scarlet, Palatinate purple and white.
B.D.S.	Rose, ivory and white fur edging.
M.D.S.	Rose and ivory.
B.Com.	Black and cerise and white fur edging.
M.Com.	Black and cerise silk lining.
B.Arch.	Black, blue and white fur edging.

and 1 Diploma (*not* Degree):—L.Th.

Note:—Palatinate purple silk, cloth, or cassimere is peculiar to this University: it is in fact a soft lilac shade.

Edinburgh

B.Arch.	Black silk, lined with orange-brown silk, and edged with white fur.
B.Com.	Black silk, lined with pale primrose yellow silk, and edged with white fur.
B.D.	Black silk, lined with purple silk, and bordered with white fur.
B.D.S.	Black stuff, lined crimson silk bordered ivory poplin 3″ broad, edged white fur showing 3″ crimson silk at front of neckband.
B.Ed.	Black silk, lined with pale blue silk, and edged with white fur.
B.Mus.	Scarlet silk, with white silk lining, and edged with white fur.
B.Sc.	Black silk, lined with green silk, and bordered with white fur.
B.V.M. & S.	Black silk, lined maroon silk bordered golden yellow 3″ broad, edged white fur.
Ch.M.	Black velvet, lined with golden silk.
D.D.	Black cloth, with appended cape, lined and faced with purple silk.
D.Litt.	Black cloth, lined with royal blue silk shot with maize-colour.
D.Mus.	Rich scarlet cloth, lined with rich white corded silk.
D.Sc.	Black cloth, lined with green silk.
D.V.M. & S.	Black silk, lined with maroon silk bordered with golden yellow 3″ broad.
LL.B.	Black silk, lined with blue silk, and bordered with white fur.
LL.D.	Black cloth, with appended cape, lined and faced with blue silk.
M.A.	Black silk, lined with white silk.
M.Arch.	Black silk, lined with orange-brown silk.
M.B., Ch.B.	Black silk, lined with crimson silk bordered with white fur.
M.D.	Black silk, with appended cape, lined and faced with crimson silk.
M.D.S.	Black cloth, lined crimson silk bordered ivory poplin 3″ broad, showing 3″ crimson silk at front of neckband.
M.Sc.	Black silk, lined white silk bordered green silk 3″ broad, showing 3″ green silk at front of neckband.
Ph.D.	Black cloth, lined blue silk shot brown.

Exeter

B.A.	Dove grey cloth edged Faculty colour silk.
M.A.	Dove grey cloth lined Faculty colour silk.
D.Litt.	Scarlet superfine cloth lined dove grey cloth, edged with Faculty colour.
LL.B.	Dove grey cloth edged Faculty colour silk.
LL.M.	Dove grey cloth lined Faculty colour silk.
LL.D.	Scarlet superfine cloth lined dove grey, edged with Faculty colour.
B.Sc.	Dove grey cloth edged Faculty colour silk.
M.Sc.	Dove grey cloth lined Faculty colour silk.
D.Sc.	Scarlet superfine cloth lined dove grey, edged with Faculty colour.
B.A. (Social Studies).	Dove grey cloth edged Faculty colour silk.
M.A. (Social Studies).	Dove grey cloth lined Faculty colour silk.
Ph.D. (all Faculties).	Dove grey cloth lined with scarlet.

The Faculty colours are:—

Arts	Kingfisher blue.	Science	Turquoise blue.
Law	Purple.	Social Studies	Dark blue.

Note:—All bachelors have theological college style hoods unlined, all the seams show, and the hood proper is merely edged with the Faculty colour 2″ both inside and outside the cowl portion. All Doctors' hoods (incl. Ph.D.) are very heavy, being made of cloth and fully lined with cloth—no silk. All hoods are of the full shape similar to Cambridge. The Ph.D. hood is the Higher Doctors' hood inside out.

Glasgow

M.A.	Black lined and edged with purple silk.
B.D.	Black, lined with cherry silk, cherry, and scarlet cloth border.
D.D.	Scarlet, lined with white silk.
B.L.	Black and red (Venetian red silk).
LL.B.	Black, lined with Venetian red silk, and scarlet cloth border.
LL.D.	Scarlet lined with red (Venetian red silk).
M.B., Ch.B.	Black, lined with scarlet silk and scarlet cord border.
Ch.M.	Black silk lined and edged with scarlet silk.
M.D.	Scarlet cloth lined with scarlet silk.
B.Mus.	Black, lined with azure blue silk, with scarlet cord border.
D.Mus.	Scarlet, lined with azure blue silk.
Ph.D.	Black, lined and edged with crimson silk.
B.Sc.	Black, lined with gold silk, scarlet cloth border.
D.Sc.	Scarlet, lined with gold silk.
B.Litt.	Black, lined with white silk, scarlet cloth border.
D.Litt.	Scarlet, lined with purple silk.
B.D.S.	Black, lined with emerald green silk, scarlet cloth border.
M.D.S.	Black, lined and edged with emerald green silk.
B.V.M.S.	Black, lined with terra-cotta silk, scarlet cloth border.
M.V.S.	Black, lined and edged with terra-cotta silk.
D.V.M.	Scarlet, lined with terra-cotta silk.
Ed.B.	Black, lined with blue silk with scarlet cloth border.
M.Sc.	Black, lined and edged with gold silk.

Note:—All hoods are of the full shape with well-rounded capes.

Hull

B.A.
M.A.
D.Litt.
B.D.
D.D.
LL.B.
LL.M.
LL.D.
B.Mus.
D.Mus.
B.Sc.
M.Sc.
D.Sc.
B.Sc.(Econ.)
M.Sc.(Econ.)
D.Sc.(Econ.)
M.Ed.
Ph.D.
(in all Faculties)

All hoods are lined throughout with the University silk, a turquoise blue taffeta. All Bachelors' hoods (other than B.D. and B.Mus.) are of black ribbed rayon, of the improved Oxford Burgon shape. The B.D. is of black superfine cloth of the same shape as the Doctors'. The B.Mus. is of the same shape as the B.A., LL.B. and B.Sc., but is of cream figured damask silk. The Doctors' hoods are of the improved Oxford Doctors' shape with semi-circular cape. The Ph.D. is of claret coloured cloth and the D.Mus. of cream figured damask silk; all the other Doctors' hoods are of scarlet superfine cloth. The necks of all hoods are cut in one piece with a single central seam and no neck bands are let in. Edging of all hoods is forbidden except that Masters' hoods are ordered to be edged $\frac{3}{8}$″ with the lining silk (turquoise blue) round the cape portion only: all Masters' hoods are of the London shape, with well-rounded cape.

Keele

B.A.	Black, faced inside with gold taffeta and piped along outer edges with scarlet.

Lancaster

B.A.	Black lined with grey taffeta with $\frac{1}{2}$″ inside edging of red taffeta.
M.A.	Black lined with red taffeta with $1\frac{1}{2}$″ grey border.
M. Litt.	Black lined with red taffeta with $1\frac{1}{2}$″ blue taffeta border.
M.Sc.	Black lined with red taffeta with $1\frac{1}{2}$″ gold taffeta border.
Ph.D.	Red lined with red taffeta.
D.Litt	Red lined with blue taffeta.
D.Sc.	Red lined with gold taffeta.
LL.D.	Red lined with grey taffeta.

Note:—The B.A. hood is of the simple shape; all other hoods are of the full shape.

Leeds

B.A.	Dark green.
M.A.	Dark green and white.
B.D.	Dark green, scarlet and white.

D.D.	Scarlet, dark green and white.
LL.B.	Light green.
LL.M.	Light green and white.
LL.D.	Scarlet and light green.
M.B., Ch.B.	Dark green and light green.
Ch.M.	Dark green, white and light green.
M.D.	Scarlet, dark green and light green.
B.Mus.	Dark green and white.
Ph.D.	Green and scarlet.
B.Ch.D.	Dark green and middle green.
M.Ch.D.	Dark green, white and middle green.
B.Sc.	Middle green.
M.Sc.	Middle green and white.
D.Sc.	Scarlet and middle green.
D.Litt.	Scarlet and dark green.
M.Ed.	Dark green, white and middle green 1" laid on the lining.
B.Com.	Light green and dark green.
M.Com.	Light green, white and dark green.

Note:—Bachelors' and Masters' hoods are of the simple shape and Doctors' hoods are of the full shape.

Leicester

B.A.	Red, lined with silver grey.
B.Sc.	Red, lined with royal blue.
M.A.	Red, lined with silver grey.
M.Sc.	Red, lined with royal blue.
M.Ed.	Red, lined with tartan green.
Ph.D.	Red, lined with a watered taffeta of lighter shade.
D.Litt.	Silver grey, lined red.
D.Sc.	Royal blue, lined red.
LL.D.	Black, lined red.

Note:—Bachelors' hoods are of a special simple shape, and all other hoods are of a specific small full shape.

Liverpool

B.A.	Black cloth, lined with apple-blossom silk, and bordered with white fur.
B.Com.	Black cloth, lined with citron silk, and bordered with white fur.
B.Arch.	Black cloth, lined with white silk, edged with two narrow lines of black velvet, and bordered with white fur.
M.A.	Black silk or cloth, lined with apple-blossom silk.
M.Ed.	Black silk or cloth, lined with green silk.
M.Arch.	Black silk or cloth, lined white silk, edged with two narrow lines of black velvet.
M.C.D.	Black silk or cloth, lined white silk, edged with one broad line of black velvet.
M.Com.	Black silk or cloth, lined with citron silk.
Litt.D.	Scarlet cloth, lined with apple-blossom silk.
B.Sc.	Black cloth, lined with slate-blue silk, and bordered with white fur.
M.Sc.	Black silk or cloth, lined with slate-blue silk.
D.Sc.	Scarlet cloth, lined with slate-blue silk.
M.B., Ch.B.	Black cloth, lined with lavender silk, and bordered with white fur.
Ch.M., M.Ch.(Orth.), M.Rad.	Black silk or cloth, lined with lavender silk.
M.D.	Scarlet cloth, lined with lavender silk.
B.D.S.	Black cloth, lined with dark red silk, and bordered with white fur.
M.D.S.	Black silk or cloth, lined dark red silk.
LL.B.	Black cloth, lined with bronze silk, and bordered with white fur.
LL.M.	Black silk or cloth, lined with bronze silk.
LL.D.	Scarlet cloth, lined with bronze silk.
B.Eng.	Black cloth, lined with orange silk, and bordered with white fur.
M.Eng.	Black silk or cloth, lined with orange silk.
D.Eng.	Scarlet cloth, lined with orange silk.
B.V.Sc.	Black cloth, lined with grey silk, and bordered with white fur.
M.V.Sc.	Black silk or cloth, lined with grey silk.
D.V.Sc.	Scarlet cloth, lined with grey silk.
Ph.D.	Scarlet cloth or cord, lined with black silk, and trimmed with scarlet velvet.

Note:—All hoods of this University are of the simple shape.

London

B.D., M.Th., D.D.	Sarum red.
B.A., M.A., D.Lit.	Russet-brown.
LL.B., LL.M., LL.D.	Blue.
B.Mus., D.Mus.	White (watered silk).
M.B., B.S., M.S., M.D.	Violet.
B.D.S., M.D.S.	Olive green (corded).
B.Pharm., M.Pharm.	Old gold.
B.Vet.Med., M.Vet.Med.	Lilac.
B.Sc., M.Sc., D.Sc.	Gold.
B.Sc.(Eng.), M.Sc.(Eng.), D.Sc.(Eng.)	Gold.
B.Sc.(Econ.), M.Sc.(Econ.), D.Sc.(Econ.)	Gold.
B.Sc.(Est.Man.), M.Sc.(Est.Man.)	Gold.

Note:—All London hoods are of identical shape (full shape with rounded cape). With the exception of B.Mus., for whom the hood is of light blue corded silk, Bachelors' hoods are of black silk or stuff edged on the inside with silk of the faculty colour 3" only. Bachelors who are members of Convocation are entitled to wear hoods lined with white silk and edged with silk of the faculty colour. Masters' hoods are of black corded silk, with a silk lining of the faculty colour. Masters who are members of Convocation are entitled to wear hoods with a facing, 1½" wide, of white silk. The Ph.D. hood is of claret-coloured cloth, lined with silk of a lighter shade of claret, with a piping of the faculty colour about ⅛" wide between the cloth and silk. Doctors' hoods are of scarlet cloth lined with silk of the faculty colour.

Manchester (Victoria University)

B.A.	Black, blue and fur.
M.A.	Black and blue.
B.D.	Black, heliotrope and fur.
D.D.	Gold and gold.
LL.B.	Black and violet.
LL.M.	Black and violet.
LL.D.	Gold and gold.
M.B., Ch.B.	Black and red.
Ch.M.	Black and red.
M.D.	Gold and gold.
Mus.B.	Dark and light blue.
Mus.D.	Gold and gold.
Ph.D.	Gold and gold.
B.Sc.	Black, salmon and fur.
M.Sc.	Black and salmon.
D.Sc.	Gold and gold.
D.Litt.	Gold and gold.
B.D.S.	Black, fawn and fur.
M.D.S.	Black and fawn.
D.D.S.	Gold and gold.
B.A.(Theol.), B.A.(Mus.)	Black, blue and fur.
B.A.(Econ.), B.A.(Admin.), B.A.(Com.)	Black, orange and fur.
M.A.(Econ.), M.A.(Admin.), M.A.(Com.)	Black and orange.
B.Sc. Tech.	Black, terra-cotta and fur.
M.Sc. Tech.	Black and terra-cotta.
M.Ed.	Black and bluish-green.

Note:—All hoods are of the simple shape and are worn back to front with the tippet or liripipe outwards.

Newcastle upon Tyne

M.B., B.S.	Scarlet, Palatinate purple and white fur edging.
M.D.	Scarlet, scarlet and Palatinate purple.
M.S.	Rose and Palatinate purple.
D.Hy.	Scarlet, scarlet, Palatinate purple and white.
D.Ch.	Scarlet, rose and Palatinate purple.
B.D.S.	Rose, ivory and white fur edging.
M.D.S.	Rose and ivory.
D.D.Sc.	Scarlet, rose and ivory white edging.
B.A.	Black, white fur, old gold edging.
B.Arch.	Same as B.A.
M.A.	Black and old gold.
M.Ed.	Same as M.A.
D.Litt.	Scarlet, white and old gold edging.
LL.B.	Maroon, Palatinate purple and white fur edging.
LL.M.	Maroon and Palatinate purple.
LL.D.	Scarlet and maroon.
D.C.L.	Scarlet and white.
B.Sc.	Black, white fur, royal blue edging.
M.Sc.	Black and royal blue.
D.Sc.	Scarlet, white and royal blue edging.
Ph.D.	Scarlet and scarlet.

Nottingham

B.A., M.A.	Light blue and cherry and black.
B.D.	Light blue and purple and black.
D.D.	Light blue and purple and scarlet.
LL.B., LL.M	Light blue and maroon and black.

LL.D.	Light blue and maroon and scarlet.
B.Mus.	Light blue and pink and black.
D.Litt.	Light blue and cherry and scarlet.
B.Sc. / M.Sc.	Light blue and royal blue and black.
D.Sc.	Light blue and royal blue and scarlet.
Ph.D.	Light blue and Faculty colour and claret.
B.Sc.(Agric.) / M.Sc.(Agric.)	Light blue and green and black.
D.Sc.(Agric.)	Light blue and green and scarlet.
B.Sc.(Eng.) / M.Sc.(Eng.)	Light blue and light navy and black.
D.Sc.(Eng.)	Light blue and light navy and scarlet.
B.Pharm.	Light blue and grey and black.
M.Pharm.	Black, light blue and grey.
M.Ed.	Light blue and lilac and black.

Note:—All hoods of this University are of the full, Cambridge shape. All Bachelors' hoods are of black stuff, lined for 3" only with light blue silk. The hoods of all Masters and of Bachelors in Divinity are of black silk, and lined throughout with light blue silk.

The hoods of Doctors in Philosophy are of claret coloured silk or cloth lined throughout with light blue silk. The hoods of the Higher Doctors are of scarlet superfine cloth lined throughout with light blue silk.

All hoods of this University are bound (cowl portion only) with a ribbon of the appropriate colour. The colours are:—

Arts	Cherry red.	Pharmacy	Dove grey.
Theology	Purple.	Agriculture and Horticulture	Green
Law	Maroon.		
Music	Pink.	Engineering and Mining	Light navy blue.
Education	Lilac.		
Science	Royal blue.		

Oxford

B.A.	Black, half-lined and edged with white fur.
M.A.	Black silk, lined crimson or shot crimson silk.
B.D.	Black, lined fine ribbed black silk.
D.D.	Scarlet superfine cloth, lined fine ribbed black silk.
B.C.L.	Medium blue silk, lined or trimmed with white fur.
D.C.L.	Scarlet superfine cloth, lined crimson silk.
B.M., B.Ch.	Medium blue, half-lined and edged with white fur.
M.Ch.	Black silk, lined and edged with blue silk.
D.M.	Scarlet superfine cloth, lined crimson silk.
B.Mus.	Lilac silk, half-lined and edged white fur.
D.Mus.	Cream silk brocade, with apple-blossom embroidery, lined cherry crimson silk.
D.Litt. / D.Sc.	Scarlet superfine cloth, lined with grey silk.
B.Litt.	Light blue, half-lined and edged white fur.
B.Sc.	Same as B.Litt.
B.Phil.	Dark blue silk, lined with white silk.
D.Phil.	Scarlet superfine cloth, lined navy-blue silk.

Note:—The Oxford Bachelors' hoods (except B.D. & B.Phil.) and the M.A. hood are either of Burgon or Oxford shape. The B.Phil. and M.Ch. hoods are always of Oxford shape. The B.D. and all Doctors' hoods are of the correct full apron shape. B.A., M.A., M.Ch., and B.D. hoods are of corded black silk; the other Bachelors' hoods are of corded or ribbed silk of the colour shown, lined or trimmed with white fur. When the Burgon shape is used the hood is half-lined and edged with fur, but for the Oxford shape only an edging of fur is used.

Reading

B.A., M.A., M.Ed., D.Litt., B.Sc., M.Sc., M.Agr.Sc., D.Sc., Ph.D.

All Reading hoods are lined with cream coloured silk. Bachelors' hoods are of dark blue lined with cream silk to a depth of 3". All hoods are full shape. All Doctors' hoods are of scarlet superfine cloth fully lined with cream silk, of the full shape, except Ph.D., which is of crimson cloth lined with cream silk (maroon Russell-Cord is generally used).

St. Andrews

M.A.	Black, cherry lining.
B.D.	Wood violet, white fur edging.
D.D.	Wood violet, white lining (satin).
M.B., Ch.B.	Medici crimson, white fur edging.
Ch.M.	Medici crimson.
M.D.	Medici crimson, white lining (satin).
B.L.	Pimento, white edging.
LL.B.	Pimento, white fur edging.
LL.D.	Pimento, white lining (satin).
Mus.D.	Cerulean blue silk or cloth with a white lining (satin).
Ph.D.	Nanking blue, white lining (satin).
B.Sc.	Purple lilac, white fur edging.
D.Sc.	Purple lilac, white lining (satin).
B.Litt.	Saffron yellow, white fur edging.
D.Litt.	Saffron yellow, white lining (silk).
B.D.S.	Claret, white fur edging.
M.D.S.	Claret.
D.D.Sc.	Claret, white lining (satin).
B.Phil.	Gold, white fur edging.
M.A. (Soc.Sc.)	Black, shamrock-green lining.
M.Sc.	Black, purple-lilac lining.
B.Sc. (App.Sc.)	Grotto-blue, white fur edging.
M.Sc. (App.Sc.)	Black, grotto-blue lining.
D.Sc. (App.Sc.)	Grotto-blue, white lining.
B.Ed.	Black primrose lining, white fur edging.

Note:—All hoods of this University are of the full shape with well-rounded capes.

Sheffield

B.A.	Green, white fur and crushed strawberry.
M.A.	Green and crushed strawberry.
Litt.D.	Red and crushed strawberry.
B.Mus.	Green, white fur and cream (brocade).
D.Mus.	Red and cream (brocade).
B.Ed.	Green, white fur and crushed strawberry (Arts) or apricot (Pure Science).
B.Sc.	Green, white fur and apricot.
M.Sc.	Green and apricot.
D.Sc.	Red and apricot.
M.B., Ch.B.	Green, white fur and red.
Ch.M.	Green and red.
M.D.	Red and red.
B.D.S.	Green, white fur and pale rose pink.
M.D.S.	Green and pale rose pink.
LL.B.	Green, white fur and pale green.
LL.M.	Green and pale green.
LL.D.	Red and pale green.
B.Jur.	Green, white fur and olive green.
B.Eng.	Green, white fur and purple.
M.Eng.	Green and purple.
D.Eng.	Red and purple.
B.Met.	Green, white fur and steel grey.
M.Met.	Green and steel grey.
D.Met.	Red and steel grey.
B.Sc.Tech.	Green, white fur and lilac.
M.Sc.Tech.	Green and lilac.
D.Sc.Tech.	Red and lilac.
B.A.Econ.	Green, white fur and lemon yellow
M.A.Econ.	Green and lemon yellow.
Litt.D.Econ.	Red and lemon yellow.
B.A.	(Arch. Studies) Green, white fur and old gold.
M.A.	(Arch. Studies) Green and old gold.
Ph.D.	Red and dark green.

Note:—All hoods of this University are of the full shape.

Southampton

Faculty colours:-

Arts	Mid-cerise	Engineering	Orange
Law	Blue (Univ. silk)	Social Sciences	Light green
Science	Rich gold	Education	White

B.A., M.A., D.Litt., B.A.(Law), LL.B., LL.M., LL.D., B.Sc., M.Sc., D.Sc., B.Sc.(Eng.), M.Sc.(Eng.), D.Sc., B.Sc. (Social Sciences), M.Sc. (Social Sciences), D.Sc. (Social Sciences), M.A.(Ed.), Ph.D. (in all Faculties)

All hoods are lined throughout with the University silk, a peacock blue. All Bachelors' hoods are of black ribbed rayon of the improved Oxford Burgon shape. The cowl portion only is edged inside and outside with $\frac{3}{8}$" of the Faculty colour, except in Law, in which case the lining is turned over $\frac{3}{8}$" on to the outside to form the edging, and B.A.(Law) which has an added edging of mid-cerise of $\frac{3}{8}$" on the outside of the cowl portion. All Masters' hoods are of the London shape, but with well rounded cape, the cowl portion is edged $\frac{3}{8}$" inside and outside with the Faculty colour except LL.M., in which case the lining silk is turned over $\frac{3}{8}$" on the outside to make the edging. The cape of Masters' hoods is edged $\frac{3}{8}$" with the peacock-blue lining silk. All Ph.D. hoods are of claret-coloured cloth fully lined with peacock-blue silk. All the Higher Doctors' hoods are of scarlet superfine cloth fully lined with peacock-blue silk. All Doctors' hoods (incl. Ph.D.) are of the improved Oxford D.D. shape. Neck bands are prohibited for all hoods, the neck of which must be cut on the curve in one piece with a single central seam.

Strathclyde

B.A.	Blue, lined with white silk.
B.Sc.	Blue, lined with gold silk.
B.Arch.	Blue, lined with gold silk, bound with scarlet cord.
M.A.	Blue, lined with white silk with a $\frac{3}{4}$" edging of white silk.
M.Sc.	Blue, lined with gold silk with a $\frac{3}{4}$" edging of gold silk
M.Litt.	Blue, lined with white silk, bound with black cord.
M.Arch.	Blue, lined with white silk with a $\frac{3}{4}$" edging of white silk.
Ph.D.	As for B.A., B.Sc., B.Arch. (as appropriate).
D.Sc.	As for B.Sc., B.Arch. (as appropriate).
D.Litt.	As for B.A.

LL.D. (*honoris causa* only) Blue, lined with white silk, bound with scarlet cord.

Note:—All hoods are of the full shape, of saltire blue (*i.e.*, the blue of the St. Andrew flag).

Sussex

B.A. B.Sc.	Black cloth lined with grey fur in squares and edged with 1″ band of silk in school colour.
M.A. M.Sc.	Black alpaca lined with dove grey silk with edge bound in school colour.
M.Phil.	Black alpaca lined with dove grey silk with 1″ band of scarlet silk over lining set in ¼″ from edge.
D.Phil. LL.D. D.Sc. D.Litt.	No hood but a distinctive gown is prescribed.

Wales

B.A.	Black and green shot blue (3″).
M.A.	Black and green shot blue.
LL.B.	Black and purple shot red (3″).
LL.M.	Black silk lined with red silk shot with purple.
LL.D.	Scarlet and purple shot red.
M.B., B.Ch.	Black and black shot green and white.
M.Ch.	Black and shot green edged white.
M.D.	Scarlet and black shot green and white.
B.Mus.	Blue and pearl silk lining to a depth of 3″.
M.Mus.	Blue silk fully lined with pearl-coloured silk.
B.D.S. M.D.S.	Black and shot saxe blue edged purple.
B.Pharm. M.Pharm.	Black and shot saxe blue.
D.Mus.	Scarlet and pearl.
B.Sc.	Black and black shot yellow.
M.Sc.	Black and black shot yellow (3″).
D.Sc.	Scarlet and black shot yellow.
Ph.D.	Crimson and Faculty colour.
D.Litt.	Scarlet and green shot blue.

Note:—Bachelors' hoods are of the simple shape, Masters' and Doctors' hoods are of the full shape.

St. David's College, Lampeter.

B.D.	Black silk, lined with violet and edged with white silk.
B.A.	Black stuff or silk, edged on inside and bound with miniver.

Note:—Both of Cambridge pattern.

York

B.A.	Grey with white edging.
B.Phil.	Grey with red edging.
M.Phil.	Red with grey edging.
D.Phil.	Red with grey lining.
D.Univ.	Red with grey lining. (hon. degree)

Note:—Academical robes of the new Universities of East Anglia, Essex, Kent, and Warwick had not been settled at the time of going to press.

MISCELLANEOUS DATA.

1 litre of water weighs 1 kg.; 1 c. ft. of water weighs 62·3 lbs.
1 gallon of water weighs 10 lbs.
A circle of a radius r has a circumference $2\pi r$ and an area πr^2, where $\pi = 3{\cdot}1416$, $\frac{1}{\pi} = 0{\cdot}3183$, $\pi^2 = 9{\cdot}8696$.
Base of natural logarithms is $e = 2{\cdot}7183$.
The acceleration of a falling body is 32·2 feet per sec. per sec., or 981 cm. per sec. per sec.
1 horse-power = 550 foot pounds per second = 746 watts.
1 atmosphere = 760 mm. of mercury (30 in.) = 1·03 Kg. per sq. cm. = 14·7 lbs. per sq. inch = 1010 millibars.
1 sea mile = 6080 feet = approx. 2000 yds.
1 cable = $\frac{1}{10}$ sea mile.
1 shackle = $\frac{1}{8}$ cable.
1 knot = 1 sea mile per hr. = approx. 100 ft. per min.
1 ton (ship capacity) = 100 c. ft. of water.

UNITS AND DIMENSIONS

	Symbol.	Dimension.	Absolute Unit.	Practical Unit.	Ratio.
Length	l	L	centimetre	micro-millimetre	10^{-7}
				light-year	946×10^{15}
			foot	mile	5280
Mass	m	M	gram	—	
			pound	—	
Time	t	T	second	—	
Velocity	v	LT^{-1}	cm. per sec.	—	
			ft. per sec.	miles per hr.	1·47
				knots	
Acceleration	f	LT^{-2}	cm. per sec. per sec.	—	
			ft. per sec. per sec.	—	
Momentum	mv	MLT^{-1}			
Force	F	MLT^{-2}	Dyne	—	
			poundal	poundweight	32·2
Work, Energy	U	ML^2T^{-2}	erg	joule	10^7
			foot-poundal	foot-pound	32·2
Power	P	ML^2T^{-3}	ergs per sec.	watt	10^7
			foot-poundals per sec.	foot-pounds per sec.	32·2
				horse-power	$1{\cdot}77 \times 10^4$

CHEMICAL NAMES OF COMMON SUBSTANCES

Alcohol	= Ethyl Alcohol (C_2H_5OH).
Alum	= Potassium Aluminium Sulphate ($K_2SO_4, Al_2[SO_4]_3, 24H_2O$).
Aqua fortis	= Nitric Acid (HNO_3).
Bi-Carbonate of Soda	= Sodium Hydrogen Carbonate ($NaHCO_3$).
Blue Vitriol (Blue Stone)	= Copper Sulphate ($CuSO_4, 5H_2O$).
Boracic Acid	= Boric Acid (H_3BO_3).
Borax	= Sodium Borate ($Na_2B_4O_7, 10H_2O$).
Calomel	= Mercurous Chloride (Hg_2Cl_2) (laxative, non-poisonous).
Chalk	= Calcium Carbonate ($CaCO_3$).
Common Salt	= Sodium Chloride (NaCl).
Corrosive Sublimate	= Mercuric Chloride ($HgCl_2$) (violently poisonous).
Epsom Salts	= Magnesium Sulphate ($MgSO_4, 7H_2O$).
Fire Damp	= Methane (CH_4) + air.
Glauber Salts	= Sodium Sulphate ($Na_2SO_4, 10H_2O$).
Green Vitriol	= Ferrous Sulphate ($FeSO_4, 7H_2O$).
Hypo	= Sodium Thiosulphate ($Na_2S_2O_3, 5H_2O$).
Lime	= Calcium Oxide (CaO).
Oil of Vitriol	= Sulphuric Acid (H_2SO_4).
Plaster of Paris	= Calcium Sulphate ($(CaSO_4)_2H_2O$).
Red Lead	= Triplumbic Tetroxide (Pb_3O_4).
Sal Ammoniac	= Ammonium Chloride (NH_4Cl).
Sal Volatile	= Impure Ammonium Carbonate ($[NH_4]_2CO_3$).
Saltpetre	= Potassium Nitrate (KNO_3).
Salts of Lemon	= Potassium Hydrogen Oxalate (KHC_2O_4).
Spirit of Salt	= Hydrochloric Acid (HCl).
Sugar of Lead	= Lead Acetate ($Pb[C_2H_3O_2]_2, 3H_2O$).
Verdigris	= Basic Copper Acetate ($-Cu[C_2H_3O_2]_2, Cu[OH]_2$).
Vinegar	= Dilute Acetic Acid ($C_2H_4O_2$).
Washing Soda	= Crystalline Sodium Carbonate ($Na_2CO_3, 10H_2O$).
White Lead	= Basic Lead Carbonate ($2PbCO_3, Pb[OH]_2$).

ELEMENTS

Element (Symbol)	Atomic Number	Atomic Weight	Valency
actinium (Ac)*	89	227	
aluminium (Al)	13	26·9815	3
americium (Am)*	95	243	3, 4, 5, 6
antimony (Sb)	51	121·75	3, 5
argon (A)	18	39·948	0
arsenic (As)	33	74·9216	3, 5
astatine (At)*	85	210	1, 3, 5, 7
barium (Ba)	56	137·34	2
berkelium (Bk)*	97	249	3, 4
beryllium (Be)	4	9·0122	2
bismuth (Bi)	83	208·980	3, 5
boron (B)	5	10·811	3
bromine (Br)	35	79·909	1, 3, 5, 7
cadmium (Cd)	48	112·40	2
calcium (Ca)	20	40·08	2
californium (Cf)*	98	249	
carbon (C)	6	12·01115	2, 4
cerium (Ce)	58	140·12	3, 4
caesium (Cs)	55	132·905	1
chlorine (Cl)	17	35·453	1, 3, 5, 7
chromium (Cr)	24	51·996	2, 3, 6
cobalt (Co)	27	58·9332	2, 3
copper (Cu)	29	63·54	1, 2
curium (Cm)*	96	245	3
dysprosium (Dy)	66	162·50	3
einsteinium (Es)*	99	254	
erbium (Er)	68	167·26	3
europium (Eu)	63	151·96	2, 3
fermium (Fm)*	100	252	
fluorine (F)	9	18·9984	1
francium (Fr)*	87	223	1
gadolinium (Gd)	64	157·25	3
gallium (Ga)	31	69·72	2, 3
germanium (Ge)	32	72·59	4
gold (Au)	79	196·967	1, 3
hafnium (Hf)	72	178·49	4
helium (He)	2	4·0026	0
holmium (Ho)	67	164·930	3
hydrogen (H)	1	1·00797	1
indium (In)	49	114·82	3
iodine (I)	53	126·9044	1, 3, 5, 7
iridium (Ir)	77	192·2	3, 4
iron (Fe)	26	55·847	2, 3
krypton (Kr)	36	83·8	0
lanthanum (La)	57	138·91	3
lawrencium (Lw)*	103	257	
lead (Pb)	82	207·19	2, 4
lithium (Li)	3	6·939	1
lutetium (Lu)	71	174·97	3
magnesium (Mg)	12	24·312	2
manganese (Mn)	25	54·9380	2, 3, 4, 6, 7
mendeleevium (Mv)*	101	256	
mercury (Hg)	80	200·59	1, 2
molybdenum (Mo)	42	95·94	3, 4, 6
neodymium (Nd)	60	144·24	3
neon (Ne)	10	20·183	0
neptunium (Np)*	93	237	4, 5, 6
nickel (Ni)	28	58·71	2, 3
niobium (Nb)	41	92·906	3, 5
nitrogen (N)	7	14·0067	3, 5
nobelium (No)*	102	254	
osmium (Os)	76	190·2	2, 3, 4, 8
oxygen (O)	8	15·9994	2
palladium (Pd)	46	106·4	2, 4, 6
phosphorus (P)	15	30·9738	3, 5
platinum (Pt)	78	195·09	2, 4
plutonium (Pu)*	94	242	3, 4, 5, 6
polonium (Po)*	84	242	
potassium (K)	19	39·102	1
praseodymium (Pr)	59	140·907	3
promethium (Pm)*	61	145	3
protactinium (Pa)*	91	231	
radium (Ra)*	88	226	2
radon (Rn)*	86	222	0
rhenium (Re)	75	186·2	
rhodium (Rh)	45	102·905	3
rubidium (Rb)	37	85·47	1
ruthenium (Ru)	44	101·07	3, 4, 6, 8
samarium (Sm)	62	150·35	2, 3
scandium (Sc)	21	44·956	3
selenium (Se)	34	78·96	2, 4, 6
silicon (Si)	14	28·086	4
silver (Ag)	47	107·870	1
sodium (Na)	11	22·9898	1
strontium (Sr)	38	87·62	2
sulphur (S)	16	32·064	2, 4, 6
tantalum (Ta)	73	180·948	5
technetium (Tc)*	43	99	6, 7
tellurium (Te)	52	127·60	2, 4, 6
terbium (Tb)	65	158·924	3
thalium (Tl)	81	204·37	1, 3
thorium (Th)	90	232·038	4
thulium (Tm)	69	168·934	3
tin (Sn)	50	118·69	2, 4
titanium (Ti)	22	47·90	3, 4
tungsten (*see* wolfram)			
uranium (U)	92	238·03	4, 6
vanadium (V)	23	50·942	3, 5
wolfram (W)	74	183·85	6
xenon (Xe)	54	131·30	0
ytterbium (Yb)	70	173·04	2, 3
yttrium (Y)	39	88·905	3
zinc (Zn)	30	65·37	2
zirconium (Zr)	40	91·22	4

* In the cases of these elements, which are very rare or not found in nature, but have been artificially prepared, atomic weight in the chemical sense is meaningless; the integral mass of the most stable isotope known is given.

Note: In 1961 the isotope of Carbon-14 replaced Oxygen as a standard, the weight of its atom being taken as exactly 12. This change of standard has meant a slight adjustment in atomic weights from the old chemical scale.

The new elements with an atomic number higher than that of uranium 238 (element 92) are termed Transuranics.

GAS LAWS

Boyle's Law (1662) pV = constant.

Charles' Law (1787) $\frac{pV}{T}$ = constant.

Van der Waal's equation $\left(p+\frac{a}{V^2}\right)(V-b) = RT$ where a and b are constants.

Adiabatic expansion of a gas pV^{γ} = constant where $\gamma = \frac{C_p}{C_v}$.

MEDICAL MATTERS

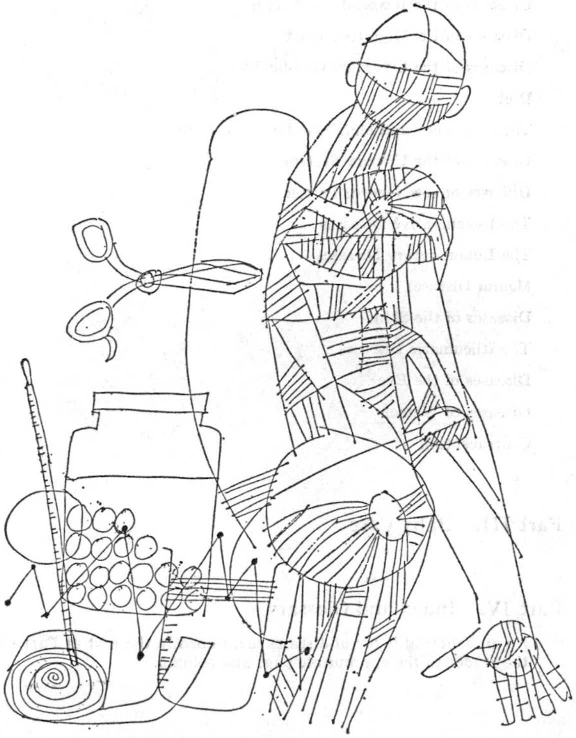

TABLE OF CONTENTS

MEDICAL MATTERS

PART I. INTRODUCTION.

(a) HOW TO USE THE SECTION.

Diseases do not exist in watertight compartments, but doctors arrange them according either to their cause or the area of the body affected. This plan has been followed here, and at the beginning of each part an account of the group of diseases under discussion is given. Unless you know enough already, you would be wise to read it.

Here is some advice about your attitude to disease in general, and your use of this section in particular.

First of all, and obviously, no book is a substitute for the doctor, and when you are ill you must see him. There are good and bad doctors, competent and incompetent ones, just as in any other profession or trade; so choose a doctor you can trust, *and then believe what he tells you and carry out his advice*. There is no use complaining about the whole medical profession just because you are dissatisfied with your own G.P. If you are, you should change him.

Secondly, *never* believe what you hear from non-medical sources. Literally millions of people are made miserable every year by taking to heart nonsense told them by others, who may well be quite unaware of the harm they do, or even have the very best intentions. In any medical matter ask your doctor, and ignore your next-door neighbour's asked-for or unasked-for advice. Doctors are sometimes wrong, but they are much less likely to be wrong than someone without a medical education. Remember, too, that the statement that there is no cure for a disease does not necessarily mean that it is deadly: and it never means that nothing can be done to make it more tolerable. There is much more to modern doctoring than simply curing the curable.

Thirdly, don't try to diagnose your own trouble or decide what treatment you think you should have. This section will have failed completely in its intentions if it puts you in the position of a character described by an English humourist, who, from a medical dictionary, discovered that he had every disease listed in it with the solitary exception of housemaid's knee. Diseases which appear to the layman to have the "same" symptoms may be vastly different in seriousness: influenza and poliomyelitis, for example, may in, the initial stages, appear very similar. So also may stomach ulcer and cancer of the stomach. No human being is infallible, but it is most important that you should go to the person who is best fitted to know—your doctor.

Lastly, you should not be misled into thinking that you can always tell the seriousness of a disease by the general appearance of the patient. Children, in particular, may have a high temperature, or even be delirious, on one day, and the next be out of bed and wanting to get back to school. On the other hand, many of the most dangerous fevers (as we shall see later) are accompanied by a low temperature and do not appear particularly dramatic in the initial stages. Thus a young woman who may be aware of nothing wrong but lack of energy and getting easily tired may be dangerously ill with tuberculosis of the lungs.

The best rule is to seek medical advice either when you have suddenly become ill with symptoms you don't understand or (and this is equally important) if you have gradually been feeling less fit over a period of time. Perhaps, too, it is wise to call your doctor if you have been ill with *anything* for more than three days. You should *not* call in a specialist before seeing your G.P., as is so often done in America and on the Continent. Specialists are very clever, but are naturally prejudiced in favour of their own subject; for example, an eye specialist will be predisposed to think of your headache in terms of eyestrain, an ear, nose, and throat specialist in terms of sinus trouble, and a psychiatrist in terms of mother-in-law trouble. Therefore you should first have a check from your G.P., who knows a little of all these things and probably a great deal about you and your past history. He will then advise you about a specialist if necessary.

(b) NEW VIEWS ON MEDICINE

(1) Body and Mind. In former times, or, at least during the nineteenth century, the body was regarded as a sort of machine belonging to you in much the same way that you own your watch. You went to your doctor and, in effect, said: "Now what on earth are you going to do about my stomach?"—and you spoke as if, somehow, your stomach didn't have anything to do with the *real* you—it was just an awkward thing that happened to be annoying you. But we know now that this is not so—that your body *is* you, that it is a fort fighting against such enemies as poisons, parasites, germs, cancer, and injuries. The defences are seriously weakened by not enough of the right kind of food, insufficient sleep, or by anxiety. Your anxieties and worries can kill you just as surely as the other agents, and can prevent recovery or retard it when you are already ill.

A stomach ulcer therefore is not just something that is happening to you, you are happening to it. Your fears, your jealousies, your hatreds, your inability to get on in life, can be (in some cases) just as harmful as germs or poisons—in fact, they act by setting free glandular poisons in your blood-stream. Scientists have discovered a reaction which they call the "stress response," and we now know that stress can ultimately lead to sickness or death without any bodily injury at all. Thus, Dr. L. J. Saul, a leading American doctor, writes: "Emotional stress in which there is no physical damage can produce responses which lead to actual damage and even to death." Rats in the laboratory can be killed through long exposure to fear caused by loud noises or other forms of shock without even being touched.

This stress factor is emphasised not because it is more important that the other enemies of the body or mind (it would be better to say body-mind), but because, as we shall see later, it does cause serious diseases, and, secondly, as mentioned already, it influences the process of recovery. A person who is afraid or has no hope is less likely to recover from pneumonia or another disease than one who is hopeful, who has peace of mind and confidence.

(2) New Views about Health. A great deal of nonsense has been talked about the healthy life; at one time we were told to take eighteen chews to each bite, to do deep breathing, to take plenty of exercise, to get lots of fresh air, to eat regularly (or to indulge in peculiar diets). But more recently, eminent doctors have cast doubt on most of these fancies. Moderate exercise is necessary to health, but athletes who indulge in violent exercise have not always been noted for longevity. Fresh air is pleasant and stimulating, but, where actual breathing is concerned, it is no better than the air in most rooms. Certainly, one of the problems of our time is air pollution by smoke and Diesel fumes, which are highly dangerous, but at present we are considering ordinary fresh air in comparison with the air indoors, and, in this case, the experts say there is little difference so far as health is concerned.

A balanced diet containing correct amounts of the basic food substances is essential, but there is no evidence that when, or at what intervals, you eat makes the slightest difference—unless you are a sufferer from stomach ulcer, in which case it is necessary that the intervals between meals should not be too long. The whole business of having meals at fixed intervals is nothing but a social convention, and in modern life obviously a matter of convenience.

Sleep, too, is a necessity. But different people require vastly different amounts of sleep. Some manage on as little as three hours, others seem to believe that they need ten or more, and there are well-authenticated records of people who never sleep at all. For example, a certain Dr. Pavoni in Northern Italy did not sleep for sixty years and made a virtue of necessity by specialising in night calls! Insomnia is unpleasant, but its only harmful effect results not from sleeplessness itself but from worry about it; for many people seem to believe that if they do not sleep they will go mad or at least become seriously ill. This is quite untrue.

In a number of studies of men and women who lived to a ripe old age it was found that the only factors in common between them were that they had a good balanced diet of healthy food, that they had contented minds, and that they were interested in something which gave them an aim in life. They also came of long-lived families—for living a long and healthy life depends partly upon heredity.

So the main rules of health are: do not think too much about your health unless it gives you trouble; have an interest in life and be prepared to sacrifice a lot for it (nothing useful has ever been done by those who are always "taking care" and being over-cautious); eat a good balanced diet; do not worry, and have a contented mind.

(3) New Drugs. A great surgeon, the first of the moderns, was Ambrose Paré, who died in 1590, and one of his best known sayings was: "I apply the dressing, but God heals the wound." He was quite right; for until about forty years ago, or even less, all the physician could do was to put the patient in as favourable a state as possible to enable his body to cure itself. That is to say, there were hardly any specific drugs—drugs that had a direct effect on the disease. There was quinine, discovered by the Spaniards in America, which was specific for malaria, and there were iron (specific for anæmia) and digitalis (specific for certain types of heart disease), but otherwise nothing until the nineteenth century, when Paul Ehrlich discovered salvarsan, which is specific for syphilis. Ehrlich died in 1914, having conceived the brilliant idea of drugs which he described as "magic bullets"—*i.e.*, drugs which, like bullets, would be aimed at the real cause of the disease. They would, that is to say, be specific.

Since then a large number of such drugs have been discovered. For example, the antibiotics, such as penicillin, discovered in 1928 by Fleming at St. Mary's Hospital, Paddington. Later, Florey and Chain in Oxford, helped in the war years by the vast resources of the American pharmaceutical industry, were able to make penicillin available to the public in sufficient quantities by new techniques of production. Penicillin is practically non-poisonous (although it is possible to become allergic to it, sometimes with serious results). It can kill some germs in a dilution of one part of pencillin to one hundred million parts of water; it is effective against streptococci, the cause of blood-poisoning, sepsis in wounds, and many other diseases: and also against the germs of anthrax, gonorrhœa, meningitis of some types, syphilis—a whole list of plagues which have troubled man for centuries. Blood-poisoning, whether from wounds or childirth, used to be almost incurable—now the rate of cure is 80–90 per cent.; anthrax and gonorrhœa have an almost 100 per cent. rate of cure. In pneumonia the rate is about 90 per cent., and early syphilis can be cured in a week, instead of the previous two to three years.

But this was only the beginning. Other antibiotics—streptomycin, tetracycline, erythromycin, and many others—are helping to wipe out the terrible scourges of the human race, in particular, in the case of streptomycin, tuberculosis. The sulpha group of drugs—sulphadiazine, sulphadimidine, etc.—have also proved a great boon. Then there are the new drugs which have created a revolution in psychiatry—the tranquillisers which relieve anxiety, the drugs which clear up certain types of depression, and substances such as chlorpromazine which make it possible to nurse formerly violent patients in the wards of a general hospital. The antihistamine drugs help in many cases of allergy, the anticoagulants prevent further attacks of coronary thrombosis, and every year new and powerful aids in the fight against disease are discovered.

Of course, these potent new drugs are not without their concomitant risks. The doctor is trained to weigh the harm they can do against the disadvantages of *not* using them in any particular case. He should not use them for every trivial illness in which their only effect may be to shorten slightly the course of a condition which, left alone, would recover of itself. Yet in Britain and other technically-advanced countries indiscriminate prescribing is common, largely because of pressure on the doctor from his patients and the drug firms. The busy mother whose child has a mild sore throat is not going to see the child sweat it out when she knows from past experience that a dose of penicillin can remove the fever and most of the symptoms within twenty-four hours. She is unlikely to listen to the argument that the slower process is capable of increasing the body's resistance to future attacks, or that repeated administration of penicillin may create germs which are insensitive to it in a future emergency, or, worse still, produce an allergy to the drug. The thalidomide tragedy of 1962–3, when a new sedative, hailed as being both effective and safe (cases were quoted of would-be suicides who had taken up to 100 of the tablets without loss of life), resulted in the birth of children with undeveloped arms and legs to mothers who had used the drug in early pregnancy, and prolonged neuritis in some adults, has been quoted against the drug industry as an example of cut-throat competition allowing new preparations on the market before they had been exhaustively tested. But the truth is not quite so simple. There can be no reasonable question that the drug industry needs to be under stricter control; that its methods of advertising its wares to the doctor are wasteful, importunate, and often in bad taste; that different firms put out what is virtually the same drug under various trade names which merely leads to confusion; that the "authorities" quoted in the advertising of some drugs are often obscure individuals in countries not noted for the high standard of their practice of medicine writing in equally obscure journals; and that many drug firms make grossly inflated profits at the expense of our National Health Service. On the other hand, it must be remembered that some of the best drug firms have played a major part in medical progress. But they must constantly check their commercial instincts where these conflict (as they sometimes do) with your interests as the patient-consumer. To be fair about thalidomide, the fact is that nobody previously had seriously considered the possibility of a drug capable of causing deformity in the unborn child, and, if they had done, it is quite likely that the danger would still have been undiscovered, since only certain laborator animals respond to thalidomide in a similar way to man. The drug had been exhaustively tested by all ordinary methods before being put on the market, and for a number of years (during which, in Germany, it was on sale to the public without prescription because of its apparent safety), millions of people took it without any ill-effects either immediately or subsequently. Its terrible side-effects were, in fact, limited to those mothers who used it in early, not later, pregnancy, and in a lesser degree to a small proportion of adults who developed unpleasant, but not dangerous, symptoms of neuritis.

The taking of any effective drug is always a calculated risk. We have mentioned that the use of penicillin—a drug which is almost completely non-poisonous—may nevertheless cause other germs and fungi to multiply in the body with unpleasant results. This is because penicillin wipes out, not only the disease-producing germs it is being used to destroy, but the penicillin-sensitive harmless germs which hold the other potentially harmful germs at bay. Thus those who keep on sucking penicillin lozenges for a real or imaginary sore throat may develop a black tongue due to the spread of a fungus normally present but kept under control. Other antibiotics, described as "wide spectrum" because they wipe out an even greater variety of germs than penicillin, also kill the organisms responsible for the absorption and possibly the creation of vitamin B in the body, thus causing severe vitamin deficiency. Tranquillisers made by various firms vary from the wholly useless to the very useful, but both can have unpleasant side-effects. One type is prone to lead in a small number of cases to severe depression, others may lower the blood-pressure to a degree that causes fainting attacks, and serious blood and liver diseases are not unknown if not common. Both tranquillisers and the antihistamine drugs can cause some people to become extremely drowsy—an obvious danger if one drives a car or works on heights. Even aspirin causes gastric hæmorrhages which have sometimes been very severe and even lethal, particularly in those with peptic ulceration of the stomach and duodenum. Aspirin, one of the most useful and safest of drugs should never be taken for an "upset stomach", or by people with known stomach trouble. Such patients should be warned that about 150 preparations including some hang-over remedies widely advertised for "upset stomach", contain arge quantities of aspirin (acetyl salicylic acid).

None of this should deter the patient from being advised by a doctor he trusts to use whatever drugs are prescribed; it *should* deter him from putting emotional pressure on his doctor to obtain drugs unwillingly given. It is high time that we gave up the notion that no patient should leave the consulting-room without a prescription for some pill or potion; for something like 40 per cent. of patients simply require advice about the conduct of their life from their diet to their relationships with others rather than medicine of any kind. The housing shortage, a bullying boss, or a nagging mother-in-law cannot be removed by a tranquilliser—in fact, a tranquilliser, by making a man or woman feel better, may prevent them from constructively solving problems which exist in the real world. We should all learn to rely as little on drugs as possible: stop taking tranquillisers or pep pills when we are merely worried about something that any normal person would worry about, or because we are just "fed-up"; stop using antibiotics (which are badly needed elsewhere in the world) for trivial infections in which they are anyhow useless; stop swallowing vitamin pills which do not relieve tiredness and are merely wasted on this overfed nation; stop buying any patent medicine whatever. Modern drugs are potent and effective; they are a dagger to destroy the enemy of disease. But, like a dagger, those who play about with them incompetently and unnecessarily are liable to get badly hurt.

(4) New Methods in Surgery. Only a few years before the Second World War many surgeons were saying that surgery had reached its extreme limits. It was impossible, they believed, to improve on the delicate techniques then reached. But events have proved them wrong. Operations on the heart, for example, which would have been inconceivable a short time ago are now carried out daily—the heart can be opened and defects of the all-important valves made good. "Blue-Babies" or adults with a heart disease which might have led to their death in a few years are now cured by surgery, and it is possible during such operations to cut off all the blood from the heart by deflecting it through tubes to an artificial heart outside the body—a machine which pumps the blood round the body whilst the real heart is at rest.

This however, will be described in more detail later.

Then there are the new anæsthetics, such as Pentothal, which are injected into a vein in the arm instead of being breathed in through a mask, as were ether and chloroform or ethyl chloride. Pentothal is much safer, and avoids the unpleasant after-effects of vomiting and nausea, which usually followed the old type of anæsthetic. Most curious of all anæsthetists use the poison curare, used by South American Indians to poison their arrow-heads. Curare produces paralysis, but in small doses merely gives the degree of muscle relaxation which is so important to the surgeon when he is operating.

Lastly, we might mention the new techniques of plastic surgery. Thus large areas of skin which have been destroyed by severe burns can be replaced by shaving off thin layers from another part of the body. These do not need to cover completely the whole damaged area: small pieces are scattered over the wound and gradually grow together. Corneal disease (the cornea is part of the "window" of the eye, and when it becomes opaque the patient cannot see) is treated by removing the diseased cornea and replacing it by a cornea removed from a dead body, or sometimes from an eye which has had to be removed from a live patient for other reasons. There are, in fact "cornea banks" where corneas are kept in refrigeration for future use, just as there are "blood banks" for use in blood transfusions. Other advances in surgery will be described elsewhere in the section.

(5) New Approaches in Social Medicine. Medicine has passed through many phases from the time when disease was regarded as a punishment from the gods or a sign of devil possession to the present era, when increasingly there is a tendency to look on society as the patient. Indeed, one commonly hears doctors and sociologists nowadays talking about "the sick society."

The early primitive stage came to an end—at least in one part of the world—when in Greece, five centuries before Christ, Hippocrates and others began to teach that all diseases were due to natural causes. But after the first ray of hope the outlook began to deteriorate when, during the Middle and Dark Ages (that is, from the fall of the Roman Empire right up to the fifteenth century), there was a return to the belief in devil possession and supernatural causes.

Eighteenth-century medicine in Europe was materialistic, regarding the body as a machine. It was founded upon a sort of pseudo-science—although, of course, there were always individual exceptions, physicians such as Sydenham in England, who, avoiding all theories, based their work on observation of the patient. This mechanistic approach persisted right through the nineteenth century, but medicine became more and more truly scientific, and the century saw the most rapid advances in the field ever known until our own times: the discovery of germs by Pasteur, of antiseptics to combat them by Lister, of vaccination by Jenner and anæsthetics by the American Wells and the Scot Simpson. The use of the microscope by Virchow, who was a German, brought great advances in the understanding of disease and Ehrlich, another German, conceived, as we have already seen, the idea of "magic bullets" which would attack the germs at the root of a disease without harming the patient. But one of the greatest of all these great men is perhaps the least known. His name was Edwin Chadwick.

From the earliest period of recorded history human communities had been constantly ravaged by great plagues which swept over their lands year after year, killing untold millions. Such plagues are recorded in the Bible and other ancient books, but, when town life became more and more common, as during the Roman Empire and the Middle Ages in Europe, the overcrowded conditions were even more favourable to the spread of disease. The Black Death of 1348–9 wiped out almost half the population of Europe. But, even in the first quarter of the nineteenth century in London, tens of thousands died from typhus, typhoid, and smallpox—and not only these, for periodically cholera would be brought into the country by travellers from abroad.

In the face of these terrible visitations the individual physician was helpless. He could not treat each one of the many sick even had he known how, and Chadwick's claim to fame rests on the fact that he was the first man to think in terms of *social* control of diseases, by so dealing with their causes that they were prevented from arising at all. In order to wipe out typhoid and cholera, he argued, we must ensure clean water supplies; for these diseases are caused by germs carried in polluted water. In order to attack typhus and plague, one must get rid of the lice which carry the germs of typhus and the rat-fleas which carry the germs of plague (including, of course, the rats, which, in turn, carry the fleas).

In the past, some attempts had been made to segregate the sick to prevent the spread of disease—for example, in the case of leprosy (which, strangely enough, we now know to be less infectious than most germ-borne diseases). But segregating those who are sick with typhoid or cholera is of little use if others are still drinking polluted water, just as it is of little use segregating plague cases if rats with their infected fleas are allowed to run at large. So these early attempts met with little success, due to lack of understanding of how the infections were passed on.

Chadwick was born in a Lancashire farmhouse where the children were washed every day all over, and he ruthlessly drove an obsession with cleanliness into the heads of his countrymen until, later in the century, it was possible for the German philosopher Treitschke to tell his class in Berlin: "The English think soap is civilisation." Although this remark was meant cynically, there is little doubt that soap, if it is not civilisation in itself, has played a greater part in making civilisation possible than many more elaborate remedies. A population riddled with chronic infectious illness has neither the time nor the energy to apply to the arts or sciences, and soap did a great deal to reduce infection.

One of the first Public Health measures was introduced by Chadwick and others when they brought in legislation to purify the water supply of London. Previously, the citizens had used water from the Thames (they still do, but only after it has been filtered and sterilised at the waterworks!), and from filthy, refuse-laden ponds and springs. Later, Chadwick helped to found the Poor Law Commission, and produced a Report in 1842, the principal suggestions of which were: a municipal water supply for all towns; scientific drainage both in town and country; and an independent health service with large powers for dealing with those who endangered the lives of others by polluting water or causing nuisances. He also proposed a national service for interment of the dead; for in those days bodies often remained for days in the overcrowded homes of the poor without burial.

What has the twentieth century contributed to the concept of social health? Well, of course, there has been a great deal of legislation along the lines initiated by Chadwick to control disease, and a great many other measures have been introduced concerned with the idea of positive health—not merely preventing bad health, but trying to bring about the highest possible state of good health. Orange juice, milk, and good meals for schoolchildren have brought about a transformation in child health which has become apparent to the least observant in the last ten or fifteen years. And the National Health Service is in the direct line of descent from early nineteenth-century legislation.

But in future years it is probable that the main achievement of the twentieth century in social medicine will prove to be its extension of the term "social health" to cover every aspect of community life, not only in such subjects as bodily health and its control of social means, but also such problems as mental illness, crime, delinquency, drug addiction, and so on. What we are now asking ourselves is: how far are these problems produced by society itself, and if this is the case, how far can we go in preventing them by social means?

Social medicine takes the view that these problems can never be dealt with solely by moralising and retribution, but only by dispassionately analysing causes and dealing with them. In this century we have developed a social conscience. Not always, it is true, a very well-informed social conscience, but at least this is a good beginning. There are organisations for dealing scientifically with delinquency, for dealing with problem children, for spreading knowledge about cancer in order to show people that it can be successfully treated if taken in time. The organisation known as "Alcoholics Anonymous" has, on the whole, been more successful in treating alcoholics by social means than have any of the individual medical methods. Mental illness is also treated by group methods, which, together with the new drugs, have revolutionised the position in mental hospitals. We can well say with John Donne, who died in 1631, that "no man is an island . . . every man's death diminisheth me; for I am involved in mankind." This is the attitude of twentieth-century social medicine.

Summary. Perhaps we can sum up our progress in the past hundred years more dramatically in terms of hard facts.

One hundred years ago, a surgical operation was never undertaken except under the gravest circumstances. There were no anæsthetics and no antiseptics, and the operation was carried out by a surgeon in a filthy tail-coat, stained with the congealed blood of countless operations (indeed the surgeons of that time took pride in the dirty condition of their coat as showing how much experience they had previously had). Germs and the part they play in producing disease were unknown, and Paul Ehrlich had not yet been born, so there were no "magic bullets" to attack syphilis, or sera for diphtheria and other diseases. The mentally ill were simply locked up with little treatment and subjected to such indignities as the strait-jacket and the padded cell; now they are given treatment which becomes more effective each year, the padded cell and strait-jacket have gone, and in the more progressive hospitals even the ward doors are not locked.

Only thirty years ago you would very likely have died if you had developed pneumonia, "childbed fever" after the birth of a child, meningitis, dysentery, typhoid, or tuberculosis. With such infections as blood-poisoning you would have had practically no chance at all. Today, the sulpha drugs and the antibiotics have changed all that. Syphilis and gonorrhœa were lifelong tragedies both to the patient and his family, but now they, too, can be conquered.

The National Health Service has brought the possibility of good treatment equally to all, and other bodies—some of them privately run—deal with alcoholism and neurosis, with rehabilitation of the mentally and physically ill, with spastics, birth control, and marriage guidance. It is up to us to see that all these facilities are used to the full by all who need them.

PART II. DISEASES ARRANGED ACCORDING EITHER TO THEIR CAUSE OR THE AREA OF THE BODY AFFECTED.

THE INFECTIOUS DISEASES
INTRODUCTION.

INFECTIOUS diseases are those which are caused by an invasion of the body by organisms from outside (the word "organism" simply means other living things, and we are using this word because, as will be seen later, it is not only what are known as "germs" which can cause infection). We know, too, that what is generally typical about this group is: (*a*) that the disease can be passed on from one person to another, and (*b*) that it is usually accompanied by a raised temperature or fever. Now (*a*), of course, is always true, because the definition of an infectious disease is one that can be passed on to others, but (*b*) is not always true, because a few infections produce little or no temperature, and also because it is possible to have a raised temperature (again in only a few cases) without any infection. For example, certain types of brain injury, tumour, or hæmorrhage can produce a raised—or lowered—temperature, and so can the injection of some foreign substance such as milk into the muscles. This is known as "protein shock," and was at one time used in the treatment of certain illnesses. Finally, solutions of dead germs, such as the anti-typhoid vaccine given to protect troops during the War, may lead when injected to very high temperatures. But, by and large, we are entitled to suppose that the patient with a raised temperature is probably suffering from an infection.

Types of Infection.

As we have seen, it is not only germs which cause infections—so from now on we shall give germs their proper name of "bacteria." Here is a list of the chief offenders which are liable to attack our bodies: bacteria, spirochætes, viruses, fungi, amœbæ, worms and other parasites. Of these, bacteria and viruses are by far the most important, but let us look at them all more closely.

Bacteria are tiny living things which can be seen only under a fairly powerful microscope. Some are grouped like bunches of grapes (staphylococci) or in strings or chains (streptococci). They are given these names because "staphylos" is the Greek word for a bunch of grapes, and "streptos" means a chain. Yet others are comma-shaped (such as the cholera vibrio), or shaped like a drumstick—a rod with a small knob at the end (the tetanus bacillus, which causes lockjaw).

It would be a mistake to think that all bacteria are harmful; for without some species we could not survive for long. Bacteriologists divide them according to their behaviour in the human body into three groups: saprophytic, parasitic or pathogenic, and symbiotic. The *saprophytic* organisms are the bacteria normally found in the skin, mouth, and intestines; they do us neither harm nor good. The *parasitic*, or as they are more usually called, pathogenic (*i.e.*, disease-producing) organisms, are the harmful ones with which we are naturally more concerned. Lastly, there are the *symbiotic* organisms, which, whilst taking something from the body, give something in return. For example, cattle would not be able to digest the cellulose of the grass they eat were it not for helpful bacteria in the lower parts of the intestines, and there are certain bacteria in the large intestine of man which build up vitamin B2.

Bacteria have two peculiar characteristics: each reproduces by splitting into two separate individuals as often as every twenty minutes in favourable circumstances like an open wound. If no bacterium were destroyed, one individual could produce a mass of bacteria larger than the whole world in a matter of a few weeks (since each of the offspring also divides into two, which in turn divide again—the progression goes: one gives birth to two, these two to four, the four to eight, eight to sixteen, sixteen to thirty-two, and so on—you will see, if you work it out, that in a short period the figure becomes astronomical). Fortunately, many bacteria have accidents, so for the present the world is safe! The other curious thing about bacteria is that, barring accidents, they are potentially immortal. Under ideal conditions in which no bacteria were killed, none would die; for a bacterium there is no death from old age, no corpse except when it is actively destroyed. It simply goes on dividing, dividing, and subdividing for ever.

How, then, are bacteria destroyed? Briefly, the answer is that most are destroyed by the natural defences of the body of whatever host they are preying on; others are destroyed by antiseptics and the new drugs; and many are destroyed when they are excreted from the body in the sputum or through the bowels and land in places where they are dried up and cannot survive—although some bacteria in such circumstances can form what are called "spores," rather like the seed of plants, so making it possible for them to survive in a state of suspended animation for months on end until picked up accidentally by another unfortunate host. Finally, bacteria, in addition to all these possibilities, face another danger: they may themselves develop disease. This disease is caused by even more minute organisms known as bacteriophages (viruses which affect bacteria), discovered by the French bacteriologist d'Hérelle a good many years ago. Attack by bacteriophage causes whole groups of bacteria (known as "colonies") to disintegrate and become harmless.

Although bacteriophage has been used in the treatment of some diseases in human beings, this method has now been largely given up, since the new drugs are infinitely more effective.

Spirochaetes. Spirochætes, like bacteria, are minute organisms, but differ in being shaped somewhat like a corkscrew and in being able to move (which many bacteria cannot do). Their progress is produced by a sideways wriggling motion. The two main diseases caused by spirochætes are syphilis and spirochætal jaundice. Spirochætal jaundice is carried by rats, and is common in those who work in mines. It is now rare in Britain, but still occurs in Japan, Egypt, and Malaya; the infection is passed through the skin where the excreta of infected rats mingles with water on damp ground in the mine where miners kneel. Infection may also occur through eating infected food.

Viruses. Unlike bacteria, viruses are too small to be seen under an ordinary microscope. They can, however, be photographed in some cases under an electron microscope, which uses a magnetic field instead of a glass lens and a stream of electrons in place of a beam of light. Viruses cause such diseases as typhus, measles, mumps, poliomyelitis, smallpox, and chickenpox—not to mention such plant and animal diseases as tobacco mosaic disease and foot-and-mouth disease, which often have serious economic consequences. Other virus diseases are psittacosis (an infection of parrots and similar birds which can be transmitted to Man), swine fever in pigs, influenza in Man, and myxomatosis in rabbits. They also cause, it is believed, the common cold.

The main characteristics of viruses are, first, that they can only grow in living cells—unlike bacteria, which readily grow in the laboratory on plates containing a jelly made from meat broth, gelatin, milk, and other delicacies. The scientist, therefore, must keep them in portions of living tissue kept alive outside the body. Secondly, they are so small that they pass through the pores of the finest filter. Thirdly, a first attack usually produces immunity for life. Second attacks of the common virus diseases mentioned above are very rare; but unfortunately, this rule does not apply to influenza or the common cold. Fourthly, there is reason to believe that viruses represent an extraordinary intermediate stage between the living and non-living; they can, for instance, be produced in crystalline form and yet are just as dangerous when "thawed out." Lastly, the virus diseases have proved for the most part to be little affected by the new antibiotics and other drugs, although vaccination in smallpox and the injection of sera from infected patients in other infections may give immunity for longer or shorter periods.

The two great practical problems that doctors face with viruses are: (i) many viruses are unknown because of the difficulty of growing them outside the body in suitable tissue culture. They cannot therefore be conveniently identified in specimens from the patient, as bacteria can; and (ii) they are unaffected by antibiotics like penicillin. It has been a great step forward to grow viruses artificially in tissue culture, in which they are identified indirectly by the effects they have on the cultured *cells*. But since we do not know exactly how to grow some viruses (like those of infective hepatitis) they have still not been seen.

When we recover from a viral illness like chickenpox, we probably do so by producing virus-killing substances inside our own cells. Scientists are currently searching for these substances in case they can be used, like penicillin, to cure viral disease.

Fungi. Some infections are caused by fungi—that is to say organisms belonging to the same group as moulds, mushrooms, and toadstools. Penicillin and some other antibiotics are produced from moulds, so, as in the case of bacteria, some fungi are helpful; they even help to destroy each other, as bacteria do. For example actinomyces, which can cause infection of the jaw and other tissues, is destroyed by other tissues.

Most fungal infections are trivial and limited to the skin. But, although trivial, they can be unsightly and uncomfortable. Ringworm of the scalp, dhobie itch—an infection of the groin spread by infected underclothing—and so-called "athlete's foot" are caused by a fungus.

Amœbae. Amœbæ are small, single-cell organisms, the largest of which (a harmless type found in stagnant ponds in Britain and elsewhere) is just visible to the naked eye. It is about the size of the head of a pin. Amœbæ move, in the species which are capable of moving, by pushing forward a part of the cell in the appropriate direction and causing the rest to flow into the advancing portion. Like bacteria, they reproduce by dividing into halves, each of which becomes a new amœba.

The main human disease caused by amœbæ is amœbic dysentery (not to be confused with bacillary dysentery).

Parasites. These may live on the skin like lice (which can carry typhus) or fleas (carriers of plague), or the parasites of scabies which burrow into the skin, or they may live part of their time in the blood or other tissues, like malaria. They often have complicated life-cycles involving other hosts (like mosquitoes) at certain stages of development.

Worms. Worms are intestinal parasites, but the only common types found in Britain are threadworms, the tiny thread-like worms which cause irritability and itching in the skin of children, less often in adults; round-worms, somewhat resembling the ordinary garden earthworm, which seldom lead to symptoms; and tapeworms, which may reach a length of 10 or even 20 ft. Many parasitic worms (like parasites elsewhere) lead a double life—they spend part of their life in the human intestine and the other part in the muscles of another animal. The tapeworm, for example, whilst in the human intestine, lays eggs which pass out of the body in the excreta, and are then swallowed by pigs, especially in those parts of the world where human excreta are used as manure in the fields. In the pig, the eggs form cysts in the muscles—meat infected in this way is known as "measly pork"—and when, in turn, the meat is eaten by man, the process in the intestine begins all over again.

Less common types, from our point of view, are the Russian tape-worm (which, as befits a Russian, grows to nearly 30 ft.!); this type is spread by caviare or undercooked infected fish. The small, leaf-shaped liver fluke, lays eggs which are passed into canals or pools in tropical countries in the urine of infected people, hatch out and enter a water snail, and finally leave the snail in the form of small parasites which pierce the skin of bathers, whence they pass to the liver and subsequently the bladder and rectum. This is a serious condition, as is also filariasis (another tropical disease), for which, unlike bilharzia—caused by the liver fluke—no cure is known. The tropical disease known as loa-loa is caused by a variety of filaria.

How the Infection is Spread.

Infection is spread in many ways, some of which have already been mentioned. In the common fevers found in Europe and elsewhere one of the most frequent ways is by *droplet infection*—that is to say, by minute drops carrying the germs which are coughed or sneezed into the air by someone already suffering from the disease. Such droplets can be projected into the air for 10 ft. or more, and when breathed in by someone within range infection may result. Next commonest mode of spread is perhaps by *infected food, water*, and the dirty hands of those who prepare food: cholera, dysentery, food-poisoning, and typhoid are spread in this way. Spread by *direct contact* is found in the venereal diseases (usually, but not always, spread by sexual intercourse with someone who already has the disease), and, of course, lice, fleas, and other parasites, including the scabies mite, are spread by contact with the infested individual—or sometimes with his clothes or bed linen. Spread through an *intermediary host*, whether it be lice, fleas, or mosquitoes carrying infection, or the various means adopted by worms, has already been described above, so no more need be said. Lastly, the infection may result from *bacteria already within the body*; for example, the bacillus coli which lives in the large intestine is there harmless, but if it gets into the bladder or the ureters (the tubes leading from kidney to bladder) a quite unpleasant result may follow in the form of cystitis or pyelitis.

How the Body Deals with Infection.

The body has many mechanisms of defence against intruders, but suffice it to say here that there are two main ones. First, substances known as antibodies and antitoxins are produced in the blood—the antitoxins to neutralise the poisons produced by the invaders, the antibodies to render them helpless, for example, by causing them to clump together so that they can more easily be dealt with by the second defence mechanism. This second mechanism is provided by the white cells in the blood, some of which (the phagocytes) act like amœbæ and swallow up and destroy the germs. Antibodies and antitoxins can be transferred from one individual to another and are used in medicine both to prevent infection and to cure it. This is known as immunisation, and can be active or passive. Active immunisation is produced by injecting either a solution of dead bacteria, as in the case of anti-typhoid injections, or by injecting live, but weakened, strains of the organism, as in the case of smallpox vaccination. In both cases the body is stimulated to produce its own immune substances. Passive immunisation is used either for people who have been in recent contact with infection or who are already ill, and in this case the antitoxins produced in another person who has had the illness are injected in the form of serum—*i.e.*, the liquid part of the blood without the blood cells. All these natural defences are inefficient in the ill, the underfed, the very young, and the very old.

Antiseptics.

We have already discussed the other ways in which bacteria are destroyed, and now need only make brief mention of antiseptics, and antibiotics. The earliest antiseptic was carbolic acid, used by Lister in his operating-theatre in the form of a fine spray directed throughout the operation on the wound, or sometimes in the form of steam from a kettle containing a solution of carbolic. But carbolic is dangerous, and since Lister's time many more useful antiseptics have been discovered. Acriflavine, thymol, and other old favourites have been discarded too. The various forms of carbolic are still used to disinfect drains but, to tell the truth, the use of antiseptics nowadays is very limited. In surgery the *antiseptic* method has given way to the *aseptic* method—instead of fighting sepsis we see to it that no possibility of sepsis is present before operating: all instruments, the surgeons' and nurses' hands, the skin, are sterilised—the instruments by boiling, the dressings by dry heat, the hands by soap and water, and almost the only antiseptic used is to clean the patient's skin in the area to be operated on.

Antiseptics are used as first-aid treatment for cuts and wounds, but should be applied only once as a general rule—that is, when the wound is first received. The trouble with antiseptics is that as well as killing germs they also kill the surrounding tissues, which antibiotics never do.

Antiseptic sprays to purify the air of a room or to destroy germs lurking in the dust on the sick-room floor—or any other floor—are practically useless. To quote the *British Medical Journal*: "There is no good scientific evidence that any of the chemical air-disinfectants can control the spread of infection in places such as schools, offices, or cinemas. Nor is there good evidence that any substantial effect on the spread of illness can be obtained by disinfection of dust."

Neither is there any good reason to believe that mouth-washes and gargles have any effect other than making the mouth feel fresher and (temporarily) removing mouth odour—by covering it up with the scent of the antiseptic. Mouth-washes are in contact with the bacteria for far too short a time to have any damaging result, and, in the case of tonsillitis and other diseases, all the important bacteria are hidden far out of any danger from gargles.

Antibiotics.

The antibiotics—penicillin, streptomycin, erythromycin, terramycin, aureomycin, and chloramphenicol—have already been dealt with, and only two important practical points need to be mentioned. These are that although most of such drugs are entirely safe under ordinary conditions, it is extremely dangerous for the layman to use them without medical guidance. If, for example, people get into the undesirable habit of sucking penicillin lozenges for sore throat and keep on doing this every time the sore throat returns, they may become sensitised to penicillin so that, when they become really ill—say, with pneumonia—the serious illness no longer responds to the drug. Or the same habit may make them allergic or hypersensitive to penicillin, and an injection given later may have serious and even fatal results.

Doctors no longer use the lozenges anyway, because of this danger and another one which is that excessive use of antibiotics may kill not only the dangerous bacteria, but also the ones which are helpful to the body. When this happens, other types of organism which are not affected by antibiotics will multiply in the absence of the bacteria which normally keep them under control. Thus chloramphenicol or aureomycin, by killing useful germs in the large intestine, may cause vitamin B deficiency, and when the non-sensitive organisms have their natural enemies removed they may step in and multiply, causing inflammation of the mouth, diarrhœa, and occasionally a fatal bowel infection. Chloramphenicol is too dangerous for general use.

General Treatment of Fevers.

Fevers are ordinarily heralded in by a rise in temperature which is noticeable either by a flushed face or by alternate sensations of heat and cold. A patient with a high temperature may have shivering attacks known as "rigors." Tell the doctor.

A high temperature does not necessarily (especially in a child) mean that the trouble is serious but the lay person should always treat it as such and certainly call a doctor if the patient is a child or an elderly person.

Even the trained physician finds it difficult to tell one fever from another in the early days; for most of the common fevers begin in more or less the same way. It is only when a rash or some other more definite sign becomes evident that a certain diagnosis can be made, and these may not show themselves until the patient has been feeling "run-down" and fevered for some days. Incidentally, although a clinical thermometer is a very useful thing when properly used, many a doctor must feel that, in unskilled hands, it is a menace. The "fussy" type of mother who is constantly taking her child's temperature whenever it looks in the slightest degree different from usual (probably it is simply feeling justifiably bored with its parents), not only causes anxiety to herself but also gives the habit of anxiety to her child. The child is made to feel that the world is a dangerous place, full of germs and all sorts of causes for fear—as indeed it is, but one needs a sense of proportion, and other dangers which we think much less about are at least as frightening and twice as deadly as most germs. Whatever you do, don't get the thermometer habit; your child, so far as fevers are concerned, is a good deal tougher than you.

Briefly, then, the way to treat a fever in the early stages before the doctor comes, and before one knows exactly what is wrong, is as follows:

(1) Put the patient to bed.

(2) Give little, and easily digested, food; if the patient wants none, give none.

(3) Give plenty to drink—the proprietary preparations containing lemonade and glucose are excellent, but water, weak tea with sugar, or home-made lemonade with squeezed-out lemon juice and sugar, whichever the patient likes best, are at least as good.

(4) Aspirin is useful to relieve headache or other pains and will reduce fever for two or three hours. But it will cure nothing. The patient will be more comfortable, but his illness will not be cured by aspirin except in certain very special cases. Soluble aspirin is best. Do not have special children's aspirins in the house. They are often nicely flavoured, the children are tempted to eat them like sweets, and there have been serious cases of poisoning. For small children, use suitably small quantities of ordinary adult soluble aspirin, having checked the dose with your doctor. Other methods of cooling seriously fevered patients such as bathing, tepid sponging, etc., are strictly for the doctor to prescribe. A patient as hot as that should be in a doctor's hands anyway.

THE INFECTIOUS FEVERS.

The remarks made above apply to the management of *any* fever, and we are now going to discuss particular infectious diseases, beginning with the common childhood fevers, then passing on to less common ones, tropical diseases, and worm and parasitic infestations.

The common infectious fevers are caused by bacteria or viruses, and it is useful to know the meaning of the following terms: *incubation period* is the time which elapses between being infected and developing symptoms; *prodromal period* is the time which elapses between the end of the incubation period and the appearance of a rash; *quarantine period*, the maximum time during which a person who has been in contact with the infection may develop the disease—it is usually two days more than the incubation period; *isolation period*, the time a patient is supposed to be isolated.

Views regarding the common infectious fevers have changed a good deal in recent years. Disinfection of rooms is now regarded as almost useless, and more cases are treated at home. Quarantine in the case of the common fevers is thought by a good many doctors to be a waste of time, since all it can do is to postpone infection from early childhood to early adult life, when it is likely to be more serious. For it is a characteristic of these fevers that they affect the adult much more violently than they do the child. However, on this, and all other points, you will have to be guided by the opinion of your family doctor.

Virus Diseases.

First, we shall take the common virus diseases, measles, chickenpox, and rubella or German measles, then the other virus diseases, mumps, infective hepatitis, virus pneumonia, and some less common conditions which do not always produce a typical rash as in the case of the first three.

In nearly all of these fevers there is a long incubation period, and one infection gives immunity for life.

Measles. The incubation period is 10–11 days. The first sign is the appearance of symptoms rather like a severe cold. The eyes become red, and exposure to light is unpleasant, the nose runs, the throat becomes inflamed, and a dry, harsh cough develops. There may be headache, and the temperature rises to 102° or more. Usually the patient is a child, and especially typical is the development of so-called Koplik's spots, which are small, bluish-white, raised spots seen on the inside of the cheek at the back of the mouth. The rash begins on the fourth day of the prodomal period, *i.e.*, 14 days after the initial infection. It shows on the forehead and behind the ears, spreading within a day downwards over the whole body; in another two days it starts to disappear, but often leaves behind a sort of brownish staining which may last for one to two weeks.

Measles can be serious, especially in very young children because of its complications, such as bronchopneumonia and infection of the ear, which can now be treated with antibiotics. These drugs have no effect on the measles virus, but only on the secondarily invading bacteria which have invaded the lungs and ear during the illness. The illness can be attenuated or lessened by injection of antibodies (gamma globulin) from an immune adult, and this is often worth while in the very young.

Rubella or German Measles. Incubation period 14–19 days. A mild fever, similar to measles except that the rash is usually the first sign that anything is wrong, and the temperature is rarely above 100°. The eyes may be pink, and there are enlarged glands at the back of the neck. The rash disappears completely in thirty-six hours. There are no complications.

German measles, in itself, is harmless, but if a woman gets the disease in the early months of pregnancy malformations in the child may appear at birth. Hence some doctors believe that girls particularly should have the opportunity of contracting German measles before they grow up. There is no special treatment, except the general rules for fevers given above.

Chickenpox. Incubation period 14–15 days, but may be more variable. In children chickenpox is a mild fever which begins with the appearance of tiny blisters on the chest and back. These later spread outwards to the legs, arms and face, and cause itching. Treatment is the general one for fevers already described. Calamine lotion or dusting powder will be helpful for the irritation, and the child's nails should be cut short to prevent scratching and infection of the spots. Whereas children are usually little bothered by chickenpox, young adults may be much more drastically affected—a temperature of 104° is not uncommon, and there may be severe headache.

Mumps. Incubation period 17–18 days. Everyone knows the typical appearance of the patient with mumps—the swelling in the salivary glands in front of the ears which makes the face look full. This causes pain later on, and it may be difficult to open the mouth. Temperature is not usually high (about 101°). Although uncomfortable, mumps is rarely dangerous, but orchitis—swelling of the testicles—is sometimes a complication. Fluid diet should be given if eating is painful, with mouth-washes, and rest in bed.

Infective Hepatitis. "Hepatitis" means inflammation of the liver, and infective hepatitis, which is much the commonest cause of jaundice in young adults, is a virus infection of the liver. In fact, this disease caused serious difficulties during the Italian campaign of 1943, and has probably become more frequent (or, at any rate, more frequently recognised) in this country since the War. The main symptoms are fever, followed by jaundice, which is first noticed in the whites of the eyes as yellow staining, then in the skin. The urine becomes coloured also, and this is most easily noticed if, on shaking in a bottle, the froth shows coloration. If the froth remains white, no jaundice is present. Treatment is a matter for the doctor, but great care should be taken, both by the patient and those in contact with him, to wash the hands thoroughly after urinating or defæcating, after handling utensils from the sick-room, and both before and after eating; for the disease is very infectious.

Virus Pneumonia. Pneumonia is usually caused by bacteria, and when we speak of pneumonia, that is the type we ordinarily refer to. Virus pneumonia is known by doctors as "pneumonitis," and is believed to be closely related to influenza. There is no specific treatment so far, and since diagnosis is a specialist matter, little more need be said except that the symptoms in general resemble those of ordinary pneumonia. Psittacosis, another virus disease, can also lead to pneumonia, and although there is no specific treatment for virus infections of the lungs, it is always worth while trying the antibiotics or sulpha drugs in view of the possibility that the lung condition may be caused by a secondary invasion by bacteria.

Influenza. While serious epidemics of influenza take the form of a very dramatic and often fatal disease—for example, the epidemic of "Spanish 'flu" which followed the First World War killed more people than the actual fighting—the milder type more usually seen is difficult to distinguish from the common cold. In fact, many people who complain of "a dose of the 'flu" are suffering from simple colds.

However, a sudden onset, aching in the muscles of the back and legs, and redness of the eyes, would suggest influenza, and especially typical is the depression and weakness which follow influenza but not a cold. The measures suggested above for the general treatment of fever should be applied; but the depression and weakness which follow influenza may need special treatment by the doctor.

Colds. Although everyone thinks he, or she knows what a "cold" is, the issue is not so simple for the symptoms of fever, running nose, and a run-down, "headachy" feeling are found in many illnesses. They may be observed, as we have seen, in the early stages of measles before the arrival of the rash, or in a number of other fevers, such as whooping cough. Mild attacks of influenza (see above) may resemble the common cold, and blocking of the nose with discharge and fever may be due to sinusitis—although here there is usually pain above, between, or below the eyes. Colds can be caused by any one of thirty different viruses known as "rhinoviruses" as well as by others which cause influenza, or infect glands (adenoviruses). This is why a single cold does not confer immunity on the sufferer. It is probable that you will not catch a cold from the same virus, at least for the rest of the year, but there are all those others waiting to infect you with other colds in buses, tubes, and other crowded places. Like all infections, do not forget that the best way to avoid them is to keep generally well, and in a good nutritional state. Do not spend money on injections or other vaccines. They do not work, probably because of the multiplicity of viruses involved. It is also unlikely that added vitamins or other expensive additions to the normal diet will do any good at all provided you are eating sensibly. There has recently been a vogue for treating colds with massive doses of Vitamin C. This doesn't work either, as has recently been proved.

Poliomyelitis. "Polio," or infantile paralysis as it used to be called, is a virus infection of the motor nerves—the nerves of movement—at the point where they leave the spinal cord. Fortunately, all the nerves are never affected, but only a few controlling one or more muscle groups

If these groups happen to be the ones controlling breathing or swallowing (which, fortunately, is not very common) the results may be serious, but ordinarily the muscles affected are those of the legs or arms. Poliomyelitis is almost as common now in adults as in children. Usually it occurs in small epidemics after hot weather, that is in Summer or Autumn, and it often seems to strike at fairly healthy normal people. This, however, is not because healthy people are specially prone as such, but because those living under less hygienic conditions are more likely to have developed immunity. In point of fact, the majority of cases of polio are so mild that they are never discovered at all, and paralysis does not develop; such people are specially dangerous, precisely because they pass unnoticed and spread the disease to others.

Like many other infections, polio begins with sore throat, fever, and sometimes vomiting five to ten days after contact. There may be severe headache and rigidity of the neck muscles. Paralysis is noted about the second or third day after this, and is usually at its maximum from the start, although this is not always the case. This stage lasts two or three weeks, by which time the temperature is down and the paralysis greatly improved, although further improvement may go on up to eighteen months after the acute stage.

This is another disease which has been dramatically reduced and even wiped out in many areas by the widespread use of vaccine. However, when the illness is already present attention is directed to relief of discomfort, resting and splinting the affected limbs, and preventing spread of infection to others. The Kenny method, devised by Nurse Kenny, and much publicised as a means of reducing permanent paralysis, is not believed by most doctors to be any improvement upon orthodox methods. The use of the iron lung is restricted to cases where the muscles controlling breathing are attacked, and any permanent paralysis of the limbs can often be helped by surgical operation.

Encephalitis. This is an infection of the brain caused by a virus, first noted in Vienna in 1916. There was an epidemic in London in 1918, but it is not very common today.

Smallpox. Smallpox was once common in Western Europe, and, as late as the early nineteenth century, was not unknown in Britain. Now, since the introduction of vaccination, it is comparatively rare in industrialised countries, although minor epidemics have occurred here recently. Jenner, who introduced vaccination, noted that dairy-maids who had suffered from the mild disease known as "cow-pox," contracted from the udders of infected cows, and transmitted to the hand of the dairy-maid, did not develop smallpox. In fact, cow-pox is a mild form of smallpox modified by transmission through cattle. Vaccination should be carried out at the age of three months, and repeated at the ages of seven, fourteen, and twenty-one years—also at any time when an epidemic occurs, or when travelling to any part of the world where smallpox is prevalent, or where immigration laws stipulate that it must be done. Many countries insist on an international certificate of recent vaccination before landing. Your family doctor will make out the certificate (he is entitled to charge you for it) and your local Medical Officer of Health will countersign it. Smallpox is one of the diseases which can very readily be spread from countries where it is prevalent because of the great increase in numbers of people travelling about the world by air.

Smallpox attacks people of all ages and is carried by excreta and droplet infection, but particularly by the dried scales on the skins of convalescent patients; it is now most common in the tropics.

Smallpox is similar in many ways to chickenpox. Typical cases are easy for the qualified doctor to distinguish from one another, but one of the difficulties of vaccination (as with Typhoid, and other artificially conferred immunities) is that the typical signs are often modified. Differential diagnosis is a job for the expert, and if your own doctor is in any doubt, he will consult with the local health authorities. The disease begins with shivering, headache, and backache, and the temperature is raised to 102–104°. On the third day a rash appears, which turns into small blisters on the sixth day, and the blisters become filled with pus by the ninth day. On the twelfth day they burst and form crusts. Unlike chickenpox, in which the rash starts in the middle of the body and works towards the outer parts, smallpox produces a rash which begins in the scalp, forehead, wrists, and feet and then moves towards the middle.

Smallpox is a serious disease, and the result depends largely upon whether the patient has been vaccinated within seven years of the attack. Contacts should be vaccinated and kept under observation for sixteen days; the patient must be isolated until all the scabs have separated and the skin healed. An effective drug has recently been announced.

Glandular Fever. This is sometimes called infective mononucleosis, since one of its features is an increase in certain mononuclear white cells and an alteration in their appearance. Another feature is an apparent infectivity. Beyond this the disease is a great mystery, and although it is probably caused by a virus, it may even be related to other (malignant) diseases of white cells. This one, however, is not dangerous although it often causes a lot of trouble by dragging on for many weeks. The main symptoms are fever, enlargement of lymph glands and sore throat. The patient feels very debilitated and often very depressed. Diagnosis is often very difficult, but there is a blood test known as the "Paul-Bunnell" test which is almost specific for the disease. The patient is usually presented as a case known to doctors as "P.U.O.," meaning Pyrexia (fever) of Unknown Origin. He has often been treated with several antibiotics, one after another, without effect, because the causal agent is not affected by these drugs. He is only very mildly infective, and it is unusual to insist on isolation or quarantine.

Typhus. This disease used to be known as "jail fever," because it was frequent in prisons; but overcrowding, poverty, and bad hygienic surroundings anywhere are suitable conditions for epidemics of typhus. Improved conditions in industrialised countries have made it unusual, since typhus is carried by a virus carried from one person to another by lice, and where lice are absent the virus is powerless to enter the human body.

Typhus comes on suddenly with a rise in temperature of about 102°, but within four days it may be as high as 107°. There may, or may not, be a rash at this time, and in the second week, when the temperature is at its highest, there is delirium, weakness, and a feeble pulse. The typical typhus rash appears about the fifth day as reddish blotches on the chest, abdomen, and wrists.

Typhus is, needless to say, very serious but responds to such modern antibiotics as chloramphenicol, aureomycin, and terramycin. Preventive measures are directed towards destroying all lice with D.D.T.

Rabies. Finally, we shall deal very briefly with a number of less common virus diseases, beginning, as is appropriate, with *hydrophobia or rabies*, since it was in this infection that the great French scientist Louis Pasteur (1822-95) showed the possibility of prevention by vaccination. Unlike Jenner, with his ready-made cowpox virus, which we have seen to be the virus of smallpox weakened by natural passage through cows, Pasteur had to weaken the rabies virus by passing it through rabbits. The rabbits were infected, and after death the spinal cord was dried and powdered, a solution passed through another rabbit, and so on until the virus was sufficiently weakened.

Rabies is spread by the bite of infected animals, usually dogs, cats, or wolves, who are driven mad by the disease; in Trinidad, however, it has been spread by vampire bats. Those who are bitten usually show no symptoms for six weeks or more, but sooner or later convulsions and delirium arise, which within four to five days are fatal.

There is no cure once the symptoms have developed, but Pasteur's serum, if given soon after the bite, prevents illness in the vast majority of cases—the sooner after the bite, the better the outlook. Dogs should be muzzled in areas where the disease is common, but quarantining imported dogs has made the infection almost unknown here.

Psittacosis. This is another virus disease which is of interest mainly in that it is spread by birds of the parrot group, such as parrots, love-birds, macaws, and the rest. It occasionally occurs here in people who have been in contact with birds of this type, and is serious both to the bird and its owner. As in the case of rabies, quarantine regulations have greatly reduced the likelihood of infection in Britain.

The symptoms of psittacosis are fever, cough, and bronchitis. The disease is especially dangerous to old people, but it responds to the same antibiotics as typhus.

Sandfly Fever, or phlebotomus fever, *Dengue*, or breakbone fever, and *Trench Fever* are all somewhat similar conditions in that they resemble influenza and are rarely fatal. They are all due to viruses, spread in the first case by sandflies in tropical climates; in the second by mosquitoes in tropical climates; and in the third by lice in temperate climates. They are all typical "soldiers' diseases"; the first two were common in the Middle East and Far East during the last War, the third during the First World War in France.

Yellow Fever. Of all the virus diseases, only four can be prevented by vaccination—smallpox, hydrophobia, yellow fever, and poliomyelitis. Yellow fever is carried by a mosquito known as Stegomyia, common in South and Central America and in African ports. For its spread, it therefore needs: a hot climate, the stegomyia mosquito, and an infected person.

In 1898 the United States was at war with Spain in Central America, where yellow fever was a serious problem. Following this war the United States, by this time acutely aware of this terrible disease, asked a Dr. G. E. Waring to deal with it in Havana, where it was rife. But Waring died of yellow fever, as had many millions before him, without knowing its cause, and it was left to Walter Reed, who died in 1902, to prove the connection between the mosquito and yellow fever. By a vigorous war on the mosquito, the disease has been eradicated from Havana and the West Indian islands, and Reed's discovery made possible the building of the Panama Canal (Ferdinand de Lesseps, the builder of the Suez Canal, had made a similar attempt in Panama, but had been beaten, amongst other factors, by yellow fever).

In yellow fever there is a sudden high temperature, aching of limbs and head, jaundice, and black vomit; the pulse-rate falls as the fever rises. Previous vaccination seems to be preventive if undertaken in time.

Conclusion.

All these virus diseases have this in common: that for many there is no specific cure, although smallpox, rabies, yellow fever, and poliomyelitis can be prevented by vaccination, or by the social control of the creatures carrying the virus. Some of the larger viruses (psittacosis, whooping cough) are destroyed by certain antibiotics. There is usually a long incubation period. Finally the question will sometimes arise of protecting some people from German measles or measles with gamma globulin containing another person's antibodies to the disease. This may be considered for measles in very young patients or to protect the fœtus in pregnant mothers in contact with German measles.

Bacterial Diseases.

Bacterial diseases differ from virus infections in a number of respects: their incubation period tends to be shorter; having the disease once does not often confer lifelong protection; and unlike virus diseases, most bacterial diseases respond to one of the antibiotics or sulphonamides. In many cases it is possible to inoculate against the disease to prevent it occurring, as we have seen is possible with only a few of the virus diseases.

Scarlet Fever and Other Streptococcal Infections. In the days, not so long ago, before the arrival of chemotherapy (sulphonamides) and antibiotics, streptococci were very much feared and even caused a high mortality, particularly in such susceptible groups as children, and mothers and babies in maternity hospitals. They are still taken very seriously in the latter and rightly so, although one wonders how much of the mystique is simply a hang over from the days, thirty years ago, when many mothers died from "childbed fever." All signs of infection, such as fever, during the puerperium (the period following childbirth) must be promptly dealt with by a doctor, and only occasionally now is there real cause for anxiety provided treatment is prompt and rigorous.

Scarlet fever is much less common and very much less serious an illness than it used to be, partly because of the effective treatments available today, but also because of a definite but unexplained reduction in its severity. Perhaps the streptococcus has changed, and certainly the improved physical condition of people who are now much better fed and housed than they were, has helped to ward off the terrors of this disease as of so many other infections. The classical picture of signs and symptoms is now so rarely seen that it will not be further described.

The importance of streptococcal infections has shifted from the initial infection, such as a sore throat, to some serious conditions which occasionally arise as a result of some form of delayed sensitivity to the bacteria. Acute rheumatism or rheumatic fever (not to be confused with ordinary aches and pains nor with rheumatoid arthritis) occasionally arise in people who have had a sore throat a few weeks before. Since the streptococcus is not the direct cause of the damage which may consequently occur in the heart or kidney, the antibiotics are no answer except sometimes to keep off further streptococcal invasions.

Diphtheria. This used to be an extremely serious disease, but immunisation has made it almost unknown; it is important, therefore, that all children should be immunised. There are many modern and up-to-date doctors who have qualified since the war who have never seen a case because it has become so rare, and in spite of the propaganda of certain ill-informed people this saving of children's lives is entirely the result of nationwide inoculation during the war and since. The following description is of historic interest only, and will remain so if a high level of inoculation is kept up by parents.

In a typical case of diphtheria the incubation period is about three days; the patient is a child who becomes ill and pale-looking (*i.e.*, the onset is not sudden, as in many fevers, but insidious); the temperature is only slightly raised to, perhaps, 99° or 101°, and although there may be no complaint of sore throat, examination will reveal inflammation with—and this is typical of diphtheria —a grey membrane spread over the tonsils, the palate, and the back of the mouth generally. The diphtheria germ does not spread within the body. It stays at the place where it entered (in this case the throat) and sends its toxins throughout the body.

Even after the acute phase is over the patient must not be allowed to walk, because the diphtheria toxin is particularly poisonous to the heart. The ordinary rule is at least one or two months in bed.

Diphtheria also occurs in the larynx—in pre-inoculation days many children choked to death with this form of the infection; in the nose; and, although this is not generally known, wounds can be infected. The so-called "Desert sores" of the North African campaign seem to have been caused by diphtheria-like organisms.

Diphtheria may lead to paralysis of the throat, with difficulty in speaking or swallowing, and paralysis of the eyes or limbs; these are due to neuritis caused by the influence of the toxin on the nerves.

Whooping Cough. For many years whooping cough has been regarded merely as a bother to the patient and a nuisance to others, as, in fact, a trivial disease. Unfortunately, this is not so: because statistics show that it causes more deaths than polio, diphtheria, scarlet fever, and measles all put together.

Whooping cough begins in a child as an ordinary cold with cough and slight fever, and this stage lasts for a week or ten days. Then the "paroxysmal stage" begins as a series of coughs following in rapid succession, during which time the patient is unable to breathe. The "whoop" is caused by the noisy indrawing of breath when the fit stops. The face may become blue and congested. Bronchitis is usually present, and bronchopneumonia may result as a complication, so inoculation of all children before the disease has a chance to strike them is most important.

Once whooping cough has begun, there is no specific treatment, although modern drugs can reduce the frequency of the fits of coughing. The antibiotic chloramphenicol has been used for this disease, but the general opinion is that it is ordinarily of little benefit. Chinese physicians once described whooping cough as the "hundred-days cough," and the cough may, indeed, continue for at least a hundred days.

Food Poisoning Diseases.

Strictly speaking, there is no such thing as "food poisoning" if one is thinking of "poisoning" in terms of anything apart from germs. But not so long ago it used to be thought that decomposition of food in itself produced poisons known as "ptomaines" which were deadly to those who swallowed them. All food poisoning is caused by infection of food with bacteria and by no other cause—unless, of course, we are thinking of the kind of poisoning which is the concern of the lawyer rather than the medical man.

Here we are considering those diseases which are commonly spread by contaminated food or drink. The classification is not scientific, but then no scientific classification has as yet been devised. First, we shall deal with typhoid, paratyphoid, and dysentery—uncommon here in Britain, although Sonné dysentery is fairly frequent. Then there is gastro-enteritis (which means irritation of the stomach and intestines), which is caused by staphylococci and the germs of the salmonella group, and lastly, botulism, which is rare.

Typhoid and Paratyphoid. These diseases are spread by infected water, food, or hands—especially uncooked food, such as milk, salads, oysters, and shellfish. Flies, too, play some part in spreading the disease. Some people are "carriers" and carry and excrete the germs without being themselves affected; for example, "Typhoid Mary," a carrier in the United States in the early years of this century, spent a large part of her life in custody as a public danger, although she did not show any symptoms of typhoid. Nevertheless, this woman caused a great deal of illness in others in her chosen profession of cook.

The influence of Chadwick's propaganda for pure water supplies is shown by the fact that deaths from typhoid, still 332 per 1,000,000 in 1870, fell to 198 per 1,000,000 at the beginning of this century. In the 1920s the death-rate was only 25 per 1,000,000, and now it is even less.

Typhoid fever begins like most fevers with headache, raised temperature, and general feeling of unwellness. This stage lasts about a week, and then the rash appears in the form of rose-red spots on the front of the chest and abdomen and on the back. In the second week there is great weakness, sometimes diarrhœa, flatulence, and mental dullness, together with dry and cracked lips and tongue. The third week is the week, in hopeful cases, of gradual decrease in temperature and other symptoms, and the fourth week is the week of convalescence.

Complications are perforation of the intestine (which needs surgical treatment), delirium, and bronchitis.

Paratyphoid fever is a milder form of typhoid (there are two forms, A and B); ordinarily it can be diagnosed only by scientific tests. The main thing is to inoculate contacts with T.A.B. vaccine and to protect food supplies; treatment is with chloramphenicol.

Dysentery. Dysentery may be caused *either* by a bacterium or an amœba; the first type is known as bacillary dysentery, the latter as amœbic dysentery (which is dealt with under tropical diseases). Infection is spread in much the same way as in typhoid. There is high fever, abdominal pain, and diarrhœa, at first consisting of fæcal matter, then blood and mucus. In severe cases the death-rate used to be over 20 per cent.

Various bacilli cause dysentery. The common tropical types are the Shiga and Flexner groups, but in this country most epidemics are due to the milder Sonné group.

However, in all these infections sulphaguanidine, one of the sulpha drugs, brings rapid relief, but care must be taken to avoid infection of other people.

Diarrhœa and Vomiting. Leaving out typhoid and paratyphoid fevers and dysentery, there is a group of infections known as "D. & V."—diarrhœa and vomiting. In Britain D. & V. is mostly due to:

(1) Salmonella infection.
(2) Staphylococcal infections.
(3) Other bacteria, ordinarily harmless, such as bacillus coli, when present in sufficient quantity.

Salmonella Infections are the most serious of this group; they affect the small intestine and produce vomiting, severe abdominal pain, and diarrhœa. These symptoms occur about one day after eating infected food and usually clear up within about two weeks, but occasionally death results. Salmonella bacteria are most likely to be found in meat, egg powder, vegetables, and ducks' eggs, but staphylococci are liable to grow in milk products, such as ice-cream and cream buns. Food poisoning from staphylococci is seldom severe, and recovery takes place in about a week. Nevertheless, it is extremely infectious, and causes a great deal of lost time in industry and temporary illness in institutions; for it is in such situations that it is most likely to occur.

Staphylococcal Food Poisoning has greatly increased in recent years, so it is important to know what circumstances are likely to cause it. The reason for its increase has nothing to do, as many people suppose, with the greater use of canned foods, but it has much to do with the greater use of communal feeding and canteen meals. It is *possible* for bacterial toxins in infected food to bring about illness even when the canning process has killed the bacteria, but it is certainly extremely rare. Canned foods, in fact, are much safer than so-called "fresh" foods in this respect—except when they have been opened, left about, and then re-heated. The same applies to the re-heating of any kind of food.

The real enemy is the canteen worker with a boil, a discharging nose, dirty hands, or a septic finger. Occasionally food may be infected in the larder by rats or mice, but the sort of canteen or restaurant where this can happen has little to commend it! Frankly, these infections are caused by dirty or stupid people who do not realise that their sore finger or boil can become someone else's diarrhœa and vomiting. Where children are concerned, the outlook is potentially more serious, and in the early part of this century the Summer-time "procession of baby coffins" was all too familiar. Infection is much more common in artificially fed babies or in older children who eat infected ice-cream. However trivial the condition may seem, diarrhœa and vomiting with fever in a child should never be ignored. Those in charge of canteens or restaurants must ensure that staff is supervised, that anyone with a septic infection is put off duty, and that all know about washing after visiting the lavatory and absolute cleanliness.

Bacilli normally present in the intestine, such

as bacillus coli, can cause infections if absorbed in large amounts, or if of a different strain from those in the patient's intestine. They are not usually serious.

Botulism. Now uncommon, this is the disease which used to be known as "ptomaine poisoning" on the theory that it was caused by poisons produced by bad food apart from germs. In the 1920s a party of picnickers at Loch Maree in the Scottish Highlands developed botulism and a number died, with the result that the disease attracted much public attention. Botulism is caused by a germ, the bacillus botulinus, which is peculiar in that, like tetanus, its poison attacks the nervous system rather than the intestines, resulting in fits, double vision, paralysis beginning in the face and spreading downwards, and difficulty in swallowing. It is found in tinned fruits or vegetables containing the toxin even when the germ has been killed, but, as we have already seen, the toxin comes from the bacilli, not from decomposition of food as such (in fact, food does not decompose in the absence of germs). Death is common in botulism, but an antitoxin is now available which, if used in time, can cure the disease.

Tuberculosis. No disease causes more public concern, and no disease is more difficult to describe, than tuberculosis; for, like the streptococcus or the staphylococcus, the tubercle germ can attack many different parts of the body and manifest itself in many ways. Furthermore, it is a widely spread disease, infecting not only humans but also cattle, birds, and reptiles. But here we shall be concerned with those types common to Man—the human and bovine (*i.e.*, the type occurring in cattle which can be spread to man by infected milk).

The tubercle bacillus is particularly hardy, so that when coughed or spat out on the ground it continues to be infectious for a long time. Infection is therefore caused by: (*a*) drinking infected milk; (*b*) droplet infection through having germs coughed in the face; (*c*) breathing in infected dust. In other words, tuberculosis is caused by absorption through either the lungs or the intestines; the former is common in adults, the latter in children.

But there is a good deal more to the problem than this; we know, for example, that over 90 per cent. of people in industrialised countries have been infected with T.B. in early life and have conquered the infection. So the question arises: what conditions predispose to T.B.—why do some people get over the early infection and others not? There are two answers to this question: one is certain—that those who are impoverished and do not get enough food are liable to T.B.; the second is not so certain—that mental stress plays some part. Yet there is reasonably good evidence that such stress as a broken love-affair can cause lowered resistance to breakdown so that when germs are encountered infection will occur.

In children, lung tuberculosis is not common, but tuberculosis of the bones and glands is, as is also infection in the abdomen, the kidney or spine, and, worst of all, tuberculous meningitis. These are often of the bovine type from infected milk. Ordinarily, T.B. in children is less serious than adult infections; but tuberculous meningitis used to be almost invariably fatal until streptomycin was discovered.

Adult tuberculosis usually occurs in the lungs or the pleura—the thin membrane surrounding the lungs. In younger people miliary tuberculosis, which is a form of T.B. blood-poisoning or septicæmia, is a very serious condition, and the infection spreads throughout the whole body in a few weeks.

Lung infection begins gradually in someone who has previously felt unwell. There may be cough, and later blood-stained sputum (although blood which is coughed up does not necessarily prove that T.B. is present). Whatever means of treatment are used, the struggle between disease and patient is likely to be fairly long, but the outlook is now good. The closure of the Swiss sanatoria is due partly to modern disbelief that air in one place is better than that in another, but mainly to improved treatment.

Prevention depends on legal action ensuring tuberculosis-free herds of cattle; on control of spread of the disease by those "open" cases who carry germs in their sputum; on the use of vaccination in childhood with B.C.G. vaccine (which you can ask your doctor about).

Many methods are used in treatment: new drugs, such as streptomycin, isoniazid, and P.A.S., lung surgery, rest, and so on. At any rate, tuberculosis is being got under control, but anyone who is worried can get a free X-ray at the nearest Mass Radiography Centre. For children, there are skin tests to show whether there is suceptibility to T.B.

Septicaemia. Commonly known as "blood-poisoning," is one of those diseases of which textbooks prior to the Second World war used to say: "death usually occurs."

Blood-poisoning occurs generally by spread from some septic area such as a wound (or even a small prick), after childbirth, or any place where certain germs have got admission to the body. The most usual germ is the streptococcus, although the pneumococcus—which ordinarily causes pneumonia—and the staphylococcus may also cause septicæmia.

Fever comes on suddenly and rises rapidly with headaches, sweating, and shivering. The patient is obviously very ill, and later there is wasting and delirium. The white blood cells increase in number. Septicæmia sometimes occurs without any apparent local infection in those who are weak and debilitated.

Pyaemia is a type of septicæmia which leads to the formation of numerous abscesses throughout the body. Its symptoms are the same as described above, except that the causative germ is usually the staphylococcus, and abscesses are found which may need surgical treatment.

However, in both conditions the state of affairs has been revolutionised by the use of the sulpha drugs and antibiotics; cure is now the rule rather than the exception.

Septicæmia should be suspected when any small wound or cut is followed by high temperature and the symptoms described above.

The word "*Toxaemia*" is used when the germs stay in their original position and produce symptoms by spreading their toxins throughout the body. Tetanus, diphtheria, and some kinds of childbirth infection come into this category; the symptoms may vary from mild disturbance to severe illness.

Meningitis means inflammation of the meninges, the covering which, like a layer of plastic, lies over the brain and spinal cord, just as the pleura covers the lungs and the peritoneum covers internal organs in the abdomen. (Hence inflammation of the pleura is known as pleurisy, and inflammation of the peritoneum as peritonitis.)

Various germs may cause meningitis, for example, the bacillus of tuberculosis, the pneumococcus, which ordinarily causes pneumonia, and the streptococcus or staphylococcus, but ordinarily the word refers to *Cerebrospinal Meningitis* or "spotted fever" caused by the meningococcus and occurring at times as an epidemic. It is commonest in the years from infancy to the early twenties, and begins suddenly with headache, vomiting, and fever. The temperature rises quickly, and pain develops in the back and legs; on the second or third day a rash appears on the body, and particularly on the inside of the thighs. Later there is stiffness of the neck, the head may be drawn back, vomiting persists, and the headache can be so severe as to cause the patient to scream with pain.

Fortunately, this type of meningitis (and most of the others) respond to treatment with antibiotics or the sulpha drugs, so the risks are very much less than formerly.

Pneumococcal Meningitis is an unusual complication of pneumonia, and the septic types (*streptococcal or staphylococcal*) arise either following an infected fracture of the skull or from infection of the ear or mastoid.

Tuberculous Meningitis has already been mentioned; originally always fatal, it is now treatable with streptomycin.

All these diseases are very much a matter for

specialist and hospital treatment, but it is worth while mentioning *benign lymphocytic meningitis*, in which, although all the symptoms of meningitis are present, recovery without specific treatment is invariable. Meningitis, which was during the First World War and after what polio is to us now, is no longer common, and when taken in time is easily treated.

Tetanus is usually known as "lockjaw" because there may be difficulty in opening the mouth, although this is simply part of a spasm of all the muscles of the body. The tetanus bacillus is found in rich soil—hence the disease is less common in desert areas—and tetanus resembles rabies in that: (*a*) it enters at a wound; (*b*) it affects the nervous system; (*c*) it results in fits and ultimately death.

However, active immunisation with T.T. (tetanus toxoid) has resulted in the disease becoming uncommon, and even when developed, treatment with antitoxin, anæsthetics, and curare may lead to cure.

The bacillus is anærobic (*i.e.*, does not use oxygen) and is most likely to occur in such situations as when a man digging manure or working in his garden sticks a fork through his foot, or, in war-time, when he is wounded in soil contaminated with manure.

Undulant fever, also known as Malta fever or abortus fever, falls into two types: melitensis, which infects goats, and abortus, cattle and pigs. Man gets the disease by reason of close contact with or drinking the milk of infected animals. (The name abortus is given because abortion is produced in cattle and sows.)

In Undulant Fever, as one would suppose, the fever goes up and down for two to three weeks; it may then go down and rise again, persisting for many months. The disease may occur in Britain, but modern drugs are on the whole successful in dealing with it. A striking feature of the disease is the combination of a high temperature with an appearance of relative well-being.

Another disease carried by mammals is *Glanders* or *Farcy*, spread by horses. In glanders there is discharge from the nose and sometimes pneumonia. Occasionally the disease is fatal. In farcy abscesses form, usually along the lymph vessels. Both conditions are very contagious, and treatment is a matter for a specialist; infected horses should be destroyed.

Cholera. Cholera could be classified under the head of food-poisoning, because it is mainly spread by infected water (however, like typhoid, it can also be spread by flies, infected food, and carriers); it could also be classified as a tropical disease, since, although it used to be found in Europe, it is now mainly rife in India.

Also like typhoid, cholera is caused by a bacillus, and can be prevented by early innoculation and care over food supplies—boiling water and milk, washing uncooked foods in chlorinated water, and keeping flies away.

The fever begins in the usual way with a short incubation period, followed by abdominal pain, severe vomiting, and diarrhœa. Later with the loss of fluid from the body there may be cramps in the muscles, diarrhœa increases, and the motions become of the typical "rice-water" type —*i.e.*, there is no solid matter, and the appearance is that of water to which a little milk has been added. This stage is followed by collapse, with low pulse and cold hands and feet. Death, if adequate treatment is not available, results in about 70 per cent. of cases.

Anthrax. The bacillus of anthrax, like that of tuberculosis, can exist outside the body for long periods, and, like that of tetanus, then takes the form of spores or seed-like bodies. It is spread by infected cattle and horses, which get the disease from eating grass containing spores.

In human beings the form the disease takes depends on where the germ alights; sometimes it comes from infected shaving-brushes, when it causes a large sore, like a boil, on the face, known as "malignant pustule"; sometimes it develops in those who inhale the dust from infected hides or wool (hence the name "wool-sorters' disease," which is a form of bronchitis with blood-stained sputum); lastly, it may arise through eating infected meat, when the result is intestinal anthrax.

In all cases the outlook is serious. Death is common, preceded by a high temperature, skin symptoms in the first instance, lung symptoms in the second, and food-poisoning symptoms in the third. Serum and arsenical preparations were formerly used, but now the sulpha drugs seem to offer more promise.

Diseases Caused by Fungi.

There are only two important groups of disease caused by fungus: the serious *actinomycosis* and the relatively harmless, if unpleasant, *ringworm*. Ringworm or tinea will be dealt with later; it affects the hair, the body, the groin (dhobie itch, already referred to), and the feet (athlete's foot). Actinomycosis is spread by a fungus in barley and grasses which may reach the human mouth, settle around bad teeth, and thence pass to the lungs, the bone of the jaw, and even to the intestines or brain. Fortunately, this unpleasant fungus, which was once difficult to eradicate, has proved susceptible to penicillin.

The Venereal Diseases.

The venereal diseases are those caused—or at least that is what the name means—by the goddess of love, Venus. Venus, of course, causes a great deal of trouble, but venereal disease is not necessarily the worst she can do. There are two diseases usually caused by sexual intercourse, and therefore described as venereal; others can be caused in this way, but are not usually so described.

Gonorrhoea is the result of an infection by the gonococcus (*Neisseria gonorrhoea*) and ordinarily comes on after a period of three to seven days following intercourse. However, babies can get an infection of the eyes, known as ophthalmia, from their mother if she is infected, and gonorrhoea in young children is often the result of being in contact with infected towels or clothes. The disease in adults is evident when there is a thick, creamy discharge from the sexual organs and sometimes pain on passing water; in infants ophthalmia is prevented by the use of silver nitrate eye-drops at birth. Gonorrhœa is fairly easily cured by the use of sulpha drugs or penicillin; but unfortunately venereal disease is increasing in recent years and drug-resistant forms are becoming more common.

Syphilis is more serious, and is nearly always caused by sexual intercourse. Stories about lavatory seats are simply stories, although it is occasionally possible to get syphilis by other than sexual means: for example, it has happened that a man playing football has been infected through his hand being grazed by the teeth of someone with syphilis. But this is very unusual, although kissing can spread the disease. Children, too, can be born with syphilis (the so-called congenital syphilis).

Adult syphilis begins with a sore, known as a hard chancre, at the point where the spirochæte of syphilis has entered; this may be on the lips, through kissing; on the sexual organs, through intercourse; and very rarely, as explained above, elsewhere. In a short time the chancre disappears and all may seem to be well, but this primary stage is followed by a secondary stage with sore throat, a rash, headache, and enlargement of glands. This, if left alone, also clears up, but is followed by the tertiary stage, in which a chronic infection develops in some part of the body which, presumably, is most susceptible in the particular individual. Thus there may be chronic syphilis of the skin, the bones, the heart, liver, or nervous system.

In the nervous system, the commonest forms are the two diseases of *tabes dorsalis*, in which the spinal cord is infected, and G.P.I. (general paralysis of the insane), in which the brain and mind are affected. These will be discussed under Nervous Diseases.

In congenital syphilis the pregnant mother gives her child syphilis. Such infants are often stillborn or premature, they look wizened, like a little old man, and amongst other symptoms are eye disease, "snuffles," a flattened nose, and when the adult teeth appear the front ones may be notched at the biting surface.

The treatment, of course, is very much a matter for a specialist, but diagnosis is usually made through the Wassermann blood test. It was for syphilis that Ehrlich produced his "magic bullet"—an arsenical drug, known as salvarsan, which could attack the organism selectively without harming the body and was the first of the modern specific drugs. Present-day treatment is with penicillin. G.P.I., once hopeless, is now dealt with by malarial therapy with a good deal of success. Penicillin alone is often adequate.

It is important to understand about venereal disease in general: (1) that it happens to many people who are no worse than anyone else; (2) that many patients believe themselves to have V.D. when, in fact, they have not; (3) that the best thing to do is to see your doctor as soon as possible—he is not concerned with your morals, and the sooner you go, the sooner you will get well; (4) every sore in the sexual area need not be V.D. There are other diseases which may be contracted as venereal infections.

Chancroid produces small septic ulcers around the sex organs, with swelling of the local glands in the groin, which may suppurate. It is caused by a bacillus, and can usually be cleared up by sulpha drugs within a week. Scabies and lice often pass from one body to another during sexual intercourse, but are not usually thought of as venereal in origin, although in many cases they are.

Tropical Diseases.

Nothing is more difficult than to define the term "tropical diseases." One might define them as the diseases which occur in tropical climates—but then measles occurs there too; and if they are defined as those diseases which are found *only* in the tropics, the solution is no easier, since leprosy, cholera, smallpox, and typhus are usually listed as tropical diseases, yet were found in this country until fairly recently—and the odd case still is.

But what a story could be told about the conquest of those infections which were—and many still are—the scourge of humanity! One day when generals and dictators are forgotten we shall remember that great international army of physicians and bacteriologists who have saved millions of lives and infinitely reduced human suffering: Koch and Ehrlich of Germany, Pasteur and Roux of France, Ross and Jenner of Britain, Reed of America, Noguchi of Japan, and many others. We shall remember how the Jesuit priests brought quinine from Peru to Europe in 1638, the first drug to save people from malaria; how in tropical heat Ronald Ross (1857–1932) peered for hours through his microscope to discover the connection between malaria and the mosquito until the sweat running from his brow rusted the instrument; how Major Walter Reed's work in Havana (1851–1902) made possible the building of the Panama Canal, and think, too, of the American soldiers who died in helping him to find the cause of yellow fever. In mentioning Jenner once more, we should recall Lady Mary Montagu (1689–1762), who brought the practice of vaccination to England from Turkey—or, rather, the practice of "variolation," which meant inoculating with the pus from smallpox cases. This was, of course, a dangerous practice, but the idea was there. Noguchi, one of the great bacteriologists of the nineteenth century, was the son of a poor peasant. He often had to steal to get enough bread even to keep alive, but was later to help in our understanding of syphilis and many tropical diseases.

Yet there is still much to do. Take, for example, the case of Egypt, one of the world's poorest countries, supporting with the help of water from the Nile about 24 million people. But if the river gives food and drink it does other things; for it carries the disease of bilharzia, which kills thousands of peasants yearly. In the villages of Egypt as many as 90–100 per cent. of the population suffer from this terrible disease. The infantile mortality rate is the second highest in the world—29·5 per cent.—seven times higher than that of Holland; the average expectation of life amongst the lower classes is thirty-one years, of the upper classes fifty to sixty years. The country is ridden with bilharzia, ankylostomiasis, malaria, plague, amœbic dysentery, typhus, tuberculosis, and pellagra. Blindness, due to trachoma and other diseases, affects tens of thousands. Such a situation cannot be treated simply by pouring drugs into the country; what is necessary is social control, to enforce purification of the water supplies, the use of insecticides such as D.D.T. to kill the disease-bearing pests, and removal of the causes of extreme poverty (tuberculosis and vitamin deficiencies which are common in Egypt are diseases of malnutrition).

Relapsing Fever, common in India and Africa, is caused by bad hygiene (rubbing infected lice into the skin); the germ is a spirochæte, similar to that of syphilis, but the disease is non-venereal. Relapsing fever gets its name from the fact that the temperature remains high (103–106°) for about a week, returns to normal for a week, and rises again. There may be three to five relapses of this sort. Cure can be brought about by the arseno-benzol drugs used in syphilis. Lice, of course, should be dealt with.

Epidemic Jaundice (also known as Weil's disease or—if you prefer it—ictero-hæmorrhagica spirochætosis), is also caused by a spirochæte, and spread by rats. Now it is rarely found in Europe, although it occurred in the trenches during the First World War, in men working in sewers, and in the women who worked in the fish market of Aberdeen, which at one time was rat-infested. It is rarely fatal, but leads to high fever and jaundice. Anti-syphilitic drugs are useless, but some of the new antibiotics may help.

Yaws is also a spirochætal disease, common in the tropics and particularly in children. It is unpleasant, but not serious, and tends to clear up in a year or so. There are raspberry-like growths on the skin, which disappear with the drugs used in syphilis (although the condition is non-venereal). The Wassermann reaction, positive in syphilis, is also positive in yaws.

Leprosy. Whereas syphilis, relapsing fever, epidemic jaundice, and yaws are caused by spirochætes, leprosy is caused by a bacillus resembling the bacillus of tuberculosis. Leprosy, in fact, should not be included here at all, for it is non-spirochætal, and not necessarily a tropical infection. But, apart from all the difficulties of classification already mentioned, leprosy *is* usually thought of as a tropical disease (although it is fairly common in Iceland and used to be so in Western Europe); it *is* thought to be deadly contagious (although it is, in fact, only very slightly contagious); and it *is* thought to be incurable (although young ladies with a mission in life who wish to go to a leper colony will find that it can be cured). One wonders why leper colonies exercise so much more attraction over some people than mental hospitals, T.B. sanatoria, or cancer clinics; but there it is. So there are many misunderstandings about this disease, and placing it in the wrong part of the medical section is probably the least.

Leprosy is not hereditary, and not very infectious without intimate contact, and this need not necessarily be sexual. It takes the form of nodules under the skin which show ulcers and can lead to the loss of a finger or toe. At first there is fever and large red patches which coalesce to form swellings with loss of sensation. The patches are on the face, forearms, and thighs; on the face they give a "leonine" appearance—*i.e.*, resembling the face of a lion. In other cases the main nerves in the forearm are affected, so that, as in the first type, the fingers and toes may drop off. Leprosy may go on for thirty or more years, sometimes getting better and then relapsing; occasionally recovery without treatment occurs. The treatment is an old Indian one in a modified form—chaulmoogra oil—but today promin and diasone are used more successfully.

Plague is another disease caused by bacteria, common in Europe at one time, but now largely restricted to Asia. Nevertheless, it caused millions of deaths in Europe during the years

1348–49 and 1665 and was the "Black Death," which, indeed, changed the course of history. Interested readers may read Hans Zinnser's *Rats, Lice, and History* about this aspect of the disease. Plague is carried by the bite of the rat flea, but, once people become infected, spread may occur from one to the other by droplet infection—*i.e.*, by coughing and sneezing. After an incubation period of two to ten days, fever develops, rather like severe influenza, and in a day or two the glands in the groin begin to swell, followed perhaps by swelling of the glands elsewhere. This is the usual type of plague, but it is also possible to get disease of the lungs from droplet infection and blood-poisoning from infection of the blood-stream. Both the latter types are almost invariably fatal, and even the glandular type (bubonic plague) has a mortality of about 80 per cent. The vaccine has given place to streptomycin and sulpha drugs which are also used on contacts.

Although we have little space to discuss the subject of plagues and epidemics in general, it is worth noting that serious epidemics have almost always followed wars, revolutions, and economic and political collapse. Thus the Black Death followed the break-up of the Roman Empire, and, in the fourteenth century, accompanied the end of mediæval civilisation. The Napoleonic wars were followed by other epidemics, and the wars of the 1830s in Europe were followed by influenza. In the most widespread outburst of influenza after the First World War, more people were killed by the disease than in all the fighting of four years. It is a reflection on the peculiar mentality of Man that this devastating epidemic, which affected almost the whole world, occupies little space in his history books—we still, with few exceptions, regard history as the doings of kings, queens, and generals. Yet, in 1918, 20 million men, and women, and children died from influenza, and no cure has, as yet, been found! Later we shall see that many millions of people die yearly from starvation or vitamin deficiencies. But these facts—the real facts of life—we rarely hear about.

Protozoal Diseases.

Nearly all the diseases caused by protozoa are tropical diseases, although one of the best-known protozoans is the harmless amœba found in British ponds. Protozoal diseases are caused by these organisms, large in comparison with bacteria which are really one-celled plants. Viruses are neither animals nor plants, are much smaller than the other two groups, and have some distinctive characteristics described elsewhere.

The only important diseases caused by protozoa are sleeping sickness or tryanosomiasis, malaria, and amœbic dysentery (as contrasted with bacillary dysentery), another disease, leishmaniasis—also known by the numerous names of kala-azar, dum-dum fever, and, in milder form, Delhi boil, Oriental sore, or Bagdad sore—will also be mentioned briefly. These infections are few, but important in their influence on Man; for, as Dr. Clark-Kennedy has pointed out, malaria until recently was responsible for one-fifth of all human sickness, sleeping sickness not so long ago caused a large part of Central Africa to be uninhabitable, and in some areas of the tropics there are probably more people with, than without, amœbic dysentery.

Malaria. The word, of course, means "bad air," just as "influenza" means "influence"—in Italian *influenza di freddo*—the influence of cold. Human beings have a natural tendency to suppose that, when two events occur together, then one must be caused by the other. Yet, although malaria and "bad air" may often go together, and influenza and cold, it does not follow that bad air (whatever that may be) causes malaria nor that cold causes influenza. In fact, the anopheles mosquito carries the amœba of malaria, and the mosquito prefers climates which some people might describe as "bad," but it is the amœba, not the air, which causes the disease. Anyhow, the unfortunate mosquito might well use the phrase honoured by many generations of schoolmasters: "It hurts me more than it hurts you!" For the mosquito, too, is sick, and passes on its sickness to the person it bites.

There are several types of plasmodium—which is the scientific name for this amœba—producing attacks of fever varying in severity and frequency: benign tertian, quartan, and malignant quartan. Entering the body from the mosquito bite, the parasites penetrate the blood cells, multiply there, and finally burst into the blood stream. When this happens the temperature rises, and then they return to the cells to carry out once more the same procedure. Depending on the type, the attacks of fever may be at intervals of three or four days, severe or milder. When someone with malaria is bitten by a mosquito the infection can be transmitted to the next person it meets, but malaria is not infectious from one person to another directly. Quinine, of course, is the time-honoured remedy, but many other drugs are now available: mepacrine, palmaquine, atebrin, and even a sulphonamide derivative known as promin have been tried. The drug must be taken long enough for the infection to die out, otherwise relapses can occur even after leaving a malarial country (but it is only fair to say that, just as some people continue to give themselves the title of "Major" when they have left the Army, so others long in Britain continue to describe attacks of cold or 'flu as "my old malaria again," when, to say the least of it, they are exaggerating).

Important as are the drugs used in the treatment of malaria, even more so is the control of the parasite-bearing mosquito. The eggs of mosquitoes hatch in water, and there the young or larval forms can be attacked by pouring oil on the surface of pools so that they are unable to breathe, or by introducing small fish which have a partiality for them. Adult mosquitoes can be killed by D.D.T. and other insecticides or kept away by nets over beds and skin creams. Finally, anti-malarial drugs can be taken in dangerous areas. Whereas anopheline mosquitoes were once well on the way to getting rid of Man, now Man is well on the way to getting rid of mosquitoes.

Blackwater Fever is a sequel to malaria in tropical Africa and some parts of India. Rather illogically, it is described as "Blackwater," although the urine is red and the skin is yellow but the result is due to breaking down of the red blood cells by some malarial toxin. Possibly too much quinine may help in producing the illness. Treatment is to give plenty of fluids and no quinine or any other anti-malarial drugs in the early stages. The death-rate is about 25 per cent.

Trypanosomiasis or sleeping sickness—not to be confused with *sleepy* sickness, which has already been dealt with under the name of encephalitis lethargica—is essentially an African disease (although also found in tropical America) spread by the tsetse fly. Its cause is the type of protozoan known as a trypanosome, almond-shaped with vibrating membranes at the sides which enable it to move through the blood-stream, rather like a flat fish in the water.

There are three stages of the disease: first, the stage of fever with enlarged glands and a rapid pulse, which may continue off and on for three years; secondly, the stage of trembling hands, legs, and tongue, vacant expression, and slow and stumbling speech; thirdly, and lastly, the stage of low temperature, apathy, wasting of the muscles, and possibly death.

Treatment is with arsenical drugs—such as tryparsamide or Bayer 205—which give good results in early cases. Preventive measures in infected areas include the destruction of tsetse flies by insecticides, the cutting down of forests near rivers which are inhabited by tsetse flies, and some authorities have suggested the shooting of big game which may form a "reservoir" of the parasites, whence tsetse flies can carry them to human beings. For similar reasons infected people should not be allowed to move to non-infected areas.

Amœbic Dysentery, also known as *Amœbiasis*, is caused by the *Entamœba histolytica*, an amœba whose cysts are found in food, water, or spread by infected fingers or flies. There is mild fever and diarrhœa which contains blood. The disease may become chronic, and can cause abscesses, usually in the liver but sometimes in the lungs. Amœbiasis is treated and usually cured by injections of emetine hydrochloride, but in the chronic phase the drug known as Yatren is used in the form of an enema.

Leishmaniasis, kala-azar, or dum-dum fever, is another amœbic disease, probably spread in this instance by the bite of sandflies. It is also known as tropical splenomegaly—enlargement of the spleen in ordinary language—since infection results in enlargement of the spleen and liver, low, irregular fever, and death within a year or so. A milder form, affecting the skin, is known as Delhi boil, Oriental sore, or Bagdad sore, does not lead to kala-azar, and is fairly readily cured. The cure for both conditions is to give injections of tartar emetic, which reduces the death-rate from kala-azar from 80 per cent. to about 5 per cent.

Diseases Caused by Parasitic Worms.

Many types of worms infest human beings and other animals. They are interesting for such reasons as their size (which may range from the almost invisible to 30 ft. or more), their life histories, and their serious or trivial consequences on their hosts. We shall mention only a few groups here, and mainly the ones likely to be met with in Europe—the tapeworms, the roundworms, and the threadworms—although some tropical types will be described briefly.

Tapeworms, as we have seen earlier, like many other types of intestinal worm, lead a double life. What usually happens is that the worm breeds in the human intestine, the eggs pass out in the fæces, and are then swallowed by animals eating contaminated material. In the animal the eggs hatch out into larvæ—primitive forms which penetrate the muscle, forming cysts—and Man is infected in turn by eating its meat. Thus *Taenia Solium* gets into the flesh of pigs, which, if imperfectly cooked (measly pork), causes infestation of the intestine in Man. It reaches a length of about 10 ft. *Taenia saginata*, which reaches a length of about 20 ft., is spread in imperfectly cooked beef, and in Baltic countries *dibothriocephalus latus* gets into the human intestine from caviare or undercooked fish. It reaches the awesome length of 30 ft.

Now all the worms we have mentioned so far are found in the human intestine, and the cysts, which are much more dangerous and unpleasant, in the animal's muscles. But in some worms the reverse happens, with the adult in the animal's intestines and the cysts in Man. Thus in Australia the dog tapeworm (*taenia echinococcus*) produces cysts in both sheep and Man. This is known as hydatid disease, and may remain unsuspected until cysts in the lungs, liver, or elsewhere become infected or rupture. *Trichinella spiralis* is similar in action, being found in the intestines of pigs and getting into the muscles or other organs of Man. The main difference is that this worm migrates from the pig's intestines into its muscles, whence it reaches Man in undercooked pork meat or sausages. The muscular cysts cause swellings and sometimes pain. There are changes in the blood, swelling of the face and leg in the early stages, and fever. A minor epidemic occurred in England in 1941. *Taenia echinococcus* and *trichinella spiralis* are small—not more than ¼ in. in length—but are more serious in their consequences than the large worms. Treatment is very difficult, and ordinarily all that can be done is to deal with individual cysts when they make themselves apparent.

The large tapeworms, *taenia solium* and *saginata* and *dibothriocephalus latus*, produce varying symptoms or none at all. Usually they are not discovered until some segments of the worm are excreted, but there may be mild indigestion, excessive hunger, and occasionally anæmia. However, when the worm is discovered the patient, not unnaturally, is likely to become anxious and uncomfortable at the thought of "having" a tapeworm; these symptoms are caused by the worry rather than the worm.

Treatment is, of course, a matter for a doctor, but purging followed by extract of male fern is usually successful. One has to make sure that the head of the worm has been removed, otherwise it will continue to grow.

Roundworms are similar both in appearance and size to ordinary earth-worms and the eggs reach Man, not from an animal, but from the contaminated fingers of someone else who handles food. They give rise to no symptoms, and are noticed only when discharged in the fæces or occasionally vomited up. They can be removed by the use of santonin.

Threadworms, as the name suggests, are like small ¼–½-inch-long pieces of white thread. They are very common in children, and live mainly in the cæcum—*i.e.*, the part of the large intestine near the appendix. The males, which are the smaller ones, remain there, but the females pass down towards the rectum at night-time and lay their eggs in the area around the anus. Infection is by contaminated hands handling food—especially uncooked food—and water. Threadworms are not serious, and cause few symptoms other than itching around the anus and between the legs, but heavily infected children may show symptoms of anæmia. The nervousness often shown by such children is usually the result of the irritation produced by the worms in the anal region. Infection is not common in adults, and in children tends to disappear at puberty.

Treatment is, in theory, simple; for the worms are easily destroyed by a number of drugs, such as gentian violet, thymol, or one of the proprietary remedies. Ointment is applied to the itching area, and the child should be prevented from scratching. However, since the eggs may lie about the house for some time, reinfection often happens, especially if there are several small children in the home who may pass the disease from one to another.

The idea that intestinal worms in general are likely to cause loss of weight by absorbing food eaten by the patient is largely mistaken: for, although it is true that they do live on this food, the amount taken is certainly not enough to be significant.

Tropical Worms. *Bilharzia* has been mentioned before in connection with its frequency in Egypt, although it is also found in other parts of Africa, Arabia, and Iraq. There are two main types: one infecting the bladder (*schistosomum haematobium*), the other the rectum (*schistosomum mansoni*). Bilharzia is more correctly known as schistosomiasis.

The parasite's fantastic life-history begins when a man bathes in infected water, and the small swimming forms known as cercariæ pierce and enter his skin—or they may enter the body by drinking infected water. From the skin they pass to the portal vein below the liver, remain there six weeks until they become adult and then swim against the blood-stream down to the pelvis, where the female lays eggs which have a sharp spine. The eggs penetrate into the bladder or rectum—depending on the type of fluke—and pass out in the fæces or urine. If they enter water they hatch out into small moving forms which seek out a water-snail, develop further in its body, and leave it in the form of cercariæ ready to find a new human victim. The female fluke is slender and round, about 1 in. in length, the male, flat and leaf-shaped, is about ¾ in. long, and as we have seen, their grisly courting takes place in the portal vein, whence the impregnated female passes to the bladder (hæmatobium) or rectum (mansoni) to lay her eggs.

Infection results in raised temperature and, in the urinary type, blood in the urine; in the intestinal type blood is found in the fæces, and there are symptoms resembling dysentery—*e.g.*, diarrhœa. Treatment in both cases is by injections of antimony tartrate. Needless to say, attempts should be made at prevention by telling people to avoid infected canals (usually easier said than done), and by periodically cutting off the water supply to the canals to kill the snails.

Hookworm Disease, or ankylostomiasis, is found in many parts of the world, especially in miners who work on damp ground. The tiny worm enters the body usually through the feet, passes through the blood-stream to the lungs, eats through into one of the bronchial tubes, climbs the windpipe, and passes down the œsophagus into the stomach to end up in the duodenum. It causes anæmia, can be fairly readily cured, but is occasionally fatal.

Elephantiasis. Some types of parasitic worm are spread by insects. Thus in *Filiarisis* mosquitoes inject by their bites the infantile forms of a tiny worm which enters the lymphatic channels; there the blockade they cause leads to the swelling of the legs and the lower part of the body, known as elephantiasis.

PHYSICAL INJURIES

INTRODUCTION.

In this section we shall inevitably discuss much that could be described as Principles of First Aid. You cannot learn First Aid from a book, even if you read one of the excellent first aid manuals, like those published by the St. John Ambulance Association. The only way is to join one of their many classes of practical and theoretical instruction which are held in all parts of this country and many others. There is much to be said for many more people receiving instruction, to judge by the level of general ignorance and ineffectiveness to be witnessed at most road accidents before the ambulance comes.

The most difficult thing to learn is what *not* to do. When a patient is knocked down in the road, people instinctively seem to want to drag him immediately to his feet, or otherwise pull him on to the pavement away from the traffic. Someone will have entered the nearest shop and be emerging with a chair so that the casualty can sit down. Before long a hot strong sweet cup of tea has arrived, and this or some other beverage is being poured into him. All this is instinctive, and all of it is wrong. Do *not* move the patient until you are sure he has no fracture which will be further aggravated by movement. To take an extreme case, a fractured spine clumsily moved may result in permanent widespread paralysis. Guard your patient from the traffic but only move him when you are certain it is safe to do so. If he has any injury which is likely to require a general anaesthetic on arrival in hospital (and this applies to most fractures) do not give anything at all by mouth. No anaesthetic can be given to a patient who has eaten or drunk anything in the previous three hours, in case he vomits while unconscious and dies of obstruction of his airway. Keep your patient warm (do *not* warm him up artificially) keep his head low, and unless he is bleeding severely or has stopped breathing, do nothing but protect him from the ministrations of the uninstructed until the ambulance comes.

Injuries to the Head and Back.

The head contains the brain, an organ with a number of inconvenient properties from the point of view of injury. Its very great importance is matched by its very great vulnerability as a tissue. Its consistency is that of stiff junket. It is quite incapable of repair once damaged and cannot heal by growing new parts in the way that skin and bone can. So it has to be totally enclosed by protective bone which means it cannot swell without compressing itself dangerously within its box—and this not infrequently happens after injury. Furthermore, any bleeding into the interior of the skull can only occur at the expense of compressing the brain, since the brain box is already fully occupied by the brain. There is a story in first aid known as "Concussion and Compression." It begins with a knock-out blow to the head and this is known as concussion. The patient struck a hard enough blow to the head will lose consciousness, if only for a short time, due to the brain being shaken up. Even slight knocks would do this if the brain were not cushioned by a thin layer of cerebrospinal fluid. Most concussed patients quickly regain consciousness, and for the great majority that is the end of the affair except for a sore head and a headache for a few days. Unfortunately for a minority, even though there may have been no fracture, the blow that knocked them out will also have damaged a small blood vessel on the surface of the brain. These patients may be indistinguishable from the luckier ones at first. They may have regained consciousness and will be just as anxious to go home. They will often be quite lucid for some hours. Surgeons call this the "lucid interval." However, when more than a certain amount of blood has accumulated in the head, and the brain is sufficiently compressed by it the patient loses consciousness slowly, for a second time, and from this phase of "compression" he will not recover unless something is done. The lucid interval can last some hours. Brain surgeons can relieve the compression and save the life of the patient only if they have him in their care when it occurs. This is why *all* cases of head injury who have once lost consciousness (concussion), for however short a period of time, and however lucid they may subsequently appear, *all* must be seen by a doctor and, if thought necessary, observed overnight in hospital, in case they are bleeding and proceeding to compression. There is no way of saving these avoidable fatalities other than by treating all cases of concussion seriously. Fractured skull is potentially even more serious, because the blow will have been harder and, the brain is therefore more seriously at risk.

The spinal cord can be regarded as an extension of the brain which runs down the middle of the spinal bones of the vertebral column. It has the same delicate consistency, and the same inability to recover from injury as the brain. Injury is usually the result of a fracture-dislocation of the spine. The consequences of injury are due to a permanent interruption of its two main functions. All movements of the voluntary muscles are only possible if they are connected by nerves to the brain. Except for muscles in the head, all these "motor" nerves run in the spinal cord. The nerve pathways leave the skull through a large hole in its base and run down in the spinal cord to the required level. They then emerge between the spinal bones and travel in bundles to reach the muscles. Motor nerves for the arm leave the cord between the vertebrae of the neck. Those for the leg leave the cord in the lumbar region in the small of the back. If the nerve supply is damaged in any part of its course, the muscles being supplied become paralysed and are unable to move. It follows that if the spinal cord is damaged, all muscles below the point of damage have been cut off from the brain, and will be paralysed, and this will be permanent because the cord cannot be repaired. Damage to the nerve pathway *after* it has left the cord can often be repaired. Permanent paralysis is only one of the consequences of cord damage, since there is another whole series of nerves running in the cord which carry sensations from all parts of the body to the brain. Therefore there will be loss of sensation as well as paralysis below the point of injury.

It is emphasised that fracture of the spinal bones can occur without damage to the cord taking place. It is when these bones move one over the other, or "dislocate," that permanent cord damage occurs. It is therefore extremely important that cases of back injury be moved very carefully indeed in order to avoid such a disaster, and special ways of moving such patients are taught in First Aid classes.

Haemorrhage and Shock.

Every part of the body must have a blood supply, or else it will die. It is possible to stop the blood supply to a leg, for example, by fastening a wide rubber bandage tightly around the top of the thigh. This so-called " constrictive bandage " is still mentioned in First Aid books as a desperate means of controlling haemorrhage in a limb. It should hardly ever be used, because by stopping all circulation of blood, the entire limb will die in the course of time. Besides, most haemorrhage can be stemmed by direct pressure on the bleeding point. The tissues of the leg, such as its muscle and skin and bone will begin to die in a little more than half an hour after cutting off the blood supply. The brain, however, will begin to suffer within three *seconds* of its blood supply being cut off, and will die in about three minutes. Thus it can be seen that some parts of the body are more susceptible than others to a failure of the blood supply and the brain suffers earliest of all. Since the brain is where most of the vital functions of the body are controlled, it follows that a shortage of blood to the brain is likely to lead to a " depression of the vital functions "—a state of affairs known to First Aiders as "'shock."

Shock occurs in a number of conditions, but is always due to a failure of the supply of blood to the vital functions of the brain for one reason or another. Its usual causes are:

(1) haemorrhage, when there is a general shortage, but the brain feels it most;

(2) severe burns, in which much fluid is lost from the blood as will be seen later; and

(3) certain medical conditions causing acute heart failure in which there is a failure to pump blood to the brain because the pump has failed.

The treatment for shock consists basically of restoring the blood supply to the brain, and where it is caused by loss of blood or other fluid, the treatment is transfusion. Finally, it must be emphasised that treatment is always urgent, since the brain cannot function for long without its blood supply, and once damaged by the shortage, can never be repaired. No attempt is made here to describe such treatment completely, but the most important things are to keep the head low so as to reduce the work the heart must do to drive blood to the brain; and to avoid artificial heating of the body by hot water bottles, etc., which only diverts blood away from the brain where it is needed, into the skin where it is not.

The treatment of severe haemorrhage is to stop the bleeding, usually by firm, direct pressure, and then to remember above all things that even though the bleeding has stopped, there may be a dangerous state of shock from which the patient could die. This can only be prevented by restoring the circulation to the brain, usually by transfusion; so, having stopped the bleeding drive him fast to hospital for the second part of the treatment which may be as necessary to save his life as the first.

There is great confusion over the use of the word " shock." In the lay mind it is a shake-up of the nervous system caused by a fright, or some bad news, or the sight of something nasty in the woodshed. Even in the medical mind it is sometimes confused, and some of the First Aid books confuse it still further. Too frequently they give the treatment as " loosen all tight clothing from neck, chest, and waist; reassure the casualty and ensure a good supply of air." All this, together with grandmother's hot strong sweet tea is perfectly good enough if the patient is only " shaken-up " by a fright or a fall, but it will be dangerously negligent and time-wasting if he is suffering from true shock due to a failure of blood supply to the brain.

Fainting is a special case which can be prevented by keeping the head low in those who feel faint. It is usually self-curing due to the patient automatically falling into a position in which the head is low. If the faint, however, is due to severe blood loss, this is the same as shock in our proper meaning of the word and must be treated accordingly.

Haemorrhage can therefore be a difficult problem. It is even more so when it is internal. This may be in *medical* cases such as in occasional cases of peptic ulceration in which the blood will be vomited and also passed in the stool. Or it may be *surgical*, in the sense of being caused by injury to internal organs. The blood may emerge from one or other of the various orifices of the body, or it may be entirely concealed within the body. Rupture of internal abdominal organs such as the spleen, kidney and liver can occur with surprisingly little to show in the way of external injury. A fractured thigh bone can pierce the main artery of the leg and cause lethal internal haemorrhage without a drop of blood being visible. In all these cases diagnosis is urgent, followed by emergency blood transfusion if the brain, and hence the patient's life, is to be saved.

Means of detecting the presence of severe haemorrhage without seeing any blood are taught in First Aid Classes as the Signs of Haemorrhage. They are in fact manifestations of the reactions of the body in its attempts to save the failing brain, and are therefore the same as the signs of shock. The main ones are a rapid, feeble pulse, getting more rapid and more feeble as time goes on in a desperate attempt to get the remaining blood to the brain; skin pallor caused by constriction of blood vessels near the surface so that the blood which remains is shunted to the brain away from the less vulnerable skin; and finally, just before death, restlessness and air hunger.

A word of warning about the First Aid treatment of shock due to heart attack (coronary thrombosis). These patients must be transported at complete rest, but many of them react very badly to being made to lie down, since they have great difficulty in breathing in this position. Transport them relaxed, in a sitting position, supported by a large comfortable back rest.

It cannot be too strongly emphasised that with haemorrhage and shock, as with so many First Aid emergencies, the importance of protecting the brain is paramount.

Asphyxia.

The previous section was concerned with maintaining an adequate supply of blood to the brain. This is needed in order to supply the brain's only possible fuel—glucose—and the oxygen with which to burn it. Many different circumstances can conspire to reduce the oxygen content of the blood, and the result in each case is asphyxia. Normally, air is taken into the lungs through the air passages and brought into contact with all the circulating blood. It diffuses from the lungs into the blood, where it enters into a special relationship with the pigment of the red cells—haemoglobin. At the same time, the waste gas carbon dioxide enters the lungs from the blood and is breathed out. The revitalised blood is passed through the heart to build up sufficient pressure to drive it into all the tissues of the body, and in particular into the brain. A special system in the brain—the respiratory centre—controls the complicated machinery of respiration and is itself, of course, kept alive by the products of the very mechanism it controls. This mechanism consists of all the muscles of respiration—those which lift the ribs, the diaphragm and many other so-called accessory muscles. They all have to be finely co-ordinated by means of nerve impulses which begin in the brain, pass down the spinal cord and out to the muscles. Information of many kinds comes along sensory nerve pathways to the respiratory centre so that breathing can be automatically adjusted to the changing needs of the moment. In order that life may continue there must be:

(1) a functioning breathing mechanism to revitalise the blood; and

(2) a circulation to carry the revitalised blood to the brain and other tissues.

In many cases when breathing stops and unconsciousness supervenes as brain function is depressed, the heart will go on beating for some time longer. The aim of First Aid is to restore the breathing by artificial respiration *before the heart stops*. Once the heart stops—and it eventually does so abruptly and without warning—the brain is dead within the usual few minutes unless *both* the heart and the breathing are restarted; and this is a very much more difficult proposition than artificial respiration alone.

For these reasons, a patient whose breathing has stopped must have it started again without any delay. Here, as in the case of severe haemorrhage, it is no use telephoning the doctor or even putting the patient in an ambulance. The First Aider must act himself, because he is on the spot and the only one in a position to save life. Both actions require elementary First Aid training, and even school children can accomplish them if they have been well taught.

Asphyxia is the name given to a failure of the oxygen supply to the brain and is due to a breakdown in some part of the complicated breathing mechanism outlined above. One of its chief causes is a blockage of the airway by (*a*) solids or (*b*) liquids. Any foreign body of the right shape and size will block the airway, as also will the tongue in the unconscious patient. Remember how much more easily the child's airway can become blocked because it is so much smaller. Blockage by a liquid, is of course, drowning. Remember that if a patient drowns in the entire ocean, it is only about half a cupful which is doing him any harm—as it only takes this amount to fill the airway. The same goes for the amount of tea, or vomit, required to kill an unconscious patient if it gets down the " wrong way "—as it will unless someone prevents it.

Another very common cause of asphyxia is carbon monoxide poisoning. Carbon monoxide is a lethal component of car exhaust fumes, incompletely burning and badly ventilated fires and stoves, and domestic coal gas. One of the inconvenient properties of haemoglobin is that it combines with carbon monoxide very much more eagerly than with oxygen. Prolonged contact with even a very slightly contaminated atmosphere can build up a concentration of carbon monoxide in the blood which will prevent the blood from carrying sufficient oxygen—and this is in fact how it kills. It takes a very short time for this to happen if the atmosphere is heavily contaminated. Remember the danger of even a very slight leak of the gas either in the kitchen, or into a car from a faulty exhaust pipe or silencer. Many elderly people die of coal gas poisoning every day because their sense of smell is poor and they do not detect the leak.

Other causes of asphyxia are lack of oxygen in the atmosphere, as occurs at high altitudes; crushing of the chest so that the ribs cannot move; paralysis of the muscles of breathing by interference with their nerve supply, usually in First Aid, as a result of a broken neck and consequent damage to the spinal cord (poliomyelitis can occasionally produce the same effect by attacking the nerves just before they leave the spine); and depressing the respiratory centre in the brain, most commonly nowadays by barbiturate poisoning.

The only really effective method of artificial respiration, which all members of any civilised community should be able to carry out, can be learned in half an hour at a good First Aid class. This is the direct, mouth-to-mouth method, sometimes dramatised by journalists as the " kiss of life." The method is taught with the aid of models and cannot be satisfactorily learned by only reading about it.

In discussing asphyxia, we have again had to consider the particularly vulnerable situation of the brain.

Fractures.

Broken bones are not the most serious possible consequences of injuries causing fractures. It is usually more to be feared that further damage will be done by the broken ends of the bones to tissues and organs in the neighbourhood of the fracture. The First Aid treatment of immobilising the part before transporting the casualty is designed to avoid this.

Six types of fracture are commonly taught, but some of them may co-exist in the same injury and the division is only for descriptive purposes. In addition there are two special fractures of the skull.

A " simple " or " closed " fracture is where only the bone is broken, without damage to surrounding tissues and without a wound. A " compound " or " open " fracture is one in which air, and hence germs, can get at the broken bone. This may be through a wound, in whose depths lies the broken bone; or the bone may have been pushed out through the skin; or a bullet track may lead down to the fracture. All these are examples of compound fracture and the great danger is that the bone will become infected. Even now that infections are less feared than before the days of antibiotics, it is still a grave matter for bone to get infected. However the antibiotic is given, we rely on the blood supply to carry it into the infected tissue, and bone has only a very small blood supply. If the infection is not successfully treated it can smoulder for a long time and become a " chronic osteomyelitis " which might ultimately necessitate amputation of the limb—and all because the original fracture was compound or open.

A " complicated " fracture is one in which the broken ends of the bone have damaged some important organ or tissue in the region. For example, a complicated fracture of the ribs is one in which the lung tissue, close behind the inner surface of the rib, has been pierced, and the patient will be coughing up small amounts of bright red, frothy blood. A " comminuted " fracture is one where the bone is broken into several pieces, and an " impacted " fracture is one in which the broken ends have been driven into each other and are firmly impacted. Finally a " greenstick " fracture occurs sometimes in children because their bones are not brittle and do not always break clean across. They partly break like a green stick.

" Depressed " fracture of the skull is where the vault of the skull has been struck and dinted. Many problems arise, since the brain is inevitably compressed and no dressing of the accompanying wound should be allowed to press on the brain. The dangers of infection here are not only to the broken bone, but to the meninges covering the brain, causing meningitis.

Fractured base of skull often passes through that part of the base through which the internal ear channel runs. Thus it frequently results in blood, or cerebrospinal fluid, or a mixture of both, emerging from the ear. The gravity of this fracture lies in the severity of the impact necessary to produce it, which will probably have also caused great destruction of delicate brain tissue. The outlook is usually very poor.

Remember that most casualties with fractures will require a general anaesthetic on arrival in hospital so that their fracture can be set in plaster or otherwise treated. Avoid giving them things by mouth such as drinks, which will mean a three-hour wait before anaesthetic can be administered.

Burns and Scalds.

The severity of a burn or scald depends largely on its surface area. If a patient dies of a burn, the cause of death is either infection or shock, the latter being due to fluid loss from the surface. Both hazards depend on surface area, since the bigger the surface the more germs are able to enter, and the more fluid can be lost. It follows that the small burn on the hand or arm is seldom a threat to life, however deep the injury; and we shall therefore confine our attention to the larger burns of the whole surface of the limb or trunk. Smaller bodies have a relatively larger surface area, and so a burn of the surface of a child's limb or trunk represents an even greater risk from fluid loss than a corresponding burn in the adult. Everyone has seen the fluid form in the blister of an ordinary small burn. It comes from the fluid part or "plasma" of the blood stream and the loss into such a blister may amount to a thimbleful. This will not hurt anyone. But the loss of similar fluid from the surface of a large burn may amount to many pints. The resultant shock will be partly due to this fluid loss from the blood stream resulting in a reduction in blood supply to the brain. Thus shock from burns has common features with shock from haemorrhage, and it is treated similarly, by transfusion. This time it is not a transfusion of blood but of plasma or some plasma substitute. In practice it is not only water that has been lost but a number of important chemicals dissolved in it as well, so that transfusion solutions have to contain sufficient of each individual substance to restore the deficit. The arrangements for replacing the lost materials are complex and urgent; every bit as urgent as after a haemorrhage and for the same reason. The brain cannot be left too long in need. In general, the First Aid treatment of burns of large surface area is to keep them clean with a dry dressing and get them very quickly to hospital. Life-saving treatment by transfusion cannot start until they arrive. The only permissible delay is in the case of burns caused by corrosive chemicals which must be thoroughly washed off before transport, so that they do not continue to burn the patient on the way.

Unconsciousness.

It is not sufficiently appreciated that the dangers of being unconscious can often far outweigh the dangers from the cause of the unconsciousness. For example it is known that as many as half the deaths from head injuries are due to the airway becoming obstructed and not to the injury itself. The most important thing in managing the unconscious patient from any cause is to preserve an airway. Particularly if the patient is lying on his back it is likely to get blocked:

(*a*) by his own tongue as the lower jaw sags backwards;

(*b*) by his dentures (so remove them);

(*c*) by vomit; and

(*d*) by anything anyone may be tempted to give him by mouth.

Nothing whatever should be given by mouth in any circumstances to the unconscious patient, since he cannot swallow and it will inevitably go into his lungs.

Many of these dangers can be very much reduced by not having him on his back. Place him instead in the semi-prone position: half on his side, half on his front, with the upper leg drawn up to prevent him from rolling about. In this position the head will be inclined downwards. The jaw will tend to sag forwards and the tongue with it, away from the back of the throat. Any vomit will also come forwards. If the tongue does get in the way of the breathing the airway can usually be cleared by bending the head backwards as far as it will go and pushing the whole lower jaw forwards, by pushing from behind the angle of the jaw on both sides.

DRUG ABUSE AND DRUG DEPENDENCE.

This section of earlier editions of *Pears* was simply called "Addiction." This word is still much used, but is gradually being replaced by the terms in the present title, because ideas about the nature of the problem and methods of dealing with it are changing. Addiction is a word that conjures up rather 19th century ideas in the minds of readers: opium dens, inscrutable orientals, Sherlock Holmes injecting himself with cocaine—basically a phenomenon of foreign origin, rather frightening if its implications were not literary rather than factual, and not of great significance in Great Britain.

Drug Abuse.

It is now realised by doctors, research scientists, social workers, and the police—if still not by society as a whole—that the truth is quite different. The *abuse* of drugs in this country is at present of large proportions, increasing rapidly and showing no signs of diminishing. It is responsible each year for thousands of deaths by suicide and by accidental overdosage; for an enormous but virtually unmeasurable amount of private suffering; and for the loss to society, in terms of reduced working efficiency, of millions of man-hours every year. It has nothing to do with opium smoking which was never in any case more than the eccentricity of the few. Opium is virtually unused in medicine these days and the amount of smuggling, always small, is now negligible. The problems today arise chiefly from the misuse of drugs given by doctors for their effects on the central nervous system—the pain-killers, sleeping pills, "stimulants," and "tranquillisers."

Drugs and Medicines.

To the doctor, any substance is a drug that can be introduced into the body from outside, and that is capable of producing some detectable effect. Most such substances have a beneficial use. They are "medicines," and as such are given by doctors in suitable cases. Others, for example, nicotine (in cigarettes), alcohol (in beer, wine, or spirits), and carbon monoxide (in coal gas), are of doubtful benefit and of certain harm and are used by doctors, if at all, only under certain very special and usually experimental conditions.

Medicines may be classified under four main headings. First, there are those like quinine, or penicillin and other so-called antibiotics, that actually cure diseases by eradicating the organism (bacteria or other parasites) that cause disturbance of normal bodily function. Second, drugs such as insulin or the steroids overcome in the unhealthy the lack of some necessary substance a healthy body manufactures for itself: they must usually continue to be given for life. Third are the drugs which relieve the signs of disease—for example, there are many new drugs that lower the blood pressure or increase the output of urine—without being able to put right the disturbed basic situation which is the cause of the trouble. Fourth are drugs to relieve the patient's symptoms—which make him feel better, less breathless, take away his pain, help him to sleep, and so on—although we seldom know why they are able to do this. Indeed, in many cases we suspect that they are acting mainly as a token of help from doctor to patient, and so encouraging his body to fight a more successful battle on its own behalf. (There is in fact a fifth class of drugs, which includes the majority of those on the market at any time, the members of which are devoid of any action whatsoever except that of enriching those who manufacture and sell them; but we are not concerned with these at the moment. They constitute a related, but different, kind of problem.)

There is no doubt that the genuine advances in beneficial drugs during the last thirty years have been enormous; but the very successes of the penicillins, tetracyclines, antimalarials, hormones, and so on have bred in the public and in the medical profession itself an attitude of uncritical wonder. There have been relatively few drugs in the first and second categories mentioned above: and in the field of mental health, the importance of which is now so rightly emphasised, there are virtually none. Yet drugs which act upon the brain are often received as if they were curative although they may pose fresh problems rather than solve the old. Thus, although there are many drugs which act upon the mind, few do this in any fundamental sense: they relieve pain and anxiety, bring sleep and lessening of stress, and may allow the patient to recuperate himself during the relief they provide. But often this deeper change does not occur—sometimes because the doctor has not clearly seen his part in helping to bring it about—and then the symptomatic relief may come to be sought for its own sake.

New and old drugs are still prescribed for their effects upon the mind—less so now than even a few years ago, before the thalidomide disaster—without sufficient attention to possible long-term dangers, of which there are in effect four.

Dangers of Long-term Medication with Drugs acting on the Brain.

1. *Toxic effects.* Drugs which act upon the nervous system, like any others, have characteristic toxic or unwanted effects of their own (incidentally, these may become apparent rapidly; even, on rare occasions, after only a single dose). Such effects may have little or nothing to do with the desired effects for which they are being prescribed and taken. For example, it has only come to be realised quite recently that aspirin is liable to cause bleeding, which is occasionally serious, from the lining of the stomach in a large proportion of people who take aspirin regularly; or that phenacetin, another substance very frequently present in pain-killers that can be bought from chemists without prescription, leads (after prolonged use) to kidney damage. Some drugs may cause rashes and other allergic reactions in susceptible subjects; and jaundice, fainting, tremors, and motor disorders are known to occur in some patients taking a variety of other drugs.

2. "*Rebound.*" The body works in such a way, over a variety of its activities, that it tends to return to a "neutral" position after it has departed from this for any reason. For example, over-eating tends to be followed by a lessening of appetite, at least for a time; the runner makes up for his air-deficit during the race by breathing more deeply thereafter; and if, at rest, you breathe for a time more rapidly and deeply than you need, this period will be followed by one in which you breathe *less* often than usual until the balance is restored. These illustrations—and there are others—have nothing to do with drugs: but in a similar way, it seems that if a continued pain, or an unpleasant emotional state such as anxiety or depression is changed into its opposite, or removed altogether by the use of a drug, the prior state may return with increased force when the drug is no longer taken. The "rebound" phenomenon, naturally, encourages the patient to take another dose, and so on.

3. *Habit formation.* This alternation of mood-changed-by-drug with the disturbed mood itself leads to the habit of taking the drug. The patient comes to rely upon it and to take it anyway, even before the unpleasant state has returned. At this stage he is said to be "habituated": he has a psychological need for the drug, and later may become disturbed at the possibility that it will not be available when he needs it. This might not matter so greatly, if it were not that continued use of drugs in this way has physical consequences as well.

4. *Tolerance and habituation.* The body also tends to restore its own balance when drugs are given, too. It "learns" surprisingly quickly how to deal with substances with which it has never before been confronted, so that it eliminates subsequent doses more and more quickly and completely. Thus the effect of each successive dose is smaller and lasts for progressively shorter periods of time. To counter this, the patient tends to increase the dose: and the vicious circle continues. At this point he has become physically dependent upon the drug: and he may suffer physically—sometimes so severely that he dies—if supplies are not continued.

As he increases the dose in this way, so his tolerance of its effects increases, to such an extent that after prolonged use he may be taking doses of a drug that are five or ten times greater than those which will kill somebody not dependent upon them in this way. It sometimes happens that a patient develops a renewed craving at some point after a course of treatment, in which the dose of drug has been reduced without removing the underlying cause of his dependence. He may then obtain and use the dose he habitually took before treatment, not knowing that his body will have lost its tolerance of such doses. That dose is now as high for him as for any other person and so may be lethal. There has been a number of deaths for this reason.

Factors in the Causation of Dependence.

The risk of becoming dependent upon a drug is governed by three main factors: the drug itself, the personality of the individual who takes it, and the circumstances in which it is taken. Most adults have taken alcohol at one time or another, unless it is against their code to do so; yet *relatively* few are dependent upon it (relatively few, but many too many: perhaps half a million in the United Kingdom alone). Many of us have had morphine or some other strong pain-killer for medical reasons, without becoming dependent upon it (whatever so-called addicts say, it is extremely rare for anyone to become dependent on an opiate because he was introduced to it in a medical setting). On the other hand, if we start to take such a drug "for kicks"—as more and more people, particularly teen-agers and young adults are doing—it is extremely probable the we shall become dependent upon it, and sooner rather than later at that. It is also probable that each one of us would become dependent, were he obliged to take it regularly, for long enough, and in sufficient dosage. Thus, although there are personalities—psychopathic, immature, or unstable—that are more prone than others to become dependent if they are exposed to the drug, there are also drugs that are more likely than others to cause such dependence no matter to whom they are given. The extent of the dependence will vary: with some, it is never physiological but remains psychological (but not the less real or disturbing for that). Also, the rate at which dependence develops may vary; and the picture presented by the dependent subject—the extent to which his normal life is impaired, or to which he becomes dangerous to himself or others—varies as well. In a very much oversimplified way, some of these relationships will now be summarised for certain substances.

Heroin, morphine and cocaine are usually injected. Barbiturates (sleeping pills) and Amphetamine ("Benzedrine") are tablets or capsules, and Marihuana ("reefers," hashish) is smoked in cigarettes. Heroin and cocaine are now usually taken together. Combinations of drugs often act differently from their individual constituents and patients dependent upon them are even more difficult to treat. Barbiturate and amphetamine, also, are often mixed (as in "purple hearts"). There is considerable *psychological* dependence on heroin, morphine, cocaine, and amphetamine, but much less with marihuana. *Physiological* dependence is great with heroin and morphine, less with barbiturates, alcohol, and amphetamine in that order, and virtually nil with cocaine and marihuana. Personality plays a greater part in initiating dependence on alcohol, marihuana, and barbiturates than with the others. Heroin, cocaine, and morphine are the cause of more antisocial tendencies in dependent people than alcohol, barbiturates, and amphetamine. The chief danger of marihuana (mere possession of which is illegal) seems to be that the search for it will lead the searcher into localities where his risk of exposure to even more dangerous influences is greatly increased. It is thus sometimes argued that if it were legal to consume marihuana, the number of young people who yearly become dependent upon the other more dangerous drugs would in fact decrease. There is as yet no evidence for or against this proposition. The number of drug dependent people in U.K. is rising fast for heroin and cocaine. This number is very large for alcohol, and is increasing in the case of barbiturates and marihuana. Very few people are dependent on morphine, and the number is not growing.

Treatment.

Exhortations, imprisonment, and other moralistic or legalistic approaches are useless. Treatment of any person dependent upon a drug is a matter for a qualified psychotherapist. It is liable to be time-consuming and frustrating for patient and doctor, and it is frequently unsuccessful. At present, there are too few specialists or centres where treatment can be obtained, although it is to be hoped that this situation will change as the problem is increasingly seen by our society to be of exceptional gravity.

When there is little or no chance of cure, prevention is certainly the best treatment. Drugs should only be taken on the prescription of a doctor: and the patient should remind him from time to time, if this be necessary, that he would like to dispense with his drugs as soon as the doctor thinks it possible. It should also be remembered that there is often no need to reach for the aspirin (or any other drug that anyone can buy from the chemist without prescription) at the first sign of a headache—or to reach for it at all to help one sleep or relax, for which purpose such drugs are in any case pharmacologically useless. A wait for ten minutes is good discipline, and will frequently resolve the problem to an extent that makes a drug unnecessary.

DISEASES OF THE BLOOD

INTRODUCTION.

The blood-stream is the canal system of the body which carries from one part to the other various substances essential to life. Thus it carries, partly in the red blood cells and partly in solution in the liquid part of the blood, the oxygen breathed into the lungs, and returns to the lungs to be breathed out the waste product known as carbon dioxide. From the intestines it carries the digested foodstuffs through a large system of veins (the portal system) to the liver, where they are changed in many ways to make them suitable for absorption by the cells of the body.

Blood consists of a liquid part, known as plasma, and floating in this are the red and white cells. A cubic millimetre—that is, an area about the size of a pin's head—of this contains about 5 million red cells, mainly concerned with the transport of oxygen, and about 5,000 white cells, concerned with resistance to infection. There are different types of white cells—for example, the lymphocytes, the leucocytes, and the eosinophils (these are all given various names and subdivided in many ways). The red cells are usually known as erythrocytes. From examination of the blood, doctors can tell a great deal about the patient; thus less than the usual number of red cells signifies anæmia, too many, polycythæmia. If the red cells are reduced in number, but too large, pernicious anæmia is possible; when they are reduced in number but too small, simple anæmia is the probable answer. In acute septic conditions or infections there is great increase in leucocytes—up to 30,000 or more—in some chronic infections or certain diseases, such as whooping cough and glandular fever, there may be increase in lymphocytes. Eosinophils are increased in many allergic diseases.

Doctors also consider such factors as the number of platelets (which are very tiny cells connected with clotting), the fragility of the red cells, and the sedimentation rate, which is the length of time it takes the red cells to sink to the bottom of a tube of blood. The time taken to coagulate is also important.

Blood diseases can be divided into various general groups: (1) those due to nutritional defects, such as pernicious anæmia, which is caused by lack of the anti-anæmic factor to be discussed later, or the simple anæmia caused by lack of iron and other substances in the food; (2) anæmia due to hæmorrhage or loss of blood in any form; (3) anæmia due to breaking-up of the red cells, as in blackwater fever following malaria; (4) anæmia caused by such damage to the bone-marrow that new blood cells are not produced; (5) a final group of little-understood diseases of the blood cells or lymphatic system. We shall consider these in turn.

NUTRITIONAL DEFICIENCY ANÆMIAS.

Pernicious anaemia is due to lack of something within the body, known as the "intrinsic factor," which is normally secreted by certain glands in the duodenum and at the lower end of the stomach. Together with the "extrinsic factor," taken into the body in protein foods, the two form a substance stored in the liver without which blood formation does not occur. No matter how much of the extrinsic factor is taken in, it is of no avail if the intrinsic factor is not secreted. The red blood cells are greatly reduced in number, but each cell is larger than normal, and the size of the spleen and liver may be increased. In this disease the stomach does not secrete hydrochloric acid. Formerly this type of anæmia was invariably fatal in a period varying from a few months to one or two years, but in 1924 Dr. Minot of Boston in America began to give raw liver to some seriously ill patients, and found that they recovered. The raw liver supplied the intrinsic factor, and, so, it was found, did dried stomach extract. Nowadays, nobody need die of pernicious anæmia, which is treated with concentrated liver extracts and vitamin B12. If, however, the anæmia has gone on for a long time without treatment, there may be signs of damage to the spinal cord with weakness of the legs and areas of loss of feeling.

Simple Anaemia is due to inadequate diet so far as iron, vitamin C, and other substances are concerned. The red cells are reduced in number, but they are not, as in pernicious anæmia, enlarged. This is the commonest type of anæmia in this country, and is what is usually described as "bloodlessness." Unlike pernicious anæmia, ordinary anæmia is *not* helped by liver extract, and *is* cured by iron tablets. It is important to realise that the fact that people look pale does not prove that they are anæmic. One can tell more effectively by finding pallor on the inner side of the lower eyelid, or by having a blood test taken, but, ordinarily, paleness, breathlessness, and swelling of the ankles denote anæmia. There are so many medicines containing iron on sale that you had better ask your doctor's advice before taking them.

Anaemia after Haemorrhage might seem to refer only to loss of blood after an injury, and so it often is. But in this case unless the blood loss is great it will soon be replaced by the bone-marrow. Perhaps more important, because less obvious, is the simple sort of anæmia caused in women by excessive menstrual loss. This demands treatment of the basic cause by a doctor. Usually in bad wounds blood transfusion is necessary; in chronic loss in women giving iron and preventing the loss is the correct treatment.

Anaemia Due to Breaking-up of the Red Cells is found in many conditions, most of them unknown in Britain. The best-known is blackwater fever, already described, in which the red cells are damaged in malaria and dark blood pigment appears in the urine—hence the name "blackwater." None of them has any importance here, and, in any case, medical advice is necessary.

OTHER DISEASES OF THE BLOOD.

Some blood diseases are due to the inability of the bone-marrow to produce more blood cells. Two important ones are *aplastic anaemia* and *agranulocytosis*. The first may happen without apparent cause, or be produced by X-rays, radium, some antibiotics, and some sulpha drugs—indeed by many drugs; in the long run, it is fatal. Agranulocytosis, if discovered in time, can be cured. The main obvious distinction between the two is the severe ulceration of the throat found in agranulocytosis and not in aplastic anæmia, and, although agranulocytosis can be caused by over-indulgence in certain drugs, it is more usually a sequel to such severe infections as tonsillitis, pneumonia, or septicæmia. Other diseases are due to something which has gone wrong with the production of white blood cells, and chief ones being the leucocytes, which are manufactured in the bone-marrow, and the lymphocytes, made in the bone-marrow and partially in the lymph glands. Disease of these cells, in which they increase vastly in number at the expense of the red cells, is called *leukaemia*, and there are three types.

(1) *Chronic Myeloid Leukaemia*, where disease of the bone-marrow causes decrease in the number of red cells and increase in the number of leucocytes—perhaps to half a million per cubic millimetre (you will recall the normal figure is about 5,000–6,000). The spleen is much enlarged and the patient, commonly a man between twenty-five and forty years, suffers from weakness, swelling of the legs, and bleeding from the nose.

(2) *Chronic Lymphatic Leukaemia* is a similar state of affairs in which the number of red cells is reduced, although less so than in the first case. The spleen is also not so much enlarged, but the lymph glands are, and the number of lymphocytes in the blood is enormously increased. In this disease the patient is usually over middle age, but otherwise the symptoms are much the same as in chronic myeloid leukæmia.

Both diseases are treated by X-rays, and although the ultimate outlook is not good, the patient may have many years of reasonably fair health to look forward to.

Acute Leukaemia is found in younger people, and is usually due to increase—very rapid in this case—in the number of the leucocytes. It is quickly fatal.

A similar condition, in which the *red* blood cells increase in number, is *polycythaemia*. The increase may be from the normal 5 million per cubic millimetre to something like 8 million. The patient has an enlarged liver and spleen, looks blue and congested, and his fingers may become clubbed at the tips. He can lead a fairly normal life for many years with the help of drugs which reduce the production of red cells. However, thrombosis (clotting) may happen at any time, or the bone-marrow may suddenly give out through overwork, so that death is caused by aplastic anæmia.

All these diseases have this in common, that the blood cells of one type or another are produced in excess; they are, in effect, a form of cancer of the blood. Their recent increase may bear some relation to increased radioactivity.

Hodgkin's Disease is another curious condition, very similar in appearance to chronic lymphatic leukæmia. Here, however, most cases appear in young people, and, although the lymph glands enlarge, there is relatively little change in the blood. There is, too, likely to be an intermittent temperature which goes up and down at intervals of about ten days. Finally, all the glands of the body (within the chest and abdomen, as well as in the more superficial areas) become enlarged and may interfere with eating, speaking, or breathing. In the later stages severe anæmia develops, but, as we have already seen, there is little to note in this respect to begin with. Hodgkin's disease is, in fact, a disease of the lymph glands rather than of the blood. The outlook is always serious, but X-rays and certain drugs are helpful in slowing down the process.

Purpura is one of quite a number of conditions in which there are hæmorrhages under the skin, usually resembling small purple spots. Often such spots are not a disease in themselves, but simply the result of some other condition. For example, many of the ordinary fevers, septic conditions, leukæmia, jaundice, and the later stages of cancer or kidney disease may bring about this type of purpura, known as secondary because of the reason given above. Purpura may also occur after epileptic fits or bouts of whooping cough due to the strain of the spasms, and following the use of certain drugs.

Primary purpura, which is the genuine article, includes a group of diseases, some serious, others mild, and the main members of this group are:

Purpura Simplex, a mild condition in children associated with small hæmorrhages into the skin of the shins, sometimes diarrhœa, fever, general "run-down" feeling, and muscle pains. It may sometimes be connected with deficiency of vitamin P, but clears up in two to three weeks.

Purpura Haemorrhagica or Thrombocytopenic Purpura is much more serious, although in some respects its symptoms are merely an exaggeration of the above. It is found in children and young women; the hæmorrhages are severe and occur not only under the skin but also from the gums, nose, and bowels, so that anæmia soon develops. There is high fever, often with delirium. Unlike purpura simplex, in which the blood is unchanged, this disease is caused by some defect in the spleen which continues to destroy the blood platelets which play a part in clotting. Blood transfusions are given, but if the condition becomes serious the spleen may have to be removed.

Henoch's Purpura: this is a disease usually associated with infants and children. Blood and mucus are secreted into the intestine, there is colic, vomiting and diarrhœa containing blood. The main importance of this disease is that it so closely resembles a number of abdominal conditions for which surgery is necessary that it may be referred to a surgeon. The fact that it is a form of purpura becomes evident when the tell-tale spots appear on the skin. An attack clears up in about two days, but may recur and become dangerous.

Haemophilia—Bleeding and Clotting. As is well known, there are some people whose blood fails to clot in the normal time when a wound occurs. When this is so, even a small wound may cause the patient to bleed to death—a tooth extraction, a slight cut, a bruise, all become major emergencies. Since these minor injuries are happening to most of us many times each year, the life of a hæmophiliac is a risky one. Many hæmophiliacs, indeed, in their early twenties, have been given as many as two hundred blood transfusions to save their lives in injuries which would have been unimportant to anyone else.

Hæmophilia is hereditary, and is passed on to the male members of a family by the mother who is not a "bleeder," but whose father was. The mother is the carrier who hands on the disease to her sons. Perhaps the most famous example was Queen Victoria, who had four sons and five daughters; one son (Prince Leopold) died of the disease, and two daughters (Princess Alice and Princess Beatrice) became carriers. Princess Beatrice married and produced two sons with hæmophilia and one carrier daughter—a daughter who married King Alfonso of Spain, and out of four sons two had hæmophilia. Princess Alice married Prince Louis of Hesse, and had one son, who died of bleeding in his fourth year, and two carrier daughters, one of whom became the Czarina of Russia. Her only son was the unfortunate little boy who, by reason of his hæmophilia, was the main reason for the introduction of the self-styled "healer" Rasputin into the family and the source of his malign influence over the royal house.

Hæmophilia is only one disease in which there is a tendency to bleed, in this case caused by delayed clotting. But a similar tendency may be caused by inadequate clotting, when the clot formed over a wound is soft, jelly-like, and fails to harden, or, as in the case of some types of purpura, when the capillaries are so fragile that they are easily broken by a relatively slight injury. What are the factors which bring about clotting? When bleeding occurs, the platelets in the blood-stream move to the area, disintegrate, and release a substance known as thromboplastin, which, together with two other substances in the blood—calcium and prothrombin—form thrombin. (The prothrombin is manufactured in the liver, and vitamin K is an essential in its formation.) Thrombin, however, is not the final product; for it interacts with something else in the blood, known as fibrinogen, to form *fibrin*, the actual clot, and, as we have seen, the fibrin forms long, thread-like fibres which fill in the gap and ultimately draw the edges of the wound together. Clearly, then, the tendency to bleeding may result from lack of any one of these substances; most often from lack of prothrombin (due to liver disease, blocking of the bile-duct, or lack of vitamin K) and very rarely from calcium deficiency. Almost equally rare is deficiency of fibrinogen, so the remaining types are caused by lack of thromboplastin, either because the number of platelets is reduced, the amount of thromboplastin in the platelets is insufficient, or, most commonly, because the platelets are so tough that they fail to break up at the site of the bleeding.

There are many different treatments used in bleeding diseases, and obviously the treatment will depend on what specifically is missing. But, in any case, the outlook is much better than it once was.

BLOOD TRANSFUSION.

When, in the early seventeenth century, William Harvey discovered the fact of the circulation of the blood, he became the predecessor of many great men in the England of his time; England was in the process of a scientific renaissance, one expression of which was the formation of the Royal Society under the patronage of Charles II—a society with such members as Sir Christopher Wren, Robert Hooke, the greatest microscopist of his time, Boyle the physicist, Sir Isaac Newton, Pepys, and others. All these men had an insatiable curiosity which extended far beyond the bounds of their particular subject, and thus it was Wren the architect who first suggested the possibility of intravenous injection of drugs (*i.e.*, injecting them directly through a syringe into a vein), and who carried out with other members the first experiments on blood transfusion. They transfused blood from one dog to another, from a sheep to a man, and from a young man to an old man—the fact that no human fatalities seem to have occurred points more to luck than good guidance, since, as we now know, there are four well-defined types of human blood, and some types are so incompatible that mixing will cause acute distress and possibly death. Before transfusion, therefore, it is necessary to know that the blood types of both donor and recipient are compatible.

Blood transfusion is much more frequently used now than formerly, as knowledge of the technique has increased. Whereas it was at one time regarded almost as a last resort, it is now used before, during, and after surgical operations if necessary. Blood transfusion, in fact, has become the most important weapon in the prevention and treatment of shock and has saved millions of lives. The blood taken from donors is stored in " banks " according to type, but when whole blood is not available plasma (usually in the form of dried powder which, like powdered soups, can be " reconstituted " with sterile water) or intravenous saline is also useful.

DISEASES OF THE HEART AND BLOOD-VESSELS

DISEASES OF THE HEART.

The heart lies in the centre of the chest and slightly to the left side between the lungs. Its shape is familiar from the hearts seen in butcher's shops, or, if you are a vegetarian, from the hearts on playing-cards (which are, however, a somewhat idealised version). There are four chambers in the heart, the right and left auricles and the right and left ventricles, the auricles being the ones at the upper part, the ventricles the ones below. The chambers are separated by valves which permit only a one-way flow of blood.

Circulation of the blood is, of course, continuous, and does not begin anywhere, but for purposes of description we may conveniently begin at the left ventricle, which pumps the blood through the aortic valve into the aorta, the largest artery in the body, and thence throughout all the other arteries. After passing to the arterioles (the smallest arteries), and to the capillaries, where the blood does its work of supplying oxygen and food to the tissues, it passes into the small veins or venules and then to larger and larger veins until, having given up its oxygen and food and absorbed waste products such as carbon dioxide (breathed out in the lungs) and soluble food wastes which are filtered out by the kidneys, it passes into the largest vein, the *vena cava*. The *vena cava* enters the right auricle, which pumps the blood through the tricuspid valve into the right ventricle, from which it passes through the lungs to get rid of its carbon dioxide and take in more oxygen. From the lungs, the blood goes to the left auricle, and thence, through the mitral valve, to the left ventricle to begin the cycle once more. The tricuspid valve, as the name implies, has three cusps or flaps; the mitral valve, shaped like a bishop's mitre, has only two.

Like other internal organs, the heart is covered in a thin, double, transparent covering or sac, rather like the plastic bags in which food is sold, and this contains a layer of fluid to prevent friction as the pumping motion is carried on; it is known as the pericardium.

There are three different tissues in the heart: the pericardium, which has just been described; the myocardium, or muscle, which forms the main bulk; and the endocardium or lining of the chambers, including the valves. Any one of these tissues may be attacked by disease, as also may the small blood-vessels, known as the coronary vessels, which supply blood to the heart muscle (for the heart, no less than any other part of the body, has to have a blood supply).

In general, heart disease belongs to one or other of three types: *congenital*, due to defects of the heart at birth; *infective*, due either to actual infection or its after-effects; *degenerative*, due to the changes of old age—which come on at different ages, depending on the individual. Now, strictly speaking, heart diseases are not curable in the sense that in most cases we cannot say that the heart has returned to its previous condition. What we can say is that the heart has a great ability to compensate for its defects, both by natural processes and with the aid of modern medicine and surgery. Only a score of years ago people were turned down for Life Insurance because they had a " murmur " in the heart (*i.e.*, the sound a doctor hears with his stethoscope if a valve is defective). But today judgement is based on much wider information; for it is realised that what is heard through a stethoscope is not in itself justification for making a hard-and-fast diagnosis. We must consider also the results given by electrocardiograms and, above all, by the individual patient's performance and symptoms.

The electrocardiograph is an instrument which measures the electrical currents passing through the heart muscle as it beats and shows them up on a chart. It gives in this way a pretty accurate estimate of the heart's efficiency. But, important as these results are, we are much more interested in the actual observation of what the heart can *do*, how it in fact *works*.

The following story—which is true—gives an indication of the modern medical attitude towards heart disease: A wealthy patient, who believed something to be wrong with his heart, made an appointment with a famous heart specialist. On reaching the hospital, he found that the doctor's office was on the third floor, and that the lift was not working. He was therefore compelled to walk up three flights of stairs, and finally knocked on the door of the specialist's office. When the door was opened the doctor looked at him and asked: " You walked up the stairs because the lift is broken?" " Yes," replied the patient. " Then your heart is perfectly normal. Good afternoon!" said the doctor.

What this story illustrates is that, generally speaking, the basic criterion of the heart's efficiency is whether it works satisfactorily. It is rarely possible to have heart disease in the presence of the ability to lead a normal life, except in the case of such conditions as coronary thrombosis or angina pectoris, which may remain undiscovered even by the most refined methods of investigation until they are upon us. In conclusion, it should be noted that symptoms related to the heart in an obvious manner, such as pain, discomfort, or palpitation, are rarely signs of heart disease, and are more likely to be nervous in origin or due to indigestion, fibrositis, pleurisy, or other causes.

Pericarditis is to the heart what pleurisy is to the lungs—an inflammation of the covering layer. The vast majority of cases result from acute rheumatism, but they can also be associated with other fevers, septicæmia, and generalised tuberculosis. Pericarditis may be an extension from local disease, such as pneumonia, pleurisy, or chest wounds.

When this happens inflammation develops between the two layers of the pericardium, so that instead of moving smoothly against each other when the heart beats they "scrape." If acute rheumatism is already present the temperature increases, there is pain over the heart, difficulty in breathing and restlessness, and the pulse rate goes up. This condition is known as "dry" pericarditis, but may develop into pericarditis with effusion in which fluid is secreted between the layers; when this happens, the pain disappears but breathlessness increases. The treatment of both types is that of the condition causing them (*e.g.*, rheumatic or scarlet fever), rest, and, if fluid is formed, it may have to be drawn off. Ordinarily the outlook is good, but adhesions between the pericardium and surrounding structures may occasionally give trouble.

Myocarditis, or disease of the heart muscle, results from a number of causes: first of all there is the great enemy rheumatic fever, and in a lesser degree diphtheria, typhoid, and chronic syphilis—all these infections poison and weaken the heart in varying degrees. Or the muscle may degenerate in pernicious anæmia, hyperthyroidism poisoning from phosphorus and other substances, or when the blood supply is affected, as in coronary thrombosis. In some cases of myocarditis damage is slight and gradual in onset, in others—such as after coronary thrombosis—it may be sudden and severe. The result in mild cases will be *compensation* when the heart is able to overcome its defects, but in severe cases *heart failure* may develop. This applies, too, to the later results of valvular disease of the heart, in which, again, there may be compensation or failure.

The condition of the heart muscle is the main factor in determining the ability of the heart to overcome any sort of damage; for it is the muscle which does the compensating. Thus, when one of the valves becomes narrowed by disease the muscle in the chamber below increases in size and thickness to force the blood through, but when the myocardium itself is degenerated this cannot take place, and sooner or later heart failure of varying degrees occurs. By and large, the symptoms of heart failure are those of most heart diseases: breathlessness (at first on mild exertion, later even when lying down), occasional coughing up of small amounts of blood, swelling of the feet (which in the later stages may extend upwards), and cyanosis—blueness of the skin. Obviously, the treatment is a matter for the doctor, who will prescribe drugs suitable to the exact condition, rest in bed, and other measures.

One of the main causes of myocarditis, as we have seen, is coronary artery thrombosis—that is to say, clotting of blood in one of the small arteries supplying the heart muscle.

Coronary Thrombosis is interesting in that: (*a*) it occurs mostly in men over forty-five; (*b*) it is more frequent in industrialised countries; and (*c*) it is more frequent in the wealthier classes. These facts have been used to support two separate theories as to its cause: first, that it is due to long periods of emotional stress in the ambitious, striving type of personality, and secondly, that it is due to over-indulgence in animal fats (not vegetable or fish oils), which causes the laying down of a substance known as cholesterol in the coronary vessels and their ultimate closure. Coronary thrombosis, then, is regarded according to one's viewpoint as an emotional or a dietary problem, but both schools of thought realise that some predisposition lies behind whatever the immediate cause may happen to be.

There is certainly some support for the view that animal fats, including milk, may play some part in predisposed individuals in bringing about coronary thrombosis. For example, the incidence of the disease went down during the War in Norway when meat was rationed; it is uncommon amongst fish-eating people, such as the Eskimos, or those who eat little meat—because they cannot afford it—such as the peasants of Southern Italy. But, of course, the "stress" school of thought can point out that these peoples are not, on the whole, subjected to the strains of a highly competitive society. High living and a tense emotional life often (if not always) tend to go together, and it is quite possible that both theories of the causation of coronary thrombosis are true: that emotional stress is the predisposing factor which disturbs the workings of the body and makes animal fats dangerous to the individual.

Thrombosis occurs when the building-up of cholesterol derived from such fats suddenly leads to clotting in one or other of the coronary arteries so that the blood cannot get through. The result is immediate and severe pain over the heart, which lasts for several days; there is breathlessness and shock, sweating, rapid and weak pulse, and later low fever. In about half the number of cases death occurs immediately, but in those who recover from the attack the outlook is reasonably good. The treatment is, naturally, a matter for the doctor, but will include rest in bed for six to eight weeks, a gradual resumption of work, depending on the state of the heart, reducing if overweight, and possibly dietary restrictions. Drugs are used to strengthen the heart.

Thrombosis in other parts of the body will be discussed later, but here it may be of interest to mention the anti-coagulant drugs which have the effect of preventing clotting. They are chemicals which have been known in Nature for a long time. Thus a leech, in order to liquefy the blood it sucks from its victim, secretes "hirudin," which prevents clotting, and the livers of dogs and oxen contain "heparin," which has a similar effect. But the greatest advance in this field came from the study of a bleeding disease in cattle, often ending fatally, which had long been familiar to veterinary surgeons. In 1921 Schofield of Canada found that the cause of this disease was the eating of spoiled sweet-clover, and in 1941 the chemical responsible for the bleeding was isolated from clover by Link in America. It is found in sweet-clover which has been spoiled by storage as hay, and is known as "dicoumarin." If given in large amounts dicoumarin produces symptoms identical with those of the bleeding diseases: purpuric spots and hæmorrhage from the gums and internal organs. It is obviously the ideal drug for dealing with diseases in which clotting takes place too readily—coronary thrombosis, phlebitis, and pulmonary embolism. Dicoumarin, however, has to be used with care and under medical supervision.

Angina Pectoris. A disease which is in many respects similar to coronary thrombosis is *angina pectoris*, but here, although the arteries may be narrowed, the immediate cause of an attack is spasm of the blood-vessels, which are therefore only temporarily closed. The symptoms are the same as in coronary disease except that the pain over the heart (which frequently passes up the neck or down the inner side of the left arm) is: (*a*) brought on by exercise, whereas thrombosis can occur whilst resting; and (*b*) wears off in a comparatively short time—usually after the exertion ceases. Death may occur during an attack, but medical care can do a great deal when the condition is discovered in time. Drugs are given which prevent spasm (usually nitro-glycerine, known in a more sinister sphere as a high explosive). During an attack, relief is obtained from amyl nitrite, which is inhaled from a capsule. Otherwise, the treatment is as for coronary thrombosis.

Valvular Disease of the Heart, or endocarditis, has a rather frightening sound which is not always justified in view of the heart's ability to compensate. The main enemy of the heart is acute rheumatism and streptococcal infections generally (scarlet fever, tonsillitis), and other conditions predisposing to endocarditis have been mentioned. Curiously enough, rheumatic fever is now a rather rare disease, although this may not be so strange when we consider the statement in a pre-war text-book that it is "relatively an uncommon disease amongst the well-to-do, and evidence is being brought forward that overcrowding in damp houses is the biggest factor of all." Higher standards of living and the much-abused Welfare State have, there can be little doubt, brought about this result.

The valves of the heart are the pulmonary, the tricuspid, the mitral, and the aortic, and each valve may be damaged in one of two ways—by narrowing, so that the blood cannot easily be forced through, or by leaking, so that the blood pumped through slips back again. The first is known as stenosis, the second as regurgitation, and when one or more of the valves are damaged in either way the heart, as we have seen, first tries to compensate. For example, in incompetence of the aortic valve between the left ventricle and the aorta, the blood is pumped out, but since the valve cannot close properly, some of it slips back into the ventricle. In order to deal with this problem, the ventricle becomes greatly enlarged, but, if this action fails, the increased pressure in a chamber which is unable to empty itself completely is passed back through the rest of the circulation. The left auricle overfills, the lungs become congested, and finally the right side of the heart is affected, ultimately leading to varying degrees of heart failure.

Since rheumatic fever is no longer so common as it once was, and diphtheria and chronic syphilis are equally rare, the most usual sequence of events today is as follows: a child or young adult develops a streptococcal sore throat, which may simply clear up without more ado, as it does in the vast majority of cases. But sometimes the infection is followed within about ten days by pains moving from one joint to another, and this, too, clears up shortly. A similar episode may follow at a later date, and, still later, it may be found that these apparently unimportant events have damaged the heart; the damage may be discovered accidentally at a routine medical examination or because the patient complains of breathlessness or some other symptom.

This, rather than the more dramatic form which was once so common, is the way that, in these times, rheumatic disease manifests itself. It has long been known that rheumatic fever was associated with streptococcal sore throat, but it is now clear that acute rheumatism is not a simple infection; for streptococci are never found in the heart or in the joints. Apparently, it is a condition in which the individual has become allergic to the toxins of the streptococcus, which then damage the joints, the heart muscle, and the valves.

Irregularities of the Heart-beat.

Like other muscles in the body, the heart cannot move without messages being passed to it from the nerves, but the nerves supplying it belong to the automatic nervous system. The vagus nerve, belonging to the parasympathetic system, slows the beats, and the sympathetic nerves quicken them. Both these groups of nerves meet at the point where the great veins enter the heart at the right auricle, and this point is known as the pacemaker; from there, they send impulses around the auricles and meet again at the auriculo-ventricular bundle at the junction of auricles and ventricles; lastly, they pass down between the ventricles, dividing into two bundles to supply both sides. Obviously, any sort of irregularity can arise: (*a*) in the lower centres of the brain, where the impulses originate; (*b*) at the pacemaker; (*c*) at the junction of auricles and ventricles.

Tachycardia means that the heart beats too rapidly, and this it does in many circumstances: after exercise, when emotionally excited, in fever when the temperature is raised, in chronic infections, or in anæmia. Rapid heart-beat is also found in thyroid disease. However, there can be little doubt that attacks of palpitation, as contrasted with prolonged rapid pulse, are nearly always due to emotional causes. Palpitation *can* be a symptom of heart disease, but most usually it is a sign of "nerves"; in the absence of other signs of heart disease such attacks can be assumed to be due to over-stimulation of the nervous centres in the brain which are concerned both with the emotions and control of the heart. An example of emotionally caused illness in a normal enough heart is what used to be called "*D.A.H.*" (*i.e.*, "disordered action of the heart") during the First World War and "*Effort syndrome*" during the Second. The commonest symptoms are breathlessness, palpitation, nervousness, dizziness, and pain over the heart—all the symptoms that would suggest heart disease to the layman. It is, in fact, a neurosis, pure and simple, and the abnormal impulses which cause the symptoms arise in the lower centres of the brain as the result of emotional tension.

When the irregularity arises at the pacemaker or in the auricles there may occur the not uncommon phenomenon of feeling the heart stop for a moment which is described medically as an *extra-systole*. They are commonly associated with disease of the myocardium in middle age, or, less frequently, in young adults, when they are (rather dubiously) asserted to be due to over-smoking. However, the most serious disease of this type is *auricular fibrillation*, in which so many impulses pass down through the auricles that they beat rapidly and irregularly and the ventricles respond to the shower of messages as best they may. Auricular fibrillation is usually a sequel to mitral stenosis, but can also result from hyperthyroidism and myocarditis. There is palpitation, rapid and completely irregular pulse (140–180 to the minute), and, ultimately, signs of heart failure. The treatment is with such drugs as digitalis and its derivatives or quinidine, which is a derivative of quinine. *Digitalis* is a drug, known for many years, obtained from the purple foxglove when the leaves are dried and powdered; it has the double effect of slowing the heart beat by acting on the brain centres, and strengthening the contraction of the muscle by direct action. *Stropanthin* acts in a similar way. Although digitalis and stropanthin are the main drugs used in heart disease, doctors are nowadays much more selective in using them; for it is evident that they are not helpful in all heart conditions. In fact, their main use is in auricular fibillation and congestive heart failure—in other conditions they do little good.

In *heart block* the trouble arises at the junction of the auricles and ventricles because the nerves which pass on the impulse have been damaged by one or other of the conditions described under the heading of myocarditis. When the block is complete the ventricles beat entirely independently of the auricles at a rate of about 30–40, and occasionally there are attacks in which the ventricles either cease beating for a few seconds or beat very slowly. This may be associated with attacks somewhat resembling epilepsy, known as the Stokes–Adams' syndrome. In partial heart block the ventricle misses a beat entirely—often every third or fourth beat. The treatment for both conditions is a matter for the specialist: digitalis is *not* used.

The Blood-pressure.

There are two types of raised blood-pressure, the type known as secondary hypertension (hyperpiesis), which is due to a number of diseases such as kidney disease and diseases of the glands, blood disorders such as polycythæmia, and hardening of the arteries, and the type known as primary or essential hypertension (hyperpiesia), which is not the result of illness elsewhere. In the treatment of secondary hypertension the doctor's attention will naturally be directed to the disease causing the raised pressure, but essential hypertension, although it is extremely common, is not so easily dealt with. Its immediate cause appears to be a spasm of the arterioles, or small arteries, throughout the body. At first this is periodic, but later becomes permanent, with the result that the pressure remains raised. At one time it was supposed that such factors as septic areas in the body, tobacco, and a too rich diet played some part, but now it is fairly clear that essential hypertension is the result of two main factors: heredity and stress. What part each of the factors plays is unknown; for, although it is often found that relatives of the patient have suffered from the condition, this by no means proves that heredity is the cause. Obviously, someone brought up in a certain kind of mental environment will tend to adopt similar attitudes to those of his relatives, heredity or no heredity. Stress, then, is the most important factor in the sort of high blood-pressure which is not the result of another disease, but "stress" does not simply mean anxiety or fear (which, after all, have been common to most human beings throughout the centuries), and if anxiety in itself had the power to cause illness we should be in an even worse state than we are now. It seems that what matters is "bottled-up" emotional tension —worrying inwardly, which is quite consistent with not being at all consciously upset. In short, heredity may supply the sort of temperament which is prone to worry, but events cause the worry itself. The treatment of essential hypertension depends on its severity; in some cases drugs will help (for example, rauwolfia or "Serpasil" and some more powerful agents), but in others an operation which divides the nerves causing the spasm is necessary. Sedatives may also be used, but there is little evidence that dietary or other factors play any important part in essential hypertension.

Most people seem to believe that certain symptoms almost infallibly suggest the existence of high-blood pressure, but in point of fact there is no reason to suppose that any of these symptoms —headaches, giddiness, noises in the ears, lack of concentration or poor memory—indicate any specific condition, least of all high blood-pressure. Nor is it true that patients tend to be the broad, muscular, red-faced type they are so often imagined to be. By and large, hypertension is discovered largely by accident, and the sufferers are just as likely to be small, thin, and pale, as large, fat, and ruby-complexioned.

Low blood-pressure is not a disease at all, although like normal or high blood-pressure it may be found in association with other diseases. No treatment for low blood-pressure in itself is necessary.

DISEASES OF THE BLOOD-VESSELS.

Arteriosclerosis or "hardening of the arteries" is one of the commonest diseases. The aorta and the main blood-vessels become narrowed by the deposition of cholesterin, and the result is most evident in the coronary arteries supplying the heart muscle or in the arteries supplying the brain. The first may lead to degeneration of the heart muscle, the second to such symptoms as forgetfulness, confusion, and dizziness. Arteriosclerosis, like coronary thrombosis, may be due to stress, or, more probably, to a diet over-rich in cholesterol in those already predisposed by heredity. Arteriosclerotic changes happen to most people as they grow older, but not necessarily to a degree that makes them noticeable. The treatment is to regulate the diet, and lead a quiet, steady life.

Thromboangeitis Obliterans, or Bürger's disease, is a rather uncommon disease in which there is spasm of the blood-vessels and perhaps clotting which may lead to gangrene. It begins with cramp in the legs brought on by exercise, ceasing when the legs are rested, but afterwards there develops redness and a shiny appearance of the feet as the vessels become entirely blocked. The pain becomes severe and continuous, and may prevent sleep.

The disease appears to be due to an allergy to tobacco, and the patients are always heavy cigarette smokers. Treatment is rest in bed, and smoking should be given up; in severe cases it may be necessary to operate on the nerves causing the spasm, or, if gangrene has supervened, to amputate the affected part.

Extreme cold, as we have seen, can affect the tissues in the form of frostbite. But some people are particularly sensitive to even mild degrees of cold and suffer in winter from *chilblains*, which, although often described under the heading of skin diseases, are really connected with the circulation. People with chilblains should take plenty of nourishing food and wear woollen socks and woollen gloves in cold weather. Sometimes vitamin K, "Pernivite," or nicotinic acid have proved helpful.

In *Raynaud's disease* the response to cold is more dramatic, and the hands or feet become dead white during attacks. In a severe case the fingers, particularly, may later become blue or black, with severe pain or even gangrene. Occasionally the ears and nose are affected. Drugs may help, or it may be necessary, as in thromboangeitis obliterans, to cut the nerves producing the spasm. Persistent exposure to cold and damp leads to circulatory trouble in anyone, and *trench foot* was common during the First World War; its counterpart in the Second World War was "*immersion foot*" in men who had been drifting for weeks in open boats with their feet in bilge-water. Frostbite, trench foot, and immersion foot are more or less normal reactions to extreme cold; chilblains and Raynaud's disease occur only in those who are specially sensitive to cold, whose blood-vessels under its influence readily go into spasm.

Aneurism happens when the muscular lining of an artery becomes weakened and then the outer lining "blows out" like a balloon, forming a large swelling on the side of the vessel. This may be caused by injury, or strain, or arteriosclerosis, but in 95 per cent. of cases is due to syphilitic disease. Aneurism used to be very common, but is now rather unusual. It is treated by drugs or by operation.

Embolism and Thrombosis are closely associated with each other; for a thrombosis occurs when the blood in a vessel clots, and, if the clot is set free to pass through the system until it finally blocks some part of it, it is described as an embolus. This clotting ordinarily occurs when the blood flows over injured tissues, but may also occur when the inside lining of the blood-vessels have degenerated, or after an operation when the patient is lying in bed for a long period and the circulation is abnormally slow. It can also occur in cases of infection in a vein, which is known as *phlebitis*. If the clot stays in the original position, the blood-vessel is closed, and in the limbs there will be swelling due to the pressure in the vein beyond (obviously the degree of upset will depend upon the size and importance of the blocked vein —in the brain it may have serious effects in even quite a small vessel, in the leg, the blocking of a small vessel might not cause much trouble). However, if the blood clots in one of the large veins of the leg after an operation the result may be a *pulmonary embolism*, when the clot separates itself and passes through the blood-stream to the right auricle, and thence to the pulmonary artery, which it blocks, causing sudden death in someone who appeared to be getting on quite well. Nowadays this danger is much reduced by getting patients out of bed as soon as possible after a major operation.

When you think about it, you will realise that, although the heart can fairly easily pump blood down to the legs, it is not so simple for the blood to return. Having passed through the capillaries it is not just pushed back up the veins by the pressure from the heart—on the contrary, it has to be *massaged* upwards by the leg muscles during exercise. To avoid the blood falling back, the veins are provided with valves somewhat like those in the heart, which prevent the backward flow. Now, especially in people who have jobs involving long hours of standing or in women who have had a number of pregnancies, the congestion produced makes it even more difficult for the valves to operate effectively, especially if they are already not too competent, and *varicose veins* may develop.

In the early stages an elastic bandage or stocking may help, but, later, injections to produce clotting in the superficial veins, or an operation involving tying the main superficial vein at the inside of the thigh, may be necessary. *Varicose ulcer* is prone to develop just above the ankle because of the failure of the tissues to get a proper blood-supply. Apart from the measures already mentioned, it is important that people with varicose veins should stand as little as possible and should rest with their feet raised; this is much more important than ointments and bandages.

HEART SURGERY.

Only about sixty years ago an eminent British surgeon stated that "surgery of the heart has probably reached the limits set by Nature to all surgery; no new method and no new discovery can overcome the natural difficulties that attend a wound of the heart." He was, however, wrong; for new methods have made it possible to operate even within the chambers of the heart. Here it is only possible to describe briefly some of the processes which can be carried out. In stenosis, or narrowing of a valve, the heart can be opened and the valve stretched, or, if the valve is leaky, it can be replaced by an additional valve, a plastic ball covered with silicone rubber which stops the back-flow when the heart relaxes. Coronary thrombosis, too, can be dealt with either by scraping out the diseased lining of the arteries or by restoring the blood-flow from somewhere else by attaching to the heart a piece of tissue from the chest wall.

Of course, some of these operations are only in the experimental state, but they are perhaps of greatest interest in the case of blue babies—those children born with heart defects which, because the blood does not get properly oxygenated, cause them to appear blue or cyanosed, as a doctor would say. Such a child may be born with the main blood-vessels turned the wrong way round, with a hole connecting the two auricles or the two ventricles, with a narrowed pulmonary valve, or with other defects which greatly shorten the expectation of life. It is in such disease that surgery has proved most successful.

Some operations can be done without opening up the heart itself, but if this becomes necessary a serious problem arises; for if the circulation is interfered with for more than four minutes the brain (which is the most delicate organ of the body) suffers irreparable damage. The problem was partially solved by C. H. Bailey in the United States, when, knowing that if the body temperature is lowered the tissues need less blood, he conceived the idea of freezing the patient in a bath packed with ice. In this way the normal body temperature of 98·4° was reduced to 75°, which gave him exactly double the time—eight minutes—to carry out his operation. But eight minutes is not enough for all heart surgery, and other techniques have had to be devised to solve the problem of how to make the blood circulate whilst the heart is not working.

One method used with blue babies was the rather dangerous method of connecting the child's circulatory system with that of someone else (usually the father), so that whilst the child's heart was out of action the donor's heart and lungs took over. But such solutions are no longer necessary because, largely in America, machines have been devised which draw the blood from the heart, pass it through an artificial lung so that it becomes oxygenated, and return it to the body whilst an operation on the heart is carried out. The difficulty of devising such a machine was primarily that the blood must be oxygenated without any bubbles getting into it; for if this occurs one of the bubbles may get into the circulation and, passing to the brain, act as an embolus causing death or paralysis in the same way as a blood-clot. So the earliest type of machine drew the blood from the heart and passed it over a series of thin plates in chambers containing oxygen, but it has since been found that oxygen can be bubbled through the blood in the machine, the mixture allowed to settle, and any excess bubbles removed by passing through a reservoir coated with a substance long used by brewers for removing froth in the manufacture of beer.

Here is a summary of some facts people may wish to know about heart surgery.

The operations are dangerous, but new methods are making them safer. They are not carried out unless the existing condition creates more risk than the operation, and the death-rates of the more important operations are as follows: blue-baby operations, 20–25 per cent.; coronary artery disease, 10–15 per cent.; narrowing of valve, 5–10 per cent.

Needless to say, only a small number of patients with heart disease ever need surgical treatment, and in fact there are not many people of over forty who do not have "heart trouble" in some degree or another. Those who are operated on successfully are improved to a considerable extent, but this does not mean to say that they can afterwards lead a perfectly normal life; they will live longer if they take reasonable precautions. Operations on blue babies are ordinarily carried out because the patient would not survive without the operation, but surgical treatment of coronary disease, and valvular stenosis or incompetence, is still in the experimental stage; it is only carried out in fairly exceptional cases.

DISEASES OF THE RESPIRATORY SYSTEM

INTRODUCTION.

The respiratory system is concerned with taking into the body the oxygen which is necessary to life and getting rid of the carbon dioxide which is a waste product. It begins at the nose, which is intended (although not always used, since there are many mouth-breathers) as a filter and air-conditioner. The hairs in the nose keep—or are intended to keep—dust particles from the throat, and its sticky lining, warmed by the blood-vessels in which it is so rich, has the double function of removing the finer dust and germs and warming the air taken in.

After this process, the air passes down from the back of the nose to the space behind the mouth and then down the windpipe or trachea into the lungs. On the way it goes through the larynx or voice-box (above the trachea), which makes speech possible with its mechanism of vocal cords; the vocal cords separate during breathing in order to let the air through. Lastly, in the chest the windpipe divides to right and left and goes into the lungs; these main divisions are the bronchi, and within the lungs they subdivide, rather like the arterial system, into smaller and smaller tubes, known as bronchioles, which end up by entering the air-spaces of the lung tissue. There, in the thin, spongy spaces lined with blood-vessels, the breathed-in air gives up its oxygen to the blood.

The two lungs, right and left, lie within the chest attached to the bronchial tubes and the large blood-vessels. These are their "roots." They are, like the heart, covered with a double layer of thin, plastic-like material, the pleura (the part which is affected in pleurisy), and they contract and expand with the movements of breathing. But breathing is not carried out by the lungs themselves—it happens when the muscles between the ribs draw the ribs up and so expand the space within the chest that air is sucked in. Normally the pressure within the chest is less than that of the air outside, so that if the chest is punctured the lung collapses. This is important both in chest surgery and in certain conditions where, as we shall see later, it is desirable to collapse the lung in order to rest it. The left lung is divided into two portions or lobes, the right into three.

When one thinks of the nose, certainly if one thinks of it in medical terms, the first disease that comes to mind is the *common cold*, about which we know so much and yet so little. Colds are a virus infection which, even if trivial, cause considerable discomfort and much wasted time; but research seems to show that a great deal depends upon the type of person in whom the virus arrives. Thus people sent out in thin sports clothes to run for long distances in the rain and then made to rest in their wet apparel showed no special liability to catch cold, but it seems possible that sudden changes of temperature may have some effect. For example, in America, where central heating in some areas is very hot and the weather outside may be very cold, nose infections are common.

Even more perplexing, however, is the fact that, like the judges we read of in the daily papers, we often have to ask: "What *is* a cold?" Everyone who has a running nose or even a temperature is not necessarily suffering from coryza, the scientific name for the common cold; they may have *allergic rhinitis*, similar to hay fever, which has no connection at all with infection. In this case the symptoms are produced by dust, pollen, or some other material to which the person is sensitive. Nasal discharge and temperature may also be brought about by *sinusitis*—that is to say, an infection of the spaces within the bone of the skull which communicate by small openings with the inside of the nose. These are the frontal sinuses just behind the eyebrows, the maxillary sinuses below the eyes, the ethmoid sinuses in the corner of the eyes on either side of the nose, and the more deep-seated sphenoid sinus right at the back of the nose. When these cavities are infected pus forms and naturally discharges into the nose, but if the lining of the nose swells up (as it does, for example, in a hot room) the openings into the nose may be blocked, the pus accumulates, and there is severe pain over the site of the sinus. Sinusitis may respond to the sulpha drugs or to antibiotics, but it is sometimes necessary to make a new opening into the nose and wash them out or to operate.

Whenever anything goes wrong with the nose, whether it be a virus infection an allergic irritation, or discharge from the sinuses, there is always a secondary invasion by germs which are the result rather than the cause of the trouble; the thick pus which comes from the nose in the later stages of a "cold" is largely due to them. There are no injections or inoculations against colds, but conceivably *some* of the many available may prevent colds getting worse by dealing with the secondary invaders; they certainly do not deal with the original cause, the virus. Capsules taken by mouth are, there is every reason to think, completely valueless, and, so far, the treatment of a cold is simply the treatment of the symptoms: aspirin relieves pain when it exists, it reduces the fever, and it does nothing else. Nor has whisky any special effect, although it is so often prescribed as a cure, but it probably has some effect on devotees in making a cold more bearable.

Hay Fever is an allergic condition due to hypersensitiveness to the pollens of certain grasses. Its symptoms have already been described so far as the nose is concerned (see allergic rhinitis), but there may be other signs of allergy, such as redness of the eyes and itching of the skin. Hay fever is helped by desensitisation with increasing strengths of the substance responsible; since cases occur mainly in May or June, the course of injections should be given early in the year. It usually has to be repeated each year. An alternative is the use of one of the antihistamine drugs, which seem to afford relief—but not cure—to many people.

Epistaxis. Another condition which is not really a disease in itself but may be a symptom of one is *epistaxis* or nose-bleeding. Bleeding may be caused by injury, by nose-picking in children (who frequently put beads or other small objects in their noses), by polypi (similar to varicose veins), and by a number of general illnesses, such as high blood-pressure, blood diseases, and fevers. It sometimes occurs in women during their periods and in people at high altitudes, flying or mountaineering. Usually no special treatment is necessary, but if the bleeding becomes troublesome a doctor will probably pack the nostrils with gauze soaked in adrenalin. In ordinary cases cold compresses and lying down should suffice.

Tonsils and Adenoids. The commonest operation in the whole field of surgery is the removal of tonsils and adenoids. Indeed, in some places, and notably in America, it was formerly almost a routine to advocate the operation when children reached the age of three to five. The tonsils, one on each side, lie at the back of the throat, and are easily visible when the mouth is opened wide; the adenoids cannot be seen, since they lie at the back of the throat behind the nose. *Acute tonsillitis* is usually, but not always, caused by the streptococcus, and it results in sore throat, high fever, and difficulty in swallowing. But, as we saw elsewhere, its main danger is that it may become chronic and cause damage to the heart and other organs. Tonsillitis responds to antibiotics and the sulpha drugs. Adenoids, when they become infected, swell to an extent which may cause difficulty in breathing and block the air passage between the nose and throat—the Eustachian tube—leading to ear infection or loss of hearing. This produces a typical facial expression: the child looks dull and listless, breathes through its mouth, which is therefore constantly open, and talks in the manner of someone with a cold. It must be remembered that this occurs only in severe cases, that most children have some trouble with their tonsils and adenoids in early life, and that after the tenth year the tissues tend to shrink, so that difficulties after that time are much less frequent.

Although the operation is still common, it is probably true to say that it is less commonly advocated than before. In part this is due to the new drugs, which can nip infection in the bud, but it is also due to the realisation that the tonsils and adenoids are there for a purpose, that they act as a barrier to infection from germs entering the nose and throat. However, when they are badly infected there can be no useful purpose in keeping them and many good reasons why one should not.

Laryngitis, Pharyngitis, and Bronchitis. One of the difficulties created by infections in the upper part of the respiratory tract—the nose and throat—is that they can extend downwards, causing laryngitis, pharyngitis, or bronchitis. In laryngitis the voice-box is infected, there is a tickling cough and difficulty in speaking; the vocal cords are swollen and red. (It should be added that the same symptoms may also be due to too much talking, to neurosis, and, so non-smokers say, to too much smoking.) In simple cases it may help to inhale the vapour of Friar's Balsam, a half teaspoonful to a pint of water, but in more persistent cases a doctor should be called. Chronic laryngitis is a matter for an ear, nose, and throat specialist.

In pharyngitis there is pain on swallowing, the lymph glands in the neck may be swollen, and there is a rise in temperature; ordinary cases will respond to aspirin and gargles.

Bronchitis, however, is another matter, although it is perhaps less common than is often supposed. Every cough does not signify bronchitis; for it may be laryngitis, *tracheitis* (*i.e.*, inflammation of the windpipe), or the result of what is popularly known as "catarrh," when discharge from the back of the nose trickles down the throat. Some coughs may even have nothing to do with the breathing system at all, for example, wax in the ear may stimulate the coughing centre in the brain and produce a cough which is stopped when the wax is washed out. Bronchitis is ordinarily found only in the very young, the very old, or as a complication of other diseases, such as measles and influenza; it is not caused by any one germ, and the bacteria found may be streptococci, staphylococci, and others—or more usually a mixture. Acute bronchitis is rarely dangerous in itself, but it can spread (if you recall the anatomy of the respiratory system) down the larger tubes into the smaller ones, and thence into the lungs, causing *broncho-pneumonia*. In broncho-pneumonia the parts of the lungs affected are those near the ends of the bronchi, so there are patches of infection scattered throughout the lungs, and this is quite unlike *lobar pneumonia*, which: (*a*) is caused by one kind of germ, the pneumococcus; (*b*) affects a whole lobe of a lung at one time; and (*c*) can happen to anyone, of any age, at any time. In any kind of pneumonia there is fever, breathlessness, and ordinarily the disease responds to penicillin or the sulpha drugs. Lobar pneumonia, when untreated by the new drugs, used to show a "crisis" in seven to ten days—the temperature suddenly went down; in broncho-pneumonia there is no crisis, but it is equally responsive to the new drugs.

Chronic Bronchitis is typically a disease of the old, or at any rate of those in later life. It is something which is always " there," but becomes worse in winter, in cities where there are fogs, in children with adenoids, and in older people who work in occupations where they are exposed to dust. Chronic bronchitis develops gradually as the result of many previous attacks and, since the lung tissues sooner or later become involved, are no longer elastic, and show *emphysema* or degeneration of the spongy substances which absorb oxygen, it would be wrong to pretend that there is any cure. People with chronic bronchitis may be helped by certain drugs, but they are not cured when irreversible changes have occurred. In this case, a large part will be played by cough mixtures, and it is important to realise that these are of two types: sedative and expectorant. A sedative mixture is intended to stop irritation which is useless, and does not perform the function of a cough in bringing up secretion. For instance, in laryngitis there is an irritating cough which is simply caused by stimulation of the tissues when there is no secretion to get rid of, and in this case it would be reasonable to give medicine which stops the cough, but when secretion is present it has to be removed, and here one has to take some drug which will make one cough more effectively. A stimulant mixture is one designed to liquefy the sputum and help to get it out of the system. (Incidentally, one of the best—even in these days of " wonder drugs "—is the solution of common salt used in Brompton Chest Hospital.) There are numerous good means of suppressing coughs, but probably very few good expectorants, although each patient swears by his own special mixture; and he may be right.

If lung or bronchial disease has been present for some time there may develop certain degenerative changes, such as *bronchiectasis* or *emphysema.* In bronchiectasis the bronchial tubes become dilated, first of all in a single lobe of one lung and then elsewhere, with the result that the stagnant and infected secretions are retained very largely within the chest, damage further the bronchial linings and the lung tissue, and end up in a vicious circle: pus accumulating, bronchitis, more pus, and more bronchitis. All the signs of chronic bronchitis are present, but what is typical is the large amounts of foul-smelling pus which are brought up. Bronchiectasis is a serious disease, but the antibiotics and the sulpha drugs have improved the outlook, and lung surgery (lobectomy or removal of a lobe and pneumothorax or collapsing of the lung) is also used in suitable cases. In emphysema the deterioration takes place in the lung tissue, and if you recall that the lung is the place where the oxygen of the air taken in meets the blood within the internal surfaces, you will see that the amount of surface available is of great importance. In fact, the normal lung internal surfaces are about the size—if they were spread out—of a tennis-court. But in emphysema the elastic tissue between the cells begins to give way, the surface available for oxygenising becomes smaller, and, as the walls of the cells collapse, so do the number of capillaries. In order to get the same amount of oxygen into the blood, the heart has to work much harder. So emphysema, like most chronic lung disease, leads to heart trouble—the heart has to work harder to get the blood through.

LUNG SURGERY.

Like heart surgery, lung surgery has greatly developed in recent years and is used in four main categories of disease: infections, cysts, tumours, and in wounds. Infection is mainly due to bronchiectasis and tuberculosis—although other infections may arise; cysts are not very common, and need not necessarily give trouble unless they become infected; tumours, if malignant, obviously have to be removed; and how a wound is treated depends on its severity. Generally speaking, the operations performed are: (1) drainage; (2) removal of part of the lung; or (3) collapse of the lung. *Drainage* is carried out when—as in the case of an abscess or infected cyst—there is an area containing pus, and the purpose of the procedure is to let the pus out. *Removal of part of the lung,* or in some cases a whole lung, is carried out where there exists bronchiectasis or tuberculosis or cancer limited to a particular area; clearly such an operation is serious, but the results today are good, although, of course, this depends in part upon the initial condition from which the patient was suffering. *Lung collapse* is carried out when infection is present, but it is thought that recovery might occur after a " rest "; for collapse means that the affected lung is put out of action and is not used for breathing. Collapse is carried out in various ways. In *pneumothorax* air is injected into the chest by a simple procedure, causing collapse; in *pneumoperitoneum* air is injected into the abdomen, with the same result, since by pushing up the diaphragm it causes collapse; in *phrenic nerve crush* the nerve supplying the diaphragm is crushed under a local anæsthetic where it passes through the neck. In more serious cases *thoracoplasty*—the removal of all or portions of the upper ribs—may be performed under a general anæsthetic.

Lung Cancer is one of the most obvious reasons for surgery, and as most people know by now, it has been established that there is some connection between lung cancer and tobacco-smoking. The facts, as known, are complicated, but some of the more important are these:

(*a*) Between the ages of fifty and sixty-four those who smoke more than twenty cigarettes a day have a death-rate more than twice as high as non-smokers (although not necessarily from lung cancer).

(*b*) Five moderate smokers die of lung cancer to every one non-smoker and fifteen or sixteen heavy smokers.

(*c*) It seems certain that other factors are important. For example, the death-rate from lung cancer is very much higher in cities than in the country, the incidence is higher amongst cigarette smokers than amongst pipe or cigar smokers. Diesel fumes and smog probably play a quite important part, and the considerable increase in cancer (which is, however, commoner in men than in women) runs parallel both with increased cigarette smoking and increased fumes from car exhausts—particularly Diesel fumes.

(*d*) As in the case of coronary thrombosis, we can see that it is not easy to analyse out the real cause of the trouble in lung cancer. We have to consider the soil—the person affected. Is there, perhaps, something within the individual which predisposes him to cancer, and that smoking merely determines *where* he will get it? We do not know, but it is a possibility.

There are few early symptoms and the condition is usually discovered by accident at a mass X-ray centre. Pain in the chest, loss of weight, and coughing blood are late symptoms. The only treatment, if the disease is found in time, is removal of the whole or part of the affected lung.

Asthma is a chest disease which we will discuss at this point, since it will serve to introduce the general problem of *allergy,* although other allergic diseases will be mentioned elsewhere according to the part of the body affected. The causes of asthma are mainly three: allergy, chronic bronchitis, and emotional disturbances, although in varying degrees they go together in any one person; there is a likelihood that allergy and emotional sensitivity are related and that in cases with bronchitis the patient may be allergic to his own germs. People may be allergic to all sorts of things: to pollens, feathers, and numerous particles present in the form of dust in any house or any city street; to foods such as shellfish, to penicillin, to injections given them at the doctor's, and a case was even reported from America in which a man got a divorce because he was allergic to his wife and developed a skin-rash whenever she embraced him! Asthma is simply one form of allergy, in this case affecting the bronchi, which go into spasm when the person comes into contact with the stuff to which he is sensitive. But allergy can affect the nose and eyes, as in hay fever, the skin, as in dermatitis, the joints, and the bowels. In an asthma attack the patient finds it more and more difficult to breathe, his chest is widely expanded, and the main trouble is in breathing out. Such attacks often come on at night, and may occur almost daily, or as infrequently as one every few months. Although asthma is an allergic disease, the attacks are very often set off by emotional crises of rage or resentment. In some cases the emotional element is even more obvious, as when a woman allergic to roses developed an attack when shown into a room in which there was a bunch of roses on the table, which were, in fact, artificial! The immediate treatment for an attack is to give something which will relax the tubes, usually adrenalin injections or ephedrene taken as tablets by mouth. The long-term treatment is directed towards finding the substance to which the patient is sensitive and by a course of injections attempting to desensitise him. Unfortunately this does not always work, but in some cases antihistamine drugs may help. However, the trouble with asthma, as with other chronic lung diseases, is that when it has existed for some time changes occur which are irreversible, such as chronic bronchitis or emphysema. When this stage is reached the best that can be done (and it is a great deal) is nevertheless palliation.

Allergy is to be understood as a perversion of the normal body reactions towards certain substances—mainly, but not always, proteins. Such substances act, just as do the toxins of germs, as antigens: that is to say they cause the formation of counter-substances designed to neutralise their influence, and these counter-substances are known as antibodies. Normally, this takes place successfully within the blood, and when a second dose of the foreign protein gets into the body its effect is neutralised. But when, due to some unknown cause, this does not happen, the antigen, or foreign substance, gets into the body cells and causes the liberation of a poisonous chemical known as histamine. It is this which causes the symptoms in allergic diseases, and which is sometimes countered by the antihistamine drugs. In extreme and rather rare cases a person with this sort of disability may get an injection, and if there has not been sufficient time for antibodies to form, a second injection of a completely harmless stuff, such as a serum, may lead to sudden death. This is known as *anaphylactic shock*.

Allergy, then, is due to an inability to produce antibodies, and this, in turn, is the result of: (*a*) heredity—for such diseases run in families; (*b*) to the person's physical condition at the time; and (*c*) to emotional causes which can interfere with antibody formation.

DISEASES OF THE DIGESTIVE TRACT

INTRODUCTION.

The digestive tract begins at the mouth and ends at the rectum, where the waste products are excreted. The food taken in at the mouth is moistened with saliva secreted by the salivary glands, of which the largest are the parotid glands —they are the ones which become swollen in mumps. The smaller glands are the submaxillary (under the jaw) and the sublingual (under the tongue). The act of chewing breaks the food down and helps to mix it with the saliva. Saliva contains an enzyme called ptyalin, which starts the digestion of starchy foods, and the food thus reduced to a pulp passes down the œsophagus, a tube about 2 ft. long leading through the chest down to the stomach, where the main part of digestion begins. The gastric juice, as everyone knows, contains hydrochloric acid, which in concentrated form is a dangerous caustic and will burn holes in carpets or anything else if allowed to —as certain advertisers at one time were not slow to point out. Advertisements used to show the dreadful effect of the acid on a carpet, and invite the gullible to consider what would be the effect on the much more delicate stomach; the effect would, of course, be neutralised by "Biffo" or whatever was the name of the stomach powder. This, needless to say, is a piece of nonsense; hydrochloric acid in the stomach is important for digestion (although some seem to manage without it), and it exists in such a diluted state that it could not burn a hole in a piece of tissue paper. However, the details of this will be discussed later when we are talking about ulcers. Suffice it to say that the acid is intended to be there, and causes harm only when something else has gone wrong with the stomach.

Also in the juices secreted by glands in the stomach lining are the substances known as enzymes, which are found not only there but play a large part in all body processes. By bringing about chemical changes they make life possible, and we have already mentioned one, ptyalin, which functions in the saliva to break down starch into sugar. The word enzyme is derived from two Greek words meaning "in yeast," because the first enzyme known to Man was the one in yeast which breaks down starchy foods into sugar and, given time, as brewers and some less-respectable gentlemen know, into alcohol. In the stomach the main enzymes are pepsin, which changes insoluble proteins in food into peptones, in which form absorption through mucous membranes is possible, and rennin (essence of rennet obtained from the cow's stomach is the stuff used to make curds and whey). In the small intestine the food comes under the influence of the alkaline juices, secreted partly by the intestine itself and partly by the pancreas; the most important enzymes here are trypsin, which breaks down proteins, amylase, which continues the work of breaking down starches, and lipase, which breaks down fats.

The end result is that by the time it reaches the end of the small intestine all the food we have eaten, however varied, is broken down into very simple chemicals: the proteins into substances known as amino-acids, the fats into glycerine and fatty acids, and the starches and sugars into glucose. The fact that glucose does not have to be digested, and that carbohydrates generally are the fuel of the body give rise to the quaint notion that glucose makes you energetic (hence all the tablets, drinks, and so on containing glucose which, from the remarks made about them by advertisers, one might suppose to be the elixir of life). Unfortunately, although glucose is useful as a temporary food in those who cannot—as after an operation—absorb anything else, there are very few people who need any extra. Most of us don't need more energy; we need more brains to make use of what energy we have. A spoonful of glucose is no better and no worse than a couple of lumps of ordinary sugar or a slice of bread so far as giving energy is concerned, for the simple reason that all end up in the same way; as glucose.

After being thus broken down, the fatty acids and glycerine enter the lymph channels passing from the intestinal walls and so get into the blood and thence to the areas under the skin which give some ladies their "vital statistics" and many men and women their "middle-aged spread," but the amino-acids and glucose pass through a special system of veins, the portal system, to the liver to be stored until they are needed.

The small intestine includes the duodenum, which joins the stomach at the lower end, where there is a sort of valve known as the pylorus. The duodenum is about a foot long and continues into the jejunum and ileum, which together are about 23 ft. long. At the end of the ileum the small intestine joins the large intestine or colon, and this, at the right-hand lower corner of the abdomen, is the site of the appendix. Finally, the 5-ft.-long large intestine passes to the rectum, which is only 6 in. long and leads to the anus, the band of muscle which ends the digestive tract.

Later on we shall deal with problems of diet and nutrition, but at present it is more convenient to wend our way down the length of the alimentary canal and discuss the various diseases which can affect it. Little need be said about the teeth, since most people know about the principles of dental care, although they do not always carry them out with any degree of completeness. Briefly these are: brushing the teeth at least twice a day, but preferably after every meal; avoiding too much sweet food, and especially the kind of nauseous confections which stick to the teeth; and going to the dentist every six months. A *gumboil* is an abscess at the root of a tooth which causes the all-too-familiar swelling of the face.

The only first-aid treatment for this is the old one of heat applied outside, aspirin for pain, and hot mouth-washes. Sooner or later the dentist will have to be consulted.

Elsewhere we have mentioned *tonsillitis* and *pharyngitis*, and so far as this region is concerned the other "ituses" are *stomatitis*, a general infection of the mouth, and *glossitis*, an infection of the tongue. Stomatitis can be due to many causes: to a fungus infection common in babies whose mothers take insufficient care in the hygiene of feeding (this is known as "thrush"); to various other sorts of infection often predisposed to by malnutrition; and to certain drugs, such as mercury.

In thrush, white patches form within the mouth, but the condition can easily be treated by a doctor. The other types are usually characterised by a bad taste in the mouth, bad breath, excessive salivation, and sometimes by a burning sensation. Their treatment depends upon the cause, and they should therefore be referred to the G.P. Glossitis, too, may be the end result of many influences, and shows itself by some unusual appearance of the tongue: redness, soreness, white or black patches, or ulcers. Sometimes the patches are in a form resembling a map, which doctors with their irrepressible sense of humour—not always shared by their patients—describe as "geographical tongue." Sometimes, and paradoxically, the cause may be the use of penicillin, which, by killing some germs, encourages the growth of others; sometimes it is the result of oral sepsis. But all these conditions, if they last any length of time, should be referred to a doctor, especially in older people, and especially if ulcers are present. *Ulcers of the tongue, although they are often of little significance, may be serious, and it is not worth while taking risks.* The œsophagus, too, may be affected by a number of diseases usually characterised by pain or difficulty in swallowing. This is known as *œsophagitis*, and may be due to the passage of burning, hot, or caustic liquids. Or there may be paralysis of the nerves supplying the muscle, which also leads to difficulty in swallowing. But the most important disease which can affect this area is *cancer of the œsophagus*. It is estimated that about 1 per cent. of all cancer deaths are due to this cause, that it affects men more often than women, and ordinarily men between fifty and seventy. The symptoms are difficulty in swallowing and loss of weight. Until recently, the outlook in the condition was absolutely hopeless, and doctors and relatives had to stand helplessly by whilst the patient virtually starved before their eyes. But now advances in chest surgery make it possible for an operation to be carried out in which the diseased area is cut out, the stomach brought up into the chest, and stitched to the remaining part of the œsophagus. Still more recently, almost the whole œsophagus has been removed and replaced with a plastic tube. Of course, this can be done only when the disease is caught in time.

Often difficulty in swallowing or a sensation of choking is due to solely emotional causes. This is known as *globus hystericus*, and requires to be treated psychologically. Lastly, there sometimes develops in the œsophagus what is described as a *diverticulum*, which is to this area what an aneurism is to an artery: *i.e.*, it is a bulging out of the wall which creates a sac. A diverticulum does not necessarily cause trouble, but the larger ones do in three ways: (1) they collect food which every now and then comes back into the mouth; (2) they may become large enough to cause obstruction; and (3) they are likely when their contents become infected to cause lung disease. If they are at this stage the only treatment is surgery, in which the "ballooning" part is tied off at the base. The operation is obviously a major one, but recovery is almost invariable.

Peptic Ulcer is a name covering two separate conditions—*gastric ulcer*, which is an ulcer in the stomach, and *duodenal ulcer* in the duodenum. The immediate cause of ulceration is that the digestive juices have, for some reason or another, digested away a part of the wall of the tract. It appears that ordinarily, although the stomach can digest protein from outside, it does not digest itself, because there are chemicals in the lining—known tentatively as "anti-enzymes"—which neutralise the effect of the hydrochloric acid and the enzymes. Why does this protection break down?

This is an important disease because it is so common, and perhaps we had better have some facts:

(*a*) About 10 per cent. of all adults have had at one time or another an ulcer of the stomach or duodenum.

(*b*) Nearly 90 per cent. of these ulcers clear up by purely medical attention, without surgery.

(*c*) When people say they have "an ulcer in the stomach" they usually mean an ulcer in the duodenum. Only one out of twelve ulcers are in the stomach.

(*d*) The indications for operation are, in general: (1) when the ulcer is chronic and medical treatment has failed; (2) when there is severe bleeding caused by the ulcer eating into a blood-vessel; (3) when, as sometimes happens, the ulcer forms scar tissue which contracts and obstructs the passage of food; (4) when an ulcer perforates.

A perforated ulcer is one which has eaten right through the stomach wall, and in these circumstances an emergency operation is necessary, for the stomach contents pass into the abdominal cavity, causing *peritonitis*—*i.e.*, a septic infection of the peritoneum, the delicate lining which covers the abdominal organs as the pericardium covers the heart and the pleura the lungs.

Typically, ulcer pain is in the upper abdomen, comes on about half an hour to two hours (depending upon its site) after meals, and is relieved to a greater or lesser extent by alkalis or taking more food. The medical treatment consists in dieting on easily digested foods taken "little and often" so that the stomach is never empty but never full. Alkaline powders are usually prescribed by the doctor, and sometimes muscle relaxants such as atropine are used to relieve the spasm which is the immediate cause of pain. It cannot be too strongly emphasised that symptoms such as those described above if they persist for any length of time should be referred to a doctor. Self-treatment is very risky.

Operative treatment is designed to reduce the hyperacidity which causes the trouble. The two main operations performed are *gastrojejunostomy*, in which part of the jejunum is stitched to the stomach so that the alkaline juices of the small intestine can enter the stomach and partially neutralise the excess acid, and, much more frequent nowadays, *partial gastrectomy*. In this operation the part of the stomach which contains the acid-secreting glands—the lower three-quarters—is removed, the duodenum is closed and the remaining quarter of the stomach is stitched to the small intestine. This operation is very successful, and only about 1 per cent. of cases have any further symptoms. Finally, *vagotomy* is sometimes performed—*i.e.*, cutting of the vagus nerve, which passes down from the brain through the neck and chest to the stomach; for it is the impulses passing down this nerve which are responsible for the over-secretion of acid.

Why is peptic ulcer becoming so common? Most doctors would agree that it is one of the diseases caused by stress and the problems facing us in an age of anxiety. It is more common in industrial communities than in peasant ones and in people whose work is a source of worry—who are continually tense. There is no reason at all to suppose that irregular meals and the other dietary reasons often given have any influence in producing an ulcer, although one must, naturally, be careful about these when an ulcer is present. Duodenal ulcer is common in the fairly young and fit, stomach ulcer in the old and poorly. For some reason, although duodenal ulcers almost never become malignant, about 10 per cent. of stomach ulcers do so, even although there may have been no previous history of dyspepsia.

Cancer of the Stomach is found most frequently in men between forty-five and sixty. The pain of cancer tends to be constant rather than periodic, and there is increasing loss of weight and anæmia. Operation is necessary, but the outlook is good if the condition is discovered in time. There would be much less risk of cancer getting beyond the stage where operation can help if people with "indigestion" lasting any length of time would put themselves immediately under medical care with periodic check-ups. A curious feature of cancer of the stomach is that hydrochloric acid is completely absent.

Gastritis means inflammation of the stomach lining; it may be acute or chronic. In acute gastritis eating too much food or eating unsuitable food in a person with a sensitive stomach may lead to symptoms, but the most frequent cause is too much alcohol. The symptoms, in general, are those of a "hangover": headache, depression, loss of appetite, and, as P. G. Wodehouse puts it, "a feeling that you're going to die in about five minutes." In more severe cases there may be a raised temperature and diarrhœa. The treatment is to avoid irritating the stomach further, to eat only as much bland food as one feels inclined to, and to take some alkaline medicine—"fizzy" salts are suitable for this. Since "gastritis," strictly speaking, refers to any form of irritation of the stomach lining, it can also be applied to serious conditions, as when poisons such as strong acids or other corrosives are swallowed, intentionally or otherwise. Here we are discussing only the condition which is ordinarily understood when the word is used.

Chronic gastritis, although it may be associated with kidney, lung, heart, or blood diseases, and with diabetes, is usually the sequel to frequent attacks of acute gastritis. Here, again, the appetite is poor, there is depression and a feeling of discomfort rather than pain after taking food. Headache, flatulence, and vomiting or nausea in the morning are common features. Although one is inclined to picture the case of chronic gastritis as typically a retired colonel from India or some other tropical spot who has subsisted for years on curries and alcohol, there is no reason to suppose that curries have anything to do with it. Even alcohol can be taken in large amounts without doing any harm (except to one's pocket!) provided it is taken diluted and with meals. In fact, many elderly ladies of irreproachable character suffer from chronic gastritis, and it is well to remember that strong tea taken too frequently causes red noses more frequently than strong drink. Chronic gastritis requires special medical attention.

Nervous or Functional Dyspepsia is a term used by doctors which means, first, that the condition is basically a sign of general neurosis and, as such, needs a psychological rather than a physical approach, and secondly, that no signs of organic disease of the stomach have been found on examination. This, of course, does not make the discomfort any easier to bear from the point of view of the patient. The symptoms tend to be different from the more or less cut-and-dried ones of ulcer: for example, flatulence and nervous vomiting are frequent. *Flatulence* is a gastric neurosis due to the habit of swallowing air; for no "gas" is formed in the stomach, and all that is brought up has previously been unconsciously swallowed. Trying to "bring it up" as many people do to the distress of those near by, only results in more air being swallowed, so the desire should be resisted. *Anorexia nervosa* is another gastric neurosis in which the patient refuses to take food or vomits it up when it has been taken. In some cases even death may result from self-imposed starvation of this type, for which psychological treatment is necessary.

The end of the stomach where it joins the duodenum is known as the pylorus, a ring of muscle which acts as a valve and allows the partially digested food to pass from the stomach only when it is ready for further digestion by the intestinal juices. In newly born babies the pylorus muscle may be too thick or it may tend to go into spasm easily, with the result that food cannot get out of the stomach and is vomited up. This is known as *pyloric stenosis*, and is quite common in babies of two or three weeks of age—three times more frequently in boys than in girls. Without treatment the continued vomiting, which is very forceful in character, would lead to death through malnutrition and lack of fluids, but fortunately treatment is relatively simple. In some cases, injections of a drug to relax the spasm is sufficient, but more often an operation is necessary. A small incision is made under an anæsthetic, and the pylorus muscle is slit down its entire length (of course, only the muscle fibres are cut, not the inner lining of the stomach). The operation is very safe, and the wound heals within about a week, after which the infant has no further trouble.

The small intestine can be affected by a number of diseases, although much less frequently than the stomach and duodenum. Here we shall mention only two of the more common conditions: regional ileitis and intestinal obstruction.

Regional Ileitis is an inflammation of the small intestine frequently found in young men and women. The cause is unknown, but it leads to ulceration and small perforations which cause adhesions between the affected area and other parts of the small intestine. Such a condition requires surgical treatment, which usually takes the form of short-circuiting the diseased area and joining together the healthy ends of the loop. Sometimes the diseased area is cut away altogether and the healthy end joined to the large intestine. By this means the vast majority of cases can be cured.

Intestinal Obstruction can be caused by a tumour, by a loop of intestine becoming twisted on itself (volvulus), by the bowel being caught in a hernial sac, or by the contraction of old adhesions. Here, too, the surgeon will either by-pass the area or if the intestine has become damaged and gangrene has set in he will remove the whole of the affected part. Acute (*i.e.*, sudden) obstruction is a surgical emergency, and if an operation is not performed death will occur in a few days. The symptoms are severe colic, profuse vomiting, distended abdomen, and collapse; no bowel motions are passed. Chronic obstruction, in which the blockage is gradual, is usually due to a tumour; the symptoms are periodic attacks of vomiting, constipation alternating with diarrhœa, and loss of weight.

In children, *intussusception* is not uncommon, especially in boys under the age of two. Here one part of bowel becomes telescoped into another, leading to colic and the passage of motions consisting of blood and mucus. Later there will be vomiting and collapse. Operation, of course, is necessary.

Constipation. Here, perhaps, we had better mention the question of constipation, about which so many people hold such pronounced views. They believe that constipation is the root of all evil, that it causes a mysterious condition known to them (although, alas, not to doctors) as "auto-intoxication." Sedulously fostered by the manufacturers of patent medicines, their beliefs range from the notion that headaches, spotty skin, muddy skin, and tiredness are caused by constipation, to the more extreme idea that the whole system is being poisoned and that, if the bowels do not work, the individual will shortly die. Of course, all this is the merest rubbish; for, as Professor Samson Wright, whose *Applied Physiology* is one of the most famous of medical text-books, has pointed out, there is no such thing as absorption of poisonous products from the bowel. There is no such thing as "auto-intoxication." "The symptoms of constipation," he writes, "are largely due to distension and mechanical irritation of the rectum." It has been shown that an enema removes these symptoms *immediately*, which would not be the case if they were due to poisons in the blood, and exactly the same symptoms can be produced by packing the rectum with cotton-wool. Wright mentions the case of a man who went for just over a year without a bowel motion, and at the end of that time, although his abdomen was distended and he felt some discomfort, he was not noticeably ill. Needless to say, telling these facts to the purgative addict will only make him annoyed, but it is as well to note that if no known diseases are due to constipation (although constipation may be a symptom of another disease), the regular use of purgatives *can* cause disease.

Constipation should be treated first by diet

containing plenty of roughage—bran and oatmeal are excellent—plenty of stewed and fresh fruits, and at least three pints of fluid should be taken daily. Failing that, one of the best things to take is "Senokot," a proprietary product prepared from senna pods. Never to be taken regularly are liquid paraffin, since there is some evidence that it may cause cancer, castor oil, preparations of aloes, Epsom salts, and all the other dreadful stuff that people swill down.

An extreme form of constipation is *Hirschsprung's disease*, which is found in children, usually males, and leads to constipation over long periods, so that motions may occur only every few months. The condition is probably due to spasm in the intestine, and can be relieved by an operation in which the nerves producing the spasm are divided.

Diarrhœa has already been discussed under the heading of infectious diseases, and the types due to infection will be found there. However, diarrhœa can be the result of other influences: food that "hasn't agreed" with one; certain poisons, such as mercury, arsenic, and purgatives; and to nervous tension. The treatment depends on the cause, but in mild cases a single large dose of castor oil is a good idea. This gets rid of whatever is causing the trouble (provided that it is not a serious infection or nervous diarrhœa we are dealing with), and it has a slightly constipating after-effect. Other mixtures given by doctors are chalk and opium or kaolin and morphia—the opium and morphia are in very small quantities.

DISEASES OF THE LARGE INTESTINE.

The large intestine consists of the colon and the rectum. If you put your hand down in the right-hand lower part of the abdomen, then you are covering the area where the small intestine meets the colon, and also where the appendix, a small, blind tube about 2 in. long, hangs from the beginning of the colon. Now move your hand upwards to the margin of the ribs, then straight across the abdomen at the level of the stomach and down the other side to the corresponding place on the left side from where you began. The path you will have mapped out is that of the colon, which, as the name implies, is much wider than the small intestine.

The colon is just as subject to disease as the stomach. In fact, Dr. Clark Kennedy says that most so-called indigestion "is not due to duodenal or gastric ulceration . . . but to disorder of the mechanics of the large bowel aggravated by introspection and *again and again by the misuse of aperients*" (the writer's italics). Irritation of the colon is known as colitis, and there are two types: ulcerative colitis and mucous colitis. As in the case of stomach and duodenal ulcers, mental factors play a large part, but, since not everyone with anxiety or who is under stress develops colitis, we have to assume that this condition, and indeed the other stress diseases, are caused by an interplay between hereditary disposition, certain physical factors not yet completely understood, and stress.

Ulcerative Colitis is a serious disease in which there is not only inflammation of the intestinal wall but also ulceration. The patient, usually an adult between twenty and forty, and most commonly a woman, develops diarrhœa, with passage of blood, pus, and mucus; there is an irregular fever, although no germs have ever been conclusively found to account for this. Sometimes the disease begins abruptly and ends in quite a short time in death, but more often it runs a course of many months in a milder form. Medical treatment, such as washing out the colon, may be used, and various drugs have been tried, and in about 75 per cent. of cases these prove adequate. But in the remaining 25 per cent. of cases operation is necessary. The operation performed is *ileostomy*, in which the end of the small intestine is brought out on the abdominal wall so that the motions pass out there, the colon is thus put out of action and can be rested. In about 10 per cent. of cases the ulceration heals and the small and large intestines can be joined up again by closing the opening on the abdomen, but more often the opening must be permanent. If, in spite of this, the bleeding and diarrhœa persist, the only possibility is to perform a *colectomy*—*i.e.*, to remove the whole of the colon. Although this is a large-scale operation, the recovery rate is well over 90 per cent.

Mucous Colitis is a less serious disease which appears to be almost entirely nervous in origin. As in the other type, there are attacks of diarrhœa, in which quantities of mucus and membranous material—actually parts of the lining of the bowel—are passed. There is no blood, and the treatment is medical, with sedatives and antispasmodics, drugs which relax the spasm in the colon.

Appendicitis is a disease which mysteriously became popular towards the beginning of this century. Appendicitis begins with pain over the stomach (*i.e.*, in the *upper* part of the abdomen, and not over the site of the appendix). The pain remains there for some hours and then moves to the right lower part of the abdomen; there is usually fever and sometimes vomiting. It is important to realise that in any case of abdominal pain purges should never on any account be given; in appendicitis particularly purges may lead to death from peritonitis. The treatment of appendicitis is nearly always surgical, but in a few cases antibiotics may be used.

Bleeding from the Rectum is a common symptom which may be due to a number of causes: hæmorrhoids, dysentery, typhoid, some blood diseases such as purpura, and tumours. Bleeding from a gastric or duodenal ulcer leads to black motions or *melæna*. The blood in this case is black because it has been changed in its passage through the digestive tract, and although black motions may result from harmless causes—*e.g.*, when iron-containing medicines or bismuth are being taken—it should always be referred to a doctor. In fact, any bleeding from the rectum should be investigated.

Visceroptosis occurs when the bands of tissue holding up any of the abdominal organs begin to sag so that the organs sink downwards. The symptoms are vague: dyspeptic tendencies, constipation, and a general feeling of being unwell. Although it often occurs in young women who have had too many pregnancies too quickly, there is a large neurotic element involved. Treatment is directed towards the neurotic condition accompanied by exercises and perhaps the use of an abdominal belt to support the sagging muscles.

Cœliac Disease. Some children are born with an innate difficulty in absorbing fats from the small intestine. They suffer from diarrhœa, in which large quantities of partly digested fats are passed from the body. The passage of fats in this way is known as *steatorrhœa*, and the disease is described as *cœliac disease* (Gee's disease), or, if it occurs in the tropics, *tropical sprue*. Adults, too, may suffer from the disease, but in children the important factor is that the disease is also associated with defective absorption of iron and calcium, so they tend to become anæmic and may develop rickets. It is necessary to give a fat-free diet, vitamins and calcium, and plenty of protein. "Sprulac," which is a dried defatted milk powder, is frequently given. The condition may go on for years, but the outlook is quite good. Tropical sprue is not caused by living in the tropics, but tropical conditions may bring out a latent tendency to steatorrhœa.

Diverticulitis. In diverticulitis an inborn weakness of the large intestine leads to weakness of the muscular wall of the large intestine, and through the weakened areas the mucous membrane or lining of the bowel pushes through. Probably at least 5–10 per cent. of all people have some diverticulæ, but they give trouble only when they become inflamed through some of the fæcal contents of the intestine getting trapped within them. There is pain, usually in the left lower part of the abdomen, slight fever, and general abdominal tenderness. Diverticulitis can usually be treated by dieting, rest, and antibiotics or sulpha drugs. The vast majority of cases can be dealt with in this way; but if they do not respond, it may be necessary to remove the affected area.

Cancer of the Large Intestine. The large intestine is one of the commonest sites for cancer. The symptoms, which usually occur from forty to sixty, are twice as common in men as in women, and, in general (although this depends upon the part of the colon affected), they are: passing of blood from the rectum, loss of weight, anæmia, and increasing constipation. Pain occurs as the obstruction increases, and finally the signs of acute obstruction already described make their appearance. Fortunately, symptoms usually appear early in the disease, so it can frequently be caught in time. Surgery is the only remedy, and in early cases may be done in one stage by removal of the affected part, but if obstruction has begun it is necessary to perform an operation—*colostomy*—in which a part of the intestine, as in ileostomy, is brought out on to the abdominal wall, so that the fæces discharge from the side of the abdomen instead of through the rectum. This operation is followed a few weeks later by removal of the part containing the tumour.

Hernia. The body, unfortunately, is supplied with many weak areas in the abdominal wall and elsewhere through which structures such as the intestines can thrust their way to where they are not supposed to be. This condition is known as hernia. There are numerous different types of hernias; for example, they may occur in the canal below the groin through which the large blood-vessels pass back and forth between the legs and abdomen or in the larger inguinal canal just above. They are also found at the umbilicus, a weak area through which before birth the child was supplied with all its needs from its mother's circulation, or right in the middle of the abdomen below the umbilicus, where the two vertical bands of muscle which form the abdominal wall come together but often leave a weakness in between. There may also be hernias internally, or in the diaphragm, or over the site of an operation scar. In the groin we speak of *inguinal hernia*, in the area where the vessels pass between abdomen and legs slightly below the groin we speak of *femoral hernia*, at the umbilicus, *umbilical hernia*, and between the two abdominal muscles, *ventral hernia*. A *diaphragmatic hernia* is one in which the stomach pushes its way into the chest through a weak part of the diaphragm.

Hernias may occur at any age, and indeed many children are born with them. In later life they are generally caused by a combination of developmental weaknesses in the area concerned, flabby muscles, and sudden strains, such as lifting heavy weights. The main danger from a hernia, apart from its inconvenience, is that it may become *strangulated*—that is, a part of the intestine may become caught in the hernial sac, and becoming filled with intestinal contents, swell up and be unable to escape. This causes all the symptoms of intestinal obstruction and has to be treated as an emergency, or else gangrene of the part which is caught and possibly peritonitis will occur.

Although many people, fearing surgery, wear a truss—that is a belt which by pressing on the part keeps the weak area compressed—there is no doubt that hernias, except in the old and infirm, should be operated on. No matter how comfortable the truss may be, it is a continual nuisance and interferes with many activities, such as swimming; nor are trusses always adequate in performing their function. The operation involves replacing the herniated organs back into the abdominal cavity, removing the sac of peritoneum (*i.e.*, the thin lining of the abdomen which has been pushed out by the organ), and then repairing the muscle wall where it was weakened. The main sign that a hernia exists (at least so far as femoral, inguinal, umbilical, ventral, or scar hernias are concerned) is a soft swelling over the place where the weakness exists. Unless strangulation occurs, there need be no other symptoms. But any bulge in the groin or upper thigh or, indeed, anywhere, should be immediately referred to a doctor.

Cancer of the Rectum. The rectum and anus are afflicted by two common diseases: cancer of the rectum and hæmorrhoids. In cancer of the rectum the symptoms are similar to those described under cancer of the large intestine. Operation is imperative as soon as possible, and it is usual to remove the anus, rectum, and the lower part of the colon, subsequently creating a permanent colostomy.

The anus, the last inch of the intestinal canal, is a sphincter, a band of muscle which controls the exit of fæces from the bowels. In addition to hæmorrhoids, the anus may be the site of fissures (*i.e.*, ulcers of the lining), fistulas (abnormal tracts leading from the lower rectum to the skin), and polyps (non-malignant growths). *Fissures* are elongated ulcers rather like a crack in the mucous lining which cause pain every time the bowels are moved. They tend, if untreated, to get deeper and more inflamed. Treatment is surgical, by cutting the sphincter muscle to allow relaxing and healing. A *fistula*, as has been mentioned, is an abnormal channel between the lower rectum and the skin—*i.e.*, it comes out somewhere around the anus. Nearly always it is the result of a previous infection, such as a boil or abscess, in the region of the anus. The treatment is surgical, as a fistula rarely clears up by itself. The channel is opened and cleared out, then packing is put in to enable it to heal from the bottom up. *Polyps* may vary in size from a pea to a golf ball, and the first sign may be fairly severe hæmorrhage from the rectum. Sometimes there is no bleeding, but the polyp suddenly appears protruding from the anus after a bowel movement. It is painless, and not in itself serious, but should nevertheless always be removed (this can often be done by cauterising without an anæsthetic), since some authorities believe that such growths may become cancerous.

Hæmorrhoids are simply varicose veins in the rectal and anal regions. They are very common, and are caused probably in about equal degrees by inherited weakness of the veins, strain such as heavy lifting, and constipation (this is one of the very few conditions in which constipation may do some damage, due to the mechanical pressure of hardened fæces in the rectum on the veins). Pregnant women are liable to develop hæmorrhoids or "*piles*," as they are commonly called, owing to the pressure of the baby's head in the pelvis. Hæmorrhoids may be external or internal, the former being in the anal region below the sphincter, the latter in the rectum; the two usually go together. There may be no symptoms, but the veins are liable to bleed, to get thrombosed (*i.e.*, a clot forms within) or to become infected. When clotting or infection occurs the piles enlarge and tend to be pushed out through the anus during defæcation, when they form extremely painful external swellings. Treatment in simple cases may be by the use of suppositories—cones of a firm grease containing suitable medicaments which are inserted in the rectum—in other cases the veins may be injected, as with varicose veins of the leg, in order to close them, but when there is much bleeding, thrombosis, infection, or interference with bowel movements they should be removed surgically.

DISEASES OF THE LIVER AND GALL-BLADDER.

The functions and site of the liver have been described elsewhere, so no more need be said about these. Presumably the most common associations of the layman in relation to the liver would be the two words "liverish" and "jaundice." Feeling *liverish*, one gathers, produces a sort of sensation like a hangover (which it frequently is), but there is no medical term corresponding to the word, nor is there any reason at all to suppose that it has anything whatever to do with the liver. Most likely it is an attack of mild gastritis, and should be treated as such.

Jaundice is easily recognised by the yellowish skin, the degree of colouring depending upon the severity of the case. In mild cases it may only be noticeable in the whites of the eyes. Less well-known symptoms of jaundice are itching of the skin, dark-coloured urine and pale motions, depression, loss of appetite, and tiredness. Jaundice, however, is not in itself a disease; rather it is a symptom of many diseases, amongst which some of the commonest are:

(1) Blockage of the bile ducts, which normally carry the bile and its pigments into the intestines (it is the pigments which produce the yellow coloration). The blockage may be caused by gall-stones, parasites, tumours, or in the liver itself when cirrhosis is present. The bile pigments, unable to get through the duct into the intestine—hence the pale motions—pass backwards into the blood-stream and are filtered into the urine, which therefore becomes stained, and into the skin. This is known as *obstructive jaundice*.

(2) *Infective jaundice*, on the other hand, results from various types of organism such as spirochætes and viruses. Examples are infective hepatitis, spirochætal jaundice, yellow fever, malaria, and some cases of syphilis. Certain poisons, such as chloroform, arsenic, phosphorus, and snake venom, can also cause jaundice, which in this case is due to damage to the liver.

(3) *Haemolytic jaundice* is found is some blood diseases, such as pernicious anæmia, acholuric jaundice, and blackwater fever. Its immediate cause is breaking down of the red cells at a rate too rapid for the liver to absorb the products.

The treatment of jaundice depends entirely upon its cause. The infective and hæmolytic types have already been dealt with under infectious diseases and diseases of the blood respectively, so it only remains to deal with obstructive jaundice, and this leads us to the subject of the gall-bladder and *gall-stones*. Doctors in their perverse way refer to inflammation of the gall-bladder as *cholecystitis* and to the condition of having gall-stones as *cholelithiasis* (just as Americans refer to typists as "stenographers" and lifts as "elevators").

The gall-bladder is pear-shaped and lies below the liver. It ends, at the "stalk" of the pear, in a tube called the cystic duct, which enters the main bile duct passing from the liver into the beginning of the duodenum. Bile is essential to the digestion of fats, and when a meal is eaten a supply of dilute bile moves down the main duct from the liver, whilst more concentrated bile is squeezed into the same duct from the gall-bladder. The bile, both dilute and concentrated, then enters the duodenum to do its work. In cholecystitis, which may be acute or chronic, the walls of the gall-bladder become infected, usually by streptococci or the bacillus coli, and severe pain develops over the liver area, typically spreading back to the right shoulder-blade. If the infection becomes worse and pus is formed there may be a high fever. Gall-stones may, as some physicians believe, be the aftermath of such an infection, although others think that they are formed because of some defect in the ability of the body to deal with fat and cholesterol. In any case, gall-stones are formed in the gall-bladder, and may number anything from one or two to several hundred; their size varies from that of a grain of corn to that of a golf ball. Stones may be present without causing any trouble at all, but usually sooner or later the following symptoms develop: indigestion after eating fatty foods, heartburn, nausea, and attacks of pain. The pain of gall-bladder disease, whether in the case of simple infection or gall-stones, is more or less the same—over the gall-bladder area and passing to the right shoulder-blade. Such pain signifies either infection, which, of course, may occur without stones, or else that a stone formerly lying quietly within the gall-bladder has passed into the bile duct and got stuck.

Typically, gall-bladder disease is found in men and women in middle age, but it is three times commoner in women. As an aid to examinations, students are told (or used to be told) that the typical case is a woman who is "fat, fair, forty, and fertile," for there can be little doubt that pregnancy plays some part in upsetting the secretion of bile in some people. But it is also entirely possible for thin men to develop the disease, so there is no general rule.

When the stone blocks the cystic duct (*i.e.*, the one leading from the gall-bladder to the main duct) there is pain, which may be relieved when the stone either moves back into the bladder or passes into the main duct. The next problem is whether it can negotiate the opening of the main duct into the intestine; for if this duct is blocked *none* of the bile can escape and, passing back into the blood-stream, it produces jaundice.

Operation is necessary when acute inflammation is present, when there are frequent attacks of severe colic and other symptoms causing discomfort, or when jaundice is present. Drugs can cause only temporary relief when a gall-bladder becomes troublesome. There is no such thing as a drug which dissolves gall-stones.

The liver may be the site of cancer, but this is nearly always secondary to cancer elsewhere. Primary cancer, that is cancer originating in the liver, is not common. So, too, the liver may become enlarged, sometimes very considerably so, as a result of events elsewhere in the body: heart failure, leukæmia and other blood diseases, and even rickets can cause enlargement. In the liver itself enlargement may be due to cancer, cirrhosis, abscesses, and cysts (the former usually caused by amœbic dysentery, the latter by parasitic worms; both of which are described elsewhere). Abscesses are usually aspirated—which means that a needle attached to a syringe is passed in and the pus drawn off—cysts have to be surgically removed.

Cirrhosis of the Liver is a condition in which more and more of the liver cells become replaced by fibrous tissue. Now, as we have seen, the whole portal system which carries away the end-products of digestion passes into the liver, so when the liver becomes fibrosed there is serious obstruction to the portal circulation, leading to back-pressure in the veins, and therefore the liquid part of the blood, the plasma, oozes out through the walls into the abdominal cavity. This is known as *ascites*, and it is also found in some cases of heart failure, kidney disease, and chronic peritonitis. Formerly the fluid was removed by tapping the abdominal cavity but modern drugs for increasing fluid loss by the urine are usually successful.

Cirrhosis is always a serious disease; for, although Nature is so generous as to give us 80 per cent. more liver than we need to preserve life, the common type of cirrhosis extends right through the liver, and the secondary effect of portal obstruction with ascites complicates the matter. The disease in the West is often associated with alcoholism, especially in those who drink large quantities of spirits (there are other types of cirrhosis which need not be mentioned here); but the problem is more complicated than might appear, for everyone who drinks to excess does not develop cirrhosis. In fact, cirrhosis is not at all common, and some seem more liable to it than others. It is believed that another unknown factor, possibly malnutrition, is involved and the disease is not due solely to alcohol as such.

Symptoms are: chronic gastritis, morning sickness, constipation. Later, when the portal system has been seriously obstructed, large veins are seen on the abdominal wall, especially around the umbilicus. These develop in an attempt to compensate for the blocked portal circulation. Ascites and slight jaundice are later symptoms. Treatment is a matter for the specialist, but obviously alcohol should be banned. Recently, an operation has been devised in which the portal vein, instead of going to the liver, is sutured to the *vena cava*—the largest vein in the body, which passes up the centre of the abdomen just in front of the backbone on its way to the heart. This operation is known as *porta-caval shunt*. Not infrequently the first sign of cirrhosis is serious hæmorrhage from the mouth due to the rupture of "varices" (*i.e.* varicose veins) at the end of the œsophagus.

The Pancreas.

This is a soft, elongated gland lying behind the stomach; it is about 5 in. long and 2 in. wide.

Within its tissues lies the duct, which, when it leaves the pancreas, passes into the duodenum near the point of entry of the bile-duct. This duct transmits the juices containing enzymes which aid in the digestion in the small intestine. The pancreas, however, has two main functions: not only does it manufacture these important digestive juices, but in certain specialised areas, known as the islets of Langerhans, it manufactures insulin. The functions of insulin will be discussed shortly when we are dealing with diabetes.

Like the liver, the pancreas may be the site of cysts or tumours. The only other condition which need be mentioned is *acute pancreatitis*. This is a not very common disease which is caused by a small gall-stone becoming stuck in the opening of the duct. When this occurs, bacteria come in to infect the pancreas, and the blocking of the duct prevents the digestive juices from leaving, with the result that the organ is digested by its own enzymes. There are all the signs of an acute abdominal disturbance: sudden severe pain, vomiting, and fever. Pancreatitis is difficult, even for the expert, to diagnose, and formerly was always treated surgically, but today it is often possible to clear it up with medical treatment and the use of penicillin or other antibiotics.

Diabetes. Although we know so much about diabetes, we still have not the faintest notion as to what causes it. Its immediate cause is a failure in varying degrees of the pancreas to produce insulin, but examination of the pancreas rarely reveals any significant changes. The disease is commonest between thirty and sixty years, but may occur even in children. Now, insulin is the substance which makes it possible for the body to make use of sugar—the glucose which is the end-product of carbohydrate digestion. So in its absence the glucose, although there to be used, is useless to the body and accumulates in the blood, finally passing out in the urine. (The fundamental test for diabetes is the discovery of sugar in the urine by the use of certain simple procedures.) The diabetic, then, is being starved of sugar no matter how much he takes in, and the excess sugar in the blood which cannot be used acts as a poison, which, in extreme cases, sends the patient into coma and may—indeed, in former times, usually did—result in death. The symptoms of diabetes vary, of course, with its severity, but in the main they are: increasing appetite in an attempt on the part of the body to supply the sugar which is there but so tantalisingly unavailable, great thirst, because this useless sugar has to be excreted, and the production of urine demands water, frequency in passing urine, and increasing loss of weight in spite of all that is taken in. In severe and untreated cases boils, itching of the skin, gangrene of the limbs, and finally coma and death may occur.

Although mild cases of diabetes could, and still can, be treated by dieting alone, by reducing the intake of carbohydrate, the diagnosis of diabetes prior to 1922 amounted almost to a death-warrant. In that year, however, the Canadian physicians Banting and Best separated out the secretion of the islets of Langerhans and named it " insulin "; they showed that insulin taken from the pancreas of animals and injected into the diabetic patient was just as effective as the home-made article.

Since a diabetic regime has to be decided on by the doctor according to the severity of the disease, no useful purpose would be served by discussing the details of diet or dosage of insulin, which vary from one person to another. On the whole, diabetes is more severe in young people than in the elderly, but with correct treatment it is possible for all cases to lead a perfectly normal life except in so far as dietary restrictions and insulin injections are concerned. Many famous people are, or have been, diabetics—for example, H. G. Wells—and have lived to a ripe old age. Recently, a drug has been discovered which has the great benefit that, unlike insulin, it can be taken by mouth.

Whereas the type of diabetes we have been describing, the disease ordinarily known by that name, is properly known as *diabetes mellitus*, there is another disease known as *diabetes insipidus*, which, in fact, has no real relation to the other at all. In this disease there is no sugar in the urine, nor has it anything to do with the pancreas. Diabetes insipidus is a rare disease characterised by the passage of large amounts of dilute urine and appears to be due to deficiency of the secretion of the posterior part of the pituitary gland at the base of the brain. It can be partially controlled by the use of pituitrin.

Peritonitis is an infection of the peritoneum, the thin, transparent lining which covers all the abdominal organs. Acute peritonitis may occur at the end of serious chronic diseases, but more commonly it arises from perforation of some part of the intestines or stomach which allows septic material to flow into the abdominal cavity, or from extension of infection from the Fallopian tubes (the tubes passing between ovaries and womb in women). Wounds of the abdomen are also a possible cause. There is severe pain, vomiting, constipation, fever, and the abdomen is distended. The coils of intestine become matted together by infected lymph, produced by the germs which, while harmless within the intestine, are dangerous to life outside them. Treatment may be by antibiotics or surgery or both.

Chronic peritonitis is usually tuberculous in origin, and is commonest in young children. It is usually caused by the bovine type of bacillus, and usually there is ascites (*i.e.*, free fluid in the abdomen), with slight fever. Matting together of the intestines may threaten to produce obstruction. Unlike acute peritonitis, in which death will occur within two or three days without treatment, chronic peritonitis is a long-drawn-out disease which is usually treated medically.

DIET.

Food, like alcohol, tobacco, and constipation, is one of those subjects which people tend to have a " thing " about. In point of fact, what we know at present about this subject may be summarised as follows: Any diet to be adequate must first of all provide enough energy, and energy is measured in terms of Calories (for definition of a Calorie see **Gen. Inf.**). Thus a ten-stone man leading a moderately active life will require about 3,000 Calories daily; that is the amount of energy he requires in order to carry out his work and avoid living on himself, on his stored-up food. The amount of Calories required varies with age, size, and the amount of work done, from 1,500 Calories for the light-weight sedentary worker to three or more times this amount for the heavy manual worker.

Now, in theory, the adequate amount of Calories could be supplied from carbohydrate and fats alone, since, as we have seen, Calories are merely a measure of energy and can be supplied by any food. But in this case the individual would not live long, because he needs for body maintenance certain kinds of food in adequate proportions. Just as you cannot run a car for long simply by putting in petrol and ignoring lubricating oil and maintenance of the engine, so you cannot run your body simply by taking in enough Calories. There must be adequate proportions of the three basic foodstuffs: carbohydrates (the fuel), fats (for insulation and other purposes), and proteins (for body-building purposes). Proteins are necessary to replace the parts of the body, which is largely a protein structure, when they become run-down In addition to being a ready source of energy, carbohydrate is converted into fat within the body, a fact within the knowledge of everyone, for it is by reducing the consumption of sweets, potatoes, and bread, which are starch and sugar-containing foods, that a tendency to put on weight is reduced. Proteins cannot be manufactured from carbohydrates or fats since proteins contain nitrogen and the others do not. One could even live on a diet of nothing but protein, but not on a diet of fat or sugar; proteins are a biological necessity. It is generally agreed that a well-balanced diet should provide 25 per cent of its energy from fats, 10–15 per cent from proteins, and the remainder, 60–65 per cent, from carbohydrates.

Here are some foods classified according to the predominating basic foodstuff they contain:

(1) *Carbohydrates:* bread, sugar, and all starchy foods or sweet things such as confectionery, puddings, and cakes.

(2) *Fats*: animal fats, such as dripping, fat meat, fried foods, butter, margarine, and vegetable oils, such as olive oil, or fish oils, which are found more in some fish than others —*e.g.*, herring.

(3) *Proteins*: lean meat, cheese, non-fatty fish, nuts, oatmeal.

In addition to these basic foods, the body must also have adequate supplies of vitamins (P42, 62) and certain minerals, such as iron, manganese, calcium, copper, sodium, potassium, iodine, and phosphate.

Obesity. Many people worry because they are overweight, and statistics show that the expectation of life is shorter in fat people than in thin ones. This, however, is a statistical view, and need not apply to any single person. Thus a famous French gourmet who weighed twenty stone died recently at the age of eighty-two—through falling out of a window. When one sees people who are constantly worrying about their health and diet one recalls the statement attributed to Winston Churchill as a recipe for a long life: drink too much, smoke too much, and work hard. He might have added ". . . and stop worrying." There are few people more pathetic than those who, by rigidly adhering to the so-called rules of health, seek to eke out a life which, if it does not actually last longer than that of the more care-free individual, will certainly seem much longer.

Being overweight is due to one cause—eating too much, and especially eating too much of the wrong kinds of food. There are, obviously, some people who can eat to their heart's content without becoming fat, perhaps because their bodies burn up the food more quickly. Their *basal metabolic rate*, which is the measure of the speed at which their body cells work, is higher than normal, and the basal metabolic rate is largely dependent on the functioning of the glands—in particular, the thyroid. Nevertheless, being overweight means that you are eating too much for you; that your intake of Calories is greater than your output.

Reducing is not difficult, but it does require an effort of will. Basically it depends on: (*a*) taking less food, and (*b*) taking food which is not fat-producing. In practice, this means taking a high-protein diet, little fat, and no sugars or starches. Such a diet would be somewhat as follows: coffee or tea with milk, but *no sugar* for breakfast, and if desired, Energen rolls or Energen crispbread, whether of rye or wheat, but *no white or brown bread*. A small amount of butter or jam may be taken with the crispbread. At lunch, grilled lean steak or an egg dish and salad, followed by jellies or fruit or crispbread and cheese—but *no potatoes*. The evening meal may consist of grilled or steamed fish, clear soup, cheese, fruit, but there must be no fried foods and no sweets at any time. This diet is merely to give an indication of general principles: more interesting ones will be found in the pages of most women's magazines or from time to time in the daily papers. The basic principles are obvious: plenty of lean meat, non-fatty fish, eggs, cheese, fruit, Energen rolls or crispbread (the ordinary crispbread is just as fattening as bread itself), but no fried foods, fat meat or fish, bread, potatoes, sweets, or cakes. However, small amounts of butter and quite a lot of milk are permissible, and the modern tendency is to ignore fat intake which, by reason of its nature, is self-limiting.

Obesity may have a psychological basis, and excessive eating is often a substitute for affection in individuals who have been spoilt as children. But, however this may be, most people find it as difficult to stick to a reducing diet as they do to give up smoking. For such people there are certain drugs which may help. Thyroid tablets, once generally used for reducing, are little used now, and should be used only when the thyroid gland is underactive; otherwise they simply increase appetite, and although they speed up the combustion in the body (the basal metabolic rate), the effect is cancelled out by the increased appetite. Dexedrene, one of the derivatives of benzedrene or amphetamine, acts by reducing the appetite, but in some people of a nervous disposition it may have the effect of causing a feeling of tenseness, and they may even have difficulty in sleeping. Finally, there is a substance obtainable at chemists' shops without prescription either in the form of granules or biscuits which does not exercise any chemical effect on the body; what it does is to swell up into a gelatinous mass within the stomach under the influence of water, which is drunk later, and this gives the impression of a "full stomach" and allays the pangs of hunger.

There are, as has already been mentioned, many fads about food, although one is treading on dangerous ground when one mentions them; for every faddist is a fanatic, and every argument one may put before him is seen as an attack on himself. For example, there was the "Hay diet," now, it appears, largely forgotten; then the "Gaylord Hauser diet" much favoured by Americans, which seems to be based largely on large quantities of molasses and brewer's yeast; and there was not so long ago a gentleman who lived on grass freshly clipped each morning from Hyde Park—it would be interesting to know whether he has survived his self-imposed ordeal. However, few doctors would deny that, although diet in some cases is an adjunct to the cure of disease (for example, peptic ulcer, diabetes, sprue), it is not a cure for disease, and those who make such claims are claiming a great deal too much. It must be repeated that, so long as a diet contains adequate amounts of the basic foodstuffs, adequate amounts of vitamins and the necessary minerals, and so long as it supplies adequate Calories for the build of the individual and the amount of work he does, it matters very little how these needs are supplied.

Vegetarianism.

This can hardly be called a fad, although it cannot be denied that many of its adherents are faddists. It apparently has two main sources. There are those who abstain from animal food for moral reasons because they believe that killing is wrong, even for food; and there are others who believe that vegetable food is more healthy than animal food. Some vegetarians live almost entirely on vegetables and fruits, whilst others allow themselves milk, eggs, and cheese. The moral issue cannot be argued here, although it must be admitted that few people who have visited a slaughter-house for the first time have as much appetite for their steak the day after, so we shall only discuss the health aspects of vegetarianism. On the negative side, it must be said that, in general, vegetable foods are much less rich in protein than animal foods, so one has to eat a great deal more in order to get an adequate amount. If, however, one includes in a vegetarian diet cheese, milk, and nuts or eggs this difficulty is largely obviated. Cows and other animals living on grass or vegetable matter have to spend practically their whole lives eating, precisely because they would not otherwise get sufficient protein. On the positive side we have the as yet unconfirmed assumption that, in predisposed people over forty, excess of animal fats can lead to cholesterol being deposited in the blood-vessels, notably the coronary vessels in the heart, and thus to coronary thrombosis. Vegetable and fish oils do not seem to have this effect, hence the infrequency of thrombosis amongst those peasants in Europe who are too poor to afford much meat and amongst the Eskimos who eat fish. From the point of view of evolution it would seem that Man is designed to be both carnivorous and vegetarian; for he has sharp, cutting teeth in the front for tearing meat and flat, grinding teeth at the back for dealing with grains. We must conclude that those who are vegetarians for moral reasons should have all our respect; for killing is not a pleasant thing, and we have already too much of it. From the merely medical point of view vegetarianism has both advantages and disadvantages. Nobody will suffer from being vegetarian, but, apart from the exceptions mentioned, there is little reason to suppose that their health will be any better than that of meat-eaters. We are less able to influence our fates than we often suppose, since longevity and good health are much more a matter of heredity than is ordinarily believed.

THE DEFICIENCY AND METABOLIC DISEASES

INTRODUCTION.

If you have read earlier parts of this section you will know that there can be two types of malnutrition; the first, of course, is the type we ordinarily think of when the word is mentioned, and in this case the individual is simply not getting enough food or enough of the right kind of food. The second type might well not be regarded by most people as malnutrition; for here we are referring to diseases such as diabetes and sprue, in which, although there is adequate supply of certain foods, the body, owing to some deficiency, is unable to make use of them. The patient with diabetes cannot make use of sugar, the patient with sprue of fat—they are starving in the midst of plenty, as is shown by the fact that in both cases one of the prominent symptoms is wasting.

We shall deal first with the ordinary type of malnutrition and later with the second. Since diabetes and sprue have already been mentioned, we shall be looking at some other conditions in which something or other is missing or is present in the wrong amounts, as in the diseases of the endocrine glands.

Two-thirds of the population of the entire world are undernourished, and particularly in Asia famines are common—famines like the one in Bengal in 1943, in which 3 million people died of starvation. In Europe such conditions exist only when war dislocates food supplies, but nevertheless individual cases of malnutrition can occur. For example, the lazy or ignorant mother of a large family may feed them largely on bread and margarine, with no fresh fruit or vegetables and only tinned meat because she "can't be bothered" cooking. Or the self-sacrificing mother of a large family may give all the meat and protein food to her working husband (somehow or other many men fail to notice that a housewife works!) and her children. Then old people or people living alone are liable to neglect their food, either because they have lost heart, because they are too frail, or because they cannot afford to buy enough good food. Lastly, those who are addicted to alcohol neglect their food and, drinking on an empty stomach, soon get such a degree of gastritis that they find it difficult to eat even when they need to.

A human being can live about six weeks without food, and a much shorter time—a week or ten days—without water. Naturally, human nature being as it is, there have been many claims to longer periods of starvation, and some of the more enthusiastic claim not to eat at all! Thus, in the sixteenth century Eve Fliegen of Brabant appears to have lived for fourteen years solely on the smell of a rose, and, coming nearer our own time, Mollie Fancher of Brooklyn, who died in 1916, similarly lived for fourteen years without eating, and in 1864 even stopped breathing. However, presumably becoming bored with this, she resumed her respirations after only fourteen weeks.

These people, needless to say, were humbugs, as is revealed by the grim case of Sarah Jacob "the Welsh Fasting Girl," who towards the end of last century allegedly took no nourishment whatever for two years, two months, and one week. The one week, at any rate, is certain; for, at the invitation of the local vicar, who was convinced of her genuineness, a number of doctors from London came to observe her. They put relays of nurses to sit by her bed day and night to note whether she ate, but in a few days she began to decline so alarmingly that the doctors begged the parents to feed her. This they refused to do, and Sarah would not ask for food. She died within a week on December 17th. The most famous non-eater of today is Theresa Neumann, who lives in Bavaria and claims that nothing but the wafer, the Eucharist, at Holy Communion has passed her lips since 1927. The Roman Catholic Church, however, has been careful never officially to recognise her claims as true. So we shall still assert that six weeks, more or less, is the longest period a human being can go without eating.

DEFICIENCY DISEASES

The materials which are necessary to the body have been mentioned elsewhere, and, we can now look at some of the diseases (other than those already discussed) which result from their lack.

Lack of iron leads to anæmia, but less well known is the type of deficiency caused by lack of iodine. Iodine is found in large amounts in seaweed, which obtains it from the sea surrounding it and concentrates it in its fronds. But ordinary water contains enough for our needs. In some districts, however, especially where the main rock is limestone—Derbyshire and some valleys in Switzerland and the Himalayas—the water contains very little iodine, and there the inhabitants are prone to develop goitre. There are several types of goitre, but this type is caused by lack of the iodine which is necessary to build up thyroxin, the secretion of the thyroid gland. It is a deficiency goitre known in adults as myxœdema, but in those parts where iodine is lacking in the water supplies the disease develops in childhood and the children become, although perfectly normal when born, dull, gross, and stupid—they become idiots or, as they are more correctly described, cretins. This is one of the commonest types of mental deficiency in children, and, if noted in time, they can become completely normal by the use of thyroxin or thyroid tablets. But prevention is better than cure, and this terrible disease has now been almost eliminated in the districts where it used to be prevalent by adding iodine to the water supply of towns and villages, by giving iodised chocolate at schools, or otherwise supplying the missing element.

In this country cretinism and myxœdema are found in individual cases for reasons other than lack of iodine: in children, cretinism may be due to congenital lack of the thyroid gland or early failure, in adults myxœdema may occur when the gland, usually in the middle period of life, runs down. Both conditions can be treated by thyroid tablets, which, like insulin, have to be taken for the rest of the patient's life.

Lack of calcium is less common in this country than it once was. Calcium is necessary for building the bones: it is calcium, in fact, that makes the bones hard. Actual lack of calcium in the diet is very rare, because calcium is one of the commonest elements in Nature, and what usually happens is that lack of vitamin D or calciferol, without which calcium cannot be utilised or absorbed, causes the deficiency.

The two main diseases caused by calcium, or rather vitamin D, deficiency are rickets and osteomalacia. Vitamin D is found in fats—but only animal fats such as are found in meat, fish, and milk; it is not found in vegetables, plants, or fruit. A second source of the vitamin is sunshine or ultra-violet light, which manufactures it in the skin; hence, in spite of inferior diet, rickets and osteomalacia are perhaps less common in sunny countries. In *rickets*, a child during the period when its bones are developing does not get enough vitamin D and cannot make use of the calcium taken in. Its bones become soft and are liable to bend, producing defects such as bow legs, curvature of the spine, and deformities of the chest (pigeon chest, funnel chest). In bad cases the skull is deformed and assumes a square shape. Rickets is rare today, at least in Britain; it is prevented by taking vitamin-D-rich oils, such as cod- or halibut-liver oil, or the vitamin can be taken in a more or less pure form in capsules.

In these days when diets are adequate, when children get cod-liver oil at home or school, and when they are much more often in the sunshine than used to be the case, it is not always realised that *overdosage* of vitamins, especially vitamin D, is possible. In its extreme form this is a rare condition, but children have died from overdoses which caused calcium to be laid down where it did not belong—in the kidneys and elsewhere. It is possible to have too much of anything.

Rickets is uncommon in adult life because the demand for calcium is less than in the growing child. But in pregnancy the demand increases, and especially in Eastern lands, where famine is frequent and where, although there is plenty of sunshine, the women are veiled from any of the sun's rays, there may occur the disease of *osteomalacia*. In this disease the bones soften and deformities occur which are particularly important in the case of women, in whom the pelvis becomes deformed, with resultant difficulties in child-birth. Osteomalacia is a main cause of the high maternal and infant mortality in such countries as India.

In old people who do not get enough food, lack of vitamin D causes no deformity, but leads to the condition known as *osteoporosis*, in which the bones, through lack of available calcium, become brittle and break easily.

Scurvy is another once-common deficiency disease which is now rare except under such unusual conditions (or perhaps not so unusual in these days) as life in concentration camps or amongst prisoners-of-war. It is due to lack of vitamin C, which is found in fruits and vegetables, particularly in lemons, oranges, tomatoes, and turnips. In scurvy the gums swell and bleed, there is increasing anæmia, and spontaneous bruises, due to hæmorrhage under the skin, occur. In former times the disease was the bugbear of sailors and travellers, because on long journeys or voyages before means of preserving food were known other than drying or salting no fresh fruit was available. It was no less a personality than Captain Cook who on his long voyages found that the simple use of lemons or limes would prevent the disease. Hence the almost international description of Englishmen as "Limeys"—a name which is not always used flatteringly, but of which we have every reason to be proud. Minor degrees of scurvy may occur in British children even today through faulty diet, but this is much less common since orange, blackcurrant, or rose-hips syrups became available to all.

We now come to the B group of vitamins. There are, regrettably, many members of the vitamin B family, but we shall mainly deal with vitamins B1 and B2.

Beri-beri is caused by lack of vitamin B1, which is found in most grains, principally in the embryo and the outer covering. Now, since many people are snobs, who prefer white bread to wholemeal and polished rice to the crude article, it has become the habit to remove the precious outer covering of the grain and its embryo which contain the vitamin: white bread and polished rice *look* so much better. Thus, in those parts of Asia where rice is the staple diet, it was frequently machine-milled, with loss of the vitamin, and the result was the serious form of neuritis known as beri-beri. Just as Captain Cook eradicated scurvy from his men by the use of citrus fruits, so, in 1882, Takaki eliminated beri-beri from the Japanese Navy by giving a good mixed diet. This led two Dutchmen, Eijkman and Grijns, to study the disease experimentally. They found that fowls fed on polished rice developed the disease, whereas those fed on rice with the husk did not. In this country we are still in the rather foolish position of carefully removing the vitamin by "refining" the flour and then replacing it chemically. However, although whole-meal bread is probably better, there is really little risk of any European diet lacking vitamin B1.

The symptoms of beri-beri are neuritis (*i.e.*, degeneration of the nerves), which leads to weakness of the muscles, wasting, and sensations of "pins and needles"; the heart muscle is also affected and œdema—swelling of the limbs—or ascities (fluid in the abdomen) occurs.

Pellagra. Vitamin B2, or rather the vitamins of the B2 group, of which the main ones are riboflavin and nicotinic acid, is another substance deficiency of which in this case leads to pellagra. Pellagra is found in those parts of the world where maize is a staple diet, that is in parts of America and the Far East and round the Mediterranean. Maize does not contain the vitamin which, like vitamin B1, is found in most other grains and vegetables, but, since vitamin B2 is also normally produced by the action of bacteria in the human colon, it would appear that there is some other factor than the mere absence of the substance from the diet. Probably maize contains a substance which prevents the absorption of the vitamin from the colon.

In pellagra there is wasting, soreness of the mouth, diarrhœa, skin rashes on the hands, forearms, face, and neck. In severe cases insanity may occur. The disease does not occur in this country in its full-blown form, but minor degrees may develop with the use of certain antibiotics, such as chloramphenicol and aureomycin, which kill the "good" vitamin-producing bacteria in the intestine as well as the disease-producing ones.

Vitamins.

Whereas vitamins B and C are found mainly in vegetables and fruits, vitamins A and D are found in oils and fats. Vitamin A is, indeed, found in the form of carotene in all green vegetables, but it is not much use to us until it has become concentrated in the fat and milk of the animals who eat the vegetables. Lack of the vitamin leads to *night-blindness*, to difficulty in seeing in the dusk. This is because the retina, the "mirror" at the back of the eye, requires adequate amounts of a substance known as visual purple for its full efficiency, and visual purple is manufactured from vitamin A. (It must be noted, however, that not all cases of night-blindness are due to lack of vitamin A—there is often a very large neurotic element, and it was frequently found during the War that men who on this account pleaded their inability to carry out sentry duties at night might show a very considerable talent for seeing their girl-friend at the camp gate even in pitch darkness.) Vitamin A is also connected with the health of the skin and the ability of the body to resist diseases of the respiratory tract such as bronchitis. Like vitamin D, it is most easily obtained from fish oils, such as halibut-liver oil.

Lesser-known vitamins are vitamins E and K. The former, found in wheat-germ oil, influences fertility; the latter influences the clotting power of the blood and the healing of wounds. Most vitamins can now be produced in the laboratory synthetically; in the case of vitamin B1 from coal-tar.

It is important to realise that vitamins, although necessary to health, are not cure-alls. There are few sights more ridiculous than the fad of over-fed individuals taking vitamin pills as a tonic to keep themselves up to scratch. Any vitamins taken in excess of requirements may either cause damage—as in the case of vitamin D—or else are simply excreted from the body. Extra vitamins are not a tonic, those who take them in excess are simply wasting their money, and if one eats a good mixed diet they are totally unnecessary.

GLANDULAR DISEASES.

The Endocrine Glands.

The workings of the body are regulated in all sorts of different ways—by the nervous system, the circulation, and by the endocrine glands or ductless glands, as they are sometimes called. We have already seen that there are glands, such as the liver (the largest gland in the body) and the pancreas, which manufacture substances and pass them through a duct or tube to their destination. But the ductless glands, as their name implies, have no duct and pass their secretion directly into the blood; the pancreas, for example, discharges the pancreatic fluid down a duct, but it also produces insulin, which is secreted directly into the blood. It is thus partly an endocrine gland and partly an ordinary one. The other endocrine glands are particularly important in that they produce hormones (the word means "chemical messenger"), which have a great deal to do with personality and health.

Myxœdema, we saw, is due to lack of thyroid hormone either because the gland, which is situated at the base of the neck astride the windpipe, has failed or because it has insufficient iodine to manufacture its product. The opposite effect occurs when the gland becomes overactive, and then we get a quite different state of affairs: instead of being dull, slow-witted, and flabby-looking, the patient with an overactive gland—*exophthalmic goitre* or *thyrotoxicosis* is excitable, nervous, flushed, and thin. The eyes become prominent and bulge forward, giving a staring, scared look. The disease is commonest in young adults, mostly women, and its origin is often associated with an emotional shock. Thyrotoxicosis is not primarily a disorder of the thyroid gland, and it is likely that the sequence of events is: emotional shock, which influences the nerves supplying the pituitary gland at the base of the brain, overactivity of the pituitary with overproduction of the hormones, which in turn affect the thyroid. (The pituitary is the main endocrine gland in the body and gives off hormones which control all the other glands—it has been called the "conductor of the endocrine orchestra.") All the body processes—the basal metabolism—are speeded up in this disease, which, however, cannot be treated at its roots in the pituitary. Sometimes it can be treated medically by the drug thiouracil, which damps down the activity of the thyroid, but more usually an operation is necessary to remove part of the gland. It is also possible in suitable cases to give the patient radioactive iodine—a radio-isotope which is carried, as all iodine is, to the gland, where it destroys some of the overactive tissues. The results of these procedures are good, but any exophthalmos, the prominence of the eyes, which may be present always remains.

A similar condition, appearing in middle age, may result, not from shock or from an overall enlargement of the gland, but from a *toxic adenoma*, which is a simple, non-malignant tumour. In this case exopthalmos does not occur, but the tumour should be removed. Malignant tumours also occur.

The Parathyroid Glands.

We have already discussed the importance of calcium in the body and seen how vitamin D is necessary for its utilisation. But the calcium content of the body is controlled by another factor, the parathyroid glands—two pairs of small glands lying behind the thyroid. Now, calcium, in addition to building the hard structure of bones, has another function in that it acts as a kind of sedative, damping down the nerves and preventing overexcitability. When the parathyroid glands do not work properly, or when they have been partially removed during a thyroid operation, *tetany* (not to be confused with tetanus) arises. The hands and feet go into spasm and there may be generalised convulsions. Tetany can be produced in a number of other ways which influence the amount of calcium in the blood: for example, alkalosis when people have taken too much alkali for stomach disease, or when they have lost acid through persistent vomiting, or even by overbreathing—*i.e.*, persistent deep and rapid breathing, which causes the body to lose carbon dioxide—a condition which may occur in hysterical or neurotic patients. The treatment is to give large amounts of calcium and vitamin D.

Overactivity of the parathyroid glands, usually due to a tumour, causes the reverse effects. The blood calcium is high, but this calcium has been withdrawn from the bones, and a disease known as *generalised osteitis fibrosa* arises, in which the bones become soft and there is pain, fractures, and deformities. Sometimes cysts form in the bones. The treatment is operative removal of the tumour.

Salt is very important in the running of our bodies. Indeed, our blood has been described as an "inner sea"; for, whereas primitive creatures in the ocean, such as sea-anemones and sponges, get their sustenance from the sea surrounding them and do not need a blood-stream within, in the course of evolution the situation gradually changed. As sea-animals grew bigger, the water outside did not suffice, and they had to develop some sort of circulation within; even more so, when they developed into land animals they had to carry their sea about with them. Loss of the salt in this inner ocean is occurring all the time, both through the urine and through sweating. Workers who do heavy jobs in a hot atmosphere lose a great deal of salt through sweating, and if afterwards they drink a great deal of water the remaining salt in the body becomes even more diluted, with the result that they will get painful cramps. Similarly, diarrhœa or prolonged vomiting can bring about the same result through loss of salt from the body. After long periods of exercise it is much more refreshing to take water with added salt than to take pure water, which will increase rather than diminish our fatigue.

Suprarenal Glands.

A glandular disease which influences the balance of salt in the body is *Addison's disease*, named after the famous English physician who first described it. This disease is characterised by great weakness of the muscles, tiredness, loss of weight, low blood-pressure, and a brown pigmentation of the skin. Until recently it was always fatal. Addison's disease is caused by damage to the suprarenal glands, two small glands which sit one on top of each kidney like little cocked hats. These glands produce a number of hormones, one of which controls the excretion of salt from the body; if it is lacking, too much salt escapes, with the results described above. The disease is now treatable by the use of cortisone, one of the suprarenal hormones.

These glands consist of an inner part or medulla which secretes a hormone known as adrenalin—the substance which, when released into the blood, prepares us for states of emergency. It reinforces states of anger or fear, and aids in the process of fighting back or running away. The cortex (the word means "bark of a tree"), on the other hand, secretes a number of hormones, one of which, as we have seen, is connected with the salt content of the body and another which plays some part in sexual development. Thus a tumour of this area may bring about a state of *hyperadrenia*, in which excessive secretion leads to premature or excessive development of masculine sexual traits. Boys show precocious sexual development, their voice breaks, and their muscular development increases. Girls assume male characteristics. This is known as the *adreno-genital syndrome*.

The Pituitary Gland.

The pituitary gland, lying at the base of the brain, is only about the size of a small cherry, yet it not only regulates the behaviour of all the other glands but is responsible for sexual development and growth. It consists of two parts, the anterior (which does all the interesting things), and the posterior, which secretes a hormone known as pituitrin, thus raising the blood-pressure and causing the muscle of the uterus to contract. Many conditions are described in which the anterior part of the gland either produces too much or too little of its hormones. For example, when this part overacts in early life the result is a giant—*i.e.*, anyone over 6 ft. 8 in. In later life, when the bones are set, the result of overaction is *acromegaly*, in which the face is elongated, the hands are relatively huge, as also are the feet. The head, too, is large, and the patient gives a somewhat gorilla-like impression.

When the anterior part of the pituitary underacts there are many unpleasant possibilities: the individual may develop into a fat boy, like the one in *Pickwick Papers*, sleepy, greedy, and monstrously fat; or into a human skeleton who appears to have hardly any flesh at all; or there may develop painful masses of fat in the wrong places, a condition described as *adiposis dolorosa*; or again, dwarfism may result and the individual retain the appearance and size of a child with normal adult mentality. These conditions are known by the various names of *Frölich's syndrome* in the fat-boy type, *Simmond's disease* in the human skeleton, *Dercum's disease* in the case of adiposis dolorosa, and *Lorrain's disease* in the case of dwarfism.

The Sex Glands.

In women these are the ovaries, and in man the testes. The ovaries produce two hormones, one of which, œstrin, brings about, under the influence of the pituitary, the normal sex changes at puberty, controls the release of the ovum from the ovary, and, in animals, produces sexual excitement. The other, also controlled by the pituitary, is progesterone, which in general has a sedative effect: it prepares the uterus for pregnancy, and, when a pregnancy exists, maintains it.

The internal secretion of the male sex glands is testesterone, and it, like œstrin, produces the sex changes at puberty. The problems of sex, however, will be discussed later.

DISEASES OF THE URINARY SYSTEM.

Everyone knows what kidneys look like—in fact, the term "kidney-shaped" is used to describe other objects. Within the kidneys the blood-vessels carrying waste materials subdivide and finally end up in little coils or glomeruli through which waste products are filtered into the other system, the system of tubes which, beginning as tiny cups around the glomeruli, become larger and larger until they join the ureter passing out at the oot of the kidney, the hilum, a point at which both the veins and tubes enter and leave. The kidneys, of course, lie one on each side in the loins, so that if one puts one's hands on the hips and then slides them farther back they will cover the area over the left and right kidney. The ureters pass down on each side to the bladder, which is the storage tank of the products excreted by the kidneys, and lies in the mid-line down low in the abdomen; it is somewhat pear-shaped, and at its base in men there lies the prostate gland—a gland which apparently has few functions but can be a nuisance. Its only known function is that it adds something to the semen from the testes without which the semen would be sterile. Then, from the base of the bladder a single tube, the urethra, passes to the outside. One can, in fact, visualise the urinary system as a capital **Y**, in which the two upper limbs are the ureters, the place where they meet is the bladder, and the single limb at the foot is the urethra. Clearly, then, there may be diseases of the kidneys, of the ureters, of the bladder, of the prostate gland, or of the urethra.

The amount of urine may be increased or diminished. It is *increased* in the following conditions: after drinking excess of fluids; after taking drugs (known as *diuretics*) which are given to increase the flow; in diabetes of both types—mellitus and insipidus; in some types of chronic kidney disease; and finally, in emotional states of excitement. It is *decreased* in the following conditions: acute nephritis; any disease in which fluid is being lost in other ways, such as diarrhœa or sweating in fevers; when the fluid intake is small; and when both ureters are blocked by stones. Passing a great deal of urine is known as *polyuria*, passing very little as *oligouria*, passing frequent small amounts is simply called *frequency*. Normally, the urine is acid, but in infections of the bladder it may become alkaline owing to decomposition by bacteria. Abnormal substances, or normal substances in abnormal quantities, may occur in the urine and give the doctor an indication of what is wrong. In fact. urine analysis is a very important part of medical diagnosis. Thus urea is a normal content of urine which is increased in fevers, wasting diseases, or diabetes; the amount of urea is to some extent a measure of the degree of tissue breakdown. Uric acid is found in small quantities in normal urine, but the amount is increased in fevers and after an attack of gout (uric acid is important in the causation of gout, but has nothing at all to do with rheumatism in general, so one may disregard the advertisements in the popular Press showing unpleasant pictures of joints with sharp crystals of uric acid which are alleged to cause the pain of rheumatic disease). Oxalates are not ordinarily found in urine, but, since they occur in such foods as rhubarb and strawberries, and some people are unable to deal with them, such individuals may develop stones or have pain on passing urine after eating oxalate-containing fruits.

Two very important substances which ought not to be in normal urine are albumen and sugar. Albumen is a protein, and its presence in the urine indicates that the filters of the kidney are leaking—they are allowing protein to pass out which ought to remain in the body. Albumen is easily tested for, and its presence may indicate kidney disease or nephritis as it is usually called by doctors. On the other hand, small amounts of albumen occur in fevers and in nervous conditions—*functional albuminuria*. Sugar, too, should not be present, but its presence does not necessarily indicate diabetes; for small amounts may occur in nervous conditions or in some people after taking large quantities of carbohydrate.

Blood in the urine may give it an appearance which varies from bright red to a dark, smoky colour. It is found in many diseases: acute nephritis, stone, tumours, poisoning by certain drugs, infections such as bilharzia or malaria, papilloma (*i.e.*, non-malignant tumour of the bladder), after injury, in high blood-pressure, scurvy, and blood diseases. Sometimes it cocurs for no known reason at all.

It will be remembered (or if it is not, you can look it up on p. 28 (1)) that streptococcal infection of the throat may cause in some people disease of the valves in the heart or endocarditis. In such cases, although the germ is found in the throat, it is not found in the heart or indeed anywhere else in the body. *Acute nephritis* occurs in the same circumstances, with the sole difference that the kidneys instead of the heart are affected. The disease appears to be an allergic reaction to the toxins of the streptococcus. The patient, often a child, has a sore throat (and even this may be absent or fail to be noticed) or sometimes the infection may arise in other sites: after scarlet fever, erysipelas, burns, and disease of the ear. A few days later there is headache, vomiting, pain in the loins, slight rise in temperature, and especially typical is *dropsy* or œdema. This begins in the face, first around the eyelids, and then affects the ankles; later it may become more general and affect the rest of the body. Blood and albumen are found in the urine, and the blood-pressure is slightly raised. The outlook is usually good if the kidneys are rested by reducing the amount of protein taken in and also the amounts of salt and water. When this is done, the inflammation soon goes and no permanent harm results. In other cases, however, if treatment is inadequate or the condition severe, the symptoms may go, but the albumen found in the urine persists. This means that permanent damage has been done, and although there may be nothing else to show for many years, *chronic nephriti*[s] develops. In this case, the blood-pressure continues to rise, and since the filters of the kidney[s] no longer work efficiently, urea, the principa[l] waste-product of the body to be excreted in th[e] urine, is retained in the blood and only smal[l] amounts escape from the system. Hence chroni[c] nephritis sooner or later leads to heart failure o[r] hæmorrhage in the brain from the rising blood pressure, or to the form of poisoning known a[s] *uræmia* which results from the retention of ure[a] in the blood. Uræmia may come on suddenly o[r] gradually, but ends in progressive coma, drowsiness, and unconsciousness. There may be convulsions similar to those of epilepsy, high fever and difficulty in breathing to complicate the picture.

Another type of nephritis which seems to hav[e] nothing at all to do with streptococcal infection[s] and the cause of which is completely unknown, i[s] *nephrosis*. Developing in early adult life, it[s] onset is insidious, and the patient first shows sign[s] of œdema in his white and puffy face and th[e] swelling of his legs. (It should be said here tha[t] if you have swelling of the ankles or elsewhere, yo[u] would be foolish to jump to conclusions; for suc[h] swelling is common in many diseases—in hea[rt] disease, in allergic conditions, in neurotic illnes[s] and even just from hot weather.) When th[e] urine is examined in a case of nephrosis it is foun[d] to be full of albumen and, as in chronic nephriti[s] the blood urea starts to rise. The end-results [of] nephrosis are the same as those of chronic nephrit[is] and depend upon the damage originally done.

The modern diuretics of the chlorothiazid[e] group help to control the œdema and, provide[d] enough healthy tissue remains, remove both th[e] fluid and the waste-products. In advanced [or] more serious cases artificial kidneys can be use[d] but as yet the transplantation of a kidney is large[ly] in the experimental stage.

Pyelitis is an infection of the pelvis of th[e] kidney, that is to say, of the part where the ureter leaves the kidney. It is usually caused by th[e] bacillus coli, which is normally present in th[e] body, or by the streptococcus. These germs may reach the ureter through the blood-stream or may pass upwards from the bladder. Obstruction anywhere in the urinary tract which causes the urine to stagnate is liable to cause pyelitis. Symptoms come on suddenly, with high fever, pain in the loin (the infection is usually on one side only, and is commoner in women), and pain in the abdomen. When urine is passed there is a burning sensation, and it is passed frequently and in small amounts. On examination, the urine is found to be highly acid and full of bacillus coli or whatever the causative germ may be. Pyelitis is fairly readily treated by the antibiotics or sulpha drugs. Plenty of fluids should be given and the urine made alkaline by administration of alkalis.

Cystitis means inflammation of the bladder, either acute or chronic, and its causes are much the same as in the case of pyelitis. There is pain over the lower abdomen, frequency, and sometimes slight fever. The treatment is as for pyelitis. *Urethritis* is an inflammation of the urethra, with burning pain on passing water and frequency. The most serious cause (although it can usually be easily dealt with now) is gonorrhœa. But non-specific urethritis is common, and in this case various germs or none may bring about pain and frequency; there is often a large neurotic element. Urethritis should be regarded as probably due to gonorrhœa, which has already been discussed elsewhere, when there is a thick, creamy discharge from the penis or discharge in women following sexual intercourse with an infected person.

Kidney stones or Renal calculi sometimes form, and, as in the case of gall-stones, what causes them is not certain. They may be caused by disorders of metabolism—that is, in the inability of the body to deal with calcium, proteins, uric acid, and other products; or by vitamin deficiency obstruction in the urinary tract, and urinary infections. But when a stone or stones are formed various events may occur: thus it may remain in the kidney and cause no symptoms; or it may cause repeated attacks of pain, infection, and blood in the urine (hæmaturia); or it may completely block the passage of urine from the kidney to such a degree that it degenerates and becomes useless; or, lastly, it may pass into the ureter, and when this occurs very severe pain, known as *renal colic*, will occur. A stone passing down the ureter into the bladder may become stuck in the urethra, although this is uncommon, since a stone small enough to get down the ureters is likely to be capable of manœuvring through the rest of the tract. In fact, about 80–90 per cent. of stones are passed spontaneously. Stones not passed spontaneously may have to be removed by operation, but whether this is undertaken or not depends on various factors, such as the general health of the patient, the amount of trouble caused by the stone, and the health of the other kidney —for it is dangerous to operate on one kidney unless one is sure that the other is functioning efficiently.

If a stone blocks the passage of urine on one side for any length of time *hydronephrosis* may result, in which the part where the ureter enters the kidney swells with the retained urine. Ultimately much of the kidney may be destroyed by the back-pressure. The same effect may be produced by kinking of the ureter or anything else which causes obstruction. Sometimes children are born with hydronephrosis, and when the dilation is due to kinking of the tube the condition may be intermittent, with attacks of renal colic during which only small amounts of urine are passed; this is followed with relief and the passage of large quantities.

Tumours and Cysts. The kidney may also be the site of tumours and cysts which produce pain in the loins, sometimes a lump over the kidney which can be felt, and blood in the urine. Cancer of the bladder is a serious condition in which the bladder may have to be removed, so the urinary flow has then to be directed elsewhere. Either the ureters are brought out on to the skin surface, a procedure known as *cutaneous ureterostomy*, or they are implanted in the large bowel, so that the urine flows out with the fæces. This is described as *uretero-colostomy*.

There may also be benign tumours of the bladder or *papillomas*, which are soft and bleed easily; a great deal of blood is passed, but there is usually little or no pain. In this, and similar, diseases of the bladder examination of the inside of the organ is carried out by means of a cystoscope, a thin tube which is passed up the urethra and has a small electric light at the end which enables the surgeon to see what is going on. Instruments may also be passed through the tube, and simple papillomas can be cauterised. Similar instruments are used in the examination of the stomach (gastroscope) and the bronchial tubes (bronchoscope). When some obstruction in the outlet of the bladder or in the urethra occurs the bladder, of course, fills with urine, which cannot be passed, and very painful dilation occurs. In this case an attempt may be made to pass a catheter, a thin rubber tube, into the bladder to relieve the tension, or if this fails a *suprapubic cystomy* is performed—an incision is made in the abdomen over the bladder and a tube inserted into it, through which the urine escapes. This is ordinarily a temporary expedient, and later when the patient's health has improved an attempt will be made to remove the cause of obstruction. The most common cause of such obstruction is *enlargement of the prostate gland* at the base of the bladder, which surrounds this area and the beginning of the ureter. About 40 per cent. of men over sixty have some degree of obstruction due to this cause, and about 20 per cent. of these require operation. The gland is about the size of a walnut, and, as we have seen, its function is to supply part of the fluid which makes up the semen, the male sex secretion. Enlargement of the prostate may be benign or maligannt, and, although nobody knows just why, such benign enlargement tends to occur in most men in later life. There may be no symptoms, but characteristically there is frequency during the day and the need to get up at night to pass water. The flow of urine being impeded by constriction of the urethra, the passage is less forceful than normal, and there is a tendency for dribbling to occur. If the obstruction is severe and not relieved the back-pressure may be transmitted to the ureters and kidneys, resulting finally in kidney failure and uræmia. The prostate, except in cases of very mild enlargement, has to be removed either through the abdomen or through the perineum (the part of the body lying between the sex organs and the anus). Sometimes, in less serious cases, it is possible without an incision to cut away the obstructing part by an electrocautery inserted, as is a cystoscope, through the urethra. Prostatectomy was once a serious operation, all the more so because the patient was usually elderly and not in good condition, but new techniques and the use of antibiotics have greatly improved the outlook.

Cancer of the Prostate is always serious, but if discovered in time it can be operated on successfully. The gland, of course, has to be completely removed; in inoperable cases, or in patients unfit to stand operation, the tumour may be treated by means of female sex hormones, which cause it to shrink and may prolong life by some years.

DISEASES OF THE NERVOUS SYSTEM.

The brain and nervous system are like a telephone exchange which sends out and receives messages from the rest of the body. Essentially it consists of two levels, the lower centres, where primitive emotions are felt, the viscera controlled, and simple actions initiated, and the true brain, which holds the lower centres under control. When, for example, one is pricked with a pin, a message is passed up the nerves (the sensory nerves or nerves of feeling) to the lower centres in the spinal cord, which return a message through the motor nerves (the nerves dealing with movement), causing the hand to jerk away. All this takes place without any conscious interference, and can, in fact, happen even when the true brain has been removed. It is, of course, possible for the movement which jerks the hand away to be inhibited, because in this case the brain intervenes; all mental life is a constant interaction between the lower and higher centres.

When we become angry, for instance, the anger originates in the lower centres, but may be inhibited by the higher ones. To some extent, the former correspond to what a psychologist would describe as the unconscious mind, the latter to the conscious mind.

The nervous system is made up of nerve cells which are smaller than the head of a pin but end in a long, thin fibre, which may be several feet long. These fibres form the nerves of the body, and they end in the motor nerves, which bring about muscular movement, or in the skin, where there are separate nerve-endings dealing with pressure, heat, cold, pain, and so on. It used to be supposed that there were areas in the brain dealing with such mental faculties as acquisitiveness, conscientiousness, and other abilities; but this is known to be quite untrue. There are, indeed, areas dealing with movement, sight, hearing, speech, feeling, and thought, but certainly none dealing specifically with the more complex mental faculties. Nor is it correct to suppose that each nerve cell carries some particular thought or feeling; for it appears that thinking and feeling are represented by nervous circuits in the brain and are not isolated in any special area. Thus large parts of the brain can be removed without interfering with mental activity.

The most primitive part of the nervous system is the autonomic nervous system, which has its "brain" in the hypothalamus at the base of the true brain. It is divided into two parts: the sympathetic nervous system, which supplies the viscera with impulses which prepare the body for flight or fight (causing the heart to beat faster, the muscles to become congested with blood, the skin to become pale, and the blood-sugar to rise whilst the intestines become less active), and the parasympathetic nervous system, which, in general, produces relaxation. When the parasympathetic system acts, the heart beats more slowly, the skin becomes flushed, the intestines digest food, and the body is prepared for rest. Since, as we have seen, the lower centres are the centres controlling both emotion and the internal organs, it is clear that emotional states will influence the action of the body. This is the basis of psychosomatic medicine.

The brain and the spinal cord, which passes down the bony canal within the spine, are covered with the thin layer of tissue known as the meninges and surrounded with cerebro-spinal fluid, which is also found in the cavities of the brain known as ventricles. A specimen of cerebro-spinal fluid, or C.S.F., may be removed by pushing a hollow needle between the vertebræ in the lumbar region, and such specimens can give a great deal of information about what is going on in the nervous system.

The diseases of the nervous system can be divided into various groups: there are those due to injuries, such as fractures of the skull or divided nerves; the infectious diseases, most of which have been discussed already; the diseases due to hæmorrhage or embolism; tumours; and, perhaps the biggest group, the degenerative diseases.

The blood-vessels of the brain are one of the common sites of *aneurisms*, bulges like small berries, often at the base of the brain, caused by weakness of the vessel wall. This is sometimes the result of arteriosclerosis, syphilitis infection, or injury, but perhaps most often the aneurisms are congenital—*i.e.*, the individual is born with them. There are usually no symptoms, although if the aneurism is large enough it may press upon other structures and cause symptoms recognisable by the specialist. In most cases the diagnosis is apparent only when the aneurism, as may occur, ruptures. When this happens the symptoms are those of brain hæmorrhage. There is severe headache, vomiting, and loss of consciousness, the patient breathes heavily, and when the doctor does a lumbar puncture the C.S.F. is stained with blood. Such an event is very serious, and ordinarily all that can be done is to rest the patient; nevertheless, over 60 per cent. of cases are fatal.

When, in the few cases in which symptoms occur *before* hæmorrhage, the presence of an aneurism is suspected, this may be confirmed by X-ray. Since soft tissues are not seen in X-ray pictures, it is necessary (for example, in the gall-bladder, the kidneys, the bronchi, or the blood-vessels of the brain) to inject some radio-opaque substance which outlines them. In the brain this is known as arteriography, and when by this means aneurisms or other abnormalities are found surgery is sometimes possible. Hæmorrhage into the brain substance produces what is generally known as a *stroke*. The artery affected is usually the middle cerebral, when in later adult life it has been strained and weakened by high blood-pressure or arterosclerosis. It can, however, be caused by bleeding into a tumour, or in children by birth injuries. Hæmorrhages may also result in the small veins from the strain of coughing in whooping cough.

A stroke comes on suddenly, and the patient is flushed with a bluish tinge. He breathes heavily and, as he breathes, the cheek on the affected side may be blown in and out. Since the left side of the brain supplies the right side of the body, and *vice versa*, the side of the body on the opposite side from the hæmorrhage is paralysed. The limbs and face right down the affected area are flaccid and useless, but if the patient survives they will at a later stage become spastic. There are, therefore, two types of paralysis: flaccid and spastic. In the first, the limb is incapable of movement, and when lifted it falls back like a dead weight; there are no reflexes, so that when the knee-cap is tapped to elicit the knee-jerk there is no response. Flaccid paralysis is typical of injury to the lower parts of the nervous system, and it means that no impulses are getting through. Spastic paralysis, on the contrary, is characterised by rigidity of the limb, overactive reflexes, and even when movement is possible it is out of control. This, in fact, is what has occurred; for spastic paralysis indicates that, although the lower nerves are undamaged, the controlling centre in the brain has been affected.

If the patient survives, there may be varying degrees of improvement in the paralysis, which is always at its greatest in the beginning.

When such an emergency occurs it is best to leave the patient where he is, keep him warm, take out his dentures if any, call the doctor, and on no account to give him any fluids or alcohol. No patient in coma should ever have fluids poured down his throat. Other causes of coma are diabetes, alcohol, uræmia, acute hypertensive (high blood-pressure) attacks, and thrombosis or embolism.

In thrombosis and embolism a similar picture to that of hæmorrhage occurs. Embolism comes on suddenly like a hæmorrhage, but in thrombosis or clotting the onset may be more gradual, with premonitory symptoms of headache, giddiness and numbness or pins and needles in the limbs. There may be difficulty in speaking.

Tumours and Abscesses. The brain is soft greyish white in colour, and from the upper surface closely resembles a huge walnut in that it has two sides joined across the middle by a smaller part known, in the brain, as the corpus callosum. It resembles a walnut, too, in that its surface is crumpled up into convolutions. Investigation of the brain has become more and more refined in recent years, the following being some of the techniques employed:

(1) Straight X-rays.

(2) Arteriograms, which have already been described.

(3) Encephalograms or ventriculograms, in which some of the fluid, the C.S.F. surrounding the brain or in the cavities known as ventricles within the brain substance, is removed and replaced by gas. The gas may be helium or oxygen, and it has the effect in an X-ray picture of outlining the brain and ventricles so that any distortion of shape due to a tumour or abscess is outlined.

(4) Electroencephalograms are pictures made of the electrical brain waves produced by the brain, just as the electrocardiograph takes pictures of the similar waves produced by the heart. Electrodes attached to the scalp may show abnormal waves over the site of a tumour or abscess.

(5) Still more recently, radioisotopes have been used to locate tumours, since radio-

active substance become concentrated in the area of the abnormal tissues.

The main symptoms of brain tumour are severe headache, vomiting, and disturbances of vision; such symptoms must be referred to a doctor at once. The pulse-rate is usually slow. All these symptoms are caused by increasing pressure within the brain because of the space taken up by the tumour.

The popular belief that a brain tumour is tantamount to a death warrant is simply untrue; for at least 80–90 per cent. of cases recover. The main types of tumour are meningiomas (*i.e.*, tumours of the brain coverings or meninges); tumours of the nerve fibres within the brain or neurofibromas; tumours of the pituitary gland; and gliomas, which are tumours of the background substance. The outlook for all of these is good, except in the case of the glioma, which is a type of tumour which tends to infiltrate into the rest of the brain fairly rapidly. It is not localised, and therefore complete removal is not always possible.

Brain abscesses may be spread from the blood-stream in people with bronchiectasis, osteomyelitis, infected sinuses, or chronic ear disease. The symptoms are similar to those of tumour, but there is also fever and drowsiness.

Aphasia is a disturbance of the ability to speak, write, or to understand spoken or written words. It is usually due to a tumour, abscess, thrombosis, or embolism of the speech area in the brain. In motor aphasia the muscles of speech are normal, but the patient is unable to speak intelligibly. In nominal aphasia the patient cannot name objects, which he nevertheless is able to recognise. In agraphia the patient cannot write, although his muscles are normal. In word-blindness and word-deafness the patient cannot understand written or spoken words respectively. Treatment depends upon the cause, but in hopeful cases re-education is sometimes possible.

Headaches. This seems a convenient point to say something about headache, which must surely be one of the commonest symptoms suffered by the human race. We shall begin by noting that at least 90 per cent. of all headaches are nervous in origin or the result of such other minor troubles as gastric upset. It is doubtful whether headache is as frequently brought about by eye-strain as is often supposed, but there is certainly no harm in having one's eyes tested if frequent headaches are present.

A doctor will first try to distinguish between headaches due to mental causes and those due to organic or physical ones. When the cause is physical the headache is often very severe, usually located sharply in one area (for example, on one side of the head), and it is likely to be accompanied by other symptoms, such as vomiting and eye-disturbances. The person with this type of pain often tries to minimise the pain he suffers, but his behaviour—for example, his obvious fear of moving his head—belies him. The neurotic person, on the other hand, suffers from headaches which are "terrible," "awful," "unbearable," vague in their location (they are "all over"), and, if they are accompanied by other nervous symptoms, the diagnosis is clear. Apart from the neurotic type, headaches are caused by migraine, increased pressure within the skull, as in brain tumour or abscess, sinus disease, and eye diseases. Treatment obviously depends on the cause, and the sensible thing to do is to go to a doctor, believe what he says, and take his advice. Neurotic headaches may be dealt with by investigation of the sources of worry, frustration, and so on which cause the pain, or by taking aspirin or other pain-relieving drugs. (Pain, in fact, is one of the very few things aspirin is good for, and as has already been said elsewhere, those who believe that it is good for "nerves," insomnia, and all the various conditions which make aspirin an almost universal cure in the minds of many, are deluding themselves.)

Migraine is a disorder which many claim to possess and not so many really do; if all the people who claim this dubious honour—often those who have little better to do than be bored with themselves—if all these were put end to end, or even stood upright in a line, they would surely encircle the Earth. True migraine, however, is a very clear-cut disease, and happens in a very definite type of person. The owner of the migraine tends to be a highly intelligent and conscientious—even over-conscientious—individual (not at all like Mrs. Jones, who says she suffers from it and could by no stretch of the imagination be described either as intelligent or over-conscientious). The headaches are severe, usually on one side of the head only, occur in periodic attacks, and are not, like the headaches suffered by Mrs. Jones, "there all the time." Vision is affected so that there may be hemianopia (*i.e.*, half-vision), flashes of light before the eyes, and the so-called fortification spectra (*i.e.*, zig-zag patterns in the field of vision). The pain is often prostrating, and is usually followed by attacks of vomiting. Migraine is a mystery disease which apparently has something to do with the personality, with emotional stresses, and conceivably in some cases with allergy; the actual pain appears to be caused by spasm of the blood-vessels in the brain. The usual treatment is with tablets of ergotamine (Fermergin), but other remedies are also helpful in different cases.

There are a number of other nervous diseases the cause of which remains a mystery, and of these we shall mention epilepsy, chorea, and pink disease.

Epilepsy is a symptom, not a disease, which is common at all ages but especially children. It has been attributed to St. Paul, Julius Caesar, Napoleon, and (with more justice perhaps) to Dostoievsky. Many varieties of attack occur often in the same patient, the commonest and best known being the *grand mal* or major seizure. In this the patient falls down unconscious and rigid and the jaw is clenched, so that there is danger of the tongue being bitten. This so-called tonic phase is followed, within a minute or so, by a clonic phase in which the limbs contract rhythmically. The attack ends with the patient going limp and gradually recovering consciousness, a process which may take up to an hour. Occasionally the patient has a brief warning, most often an indescribable feeling in the stomach. There are two common forms of minor seizure, one occurring mainly in children and the other more often in adults. The common minor attacks in children are often called *petit mal* or *absence*, which well describes the instantaneous and brief loss of consciousness often unaccompanied by any change in posture. Recovery is equally instantaneous. On the other hand, in the other forms of epilepsy which arise from various parts of the brain, but especially from the lobe under the temporal region, there is often a warning similar to that which may precede a major seizure. In these cases the patient shows only confusion, no definite loss of posture, but automatic activity such as fumbling with buttons, muttering, and grimacing. Following these attacks there may be a quite prolonged period of confusion in which the patient may wander away and occasionally may be violent. Criminal acts are very rarely carried out in this state.

A large number of people have had one or two fits in their lives, particularly at times of physical or psychological stress. "Fever" or "Febrile" convulsions (often called teething fits in the past) are extremely common in young children and are often thought of as something different from epilepsy since the attacks rarely continue in later years. This form of epilepsy and some cases of *petit mal* are the only forms in which hereditary factors are important in the causation, and these are the least serious forms of epilepsy. They are very rarely associated with serious physical or psychological disturbances. Most other forms of epilepsy are due to a scar or other area of brain damage. It is a proportion of these cases which develop the psychological disturbances that are occasionally very serious.

Not every patient who has had one or two fits need necessarily take regular anticonvulsant drugs; that is drugs which damp down the abnormal excessive activity of the brain that leads to the attacks. Many drugs are available of which the most important are phenobarbitone, phenytoin, succinimides, and troxidones, the last two being effective only against minor seizures. Which one to use and whether to use one at all is, of course, quite a complicated judgment, and must be left to the doctor. Epileptics often find it difficult to get work because of the reluctance of employers to take on someone who may be more prone to accidents and whose fits may distress other workers. Obviously there are some jobs which epileptics should not do because of the danger involved, (from, for example, moving machinery), and they should not drive a car. A few cases are so severe that work is almost impossible, but employers have a duty whenever possible to employ these people whose mental health may suffer greatly if they are made to feel outcasts and who ordinarily are as efficient, or even more so, as the next man. It is also hoped that employees will become less prejudiced about epilepsy as the general public become less ignorant about medical matters. In this way epileptics will come to be accepted in all those kinds of employment for which they are well suited. If some of the famous men who have suffered from this disease had had to rely on the charity of some employers today the world would have been much the poorer, although possibly we could have managed without the generals.

The British Epilepsy Association exists to give guidance to people with epilepsy, their families, and friends. It provides a full-time welfare service and a chain of social clubs. It is concerned by means of books, films, courses, and lectures to make known the true facts about epilepsy. It seeks to share its knowledge with organisations in other countries. Its offices are at 3–6 Alfred Place, London, W.C.1. Tel. LAN 2704/5.

Chorea, or St. Vitus' Dance, is connected in some way with rheumatism, especially with rheumatic fever. It is much less common than formerly, and is also known as Sydenham's chorea, after the English physician who first described it and to distinguish it from Huntington's chorea, a serious hereditary and incurable degenerative disease which leads to progressive mental deterioration. Fortunately, Huntington's chorea is rather rare. The patient with Sydenham's chorea is a child, most often a girl, and one who has been rather delicate and nervous. She shows an inability to keep still and makes purposeless movements, such as writhing and twitching of the limbs and grimaces of the face. The speech may be affected, and the muscular inco-ordination may be so pronounced that dishes or other objects fall from the hands when lifted. The treatment for chorea is that for acute rheumatism with the addition of sedatives. The heart may be affected.

Pink Disease is a disease of young children between the ages of six months and three years. Why it should be included here is not certain: for its cause is unknown, and the theories to explain its origin range from the supposition that it is a vitamin-deficiency disorder, an infection, or the result of poisoning by mercury in teething powders, to the more probable theory that it is a vasomotor disorder like chilblains brought about by the nerves which control the diameter of the arteries. (Here it should be said that "teething powders," whether or not they play any part in causing this disease, should never be used anyhow, since in the first place—doubtless to the great indignation of mothers who, of course, always know best—one must say that it is extremely uncertain whether the many disturbances allegedly due to teething have anything to do with teeth at all, and secondly, that whether or not teething causes anything, it is certain that the numerous powders available in the shops can do nothing about it.) Pink disease was first described in Australia in 1914, and the general picture is that of a child in acute misery with itching or burning of the hands and feet, which are swollen and pink in appearance. Sometimes the face, ears, and nose are affected, there is loss of appetite, sweating, insomnia, and thirst. The treatment of the condition, which may last many months but with an ultimately good outlook, is injection of the B vitamins, especially B12, rest, and sedatives.

Angio-neurotic œdema. Another mysterious disease, common to both children and adults, and mentioned here because it, too, seems to be caused by malfunctioning of the nerves controlling the blood-vessels, is angio-neurotic œdema in which attacks of œdema (swelling) occur in various parts of the body, but are most apparent in the face. Undoubtedly allergy to various foodstuffs can play some part, but emotional factors are at least equally important. Very frequently, without any warning at all—but often after an emotional outburst—the face within a short time swells so that the patient is almost literally unrecognisable. Sometimes the swelling is so severe that breathing is endangered by œdema of the glottis, the entry to the windpipe. An immediate injection of adrenalin usually starts to clear up the condition, and for later use the antihistamine drugs have proved helpful.

THE DEGENERATIVE DISEASES.

There are very many conditions coming into this category, and they are given different names according to the parts of the nervous system affected. However, they all have this in common, that they are the result of a degeneration of groups of nerve cells, usually for no known reason, and, since nerve cells once destroyed can never regenerate, the diseases are usually irreversible and progressive. In a few cases, however, they can be arrested or simply die out.

It would be impossible to deal even briefly with all these diseases, so here only a few of the more common ones will be discussed. The ones we shall mention are: muscular atrophy, amyotrophic lateral sclerosis, disseminated sclerosis, syringomyelia, and subacute combined degeneration.

Muscular atrophy is, in fact, a whole group of diseases in which there is some damage to the lower parts of the nervous system, usually in the nerve cells at the point where they leave the spinal cord. The common type, *progressive muscular atrophy*, occurs in middle age or over, and the patient begins to note wasting of the muscles in first one hand and then the other. Ultimately, the hand becomes claw-shaped, and some wasting may spread up the forearm. It may finally spread up to the base of the brain, with fatal results. There is no known cure. In children a similar condition is *peroneal muscular atrophy*, in which degeneration of the nerve cells in the spinal cord leads to wasting both of the hands and legs. In this case the disease may stop of itself after several years.

Amyotrophic lateral sclerosis affects both the lower and higher nerve cells. There is wasting of the hands and arms, with increasing weakness, and the legs show a spastic type of paralysis, *i.e.*, they do not waste, but the muscles are in varying degrees of spasm and the knee-jerk and other reflexes are increased. The disease has been treated with concentrated vitamin E, but the results are uncertain. It should be noted that to say that a disease is incurable is not at all the same thing as saying that the patient is going to die from it. Some of these diseases progress very slowly, or may stop of themselves, and any disease process tends to go slower as one gets older. For example, many old people with cancer die of old age long before they are in danger of dying from the disease.

Disseminated sclerosis—sclerosis means hardening of the affected parts of the nervous system—is a progressive condition which goes on with periodic intermissions of improvement. Often the first symptom is double vision or sudden weakness in a limb, but the later symptoms are largely those resulting from loss of muscular co-ordination; thus, when the patient is asked to shut the eyes, stretch out the arm at right-angles to the body and then touch the tip of his nose, he manages the first part of the movement fairly adequately, but as the finger nears the nose it starts to wobble and fails to reach its goal. There is thus some loss of sense of position and difficulty in carrying out such actions as drinking tea from a cup. Another typical symptom is nystagmus in which, when he is asked to look to one side, the patient's eyes jerk back and forth (this condition is, of course, also a feature of so-called "miner's nystagmus," which appears to have a large psychological element and certainly has nothing to do with disseminated sclerosis). In later stages the spinal cord becomes affected and there are varying degrees of paralysis in the lower half of the body so that the legs are useless and there is loss of control of bladder and bowels. Thus, although disseminated sclerosis is not by itself a fatal disease, it does result in the long run in the patient becoming increasingly bed-ridden. Examination of the nervous system reveals that the covering of the nerve fibres—which have a sort of insulating layer much the same as in the case of electric wires—has been damaged and the underlying fibres have degenerated themselves. Where this damage occurs, and this appears to be completely fortuitous, determines the nature of the symptoms and where they occur. Many treatments have been tried, but their number only emphasises how little we know. The disease may be the result of inborn weakness in the fibres, of allergy, or of a virus infection with a so far undiscovered virus, but since it occurs in young adults in the prime of their life it is a particularly tragic disorder. Strangely enough, it is confined almost entirely to Europeans, and is rare elsewhere in the world.

Syringomyelia, another degenerative disease, is caused by the formation of small cavities in the upper parts of the spinal cord in the neck and chest regions. These cavities become surrounded with scar tissue, and hence interfere with nerve impulses passing down the areas where they occur. The patient may be any age between ten and thirty, and suffers from both sensory and motor symptoms. There is wasting of the muscles of the hand, and sometimes of the arm and shoulder, and specially typical is loss of the sense of pain with retention of the sense of touch. Because of this, the patient may burn or cut his fingers without noticing anything. The disease is slowly progressive over a long period of time, and there is no known effective treatment.

One of the few degenerative diseases which can be treated is *subacute combined degeneration*, which is invariably associated with pernicious anæmia. A middle-aged patient notices numbness, pins and needles, and so-called lightning pains in the fingers and toes and later in the limbs. The muscles are weak, and the tongue is smooth and glossy. On examination, the symptoms of pernicious anæmia are found. Treatment for the anæmia puts a stop to the disease, although damage already done may remain.

INFLAMMATORY DISEASES.

These are those, such as shingles or neuritis, which may be due, as is shingles, to virus infection, or to various causes, as is neuritis. The virus causing *shingles* is apparently the same as that causing chickenpox. Shingles, or to give it its proper title *herpes zoster* (it must not be confused with *herpes labialis* or cold sore of the lips, with which it has no connection whatever), shows itself in the form of a band of pain surrounding the upper abdomen or chest, which is then followed by an eruption with blisters in the affected area. There is no specific treatment; aspirin may be given for the pain and the reuption painted collodion or "New Skin." Ordinarily the condition clears up fairly quickly, but the pain may persist for a long time. Injections of vitamin B12 are sometimes helpful.

The word "neuritis," meaning inflammation of a nerve, covers many different types of illness: polyneuritis, simple neuritis, neuralgia, sciatica, prolapsed vertebral disc, and other conditions. All they have in common is nerve pain; for, as in the case of "colds," one cannot assume that because a condition has one name it represents one disease or has even one cause.

Multiple, peripheral, or polyneuritis is, as the name indicates, a condition in which numerous of the peripheral nerves, mainly in the limbs, are affected. The symptoms will vary according to whether motor or sensory nerves are attacked. The causes are various: poisons, such as lead, arsenic, or alcohol; bacterial poisons, such as those of diphtheria, typhoid, or gonorrhœa; vitamin deficiencies, as in beri-beri; and, finally diseases of metabolism, such as diabetes. Rarely, an infection known as acute infective polyneuritis causes the symptoms. The parts affected depend to some extent on the cause. Thus alcohol brings about, when taken in excess, pain in the calves and foot-drop (*i.e.*, the foot hangs down and cannot be raised to its normal position); neuritis due to diabetes and arsenic shows similar symptoms, whereas in lead poisoning not only the foot but also the wrist may be affected. Diphtheria tends to attack the palate and the eyes, causing difficulty in swallowing and in vision.

The ordinary type of neuritis, however, is localised—and here it should be said that many pains described as neuritic are nothing of the sort, being probably caused by fibrositis or muscle and joint disorders. Typical of localised neuritis is *Bell's palsy*, neuritis of the facial nerve, in which one side of the face is paralysed so that the eye on the affected side will not shut, and the mouth droops down. Asked to whistle or blow out his cheeks, the patient with facial paralysis is unable to do so. The usual cause of Bell's palsy is cold—for example, it is common to find that the patient has been driving with the car window open in cold weather. But facial paralysis may also be caused by infection in the middle ear. Most cases clear up in a fairly short time, but in a few instances the palsy is permanent. There is very little evidence that the treatments usually employed, such as electrical stimulation, have any effect, but injections of concentrated vitamins B may be used.

Other familiar types of neuritis are *sciatica* and neuritis in the arm. They can be caused by fractures, or pressure from tumours, or the callus (excess bone) in badly healed fractures; cold, too, is said to be a factor, and then there is always "idiopathic neuritis"—which, in everyday language, means that one does not know the cause. Most cases, regrettably, are idiopathic. In sciatica, we have a condition which is not a disease but rather a symptom. The familiar pain down the back of the leg may be caused by alcohol, rheumatism, diabetes, tumour, fibrositis, "slipped disc," arthritis of the hip joint, dislocated sacro-iliac joint, infection such as tonsillitis, and so on. Treatment depends on the cause, which frequently is never found.

Prolapsed Intervertebral disc is a popular disease in these days. It causes a sciatica-like type of pain, and is brought about by the bulging of an intervertebral disc (the shock-absorbers, which lie between the vertebræ of the spinal column) into the area where it can press upon the nerve root. Treatment is first by rest and pain-relieving drugs; if this is not enough laminectomy is performed and the protruding part of the disc removed.

Paralysis agitans or *Parkinson's disease* may result in young adults following an attack of encephalitis, or in older people, in whom the part of the brain concerned simply deteriorates. The face becomes expressionless, the movements stiff and slow, the gait shows a shuffling tendency, in which the patient bends forward and seems to be running to catch up with himself. There is tremor of the fingers and the so-called "pill-rolling" movements, in which the thumb and fingers are constantly moving against each other. Treatment is by drugs, such as hyoscine or more modern proprietary ones; in some cases surgical operation has been used with varying degrees of success. The disease is also known as "shaking palsy."

MENTAL DISEASES.

Psychosis.

Mental diseases are divided into psychoses (*i.e.*, insanity) and neuroses (*i.e.*, what is ordinarily known as "nerves"). Psychoses, in their turn, are divided into organic and functional—those due to physical disease and those in which no physical cause has been discovered. In point of fact, the distinction into organic and functional is rather meaningless; for if we accept the modern view of psychosomatic medicine which regards the body and mind as a single unit it is clear that organic disease brings out psychological defects which were already there and that functional disease must, in the final analysis, be the result of physico-chemical causes, even if this is brought about by mental stress.

Organic disease results from poisoning of the nervous system by such poisons as alcohol, carbon monoxide, or lead; vitamin deficiencies, as in pellagra; infections such as syphilis; and degeneration of the brain, either primary or as a result of poor blood supply. In all cases its main symptoms are confusion, signs of other disease, and loss of memory. Alcohol leads to various conditions: in *delirium tremens* heavy bouts of drinking end in delirium ("D.T.s"), confusion, hallucination—although not necessarily of pink elephants or rats. It is a serious disease, but the outlook is much improved since it was discovered that injections of concentrated vitamins B and C in the form of "Parentrovite" can help. In more chronic cases *Korsakov's syndrome* manifests itself in the form of mental deterioration and memory defects. There can be little doubt that previously existing mental instability is a predisposing factor in these conditions. The same may be said of *general paralysis of the insane* or G.P.I., and in this case the immediate cause is syphilitic infection of the nervous system. Nevertheless, of all the patients with chronic syphilis, only a small number get syphilis of the nervous system. G.P.I. is typically associated with the usual symptoms of organic disease and delusions of grandeur; for example, a man with this disease may go out and buy several expensive cars in one day. However, it is not uncommon to find G.P.I. associated with severe depression—again the picture depends on the previous personality. At one time G.P.I. was considered hopeless, but treatment by malaria (that is, deliberate injection of malarial germs) was found to be helpful. Today, although in some places the treatment is still used, penicillin is found to be adequate. The association of the above symptoms with a positive Wasserman test—which proves the presence of the spirochæte in the blood—indicates neurosyphilis. When the lower centres of the nervous system are affected the disease is known as *tabes dorsalis*, in which there is difficulty in passing urine, limb pains, inability to stand when the eyes are closed, and finally difficulty in walking. The patient becomes paralysed and ultimately bedridden. Treatment is with penicillin.

People age at varying rates, so that some are hale and hearty at eighty or ninety whereas others are old at sixty or seventy. They present the typical picture of old age: "second childishness and mere oblivion, sans eyes, sans teeth, sans everything." When this condition, which is caused by degenerative changes in the brain or by defective blood-supply resulting from arteriosclerosis, is pronounced we speak of *senile psychosis*. There is mental confusion, forgetfulness, and delusions, in which the previous personality defects which we all have are accentuated. Such patients may have to be put under special care, but the process is largely irreversible.

The functional psychoses are two in number: schizophrenia and manic-depressive insanity. In *schizophrenia*, which, when it occurs in early adult life, is known (or used to be known) as *dementia præcox*, the symptoms are bizarre. There are delusions and hallucinations, so that the patient often believes himself to be persecuted and hears voices which say objectionable things to him. Sometimes the schizophrenic is wildly excited, and in other cases he goes into a state of stupor which is described as a catatonic state. Although the disease is described as functional, recent discoveries seem to suggest that there is some derangement of the blood chemistry. Treatment by insulin and the new tranquillising drugs has revolutionised the outlook in this admittedly serious disease. Indeed, some cases of psychosis are more easily treated than neurotic patients, since the former respond to physical methods, whereas the latter may require fairly prolonged psychotherapy (psychological treatment) and are less responsive to drugs.

In cases which do not respond to other methods, the brain operation known as *leucotomy* may be performed. Leucotomy is also performed to alleviate intractable pain, as in incurable cancer, but some of the ataraxic drugs (tranquillisers) are probably equally useful for this purpose. Leucotomy involves the severing of the connecting nerve fibres between certain areas of the brain, and the results are often favourable, but in fact the operation should be performed only in cases where the outlook is otherwise very poor; chronic severe neuroses, frequent attacks of manic depressive psychosis, severe chronic depression, and schizophrenia which has not responded to other forms of treatment. The operation reduces anxiety, fear, aggressiveness, and agitation, but may result in the less-desirable symptoms of apathy, impaired judgment, lack of self-control, and loss of initiative.

Schizophrenia developing in later life is likely to be less dramatic in origin, and the delusions tend to be more systematised—that is, they take a persistent form, which does not change from day to day. This type of the disease is known as *paraphrenia*. In those beyond middle age the rare but dangerous condition described as *paranoia* may develop in which there are no hallucinations and the only symptom is a completely systematised collection of persecutory delusions, which on recital may sound entirely convincing even to the ordinary doctor. Such people are dangerous precisely because they are so plausible, and they fill the ranks of the litigious, the trouble-makers, and the political and religious eccentrics. One such patient known to the writer spent his life in a mental hospital from which he had parole, employing this to form a society propagating highly eccentric sexual and political beliefs. It says little for the intelligence of the general population that his meetings were invariably crowded out (although, of course, when one reads of the people who apparently believe that the various fictitious families on radio or television—the Groves, the Archers, and the like—really exist, one need not be surprised at such examples of communal dottiness, even if one may despair of democracy).

Manic-depressive insanity is characterised by mood swings in which the emotions alternate between wild elation without obvious cause and equally causeless depression. However, the picture is not quite as simple as this; for phases of mania or excitement may occur without depression obviously following, or there may be a single attack of depression with no manic phases. The disease may be absolutely incapacitating, or there may be periods of relative normality; typically, then, manic-depressive insanity is a disease of alternating moods. The depression responds to electroconvulsive therapy or E.C.T., but mania is less responsive to treatment. However, it ordinarily remits of itself. Sometimes in middle age *involutional depression* occurs, and this in the vast majority of cases is cured by E.C.T. As in the case of schizophrenia drugs are increasingly used for depression. Chlorpromazine in the former case and in depression Nardil or Tofranil, etc. The ever-present risk in depression is suicide.

Neurosis.

The main neuroses are anxiety neurosis, hysteria, and obsessional neurosis. *Anxiety neurosis* is an illness in which the main symptom (as the name implies) is anxiety. There is fear which rationally the patient knows to be groundless; there may be anxiety attacks, in which the heart pounds, the patient feels he is going mad, is unable to sleep, and worries "for no reason at all." In hysteria, anxiety is largely absent, but there may be apparently physical symptoms ranging from paralysis of the limbs to blindness, deafness, inability to write, and lapses of memory (the so-called hysterical fugues or loss of memory). Typical of *hysteria* is the fact that the patient is less worried by his symptoms than would be expected from their apparent seriousness; this is what the early psychiatrists described as "la belle indifference." The reason for the indifference is simple—it is that the paralysed individual *wants* to be paralysed, the blind *want* to be blind, the deaf to be deaf (there are none so blind—or deaf—as those who don't want to see, or hear), and the person who doesn't want to write conveniently finds that he cannot.

Generally speaking, neurotic people are suffering from a failure to face up to reality. They are not physically ill and are largely the end result of a faulty upbringing. It is wrong to suppose that the only bad families are those in which the children are ill-treated; much the worst ones are those in which children are spoilt, the parents possessive, and the wrong kind of love is dispensed. Neuroses are the result of a conflict between primitive desires and what the individual has been brought up to believe he should be. For example, before an examination a student may develop a nervous breakdown because he fears failure when he has been brought up to expect success. The excuse, of course, is "overwork"—an entirely non-existent condition. With his breakdown he solves his problem, he avoids the fear of failing and preserves his self-respect: he has been ill. Similarly, the soldier with "shell shock" (another non-existent condition) has a conflict between his sense of duty and his fear of death, which again is solved by becoming ill. Or, to take a final example, a woman feels the duty to look after her ageing mother. But she also wants to get married. So she unconsciously develops a neurosis which says, in effect, "I should like to do my duty in looking after my mother, but unfortunately I am unable to." There is an unconscious rebellion on the part of the mind.

Neurosis, in effect, is not a disease—it is a self-inflicted injury, a form of maladaptation to life. The neurotic, no matter how much he suffers, does not want to get well; he has found some way of getting along, even if a foolish way, and he intends to keep it. Often his symptoms are the sort of excuse that say: "If only I wasn't ill what wouldn't I be able to do!" The neurotic is a person who is different and is afraid to be himself; his problem is a conflict between being "ordinary," "like other people," and being what he was supposed to be. You will find some further references to neurosis in **Section Q, Part II.**

Obsessional Neurosis is a more severe type of neurotic illness; for although in anxiety neurosis we find such symptoms as phobias—irrational fears of open spaces, closed spaces, animals, and so on—obsessional states are characterised by compulsive feelings that certain acts must be performed or certain thoughts thought. In a mild form we all have obsessions: we feel that we must walk on the spaces between paving-stones, that we must touch lamp-posts, and so on. But when this type of compulsion gets to the stage when we must go back several times to make sure the lights have been put out, when we feel the need to wash our hands every few minutes, become obsessed with numbers on cars or dates on coins, then it becomes a nuisance and requires treatment. Usually the treatment is psychotherapy—whether psychoanalysis according to the method of Freud or shorter methods—and, in serious cases, physical methods such as L.S.D. (lysergic acid) or leucotomy. The obsessional neurotic is a person who feels that life must be controlled; he is "a creature who moves in predestinate grooves—he's not even a bus but a tram." His symptoms are an attempt to devise self-imposed rules which will control the unconscious desires of which he is so afraid.

Neurasthenia is an entirely imaginary condition allegedly due to exhaustion of the nervous system. Since no such condition exists, we need not bother with it. Neuroses cannot be treated by feeding the nerves (which are perfectly normal). They can be helped by such things as sedatives, but not cured. *Neurosis has nothing at all to do with disease of the physical nerves, so nerve tonics do not exist, and anyone who asserts that they do is a humbug.* Glycerophosphates and the usual contents of tonics are excreted almost as soon as they are taken in, and tonic wines are one of the best ways of becoming an alcoholic. The one reason for not taking alcohol is when one craves it, and many a "respectable" old lady has required several dust-carts to carry away the store of empty bottles left behind when she died.

Psychopathic Personality is the term given to anyone who has different standards of behaviour from those generally accepted by society. Some of these unfortunates may be *inadequate*, that is to say, although perfectly intelligent, unable to earn their own living. Others are the *creative* people, who, as in the case of Van Gogh, did many eccentric things but also many productive things—Van Gogh was gifted, or cursed, with an intense sensitivity. Lastly, there are those who have what others regard as peculiar sexual habits. Of the first two classes nothing more need be said, and all that is necessary is to mention certain of the so-called sexual perversions. (When we say so called the implication is not that none of these forms of behaviour is perverse but that some of them are carried out by otherwise quite ordinary people.) *Sadism* and *Masochism* refer to, in the first place, pleasure in inflicting pain and, in the second, to receiving pain. The pleasure is sexual, and it is incorrect to talk of cruelty in itself as sadism. Sadism is named after the Marquis de Sade, who suffered from this perversion, although he certainly did much less harm in his small way than numerous politicians or generals of our time, and masochism is named after the Austrian novelist Sacher-Masoch, who wrote books which, although unpleasant, were not notably more so than certain Sunday newspapers of today.

Masturbation is sexual self-stimulation. Needless to say, it produces no more *physical* harm than ordinary sexual intercourse—that is to say, none at all, although some people have the strange belief that every act of intercourse weakens the body and it has even been believed that each act shortens life by a specific length of time. This is rather illogical in view of the fact that most of the famous rakes have been noted for their longevity! Masturbation is almost universal in infancy, adolescence, or even in later life when other outlets are not available. It need only be a matter of concern: (*a*) when it is chosen in preference to normal sexual activity, or (*b*) when it is compulsive and excessive, since then it is a sign, not of sexual desire, but of severe underlying anxiety.

Homosexuality is, as presumably most people now know, an attraction between individuals of the same sex. Feminine homosexuality is not illegal in Britain, but male homosexuality is. The Wolfenden Report of 1957 takes a much more tolerant view of the problem than has been hitherto current, recommending, in effect, that homosexual acts between consenting adults should be legalised. Homosexuality is, so far as is known, not inherited, and is the result of psychological difficulties in early development; occasionally it can be treated by psychotherapy, but it is doubtful whether those "cured" in this way were ever genuine homosexuals. To any humane person it must seem that the Wolfenden Report gives a sensible solution to the problem; for it is difficult to see why the homosexual should be treated differently from the heterosexual offender. That is to say, what adults do (with consent) together is their own business, but the male homosexual who seduces a boy under age should be treated in no way differently from the man who seduces an under-age girl.

All that remains to be said is that many of these conditions are treatable or, if not treatable so far as cure is concerned, they can at least be relieved. The world is full of people who are "different"; there are those who are different in the right way, who should take satisfaction from their achievements, and those who are different in the wrong way, who should seek expert advice. Since psychological treatment is time-consuming, it is not very easy to obtain it within the National

Health Service, although group treatment has simplified the problem. However, any person with such difficulties would probably benefit from a discussion with his family doctor.

DISEASES OF THE SKIN.

The skin in the course of development before birth is particularly closely associated with the nervous system. It is therefore not surprising that so many skin diseases are influenced by emotional states. Other causes of skin disease are infections, glandular disorders, vitamin deficiencies, and the numerous conditions for which no cause has been discovered, but which presumably are due to metabolic disorders.

One of the commonest skin symptoms is *itching or pruritus*. It may accompany many different general diseases, for example diabetes and jaundice. It may also be troublesome during the menopause (the change of life in women), in old age, or in nervous conditions. Sedatives and sex hormones sometimes help the itching during the menopause, and there are ointments which may be useful.

Itching in the region of the anus and genital organs is relatively common. It may be caused by worms, by irritating vaginal discharge, or by sugar in the urine, as in diabetes. The alteration in the normal bacteria of the bowel which follows treatment with various antibiotics also often causes anal pruritus and soreness. In many cases however the itching has some psychological cause. In treatment it is important to avoid ointments and creams which contain a local anæsthetic, because these substances can cause severe allergic reactions if used for longer than a few days, and may thus make the condition much worse. Treatment with a local corticosteroid application is more effective and safer.

Parasites, such as the *scabies* mite or *lice* can cause severe and persistent itching. The scabies mite is very small, and since it burrows under the skin surface, is unlikely to be seen; it is the cause of itching most commonly between the fingers and on the front of the wrists. The itching is worst when the body becomes heated, as in bed. Treatment consists of painting the body from head to foot with benzyl benzoate application, followed the next day by a hot bath. Since scabies is contracted through close personal contact with an infested person it is often desirable for several or all members of a family to be treated at the same time, even though only one of them may be affected. Lice are specialists, one type of which affects the scalp, another the body, and a third the genital area. Head lice are destroyed by lethane, body lice by D.D.T (dicophane) powder, and genital (pubic) lice by shaving off hair and washing. Obviously, the clothes, especially in the case of body lice, should be disinfested, either by the use of D.D.T. or, if this is not available, by using a hot iron over the seams, which lice (for some inexplicable reason) seem to favour. Apart from the discomfort they cause, lice are dangerous as potential carriers of typhus fever.

Baldness, or Alopecia, is a very common condition, as is manifested by the extraordinary number of preparations advertised as curing it. When many preparations are offered for the treatment of one condition it is a fair judgment to assume that none of them is likely to be effective. There are, in fact, two types of baldness; one, which is much the commoner, is hereditary, and cannot be influenced in the slightest by any treatment, the other, *alopecia areata*, is caused by nervous stress, and would recover in most cases by itself, whether one used a solution of soot and water or the most expensive " hair food." There is no such thing as a hair food, any more than there is such a thing as a nerve food, and although it is probable that hair hygiene may delay baldness, it certainly cannot prevent it. All hair tonics and " foods " are useless, and their uselessness is only equalled by their costliness. Those who have lost their hair and find it growing again after using some alleged tonic are people who have had *alopecia areata* and whose hair would have grown back anyhow. In women the hair often thins out soon after a pregnancy, but a few months later it usually returns to normal.

Seborrhœa is a condition in which there is overactivity of the sebaceous glands. The most usual form it takes is *dandruff*. However, it takes other forms, and those who have dandruff may also have rashes on the face, shoulders, and chest. In these areas there is a patchy, greasy, and often itchy, rash which does not clear up until the primary condition in the scalp is dealt with. The scalp should be washed with one of the modern sulphur-containing shampoos at least twice a week, and the affected parts on the face and chest can be dealt with by the use of a sulphur lotion (*not* on any account by greasy ointments). Seborrhœa is not in itself difficult to treat, but, since the condition depends on over-secretion of sebum, the skin lubricant, treatment may have to be persisted in during the years of early adulthood, when it is most active.

Erythema Intertrigo is, quite simply, the sort of irritation which occurs usually from excessive sweating under the armpits, between the legs, and under the breasts in women. All that need be done is to wash frequently and to dust the affected areas after washing with powder. This is the condition which, in the tropics, is known as " prickly heat " and elswhere as a " sweat rash." In some people *hyperidrosis* or *excessive sweating* is a problem, especially when the sweating is accompanied with body odour—the sort of thing that, according to the advertisements, " even your best friends won't tell you." There is little need for anyone in these days to suffer in this way: for the cosmetic firms have produced many highly efficient deodorants which not only control odour but also control the amount of sweating. Chlorophyll, which has been much advertised as removing odours, is effective when applied directly to surfaces which give off an unpleasant smell. It is however ineffective when taken by mouth, and does not prevent body odours. Stale sweat smells bad because it is decomposed by bacteria, and this type of body odour can be largely prevented by preparations containing a harmless antiseptic such as hexachlorophane and an antiperspirant such as aluminium chloride (see *Which*, February 1960).

Erysipelas is an infection of the skin caused by the hæmolytic streptococcus. It begins as a red, raised area anywhere on the body where the germs have been able to enter through a small crack or cut in the skin. The red area advances and spreads over the body until the disease is got under control. Erysipelas is very infectious, and those who look after the patient should wash their hands throughly after contact. At one time the disease used to spread as an epidemic throughout the hospital wards, but this is very rare nowadays. Treatment is, of course, a matter for the doctor.

Chilblains are common in cold weather, especially in those with poor circulation. Ordinarily they occur in the toes and fingers, but may appear on the nose and ears. The part affected becomes swollen, dusky, and there is pain and itching, sometimes leading to ulceration. Protection of the body, especially the hands and feet, from cold is the best and the only really effective way of preventing chilblains. Warm lined gloves and footwear, and warm stockings or trousers should be worn outdoors. Adequate heating of rooms is essential: a temperature between 18° and 21°C is recommended (65°–78°F). Most tablets, medicines, ointments, or creams for chilblains are useless. A skin affection caused by heat is rather grandiosely described as *erythema ab igne*, and is frequently seen on the legs of ladies addicted to roasting their legs before the fire. It takes the form of red patches on the front of the legs, and can be removed only by avoiding the cause.

Dermatitis means " inflammation of the skin," and therefore the word could be, strictly speaking, applied to any skin disease. In fact the term is used almost interchangeably with the term *eczema*. There are three main types of dermatitis or eczema. The first, *primary irritant dermatitis* results from injury of the skin by some powerful chemical, such as strong alkali or turpentine. The second, *contact dermatitis* is due to sensitisation of the skin to some substance which is normally liable to cause this type of allergic sensitivity; examples are nickel (in jewellery and suspender buckles), epoxy resins, rubber additives, primulas and chrysanthemums, and even ingredients of cosmetics. Contact dermatitis may continue for a long time, even after the patient is no longer in contact with the offending material. The third type is often called *constitutional eczema*. Although the skin is apt to react adversely to various irritants and sensitisers the major part is played by the personality, and there is often a history of eczema, hay fever or asthma in the family. Treatment is more difficult, but local corticosteroids and tar, sedatives and psychological treatment can be of great help. Infantile eczema also belongs in this category, but in most patients it disappears as the child grows up.

Impetigo is an infectious skin disease caused primarily by the streptococcus, but later often infected with staphylococci. It usually occurs on the face, and takes the form of blisters filled with pus on a red base; when the blisters burst their place is taken by yellow crusts. Impetigo is very infectious and easily spread by the fingers, dirty towels, or cloths; therefore, one of the first necessities is to prevent infection of others or reinfection of oneself by avoiding scratching and using a different towel each day, which must on no account be used by anyone else. Treatment is simple with an antibacterial ointment, so the main issue is prevention of contamination.

Sycosis or " Barber's Rash " occurs in men, and is similarly treated.

Urticaria or *Nettlerash* is a familiar skin disease in which itching weals appear on the skin, usually for no obvious reason. It is not infectious, and can be caused by nervous stress, certain drugs, allergy to some foods, or even exposure of the skin to cold. In some people it is possible to write on the skin with a fingernail: the " writing " appears in the form of weals. This is known as *dermographism*; it occurs in many normal persons as well as in many patients with urticaria. The antihistamine drugs are the most useful in the treatment of urticaria. Urticarial swelling of the tongue or throat must however be relieved at once and is treated by an injection of adrenaline.

Acne, or " *Blackheads*," is a condition found on the face and shoulders; its appearance is so familiar that no description is necessary. Acne is one of those conditions which is the end result of many factors. There is, first, a greasy skin, the result of glandular upset (which is why the disease usually occurs in adolescence); secondly, there is infection of the skin; and thirdly, there is blockage of the sebaceous ducts, which ordinarily allow the grease from the skin to pass out on to the surface. Since the condition starts with excess secretion of grease, ointments should never be used, and probably the best applications are drying lotions containing some sulphur preparation which inhibits secretion of grease. The face should be frequently washed, and it is possible now to obtain detergent solutions which are both antiseptic and prevent grease formation. In severe cases ultraviolet ray treatment may be necessary.

Rosacea. As has already been implied elsewhere, although the wages of sin may be extremely unpleasant, the wages of extreme virtue may be no less troublesome. Thus *rosacea*, in which the nose and cheeks become red and greasy and the skin coarsened, occurs alike in chronic alcoholics and elderly ladies with no vices other than a preference for strong tea. Both cases are associated with indigestion, since, regrettable as it may seem, strong tea and alcohol are about equally liable to cause the gastritis which may be at the root of this complaint. However, in many patients the chronic flushing is caused in other ways and psychological factors are important.

Lichen Planus is one of the numerous skin diseases which seem to be due to nervous states of tension. It may occur on any part of the body, but is most common on the front of the forearms and legs. The rash takes the form of nodules which are lilac in colour and have a dent on the top; when these disappear a stain is left behind. There is severe itching. Treatment is a matter for a doctor, as it also is in the case of *psoriasis*, a very common disease of largely unknown origin, which is extremely resistant to treatment. It tends to run in families. It takes the form of slightly raised papules, usually on the elbows and knees; typically the papules are covered with dry, silvery-looking scales. Apart from the rash, the patient is usually in perfectly good health and there is no itching. Many drugs have been used in psoriasis, notably chrysarobin, and while it is not difficult to cause the rash (which may occur anywhere on the body) to disappear in one area or even in all areas for a time it has a strong tendency to return.

Warts, or *Verrucae* are familiar enough. They are caused by a virus, and are, theoretically at least, contagious (although having removed many warts, the writer has never found them contagious). Most frequently they are found on the hands, but may occur elsewhere. Treatment is best carried out by a doctor, who will use a cautery, a caustic carbon dioxide frozen into " snow ". A curious feature of the common wart is that it can sometimes be caused to disappear by suggestion, which is presumably why so many old wives charms are not necessarily without effect. Different altogether from the common wart is the *plantar wart*, which occurs on the soles of the feet and often causes a good deal of discomfort. It is best dealt with by a chiropodist or in bad cases by a skin specialist since it is highly infectious.

Icthyosis is a disorder of horn formation with which some unfortunate people are born. The oil and sweat-producing glands do not function well and the skin is dry and scaly like the skin of a fish. It is, however, possible to help the condition, which does not affect the general health, by frequent alkaline baths to wash off the scales, and the subsequent use of lanolin to replace the lacking oil. Large doses of vitamin A seem to help in some cases, and there have been reports in the medical Press of cases being helped by hypnosis; this, however, is very much a matter for speculation.

Cancer, Rodent Ulcer, and Cysts. Cancer of the skin occurs mostly in old people, and takes the form of what is described as an *epithelioma*. It is most common on the face or hands, and usually appears as a nodule which breaks down and produces an ulcer. The glands may later be affected, but such cancers can almost invariably be cured unless a considerable time has elapsed during which they have been neglected. *Rodent ulcer* is a form of ulcer which appears on the inner corner of the eye or the side of the nose in old people. It does not spread over the body, but acts by eating into the tissues in the area where it has started. X-ray or operation is necessary, but the outlook is good. *Cysts* on the skin are due to blockage of the sebaceous glands. They may become very large, and are best removed, as they may become infected. They do not turn into cancer, and there is no such thing as " male " and " female " cysts. It does sometimes happen that *moles*, especially of the bluish-black type, may become malignant, so it is perhaps best to have them removed surgically when they exist. *All moles which change in appearance or size should be at once referred to a doctor.*

Skin Grafts.

These are a very complex subject which can be only briefly discussed here. They are used basically for a number of conditions in which large areas of skin have been removed from the body, as in burns or serious accidents. In other cases, as in plastic surgery, grafts may be used to make a new nose, eyelids, and so on. The following are the main types:

Pinch Grafts are small, circular pieces of skin cut from some other part of the body. (The former method of using grafts from another person has been given up almost completely, since such grafts—except in the case of identical twins—never " take.") The small pieces are laid on the area without skin and gradually grow together. *Split-thickness grafts* are grafts removed from another part of the body by an instrument known as a dermatome, which cuts sections about 4 in. by 8 in. containing part of the deep layers of the skin.

In *Full-thickness Grafts*, on the other hand, the whole thickness of the skin is removed from elsewhere and applied to an area which has to bear friction or heavy weights, such as the hand or the foot. Lastly, and this is largely used in plastic surgery, there is the *Pedicle graft*, which, unfortunately, although it is certainly the most exciting type, is rather difficult to describe. Briefly, if one, for example, wants to make a new nose, one cuts an area of skin and underlying fat about 2 in. wide and 5 or 6 in. long in the abdomen. One end, however, remains attached so that it gets adequate blood-supply. The problem is how to get this tissue to the nose, and this is done by a complicated process of leap-frog. First, the free end of the graft is attached to the forearm, whilst its " root " remains in the original site, and when it begins to grow and get its blood-supply from the arm, the original " root " is cut. So we now have a " sausage " of tissue attached to the arm. The arm is then lifted to the face and kept firmly in position there until the new free part becomes attached. It is then detached from the arm, modelled to the correct shape, and grows where the nose used to be!

THE RHEUMATIC DISEASES.

The main rheumatic diseases (or so they are described, although they seem to have little relationship one with the other), are *rheumatic fever*, the acute form, which has already been dealt with; *chorea*, or rheumatism of the nervous system, also mentioned; *rheumatoid arthritis*; *osteoarthritis*; *gout;* and *fibrositis*. The only thing these diseases seem to have in common is that most seem to be associated with the connective tissues, muscles or joints—this, of course, with the single exception of chorea. Apart from this, there is very little similarity.

Rheumatoid arthritis often starts without evident cause in early adult life, and affects the small joints of the fingers and toes, causing swelling and pain. No infective process has been discovered, yet the disease goes on and on, sometimes better, sometimes worse. It is (and this is all one can say) a disease commoner in women, commoner in temperate climates, commoner following emotional stress. Although, as we have seen, rheumatoid arthritis is a disease characterised by frequent remissions, it takes a considerable time to burn itself out. The most likely explanation for its occurrence is that stress reactions act on the suprarenal glands and the secretion of cortisone is inadequate to play its usual part in preventing the body from responding too severely to injury. However, the injection of cortisone has proved, on the whole, less useful than might have been expected, and there is little reason to suppose that in most cases it is any better than aspirin.

Osteoarthritis is essentially a degenerative disease of old people. The bones affected are ordinarily the larger joints: the shoulders, the hips, or the spine. There is no disease in the ordinary sense, and essentially what has happened is that these joints have got " old " and the bone has overgrown so that movement is less simple than it once was. Osteoarthritis is not curable, but can be relieved by drugs and physiotherapy.

Gout, so far as one knows, has nothing at all to do with rheumatism. It is a metabolic disease caused by the inability of the body to deal with certain protein breakdown substances, such as uric acid. Typically, the pain develops in the big toe, and the foods concerned are such luscious products as wines, spirits, liver, sweetbreads. Although drugs such as cinchophen can help, the plain fact is that those liable to gout cannot have sweetbreads and wine, liver and spirits, without having gout as well. Most people, perhaps, would prefer the food and wine, but those who dislike gout must abstain.

Fibrositis. All diseases are annoying to the patient, but fibrositis is just about equally annoying to the doctor. Fibrositis, in fact, is a condition in which people come along (and how often they do so!) with muscular pain which may be caused by anything from falling down the stairs to quarrelling with their mother-in-law. Although at one time, and perhaps even now, it used to be said that those with fibrositis could be diagnosed by the presence of " nodules " in their muscles, it is almost certain: (*a*) that there are no such nodules, and (*b*) that muscular pain may be due to many causes and very largely to psychological ones.

DISEASES OF THE EYE.

The Eye.

The eye is frequently compared to a camera, and in a general sort of way there is some resemblance. The eyeball consists of 3 coats within which are contained the refraction media: (1) The outermost layer, the main support of the eyeball, comprising the sclera (opaque) and the cornea (transparent, covering the front of the eyeball). The conjunctiva (the part which gets inflamed when you get germs or dust on the surface of the eye) is a thin protective membrane covering the sclera and doubles back to line the inside of the upper and lower lids. It stops at the junction of the sclera and cornea. (2) The middle layer containing many blood vessels which forms the choroid and, in front, the iris (the coloured part of the eye). The muscle in the iris enables its central aperture, the pupil, to contract in bright light, and to dilate in dim light. (3) The innermost layer of nervous tissue, the retina. The retina contains the expanded termination of the optic nerve which is part of the brain. Behind the iris is the lens, which is controlled by a series of muscles which increase or diminish its curvature, and thus produce, according to the nearness or distance of the object, a clear picture on the retina. Some of these parts may, of course, be affected by disease. Here we shall deal only with a few of the more common diseases.

Blepharitis is an infection of the eyelids which is easily recognisable from the red, sore appearance at the margins, the formation of crusts, and the falling-out of the eyelashes. If it has just developed, an attempt may be made to treat it at home with hot bathing and the so-called Golden Eye Ointment, but *blepharitis* is liable to become a chronic disease, and it is wiser to see a doctor. Penicillin cream or ointment can cure the disease, but must *never* be used save under medical advice; allergy to penicillin is commoner in the eyes than anywhere else, and in some cases patients have lost their sight through its use in this way.

Conjunctivitis is the result of infection of the conjunctiva, and the symptoms are the familiar ones of a feeling as if some grit had got into the eye, running from the eye, and frequently gummed-together eyelids in the morning. In some cases it can be treated by hot bathing and eye-baths with one of the proprietary lotions on the market, but it is much wiser to see your doctor, who can supply much more effective remedies and may save you a lot of unnecessary discomfort.

Other Eye Diseases. We can only mention briefly *keratis*, inflammation of the cornea;

iritis, inflammation of the iris; and *glaucoma*. These are all potentially serious diseases, and should not be diagnosed or treated by the layman. Glaucoma, in particular, may lead to blndness if help is not sought in time. If there is redness and congestion over the eye, dimness of vision, *severe* pain (as contrasted with the irritation caused by conjunctivitis), and perhaps even vomiting, the doctor must be called immediately.

The main disease of the lens is *cataract*, in which the lens becomes opaque and varying degrees of blindness result. Ordinarily, cararact is a condition found in people after middle age, but sometimes it is found in children at birth. The treatment is by operation—one which has been carried out for centuries—in which the opaque lens is removed. The patient thereafter has to wear glasses, but the vast majority of patients obtain good vision.

In *retinitis*, however, where the "screen" at the back of the eye is affected, the general outlook is more serious. This is because, whereas cataract is a localised disease, retinitis often signifies some bodily illness: infection, hardening of the arteries leading to hæmorrhage, diabetes, or kidney disorders. Sometimes the retina becomes detached, leading to blindness. As has been suggested above, except in very minor conditions such as styes (a localised infection treated in the same way as blepharitis), or conjunctivitis, the doctor should always be consulted. He should be consulted, too, when a foreign body gets into the eye unless it can be removed by very gentle manipulation with a handkerchief, for it must be remembered that such "poking about" on the surface of the eye may do much more harm than the original condition. So, if a couple of minutes fail to remove the grit, give up, and go to the surgery.

DISEASES OF WOMEN.

The *internal sexual organs* of a woman, like the urinary system, can best be described as shaped like a capital Y. At the tips of the arms of the Y are the female sex glands, the ovaries: the two arms running downwards are the Fallopian tubes: the point where the arms meet is the womb or uterus: the single leg of the Y is the vagina. These are the *primary sexual organs* of a woman and they undergo regular cyclical changes in response to the control exercised over them by the pituitary gland, situated in the base of the skull. This control is mediated by chemical messengers (hormones) secreted into the circulation. The ovaries also secrete hormones, œstrogen, and progesterone, and a delicate hormonal balance is maintained between the pituitary gland and the ovaries. Each month an egg cell (ovum) matures and is released from the ovary, usually midway between two menstrual periods: the ovum is wafted along the Fallopian tubes by waves of contraction and if fertilised embeds in the lining of the uterus which has been conditioned to nourish it by the ovarian hormones. If it is not fertilised the ovum escapes from the uterus, altered hormone levels then cause the lining of the uterus to be shed (this is menstruation), usually about 14 days after ovulation. After menstruation a new cycle begins: another ovum matures and a fresh lining grows in the uterus. These cyclical changes recur from puberty to the menopause. Menstruation does not occur during pregnancy, of which a missed period is often the first sign. However, women do miss periods even though they are not pregnant, and this usually means that some minor and temporary change has occurred in the hormone balance. If three consecutive periods are missed it is wise to consult a doctor.

The *breasts* are called *secondary sexual organs* and are also under the influence of the ovarian hormones. Women are sometimes worried because they believe that their breasts are either too small or too large. However, small breasts cannot be made larger and are just as efficient for feeding babies as large ones, which are not always as effective as they appear. If breasts become too large they can be dealt with by plastic surgery. Two conditions which do need treatment are *mastitis* and *cancer of the breast*, both of which are characterised by lumps within the breast tissue. Mastitis may be uncomfortable but is not dangerous and can be treated medically, whereas cancer is more serious. The distinction between mastitis and cancer can only be made by a doctor and any woman who discovers a lump in her breast must seek medical aid *at once*.

Abscesses also occur in the breast, nearly always when the mother is feeding her child. Here again, a lump appears, the breast becomes red and very tender, and the woman may be feverish. Treatment with antibiotics is sometimes successful, especially if the mother consults her doctor quickly, otherwise treatment is by a small operation.

The Ovaries. The two commonest diseases of the ovaries are cysts and disorders arising from hormonal imbalance. The symptoms of ovarian disease are usually abdominal or low back pains, and heavy and painful loss during the periods, which may become irregular. These signs should be taken as a warning to consult a doctor.

The Fallopian Tubes. Infection of the Fallopian tubes is called salpingitis. The membrane lining the tubes is continuous with the lining of the uterus, hence an infection is rarely confined to a circumscribed area in either the tubes or the uterus, and pelvic inflammatory disease is a better name for this condition. Pelvic inflammatory disease often follows an abortion, or childbirth where part of the afterbirth (placenta) has been retained, or can spread from an infection in a nearby organ, for example the appendix. Infection is sometimes conveyed by the blood from another septic source in the body. The gonococcus is another cause of infection. The disease is characterised by pain and tenderness in the lower part of the abdomen, accompanied by fever, general malaise and frequently (but not invariably) a vaginal discharge. The treatment of pelvic inflammatory disease is usually medical and is the same irrespective of the primary site of infection. Before the introduction of antibiotics the disease often became chronic and the Fallopian tubes were frequently blocked by a cicatrising scar, a cause of subsequent sterility.

The Uterus. This is a hollow muscular organ and both its musculature and its lining membrane can be the site of disease. *Fibroids* are non-malignant muscular tumours which develop in many women. The main symptom is a heavy menstrual loss and surgical removal of the uterus (hysterectomy) is often necessary. This is a major operation, but modern anæsthesia and operative techniques minimise the discomfort. Hysterectomy does not impair sexual pleasure, but no more babies can be conceived. Infection of the lining of the uterus is usually part of a generalised pelvic inflammatory disease (*see* Fallopian tubes).

Cancer of the Uterus and Cervical Smears. The uterus is pear-shaped and consists of a body and neck. The wide end is uppermost (the body) and the narrow neck (cervix) projects into the top of the vagina. Cancer of the cervix is commonest in middle-aged women who have married young and have had a large family; cancer of the body of the uterus usually occurs after the menopause and is most common in childless women. The symptoms are variable and it is sufficient to emphasise that any woman who has unexpected bleeding, especially after intercourse, whether her periods have stopped or not, *must* see her doctor at once. The treatment depends on individual circumstances, but is usually by operation. It is now possible to detect cancer of the cervix long before symptoms develop and at a stage when the disease can be eradicated by a relatively small operation. This early detection has been made possible by the development of exfoliative cytology. Cells taken from the cervix (without discomfort to the woman) are examined under a microscope. This test is popularly known as the "cancer test" or "cervical smear." A cervical smear is often taken as part of the routine gynæcological examination by consultants, general practitioners, and family planning doctors, and is also being included in some population screening programmes. It is a big step forward in preventive medicine and may ultimately solve the problem of cancer of the cervix. Every woman between the ages of 25 and 60 should seize any chance to have this test done.

Prolapse means a sagging down of the uterus into the vagina and the cervix may even appear at the outside. It is a result of frequent childbirth and laxness of the ligaments which support the uterus: weakness of the vaginal walls often occurs at the same time. The symptoms of uterine prolapse are low back pain and a heavy dragging feeling in the lower abdomen: these are often overshadowed by the distressingly embarrassing incontinence which results from lax vaginal walls. The stress of only a sneeze, a cough, or a giggle often causes the involuntary escape of urine. The cure is operative and very rewarding.

Discharge (*Leucorrhœa*). A white discharge is called leucorrhœa. It is normal for a woman to have a white odourless discharge: medical help should be sought if a discharge becomes offensive, is unduly watery, is bloodstained or causes irritation. A discharge can originate in the Fallopian tubes and uterus, for example in pelvic inflammatory disease, but is more commonly due to an infection of the vagina by bacteria or fungi. A vaginal discharge causes the patient a great deal of discomfort and misery but as soon as the exact cause has been found treatment is speedily followed by cure.

The change of life or *Menopause* is the outward manifestation of a change in the hormonal balance in a woman's body: the periods stop and she can no longer conceive. Many women are very troubled at the prospect of the menopause, and this is not unnatural for nobody likes growing older. This natural apprehension is overlaid with all sorts of irrational fears largely based on "old wives' tales." Heavy losses of blood, growth of facial hair, depression, loss of sexual pleasure, and frequent hot flushes are not an inevitable burden. The commonest symptoms are hot flushes and depression, but both are usually rapidly relieved by small doses of hormones, especially if the woman consults her doctor when her symptoms first appear. At the menopause periods may stop rapidly or become irregular and finally cease: sometimes a woman misses one or more periods, then periods re-start and this cycle may be repeated several times before menstruation finally stops. The pattern at the menopause is as varied as woman herself—but if a woman has had no period for two years and then notices spotting or bleeding she should consult her doctor to make sure that all is well. The menopause has no influence whatever on sexual life (although naturally it has on fertility) and desire is not affected. It is recounted that a famous courtesan, at the age of 80, on being asked by Voltaire when women ceased to feel desire, replied, "I don't know—I haven't lived long enough."

Dysmenorrhœa or pain with the periods, is very common and most women experience this symptom at some time or another. Very often a girl's first periods are troublefree, but dysmenorrhœa develops after a year or two: this suggests that a psychological element is involved. Dysmenorrhœa is a symptom which has many varying causes, and the sensible thing to do, if pain is troublesome, is to see a doctor.

Amenorrhœa means stopping of the periods in a young woman. It may signify pregnancy or glandular disease or it can be purely psychological.

Abortion is a word which does not necessarily signify any criminal act, for abortion, or its more acceptable name, miscarriage, describes the spontaneous or induced termination of a pregnancy before the fœtus (baby) is able to survive. A baby cannot live unless it is born after the twenty-eighth week of pregnancy, though many infants born at this time die. The two main symptoms of abortion are bleeding and abdominal pain. Any bleeding occurring during pregnancy ought to be reported at once. Pain starts in the back and lower abdomen and is usually spasmodic in character, and like colic it works up to a peak and then temporarily passes off. Any pregnant woman with pain and bleeding should go to bed at once and send for her doctor. *Criminal abortion* is brought about deliberately either by the use of drugs or by injecting substances into the womb. Both these practices are extremely dangerous: there are no drugs which can produce an abortion without also endangering life, and an injection into the womb is likely to cause a serious infection (pelvic inflammatory disease) and sometimes death. The immediate risk to life and the not inconsiderable risk of sterility and chronic ill-health is too often the price of a criminal abortion: the price is too high and should never be paid. When doctors are convinced that a pregnancy may endanger the health of the mother then an abortion by safe surgical means may legally be performed in hospital.

CONTRACEPTION.

If a couple intends to practice birth control expert advice should be obtained from their family doctor or family planning clinic. The matter of whether or not a baby is born is too important to leave to chance. The method chosen must be effective as well as acceptable to the couple concerned, and the extent of the choice only emphasises the fact that the ideal contraceptive which is best for every couple at all times has yet to be discovered. The only method which is 100 per cent reliable is abstinence. If the male seed (sperm) fertilises the female seed (ovum) then pregnancy results. Contraception is only effective if this union is prevented. A couple can achieve a measure of contraception without the help of pills or appliances if the husband practices *coitus interruptus* or they rely on the wife's "safe period." *Coitus interruptus* (when the man withdraws before emission occurs) is a thoroughly unreliable method which often leads to psychological difficulties in both partners. The "rhythm" or "safe period" method relies on estimating the time of ovulation and abstaining from intercourse during this time. This is at best unreliable, though its effectiveness can be improved by keeping careful records of the body temperature on waking each morning as the temperature rises once ovulation has occurred. The interpretation of these temperature records needs care and couples who must rely on this method can obtain expert advice from, for example, The Catholic Marriage Advisory Council, or a family planning clinic. *Barrier methods* prevent the sperms from reaching the ovum and can be used by the man (sheath or condom) or woman (cap or diaphragm): the reliability of the barrier is greatly increased if it is used in conjunction with a spermicidal cream, jelly, or pessary. A great many women have found that the *oral contraceptive pill* is ideal for their needs: it is the mose æsthetic means of contraception and offers the most complete protection against pregnancy. Oral contraceptive pills contain chemical substances (œstrogen and progestagen) which replace the hormones normally released from the ovary while an ovum is developing. Ovulation does not occur, and without an ovum there can be no pregnancy. Pills must be taken strictly as directed as the dose is the lowest that will provide effective contraception and missing a tablet may result in pregnancy. Side effects sometimes occur (for example, nausea, breast discomfort, headaches,) but usually decrease after a few cycles of medication. Newspaper reports of the deaths of young women taking the pill have caused widespread concern. These tragedies have followed blockage of a blood vessel (by thrombosis or embolism) and have been carefully investigated, and the conclusions are that the number of such deaths is small and does not differ from the number which would probably have occurred in any case. No satisfactory pill for a man has yet been developed. In the newest method of contraception a small plastic *intra-uterine device* (loop, bow, or coil) is inserted into the womb. Once inserted it can be forgotten: a tremendous advantage to many different peoples and societies. It is not as effective as the pill but is more satisfactory than barrier methods. This intra-uterine device is not suitable for all women and is usually not recommended to women who have borne no children or who have very heavy periods. However, careful selection of suitable women has resulted in a high proportion of satisfied users. The search for the ideal contraceptive continues.

PART III. BABY CARE

The Health of the Mother.

The health of a baby during its early years of life is so bound up with the health of the mother that the two must be considered together. Indeed the intimate relationship which exists between the two before birth is, in normal circumstances, continued after birth and throughout the whole of the first year. It is therefore necessary to consider first the health of the mother before the birth of the child.

It has now been established beyond doubt that the health of the expectant and nursing mother affects profoundly the health and well-being of her infant. It is not merely a question of good bodily health. Mental contentment and freedom from anxiety are also important. It is necessary, therefore, to encourage a placid state of mind from the outset. This can best be done by making the arrangements for adequate care and supervision as early as possible. As soon, therefore, as pregnancy is suspected the mother should seek the advice of her family doctor.

When the pregnancy is confirmed the question whether to have the baby at home or in hospital must be decided. Much will depend on the opinion of the doctor, who may consider confinement in hospital advisable on medical grounds. Other considerations will also enter into this decision, such as the suitability of home conditions, the care of other children in the family, the availability of domestic help and so on. If it is decided to have the baby at home, arrangements must be made for securing the services of a midwife. The sooner these arrangements are made, and other matters such as the provision of home help and care for the other children decided, the sooner will the mother be able to settle contentedly to prepare for the baby. Subject to the advice given by the doctor and midwife the more natural the life the expectant mother lives the better.

Experience in a number of countries, including Great Britain, in the Second World War, confirmed the view that the nutrition of the expectant mother is of vital importance, both to her own health and to that of the baby. That is so throughout pregnancy, and especially in the earlier months. From the moment that pregnancy is diagnosed, therefore, it is essential that the mother should have a good and varied diet, with plenty of fruit, salads, and vegetables, in addition to fresh meat and fish, milk, butter, eggs, and cheese, for it is from these materials that the essential proteins, the fats, carbohydrates, and mineral salts required by the developing infant are drawn. Adequate supplies of vitamins are also required, especially when the baby is growing rapidly in the later months of pregnancy, and these are usually supplied in the form of cod-liver oil or halibut-liver oil which contains vitamins A and D, and fresh orange or tomato juice or concentrated orange juice, rose-hip syrup, blackcurrant syrup, etc., which contain vitamin C. Multi-vitamin preparations containing a number of vitamins may be taken on the recommendation of the doctor or welfare centre.

Mineral salts, and especially calcium and iron, are essential for both the mother and the child, especially during lactation. Calcium is supplied naturally by means of milk, cheese, and vegetables, and iron by way of green vegetables, egg yolk, liver, peas, beans and lentils, oatmeal, and wholemeal flour.

The old tradition that the expectant mother should attempt to eat enough for two people is, of course, a fallacy. A good, well-nourishing diet taken at regular meal-times is all that is required. Similarly, the other elementary principles of healthy living should be followed, with adequate fresh air, exercise and sleep, and a rest during the day. Before attempting anything exceptional, such as hard exercise or swimming, medical advice should be taken.

Medical Services.

It is no part of these notes to describe the arrangements for the confinement, but it is obvious that this will be made much easier if adequate preparation has been made. The expectant mother should therefore make sure that she is getting all the help which the health and welfare services can give. These services are now very extensive, and they are available to everyone. Under the National Health Service, for example, the help and advice of a doctor and midwife are freely available, and so also are the welfare clinics of the local authority and the expert care of the hospitals.

The Local Health Authorities now provide a free ambulance service for those who may need it, and also a home help service whereby a helper experienced in the running of a home can come to assist the family during the time of confinement, and also if necessary during the nursing period. Local Health Authorities may make a charge for this home-help service.

If there are other young children in the family it may be possible to make use of day or residential nurseries where these are provided by the Local Health Authority, and old people in the house may be encouraged to go to an old people's club during the day or be found temporary residential accommodation elsewhere. In making these arrangements the advice of the health visitor will be valuable. Local Health Authorities are empowered, under the National Health Service Act, to provide nursing equipment and additional comforts in the home. These may take the form of bedding and blankets, and nursing equipment may include such items as bed-pans, macintosh sheeting, air-rings, and bed cradles. Local authorities can make a charge for lending this equipment. Another helpful provision is that of a recuperative holiday after confinement.

It goes without saying that regular examinations of the expectant mother's health should be made, and these ante-natal examinations may be carried out by the general practitioner, at the welfare centre, or at hospital. Similarly, an examination to detect that no minor disability remains as a result of the confinement is also essential to prevent subsequent ill-health. This post-natal examination, which is usually made about six weeks after the confinement, may be undertaken by the family doctor or at the welfare clinic or the hospital.

General Preparation.

Two of the important things to prepare in advance are the baby's clothing, and equipment and furniture.

Clothes have undergone revolutionary changes in the past thirty years. Whereas it was formerly the fashion to provide elaborate sets of clothing, often in three or four layers, the objective to-day is to provide the simplest and lightest clothes which will keep the baby warm and comfortable and at the same time allow free movement and exercise. It is essential to remember when buying or making baby's clothes, and also later on when washing them, that a baby's skin is very sensitive and liable to chafe easily. The under-garments must be of soft and fine material that will wash and wear well, and the layer next to the baby's skin should be the same in summer and in winter and night as well as day. A common mistake is to put too many clothes on the body. A baby loses heat quickly from the whole skin, including the legs, and in cold weather the legs should be covered. The old tradition of wearing bonnets is now nearly dead. Provided that the baby is not directly exposed to draughts and keen winds, there is no need to wear any head covering except in very cold weather, when a woollen bonnet which covers the ears should be worn out of doors.

Vests should be of soft, fine wool, silk or silk merino, and long enough in the body to ensure that there is no gap between vest and napkin. A wide piece of tape can be sewn to the bottom of the front of the vest so that the napkin can be pinned to the vest without tearing it. The neck of the vest should be wide enough to go over the baby's head without force.

Napkins are usually of two kinds; soft muslin squares to be worn next to the skin, and turkish towelling worn over these as an added protection. The various ways of putting on and changing napkins are best learnt by demonstration by the midwife or at the clinic.

In cold weather the baby will need, in addition to vest and napkin, a woollen jersey and knickers and good woollen socks long enough to reach almost to the knee. As woollen socks are easily kicked off they should be drawn in by a ribbon and tied above the ankle. In really cold weather a long-sleeved double-breasted matinee coat of wool should be worn.

In hot weather the baby may need only vest and napkin, but care must be taken to add clothes as soon as it turns cooler. Incidentally it is wiser not to speak of summer and winter clothes when dealing with young children. In the British Isles, at any rate, a winter day can be warm and cold spells occur in the summer. If the system is adopted of adding warm garments to the foundation of vest and napkin according to the temperature indoors or outdoors, the child will be most comfortable. In this, as in all other matters relating to the care of the baby, common sense plays a very large part.

Bibs are needed to save the clothes when the child dribbles or regurgitates its food after feeding. They should be of soft, absorbent material, such as drill or cotton, with tapes to tie round the neck and the waist. Bibs made of plastic material are not recommended, as they may cover the child's face if he falls asleep, and a young baby was stifled in this manner not long ago.

Binders are *not* necessary after the first ten days of the baby's life. Once the stump of the umbilical cord has separated and the scar at the navel has healed the binder should be discarded.

The equipment and furniture required are simple and will vary with the type of home and financial circumstances, but the underlying principles are the same for all homes. The first essential is cleanliness. This means not only provision for bathing the baby, but also facilities for washing the baby's clothes and napkins, and for the clean preparation of the baby's food and clean surroundings generally. It is essential also that the mother should be able to see to her own cleanliness and in particular the care of her clothes and hands.

A low chair on which the mother can sit to nurse and bath the baby is useful, and this can be improvised by cutting down an ordinary wooden chair. It can be painted a bright colour and it should be scrubbed at regular intervals—for example, once a month.

The cot for the young baby can, if necessary, be improvised from such things as a wicker basket. During the late war, cots were even improvised from orange boxes! It is, however, worth while to buy a wicker cradle and later a large dropside cot, as this will last well into infancy. A point to be remembered about cots and also about play-pens is that the bars should not be more than 3 inches apart, so that the baby cannot get his head through. Also there should be no collapsible parts which can suddenly give way and trap the fingers.

Bedding for the cot will include a blanket to go under the mattress. Next comes the under-blanket on top of the mattress. Over this comes the macintosh or other waterproof material with the flannelette drawsheet over it. The baby is wrapped in a shawl or soft blanket and covered with a top blanket. An extra blanket may be needed in cold weather. Many leading authorities on baby care recommend that a pillow should never be used, and certainly not a soft pillow, for babies have been known to be suffocated by these. When discussing later on the preparation of food, the washing of the baby and the washing of baby's clothes, reference will be made to some other items of equipment required.

With quiet and orderly preparation for the coming of the baby, pregnancy can be a very happy time. Indeed, that is what Nature intended it to be, and most women are never so well as during the months of pregnancy.

The Health of the Baby.

So far these notes have dealt primarily with the health of the mother. Independent life begins for the baby from the moment he is born. The stimulus of the external air makes him draw his first breath, and immediately his own circulation replaces that of the mother on which he has been dependent for the past nine months. But a new association begins. It is the baby's birth-right that he should be nursed and fed by his mother, and the intimate relations which exist between mother and baby render them, in effect, one person for nearly the whole of the first year of life. The more the mother knows about babies in general, and her own baby in particular, the better.

Care of the Newly Born Baby.

This is, of course, the province of the midwife, who, in addition to cleaning the eyes and freeing the mouth from mucus, will bath the baby and wrap him up carefully to prevent chilling. After weighing, the baby is put into his cot while the midwife looks after the mother.

The Cord. Before birth the baby gets his nourishment from the mother through a cord which enters his body at the navel and at the other end is fixed to a large sponge-like structure (the placenta) attached to the inner wall of the mother's womb. Although the bloods of mother and baby do not intermingle, oxygen and nutritive substances in the mother's blood pass via the placenta into the baby's circulation and waste products are transferred from the fœtus to the mother's blood. The baby is part of the mother. That is one reason why the expectant mother should not over-indulge in tobacco or alcohol!

Directly after birth the midwife or doctor ties off the cord and the stump falls off in about seven days. The scar at the navel heals about the tenth day. If strict cleanliness is not observed in handling the baby during that time the cord stump may become septic and the baby's life be endangered. The directions of the doctor and midwife must therefore be followed carefully.

Weight and Length. The weight at birth varies usually between 6½ and 8 lb. It is sometimes as high as 10 lb. or as low as 5 lb. Boys usually weigh more than girls; the length of a baby at birth is usually 19 to 20 in.

The premature baby is not necessarily one which is born before the end of the normal pregnancy, and often babies born three weeks before they are expected are normal in size and do not require special care. The newly born baby weighing less than 5½ lb. is usually regarded as premature and treated accordingly. Premature babies have not got the natural resistance of the normal baby and require special care. For example, the results of a cold or influenza, or any septic infection, are more serious in these babies, and it is therefore necessary to exercise strict watch over them and keep them apart from other children and adults. Again, the body temperature of these babies is often low and requires to be kept up to normal by artificial means, such as hot bottles and extra clothing or electric blankets. Some babies are so small and delicate that they have to be nursed in an incubator. Premature babies are difficult to feed and they do not suck so vigorously as a normal infant. On the other hand, it is even more important that they should be breast-fed, if possible, than with normal infants. Extra care is therefore necessary with the premature infant, and many Local Health Authorities have arrangements for nursing these babies either at hospital or at home with a specially experienced nurse. It is important to remember that premature babies need special attention throughout the first year of life, for if neglected they are especially liable to bronchitis and pneumonia. The care taken by health and hospital authorities to save such babies is well worth while, for once they pass the critical early months they develop fully, both in mind and body, into normal healthy people.

The Skin. At birth the skin of a baby is red and covered with a protective fatty substance which comes off with the first bath; the redness persists for a few days. The skin of a baby is extremely delicate and needs very careful attention. This will be emphasised later when the question of washing and bathing is considered.

The Head of the new-born baby may look a little out of shape. This is because of the pressure during birth and it rapidly becomes normal. The bones of the skull are separated from each other in the new-born baby, and on the middle of the top of the head there are two diamond-shaped soft spaces where the skull bones meet. The space towards the front of the top of the head is known as the anterior fontanelle, and the doctor and midwife often gain useful information on the child's condition from the bulging or depression of this area. The other opening towards the back of the skull is smaller and is known as the posterior fontanelle. This closes in six or eight weeks, but the anterior fontanelle remains open for about eleven to eighteen months.

Chest and Abdomen. No special comment is needed concerning the chest of the baby, but the abdomen is normally more prominent than in older children. This is due partly to the very large liver of the young baby and also to the fact that the stomach stretches to take in as much as 3 or 4 oz. of milk at one feed.

Nervous system. Even a newly born baby can grasp an object and hold it. It can also suck and swallow from birth, but the special senses are not well developed. Loud noises will startle the baby, but he cannot at first recognise where a particular noise comes from. Babies are particularly sensitive to bright lights, but for some time cannot properly control the movements of the eyes and head so as to be able to gaze steadily at anything. The sense of smell and taste develop in a few days. Movements of arms and legs are not co-ordinated at first, but at the end of the third or fourth month of life the child can usually hold up his head. At the end of five or six months the baby makes an attempt to sit up, although this may be delayed until the seventh or eighth month. By the ninth month the child begins to crawl and can usually stand at the end of ten months. At twelve or fourteen months he walks. The young baby is very sensitive to his surroundings. If these are unfamiliar he may, for example, refuse to feed. Also if the mother or a relative is nervous in handling him he will immediately become frightened. It is therefore very important to learn how to handle a baby properly and firmly so as to gain and hold the child's confidence.

Speech. Sounds are made a few weeks after birth, but single words are only said towards the end of the first year. Real talk does not occur until about twenty months or two years.

The Teeth. One of the reasons why it is important to ensure the adequate nutrition of the mother during pregnancy is that the infant's first, or milk teeth, are developing at this time, so that they are already present within the gums at birth. They appear through the gums in the following order :—

Lower central incisors .	5th to 6th month
Upper central and outer incisors	7th to 8th month
Lower outer incisors .	10th to 12th month
First molars . . .	14th to 16th month
Canine teeth (eye teeth) .	17th to 18th month
Second molars . . .	24th to 30th month

Although there are wide variations in the time of appearance of teeth, eight teeth should be present by the end of the first year, and all twenty of the milk teeth by the end of the second year.

The prevention of dental decay depends, therefore, partly on the good nutrition of the mother, but also on freedom from illness of the infant, especially one which affects the intake of food for any length of time. The preservation of the teeth depends on the presence of an adequate supply of mineral salts, and especially calcium, and also of vitamin D. Exercise for the jaws by the gnawing of hard crusts, or rusks, is also necessary.

General Management.

It is important to have a clear idea of the needs of the young baby, in order that a regular routine may be worked out which will place the least strain on the mother and give the baby the maximum degree of comfort and security. It is also necessary to know where to turn for guidance and advice in a difficulty. The family doctor is, of course, the stand-by in emergency and if illness is suspected. He is, however, a very busy man, and the young mother may not want to worry him with enquiries which, although important to her, are relatively trivial to him. The midwife, the health visitor, the home nurse, and the Welfare Centre are all available to advise. When in doubt do not hesitate to ask for advice. The mere sharing of an anxiety with another is helpful.

The baby's material requirements are simple. They are food, cleanliness, warmth, and sleep and, above all, an orderly routine.

The Daily Routine.

Opinion varies as to the frequency of baths for the newly-born infants, but it is now a common practice to bath the baby immediately after birth, and then to leave him until the stump of the cord has separated, at the seventh to the tenth day, the skin being cleaned, when necessary, with olive oil.
After this time the baby will take a bath each day.

A baby's skin is very sensitive and will quickly chafe and get sore if roughly handled. It is therefore necessary to exercise the greatest care in the choice of materials used for washing and in the handling and drying of the skin. Great care should be taken to select the finest soap and the softest of washing flannels or sponges. Towels must be soft, dry, and clean, so that the skin can be dried thoroughly by gentle rubbing. Gentle handling is particularly necessary for the creases of the skin and behind the ears. Some experts say that powder is unnecessary after bathing, but there is little doubt that a good dusting powder helps to preserve and soothe the baby's skin and to keep it dry.

If the skin becomes inflamed and sore expert advice should be sought, as the baby is very susceptible to septic infections which can enter through small abrasions or cracks in the skin.

Sun and Air.

Many skin conditions in infancy, and indeed other illnesses, are predisposed to either by neglect or excessive care. Leaving the baby to lie in wet and dirty napkins is one example, and at the other extreme is the failure to allow free access of air and sunlight to the skin by over clothing. The human skin has many important functions, including the maintenance of the temperature of the body, and it is also concerned with the manufacture of vitamin D by the action of sunlight on the skin. It is therefore essential that the body should obtain a reasonable amount of fresh air and sunlight.

Sore Buttocks. The best way to prevent a baby from developing soreness of the skin of the buttocks is early training in clean habits, as in many instances the inflammation of the skin is due to irritation set up by the child's urine or motions. Obviously a clean dry napkin will not cause this soreness, and the well-trained child soon learns to keep clean and dry. Accidents will, of course, happen and some little upset in the diet may cause frequent stools. It is therefore essential to change the napkins regularly and to clean the buttocks thoroughly after a motion. All fæcal matter should be removed with cotton wool swabs (which are put immediately into the "dirty" bucket), and the buttocks are then cleaned gently with warm water, dried and powdered. If the skin is red and sore, olive oil may be used for cleaning instead of water, and zinc and castor oil ointment or cold cream instead of powder. If the soreness is marked the daily bath can be stopped for a day or two, but expert advice should be sought if it does not clear up quickly.

Care of the Clothes.

Apart from the fact that every mother likes her baby to look clean and neat it is essential to keep the clothes clean because of the sensitiveness of the young infant to infection of all kinds. Cracks or abrasions of the skin may turn septic if dirt comes in contact with them, and dirty clothes or towels are particularly liable to cause infections of this kind. Apart from this, badly washed clothes may also set up inflammation of the skin by being hard, and thereby chafing the skin, or because irritating fatty acids from the wrong kind of soap have not been completely rinsed out. The first essential is therefore to wash all articles which may come into contact with the baby regularly and frequently

The mother must see that her own clothes and body are clean and in particular that her hands are washed thoroughly before the baby is handled. Her aprons and overalls should be washed frequently and discarded at once if soiled. This is particularly important if soiling takes place when the baby's napkins are changed.

Towels must be clean, soft, and thoroughly dry, before they are used.

Flannels and sponges should be washed frequently in hot water and thoroughly rinsed free of soap. Face flannels should be boiled once a week

Napkins require special care. They should first be sluiced under running water to wash out all solid matter, and then left in a bucket of cold water until ready for washing. Washing should be done in warm water with a good soap lather with thorough rubbing, and rinsed in several lots of water until all the soap is rinsed out. After wringing they are hung up to dry. Drying should not take place too quickly, as the napkins will then be hard. For this reason it is best to dry them out of doors. Mangling will help to make the napkins soft after drying.

Baby s Clothes. Different materials require different methods of washing, but the principles set out above hold good for all clothes. The washing must be thorough, in water which is hot enough to enable dirt to be removed but not so hot that the clothes cannot be well cleaned by hand. It is particularly necessary to see that neck and cuffs are cleaned properly, and the same comment applies to the lower edge of the vest which may be soiled from the napkin.

Bibs should be boiled at regular intervals, as they are liable to get smelly from regurgitated milk.

Sleep.

If a baby is warm and comfortable and well fed its natural reaction is to sleep. The newborn infant sleeps for eighteen to twenty hours each day, waking only to be fed, and even at twelve months he will require fourteen or fifteen hours sleep each day. Sound sleep is essential to good health, and bad management of the young baby may result in faulty habits which last throughout life. Thus undue excitement before being put down to sleep, or irregular hours, may sow the seeds of insomnia. Ideally the baby should be made so comfortable that he will sleep from ten o'clock at night until six o'clock the next morning, but hunger may prevent this, and feeds may require to be re-arranged accordingly.

Restless sleep, with sudden nervous starts, is not a normal condition, and expert advice should be sought if this persists. A common cause is some digestive upset, such as colic or constipation, and coughs and colds also disturb the normal sleep rhythm, especially if there is a rise of temperature. It may then take a few days for the normal sleep habit to return.

Crying.

It is normal for the young baby to cry, and a lusty yell is a good way to expand the lungs. Attacks of crying and screaming do not always signify pain or colic. Although it is a mistake to pick up a baby every time he cries, it is necessary to exclude sources of discomfort, such as hunger, a wet napkin, colic, constipation, and pain. Apart from these, the child may quite easily get into the habit of crying, or the baby, even the very young baby, may realise that he can readily attract attention by a display of tears or temper and thus be spoilt. It is advisable to seek expert advice if the fits of crying persist without apparent cause.

Care of the Mouth, Nose, and Ears.

Common sense applies in the cleanliness of the mouth, nose, and ears, just as in all other matters relating to the care of the baby. The lining of the mouth is very delicate and easily scratched It should not, therefore, be cleaned. Indeed, any attempt to clean the mouth may result in an infection which will result in difficulty in feeding and fretfulness. As mentioned earlier, the nostril must be cleaned regularly, but this only means th entrance to the nostrils. Sneezing and discomfort are caused if the cotton wool is pushed up too far. The cotton wool swabs used to clean the nose should be moistened in warm water and twisted to a point. The ears may also be cleaned gently in the same manner as the nostrils, but no attempt to remove dirt or wax with a solid instrument, like a match-stick or hair-pin, must be made. Permanent injury to the ear-drum and hearing may easily result.

Breast-feeding.

Every baby has the right to expect that his mother will feed him herself. That is the natural way and has advantages to both mother and baby. The baby gets the best possible food without any of the risks of contamination that may occur with the preparation of artificial food. The temperature of breast milk is that of the infant's body and it contains various protective substances which help to shield the baby from infection.

The mother, for her part, has the satisfaction of knowing that she is " mothering " her baby in the fullest sense. Incidentally, breast-feeding costs nothing, whereas artificial feeding can be quite an expensive matter. There are certain medical conditions where a mother should not feed her baby herself, but they are very few in number.

As in everything else in life confidence arises from the knowledge of the right way to do a thing. Breast-feeding is no exception to this rule, but it is particularly important that the mother should have full confidence in her ability to feed the baby, as any nervousness and anxiety on her part are soon transmitted to the child. This is one of the reasons why regular visits should be made during pregnancy to the doctor or clinic, in order that the mother's general health may be investigated and such important details as the care of the nipples attended to. The midwife will see that a regular routine is taught during the first fortnight of the baby's life, so that by the time the mother assumes full responsibility for the baby she will have had quite a lot of experience.

The general rules are, of course, quite simple. A regular routine is desirable both for the sake of mother and baby. The latter must be able to have his food at the same times each day, and the regular routine helps the mother to lead her normal life. The mother will already have had instruction on the care of the breasts, and in particular the preparation of the nipples so that they will not become tender when the baby starts feeding. The next essential is, of course, cleanliness. The nipples must be carefully washed before and after feeding and particular care should be taken in drying after feeding, as a little crack or fissure in the skin of the nipple, in addition to causing pain and discomfort, may let organisms enter to cause a breast abscess.

The third essential is to persevere. Many young mothers get discouraged at what proves to be in fact only a temporary upset. For example, the baby with a cold in the nose has difficulty in breathing and feeding at the same time, but a little patience will soon ensure that he does not suffer, by taking a little longer at each feed.

The last great requisite is calmness. Breast-feeding is a natural process, and countless millions of women have successfully fed their babies since the world began. It is not therefore a matter for nervous speculation and anticipation. Any nervousness or sense of strain on the part of the mother is quickly felt by the infant, who will in turn be restless and irritable. A comfortable position in quiet surroundings, and a regular routine, will ensure that the baby can give his entire attention to feeding, and the supply of milk almost invariably keeps pace with the demand. If any little anxiety or doubt arises in the mother's mind she should seek competent advice and not listen to " old wives' tales." The doctor, midwife, or health visitor, are the best people to advise.

Weaning.

No sensible grown-up person would contemplate changing suddenly from a normal diet to one entirely different. In the same way, weaning should be a gradual process. Between the sixth and twelfth month of life the baby will be changing from four-hourly feeds to the " three good meals a day " routine which he will hope to continue for the rest of his life. To begin with, therefore, it will be natural to change his diet by altering *one* of his feeds, for example that at 10 a.m. This may be at first one of the recognised proprietary milk foods, and later such items as milk pudding, potato and gravy, and green vegetables, may be given. From the sixth month onwards, the baby will want to nibble a rusk or hard-baked crust, which may be smeared with butter, egg, honey, etc. It is not necessary to continue breast-feeding beyond the ninth month and many mothers stop earlier. Much depends on the health and energy of the mother. Generally speaking she should try and continue breast-feeding during the hot weather and not wean until the autumn. By this means the anxiety of protecting the baby's food from contamination during the summer months is avoided. It is also inadvisable to wean if the baby is suffering from illness. It is much better to continue with breast-feeding until he is well. It is sometimes necessary suddenly to wean a baby. For example, the illness of the mother may make this imperative. In that event expert advice should be taken, as the sudden transfer to an unsuitable food may upset the baby's digestion. Again, the amounts of food taken by different babies vary very much, and one may take several ounces more than another in the course of twenty-four hours. It may therefore be necessary to try different kinds and amounts of artificial food before the right one is found, and expert advice on this is most helpful.

Artificial Feeding.

It would be unwise in these notes to attempt to describe the various kinds of artificial food for a baby. Babies vary in their likes and dislikes from one to another just as grown up people do. The basis of artificial food is cow's milk modified in various ways. Very few infants will tolerate whole cow's milk as the amounts and nature of the fat, sugar, and protein, are different from human milk. Expert advice should be sought on the best type of artificial food for the baby, but there are certain fundamental rules which must be followed in all cases. In addition to the essentials already set out for breast-feeding, namely, a regular routine, quiet surroundings, and personal care all the time the baby is being fed, particular attention must he paid to cleanliness. It is very easy to contaminate the baby's food in the course of artificial feeding and infections caused in this way may prove to be serious.

First, the mother must make sure that her own hands are clean by scrubbing with soap and water and drying on a clean towel before each feed is prepared. This precaution is particularly necessary if the mother or one of the other members of the family has an intestinal upset, such as diarrhœa. Next, the room in which the food is prepared must be scrupulously clean and free from dust and dirt. The outside of tins and containers must be cleaned before they are opened and so must the table or tray on which the food is kept. Much time is saved by neat and methodical preparation. If everything required is kept always in the same place, and used articles are cleaned and replaced immediately, the risk of contamination by constant handling of unnecessary articles is thereby reduced. Saucepans and bowls and basins must also be absolutely clean, but the most frequent source of infection is in the feeding-bottles and teats. If these are not cleaned properly after each feed the film of milk left behind makes an ideal breeding-ground for bacteria. Feeding-bottles should be washed after each feed, rinsed, and kept in cold boiled water until required again. They should also be boiled for five or ten minutes every twenty-four hours. Teats should be turned inside out and cleaned thoroughly after each feed, and boiled once a day in water to which a little salt has been added: the salt helps to preserve the rubber. Between feeds they also should be kept in cold boiled water.

It is advisable to boil all milk for babies, especially in hot weather. Indeed, where there are no proper facilities for keeping fresh milk, it may be wiser to use dried milk in very hot weather. It is also essential to see that jugs and bottles containing milk are securely covered to keep out dust and flies.

The actual feeding of the infant should follow the same routine as for breast-feeding. The baby feeds best when he is quiet and comfortable, and the napkin should therefore be changed before feeding. In no circumstances must the baby be given a bottle and left to his own devices. The mother should stay during the whole feed and hold the bottle herself. Only by this means can the little encouragement and attention which mean so much to the health of the infant be given.

Vitamins.

Milk, fruit, and vegetables make the basis of the baby's diet, but by the age of nine months he is able to digest tender and finely divided meat, and also fish. At this age all fruits can be eaten, but fruit with pips and skins, *e.g.*, black and red currants and gooseberries, require to be strained and given in the form of gooseberry fool, etc.

Similarly, all vegetables can be taken, provided that they are young and tender and well cooked, and small amounts of lettuce, carrot, and other salads can be given, provided that they are finely divided.

It is essential to ensure that the infant receives an adequate supply of vitamins, especially in the winter. This may be done by adding fresh or concentrated orange juice or rose-hip syrup, and cod-liver oil or halibut-liver oil, to the diet, or by means of vitamin concentrates. It is advisable to take expert advice on the most suitable way of supplementing the vitamin content of the diet especially following an infection, for coughs, colds, and other infections, tend rapidly to lower the reserves of vitamins in the body.

Foods containing iron include green vegetables, and bone and vegetable broths. Calcium, so important for bone formation, is supplied with the milk in the diet.

The Symptoms and Signs of Ill-health.

It is, of course, essential to seek advice immediately illness is suspected. The signs and symptoms of illness in the baby are not so clearly defined as in grown-ups, nor can the baby tell where he has pain or discomfort. Again, anxiety or doubt in the mother's mind is best shared with an expert as soon as possible. The following notes may, however, serve as a guide in interpreting some early departures from the normal.

Temperature. A young child will often develop a rise of temperature for no apparent reason, as the mechanism for controlling the heat of the body is not so well regulated as in older people. A slight temporary rise in temperature may not therefore be so significant as in older children, but if at the same time the child is restless, irritable and "off his food," it should not be neglected. The thermometer should be placed under the armpit with the arm held closely to the side, or in the fold of the groin with the legs held closely together. As the skin temperature is a little lower than the body temperature it should be kept in position for five minutes before reading the result. The normal temperature is 98·4° F. *See also* **P9**.

General Appearance. The mother will be able to tell when a child is ailing, as she sees the baby constantly. Restlessness, irritability, pallor or undue flush, sweating, crying and unusual movements or positions, may all give an indication that the child is unwell. Colic, or vomiting and diarrhœa or constipation, may also help to show abnormalities.

Restlessness and disturbed sleep in a baby who had previously been sleeping and eating well are obviously indications that there is something not quite right. This is especially the case if at the same time there are other symptoms, such as sweating and a rise in temperature. Lying in an abnormal position, or the development of rigidity in the back or neck, should be enough to seek expert advice at once.

The Air Passages. The common cold may be quite a serious matter in the young baby. In addition to making him feverish and fretful it interferes with his feeding because the nose is stuffed up. A cold in the head should not be treated lightly and every effort should be made to keep away people who have a cold so that the baby does not catch it. When nursing a child with a simple cold make sure that he has plenty of fresh air. A stuffy atmosphere delays recovery, and the child will come to no harm if he is warmly clad. Patience in feeding is required, as he will need frequent rests to get his breath. Plenty of warm, sweetened, boiled water will help to relieve thirst. The nostrils should be kept clean and soreness prevented by lightly rubbing vaseline round the nose and upper lip.

Cough and Shortness of Breath. If the baby develops cough, and shortness of breath, expert advice should be sought at once. There is, of course no need to assume that the child has some serious condition such as pneumonia. Probably he has some simple condition which will get better in a few days with expert treatment. On the other hand, it would be sheer stupidity not to take advice, as even a simple bronchitis can cause the baby distress and interfere considerably with his feeding.

Refusal of Food. A young child refuses food either because he does not want it, or he is "full up," or because he is not feeling well, or because he is feeling cantankerous and is "playing up" in consequence. The first and last reasons are soon cured by hunger, but the onset of illness, and especially the early stages of infection, are not easy to detect, and it is inadvisable to delay too long before seeking advice.

Vomiting and Diarrhœa occurring together should lead the mother to seek advice at once, particularly if this happens during the hot weather and other cases are known to have occurred in the neighbourhood.

Vomiting without Diarrhœa. It is normal for the child to regurgitate a little food after feeding particularly if he has had too much. Again he may bring up a little milk with the wind, but the vomiting of sour curdled milk is not a normal event. Persistent vomiting, particularly if "explosive," or not related to food, will need expert advice, as it may be the first symptom of illness.

Diarrhœa. Slight changes from the normal, righting themselves in a few hours, are only to be expected from time to time. If diarrhœa persists, and particularly if the child is also out of sorts, expert advice must be taken. A change of colour of the motions from orange-yellow to a green slimy stool is an indication for seeking advice at once. In any attack of diarrhœa, however slight, particular attention should be paid to the skin of the buttocks, as this readily becomes inflamed and sore. The treatment for sore buttocks is described earlier in this article.

Constipation is not a cause for anxiety unless it is persistent, or the child is ill in other respects. In fact many babies tend to be constipated. Drastic measures are not called for. It is, of course, essential to persevere with the regular routine each day in order that regular habits may be acquired. The first essential in treatment is to see that the baby is getting enough food, and adequate exercise, together with plenty of sweetened water, or fruit juice and water to drink. Constipation is more frequent in the older infant who is taking mixed or artificial food, and he can be given such simple (and usually effective) remedies as a teaspoonful of prune juice or a teaspoonful of honey in warm water. Persistent constipation requires expert advice, and remedies such as glycerin suppositories or enemas should not be given without that advice.

Feeding Troubles. In addition to the above indications of ill-health there are other signs and symptoms which help to show when the baby is not feeding properly. Distention and discomfort may be indications that all is not normal. Some distention after a feed is not abnormal, but it should subside before the next feed. Persistent distention, especially if it is increasing, should lead the mother to seek expert advice.

Discomfort after feeding is not normal. It may vary from mild restlessness and fretfulness to attacks of colic with screaming and the legs drawn up. Examination of the motions may show that they are loose and green or contain white undigested lumps, in which case expert advice should be sought.

Failure to Gain Weight and Wasting. It is essential to remember that babies are not machine made. Therefore they vary from one to another. One may be big and sturdy with a loud cry and a lusty appetite. Another may be small and quiet with only slow gain in weight. Too much attention must not be paid, therefore, to the weighing machine. If the baby is placid, healthy, and sleeping well, the fact that he is not gaining rapidly in weight does not matter. If, on the other hand, the child looks tired and thin with sunken eyes and the fontanelle on top of the head drawn in, expert advice must be sought. If he also has diarrhœa and is irritable or apathetic, then expert advice should be sought immediately.

Teething. There is no doubt that teething causes temporary disturbances in most babies, but it is important that illness due to other causes should not be dismissed as teething trouble. It is safer, therefore, to assume that any illness is not due to teething and to seek advice. The kinds of disturbance that may occur in teething are local and general. The local symptoms are pain in the mouth with sore and inflamed gums. The child resents any attempt to see the teeth. There may also be dribbling, and enlargement of the glands in the neck. The general symptoms may include a tendency to eczema, and bronchitis, and nervous symptoms, such as fretfulness, irritability, sleeplessness and convulsions. Expert advice should be sought for such conditions as eczema, bronchitis or convulsions. Beyond this no treatment is required except patience and watchful care. Common sense will show the wisdom of studying the child's needs for soft and easily digested food, and avoiding hard crusts and rusks until the tooth is through.

Convulsions. The occurrence of convulsions is a danger signal indicating the need for immediate medical advice. In many instances the cause and the remedy are simple, such as faulty feeding with insufficient vitamins in the diet. On the other hand, they may be an indication of the onset of an acute infection, or some other condition requiring careful investigation. Fortunately convulsions are rarely fatal, and the first-aid treatment is to put the baby in his cot in a quiet corner of the room and send at once for the doctor.

Head Injuries. Babies and young children can fall in the most alarming manner without sustaining anything more serious than a bruise. If, however, following a head injury, the baby is pale and drowsy with vomiting, then expert advice must be sought immediately.

Prevention of Accidents.

Each year about 6,000 people die, in England and Wales alone, as the result of accidents in the home. More than one-quarter of these are children under the age of fifteen, and between the ages of one and five years a fatal accident in the home is the third most frequent cause of death. Many of these are either due to accidental suffocation or to burns and scalds.

Down pillows for small babies were formerly a common cause of suffocation. Burns and scalds may result from an unguarded fire, or one in which the fire-guard is faulty. Electric flex with worn insulation is a particular danger to the toddler, for he may fall over it, or get an electric shock if he plays with it. A saucepan handle put within easy reach of the child, or an over-hanging table-cloth with a tea-pot on the edge of the table, may result in a bad scald if the child can reach to pull it down.

Medicines or garden chemicals, etc., left lying about may tempt the child to eat them, and in this connection it should be remembered that young children are more susceptible to poisons than adults.

Finally, a very young child, like an old person, falls readily, and care should be taken not to put obstacles in its path, such as a loose mat on a slippery floor, or a worn carpet with loose strands.

The young baby should be so well protected that accidents do not happen, but they do sometimes occur, even in the best regulated families! The first essential is, of course, prevention, and the wise parent will look carefully round the rooms in which the baby lives to see that all fires are protected by guards, electric light and power flexes and switches are not exposed, and that hot kettles and taps are out of reach. The table must be so laid that sharp knives cannot be touched and table-cloths cannot be pulled, and tea-pots, and other vessels containing hot liquids, thereby spilled over the infant.

Protection against Smallpox, Diphtheria, Whooping Cough, and Poliomyelitis.

Smallpox is now rare in the British Isles because of the care taken at the sea and airports to keep it out of the country, and because vaccination prevents it from spreading if it is introduced. It is a very serious disease with a high mortality, particularly in young children.

Although compulsory vaccination has been abolished it is still essential that every baby should be vaccinated. This can be done either by the family doctor or at the Welfare Centre.

Diphtheria, Whooping Cough, and Poliomyelitis. During the late war the diphtheria immunisation campaign was so successful that the number of cases and the deaths from diphtheria were reduced beyond all expectation. Diphtheria remains, however, a very serious disease and the baby must be protected against it. Immunisation is a simple procedure and does not leave any after-effects. It can be done by the family doctor or at the Welfare Centre. It is now possible to immunise also against whooping cough, and poliomyelitis, and it is a wise precaution to take medical advice on protection against these serious diseases.

PART IV. INDEX AND GLOSSARY

Abdomen. The part of the body below the chest and above the thighs.

Abortion. The termination of pregnancy, from whatever cause, before the child is capable of independent existence, 56 (1).

Abortus fever. An infectious disease known as undulant fever, 15 (1).

Abrasion. Any injury which rubs off the surface skin.

Abscess. A collection of pus enclosed anywhere in the body.

Acidity. *See under* **Peptic ulcer**, 34 (2).

Acne, 53 (1).

Acromegaly. A state of excessive growth of the body caused by overaction of the pituitary gland in the base of the brain, 43 (2).

ACTH. An abbreviation for adreno-cortico-trophic-hormone, a drug related to cortisone.

Actinomycosis, 15 (2).

Acute nephritis, 44 (2).

Addiction to drugs. *See* **Drug abuse**, 22.

Addison's disease, 43 (2).

Adenoids, 31 (1).

Adhesions. An occasional cause of pain after operations when abraded areas adhere to each other.

Adreno-genital syndrome, 43 (2).

Air we breathe, 4 (1).

Agranulocytosis, 25 (1).

Alcoholics Anonymous, 6 (2).

Allergic rhinitis, 31 (1).

Allergy. Abnormal sensitivity to any substance which does not affect normal people, 33 (1).

Alopecia, 52 (1).

Amenorrhœa, 56 (1).

Amnesia. Loss of memory, *see under* **Neurosis**, 50 (2).

Amœbæ, 8 (1).

Amœbic dysentery, 17 (2).

Amphetamine, 23 (2).

Amyotrophic lateral sclerosis, 48 (2).

Anæmias, 24–25.

Anæsthetic. Any drug used by surgeons to remove pain during an operation.

Aneurism, 29 (2), 46 (1).

Angina pectoris, 27 (2).

Angio-neurotic œdema, 48 (2).

Ankylosis. Partial or complete fixation of a joint as after some types of arthritis. In other cases deliberately produced by surgery.

Ankylostomiasis, 16 (2).

Anorexia. Loss of appetite.

Anthrax, 15 (1), 9 (1), 4 (2).

Antibiotics, 9, 4, 22 (2).

Anticoagulants. *See under* **Coronary thrombosis**, 27 (2).

Antihistamine drugs, 4 (2), 5 (1).

Antiseptics, 8 (2).

Antitoxins. *See under* **How the Body Deals with Infection**, 8 (2).

Anxiety neurosis, 50 (2).

Aphasia, 47 (1).

Aplastic anæmia, 25 (1).

Apoplexy, 46 (2).

Appendicitis, 36 (2).

Arteriography, 46 (2).

Arteriosclerosis, 29 (1).

Arthritis, 54 (1).

Artificial respiration (kiss of life), 21 (1).

Ascites, 38 (2).

Asphyxia, 20 (2).

Aspirin and "upset stomach", 5 (1), 23 (1).

Asthma, 32–33.

Athlete's foot, 8 (1), 15 (2).

Auricular fibrillation, 28 (2).

Auscultation. The method used by a doctor when he listens for signs of disease inside the body by means of a stethoscope.

Autonomic Nervous System, 46 (1).

Baby Care, 57–63.

Backache. A symptom which may be caused by many different diseases—sometimes disease of the vertebræ themselves, sometimes strain of the ligaments, and sometimes inflammation or spasm of the surrounding muscles. "Lumbago" is usually due to inflammation of the muscles in the small of the back. Backache from purely local causes may be treated temporarily by applying heat in the form of a kaolin poultice or a rubber hot-water bottle and taking two aspirin tablets a day. On the other hand, many cases of backache are due to disease elsewhere. The most important thing is to find out the cause, and therefore a doctor should be consulted. *See also* **Fibrositis** 54 (2).

Bacteria, 7 (1). **Bacterial diseases**, 12–15.

Bacteriophage, 7 (2).

Baldness, 52 (1).

Barber's rash, 53 (1).

Barbiturates, 23 (2).

Bell's palsy, 49 (2).

Benzedrine. The proprietary name of a drug known as amphetamine. *See* 23 (2).

Beri-beri, 42 (1).

Bilharzia, 18 (2), 16 (1).

Birth control, 56 (2).

Blackwater fever, 17 (2), 24 (2).

Bladder. *See under* **Urinary diseases**, 44 (1).

Blepharitis, 54 (2).

Blood, function of the, 23–24.

Blood, circulation of the, 26 (2).

Blood, diseases of the, 24.

Blood poisoning (septicæmia), 14 (2).

Blood-pressure, 28–29.

Blood transfusion, 26 (1).

Blood-vessels, diseases of the, 29–30.

Blue babies, 30 (1), 5 (2).

Boils. A boil is an infection of the skin, and is caused by three separate factors: (1) the presence of germs on the surface of the skin; (2) lowered bodily resistance to these particular germs; and (3) the existence of pressure or friction causing the germs to be rubbed into small cracks in the skin. Boils are therefore commonest where such pressure exists, *e.g.*, on the neck where the collar rubs, on the wrists beneath the cuffs, in the armpit, and on the buttocks. The treatment is directed to the causes: (1) keep the skin clean with frequent washing with soap and water; (2) increase bodily resistance by taking yeast tablets; (3) avoid pressure and friction, and ensure that collars and other clothing compressing the skin are frequently changed. It should not be forgotten that, when many boils occur, this may be a sign of diabetes or other chronic disease.

Botulism, 14 (1).

Brain. *See under* **Nervous system**, 45–46, **Physical injuries**, 19.

Brain abscess, 47 (2).

Brain tumour, 47 (2).

Breasts, 55 (1).

Bronchiectasis, 32 (1).

Bronchitis, 31–32.

Broncho-pneumonia, 31 (2).

Bruises and abrasions, 19 (2).

Bürger's disease, 29 (1).

Burns and scalds, 21 (2).

Cachexia. Extreme wasting due to disease.

Cæsarean operation. When the abdomen has to be opened to remove the child, named after

HUMAN RELATIONS

TABLE OF CONTENTS

HUMAN RELATIONS

IN this section we have tried to give the reader an understanding of modern society and of the forces which motivate behaviour so that he can interpret what is going on around him and in his own mind. An effort has also been made to provide that help which understanding alone can give not only in the working out of one's own problems but in extending tolerance towards the shortcomings of others.

The section is in three parts:

I. The Self (i.e., the individual and his development and the way he meets the problems of life in the process of growing up).

II. Society (i.e., our relationships with other people from the family to the larger social groups and the problems created by changing social patterns).

III. Work (i.e., all the many factors that affect the worker in an industrial society).

These categories overlap to some extent since we are not isolated individuals but involved with people from the earliest days, and work is an integral part of everyone's life, so each part flows into the next, occasionally making a little repetition inevitable.

INTRODUCTION.

All societies have had their problems and their times of crisis and modern society is no exception. What is special about our problems is that they are of an entirely different nature from those which faced our forefathers. For them, as over vast areas of the earth even today, the main hazards came from an untamed natural environment in which plagues were rampant and malnutrition the rule, in which crops and livestock could be ravaged by adverse weather or disease, bringing starvation and death just as surely as the plagues afflicting man himself. This is still the state of affairs in many of the technically underdeveloped countries of the world where epidemic diseases, chronic infections such as malaria and tuberculosis, hunger, poverty, and malnutrition still need immediate action. To improve the human environment calls for efforts by the community as a whole which these poorer countries are, as yet, incapable of making by themselves, for their people have neither the necessary knowledge, wealth, nor organisation to do so, and, most difficult of all, they need to change long-established habits and attitudes.

The peoples of the Western countries have so modified their environment that they have succeeded in adding many years to their average expectation of life, yet it is not so long ago that they had to face similar problems. For example, it is little more than a hundred years ago (1848), when the appalling living conditions resulting from the industrial revolution threatened to spread disease throughout Britain, that the first public health measures were taken to deal with the fearful cholera and smallpox epidemics which were then prevalent. In Ireland, failure of the potato crop led to the great famine of the 1840s when a million people died of starvation and a million and a quarter were forced to emigrate. During the influenza epidemic which followed the First World War more people died in a single year than were killed on all the fronts in four years of devastating war. In 1962 only 882 cases of malaria were detected among 648 million people in Europe (including Russia) compared with 10 million at the end of the Second World War. The expectation of life in Britain has increased by 25 years since the turn of the century: a baby boy may now expect to live to 68 years and a girl to 74. By a process which began gradually about a hundred years ago and accelerated in recent times until it has become an explosion, our circumstances have radically changed as technology has advanced and along with the truly wonderful scientific achievements of our civilisation have come new and unheralded dangers. We are living largely in a synthetic environment created by our own technology and our most serious problems today are caused not by nature but by ourselves. This is perhaps a depressing fact, but it is also a hopeful one; for we are now at little risk from the physical world around us and it might be thought that the minds which created the new environment are surely capable of solving the problems which come in its wake.

Unfortunately the situation is not quite so simple because, though we know a good deal about the physical universe and how to bring it under control, we know rather less about ourselves and what information is available does not suggest that human problems are as easy to solve as technical ones. Most of us are able to handle things with some measure of efficiency, but we are likely to be much less skilled when it comes to human relationships and, in the long run, even things become tied up with personal emotions. Thus there are not *two* sets of problems, the one concerned with science and technology and the other with mental life, because science and technology *in themselves* create no problems at all—there is really only one problem and that is the uses to which we put our knowledge. Man uses his reason to find out about the physical universe but all too often what he does with his discoveries is determined not by reason but by false beliefs, old traditions, and emotional prejudice.

Among the major problems in the world today are racial and national hatred, undernourishment, over-population, the control of disease in impoverished countries, the prevention of nuclear war, superstition, illiteracy and poor educational standards. Most of the causes of these are already known and in many cases the remedies are not only known but capable of being put into practice immediately. What stops them from being effectively dealt with is not lack of knowledge but the fact that we are unable to understand or control ourselves; the problems are not outside but inside man—his stupidity, greed, aggressiveness, suspicions and prejudices. These are the concern of the psychologist, because psychology is the scientific study of human behaviour, emotions, and thoughts. In the pages that follow we shall be dealing mainly with those aspects of the subject which are most relevant to the individual citizen in the Western world today but it is hoped that the reader will gain some insight into the forces which motivate all men irrespective of politics, race, or creed.

Adjusting to Inevitable Change.

Broadly speaking, the problems of the West are those of the Welfare State or what has been described as the Affluent Society (the two are not quite the same because, though a welfare state may be affluent, an affluent society like America is certainly not a welfare state). Along with very real benefits such as comparative economic security, improved material well-being, freedom from many of the killing diseases which once plagued us, greater social mobility, and better opportunities for higher education, have come other features which cannot be cured by more affluence. Many people are bored, rebellious, perplexed, and downright unhappy, and some would ascribe this to the 'spiritual sickness of our time' brought about by the loss of traditional values. Perhaps they are right. The only trouble about this analysis is that it is not a very helpful approach because traditional values cannot be brought back by legislation, nor is it desirable that they should be brought back at all. Our real problem is that we have failed to adjust to a rapidly-changing technological environment, which demands a new set of values and fresh attitudes. More than a century and a half ago a famous philosopher wrote that "man, insofar as he acts to change his environment, acts to change himself," and herein lies our failure; we have created a new environment but have failed to make new adjustments to it though the essence of normality is the ability to see and react appropriately to life as it is. The authoritarian family has gone, woman's place in relation to home and work has changed, traditional attitudes in industry are dying, and the gulf in understanding between parents and children has increased because the pre-war world is not the world of today. All these issues will be discussed here.

I. THE SELF

1. THE FOUNDATIONS.

What is Personality?

Personality may be defined as that arrangement of traits which are relatively consistent and enduring attributes of an individual's behaviour. Thus if one man is aggressive in any and every situation and another gentle and thoughtful towards everyone he meets, then we are entitled to assume that these are fundamental and relatively fixed aspects of their personalities.

On the other hand, it is easy to see that whilst some aspects of behaviour are comparatively stable, people's actions are also variable—they may be shy in one set of circumstances and not in another, dominating within one group and submissive elsewhere. This is because these traits are not something *in* the individual, but are simply a response to the social circumstances he is facing at the moment. In more technical terms, they are not a function of his personality but rather a function of the role he is playing as a member of a group facing a specific situation.

So it often happens that we attribute certain characteristics of a person to his innate traits when, in fact, they only appear to be fixed because we always meet him in the same social surroundings. For example, a supervisor in a factory who finds that one of his workers is always resentful is liable to suppose that he is just resentful by nature, whereas, if he saw the man at home he might be surprised to discover that his family and neighbours regard him as kindly and generous to a fault. The reason is, of course, that the worker is resentful in response to the factory situation which, being the kind of person he is, he finds frustrating because it does not permit free expression to his real abilities. Thus what might be described as the 'core' personality is rigid in structure and resists change, whilst the more superficial aspects of personality, of which the above is an instance, change very rapidly as the individual moves from one group to another, and these aspects are described as relating to the 'peripheral', 'public', or 'social' personality. The practical significance of this distinction will be seen later, but it is obvious that if we are dealing with a social problem such as juvenile delinquency it is absolutely necessary to know whether, in a given case, we are faced with an attitude which is firmly ingrained in the youth or whether he is simply responding to a frustrating environment.

Some aspects of personality are therefore relatively fixed whilst others merely reflect responses to a particular environment, but the two cannot be entirely separated because most of the time people tend to respond, not to the environment as it really is but *to the environment as they interpret it* and this naturally depends upon the nature of their core personality. In the example of the worker quoted above, it is obvious that he was suspicious, not merely because of the objective situation (which of course first aroused his suspicions) but because he was the sort of person who might be expected to feel that way in those circumstances. Perhaps his innate intelligence and the fact that he had been brought up with the ambition to better himself made the situation more intolerable to him than to his mates (though in some factories things may be so bad that nearly everyone feels dissatisfied). But this does not alter the fact that a change to a more satisfying job would change the behaviour of this particular man, whilst, in other cases, suspiciousness may be an ingrained trait which appears in any situation.

How is Personality Fashioned?

Where, then, do these fixed traits come from? Broadly speaking, they arise from three distinct but interacting sources: temperament, the child-rearing patterns of the first five or six years of life, and the culture in which the individual is brought up. Temperament is what we inherit, and child-rearing patterns are based on the way in which the parents attempt to pass on the culture to which they and their children belong. The family, it has been said, is the personality-factory of society which attempts with greater or lesser success to inculcate the ideals of a particular group into each new generation. To use another metaphor, we come into the world as an undifferentiated lump of clay which nevertheless has its own particular properties, the family is the potter, and culture supplies the design. If our society values conquest, we shall be brought up to admire and try to emulate war-like men; if it measures success in terms of money we shall see acquisitiveness and wealth as our goal; and, in a caste society, we must learn to behave in all ways according to the position into which we are born. This ideal pattern is the *basic personality structure* and represents those aspects of personality which distinguish the members of one cultural group from another and defines what is considered as 'normal' in a given society. The variations on this common theme which differentiate one member of the group from any other member making him, to some extent, a unique individual, are what is described as 'character'. Since the interplay between these various factors is very subtle, it is necessary to discuss them in more detail.

Temperament.

Just a century ago the Austrian monk Gregor Mendel was able to show that the physical characteristics of plants are passed on from one generation to the next according to certain definite laws (*see* **Section F, Part II**). It is known that such factors as body-build, hair and eye colour, height, and the rest are inherited in this way, and there are a few diseases (probably not more than can be counted on the fingers of one hand) such as hæmophilia, which are also known to be hereditary. But when it comes to mental traits, we are on much less secure ground, largely because it is difficult to distinguish between what has been inherited and what has been learnt. Nearly all psychologists believe that if a son is fussy and punctilious like his father this is because he has been taught to behave in this way or has learned it by imitation, and whilst many psychiatrists (*i.e.*, physicians who specialise in treating mental disorders) believe that a *tendency* to certain forms of insanity is inherited, few would accept that this is true of the minor forms of neurosis. It is known for certain that general intelligence is determined at the moment of conception, and quite likely that the traits collectively described as 'temperament' are largely inherited because they seem to be correlated with body-build. The short stocky individual with a tendency to run to fat is usually cheerful and outgoing—one of those described by Shakespeare when he referred to "men that are fat, sleek-headed men and such as sleep o'nights" and compared them to Cassius with his "lean and hungry look" who "thinks too much—such men are dangerous". The former type of body-build is the 'pyknic' and his temperament is 'cyclothyme' or 'extraverted', the latter has an 'æsthenic' build associated with a 'schizoid' or 'introverted' temperament. (*See also* **Characterology, J8.**)

The Interplay of Heredity and Environment.

But all this has to be modified because the introvert and extravert are obviously at the extreme ends of a normal curve of distribution so most people fall in between the two and both attitudes can be considerably modified by cultural factors. An extravert, who would naturally be given to talkativeness and the strong expression of his emotions, if born into a Red Indian tribe, where the approved basic personality structure is the impassive and silent man, would become just as impassive as the rest. Even intelligence, the only mental trait which we know *for certain* to be inherited, can be considerably modified by environmental factors which encourage or discourage its full development. Furthermore, there are two other considerations to be taken into account: first, not every trait that a child is born with is inherited, and second, heredity may have an indirect as well as a direct effect on character. What a child is born with is congenital, but congenital traits are not always inherited or determined at the moment of conception; for we know that what takes place whilst the child is developing within the womb also has a potent influence on its future life, usually for the worse. Thus German measles in the mother, birth injury, and drugs such as thalidomide taken in the early weeks of pregnancy (*see* **P4**) can cause severe mental defect or physical deformity. Again, the effect of inherited characteristics may be indirect depending upon how they are regarded by the society into which the child is born and the way the child reacts to the views of his society. For example, a mentally-retarded or brain-damaged person may be regarded with contempt or pity in one group or be thrust into a position of high status as a witch-doctor or sorcerer in another. A boy who is short in stature may become neurotic and a failure when he is teased by his associates or, on the other hand, may compensate by becoming powerful and dominating to cover up his deficiency. The influence of heredity is therefore very complex and even the most fixed traits may be considerably modified by environment; stature is inherited, but without adequate diet the full stature will not be reached, whereas given better nourishment it will. The youth of Britain today are on the average considerably taller than their grandparents, and the Japanese who were always regarded as 'naturally' small are becoming taller as the economic position of their country improves. Heredity, by and large, does not determine the details—it merely sets the limits.

Child-rearing Patterns.

It follows that, though we are prone to think of the child as a pre-fabricated structure waiting at birth to be erected, for better or worse, by the adults who look after it, this is a wholly mistaken belief, because *prior to an infant's earliest contacts with other human beings it simply does not exist as a 'person' at all.* All we have is a living thing with certain physical characteristics, a *potential* intellectual level which, again, without the intervention of people could not raise him above the level of an idiot or a chimpanzee, and a bundle of biological drives such as hunger, thirst, sex, and the needs for sleep and warmth which only others can satisfy. Human beings are unlike animals in their prolonged period of helplessness, in their ability to communicate by speech, in the possession of an opposable thumb which makes it possible to carry out delicate manipulations, in the fact that they alone can hand on knowledge or culture from one generation to the next and, above all, in having no instincts. Correctly used, the word 'instinct' refers to behaviour inherited in the structure of the nervous system, unlearned, and relatively unmodifiable; it is typical of the lower animals which automatically carry out quite complicated actions such as nest-building, yearly migrations, courting behaviour, and so on, without having been taught how to do so. In the higher animals such as apes this is already a disappearing category and, so far as human beings are concerned, it has disappeared altogether, being replaced by undifferentiated drives or needs that are inherited, but require the help of a family before they develop into the patterns for satisfying them approved in a given society.

The Sense of Self.

The need for food like the need for sleep, is innate but from a very early age the child learns not merely to demand food or sleep as such, but certain kinds of food and certain hours of sleep which it has been taught are 'right' and 'good'. The basic psychological process occurs in a particular direction: the infant has physical needs which demand satisfaction, it becomes aware of the world around it, interprets it, responds to it, finally responds to the results of its own response. It feels sensations of hunger, becomes aware of the breast, interprets it as a source of food, sucks it, and depending upon whether its experience is satisfying or not, feels pleasure, anger, or anxiety. Because the way in which people or things respond to our approaches to them influences our attitude towards ourselves, it has been said that the self is based on "the reflected appraisal of other people", or more dramatically by an Italian novelist, that "the self is the meeting-place of all relationships". In other words, we do not just *have* experiences, we *are* our experiences and in later life we treat others as we interpret the way they treated us during the formative years, and value or dislike ourselves as we believe we were valued or otherwise. This too is important in understanding certain types of delinquency, because one can only give as much love as one has received, and a delinquent who has suffered from parental neglect may become what is known as a 'loveless character' because he literally has no love to give and can only respond with hate. The selfish person does not care for others, but he does not care for himself either.

2. THE FORMATIVE YEARS.

The Fundamental Need for Love and Protection.

The biological needs of hunger, thirst, and the rest, by reason of the utter helplessness of the human infant, cannot be satisfied unaided, so there arises very early in life the most fundamental of psychological needs—the need to be loved, protected, and cared for. Love is not something we are born with; it develops through a series of stages from mere cupboard love to a mature and disinterested affection for other people. Hate is an emotion which arises when certain needs are frustrated—in fact, it might almost be said to be a derivative of love since, together with anxiety, it is initially aroused by fear of loss of love. This need to be cared for leads in later life to the need for personal affection and subsequently to a desire for the approval of society so, as one psychologist puts it, love forms "the underpinning on which all the later motives and the cultural imperatives are constructed".

The Formation of Basic Attitudes.

During the first five years of life the child begins to learn, not only by the process of conditioning whereby it comes to associate two quite different stimuli together as a dog learns to associate the the sound of a whistle with food because one has always followed the other, whilst ignoring the sound of a bell which has been unrelated to food, but also by a process of trial and error and by imitating its parents. Habits are established by differential reward and punishment, indulgence and deprivation, or the implied threat of deprivation of affection on the part of the parents who make use of the infant's needs to avoid harm and obtain approval and the satisfaction of its biological drives to this end. The habits acquired at this stage relate to sleeping and feeding, bowel and bladder control and the child's early loves and hates (Œdipus complex) within the family circle. Throughout this period it develops attitudes towards its father and mother, brothers and sisters, which becomes the model of its attitudes towards all the people it meets subsequently. So, whilst the core personality is being laid down, the child is not only learning control of its excretory and feeding functions but also how to deal with people; if it is not given affection freely, consistently, and unconditionally, it will soon discover more devious ways of getting attention. If being sick produces the required results, the child will grow up into the sort of person who tries to get affection by taking refuge in real or imaginary illnesses when trouble threatens. If keeping to oneself works ("If I leave people alone they won't harm me"), he will be unsociable, and if a domineering or aggressive attitude works that is what he will become. Naughty and ultimately delinquent behaviour sometimes arises from the child's feeling that he is not cared for ("All right, if you don't love me, at least I'll see to it that you have to give me *some* sort of attention")

The important point is that all our most basic attitudes arise because at one time they demonstrably worked. As a child psychiatrist expresses it: "We become acceptable or non-acceptable, helpless or capable, important or insignificant, passive or aggressive, busy or lazy, resourceful, or cautious, or sweet, or clever, or polite, or thoughtful, or obedient, or demanding, or a thousand and one other characteristics. These are the traits which are produced by the child and structuralised into his very self because of their *functional* value to him in the earliest years of life. Each one was the trait that worked best and got the best results in the particular setting in which he was placed."

How the Personality Develops.

Parents usually think of child-rearing as a simple—or at least theoretically simple—and direct process whereby 'good' behaviour is inculcated and 'bad' behaviour discouraged by reward and punishment, personal example, and later by speech. Unfortunately this is not the case because, though these are important, other facts must be taken into consideration. To begin with, character formation starts from the very earliest weeks and those traits which are learned then are the most potent by reason of the Law of Primacy which states that the earlier an experience the greater its effect. This is because from birth onwards the way we interpret a new experience depends on our previous mental state; for example, though a child will certainly have no conscious memory of satisfying or unsatisfying emotions at the breast, these are nevertheless built into its brain structure and cause it to see later events in a hopeful or depressing light.

Early Infancy.

There is very good evidence that in the first six months of infancy we have already acquired basic traits which make for an authoritarian or humanitarian outlook and, in fact, the words of the song by Gilbert and Sullivan to the effect that "every boy and every girl that's born into this world alive is either a little Liberal or else a little Conservative" are quite literally true with the single modification that we are not born that way but learn these attitudes at the breast. Of course, like the introvert–extravert scale and the level of intelligence, these attitudes are distributed over a normal curve so that most people fall somewhere about the middle, and the radical-conservative scale is not meant to refer to any political party, though it will clearly influence later political beliefs.

Again, it is almost certain that such traits as fussiness, punctuality, belief in discipline, excessive concern with cleanliness, and extreme (but repressed) aggressiveness are learned, not by direct example, but are intercorrelated attitudes associated with an over-strict emphasis on bowel training. Those nations which value punctiliousness, obedience, and strict hygiene (*e.g.*, the Teutonic nations) are also likely to be aggressive, obsessed with bowel functions (*c.f.*, Martin Luther), and to make jokes, not as in other countries about sex, but about lavatories.

The Beginnings of Conscience.

At a later stage, about the age of five or six, the child normally passes through what is known as the Œdipus complex when it loves the parent of the opposite sex and feels correspondingly jealous of the parent of the same sex as a rival and this influences its attitudes towards the opposite sex throughout life. But quite soon it begins to realise the futility of this state of affairs and from then on two important things happen. First, the child leaves behind the stage when its moral controls came from outside, from the orders of its parents, and by a process known as 'introjection' takes the parent's moral attitudes inside itself. This is the earliest beginnings of the adult conscience which initially starts as an 'internalised parent' exercising control from within instead of having it superimposed from without. Second, the child now begins to imitate the parent of the *same* sex, and in this way the boy learns how to play the masculine role as defined in his society, the girl to play the feminine role. This is a very important stage and in households where the father is absent, badly behaved, or a weakling, the boy may imitate his mother and develop homosexual tendencies in later life.

Child–Parent Relationship.

There are therefore two parallel processes involved in child-rearing, the one conscious and deliberate in which the child is taught to behave according to the rules of its society and also learns in the academic sense, but the more significant one is an unconscious process because, as we have seen, many of our most deep-rooted traits arise during the period when the child cannot understand speech and are the result of an interaction between parent and child at a time when the parent is unlikely to realise the values he or she is actually inculcating. In short, the child is responding more to what his parents *are* than to what they *say*, and therefore *the basic rule in bringing up a child is to give it unconditional, secure, and consistent affection.* But it is only the normal parent who is able to do this and, since not many of us have reached full emotional maturity, our children may appear to be getting plenty of affection, but the true reasons for the mother's behaviour may be guilt at not feeling enough love or, if she is unhappy with her husband, she may be displacing her frustrated affections on her son—in neither case is the love healthy or genuine and the child will suffer.

Even the formal educational process is influenced by these emotional undercurrents which the parents neither understand nor are capable of controlling, and the child will accept or reject what it is deliberately taught, not in terms of its truth or real value, but rather in terms of his unconscious (or sometimes conscious) feelings towards the parent who tries to inculcate them. The boy who either unconsciously resents his father or is striving to become independent of unduly possessive parents (or even, as sometimes happens, trying to avoid being overwhelmed by the reputation of a well-loved but very famous father) is more likely to reject his father's religious, philosophical, or political views than to accept them. One little boy whose very tolerant parents had never uttered a word of condemnation against his lack of interest in books were distressed to hear him say when he thought they were not listening, "Of course, I'm the idiot of the family"—they had *said* nothing, but the walls of their home covered with bookshelves filled with books, many of which they themselves had written, had said a great deal. The boy excelled at getting on with his schoolmates and at sport, but until the reasons for his attitude against learning were pointed out to him, he did not do well academically. Once he had learned what was going on in his unconscious, he became one of the best scholars in his college.

3. THE UNCONSCIOUS PROCESSES SHAPING PERSONALITY

The Repression of Emotions.

In general, we only pay attention to those elements of our environment which (*a*) fit in with the rest of our beliefs, and (*b*) help to further the action in hand at the moment. Freud, the founder of psychoanalysis, pointed out that all those emotions and thoughts which are repugnant to the individual are either pushed into his unconscious or never allowed to leave it. They are, as Freud said, "repressed"—a term which does not mean the conscious *suppression* of anti-social desires, but the refusal even to recognise their existence. (*See also* **Freudian Theory, Section F, Part III.**) However, as others have pointed out since, it is not only those aspects of personality which are regarded as morally objectionable that come to be repressed, but traits which, whilst not necessarily 'bad' in themselves, do not fit in with conscious attitudes. Charles Darwin, for example, admitted that, as he became more and more absorbed in reasoning and scientific pursuits, he lost the ability to enjoy, as he once had done, the pleasures of poetry and literature. We shall see later that one of the great barriers to changing attitudes from whatever motive is the fact that, after they have grown up, people do not tend to seek new experiences but rather to reinforce existing prejudices.

For the moment, however, we are concerned with those emotions and desires which are repressed in the original Freudian sense. When such emotions are repressed they do not cease to exist and sometimes have quite devastating effects on the individual and his associates. Thus those who have been brought up to refuse to recognise their aggressiveness may repress it and, by the process known as 'reaction-formation', become compulsively 'gentle'. Their assumed 'gentleness' is adopted in order to fight their 'bad' aggressive side; and so we often find (and this is the tragedy of these movements) that those who are pacifists, vegetarians, and against cruelty to animals or children cannot help their latent aggressiveness from leaking out. This leads to such unpleasant phenomena as the obvious tendency to fragmentation and quarrelsomeness within pacifist movements, an unhealthy absorption in cruelty quite frequently in situations where others see none, and extreme intolerance. Jung described this unrecognised aspect of a man's nature as his "shadow", giving as an example a man he had once met, a Quaker, who could not imagine that he had ever done anything wrong in his life. "And do you know what happened to his children?" Jung asked. "The son became a thief, and the daughter a prostitute. Because the father would not take on his shadow, his share in the imperfection of human nature, his children were compelled to live out the dark side which he had ignored." Thus unconscious attitudes in the parents are sometimes more potent in influencing their children than the respectable conscious ones.

Mental Mechanisms to Guard Our Self-Esteem.

Since everyone has had to repress quite a lot of unacceptable material (and, of course, the individual has been *taught* to reject it though it may be harmless enough in itself and infinitely more dangerous repressed than openly recognised), the mind has learned many tricks for concealing those traits or memories from awareness. These forms of self-deception are what Freud described as "mental mechanisms" which permit some form of expression without allowing knowledge of its source. These are explained under **Freudian Theory, Section F, Part III.** The lesson to be learned is that the proper way of dealing with repressed emotions is (*a*) to recognise them, and (*b*) to sublimate them—*i.e., consciously* direct them towards socially useful ends. Many who have helped the poor and sick have been stimulated to do so because of their own unhappy childhood experiences and those who have done something useful on behalf of small underprivileged nations or classes have usually been well aware that it was their own early experience of being underprivileged that caused them to do so.

The Nature of Aggression.

Hardly any subject in the whole field of psychology is more important than the problem of aggression, and it is doubtful if any is less understood by the layman. This is little short of tragic since it is obvious that what is generally comprehended under the name of aggression is responsible for many of the issues facing us today: for example, warfare between nations, crimes of violence, race prejudice, and the concern felt by many about violence on television or in children's 'comics', all reflect the necessity for taking the matter seriously. What stands in the way of genuine understanding is the fact that, as is so often the case in psychology, most people are not only convinced that they already know all that needs to be known but, worse still, they are confident that they know the solutions. What could be more apparent than that war is caused by the 'instinct' of aggression, that violent crimes can be cured by violence, or that horror scenes in comics or on television are a cause of juvenile delinquency which can therefore be reduced by preventing children from being exposed to them? Naturally enough, anyone who is rash enough to attempt to show that these are dangerous delusions or that, to say the least, the problem is much more complex than is often supposed, is immediately suspect of blinding himself to realities or of being 'soft' when the correct attitude is to be 'hard' and 'objective'. However, the reader is invited to try to see the other side of the picture.

Life Energy or Drive.

In the first place, 'aggression' is not a simple entity synonymous with 'hate', and this confusion leads to the belief that what is a perfectly natural and inborn tendency is, without qualification, evil. Actually, as Dr. D. W. Winnicott, who is one of the most eminent British psychoanalysts (*i.e.*, those who treat patients by the methods based on the theories of Freud) has pointed out, "at origin aggressiveness is almost synonymous with activity". It is not an 'instinct' nor even a specific drive but the natural tendency to overcome obstacles to the attainment of goals without which life itself could not exist; thus we talk about 'attacking' a problem, 'struggling with' and 'overcoming' a difficulty, 'mastering' a subject or 'getting one's teeth into it'.

Hate or Anger.

In this sense aggressiveness is simply life-energy which, when it meets a barrier to satisfaction (whether the need for satisfaction involves solving a mental problem or looking for one's next meal) accumulates in order to summon up enough power to overcome it. This sort of behaviour is happening to everybody at every hour of the day and usually the barrier is successfully overcome and the organism returns briefly to the original resting state. But if it proves insurmountable, a state of frustration develops which leads to emotions which can be described as 'aggression' in the more limited sense of the word implying anger, anxiety, and hate. Hate arises in interpersonal situations, that is to say, it is something we feel towards *people*, arising originally from fear of loss of love which threatened our security in infancy because an unloving mother could not be relied upon to satisfy our physical needs, and subsequently it arises in situations where security is threatened either in the emotional sense or when there exists a real or imagined physical danger to status, life, or property. For example, rejection in love threatens our self-image by damaging that personal esteem which is the badge of psychological security, and the fear of attack from other individuals, groups, or nations threatens our physical security, so both are prone to lead to hate. *Since hatred is so closely linked with anxiety, anxious and insecure people are particularly prone to irrational hatred.* Thus revolutions are not made by the secure ruling classes who have nothing to gain, nor (as the Communists have learned to their cost) by the very poor who have nothing to lose, but by the insecure lower middle classes; those who incite race riots in the southern states of America are not the well-to-do or the old 'aristocracy' who are often, in private, quite liberal in their views, but the 'poor whites' whose only claim to superiority rests on their colour. Anger, though often directed against people, is also aroused by situations or things which frustrate the individual, such as the car that fails to start; hate always involves people, anger does not.

How Aggression is Dealt With.

When a great deal of anger or hatred (*i.e.*, aggression in the narrower sense of the word) has been aroused, various possibilities of handling it arise. The normal reaction is to assess the situation rationally and consciously recognise one's feelings for what they are; from this point one may feel that by an increased effort the barrier to satisfaction may be overcome and decide to carry on, or that the barrier is genuinely insuperable so that further effort would be wasted and that, failure being no disgrace in the circumstances, one can without loss of self-respect redirect one's efforts elsewhere. Unfortunately, in our own culture children are often brought up to believe that anger, aggression, or even normal self-assertion are 'bad' emotions to be suppressed just as much as 'evil' sexual desires. When this happens, what was once consciously suppressed by the threat of punishment or loss of love in childhood soon comes to be automatically and unconsciously repressed in later life. In this case our aggressive feelings (which, as mentioned above, may sometimes extend to what is merely self-assertiveness or the right to develop oneself as an independent individual) are dealt with by *denial*—we deny that they exist at all, or assert that they exist in other people but not in ourselves, or direct them against a socially-accepted scapegoat. That is to say, they are repressed, projected, or displaced, and this is the cause of most of the troubles facing the modern world. Those who lead campaigns for peace, if in many cases genuinely gentle people or motivated by a commonsense realisation that the human race must choose between international peace or total destruction, are all too frequently individuals who are compulsively 'gentle' in a neurotic attempt to deny their own destructive tendencies. But the denial of such tendencies does not prevent their manifesting themselves in such a way as to frustrate the achievement of the avowed goals of the movement and, to quote Dr. Winnicott once more: "*If society is in danger, it is not because of man's aggressiveness, but because of the repression of personal aggressiveness in individuals.*"

The Effects of Repressing Aggressive Feelings.

Normal sexual or aggressive feelings when denied give rise to those horrible sexual and aggressive fantasies which, when projected upon the outer world, lead to that race hatred when the victim of what is in fact a diseased imagination pictures his womenfolk being raped by Negroes or himself being dominated by designing Jews. The problem of war will be discussed elsewhere, but it is worth while noting here that one of the main reasons why warfare occurs is that for masses of frustrated people it is the most obvious way out of their frustrations; in fact, if we do not exactly *want* wars there are millions who *need* them. Freud pointed out the apparent paradox that a nation is never so much at peace within itself as when it is fighting an external enemy, from which it follows that countries which have long been living peacefully with their neighbours will have more aggression to direct inwardly. That this contains more than a grain of truth is evinced by the high suicide rate in such countries as Sweden and Switzerland, and Jung, himself a Swiss, referring to the peculiar bitterness of Swiss internal politics, made the remark that his people had "introverted war".

But there are some people in whom any self-assertive or aggressive manifestations have been so thoroughly repressed that they are permitted hardly any expression even in the forms described above; such individuals are as embarrassed and anxious at the least sign of anger or self-assertion in quite normal circumstances as the prude is upset by things with a sexual connotation which the ordinary person simply does not notice. When this occurs the only possible solution is to *introject* the aggression (*i.e.*, turn it against the self), and this leads to severe states of depression—which is really self-hatred—to actual suicide, or to psychosomatic disorders such as high blood-pressure brought about by prolonged stress. Finally, it must be remembered that suicide is not the only form of self-destruction, that chronic alcoholism, drug addiction, accident-proneness, and other conditions are often unconscious attempts to walk slowly or rapidly along the road to death and failure, resulting from inwardly-directed aggression. These are, of course, states that *may* be brought about by introjection, though since different people have different levels of tolerance and stamina they do not invariably occur; what we can safely say is that, as aggression in its original aspect is a manifestation of the drive towards self-assertion and self-realisation, its repression will *inevitably* lead to impoverishment and inadequacy of the personality.

4. THE FIVE AGES OF MAN.

Disregarding Shakespeare's account of the seven ages of man, we shall describe for the sake of convenience a mere five: childhood, adolescence, the period during which we can still hopefully expect to be described as a young bachelor or married couple, middle age, and old age. Each of these age groups has its own special problems, so it is necessary to observe the process of development and the satisfactions and difficulties arising at each stage whilst remembering that many, if not most, of these difficulties arise in a social context and cannot be usefully considered in terms of the non-existent isolated individual. For example, though we in the West commonly (and not without justice) regard adolescence as a period of 'storm and stress', this is not the case in other societies, and therefore must be regarded as a socially-conditioned phenomenon. But since most people tend to regard their particular problems as unique and 'inside' themselves, some of these will be mentioned here, whilst in Part II other problems will be discussed and it will become evident that, in fact, *all personal problems are also social problems.*

The childhood years are the formative years and what we later become can only be discussed in their light; furthermore, the child only experiences society indirectly through the medium of the family and, initially at least, is the only true individualist until moulded into the image of society. What we have so far been discussing are the basic principles of dynamic psychology without which none of the rest of this section could be understood. Whilst the problems of the child are to some extent peculiar to the particular family even when it acts under social pressures, those of the other age groups result from interaction at first hand with society. The difficulties of the other age groups are not *related* to society, but in large measure *created* by society. So, whilst adolescence, young married life or bachelorhood, and old age have their problems, they cannot usefully be discussed outside their social context and properly belong to Part II. How true this is will be shown in what follows.

THE CHILD.

From the point of view of its physical development the child is described as a *neonate* from birth to the end of the first month, an *infant* from one month until he is able to walk at fifteen or sixteen months, a *toddler* from fifteen months to the age of 2½, a *preschool* child from 2½ years to 5 or 6 years, and a *child in middle years* from 6 to about 12 years. About the latter period he has, with fairly wide variations, reached *physical* maturity, but it is not until the end of adolescence that he has reached *social* maturity. He can follow a moving object with his eyes at about 4 weeks, control his head about 16, grasp and manipulate objects at about 28, crawl and sit about 40, and stand and move around at 52 weeks or slightly later. At the tenth month the average vocabulary of an average child is one word; at two years the average is 272 words; and by the sixth year the average has risen to 2,562 words.

Parental Behaviour and its Effects on the Personality of the Child.

Something has already been said about the way in which the personality develops and there is good evidence that important traits have arisen long before the child is able to speak or understand speech; whether he tends to be tolerant of himself and others is probably determined in the first six months of life. Then, and even after acquiring speech, he responds more to what the parent is than to what she (because at that time it is the mother who is the important person) deliberately tries to inculcate. For example, a nervous and tense mother or one who secretly dislikes the process of breast-feeding cannot help but convey these impressions to the child through body tensions and the adequacy or otherwise of the flow of milk. The two problems facing the infant at the breast are, first, that it is unable to foresee the future and so it takes some time before it comes to learn that its hunger and thirst will sooner or later be reliably appeased; second, that its emotions are of the all-or-none type which it is not yet able to deal with and therefore even momentary frustration of its needs brings about outbursts of uncontrollable rage. In short, it alternates between states of satisfaction and fury, and the latter are so frightening that it may *introject* them (in which case it feels that there is something 'bad' inside itself) or *project* them against the frustrating breast or mother (in which case it will feel that mother is 'bad').

The Mature Personality.

All of us employ both of these mechanisms to deal with infantile aggression and what we later become is influenced by which one predominated; there is at one extreme the type of person who, when things go wrong, tends to feel 'I am bad' and at the other the type who will tend to blame others. The former will develop the sort of conscience based upon fear of having disappointed or hurt something that is loved (*i.e.*, will have humanistic attitudes), the latter will have the sort of conscience based upon fear of punishment (*i.e.*, he will have authoritarian attitudes). As we shall see in more detail later, both of these extremes are undesirable; for it cannot be too often emphasised that the fully mature personality is one whose relationships are neither self-denying nor denying the rights of others but one *based on mutual acceptance and respect*. The man or woman who denies his or her own rights as an individual and becomes dedicated to 'helping' others merely in order to assuage personal guilt-feelings is just as abnormal as the one who projects his 'bad' emotions into the outer world; neither is motivated by anything better than a neurotic attempt to solve personal tensions. Genuinely helpful people are motivated by that overflow of love for humanity which can only arise from love and respect for themselves and that, as we have seen, comes from the experience of deep and satisfying parental affection in childhood.

The Neurotic Personality.

The effects upon the personality of over-strict bowel control have already been mentioned and this sort of parental behaviour leads to the obsessional type of basic personality structure shown in some of the peoples of northern Europe where the approved attitudes are seriousness, hard work, punctuality, acquisitiveness, authoritarian-submissiveness (*i.e.*, a heirarchy in which one does not mind being kicked so long as there is an inferior who can be kicked in return), and repressed aggression manifesting itself in a superficial sentimentality or the search for a scapegoat. Heinrich Himmler, whilst responsible for the murder of six million Jews, was also a leader in the society for prevention of cruelty to animals in Germany. In southern Europe, on the other hand, where parents are more lenient in this respect, the general attitude is easy-going, impulsive, warm, and not over-concerned about the passage of time. It is true that many Latins are indifferent to animals, but they have no need (as in some other countries) for a society for the prevention of cruelty to children. It should hardly be necessary to repeat that nobody asserts (*a*) that all people who are kind to animals are necessarily motivated by a 'gentleness' which is merely a cover-up for concealed sadism, since many of them are just naturally gentle people to man and beast alike; nor (*b*) is it asserted that there is necessarily an inverse relationship between the degree of affection shown to animals and that shown to people. Obviously the ideal is to be kind to both. But nobody who uses his eyes can fail to see that some people love animals to the exclusion of human beings and that many gentlewomen who are good to their cats are very vocal in informing us that they would "beat a man to death" for whipping a horse, and regular in their attendance at conferences where motions are proposed for bringing back the birch and retaining capital punishment. Of course, they are perfectly entitled to these views; but they are certainly not entitled to regard themselves as kind and loving or opposed to aggression. Such people are merely displacing the affection normally felt for their fellow men on to animals as a substitute object, or displacing their aggression from its true cause in their personal frustrations towards other substitute objects which happen to be the socially accepted scapegoats of society.

Sexual Development.

Just as 'aggression' has a general application signifying life-energy or drive and the narrower and more common application meaning hatred or anger, so the word 'sex' has a general and a particular meaning. The former is more or less synonymous with 'desire' and this type of sexuality is present from birth, manifesting itself first in the pleasure of sucking where the source of pleasure is the mouth, later in the interest in bowel motions which children experience during the 'house-training' period, and subsequently in the more overtly sexual feelings of the young boy towards his mother and the young girl towards her father at the Œdipus stage. At this stage, about the age of five or six years, the child becomes interested in its sexual organs—though even quite young babies often show a similar interest. All these stages of immature sexuality are described as 'autoerotic' because the main object of love is the self and other people are seen in terms of the degree to which they satisfy or frustrate the child's self-love. Masturbation is natural at this time and later attitudes to sex will be strongly influenced by parental attitudes of permissiveness or severe prohibition since the latter may cause the individual throughout life to feel that sex is something 'dirty' and 'sinful'—a belief which has ruined many a married life. The question of masturbation in later life will be dealt with when adolescence is discussed.

With the passing of the Œdipus stage, the adult conscience begins to develop on the foundations already laid in the early months of life and the parents' values are internalised as the 'still small voice'. However, it must not be thought that this is the whole of conscience because it is still primitive and in later life continues to develop with the formation of an 'ego-ideal' when we consciously try to imitate the behaviour of those we admire and respect. With puberty the sexual drive becomes directed towards the other sex and the child is physically mature, but this level is preceded by a homosexual phase in which the object of love belongs to the same sex. This does not mean that overt homosexual behaviour necessarily occurs, though it is not infrequent, and according to the Kinsey report, the majority of American males reported such experiences, but in this country its most obvious manifestation is the 'crushes' felt by schoolgirls towards attractive teachers or senior girls and the similar behaviour among boys when they admire other schoolboy friends and think girls silly. However, what actually happens depends upon social factors; homosexuality is common in public schools whether overtly or in a more sublimated form, and much less frequent among those who have been lucky enough to be reared in a more natural environment where extreme segregation of the sexes does not occur.

Thus the course of sexual development is a gradually moving away from self-love (autoerotic), by way of love of someone of the same sex (homosexual), towards the wholly other (heterosexual). But since nobody completely leaves behind all the manifestations of the various stages through which he has passed, everyone has homosexual and autoerotic elements in his or her personality.

The Subjective Life of the Child: Fantasies.

No child can avoid the various conflicting situations which are part of the process of growing up from infancy to puberty and after; for, to take the more superficial difficulties first, every child must feel small and helpless in the great world of adults, feel jealous of older brothers or sisters, and even more so of the new baby who intrudes upon his supremacy in his parents' attention, just as the new baby will later feel a particular need to clamour for attention in face of the existing competition.

Now these are some of the situations that are dramatised in fairy-tales and the ancient myths (which have been described as the "dreams of a people"), and form part of much great literature and art. Whilst an obvious function of art is its aesthetic aspect when the artist creates something of beauty, it has another function which Aristotle describes as 'catharsis' (*see also* **I6**)—that is, by moving people to pity, love, or terror, it helps them to discharge emotional tensions and even to resolve their conflicts by enabling them to see that their individual problem is part of the whole human situation, and by pointing out reassuring solutions. Thus art is a form of psychotherapy and, of course, is often deliberately used to that end in the treatment of mental illness. Keeping at the superficial level, it is easy to see that two very pervasive and readily interpreted themes in fairy-tales are the giant-killer theme which reassures the child that the frequently awe-inspiring 'giants' of the adult world are capable of being dealt with and have their weaknesses, and the theme which pictures the youngest son as the 'hero' who accomplishes all the tasks the older brothers have failed in and wins the hand of the fairy princess. But at a much deeper level there lies a darker and more sinister set of fantasies shared by all of us in a world peopled by demons, witches with iron teeth who devour children, the wicked stepmother who wishes to poison her lovely stepdaughter, all of which are depicted in such tales as 'Hansel and Gretel', 'Snow-white', 'Rumplestiltskin', and the rest. The great Greek plays centre around such incredible plots as that of King Œdipus who kills his father and marries his mother, or Princess Electra who connives at the death of her mother who had murdered her father Agamemnon (*see* **H24**), and the myths of all countries tell of infants born out of the mouth or navel, of castration, incest, and milder stories such as that of the unknown child reared by simple folk who turns out to be of royal blood.

These horror-comic themes, in short, are universal not because some eccentric invented them but *because we have all experienced them in real life.* The child unsatisfied at the breast has fantasies of devouring the breast and, when these are projected, they reappear as the mother who wishes to devour the child; the mother in one stage of infancy is divided into the good satisfying mother and the bad devouring one, the former becoming the 'fairy godmother' and the latter the witch or evil 'stepmother'. Shakespeare's *Hamlet*, incidentally, is a good example of this mechanism because Hamlet was actually jealous of his late father's possession of his mother but, being unable to accept that the father he also loved could be hated, the wicked uncle-stepfather is made to bear the hated side; psychologically speaking, the bad stepfather and the good murdered father are different aspects of the same person and Hamlet has projected his own incestuous desires for his mother upon the stepfather. Many children quite consciously have the feeling that their mother is not their true parent and that they have more exalted origins. This necessity to think in terms of a good parent and a bad one is later replaced by the realisation that there is simply one individual who is sometimes lovable and sometimes hateful and this ambivalence, *i.e.*, having mixed feelings for the same person, is a step towards maturity, though later it will be replaced by a more discriminating picture of goodness and badness based, not on how people react to us in satisfying or unsatisfying terms, but on more objective standards.

There are two main conclusions to be drawn from this analysis of the fantasies of the child:

(1) that children are far from 'innocent' in the Victorian sense and have experienced far greater horrors in their own minds than can be introduced from outside. They enjoy, for example, Grimm's fairy-tales because *in an atmosphere of security* at the mother's knee or by the nursery fireside, their conflicts are objectified and the story has a satisfying ending which helps to resolve them.

(2) that the normal child is the ambivalent child who has received enough sense of security from its parents to be able to express openly its alternate affection and resentment which, beginning at an early age, becomes increasingly evident as it grows older when a conflict arises between the need for dependency and its ever-increasing need for independence and self-realisation. Large-scale studies have shown beyond shadow of doubt that ambivalence is characteristic of the normal child; obedience, dependence, and unnatural 'goodness' or compliance are characteristic of the neurotic child; and complete lack of feeling is typical of the potential delinquent.

Intelligence.

Since we are discussing fundamentals rather than techniques or applications (many of which are left for the reader to decide, on the basis of what has been said here, for himself) little will be said of the way intelligence tests are carried out nor of the actual process of education about which so many different views are held. The writer can only state his personal disapproval of the 11-plus examination, and his preference for the comprehensive and mixed school, but others doubtless have equally good reasons for their contrary opinions. So all that will be considered at this point is the general validity of intelligence tests and the factors which may influence their results together with some significant facts and fallacies about intelligence.

Intelligence is simply defined as that which intelligence tests test and, by and large, such tests are correlated with school success—though it would be more accurate to say that these correlations are sufficiently high to be useful but not so high as to exclude other factors in which the personality is involved as predictors to success. As one authority puts it, what is tested are those qualities that happen to be useful or regarded as valuable in the industrial society in which we live. Recent work seems to suggest that most of those who do well at school are almost certain to do well (other things being equal) in fairly pedestrian and conventional jobs in which hard work, knowledge, intelligence, and not too much imagination are required, whereas genuinely brilliant children with novel ideas may do rather badly simply because, though equally intelligent, they are original and rebel against discipline. This does not mean that many geniuses have not shown consistent success from their earliest days, but there are also those in whom failure to do well at school has been almost a hall-mark of their later success. Intelligence is defined (*a*) in terms of mental age or M.A., and (*b*) in terms of the intelligence quotient or I.Q. (These terms are explained in **Section L** under **Intelligence.**)

Measurement of Mental Ability.

Since intelligence, like other dimensions of personality, is distributed in a bell-shaped curve with the average people at the top and the very intelligent or very dull at either end, we can say that the *normal* category (including 50 per cent of the population) has I.Q.s from 90–110. Those with an I.Q. of more than 110 are in the upper fourth of the population. I.Q.s from 110–120 place the individual in a *superior* category, 120–130 in the very superior category, and from 130–

140 in that of the *near-geniuses*. Geniuses (in the technical, not the popular, sense of the word) are those with I.Q.s of over 140 and include less than 1 per cent of the population. At the other end of the scale are the *dull normals* (80–90), the *borderline mentally deficient* (70–80) and the *mentally deficient* (70 and below). The latter group includes the dull and backward or *morons* (50–70), *imbeciles* (20–40), and the *idiots* who fall below 20.

Mental ability, as measured by intelligence tests, reaches its peak between the ages of 14 and 20 and subsequently declines slowly until old age, though no great decline appears before 50 and even then it is not marked. However, this slow decline in intelligence is compensated for by greater ability due to increasing knowledge and experience, so whilst John Stuart Mill was obviously a genius by the age of three and most scientists who achieve anything do so by the age of thirty, Verdi's greatest operas were composed when he was over eighty. Nor is there any necessary correlation between greatness and high intelligence; for though such men as Mill, Coleridge, Macaulay, Pope, and Voltaire, according to retrospective estimates, would have had I.Q.s in the region of the 170–180 group, those with I.Q.s of 100–110 would have included John Bunyan, Cervantes, Luther, Rembrandt, William Cobbett, and the poet Dryden.

Influential Factors.

Among the factors known to influence the result of intelligence tests are learning how to do such tests (in other words, this is an ability which to some extent can be acquired); better education, because it has often been demonstrated that even identical twins with the same heredity and therefore the same basic intelligence can have different I.Q.s, the twin with the better education sometimes having an I.Q. of ten or more points above the other; city children do better than country children with an average I.Q. difference of 6½ points because the city child is exposed to more stimulation; foster-children sent to poor homes may show a *loss* of their initial I.Q. of up to 47 points, whilst foster-children placed in good homes may gain 20 or more. Psychological factors are also important and those with so-called obsessional traits of carefulness who are always looking back to see if their previous answers were correct are penalised in comparison with the confident child who works fast. As regards sexual differences, and those connected with race, we know there are no significant differences between the sexes in overall intelligence and that men do better on some tests, women on others; northern Negroes in America score as well or better than southern whites, northern whites higher than southern whites, and southern Negro children moved into northern schools show an increase in I.Q. One of the highest I.Q. scores ever recorded was that of a Negro girl in North America.

Elsewhere we have noted the importance of the child's attitude towards education in relation to parental attitudes towards the child, and when we come to discuss industry it will become apparent that many countries remain backward in spite of technical and other aid because of their emotional and social attitudes to such matters as ambition, working to the clock, financial incentives, and social change. Those who have always thought of society as essentially static and of life as being determined by fate, require to change these attitudes before they can bring about their industrial revolution. It is not lack of intelligence, but socially-conditioned indifference that causes their problems. Other psychological tests which measure special aptitudes or the personality will be dealt with in Part III.

ADOLESCENCE.

Adolescence is manifestly brought about by physical changes in the body due to changes in the sex and other glands such as the pituitary and the adrenal glands on top of the kidneys. Obvious bodily developments begin to take place: menstruation, the development of the breasts, and the increasingly rounded contours of the figure in girls, the breaking of the voice, development of the muscles, and the production of semen in boys, together with the growth of the beard in boys and growth of hair under the armpits and in the genital region in both sexes. But even these manifestly organic changes are influenced by social factors, both psychological and nutritional, and within the present century the average height of each younger generation has increased and sexual maturity, particularly in girls, begins at an earlier age. Therefore, though these physiological reactions *started* the process, it is very important to avoid ascribing to adolescents in general features which are merely typical of our own and a few other societies. On the other hand, once they have been recognised as non-universal, it is still necessary to consider the characteristics of adolescence in the technologically advanced countries and try to discover their social causes.

The Characteristics of Adolescence in the Technically Advanced Countries.

We can begin by taking two accounts of the traits said to be typical of the adolescent in America, one dating back to G. Stanley Hall in 1908, the other to E. B. Hurlock in 1953. Stanley Hall's list includes (with particular reference to the immediately post-pubertal period): inner absorption and reverie; the birth of imagination, illusions, dreams, etc.; self-criticism, scruples; the over-assertion of individuality; a strong tendency to imitation; the assumption of dramatic poses, roles, affectations; folly, absurdities, freakishness; new speech consciousness; absorption in friendship; intense fluctuations in energy and emotional and intellectual plasticity. Hall likened the manifestations of adolescence to the symptoms of hysteria and insanity, and considered it a period particularly prone to religious conversion and other violent personality changes. Hurlock describes the emotional life of the adolescent as characterised by intensity, lack of control, inconsistency, prevalence of long-drawn-out emotions or moods, and the growth of such sentiments as patriotism, loyalty, and reverence.

Comparison with Other Cultures.

Unfortunately both these catalogues of traits, and particularly that of Hall, show by the very language in which they are expressed the lack of sympathy which, in part, makes the adolescent what he or she is: freakish, given to absurdities, self-conscious about his speech, too individualistic and yet given to self-criticism, lack of control, and the rest. Yet, if some of the features mentioned are dated (*e.g.*, proneness to religious conversion and patriotism are less common than they used to be) and others are obviously more typical of the middle- than the working-class adolescent, as a whole they are recognisably true of our society. That they are far from being true of all, or even many, societies is shown by Margaret Mead's study of Samoa where adolescence brings about no conflict or revolt and no neurotic worries; all children from the earliest age have freely engaged in sexual play and, on the arrival of puberty, the girl engages in a series of affairs with the boys of the community each of which is short-lasting. There are no rules which allow members of certain age-groups definite rights and privileges and in this respect nobody may progress faster than anybody else. So far as sex is concerned, the adults are perfectly well aware of what is going on and make no criticisms nor attempt to interfere in any way.

If one looks behind the lists of traits supposedly typical of the adolescent in our society, it will be found that they can all be compressed into a few fundamental problems or conflicts: there is the quest for identity, the answer to the question, "Who am I?"; the exaggeration of the conflict between dependency and self-sufficiency; and, if frequently the subject of prurient interest on the part of certain adults, the rather less significant sexual problems which do not actually arise at this time, though there is more opportunity to accept or refuse approaches from the other sex, to engage or not to engage in overtly sexual affairs.

No Fixed Rules.

The adolescent in our society is in a confused and precarious position. His childish behaviours are no longer adequate or tolerated and the apparently secure and settled ways of the adult have not yet been learned—in short, he is playing a game with no fixed rules. Now this is not so elsewhere, nor was it always so here; in mediæval society everyone had a fixed role to play according to age, sex, and social status just as in Samoa, and even just prior to the last war few problems of this sort bothered the middle-class child. A girl was a girl until she left school, possibly at the age of eighteen or more; a boy was a boy until he went to university or started in a job. This, indeed, is still the case in less sophisticated societies where a boy becomes a man at a specific age and the occasion is marked by initiation rites following which he *knows* that he is a man with full adult rights. In many European peasant communities one can tell an individual's position from his (or her) dress: the unmarried girl, the widow, the bachelor, the married couple, all have sartorial indications of their state. Today none of this exists in the technically developed countries: according to traditional morality, sexual intercourse is forbidden before marriage (at least to girls) and yet the period between the attainment of sexual maturity and the possibility of marriage increases for those who wish to advance themselves. There are no fixed rules regarding the age at which certain privileges are automatically obtained; for example, one piece of research showed that in a suburb in a large American city the age at which parents permitted their daughters to go out unaccompanied varied from fourteen to twenty. The law decides when children may buy cigarettes, parents make their own widely differing regulations and it is understandable that those who see this behaviour permitted in others of their own age-group will feel deprived and embarrassed if it is forbidden to themselves.

Moral Standards

The period at which an adolescent ceases to be a child and becomes an adult not only varies widely in general but even varies in relation to specific activities; it is possible to be a 'child' in one field and an 'adult' in others. Hence the adolescent's search for identity, role-playing, imitation of heroes or pop-singers of his own age, self-searching, and resentment of adults. The latter is increased by the ardent moving away from childhood status towards self-realisation as the individual interprets it, and both lead to adolescent assertion, aggressiveness, and the feeling that he is not 'understood'. Nor is he understood, because technical progress and the changes it has brought about in social patterns make even the young parent useless as a model for youth to follow—there is an ever-increasing gap between the generations who cannot understand that each is literally living in a different world and the old rules of even twenty years ago are not always applicable now. Sexual behaviour is as much a sign of revolt and defiance as of genuine sexuality, and having a sexual affair is often regarded as a status-symbol just as smoking in school was a status-symbol before the war. Modern youth is much more knowledgeable about sex than formerly (though still not sufficiently instructed) and therefore less prone to genuinely sexual conflicts than previous generations. Few indeed worry about masturbation, that object of baseless terror to their parents; for they know that it is largely universal and entirely harmless. Of course, many moralists regard it as wicked as they are perfectly entitled to do, but that it is harmless is a medical *fact* which they are not entitled to query. Indeed, the main cause of excessive masturbation is not overdeveloped sexuality but anxiety brought about by threats of this sort.

Good Morals begin with Right Attitudes to Others.

The trouble about sexual morality is that, though some may believe that there are certain fixed standards which determine what is 'right' or 'wrong' in this field—and it is impossible to contradict them because this is not a matter science can usefully discuss—in reality all moral standards have varied widely from one place or time to another. It is clear that the basic revolution brought about by Jesus Christ was a realisation that good morals begin with right *attitudes* to other people and cannot be codified in a fixed set of rules that tell people what they must *not* do, and we have given numerous examples from modern psychology to show that when people do the 'right' thing for the wrong reason they are not likely to be successful in achieving their goal. Saint Augustine put it even more bluntly when he said: "Love God and do what you like"—or as some might say, "If you genuinely care for other people in their own right you't can go far wrong."

ADULTHOOD AND MATURITY.

Psychological Maturity.

It is evident that society decides when a person shall be regarded as adult and that, on the whole, this bears little relationship to biological maturity—much less to psychological maturity which is achieved by few. Among the qualities which are the signs of psychological maturity one must take into account:

(1) Emotional control, which implies that the truly adult person has to learn to defer immediate gratification of his wishes or expressions of his feelings which must become subject to his total way of life—he will learn that it is not worth while giving way momentarily to a form of behaviour which will only be followed by shame or is likely to ruin all that he has regarded as his highest ideals.

(2) The appropriateness of his emotions—that is to say that, broadly speaking, a mature person's emotional responses are objectively relevant to the actual situation facing him and his expression of feelings shows an awareness of those of others. The problem of achieving emotional maturity is not solved by stamping out or denying emotions, however strong or unpleasant they may be; it is a problem of learning to live with emotions, keeping them within reasonable bounds, and of turning them, whenever possible, to the ends of survival of ourselves and others in this complicated world.

(3) The richness and variety of experience, whereby the all-or-none emotions of the infant become highly differentiated, varying from righteous anger or disgust, to wry amusement and the most subtle æsthetic pleasures. Unfortunately most of us, partly from psychological distortions arising in childhood and partly from lack of stimulation from the environment such as inadequate education, never wholly reach this stage and it is obvious that some of the greatest geniuses, whilst adding to our own capacity for æsthetic pleasures, still remained emotionally childish—not with the *child-like* simplicity of a poet such as Blake, but often with the vicious childishness of the antisemitic Wagner or the woman-obsessed yet woman-terrified Strindberg.

Most people are immature in various ways and must simply try to make the best of things and it is probably true to say that many live lives of quiet desperation. Marriage takes place for the wrong reasons because of modern society's obsession with sex and its failure to see that sex without comradeship, compatibility of temperament, and the appreciation and respect due to a partner who is a human being in his or her own right, is bound to fail. Men marry women sometimes as lovely status-symbols, sometimes as mother-substitutes, and sometimes as someone to boss for the lack of any other means of expressing their power obsessions—yet, strangely enough, marriage survives and perhaps has never been in a stronger position as a social institution. But, again, society determines the form of marriage and the structure of the family and exerts pressures upon it for good or ill that must be considered later. Even when the change of life, which is biologically conditioned, makes its appearance in the course of time how it is experienced is socially influenced. Like adolescence, it may become a period of storm and stress, or, on the other hand, the prelude to a contented retirement with enhanced powers of enjoyment both sexual and æsthetic; its connection with cultural factors is demonstrated even within the bounds of our own country where serious depressive states in middle age are much commoner in the more puritanical north than in the more permissive south.

OLD AGE.

Biological Factors.

Anyone can see that not only do the signs of old age come on at very varying times, being sometimes relatively early and in other cases hardly apparent at all even in advanced years, but also that, when the signs do come, they assume a form which is the same for all peoples and at all places. This is because old age, like puberty and the change of life but even more so, is brought about by basically biological factors. These include glandular changes, though the most obvious results of senility arise from a deterioration of the substance of the brain caused either by a primary degeneration of the cells in the nervous tissues or a secondary degeneration which produces the same result by reducing their blood supply when ageing arteries become hardened and narrow. The effects of these changes can be summarised by saying that senile deterioration leads in varying degrees to memory changes such that memory for recent events is poor whilst that for long past events is usually retained or even emphasised and dwelt on; that the individual tends to become emotionally unstable and, for example, more easily moved to tears; and that there may be apparent changes in personality.

Social Influences.

These changes are more apparent than real, for what actually happens is that, with the deterioration of the higher centres of control, features such as jealousy, greed, or meanness, which have hitherto been kept under control, are released. In other words, the senile person 'becomes himself, only more so'. But even in the presence of such changes as are clearly due to biological factors, social influences are very much in evidence —for example, in our form of society where old people are often regarded as a problem or a nuisance, it is hardly surprising that they tend to become suspicious, irritable, and self-centred.

Technical change has brought a situation in which, unlike that in the old peasant or agrarian community, old people and schoolchildren, up to quite a later age, are unproductive. Whereas in the changing rural communities of today and even in the old East End of London, the grandparents played an important part in the life of the community, looking after the grandchildren whilst their mother and father were at work, advising their own children about matters in which their long life had given them the experience to guide, and acting as the respected elders of the village or suburban group, they now find themselves unwanted. The younger generation is moved out to satellite towns whilst the old people are left behind, alone and lost in a world they no longer understand. What seemed to be eternal verities have gone, and these are needs that even the best treatment in an old people's home cannot satisfy.

Here is another clear example of a biological problem which is also a personal one and at the same time very much a social one to be solved not by charity and misplaced sympathy but by the understanding that comes from a combination of science and caring which are more closely related than is always realised. As Leonardo da Vinci wrote in his 'Treatise on Painting': "In truth great love springs from great knowledge of the beloved object, and if you know it but little you will be able to love it only a little or not at all." Or in the language of Freud, even the most abstract study of the universe requires that the object of our study should be invested with the love we have projected upon it; when hate is projected hate is what is reflected back and we understand nothing.

II. SOCIETY

1. SOCIETY AND CULTURE.

A society is a more or less permanent group of people living together and sharing a common way of life and common attitudes and beliefs. Its culture is the name given to this way of life, and the term *physical culture* refers to objects such as weapons, bowls, art, and in more complex societies, an elaborate technology. The people who make a special study of different cultures are known as social anthropologists and when they first began to take their work seriously and carry out field studies by living among the people they were studying, it was natural that they should choose primitive tribes as being the most convenient because (at any rate at that time, from the beginning of the present century to just before the last war) there were many of these primitive groups which had lived in comparative isolation and therefore showed the culture in an almost unadulterated form. The culture had remained unchanged for many centuries, and among these people the social structure was much more rigid and easily defined than in the larger and more complex industrial societies. Nowadays, however, a social anthropologist may study any sort of culture, for example, a Yorkshire mining community, or a working-class community such as Dagenham, a study which is mentioned in Part III.

Basic Personality Structure of a Society.

Enough has already been said to show that there are great variations among different cultures as to what people consider 'normal' behaviour and the different roles its members ought to play in relation to the rest. Culture not only imposes general beliefs which are expected to be shared by all members of a society (for example, its religion and mythology, or its economic and political system) but defines the part men and women must take in the division of labour or rearing the family together with accepted methods of doing so, and the rules children must follow in dealing with each other and their parents or elders. This results in what has been described as the 'basic personality structure' of a society, the blueprint for parents to adopt when bringing up their children.

Studies of Primitive Societies.

A brief glance at some of these various cultural ideals in primitive societies is necessary because they are of great practical interest to psychologists and psychiatrists to whom they have given an entirely different view of the potentialities of 'human nature' and caused the psychiatrist, in particular, to re-think what he means when he talks about 'normality', and even what he means by 'mental disease'. Thus the great majority of psychiatrists up to the late nineteenth century, and a certain number at the present day, have taken the view that mental disease is brain disease but this belief requires considerable modification if one finds that serious depression leading to suicide is totally unknown in some communities, that people in one tribal group show many of the symptoms of what in Europe would be regarded as schizophrenia, that the neurosis known as 'conversion hysteria' is commoner in technically backward parts of the world and, even in Europe, begins to disappear as technology advances. Similarly, those who have always supposed that certain behaviour is typical of women and that women are socially and intellectually inferior to men because of their allegedly innate physical weakness and their peculiar glandular structure, will have to reconsider their belief when they find that in some societies women are the dominant sex.

The Researches of Ruth Benedict and Margaret Mead.

Two American anthropologists, Ruth Benedict and Margaret Mead (who has already been mentoned in relation to her study of adolescence in Samoa), began in the 1930s to study various primitive tribes and the differences in basic personality structure that they discovered were striking. To take a few examples: among neighbouring tribes in New Guinea Mead found the following differences in sexual attitudes. One tribe, the Arapesh, had as its ideal the mild responsive man married to the mild responsive woman; another, the Mundugumor, valued the violent aggressive man and the corresponding aggressive woman—in fact, aggressiveness was so strong a feature of this tribe that literally every man hated and feared every other man and the only possible relationship between two men was one mediated by a woman; a third tribe, the Tshambuli, showed a complete reversal of the sexual attitudes regarded by us as 'normal' with the husband the mild submissive partner who sat at home dressing himself up and applying cosmetics whilst the wife was impersonal, dominant, and managing, doing most of the work outside the home. Benedict found that the Zuni Indians of New Mexico had such a distaste for aggression or even self-assertion that the polite thing to do was to try to lose at competitive games, and leaders could only be elected by locking up some of the nastier members of the group until they broke down and agreed to act as chiefs; once elected, they were regarded with contempt and, at the least sign of self-assertion, would be hung up by their thumbs until they confessed and promised not to behave in that way again. The Arapesh, too, are so unaggressive that the sign of anyone in a rage shocks them as much as any discussion of sex shocked our Victorian forebears. The Dobu of New Guinea live in such a state of persecutory suspicion that a Western psychiatrist would unhesitatingly diagnose them as paranoiacs just as he might diagnose a typical Balinese as schizophrenic, and whilst the Western industrialist tries to acquire wealth, the Kwakiutl Indians of Puget Sound hold ceremonies at which the men compete to discover who can destroy the greatest amount of money in the shortest possible time.

Many societies, like the Greeks of classical times, have valued homosexuality as being a more spiritual form of love than sexual relations with women who exist only to do domestic work and bear children. In the words of Benedict, we have come to realise that "most of these organisations of personality that seem to us most incontrovertibly abnormal, have been used by different civilisations in the very foundations of their institutional life. Conversely, the most valued traits of our normal individuals have been looked upon in differently organised cultures as abnormal. Normality, in short, within a very wide range, is culturally defined."

Cultural Change.

Two important questions arise from these observations, the first is how these various cultures arose and took the particular form they did, the second is the problem of what makes cultures change. The answer to the first question is fairly simple; it is that each culture is a way of life suited to a particular group with certain historical traditions and adapted to a specific physical environment. It is both unconsciously and deliberately passed on from one generation to the next by specific methods of child rearing. "Systems of child training", writes Erikson, "represent unconscious attempts at creating out of human raw material that configuration of attitudes which is (or once was) the optimum under the tribe's particular natural conditions and economic-historic necessities."

As will be seen in more detail later, the basic personality structure of Western Europe completely changed about the time of the Renaissance from a state of affairs in which conformity and a static social structure was the ideal to one which valued the most extreme expressions of individualism, personal aggrandisement, acquisitiveness, and social mobility. No living things are so variable as human beings and, though the existence of their innate needs explains why they *initiate* certain actions (*e.g.*, why they want to eat, drink, or obtain sexual satisfaction), it does not in any way explain *how* they do these things, why they sometimes do them when they do not wish to, or do not do them when they do wish to; biology becomes subservient to culture and even the most pressing physical needs may become secondary to social needs. Thus in an American town during the depression of the early 1930s, purchases of food declined markedly whilst petrol sales remained at the normal level—obviously the social prestige associated with running a car was more important to many impoverished citizens than having regular and satisfying meals.

Causes of Technical Backwardness.

Whilst such societies as the primitive tribes we have been discussing have shown little change over many centuries, the technically advanced societies are subject to ever-accelerating social change and, of course, under the impact of Western technology, even the primitive communities are beginning to enter a new state of development. It has often been thought that the backwardness of certain peoples was due to some sort of innate inferiority, but the reasons for their apparent backwardness are quite unrelated to any such factors. First, the use of this term is, to some degree, a value judgment—for who is to say whether our society with all its many human problems is 'superior' or not to simpler societies where, for example, suicide and war may be inconceivable? Second, two of the reasons for technical backwardness are quite evident: thus the Eskimos never entered an iron age for the sole reason that they had no iron, and brains are of little avail without the appropriate material conditions to work on; furthermore, until recent times, few of these peoples ever had the stimulus of meeting more complex civilisations. We ourselves lived in a state of comparative backwardness until we were invaded and occupied by the Romans. Third, there may be some truth in Arnold Toynbee's suggestion that cultures need some environmental stimulus to set them moving on the path to progress, and it is of interest to note that nearly all the great civilisations have developed in temperate lands where nature was not so harsh as to prevent any elaborate culture from arising nor so lavish as to make such attempts unnecessary.

Technological Change.

Primarily, says W. F. Ogburn of Chicago, "the cause of social change is the making of inventions mechanical or otherwise, and secondarily, the diffusion of inventions already made." Whilst new *discoveries* are by their very nature quite original, *e.g.*, the discovery of how to make bronze (the first alloy known to man) from its constituent metals of copper and tin, was something entirely novel in man's history, new *inventions* are for the most part a combination of old elements—that is, they are dependent upon already-known principles. It follows that the more of such elements or principles existing in a particular culture the greater will be the number of possible new inventions. So although a simple kind of steam-engine was devised by Hero of Alexandria (*fl.* A.D. 62) nearly two thousand years ago, it was of no practical use because before the steam-engine of the eighteenth century could be produced it was necessary to know about new ways of treating iron to make it harder, the principle of transmitting power from shaft to shaft and from one direction to another which involves knowledge of the toothed wheel or gear, the idea of vehicles travelling on rails, and many other elements. Today, even a complicated piece of machinery such as the electronic computer was readily put together by utilising and recombining a large number of elements and principles already known. Technical progress moves at an ever-increasing rate for just this reason, and as Ogburn has pointed out material culture grows according to the exponential principle, *i.e.*, like compound interest.

The Social Effects of Technical Change.

Since culture is an attempt to adjust to a particular environment which is now almost entirely of our own making, it follows that the culture of modern society is an attempt to adjust to our man-made environment and reflects this material background, and also that, since the pace of development is rapidly increasing, adjustment becomes ever more difficult. This has been noted already in the gulf of understanding between generations; for even the most modern youth is barely adjusting to the changes of ten years earlier. The situation is very similar to that described by Karl Marx, who whatever one may think of his economic theories, was one of the greatest sociologists who ever lived. Marx described a substructure or *Unterbau* which he believed to be the economic system of a society, and pointed out that upon this is built the religious attitudes, ethics, laws, and institutions which form the *Oberbau* or superstructure of society. (*See* **J27**). In fact, the less a body of thought is subject to objective verification, the more is it likely to reflect the substructure of society which modern sociologists regard as its technology. Whilst science is comparatively culture-free, existing religious attitudes or philosophical systems or ethical beliefs are very strongly influenced in this way; for example, the Reformation (**J38**) was not brought about by Luther's distaste for the corruption of Rome, since movements dating back to the thirteenth century or earlier (the Waldenses (**J45**), the Albigenses (**J2**), and that led by Wyclif in England) had felt just the same—it happened *at that time* because Luther's ideas fitted in very well with new individualist attitudes resulting from the early stirrings of the industrial revolution and German nationalism. Again, slavery would have been abolished in America even if William Lloyd Garrison had never been born and *Uncle Tom's Cabin* had never been written; slavery disappeared because it was becoming useless as a means of production, just as it had previously been supported by moralists so long as it was useful. Reformers need to learn that one can rarely start a trend without pre-existing foundations, frequently accelerate one that already exists, but never reverse trends already moving in a particular direction in response to environmental pressures.

The Stages of Cultural Change.

The development from technical changes to changes in the ideological superstructure takes place in four stages:

(1) The material invention or discovery.

(2) Changes in the economic and social structure.

(3) Changes in the other parts of the social structure.

(4) Change in cultural attitudes and popular ideology.

Let us take as an example the influence of the steam-engine on woman's position in society. First, the various types of steam-engine led to the development of more efficient and specialised power-driven machinery on the railroads, in the factory, and ultimately in the home; transport is made easier and therefore cities grow larger, industrial work is made lighter, and house-work less onerous. As a result of this the greater physical strength of men becomes less important in many forms of work and women become as efficient as men over a wider field; they are increasingly employed in industry, work becomes separated from home, and gradually there arises an improved standard of living, increased consumption, and a more easy-going attitude to life.

Changes in other parts of the social structure develop more slowly: the modern family is no longer an economic unit as in the agrarian society, and it is losing its rigid social control over its individual members whilst, as Folsom puts it, " elaborating other functions, most important of which is the more complete satisfaction of the love-wish, both with regard to marital and parent–child love". There is no longer one single accepted family-pattern, the patriarchal family, but wide variations from the mother-centred family to the egalitarian family and even the filiocentric family, so that power is no longer centred exclusively upon the father and the family is becoming more democratic. Of course, all these developments arose not from any single cause but were helped along by such other technical inventions as gas and subsequently electric lighting in the streets and home, the wider knowledge and use of contraceptives, and the mass media which (in one of their aspects) led to a wider and faster spreading of knowledge and a levelling in cultural standards.

Cultural Lag.

Traditional attitudes and old ways of thinking, however, tend to persist much longer, largely because they are identified with values which are very deep-seated and any attempt to modify these is likely to be described as " a lowering of moral standards " or in such terms as " the moral crisis of our time". Of course, there is a moral crisis, but it is due not to change but precisely to the failure to change; it is caused by the ' cultural lag ' between old attitudes and a new environment. Thus the so-called ' equality of the sexes ' to which all but the least-enlightened pay lip-service is more nominal than real; for what has happened is that, whilst women have gained many new functions, they have lost few of their old ones. The girl who comes back from work at the factory is still expected to do some of the housework whilst her brother is not. There is even an attempt to drag women back to their more ' feminine ' role with the appeal of cosmetic, fashion, and home-decoration advertising; papers of good standing intended for both sexes nevertheless have a special section for women as though they were social oddities in a way that men are not; and there is the tremendous number of women's magazines catering for all that is most infantile and written in a kind of baby-talk, stories of how the heroine succeeds in marrying her boss, columns dealing with how to dress, solving one's love-problems, and the rest. As Dr. Viola Klein says, the state of women at the present time is characterised by a dilemma, which is another of the many conflicts inherent in our present cultural situation. " It results from the contrast between a materially changed situation and the simultaneous survival of traditional ideologies and attitudes." One has only to think of the fuss made by many men teachers at any suggestion that women should get equal pay for equal work, to see how true this statement is.

Cultural Change in the Underdeveloped Countries.

In the more technically backward societies, the impact of industrialisation and new mass-production techniques has been even more dramatic. Drucker has shown how " the sweep of mass-production technology is undermining and exploding societies and civilisations which have no resistance to the new forces, no background or habit-pattern of industrial life to cushion the shock. In China the mass-production principle, swept into the hinterland from the coastal cities by the forced migration of industries during the Japanese invasion, is destroying the world's oldest and hitherto its stablest institution: the Chinese family. In India industrialisation has begun to corrode the Hindu caste system: ritual restrictions on proximity and intercourse between castes simply cannot be maintained under factory conditions. In America the Old South, hitherto least touched by industry and still living in the ruins of its ante-bellum order is speedily being ' tractored off '. Indeed, conversion of the Southern farm into a rural assembly-line seems on the verge of ' solving ' the Southern race problem in a manner never dreamed of by either Southern Liberal or Southern Reactionary: by pushing the Negro off the land into the industrial cities."

Whilst we in Britain have had ample time to adjust to the results of the industrial revolution and have not yet succeeded in completely doing so, the danger in these new societies is that what took more than two centuries here is being compressed into a matter of a few years with a consequent risk of serious conflict and the uprooting of old values with nothing to take their place. Unless social scientists work alongside technicians to ensure that social change is smooth, the persistence of traditional attitudes against a new material background may have dangerous results.

Since the end of the last war the introduction of modern medicine to Ceylon has halved the death-rate, largely by virtually wiping out malaria with drugs and DDT; it was reduced from 22 to 11 per thousand in less than ten years—but the birth-rate remains the same and, at the present rate, the population will more than double every 25 years. The failure to make psychological adjustments to situations of this sort has resulted in the great benefits made possible by science in the form of better health, better nutrition and higher standards of living being nullified as quickly as they are being developed.

All over the world man's greed has led, in the words of Julian Huxley, to the despoiling of nature at an appalling rate. " Wildlife is being exterminated; forests are being cut down, mountains gashed by hydroelectric projects, wildernesses plastered with mine shafts and tourist camps, fields and meadows stripped away for roads and airports." Processes such as these are not planned with a view to the greater benefit of people in general but motivated by a blind and stupid acquisitiveness.

2. THE MODERN SOCIETY.

The large-scale modern society differs from the primitive societies, first investigated, in some important respects which will now be discussed.

The Social Structure: Sub-cultures.

The social structure of modern society is much more complex due to the existence of class differences, regional groupings, and different racial and religious or political groups within the national boundaries. These are described as sub-cultures and require to be considered separately against the overall culture of the state. Thus, though all Britons share some attitudes in common which can be described as the national character, a Roman Catholic Briton does not share all the values of a Protestant one; a middle-class Briton has very different attitudes to many things compared with a working-class one; and a Yorkshireman differs culturally from a Welshman. It is necessary to understand this when we are trying to unravel the causes of racial disturbances, industrial unrest, and other problems in which there are two opposed groups failing to communicate because they are simply not talking the same language and see the same events in a totally different light.

We must repeat, too, that national character is not fixed nor is it innate, but like other constellations of traits has social and historical roots. In spite of the complexity of these national groups more or less successful attempts have been made to understand their overall culture: Mead and Gorer have written studies of the American national character, Gorer of the Greater Russians, and Benedict of the Japanese. The usefulness of these studies is shown by the fact that Benedict was able successfully to predict how the Japanese would react to defeat and occupation at the end of the last war. Much of the American national character can be explained in terms of the rejection of the alien father by the children of first-generation immigrants and the fact that most American males are almost entirely reared by women from the possessive mother whose cult has been described as 'momism' to school education which is carried out largely by women teachers. Hence the American suspicion of 'foreigners', their rejection of Europe towards which many have a love–hate relationship, their constant affirmation of manliness and being 'red-blooded Americans' and their terror of homosexuality—the latter attitudes arising from a deep-seated fear of the sometimes overwhelming females who reared them causing a need constantly to affirm their maleness, and the already-noted fact that boys brought up mainly by women often develop latent or overt homosexual tendencies against which they attempt to defend themselves. Jess Stearn's book *The Sixth Man* which asserts that "one out of every six men in America is a homosexual" demonstrates this fear to an almost paranoiac degree and, although almost entirely nonsensical, became a best-seller showing how widespread is this anxiety in the United States.

Rapid Social Change and Social Status.

Another respect in which modern society differs from primitive societies is the rapidity of social change which leads to the discrepancy between old traditions and present realities with results which have already been discussed. In a society of rapid change social status is not only subject to fluctuation as the individual moves up or down a scale created by extreme social mobility, but quite often status is not (as it is in more primitive groups) very clearly defined, and this leads to feelings of insecurity. Since social status is a kind of transference of the child's need for maternal approval towards the need for the approval of society in later life, we can say that the desire for status is one of the most fundamental of human drives and its absence or loss is a common precipitating factor in neurosis.

In the first part of this section we saw how many of the individual's attitudes are derived from the groups to which he belongs, and it is these which are his main source of status, from the small, primary, informal groups such as the family, the play-group, the work-group, the group of village elders, the group of housewives who regularly meet for a cup of coffee, to the large and more impersonal secondary institutions which confer formal status, *e.g.*, the army, the professions, industry, the churches, and so on. If the primary groups break up, status is in peril.

The Sick Society Concept.

Now, in the view of some authorities, this is just what is happening. The old primary groupings are allegedly disintegrating in what has become a mass society, and the family, the working group, the village council, are being replaced by huge anonymous bodies in relation to which personal status, useful function, and individual significance are lost. It is further claimed that more than any previous society ours is one which persistently stimulates people's desires without being able to satisfy them, and that it is based on conflicting ideals which the individual finds it impossible to reconcile. Whilst accepting the two latter statements with reservations, the present writer, for reasons to be discussed elsewhere, does not wholly accept the first. Nevertheless it is obvious that many supposedly personal conflicts are really imposed upon us by society, and the psychoanalyst Karen Horney believed that the conflicts found in the neuroses are simply a microcosm of social conflicts. From such considerations as these has arisen the concept of the 'sick society', elaborated on by Halliday in this country and Frank in America, which suggests that since all our most pressing problems are simply facets of a more fundamental problem lying at the very heart of modern society, they can be dealt with constructively only at the social level. Frank expresses his views as follows: "Instead of thinking of a multiplicity of so-called social problems, each demanding special attention and a different remedy, we can view all of them as different symptoms of the same disease. If, for example, we would regard crime, mental disorders, family disorganisation, juvenile delinquency, prostitution and sex offenses, and much that now passes as the result of pathological processes (for example, gastric ulcer) as evidence not of individual wickedness, incompetence, perversity, or pathology, but as human reactions to cultural disintegration, a forward step would be taken." This is tantamount to saying—as is quite true—that malaria is most suitably dealt with by killing mosquitoes with DDT or typhoid fever by ensuring a pure water supply, but it does not alter the fact that, once individual cases have been infected, the physician must have recourse to quinine and penicillin. Certainly we are made what we are by social pressures, but as individuals we have to learn to live with these pressures and in what follows an attempt will be made to show that individual responsibility must still play a part and that we personally can do something to help ourselves.

The sick society concept is both true and useful and, practically speaking, it does three things:

(1) It makes us realise that it is not profitable to try to help people by blaming them and that an additional reason for not doing so is that society (which is another name for ourselves) has played some part in making them what they are. One has only to think of the many moralists who have supported prostitution in the past because it upheld the 'sanctity' of the family, maintained the 'purity' of the middle-class girl, and reduced what might otherwise have resulted in emotional tensions.

(2) It makes us realise that our own problems, if often peculiar, are never unique.

(3) It helps not only in discovering what these problems are but, by revealing their social background, enables us to see them more constructively, less uncharitably, and points to possible solutions.

If we recall Jung's case of the Quaker who could not imagine that he had ever done anything wrong, yet whose son became a thief and his daughter a prostitute, we may see therein a parable showing how the respectable members of society are not guiltless of creating juvenile delinquency and prostitution because those who engage in these activities represent the dark aspects of society and act as our scapegoats. In a perfectly real sense, we are enabled to remain 'good' because they are 'bad'.

3. THE FAMILY.

Family Conflicts.

The original family was the extended family of agrarian communities which included not only both pairs of grandparents but also various uncles and aunts and assorted relatives. It was an economic unit in which throughout life each member had a useful part to play; moreover being large, family tensions were less prolonged if often no less acute than in the family of today.

The modern family is usually small because children, until they go to work, and the old who have finished working, are economic liabilities, but this very smallness leads to more intense and chronic disagreements, the more obvious sources of which have already been mentioned: jealousies between children, parental conflicts, conflicts between parents and children as the latter try to assert their independence, and between grandparents, who feel useless and unwanted, and their children and grandchildren. Other sources of difficulty arising from without the family are modern society's obsession with commercial sex which incessantly stimulates desire whilst conventional morals deny it outlet, and the no less stupid obsession with the achievement of complete sexual satisfaction as a necessity for a happy marriage. Working mothers in addition to their other worries are told by reputable psychiatrists that by going out to work they are turning their children into potential delinquents; many men still refuse to recognise the changing role of women in society and attempt to reverse the trend by reverting to the 'baby doll' image of womanhood; the 'housebound housewife' feels the boredom that only increases with affluence. All these are real problems yet it is undoubtedly true that at no time has the British family been so stable and so mature in its relationships. We hear about the failures because they are newsworthy and most widely discussed by experts and, as Michael Young and Peter Willmott have shown in their study of the family in Bethnal Green, all that is written about broken marriages, juvenile delinquency, child neglect, and problem families has "created an impression that working-class families are disunited, unsocial, and unhappy".

The Present Status of the Family.

We have no space to discuss the fallacies involved in this belief, but perhaps this is best done by quoting from two of the most detailed accounts of current attitudes towards the family: the study mentioned above on working-class attitudes, *Family and Kinship in East London*, and Gorer's more inclusive book, *Exploring English Character*. Of the modern working-class family Young and Willmott write: "(Our) impressions suggest that the old style of working-class family is fast disappearing . . . in place of the old comes a new kind of companionship between man and woman, reflecting the rise in status of the young wife and children which is one of the great transformations of our time. There is now a nearer approach to equality between the sexes and, though each has a peculiar role, its boundaries are no longer so rigidly defined nor is it performed without consultation."

In a survey which covered all classes in England, Gorer discovered that half the married population of the country have had no sexual relationships either before or after marriage with anyone else but their spouse, and continues: "What seems to me most noteworthy is the high seriousness with which the great majority of English people approach and regard marriage. Whether premarital experience is advocated or reprobated, the effect on the future marriage is the preponderating consideration. Secondly, the high valuation put on virginity for both sexes is remarkable and I should suspect specifically English." Neither sex pays any appreciable heed to the æsthetic qualities of the other, and when asked to give their opinions on the factors making for happiness in marriage most people mentioned "give and take, understanding, love, mutual trust, equanimity, sexual compatibility, comradeship, a decent income, mutual interests, happy home life, and no money difficulties." One of the biggest surprises in this study was the small number of people who thought that infidelity was a significant cause of marital unhappiness, and most believed that adultery "should not terminate the marriage (if that can possibly be avoided) and does not justify the wronged spouse in adopting violent or aggressive behaviour". This view was accepted by more than half the men and nearly three-quarters of the women. Furthermore, as Gorer says, "there is at least as much tendency to blame oneself for a spouse's derelection as to blame or punish the offending spouse." He suggests that such attitudes imply a relatively low valuation of 'love' and a very high estimation of the institution of marriage, and concludes: "(I) have I hope illustrated the great importance for English men and women of the institution of marriage and the seriousness with which they consider it. It is marriage itself which is important, not, I think, love or sexual gratification; and marriage is living together, making a home together, making a life together, and raising children. Perhaps even more for Englishmen than for English women, parenthood is the greatest joy and greatest responsibility of adult life."

The Married Couple.

There is therefore ample reason to suppose that most married couples in this country are reasonably satisfied with their own lot even if the new society has also given rise to problems. Here we are going to discuss some of those involved in the husband–wife relationship, and it is convenient to do so under the three headings of personal relationships, sex, and work. But before going into details, it is important to consider what exactly is meant by 'happiness', the goal towards which most people seem to be so fervently striving. Indeed, the word 'striving' sums up very clearly what 'happiness' implies; it is, as one psychologist has said, "the state of going someplace". A person is happy when he or she has certain goals which they are on the way towards achieving, no matter how slowly or with what difficulty. Happiness means movement towards, and the pleasure is in the moving rather than in the achieving—which sometimes comes as rather a disappointment. When the philosopher Schopenhauer said that the lot of man must inevitably be a wretched one because he could only be happy in relation to a previous state of comparative unhappiness, he was perhaps being unduly pessimistic but at the same time he was expressing a profound truth: that there is no absolute happiness, but only happiness *in relation to how we felt before*. Thus a crust to a starving man provides more pleasure than another million pounds to a millionaire.

This was strikingly illustrated in a social survey in the United States where many people of all income-groups were asked by what percentage their annual income would require to be increased in order to make them entirely satisfied. The result showed that *all* income-groups produced practically the same figure; both the fifty-dollar-a-week man and the five-hundred-a-week man agreed that an increase of 25 per cent would be adequate. People talk glibly of the 'essentials of life' or the 'basic essentials', but there is, of course, no such thing; what we already have are the basic essentials for us and we usually want a little more. No amount of affluence can make us happy because happiness is a state of striving for more—it may be more money, more household appliances, more children, more rooms and space or more knowledge and virtue, but it is always more of something. Happiness is quite different from contentment which is a state of not wanting, of being satisfied with what we already have, and it is probable that static communities such as the so-called 'backward' countries or the Europe of the Middle Ages contain more contented people because they can move neither up nor down the social scale nor very easily change their position geographically. Doctors and psychiatrists see plenty of people who 'only' want happiness when what they really mean is that they want peace of mind (which is contentment) or that they want happiness but are not prepared to accept that, since this involves striving, it also means the acceptance of much pain and frustration and hard work. Those who think that happiness is something they are *entitled* to—as the Welfare State or the Affluent Society often leads them to believe—had better think again; the *means* to contentment, yes, the *right* to happiness, no. Men or women who set their aim far above what they are humanly likely to achieve should remember the equation which reads: expectation minus realisation equals neurosis.

Personal Relationships in Marriage.

Now this applies with particular force to marriage; for those who have been dazzled by silly romantic stories or commercial advertising into thinking that they are entering a state of undiluted bliss, and, if that fails, there is always a new washing machine to create happiness by lightening their labour, are living in a fool's paradise. Marriage is a constant struggle throughout life to become more mature, better adjusted to one's partner, more tolerant, but above all it is a constant process of education in human relationships. Maturity has already been defined as a state in which relationships are neither self-denying nor denying the rights of others but based on mutual acceptance and respect, and this is the key to satisfaction in marriage. Nobody is more pathetic and in the end, more distasteful, than the mother who is continually telling her husband or her children or her own mother how she has 'sacrificed herself' for them; for in doing so she is either demonstrating her own insincerity (since what one gives up *willingly* for the sake of others is not a sacrifice any more than it is a sacrifice for a man to give up his game of darts at the local in order to give more attention to his pigeons or the new baby which he finds much more interesting), or revealing her masochism, her stupidity, and, almost always, her malice. What she really wants is to make the others feel dependent on her, to inflate her own ego, show her spite, or cause them to feel guilty. Nobody can usefully help by relinquishing personal rights *unwillingly and unnecessarily* for the supposed rights of others, *because love for humanity begins with genuine self-love and self-respect.* In other words, whilst situations frequently arise in which one must consciously and deliberately give up some personal rights, this is totally different from the case of the mother who keeps on harping about her total self-sacrifice because, as we have seen, her action is not motivated by the desire to be helpful but rather by a neurotic compulsion to feel 'put upon'. Now this kind of behaviour leads to a vicious circle; for the woman's self-induced limitation of her rights as a person naturally makes her increasingly resentful of those who are felt to be responsible for her frustrations and since this resentment must remain unconscious (because it would clash with her self-picture of martyrdom), she can only respond by making herself even more of a martyr in ways which other people will easily recognise to be motivated by malice and spite. She is not only tormenting herself, but everybody else in her family.

The Housebound Housewife.

In order to distinguish between the normal and the neurotic giving up of individual rights, let us take an example from the so-called 'housebound housewife'. Here is a woman who feels lonely and depressed for various reasons discussed elsewhere but, in general, because she has been used to company before marriage and feels isolated when tied to the home looking after young children, or perhaps because she is ambitious and feels that her present position does not give sufficient scope for her abilities. There is nothing surprising or reprehensible about feeling this way in the circumstances, and the normal approach is that she should begin by being fully aware of the total situation and honest about her feelings in relation to it, subsequently doing something practical to alter the actual situation or herself.

Three solutions immediately present themselves:

(1) After discussion with the other members of the family, and having made suitable arrangements for the children, decide that a part- or full-time job is the answer.

(2) To look around for work, studies, interests, or hobbies that can be carried out in the home to alleviate boredom and possibly prepare the path for more interesting work in the future.

(3) To accept the situation and, after careful thought, change her own attitude towards it, arguing, for example, that looking after the home and her young family should be a rewarding and important period of life which will all too soon be over leaving her free to do as she pleases.

At the other extreme is the neurotic solution which occurs with the type of woman who refuses to face the situation constructively and thinks of it in 'moral' terms, denying that she wants to leave the home at all or that the children tie her down and limit her freedom of movement; she is so 'self-sacrificing' that she does not realise that normal love is always ambivalent in which love and anger or hate are parts of the mixture. Her world is composed of black and white, not as in the real world of varying shades of grey. This may lead to the not uncommon type of neurosis which has as its main symptom the fear of leaving the house even for a single moment, because as was seen earlier a conscious fear is often the expression of an unconscious wish. Immediately she puts her foot outside the door or attempts to cross the street, she is suddenly overwhelmed by attacks of sheer panic. What are the consequences of this 'solution'? First, her neurosis prevents her doing what she really wants but refuses to admit to wanting; second, she is punishing herself for her 'wicked' desires but, being frustrated, her unconscious resentment increases and with it her conscious anxiety; third, she is punishing the rest of the family by being 'ill', becoming a professional martyr probably requiring psychiatric treatment, and fills them with guilt both by snide remarks inferring that her condition is caused by overwork, and by coldness towards them, or perhaps by outbursts of irrational and uncontrollable rage. Certainly she is frustrated, but the cause of the frustration lies not in her objective surroundings but in the way she interprets them.

Truth and Honesty.

Normality in personal relationships can be judged by the degree to which one is aware of the objective situation and able to appreciate the nature of unconscious factors motivating behaviour. So far as humanly possible, one is true to one's own nature and truthful in most circumstances. The more mature a married couple are, the more will it be possible for them to be completely truthful with each other but, since no one is completely mature, it is not always wise to tell the truth regardless of circumstances because those who do so are not always motivated by a desire for truth but by unconscious motives ranging from the need to purge personal feelings of guilt without the least regard for the feelings of others to the desire to wound. One of the commonest questions appearing in the personal problems columns of women's magazines is whether some sexual peccadillo in the individual's past should be revealed to the husband, to which (unless the act had repercussions which are still having an effect) the simple answer is: certainly not. Assuming that the person is moved to tell because of continuing feelings of guilt or shame then we can only say:

(1) that such feelings, like those of so-called self-sacrifice, are very often a sign of a concealed but overweening conceit demonstrating to the individual's own satisfaction what a tender conscience he (or she) must possess.

(2) that the correct solution to guilt is surely not to permit what cannot be undone to spoil the present—which is a much more practical reason for feeling guilty—but t

resolve to learn from experience and employ it in avoiding similar mistakes in the future;

(3) that if the act must be confessed, then the best person to confess to is someone who is not emotionally involved, such as a priest, physician, psychiatrist or even a sympathetic, reliable and impartial friend;

(4) that the woman (or man) concerned should consider very seriously the *real* motives lying beneath the need to confess, which, as suggested above, are not infrequently the desire to attract attention or even to wound the other partner.

The only circumstances in which these rules would not always apply are those in which the wrong can still be undone or partly undone in which case the individual's duty is clear, or those in which news of the act is likely to reach the ears of the partner sooner or later from some other source, when it is usually wisest to consider making a clean breast of it (though, even then, it would be wise to be sure of one's correct estimation of the objective situation and the probable response of the other).

Knowing Oneself.

The fundamental rules for close personal relationships within or without marriage are: mature affection (which has already been defined), sincerity, as much honesty as is wise judged by the criteria above and, most of all, self-knowledge. One of the ways in which we can become more self-aware is by observing not merely what we believe to be our conscious motives, but the consequences of our actions. If a husband or wife resolves to be pleasant and friendly when the other returns from work yet every time the evening is spent in constant bickering, then there must be some underlying resentment which it would be more helpful to bring out into the open and discuss frankly, than to continue making futile resolutions that are never kept. If a particular emotion or type of event always seems to keep on recurring; for example, if in all our relationships we invariably end up by feeling 'put upon', if we can never maintain a friendship for long, if a woman says that her dearest wish is to get married yet she fails to do so, if one allegedly loves a child yet is constantly losing one's temper with it, if other people always seem unfriendly and shop assistants rude, if we are frequently depressed or anxious without apparent cause, then the causes must be sought inside ourselves, since it is impossible that the environment is always to blame. The woman who believes that she wants to get married yet never finds the 'right' man, has affairs which invariably come to an end, or somehow inevitably seems to fall in love with unsuitable people—married men, confirmed bachelors, or those with latent homosexual tendencies, is obviously not being quite truthful with herself. Perhaps she wants to marry but fears the loss of her independence, perhaps she feels incapable of any close relationship with another, or perhaps she is afraid of sex and motherhood; for the fact is that even the plainest woman can get married if she wishes, and whether one falls in love or not depends less on that person's objective qualities than on our own deepest needs. In other words, a person who really wants love and marriage can't help falling in love. If we are constantly quarrelling with a loved one, it is because we refuse to admit that in certain respects we also resent him, and it is sensible to recall Dr. Winnicott's dictum that the danger arises, not from aggressiveness in itself, but from the repression of personal aggressiveness in individuals. Or, as the poet Blake expressed it:

"I was angry with my friend,
I told my wrath, the wrath did end;
I was angry with my foe,
I told it not, the wrath did grow."

Indeed, as the poem continues, the wrath was lovingly nurtured and increased until it finally ended in murder. Anger and aggression must often be consciously suppressed in ordinary social situations in which emotion would be inappropriate, but in personal relationships it should never be repressed but admitted and talked out.

Sexual Relationships.

The belief so assiduously spread by specialists during the 1930s that complete sexual satisfaction in both partners is not only necessary but inevitably results in a happy married life turned the truth upside down; for the fact is that, in general, a happy married life based on love and respect is the cause rather than the effect of good sexual relations. Every psychiatrist has seen many cases of marriages in which physical relations were perfect and yet the marriage ended in divorce, and even more in which the sexual life was not wholly satisfactory but the marriage as a whole was.

The causes of sexual difficulties are rarely anatomical but have their origin in unconscious fears, guilt, and sometimes in ignorance. But ignorance is not as common a cause as used to be thought, not because it does not exist, but because a genuinely loving couple will find it easy in the course of time to make adjustments and discover for themselves. The bogey set up by these foolish 'experts' that women who do not always achieve complete satisfaction are in some way abnormal may have some sort of theoretical background, but it has very little relationship to the real state of affairs in which a majority of women may achieve orgasm fairly frequently, only occasionally, or not at all throughout their married life. Men who are always impotent are not very common and need medical or psychiatric help, but for women the state of affairs is quite different. Most men experience sexual desire initially as a physical need like hunger, whilst women for obvious biological reasons experience desire in a much more complex form which cannot be separated from emotional security; for a man sex begins and ends with the act, for a woman it only begins with the act since she has to think of (and normally look forward to) future consequences. Of course, this is not true of all women, and as contraceptive measures become more efficient and women more socially independent, many regard sex in pretty much the same light as men. But women even more than men have been brought up to feel that sex is unpleasant or dirty, and many people of both sexes are afraid to give themselves completely in love (the childhood mechanism: "If I don't give all of myself to others, then they can't hurt me"), so it is hardly surprising that comparatively few lead a completely satisfying sexual life. In any case, mutual adjustment usually takes some time and many men and women may take years to accomplish this. However, with or without complete sexual satisfaction most couples as we have seen lead reasonably happy lives together because their goal is not sex alone but the maintenance of a marriage and a home.

There are some cases in which this is not so and the help of a psychiatrist or Marriage Guidance Council is required: if intercourse is completely impossible, if one of the partners finds it totally repulsive, if the couple desire to have children and fail to do so, or if, as sometimes happens in women, the act by arousing desires which they are ashamed of leads not only to non-completion but to anxiety and emotional tension. When this happens, the wife may find that following intercourse her nervous tension brings about irritability and this in turn may lead to constant bickering that may threaten to wreck the marriage. All these cases require skilled advice though, of course, they are no ground for worry on physical grounds alone nor are they anything to feel ashamed about. Everybody fails from time to time in some aspect of their lives and, if it cannot be dealt with by ordinary means, the sensible thing to do is to seek expert advice; there is no more need to feel embarrassed about seeking help from a psychiatrist in these circumstances than in seeking help from a lawyer or house-surveyor in others.

The Goal of Self-Realisation.

Gordon Allport, a leading American psychologist, has emphasised that every living being is trying to complete his own nature—in the terms already used here, he is striving towards self-realisation. But his search, depending upon parental attitudes, may take one of two roads.

One road seeks safety through exclusion, through a restrictive and rejective equilibrium employing the mechanism of repression and denial, yet, because the more we repress the more we must continue to repress, the personality inevitably becomes impoverished and incapable of free self-expression. The person clings to a narrow island, restricts his circle, sharply selects what reassures him and rejects what seems to threaten him. The other road is one of relaxation, self-trust, and therefore trust of others. "There is no need to exclude strangers from one's gathering. Self-love is compatible with love of others. This tolerant orientation is possible because security has been experienced in the realistic handling of inner conflicts and social transactions. Unlike the authoritarian and prejudiced person, the tolerant person does not perceive the world as a jungle where men are basically evil and dangerous."

Teaching Morals.

The disasters arising from a restrictive upbringing have to do with the child's early failure to live with his own impulses; he is made to feel guilty and punished whenever he soils himself or is found handling his own genitals. (Incidentally, research has demonstrated that mothers of prejudiced children are mostly likely to punish the child for this offence.) He is punished or made to feel guilty too—and only a child can tell what guilt and pain can be aroused by the hurt and suffering expression on a mother's face which is much worse than a physical blow—whenever he has a tantrum or strikes a parent or other relative. A child who finds his every impulse, even his desire to self-expression, wicked, and feels that he is unloved when he gives way to it—is likely to grow up hating himself for his many transgressions. Says Allport: "He carries a burden of infantile guilt. As a consequence, when he sees any lapses from the conventional code in others he grows anxious. He wishes to punish the transgressor, just as he himself was punished. He develops a dread of the very impulses that trouble him. When a person grows overconcerned with sin in others, the tendency may be viewed as a 'reaction formation'. Having had to fight unholy impulses in himself, he cannot be permissive and lenient toward others. (This) moralism is only surface compliance; it does not solve the conflicts within. It is tense, compulsive, projective. True morality is more relaxed, integral, and congruent with the life pattern as a whole."

The Development of Normality and True Morality.

The way to avoid these developments is obvious. In addition to the fundamental parental attitudes already mentioned, the basic rule is *never to apply prohibitions to a child until it is capable of carrying them out and understanding them.* For example, the senseless attempt to 'train' a child in potting habits before the muscle controlling bowel movements has even been developed is something which is carried out to suit the parents' convenience rather than for the child's own benefit as, alas, in many cases are the sleeping habits and regular feeding habits imposed upon the infant. What parents should realise is that to a considerable extent normality and genuine moral attitudes are developed by a process of internal maturation rather than by any sort of direct intervention on the part of the father or mother whose real job in the early years is to provide the right emotional background. The child who is fed 'on demand', that is, whenever it wants, does not become an anarchist but in a few weeks develops as regular a rhythm as the unfortunate who has regular feeding imposed upon it; the child who is left alone so far as bowel-training is concerned learns control by itself in the course of time.

Young children naturally play with their genitals which, after all, are an interesting part of the body and, quite apart from sex, an obvious object for attention; they should be left alone to do so unless the parents prefer that the child should learn to do the same thing in secret or, worse still, that it should learn that sex is dirty and sinful and therefore to be repressed. In fact the young child's genital play is not initially sexual at all but merely natural curiosity, and it is only the guilt-ridden adult who interprets it in this way.

The Good Parent.

A permissive attitude on the part of parents is the only sensible one because it is impossible to destroy a desire but only to drive it underground when it will reappear in far less desirable forms. Aggression, even more than sex, is dangerous if not permitted free expression in the early years; the child with a temper-tantrum should be hugged and reassured because it is frightened by its inability to control this terrifying emotion. Training, until the child has acquired the ability to understand what he is told, is a matter of living and leaving well alone. (Obviously, this does not apply to situations where the child is in physical danger of falling or touching dangerous objects, but even then the minor accident should be minimised as far as possible because the mother who shows her excessive anxiety infects her child with it and causes it to feel that the world is a dangerous place. It is, but one can handle it better when unafraid.) Thus the good parent must strike a useful balance between sincere love and concern for the child and the avoidance of inducing too much anxiety by undue fussing about risks and illness. So far as dangerous situations are concerned, the sensible thing to do is to remove or guard against any potential source of danger rather than worry the child about it.

Sex Education.

Sex education has often been conceived as a process whereby the child—hitherto assumed to be totally ignorant of sex—is, at a certain age (usually puberty), taken aside and given a serious talk either by the parent, or (as some seem to suppose) by the biology teacher at school whose duty it is naïvely believed to be. This, of course, is simply nonsense. Sex education begins at birth by supplying the child's physical needs, its psychological need for love, and otherwise leaving it alone to explore its body as it pleases. Later, when it acquires speech, the child who trusts its parents and has not been made to feel that there is anything 'bad' about its natural processes, will start to ask questions. The rules which should be followed by the parents at this stage are clear:

(1) Every question should be answered *honestly* in a way the child at that age can comprehend;

(2) The answer should be a simple and *brief* reply to what has actually been asked;

(3) Formal sex education, in the sense of a more detailed and scientific account, belongs only to the later years of childhood when the parents should continue to answer all questions honestly and in the greater detail the child now requires, discussing the *social* implications of sex insofar as they are capable of doing so;

(4) Sex will finally become something to be taught by the teacher as part of a course in general biology.

The reasons for this approach are clear: we have seen that in the early months it is useless—and worse than useless—to apply prohibitions which the child is unable to understand. When it acquires speech and subsequently goes to school, it will inevitably obtain some sort of sexual information anyhow, so the parents' choice is not between some knowledge and none at all but between garbled and often nasty information and that which is decent and honest. In fact, the child whose questions have been answered briefly and truthfully becomes *less* interested in sex except as one feature of life as a whole than the one who has been told nothing, to whom the secret and forbidden knowledge becomes both a private obsession and a status symbol.

Everybody has a particular desire to acquire knowledge which he or she knows to exist, but which has clearly been withheld because it is supposedly 'naughty' and 'dirty'. Thus sex education is a continual process, inseparable from education in general; it is, in fact, merely one aspect of personal relationships and should be taught as such. What the child should learn is that, since no form of sex is harmful *in itself*, the only practical considerations to be taken into account are whether any given sex act is hurtful to either person involved, a breach of their self-respect, or a risk to their future happiness—as, for example, an unwanted pregnancy. It would be wrong therefore to encourage someone to engage in any sort of behaviour which their religion teaches them to be evil, even if we ourselves believe it to be harmless or even good.

Pre-marital Relationships.

There are social reasons already mentioned why pre-martial relationships *may* be more frequent, and it seems likely that this trend may continue to increase. But we might well wonder whether those who are so alarmed about it (and no decision as to its moral desirability can be made here, since this must be left to the reader) are fully aware of its background. It is usually assumed that morals are becoming more lax in this respect, whereas a large part of the truth is that people are simply more frank and at less pains to conceal what they do. Again, the kind of behaviour condemned by the moralists is very far from being new: for instance, in the heyday of the Church during the Middle Ages what was then more kindly described as the 'natural' child was not only as well treated as the child born in wedlock, but the term 'bastard' was applied to many exalted people as an honourable title. In agricultural societies—including our own—when children were regarded as an important asset, engaged couples deliberately sought pregnancy because the man wanted to make sure that the woman was fertile before marriage. Another obvious reason for the apparent increase in illegitimacy is that the 'shotgun' marriage is less frequent, and a woman who has become pregnant will not marry her lover if she subsequently decides that he is unsuitable; this is surely a tendency in the right direction since no good can come of an enforced marriage and, in view of the stigma still attached to illegitimacy, shows that the young take these matters more seriously today.

4. SOCIAL PATHOLOGY.

We are now going to glance very briefly at certain aspects of what are regarded as some of the more important problems of our day and, since it is only possible to select a few, those chosen are juvenile delinquency, neurosis and the stress diseases, and what appears to be an increase in boredom and discontent.

Changing Social Attitudes.

Take first of all the background. There is a tremendous technical revolution going on in which there exists a lag between the actual environment in which we live and our ability to adjust to it; the real enemy, however, is not so much lack of ability as ignorance and superstition. For example, it is indeed true that malnutrition is a world-wide problem, but it is necessary to realise that the causes of hunger are just as often political and religious as the result of any lack in foodstuff. In Asia, one of the main drawbacks to an adequate diet is the caste system of India which prevents certain foods from being eaten and in communities in both Asia and Africa, as people earn more money, they frequently spend it, not on food, but on clothes and bicycles. Attitudes require changing at least as much as the agricultural system; *for all the attitudes which we regard as special problems are common to every country in which industrialisation and democratisation are taking place* and the mass media are not the cause but merely a single symptom of this total process. Rebellious youth, for instance, and the search for more possessions and affluence is as much in evidence in the Communist countries where the media have been used not only to indoctrinate but also to improve, and they are just as common in the new countries where the mass media hardly exist. In our own country the working class are doing exactly what the middle class were doing when they first got into power, only more obviously so because of the narrowed time-scale within which social change takes place: gambling, buying rather tasteless objects, building rather ghastly houses and fitting them with equally ghastly furniture, reading bad books (the women's magazines of today are really no worse than the writings of Ethel M. Dell and Ouida) and horror comics (which were invented in the late eighteenth century, and the most famous, *Frankenstein*, was written by the wife of Shelley). Of course, the middle class to a considerable extent are still doing these things—but they dislike the working class having the same freedom. Just as one can well imagine the first time that the well-to-do on the Riviera looked with distaste on the newly affluent grocers and 'tradesmen' who were beginning to flood into 'their' preserve, so today the descendants of the grocers and tradesmen view with the same distaste each favourite resort as it becomes flooded with newly affluent workers.

The Cost of Affluence.

But affluence is a state for which a price has to be paid, particularly by youth. In modern society teenagers for the first time have money to spare, are socially emancipated, reach puberty earlier, and have far greater possibilities for success (and failure) than their forebears ever had. A society based on the concept of social mobility, whether the goal is wealth, affluence, or status, must necessarily be associated with striving and the more sensitive members will feel more strongly than others the pressure to achieve, to avoid failure, or even to maintain their present position. In addition, if one has been indoctrinated with the belief that success is essential to self-respect and that affluence is 'normal', it is not surprising that the failures will try to walk round the ladder if they are unable to climb it, *i.e.*, they may attempt the devious way of criminality. Whereas in former times people stole because in some sense they were genuinely deprived, today they do so because they feel relatively deprived. Since happiness is not an absolute, the affluent society aided by the power of commercial advertising ensures a state of affairs in which there is always a gulf between what people have and what they think they are entitled to. Crime and neurosis are the two sides of this single penny; for, as Freud pointed out, whilst the criminal is in open rebellion against his society, the neurotic is in a state of unconscious rebellion. Which 'solution' is selected depends upon a number of factors, one of the most important being social class; for the unsatisfactory upbringing that will tend to make the middle-class boy neurotic will tend to make the working-class boy *living in an area where delinquency is a socially-accepted pattern, or at least not a wholly condemned one*, into a delinquent. Here, of course, we are referring, not to the whole working class, but to specifically delinquent areas.

The Delinquent.

Among the most striking facts about crime are (*a*) that it is predominantly a male, adolescent, and working-class activity; (*b*) that it is at its height in the 14–17 age-group; and (*c*) that, not only do crimes become less violent after the age of 30, but they tend to cease altogether in the majority of cases. An obviously important conclusion of (*c*) is that the majority of delinquents would stop their behaviour regardless of what was done whether by way of punishment or 'treatment'.

It is completely fallacious to suppose that a large majority of criminals of all categories are suffering from some form of mental disturbance, and for the sake of convenience it is useful to consider the following categories: mere wildness and 'proving offences', the disturbed and violent delinquent, the sexual offender, and the professional criminal or old lag. Of course, there are other groups such as those who habitually engage in fraud, blackmail, and shady financial transactions, but these can be fitted into the last of the above categories.

The first type of case is very often a perfectly normal boy who is simply engaged in 'working off steam' and doing the sort of things most of the rest of us have done, since aggressiveness and a certain amount of destructiveness are usual accompaniments of adolescence, or, in the case of the 'proving' offence, he feels the need to demonstrate his toughness or lack of fear by engaging in crimes which are clearly not carried out primarily for personal gain. Typical of these are those who smash street lamps, steal apples or other goods, damage railway property, and so on, or the group of boys who break and enter an office yet, whilst smashing up some of the furniture, steal nothing but a few pencils or other worthless objects. These form the vast majority of all cases and the act, as a German criminologist puts it, is "an episode rather than a symptom", *i.e.*, most of these cases are normal and will develop into perfectly good citizens. More dangerous is the delinquent who takes crime seriously and is often violent towards his victim. Whilst the first group can belong to any class, this group usually comes from a disturbed home and a delinquency area—which is not at all the same thing as saying that he is necessarily abnormal though he may need help: nevertheless, except in grave cases, even this type tends to outgrow his criminal tendencies or, at least, to become less violent after the late twenties. In other instances he may develop into the old lag.

Sexual perversions are, of course, the concern of the psychiatrist and need not be discussed here, but it should be noted that most perverts are suffering from a lack of sexual drive rather than, as popular belief would have it, a state of being 'oversexed'. They are rarely dangerous and most are sexually impotent in normal relationships, but even those who murder with a sexual motive tend to have the same incapacity and a surprising number (*e.g.*, Christie and Haigh) have been brought up in oppressively religious households. The professional criminal is frequently just that, and those who seek complicated psychiatric explanations for his behaviour are usually wasting their time; few people seem to realise that there are those who take to crime as a 'career' just as others become doctors or carpenters. In many instances they are merely 'following the dear old dad'. The old lags or recidivists who form such a large proportion of our prison population are commonly dullards but it is doubtful if many are in the clinical sense mentally ill. As the late Sir Norwood East, one of Britain's leading criminologists, said: "As the result of more than fifty years' practical experience of crime I am unable to regard crime as a disease, although sometimes the result of it."

Crime and Punishment.

Since the great majority of criminals who show early delinquent tendencies simply grow out of them, it is doubtful whether punishment (or for that matter, psychiatric treatment) has any great influence upon the course of events, though detention may often be necessary. But it is really more than doubtful whether punishment has any preventive effect at all. On the contrary, we know that severe corporal punishment can often arouse such a store of resentment as to last through a lifetime of violence and it is also well known that many people commit crimes in order to be found out because they are unconsciously seeking punishment.

How many, one wonders, are aware of the following facts: that the annual average of murders per million of the population in Britain has increased from 3·2 in 1931–40 to 3·3 in 1951–60; that over a fifth of male murderers commit suicide; that between 1955 and 1960 only 31 per cent of offenders were wholly responsible for their actions and that a number of those sentenced to life imprisonment subsequently had to be sent to mental hospitals; that about half the male offenders killed wives, children, or parents, 10 per cent girl friends, and about a quarter strangers (*i.e.* murder is largely a family affair); that, of about 150 murders a year, less than a dozen are not cleared up; and that murders with a sexual motive average 8 a year. Murder is therefore very unlike any other form of crime in that its incidence hardly changes from year to year, the number of mentally disturbed cases is large, the vast majority of murders are due to family or intimate quarrels where gain is seldom the motive, and (except for the occasional psychopathic murderer) the crime is unlikely to be committed again. *See* **D34–37**.

Stress and Mental Illness.

Before discussing this problem we must say something about the nature of mental illness, and the first point to note is that, apart from the fact that all cases of mental illness show symptoms of disturbance in thought, emotion, or behaviour, this is the only factor that they do have in common. Without encroaching too far on the material presented by the writer of the Medical Section, mental disorders can be roughly classified as psychoses (*i.e.*, the insanities), the neuroses, which are minor if very uncomfortable conditions differing from the psychoses mainly in that the psychotic patient does not realise that he is ill, whereas the neurotic is all too aware of the fact; the psychopathic personalities who are people that are more of a trouble to society than to themselves; the mental defectives suffering from a defect of intelligence; and the psychosomatic diseases in which actual physical disease has been brought about by mental stress.

The causes of these conditions are very various, some like the so-called organic psychoses being really physical diseases with mental symptoms brought about by infections such as syphilis or toxins such as alcohol, others such as mental defect being either inherited or caused by damage to the child before birth. The functional psychoses, such as schizophrenia or manic-depressive insanity, have no known physical cause though some authorities believe that they have discovered abnormal substances in the body fluids of schizophrenics. But with these exceptions (and possibly a few cases of so-called psychopathic personality), we have to realise that '*mental diseases' are not in any meaningful sense diseases at all but cases of social maladjustments.* From this fact the following important conclusions can be drawn:

(1) that the neuroses and the psychopathic conditions—insofar as the latter term has any meaning at all—are really the result of a faulty upbringing resulting in a basic defect in interpersonal relations and the symptoms are usually brought on by a precipitating cause when the individual is confronted by a problem which, by reason of his early experiences, he is unable to face;

(2) that, unlike ordinary diseases, a neurosis is not something that one 'has' but something that one 'is';

(3) that, since nobody has had a completely perfect upbringing, everybody is in some degree neurotic and it is therefore meaningless to suggest that a person is either neurotic or not—what we usually mean is that he (or she) is neurotic to a degree which troubles him (or her) or troubles others.

The latter is the criterion upon which the person is declared to be suffering from a neurosis and, since this is obviously a matter of individual judgment, it follows that all statistics purporting to tell us the incidence of neurosis in a given community are to a large extent based on value judgments and of very dubious validity.

The figures are made even more absurd by the fact that there must be countless thousands suffering, for example, from a fear of enclosed spaces (claustrophobia) who have never seen a doctor in their lives and simply solve their problem by travelling by bus and avoiding the underground, and even more who are not aware that they are neurotic at all; they may have 'nervous indigestion' for which they medicate themselves with pills, or believe—as plenty of people do—that the state of 'nerves' is a physical one brought on by overwork and curable by a 'nerve tonic' or 'nerve food'. These, too, may never see a doctor because they are perfectly satisfied with their own medicine. Again, perhaps the sort of neurosis that does most harm is the sort of behaviour described earlier when we were discussing harmful influences on children: the possessive and jealous, the mother-in-law who cannot leave well alone, the suspicious wife or husband, those with a profound sense of guilt with which they may infect others. All these are suffering from behaviour disorders but few indeed see a psychiatrist.

The Structure of a Neurosis.

We must distinguish between the early roots of neurosis which are laid in childhood, *e.g.*, the unsatisfied need for love and security, resentment against authority, and other undesirable patterns of behaviour which, being unsatisfied, continue to repeat themselves throughout life, and the immediate cause of a breakdown which is the result of the individual's applying these outdated patterns to new situations. The main difference between the relatively neurotic and the relatively normal is that the neurotic tries to apply old solutions to new situations whereas the normal person takes every new situation on its own merits. Thus the man who has had a conflict between his desire for self-realisation and the authority of a repressive father does not distinguish between different authorities in later life, continues to act on the belief that all authority is bad, and naturally frequently finds himself in trouble. The man or woman who has felt some denial of love in childhood, continues to seek the symbols of love throughout life in stereotyped ways even if these take many different forms. The individual may become promiscuous, feel victimised, become parasitic upon others, overeat, or constantly strive for more goods or status. It is not that all these forms of self-expression are necessarily bad in themselves: what makes them neurotic is that they are compulsive. Broadly speaking, then, there are two main types of conflict, that which shows itself in the search for approval, love, status, and goods, and the other type which is a crisis of self-expression, the freedom to assert oneself. The one is shown in the person who looks for affluence, the other in the person who seeks for power, even if both have a common root, the search for security.

Boredom and Anomie.

Many people are bored today because, instead of seeking contentment within, they are in the position of a spoilt child who has been offered so many things that he does not know what to do with them since none is a substitute for love. Whatever point he reaches, there is always something more to desire and each goal as it is reached is less satisfactory than the last. Not only is success less satisfying than it once appeared, there is also the danger of falling from the position achieved, and those who want what they cannot have may become no less neurotic than those who have got what they wanted and are afraid of losing it. It is not only people who want who develop a neurosis but those who have achieved their dreams: the East End family moved to a new town is often troubled by the idea that they will be unable to keep up with the higher standard set by others—there is a 'success' no less than a 'failure' neurosis.

A feature of modern society was described by the French sociologist Durkheim as *anomie*, the feeling of futility and not-belonging as old groups are broken up and the mass becomes the 'lonely crowd'. Social mobility has introduced the working-class student to new ways of life which often arouse a conflict between his attitudes towards his family and the atmosphere of Oxbridge; the worker's new desire to get on often alienates him from his mates; and the housewife stranded at home knows, unlike her predecessors, what she is missing—life is passing her by. There is a gulf between what we want and can have, between what we are and what we want to be; our society is characterised by a never-ending search for the end of the rainbow and for security that will never be ours. The only solution is to learn to live with conflict by seeing our own personal problems as problems to be shared and understood together.

III. WORK

1. THE SATISFACTIONS OF WORK.

Work, no matter how we define it, is not simply something that we have to do in order to make money to do something else; it is the main source in modern society of status—the sign of approval of other people. In the words of an industrial psychologist: "Work is the source of man's most basic satisfactions, it is his social catalyst—the purveyor *par excellence* of his status and prestige among his fellows." In former times, status came from one's social position, rank, position in the church, craftsmanship, or some special ability; but few of us today are lords, churchmen, or craftsmen and it is our job that tells others what we are. Even from the psychological point of view, it is desirable that our aggressive or creative drives should find expression in doing the sort of work that fulfils and helps towards the goal of self-realisation. Of course, many people are actively dissatisfied in their work, many more satisfied, and others feel that, however well they have done, they might have done better. So it is worth discussing, first, what is satisfying about work, and second, the process of education and selection for work.

Work and boredom are not necessarily related, because from the earliest times work has often been objectively boring but subjectively interesting. To the woman washing clothes in the stream, or to the man planting rice-shoots, boredom was unknown because what they were doing made sense to them. The craftsman in mediæval times took pride in producing a good and useful article. One unfortunate result of the industrial revolution was that, while in the long run it created more wealth and goods and benefited more people than any comparable period in history, it was a first step for the majority of workers in the direction of taking the meaning out of work. As Christopher Salmon has said: "Because the Victorians regarded work in industry as necessarily hard and disagreeable, they made little effort to introduce tolerable conditions into mines and mills, and foundries, and were content to think of industry itself as an economic necessity instead of as an element in society."

For work to be agreeable it should be meaningful, and, since most people are sociable to a greater or less degree, the company of one's workmates is important. These are two of the factors which, apart from material rewards, the manager or the industrial psychologist has to consider, and some of the modern views on the subject of incentives will be mentioned later. It will become evident that conditions have much improved in the course of this century, but there is no doubt that they might be very considerably better. The fact that work is not only necessary to man but necessary to most people's mental health as well as being an activity that it is normal to like, stands out in odd contrast to a background of industrial unrest. We shall have to ask ourselves what it is that transforms a necessary and ordinarily pleasant activity into a source of strife.

2. EDUCATION AND SELECTION.

The Past.

In former times education was a privilege of the few and compulsory education was not introduced into this country until as late as 1870. The sort of training given by well-to-do parents to their boys was based on the classics and its intention was to create the cultured gentleman at ease in company and able to discourse intelligently on as many subjects as possible without appearing to be too uncomfortably intelligent. Since science was not regarded as a very cultural pursuit and, until the seventeenth and eighteenth centuries, chemistry and physics were still 'natural philosophy' and hardly existed as sciences in the modern sense, it was little taught at school. Those who practised it were comfortably-off gentlemen who, living more or less in isolation, became interested in it as a hobby. It was only the founding of the Royal Society in 1660 that began to bring these people together to exchange ideas and, since the Society was given a Royal Charter by Charles II, science began to be respectable. Its respectability, however, was conditional and the condition was that it should remain theoretical because gentlemen were not expected to work towards practical ends.

From this attitude there arose the unfortunate distinction between pure science and technology which still bedevils British science and causes parents to feel that technical schools and colleges are somehow inferior to the universities and grammar schools. Of course, another unfortunate result has been that, whereas Britain has never been short of ideas, their serious application has often been carried out in other countries: obvious examples are the jet engine and penicillin. Until much more recently girls, apart from a smattering of languages, music, and drawing, were taught almost entirely such crafts as might be expected to make them good housewives, and the daughters of wealthy parents were not even taught the domestic arts—indeed, since it was believed that any sign of intelligence was likely to put off a prospective suitor, many manuals of instruction suggested that they should actively conceal what intelligence they had.

The Modern Educational Outlook.

Much of this has changed with the acceptance, at least in theory, of the equality of the sexes and the realisation that, as a nation, we cannot afford to waste our human resources. Children are carefully selected at an early age in terms of their abilities and the intelligent child, regardless of his origins, has the opportunity to reach a position consonant with his gifts. But, just as the science-technology dichotomy still persists, whatever governments may say, so other traces of past attitudes make freedom of opportunity less real than might at first appear. Women have not yet gained full equality and we have already seen that what they have gained is more by way of an addition to their traditional tasks than a release from them. One of the greatest barriers to social equality is less any sort of physical barrier confronting the working-class child than the traditional attitudes of his class. It is easy to see why history has made solidarity a traditional working-class virtue and why the boy who tries to better himself is often regarded as a traitor to his class, nor is it unnatural that many workers regard education as synonymous with childhood as work is synonymous with manhood. High culture is still regarded with suspicion as the special province of the ruling class in spite of the fact that, at least since Elizabethan times, most of our great writers and artists have been of comparatively humble origin. These intangible attitudes are obviously a serious barrier to working-class children, as are also the difficulty of finding sufficient privacy to study, the pressures of the affluent society which cause them to want as much money as possible as soon as possible, and the not infrequent family problems centring around the cultural gulf between the university-trained youth and his relatively uneducated parents. Lastly, there is the problem peculiar to England where accent (at least in the south-east) is class rather than regional, and, as Bernard Shaw once said, the child cannot open his mouth without revealing his origins. In a country in which social snobbery is still very real, many can forgive a Scottish, Irish, or Welsh accent, but not a Cockney one. Physical barriers exist, too, because the smaller classes, sometimes the better quality of the teaching, and the limited number of university places in some areas favour the public school child and it is well known that certain universities or colleges prefer the products of particular schools.

Early Specialisation.

The whole concept of education has radically changed, mainly in the direction of very early selection in terms of intelligence and learning ability, and the tendency to early specialisation. We have moved far from the education of the cultured gentleman when John Vaizey can write that " it is worth spending money on education because it assists the economy, because it provides a skilled and resilient body of workers at all levels, who help to keep a highly fluid economy going ". Children are put into various ' streams ' and sent to grammar schools, secondary modern schools, and secondary technical schools. Though the original intention was that there should be no question of any of these schools being superior or inferior to the other the fact remains that parents are often very upset when their child fails to obtain a grammar-school place and this puts a great deal of tension upon family relationships when both parents and children become obsessed with school marks and examinations.

The Need for Generalists as well as Specialists.

The situation has arisen out of our need for experts and many authorities obviously believe that this is the best way to obtain them. On the other hand, many others are clearly worried about what is happening, the tensions and disappointments and discrimination that it leads to, and are even beginning to doubt whether excessive specialisation is a good thing. Like Sir Charles Snow, they see our nation as coming to be divided into two cultures—the world of the arts and humanities and the world of science and technology. We need the specialists but we need ' generalists ' too if only because the really creative ideas—the discoveries rather than the inventions —have been produced by men who had wide-ranging minds, and though a study of the humanities does not guarantee that one will be humane it is rather terrifying to contemplate men specialising in germ-warfare or inventing nerve-gases, totally lacking in any knowledge of the men and the human and natural beauty of the world they are being employed to destroy.

The 11-Plus.

The doubts of the value of attaching too much importance to the results of intelligence tests and early progress at school are bringing about a movement in favour of abolishing the 11-plus examination and making more use of the comprehensive school. London, for example, has decided to abolish the 11-plus or any sort of single test which decides whether children should go to grammar school or not, and this, in part, is due to the great success of the comprehensive school. In the comprehensive schools in the area, the grammar school, secondary modern, and technical streams study under the same roof and since these children get equal education the need to select at an early age is disappearing. Outmoded ideas are rapidly being broken down.

Selection Procedures.

Some fortunate people are able to select freely the sort of work they would like to do—writers and artists, for example—and others simply slide in and out of unskilled jobs, going where the pay is best but the prospects less satisfactory. Today, however, the vast majority of people, including those who are going to fall into the above categories, have to go through at some time or another in their lives various tests to discover their abilities. The justification for these tests is (*a*) the present need for able people with particular qualifications; (*b*) the need to avoid wastage by attempting to train people who cannot be trained to the necessary level; and (*c*) the obvious fact that it is a good idea to have a square peg in a square hole and a worker who is not only suited to his job but satisfied with it.

There are three aspects of personality which can be tested in this way: general intelligence, special abilities such as manual dexterity, engineering ability, speed of reaction, the absence of colour blindness, and so on, and tests of personality itself —that is to say, the individual's attitudes.

Intelligence tests have already been discussed, and we have seen that they are by no means infallible; perhaps their main value is negative rather than positive in the sense that, whilst a high IQ does not *guarantee* academic success, we know that anybody with an IQ lower than about 120 is unlikely to get far in a university. Aptitude tests are less likely to be met with by the average citizen, being mainly employed where a specific job requires specific abilities (*i.e.*, in situations where we know that before the individual is taken into the job he requires a certain minimum of quality x unless time is to be wasted, efficiency diminished, or danger incurred.) Obviously an air pilot must be able to react quickly, an engine driver capable of distinguishing between green and red signals, a musician possess a good ear for tone, and so on. Most of these tests are very accurate and nobody who fails them need feel 'let down' because they are in his or her own interests as well as those of others.

Personality Tests.

The personality test is a procedure which, when applied outside its original field of psychiatry, has given rise to a good deal of controversy. One of its earliest forms, still used in conjunction with the lie-detector employed in criminology, was the word-association test devised by Jung at the beginning of the century to discover hidden complexes. In this a list of words, some neutral and others which are believed to have special significance for the patient, is slowly read out and the testee is asked to respond as quickly as possible with the first word that comes into his head. His reaction-time is measured with a stop-watch, and any delay or hesitation or any unusual responses noted. These give clues to unconscious problems.

Today, however, the usual form of personality test is what is known as a projection test, now widely employed in industry as well as in psychiatry to discover much more accurately personality traits of which the individual is probably totally unaware himself—indeed, his unconsciousness of the traits is almost a necessity for the use of the test. The three tests of this sort which the reader is most likely to come across are the Rorschach or 'inkblot' test, the Szondi test with its photographs of oddly-assorted individuals, and the TAT or thematic apperception test in which the outlines of vague human figures in various postures in relation to each other are shown. In the first, the testee is asked to say what he imagines himself to 'see' in the multicoloured inkblot, in the second, he is asked to say which of the people in the photograph he would prefer to sit with in a railway carriage and which he would most dislike in these circumstances, and in the third he is asked to write a story about the shadowy figures. As the name indicates, all three tests are based on the same idea—that, presented with a vague situation to which he has no outward clues, the testee will project upon the figures or shapes his own attitudes. When a picture of an apple is presented to anyone, he has no choice but to recognise it for what it is, but when he is presented with a Rorschach inkblot what he 'sees' in it must come from himself. In this way, such traits as introversion or extraversion, authoritarianism or humanitarianism, latent homosexuality, sado-masochistic trends, and the degree of integration or otherwise of the mind can be fairly reliably assessed.

Criticisms of Personality Tests.

These procedures are widely used in the selection of management in America and have been severely criticised. The most cogent of these criticisms are: (*a*) the moral one that it is an invasion of privacy and that no one at a man's place of work has any right to knowledge of the most intimate type about himself which, if he knew, he would not wish to be communicated; (*b*) the factual one that, although the tests are probably scientific, the uses to which they are put in industry are not, since nobody knows what makes a good manager good (in other words, unlike aptitude tests in which one knows what one is looking for, projection tests reveal material which is only of interest to the psychiatrist); (*c*) the fact that, given knowledge of the technique of the tests, it is very easy to cheat at them. (Those who wish to learn how to do so should consult W. H. Whyte's book *The Organisation Man.*) All that is necessary is to imagine that one is moderate in all things, has no unduly strong feelings either for or against parents and relatives, has conservative views on politics and religion, and has been good—but not too good—at all the tasks one has been presented with throughout life. That, to sum up, one is an insufferable prig and a complete bore.

Group Tests.

Another type of test, or rather group of tests, is that carried out in management selection and at officer selection boards for the army. Here a group of about ten applicants are asked to spend a week-end at a country house (in the case of industry); they are given batteries of tests from intelligence tests to TAT personality tests, are in some cases seen by a psychiatrist who has the test results, and are carefully observed as unobtrusively as possible by trained observers as they interact with each other. The fundamental part of the programme is the group task in which various assignments are given to the group as a whole and, in the course of time, it will be found that, in the discussions as to how these tasks are to be accomplished, those who have superior organising abilities and other useful qualities come to be recognised by the group as its informal leader. Thus in this type of test, it is the group itself which chooses (consciously or unconsciously) the most suitable applicant—not, of course, by votes or words but by behaviour. He is the person who is most frequently turned to for advice during the carrying out of the task, which naturally is related to the activities for which the group is being tested. In the case of industry, for example, it will be the solving of an imaginary business problem, in the army it is usually a problem involving doing things of a para-military nature. All that one can say of this method is that it gives the candidate a better opportunity than the individual interview, since he is checked by a fair number of people and this eliminates the prejudices of selection by one person.

3. THE PROBLEM OF LEADERSHIP IN MODERN SOCIETY.

What has been said above leads us directly to the question of leadership, not necessarily in industry, but in modern society as a whole. We have seen that in many cases there still exists the belief that 'leadership' is a psychological trait which is somehow situated inside a person, being either there or not. Oddly enough, so far as industry and the services are concerned, this innate quality is most frequently found in those who have had a public school education—indeed, one of the mainstays of the argument for retaining public schools is that they train the 'character' and produce qualities of 'leadership' denied to lesser breeds. Scientifically speaking, this is the merest nonsense (*a*) because one can no more train character in a public school than in a borstal or any other place—that has, for better or worse, occurred in the home in the early years of life, and (*b*) because there is no such quality as leadership within a particular man or woman, only the ability possessed by nearly everyone to be a leader in a given situation. Many pieces of psychological research have shown that the only common factor found in those who become leaders in a particular field is their superior competence or knowledge in that area. Of course, many people are thrust into positions of leadership by reason of their social position, their wealth, their education (not what they have *done*, but *where* they have *been*), but these are leaders only in the formal sense and, if many products of our public schools have made good army officers, that is first because they have supreme self-confidence and, second, because they were acting within an authoritarian network in which even the less competent had the full backing of authority behind them. Even the self-assurance is more likely to have been derived from the social background of which their school is only one aspect than from any training within the school itself. This sort of leadership is all very well for the army which of its very nature must be authoritarian, but it is of no use at all in a modern democracy in which a leader must be chosen because he represents the feelings and views of the group he leads. The reason for saying this is not a sentimental one or based on political faith in democracy; it is simply that, in a society which is not authoritarian and where there is more or less full employment, there are no means open to a leader to get his subordinates to work effectively or even to stay with him than by possessing their confidence and respect.

Leadership as a Function of the Working Environment.

We have seen that leadership is a function of the situation confronting the group, so it follows that if the situation changes the leader may have to change too. This is well illustrated in the following case: a factory manager who had been well liked and respected retired and his place was taken by a bumptious, self-assertive man who did not believe in consulting his subordinates. Hitherto, the supervisors had formed their own group which elected one of their members to deal with their interests or problems when he took them to the factory manager for advice, help, or information. Throughout the period of office of the first manager, the supervisors' leader was a quiet, sensible man and the two got on very well together and with the rest of the men. But when it was seen what the new manager was like, resentment began to grow and, at the next election, the old leader was ousted and the man put in his place was an agitator who had up till then been regarded by most of the supervisors as aggressive, unpleasant, and even a little ' cracked '. Year after year the same man continued to be elected in spite of the fact that each member of the group still continued to dislike him, and when they were asked why the answer was: " Well, you see, he's the only man amongst us who is capable of dealing with that (unmentionable) manager."

A Taoist philosopher, about five or six hundred years B.C., made the observation that the great ruler is one whose people do not even notice his existence, the lesser one is feared, and the still lesser one despised. This is confirmed by the leading American authority on management, C. I. Barnard, who wrote that the good leader in industry in a democratic society may sometimes give the impression that he is a " rather stupid fellow, a mere channel of communications, and a filcher of ideas. In a measure this is correct. He has to be stupid enough to listen a great deal, he certainly must arbitrate to maintain order, but he has at times to be a mere centre of communication. If he used only his own ideas he would be somewhat like a one-man orchestra, rather than a good conductor, who is a very high type of leader." Or, as the same Chinese philosopher wrote:

> The best employer of men keeps himself below them.
> This is called the virtue of not contending;
> This is called the ability of using men.

In a democracy politics is ' the practice of the possible ' because the leader can never be too far ahead of the desires and attitudes of the people.

The Nature of Democratic Society.

A democratic society is, of course, in one of its aspects a society which elects its leaders by secret and universal voting; but this is not the only, or even the most important part of democracy. In modern societies it is often necessary to put people in high positions because of their specialist knowledge—government by amateurs is now no longer possible in all fields, and in industry and other spheres such as the armed forces it is not always possible to elect leaders. What is much more important is (*a*) that the leaders at all levels even when they have been chosen primarily because of their technical qualifications should be able to make themselves acceptable to those under them, and (*b*) that there should be free flow of information both up and down the channels of communication. This is not achieved by manipulating others on the model of Dale Carnegie's book *How to Make Friends and Influence People*—which is often used as a means of influencing people without necessarily making friends of them—but by being the sort of leader described by Barnard who acts, not on his own decisions taken in isolation, but with regard to the feelings of others and an ear to their opinions. There would be far fewer strikes if management employed genuine joint consultation in which no major decisions were taken on matters affecting the workers without consulting them about the decisions beforehand, seeking their cooperation and advice as to how they should be carried out—and this not because of common decency alone but because management *in fact* cannot act without the cooperation of their employees. Indeed, many strikes happen not because the workers object to the decisions as such, but because their human dignity is affronted by not being told about them. Sometimes it is necessary to make decisions, for example, about redundancy, which on the one hand may be inevitable and on the other hardly likely to be pleasant to the workers, but in these cases there is all the more reason why they should be kept informed from the earliest stages and allowed, at least, to express their views as to how the process can be carried out with least hardship.

An Effective Communication System.

One of the secrets of good management is an effective communication system; for workers will do their job efficiently only when they are able to identify themselves with their firm and feel that they are taking part in joint enterprise rather than being used as mere tools. Thus it must be possible for all grievances to be dealt with openly at the earliest moment and everybody in a factory ought to know what he is doing, for whom he is doing it, and why—the days of ' You're not paid to think: do what you're damn well told,' are, or should be, long past. The widest publicity must be given to the firm's finances, its future projects, its exports, and sales within the country because, as we have seen, nobody works satisfactorily unless he can feel that his work is meaningful. The real essence of democracy is not any special technique but the confidence of the ruled that they can influence their rulers, trust them, and receive justice at their hands.

Social Mobility.

Social mobility is another characteristic of a democracy, and we have seen that in England the barriers to the right man finding the right job and attaining the highest status of which he is capable are psychological and based on traditions rather than the result of any legal or physical hindrances. Indeed, it is surprising to note that social mobility in Britain is freer than in the United States in spite of the latter country's tradition of ' from log cabin to White House '. Probably the main reason for this, as Vance Packard has suggested, is that the American manager has little chance of success unless he is a WASP (White, Anglo-Saxon, Protestant) and, of course, industry is the main field controlling social mobility and status. In Britain the main obstacles for a man are the dying ' old boy ' tradition and the worker's fear of leaving his class, but for a woman the sole obstacle is simply the fact of being a woman.

4. THE DEVELOPMENT OF INDUSTRIAL PSYCHOLOGY.

We turn now to a brief account of the discoveries in the field of industrial psychology which had its beginnings in the United States at the turn of the century. One of its first exponents was a man known as Frederick Winslow Taylor who was to become famous—and, in the eyes of some, notorious—as the founder of the system described as ' Taylorism '. The principles of this system were simple:

(1) to select the best man for the job;

(2) to instruct him in the most efficient methods and the most effective movements to employ in his job;

(3) to give incentives in the form of higher wages to the best workers.

By applying these principles—which, in a more humane form, were to develop into modern Time and Motion Study—Taylor was able to reduce the number of workers needed to load wagons at his firm, the Bethlehem Steel Company, from 500 to 140, increase daily earnings of those who remained by 60 per cent, and save his bosses about 75,000 dollars a year. He was, not unnaturally, unpopular with the workers who, to this day, have always tended to dislike the man with the stop-watch and if Taylor as a sincere Quaker was basically a humane man and hoped that his system would benefit all, he nevertheless held the very odd philosophy that "all employees should bear in mind that each shop exists first, last, and all the time, for the purpose of paying dividends to its owners".

About the same time Frank B. Gilbreth was encouraging the fragmentation of work which, as we have seen, was already an increasing tendency throughout the middle period of the industrial revolution in an attempt to increase efficiency and, to be fair, decrease the amount of hard work necessary. Like Taylor, his ideal was to make work so simple that "it could be carried out by a trained chimpanzee". Neither of these two men were trained psychologists, who only entered the field about the time of the First World War and concerned themselves mainly with experimenting on such environmental factors as the influence of temperature, humidity, noise and so on, on efficiency, but the total effect of all this early work was to increase the meaninglessness of the job, arouse resentments in many cases, and cause the workers to feel that they were being exploited. Since it is necessary to most workers to feel that what they are doing is meaningful and worthwhile, it is now generally admitted that if, from the economic point of view, many of these researches were really successful, the early investigators took a far too simple and mechanistic view of the nature of the problem. The philosophy lying behind them implied the beliefs (*a*) that man was a machine or, at any rate, that his mind could be ignored since the real problem lay in adjusting the physical environment or the way of doing the job; (*b*) that the only incentives were 'the carrot or the stick'—that is money or the negative incentive of fear of losing one's job; (*c*) that these propositions were self-evident because only a privileged few ever learn to like their work.

The Hawthorne Researches.

These assumptions were to receive a rude shock with the so-called researches carried out in the early 1930s by Elton Mayo and others at the works of the Western Electric Company in the United States. Mayo was an Australian working at Harvard University who initially started off with the same assumptions as his predecessors and contemporaries—basically, that the main factors in improving output were the conditions in the physical environment of the work-room and, when Western Electric called on him because they were having labour problems, he proceeded to put them into force. In a work-room where a number of girls were assembling telephone relays, Mayo and his colleages began by altering the lighting in the room and, after a time, were gratified to find that productivity went up. Subsequently various other improvements were made in the way of rest-breaks, atmospheric conditions, and new wage plans and, following each improvement, the higher output continued to rise steadily. Whilst carrying out these researches, the group of psychologists had kept on talking to the workers, asking for their views and even for advice, thus arousing a real interest in what was going on. However, as a good scientist, Mayo did not merely accept as others had done before him the satisfactory results of his work and decided to put them to more rigorous tests. The environmental 'improvements', the breaks, the better wages plans, were removed one by one and, when all had been removed and the girls were working in their room with lighting which was of about the intensity of bright moonlight, it was found that production figures soared far beyond the highest level ever recorded. The conclusions of this piece of work were the now commonplace ones that the rise in productivity and efficiency had nothing whatever to do with environmental changes but were due to social factors such as the girls' attitudes towards each other. Approval, antagonism, or indifference directly affected production, whereas a feeling of importance at being selected for the study, a sense of responsibility and mutual co-operation with the researchers, and growing congeniality among themselves caused a general improvement. In short, it was conclusively proved that human relationships between one worker and another and between all and management motivated them more strongly than financial incentives or good working conditions.

Incentives.

Social surveys carried out by numerous workers in this country and the United States under the influence of Mayo showed that *in all cases money was one of the least powerful incentives*—to take a single example typical of many, the 17,000 employees of Joseph Lucas Ltd. in England put security first and high earnings fourth in a list of seven items which they were asked to place in order of importance. Of course, it has to be remembered that this may change when inflation occurs and prices rise and it may even be the case that, in an affluent society, workers may want more money as an aim in itself, but generally speaking the demand for higher wages is more likely to reflect either dissatisfaction with the firm or a concern with 'differentials'. That is to say, since the workers have their own informal status hierarchy, one group may feel aggrieved if those of a lower status have their wages increased in such a way as to lower the relative prestige of the other—it is the prestige rather than the money that matters, *e.g.*, when the very low wages of the lower grades of railway workers were raised, the engine drivers demanded correspondingly more, not because they begrudged their work-mates their increased affluence, but because their self-esteem had been hurt. The following are some of the relevant facts about incentives in general:

(1) There is no single ideal incentive, because incentives vary greatly from one culture to another (we have seen elsewhere that one of the difficulties in motivating workers in South America and the Afro-Asian countries is their lack of interest in bettering their material conditions), and from one individual to another (*e.g.*, one man may value money whilst another may find more leisure or opportunity for promotion a stronger stimulus to work);

(2) The law of diminishing returns applies to all material incentives, *i.e.*, as the reward increases the desire for further reward decreases until it reaches vanishing-point. Thus the miners, when given higher wages, increased their absenteeism, because the point had been reached at which the need for more money had become secondary to the need for more leisure;

(3) Incentives may conflict with each other; for the worker may ignore financial incentives if he fears that the rate for the job may be cut or that he may work himself out of a job;

(4) It is necessary to realise that in our own culture all motives tend to become 'monetised' since people have subconsciously been taught to believe that money is the key to satisfaction and, when they feel that something is wrong, naturally ask for more money—as Gordon Rattray Taylor has noted "a demand for money undoubtedly indicates that they want *something*, but it does not tell us what".

Restrictive Practices.

We have already seen that incentives can conflict with each other, and one of Mayo's researches demonstrated very clearly the phenomenon of restrictive practices arising from such conflicts. In what was known as the 'bank-wiring room' of the Western Electric Company, he found a group of male workers who completely disregarded all financial incentives and, though the incentive plan provided that the more work a worker did the more money he received, productivity remained at 6,000 units a day in spite of the fact that without the least difficulty the group could have produced 7,000. Here Mayo found that the informal group, which he believed to be the basic unit in industry (it has been described elsewhere as the 'primary group'), had selected an informal leader who was not the same person as the official one. There was an unofficial code of behaviour which exerted a strong influence over group members and impressed upon them the following rules: "You should not turn out too much work, otherwise you will be a 'chiseller'." "You should not tell a supervisor anything to the detriment of a work-mate, otherwise you will be a 'squealer'." "You should not 'act officious'—if you are an inspector, for example, you should not act like one." These are, of course, as Sargant Florence points out, the same sort of principles as are found in the English public school: "Rate-busters have been called 'swots', chisellers, 'slackers', squealers, 'sneaks'. Americans apparently had no name for the form of behaviour described as 'acting officious', but familiar English slang is 'swank'." These form the basis for restrictive practices in industry though here the need to maintain status and avoid the traditional fear of insecurity plays a greater part.

Summary of Mayo's Researches.

Mayo's important conclusions can be summarised as follows:

(1) Work is a social activity in the sense that, even when working in physical isolation as in the case of the artist, what is done is carried out either in society or for society.

(2) The social world of the adult is primarily patterned around work activity.

(3) The need for recognition, security, and sense of belonging is more important in determining workers' morale and productivity than the physical conditions under which the work is carried out.

(4) A complaint is not necessarily an objective recital of facts; it is commonly a *symptom* manifesting disturbance of an individual's status position. Contrary to general belief, the majority of strikes are not about wage claims, but about matters in which the workers feel their status or self-respect to be threatened.

(5) The worker is a person whose attitudes and effectiveness are conditioned by social demands from both inside and outside the work plant.

(6) The change from an established to an adaptive society—*i.e.*, one in which there is great social and geographical mobility, and where a traditionally static society has given way to mass democracy—tends continually to disrupt the social organisation of factories and industry generally.

Two of the dangers of high geographical mobility are (*a*) that a constantly mobile population never has the time to develop loyalty to individual members or individual firms—as one supervisor said, his department was more like a procession than a work-room because its members were continually changing; (*b*) since social control by the superego or conscience is less effective in many fields than control by group-membership, those who never stay in a community long enough are apt to become 'rootless' with a subsequent weakening in moral control. This, of course, is one of the reasons why immigrants are peculiarly liable to get into trouble. It is not their innate wickedness, but the fact that they have left the community which originally supported their moral beliefs, their old cultural imperatives have weakened, and they have not become sufficiently identified with their new surroundings to accept the current mores. Hence the social phenomenon of gangsterism during the 1930s in America was almost exclusively an Italian or Irish one—in fact, even now, the old secret society founded in Sicily and known as the Mafia, virtually rules a large sector of modern gangsterism.

(7) Group collaboration does not occur by accident; it must be planned for and developed. If group collaboration is achieved, a cohesion may result which resists the disrupting effects of the mass society.

CONCLUSIONS.

What we have found in this brief survey is that society is constantly changing in order to adapt itself to a new environment which itself alters with disconcerting and ever-accelerating speed. It follows that it is incorrect to say that 'human nature' is always the same and that moral standards never change—on the contrary, it should be evident by now that changes in these fields are not only inevitable but desirable. Of course, there are a few basic laws which are 'absolute' in the sense that they are firmly based on the nature of society—*e.g.*, "Love thy neighbour as thyself" is a fundamental rule simply because society, by definition, is a state of affairs in which most people are neighbourly, and Stuart Chase has said that if more than 10 per cent of any community failed to cooperate, the community would simply collapse.

'Free competition' may well have been in the interests of society as a whole in a developing economy, but it is neither possible nor desirable now—in fact, it was brought to an end some time ago, not by the machinations of wicked socialists, but because capitalists could not keep up with the pace and began to combine to protect their own interests.

Again, though we have not presumed to prescribe in what direction sexual morality should change, there is not the slightest doubt that it is changing and will continue to do so. What we have suggested is that sexual relations must be based on mutual respect and, when that is done, nothing serious is likely to go wrong. This was the fundamental meaning of the teachings of Christ when he shifted the emphasis from the externally applied laws of the Ten Commandments to inward intentions and motives. However, no matter how important sexual morality may be, it is very far from being the whole of morality and we might guess that one of the reasons for the general decline of interest in the churches has been their tendency to equate sex with sin to the exclusion of the social injustices which people feel to be among the major issues of our times. If this does not always apply to individual churchmen, it does in general apply to their churches. Very often their influence has been on the side of reaction as in Spain, and it was an Anglican clergyman who described his church as "the Tory party at prayer" but, again, there are many exceptions, such as the attitude of the Church of Scotland to African affairs and the last Encyclical of Pope John.

In the field of industry what has been said here may be summarised in the words of Goronwy Rees: "It seems sometimes, today, as if the grand committee of management which has for so long conducted the affairs of the country has at last become conscious of its failure and seeks desperately for a cure. Hence the 'lofty symbols', the 'admonitions', the 'signals for a change of heart', which we are offered daily. But how are our managers to cure themselves, and where, in the short time that may be left to us, are they to discover either the knowledge and competence, or the powers of will, energy, and creativeness, which today so many of them conspicuously lack?" Much the same might be said of some of the workers' leaders who cannot divest themselves of wholly outdated notions and superstitions.

We have tried to show that there is a more hopeful side to the picture presented, notably in the field of education; but what is clear is that radical changes in attitudes are needed on all fronts. What mainly hinders this is not only the backward-looking traditionalist mentality but, oddly enough, the 'affluent society' which, along with its many benefits, has brought about the state of affairs described by J. K. Galbraith, the eminent economist, and until recently American Ambassador to India, when he pointed out that "in a country where well-being is general, the astute politician will be the one who stalwartly promises to defend the status quo".

A GUIDE TO MODERN GARDENING

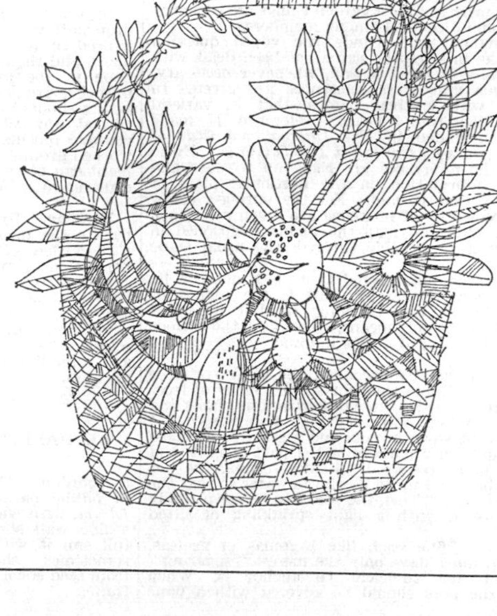

MODERN GARDENING

CULTIVATION OF FLOWERS.

Throughout this section the notes must be taken to refer to cultural conditions in the British Isles, although in many cases the information can be adopted to suit the necessity of readers living abroad. Undoubtedly, in many temperate parts of the world interest in gardening has increased enormously during the past decade or so, despite the fact that numbers of large gardens have ceased to exist and that few people can afford to pay for full-time help in their gardens. To counteract this, the all important labour-saving garden has come into its own; shrubby plants have replaced annual bedding schemes and large lawns put down instead of herbaceous borders or beds of particular plants.

In addition, the owner-gardener is anxious to avail himself of the excellent selection of modern tools; thus the conventional hoe is being replaced by the "Swoe" or the Wolf pattern of Dutch weeder, both of which are very easy to use, and digging can be done quickly—and with much less effort—by using a German digger called a "Terrex" spade. For grass mowing, the work is easily done with motor mowers like the "Rotoscythe," or battery-driven patterns.

For greenhouse work, smaller houses are being used and one, say, 12 ft. by 8 ft., can be run economically with a minimum winter temperature of 40° Fahrenheit by the introduction of trouble-free, thermostatic heaters or the turbo-heaters. At the moment, besides automatic heating, the prototypes for automatic ventilation and watering are making an appearance.

While advocating the use of such appliances, it must be pointed out that there are also to be found tools, sundries, and fertilisers of little value, and many of which have never been properly tested prior to being put on the market. It is, therefore, a good plan to discuss the comparative merits of any appliance or horticultural sundry with a competent horticulturist or to contact a public authority. In particular, many local horticultural societies have special trading facilities, and the merits of most garden things are generally known and discussed among members.

Throughout this Guide the vexed question of change in scientific name has been dealt with as liberally as possible and, whenever necessary, synonyms and cross references are given. In dealing with cultivar names, that is, varietal names like rose 'Peace,' reference is made as recommended in *The International Code of Nomenclature for Cultivated Plants* (1961). By so doing, the references are right up to date and further information on any particular plant or subject is easy to find. For the purpose, a few standard works of reference are given after each section. Normally, all the plants mentioned in the text are available through the usual trade channels.

After each plant listed there is a note on its propagation. Generally, this is the easiest or most efficient way of doing so, but it is not necessarily the only means. Details of the various methods employed are as follows:

Seed. Generally speaking, the early spring is the most suitable time for sowing seeds of trees and shrubs besides those of herbaceous plants and alpines. Where only a few plants are needed, the seed can be sown in pots and a suitable compost made up with 2 parts of soil, 1 part of peat, and 1 part of coarse sand. Before sowing, the pot should be stood up to its rim in water so that the soil is soaked. Then the seed can be sown thinly and covered with a light sprinkling of sifted compost.

For very fine seed, like begonias or azaleas, the seed must have only the merest "sugaring" of sand just sufficient to anchor it. When sown, the pots should be covered with a pane of glass (to prevent evaporation) and kept, if possible, in a warm greenhouse or frame. With this method of propagation it is important to remember that failure will result if the seed is sown too deeply, if the temperature is too low, or if the soil is too dry.

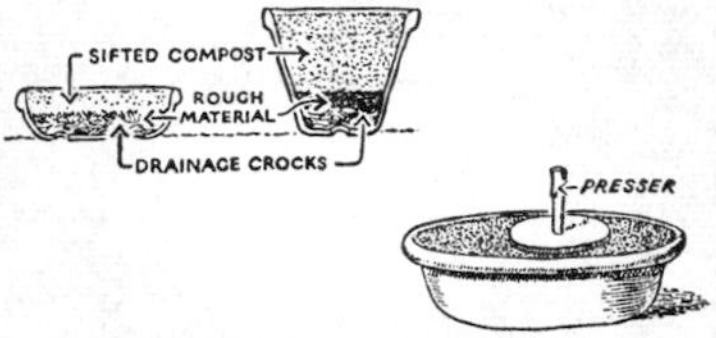

CORRECT PREPARATION OF SEED POTS AND PANS—Note provision for ample drainage and compost to rim of its container. After sowing, the containers are covered with a sheet of glass.

Cuttings. There are two main types of cutting: soft-wood cuttings made from fresh, green shoots in the spring and summer and hard-wood cuttings made of mature or semi-mature woody shoots in the autumn. A soft cutting is taken about 3 in. long, the lower leaves removed and a clean cut made through a node in the stem. These are then inserted in pots containing a light, sandy soil or a rooting medium such as horticultural vermiculite, well watered, and covered with a bell jar or plastic bag. Delphiniums, hydrangeas, and lupins are all propagated in this way.

Hard-wood cuttings are taken in the autumn and made from shoots about 8–12 in. long. These are inserted in a sandy soil out of doors or in a cold frame, and left to develop for a year. Black-currants, forsythia, and roses can be propagated by this means.

Layering. This is one of the easiest ways of propagating the majority of woody plants, and is used to increase stocks of plants like clematis, lilacs, and rhododendrons. Normally, layering is done in the autumn or spring when suitable branches are pegged down. On each of these the young shoots are, in turn, pegged down and tips turned upwards and tied in position. To encourage rooting, gritty sand and peat should be worked around each layer, and usually the young plant can be severed from the parent after about eighteen months.

Division. By this method it is easy to propagate the majority of herbaceous plants, some rock-garden plants, and a few shrubs. A few herbaceous plants, like delphinium and paeony, are slow to get established after moving, and here the method should not be employed. In any case, old plants should not be split up in a wholesale manner; instead, it is far better to select a few young healthy plants, divide these, and replant the best of the young shoots, in the autumn.

ALPHABETICAL LIST OF ORNAMENTAL PLANTS.

Abutilon.—The greenhouse species is often used in public parks for bedding schemes. *A. vitifolium*, with white, mauve, or blue flowers makes a fine wall shrub for warm gardens. If given full sun it will quickly reach 10–15 ft., but is sometimes short-lived. *Prop.*—Easily raised from seed sown in March in a warm greenhouse or frame.

Acer (Maple).—Hardy, ornamental trees; the Norway maple is often planted for its magnificent autumn colour and as a lawn tree. *A. palmatum* and vars. constitute the Japanese maples; all colour brilliantly in the autumn but do not grow freely unless given some shade and a light soil rich in humus. *Prop.*—Seed, layering, or budding.

Achillea (Yarrow).—Grey-leaved perennials for open border or, dwarf species, for rock garden. Valued as a cut flower, particularly *A. ptarmica* 'Perry's White,' with double, white flowers and *A. eupatorium* 'Gold Plate,' with large, flat, yellow flower heads. *A. millefolium* is a pernicious weed of turf (**T33**). *Prop.*—Division in autumn.

Acidanthera.—Scented, bulbous plant introduced from Abyssinia. It is not difficult to grow if the corms are planted in the spring and lifted in the autumn for storing in a frost-proof shed. It requires a sunny position and plenty of water in the summer. *Prop.*—Offsets removed when the old crop of bulbs is lifted.

Aconitum (Monkshood).—Blue-flowered perennial plants particularly useful for lightly shaded positions or full sun; flowers from May to July, height 3–5 ft.; roots poisonous. *Prop.*—Seed or division.

Adiantum.—*See* **Ferns.**

A Well-Grown Agapanthus—In winter the pot should be kept in a cold greenhouse or some protected place; in summer afforded full sun.

Agapanthus.—A bulbous plant, native of South Africa, usually found in seaside gardens and sometimes grown in tubs; flowers blue, violet, or white. It needs winter protection in the form of a covering of bracken or straw and a light soil heavily enriched with manure. Worthy of wider cultivation. *Prop.*—Seed or division in March.

Ageratum.—Blue-flowered carpeting plant. *See* **Annuals.**

Allium (Flowering Onion).—A genus of nearly 300 species of bulbous plants widely distributed over the Northern Hemisphere. The foliage has the distinctive smell of garlic, but some species are grown for garden ornamentation; in particular *A. roseum*, valuable late-flowering rock plant for dry positions. *Prop.*—Offsets, taken from parent bulbs in the spring.

Alstroemeria aurantiaca (Peruvian Lily).—This tuberous-rooted, herbaceous plant is often grown for cutting. Flowers orange-red and height 2–3 ft.; of easy culture if afforded a sunny position and left undisturbed. For best results apply liquid manure or soot water when growth starts. *Prop.*—Seed or division.

Althaea (Hollyhock).—A truly delightful, old-world plant, but not often seen, as modern hybrids have given way to rust disease. Best grown in a rich, heavy loam. Mulch with manure of any sort and stake as necessary. *Prop.*—Seed in June, thin out, and transfer to flowering position in September. Although a perennial, in some localities the best results are obtained by treating it as a biennial and raising a small supply annually.

Alyssum.—Low-growing annuals and perennials for rock garden and sunny border. The perennial, *A. saxatile*, is deservedly popular by reason of its bright, spring flowers and value as a wall plant. The variety 'Citrinum' is bright yellow and 'Dudley Neville' biscuit-yellow. *Prop.*—Perennial sorts by cuttings in June.

Amaryllis belladonna.—Often this plant is confused with the greenhouse, bulbous plant, *Hippeastrum*. The true amaryllis is a half-hardy bulb for planting at the foot of a warm wall; it has white to pinkish-red flowers. When planting, cover neck of bulb with an inch of soil and leave undisturbed, as the plant resents moving and is slow to get established. Lack of flowering is generally due to planting too deep. Established clumps may be fed with hoof and horn meal at 2 oz. per sq. yd. in July. *Prop.*—Divide and replant clumps in early July.

Amelanchier canadensis.—A large shrub or small tree; valuable for its spring flowers and autumn colour. As it will grow almost anywhere in sun or shade, it makes a good plant for informal screening. *Prop.*—Seed or layers.

Amepelopsis.—*See* **Parthenocissus.**

Anchusa italica.—A blue-flowered perennial with fleshy roots, growing to a height of about 3 ft. Responds to feeding and needs a position in full sun. *Prop.*—Root cuttings in the spring; division in the autumn.

Anemone.—The tuberous-rooted section includes the 'Caen' and 'St. Brigid' strains. These are best grown in an open position in light, rich soil; plant in October, lift and store when foliage dies. The hardy, fibrous-rooted perennials are varieties of *A. hybrida* (syn. *japonica*) and constitute one of the most accommodating of perennials, being particularly useful for damp, shady positions. Worthy of wider attention from gardeners. *Prop.*—Perennial sorts by division in autumn.

Annuals.—These are plants which develop from seed, flower, fruit, and die within a year. Additionally, some perennials, like antirrhinums, may be treated as annuals for the convenience of their cultivation. Sunny borders may be planted solely with annuals, they may be interplanted with perennials, used for window boxes, or, occasionally, in the rock garden. All sorts do best in well-worked, light loam enriched each year with a dressing of fish meal at 3 oz. per sq. yd., ten days before sowing or planting.

In the division of the group Hardy Annuals may be sown in the open ground as soon as conditions permit during March or April where the plants are to flower. Wet or cold soils will give many failures, and fine seed should be covered only with the lightest sugaring of soil. Often surprising—but delightful—results may be obtained by sowing broadcast mixed seed of annuals specially offered by some trade houses.

To raise Half Hardy Annuals, seed may be sown in early March in a warm greenhouse and the seedlings pricked out into boxes. Subsequently, the plants are grown on in a cold frame, gradually hardened off, and then transferred to their flowering positions towards the end of May.

Anthemis tinctoria.—Hardy perennial with feathery, grey foliage and flowers in varying shades of yellow. Height 2–3 ft., needs full sun and good for cutting. *Prop.*—Division in the autumn. *Anthemis nobilis* is the chamomile sometimes unwisely used to make lawns.

Antirrhinum (Snapdragon).—The popular bedding plant requiring a good soil and position in full sun now largely in disfavour owing to rust disease; planting should be restricted to rust-resistant varieties. *See* Annuals.

Aphelandra squarrosa.—An evergreen, perennial plant introduced from Brazil. Often sold as a house plant, albeit a warm temperature and a high humidity are necessary for its cultivation. When grown indoors it is best discarded when the flowers fade and the foliage starts to wither, as it cannot be successfully grown on from year to year under normal conditions indoors.

Aquilegia.—The modern race of hybrids are the result of much interbreeding with wild forms to give a wide range of colours. Best when planted in light shade where soil is naturally moist. *Prop.*—Seed in late spring; transplant to flowering position for following year.

Arabis caucasica.—Once known as *A. albida*, this common rock plant is often used on dry walls. The double-flowered form is particularly good. *Prop.*—Cuttings in July; a fresh stock should be raised regularly as the special forms tend to die out.

Araucaria (Monkey Puzzle).—This tree was introduced from Chile, where it forms large natural forests, and widely planted in Victorian days. Browning of foliage suggests lack of water in the summer or, occasionally, effects of very cold weather. It should be planted in a position protected from the prevailing wind. *Prop.*—Seed in a warm greenhouse.

Armeria maritima.—A hardy perennial with pink or red flowers in the spring; must be grown in full sun where the soil is dry. *Prop.*—Division after flowering.

Artemisia.—A genus of shrubs and perennials suitable for sunny borders or rockeries. *A. lactiflora* is among the best of the herbaceous species, having grey foliage and creamy-white flowers. *A. abrotanum* (lad's love) in the shrubby section has grey, fragrant foliage. *Prop.*—Herbaceous section by division; shrubs by cuttings in the early summer.

Arundinaria.—*See* Bamboo.

Aster (Michaelmas Daisy).—By careful breeding this plant has been improved out of all recognition, and many first-class varieties are available in the trade. Responsive to good cultivation, it is used for its colour late in season and properties as a cut flower, particularly *A. yunnanensis* 'Napsbury' and *A.* 'Barr's Pink.' A wide range of colours are available besides some fine, low-growing forms. In the border one pleasing combination can be made with *A.* 'Harrington's Pink' and *Scabious* 'Dinkie.' *Prop.*—The clumps should be split up *annually* in the spring, and only the plumpest pieces of outer root replanted.

Aster, China or Common.—*See* Callistephus.

Astilbe.—Allied to the *Spiraea* and useful for planting in moist, rich soils; flowers white, pink, and crimson; height 2 ft. *Prop.*—Division of clumps.

Aubrieta.—A name often misspelt. Throughout the country it is used as edging or for dry walls. Many lovely sorts available apart from the commonly found, pale-blue variety. It is a lime lover. *Prop.*—After flowering the plants should be severely trimmed and, as necessary, stock increased by division.

Aucuba japonica.—Much maligned and overplanted shrub, but one tolerant of neglect and sunless or smoky conditions. Interesting variants of the type, like 'Crotonifolia,' may be found in trade lists. *Prop.*—Cuttings rooted in the open in July.

Auricula.—Correctly known botanically as *Primula auricula*. Flowers of alpine auriculas are white or yellow, while in those of florists' auriculas are to be found some of the most delicate colourings among hardy plants Choice varieties are grown in pots under glass; others in moist, shady borders. *Prop.*—Seed or division in the spring.

Azalea.—*See* Rhododendron.

Bamboo.—The common name for the large group of woody grasses, reference to which is difficult owing to the confusion in their nomenclature. Often grown for screening and wind breaks, and is a favourite shelter for small birds; the best for home-grown canes are *Phyllostachys viridi-glaucescens* and *Sinarundinaria nitida*. An interesting account of bamboo growing is found in the *Jour. Roy. Hort. Soc.* (June 1957). Growth can be encouraged by feeding with sulphate of ammonia and mulching with leaf-mould in the spring. *Prop.*—Division of clumps in late spring; transplants must be kept watered until established.

Begonia.—A genus showing wide diversity of form and much horticultural value. Of particular interest is the tuberous-rooted section, of which many of the loveliest varieties have originated in the nurseries of Messrs. Blackmore and Landon at Bath. For bedding schemes, the tubers are started in boxes of rich soil under glass in late March and planted out 9 in. apart in June. During the summer feed with liquid manure of any sort and keep moist in dry periods. *Prop.*—Cuttings in early spring in a warm case.

Berberis.—An extensive genus of beautiful and easily grown shrubs, evergeen and deciduous; the former used mainly for beauty of flower, and the latter for autumn colouring and ornamental fruits. *B. stenophylla* makes a fine evergreen hedge; invaluable for preventing illicit entry by dogs and, even, unruly children. *B. aggregata* and *B. jamesiana* are among the best berrying kinds. Prune in the winter by removing old wood. *Prop.*—Seed in spring or layering in autumn.

Buddleia.—Deciduous shrubs of easy culture for sunny positions. Varieties of *B. davidii* available in range of colours from purple to white; best when pruned hard by cutting all previous year's growth back to main stems in February. The weeping species, *B. alternifolia*, often grown as a standard; good specimens at R.H.S. Gardens, Wisley. This sort must be pruned in the summer by cutting off the dead flowering stems. *Prop.*—Cuttings in July–August in cold frame.

Cactus.—In the main grown in cool greenhouses or as house plants and, if cultivated well, many will flower every year. As a general guide, plants should be watered fairly freely in the summer and little in the winter, but there are exceptions. A detailed account of growing these fascinating plants will be found in *The Cactus Grower's Guide*, by Vera Higgings (Latimer House), 1946.

Calceolaria.—Seed of the greenhouse biennials sown in June or July for flowering in the following year. Mixed seed provides a wide range of colour. *C. integrifolia* is a half-hardy perennial, raised by cuttings or seed, for greenhouse or bedding work.

Calendula (Marigold).—This common hardy annual is freely raised from seed sown in August. Of easy culture in any sort of soil, although it is worth getting seed of new varieties now available. *See* Annuals.

Callistephus.—The China asters are among the best half-hardy annuals for garden and indoor decoration, but good soil and full sun are necessary for best results. *See* Annuals.

Camellia japonica.—Hardy, evergreen shrub rightly beloved by connoisseurs and cultivated in gardens for many centuries. May be grown in cold greenhouses, woodland gardens, and against north- and west-facing walls; under all conditions camellias must have a moist, acid soil. Best varieties for outdoors are 'Althaeaflora' (dark red), 'Donckelarii' (red, white marbling), and 'C. M. Wilson' (pink). Of recent introduction is the desirable *C. williamsii* bred from *C. japonica* in part; often the subject of television and gardening notes. The dropping of buds is thought due to dryness at the roots at some time or sharp fluctuation in temperature. *Prop.*—Named varieties by cuttings under glass in early July. Otherwise plants easily raised from seeds if sown in the autumn immediately they are ripe, in acidic peat and kept moist.

Campsis grandiflora.—Sometimes found listed as *Bignonia* or *Tecoma*; choice deciduous climber for warm wall, large reddish-orange flowers in autumn. To encourage flowering growth, prune hard back to old growth in spring. *Prop.*—Cuttings in April struck in a warm case.

Canary Creeper.—*See* **Tropaeolum.**

Candytuft.—Hardy annual (*q.v.*) and perennials with white, crimson, blue, or purple flowers. The perennial—*Iberis sempervirens*—is a fine plant for a rock wall. *Prop.*—Seed or, perennials, from cuttings.

Carnation.—*See* **Dianthus.**

Centaurea (Cornflower).—The perennial species are valuable for cutting and border use, and may be found in such colours as pink, crimson, and yellow. *Prop.*—Lift and divide every third or fourth year. The hardy annual, *C. cyanus*, is often sold as a cut flower. *See* **Annuals.**

Cheiranthus cheiri (Wallflower).—Among the finest displays of this biennial are those found each year in the public gardens of Southend-on-Sea, where it is used in conjunction with bulbs and forget-me-nots. *Prop.*—Seed sown thinly in rows in May and seedlings thinned or lined out and then transplanted in late autumn. The so-called Siberian wallflower, *Erysimun asperum*, which has bright orange flowers, is grown in the same way, but it is intolerant of wet soils. Both sorts are lime lovers, and on acid soils plants may receive treatment with 1 oz. of lime in a gallon of water.

Chimonanthus (Winter Sweet).—Hardy, winter-flowering shrub with heavily scented flowers. Although brought to this country from the Far East in the mid-eighteenth century its garden value is not widely appreciated. The large-flowered, yellow sort, *C. praecox*, is particularly fine, but like all the varieties, it is best grown against a sunny wall and where the soil tends to be poor. If growth is excessive and flowering poor, trim back young growth severely in March to encourage short, spur-like shoots. *Prop.*—Easily raised from seed or layers.

Chionodoxa.—Blue-flowered bulbs useful for under-planting shrubs such as forsythia. Will tolerate shade and may be left undisturbed to naturalise. Height 6 in.

Christmas Rose.—*See* **Helleborus.**

Chrysanthemum.—Hardy annual sorts are available in a wide range of colours and give a fine display in the summer months. *See* **Annuals.** There are also a number of perennials such as the shafta daisy and the oxeye daisy for sunny, herbaceous borders; all do well in ordinary soil, but should be lifted and split up about every three years. The plant sold by florists in the autumn is the Japanese chrysanthemum. Many are hardy out-of-doors, but no plant is more responsive to good cultivation and normally is best left to the specialist grower. For ordinary garden work, the best sorts are the Korean and Otley types. Under a brief reference the interesting details of cultivation cannot be dealt with fairly, and reference to specialist books is recommended.

Cistus.—Hardy and half-hardy evergreen shrubs, mainly native of Southern Europe. Well worth growing in light, sandy soils in reasonably sheltered positions. Pruning should be limited to the removal of any shoots killed in the winter. Among the hardiest sorts are *C. laurifolius*, white flowers, 6 ft., and *C. purpureus* 'Silver Pink,' –4 ft. *Prop.*—Easily raised from seed.

Clarkia elegans.—A Californian, hardy annual of easy culture and mixed seeds will give a wide range of colours in white, pink, scarlet, and crimson. *See* **Annuals.**

Clematis.—A hardy climber for walls, screens, pergolas, and the like. Best kinds are to be found among named varieties in nurserymen's lists. A light, well-drained soil is necessary and if fed annually with a bucketful of manure or compost the plant will thrive for many years. Occasionally plants will be found on north walls, and if grown in full sun some light protection from the sun is desirable for the roots. Varieties which flower on the *current* season's growth, like *C. jackmanii*, should be pruned in late February to within a foot of the ground; other sorts should have sufficient old growth removed, after flowering, to keep them within bounds.

Unfortunately, the climber is sometimes killed by clematis wilt, a disease about which very little is known, and the premature death of young plants should not be blamed automatically on the supplier. *Prop.*—Layering, by which means one shoot will often give three or four plants.

Convallaria majalis (Lily of the Valley).—Well-known perennial that will thrive in any damp, shady position. For best results lift every four or five years and mulch annually with old manure. *Prop.*—Division when foliage fades.

Coreopsis.—The hardy annuals are found in catalogues under "Callipsis," and all will thrive in ordinary soil. The flowers are mainly bright yellow, and many are good for cutting. *See* **Annuals.** Similarly, the perennials have the same predominant colour and are useful because of their long flowering season and abundance of flower. *Prop.*—Division.

Cornflower.—*See* **Centaurea.**

Cosmos.—Tall-growing, half-hardy annuals that are best grown in full sun in a dryish border. The large, daisy-like flowers can be had in a variety of colours, including white, yellow, pink, and crimson. *See* **Annuals.**

Cotoneaster.—Hardy evergreen and deciduous shrubs or small trees bearing scarlet or sometimes yellow berries in the autumn. All may be grown in ordinary or poor soil and planted in open or shady shrubberies and trailing species used against walls, over banks, or as ground cover. For shrubberies *C. lacteus* and *C.* 'Cornubia' with red berries and *C. rothchildianus* with yellow berries are among the best sorts; *C. conspicuus* 'Decora' is a strong grower for banks, while *C. horizontalis* is an excellent cover for any wall. Planting may be done in the autumn or spring, and no pruning, apart from occasional shaping, is required. *Prop.*—Seeds and layering.

Crataegus (Hawthorn).—There are many good varieties of our British hawthorn, *C. oxyacantha*, worthy of attention, particularly 'Coccinea' (crimson) and 'Paulii' (double, red). All will do well on poor soils, and no pruning is required. The common hawthorn makes a stout, impenetrable hedge planted 9 in. apart in a double row 9 in. asunder. *Prop.*—Common sort by seed; choice varieties by budding.

Crocus.—A hardy bulb of great beauty which was studied for many years by one of the greatest horticulturists of the twentieth century, the late E. A. Bowles. Does best in rich soil planted in bold groups around margins of beds or borders and naturalised in grass. When required, feed in early spring with bone meal at 2 oz. per sq. yd. *C. sieberi* and *C. tomasinianus* very early flowering; large-flowered, garden forms about three weeks later. *C. zonatus* flowers in the autumn and is often naturalised in grass. *Prop.*—Clumps may be lifted and divided about every five years, in July. The so-called autumn crocus is *Colchicum autumnale.* This bears large, lustrous leaves in the summer, followed by mauve or white flowers—of fleeting duration—in the autumn.

Crown Imperial.—*See* **Fritillaria.**

Cyclamen.—*See* **House plants (T40).**

Cytisus (Broom).—Only does really well in dry, poor soils in full sun; choice, procumbent sorts, like *C. kewensis*, used in rock gardens and tall ones in open shrubberies. Pruning is important; shoots should be shortened after flowering, but old wood must never be cut. *Prop.*—Seed and cuttings in August in a sandy soil.

Daffodil.—*See* **Narcissus.**

Dahlia.—The cultivation of this plant is a special study, and there are probably more garden varieties of it than any other plant. Ordinary soil enriched with manure and an open position is required. Tubers may be planted 3 in. deep in April or young plants in late May. During the summer feed with soot water and liquid manure. After the first frosts lift, dry, and then store tubers in peat or straw in frost-proof place. Many stocks of dahlia are affected by virus (**T30**), and purchasers should be careful to check source of supply.

Daphne.—Shrubby plants, giving some of the most richly scented of all flowers. In particular, there is *D. mezereum*, which requires a damp soil; failure with the shrub is due usually to root disturbance or virus disease (**T30**) *D. odora* is one of the evergreen, fragrant species. Some references have suggested that this lovely shrub is not hardy, but there is no evidence to support the supposition. *Prop.*—Seed or layering.

Delphinium.—Hardy annuals and perennials. The latter sorts have gained popularity enormously since the War, due in the main to the activities of the Delphinium Society but also to the introduction of many very fine new varieties. American hybrids, like the 'Pacific Strain,' are very large but tend to die out and, consequently, lack the true, perennial habit of European sorts, albeit some of these have been weakened by the introduction of poor lines. It is important therefore to select stocks of strong constitution. Delphiniums need a deep, rich soil and a sunny position protected from wind. Plant in autumn 3 ft. apart, feed in the summer with liquid soot water, and mulch with decayed compost or manure in the spring. When growth starts, thin out weak growths to leave not more than five stems per plant. In winter take steps against possible slug damage (**T28**), and on this point it is beneficial to protect crowns with a covering of ashes. *Prop.*—Cuttings in the spring or seed; division of clumps is a poor alternative.

The hardy annual sorts are the well-known larkspurs, which grow to a height of 18 in. to 2 ft. and may be found in a range of colours including pink, red, white, and shades of blue. *See* **Annuals.**

Deutzia.—Hardy deciduous shrubs thriving in any soil and valuable for their summer flowers of white or whitish-pink shade. To keep the plants vigorous, shoots should be shortened after flowering and old or weak wood cut out. *D. scabra* is of robust habit, reaching about 7 ft., and *D. elegantissima* 'Fasciculata' proves a graceful shrub some 5 ft. tall with clusters of about twenty flowers coloured rosy-pink and each nearly an inch across. *Prop.*—Cuttings made from firm young growths about 10 in. long in sandy soil out-of-doors.

Dianthus.—This name covers a wide range of annual, biennial, and perennial plants. At one time often grown for their fragrance, but to a large extent this has been lost with the introduction of wider ranges of colour. Border carnations and picotees grown out-of-doors need a limy, fairly rich soil in full sun. Plant in the autumn or spring and, as the buds appear, feed with soot water or liquid animal manure, if necessary. These groups are *not* of good perennial habit and should be propagated annually to ensure continuation of stock.

The common pink requires the same soil conditions, and should be propagated when the stock gets weak; good scented varieties should be sought, and include the 'Imperial Pinks,' 'Mrs. Simkins,' and 'White Ladies.' *Prop.*—The best method is by layering in July so that the new plants can be put in their flowering position by mid-September. The lower leaves are pulled off selected shoots and a slit passing through a joint is made in the stem. Each layer is then pegged down with a hair-pin, the pin being placed above the cut. The layers are then covered with an inch of sandy compost and well watered.

In this genus is the sweet william; although truly a perennial, it is generally grown as a biennial and, consequently, the plant is raised from seed in May out-of-doors. In gardens where it is prone to rust disease control is most difficult and it is not worth a place.

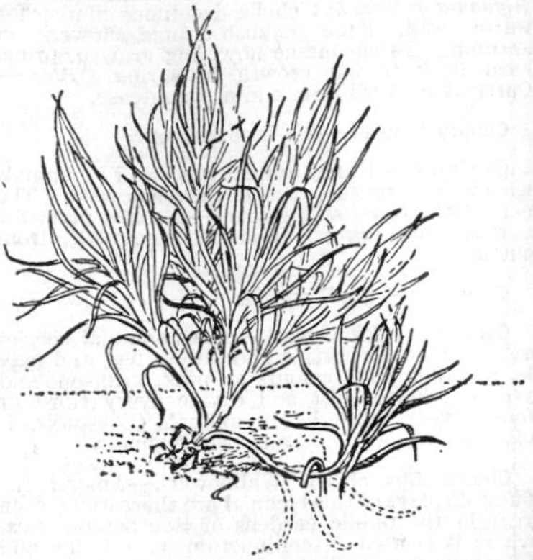

LAYERING CARNATIONS—This is a typical example of how many plants can be propagated. A strong, new growth is pegged down into sandy soil after a cut has been made in the stem, at the point of pegging. Once rooted the layer can be severed from the parent and transplanted a week or two later.

Digitalis.—The biennial sort generally found in gardens is the common foxglove, which is grown in light shade in fairly rich, moist soil. In the past many named forms have been offered in the trade, but undoubtedly the best one is *D.* 'Sutton's Excelsior.' *Prop.*—Seed sown in May out-of-doors.

Doronicum.—Hardy perennials with yellow flowers; warrants wider planting, as they are among the earliest perennials to bloom and will thrive in poor soil or in some shade. The best is *D. austriacum* flowering in March, height 9 in. *Prop.*—Division after flowering.

Echinops.—Name appropriately derived from *echinos*, a hedgehog, in reference to the spiny, long scales of the flowers. The plant does well in an open position, where the globular heads of steely-blue flowers can be seen to advantage. *Prop.*—Division in March, but best left undisturbed as long as possible, as it must be moved with care.

Elaeagnus.—Hardy deciduous and evergreen shrubs generally grown in rather dry positions as foliage plants. Of the evergreen sort, *E. pungens* 'Aureo-Variegata' has bright golden variegation, and is therefore valuable for indoor decoration during the winter. *Prop.*—Layering in late summer.

Erica.—The heathers are native plants to Britain, and many variants found in the wild have been introduced into gardens to good purpose. Indeed, heathers have become so popular that special Heather Gardens have been made, and two fine examples may be found in the Royal Gardens, Windsor, where the planting is new and the Royal Horticultural Society's Gardens, Wisley. Here different sorts reaching the dimensions of small trees, dwarf kinds, and many scores of interesting variants, to supply flower throughout the year will be found.

The Scottish heather is, botanically, *Calluna vulgaris*, and, like all British heathers, it is intolerant of lime or chalk. Where alkaline conditions exist, planters can try *E. carnea*—a winter-flowering heather—or *E. darleyensis*, but the results are usually disappointing. When planting all heathers, clumps must be well firmed and after wards kept moist; subsequently, mulch all types annually with peat. *Prop.*—Division and layering.

Erigeron.—Hardy perennial for sunny borders; daisy-like flowers freely develop and are good for cutting. *Prop.*—Division in the autumn.

Escallonia.—Slightly tender evergreen and deciduous shrubs. In the Midlands protection of a south wall is necessary; suitable for open shrubbery in the South. Ideal for maritime conditions, and here may be used to good effect as hedges. Many of the best varieties originated in the nursery of Messrs. The Slieve Donard Co. in County Down. *Prop.*—Cuttings under a glass jar in summer; layers in September.

Eschscholzia californica.—A hardy annual of easy culture; height 18 in., flowers mainly shades of orange. *See* **Annuals.**

Everlasting Flowers.—*See* **Helichrysum.**

Ferns.—A large number of plants are included under this name and, as they grow wild in many parts of the world, some need hothouse conditions. They are distinguished from flowering plants by their method of reproduction; instead of producing seeds, ferns develop spores, usually on the back of their leaves. The hardy kinds may be grown in equal parts of leaf-mould and soil, and the fronds of leaf-losing kinds should not be removed until the spring, as they offer some protection from the cold. Tender ferns should be repotted when new growth starts in the spring in a compost of equal parts soil, leaf-mould, and sand, using a pot just large enough for the purpose. During the growing season, in particular, keep the roots moist and plants free from a dry or smokey atmosphere. *Prop.*—Division of clumps when growth starts in the spring.

Forget-me-nots.—*See* **Myosotis.**

Forsythia.—Commonly found in many gardens, as it is of easy culture in any soil. Flowers bright yellow in early spring. To keep in good shape prune directly after flowering by cutting out old wood. *F. intermedia* 'Lynwood' is upright in growth and *F. suspensa* of weeping habit; both types make good wall plants for North aspects. *Prop.*—Cuttings in the autumn.

Foxglove.—*See* **Digitalis.**

Freesia.—Greenhouse bulbous plant and, if grown for scent, care must be taken to select fragrant varieties. Pot in the autumn in a fairly rich compost and keep as cold as possible until growth is seen. Then bring into a frost-free greenhouse and water freely. When flower stems appear, feed with liquid manure; after flowering, gradually dry-off until time for repotting. Failures almost invariably traced to premature forcing before root growth has been made or growing in excessively high temperature. *Prop.*—Offsets at potting time.

Fritillaria.—The one mainly used in gardens is *F. imperialis*, a handsome, spring-flowering bulb. To grow it *really* well, this species must be given a deep, rich soil and, contrary to some views, it is best lifted every year as soon as the foliage fades. If growth is poor or plants do not flower, feed when growth starts in the following spring with equal parts of bone meal and superphosphate at 3 oz. per sq. yd. *Prop.*—Offsets removed from parent bulb at lifting time. The old bulb should then be replanted at once and any offsets lined out in a nursery row.

Fuchsia.—Greenhouse and tender flowering shrubs. The outdoor sorts (of which *F. riccartonii* is the best) may be grown in light soil in full sun. In the spring prune all growth down to ground level; protect, if necessary, in winter with covering of cut bracken or dry straw. Greenhouse varieties are potted firmly before growth starts in the spring and, when buds burst, all the previous year's growth can be cut back hard. To encourage flowering, feed with a liquid manure, such as dried blood, and syringe foliage in hot weather. During the winter keep plants dry and house in a cool greenhouse. *Prop.*—Cuttings of new growth taken about 1 in. long and inserted in sand under a bell jar.

Gaillardia.—Hardy annuals and perennials 18 in. to 3 ft. high which bear large, richly coloured flowers invaluable for cutting in mid- and late-summer. Unfortunately, on heavy soil the perennials are liable to die after flowering, and even on well-drained soils they cannot be considered long-lived plants. *Prop.*—Normally it is necessary to raise a fresh stock in alternate years; seed is sown in May in a cold frame and the young plants lined out in a reserve border prior to planting in the autumn.

Galanthus (Snowdrop).—Hardy bulbs well worth growing if given a moist, shady position where stock can be left undisturbed. Planting should be done in fairly bold clumps; bulbs are not expensive, and many variants, like double-flowered and tall-stemmed ones, are well worth a trial. *Prop.*—Lift and divide clumps in August.

Gentiana.—The gentians comprise some of the most fascinating of all rock-garden plants partly, perhaps, because some are difficult to manage. In particular, *G. acaulis*—which has true "gentian blue" flowers—is exacting in its requirements, and in many gardens flowering can never be induced. What controls flowering has not been discovered, and the plant can be grown well in acid or limy soils. On the other hand, *G. sino-ornata* must have an acid soil and is best in a position out of the direct sun. Beginners with the genus are advised to start with easily grown sorts, like *G. lagodechina* and *G. septemfida*. *Prop.*—Seed sown in cold frame in March or division in early spring.

Geranium.—The true geranium or cranesbill is a hardy floriferous perennial for rock garden or open border. In the latter case *G. ibericum* (blue flowers) and *G. sanguineum* 'Lancastriense' (rosy-pink flowers) are exceptionally good, and both do well in dry, sunny positions. The so-called "bedding" or "greenhouse" geranium is a pelargonium (*q.v.*). *Prop.*—Seed in March.

Gladiolus.—Dutch hybridists have done much work on this bulbous plant, and many new and lovely varieties are now available. The plant is responsive to good cultivation, and corms may be planted 4 in. deep and 6 in. apart during the spring in well-prepared ground. When the blooms fade remove the dead spikes of flower and lift the corms in September. After a month—and this point is important—pull off the old shrivelled corm and clean the new one. By doing this there is less likelihood of spores of diseases overwintering on the new stock. Finally, the corms should be stored in a dry, frost-free shed, and if given proper attention can be kept for a number of years. *Prop.*—Bulbils, removed when the corms are cleaned, can be sown in the spring in nursery rows and will flower within two years.

Godetia.—Hardy annual of easy culture and tolerant of poor soil conditions and even some shade. There are many varieties, mainly with bright flowers of rosy-pink and crimson. *See* **Annuals.**

Guernsey Lily.—*See* **Nerine.**

Gypsophila.—The favourite sort is *G. paniculata*, which is often grown for cutting, together with its double-flowered form, 'Bristol Fairy.' To do well gypsophila must be given a dryish soil which the roots can penetrate undisturbed; if growth is poor mulch in the spring with animal manure. *Prop.*—Generally done by seed in spring; special forms by grafting.

Hamamelis.—A lovely, but little grown, winter-flowering, heavily-scented shrub. The delicate, lemon-coloured flowers appear interminably from December to February. Although it flowers in its young stage, hamamelis is slow to get established and must be left free of root disturbance. The best sort is *H. mollis* introduced from China in 1879. *Prop.*—Usually by grafting; can be layered.

Heather.—*See* Erica.

Hedera.—Although ivy is seldom planted nowadays, there are a few evergreens to equal it for covering buildings. The large-leaved ivy with golden variegation, *H. colchica* 'Dentato-Variegata,' is invaluable for cold or shady walls. *Prop.*—Cuttings in August in shady border out-of-doors.

Helianthus.—The perennial sunflowers are tall, yellow-flowered plants of vigorous habit. They spread quickly and become a nuisance, and therefore clumps should be lifted and single, rooted pieces replanted every other year. The annual sunflower may reach a height of 10 ft. or so; seed is sown out-of-doors in April or seedlings raised under glass in the spring. When the flower bud appears, feed with soot water. The seed may be used as food for large birds like parrots.

Helichrysum.—Although this is a large group of plants, the most interesting is the half-hardy annual, *H. bracteatum*, the everlasting flower. When the flowers are fully developed they are cut with long stems and hung up to dry for winter decoration. *See* **Annuals.**

Heliotropium peruvianum (**Cherry Pie**).—Scented, shrubby plants used for greenhouse decoration or summer bedding. *H.* 'Sir Edward Fry' is among the scented varieties and *H.* 'Princess Marina' is the best dark-purple variety. For really good results, heliotropes need a rich soil and plenty of water in summer. *Prop.*—Cuttings 2–3 in. long in early autumn or spring, struck in sandy loam in a warm greenhouse.

Helleborus.—The Christmas rose, *H. niger*, should be planted out of the direct sun in a moist soil which has been liberally enriched with leaf-mould and old manure and here left free from root disturbance. Its large, white flowers appear irregularly from December to February with early flowering encouraged by protection with cloches. The Lenten rose, *H. orientalis*, flowers from February to April, and it is well worth searching nurserymens' lists for varieties with a wide range of colours. *Prop.*—Division of clumps in the spring, with each piece having four or five growth buds; the clumps should not be split into small pieces.

Hemerocallis.—Hardy perennial for moist border either open or slightly shaded. Mulch established clumps in the spring with compost or manure. Many new varieties are coming on the market as a result of introductions from America, where the plant is popular. *Prop.*—Division.

Hibiscus.—The evergreen, shrubby sorts with large exotic flowers are widely grown in the tropics and can be seen under glass in botanic gardens in Britain. *H. syriacus* is a deciduous, hardy species; little pruning is required, and in full sun it will reach 8–10 ft. Normally, it is a free-flowering plant of great beauty and, in cases where the flowers fail to develop, the stock is best replaced with good varieties, like 'Coeleste' (single, blue) and 'Woodbridge' (single, red). *Prop.*—Cuttings under glass; grafting.

Holly.—*See* **Ilex.**

Hollyhock.—*See* **Althaea.**

Honeysuckle.—*See* **Lonicera.**

House Leek.—*See* **Sempervivum.**

Hyacinth.—Bulbs generally used for bowl culture; often results are disappointing, but responsibility does not necessarily rest with the nurseryman, as poor cultivation is the most probable cause. Plant in September–early October (not later) in peat, loam, and sand, and keep as cool as possible until growth starts, when bowls may be brought into a warm room. Care must be taken with watering, as the bulbs must not dry out nor the compost allowed to become wet and soggy. After flowering, plant out-of-doors and lift annually in June for replanting in the autumn; for bowls a fresh stock is required every year. Failures are mostly due to late planting or faulty watering.

Hydrangea.—A favourite shrub introduced from the Far East. Of the many forms, the one offered by florists, *H. macrophylla*, is the most popular. This can be bought in a wide range of shades, from white and pink through to crimson and blue. The colour will depend on soil reaction; in alkaline or neutral soils *only* white and pink shades can be grown, and blue flowers will be found *only* on acid soil. The intensity of colour can be improved by adding lime in the first instance and flowers of sulphur in the second, but it is not possible to make an alkaline garden soil acid in reaction. Lack of flower is generally the result of buds being killed by cold weather. For this reason, hydrangeas are best not pruned until the late spring; then old flower-heads and any weak or unwanted growth can be cut out. During the summer the plants must not suffer from lack of water.

Among the many other sorts are *H. paniculata*, with large, cone-shaped panicles of flower and *H. petiolaris*. The latter plant is a vigorous climber, well suited to cover cold walls or for climbing over dead trees. *Prop.*—Cuttings in July–August in a cold frame.

Iberis (**Candytuft**).—The hardy annual sorts will thrive in any soil, and may be had in a range of colours. *See* **Annuals.** The perennial candytuft (*I. sempervirens*) is a good plant for a rock wall and has white flowers in early spring. *Prop.*—Seeds in spring and cuttings in summer.

Ilex.—The ornamental value of our native holly is rarely fully appreciated, bearing in mind that, on good varieties, the berries sometimes persist until March. The greenish flowers are sometimes bisexual, and sometimes male and female flowers are on *separate* plants. For this reason hollies should be planted in groups, and at least one plant of good berrying habit, like *I. aquifolium* 'Pyramidalis,' grown. Some varieties have yellow berries and gold or silver variegations on their leaves. *Prop.*—Seed; special forms by budding.

Iris.—This plant is divided into two main sections: those types which grow from bulbs and those which grow from fleshy rhizomes, with many subdivisions in each of them. Of the latter type, there are the commonly grown bearded flag irises, which, owing to their ease of cultivation and wide range of colours, are appropriately known as the poor man's orchid. Notwithstanding, these irises respond to good treatment, doing best in well-dug soil to which a little manure has been added and a dressing of rough chalk forked into the surface. The site should be in full sun for preference and one that never lies wet in winter. Planting or division of established clumps is done in July, setting the rhizome on the surface of the soil but firming the roots well. To maintain growth and flower, feed annually in the spring with equal parts of superphosphate and bone meal at 3–4 oz. per sq. yd. Iris gardens are not often seen nowadays, but the fine example still maintained at Kew is well worth close inspection.

In the bulbous section the Siberian iris is a graceful plant with delicate foliage, though much smaller-flowered than the flags. They make a fine waterside planting or may be grown in the herbaceous border. The Japanese iris is another water lover, and this has delicate-coloured, clematis-like flowers. On the other hand, for dry, poor, stony soils in full sun the lovely, winter-flowering, Algerian iris, *I. unguicularis* (*stylosa*), is an ideal plant, flowering as it does in December and January. This is a plant which must be left undisturbed after planting in June and if leafy growth is excessive the foliage can be cut back by half in August. Spanish, Dutch, and English types of bulbous iris are often used as cut flowers. These may be planted in ordinary garden soil in the autumn and left undisturbed until signs of deterioration are found.

Japonica.—Common misnomer of *Chaenomeles.* (*q.v.*).

Jasminum.—The yellow-flowered, sweetly scented winter jasmine blooms intermittently from November to February. It grows in any soil, and is best trained up a wall or grown on a trellis. Pruning consists of cutting out the flowering shoots as soon as the blossoms fade. The summer jasmine is a vigorous climbing plant with white, scented flowers. It needs a sunny position and should be well thinned after flowering. *Prop.*—Layering in summer.

Kalmia.—Hardy American shrubs with clusters of waxy, rose or pink blossoms in early summer. Although slow to get established and requiring a damp, acid soil, the plant is well worth growing. It constitutes a feature of the gardens of the National Trust at Sheffield Park, Sussex. *Prop.*—Seed or layering.

Kerria japonica.—A hardy shrub which will thrive in any garden but is best fed with manure to encourage strong growth. When the yellow flowers fade, the stock should be kept vigorous by cutting out old or weak growth. The plant is named after William Kerr, a young man despatched from Kew to collect plants in China. *Prop.*—Division in autumn.

Kniphofia (Red-hot Poker).—Although these plants are so commonly seen, their full value as late-flowering subjects is not often fully explored. There are a number of good varieties worth growing, such as 'Maid of Orleans' (white, 4 ft.), 'Mount Etna' (scarlet, 5 ft.), and 'Royal Standard' (gold and scarlet, 4 ft.). Of equal value is the dwarf variety with grass-like foliage, *K. nelsonii*. *Prop.*—Division in March; easily raised from seed if so desired.

Laburnum.—Handsome trees with long racemes of yellow flowers the seeds of which are very poisonous. It is not advisable to remove branches, as wounds do not heal well or quickly, and once a specimen shows signs of deterioration it is best replaced with little delay. *Prop.*—Seed or grafting.

Larkspur.—*See* **Delphinium.**

Lathyrus (Sweet Pea).—For general garden decoration, seed may be sown in pots in a warm greenhouse in early February prior to transplanting out-of-doors in April. When heat is not available sowing can be done in the open in October, setting the seed 4–6 in. apart and 2 in. deep where the plants are to grow. In this case the rows are best protected by cloches. As the plants flower with great freedom and make strong growth, a rich, deep soil is required. During the summer water should be given freely and liquid animal manure or soot water applied weekly when flowering starts. When raised for exhibition, special cultural treatment is necessary. The cause of the condition referred to as bud drop is not known, but it is thought to be connected with low temperature and faulty root action.

There is also the hardy, perennial sweet pea, an old-world plant usually seen at its best in cottage gardens. This plant requires the same cultural conditions, except that the old stems are cut down in the autumn. Three or four different species are available, and all are easily raised from seed sown in the spring.

Lavandula.—The lavender is one of the best known of garden plants. It thrives in full sun in a light soil; old flower heads should be clipped off in the summer, but any cutting back into old growth must be left until the spring. The best garden form is *L. spica* 'Nana Atropurpurea'; it has a neat, dwarf habit, with deep purple flowers, and is available from leading nurserymen. *Prop.*—Cuttings out-of-doors in August–September.

Leucojum.—The spring snowflake flowers in February and is a charming plant for any damp, shady border. Although it has a large flower, it has never become as popular as the snowdrop, despite its ease of culture. It should be grown by everyone who values early spring flowers. *Prop.*—Lift clumps and replant after removing offsets in August.

Lilac.—*See* **Syringa.**

Lilium.—The lilies constitute a large genus of plants, some of easy culture, some demanding the most exacting of conditions. For a soil containing chalk two of the best lilies are *L. candidum*, the Madonna lily, and *L. regale*. The former is a feature of many gardens in South Wales, where bulbs are planted near the surface of the soil and the clumps eventually left to develop undisturbed. Only the easiest-grown lilies are suitable for the herbaceous border and, here, apart from the Madonna lily, the tiger and martagon lilies should be first choices for beginners in the cultivation of this genus. *Prop.*—Those referred to above may all be raised from seed sown out-of-doors (or in deep boxes in a cold frame) in the spring. In the following April line out into nursery rows prior to transplanting to flowering positions. Also propagated by offsets and bulbils.

Lily of the Valley.—*See* **Convallaria.**

Lobelia.—The bedding lobelias are perennial plants best raised as annuals (*q.v.*). They do well in a light soil, but should be firmed at planting time to prevent plants dying off during a hot spell. The handsome, tall-growing lobelias with scarlet flowers, like *L. fulgens* 'Huntsman,' may be used in herbaceous borders with great effect, but the roots must be lifted and overwintered in a cold frame. These sorts grow to a height of 2–3 ft. and will do well only on a wet, heavily manured soil.

Lonicera.—The honeysuckles make effective climbing plants if grown on the shady side of arches or tree stumps or against north or west walls. Care should be taken to train young growth before it becomes hard. Old shoots may be cut out each spring to keep the plant within bounds, although space must be available for free development. If growth and flowering is poor mulch the roots in the spring with old manure. *Prop.*—Easily done by layering in late summer.

Lupins.—There are two sorts of lupins, perennial and annual. The herbaceous perennials are among the most colourful of plants as a result of the famous 'Russell' strain being introduced. Of late years, however, the constitution of the plant has been weakened through, perhaps, breeding and virus diseases, and it should be taken for granted that most stocks have to be replaced every two years or even annually in some cases. The plant requires a rich soil and is best in ground free of lime. Conversely, in poor soil the tree lupin thrives and will reach a height of 7–9 ft.; plant in full sun and lightly prune into shape after flowering. *Prop.*—Both sorts are best raised from seed sown in May out-of-doors and transferred to flowering positions in October. The annual lupin may be obtained in a range of colours, and should be grown in full sun. *See* **Annuals.**

Magnolia.—Rightly said to be one of the most beautiful of all flowering plants. Contrary to popular belief, some kinds are of easy culture, flowering when young and suitable for small gardens. Of course, careful selection is necessary and for a specimen on a lawn *M.* 'Soulangeana' (large, white or white, purple-stained flowers) is ideal. *M. stellata* freely flowers in the young stage, and may be planted in an ordinary border if the soil is lime free. To encourage growth, mulch annually with peat or leaf mould, but never dig near the roots. The evergreen magnolia is often seen as a fine wall plant in old gardens. This is the only species which may be pruned, and long shoots can be cut back hard in April. There are a number of non-flowering strains of the evergreen one, and unsatisfactory plants are best destroyed, as flowering cannot be induced; in buying a replacement care is necessary in order to avoid *another* dud. *Prop.*—Seed sown as soon as it is ripe in October; layering.

Mahonia.—Hardy evergreen shrub. *M. aquifolium* is useful as ground cover, and will thrive in any soil and in any cold, shady position providing the soil is not waterlogged. *M. japonica* has long racemes of lemon-scented flowers in the winter; inferior sorts are often offered by nurserymen under this name. *Prop.*—Seed, suckers, and layers.

Marigold.—*See* **Calandula.**

Mathiola.—The night-scented stock is a hardy annual with insignificant purplish flowers which open at dusk; grown primarily for its perfume. Conversely, the so-called Ten-Week stocks and a selection of these, the East Lothian stocks, have a wide range of colours. If sown in March they may be used for summer bedding or if sown in August overwintered in a sunny frame and grown as a biennial.

Brompton stocks flower earlier than the other sorts, and are grown as a biennial by sowing seed in June or early July and, after pricking out into boxes, are overwintered in a sunny frame. In mild districts, if the soil is well drained, stocks may be planted out-of-doors in the autumn, but a reserve should be kept for filling up gaps in the spring.

Meconopsis.—This genus includes the famous "blue poppy," introduced from the Himalayas. It is not a plant of easy culture, albeit large groups are grown in many woodland gardens where soil conditions permit. After flowering the plants generally die, although an occasional plant may persist. *Prop.*—Seed sown in March.

Michaelmas Daisy.—*See* **Aster.**

Montbretia.—This bulbous plant is of easy culture and has a long season of flowering. Many new varieties with large flowers are now available, and growth can be kept vigorous by lifting and dividing the clumps every three or four years. Plant in early spring 4 in. deep and 6 in. apart and in cold gardens protect clumps in winter with a covering of ashes.

Myosotis.—The forget-me-not is grown as a biennial by sowing seed in May and planting out in the autumn in conjunction with spring-flowering bulbs and wallflowers. Poor varieties freely establish themselves, and these should be destroyed before planting any of the really good sorts offered by seedsmen.

Narcissus.—This botanical name includes plants commonly known as "daffodil" and "narcissus." Although often grown, the wide garden value of these spring-flowering bulbs is not fully realised, as by careful selection of varieties a long season of flower can be obtained when they are grown in formal borders or naturalised. Thus, a season may be extended with 'Peeping Tom' and 'Covent Garden' (early) and 'Geranium' and 'Buttermilk' (late). The bulbs can be left undisturbed until flowering is affected by over-crowding; the clumps should then be lifted and be divided in the late summer. To maintain vigour, feed annually in February with 2 parts bone meal, 1 part hoof and horn meal, and 1 part sulphate of potash at 2 oz. per sq. yd. The chief troubles with narcissi are due to eelworm (**T29**) and the narcissus bulb fly (**T28**). For indoor work, plant in bowls in October and keep in cold place until growth is an inch high; failure is invariably due to premature forcing or faulty watering.

Nasturtium.—*See* **Tropaeolum.**

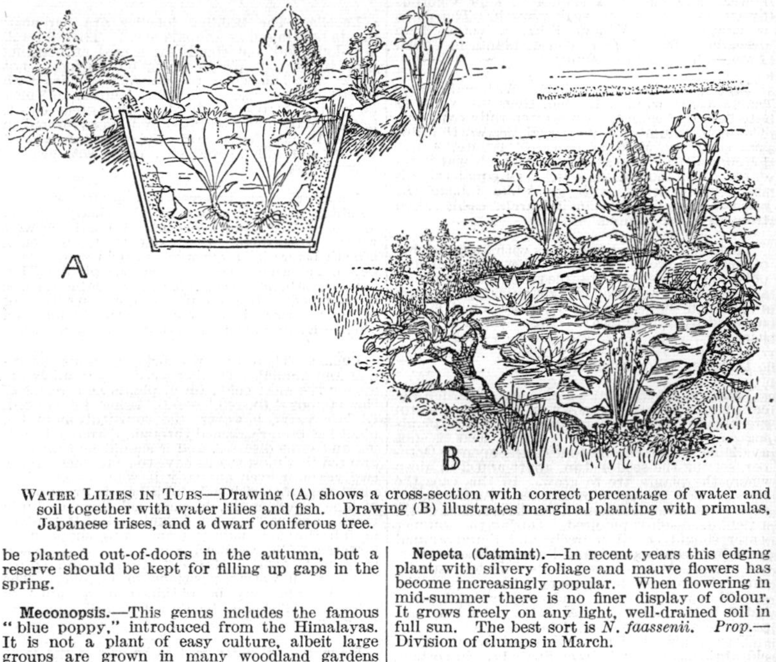

WATER LILIES IN TUBS—Drawing (A) shows a cross-section with correct percentage of water and soil together with water lilies and fish. Drawing (B) illustrates marginal planting with primulas, Japanese irises, and a dwarf coniferous tree.

Nepeta (Catmint).—In recent years this edging plant with silvery foliage and mauve flowers has become increasingly popular. When flowering in mid-summer there is no finer display of colour. It grows freely on any light, well-drained soil in full sun. The best sort is *N. faassenii*. *Prop.*—Division of clumps in March.

Nerine.—Lately this lovely bulbous plant has increased in popularity mainly through the varieties introduced from the late Lionel de Rothschild's garden at Exbury. The hardy sort *N. bowdenii* flowers in the autumn and should be planted at the foot of a warm wall in August or September and left undisturbed for many years. As the bulbs gradually multiply and work to the surface, a light dressing of sandy compost, to which has been added a little bone meal, can be applied. *Prop.*—Separation of bulbs in August.

Nicotiana (Tobacco Plant).—This half-hardy annual is grown mainly for its heavily scented flowers, which open in the evening. It is worth remembering that the white-flowered sorts are the best in this respect; scarlets and pinks are very much inferior. *See* **Annuals.** The tobacco of commerce is a different plant, namely, *N. tabacum.*

Nymphaea.—No branch of gardening is more fascinating than the water garden, and for it the chief plant must be the water lily. Basically, the main reason for failure is in the fact that in most pools the *average* depth of water is less than 18 in.; this means that the water is liable to be adversely affected by extremes of temperature. All nymphaeas should be grown in full sun and where the water is still; in streams it is necessary to utilise a little backwater out of the current. Water lilies are planted in May in large wicker baskets with a compost of three-quarters of loam and a quarter of peat; alternatively, planting sites can be built up with bricks to the desired height. If growth is poor, mould Clay's Fertiliser into the size of pigeons' eggs and drop one around each clump. To maintain a healthy condition in the water, fish should be introduced as soon as the plants are established. *Prop.*—Division of tuberous roots in late May.

Orchids.—In the main, this large group of plants needs greenhouse conditions and specialised knowledge. Their cultivation has attracted the attention of some of the greatest of horticulturists, and detailed references may be found in books like *Orchids, their Description and Cultivation*, by C. H. Curtis (Putnam), 1950.

Paeonia.—There are two sorts of paeony, the tree paeony and the herbaceous paeony. The former needs a sheltered, warm position and takes about three years to flower from planting time. The latter sort needs a moist, rich soil, and should be mulched annually in the spring with well-rotted manure; some are known not to flower, and as such plants cannot be induced to do so they should be destroyed. The old-fashioned variety of paeony has been superseded by many fine new varieties found listed by specialists. *Prop.*—Tree paeonies by layering or seed sown in the autumn; herbaceous sorts by seed or division.

Pansy.—*See* **Viola.**

Papaver (Poppy).—The oriental poppy is a hardy herbaceous perennial with striking flowers, intolerant of shade and root disturbance. As it blooms early, it should be set near the back of a border, as the large leaves look untidy later in the year. Apart from the commonly grown, red-flowered sort there are others in shades of crimson, pink, and lavender. *Prop.*—A wide range of colours can be obtained by sowing mixed seeds in May. This is a better method than division. The Shirley poppy is a hardy annual (*q.v.*), while *P. nudicale* is a biennial needing a warm, sheltered position.

Parthenocissus (Virginia Creeper).—This climber, with its brilliantly-coloured leaves, makes a fine sight in the autumn, and there is no better plant for covering brickwork or unsightly buildings with a south or west aspect. It has been suggested (mainly by builders) that the plant will damage stonework or cause dampness. There is little evidence to support these suppositions, and reasons for damage can usually be traced—often without difficulty—to other sources. The plant has had a number of names—*Ampelopsis veitchii* is one—but up-to-date nurserymen are listing it correctly as *P. tricuspidata*. *Prop.*—Cuttings out-of-doors in the late summer; layering.

Passiflora caerulea (Passion Flower).—A south wall in favoured gardens is needed to grow this plant. It is of vigorous habit and, once the framework of branches has been produced, it should be pruned annually in the early spring, by cutting back all the previous season's growth to 2–3 in. of the main stem. *Prop.*—Layering.

Pelargonium (Geranium).—So-called "bedding geraniums," such as 'Paul Crampel,' are really zonal pelargoniums. To maintain a stock, take cuttings in early August and insert in sandy soil around the edge of a pot and overwinter in a frost-free greenhouse. In the spring pot-up singly and use for bedding. Otherwise pot-on after two months and, if early buds are nipped off, plants can be adopted for late flowering indoors. Pelargoniums are easy to grow, but for best results a position in full sun is necessary, and cuttings should be rooted *before* the autumn so that overwintering constitutes no great difficulty.

Petunia.—Although really perennials, these plants, native of South America, are treated as annuals (*q.v.*). They are sun lovers and do best on light soils. Petunias make fine plants for sunny window boxes, and particularly happy combinations can be made by planting together varieties such as 'Violacea' (deep violet) and 'Cheerful' (pale pink) or 'Flaming Velvet' (crimson) and 'Cream Star' (pale cream). The violet-flowered sorts are faintly scented.

Philadelphus (Mock Orange).—Although some fine varieties of this shrub are available in the trade, it is not grown as widely as its merit deserves. As a scented shrub it has few equals, while it is tolerant of poor soil conditions and shade. Particularly good sorts worth searching for are 'Albatre' (double), 'Beauclerk' (single), and 'Sybille,' which, at 3 ft., is about half the height of the others. After flowering, prune annually by removing as much old flowering wood as possible. *Prop.*—Hard-wood cuttings out-of-doors in November.

Phlox.—A wide range of varieties of the border phlox are offered to make an impressive display late in the season. If grown on light soils some shade is desirable, as phloxes do well where only the soil is damp. For this reason, mulching should be done annually in the spring with compost or animal manure. Failures are usually due to eelworm (**T29**). *Prop.*—Seeds in autumn; division.

Poppy.—*See* **Papaver.**

Polyanthus.—*See* **Primula.**

Polygonium.—In the main these plants are weeds of gardens, although originally they were introduced from the Orient for ornamental purposes at a time when their invasive habits were not fully appreciated. The one woody climber in the genus, *P. baldschuanicum*, makes an admirable cover where a very vigorous plant is wanted. Rampant and unwanted species may be eradicated by hormone treatment (**T33**).

Primula.—Polyanthuses, primroses, greenhouse primulas, and the hardy primulas all belong in this genus. The first two are the most popular; both will do well only in damp soil and respond to generous manurial treatment; both are available in a wide range of colours. *Prop.*—The Blackmore and Langdon strains of seed will give a magnificent display of mixed colours. Sow in warm greenhouse in early March or cold frame in April; prick out into boxes and transfer to flowering positions in the autumn.

Prunus.—A large genus which includes the flowering peaches, Japanese cherries, and flowering almonds. All of them are best left to develop naturally and are not responsive to pruning or cutting back in any way. A few sorts are overplanted in gardens and as street trees (by Park Superintendents), but anybody wishing to be a little out of the ordinary would do well to see the wide range of some of these lovely trees flowering in April and May in our botanic gardens and many of the large gardens now under the jurisdiction of the National Trust. The selection offered by nurserymen is often strictly along conventional lines. Lack of flower in some seasons can often be traced to bird damage.

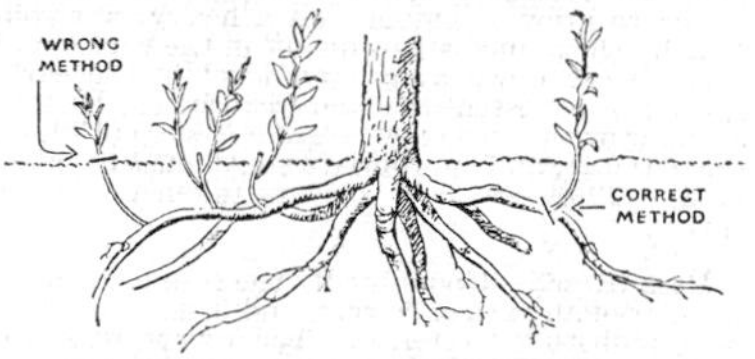

REMOVAL OF SUCKERS—As illustrated, these must be sawn off into the root or pulled off the root with a sharp tug and never so removed that dormant buds are left.

Red-hot Poker.—*See* **Kniphofia.**

Rhododendron.—Greenhouse and hardy, evergreen and deciduous shrubs, including *Azalea.* With something like ten thousand different sorts, it is impossible to deal with individual requirements. General cultivation: an acidic soil is essential, with adequate moisture in summer. If growth is poor on established plants, mulch liberally with animal manure. Beginners should plant from the accepted list of hardy garden hybrids. Since the turn of the century widely planted and fine examples are to be found, for instance, in many gardens of the National Trust. *Prop.*—Seed and layering.

Romneya.—Since its introduction from California in about 1850 the plant has proved a fascination to gardeners, as sometimes it fails completely or does exceedingly well. It apears to require a light soil and a sheltered position, preferably against a sunny wall, and there is no point in trying to grow a romneya on a heavy, wet soil. Usually the annual stems die off in the winter and may be cut down at ground level in the early spring; if persistent the stems can be cut back to sound growth. The new growth is susceptible to slug damage, and appropriate steps must be taken (T28). *Prop.*—Seed or suckers taken off in the spring.

Rosa (Rose).—Undoubtedly the rose is the most popular of all garden flowers, and it may be found in a multitude of forms. The dwarf roses for bedding may be grown on most soils, but are best on a rich, heavy loam. Planting is done from early November onwards when soil conditions permit and the first pruning carried out in the following spring, when the extent of any winter damage can be seen. Opinions differ sharply on pruning; a sound, general rule is to do the work in March and—unless there are special circumstances—to prune on the light side. Thus, for Hybrid Teas and the like, reduce strong stems by about one-third of their length, medium ones by a half, and weak ones to within two or three buds of the main stem.

Whatever sorts of soil roses are grown in, feeding is important, but, of course, it is particularly so on poor ones. It is in soils of *low* fertility that diseases such as rust and black spot are most prevalent and, in some measure, persistence of the disease is due to bad cultivation and lack of treatment with fertilisers. Where black spot is established, spray with "Captan." For a manurial programme, an application of 2 parts of superphosphate and 1 part of sulphate of potash can be applied at 3 oz. per sq. yd. after pruning. Following this, a surface mulch of animal manure, compost, peat, or leaf-mould or a mixture of all of them is given about 2–3 in. thick. Subsequently, if growth is poor, a dressing of nitro-chalk can be made at 1 oz. per sq. yd. Some other manurial treatments, like the so-called "Foliar Feeding" and use of "special" (and often expensive) compounds, have little to commend them

Where soil conditions are poor and disease prevalent, it is important to buy plants only from nurserymen who take special precautions to ensure that their customers have disease-free stock. Likewise, varieties of robust constitution are essential, and a selection list may include: *Hybrid Teas:* 'Christopher Stone' (crimson), 'Dame Edith Helen' (pink), 'Eden Rose' (magenta pink), 'Granmere Jenny' (yellow, rose-pink flush), 'Madam Henri Guillot' (salmon pink), 'Quebec' (yellow), and 'Tzigane' (bicolor; vermilion and yellow). *Floribundas:* 'Dainty Maid' (rose pink), 'Dusky Maiden' (dark red), 'Tantau's Surprise' (deep crimson), and 'Yellow Holstein' (yellow).

In most of the modern hybrids scent is almost absent. The true rose perfume is found only in the Old Fashion or shrub roses and, normally, these are planted in a mixed shrub border. For the richest perfume varieties like 'Mrs. John Laing' and 'Conrad F. Meyer' should be sought. *Prop.*—Nurserymen's plants are budded; many varieties are easily raised from cuttings taken in the autumn and struck in sandy soil out-of-doors.

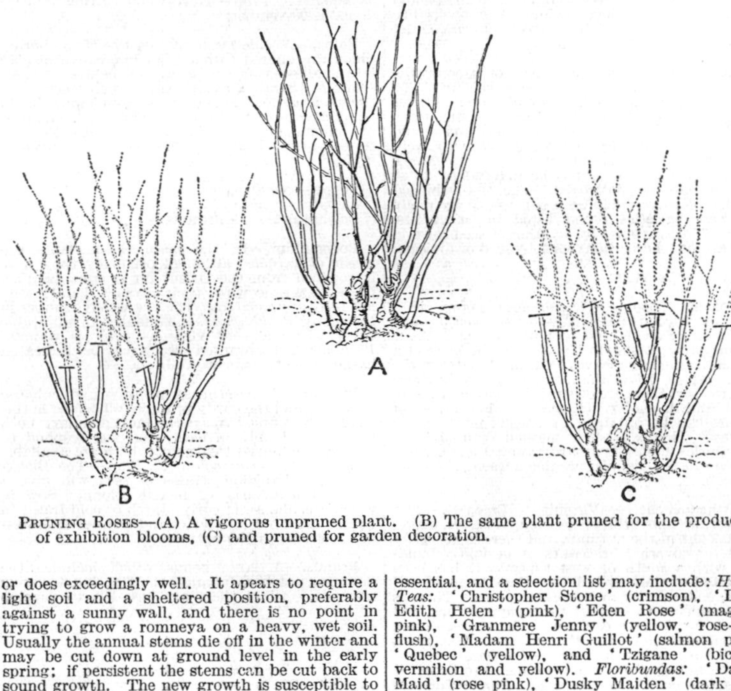

PRUNING ROSES—(A) A vigorous unpruned plant. (B) The same plant pruned for the production of exhibition blooms, (C) and pruned for garden decoration.

Salvia.—Annuals, perennials, and tender shrubs. The most popular one is the scarlet sort used for bedding. It requires careful attention, and seed should be sown in February in a temperature of 60° Fahrenheit and seedlings put into single pots when large enough. Gradually the young plants are hardened off and finally planted out in rich soil in a sunny bed.

Saxifraga.—A large genus of plants suitable for the rock garden and valued for their bright flowers in the spring. The encrusted saxifrages are cushion-forming plants requiring sharp, surface drainage and an open position out of the direct sun. The mossy saxifrages are mat-forming in growth and of easy culture. In time old clumps develop brown patches and then require splitting up and replanting in the spring.

Scabiosa.—The commonly grown perennial sort is *S. caucasica* and is invaluable as a cut flower. It is not at home on all soils, and only does really well in a deep, rich loam containing plenty of chalk. In addition, it must be grown in full sun and particular care taken against slugs. *Prop.*—Old plants divided in the spring and rooted pieces replanted in their flowering positions. A wide range of shades in white, blue, and purple can be had normally from sowing mixed seed in April.

Sedum.—The stonecrops make up a large group of hardy and tender plants, but comparatively few are of horticultural value. Notwithstanding, *Sedum spectabile* is to be found in most herbaceous borders, where its fine, flat heads of pink flowers are a feature for many weeks. It is beloved by bees and butterflies. *S. sieboldii* was introduced from Japan about 100 years ago and, although hardy, it is usually grown as a house plant. In the winter it can be stood out-of-doors, and every two or three years repotted in the spring; keep well watered during the summer and feed with liquid manure occasionally. *Prop.*—Division in the spring.

Sempervivum (House leek).—These hardy plants with succulent leaves often decorate the crevices of old walls and are regular features of trough or sink gardens. If given a light, poor soil and a position in full sun a fascinating collection of house leeks can be built up. The species which gives the plant its common name can be established easily on a sunny roof by planting in a mixture of cow manure and clay during the spring. *Prop.*—Division in the spring.

Skimmia.—A hardy evergreen 2–3 ft. tall which is tolerant of shade and some degree of dryness. If growth is poor water with a liquid manure and mulch with peat or leaf mould. Some forms bear only male flowers and to ensure a good crop of berries plant an hermaphrodite like *S. foremanii*. *Prop.*—Layering in the autumn.

Snowdrop.—*See* **Galanthus.**

Snowflake.—*See* **Leucojum.**

Solanum capsicastrum (Winter Cherry).—A berrying plant with bright-red fruits which is often used for house decoration. To maintain the plant in a healthy condition it should be clear of draughts and fumes of gas fires and the foliage kept fresh and free of dust by vigorous syringing. If the stock is to be kept for more than one season water should be given only sparingly in the New Year, and in early March all the side shoots pruned back hard to within a bud or two of the main stems. As new growth develops, water can be given more freely and syringing started when the flowers first appear; liquid manure will prove beneficial when berries develop.

Spiraea.—Hardy deciduous shrubs for open borders; tolerant of poor soil conditions. The commonly grown one is *Spiraea bumalda* (syn. *japonica*). After flowering, a percentage of the old wood should be removed together with any weak growth, and development of new shoots encouraged by mulching with compost or animal manure. *Prop.*—Cuttings rooted in sandy soil under a hand light in summer; suckers thinned out in winter.

Stocks.—*See* **Mathiola.**

Sunflower.—*See* **Helianthus.**

Sweet William.—*See* **Dianthus.**

Symphoricarpos (Snowberry).—Often found existing in deep shade and in competition with roots of overhanging trees, presumably as a result of the generalisation that the shrub is a shade lover. Certainly a useful one in this respect, but it is responsive to good treatment. Given an average soil and if growth is thinned annually in the early spring, then *S. albus* 'Laevigatus' is well worth having. Its large white fruits are untouched by birds and hang well into the winter, and are thus beloved by the floral decorator. *Prop.*—Suckers removed in the winter.

Syringa (Lilac).—The botanical name of *Syringa* is often erroneously applied to the Mock Orange, correctly named *Philadelphus* (*q.v.*). A wide selection of first-class varieties are available in nurserymen's lists. To obtain heavy crops of flowers nip off all dead flower-heads as the blossom fades, but do *not* cut back into the old stem, as this will prevent flowering. At the same time any branches causing overcrowding can be removed. Annually feed with "National Growmore" at 2 oz. per sq. yd. and on poor soils mulch with any sort of manure or compost. *Prop.*—Layering in the autumn.

Tagetes (African and French Marigolds).—Half-hardy annuals of free-flowering habit and easiest culture. Best if fed generously with soot water or other nitrogenous manure during growing season. *See* **Annuals.**

Tropaeolum.—The common nasturtium and the flame flower (*T. speciosum*) belong to this genus. The former is easily grown from seed sown in May in a sunny position. The latter is a very difficult plant to grow outside the conditions which it demands. To be successful, this perennial climber must be planted in acid soil which is naturally damp and lightly shaded but yet where the new growth can reach full sun. Much disappointment often results from planting it in eastern England, for instance, after seeing it flourishing almost as a weed where the rainfall is high in Ireland and the west of Scotland.

In the genus will also be found the canary creeper, which can be used for screening purposes and will thrive in full sun or shade. Seed is sown in May in open ground and light supports supplied by way of pea sticks or strings; failure is normally due to nothing more than lack of moisture.

Tulipa (Tulip).—Thrives in a deep, rich loam, but will do well for one season in ordinary garden soil. When used for bedding, bulbs must be lifted after flowering, replanted in a trench, and thoroughly watered. Sometimes tulips may be left in the ground *if* conditions are favourable, and then the stock only needs lifting and replanting every three years. To check the incidence of tulip fire plant in late November or early December, covering the bulbs with 4–5 in. of soil and treat the ground with a fungicide like "Botrilex." Before doing so rake in a dressing of 2 oz. superphosphate and 1 oz. sulphate of potash per square yard. A small collection of wild tulips is being got together at Cambridge and grown there in the University Botanic Garden.

Viola.—This name embraces pansies, violas, and violets. Although the viola has not got the rich colours of the pansy (or its attractive markings), it has got a remarkably long season of flower, and for this reason it is invaluable as an edging plant or as ground cover for roses. *Prop.*—Both plants are easily raised from seed sown in a frame in the spring, pricked out, and then transferred to their flowering positions in late May. Alternatively, seed may be sown in July for planting out in October. Named varieties increased by cuttings in a frame in late summer.

Virginia creeper.—*See* **Parthenocissus.**

Wallflower.—*See* **Cheiranthus.**

Water Lily.—*See* **Nymphaea.**

Winter Sweet.—*See* **Chimonanthus.**

Wisteria.—One of the finest of all climbing plants for south or west walls or stout pergolas. Plants which do not flower, or only do so poorly, are probably seedlings and the true flowering habit cannot be induced; the only solution is to replace with a *grafted* plant of known flowering capacity from a reliable nurseryman. All young shoots not required for the extension of branches should be shortened to within 3 in. of the old stem in the autumn. Wisterias growing over trees do not require pruning. *Prop.*—Layer shoots of current season's growth in the autumn.

Zinnia.—Half-hardy annual, ideally grown on moist, deep loam liberally enriched with well-decayed manure. Mulch with manure after planting and apply liquid fertiliser as buds appear; plants must not suffer from lack of water. *See* **Annuals.**

Standard References.

Chrysanthemums, by Frank Kyle (Ward Lock), 1952 (15*s.*).

Collins Guide to Roses, by Bartram Park (Collins), 1956 (25*s.*).

Hortus Second, by L. H. Bailey and Ethel Zoe Bailey (Macmillan), 1947 (40*s.*).

R.H.S. *Dictionary of Gardening*, edited by F. J. Chittenden (Oxford), 1956 (14 guineas).

Sanders' *Encyclopaedia of Gardening*, revised by A. G. L. Hellyer (Collingridge), 1952 (21*s.*).

MAKING A LAWN

In almost every garden the most prominent feature is the lawn, and often a lot of work is put into making one without any great measure of success. Usually, the reason for failure may be found in faulty preparation of the soil or premature sowing, albeit the blame is often placed on bird damage or poor seed.

For anything like a reasonable turf, the site must be thoroughly dug and the content of organic matter increased by incorporating generous quantities of materials like peat, leaf-mould, compost, sewage sludge, and animal manure. A dressing of these ingredients can be applied in a layer 3–4 in. thick and buried in the bottom of the top spit of soil. As the ground is dug to incorporate the organic matter, roots of perennial weeds should be removed.

If the site is one on which water tends to lie or if the soil is heavy, then surface drainage should be sharpened by forking into the top 2 or 3 in. a liberal application of some coarse material such as builders' rubble, road grit, screened ashes, or coarse sand. In some cases this treatment will not be sufficient, and then the installation of land drains must be resorted to. This particular task is not as difficult as is sometimes imagined, but, before a start is made, it is always a good plan to discuss the matter with an experienced man.

After the initial work a fine tilth on the soil may be obtained by thoroughly raking and cross-raking and at the same time establishing a level surface. On this point, it should be remembered that good lawns can be made on undulating ground or on natural slopes, but the things to avoid are the shallow depressions where water will naturally tend to lie. Finally, ten to fourteen days before sowing the subsequent growth of grass can be encouraged by making an application of "National Growmore" at 2 oz. per sq. yd.

Sowing is best done in the late summer at a time when the soil is moist. For the purpose, a good mixture of seed should be obtained from a reliable seedsman, and it is worth paying a reasonable price for it, as, by and large, the coarsest and roughest grasses have the largest and heaviest seeds. Opinions differ on rates of sowing, but, with care and in a well-prepared soil, 1 oz. per sq. yd. is ample; heavier rates may give quicker results, but the density of seedlings in such cases often leads to the finer grasses being choked by the coarser ones.

After sowing, the ground should be lightly raked, but not rolled. At this stage the important point is to protect the seed bed from birds by the use of hazel sticks, strings of papers tied to stakes after they have been dipped in lime-wash, and strands of black cotton. Subsequently, annual weeds may appear in quantity; these are of no consequence, and they will be eliminated once the grass is cut regularly. Until a good turf is formed—usually about twelve months after sowing—it is not desirable (or probably necessary) to use hormone weed-killers. *See* T32.

Care of Established Lawns.

Most turf is never manured from year to year, and the soil may seriously lack plant foods. In the first place this can be corrected by making an application annually in the spring of "National Growmore" at 1 oz. per sq. yd. Subsequently, if growth is below par in the early part of the year an application of sulphate of ammonia can be made at the same rate. To avoid scorching or blackening of the foliage, each fertiliser can be mixed with equal parts of dry soil or sand as a carrier to ensure even distribution and, what is most important, each one should be applied only when the turf is wet and there is the prospect of rain to follow. Linked with this treatment, turf is always responsive to top dressings. A compost for the purpose can be made up with:

2 parts of loam;
1 part of sieved compost;
1 part of fine peat or leaf soil.

This may be used in the spring at 3–5 lb. per sq. yd. and if the soil is heavy 1–2 parts of gritty sand may be added.

With the introduction of new designs in motor mowers, most lawns are seriously overcut, and this has led to a sharp decline in the quality of the grass and the appearance of one or two pernicious weeds. It is appreciated that special turf, such as that found on a bowling green, may be shaved off to $\frac{1}{16}$ in., but if a utility lawn is cut below half to 1 in., then the quality of the grass will deteriorate. Of course, it is a good thing to occasionally cut the grass very short, but, conversely, if the blades of the mower are set as low as possible and left like it throughout the season nothing but harm can result. The reason for this hard fact is that when the turf is cut very close the grasses simply cannot develop and spread, and weeds will gradually establish themselves. Eventually the cultivator will be faced with the difficult problem of trying to deal with such plants as pearlwort, yarrow, and various mosses, all of which are resistant to hormones.

As for the vexed question of whether or not to remove the mowings, there is no doubt that the best turf is found where the mowings are collected up, although in very dry weather they can be left on the surface. If the clippings are not removed the surface of the turf tends to become choked with semi-decayed organic matter, and conditions are brought about which are inducive to the spread of moss.

Finally, it is worth noting that the finest turf is found on acidic—not alkaline—soils. For this reason, lime should not be applied as a general rule, for apart from helping the development of coarse grasses, it encourages the growth of clover. Of course, there are times when lime is necessary, but the occasions are rare and before it is used it is a good plan to test the soil by chemical means.

THE FRUIT GARDEN.

The guidance of an expert is probably more important in the growing of fruit than for most of the commoner vegetables and ornamentals. This is primarily because the majority of fruit trees and bushes are long-lived, and only in the case of strawberries can a change of site or variety be made easily and inexpensively.

Gardens which are low-lying are very prone to damage from spring frosts, and should not have too much space devoted to fruit, as returns may well prove unprofitable. Here, as with the selection of varieties, advice of a local expert is invaluable. Some varieties do better in certain localities and on certain soils than others, although personal preferences will naturally be met where possible. Varieties chosen should cover as long a season as is practicable so that the fruit can be used and enjoyed to the full.

Tree fruits are grown on a rootstock, and for apples and pears special dwarfing stocks make these a possibility for the small garden. It is therefore important to explain to the nurseryman what type of tree is required. As a general rule, however, the smaller gardens will gain by concentrating on currants, gooseberries, raspberries, and strawberries. Plums and cherries have no dwarfing stocks, and should be included only where sufficient room is available.

Adequate preparation of the ground is important, and this, followed by good management, can result in worth-while crops from most soils, providing they are reasonably free of frost, well-drained, and sufficiently sunny.

Apples.—Can be grown on most soils. Manure should not be used when planting, except in sandy and chalky gardens. Obtain trees on dwarfing rootstocks, such as M.IX, M.VII, or MM.106. Always stake trees on M.IX, otherwise this practice is necessary only in exposed sites. The tie must be rigid, with a "cushion" between tree and stake to avoid chafing, and must be renewed annually to avoid constriction. Plant between late October and early March, preferably before Christmas if soil and weather allow. Make the hole large enough to spread the roots evenly; firm thoroughly while filling in and plant level with the nursery soil mark already on the tree. Mulch around each tree with manure or compost, mainly to avoid drying out, and supplement with watering during the summer when necessary.

In the first year any flowers produced are best pinched out to encourage root and shoot development. For walls or fences use oblique cordons or espaliers; these are also useful for flanking paths and lawns. Plant cordons 2½ ft. apart with 6 ft. between rows, and espaliers 12–15 ft. apart. For larger areas use bush trees 12–15 ft. apart.

Manuring for cropping trees should be varied according to growth. Generally apply 1 oz. sulphate of ammonia (or nitro chalk on acid soils) in early March, repeating this in early April if trees are growing in grass. Give ½ oz. sulphate of potash in February and add 3 oz. of superphosphate every third year. The above rates are per square yard, and a complete fertiliser can be used in lieu if preferred.

Young bush trees should have main shoots reduced by half in early years to produce strong branches. Thereafter prune side shoots to three to six buds. For weak growers prune harder, and for strong growers prune less. It is wiser to leave a strong tree unpruned than to prune it too severely, the latter merely encouraging even stronger growth. A few varieties (*e.g.*, 'Bramley's Seedling,' 'Worcester Pearmain') fruit at shoot tips, and here a proportion of side shoots should be left unpruned. Summer pruning is advisable on restricted trees, such as cordons; for details see pears. Very few varieties are self-fertile, and at least two sorts should be planted to ensure satisfactory crops. Good combinations are 'Cox's Orange Pippin' with 'Laxton's Fortune' and 'Winston' with the cooker 'Lord Derby.' Seek expert advice on pairings if in doubt.

Apricots.—These are often an unreliable fruit to grow, needing a well-drained, calcareous loam and a warm wall for success. Train the tree as a fan, and once established pinch unwanted side shoots to four leaves in summer. Thin fruits when young, these developing mainly on spurs on older wood. 'Moor Park' and 'Hemskirk' are good varieties.

Blackberries.—Allow plenty of room and train against fences or wires. Autumn planting is preferable, using good, well-manured soil and cutting back the cane to 9 in. from the ground. Mulch with manure each spring, water freely in drought, and cut out old canes as soon as they have fruited. Good varieties are 'Himalaya,' 'Merton Thornless,' and the parsley-leaved blackberry. Increase by tip layering.

Cherries.—Sweet cherries are unsuited to most gardens. The trees become too large, and *must* be planted in selected pairs to fruit satisfactorily, as all varieties are self-sterile. Large wall spaces are ideal for fan trees, as the fruit can then be protected from birds by the use of nets. Pinch side shoots on fans to four leaves in July; further pruning details being as for plums. Expert advice is essential to ensure that suitable varieties are grown together, the factors involved being complicated. 'Early Rivers' with 'Bigarreau Schrecken' and 'Merton Heart' with 'Waterloo' are good combinations.

For the small garden the dwarf-growing, acid 'Morello' cherry is more useful, being infinitely superior for preserves as well as self-fertile. It also succeeds on a north wall, but unlike sweet varieties, fruits *only* on one-year-old wood.

Currants, Black.—These are perhaps the most valuable of all hardy fruits, and bushes will give up to 10 lb. and more of currants with correct treatment. Plant from November to February, preferably autumn, at 5 ft. square on clean, heavily manured ground. Then cut all shoots to one bud above soil level. Mulch each spring with well-rotted manure and supplement with fertilisers if necessary. The mulch is essential as much for keeping the soil moist as for a general feed.

On established bushes prune preferably after fruiting or in winter, retaining strong young wood and cutting out older shoots, where possible from ground level. If necessary, alternate bushes can be cut down completely every other year to maintain vigour, as the bulk of the crop is always borne on young wood. Increase by 8-in. cuttings of one-year-old wood taken in late September from healthy bushes. Remove lower leaves and insert firmly with one bud above ground. Good varieties: 'Boskoop Giant,' 'Wellington XXX,' 'Baldwin.'

Currants, Red and White.—One or two well-grown bushes are usually sufficient for the average household. Plant between November and March at a minimum of 5 ft. square on well-manured ground and mulch each spring. Supplement with fertilisers if necessary, potash being particularly important in the form of sulphate of potash at 1 oz. per sq. yd. in February. Can be grown as cordons or fans against walls or fences, on which the pinching of young side shoots to four leaves in mid-June is essential. Winter pruning of all types simply involves cutting side shoots to one bud and tip pruning branch leaders. Propagate by 12-in. cuttings of young shoots in late September inserted to half their length with all buds removed except the top four. This enables the bush to be grown on a "leg." A permanent framework of branches is then developed, as, in contrast to the black currant, fruit is borne on spurs on the old wood. Good varieties: 'Laxton's No. 1,' 'Red Lake,' 'White Grape.'

Damson.—*See* **Plums.**

Figs.—A warm south wall is usually essential, 'Brown Turkey' being one of the few reliable outdoor varieties. Plant in a brick or concrete trough (with drainage holes) about 2½ ft. wide, 5 ft. long, and 2½ ft. deep so that the root run is restricted. This will curb excessive growth (which otherwise is difficult to control) and encourage fruiting. Plant in March for preference, to avoid frost injury to young shoots, and then train fan-wise. A rich soil is not essential. Figs visible as such in the autumn will never over-winter, and should be rubbed out. Those the size of a pea and less at the tips of short, well-ripened shoots, on the other hand, are the potential crop for the following year, and should be covered in severe weather to avoid frost damage. To encourage the formation of these embryo fruits pinch young shoots back to the fifth leaf in late August. Winter prune in March, removing any wood that is frosted, overcrowded, or worn out; growths should be spaced at about 1 ft. Apply a spring mulch and water freely when required to avoid premature fruit drop.

Gooseberries.—Need conditions and spacing very similar to red currants, but with rather more moisture to ensure ample new wood, as this bears fruit as well as the older wood. Apply sulphate of ammonia and sulphate of potash annually in late February at up to 1 oz. per sq. yd. of each in addition to mulching. Can also be grown as cordons, etc., as for red currants. Pruning is also similar, though not quite so severe, as the young wood is productive of fruit. Cuttings are more difficult to root, and for best results should be taken in mid-September, again as for red currants. Good varieties: 'Lancer,' 'Leveller,' 'Whinham's Industry.'

Grapes.—Outdoor vines should be grown against a warm south- or south-west-facing wall. With good cultivation, the grapes should then ripen successfully providing suitable varieties are chosen. In preparing the site ensure that it is well drained and break up the soil to a depth of about 2 ft. Add bone meal to the top few inches at 4 oz. per sq. yd. and incorporate mortar rubble, particularly on the heavier soils. Do not dig in any manure except on poor, light soils, but always apply some as a mulch after planting, repeating this every spring. On poor, hungry soils the importation of some fibrous loam is advisable where possible.

Plant in November or, failing this, before early March, with the stem about 6–9 in. away from the wall. Firm well and then wait a further two months before tying to any wires or stakes, in case of soil sinkage. Cut the vine back in winter to well-ripened wood and to just above a bud. The training of subsequent growth will then depend on the space available, single and double cordons being the most convenient. Unwanted shoots should be pinched at about 2 ft. in summer and leading shoots carefully tied in to wire or bamboo supports. The following winter (December) prune leading shoots back to well-ripened wood so as to leave 3–4 ft. of new growth. Then cut all laterals hard back to one bud. In spring reduce young side shoots to one at each bud, stop laterals at about 12 in., and pinch any sub-laterals that may develop to the first leaf. Do not allow any crop to develop, except perhaps one bunch if growth is adequate; others should be pinched off. As fruit develops, thinning should be done as required. Winter prune as before, and then in the third summer four or five bunches of grapes can be allowed if the vine is healthy, the crop then increasing annually. Shoots carrying bunches should be pinched to two leaves beyond the bunch. Winter pruning is repeated each year as already described. Sour top-soil should be carefully removed when necessary and replaced with good loam while the vine is dormant. Good varieties: 'Black Hamburgh' and 'Foster's Seedling.'

Loganberries.—A very popular hybrid berry which should be treated as for blackberries. A thornless form is now available. Suitable for a north wall.

Medlars.—A tree of spreading habit, the peculiar fruits of which are best used for jelly before they are fully ripened. Most soils are suitable, and no pruning is needed except to keep in shape.

Nectarines.—A fruit very closely allied to the peach but with a richer flavour and needing rather more warmth. The skin is smooth, as distinct from the hairiness of the peach. For full details see Peach.

Nuts.—The most important kinds grown are cobnuts, the closely related filberts, and walnuts, but none of these is cultivated to any great extent. The two former kinds flower very early in February, and are therefore predisposed to frost damage; similarly, the young shoots of walnuts are easily injured by spring frosts, and all are therefore inadvisable for frosty areas.

Cobnuts and filberts.—Highly developed forms of the ordinary hazel nut. The nut of a cob is only partially covered by the husk, whereas a filbert is completely enclosed by it, this being the essential difference between the two. Will grow on most soils, including the poorer ones, and spacing should be about 15 ft., choosing sites sheltered from the colder winds. Plant during the autumn. Prune established bushes in March, cutting back shoots that have borne nuts to two or three buds; strong young shoots are cut back to a catkin near their base, and the weaker ones are left untouched. In August any strong new side growths are "brutted"—that is, broken off—and left hanging until the March pruning. Gather the nuts as they fall and allow to dry. Then store in jars for Christmas use, packing salt and coconut fibre between each layer of nuts.

Walnuts.—Special, grafted varieties are now available which produce early crops compared with the unreliable seedling trees that used to be planted. Plant between October and March and water well in spring and summer. Do not prune, as walnuts bleed badly. Gather nuts in mid-July for pickling. For storing allow to drop naturally and remove outer husk immediately, scrubbing the shell clean and then drying thoroughly. The shells can be bleached if necessary before storing the nuts as for cobs above.

Peaches.—This fruit along with its close ally, the nectarine, is best grown against a warm south or south-west wall, but two varieties of peach, 'Peregrine' and more particularly 'Rochester,' will succeed as bushes in the open in southern England. The fan-trained peach is one of the most difficult trees to keep in order, as sufficient new shoots must be retained annually to replace old wood. This is essential, as it is only the previous year's shoots which bear fruit. Badly placed shoots are rubbed out when only an inch long, and the principle is to allow one young replacement shoot to develop near the base of each fruiting shoot, pruning back to the former and tying it in as soon as all fruit has been picked. Other shoots may be used to extend the fan where space allows or to replace any branches or parts of them which may have become worn out. Other unwanted shoots are bound to arise during each summer, and these are either removed immediately or pinched to three leaves and then removed when pruning in late summer. Those shoots retained are spaced at about 4 in. apart.

Most peaches are self-fertile, but hand-pollinating on sunny days can improve the set. Excessive feeding should be avoided, varying this according to each tree's performance, but as a general rule a surface mulch of well-rotted manure or compost should always be given each spring, together with sulphate of potash at ½ oz. per sq. yd. Prick over and rake off top-soil and replace with good loam every few years. Never allow the sub-soil to dry out—this can quickly occur against warm walls—and water thoroughly when doing so to ensure an even distribution of moisture. On the other hand, drainage must be satisfactory to avoid waterlogging.

There are numerous other essential operations in the growing of trained peach trees (for example, fruit thinning), and it is impossible to deal with these adequately in brief notes. Would-be growers should therefore seek expert advice and obtain literature dealing specifically with the crop rather than risk disappointment. Good varieties for outside wall training include: *Peaches:* 'Peregrine,' 'Bellegarde.' *Nectarines:* 'Early Rivers,' 'Lord Napier.'

Pears.—The requirements for pears are similar to those for apples, but the necessity for adequate summer and autumn warmth rules out many varieties for northern areas. In these less favoured localities enquire which varieites do succeed, and where possible make use of a warm, south-facing wall. Protection from wind is very important, particularly from the cold easterlies of spring. Many soil types grow pears satisfactorily providing drainage is good and the trees are looked after. Plant as for apples. Fertiliser requirements are also similar once cropping commences, except that pears may require a little more nitrogen.

Pruning (winter) is comparatively simple, the spur pruning given for apples suiting all except a very few pears. Initial shaping is essential, cutting the stronger shoots selected to form branches by about half their length and keeping the centre of the tree open. For cordons and other restricted forms of tree, to which pears lend themselves particularly well, summer pruning is advisable. This involves shortening all young shoots more than 10 in. in length to about 5 in. from the base. Do this when the base of such shoots is hardening and turning brown in colour, usually late July-early August. Pruned shoots may then be further reduced in winter. Such summer treatment may also be given to trained apple trees with advantage during August.

Only a few pears are self-fertile and 'Con

ference' is the most reliable if only one tree can be planted. Good pollinating pairings include 'Laxton's Superb' with 'Doyenné du Comice' and 'Conference' with 'Williams' Bon Chrétien.' Early varieties should be picked a little before ripening and used quickly.

Plums.—This general term includes gages and damsons. Numerous varieties are easy to grow but are unsuited to small gardens because of the amount of space required. Unlike apples and pears, there are no dwarfing rootstocks, and a minimum spacing of 14 ft. should be allowed for, growing the trees as half standards, or fan-trained against a south or west wall. Flowering is during April, and frost damage can be serious in some seasons. Plant preferably in the autumn, and by early March at the latest, using no manure unless soil is distinctly poor. Young trees should be staked during their early years, and must not be allowed to rub against the support.

Pruning should be reduced to a minimum, as the spores of silver leaf disease gain entry through wounds such as pruning cuts and stake rubs. Shorten branch leaders on young trees just as buds are bursting, but on older trees prune only when branches become overcrowded. Do this between June and August, when the risk of silver leaf is at a minimum. Cut cleanly and coat the wounds thoroughly with a bituminous paint; treat broken branches similarly immediately they are noticed. Trees fruiting heavily should have the branches supported and the fruit thinned in late June. Side shoots on fans must be cut to four to five leaves in late June and reduced still further following picking if necessary. Feed cropping trees regularly to encourage new growth, using well-rotted manure or sulphate of ammonia at 1 oz. per sq. yd. in early spring. Some varieties are self-fertile including 'Victoria,' 'Oullin's Golden Gage,' and 'Merryweather Damson.'

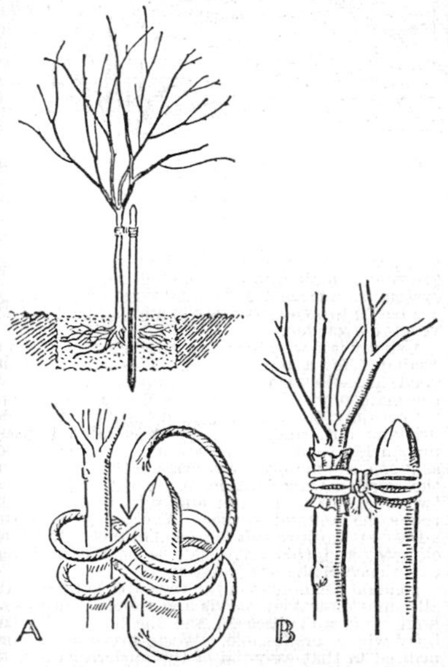

A WELL-PLANTED TREE, illustrating (A) a good method of tying and (B) sapling firmly secured with sacking around the trunk and held with stout cord.

Raspberries.—These are an ideal fruit for the small garden, but because of virus disease always buy certified canes from a fruit nursery. Plant between November and March on clean, well-manured ground, allowing 18 in. between canes and 6 ft. between rows. After planting prune each cane back to 12 in. Do not attempt to crop them in their first year, or the production of young canes for the following year's fruit will suffer.

A semi-shaded position will answer, but full sun is preferable for quality fruit. New canes should be looped with string to a post-and-wire fence and later tied individually to each wire when fully hardened. Space them at about 4 in. and remove any weak or diseased canes at ground level. In late February cut each cane to just above the top wire, which is usually 5–6 ft. high. This removes any damaged tips and may encourage fruiting over a longer length of cane. In the second summer a fair crop should result, and netting against birds is essential. Regular watering is imperative in dry weather, and spring and summer mulches of well-rotted manure or compost should always be applied. Supplement this in March with nitrogen and potash (fertilisers) if required, this depending on how well the ground was manured before planting. After fruiting cut out all old canes and tie in the new ones as already described. 'Malling Promise' and 'Lloyd George' are good varieties.

For autumn-fruiting varieties prune all canes to the ground in late February and tie in the best during the summer for cropping in September–October. 'September' is a good variety, and 'Lloyd George' can also be used.

Strawberries.—This is the one fruit that should be included in the vegetable garden. Fresh ground can then be used regularly for establishing new beds. Plants more than two years old are seldom profitable, and the best fruit is always picked from healthy one-year-olds planted the previous August or September. Runners put in later than early October should be deblossomed the following spring, the reward being a much heavier crop in the second year. This wastes ground, however, and early planting is preferable on all counts. Prepare the ground well in advance of planting and dig in plenty of well-rotted manure or compost or both, as this is the key to success.

Because of virus diseases order certified plants from a fruit nursery and burn any unhealthy ones in old beds before planting. Insert firmly with the base of the crown of each plant just at soil level and refirm after winter frosts; space at 20 in. in rows and 2 ft. 6 in. between rows (3 ft. if possible). A mulch of rotted manure or compost is beneficial each autumn, and if this is lacking apply sulphate of potash at 1 oz. per sq. yd. instead. Bonemeal is also advisable in spring and again in July, but quick-acting *nitrogenous* fertilisers should normally be avoided.

During flowering cover the plants where possible to guard against frost damage reducing the crop. Keep the ground weed-free and remove runners regularly; a few plants should always be grown away from the main bed, deblossomed and kept purely for runner production, as this then helps to reduce the spread of virus. Ruthlessly burn any plant that remains stunted, including its runners, as this is usually a symptom of virus disease. When the young fruits are just forming spread clean straw underneath them to avoid splashing from the soil; it is a mistake to do this too early, as it increases the risk of frost damage. Net the fruit against birds and remove any rotting specimens when picking.

After fruiting remove and burn all old foliage, weeds, and straw, and feed as already described. Plant a percentage of new, vigorous runners each year on fresh ground, at the same time burning the old ones they are replacing. Good varieties include 'Royal Sovereign,' 'Cambridge Favourite,' and 'Talisman.'

Alpine strawberries require similar treatment, preferably with a semi-shaded position, and should be raised from seed. Perpetual fruiting types continue fruiting on and off well into the autumn, and should be treated as for ordinary varieties. In all cases cloches can be used from late February onwards to obtain early fruit.

Standard References:

Tree Fruit Growing, by Raymond Bush, revised by E. G. Gilbert, N.D.H. (Penguin) 1962 (12*s*. 6*d*.)

The Fruit Garden Displayed (Royal Horticultural Society), 1951 (6*s*. 6*d*.).

THE VEGETABLE GARDEN.

The vegetable garden is, or should be, an integral part of home economy nowadays. Home-grown vegetables, although requiring considerable labour, are cheaper and fresher than most shop supplies. The ideal site is in an open, sunny position sheltered from cold winds with the soil a deep, rich loam well supplied with humus; quite obviously very few gardens have the ideal site, and we have to do the best we can with the ground available. In laying out the vegetable plot, ease of working should be considered; the lines of vegetables should go from north to south, and paths should be wide enough for a barrow to pass. The vegetable lines should not be too long, or the soil will be trodden down too much.

Each individual will have to decide the size of his plot according to the amount and types of vegetables required, and the land available. Shelter from a hedge or wall is desirable, and a plot about 90 ft. by 30 ft. can be made to produce a succession of vegetables to feed an average family over the year. Land preparation is important; on a new site the weeds should be cut down and removed, but any turf can be left and dug in. The land should be dug two spits deep ("double digging") in winter, and for this the plot is divided into two longitudinally and a trench 2 ft. wide and 10 in. deep is dug out at one end, as shown on the accompanying diagram. The sub-soil below the trench is then broken up and manure or compost incorporated (or turf if grassland is being dug). The next strip is then dealt with in a similar manner, and this continues down the plot until the last trench, which is then filled with the loose soil from the first trench.

Clay soils which are sticky are much improved by humus and constant working, but should not be dug in wet weather. Sandy soils also require plenty of humus to conserve moisture, but are less fertile, though often warmer and earlier. For the majority of vegetables a slightly acid soil is best, and a dressing of lime is only desirable if the soil is too acid. Double digging is not necessary each year, and single digging, carried out in a similar manner without breaking up the second spit, or a light forking over is sufficient for some crops, provided the ground has been well cultivated previously.

The lay-out with vegetables must be designed to provide a succession through the year and to utilise the full capacity of the ground by catch crops and a suitable succession. The land can be divided into four plots; one is used for the more or less permanent crops, such as asparagus, rhubarb, and globe artichokes, and the other three will provide a rotation. This is used to stop any group of vegetables being grown on the same land more than once in every three years, so preventing the carry-over of some pests and diseases and providing for a full use of the manures in the soil, as different groups of vegetables need more of some nutrients than others. It also allows the clearance of one section to enable winter digging and manuring to be carried out. On this freshly manured plot peas, beans, onions, leeks, and lettuces, all revelling in rich ground, should be grown. The next plot, manured for the *previous* crop, can be used for root crops—early potatoes, carrots, parsnip, and beet. A light dressing of artificial fertiliser such as "National Growmore" should be applied before sowing. On the third plot the green vegetables should be grown; a dressing of fertilisers is desirable, and lime should also be applied.

In the following season the root crops can be grown on the plot which was manured the previous year, and the brassicas grown on the land vacated by the root crops. The plot on which the brassicas were growing is double dug and manured ready for the peas, beans, and onions. A system of this type proves very satisfactory, but numerous variations can be devised, and it is really a matter for the gardener to decide his best method. The growing of maincrop potatoes will complicate the system, as a large area is usually required. They are better grown separately in another part of the vegetable garden.

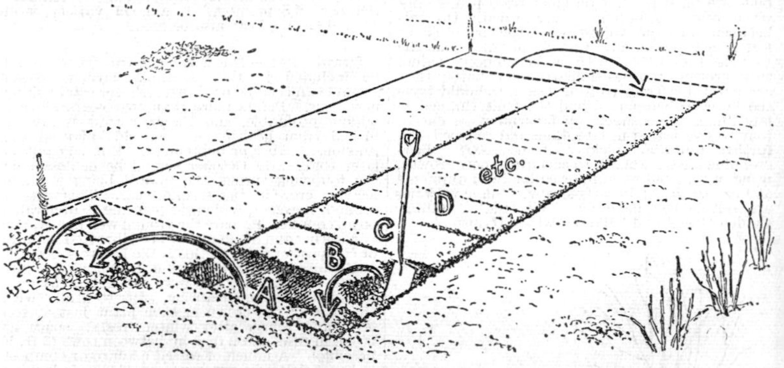

DOUBLE DIGGING—A sound cultural practice. A trench 2 ft. wide and the depth of a spade is taken out at A and placed as shown. The bottom of trench A is then forked up and filled in with soil from B and the process repeated with C and D, etc. In double digging the sub-soil is *always* left on the bottom and never brought to the surface.

Usually it is wise to have a small piece of ground available for a nursery bed. This should be of good, fine soil in which seeds can be sown to supply the main plot. In all cases seed should be sown very thinly to prevent the necessity for much pricking out, and a slug-killer is often a wise precaution to use before sowing. Sowing dates, as given, are mainly for growers in the South. In the North sowing dates in spring will be generally two weeks or more later and autumn operations the same amount earlier. Any gardener must adjust his work to suit local conditions of soil and climate, and this knowledge is only gained by experience of the particular area.

General cleanliness in the vegetable garden is at all times desirable; weeds and rubbish only harbour pests and diseases, and the hoe should be busy whenever possible. Waste material can be utilised in that essential of the modern garden—the compost heap. *See* **Manures and Fertilisers** for description.

Frames and Cloches.—The gardener is able to extend the season of many crops by protecting them under frames and cloches; this is particularly useful where spring or early autumn frosts are prevalent. The use of frames is limited, as they are in a fixed position, but nevertheless they are very useful for obtaining out-of-season salad crops, especially if they are heated by electricity or a hot bed.

Cloches have the advantage of mobility and can be used on a number of crops in succession. Essentially, each is a number of pieces of glass in a tent or barn shape held together by wire. Pattern, size, and height vary according to the crop to be covered and the manufacturer's design. A good cloche should be of simple design, rigid and capable of standing up to ordinary winds, easily transported, and well ventilated.

The low barn cloche is probably the most economical type. This is 23 in. wide and 13 in. high when erected, and will allow two rows of lettuce to be grown, with an intercrop of another vegetable. The large barn or barn cloche of similar design, but with 12-in. side is 19 in. high in the centre, enabling taller crops, *e.g.*, peas and dwarf beans, to be grown on, almost to maturity.

Dwarf varieties should be used for growing under cloches, although methods of raising the cloches another foot or so have been devised and are on the market, which allow the use of taller growing varieties. Many different vegetables can be helped to some extent in the early stages, besides those crops which can be grown entirely under cloches; the grower must decide what crops he needs and fit a rotation to cover as many crops as possible with the cloches available. This is mainly a matter of experience, but books on the subject will suggest many variations that can be tried. Intercropping with quick-maturing crops can also be practised. As instances, radish or mustard and cress can be cropped between two rows of lettuce, or a row of cos lettuce can be grown between two rows of cabbage lettuce.

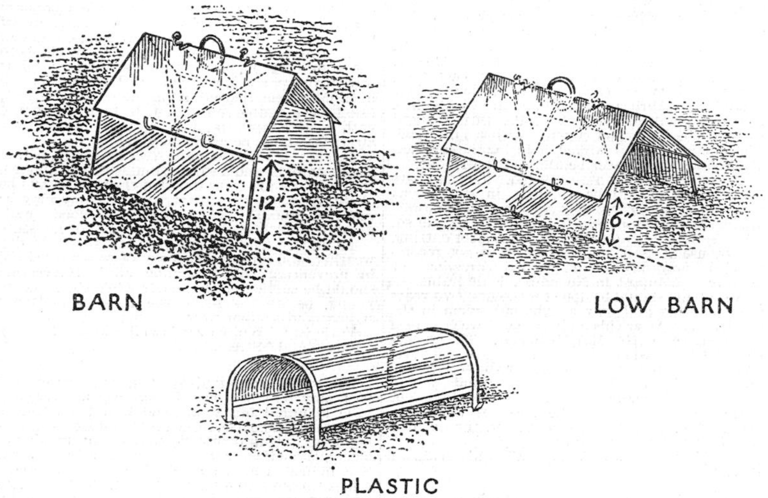

TYPES OF CLOCHES—The most popular is the barn cloche; with 12-in. sides it will cover strawberries and peas and beans in their early stages. The low barn will accommodate three rows of lettuce in winter and cucumbers in the summer. Plastic cloches are growing in popularity, especially those patterns using toughened plastic, and have some decided advantages over glass ones.

The tomato cloche has sides 24 in. square and a basal width of 26 in. Many others of various shapes and sizes are offered; the amateur should buy to suit his own requirements. Other materials have been tried instead of glass with varying success. Plastic cloches are on the market, but their lightness entails very safe anchoring, and at the moment glass still seems to be the best material in most instances.

Gardening under cloches obviously is a subject too large to be dealt with in a few sentences, and the reader would be well advised to refer to one of the books mentioned in the bibliography for fuller information. A few of the main points are mentioned here and also under the individual crops.

Cloche cultivation is an intensive method of production, and this means that the land must be well cultivated and manured to ensure good-quality crops at all times. About ten days before crops are sown or planted the cloches should be put in the position where they are to be used, to warm the soil. The crop is sometimes sown a month before the normal date, and this prewarming ensures that the soil can be cultivated to a good tilth, as well as giving the plants a good start. Watering is a problem that often bothers the amateur. Provided the soil is well watered at sowing time, there should be no need to decloche to water. Rain seeping under the cloches and a spray directed over them occasionally will provide enough for the crop in normal weather; on dry, sandy soils it may be necessary to spray over the cloches more often. A mulch of compost is also very useful to help retain water.

It must be remembered that the glass of cloches will need cleaning from time to time; the crop still needs the maximum light available, although shading of certain crops may be necessary in hot sun.

Artichokes.—Two different plants are grown as artichokes. One, the Jerusalem artichoke (*Helianthus tuberosus*), is related to the sunflower and is grown for its tuberous roots, which are second in food value only to the potato. It will grow in poor soil, but amply repays good cultivation, and may be placed at the more exposed end of the vegetable plot as a windbreak and screen. Tubers should be planted during February or March, on well-manured ground in drills 4–6 in. deep, and 2 ft. 6 in. apart, with 15 in. between the tubers. Hoe frequently during the summer and cut the stalks down in early winter. The tubers may then be lifted and stored, or better dug as required, reserving a number for replanting the following February.

The other type, the globe artichoke (*Cynara scolymus*), is often grown as an ornamental plant, but is esteemed as a vegetable for its young, fleshy flower-heads, which must be cut before the scales begin to open, after which they become hard and unpalatable. A deep, rich, well-manured soil is required, and after planting in early spring in rows 4 ft. apart, with 2 ft. between the plants, a compost or manure mulch is beneficial. A good crop may be expected for five or six years provided an annual dressing of manure is applied. After this time they should be replaced by young suckers, planted in a fresh position. A covering of straw or bracken on the crowns is advisable during winter.

Asparagus.—This will grow on most types of soil provided that drainage is good and that plenty of organic matter is available. The site for the asparagus bed should be double dug in the autumn prior to planting, and a generous dressing of about half a barrow load of manure per square yard incorporated. Crowns up to three years old may be bought, but it is found that one-year-old crowns give the best results. Plants may be obtained cheaply by sowing seed in late March in drills 1½ in. deep and 18 in. apart and thinning the seedlings to 4 in. apart. It is thought that male plants produce more stalks of better quality than female plants, but at present no supplies of male crowns alone are available.

Planting may be on the single-row system or the wide-bed system. In the single-row system crowns are planted 18 in. apart in rows 4½ ft. apart; the wide-bed system consists of 5-ft. beds, with three rows of crowns 15 in. apart each way, and 2 ft. between each bed. Planting is best done during April and the plants are placed in a trench 8 in. deep and 1 ft. wide, with a slight ridge at the base, and covered with 3 in. of soil. The remaining soil is worked in during the summer. The roots should never be allowed to dry out.

The following March 2 oz. per sq. yd. of sulphate of ammonia should be applied; in subsequent years 3 oz. per sq. yd. of "National Growmore" applied at the same time, followed by 2 oz. per sq. yd. of sulphate of ammonia in June, after cutting, can be used. Salt, as a fertiliser, is not recommended nowadays. An annual dressing of manure or compost in November is desirable.

No cutting should be done for the first two years after planting and only a light cut taken in the third year. After this a six-to-eight-week season beginning in early May is usual. The spears should be cut when about 4 in. above soil level and severed about 2 or 3 in. below the soil, giving an overall length of 6–7 in. The fronds should be cut in October before the seeds drop, but not during the summer, as the plant is weakened. Weeds should be kept down and in the autumn the plant may be earthed up.

Varieties: 'Connover's Colossal' and 'Kidner's Pedigree.'

Beans. Three types are commonly grown, as follows:

Broad Beans are the hardiest and can, in warm gardens, be sown during autumn to obtain an early crop. Little is gained by this as a rule, and sowing in well-manured ground in February, when the soil is frost free, with successional sowings during March and April, is generally better in most gardens. The soil is broken down, finely raked, and the seed sown 9 in. apart in drills 3 in. deep, with 18 in. between each row. If double rows are sown 10 in. should be left between the rows, and 2 ft. between each pair of rows. Staking may be necessary. Plants from sowings under glass or under cloches in January may be used to obtain an earlier crop; the cloches should be removed in March and a further crop sown, and recloched.

Black aphis was a serious pest, but is now easily checked by pinching out the young tips and applying malathion or lindane as soon as any are seen. The pods may be used before the beans are fully developed and sliced as are runner beans, but normally they are picked when the beans are well formed but not tough.

Varieties: 'Aquadulce' and 'Green Masterpiece.'

Dwarf Beans (which include French, Kidney, and Haricot Beans) may be either used as young pods in a similar manner to runner beans or ripened in the pod for winter use. A rich well-manured soil gives the best results, and seeds sown during the first week in May, 2 in. deep and 6 in. apart, in drills 18 in. apart, may be followed by a second sowing at the end of May. The young plants should be thinned out to 1 ft. apart and small twigs used to stake them. If sown earlier, frost damage may occur. Seeds may also be sown in the greenhouse and the seedlings transplanted, or sown under cloches in the last week in March, provided the soil has been prewarmed.

The plants, as long as the pods are picked over frequently, will continue to bear until the frosts; a little liquid manure will be beneficial during the summer. A late sowing in July, cloched in September, will continue the season into the autumn.

If required for winter use (Haricot varieties) certain plants should be left unpicked and the pods allowed to ripen on the plants. They should not be picked green; if unripe when frosts come, the plants should be pulled up and dried in a shed.

Varieties: 'The Prince' (Cloche), 'Masterpiece,' and 'Comtesse de Chambord' (Haricot).

Runner Beans are the most popular type, and can be grown in two ways: either without stakes, in which case the tips of main and side shoots are regularly pinched out to make a bushy, dwarf plant, a method often used by farmers, or staked, with cross poles, allowing the plants to climb to the tops of the poles before pinching. Seed is sown from early May (mid-April under cloches) until late June, depending on the danger of frost, usually in a double row with drills 15 in. apart, and with seeds 3 in. deep and 6 in. apart in the rows, alternate plants being removed later.

Staking should be done as soon as the first pair of leaves unfolds, and a surface mulch is then applied. If the beans are to be dwarfed the rows should be about 18 in. or 2 ft. apart, and pinching may be required about once a week. A good, well-manured soil is essential, and plenty of moisture is required. The flowers may fail to set in dry weather, and an evening spray of water is helpful in preventing this "running off." Harvesting should be carried out regularly while the pods are young, before the seeds swell; older pods are stringy and seldom worth eating.

Varieties: 'White Czar' (white-flowered, heavy cropper) and 'Streamline.'

Beetroot.—From mid-April onwards varieties of beet may be sown on soil that has not recently been manured but is in good heart; on freshly manured soils coarse, forked roots subject to cracking occur. If in poor condition a light dressing of a complete fertiliser should be given before sowing. Sow in drills 1 in. deep and 12 in. apart and make a first thinning to 4 in. apart when the first rough leaf appears, and a second later, leaving 9 in. between the plants. Transplanting is inadvisable. Early roots for summer pulling may be obtained from a sowing of a Globe type in mid-April, and the main sowing should be made during May or early June for the winter supply. A sowing under cloches in late February will provide roots for pulling in late May.

On a heavy soil the oval-rooted types are best, but on a lighter soil the long-rooted types may be used. A sowing in late July of the Globe type will provide beet for use at the end of winter. Salad beet from early sowings may be pulled as required; the main crop should be allowed to mature and is lifted in October before the roots become woody and tough. Any damaged roots should not be stored. Twist off the tops just above the roots, shake the soil from the roots, and store in boxes of sand or peat in a frost-free shed. If clamped outside, straw and a thick layer of soil should be used; if frost reaches them they are spoilt.

Varieties: globe—'Detroit Red,' 'Red Globe, and 'Crimson Globe'; oval—'Cobham Early'; long—'Cheltenham Green Top.'

Sugar beet is similar but is white, not red-fleshed, and is mainly a farm crop; if desired it may be grown in a similar manner. Care should be taken in hoeing all beet crops to avoid damage to the small surface roots which feed the swollen rootstock.

Borecole.—*See* **Kale.**

Brassica.—A generic name of vegetables usually known to gardeners as "greens." This group includes brussels sprouts, cabbages, cauliflowers, kale, turnips, kohl-rabi, broccoli, and couve tronchuda. As they are all related, similar soil and cultural treatment is needed, and many pests and diseases are common to them. Each is dealt with under a separate heading.

Broccoli.—*See* Cauliflower.

Brussels Sprouts.—Young plants from seed sown thinly in a nursery seed bed during mid-March can be transplanted during May or June. The soil should be firm, well drained, in good heart, and contain adequate lime, some manure preferably having been dug in during the winter; a supplementary dressing of 2 oz. superphosphate and 1 oz. of sulphate of potash per square yard is given before planting. The young plants should be set out 3 ft. apart both ways, planted firmly, and watered in thoroughly. Regular hoeing is necessary, and about a month after planting a little soil should be drawn round the stems.

If growth seems weak a top dressing of nitro-chalk should be given and this repeated in early September. As the lower leaves yellow, cut them off and gather the sprouts as they mature, picking from the bottom of the stem. Where space is available a succession of sowings from March to June can be made to lengthen the cropping period.

Club root, the worst disease of brassicas, is kept in check by only using well-limed, well-drained soil, and dipping the roots in 4% calomel before planting, and cabbage root fly, a frequent insect pest, by using dieldrin.

Varieties: early—'Cambridge No. 1'; mid-season—'Rous Lench' and 'Triumph' (dark foliage, distinct).

Cabbage.—Sowings in March and April for summer use, in May or June for winter use, and in late July or August for spring use will give a succession of cabbages all the year round. Seed is sown thinly in a nursery bed of well-firmed, limed soil, clear of weeds, in drills ¾ in. deep and 6 in. apart, and the seedlings are dusted with D.D.T. to check flea beetle attack (prevalent with all brassica seedlings). All cabbages are gross feeders, and a well-drained soil in good heart, with adequate lime, is required.

"Spring cabbage" should be sown during late July (north) and August (south). If sown too early the plants may "bolt" without making a heart. The young plants are set out in mid-September 18 in. apart and with 18 in. between the rows if for hearting, or 9 in. apart with 18 in. between the rows, in which case the alternate plants are cut for "spring greens." On a heavy soil ridging along the rows of plants keeps the soil round the roots drained and helps to prevent loosening by frosts. In cold districts cloches may be used with advantage to help plants through the winter. In early March a dressing of 1 oz. per sq. yd. of sulphate of ammonia or nitro-chalk is a good stimulant.

Seed of "summer" and "autumn cabbage" is sown in March and April and planted during late May and June, 18 in. to 2 ft. each way between the plants, depending on the variety. The plants should be thoroughly watered, both before and after transplanting. A top dressing of 1 oz. per sq. yd. nitro-chalk may be given if required.

"Winter cabbage," maturing from October to February from sowings during May and early June, are set out 2 ft. apart each way in July or early August, usually on ground which has been cropped with early potatoes or peas. No nitrogen fertiliser should be given late in the season, as soft growth, liable to frost damage, is encouraged. A balanced fertiliser, such as "National Growmore," may be used if needed. When the stalks of cabbage are left standing over winter a common practice is to cut across the tops to obtain bunches of leaves, for use as greens during early spring.

"Savoy cabbages" mature during winter and early spring from seed sown in May. Seedlings are transplanted in late July and early August on to land manured for the previous crop, to which a dressing of 2 oz. superphosphate and 1 oz. sulphate of potash per square yard has been given. The young plants should be set out 2 ft. apart each way; they are exceptionally hardy, and should be grown in every garden in case of a hard winter.

Varieties: Spring sowing—autumn cutting, Greyhound' (early), 'Winningstradt.' Autumn sowing—spring cutting, 'April,' 'Wheeler's Imperial.' Savoy 'Ormskirk Late Green.'

Red Cabbage is slow to mature; plants from sowings in August are transplanted 6 in. each way in autumn and set out in early spring 18 in. each way. They are ready to cut in late summer.

Cardoon (Cynara cardunculus).—Closely related to the globe artichoke and grown for the blanched hearts. Seed is sown in trenches 18 in. wide and 1 ft. deep; 3 in. of manure is worked into the bottom soil and covered with 3 in. of fine soil. Three or four seeds are dibbled in every 18 in. and covered with a flower pot till visible, and then thinned out, leaving one strong seedling at each station. Protection from sun and late frosts is provided by twigs over the trench, and copious watering is given during the summer. On a fine day in September the plants are blanched by tieing the leaves together and covering with dry hay, 3 in. thick, kept in position by raffia, and earthed up in the same way as celery. Blanching is completed in about a month. Litter over the top protects them from frost.

Carrots.—A light, well-drained soil, enriched with decayed organic matter, is suitable for carrots. No fresh manure should be given, but a light dressing of "National Growmore" fertiliser can be applied prior to sowing. The surface is left rough until sowing time and then broken down to a fine tilth. The first sowing is made in early April in drills ¾ in. deep and 12 in. apart, and a succession is obtained by sowing at intervals of a month until the end of July.

On heavy, unfavourable soils stump-rooted varieties are best grown, long-rooted varieties needing a light soil. Thin out the stump-rooted varieties to 4 in. apart and the longer varieties to 6 in. Thinnings should be removed and the soil pressed firmly back to minimise damage by carrot fly. The early sowings are pulled as required, but the later sowings for winter use should be lifted in October and stored in slightly damp sand in a frost-proof shed or clamped in the open.

Frames and cloches are sometimes used to obtain early and late carrots. Seed of a quick-growing variety, such as 'Amsterdam Forcing' or 'Early Nantes,' sown in late January under cloches or in frames will provide an early crop; the same varieties sown in frames or cloches in early August will provide young carrots for the autumn. Carrot fly is a bad pest, especially on light soils; the seedlings should be dusted with lindane or dieldrin when 2–4 in. high to prevent the flies from egg laying.

Varieties: globular—'Early Gem'; stump-rooted—'French Short Horn'; intermediate—'Amsterdam Forcing' and 'Early Nantes'; long—'St. Valery' and 'Long Red Surrey.'

Catch Crops.—A term used for quick-growing crops interplanted between rows of other crops. Radishes between rows of broad beans, and lettuce between celery rows provide examples. In this way the best use of a limited amount of land can be made.

Cauliflower.—Broccoli is for all practical purposes a hardy winter cauliflower. Seed is sown ¾ in. deep in a nursery bed from mid-April to mid-May, depending on the variety, and transplanted during June and July on to firm soil, well manured for the previous crop. The plants are set out 2 ft. apart each way; 2 oz. superphosphate and ¾ oz. of sulphate of potash per square yard may be hoed in before transplanting. No nitrogenous manure should be given late in the year.

Varieties: cauliflower—'Snowball' (summer), 'Majestic' (autumn). Broccoli—'Snow's Winter White' (winter), 'St. George' (early spring). Sprouting broccoli—'Nine Star Perennial' (a many-headed sort).

Sprouting broccoli is very hardy, has a more leafy head, and is cultivated in the same way. Purple- and green-sprouting varieties are grown.

Summer cauliflowers require a soil which has been limed and manured during the winter; 1–2 oz. per sq. yd. of superphosphate should be given before transplanting. An early sowing in frames in February or March will provide plants for cropping in June. These should be hardened off and planted in March or April from 18 to 24 in. square, depending on the variety. Seed sown outdoors in April in drills ¾ in. deep will give plants for transplanting in May or June, for cropping from late July onwards. If growth is slow a dressing of 1 oz. per sq. yd. of sulphate of ammonia should be given. Leaves broken over the curds will help to prevent any damage from early frosts. Varieties given in previous paragraph.

Celeriac.—A plant allied to celery grown for its edible root, which resembles a turnip but has the flavour of celery; the stems are bitter to the taste and are not eaten. It is used in salads or boiled as other root crops. Seed is sown in gentle heat in March and seedlings pricked out into seed-boxes, 2 in. apart each way. In June, after hardening off, the seedlings are planted out in shallow drills 18 in. apart, leaving 12 in. between each plant in the row. Water freely during the summer and remove side shoots as they appear. Lift the roots in October or November and store in a frost-free shed.

Celery.—Richly prepared ground is required. A trench 15 in. wide and 1 ft. deep is taken out and manure worked into the bottom of the trench. The soil is then returned to within 3 in. of the ground level. Seed should be sown in early March at about 60° Fahrenheit and the seedlings pricked out in deep boxes 3 in. each way and gradually hardened off. Celery seed is very fine, and care should be taken to cover it with only a fine layer of soil; if covered too deeply it may not germinate.

In late May or June set the plants out in staggered double rows 1 ft. apart, with 10 in. between the plants, and water them in. Frequent watering during the summer is required, and a light dressing of nitrate of soda will stimulate them if growth is poor. Before earthing up to blanch the plants, tie the stems loosely below the leaves and remove any suckers. Earthing up begins when the plants are about 15 in. high; the ground should be moist, and the first earthing should only be slight. The second and third earthings, at intervals of about three weeks, should be more generous, but should never reach higher than the base of the leaves, and no earth should fall into the heart. For exhibition purposes brown-paper collars may be tied round the stalks before earthing. The final earthing should cover all the stems right up to the leaves, and the soil should slope away neatly. In winter litter or bracken spread over the plants will help protect them from frost.

Celery fly is a serious pest, and the brown leaf-blisters should be pinched to kill the maggot inside and lindane applied two or three times at fornightly intervals. Slugs should be discouraged with a good slug killer. Leaf spot, a seed-borne disease, can be prevented by spraying with Bordeaux mixture.

Varieties: white—'Solid White'; pink—'Clayworth Prize Pink'; red—'Standard Bearer' self-blanching—'Golden Self-Blanching.'

Chervil.—An annual herb sown during March in drills 10 in. apart, and thinned to 6 in. in the rows. Further sowings can be made during the summer. Used in salads and soups.

Chicory.—The young, blanched growths are used in winter salads. Seeds are sown in drills 1 ft. apart in May; the young seedlings are thinned to 8 in. apart and grown on until October or November, when they are lifted and the roots trimmed to 8 or 10 in. long. They are then planted in deep boxes in a moist, sandy soil 5 in. apart each way, leaving 1 in. above the soil surface, and the boxes put in a warm greenhouse or cellar. No light must reach the crowns; one method sometimes used is to cover the crowns with 6 in. of sand. When the blanched growths show through they are about 6 in. high and ready for cutting.

Chives.—These are like small onions, and the leaves are used for flavouring salads and soups. They are easily grown in window boxes and town gardens. Bulbs can be planted in March 6 in. apart and divided when the clusters become too large.

Corn Salad or Lamb's Lettuce.—Occasionally grown for the leaves, which are used in early spring salads. Seed sown from August to October will provide plants for winter and spring use.

Couve Tronchuda.—A large brassica known as "Portugal cabbage," not generally suitable for smaller gardens. Seed is sown in March and the plants set out 2–3 ft. apart each way. The hearts may be cooked in the same way as cabbage.

Cress.—An annual growing rapidly from seed and used as a salad when only the seed leaves have developed. Seed sown as required, in boxes of light, moist soil and covered with brown paper until germination, when it is removed, will provide salad all the year round. The seed is merely pressed into the soil and the boxes kept moist. Cress may even be grown on damp flannel in a window.

Cucumber.—The cucumber of the shops is grown as a specialist crop under glass. Temperatures of 85° Fahrenheit or more may be required, and only occasionally are they grown by the amateur, although cloche and frame culture is now popular.

Ridge cucumbers, which are smaller and prickly outside, may be grown outdoors in summer. Plants from seed sown singly in pots under glass can be planted during late May on ridges of good, well-manured soil or, alternatively, sown on the ridges 1 in. deep at the same date. Water freely during the summer and cut the cucumbers while young to encourage further production.

If cloches are available greenhouse-raised cucumbers can be planted under them, in mid-April. Frame cucumbers are less hardy, but young plants raised under glass can be planted under cloches in early May.

Varieties: ridge—'King of the Ridge' and 'Stockwood Ridge'; frame—'Conqueror' and 'Telegraph.'

Endive.—Used in winter or autumn salads. Seed is sown during April in drills 18 in. apart and the seedlings thinned to 12–15 in. apart. Sowings in June and August will provide a succession. A rich soil and plenty of moisture are the main requirements; before eating blanching is necessary, as the leaves are very bitter. This is achieved by tieing the leaves loosely together and covering the plants with inverted flower pots (with the holes blocked) to exclude the light; frost should be kept out by piling litter over the pots in winter. If cloches are used they can be coated inside with lime-wash to achieve the same effect. Alternatively, plants may be lifted in October and blanched in darkened frames.

Varieties: summer—'Green Curled'; winter—'Batavian Broad Leaved.'

Fennel.—A perennial culinary herb used in fish sauces and salads. Blanched stems may also be cooked in the same way as celery. Seed is sown in drills 2 ft. apart in rich soil and the seedlings thinned to 18 in.

French Beans.—*See* **Dwarf Beans.**

Garlic.—One or two "cloves" planted in February, 9 in. apart, will provide ample garlic for salads, as only a little is required. After growth is complete in summer the bulbs can be lifted, dried, and stored and some saved for replanting.

Haricot Beans.—*See* **Dwarf Beans.**

Herbs.—Many herbs are useful in small quantities for flavouring and garnishing, as well as being decorative. If possible, a separate herb garden should be made as a feature in the garden, or they may be used as edging plants. Perennial herbs, of which borage, caraway, chamomile, chives, fennel, garlic, horseradish, lavender, mint, pennyroyal, marjoram, rosemary, rue, sage, tansy, tarragon, and thymes are the main types grown, should be given a permanent position. Those grown as annuals—anise, basil, coriander, dill, parsley, purslane, and summer savory—can be used as "fill-ins" on the vegetable garden. Brick and cobble paths associate well with herbs, imparting something of the character of the gardens of bygone days, when herb gardens were considered one of the most important features.

Horseradish.—A deep-rooting perennial herb which appreciates a well-manured, moist soil. It is easily propagated from root cuttings and can become a nuisance, as pieces of root left in the soil will make a new plant; care should be taken to lift the complete root when digging it for use. Straight roots planted in spring with the crowns 6 in. below soil level and 1 ft. apart can be lifted for use in autumn; no further treatment is required, apart from keeping weeds in check. Some of the roots should be kept for planting the following spring.

Kale.—Very useful during a cold winter, when other green vegetables are scarce, because of its hardiness. Seed sown in April or May will provide young plants for transplanting 18 in. apart each way in July or early August, on to a site used for peas or early potatoes, in good heart. A catch crop of lettuce can usually be taken from between the rows. The variety 'Hungry Gap' is usually sown in rows 18 in. apart where it is to mature and thinned, leaving 18 in. between the plants. There are many varieties; which types are grown is a matter of personal preference.

Varieties: 'Cottager's' and 'Hungry Gap.'

Kidney Beans.—*See* **Dwarf Beans.**

Kohl Rabi.—A brassica with a swollen stem base, in flavour and appearance something between a turnip and a cabbage. Seeds sown in April in rows 1 ft. apart are thinned to 1 ft. apart in the rows, and the swollen stem harvested when about the size of a tennis ball. If left to grow it becomes coarse.

Lamb's Lettuce.—*See* **Corn Salad.**

Leeks.—A vegetable which repays planting on a well-manured soil. If they are to follow winter greens, then manure or compost should be dug in after the previous crop is cleared. Leeks may be sown from early March to April in lines 8 in. apart on a prepared seed bed, and the seedlings transplanted as land becomes available during June and July, when about 6 in. high. Thinning in the seed bed should be unnecessary provided the sowing has been correct. The seedlings are set out 9 in. apart in rows 15 in. apart; a hole is made with a dibber, and each seedling dropped in and watered thoroughly. No firming is needed, the watering should tighten the plants sufficiently. Alternatively, drills 4 in. deep and 15 in. apart can be drawn out with a hoe and the plants put in 9 in. apart in the drills.

Regular hoeing is required, and a feed of sulphate of ammonia (1 oz. per gallon of water) can be applied if in poor growth. In September a little earth should be drawn up around the roots, which should, by then, be almost full grown. Leeks are very hardy and can be left in the soil until required for use.

Varieties: 'Lyon' and 'Musselburgh.'

Lettuce.—Two main types are grown: cos lettuce, a summer crop with long, straight leaves that curl inwards naturally or are tied in so that the heart is more or less blanched; and cabbage lettuce, which are broad and spreading, with round cabbage-like hearts, and are grown to supply salad all the year round. Lettuce should be grown on ground manured during autumn or winter, dug and left rough till planting time, when it is broken down and raked to a fine tilth.

Seed, sown in January in frames and cloches, or outdoors in March and at fortnightly intervals thereafter, a little at a time, until September outdoors, or October in frames and cloches will provide lettuce for most of the year. Sow thinly in drills ½ in. deep, in rows 1 ft. apart, and thin out or transplant young seedlings so that they are 9–12 in. apart, depending on the variety. Quick, unchecked growth with adequate moisture is required; a dressing of bonemeal worked into the soil before planting and a light dressing of sulphate of ammonia in water on poor soils will help growth considerably. Aphids may be troublesome, and should be checked by using lindane or malathion.

Varieties: summer—'All the Year Round' and 'Continuity'; early spring—'Arctic King' and 'Cobham Green.'

Maize.—*See* **Sweet Corn.**

Marrows.—Pumpkins, gourds, bush, and trailing marrows all require similar treatment; plenty of sun and water and a rich soil, such as an old hotbed or compost heap, which will provide a porous medium of humus. Seed can be sown singly in pots under glass in March, or outdoors on the site in May. For cloches a bush variety must be used, and greenhouse-raised plants are cloched in mid-April. Plant four or five seeds in groups about 6 in. apart and 1 in. deep and finally thin to two plants 15 in. apart. Protection from late frosts may be necessary. Water copiously and hoe regularly. Cut marrows when about 12 in. long to encourage further fruits. Some can be left until they are full size and cut before the frosts, for storing in a dry, frost-proof place.

Varieties: bush—'Green Bush' and 'White Bush'; trailing—'Long Green Trailing.'

Melons.—Although usually a glasshouse crop, melons can be grown outdoors under cloches and in frames. Seed is sown under glass in April at 60° Fahrenheit, and seedlings can be set out 3 ft. apart in early May. The soil should be manured generously and the seedlings planted on a mound of compost mixed with soil. The plants must be stopped at the fourth or fifth leaf to encourage laterals. Two can be selected to grow on and, when 18 in. long, pinched out to obtain sub-laterals, which will bear the fruit. The female flowers may require pollinating, and on a sunny day a male flower or rabbit's tail can be used to transfer the pollen; as soon as the young fruits swell, remove all but two or three per plant and pinch back the laterals bearing fruit to two leaves from the melon. A feed of dried blood once a week, with plenty of watering (though not saturation!) will help the developing fruits. Light shading may be necessary.

Varieties: 'Dutch Net' and 'Tiger.'

Mint.—Easily grown from suckers in any soil. For winter use a few pieces can be planted in a frame. A number of varieties—'Apple Mint,' 'Peppermint,' and 'Spearmint'—can be grown besides common mint.

Mushrooms.—Growing mushrooms is really a specialist occupation. For the experimental amateur, beds of composted stable-manure are made up in a warm, damp cellar or disused air-raid shelter. Pieces of spawn are inserted when the temperature of the compost has dropped to about 70° Fahrenheit and the whole bed covered with an inch of inert sub-soil. The air temperature should be from 60° to 70° Fahrenheit, and in a few weeks mushrooms may appear. Full instructions will be given with the spawn, but it is advisable to consult a text-book dealing with the culture, as even for professional growers a crop is never certain.

Mustard.—Grown exactly in the same way as cress, but is ready two or three days earlier. If used together, mustard seed should be sown two or three days after cress. Again it is the seed leaves which are eaten.

Onions.—These respond well to good cultivation. The site is dug deeply in winter, manure incorporated, and left rough until February, when it is broken down to a fine tilth and firmed well. Seed can be sown ¾ in. deep in drills during August and planted in March for exhibition onions, but the usual practice is to sow seed in late February outdoors or under glass in January and transplant during April in rows 12 in. apart with 6 in. between the onions, taking care to keep the bases about ¼ in. below the surface. If sown outdoors and thinned the thinnings may be used in salads. Autumn-sown onions are liable to bolt, but less liable to attack by onion fly than spring-sown plants.

Dressings of sulphate of ammonia or nitrate of potash may be given during the growing season, but not later than July. In August the tops are bent over to hasten ripening and the bulbs harvested in a dry spell at the end of the month, first laying them on the ground for a day or two to dry off. They should be stored in a dry, airy place. The chief pest is onion fly, controlled by dusting the seedlings with aldrin at the loop stage. Onion sets are small onions produced the previous summer, stored and replanted in spring to obtain very large bulbs. They are particularly valuable on poor soils.

Varieties: spring sowing—'Bedfordshire Champion,' 'Best of All,' and 'White Silverskin' (pickling); autumn sowing—'Giant Zittau,' 'Sutton's Solidity,' and 'White Lisbon' (salad onions); sets—'Ebenezer' and 'Stuttgarter Reisen.'

Parsley.—Sow thinly in rows 8 in. apart during March and again in July for a succession of young foliage; thin to 4 in. between plants.

Parsnip.—Grow parsnips on ground manured for a previous crop; if given fresh manure splitting and forked roots occur. Dig the soil deeply, and at sowing time in March, work the soil to a fine tilth. On a soil unsuitable for deep-rooted crops special holes 10–12 in. apart, filled with sifted soil, may be prepared. If this method has to be used four or five seeds are sown per hole; normally drills 15 in. apart and 1 in. deep are made and four or five seeds sown every 9 in. The seedlings are thinned, leaving one at each station. Parsnips should be left in the ground until needed; litter over the rows will ease lifting in frosty weather.

Varieties: 'Evesham' and 'Student.'

Peas.—Dig the ground well in autumn and add a generous amount of manure or compost. Seed sowing begins at the end of February, and can be continued at three-weekly intervals until early July. Under cloches sowings in January and October will lengthen the season. Both early and late sowings should be of a quick-maturing variety. Seed is sown in drills 6–8 in. wide and 3 in. deep, with 2 ft. between drills; the seeds can be scattered thinly in the drill or spaced 3 in. apart in a treble row. Cover with 2 or 3 in. of soil and as soon as the peas are about 2 in. high stake with twigs.

Failures are often due to attacks by birds and field-mice. The former should be discouraged by netting and the latter by trapping. Pea-sticks will be necessary for the taller varieties which should have 3–4 ft. between the rows. With limited space only the dwarf quick-maturing varieties should be used. A summer mulch will keep the soil moist, and picking should be done regularly.

Varieties: 1½–2 ft.—'Kelvedon Wonder,' 'Kelvedon Triumph,' and 'Meteor' (cloches); 2½ ft.—'Onward'; 3½–4 ft.—'Gladstone.'

Potatoes.—In general, it is only economic for the amateur to produce an early crop; the main winter supply can be grown if room and labour are available. They should be grown on land well manured the previous season, dressed at planting time with a mixed fertiliser, such as "National Growmore," at a rate of 1½ lb. to a 30-yd. row. The soil should not contain too much lime, as the damage of scab disease is increased.

"Seed" tubers about the size of a large egg are best used, and these can be bought or saved from the previous season's crop. Large potatoes may be cut leaving about three eyes to each part. New stocks should be bought occasionally if the "seed" is home saved to obviate risk of virus. "Seed" should be put in trays during February in a frost-proof shed to sprout, and in early April the "first-earlies" can be planted.

Drills 2 ft. apart and 4–5 in. deep are taken out and the sprouting "seed" planted 12 in. apart in the rows. Maincrop varieties are planted in early May 15 in. apart. The young growths should be protected from frost by earthing up slightly, and a further earthing is done as the potatoes mature. This practice of earthing prevents the tubers near the surface from becoming green when exposed to light, keeps weeds down, and protects the tubers from spores of potato blight, which are washed into the gullies. If growth is poor sulphate of ammonia can be applied at a rate of ¼ lb. per 30-yd. row. Early varieties should mature in late July and later varieties in September and October; when the tops (haulm) turn yellow the crop can be lifted, dried for a few hours (too much light will turn them green), and stored in boxes in a frost-proof shed or clamps. No damaged tubers should be stored. Clamps outside can be made by laying straw on a flat site and building the potatoes into a ridge-shaped heap; this is then covered with a thick layer of straw and then by a 6-in. layer of soil, interspersed with straw "chimneys" to aerate the clamp.

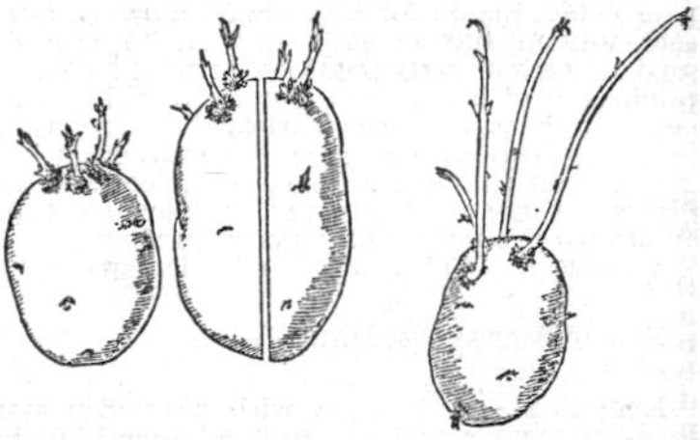

SEED POTATOES—Good seed is essential for first-rate crops. Illustration shows (*left*) a well-sprouted tuber, (*centre*) a large well-sprouted tuber suitable for cutting, and (*right*) a poor, badly sprouted tuber.

Potato blight is a common disease, and control by spraying with "Bouisol" before the leaves touch in the rows is effective. Virus diseases, spread by greenfly, are checked by using "seed" from Scotland, where greenfly is less troublesome because of the lower temperatures. Colorado beetle should be watched for, and if found notified to the Ministry of Agriculture.

Varieties: early—'Arran Pilot,' 'Duke of York,' and 'Epicure'; main—'Arran Banner,' 'King Edward,' and 'Majestic.'

Pumpkin.—*See* **Melon.**

Radish.—Most cultivated ground is suitable for growing radishes; successional sowings at fortnightly intervals from early March until May in drills ½ in. deep should be made. Summer-sown radishes bolt and are hot and tough, but autumn sowings for late salads can be made. As radishes germinate very quickly, they can be sown together with another crop and used quickly, and also enable the rows to be seen and hoed early.

Varieties: 'French Breakfast' and 'Scarlet Globe.'

Rhubarb.—Before planting the ground should be generously manured and deeply dug. Crowns are planted in March, 3–4 ft. apart each way and mulched, but no rhubarb should be pulled until the following year, when a light pull can be taken. Remove any flowering shoots and give a dressing of sulphate of ammonia if growth is weak. Manure well each winter; if early supplies are needed, some of the crowns can be covered with inverted boxes or barrels and a packing of loose straw or bracken. An established, well-cultivated bed will continue almost indefinitely.

Sage.—A hardy shrub for the herb garden easily raised from cuttings. The leaves are harvested and dried in summer.

Salsify (Oyster Plant).—A winter root rather like a parsnip which requires similar growing conditions.

Savoy.—*See* **Cabbage.**

Scorzonera.—A winter root cultivated in the same way as salsify. It has a purplish root instead of the yellow-green one of salsify.

Sea-kale.—A perennial plant native to our sea-shores, which can be either grown from seed sown in March and left for two years to produce forcing crowns or from bought thongs, which are planted during March, 9 in. apart in groups of three, leaving 3 ft. between groups. During summer a manure mulch and nitrogenous fertiliser can be applied. When the tops die down in autumn the crowns are covered with boxes to force and blanch the new growths. Crowns can be covered in succession to keep a supply. Earlier sea-kale can be obtained by lifting crowns in November. These are planted in batches five or six to a pot, watered well, and a second pot, with the hole blocked, placed over them. In a warm green-house or similar position they should develop sufficiently for cutting in about three weeks. Slugs are the chief pest outside, and should be kept in check by a proprietary slug-killer.

Shallots.—A popular crop for the small garden. Shallots are purchased as bulbs, like small onions. A deep, well-manured soil is required, as for onions, and they are planted during February, the bulbs being pressed about half their length into soft soil, 6 in. apart in the rows, leaving 1 ft. between rows. In mid-July the little bunches of bulbs can be lifted. Leave them on the surface to dry for a few days and then store in a dry, frost-proof shed. Some, about the size of a shilling, should be kept for planting the following year.

Spinach.—Sowings in February to April on a well-manured soil will provide a succession during the summer. Sow in drills 1 in. deep and 12 in. apart and thin the young plants to 3 in., and then to 6 in., using the second thinning to eat. A sowing of the prickly variety in August at the same distances will provide a winter crop. When picking gather a few leaves from each plant in the row.

Varieties: 'America' and 'Giant Prickly.'

Sprouting Broccoli.—*See* **Cauliflower.**

Sugar Beet.—*See* **Beetroot.**

Swede.—*See* **Turnip.**

Sweet Corn (Maize).—Gardeners should distinguish between the types of maize used for poultry food and those which supply sweet corn for human consumption. It is wise to use cloches for growing sweet corn, as it is only half-hardy and resents transplanting. Seeds sown under cloches in mid-April in two drills 12 in. apart and 1½ in. deep should be placed 1 ft. apart in staggered positions in the rows. More robust varieties may need 15 in. from plant to plant. A soil well manured for the previous crop is best used, and a mulch can be given as soon as the plants are a few inches high. The first cobs should be ready by mid-July, and should be eaten when the cob is milky.

Variety recommended: 'John Innes Hybrid.'

Tarragon.—A herb used for flavouring vinegar. Raised by root division in spring. Cut down and dried for use in winter.

Tomato.—A sunny, sheltered site is required, otherwise ripening outdoors in our climate is uncertain. Sow seeds under glass in late March and harden off the plants in a cold frame or buy plants for setting out in late May or early June. The soil should be thoroughly dug and some artificial manure applied before planting. Allow 18 in. between plants and 2½ ft. between rows, and put in a strong stake with each plant. Keep to a single stem, pinching out side shoots regularly. When four or five trusses are set pinch out the top of the main shoot.

Feed with a liquid manure during summer. Fruit which fails to ripen outdoors can be gathered and stored at about 50° Fahrenheit or the plants laid flat on the ground and covered with cloches, when the tomatoes should ripen. Under cloches plants can be planted out in mid-April instead of late May, gaining six weeks growing time, and the Cloches removed when they become too large.

Potato blight attacks tomatoes, and a spray of "Bouisol" during the first week in August and repeated after fourteen days will give a control.

Varieties: 'Market King' and 'Money-maker'; some heavy-cropping sorts have little or no flavour and a thick skin.

Turnips.—Ground manured the previous season should be dug well and dressed with 2 oz. super-phosphate per square yard. An early variety can be sown during April in drills ¾ in. deep and 15 in. apart, followed by successional sowings at three-week intervals as required. The main crop for storage is sown in July and August, and seed-lings should be thinned gradually to 10 in. apart. Use when about the size of tennis balls. A sowing can be made in September, left almost unthinned and the tops used as "greens" in spring. In autumn the storage crop is lifted and all un-damaged roots put in sand in a shed or clamped. Flea beetle and turnip fly can be checked by D.D.T. at the seedling stage.

Swedes are grown in a similar manner.

Varieties: turnips—'Early Milan' (summer) and 'Green Top Stone' (winter storage); swedes—'Purple Top.'

Standard References.

Cloche Gardening, by J. L. H. Chase (Faber) (1948) (15*s*.).

Gardening with Cloches, by Louis Flawn (Gifford) (1957) (16*s*.).

Vegetable Garden Displayed (R.H.S.) (1961) (6*s*.).

FERTILISERS AND ORGANIC MANURES.

The elements essential for healthy plant growth may be roughly grouped into classes—first, those required in some quantity, the major elements, nitrogen, potassium, and phosphorus; secondly, calcium, magnesium, and sulphur, which are required in lesser quantities; and thirdly, the trace elements, boron, manganese, iron, zinc, copper, and molybdenum, of which only minute quantities are needed. As well as the elements mentioned, others, such as silicon, aluminium, chlorine, nickel, and sodium, are often found on plant analysis, but the evidence that these are essential is inconclusive, though they may be beneficial to certain crops.

It is important to remember, when adding fertilisers to the soil, that different crops may require relatively more of one element than another, but a balance between all the elements is essential. As an instance, brassicas (the cabbage family) are gross nitrogen feeders, while root crops (*e.g.*, carrots) require far less nitrogen, and an excess may be harmful. A further point to notice is that although an element may be present in the soil the plant may be unable to absorb any because it is being kept in an insoluble state by excess of another element. An instance of this is the frequent yellow and sickly appearance of plants on very chalky soils due to lack of iron, which is present, but locked in an insoluble state by too much calcium.

The elements needed by the plant are in the form of various compounds, such as nitrates and phosphates, and may be applied as artificial fertilisers, which are manufactured, or as humus, which contains most of the foods required and also provides the essential soil micro-organisms or bacteria, without which the soil would be inert and no plants would grow. Bacteria break down the complicated animal and vegetable matter of which humus is composed to soluble compounds which plants can absorb. Humus can be supplied as farmyard and poultry manure, leaf mould, compost, sewage sludge, spent hops, and from animal by-products like hoof and horn, dried blood, meat and bone meal, and many others.

Nitrogen is mainly concerned with vegetative growth, encouraging leaf and stem formation. It is also contained in chlorophyll, the green colouring matter of the plant, and one of the symptoms of nitrogen starvation is a pale-green colour to the leaf, indicating a lack of chlorophyll. Most of the nitrogen compounds used are soluble, and it is a wise maxim to apply "little and often"; if given in large doses much is washed through the soil and wasted.

Nitrogenous fertiliser should not be given to any plant late in the season, as sappy growth, easily damaged by winter cold and frosts, is encouraged. Similarly, at no time should large quantities be given to any plant, as this results in an excess of leafy growth, which is very susceptible to disease and adverse conditions of drought and cold; also plants tend to be later flowering.

Sulphate of ammonia is the most used inorganic nitrogenous fertiliser, and is excellent for spring use on seed beds, lawns, and early crops, and it is contained in most fertiliser mixtures. It makes soils acid in reaction, and if both lime and nitrogen are required, nitro-chalk should be used instead. Other nitrogen fertilisers used are potassium nitrate, which has the advantage of supplying two major elements at once, and is very soluble, and nitrate of soda, often used on beet and mangolds. The latter chemical should not be applied in excess, as too much sodium has a bad effect on soil structure. These inorganic fertilisers are all soluble and quick acting. As a general guide, 1 oz. of the fertiliser to a gallon of water, applied at 1 oz. to a square yard, is a good general summer dressing, given at intervals of two or three weeks. It should always be given after rain or watering, and should be applied to the soil and not to the foliage.

Among organic fertilisers containing a percentage of easily available nitrogen are dried blood, soot, and meat and fish meals. Slower to decompose, and so having a more lasting effect, are shoddy (wool waste) and hoof and horn.

Phosphorus is concerned in the plant with the production of young cells of the root and shoot, and also encourages flower and fruit production and early ripening. Most of the compounds are relatively insoluble (rendering absorption by the plant difficult), and so large amounts can be supplied without deleterious effects, especially on acid soils, where the availability is less than on alkaline soils.

Phosphorus is generally applied to the soil in the form of phosphates, and among these superphosphate of lime is quick acting, and is usually applied at 2–3 oz. per sq. yd. in spring and summer, when the need is greatest. More slow acting is basic slag, a by-product of the steel industry, sold as a fine black powder and containing, besides phosphates, many of the trace elements, as well as a considerable percentage of lime. This is good for application to acid, wet soils, but should not be applied to potatoes owing to the risk of scab disease with the increase in the content of lime. It should not be applied with sulphate of ammonia. Bonemeal is also slow acting and also contains some nitrogen. It is excellent for crops like tomatoes, and is also used extensively for ornamental and pot plants.

Potassium, the third major element, is essential for good flower colour and ripeness in fruits. Dessert apples, potatoes, cereals, and root crops all need potash in some quantity, and if excess nitrogen has been applied a dressing of potash may counterbalance the effect. Sulphate of potash is the main inorganic compound in use. Muriate of potash (potassium chloride), to which some crops are sensitive, is much less used; it should be applied as a winter dressing before the crop is sown to lose the impurities by weathering. Sulphate of potash is purer, and may be applied during the growing season at 1 oz. per sq. yd. on the vegetable plot, and is used in many proprietary fertiliser mixtures.

Wood ash contains variable quantities of potassium, and provided that the ash has not been washed by rain and the potassium leached out, is a useful addition to the soil; bracken, cut during June and July, when large amounts of potassium are present in the foliage, can be composted when green to provide a good supply of the element.

Elements Required in Lesser Quantity.—Calcium, although required in small quantities in the plant, has profound effects on the soil. Its main function in the plant is in the production of the cell walls, but in the soil it helps to bind light soils together and to make the structure of sticky clay soils finer and more workable. Also soils without calcium are acid and tend to lock up some elements in an insoluble form. Addition of calcium changes the acidity, making it slightly alkaline or neutral, and releases the locked elements.

Calcium is applied as some form or derivative of calcium carbonate, commonly known as lime, which can be obtained in various forms. Hydrated or slaked lime (calcium hydroxide) is commonly used on clay soils, and chalk or ground limestone on lighter soils. Calcium is gradually leached from the soil, and it is necessary to replace it, or the soil becomes too acid and many crops will fail to grow. A normal dressing of lime for a vegetable garden is about 4 oz. lime or ½ lb. chalk per square yard every two or three years, and is best applied in autumn as a surface dressing after digging. It should not be applied together with other fertilisers. The amount of lime will depend on the type of soil, but it must be remembered that most vegetables grow best on a slightly acid soil.

Gypsum, or calcium sulphate, is sometimes recommended to supply calcium, but its solubility is negligible, and it is preferable to chalk or limestone only on soils containing salt due to sea flooding. It has been used to help reclaim parts of East Anglia flooded by sea-water during recent years by improving the soil structure. Sulphur, as sulphates, and magnesium, as an impurity in limestone, are usually present in sufficient quantities for the plants' needs.

Trace Elements.—In the case of the trace elements most soils contain enough for the plant, but in certain circumstances deficiencies occur. Iron on very alkaline soils is insoluble and, as it is essential for the production of chlorophyll, deficiency results in the chlorosis of the leaves. It can be rectified by spraying the leaves with "Sequestrene Plus," as can the lack of magnesium and manganese, which may also be deficient on acid soils.

Chlorosis in brassicas and marsh spot of peas are due to magnesium deficiency. Boron deficiency, often occurring on light, calcareous soils, is responsible for brown heart of cauliflower and several other "diseases," mainly affecting the growing point. It can be rectified by applying borax to the soil at about 1 oz. per 15 sq. yd. Zinc and copper deficiencies are unusual in England, but lack of molybdenum has caused whiptail disease of cauliflower. Only minute quantities of the last three are required; more may be poisonous to plants and animals.

Organic Manures.—It should be noted that most of the deficiencies will not concern the amateur, especially if he keeps the ground in good heart with ample organic manure, which contains all the plant foods necessary. Well-rotted farmyard manure from cows and pigs is by far the best organic food, but is scarce now, good farmers returning it to their own land, and generally the material offered is low in nutrients. Poultry manure, which is rich in soluble nitrogen salts, is excellent either applied direct to the soil (not to the growing crop for fear of damage) or composted with straw.

Many substitutes have been devised to use in place of manure, among them sewage sludge, best applied some time before growing the crop, spent hops from breweries, dried seaweed, excellent for potatoes when supplemented by superphosphate, soot, rich in nitrogen, composted town refuse, and the waste organic animal products mentioned earlier. The organic matter in all these materials is essential for maintaining the soil structure and cannot be replaced simply by artificial fertilisers.

Liquid manure, produced by suspending an old sack of animal manure or soot in water for a few days, is useful for the amateur to apply to pot plants and to individual crops like sweet peas, tomatoes, and chrysanthemums. Leaf mould and peat can be used as a mulch and also to supply organic matter to the soil. Sawdust in a well-rotted condition is also useful for inclusion in compost and as a mulch. It is emphasised that it must be well-rotted, and it is advisable to apply a nitrogen fertiliser, such as sulphate of ammonia, at the same time.

Composting of organic refuse from house and garden is much practised by the amateur nowadays.

Compost-making.—The methods developed for making compost heaps are many and various; they depend on three basic principles, good aeration, plenty of moisture, and a nitrogen supply for the decomposition bacteria. A fairly simple method by which much garden and house refuse can be utilised is as follows. An area about 9 ft. by 4 ft. is marked out and all waste vegetable matter—weeds, lawn mowings, cabbage leaves, pea haulm, straw, dead leaves, and hedge clippings—are put in this area and trodden down. Care should be taken not to use diseased material but grass clippings and weeds which have been recently treated with hormone weed-killers may be applied. When the heap is about 9 in. thick it is sprinkled with sulphate of ammonia and superphosphate, at ½ oz. of each per square yard (2 oz. of each for a 9-ft. by 4-ft. plot) and any wood ash available, and then sprinkled with 4 gallons of water and covered with an inch of soil. This process is repeated with 9-in. layers of rubbish until the heap is about 4 ft. high, when it is better to begin a second heap. A sprinkling of ground lime may be given as each layer is added, but should not be applied until after watering to avoid reaction with the sulphate of ammonia.

The completed heap should be watered occasionally, and after about a month or six weeks, if time permits, it can be turned completely over, watered again, and re-covered with soil. The heap may then be left until rotted, and the compost can be dug in as required; any unrotted material can be used as a basis for a new heap. The time taken for rotting will vary with the time of year and material used, but generally a compost heap made during the summer should be available for autumn use, and one made during the autumn ready for spring use.

There are a number of compounds on the market, known as compost makers, which are said to accelerate the decomposition, but in general a heap made in the way described is eminently satisfactory, and although requiring a certain amount of labour, is the least expensive way of obtaining humus for the garden. This latter point is extremely important nowadays with the scarcity of animal manure and the high costs of both inorganic and organic fertilisers. Prices are, of course, not static, but comparatively the organic manures, such as dried blood, hoof and horn, and guano, are more expensive than the inorganic salts, but these lack humus, which is an essential of a well-cultivated soil.

General Fertiliser.—Many firms supply compound fertilisers containing given amounts of the main nutrients needed, in either liquid or powder form, and some are made up with quantities of nitrogen, potassium, and phosphorus suitable for specific crops like roses, tomatoes, and chrysanthemums. A general fertiliser which can be made up by the amateur is as follows:

7 parts by weight superphosphate.
5 parts by weight sulphate of ammonia.
2 parts by weight sulphate of potash.

All the ingredients are easily obtained from local sundriesmen, and a mixture of this sort will supply a good general feed.

Green Manuring.—Another method of enriching the soil with organic matter is green manuring, which has been practised for some time by farmers and can no doubt be adapted to the gardener's purpose. Green manuring consists of planting a fast-growing catch-crop and ploughing the mature crop back into the soil. Legumes are especially good for this, as certain bacteria in their roots can "fix" the nitrogen in the air. Field peas, sown at 4 oz. per sq. yd. and Italian rye grass at 2 oz. per sq. yd. are commonly used, and clover and annual lupins are also suitable.

If sown after an early crop on land needing organic matter the green manure may be dug in during late summer. Alternatively, if the land is not being cropped at all during the year two green-manure crops may be grown; an early sowing of field peas in April may be dug in during July, and a further sowing of field peas or Italian rye grass sown immediately after may be dug in following the first few frosts.

New chemicals often appear on the market at exorbitant prices and with fantastic claims as to their value as "soil conditioners" and the like. Contrary to this generalisation, in recent years a chemical known as "Gibberellin" has been used to increase the growth of certain plants. It is now available to the amateur, but should be used with care and mainly in a spirit of experimentation, as no conclusive proof of its efficacy has yet been put forward.

Standard References.

Gardener's Earth, by S. B. Whitehead (Dent), revised ed. 1952 (9*s*. 6*d*.). *Manures and Fertilisers*, by A. M. Smith (Nelson), 1952 (15*s*.). *Seed and Potting Composts*, by Lawrence and Newell (Allen and Unwin) (9*s*. 6*d*.).

GARDEN PESTS.

Every garden abounds in insects and other small creatures, but comparatively few species are pests which feed on plants. The great majority are quite harmless, while many are positively beneficial and help to keep the number of pests under control by catching and eating them. Every good gardener should make it his business to be able to differentiate between friend and foe. This is not always easy, but the speed of a creature's movements may often provide a clue. Fast-running, active creatures, such as the black ground-beetle or the centipede, are usually beneficial, while the slow-moving and sluggish ones, *e.g.*, wireworms, aphids and caterpillars, are usually pests. This is by no means an infallible rule, but it is handy to remember when in doubt.

The good gardener should also get to know the pests which are most prevalent in his district and which can be expected to crop up year after year. The first principle of good control measures is to act while an infestation is still in its early stages and before a great deal of damage is done. When one knows what to expect, steps can be taken to prevent an attack or to stop it developing to serious proportions.

Also, from the experience of past years one can often forecast whether a pest is likely to become numerous enough to make chemical treatment worthwhile. Remember, insecticides can become an expensive item, and there is little point in using them if the damage is negligible. In these circumstances insecticides may eventually increase the numbers of pests, since the treatment will also have killed off many of their natural enemies which had hitherto kept the pests under adequate control. In addition, good cultivation and general garden hygiene helps to reduce the numbers of pests.

The common pests of garden plants can be roughly divided into four main groups.

I. Root Pests.—These destroy the feeding mechanism of plants or tunnel into fleshy tap roots, tubers, and bulbs. Attacked plants make poor growth, and may eventually wilt and die.

Some insects are general root-feeders. These include (*a*) **Swift Moth Caterpillars**, soft, white caterpillars with reddish-brown heads; (*b*) **Chafer Grubs**, large, C-shaped, whitish grubs with chestnut-brown heads; (*c*) **Wireworms**, long, cylindrical, yellowish-brown grubs with a hard shiny skin; and (*d*) **Leatherjackets**, greyish-black grubs with a wrinkled, leathery skin. These are particularly prevalent in recently cultivated grassland or in gardens surrounded by fields, and will attack the roots of a wide range of plants. Chafer grubs, however, are particularly fond of the roots of shrubs, and wireworms will often tunnel in potato tubers and other fleshy roots, whereas leatherjackets prefer the roots of grasses, and may cause browning on large patches of lawn.

Badly infested ground should be dressed with lindane dust when cultivating, working the dust into the top 4 in. of soil. Where this is not possible, *i.e.*, on lawns or around established shrubs, the liquid form of the insecticide should be watered into the soil.

Cutworms are stout, fleshy caterpillars, varying in colour from greyish-brown to dingy green. They feed on roots during the day, but at night come to the surface and feed at the base of the stems of plants, causing them suddenly to collapse and wither. Brassicas and lettuce are commonly damaged in this way. Infested ground should be dusted with D.D.T.

Millepedes are hard-skinned, cylindrical creatures, brown or black, with numerous short, hair-like legs. They are slow-moving and curl up when disturbed. They should not be confused with the active, long-legged centipedes, which are beneficial. Millepedes commonly extend the damage made by other pests, such as slugs and wireworms. They also bore into the sown seeds of peas and beans. During the day they hide in dark, damp places, such as long vegetation or under stones and pieces of wood. Such hiding-places should be removed or dusted with lindane. Drills for pea and bean seed should also be dusted before covering.

Weevil Grubs, small, curved, white grubs, may infest the roots of pot plants and plants in rockeries. Such plants should be removed, the roots cleaned, and replanted in soil which has been dressed or mixed with lindane dust. Where it is not practicable to remove the plants they should be watered copiously with a liquid form of these insecticides and soil dressed properly at the earliest opportunity.

Slugs need no description. They vary greatly in colour. The most destructive are the underground keeled slugs, small, grey-black in colour, which tunnel in roots, tubers, and bulbs. There are also several foliage-feeding species which rasp holes in the top parts of plants. Slugs like wet conditions, and much can be done to control them by ensuring that the soil is well-drained and that long, tangled vegetation is removed.

Poison baits can be bought or made by mixing 1 oz. metaldehyde with 3 lb. bran (or bonemeal for keeled slugs). The bait is sprinkled over the infested ground or distributed in small heaps and protected from the rain. There is also available on the market a metaldehyde spray for dealing with the foliage-feeding types.

Cabbage Root Fly attacks brassicas and wallflowers. The small white maggot eats away the side roots and tunnels in the main root, causing the plant to wilt and collapse. The roots of young seedlings should be dipped in lindane before planting out. Alternatively, the plants can be given a drench of lindane within four days of planting out.

The maggots also tunnel in radishes and turnips, and this can be avoided by dusting the seed drills with lindane.

Carrot Fly.—The maggot of this fly tunnels in carrots and parsnips. Where the pest is serious it is best to delay sowing until the end of May. If possible, seeds should be sown in exposed, windy places, which are avoided by the egg-laying flies. Seedlings should be dusted or sprayed with lindane when 2–4 in. high, particularly in late May or early August, the peak periods for egg-laying.

Onion Fly maggots tunnel into the bulbs of onions, leeks, and shallots, causing the foliage to collapse. Dig out attacked plants carefully, ensuring that parts of them are not left in the soil, and burn them. To prevent attacks dust around the seedlings with lindane when they are at the "loop" stage, *i.e.*, about 1 in. high, and again ten days later.

Narcissus Bulb Flies are serious pests of narcissi and also snowdrops and other bulbous plants. The maggots burrow in the centre of the bulbs, causing them to rot. All soft bulbs should be burned and the remainder immersed for three hours in a solution of lindane containing a wetter. To prevent future attacks and a reinfestation, dust around the necks of growing bulbs with lindane at fortnightly intervals from the end of April until the end of June.

Insects which feed above ground include:

II. Sucking Pests pierce the tissues of plants with needle-like mouth parts and suck the sap. This devitalises the plant, checks growth, and causes wilting. Some species cause distortion of leaves and young shoots, and aphids, suckers, scale insects, and mealy bugs excrete a sugary fluid which disfigures the foliage, attracts ants, and allows the growth of sooty moulds.

Aphids, *i.e.*, blackfly, greenfly, etc., are serious pests which attack almost all plants and multiply rapidly in warm weather. They feed on the shoots and undersides of the leaves, and many species are responsible for the transmission of virus diseases. Infestations should be treated as early as possible. Malathion, lindane, D.D.T. emulsion, and nicotine are all good sprays to use, and should be applied to the undersides of the leaves. With the advent of these sprays the control of aphids on roses and broad beans, for example, is no longer a serious problem.

Tree fruits should be sprayed when the buds are bursting and again when the flower buds are still green. Currants should be treated at the "grape" stage, but lindane should not be used on this fruit. Tar oil, applied to deciduous woody plants while they are completely dormant, will kill the overwintering stages of these and many other pests. It does not, however, give a good winter control for **Woolly Aphid** on apples. This pest is best controlled by spraying at the pink-bud stage with B.H.C. with a succinate spreader added. Small colonies on the bark can be eradicated by painting with 10% tar oil.

Some aphids feed underground on roots, particularly of lettuces, currants, and cacti. Where practicable, infested plants should be lifted and the roots cleaned and sprayed before replanting in clean soil. Otherwise water them copiously with malathion or lindane.

Scale Insects are often found in greenhouses, but also occur out-of-doors on trees and shrubs. Flat or dome-shaped, these creatures spend most of their lives immobile, and they do not at all resemble insects, or even appear to be alive. Again tar oil is useful for killing the overwintering stages on deciduous woody shrubs which are dormant. Plants which are in leaf should be sprayed with malathion or nicotine/white oil emulsion two or three times at fortnightly intervals. These substances are more effective if as much as possible of the scale is first removed by means of a sponge, brush, or scraper with water in which soft soap has been dissolved. **Mealy Bugs** are common pests of greenhouse plants, and should be given the same treatment as scale insects.

Capsid Bugs are very active insects which cause considerable damage to fruit trees and bushes and also to various ornamental plants, principally chrysanthemums and dahlias. They feed on the young leaves, causing distortion and raggedness, and on the buds, which later produce misshapen blooms. These insects, green or reddish in colour, can be controlled by spraying with lindane or D.D.T. when the flower buds are still green (tree fruit) or with D.D.T. at the " grape " stage (currants). Herbaceous plants should be sprayed two or three times at three-weekly intervals, starting when the plants are young and before the damage is seen. The ground under the plants should also be sprayed to kill those insects which fall off during treatment.

Leafhoppers are small, yellowish-green insects like aphids but much more active. They feed on the undersides of the leaves of a variety of plants, causing them to become speckled with yellow. Roses are commonly attacked. The treatment given to capsids on herbaceous plants will control these also, the sprays being directed to the undersides of the leaves.

Whiteflies are serious pests in greenhouses, and also occur out-of-doors on rhododendrons and other evergreen shrubs. The adults are like miniature moths with white wings, and the young are small, scale-like creatures, generally greenish in colour, which feed without movement on the undersides of the leaves. To control this pest D.D.T., lindane, or malathion should be used as a spray or smoke, two to three applications being given at fortnightly intervals.

Red Spider Mites are extremely small creatures, red or greenish in colour and just visible with the naked eye. They feed on the undersides of the leaves of many greenhouse and outdoor plants, including fruit, causing the leaves to turn sickly yellow. Control is difficult, the most effective materials being malathion, derris, summer ovicides, or azobenzene smoke. The directions on the labels of these products should be followed carefully.

III. Biting Insects have chewing and biting mouth parts which are used to cut away pieces of plants.

Caterpillars (the young stages of moths and butterflies) are the best-known pests in this group. They vary in size and colour according to the species, and most plants are liable to be attacked. These should be sprayed or dusted with D.D.T. or derris as soon as damage is seen. On fruit trees D.D.T. should be used when the fruit buds are still green, and again at the pink-bud stage if the infestation is serious.

The Codling Caterpillar, which tunnels in apples, is controlled by spraying with D.D.T. at the end of June and again three weeks later. Since this latter treatment tends to encourage red spider mites, it is advisable to add to the D.D.T. one of the materials recommended for these pests.

Sawfly Caterpillars are very similar to those above, and commonly attack gooseberry and rose foliage. They can be controlled by spraying with D.D.T., derris, or lindane. Attacks by the **Apple Sawfly**, which burrows in young apples and forms ribbon-like scars on the skin, can be prevented by spraying with lindane seven days after 80% of the blossom has fallen.

Beetles and Weevils which feed on foliage are usually best controlled by spraying or dusting with D.D.T. To kill the tiny **Flea-beetles** which eat small holes in the seedlings of brassicas and turnips, treat the plants at fourteen-day intervals until they reach the " rough-leaf " stage.

The golden-brown **Raspberry Beetle**, which feeds on the flowers and whose grub tunnels in the fruit, is eradicated by D.D.T. or derris applied ten days after full bloom and again ten days later. For other common pests in this group, *e.g.*, **Vine Weevil, Clay-coloured Weevil, Pea and Bean Weevil**, etc., apply the D.D.T. as soon as the damage is first seen.

Earwigs feed at night on the foliage and flower petals of many plants. They hide by day inside flowers, in the folds of leaves, and in nooks and crannies on the ground, under flat stones, etc. These pests are killed by D.D.T., applied to the plants (but not to open flowers) and to their hiding-places.

Leaf Miners are very small grubs which tunnel between the upper and lower surfaces of leaves, forming pale blisters, as on lilac, holly, celery, etc., or long, twisting galleries, as on chrysanthemum, pea, and tomato. In small infestations the affected leaves should be picked off and burned. Otherwise spray with lindane as soon as the damage starts, giving three applications at fourteen-day intervals.

IV. Eelworms are microscopic pests which are invisible to the naked eye. They are able to live for very long periods without food and are extremely difficult to eradicate. The most common species are:

Stem and Bulb Eelworm, which infests narcissus, phlox, strawberry, hyacinth, onion, and other plants. Infested plants show distorted foliage and dwarfing and gradually deteriorate. They can only be sterilised by immersion in hot water kept at well-defined temperatures for one to three hours, but expert diagnosis and advice should be obtained before this or any other control is attempted. Infested ground must be kept clear of any host plants for at least three years to starve out the eelworms.

Chrysanthemum Eelworm causes the formation of yellowish blotches between the veins of chrysanthemum leaves, which later turn black and drop off. In severe infestations the blooms are undersized and malformed. Expert advice should be obtained before control measures are attempted.

Potato Root Eelworm is a serious and widespread pest of potatoes, causing the plants to become stunted and sickly, giving very poor yields. The pest can only be kept in check by crop rotation, potatoes being grown on the same ground only once in four years. This is difficult in small gardens, and where land becomes heavily infested the only remedy is to rest it from potatoes for at least five years.

The Purchase and Use of Insecticides.—To ensure that an insecticide will do what the maker claims, it is advisable only to buy brands which have been tested and approved by the Ministry of Agriculture. This can be ascertained by the presence of an Approval Mark (**T30**) on the label. Read the directions and follow them carefully. Over-strength insecticides can cause damage to plants, and certain plants (usually listed) can be injured by some insecticides at any concentration, *e.g.*, cucumbers, marrows, etc., by D.D.T. and lindane. Never apply insecticides to flowers in full bloom, otherwise many valuable pollinating insects will be killed.

Standard References.

Encyclopaedia of Garden Pests and Diseases, by van Konynenburg and Lawfield (Collingridge), 1958 (42*s*.).

Horticultural Pests: Detection and Control, by G. Fox Wilson, revised by P. Becker (Crosby Lockwood), 1960 (25*s*.).

DISEASES OF PLANTS.

Plant diseases are important because they can cause great loss not only in growing crops but also in the produce after it has been harvested and stored. The skill in growing crops is wasted if they are destroyed by disease, and many people know the wastage of potatoes through blight disease in winter stores and rotting of onions when they decay through neck rot disease. For these reasons the keen gardener must take notice of diseases and use the knowledge available to him in checking them wherever possible.

The most important point to remember about plant diseases is to recognise the first signs so that the remedy can be applied at once. In greenhouses this is of great importance because the atmosphere is warm and moist, and in such conditions diseases flourish. It must also be remembered that the same crop is often grown in the same soil in a greenhouse so that we get a build-up of disease, and this causes the well-known "soil sickness." This means that new soil must be brought in or the old soil enriched and also sterilised by steam or by chemicals. Even frames and propagating pits require periodic cleaning up by a disinfection treatment.

Unlike insect pests, the actual cause of a plant disease cannot be seen with the naked eye, and microscopic examination is required for its detection. The scientists who study diseases are called plant pathologists, and these are stationed

THE APPROVAL MARK—An officially approved crop-protection product shows on its label this design.

at universities and other institutes throughout the country, where they carry out research on various plant troubles and advise on suitable remedies for checking them. It is obviously necessary to understand the exact cause of a disease and how that cause operates before a means of checking the trouble can be devised. The advice can then be passed on to growers, farmers, and the gardening public.

The presence of disease in most cases can only be detected by the symptoms shown by the affected plant, which is called the "host" plant. The actual cause must then be determined by careful examination in the laboratory, which is done by the pathologist.

Plant diseases in general are divided into three classes as follows: 1. Fungus and Bacterial. 2. Virus. 3. Functional Disorders.

1. Fungus and Bacterial Diseases.—The first kind called fungus diseases are caused by the attack of fungus parasites; examples being the well-known club root of cabbages, potato scab, apple scab, and plum brown rot. These parasitic fungi are microscopic and composed of fine threads, but they attack plants and penetrate them either through wounds (insect bites, hail damage, pruning cuts) or directly through the surface cells (epidermis). The threads grow into the plant, killing the cells and absorbing their contents. There is usually some discoloration or even decay of the tissues around the point of infection, but it is possible for the plant to show distress in one part although the parasite is at work some distance away. Examples are silver leaf in plums and the honey fungus, which kills trees by attacking the roots.

The fungus spreads by means of spores which are equivalent to seeds in flowering plants but which are microscopic in size. These spores are produced on the surface of the plant in enormous numbers and are blown (wind), splashed (rain), or carried (insects, etc.) in all directions to alight on other healthy plants, where they germinate and spread the disease. This occurs in the growing season, but when winter approaches, the parasite forms tough, resting bodies of one kind or another, and these are resistant to extreme cold.

They overwinter in the soil or in the surface of tree bark, etc., so that in the following spring they can germinate and cause disease again. So we get the reappearance of such troubles as damping off in seedlings, scab in apples, brown rot in apples and plums, foot rot in peas, wart disease in potatoes, mildews on all kinds of plants, and so on. This question of soil contamination by overwintering spores is one of the most serious in the fight against plant disease.

The signs of fungus and bacterial diseases are varied, and may show as yellowing, silvering, brown spotting, or blackening of leaves (potato blight, rose black spot, celery leaf spot, antirrhinum rust), as stunting (cabbage wire stem), as pustules and cankers in stems (coral spot, apple canker), as gumming or dieback in branches (rose canker, plum dieback), as galls, warts, witches brooms, or other malformation (club root in cabbages, crown gall, leafy gall, peach leaf curl), as dry or soft rots of fruits, tubers, vegetable bulbs, and corms (gladiolus dry rot, potato dry rot, iris rhizome rot, celery heart rot), and many other abnormal conditions. Sometimes only a part of the plant is affected and can be removed, *e.g.*, branches showing attack by coral spot or one of the large bracket fungi seen on trees, these having gained entrance through a wound.

2. Virus Diseases.—This class of disease is becoming increasingly important as more is discovered about them, although research on them is a comparatively recent development. A virus disease is caused by infection with a virus, and the exact nature of this is not yet clearly understood, but it is so small that it cannot be seen with ordinary microscopes. Its detection is therefore not easy, but when the sap of a virus-diseased plant is injected into a healthy one it causes the disease.

In nature this spread is brought about by biting and sucking insects, which are referred to as **Vectors.** They transmit the virus by feeding on infected plants and then travelling to healthy ones, on which they feed and so spread the disease. Most viruses are transmitted by aphids (greenflies).

In the garden and nursery they can be carried from plant to plant by pruning knives or by the fingers in the process of trimming plants such as tomatoes, melons, and cucumbers or by the use of the knife in taking cuttings. In general, the virus does not kill a plant quickly but tends to cripple it and cause a slow deterioration. Infected plants cannot recover but remain, sometimes for years, as sources of infection on which insects feed and carry on the disease. So viruses may increase in lily stocks, strawberry beds, and raspberry plantations unless virus-infected plants are removed and aphids strictly suppressed.

The signs of virus disease are of different kinds, but the commonest are those of the type called mosaic, in which the leaves show a mottling with light-green or yellow patches scattered in irregular fashion on the darker green of the leaf. There may be also some reduction in the leaf blades. These symptoms can be seen in the mosaic of cucumber, vegetable marrow, lettuce, cabbage, turnip, tomato, delphinium, primula, dahlia, apple, raspberry, and many other common plants. In some, such as lilies, daffodils, and onions, the mosaic is more in the form of stripes down the leaf blades.

Another virus symptom is flower "breaking," where the normal colour of the petals is broken by streaks and spots of white, and this can be seen in tulip, wallflower, pansy, stocks, or carnations affected by the mosaic virus. Other viruses cause bronzing of the top leaves (as in tomato spotted wilt) or small light-coloured rings arranged in concentric circles (as in dahlia ring spot) or even reduction of leaves until they are tendril like (as in tomato fern leaf). Sometimes there is malformation or even proliferation, producing innumerable stunted shoots, as in blackberry dwarf disease.

The important point to note about these virus diseases is that every part of the plant is quickly infected, so that the sap is infectious to other plants of the same kind. The virus is present in all parts, and for this reason it is useless to propagate from a virus-infected plant. This means that all the scales and offsets from bulbs such as lilies and tulips, all the tubers from potatoes, and all cuttings from herbaceous plants which are taken from a virus-infected plant are useless, because they will carry the virus. They should be destroyed, and the only exception is where the plant is greatly valued, in which case seed can be taken from it before it is destroyed. In general, viruses do not travel in the seed, and only in one or two cases is seed infected, and this only in negligible quantity.

3. Functional Disorders.—This third class of disease is often called non-parasitic, because unlike the previous two kinds there is no parasite involved, and these troubles are therefore not infectious. They are due to faulty cultivation or unsuitable environment, in which soil conditions or climate affect the plants adversely. In this group we include cases of unsatisfactory growth due to waterlogging, drought, frost, high temperature, damage by fumes or atmospheric pollution, or even excess lime.

Perhaps the most important kinds of trouble in this class are the so called **Deficiency Diseases**, where the plants suffer from shortage of some important food. This may be one of the common food substances, such as nitrogen, potash, or phosphate, and details will be found under the section on manures and fertilisers (**T25**).

CONTROL OF DISEASES.

1. Garden Hygiene.—The control of plant diseases can be dealt with only briefly, but to begin with we must emphasise the value of good cultivation as an insurance against losses from disease. Robust plants are better able to stand up to disease than sickly ones, and everything in the way of proper drainage, soil aeration, proper spacing, sensible feeding, and so on, will help to keep the plants vigorous, and this is the first line of defence against diseases. Garden hygiene is important, weeds need to be kept down, wounds in trees and shrubs covered with a good paint against infection, new stocks examined carefully, seed bought only from reliable sources, diseased plants burnt, and dead material regularly removed from plants, especially in greenhouses.

2. Soil Sterilisation.—There are other precautions, among which the sterilisation of the soil in greenhouses by means of steam or chemicals is of some importance. Outdoors this is not possible, but rotation of crops is a most useful system in helping to avoid disease. Disinfection of frames, propagating pits, and seed boxes by formalin or cresylic acid are other useful measures.

All these operations aim at destroying the resting spores of fungus parasites responsible for such diseases as tomato leaf mould, gladiolus dry rot, damping off in seedlings, root rots, and downy mildews of many kinds in young plants such as stocks, cheiranthus, cineraria, tomato, aster, and calceolaria when grown in boxes or pots.

3. Disease Resistant Plants.—The use of disease-resistant varieties of plants is very desirable, but there are not many kinds available, and often the resistant kind does not possess flowers or fruit of such fine quality or flavour as the more susceptible kind. The outstanding success of this kind is that of potatoes immune to the dreaded wart disease, and these can be grown safely in the most heavily infected land. There are antirrhinums resistant to rust disease, and there is resistance in some degree in the case of delphinium mildew, potato blight, tomato leaf mould, and some others. Research goes on to discover still more, because any such plants are always worth a trial.

4. Treatment of Seeds and Bulbs.—For seed-borne diseases seed treatments may be done with an organo-mercurial seed dressing, or even by immersion of the infected seed in warm water.

In some diseases, for example, tulip fire, we can protect the bulbs from the danger of infected soil by raking in a powder such as "Botrolex" when planting the bulbs, and a similar treatment is done with calomel dust against club root in beds intended for sowing brassica seeds.

5. Fungicides.—Even after all this, a disease may still appear in the crop, and more direct action must be taken. It is then necessary to protect the plants by means of a **Fungicide**. This is a chemical which is poisonous to fungus parasites but which will not harm the crop plant (host). Fungicides are used as wet sprays or in powder form as dusts, and they are sprayed or dusted all over the plants to protect them from infection by diseases.

The object of the treatment is to cover the plants with a film of the fungicide so as to protect the still healthy ones. To help the spray fluid to spread over and adhere to the foliage another substance, called a wetter, spreader, or sticker, is added to the spray, but sometimes this is already included by the manufacturer.

5. (*a*) Sprays.—Sprays are applied by means of machines called sprayers which vary from small, hand-syringe types giving a continuous jet of spray to those pumped up to a pressure and carried on the back (knapsack machines), and so on to the large machines driven by a petrol engine, which deliver the spray at a high pressure. It is necessary to have a suitable nozzle giving a fine mist-like cone of spray which settles on the foliage and is not wasted.

5. (*b*) Dusts.—Dusts are similar chemicals produced in such finely divided form that the powder can be blown over and on the foliage almost like a fog. This is best done after a shower of rain or after a heavy dew. The machines used are far more varied in design than spraying machines. There are small hand dusters worked either like a small pump or like a bellows, of which the "Acme" is a good example, and there are those which are carried on the back and worked as a double-bellows action or on the front of the body with a rotary-fan action. It is important in gardens to clean and dry the machines after use, and small sprayers may be best put upside down to drain for a time after use.

The substances used as sprays and dusts against plant diseases for many years have been copper and sulphur and their compounds. Perhaps the best known copper-containing spray is "Bordeaux Mixture," which is still a good spray, but which has been largely replaced by colloidal copper available under trade names like "Coppicide" for such diseases as tomato blight, etc. Sulphur is used extensively as lime-sulphur against apple scab and as colloidal sulphur against the powdery mildew diseases. As dusts, copper is mixed with lime to give copper–lime dust and sulphur is used alone either as flowers of sulphur or green sulphur.

5. (*c*) The Newer Fungicides.—In recent years much research has been carried out in tests to see whether other chemicals have value as fungicides, and the search has been in the field of organic chemistry and among all kinds of these chemicals. Tests of this kind take a long time, but a few substances have already been picked out as showing great promise, and we can mention "Captan," which is so good against apple and pear scab, "Zineb" aginst tomato leaf mould, onion mildew, and tulip fire, "Karathane" against any of the powdery mildews, such as american gooseberry mildew, strawberry mildew, vine and peach mildews, as well as the same diseases on ornamental roses, delphiniums, michaelmas daisies, and the like.

6. Control of Viruses.—The control of virus diseases is very different, because in this case the only spray treatments likely to be of use are those designed to keep down insects. The other necessary control measure is to remove and destroy the virus-infected plants, which are a danger as sources of infection.

This is best done when the plants are young, so that any young marrows, cucumbers, dahlias, delphiniums, sweet peas, lupins, lilies, etc., which show virus symptoms as commonly revealed in leaf mottling and poor growth should be removed as soon as detected. Propagation should be done carefully, so that young stock is not propagated from stocks of strawberries, raspberries, and all kinds of herbaceous perennials which show signs of virus infection. Even the knife used for taking cuttings should be wiped occasionally on a rag dipped in a good disinfectant.

7. Prevention of Functional Disorders.—In the case of Functional Disorders (non-parasitic diseases) it is not always easy to advise remedies. Where the soil conditions are faulty attention can be directed to improving drainage if necessary or counteracting dryness by digging in humus, irrigating, and general mulching. Dryness at the roots of tomatoes causes loss of fruit, and so does extreme dryness in the air of the greenhouse, but these should be adjusted fairly easily.

Hail damage can spoil many crops, but robust foliage may help a little to lessen the damage. Late frost damage to fruit in some areas can be lessened by various methods of cultivation and planting. The effects of drought can be aggravated by shortage of certain foods, especially potash, so that even here some attempt can be made to avoid loss. Excess liming may cause food shortages by causing the appearance, in the leaves, of a yellowish or even whitish colour, which is known as lime-induced chlorosis. The real reason may be lack of iron or manganese due to the excess lime in the soil, but recently very good results at counteracting this condition have been obtained by using the substance known as "Sequestrene Plus."

Another method of treating these food shortages is to spray the young foliage in early summer with the required element in a very weak solution. They can even be included in sprays used for keeping down diseases or pests. It must not be forgotten that even the ordinary foods, such as nitrogen, potash, and phosphate, may sometimes be in short supply, and the effect can be seen by the trained plant pathologist. In these cases the effect may not always show clearly in the growing crop, but may appear long afterwards in the stored fruits and vegetables, which as a result deteriorate and break down long before they are required for use.

The present-day methods of cultivating large numbers of the same plant in one spot tend to increase the risk of large-scale disease attacks. Modern plants may be highly bred and selected for great purity of strain. Indeed, they have often been chosen for fine quality and flavour, with little regard to their ability to resist disease, so that the gardener must always be ready to give them the protection they may need.

Standard References.

Diseases of Vegetables, by Donald E. Green (Macmillan), 1946 (8*s*. 6*d*.).

Plant Diseases, by F. T. Brooks (Oxford), 1953 (38*s*.).

Diseases of Fruit and Hops, by H. Wormald (Crosby Lockwood), 1955 (25*s*.).

USES OF MODERN WEEDKILLERS

The eradication of weeds by chemical means is one of the greatest advances of recent years albeit the value of herbicides is still unappreciated by most gardeners. With a planned programme, all cultivated ground and lawns can be kept free of weeds without hoeing or any other sort of manual cultivation.

Occasionally troubles have arisen in not following makers' instructions. Sometimes the damage has been most unfortunate, as the majority of herbicides are toxic, in varying degrees, to a wide range of plant life. In the main, controls are determined by circumstance, as typified in the following cases:

Asparagus Beds.—Annuals and top growth of perennial weeds can be controlled with cresylic acid in the autumn and before the asparagus appears in the spring. In beds free of perennials, a first-class control of weeds can be maintained with Simazine applied in the early spring.

Where annual and perennial grasses predominate, Dalapon or Diquat will give good control. As for bindweed, this may be eradicated by watering the foliage with 2,4-D in late July or August taking care to avoid contact with the asparagus stems and particularly the fern.

Fruit Garden.—Around blackcurrants, gooseberries, raspberries, apples, and pears, grasses can be killed with Dalapon. Once clear of perennial weeds, annuals may be controlled effectively with Simazine. Alternatively, weeds may be killed with Diquat, making applications as necessary throughout the season.

Garden Paths.—On any surfaced path or drive a first-rate control of weeds can be maintained by watering with a residual herbicide such as Simazine. As this preparation is virtually insoluble in water, it does not seep through the soil as sodium chlorate would, and therefore it can be used near garden crops and grass edgings. Further to this, it is not easily washed from the soil and remains active near the surface for up to twelve months. Notwithstanding, the herbicide must be used with proper care.

A dilute solution of sodium chlorate with 4–6 ozs. to a gallon of water may be applied, but it is liable to affect plants near by and, for this reason, application should be confined to the centre of the path, thereby leaving room for the chlorate to seep through the soil.

Lawns.—The majority of weeds in turf can be eradicated easily with formulations of 2,4-D or M.C.P.A. (*see* **Finding List**). In particular, daisies, dandelions, plantains, and most broad-leaved weeds are susceptible although it may be necessary to repeat the dose after 10 days. The best time to do the work is on a warm, fine day in the spring when the plants are growing actively and there is the prospect of fine weather to follow for twenty-four hours. The action of the herbicides is rapid, and grass may be cut after a couple of days, composting with mowings in the normal way. It appears that the hormones are not injurious to bacterial life in the soil and in a few weeks break down into harmless substances.

Where bulbs are naturalised in grass, steps to control weeds should not be taken until the foliage of the bulbs has died down and the bulbs are dormant. Thus, as a general rule, control measures are best applied throughout July.

To deal with weeds in turf where there arises the danger of the spray—or even a drift from it—touching cultivated plants near by, as, for instance, on grass paths in a rose garden, then a wax bar impregnated with a hormone can be lightly drawn over the turf. Such bars are available at a reasonable price under trade names like "Supplex Touchweeder."

Some weeds are resistant to normal doses of hormones and need special treatment. These are mostly mat-forming plants of low-growing habit which are not cut off by mowing. Typical examples include mosses of all sorts, pearlwort, speedwell or veronica, yarrow, and yellow-flowered clover. Here, the main control must be in the use of lawn sand, a good mixture of which can be made up with:

2 parts by weight sulphate of ammonia.
1 part by weight sulphate of iron.
13 parts by weight LIME-FREE sand.

Where moss is the most prevalent weed, to the mixture should be added sufficient superphosphate to give 1 oz. of it per sq. yd. for the area to be treated. A hundredweight of the lawn sand plus superphosphate can be made up for about 17*s*. and is sufficient to treat about 450 sq. yds. at 4 oz. per sq. yd.

Applications to patches of the weeds should be made when the turf is damp and there is the prospect of fine weather; if a period of drought follows an application, then water should be applied to avoid serious scorching. Repeat the treatment as necessary throughout the growing season. Linked with this "spot" treatment, the growth of grass must be encouraged, as this will tend to smother low-growing weeds. Thus, in the early spring when the turf is wet, feed with a mixture of equal parts of superphosphate, sulphate of ammonia and dry soil at 2 oz. per sq. yd. over the whole area and repeat after a month, if desirable. In addition, do *not* shave off the grass by close cutting; instead, the blades of the mower should be set reasonably high for a whole season.

Where fertility is low, clovers often predominate in turf. The Dutch clovers with white—or pink—flowers and a white-angled band towards the base of each leaflet, can be eradicated with Mecoprop. Afterwards the turf should be fed with nitrogenous fertilisers like soot and sulphate of ammonia, to discourage reinfestation. Other types of clover found in turf are species of *Trifolium*. Compared to the Dutch clover, these have a tight, bunched habit of growth and yellow flowers. All of them are resistant to hormones and, in addition to manurial treatment, should be treated with lawn sand.

Lakes.—It sometimes happens that aquatic plants with large floating leaves, such as water lilies, get out of hand. Here, control can be established by cutting off the foliage with a long-handled appliance like the "Corypu Water Scythe." The work should be done early in June and repeated as often as any fresh growth is seen.

Bulrushes are difficult to eliminate, but can be destroyed by digging out the roots when the level of the water permits. Dalapon has been found to give a control; applications should be made, with a wetting agent added, when the rushes reach maturity.

Ponds.—Problems of weed control in ornamental ponds are often not easy to solve. Where duckweed is prevalent this small floating plant can be eliminated by sweeping the surface of the water at regular intervals. If this practice is carried out thoroughly much of the vegetative growth will be eliminated, and the plant will not be able to form resting bodies whereby it overwinters. Once a control has been established, further spread of the plant can be prevented by introducing a few moorhens or ornamental ducks.

The most common of unwanted plants in pools is blanket weed. There is no single means of dealing with this plant, for its spread is governed, to a certain extent, by unbalanced plant and anima life in the water. With this fact in mind, water lilies should be established so that their foliage shades about 25 per cent of the water. In addition, a few oxygenating plants should be introduced from local ponds or streams and a supply of goldfish added. Blanket weed is usually found in pools where the water gets overheated in summer; for this reason, the average depth of garden ponds should be a minimum of 2 ft. and preferably a minimum of 3 ft.

Rose Beds.—A complete control of annual weeds among roses can be obtained with Simazine. Here, the salient point is to apply the herbicide immediately after pruning in March *before* any weed growth starts. Alternatively, Diquat can be used in April or early May and the application repeated as necessary.

Shrubberies.—With a shortage of labour, beds of shrubs are often weed infested. Perennials can be eradicated with Diquat and annuals controlled by this treatment as they appear. Alternatively, once the perennials are removed, the ground can be kept clear with Simazine used in the early spring.

Much to check weeds in shrubberies can be done by mulching the surface of the soil with heavy dressings of peat, fallen leaves, or sawdust; if the weeds push through the mulch, a second application should be made at once.

Vacant Ground.—On land free of crops all plants can be killed by watering the herbage with sodium chlorate at 1 lb. to a gallon of water. In some cases repetition may be necessary. When using this method it should be remembered that treated ground will remain toxic to plant life for a period of up to six months; if doubt exists about the persistence of the chlorate in the soil, then it is advisable to wait for the appearance of annual weeds before planting.

Apart from its persistence, sodium chlorate is prone to seep through soil and affect plants for some distance away. To avoid danger of fire from clothes being soaked in a solution of the chlorate and then dried, it is prudent to use a formulation with an additive to reduce the risk of fire. (*See* **Finding List.**) Where couch grass is predominant then the best control is to be obtained with Dalapon.

SPECIAL PROBLEMS OF WEED CONTROL

Bindweed.—Probably the most ubiquitous of all garden weeds. Up to the present time the main control has been to carefully fork out the roots as new growth is seen; if this is done methodically the plant can be eliminated within a reasonable time.

Lately, chemicals have come to the fore, and bindweed may now be eliminated by watering or painting the foliage with a formulation of 2,4-D when the annual growth has nearly reached maturity. Thus, first applications can be applied in July and the treatment repeated, if necessary, to good effect. Where the weed is among cultivated plants, the herbicides must be applied with a paint brush or the foliage rubbed with a cloth damped in a solution. When doing this rubber gloves should be worn.

Blanket Weed.—*See* **Ponds.**

Bracken.—Horticulturally, control is not a big problem, and in limited areas it is easily dealt with by repeatedly cutting the aerial stems with a grass hook as the first fronds open. This practice will exhaust the underground food supply of the plant, and gradually it will die out. The young fronds are rich in plant food and, while still green and fresh, they should be composted. No chemicals will offer a reasonable control of this plant and, indeed, it is best dealt with by cutting and final digging out of the roots.

Couch Grass.—Where the soil is light and tends to be low in fertility, it is often found that this is a difficult plant to eradicate by cultural means. If the long, underground stems are forked out in the conventional manner and left on the surface to dry, the roots may be composted to advantage and a good control established. To prevent reinfestation, manures and fertilisers should be applied generously and the ground kept hoed regularly.

Chemically, couch grass can be killed easily by watering the foliage with Dalapon.

Ground Elder.—Without question this is one of the worst garden weeds and, whether or not the fact is pleasant or acceptable, it is indubitably a weed of neglected ground. In varying degrees it is resistant to hormone weed-killers of all sorts. On ground free of crops it may be reduced by an application of sodium chlorate, as explained in the paragraph **Vacant Ground.** The first treatment should be made as soon as growth starts in the spring and repeated if the desired effect is not abundantly clear. When ground elder is to be found among herbaceous plants the cultivated plants must be lifted out and the weed removed by repeated hand-forking.

In shrubberies reasonable control can be had by smothering the young growth in the spring with a thick dressing of peat, leaf mould, baled straw, or sawdust. If growth penetrates the surface dressing it will be found that the etiolated shoots are not difficult to remove by hand, or a second layer can be applied to complete the treatment.

Alternatively, the foliage of ground elder can be watered with Diquat and the treatment repeated once or twice during the growing season.

Horsetail.—This is sometimes erroneously called marestail and on poor, sandy soils it is often a common weed. Fortunately, recent experiments have proved that it can be easily controlled by spraying or painting the *mature* growths with a formulation of 2,4-D, taking care, of course, to keep the spray off cultivated plants near by. As the appearance of horsetail is symptomatic of low fertility, manurial treatment should be carried out on a generous scale. Where the weed is growing among cultivated crops, individual stems must be treated separately as recommended for bindweed.

Marestail.—*See* **Horsetail.**

Moss.—*See* **Lawns (T32).**

Nettles.—It is difficult to understand why the perennial nettle is so abundant as it is immediately responsive to applications of 2,4-D and 2,4,5-T made any time during the growing season.
The annual nettle is usually proved a denizen of rich, light soils and may be eradicated with cresylic acid, Diquat or 2,4-D.

Oxalis.—Of all weeds this is probably the most difficult to destroy. It is easily identified by its large, trifoliolate leaves like that of clover. Unlike other weeds, oxalis cannot be efficiently removed by hand, as this disturbs the bulbils clustered around the base of the stem of mature plants. On ground free of crops, sodium chlorate can be applied in March (*see* **Vacant Ground**). Perhaps a second application may be necessary, but, even so, control may not be complete. Among shrubby plants, it may be possible to eradicate the weed by smothering, as suggested in the paragraph on ground elder.
The foliage can be killed with Diquat and, by repeated applications, this may constitute the best means of control.

Speedwell.—*See* **Veronica.**

Veronica.—This procumbent, blue-flowered weed of turf is sometimes know as speedwell. Being resistant to hormones, its control may only be established with lawn sand. *See also* **Lawns.**

Woody Plants.—With or without the addition of 2,4-D, these may be killed with 2,4,5-T. This hormone is particularly useful on bramble, gorse, ivy, and other unwanted shrubby plants. It is necessary to thoroughly saturate the foliage of deciduous trees, and the best results are obtainable when the leaves are fully mature but not starting to die off. In the case of ivy, the dormant shoots should be generously sprayed for the best results.

Yarrow.—A weed found in many lawns where its presence often signifies low fertility. Control is with lawn sand. *See* **Lawns (T32).**

Summary.—From these notes it will be seen that there are many aids for dealing with weeds. The salient point is to get the *right* method for *each* plant. Equally important is to check the reason why certain weeds grow profusely under some conditions. Very often this natural tendency can be counteracted as in the case of phosphatic fertilisers against moss and in the application of organic manures and chemical fertilizers where horsetail and yarrow are concerned. *See* **T35.**

Standard References.

Chemicals for the Gardener, H.M. Stationery Office, 1965 (1*s.* 7*d.* incl. postage).

List of Approved Products for Farmers and Growers (published annually), copies free from Ministry of Agriculture, Fisheries, and Food (Publications), Tolcarne Drive, Pinner, Middlesex.

Weed Control Handbook, issued by the British Weed Control Council (Blackwell), 1963 (21*s.*).

HORTICULTURAL SOCIETIES.

There are many specialist societies in Britain. Detailed information on particular plants is normally available from them, and membership is open to all wishing to join. The most prominent societies are:

Alpine Garden Society
Sec. Michael Upward, 58 Denison House, 296 Vauxhall Bridge Road, S.W.1.

Auricula and Primula Society, The National
Sec. A. Marlow, 52 Epsom Lane North, Epsom, Surrey.

Begonia Society, The National Society of England and Wales
Sec. F. J. Martin, 50 Woodlands Farm Road, Erdington, Birmingham 24.

Cactus and Succulent Society of Great Britain
Sec. K. H. Walden, 152 Ardgowan Road, Catford, S.E.6.

Camellia Society, The International
Sec. Charles E. Puddle, V.M.H., Bodnant, Tal-y-Cafn, Denbighshire.

Carnation Society, The British National
Sec. E. G. Cook, 1 Evelyn Rd., Worthing, Sussex.

Chrysanthemum Society, The National
Sec. S. G. Gosling, 65 St. Margaret's Avenue, Whetstone, N.20.

Daffodil Society
Sec. D. J. Pearce, College of Ascension, Selly Oak, Birmingham, 29.

Dahlia Society, The National
Sec. H. F. Newson, 93 Byng Road, High Barnet, Herts.

Delphinium Society, The
Sec. C. J. H. Topping, B.A., Ph.D., 5 Park Lane, Sevenoaks, Kent.

Floral Arrangement Societies of Great Britain National Association of
Sec. Mrs. F. C. Dobson, 21A Denbigh Street, London, S.W.1.

Floral Decoration Society, The London
Sec. Mrs. C. Heaven, 22 St. Luke's Mews, London, W.11.

Fuchsia Society, The British
Sec. W. G. Sharp, Rydal, The Green, Gt. Bentley, Colchester, Essex.

Gladiolus Society, The British
Sec. J. G. Lord, 25 Kimpton Avenue, Brentwood, Essex.

Hardy Plant Society
Sec. Miss B. White, 10 St. Barnabas Rd., Emmer Green, Reading, Berks.

Heather Society, The
Sec. Mrs. C. I. MacLeod, Yew Trees, Horley Row, Horley, Surrey.

Iris Society, The British
Sec. Mrs. E. G. Osborn, 114 Ellison Road, Streatham, S.W.16.

Pansy and Viola Society, The North of England
Sec. F. C. Marshland, 2 Jubilee Mount, West Lillands, Brighouse, Yorks.

Pansy „nd Viola Society, The Scottish
Sec. Hugh Campbell, O.B.E., 960 Dumbarton Road, Dalmuir, Glasgow.

Pelargonium and Geranium Society, The British
Sec. Miss E. D. James, 22 Lanercost Rd., London, S.W.2.

Pteridological Society, The British
Sec. J. W. Dyle, 46 Sedley Rise, Loughton, Essex.

Rose Society, The Royal National
Sec. L. G. Turner, Chiswell Green Lane, St. Albans, Herts.

Royal Horticultural Society
Sec. John Hamer, M.B.E., B.A., Royal Horticultural Society's Offices, Vincent Square, S.W.1.

Royal Caledonian Horticultural Society
Sec. John Turnbull, D.S.O., D.F.C., C.A., Royal Caledonian Horticultural Society, 44 Melville Street, Edinburgh 3.

Saintpaulia and Houseplant Society
Sec. The Secretary, 54 Queensborough Terrace, London, W.2.

Scottish Rock Garden Club
Sec. Sqdn-Ldr. J. J. Boyd-Harvey, Boonslie, Dirleton, East Lothian.

Sweet Pea Society, The National
Sec. R. J. Huntley, 431 Wokingham Road, Earley, Reading, Berks.

FINDING LIST FOR WEEDKILLERS

All the herbicides in this list are first-class chemicals which have been approved by the Ministry of Agriculture and are available in small packs designed for use by amateur gardeners. In case of difficulty in obtaining any of them, the manufacturers should be contacted.

The list may appear unnecessarily long but the pipe dream of multipurpose herbicides is not a reality and the full extent and value of chemical weed controls are only obtained by using herbicides for their specific purposes; as such, they constitute an efficient and economic method of eradicating unwanted plants of all sorts.

Trade names	Chemicals	Manufacturers	Type of action	Plants controlled	Notes and precautions
			WEED KILLERS FOR USE ON TURF		
"Bugges 2,4-D" "Dicotox" "Shell Weed-kill"	2,4-D	Bugges Insecticides Ltd., London Rd., Sittingbourne, Kent. May and Baker Ltd., Dagenham, Essex Shell Chemical Co. Ltd., 15–17 Gt. Marlborough St., W.1.	Hormone growth regulator trans-located throughout the plant.	Many broad-leafed weeds and some perennial ones. Best hormone type for killing daisies, dandelions and plantains.	Primarily for use on lawns Beware of drift.
"Bugges M.C.P.A." "Weed-a-Lawn"	M.C.P.A.	Bugges Insecticides Ltd., London Rd., Sittingbourne, Kent. Pan Britannia Industries Ltd., Britannia House, Waltham Cross, Herts.	Hormone growth regulator trans-located throughout the plant.	Many broad-leafed weeds and some perennial ones. Best hormone type for killing creeping buttercup. Useful against pearlwort with repeated applications.	Primarily for use on lawns Beware of drift.
"Clovotox"	Mecoprop	May and Baker Ltd., Dagenham, Essex.	Hormone growth regulator trans-located throughout the plant.	Best control for white-flowered clover, chickweeds and field woodrush. Useful against pearlwort with repeated applications.	Primarily for use on lawns Beware of drift.
Lawn sand	*See* T32(2).	Usually home made.	Scorching of annual growth. Of herbicidal and manurial value.	Invaluable against weeds resistant or semi-resistant to hormones, like pearlwort, moss, veronica (speedwell), yellow-flowered clover, and yarrow.	*See* **Lawns** (**T32(2)**) for detailed information.
			WEEDKILLERS FOR GARDEN USE		
"Nova Soil Steriliser"	Cresylic Acid	The Murphy Chemical Co. Ltd., Wheathampsted, St. Albans, Herts.	Contact herbicide.	For destruction of growth of annual weeds and top growth of perennials.	Particularly valuable on asparagus beds and where annual weeds have to be controlled. Also used as a soil sterilant.
"Bugges Dalapon"	Dalapon	Bugges Insecticides Ltd., London Rd., Sittingbourne, Kent.	Translocated throughout the plant, killing vegetation by movement from leaves to roots.	Annual grasses, couch grass, sedges, reeds, and bulrushes.	Delay planting for 40 days after application. May be used, upon makers' instructions as a *selective* herbicide on asparagus, shrubberies, fruit gardens, etc.
"Weedol"	Diquat Salt	Plant Protection Ltd., Yalding, Kent.	Translocated throughout the plant but with scorching effect similar to contact herbicides.	Kills annual weeds and top growth of perennials. One of the few herbicides to give a good control of ground elder. Selective only by application, *i.e.*, kills all foliage it contacts.	Undoubtedly one of the most valuable and interesting herbicides to be introduced. Inactivated upon contact with soil; no residual effects. Available in small packs. Can be stored from season to season.
"Weedex"	Simazine	Fisons Horticultural Ltd., Harvest House, Felixstowe, Suffolk.	Soil acting, killing seedling vegetation by uptake through roots.	Controls germinating seeds of many weeds over a long period.	Apply when ground is wet in early spring on asparagus, apples, pears (not plums), soft fruit, ornamental trees, and shrubs including roses. Slow acting.
"Polybor-Chlorate"	Sodium Chlorate	Borax Consolidated Ltd., Borax House, Carlisle Place, S.W.1.	Translocated throughout the plant and soil acting.	Toxic in varying degrees to all plants except mosses. The best chemical for killing tree stumps.	To a large extent superseded by other chemicals. Can be used on paths, drives, and vacant ground.
"Boots Bramble, Brushwood and Nettle Killer"	2,4,5-T	Boots Pure Drug Co. Ltd., Station Street, Nottingham.	Hormone growth regulator trans-located throughout the plant.	Special value in control of woody plants like brambles, brushwood, and ivy. Also good against nettles.	Beware of drift.

THE GARDEN CALENDAR.

January.—All digging should be finished this month. As the work is done, so generous applications of organic matter such as peat, compost, sewage sludge, leaf mould, animal manure, or a mixture of any of them, should be incorporated into the ground. On clay soils the physical condition can be improved by raking into the surface dressings of rough materials like screened ashes, road grit, or coarse sand.

Fork over ground between rows of fruit trees and in shrubberies and bury annual weeds; if land is not free of weeds in January it is unlikely to be so throughout the year.

A trench for runner beans can be made, the bottom forked over, a thick dressing of compost or kitchen waste added, and the soil replaced.

Rhubarb will require protection with compost or straw and early growth forced by covering with small tubs.

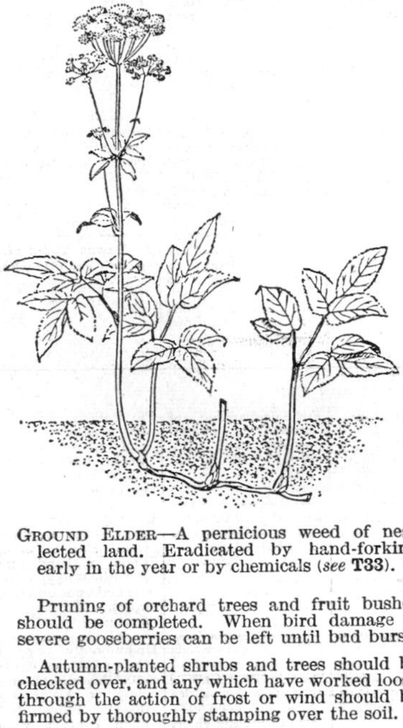

GROUND ELDER—A pernicious weed of neglected land. Eradicated by hand-forking early in the year or by chemicals (*see* **T33**).

Pruning of orchard trees and fruit bushes should be completed. When bird damage is severe gooseberries can be left until bud burst.

Autumn-planted shrubs and trees should be checked over, and any which have worked loose through the action of frost or wind should be firmed by thoroughly stamping over the soil.

February.—Broad beans can be sown if conditions are favourable and shallots planted by pressing the bulbs into the soil until only the tips show.

Jerusalem artichokes are an unusual crop well worth growing; plant tubers as early as possible to give a long season for maturity.

Parsnips should be lifted to check new growth and stored on the north side of a wall or fence.

"Seed" potatoes can be arranged in boxes and kept in a frost-proof shed; a light, airy position will encourage short, sturdy shoots.

Protective covering on half-hardy shrubs, like fuchsias and mimosa, should be removed as early as possible.

Herbaceous plants which do not over winter easily, such as delphiniums and gaillardias, may be planted at the end of the month.

Turf may be laid in February so that the grass can be established before the ground starts to dry out in the spring. Before laying, rake in a dressing of "National Growmore" at 1½ oz. per sq. yd. to encourage root action.

Vines under glass should still be kept as *cold* as possible to maintain the dormant period. As the buds swell the temperature can be higher, but ventilation must be increased if it reaches 45° Fahrenheit.

Fuchsias grown under glass should be pruned hard by cutting back all of last season's growth to within a bud or two of the old stems. Later, as new growth appears, take cuttings which will root easily in sand under a plastic bag.

Shrubby plants like the india-rubber plant and most pot plants grown indoors or under glass should be repotted or top dressed with fresh potting compost.

Early strawberries can be obtained by cloching rows at the beginning of the month.

March.—Sow round-seeded spinach and broad beans for a succession in cropping.

Brussels sprouts, cabbage, lettuce, leeks, onions, parsley, parsnips, peas, and radish should all be sown as the soil gradually warms up

Asparagus is easily raised from seed sown this month. Sow the seeds individually 1 in. apart and mark the rows by sowing a pinch or two of radish seed at intervals, as the asparagus is slow to germinate.

Onion sets can be planted as early as possible on well-manured ground.

Spring cabbage will respond in the spring to an application of nitrate of soda at 1 oz. per sq. yd.

Tomato seed may be sown in a warm greenhouse at the end of the month. It is a mistake to sow early in the year, as then seedlings get drawn and weak before it is time for planting outdoors.

Seed of half-hardy annuals, such as antirrhinums, China asters and *Phlox drummondii*, may all be sown in a greenhouse or frame. Remember the seed should only be covered with a sugaring of fine soil sufficient to "anchor" the seedlings and to sow thinly.

Hedges, and particularly evergreen sorts which have outgrown their stations, should be cut back, and this is the *best* month for doing so. Often drastic reduction is necessary, and such treatment will save endless, unnecessary work in trimming later on in the year. As an example, privet may be safely reduced to a width of 9 in. and a height of 4–5 ft.

Evergreen shrubs, like some daphnes, rhododendrons, and hollies, may be planted and—what is most important—kept moist until growing freely.

Over-grown lavender may be reduced in size by cutting back into old wood.

Lawns should be fed with fertilisers to encourage new, strong growth when the turf is damp.

As buds burst on roses, so pruning and manuring can be started.

Planting time for all fruit trees is nearly over, and should be completed without delay.

As buds burst on early planted raspberries, so the already shortened canes can be cut down to just above the lowest bud in growth; as further growth develops so the old stems can be shortened further until, finally, cut to ground level.

April.—Potato planting for an early crop is done this month using well-sprouted "seed." Protect from late frosts by covering the first shoots with earth and, if necessary, applying a coating of straw or sacking.

Onions raised under glass in boxes can be planted outdoors.

Watch for germination of asparagus seed; as the fern-like growths appear, hand weed the rows with great care and thin seedlings to 2–3 in. apart.

Hardy annuals can be sown outdoors when soil conditions are right; lightly cover and protect from birds. Half-hardy sorts must be grown-on in frames.

New stocks of carnations, chrysanthemums, and violas may be planted outdoors.

Transplant autumn-raised sweet peas to open garden early in the month.

Lawns may be sown as the soil warms up, and a good surface tilth can be obtained by raking; *prior* to sowing, make arrangements to protect the seed bed from birds by use of pea sticks, wire netting, strips of newspaper dipped into lime-wash, or "Glitterbangs" or a combination of these scarers.

Evergreen shrubs, like bamboos, hollies, and rhododendrons, should be planted and kept moist until well established.

Gladioli and montbretias can be planted in sunny positions where soil is in good heart.

Prune winter-flowering shrubs, such as winter jasmine and forsythia, by cutting off the old flowering stems.

Weeds will be appearing on garden paths and drives; establish an early and efficient control by watering with "Weedex."

Early planted fruit trees should be mulched with organic matter to conserve moisture in the soil.

May.—Brussels sprouts should be planted early in the month and also late potatoes. Watch out for blackfly on broad beans, as the first infestations are the important ones to deal with promptly.

Encourage growth on leafy vegetables, like lettuce and spinach, by a dressing of nitrate of soda at 1 oz. per sq. yd.

Towards the end of month plant out tomatoes, or in the first week if cloches are available.

Sow sweet corn and vegetable marrows in the open. Bedding plants and half-hardy annuals may all be planted outdoors.

Roses should be checked over for first signs of greenfly infestation; spray with nicotine if necessary.

Garden pools in need of cleaning should be dealt with thoroughly. At the same time water lilies may be lifted and divided when growth in the previous year was excessive.

Delphiniums now develop rapidly; for best results cut out thin shoots to leave five to seven strong growths to each plant. Stake and tie each one and encourage healthy growth by feeding with liquid animal manure or soot water on one or two occasions.

Faded blooms on azaleas, lilacs, and rhododendrons should be removed.

Agapanthuses and hydrangeas grown in tubs can be brought into a sunny position. If repotting has not been necessary remove top 2 in. of soil and replace with fresh compost. Encourage new growth with applications of liquid animal manure.

Window boxes should be repaired, filled with fresh compost, and replanted. Remember a generous layer of peat or leaf soil placed in the bottom will do much to conserve moisture.

Lawns will need attention, and broad-leaved weeds can be eliminated by treatment with hormone weed-killers.

Small greenhouses are liable to get very hot and plants suffer accordingly especially if short of water; therefore keep staging and floors well damped. Conversely, sharp falls in temperature may be experienced and every day the ventilators should be shut down in the late afternoon in order to conserve the heat from the sun.

June.—Plant cabbages, cauliflower, celery, marrows, and tomatoes.

Sow seed of garden swedes.

After thinning beet, carrots, onions, and parsnips, feed with nitrate of soda at ½ oz. per yd. run.

Asparagus raised from seed must be kept clear of weeds and watered thoroughly at the least sign of being dry. Beds cropping in their third season should not be cut after June 1st; on old beds cutting may continue until the third week of June.

Sweet corn should be thinned and a surface dressing of compost applied.

Aubrietas now past their best should be clipped back hard to the old stems, with a pair of shears.

Seed of delphiniums, hollyhocks, lupins, and wallflowers may be sown.

Phloxes, especially if grown on light soil, should be mulched with compost and watered when necessary.

Herbaceous plants of all sorts respond to feeding if growth is below par; individual species may be fed with soot water or large beds given an application of sulphate of ammonia at 1 oz. per sq. yd., taking care to keep the crystals off the foliage of plants.

Old flower-heads on roses should be removed regularly by cutting back old flowering stems to within 4 or 5 in. of the mature wood.

Raspberries and similar berries should be mulched with compost or old manure to encourage new growth.

Strawberries may be layered if the stock is healthy and growth vigorous.

July.—Plant winter cabbage, leeks, sprouting broccoli, and kales as ground becomes available.

Sow prickly spinach and turnips for autumn and winter use.

Water celery, marrows, and runner beans at first sign of dryness. If setting is poor, beans should be sprayed vigorously with water from a hose.

Shallots may be lifted and dried off as foliage gradually yellows.

Carnations may be layered as sturdy young shoots develop; remove sufficient leaves to make a horizontal cut up the stem passing through a joint, and peg down.

Flag irises can be lifted and divided as flowering finishes. After replanting, the tubers should be showing above ground but, nevertheless, firmly in the soil.

Wallflowers may be lined out in nursery rows. To avoid sappy, lush growth do not plant on rich soil. Where ground is acid water plants with lime-water (a large handful to a gallon).

Hydrangeas can be easily propagated in July by cuttings of short flowerless shoots. These should be inserted in pots in a sandy compost and kept under a plastic bag or hand light until rooted.

Transplant into nursery rows, seedlings of biennials and perennials sown earlier in the year.

Order supplies of daffodils, hyacinths, and other bulbous plants for delivering in September. Stocks in good trade houses are often soon exhausted.

Late in the month hedges of beech, holly, hornbeam, and yew can be clipped.

August.—Runner beans are now in full bearing, and the pods should be gathered while still young, to encourage further croppings; often beans are picked much too old. Water and feed with nitro-chalk at 2 oz. per yd. run if necessary. If properly grown this is one of the most profitable of *all* crops.

Marrows should also be gathered while still young and fresh; early development of seeds checks fruiting.

Strawberries layered in pots earlier in the year may be planted when the soil conditions are right. Use a well-manured site and plant at approved distances.

Raspberries and loganberries will now have finished cropping, and all the old fruiting canes may be cut out at ground level.

September.—Tomatoes can be gathered while still green and ripened easily and quickly by storing in open boxes, out of the direct sun, in a warm kitchen. Such a practice is better than putting the fruit in a dark, airless cupboard.

Ground recently cleared of onions and potatoes is admirable for planting out cabbages for spring cutting. Apart from removing any weeds, no preparation is desirable.

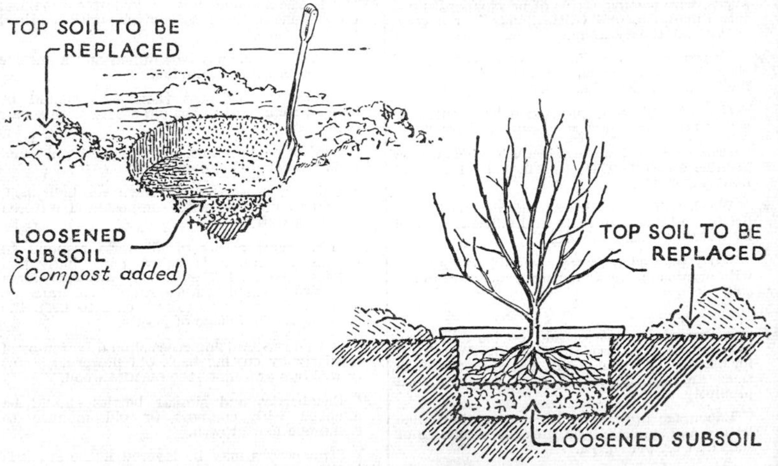

CORRECTLY PLANTED SHRUB, showing planting hole and bush in position. The loosened sub-soil must be firmed prior to planting, and any tree or shrub must never be planted deeper than it was in its previous position or nursery row.

Seed of prickly spinach—a valuable winter crop—may be sown. As seedlings develop, thin out and on acid soils apply lime-water.

Tomatoes should be sprayed with "Bouisol" at fortnightly intervals to prevent potato blight.

Winter greens, if not already planted, should be put in as soon as possible.

Pelargoniums ("Geraniums") should be propagated by cuttings taken throughout the month as young, short side-shoots develop. Rooting soon starts if the cuttings are inserted in sand or a mixture of sand and peat.

Border carnations may be layered; encourage rooting by not allowing the plants to suffer from a lack of water.

Madonna lilies may be planted this month in an open position where they will not be disturbed.

Flowering shrubs of a wide range may be propagated in August. Short side-shoots of the current season's growth should be taken off with a heel when the wood is still young but starting to harden at the base. Insert in sand and cover with a plastic bag.

Grass seed is best sown this month whenever the soil is moist but not wet, as in the notes for April. Before sowing, any perennial weeds must be removed by hand forking.

Brussel sprouts are heavy feeders and growth should be encouraged by an application of nitro-chalk at 1 oz. per sq. yd. early in the month.

Carnation layers will now be rooted and the young plants may be severed from the parents and transferred to their flowering positions.

Crocuses, daffodils, and snowdrops are often planted too late; September is the time for the job. Similarly, these, together with hyacinths, may all be planted in bowls for indoor decoration before the end of the month.

Lavender bushes can be trimmed when the flowers fade; do not, however, trim or cut back in any way the old stems or foliage.

Grass seed not sown last month should be put in without delay.

Roses of nearly every sort can be propagated by inserting cuttings 8–10 in. long in a shallow trench outdoors. A sprinkling of sand should be put in the bottom of the trench and the cuttings firmed well.

Brown rot is often prevalent on fruit. There is no remedy for the disease, and brown, rotten fruit on apple and other trees should be picked off and burnt.

October.—Jerusalem artichokes are safe left in the ground, but the stems should be cut down.

If a regular supply is wanted, then a store of tubers may be lifted to ensure against hard frost.

Parsnips may, similarly, be left in the ground until needed.

Asparagus stems should be cut down before the seeds drop. If "fern" is cut during the summer for indoor decoration, subsequent cropping is affected.

Lettuce for early cutting next spring should be sown, late in the month, under cloches.

Virgin ground which is to be taken into cultivation should be dug as soon as possible in order that it may be exposed to a *full* season of winter frosts. There is no doubt that the maximum value in digging virgin land can only be had if the work is completed well before Christmas.

Evergreen shrubs should be planted before the weather turns severely cold.

Lily-of-the-valley will respond to a top dressing of old animal manure or an application of bone meal at 2 oz. per sq. yd. followed by a mulch of leaf soil.

Clematis grown in pots may be planted in their permanent positions.

Lilies of various sorts can be planted early in the month.

Gladioli should be lifted, cleaned, and stored in a dry, frost-proof shed.

Polyanthuses and all sorts of primroses may be planted in moist, rich soil for flowering in the spring.

Sweet Williams and pansies may be transferred from nursery rows to their flowering positions.

Wallflowers should be planted without delay, firming the plants well. Forget-me-nots and daffodils may be used in conjunction with them and planted at the same time.

Most plants grown indoors have been watered freely during the summer; from now on care must be taken in applying water, as soil only dries out slowly in winter, and growth has virtually stopped.

Bulbs in bowls must be kept as cold as possible, and up to early November not more than about ½ in. of growth should be showing. Damp the peat as it shows signs of drying out.

Black and red currants and gooseberries may all be propagated by cuttings.

November.—Runner beans can be cleared and the haulms used for compost; the old roots can be left in the ground and later dug-in. If the sticks are pulled up early and stored they will last for some years.

Broad beans may be sown outdoors in districts where they are known to succeed; an allowance for losses should be made by sowing 3 in. apart.

Asparagus responds well to a top dressing of animal manure or compost; if supplies are short, aim to apply once in three years.

Lettuce sown last month under cloches can be transplanted and, under wide barn cloches, three rows can be grown easily for cutting in the spring. Slugs may cause serious losses, so water with "Slugit" at planting time and keep a few spare seedlings to fill any gaps.

Tulips may be planted throughout November.

Heaths and heathers of all sorts can be planted in peaty soils. Large clumps may be split up and replanted.

Roses and all deciduous shrubs and trees, including fruit trees of all sorts, should be planted as soon as possible. Always firm the soil well, but do not plant too deeply.

Where necessary, herbaceous borders can be replanted. Large clumps of perennials can be split up and the strong pieces from outside of the clump replanted; the centre of the clump should be discarded.

Continue to keep indoor bulbs as cold as possible. By the second week in November, growth should be about an inch high. Towards the end of the month, transfer to a cool, light position.

Throughout the winter continue digging and incorporating organic matter like compost, spent hops, and coffee grounds.

Vines grown in a cold greenhouse should be given full ventilation night and day. After leaf fall cut back annual growth to one bud.

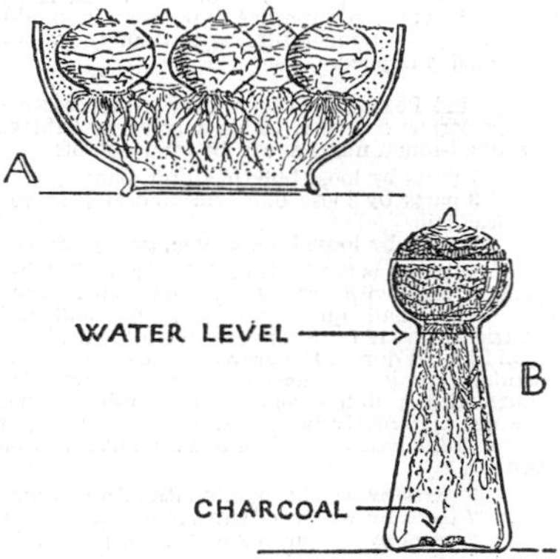

Bulbs Indoors—Note strong root development before leaves appear. This factor can only be brought about by early planting (*see* September notes). In both bowl (A) and glass (B) a little bonfire charcoal is necessary for healthy growth.

December.—Decaying leaves on winter greens should be removed to give free circulation of air around the plants.

Bird damage may be prevalent on spring cabbages because of pigeons. In serious cases it is worthwhile to erect fish netting.

When frost makes cultivations impossible, pruning of fruit trees should be done. The only exception may be red currants and gooseberries, because in districts where bird damage is serious any pruning is best left until the spring.

Deciduous hedges of beech, hawthorn, and the like can all be cut back hard where the plants have got out of hand, with a view to reducing work of trimming during the growing season.

Well-berried holly is always in demand, and a variety of regular fruiting habit to fulfil the requirement is *Ilex aquifolium* 'Pyramidalis.'

For those wanting mistletoe, the seed should be planted on apple trees in the spring—not in December.

Early in the month, hyacinths can be brought into full light and warmth for Christmas flowering. If growth is a little stunted cover plants with a sheet of newspaper and give more warmth; if growth is poor look to the cultivator not the supplier.

Christmas trees to be brought indoors in pots should be thoroughly watered first, to check the needles falling through lack of moisture in hot, stuffy rooms.

CARE OF INDOOR PLANTS

Cultural Conditions.—Ideally, the temperature should be kept as constant as possible, and in cold weather plants grown in window-boxes are best moved nightly into the centre of the room to avoid damage by frost. Linked with temperature is the question of humidity, for plants respond well to a moist atmosphere. Pots may be stood on a layer of gravel which can be kept damp without allowing water to seep through the bottom of the pot and thereby saturating the soil. Gas fumes and draughts must be avoided. Plants with large leaves should be sponged regularly with soapy water. Others, with hairy leaves, like saintpaulia, may be gently sprayed, but the water must not be allowed to remain on the foliage, as it may lead to scorching or rotting.

Of all cultural practices, the most important is watering. As a general guide, plants may become *nearly* dry before watering and then be given a *thorough* soak by standing the pots up to their rims in a bucket of water. For all plants, rainwater is best; if tap water has to be used, it should reach the same temperature as that of the room before being applied.

Soils and Potting.—The important factor is to get the correct compost. This may vary slightly, but an all-round mixture can be made up of:

7 parts by loose bulk medium loam
3 parts by loose bulk granulated peat (or leaf soil)
2 parts by loose bulk coarse, gritty sand

This mixture is the basis of John Innes Potting Compost and, with fertilisers added, can be purchased in small quantities from horticultural sundriesmen. If fertilisers are not added, plants should be fed during the growing season at about fortnightly intervals (depending on the particular plant) with a dilute solution of liquid animal manure; alternatively, 2 oz. of the following mixture dissolved in a gallon of rain-water can be used:

5 parts by weight of sulphate of ammonia
7 parts by weight of superphosphate
2 parts by weight of sulphate of potash

Normally a plant will grow satisfactorily in the same soil for three or four years. After this annual growth may be poor together with yellowing or dropping of the foliage. The plant is then in immediate need of repotting. To do this a large crock should be put into the bottom of the new pot—which should be generally a shade larger—followed by a little compost. Then the matted roots of the plant can be teased out with a pointed stick, put in the pot and more compost worked firmly around the roots. When repotting is not absolutely necessary, the top inch of soil can be taken off annually and the pot top-dressed with fresh compost. Both repotting and top-dressing are best done before growth starts in the spring.

Florists' Plants.—Plants like cyclamen and cinerarias, which are purchased in flower and usually discarded when flowering has finished, are forced for seasonal trade in the moist atmosphere of a heated greenhouse, so do not respond kindly to treatment indoors. One of the loveliest of these plants in *Azalea indica*, the Indian or evergreen azalea. After flowering it can be kept in a cool greenhouse. It needs plenty of moisture, and as it is a calcifuge, only rain-water can be used. To encourage growth after flowering, spray the foliage regularly and apply dilute, liquid animal manure or dilute soot water. Cyclamen is difficult to grow really well, and cultural notes should be followed. With expert attention old plants can be flowered for ten years or more, although the best results are obtained from one-year seedlings. On the other hand, varieties of cineraria are grown as biennials. These need cool, airy conditions, and should be watered freely but, at the same time, with care not to over-water.

At Christmas-time numerous varieties of primula will be offered for sale. All of them are of comparatively easy culture, and if top-dressed and fed can be grown-on for a year or two. Some varieties, particularly those of *Primula obconica*, can cause a rash on those susceptible to it. Other plants which can be kept after flowering are the varieties of *Solanum capsicastrum*, the winter cherry.

Indoor Plants.—The ones listed are among those which can be grown as permanent features in most homes if given reasonable care.

Begonia.—An enormous genus of plants of world-wide distribution, many being suitable for indoor cultivation. Of particular interest are *B. heracleifolia* and *B. manicata*, both being easy to propagate from cuttings under a tumbler.

Billbergia nutans.—This is a member of the pineapple family, the Bromeliads, having typically narrow, spiny-edged leaves. Nearly hardy, and will flower in a warm room. Do not repot unless absolutely necessary, as the roots are best confined.

Campanula isophylla (Harebell).—A charming blue-flowered plant with a long flowering period. Easily grown in cool conditions, and its pendulous habit makes it useful for a basket. After flowering, remove dead flower-heads and trim straggly shoots. There is a good white form, 'Alba.'

Cacti.—Innumerable sorts are used as house plants. In the main, all should be grown in a sandy, gritty soil with sharp drainage; water may be given freely in the summer, but withheld in winter, except to prevent the soil drying out. Two cacti which will flower freely and are particularly worthy of cultivation are *Aporocactus flagelliformis*, the rat's tail cactus, and *Epiphyllum ackermanii*. Both are tolerant of poor conditions and neglect. Mention should also be made of the old-fashioned Christmas cactus, *Schlumbergera bridgesii*, as a great favourite, but an infinitely more exciting one of a similar type is the rare *Rhipsalidopsis gaertneri* with bright-red flowers.

Crassula.—Shrubby members of this genus make fine house plants, growing well in light soil in full sun. Particularly valuable are *C. lactea*—which has white flowers annually and large, succulent, spoon-shaped foliage—and *C. falcata*, a choice plant with red and yellow flowers.

Ivy.—Common in many continental houses, for ivies show an interesting range of colour, shape, and size in their foliage. Invaluable as climbing plants and in warm rooms, the Canary Island ivy is worth trying. A related plant raised in France is *Fatshedera lizei*. All of these prefer a damp, leafy soil, and the foliage should be sprayed occasionally.

Monstera deliciosa.—A striking plant with large, deeply-cut leaves and long, thick, aerial roots, many of which do not reach the ground. Often seen as a prominent decorative feature of continental homes. Requires a leafy soil and generous watering. Spray or sponge foliage regularly and avoid fluctuation of temperature in its cultivation.

Pelargonium (Geranium).—Ease of cultivation and beauty are found in this plant and its infinite varieties. Some of these, like 'Mrs. Cox,' have multi-coloured leaves and are well worth hunting for in trade lists. During the summer feed generously and keep the stock vigorous by rooting cuttings annually in the late summer.

Philodendron.—Most climbing plants with aerial roots and represented by a number of species from tropical America. Fairly tolerant of adverse conditions, but dislike draughts and require light shade, free watering, and a rich, open soil. *P. scandens* with heart-shaped leaves, is typical of the climbing group; *P. bipinnatifidum*, with broad, incised leaves, of the non-climbers.

Saintpaulia (African violet).—A charming, dwarf plant with hairy leaves and pretty single and double flowers in many colours. It is a *difficult* plant to grow well, as it thrives in a steady temperature of 65–70° F. and a wet atmosphere. Water from below. Rotting of leaves is due to excess of moisture, draughts, cold, or gas fumes.

GAMES & RECREATIONS

GAMES AND RECREATIONS

INTRODUCTION.

THE people of Britain have always been fond of spending their leisure hours in pursuits requiring physical effort or mental effort or both, and of thinking out special ways of celebrating special occasions. The result of this is a long history of games, recreations, and customs, some based vaguely on the pastimes of very ancient races, others appearing from time to time as the years and centuries passed; and, in a country with a strong sense of tradition, many activities of long ago still remain virtually unaltered, while many others retain much more than a trace of distant origins. For many years, most of the more highly organised pastimes were restricted to the nobility, but the ordinary people often contrived simplified or less formal versions of them, and always had plenty of recreations of their own. While the nobility took part in the joust that was the forerunner of fencing, the people took part in wrestling that remains wrestling; while the nobility enjoyed casting the bar that became throwing the hammer, the people enjoyed throwing the javelin that remains throwing the javelin; while the nobility performed masques and court dances, the people performed country dances, both sections of the populace thus playing their parts in paving the way for the theatre and the ballet.

About a century ago, games began to show more signs of organisation, with governing bodies coming into being to control them, and rules becoming fixed and codified. The object of these measures was to make the games available to more people, but the effects were, firstly, to make them more formal and less spontaneous, and secondly, to make the eventual classification of players of them according to ability at them inevitable. The next stage was probably equally inevitable. If you have classes, you have a top class, and the top class is presumably worth watching. People began to spend the leisure time that had been used for playing games in watching others play them. This development began about seventy years ago, and reached its climax between the first and second world wars, when not only games but also entertainments had multiplied and reached such high standards that they attracted as spectators those who, feeling that they were not good enough to participate, began to lose the desire to do so.

The second world war changed that, and started to swing the pendulum back again. It was a testing time that might have driven all thoughts of games and recreations out of people's minds, but it actually had the reverse effect. People needed recreational activities and entertainments as a relaxation, and a great many people were stationed in remote areas where, if they wanted these things, they had to provide them for themselves. Many, forced into a more active life than they had led for years, returned to games they had not played for years; and many, starved of entertainment, took to providing entertainments for their fellows. In many cases, the taste for these activities acquired during the war was retained after it, and it was helped and strengthened by various developments. On the one hand, there was a definite effort by certain associations and bodies to bring recreational activities, including some that had previously been the prerogative of the wealthy, within the reach of all, and to provide facilities and instruction in them; on the other hand, there was television. Television has been accused of restricting social activities by an ability to hypnotise people and keep them tied to their sets. It may well deserve some of these strictures, but there is also something to be said on the other side. It brings demonstrations of various activities to people who have never seen them before, and who, having seen them, often feel that they would like to try them; and, by bringing top-class sport to people's homes, often at times other than those normally used for outdoor recreation, it frees people who want to see the events from the necessity of giving up their own outdoor activities to watch them. This showing of major events at times more compatible with viewers' own recreational activities is achieved in two ways: one being the use of telefilms, and the other because of yet another post-war development, that of the playing of first-class fixtures in the evening by floodlight. Still another factor in the move back to practical, physical recreation is, of course, the increased leisure provided by shorter working hours. To-day, there are more people about than there ever were before; there is more spare time than there ever was before; and there are more recreational activities than there ever were before.

Any attempt at a thorough coverage of the present vast field of games and recreations in one section of this volume would be doomed to failure unless some limitations were applied. There is, therefore, no mention of sports in which the participant is largely dependent on mechanical aids, and none of racing, in which only a comparatively few people can actually take part as riders. There is, however, some mention of most sports and games popular in Britain, including fairly recent importations from abroad, and including also some overseas games that have not yet reached Britain. Indoor games are also included, though one section of them, card games, has had to be restricted to what might be called the major and most popular games of skill. Mention is also made of various non-competitive recreations, indoor and out; of children's games, again indoor and out; and of old games and customs in Britain and elsewhere, some of which survive to-day in whole or in part.

One problem that confronts those keen to try some game or recreation is how to set about it. In many cases, the simplest way of finding out what facilities exist in a particular area is to enquire at a local newspaper office, which will have particulars of all sports clubs, dramatic societies, and other recreational bodies in the area. A few addresses that might be useful to those with certain specialised interests appear at the appropriate places in the text, and a valuable source of helpful information on many games and recreations is the Central Council of Physical Recreation, which has English, Scottish, Welsh, and Northern Irish addresses as follows: England, 6 Bedford Square, London, W.C.1; Scotland, 4 Queensferry Street, Edinburgh, 2; Wales, 18 Windsor Place, Cardiff; and Northern Ireland, 45 Arthur Street, Belfast. Those keen on touring the country at moderate cost might appreciate the services provided by the Youth Hostels Association, which has addresses as follows: England and Wales, Trevelyan House, St. Albans, Herts, with a London office at 22 Gordon Square, London, W.C.1; Scotland, 7 Bruntsfield Crescent, Edinburgh, 10; Northern Ireland, 28 Bedford Street, Belfast; and the Irish Republic, 39 Mountjoy Square, Dublin.

American Football.

American Football is played eleven-aside on a pitch marked by a line across it every 5 yards, and with goals and a ball resembling those used in Rugby Football (*q.v.*), though the ball is smaller. Scoring is by "touchdowns," which are like Rugby tries, but count six; goals after touchdowns, which count one; field goals during play, which count three; and "safeties," which give the attacking side two points if the defenders carry the ball over their own goal-line and touch it down. The ball is advanced by carrying it, forward passing, and kicking. The game consists of a series of "plays" or "downs," the ball becoming dead when the ball-carrier is tackled. A team must advance 10 yards in four downs or give up the ball to their opponents. Players can run ahead of the ball-carrier to protect him by "blocking" opponents. Penalties take the form of distance, usually 5 or 15 yards, lost. A game lasts 60 minutes, divided into four 15-minute quarters.

Angling.

Angling, which is catching fish with rod, line, and hook, goes back to beyond the beginning of history, for it was known to the Greeks and Romans. It is now a recreation, for, though the catch may subsequently be cooked, it is not primarily fishing for the pot. It has its competitive side, with competitions offering prizes for the biggest catch, and there are angling clubs, but many people prefer to use it as a recreation to be enjoyed alone in quiet surroundings. It is actually not so much a recreation as many recreations, for fishing can take place in the sea, rivers, lakes, ponds, and even canals, and there are several entirely different kinds of angling. The most obvious divisions are fresh-water fishing, including coarse and fly-fishing, and sea angling, including fishing from piers and the shore and big-game fishing.

The biggest branch of angling is fresh-water fishing for general or "coarse" fish, which are so called to distinguish them from "game" fish like salmon. Coarse fishing is bait fishing, or, in the case of pike, spinning, groundbait also being thrown in before and during fishing. It covers many varieties of fish, and the bag may be a very mixed one. Certain fish, of course, are known to frequent certain localities or types of locality, but, though the angler may know exactly the kind of fish he is after, he rarely knows if his catch will consist entirely of that kind of fish, or even if it will include any of that kind. Coarse fish do not generally make good eating.

Fly-fishing for salmon and trout differ widely from coarse fishing, and from each other. As the name implies, artificial flies are used, but those used for trout are quite different from those that attract salmon. In the case of trout, a fly is made to resemble a real insect as closely as possible, but, with salmon, this is not necessary. Salmon rarely, if ever, feed in fresh water, and, when in that type of water, they are usually irritable. They will dart wildly at any objects that attract their attention, so salmon flies are simply bright objects designed to draw them on. Fly-fishing is rather an expensive sport, for it means hiring beats on private water. In both coarse and fly-fishing the angler would be well advised to keep out of sight of the quarry as much as possible.

Old though angling itself is, sea angling is a comparatively recent development of it, really dating back only to the nineties of the nineteenth century. It is now the most competitive form of angling, with sea-angling festivals and competitions plentiful during the holiday season. As with coarse fresh-water fishing, the catch can be a very mixed one. Sea angling has what might be called its equivalent of fly-fishing in fishing with feathers, which attract several kinds of fish.

The sea is also the scene of the greatest of all forms of fishing, big-game fishing, when a single bite can mean a catch of 1000 lb., if the angler can win the terrific battle to land it. Big-game fishing takes place from a motor-launch, which is not towed by the hooked fish, but follows it, so that the ensuing fight is between man and fish, and not between the fish and the dead weight of the boat. Such a fight could last for 12 hours, and it is never certain that the angler will win it. With fish of this size, some of them with a terrifying armoury of razor-sharp teeth, liable to turn back on the boat or leap clear of the water, big-game fishing can sometimes be as dangerous as the most adventurous sportsman could wish.

Archery. *See* **Old English Games and Customs.**

Association Football.

Games that may have resembled football were played by very ancient races, and games that certainly were football of a kind were played in the England of several centuries ago, but the Association Football that is the most popular game in Britain, and perhaps the world, to-day had its origins in the games played at English Public Schools in the days before sport became organised.

It was not surprising that some of those who had played football of one kind or another at school should want to go on playing after they left, but, before they could do so, it was necessary to work out a set of rules that would be universally understood and accepted. Meetings were organised by those interested, and, as the universities were natural meeting-places for boys from many schools, it was there, particularly Cambridge, that these took place.

It was soon evident that there was a major difference of opinion between those who wanted handling permitted and those who opposed this. The rival factions proved irreconcilable, so they went their separate ways. The handling enthusiasts based their rules on those in force at Rugby School, and thus pioneered Rugby Football (*q.v.*). Those who felt that football should be played primarily with the foot brought into being the game that was to take its name from the Association that was formed, in 1863, to govern it, and became Association Football, often called by the abbreviation, "Soccer."

Soccer is played with a round, leather-covered ball weighing from 14 to 16 ounces, and with a circumference of from 27 to 28 inches, on a pitch marked out as in the accompanying diagram. It is played eleven-aside, the positions being goalkeeper; right and left full-backs; right, centre, and left half-backs; and five forwards, playing at outside-right, inside-right, centre-forward, inside-left, and outside-left. The object is to score goals by putting the ball between uprights 8 yards apart and under a crossbar 8 feet high. The ball is advanced by kicking or heading, but only the goalkeeper when in his own penalty area may handle it, and he may not carry it. A game lasts for 90 minutes, divided into two halves.

The game is started by a kick-off from the centre, with all the opposing players outside the centre circle and in their own half. The ball must travel at least its own circumference into the opponents' half, and the kicker may not play it again until someone else has done so. The right to kick-off is decided by a toss that gives the winner the option of kicking or choosing which goal he will defend. Ends are changed at half-time, after which the ball is kicked-off by the side that did not do so at the start. The game is restarted in this way after each goal, the non-scorers kicking-off.

If the ball crosses the touch-line it is thrown in by a player of the side that did not put it out, the throw being two-handed. If it crosses the goal-line wide of the goal it is kicked-off by a defender from the 6-yards line if the attackers were responsible, and by an attacker from the intersection of the goal-line and the touch-line if the defenders were responsible.

Infringements are penalised by free kicks, which may be "direct" or "indirect." Direct free kicks, from which a goal may be scored, follow deliberate infringements, indirect free kicks, from which a goal cannot be scored, being for more technical offences. Offences by defenders in the penalty area are generally penalised by a penalty kick, which is a shot from a spot 12 yards out from the centre of the goal, with only the kicker and the goalkeeper in the penalty area, and the goalkeeper barred from moving until the ball has been kicked. However, certain offences in the penalty area, such as carrying by the goalkeeper and obstruction, are penalised only by an indirect free kick.

A player is "offside"—called "sneaking" in the school games from which the rule came—if he is nearer the opponents' goal-line than is the ball unless there are two opponents between him and the goal-line, or unless the ball was last played by an opponent. He cannot, however, be offside in his own half, from a corner kick, or from a throw-in. If a player in an offside position interferes with the game, a free kick is awarded.

A game is controlled by a referee, who has the assistance of two linesmen. These may signal infringements, but the referee is not bound to act on such signals.

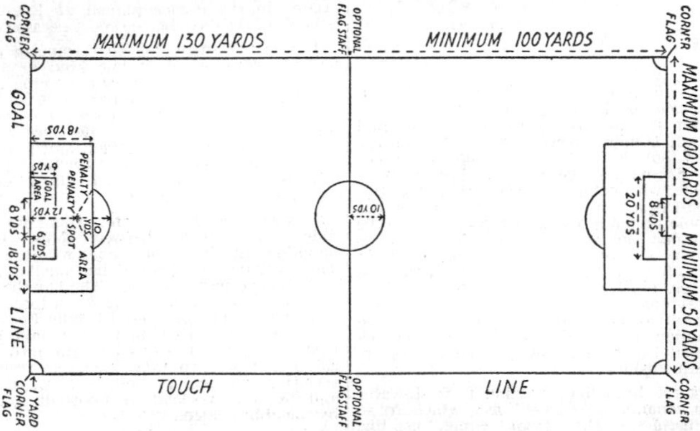

In Britain, soccer is a winter game, the season lasting from August until May, though, in Scotland, it continues even during the short summer season in the form of five-aside football, known as the "short" game. British soccer is highly organised, ranging from the fully professional Football League of four divisions and the equivalent, though slightly smaller, Scottish League through minor professional leagues to amateur leagues. There are also many cup competitions, from the Football Association Challenge Cup and the Scottish Cup downwards.

The game has also spread almost all over the world, being extraordinarily popular all over Europe and in South America, and played to some extent in the United States, Canada, South Africa, Australia, and other areas. There is a World Cup competition that is played for every four years, and an annual European Cup competition played for by the top club of almost every European country. Soccer is also included in the Olympic Games.

Athletics.

The sport of Athletics, which includes running, walking, jumping, and throwing, is probably the most natural of all sports, and certainly one of the oldest, for it began in the days of pre-history or of mythology. Details of the Olympic Games of 776 B.C. are known, and it is certain that the Games were being held long before that. The story of Athletics is not, however, a continuous one, for the Romans discontinued the Games.

A later starting-point might be found in the country sports of various periods of English history, but, though these included some events that might be regarded as the ancestors of certain modern athletic events, they were mainly concerned with activities far removed from Athletics.

Modern Athletics probably really began in 1849, when the Royal Military Academy instituted a meeting that was followed by a similar meeting at Exeter College, Oxford, and, subsequently, at other Oxford and Cambridge Colleges. The Civil Service were also early in the field; and the first athletic club was the Mincing Lane Athletic Club, now the London Athletic Club. There was also the Amateur Athletic Club, which organised an annual championship meeting, and acted as a governing body for both athletics and amateur boxing.

In 1880 the Amateur Athletic Association was formed as a governing body. Other countries, particularly the United States, took to the sports and in 1896 the first modern Olympic Games were held at Athens. Other international meetings and matches followed, and championships and competitions of all standards were started in many countries. Women came into the sport in the early 1920s, and were included in the Olympic Games in 1928. There is now a long list of internationally agreed standard events, including distances measured in yards and miles, and also their metric equivalents; and including also a major all-round test, the ten-event Decathlon.

The longest strictly standard distances are the Marathon of 26 miles 385 yards for runners, and 50,000 metres for walkers, but there are regularly held longer events. For runners, the longest annual race is between Durban and Maritzburg, about 55 miles, the longest in Britain being from London to Brighton, about 53 miles; but there are occasional 100-mile and 24-hour events. For walkers, there are annual 100-mile races and fairly regular 24-hour ones.

The Marathon is not, as might be expected, a revival of an ancient Greek race, for the Greeks had no races longer than 3 miles. It does, however, commemorate an ancient Greek event that is quite possibly no more than a legend: the supposed run by Pheidippides to take the news of the Battle of Marathon to Athens in 490 B.C. The first Marathon race, in 1896, was from Marathon to Athens, but the standard distance of the race is that of the 1908 Olympic Marathon from Windsor to the White City, London, which had just been held when it was thought advisable to have an exact standard distance. All Marathons commemorate the Battle of Marathon, but the oldest annual Marathon, the Boston Marathon, also commemorates the Battle of Lexington (the first battle of the American Revolution), and, more particularly, the ride by Paul Revere that preceded it.

Athletics is entirely an amateur sport. There are some professional races, but this side of the sport is called, not athletics, but pedestrianism.

There is a famous annual professional meeting at the Powderhall Grounds, Edinburgh, and there are other events in Scotland and the North of England. There are also professional meetings in Australia, chiefly in Victoria.

Cross-Country. Athletics is mainly a summer sport, but in cross-country running it has an extremely popular winter branch.

Cross-country originated in the traditional runs at various English Public Schools, particularly Rugby and Shrewsbury; and came into wider prominence when it was adopted by the Thames Rowing Club as winter training. It is still used as training by many sportsmen of all kinds, but it is now also a thriving competitive sport in its own right. There is an International Championship, but this is not yet fully representative, being virtually confined to Western European nations. Major cross-country championships are over courses of 9 or 10 miles.

Badminton might be described as an indoor version of Lawn Tennis (*q.v*) in that it is played over a net, and can consist of either singles or doubles. There, however, the resemblance ceases. Scoring is by single points, and only the servers score, winning shorts by the receivers ending service sequences. The equipment used is lighter than that of Lawn Tennis, particularly the " shuttles " or " birds " that replace the ball. These are half-circles of cork in which feathers are fixed, and, as they do not bounce, all shots are volleys. Unlike Lawn Tennis, shots are made with the wrist, rather than the whole arm.

It is often said that it is impossible to play both Lawn Tennis and Badminton well, but this is not really true. Though the techniques differ, the eye for the moving object is the main requisite of both games. Badminton is a winter game, and many Lawn Tennis players turn to it during that season.

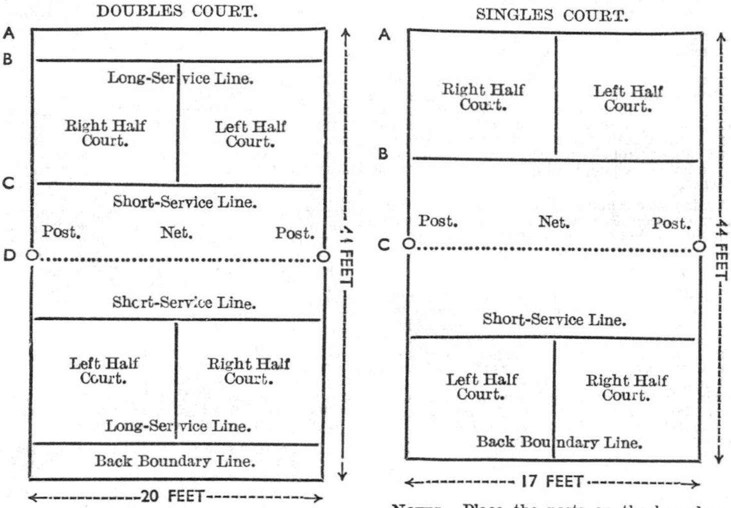

NOTE.—If it is practicable place the posts on the side boundary lines; failing this, place them at any distance not more than 2 ft. outside these lines.

A to B 2 ft. 6 in. A to C 15 ft. 6 in.
A to D 22 ft.

NOTES.—Place the posts on the boundary lines or not more than 2 ft. outside these lines.

The back boundary lines become the long-service lines.

A to B 15 ft. 6 in. B to C 6 ft. 6 in.

Top of net 5 ft. from ground at centre and 5 ft. 1 in. at posts.

Diagram of Ground as marked out for Badminton.

Australian Rules Football.

Australian Rules Football is played 18-aside on large, oval grounds. There is no offside, and scoring in goals and behinds (near misses) is high. It is played to the practical exclusion of all other forms of football in the southern half of Australia.

Badminton.

Badminton is said to have been invented by two guests at the Duke of Beaufort's house at Badminton in Gloucestershire, who spent a wet afternoon playing with the children's battledores and shuttlecocks. It seems certain that the game we know to-day did take shape at Badminton, from which it takes its name, but it is likely that its basis was a game originally played in the Orient.

Ballroom Dancing.

Though the actual dances have changed from time to time, Ballroom Dancing has been one of the most popular of all recreations for a very long time; and while, in recent years, some other evening activities and entertainments have declined in popularity owing to the growing interest in television, the popularity of dancing has actually increased to a remarkable extent.

For many years, the " standard " ballroom dances have been the foxtrot, the quickstep, the waltz, and the tango; but these have frequently been augmented by various other dances, often novelty dances, that have been the subjects of sudden, and generally short-lived, crazes. A stronger challenge, however, has come from Latin America, which has exported quite a number of dances, most of them arousing some interest, and some of them winning and holding firm places. Many of them are ballroom versions of old native and folk dances, which were often solo dances in their original form.

Dancing is highly organised, with its "governing body" composed of qualified teachers, and each dance has its recognised and approved fundamental steps and variations on those steps. If the popularity of a new dance justifies it, the authorities recognise it and approve step sequences. Many people dance regularly without ever having a dancing lesson, but, for the many others who really want to know all about the different dances and steps, there are countless dancing schools all over the country, where dancing is taught both in classes and in private lessons, and where special classes are arranged to teach any new dances that appear. These schools cater for absolute beginners absolutely regardless of age, and also for experienced dancers who want to rise to still higher standards.

A great many people dance purely for pleasure, and never think of dancing as a competitive activity. It is one, though; and there is a link between purely recreational dancing and competitive dancing in the system of medal tests. In these, dancers do not compete with other dancers, but simply try to achieve a certain standard. Beyond these tests, there are numerous competitions, ranging from local ones to world professional and amateur championships and international matches.

A fairly recent and very popular ballroom dancing innovation is formation dancing, in which teams consisting of a number of couples perform dances either as exhibitions or in competitions.

Old-Time Dancing. The most striking and, in some ways, surprising dancing development of recent years has been a tremendous increase in the popularity of Old-Time (often described as Old-Tyme) Dancing. A few old dances, such as the veleta, which, despite its name, is of English origin, had always retained at least a small place in dancing, but the organisation of dances in which every dance was of what might be called approximately veleta vintage was a new idea that seemed destined to enjoy at most the short-lived success that is the reward of novelties. That, however, was not the case. Interest in this type of dancing increased, and it has long since become firmly established, even to the extent of offering competitions. It is, in fact, no longer really true to describe it as old-time, for it is definitely part of the dancing of to-day.

This popularity is not, after all, so very surprising, for an old-time programme offers a wide variety of dances, most of them accompanied by exceptionally tuneful music. The dances are really similar to what, in some other countries, such as, for instance, Scotland, would be called country dancing, and include ordinary "pair" dances, sequence dances, progressive dances, and set or square dances. The veleta holds its place, as do several kinds of tango and many kinds of waltz, as well as the Canadian barn dance, the Boston two-step, the maxina, the lancers, and cotillions and quadrilles. Strangely enough, the cheerful Bohemian dance, the polka, is rarely seen. Old-time dancing provides no scope for just "walking round." The steps are in regular sequences, and all the dancers are making the same movements at the same time.

Bandy. *See* **Skating.**

Baseball.

The invention of Baseball, a summer game played from April until October, and the national game of the United States, is generally credited to an Army officer, its origins being old country games called "One Old Cat" and "Two Old Cat."

Teams are nine-aside, and bat and field in turn. The main part of the ground, the "diamond," has a "base," marked by a sack, at each corner, the lines from sack to sack being the "base paths." One base is "home," and there the batter stands, by a square of rubber on the ground, called the "plate." The base forward and to the right of a right-handed batter is "first," the one straight ahead of him is "second," and the one forward and to his left is "third," the distance from one base to the next being 30 yards. 20 yards out straight in front of the plate is the pitcher's "mound." The lines from home to first and from home to third are continued beyond these bases, and are the "foul lines."

It is the object of the batting side, using a bat which resembles a long, heavy Indian club with which to hit a hard, white ball weighing 5 ounces, to score runs, one being scored each time a player completes a circuit of the bases, not necessarily from one hit. When a batter leaves the plate, either "out" or to proceed along the base paths, the next man comes in, the team's innings lasting until three men are out. Nine such innings complete the game, and, in each innings, the batting side carries on at the point in the batting order reached in the previous innings. There is no toss for first innings, the visiting side always batting first.

The pitched ball reaches the batter without touching the ground, and, if not hit, it should pass over the plate between the batter's shoulders and knees. If it does so, it is a "strike," and three such strikes dismiss the batter. If it does not, it is a strike only if the batter swings at it; otherwise it is a "ball," and four balls give the batter a free passage to first base, called a "walk." A batter also walks if he is hit by a pitched ball. Other ways in which the batter can be dismissed are by being caught, and by being "put out" while on the base paths by failing to reach the base to which he is running before the ball. When an out is made, the ball does not become "dead." If there is more than one runner on the base paths, then, if the ball can be relayed quickly enough, two, or even three, men can be put out on the same "play."

If the batter hits fairly, he must run, but, to be fair, the hit must be in front of him and between the foul lines. A "foul hit" counts as a strike against him, except that the third strike, which actually dismisses him, must be a clean one across the plate. If a foul is caught, he is out.

The fielding side is divided into three sections, the "battery," the "infield," and the "outfield." The battery consists of the pitcher and the catcher, who stands behind the plate and gives signals indicating the kind of ball he thinks the pitcher should deliver: for, though the pitched ball does not touch the ground, pitchers can produce a wide variety of deliveries, including various kinds of curve. The infield consists of the first baseman, at or near first; the second baseman, between first and second; the shortstop, between second and third; and the third baseman, at or near third. The outfield covers the ground beyond the infield, the three remaining fielders taking the right, centre, and left sections of it. Catchers wear a large glove on the non-throwing hand, a mask, a chest protector, and leg-guards. All the other fielders wear a glove on the non-throwing hand, the first baseman's being larger than the others. The batter wears no protective gear.

Substitutes are permitted, pitchers frequently being changed if they are being hit, and "pinch hitters" being sent in instead of weak batters if a hit is desperately needed. If this happens, the man replaced, often the pitcher, cannot return when his side fields again, though his field replacement need not be the man who batted for him.

As with Cricket (*q.v.*) batting averages are recorded, these being calculated by dividing the number of times at bat into the number of hits. An average of 0·400, referred to as "four hundred," would be exceptionally good. "Hits" mean safe hits on which the batter achieved one or more bases without giving a chance. If he reaches base because a catch was dropped or a ball misfielded, he plays on from there in the usual way, but is not credited with a hit. Pitchers are graded according to the number of games won and lost. Recorded fielding statistics include each man's "put outs," "assists," which are throws from which a team-mate made a put out, and "errors."

In the United States there are clubs and leagues of all standards, from professionals of various classes through semi-professionals to amateurs, called "sandlotters," and boys. The top class of all consists of two major leagues, the National and the American, each with eight clubs. The champions of these two leagues meet in a best-of-seven-games series for the "Championship of the World," always known as the World Series.

Baseball is also the chief summer game of Canada, and it is quite widely played in some other countries, including Australia, Britain, and Japan.

Softball. Similar to Baseball is Softball, which is popular in the United States with girls as well as men, and which was demonstrated in Britain during the War by American and Canadian servicemen. The ball is not particularly soft, but it is larger than a baseball, and pitching is under-arm. Distances between bases, and between the plate and the mound, are shorter than in the parent game.

Basketball.

Basketball was invented by an American Y.M.C.A. official at Springfield, Massachusetts, as a winter team game that could be played indoors. It can be played in almost any gymnasium or hall, and it can also be played outdoors on an asphalt court. In America it is played by teams of all standards from schoolboys to professionals, and it is watched by more spectators than any other game. It has also spread to almost as many other countries as has Association Football (*q.v*), and it is included in the Olympic Games. It has been established for some years in Britain, where it has been encouraged by the Services and the Y.M.C.A.

Basketball is played five-aside, substitutes being permitted, with a ball resembling that used in Association Football, and goals consisting of posts that have iron rings with short nets attached to them and backboards. It is purely a handling game, and the ball is advanced by dribbling, which means bouncing, and by passing. Deliberate bodily contact is not allowed. Goals thrown during play count two points, and goals thrown from free throws after infringements one point. Height is an asset in the game, which demands stamina and agility, and which has been highly recommended as an ideal training activity by coaches of other sports, particularly Athletics (*q.v.*).

Girls also play Basketball, and, in Britain, there are national championships for clubs and schools, and international matches between England and Scotland.

Billiards.

Billiards, which originated in France, is a game of angles, and of very great skill. It is played on a table measuring 12 feet by 6 feet 1½ inches, having six pockets, one at each corner, and one in the middle of each side. The table is covered with green baize, the edges being of cloth-covered rubber, called "cushions." Across the table, 2 feet 5 inches from the bottom edge, is a line, called the "baulk" line, the space between the line and the bottom of the table being "baulk." On the baulk side of the line there is a semi-circle with a radius of 11½ inches from the centre of the line. Down the centre of the table are four "spots," one 12¾ inches from the top, one midway between the top and the centre, one in the centre, and one in the middle of the baulk line. Two white balls, one with a spot for identification purposes, and one red one, are used, the balls being played with "cues" that taper down to a striking tip. The remaining equipment includes a long, cue-like stick with a metal cross fixed diagonally on the end, called a "rest" or "jigger," and a special long cue, these being used when the player cannot reach his ball in the ordinary way. Most games are "singles," though "doubles" can be played, the object of the game being to score points according to fixed rules, an agreed number of points making the game.

To decide who is to start, players "string" by playing their balls simultaneously from baulk up to the top cushion, the ball which returns nearer to the bottom cushion winning. At the start, the red ball is "spotted" on the top spot, and players start from the baulk circle. Scoring is three for pocketing, or "potting," the red or going in off the red; two for potting the white, which is, of course, the opponent's ball, or going in off the white; and two for a cannon, which is hitting both the other balls. A player whose shot hits no other balls at all gives one point to his opponent, unless his ball goes into a pocket, when he forfeits three. A player's turn, called a "break," continues as long as he is actually scoring. When the red is potted, it is immediately respotted.

Snooker. Also played on a billiard table, and perhaps even more popular, is Snooker, which uses 22 balls, positioned as follows: 15 reds in the form of a triangle with its apex on the second spot from the top, and its base at the top end; a black on the top spot; a pink touching the apex ball of the triangle; a blue on the centre spot; a brown in the middle of the baulk line, with a green beside it on the left end of the baulk circle, and a yellow on the right end; and a white, which is the cue-ball to be played. The points values of the balls are from one for red, through yellow, green, brown, blue, and pink, to seven for black. A player's turn continues as long as he scores, his first shot being at a red, when, if he pots one, he plays at one of the other colours, play being at reds and colours alternately as long as balls are being potted, and as long as there are reds on the table, after which the remaining colours are played in ascending order of value.

A variation of Snooker is Snooker Plus. This uses two additional balls, an orange, placed between the pink and the blue and valued at eight points, and a purple, placed between the blue and the brown and valued at ten points.

Pool, Russian Pool, and Pyramids. Other games played on a billiard table include Pool, Russian Pool, and Pyramids. In Pool each player has a ball of a different colour, the order of play being white, red, yellow, green, brown, blue, pink, black. Each player plays at the ball of his predecessor, and tries to pot it, the game starting with white spotting his ball on the top spot, so that red is actually the first to play. A player whose ball is potted loses a life, players losing three lives dropping out of the game. A turn continues as long as a player is potting balls, and if he clears all the balls on the table he then spots his own ball for the next player.

Russian Pool uses the yellow, green, blue, and black balls, with the white as cue-ball, the black being placed on the top spot, the blue on the centre spot, the green on the left side of the baulk circle, and the yellow on the right side. A player's first shot must hit the black, after which he can play at will. Scoring is by potting balls, by going in off balls, and by cannons, but the black can be used only for the top pockets, the blue for the middle pockets, and the green and the yellow for the bottom pockets. Cannons count two, potting or going in off counting nine for the black, seven for the blue, five for the green, and three for the yellow. A player's turn continues as long as he is scoring, but consecutive cannons on the same balls are limited to 25, and the same ball must not be potted from the same spot more than three times in succession. A complete miss forfeits three points. A variation of Russian Pool adds the pink ball, which is spotted on the second spot from the top, counts six, and can be used with any pocket.

Pyramids uses the 15 reds, starting in their triangle, and a white cue-ball, the object being to pot the reds. A turn continues while a player is scoring, 8 balls potted ending the game.

Bird-watching.

Mention of Bird-watching might well bring thoughts of uncomfortable, and even hazardous, journeys to remote islands off the coast of Scotland, or at least to desolate parts of the Scottish mainland; but, while it is true that expert bird-watchers of long experience do frequent these localities, as well, of course, as less-remote places like the Norfolk Broads, bird-watching can be practised, and should certainly be started, much nearer home, and with birds seen by almost everybody, though properly observed by very few, every day.

Bird-watching means exactly what it says: watching birds flying; watching two birds to see if they are, in fact, a pair, or if they are two males competing for the attentions of a hen-bird, which may be near by; watching where and how and with what materials they build nests; watching what they eat and how they get it; watching a pair in a nest to see if the male plays a full part in their domestic life, or if he just sits on a branch singing while the female does it all. If the bird-watcher really wants to increase his knowledge, and perhaps that of other people, careful observation accompanied by careful note-taking is essential, and will reveal some surprising facts. It has, for instance, been discovered that a pair of quite ordinary "garden" birds may fly sixty miles a day for every hundred yards their source of food is from the nest, and that the collecting of materials for building a nest may mean a total of six hundred miles flying. In time, the bird-watcher may wish to go in search of more unusual birds in remote places, but if he is anxious to increase the general knowledge of birds he might do better to remain close to his home; for, so keen have the experts been to track down the rarer birds, that far more is now known about them than is known about "ordinary" birds like the blackbird and the thrush.

Bird-watchers who would like to contact and compare notes with those with similar interests can do so by joining a Natural History Society, of which there is at least one in almost every county, full particulars generally being available at public libraries.

Boat Races.

Race rowing is a strenuous sport that makes no pretence of attracting as many active participants as some other sports and games; yet its long history includes races with unusual stories about them; races that are amongst the greatest annual international sporting events; and one race that provides what is probably the most enthusiastically supported free sporting spectacle in the world.

That, of course, is the Oxford and Cambridge University boat race, rowed on the Thames from Putney to Mortlake. First rowed in 1829, it has offered its excited public, which includes thousands of people with no connection of any kind with either university, everything, including runaway victories, dead heats, and even sinking boats. To all intents and purposes, this is a regular annual event, and has been so since 1856; but, in actual fact, every race is the result of a separate special challenge from the losers of the previous race to the winners of it. The race has an interesting parallel in the United States, where Yale University, whose colours are dark blue, annually meet Harvard University, which is at Cambridge, on a river called the Thames.

The Oxford and Cambridge race is the best-known annual race on the Putney–Mortlake stretch of the Thames, but it is by no means the only one. There are other races that attract entries sometimes numbered in hundreds: entries that are far too big to race abreast on the Thames, and so race in single file, with crews following each other at fixed intervals in what are known as the Head of the River races. The biggest of these is for crews of eight, but there are other Head of the River races for women's crews, who cover only part of this famous stretch of water, and for single scullers. Single scullers also cover this course in a straightforward race in the Wingfield Sculls event, which ranks as the English Amateur Championship, and which was first held one year after the first Oxford and Cambridge race, in 1830.

Head of the River races, but with a difference, are also held between the colleges of Oxford and Cambridge, where the Isis and the Cam, respectively, are much too narrow to permit straightforward racing. These are the Bump Races, in which each crew endeavours to catch and bump the crew ahead of it, except for the leading crew, which can concentrate on staying in front. When a bump is achieved, the two crews pull into the bank, and change places for the next day's racing. The racing goes on for four days, and it is, of course, the ambition of each crew, apart from the leaders, to register a bump on each day.

Back on the Thames, but farther down it towards the port and docks of London, is the scene of a race that makes the Oxford and Cambridge race and the Wingfield Sculls look like recent innovations. This is the annual race from London Bridge to Chelsea for the Doggett's Coat and Badge, a single sculling event open only to young watermen who are within twelve months of completing their apprenticeship. It was founded in 1715 in honour of the House of Hanover, and to commemorate the anniversary of "King George I's happy accession to the throne of Great Britain," by Thomas Doggett, a Dublin-born actor connected with the Drury Lane and Haymarket theatres, who regularly travelled on the Thames in preference to using the roads, and who left a sum of money to perpetuate the race, which is now controlled by the Fishmongers' Company.

This race is more truly an annual one than almost any other event; for, while most so-called annual races have been subjected to long interruptions because of the two World Wars, those qualified for the Doggett races during those years were subsequently traced, and the races duly decided after the wars. The event is a colourful one, always followed by a barge carrying a batch of past winners wearing the Coat and Badge, and also the cap, breeches, silk stockings, and buckled shoes that go with them. The scarlet, pleated, quilted Coat, with its silver buttons and the large silver arm Badge bearing the White Horse of Hanover and the word "Liberty", are presented at the Fishmongers' Hall, where the winner is greeted with a salute of trumpets and the tune, "See the Conquering Hero Comes."

For a rowing event of a very different kind, dating back "only" to 1839, one must go up the Thames, far beyond the end of the Tideway, to Henley, for the annual Royal Regatta. This consists of events open to the world and others closed to English colleges and schools for eights, fours, pairs, double sculls, and single sculls, the most famous of its races being the Grand Challenge Cup for eights and the Diamond Sculls.

A journey far from the Thames will bring to light the story of a rowing trophy that first appeared sixteen years before Oxford first met Cambridge. The Carrow Cup was awarded for a four-oared race on the River Yare, in Norfolk, from Carrow Bridge to Whitlingham and back in 1813. Sometime during the 1840s that cup disappeared: to reappear in 1890—in Australia. In 1947 it came into the possession of the Victoria Rowing Association, which made it the trophy for a pair-oared race, but sent it to England for exhibition in the 1948 Olympic rowing museum. There it was recognised as a Norfolk trophy, and, though it returned to Victoria, it came home again in 1950, when the Melbourne club gave it to the Norwich Rowing Committee, which now annually awards it to "the Norwich club whose general performance, judged by a points system in Regattas, shall be best."

Bobsleigh Riding. *See* **Winter Sports.**

Bowls.

Bowls, one of the oldest of all games, was once regarded as "an old man's game," but it actually has many devotees of all ages and both sexes, and is played indoors as well as outdoors. It certainly goes back to the thirteenth century, when it popularity made it one of the games legislated against as likely to draw people away from archery. Henry VIII played; and the famous game on Plymouth Hoe, in which Sir John Hawkins stayed to beat Sir Francis Drake even after the Armada had been sighted, if not definitely authenticated, is accepted as fact by several historians. It is interesting to note that, if this game was played, it would have been almost identical with a game of to-day, for it was in that century that the "bias" that is a leading feature of the bowls or "woods" was introduced. A century later, however, Bowls, which was largely played on greens attached to taverns, acquired a reputation as being merely an adjunct to pot-house revelry, but it was revived on a higher level in Scotland, and never again came so near to oblivion.

There are actually two games of Bowls, the Rink or Level Green game and the Crown Green game, and it is the rinks rather than the objectives that differ. The Level Green game is the more widely played, and it takes place on a perfectly flat piece of well-cared-for turf. The Crown Green game, which is popular in the North and Midlands, is played on a green of which the centre is 6 inches or more higher than the corners. The games differ—for instance, in the putting into play of the object ball—but only slightly, so it will be appreciated that the Crown Green game demands a good deal of experience and skill. It is mainly a singles game, whereas the Level Green game is played between sides consisting of one, two, three, or four players.

Bowls looks a simple game, the object being simply to place the bowls as near as possible to the object ball, or "jack." The bowls, however, are "biased," and the game is actually one of considerable skill. When bias was introduced, it took the form of weighting with lead, but it is now achieved by turning one side of the bowl less round than the other. Level Green bowls weigh up to 3½ lb., but Crown Green bowls are smaller and less biased. On the Crown Green, however, the jack, which is played into position by the first player, is also biased.

Players normally use two bowls in a game, or four in singles, and the side with the best record of bowls near the jack wins the "end," and the best record of shots in an agreed number of ends the game.

A Bowls green is such a perfect piece of grass that it might be thought that the expression "rub of the green," used to describe an unavoidable piece of bad luck, comes from this game. In actual fact, though, it would probably be more correct to attribute this phrase to Golf (*q.v.*).

Boxing.

Boxing, sometimes called "The Noble Art of Self Defence," though actually aggression is its keynote and defence an incidental, is a modern continuation of the old sport of prize-fighting, which, though always illegal, was popular from the time of the Regency until it was succeeded by the present-day glove-fighting at the end of the nineteenth century.

In prize-fighting bare fists were used, and wrestling holds were allowed. Rounds ended when a fighter went down, and fights continued until, following a knockdown, a man failed to come up to the scratch line in 30 seconds.

In modern boxing, gloves are worn, and no wrestling is allowed. Rounds last for a fixed time, generally 3 minutes with 1 minute between rounds, and fights last only for a fixed number of rounds, never more than fifteen. A knockdown does not end a round, the man who is down having 10 seconds in which to rise. If he fails to do so, his opponent wins by a knock-out. If a man fails to come up at the beginning of a round or if the fight is stopped to save a man from further injury, the victory is by a technical knock-out. If, however, both men are still on their feet at the end of the stipulated number of rounds, a decision is given on points. Boxing is therefore technically a contest of skill for points, and, as such, far removed from prize-fights to a finish.

Fights are controlled by a referee, and, in British professional boxing, he is solely responsible for any points decision. In amateur boxing the decision is given by several judges, who sit apart from each other. The difference between a good professional and a good amateur is probably more marked in boxing than in any other sport

Boxing contests are arranged in classes according to weight, the divisions being: fly-weight, up to 8 stone; bantam-weight, up to 8 stone 6 lb.; feather-weight, up to 9 stone; light-weight, up to 9 stone 9 lb.; welter-weight, up to 10 stone 7 lb.; middle-weight, up to 11 stone 6 lb.; light-heavy or cruiser-weight, up to 12 stone 7 lb.; and heavy-weight, any weight. In amateur boxing some of these weights are slightly different, and there are two additional classes, light-welter-weight, up to 10 stone, and light-middle-weight, up to 11 stone.

Prize-fighting was governed successively by "Broughton's Code," the "New Rules of the Ring," and the "London Rules." Then, in 1867, the eighth Marquess of Queensberry and Mr. J. G. Chambers drew up the rules that have been the basis of boxing ever since. British professional boxing has been controlled since 1929 by the British Boxing Board of Control. The Amateur Boxing Association has governed amateur boxing since 1884, when it took over from the Amateur Athletic Club, which had looked after both boxing and athletics.

Prize-fighting is finished, but it has left a legacy, not only in modern boxing, but through an expression that has become part of the language, for the phrase "come up to scratch" originally referred to a prize-fighter stepping up for a new round.

Bridge.

Auction. Auction Bridge is a card game in which two partnerships of two oppose each other, each player facing his partner. A complete pack is used, the suits having special values, ranging from 6 points per trick for Clubs, through Diamonds, Hearts, and Spades, to 10 points per trick for No-trumps. When bidding, it is the points value of the bid, and not the number of tricks bid, that decides seniority, though the highest number of tricks prevails when the points values are equal. If a bid, or contract, is doubled or redoubled, the trick score is doubled or redoubled.

A player may pass, but, should he bid under the previous bid, he can be penalised, the player on his left having the option of closing the bidding at the previous bid or demanding that the offender make a proper bid. In this case, his partner is barred from bidding again unless the opponents do so. Should a player bid out of turn, the player on his left can demand a new deal.

Points are counted in two ways, below the line and above it. Points below count towards game (30 points), and are awarded for all tricks over six made by the contracting side. Points above the line are gained in various ways, and count in the final score, but not towards game. The first side to win two games wins the rubber, and 250 extra points above the line. The holding of honours also wins points above the line, as follows: three honours, twice the suit value; four, four times the suit value; five, five times the suit value; four in one hand, eight times the suit value, four in one hand and one in partner's, nine times the suit value; five in one hand, ten times the suit value. At No-trumps the honours count for Aces is 30 points for three, 40 for four, and 100 for four in one hand. The points for defeating a contract are 50 for each trick by which the contract fails. Extra points for making a doubled or redoubled contract are 50 for the contract plus 50 for each trick over when doubled, and 100 for the contract plus 100 for each trick over when redoubled. 50 points are awarded for a little slam, which is 12 tricks, and 100 for a grand slam, all 13 tricks.

The player who first named the contract suit is the declarer, and his partner is dummy. After the lead, which comes from the player on declarer's left, dummy lays his hand face upwards on the table, and it is played by declarer, dummy having only limited rights of intervention. If his partner fails to follow suit, he can ask him if he has no cards in the appropriate suit; he can draw attention if too few or too many cards are played in a trick, or if the wrong side gathers up the trick; he can discuss questions of fact, and correct any claims made by the opponents to which they are not entitled. He cannot draw attention to any revoke; he cannot claim any penalty; and he cannot warn his partner against leading from the wrong hand.

Revoking is failing to follow suit when this is possible, the revoke becoming established when the player or his partner plays to the next trick. Up to then, the offender may correct it. The penalty is 2 tricks for the first revoke, and one for subsequent revokes, the penalty tricks to be taken only from the trick in which the revoke occurred or later ones.

A lead from the wrong hand may not be withdrawn unless the opponents request this. If they do, the card is replaced, and play continues. If declarer's opponents lead from the wrong hand, declarer may either demand a lead in a particular suit from the right hand or reserve the right to have the exposed card played whenever he chooses to call for it. In this case, though, the offender may play the card before it is called, if he has an opportunity.

Contract. At Contract Bridge only the tricks contracted for are scored below the line, over-tricks being recorded above it. The score for tricks is 30 in a major suit (Spades or Hearts) and 20 in a minor suit (Diamonds or Clubs). In No-trumps the first trick counts 40 and subsequent tricks 30. In bidding, the highest number of tricks prevails, regardless of suit values.

A game is 100 points, two games won constituting a rubber, which carries a bonus of 700 points, if the opponents have not won a game. In an unfinished rubber, a game gains 300 points and a part score 50, provided the opponents have no part score at all. A side winning a game becomes vulnerable, and this affects subsequent scoring.

Penalties for failing to make a contract are 50 points per undertrick if the declarer is not vulnerable and 100 points per undertrick if he is. If an opponent has doubled, the penalties are 100 for the first undertrick and 200 for subsequent ones if not vulnerable, and 200 for the first undertrick and 300 for subsequent ones if vulnerable. If the declarer has redoubled, these penalties are doubled. In successful contracts doubled, over-tricks score 100 if declarer is not vulnerable and 200 if he is. A successful doubled or redoubled contract wins a bonus of 50 points. Bonuses are awarded for making slams, if they have been bid. If declarer is not vulnerable, the bonuses are 500 for a small slam (12 tricks) and 1000 for a grand slam (13 tricks). If vulnerable, the bonuses are 750 and 1500. Honours points are 100 for four honours in the contract suit in one hand; 150 for five honours in one hand; and, in No-trumps, 150 for four Aces in one hand.

A player making an insufficient bid may be required either to pass or to make a sufficient bid. If he passes or makes a sufficient bid in a different suit, his partner is barred from further bidding. A call out of turn is void, but, if it was a pass, the offender must pass in his turn, and, if it was not a pass, his partner is barred from further bidding. A player has no redress if he misunderstands a bid, though he can ask for a bid or a sequence of bids to be repeated. When three successive players have passed, the contract is fixed, declarer being the first player on the contracting side to nominate the suit, and dummy being his partner.

Dummy is entitled to ask for or give information on the laws, to point out revokes and try to prevent those about to occur, and to remind his partner from which hand he should lead. If, however, he looks at any hand other than his own, he forfeits these rights.

If declarer leads from the wrong hand the opponents can demand a lead from the correct hand; and, if it is possible, this must be in the same suit. If a defender leads when it is the declarer's turn, the card becomes a penalty card. If a defender leads when it is his partner's turn, declarer may either bar a lead in that suit or make the exposed card a penalty card. A penalty card must be played at the first legal opportunity.

Contract Bridge is a game of systems. There are systems for assessing the value of a hand, and there are more important and more involved systems governing bidding, the object of these being the interchange of information between partners.

Bumping Races. *See* **Boat Races.**

Camping.

For those whose holiday requirements are a maximum of fresh air and a minimum of formality, Camping is the ideal solution. Choice of equipment, such as tents, tent furniture, and cooking accessories, is entirely a matter for the camper, the only difficulty in this department being making a selection from the very wide variety available. The choice will, of course, depend to some extent on the type of camping holiday planned, for Camping can take several forms. It can, for instance, be static, or it can be combined with motoring, canoeing, cycling, or walking. The more static the camp or the heavier the transport, the more elaborate the equipment that can be taken, cyclists and walkers being restricted to the lightest, though not necessarily the least comfortable, gear.

Practically all suitable camp sites are privately owned, so permission to use them must, of course, be obtained. The choice of site is of major importance, and should combine proximity to water with shelter from winds. The pitching of the tent or tents is also important, as, if the campers intend to keep the tent "door" open at night, they will not want to face east, and be wakened unduly early by the rising sun. If the camp is static, tents should not be allowed to remain too long in one position, as this is not good for the ground on which they are pitched; and the hallmark of the experienced camper is that he leaves the site exactly as he found it. Rain is always a possibility, and demands certain precautions, particularly the slackening of the guy ropes, which might otherwise become taut enough to pull out the pegs, in which case the tent would probably be blown away. In wet weather the tent walls and roof should not be touched from the inside, as this tends to cause, or to reveal, leaks.

Several organisations exist to assist campers, including the Camping Club of Great Britain and Ireland, of 35 Old Kent Road, London, S.E.1, which specialises in lightweight camping, and has done much to develop suitable equipment and to obtain and list sites. There is also the Youth Camping Association, of 106 Ashurst Road, Cockfosters, Herts; and canoe-campers have an organisation of their own in the Canoe Camping Club, of 4 Felstead Road, Wanstead, London, E.11.

Canadian Football.

Canadian Football resembles American (*q.v.*), but is twelve-aside, uses only three downs, and limits blocking.

Canoeing.

Canoeing is both a recreation and an organised competitive sport.

As a recreation, it can take the form either of simply taking a canoe out and "paddling about" for a short period or, by combining it with Camping (*q.v.*), of a lengthy and interesting river trip, the canoe-camper proceeding, of course, at his own pace, and giving as much time as he wishes to sightseeing.

As a sport, Canoeing has Olympic Games status. In Britain it has its headquarters on the Thames at Teddington in Middlesex, the governing body being the British Canoe Union. There are races for singles and pairs, including events for women. There is also one long annual race for pairs that really combines Canoeing with Camping. The course is from Devizes in Wiltshire to London, and the competitors have to negotiate a long series of locks.

There are two types of canoe: Canadian canoes, like those used for many years by Red Indians, and kayaks, the very light Eskimo-type canoes, in which an expert, but not a beginner, can turn a complete circle into the water and out again without losing his seat in his craft. Both types are catered for in the Olympic Games, but most of the Canoeing in Britain is in kayaks.

Card Games. *See* **Bridge; Patience; Solo Whist; Whist.**

Chess.

Chess, greatest of all board games and a game of pure skill, has a known history of some 1500 years. Eastern players, who originated it, reached a high standard, but the game's greatest advances were made in Italy in the fifteenth and sixteenth centuries. In the early days the value of the pieces and their moves underwent periodical changes, but the game we know to-day dates from the sixteenth century.

The board has 64 squares in eight rows of eight, and each player has 16 pieces, one set being white and the other black or red, but always referred to as black. A toss decides possession of white, which always starts. The object is the capture of the opponent's King, no matter how many pieces are lost in doing so, nor how many opposing pieces remain untaken. If the King could be captured on the next move, it is in "check." It must move out of check, and, if it cannot, it is "checkmate." and the game is over. If the King is not in check, but cannot move except into check, and the player has no other pieces he can move, it is "stalemate," and a draw. Games may also be drawn if neither player has sufficient pieces to force a win.

In addition to the King, each player has a Queen, two Bishops, two Rooks—sometimes wrongly called Castles—two Knights, and eight Pawns, and all these move in accordance with rigid rules. The following diagram shows the pieces at the start of a game:

BLACK

QR QKt QB Q K KB KKt KR

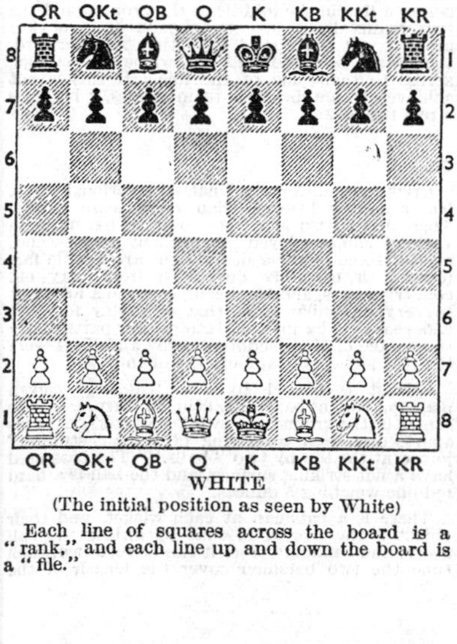

QR QKt QB Q K KB KKt KR

WHITE

(The initial position as seen by White)

Each line of squares across the board is a "rank," and each line up and down the board is a "file."

The permitted moves are as follows:—

The King  can move one square at a time in any direction.

The Queen  can move in accordance with the powers described below for both Bishops and Rooks.

The Bishops  move diagonally as many squares as desired.

The Rooks  move straight along the ranks or files as far as desired.

The Knights  move as shown in the following diagram:—

(The Knight's Move)

Stationed away from the side of the board, and on a black square, the Knight illustrated can move to any of the numbered white squares. The move is one square along rank or file in the desired direction, and one square diagonally. The Pawns  move straight forward, one square at a time, but may move two squares when moved for the first time. They capture by moving one square diagonally forwards. A Pawn reaching the eighth rank may be replaced by any other piece.

Once during a game, a player may "Castle," by moving the King two squares towards the Rook, which is placed on the last square passed over by the King. This move cannot be made if either the King or any of the squares he would pass over are in check. Neither King nor Rook must have moved previously.

Games of Chess can be recorded, so players can play over great "Masters" games, and record their own games.

Draughts. Draughts—called Checkers in America—is also played on a chess board. Possibly older even than Chess, it is much simpler, but not devoid of skill.

Each player has twelve pieces or "men," all alike. Squares of one colour only are used, the men starting on the first three rows on the board. The move is one square diagonally forward, but a man reaching the eighth row becomes a "King," and may then move forward or backward. The object is the capture of all the opposing men by jumping over them. If the arrangement of the men permits it, more than one man may be captured in a single move. A man which can effect a capture but does not do so is removed from the board, or "huffed."

Children's Games.

Amongst the many sports and games that have come into being through the years and the centuries is a lengthy list of what, for lack of a more precise name, might be called Children's

Games, suitable for playgrounds or, indeed, practically any open space. Almost without exception, they are simple; they require little or no equipment; they can be adapted to almost any number of players; and they are good fun and good exercise. Most of them are also very old; few of them have any " official " name; and many of them have had many names.

The " basic " playground game is Tag, in which one player, called " it," chases the others, any player he touches becoming " it." A variation of this allows players to rest without being tagged if they can find a piece of wood to touch; but there are many more variations that make more interesting games. In Imitation Tag " it " can follow any mode of progression he chooses, such as running, walking, running or walking backwards, hopping, or crawling on all fours; and whatever he does the other players must do, too. In Partner Tag all the players except " it " and one other stand about in pairs with their arms linked. " It " chases the other free player, who may link up with any pair, when the player at the other end of the link becomes " it's " quarry. For Chase Tag, all the players except " it " and one other form a circle, each player just touching his neighbour's shoulder with one outstretched arm. " It " and his quarry start at opposite sides of the circle, and the quarry may dive in and out under the outstretched arms, " it " being compelled to follow exactly the same route. A variation of this has three players running, with the second chasing the first, and the third chasing the second. Pursuit Race is a form of tag in which every player is both chaser and chased. Players station themselves in a very large circle, all facing either clockwise or anti-clockwise, and with approximately the same distance between each. At the word " Go," each player sets off after the one in front of him, tagged players dropping out.

Marching Tag also starts with the players in a circle facing clockwise or anti-clockwise, but they are close behind each other, and there is an " it " inside the circle. " It " announces a number, and then starts counting steadily up to it. As he does so, the others march round in their circle, but when he reaches the chosen number, they all dash away to a " home " line 25 or 30 yards away, with " it " in pursuit. Listen Tag starts with the players in a circle, facing inwards, and with " it " and one other player inside the circle. This other player announces a word, and then goes on talking or telling a story, in the middle of which he casually introduces the word. When he does so, the players dash for the home line, with " it " either in pursuit or calmly tagging some player who has missed the word and is still listening to the story. Numbers Tag has the players in two teams, who form rows, one behind the other, and both with their backs to the home line. The front team agree on a number that their rivals do not know, and a member of the rear team then calls out numbers in any order. If he hits on the agreed number, the front team swing round, each man trying to tag the man behind him before that player realises what is happening and dashes for the home line. Hidden Numbers Tag starts similarly, except that the teams face the home line, each player in the front team having a number that is unknown to the rear team. A player in the rear team calls out a number, and the player with that number dashes for the home line with the caller in pursuit. This goes on until everyone has gone, the last front-team player being allowed to run immediately his predecessor is either safe or tagged.

Bucket Tag has all the players in a line with their backs to the home line, " it," who is in the middle of the line, having a bucket several yards in front of him. He tries to toss a tennis ball or a rubber ball into the bucket, and the moment he succeeds, everyone dashes for the home line with " it " in pursuit. Ball Tag and Football Tag are like ordinary tag, except that, in ball tag, " it " must hit his quarry with a tennis ball or a rubber ball, which he throws, and in football tag he must hit him with a football, which he kicks. Another form of Ball Tag is between teams, and uses a football, which is thrown. The area is divided into two halves, one team being in each, and each half having an additional, narrow zone behind it. A non-player should act as referee, and start the game by throwing the ball up over the centre line, which no player must cross. The game consists of trying to hit opponents on the legs with the ball, any player who is hit retiring to the zone behind the other team, from where he can still take part in the game by throwing the ball at his opponents from behind if it should come through to him. The game continues until one half has been cleared. This " pitch " also serves for End to End Ball, in which half of each team starts off in the zone behind their opponents, and the ball is not thrown at opposing players, but through to team-mates behind the other team, each successful effort counting as a goal.

There are several popular " combat " games, in which players take part two at a time. Two are described, not very accurately, as Indian Wrestling. In one, the two opponents face each other, clasp their right hands, and press their right feet against each other, the " fight " consisting of an attempt to make the opponent move his foot by pushing with the clasped hand. In the other method opponents face each other, each with his hands pressed against his rival's shoulders, and with some object, such as an Indian club, a skittle, or even a stone bottle, on the ground between them, the object being to push the opponent in such a way that he will knock the object over. In Cock-Fighting two players with arms folded hop, each trying to make the other put his raised foot to the ground by pushing into him with his shoulder. Hat Snatch is more tag than combat, unless it is a combat of wits. Two teams face each other, some way apart, and having a hat or cap or some other suitable object on the ground between them. Each player has a number, the same numbers being used for both teams. A non-player acting as referee calls a number, and the players concerned, one from each team, try to snatch the object and carry it back to their own team, the one who does not get it trying to tag his opponent before he reaches safety.

Finally, three Tug-of-War variations. In Elbow Tug two players stand back to back with their elbows linked, each having in front of him a line, across which he tries to pull his opponent. In Rope Tug three players grasp a rope that has been tied so that it is actually a circle. The players are outside the circle of the rope, holding it with one hand, and having their backs to it. In front of each player is a small stick, which he tries to pick up, without letting go of the rope, before his rivals can pick up their sticks. Sprint Tug may end up as an ordinary tug-of-war, but it starts with the rope being placed at right angles across a line in the middle of the ground, and the two teams lined up at opposite ends of the ground. At the word " Go " they rush forward, the object being to pull the whole of the rope across to their side of the line. If this is not achieved before the other team arrives, it becomes a real tug-of-war.

Cricket.

Cricket, traditionally England's national game, has a longer history than most team games. There have been attempts to trace its origin in various games played by ancient races; and, even if some of these derivations are a little far-fetched, it certainly developed from very old country games, and has been played in a form not so very dissimilar from that of to-day for over 250 years. The men of Hampshire, particularly the village of Hambledon, Surrey and Kent were the real pioneers of the cricket of to-day.

Cricket is played by two teams of eleven players, which bat and field in turn. In the centre of the ground are two " wickets," 22 yards apart, and each consisting of three " stumps," joined at the top by two " bails." The bats used have a flat striking surface, and the ball is a hard red one weighing 5 ounces.

There is a batsman at each wicket, and their object is the scoring of runs by hitting the ball away, and running before it can be returned, each time the two batsmen cover the length of the pitch counting as one run. Should the ball be hit beyond the boundary line round the ground, it counts four or, if it crosses the line without touching the ground, six.

The ball is "bowled" from one wicket to the batsman at the other, six balls, or, in some cases, eight, which comprise an "over," being bowled from each end in turn. The object of the fielding side is to get the batsmen "out," ten dismissals completing the "innings," as the eleventh man is left without a partner.

A batsman can be dismissed in several ways. If he misses the ball and it hits the wicket, or if he plays it on to the wicket, he is out "bowled." If he leaves his ground, indicated by a line in front of the wicket, misses the ball, and has the wicket "broken" by the wicket-keeper he is out "stumped." If he hits the wicket with his bat he is out "hit wicket." If his hit is caught he is out "caught." If, when running, he fails to reach his ground before the wicket is "broken" he is out "run out." If a ball, when bowled, would have hit his wicket, but hits his leg instead, then, subject to certain provisions regarding where the ball actually pitched, he is out "leg-before-wicket." A batsman may also be given out if he handles the ball or obstructs the fielding side, but these are rare occurrences.

In addition to runs hit by the batsmen, there are certain "extras." If the ball passes the bat, misses the wicket, and goes far enough for the batsmen to run, it is a "bye." If, however, it goes off the batsman's leg it is a "leg-bye," but leg-byes cannot be run unless the batsman was definitely attempting a stroke. If it is bowled so wide that the batsman cannot reach it, it is a "wide." If the bowler comes in front of his wicket before releasing the ball, or if he throws it, it is a "no-ball," in which case the umpire calls it as quickly as he can, for the batsman can hit such a ball, but he cannot be out to it, unless he is run out. If he does not score, one extra is added.

Of the fielding side, one, of course, is the bowler, and another, placed behind the batsman's wicket, is the wicket-keeper. The others will be placed as the bowler and his captain decide, for there are far more recognised positions than can be occupied at one time. To gain some idea of these positions, imagine a right-handed batsman at the wicket, his left side towards the bowler. The side of the wicket in front of him, nearer to his bat than to his body, is the "off" side; the side behind him, nearer to his body than to his bat, the "leg" side. On the off, behind the wicket and close to it, are the "slips," and, behind them, "third man." Farther round, but still behind the bat and close to it, is "gully." Level with the bat is "point" or, if he is some way from the bat, "deep point." In front of the bat, but in front also of the bowler's wicket, is "cover" and "extra cover." Roughly level with the bowler's wicket is "mid-off," with, behind him, "long off." Similarly on the leg side, where "long on" is the equivalent of "long off," "mid-on" of "mid-off," "mid-wicket" and "deep mid-wicket" of "cover" and "extra cover," "square leg" and "deep square leg" of "point" and "deep point," "short leg" of "gully," "long leg" of "third man," and "leg slip" of "slip."

First-class cricket matches last for three six-hour days or longer, but there are also two-day, one-day, and half-day matches. Matches of two days or more are two-innings games; of one day or half a day, one innings. If the side batting first, which is decided by a toss that gives the winner the choice of batting or fielding first, dismisses the opposing side for a smaller score, the victory is by the number of runs by which the smaller score was exceeded. If the side batting second pass the other total, the game ends, and the victory is by the number of wickets the second side still have standing. In a two-innings match, should the side batting first gain a first-innings lead of a certain size, normally 150 runs in a three-day match, it can require the other side to follow straight on with its second innings, the leading team keeping its second innings in reserve, to be played if needed. If a batting side has sufficient runs, and is anxious to see the other side batting while there is still plenty of time to dismiss it, it can declare its innings closed. In this case, should the second team score enough runs to win, it does, in fact, win, even though it may have lost more wickets than had the declaring side.

Cricket is not a fast-moving game, and for years views have been expressed to the effect that it must be "brightened up" if it is not to die out. Periodically, small changes in the rules are made; but, for the most part, the game just goes steadily on, easily retaining a large following that is satisfied with it as it is, and still able, when big international matches take place, to command a place, not only on the sports pages, but on the front pages of the Press.

The game is unusual in that it has no really official governing body. It is ruled by the M.C.C., which stands simply for Marylebone Cricket Club, from its headquarters at Lord's ground in London; and the M.C.C.'s pronouncements are accepted almost without question.

Outside England, the development of cricket has been peculiar. Even as near at hand as Scotland and Ireland, the game has never aroused much enthusiasm; and in Continental Europe, where many British games have won great acclaim, cricket has gained a real foothold only in the Netherlands. In the United States and Canada it is played, but only to a small extent. However, in the other Commonwealth countries of Australia, South Africa, New Zealand, the West Indies, India, and Pakistan, it is extremely popular; and the national teams of these countries, together with England, provide the top-class international sides of the game. They meet regularly in "Test Matches," a "rubber" normally being decided in a series of five Tests.

Cricket is rich in technical terms and expressions, which are seen and heard frequently through newspapers, television, and radio when a Test series is in progress. Many of these are almost self-explanatory, but a few never fail to puzzle less-experienced readers, viewers, and listeners. Prominent amongst these are three types of ball used by bowlers, the "yorker," the "googly," and the "chinaman."

A yorker is a fast ball that pitches just in the batsman's block-hole, and often passes under his defensive stroke. The term is believed to have originated in Yorkshire, but the only known explanation of it is that attributed to a Yorkshire cricketer, who, asked why a yorker was so called, replied simply, "Well, what else would you call it?" There is an answer to that, for the yorker was originally known as a "tice." A googly is an off-break or a leg-break which is disguised, because the bowler has delivered the one with the action of the other. A chinaman is an off-break bowled by a left-handed bowler to a right-handed batsman. These words also lack an authentic derivation.

Cricket has provided one expression that is now heard in many connections. That is "hat-trick," which dates back to the days when cricketers wore top-hats, and any player who took three wickets with three successive balls was presented with a white top-hat. Now, he is usually given the ball.

Croquet.

Croquet originated in France, and has been played in Britain for about a century. The governing body, the All-England Croquet Club, was founded in 1868, with headquarters at Wimbledon. Soon afterwards, this also became the headquarters of Lawn Tennis (*q.v.*), and it is probable that the rapid growth of that game was a factor that restricted the development of Croquet. Croquet, however, still retains a following, and, in addition to Championships and tournaments, it is widely played on private lawns.

The equipment consists of four balls, coloured blue, black, yellow, and red; four mallets, usually marked with the same colours; six hoops; and a peg. The playing area is 35 yards by 28 yards, but this can be reduced, provided that the proportion remains 5 to 4. The hoops, which stand 1 foot out of the ground, and the peg are placed as shown in the diagram. Generally two players, taking the blue and black balls, oppose two using

STANDARD SETTING.

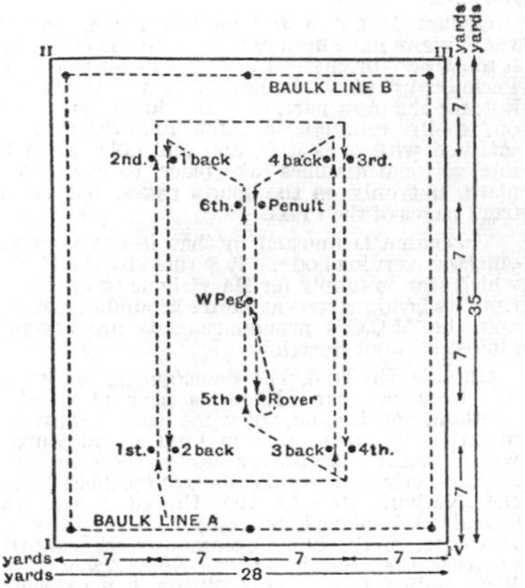

Only those portions indicated by a continuous line need be marked on the court.

The order of making the points is indicated by the arrows.

the yellow and red, but singles can be played, each player using two balls, blue being paired with black, and yellow with red. Each player completes the circuit of hoops twice, finishing by hitting the peg.

Croquet is a game of skill, and players can earn extra turns in various ways, such as hitting another ball with their own or passing through hoops. While making their own circuits, players also concentrate on leaving their opponents at a disadvantage. Handicap matches are possible through the giving of extra turns, or "bisques." A "half-bisque" is an extra turn in which no hoop may be scored.

Croquet can, perhaps, claim some credit for a phrase used in everyday life. "Pegging out" has the rather sinister meaning of "dying" or "finishing," but it is actually the term used for finishing a Croquet round by hitting the peg.

Cross-country. *See* **Athletics.**

Cycling.

That few inventions have been so widely adopted so rapidly as the bicycle is not surprising, for this comparatively simple machine is at once a useful method of transport, a means of healthy and enjoyable recreation, and, for those who desire it, the "key" to participation in a thrilling and well-organised competitive sport.

The earliest cyclists aroused considerable hostility on the roads; but as cycling progressed through a series of unwieldy and dangerous machines to the present "safety" models, more and more people realised its many advantages, with few counterbalancing disadvantages, and it soon became established and accepted. A bicycle is not expensive, it should have a long life, and the riding of it is not difficult to learn.

From a utilitarian point of view alone, a bicycle can be extremely useful. A small amount of "luggage" can be carried, so it can be used for shopping, as well as for travelling to and from work, and for any necessary journey of reasonable length. Like walking, it provides exercise, but the cyclist can travel three or four times as fast as when walking. The rider is also independent of local transport services, while probably travelling, at least in towns, as fast as the public transport.

As a pleasant recreation, cycling offers a wide range of possibilities. Outings can be for a day or part of a day, or they can be tours of any length the rider wishes, with the overnight halts spent in hotels or hostels or Camping (*q.v.*), which can easily be combined with cycling. The cycle tourist has distinct advantages over both the walker and the motorist. The walker gets exercise and a good view of the country, but covers only a limited distance. The motorist covers plenty of ground, but sees little and gets no exercise. The cyclist, however, gets exercise while covering a distance which, if much less than the motorist's, is four times the walker's at a pace that still enables him to see the country, and spot places worth a stop for a closer investigation. Progress can be fast or slow, and exercise strenuous or leisurely, as the rider wishes.

As a competitive sport, cycling offers a remarkable variety, for no other form of racing provides events of so many different types. On the Continent, cycle racing is by far the most popular sport, and the leading riders are national heroes. The sport, which caters for both amateurs and professionals, also has a large following in Britain, where it would soon progress still farther if there were more tracks suitable for big events available.

Cycle races are held on banked tracks rather like motor-racing tracks, on flat grass tracks, on cinder tracks, on indoor banked board tracks, on roads, and even across country. There are races at all distances, from short sprints to road tours divided into daily stages lasting for several weeks. There are massed-start races, in which all the competitors start together; races in which competitors are drawn in twos or threes through several rounds up to a final; and time trials, in which each rider starts alone. Track races may be straightforward races or time trials; or motor-paced, with the riders behind motor-cycles; or tandem-paced; or pursuit races, with riders or teams of riders starting on opposite sides of or spaced round the track; or point-to-point, with points awarded to the leaders at the end of each lap; or courses des primes, with a prize for the leader at the end of each lap; or Madison races, for teams of two, and occasionally three, riding one at a time, and relieving each other at will. There are also races for tandems and tricycles; and the sport includes races on both track and road for women as well as men.

In the cross-country side of cycle racing, called Cyclo-Cross, riders cover a cross-country course of perhaps 10 miles, riding when they can and carrying their machines where riding is impossible. Still another form of cycle racing is roller racing. In this, the cycles are fixed on rollers, and do not move at all, the distance the riders pedal being registered on large dials. There is also cycle speedway, a sport devised by youths, and practised only by youths. Events take the form of team matches, generally on rough cinder tracks constructed on waste ground by the youths themselves, with pairs of riders opposing rival pairs in a series of races, and points awarded to the leaders in each race. Corners have to be "skidded" round, as they sometimes are in ordinary grass-track cycle racing. Very different, but still competitive in a way, is a form of event that provides a link between the sporting side of cycling and the more purely recreational side, the reliability trial or attempt to achieve a fixed standard.

Cycling also has its team game in Bicycle Polo, a hard game requiring a high level of cycling skill and considerable nerve.

Taking up cycling is simply a matter of purchasing a bicycle and devoting a short time to learning to ride it. After that, it is for the individual cyclist to decide for what purposes he wishes to use his machine, and whether he prefers to ride alone or in company. If he likes company there are many clubs which provide facilities for touring cyclists of all degrees of energy and ambition, as well as for racing cyclists.

There is also an organisation that caters especially for the distance tourist in the Cyclists

Touring Club, which keeps a check on premises offering accommodation to cycle tourists, and provides a sign for use on approved accommodation. It is interesting to note that the Automobile Association, which offers similar services to motorists, but which is not as long-established as the C.T.C., originally based its methods on those of the C.T.C. The C.T.C. address, for those who might be interested in joining, is 3 Craven Hill, London, W.2.

Dancing. *See* **Ballroom Dancing; Folk Dancing.**

Darts.

Originally just a casual amusement confined almost entirely to public-houses, the game of Darts is now one of Britain's most popular pastimes. Public-houses still provide facilities for it, but to-day clubs, canteens, factories, offices, and private houses also have their boards, and there are numerous team and individual competitions, including a National Championship. The prizes rival those of any other game for value, matches are widely reported, and the attendance for the bigger contests is limited only by the size of the hall. This enthusiasm is not misplaced, for the game is a test of skill, and luck plays little part in it.

The circular board has a diameter of 18 inches, and is divided into segments numbered from 1 to 20, but not consecutively. In addition, there are two rings, each ⅜ inch wide, that go right round the board and through each segment. These are the " double " ring, at the extremity of the board, and the " treble " ring, near the centre of the board, darts in these rings counting double or treble the value of the segment. In the centre of the board there are two small rings, the " bull " or " dosser," counting 50, and the " outer," counting 25. The bull is 5 feet 8 inches from the ground, and the wooden or metal feathered darts are thrown from a line, called the " hockey," 9 feet away.

Matches may be singles, doubles, or between teams of four or eight players. Games are for a certain number of points, usually 101, 201, 301, 501, 801 or 1001, the lower totals being used for individual, and the higher for team contests, and matches are generally the best two out of three games or " legs." Conditions for matches vary, but normally stipulate either " straight start and finish on a double " or " start and finish on a double." In the first case players score from the start, but in the second they do not score until one double has been registered. In both cases they must finish on a double, and they must finish with the exact number they require. Scores are counted downwards, players being told how many they need, rather than how many they have scored.

In addition to the straightforward game, there are many Darts variations. In one, " Round the Clock," a player has to throw one dart into each segment from 1 to either 20 or the bull, his turn continuing until he throws three darts unsuccessfully. In " Shanghai," players start with a complete throw of three darts at number 1, and continue with a throw at every number up to 9, but players who fail to score at number 5 drop out. In " Cricket," one player " bats," throwing normally, and counting everything over 40, while the other " bowls," throwing only at the bull, and counting one wicket for every " outer " and two for every " bull," five wickets ending his opponent's " innings." In a Darts version of Shove-Ha'penny players have to get three darts in each segment from 1 to 9, and three in the centre. In " Fives," players score only if their total is divisible by five.

Diving. *See* **Swimming.**

Dramatics.

For many years, " amateur theatricals " were a popular indoor pastime; but they were a recreation for the performers, offering little in the way of real entertainment to the spectators, and relying for their audiences on relatives and friends who had little option but to attend. In no sense were they either connected with or comparable to the professional stage.

There may still be a few " entertainments " of this kind, but the vast bulk of amateur drama today is something very different. It is something that is taken really seriously, that is worked at, and that can entertain a paying audience on its merits. Relatives and friends still attend, of course, but so do strangers in search of entertainment, many productions, particularly big musical ones, depending on public audiences to cover their heavy expenses. The change from lightheartedness to seriousness, and from play to work, far from driving performers to seek recreation elsewhere, has increased the popularity of this particular recreation to a phenomenal extent. Nobody can say with certainty how many amateur groups there are in Britain at any one time, for new ones are springing up all the time, but there are certainly thousands.

Surprising though it may seem, the amateur theatre movement made tremendous advances through the Services in the Second World War. There was a certain amount of professional entertainment available to servicemen, but, for much of the time, service units had to provide their own entertainment. In many cases a few enthusiasts who knew something about entertaining were found to start things moving, and these soon built up casts by " conscripting " those in whom they thought they saw talent, and, often with considerable ingenuity, staged some excellent shows under very difficult conditions. Many of those who were " forced " into amateur entertaining during those days remained in it after the War, and many of the things that producers of those shows had to teach themselves by experiment and trial and error have contributed to better productions since then.

People often query whether or not it is fair to judge amateur actors by a severe standard, or to compare them with professionals. Generally speaking, it is perfectly fair to do both. Though amateurs are acting voluntarily, and because they like it, they are, nevertheless, setting out to entertain audiences whom they charge for admission. This renders them liable to criticism, and most serious amateur performers would not want it otherwise. With regard to comparisons with professionals, amateurs cannot, of course, fairly be compared with the best professionals, but they can be compared with, say, professional repertory companies, and they should emerge from such comparisons with distinction. Professional repertory actors generally perform a different play every week, rehearsing each play while they are acting another, and rehearsing only for a short time. Amateurs usually rehearse for a long time, and with only one play to think about. They should, therefore, if they are of any standard at all, give a better performance than the harassed repertory players.

The connection between the professional and amateur stage to-day goes beyond the mere making of comparisons. Professional theatre people sometimes assist at summer and week-end schools for amateur actors, and many amateurs have helped out both repertory and touring companies by playing small parts and appearing as " supers." Many young amateurs particularly in musical shows, hope that the amateur stage might prove the first step towards a professional career, and some amateur groups include former professionals who, for one reason or another, have left the theatre.

There are several ways in which the amateur theatre can be of real assistance to the theatre as a whole, particularly in that amateurs can try out new or experimental plays that the professional, commercial theatre dare not risk. Many amateur groups conduct vigorous and useful theatrical experiments, and this also applies to some musical groups. Other companies, both straight and musical, prefer to concentrate on proved successes.

The days when the first consideration in choosing a play was that it should have parts for every member of the group are gone. Groups now normally select plays on their merits, and often cast them, as in the professional theatre, by competitive audition. This, however, need not discourage those who might feel that, if parts have to be "won," they would never get any. Even these more ambitious groups often, in addition to their main plays, stage supplementary programmes consisting, perhaps, of three or four one-act plays, which are cast from those omitted from the bigger productions; while some groups definitely pick an occasional play, possibly a costume drama, that has a long cast. There are also plenty of small groups that often find themselves with too few people for the play they want to do. A newcomer can always find a welcome somewhere. Many amateurs start with small groups, and either remain with them or move farther up the tree, as their particular ambitions or talents may suggest.

There is also a vast field for enjoyable and useful activity behind the scenes. Many of those in the amateur theatre movement never appear on the stage at all, preferring to concentrate on producing, stage-managing, set designing, lighting, or one or other of many essential jobs; and anyone whose ambitions follow these lines is always welcome. Producing plays is, of course, an extremely important and satisfying activity. Small groups will often let a new producer try his hand, while the more ambitious groups will offer opportunities to new producers in the supplementary programmes which they also use to give newcomers acting opportunities.

Straight plays and musical comedies, comic operas or operettas are the best-known branches of the amateur theatre, but amateur revues are also frequently seen. Many of the improvised Services shows were of this type, and the taste for them has increased. They provide opportunities of many kinds, not only in singing, dancing, and acting, but also in composing, song-writing, and writing sketches. Still another type of amateur entertainment born during the War is the radio-style play, which was first tried in prisoner-of-war camps, when no other type of play was possible. In this, performers read their parts behind a curtain, submitting themselves to the severe test of holding their audiences by the voice alone.

Another branch of "home-made" entertainment well worth considering is folk-singing. Many people think folk-songs are just old country songs, but these form only a fraction of what is actually a big field of activity. As industries and towns grew in size and number, urban songs were added to the rural ones; and there are also work songs of many occupations and songs of many races. Many serious composers have used folk themes, and some, like Bartok and Kodaly, made detailed studies of folk-song. Folk-songs often describe actual events, set out particular problems or express political viewpoints; and, though many old songs remain popular, new ones are still appearing, some consisting of new words set to old tunes. Most folk-singers accompany themselves, and many are brilliant instrumentalists. Some songs, however, have very simple accompaniments, and others are almost "talked", rather than sung. Traditional instruments include guitars, banjos, mouth-organs, concertinas, pipes, "penny" whistles, and harps and dulcimers of various kinds. Folk-singing attracts people of all ages and all types, and the number of folk-song clubs, already large, is constantly increasing.

Film-making. While it is not too difficult for amateurs to present their own plays, it might seem that amateur film-making, apart from purely private records of things like family holidays, is too ambitious a project to be seriously considered. This, however, is not the case; and if those whose ambitions are to act, direct, and write for films have fewer opportunities than their stage counterparts, they nevertheless have opportunities, and a growing number of them, in the various film societies, now more often called ciné clubs. These clubs make their own films, including fiction films, documentaries, and cartoons, and many of them attract attention far beyond the club that made them. The clubs also show members films other than those made by themselves, including some made by other clubs; and they periodically entertain and visit other clubs.

Draughts. *See* **Chess.**

Eton Fives. *See* **Fives.**

Fencing.

Fencing can claim a longer history than most sports, for it is the modern equivalent of duelling. In mediæval tournaments mounted knights fought with lances, and, in addition to actual fights to the death, they also met with special, less lethal lances purely for sport. Later, duels were fought dismounted, and with different weapons. In Elizabethan days duellists used a sword, for attacking, in the right hand, and a dagger, for defence, in the left. Later still, the dagger was discarded, and duels were fought, as are fencing bouts to-day, with a sword only.

Duelling declined in Britain during the Regency period, when it became fashionable for gentlemen to learn to fight with their fists, but they continued to learn swordsmanship, and to fence with the practice weapon, the foil. Eventually, duelling became illegal almost throughout the world, but swordsmen of other countries similarly continued to fence with the foil. Even before Britain took to fist-fighting, most of the advances in fencing technique had been made in France and Italy, and the fencers of these and other Continental countries are still the best in the world, countries like Britain and the United States relying largely on fencers of Continental European descent.

Duelling was restricted to "gentlemen," and something of this restricted atmosphere pervaded the early days of fencing as a sport, clubs being few, expensive, and rather exclusive. Now, however, that has changed, and widespread class tuition in fencing has opened the sport to anyone.

Modern fencing includes contests with three weapons: the foil, which is the only one used by women; the epée, the real duelling sword; and the sabre, which cuts as well as thrusts. These weapons have "buttons" on the points, but fencers wear a special glove, a padded jacket, and a mask. Fencing requires grace of movement, lightness of foot, agility, strength of wrist and forearm, quick mental reactions, and good eyesight; and it will do much to develop these qualities, including the eyesight. As masks are worn, it is perfectly practicable to fence wearing glasses.

The language of fencing is French, all the terms used, many of them traditional, being French.

Figure Skating. *See* **Skating.**

Film-making. *See* **Dramatics.**

Fives.

There are two games of Fives, Eton Fives and Rugby Fives. They are court games using walls, but an Eton Fives court has the addition of a buttress or "pepper" jutting out from one side wall. The striking implement is the gloved hand. Eton Fives is a doubles game, but both singles and doubles are played in Rugby Fives.

Folk Dancing.

From the ballet, by way of the less-serious stage and the ballroom, to country and folk dancing, there are many forms of dancing, and it is easy to trace links from one kind to another, but much harder to say definitely exactly where one kind stops and another starts. Of all types of dancing, perhaps Folk Dancing is the most difficult to pinpoint. Its name implies that it would be found chiefly in remote areas, where it would be performed, almost instinctively, by simple country people. Originally, it was, and, to some extent, it still is; but it is now also to be seen in ballet and in the ballroom in adaptations that may or may not have retained the main features of the original, but that have almost certainly lost the spirit of it. To many people, thoughts of folk dancing mean thoughts of Central Europe; of places like Bohemia with its polkas. Central Europe, however, by no means covers the subject. Italy, for example, is rich in gay dances, and in dances with folk-lore-type stories behind them, like the famous tarantella, which is reputed to induce enough perspiration to cure the bite of the tarantula. Latin America, too, has its rumbas and other native dances that were originally solos, but are now known mainly in their ballroom versions.

There are good grounds for regarding the term "folk dancing" as nearly synonymous with country dancing; for if country dances differ, as they do, in different countries, they are not only countryside dances, but dances of a particular country, and therefore of its people. Almost every country has its country or folk dances, though it has been said that England is an exception. It is, however, nothing of the kind, for English Morris dancing has been a part of England, and of England's holiday festivals and customs, for centuries, and remains so to-day, about fifty different teams or groups now being affiliated to the Morris Ring of England.

The origins of Morris dancing, and even of its name, are shrouded in mysteries that will probably never now be solved. The name probably comes from the word "Moorish," and it was certainly used to mean Moorish by Shakespeare. Morris dancing, though, dates from long before Shakespeare's time, so, while the word may be the same as Moorish, it is probably used in the mediæval meaning of Moorish, which was simply "pagan." It may be, therefore, that Morris dancing was based on rituals of the old religion, and that the facial disguises that figure in it were originally necessary if the dancer was to avoid persecution and prosecution. A theory that Moorish was used in its more normal sense because the dancers blacked their faces falls down on the fact that only a minority of Morris dancers ever did this. To-day, only the Lancashire Coconut Dancers do so. For centuries, Morris dancing was mainly associated with England's May-day revels, but it was, and is, also seen at other times, such as for instance, Boxing Day.

There are many different Morris dances, including handkerchief dances; stick dances, using either 3-foot quarter-staves or seed-planting sticks of half that length; and jigs. Most of the dances are for teams of six, but some of the jigs are danced as solos. The accompaniment was originally on pipe and tabor, both being played by one man, but is now mostly on accordions and violins. The dancers are generally preceded by their Fool, armed with a stick and bladder, with which he clears a space for the dancing.

Scottish dancing is famous; but what is less generally realised is that there are two distinct kinds of it, Highland dancing and Scottish country dancing. Highland dancing consists of dances like the sword dance, or Gillie Callum; the fling; and the seann triubhas (which means "old trousers"). It is solo dancing, and though many girls now take part, it should really be danced only by men. Highland dances are danced mainly, though not quite entirely, on the ball of the foot.

Scottish country dancing includes set dances, such as reels and the similar but generally slower, strathspeys, and also jigs and progressive dances, during which each dancer meets practically every other dancer. Highland dancing is normally accompanied by a single piper, but the accompaniment for Scottish country dancing should be built round Scotland's national musical instrument, the violin. Scotland is also the home of the unusual "mouth music." This is, of course, vocal, but it is not song, being, in fact, an entirely practicable substitute that can be used when no musical instruments are available to accompany dancing.

Ireland also has its reels and its jigs, also normally performed to an accompaniment led by a violin. With lesser-known tunes, people who are not Celtic sometimes find it almost impossible to tell the difference between Scottish and Irish country dance music.

A country that does not spring very readily to mind when one thinks of folk dancing is the United States, but it has its country square-dancing, and, here again, the violin is the prominent accompanying instrument. Many of the tunes used are clearly based on old Scottish and Irish airs that were taken across the Atlantic by emigrants many years ago.

Football. *See* **American Football; Association Football; Australian Rules Football; Canadian Football; Gaelic Football; Public-School Football; Rugby Football.**

Gaelic Football.

Gaelic Football is seldom played by anyone who is not Irish, but it is frequently played outside Ireland, for Irishmen have taken it with them to Britain, the United States, Australia, and South Africa.

Played fifteen-aside, it is a blend of Association and Rugby Football (*q.v.*), the goals having the uprights, cross-bar, and net, exactly as in Association, but having the uprights extended above the cross-bar, as in Rugby. If the ball goes under the cross-bar it is a goal, and if it goes over it is a point, a goal equalling three points. The ball is round, and it may be kicked or caught, but not thrown forward, nor carried, though it may be dribbled by bouncing it. In its essentials, it is probably simpler than most other forms of football, but it is fast and involves frequent hard bodily contact. Substitutes are permitted in case of injury.

Gaelic Football joins with Hurling (*q.v.*) in coming under the old-established Gaelic Athletic Association.

Gliding.

The first serious efforts to develop Gliding, which is flying in engineless aircraft or sailplanes, took place in Germany in 1919, and were successful enough to lead to experiments in France and England, where it arrived in 1922. At that time, however, it failed to gain much support, and the real history of gliding in Britain dates from a second attempt to encourage it in 1929. Little more than ten years later, gliding had advanced sufficiently to be a real factor in the Second World War.

Normally launched from hills and by catapult, gliders at first achieved nothing more than small hops. These were followed by steady descents from high hills, and, eventually, by the achievement that ensured the success of the idea, ascents to points higher than the starting-point; for, with altitude, flights of considerable duration, and also over considerable distances, became possible. The altitude is gained by using air currents, which, when the wind strikes the hills that are the ideal starting-points, must rise, and must, if the force of the wind is strong enough to overcome the sinking speed of the glider, carry the glider upwards. Skilful use of air currents enables the glider pilot to stay up, and skilful use of the rising currents beneath clouds enables him to cover long distances by hopping from cloud to cloud.

The extent to which gliding has developed can be gathered from the fact that world championships now take place, and that, in Britain in one recent year, gliding enthusiasts made over 180,000 flights of a total duration of nearly 25,000 hours, and covering altogether over 56,000 miles. Gliders can now reach altitudes of over 40,000 feet, stay in the air for over 50 hours, and carry out flights of hundreds of miles. Both men and women pilot gliders, and the best pilots are often people in their forties and fifties.

Golf.

Golf, a game of great antiquity, originated in Scotland, and is now widely popular in many countries. It consists of using a set of clubs with which to play a small white ball over a cross-country course of eighteen holes. Each hole will be several hundred yards long, and will have its fixed starting-point and its finish with an actual hole in the ground, the object being to complete the course, which will be several miles long, in as few strokes as possible.

The playing of each hole falls into three sections, driving, approaching, and putting. The starting-point will be a flat piece of ground on which the player will "tee up" his ball on a small rubber peg, or "tee," which he will carry round with him. He will then hit the ball towards the hole, concentrating on achieving distance. From the tee to near the hole is the "fairway," which will consist of fairly smooth ground, not entirely devoid of natural obstacles, and probably containing some sand traps, or "bunkers." On each side of the fairway is the "rough," which may consist of long grass, shrubs, woods, or even roads. The player will continue to play his ball towards the hole, concentrating now chiefly on direction. On the fairway or off it, he should always play his ball where it lies, but, should it be quite unplayable, or even lost, he may drop it or a new one, and pay a stroke penalty for the privilege. The actual hole will be on the "green," a rough circle of exceptionally well tended grass, and, once on it, the player will cover the last few yards by the more delicate art of "putting."

There are many different types of club, players being limited to fourteen. The shafts are generally steel, the striking surfaces being iron or, in the case of drivers, wood. The different "irons" have numbers, but golf clubs used to have special names, often descriptive of their functions, for instance, lofter, cleek, mashie, niblick, and even blaster. Originally, most golf courses were by the sea, and these were called "links," a term now loosely applied to any course.

There are two actual methods of competitive play, match play and medal play. Match play is by holes, a player completing any hole in fewer strokes than his opponent winning that hole. Once a player leads by more holes than there are still to play, the game finishes, the victory being by *X* and *Y*, where *X* is the number of holes he is "up," and *Y* the lesser number of unplayed holes. When a player leads by the same number of holes as there are still to play he is said to be "dormy" so many. Opponents level after eighteen holes proceed to the first hole, and play on until one is one hole up, when he is said to have won at the 19th, 20th, or whatever it may be. Some important match-play events are over 36 holes, or two complete rounds. Medal play is simply stroke play, the result depending on the number of strokes needed to complete the course. This demands a higher level of consistency, for one bad spell can ruin the total, whereas, in match play, it may cost only one hole. In play after the initial drive, the player farthest from the hole normally plays before his opponent.

In match-play championships and tournaments players are drawn against each other, the winners going on to the next round, and so on up to the final. In medal-play events players go round in pairs, but each is, of course, playing against the whole field. Team matches consist of singles and foursomes, in which the partners play shots in turn. Other, less-formal forms of golf are four-ball foursomes, in which each player plays his own ball; best-ball foursomes, in which both partners drive, but, thereafter, play in turn only at the most successfully driven ball; and threesomes, in which each player plays for himself against the others. During a match, a player must not receive advice from anyone except his "caddie," if he has one, the caddie being an attendant who makes a profession of carrying golfers' clubs round.

Every course has its "bogey" and "par" figures, these being scores, with par representing the higher standard that a first-class player might achieve for the course. By assessing a member's own scores against these figures, clubs can allocate a handicap which indicates the player's standard. There are many minor competitions in which golfers play, not on level terms, but from their handicaps, which also serve as a perpetual incentive to players to improve their game, and therefore their handicaps. The possession of a handicap also makes it easier for players to arrange even matches with strangers. Handicaps are subject to alteration as a player's standard changes, and such alterations may be in either direction. The operation of the handicap in play takes the form of strokes deducted from the actual score at certain holes, in accordance with the arrangements in force at any particular club.

Golf offers a tremendous number of competitions of all standards, as well as championships and team matches. Probably the four most important individual championships are the British Open, the British Amateur, the American Open, and the American Amateur. These are long-established, but the two major international team events are quite new. They are the Canada Cup, open to teams of two professionals from any country, and the Eisenhower Cup, for teams of four amateurs, the three best scores counting, from any country. Other, much older international team events include the Ryder, Walker, and Curtis Cups, which are contests between Britain and the United States for professionals, amateurs, and women, respectively; though it is interesting to note that the actual inscription on the Curtis Cup indicates that this trophy is open to women golfers of any country.

Golf is ruled by the Royal and Ancient Club of St. Andrews, Scotland, which is recognised all over the world as the game's headquarters. There was an unusual illustration of this widespread recognition when the Eisenhower Cup competition was instituted by the United States in 1958, for, at the special request of the American organisers, the first meeting took place, not in the United States, but at St. Andrews. The Royal and Ancient Club makes the rules of golf, but these are generally supplemented by local rules in force at particular clubs.

The popular expression "rub of the green," used to describe an unexpected and unavoidable mischance, comes from golf, where it is used when a putt fails to take the expected line because of a slight flaw in the normally perfect turf of the green.

Gymnastics.

Gymnastics is a system of exercising with apparatus, and also a competitive sport, the chief items of apparatus used being the horizontal bar, the parallel bars, rings, ropes, ladders, and the vaulting horse. The horizontal bar, the parallel bars, and the rings can all be used for similar exercises, some being fast swings and others slow movements requiring considerable strength. Strength and swinging also come into ladder exercises; and the rope, which can be climbed in several different ways, is a simple form of apparatus that demands, and will develop, strength. The horse can be used for a variety of vaults, in either the lengthways or sideways position, and still others are possible when pommels are fitted to it. In addition to those who specialise in gymnastics, many sportsmen of various kinds regularly attend gymnastic classes as part of their training for their own particular activities.

Head of the River Races. *See* **Boat Races.**

Henley Royal Regatta. *See* **Boat Races.**

Highland Dancing. *See* **Folk Dancing.**

Highland Games. *See* **Traditional Games and Customs.**

Hockey.

Hockey originated about three-quarters of a century ago as a game confined to Britain, but with rules that varied in each of the home countries. However, in 1900, England, Ireland, and Wales combined to form the International Hockey Board, with a view to formulating rules that would apply wherever the game was played, and, two years later, Scotland joined the alliance. The game was also taken up with terrific enthusiasm in India, and Indian players became, and remain, the best players in the world. Their enthusiasm extended to what is now Pakistan, so the division that brought that country into existence also added one more to the list of hockey-playing countries, and without noticeably weakening India's own national team.

Hockey is now played in many other countries, but, for some time, it made little progress on the Continent. Eventually, though, it was tried, liked, and adopted in a number of European countries, and one of these, the Netherlands, has now established a right to a place alongside India, Pakistan, and Britain as the game's top layer. Hockey has, and has long had, Olympic Games status.

Hockey is played eleven-aside on a pitch marked out as in the accompanying diagram, the normal positions of the players being a goalkeeper, two full-backs, three half-backs, and five forwards, exactly as in Association Football (*q.v.*). The white ball can be either sewn, as is a cricket ball, or seamless, and it must weigh from $5\frac{1}{2}$ to $5\frac{3}{4}$ ounces. Sticks must weigh from 12 to 28 ounces, and have a handle that can be passed through a ring with an inside diameter of 2 inches. They have a striking surface on the left side only, left-handed sticks not being permitted. A game consists of two 35-minute halves, unless the captains have agreed on a shorter period.

The game is started, and restarted after half-time and after a goal, by a bully at the centre of the ground. The players bullying stand facing the side-line, each with his own goal on his right. Each taps the ground between the ball and his own goal and his opponent's stick over the ball three times alternately, after which one of them must play the ball. At any bully, all the other players must be 5 yards from the ball, and between it and their own goal.

In play, the ball must be propelled only by the stick, and it must not be stopped with any part of the body except the hand, in which case it must only be stopped, and not caught or knocked forward. These prohibitions, however, do not apply to goalkeepers, who may stop the ball with any part of their body, and also kick it, when in their circle. No part of a player's stick must be raised above the shoulder either at the beginning or end of a stroke, or to stop the ball. Hitting the bal in the air and scooping it are allowed, but deliberate undercutting is not, and umpires can penalise any hit which they judge to be dangerous. Interfering with an opponent's stick, running between an opponent and the ball; and charging or other bodily contact are not allowed. Players must not tackle from the left unless they can play the ball without touching the opponent or his stick.

A player is "offside" if there are fewer than three opponents between him and the goal-line, unless he is in his own half, or unless a team-mate playing the ball is nearer to the goal-line than he is. A player who is offside is put onside if an opponent plays the ball, but not if the ball merely touches or glances off the opponent. Players who are offside are not penalised if they do not interfere with the play.

If the ball crosses the side-line it is rolled in by a player of the side that did not put it out. This player must have his hands, feet, and stick outside the field of play, and he must not play the ball again until someone else has done so. All the other players must have their feet and sticks inside the 7-yard line until the ball leaves the roller's hand.

If the ball is sent across the goal-line wide of the goal by an attacker, or, unintentionally, by a defender who is more than 25 yards from the goal-line, the restart is by a bully on the 25-yard line. If it is hit behind unintentionally by a defender who is within 25 yards of the goal-line, a corner is awarded to the attacking side. If it is hit behind intentionally by a defender from any part of the ground, a short, or penalty, corner is awarded to the attacking side. A corner is a hit from a point on either the goal-line or the side-line within 3 yards of the corner flag, while a short corner is a hit from a point on the goal-line 10 yards from the nearer goal-post. At a corner, all the defenders must be behind the goal-line, and all the attackers outside the circle. When the corner hit comes into the circle, attackers are not allowed to take a first-time shot, but must first stop the ball or slow it down. At no time during the game can a goal be scored unless it was hit from inside the circle.

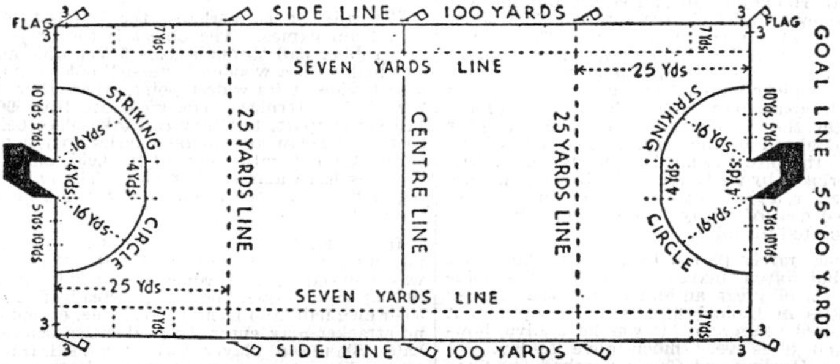

Ground.—100 yards by 55 to 60 yards. **Opening of Goal.**—7 feet by 12 feet.

Diagram of Ground as marked out for Hockey.

Penalties for infringements outside the circles are generally free hits. Penalties for infringements inside the circle by defenders are short corners, unless they have been deliberately committed to prevent a goal, or have, in fact, prevented a goal, in which cases a penalty bully is awarded. In extreme cases, both short corners and penalty bullies can be awarded for offences anywhere behind the 25-yard line.

A penalty bully is a duel between the offender and one opponent, taking place in the circle, and with all the other players, including the goal-keeper, if he is not the offender, beyond the 25-yard line. The players bully 5 yards from the centre of the goal, and play between them continues until either the attacker scores or hits the ball behind or hits the ball out of the circle, or the defender hits it out of the circle. If the defender hits it behind, the bully is restarted. If no goal results, the game is restarted by a bully on the 25-yard line.

A game is controlled by two umpires, each of whom takes one half of the field and one complete side-line. Substitutes are not permitted in hockey.

Hockey is entirely an amateur game. Almost every match is a friendly, for, in Britain, there are no leagues and only a very few rather specialised cup competitions. There are, however, a great many representative games, from county matches up to internationals.

A major feature of the hockey season, which normally lasts from October until March, is the end-of-season Easter Hockey Festival. There are actually several festivals, most of them taking place at seaside resorts. Teams go to them from many different areas, including the Continent, and play three or four matches in four days against opponents whom they would not normally meet. Six-aside tournaments also take place occasionally during the season.

Hockey is played by women, as well as men, and there is a certain amount of mixed hockey between teams composed of both men and women.

Hurling.

Hurling, which might loosely be called the Irish brand of Hockey (*q.v.*), is played fifteen-aside, and has been described as the fastest game using a ball in the world. The ball, called the "slitter," and the sticks, called "hurleys," bear some resemblance to Hockey's ball and sticks, but nothing like Hockey's "sticks" rule applies. The slitter may be hit at any height, and with either side of the hurley, and it may be kicked or caught, though it must not be carried more than three steps, nor picked up off the ground. There is no offside, apart from the fact that attackers must not enter the parallelogram marked out near the goal ahead of the slitter. The goals have uprights that are extended above the cross-bar, and scoring is by goals, under the bar, and points, over the bar, a goal equalling three points. There is a good deal of bodily contact, and substitutes are permitted for injured players.

Hurling, rarely played by anyone who is not Irish, but often played by Irishmen outside Ireland, is of great antiquity, and the English authorities in Ireland first tried to suppress it six hundred years ago. It was kept alive, however, and it is very much alive to-day. To Irishmen, Hurling and Gaelic Football (*q.v.*) are symbols of nationalism and patriotism. They are governed by the Gaelic Athletic Association, which has a rule that states: "Any member who plays or encourages Rugby, Association Football, Hockey or Cricket by that very fact incurs immediate suspension from membership of the Association."

A form of Hurling with slightly different rules, called Shinty, is still preserved in another Celtic country, Scotland.

Ice-Hockey. *See* **Skating.**

Ice Skating. *See* **Skating.**

Judo. *See* **Wrestling.**

Knur and Spell. *See* **Old English Games and Customs.**

Korfball

Korfball is a team game with several unique features, the most striking being that it is a mixed game, a team consisting of twelve players—six men and six women. The game resembles Basketball (*q.v.*) in some ways, the goals, which are 11½ feet high, and the scoring of goals being similar. It can be played on any firm surface, the pitch measuring 300 feet by 133 feet, though a smaller pitch can be used, provided that length and width are reduced in proportion. The pitch is divided into three sections, and players do not move from one sector to another during actual play. They must, however, change to another zone after every two goals. This encourages all-round attacking and defensive ability, and ensures that, even in a one-sided match, every player gets a fair share of the game. Four players from each team play in each section, and players always mark opponents of their own sex. Players must not run with the ball which is advanced purely by passing. There is no tackling, and the ball can only pass from one team to the other by interception. Players may not score if there is an opponent within arm's length. A game lasts for 90 minutes, divided into two halves.

Korfball originated in the Netherlands, where it was first played in 1902. It spread to Belgium in 1927, and reached England in 1947. There is an International Board, on which the Netherlands, Belgium, and England are represented. International inter-club matches are a regular feature of the game. Though really a winter game, Korfball is actually played all the year round, the international games between clubs from the three Korfball countries taking place during the summer.

Lacrosse.

Lacrosse, which originated from a game played by the Red Indians, was introduced into England from Canada in 1867, and has been played here ever since.

Basically, it is, perhaps, the simplest of all field team games. The object is the propelling of a rubber ball through goals 6 feet wide and 6 feet high with a wooden "crosse" not more than a foot wide at its widest point, where there is a "mesh" of strings. The goals are from 90 to 110 yards apart, but play can take place behind them, for there are no boundaries to the pitch except the natural borders of the field, unless the captains have agreed otherwise. The only lines required are the centre circle, the goal-lines, and the goal-creases.

In England teams consist of twelve players, but in Canada and the United States the number was reduced to ten some years ago. Players line up right down the field, instead of only in their own half, and there is no offside, except that no attacker may enter the goal-crease before the ball. Should a player leave the field through injury, his opponents must also withdraw a man.

A game consists of four 20-minute periods, but the captains can agree to vary this, either to two 45-minute halves or otherwise. The game is started or re-started after a stoppage by one player from each side "facing" by placing the ball on the ground between the backs of the two crosses, and then drawing them apart, after which the ball is in play. It can then be advanced by running with it on the crosse, throwing it from the crosse, or kicking it, though no goal, except an "own goal," can be scored by a kick. Only the goalkeeper, who can deflect the ball with his hand, but not catch or throw it, may handle the ball. Players can shoulder opponents when trying to get the ball off the ground, and "body check" them by simply standing in front of them to impede them. A player can also check an opponent's crosse with his own crosse if the opponent has the ball. A foul is penalised by giving the non-offending player a "free position," which means that he is given the ball, and the game is then re-started.

Lacrosse demands speed and stamina, and a high level of skill demands practice, but it is not hard for a beginner to grasp the main objects or master the comparatively simple rules.

It is interesting to note that Lacrosse, which can be one of the roughest of all games, has been made a suitable game for women by very simple measures, such as the elimination of the body check; and that there are now more women playing than there are men.

Lawn Tennis.

Originally called Sphairistike—or "Sticky" by those who disliked it—Lawn Tennis was invented in the seventies of the last century as a simplified, outdoor version of Real Tennis (q.v.), using a net, but no walls. It is now far more widely played than the parent game, being popular almost all over the world. As its name implies, it was originally intended to be played on grass, but it is now also played on hard courts of various surfaces, and indoors on wood.

The court is as shown in the accompanying diagram, the outer long boundary lines being the limitations for doubles, and those parallel to them being the boundaries for singles. Both server and receiver score, four points making a game, six games won a set, and two out of three or three out of five sets won a match. Game points are scored "15," "30," "40," and "Game." The system of "vantage" games and sets is used. This means that, if 40-all—called "deuce"—is reached, a player must gain a clear lead of two points to win the game, the winner of the first point after deuce being said to have the "advantage." If the games reach 5-all, the set continues until one player has a clear lead of two games.

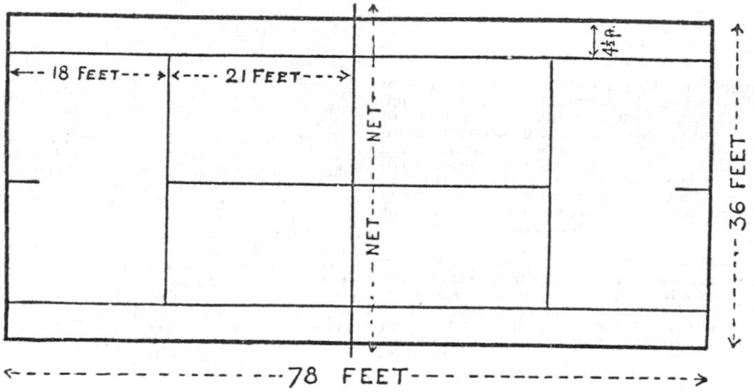

NET:—Height 3 ft. 6 in. at posts, 3 ft. at centre.
Diagram of Ground as marked out for Lawn Tennis.

When the game began, there was considerable discussion before this scoring, which is taken from Tennis, was given preference over the straightforward one-two-three system of Rackets (*q.v.*). Much more recently, experiments have been made with the equally straightforward system of Table Tennis (*q.v.*), but the Tennis system survived these, and remains in force.

Service is almost invariably overhand, and the receiver plays the service after one bounce. Thereafter, strokes may be "ground" strokes, played after one bounce, or volleys, played before any bounce. In doubles, either partner may play the ball, but each must serve in turn.

In addition to being played by thousands of people, Lawn Tennis attracts large crowds of spectators. The big annual tournaments, such as Wimbledon, Forest Hills, and Paris, are amongst the major sporting events of the year; as are the Davis Cup competition, open to teams of men from every country in the world, and the Wightman Cup, a women's contest between Britain and the United States. All these events are amateur; but the game also has a top layer of professionals, whose annual world tours are a great attraction.

Marbles. *See* **Old English Games and Customs.**

Modern Pentathlon.

Imagine a king's messenger riding with an important dispatch, and being hotly pursued. His horse is shot, and he has to engage his pursuers, first with his revolver, and then with the sword. Eventually, he breaks away, swims a river, and finishes his journey on foot and running.

That is the "plot" on which is based one of the most interesting, exciting, and testing of all sporting events, the Modern Pentathlon. Often wrongly thought to be a part of Athletics, the Pentathlon is a separate sport, but one that actually consists of five different sports: the five activities, in fact, of the king's messenger in the story, riding, revolver shooting, fencing, swimming, and running. True, the Pentathlon competitor does not have to carry them out one after the other, but he does have to take part in them in that order, one on each of five successive days, both riding and running being across country, the riding on a horse strange to him.

The Pentathlon first appeared in the Olympic Games of 1912, but, in recent years, it has become so popular that, in addition to the Olympic event every four years, there are now annual world championships, as well as national championships in many countries, including Britain. The event was originally designed as one suitable for Army officers, and, though present-day Army training is rather different, most Pentathlon competitors are still servicemen, though they are not all officers. However, a civilian has won the Olympic event, and, in Britain, the Army authorities are willing to provide training facilities for civilian competitors who show signs of reaching a high standard. Many people believe that the "keys" to success in the Modern Pentathlon are swimming and running, and that competitors who are good at them can be taught the riding, shooting, and fencing without too much difficulty.

Morris Dancing. *See* **Folk Dancing.**

Mountaineering.

It is difficult to say when Mountaineering, which is the climbing of mountains, not for any scientific reason, but purely for the sense of achievement and for sport, began, but, by the middle of the sixteenth century, Zürich students had formed an Alpine club, and the value and uses of ropes and even dark glasses were known. Amongst famous peaks, Mont Blanc was first conquered in 1786, the Jungfrau in 1811, and the Wetterhorn in 1854. By then, Mountaineering was becoming organised, and there were systematic assaults on the Alps; in Norway, the Caucasus, and Corsica; in the Rockies and the Andes; in Japan, New Zealand, and Kenya; and, of course, in the Himalayas, where over thirty years passed between the first assault on Everest and its conquest. There are still unconquered peaks in the Himalayas, but it is not only first ascents that interest mountaineers, who can find exciting sport in many parts of the world.

The way to master Mountaineering is to accompany and watch experts. The essential qualities include perfect physical fitness and perfect nervous fitness, and to them must eventually be added a detailed knowledge of snow, ice, avalanches, glaciers, crevasses, and cornices, as well as of the different techniques of ascending, descending, and traversing. Also to be learned is step-cutting, which is hard manual labour carried out under difficult conditions that are also conditions that make perfect workmanship literally a matter of life and death. Clothing, including properly nailed boots, and equipment, including ropes, ice axes, knives, maps, compasses, medical supplies, and a number of other things, must be of the best, and yet, at the same time, it must be light.

Apart from the more obvious dangers, one of the ills to which the mountaineer is heir is mountain sickness, which may take one or more of several forms, including actual sickness, headaches, drowsiness, shortness of breath and palpitations, and general bodily weakness, particularly in the legs. These are about the last sensations that a man engaged in an ascent would choose to experience, but, at high altitudes, the only way to avoid them is by using oxygen.

Rock-climbing. Mountaineering is generally taken to mean snow and ice climbing, but allied to it is Rock-climbing, which demands the same perfect physical and nervous condition, and, in place of knowledge of snow and ice, knowledge of several very different kinds of rock. Ascending, descending, and traversing all apply, and so do ropes, and the rock-climber should, in fact, be something of a knot expert. Light, rope-soled shoes replace the mountaineer's nailed boots. Skye is a favourite haunt of rock-climbers, and, in view of what might justifiably be called the antiquity of climbing, it is surprising to note that the highest peak in Skye, Sgurr Alasdair, was not conquered until 1873.

Netball.

Netball, which is played exclusively by women, is similar to Basketball (*q.v.*), but it is played seven-aside, does not allow substitutes, and the goals have no backboards. It is almost always played outdoors on asphalt or grass.

Nine Men's Morris. *See* **Old English Games and Customs.**

Old English Games and Customs.

The story of England had its beginnings a very long time ago, and many of England's present-day customs, recreations, sports, and games can be traced far back in that story. Some, of course, have undergone very considerable changes, but the links with the past are still clear.

On 1 May, for instance, girls still awake in some villages to the realisation that they are to be May Queens, and to reign for a day, though they may not realise that they are preserving a custom that can point to origins in the days of the Druids, and that, in Tudor times, would have sent them and their fellow villagers out to spend the preceding night in the woods, gathering branches of trees and flowers with which to decorate their houses. Maypoles and morris dancers also belonged to May Day, and they can still be seen in England, and not only on that day.

More local, even quainter, but equally traditional is the trial for the Dunmow Flitch of Bacon in the village of Dunmow in Essex. The original conditions offer this award to any married couple who will go to the twelfth-century Augustinian priory, and there kneel on two sharp-pointed stones and swear that they have neither quarrelled nor repented of their marriage within a year and a day of its celebration. This award has lasted into modern times, not annually, it is true; but then it never was given annually, for it was instituted in 1244, and first claimed in 1445.

One annual event that is as traditional as it is strenuous in the Whit Monday cheese-chase at the village of Brockworth, near Gloucester. Records of this go back to the days of the Stuarts, for that was when they started to keep records of a custom that was already old then: so old that its origins are unknown, though they had to do with the villagers' cattle-grazing rights. A massive round cheese is rolled down nearby Coopers Hill, which has a gradient of one in four throughout its 150 yards; and, with a certain amount of risk to life and limb, the chasers tear down after it, the cheese being the prize for whoever catches it. Sometimes, the cheese hits a bump, and literally leaps out of reach over the hedge at the bottom of the hill, but the chase continues, the prize going to the first pursuer to reach the hedge, where "catchers" wait to halt the headlong rush of the runners. Despite the obvious dangers, the records to date mention nothing worse than a sprained ankle.

This brings us to sports and games; and, though today's most popular game, Football, is, in anything like its present form a comparatively recent growth, it can perhaps claim some relationship with Harpastum and Campball, which existed before the Norman Conquest; and it was one of the popular recreations banned in the interests of Archery. The football of those and later days, however, took the form of struggles between whole villages, the players battling *en masse* over a cross-country course of several miles. People past whose houses the battle was likely to rage prudently barred and shuttered all windows and doors, awaited the cessation of hostilities with anxiety, and probably helped to push this particular custom into oblivion.

The oldest English games are old indeed, and Cricket, too, had remote ancestors, from which the descent to today can be traced more directly. They included Bat and Trap, Creag, Cat and Dog, and Rounders. In Bat and Trap, the batsman hit a ball released from a trap between two posts. His opponent rolled it back underarm at the trap flap. If he knocked it down, the batsman was out: if not, the batsman scored one run and had another hit. This game is still played in Kent. Creag, which was played at the time of Edward II, used a curved stick, called a "cryc," as a bat, and a tree-stump as a wicket. Cat and Dog, which came later, was a game for three, two batsmen defending holes 13 yards apart, and trying to hit away the piece of wood that the third player aimed at the holes, the bats being the "dogs" and the piece of wood the "cat." It is worth noting that Baseball's accepted ancestors are games called One Old Cat and Two Old Cat, which clearly indicates a common origin for Cricket and Baseball. Some of the games in Cricket's ancestry remained popular after Cricket arrived, and Rounders is still a popular children's game.

The beginning of Athletics can also be found in old England. Putting the weight and casting the bar, a forerunner of throwing the hammer, were popular with the courtiers in Tudor days, while other events, including javelin throwing, were practised by ordinary people of the same period. Later, the early hammer throwing spread beyond the Court, and was even attempted by women, which modern hammer throwing is not.

Tournaments and jousts were popular from the Middle Ages until Tudor times. These were combats between mounted men, a joust being single combat, while a tournament involved many contestants. They were succeeded by dismounted combats, which still take place today in the sport of Fencing. Those taking part in tournaments and jousts were required to swear an oath to the effect that they were competing purely for sport; and those taking part in the Olympic Games and certain other big sports meetings to-day swear an almost identical oath. Somewhat similar to jousting, but not restricted, as jousting was, to the nobility, was Tilting at the Quintain, which was practised both mounted and on foot, and in which a lance was thrust at a wooden target, which, if not struck accurately, swung round and struck the tilter.

Other old games, clearly the ancestors of modern ones, included Handball, which became Fives, but which is still handball in the United States; Battledore and Shuttlecock, still a children's game, but now developed by adults into Badminton; and Shovelboard, an elaborate game, for the nobility, which consisted of sliding weights down a long table marked with lines, and which is certainly a forerunner of Shove-Ha'-penny. Another probable ancestor of Shove-Ha'penny was Squails, in which a coin was placed in the centre of a round table, and players tried to push their "squails," or discs, as close to the coin as possible, distances being measured by an instrument called a "swoggle." Also known as Skayles and Keels, this game appeared in the sixteenth century, lasted into the nineteenth century, and, under the name of Keels, achieved a poetic mention in Sidney's "Arcadia."

Archery. Archery goes back hundreds of years, to the days when the bow was the chief weapon of war, and, because of that, practice shooting and contests were officially encouraged: encouraged, in fact, to the extent that other popular recreations, like Football, Quoits, and Bowls, that might have interfered with it were banned, though the bans were always largely ignored. Eventually, the bow disappeared from the battlefields, but, to this day, it has remained popular as a means of recreation and sport. Through the centuries, archery contests were generally of three kinds: shooting at a mark, or target; shooting purely for distance, though this was more popular abroad, in countries like Turkey, than in Britain; and shooting at "rovers," in which two or three archers would cover a cross-country course, taking it in turns to select a mark at which to shoot. To-day, archery, which retains enough of tradition in its terminology to remind the archer that he is following in a very long line, consists of shooting at a target containing rings coloured, going from the centre outwards, gold, red, blue, black, and white, the values being respectively, nine, seven, five, three, and one.

Knur and Spell. Knur and Spell belongs to Lancashire and Yorkshire, and originated in a children's game called Trap and Ball. The player uses a wooden club, the striking end of which, called the "pommel," is shaped something like a bottle, though it has a flat hitting surface, with which to hit a small ball, which he himself releases from a trap by means of a trigger. The ball, which is the "knur," weighs ½ ounce, measures 1 inch in diameter, and was originally wooden, though, later, porcelain was used. The trap is the "spell," and consists of a small brass cup with a strong spring, which is kept down by the trigger. The fixing of the spell is an elaborate process requiring the use of a spirit level, and, when it is in position, a player is allowed 10 minutes to adjust the tension of the spring. Players generally have their own spells. Each player has five consecutive hits, or "rises," and scores one point for every 20 yards covered.

Marbles. Marbles is supposed to have been played in ancient Egypt, but its popularity, with adults as well as children, in the England of the Middle Ages entitles it to count as an old English game. Marbles are often made of clay, but better ones are glass, and the best are pure marble. These are called "alleys," or "alley taws." There are several games of marbles, but they all involve the aiming of a marble at a target, which may be another marble or an opening, by bowling or "shooting" it along the ground. In shooting, the marble is held between the thumb and forefinger, with the knuckle of the forefinger on the ground, and is then flicked away.

Perhaps the best-known game is Ring Taw, in which players shoot from one circle at marbles placed in another about 6 feet away. Fortifications and Increase Pound use concentric circles, players shooting at marbles in each circle in turn. Three Holes and Handers involve shooting at holes in the ground; Arch Board or Bridge, at arches in an upright board; and Die Shot, at another marble on which a numbered die is balanced.

Nine Men's Morris. Nine Men's Morris is a fourteenth-century game for two, usually played outdoors on a diagram marked on the ground, but sometimes played indoors on a board. The diagram consists of three squares drawn inside each other. In addition to the outlines of each square, there are lines from the centre of each side of the inmost square, through the centre of the sides of the middle square, to the centre of the sides of the outermost square. The corner of each square and the centre of each side are the 24 points of importance in the game. Each player has nine men, often counters, and they play in turn, placing a man at an unoccupied point, and endeavouring to place three men in one row, continuing, when all the men are placed, to try to form rows by moving men along the lines. The completion of a row entitles a player to remove, or "pound," one of his opponent's men, the object of the game being either the capture of all the opposing men or blocking them so that they cannot move. The game has many variations, and many names, including ninepenny morris; fivepenny morris, for a version played with five men; and merils, marls, marrels, morals, morris and miracles, all for a version played with three men.

Pall-Mall. Two London thoroughfares, Pall Mall and the Mall, are reminders that Pall-Mall was once popular. Often described as a forerunner of Croquet, it was really more like a form of Golf, a game that arrived at about the same time, both having a common, if remote, ancestor in the Roman game, Paganica. In Paganica players walked across fields hitting a small, leather ball at trees with a curved stick, the object being to reach the target in the fewest possible strokes. It was played by country people, whereas pall-mall, which achieved rapid popularity in the seventeenth century, was a game for the nobility, though other people played simplified versions of it. Pall-Mall was played in special alleys, sometimes ½ mile long, and often surrounded by walls. A boxwood ball a foot in circumference had to be played down the alley, in which were a number of iron arches, in the fewest possible strokes. The player drove off as in golf, but, on reaching the arches, not only changed his club, but also substituted a small steel ball for the boxwood one.

Quoits. Dating back to the fifteenth century, Quoits is one of those ancient games that had the distinction of being banned because its popularity was such that it was believed to be keeping people from archery practice. The ban was not effective, and it continues to this day, though it is now less played than it used to be, Scotland, the North of England, and Suffolk being, perhaps, the last main strongholds. The pitch consists of two circles or squares of clay, 18 yards apart, and each having in its centre an iron pin, called the "hub," 1 inch of which remains above the surface. The quoits are iron rings with a diameter that must not exceed 8⅝ inches. The weight is not fixed, but is often 3 lb. or more. The object of the game, which can be either "singles" or "doubles," is to throw the quoit over or near the hub from the opposite point, 18 yards away, one point being scored for each quoit nearer the hub than the opponent's quoits, and two being awarded for a quoit that drops over the hub, called a "ringer." No points are awarded if opposing quoits are the same distance from the hub, and none are awarded if each side has a ringer. A game is 11 points in "singles," and 15 points in "doubles." Quoits developed from pitching actual horseshoes, and, to this day, some players make their first practice attempts at it with horseshoes. It is, in fact, to the large-scale disappearance of horses, and, therefore of horseshoes, from country life that some people attribute the drop in the popularity of quoits. It is interesting to note that, in the United States, horseshoe pitching itself is a game, and one that is still popular.

Shove-Ha'penny. Shove-Ha'penny, an old English game that is still popular, uses a cushioned wood or slate board, divided by parallel lines across it into nine "beds." The "halfpennies" may be actual halfpennies, but are generally round metal discs. The object of the game is to shove the halfpennies into one of the nine beds, the shoving usually being done with the ball of the thumb, though any part of the hand may be used. First turn is decided by shoving halfpennies at the number nine bed, the best attempt winning. A turn consists of five halfpennies, and the winner is the first player to shove three halfpennies into each bed, halfpennies that touch the cushion not counting. Should a player place more than three halfpennies in any bed, his opponent can claim the excess, if he needs them, but cannot win the final point of a game in this way. Push-Penny, a similar game using three coins is played in some parts of the country, mainly in Lincolnshire.

Skittles. There are several variations of the ancient game of Skittles, but all consist of throwing a ball down a level alley at a set of pins. The ball is generally a flat-sided wooden object called a "cheese," but some games use a round ball. The number of pins has varied between 3 and 17, but the "normal" number is 9, though some parts of England have always preferred 10. Scoring is by knocking down as many pins as possible in a fixed number of throws, by knocking down 31 in the fewest possible throws, or by knocking down 9 in three or fewer throws. In some games, the centre pin must be hit first. Skittles became popular in the United States as Ninepins, but was made illegal because of the gambling on it. It survived, however, as Bowling, using 10 pins, and this version is now also played in Britain.

Stoolball. Yet another ancestor of Cricket, Stoolball is still a popular girls' game. The wicket is a board a foot square on a pole 4 feet 8 inches high, the bat has a round striking surface, and the ball is rubber. Wickets are 16 yards apart and eight balls constitute an over.

Old-time Dancing. *See* **Ballroom Dancing.**

Oxford and Cambridge Boat Race. *See* **Boat Races.**

Pall-Mall. *See* **Old English Games and Customs.**

Parachute Jumping.

Parachute jumping is generally regarded as a last-resort safety measure, to be undertaken only in a supreme emergency, and with considerable anxiety; but it is now also a recreation and a competitive sport, practised entirely voluntarily, and for enjoyment. This form of jumping may be said to have grown out of the Second World War, in which jumping was used to a far greater extent than ever before, and not only for escape in an emergency. Now, international competitions take place, and the sport has an enthusiastic following in Britain.

Parachute jumping as a sport involves jumps of particular kinds, including landings in a certain area, marked by a circle, and demonstrating turns and body control in the air, the parachutist regulating his direction by pulling down the lines of the parachute. Jumps of this kind may be made from about 6000 feet.

The first point that occurs to many people when they think about Parachute Jumping is that it is extremely dangerous. However, those who jump as a recreation maintain that this is not so, and that it is about as dangerous as skiing. Injuries are few and slight, and, in three years, none of the hundred-odd members of the British Parachute Club, of Fairoaks, Surrey, suffered anything worse than a sprained ankle. The parachutes used are so reliable that they still work even if they have been badly packed. A parachute consists of twenty-eight sections, called "gores," each divided into four panels, so that, even if a hole should stretch right across one gore, which is rare, the remainder of the parachute remains intact, and will bring the jumper down safely. As an additional precaution, jumpers wear a small reserve parachute on the chest, but this is hardly ever needed.

Training, which generally takes place at weekends, starts with a period of learning how to fall, how to judge wind direction and speed, and how to pack a parachute. The first actual jumps are from 1500 feet. Both men and women take part in Parachute Jumping.

Party Games.

Parties can be for any of quite a number of age groups; and, when it comes to Party Games, it is not easy to say at what age a particular game ceases or starts to be fun. However, given a number of games from which to choose, the organiser of a party should be able to select those suitable for the occasion and the guests.

Many years of popularity perhaps confer the right to first mention on a batch of "classic" games suitable for young children, starting with Musical Chairs and a less-well-known variation of it. Musical chairs requires a line of chairs, one facing one way, and the next one the opposite way, and so on. Someone starts playing the piano, and the players, who should number one more than the chairs, move round and round them. When the music stops, they sit down quickly, the odd one out dropping out. The game continues with one chair removed, and carries on until the last two players are contending for the last chair. The variation is Going to Jerusalem, which needs a line of chairs similarly placed, and numbering one less than the players, and also a piano accompaniment. The players start seated, the remaining one walking round and round them, chanting "I'm going to Jerusalem." Every now and again, he knocks on the floor behind a chair, and the player seated there must rise and follow him. He carries on, reversing his direction at will, until all the players are following, after which the game is exactly the same as musical chairs.

Hunt the Slipper has all the players except one seated in a circle, with their knees raised so that the slipper can be passed underneath them. The extra player stands either outside or inside the circle, and tries to spot the slipper, and tap a player when he is in possession of it. For Hunt the Thimble, all the players except one go out of the room while the selected player hides the thimble in such a way that it is visible without anything having to be moved. He then summons the others with the formula, "Hot beans and melted butter, ladies and gentlemen, come to supper." The others then search for the thimble, being told if they are "hot," "warm," or "cold." As each player spots it, he sits down quietly, and lets the others continue their search. Up Jenkins has two teams seated on opposite sides of a table, one team having a small coin, which one player holds. The leader of the other side then says, "Up Jenkins," at which the first team hold their hands, with fists clenched, above the table. Next comes a command, which is either "Smash," at which the hands come down flat on the table, or "Crawl," at which they come down clenched and then slowly spread the fingers, the coin holder always complying, but trying to conceal that he has it. The other side then order various hands to be removed, the object being to remove all but the one with the coin.

In Charades a group of players go out of the room and select a word for the others to guess. This should have two syllables, each itself a word. The group then act three short scenes, the first representing the first half of the word, the second the other half, and the third the whole word. There are several ways of acting Charades. In one, each scene actually represents the word or syllable in some way; in another, it has nothing to do with it, but the word or syllable is mentioned; and in still another, it is both represented and mentioned. In historical Charades a well-known figure of fact or fiction with a name containing about five letters is selected, and short scenes are acted about different characters whose names begin with the various letters in the chosen name. Similar to Charades is Dumb Crambo, in which those in the room select two rhyming words, decide on one to be acted, then call in the "actors" and tell them the other. If they start to act a wrong word, the spectators hiss, but, when the right word is reached, they clap. Both actors and audience remain silent. The similarly named Crambo requires each player to write a noun and a question on separate pieces of paper, put them into two hats, draw another paper out of each, and write an answer to the question on one bringing in the noun on the other. Capping Verses is a rhyming game in which one player invents a line, and the others have to supply a rhyming line in the same metre.

Perhaps the most famous of all paper games is Consequences. Each player has a sheet of paper divided into columns, writes an adjective applicable to a man in the first column, folds it over, and passes it on. He then writes a man's name in the second column of the paper he receives, folds and passes it, and carries on with an adjective applicable to a woman, a woman's name, a place, a remark by a man, a remark by a woman, what the consequence was, and what the world said; after which, the papers are read out. Lost and Found is a variation, in which the items required are the object lost, by whom, when, where, by whom it was found, in what condition, where, and what the reward was. A simple paper game is Squares, in which several lines of dots are marked on a sheet of paper. Each player in turn joins two dots with a line, the object being to collect squares, which go to the player who makes the line that completes them. Advertisements has sections of well-known advertisements displayed with the name of the product omitted, players having to write down as many of the names as they can. This is an observation test, as is Kim's Game, in which a number of small objects on a table or a tray are displayed for one minute, after which the players write down as many of them as they can.

Verbal guessing games are numerous. In Proverbs, one player goes out of the room while the others choose a proverb, and allocate one word of it to each person. The player then returns and asks questions, the answers to which must include the speaker's particular word. In Guess Who, a character of fact or fiction is chosen, and has to be guessed by questions that must be answered "Yes" or "No." In How, When, and Where, a noun with several different meanings has to be guessed by questions that are restricted to "How do you like it?" "When do you like it?" and "Where do you like it?" Biographies is a game generally popular with children. An adult tells a brief, but accurate, life story of some famous historical character, omitting any mention of the character's surname. The winner is the first listener to interrupt the story by calling out the missing name.

Perhaps the most popular of all question-and-answer games is Murder, which starts with cards being dealt round so that only the recipients can see them. This is to allot the "parts," one particular card indicating the murderer, and another the detective. The detective announces himself at once, but the murderer keeps quiet. All the lights are then turned out, and the players disperse about the house. The murderer counts fifty, and then commits his murder by pretending to stab another player, who must stand still and count fifteen before screaming to announce the murder. The scream brings the detective, who puts the lights on, and makes what mental notes he wishes of the various players' positions, which, with the exception of the murderer's, must remain unaltered from the moment of the scream. The detective then gathers the players together, and questions them, everyone being compelled to answer truthfully, except the murderer, who can lie as much as he likes, unless he is directly accused by the detective, when he must own up. The detective is allowed three direct accusations. A variation gives an additional part to a detective's assistant, who does the gathering in of the suspects, and reports on their respective positions to the detective.

Finally two word games that generally amuse children. In What's the Word two players quietly select a word with several meanings, and start to discuss one of its meanings, without mentioning the word, soon switching to another meaning, and then another, or else back to the first. If another player thinks he has guessed the word, he joins in the conversation. He is soon proved wrong or right; and, if wrong, he drops out again, but, if right, he then takes over with a partner whom he chooses. Travels gives one player a special part, another acting as an intermediary between him and the others. The player whispers to the intermediary the name of a place, which may be anywhere in the world, to which he intends to travel. The intermediary then asks three others, who do not know the place, one question each, these being "How is he to go there?" "How is he to travel about when he gets there?" and "How is he to come home again?" The answers must be methods of transport, and the first player then tells a brief story of his journeys and adventures, during which he must abide by the means of travel suggested.

Patience.

Patience is a card game for one person, and, though there are few different games for one, there are countless different forms of Patience. There are some using one pack, and others using two, almost all of them starting with the setting out of the cards on the table according to fixed rules, and having as their object the building up of the four suits on their aces.

The game that might almost be called the basic form of single-pack patience starts with a row of seven cards, only the left-hand one being exposed. Underneath this, and overlapping it, comes a row of six cards with the left-hand one exposed, and so on down to a "row" consisting of only a single exposed card, the exposed cards being left uncovered in each decreasing row. The object is to take out first the aces, and then the cards from two up to king, building each suit on its ace. From the "lay out," exposed cards can be moved when it is possible to put one on a card one pip higher in value of the opposite colour, when any card left uncovered by an exposed card can itself be exposed. The undealt cards can be played three at a time, the top one of each three being "playable," with the one underneath becoming "playable," if the top one is, in fact, played. The undealt cards can be played through three at a time in this manner as often as desired. A slight variation of this game allows the undealt cards to be played through one at a time, but this can be done only once.

Another single-pack game starts with a row of nine exposed cards, with, below it and overlapping, a row of eight, and so on down to one, all the cards being exposed, and the right-hand one being left uncovered in each decreasing row. The remaining seven cards form a separate row at the bottom. The object and the "move" are the same as in the previous game, only one card being moved at a time, and any card being eligible to fill any vacancy that might occur in the top row. Cards in the separate row can be played as required, but, once in the "lay out," they must remain there. This game is called King of the Belgians, and the last seven cards are referred to as the Belgian Reserve.

One to Six is a two-pack game. The player deals out a row of four cards, then discards two to a rubbish heap, and carries on like this until all the cards have been used. If, however, while doing it, he comes across any aces or kings, he takes them out, up to one of each from each suit, subsequently also taking out any that will fit on to these, building up from the aces and down from the kings. Then he goes through the rubbish heap, extracting any cards that will fit on the eight piles. The dealt-out cards, with the rubbish-heap cards, are then dealt again in the same way, the object being to complete the eight built-up suits in three rounds of dealing.

At first sight, it might appear that there is little point in Patience, which does nothing to inculcate "card sense" that might prove useful in ordinary card games. However, the fact that it has its own fascination is shown by the countless thousands who play it at one time or another, and by the virtual inability of anyone seeing a game of Patience in progress to refrain from studying the "lay out," and offering advice. There is scope for a certain amount of skill in the management of the cards, as, for instance, in the first two games described above, in which it is advisable to build up the suit-piles fairly evenly, as a long run in one suit will leave a disproportionate number of cards of one colour, thus restricting further moves.

Polo.

Polo, one of the oldest of all games, originated in Persia, then spread in one form or another to China, Japan, and India, eventually being brought from India to England by cavalry officers in the second half of the nineteenth century. Later, it was enthusiastically taken up in the United States and Argentina. Played four-aside, and mounted, on a pitch that should measure 300 yards by 160 yards, its object is to score goals by hitting a 5-ounce ball through goals 24 feet wide with a stick consisting of a long cane fixed at a slight angle into a wooden or bambo striking head. The game is divided into periods, called "chukkas," the number of periods varying slightly, as may be agreed for particular games.

Formerly, Polo was a game for the wealthy, for it entailed owning and maintaining a string of trained ponies. In recent years, however, certain stables and riding schools have provided facilities for playing and practising Polo, and these facilities include the hiring out of ponies. This apparently simple and obvious step is actually quite a revolutionary innovation that has brought Polo within the reach of almost anyone who wants to play, and thereby increased the popularity of an ancient and exciting game that might otherwise have died out because of the expense involved.

Pot-holing.

Pot-holing might almost be described as mountaineering in reverse, for it consists of the descent, perhaps to a depth of 80 or 90 feet or more, and probably by a precarious rope-ladder, of pot-holes caused by the action of carbon-charged water on rocks of the chalk or limestone type. Pot-holing is pursued as a recreation, but it can also lead to extremely useful geographical and geological discoveries, and it certainly does not lack danger.

Pot-holes are plentiful in Britain, particularly in Derbyshire and Yorkshire, for there are many instances of streams plunging into the earth, to reappear many miles away. While underground, they may alter course considerably, even to the extent of turning almost back on themselves, and they may cross other underground streams. Where many of them reappear, or where many of those that appear start from, is still unknown, for the exploration of these underground courses is of comparatively recent origin, and is still far from complete. It is, in fact, exploration of this type that pot-holers undertake, and, if, in doing it, they subject themselves to considerable discomfort and some danger, they also discover a fascinating, and even beautiful underground world. Once below the ground, even quite small pot-holes often lead to winding passages, tunnels, and underground caverns containing icicle-like formations both descending from the roof and ascending from the ground. Called stalactites and stalagmites, respectively, these sometimes meet to form weird columns and pillars, all these and other strange formations being caused by calcium deposits. Seen in the light of the pot-holers' torches, some of these caverns are wonderful sights, and new tunnels and caverns are always being discovered.

For those who have the nerve for it, Pot-holing can be an enthralling, and also useful, recreation, but it is one that the newcomer should practise only in company with experienced pot-holers, and it is one in which the loss of a torch can be a major disaster.

Public School Football.

All the forms of football popular to-day grew out of the games played at various English Public Schools a century and more ago. These games differed widely, the rules often depending on purely local considerations imposed by the available space. The Rugby game (*q.v.*) in its modern form is, of course, still played, both at that school and far beyond it; and other games that still survive at the schools that originated them are the Eton Field Game, the Eton Wall Game, the Harrow Base Game, and Winchester College Football.

Punting.

Punting consists of propelling a long, narrow, flat-bottomed boat with a pole, the punter standing up; and it can be either a pleasant, leisurely recreation or a fairly strenuous competitive sport. The sporting side is governed by the Thames Punting Club, which has headquarters on the Thames at Staines in Middlesex. Women, as well as men, take part in competitive events.

Punting as a sport has the unique distinction of being confined, not only to one country, Britain, but to one river, the Thames; though in some parts of the world boats poled from a standing position are used for various purposes. There have been rumours that Japan has, or had, a similar sport, but these have never been authenticated.

Quoits. *See* **Old English Games and Customs.**

Race Walking. *See* **Athletics, Walking.**

Rackets.

Rackets is a fast, racket-and-ball game, played on a court measuring 62 feet by 31 feet, and using walls. A game consists of 15 points, unless 13-all is reached, when the non-server can set the game to 3 or 5, or 14-all is reached, when the non-server can set the game to 3, the game going to the first player to score the prescribed number of points. Only the server scores, the receiver taking over service when he makes a winning shot. When served, the ball must strike the front wall above a line called the "cut" line before striking any other part of the court, but, in play, it may be played either on the volley or after one bounce. If a player impedes his opponent, it is a "let," and the point is re-started.

Real Tennis.

Tennis, sometimes called "Real," "Royal," or "Court" Tennis, is a court game played with rackets and balls that has been called the King of Games, and that was once certainly the game of kings. Henry VIII played, and it is mentioned in Shakespeare's *Henry V*; but the first kings to play were of France, where the game originated.

It is a complicated game, and no description could give anyone who had never seen it an accurate idea of what it is like. Most racket-and-ball games use either a net, over which the ball is hit, or walls, against which it is hit, but Tennis uses both. Also, in most racket games, players change ends after so many games, but, in Tennis, they may do so during a game. Matches are in games and sets, a player winning six games completing a set towards the two out of three or three out of five that will make the match.

There are not many Tennis players in the country—there are only about a dozen courts—and very few women have ever played. People who do play, however, most of whom play other games as well, are almost unanimous in voting it the best of all games.

It is said that the term " love," used in so many games to indicate " nought," comes from Tennis, the original French term being " l'œuf," which, in that language, actually means " egg ": an egg being, of course, something like the figure used for " nought." This derivation is not sufficiently well documented to be accepted as definite fact; but it is interesting to note that, in Cricket (*q.v.*), the term used for a score of " nought " is a " duck," or, in full, a " duck's egg."

Revolver Shooting. *See* **Rifle Shooting.**

Riding and Show-jumping.

The almost complete disappearance of the horse from everyday life has been followed by an increase of interest in Riding as a recreation. This is at least partly due to the great attention paid in recent years by both Press and television to one particular branch of horsemanship, Show-jumping. Before learning to jump, however, it is necessary to learn to ride, and many people never go, and have no wish to go, beyond the ordinary, unspectacular riding for pleasure that is called " hacking."

A great deal has been said and written about " correct " riding style, but, in actual fact, there are many different styles. The cavalryman, for instance, bends the leg to some extent; the Red Indian bends it to a much greater extent, more or less in the style that has been adopted by American jockeys; and the cowboy rides with an absolutely straight leg. Yet all these are expert horsemen. To assist in acquiring the normal English style, which is very close to that of the cavalryman, there is an old jingle that is now much less heard than it used to be, but is probably none the less helpful or accurate for that. It runs: " Your head and your heart keep up. Your hands and your heels keep down. Your knees keep close to your horse's sides, and your elbows close to your own." Old or not, anyone who learns it, and then builds up a certain amount of experience of putting it into actual practice is well on the way to becoming a rider.

It has been said that Riding is excellent exercise for the horse, but, whatever its merits or demerits as a medium of actual physical exercise for the rider, it certainly provides him or her with a delightful and beneficial form of recreation in the open air. For those who like the idea of Riding, no matter how inexperienced they may be, there are " pony trekking " holidays. These take place at fixed centres, where about two days are spent in simple instruction in such elementary things as saddling, mounting, starting, and stopping the horse, after which day expeditions cover the surrounding countryside. Those who feel they would like to combine their Riding with something competitive might start with gymkhanas, which are sports meetings that generally include mounted equivalents of such novelty events as obstacle races and needle-threading races. For the more ambitious, gymkhanas could even be the first step towards the top-class competitive sport of Show-jumping.

Show-jumping. A Show-jumping contest is a mounted competition over a circuit of jumps, which the entrants attempt one at a time, each having the field to himself or herself, and being free to concentrate entirely on the jumps, without having to worry about other riders. The jumps, which have to be taken in a certain order, are of many kinds, including fences, double fences, walls, and water. Scoring is by points against, called " faults," so many being debited against an entrant for falling, knocking down an obstacle or displacing part of it, refusing, and other mistakes. Though the event is in no sense a race, there is normally a time limit that must not be exceeded, and, in some events, bonus points are awarded for fast rounds. Show-jumping is not restricted to riders who own their own horses, for some owners do not want to compete themselves, and are only too pleased to let good horsemen take their jumpers round for them. Incidentally, inexperienced riders taking up jumping for the first time will probably find it advisable to make some slight changes in their method of sitting in the saddle. Jumping needs a firm seat, and the novice rider may find it necessary to shorten the stirrups a little.

Allied to Show-jumping, and coupled with it in the difficult three-day competitions, is dressage. This is simply a mounted display revealing that the horse is obedient, balanced, supple, and, in a word, trained; and is a simplified form of the better-known " haute école," or highly-schooled riding. Good riders who seek absolute perfection can, if they are willing to pay for it, take an intensive course of haute école riding and all forms of horsemanship at the most famous of all riding schools, the Spanish Riding School in Vienna. Courses, which are conducted in German, consist of eight hours training a day for six months, and informality is not encouraged, the regulation dress for students being a bowler hat, black jacket, and white breeches. Riders who fall are immediately assisted by an attendant armed, not with a stretcher, but with a clothes brush.

Rifle Shooting.

Considered as a sport, Rifle Shooting, which might almost be called the modern equivalent of archery, had its origins in virtually the same conditions and circumstances that had popularised the older weapon five hundred years previously; though, unlike archery, it did not enjoy legislation aimed at abolishing other recreations in its favour. Both were encouraged because, in their respective periods, efficiency at them meant, not only success in competitions, but also the most effective defence in time of war, the great period of the rifle's encouragement for this reason being the latter half of the nineteenth century. Archery as a sport survives to the present day, and Rifle Shooting as a sport continues, though it can no longer be regarded as the most effective weapon.

With a normal rifle, with a calibre of about ·300 inch, competitive shooting is at ranges from 200 yards to 1000 yards, and there are many competitions, the greatest of them being the annual contest at Bisley, Surrey, for the Queen's Prize. Almost equally popular, however, is small-bore shooting, with a calibre of ·22 inch, and this, too, offers many annual competitions.

Revolver Shooting. Revolver shooting, often called pistol shooting, is also a competitive sport, and a very difficult one. Impressions gained from cinema and television screens might lead anyone who has never fired one to think that the revolver is an easy weapon to fire without fuss and with devastating effect. It is the very reverse of this. It is fired, not from the hip, but with the extended arm raised, which is how, in real life, it was generally fired in the old West. It is extremely difficult to hit even a man-size target at 10 yards, and very few people can call themselves good revolver shots, just as few of the old Westerners were good revolver shots. The difficulty is caused by the tremendous " kick " of a weapon that is held, not by both hands and pressed into the shoulder, as a rifle is, but by one hand. A revolver has sights, but the normal method of aiming is by using the " instinctive pointing sense," which is based on the fact that, if you point your finger at an object in the ordinary way, without, of course, taking a careful sight along it, you will, in fact, be pointing accurately. The same applies when pointing a revolver.

Rink Hockey. *See* **Skating.**

Rock Climbing. *See* **Mountaineering.**

Roller Skating. *See* **Skating.**

Rowing.

Rowing, meaning simply taking a boat out on the sea or a river for a short period, is a pleasant recreation and a healthy exercise, but competitive rowing is one of the most strenuous of all sports.

A racing oarsman either rows, which means that he uses one oar, or sculls, which means two oars. Races are of various kinds, the best-known being for crews of eight oarsmen with a cox. Then there are races for crews of four with cox, and for crews of four without cox. There are also events for pairs with cox, pairs without cox, double sculls, and single sculls. Eights, fours, and pairs row, while double and single scullers, of course, scull. In fours and pairs without cox, and in all sculling, the oarsmen steer themselves.

Race Rowing is mainly a river sport, but there are races on the sea. For these, crews are usually fours with cox, and they use heavier boats than the normal racing "shell." (*See also* **Boat Races.**)

Rugby Fives. *See* **Fives.**

Rugby Football.

As its name implies, Rugby Football is based on the game played at Rugby School in the days when football was not organised and various schools played to their own rules. The story of how the Rugby game originated is well known and widely accepted, but it is definitely not accurate and possibly almost entirely apocryphal.

The story is that, in 1823, a boy named William Webb Ellis disregarded the rules of that time by handling the ball, and that handling was subsequently made legal. In fact, handling the ball by catching it was allowed at Rugby before 1823, so, if Ellis was responsible for an innovation, it was not by handling the ball, but by running with it after catching it. Running with the ball certainly became, and remains, the leading feature of Rugby Football; but the story that Ellis was responsible, though commemorated by a plaque at the school, was first heard years after Ellis's death, and he never knew of the fame that became his. He was definitely at Rugby at the time, though, and, a few years later, he played in the first-ever Oxford and Cambridge cricket match.

The spread of the game beyond the school that originated it has led to, not one, but two games of Rugby Football, Rugby Union and Rugby League. About twenty-five years after the game had become organised, with the Rugby Union as its governing body, there was a dispute on the question of legalising payment for time lost from work by players. The Union would not agree to this, so twenty-two clubs, mainly in Yorkshire, seceded and formed the Northern Union, now the Rugby League. Both bodies originally played the same game, but now, after over sixty years of independent existence, during which each has made various rule changes, there are some important differences.

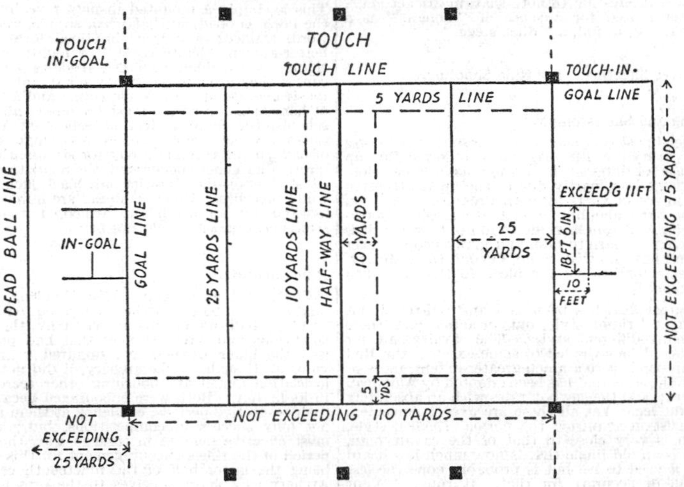

NOTES:—

■ Indicates Post with Flag. Length and breadth of field to be as near to dimensions indicated as possible.

– – – These broken lines indicate 10 yards and 5 yards from half-way and touch lines respectively.

Goal dimensions.—10 feet is taken from the ground to the top edge of the crossbar and 18 feet 6 inches from inside to inside of the goal posts.

Rugby was originally played twenty-aside, but it is now fifteen-aside in R.U. and thirteen-aside in R.L., the positions being seven backs and eight forwards in R.U. and seven backs and six forwards in R.L. Played on a pitch marked out as in the diagram, and with an oval ball, Rugby is mainly a handling game, the chief object being the grounding of the ball behind the opponents' goal-line. This is a "try," which counts three points, and entitles the scoring side to an attempt to score a goal by kicking the ball over the cross-bar from a point measured in a straight line from where the ball was grounded. Other forms of goal are penalties, which may be awarded anywhere, dropped goals during play, and goals from a "mark," after a player has signalled a "fair catch" of the ball during play by shouting, "Mark." In R.U. goals following tries, called "conversions," count two, and other goals three.

In R.L. any goal counts two, but goals from a "mark" are not allowed.

The game is started, and restarted after a score, by a kick-off from the centre; and, thereafter, the ball may be advanced by kicking or carrying. It may also be passed from hand, but not forward. Ball carriers may be tackled and thrown down, and they may "hand off" tacklers with the unclenched hand. A frequent method of restarting after a stoppage is the "scrummage," in which the forwards bend down and push against each other, three from each side constituting a front row, and the remainder two subsequent rows. The ball is then put into the tunnel between the front rows, the centre man of each, the "hooker," endeavouring to gain possession by hooking it back into, and generally right through, his "scrum." In R.L. this method of restarting is used whenever the ball goes out over the touch-line; but in R.U. the ball is thrown in straight along a "line out" of both sets of forwards, unless the side whose throw it is demand a scrummage. In R.L. kicking the ball straight out over the touch-line is allowed only from a free-kick, the penalty being a scrummage at the point from which the ball was kicked. The effect of the differences between the two games is that R.L. is faster and more open, and the ball is more continuously in play. A game lasts for eighty minutes, divided into two halves.

In addition to Britain, both forms of Rugby are played in France, New Zealand, and Australia, and R.U. is played in South Africa. Both codes also have other, smaller "outposts" in various European countries, and there are minor R.U. centres in North and South America. R.U. is entirely an amateur game, and R.L. primarily so, though there is a top layer of clubs using part-time professionals.

Sailing.

Mention of Sailing tends, perhaps, to conjure up visions of large, graceful yachts, beautiful to see, but clearly to be owned only by the wealthy. Sailing to-day, though, is very different from that. It is mainly sailing in small boats, many of them wholly or partly built by their owners. At first glance the building of a boat might seem a tremendous and highly skilled task, but, in actual fact, it can be as big and as hard or as small and as easy as the builder wishes. Some amateur builders start from the very beginning, acquiring the various materials needed bit by bit, and gradually bringing their boats into being. However, those who either lack the time for this or doubt their ability to construct a boat in which they would feel safe on the water can buy complete boat-building kits; and they can buy them at any stage of construction they choose from hardly started to complete except for a coat of paint. It is more economical to build a boat than to buy one complete and ready for launching, and the earlier the stage of construction at which the owner takes over, the greater the saving. Some owners claim that they enjoy the building as much as the sailing, and it is probably true that the owner who has done some work on his boat, however little, takes more interest and pride in the finished article.

The fact that boat-building is now within the reach of practically everyone means, of course, that the end to which it is a means, Sailing, is also within the reach of practically everyone, for few people are far from some suitable stretch of water. Where there is sailing, there are clubs, which the boat owner can join for quite reasonable fees, and which provide either sheltered moorings or "dinghy parks" where the boat can be kept.

Eventually, the small-boat owner may want to try racing his craft, and there are many events for boats of all classes and sizes. Racing is an enthralling pastime, for, though races are, of course, tests of speed, they are also very much more than that. There is tremendous scope for tactics, and the sport is in every sense a highly skilled one, as well, incidentally, as one with an interesting history behind it.

Yacht Racing. The first recorded sailing contest was a race from Greenwich to Gravesend on 1 October 1661, between Charles II, who won, and his brother, the Duke of York. In those days, such contests generally took the form of manœuvring for positions of advantage, rather than straightforward racing, for the Royal Navy also relied on sailing, and every privately owned vessel was a potentially useful naval auxiliary: a fact that emphasises the appropriateness of the right of England's most famous yacht club, the Royal Yacht Squadron, to fly the White Ensign. The club was founded as the Yacht Club in 1815, becoming the Royal Yacht Club in 1817, when the Prince Regent joined, and taking its present name in 1832. In 1851 the club put up for competition a 137-ounce, 100-guinea cup that has become the most famous trophy in yachting, and one of the most famous in sport.

In that year a schooner of the then famous New York pilot-cutter type, called the *America*, sailed across the Atlantic, and her commander challenged the Royal Yacht Squadron to find a schooner or schooners to race against her. There were no takers, so the *America*'s commander made a more tempting offer. Though the schooner rig was considered slow, and was generally given a time allowance in races, he offered to race on level terms against vessels of any rig, and to back his ship for anything up to 10,000 guineas. There were still no takers, so the commander entered for the 53-mile race round the Isle of Wight for the new cup, though he knew that some of the seventeen other yachts in the race were twice the size of the *America*. Despite that, the *America* won by eight minutes.

Subsequently, the *America* was sold to an Englishman, who cut 5 feet off the masts, and then wondered why she did not win races. She was rebuilt in a Thames boatyard, and, when the war between the States broke out, became a Confederate blockade-runner, but was trapped in the St. John's River, Florida, and scuttled. However, she was raised and repaired, and finished the war as part of the Union Navy, after which she returned to racing, which brings us back to the story of her cup.

The cup, now called the *America*'s Cup, had been given to the New York Yacht Club for perpetual competition between different countries, and the first challenge for it came in 1870. The challenger was defeated, and by the *America*. To date, there have been nineteen challenges, sixteen by Great Britain, two by Canada, and one by Australia, but not one of them has succeeded. Britain's 1958 challenge, which was the seventeenth, pointed the present trend in yachting, which is towards smaller vessels. Previously, the America's Cup conditions stipulated that the races must be between very large yachts of the "J" or 21-metre type, and that, if the challenge was from across the Atlantic, the challenger must sail across. In 1958, the rule about sailing across the Atlantic was waived, and the event was between yachts of the 12-metre class.

Large vessels are still seen in the famous Bermuda Race, but the modern trend is very evident in the growing popularity of the annual Folkestone Dinghy Race across the Channel, which also has a class for catamarans, very fast and very popular boats that consist of two boats side by side joined by a kind of raft.

Sculling. *See* **Rowing.**

Shove-Ha'penny. *See* **Old English Games and Customs.**

Show-Jumping. *See* **Racing and Show-Jumping.**

Skating.

At first glance, ice-skating would not appear to be a normal activity for British people, for it is a part of Winter Sports (*q.v.*), which are possible in Britain only rarely and to a very small extent, and it was formerly restricted to brief periods when rivers, lakes, and ponds were frozen. Despite this, however, the people of this country have always appeared to possess a natural talent for it, and they have practised it whenever opportunity offered. The history of British Skating goes back a very long way, and includes occasions when Skating was possible, and took place, on the Thames, as well as many, more regular instances in the Fen district and other places. In recent years this wish to skate on ice has been catered for by the opening of many indoor rinks, which make the skater independent of weather and daylight, and enable Skating to be carried on throughout the year.

Many people ice-skate just for recreation, health, and amusement, but anyone keen to carry Skating a stage farther and acquire a higher level of skill can find a wide range of opportunities from which to choose. Figure-skating is very popular, and for those anxious to test their skill at it there is a series of medal tests, in which the skater is not in competition with anybody, but is attempting only to reach a fixed standard. Beyond these, there are many competitions and championships. Dancing on skates also attracts many people; and also offers those interested standard medal tests and competitions.

Another popular skating activity is speed-skating, which takes place indoors and, whenever possible, outdoors as well, though the methods and techniques of the two forms of racing differ widely. Outdoors, the skaters normally race in pairs, though each man is timed, and is actually racing against the whole field. Much of the racing is on long, straight stretches of ice. Indoors, skaters race perhaps four at a time, and are directly opposed to those on the ice with them. These races are on small tracks, a lap sometimes being no more than 130 yards. Standard outdoor distances range from 500 to 10,000 metres, while indoor races go from 440 yards to 2 miles. There are also indoor relays, generally of 3 miles, in which teams of four race on the "Madison" method, relieving each other, not at fixed points, but at will. In addition to competitions and championships, speed-skaters also have their standard medal tests.

Ice, however, is not the only surface on which Skating takes place, for, following an unusual history, roller-skating also maintains a large following. Roller-skating was originally introduced long before the arrival of the indoor ice rinks purely to provide ice-skaters with some kind of substitute when no natural ice was available. It progressed by fits and starts, varying from extraordinary "crazes" when it seemed that everybody was roller-skating, to periods when nobody appeared to be doing so. Eventually, it settled down to a steady existence as a popular recreation in its own right that has in no sense been pushed into the background by the increased facilities for ice-skating. The opportunities it offers are almost identical with those of ice-skating, for they include figure-skating, dancing, and speed-skating, with championships, competitions, and standard medal tests in all branches.

Both forms of Skating also offer a team game, and in both it is hockey. Ice-hockey, which is called simply hockey in Canada, where it originated, and the United States, is played six-aside, with substitutes permitted, and with a rubber disc, called a "puck," instead of a ball. It first began to win popularity in Britain soon after the First World War, and since then has had rather a chequered career, helped forward by the semi-professional players from Canada, who play in the National League teams, and held back by the lack of facilities for British youngsters to practise; for practice sessions mean closing rinks to all the other forms of Skating for certain periods. The game should, however, survive, for there is a definite demand for it.

Roller-hockey, generally known as rink-hockey, bears a closer resemblance to its parent game, outdoor field hockey, than does ice-hockey. It is played with a ball, and is five-aside, with one substitute permitted. Its popularity is such that it is now played throughout the year.

There is a form of hockey on ice that closely resembles outdoor hockey. This is Bandy, which originated in England but is no longer played here, though it is popular in Sweden and the U.S.S.R. Some other games have been tried on skates from time to time. One is Badminton, which has been played on ice, but only as a stage exhibition. Basketball on roller-skates has been tried in several countries, and might well develop and spread.

Skating is not so much a recreation, sport, or game as a whole series of different recreations, sports, and games. Each has its following, and, while there are enthusiasts who are interested in both ice- and roller-skating, or in more than one branch of one or both of them, there are many ice-skaters who have no interest in or knowledge of roller-skating, and vice versa, and many keen supporters of just one branch of Skating who hardly know that the many other branches exist. It is, of course, quite possible to take part in both ice- and roller-skating, and in more than one branch of Skating, and greatly to increase one's enjoyment by doing so.

It is not particularly hard to learn to skate. It requires strong ankles, a good sense of balance, and plenty of confidence; and it is possible to start practising, at least to a limited extent, at home, for instance, by getting used to standing on skates. Skating is probably more easily mastered when young, but many adults have successfully taken it up.

Skiing. *See* **Winter Sports.**

Ski-Joring. *See* **Winter Sports.**

Ski-Jumping. *See* **Winter Sports.**

Skittles. *See* **Old English Games and Customs.**

Snooker. *See* **Billiards.**

Snowshoe Running. *See* **Winter Sports.**

Softball. *See* **Baseball.**

Solo Whist.

Solo Whist is a card game for four players, who normally act independently. Play is as at Whist (*q.v.*), but the cards are dealt in threes, the final round being dealt singly, and the dealer exposing his last card to indicate trumps.

Players then "declare" in turn, starting with the player on the dealer's left. The lowest call is "I propose," which entails making eight tricks with a partner, any one of the other players being eligible to "accept" in his turn. The next call is "Solo," which requires five tricks to be made unassisted. Next comes "Misère," in which every trick must be lost, and then comes "Abondance," in which nine tricks must be made. Higher still is "Misère Ouverte," in which every trick must be lost with the player's hand exposed, and highest of all is "Abondance Declarée," in which every trick must be made. Any player may "Pass," and, once a call has been made, later callers must make a higher call or pass.

Though calls are made with trumps already nominated, certain calls may alter the trumps; and, with regard to these, there are several views, all quite widely held, as to the rules that should apply. A player calling Abondance can choose his own trumps, though Abondance in the nominated trumps—called Royal Abondance—takes precedence over the same call in another suit. In Abondance one school of thought holds that the first round is played on the nominated trumps, while another takes the view that the first card only is played on the nominated trumps. In either of these circumstances a player making this call should not announce his trumps until the round or card has been played, unless it is necessary to announce Royal Abondance to overcall. There is, however, a third view, and it is the view of the majority of authorities who have actually written about the game, that the new trumps should be announced before the hand starts. Also the subject of differing views is Abondance Declarée, one view being that the caller can choose his own trumps, and another that, in this call, there are no trumps, though both views agree that this call confers the right to lead. A good player can easily adapt himself to any of these variations, the important thing being to check which versions are being used before starting to play. On the Misère calls there are no trumps, and in Misère Ouverte the player need not expose his hand until the first round has been played.

Speed-Skating. *See* **Skating.**

Squash Rackets.

Squash Rackets was designed as a preliminary preparation for the game of Rackets (*q.v.*), but it is now a popular game in its own right, played by men who have no intention of playing Rackets, and by women who never play Rackets. The game is similar to Rackets, but the court is smaller and most matches are singles. Doubles, however, can be played, and in the United States there are special doubles courts slightly larger than the normal Squash court.

Stoolball. *See* **Old English Games and Customs.**

Strand-Pulling. *See* **Weight-lifting.**

Surf Riding. *See* **Swimming.**

Swimming.

Swimming is an extremely popular pastime that also shares with walking the distinction of being a perfect exercise for health, as it exercises the whole body, and can be carried out as easily or as strenuously as the swimmer wishes. It is also a very useful accomplishment that may at any time put its possessor in a position to save a life.

There are several different swimming strokes, the basic stroke being the breast-stroke, now often seen in an alternative method, the butterfly. Faster strokes include the side-arm, the overarm, the trudgeon, and the crawl, but each of these attempts to speed up progress through the water has really superseded its predecessor, and the crawl is now almost universal. There are also two strokes used in swimming on the back, one being a back equivalent of the breast-stroke, and the other a back crawl. It is possible to swim under the water, using the breast-stroke, and to keep the eyes open while doing so. It is also possible to swim down through the water to retrieve objects that may have been dropped. Ascending through the water is automatic, though it can be hastened by a kick. Remaining stationary in deep water can be achieved either by floating on the back or by treading water, which simply means moving the legs gently up and down.

It is not difficult to teach oneself to swim, and, like cycling, it is an accomplishment which, once learned, is never forgotten. The main thing is confidence, or an absence of any fear of the water. Such fears are quite unnecessary, for water is an element that always tends to keep a human being on the surface, and not to draw him under. Going underneath the water, and staying underneath, requires a definite physical effort, and, if that effort ceases, the swimmer is automatically brought to the surface again. Many non-swimmers who get into difficulties increase these by struggling wildly, for, by doing so, they may easily take and keep themselves under. If they would make only the gentle movements of treading water, they would both stay afloat much longer and present far fewer problems to any swimmer who might be trying to save them.

Saving life in the water is the object of the Royal Life-Saving Society, which teaches the best methods of bringing people who are in difficulties ashore, and also methods of artificial respiration for use in reviving the apparently drowned. Every swimmer should acquire some knowledge of life-saving, for even a strong swimmer may experience considerable difficulty in saving anyone unless he or she has some idea of the best way of setting about it. Many swimmers, for instance, normally use only the crawl and the back crawl, whereas, to save anyone, it is almost essential to use either the breast-stroke or its back equivalent.

Swimming has a well-organised competitive side, with many competitions and championships right up to the Olympic Games. Most races take place in baths, but there are some river and sea events, and the greatest competitive challenge to any swimmer is, of course, the English Channel. Although this has been conquered many times, the swimming of it remains, and will always remain, a wonderful achievement.

Diving. Generally accepted as being akin to Swimming, though actually it is quite a different sport, is Diving. Competition Diving means using boards of various heights, performing certain set dives, and choosing additional ones from an approved list. Diving requires a certain amount of nerve, and also gymnastic ability, including the ability to control the body in the air. Whereas strong swimmers are generally fairly big, divers are often much smaller and more compactly built.

Water Polo. In view of the popularity of Swimming, it is not surprising that there is a water team game, this being Water Polo, in which the object is the scoring of goals, the ball and the goals resembling those used in Soccer, though all shots and passes are, of course, thrown. Throughout a history of nearly eighty years, Water Polo has been beset by rule trouble, and has probably been the subject of more codes of rules than almost any other game. The difficulty is the detection of fouls under the water; the ideal, a game of the basketball type, free of bodily contact.

Surf Riding. Though straightforward Swimming, Diving, and Water Polo are the chief competitive water sports, there are other water activities with large and, in some cases, growing followings, some of them also having their competitive side. Fairly old-established is the Hawaiian sport of Surf Riding, which has been seen, though generally in a rather milder form, in many parts of the world. It consists of placing a flat board on the water, and then lying, or, more rarely, kneeling or standing on it, and being carried ashore on the crest of a wave.

Water-Skiing. A growing water sport, and one in which contests are held, is Water-Skiing, which is of more recent origin than Surf Riding, from which, in fact, its development can be traced. Surf Riding led to Aquaplaning, in which the board was towed by a motor-boat, with the rider standing. A further development saw the board giving place to actual skis, and Water-Skiing was born. This sport owes some of its popularity in Britain to television, for, when still in its infancy, it was demonstrated on the screen, and this led directly to several new water-skiing centres being opened up in various parts of the country.

Underwater Swimming. Undoubtedly the fastest growing of all swimming activities is Underwater Swimming, which is a link between ordinary diving and swimming under water, with the swimmer, depending on his own lungs, able to remain below for only a few seconds, and fully-fledged deep-sea diving, with the diver weighed down with equipment and receiving assistance from the surface. The underwater swimmer receives no surface assistance, but he does use light equipment, consisting of an artificial "lung" and breathing tubes, and also a mask and flippers. This type of swimming developed during the Second World War, in which Naval underwater swimmers, called "frogmen," rendered great services. Frogmen can also render useful services in peacetime, in, for instance, the sometimes necessary searching of rivers and canals; in underwater photography; and in exploring wrecks, and even old, lost cities, now under water. There is also a vast amount of knowledge, excitement, and pleasure to be gained from a "close-up" study of the many fascinating aspects of the underwater world.

It might be thought that the first step towards becoming an underwater expert was to become an expert swimmer, but it is not essential for an underwater swimmer to be a surface swimmer of anything like championship class. There are, of course, dangers, and the newcomer to Underwater Swimming should not go down too deep until he has had a good deal of practice and gained a certain amount of experience. Preferably, the first descents to any depth should not be undertaken alone, and if the swimmer has gone at all deep he should come up slowly, otherwise he risks getting the "bends," which is caisson disease, and means that reduced air pressure has caused nitrogen bubbles to form in the tissues. There may also be danger from large fish, and underwater swimmers should not venture into undersea caverns without a light. It is always advisable to collect as much local information as possible before diving in a strange area. Though all kinds of equipment, including cameras, harpoons, knives, and torches, can be carried, the beginner will make a better start if he dives without encumbrances. Most of the dangers can be avoided or circumvented with care, and the reward for those who master Underwater Swimming is a whole new world to explore.

Table Tennis.

Originally simply an amusing parlour game known as "Ping-Pong," Table Tennis is now a serious, world-wide, competitive sport, with many championships and tournaments, and the ability to attract crowds of 10,000 spectators.

Resembling a miniature game of Lawn Tennis (*q.v.*), the net is set on a table 9 feet long by 5 feet wide, and the ball is a very light celluloid one. Players serve series of five balls in turn, both server and receiver scoring. The service has to bounce first on the server's side of the net, and then on the other, and, thereafter, all strokes are "ground" strokes, volleying not being allowed. A game is 21 points, and matches are usually the best two out of three or three out of five games. "Vantage" games are played, as, if the score reaches 20-all, each player serves once in turn until one has a clear lead of two points. Both singles and doubles are played.

Table Tennis requires perfect fitness and split-second reactions. Many Lawn Tennis players also play Table Tennis, and several of these have found it desirable to retire from the fast table game before giving up the outdoor game.

Tennis. *See* Lawn Tennis, Real Tennis.

Tobogganing. *See* Winter Sports.

Traditional Games and Customs.

Traditional and unusual sporting events are plentiful in many parts of the world, but few have a longer tradition behind them than the Calcio in Livrea that can still be seen, over 500 years after its inception, in the Italian city of Florence. It is a version of Football, based on an ancient Greek game called Episkuros and the old Roman game of Harpastum. Played twenty-seven-aside on a pitch rather smaller than an Association football pitch, it was originally restricted to the nobility, and in 1672 a game was cancelled when it was discovered that the selected teams included players who were only "gentlemen." The ordinary people did play, but the game as played by them was called Calcio Divisi, and was not regarded as the same thing. The playing of Calcio in Livrea faded out in 1739, but was revived in 1898, to stop again in 1902, only to be revived once more in 1930. To-day, there are generally two games a year between teams no longer restricted to the nobility and representing the four quarters of Florence. They are wonderful spectacles, for the players, and also numerous officials and attendants, wear fourteenth-century costume, and the games are preceded by ceremonial processions, and by a special address to the most distinguished person present. The trophy for the games is traditionally a white calf.

Another ancient Italian sporting event that still survives is found in Siena, and consists of horse-racing in the city. It is a wild and fierce form of racing in which virtually anything that might further the cause of victory goes on between the riders. Riding events, many of them of great antiquity, figure prominently in countries in which great horsemanship is an age-old tradition. Russia offers Kop-Karri, a fifteen-aside mounted game that is a battle for possession of a sheep's pelt. Riders carry their reins in their teeth to leave their hands free for the fight, and anyone who gets the pelt is soon downed in what is one of the roughest and toughest games of all time. Played now by Kazakhs from the Steppes and Tadjiks from the Afghanistan border, this game originated in China, and was brought out of that country by the riders of the Golden Hordes of Genghis Khan. Also found in Russia is the mounted Kissing Game, in which a galloping male horseman seeks to snatch a kiss from a girl rider armed with a whip.

Horses are also prominent in North American Rodeos, which consist of competitions in cowboy skills, such as riding, roping, steer-wrestling, and chuck-wagon racing, which can still be seen annually in rodeos like the famous Stampede at Calgary in Alberta. Rather different are Chilean Rodeos, which consist mainly of displays involving horses and young bulls, and the Topeadura, in which two mounted teams push against a long log suspended horizontally between them. Chilean Rodeos carefully avoid anything that might harm the animals, which enter into things with excitement and enjoyment. This also applies to the bull races at Pamekasan in the Indonesian island of Madura. Based on the local method of ploughing, these consist of races in which a driver stands barefooted on a small wooden sled harnessed to a pair of bulls, though these need little driving. In India, elephant racing may be as much as a thousand years old, but it is now being allowed to decline because of reputed "feudal" associations. Recently, there was a not-very-serious attempt to introduce it into the United States, which is, however, more at home with events like Florida's Swamp Buggy Derby, in which vehicles carrying two hunters and their equipment must cover a figure-eight course of a mile within ten minutes.

Differing widely from these events in everything but speed is Pelota, or Jai Alai. Played in Spain, France, Portugal, North Africa, and South and Central America, pelota is a traditional Basque game that developed from a mediæval form of handball that was played against village church walls. To this day, many pelota courts, called "canchas," are next to churches, the wall, or "fronton," which is an integral part of the game being that of the church, and the priest very often being one of the best of the local players. The game, which is very fast and exhausting, can be between two players or between teams of two or three, and consists of playing a ball that is rather smaller than a tennis ball against a wall with either the hand or, in the case of the most popular form of the game, the Grand Chistera, with a long, narrow, wicker basket, called a "chistera," that is strapped to the player's hand and arm.

Personal combat sports have always been popular, and Switzerland has a national sport of this type that had its first big tournament in 1905 in Das Schwingen, which means "The Swinging." It is a form of wrestling, in which the contestants, normally very powerful Alpine herdsmen, wear special belts and shorts by which holds are taken. The traditional prize for the winner of the annual Swiss championship is a two-year-old heifer. Iceland has a rather similar form of wrestling, called Glima. Much less similar is the Siamese form of boxing. Competitors in this wear, and use, ordinary boxing gloves, but they are also allowed to use their elbows, knees, and feet, which are bare.

Next, a group of recreations in which the feet are used less lethally, starting with the Netherlands, and the Nijmegen Marches. Over half a century old, these are international long-distance walks that are not races, but reliability trials, in which complete teams must start and finish together within a certain time. The marches take four days, the distance to be covered each day varying between 25 and 30 miles according to the class. Classes catered for include men, women, and also police teams, walking in uniform, and military teams, carrying equipment. The walks, which attract over 10,000 competitors every July, are an unusual and colourful spectacle, and the opening ceremony is as well worth watching as that of the Olympic Games. British walkers, civilian, police, and military, regularly take part. Though called marches, they are really walks; and it is unlikely that many men would consider real precision marching as a recreation. However, women do in at least one country. This is New Zealand, where marching competitions are held between teams of twelve, with a leader, each team wearing a special uniform, and carrying out a three-minute routine to the music of a pipe band. Points are awarded, not only for the marching, but also for the costumes and the leading. Though the competitions are confined to women, teams are generally trained and drilled by men. This type of marching was seen in Britain a few years ago, when the Blair Atholl team toured the country giving demonstrations.

About fifty years old in its own country, Sweden, and quite likely to spread to other countries in the future is Orienteering, which consists of finding one's way about the country from one control point to another by using maps and compasses. Generally carried out on foot, and in wild country, it can also be done on horses, bicycles, motor-cycles, skis, and skates, and in cars and canoes, and in any kind of country, including urban areas. During the Second World War, in which Sweden, though not involved, had to be ready, Orienteering was extensively used in military and civil defence training; and it was then that night Orienteering began, with competitors wearing lamps strapped to their foreheads. Probably the most strenuous annual event in Orienteering is the Swedish three-day mountain race, in which contestants, working in teams of two, have to cover 60 miles of mountains, forests, and swamps on foot, carrying equipment that must include tents and food. Though mainly confined to Sweden, Orienteering has been successfully tried in Canada and the United States, where it acquired its English-language name.

Non-English recreations that English people do not have to travel very far to see are the many and various activities that go to make up Scotland's Highland Games. Highland Games meetings, or gatherings, are sports meetings, but sports meetings with their own definite and extremely colourful and spectacular characteristics. The chief sporting events at them are the "heavy-weight" events, including tossing the caber, throwing the hammer in the Scots style, putting and throwing weights of various sizes, and wrestling. In addition, there are competitions in Highland dancing and piping, and often for pipe bands, all playing their parts in a spectacle that can hold its own with any of the many spectacular events that love of tradition and love of sport have combined to produce all over the world. (*See also* **Old English Games and Customs.**)

Tug-of-War.

A Tug-of-War is one of the least complicated and one of the most strenuous events in sport. It consists of eight men pulling on a rope against another set of eight pulling in the opposite direction, each team trying to pull the other forward across a line, and each helped by a coach, who instructs them when to "heave" and when to concentrate on resisting the opponents' heaves. A pull may be over in a few seconds, or it may take many minutes. Contests are generally the best two out of three pulls, and a competition may involve three such contests in one afternoon. Competitions may be at "catchweights," which means that there is no weight limit, or they may restrict the eight men to a total weight of, say, 104 stone or 100 stone. The Tug-of-War requires, and will help to develop, great strength.

A popular event that always arouses great enthusiasm amongst the spectators, the Tug-of-War fully merits this position, but it owes some of its success to the fact that it was introduced into the right place at the right time. In the nineteenth century, before athletic sports were really organised, most country sports meetings included events like obstacle races, sack races, and egg-and-spoon races. These, however, though they are found to this day in some children's and local sports, grew less popular, and began to give place to more "serious" ones, favourite replacement for them being the Tug-of-War. Then athletic sports became organised, and the Amateur Athletic Association was founded, and instituted its famous annual championships, including two Tug-of-War championships that still exist, where, a few years earlier, there might have been obstacle-race and sack-race championships.

For years, service units and police forces provided the leading Tug-of-War teams, but, more recently, they have been challenged by teams from big firms. A still later development has been the formation of clubs concentrating entirely on the Tug-of-War. Organisations and clubs with Tug-of-War teams now have their own association, and their own annual championship meeting.

Underwater Swimming. *See* Swimming.

Underwater Watching.

In recent years there has been a considerable increase of interest in the undersea world; and some participation in this has been brought within the reach of those who are unwilling or unable to take part in underwater swimming and diving by the use of glass-bottomed boats, often boats in which the viewer slides back a wooden panel at his feet to reveal the glass viewing panel. Such boats, of course, can only be of use where the water is exceptionally clear and transparent, but, where conditions are suitable, a surprising amount of the life and colour of the world beneath the seas can be seen, and without any of the strain or danger of diving.

Much of the Mediterranean Sea fulfils the necessary conditions of clarity and transparency, particularly, perhaps, the coasts of Corsica, Sardinia, Sicily, and Italy itself. Greek and Egyptian waters are also clear, as are the waters of the Spanish Costa Brava and the Balearic Islands. Going farther afield, there are very transparent waters off parts of the Australian coast, and, of course, in the West Indies.

Volleyball.

Long-established in the United States, and played also in some other countries, Volleyball is a comparatively recent arrival in Britain, where it has been encouraged by leading personalities from the sport of Athletics, who saw in it an ideal game for maintaining fitness, and formed a governing body to organise and control it. A league started in London owed much of its early success to players of nationalities other than British, but the game took a big step forward when it was adopted by the London Fire Brigade as an effective method of physical training.

Volleyball might be compared with Basketball (*q.v.*) in that it is a team game that can be played indoors, though it can also be played on outdoor courts. The actual game, however, differs widely from Basketball. Played six-aside on a rectangular court that should not exceed 60 feet by 30 feet, it consists of "volleying" an inflated ball across a net 8 feet high with the hands, the object being to make it touch the ground in the opponents' court, while preventing it doing so in your own.

Water Polo. *See* **Swimming.**

Water Skiing. *See* **Swimming.**

Walking.

Walking comes so naturally that few people ever think about it. It is, however, worth thinking about, for it is the basis, not only of everyday life, but also of every physical, as opposed to purely mental, recreation, sport, and game, all of which involve, if not actual walking, then running, which is an equally natural step beyond walking. It is also the basis of training, either for health and fitness or for a strenuous sport. It has been said that it is impossible to walk too much; and, while those who have done little walking would, of course, have to increase the distance gradually, there is no doubt that a regular, daily two- or three-mile walk would in itself prove an effective method of maintaining health and fitness.

Walking is also a pleasant recreation in its own right, in the form either of long walks or of actual walking tours, on which the walker can regulate the pace, distance, and halts to suit himself. There are different styles of walking, and some are better than others. It is, for instance, better to point the toes straight ahead, or even to turn them in slightly, as the very fit and active Red Indians did, than to turn them out. Everyone, however, has his or her own natural way of walking, and it is probably better to continue walking naturally than to set out deliberately to alter the style.

Something about the opportunities open in race walking will be found under the heading Athletics, but it might be as well to say a few words about race-walking style, and to clear up a popular fallacy. This is that race walking is unnatural, and quite remote from ordinary walking. It is not; and the fallacy has arisen largely because the walking races seen by the largest audiences are the short ones that take place in arenas during athletic meetings. An attempt to walk a short distance as fast as possible does lead to an exaggerated action, and is unnatural to the extent that anyone who really wanted to cover a limited distance as quickly as possible in ordinary life would run. The longer the distance, however, the smaller the difference between race walking and ordinary walking, competitors in, for instance, a 100-mile race being virtually indistinguishable from ordinary "hikers."

If you walk along in the ordinary way, and then try to walk faster and faster, adding to your speed by pointing the toes straight ahead, swinging the arms vigorously, and swinging the hips so that each foot falls more or less straight in front of the other, you are race walking. The official definition of race walking is so uncomplicated that it is contained in a single sentence that simply requires that contact with the ground should always be maintained, as it normally is in all walking.

Weight-lifting.

Weight-lifting is a method of exercising to maintain health and develop strength; a system of training that can usefully be at least a part of the preparation for almost any sport or game; and a highly organised and very popular competitive sport in its own right. Once, quite erroneously, thought to be an over-strenuous and "dangerous" activity, it has now, in more enlightened days, seen the pendulum swing completely in the opposite direction, with professional and amateur sportsmen of all kinds freely admitting how much they owe to it, and a large following of seekers after health and fitness, including women, many of them actresses, models, and others whose work demands a near-perfect figure.

When it is used as exercise and training, the strenuousness of it depends entirely on the wishes of the lifter or his or her adviser; for training with weights does not mean lifting as heavy a weight as possible, but carrying out a certain number of repetitions in various styles with weights well within the lifter's capacity. For those keen to develop the maximum strength of which, according to their build, they are capable, weight-lifting is certainly the quickest, and perhaps the only, way of achieving this. One of the charges levelled against it is that it makes one slow, but this is just another fallacy. It does not; and competitive weight-lifters actually make some of the fastest movements known in sport.

As a competitive sport, Weight-lifting is divided into weight classes, and there are many international and national championships and competitions. The sport is popular almost all over the world, and has been firmly established in Britain for many years.

Strand-Pulling. Akin to Weight-lifting in that it is a method of keeping fit and developing strength that is also a competitive sport is Strand-pulling, using a steel or rubber expander. Various different "pulls" are possible, and the strength and resistance of the expander can be altered at will. Many people use this old-established system of exercising for health and strength; and, for those interested, there are many strand-pulling championships and competitions.

Whist.

Whist might be called the standard card game. It has never excited quite the furore of Bridge (*q.v.*), but it is long established and popular, both at home and at Whist Drives. It is probably the first card game, apart, perhaps, from a few simple games depending on luck, that most people learn, and it provides a sound foundation for the embryo card player.

It is played by four people, two partnerships of two opposing each other, and with a normal pack of cards. The partners sit opposite each other; and the pack is shuffled, cut for trumps, and dealt out singly. The cards are then played out in thirteen tricks of four each, the player on the dealer's left having first lead, and the winner of each trick leading in the next. Ace counts as the highest card—except in cutting, when it counts as the lowest—and it is followed by king, queen, knave, and then on from ten downwards. The higher card of any suit takes the lower, unless it is trumped by a player unable to follow suit, the tricks being gathered up by the winner as made.

It is necessary to concentrate, to watch the cards played, and to endeavour to "place" the unplayed cards. This comes with experience, as does an understanding of such unwritten rules as "Second in hand plays low" and "Third in hand plays high," and a knowledge of when to disregard these.

Three-handed Whist is possible, one suit being discarded.

Winter Sports.

There are few fields of recreational or sporting activity to which, given the opportunity, British people take more eagerly than Winter Sports. Enthusiasts from Britain were going abroad to find, and in some cases start, them before the turn of the century; and to-day there are probably a hundred travellers for every one who went sixty years ago. Most of this tremendous increase has been added since the Second World War, and the numbers grow every year. Switzerland is, of course, the traditional objective, but there is actually a wide choice, for facilities exist in Norway, Austria, Italy, France, Germany, and Czechoslovakia. There are opportunities to suit most purses, and to suit both those who want only sport and those who want sport combined with entertainment.

The most popular winter sport is Skiing; and, for those whose time and experience are both limited, it is normally skiing of the downhill variety, rather than the lengthy journeys on the level as well as on hills, and up as well as down, at which many Continental, and particularly Scandinavian, skiers are adept. Greatly increased facilities in the way of ski-lifts enable the holiday skier to work in three times as many descents as the skier of only a few years ago. Almost every resort has a ski-school with an English-speaking instructor, and it is always advisable for a novice to join this. It is also advisable for novices to start training for a ski holiday some time in advance, both by ordinary physical training and by attending a dry ski-school. The air in winter sports resorts encourages more activity than is good for a completely untrained person, and the fitter the skier, the less his chance of being injured. Skiing accidents are plentiful, but many of them could be avoided by the exercise of a few simple precautions. Having lessons is one; being fit is another; short skis with safety bindings are still another; and refusing to ski late, which may be any time after four o'clock, is yet another, for, as the light fades, it is replaced by a bluish light that makes uneven patches difficult to see, and the snow tends to ice over. Most winter sports equipment can be hired, but hired or bought, and regardless of the extent to which fashionable skiing clothing may be advertised, the most important items are the boots. The winter sports season lasts from December until March, but the snow is sometimes late, and, while Christmas and New Year should be safe enough, February offers the certainty of snow, combined with longer days.

Ski-jumping is a separate sport, and one for experts. The jumper takes-off down a steep slope and over a platform, which he leaves at a speed of about 50 m.p.h., to land something like 150 feet below his take-off, and more than that distance out in front of it. Ski-Joring is really ski-racing behind unridden horses, but the term is also applied to quite gentle ski-trips behind ridden horses, horse-drawn vehicles, and mechanical vehicles.

Bobsleigh Riding and Tobogganing consist of riding and racing down ice runs at terrific speeds on sleighs, the bobsleigh being for two, four, or five riders, and the toboggan, which takes its name, not from anywhere in Europe, but from a Red Indian language, being for one rider. Bobsleigh crews sit, the first man steering by a wheel or ropes, and the last man operating the brake with which the sleigh is fitted. Toboggan riders lie face downwards, and brake through special spikes on their boots. Both sports are exceptionally thrilling, and both can be dangerous.

At the opposite extreme from the point of view of speed is the 400-year-old Scottish game of Curling, which is played on ice, but not on skates. It resembles Bowls (*q.v.*), but the implements used are curling stones weighing about 35 lb., and having handles. Slow, but still-moving stones are encouraged by sweeping the ice in front of them with brooms.

Not a European winter sport, but nevertheless a snow sport in Canada is Snowshoe Running. Like skiing, this is a useful method of travelling about on snow that has been made the subject of races. The Canadian side of the Atlantic is also the home of Snow Snakes, a Red Indian game that consists of throwing a polished wooden stick along an ice trough in the snow. These "snakes" have been known to go for over a mile and to travel at 120 m.p.h. (*See also* **Skating.**)

Wingfield Sculls. *See* **Boat Races.**

Wrestling.

Wrestling, an individual combat in which competitors, using only their bare hands, endeavour to throw each other, is one of the most natural sports, and also one of the oldest. It is practised in many countries, and in many different styles, in most of which the wrestlers are divided into classes by weight.

In Britain, probably the most popular style is Catch-As-Catch-Can, in which the wrestlers start apart, and may try to throw their opponents by grasping them with the hands or by various kinds of trip. During the bout, the competitors may be either on their feet or down on the mat, and the rules contain various provisions to prevent the bout lasting for an indefinite time. Wrestlers reaching a deadlock on the mat may be ordered to stand up and start again, and points decisions after a certain time are also possible. Certain dangerous holds are barred.

Another style is Cumberland and Westmorland Wrestling, which is extremely popular in those counties, and in Scotland. In this, the wrestler clasps his hands together behind his opponent's back, and all throwing is done by the legs, the breaking of the opponent's clasp constituting the fall. The initial hold is, therefore, of major importance, and the taking of it often takes longer than the actual bout.

A further form of British wrestling is Cornish Wrestling, in which the wrestlers wear canvas jackets, by which all holds are taken. A similar form of wrestling is found in Brittany.

In Græco-Roman Wrestling, which has always been very popular on the Continent, though less so in Britain, wrestlers start apart, and may take hold only above the waist. Bouts in this style may take a considerable time. At one time, there were many Græco-Roman handicap matches, in which a top-class wrestler undertook to win a fall, or a number of falls, in a fixed time.

Græco-Roman was formerly the style used in professional wrestling, but, in recent years, professionals have used the "Free" or "All-In" style. This has rules, but it is not always very clear just what they are, and this, combined with widespread suspicions that bouts are not really genuine contests, has led to the quite large following that it retains going to see it more as an amusing "stunt" than as a serious sporting event. In the United States efforts to widen interest in it have taken the form of staging bouts in a ring that has been turned into a sea of mud, or that has been filled with fish. All this has, of course, done considerable harm to the reputation of what is really a fine sport and a healthy exercise.

Judo. Wrestling has been popular for centuries in Oriental countries such as India, China, and Japan. Of the various styles, one from Japan has won popularity in many countries, including Britain.

This is Judo, which derives from the more elaborate Ju-Jitsu. Governed largely by rituals, and with wrestlers graded according to ability, Judo is now an international competitive sport: but it is still often taken up as an effective method of defence against a stronger or better-armed attacker. Requiring a knowledge of anatomy, it consists partly of defence by knowing how to fall, and partly of attack by locks which give the opponent a choice between capitulation and a broken bone, and by paralysing nerve centres. The various locks are potentially dangerous, and, when practising, should be released immediately the opponent requests this. Also developed in Japan, though it originated in China, is Karate, a combat system so potentially dangerous that, when practised as a sport, attacking moves must only be indicated, and never pressed home.

Yachting. *See* **Sailing.**

ATHLETICS

1964 OLYMPIC GAMES WINNERS (HELD AT TOKYO).

100 metres, R. Hayes, U.S.A., 10 sec.
200 metres, H. Carr, U.S.A., 20·3 sec.
400 metres, M. Larrabee, U.S.A., 45·1 sec.
800 metres, P. Snell, New Zealand, 1 min. 45·1 sec.
1500 metres, P. Snell, New Zealand, 3 min. 38·1 sec.
5000 metres, R. Schul, U.S.A., 13 min. 48·8 sec.
10,000 metres, W. Mills, U.S.A., 28 min. 24·4 sec.
Marathon, B. Abebe, Ethiopia, 2 hr. 12 min. 11·2 sec.
4 × 100 metres Relay, U.S.A., 39 sec.
4 × 400 metres Relay, U.S.A., 3 min. 0·7 sec.
110 metres Hurdles, H. Jones, U.S.A., 13·6 sec.
400 metres Hurdles, R. Cawley, U.S.A., 49·6 sec.
3000 metres Steeplechase, G. Roelants, Belgium, 8 min. 30·8 sec.
20,000 metres Walk, K. Matthews, Great Britain and Northern Ireland, 1 hr. 29 min. 34 sec.
50,000 metres Walk, A. Pamich, Italy, 4 hr. 11 min. 12·4 sec.
High Jump, V. Brumel, U.S.S.R., 7 ft. 1¾ in.
Long Jump, L. Davies, Great Britain and Northern Ireland, 26 ft. 5½ in.
Triple Jump, J. Schmidt, Poland, 55 ft. 3¼ in.
Pole Vault, F. Hansen, U.S.A., 16 ft. 9 in.
Putting the Shot, D. Long, U.S.A., 66 ft 8½ in.
Throwing the Discus, A. Oerter, U.S.A., 200 ft. 1½ in.
Throwing the Javelin, P. Nevala, Finland, 271 ft. 2¼ in.
Throwing the Hammer, R. Klim, U.S.S.R., 228 ft. 10¾ in.
Decathlon, W. Holdorf, Germany, 7887 pts.
100 metres (Women), W. Tyus, U.S.A., 11·4 sec.
200 metres (Women), E. McGuire, U.S.A., 23 sec.
400 metres (Women), B. Cuthbert, Australia, 52 sec.
800 metres (Women), A. Packer, Great Britain and Northern Ireland, 2 min. 1·1 sec.
4 × 100 metres Relay (Women), Poland, 43·6 sec.
80 metres Hurdles (Women), K. Balzer, Germany, 10·5 sec.
High Jump (Women), I. Balas, Rumania, 6 ft. 2¾ in.
Long Jump (Women), M. Rand, Great Britain and Northern Ireland, 22 ft. 2 in.
Putting the Shot (Women), T. Press, U.S.S.R. 59 ft. 6 in.
Throwing the Discus (Women), T. Press, U.S.S.R., 187 ft. 10¾ in.
Throwing the Javelin (Women), M. Penes, Rumania, 198 ft. 7½ in.
Pentathlon (Women), I. Press, U.S.S.R., 5246 pts.

1962 EUROPEAN CHAMPIONSHIPS WINNERS (HELD AT BELGRADE).

100 metres, C. Piquemal, France, 10·4 sec.
200 metres, O. Jonsson, Sweden, 20·7 sec.
400 metres, R. Brightwell, Great Britain and Northern Ireland, 45·9 sec.
800 metres, M. Matuschewski, Germany, 1 min. 50·5 sec.
1500 metres, M. Jazy, France, 3 min. 40·9 sec.
5000 metres, B. Tulloh, Great Britain and Northern Ireland, 14 min. 0·6 sec.
10,000 metres, P. Bolotnikov, U.S.S.R., 28 min. 54·0 sec.
Marathon, B. Kilby, Great Britain and Northern Ireland, 2 hr. 23 min. 18·8 sec.
4 × 100 metres Relay, Germany, 39·5 sec.
4 × 400 metres Relay, Germany, 3 min. 5·8 sec.
110 metres Hurdles, A. Mikhailov, U.S.S.R., 13·8 sec.
400 metres Hurdles, S. Morale, Italy, 49·2 sec.
3000 metres Steeplechase, G. Roelants, Belgium, 8 min. 32·6 sec.
20,000 metres Walk, K. Matthews, Great Britain and Northern Ireland, 1 hr. 35 min. 54·8 sec.
50,000 metres Walk, A. Pamich, Italy, 4 hr. 18 min. 46·6 sec.
High Jump, V. Brumel, U.S.S.R., 7 ft. 3 in.
Long Jump, I. Ter-Ovanesyan, U.S.S.R., 26 ft. 10¼ in.
Triple Jump, J. Schmidt, Poland, 54 ft. 3½ in.
Pole Vault, P. Nikula, Finland, 15 ft. 8¾ in.
Putting the Shot, V. Varju, Hungary, 62 ft. 4¾ in.
Throwing the Discus, V. Trusenyov, U.S.S.R., 187 ft. 4 in.
Throwing the Javelin, J. Lusis, U.S.S.R., 269 ft. 1½ in.
Throwing the Hammer, G. Zsivotzky, Hungary, 228 ft. 5½ in.
Decathlon, V. Kuzyetsov, U.S.S.R., 8026 pts.
100 metres (Women), D. Hyman, Great Britain and Northern Ireland, 11·3 sec.
200 metres (Women), J. Heine, Germany, 23·5 sec.
400 metres (Women), M. Itkina, U.S.S.R., 53·4 sec.
800 metres (Women), G. Kraan, Netherlands, 2 min. 2·8 sec.
4 × 100 metres Relay (Women), Poland, 44·5 sec.
80 metres Hurdles (Women), T. Ciepla, Poland, 10·6 sec.
High Jump (Women), I. Balas, Rumania, 6 ft. 0 in.
Long Jump (Women), T. Shchelkanova, U.S.S.R., 20 ft. 10⅜ in.
Putting the Shot (Women), T. Press, U.S.S.R., 60 ft. 10¼ in.
Throwing the Discus (Women), T. Press, U.S.S.R., 186 ft. 8½ in.
Throwing the Javelin (Women), E. Ozolina, U.S.S.R., 180 ft. 2½ in.
Pentathlon (Women), G. Bystrova, U.S.S.R., 4833 pts.

1962 EMPIRE AND COMMONWEALTH GAMES WINNERS (HELD AT PERTH, W. AUSTRALIA).

100 yards, S. Antao, Kenya, 9·5 sec.
220 yards, S. Antao, Kenya, 21·1 sec.
440 yards, G. Kerr, Jamaica, 46·7 sec.
880 yards, P. Snell, New Zealand, 1 min. 47·6 sec.
1 mile, P. Snell, New Zealand, 4 min. 4·6 sec.
3 miles, M. Halberg, New Zealand, 13 min. 34·2 sec.
6 miles, B. Kidd, Canada, 28 min. 26·6 sec.
Marathon, B. Kilby, England, 2 hr. 21 min. 17 sec.
4 × 110 yards Relay, England, 40·6 sec.
4 × 440 yards Relay, Jamaica, 3 min. 10·2 sec.
120 yards Hurdles, G. Raziq, Pakistan, 14·3 sec.
440 yards Hurdles, K. Roche, Australia, 51·5 sec.
3000 metres Steeplechase, T. Vincent, Australia, 8 min. 43·4 sec.
High Jump, P. Hobson, Australia, 6 ft. 11 in.
Long Jump, M. Ahey, Ghana, 26 ft. 5 in.
Triple Jump, I. Tomlinson, Australia, 53 ft. 2 in.
Pole Vault, T. Bickle, Australia, 14 ft. 9 in.
Putting the Shot, M. Lucking, England, 59 ft. 4 in.
Throwing the Discus, W. Selvey, Australia, 185 ft. 3½ in.
Throwing the Javelin, A. Mitchell, Australia, 256 ft. 3 in.
Throwing the Hammer, A. Payne, England, 202 ft. 3 in.
100 yards (Women), D. Hyman, England, 11·2 sec.
220 yards (Women), D. Hyman, England, 23·8 sec.
880 yards (Women), D. Willis, Australia, 2 min. 3·7 sec.
4 × 110 yards Relay (Women), Australia, 46·6 sec.
80 metres Hurdles (Women), P. Kilborn, Australia, 10·9 sec.
High Jump (Women), R. Woodhouse, Australia, 5 ft. 10 in.
Long Jump (Women), P. Kilborn, Australia, 20 ft. 6¾ in.
Putting the Shot (Women), V. Young, New Zealand, 49 ft. 11½ in.
Throwing the Discus (Women), V. Young, New Zealand, 164 ft. 8½ in.
Throwing the Javelin (Women), S. Platt, England, 164 ft. 10½ in.

THE DERBY

	Horse.	Jockey.	Owner.
1947	Pearl Diver	G. Bridgland	Baron G. de Waldner.
1948	My Love	W. Johnstone	The Aga Khan. M. L. Volterra.
1949	Nimbus	E. Elliott	Mrs. M. Glenister.
1950	Galcador	W. Johnstone	M. Boussac.
1951	Arctic Prince	C. Spares	Mr. J. McGrath.
1952	Tulyar	C. Smirke	The Aga Khan.
1953	Pinza	G. Richards	Sir V. Sassoon.
1954	Never Say Die	L. Piggott	Mr. R. S. Clark.
1955	Phil Drake	F. Palmer	Mme. Volterra.
1956	Lavandin	W. Johnstone	M. Wertheimer.
1957	Crepello	L. Piggott	Sir V. Sassoon.
1958	Hard Ridden	C. Smirke	Sir V. Sassoon.
1959	Parthia	H. Carr	Sir H. de Trafford.
1960	St. Paddy	L. Piggott	Sir V. Sassoon.
1961	Psidium	R. Poincelet	Mrs. Arpad Plesch.
1962	Larkspur	N. Sellwood	Mr. R. Guest.
1963	Relko	Y. Saint-Martin	M. F. Dupré.
1964	Santa Claus	A. Breasley	Mr. J. Ismay.
1965	Sea Bird II	P. Glennon	M. J. Ternynck.

CRICKET

TEST MATCHES.

England *v.* Australia.
(first played 1876)
Won: England 65. Australia 79. Drawn: 54.

England *v.* South Africa.
(first played 1888)
Won: England 46. South Africa 18. Drawn: 28.

England *v.* West Indies.
(first played 1928)
(not including 1966 Series)
Won: England 16. West Indies 13. Drawn: 16.

England *v.* New Zealand.
(first played 1929)
Won: England 17. New Zealand 0. Drawn: 20.

England *v.* India.
(first played 1932)
Won: England 15. India 3. Drawn: 16.

England *v.* Pakistan.
(first played 1954)
Won: England 6. Pakistan 1. Drawn: 5.

COUNTY CHAMPIONSHIP.

1948 Glamorgan.
1949 Middlesex and Yorkshire.
1950 Surrey and Lancashire.
1951 Warwickshire.
1952 Surrey.
1953 Surrey.
1954 Surrey.
1955 Surrey.
1956 Surrey.
1957 Surrey.
1958 Surrey.
1959 Yorkshire.
1960 Yorkshire.
1961 Hampshire.
1962 Yorkshire.
1963 Yorkshire.
1964 Worcestershire
1965 Worcestershire.

ASSOCIATION FOOTBALL

WORLD CUP WINNERS.

1930 Uruguay.
1934 Italy.
1938 Italy.
1950 Uruguay.
1954 Western Germany.
1958 Brazil.
1962 Brazil.

EUROPEAN CHAMPION CLUBS CUP WINNERS.

1957 Real Madrid.
1958 Real Madrid.
1959 Real Madrid.
1960 Real Madrid.
1961 Benfica.
1962 Benfica.
1963 Milano.
1964 Inter-Milan.
1965 Inter-Milan.

EUROPEAN NATIONAL CUP HOLDERS CUP WINNERS

1963 Tottenham Hotspur.
1964 S.C., Lisbon.
1965 West Ham United.

F.A. CUP WINNERS.

1947 Charlton Athletic.
1948 Manchester United.
1949 Wolverhampton Wanderers.
1950 Arsenal.
1951 Newcastle United.
1952 Newcastle United.
1953 Blackpool.
1954 West Bromwich Albion.
1955 Newcastle United.
1956 Manchester City.
1957 Aston Villa.
1958 Bolton Wanderers.
1959 Nottingham Forest.
1960 Wolverhampton Wanderers.
1961 Tottenham Hotspur.
1962 Tottenham Hotspur.
1963 Manchester United.
1964 West Ham United.
1965 Liverpool.

SCOTTISH CUP WINNERS.

1948 Rangers.
1949 Rangers.
1950 Rangers.
1951 Celtic.
1952 Motherwell.
1953 Rangers.
1954 Celtic.
1955 Clyde.
1956 Heart of Midlothian.
1957 Falkirk.
1958 Clyde.
1959 St. Mirren.
1960 Rangers.
1961 Dunfermline Athletic.
1962 Rangers.
1963 Rangers.
1964 Rangers.
1965 Celtic.

OLYMPIC GAMES WINNERS.

1908 United Kingdom.
1912 United Kingdom.
1920 Belgium.
1924 Uruguay.
1928 Uruguay.
1932 No Competition.
1936 Italy.
1948 Sweden.
1952 Hungary.
1956 U.S.S.R.
1960 Yugoslavia.
1964 Hungary.

RUGBY LEAGUE FOOTBALL

WORLD CUP WINNERS.

1954 Great Britain.
1957 Australia.
1960 Great Britain.

R.L. CUP WINNERS.

1948 Wigan
1949 Bradford Northern.
1950 Warrington.
1951 Wigan.
1952 Workington Town.
1953 Huddersfield.
1954 Warrington.
1955 Barrow.
1956 St. Helens.
1957 Leeds.
1958 Wigan.
1959 Wigan.
1960 Wakefield Trinity.
1961 St. Helens.
1962 Wakefield Trinity.
1963 Wakefield Trinity.
1964 Widnes.
1965 Wigan.

ROWING AND SCULLING

THE UNIVERSITY BOAT RACE.

		min.	sec.	Lengths.			min.	sec.	Lengths.
1948	Cambridge	17	50	5	1958	Cambridge	18	15	3½
1949	Cambridge	18	57	¼	1959	Oxford	18	52	6
1950	Cambridge	20	15	3½	1960	Oxford	18	59	1¼
1951	Cambridge	20	50	12	1961	Cambridge	19	22	4¼
1952	Oxford	20	23	canvas	1962	Cambridge	19	46	5
1953	Cambridge	19	54	8	1963	Oxford	20	47	5
1954	Oxford	20	23	4½	1964	Cambridge	19	18	6½
1955	Cambridge	19	10	16	1965	Oxford	18	7	4
1956	Cambridge	18	36	1¼	1966	Oxford	19	12	3¾
1957	Cambridge	19	1	2					

DOGGETT'S COAT AND BADGE.

1954	K. Everest.	1957	K. Collins.	1960	R. Easterling.	1963	D. Allen.
1955	J. Goulding.	1958	R. Crouch.	1961	K. Usher.	1964	F. Walker
1956	C. Williams.	1959	G. Saunders.	1962	C. Dearsley.	1965	A. Collins

1964 OLYMPIC GAMES WINNERS (HELD AT TOKYO).

Single Sculls, V. Ivanov, U.S.S.R.
Double Sculls, U.S.S.R.
Coxwainless Pairs, Canada.
Coxed Pairs, U.S.A.
Coxwainless Fours, Denmark.
Coxed Fours, Germany.
Eights, U.S.A.

SWIMMING

1964 OLYMPIC GAMES WINNERS (HELD AT TOKYO).

100 metres free-style, D. Schollander, U.S.A., 53·4 sec.
400 metres free-style, D. Schollander, U.S.A., 4 min. 12·2 sec.
1500 metres free-style, R. Windle, Australia, 17 min. 1·7 sec.
200 metres back-stroke, J. Graef, U.S.A., 2 min. 10·3 sec.
200 metres breast-stroke, I. O'Brien, Australia, 2 min. 27·8 sec.
200 metres butterfly, K. Berry, Australia, 2 min. 6·6 sec.
400 metres medley, R. Roth, U.S.A., 4 min. 45·4 sec.
4 × 100 metres free-style Relay, U.S.A., 3 min. 33·2 sec.
4 × 100 metres medley Relay, U.S.A., 3 min. 58·4 sec.
4 × 200 metres free-style Relay, U.S.A., 7 min. 52·1 sec.
Highbd. Diving, R. Webster, U.S.A., 148·58 pts.
Springbd. Div., K. Sitzberger, U.S.A., 159·90 pts.
Water Polo, Hungary.
100 metres free-style (Women), D. Fraser, Australia, 59·5 sec.
400 metres free-style (Women), V. Duenkel, U.S.A., 4 min. 43·3 sec.
100 metres back-stroke (Women), C. Ferguson, U.S.A., 1 min. 7·7 sec.
200 metres breast-stroke (Women), G. Prozumenschikova, U.S.S.R., 2 min. 46·4 sec.
100 metres butterfly (Women), S. Stouder, U.S.A., 1 min. 4·7 sec.
400 metres medley (Women), D. De Varona, U.S.A., 5 min. 18·7 sec.
4 × 100 metres free-style Relay (Women), U.S.A., 4 min. 3·8 sec.
4 × 100 metres medley Relay (Women), U.S.A., 4 min. 33·9 sec.
Highbd. Div. (Women), J. Bush, U.S.A., 99·80 pts.
Springboard Diving (Women), I. Engel-Kramer. Germany, 145 pts.

CROSS-COUNTRY

THE INTERNATIONAL CHAMPIONSHIP.

1947	France.	1952	France.	1957	Belgium.	1962	England.
1948	Belgium.	1953	England.	1958	England.	1963	Belgium.
1949	France.	1954	England.	1959	England.	1964	England.
1950	France.	1955	England.	1960	England.	1965	England.
1951	England.	1956	France.	1961	Belgium.	1966	England.

HOCKEY

OLYMPIC GAMES WINNERS.

1920	Great Britain.	1936	India.	1956	India.
1928	India.	1948	India.	1960	Pakistan.
1932	India.	1952	India.	1964	India.

BASKETBALL

OLYMPIC GAMES WINNERS.

1936	U.S.A.	1952	U.S.A.	1960	U.S.A.
1948	U.S.A.	1956	U.S.A.	1964	U.S.A.

GOLF

CANADA CUP.

1954	Australia.	1958	Ireland.	1962	U.S.A.
1955	U.S.A.	1959	Australia.	1963	U.S.A.
1956	U.S.A.	1960	U.S.A.	1964	U.S.A.
1957	Japan.	1961	U.S.A.	1965	South Africa.

LAWN TENNIS

DAVIS CUP.

1948	U.S.A.	1954	U.S.A.	1960	Australia.
1949	U.S.A.	1955	Australia.	1961	Australia.
1950	Australia.	1956	Australia.	1962	Australia.
1951	Australia.	1957	Australia.	1963	U.S.A.
1952	Australia.	1958	U.S.A.	1964	Australia.
1953	Australia.	1959	Australia.	1965	Australia.

BASEBALL

WORLD SERIES WINNERS.

1957	Milwaukee Braves.	1960	Pittsburgh Pirates.	1963	Los Angeles Dodgers.
1958	New York Yankees.	1961	New York Yankees.	1964	St. Louis Cardinals.
1959	Los Angeles Dodgers.	1962	New York Yankees.	1965	Los Angeles Dodgers.

DOMESTIC PETS

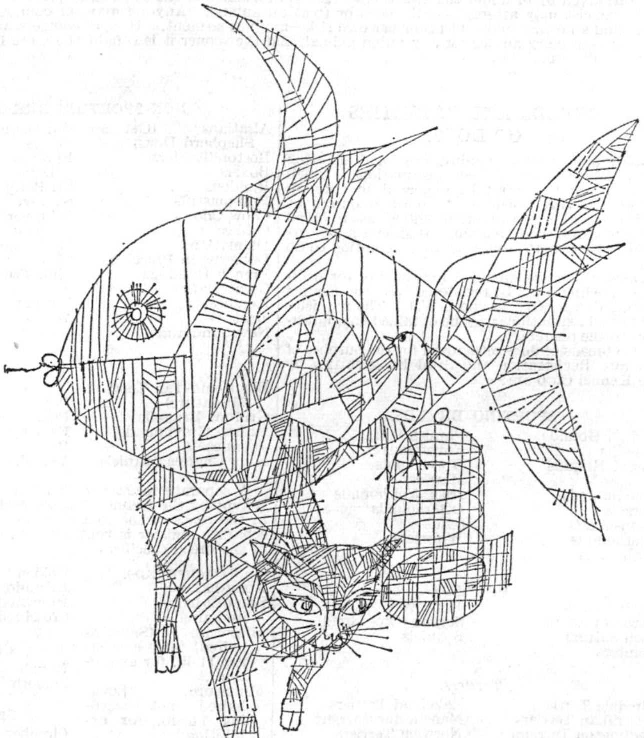

DOMESTIC PETS

By ALASTAIR N. WORDEN, M.A., (Cantab)., F.R.I.C., formerly Milford Research Professor in the University of Wales.

This section attempts to deal not with all the many hundreds of animals that may be kept as pets, but only with those that are best suited to average homes in Great Britain. The maintenance of monkeys, squirrels, bats, mongooses, and snakes, while quite feasible to those with experience and facilities, requires considerable time and—in some instances—expense. Those who contemplate such exotic pets should consult works of reference, study the methods adopted in zoological gardens, and discuss the matter with experts. Even in the case of the more common animals, the information provided in the following pages is to be regarded only as a beginning, to be supplemented so far as possible by practical experience, discussions with more knowledgeable owners, and the study of more detailed writings.

Certain considerations are basic. Never keep a pet unless you are really interested in it and are prepared to give it due—and regular—care and attention. Don't keep a pet you cannot afford to maintain in health and comfort. Scrupulous attention to cleanliness is essential, and wise feeding is one of the most important factors in avoiding illness and loss of condition.

Since the passing of the Veterinary Surgeons Act of 1948 it is illegal for anyone to practise the diagnosis and treatment of animal diseases unless he or she is: (1) a veterinary surgeon; or (2) a person whose name has been placed on the Supplementary Veterinary Register. (Certain employees of Animal Welfare Societies are specially licensed, but it is intended that in future all animal treatment shall be given by or under the direct supervision of members of the veterinary profession.) Not even a pharmacist may attempt to diagnose or treat an animal. Anyone may, of course, render "first aid," and an owner may—at his or her own risk—apply treatment. It is, of course, a wise precaution to seek veterinary advice for any ailing animal, and the sooner it is sought the more likely it is that good results will follow.

BREEDS AND VARIETIES OF DOGS.

Of recent years, dog-breeding and showing have become specialised occupations, which average people cannot be expected to take up without having adequate time or resources at their disposal. Any amateur who wishes to breed for profit from pedigree animals should most certainly seek expert advice before attempting to do so.

Dogs which are intended for show or for pedigree breeding must be registered with the Kennel Club, 1 Clarges St., London, W.1. The requisite forms and regulations may be obtained on application to the Secretary.

The breeds of dogs recognised for the purpose of separate Registration and Stud Book entries by the Kennel Club are:—

SPORTING BREEDS.

Afghan Hounds	Finnish Spitz
Besenjis	Foxhounds
Basset Hounds	Greyhounds
Beagles	Harriers
Bloodhounds	Irish Wolfhounds
Borzois	Otterhounds
Dachshunds	Salukis
Deerhounds	Whippets
Elkhounds	

Gun-dogs.

English Setters	Retrievers
Gordon Setters	Setters (Cross-bred)
Irish Setters	Spaniels
Pointers	

Terriers.

Airedale Terriers	Lakeland Terriers
Australian Terriers	Manchester Terriers
Bedlington Terriers	Norwich Terriers
Border Terriers	Scottish Terriers
Bull Terriers	Sealyham Terriers
Cairn Terriers	Skye Terriers
Dandie Dinmont Terriers	Staffordshire Bull Terriers
Fox Terriers	Welsh Terriers
Irish Terriers	West Highland White Terriers
Kerry Blue Terriers	

NON-SPORTING BREEDS.

Alsatians (German Shepherd Dogs)	Old English Sheepdogs
Boston Terriers	Poodles
Boxers	Pyrenean Mountain Dogs
Bulldogs	St. Bernards
Bull-mastiffs	Samoyeds
Chow Chows	Schipperkes
Collies	Schnauzers
Dalmatians	Miniature Schnauzers
Dobermann Pinschers	Shetland Sheepdogs
French Bulldogs	Shih Tzus
Great Danes	Tibetan Terriers
Keeshonds	Welsh Corgis (Cardigan)
Mastiffs	Welsh Corgis (Pembroke)
Newfoundlands	

Toys.

Black-and-Tan Terriers (Miniature)	Maltese
Griffons Bruxellois	Papillons
Italian Greyhounds	Pekingese
Japanese	Pomeranians
King Charles Spaniels	Pugs
	Yorkshire Terriers

A separate register, called the Breed Register, is kept by the Kennel Club for each breed, except in the cases of the following breeds, for which a separate register is kept for each of the varieties of the breed specified.

DACHSHUNDS.
Long-haired
Smooth-haired
Wire-haired
Miniature (Smooth-haired) not exceeding 11 lb. for exhibition).
Miniature (Long-haired) (not exceeding 11 lb. for exhibition.)

IRISH SETTERS.
Red
Whiteand Red (A.O.V.)

RETRIEVERS.
Curly-coated
Flat-coated
Golden
Labrador
Interbred
Crossbred

COLLIES.
Rough
Smooth

SPANIELS.
Clumber
Cocker
Field
Irish Water
Springer, English
Springer, Welsh
Sussex
Interbred
Crossbred

BULL TERRIERS.
Bull Terriers
Bull Terriers (Miniature).

FOX TERRIERS.
Smooth
Wire

POODLES.
Not under 15 in.
Miniature, under 15 in.

TOY SPANIELS.
Cavalier King Charles Spaniels.
King Charles Spaniels

The Committee of the Kennel Club has decided to classify those breeds which at present have no separate register, but are included under the heading "Any Other Variety." The classification is as follows:—

HOUNDS.
Dachsbracke
Dachshund Miniature (Wire-haired)
Rhodesian Ridgeback Lion Dog

GUN-DOGS.
Chesapeake Bay Retriever
Kleine Munsterlander
Pointer German Short-haired
Pointer German Long-haired
Pointer German Wire-haired
Pointer Griffon Wire-haired
Setter German Long-haired
Weimaraner

TERRIERS.
Soft-coated Wheaten Terrier
Sydney Silkie

NON-SPORTING.
Bearded Collies
Bouvier de Flandres
Groenendael
Husky
Leonberger
Lhasa Apso
Maremma Italian Sheep-dog
Norwegian Buhund
Polish Sheepdog
Reisenschnauzer
Tibetan Mastiff
Tibetan Spaniel
Volpino
Wolf Spitz

TOYS.
Chihuahua
Penscher Miniature

In the limited space available it is impossible to describe the special characteristics of the different breeds. The breeds recognised in Great Britain are subject to constant review by the Kennel Club, and it is probable that the number will continue to be added to from time to time.

The dog was probably the first animal to be domesticated in the true sense of the word, and the uses to which he has been put by man are almost legion. Throughout the world dogs are employed to help protect herds and flocks, and indeed the dog trained for shepherding plays an integral part in sheep management. The names Foxhound, Deerhound, and Otterhound all indicate the specific uses to which dogs have been put in the Chase. Greyhounds and Whippets are used in coursing, and work singly or in pairs, rather than in packs. As their names indicate, the various Setters and Pointers are employed to indicate the exact whereabouts of game, and Spaniels also are widely used as gun-dogs. The other uses to which dogs have been put in field sports include hunting over rough and difficult country by small terriers, and going to earth to kill or hold badgers, foxes, and otters. Fox Terriers, Dachshunds, Dandie Dinmonts, and Scottish Terriers are among the types which have been so employed. Dogs have played their part also in entertainment: thus there are performing dogs, notably the Poodle, and racing Whippets and Greyhounds, while in former times various types of fighting, including the baiting of bulls by Bulldogs, were to be seen. The use of sledge-dogs is well known, while in Belgium and elsewhere dogs were at one time widely used as traction animals. In coaching days, the Dalmatian was a carriage dog, and modern scientists have recently suggested, as a result of experiments, that the position under or behind a coach which a Dalmatian automatically takes is determined by heredity! Perhaps the most exacting use to which man has ever put dog was in China, where the Chow-Chow was once maintained as a source of meat and fur! In Portugal, fishermen employ a race of dog to accompany their fleets. The dogs in question (Portuguese Water Dogs) will dive into the sea to retrieve a broken net or an escaped fish, and will even swim from one smack to another to convey messages! In New Guinea native dogs act as scavengers, while in various countries on the Continent of Europe "truffle dogs" are employed to locate the fungi known as truffles, relished as a table delicacy.

The above paragraph is far from exhaustive, and for those who wish to know more of the characteristics of the different varieties of dogs, reference should be made to such volumes as *Book of the Dog* by Brian Vesey-Fitzgerald (Nicholson and Watson, London; 2 guineas) or *Working Dogs of the World* by C. L. B. Hubbard (Sidgwick and Jackson Ltd., London; 16s.) For general guidance on dog management, see *The Right Way to Keep Dogs* by R. C. G. Hancock (Elliott, Kingswood, Surrey; 5s.)

For present purposes it is, however, as a pet or companion that we are considering the dog, and it must be agreed that many of the most successful animals for this purpose are cross-breeds or "mongrels." There are many fallacies or unsubstantiated generalisations regarding the relative merits of pure-breds and mongrels. This is in fact an intricate scientific problem, and probably the simplest way of summarising the true position would be to say that, from the point of view of health and temperament, there are good, bad, and indifferent specimens among pure-bred and cross-bred animals. It is true that within a breed (or within a local community of mongrels for that matter) certain weaknesses or undesirable traits may arise from hereditary defects.

It may be noted that the word "dog" is applied to the whole species, although it is used also to denote the male as opposed to the female, for which the correct term is "bitch." Young animals are referred to as "dog puppies" or "bitch puppies" respectively. A male animal employed regularly for breeding is known as a "stud dog," and the corresponding female as a "brood bitch." In hunting circles the Foxhound is referred to as a "hound," and the term dog and bitch are employed only as prefixes to denote the sex.

CHOICE OF DOG.

However attractive the idea of keeping a dog may be, it is unwise and unkind to purchase or to accept one without very careful consideration. Dogs require regular feeding, grooming, and exercise and, if they are to be allowed to show their full capabilities, constant companionship and attention. Nothing is more pathetic than the unwanted dog, which may have been purchased because of a passing whim, and with which no one appears to have the courage to part. If, on the other hand, one is prepared to give all the necessary time and trouble to the proper care of the dog, the reward will be ample.

The size of the choice is important. Many people keep dogs which are far too large for their houses and for their purses. The smaller the dog, the less food, exercise, and house-room will he need, and the many varieties of terrier provide a range from which suitable choices for most households may be made. In any event, a very large dog should not be chosen unless expert advice has been taken about his feeding and other requirements.

Household dogs of six months of age or over must be licensed. Licences may be obtained from any post office (7s. 6d. at present).

MANAGEMENT OF THE DOG.

Accommodation.—Up till comparatively recently most dogs were kennelled down out of doors. This practice has its advantages, but today the majority of pet dogs are allowed more or less the run of the house. A warm sleeping-place, such as a box or basket, should be provided, and should contain removable bedding. Newspaper is an excellent non-conductor of heat. It is a very useful material to place at the bottom of a dog's box; and on two or three thicknesses may be placed a rug or blanket on which the animal may lie. It is astonishing the amount of grit and dust a dog can bring into a house on his limbs and the lower part of his body. His bedding will require frequent shaking out and renewal, and paper is easily changed. The box or basket in which the dog lies should be allowed a place free from draughts, and requires airing daily when the dog leaves its bed in the morning. Wood-wool makes excellent bedding in outhouses or where a special structure is provided by way of dog-kennel, but is inclined to be messy about the house, as a dog will draw portions of it about the room as he leaves his bed. If straw is used, it is best stuffed into a sack and made into a kind of mattress. An odd piece of linoleum forms an excellent foundation to the dog's sleeping-box or kennel; it does not strike cold to the skin, is a slow conductor of heat, and has the advantage of being easily kept clean, particularly during illness, when there may be discharges and messes to be frequently cleaned up, until the animal can once more go out of doors.

Exercise.—Every dog should be exercised regularly, but there is no need to over-exercise, and the practice of allowing a dog (other than a large and athletic animal) to run behind a bicycle for mile after mile cannot be too strongly deprecated. Two or three fairly short walks a day are sufficient for a small terrier, always provided that there is a garden in which he can play on fine days and some open space where he can run freely for a short time. While still in the puppyhood stages, a dog should be trained to walk to heel and to beware of traffic. Even so, it is usually safer to put him on a lead in busy thoroughfares. One point which, to the annoyance of the public, many dog-owners fail to realise, is that their animals would show much less tendency to fight if allowed to investigate one another off the lead. A dog naturally feels aggressive if put on the lead immediately a rival hails in sight. There are, of course, certain dogs which attack others at sight; these are a public nuisance, and should never be allowed loose on the streets.

The practice of allowing a dog to take his own exercise is to be deprecated, especially in towns and suburbs. The animal will be tempted to sniff into dustbins, and, if a male, will tend to follow a bitch in season or to take part in the unsavoury "dog parties" which are so often to be seen. Furthermore, such an animal is usually responsible for the disgusting habit of fouling the pavements and gateways. In this connection, it should be emphasised that dogs may quite easily be trained to defæcate in the gutter, or on the grass verge, and so avoid contamination of the pavement or carriage-way. In some districts owners are liable to a fine if their dogs foul the pavement.

Training.—Patience combined with the gift of putting yourself in the dog's place is the chief requisite for successful education. It is most important to encourage regularity of habit, as an animal will obviously learn very much more quickly if his daily walks, meals, and grooming take place at fairly constant times. A quiet firmness is the ideal method, and a puppy should learn early that a command *is* a command, and must be obeyed. There is no need to shout and make an exhibition of oneself, or to race in circles after a disobedient puppy; if these things are done, the animal will never become so well trained as it otherwise would. Again, it is rather ridiculous to chastise a puppy *after* he has somewhat belatedly decided to come to heel: quite obviously, he will then be liable to think that he has done wrong in actually coming to heel. Whatever happens, it must never be that the dog becomes master; there is no more unbecoming sight than that of a person with a frankly disobedient dog, and if the animal be large and powerful it may prove a menace to its owner and to the public.

Puppies should be house-trained at an early stage. If care and thought are given to the matter, the animal will soon learn not to make messes in the house. However, it is very stupid to forget all about a puppy or dog for many hours, and then, out of sheer vexation, chastise it for having made a mess. If puppies are let out every two hours or so at first, they will soon learn not to make a mess. Encourage them for performing in the right place rather than scold them for doing so in the wrong one. Physical punishment should be administered only where strictly necessary, and then in a sensible fashion. The most effective method is to grasp the dog or puppy by the skin of its neck and to shake it.

Grooming and Washing.—Whilst short-haired breeds need little or no attention to the coat, bar an occasional brisk rub down with a brush or rough towel (which incidentally puts a pleasant gloss on the smooth-haired breeds), yet with the long-haired breeds grooming should be carried out regularly, and if the habit is made a daily one it will not be forgotten so readily. Nearly all dogs love this procedure, and most dogs will actually ask for their daily groom by jumping on the table or bench on which it is carried out. Steel combs and brushes are sold by many shops, principally corn chandlers, though some store chemists also provide a suitable range of grooming kit for all breeds. There is a curious fetish current among many breeders that dogs should not be washed. There is no reason why, with a few simple precautions, a dog should not be washed whenever it is socially necessary. The first precaution is to use a soap that does not contain an excess of soda. The strong washing-up soaps, excellent as they are for certain purposes, are too irritant for a dog's skin. While some of the toilet soaps suitable for human use may be employed for dogs, the special dog soaps and shampoos are much better for the purpose. They are more suited to the dog's skin and coat, and have better detergent properties. It is important not to have water that is too hot—as with a baby's bath, it should be possible to dip the point of one's elbow into the water and find that it gives a pleasantly warm sensation but is easily bearable, *i.e.*, it should not be above 95–100° F. On emerging from a bath a dog will shake himself thoroughly, and then, if not curbed, will roll on the floor or ground and speedily cover himself with dust or dirt! It is therefore necessary to give him a brisk rub down with old (but clean) towelling, whereupon he may be allowed to dry off in a warm place free from draughts or, in good weather, put on a lead and taken for a brisk walk. In the case of many of the long-coated breeds it is customary to have them trimmed at the beginning of summer, and this is a sensible precaution that may avoid a good deal of distress during hot weather. The smaller long-haired dogs in particular, such as Scottish Terriers, suffer unduly from the heat if their coats are grown too long.

FEEDING OF THE DOG.

Meat, usually beef, is generally regarded as the staple article of the dog's diet. It must be pointed out, however, that although the dog is naturally a carnivore (flesh-eater), ordinary meat (muscle or "flesh") is not a completely adequate diet, and lacks certain factors which the wild dog would find in the blood, bones, liver, and other organs of his prey. Furthermore, it has been proved scientifically that dogs can thrive on a meatless diet. In spite of these reservations, however, meat must be regarded as an excellent article of food, and if properly supplemented will prove very satisfactory. In recommendations which have recently been made in America (Dr. S. R. Speelman, of the U.S. Department of Agriculture) it is suggested that meat (beef, lamb, mutton, or horseflesh, providing that the last is fed regularly and not spasmodically) or meat substitutes (fish, milk, eggs, etc.) should constitute one-half of the daily ration, and that the remainder should comprise approximately equal parts of cereal substances (bread, biscuits) and of vegetables (carrots, spinach, onion, beet, etc.). It is pointed out that many dogs do not accept the vegetable material readily. On this basis, the approximate quantities of food required by adult dogs have been calculated as follows:—

Weight of dog.	*Total food per day.*
1 lb.	2 oz.
10 lb.	12 oz.
25 lb.	1½ lb.
50 lb.	2 lb.
75 lb.	3½ lb.
100 lb.	4¼ lb.
150 lb.	5¼ lb.
225 lb.	7 lb.

(Weights of up to 10 lb. would include the toy breeds, 25 lb. would correspond to a Fox Terrier; Airedale Terriers and Retrievers would fall into the 50–75-lb. class, and the larger weights would be those of the very big breeds, such as the St. Bernard.) The quantities given are, of course, an *approximation* and no more. Dogs which lead a very active life will require more, while those which take little exercise, or which tend to put on fat easily, will require less. Common sense is necessary, and great care must be taken not to over-feed or to under-nourish.

Meat is probably best fed raw, or lightly cooked, but many animals appear to have a preference (probably through habit) for well-cooked meat. In any event, the meat should not be "over-done," as there is substantial evidence that prolonged heating destroys much of the food value of the meat protein. *Fish* is an excellent substitute. There need be no anxiety about the greed with which a dog swallows lumps of meat and also neglects to masticate them. The teeth of the dog are for tearing meat, he is not concerned with biting his food up small; indeed, his salivary glands contain no digestive ferments, as is the case with some other animals.

Milk is almost essential during pregnancy and lactation (see below), and may well be included in normal dietaries. Whether or not *bones* should be fed is a matter which has been hotly debated, but for mature household dogs the evidence suggests that they are unnecessary. (The teeth of racing greyhounds, which receive a "sloppy" diet, are quite as good as those of the average household dog.) Bone-feeding is responsible for much trouble, including constipation, actual impaction of the rectum, and lodgement of pieces of bone in the mouth or throat. The value of bones is, of course, that they contain large quantities of essential mineral substances, and for this reason the inclusion in the diet of bone-meal, or of steamed *bone-flour*, or, preferably, a mineral supplement, is recommended. Only very small quantities of these substances are required.

Bread is an article of food which is often overlooked in the case of the dog, but there is no doubt that wholemeal bread is very suitable indeed, provided it is not fed to excess.

The answer to the question whether a dog requires vegetables is, in the main, no. From the Vitamin C standpoint they are quite unnecessary, since it has been shown that a dog manufactures this vitamin for itself, but the fact remains that many dogs, particularly of the toy variety, enjoy a few slices of banana or apple, and there is no harm in letting them pander to their taste. Vegetables do help, however, to provide roughage, and cooked (*not* raw) *potatoes* may be used in place of bread or biscuits. The dog—like many other animals—cannot digest raw starch properly. *Flaked maize* and *oatmeal* are other substitutes, but it must be remembered that the energy value of maize is high and that the dogs must never be overfed. *Dog biscuits* are an item that were long is disfavour with some professional people on account of their often having been made from agenised white flour (see section on Canine Hysteria), but now that this factor has been overcome, and the biscuits themselves are being improved in other ways, their use for the non-meat portion of the diet may be recommended.

Clean fresh *water* must be provided at all times.

In addition to the diets recommended above, there are on the market several tinned dog foods which claim to be complete, or almost complete, diets for the dog. It must be said that many dogs (including those of the writer) have remained in excellent health when receiving one of these foods as a large part of the diet over long periods. There is, therefore, little that may be said against the widespread use of the better varieties of such products. Again, it is a matter for common sense; if an owner finds that his animal is thriving on such a diet, he is wise to continue to use it.

It is customary to give dogs two meals a day. There is no need to give more than two to healthy adults, for the dog's stomach is exceedingly capacious and adapted to long gaps between meals. Many dogs thrive on only one meal in twenty-four hours. Whatever plan is decided on, regularity should be adhered to, and a meal or meals given at the same times every day. Dogs require vitamins A and D and B complex. There are several ways of administering these, but the special commercial preparations, including the modern form of condition-powder tablet, are the most convenient.

The *pregnant* and *lactating bitch* require special consideration. The food requirements are very much increased in a bitch which is carrying puppies, especially towards the end of the period. Normally, appetite is not a complete guide to a dog's food requirements, but in pregnancy and lactation the bitch must not be allowed to go hungry. It is quite normal for a heavily pregnant bitch to require over one and a half times her normal amount of food, and in lactation her requirements will increase still further. Milk is a most excellent article of diet at this time; indeed, there is no better way (apart from commercial preparations) of replacing the milk which the bitch is giving to her own puppies.

Up to the age of three weeks or so, *puppies* need have mother's milk only, but at any time after this it is a sound policy to give them additional food, and so spare the mother and also render weaning (at from six to eight weeks) a *gradual* process. At first a little cow's milk or one of the commercial "dog-milk" preparations may be given, and gradually the puppies should be encouraged to eat solid food. Eggs (if they can be spared), wholemeal bread in milk, or even finely minced meat may be given, at first in very small amounts but later in larger quantities. If this process is carefully carried out, there will be far less trouble at and after weaning time. After weaning, puppies should receive five or six meals a day, and this number may be cut down gradually until two or three only are given to the fully grown dog. (The smaller breeds are fully grown at about a year.) *More* meat or meat substitutes and milk, and *less* cereal or vegetable matter, should be fed to the growing dog as compared with the adult. This fact is important, as the substances present in meat and milk are required for laying down the growing tissues. Nevertheless, the energy portion of the ration is important, and the cereal or vegetable should be nutritious and not fibrous. It is possible to rear puppies by hand from birth if the bitch for any reason should die. It requires great patience for the first two or three weeks, as naturally the puppies will require feeding once or twice during the night. Special milks for puppies are to be recommended. Cow's milk requires enriching with fat and sugar to approximate to the composition of bitch's milk. Feeding will have to be done at every two or three hours, and a very useful gadget is a fountain-pen filler attached to cycle-valve tubing. Very small quantities are required for the first two or three days, and a level teaspoonful of milk is more than sufficient for the average terrier at first. Even with the best care in the world hand-fed puppies tend to be weaklings and do not grow as fast as those naturally fed. A foster bitch, if obtainable, is much to be preferred.

BREEDING OF DOGS.

It is natural for adult dogs of both sexes to wish to breed, and in the case of the female especially it is an excellent thing if one can arrange for a suitable mating to take place. Bitches come "into season" or "on heat" (lay terms for œstrus) at approximately six-monthly intervals, but it is not advisable to breed from the first season which occurs usually at about eight to nine months of age, but over a wide range of age according to breed and other factors. The periods of season often occur between January and March and in early Autumn, but there is no fixed rule. Each season lasts for three weeks. For the first seven days, approximately (pro-œstrus), a bitch does not permit mating, though during this time she is a source of strong attraction to all males in the neighbourhood. At about the seventh to the tenth day the blood-stained discharge, which ushers in the heat, stops; this is usually taken by the breeder as an indication that the bitch will stand to service. If possible, it is always better when puppies are wanted to allow mating to occur more than once. Under natural conditions a dog and bitch are usually strictly monogamous and mate for life, and during the period of œstrus will mate many times. A dog and bitch that are kept together all the time will probably behave naturally, but under domestication both dogs and bitches usually become promiscuous. Many bitches will in fact accept service from different males on different days, and the phenomenon of superfecundation, *i.e.*, the production of a litter that is fathered by *two* males, may occur. It is therefore wise to retain strict control of the bitch throughout the whole of the three weeks or so she is in season. At the end of season the bitch passes into a state of " metœstrus " if she has not conceived.

If a bitch conceives, she carries her puppies for a period of about nine weeks. There is, however, a normal variation of fifty-eight to seventy days, and puppies born before the fifty-eighth day sometimes live. The number of puppies born varies with breed; in the smaller terriers it is usually from four to six, but in Airedales and Alsatians the number may be eight to ten, and the larger breeds tend to have even more offspring at a time. Birth usually takes place fairly easily in the larger breeds, but there is often much difficulty in the case of the short-legged breeds, such as Scottish and Sealyham Terriers, Pekingese and Dachshunds. In some breeds, in fact, the problem is one that is giving serious concern to veterinary surgeons and breeders.

A short while before her puppies are due, a bitch will " make her bed." Owners are often amazed at the destruction of soft furnishings, or even of wall-paper, that a previously well-behaved bitch may carry out at this time; it is therefore by far the best to provide a suitable box (if the animal has not one already). A smooth flooring such as a strip of linoleum serves for the bitch to give birth to her puppies. Her instinct to tear up everything given to her for bedding may lead to suffocation of the puppies by pieces of bedding. Provided labour occurs in a warm room, it is sometimes better—according to the temperament of the bitch—to remove each puppy as it is born, placing a warm bottle underneath, and bring it back to the mother when the last birth has occurred. At this time the bitch should be watched carefully for any discharge from the vulva or for any evidence of straining. If either of these occurs without results, it is advisable to send for help as early as possible, especially in the case of the smaller breeds. Many hundreds of bitches are lost through neglect at this time, and usually because it was not suspected that anything was wrong. If the discharge becomes bloody, or green, help should be obtained *at once* if no puppy is delivered. Similarly, any great delay between births is a matter for concern. The afterbirth usually follows the puppy within a few minutes, but puppies are sometimes delivered in their fœtal membranes, and in this case the latter should be gently but quickly removed. It is quite normal for the umbilical cord to remain attached to the puppy, but the bitch will normally break it by biting through it.

The mother will wash and attend to the new born puppies, and after the last is born it is a good idea to burn all the mess and to provide clean newspaper, but do not worry or frighten the bitch more than is necessary. For the care and feeding of the bitch and her puppies see the sections on Management and Feeding. Puppies, like kittens, are born with their eyes closed, but open them after about nine days—there again being considerable variation.

The phenomenon of pseudopregnancy is common in bitches, and indeed to a minor degree it is probably present in most bitches following an œstrus without conception. In some bitches, however, presumably those with strong maternal drives, the changes in the ovary may be accompanied by external signs of " phantom " or " ghost " pregnancy. These may include not only enlargement but actual functioning of the mammary glands, and the making of a " nest " by the bitch just as if her puppies were really due. The average duration of pseudopregnancy is usually given as about two months, and although variable, it is often sufficiently near to the correct time after œstrus that everyone suspects the bitch to be truly pregnant. The condition may be suppressed with the aid of modern drugs, but in some instances it is not realised that the condition is not real. In many cases only professional advice can solve the mystery, and radiographical examinations have often proved necessary to ascertain the truth, particularly in fat bitches of the heavier breeds. It might be well to note, at this point, that there is another condition of the older bitch that is known as *Pyometra*. This condition usually reveals itself at the same time as the ghost pregnancy (and is sometimes a pathological extension of it) but is accompanied by considerable disturbance of health, coupled in many instances with purulent discharge from the vagina. A bitch which is off-colour in the weeks following pregnancy, or which develops a discharge from the vulva (especially one which is dark in colour), may well be a pyometra subject. The disease is most serious, and often requires surgical intervention. As the best chance of success is to operate or otherwise deal with early, a veterinary surgeon should be consulted immediately.

DISEASES AND INJURIES OF THE DOG.

Canine Distemper and " Para-distemper " (Including so-called " Hard-pad ").—It has long been recognised that the commonest and most serious disease of dogs throughout the world is canine distemper. Dogs of all ages and breeds are susceptible, and no dog is free from the risk of infection unless it has recovered from the disease or has acquired an immunity for other reasons (*see* **P8**(2). The disease is caused primarily by a minute agent known as a filterable virus (*see* **P7**(2). which may be of varying type in that it will attack the body in different ways. Thus some strains of the virus are known as " neurotropic " because they show an affinity for the nervous system. Sometimes a dog will apparently recover from an attack of distemper, only to succumb later to " fits " or other nervous manifestations due to permanent damage to the central nervous system by the virus. Often, however, the virus is not fatal in itself, but will lower the dog's resistance and permit the entry or the activity of bacteria that may lead to pneumonia or other serious effects. These so-called " secondary invaders," as the bacteria are termed, may prove as harmful as the original virus. Indeed, once these bacteria have set to work it is too late to expect the best results from the use of serum, and whether or not the dog will live through will depend upon the severity of the attack, the dog's powers of resistance, and good nursing. It is therefore most important either to prevent the disease by vaccination or to be able to send for veterinary attention (and hence for an injection of serum) *immediately* an attack is suspected. Any puppy which is listless or off its food, or which may throw a fit, or which is obviously unwell with other symptoms (*e.g.*, cough or diarrhœa) may well be in the early stages of distemper, and it is *then* (not the next day) that help should be sought. Many thousands of puppies (and older dogs) that have been injected with serum in the early stages of the disease have become perfectly normal within forty-eight hours. On the other hand, the number of dogs that die in Great Britain alone from distemper and distemper-like infections must assume enormous proportions. Distemper is a highly infectious disease, and it is important that the owner of an infected animal should do his best to avoid contact with other dogs, ferrets, or mink. Ferrets and mink are very susceptible to canine distemper. On the other hand, human beings and cats are *not* susceptible to canine distemper, and the so-called distemper of cats is quite a distinct disease.

A highly satisfactory means of vaccinating puppies against distemper was worked out about 1926–30, and this—named the " Laidlaw–Dunkin " after its two inventors—has since afforded protection to thousands of animals. Modern vaccines are based on a virus which has been modified by growth on developing egg embryos; or, more recently, in tissue culture. Puppies should be vaccinated when they are 10–12 weeks; prior to this age the immunity induced by the vaccine may not develop satisfactorily. After vaccination the puppy requires some time, possibly 2 weeks, before an immunity is established. Sometimes vaccinated dogs suffer distemper or distemper-like signs due to "secondary invaders" causing disease on their own account; or because they were already infected when vaccinated. Variants of distemper of which "hard pad" is an example may also overwhelm a vaccinated dog's immunity, alhough this is uncommon with modern vaccines, since several distemper strains are used in their production. Hyperimmune serum, which is collected from animals previously hyperimmunised against distemper, is available and can immediately aid the dog suffering from distemper but its effect is short-lived (7–10 days).

Infectious Hepatitis or Rubarth's Disease.—Another virus disease of dogs (and foxes) is known as Rubarth's disease, after one of its discoverers, now known as infectious hepatitis. This disease has been recognised in Sweden ever since the 1930s, but in Great Britain only since the end of the war. The condition is extremely sudden in onset, and an affected dog may be found dead. Many cases are, however, mild, and in some instances only one or two out of a large group of dogs have been affected. The changes seen after death vary, but the findings in the liver cells are usually characteristic. Specific treatment is not yet established as in the case of the distemper-like conditions, although the administration of antibiotics (*see* **P9**) may prevent the effects of secondary infection. An effective vaccine is now produced and often combined with the distemper chick embryo vaccine. A dog is thereby protected against both these diseases.

Canine Hysteria (called "fright disease" or "running fits" in the U.S.A.) is an alarming but not necessarily serious condition (in that it can often be cured very readily) which appears to arise from a variety of exciting causes. The affected animal rushes around wildly, often screaming and howling, and obviously loses all sense of whereabouts or ability to recognise people. After a more severe attack (and there are all degrees up to a full epileptiform fit) the dog may appear quite exhausted, but returns to normal. Sometimes there are many attacks in one day. The dog will not wilfully attack people during a bout of hysteria—at least, that has been the experience of the writer—but is very difficult to control. Apart from ensuring that the dog does itself no grievous bodily harm, there is little that can be done until the attack has subsided. Then the animal should be kept as quiet as possible and given a tranquilliser.

Hysteria may be an hereditary taint, derived from one or other parent. In certain circumstances, however, it may arise in apparently normal animals. There are several possible causes (including parasites), but a definite one is the bleaching agent—nitrogen trichloride or "agene"—employed for some years in the manufacture of flour, and hence present in white bread and certain dog biscuits. Indeed, the clear demonstration that agene could set up hysteria in dogs, and subsequent scientific work, has led to the introduction of regulations that have led to its abandonment as a bleaching agent in favour of other methods which have been found not to cause hysteria. There has already been a marked decline in the incidence of hysteria due to dietary factors.

Rabies is a fatal disease of dogs, and is also due to a "filterable virus." It is transmissible to the human being and to many other species, but has fortunately been absent from Great Britain for many years. Stringent precautions are taken to prevent its entry, and dogs which are brought into Great Britain must spend a long period in quarantine. A vaccine is available and people taking dogs to countries where rabies occurs should have their animals protected. Many countries insist on this prodceure.

Tonsilitis appears quite frequently in dogs, and seems in many cases to be part of a more generalised infection. It demands expert treatment, but although it may persist for a long time, it usually yields to treatment.

Nephritis.—Inflammation of the kidneys is unfortunately all too common in dogs, and in adult males in particular there is a high incidence of chronic kidney damage. One of the symptoms is a marked thirst. Sometimes this condition is a sequel to an infection known as *leptospirosis*, which calls for prompt veterinary treatment if death or permanent damage is not to follow. It is always worth while seeking professional advice for a dog that drinks excessively or has a somewhat characteristic type of bad breath. A vaccine which gives a good immunity against the two common forms of *leptospirosis* is available.

Anal Glands, which are found in the dog and in other carnivora, often give rise to trouble. Animals which "rub themselves along the ground" are not necessarily affected with "worms," but with impaction of these two little glands, which are situated one on each side of the anus. They secrete a peculiar dark-coloured, very offensive fluid, which sometimes is not discharged properly and causes the animal great discomfort. The glands in such cases should be relieved periodically. Those who do not mind this somewhat dirty task may perhaps learn how to do it themselves. Occasionally, segments of tapeworm are responsible for the impaction, but usually the trouble has nothing to do with worms. Whenever a dog pays considerable attention to his anus, this impaction should be suspected. Actual infection of the glands is also fairly common, and demands expert attention.

Diseases of the Ear, especially of the outer ear, are very common in dogs. The dog's outer ear is somewhat more complicated than is our own, and the drum is set more deeply. Hence it is easy for wax and dirt to accumulate, for various parasites to establish themselves, and for inflammatory conditions to result. The word "canker" (which has no precise scientific meaning) is sometimes applied by lay people to the more serious or chronic forms of inflammation of the outer ear canal. It is not difficult to diagnose "ear trouble," as the affected animal usually shakes its head or worries or scratches its ear and rubs it along the ground. The ears should be inspected regularly to see that there is no great accumulation of wax or dirt. Cotton-wool twisted on to the end of a match-stick or orange-stick is quite satisfactory for cleaning out the ear, providing care is taken. A dog which is continually worrying its ear, or which has ears which are obviously diseased, should not be neglected, as the sooner expert treatment is begun the more readily will the condition be cured. Even if the lining of the ear is greatly thickened through inflammatory reaction, and the lumen nearly occluded, it is still possible for a plastic operation to be performed. Many hundreds of such cases have been successfully treated in this way. A percentage of inflammatory conditions of the outer ear is associated with ear mange mites. In such an event treatment with modern anti-mange preparations should be carried out.

Deafness in certain white dogs (*e.g.*, in some Bull Terriers) appears to be hereditary, and is quite incurable. Old dogs often become deaf, and deafness has been produced experimentally in young puppies by feeding them on a deficient diet.

Diseases of the Eye are very common in dogs, and are often the result of injury. Except for minor discharges from the corners of their eyes (and in younger dogs especially it must be ascertained that these are not a symptom of distemper) any eye disease is sufficiently serious to merit professional advice. Boracic lotion is not suitable for the eyes of dogs. It is slightly irritant, and dogs are apt to scratch and make the eyes raw after application. Colloidal silver eye lotions and ointments are far more suitable pending the advice of a veterinary surgeon. In eye inflammation avoid sunlight and wind. For some days in the early stages of inflamed eyes, the light in the room should be subdued. Pekingese seem to be especially prone to eye disease, but the remarkably unwholesome appearance of some affected eyes in this breed is not necessarily evidence that recovery is unlikely. Steps should be taken to ensure that the dog does not inflict further injury on an already diseased eye. Cat scratches are a frequent source of inflammatory conditions of the dog's eye. Eyes must never be neglected, for the consequences are serious.

Skin Diseases are common in dogs, and may be contagious. Among the common contagious causes of skin disease are lice, mange mites and fleas. Lice and mange mites (except for demodex) are killed by modern insecticides such as benzene hexachloride (gammexane) although two applications at a 10–14 day interval are required to destroy the young stages which are within the insecticide-resistant eggs at the first dressing. The flea actually on the dog, is only one of four stages in the life cycle of the flea; the others are in the house or dog's bedding. Insecticides used for flea control should therefore be applied every week or 10 days during the summer to kill the young fleas as they hatch and infest the dog. The dog's bedding should be discarded or cleaned. The dog also suffers from other skin diseases caused by systemic disorders for which expert attention is required.

Diseases of the Teeth and Gums are very common in household dogs. A serious systemic disease, such as distemper, may leave the enamel of the teeth permanently pitted, hence "distemper teeth." More serious than this, however, is a form of pyorrhœa, which is really a disease of the gums rather than a primary disease of the teeth themselves. The margins of the gums become red and swollen, and may bleed easily. As the condition progresses the teeth may become loosened. Particles of food become lodged between the teeth or between teeth and gums, and add to the inflammation and to the smell of the breath.

This disease may, if unchecked, become very serious. In many cases extraction of one or more teeth is indicated, but unfortunately it is not always possible to do this. The condition demands expert attention.

Another common condition of dogs' teeth is the deposition around them of "tartar." This should be removed by scaling or by special use of dental forceps. Some breeders and others may themselves have learnt how to carry out these operations with the requisite skill and care, but they are not easy to the amateur, and it is essential that no harm be done to the animal's soft tissues by injudicious use of the instruments. Ordinary dog-owners are strongly advised to take their dogs to a veterinary surgeon in order to have the "tartar" removed.

Most puppies lose their first or "milk" teeth quite regularly between the ages of three and five months, but sometimes there is difficulty and the primary teeth are not shed properly. These cases should be treated by a veterinary surgeon before the permanent teeth are thrown out of their proper alignment.

One hears very much about "teething fits" in puppies, and while these occur, owners should be *very* careful to ensure that a "teething fit" is not a sign of distemper, which often starts with a fit. As puppies of this age are so susceptible to distemper, it is advisable to seek professional advice should any form of fit occur. It may save much time, money, and trouble, and even the animal's life.

Internal Parasites: "Worms."—It is probable that more nonsense has been talked and written about "worms" in dogs than about any other canine subject. According to some people, "worms" are the root of nearly all doggy evil, and so long as a dog is regularly "wormed" all will go well with him. These beliefs are frankly absurd. The real facts are very different, and are stated in as brief a fashion as possible in the following sentences. In this country dogs are infested by a species of "roundworm" (a creature which is a dirty-white colour and in shape somewhat resembles the common earthworm) and by several species of "tapeworm," which are also whitish but which are flat and are made up of many small segments joined to a little "head" which is attached to the lining of the gut. In spite of all that is said, tapeworms as such are rarely responsible for much harm to the dog, although they can, of course, prove debilitating and should be removed. They are a nuisance, and attempts to remove them should be made by administration of the appropriate drug. Occasionally, segments of worm are responsible for impaction of the ducts of the *anal glands* (see above).

The roundworms may be extremely serious in young puppies, in which they cause stunting, "pot-belly," harshness of coat and dangerous or fatal illness. Fortunately, modern anti-roundworm preparations are available for animals of this age. Once over the age of 4–8 months dogs rarely suffer serious illness from roundworms, although these may cause occasional vomiting, or even diarrhoea, and some loss of coat and bodily condition. It is now known that puppies are infected before birth from their mother. It is therefore desirable to keep down the incidence of roundworms in the mother—and in dogs generally—and fortunately the modern preparations are—unlike some of the old-fashioned ones—safe in use and unlikely to cause digestive disturbances. From all that has been said above owners will realise the necessity of taking professional advice about young dogs which are ill, and any signs of "worms" in young puppies—either in the stools or by some obvious intestinal upset or bloated appearance of the belly—should be acted upon. One last word about this aspect of worms—do not assume that your adult dog has "tapeworms" unless you see some evidence in his stools. There are so many "signs of worms" that veterinary surgeons must at times get a little tired of being assured that "My dog has worms" because of some trivial habit connected with appetite.

There is, however, another side to the study of tapeworms, and one which is not generally realised. The tapeworm which is found in the dog represents one stage in the life-cycle. The eggs, which are present in the ripe segment passed by the dog, develop, not in the outside world, but in another animal altogether. Thus one of the commonest tapeworms in this country has an intermediate stage, as it is called, in the flea, and it is when the flea is eaten by the dog that this intermediate stage develops further to become a tapeworm. Another tapeworm has an intermediate stage which develops in the sheep, and a third has one which develops in the ox. There is a fourth tapeworm which has an intermediate stage which *may* develop in man, to set up serious diseases in certain cases. Children may become infected through handling the dog, and so picking up the eggs, which may then be eaten through putting the hands in the mouth. The dogs which are most likely to be infested are those which have the opportunity to eat freshly killed sheep and other food-animals. An ordinary household dog is not likely to be infested, and people should not worry unduly in this connection, provided they do not allow their dogs to stray into the wrong places. It is illegal to allow dogs to enter a slaughter-house, but unfortunately one often sees dogs in such places. The routine worming of dogs is justified if evidence of infection exists, and certainly in country areas where opportunities of tapeworm re-infection may be plentiful.

Tumours, including malignant tumours ("cancers") are relatively very common in the dog—probably as common as in the human subject. Space does not permit of a detailed account, but the following examples of growths may be mentioned: a proliferation of warts on the skin of puppies (usually disappear spontaneously); a true cancer of the tonsil in middle-aged and older dogs of both sexes; cancer of the mammary glands in bitches (both incurable); fatty growths of the vagina of bitches (amenable to operation).

Space does not allow of the discussion of other

diseases, but it should be pointed out that dogs are susceptible to human and bovine forms of *tuberculosis*, especially the former. In a household which contains a tubercular person, the dog should be watched for any signs of illness, and the thought entertained that he might be responsible for the further spread of the disease. For a discussion on ringworm see the appropriate heading in the section on the cat (Z12).

Accidents and Injuries.—In these days of swiftly moving motor transport, street accidents to dogs are extremely common. Many could be prevented by training the animal to walk to heel, by the use of a lead in busy thoroughfares, and by not allowing dogs to roam the streets unaccompanied—a thoroughly bad habit. Sometimes the victim escapes with a scare and a few bruises, and at others death is mercifully swift. In the vast majority of accidents, however, a more or less serious injury is incurred, and if the animal is unable to move, the police should be notified immediately. The dog is best left quiet, and it is not recommended that attempts be made to administer brandy or other supposed "stimulants" unless help is markedly delayed. Excessive hæmorrhage may in some instances be prevented by common-sense application of principles learnt in first-aid courses.

One of the commonest accidents to dogs, especially to young dogs, is a fracture involving the head of the femur, or thigh-bone. Inability to put one of the hind legs to the ground, or to bear any weight on this limb, is an indication of such an injury. (This injury may occur also from falling off a chair or wall.) Professional help is, of course, required in such cases.

Cuts and Bruises, if not serious, may be treated at home as in the case of human beings. The indiscriminate use of tincture of iodine is not to be recommended, and spirit alone makes a more satisfactory dressing in most cases. Simple washing and removal of dirt are usually sufficient, combined, perhaps, with modern antiseptic ointments or other preparations. The dog (and also the cat) are very liable to sepsis, and it is best in such cases to send for proper assistance early, or there may be grave trouble. It is probable that in nature many of the flesh-eating animals end their lives as victims of the sepsis following wounds.

Injuries from cat-scratches are exceedingly common, as are bites from other dogs. These are serious, as they more readily result in septic places. The scratch or bite sometimes penetrates quite deeply, leaving a pocket which fills up with pus. This pus may spread under the skin to form sinuses. Never neglect such places.

Conclusion.—There are a few concluding remarks on the treatment of the diseases of the dog:—

(1) It is not correct that "water should be withheld from a sick dog." It is true that an animal which is using water only to vomit, or which is drinking excessively, should have its water intake restricted, but it is wrong to deprive a dog altogether.

(2) There have been such wonderful advances in the field of veterinary anæsthetics that there is nowadays little to fear in this connection from operations to dogs and cats. The records over the past years at the Royal Veterinary College, London and at other centres have been most encouraging, and the anæsthetic risk is now small indeed.

(3) When a dog's life is a burden to him, it is unfair to keep him alive, and he should be put to sleep. It must be realised, however, that putting a dog to sleep is a very skilled task. It is made much easier if an owner will allow his veterinary surgeon to administer an anæsthetic and not allow the animal "to come round," and shooting is also straightforward and painless if *skilfully* carried out. There are no "magical ways" of destroying human or animal life, and an owner must not expect his veterinary surgeon to be able to bring about death merely by holding a pad to the dog's face. It is far better that the task be carried out at a veterinary surgeon's own premises, where there is skilled assistance.

CATS.

Many of the general remarks in the preceding section apply equally to cats, and will not be repeated unnecessarily in the following paragraphs.

BREEDS AND VARIETIES OF CAT.

The following breeds and varieties are recognised for registration purposes by the Governing Council of the Cat Fancy:—

Long-haired Cats.

Black	Tortoiseshell
White (Blue-eyed)	Tortoiseshell-and-White
White (Orange-eyed)	Blue Cream
Blue	Brown Tabby
Red Tabby	Chinchilla
Red Self	Smoke
Cream	Silver Tabby

Short-haired Cats.

Black	Spotted
White	Russian Blue
British Blue	Manx
Cream	Abyssinian
Tortoiseshell	Siamese (Seal-pointed)
Tortoiseshell-and-White	Siamese (Blue-pointed)
Silver Tabby	Siamese (Chocolate-pointed)
Brown Tabby	Burmese
Red Tabby	
Mackerel-striped Tabby	

Pedigree breeding and showing are practised with a very small fraction of the total cat population of Great Britain, and the majority of these remarks will be concerned with the ordinary household cat. Nevertheless, in recent years there appears to have been a considerable increase in pedigree cat breeding. Registration—which is essential for showing and pedigree purposes—is controlled by the Governing Council of the Cat Fancy, of which the secretary (1962) is S. E. Barnes, O.B.E., 4 Elim Court Gardens, London Road, Crowborough, Sussex. Many of the breeds listed above have their own societies, which are affiliated to the Governing Council. The addresses and particulars of these and other cat societies and clubs may be had on application to the secretary of the Governing Council. The two most popular varieties of cat are the Blue Persian and the Siamese, and an exclusive show is held for each of them. In addition to these shows there are five big Championship Shows open to every variety of long- and short-haired cat, while there are classes for cats and kittens at some of the Agricultural Shows.

CHOICE OF CAT.

Although there are, as noted above, many varieties of cat, most people are content to accept an ordinary kitten, and for them the chief points to consider will be: (*a*) whether to have a long-haired or a short-haired animal, (*b*) whether to have a male or female, (*c*) whether or not to have the kitten "doctored" (*i.e.*, castrated or spayed). As a general rule, short-haired cats are probably more suitable for the average household, since their fur does not become shed so noticeably and they probably suffer less from "fur-balling." Nevertheless, many long-haired cats are so attractive that they will obviously be preferred, and there is no reason why they should not be chosen. Sex is a rather more important question, although, as may be seen in the section on management, it is possible to have both males and females "doctored." Male cats which are kept as entires are often a nuisance in that they make abominable smells in the house and spend much of their time in fighting. These characteristics are by no means invariable; but they are so common as to justify the castration of the majority of males. Siamese males in particular may be a liability. Females are generally credited with a greater attachment to the home (although they wander when "in season") and with being better mousers. The principal objection to females is that they seem to be bearing kittens almost continuously. In normal circumstances it is, of course, quite impossible to prevent cats from mating by keeping the female in confinement during her season, a practice which is frequently adopted in the case of the dog. For one thing, most people are never aware when their female cats are in season.

Whatever animal is chosen, it is essential to pick a healthy and preferably a fairly young—but *not* too young—kitten. It is best not to accept a kitten under about eight weeks of age.

For those who wish for something a little out of the ordinary, Siamese cats make excellent and highly intelligent pets. Siamese kittens are born white, but gradually develop their even pale fawn colour, with cream on belly and chest and with "seal brown" mask, ears, legs, feet, and tail. The coat is very short, and the eyes are blue. There has long been a popular belief that Siamese cats are delicate creatures, but the present writer has seen healthy specimens, kept under ordinary household conditions, living to a mature age. It is not wise to keep a male Siamese as a household pet. The male is a fierce fighter, and is generally a worse offender in the house than the males of other breeds, and should therefore be castrated if it is to be kept as a pet.

Many people find Manx cats attractive. Instead of the normal large number of tail bones, they have but three, and hence appear almost tailless. One should beware against fraudulent amputation of the tail of ordinary cats, which are then described as "Manx."

MANAGEMENT OF THE CAT.

The cat is an independent creature, so much so that one may say that to a large extent it manages its own affairs. This, however, is not true of all cats, and every reasonable attempt should be made to provide the cat with a comfortable and friendly home. Cats are highly intelligent, and if sufficient patience is exercised they will respond to a very great degree to human attention. Kittens should not be neglected, but should be talked to and played with just as are puppies. Many cats, especially young cats, make excellent playmates for children.

In order to prevent to a large extent their nocturnal wanderings, many cats of both sexes are castrated or spayed (the popular lay expression for this is "doctored"). In the male cat the testicles are removed by an operation which is almost always safe and simple if carried out skilfully. From three to four months is a good age at which to have this done. Female cats may also be "doctored." As the female glands or ovaries lie within the body cavity, this operation is a major one, but it is nevertheless quite a straightforward, though a more expensive, procedure if conducted at the right age (about five months). Very many thousands of female cats have been so operated upon and the subsequent health of these cats has been excellent. Indeed, it has been said that a spayed female makes one of the best of all household cats.

Cats may choose to sleep in a variety of places, and will often lie on beds, chairs, mats, and other warm places. It is a sound policy to provide them with a box or basket, and to encourage them to use newspaper as a bedding. Most cats will take well to newspaper. The bed should be placed in a warm site—it is of little use putting it in a cold corner of a room and expecting the cat to lie in it.

Owing to the fact that, even in play, a cat's claws may inflict serious injury, dogs and cats do not always make the best of house companions. Nevertheless, the traditional enmity of cat and dog is often overcome, and if the two are brought up together they often make firm friends, sharing the same basket or hearth-rug and feeding together without serious consequences.

A cat normally attends to its own toilet, and everyone must be aware that a cat devotes long periods each day to cleaning and washing itself. Except in special cases, therefore, bathing is quite unnecessary, while in short-haired cats especially, grooming, too, is superfluous (this does not apply to show-cats). For some reason (and sometimes, apparently, because an owner attempts to assist in the daily grooming) an occasional cat may cease to wash or care for itself. Such an animal is a dejected sight, and should be taken to a veterinary surgeon to have its matted fur cut or combed, and its dirt removed. Such animals (unless they completely re-acquire their self-respect) must be groomed regularly if they are to be kept at all.

All household cats are accustomed to take their own exercise, and it is advisable (except in any special circumstances) to allow them free access to and from the outer world. Do not shut your cat in the house for a long period and then blame it for making a mess. Cats are clean creatures; they normally dig small holes in which to defæcate or urinate, and subsequently cover the deposit with earth. If, therefore, they are for some reason debarred temporarily or permanently from access to a garden, they should be provided with a box or tray containing soil or cinders. Indeed, in many types of houses it is a good plan to encourage kittens to use such a device. (Note the corresponding remarks about puppies.)

It is generally stated that "cats never forget a blow," and for that reason it is recommended that cats are not chastised. It may be said that, if a cat (or dog) be brought up conscientiously and well, it should never, or very rarely, require such punishment. An animal which has been brought up properly seems to develop a fair sense of what is right and what is wrong.

For pedigree cats, or those kept in confinement for other reasons, see the relevent remarks in the section on breeding.

FEEDING THE CAT.

Although most cats are capable of supplementing their diet by catching small rodents or birds, it is unwise to rely on this as a regular source of food. The idea that hungry cats make the best mousers is by no means always correct. Indeed, animals that are in poor condition are less likely to be successful hunters. Moreover, while the riddance of pests is an excellent matter from the human point of view—and one of the reasons why the keeping of cats is economically justified—the "cruel" fashion in which most cats tackle their prey is repulsive to most of us.

It is therefore necessary and desirable to provide regular daily feeding. Kittens should receive several meals a day, but by the time they are six months old the number of daily feeds should be reduced to one, or at most two. Most cats (many Siamese are exceptions) are extremely fond of *milk*, especially if it is creamy, and the cat's love of *fish* is well known. Many *meats*, especially *rabbit meat*, are relished, and a diet high in "animal protein" is indeed the aim, always provided that it contains sufficient "dietary energy." It is significant that cat's milk has a higher content of fat and sugar than cow's milk, *i.e.*, it is a richer source of energy. Some of the proprietary bitch-milk substitutes are nearer to cat's milk in composition than is cow's milk.

Many hundreds of cats have been reared and bred successfully in experimental laboratories on a diet consisting, in the main, of one part of fish or meat and two parts of *cooked potatoes*. This is relatively inexpensive, and may be supplemented by milk and by some of the proprietary cat foods.

Cats are also extremely fond of liver. Some of the proprietary cat foods—the better ones of which are excellent—and vitamin tablets contain liver, which is a rich source of the vitamin B complex.

Within reason a healthy kitten should be fed to appetite, always provided good-quality foods are available. The amount should be restricted when they are adult, however, except for pregnant and lactating cats, which are sometimes referred to as "queens" as opposed to the male "toms." An average daily allowance of solid food for a healthy non-pregnant adult cat should be of the order of $\frac{1}{2}$ oz. per 1 lb. body-weight.

Cats are fastidious eaters; they usually sniff and examine carefully any strange or doubtful food. At the same time they are often greedy especially with relished food to which they are accustomed, but fortunately they can, like dogs, vomit very readily. Here, incidentally, is one very good tip—an excellent emetic for both cat and dog is a small crystal of washing-soda, given as a pill. People are usually amazed at the way this simple device results in a dog's or a cat's bringing up undesirable food.

It is important not to overfeed cats, and it is

almost equally important to prepare all food in a clean manner, and to make it as attractive as possible. Cats will greatly appreciate this care. While milk is an excellent food for kittens (see under breeding), and is relished by most adult cats, it must be supplemented by solid food.

Clean fresh water should be provided at all times, even if the cat appears to drink it but little.

BREEDING OF CATS.

Pedigree animals are normally confined, and their breeding is strictly controlled. Ordinary household cats are at the opposite extreme, and there is little that can be done to prevent their mating. The length and scope of this article does not permit of a discussion of controlled mating.

Scientifically, there is as yet a good deal to learn about the reproductive behaviour of the cat. As an American physiologist has succinctly put it in a description of the reproductive cycle of the female cat, "no two authors agree." In Northern Europe there are two main heat periods a year, in spring and early autumn, but some animals may appear in heat at any time from January to July, and those who keep female cats in confinement describe their charges as "calling" quite frequently if not mated. A cat which is "in season" or "on heat" is often observed to be behaving in a quite characteristic fashion, rolling about on the floor and making peculiar sounds. The periods of heat, which commence usually at about eight months of age, may last for several days, and during this time the female will make every attempt to find a mate.

Gestation lasts about nine weeks, as in the case of the bitch, but here again there is a considerable variation. As most owners are quite unaware of the time at which their cats were mated, it is difficult to talk of "going overtime," but if there is any evidence of trouble during pregnancy, or at birth, veterinary advice should be obtained. As soon as a cat is obviously pregnant, her food allowance should be increased, and she should be allowed plenty of milk. It is highly important to increase her food and milk ration still further after the kittens are born, as lactation is a great drain on the mother.

Cats sometimes choose strange, out-of-the-way places in which to litter, and many healthy litters are born and reared out of doors. Rats are a source of danger, and will often destroy very young kittens during the mother's absence. For this and other reasons it is better in town and suburban areas to have the litter comfortably housed indoors. A wooden box containing newspaper is ideal, provided it is kept in a fairly warm place and out of the way of draughts. An average litter consists of three to six kittens, which are born blind, but which normally open their eyes after eight or nine days. There is no need to be alarmed if the eyes remain closed for a few days longer. Kittens which are born dead should be removed and buried or burnt. If the whole litter is born dead, the mother's food supply should be cut down considerably, and little milk given for a few days. If the mamary glands become inflamed, they may be bathed in a cold solution of alum. The glands normally return to their former size within a short space of time if they are not milked, but if there is persistent trouble veterinary advice should be sought.

While many pedigree owners wean kittens at four to five weeks of age, it is strongly advised that the household cat be allowed to continue to feed her family for a longer period, and eight weeks is not too long if the mother is still in good bodily condition. She *must*, however, be well fed and be allowed plenty of milk. As in the case of puppies, it is an excellent idea to provide the kittens with a little solid food as from a few weeks of age. It is very wrong to remove a kitten from its mother too early, and such an animal is often weakly, develops an intestinal infection, and dies as a miserable bedraggled creature. Moreover, during the period following weaning the mother educates her offspring in the art of living, particularly ratting and mousing.

As many litters are unwanted, some people get rid of all the kittens as soon as possible after birth. Drowning is frequently practised, but it is not recommended as a merciful death. Indeed, a hard blow on the back of the head is more humane if given accurately. It is much better to take the kittens to a veterinary surgeon or clinic.

DISEASES AND INJURIES OF THE CAT.

The principal infectious diseases of cats are still in need of much scientific study. It is now clear, however, that there are at least two major cat plagues. Both have been given many names, and there is much confusion between them.

Feline Enteritis or Panleucopenia.—This is a highly infectious disease, due to a filterable virus. The symptoms include loss of appetite, sometimes accompanied by a rise in body temperature, followed by listlessness, usually vomiting, sometimes diarrhoea, and a marked tendency to show tenderness or pain on being handled. This tenderness or pain is due to a developing peritonitis. The poor animal may become seriously ill, with loss of water from the tissues or dehydration, prostrate and dead within 48 hours or less from the time of the first symptoms. The incubation period of the disease is believed to be from 4 to 8 days, or sometimes longer. There is a fall in the white-cell count of the blood, hence the term "panleucopenia." Some cats recover, the recovery rate in different outbreaks that have been studied ranging from 30 to 80 per cent., and recovered animals are probably immune to further attacks. Cats that are able to take a little food during the early stages of recovery have the best chance of recovery, but require careful nursing. There may be complications during the convalescent stage due to secondary bacterial infections or to vitamin deficiency, and a light nourishing diet, combined with vitamin preparations, is recommended. Fleas may transmit the disease to other cats, as may contact with infected materials. It has been shown that bedding and dirt trays from sick cats were infectious for other cats for up to 16 days. The disease is not transmissible to dogs or to human beings. There is nowadays a protective vaccine, and it is a wise precaution to have your pet vaccinated.

Feline Pneumonitis.—This disease is sometimes called "cat distemper"—as indeed is feline enteritis—but it has no connection with dog distemper, and is not transmissible to dogs or to human beings. Both mild and severe forms occur, and the incubation period varies from 5 to 8 days. The mild form may seem like a cold, and there is a weeping from the eyes and a varying degree of conjunctivitis. There is a thin, clear discharge from the nose, with a characteristic sneezing. Provided that the animals can be made to continue eating, and are kept in warm and dry but ventilated conditions, recovery may be rapid and not entail serious loss of condition. The eyes should be treated with a suitable preparation, such as silver vitellin. There may be secondary bacterial infection in cases that are neglected.

The severe form of the disease has similar, although more severe, commencing symptoms, but the nasal discharge becomes purulent and there is often profuse salivation, with much spreading of the long ropes of saliva. The cat is listless, dislikes strong light, and seems to resent being disturbed. It loses its appetite, and rapidly becomes thinner over a period of from 2 to 5 days or so. Breathing becomes laboured, and a bronchopneumonia develops. There may be a high death rate in young kittens, and pregnant females may abort. Recovery tends to be slow, and is often complicated by bacterial infection. Some of the modern antibiotics appear to be highly effective in the treatment of many cases of this disease, but they must, of course, be given under veterinary supervision.

Tuberculosis.—The cat, like the dog, can contract tuberculosis, but so far as is known only the bovine form has been known to infect it. The infections usually comes, of course, from milk, and the elimination of bovine tuberculosis from this country will stop the incidence of the disease in cats. The disease commences in the abdomen, but may spread to the lungs. There is general wasting.

Skin Diseases.—As in the case of the dog, skin disease in the cat is usually of parasitic origin, and fleas and mange mites are again the chief source of trouble in Great Britain. Cats do so much of their own toilet that the average household cat has probably a cleaner skin than its canine counterpart. When skin disease does develop, it is strongly advised that the animal be taken to a veterinary surgeon for appropriate treatment. As a rule cats greatly resent the interference which must accompany any attempt to bathe or dress an affected place, and for this reason it is usually unwise for an owner to attempt to do other than make an inspection. Very small patches of skin eruption may clear satisfactorily if the surrounding hair is clipped away with curved scissors, but generally speaking skin disease calls for professional attention. The cat flea has a similar life cycle to the dog flea (*see* Z8).

Diseases of the Ear.—The outer ear of the cat is frequently affected, and in a great many cases a form of mange mite is responsible. The animal provides evidence of the trouble by scratching and shaking its ear and generally showing its discomfort. It will not always be possible for an owner to make a thorough examination, as in many cases the cat objects, but if it is possible to look inside the ear it will be seen that there is a dirty and usually brownish mess of tissue, sometimes mixed with dried blood or pus. Not all cases are as bad as this, of course, but if a cat persistently worries its ear it should be taken to a veterinary surgeon. There are satisfactory dressings for this condition, and owners will be able to dress their cats if the latter are docile. Otherwise it is necessary to have the ears dressed by a veterinary surgeon or by one of his staff.

A cat's ear is frequently the site of a blood blister, or hæmatoma. This is usually the sequel to a blow, such as a slamming door, and shows itself as a large, tense swelling, which when opened by the surgeon proves to be an accumulation of serum usually tinged with blood. Some cases become infected at the time of injury, some after with the patient's rubbing. With the greatest surgical skill in the world one must expect a slight deformity, and the cat develops a puckered ear, much the same as the human boxer.

Disease of the Bladder.—The bladder is a common seat of disease in cats, and is frequently affected through the blocking of the natural water-passage by small sand-like calculi. Naturally, male cats are more often affected, as the terminal end of the urinary tracts is wider and more dilatable in females. The urine is unable to escape, and the bladder becomes filled with a mixture of urine and the sandy calcular matter. The condition may be diagnosed quite readily, as the cat usually collapses, or partially collapses, and one may easily feel the distended bladder through the walls of the abdomen (belly). It is necessary to send for professional help immediately, and, while no relief can be guaranteed, it is often possible to relieve the condition by judicious manipulation. Owners should not attempt to do this themselves (unless help cannot be obtained), as they may easily burst the bladder. As the animal is usually in a state of collapse when the condition is discovered, it makes a bad risk for actual operation, and relief by *skilled* pressure is usually to be recommended.

Ringworm.—There are two common kinds of ringworm in the cat (a third, which may also infect the dog, is more rare; it is the trichophyton which is usually found on cattle). The first kind is acquired from rats and mice, and is most commonly to be found at the bases of the claws, from where it may spread to the ears and face. The individual lesions are circular and yellow in colour, and consist largely of a scabby material. This kind of ringworm is known as "favus."

The second type of ringworm (microsporon) is more important, because it is more readily transmissible to human beings. Whereas this form usually sets up circular scaly lesions in the dog, it often infects cats without there being much naked-eye evidence of its presence. Indeed, in the cat the condition is often unsuspected until the owner himself becomes infected and consults his doctor.

Ringworm should be treated or dealt with by a veterinary surgeon, who will also confirm or refute by special methods the presence of microsporon in cats.

Intestinal Parasites—" Worms."—The cat also is subject to both roundworms and tapeworms. The roundworm which parasitises cats in this country is similar to that of the dog (although a different species) and is also much more harmful to the young than to the adult animal. In kittens the symptoms are a general unthriftiness, staring coat, and in some cases diarrhœa and a " pot-bellied " appearance.

The commonest cat tapeworm in this country is one which passes its intermediate stage in the rat or mouse, or sometimes in other rodents. The tapeworm, which, as mentioned under the section on dogs, is dangerous to man, is sometimes found in the cat also.

Accidents and Injuries.—Despite their sagacity and alertness in many ways, cats seem curiously unable, in many instances, to acquire road-sense. They are dazed by a car's head-lights, while if a motorist sounds his horn they tend to stop still in their tracks.

Injuries from traps, *e.g.*, gin-traps, are very common, and it is probable that many thousands of cats annually are maimed in this fashion. Cats suffer injury from shooting, from stoning, and from blows with sticks. Since they are predatory animals, they have often to pay the penalty inflicted on them by wrathful people. Needless to say, cats which survive to return home usually require expert treatment.

Poisoning may be included under this heading. Although there are doubtless many deliberate attempts to poison marauding cats, alleged " poisoning " is often no more than a case of feline enteritis, and owners should not claim glibly that their cats have been poisoned until they have expert evidence to back their judgment.

Fur-balling, as it has been termed, may be mentioned here. Cats, especially the long-haired varieties, must often ingest hair during their toilet, and occasionally serious trouble (a stoppage of the bowels) is brought about by a mass of such hair which has collected in a part of the bowel. There is constipation, loss of condition, and often evidence of considerable pain. Such cats should be taken to a veterinary surgeon.

Bites and scratches are even more common in the cat than they are in the dog, and subsequent sepsis is equally likely.

FERRETS.

Description.—The ferret is probably a domesticated form of the pole-cat (*Mustela putorius*), and is known sometimes by that name and sometimes as *Mustela furo*. Most tame ferrets have pink eyes and yellowish-white fur, but there are darker forms believed to have resulted from crossing in previous generations with wild pole-cats. Indeed, these darker forms are popularly termed " pole-cat ferrets." They are of two main kinds, the first having creamy under fur and black guard hairs, and the second being a chocolate-brown colour, with brown upper parts and black under parts, and a few scattered light hairs on the face.

Ferrets are long creatures in relation to their body weight, and when fully-grown may have a body 14 in. long or more and a tail of 5 in. Some strains grow appreciably larger. The main use of the ferret is, of course, in rabbiting, for which purpose they have been employed for many centuries. Although they can become fierce if not accustomed to regular handling or kind treatment, and are capable of inflicting a nasty bite, they may nevertheless be made into docile and highly intelligent pets. It is most important to win their confidence from the beginning and to accustom them to regular handling from the time they are young " kittens."

Accommodation.—Ferrets must have dry, clean accommodation in a room free from draughts but well ventilated. Wood is warmer than metal, but more difficult to clean, and is best lined with hard asbestos sheeting, which is resistant to water. The most suitable accommodation comprises a sleeping compartment of similar proportions to a small kennel, leading by a small doorway or "pop-hole" to a wire-netting exercising run, which should be as large as possible compatible with cleanliness. It is a good idea to have a means of closing the doorway so that the ferret or ferrets may be confined within the sleeping-compartment if necessary. Wood-wool makes an excellent bedding, but if difficult to obtain newspaper may be provided for the ferret to lie on. The floor of the run may have a false bottom or may be sprinkled with sawdust. It is imperative to keep the whole of the accommodation clean and dry, not only to avoid smell but also to prevent the ferrets from developing a very serious necrotic infection of the feet known as "foot-rot."

Feeding.—Many ferrets are unfortunately not fed adequately. It must be appreciated that basically they are carnivorous animals, and that their food requirements are more similar to those of the dog and cat than those of rodents. Indeed, many of the general remarks made about the principles of feeding dogs and cats apply to ferrets also.

Most ferrets like bread-and-milk, and while this is an excellent article of diet, it is in itself inadequate. Up to about 4 oz. of raw meat (minced for younger animals) daily is an excellent basis, and this may be replaced by fish. Liver, especially raw liver, is an excellent source of many factors, and there is good reason to provide some at least weekly if it can be obtained. Failing this, it is advisable to add 1–2 per cent. of whole dry liver to the diet. Once ferrets are grown, one feeding daily—at a fixed time—is sufficient. The female (jill) should have ample supplies of milk just prior to the birth of her young and while she is suckling them.

Breeding.—In the northern hemisphere the female ferret usually comes into œstrus (season) in early March of the year following that in which it is born. If the jill does not conceive during this œstrus she will have a further œstral period in July or August The desire of the jill to mate is very strong, and if not allowed to do so, some animals sometimes have been found to waste and pine. The act of mating is prefaced by very vigorous behaviour on the part of the male (hob), and anyone not appreciating the performance might think that he was out to kill his mate! The mating act itself is usually prolonged, and may take up to three hours. If left together the hob and jill will probably mate from two to four times during the course of a couple of days. As in the cat and rabbit, ovulation or the shedding of the egg from the ovary takes place as a result of mating, and not spontaneously. The period of gestation is forty-two days, and the numbers of young born usually varies from five to thirteen, the average litter being six to eight. Pseudo-pregnancy occurs if the jill is not mated, and may become outwardly obvious as in the case of certain bitches.

Males also have a seasonal rhythm, their capacity to fertilise being greatest from early March to August. Young hobs seem to be active about a month earlier than older ones. The length of daylight or, rather, the incrementation in light from day to day, has an important bearing on breeding capacity in both sexes, and by the use of artificial light it has proved possible to induce either œstrus or male activity at different times of the year.

The young are hairless and blind, and weigh on the average under ½ oz. at birth. Their eyes open at about four weeks, and they can then commence to eat small pieces of solid food to supplement their mother's milk. They may be weaned at from six to eight weeks.

Diseases.—The most serious disease of ferrets is *canine distemper*, and the variant known as "hard pad" (see under dog) is equally capable of infecting ferrets. Such infections can wipe out entire stocks, and every care should be taken to prevent their spread from dogs to ferrets—and vice versa. A veterinary surgeon should be consulted immediately when a ferret becomes ill or out of sorts. Ferrets are also susceptible to some strains of *human* influenza, and should not be tended by persons with colds or with any indications of "flu." The feeding of infected milk may give rise to *tuberculosis* (now unlikely in Britain). *Foot-rot* has already been mentioned, and must on no account be neglected. *Mange* or "scabies" of the back and tail region should be dealt with promptly, employing modern preparations. Abscesses of the neck region are often encountered, and should receive professional treatment if they do not clear up rapidly, for they may spread with dire consequences.

RATS.

Description.—Tame rats are domesticated varieties of the wild Norway or "brown" rat (*Rattus norvegicus*). Such rats are usually albinos or black-and-white, although other colours have been bred. The hooded varieties are those in which the head and foreparts are mainly black or chocolate and the remainder of the body, apart from small patches the same colours as the hood, is white. Tame rats differ materially from wild ones in disposition, and properly managed are extremely tractable. Healthy specimens accustomed to handling bite only when frightened, *e.g.*, when a sudden movement is made in front of them. Males appear to live longer than females, but three years is a good age.

"Black" rats, *i.e.*, the species (*Rattus rattus*) sometimes known as the ship or Alexandrine rat, have been bred in captivity, but tame strains are not generally available.

Housing.—Tame rats require a warm, even temperature—65–70° F. all the year round—and draughts or lowered temperature may precipitate lung disease or other disorders. It is best to have a complete spare set of boxes or cages, and to change to fresh quarters weekly except when the females have unweaned young with them. Empty cages should be cleaned and disinfected thoroughly before being used again. Provided the temperature conditions are suitable—and this is essential—metal cages of the types employed in scientific laboratories are best, with wire-mesh false bottoms and trays containing sawdust to catch the droppings. Accommodation should be

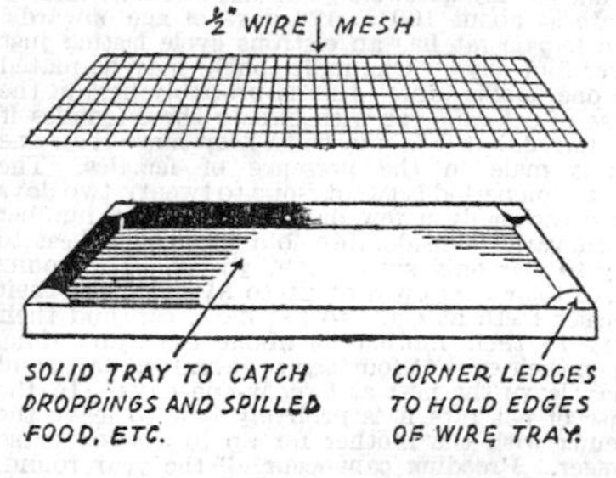

ample, and even for a pair of pet rats the cage should measure about 30 in. × 18 in. × 18 in. If wooden boxes are employed it may be desirable to line them with hard asbestos sheeting or galvanised metal to prevent damage from gnawing.

Small, dark "shelters" and exercising devices, *e.g.*, wheels or ladders, are appreciated by the rats, but must be kept clean. Wood-wool makes the best bedding.

Feeding.—Rats may take a wide variety of foods, including many of our own, and there are several successful ways of feeding them, including the provision of specially formulated "rat-cubes," of the same type as that described below for mice. A good daily diet is wholemeal bread, mixed cereals (*e.g.*, oats, wheat, hempseed), with about

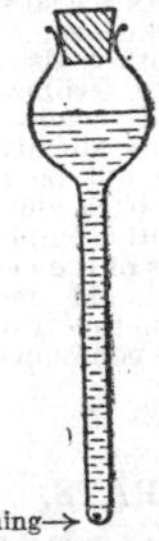

WATER BULB SUITABLE FOR USE WITH PET RODENTS

5 per cent. dried brewers' yeast and milk either fed separately or mixed with the rest of the food. Twice weekly each rat should be given up to ½ oz. or more of meat, liver, fish, or other "animal protein." A little fresh greenfood (even grass) is appreciated, and in winter especially some supplement containing vitamins A and D is desirable. Expectant and nursing mothers should have as much milk as they require. Never overfeed or allow uneaten food residues to remain in the cage. Fresh water (preferably in bulbs or bottles) should be available at all times. Far cleaner than open dishes are the special but simple type of water bulbs suspended on or in front of the cage or box so that the rat can drink from the rounded end of the spout. A simple substitute is a medicine "flat" bottle—or even a ¼- or ⅛-pint milk-type bottle. This should be fitted with a cork—or, better, a rubber bung—pierced for a piece of bent glass tubing. Provided that the free end of the glass tubing is not sharp, and is chosen so that the aperture is considerably smaller than that of the tube itself, the water will not run out unless sucked out by the rat. The spout should, of course, be within easy access of the rat, which will soon learn to drink from it.

Breeding.—Rats can breed at quite a young age (usually being capable of mating when fifty to sixty days old), but it is better to separate the sexes within a fortnight or so of weaning (weaning being usually at twenty-one days of age) and to mate at about 100 to 120 days of age onwards. the female rat has an œstrous cycle lasting just over four days. One male (buck) may be mated to one female (doe)—this is probably best in the case of pet rats—or with two or three females if preferred, but it is unwise to keep more than one adult male in the presence of females. The gestation period is twenty-one to twenty-two days or occasionally a few days longer. The number born varies considerably, but often it is best to try to rear only six to eight young. The young have their ears open at 2½ to 3½ days, cut their incisor teeth at eight to ten days, can find their way to their mother at about the same time, open their eyes at fourteen to seventeen days, and may leave the nest at twenty-one days. In the case of pet rats it is probably best to leave the young with the mother for up to a week or so longer. Breeding can occur all the year round, but takes place less readily in winter.

Handling.—Rats should not be "tailed," or the skin may slough off. Regular handling after weaning is excellent and promotes docility. The weight of the body should be supported.

Diseases.—On the whole rats are much less liable to disease than mice, provided temperature conditions are suitable. The commonest infection is *broncho-pneumonia*, often precipitated through draughts or cold. *Mange* (especially of the ear) and infestation with *lice* may occur, and should be dealt with promptly by means of modern insecticides. Avoid contact with wild rodents, or the use of food or bedding that may have been contaminated by wild rats and mice.

MICE.

Description.—Tame mice are descended from the common house mouse (*Mus musculus*), and it is believed that mice have been domesticated for over 3,000 years. Apart from albino or "white mice," there are many varieties that have been bred by the extensive "mouse fancy," and there is a wide range of coat colour and also different types of coat, *e.g.*, long-haired, short-haired, and rex. "Waltzing mice" have an abnormality of that part of the inner ear concerned with balance. Mice may live up to thirty months, and in exceptional cases attain the age of three years or more.

Housing.—Although strains vary, most tame mice require a warm even temperature and the same general remarks concerning temperature range, bedding, and wooden or metal cages apply as in the case of rats. If a solid floor is used, this should be covered with clean sawdust. It is a good plan to change to a clean cage regularly, except when the female (doe) is nursing her young. If the cage is large (as in the case of pet mice it should be, with a floor space of say 24 in. × 12 in. × 12 in. for a group of mice), inner nest-boxes should be provided—one for each doe if breeding is taking place, although two does will often share the same nest-box. (In changing to fresh cages the nest-box, with mother and young inside, may, of course, be moved over.) A "two-storey" cage, with a ladder or "staircase" to the upper part, is an attractive variation, although difficult to keep clean. Mice should be kept well out of reach of wild rodents, from which they may all too readily contract disease.

Feeding.—Mice have not quite such a wide dietary range as rats, but there are several different ways of feeding them, including the provision of special "mouse cubes." These mouse cubes are of varying composition. One of the most successful, devised by workers in the Medical Research Council's laboratories, is known as "Diet 41," and is made up of the following parts by weight: wholemeal flour, 45; Sussex ground oats, 40; fish meal, 8; dried yeast, 1; dried skimmed milk, 3; cod-liver oil, 1; and common salt, 1. Diet 41 has also been employed for rats and monkeys, although for the latter particularly it requires supplementing. It is perhaps worth emphasising that cod-liver oil must not be fed in excess (½% of the diet is quite sufficient, and should not be exceeded), or it may prevent breeding and possibly have other harmful effects. Cubed diets are best fed from a wire basket through which the mice enjoy gnawing and eventually pulling out the pieces. Wholemeal bread is excellent if not allowed to become stale, but it should not form the sole article of diet, and it is a good idea to feed it alternately with a grain mixture (made up of rolled oats, wheat and other cereal grains, or mixed bird seed). Up to about 5 per cent. dried brewers' yeast is excellent, and so is fresh or dried milk, especially for mothers that are carrying or nursing young. Cheese is relished, but may smell if not fed carefully. Mice sometimes like an occasional pinch of marmalade, and it is a good idea to provide lettuce or other greenfood every week or so. There should be a constant supply of fresh water, preferably from bulbs or bottles as described for rats.

Breeding.—Young mice may be weaned at twenty-one days, although it is usually preferable to leave them with their mother for a further week. The age at which mice are capable of mating varies considerably from one strain or individual to another, and while the average is six to eight weeks, it may be much younger. It is therefore desirable to separate the males from the females at or shortly after weaning.

Mice may be mated up at two to three months of age, and the best arrangements are one male (buck) to one or two females. A pair of mice or a "bigynous trio" makes a successful combination. The œstrus cycle is similar to that of the rat, but its length appears to vary with coat colour, being longest in the brown mice and shortest in blacks and albinos. The gestation period is usually from eighteen to twenty days, but may be prolonged if the female was still suckling her previous litter when she conceived. There may be up to twelve or more young in a litter, but the average litter size is from five to seven. The second litter is usually the largest, and subsequent litters tend to decrease in numbers, so that the sixth is usually smaller than the first. Breeding may take place all the year round, although, as with rats, fertility is higher during the summer months.

Handling.—Any rapid or rough movement may frighten mice and cause them to bite through fear. Mice should be lifted by the tail—not too near the tip—and may be held in the palm of the hand, where they may be suitably restrained by keeping the tail between two fingers.

Diseases.—Mice are unfortunately prone to many diseases, although the risks will be much lower if they are kept in suitable surroundings, great care is taken to avoid infection, scrupulous cleanliness is observed, and the standard of feeding is good. One common source of infection is the presence of the excreta of wild rodents on bedding or foodstuffs. A common disease is that sometimes called "*mouse typhoid*," caused by organisms of the Salmonella group. Although some mice recover, they may remain carriers of infection, and once this disease is diagnosed it is best to destroy the affected mice and those in contact with them, and not to employ any of the cages or utensils for fresh mice without adequate sterilisation. There are other septicæmia diseases of mice, and also virus diseases, including certain types of *pneumonia* and a condition known as *infectious ectromelia*. The accurate diagnosis of these calls for expert opinion and often for special bacteriological or other examinations. The mouse-owner should, however, be able to recognise signs of ill-health or departure from normal, one of the commonest being loss of appetite. In young mice the coat should be smooth and glossy. As mice get older there may be loss of pigmentation (in coloured mice) or even loss of fur. A sick mouse usually sits hunched up and has a ruffled coat, while the eyes may be partially closed or have some discharge. A healthy mouse will usually catch on to suitable objects when held by its tail and is capable of pulling quite hard, whereas the pull of a sick mouse is much weaker. If one or more mice die it is best to destroy at once any cage-mates that appear seedy. As in the case of rats, external parasites should be dealt with promptly with the aid of modern insecticidal preparations.

GOLDEN HAMSTERS.

Description.—There are many species of hamsters in the world, and more than one kind can now be bred in captivity. The one referred to, however, is the Golden Hamster (*Mesocricetus auratus*), a delightful little creature of which a full-grown female (females are larger than males) rarely exceeds 7 in. in length. This history of the domestication of the golden hamster is quite remarkable, for prior to 1930 only museum specimens were known. In that year a mother and her twelve young were dug up in a field near Aleppo and were taken to the Hebrew University, Jerusalem, and from that one family have been bred the hundreds of thousands of golden hamsters now employed as pets or as laboratory animals in many parts of the world. The species has taken well to captivity and, although capable of inflicting a nasty little bite if frightened or handled roughly, becomes docile and friendly when properly cared for. Characteristic features are the soft, smooth fur, the large black eyes, the "cheek pouches" in which food is stored and which may become enormously distended after a meal, the short, stumpy tail, and the extremely loose skin, inside which the hamster can turn round to a considerable degree.

Housing.—The same remarks about accommodation, environmental temperature, freedom from draughts, fittings, and other general considerations (including cleanliness) apply as in the case of rats and mice. For breeding purposes a dark inner chamber or nest-box is desirable. Several hamsters may be kept together, but the introduction of a stranger (or even the re-introduction of a former cage-mate that has been removed for some time) may lead to fighting.

Feeding.—Satisfactory diets include the following: (1) rat cubes (*e.g.*, "Diet 41"), carrots, greenfood, and milk; (2) cereal grains and/or wholemeal bread, carrots, greenfood, and milk; (3) steamed Rangoon beans, wheat, maize meal bread, a little Marmite, and milk. Care must be taken not to allow storage of excess food, which will deteriorate and cause a smell. Grass is a suitable source of greenfood during its growing season. Apples and other fruits are often relished. Water, preferably in bulbs or bottles as described for rats, should always be available.

Breeding.—Golden Hamsters attain puberty at from ten to fifteen weeks of age, or even younger, males being usually earlier. Generally speaking, it is best to defer breeding until after fifteen weeks of age. There is an œstrus cycle of about four days, and the gestation period is very short, averaging sixteen days, although sometimes up to nineteen days. Mating not followed by conception results in phantom or pseudopregnancy. Litter size varies from one to fifteen, but the average is six to seven. Not many females have more than four litters and although both sexes may live up to two years, breeding by the female is rare after nine months. The young are naked and blind at birth. Hair first appears at five days, and covers the whole body at eight days. The eyes open at about eleven days, and soon after this the young begin to take food for themselves and may be weaned at three to four weeks. Care must be taken that the female does not injure the male, and for safety's sake it is probably better to keep only one female and one male together and to remove the male before the young are born.

Handling.—Gentleness is essential, and sudden movements should be avoided. The tail is much too short to use, and the easiest way is to lift them by the loose skin over the back and shoulders. As already noted, they can twist easily within their skins, unless a substantial amount is taken in the hand. After picking up they may be allowed to sit on the palm of the hand.

Diseases.—Several diseases of hamsters are now known, and, like most rodents, they are susceptible to *Salmonellosis* (see notes under "mouse typhoid" and "paratyphoid" in guinea-pigs). One of the most prevalent conditions is *ear mange*, in severe cases of which the condition spreads from the ears to other parts of the body. Modern anti-mange preparations are highly effective.

CAVIES (GUINEA-PIGS).

Description.—Cavies or guinea-pigs (*Cavia porcellus*) are rodents, and are descended from one or more of the several kinds of wild cavy found in South America. They are believed to have been domesticated by the Incas long before Europeans "discovered" that part of the world. They make excellent pets, but are easily frightened, and should be treated gently and quietly. They usually behave quietly, although there may be fighting between adult males ("boars"), while the arrival of food—or the entry of a person into a room, which fact is obviously connected with feeding-time—usually sets up a chorus of chirruping squeaks. There is to-day a considerable cavy "fancy" in Great Britain and other countries, and many varieties are recognised, including rough-coated and smooth-coated types. Among recognised colours are the agouti (banded hairs), brindle, cinnamon, tortoiseshell (tricoloured), and Himalayan (white with attractive black points). The long-haired Peruvian and rosette-haired Abyssinian breeds are popular. Guinea-pigs may live up to two to three years. There is a small tail (composed of from five to seven caudal vertebræ), but usually this is so short that it does not project outside the body. There are four toes on each of the fore-feet and three on each hind foot. An adult guinea-pig may measure up to 10 in. or more in length, and sometimes its weight is well over 2 lb.

Housing.—Guinea-pigs may be kept outside or inside. If outside conditions are favoured, great care must be taken to protect them from dogs, cats, and rats. The last-named may be a danger also in conveying disease. The run should be in a sheltered position away from wind and direct summer sunlight. Tent-shaped waterproof shelters, with wooden floors covered by cleaning trays, have been found satisfactory. Another method is to keep them in hutches of the same type employed for rabbits and when conditions are suitable to let them out into a temporary run on the lawn surrounded by ½ in.-mesh wire-netting that is at least 12 in. high. (N.B. This will keep dogs or cats out.) Guinea-pigs will crop the grass and help to keep the lawn smooth. Great care should be taken not to allow the ground or floor to become so contaminated by guinea-pig excreta that it conveys disease from one animal to another.

If indoor methods are selected, an even, preferably warm temperature is desirable, and there should be freedom from draughts. Guinea-pigs have been found to thrive best at about 65° F. with a humidity range of 45–55 per cent. Provided warm conditions are available, metal cages are easier to keep clean than wooden ones, while a false bottom of wire mesh, above the cleaning tray, is helpful. Wood-wool is again the best bedding. Cages must not be too small, and a pair of pet guinea-pigs should have about 14 sq. ft. of floor space. It is a sound principle, as with rats and mice, to change frequently to a clean cage, the used one being cleaned and disinfected thoroughly before being used again.

Feeding.—Guinea-pigs, like human beings, apes, and monkeys, require a source of vitamin C (ascorbic acid). Normally they obtain this from greenfood, but in winter especially they may not secure enough in this way. The daily requirement of an adult guinea-pig is about 2 milligrammes, and supplies can be obtained from a chemist's shop.

There are many different methods of feeding guinea-pigs. Among cubed or pelleted diets is that known as "Diet 18," which is employed also for rabbits. It contains the following parts by weight: wheat feed, 15; grass meal, 30; decorticated groundnut meal, 15; linseed cake, 10; barley meal, 20; common salt, 1; and chalk, 1. This is fed together with fresh greenfood to supply vitamin C. For feeding without the use of compressed diets a good plan is to provide a daily "concentrate ration" of about 1 oz. per head of a mixture of 2 parts bran and 1 part crushed oats, and to feed in addition ample amounts of cabbage, lettuce or other greenfood, meadow hay of good quality, grass, and raw vegetables. Although guinea-pigs normally derive moisture from fresh greenfood, and may appear to take little or no water for long periods, it is a mistake not to provide a fresh supply, preferably from water bulbs, or from inverted bottles fitted with a stopper and drinking-spout. A little dried brewers' yeast makes an excellent addition to the diet, while for females ("sows") when pregnant or lactating, milk is excellent. Dead foliage should be removed from greenfood, and soil and dirt cleaned off. Frosted greenfood should be soaked in warm water before it is given to guinea-pigs. Unfortunately, hay may be contaminated by wild rodents, but it forms an excellent article of diet. Never allow food residues to remain in the cage.

Breeding.—The lactation period of the guinea-pig is a short one. The gestation period averages sixty-three to seventy-five days, although variations of fifty-eight to seventy-two days are known, and the young are born in an advanced state, with their eyes already open. They can run freely with their mother shortly after birth. They are able to nibble a little food as early as the second day, and by the time they are two to three weeks old they are completely independent and are neglected by their mother. A sow will often mate again the day the young are born, or shortly after, so that a rapid succession of litters often occurs.

Guinea-pigs are capable of mating from about fifty-five days of age, or even younger in certain circumstances, which include the provision of a high plane of nutrition. The œstrous cycle averages fifteen to seventeen days, although it may vary from thirteen to twenty-five days. The actual period during which mating may occur usually lasts only from about six to eleven hours. One boar may run with as many as twenty sows if so desired, but in the case of pets it is much more interesting to run a boar with only one sow, in which case she need not usually be removed to a separate cage before the young are born. The young guinea-pigs should be separated from the older ones shortly after weaning, and the sexes separated at four to five weeks of age if they are not to breed prematurely. It is better to wait until the animals are approaching six months of age or so before they are mated, for they do not become fully grown and "filled out" until they are between six and nine months.

Handling.—Guinea-pigs are timid creatures, and should be handled gently. They are best picked up with both hands. If a guinea-pig is to be held in order to examine it for any purpose, a good method is to place one hand over the animal's shoulders, with the fingers and thumb around its neck, and to extend its hind limbs with the other hand.

Diseases.—The most important infectious disease of guinea-pigs is, like "mouse typhoid," caused by organisms of the Salmonella group, and it may be contracted from wild rodents or from food or bedding contaminated by them. In guinea-pigs the disease is known usually as "*paratyphoid*" (or sometimes as "*salmonellosis*") and it may take an acute form, causing death within a few days, or a more chronic form in which many animals recover to become symptomless carriers of disease. Outwardly healthy, they may infect susceptible guinea-pigs with which they are placed. Cold or other environmental variations, and faulty feeding, can help to set off an outbreak, for there are few stocks in which the organisms are not lurking in some "latent carriers." *Coccidiosis* is common, but is a much less serious threat than in the case of rabbits. It has been set up in infected stocks by feeding inadequate diets, and provided that nutrition and hygiene are adequate there is rarely serious trouble from this disease. *Infections of the respiratory tract* may occur, but are uncommon except when there is overcrowding, high humidity, or damp bedding. Sometimes organisms of the Pneumococcus group cause not only disease of the respiratory tract but also a generalised infection of the serous membranes of the body. When this disease occurs it may produce death without much warning. It is possible that the infection sometimes comes from human beings. The disease known as *pseudotuberculosis*, and described under rabbits, occurs in guinea-pigs also. Again, environmental conditions and faulty feeding may predispose towards active infection.

With good fortune and sound management, trouble from these serious infections may never occur. *External parasites* should be dealt with promptly by insecticides. Sometimes *non-parasitic skin disorders* occur when the diet is faulty, *e.g.*, too dry or lacking in sufficient fresh greenfood of good quality.

RABBITS.

Description.—Domesticated varieties of the wild European rabbit (*Oryctolagus cuniculus*) are now kept in many countries. The wild rabbit is believed to have been introduced into Great Britain in the 12th cent. Tame rabbits have been bred for centuries, and the breeds and strains produced differ appreciably in size, colour, and habits from the common wild form. Some breeds have been specially bred for table purposes, while others (*e.g.*, the Angora, Sitka, and Argente de Champagne) have been developed for their fur. In addition, many varieties are produced for show purposes by the extensive rabbit "fancy." The small hardy Dutch rabbit (usually black and white) is one of the kinds suitable for beginners. Among well-known categories are the English, Japanese, Himalayan, Belgian Hare (really a rabbit), Flemish Giant, Beveren, Blue Imperial, Polish, Havana, Lop, Half-Lop, Chinchilla, and New Zealand White. The Copenhagen rabbit appears to be identical with the New Zealand White. The smaller breeds weigh only 4–6 lb. when fully grown, whereas some specimens of some of the giant breeds attain a weight of 20 lb. or more.

Rabbits and hares were formerly classified with the rodents, but are now placed in a separate Order of mammals, known as the Lagomorphs. Young rabbits (in contrast to leverets or young hares) are blind and helpless for some time after birth. Tame specimens may live for 4–5 years, and individuals have lived for up to 13 years.

Housing.—Since rabbits are kept for commercial purposes, various systems have been devised, including the use of movable ark-huts, with covered runs, that can be moved regularly to fresh ground. If kept indoors rabbits do not need special heating, but freedom from draughts, damp, excessive cold, and access by wild rodents is most desirable. A garage is regarded as an unsuitable place, owing to the susceptibility of rabbits to exhaust or engine fumes. One of the great difficulties of rabbit-keeping is coccidiosis, which is a serious disease in rabbits and hares. (European hares could never be bred successfully in captivity until means of overcoming coccidiosis were discovered.) With young rabbits especially (*i.e.*, those that have left the nest and are able to run about freely) it is a sound principle to move them to a clean floor or fresh ground every two days, so as to "break" the life-cycle of the coccidial parasite. One way of doing this is to have "back-to-back" cages or hutches, from one to the other of which the rabbits may be transferred easily. The empty cage or hutch may then be cleaned and disinfected thoroughly and allowed to dry out before the rabbits are returned to it. Wood-wool makes a suitable bedding material, although the female (doe) will pluck her own fur to line the nest when her litter is due to be born. Wire-mesh floors with a tray beneath are convenient, but if solid floors are used these should be sprinkled with fresh sawdust daily or every other day. Provided the standard of hygiene can be maintained, cages or hutches and their runs should be large. The absolute minimum is "1 sq. ft. of floor space for each 1 lb. weight of adult rabbit," *i.e.*, if there are two rabbits totalling 12 lb. in weight there must be at least 12 sq. ft. of floor space. If cages or hutches are stacked one on top of the other the lowest should be well clear of the ground, and if there is only one hutch this, for convenience and safety from wild rodents, should be 2–3 ft. off the floor.

Feeding.—The wild rabbit grazes at dusk and dawn, and it is preferable to feed tame rabbits twice daily, while pregnant or lactating does and young rabbits benefit from three meals a day. As in the case of guinea-pigs, the ration may be thought of as consisting of two parts, a concentrate portion and a portion consisting of greenfood and other succulent material. The concentrate portion consists usually of a mixture of cereal grains or of some other form of mash. Successful mashes, of which there are many, include: (1) a mixture of 4 parts cereal grains and 1 part dairy cake; (2) equal parts of bran, weatings, flaked maize—or barley meal—and fish meal. This second is useful for breeding. If materials for the mash are in short supply they may in part be replaced by cooked potatoes. An average daily food allowance for a resting (non-breeding) adult of medium size would be: greenfood (grass, clover, weeds, lettuce, etc.) and/or roots, 12–16 oz.; hay (good quality), 2–3 oz.; and concentrates (cereal grain or meal mash), 2 oz. If cooked potatoes are used they should be fed at the rate of 4 parts to each 1 part of cereal that they replace. For a doe nursing her litter a suitable diet would comprise: greenfood to appetite, hay (good quality and preferably containing clover or other legume), 2–4 oz.; concentrates (preferably with fish meal or some other suitable source of "animal protein"), 4–6 oz.; and common salt at the level of up to 1 per cent. of the ration. A mineral mixture is preferable to salt alone. Excessive greenfood, especially in the form of cabbage and other Brassica plants, may cause polyuria, *i.e.*, the passage of excessive quantities of urine. No matter how much fresh greenfood rabbits may have available, a supply of fresh water should always be provided. The daily water requirement of the rabbit is quite high, and certain bad habits such as urine drinking or even cannibalism may result from an inadequate intake of water. Pots that cannot be overturned or, preferably, water bulbs or bottles as described for guinea-pigs, are the most suitable means of providing water.

"Diet 18," described under guinea-pigs, is one of several types of compressed diet successfully employed for rabbits. Fresh greenfood is preferably fed in addition, while the water requirement with diets of this kind is considerable.

Breeding.—The age of puberty varies with the breed, and also with the time of year at which the individual rabbit was born. Rabbits born in spring are usually capable of breeding at a younger age than those born in the autumn. In Great Britain the wild rabbit has a fairly sharply defined main breeding season, lasting from January to June, but some degree of "out-of-season" breeding may take place at almost all other times. Tame rabbits may not breed freely during the winter months, especially if environmental conditions are cold. Mating may take place as early as four months of age, and although this does not often result in pregnancy, it is accompanied by competition and fighting between individuals of the same sex. Males (bucks) and females should therefore be separated at weaning, or at least before they are four months old. Fertile matings may occur at from about 5½ months of age onwards, but it is wise to defer breeding until later—say seven to eight months for most breeds. The female does not ovulate or shed her eggs from the ovary spontaneously as do most domestic mammals, but, like the cat and ferret, does so in response to the act of mating or some other strong stimulus. Even playing between two does may precipitate ovulation, in which case a so-called "phantom pregnancy" (pseudopregnancy) may result, the doe that has ovulated appearing pregnant and even developing lactating mammary glands. There is not therefore an obvious regularly recurring œstrus cycle as in the domestic rat, mouse, and guinea-pig, and in summer at least the doe may be ready to mate at almost any time. Observation suggests, however, that there are fluctuations in the desire to mate. The act of mating in rabbits sometimes causes alarm that all is not well to those that have not hitherto witnessed it, for the buck usually emits a peculiar cry and loses his balance to fall over sideways. It is usually best to separate the buck from the doe before the young are born. The gestation period is usually thirty to thirty-two days. In wild rabbits a high percentage of embryos die and are "resorbed," and are therefore never born. In some populations it appears that about two-thirds of all rabbits conceived (including about 60 per cent. of total litters) are lost before birth in this way. Losses from this cause are probably much less common in domesticated rabbits, especially when the standards of feeding and management are high. Litter size is variable, and depends in part on the breed or strain. In some strains mean litter sizes up to eight or nine have been obtained, but a mean of four or so is more common. Does that do not prepare the nest or rear their young properly should not be selected for further breeding. The doe with her new-born litter should not be disturbed unduly, or she may desert her young, which are blind and helpless at birth and are entirely dependent on her for at least three weeks, after which they begin to nibble food to supplement the milk that they receive from her. The eyes open at about fourteen days. Weaning should be carried out at between six and eight weeks of age, by which time the young should be able to fend for themselves completely.

Handling.—Rabbits should never be lifted by the ears alone. One good way of lifting them is to grip the ears firmly but gently with one hand and to place the other hand under the rump to take the weight of the rabbit's body. Alternatively, one hand may be placed flat under the rabbit's belly, but this requires more care, and may be a risky procedure with pregnant does. Another convenient way to handle rabbits, especially young ones, is to lift them by the loose skin over the shoulders. Rabbits can inflict quite nasty scratches with the nails of the hind feet. It is incidentally a good plan to examine the nails of all four feet and to trim them if they are too long. A stout pair of scissors, or preferably a pair of clippers, is used, and care should be taken not to cut back as far as the "quick," *i.e.*, the bluish portion at the base of the nail that contains blood vessels and will bleed freely if damaged.

Diseases.—As already indicated, *coccidiosis* is a highly important disease of young rabbits. It may be either of the "hepatic type," affecting principally the liver, or the "intestinal type," affecting principally the gut. Even in the case of the hepatic type, however, the coccidial parasites are picked up by mouth and after penetrating the intestinal walls make their way via the blood-stream to the liver. Hygienic measures are the best means of preventing the disease (see under **Housing**), but should it break out, prompt treatment with certain sulphonamides or other anti-coccidial drugs may prove effective. In certain rabbitries in which coccidiosis is a constant problem, protection has been obtained by feeding a dilute solution of one of the soluble sulphonamides in place of drinking-water. There are certain types of digestive disturbance that may resemble coccidiosis, and one of these, the cause of which has not yet been established with certainty, is known as *mucoid enteritis*. Some such cases are probably variations of "*bloat*" ("the blows") a condition the cause of which is again not fully established, although there may in fact be several factors. A rabbit may, of course, "blow" after eating fermentative food, but cases of "bloat" can occur independently of this, and some may be due to a virus. "*Snuffles*" is characterised by a nasal discharge, and is not always associated with the same organism. In its milder forms it is not a severe disease, but with the more chronic forms the nasal discharge becomes marked and gives rise to a typical snuffling noise. Severe chronic cases become progressively worse and die of a terminal pneumonia. There is also a severe acute form, in which the rabbit dies so rapidly that the condition is sometimes not recognised. Acute cases that are treated in time with certain sulphonamides may respond well, but chronic snufflers are difficult to treat and go on spreading the infection, and hence are better destroyed. Correct environmental conditions are a great help in preventing this disease. A chronic type of infection is known as *pseudotuberculosis*, which is usually acquired from eating material contaminated by wild rodents or by other infected rabbits. It is caused by quite a different organism from that of true tuberculosis, which is much rarer in rabbits. Clinical cases should be killed, and prevention lies in hygienic measures. Infected wounds or skin abscesses may lead to a disease caused by the "necrosis bacillus" (*Fusiformis necrophorus*) and known sometimes as *necrobacillosis* It is usually characterised by subcutaneous swellings distributed irregularly over the head and body. Although in the early stages the affected rabbit may remain in apparently good health, the spread of the disease is insidious and usually fatal, and in most instances it is kinder and safer to destroy a case before it progresses too far. There are unfortunately several other infectious conditions occurring in rabbits, but all call for expert help in diagnosis and treatment. Generally speaking, it is a bad policy not to cull an ailing rabbit immediately, and one that is ill should certainly be isolated at once and not fed or tended before the person looking after it touches the healthy rabbits.

Among non-infectious conditions *pregnancy toxæmia* is not uncommon in does during the very late pregnancy, and usually proves fatal within two to three days. It is a "metabolic disorder," *i.e.*, it is associated with some functional derangement of the endocrine or ductless glands or with the inability to control properly the utilisation of its food. Faulty feeding is probably a contributory cause. Diseases of the *heart and blood* may arise occasionally, and can be aggravated by faulty feeding.

Among external parasites, *ringworm* is not common, but may be acquired from rodents. Affected rabbits that are to be treated must be isolated. *Ear mange* (known usually as *ear canker*) is common, and may be treated by strict attention to hygiene, with thorough disinfection of the hut or cage, and by dressing with a modern anti-mange preparation. *Body mange* is much less common but far more difficult to treat.

Among internal parasites, so-called "*bladder worms*," *i.e.*, the larval stages of two dog tapeworms (*Taenia pisiformis* and *Taenia serialis*) are quite common, although rarely fatal. The feeding of grass or other greenstuff to which dogs have had access should be avoided, as well as the contamination of the drinking-water with dog fæces.

Domestic rabbits are susceptible to myxomatosis, and it is a wise precaution to have them vaccinated. The vaccine is inexpensive, and may be obtained through veterinary surgeons and pharmacists.

HEDGEHOGS.

Description.—The European hedgehog (*Erinaceus europaceus*), found throughout Great Britain, belongs to the Order Insectivora, of which moles and shrews are also members. Its diet is, however, by no means restricted to insects, although in nature a considerable portion is probably made up of small invertebrates. There is a good deal of prejudice against them as pets, owing to the fact that freshly caught specimens are usually infested with fleas or other external parasites. The spines of the hedgehog, being well-spaced, make the presence of external parasites more obvious than is the case in animals with a coat of close fur. The hedgehog's spines form its defence, and its capacity to roll up into a prickly ball at the threat of danger is well known. This defence reaction is unfortunately of no avail to it when the danger is an oncoming car or lorry, and thousands of hedgehogs die every years as a result of being killed by vehicles on the roads. Many other species of mammals wander on to the roads, but most attempt to flee when they sense the approach of a vehicle. The capacity to roll up is not secure defence even against animal enemies. There are some foxes, dogs, and cats that have learned to "uncurl" a hedgehog, and subsequently eat it.

Provided that care is taken, a hedgehog makes an excellent pet, especially if given a suitable enclosure in the garden. For a variable time during winter hedgehogs hibernate, and during this time they must not be disturbed. Should they emerge at any time however, food must be provided. Some specimens have lived for five years or more in captivity.

Accommodation.—The most satisfactory way to maintain a pet hedgehog is to provide it with a large "run" in part of the garden. If wire-netting is employed it should be sunk under the ground to a depth of several inches, or the hedgehog will burrow underneath and escape. The top of the run must be wired in, or alternatively there must be a "baffle board" or wire-frame (at least 9 in. wide) near the tops of the sides to prevent escape that way, for hedgehogs can scale wire-netting—and some other types of fence—with ease. There should be a warm, dry box for shelter, containing wood-wool or other bedding material. A simple but suitable shelter may be made out of a soap-box, preferably lined with asbestos sheeting or some other material impervious to water. A shallow sunken bath in the enclosure may be of interest, for hedgehogs take well to water, but the edges should be such that the hedgehog can get out easily.

If it is decided to keep a hedgehog indoors, then the best accommodation is probably similar to that described for ferrets.

Feeding.—The simplest diet consists of milk, some bread, and minced lean meat. Cooked meat is preferred to raw, but raw liver should be given occasionally. Another satisfactory diet comprises meat offals, "root" vegetables (*e.g.*, carrot, potato, and swede), and wheaten wholemeal biscuit, steamed together until cooked, and then mixed and minced with a small proportion of raw liver. A small quantity (say 1–2 per cent.) of mineral mixture is also desirable, and milk should be given freely. Although hedgehogs appear to drink but little water, a fresh supply should always be provided.

Breeding.—During the breeding season marked changes occur in both males and females, and the structures associated with reproduction increase enormously in size from about March onwards. The female is capable of having two litters a year, the first in May or June and the second in August or September. The period of gestation has not been determined exactly, but is believed to be thirty-five days, possibly with variations of up to well over forty days. During the breeding season the males are very pugnacious towards each other if females are with them, and may do each other considerable damage. (The mixing of strange hedgehogs is often a difficult procedure anyway, for they often fight and inflict nasty bites on one another's feet.)

The litter size is usually four to six, and the young, which have "soft" spines, are suckled by their mother for nearly six weeks. The young can partake of some solid food at about three weeks, and there is some evidence that if left with their mother for longer than six weeks she may compete unfairly with them for food!

Diseases.—Hedgehogs in captivity are susceptible to *respiratory infections*, and can sometimes contract certain strains of *human influenza.* They are susceptible also to *Salmonellosis* (see under mice and guinea-pigs). Fleas and other external parasites have been mentioned; these often disappear spontaneously as the hedgehog begins to thrive in captivity, but if not they should be dealt with by modern methods. The nails of a hedgehog may need trimming. (*See* **Rabbits.**)

LAND TORTOISES.

Tortoises are popular pets, but although many are kept with great success in Great Britain, the majority of those that are imported each year are never looked after adequately, or fail to thrive for other reasons.

Most land tortoises that are imported into Great Britain for sale through dealers are: (1) the Spur-thighed Mediterranean Land Tortoise (*Testudo graeca*), commonly known as the "Moroccan tortoise" and sometimes as the "Iberian" or "Algerian"; or (2) Hermann's Tortoise (*Testudo hermanni*). The second is distributed in Southern France, Southern Italy, the larger islands of the Western Mediterranean, and parts of Yugoslavia, Albania, and Greece. There is a species found in Greece, the Margined Tortoise (*Testudo marginata*), but while adaptable to life in Great Britain, it is more difficult to acquire. The two common species differ in several ways, the "Moroccan tortoise" having a small bony spur on the back of the thigh. (The upper part of the shell is termed the carapace and the ventral portion the plastron.)

In selecting a tortoise one should ensure that the animal appears healthy. It should be active and withdraw quickly into its shell on being disturbed. Its legs should be firm and not limp, and there should be no abnormal discharge from the eyes or nostrils. The shell and limbs should be uninjured. Females are generally larger and have a shorter tail than the male. The shield above the tail is flat in the former and curved in the male. It is a good idea to obtain a pair or more of tortoises, but not more than can be looked after with care. On being purchased they should be washed in tepid water.

Many tortoises are given free range in gardens, but this is not advised with all, as they eat a wide variety of vegetables and young plants, and being wandering animals are liable to get lost if the garden is not completely fenced or walled. They should be provided with as large a "pen" or "run" as possible, the walls or wire netting of which should be high enough to prevent their climbing over. The practice of tethering tortoises by a hole in the shell should be discouraged. They should always be provided with a box or shelter, the cheapest form being a wooden soap box turned on one side and with a sufficiently wide entrance, the wood being creosoted and covered with roofing felt. It can be lined with asbestos sheeting if desired, and have its floor covered with dry leaves or other bedding material. Some other shelter should also be provided in the run. The tortoises should be bathed during the hot weather. The occasional application of olive oil will keep the shell polished.

Land tortoises must be fed daily, and it is important to allow them to build up good reserves to enable them to hibernate through the winter successfully. Suitable foods include lettuce, young cabbage, peas, clover, dandelions, and a wide variety of green plants and ripe, sweet fruits. Generally bread and milk should be avoided. For young tortoises especially, it is recommended that once weekly or so the food should be sprinkled with powdered cuttlefish bone, or better still a small quantity of powered calcium gluconate or cod-liver oil. Fresh water in a shallow tray, or even a saucer, should always be provided.

One of the most difficult problems in tortoise keeping is hibernation. Some persons avoid allowing their pets to hibernate by transferring them to a warm place, such as a heated greenhouse; if this is done they must be kept well fed and their place maintained at a summer temperature. It is imperative to do one thing or the other—the half-torpid tortoise that is neither hibernating nor kept at summer temperature will die. Moreover, a tortoise that is allowed to hibernate must not be disturbed.

Signs of pending hibernation, including sluggishness and lowered appetite, are usually evident late in September or early in October. Tortoises living in the garden may commence to bury themselves. If this is allowed they must be well covered, else they may be killed by the ensuing frost. It is, though, more convenient and perhaps provides a greater chance of survival, due to the changeable winter conditions in Britain, to place the animal in a large box, which should be packed with straw, leaves, or hay. The box should be stored in a cool but frostproof place, such as out-building, cellar, or attic. It is important not to create conditions that will awaken the tortoise or tempt it to emerge before the following spring. Rats have been known to attack hibernating tortoises, and so due precautions should be taken.

On emerging from hibernation the eyes and nostrils are somewhat sealed, and should be released by bathing with a 4 per cent. boric acid solution and warm water.

Recently imported female tortoises frequently lay eggs, but it is not a common occurrence for pairs to breed freely in Britain. During the early part of the summer the male is sometimes seen butting the shell of the female, this being a courtship action. If eggs are laid it is unlikely that they will be fertile, and less likely that they can be hatched. They have been hatched by placing them on damp sand and storing them in a warm place—a heated greenhouse or airing cupboard. The eggs should not be disturbed or "turned" once incubation has commenced.

Tortoise ticks are often present on freshly imported specimens, and may best be removed by damping the tick with paraffin or methylated spirits and then removing it gently with tweezers. Round worms are very numerous in tortoises, and should they be seen in the faecal matter the remainder may be eliminated by sprinkling up to one grain of powdered santonin on the food once a week for six weeks. Possibly, some of the newer, safe anthelmintic preparations containing piperazine derivatives may be equally effective. Eye infections are common, and are usually remedied by bathing the eye well with a 4 per cent. boric acid solution or warm cod-liver oil. Continuous discharge from the nose indicates lung infection, and as a primary measure the animal should be kept warm. Bleeding can be stopped by using Friar's Balsam, and care should be taken to prevent insects settling on open wounds.

WATER TORTOISES (TERRAPINS).

In Great Britain the tortoises that have become adapted to life in ponds and rivers are usually termed " terrapins," the name turtle being applied to marine forms. In the U.S.A. and Canada, however, not only the marine species but also terrapins and tortoises are all termed " turtles."

Several kinds of terrapin are available and capable of thriving in Great Britain. These include several American species, the European Pond Tortoise (*Emys orbicularis*), the Spanish Terrapin (*Clemmys leprosa*), the Caspian Terrapin (*Clemmys caspica*), and the Reeves' Terrapin (*Chinemys reevesii*), which hails from China and Japan.

The ideal place in which to keep terrapins is a garden pond within an enclosure. The pond should contain an " island " of dry ground on to which the animals can climb easily. The water should vary in depth, and at one point be at least 2 ft. deep. Provided that there is a suitable " island " the boundary walls of the pond can be upright to prevent escape. The final coat of cement should be smooth and mixed with a waterproofing agent. Shade should be available, not only on the island but also in some parts of the water. This may be provided by suitable plants.

Terrapins are almost entirely carnivorous, although the young of some species may take a little lettuce or other vegetable food. Suitable foods include *small* pieces of raw meat, raw liver (this should certainly be given from time to time), fish, and earthworms. Terrapins prefer to take their food in the water, and it is best to feed them individually if there are several, to ensure that each receives his proper share.

Water tortoises also hibernate. Some bury themselves in mud or sand at the bottom of their ponds, others will dig themselves into the earth in the island or banks of their pond, while others again may go to sleep in the box that, as in the case of land tortoises, should preferably be provided for them on part of ther " land." Should they sleep at the bottom of the pond, it is as well to prevent freezing of the water. One means of doing this is to leave a log or logs floating on the surface. Moving these logs on cold mornings will help to break any ice formed and to prevent total freezing.

AQUARIUM FISH.

There are two types of aquaria—the cold-water, for fish from this and other temperate countries, and the heated, for tropical varieties of fish. Apart from the fact that a suitable heating mechanism—usually electric, with thermostatic control—has to be maintained for tropical aquaria, the general principles governing the two types are much the same. There is a certain amount of additional initial expense in setting up a heated aquarium—the running costs are not high—but in some respects tropical fish are easier to maintain than many of the cold-water varieties.

It should be emphasised at the outset that those who want to keep fish should invest in a proper aquarium and not in a " goldfish bowl," unless the latter be very large in relation to the fish to be kept. Far too many fish suffer from overcrowding or from lack of sufficient water surface. In the case of cold freshwater fish such as carp and goldfish (which need quite different conditions from tropical fish) it has been calculated that every " 1 in. of body " requires 1 sq. ft. of water surface in order to obtain sufficient oxygen for respiration. Thus a fish the body of which (*i.e.*, the length minus the tail fins) is 4 in. will require at least 4 sq. ft. of water surface, *i.e.*, an area of 2 ft. × 2 ft. Two such fish will require twice this area, and so on. In *The Right Way to Keep Pet Fish* by R. Dutta (6*s.*), it is pointed out that a goldfish should normally live for twenty-five years in a suitable pond, and grow to its full length of over 14 in. There are few indoor aquaria capable of supporting many full-grown goldfish in adequate conditions, and indeed it is recommended that domestic varieties of goldfish such as shubunkins, fantails, veiltails, and orandas, which grow more slowly, are far better adapted to cold-water aquaria. Tropical fish of the varieties kept in aquaria are usually much smaller, differ in their oxygen requirements, and can be kept in more crowded conditions. Many have an average body length of only about 1½ in., and eighteen such fish may be maintained in a suitably heated tank with an area of water surface of 18 in. × 12 in.

A beginner should not only read good books on the subject (including *Water Life* publications) but also consult experts and his local aquarist or dealer. Whatever aquarium is chosen, the conditions should be correct *before* any fish are introduced. Should fish be suddenly acquired, before a proper aquarium has been fitted up for them, they should be kept in some temporary (but sufficiently capacious) quarters until the aquarium is ready.

The instructions for installing and fitting up an aquarium are usually supplied, and should be followed carefully. The sand that is usually placed on the bottom should be thoroughly washed, and is best put in a little at a time. Make sure that the inside of the aquarium is thoroughly clean before anything at all is put into it. Ornamental rocks may next be introduced, and great care should be taken to ensure that these are of the correct type, unlikely to harm the fish physically or chemically. Water is then added very gently indeed, and suitable plants set. In the case of large tanks the planting is best done when the tank is only partly filled with water, but in any event the plants themselves should be kept wet all the time, or they may quickly shrivel up. In the case of cold-water aquaria everything may now be left for a few days—preferably a week or more—to ensure that all is well, and to allow certain micro-organisms that help form the food of the fish to develop. In the case of heated aquaria it is necessary also to ensure that the thermostat is working correctly and that the temperature is remaining constant or within very narrow limits. Here again it is advisable to wait at least a week before introducing any fish. Should conditions " go wrong " before or after the fish are introduced, it is best to start filling the tank all over again.

Fish should not be overfed, although regular feeding is essential. Attention must be paid to the feeding instructions issued with prepared fish foods, and to details given by the supplier of " live " foods. Provided fish are neither overcrowded not overfed, the amount of sediment that accumulates in the tank will not be excessive, but it should be siphoned away gently every month, or more often if necessary. Water lost by evaporation should be replaced, and in the case of heated tanks especially, it is most desirable that the added water be of the same temperature as that already in the tanks.

Certain species of water snail are often placed in aquaria to act as scavengers. It is necessary to ensure that, if snails are kept, they are of the right type, and it is important to consult experts on this matter.

Breeding is an interesting topic, there being both egg-laying and viviparous or " live-bearing " fish. The beginner is well advised to learn first how to keep fish in healthy condition in his aquarium before indulging in any planned breeding, and he should study the relevant information in books on the subject.

An aeration plant is often recommended on the grounds that it will increase the fish-carrying capacity of the aquarium. This is true up to a point, but overcrowding may bring other troubles besides those connected with lack of sufficient oxygen, and the golden rule is never to keep too many fish for the size of aquarium in question. Another factor to be remembered is that should the aerator break down it may leave the fish with less oxygen than their proper requirement. It has been recommended that an aerator is best thought of as a stand-by, to be employed only in emergencies, *e.g.*, when for some reason extra fish have to be added to a tank already holding all or almost all its proper capacity.

There are unfortunately many diseases of fish, and as yet scientific knowledge concerning many of them is far less detailed than it should be. It is clear, however, that environmental factors are responsible for many deaths or cases of unthriftiness, and among the factors concerned may be listed: overcrowding, overfeeding, the provision of a diet that is qualitatively inadequate, lack of "balance" in the aquarium leading to unsuitable conditions, dirt, too strong light, lead paint and noxious substances, that may somehow have come into contact with the water (*e.g.*, from the hands of the person tending them) or been absorbed from the atmosphere. One must be careful of such things as disinfectants, soaps, petrol, etc. In the case of tropical fish the temperature of the water may be incorrect. Should fish troubles occur, therefore, it is as well to consider these various possibilities, although one should not hesitate to seek professional advice where there appears to be a case of infectious disease. An ailing fish should certainly be removed from the tank (assuming that there are other fish present) and given separate quarters of its own if such a course is feasible.

It is not intended to provide a description of the separate diseases, although it may be mentioned that such signs as the appearance of material resembling cotton-wool (actual fungal growths) and "rotting" of the tail or fins, are among those that should lead the owner to isolate affected fish and to seek help immediately.

No attempt is made here to describe any of the many different species and varieties of fish suitable for private aquaria. Some of the "points"

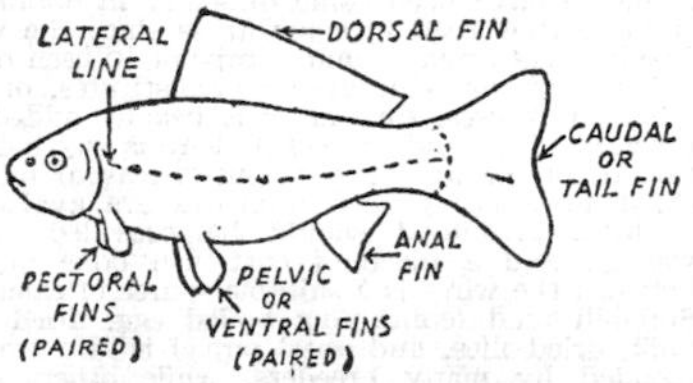

of a fish are shown in the accompanying illustration. Great care must be taken in mixing species, *e.g.*, "hard mouthed" and "soft mouthed" kinds should not be kept together. The temptation to put other species (*e.g.*, newts) with aquarium fish must likewise be avoided.

CAGE BIRDS.

Very many species and varieties of birds are now maintained successfully in captivity, and there exists in Great Britain a large and expanding "cage-bird fancy," that caters for a considerable proportion of the smaller birds adapted to cage or aviary life. The increase in the numbers of budgerigars since the end of the Second World War has been phenomenal, and it was estimated during 1957 that the numbers of the species alone in the United Kingdom exceeded 6 millions, the corresponding figure for the U.S.A.—where the popular name is "parakeets"—being over 18 millions.

The different types and sizes of birds have different requirements, and in the space available it is not possible to do more than cover the general principles and to deal briefly with the special characteristics of the management of the more easily maintained species. The beginner is advised to restrict his attention to one of the better-known species, *e.g.*, canaries or budgerigars, and not to attempt to maintain exotic varieties until he has acquired considerable experience.

Most species thrive best in aviaries, which may be indoor, outdoor, or of the combined "outdoor-indoor" type. An indoor aviary is usually all-wire and portable. The criticism of many such aviaries is that they tend to be high and narrow, whereas a fairly large floor-space is desirable. They should not be placed in cold or draughty places, nor too near a fire. If sited so as to receive much direct sunlight they must have adequate shelter. The wires must be close together, especially if smaller species are kept, a distance between them of about ⅜ in. being generally suitable. An outdoor aviary—suitable only for some species or at certain times in the case of others—should occupy a sunny position, although it too must include shade, and must be protected from winds. There ought in fact to be a sheltered portion, dry and well protected from the elements. The aviary must be strongly made and safe from all predators, including rats and mice. While it is often considered desirable to allow herbage to protrude through the wire-mesh floor, it is essential that the birds are never in close contact with wild rodents or their droppings. Most birds are highly susceptible to some forms of *salmonellosis* (see under mice and guinea-pigs), and can contract them in this way. It is advisable also that the roof of the aviary is solid: corrugated asbestos sheeting, projecting well clear of the edges of the uprights so as to prevent water and other matter from entering the interior, is excellent. The droppings of wild birds may be a potent source of bacterial infection or of internal parasites. To prevent close contact otherwise with wild birds, the wire or wire-netting "walls" of the aviary may be double. If an "outdoor-indoor" aviary is employed, there is usually an indoor flight cage, separated from the external portion either by a very light hanging door of suitable size, through which the birds can easily push their way, or by a sliding partition that the owner can operate as required.

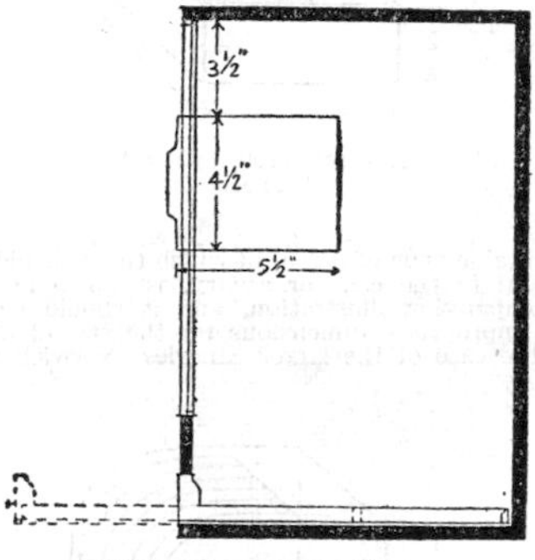

Section through Cage.

If an aviary is out of the question, then a suitable cage should be purchased or constructed. The cage need not be ornate—indeed simplicity of design usually facilitates the highly important task of keeping everything clean—but it must be large enough. A cross-section through a breeding-cage suitable for canaries, and for many other species, is shown in the accompanying illustration. Such a cage should measure about 40 in. in length × 12 in. wide × 18 in. high. It is constructed of wood or some suitable sheeting except for the front, which consists of vertical wires with horizontal stays, and can be divided into two parts by means of a suitable partition containing a removable section made of wire. By this means the cock and hen canaries can be introduced into the separate sections and develop a courtship before being allowed to be together for actual mating. The cross-section indicates the site and size of the removable portion of the partition, and it shows also the removable tray that is such an excellent fitting for almost any type of cage, and which greatly facilitates cleaning.

Whether an aviary or a cage is employed, it is essential to have proper fittings, including conveniently placed drinking-troughs, feeding-trays and bird-baths, and good perches. Much unnecessary discomfort is brought about through the use of unsuitable perches, or ones that are incorrectly situated or not sufficiently "firm."

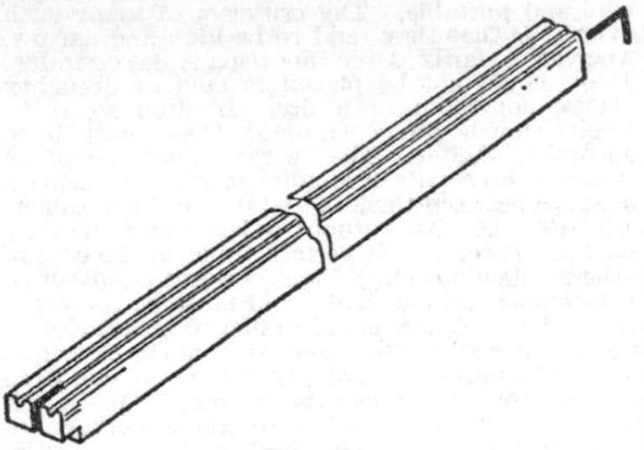

PERCH.

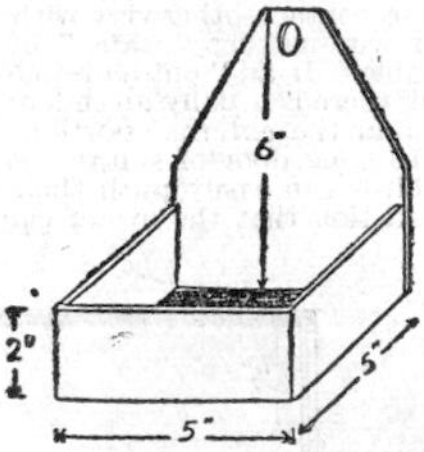

NESTING-BOX WITH PLAIN WOOD BOTTOM.

A suitable type of perch, of which there should be several in the cage or aviary, is shown in the accompanying illustration, and it should be of the appropriate dimensions for the size of bird. In the case of the larger canaries (Norwich and Yorkshire), *e.g.*, the sectional measurements should be $\frac{5}{8}$ in. × $\frac{3}{4}$ in., whereas for a smaller canary (Border) they should be $\frac{1}{2}$ in. × $\frac{3}{4}$ in. The type of perch shown is easy to clean and does not possess awkward corners in which parasites may be harboured. The dimensions of a nesting box a bird-bath, and a feeding-tray suitable for canaries are also given in the accompanying illustrations.

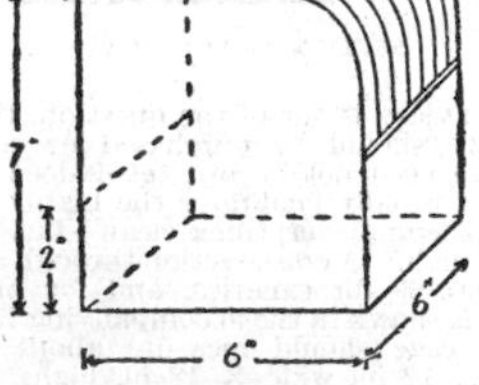

BIRD BATH.

While wood is a convenient material for aviary and cage construction, it has, of course, several disadvantages. Out of doors it is best creosoted (lead paint must never be used for places in which birds or other small animals are kept), and indoors it is better lined with hard asbestos sheeting. Metal is suitable—provided that it does not rust or corrode and that the environmental conditions are warm enough.

In all cases a supply of clean, fresh water should be available. Strict cleanliness should be observed, and professional advice taken immediately if a bird is not thriving.

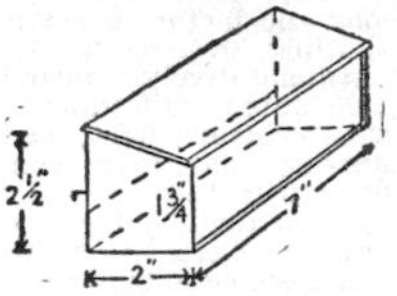

SEED TROUGH.

CANARIES (*Serinus canarius*).—These are domesticated forms of the race of wild serin found in the Canary Islands, and may live up to twenty-five years. Many varieties are known, and although most individuals are "canary yellow," other colours have been developed by fanciers. Many books have been written about the canary, although there is still much to be learned concerning its feeding and diseases—as is indeed the case with almost all cage-birds. The system of feeding generally recommended is based upon a mixture of 2 or 3 parts of canary seed (which is rich in energy, and which is sometimes mixed with a little millet seed) to 1 part of summer rape seed, which is high in fat and protein. There seems to have been some difficulty in obtaining suitable rape seed in some areas since the war. The best is German summer rape or Rübsen rape. Other seeds are employed as substitutes, or for special purposes, *e.g.*, niger is usually added at breeding time, and linseed if there is any indication of premature or soft (out-of-season) moult. Good proprietary seed mixtures are available. A little greenfood should be provided twice weekly, and a piece of cuttlefish bone placed between the wires is a suitable source of calcium. Soft-bill food (containing boiled egg, dried egg yolk, dried flies, and ants' pupæ) is also recommended by many breeders, while others give chopped egg alone. Others again favour milk, especially for young birds.

Breeding is usually started late in March or early in April, but not unless the daily shade temperature is at least 50° F. The pairs should be selected earlier than this and transferred to breeding-cages, with the partition in position. By the middle of February the wire partition may be installed so that the two birds can see one another. A little niger seed is usually added to the diet, while finely ground oystershell or eggshell may be sprinkled on the floor. (Otherwise the floor may be covered with washed sand that is not too fine and is free from dust.) When the birds begin to feed one another through the wire they are ready for mating, and the partition may be removed. The nest-box can then be inserted and suitable nesting materials, *e.g.*, cow hair and moss, placed in the cage. The incubation period is thirteen to fourteen days. After the eggs are laid some owners prefer to separate the cock and the hen, but allow him to rejoin her after the young are all about eight to nine days old and have opened their eyes. If it is desired that all the chicks be hatched together, then one can remove the first three eggs that are laid—usually one egg is laid daily—and keep them in a box at room temperature, substituting dummy eggs for them in the nest-box. On the afternoon of the third day of laying they are returned to the nest-box in place of the dummies.

When the young chicks are able to feed for themselves they should be provided with special food, such as egg and bread crumbs and a little cracked canary seed. If the cock bird interferes with them, or causes the hen to neglect them, he must be returned to his own section. Usually, however, all goes well, and the hen will go to the nest again when the first chicks are almost sixteen days old. Some three or four broods may be raised in a season.

WAXBILLS, FINCHES, AND OTHER SEED-EATERS.—The canary is of course a finch, but most of the other "foreign finches" are considered by dealers and writers together with other types of seed-eating birds. Well over 30 species of *Avadavats*, *Buntings*, *Mannikins*, *Cardinals*, *Whydahs*, *Weavers*, and *Finches* of various descriptions have been maintained successfully in capitivity in Great Britain. One of the most popular is the *Zebra finch* (*Taeniopygia castanotis*), from Australia, which has bred so successfully in this country that supplies no longer depend upon fresh importations, and which is already appearing in several varieties. The native bird, and many of its descendants, are grey and white, with red beaks. The male bird has orange cheek-patches, and orange flanks with white markings. The throat has black barring on a white background, and indeed the characteristic markings of the male have been the subject of interesting behaviour studies. The female lacks these special markings. The species is hardy, and is capable of living in outdoor aviaries all the year round, so long as it has shelter from draughts or strong winds and adequate facilities for roosting. If provided with nest-boxes, the birds will attempt—often successfully—to breed all the year round, so to avoid overbreeding it is better to remove these boxes in winter. A mixture of millet and canary seed forms the basis of their diet, which should be supplemented with fresh greenfood, millet sprays, fine grit, and cuttlebone—and, of course, fresh water should be available. Another bird suitable for the relatively uninitiated bird-keeper is the *Bengalese* (a domestic variety of *Munia striata*). It seems that these birds are the result of careful breeding by the Japanese, and may be regarded as fertile hybrids. Three main forms, the Chocolate-and-White, the Fawn-and-White, and the White, have been developed. These birds will thrive in cages or in aviaries. As in the case of Zebra Finches, they will attempt to breed all the year round if provided with nest-boxes. Bengalese are sociable birds, sometimes known in the U.S.A. as Society Finches. They appear to require less additional food than most species, thriving on a mixture of canary and millet seed, together with grit, cuttlebone, and an occasional millet spray or item of greenstuff.

For details of these birds, and of the many others from which a selection may be made, works of reference should be consulted. Three very useful books, all published by Cage Birds, London, are *Foreign Bird Keeping*, by Edward J. Boosey (63*s*.), *Foreign Birds for Beginners*, by D. H. S. Risdon (10*s*. 6*d*.), and *Foreign Birds for Garden Aviaries*, by Alec Brooksbank (10*s*. 6*d*.).

BUDGERIGARS.—The increase in the popularity of this bird has been phenomenal, although to those who have experience of other birds as pets the reasons are soon fairly obvious. Apart from the capacity to talk, shown by many birds—especially males—kept alone and trained, there is a liveliness, almost a "cheekiness," and an apparent like of human companionship. The wild green budgerigar (*Melopsittacus undulatus*) exists in large numbers in the grassland and desert shrub regions of Australia. The usual colour is grass green—it is frequently known as the Grass Parakeet—with a yellow mask, with three black spots on either side. As a result of intensive breeding, a considerable number of colour varieties has been produced, and the genetics of colour are a constant source of interest to budgerigar breeders. A vast budgerigar "fancy" has been built up in the United Kingdom, the U.S.A., and other countries, and World Budgerigar Congresses are held every few years. Budgerigars will thrive in outdoor aviaries all the year round, but the vast majority are kept as indoor pets in cages or small aviaries. The cages can be similar to those used for canaries, and care should be taken that the perches are of the correct diameter. If nest-boxes are put up, and the environmental conditions are suitable, budgerigars suitably paired will breed at almost any time of the year. It is customary, however, to restrict breeding to the spring, summer, and early autumn. Overbreeding may lead to difficulties, including the production of "runners" or "French moult." The sexes may normally be distinguished, at any rate in mature individuals, by the colour of the cere at the base of the beak, which is blue in males and brown in females. Males may lose their colour if not in good condition and for other reasons.

There are now many proprietary seeds mixtures, but some owners prefer to make up their own mixtures of millet (usually mixing small yellow and large white varieties) and canary seed. Millet sprays, fresh greenfood, good grit, and cuttlebone are all desirable, and it is important that the correct size and consistency of grit be chosen. Variety in "extras" to the basal seeds diet is probably important, for the captive bird has not the same opportunities as its wild ancestors for ranging widely for, possibly, important trace items of food. Breeding birds secrete a "milk," comparable with the crop milk of pigeons and some other birds, and this is of importance in the early feeding of the young.

Most healthy budgerigars seem to live to the age of 5–7 years or more, and considerably greater ages have been attained in captivity.

Such is the development of the budgerigar fancy that most equipment as well as food can be obtained ready for use. The playful habits of budgerigars have led to their being given table-tennis balls or a variety of small toys to play with, while some forms of food are supplied as budgerigar bells or otherwise in special shapes that seem to amuse the birds as they take the constituent seed from them.

The study of budgerigar diseases is in its infancy, but already some important facts have become realised. *French moult* is certainly reproducible by overbreeding, and may be linked with deficiencies in the ability of the parent birds to feed their young—or to hand over to them at the time of laying sufficient nutritional reserves to carry them through hatching and parental feeding until the time that they can fend for themselves. A deficiency in the "milk" has been shown in some cases, and may be generally true. Large chicks can be produced by killing off or removing all but a single member of the clutch, and allowing the parents to deal with it alone.

A mite infestation, due to *Cnemidocoptes pilae*, may give rise to *Scaly face*, *Scaly beak*, or *Scaly leg*, for which veterinary treatment is now available. Another condition, known as *Brown hypertrophy of the cere*, is characterised by thickening and darkening of the surface of the cere. In the early stages it is sometimes thought that the bird is changing its sex. There is no known successful treatment at the time of writing, and if the overgrowth is cut away it will only reform. There are various disturbances of the *digestive tract*, and some of these may be associated with inability to stand properly.

There are many treatises on the budgerigar. A useful little work is *Budgerigar Guide*, by Cessa Feyerbrand (Fond du Lac, Wisconsin: All-Pets Magazine).

LOVEBIRDS AND PARROTLETS are also members of the parrot family, and while they are unlikely to equal the budgerigar in popularity, they are nevertheless interesting birds that are being kept in increasing numbers as pets. Lovebirds, of the genus *Agapornis*, are African in origin, and some six species are commonly kept in captivity. Parrotlets derive from South America, the commonest species being the Guiana Parrotlet, *Forpus passerinus*. Both types of bird are relatively simple to maintain in aviaries or large cages, and their basal diet (which should be supplemented widely) is a mixture of millet and canary seed. They are hardy and vigorous creatures, many details of which are to be found in condensed form in *Lovebirds and Parrotlets*, by C. P. Luke (London: Cage Birds, 8*s*. 6*d*.).

CALENDAR FOR 1966.

January

S	M	T	W	T	F	S
.	.	.	.	.	.	1
2	3	4	5	6	7	8
9	10	11	12	13	14	15
16	17	18	19	20	21	22
23	24	25	26	27	28	29
30	31	.	.	.	.	.

February

S	M	T	W	T	F	S
.	.	1	2	3	4	5
6	7	8	9	10	11	12
13	14	15	16	17	18	19
20	21	22	23	24	25	26
27	28	.	.	.	.	.
.	.	.	.	.	.	.

March

S	M	T	W	T	F	S
.	.	1	2	3	4	5
6	7	8	9	10	11	12
13	14	15	16	17	18	19
20	21	22	23	24	25	26
27	28	29	30	31	.	.
.	.	.	.	.	.	.

April

S	M	T	W	T	F	S
.	.	.	.	.	1	2
3	4	5	6	7	8	9
10	11	12	13	14	15	16
17	18	19	20	21	22	23
24	25	26	27	28	29	30
.	.	.	.	.	.	.

May

S	M	T	W	T	F	S
1	2	3	4	5	6	7
8	9	10	11	12	13	14
15	16	17	18	19	20	21
22	23	24	25	26	27	28
29	30	31	.	.	.	.
.	.	.	.	.	.	.

June

S	M	T	W	T	F	S
.	.	.	1	2	3	4
5	6	7	8	9	10	11
12	13	14	15	16	17	18
19	20	21	22	23	24	25
26	27	28	29	30	.	.
.	.	.	.	.	.	.

July

S	M	T	W	T	F	S
.	.	.	.	.	1	2
3	4	5	6	7	8	9
10	11	12	13	14	15	16
17	18	19	20	21	22	23
24	25	26	27	28	29	30
31	.	.	.	.	.	.

August

S	M	T	W	T	F	S
.	1	2	3	4	5	6
7	8	9	10	11	12	13
14	15	16	17	18	19	20
21	22	23	24	25	26	27
28	29	30	31	.	.	.
.	.	.	.	.	.	.

September

S	M	T	W	T	F	S
.	.	.	.	1	2	3
4	5	6	7	8	9	10
11	12	13	14	15	16	17
18	19	20	21	22	23	24
25	26	27	28	29	30	.
.	.	.	.	.	.	.

October

S	M	T	W	T	F	S
.	.	.	.	.	.	1
2	3	4	5	6	7	8
9	10	11	12	13	14	15
16	17	18	19	20	21	22
23	24	25	26	27	28	29
30	31	.	.	.	.	.

November

S	M	T	W	T	F	S
.	.	1	2	3	4	5
6	7	8	9	10	11	12
13	14	15	16	17	18	19
20	21	22	23	24	25	26
27	28	29	30	.	.	.
.	.	.	.	.	.	.

December

S	M	T	W	T	F	S
.	.	.	.	1	2	3
4	5	6	7	8	9	10
11	12	13	14	15	16	17
18	19	20	21	22	23	24
25	26	27	28	29	30	31
.	.	.	.	.	.	.

CALENDAR FOR 1967.

January

S	M	T	W	T	F	S
1	2	3	4	5	6	7
8	9	10	11	12	13	14
15	16	17	18	19	20	21
22	23	24	25	26	27	28
29	30	31	.	.	.	.
.	.	.	.	.	.	.

February

S	M	T	W	T	F	S
.	.	.	1	2	3	4
5	6	7	8	9	10	11
12	13	14	15	16	17	18
19	20	21	22	23	24	25
26	27	28	.	.	.	.
.	.	.	.	.	.	.

March

S	M	T	W	T	F	S
.	.	.	1	2	3	4
5	6	7	8	9	10	11
12	13	14	15	16	17	18
19	20	21	22	23	24	25
26	27	28	29	30	31	.
.	.	.	.	.	.	.

April

S	M	T	W	T	F	S
.	.	.	.	.	.	1
2	3	4	5	6	7	8
9	10	11	12	13	14	15
16	17	18	19	20	21	22
23	24	25	26	27	28	29
30	.	.	.	.	.	.

May

S	M	T	W	T	F	S
.	1	2	3	4	5	6
7	8	9	10	11	12	13
14	15	16	17	18	19	20
21	22	23	24	25	26	27
28	29	30	31	.	.	.
.	.	.	.	.	.	.

June

S	M	T	W	T	F	S
.	.	.	.	1	2	3
4	5	6	7	8	9	10
11	12	13	14	15	16	17
18	19	20	21	22	23	24
25	26	27	28	29	30	.
.	.	.	.	.	.	.

July

S	M	T	W	T	F	S
.	.	.	.	.	.	1
2	3	4	5	6	7	8
9	10	11	12	13	14	15
16	17	18	19	20	21	22
23	24	25	26	27	28	29
30	31	.	.	.	.	.

August

S	M	T	W	T	F	S
.	.	1	2	3	4	5
6	7	8	9	10	11	12
13	14	15	16	17	18	19
20	21	22	23	24	25	26
27	28	29	30	31	.	.
.	.	.	.	.	.	.

September

S	M	T	W	T	F	S
.	.	.	.	.	1	2
3	4	5	6	7	8	9
10	11	12	13	14	15	16
17	18	19	20	21	22	23
24	25	26	27	28	29	30
.	.	.	.	.	.	.

October

S	M	T	W	T	F	S
1	2	3	4	5	6	7
8	9	10	11	12	13	14
15	16	17	18	19	20	21
22	23	24	25	26	27	28
29	30	31	.	.	.	.
.	.	.	.	.	.	.

November

S	M	T	W	T	F	S
.	.	.	1	2	3	4
5	6	7	8	9	10	11
12	13	14	15	16	17	18
19	20	21	22	23	24	25
26	27	28	29	30	.	.
.	.	.	.	.	.	.

December

S	M	T	W	T	F	S
.	.	.	.	.	1	2
3	4	5	6	7	8	9
10	11	12	13	14	15	16
17	18	19	20	21	22	23
24	25	26	27	28	29	30
31	.	.	.	.	.	.

CALENDAR FOR 1968.

January

S	M	T	W	T	F	S
.	1	2	3	4	5	6
7	8	9	10	11	12	13
14	15	16	17	18	19	20
21	22	23	24	25	26	27
28	29	30	31	.	.	.
.	.	.	.	.	.	.

February

S	M	T	W	T	F	S
.	.	.	.	1	2	3
4	5	6	7	8	9	10
11	12	13	14	15	16	17
18	19	20	21	22	23	24
25	26	27	28	29	.	.
.	.	.	.	.	.	.

March

S	M	T	W	T	F	S
.	.	.	.	.	1	2
3	4	5	6	7	8	9
10	11	12	13	14	15	16
17	18	19	20	21	22	23
24	25	26	27	28	29	30
31	.	.	.	.	.	.

April

S	M	T	W	T	F	S
.	1	2	3	4	5	6
7	8	9	10	11	12	13
14	15	16	17	18	19	20
21	22	23	24	25	26	27
28	29	30	.	.	.	.
.	.	.	.	.	.	.

May

S	M	T	W	T	F	S
.	.	.	1	2	3	4
5	6	7	8	9	10	11
12	13	14	15	16	17	18
19	20	21	22	23	24	25
26	27	28	29	30	31	.
.	.	.	.	.	.	.

June

S	M	T	W	T	F	S
.	.	.	.	.	.	1
2	3	4	5	6	7	8
9	10	11	12	13	14	15
16	17	18	19	20	21	22
23	24	25	26	27	28	29
30	.	.	.	.	.	.

July

S	M	T	W	T	F	S
.	1	2	3	4	5	6
7	8	9	10	11	12	13
14	15	16	17	18	19	20
21	22	23	24	25	26	27
28	29	30	31	.	.	.
.	.	.	.	.	.	.

August

S	M	T	W	T	F	S
.	.	.	.	1	2	3
4	5	6	7	8	9	10
11	12	13	14	15	16	17
18	19	20	21	22	23	24
25	26	27	28	29	30	31
.	.	.	.	.	.	.

September

S	M	T	W	T	F	S
1	2	3	4	5	6	7
8	9	10	11	12	13	14
15	16	17	18	19	20	21
22	23	24	25	26	27	28
29	30	.	.	.	.	.
.	.	.	.	.	.	.

October

S	M	T	W	T	F	S
.	.	1	2	3	4	5
6	7	8	9	10	11	12
13	14	15	16	17	18	19
20	21	22	23	24	25	26
27	28	29	30	31	.	.
.	.	.	.	.	.	.

November

S	M	T	W	T	F	S
.	.	.	.	.	1	2
3	4	5	6	7	8	9
10	11	12	13	14	15	16
17	18	19	20	21	22	23
24	25	26	27	28	29	30
.	.	.	.	.	.	.

December

S	M	T	W	T	F	S
1	2	3	4	5	6	7
8	9	10	11	12	13	14
15	16	17	18	19	20	21
22	23	24	25	26	27	28
29	30	31	.	.	.	.
.	.	.	.	.	.	.

CALENDAR FOR 1969.

January

S	M	T	W	T	F	S
.	.	.	1	2	3	4
5	6	7	8	9	10	11
12	13	14	15	16	17	18
19	20	21	22	23	24	25
26	27	28	29	30	31	.
.	.	.	.	.	.	.

February

S	M	T	W	T	F	S
.	.	.	.	.	.	1
2	3	4	5	6	7	8
9	10	11	12	13	14	15
16	17	18	19	20	21	22
23	24	25	26	27	28	.
.	.	.	.	.	.	.

March

S	M	T	W	T	F	S
.	.	.	.	.	.	1
2	3	4	5	6	7	8
9	10	11	12	13	14	15
16	17	18	19	20	21	22
23	24	25	26	27	28	29
30	31	.	.	.	.	.

April

S	M	T	W	T	F	S
.	.	1	2	3	4	5
6	7	8	9	10	11	12
13	14	15	16	17	18	19
20	21	22	23	24	25	26
27	28	29	30	.	.	.
.	.	.	.	.	.	.

May

S	M	T	W	T	F	S
.	.	.	.	1	2	3
4	5	6	7	8	9	10
11	12	13	14	15	16	17
18	19	20	21	22	23	24
25	26	27	28	29	30	31
.	.	.	.	.	.	.

June

S	M	T	W	T	F	S
1	2	3	4	5	6	7
8	9	10	11	12	13	14
15	16	17	18	19	20	21
22	23	24	25	26	27	28
29	30	.	.	.	.	.
.	.	.	.	.	.	.

July

S	M	T	W	T	F	S
.	.	1	2	3	4	5
6	7	8	9	10	11	12
13	14	15	16	17	18	19
20	21	22	23	24	25	26
27	28	29	30	31	.	.
.	.	.	.	.	.	.

August

S	M	T	W	T	F	S
.	.	.	.	.	1	2
3	4	5	6	7	8	9
10	11	12	13	14	15	16
17	18	19	20	21	22	23
24	25	26	27	28	29	30
31	.	.	.	.	.	.

September

S	M	T	W	T	F	S
.	1	2	3	4	5	6
7	8	9	10	11	12	13
14	15	16	17	18	19	20
21	22	23	24	25	26	27
28	29	30	.	.	.	.
.	.	.	.	.	.	.

October

S	M	T	W	T	F	S
.	.	.	1	2	3	4
5	6	7	8	9	10	11
12	13	14	15	16	17	18
19	20	21	22	23	24	25
26	27	28	29	30	31	.
.	.	.	.	.	.	.

November

S	M	T	W	T	F	S
.	.	.	.	.	.	1
2	3	4	5	6	7	8
9	10	11	12	13	14	15
16	17	18	19	20	21	22
23	24	25	26	27	28	29
30	.	.	.	.	.	.

December

S	M	T	W	T	F	S
.	1	2	3	4	5	6
7	8	9	10	11	12	13
14	15	16	17	18	19	20
21	22	23	24	25	26	27
28	29	30	31	.	.	.
.	.	.	.	.	.	.

ATLAS OF THE WORLD

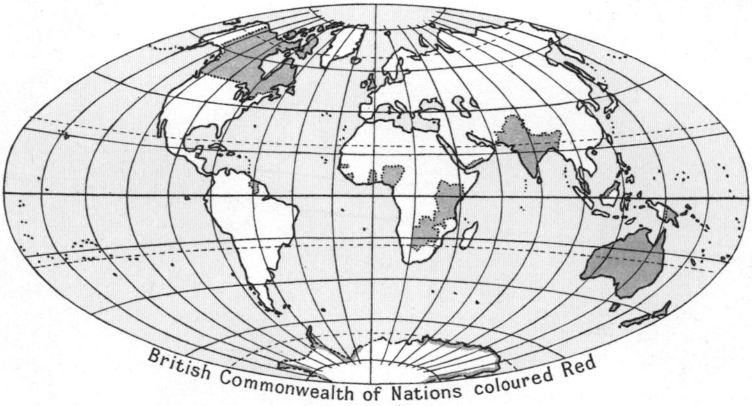

CONTENTS

PRINTED BY JOHN BARTHOLOMEW AND SON, LTD.,
AT THE GEOGRAPHICAL INSTITUTE, EDINBURGH

2824

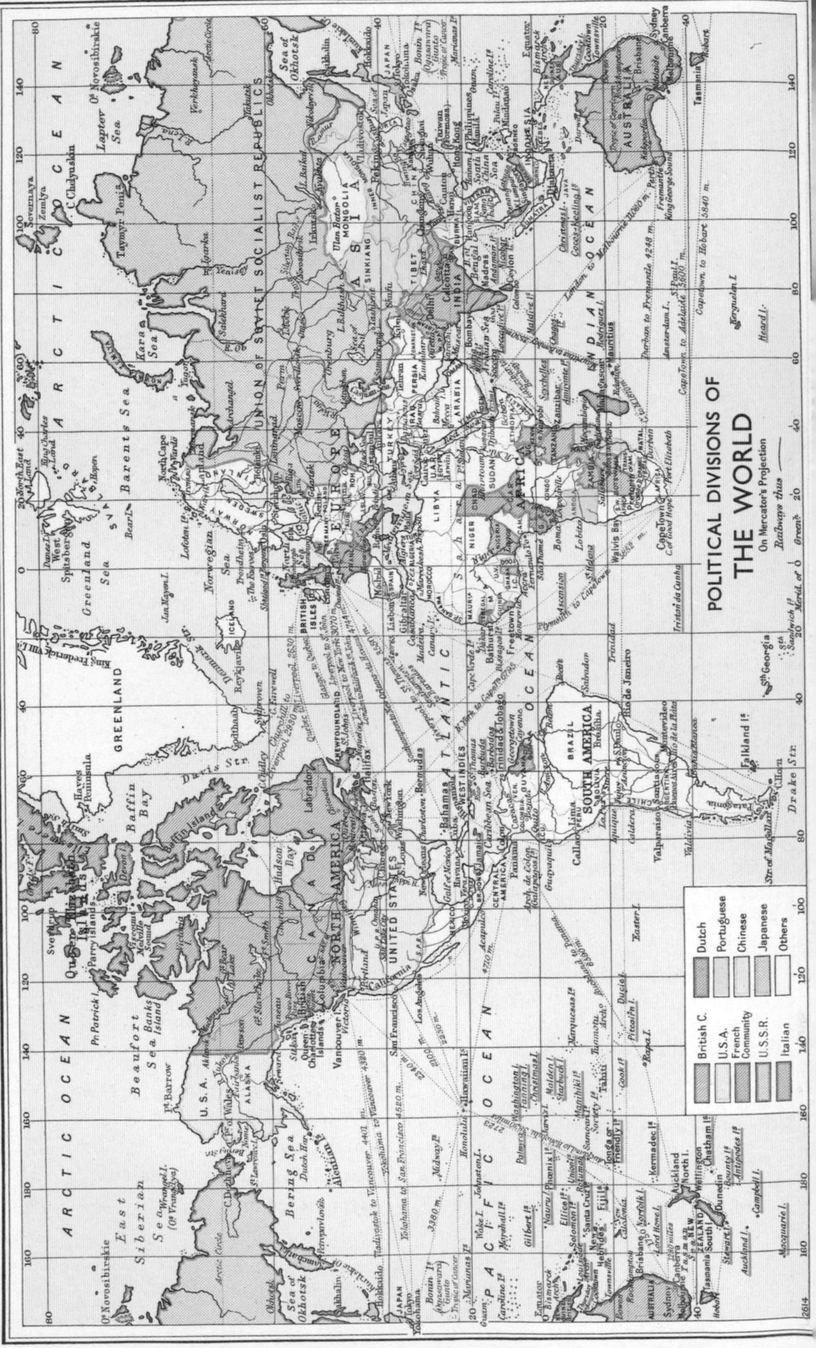
POLITICAL DIVISIONS OF
THE WORLD
On Mercator's Projection
Railways thus
British C.
U.S.A.
French Community
U.S.S.R.
Italian
Dutch
Portuguese
Chinese
Japanese
Others

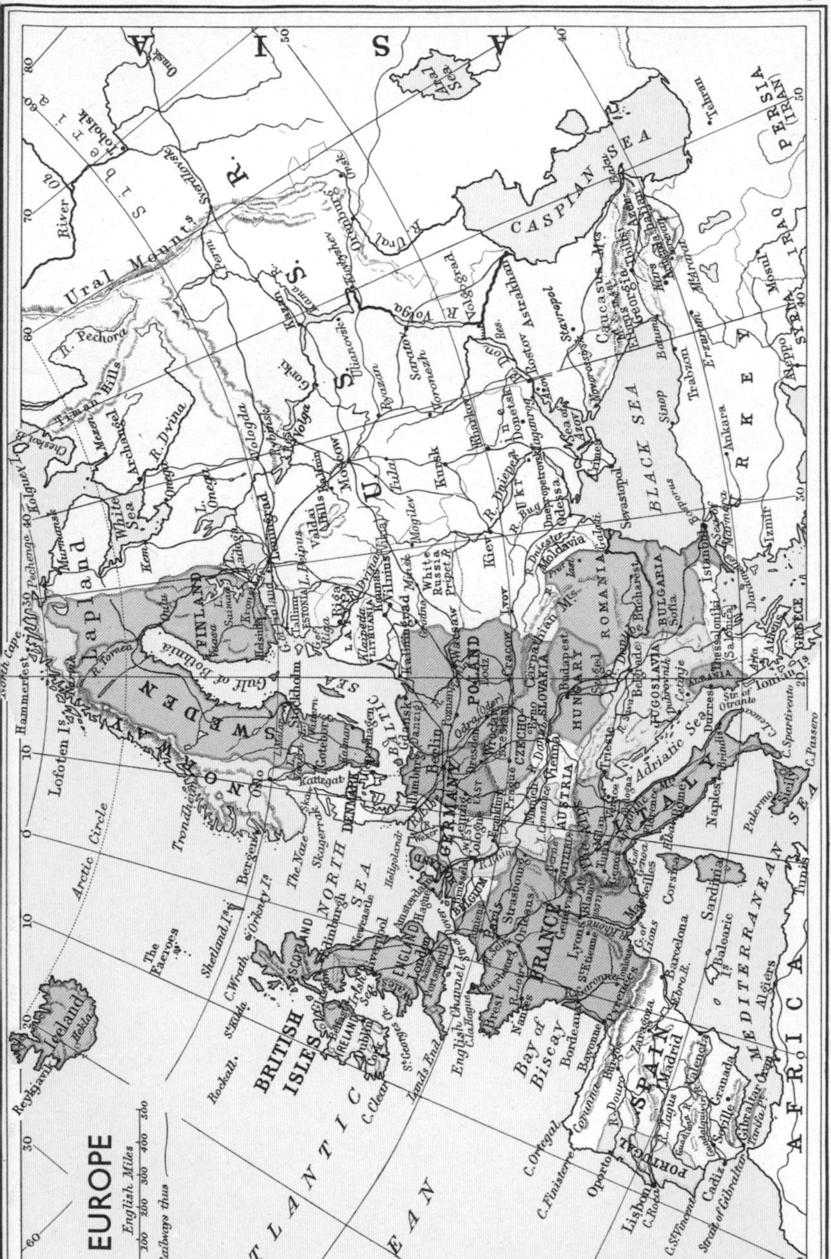
EUROPE
English Miles
0 100 200 300 400 500
Railways thus
ATLANTIC
OCEAN
BRITISH ISLES
NORTH SEA
BALTIC SEA
BLACK SEA
CASPIAN SEA
MEDITERRANEAN SEA
AFRICA
Adriatic Sea
Bay of Biscay
Arctic Circle
Iceland
SCOTLAND
ENGLAND
IRELAND
FRANCE
SPAIN
PORTUGAL
ITALY
GERMANY
POLAND
CZECHOSLOVAKIA
AUSTRIA
HUNGARY
ROMANIA
BULGARIA
YUGOSLAVIA
ALBANIA
GREECE
DENMARK
NORWAY
SWEDEN
FINLAND
Lapland
ESTONIA
LATVIA
LITHUANIA
BELGIUM
SWITZERLAND
TURKEY
PERSIA (IRAN)
IRAQ
SYRIA
U.S.S.R.
Siberia
Ural Mounts
Caucasus Mts
Aral Sea
Moscow
Leningrad
Kiev
Berlin
Paris
London
Madrid
Lisbon
Rome
Vienna
Budapest
Warsaw
Stockholm
Oslo
Helsinki
Istanbul
Ankara
Athens
Sofia
Belgrade
Bucharest
Prague
Copenhagen
Reykjavik
Tehran

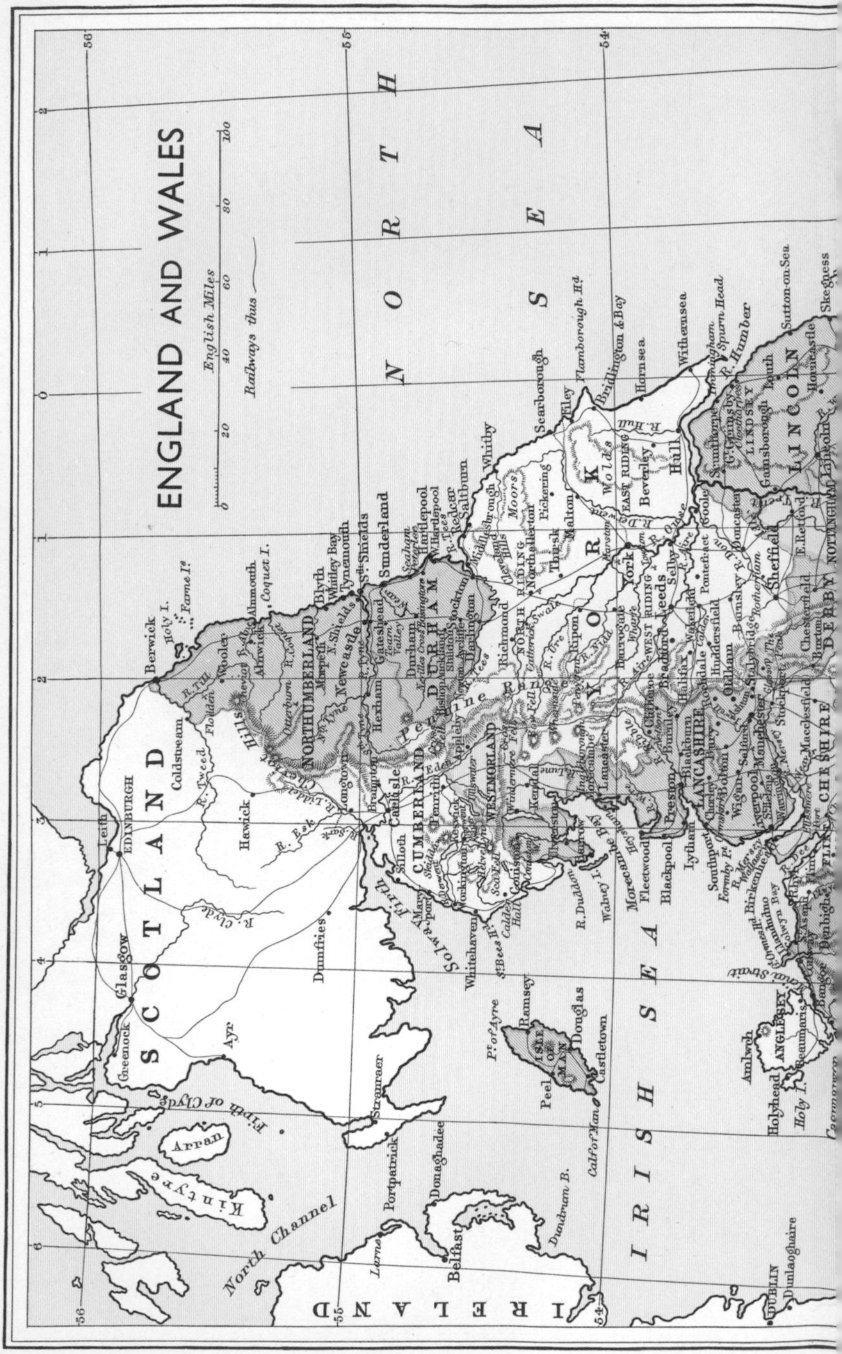
ENGLAND AND WALES
English Miles
0
20
40
60
80
100
Railways thus
NORTH SEA
IRISH SEA
SCOTLAND
IRELAND
North Channel
Firth of Clyde
Arran
Kintyre
Solway Firth
ISLE OF MAN
NORTHUMBERLAND
DURHAM
CUMBERLAND
WESTMORLAND
LANCASHIRE
CHESHIRE
DERBY
NOTTINGHAM
LINCOLN
LINDSEY
FLINT
ANGLESEY
NORTH RIDING
EAST RIDING
WEST RIDING
YORK
Pennine Range
Cheviot Hills
Edinburgh
Leith
Glasgow
Greenock
Ayr
Dumfries
Stranraer
Portpatrick
Donaghadee
Belfast
Larne
Dublin
Dunlaoghaire
Berwick
Holy I.
Farne Is
Coquet I.
Alnmouth
Alnwick
Wooler
Coldstream
Hawick
Blyth
Whitley Bay
Tynemouth
St. Shields
Sunderland
Newcastle
Gateshead
Hexham
Morpeth
Durham
Hartlepool
Redcar
Saltburn
Whitby
Stockton
Darlington
Middlesbrough
Carlisle
Longtown
Brampton
Silloth
Penrith
Keswick
Cockermouth
Workington
Whitehaven
St. Bees Hd.
Appleby
Kendal
Windermere
Coniston
Barrow
Ulverston
Walney I.
Lancaster
Morecambe
Morecambe Bay
Fleetwood
Blackpool
Preston
Lytham
Southport
Blackburn
Burnley
Bolton
Wigan
Liverpool
Birkenhead
Manchester
Oldham
Rochdale
Halifax
Huddersfield
Bradford
Leeds
Wakefield
Barnsley
Sheffield
Rotherham
Doncaster
Goole
Selby
York
Harrogate
Ripon
Thirsk
Northallerton
Richmond
Malton
Pickering
Scarborough
Filey
Flamborough Hd.
Bridlington Bay
Hornsea
Beverley
Hull
Withernsea
Spurn Head
R. Humber
Grimsby
Louth
Horncastle
Lincoln
Sutton-on-Sea
Skegness
Chesterfield
Macclesfield
Stockport
Ramsey
Douglas
Peel
Castletown
Calf of Man
Pt. of Ayre
Holyhead
Holy I.
Amlwch
Beaumaris
Bangor
Conway
Denbigh
Menai Strait
Dundrum B.
R. Tweed
R. Tyne
R. Tees
R. Eden
R. Esk
R. Clyde
R. Ouse
R. Derwent
R. Mersey
R. Dee
R. Hull
Moors
Wolds

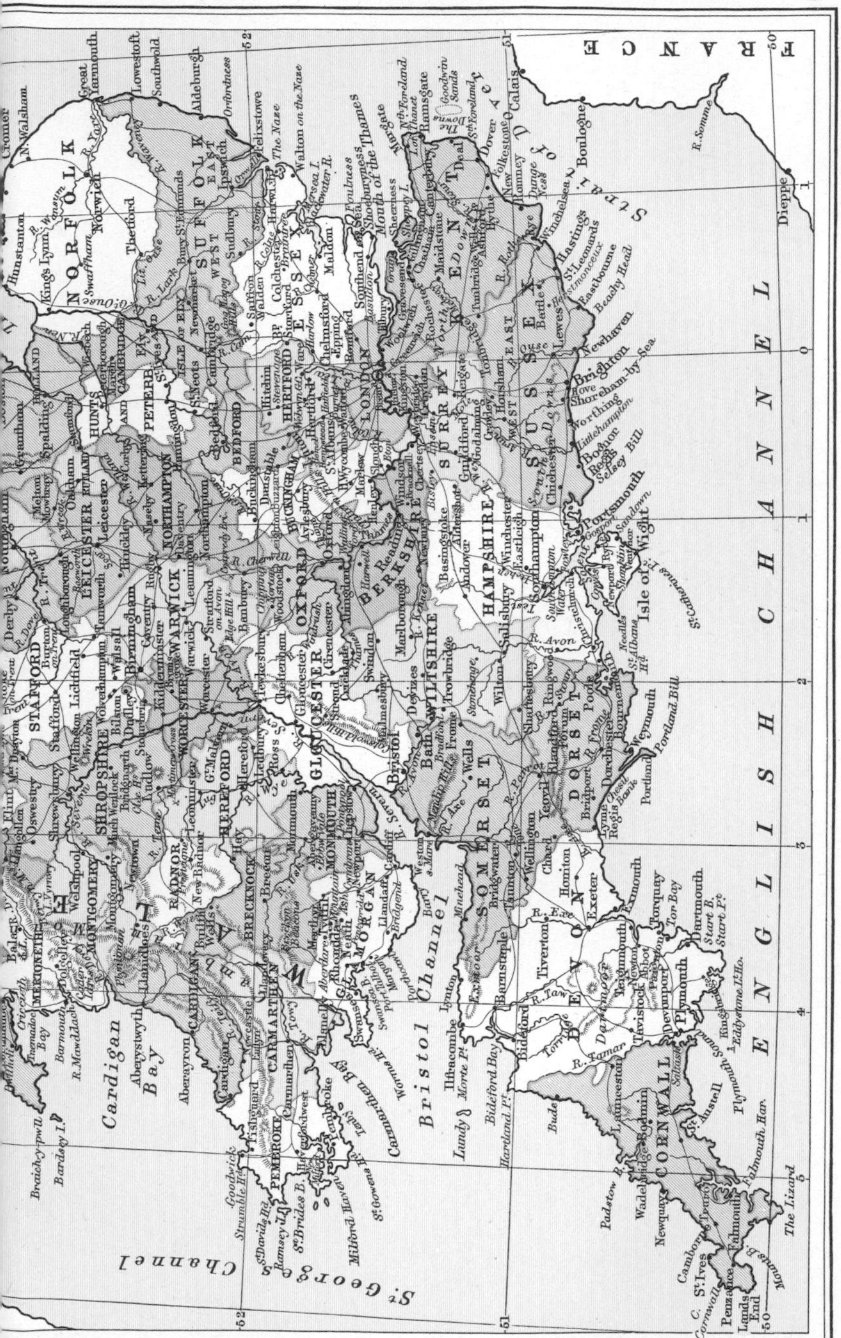
ENGLISH CHANNEL
FRANCE
Strait of Dover
Bristol Channel
Cardigan Bay
St. George's Channel
Carmarthen Bay
Bideford Bay
NORFOLK
SUFFOLK
ESSEX
KENT
SUSSEX
SURREY
HAMPSHIRE
DORSET
DEVON
CORNWALL
SOMERSET
WILTSHIRE
BERKSHIRE
OXFORD
GLOUCESTER
MONMOUTH
HEREFORD
WORCESTER
WARWICK
NORTHAMPTON
LEICESTER
STAFFORD
SHROPSHIRE
BEDFORD
HERTFORD
HUNTS
LONDON
Isle of Wight
Mouth of the Thames

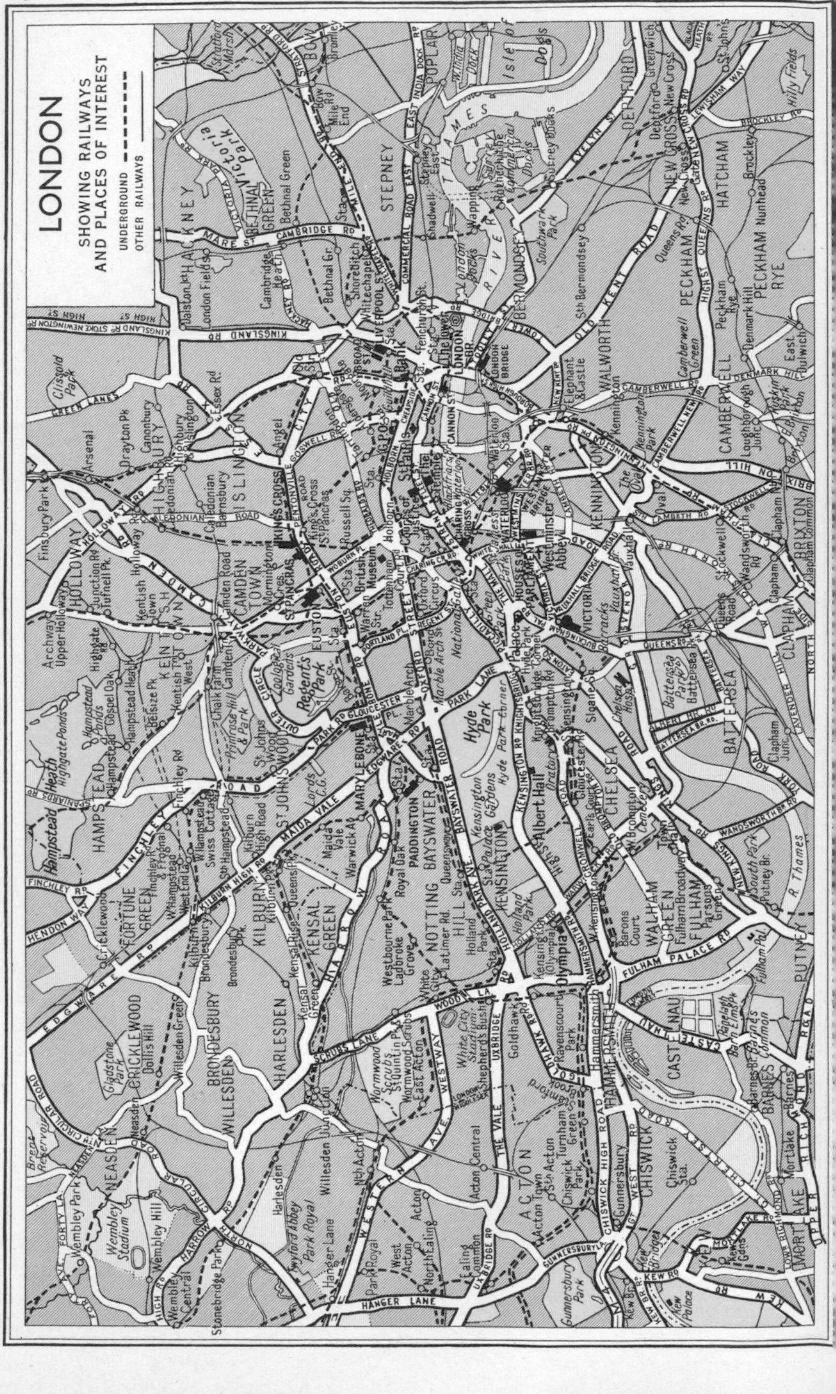
LONDON
SHOWING RAILWAYS AND PLACES OF INTEREST
UNDERGROUND
OTHER RAILWAYS
HAMPSTEAD
Hampstead Heath
HIGHGATE
HOLLOWAY
ISLINGTON
HACKNEY
Victoria Park
BETHNAL GREEN
STEPNEY
POPLAR
Isle of Dogs
RIVER THAMES
DEPTFORD
NEW CROSS
BERMONDSEY
WALWORTH
PECKHAM
HATCHAM
CAMBERWELL
PECKHAM RYE
KENNINGTON
BRIXTON
CLAPHAM
BATTERSEA
Battersea Park
CHELSEA
KENSINGTON
Albert Hall
Hyde Park
Kensington Gardens
BAYSWATER
PADDINGTON
NOTTING HILL
MARYLEBONE
Regent's Park
ST JOHNS WOOD
KILBURN
KENSAL GREEN
FORTUNE GREEN
CRICKLEWOOD
BRONDESBURY
WILLESDEN
HARLESDEN
NEASDEN
Wembley Stadium
ACTON
HAMMERSMITH
CHISWICK
CASTELNAU
BARNES
MORTLAKE
KEW
PUTNEY
FULHAM
WALHAM GREEN
Olympia
CAMDEN TOWN
KENTISH TOWN
KINGS CROSS
ST PANCRAS
EUSTON
British Museum
Westminster Abbey
HOUSES OF PARLIAMENT
VICTORIA
WATERLOO
LONDON BRIDGE
Tower
Bank
LIVERPOOL ST.
White City Stadium
Wormwood Scrubs
R. Thames

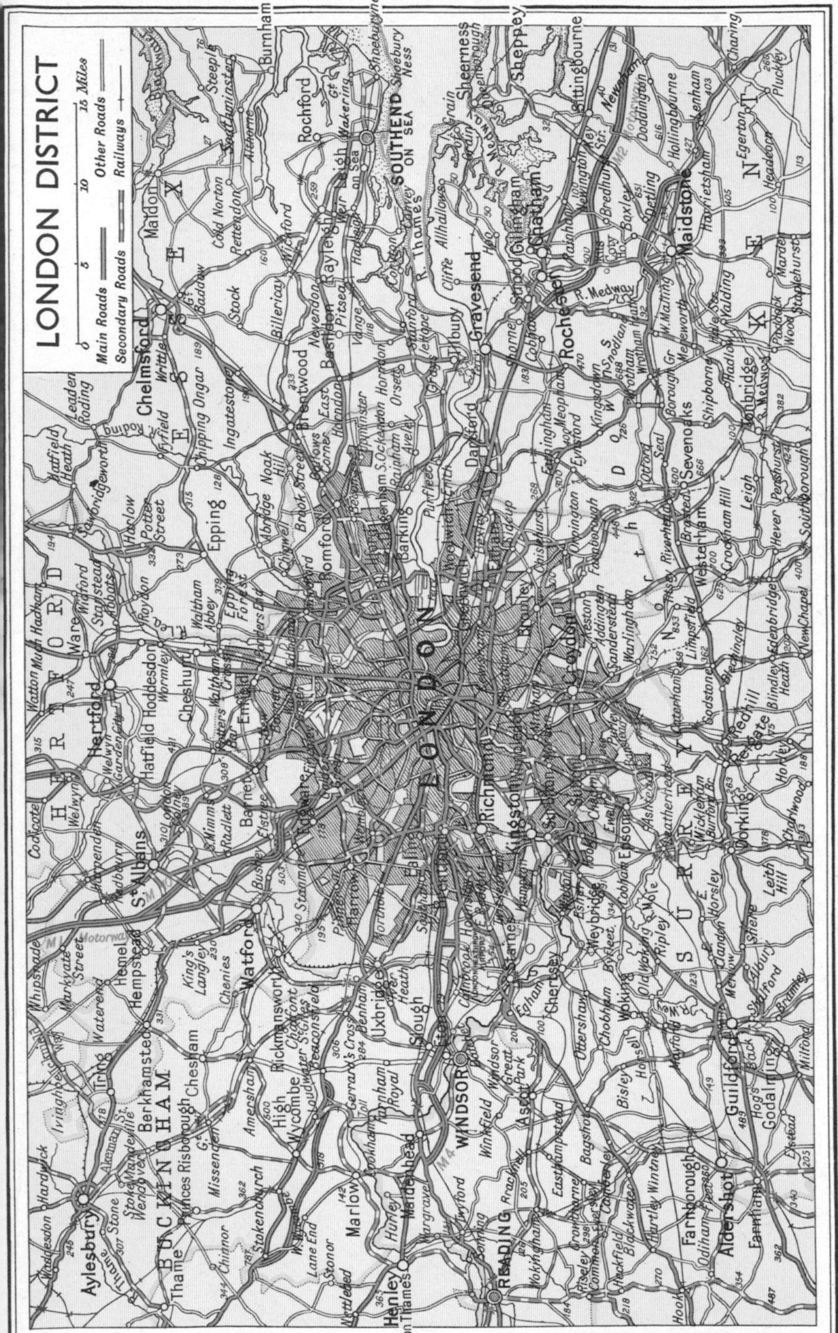
LONDON DISTRICT
Main Roads
Secondary Roads
Other Roads
Railways
0 5 10 15 Miles
LONDON

SCOTLAND
English Miles
0 10 20 30 40
Railways thus
Same Scale
SHETLAND
Unst
Yell
Fetlar
Whalsey
Lerwick
Bressay
Fitful Hd.
Sumburgh Hd.
ORKNEY
Westray
Rousay
Eday
Sanday
Stronsay
Shapinsay
Nth. Ronaldsay
Stromness
Kirkwall
Hoy
Sth. Ronaldsay
Pentland Firth
Dunnet Hd.
Duncansby Hd.
John O'Groats Ho.
Noss Hd.
Nth. Rona
Sula Sgeir
Butt of Lewis
C. Wrath
L. Eriboll
Kyle of Tongue
Strathy Pt.
Scrabster
Thurso
Dounreay
CAITHNESS
Wick
Morven
NORTH SEA
L. Laxford
L. Naver
SUTHERLAND
Eddrachillis Bay
Pt. of Stoer
L. Assynt
L. Shin
L. Enard
Lochinver
Ben More Assynt
Helmsdale
Brora
Lairg
Golspie
Dornoch
Dornoch Firth
Tarbat Ness
Tain
Stornoway
Lewis
North Minch
Harris
Tarbert
L. Broom
L. Gruinard
L. Ewe
Ullapool
Ben Dearg
Gairloch
L. Maree
L. Fannich
Ben Wyvis
Dingwall
Cromarty Firth
Cromarty
Fortrose
Moray Firth
Lossiemouth
R. Lossie
Buckie
Cullen
Portsoy
Macduff
Kinnaird Hd.
Banff
Fraserburgh
Elgin
Forres
Fochabers
Keith
Nairn
NAIRN
MORAY
R. Deveron
R. Ugie
Peterhead
Buchan Ness
Huntly
BANFF
ABERDEEN
Inverurie
R. Ythan
R. Don
Aberdeen
Girdle Ness
OUTER HEBRIDES
Little Minch
Pt. of Aird
L. Torridon
Sd. of Harris
Nth. Uist
Lochmaddy
Benbecula
South Uist
Uig
ROSS & CROMARTY
Beauly
Conan
Inverness
Raasay
Portree
Skye
L. Bracadale
Cuillin Hills
Scalpa
Kyle of Lochalsh
L. Carron
Ben Attow
Glen Affric
Loch Ness
R. Nairn
R. Findhorn
Grantown
R. Spey
R. Avon
Aviemore
Cairn Gorms
Kingussie
Fort Augustus
L. Oich
Canna
Eriskay
Barra
Barra Hd.
Rum
Eigg
Muck
Sleat Pt.
Sound of Sleat
Mallaig
INVERNESS
Ben Macdhui
Newtonmore
Braemar
Balmoral Castle
Lochnagar
Ballater
Aboyne
Banchory
R. Dee
Stonehaven
KINCARDINE
Inverbervie
L. Arkaig
Loch Lochy
L. Laggan
Grampian Mountains
L. Eil
Fort William
Ben Nevis 4406
Kinlochleven
L. Shiel
L. Linnhe
L. Sunart
Ballachulish
Ardnamurchan Pt.
Coll
Tiree
Tobermory
Sound of Mull
Mull
Ben More
Staffa
Iona
Skerryvore L.H.
L. Ericht
L. Rannoch
Schiehallion
Ben Gloe
Blair Atholl
Killiecrankie Pass
Pitlochry
Aberfeldy
L. Tay
Ben Lawers
Killin
Dunkeld
Blairgowrie
Coupar Angus
Forfar
ANGUS
Brechin
Montrose
Clova
R. Isla
Arbroath
Carnoustie
Sidlaw Hills
Dundee
Broughty Ferry
Firth of Tay
Bell Rock L.H.
PERTH
Perth
Scone
Crieff
L. Earn
Ben Vorlich
Ben Ledi
Callander
L. Katrine
L. Leven
L. Etive
Lismore
Oban
Ben Cruachan
ARGYLL
Loch Awe
Inveraray
Firth of Lorne
Scarba
Strait of Corryvreckan
Colonsay
Oronsay
Jura
Sound of Jura
Islay
Bowmore
Port Ellen
Mull of Oa
Gigha
Loch Fyne
Loch Long
Tarbert
ATLANTIC OCEAN
INNER HEBRIDES
Ochil Hills
Dunblane
Aberfoyle
Ben Lomond
R. Forth
L. Lomond
DUNBARTON
Stirling
Bannockburn
STIRLING
CLACKMANNAN
KINROSS
Glenrothes
Alloa
Clackmannan
Dunfermline
Kirkcaldy
Leven
Methil
FIFE
Cupar
St. Andrews
Fife Ness
I. of May
Firth of Forth
Nth. Berwick
Burntisland
Dunbar
Haddington
E. LOTHIAN
St. Abbs Hd.
Eyemouth
Falkirk
Linlithgow
Leith
Edinburgh
W. LOTHIAN
MIDLOTHIAN
Penicuik
Pentland Hills
Dumbarton
Greenock
Gourock
Glasgow
Renfrew
Paisley
Airdrie
Bathgate
Wishaw
Hamilton
RENFREW
Rothesay
Bute
Cumbrae
Barrhead
Ardrossan
Kilmarnock
LANARK
Lanark
Goat Fell
Brodick
Arran
Kilbrannan Sound
Kintyre
Firth of Clyde
Irvine
Prestwick
Ayr
R. Ayr
AYR
Campbeltown
Machrihanish
Mull of Kintyre
Sanda
Turnberry Pt.
Ailsa Craig
Maybole
R. Doon
Girvan
L. Doon
Ballantrae
L. Ryan
Stinchar
Merrick
North Channel
Corsewall Pt.
Stranraer
Portpatrick
Newton Stewart
WIGTOWN
Wigtown
Luce Bay
Burrow Hd.
Mull of Galloway
Wigtown Bay
Kirkcudbright
KIRKCUDBRIGHT
L. Ken
R. Ken
R. Dee
Castle Douglas
Southerness
Solway Firth
Dumfries
Annan
Lockerbie
DUMFRIES
Langholm
R. Esk
R. Nith
Sanquhar
Lowther Hills
Leadhills
Tinto
Moffat
Tweedsmuir Hills
PEEBLES
Peebles
Broad Law
Selkirk
SELKIRK
ROXBURGH
Hawick
Jedburgh
Kelso
Melrose
Galashiels
Coldstream
Greenlaw
BERWICK
Duns
Lammermuir Hills
Moorfoot Hills
R. Tweed
R. Teviot
Cheviot Hills
Carlisle
ENGLAND
IRELAND
Londonderry
Larne
Belfast
58
57
56
55
59
7 6 5 4 3 2

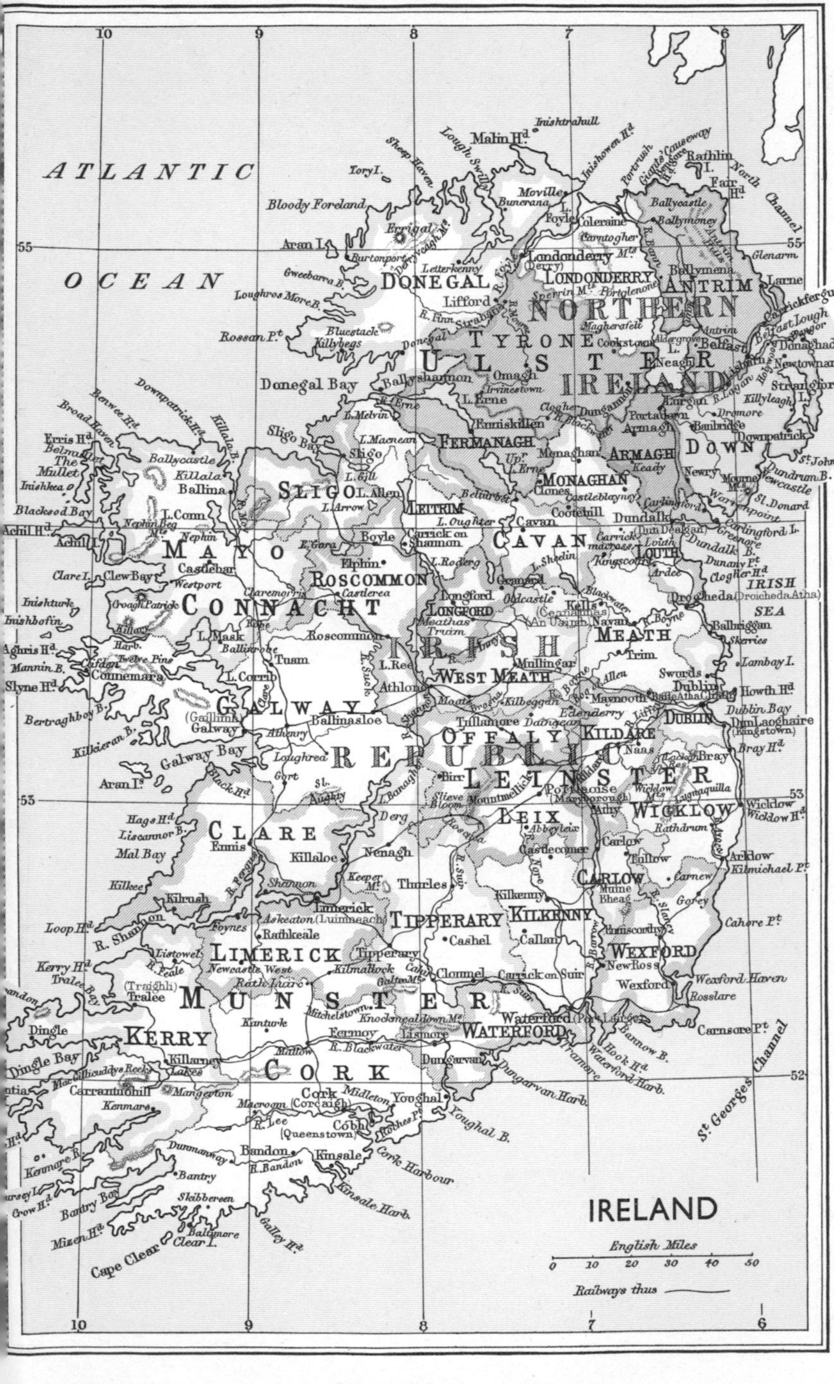
IRELAND
English Miles
0 10 20 30 40 50
Railways thus
ATLANTIC
OCEAN
IRISH
SEA
North Channel
St. Georges Channel
NORTHERN
IRELAND
ULSTER
IRISH
REPUBLIC
CONNACHT
LEINSTER
MUNSTER
DONEGAL
LONDONDERRY
ANTRIM
TYRONE
FERMANAGH
ARMAGH
DOWN
MONAGHAN
CAVAN
LOUTH
MEATH
SLIGO
LEITRIM
MAYO
ROSCOMMON
LONGFORD
WEST MEATH
DUBLIN
GALWAY
OFFALY
KILDARE
WICKLOW
LEIX
CARLOW
CLARE
TIPPERARY
KILKENNY
WEXFORD
LIMERICK
KERRY
CORK
WATERFORD
Malin Hd.
Inishtrahull
Rathlin I.
Fair Hd.
Tory I.
Bloody Foreland
Aran I.
Errigal
Burtonport
Letterkenny
Lifford
Londonderry
(Derry)
Coleraine
Ballycastle
Ballymoney
Ballymena
Glenarm
Larne
Carrickfergus
Belfast Lough
Bangor
Donaghadee
Newtownards
Belfast
Lisburn
Strangford
Dromore
Banbridge
Downpatrick
Dundrum B.
Newcastle
Newry
Armagh
Dungannon
Omagh
Irvinestown
Enniskillen
Strabane
Cookstown
Magherafelt
Portglenone
Sperrin Mts.
Killybegs
Donegal
Donegal Bay
Ballyshannon
Rossan Pt.
Sligo Bay
Sligo
Killala
Ballina
Ballycastle
Belmullet
Erris Hd.
Achill Hd.
Achill I.
Blacksod Bay
Clew Bay
Westport
Castlebar
Croagh Patrick
Clare I.
Inishturk
Inishbofin
Killary Harb.
Clifden
Twelve Pins
Connemara
Slyne Hd.
L. Mask
L. Corrib
Ballinrobe
Tuam
Claremorris
Castlerea
Boyle
Carrick on Shannon
Elphin
Roscommon
Athlone
L. Ree
Longford
Mullingar
Kells
Navan
Trim
Cavan
Cootehill
Clones
Monaghan
Castleblayney
Dundalk
Dundalk B.
Carlingford L.
Drogheda
Balbriggan
Skerries
Lambay I.
Swords
Dublin
Howth Hd.
Dublin Bay
Dun Laoghaire
(Kingstown)
Bray
Bray Hd.
Maynooth
Edenderry
Naas
Tullamore
Kilbeggan
Moate
Ballinasloe
Galway
(Gaillimh)
Galway Bay
Athenry
Loughrea
Gort
Aran Is.
Black Hd.
Hags Hd.
Liscannor B.
Mal Bay
Ennis
Kilkee
Kilrush
Killaloe
Nenagh
Birr
Mountmellick
Portlaoise
(Maryborough)
Athy
Abbeyleix
Castlecomer
Carlow
Tullow
Rathdrum
Lugnaquilla
Wicklow
Wicklow Hd.
Arklow
Gorey
Enniscorthy
Wexford
Wexford Haven
Rosslare
Carnsore Pt.
New Ross
Kilkenny
Callan
Thurles
Cashel
Tipperary
Clonmel
Carrick on Suir
Waterford
Tramore
Dungarvan
Youghal
Lismore
Fermoy
Mitchelstown
Limerick
(Luimneach)
Askeaton
Foynes
Rathkeale
Listowel
Newcastle West
Kilmallock
Loop Hd.
R. Shannon
Kerry Hd.
Tralee
Tralee Bay
Dingle
Dingle Bay
Killarney
Lakes
Carrantuohill
Mangerton
Kenmare
Mallow
Kanturk
Macroom
Cork
(Corcaigh)
Midleton
Cobh
(Queenstown)
Cork Harbour
Kinsale
Kinsale Harb.
Bandon
Dunmanway
Bantry
Bantry Bay
Skibbereen
Baltimore
Clear I.
Cape Clear
Mizen Hd.
Galley Hd.

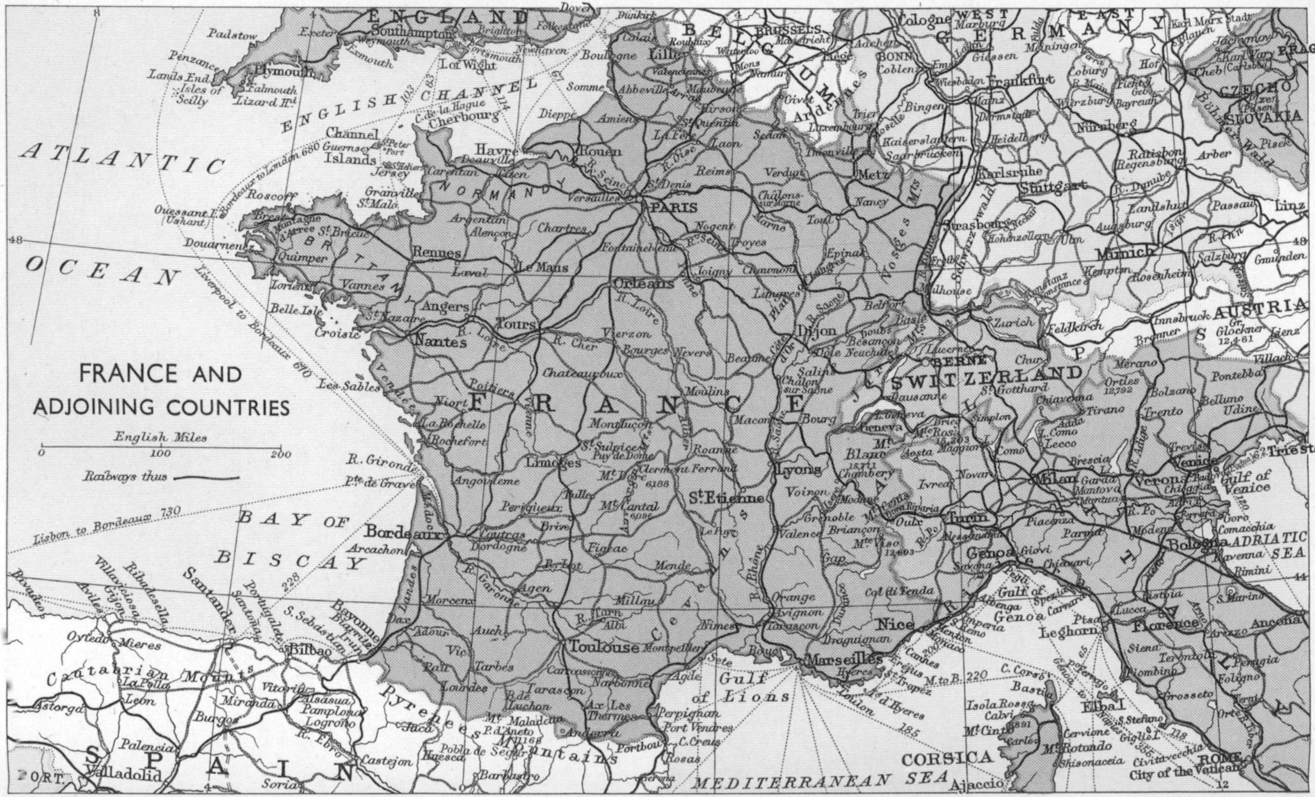
FRANCE AND
ADJOINING COUNTRIES
English Miles
0
100
200
Railways thus
ATLANTIC
OCEAN
ENGLAND
ENGLISH CHANNEL
BAY OF
BISCAY
FRANCE
BELGIUM
WEST GERMANY
EAST
SWITZERLAND
AUSTRIA
CZECHO SLOVAKIA
ITALY
SPAIN
CORSICA
Gulf of Lions
MEDITERRANEAN SEA
ADRIATIC SEA
Gulf of Venice
Pyrenees Mountains
Cantabrian Mounts
NORMANDY
BRITTANY
PARIS
Lyons
Marseilles
Bordeaux
Toulouse
Nantes
Orleans
Rouen
Havre
Cherbourg
Rennes
Le Mans
Tours
Limoges
St Etienne
Dijon
Nice
Metz
Nancy
Strasbourg
Lille
BRUSSELS
BONN
Cologne
Frankfurt
Stuttgart
Munich
PRAGUE
BERNE
Geneva
Milan
Turin
Genoa
Venice
Verona
Bologna
Florence
Leghorn
ROME
City of the Vatican
Trieste
Santander
Bilbao
Bayonne
Plymouth
Southampton
Dover
Liverpool to Bordeaux 670
Bordeaux to London 680
Lisbon to Bordeaux 730

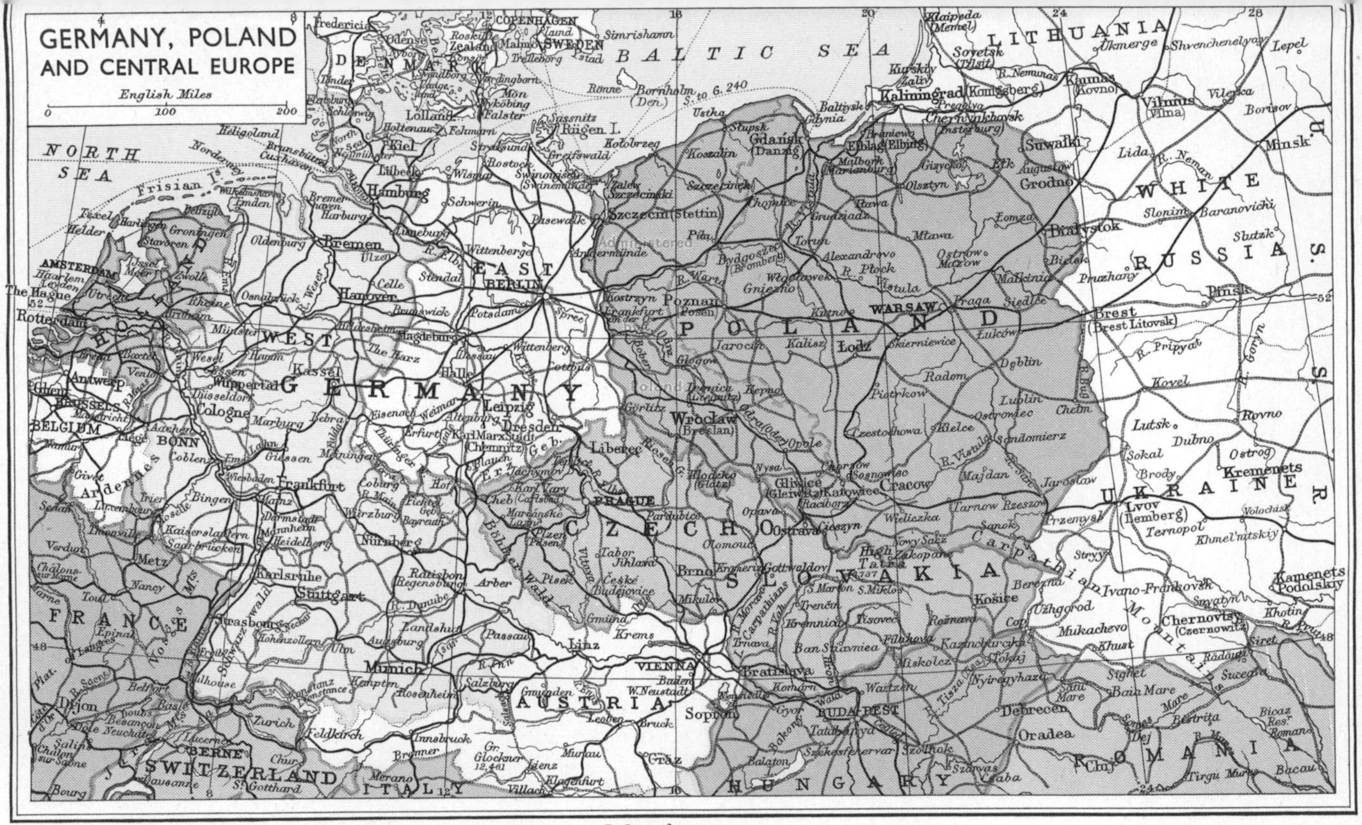

Railways thus

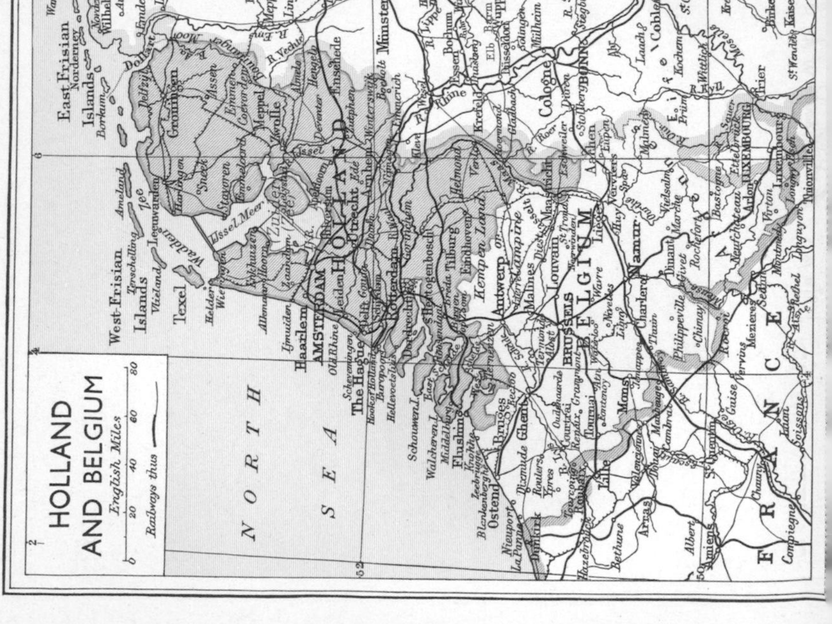
HOLLAND AND BELGIUM
English Miles
0 20 40 60 80
Railways thus
NORTH SEA
West-Frisian Islands
East Frisian Islands
Texel
Ameland
Amsterdam
The Hague
Rotterdam
Utrecht
Haarlem
Leiden
Dordrecht
Arnhem
Zwolle
Groningen
Enschede
HOLLAND
BELGIUM
Brussels
Antwerp
Ghent
Bruges
Ostend
Louvain
Malines
Namur
Liège
Charleroi
Mons
Flushing
Luxembourg
Aachen
Cologne
Bonn
Düsseldorf
Münster
Emden
Coblenz
Trier
Lille
Arras
Amiens
St. Quentin
FRANCE
GERMANY

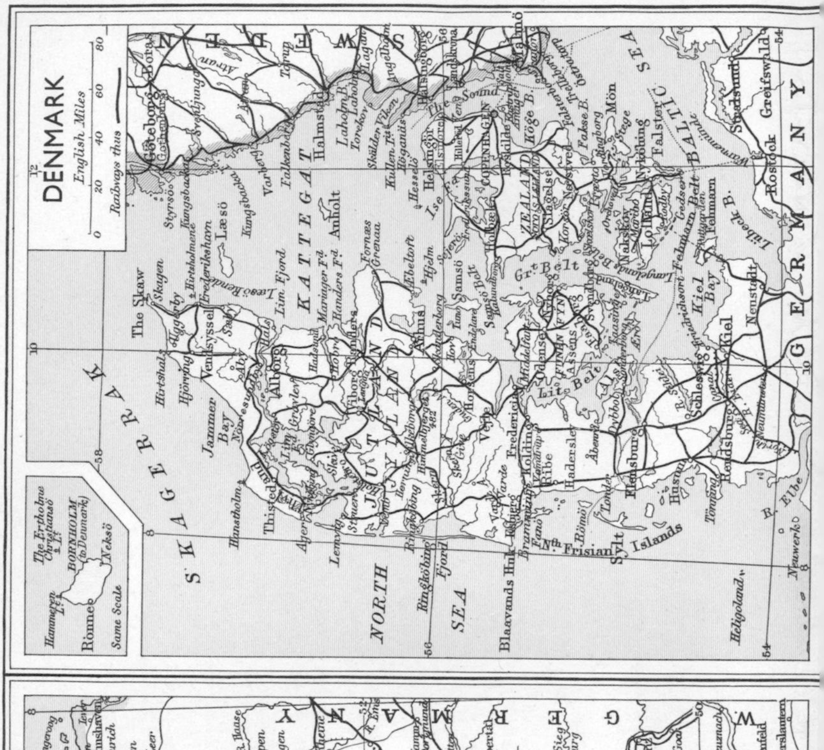
DENMARK
English Miles
0 20 40 60 80
Railways thus
The Ertholme
Christiansö
BORNHOLM (to Denmark)
Hammeren
Rönne
Neksö
Same Scale
SKAGERRAK
KATTEGAT
NORTH SEA
BALTIC SEA
The Skaw
Skagen
Frederikshavn
Læsö
Anholt
Hirtshals
Hjörring
Vendsyssel
Jammer Bay
Thisted
Aalborg
Viborg
Randers
Grenaa
Aarhus
Horsens
Vejle
Fredericia
Kolding
Ribe
Esbjerg
Ringkjöbing
Ringkjöbing Fjord
Blaavands Huk
JUTLAND
Odense
FYN
FUNEN
Svendborg
Lit. Belt
Gr. Belt
Samsö
ZEALAND
Helsingör
COPENHAGEN
Roskilde
Köge B.
Slagelse
Naestved
Mön
Falster
Lolland
Nakskov
The Sound
Helsingborg
Malmö
Göteborg
Halmstad
Varberg
SWEDEN
Haderslev
Flensburg
Schleswig
Kiel
Kiel Bay
Rendsburg
Husum
Sylt
Nth. Frisian Islands
Heligoland
R. Elbe
Lübeck B.
Rostock
Stralsund
Greifswald
GERMANY

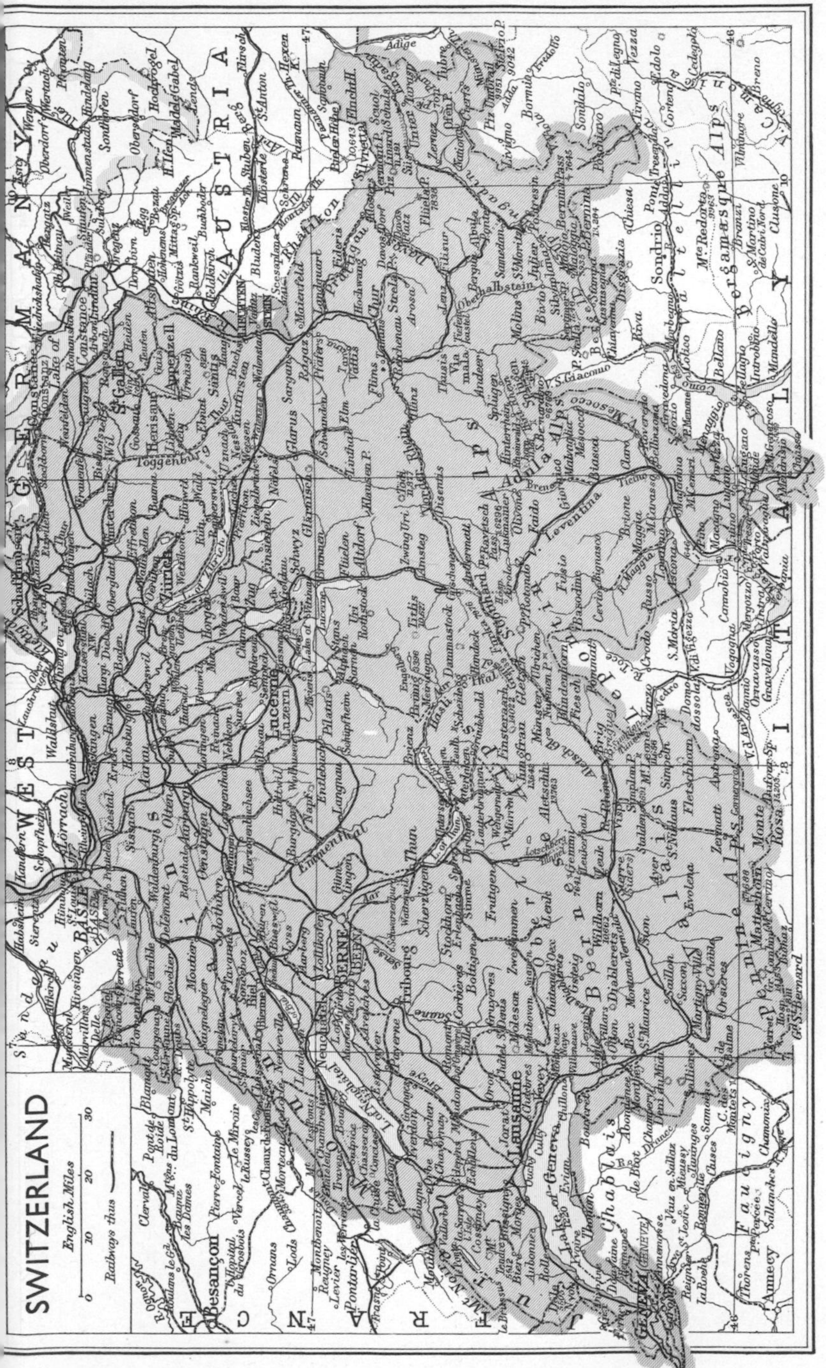
SWITZERLAND
English Miles
0 10 20 30
Railways thus
GERMANY
AUSTRIA
FRANCE
ITALY

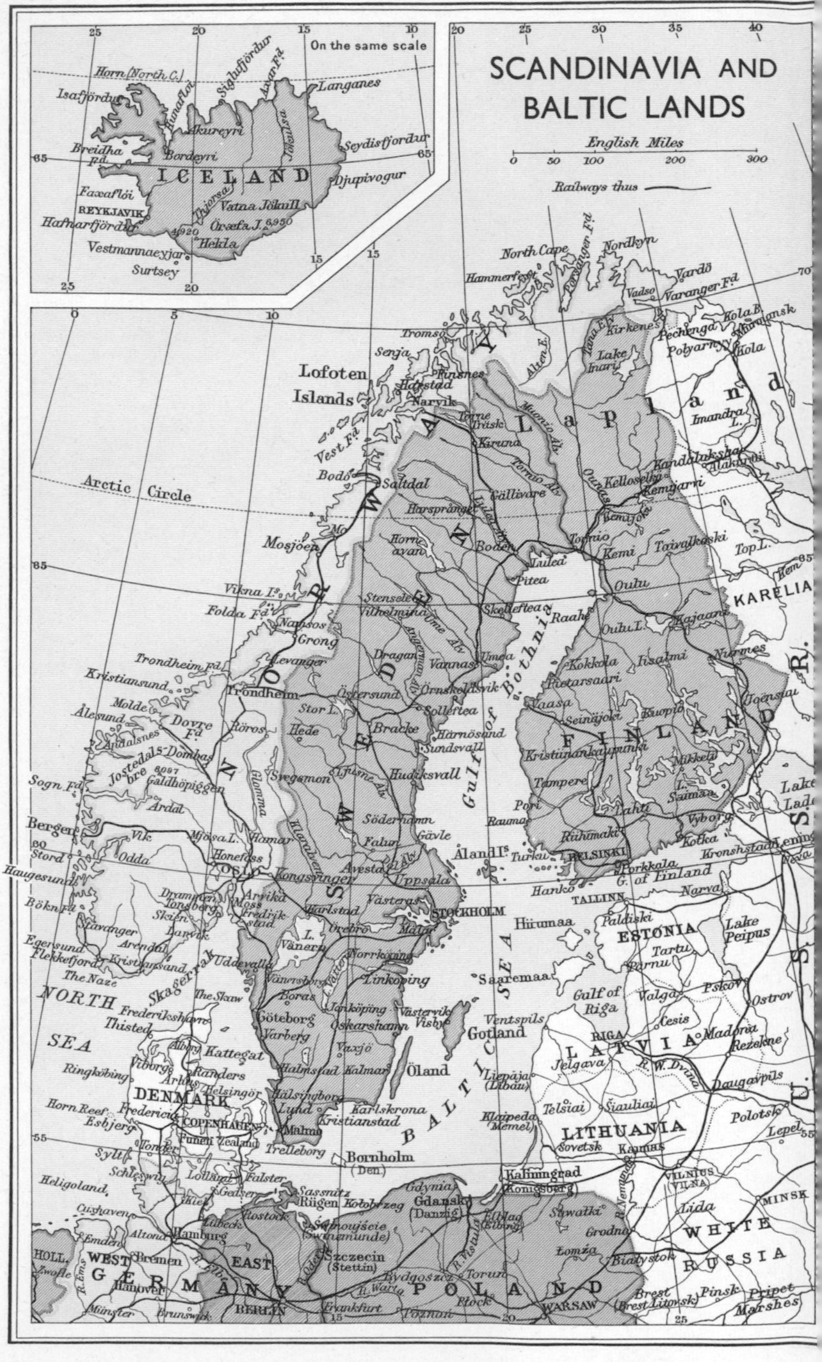
SCANDINAVIA AND BALTIC LANDS
English Miles
0 50 100 200 300
Railways thus
On the same scale
ICELAND
REYKJAVIK
Akureyri
Isafjördur
Siglufjördur
Langanes
Seydisfjordur
Djupivogur
Faxaflói
Hafnarfjördur
Vatna Jökull
Hekla
Vestmannaeyjar
Surtsey
Horn (North C.)
Breidha Fd.
Bordeyri
Lofoten Islands
Arctic Circle
NORWAY
SWEDEN
FINLAND
Lapland
KARELIA
North Cape
Hammerfest
Nordkyn
Vardö
Vadso
Varanger Fd.
Kirkenes
Pechenga
Polyarnyy
Murmansk
Kola
Lake Inari
Tromsø
Senja
Narvik
Kiruna
Gällivare
Bodø
Saltdal
Mosjöen
Luleå
Piteå
Tornio
Kemi
Oulu
Raahe
Umeå
Trondheim
Kristiansund
Molde
Ålesund
Östersund
Sollefteå
Härnösand
Sundsvall
Hudiksvall
Söderhamn
Gävle
Falun
Uppsala
Västerås
STOCKHOLM
Bergen
Stord
Haugesund
Odda
Hamar
OSLO
Stavanger
Kristiansand
Arendal
Kongsvinger
Karlstad
Örebro
L. Vänern
Norrköping
Linköping
Jönköping
Göteborg
Varberg
Halmstad
Kalmar
Växjö
Karlskrona
Kristianstad
Helsingborg
Lund
Malmö
Trelleborg
Bornholm (Den.)
Öland
Gotland
Gulf of Bothnia
BALTIC SEA
Åland Is.
Turku
HELSINKI
Porkkala
G. of Finland
Hanko
Tampere
Pori
Vaasa
Kokkola
Kuopio
Mikkeli
Lahti
Vyborg
Kotka
Kronshtadt
Joensuu
Iisalmi
Kajaani
TALLINN
Paldiski
Hiiumaa
Saaremaa
ESTONIA
Tartu
Pärnu
Narva
Lake Peipus
Gulf of Riga
RIGA
LATVIA
Jelgava
Liepāja (Libau)
Ventspils
Daugavpils
R.W. Dvina
Pskov
Ostrov
LITHUANIA
Klaipeda (Memel)
Kaunas
Sovetsk
VILNIUS (VILNA)
Kaliningrad (Königsberg)
Gdynia
Gdansk (Danzig)
Elblag (Elbing)
Szczecin (Stettin)
Bydgoszcz
Torun
Poznan
WARSAW
POLAND
Grodno
Bialystok
Brest (Brest Litovsk)
Pinsk
Pripet Marshes
Lida
MINSK
Polotsk
Lepel
WHITE RUSSIA
DENMARK
COPENHAGEN
Esbjerg
Fredericia
Randers
Ringköbing
Horn Reef
Kattegat
Skagerrak
The Skaw
NORTH SEA
Sylt
Schleswig
Kiel
Lübeck
Rostock
Hamburg
Altona
Bremen
Cuxhaven
Emden
Heligoland
WEST GERMANY
EAST
BERLIN
Frankfurt
Hanover
Brunswick
Münster
HOLL.

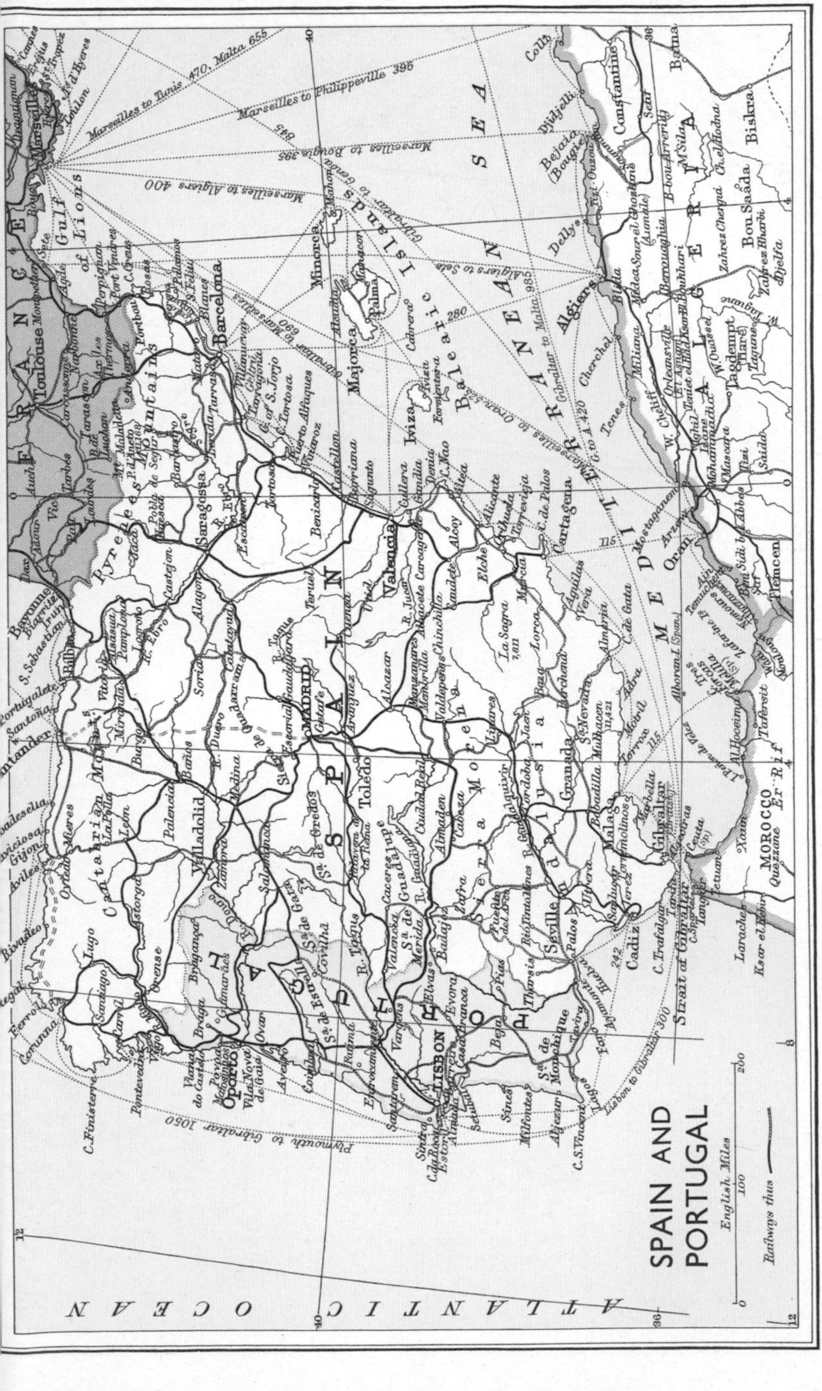
SPAIN AND PORTUGAL
English Miles
0
100
200
Railways thus
ATLANTIC OCEAN
MEDITERRANEAN SEA
Balearic Islands
Gulf of Lions
SPAIN
PORTUGAL
FRANCE
ALGERIA
MOROCCO
Pyrenees Mountains
Cantabrian Mountains
Sierra Morena
Andalusia
Strait of Gibraltar
MADRID
LISBON
Oporto
Barcelona
Valencia
Seville
Granada
Malaga
Cadiz
Gibraltar
Cartagena
Zaragossa
Valladolid
Toledo
Bilbao
Santander
Corunna
Majorca
Minorca
Iviza
Palma
Toulouse
Marseilles
Algiers
Oran
Constantine
Marseilles to Algiers 400
Plymouth to Gibraltar 1050
Lisbon to Gibraltar 300

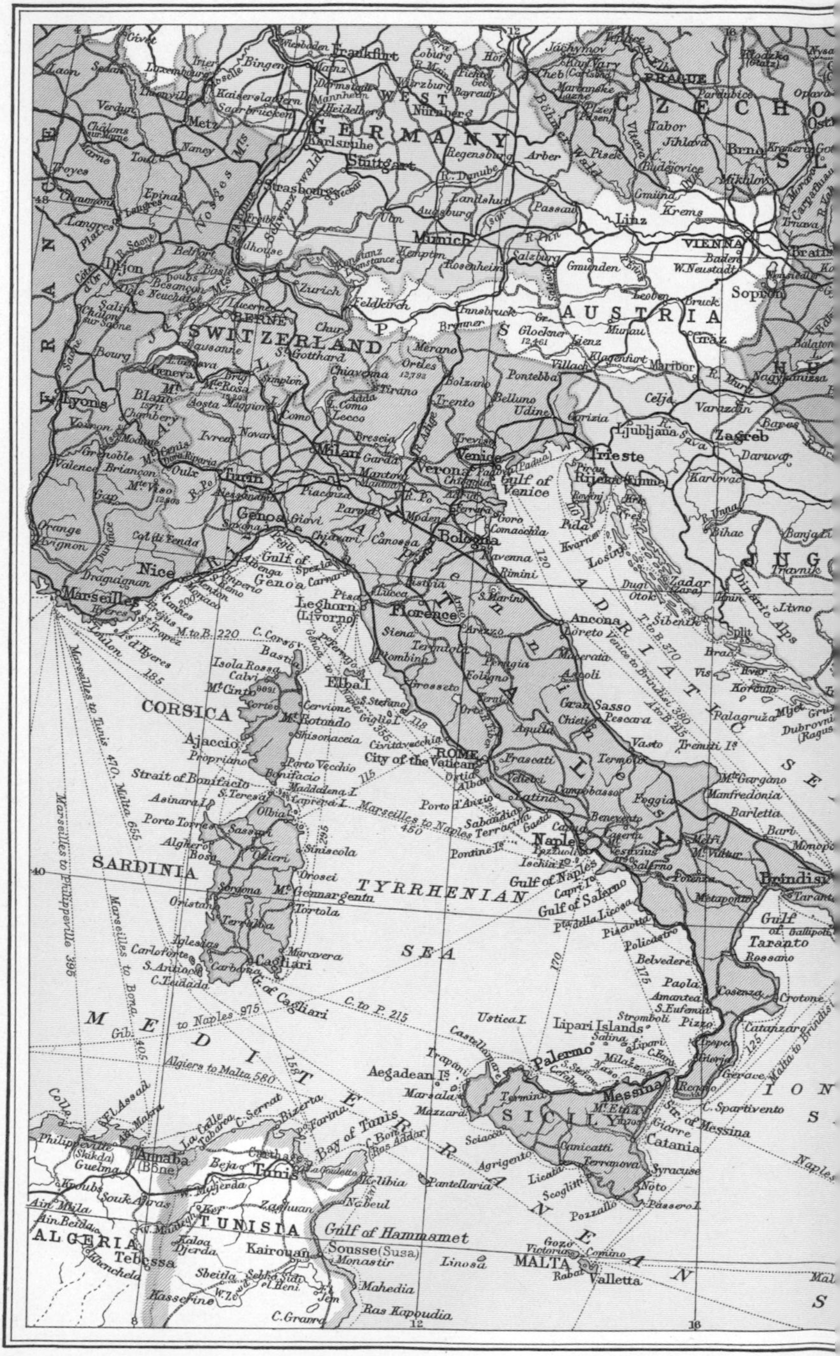
GERMANY
FRANCE
SWITZERLAND
AUSTRIA
CZECHOSLOVAKIA
ITALY
CORSICA
SARDINIA
SICILY
TUNISIA
ALGERIA
MALTA
TYRRHENIAN SEA
ADRIATIC SEA
MEDITERRANEAN
IONIAN SEA
ALPS
APENNINES
Frankfurt
Stuttgart
Munich
Strasbourg
Zurich
Berne
Lyons
Marseilles
Nice
Turin
Milan
Genoa
Venice
Verona
Bologna
Florence
Leghorn (Livorno)
Rome
City of the Vatican
Naples
Palermo
Messina
Catania
Syracuse
Trieste
Zagreb
Vienna
Prague
Linz
Graz
Ancona
Brindisi
Taranto
Ajaccio
Cagliari
Tunis
Bizerta
Annaba (Bône)
Valletta
Gulf of Genoa
Gulf of Venice
Gulf of Naples
Gulf of Salerno
Gulf of Taranto
Gulf of Hammamet
Bay of Tunis
Strait of Bonifacio
Str. of Messina
Lipari Islands
Aegadean Is.
Elba I.
Marseilles to Naples 450
Marseilles to Tunis 470. Malta 655
Marseilles to Philippeville 395
Algiers to Malta 580
Venice to Brindisi 380
Malta to Brindisi

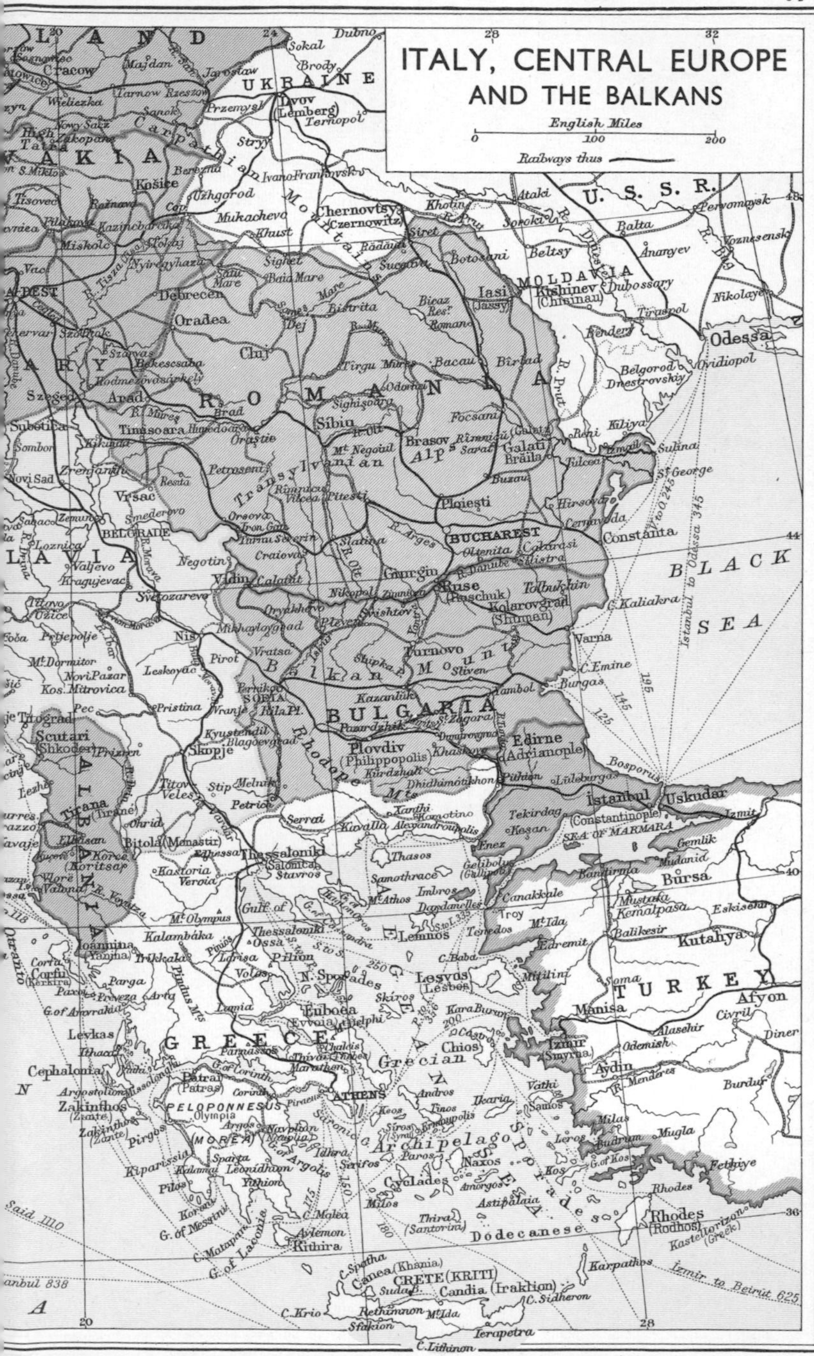
ITALY, CENTRAL EUROPE
AND THE BALKANS
English Miles
0 100 200
Railways thus
U K R A I N E
U. S. S. R.
MOLDAVIA
R O M A N I A
BULGARIA
GREECE
TURKEY
BLACK SEA
SEA OF MARMARA
Grecian Archipelago
Dodecanese
Cracow
Lvov (Lemberg)
Ternopol
Chernovtsy (Czernowitz)
Carpathian Mountains
Uzhgorod
Mukachevo
Košice
Miskolc
Debrecen
Oradea
Cluj
Szeged
Arad
Timisoara
Sibiu
Brasov
Transylvanian Alps
Iasi (Jassy)
Kishinev (Chisinau)
Odessa
Galati
Braila
Ploiești
BUCHAREST
Constanta
Craiova
Vidin
Ruse (Ruschuk)
Kolarovgrad (Shumen)
Varna
Burgas
Turnovo
Balkan Mountains
SOFIA
Plovdiv (Philippopolis)
Rhodope Mts
Edirne (Adrianople)
Istanbul (Constantinople)
Uskudar
Izmit
Bursa
Canakkale
Troy
BELGRADE
Nis
Skopje
Scutari (Shkoder)
Tirana (Tiranë)
Bitola (Monastir)
Thessaloniki (Salonica)
Mt Olympus
Ioannina (Yanina)
Corfu (Kerkira)
Larisa
Lemnos
Lesvos (Lesbos)
Chios
Izmir (Smyrna)
Manisa
Afyon
Aydin
Euboea (Evvoia)
Patrai (Patras)
ATHENS
PELOPONNESUS
Olympia
(MOREA)
Sparta
Cyclades
Naxos
Rhodes (Rodhos)
Kithira
CRETE (KRITI)
Canea (Khania)
Candia (Iraklion)
Istanbul to Odessa 345
Izmir to Beirut 625

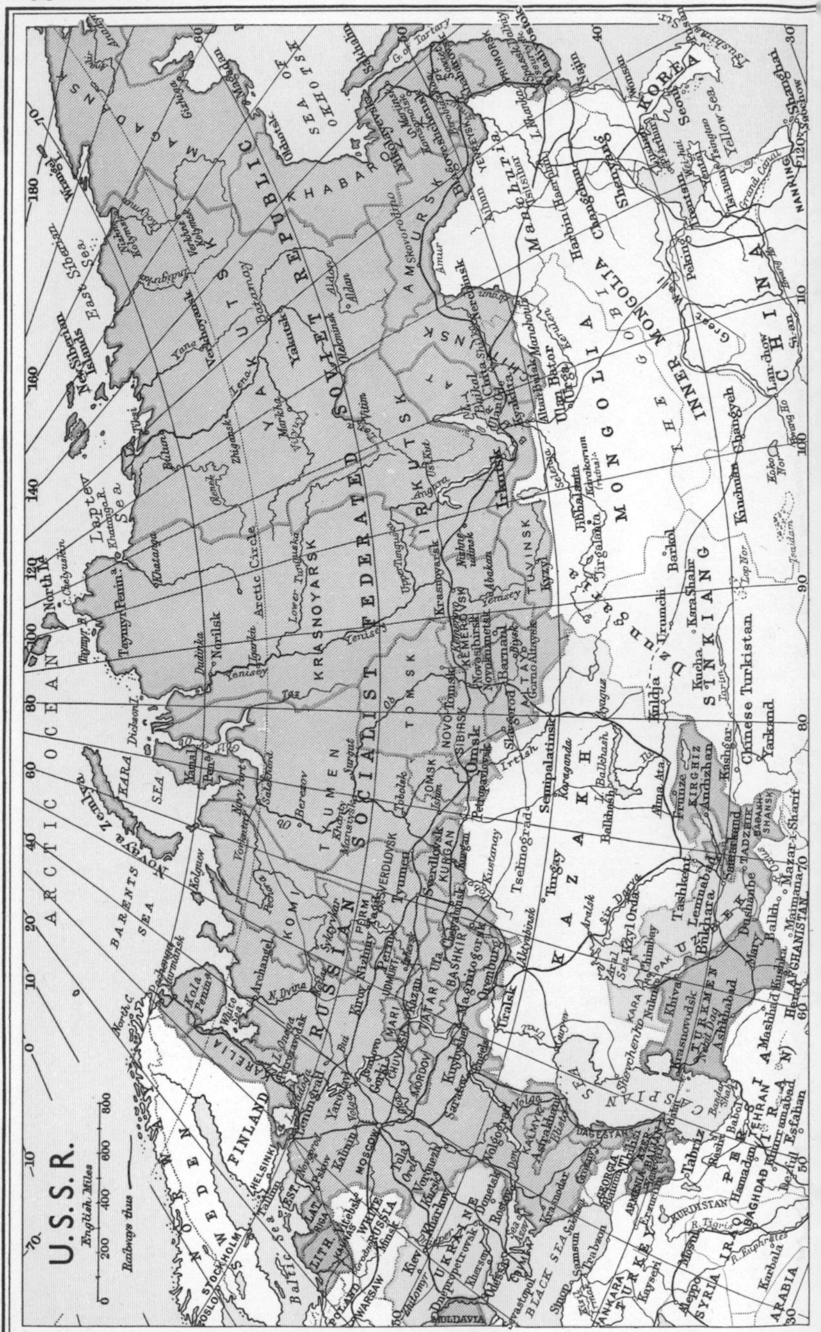
U.S.S.R.
English Miles
0 200 400 600 800
Railways thus
ARCTIC OCEAN
BARENTS SEA
KARA SEA
Laptev Sea
East Siberian Sea
SEA OF OKHOTSK
Novaya Zemlya
New Siberian Islands
RUSSIAN SOVIET FEDERATED SOCIALIST REPUBLIC
KRASNOYARSK
TOMSK
TYUMEN
KOMI
IRKUTSK
YAKUTSK
KHABAROVSK
MAGADAN
Arctic Circle
KAZAKH
UZBEK
TURKMEN
KIRGHIZ
TADZHIK
UKRAINE
WHITE RUSSIA
KARELIA
FINLAND
SWEDEN
MONGOLIA
INNER MONGOLIA
SINKIANG
Chinese Turkistan
CHINA
Manchuria
KOREA
IRAN (PERSIA)
AFGHANISTAN
TURKEY
IRAQ
SYRIA
ARABIA
CASPIAN SEA
BLACK SEA
Aral Sea
Moscow
Leningrad
Kiev
Kharkov
Gorki
Kazan
Sverdlovsk
Omsk
Novosibirsk
Krasnoyarsk
Irkutsk
Yakutsk
Tashkent
Alma Ata
Semipalatinsk
Karaganda
Vladivostok
Khabarovsk
Ulan Bator
Peking
Tehran
Baghdad
MOLDAVIA

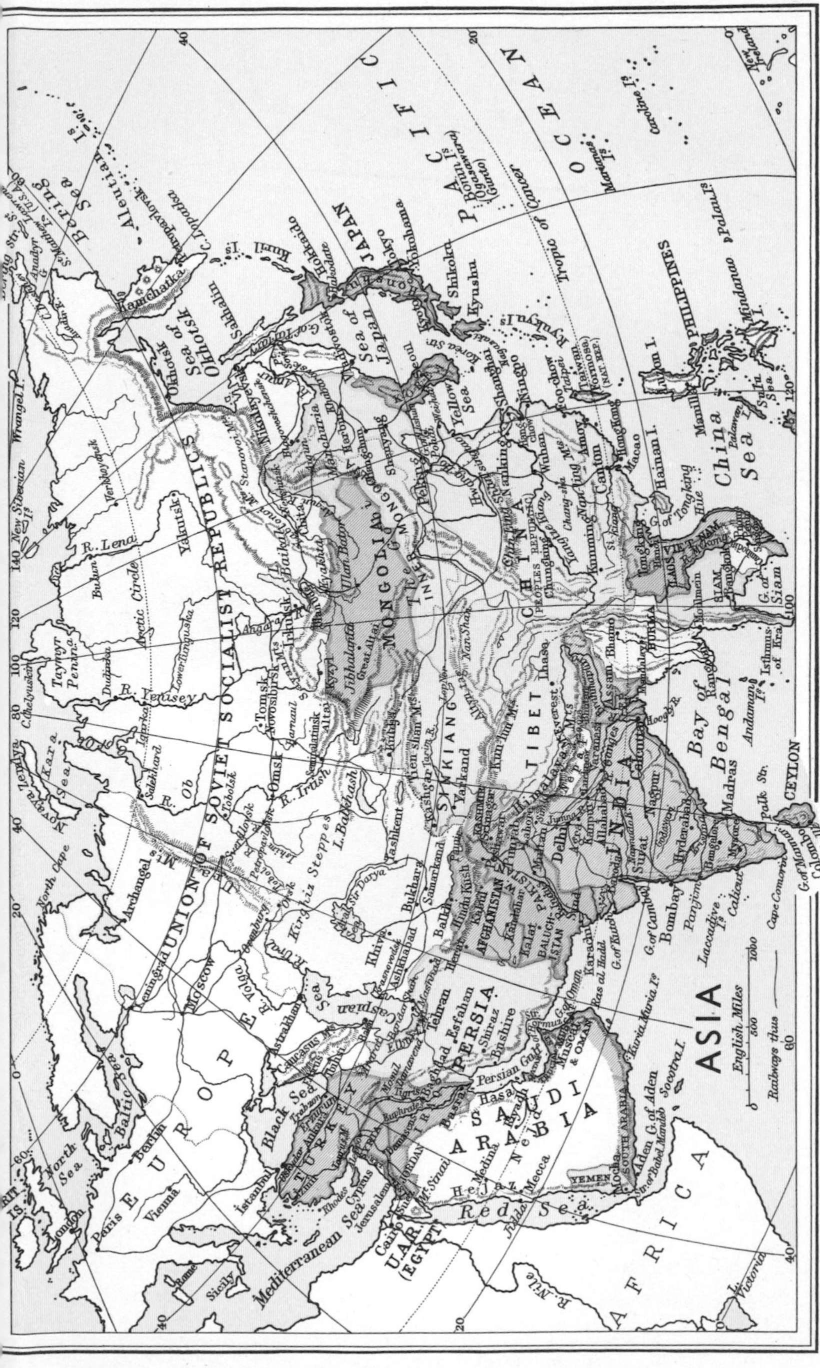
ASIA
English Miles
0
500
1000
Railways thus
UNION OF SOVIET SOCIALIST REPUBLICS
E U R O P E
A F R I C A
P A C I F I C
O C E A N
Tropic of Cancer
Arctic Circle
MONGOLIA
CHINA
(PEOPLES REPUBLIC)
INNER MONGOLIA
TIBET
SINKIANG
INDIA
PAKISTAN
AFGHANISTAN
PERSIA
TURKEY
SAUDI ARABIA
BURMA
SIAM
LAOS
VIET NAM
JAPAN
PHILIPPINES
CEYLON
YEMEN
SOUTH ARABIA
IRAQ
SYRIA
JORDAN
U.A.R. (EGYPT)
BALUCHISTAN
Manchuria
Korea
Bering Sea
Bering Str.
Sea of Okhotsk
Sea of Japan
Yellow Sea
China Sea
Bay of Bengal
Arabian Sea
Red Sea
Persian Gulf
Caspian Sea
Black Sea
Mediterranean Sea
Baltic Sea
North Sea
Kara Sea
L. Balkhash
L. Baikal
Aral Sea
R. Lena
R. Yenisey
R. Ob
R. Irtish
R. Amur
R. Volga
R. Ural
R. Nile
Euphrates
Tigris
Ganges
Himalaya Mts
Kun Lun Mts
Tien Shan Mts
Altai Mts
Caucasus Mts
Ural Mts
Hindu Kush
Kamchatka
Sakhalin
Kuril Is
Aleutian Is
New Siberian Is
Wrangel I.
Novaya Zemlya
Taymyr Penin.
Hokkaido
Honshu
Shikoku
Kyushu
Ryukyu Is
Formosa
Hainan I.
Mindanao
Luzon I.
Palau Is
Caroline Is
Mariana Is
Bonin Is
Andaman Is
Laccadive Is
Socotra I.
Cyprus
Rhodes
Sicily
Moscow
Leningrad
Archangel
Sverdlovsk
Omsk
Novosibirsk
Tomsk
Tobolsk
Irkutsk
Chita
Yakutsk
Verkhoyansk
Okhotsk
Vladivostok
Khabarovsk
Tashkent
Samarkand
Bukhara
Khiva
Ashkhabad
Astrakhan
Baku
Tbilisi
Istanbul
Ankara
Berlin
Vienna
Paris
London
Rome
Cairo
Jerusalem
Damascus
Baghdad
Basra
Tehran
Esfahan
Shiraz
Bushire
Mecca
Medina
Riyadh
Aden
Mocha
Muscat & Oman
Karachi
Lahore
Delhi
Bombay
Madras
Calcutta
Colombo
Kabul
Kandahar
Herat
Kashgar
Yarkand
Lhasa
Rangoon
Mandalay
Bangkok
Hanoi
Hue
Peking
Tientsin
Shanghai
Nanking
Wuhan
Canton
Hong Kong
Macao
Amoy
Foochow
Ningpo
Chungking
Kunming
Harbin
Mukden
Seoul
Tokyo
Yokohama
Kyoto
Manila
Ulan Bator

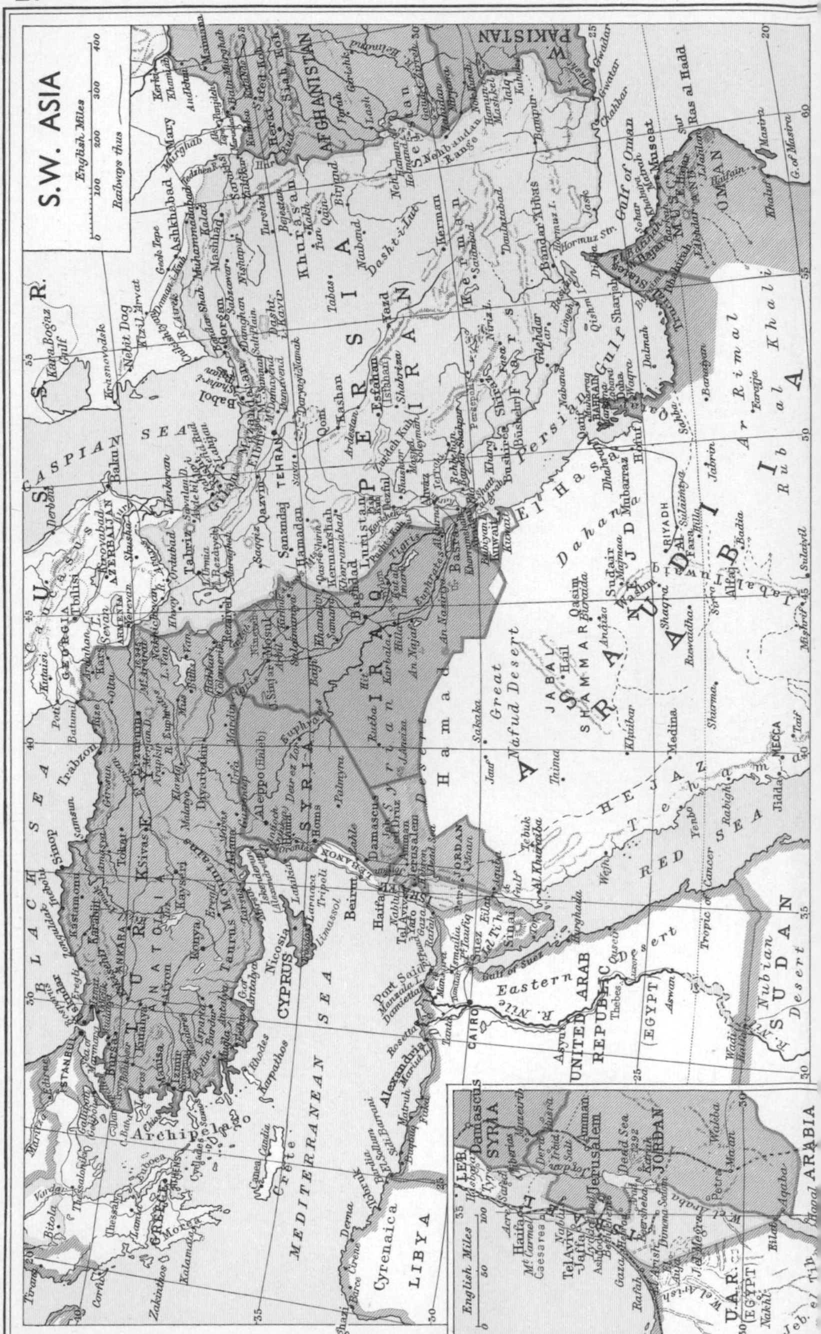
S.W. ASIA
English Miles
100 200 300 400
Railways thus
U. S. S. R.
CASPIAN SEA
BLACK SEA
MEDITERRANEAN SEA
Archipelago
CYPRUS
Nicosia
T U R K E Y
A N A T O L I A
ANKARA
ISTANBUL
GEORGIA
ARMENIA
AZERBAIJAN
Tbilisi
Baku
S Y R I A
Aleppo (Haleb)
Damascus
Homs
LEBANON
Beirut
ISRAEL
Jerusalem
Haifa
Tel Aviv
Amman
JORDAN
I R A Q
Baghdad
Mosul
Basra
P E R S I A (I R A N)
TEHRAN
Tabriz
Esfahan
Shiraz
Mashhad
Kerman
Yazd
Persian Gulf
Gulf of Oman
Muscat
OMAN
AFGHANISTAN
Herat
W. PAKISTAN
S A U D I A R A B I A
RIYADH
Medina
MECCA
Jidda
HEJAZ
Great Nafud Desert
Ar Rimal
Rub al Khali
RED SEA
Tropic of Cancer
Kuwait
BAHRAIN
Qatar
Dahana
UNITED ARAB REPUBLIC
EGYPT
CAIRO
Alexandria
Port Said
Suez
Sinai
Eastern Desert
Nile
Aswan
SUDAN
Nubian Desert
LIBYA
Cyrenaica
Benghazi
Crete
Rhodes
GREECE
ATHENS
U.A.R. (EGYPT)
ARABIA
Dead Sea
Gaza
Beersheba
Aqaba
Petra

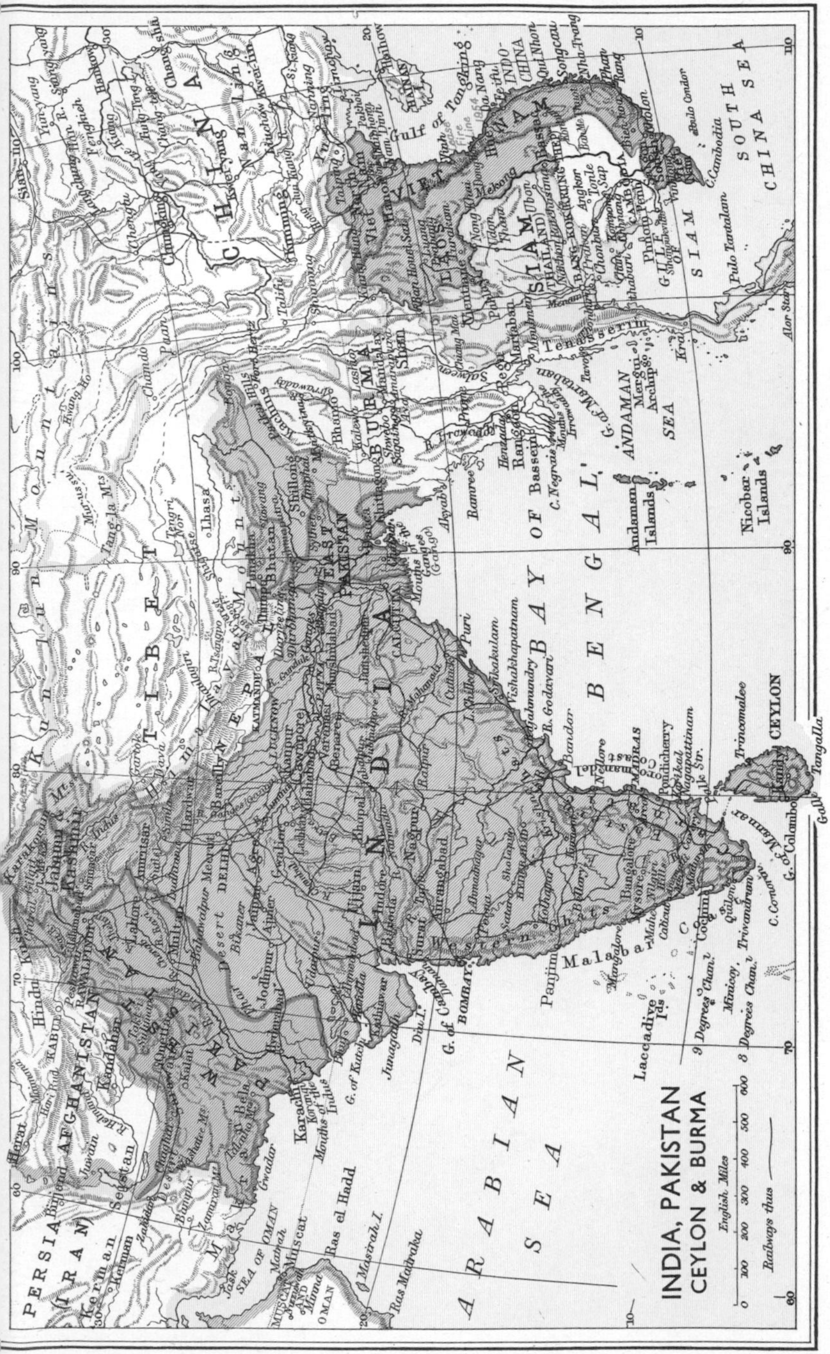
INDIA, PAKISTAN
CEYLON & BURMA
English Miles
0 100 200 300 400 500 600
Railways thus
ARABIAN SEA
BAY OF BENGAL
ANDAMAN SEA
SOUTH CHINA SEA
GULF OF SIAM
Gulf of Tongking
SEA OF OMAN
TIBET
CHINA
INDIA
PAKISTAN
EAST PAKISTAN
BURMA
NEPAL
Bhutan
SIAM
THAILAND
LAOS
VIET NAM
CAMBODIA
INDO-CHINA
CEYLON
AFGHANISTAN
PERSIA (IRAN)
OMAN
MUSCAT AND OMAN
Jammu & Kashmir
Kunlun Mts.
Hindu Kush
Karakoram
Tangla Mts.
Western Ghats
Malabar
Coromandel Coast
Laccadive Ids.
Andaman Islands
Nicobar Islands
Mergui Archip.
Tenasserim
Desert
DELHI
BOMBAY
CALCUTTA
MADRAS
KARACHI
Lhasa
KATMANDU
Rangoon
Mandalay
Colombo
Kandy
Trincomalee
Hanoi
Saigon
Bangkok
Kunming
Chungking
Ras el Hadd
Masirah I.
Ras Madraka
G. of Cambay
G. of Kutch
G. of Manaar
C. Comorin
Mouths of the Ganges
Mouths of Indus
9 Degrees Chan.
8 Degrees Chan.
Minicoy
Pulo Tantalan
Pulo Condor
C. Cambodia

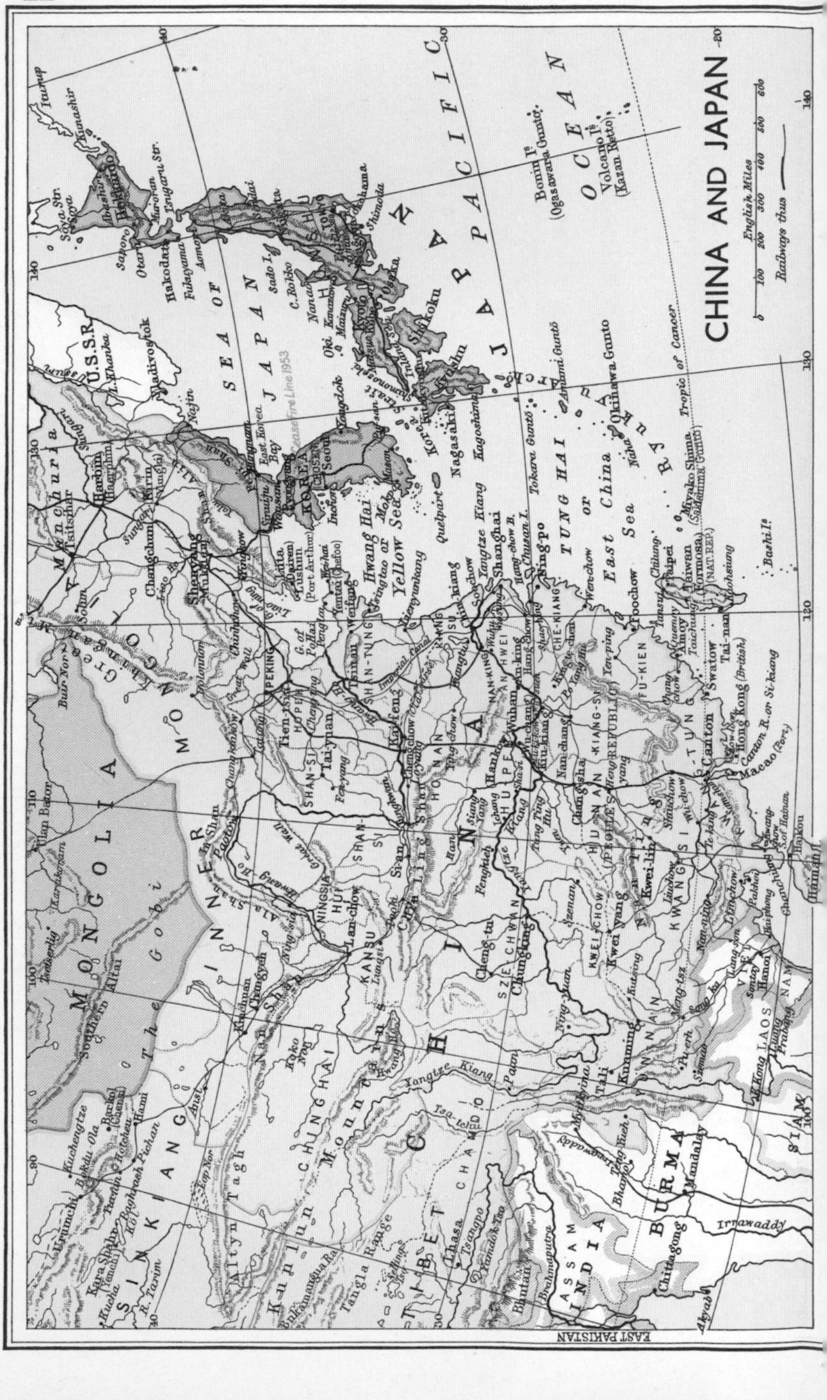
CHINA AND JAPAN
English Miles
0 100 200 300 400 500 600
Railways thus
MONGOLIA
Manchuria
INNER MONGOLIA
SINKIANG
TIBET
CHINA
KOREA (CHOSEN)
JAPAN
SEA OF JAPAN
PACIFIC OCEAN
HWANG HAI or Yellow Sea
TUNG HAI or East China Sea
Ryukyu Arch.
Formosa (NAT. REP.)
U.S.S.R.
BURMA
INDIA
ASSAM
EAST PAKISTAN
SIAM
LAOS
VIET NAM
PEKING
Tien-tsin
Shanghai
Nanking
Hankow
Canton
Hong Kong (British)
Macao (Port.)
Chungking
Lhasa
Tokyo
Osaka
Kyoto
Seoul
Mukden
Harbin
Vladivostok
Hokkaido
Honshu
Shikoku
Kyushu
Bonin Is. (Ogasawara Gunto)
Volcano Is. (Kazan Retto)
Tropic of Cancer
Cease Fire Line 1953
The Gobi
Kunlun Mountains
Yangtze Kiang
Hwang Ho
Irrawaddy
Brahmaputra
CHINGHAI
KANSU
SZECHWAN
YUNNAN
KWEICHOW
KWANGSI
KWANGTUNG
FUKIEN
CHEKIANG
KIANGSI
HUNAN
HUPEH
HONAN
SHANTUNG
HOPEH
SHANSI
SHENSI
NINGSIA HUI
ANHWEI
KIANGSU

S.E. ASIA
English Miles
0 100 200 300 400 500 600
Railways thus
PACIFIC OCEAN
INDIAN OCEAN
SOUTH CHINA SEA
SULU SEA
CELÉBES SEA
JAVA SEA
BANDA SEA
ARAFURA SEA
TIMOR SEA
CORAL SEA
MARIANAS OR LADRONES ISLANDS
CAROLINE ISLANDS
(U.S.A. Trust Terr.)
PHILIPPINES
LUZON
MANILA
MINDANAO
SIAM (THAILAND)
LAOS
VIET NAM
INDO-CHINA
CAMBODIA
MALAYA
MALAYSIA
SABAH
BORNEO (KALIMANTAN)
SARAWAK
SINGAPORE
INDONESIA
JAVA
DJAKARTA
CELEBES (SULAWESI)
MOLUCCAS
WEST IRIAN
NEW GUINEA (AUST)
AUSTRALIA
Equator

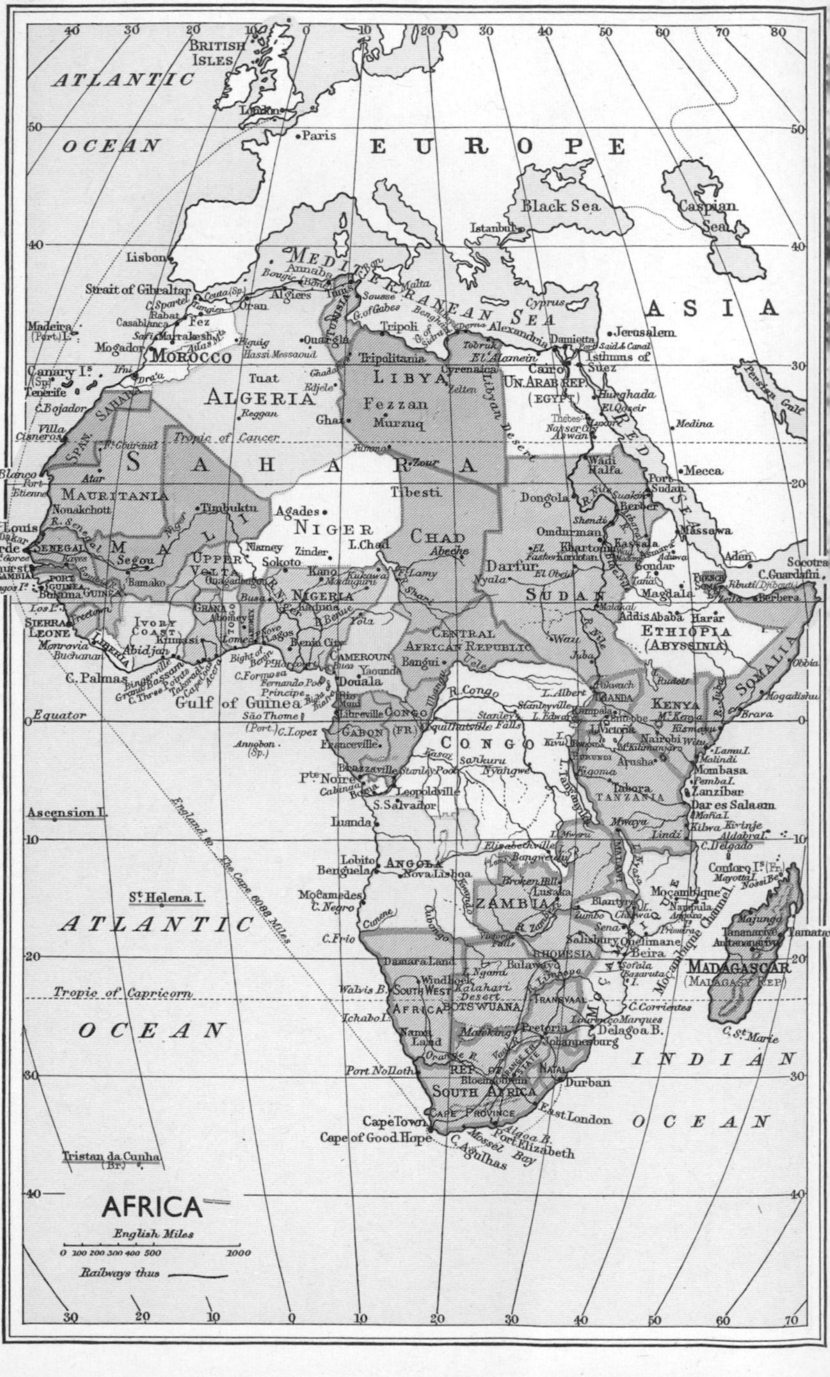
AFRICA
English Miles
0 100 200 300 400 500 1000
Railways thus
ATLANTIC
OCEAN
EUROPE
ASIA
BRITISH ISLES
London
Paris
Black Sea
Caspian Sea
Istanbul
MEDITERRANEAN SEA
Lisbon
Strait of Gibraltar
Madeira (Port.) I.
Canary I.s (Sp.)
Tenerife
C. Bojador
Villa Cisneros
C. Blanco
Port Etienne
Casablanca
Rabat
Fez
Marrakesh
Mogador
MOROCCO
Oran
Algiers
Tunis
TUNISIA
Tripoli
Tripolitania
LIBYA
Fezzan
Murzuq
Cyrenaica
Benghazi
Tobruk
El Alamein
Alexandria
Cairo
UN. ARAB REP. (EGYPT)
Cyprus
Jerusalem
Isthmus of Suez
Port Said & Canal
Damietta
Libyan Desert
Aswan
Thebes
Luxor
Wadi Halfa
Medina
Mecca
Port Sudan
RED SEA
Persian Gulf
Ouargla
Tuat
ALGERIA
Reggan
Ghat
SAHARA
Tropic of Cancer
SPAN. SAHARA
Atar
MAURITANIA
Nouakchott
St. Louis
Dakar
C. Verde
SENEGAL
GAMBIA
Bathurst
PORT. GUINEA
Bissagos I.s
Bolama
GUINEA
SIERRA LEONE
Freetown
Monrovia
LIBERIA
C. Palmas
IVORY COAST
Abidjan
GHANA
Kumasi
Accra
TOGO
Lome
DAHOMEY
Lagos
NIGERIA
Kano
Benin City
Bight of Benin
Bight of Biafra
Timbuktu
MALI
Bamako
Segou
UPPER VOLTA
Ouagadougou
Niamey
Zinder
Sokoto
Agades
NIGER
L. Chad
CHAD
Tibesti
Abeche
Ft. Lamy
Gulf of Guinea
Fernando Po
Principe
São Thome (Port.)
Annobon (Sp.)
C. Lopez
Equator
CAMEROUN
Douala
Yaounde
Libreville
GABON
Franceville
Brazzaville
Pte. Noire
CONGO (FR.)
CENTRAL AFRICAN REPUBLIC
Bangui
R. Congo
CONGO
Leopoldville
S. Salvador
Luanda
Lobito
Benguela
ANGOLA
Nova Lisboa
Moçamedes
C. Negro
C. Frio
Dongola
Omdurman
Khartoum
Berber
Kassala
Massawa
Darfur
El Obeid
SUDAN
Gondar
Magdala
Addis Ababa
Harar
ETHIOPIA (ABYSSINIA)
Aden
C. Guardafui
Socotra
FRENCH SOM.
Djibouti
Berbera
Zeila
SOMALIA
Mogadishu
Obbia
Juba
L. Albert
UGANDA
Kampala
L. Victoria
KENYA
Nairobi
Mombasa
Kilimanjaro
Arusha
Tabora
TANZANIA
Zanzibar
Dar es Salaam
Mafia I.
Kilwa
Lindi
L. Tanganyika
Elisabethville
ZAMBIA
Lusaka
Broken Hill
MALAWI
Blantyre
Salisbury
RHODESIA
Bulawayo
Quelimane
Beira
Moçambique
Mozambique Channel
Comoro I.s (Fr.)
MADAGASCAR (MALAGASY REP.)
Tananarive
Majunga
Tamatave
C. St. Marie
Ascension I.
St. Helena I.
England to The Cape 6088 Miles
Damara Land
Windhoek
Walvis B.
SOUTH WEST AFRICA
Kalahari Desert
BOTSWANA
Ichabo I.
Nama Land
Orange R.
Port Nolloth
Mafeking
Pretoria
Johannesburg
TRANSVAAL
Lourenço Marques
Delagoa B.
C. Corrientes
Tropic of Capricorn
ORANGE FR. STATE
Bloemfontein
NATAL
Durban
REP. OF SOUTH AFRICA
CAPE PROVINCE
East London
Cape Town
Cape of Good Hope
C. Agulhas
Mossel Bay
Port Elizabeth
Algoa B.
INDIAN OCEAN
Tristan da Cunha (Br.)

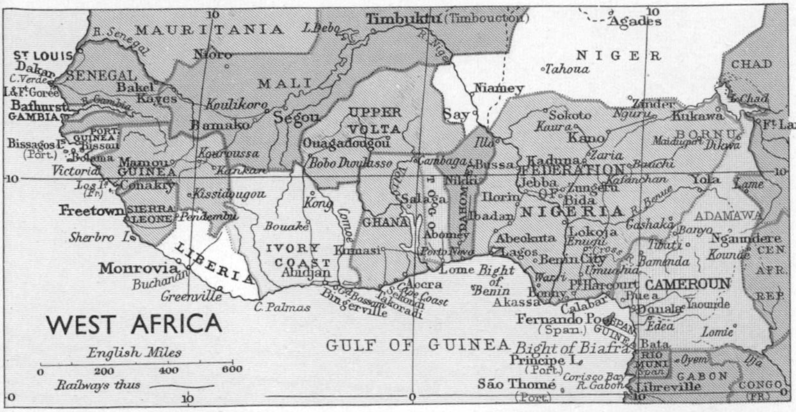
WEST AFRICA
English Miles
0 200 400 600
Railways thus
MAURITANIA
MALI
NIGER
CHAD
SENEGAL
GAMBIA
PORT. GUINEA
GUINEA
SIERRA LEONE
LIBERIA
IVORY COAST
UPPER VOLTA
GHANA
TOGO
DAHOMEY
FEDERATION OF NIGERIA
CAMEROUN
ADAMAWA
BORNU
CEN. AFR. REP.
GABON
CONGO (FR.)
RIO MUNI (Span.)
St LOUIS
Dakar
C. Verde
I.&Ft Gorée
Bathurst
Bissagos Is (Port.)
Bissau
Bolama
Victoria
Los Is (Fr.)
Conakry
Freetown
Sherbro I.
Monrovia
Buchanan
Greenville
C. Palmas
Nioro
Bakel
Kayes
Koulikoro
Bamako
Segou
Timbuktu (Timbouctou)
L. Debo
R. Senegal
R. Gambia
R. Niger
Mamou
Kouroussa
Kankan
Kissidougou
Pendembu
Ouagadougou
Bobo Dioulasso
Kong
Bouake
Comoe
Abidjan
Bingerville
Grand Bassam
Kumasi
Sekondi
Takoradi
Cape Coast
Accra
Gambaga
Salaga
Nikki
Abomey
Porto Novo
Lome
Bight of Benin
Say
Niamey
Tahoua
Agades
Sokoto
Kaura
Kano
Zaria
Zinder
Nguru
Kukawa
L. Chad
Ft Lamy
Maiduguri
Dikwa
Bauchi
Kafanchan
Yola
Lame
Illo
Bussa
Kaduna
Jebba
Zungeru
Bida
Ilorin
Ibadan
Abeokuta
Lagos
Benin City
Lokoja
Enugu
Cross R.
Umuahia
Warri
Bonny
Akassa
Pt Harcourt
Calabar
R. Benue
Gashaka
Banyo
Tibati
Bamenda
Ngaundere
Kounde
Buea
Douala
Yaounde
Edea
Lomie
Fernando Po (Span.)
Bight of Biafra
SPAN. GUINEA
Bata
Oyem
Principe I. (Port.)
São Thomé (Port.)
Corisco Bay
R. Gabon
Libreville
GULF OF GUINEA
10
0

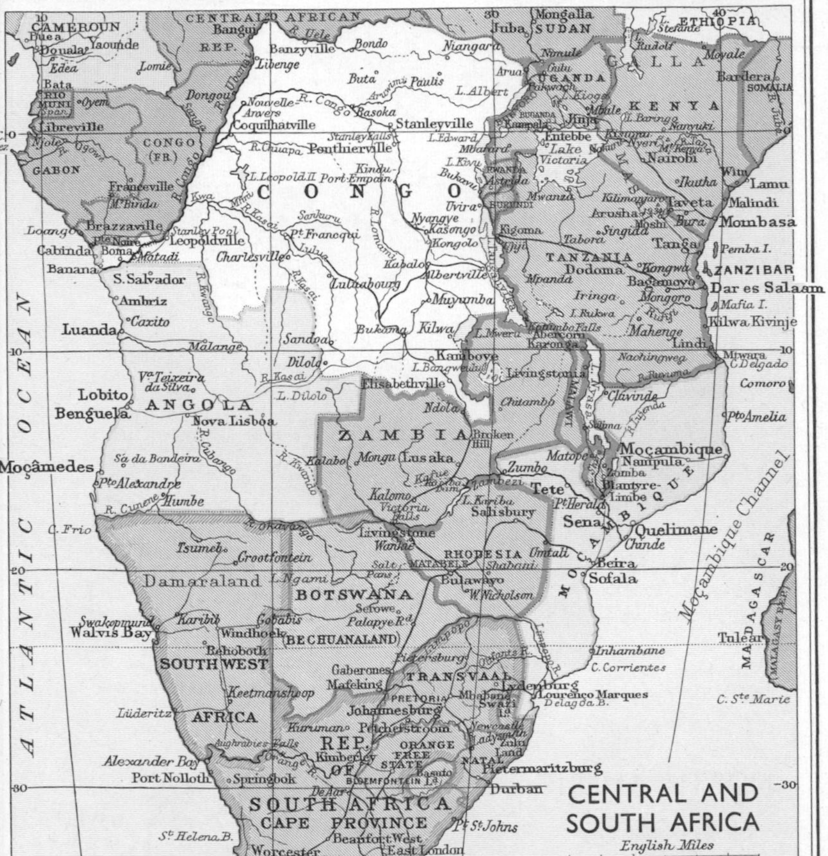
CENTRAL AND SOUTH AFRICA
English Miles
0 200 400 600
Railways thus
ATLANTIC OCEAN
CAMEROUN
CENTRAL AFRICAN REP.
SUDAN
ETHIOPIA
GALLA
SOMALIA
UGANDA
KENYA
BUGANDA
RWANDA
BURUNDI
TANZANIA
ZANZIBAR
CONGO
CONGO (FR.)
GABON
RIO MUNI (Span.)
ANGOLA
ZAMBIA
MALAWI
MOÇAMBIQUE
RHODESIA
MATABELE
BOTSWANA
(BECHUANALAND)
SOUTH WEST AFRICA
Damaraland
TRANSVAAL
ORANGE FREE STATE
NATAL
Basuto Ld
Swazi Ld
Zulu Land
REP. OF SOUTH AFRICA
CAPE PROVINCE
MADAGASCAR (MALAGASY REP.)
Moçambique Channel
Buea
Douala
Yaounde
Edea
Lomie
Bata
Oyem
Bangui
Dongou
Libreville
Njole
R. Ogowe
Franceville
M'Binda
Brazzaville
Loango
Pte Noire
Cabinda
Boma
Matadi
Banana
Stanley Pool
Leopoldville
Banzyville
Libenge
R. Uele
Bondo
Buta
Niangara
Paulis
Aruwimi
Arua
L. Albert
Nouvelle-Anvers
Coquilhatville
R. Congo
Basoka
Stanleyville
Stanley Falls
Ponthierville
R. Chuapa
L. Leopold II
Kindu-Port-Empain
L. Edward
Mbarara
L. Kivu
Bukavu
Astrida
Uvira
Kwa
Mfimi
R. Kasai
Sankuru
Pt Francqui
R. Lomami
Nyangwe
Kasongo
Kongolo
Charlesville
Lulua
Kabalo
Albertville
L. Tanganyika
Luluabourg
Muyumba
Bukama
Kilwa
Sandoa
Dilolo
L. Dilolo
Kambove
L. Bangweulu
Elisabethville
L. Mweru
S. Salvador
Ambriz
Caxito
Luanda
R. Kwango
Malange
Va Teixeira da Silva
Lobito
Benguela
Nova Lisboa
R. Cubango
R. Kwando
Moçâmedes
Sá da Bandeira
Pte Alexandre
Humbe
R. Cunene
C. Frio
R. Okavango
Juba
Mongalla
Nimule
Gulu
Pakwach
L. Kioga
Kampala
Jinja
Mbale
Entebbe
Lake Victoria
Kisumu
L. Rudolf
L. Stefanie
Moyale
Bardera
R. Juba
L. Baringo
Nanyuki
Nyeri
R. Tana
Nairobi
Witu
Lamu
Malindi
Ikutha
Kilimanjaro
Taveta
Arusha
Moshi
Bura
Mombasa
Tanga
Pemba I.
Mwanza
Tabora
Singida
Kigoma
Ujiji
Dodoma
Kongwa
Bagamoyo
Dar es Salaam
Mpanda
Iringa
Morogoro
Mafia I.
L. Rukwa
Rufiji
Mahenge
Kilwa Kivinje
Kalambo Falls
Abercorn
Karonga
Lindi
Nachingwea
Mtwara
C. Delgado
R. Ruvuma
Comoro
Livingstonia
L. Nyasa
Chitambo
Clavinde
Pto Amelia
Broken Hill
Mongu
Lusaka
Kalabo
Kafue
Kalomo
Victoria Falls
Livingstone
Wankie
L. Kariba
Salisbury
Zumbo
Matope
Nampula
Zomba
Blantyre-Limbe
Tete
Pt Herald
Sena
Quelimane
Chinde
Zambezi
Umtali
Beira
Sofala
Shabani
Bulawayo
W. Nicholson
Tsumeb
Grootfontein
L. Ngami
Salt Pans
Serowe
Palapye Rd
Swakopmund
Walvis Bay
Karibib
Gobabis
Windhoek
Rehoboth
Limpopo R.
Inhambane
C. Corrientes
Tulear
C. Ste Marie
Pietersburg
Gaberones
Mafeking
Lydenburg
PRETORIA
Mbabane
Lourenço Marques
Delagoa B.
Keetmanshoop
Johannesburg
Lüderitz
Kuruman
Potchefstroom
Newcastle
Ladysmith
Aughrabies Falls
Orange R.
Kimberley
Alexander Bay
Pietermaritzburg
Port Nolloth
Springbok
BLOEMFONTEIN
De Aar
Durban
Pt St Johns
St Helena B.
Beaufort West
Worcester
East London
Grahamstown
CAPE TOWN
Mossel Bay
Great Fish R.
Port Alfred
Cape of Good Hope
Port Elizabeth
C. Agulhas
10
20
30
0

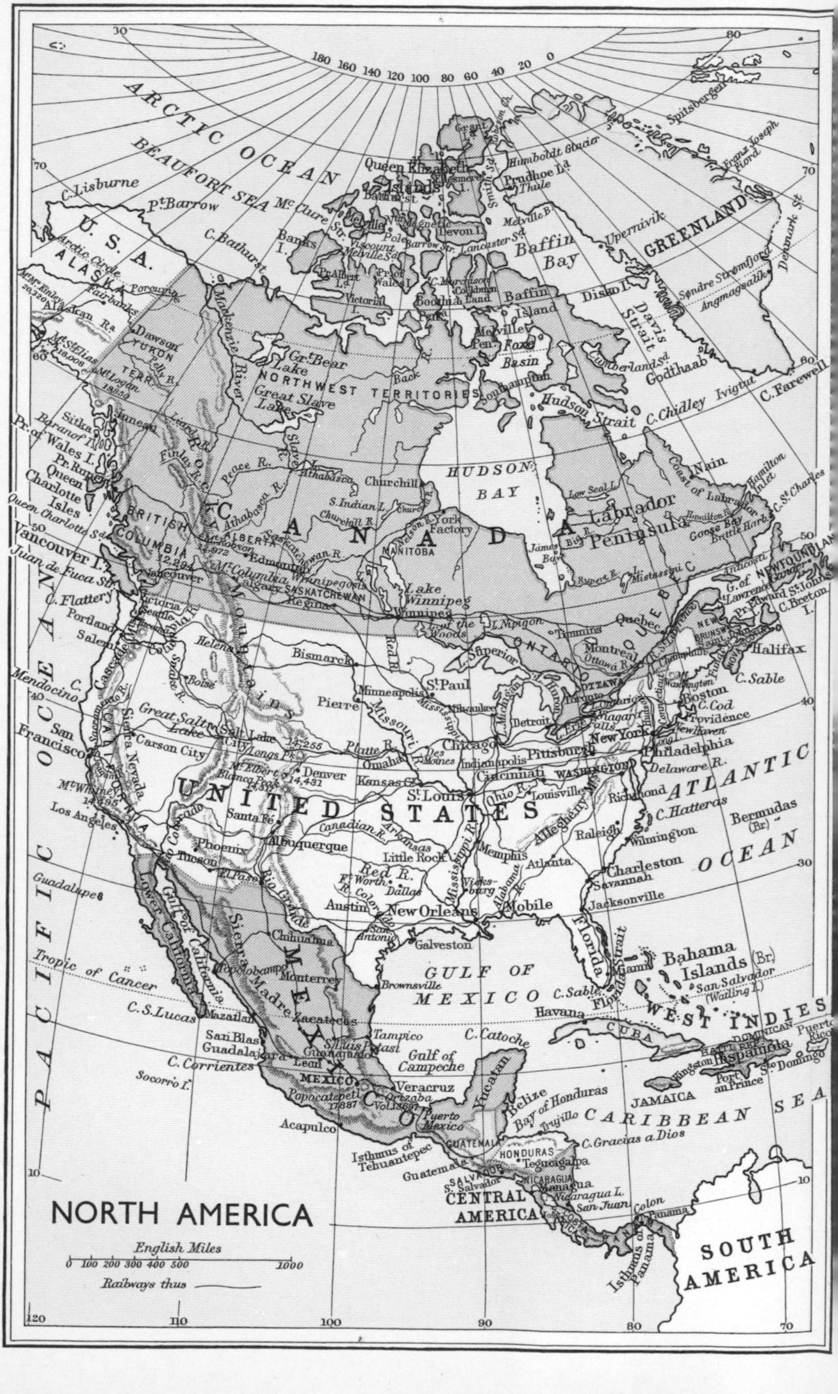
NORTH AMERICA
English Miles
0 100 200 300 400 500 1000
Railways thus
ARCTIC OCEAN
BEAUFORT SEA
GREENLAND
Baffin Bay
Davis Strait
Hudson Strait
HUDSON BAY
CANADA
NORTHWEST TERRITORIES
YUKON TERR.
BRITISH COLUMBIA
ALBERTA
SASKATCHEWAN
MANITOBA
ONTARIO
QUEBEC
Labrador Peninsula
NEWFOUNDLAND
U.S.A.
ALASKA
UNITED STATES
MEXICO
GULF OF MEXICO
CUBA
JAMAICA
Hispaniola
WEST INDIES
Bahama Islands (Br.)
Bermudas (Br.)
CARIBBEAN SEA
CENTRAL AMERICA
GUATEMALA
HONDURAS
NICARAGUA
SOUTH AMERICA
ATLANTIC OCEAN
PACIFIC OCEAN
Tropic of Cancer
Arctic Circle
Gulf of California
Lower California
Gulf of Campeche
Yucatan
Isthmus of Tehuantepec
Isthmus of Panama
Florida
Florida Strait
Rocky Mountains
Sierra Nevada
Sierra Madre
Mississippi R.
Missouri R.
Ohio R.
Red R.
Rio Grande
Colorado
Mackenzie River
Gr.t Bear Lake
Great Slave Lake
Lake Winnipeg
L. Superior
L. Michigan
L. Huron
L. Erie
L. Ontario
Ottawa
Washington
New York
Chicago
San Francisco
Los Angeles
New Orleans
Montreal
Quebec
Winnipeg
Vancouver
Mexico
Havana
Panama

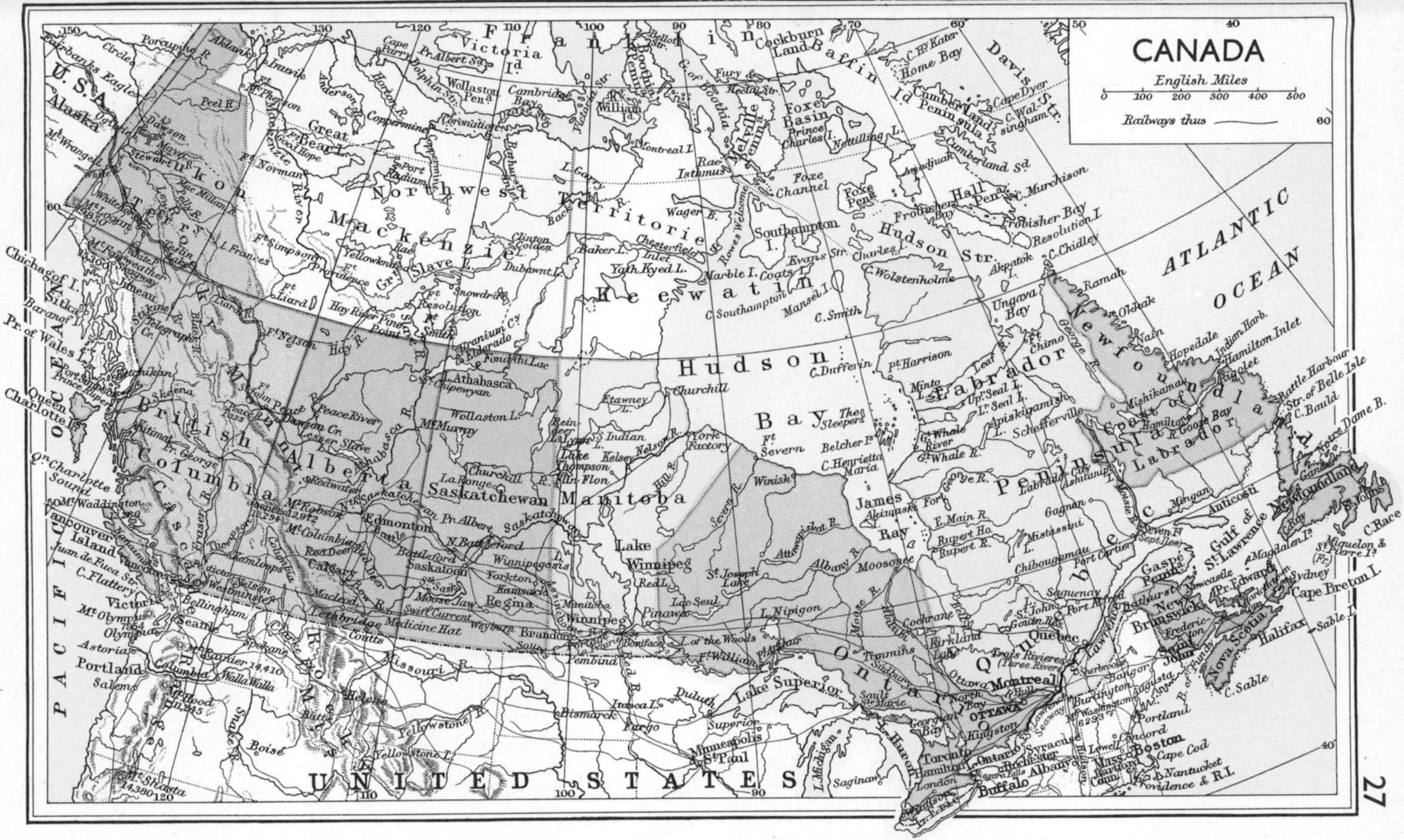
CANADA
English Miles
0 100 200 300 400 500
Railways thus
ATLANTIC OCEAN
PACIFIC OCEAN
UNITED STATES
Franklin
Victoria Id.
Baffin Id.
Davis Str.
Hudson Str.
Hudson Bay
James Bay
Keewatin
Mackenzie
Northwest Territories
Yukon Terr.
British Columbia
Alberta
Saskatchewan
Manitoba
Ontario
Quebec
Labrador
Newfoundland
New Brunswick
Nova Scotia
Pr. Edward I.
Cape Breton I.
Gulf of St. Lawrence
Anticosti
Labrador Peninsula
Southampton I.
Foxe Basin
Foxe Channel
Melville Penin.
Boothia Penin.
Great Bear L.
Gt. Slave L.
L. Athabasca
Lake Winnipeg
Lake Superior
L. Huron
L. Michigan
Ungava Bay
U.S.A. Alaska
Vancouver Island
Queen Charlotte Is.
Ottawa
Montreal
Quebec
Toronto
Winnipeg
Regina
Edmonton
Calgary
Saskatoon
Vancouver
Victoria
Halifax
St. Johns
Churchill
Boston
Buffalo
Portland
Seattle
Duluth
Minneapolis
St. Paul
Bismarck

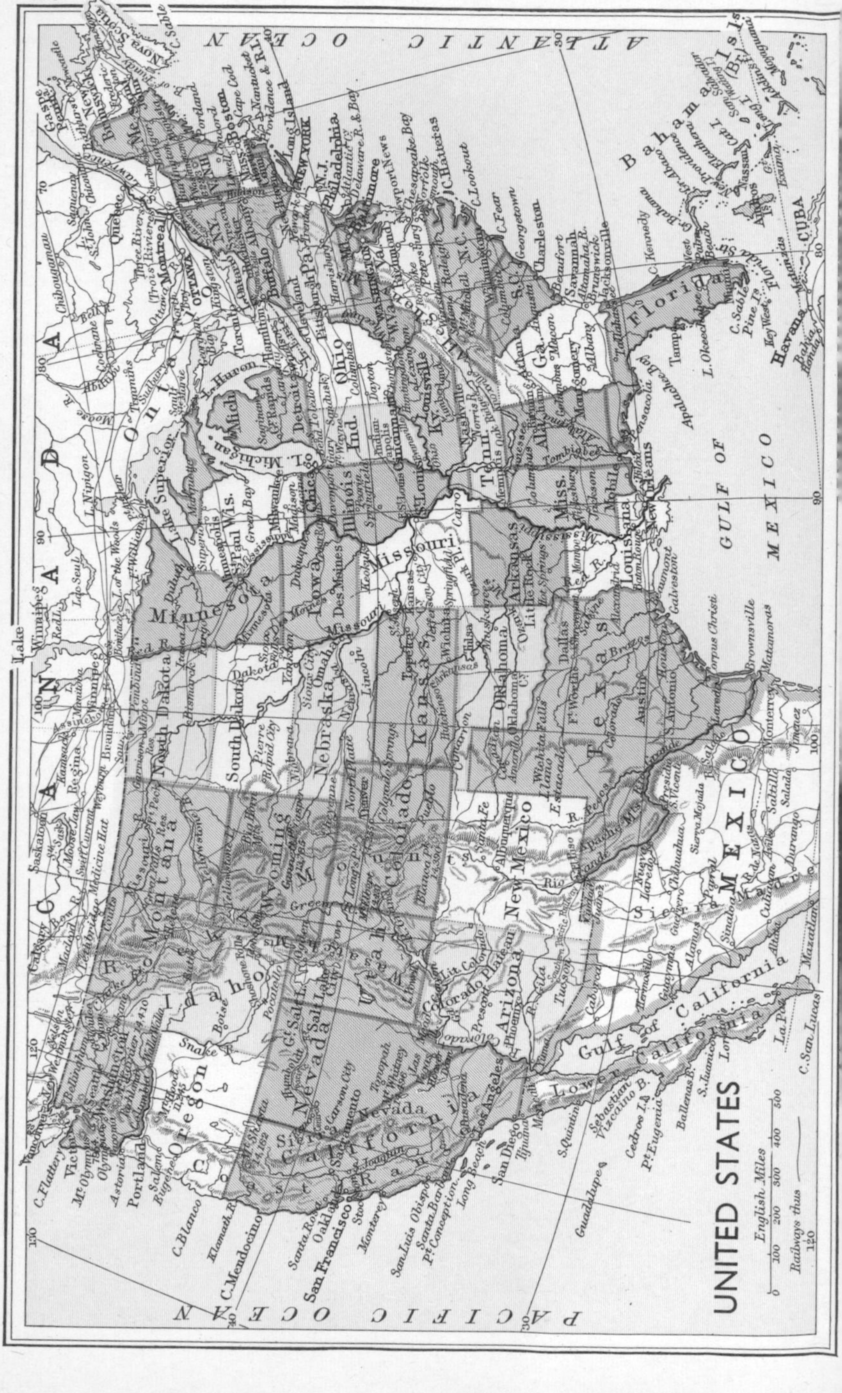
UNITED STATES
English Miles
0 100 200 300 400 500
Railways thus
C A N A D A
PACIFIC OCEAN
ATLANTIC OCEAN
GULF OF MEXICO
MEXICO
Gulf of California
Lower California
Bahama Is (Br.)
CUBA

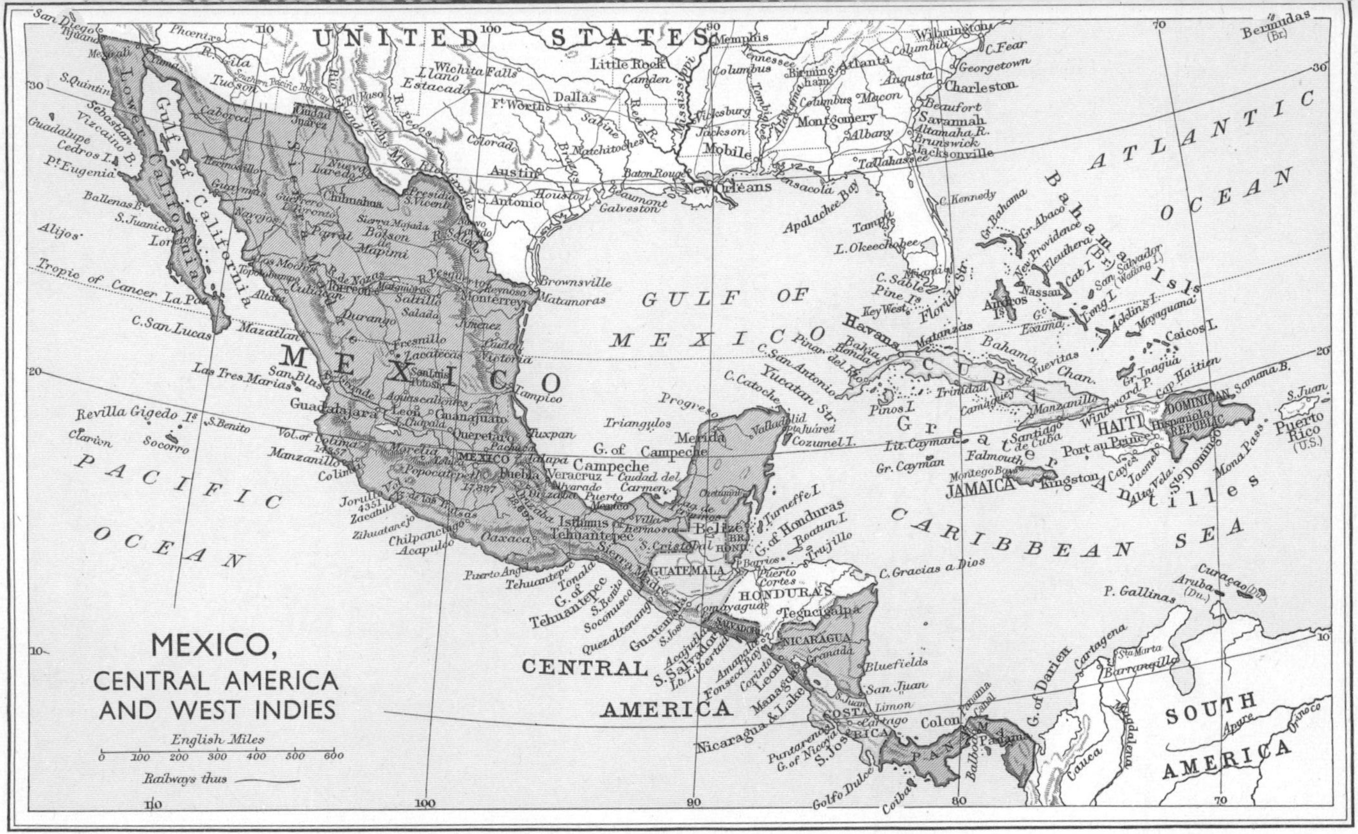

MEXICO,
CENTRAL AMERICA
AND WEST INDIES

English Miles
0 100 200 300 400 500 600

Railways thus

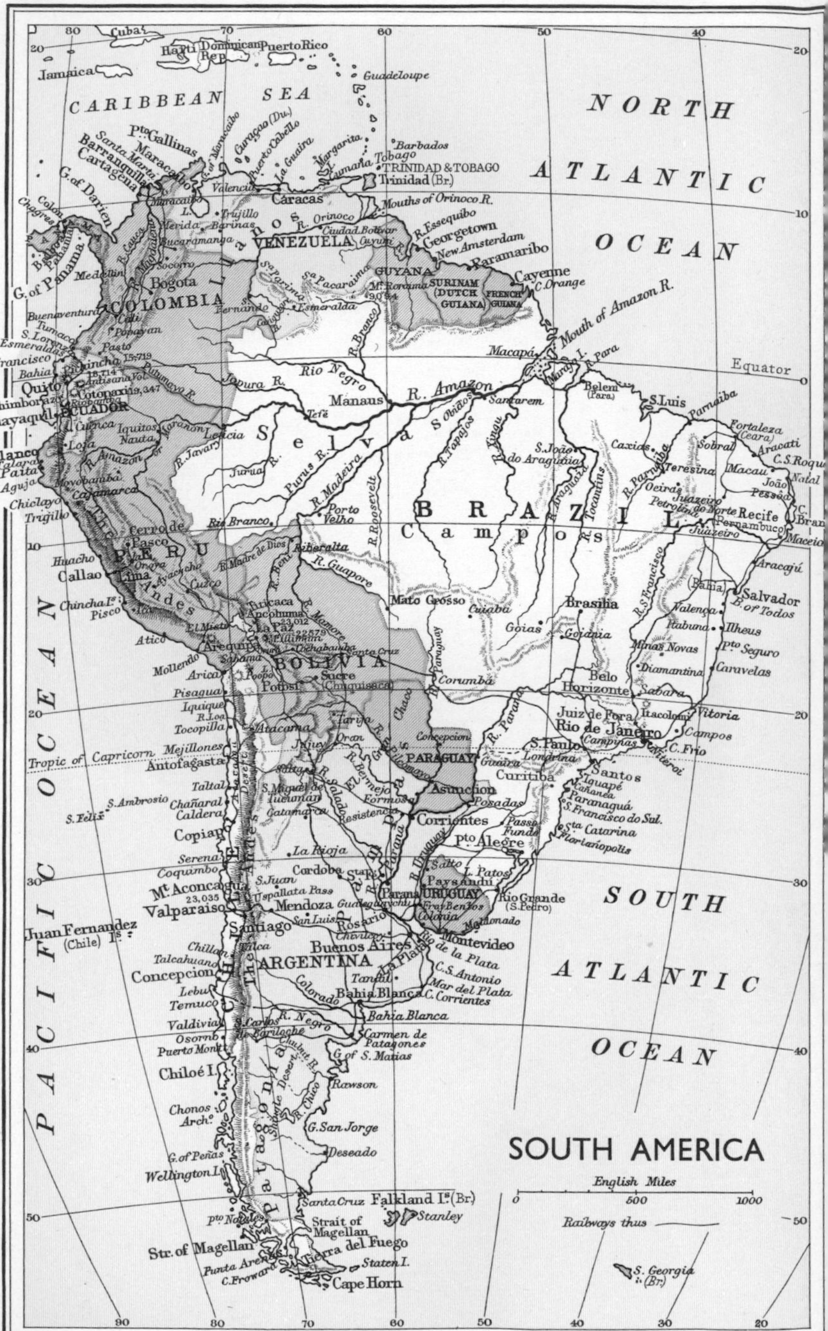
SOUTH AMERICA
English Miles
0
500
1000
Railways thus
CARIBBEAN SEA
NORTH ATLANTIC OCEAN
SOUTH ATLANTIC OCEAN
PACIFIC OCEAN
Equator
Tropic of Capricorn
Cuba
Haiti
Dominican Rep.
Puerto Rico
Jamaica
Guadeloupe
Barbados
Tobago
TRINIDAD & TOBAGO
Trinidad (Br.)
Curaçao (Du.)
Puerto Cabello
La Guaira
Margarita
Pto. Gallinas
Santa Marta
Barranquilla
Cartagena
Maracaibo
G. of Darien
Colon
Chagres
Panama
G. of Panama
Valencia
Caracas
Mouths of Orinoco R.
Trujillo
Merida
Barinas
R. Orinoco
Llanos
Ciudad Bolivar
VENEZUELA
R. Essequibo
Georgetown
New Amsterdam
Paramaribo
GUYANA
SURINAM (DUTCH GUIANA)
FRENCH GUIANA
Cayenne
C. Orange
Mt. Roraima
Bucaramanga
Socorro
Medellin
Bogota
COLOMBIA
Buenaventura
Cali
Popayan
Tumaco
Esmeraldas
Pasto
S. Francisco
Bahia
Quito
Chimborazo
Cotopaxi
Guayaquil
ECUADOR
R. Putumayo
Japura R.
Rio Negro
R. Branco
Esmeralda
Mouth of Amazon R.
Macapá
Marajo I.
R. Para
Manaus
R. Amazon
Santarem
Belem (Para)
S. Luis
Parnaiba
Fortaleza (Ceara)
Aracati
C. S. Roque
Natal
Macau
João Pessoa
Recife Pernambuco
Maceio
Tefé
Selvas
Obidos
R. Tapajos
R. Xingu
S. João do Araguaia
Caxias
Teresina
Sobral
Oeiras
Juazeiro do Norte
Petrolina
Juazeiro
Iquitos
Nauta
Leticia
R. Maranon
R. Amazon
R. Javary
Jurua R.
Purus R.
R. Madeira
R. Roosevelt
Porto Velho
Rio Branco
BRAZIL
Campos
R. Araguaia
Tocantins
R. Parnaiba
R. S. Francisco
Aracajú
Salvador (Bahia)
B. of Todos
Valença
Itabuna
Ilheus
Pto. Seguro
Caravelas
Minas Novas
Diamantina
Cuenca
Loja
C. Blanco
Talara
Paita
C. Aguja
Chiclayo
Trujillo
Moyobamba
Cajamarca
Cerro de Pasco
PERU
Huacho
Callao
Lima
Oroya
Ayacucho
Cuzco
Andes
Chincha Is.
Pisco
Ica
Atico
El Misti
Arequipa
Mollendo
Riberalta
R. Madre de Dios
R. Beni
R. Guapore
R. Mamore
Titicaca
Ancohuma
La Paz
Cochabamba
Santa Cruz
BOLIVIA
Sucre (Chuquisaca)
Potosi
Poopo
Mato Grosso
Cuiaba
Brasilia
Goias
Goiania
Belo Horizonte
Sabara
Itacolomi
Vitoria
Campos
Juiz de Fora
Rio de Janeiro
C. Frio
Niteroi
Corumba
R. Paraguay
Chaco
Arica
Pisagua
Iquique
R. Loa
Tocopilla
Atacama
Tarija
Oran
Jujuy
Concepcion
PARAGUAY
R. Parana
S. Paulo
Campinas
Londrina
Guaira
Curitiba
Santos
Iguapé
Paranaguá
S. Francisco do Sul
Sta. Catarina
Florianópolis
Mejillones
Antofagasta
Taltal
Salta
S. Miguel de Tucuman
R. Bermejo
Formosa
Asuncion
Posadas
S. Ambrosio
S. Felix
Chañaral
Caldera
Catamarca
Resistencia
Corrientes
Passo Fundo
Pto. Alegre
Copiapo
La Rioja
Serena
Coquimbo
Cordoba
Sta. Fé
Salto
L. Patos
Paysandú
URUGUAY
Rio Grande (S. Pedro)
Mt. Aconcagua
23,035
S. Juan
Uspallata Pass
Valparaiso
Mendoza
Parana
Fray Bentos
Colonia
Maldonado
Juan Fernandez (Chile) Is.
Santiago
San Luis
Rosario
Montevideo
Rio de la Plata
Buenos Aires
Chillan
Talca
Talcahuano
ARGENTINA
La Plata
C. S. Antonio
Concepcion
Tandil
Mar del Plata
Colorado
Bahia Blanca
C. Corrientes
Lebu
Temuco
Valdivia
R. Negro
Osorno
Puerto Montt
S. Carlos de Bariloche
Carmen de Patagones
G. of S. Matias
Chubut R.
Chiloé I.
Rawson
Chonos Archo.
G. San Jorge
G. of Peñas
Deseado
Wellington I.
Patagonia
Santa Cruz
Falkland Is. (Br.)
Stanley
Pto. Natales
Strait of Magellan
Str. of Magellan
Tierra del Fuego
Punta Arenas
C. Froward
Staten I.
Cape Horn
S. Georgia (Br.)

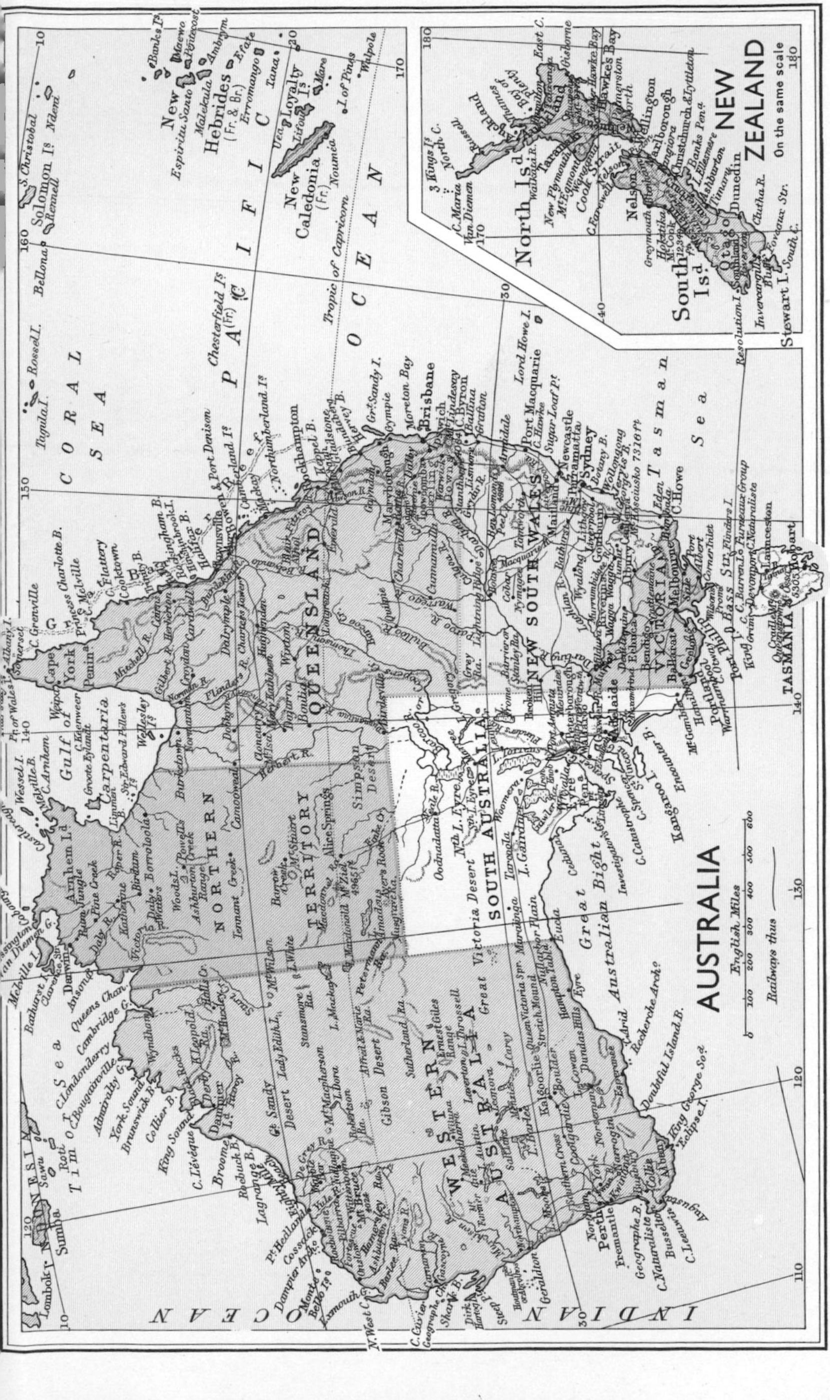
AUSTRALIA
English Miles
0 100 200 300 400 500 600
Railways thus
NEW ZEALAND
On the same scale
WESTERN AUSTRALIA
NORTHERN TERRITORY
QUEENSLAND
SOUTH AUSTRALIA
NEW SOUTH WALES
VICTORIA
TASMANIA
North Isd.
South Isd.
CORAL SEA
PACIFIC OCEAN
INDIAN OCEAN
Tasman Sea
Great Australian Bight
Timor Sea
Gulf of Carpentaria
Tropic of Capricorn
New Caledonia (Fr.)
New Hebrides (Fr. & Br.)
Loyalty Is.
Solomon Is.
Perth
Adelaide
Melbourne
Sydney
Brisbane
Hobart
Darwin
Canberra
Wellington
Auckland
Christchurch & Lyttelton
Dunedin
Nelson

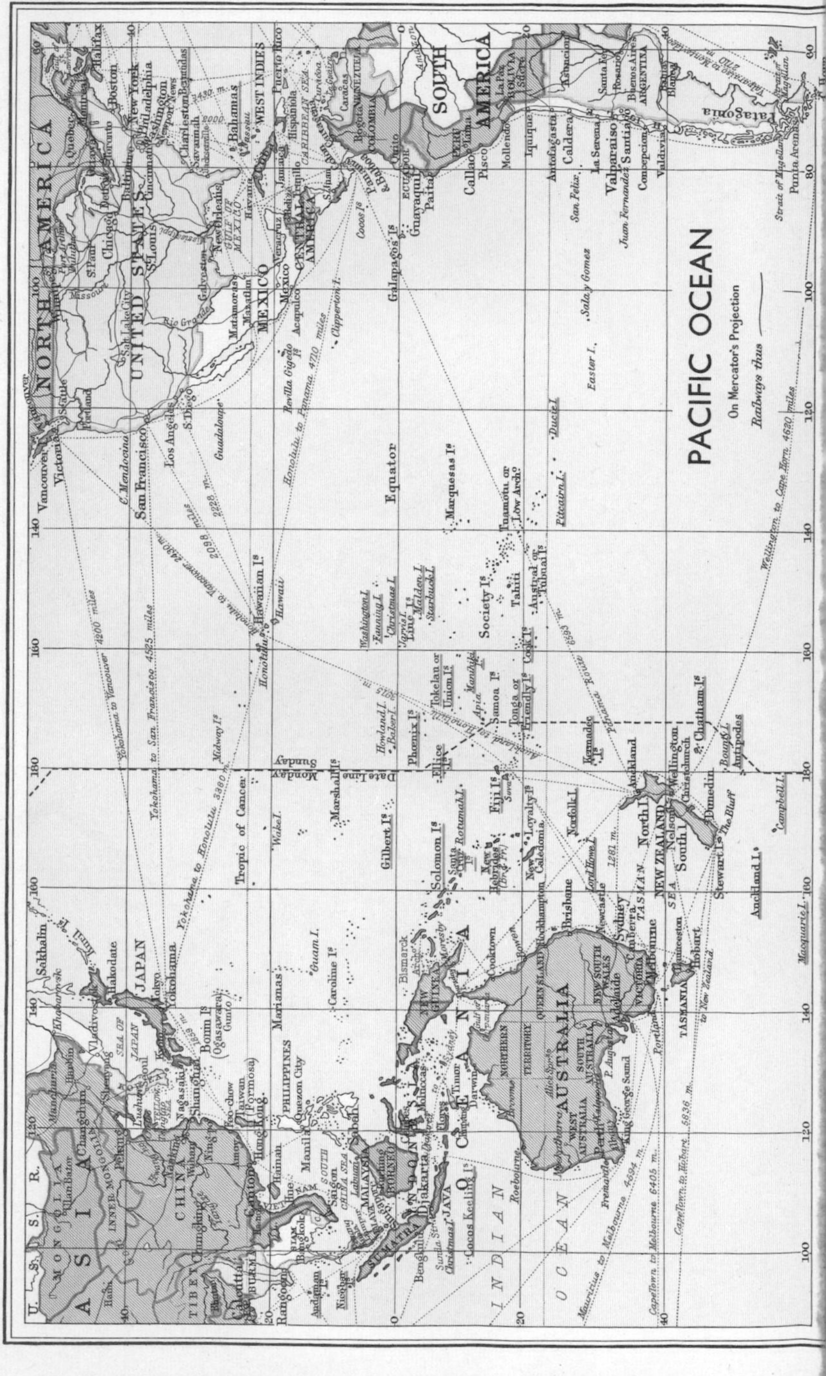
PACIFIC OCEAN
On Mercator's Projection
Railways thus
NORTH AMERICA
UNITED STATES
MEXICO
SOUTH AMERICA
ASIA
CHINA
JAPAN
AUSTRALIA
NEW ZEALAND
INDIAN OCEAN
Equator
Tropic of Cancer
Date Line